36th Edition
ULRICH'S™
INTERNATIONAL PERIODICALS DIRECTORY
1998

Ulrich's International Periodicals Directory
is compiled by
R.R. Bowker
Serials Bibliography Department

Database Publishing Group
Leigh C. Yuster-Freeman, Vice President, Database Production
Andrew Grabois, Senior Managing Director, Bibliographies

Editorial
Judith Salk, Publisher and Editorial Director
Edvika Popilskis, Managing Editor
Ewa Kowalska, Maria Mucino, Senior Editors
Zhaoxia Lian, Senior Associate Editor
Egill Halldorsson, Christopher King, Associate Editors
Thomas Berry, Gerry Milligan, Virginie Raguenaud, Diane Shpiz, Assistant Editors
Mary Crouthers, O'Sheila Delgado, Editorial Coordinators

René Bernadel, Lorraine Cantillo, Terence Carlson, Maria Christopher, Michael Dalelio,
Connie Duffy, Karl Dusza, Deborah Frail, Qingye Guo, Evelyn Irvine, Jean Kontra, Bronislaw Jan Kowalski,
Margareta Leon, Dawn Lombardy-Stoecker, Karen Lombardy, Stefan Miarka, Olga Neville,
Eline van de Poel-Becker, Noreen Riley, Alina Warda, and Lisa Wilcox, Contributing Editors

Production
Doreen Gravesande, Production Director
Myriam Nunez, Managing Editor
Barbara Holton, Frank McDermott, Senior Editors

Editorial Systems Group
Gary Aiello, Vice President, Information Technology
Rhonda Vollbrecht, Project Manager, Bibliographies
Nana Rizinashvili and Robert Michniewicz, Senior Systems Analysts

Computer Operations Group
Nick Wikowski, Director, Network/Computer Operations
Jack Murphy, Supervisor

Reed Technology and Information Services
Donna Brinkmann, Account Manager

36th Edition

INTERNATIONAL PERIODICALS DIRECTORY

1998

including
Irregular Serials & Annuals

Volume 5

Indexes
U.S. Newspapers and
Newspaper Index

THE BOWKER INTERNATIONAL SERIALS DATABASE

R.R. BOWKER
A Unit of Reed Elsevier Business Information
New Providence, New Jersey

Published by R.R. Bowker
A Unit of Reed Elsevier Business Information
121 Chanlon Rd., New Providence, NJ 07974

Neal Goff, Senior Vice President and Chief Operating Officer

Copyright © 1997 by Reed Elsevier Inc.
All rights reserved

Ulrich's Hotline (U.S. only): 1-800-346-6049
Editorial (Canada only, call collect): 1-908-665-2875
Serials Fax (overseas users): 908-771-7725
Serials E-mail: ulrichs@bowker.com
URL: http://www.bowker.com

Ulrich's is a trademark of Reed Properties Inc., used under license

No part of this publication may be reproduced or transmitted in any form or by any means, stored in any information storage and retrieval system, without prior written permission of R.R. Bowker, 121 Chanlon Rd., New Providence, New Jersey 07974, USA.

International Standard Book Number
5-Volume set: 0-8352-3967-5
Volume 1: 0-8352-3968-3
Volume 2: 0-8352-3969-1
Volume 3: 0-8352-3970-5
Volume 4: 0-8352-3971-3
Volume 5: 0-8352-3972-1

International Standard Serial Number
0000-0175

Library of Congress Catalog Card Number
32-16320

Printed and bound in the United States of America

No payment is either solicited or accepted for the inclusion of entries in this publication. R.R. Bowker has used its best efforts in collecting and preparing material for inclusion in this publication, but does not warrant that the information herein is complete or accurate, and does not assume, and hereby disclaims any liability to any person for the loss or damage caused by errors or omissions in this publication whether such errors or omissions result from negligence, accident or any other cause.

ISBN 0-8352-3967-5

Contents

BOWKER/ULRICH'S SERIALS LIBRARIANSHIP
 AWARD WINNERS... vi
PREFACE.. vii
USER'S GUIDE ix
INTERNATIONAL STANDARD SERIAL NUMBER (ISSN) xviii
ABBREVIATIONS
    General Abbreviations and Special Symbols xx
    Money Symbols... xxi
    Country of Publication Codes xxii
    Document Suppliers xxiv
    Micropublishers and Distributors.. xxvi
    Reprint Services xxx
    Wire Services xxxi
    Abstracting and Indexing Services xxxii
SUBJECT GUIDE TO ABSTRACTING AND INDEXING............................ xlv
SUBJECTS.. xlvi

VOLUME 1
CLASSIFIED LIST OF SERIALS/SUBJECTS A to D................................. 1

VOLUME 2
CLASSIFIED LIST OF SERIALS/SUBJECTS E to L................................. 2309

VOLUME 3
CLASSIFIED LIST OF SERIALS/SUBJECTS M to Z 4541

VOLUME 4
CROSS-INDEX TO SUBJECTS.. 7351
CESSATIONS... 7383
ISSN INDEX 7605
TITLE INDEX 8461
TITLE CHANGE INDEX 9697

VOLUME 5
REFEREED 9719
SERIALS AVAILABLE ON CD-ROM 9973
PRODUCER LISTING/SERIALS ON CD-ROM..................................... 10033
SERIALS AVAILABLE ONLINE 10037
VENDOR LISTING/SERIALS ONLINE 10229
INDEX TO PUBLICATIONS OF INTERNATIONAL ORGANIZATIONS 10263
    International Organizations... 10263
    International Congress Proceedings.. 10275
    European Communities... 10278
    United Nations.. 10280
CONTROLLED CIRCULATION SERIALS 10289

U.S. NEWSPAPERS
USER'S GUIDE li
ABBREVIATIONS.. liv
DAILY NEWSPAPERS — US 10415
WEEKLY NEWSPAPERS — US... 10517
TITLE INDEX 10777
DAILY NEWSPAPER INDEX 10853
WEEKLY NEWSPAPER INDEX.. 10871
GEOGRAPHIC INDEX 10929
CESSATIONS... 10997

Bowker/Ulrich's Serials Librarianship Award

Presented by the Serials Section
Association for Library Collections and Technical Services (ALCTS)
Division of the American Library Association (ALA)

Sponsored by R.R. Bowker

This annual award is given in recognition of distinguished and ongoing contributions to serials librarianship. Qualified individuals demonstrate leadership in serials-related activities through their participation in professional associations, groups, and/or library education programs; make significant contributions to serials literature; and, in general, strive to enhance our comprehension of the serials world.

AWARD RECIPIENTS

Year	Recipient
1985	Marcia Tuttle
1986	Ruth C. Carter
1987	James P. Danky
1988	Marjorie E. Bloss
1989	John E. Merriman
1990	Jean S. Cook
1991	Deana L. Astle/Charles A. Hamaker
1992	Linda K. Bartley
1993	Ann L. Okerson
1994	Tina Feick
1995	Peter Gellatly
1996	Jean L. Hirons
1997	Cindy Hepfer

Preface

Now in its 36th edition, **Ulrich's International Periodicals Directory** upholds its reputation for excellence in the provision of serials information. In the 65 years since it was first published, **Ulrich's** has established itself as the premier serials reference source in the world, providing serials users with essential bibliographic and access information.

Beginning with the 34th edition, the publication date of **Ulrich's** moved from August to November. Publication in November continues to enable us to provide thousands of updated prices for 1998. Most publishers establish prices for the upcoming year between May and September. Prices set and received by us later than mid-September did not get updated for this print edition. However, data are entered as received, so price changes and all other information received after mid-September will appear in subsequent quarterly CD-ROM versions of **Ulrich's** (**Ulrich's on Disc**™, formerly Ulrich's *PLUS*) and online versions (update monthly through Knight-Ridder Information, Inc./DIALOG file number 480; OVID Technologies/file name: ULRI; and LEXIS®-NEXIS®/library: BUSREF, file name: ULRICHS; and SilverPlatter Information, Inc.-SilverPlatter ERL).

As libraries, institutions, and researchers evaluate new opportunities and technologies that enable them to access individual articles on demand rather than to acquire serials in their entirety, our coverage of document delivery services has expanded to include CINDOC (CINDOC Suministro de Documentos Service), Ask*IEEE, KR SourceOne, and Linda Hall Library. We now identify 18 different document delivery services from which the full text of articles from serials listed in **Ulrich's** may be obtained (see pgs. xxiv-xxv). For a brief explanation of and contact information for these useful services, please refer to the section entitled "Document Suppliers" in the User's Guide of **Ulrich's**, pg. ix of the prefatory material of Volumes 1-4.

Further access to serials in **Ulrich's** is facilitated through the inclusion of nearly 250,000 indicators denoting coverage by some 800 abstracting and indexing services; 12,000 notations of reprint availability; over 30,000 e-mail addresses; and 22,000 URLs (Uniform Resource Locators on the World Wide Web). The number of URLs includes publisher sites as well as sites for individual journals.

Serials, whether in print or in an electronic medium, are as important as ever as primary sources of current information and topical news in all fields of endeavor. Though the printed serial is by no means on the wane, the proliferation of serials in electronic formats, whether online or on CD-ROM, continues unabated, especially with dramatically increased use of the Internet as a publishing medium. This edition of **Ulrich's** includes 8,762 serials available exclusively online or in addition to hard copy, and 2,903 serials available on CD-ROM. These serials are indicated by a notation and a bullet (●) in the main entry.

Ulrich's includes nearly 19,000 Rights & Permissions contact names, along with telephone contact information, if provided. Users anticipating forthcoming serial launches will find 51 titles announced for publication in 1998.

The 36th edition of **Ulrich's** contains information on over 156,000 serials published throughout the world, arranged under 869 subject headings. More than 112,000 entries have been updated to reflect the most current information available and nearly 7,000 serials have been added this year, some of which have since ceased or suspended publication. Included in this edition is cessation or suspension information which has been recorded in our database during the past three years for 9,586 titles. The ceased or suspended titles are preceded by a dagger (†) in the TITLE INDEX for instant identification.

Users can identify newer serials, over 3,571 of which are known to have begun publication since January 1, 1995, by looking for an upside-down solid triangle (▼) in both the CLASSIFIED LIST OF SERIALS and the TITLE INDEX. This symbol is also used to highlight forthcoming publications. In addition, more than 13,550 refereed serials notations; nearly 71,000 brief descriptions; almost 42,700 LC Classification Numbers; over 20,000 CODEN; and 4,421 vendor file names or numbers for 8,762 serials available in an online format appear in this edition.

Included in **Ulrich's** are serials that are currently available, issued more frequently than once a year and usually published at regular intervals, as well as publications issued annually or less frequently than once a year, or irregularly. Due to the vast number of serials, we have established certain criteria for inclusion, while maintaining our aim of maximum title coverage that will satisfy the widest range of use. We include all publications that meet the definition of a serial except administrative publications of governmental agencies below state level that can be easily found elsewhere, membership directories, comic books, and puzzle and game books.

This edition of **Ulrich's** is arranged within five volumes, as follows: the first three volumes comprise the CLASSIFIED LIST OF SERIALS; the fourth volume contains the CROSS-INDEX TO SUBJECTS, CESSATIONS INDEX, ISSN INDEX, TITLE INDEX, and TITLE CHANGE INDEX. The fifth volume comprises the remaining indexes: REFEREED SERIALS, SERIALS AVAILABLE ON CD-ROM, PRODUCER LISTING/SERIALS ON CD-ROM, SERIALS AVAILABLE ONLINE, VENDOR LISTING/ SERIALS ONLINE, INDEX TO INTERNATIONAL ORGANIZATIONS, and CONTROLLED CIRCULATION SERIALS, as well as the NEWSPAPERS section listing general-interest daily and weekly newspapers published in the United States.

International data inquiries are mailed annually to nearly 80,000 publishers to secure accurate and up-to-date information on current titles, new titles, title changes, and cessations. Updating of the database occurs daily using information received from publishers throughout the year and from serials research conducted in our editorial department. All post office returns are researched, and entries from publishers whose addresses cannot be verified are suspended from the file. Information about title changes, cessations, and new titles not received by the deadline for this edition will appear in **Ulrich's Update**, in the **Ulrich's Online** file as noted above, and **Ulrich's on Disc**™, the quarterly CD-ROM formerly known as Ulrich's *PLUS*. **Ulrich's Microfiche** was discontinued in 1997.

Your purchase and use of **Ulrich's** is complemented by some additional services. **Ulrich's Update**, provided free of charge, twice a year in March and July, is a supplemental service to the annual directory. The **Ulrich's Hotline** is a toll-free number that subscribers can call to get help in solving particular serials research problems and questions. Canadian users are asked to call a special number collect, and our overseas users are asked to use a designated fax number. (Please refer to page iv for our mailing address, telephone/fax numbers, and e-mail address.)

As we continue to research, plan, and implement enhancements to the **Ulrich's** database and our database maintenance system, we consider feedback from our users to be essential. Please contact us to let us know your thoughts. We want **Ulrich's** and its family of products to provide all necessary reference information quickly and effectively. Comments and suggestions are encouraged in order to help keep our directory of the highest quality. There are a wide variety of communication modes for you to select. You may write to us, send us a fax, call us on the telephone, or send us e-mail. Also, be sure to visit the R.R. Bowker Home Page on the World Wide Web at *www.bowker.com*. Look for a Home Page for **Ulrich's** in the future. Please refer to page iv for all contact information.

My sincere gratitude is extended to the entire staff of **Ulrich's** for their unflagging dedication and diligent work in updating and maintaining the serials database in preparation of the 36th edition of **Ulrich's**. Appreciation is also extended to all vendors and service suppliers for working with us to produce this directory. Finally, I would like to thank the various information specialists, serialists, national libraries, and serials publishers throughout the world who have aided us in updating **Ulrich's**. We consider their participation and interest in the dissemination of accurate and comprehensive serials information to be of tremendous value to **Ulrich's** and its users.

Judy Salk
Publisher and Editorial Director

User's Guide

This directory offers two primary access methods for locating periodicals: by subject in the CLASSIFIED LIST OF SERIALS (Volumes 1-3), and alphabetically in the TITLE INDEX (Volume 4). Ceased serials are listed in a separate CESSATIONS section (Volume 4) and are also accessible by means of the TITLE INDEX. Other indexes provide listings of selected periodicals in specific categories. These indexes, in Volume 5 unless otherwise noted, are REFEREED SERIALS, CONTROLLED CIRCULATION SERIALS, SERIALS AVAILABLE ON CD-ROM, PRODUCER LISTING/SERIALS ON CD-ROM, SERIALS AVAILABLE ONLINE, VENDOR LISTING/SERIALS ONLINE, PUBLICATIONS OF INTERNATIONAL ORGANIZATIONS, ISSN INDEX (Volume 4), and TITLE CHANGE INDEX (Volume 4). See the User's Guide in Volume 5 for a content description and use instructions for the U.S. NEWSPAPERS section.

In addition, separate subheadings for "Abstracting, Bibliographies and Statistics" under major subject headings provide convenient access to these types of publications. Page references for these subheadings are given in the "Subject Guide to Abstracting and Indexing" on p. xlv. This listing provides an overview of subjects for which abstracting and indexing publications have been identified.

The "User's Guide" is separated into three divisions for ease of use: (I) Section Descriptions, (II) Full Entry Content Description, and (III) Cataloging Rules for Main Entry Title.

Section Descriptions

CLASSIFIED LIST OF SERIALS

This is the main section of the book, containing bibliographic information for currently published serials classified by subject. Entries are arranged alphabetically by title within each subject heading. Subject cross-references in the text direct the user to the location of subheadings.

Volume 1 contains subjects A-D, from "Abstracting and Indexing" through "Drug Abuse and Alcoholism." Volume 2 contains subjects E-L, "Earth Sciences" through "Lumber and Wood." Volume 3 contains subjects M-Z, from "Machine Theory" through "Zoology."

A complete listing of the "Subjects" used in the CLASSIFIED LIST OF SERIALS appears on p. xlvi. To aid international users, this list is translated into four languages. For additional guidance on the subject classification scheme, the user should also consult the CROSS-INDEX TO SUBJECTS on p. 7351, which contains additional key word references.

Each serial is listed with full bibliographic information only once. If a serial covers several subjects, title cross-references appear under the related headings, directing the user to the heading where the full entry is listed.

New serials beginning publication in the past three years, as well as titles announced for publication in the coming year are highlighted by a ▼ in front of the title.

The "Cataloging Rules for Main Entry Title" section of this "User's Guide" explains the title cataloging rules followed in compiling **Ulrich's**.

CROSS-INDEX TO SUBJECTS

This index lists alphabetically all main subject headings in the **Ulrich's** Subject Heading File, as well as keyword references that direct users to main or subheadings where publications on those topics are likely to be found. The number following each subject term directs users to the page on which the subject begins within the CLASSIFIED LIST OF SERIALS.

A keyword may refer the user to more than one subject category. In this case, the subject references are listed in alphabetical order and are not necessarily listed in hierarchical order.

Main subject headings appear uppercased, e.g. AGRICULTURE. Subheadings contain the main subject term in uppercase and the specific subheading term in mixed case, e.g. AGRICULTURE—Agricultural Economics. The keywords, except for acronyms, are displayed entirely in mixed case.

CESSATIONS

In this section, entries for serials for which cessation was noted in the past three years are listed alphabetically by title. The cessation entry includes: title, Dewey Decimal

Classification number, former frequency of publication, publisher name and address, country-of-publication code, and, if available, other information such as ISSN, CODEN, LC number, subtitle, corporate author, year of first issue and year ceased. Titles which were originally planned as continuing series but which have closed are included in the CESSATIONS section although back issues may still be available.

If a title has "ceased" because a new title is being used, there will not be an entry in the CESSATIONS section. Instead, the entry is maintained in the CLASSIFIED LIST OF SERIALS under the new title, with a **"Formerly"** or **"Former titles"** indication.

ISSN INDEX

The ISSN INDEX lists serials in order by ISSN number. It includes all serials contained in the Bowker International Serials Database, whether current, ceased, or inactive, to which an ISSN has been assigned in our file. A dagger symbol (†) indicates that the title is ceased. If an ISSN appears twice, it usually indicates that the serial has split into two or more parts. Titles that have changed and for which new ISSNs have been assigned will show cross-references from one ISSN to the new ISSN. If no new ISSN has been assigned, the cross-reference is from ISSN to new title. Entries for inactive titles do not appear in the book.

Italicized type indicates the page number where a complete entry can be found for active titles. Titles for which cessation was noted in the last three years have a page reference to the listing in the CESSATIONS INDEX. If no page reference appears for a ceased title, it means that the cessation was noted more than three years ago and is not listed in this edition. ISSNs of inactive titles likewise do not have page references and are not listed in this book.

A full description of the ISSN and its use is provided on p. xviii.

TITLE INDEX

The TITLE INDEX is the second major access point for serials. To locate a serial by its title, the user should be familiar with title cataloging rules as described in the "Cataloging Rules for Main Entry Titles" paragraphs of this "User's Guide."

The TITLE INDEX lists all current and ceased serials included in this directory. **Boldface** type indicates the page number where the complete entry will be found; page numbers in roman type refer to related subject categories.

For serials with identical titles published within a country, the city of publication is added in parentheses, and sometimes the year of first publication is given to further distinguish the titles.

If a serial title consists of or contains an acronym, a cross-reference is provided from the full name to the acronym form of the title.

Cross-references are provided from former titles and variant titles, and from the alternate language titles of multi-language publications. Recent title changes are noted, with a reference to the current title. The TITLE INDEX also lists the country code for all serials, along with the ISSN, if known.

The ▼ used in the "Classified List of Serials" to indicate new serials also appears in this index, preceding the title. A (†) appears preceding the title if the publication has ceased.

TITLE CHANGE INDEX

The TITLE CHANGE INDEX lists former titles alphabetically with references to new titles. Page numbers indicate where bibliographic entries are listed in the CLASSIFIED LIST OF SERIALS. This index cumulates all title changes recorded in the **Ulrich's** database since the publication of the previous, or 35th, edition.

REFEREED SERIALS

This section is an alphabetical listing by title of all serials known to be refereed, or peer reviewed. It includes the publisher name, address, and telephone number, if known. The italicized number at the end of each entry is the page number where the full entry appears in the CLASSIFIED LIST OF SERIALS.

Omission of a title from this index does not mean that the journal is not peer-reviewed; nor does **Ulrich's** make any attempt to rate or judge the relative value of an individual journal's peer review process.

SERIALS AVAILABLE ON CD-ROM

This section is an alphabetical listing of all serials known to be available on CD-ROM, either in addition to hardcopy, or on CD-ROM only. It includes the publisher name, address, telephone and fax numbers, if known. It also includes the name of CD-ROM producers, when known. The italicized number at the end of each entry is the page number where the full entry appears in the CLASSIFIED LIST OF SERIALS.

PRODUCER LISTING/SERIALS ON CD-ROM

This section is an alphabetical listing of identified producers of serials on CD-ROM. Entries include the producer address, telephone and fax numbers, and an alphabetical listing of all serial titles known to be available. If known, the serial on CD-ROM product name is listed in parentheses after the serial title. All serials listed in this index also have full bibliographic entries in the CLASSIFIED LIST OF SERIALS. Consult the TITLE INDEX or the

SERIALS AVAILABLE ON CD-ROM listing for page numbers.

SERIALS AVAILABLE ONLINE

This section is an alphabetical listing of all serials known to be available online, either in addition to hardcopy, or online only. Entries include publisher name, address, telephone and fax numbers, plus names of online vendors and file names or numbers if known. Certain electronic journals may not have a physical mailing address listed. The number in parentheses at the end of each entry is the page number where the full entry appears in the CLASSIFIED LIST OF SERIALS.

VENDOR LISTING/SERIALS ONLINE

This section is an alphabetical listing of identified vendors of online periodicals. Entries include addresses, telephone and fax numbers for the vendor, and an alphabetical listing of all titles known to be available, with file names or numbers, if known. All serials listed in this index also have full bibliographic entries in the CLASSIFIED LIST OF SERIALS. Consult the TITLE INDEX or the SERIALS AVAILABLE ONLINE listing for page numbers.

INDEX TO PUBLICATIONS OF INTERNATIONAL ORGANIZATIONS

Complexity of corporate author structure, as well as title page variations in multilingual texts, compound the problems in cataloging publications of international organizations. This special index is provided so that the user may have one reference point for these titles. This index consists of four sections:

International Organizations
International Congress Proceedings
European Communities
United Nations

The index contains all current titles listed in the Bowker International Serials Database. The user must consult the CLASSIFIED LIST OF SERIALS for the full bibliographic information pertaining to these titles. Page references are provided.

CONTROLLED CIRCULATION SERIALS

This section is an alphabetical listing of all serials identified as having controlled circulations. It includes the publisher name and address, telephone and fax numbers, and circulation figure, if known. The italicized number at the end of each entry is a reference to the page on which the full entry appears in the CLASSIFIED LIST OF SERIALS.

Full Entry Content Description

Basic Information
The following elements are mandatory for listing and appear in all entries: main entry title, frequency of publication, publisher address, country code, and Dewey Decimal Classification number.

Certain electronic journals may not have a physical mailing address; the URL and/or E-mail address provide a means of contacting the publication.

Dewey Decimal Classification Number
The Dewey Decimal number is printed at the top left of each entry. More than one Dewey number may have been assigned if a serial covers several subjects.

LC Classification Number
The Library of Congress classification number, if known, appears directly below the Dewey Decimal number. Shelf numbers are not included.

Country Code
The Country Code is printed at the top right of each entry following the Dewey Decimal number. A complete list of country codes used will be found on p. xxii.

ISSN
The ISSN for the main entry title is printed immediately following the country code. Not all publications have been assigned an ISSN, and lack of a number does not render a publication ineligible for listing.

CODEN
The CODEN designation, if known, is printed directly below the country code and ISSN. The CODEN is an alphanumeric code, applied uniquely to a specific publication. Devised by the American Society for Testing and Materials, it is used primarily for scientific and technical titles. New CODEN are assigned by Chemical Abstracts Service.

Title Information
The main title is printed in **boldface** and upper case as the first item in the entry. Titles are catalogued according to rules described below in the "Cataloging Rules for Main Entry Title" section. For multi-language publications, the parallel language title is also printed in upper case, immediately following the main entry title, and is separated from it by a slash.

A ▼ printed before the title indicates that the title began publishing within the past three years. This symbol also appears before titles announced for publication in the coming year.

An asterisk (*) printed after the title indicates that the information in the entry was not verified by the publisher for this edition.

xii USER'S GUIDE

The subtitle is printed in lower case after the title.

Variant titles or translated edition titles are given within the entry and are labeled as such.

Former titles are given at the end of the entry, along with publication dates if known. If a former title also had an ISSN, the ISSN is listed in parentheses after the former title. Many entries contain extensive former title information, providing a history of changes which may be useful for bibliographic record-keeping.

The Key Title, which is assigned at the time of ISSN assignment by the responsible center of the International Serials Data System, is given only if it is different from the main entry title.

Year First Published
The year first published is given if provided by the publisher. If information is lacking, a volume number and specific year may be provided to indicate the approximate age of the publication.

Frequency
The frequency of publication is given in abbreviated form, such as "a." for annual, "irreg." for irregular, "m." for monthly, "3/yr." for three times per year. All abbreviations used are listed in the "General Abbreviations" on p. xx.

Price
Unless otherwise indicated, the price given is the annual price for an individual subscription in the currency of the

---

SAMPLE ENTRY

[1] 930.198 490.996   **[2]** US   **[3]** ISSN 1055-7644
[4] DZ991   **[5]** CODEN: JAAPL9
[6] JOURNAL OF ANARCTIC ARCHEOLOGY AND PROTOLINGUISTICS;   **[7]** international communications and research.   **[8]** (Supplement avail.)   **[9]** (Test in English, French, Polynesian languages)   **[10]** 1927.   **[11]** 2/yr.   **[12]** $39 to individuals; institutions $99 (includes supplement) (effective 1998); newsstand price: $20   **[13]** (Societe d'Archaeologie et de Linguistique Pacifiques-Society of Pacific Archaeology and Linguistics)   **[14]** W.A. Translations (Subsidiary of: Temporary Culture),   **[15]** Box 43072, Upper Montclair, NJ 07043-7072.   **[16]** TEL 908-665-2869.
[17] FAX 508-555-0010.   **[18]** TELEX 123458.   **[19]** E-mail:antarchaeol@miskaton.edu; URL http://www.miskaton.edu/.   **[20]** (Subscr. to: Department of Archaeology and Proto-Linguistics, 7 Old College Walk, Arkham, MA 01901-1011. TEL 508-555-0110. FAX 508-555-4112;
[21] Dist. in Europe by: Editions d'Erlette, Ch. de Kerangat, 56120 Plumelec, France. TEL 33-76-63-94. FAX 33-76-205).   **[22]** (Co-sponsor: Miskatonic University, Department of Archaeology and Proto-Linguistics)
[23] Eds. A.H. Whateley, J.M. Snyrnat;   **[24]** Pub. M.J. Smith.   **[25]** R&P contact: J.M. Snymat. TEL 508-555-0011.   **[26]** adv.: B&W page $400; trim 8-1/8x10;   **[27]** adv. contact: Arthur Dunwich.
[28] bk.rev; abstr; bibl.; illus., index;   **[29]** circ. 500 (paid); 500 (controlled).   **[30]** (also avail. in microform from SWZ, UMI; also avail. on diskette; back issues avail.; reprint service avail. from SWZ, UMI).
[31] **Indexed:** Abstr. Anthropol, Br.Archaeol.Abstr.   **[32]** (1991—), Onoma (1986—), Ref. Zh.
[33] **Document type:** academic/scholarly publication.
[34] •Also available online   **[35]** Vendor(s): UTOPIA (Miskatonic).
[36] Also available on CD-ROM.   **[37]** Producer(s): TEMPCULT (Miskatonic).
[38] –BLDSC (9999.000000); CIS   **[39]** CCC.
[40] **Supersedes (in 1986):** Miskatonic Annals of Antarctic Archaeology and Extraterrestrial Linguistics
[41] (ISSN 0055-1298).
[42] **Description:** Publishes archaeologic field research on prehistoric civilizations in the Pacific Islands and Antarctica, with relevant contributions discussing worldwide linguistic evidence of contacts among civilizations.
[43] *Refereed Serial*

KEY

[1] Dewey Decimal Classification
[2] Country Code
[3] ISSN
[4] LC Classification
[5] CODEN
[6] Main Entry Title
[7] Subtitle
[8] Bibliographic Note
[9] Language
[10] First Published
[11] Frequency
[12] Price
[13] Corporate Author
[14] Publishing Company
[15] Address
[16] Telephone
[17] Fax
[18] Telex
[19] E-mail; URL
[20] Subscription Address, Tel & Fax
[21] Distributor Address, Tel & Fax
[22] Co-sponsor
[23] Editor
[24] Publisher
[25] Rights & Permissions Contact, Telephone
[26] Advertising Rate
[27] Advertising Contact
[28] Special Features
[29] Circulation
[30] Format
[31] Indexed
[32] Years of Coverage
[33] Document Type
[34] Online Availability
[35] Online Vendor/File Name
[36] CD-ROM Availability
[37] CD-ROM Producer(s)
[38] Document Suppliers
[39] Copyright Clearance Center Registration Notation
[40] Title Changes
[41] Former ISSN
[42] Brief Description
[43] Refereed

country of origin. The price in U.S. dollars may also be given in parentheses if it is provided by the publisher. No attempt is made to convert foreign currency to U.S. dollars. Separate postage information is not given, since postal rates vary widely.

Publishing Company Information
Many serials are editorially controlled by a sponsoring organization or corporate author and published by a commercial publisher. In these instances, the commercial publishing company's name and address are given, and the name of the corporate author is given in parentheses immediately preceding. In other instances, either a sponsoring organization or a commercial publishing company has sole responsibility, and only one name is given. We avoid listing printers as publishing companies, preferring the name and address of someone with editorial responsibility. For the same reason, we avoid listing distributors as publishing companies.

If no publishing company name is given, it is assumed that the publishing company name is the same as the title.

Telephone, Fax, Telex Numbers, E-mail, and Web Site Addresses
Telephone, fax, telex numbers and e-mail as well as web site addresses (URLs) are given when provided by the publisher. U.S. and Canadian numbers are given in standard North American format. Toll-free numbers within U.S. and Canada are also included, when available. Numbers in other countries are provided in the same format as supplied by the publisher, resulting in some inconsistencies (e.g. sometimes with a country and/or city code, sometimes without). Users are advised to consult an international operator before placing calls.

Subscription or Distribution Address
A second address is given only if the address for ordering subscriptions is different from the publishing company's address. Distributors are listed only if we have been informed that a particular organization is the exclusive distributor. Additional subscription and/or distribution offices of international publishers are listed, if known. Telephone and fax numbers for subscription and/or distribution offices appear if provided by the publisher.

Editor
Only one or two names are given when known, preceded by the notation "Ed." or "Eds." Advanced degrees and titles are omitted, except for medical, military and religious titles; absence of a title does not mean that the editor has none. The abbreviation "Ed.Bd." indicates editorship by three or more persons.

Publisher
Only one or two names are given when known, preceded by the notation "Pub." or "Pubs." Advanced degrees and titles are omitted, except for medical, military and religious titles; absence of a title does not mean that the publisher has none.

If the publisher is also the editor, and no publishing company name is available, the person's name is given with the notation "Ed. & Pub."

Rights and Permissions Contact
A name is given when supplied, preceded by the notation "R&P contact". The telephone number information follows, when known and different from the main number.

Advertising Rates and Contact
When provided by the publisher, the name of the advertising contact, as well as full-page advertising rates and trim size are indicated. Most dimensions are listed in millimeters, except for U.S. publications, the dimensions of which are usually in inches.

Special Features
A listing of special features may include such items as book or other types of reviews, advertising (usually meaning commercial, not classified advertising), charts, illustrations, bibliography section, article abstracts, and an annual index to the periodical's contents.

Reprint Services
If a serial is known to be available from a reprint service, a code referring to the service appears in the entry. More than one code may be listed. For a list of reprint services and a translation of the codes, please refer to p. xxx.

Circulation
All circulation figures used are approximate. Circulation is given only if provided by the publisher. The notation "controlled" indicates that the publication is available only to the qualified persons, usually members of a particular trade or profession.

Format
Formats other than standard magazine format are noted in parentheses. Other formats may be looseleaf, duplicated (mimeographed), tabloid. If a publication is available in microform, a notation is made which includes a three-letter code for the vendor, if known. A list of names, addresses, telephone and fax numbers of micropublishers begins on p. xxvi.

Abstracting and Indexing
The notation **"Indexed:"** precedes a list of abbreviations for all abstracting and indexing services known to cover the serial on a regular basis. Years of coverage immediately follow each abstracting and indexing service code, if known. The complete names of the abstracting and indexing services are listed with their abbreviations on p. xxxii. All currently published abstracting and indexing services are also listed as entries in the CLASSIFIED LIST OF SERIALS.

USER'S GUIDE

Document Type
Notations are included to indicate type of publication, e.g. trade publication, newsletter, or abstracting/indexing. The words "**Document type:**" appear in boldface, followed by the document type description, in entries where this information is known. More than one document type may be listed for a single publication, if applicable.

Online Availability and CD-ROM Availability
If a serial is known to be available in a full-text online format and/or on CD-ROM, a bullet symbol (●) precedes the information. Online and CD-ROM availability are noted whether they exist in addition to hardcopy or in one or both formats exclusively. Online vendors and CD-ROM producers are also listed, if known.

For a listing of serials available online, consult the SERIALS AVAILABLE ONLINE index on p. 10037. Complete names and addresses of vendors, with a listing of serials known to be available through them, are in a separate index, VENDOR LISTING/SERIALS ONLINE on p. 10229.

For a listing of serials available on CD-ROM, consult the SERIALS AVAILABLE ON CD-ROM index on p. 9973. Complete names and addresses of producers, with a list of CD-ROMs known to be available through them, are in a separate index, PRODUCER LISTING/SERIALS ON CD-ROM on p. 10033.

Document Suppliers
The **Ulrich's** database and the individual databases of the following document suppliers were matched on the presence of ISSNs. When a match was successful, the appropriate document supplier code was noted. Not all serials titles in general, or in these individual databases, have ISSNs. Therefore, the absence of one or any document supplier code in an **Ulrich's** listing does not necessarily mean the title is unavailable from one or any of these suppliers.

ADONIS™
The notation, ADONIS, appearing in a serial entry indicates the availability of that serial for document delivery through ADONIS's service, by permission from the copyright owner. Such permission is subject to change without notice.

For further information, contact: ADONIS B.V., Spuistraat 112D, 1012VA Amsterdam, The Netherlands; tel: 31-20-6262629, fax: 31-20-6261437; ADONIS USA, 350 Main St., 6th fl., Malden, MA 02148-5018, USA; tel: 800-944-6415; fax: 617-876-7022; e-mail: infousa@adonis.nl; URL: http://www.adonis.nl.

Ask*IEEE
The notation, AskIEEE, appearing in a serial entry indicates that photocopies of articles from that serial are available through IEEE's document delivery service, Ask*IEEE.

For further information, contact Ask*IEEE, 75 Varick St., 9th fl., New York, NY 10013, USA; tel: 800-949-4333 (outside US & Canada: 212-301-4100); fax: 212-301-4090; e-mail: askieee@ieee.org.

British Library Document Supply Centre
The notation, BLDSC, appearing in a serial entry indicates the availability of that serial for document delivery from the British Library Document Supply Centre, by permission from the copyright owner. The BLDSC shelfmark number, a unique identifier of each serial, is preceded by an em-dash (—) which is followed by the notation "BLDSC (0000.000000)." The format of the shelfmark is four digits, a decimal point, then six digits.

For further information about BLDSC's services, contact: Customer Services, BLDSC, Boston Spa, Wetherby, LS23 7BQ, UK; tel: 44-1937-546060; fax: 44-1937-546333; e-mail: dsc-customer-services@bl.uk.

Chemical Abstracts Service
The notation, CASDDS, appearing in a serial entry indicates the availability of that serial for document delivery through Chemical Abstracts Service Document Detective Service.

For further information, contact CAS Client Services, Document Detective Service, 2540 Olentangy River Rd., P.O. Box 3012, Columbus, OH 43210-0012, USA; tel: 800-631-1884, 614-447-3870; fax: 614-447-3648; e-mail: dds@cas.org; URL: http://www.cas.org/Support/dds.html.

CINDOC
The notation, CINDOC, appearing in a serial entry indicates the availability of that serial for document delivery through CINDOC Suminstro de Documentos Service.

For further information, contact Document Delivery Service CINDOC (Servico de Suministro de Suministro de Documentos), Joaquín Costa, 22, 28002 Madrid, Spain; fax: 34-1-5642644; e-mail: bib-icyt@bib.csic.es.

CISTI
The notation, CISTI, appearing in a serial entry indicates the availability of that serial for document delivery from the Canada Institute for Scientific and Technical Information, by permission from the copyright owner. Such permission is subject to change without notice.

For further information, contact: Client Assistant, Document Delivery, CISTI, National Research Council Canada, Ottawa K1A 0S2, Canada; tel: 800-668-1222 (Canada & US) or 613-993-9251; fax: 613-993-7619; e-mail: cisti.docdel@nrc.ca.

Congressional Information Service, Inc.
The notation, CIS, appearing in a serial entry indicates the availability of that serial for document delivery through CIS

Documents on Demand Service, by permission from the copyright owner. Such permission is subject to change without notice.

For further information, contact Congressional Information Service, Inc., 4520 East-West Hwy., Ste. 800, Bethesda, MD 20814-3389, USA; tel: 301-654-1550, 800-227-2477; fax: 301-654-4033; e-mail: EAINET@US.NET; URL: http://www.cispubs.com.

EMDOCS

The notation, EMDOCS, appearing in a serial entry indicates the availability of that serial for document delivery through EMDOCS: The EMBASE Document Delivery Service, by permission from the copyright owner. Such permission is subject to change without notice.

For further information, contact EMDOCS, 75 Varick St., 9th fl., New York, NY 10013, USA; tel: 800-282-2720 or 212-301-4003; fax: 212-301-4060; e-mail: dds@work4u.artx.com.

Engineering Information Inc.

The notation, Ei, appearing in a serial entry indicates the availability of that serial for document delivery through Ei Text, the Ei Document Delivery Service, by permission from the copyright owner. Such permission is subject to change without notice.

For further information, contact Ei Text, One Castle Point Terrace, Hoboken, NJ 07030-5996, USA; tel: 800-221-1044 (USA & Canada), 201-216-8500; fax: 201-216-8557; e-mail: eitext@ei.org; URL: http://www.ei.org.

The Genuine Article

The notation, Genuine Article, appearing in a serial entry indicates the availability of that serial for document delivery through The Institute for Scientific Information's Document Solution, by permission from the copyright owner. Such permission is subject to change without notice.

For further information, contact ISI Document Solution, 3501 Market Street, Philadelphia, PA 19104, USA; tel: 215-386-4399; fax: 215-386-4343; e-mail: tga@isinet.com.

Haworth Document Delivery Service

The notation, Haworth, appearing in a serial entry indicates the availability of that serial for document delivery through The Haworth Press's Document Delivery Service. This service is available for all Haworth journals. As the copyright holder, there will be no permission fee, but other fees are applicable.

For further information, contact Haworth Document Delivery Service, 10 Alice Street, Binghamton, NY 13904-1580, USA; tel: 800-HAWORTH; fax: 800-895-0582; e-mail: getinfo@haworth.com.

KR SourceOne

The notation, KR SourceOne, appearing in a serial entry indicates the availability of that serial for document delivery through KR SourceOne. Copyright compliance is ensured through KR SourceOne's agreements with the Copyright Clearance Center.

For further information, contact KR SourceOne, 75 Varick St., 9th fl., New York, NY 10013, USA; tel: 800-239-3458 (outside US & Canada: 212-301-4000); fax: 212-301-4060; e-mail: dds@work4u.artx.com; URL: http://www.krinfo.com/krsourceone/.

Library KNAW

The notation, KNAW, appearing in a serial entry indicates the availability of that serial for document delivery through the NIWI (Netherlands Institute of Scientific Information Services). In addition, NIWI offers free access to Medline.

For further information, contact Library NIWI Customer Service, P.O. Box 95180, 1090 HD Amsterdam, The Netherlands; tel: 31-20-4628628; fax: 31-20-6639257; e-mail: info@niwi.knaw.nl; URL: http:// www.niwi.knaw.nl.

Linda Hall

The notation, Linda Hall, appearing in a serial entry indicates the availability of that serial for document delivery from Linda Hall Library of Science, Engineering and Technology.

For further information, contact: Document Services, Linda Hall Library, 5109 Cherry St., Kansas City, MO 64110-2498; tel: 800-662-1545, or 816-363-4600; fax: 816-926-8785; e-mail: requests@lhl.lib.mo.us; URL: http://www.lhl.lib.mo.us.

Petroleum Abstracts - Document Delivery Service (PADDS)

The notation, PADDS, appearing in a serial entry indicates the availability of that serial for document delivery through PADDS document delivery service, by permission from the copyright owner. Such permission is subject to change without notice.

For further information, contact Petroleum Abstracts - Document Delivery Service, University of Tulsa, McFarlin Library, 2933 E. 6th Street, Tulsa, OK 74104-3123, USA; tel: 800-247-8678; fax: 918-631-3823; e-mail: PADDS@TUred.pa.utulsa.edu.

SWETS

The notation, SWETS, appearing in a serial entry indicates the availability of that serial's table of contents in SwetScan, and document delivery through Swets, by permission from the copyright owner. Such permission is subject to change without notice.

For further information, contact Swets & Zeitlinger BV, Heereweg 347B, P.O. Box 830, 2160 SZ Lisse, The Netherlands; tel: 31-252-435111; fax: 31-252-415888; telex: 41325; e-mail: infoho@swets.nl; URL: http://www.swets.nl.

UMI

The notation, UMI, appearing in a serial entry indicates the availability of that serial for document delivery through UMI InfoStore service, by permission from the copyright owner. Such permission is subject to change without notice.

For further information, contact UMI InfoStore, 300 N. Zeeb Rd., P.O. Box 1346, Ann Arbor, MI 48106-1346, USA; tel: 800-248-0360 (US & Canada), fax: 313-761-1032; e-mail: orders@infostore.com.

The UnCover Company

The notation, UnCover, appearing in a serial entry indicates that the material is indexed in the UnCover database. Copies of articles are available through Uncover's document delivery service if the copyright owner has granted permission. Such permission is subject to change without notice.

For further information, contact the UnCover Co., 3801 E. Florida Ave., Ste. 200, Denver, CO 80210, USA; tel: 800-787-7979 (outside US & Canada: 303-758-3030); fax: 303-758-5946; e-mail: uncover@carl.org; URL: http://www.uncweb.carl.org.

Copyright Clearance Center, Inc.

The Copyright Clearance Center, Inc. (CCC) is a not-for-profit collective licensing organization. The CCC grants permissions to institutions and individuals to photocopy works of its registered publishers upon payment of publisher set royalties. The CCC does not supply copies of registered works directly to anyone.

The boldfaced **CCC** notation appears in the entries of titles for which the CCC has been authorized by the publisher to grant photocopy permissions through its Transactional Reporting Service (TRS). Additional titles may be available for certain publishers who have authorized the CCC to grant photocopy permissions on any of their works. The same inclusive country-wide coverage is available for publishers in the following countries: Canada, the Commonwealth of Independent States, Germany, New Zealand, Norway, and Spain. To register with the CCC, please contact TRS Customer Service, 222 Rosewood Dr., Danvers, MA 01923, USA; tel: 508-750-8400; fax: 508-750-4470; URL: http://www.copyright.com/

Brief Description

A brief description of the contents and editorial focus of the publication may be provided, preceded by the word **"Description:"** at the end of the entry. These descriptions were submitted by the publisher or were written by editorial staff after examination of sample copies or publisher catalogs.

Refereed Serial

The manuscript peer review and evaluation system is utilized to protect, maintain and raise the quality of scholarly material published in serials. If a serial is known to be refereed or juried, the notation "*Refereed Serial*" appears in italics at the end of the entry. This information is generally provided by the serial publisher.

Newspaper-Specific Data Elements

Ownership

The name of the owner(s) of a newspaper is listed, usually accompanied by the owner(s) address, and telephone and fax numbers. The owner address may differ from the newspaper location address. Owner information is preceded by the notation "Owner(s):."

Wire Services

If a newspaper is known to use one or more news or photo wire services, abbreviations or names of the services used are listed in the entry. Such information is preceded by the words "Wire Service(s):." Abbreviations for wire services used are listed on page xxxi of this volume.

Pages Per Issue; Columns Per Page

When known, the number of pages per issue (pp./issue:) and/or columns per page (cols./p.:) is/are noted.

Cataloging Rules for Main Entry Title

The majority of titles in the Bowker International Serials Database were cataloged according to *Anglo-American Cataloging Rules* prior to 1978, the date of the new edition of *Anglo-American Cataloging Rules*. The new *AACR II* reflects a trend toward the Key Title concept of cataloging as used by the International Serials Data System (ISDS) and published in its *International Standard Bibliographic Description for Serials* (1974).

Because recataloging a database the size of Bowker's was not feasible, our cataloging rules were modified but not radically changed. Cross-references are provided in the TITLE INDEX from variant forms of title, such as Key Title, to aid users searching by other methods.

Whenever possible, main entry title cataloging is done from a sample of the title page of the most recent issue, according to the following rules:

Articles at the beginning of titles are omitted, or are bypassed in filing.

Serials with distinctive titles are usually entered under title. For example:

Annual Bulletin of Historical Literature
Business Week
Milton Studies

If a title consists only of a generic term followed by the name of the issuing body, or if the name of the issuing body clarifies the content of the publication, entry is under the name of the issuing body. For example:

Newsletter of the American Theological Library Association

is entered as

American Theological Library Association. Newsletter

Economic Performance and Prospects, issued by the Private Development Corporation of the Philippines

is entered as

Private Development Corporation of the Philippines. Economic Performance and Prospects

A title which consists of a subject modified generic term followed by the name of the issuing body is considered nondistinctive and is entered under the name of the issuing body. For example:

Annual Meeting Scientific Proceedings of the American Animal Hospital Association

is entered as

American Animal Hospital Association. Annual Meeting Scientific Proceedings

Government publications with nondistinctive titles are entered under the name of the government jurisdiction of the issuing body, although distinctive titles of government organizations may be entered directly under title. For example:

Great Britain. Economic and Social Research Council. Annual Report

but

Statistical Abstract of Iceland

Titles which begin with the initials of the issuing body are entered under the initials. Cross-references from the full name are provided in the TITLE INDEX.

If a geographic name is part of the name of the issuing body, entry will be under the common form of the name of the body. For example:

University of the West Indies. Vice-Chancellor's Report

not

West Indies. University. Vice-Chancellor's Report

Note, however, that government publications retain similar cataloging as government jurisdiction.

Canada. Statistics Canada. Field Crop Reporting Series

Multilingual titles are entered under the first title given on the title page, or the first title reported by the publisher if the title page is not available. Titles in other languages are entered directly after the main entry title. Cross-references are provided in the TITLE INDEX for each language title.

FILING RULES

Due to the restrictions imposed by computer filing of titles, the following special filing rules should be noted.

Articles and prepositions within titles are alphabetized as words:

Journal of the West

precedes

Journal of Theological Studies

Hyphenated words are treated as separate words:

Pre-Text

precedes

Preaching

However, words indicating compass points (northeast, southwest, etc.) are filed as one word regardless of how printed:

Southeast Asia Builder
South-East Asia Stamp Catalogue
Southeast Dragster
South East Magazine

Titles entered under corporate author or government jurisdiction are sequenced before distinctive titles that begin with the same words:

British Columbia. Ministry of Energy, Mines and Petroleum Resources. Mineral Market Update

precedes

British Columbia Catholic

Acronyms and initials are treated as such and are listed at the beginning of each letter of the alphabet. Exceptions are the abbreviations of U.N. (United Nations), U.S. (United States), Gt. Britain (Great Britain), and St. (Saint), which are filed as words:

U R A M Newsletter
United Mutual Fund Sector
U.S. Environmental Protection Agency. Clean Water: Report to Congress

Titles in excess of 36 characters which are identical may not sort sequentially. The editors suggest that users scan the entire sequence of identical titles to locate specific entries.

Diacritical marks have been omitted. The German and Scandinavian umlaut has been replaced by the letter "e" following the vowels a, e, o, and u. In Danish, Norwegian and Swedish, the letter å is sequenced as "aa" and the letter ø as "oe."

International Standard Serial Number (ISSN)

1. What is the ISSN?

An internationally accepted, concise, unique, and unambiguous code for the identification of serial publications. One ISSN represents one serial title.

The ISSN consists of seven numbers with an eighth check digit calculated according to Modulus 11 and used to verify the number in computer processing. A hyphen is printed after the fourth digit, as a visual aid, and the acronym, ISSN, precedes the number.

2. How did the ISSN evolve as an international system?

The International Organization for Standardization Technical Committee 46 (ISO/TC 46) is the agency responsible for the development of the ISSN as an international standard. The organization responsible for the administration and coordination of ISSN assignments worldwide is the ISSN International Centre in Paris, which is supported by the French government and UNESCO.

ISSNs are assigned by over 50 national centers worldwide. The National Serials Data Program (NSDP) is the U.S. national center. The centers form a network which is coordinated by the ISSN International Centre located in Paris.

The implementation of the ISSN system started with the numbering of 70,000 titles in the serials database of R.R. Bowker (*Ulrich's International Periodicals Directory* and *Irregular Serials and Annuals*). The next serials database numbering was the *New Serials Titles 1950-70* cumulation listing 220,000 titles, cumulated, converted to magnetic tape, and published by R.R. Bowker in collaboration with the Serials Record Division of the Library of Congress. These two databases were used as the starting base for the implementation of the ISSN.

3. What types of publications are assigned ISSNs?

For assignment of an ISSN, a serial is defined as a publication in print or non-print form, issued in successive parts, usually having numerical or chronological designations, and intended to be continued indefinitely.

4. How is the ISSN used?

The ISSN is employed as a component of bar codes and as a tool for the communication of basic information about a serial title and for such processes as ordering, billing, inventory control, abstracting, and indexing. In library processes, the ISSN is used in operations such acquisitions, claiming, binding, accessioning, shelving, cooperative cataloguing, circulation, interlibrary loans, and retrieval of requests.

5. May a publication have an International Standard Book Number (ISBN) and an ISSN?

Yes! Monographic series (separate works issued indefinitely under a common title, generally in a uniform format with numeric designations) and annuals or titles planned to be issued indefinitely under the same title may be defined as serials. The ISSN is assigned to the serial title, while an ISBN is assigned to each individual title or monograph in the series.

A new ISBN is assigned to each volume or edition by the publisher, while the ISSN, which is assigned by the ISSN International Centre or national ISSN centers, remains the same for each issue. Both numbers should be printed on the copyright page or other appropriate page of each volume, with their acronyms or words preceding each number for immediate identification. With the availability of both an ISSN and ISBN, the problem of defining the overlap of serials and monographs has been resolved.

INTERNATIONAL STANDARD SERIAL NUMBER   xix

SAMPLE TITLE

Advances in the Biosciences
ISSN 0065-3446

Vol. 1 Proceedings: Berlin. Schering Symposium of Endocrinology, Berlin. Ed. by Gerhard Raspe. 1969. 40.00 (ISBN 0-08-013395-9). Pergamon.

Vol. 2 Proceedings. Schering Symposium on Biodynamics & Mechanisms of Action of Steroid Hormones, Berlin. Ed. by Gerhard Raspe. 1969. 41.25 (ISBN 0-08-006942-8). Pergamon.

Vol. 3 Proceedings. Schering Workshop on Steroid Metabolism "in Vitro Versus in Vivo," Berlin. Ed. by Gerhard Raspe. 1969. 41.25 (ISBN 0-08-017544-9). Pergamon.

Vol. 4 Proceedings. Schering Symposium on Mechanisms Involved in Conception. Berlin. Ed. by Gerhard Raspe. 1970. text ed. 41.25 (ISBN 0-08-017546-5). Pergamon.

Vol. 25 Development of Responsiveness to Steroid Hormones. Alvin M. Kaye & Myra Kaye et al. LC 79-42938. 1980. 66.00 (ISBN 0-08-024949-X). Pergamon.

6. Where should the ISSN appear on the serial?

In a prominent position on or in each issue of the serial, such as the front cover, back cover, masthead, title, or copyright pages. The international standard recommendation is that the ISSN of a periodical be printed, whenever possible, in the upper right corner of the front cover.

Promotional and descriptive materials about the serial should include the ISSN.

7. When a title changes, is a new ISSN assigned?

In most instances, a new ISSN is assigned when a title changes. However, the determination is made by the ISSN International Centre or the appropriate national ISSN centers. Publishers should report all the title changes to their respective centers.

8. How does a publisher apply for an ISSN?

The publisher should contact the appropriate national ISSN center or the ISSN International Centre. Centers require bibliographic evidence of a serial, including a copy of the title page and cover. There is no charge to publishers for the assignment of ISSNs.

For full information, publishers should contact the national library or bibliographic center in the country where they are publishing. The address of the ISSN International Centre is:

ISSN International Centre
20, rue Bachaumont
75002 Paris
France
Tel: +33 (1) 44 88 22 20
Fax: +33 (1) 40 26 32 43
Telex: 219847F
E-mail: issnic@issn.org
URL: http://www.issn.org

The address for the U.S. national ISSN center is:

National Serials Data Program (NSDP)
Library of Congress
Washington, DC 20540-4160
Tel: 202-707-6452
Fax: 202-707-6333
E-mail: ISSN@loc.gov
URL: http://lcweb.loc.gov/issn/

9. What is SISAC?

SISAC stands for the Serials Industry Systems Advisory Committee. SISAC is an industry group formed to develop voluntary standardized formats for electronically transmitting serials business transaction information. SISAC provides a forum where serial (particularly journal) publishers, library system vendors, and librarians can discuss mutual concerns regarding the electronic transmission of serial information and develop cooperative solutions, in the form of standardized formats, to efficiently address these concerns. *(Reprinted with permission from SISAC.)*

10. What is the SISAC Symbol (SICI) and its relationship to the ISSN?

The Serial Item and Contribution Identifier (SICI) is a serial identification code which follows the ISSN and is a string of letters and/or numbers which uniquely identify a particular issue of a serial. Encoded in the SICI are chronological and enumeration data which identify serials by date and volume/issue numbers. According to SISAC, "the ANSI* standard extends the code down to the article level by adding location number and necessary title information, plus a record validation character. Code 128 is the bar code symbology selected by SISAC for displaying this number string in scannable form. When displayed in the Code 128 symbology, the SICI is called the SISAC symbol." The SICI is the ANSI standard; the SISAC symbol is the bar code. *(Reprinted with permission from SISAC.)*

*ANSI American National Standards Institute. Organization that coordinates the voluntary standards system in the United States. U.S. member of the International Standards Organization (ISO).

Abbreviations

General Abbreviations and Special Symbols

a.	annual	no.	number
abstr.	abstracts	pat.	patents
adv.	advertising	play rev.	play reviews (theater reviews)
approx.	approximately	pp./issue	pages per issue
avail.	available	Prof.	Professor
bi-m.	bimonthly (every two months)	Pub., Pubs.	Publisher, Publishers
bi-w.	biweekly (every two weeks)	q.	quarterly
bibl.	bibliographies	R&P	Rights & Permissions
bk.rev.	book reviews	rec.rev.	record reviews
CCC	Copyright Clearance Center	s-a.	semiannually (twice annually)
c/o	care of	s-m.	semimonthly (twice monthly)
circ.	circulation	s-w.	semiweekly (twice weekly)
cols./p.	columns per page	stat.	statistics
cum.index	cumulative index	subscr.	subscription
Cy.	county	tele.rev.	television reviews
d.	daily	3/m.	3 times a month
dance rev.	dance reviews	3/yr.	3 times a year
Dir.	Director	tr.lit.	trade literature (manufacturers' catalogues, reader response cards)
dist.	distributed		
Ed., Eds.	Editor, Editors	tr.mk.	trade marks
Ed.Bd.	Editorial Board	URL	Uniform Resource Locator
film rev.	film reviews	video rev.	video reviews
fortn.	fortnightly (every two weeks)	vol.	volume
ISSN	International Standard Serial Number	w.	weekly
illus.	illustrations	*	not updated / unverified
irreg.	irregular	●	online and / or CD-ROM availability
m.	monthly	▼	new serial
mkt.	market prices	†	ceased
music rev.	music reviews		
N.S.	New Series		

Money Symbols

SYMBOL	UNIT	COUNTRY
	afghani	Afghanistan
..$	peso	Argentina
..$	dollar	Australia
	baht	Thailand
	dollar	Belize, Bermuda, Brunei Darussalam
F	franc	Belgium
	balboa	Panama
.$	peso	Bolivia
	birr	Ethiopia
	bolivar	Venezuela
	bonus do tesouro nacional	Brazil
NF	bonus do tesouro nacional fiscal	Brazil
	cordoba; dollar; peso	Nicaragua, Cayman Islands, Cuba
n.$	dollar	Canada
PF	franc	New Caledonia
$	peso	Chile
	colon	Costa Rica, El Salvador
.$	peso	Colombia
$	cruzerio	Brazil
$	cruzado	Brazil
	dalasi	Gambia
, Dh.	dirham	Morocco, United Arab Emirates
K	krone	Denmark
	mark	Germany
	dinar	Algeria, Jordan, Kuwait, Libya, Tunisia, Yugoslavia
	dollar; peso	various
	drachma	Greece
	emalageni	Swaziland
s.	shilling	East Africa, Somalia, Tanzania, Uganda
$.	dollar	Dominica, Grenada, St. Lucia, Eastern Caribbean
J	European currency unit	European Communities/European Union
K	kroon	Estonia
	escudo	Angola, Cape Verde, Mozambique, Portugal
	franc	Djibouti, France, Guadeloupe, Mali, Martinique, Monaco, Rwanda
	dollar	Fiji
	markka	Finland
	guilder; florin	Netherlands, Netherlands Antilles, Surinam
	franc	Malagasy Republic
	mark; markka	Finland
	franc	Belgium, Liechtenstein, Luxembourg, Switzerland
FA	franc	African Financial Community, Benin, Burkina Faso, Burundi, Cameroon, Central African Republic, Chad, Congo, Gabon, Ivory Coast, Niger, Reunion, Senegal, Togo
	forint	Hungary
	guarani	Paraguay
	gourde	Haiti
	franc	Guinea
	dollar	Guyana
	dollar	Hong Kong
	kuna	Croatia
	pound	Ireland
	dinar	Iran, Iraq
	riyal	Iran
	shekel	Israel
	krona	Iceland
	dollar	Jamaica
.$	dollar	Jamaica

SYMBOL	UNIT	COUNTRY
K.	kina; kwacha; kyat	Malawi, Papua New Guinea, Union of Myanmar (Burma), Zambia
Kc.	koruna	Czech Republic
Kcs.	koruny	Czechoslovakia
kip	kip	Laos
Kr.	krona; krone	Scandinavian countries
KShs.	shilling	Kenya
L.	lempira; lira	Honduras, Italy
Le.	leone	Sierra Leone
lek	lek	Albania
lei	lei	Rumania
Lit.	lira italiana	Italy
Ls.	lats	Latvia
Lt.	litas	Lithuania
lv.	lev	Bulgaria
M.$	dollar; ringgit	Malaysia
Mex.$	peso	Mexico
MKD	denar	Macedonia
$m.n.	moneda nacional	various
mt.	metical	Mozambique
N$	new Uruguay peso	Uruguay
NC.	cedi	Ghana
NOK	krone	Norway
NT.$	dollar	Republic of China (Taiwan)
N.Z.$	dollar	New Zealand
ORI.	riyal	Oman
P.	pula; pataca; peso	Botswana, Macao, Philippines, various
PG.	peso	Guinea-Bissau
QRI.	riyal	Qatar
£	pound	Ireland, Gt. Britain, Malta
£C	pound	Cyprus
£E	pound	Egypt
£L	pound; dinar	Lebanon
£N	pound; naira	Nigeria
£S	pound	Syria
ptas.	peseta	Spain
Q.	quetzal	Guatemala
R.	rand	South Africa, Lesotho, Namibia
RD.$	peso	Dominican Republic
Rps.	rupiah	Indonesia
Rs.	riel; rial; rupee	Cambodia, India, Iran, Mauritius, Nepal, Pakistan, Seychelles, Sri Lanka
Rub.	ruble	Commonwealth of Independent States
S/	sucre; sole	Ecuador, Peru
S.	schilling	Austria
S.$	dollar	Singapore, Western Samoa
SEK	krona	Sweden
SFr.	franc	Liechtenstein, Switzerland
SI$	dollar	Solomon Islands
SK.	koruna	Slovakia
SL.	pound	Sudan
SLT	talar	Slovenia
SRI.	riyal	Saudia Arabia
$T.	dollar	Tonga
TK.	taka	Bangladesh
TL.	pound; lira	Turkey
T.T.$	dollar	Trinidad and Tobago
tugrik	tugrik	Mongolia
UM	ouguiya	Mauritania
Urg.$	peso	Uruguay
vatu	vatu	Vanuatu
VN.$	dollar	Vietnam
Won	won (hwan)	Korea
Y	yuan	People's Republic of China
Yen	yen	Japan
YRI.	rial	Yemen
Z	zaire	Zaire
Z.$	dollar	Zimbabwe
Zl.	zloty	Poland

xxi

Country of Publication Codes

This list of countries and their codes has been taken from the list used by the Library of Congress in the MARC II format, 1992. The list used here is not the complete list of the MARC II format and is limited to countries and territories with publications listed in **Ulrich's**. The states of the United States, provinces and territories of Canada, and divisions of the United Kingdom are not listed separately.

The codes are mnemonic in most cases. Special codes not in the MARC format are used for publications of two international organizations: EI for European Communities and UN for United Nations and related organizations; and KR for Ukraine.

Country Code Sequence

AA	- ALBANIA	GD	- GRENADA	NZ	- NEW ZEALAND
AE	- ALGERIA	GE	- GERMANY, EAST	PE	- PERU
AF	- AFGHANISTAN	GH	- GHANA	PG	- GUINEA-BISSAU
AG	- ARGENTINA	GI	- GIBRALTAR	PH	- PHILIPPINES
AI	- ARMENIA	GL	- GREENLAND	PK	- PAKISTAN
AJ	- AZERBAIJAN	GM	- GAMBIA	PL	- POLAND
AN	- ANDORRA	GO	- GABON	PN	- PANAMA
AO	- ANGOLA	GP	- GUADELOUPE	PO	- PORTUGAL
AQ	- ANTIGUA	GR	- GREECE	PP	- PAPUA NEW GUINEA
AS	- AMERICAN SAMOA	GS	- GEORGIA	PR	- PUERTO RICO
AT	- AUSTRALIA	GT	- GUATEMALA	PY	- PARAGUAY
AU	- AUSTRIA	GU	- GUAM	QA	- QATAR
AY	- ANTARCTICA	GV	- GUINEA	RE	- REUNION
BA	- BAHRAIN	GW	- GERMANY	RH	- ZIMBABWE
BB	- BARBADOS	GY	- GUYANA	RM	- RUMANIA
BD	- BURUNDI	HK	- HONG KONG	RU	- RUSSIA
BE	- BELGIUM	HO	- HONDURAS	RW	- RWANDA
BF	- BAHAMAS	HT	- HAITI	SA	- SOUTH AFRICA
BG	- BANGLADESH	HU	- HUNGARY	SE	- SEYCHELLES
BH	- BELIZE	IC	- ICELAND	SF	- SAO TOME E PRINCIPE
BL	- BRAZIL	IE	- IRELAND	SG	- SENEGAL
BM	- BERMUDA	II	- INDIA	SI	- SINGAPORE
BN	- BOSNIA HERCEGOVINA	IO	- INDONESIA	SJ	- SUDAN
BO	- BOLIVIA	IQ	- IRAQ	SL	- SIERRA LEONE
BP	- SOLOMON ISLANDS	IR	- IRAN	SM	- SAN MARINO
BR	- UNION OF MYANMAR (FORMERLY BURMA)	IS	- ISRAEL	SO	- SOMALIA
		IT	- ITALY	SP	- SPAIN
BS	- BOTSWANA	IV	- IVORY COAST	SQ	- SWAZILAND
BT	- BHUTAN	JA	- JAPAN	SR	- SURINAM
BU	- BULGARIA	JM	- JAMAICA	SU	- SAUDI ARABIA
BW	- BELARUS	JO	- JORDAN	SW	- SWEDEN
BX	- BRUNEI DARUSSALAM	KE	- KENYA	SX	- NAMIBIA (FORMERLY SOUTH-WEST AFRICA)
CB	- CAMBODIA	KG	- KYRGYZSTAN		
CC	- CHINA, PEOPLE'S REPUBLIC OF	KN	- KOREA, NORTH	SY	- SYRIA
CD	- CHAD	KO	- KOREA, SOUTH	SZ	- SWITZERLAND
CE	- SRI LANKA	KR	- UKRAINE	TA	- TAJIKISTAN
CF	- CONGO (BRAZZAVILLE)	KU	- KUWAIT	TC	- TURKS AND CAICOS ISLANDS
CG	- CONGO, DEMOCRATIC REPUBLIC OF	KZ	- KAZAKHSTAN	TG	- TOGO
CH	- TAIWAN (REPUBLIC OF CHINA)	LB	- LIBERIA	TH	- THAILAND
CI	- CROATIA	LE	- LEBANON	TI	- TUNISIA
CJ	- CAYMAN ISLANDS	LH	- LIECHTENSTEIN	TK	- TURKMENISTAN
CK	- COLOMBIA	LI	- LITHUANIA	TO	- TONGA
CL	- CHILE	LO	- LESOTHO	TR	- TRINIDAD & TOBAGO
CM	- CAMEROON	LS	- LAOS	TS	- UNITED ARAB EMIRATES
CN	- CANADA	LU	- LUXEMBOURG	TU	- TURKEY
CQ	- COMOROS	LV	- LATVIA	TV	- TUVALU
CR	- COSTA RICA	LY	- LIBYA	TZ	- TANZANIA
CS	- CZECHOSLOVAKIA	MC	- MONACO	UA	- EGYPT (ARAB REPUBLIC OF EGYPT)
CU	- CUBA	MF	- MAURITIUS	UG	- UGANDA
CV	- CAPE VERDE	MG	- MADAGASCAR	UI	- UNITED KINGDOM MISC. ISLANDS
CX	- CENTRAL AFRICAN REPUBLIC	MH	- MACAO	UK	- UNITED KINGDOM
CY	- CYPRUS	MJ	- MONTSERRAT	UN	- UNITED NATIONS
DK	- DENMARK	MK	- OMAN	US	- UNITED STATES
DM	- BENIN	ML	- MALI	UV	- BURKINA FASO
DQ	- DOMINICA	MM	- MALTA	UY	- URUGUAY
DR	- DOMINICAN REPUBLIC	MP	- MONGOLIA	UZ	- UZBEKISTAN
EA	- ERITREA	MQ	- MARTINIQUE	VB	- BRITISH VIRGIN ISLANDS
EC	- ECUADOR	MR	- MOROCCO	VC	- VATICAN CITY
EG	- EQUATORIAL GUINEA	MU	- MAURITANIA	VE	- VENEZUELA
EI	- EUROPEAN COMMUNITIES/ EUROPEAN UNION	MV	- MOLDOVA	VI	- U.S. VIRGIN ISLANDS
		MW	- MALAWI	VN	- VIETNAM
ER	- ESTONIA	MX	- MEXICO	WS	- WESTERN SAMOA
ES	- EL SALVADOR	MY	- MALAYSIA	XC	- MALDIVE ISLANDS
ET	- ETHIOPIA	MZ	- MOZAMBIQUE	XE	- MARSHALL ISLANDS
FA	- FAEROE ISLANDS	NA	- NETHERLANDS ANTILLES	XI	- SAINT KITTS-NEVIS
FG	- FRENCH GUIANA	NE	- NETHERLANDS	XK	- SAINT LUCIA
FI	- FINLAND	NG	- NIGER	XM	- SAINT VINCENT
FJ	- FIJI	NL	- NEW CALEDONIA	XN	- MACEDONIA
FK	- FALKLAND ISLANDS	NN	- VANUATU (NEW HEBRIDES)	XO	- SLOVAKIA
FM	- FEDERATED STATES OF MICRONESIA	NO	- NORWAY	XR	- CZECH REPUBLIC
		NP	- NEPAL	XV	- SLOVENIA
FP	- FRENCH POLYNESIA	NQ	- NICARAGUA	YE	- YEMEN, REPUBLIC OF
FR	- FRANCE	NR	- NIGERIA	YU	- YUGOSLAVIA
FT	- DJIBOUTI	NU	- NAURU	ZA	- ZAMBIA
GB	- KIRIBATI	NX	- NORFOLK ISLAND	ZR	- ZAIRE

COUNTRY OF PUBLICATION CODES

Country Sequence

AFGHANISTAN - AF
ALBANIA - AA
ALGERIA - AE
AMERICAN SAMOA - AS
ANDORRA - AN
ANGOLA - AO
ANTARCTICA - AY
ANTIGUA - AQ
ARGENTINA - AG
ARMENIA - AI
AUSTRALIA - AT
AUSTRIA - AU
AZERBAIJAN - AJ
BAHAMAS - BF
BAHRAIN - BA
BANGLADESH - BG
BARBADOS - BB
BELARUS - BW
BELGIUM - BE
BELIZE - BH
BENIN - DM
BERMUDA - BM
BHUTAN - BT
BOLIVIA - BO
BOSNIA HERCEGOVINA - BN
BOTSWANA - BS
BRAZIL - BL
BRITISH VIRGIN ISLANDS - VB
BRUNEI DARUSSALAM - BX
BULGARIA - BU
BURKINA FASO - UV
BURUNDI - BD
CAMBODIA - CB
CAMEROON - CM
CANADA - CN
CAPE VERDE - CV
CAYMAN ISLANDS - CJ
CENTRAL AFRICAN REPUBLIC - CX
CHAD - CD
CHILE - CL
CHINA, PEOPLE'S REPUBLIC OF - CC
COLOMBIA - CK
COMOROS - CQ
CONGO (BRAZZAVILLE) - CF
CONGO, DEMOCRATIC REPUBLIC OF - CG
COSTA RICA - CR
CROATIA - CI
CUBA - CU
CYPRUS - CY
CZECH REPUBLIC - XR
CZECHOSLOVAKIA - CS
DENMARK - DK
DJIBOUTI - FT
DOMINICA - DQ
DOMINICAN REPUBLIC - DR
ECUADOR - EC
EGYPT (ARAB REPUBLIC OF EGYPT) - UA
EL SALVADOR - ES
EQUATORIAL GUINEA - EG
ERITREA - EA
ESTONIA - ER
ETHIOPIA - ET
EUROPEAN COMMUNITIES/
   EUROPEAN UNION - EI
FAEROE ISLANDS - FA
FALKLAND ISLANDS - FK
FEDERATED STATES OF MICRONESIA - FM
FIJI - FJ
FINLAND - FI
FRANCE - FR
FRENCH GUIANA - FG
FRENCH POLYNESIA - FP
GABON - GO
GAMBIA - GM
GEORGIA - GS
GERMANY - GW
GERMANY, EAST - GE
GHANA - GH
GIBRALTAR - GI
GREECE - GR
GREENLAND - GL
GRENADA - GD
GUADELOUPE - GP
GUAM - GU
GUATEMALA - GT
GUINEA - GV
GUINEA-BISSAU - PG
GUYANA - GY
HAITI - HT
HONDURAS - HO
HONG KONG - HK
HUNGARY - HU
ICELAND - IC
INDIA - II
INDONESIA - IO
IRAN - IR
IRAQ - IQ
IRELAND - IE
ISRAEL - IS
ITALY - IT
IVORY COAST - IV
JAMAICA - JM
JAPAN - JA
JORDAN - JO
KAZAKHSTAN - KZ
KENYA - KE
KIRIBATI - GB
KOREA, NORTH - KN
KOREA, SOUTH - KO
KUWAIT - KU
KYRGYZSTAN - KG
LAOS - LS
LATVIA - LV
LEBANON - LE
LESOTHO - LO
LIBERIA - LB
LIBYA - LY
LIECHTENSTEIN - LH
LITHUANIA - LI
LUXEMBOURG - LU
MACAO - MH
MACEDONIA - XN
MADAGASCAR - MG
MALAWI - MW
MALAYSIA - MY
MALDIVE ISLANDS - XC
MALI - ML
MALTA - MM
MARSHALL ISLANDS - XE
MARTINIQUE - MQ
MAURITANIA - MU
MAURITIUS - MF
MEXICO - MX
MOLDOVA - MV
MONACO - MC
MONGOLIA - MP
MONTSERRAT - MJ
MOROCCO - MR
MOZAMBIQUE - MZ
NAMIBIA (FORMERLY SOUTH-
   WEST AFRICA)- SX
NAURU - NU
NEPAL - NP
NETHERLANDS - NE
NETHERLANDS ANTILLES - NA
NEW CALEDONIA - NL
NEW ZEALAND - NZ
NICARAGUA - NQ
NIGER - NG
NIGERIA - NR
NORFOLK ISLAND - NX
NORWAY - NO
OMAN - MK
PAKISTAN - PK
PANAMA - PN
PAPUA NEW GUINEA - PP
PARAGUAY - PY
PERU - PE
PHILIPPINES - PH
POLAND - PL
PORTUGAL - PO
PUERTO RICO - PR
QATAR - QA
REUNION - RE
RUMANIA - RM
RUSSIA - RU
RWANDA - RW
SAINT KITTS-NEVIS - XI
SAINT LUCIA - XK
SAINT VINCENT - XM
SAN MARINO - SM
SAO TOME E PRINCIPE - SF
SAUDI ARABIA - SU
SENEGAL - SG
SEYCHELLES - SE
SIERRA LEONE - SL
SINGAPORE - SI
SLOVAKIA - XO
SLOVENIA - XV
SOLOMON ISLANDS - BP
SOMALIA - SO
SOUTH AFRICA - SA
SPAIN - SP
SRI LANKA - CE
SUDAN - SJ
SURINAM - SR
SWAZILAND - SQ
SWEDEN - SW
SWITZERLAND - SZ
SYRIA - SY
TAIWAN (REPUBLIC OF CHINA) - CH
TAJIKISTAN - TA
TANZANIA - TZ
THAILAND - TH
TOGO - TG
TONGA - TO
TRINIDAD & TOBAGO - TR
TUNISIA - TI
TURKEY - TU
TURKMENISTAN - TK
TURKS AND CAICOS ISLANDS - TC
TUVALU - TV
U.S. VIRGIN ISLANDS - VI
U.S.S.R. - UR
UGANDA - UG
UKRAINE - KR
UNION OF MYANMAR (FORMERLY
   BURMA) - BR
UNITED ARAB EMIRATES - TS
UNITED STATES - US
UNITED NATIONS - UN
UNITED KINGDOM - UK
UNITED KINGDOM MISC. ISLANDS - UI
URUGUAY - UY
UZBEKISTAN - UZ
VANUATU (NEW HEBRIDES) - NN
VATICAN CITY - VC
VENEZUELA - VE
VIETNAM - VN
WESTERN SAMOA - WS
YEMEN, REPUBLIC OF - YE
YUGOSLAVIA - YU
ZAIRE - ZR
ZAMBIA - ZA
ZIMBABWE - RH

Document Suppliers

ADONIS	ADONIS B.V. (main office) Spuistraat 112D 1012 VA Amsterdam The Netherlands **Tel:** 31-20-6262629 **Fax:** 31-20-6261437	**CIS**	**Congressional Information Service, Inc.** CIS Documents on Demand 4520 East-West Hwy., Ste. 800 Bethesda, MD 20814-3389 USA **Tel:** 301-654-1550, 800-227-2477 **Fax:** 301-654-4033 **E-mail:** EAINET@US.NET **URL:** http://www.cispubs.com
	ADONIS USA 350 Main St., 6th fl. Malden, MA 02148-5018 USA **Tel:** 800-944-6415 **Fax:** 617-388-8272 **E-mail:** infousa@adonis.nl **URL:** http://www.adonis.nl	**CISTI**	**Canada Institute for Scientific and Technical Information** Document Delivery, CISTI National Research Council Canada Ottawa K1A 0S2 Canada **Tel:** 800-668-1222 (Canada & US), or 613-993-9251 **Fax:** 613-993-7619 **E-mail:** cisti.docdel@nrc.ca
Ask*IEEE	Ask*IEEE 75 Varick St., 9th fl. New York, NY 10013 USA **Tel:** 800-949-4333 (Canada & US), or 212-301-4100 **Fax:** 212-301-4090 **E-mail:** askieee@ieee.org	**Ei**	**Engineering Information Inc.** Ei Text One Castle Point Terrace Hoboken, NJ 07030-5996 USA **Tel:** 800-221-1044 (USA & Canada), 201-216-8500 **Fax:** 201-216-8557 **E-mail:** eitext@ei.org **URL:** http://www.ei.org
BLDSC	**British Library Document Supply Centre** Customer Services Boston Spa, Wetherby W. Yorkshire LS23 7BQ England **Tel:** 44-1937-546060 **Fax:** 44-1937-546333 **E-mail:** dsc-customer-services@bl.uk	**EMDOCS**	**EMDOCS: The EMBASE Document Delivery Service** 75 Varick St., 9th fl. New York, NY 10013 USA **Tel:** 800-282-2720, 212-301-4003 **Fax:** 212-301-4060 **E-mail:** dds@work4u.artx.com
CASDDS	**CAS Client Services** Document Detective Service 2540 Olentangy River Rd. P.O. Box 3012 Columbus, OH 43210-0012 USA **Tel:** 800-631-1884; 614-447-3870 **Fax:** 614-447-3648 **E-mail:** dds@cas.org **URL:** http://www.cas.org/Support/dds.html	**Genuine Article**	**The Institute for Scientific Information** ISI Document Solution 3501 Market St. Philadelphia, PA 19104 USA **Tel:** 215-386-4399 **Fax:** 215-386-4343 **E-mail:** tga@isinet.com
CINDOC	**CINDOC Suministro de Documentos Service** Joaquín Costa, 22 28002 Madrid Spain **Fax:** 34-1-5642644 **E-mail:** bib-icyt@bib.csic.es	**Haworth**	**The Haworth Press, Inc.** Haworth Document Delivery Service 10 Alice St. Binghamton, NY 13904-1580 USA **Tel:** 800-HAWORTH **Fax:** 800-895-0582 **E-mail:** getinfo@haworth.com

DOCUMENT SUPPLIERS

KNAW
NIWI (Netherlands Institute of Scientific Information Services)
Customer Service
P.O. Box 95180
1090 HD Amsterdam
The Netherlands
Tel: 31-20-4628628
Fax: 31-20-6639257
E-mail: info@niwi.knaw.nl
URL: http://www.niwi.knaw.nl

KR SourceOne
KR SourceOne
75 Varick St., 9th fl.
New York, NY 10013
USA
Tel: 800-239-3458 (Canada & USA), or 212-301-4000
Fax: 212-301-4060
E-mail: dds@work4u.artx.com
URL: http://www.krinfo.com/krsourceone/

Linda Hall
Linda Hall Library
Document Services
5109 Cherry St.
Kansas City, MO 64110-2498
USA
Tel: 800-662-1545, 816-363-4600
Fax: 816-926-8785
E-mail: requests@lhl.lib.mo.us
URL: http://www.lhl.lib.mo.us

PADDS
Petroleum Abstracts - Document Delivery Service
University of Tulsa, McFarlin Library
2933 E. 6th St.
Tulsa, OK 74104-3123
USA
Tel: 800-247-8678
Fax: 918-631-3823
E-mail: PADDS@TUred.pa.utulsa.edu

SWETS
Swets & Zeitlinger bv
Heereweg 347B
P.O. Box 830
2160 SZ Lisse
The Netherlands
Tel: 31-252-435111
Fax: 31-252-415888
Telex: 41325
E-mail: infoho@swets.nl
URL: http://www.swets.nl

UMI
UMI InfoStore
300 N. Zeeb Rd.
P.O. Box 1346
Ann Arbor, MI 48106-1346
USA
Tel: 800-248-0360 (USA & Canada)
Fax: 313-761-1032
E-mail: orders@infostore.com

UnCover
The UnCover Co.
3801 E. Florida Ave., Ste. 200
Denver, CO 80210
USA
Tel: 800-787-7979,
(outside US & Canada: 303-758-3030)
Fax: 303-758-5946
E-mail: uncover@carl.org
URL: http://uncweb.carl.org

Micropublishers and Distributors

ACR   **A.C.R.P.P.**
(Association pour la Conservation et la Reproduction Photographique de la Presse)
B.P. 21
77313 Marne-La-Vallee Cedex 2
France
Tel: 33-1-60-17-68-10; **Fax:** 33-1-60-17-68-05

ADL   **Advanced Library Systems, Inc.**
100 Brickstone Sq.
P.O. Box 246
Andover, MA 01810-0005
USA
Tel: 508-470-0610; **Fax:** 508-472-1072

AFS   **Fertility and Sterility**
(no longer producer)
2140 11 Ave. S., Ste. 200
Birmingham, AL 35205-2800
USA
Tel: 205-933-8494; **Fax:** 205-930-9904

AGU   **American Geophysical Union**
2000 Florida Ave., N.W.
Washington, DC 20009
USA
Tel: 202-462-6900; **Fax:** 202-328-0566
E-mail: Serv@kosmos.agu.org

AIP   **American Institute of Physics**
500 Sunnyside Blvd.
Woodbury, NY 11797-2999
USA
Tel: 516-576-2270; **Fax:** 516-349-9704

AIR   **Aircraft Technical Publishers**
101 S. Hill Dr.
Brisbane, CA 94005-1203
USA
Tel: 415-468-1705; **Fax:** 415-468-1596
E-mail: inf@ATP.com

AJP   **American Jewish Periodical Center**
Hebrew Union College - Jewish Institute of Religion
3101 Clifton Ave.
Cincinnati, OH 45220
USA
Tel: 513-221-1875; **Fax:** 513-221-0519

ALP   **Alpha Com**
Sportallee 6
22335 Hamburg
Germany
Tel: 49-40-51302-123; **Fax:** 49-40-51302111

AMP   **Adam Matthew Publications**
8 Oxford St.
Marlborough, Wiltshire SN8 1AP
England
Tel: 44-1672-511921; **Fax:** 44-1672-511663

AMS   **AMS Press, Inc.**
(no longer producer)
56 E. 13th St.
New York, NY 10003
USA
Tel: 212-777-4700; **Fax:** 212-995-5413

ATL   **American Theological Library Association, Preservation Board**
820 Church St., Ste. 400
Evanston, IL 60201
USA
Tel: 847-869-7788; **Fax:** 847-869-8513
E-mail: atla.atla.com

BHP   **Brookhaven Press**
P.O. Box 2287
La Crosse, WI 54602-2287
USA
Tel: 608-781-0850; **Fax:** 608-781-3883

BIO   **BIOSIS**
2100 Arch St.
Philadelphia, PA 19103-1399
USA
Tel: 215-587-4800, 800-523-4806
Fax: 215-587-2041

BKR   **Bowker A&I Publishing**
(See: CIS)

BLC   **Bloch & Company**
P.O. Box 18058
Cleveland, OH 44118
USA
Tel: 216-371-0979

BLH   **Bell & Howell**
(Micropublishing now operated by UMI)

BLI   **Balch Institute**
Research Library
18 S. 7th St.
Philadelphia, PA 19106
USA
Tel: 215-925-8090; **Fax:** 215-925-8195
E-mail: balchlib@hslc.org

BNB   **British Library National Bibliographic Service**
Boston Spa, Wetherby
W. Yorkshire LS23 7BQ
England
Tel: 44-1937-546585; **Fax:** 44-1937-546586

BNQ   **Bibliotheque Nationale du Quebec**
Section de la Reproduction
3275 Holt
Montreal, PQ H2J 3H1
Canada
Tel: 514-873-1100; **Fax:** 514-873-9932

MICROPUBLISHERS AND DISTRIBUTORS

BWC   **Butterworth & Co., Ltd.**
88 Kingsway
London WC2B 6AB
England
Tel: 44-171-4056900; **Fax:** 44-171-4051332

CDS   **Current Digest of the Past-Soviet Press**
3857 N. High St.
Columbus, OH 43214
USA
Tel: 614-292-4234; **Fax:** 614-267-6310

CHL   **Chadwyck-Healey Ltd.**
The Quorum, Barnwell Rd.
Cambridge CB5 8SW
England
Tel: 44-1223-215512; **Fax:** 44-1223-515514
E-mail: mail@chadwyck.co.uk

Chadwyck-Healey Inc.
1101 King St.
Alexandria, VA 22314-2944
USA
Tel: 703-683-4890; **Fax:** 703-683-7589
E-mail: mktg@chadwyck.com

CIS   **Congressional Information Service, Inc.**
4520 East-West Hwy., Ste. 800
Bethesda, MD 20814-3389
USA
Tel: 301-654-1550, 800-638-8380
Fax: 301-654-4033

CLA   **Canadian Library Association**
(no longer producer)
Microfilm Department
200 Elgin St., Ste. 602
Ottawa, ON K2P 1L5
Canada
Tel: 613-232-9625; **Fax:** 613-563-9895

CLS   **CLASS**
(Cooperative Library Agency for
Systems & Services)
1415 Koll Circle, Ste. 101
San Jose, CA 95112-4698
USA
Tel: 510-444-1011; **Fax:** 510-453-5379

CMC   **Computer Microfilm Corp.**
3655 Wheeler Ave.
Alexandria, VA 22304
USA
Tel: 703-461-4400; **Fax:** 703-461-0042

CML   **Commonwealth Microfilm Products**
202 Amber St.
Markham, ON L3R 3J8
Canada
Tel: 905-415-9498; **Fax:** 905-415-9616

EDR   **Eric Document Reproduction Service**
(See: CMC)

EEE   **Institute of Electrical and Electronics Engineers Inc.**
345 E. 47th St.
New York, NY 10017
USA
Tel: 212-705-7900; **Fax:** 212-705-7682

EMP   **Emmett Publishing, Ltd.**
W. House 21, West St.
Haslemere, Surrey GU27 2AB
England
Tel: 44-1428-654443; **Fax:** 44-1428-661582

FCM   **Fairchild Books & Visuals**
7 W. 34th St.
New York, NY 10001
USA
Tel: 212-630-3880; **Fax:** 212-630-3868

GCS   **Preston Publications**
6600 W. Touhy Ave.
P.O. Box 48312
Niles, IL 60714
USA
Tel: 847-647-2900; **Fax:** 847-647-1155

GMC   **General Microfilm Co.**
(acquired by OMNISYS Corp.)

HPL   **Harvester Press Microfilm Publications Ltd.**
(Now wholly owned and operated
by Primary Source Media)

IAM   **SIAM Publications**
3600 University City Science Center
Philadelphia, PA 19104-2688
USA
Tel: 215-382-9800; **Fax:** 215-386-7999

ICS   **Editions I.C.S.**
23 Ave. Villemain
75014 Paris
France
Tel: 33-1-45392244; **Fax:** 33-1-45434680

IDC   **IDC Microform Publishers bv**
P.O. Box 11205
2301 EE Leiden
The Netherlands
Tel: 31-71-5142700; **Fax:** 31-71-5131721

IFA   **International Federation of Film Archives (FIAF)**
6 Nottingham St.
London W1M 3RB
England
Tel: 44-171-2240991; **Fax:** 44-171-2241203

ILO   **ILO Publications**
P.O. Box 753
Waldorf, MD 20604
USA
Tel: 301-638-3152; **Fax:** 301-843-0159

IMI   **Irish Microforms, Ltd.**
Unit 56
Sandyford Industrial Estate
Dublin 18
Ireland
Tel: 353-1-2893626; **Fax:** 353-1-2954270

IPC   **Institute of Paper Science & Technology, Inc.**
500 Tenth St. N.W.
Atlanta, GA 30318
USA
Tel: 404-894-5700; **Fax:** 404-894-4778

MICROPUBLISHERS AND DISTRIBUTORS

IRE   International Research and Evaluation
21098 IRE-Control Center
Eagan, MN 55121-0098
USA
Tel: 612-888-9635; Fax: 612-888-9124

ISI   Institute for Scientific Information
3501 Market St.
Philadelphia, PA 19104
USA
Tel: 215-386-0100
Fax: 215-386-6362, 215-386-2911

JOH   Johnson Reprint Microeditions
(Out of business)

JSC   J.S. Canner & Co.
(Ceased operations)
10 Charles St.
Needham Heights, MA 02194
USA
Tel: 617-449-9103; Fax: 617-449-1767

KHS   Kansas State Historical Society
Microfilm Publications
6425 S.W. Sixth Ave.
Topeka, KS 66615-1099
USA
Tel: 913-272-8681; Fax: 913-272-8682

KTO   Kraus Microform
(Micropublishing now operated by
Norman Ross Publishing, Inc.)

LCP   The Library of Congress
Photoduplication Service
Washington, DC 20540-5230
USA
Tel: 202-707-5640; Fax: 202-707-1771

LIB   Library Microfilms
1115 E. Arques Ave.
Sunnyvale, CA 94086
USA
Tel: 408-736-7444; Fax: 408-736-4397

LOP   Lomond Publications
7101 Woodville Rd.
Mt. Airy, MD 21771
USA
Tel: 301-694-0123, 800-443-6299

MCA   Microfilming Corporation of America
(Acquired by UMI;
operation phased out)

MCE   Microcard Editions
(See: CIS)

MEL   Metropolitan Library Service Agency
(MELSA)
570 Asbury St., Ste. 201
St. Paul, MN 55104-1849
USA
Tel: 612-645-5731; Fax: 612-649-3169

MIM   Elsevier Science Ltd.
The Blvd., Langford Ln.
Kidlington, Oxford OX5 1GB
England
Tel: 44-1865-843000; Fax: 44-1865-843010

MIS   Moody's Investors Service
Sales Department
99 Church St.
New York, NY 10007
USA
Tel: 212-553-0300; Fax: 212-553-4700

MML   Micromedia Limited
20 Victoria St.
Toronto, ON M5C 2N8
Canada
Tel: 416-362-5211, 800-387-2689
Fax: 416-362-6161
E-mail: info@micromedia.on.ca

MMP   McLaren Micropublishing Ltd.
P.O. Box 972, Sta. F
Toronto, ON M4Y 2N9
Canada
Tel: 416-960-4801; Fax: 416-964-3745

MUE   University Music Editions
Div. of High Density Systems, Inc.
P.O. Box 192, Ft. George Sta.
New York, NY 10040
USA
Tel: 212-569-5340, 5393; Fax: 212-569-1269

NBI   Newsbank, Inc.
58 Pine St.
New Canaan, CT 06840
USA
Tel: 203-966-1100, 800-762-8182
Fax: 203-966-6254

NRP   Norman Ross Publishing, Inc.
330 W. 58th St., Ste. 214
New York, NY 10019
USA
Tel: 212-765-8200, 800-648-8850
Fax: 212-765-2393
E-mail: inf@nross.com

NTI   National Technical Information Service
5285 Port Royal Rd.
Springfield, VA 22161
USA
Tel: 703-487-4600; Fax: 703-321-8547

NYL   New York Law Publishing Co.
345 Park Ave., S.
New York, NY 10010
USA
Tel: 212-779-9200; Fax: 212-481-8110

NYT   New York Times Information Bank
(Operation phased out)
229 W. 43rd St.
New York, NY 10036
USA
Tel: 212-556-1234

OEC	Organization for Economic Cooperation & Development, Publications & Information Center 2001 L St., N.W., Ste. 650 Washington, DC 20036-4910 USA **Tel:** 202-785-6323; **Fax:** 202-785-0350	SWZ	Swets & Zeitlinger bv Backsets Department P.O. Box 810 2160 SZ Lisse The Netherlands **Tel:** 31-252-435111; **Fax:** 31-252-415888 URL: http://www.swets.nl
OMN	OMNISYS Corp. 32 Wexford St. Needham Heights, MA 02194 USA **Tel:** 617-444-4123; **Fax:** 617-444-5590	TMI	Tennessee Microfilms P.O. Box 23075 Nashville, TN 37202 USA **Tel:** 615-242-3632
OMP	Oxford Microform Publication Ltd. (Acquired by UMI)	UMI	University Microfilms International (A Bell & Howell Company) 300 N. Zeeb Rd. Ann Arbor, MI 48103 USA **Tel:** 313-761-4700, 800-521-0600, 800-864-0019 **Fax:** 313-761-1203 E-mail: T.Youst@UMI.com
PMC	Princeton Microfilm Corp. P.O. Box 2073 Princeton, NJ 08543 USA **Tel:** 609-452-2066, 800-257-9502 **Fax:** 609-275-6201	UPD	Updata Publications, Inc. 1736 Westwood Blvd. Los Angeles, CA 90024 USA **Tel:** 310-474-5900; Fax: 310-474-4095
PSL	The Pretoria State Library P.O. Box 397 Pretoria 0001 Republic of South Africa **Tel:** 27-12-218931; **Fax:** 27-12-3255984	VCI	VCH Publishers, Inc. 303 N.W. 12th Ave. Deerfield Beach, FL 33442-1788 USA **Tel:** 305-428-5566 **Fax:** 305-428-8201, 800-367-8247
RPI	Primary Source Media 12 Lunar Dr. Woodbridge, CT 06525 USA **Tel:** 203-397-2600, 800-444-0799 **Fax:** 203-397-3893	VFN	Voltaire Foundation Ltd. 99 Banbury Rd. Oxford OX2 6JX England **Tel:** 44-1865-284600; **Fax:** 44-1865-284610
RRI	Fred B. Rothman & Co. 10368 W. Centennial Rd. Littleton, CO 80127 USA **Tel:** 303-979-5657, 800-457-1986 **Fax:** 303-978-1457	WDS	Dawson Microfiche (Distributor only) Cannon House Parkfarm Rd. Folkestone, Kent CT19 5EE England **Tel:** 44-1303-850101; **Fax:** 44-1303-850440
SAL	South African Library P.O. Box 469 Capetown 8000 Republic of South Africa **Tel:** 27-21-246320; **Fax:** 27-21-244848	WMP	World Microfilm Publications Ltd Microworld House, 2-6 Foscote Mews London W9 2HH England **Tel:** 44-171-2662202; **Fax:** 44-171-2662314
SAS	Society for Applied Spectroscopy 201-B Broadway St. Frederick, MD 21701 USA **Tel:** 301-694-8122; **Fax:** 301-694-6860	WSH	William S. Hein & Co., Inc. Hein Bldg., 1285 Main St. Buffalo, NY 14209-1987 USA **Tel:** 716-882-2600, 800-828-7571 **Fax:** 716-883-8100
SOC	Societe Canadienne du Microfilm Inc. - Canadian Microfilming Co. Ltd. 464 rue Saint-Jean Montreal, PQ H2Y 2S1 Canada **Tel:** 514-288-5404; **Fax:** 514-843-4690	WWS	Williams & Wilkins 351 W. Camden St. Baltimore, MD 21201 USA **Tel:** 410-528-8555, 800-638-6423 **Fax:** 410-528-8596

Reprint Services

CIS — **Congressional Information Service, Inc.**
4520 East-West Hwy., Ste. 800
Bethesda, MD 20814-3389
USA
Tel: 301-654-1550, 800-638-8380
Fax: 301-657-3203

CMC — **Computer Microfilm Corp.**
3655 Wheeler Ave.
Alexandria, VA 22304
USA
Tel: 703-461-4400
Fax: 703-461-0042

HAW — **The Haworth Press**
10 Alice St.
Binghamton, NY 13904
USA
Tel: 607-722-5857
Fax: 607-722-1424

IRC — **International Reprint Corp.**
968 Admiral Callaghan Ln., #268
Vallejo, CA 94590
USA
Tel: 707-746-8740
Fax: 707-746-1643
E-mail: reprints@intlreprints.com

ISI — **Institute for Scientific Information**
3501 Market St.
Philadelphia, PA 19104
USA
Tel: 215-386-0100
Fax: 215-386-6362, 215-386-2911

JOH — **Johnson Reprint Microeditions**
(out of business)

KTO — **Kraus Microform**
(reprint service acquired by
Periodicals Service Co., PSC)

NRP — **Norman Ross Publishing, Inc.**
330 W. 58th St., Ste. 214
New York, NY 10019
USA
Tel: 212-765-8200, 800-648-8850
Fax: 212-765-2393
E-mail: inf@nross.com

NTI — **National Technical Information Service**
5285 Port Royal Rd.
Springfield, VA 22161
USA
Tel: 703-487-4600
Fax: 703-321-8547

PSC — **Periodicals Service Co.**
11 Main St.
Germantown, NY 12526
USA
Tel: 518-537-4700
Fax: 518-537-5899

RPI — **Primary Source Media**
12 Lunar Dr.
Woodbridge, CT 06525
USA
Tel: 203-397-2600, 800-444-0799
Fax: 203-397-3893

RRI — **Fred B. Rothman & Co.**
10368 W. Centennial Rd.
Littleton, CO 80127
USA
Tel: 303-979-5657, 800-457-1986
Fax: 303-978-1457

SCH — **Schmidt Periodicals GmbH**
Dettendorf
D 83075 Bad Feilnbach
Germany
Tel: 49-8064221
Fax: 49-8064557

SWZ — **Swets & Zeitlinger bv**
Backsets Department
P.O. Box 810
2160 SZ Lisse
The Netherlands
Tel: 31-252-43511
Fax: 31-252-415888
Telex: 41325
URL: http://www.swets.nl

UMI — **University Microfilms International**
(A Bell & Howell Company)
300 N. Zeeb Rd.
Ann Arbor, MI 48103
USA
Tel: 313-761-4700, 800-521-0600
Fax: 313-761-1203
E-mail: T.Youst@UMI.com

WDS — **Dawson Microfiche**
Cannon House
Parkfarm Rd.
Folkestone, Kent CT19 5EE
England
Tel: 44-1303-85010
Fax: 44-1303-850440

WSH — **William S. Hein & Co., Inc.**
Hein Bldg., 1285 Main St.
Buffalo, NY 14209-1987
USA
Tel: 716-882-2600, 800-828-7571
Fax: 716-883-8100

Wire Services

P	Australian Associated Press Information Services
P	Agence France-Press
P	Algemeen Nederlands Persbureau (Netherlands Press Agency)
	Associated Press (USA)
P	Associated Press of Pakistan
S	Baltic News Service
nP	Canadian Press
E	Agencia EFE (Spain)
	Knight-Ridder Financial News
T-WP	Los Angeles Times-Washington Post News Service
A	New Zealand Associated Press
T	New York Times News Service
P	Polska Agencja Prasowa (Polish Press Agency)
	Pakistan Press International
	Reuters News Agency
PA	South African Press Association
NA	Scripps-Howard Newspaper Alliance - Scripps-Howard News Service
SS	Telegrafnoe Agentstvo Suverennykh Stran (Telegraphic Agency of the Sovereign Countries)
News	United Kingdom News
	United Press International

xxxi

Abstracting and Indexing Services

This list contains the full names of all abstracting and indexing services whose abbreviations are used in entries in the CLASSIFI… LIST OF SERIALS. For all currently published abstracting and indexing services, entries containing full bibliographic information … be found in the CLASSIFIED LIST OF SERIALS. Consult the TITLE INDEX for page numbers. (Bibliographic information on titles … which cessations were noted more than three years ago are not listed in this book. To view information on such titles, one must re… to **Ulrich's™** *on Disc* or **Ulrich's Online** services.)

A

A.A.P.P.Abstr.	Amino Acids, Peptides & Proteins Abstracts (Now: Cambridge Scientific Biochemistry Abstracts, Part 3: Amino Acids, Peptides & Proteins) (Ceased)
AAR	Accounting Articles
ABC	Abstracts in BioCommerce
A.B.C.Pol.Sci.	ABC Pol Sci; A Bibliography of Contents: Political Science and Government
ABI Inform.	A B I - INFORM
ABTICS	Abstracts and Book Title Index Card Services (Ceased)
A.D.& D.	Alcohol, Drugs and Driving: Abstracts and Reviews (Now: Alcohol, Drugs and Driving)
AESIS	A E S I S Quarterly (Australian Earth Sciences Information System)
A.I.Abstr.	Artificial Intelligence Abstracts (United States) (Ceased)
A.I.C.P.	Anthropological Index to Current Periodicals in the Library of the Museum of Mankind Library
A.I.D.Res.Dev.Abstr.	A.I.D. Research & Development Abstracts (Agency for International Development)
AIDS Abstr.	AIDS Abstracts
AIM	Abridged Index Medicus
A.I.P.P.	Annual Index to Poetry in Periodicals (Now: Roth's American Poetry Annual) (Ceased)
AIT Reports	A I T Reports and Publications on Renewable Energy Resources. Abstracts (Asian Institute of Technology) (Now: A I T Reports and Publications on Energy. Abstracts)
ALISA	A L I S A (Australian Library and Information Science Abstracts)
API Abstr.	A P I Abstracts: Literature (American Petroleum Institute) (Now: Technical Literature Abstracts)
API Catal.	A P I Abstracts: Catalysts & Catalysis (Now: Technical Literature Abstracts: Catalysts - Zeolites)
API Hlth.& Environ.	A P I Abstracts: Health & Environment (Now: Technical Literature Abstracts: Health & Environment)
API Oil.	A P I Abstracts: Oilfield Chemicals (Now… Technical Literature and Abstracts: Oilfield Chemicals)
API Pet.Ref.	A P I Abstracts: Petroleum Refining and Petrochemicals (Now: Technical Literature Abstracts: Petroleum Refin… and Petrochemicals)
API Pet.Subst.	A P I Abstracts: Petroleum Substitutes (Now: Technical Literature Abstracts… Petroleum Substitutes)
API Transport.	A P I Abstracts: Transportation and Storage (Now: Technical Literature Abstracts: Transportation and Storag…
A.S.& T.Ind.	Applied Science & Technology Index
ASCA	Automatic Subject Citation Alert (Now: Research Alert (Philadelphia))
ASEAN Manage. Abstr.	A S E A N Management Abstracts (Association of South East Asian Nations)
ASSIA	A S S I A: Applied Social Sciences Inde… Abstracts
ASTIS	A S T I S Bibliography (Arctic Science & Technology Information System)
Abr.R.G.	Abridged Readers' Guide to Periodical Literature
Abstr.Anthropol.	Abstracts in Anthropology
Abstr.Bk.Rev.Curr.Leg.Per.	Abstracts of Book Reviews in Current Legal Periodicals (Ceased)

ABSTRACTING AND INDEXING

Abstr.Bulg.Sci.Med.Lit.	Abstracts of Bulgarian Scientific Medical Literature
Abstr.Bull.Inst.Pap.Chem.	Institute of Paper Chemistry. Abstract Bulletin (Now: Institute of Paper Science and Technology. Abstract Bulletin)
Abstr.Crim.& Pen.	Abstracts on Criminology and Penology (Now: Criminology, Penology & Police Science Abstracts)
Abstr.Engl.Stud.	Abstracts of English Studies (Ceased)
Abstr.Folk.Stud.	Abstracts of Folklore Studies (Ceased)
Abstr.Health Care Manage.Stud.	Abstracts of Health Care Management Studies (Ceased)
Abstr.Hosp.Manage.Stud.	Abstracts of Hospital Management Studies (Now: Abstracts of Health Care Management Studies) (Ceased)
Abstr.Hum.Comp.Inter.	Abstracts in Human-Computer Interaction
Abstr.Hyg.	Abstracts on Hygiene and Communicable Diseases
Abstr.Inter.Med.	Abstracts in Internal Medicine (Now: Abstracts in Medicine and Key Word Index) (Ceased)
Abstr.J.Earthq.Eng.	Abstract Journal in Earthquake Engineering
Abstr.Mil.Bibl.	Abstracts of Military Bibliography
Abstr.Musl.Rel.	European Muslims and Christian-Muslim Relations. Abstracts. (Ceased)
Abstr.N.Amer.Geol.	Abstracts of North American Geology (Ceased)
Abstr.Pop.Cult.	Abstracts of Popular Culture (Ceased)
Abstr.Rural Dev.Trop.	Abstracts on Rural Development in the Tropics (Ceased)
Abstr.Soc.Geront.	Abstracts in Social Gerontology: Current Literature on Aging
Abstr.Soc.Work.	Abstracts for Social Workers (Now: Social Work Abstracts)
Abstr.Trop.Agri.	Abstracts on Tropical Agriculture
Acad.Ind.	Academic Index
Access	Access: the Supplementary Index to Periodicals
Account.& Data Proc.Abstr.	Accounting & Data Processing Abstracts (Now: Accounting & Finance Abstracts) (Also see: Anbar)
Account.Ind.	Accountant's Index (Now: Accounting and Tax Index)
Acid Pre.Dig.	Acid Precipitation Digest (Ceased)
Acid Rain Abstr.	Acid Rain Abstracts (Now: Environment Abstracts)
Acid Rain Ind.	Acid Rain Annual Index (Now: Environment Abstracts Annual)
Acoust.Abstr.	Acoustics Abstracts
Adol.Ment.Hlth.Abstr.	Adolescent Mental Health Abstracts (Ceased)
Agri.Eng.Abstr.	Agricultural Engineering Abstracts
Agri.Ind.	Agricultural Index (Now: Biological & Agricultural Index)
Agrindex	Agrindex
AgroLibex	Agro-Libex
AgroAgen	Agro-Agen
Agroforest.Abstr.	Agroforestry Abstracts
Air Un.Lib.Ind.	Air University Library Index to Military Periodicals
Alloys Ind.	Alloys Index
Alt.Press Ind.	Alternative Press Index
Amer.Bibl.Slavic & E.Ear.Stud.	American Bibliography of Slavic and East European Studies
Amer.Hist.& Life	America: History & Life
Amer.Hum.Ind.	American Humanities Index
Amer.Stat.Ind.	American Statistics Index
Anal.Abstr.	Analytical Abstracts
Anbar	Anbar Management Services Abstracts (Now: Operations & Production Management Abstracts; Marketing & Distribution Abstracts; Personnel & Training Abstracts) (Also see: Account.& Data Proc.Abstr.; also see: Computer Abstr.; also see: Top Manage.Abstr.)
Anim.Behav.Abstr.	Animal Behavior Abstracts
Anim.Breed.Abstr.	Animal Breeding Abstracts
Anthropol.Lit.	Anthropological Literature
Ap.Ind.	Apple Index
Apic.Abstr.	Apicultural Abstracts
Appl.Ecol.Abstr.	Applied Ecology Abstracts (Now: Ecology Abstracts)
Appl.Mech.Rev.	Applied Mechanics Reviews
Aqua.Sci.& Fish.Abstr.	Aquatic Sciences & Fisheries Abstracts (Parts 1, 2)
Aquacult.Abstr.	A S F A Aquaculture Abstracts
Archit.Per.Ind.	Architectural Periodicals Index (Now: Architectural Publications Index)
Arct.Bibl.	Arctic Bibliography (Ceased)
Art & Archaeol.Tech.Abstr.	Art and Archaeology Technical Abstracts
Art Ind.	Art Index
Art.Hosp.& Tour.	Articles in Hospitality and Tourism
Art.Int.Abstr.	Artificial Intelligence Abstracts (England) (Ceased)
Artbibl.	Artbibliographies Current Titles
Artbibl.Mod.	Artbibliographies Modern
Arts & Hum.Cit.Ind.	Arts & Humanities Citation Index
Ash.G.Bot.Per.	Asher's Guide to Botanical Periodicals (Now: Guide to Botanical Periodicals) (Ceased)
Asian-Pac.Econ.Lit.	Asian-Pacific Economic Literature
Astron.& Astrophys.Abstr.	Astronomy and Astrophysics Abstracts
Aus.Educ.Ind.	Australian Education Index

Aus.Leg.Mon.Dig.	Australian Legal Monthly Digest
Aus.P.A.I.S.	Australian Public Affairs Information Service (Now: APAIS: Australian Public Affairs Information Service)
Aus.Rd.Ind.	Australian Road Index (Ceased)
Aus.Sci.Ind.	Australian Science Index (Ceased)
Aus.Speleo Abstr.	Australian Speleo Abstracts
Avery Ind. Archit.Per.	Avery Index to Architectural Periodicals

B

B.C.I.R.A.	B.C.I.R.A. Abstracts of International Foundry Literature (British Cast Iron Research Association) (Now: B C I R A Abstracts on International Literature on Metal Castings Production)
BIM	Bibliography and Index of Micropaleontology
BMT	B M T Abstracts (British Maritime Technology)
BNI	B N I (British Newspaper Index)
B.P.I.	Business Periodicals Index
BPIA	Business Publications Index and Abstracts (Ceased)
B.R.I.	BioResearch Index (Now: Biological Abstracts - R R M (Reports, Reviews, Meetings))
BSL Biol.	Abstracts of Bulgarian Scientific Literature. Biology (Ceased)
BSL Econ.	Abstracts of Bulgarian Scientific Literature. Economics and Law (Ceased)
BSL Geo.	Abstracts of Bulgarian Scientific Literature. Geosciences (Ceased)
BSL Indus.	Abstracts of Bulgarian Scientific Literature. Industry, Building and Transport
BSL Math.	Abstracts of Bulgarian Scientific Literature. Mathematical and Physical Sciences (Ceased)
Bangladesh Agr. Sci.Abstr.	Bangladesh Agricultural Sciences Abstracts
Bank.Lit.Ind.	Banking Literature Index
Behav.Abstr.	Behavioural Abstracts (Ceased)
Behav.Med.Abstr.	Behavioral Medicine Abstracts (Now: Annals of Behavioral Medicine)
Ber.Biochem.Biol.	Berichte Biochemie und Biologie (Ceased)
Bibl Agri.	Bibliography of Agriculture
Bibl.& Ind.Geol.	Bibliography & Index of Geology (see: GeoRef)
Bibl.Cart.	Bibliographia Cartographica
Bibl.Dev.Med.& Child Neur.	Bibliography of Developmental Medicine & Child Neurology. Books and Articles Received (Ceased)
Bibl.Engl.Lang.& Lit.	Bibliography of English Language and Literature (Now: Annual Bibliography of English Language and Literature)
Bibl.Ind.	Bibliographic Index
Bibl.Ling.	Linguistic Bibliography/Bibliographie Linguistique
Bibl.Repro.	Bibliography of Reproduction (Now: Human Reproduction Update)
Bibliogr.Bras.Odontol.	Bibliografia Brasileira de Odontologia
Bio-Contr.News & Info.	Bio-Control News and Information
Biodet.Abstr.	Biodeterioration Abstracts
Bioeng.Abstr.	Bioengineering Abstracts
Biog.Ind.	Biography Index
Biol.Abstr.	Biological Abstracts
Biol.& Agr.Ind.	Biological & Agricultural Index
Biol.Dig.	Biology Digest
Biostat.	Biostatistica
Biotech.Abstr.	Biotechnology Research Abstracts (Now: Agricultural & Environmental Biotechnology Abstracts; Medical & Pharmaceutical Biotechnology Abstracts)
Biwk.Pap.Rad.Chem.& Photochem.	Biweekly List of Papers on Radiation Chemistry and Photochemistry (Ceased)
Bk.Rev.Dig.	Book Review Digest
Bk.Rev.Ind.	Book Review Index
Bk.Rev.Mo.	Book Reviews of the Month (Ceased)
Br.Archaeol.Abstr.	British Archaeological Abstracts (Now: British and Irish Archaeological Bibliography)
Br.Ceram.Abstr.	British Ceramic Abstracts (Now: World Ceramics Abstracts)
Br.Educ.Ind.	British Education Index
Br.Geol.Lit.	British Geological Literature
Br.Hum.Ind.	British Humanities Index
Br.Rail.Bd.	British Railways Board. Monthly Review Technical Literature (Ceased)
Br.Tech.Ind.	British Technology Index (Now: Abstract in New Technologies and Engineering)
Build.Manage.Abstr.	Building Management Abstracts (Now: Construction Information File - C I F)
Bull.Anal.Ent.Med.Vet.	Bulletin Analytique d'Entomologie Medic. et Veterinaire (Ceased)
Bull.Signal.	Bulletin Signaletique (Now: P A S C A L Explore, P A S C A L Folio, P A S C A L Thema) (Programme Applique a la Selection et la Compilation Automatic de la Literature)
Bull.Thermodyn.& Thermochem.	Bulletin of Thermodynamics & Thermochemistry (Now: Bulletin of Chemical Thermodynamics) (Ceased)
Bus.Comput.Ind.	Business Computer Index
Bus.Educ.Ind.	Business Education Index
Bus.Ind.	Business Index

C

CAD CAM Abstr.	C A D - C A M Abstracts (Ceased)
CALL	C A L L (Current Awareness—Library Literature)

ABSTRACTING AND INDEXING

C.I.Ob.Gyn.	Combined Cumulative Index to Obstetrics and Gynecology
C.I.P.	Combined Cumulative Index to Pediatrics
C.L.P.	Contents of Current Legal Periodicals (Now: Legal Contents) (Ceased)
C.M.J.	Contents of Contemporary Mathematical Journals (Now: Current Mathematical Publications)
R	Current Christian Abstracts (Now: Current Thoughts & Trends)
RDIC	Universite de Strasbourg. Centre de Recherche et de Documentation des Institutions Chretiennes. Bulletin du CERDIC (Ceased)
NI	Consumer Health & Nutrition Index (Ceased)
J.E.	Current Index to Journals in Education
AHL (also I.N.L.)	Cumulative Index to Nursing and Allied Health Literature
RF Abstr.	C I R F Abstracts (Now: T&D Abstracts) (Ceased)
S. Abstr.	C I S Abstracts (Centre International d'Information de Securite et Hygiene du Travail) (Now: Safety and Health at Work)
S. Ind.	C I S Index to Publications of the United States Congress (Congressional Information Service)
PI	Criminal Justice Periodical Index
I.	Current Law Index
OA	Current Literature on Aging (Now: Abstracts in Social Gerontology: Current Literature on Aging)
OSS	Current Literature on Science of Science
	Canadian Magazine Index (Now: Canadian Index)
I.	Current Physics Index
E.J.	Contents of Recent Economics Journals
I.Abstr.	C R I Abstracts (Cement Research Institute of India)
I.Curr.Cont.	C R I Current Contents
Ind.	Canadian Statistics Index (Now: Directory of Statistics in Canada
HM	Current Work in the History of Medicine
scan	Cadscan
Per.Ind.	California Periodicals Index
Tiss.Abstr.	Calcified Tissue Abstracts (Now: Calcium and Calcified Tissue Abstracts)
B.P.I.	Canadian Business Periodicals Index (Now: Canadian Index)
Educ.Ind.	Canadian Education Index
Lit.Ind.	Canadian Literature Index (Ceased)
Per.Ind.	Canadian Periodical Index
Rev.Comp.	Canadian Review of Comparative Literature (Abstracting discontinued)
Wom.Per.	Canadian Women's Periodicals Index (Ceased)
Canadiana	Canadiana
Canon Law Abstr.	Canon Law Abstracts
Cath.Ind.	Catholic Periodical & Literature Index
Ceram.Abstr.	Ceramic Abstracts
Chem.Abstr.	Chemical Abstracts
Chem.Cit.Ind.	Chemistry Citation Index
Chem.Eng.Abstr.	Chemical Engineering Abstracts (Now: Process and Chemical Engineering)
Chem.Infd.	Chemischer Informationsdienst (Now: ChemInform)
Chem.Titles	Chemical Titles
Chemorec.Abstr.	Chemoreception Abstracts
Chicago Psychoanal. Lit.Ind.	Chicago Psychoanalytic Literature Index (Ceased)
Chic.Per.Ind.	Chicano Periodical Index (Now: Chicano Index)
Child.Auth.& Illus.	Children's Authors and Illustrators
Child.Bk.Rev.Ind.	Children's Book Review Index
Child Devel.Abstr.	Child Development Abstracts and Bibliography
Child.Lit.Abstr.	Children's Literature Abstracts
Chr.Per.Ind.	Christian Periodical Index
Coll.Stud.Pers. Abstr.	College Student Personnel Abstracts (Now: Higher Education Abstracts)
Commun.Abstr.	Communication Abstracts
Community Ment.Health Rev.	Community Mental Health Review (Now: Journal of Prevention and Intervention in the Community)
Compumath	Compumath Citation Index
Comput.Abstr.	Computer Abstracts (Also see: Anbar)
Comput.& Info. Sys.	Computer and Information Systems Abstracts Journal
Comput.Bus.	Computer Business (Ceased)
Comput.Cont.	Computer Contents (Ceased)
Comput.Dtbs.	Computer Database
Comput.Ind.	Computer Index
Comput.Indus.Up.	Computer Industry Update (Ceased)
Comput.Lit.Ind.	Computer Literature Index
Comput.Rev.	Computing Reviews
Concr.Abstr.	Concrete Abstracts
Consum.Ind.	Consumers Index
Cont.Pg.Educ.	Contents Pages in Education
Cont.Pg.Manage.	Contents Pages in Management
Copper Abstr.	Copper Abstracts (Now: International Copper Information Bulletin) (Ceased)
Corros.Abstr.	Corrosion Abstracts
Cott.& Trop.Fibr. Abstr.	Cotton and Tropical Fibres Abstracts (Now: Cotton and Tropical Fibres)
Crim.Just.Abstr.	Criminal Justice Abstracts
Crime Delinq. Abstr.	Crime and Delinquency Abstracts (Ceased)
Crop Physiol. Abstr.	Crop Physiology Abstracts

ABSTRACTING AND INDEXING

Curr.Adv. Biochem.	Current Advances in Biochemistry (Now: Current Advances in Protein Biochemistry)
Curr.Adv.Cancer. Res.	Current Advances in Cancer Research
Curr.Adv.Cell & Devel.Biol.	Current Advances in Cell and Developmental Biology
Curr.Adv.Clin. Chem.	Current Advances in Clinical Chemistry
Curr.Adv.Ecol. Sci.	Current Advances in Ecological Sciences (Now: Current Advances in Ecological and Environmental Sciences)
Curr.Adv. Genetics & Molec.Biol.	Current Advances in Genetics and Molecular Biology
Curr.Adv. Neurosci.	Current Advances in Neuroscience
Curr.Adv.Physiol.	Current Advances in Physiology (Now: Current Advances in Endocrinology & Metabolism)
Curr.Adv.Plant Sci.	Current Advances in Plant Science
Curr.Aus.N.Z.Leg. Lit.Ind.	Current Australian and New Zealand Legal Literature Index (Ceased)
Curr.Biotech. Abstr.	Current Biotechnology Abstracts (Now: Current Biotechnology)
Curr.Bk.Rev.Cit.	Current Book Review Citations (Ceased)
Curr.Chem.React.	Current Chemical Reactions
Curr.Cont.	Current Contents consists of: Current Contents: Agriculture, Biology & Environmental Sciences Current Contents: Arts & Humanities Current Contents: Clinical Medicine Current Contents: Engineering, Computing & Technology Current Contents: Health Services Administration (Ceased) Current Contents: Life Sciences Current Contents: Physical, Chemical & Earth Sciences Current Contents: Social & Behavioral Sciences
Curr.Cont.Africa	Current Contents Africa (Ceased)
Curr.Cont.M.E.	Current Contents of Periodicals on the Middle East
Curr.Dig.Sov. Press	Current Digest of the Soviet Press (Now: Current Digest of the Post-Soviet Press)
Curr.Ind.Stat.	Current Index to Statistics
Curr.Leather Lit.	Current Leather Literature (Now: Leather Science Abstracts)
Curr.Lit.Fam. Plan.	Current Literature in Family Planning (Ceased)
Curr.Pack.Abstr.	Current Packaging Abstracts (Ceased)
Curr.Ref. Fish Res.	Current References in Fish Research
Curr.Tit.Dent.	Current Titles in Dentistry
Curr.Tit. Electrochem.	Current Titles in Electrochemistry
Curr.Tit.Ocean	Current Titles in Ocean, Coastal, Lake & Waterway Sciences (Ceased)
Cyb.Abstr.	Cybernetics Abstracts

D

DAAI	Design and Applied Arts Index
DM&T	Defense Markets and Technology (Now: Aerospace Defense Markets and Technology) (Ceased)
DNP	Digest of Neurology & Psychiatry
DSH Abstr.	DSH Abstracts (Deafness, Speech and Hearing) (Ceased)
Dairy Sci.Abstr.	Dairy Science Abstracts
Data Process.Dig.	Data Processing Digest
Deep Sea Res.& Oceanogr.Abstr.	Deep Sea Research & Oceanographic Abstracts (Now: Oceanographic Literature Review)
Dent.Abstr.	Dental Abstracts
Dent.Ind.	Index to Dental Literature
Diab.Cont.	Diabetes Contents
Diab.Lit.Ind.	Diabetes Literature Index (Ceased)
Diar.Dis.Res.	Journal of Diarrhoeal Diseases Research
Djerelo	Djerelo
Doc.Geogr.	Documentatio Geographica (Now: Dokumentation zur Raumentwicklung) (Ceased)
Documentatie- blad	Documentatieblad: The Abstracts Journal of the African Studies Centre Leiden (Now: African Studies Abstracts)
Dok.Arbeitsmed.	Dokumentation Arbeitsmedizin (Now: Arbeitsmedizin)
Dok.Raum.	Dokumentation zur Raumentwicklung (Ceased)
Dok.Str.	Dokumentation Strasse

E

E & P Hlth.	Exploration and Production Health, Safety and Environment
EC Ind.	EC Index (European Communities)
E.I.	E I (Excerpta Indonesica)
ELLIS	E L L I S (European Legal Literature Information Service)
ERIC	Eric Clearinghouse (See: C.I.J.E.)
Ecol.Abstr.	Ecological Abstracts
Ecol.Zoo.& Plant Sci.Abstr.	Essential Ecology, Zoology & Plant Science Abstracts
Econ.Abstr.	Economic Abstracts (Now: Key to Economic Science) (Ceased)
Educ.Admin. Abstr.	Educational Administration Abstracts
Educ.Ind.	Education Index
Educ.Tech.Abstr.	Educational Technology Abstracts
Ekist.Ind.	Ekistic Index of Periodicals
Electroanal.Abstr.	Electroanalytical Abstracts (Ceased)
Electron.& Communic. Abstr.J.	Electronics and Communications Abstracts Journal

ABSTRACTING AND INDEXING xxxvii

Endocrin.Ind.	Endocrinology Index (Ceased)
Energy Abstr.	Energy Abstracts
Energy Ind.	Energy Index (Now: Energy Information Abstracts Annual)
Energy Info. Abstr.	Energy Information Abstracts
Energy Res. Abstr.	Energy Research Abstracts
Energy Rev.	Energy Review (Santa Barbara) (Ceased)
Eng.Ind.	Engineering Index (Now: Engineering Index Monthly)
Eng.Mat.Abstr.	Engineered Materials Abstracts
Entomol.Abstr.	Entomology Abstracts
Environ.Abstr.	Environment Abstracts
Environ.Ind.	Environment Index (Now: Environment Abstracts Annual)
Environ.Per.Bibl.	Environmental Periodicals Bibliography
Ergon.Abstr.	Ergonomics Abstracts
Euro.LJI	European Legal Journals Index
Excpt.Child Educ.Abstr.	Exceptional Child Education Abstracts (Now: Exceptional Child Education Resources)
Excerp.Bot.	Excerpta Botanica (Sections A, B)
ExtraMED	ExtraMED
Excerp.Med.	Excerpta Medica

Section 1: Anatomy, Anthropology, Embriology & Histology
Section 2: Physiology
Section 3: Endocrinology
Section 4: Microbiology: Bacteriology, Mycology Parasitology and Virology
Section 5: General Pathology and Pathological Anatomy
Section 6: Internal Medicine
Section 7: Pediatrics and Pediatric Surgery
Section 8: Neurology and Neurosurgery
Section 9: Surgery
Section 10: Obstetrics and Gynecology
Section 11: Otorhinolaryngology
Section 12: Ophthalmology
Section 13: Dermatology and Venereology
Section 14: Radiology
Section 15: Chest Diseases, Thoracic Surgery and Tuberculosis
Section 16: Cancer
Section 17: Public Health, Social Medicine and Epidemiology
Section 18: Cardiovascular Diseases and Cardiovascular Surgery
Section 19: Rehabilitation and Physical Medicine
Section 20: Gerontology and Geriatrics
Section 21: Developmental Biology and Teratology
Section 22: Human Genetics
Section 23: Nuclear Medicine
Section 24: Anesthesiology
Section 25: Hematology
Section 26: Immunology, Serology and Transplantation
Section 27: Biophysics, Bio-Engineering and Medical Instrumentation
Section 28: Urology and Nephrology
Section 29: Clinical and Experimental Biochemistry
Section 30: Clinical and Experimental Pharmacology
Section 31: Arthritis and Rheumatism
Section 32: Psychiatry
Section 33: Orthopedic Surgery
Section 34: Plastic Surgery
Section 35: Occupational Health and Industrial Medicine
Section 36: Health Policy, Economics and Management
Section 37: Drug Literature Index
Section 38: Adverse Reactions Titles
Section 40: Drug Dependence, Alcohol Abuse and Alcoholism
Section 46: Environmental Health and Pollution Control
Section 48: Gastroenterology
Section 49: Forensic Science Abstracts
Section 50: Epilepsy Abstracts
Section 51: Mycobacterial Diseases, Leprosy, Tuberculosis and Related Subjects
Section 52: Toxicology
Section 54: AIDS
Section 130: Clinical Pharmacology

F

F.A.C.T.	Fuel Abstracts and Current Titles (Now: Fuel and Energy Abstracts)
FAMLI	F A M L I (Family Medicine Literature Index) (Ceased)
F.R.	Fanatic Reader
Fababean Abstr.	Faba Bean Abstracts (Ceased)
Fam.Ind.	Family Index
Farm & Garden Ind.	Farm & Garden Index (Ceased)
Fed Print	Fed in Print
Fem.Per.	Feminist Periodicals
Fert.Abstr.	Fertilizer Abstracts (Ceased)
Field Crop Abstr.	Field Crop Abstracts
Film Lit.Ind.	Film Literature Index
Fish.Abstr.	Essential Fisheries Abstracts
Fluidex	Fluidex

consists of:
Civil Engineering Hydraulics Abstracts (Now: Fluid Abstracts: Civil Engineering)
Current Fluid Engineering Titles (Ceased)
Fluid Flow Measurement Abstracts (Now: Fluid Abstracts: Process Engineering)
Fluid Power Abstracts (Now: Fluid Abstracts: Process Engineering)
Fluid Sealing Abstracts (Now: Fluid Abstracts: Process Engineering)
Industrial Aerodynamics Abstracts

	(Now: Fluid Abstracts: Civil Engineering)
	Industrial Jetting Report (Ceased)
	Offshore Engineering Abstracts (Now: Fluid Abstracts: Civil Engineering)
	Pipelines Abstracts (Now: Fluid Abstracts: Process Engineering)
	Pumps & Other Fluids Machinery Abstracts (Now: Fluid Abstracts: Process Engineering)
	Pumps and Turbines (Ceased)
	River and Flood Control Abstracts (Ceased)
	Solid-Liquid Flow Abstracts (Now: Fluid Abstracts: Process Engineering)
	Tribos-Tribology Abstracts (Now: Tribology & Corrosion Abstracts) (Ceased)
	World Ports and Harbours Abstracts (Now: Fluid Abstracts: Civil Engineering)
	World Ports and Harbours News (Ceased)
Food Sci.& Tech. Abstr.	Food Science and Technology Abstracts
Foreign Leg.Per.	Index to Foreign Legal Periodicals
Forest.Abstr.	Forestry Abstracts
Forest.& Wildfire Abstr.	Essential Forestry & Wildfire Abstracts
Forest Prod. Abstr.	Forest Products Abstracts
Foul.Prev.Res. Dig.	Fouling Prevention Research Digest (Now: H T F S Digest (Heat Transfer & Fluid Flow Service))
Fuel & Energy Abstr.	Fuel & Energy Abstracts
Fut.Abstr.	Future - Abstracts
Fut.Surv.	Future Survey

G

G.Indian Per.Lit.	Guide to Indian Periodical Literature
G.Perf.Arts.	Guide to the Performing Arts (Ceased)
G.Soc.Sci.& Rel. Per.Lit.	Guide to Social Sciences and Religion in Periodical Literature
Gard.Lit.	Garden Literature
Gas Abstr.	Gas Abstracts
Gas Process.& Ppl.	Gas Processing and Pipelining
Gastroenterol. Abstr.& Cit.	Gastroenterology Abstracts & Citations (Ceased)
Gdlns.	Guidelines
Gen.Phys.Adv. Abstr.	General Physics Advance Abstracts
Gen.Sci.Ind.	General Science Index
Geneal.Per.Ind.	Genealogical Periodical Annual Index
Genet.Abstr.	Genetics Abstracts
Geo.Abstr.H.G. (also Geo.Abstr.)	Geographical Abstracts: Human Geography
Geo.Abstr.P.G. (also Geo.Abstr.)	Geographical Abstracts: Physical Geography
Geol.Abstr.	Geological Abstracts
Geophys.Abstr.	Geophysical Abstracts (Ceased)
GeoRef	Bibliography and Index of Geology (Also known as GeoRef)
Geosci.Doc.	Geoscience Documentation
Geotech.Abstr.	Geotechnical Abstracts
Ger.J.Psych.	German Journal of Psychology (Now: European Psychologist) (Abstracting discontinued)
Graph.Arts Abstr.	Graphic Arts Abstracts (Now: G A T F World)
Graph.Arts Lit. Abstr.	Graphic Arts Literature Abstracts (Now: Institute of Paper Science and Technology. Graphic Arts Bulletin)

H

HMA	Healthcare Marketing Abstracts
HR Rep.	Human Rights Internet Reporter
HRIS	H R I S Abstracts (Now: T R I S Electron Bibliographic Data Base (Transportati Research Information Services))
Helminthol.Abstr.	Helminthological Abstracts. Series A (No Helminthological Abstracts)
	Helminthological Abstracts. Series B (No Nematological Abstracts)
Herb.Abstr.	Herbage Abstracts (Now: Grasslands an Forage Abstracts)
High.Educ.Abstr.	Higher Education Abstracts
High.Educ.Curr. Aware.Bull.	Higher Education Current Awareness Bulletin (Ceased)
Hisp.Amer.Per. Ind.	Hispanic American Periodicals Index
Hist.Abstr.	Historical Abstracts (Parts A, B)
Hlth.Ind.	Health Index
HongKongiana	HongKongiana
Hort.Abstr.	Horticultural Abstracts
Hosp.Abstr.	Hospital Abstracts (Now: Health Service Abstracts)
Hosp.Abstr.Serv.	Hospital Abstracts Service (Ceased)
Hosp.Lit.Ind.	Hospital Literature Index
Hospit.Ind.	Hospitality Index (Now: Hospital and Health Administration Index)
Hum.Ind.	Humanities Index
Human Resour. Abstr.	Human Resources Abstracts
Hung.Build.Bull.	Hungarian Building Bulletin (Ceased)
Hung.Lib.& Info. Sci.Abstr.	Hungarian Library and Information Scier Abstracts
Hwy.Res.Abstr.	Highway Research Abstracts (Now: Transportation Research Abstracts) (Ceased)

I

IBM PC Ind.	IBM PC Index (Personal Computer)
IBR	Internationale Bibliographie der Rezensionen Wissenschaftlicher

ABSTRACTING AND INDEXING xxxix

	Literatur/International Bibliography of Book Reviews of Scholarly Literature		Key Abstracts - Rotobics & Control
			Key Abstracts - Semiconductor Devices
Z	Internationale Bibliographie der Zeitschriftenliteratur aus allen Gebieten des Wissens/International Bibliography of Periodicals from all Fields of Knowledge		Key Abstracts - Software Engineering
			Key Abstracts - Telecommunications
			Physics Abstracts (Alternative title: INSPEC, Section A. Represents: Science Abstracts. Section A)
C.U.I.S.Abstr.	I C U I S Abstracts Service (Institute on the Church in Urban Industrial Society) (Now: I C U I S Justice Ministries) (Ceased)	I.P.A.	International Pharmaceutical Abstracts
		ISMEC	I S M E C Bulletin (Information Service in Mechanical Engineering) (Now: Mechanical Engineering Abstracts)
A	International Development Abstracts	Ind.Agri.Am.Lat. Caribe	Indice Agricole de America Latina y el Caribe (Ceased)
	Index to International Statistics		
CS	Index to Journals in Communication Studies	Ind.Amer.Per. Verse	Index of American Periodical Verse
FL	Inventory of Marriage and Family Literature (Now: Family Studies Database)	Ind.Artic.Jew. Stud.	Index of Articles on Jewish Studies
		Ind.Bk.Rev.Hum.	Index to Book Reviews in the Humanities (Ceased)
.M.Abstr.	I M M Abstracts (Institute of Mining & Metallurgy) (Now: I M M Abstracts and Index)		
		Ind.Bus.Rep.	Index to Business Reports
		Ind.Can.L.P.L.	Index to Canadian Legal Periodical Literature
.E.P.	Index to New England Periodicals		
S Atomind.	I N I S Atomindex (International Nuclear Information System)	Ind.Chem.	Index Chemicus
		Ind.Child.Mag.	Subject Index to Children's Magazines (Now: Children's Magazine Guide)
SPEC	INSPEC (The Institution of Electrical Engineers):	Ind.Curr.Urb. Doc.	Index to Current Urban Documents
	Computers & Control Abstracts (Alternative title: INSPEC, Section C. Represents: Science Abstracts. Section C)		
		Ind.Free.Per.	Index to Free Periodicals (Ceased)
		Ind.Heb.Per.	Index to Hebrew Periodicals
	Current Papers in Computers & Control	Ind.How To Do It	Index to How to Do It Information
	Current Papers in Electrical & Electronics Engineering	Ind.Hyg.Dig.	Industrial Hygiene Digest
		Ind.India	Index India
	Current Papers in Physics	Ind.Islam.	Index Islamicus
	Electrical & Electronics Abstracts (Alternative title: INSPEC, Section B. Represents: Science Abstracts. Section B.)	Ind.Jew.Per.	Index to Jewish Periodicals
		Ind.Lit.Amer. Indian	Index to Literature on the American Indian (Ceased)
	Key Abstracts - Advanced Materials		
	Key Abstracts - Antennas & Propagation	Ind.Lit.Dent.	Indice de la Literatura Dental Periodica en Castellano
	Key Abstracts - Artificial Intelligence		
	Key Abstracts - Business Automation	Ind.Little Mag.	Index to Little Magazines (Ceased)
	Key Abstracts - Computer Communication and Storage	Ind.Med.	Index Medicus
		Ind.Med.Esp.	Indice Medico Espanol
	Key Abstracts - Computing in Electronics & Power	Ind.N.Z.Per.	Index to New Zealand Periodicals (Now: Index New Zealand)
	Key Abstracts - Electronic Circuits	Ind.Per.Art.Relat. Law	Index to Periodical Articles Related to Law
	Key Abstracts - Electronic Instrumentation		
	Key Abstracts - Factory Automation	Ind.Per.Blacks	Index to Periodical Articles by and about Blacks (Now: Index to Black Periodicals)
	Key Abstracts - High-Temperature Superconductors		
		Ind.Per.Lit.	Index to Indian Periodical Literature (Ceased)
	Key Abstracts - Human-Computer Interaction		
		Ind.Per.Negroes	Index to Periodical Articles by & about Negroes (Now: Index to Black Periodicals)
	Key Abstracts - Machine Vision		
	Key Abstracts - Measurements in Physics		
		Ind.Phil.Per.	Index to Philippine Periodicals
	Key Abstracts - Microelectronics & Printed Circuits	Ind.Rheum.	Annual Index of Rheumatology (Ceased)
		Ind.S.A.Per.	Index to South African Periodicals
	Key Abstracts - Microwave Technology	Ind.Sci.Rev.	Index to Scientific Reviews
	Key Abstracts - Neural Networks		
	Key Abstracts - Optoelectronics	Ind.Sel.Per.	Index to Selected Periodicals (Now: Index to Black Periodicals)
	Key Abstracts - Power Systems & Applications		

Ind.SST.	Indice Espanol de Ciencia y Tecnologia		
Ind.U.S.Gov.Per.	Index to U.S. Government Periodicals (Now: U S Government Periodicals Index)		**J**
		JAMA	JAMA: The Journal of the American Medical Association
Ind.Vet.	Index Veterinarius	JCT	Japan Computer Technology and Applications Abstracts (Ceased)
Indian Lib.Sci. Abstr.	Indian Library Science Abstracts	JTA	Japanese Technical Abstracts (Now: Japan Technology Series) (Ceased)
Indian Psychol. Abstr.	Indian Psychological Abstracts (Now: Indian Psychological Abstracts and Reviews)	J.Cont. Quant.Meth.	Journal Contents in Quantitative Methods
Indian Sci.Abstr.	Indian Science Abstracts	J.Curr.Laser Abstr.	Journal of Current Laser Abstracts
Indian Sci.Ind.	Indian Science Index (Ceased)		
Info.Media & Tech.	Information Media and Technology (Now: Information Management & Technology)	Jewish Abstr.	Jewish Abstracts
		J.of Abstr.Int. Educ.	Journal of Abstracts in International Education
Inform.Sci.Abstr.	Information Science Abstracts		
Inpharma	InPharma (Now: InPharma Weekly)	J.of Econ.Abstr. (also: J.of Econ. Lit.)	Journal of Economic Abstracts (Now: Journal of Economic Literature)
Int.Abstr.Biol.Sci.	International Abstracts of Biological Sciences (Now: Current Awareness in Biological Sciences)		
		J.of Ferroc.	Journal of Ferrocement
Int.Abstr.Oper. Res.	International Abstracts in Operations Research	Jap.Per.Ind.	Japanese Periodicals Index (Humanities and Social Sciences Section; Medical Sciences and Pharmacology (Ceased Science and Technology)
Int.Aerosp.Abstr.	International Aerospace Abstracts		
Int.Bibl.Soc.Sci.	International Bibliography of the Social Sciences: Anthropology, Political Science, Economics, Sociology (Ceased)		
		Jun.High Mag. Abstr.	Junior High Magazine Abstracts
Int.Build.Serv. Abstr.	International Building Services Abstracts		**K**
Int.G.Class.Stud.	International Guide to Classical Studies (Ceased)	Key to Econ.Sci.	Key to Economic Science (Ceased)
		Key Word Ind. Wildl.Res.	Key Word Index of Wildlife Research
Int.Ind.Film Per.	International Index to Film Periodicals		
Int.Lab.Doc.	International Labor Documentation	Kidney	Kidney (New York, 1992)
Int.Nurs.Ind.	International Nursing Index		
Int.Packag.Abstr.	International Packaging Abstracts		**L**
Int.Polit.Sci. Abstr.	International Political Science Abstracts	LAMP	L A M P (Literature Analysis of Microcomputer Publications)
Int.Sci.Rev.	International Science Review Series (Ceased)	LCR	Literary Criticism Register
		LHTN	Library Hi Tech News
Int.Z.Bibelwiss.	Internationale Zietschriftenschau fuer Bibelwissenschaft und Grenzgebiete	L.I.I.	Life Insurance Index (Ceased)
		LISA	L I S A: Library & Information Science Abstracts
InterActions Bibl.	InterActions Bibliography (Now: Humans & Other Species)		
		LJI	Legal Journals Index
Intl.Bibl.S.S.Econ.	International Bibliography of the Social Sciences: Economics	L.R.I.	Legal Resource Index (Now: LegalTrac)
		Lab.Haz.Bull.	Laboratory Hazards Bulletin
Intl.Bibl.S.S.Pol. Sci.	International Bibliography of the Social Sciences: Political Science	Landwirt. Zentralbl.	Landwirtschaftliches Zentralblatt (Now: Agroselekt) (Ceased)
Intl.Bibl.S.S. Soc.Cult.Anthro.	International Bibliography of the Social Sciences: Anthropology	Lang.& Lang. Behav.Abstr.	Language and Language Behaviour Abstracts (Now: Linguistics and Language Behavior Abstracts)
Intl.Civil Eng. Abstr.	International Civil Engineering Abstracts		
Intl.Ind.TV.	International Index to Television Periodicals	Lang.Teach.& Ling.Abstr.	Language Teaching and Linguistics Abstracts (Now: Language Teaching)
Intl.Mgmt.Info.	International Management Information Business Digest (Ceased)	Law Ofc.Info.Svc.	Law Office Information Service
		Lead Abstr.	Lead Abstracts (Now: Leadscan)
Intl.Polym.Sci.& Tech.	International Polymer Science and Technology	Left Ind.	Left Index
		Leg.Cont.	Legal Contents (Ceased)
Iron & Steel Indus.Pr.	Iron and Steel Industry Profiles (Ceased)	Leg.Info.Manage. Ind.	Legal Information Management Index
Irr.& Drain.Abstr.	Irrigation & Drainage Abstracts		

ABSTRACTING AND INDEXING xli

Abbrev.	Full Title
eg.Per.	Index to Legal Periodicals (Now: Index to Legal Periodicals & Books)
b.Lit.	Library Literature
b.Sci.Abstr.	Library Science Abstracts (Now: L I S A: Library & Information Science Abstracts)
ng.Abstr.	Linguistics Abstracts
t.Automat.	Literature on Automation (Now: Excerpta Automatica)
od.Restr.& Tour.Ind.	Lodging, Restaurant & Tourism Index

M

Abbrev.	Full Title
EDOC	Medoc: Index to U.S. Government Publications in the Medical and Health Sciences (Ceased)
EDSOC	Medical Socioeconomic Research Sources (Ceased)
ELSA	MELSA Messenger (Metropolitan Library Service) (Ceased)
L.A.	M L A Abstracts of Articles in Scholarly Journals (Ceased)
L.A. Intl.Bibl.	M L A International Bibliography of Books and Articles on Modern Languages and Literatures
M.R.I.	Multi-Media Reviews Index (Now: Media Review Digest)
ag.Ind.	Magazine Index
ize Abstr.	Maize Abstracts
nage.Abstr.	Management Abstracts (India) (Now: Indian Management)
nage.Cont.	Management Contents
r.Aff.Bibl.	Marine Affairs Bibliography
r.Sci.Cont.Tab.	Marine Science Contents Tables (Ceased)
rk.Res.Abstr.	Market Research Abstracts
ss Spectr.Bull.	Mass Spectrometry Bulletin
t.Sci.Cit.Ind.	Materials Science Citation Index
th.R.	Mathematical Reviews
d.Abstr.	Medical Abstract Service (Ceased)
d.& Surg. ermat.	Medical & Surgical Dermatology
d.Care Rev.	Medical Care Review
dia Rev.Dig.	Media Review Digest
nt.Retard. bstr.	Mental Retardation Abstracts (Now: Developmental Disabilities Abstracts) (Ceased)
t.Abstr.	Metallurgical Abstracts (Now: Metals Abstracts)
t.Abstr.Ind.	Metals Abstracts Index
t.Finish.Abstr.	Metal Finishing Abstracts (Now: Surface Treatment Technology Abstracts)
teor.& eoastrophys. bstr.	Meteorological & Geoastrophysical Abstracts
th.Per.Ind.	Methodist Periodical Index (Now: United Methodist Periodical Index) (Ceased)
mt.& Market. bstr.	Management & Marketing Abstracts
Mich.Mag.Ind.	Michigan Magazine Index (Ceased)
Microbiol.Abstr.	Microbiological Abstracts (Sections A, B, C)
Microcomp.Ind.	Microcomputer Index (Now: Microcomputer Abstracts)
Microcomp. Indus.Up.	Microcomputer Industry Update (Ceased)
Mid.East: Abstr. & Ind.	Middle East: Abstracts and Index
Mineral.Abstr.	Mineralogical Abstracts
Mkt.Inform. Guide	Marketing Information Guide (Ceased)
Mult.Ed.Abstr.	Multicultural Education Abstracts
Multi.Scler.Abstr.	Multiple Sclerosis Indicative Abstracts (Ceased)
Music Artic. Guide	Music Article Guide (Ceased)
Music Ind.	Music Index
Mycol.Abstr.	Abstracts of Mycology

N

Abbrev.	Full Title
NAA	N A A (Nordic Archaeological Abstracts)
NBA	Notiziario Bibliografico di Audiologia ORL e Foniatria
NRN	Nutrition Research Newsletter
Neurosci.Abstr.	Neurosciences Abstracts (Now: CSA Neurosciences Abstracts)
Neurosci.Cit.Ind.	Neuroscience Citation Index
New Per.Ind.	New Periodicals Index (Ceased)
New Test.Abstr.	New Testament Abstracts
Noise Pollut. Publ.Abstr.	Noise Pollution Publications Abstracts (Ceased)
Nonfer.Met.Alert	Nonferrous Metals Alert
Nonwov.Abstr.	Nonwovens Abstracts
Nucl.Sci.Abstr.	Nuclear Science Abstracts (Now INIS Atomindex)
Numis.Lit.	Numismatic Literature
Nurs.Abstr.	Nursing Abstracts
Nurs.Res.Abstr.	Nursing Research Abstracts (Ceased)
Nutr.Abstr.	Nutrition Abstracts & Reviews (Now: Nutrition Abstracts and Reviews Series A: Human and Experimental; Nutrition Abstracts and Reviews Series B: Livestock Feeds and Feeding)

O

Abbrev.	Full Title
Ocean.Abstr.	Oceanic Abstracts
Ocean.Abstr.Bibl.	Oceanographic Abstracts and Bibliography (Now: Oceanographic Literature Review)
Ocean.Ind.	Oceanic Index (Now: Oceanic Abstracts)
Off.Tech.	Offshore Technology
Old Test.Abstr.	Old Testament Abstracts
Oncol.Abstr.	Oncology Abstracts (Ceased)
Oper.Res. Manage.Sci.	Operations Research - Management Science
Ophthal.Lit.	Ophthalmic Literature

ABSTRACTING AND INDEXING

Oral Res.Abstr.	Oral Research Abstracts (Ceased)
Ornam.Hort.	Ornamental Horticulture
Ornithol.Abstr.	Essential Ornithological Abstracts

P

P.A.I.S.	P A I S Bulletin (Public Affairs Information Service) (Now: P A I S International in Print)
P.A.I.S.For.Lang.Ind.	Public Affairs Information Service Foreign Language Index (Now: P A I S International in Print)
PC Abstr.	P C Abstracts (Personal Computing) (Ceased)
PCC Alert	Polymers, Ceramics, Composites Alert
PCR2	P C R2 (Personal Computer Review - Squared)
PHRA	Poverty & Human Resources Abstracts (Now: Human Resources Abstracts)
P.I.R.A.	P.I.R.A. Marketing Abstracts (Packaging Industry Research Association) (Now: Management and Marketing Abstracts)
P.L.E.S.A.	Quarterly Index to Periodical Literature, Eastern and Southern Africa
P.L.I.I.	Property & Liability Insurance Index (Ceased)
P.M.I.	Photography Magazine Index (Ceased)
PMR	Popular Magazine Review (Now: Magazine Article Summaries)
P.N.I.	Pharmaceutical News Index
PROMT	Predicasts Overview of Markets and Technologies
PSI	Philanthropic Studies Index
Packag.Sci.Tech.	Packaging Science and Technology Abstracts
Paper & Bd.Abstr.	Paper and Board Abstracts (Now: Paperbase Abstracts)
Past.Care & Couns.Abstr.	Pastoral Care & Counseling Abstracts (Now: Abstracts of Research in Pastoral Care and Counseling)
Peace Res.Abstr.	Peace Research Abstracts Journal
Per.Islam.	Periodica Islamica
Perf.Arts Biog.Master Ind.	Performing Arts Biography Master Index
Periodex	Periodex (Now: Point de Repere)
Pers.Lit.	Personnel Literature
Pers.Manage.Abstr.	Personnel Management Abstracts
Petrol.Abstr.	Petroleum Abstracts
Petrol.Energy B.N.I.	Petroleum - Energy Business News Index
Phil.Ind.	Philosopher's Index
Philip.Abstr.	Philippine Abstracts (Now: Philippine Science & Technology Abstracts)
Photo.Abstr.	Photographic Abstracts (Now: Imaging Abstracts)
Photo.Ind.	Photography Index
Phys.Ber.	Physikalische Berichte (Now: Physics Briefs - Physikalische Berichte) (Ceased)
Phys.Ed.Ind.	Physical Education Index
Pig News & Info.	Pig News and Information
Pinpointer	Pinpointer (Ceased)
Plant Breed.Abstr.	Plant Breeding Abstracts
Plant Grow.Reg.Abstr.	Plant Growth Regulator Abstracts
Plast.Abstr.	Plastics Abstracts (Ceased)
Pol.Tech.Abstr.	Polish Technical Abstracts (Now: Polish Technical and Economic Abstracts) (Ceased)
Polit.Sci.Abstr.	Political Science Abstracts
Pollut.Abstr.	Pollution Abstracts
Pop.Mus.Per.Ind.	Popular Music Periodicals Index (Ceased)
Pop.Per.Ind.	Popular Periodical Index
Popul.Ind.	Population Index
Potato Abstr.	Potato Abstracts
Poult.Abstr.	Poultry Abstracts
Print.Abstr.	Printing Abstracts
Protozool.Abstr.	Protozoological Abstracts
Psychoanal.Abstr.	Psychoanalysis Abstracts (Now: Psychoanalytic Abstracts)
Psychol.Abstr.	Psychological Abstracts
Psychol.R.G.	Psychological Reader's Guide (Ceased)
Psychopharmacol.Abstr.	Psychopharmacology Abstracts (Ceased)
Psycscan	Psycscan: Applied Psychology
Psycscan C.P.	Psycscan: Clinical Psychology
Psycscan D.P.	Psycscan: Developmental Psychology
Pt.de Rep.	Point de Repere (Formed by the merger Periodex and RADAR)
Pub.Admin.Abstr.	Public Administration Abstracts and Index of Articles (Now: Documentation in Public Administration)

Q

Q.Abstr.	Quality Abstracts (Ceased)
Qual.Contr.Appl.Stat.	Quality Control and Applied Statistics

R

RADAR	Repertoire Analytique d'Articles des Revues du Quebec (Now: Point de Repere)
RAPRA	R A P R A Abstracts (Rubber and Plastic Research Association of Great Britain)
R.G.	Readers' Guide to Periodical Literature
R.G.Abstr.	Readers' Guide Abstracts
RICS	R I C S Abstracts and Reviews (Now: R S Library Information Service Abstracts and Reviews) (Royal Institute of Chartered Surveyors)

ABSTRACTING AND INDEXING xliii

A	R I L A (Repertoire International de la Litterature d'Art) (Now: BHA (Bibliography of the History of Art))	SOPODA	Social Planning, Policy and Development Abstracts
		SRI	Statistical Reference Index
M	R I L M Abstracts of Music Literature (Repertoire International de la Litterature Musicale)	SSCI	Social Sciences Citation Index
		Saf.Sci.Abstr.	Safety Science Abstracts Journal (Now: Health and Safety Science Abstracts)
ac.	Reactions (Now: Reactions Weekly)	Sage Fam.Stud. Abstr.	Sage Family Studies Abstracts
.Pt.Food dus.Abstr.	Reference Point: Food Industry Abstracts		
.Sour.	Reference Sources (Ceased)	Sage Pub.Admin. Abstr.	Sage Public Administration Abstracts
.Zh.	Referativnyi Zhurnal		
ug.Abstr.	Refugee Abstracts (Now: Refugee Survey Quarterly)	Sage Race Rel.Abstr.	Sage Race Relations Abstracts
abil.Lit.	Rehabilitation Literature (Ceased)	Sage Urb.Stud. Abstr.	Sage Urban Studies Abstracts
.& Theol. ostr.	Religious & Theological Abstracts	Sci.Cit.Ind.	Science Citation Index
		Sci.Res.Abstr.	Science Research Abstracts (Now: Solid State and Superconductivity Abstracts)
.Ind.One	Religion Index One: Periodicals		
.Ind.Two	Religion Index Two: Multi-Author Works	Search	Search (Devon)
.Per.	Index to Religious Periodical Literature (Now: Religion Index One: Periodicals)	Seed Abstr.	Seed Abstracts
		Sel.J.Water.	Selected Journals on Water (Ceased)
index	Repindex	Sel. Water Res. Abstr.	Selected Water Resources Abstracts (Now: Water Resources Abstracts)
.Educ.	Research in Education (Now: Resources in Education)		
		Sh.& Vib.Dig.	Shock and Vibration Digest
.High.Educ. ostr.	Research into Higher Education Abstracts	Small Anim. Abstr.	Small Animal Abstracts (Now: Small Animals)
our.Ctr.Ind.	Resource Center Index		
.Appl. tomol.	Review of Applied Entomology. Series A (Now: Review of Agricultural Entomology) Review of Applied Entomology. Series B (Now: Review of Medical and Veterinary Entomology)	So.Pac.Per.Ind.	South Pacific Periodicals Index
		Soc.Sci.Ind.	Social Sciences Index
		Soc.Work Res.& Abstr.	Social Work Research & Abstracts (Now: Social Work Abstracts)
		Sociol.Abstr.	Sociological Abstracts
.Appl.Mycol.	Review of Applied Mycology (Now: Review of Plant Pathology)	Sociol.Educ. Abstr.	Sociology of Education Abstracts
.Med.& t.Mycol.	Review of Medical and Veterinary Mycology	Soft.Abstr.Eng.	Software Abstracts for Engineers
		Soils & Fert.	Soils & Fertilizers
.Plant Path.	Review of Plant Pathology	Solid St.Abstr.	Solid State Abstracts (Now: Solid State and Superconductivity Abstracts)
ol.Abstr.	Rheology Abstracts		
e Abstr.	Rice Abstracts	Sorghum & Millets Abstr.	Sorghum and Millets Abstracts (Now: Sorghum and Millets)
k Abstr.	Risk Abstracts		
omat.	Robomatix Reporter (Now: Robotics Abstracts) (Ceased)	South.Bap.Per. Ind.	Southern Baptist Periodical Index (Ceased)
al Devel. str.	Rural Development Abstracts	Soyabean Abstr.	Soyabean Abstracts
		Sp.Ed.Needs Abstr.	Special Education Needs Abstracts
al Ext.Educ.& .Abstr.	Rural Extension, Education and Training Abstracts (Ceased)		
		Speleol.Abstr.	Speleological Abstracts
al Recreat. ur.Abstr.	Rural Recreation and Tourism Abstracts (Now: Leisure, Recreation and Tourism Abstracts)	Sport Fish.Abstr.	Sport Fishery Abstracts (Now: Fisheries Review)
		Sports Per.Ind.	Sports Periodicals Index (Ceased)
	S	Sportsearch	Sportsearch
A	State Academies of Science Abstracts	Sri Lanka Sci. Ind.	Sri Lanka Science Index
.Waterabstr.	S.A. Waterabstracts (South Africa) (Ceased)	Stat.Theor.Meth. Abstr.	Statistical Theory and Method Abstracts
MP	S C I M P (Selective Cooperative Index of Management Periodicals) (Ceased)	Steels Alert	Steels Alert
		Stud.Wom.Abstr.	Studies on Women Abstracts
MA	School Organization & Management Abstracts	Sugar Ind.Abstr.	Sugar Industry Abstracts

ABSTRACTING AND INDEXING

T

T.C.E.A.	Theoretical Chemical Engineering Abstracts (Now: Theoretical Chemical Engineering)
THA	Tobacco & Health Abstracts
TOM	T O M (Text on Microfilm)
Tech.Educ.Abstr.	Technical Education Abstracts (Now: Technical Education & Training Abstracts)
Tel.Abstr.	Telecommunications Abstracts (Ceased)
Tel.Alert	Telecommunications Alert
Telegen	Telegen Reporter (Now: Telegen Abstracts) (Ceased)
Text.Tech.Dig.	Textile Technology Digest
Therm.Abstr.	Thermal Abstracts (Now: International Building Services Abstracts)
Tob.Abstr.	Tobacco Abstracts
Top Manage. Abstr.	Top Management Abstracts (Also see: Anbar)
Tox.Abstr.	Toxicology Abstracts
Tr.& Dev.Alert	Training and Development Alert
Tr.& Indus.Ind.	Trade & Industry Index
Trans.Res.Abstr.	Transportation Research Abstracts (Ceased)
Triticale Abstr.	Triticale Abstracts (Now: Wheat, Barley and Triticale Abstracts)
Trop.Abstr.	Tropical Abstracts (Now: Abstracts on Tropical Agriculture)
Trop.Dis.Bull.	Tropical Diseases Bulletin
Trop.Oil Seeds Abstr.	Tropical Oil Seeds Abstracts (Now: Tropical Oil Seeds)

U

Urb.Aff.Abstr.	Urban Affairs Abstracts

V

Va.Hist.Abstr.	Virginia Historical Abstracts (Ceased)
Vert.File Ind.	Vertical File Index
Vet.Bull.	Veterinary Bulletin
Viol.& Abuse Abstr.	Violence & Abuse Abstracts
Virol.Abstr.	Virology Abstracts (Now: Virology and AIDS Abstracts)
Vis.Ind.	Vision Index (Ceased)
VITIS	Vitis - Viticulture and Enology Abstracts

W

WPM	World Publishing Monitor
W.R.C.Inf.	W.R.C. Information (Water Research Centre) (Now: Aqualine Abstracts)
Water Pollut. Abstr.	Water Pollution Abstracts (Now: Aqualine Abstracts)
Water Resour. Abstr.	Water Resources Abstracts (Now: Hydro-Abstracts)
Weed Abstr.	Weed Abstracts
Wild Life Rev.	Wildlife Review (Ceased)
Wild.Rev.	Wildlife Review (Fort Collins)
Wildlife & Conserv.Biol. Abstr.	Essential Wildlife & Conservation Biology Abstracts
Wom.Stud.Abstr.	Women Studies Abstracts
Work Rel.Abstr.	Work Related Abstracts (Ceased)
World Agri.Econ. & Rural Sociol. Abstr.	World Agricultural Economics & Rural Sociology Abstracts
World Alum. Abstr.	World Aluminum Abstracts
World Bank. Abstr.	World Banking Abstracts
World Bibl.Soc. Sec.	World Bibliography of Social Security
World Fish.Abstr.	World Fisheries Abstracts (Ceased)
World Surf.Coat.	World Surface Coatings Abstracts
World Text.Abstr.	World Textile Abstracts

Y

Yrbk.Assoc.Educ. & Rehab.Blind	Association for Education and Rehabilitation of the Blind and Visually Impaired. Yearbook (Ceased)

Z

Zent.Math.	Zentralblatt fuer Mathematik und ihre Grenzgebiete
Zincscan	Zincscan
Zoo.Rec.	Zoological Record

Subject Guide to Abstracting and Indexing

The 135 subject headings listed below are major subjects which contain a sub-category headed "Abstracting, Bibliographies, Statistics." This sub-category, which follows the major subject headings in the CLASSIFIED LIST OF SERIALS, identifies publications which abstract and/or index publications in the relevant subject. Bibliographies and statistical publications pertaining to the subject are also included in this sub-category. This guide will enable users to quickly locate subject areas of interest for which abstracting and indexing publications have been identified and to build profiles by combination of relevant subject areas. Page numbers refer to the first page on which the sub-category appears.

SUBJECT CATEGORY	PAGE
Advertising and Public Relations	47
Aeronautics and Space Flight	83
Agriculture	167
Alternative Medicine	299
Animal Welfare	305
Anthropology	335
Archaeology	390
Architecture	417
Art	475
Arts and Handicrafts	485
Astronomy	503
Beauty Culture	509
Beverages	530
Biography	581
Biology	634
Birth Control	859
Building and Construction	919
Business and Economics	1014
Ceramics, Glass and Pottery	1735
Chemistry	1771
Children and Youth	1861
Civil Defense	1899
Classical Studies	1909
Cleaning and Dyeing	1912
Clothing Trade	1919
College and Alumni	1980
Communications	2010
Computers	2093
Conservation	2251
Consumer Education and Protection	2259
Criminology and Law Enforcement	2283
Dance	2295
Drug Abuse and Alcoholism	2307
Earth Sciences	2324
Education	2496
Electronics	2655
Energy	2681
Engineering	2746
Environmental Studies	2959
Ethnic Interests	3051
Fire Prevention	3059
Fish and Fisheries	3081
Folklore	3093
Food and Food Industries	3131
Forests and Forestry	3167
Funerals	3179
Gardening and Horticulture	3208
Genealogy and Heraldry	3246
Geography	3427
Gerontology and Geriatrics	3447
Handicapped	3458
Heating, Plumbing and Refrigeration	3486
History	3518
Hobbies	3680
Home Economics	3690
Homosexuality	3702
Hospitals	3721
Hotels and Restaurants	3738
Housing and Urban Planning	3764
How-to and Do-it-Yourself	3769
Humanities: Comprehensive Works	3798
Instruments	3806
Insurance	3838
Interior Design and Decoration	3851
Jewelry, Clocks and Watches	3868
Journalism	3883
Labor Unions	3902
Law	4050
Leather and Fur Industries	4147
Leisure and Recreation	4154
Library and Information Sciences	4223
Linguistics	4318
Literary and Political Reviews	4368
Literature	4493
Machinery	4554
Mathematics	4617
Matrimony	4627
Medical Sciences	4762
Meetings and Congresses	5173
Metallurgy	5216
Meteorology	5248
Metrology and Standardization	5256
Military	5292
Mines and Mining Industry	5319
Motion Pictures	5348
Museums and Art Galleries	5369
Music	5446
Numismatics	5468
Nutrition and Dietetics	5484
Occupational Health and Safety	5502
Occupations and Careers	5518
Oriental Studies	5541
Packaging	5550
Paints and Protective Coatings	5556
Paleontology	5564
Paper and Pulp	5573
Parapsychology and Occultism	5579
Patents, Trademarks and Copyrights	5592
Petroleum and Gas	5628
Pets	5644
Pharmacy and Pharmacology	5700
Philately	5715
Philosophy	5760
Photography	5776
Physical Fitness and Hygiene	5793
Physics	5833
Plastics	5886
Political Science	5982
Population Studies	6060
Printing	6087
Psychology	6160
Public Administration	6201
Public Health and Safety	6255
Publishing and Book Trade	6288
Real Estate	6316
Religions and Theology	6385
Rubber	6505
Sciences: Comprehensive Works	6587
Shoes and Boots	6597
Social Sciences: Comprehensive Works	6648
Social Services and Welfare	6695
Sociology	6739
Sound Recording and Reproduction	6746
Sports and Games	6795
Technology: Comprehensive Works	6980
Textile Industries and Fabrics	6999
Theater	7018
Tobacco	7022
Transportation	7047
Travel and Tourism	7252
Veterinary Science	7285
Water Resources	7307
Women's Health	7311
Women's Interests	7370
Women's Studies	7350

Subjects

ENGLISH	FRENCH	GERMAN	SPANISH
Abstracting and Indexing Services	Services d'Analyse et d'Indexage	Referate- und Indexdienste	Servicio de Análisis e Indización
Advertising and Public Relations	Publicité et Relations Publiques	Reklamewesen und Public Relations	Relaciones Públicas y Publicidad
Aeronautics and Space Flight	Aéronautique et Astronautique	Luft- und Raumfahrt	Aeronáutica y Vuelo Espacial
Computer Applications	Applications Informatiques	Computer Anwendung	Aplicaciones para Computadoras
Agriculture	Agriculture	Landwirtschaft	Agricultura
Agricultural Economics	Agriculture Économique	Agrarökonomie	Economía Agrícola
Agricultural Equipment	Outillage Agricole	Landwirtschaftsgeräte	Equipo para la Agricultura
Computer Applications	Applications Informatiques	Computer Anwendung	Aplicaciones para Computadoras
Crop Production and Soil	Production Végétale et Terrain	Ernte und Acker	Producción de Cosecha, Tierra
Dairying and Dairy Products	Production Laitière	Milchwirtschaft	Lechería y Productos Lácteos
Feed, Flour and Grain	Pature, Farine et Grain	Futter, Mehl und Getreide	Forraje, Granos y Harina
Poultry and Livestock	Élevage	Geflügel- und Viehwirtschaft	Ganadería
Alternative Medicine	Médecine Alternative	Alternative Heilkunde	Medicina Alternativa
Animal Welfare	Protection des Animaux	Tierschutz	Protección a los Animales
Anthropology	Anthropologie	Anthropologie	Antropología
Antiques	Antiquités	Antiquitäten	Antigüedades
Archaeology	Archeologie	Archaeologie	Arqueología
Computer Applications	Applications Informatiques	Computer Anwendung	Aplicaciones para Computadoras
Architecture	Architecture	Architektur	Arquitectura
Computer Applications	Applications Informatiques	Computer Anwendung	Aplicaciones para Computadoras
Art	Art	Kunst	Arte
Computer Applications	Applications Informatiques	Computer Anwendung	Aplicaciones para Computadoras
Arts and Handicrafts	Arts et Métiers	Kunst und Handwerk	Artesanías y Obras Manuales
Astrology	Astrologie	Astrologie	Astrología
Astronomy	Astronomie	Astronomie	Astronomía
Computer Applications	Applications Informatiques	Computer Anwendung	Aplicaciones para Computadoras
Beauty Culture	Soins de Beauté	Schönheitspflege	Belleza Personal
Perfumes and Cosmetics	Parfums et Cosmétiques	Kosmetik und Parfüme	Perfumes y Cosméticos
Beverages	Boissons	Getränke	Bebidas
Bibliographies	Bibliographies	Bibliographien	Bibliografías
Biography	Biographie	Biographie	Biografía
Biology	Biologie	Biologie	Biología
Bioengineering	Biogénie	Bioingenieurwesen	Bio-ingeniería
Biological Chemistry	Biochimie	Biochemie	Bio-química
Biophysics	Biophysique	Biophysik	Biofísica
Biotechnology	Biotechnologie	Biotechnologie	Biotecnología
Botany	Botanique	Botanik	Botánica
Computer Applications	Applications Informatiques	Computer Anwendung	Aplicaciones para Computadoras
Cytology and Histology	Cytologie et Histologie	Zytologie und Histologie	Citología e Histología
Entomology	Entomologie	Entomologie	Entomología
Genetics	Génétique	Genetik	Genética
Microbiology	Microbiologie	Mikrobiologie	Microbiología
Microscopy	Microscopie	Mikroskopie	Microscopía
Ornithology	Ornithologie	Ornithologie	Ornitología
Physiology	Physiologie	Physiologie	Fisiología
Zoology	Zoologie	Zoologie	Zoología
Birth Control	Limitation des Naissances	Geburtenregelung	Control Natal
Building and Construction	Bâtiment et Construction	Bauwesen	Edificios y Construcción
Carpentry and Woodwork	Charpenterie et Menuiserie	Zimmerhandwerk und Holzbau	Carpintería y Ebanistería
Hardware	Quincaillerie	Metallbaustoffe	Ferretería
Business and Economics	Affaires et Économie	Wirtschaft und Handel	Economía y Negocios
Accounting	Comptabilité	Rechnungswesen	Contabilidad
Banking and Finance	Banque et Finance	Bank- und Finanzwesen	Bancos y Finanzas

Banking and Finance-
    Computer Applications
	Banque et Finance-
	    Applications Informatiques
		Bank- und Finanzwesen-
		    Computer Anwendung
			Bancos y Finanzas-
			    Aplicaciones para Computadoras

Chamber of Commerce
    Publications
	Publications des Chambres
	    de Commerce
		Veröffentlichungen von Handels-
		    kammern
			Publicaciones de las Cámaras de
			    Comercio

Computer Applications	Applications Informatiques	Computer Anwendung	Aplicaciones para Computadoras
Cooperatives	Coopératives	Genossenschaften	Cooperativas
Domestic Commerce	Commerce Interieur	Binnenhandel	Comercio Interno

Economic Situation and
    Conditions
	Situations et Conditions
	    Économiques
		Wirtschaftliche Situation und
		    Verhältnisse
			Condiciones y Situaciones
			    Económicas

Economic Systems and Theories,
    Economic History
	Systèmes et Théories Économiques,
	    Histoire Économique
		Ökonomische Systeme und
		    Theorien, Wirtschafts-
		    geschichte
			Sistemas y Teorías Económicos,
			    Historia de la Economía

International Commerce	Commerce International	Aussenhandel	Comercio Internacional

International Development and
    Assistance
	Aide et Développement
	    Internationaux
		Internationale Entwicklungshilfe	Desarrollo y Asistencia Inter-
			    nacional

Investments	Investissements	Investitionen	Inversiones
Labor and Industrial Relations	Travail et Relations Industrielles	Arbeits und Industrielle Beziehungen	Trabajo y Relaciones Industriales
Macroeconomics	Macroéconomie	Makroökonomie	Macroeconomía
Management	Gestion	Betriebsführung	Administración
Marketing and Purchasing	Marketing et Achats	Marketing und Kauf	Ventas y Mercadotenica
Office Equipment and Services	Matériel et Entretien de Bureaux	Büroeinrichtung und Service	Equipo y Servicios de Oficinas
Personnel Management	Gestion du Personnel	Personal Führung	Administración de Personal
Production of Goods and Services	Production de Biens et Services	Produktion	Producción de Bienes y Servicios
Public Finance, Taxation	Tresor Publique, Fiscalité	Staatsfinanzen, Steuerwesen	Finanzas Públicas e Impuestos
Small Business	Petites et Moyennes Entreprises	Kleinbetrieb	Pequeños Negocios
Trade and Industrial Directories	Annuaires de Commerce et d'Industrie	Firmenverzeichnisse	Directorios de la Industria y el Comercio

SUBJECTS xlvii

Ceramics, Glass and Pottery	Céramique, Verrerie et Poterie	Keramik, Glas und Töpferei	Cerámica, Vidrio y Porcelana
Chemistry	Chimie	Chemie	Química
Analytical Chemistry	Chimie Analytique	Analytische Chemie	Química Analítica
Computer Applications	Applications Informatiques	Computer Anwendung	Aplicaciones para Computadoras
Crystallography	Cristallographie	Kristallographie	Cristalografía
Electrochemistry	Electrochimie	Elektrochemie	Electroquímica
Inorganic Chemistry	Chimie Inorganique	Anorganische Chemie	Química Inorgánica
Organic Chemistry	Chimie Organique	Organische Chemie	Química Orgánica
Physical Chemistry	Physicochimie	Physikalische Chemie	Fisicoquímica
Children and Youth	Enfants et Adolescents	Kinder und Jugend	Niños y Jóvenes
About	Au Sujet des	Über	Acerca
For	Pour	Für	Para
Civil Defense	Defense Civile	Ziviler Bevölkerungsschutz	Defensa Civil
Classical Studies	Etudes Classiques	Klassische Studien	Estudios Clásicos
Cleaning and Dyeing	Nettoyage et Teinturerie	Reinigen und Färben	Limpieza y Tintura
Clothing Trade	Vêtement	Bekleidungsgewerbe	Industria del Vestido
Fashions	Mode	Moden	Modas
Clubs	Clubs	Klubs	Clubes
College and Alumni	Université et Diplomés	Universitäten und Hochschulabsolventen	Universidades y Exalumnos
Communications	Communications	Nachrichtentechnik	Comunicaciones
Computer Applications	Applications Informatiques	Computer Anwendung	Aplicaciones para Computadoras
Postal Affairs	Courrier	Postwesen	Correo
Radio	Radio	Rundfunk	Radio
Telephone and Telegraph	Téléphone et Télégraphe	Telephon und Telegraph	Teléfono y Telégrafo
Television and Cable	Télévision	Fernsehen und Bildfrequenzkanal	Cable y Televisión
Video	Vidéo	Video	Video
Computers	Ordinateurs	Computer	Computadoras
Artificial Intelligence	Intelligence Artificielle	Künstliche Intelligenz	Inteligencia Artificial
Automation	Automation	Automatisierung	Automatización
Calculating Machines	Calculateurs	Rechenmaschine	Calculadoras
Circuits	Circuits	Schaltungen	Circuitos
Computer Architecture	Architecture de la Machine	Computer Architektur	Arquitectura de las Computadoras
Computer-Assisted Instruction	Enseignement Assisté par Ordinateur	Computerunterstützter Unterricht	Enseñanza con la Ayuda de las Computadoras
Computer Engineering	Technique Informatique	Computerentwicklung	Ingeniería de las Computadoras
Computer Games	Jeux sur Ordinateurs	Computer Spiele	Juegos para Computadoras
Computer Graphics	Conception Assistée par Ordinateur	Computergraphik	Diseño a través de Computadoras
Computer Industry	Industrie Informatique	Computerbetrieb	Industria de las Computadoras
Computer Industry Directories	Annuaire de l'Industrie Informatique	Computerbetriebverzeichnisse	Directorios de la Industria de las Computadoras
Computer Industry, Vocational Guidance	Industrie Informatique, Orientation Professionnelle	Computerbetrieb Berufsberatung	Guía para la Industria de las Computadoras
Computer Music	Musique sur Ordinateur	Computer Musik	Música a través de Computadoras
Computer Networks	Réseaux d'Ordinateurs	Rechnernetz	Redes de Computadoras
Computer Programming	Programmation Informatique	Computerprogrammierung	Programación de Computadoras
Computer Sales	Ventes d'Ordinateurs	Computervertrieb	Ventas de Computadoras
Computer Security	Sécurité Informatique	Computersicherheit	Seguridad en Computadoras
Computer Simulation	Simulation sur Ordinateurs	Computersimulation	Simulación a través de Computadoras
Computer Systems	Systèmes Informatiques	Computersystemen	Sistemas de Computadoras
Cybernetics	Cybernétique	Kybernetik	Cibernética
Data Base Management	Gestion de Base de Données	Datenbankverwaltung	Bases de Datos
Data Communications, Data Transmission Systems	Communication de données	Datenübertragung, Datenübertragungssystem	Comunicación y Transmisión de Datos
Electronic Data Processing	Traitement de l'Information Electronique	Elektronische Datenverarbeitung	Procesamiento Electrónico de Datos
Hardware	Matériel	Hardware	Equipo Físico
Information Science, Information Theory	Théorie de l'Information	Informationstheorie	Ciencia y Teoría de la Información
Machine Theory	Théorie de Machine	Maschinetheorie	Teoría de las Máquinas
Microcomputers	Micro-Ordinateurs	Mikrocomputer	Microcomputadoras
Minicomputers	Mini-Ordinateurs	Minicomputer	Minicomputadoras
Personal Computers	Ordinateurs Personnels	Persönlichecomputer	Computadoras Personales
Robotics	Robotique	Robotersysteme	Robótica
Software	Logiciel	SoftwareRComputertheorie	Applicaciones de Computadora
Theory of Computing	Théorie de Traitement	Textverarbeitung	Teoría de Cálculo
Word Processing	Traitement de Textes		Procesador de Textos
Conservation	Conservation	Landschaftsschutz	Conservación
Consumer Education and Protection	Protection du Consommateur	Verbraucherwirtschaftsschutz	Protección al Consumidor
Criminology and Law Enforcement	Criminologie et Police	Kriminologie und Strafvollzug	Criminología y Acción Policial
Computer Applications	Applications Informatiques	Computer Anwendung	Aplicaciones para Computadoras
Security	Securité	Sicherheit	Seguridad
Dance	Danse	Tanz	Baile
Drug Abuse and Alcoholism	Toxicomanie et Alcoolisme	Rauschgiftsucht und Alkoholismus	Alcoholismo y Drogadicción
Earth Sciences	Sciences Géologiques	Wissenschaften der Erde	Ciencias Geológicas
Computer Applications	Applications Informatiques	Computer Anwendung	Aplicaciones para Computadoras
Geology	Géologie	Geologie	Geología
Geophysics	Géophysique	Geophysik	Geofísica
Hydrology	Hydrologie	Hydrologie	Hidrología
Oceanography	Océanographie	Ozeanographie	Oceanografía
Education	Education	Bildungswesen	Educación
Adult Education	Enseignement des Adultes	Erwachsenenbildung	Educación para Adultos
Computer Applications	Applications Informatiques	Computer Anwendung	Aplicaciones para Computadoras
Guides to Schools and Colleges	Guides des Écoles et Colleges	Führer zur Schulen und Universitäten	Guías de Escuelas y Colegios
Higher Education	Enseignement Supérieur	Hochschulwesen	Educación Superior
International Education Programs	Programmes d'Éducation Internationale	Internationale Erziehungsprogramme	Programas Internacionales de Educación
School Organization and Administration	Organisation et Administration de l'École	Organisation und Verwaltung von dem Schule	Administración y Dirección de Escuelas
Special Education and Rehabilitation	Enseignement Special et Réhabilitation	Fachunterricht und Rehabilitierung	Educación Especial y Rehabilitación
Teaching Methods and Curriculum	Méthodes Pédagogiques et Programmes Scolaires	Lehrmethoden und Lehrplan	Métodos y Planes de Estudio

SUBJECTS

Electronics	Electronique	Elektronik	Electrónica
Computer Applications	Applications Informatiques	Computer Anwendung	Aplicaciones para Computadoras
Encyclopedias and General Almanacs	Encyclopédies et Almanachs Générales	Enzyklopädien und Allgemeine Nachschlagewerke	Enciclopedias y Almanaques Generales
Energy	Energie	Energie	Energía
Computer Applications	Applications Informatiques	Computer Anwendung	Aplicaciones para Computadoras
Electrical Energy	Energie Électrique	Elektrizitätsenergie	Energía Eléctrica
Geothermal Energy	Energie Géothermique	Thermalenergie	Energía Geotérmica
Hydroelectrical Energy	Energie Hydraulique	Hydroelektroenergie	Energía Hidroeléctrica
Nuclear Energy	Energie Nucléaire	Kernenergie	Energía Nuclear
Solar Energy	Energie Solaire	Sonnenenergie	Energía Solar
Wind Energy	Energie Eolienne	Windenergie	Energía de Viento
Engineering	Ingénierie	Ingenieurwesen	Ingeniería
Chemical Engineering	Génie Chimique	Chemieingenieurwesen	Ingeniería Química
Civil Engineering	Génie Civil	Bauingenieurwesen	Ingeniería Civil
Computer Applications	Applications Informatiques	Computer Anwendung	Aplicaciones para Computadoras
Electrical Engineering	Génie Électrique	Elektrotechnik	Ingeniería Eléctrica
Engineering Mechanics and Materials	Méchanique et Materiels	Ingenieurwesen Mechanik und Materialien	Ingeniería Mecanica y de Materiales
Hydraulic Engineering	Génie Hydraulique	Wasserbau	Ingeniería Hidráulica
Industrial Engineering	Génie Industriel	Industrieingenieurwesen	Ingeniería Industrial
Mechanical Engineering	Génie Mécanique	Maschinenbau	Ingeniería Mecánica
Environmental Studies	Science de l'Environnement	Umweltschutz	Estudios Ambientales
Computer Applications	Applications Informatiques	Computer Anwendung	Aplicaciones para Computadoras
Pollution	Pollution	Umweltverschmutzung	Contaminación
Toxicology and Environmental Safety	Toxicologie et Sécurité de l'Environnement	Toxokologie und Umweltsicherheit	Toxicología y Seguridad Ambiental
Waste Management	Gestion de Déchets	Abfallwirtschaft	Administración de Desperdicios
Ethnic Interests	Ethnologie	Allgemeine Völkerkunde	Publicaciones de Temas Etnicos
Fire Prevention	Prévention d'Incendie	Brandbekämpfung	Prevención del Fuego
Fish and Fisheries	Poisson et Pêche	Fische und Fischerei	Pesca y Pesquerías
Folklore	Folklore	Volkskunde	Folklore
Food and Food Industries	Alimentation et Industries Alimentaires	Nahrungsmittel und Lebensmittelindustrie	Alimentos e Industrias de Alimentos
Bakers and Confectioners	Boulangerie et Confiserie	Bäcker- und Konditorgewerbe	Panaderías y Dulcerías
Grocery Trade	Épicerie	Kolonialwarenhandel	Abacerías
Forest and Forestry	Forêts et Exploitation Forestière	Forstwesen und Waldwirtschaft	Bosques y Selvicultura
Lumber and Wood	Bois	Holz	Maderas
Funerals	Funérailles	Beerdigungen	Funerales
Gardening and Horticulture	Jardinage et Horticulture	Gartenpflege und Gartenbau	Jardinería y Horticultura
Florist Trade	Commerce des Fleurs	Blumenhandel	Comercio de Flores
Genealogy and Heraldry	Généalogie et Science Héraldique	Genealogie und Wappenkunde	Genealogía y Heráldica
Computer Applications	Applications Informatiques	Computer Anwendung	Aplicaciones para Computadoras
General Interest Periodicals (Subdivided by country)	Publications d'Intérêt Général (Selon pays)	Allgemeine Zeitschriften (nach Land)	Periódicos de Interés General (por país)
Geography	Géographie	Geographie	Geografía
Computer Applications	Applications Informatiques	Computer Anwendung	Aplicaciones para Computadoras
Gerontology and Geriatrics	Gérontologie	Gerontologie	Gerontología y Geriátrica
Giftware and Toys	Cadeaux et Jouets	Geschenkartikel und Spielwaren	Juguetes y Regalos
Handicapped	Handicapés	Behinderung	Descapacitados
Computer Applications	Applications Informatiques	Computer Anwendung	Aplicaciones para Computadoras
Hearing Impaired	Sourds	Schwerhörigkeit	Descapacitado del Oído
Physically Impaired	Handicapés Physiques	Körperbehinderung	Descapacitado Físicamente
Visually Impaired	Aveugles	Blindheit	Descapacitado Visualmente
Heating, Plumbing, and Refrigeration	Chauffage, Plomberie et Réfrigeration	Heizung, Kühlung und Installation	Calefacción, Plomería y Refrigeración
History	Histoire	Geschichte	Historia
Computer Applications	Applications Informatiques	Computer Anwendung	Aplicaciones para Computadoras
History of Africa	Histoire de l'Afrique	Geschichte-Afrika	Historia de Africa
History of Asia	Histoire de l'Asie	Geschichte-Asien	Historia de Asia
History of Australasia and Other Areas	Histoire de l'Australasie et Autres Pays	Geschichte-Australasien und Andere Gebieten	Historia de Australasia y Otras Areas
History of Europe	Histoire de l'Europe	Geschichte-Europa	Historia de la Europa
History of North and South America	Histoire de l'Amérique du Nord et du Sud	Geschichte-Nord- und Südamerika	Historia de América del Norte y del Sur
History of Near East	Histoire du Proche-Orient	Geschichte-Nahe Osten	Historia del Cercano Oriente
Hobbies	Passe-Temps	Hobbies	Pasatiempos
Home Economics	Gestion Domestique	Hauswirtschaft	Economía Doméstica
Homosexuality	Homosexualité	Homosexualität	Homosexualidad
Hospitals	Hôpitaux	Krankenhäuser	Hospitales
Computer Applications	Applications Informatiques	Computer Anwendung	Aplicaciones para Computadoras
Hotels and Restaurants	Hôtels et Restaurants	Hotels und Restaurants	Restaurantes y Hoteles
Computer Applications	Applications Informatiques	Computer Anwendung	Aplicaciones para Computadoras
Housing and Urban Planning	Logement et Urbanisme	Wohnungswesen und Stadtplanung	Planeación Urbana y Vivienda
Computer Applications	Applications Informatiques	Computer Anwendung	Aplicaciones para Computadoras
How-To and Do-It-Yourself	Bricolage	Selbstanfertigung	Cómo Hacerlo Usted Mismo
Humanities: Comprehensive Works	Humanités: Oeuvres d'Ensemble	Klassische Philologie	Humanidades: Obras Generales
Computer Applications	Applications Informatiques	Computer Anwendung	Aplicaciones para Computadoras
Instruments	Instruments	Instrumente	Instrumentos
Insurance	Assurances	Versicherungswesen	Seguros
Computer Applications	Applications Informatiques	Computer Anwendung	Aplicaciones para Computadoras
Interior Design and Decoration	Agencements Intérieurs et Décoration	Innenarchitektur und Innenausstattung	Diseño Interior y Ornamentación
Furniture and House Furnishings	Meubles et Articles pour la Maison	Möbel und Wohnungseinrichtung	Muebles y Articulos para el Hogar
Jewelry, Clocks and Watches	Bijouterie et Horlogerie	Schmuck und Uhren	Joyería y Relojería
Journalism	Journalisme	Journalismus	Periodismo

SUBJECTS xlix

bor Unions	Syndicalisme	Gewerkschaften	Sindicatos
w	Droit	Rechtswissenschaft	Derecho
Civil Law	Droit Civil	Zivilrecht	Derecho Civil
Computer Applications	Applications Informatiques	Computer Anwendung	Aplicaciones para Computadoras
Constitutional Law	Droit Constitutionel	Verfassungsrecht	Derecho Constitucional
Corporate Law	Droit Commercial	Handelsrecht	Derecho Corporativo
Criminal Law	Droit Pénal	Strafrecht	Derecho Criminal
Estate Planning	Succession	Mobiliarvermögensrecht	Planeación de Bienes Raíces
Family and Matrimonial Law	Droit Familial et Matrimonial	Ehegesetz und Familienrecht	Derecho Familial y Matrimonial
International Law	Droit International	Völkerrecht	Derecho Internacional
Judicial Systems	Système Judiciaire	Gerichtswesen	Sistemas Judiciales
Legal Aid	Assistance Judiciaire	Rechtshilfe	Ayuda Legal
Maritime Law	Droit Maritime	Seerecht	Derecho Marítimo
Military Law	Droit Militaire	Kriegsrecht	Derecho Militar
ather and Fur Industries	Maroquinerie et Fourrure	Leder und Pelz	Pieles y Cuero
sure and Recreation	Loisirs et Récréation	Freizeit und Unterhaltung	Tiempo Libre y Recreación
rary and Information Science	Bibliothéconomie et Informatique	Bibliothek- und Informations-wissenschaft	Bibliotecología y Ciencias de la Información
Computer Applications	Applications Informatiques	Computer Anwendung	Aplicaciones para Computadoras
guistics	Linguistique	Sprachwissenschaft	Lingüística
Computer Applications	Applications Informatiques	Computer Anwendung	Aplicaciones para Computadoras
erary and Political Reviews	Revues Littéraires et Politiques	Literarische und Politische Zeitschriften	Revistas Literarias y Políticas
erature	Littérature	Literatur	Literatura
Adventure and Romance	Aventure et Romance	Abenteuer und Romantik	Aventura y Romance
Mystery and Detective	Mystère et Policier	Geheimnis und Detektivroman	Misterio y Novela Policiaca
Poetry	Poésie	Poesie	Poesía
Science Fiction, Fantasy, Horror	Science-Fiction, Fantastisque, Horreur	Zukunftsroman, Phantasiegebilde, Grausen	Ciencia Ficción, Fantasía, Horror
chinery	Machines	Maschinenwesen	Maquinaria
Computer Applications	Applications Informatiques	Computer Anwendung	Aplicaciones para Computadoras
thematics	Mathématiques	Mathematik	Matemáticas
Computer Applications	Applications Informatiques	Computer Anwendung	Aplicaciones para Computadoras
trimony	Mariage	Ehestand	Matrimonio
Computer Applications	Applications Informatiques	Computer Anwendung	Aplicaciones para Computadoras
dical Sciences	Médecine	Medizinische Wissenschaften	Ciencias Médicas
Allergology and Immunology	Allergologie et Immunologie	Allergie und Immunologie	Alergología e Imunología
Anaesthesiology	Anesthésiologie	Anaesthesiologie	Anestesiología
Cardiovascular Diseases	Maladies Cardiovasculaires	Kreislauferkrankungen	Enfermedades Cardiovasculares
Chiropractic, Homeopathy, Osteopathy	Chiropraxie, Homéopathie, Ostéopathie	Chiropraktik, Homöopathie, Osteopathie	Quiropráctica, Homeopatía, Osteopatía
Communicable Diseases	Maladies Contagieuses	Infektiöse Krankheiten	Enfermedades Contagiosas
Computer Applications	Applications Informatiques	Computer Anwendung	Aplicaciones para Computadoras
Dentistry	Dentisterie	Zahnmedizin	Odontología
Dermatology and Venereology	Dermatologie et Maladies Vénériennes	Dermatologie und Geschlechtskrankheiten	Dermatología y Venereología
Endocrinology	Endocrinologie	Endokrinologie	Endocrinología
Experimental Medicine, Laboratory Technique	Médecine Expérimentale, Techniques de Laboratoire	Versuchsmedizin, Laboratoriumstechnik	Medicina Experimental, Técnicas del Laboratorio
Forensic Sciences	Médecine Légale	Gerichtliche Medizin	Ciencias Forenses
Gastroenterology	Gastroentérologie	Gastroenterologie	Gastroenterología
Hematology	Hématologie	Hämatologie	Hematología
Hypnosis	Hypnose	Hypnose	Hipnotismo
nternal Medicine	Médecine Interne	Innere Medizin	Medicina Interna
Nurses and Nursing	Personnel et Soins Infirmiers	Krankenpflege	Enfermeros y Enfermería
Obstetrics and Gynecology	Obstétrique et Gynécologie	Gynäkologie und Geburtshilfe	Obstetricia y Ginecología
Oncology	Cancer	Onkologie	Oncología
Ophthalmology and Optometry	Ophtalmologie et Optométrie	Opthalmologie und Optometrie	Oftalmología y Optometría
Orthopedics and Traumatology	Orthopédie et Traumatologie	Orthopädie und Traumatologie	Ortopedia y Traumatología
Otorhinolaryngology	Otorhinolaryngologie	Otorhinolaryngologie	Otorinolaringología
Pediatrics	Pédiatrie	Pädiatrie	Pediatría
Physical Medicine and Rehabilitation	Médecine Physique et Réhabilitation	Physikalische Heilkunde und Rehabilitation	Medicina Física y de Rehabilitación
Psychiatry and Neurology	Psychiatrie et Neurologie	Psychiatrie und Neurologie	Psiquiatría y Neurología
Radiology and Nuclear Medicine	Radiologie et Médecine Nucléaire	Radiologie und Nuklearmedizin	Radiología y Medicina Nuclear
Respiratory Diseases	Maladies Respiratoires	Atmungskrankheiten	Enfermedades Respiratorias
Rheumatology	Rhumatologie	Rheumatologie	Reumatología
Sports Medicine	Médecine du Sport	Sportmedizin	Medicina del Deporte
Surgery	Chirurgie	Chirurgie	Cirugía
Urology and Nephrology	Urologie et Néphrologie	Urologie und Nephrologie	Urología y Nefrología
etings and Congresses	Réunions et Congrès	Tagungen und Kongresse	Conferencias y Congresos
n's Health	Santé de l'Homme	Gesundheit von Männern	Salud de los Hombres
n's Interests	Publications d'Intérêt Masculin	Männer Interessen	Intereses Masculinos
n's Studies	Études de l'Homme	Männerstudien	Estudios de los Hombres
tallurgy	Métallurgie	Metallurgie	Metalurgia
Computer Applications	Applications Informatiques	Computer Anwendung	Aplicaciones para Computadoras
Welding	Soudure	Schweissen	Soldadura
teorology	Météorologie	Meteorologie	Meteorología
Computer Applications	Applications Informatiques	Computer Anwendung	Aplicaciones para Computadoras
trology and Standardization	Métrologie et Standardisation	Mass- und Gewichtskunde, Normung	Metrología y Normalización
Computer Applications	Applications Informatiques	Computer Anwendung	Aplicaciones para Computadoras
tary	Militaires	Militärwesen	Militares
es and Mining Industry	Mines et Resources Minières	Bergwesen und Bergbauindustrie	Minas e Industria Minera
Computer Applications	Applications Informatiques	Computer Anwendung	Aplicaciones para Computadoras
tion Pictures	Cinéma	Film und Kino	Películas
seums and Art Galleries	Musées et Galleries	Museen und Kunstgalerien	Museos y Galerías del Arte
sic	Musique	Musik	Música
Computer Applications	Applications Informatiques	Computer Anwendung	Aplicaciones para Computadoras
edlework	Travaux de Couture	Näherei	Bordado
w Age	New Age	New Age	Nueva Epoca
nismatics	Numismatique	Numismatik	Numismática
rition and Dietetics	Nutrition et Diététique	Ernährung und Diätetik	Dietas y Nutrición
cupational Health and Safety	Médecine du Travail et Prévention	Berufsgesundheitspflege und Sicherheit	Sanidad y Seguridad en el Trabajo
cupations and Careers	Emplois et Carrières	Berufe	Empleos y Ocupaciones
ental Studies	Études Orientales	Orientalistik	Estudios Orientales

SUBJECTS

Packaging	Emballage	Verpackung	Empaque
Computer Applications	Applications Informatiques	Computer Anwendung	Aplicaciones para Computadoras
Paints and Protective Coatings	Couleurs et Peintures	Farben und Beläge	Pinturas y Revestimientos Protectores
Paleontology	Paléontologie	Paleontologie	Paleontología
Computer Applications	Applications Informatiques	Computer Anwendung	Aplicaciones para Computadoras
Paper and Pulp	Papier et Pulpe	Papier und Papierstoff	Papel y Pulpa
Parapsychology and Occultism	Parapsychologie et Occultisme	Parapsychologie und Okkultismus	Parapsicología y Ocultismo
Patents, Trademarks and Copyrights	Brevets, Marques Commerciales et Droits d'Auteur	Patente, Schutzmarken und Urheberrechte	Patentes, Marcas Registradas y Derechos de Autor
Petroleum and Gas	Pétrole et Gas Naturel	Petroleum und Gas	Petróleo y Gas Natural
Computer Applications	Applications Informatiques	Computer Anwendung	Aplicaciones para Computadoras
Pets	Animaux Familiers	Haustiere	Mascotas
Pharmacy and Pharmacology	Pharmacie et Pharmacologie	Pharmazie und Pharmakologie	Farmacia y Farmacología
Computer Applications	Applications Informatiques	Computer Anwendung	Aplicaciones para Computadoras
Philately	Philatélie	Briefmarkenkunde	Filatelia
Philosophy	Philosophie	Philosophie	Filosofía
Photography	Photographie	Photographie	Fotografía
Computer Applications	Applications Informatiques	Computer Anwendung	Aplicaciones para Computadoras
Physical Fitness and Hygiene	Santé Physique et Hygiène	Gesundheitszustand und Hygiene	Salud Física e Higiene
Physics	Physique	Physik	Física
Computer Applications	Applications Informatiques	Computer Anwendung	Aplicaciones para Computadoras
Electricity	Electricité	Elektrizität	Electricidad
Heat	Chaleur	Wärme	Calor
Mechanics	Mécanique	Mechanik	Mecánica
Nuclear Physics	Physique Nucléaire	Kernphysik	Física Nuclear
Optics	Optique	Optik	Optica
Sound	Son	Schall	Sonido
Plastics	Plastiques	Kunststoffe	Plásticos
Computer Applications	Applications Informatiques	Computer Anwendung	Aplicaciones para Computadoras
Political Science	Sciences Politiques	Politische Wissenschafte	Ciencias Políticas
Civil Rights	Droits Civiques	Bürgerrechte	Derechos Civiles
International Relations	Relations Internationales	Internationale Beziehungen	Relaciones Internacionales
Population Studies	Démographie	Bevölkerungswissenschaft	Demografía
Printing	Imprimerie	Druck	Imprenta
Computer Applications	Applications Informatiques	Computer Anwendung	Aplicaciones para Computadoras
Psychology	Psychologie	Psychologie	Psicología
Public Administration	Administration Publique	Öffentliche Verwaltung	Administración Pública
Computer Applications	Applications Informatiques	Computer Anwendung	Aplicaciones para Computadoras
Municipal Government	Gouvernement Municipal	Kommunalverwaltung	Gobierno Municipal
Public Health and Safety	Santé Publique et Prévention	Öffentliche Gesundheitspflege	Salud y Seguridad Pública
Publishing and Book Trade	Édition et Commerce du Livre	Verlagswesen und Buchhandel	Editoriales y Ferias de Libros
Computer Applications	Applications Informatiques	Computer Anwendung	Aplicaciones para Computadoras
Real Estate	Immobiliers	Grundbesitz und Immobilien	Bienes Raíces
Computer Applications	Applications Informatiques	Computer Anwendung	Aplicaciones para Computadoras
Religions and Theology	Religions et Théologie	Religion und Theologie	Religión y Teología
Buddhist	Bouddhisme	Buddhist	Budismo
Eastern Orthodox	Églises Orthodoxes	Orthodox	Inglesias Ortodoxas
Hindu	Hindouisme	Hindu	Hinduísmo
Islamic	Islam	Islamische	Islamísmo
Judaic	Judaisme	Jüdäistische	Judaísmo
Protestant	Protestantisme	Evangelische	Iglesia Protestante
Roman Catholic	Catholicisme Romain	Römisch-katholische	Iglesia Católica
Other Denominations and Sects	Autres	Andere Bekenntnisse und Sekte	Otras Denominaciones y Sectas
Rubber	Caoutchouc	Gummi	Caucho
Computer Applications	Applications Informatiques	Computer Anwendung	Aplicaciones para Computadoras
Sciences: Comprehensive Works	Sciences: Oeuvres d'Ensemble	Wissenschaften: Umfassende Werke	Ciencias: Obras Completas
Computer Applications	Applications Informatiques	Computer Anwendung	Aplicaciones para Computadoras
Shoes and Boots	Chaussures et Bottes	Schuhe und Stiefel	Zapatos y Botas
Singles' Interests and Lifestyles	Intérêts et Style de Vie Célibataire	Ledigenstandinteressen	Intereses y Estilos de Vida de Solteros
Social Sciences: Comprehensive Works	Sciences Sociales: Oeuvres d'Ensemble	Sozialwissenschaften: Umfassende Werke	Ciencias Sociales: Obras Completas
Social Service and Welfare	Service Social et Protection Sociale	Sozialpflege und Fürsorge	Asistencia y Bienestar Social
Sociology	Sociologie	Soziologie	Sociología
Computer Applications	Applications Informatiques	Computer Anwendung	Aplicaciones para Computadoras
Sound Recording and Reproduction	Enregistrement et Reproduction du Son	Tonaufnahme und Tonwiedergabe	Grabaciones y Reproducciones Sonoras
Computer Applications	Applications Informatiques	Computer Anwendung	Aplicaciones para Computadoras
Sports and Games	Sports et Jeux	Sport und Spiele	Deportes y Juegos
Ball Games	Jeux de Balle	Ballspiele	Juegos de Pelota
Bicycles and Motorcycles	Bicyclettes et Motocyclettes	Fahrräder und Motorräder	Bicicletas y Motocicletas
Boats and Boating	Bateaux et Canotage	Boote und Bootfahren	Barcos y Canotaje
Horses and Horsemanship	Equitation	Pferde und Reitsport	Caballos y Equitación
Outdoor Life	Vie en Plein Air	Im Freien	Vida de Campo
Statistics	Statistiques	Statistik	Estadísticas
Technology: Comprehensive Works	Technologie: Oeuvres d'Ensemble	Technologie: Umfassende Werke	Tecnología: Obras Completas
Textile Industries and Fabrics	Textiles	Textil	Telas e Industria Textil
Computer Applications	Applications Informatiques	Computer Anwendung	Aplicaciones para Computadoras
Theater	Théâtre	Theater	Teatro
Tobacco	Tabac	Tabak	Tabaco
Transportation	Transports	Transport	Transporte
Air Transport	Transport Aérien	Luftverkehr	Transporte Aéreo
Automobiles	Automobiles	Kraftfahrzeugen	Automóviles
Computer Applications	Applications Informatiques	Computer Anwendung	Aplicaciones para Computadoras
Railroads	Chemins de Fer	Eisenbahnen	Ferrocarriles
Roads and Traffic	Routes et Circulation	Strassen und Strassenverkehr	Caminos y Tráfico
Ships and Shipping	Navires et Transport Maritimes	Schiffe und Schiffahrt	Barcos y Embarques
Trucks and Trucking	Transports Routiers	Lastkraftwagen	Camiones
Travel and Tourism	Voyages et Tourisme	Reisen und Tourismus	Viaje y Turismo
Airline Inflight and Hotel Inroom	Revues pour Vol de Lignes Aériennes et pour Chambres d'Hôtels	Fluggesellschaft und Hotel Veröffentlichungen	Vuelo en Aerolínea y Cuarto de Hotel
Veterinary Sciences	Science Vétérinaire	Tierheilkunde	Veterinaria
Computer Applications	Applications Informatiques	Computer Anwendung	Aplicaciones para Computadoras
Water Resources	Ressources en Eau	Wasserwirtschaft	Recursos del Agua
Computer Applications	Applications Informatiques	Computer Anwendung	Aplicaciones de los Computadoras
Women's Health	Santé de la Femme	Gesundheit von Frauen	Salud de las Mujeres
Women's Interests	Publications d'Intérêt Féminin	Fraueninteresse	Intereses Femininos
Women's Studies	Études de la Femme	Frauenstudien	Estudios de las Mujeres

Refereed Serials

A A A INVESTMENT GUIDE.
Wisebuy Publications, 25 West Cottages, London NW6 1RJ, England. TEL 44-171-433-1121. *1372*

A A C N CLINICAL ISSUES.
Lippincott - Raven Publishers, 227 E. Washington Sq., Philadelphia. TEL 215-238-4200. *4628*

A A C N NURSING SCAN IN CRITICAL CARE.
Nursecom Inc., 1211 Locust St., Philadelphia, PA 19107. TEL 215-545-7222. FAX 215-545-8107. *4762*

A A F M PROCEEDINGS OF ANNUAL MEETING.
American Association of Feed Microscopists, c/o Marjorie McCutcheon, Box 5246, Charleston, WV 25361. TEL 304-558-2208. FAX 304-558-3594. *5167*

A A M A EXECUTIVE.
American Academy of Medical Administrators, 30555 Southfield Rd., Ste. 150, Southfield, MI 48076. TEL 810-540-4310. FAX 810-645-0590. *4628*

A A P G BULLETIN.
American Association of Petroleum Geologists, Box 979, Tulsa, OK 74101. TEL 918-584-2555. FAX 918-560-2665. *5593*

A A P G STUDIES IN GEOLOGY SERIES.
American Association of Petroleum Geologists, Box 979, Tulsa, OK 74101. TEL 918-584-2555. *5594*

A A P P O JOURNAL.
Health Care Communications, Inc., 1 Bridge Plaza, Fort Lee, NJ 07024. TEL 201-947-5545. FAX 201-947-8406. *929*

A A S HISTORY SERIES.
Univelt, Inc., Box 28130, San Diego, CA 92198-0198. TEL 619-746-4005. FAX 619-746-3139. *50*

A A T T BULLETIN.
American Association of Teachers of Turkic Languages, Near Eastern Studies Department, NES 110 Jones Hall, Princeton University, Princeton, NJ 08544-1008. TEL 609-285-1435. FAX 609-258-1242. *2563*

A A V S O BULLETIN: PREDICTED DATES OF MAXIMA AND MINIMA OF LONG PERIOD VARIABLE STARS.
American Association of Variable Star Observers, 25 Birch St., Cambridge, MA 02138. TEL 617-354-0484. *487*

A A V S O REPORTS AND MONOGRAPHS.
American Association of Variable Star Observers, 25 Birch St., Cambridge, MA 02138. TEL 617-354-0484. *487*

A - B: AUTO - BIOGRAPHY STUDIES.
University of Kansas, Joyce & Elizabeth Hall Center for the Humanities, Lawrence, KS 66045-2967. TEL 913-864-4798. FAX 913-864-3884. *571*

A B N F JOURNAL.
Tucker Publications, Inc., Box 580, Lisle, IL 60532. TEL 630-969-3809. FAX 630-969-3895. *4927*

A C C A DOCKET.
American Corporate Counsel Association, 1225 Connecticut Ave., N.W., Ste. 302, Washington, DC 20036-2604. TEL 202-296-4522. FAX 202-331-7454. *4072*

A C C CURRENT JOURNAL REVIEW.
Elsevier Science Inc., Box 945, New York, NY 10159-0945. TEL 212-633-3730. FAX 212-633-3680. *4762*

A C M MONOGRAPH SERIES.
Academic Press, Inc., 525 B St., Ste. 1900, San Diego, CA 92101-4495. TEL 619-231-0926. FAX 619-699-6715. *2071*

A C O G CLINICAL REVIEW.
Elsevier Science Inc., Box 945, New York, NY 10159-0945. TEL 212-633-3730. FAX 212-633-3680. *4762*

A C S SYMPOSIUM SERIES.
American Chemical Society, 1155 16th St. N.W., Washington, DC 20036. TEL 800-227-5558. FAX 202-872-4615. *1736*

A D M.
Asociacion Dental Mexicana, A.C., Ezequiel Montes No. 92, Col. Revolucion, Delegacion Cuauhtemoc, Mexico, D.F. 06030, Mexico. TEL 52-5-29400095. FAX 52-5-2945143. *4848*

A E J M C NEWS.
Association for Education in Journalism and Mass Communications, LeConte College, Rm. 121, University of South Carolina, Columbia, SC 29208-0251. TEL 803-777-2005. *3868*

A F F H O NEWSLETTER.
Australasian Federation of Family History Organisations, 6-48 May St., Bayswater, W.A. 6053, Australia. FAX 61-8-92714311. *3210*

A F I P ATLAS OF RADIOLOGIC-PATHOLOGIC CORRELATION.
Armed Forces Institute of Pathology, 6825 16th St., N.W., Washington, DC 20306-6000. *4628*

A G A R D REPORTS.
U.S. National Aeronautics and Space Administration, Scientific and Technical Information Office, 800 Elkridge Landing Rd., Linthicum Heights, MD 21090-2934. *51*

A H A F JOURNAL.
American Handwriting Analysis Foundation, Box 6210, San Jose, CA 95150. TEL 804-979-2848. *2418*

A H P PERSPECTIVE.
Association for Humanistic Psychology, Box 1938, Sebastopol, CA 95473. TEL 415-864-8850. FAX 415-864-8853. *6088*

A I A A JOURNAL.
American Institute of Aeronautics and Astronautics, Inc., 1801 Alexander Dr., Ste. 500, Reston, VA 20191. TEL 703-264-7500. *51*

A I APPLICATIONS.
University of Idaho, Box 3066, Moscow, ID 83843. TEL 208-885-7033. FAX 208-885-6226. *2964*

A I C C M BULLETIN.
Australian Institute for the Conservation of Cultural Material, Inc., P.O. Box 1638, Canberra, A.C.T. 2601, Australia. TEL 06-243-4531. FAX 06-243-4531. *419*

A.I.CH.E. EQUIPMENT TESTING PROCEDURES SERIES.
American Institute of Chemical Engineers, 345 E. 47th St., New York, NY 10017. TEL 212-705-8100. FAX 212-705-8400. *2753*

A.I.CH.E. JOURNAL.
American Institute of Chemical Engineers, 345 E. 47th St., New York, NY 10017. TEL 212-705-8100. FAX 212-705-8400. *2753*

A I CH E M I MODULAR INSTRUCTION. SERIES A: PROCESS CONTROL.
American Institute of Chemical Engineers, 345 E. 47th St., New York, NY 10017. TEL 212-705-8100. FAX 212-705-8400. *2753*

A I CH E M I MODULAR INSTRUCTION. SERIES C: TRANSPORT.
American Institute of Chemical Engineers, 345 E. 47th St., New York, NY 10017. TEL 212-705-8100. FAX 212-705-8400. *2753*

A I CH E M I MODULAR INSTRUCTION. SERIES D: THERMODYNAMICS.
American Institute of Chemical Engineers, 345 E. 47th St., New York, NY 10017. TEL 212-705-8100. FAX 212-705-8400. *2754*

A I CH E M I MODULAR INSTRUCTION. SERIES E: KINETICS.
American Institute of Chemical Engineers, 345 E. 47th St., New York, NY 10017. TEL 212-705-8100. FAX 212-705-8400. *2754*

A I CH E M I MODULAR INSTRUCTION. SERIES F: MATERIAL AND ENERGY BALANCES.
American Institute of Chemical Engineers, 345 E. 47th St., New York, NY 10017. TEL 212-705-8100. FAX 212-705-8400. *2754*

A I CH E M I MODULAR INSTRUCTION. SERIES G: DESIGN OF EQUIPMENT.
American Institute of Chemical Engineers, 345 E. 47th St., New York, NY 10017. TEL 212-705-8100. FAX 212-705-8400. *2754*

A I CH E SYMPOSIUM SERIES.
American Institute of Chemical Engineers, 345 E. 47th St., New York, NY 10017-2395. TEL 212-705-8100. FAX 212-705-8400. *2754*

A I D VERBRAUCHERDIENST.
Auswertungs- und Informationsdienst fuer Ernaehrung, Landwirtschaft und Forsten e.V., Konstantinstr. 124, 53179 Bonn, Germany. TEL 49-228-84990. FAX 49-228-9526952. *5468*

A I M.
Association of Indian Muslims of America, 11649 Masters Run, Elliot City, MD 21042. TEL 410-730-5456. FAX 410-922-0665. *6600*

A I M INTERNATIONAL.
Africa Inland Mission International, Box 178, Pearl River, NY 10965. TEL 914-735-4014. FAX 914-735-1814. *6318*

A J A S: AUSTRALASIAN JOURNAL OF AMERICAN STUDIES.
Australian and New Zealand American Studies Association, c/o History Dept., Massey University, Palmerston N., New Zealand. TEL 64-6-3569099. FAX 64-6-3505662. *3614*

A J N R.
American Society of Neuroradiology, 2210 Midwest Rd., Ste. 207, Oak Brook, IL 60521. TEL 630-574-0220. FAX 630-574-0661. *5102*

A J R.
American Roentgen Ray Society, Attn.: Leigh Myzk, 1891 Preston White Dr., VA 22091. TEL 703-648-8992. FAX 703-264-8863. *5102*

A J S REVIEW.
Yeshiva University Press - Ktav Publishing House, Inc., 900 Jefferson St., No. 6249, Hoboken, NJ 07030-7205. TEL 201-963-9524. FAX 201-963-0102. *2993*

A L A N REVIEW.
National Council of Teachers of English, Assembly on Literature for Adolescents, Office of the Dean, College of Education & Human Development, Box 6960, Radford University, VA 24142. TEL 703-831-5439. FAX 703-831-6053. *2593*

A L T - J.
University of Wales Press, 6 Gwennyth St., Cathays, Cardiff CF2 4YD, Wales. TEL 44-1222-231919. FAX 44-1222-230908. *2514*

A M A T Y C REVIEW.
American Mathematical Association of Two-Year Colleges, c/o Joseph Browne, Ed., Onondaga Community College, Syracuse, NY 13215. TEL 315-469-2649. *2529*

A M E CHURCH REVIEW.
African Methodist Episcopal Church, 500 Eighth Ave. S., Nashville, TN 37203. TEL 615-256-7020. FAX 615-256-7092. *6411*

A M I A - ANNUAL FALL SYMPOSIUM. PROCEEDINGS.
Hanley & Belfus, Inc., 210 S. 13th St., Philadelphia, PA 19107. TEL 215-546-7293. FAX 215-790-9330. *4845*

A M I A NEWSLETTER.
Association of Moving Image Archivists, c/o National Center for Film and Video Preservation, American Film Institute, 2021 N. Western Ave., Los Angeles, CA 90027. TEL 213-856-7637. FAX 213-856-7616. *4155*

A M S STUDIES IN ANTHROPOLOGY.
A M S Press, Inc., 56 E. 13th St., New York, NY 10003. TEL 212-777-4700. FAX 212-995-5413. *305*

A N.
A N Publications, P.O. Box 23, Sunderland, Tyne and Wear SR4 6DG, England. TEL 44-191-567-3589. FAX 44-191-564-1600. *419*

A N N A JOURNAL.
Jannetti Publications, Inc., East Holly Ave., Box 56, Pitman, NJ 08071-0056. TEL 609-256-2300. FAX 609-589-7463. *4927*

A N Q: A QUARTERLY JOURNAL OF SHORT ARTICLES, NOTES AND REVIEWS.
Heldref Publications, 1319 Eighteenth St., N.W., Washington, DC 20036-1802. TEL 202-296-6267. FAX 202-296-5149. *4369*

A N R E D ALERT.
Anorexia Nervosa & Related Eating Disorders, Inc., Box 5102, Eugene, OR 97405. TEL 541-344-1144. *6088*

A N Z A NEWS.
Down-Under Publications, 3 W. 8th Ave., Vancouver, BC V5Y 1M8, Canada. TEL 604-876-7128. *3250*

A O A C INTERNATIONAL. JOURNAL.
A O A C International, 481 N. Frederick Ave., Ste. 500, Gaithersburg, MD 20877-2417. TEL 301-924-7077. FAX 301-924-7089. *1786*

A O J T NEWS.
Association of Orthodox Jewish Teachers, 1577 Coney Island Ave., Brooklyn, NY 11230. TEL 718-258-3585. FAX 718-258-3586. *2418*

A O P A MAGAZINE.
Aircraft Owners and Pilots Association of Australia, P.O. Box 1065, Fyshwick, A.C.T. 2609, Australia. TEL 61-6-2804221. FAX 61-6-2391366. *51*

A P K: EKONOMIKA, UPRAVLENIE.
AgriPress, Sadovaya-Spasskaya, 18, 107807 Moscow, Russia. TEL 7-095-2071662. FAX 7-095-2072870. *85*

A P M I S.
Munksgaard International Publishers Ltd., 35 Noerre Soegade, P.O. Box 2148, DK-1016 Copenhagen K, Denmark. TEL 45-33-127030. FAX 45-33-129387. *581*

A R A NEWSLETTER.
A R A Publications (Tempe), c/o Aleksandra Gruzinska, Ed., Foreign Languages Department, Arizona State University, Tempe, AZ 85287-0202. TEL 602-965-6281. FAX 602-965-0135. *2530*

A R E S NEWSLETTER.
American Real Estate Society, c/o James R. Webb, Cleveland State University, Dept. of Finance, College of Business, University Center, Rm. 592A, Cleveland, OH 44115. TEL 216-687-4732. FAX 216-687-9354. *6293*

A R I D O NEWSLETTER.
Association of Registered Interior Designers of Ontario (ARIDO), 717 Church St., Toronto, ON M4W 2M5, Canada. TEL 416-921-2127. FAX 416-921-3660. *3840*

A R I E L.
University of Calgary, Department of English, SS 1152, 2500 University Dr. N.W., Calgary, AB T2N 1N4, Canada. TEL 403-220-4657. FAX 403-289-1123. *4369*

A-R PERFORMER'S LIBRARY.
A-R Editions, Inc., 801 Deming Way, Madison, WI 53717. TEL 608-836-9000. FAX 608-831-8200. *5370*

A R S C JOURNAL.
Association for Recorded Sound Collections, Inc., Box 543, Annapolis, MD 21404-0543. TEL 410-757-0488. FAX 410-379-0175. *6742*

A S A E TRANSACTIONS.
American Society of Agricultural Engineers, 2950 Niles Rd., St. Joseph, MI 49085-9659. TEL 616-429-0300. FAX 616-429-3852. *85*

A S A E TRANSACTIONS. FOOD & PROCESS ENGINEERING.
American Society of Agricultural Engineers, 2950 Niles Rd., St. Joseph, MI 49085-9659. TEL 616-429-0300. FAX 616-429-3852. *3094*

A S A E TRANSACTIONS. INFORMATION AND ELECTRICAL TECHNOLOGIES - EMERGING TECHNOLOGIES.
American Society of Agricultural Engineers, 2950 Niles Rd., St. Joseph, MI 49084-9659. TEL 616-429-0300. FAX 616-429-3852. *2807*

A S A E TRANSACTIONS. POWER & MACHINERY.
American Society of Agricultural Engineers, 2950 Niles Rd., St. Joseph, MI 49085-9659. TEL 616-429-0300. FAX 616-429-3852. *204*

A S A E TRANSACTIONS. SOIL & WATER.
American Society of Agricultural Engineers, 2950 Niles Rd., St. Joseph, MI 49085-9659. TEL 616-429-0300. FAX 616-429-3852. *210*

A S A E TRANSACTIONS. STRUCTURES & ENVIRONMENT.
American Society of Agricultural Engineers, 2950 Niles Rd., St. Joseph, MI 49085-9659. TEL 616-429-0300. FAX 616-429-3852. *2776*

A S H E - E R I C HIGHER EDUCATION REPORT SERIES.
A S H E - E R I C Higher Education Reports, George Washington University, One Dupont Circle, Ste. 630, Washington, DC 20036. TEL 202-296-2597. FAX 202-452-1844. *2530*

A S H R A E JOURNAL.
American Society of Heating, Refrigerating and Air-Conditioning Engineers, Inc., 1791 Tullie Circle, N.E., Atlanta, GA 30329. TEL 404-636-8400. FAX 404-321-5478. *3476*

A T E A JOURNAL.
American Technical Education Association, Inc., North Dakota State College of Science, Wahpeton, ND 58076. TEL 701-671-2240. FAX 701-671-2260. *2418*

A T I P.
Association Technique de l'Industrie Papetiere, 154 bd. Haussmann, 75008 Paris, France. FAX 33-1-45-63-53-09. *5565*

A T P ENERGIA Y MOVIMIENTO.
Obsidiana Editores, S.A., Czda. de Tlalpan 2365, Col. Ciudad Jardin, 04370 Mexico DF, Mexico. TEL 6899133. *5128*

A.U.M.L.A.
Australian Universities Language and Literature Association (AULLA), University of Canterbury, Dept. of French, Private Bag 4800, Christchurch, New Zealand. TEL 64-3-3667001. FAX 64-3-3642999. *4235*

A V E W D NEWSLETTER. *2130*

A X I S.
Whurr Publishers Ltd., 19b Compton Terrace, London N1 2UN, England. TEL 44-171-359-5979. FAX 44-171-226-5290. *2072*

AARDRIJKSKUNDE.
Vereniging Leraars Aardrijkskunde, Instituut voor Sociale en Economische Geografie, 42 de Croylaan, 3001 Leuven-Heverlee, Belgium. TEL 32-16-322441. *3393*

AARHUS UNIVERSITET. PSYKOLOGISK SKRIFTSERIE.
Aarhus Universitet, Psykologisk Institut, DK-8000 Aarhus C, Denmark. TEL 45-89-42-49-00. FAX 45-89-42-49-01. *6089*

ABDOMINAL IMAGING.
Springer-Verlag, Medical Journals, 175 Fifth Ave., New York, NY 10010. TEL 212-460-1500. FAX 212-473-6272. *4907*

ABERDEEN LETTERS IN ECOLOGY.
University of Aberdeen, Department of Agriculture, MacRobert Bldg., 581 King St., Aberdeen AB24 5UA, Scotland. TEL 44-1224-274122. FAX 44-1224-273731. *581*

ABERTAY HISTORICAL SOCIETY. SERIES OF MONOGRAPHS.
Abertay Historical Society, Archive & Record Centre, Publications Secretary, 21 City Sq., Dundee DD1 3BY, Scotland. TEL 44-1382-434494. FAX 44-1382-434666. *3545*

AL-ABHATH.
American University of Beirut, Faculty of Arts and Sciences, AUB Post Hall 106, Beirut, Lebanon. TEL 96-1-353465. FAX 212-478-1995. *5519*

ABHIGYAN.
Foundation for Organisational Research and Education, Adhitam Kendra, B-18, Qutab Institutional Area, New Delhi 110 016, India. TEL 91-11-6863396. FAX 91-11-6856294. *6600*

ABORIGINAL HISTORY.
Aboriginal History Inc., G.P.O. Box 2837, Canberra, A.C.T. 2601, Australia. TEL 61-6-2494685. FAX 61-6-2394324. *3541*

ABRAHAM LINCOLN ASSOCIATION. JOURNAL.
University of Illinois Press, 1325 S. Oak St., Champaign, IL 61820. TEL 217-333-0950. FAX 217-244-8082. *3487*

ABSTRACTS IN ANTHROPOLOGY.
Baywood Publishing Co., Inc., 26 Austin Ave., Box 337, Amityville, NY 11701. TEL 516-691-1270. FAX 516-691-1770. *335*

ACADEMIA CHILENA DE LA HISTORIA. BOLETIN.
Academia Chilena de la Historia, Clasificador 245, Correo Central, Santiago, Chile. TEL 6399323. *3614*

ACADEMIA COLOMBIANA. BOLETIN.
Academia Colombiana de la Lengua, Carrera 3-A, Numero 17-34, Bogota, Colombia. TEL 3343152 ext. 7. *4236*

ACADEMIA ECONOMIC PAPERS.
Academia Sinica, Institute of Economics, Nankang, Taipei, Taiwan 11529, Republic of China. TEL 02-782-2791. FAX 02-785-3946. *930*

ACADEMIA SCIENTIARUM HUNGARICA. ACTA ZOOLOGICA.
Magyar Termeszettudomanyi Muzeum, Baross u. 13, 1088 Budapest, Hungary. TEL 36-1-3130035. FAX 36-1-11171669. *823*

ACADEMIC EMERGENCY MEDICINE.
Hanley & Belfus, Inc., 210 S. 13th St., Philadelphia, PA 19107. TEL 215-546-7293. FAX 215-790-9330. *5003*

ACADEMIC MEDICINE.
Association of American Medical Colleges, 2450 N St., Washington, DC 20037-1126. TEL 202-828-0416. FAX 202-828-1123. *4629*

ACADEMIC PRESS GEOLOGY SERIES.
Academic Press, Inc., 525 B St., Ste. 1900, San Diego, CA 92101-4495. TEL 619-231-0926. FAX 619-699-6715. *2329*

ACADEMIC PRESS SERIES IN COGNITION AND PERCEPTION.
Academic Press, Inc., 525 B St., Ste. 1900, San Diego, CA 92101-4495. TEL 619-231-0926. FAX 619-699-6715. *6089*

ACADEMIC PSYCHIATRY.
American Psychiatric Press, Inc., Journals Division, 1400 K St., N.W., Ste. 1101, Washington, DC 20005. TEL 202-682-6240. FAX 202-789-6341. *5047*

ACADEMIE DE DROIT INTERNATIONAL DE LA HAYE. RECUEIL DES COURS.
Kluwer Academic Publishers, Postbus 17, 3300 AA Dordrecht, Netherlands. TEL 31-78-6392392. FAX 31-78-6392254. *4104*

ACADEMIE DES SCIENCES. COMPTES RENDUS. SERIE 3: SCIENCES DE LA VIE.
John Libbey Eurotext, 127 av. de la Republique, 92120 Montrouge, France. TEL 33-1-46730660. FAX 33-1-40840999. *582*

ACADEMIE ET SOCIETE LORRAINES DE SCIENCES. BULLETIN.
Academie et Societe Lorraines des Sciences, Biologie Vegetales, B.P. 239, 54506 Vandoeuvre Cedex, France. TEL 83-91-22-53. FAX 83-91-22-53. *6508*

ACADEMIE INTERNATIONALE D'HISTOIRE DES SCIENCES. COLLECTION DES TRAVAUX.
E.J. Brill, P.O. Box 9000, 2300 PA Leiden, Netherlands. TEL 31-71-5353500. FAX 31-71-5317532. *6508*

ACADEMIE POLONAISE DES SCIENCES. CENTRE D'ARCHEOLOGIE MEDITERRANEENNE. ETUDES ET TRAVAUX.
Polska Akademia Nauk, Zaklad Archeologii Srodziemnomorskiej, Palac Kultury i Nauki, p. 2105, 00-901 Warsaw, Poland. TEL 48-22-6248593. FAX 48-22-6207651. *345*

ACADEMIE POLONAISE DES SCIENCES. CENTRE D'ARCHEOLOGIE MEDITERRANEENE. TRAVAUX.
Polska Akademia Nauk, Zaklad Archeologii Srodziemnomorskiej, Palac Kultury i Nauki, p. 2105, 00-901 Warsaw, Poland. TEL 48-22-6248593. FAX 48-22-6207651. *345*

ACADEMIE ROYALE DE MARINE DE BELGIQUE. COMMUNICATIONS.
Nationaal Scheepvaartmuseum, Steinplein 1, B-2000 Antwerp, Belgium. TEL 32-3-232-08-50. *7144*

ACADEMY FOR EVANGELISM IN THEOLOGICAL EDUCATION. JOURNAL.
Academy for Evangelism in Theological Education, c/o Richard S. Armstrong, Ed., Princeton Theological Seminary, Box 821, Princeton, NJ 08542. TEL 609-924-2997. FAX 609-924-2973. *6318*

ACADEMY FORUM.
American Academy of Psychoanalysis, 47 E. 19th St., 6th Fl., New York, NY 10003-1323. TEL 212-475-7980. FAX 212-425-8101. *6089*

ACADEMY OF MARKETING SCIENCE. JOURNAL.
Sage Publications, Inc., 2455 Teller Rd., Thousand Oaks, CA 91320. TEL 805-499-0721. FAX 805-499-0871. *1514*

ACADEMY OF MEDICINE, SINGAPORE. ANNALS.
Academy of Medicine, Singapore, 16 College Road, 01-01 College of Medicine Bldg., Singapore 169854, Singapore. TEL 65-2245166. FAX 65-2255155. *4630*

ACADEMY OF REHABILITATIVE AUDIOLOGY. JOURNAL.
Academy of Rehabilitative Audiology, c/o Robert J. Dunlop, Ph.D., JARA Circ. Mgr., Audiology Section (126A), VA Medical Center, Temple, TX 76504. TEL 817-778-4811. *5018*

ACAROLOGIA.
61 rue de Buffon, 75231 Paris Cedex 05, France. FAX 33-1-40-79-35-76. *823*

ACCADEMIA DELLE SCIENZE DI SIENA DETTA DE FISIOCRITICI. ATTI.
Accademia delle Scienze di Siena Detta de Fisiocritici, Piazza S. Agostino 5, 53100 Siena, Italy. TEL 39-577-47002. *4630*

ACCADEMIA NAZIONALE DEI LINCEI. ATTI. RENDICONTI LINCEI. MATEMATICA E APPLICAZIONI.
Accademia Nazionale dei Lincei, Via della Lungara 10, 00165 Rome, Italy. TEL 39-6-6838831. *4555*

ACCADEMIA NAZIONALE DEI LINCEI. ATTI. RENDICONTI LINCEI. SCIENZE FISICHE E NATURALI.
Accademia Nazionale dei Lincei, Via della Lungara 10, 00165 Rome, Italy. TEL 39-6-6838831. *6509*

ACCELERATORS AND STORAGE RINGS SERIES.
Gordon and Breach - Harwood Academic, Amsteldisk 166, 1st Fl., 1079 LH Amsterdam, Netherlands. *5849*

ACCESS (BELCONNEN).
Australian School Library Association, Inc., P.O. Box 450, Belconnen, A.C.T. 2616, Australia. *4156*

ACCIDENT ANALYSIS & PREVENTION.
Elsevier Science Ltd., Pergamon, P.O. Box 800, Kidlington, Oxford OX5 1DX, England. TEL 44-1865-843000. FAX 44-1865-843010. *6227*

ACCOMMODATOR.
Motels Ontario, 347 Pido Rd., Unit 2, R.R. 6, Peterborough, ON K9J 6X7, Canada. TEL 705-745-4982. FAX 705-745-4983. *3722*

ACCOUNTABILITY IN RESEARCH.
Gordon and Breach - Harwood Academic, Amsteldisk 166, 1st Fl., 1079 LH Amsterdam, Netherlands. *6509*

ACCOUNTANCY S A.
South African Institute of Chartered Accountants, P.O. Box 59875, Kengray 2100, South Africa. TEL 27-11-622-6655. FAX 27-11-622-3321. *1080*

THE ACCOUNTANT.
Institute of Certified Public Accountants of Kenya, P.O. Box 59963, Nairobi, Kenya. TEL 254-2-224629. FAX 254-2-211563. *1080*

ACCOUNTING AND BUSINESS RESEARCH.
Institute of Chartered Accountants in England and Wales, P.O. Box 433, Moorgate Pl., London EC2P 2BJ, England. TEL 44-171-920-8899. *1080*

ACCOUNTING, BUSINESS AND FINANCIAL HISTORY.
Thomson Professional, 2-6 Boundary Row, London SE1 8HN, England. TEL 44-171-865-0066. FAX 44-171-522-9621. *930*

ACCOUNTING EDUCATION.
Thomson Professional, 2-6 Boundary Row, London SE1 8HN, England. TEL 44-171-8650066. FAX 44-171-8659623. *1081*

ACCOUNTING EDUCATION.
J A I Press Inc., 55 Old Post Rd., No. 2, Box 1678, Greenwich, CT 06836-1678. TEL 203-661-7602. FAX 203-661-0792. *1081*

ACCOUNTING HISTORIANS JOURNAL.
Academy of Accounting Historians, c/o William D. Samson, Culverhouse School of Accountancy, University of Alabama, Tuscaloosa, AL 35487. TEL 205-348-2903. *1081*

ACCOUNTING HISTORY.
Garry Carnegie, Ed. & Pub., c/o School of Accounting and Finance, Faculty of Business and Law, Deakin University, Geelong, Vic. 3217, Australia. TEL 61-3-52272733. FAX 61-3-52272264. *1081*

ACCOUNTING, MANAGEMENT AND INFORMATION TECHNOLOGIES.
Elsevier Science Ltd., Pergamon, P.O. Box 800, Kidlington, Oxford OX5 1DX, England. TEL 44-1865-843000. FAX 44-1865-843010. *1082*

ACCOUNTING, ORGANIZATIONS AND SOCIETY.
Elsevier Science Ltd., Pergamon, P.O. Box 800, Kidlington, Oxford OX5 1DX, England. TEL 44-1865-843000. FAX 44-1865-843010. *1082*

ACCOUNTING RESEARCH JOURNAL.
Royal Melbourne Institute of Technology, Department of Economics and Finance, G.P.O. Box 2476V, Melbourne, Vic. 3001, Australia. *1082*

ACCOUNTS OF CHEMICAL RESEARCH.
American Chemical Society, 1155 16th St., N.W., Washington, DC 20036. TEL 202-872-4363. FAX 614-447-3671. *1736*

ACCREDITED PROFESSIONAL PROGRAMS OF COLLEGES AND SCHOOLS OF PHARMACY.
American Council on Pharmaceutical Education, 311 W. Superior St., Chicago, IL 60610. TEL 312-664-3575. FAX 312-664-4652. *5644*

9722 REFEREED SERIALS

DE ACHTTIENDE EEUW. DOCUMENTATIEBLAD WERKGROEP 18E EEUW.
Werkgroep 18e Eeuw, Institute for the History of Science, Nieuwe Gracht 187, 3512 LM Utrecht, Netherlands. TEL 31-30-2538283. FAX 31-30-2536313. *3545*

ACME.
Universita degli Studi di Milano, Facolta di Lettere e Filosofia, Via Festa del Perdono 7, Milan, Italy. TEL 39-2-58352892. FAX 39-2-58300387. *4370*

ACOUSTICAL IMAGING.
Plenum Publishing Corp., 233 Spring St., New York, NY 10013-1578. TEL 212-620-8000. FAX 212-463-0742. *5871*

ACOUSTICAL SOCIETY OF AMERICA. JOURNAL.
American Institute of Physics, One Physics Ellipse, College Park, MD 20740-3843. TEL 301-209-3100. *5871*

ACOUSTICAL SOCIETY OF JAPAN. JOURNAL.
Acoustical Society of Japan, Ikeda Bldg., 7-7, Yoyogi 2-chome, Shibuya-ku, Tokyo 151, Japan. TEL 81-3-3379-1200. FAX 81-3-3379-1456. *5871*

ACOUSTICS LETTERS.
Parjon Information Services, P.O. Box 144, Haywards Heath, Sussex RH16 2YX, England. *5871*

ACQUISITIONS LIBRARIAN.
Haworth Press, Inc., 10 Alice St., Binghamton, NY 13904. TEL 607-722-5857. FAX 607-722-6362. *4156*

ACTA ACADEMICA.
Acta Academica, c/o UOVS-Sasol-Bibliotheek, Posbus 301, 9300 Bloemfontein, South Africa. TEL 27-51-4012351. FAX 27-51-4482879. *3770*

ACTA ACUSTICA.
Editions de Physique, B.P. 112, 7, Av. du Hoggar, Zone Industrielle de Courtaboeuf, 91944 Les Ulis Cedex, France. TEL 69-07-36-88. FAX 69-28-84-91. *5871*

ACTA AGRICULTURAE SCANDINAVICA. SECTION A, ANIMAL SCIENCE.
Scandinavian University Press, P.O. Box 2959 Toeyen, N-0608 Oslo, Norway. TEL 47-22-57-54-00. FAX 47-22-57-53-53. *267*

ACTA AGRICULTURAE SCANDINAVICA. SECTION B, SOIL AND PLANT SCIENCE.
Scandinavian University Press, P.O. Box 2959 Toeyen, N-0608 Oslo, Norway. TEL 47-22-57-53-53. FAX 47-22-57-53-53. *211*

ACTA AMAZONICA.
Instituto Nacional de Pesquisas da Amazonia, Alameda Cosme Ferreira 1756, P.O. Box 478, 69083-000 Manaus, Amazonas, Brazil. TEL 55-92-643-3220. FAX 55-92-6433030. *6509*

ACTA ANAESTHESIOLOGICA SCANDINAVICA.
Munksgaard International Publishers Ltd., Noerre Soegade, P.O. Box 2148, DK-1016 Copenhagen K, Denmark. TEL 45-33-127030. FAX 45-33-129387. *4802*

ACTA ANATOMICA.
S. Karger AG, Allschwilerstr. 10, P.O. Box, CH-4009 Basel, Switzerland. TEL 41-61-3061111. FAX 41-61-3061234. *4630*

ACTA APPLICANDAE MATHEMATICAE.
Kluwer Academic Publishers, Postbus 17, 3300 AA Dordrecht, Netherlands. TEL 31-78-6392392. FAX 31-78-6392254. *4556*

ACTA ARACHNOLOGICA.
Arachnological Society of Japan, Biological Laboratory, Otemon-Gakuin University, 2-1-15 Nishiai, Ibaraki, Osaka 567, Japan. FAX 81-726-43-5427. *823*

ACTA ARCHAEOLOGICA.
Munksgaard International Publishers Ltd., 35 Noerre Soegade, P.O. Box 2148, DK-1016 Copenhagen K, Denmark. TEL 45-33-127030. FAX 45-33-129387. *345*

ACTA ARITHMETICA.
Polska Akademia Nauk, Instytut Matematyczny, Dzial Wydawnictw, Ul. Sniadeckich 8, P.O. Box 137, 00-950 Warsaw, Poland. TEL 48-22-6282471. FAX 48-22-6293997. *4556*

ACTA ASTRONAUTICA.
Elsevier Science Ltd., Pergamon, P.O. Box 800, Kidlington, Oxford OX5 1DX, England. TEL 44-1865-843000. FAX 44-1865-843010. *52*

ACTA ASTRONOMICA.
Copernicus Foundation for Polish Astronomy, Al. Ujazdowskie 4, 00-478 Warsaw, Poland. TEL 48-22-6295346. FAX 48-2-26294967. *488*

ACTA BALTICO - SLAVICA.
Slawistyczny Osrodek Wydawniczy, Al. Ujazdowskie 18 m.16, 00-478 Warsaw, Poland. TEL 48-22-6250054. FAX 48-22-6290075. *3546*

ACTA BIOLOGICA PARANAENSE.
Universidade Federal do Parana, Setor de Ciencias Biologicas, Cx. Postal 19020, 81531-990 Curitiba, Parana, Brazil. TEL 55-41-3663144 ext. 165. FAX 55-41-2662042. *582*

ACTA BIOLOGICA VENEZUELICA.
Universidad Central de Venezuela, Instituto de Zoologia Tropical, Facultad de Ciencias, Apdo. 47058, Caracas 1041-A, Venezuela. FAX 58-2-6052136. *582*

ACTA BIOTHEORETICA.
Kluwer Academic Publishers, Postbus 17, 3300 AA Dordrecht, Netherlands. TEL 31-78-6392392. FAX 31-78-6392254. *582*

ACTA BOTANICA BARCINONENSIA.
Universitat de Barcelona, Facultat de Biologia, Avda. Diagonal, 615, 08028 Barcelona, Spain. TEL 34-3-4021472. FAX 34-3-4112842. *688*

ACTA BOTANICA INDICA.
Society for the Advancement of Botany, Department of Botany, Meerut College, Meerut 250006, India. *689*

ACTA BOTANICA MALACITANA.
Universidad de Malaga, Facultad de Ciencias, Apdo. 59, 29080 Malaga, Spain. TEL 34-5-2133342. FAX 34-52-131944. *689*

ACTA BOTANICA NEERLANDICA.
Blackwell Science Ltd., Osney Mead, Oxford OX2 0EL, England. TEL 44-1865-206206. FAX 44-1865-721205. *689*

ACTA CHEMICA SCANDINAVICA.
Munksgaard International Publishers Ltd., 35 Noerre Soegade, P.O. Box 2148, DK-1016 Copenhagen K, Denmark. TEL 45-33-127030. FAX 45-33-129387. *1825*

ACTA CHIMICA SLOVENICA.
Slovensko Kemijsko Drustvo, Hajdrihova 19, 61115 Ljubljana, Slovenia. TEL 386-61-176-0200. FAX 386-61-125-9244. *1736*

ACTA CHIRURGIAE PLASTICAE.
Nakladatelske Stredisko C L S J.E. Purkyne, Sokolska 31, 120 26 Prague 2, Czech Republic. TEL 420-2-24911420. FAX 420-24911420. *5133*

ACTA CIENTIFICA VENEZOLANA.
Asociacion Venezolana para el Avance de la Ciencia, Av. Neveri, Colinas de Bello Monte, Apdo. 47286, Caracas, Venezuela. TEL 58-2-7521002. FAX 58-2-7511420. *6509*

ACTA CLASSICA.
Classical Association of South Africa, P.O. Box 392, Pretoria 0001, South Africa. TEL 27-12-429-6501. FAX 27-12-429-3221. *1899*

ACTA CLINICA BELGICA.
University Hospital Gent, Renal Division, De Pintelaan 185, B-9000 Gent, Belgium. TEL 32-9-2404402. FAX 32-2-2404403. *4630*

ACTA CRIMINOLOGICA.
Unisa Press, Periodicals, P.O. Box 392, Pretoria 0001, South Africa. TEL 27-12-4293111. FAX 27-12-4293221. *2260*

ACTA CRYSTALLOGRAPHICA. SECTION A: FOUNDATIONS OF CRYSTALLOGRAPHY.
Munksgaard International Publishers Ltd., 35 Noerre Soegade, P.O. Box 2148, DK-1016 Copenhagen K, Denmark. TEL 45-33-127030. FAX 45-33-129387. *1800*

ACTA CRYSTALLOGRAPHICA. SECTION B: STRUCTURAL SCIENCE.
Munksgaard International Publishers Ltd., 35 Noerre Soegade, P.O. Box 2148, DK-1016 Copenhagen K, Denmark. TEL 45-33-127030. FAX 45-33-129387. *1800*

ACTA CRYSTALLOGRAPHICA. SECTION C: CRYSTAL STRUCTURE COMMUNICATIONS.
Munksgaard International Publishers Ltd., 35 Noerre Soegade, P.O. Box 2148, DK-1016 Copenhagen K, Denmark. TEL 45-33-127030. FAX 45-33-129387. *1801*

ACTA CRYSTALLOGRAPHICA. SECTION D: BIOLOGICAL CRYSTALLOGRAPHY.
Munksgaard International Publishers Ltd., 35 Noerre Soegade, P.O. Box 2148, DK-1016 Copenhagen K, Denmark. TEL 45-33-127030. FAX 45-33-129387. *1801*

ACTA CYTOLOGICA.
Science Printers and Publishers, Inc., 8342 Olive Blvd., St. Louis, MO 63132. TEL 314-991-4440. FAX 314-991-4654. *735*

ACTA ENTOMOLOGICA CHILENA.
Universidad Metropolitana de Ciencias de la Educacion, Instituto de Entomologia, Casilla 147, Santiago, Chile. FAX 56-2-2392067. *745*

ACTA GASTROENTEROLOGICA LATINOAMERICANA.
Juncal 2134, Planta Baja B 1125, Buenos Aires, Argentina. TEL 541-8250050. FAX 541-8222139. *4907*

ACTA GEOLOGICA HISPANICA.
Universidad de Barcelona, Biblioteca Facultat de Geologia, Marti Franques s-n, 08028 Barcelona, Spain. TEL 34-3-4021420. FAX 34-3-4021421. *2329*

ACTA HAEMATOLOGICA.
S. Karger AG, Allschwilerstr. 10, P.O. Box, CH-4009 Basel, Switzerland. TEL 41-61-3061111. FAX 41-61-3061234. *4915*

ACTA HISTOCHEMICA ET CYTOCHEMICA.
Japan Society of Histochemistry and Cytochemistry, c/o Nakanishi Printing Co., Shimotachiuri-Ogawa, Kamikyo-ku, Kyoto 602, Japan. TEL 81-75-415-3661. FAX 81-75-415-3662. *735*

ACTA HYDROBIOLOGICA.
Polska Akademia Nauk, Zaklad Biologii Wod im. Karola Starmacha, Ul. Slawkowska 17, 31-016 Krakow, Poland. TEL 48-12-215082. FAX 48-12-222115. *583*

ACTA ICHTHYOLOGICA ET PISCATORIA.
Akademia Rolnicza w Szczecinie, Dzial Wydawnictw, Ul. Doktora Judyma 22, 71-460 Szczecin, Poland. TEL 48-91-541639. FAX 48-91-541642. *3059*

ACTA IRANICA.
E.J. Brill, P.O. Box 9000, 2300 PA Leiden, Netherlands. TEL 31-71-5353500. FAX 31-71-5317532. *3653*

ACTA MATERIALIA.
Elsevier Science Ltd., Pergamon, P.O. Box 800, Kidlington, Oxford OX5 1DX, England. TEL 44-1865-843000. FAX 44-1865-843010. *5184*

ACTA MATHEMATICA ET INFORMATICA UNIVERSITATIS OSTRAVIENSIS.
Ostravske University, Matematicka Fakulta, Brafova 7, 701 00 Ostrava, Czech Republic. TEL 420-69-225026. *4556*

ACTA MATHEMATICA HUNGARICA.
Kluwer Academic Publishers, Postbus 17, 3300 AA Dordrecht, Netherlands. TEL 31-78-6392392. FAX 31-78-6392254. *4556*

ACTA MATHEMATICA SCIENTIA.
Baltzer Science Publishers B.V., P.O. Box 221, 1400 AE Bussum, Netherlands. TEL 31-20-6370061. FAX 31-20-6323651. *4556*

ACTA MATHEMATICA SINICA, NEW SERIES.
Science Press, Marketing and Sales Department, 16 Donghuangchenggen North St., Beijing 100717, People's Republic of China. TEL 4010624. FAX 4019810. *4556*

ACTA MATHEMATICAE APPLICATAE SINICA.
Science Press, Marketing and Sales Department, 16 Donghuangchenggen North St., Beijing 100717, People's Republic of China. *4556*

ACTA MECHANICA SINICA.
Science Press, Marketing and Sales Department, 16 Donghuangchenggen North St., Beijing 100717, People's Republic of China. TEL 4010642. FAX 4012180. *5843*

ACTA MEDICA.
Karolinum - Nakladatelstvi Univerzity Karlovy, Ovocny trh 5, 116 36 Prague 1, Czech Republic. TEL 42-2-24491265. FAX 42-2-24212041. *4630*

ACTA MEDICA. SUPPLEMENTUM.
Vydavatelstvi Karolinum, Ovocny trh 5, 116 36 Prague 1, Czech Republic. TEL 42-2-24491265. FAX 42-2-24212041. *4631*

ACTA MEDICA BALTICA.
Pabst Science Publishers, Am Eichengrund 28, 49525 Lengerich, Germany. TEL 49-5484-308. FAX 49-5484-550. *4631*

ACTA MEDICA BULGARICA.
Tsentar za Informatsiia po Meditsina, 1, Sv. Georgi Sofiiski St., 1431 Sofia, Bulgaria. TEL 395-2-522342. FAX 359-2-522393. *4894*

ACTA MEDICA IRANICA.
Tehran University of Medical Sciences, Faculty of Medicine, Poursina St., Tehran 14174, Iran. TEL 98-21-6112743. FAX 98-21-6404377. *4631*

ACTA MEDICA KINKI UNIVERSITY.
Kinki University Medical Association, 2-377, Ohno-Higashi, Osaka-Sayama, Osaka 589, Japan. TEL 0723-66-0221. FAX 0723-67-8810. *4631*

ACTA MEDICA NAGASAKIENSIA.
Nagasaki Daigaku, Igakubu, 12-4 Sakamoto-machi, Nagasaki-shi, Nagasaki-ken 852, Japan. TEL 81-958-49-7353. FAX 81-958-49-7357. *4631*

ACTA METEOROLOGICA SINICA.
China Meteorological Press, 46 Baishiqiao Rd., West Suburb, Beijing 100081, People's Republic of China. TEL 86-10-6217-6428. FAX 86-10-6217-5925. *5225*

ACTA NEUROLOGICA SCANDINAVICA.
Munksgaard International Publishers Ltd., 35 Noerre Soegade, P.O. Box 1248, DK-1016 Copenhagen K, Denmark. TEL 45-33-127030. FAX 45-33-129387. *5048*

ACTA NEUROLOGICA SCANDINAVICA. SUPPLEMENTUM.
Munksgaard International Publishers Ltd., 35 Noerre Soegade, P.O. Box 2148, DK-1016 Copenhagen K, Denmark. TEL 45-33-127030. FAX 45-33-129387. *5048*

ACTA NEUROPSYCHIATRICA.
Misset, P.O. Box 1110, 3600 BC Maarssen, Netherlands. TEL 31-346-558222. FAX 31-346-554287. *5048*

ACTA OBSTETRICA ET GYNECOLOGICA SCANDINAVICA.
Munksgaard International Publishers Ltd., 35 Noerre Soegade, P.O. Box 2148, DK-1016 Copenhagen K, Denmark. TEL 45-33-127030. FAX 45-33-129387. *4951*

ACTA OCEANOLOGICA SINICA.
China Ocean Press, International Cooperation Department, Haimao Dalou, 1 Fuxingmenwai Dajie, Beijing 100860, People's Republic of China. TEL 8032211. FAX 8033515. *2398*

ACTA ORIENTALIA.
Munksgaard International Publishers Ltd., 35 Noerre Soegade, P.O Box 2148, DK-1016 Copenhagen K, Denmark. TEL 45-33-127030. FAX 45-33-129387. *5519*

ACTA ORTHOPAEDICA SCANDINAVICA.
Scandinavian University Press, P.O. Box 2959-Toeyen, N-0608 Oslo, Norway. TEL 47-22-57-54-00. FAX 47-22-57-53-53. *5003*

ACTA PAEDIATRICA SINICA.
Chinese Taipei Pediatric Association, 10F-1, No.69 Sec. 1, Hangchow S. Rd., Taipei, Taiwan, Republic of China. TEL 886-2-351-6448. FAX 886-2-351-6446. *5026*

ACTA PALAEOBOTANICA.
Polska Akademia Nauk, Instytut Botaniki im. W. Szafera, Ul. Lubicz 46, 31-512 Krakow, Poland. TEL 48-12-215144. FAX 48-12-219790. *689*

ACTA PALAEONTOLOGICA POLONICA.
Polska Akademia Nauk, Instytut Paleobiologii, Ul. Twarda 51-55, 00-114 Warsaw. TEL 48-22-69778874. FAX 48-22-6206225. *5557*

ACTA PARASITOLOGICA.
Polska Akademia Nauk, Instytut Parazytologii Witolda Stefanskiego, Ul. Pasteura 3, 00-937 Warsaw, Poland. TEL 48-22-222562. *779*

ACTA PHARMACEUTICA TURCICA.
ETAM A.S. Matbaa Tesisleri, 26470 Eskisehir, Turkey. TEL 90-222-2360051. *5644*

ACTA PHYSICA POLONICA. SERIES B: ELEMENTARY PARTICLE PHYSICS, NUCLEAR PHYSICS, STATISTICAL PHYSICS, THEORY OF RELATIVITY, FIELD THEORY.
Uniwersytet Jagiellonski, Instytut Fizyki, Reymonta 4, 30-059 Krakow, Poland. TEL 48-12-336377. *5794*

ACTA PHYSIOLOGIAE PLANTARUM.
Agencja Wydawnicza ARIES, Ul. Zorzy 22, 40-639 Warsaw, Poland. TEL 48-22-153162. FAX 48-22-153162. *689*

ACTA PHYSIOLOGICA SCANDINAVICA.
Blackwell Science Ltd., Osney Mead, Oxford OX2 OEL, England. TEL 44-1865-206206. FAX 44-1865-721205. *811*

ACTA PHYTOGEOGRAPHICA SUECICA.
Opulus Press AB, P.O. Box 25137, S-750 25 Uppsala, Sweden. TEL 46-18-32-06-62. FAX 46-18-32-13-68. *689*

ACTA POLONIAE PHARMACEUTICA.
Polskie Towarzystwo Farmaceutyczne, Ul. Dluga 16, 00-238 Warsaw, Poland. TEL 48-22-0310241. FAX 48-22-8310243. *5644*

ACTA POLYTECHNICA.
Ceske Vysoke Uceni Technicke, Zikova 4, 166 35 Prague 6, Czech Republic. TEL 420-2-24353490. FAX 420-2-24311042. *2708*

ACTA PSIQUIATRICA Y PSICOLOGICA DE AMERICA LATINA.
Fundacion Acta Fondo para la Salud Mental, Malabia 2274 13 A, 1425 Buenos Aires, Argentina. TEL 541-832-3286. FAX 541-856-7108. *5048*

ACTA PSYCHIATRICA SCANDINAVICA.
Munksgaard International Publishers Ltd., 35 Noerre Soegade, P.O. Box 2148, DK-1016 Copenhagen K. TEL 45-33-127030. FAX 45-33-129387. *5048*

ACTA PSYCHOLOGICA.
North-Holland, P.O. Box 211, 1000 AE Amsterdam, Netherlands. TEL 31-20-4853911. FAX 31-20-4853598. *6089*

ACTA RADIOLOGICA.
Munksgaard International Publishers Ltd., 35 Noerre Soegade, P.O. Box 2148, DK-1016 Copenhagen K, Denmark. TEL 45-33-127030. FAX 45-33-129387. *5102*

ACTA REPRODUCTIVA TURCICA.
Hacettepe University, Department of Gynecology and Obstetrics, Ankara, Turkey. *4952*

ACTA SEISMOLOGICA SINICA.
Seismological Society of China, c/o Institute of Geophysics, State Seismological Bureau, No. 5, Minzuxueyuan Nanlu, Haidian District, Beijing 100081, People's Republic of China. TEL 86-10-8417744. FAX 86-10-8415372. *2377*

ACTA STEREOLOGICA.
Institute of Histology and Embryology, Medical Faculty, Korytkova 2, 61105 Ljubljana, Slovenia. TEL 386-61-441121. FAX 386-61-1401294. *583*

ACTA STOMATOLOGICA CROATICA.
Hrvatski Lijecnicki Zbor, Petrinjska 34, 10000 Zagreb, Croatia. TEL 385-41-276015. FAX 385-41-276017. *4849*

ACTA SUECO-POLONICA.
Uppsala University, Centre for Multiethnic Research, Box 514, S-751 20 Uppsala, Sweden. TEL 46-18-18-27--88. FAX 46-18-18-26-63. *2993*

ACTA TECHNICA C S A V.
Ceska Akademie Ved, Ustav pro Elektrotechniku, Dolejskova 5, 182 00 Prague 8, Czech Republic. TEL 42-2-6883422. FAX 42-2-6883422. *2708*

ACTA THERIOLOGICA.
Polska Akademia Nauk, Zaklad Badania Ssakow, Ul. Gen. Waszkiewicza 1, 17-230 Bialowieza, Poland. TEL 48-835-12289. FAX 48-835-12289. *823*

ACTA TROPICA.
Elsevier Science B.V., P.O. Box 211, 1000 AE Amsterdam, Netherlands. TEL 31-20-4853911. FAX 31-20-4853598. *4830*

ACTA UNIVERSITARIA.
Universidad de Guanajuato, Direccion de Investigacion, Lascurain de Retana 5 (Centro), 36000 Guanajuato, Gto., Mexico. TEL 52-473-20006. FAX 52-473-29312. *6509*

ACTA UNIVERSITATIS PALACKIANAE OLOMUCENSIS. FACULTATIS MEDICAE.
Universita Palackeho, Olomouc, Lekarska Fakulta, Hnevotinska 3, 775 15 Olomouc, Czech Republic. TEL 42-68-5412551. FAX 42-68-541-3541. *4632*

ACTA UROLOGICA ITALICA.
Societa Italiana di Urologia, Largo Lanciani 1, 00162 Rome, Italy. TEL 39-6-86202637. FAX 39-6-86325073. *5158*

ACTA VETERINARIA BRNO.
University of Veterinary and Pharmaceutical Sciences, Palackeho 1-3, 612 42 Brno, Czech Republic. TEL 42-5-42562505. FAX 42-5-4121151. *7263*

ACTA ZOOLOGICA.
Elsevier Science Ltd., Pergamon, P.O. Box 800, Kidlington, Oxford OX5 1DX, England. TEL 44-1865-843000. FAX 44-1865-843010. *824*

ACTA ZOOLOGICA CRACOVIENSIA.
Polska Akademia Nauk, Instytut Systematyki i Ewolucji Zwierzat, Ul. Slawkowska 17, 31-016 Krakow, Poland. TEL 48-12-221891. FAX 48-12-224294. *824*

ACTION NATIONALE.
Ligue d'Action Nationale, 425 Blvd. de Maisonneuve Ouest, Montreal, PQ H3A 3G5, Canada. TEL 514-845-8533. FAX 514-845-8529. *5888*

ACTIVE AND PASSIVE ELECTRONIC COMPONENTS.
Gordon and Breach - Harwood Academic, Amsteldisk 166, 1st Fl., 1079 LH Amsterdam, Netherlands. *2807*

ACTIVE LEARNING.
Computers in Teaching Initiative Support Service, University of Oxford, 13 Banbury Rd., Oxford OX2 6NN, England. TEL 44-1865-273273. FAX 44-1865-273275. *2514*

THE ACTIVIST.
Amnesty International, Canadian Section (English Speaking), 214 Montreal Rd., Ste 401, Vanier, ON K1L 1A4, Canada. TEL 613-744-7667. FAX 613-746-2411. *5987*

ACTIVITIES, ADAPTATION & AGING.
Haworth Press, Inc., 10 Alice St., Binghamton, NY 13904. TEL 607-722-5857. FAX 607-722-6362. *3430*

ACTIVNEWS.
Activ Foundation Inc., P.O. Box 446, Jolimont, W.A. 6014, Australia. TEL 61-9-3870555. FAX 61-9-3870599. *6652*

REFEREED SERIALS

ACTUALIDAD TABAQUERA.
Tabapress, S.A., Barquillo 7, 28004 Madrid, Spain. TEL 34-1-3609050. FAX 34-1-5325562. *7019*

ACTUARIAL DIGEST.
Actuarial Digest Publishing Company, Box 1127, Ponte Vedra Beach, FL 32004-1127. TEL 904-273-1245. *3806*

ACUPUNCTURE AND ELECTRO-THERAPEUTICS RESEARCH.
Cognizant Communication Corporation, 3 Hartsdale Rd., Elmsford, NY 10523-3701. TEL 914-592-7720. FAX 914-592-8981. *294*

ACUPUNCTURE IN MEDICINE.
British Medical Acupuncture Society, Newton House, Newton Lane, Lower Whitley, Warrington, Cheshire WA4 4JA, England. TEL 44-1925-730727. FAX 44-1925-730492. *294*

ACUTE CORONARY CARE.
Kluwer Academic Publishers, Postbus 17, 3300 AA Dordrecht, Netherlands. TEL 31-78-6392392. FAX 31-78-6392254. *4808*

ADAPTED PHYSICAL ACTIVITY QUARTERLY.
Human Kinetics Publishers, Inc., Box 5076, Champaign, IL 61825-5076. TEL 217-351-5076. FAX 217-351-2674. *2580*

ADAPTIVE BEHAVIOR.
M I T Press, 5 Cambridge Center, Cambridge, MA 02142. TEL 617-253-2889. FAX 617-577-1545. *2097*

ADAY.
Mindanao State University, Mamitua Saber Research Center, P.O. Box 5594, Iligan City 9200, Philippines. *4371*

ADDICTION.
Carfax Publishing Co., P.O. Box 25, Abingdon, Oxon. OX14 3UE, England. TEL 44-1235-401000. FAX 44-1325-401550. *2297*

ADDICTIVE BEHAVIORS.
Elsevier Science Ltd., Pergamon, P.O. Box 800, Kidlington, Oxford OX5 1DX, England. TEL 44-1865-843000. FAX 44-1865-843010. *2297*

ADELAIDE LAW REVIEW.
Adelaide Law Review Association, c/o Department of Law, University of Adelaide, Adelaide, S.A. 5005, Australia. TEL 61-8-303-4440. FAX 61-8-303-4344. *3905*

ADHESION.
Elsevier Science Ltd., Books Division, P.O. Box 800, Kidlington, Oxford OX5 1DX, England. TEL 44-1865-843000. FAX 44-1865-843010. *5875*

ADICCIONES.
Socidrogalcohol, C. Rambla 15, 2a 3a, 07003 Palma de Mallorca, Spain. TEL 34-71-727434. FAX 34-71-718073. *2297*

ADIRONDACK JOURNAL OF ENVIRONMENTAL STUDIES.
Chimera Press, AJES, SSHE Division, Paul Smith's College, Paul Smiths, NY 12970. TEL 518-327-6377. FAX 518-327-6369. *2904*

ADMINISTRATION AND POLICY IN MENTAL HEALTH.
Human Sciences Press, Inc., 233 Spring St., New York, NY 10013-1578. TEL 212-620-8000. FAX 212-463-0742. *4632*

ADMINISTRATION IN SOCIAL WORK.
Haworth Press, Inc., 10 Alice St., Binghamton, NY 13904. TEL 607-722-5857. FAX 607-722-6362. *6652*

ADMINISTRATIVE RADIOLOGY.
Glendale Publishing Corp., 1305 Glenoaks Blvd., Glendale, CA 91201. TEL 818-500-1872. *5102*

ADMINISTRATIVE SCIENCE QUARTERLY.
Cornell University, Johnson Graduate School of Management, 20 Thornwood Dr., Ste. 100, Ithaca, NY 14850-1265. TEL 607-254-7143. FAX 607-254-7100. *6162*

ADMINISTRATIVE SCIENCES ASSOCIATION OF CANADA. PROCEEDINGS, ANNUAL CONFERENCE.
A S A C Publications, c/o Irene Lepine, Dept. of Administrative Sciences, Universite du Quebec a Montreal, P.O. Box 6192, Sta. Centreville, Montreal, PQ H3C 4RZ, Canada. TEL 514-987-3697. FAX 514-987-3343. *1463*

ADOBE MAGAZINE.
Adobe Systems, 411 First Ave., S., Seattle, WA 98104. TEL 206-622-5500. FAX 206-343-3273. *2208*

ADOLESCENT MEDICINE (PHILADELPHIA).
Hanley & Belfus, Inc., 210 S. 13th St., Philadelphia, PA 19107. TEL 215-546-7293. FAX 215-790-9330. *5027*

ADOLESCENT PSYCHIATRY.
University of Chicago Press, Journals Division, 5720 S. Woodlawn Ave., Chicago, IL 60637. TEL 773-753-3347. FAX 773-753-0811. *5049*

ADOPTION QUARTERLY.
Haworth Press, Inc., 10 Alice St., Binghamton, NY 13904. TEL 607-722-5857. FAX 607-722-6362. *6653*

ADORERIAN.
Nihon Adora Shinri Gakkai, 5-12-15-301 Nishinakajima, Yodogawa-ku, Osaka 532, Japan. TEL 81-6-306-4699. FAX 81-6-306-0160. *6089*

ADSORPTION.
Kluwer Academic Publishers, Postbus 17, 3300 AA Dordrecht, Netherlands. TEL 31-78-6392392. FAX 31-78-6392254. *2754*

ADSORPTION SCIENCE AND TECHNOLOGY.
Multi-Science Publishing Co. Ltd., 107 High St., Brentwood, Essex CM14 4RX, England. TEL 44-1277-224632. FAX 44-1277-223453. *2754*

ADULT EDUCATION QUARTERLY.
American Association for Adult and Continuing Education, 1200 19th St., N.W., Ste. 300, Washington, DC 20036. TEL 202-429-5131. *2506*

ADVANCE - TITAN.
Advance - Titan, 800 Algoma Blvd., Oshkosh, WI 54901. TEL 414-424-3048. FAX 414-424-0866. *1938*

ADVANCED CARDIAC LIFE SUPPORT.
American Health Consultants, Inc., 3525 Piedmont Rd., N.E., Bldg. 6, Ste. 400, Atlanta, GA 30305. TEL 800-688-2421. FAX 800-284-3291. *4808*

ADVANCED CEMENT BASED MATERIALS.
Elsevier Science Inc., Box 945, New York, NY 10159-0945. TEL 212-633-3730. FAX 212-633-3680. *2754*

ADVANCED COMPOSITE MATERIALS.
V S P, P.O. Box 346, 3700 AH Zeist, Netherlands. TEL 31-30-6925790. FAX 31-30-6932081. *2850*

ADVANCED COMPOSITES LETTERS.
Woodhead Publishing Ltd., Abington Hall, Abington, Cambridge CB1 6AH, England. TEL 44-1223-891358. FAX 44-1223-893694. *5875*

ADVANCED DRUG DELIVERY REVIEWS.
Elsevier Science B.V., P.O. Box 211, 1000 AE Amsterdam, Netherlands. TEL 31-20-4853911. FAX 31-20-4853598. *5645*

ADVANCED LABANOTATION.
Gordon and Breach - Harwood Academic, Amsteldisk 166, 1st Fl., 1079 LH Amsterdam, Netherlands. *2290*

ADVANCED MATERIALS FOR OPTICS AND ELECTRONICS.
John Wiley & Sons Ltd., Journals, Baffins Ln., Chichester, W. Sussex PO19 1UD, England. TEL 44-1243-779777. FAX 44-1243-843232. *1804*

ADVANCED PERFORMANCE MATERIALS.
Kluwer Academic Publishers, Postbus 17, 3300 AA Dordrecht, Netherlands. TEL 31-78-6392392. FAX 31-78-6392254. *2851*

ADVANCED POWDER TECHNOLOGY.
V S P, P.O. Box 346, 3700 AH Zeist, Netherlands. TEL 31-30-6925790. FAX 31-30-6932081. *2754*

ADVANCED ROBOTICS.
V S P, P.O. Box 346, 3700 AH Zeist, Netherlands. TEL 31-30-6925790. FAX 31-30-6932081. *2206*

ADVANCED SERIES IN MANAGEMENT.
Elsevier Science B.V., Books Division, P.O. Box 211, 1000 AE Amsterdam, Netherlands. TEL 31-20-4853911. FAX 31-20-4853705. *1464*

ADVANCED STUDIES IN CONTEMPORARY MATHEMATICS.
Gordon and Breach - Harwood Academic, Amsteldisk 166, 1st Fl., 1079 LH Amsterdam, Netherlands. *4557*

ADVANCED STUDIES IN THEORETICAL AND APPLIED ECONOMETRICS.
Kluwer Academic Publishers, Postbus 17, 3300 AA Dordrecht, Netherlands. TEL 31-78-6392392. FAX 31-78-6392254. *1296*

ADVANCED TEXTBOOKS IN ECONOMICS.
Elsevier Science B.V., Books Division, P.O. Box 211, 1000 AE Amsterdam, Netherlands. TEL 31-20-4853911. FAX 31-20-4853705. *1296*

ADVANCES IN AGRICULTURAL BIOTECHNOLOGY.
Kluwer Academic Publishers, Postbus 17, 3300 AA Dordrecht, Netherlands. TEL 31-78-6392392. FAX 31-78-6392254. *677*

ADVANCES IN AGRICULTURAL SCIENCES.
Akademia Rolnicza w Szczecinie, Dzial Wydawnictw, Ul. Doktora Judyma 22, 71-460 Szczecin, Poland. TEL 48-91-541639. FAX 48-91-541642. *86*

ADVANCES IN AGRONOMY.
Academic Press, Inc., 525 B St., Ste. 1900, San Diego, CA 92101-4495. TEL 619-231-0926. FAX 619-699-6715. *86*

ADVANCES IN ANATOMIC PATHOLOGY.
Lippincott - Raven Publishers, 227 E. Washington Sq., Philadelphia, PA 19106. TEL 215-238-4200. FAX 215-238-4227. *4632*

ADVANCES IN ANATOMY, EMBRYOLOGY AND CELL BIOLOGY.
Springer-Verlag, 175 Fifth Ave., New York, NY 10010. TEL 212-460-1500. FAX 212-473-6272. *584*

ADVANCES IN APPLIED MATHEMATICS.
Academic Press, Inc., Journal Division, 525 B St., Ste. 1900, San Diego, CA 92101-4495. TEL 619-230-1840. FAX 619-699-6800. *4557*

ADVANCES IN APPLIED MECHANICS.
Academic Press, Inc., 525 B St., Ste. 1900, San Diego, CA 92101-4495. TEL 619-231-0926. FAX 619-699-6715. *5843*

ADVANCES IN APPLIED MICROBIOLOGY.
Academic Press, Inc., 525 B St., Ste. 1900, San Diego, CA 92101-4495. TEL 619-231-0926. FAX 619-699-6715. *779*

ADVANCES IN APPLIED PROBABILITY.
Applied Probability Trust, School of Mathematics, University of Sheffield, Sheffield S3 7RH, England. TEL 44-114-222-3920. FAX 44-114-222-3920. *4557*

ADVANCES IN APPLIED SOCIAL PSYCHOLOGY.
Lawrence Erlbaum Associates, Inc., 10 Industrial Dr., Mahwah, NJ 07430-2262. TEL 201-236-9500. FAX 201-236-0072. *6089*

ADVANCES IN ATMOSPHERIC SCIENCES.
China Ocean Press, International Cooperation Department, Haimao Dalou, 1 Fuxingmenwai Dajie, Beijing 100860, People's Republic of China. TEL 8032211. FAX 8033515. *5226*

ADVANCES IN AUDIOLOGY.
S. Karger AG, Allschwilerstr. 10, P.O. Box, CH-4009 Basel, Switzerland. TEL 41-61-3061111. FAX 41-61-3061234. *5019*

ADVANCES IN BEHAVIORAL BIOLOGY.
Plenum Publishing Corp., 233 Spring St., New York, NY 10013-1578. TEL 212-620-8000. FAX 212-463-0742. *6089*

ADVANCES IN BIOCHEMICAL PSYCHOPHARMACOLOGY.
Lippincott - Raven Publishers, 227 E. Washington Sq., Philadelphia, PA 19106. TEL 215-238-4200. FAX 215-238-4200. *5645*

ADVANCES IN BIOENGINEERING.
American Society of Mechanical Engineers, 22 Law Dr., Fairfield, NJ 07007-2300. *645*

ADVANCES IN BIOLOGICAL PSYCHIATRY.
S. Karger AG, Allschwilerstr. 10, P.O. Box, CH-4009 Basel, Switzerland. TEL 41-61-3061111. FAX 41-61-3061234. *5049*

ADVANCES IN BIOMATERIALS.
Elsevier Science B.V., Books Division, P.O. Box 211, 1000 AE Amsterdam, Netherlands. TEL 31-20-4853911. FAX 31-20-4853705. *649*

ADVANCES IN BIOPHYSICS.
Elsevier Science Ireland Ltd., P.O. Box 85, Limerick, Ireland. TEL 353-61-471944. FAX 353-61-472144. *673*

ADVANCES IN BOTANICAL RESEARCH.
Academic Press, Inc., 525 B St., Ste. 1900, San Diego, CA 92101-4495. TEL 619-231-0926. FAX 619-699-6715. *690*

ADVANCES IN C A D FOR V L S I.
Elsevier Science B.V., Books Division, P.O. Box 211, 1000 AE Amsterdam, Netherlands. TEL 31-20-4853911. FAX 31-20-4853705. *2119*

ADVANCES IN CANCER RESEARCH.
Academic Press, Inc., 525 B St., Ste. 1900, San Diego, CA 92101-4495. TEL 619-231-0926. FAX 619-699-6715. *4969*

ADVANCES IN CARBOHYDRATE CHEMISTRY AND BIOCHEMISTRY.
Academic Press, Inc., 525 B St., Ste. 1900, San Diego, CA 92101-4495. TEL 619-231-0926. FAX 619-699-6715. *1810*

ADVANCES IN CARDIOLOGY.
S. Karger AG, Allschwilerstr. 10, P.O. Box, CH-4009 Basel, Switzerland. TEL 41-61-3061111. FAX 41-61-3061234. *4808*

ADVANCES IN CATALYSIS.
Academic Press, Inc., 525 B St., Ste. 1900, San Diego, CA 92101-4495. TEL 619-231-0926. FAX 619-699-6715. *1825*

ADVANCES IN CELLULAR AND MOLECULAR BIOLOGY OF PLANTS.
Kluwer Academic Publishers, Postbus 17, 3300 AA Dordrecht, Netherlands. TEL 31-78-6392392. FAX 31-78-6392254. *735*

ADVANCES IN CEMENT RESEARCH.
Thomas Telford Services Ltd., Thomas Telford House, 1 Heron Quay, London E14 4JD, England. TEL 44-171-987-6999. FAX 44-171-538-9620. *860*

ADVANCES IN CHEMICAL ENGINEERING.
Academic Press, Inc., 525 B St., Ste. 1900, San Diego, CA 92101-4495. TEL 619-231-0923. FAX 619-699-6715. *2755*

ADVANCES IN CHEMICAL PHYSICS.
John Wiley & Sons, Inc., 605 Third Ave., New York, NY 10158-0012. TEL 212-850-6000. FAX 212-850-6099. *5795*

ADVANCES IN CHEMISTRY SERIES.
American Chemical Society, 1155 16th St., N.W., Washington, DC 20036. TEL 800-227-5558. FAX 202-872-4615. *1737*

ADVANCES IN CHILD DEVELOPMENT AND BEHAVIOR.
Academic Press, Inc., 525 B St., Ste. 1900, San Diego, CA 92101-4495. TEL 619-231-0926. FAX 619-699-6715. *6089*

ADVANCES IN CHROMATOGRAPHY.
Marcel Dekker, Inc., 270 Madison Ave., New York, NY 10016. TEL 212-696-9000. FAX 212-685-4540. *1787*

ADVANCES IN CLINICAL CHEMISTRY.
Academic Press, Inc., 525 B St., Ste. 1900, San Diego, CA 92101-4495. TEL 619-231-0926. FAX 619-699-6715. *649*

ADVANCES IN CLINICAL CHILD PSYCHOLOGY.
Plenum Publishing Corp., 233 Spring St., New York, NY 10013-1578. TEL 212-620-8000. FAX 212-463-0742. *6090*

ADVANCES IN CLINICAL PHARMACOLOGY.
Lippincott - Raven Publishers, 227 E. Washington Sq., Philadelphia, PA 19106. TEL 215-238-4200. FAX 215-238-4227. *5645*

ADVANCES IN COLLOID AND INTERFACE SCIENCE.
Elsevier Science B.V., P.O. Box 211, 1000 AE Amsterdam, Netherlands. TEL 31-20-4853911. FAX 31-20-4853598. *1825*

ADVANCES IN COMPUTATIONAL ECONOMICS.
Kluwer Academic Publishers, Postbus 17, 3300 AA Dordrecht, Netherlands. TEL 31-78-6392392. FAX 31-78-6392254. *1198*

ADVANCES IN COMPUTATIONAL MATHEMATICS.
Baltzer Science Publishers B.V., P.O. Box 221, 1400 AE Bussum, Netherlands. TEL 31-20-6370061. FAX 31-20-6323651. *4618*

ADVANCES IN COMPUTERS.
Academic Press, Inc., 525 B St., Ste. 1900, San Diego, CA 92101-4495. TEL 619-231-0926. FAX 619-699-6715. *2072*

ADVANCES IN CONSUMER RESEARCH.
Association for Consumer Research, Brigham Young University, Graduate School of Management, 632 TNRB, Provo, UT 84602. TEL 801-378-2080. FAX 801-226-7650. *1514*

ADVANCES IN CONTRACEPTION.
Kluwer Academic Publishers, Postbus 17, 3300 AA Dordrecht, Netherlands. TEL 31-78-6392392. FAX 31-78-6392254. *856*

ADVANCES IN CONTRACEPTIVE DELIVERY SYSTEMS.
Reproductive Health Center, 78 Surfsong Rd., Kiawah Island, SC 29455. TEL 803-768-5556. FAX 803-769-6494. *856*

ADVANCES IN CRYOGENIC ENGINEERING.
Plenum Publishing Corp., 233 Spring St., New York, NY 10013-1578. TEL 212-620-8000. FAX 212-463-0742. *5839*

ADVANCES IN DESCRIPTIVE PSYCHOLOGY.
Jessica Kingsley Publishers, 116 Pentonville Rd., London N1 9JB, England. TEL 44-171-833-2307. FAX 44-171-837-2917. *6090*

ADVANCES IN DESERT AND ARID LAND TECHNOLOGY AND DEVELOPMENT SERIES.
Gordon and Breach - Harwood Academic, Amsteldisk 166, 1st Fl., 1079 LH Amsterdam, Netherlands. *3394*

ADVANCES IN DEVELOPMENTAL AND BEHAVIORAL PEDIATRICS.
Jessica Kingsley Publishers, 116 Pentonville Rd., London N1 9JB, England. TEL 44-171-833-2307. FAX 44-171-837-2917. *5027*

ADVANCES IN DEVELOPMENTAL PSYCHOLOGY.
Lawrence Erlbaum Associates, Inc., 10 Industrial Dr., Mahwah, NJ 07430-2262. TEL 201-236-9500. FAX 201-236-0072. *6090*

ADVANCES IN DIFFERENTIAL EQUATIONS.
Khayyam Publishing Company, Inc., Box 429, Athens, OH 45701. TEL 614-592-6136. FAX 614-592-1252. *4557*

ADVANCES IN DRUG RESEARCH.
Academic Press, Inc., 525 B St., Ste. 1900, San Diego, CA 92101-4495. TEL 619-231-0926. FAX 619-699-6715. *5645*

ADVANCES IN ECHO-CONTRAST.
Kluwer Academic Publishers, Postbus 17, 3300 AA Dordrecht, Netherlands. TEL 31-78-6392392. FAX 31-78-6392254. *4845*

ADVANCES IN ECOLOGICAL RESEARCH.
Academic Press, Inc., 525 B St., Ste. 1900, San Diego, CA 92101-4495. TEL 619-231-0926. FAX 619-699-6715. *2904*

ADVANCES IN ECONOMIC BOTANY.
New York Botanical Garden, Scientific Publications Department, Bronx, NY 10458-5126. TEL 718-817-8721. FAX 718-817-8842. *690*

ADVANCES IN EICOSANOID RESEARCH.
Kluwer Academic Publishers, Postbus 17, 3300 AA Dordrecht, Netherlands. TEL 31-78-6392392. FAX 31-78-6392254. *649*

ADVANCES IN ELECTROMAGNETIC FIELDS IN LIVING SYSTEMS.
Plenum Publishing Corp., 233 Spring St., New York, NY 10013-1578. TEL 212-620-8000. FAX 212-463-0742. *646*

ADVANCES IN ENGINEERING.
Swets & Zeitlinger b.v., P.O. Box 825, 2160 SZ Lisse, Netherlands. TEL 31-252-435111. FAX 31-252-415888. *2709*

ADVANCES IN ENGINEERING.
Society of Automotive Engineers, 400 Commonwealth Dr., Warrendale, PA 15096-0001. TEL 412-776-4841. FAX 412-776-3036. *7081*

ADVANCES IN ENGINEERING SOFTWARE.
Elsevier Science Ltd., P.O. Box 800, Kidlington, Oxford OX5 1DX, England. TEL 44-1865-843000. FAX 44-1865-843010. *2802*

ADVANCES IN ENVIRONMENTAL PSYCHOLOGY.
Lawrence Erlbaum Associates, Inc., 10 Industrial Dr., Mahwah, NJ 07430-2262. TEL 201-236-9500. FAX 201-236-0072. *6090*

ADVANCES IN ENVIRONMENTAL SCIENCE AND ENGINEERING.
Gordon and Breach - Harwood Academic, Amsteldisk 166, 1st Fl., 1079 LH Amsterdam, Netherlands. *2904*

ADVANCES IN ENVIRONMENTAL SCIENCE AND TECHNOLOGY.
Krieger Publishing Co., Box 9542, Melbourne, FL 32902. TEL 407-724-9542. FAX 407-951-3671. *2905*

ADVANCES IN ENZYME REGULATION.
Elsevier Science Ltd., Pergamon, P.O. Box 800, Kidlington, Oxford OX5 1DX, England. TEL 44-1865-843000. FAX 44-1865-843010. *4632*

ADVANCES IN ENZYMOLOGY AND RELATED AREAS OF MOLECULAR BIOLOGY.
John Wiley & Sons, Inc., 605 Third Ave., New York, NY 10158-0012. TEL 212-850-6800. *649*

ADVANCES IN EPILEPTOLOGY.
Lippincott - Raven Publishers, 227 E. Washington Sq., Philadelphia, PA 19106. TEL 215-238-4200. FAX 215-238-4227. *5049*

ADVANCES IN EXPERIMENTAL MEDICINE AND BIOLOGY.
Plenum Publishing Corp., 233 Spring St., New York, NY 10013-1578. TEL 212-620-8000. FAX 212-463-0742. *584*

ADVANCES IN EXPLORATION GEOPHYSICS.
Elsevier Science B.V., Books Division, P.O. Box 211, 1000 AE Amsterdam, Netherlands. TEL 31-20-4853911. FAX 31-20-4853705. *2378*

ADVANCES IN FINANCE, INVESTMENT AND BANKING.
Elsevier Science B.V., Books Division, P.O. Box 211, 1000 AE Amsterdam, Netherlands. TEL 31-20-4853911. FAX 31-20-4853705. *1372*

ADVANCES IN FLUID MECHANICS.
Computational Mechanics Publications, Ashurst Lodge, Ashurst, Southampton, SO40 7AA, England. TEL 44-1703-293223. FAX 44-1703-292853. *2709*

ADVANCES IN GENETICS.
Academic Press, Inc., 525 B St., Ste. 1900, San Diego, CA 92101-4495. TEL 619-231-0926. FAX 619-699-6715. *762*

REFEREED SERIALS

ADVANCES IN GEOPHYSICS.
Academic Press, Inc., 525 B St., Ste. 1900, San Diego, CA 92101-4495. TEL 619-231-0926. FAX 619-699-6715. *2378*

ADVANCES IN HEALTH ECONOMICS AND HEALTH SERVICES RESEARCH.
J A I Press Inc., 55 Old Post Rd., No. 2, Box 1678, Greenwich, CT 06830-1678. TEL 203-661-7602. FAX 203-661-0792. *5777*

ADVANCES IN HEALTH EDUCATION: CURRENT RESEARCH.
A M S Press, Inc., 56 E. 13th St., New York, NY 10003. TEL 212-777-4700. FAX 212-995-5413. *2593*

ADVANCES IN HEALTH SCIENCES EDUCATION.
Kluwer Academic Publishers, Postbus 17, 3300 AA Dordrecht, Netherlands. TEL 31-78-6392392. FAX 31-78-6392254. *4633*

ADVANCES IN HEAT TRANSFER.
Academic Press, Inc., 525 B St., Ste. 1900, San Diego, CA 92101-4495. TEL 619-231-0926. FAX 619-699-6715. *5839*

ADVANCES IN HETEROCYCLIC CHEMISTRY.
Academic Press, Inc., 525 B St., Ste. 1900, San Diego, CA 92101-4495. TEL 619-231-0926. FAX 619-699-6715. *1811*

ADVANCES IN HORTICULTURAL SCIENCE.
Universita degli Studi di Firenze, Dipartimento di Ortoflorofrutticoltura, Via Donizetti 6, 50144 Florence, Italy. TEL 055-333462. FAX 055-331497. *3179*

ADVANCES IN HUMAN - COMPUTER INTERACTION.
Ablex Publishing Corporation, Box 5297, Greenwich, CT 06831-0504. TEL 203-661-7602. FAX 203-661-0792. *2105*

ADVANCES IN HUMAN FACTORS - ERGONOMICS.
Elsevier Science B.V., Books Division, P.O. Box 211, 1000 AE Amsterdam, Netherlands. TEL 31-20-4853911. FAX 31-20-4853705. *6090*

ADVANCES IN HUMAN GENETICS.
Plenum Publishing Corp., 233 Spring St., New York, NY 10013-1578. TEL 212-620-8000. FAX 212-463-0742. *762*

ADVANCES IN HUMAN PSYCHOPHARMACOLOGY.
Jessica Kingsley Publishers, 116 Pentonville Rd., London N1 9JB, England. TEL 44-171-833-2307. FAX 44-171-837-2917. *5645*

ADVANCES IN IMAGING AND ELECTRON PHYSICS.
Academic Press, Inc., 525 B St., Ste. 1900, San Diego, CA 92101-4495. TEL 619-231-0926. FAX 619-699-6715. *2807*

ADVANCES IN INCLUSION SCIENCE.
Kluwer Academic Publishers, Postbus 17, 3300 AA Dordrecht, Netherlands. TEL 31-78-6392392. FAX 31-78-6392254. *1811*

ADVANCES IN INDUSTRIAL ENGINEERING.
Elsevier Science B.V., Books Division, P.O. Box 211, 1000 AE Amsterdam, Netherlands. TEL 31-20-4853911. FAX 31-20-4853705. *2875*

ADVANCES IN INFANCY RESEARCH.
Ablex Publishing Corporation, Box 5297, Greenwich, CT 06831-0504. TEL 203-661-7602. FAX 203-661-0792. *5027*

ADVANCES IN INFLAMMATION RESEARCH.
Lippincott - Raven Publishers, 227 E. Washington Sq., Philadelphia, PA 19106. TEL 215-238-4200. FAX 215-238-4227. *4633*

ADVANCES IN INORGANIC BIOCHEMISTRY.
Elsevier Science B.V., Books Division, P.O. Box 211, 1000 AE Amsterdam, Netherlands. TEL 31-20-4853911. FAX 31-20-4853705. *1806*

ADVANCES IN INORGANIC CHEMISTRY.
Academic Press, Inc., 525 B St., Ste. 1900, San Diego, CA 92101-4495. TEL 619-231-0926. FAX 619-699-6715. *1806*

ADVANCES IN INSECT PHYSIOLOGY.
Academic Press, Inc., 525 B St., Ste. 1900, San Diego, CA 92101-4495. TEL 619-231-0926. FAX 619-699-6715. *745*

ADVANCES IN INSTRUCTIONAL PSYCHOLOGY.
Lawrence Erlbaum Associates, Inc., 10 Industrial Dr., Mahwah, NJ 07430-2262. TEL 201-236-9500. FAX 201-236-0072. *6090*

ADVANCES IN INSTRUMENTATION AND CONTROL.
Instrument Society of America, 67 Alexander Dr., Box 12277, Research Triangle Park, NC 27709. TEL 919-549-8411. FAX 919-549-8288. *3800*

ADVANCES IN LEARNING AND BEHAVIORAL DISABILITIES.
J A I Press Inc., 55 Old Post Rd., No. 2, Box 1678, Greenwich, CT 06836-1678. TEL 203-661-7602. FAX 203-661-0792. *2580*

ADVANCES IN M R I - CONTRAST.
Kluwer Academic Publishers, Postbus 17, 3300 AA Dordrecht, Netherlands. TEL 31-78-6392392. FAX 31-78-6392254. *5103*

ADVANCES IN MAGNETIC AND OPTICAL RESONANCE.
Academic Press, Inc., 525 B St., Ste. 1900, San Diego, CA 92101-4495. TEL 619-231-0926. FAX 619-699-6715. *5795*

ADVANCES IN MAGNETIC RESONANCE IMAGING.
Ablex Publishing Corporation, Box 5297, Greenwich, CT 06831-0504. TEL 203-661-7602. FAX 203-661-0792. *2120*

ADVANCES IN MARINE BIOLOGY.
Academic Press, Inc., 525 B St., Ste. 1900, San Diego, CA 92101-4495. TEL 619-231-0926. FAX 619-699-6715. *584*

ADVANCES IN MATHEMATICS.
Academic Press, Inc., Journal Division, 525 B St., Ste. 1900, San Diego, CA 92101-4495. TEL 619-230-1840. FAX 619-699-6800. *4557*

ADVANCES IN MEDICAL SOCIAL SCIENCE.
Gordon and Breach - Harwood Academic, Amsteldisk 166, 1st Fl., 1079 LH Amsterdam, Netherlands. *6601*

ADVANCES IN METABOLISM.
Academic Press, Inc., 525 B St., Ste. 1900, San Diego, CA 92101-4495. TEL 619-231-0926. FAX 619-699-6715. *4882*

ADVANCES IN MICROBIAL ECOLOGY.
Plenum Publishing Corp., 233 Spring St., New York, NY 10013-1578. TEL 212-620-8000. FAX 212-463-0742. *779*

ADVANCES IN MICROBIAL PHYSIOLOGY.
Academic Press, Inc., 525 B St., Ste. 1900, San Diego, CA 92101-4495. TEL 619-231-0926. FAX 619-699-6715. *779*

ADVANCES IN MINING SCIENCE AND TECHNOLOGY.
Elsevier Science B.V., Books Division, P.O. Box 211, 1000 AE Amsterdam, Netherlands. TEL 31-20-4853911. FAX 31-20-4853705. *5293*

ADVANCES IN MODELLING & ANALYSIS. A: GENERAL MATHEMATICAL & COMPUTER TOOLS.
A M S E Press, 16 av. de Grange Blanche, 69160 Tassin-la-Demi-Lune, France. TEL 33-4-78343604. FAX 33-4-78345417. *4618*

ADVANCES IN MOLTEN SALT CHEMISTRY.
Elsevier Science B.V., Books Division, P.O. Box 211, 1000 AE Amsterdam, Netherlands. TEL 31-20-4853911. FAX 31-20-4853705. *1806*

ADVANCES IN MOTOR DEVELOPMENT RESEARCH.
A M S Press, Inc., 56 E. 13th St., New York, NY 10003. TEL 212-777-4700. FAX 212-995-5413. *5777*

ADVANCES IN NATURAL AND TECHNOLOGICAL HAZARDS RESEARCH.
Kluwer Academic Publishers, Postbus 17, 3300 AA Dordrecht, Netherlands. TEL 31-78-6392392. FAX 31-78-6392254. *6227*

ADVANCES IN NEURAL AND BEHAVIORAL DEVELOPMENT.
Ablex Publishing Corporation, Box 5297, Greenwich, CT 06831-0504. TEL 203-661-7602. FAX 203-661-0792. *6090*

ADVANCES IN NEUROCHEMISTRY.
Plenum Publishing Corp., 233 Spring St., New York, NY 10013-1578. TEL 212-620-8000. FAX 212-463-0742. *649*

ADVANCES IN NEUROLOGY.
Lippincott - Raven Publishers, 227 E. Washington Sq., Philadelphia, PA 19106. TEL 215-238-4200. FAX 215-238-4235. *5049*

ADVANCES IN NEUROPSYCHIATRY AND PSYCHOPHARMACOLOGY.
Lippincott - Raven Publishers, 227 E. Washington Sq., Philadelphia, PA 19106. TEL 215-238-4200. FAX 215-238-4227. *5049*

ADVANCES IN NEUROSCIENCE.
Lippincott - Raven Publishers, 227 E. Washington Sq., Philadelphia, PA 19106. TEL 215-238-4200. FAX 215-238-4227. *5049*

ADVANCES IN NUCLEAR PHYSICS.
Plenum Publishing Corp., 233 Spring St., New York, NY 10013-1578. TEL 212-620-8000. FAX 212-463-0742. *5850*

ADVANCES IN NUCLEAR SCIENCE AND TECHNOLOGY.
Plenum Publishing Corp., 233 Spring St., New York, NY 10013-1578. TEL 212-620-8047. *5850*

ADVANCES IN NURSING SCIENCE.
Aspen Publishers, Inc., 200 Orchard Ridge Dr., Gaithersburg, MD 20878. TEL 301-417-7500. FAX 301-417-7550. *4928*

ADVANCES IN NUTRITIONAL RESEARCH.
Plenum Publishing Corp., 233 Spring St., New York, NY 10013-1578. TEL 212-620-8000. FAX 212-463-0742. *5468*

ADVANCES IN OPTO-ELECTRONICS.
Kluwer Academic Publishers, Postbus 17, 3300 AA Dordrecht, Netherlands. TEL 31-78-6392392. FAX 31-78-6392254. *2625*

ADVANCES IN ORGANOMETALLIC CHEMISTRY.
Academic Press, Inc., 525 B St., Ste. 1900, San Diego, CA 92101-4495. TEL 619-231-0926. FAX 619-699-6715. *1811*

ADVANCES IN ORTHOPAEDIC SURGERY.
Lippincott - Raven Publishers, 227 E. Washington Sq., Philadelphia, PA 19106. TEL 215-238-4200. FAX 212-238-4227. *5003*

ADVANCES IN OTO-RHINO-LARYNGOLOGY.
S. Karger AG, Allschwilerstr. 10, P.O. Box, CH-4009 Basel, Switzerland. TEL 41-61-3061111. FAX 41-61-3061234. *5019*

ADVANCES IN PAIN RESEARCH AND THERAPY.
Lippincott - Raven Publishers, 227 E. Washington Sq., Philadelphia, PA 19106. TEL 215-238-4200. FAX 215-238-4227. *5049*

ADVANCES IN PARALLEL COMPUTING.
Elsevier Science B.V., Books Division, P.O. Box 211, 1000 AE Amsterdam, Netherlands. TEL 31-20-4853911. FAX 31-20-4853705. *2131*

ADVANCES IN PARASITOLOGY.
Academic Press, Inc., 525 B St., Ste. 1900, San Diego, CA 92101-4495. TEL 619-231-0926. FAX 619-699-6715. *824*

ADVANCES IN PERSONALITY ASSESSMENT.
Lawrence Erlbaum Associates, Inc., 10 Industrial Dr., Mahwah, NJ 07430-2262. TEL 201-236-9500. FAX 201-236-0072. *6090*

ADVANCES IN PETROLEUM GEOCHEMISTRY.
Academic Press, Inc., 525 B St., Ste. 1900, San Diego, CA 92101-4495. TEL 619-231-6616. FAX 619-699-6715. *5594*

ADVANCES IN PHARMACEUTICAL SCIENCES.
Academic Press, Inc., 525 B St., Ste. 1900, San Diego, CA 92101-4495. TEL 619-231-0926. FAX 619-699-6715. *5645*

ADVANCES IN PHARMACOLOGY.
Academic Press, Inc., 525 B St., Ste. 1900, San Diego, CA 92101-4495. TEL 619-231-0926. FAX 619-699-6715. *5645*

ADVANCES IN PHOTOCHEMISTRY.
John Wiley & Sons, Inc., 605 Third Ave., New York, NY 10158-0012. TEL 212-850-6645. *1825*

ADVANCES IN PHOTOSYNTHESIS.
Kluwer Academic Publishers, Postbus 17, 3300 AA Dordrecht, Netherlands. TEL 31-78-6392392. FAX 31-78-6392254. *690*

ADVANCES IN PHYSICAL ORGANIC CHEMISTRY.
Academic Press, Inc., 525 B St., Ste. 1900, San Diego, CA 92101-4495. TEL 619-231-0926. FAX 619-699-6715. *1825*

ADVANCES IN PHYSICS.
Taylor & Francis Ltd., 1 Gunpowder Sq., London EC4A 3DE, England. TEL 44-171-583-0490. FAX 44-171-583-0585. *5795*

ADVANCES IN PLANT PATHOLOGY.
Academic Press, Inc., 525 B St., Ste. 1900, San Diego, CA 92101-4495. TEL 305-345-2000. FAX 619-699-6715. *690*

ADVANCES IN POLYMER TECHNOLOGY.
John Wiley & Sons, Inc., Journals, 605 Third Ave., New York, NY 10158-0012. TEL 212-850-6645. FAX 212-850-6021. *5875*

ADVANCES IN POROUS MEDIA.
Elsevier Science B.V., Books Division, P.O. Box 211, 1000 AE Amsterdam, Netherlands. TEL 31-20-4853911. FAX 31-20-4853705. *2309*

ADVANCES IN PRIMATOLOGY.
Plenum Publishing Corp., 233 Spring St., New York, NY 10013-1578. TEL 212-620-8000. FAX 212-463-0742. *824*

ADVANCES IN PROSTAGLANDIN, THROMBOXANE, AND LEUKOTRIENE RESEARCH.
Lippincott - Raven Publishers, 227 E. Washington Sq., Philadelphia, PA 19106. TEL 215-238-4200. FAX 215-238-4235. *5645*

ADVANCES IN PROTEIN CHEMISTRY.
Academic Press, Inc., 525 B St., Ste. 1900, San Diego, CA 92101-4495. TEL 619-231-0926. FAX 619-699-6715. *649*

ADVANCES IN PSYCHOLOGY.
Elsevier Science B.V., Books Division, P.O. Box 211, 1000 AE Amsterdam, Netherlands. TEL 31-20-4853911. FAX 31-20-4853705. *6090*

ADVANCES IN PSYCHOSOMATIC MEDICINE.
S. Karger AG, Allschwilerstr. 10, P.O. Box, CH-4009 Basel, Switzerland. TEL 41-61-3061111. FAX 41-61-3061234. *5049*

ADVANCES IN QUANTUM CHEMISTRY.
Academic Press, Inc., 525 B St., Ste. 1900, San Diego, CA 92101-4495. TEL 619-231-0926. FAX 619-699-6715. *1737*

ADVANCES IN REGULATION OF CELL GROWTH SERIES.
Lippincott - Raven Publishers, 227 E. Washington Sq., Philadelphia, PA 19106. TEL 215-238-4200. FAX 215-238-4227. *584*

ADVANCES IN REPRODUCTIVE HEALTH CARE.
Kluwer Academic Publishers, Postbus 17, 3300 AA Dordrecht, Netherlands. TEL 31-78-6392392. FAX 31-78-6392254. *4952*

ADVANCES IN RISK ANALYSIS.
Plenum Publishing Corp., 233 Spring St., New York, NY 10013-1578. TEL 212-620-8000. FAX 212-463-0742. *6255*

ADVANCES IN SCHOOL PSYCHOLOGY.
Lawrence Erlbaum Associates, Inc., 10 Industrial Dr., Mahwah, NJ 07430-2262. TEL 201-236-9500. FAX 201-236-0072. *6090*

ADVANCES IN SECOND MESSENGER AND PHOSPHOPROTEIN RESEARCH.
Lippincott - Raven Publishers, 227 E. Washington Sq., Philadelphia, PA 19106. TEL 215-238-4200. FAX 215-238-4227. *649*

ADVANCES IN SMALL ANIMAL MEDICINE AND SURGERY.
W.B. Saunders Co., Curtis Center, 3rd Fl., Independence Sq. W., Philadelphia, PA 19106-3399. TEL 215-238-7800. FAX 215-238-6445. *7263*

ADVANCES IN SOFTWARE ENGINEERING.
J A I Press Inc., 55 Old Post Rd., No. 2, Box 1678, Greenwich, CT 06836-1678. TEL 203-661-7602. *2209*

ADVANCES IN SOFTWARE SCIENCE AND TECHNOLOGY.
Academic Press, Inc., 525 B St., Ste. 1900, San Diego, CA 92101-4495. TEL 619-231-6616. FAX 619-699-6715. *2209*

ADVANCES IN SOLAR ENERGY: AN ANNUAL REVIEW OF RESEARCH AND DEVELOPMENT.
Plenum Publishing Corp., 233 Spring St., New York, NY 10013-1578. TEL 212-620-8000. FAX 212-463-0742. *2705*

ADVANCES IN SOLID STATE TECHNOLOGY.
Kluwer Academic Publishers, Postbus 17, 3300 AA Dordrecht, Netherlands. TEL 31-78-6392392. FAX 31-78-6392254. *5795*

ADVANCES IN SPACE RESEARCH.
Elsevier Science Ltd., Pergamon, P.O. Box 800, Kidlington, Oxford OX5 1DX, England. TEL 44-1865-843000. FAX 44-1865-843010. *52*

ADVANCES IN SPATIAL REASONING.
Ablex Publishing Corporation, Box 5297, Greenwich, CT 06831-0504. TEL 203-661-7602. FAX 203-661-0792. *2097*

ADVANCES IN SUBSTANCE ABUSE: BEHAVIORAL AND BIOLOGICAL RESEARCH.
Jessica Kingsley Publishers, 116 Pentonville Rd., London N1 9JB, England. TEL 44-171-833-2307. FAX 44-171-837-2917. *2297*

ADVANCES IN SUICIDOLOGY.
E.J. Brill, P.O. Box 9000, 2300 PA Leiden, Netherlands. TEL 31-71-5353500. FAX 31-71-5317532. *5050*

ADVANCES IN THE MECHANICS AND PHYSICS OF SURFACES SERIES.
Gordon and Breach - Harwood Academic, Amsteldisk 166, 1st Fl., 1079 LH Amsterdam, Netherlands. *5843*

ADVANCES IN THE PSYCHOLOGY OF HUMAN INTELLIGENCE.
Lawrence Erlbaum Associates, Inc., 10 Industrial Dr., Mahwah, NJ 07430-2262. TEL 201-236-9500. FAX 201-236-0072. *6091*

ADVANCES IN THE STUDY OF BEHAVIOR.
Academic Press, Inc., 525 B St., Ste. 1900, San Diego, CA 92101-4495. TEL 619-231-0926. FAX 619-699-6715. *6091*

ADVANCES IN THE STUDY OF COMMUNICATION AND AFFECT.
Plenum Publishing Corp., 233 Spring St., New York, NY 10013-1578. TEL 212-620-8000. FAX 212-463-0742. *6091*

ADVANCES IN THERAPY.
Health Communications Inc., 20 Highland Ave., Metuchen, NJ 08840. TEL 908-548-9130. FAX 908-548-8555. *5645*

ADVANCES IN TRANSPORT PROCESSES.
Elsevier Science B.V., P.O. Box 211, 1000 AE Amsterdam, Netherlands. TEL 31-20-4853911. FAX 31-20-4853598. *2755*

ADVANCES IN UNDERWATER TECHNOLOGY, OCEAN SCIENCE AND OFFSHORE ENGINEERING.
Kluwer Academic Publishers, Postbus 17, 3300 AA Dordrecht, Netherlands. TEL 31-78-6392392. FAX 31-78-6392254. *2399*

ADVANCES IN URETHANE SCIENCE AND TECHNOLOGY.
Technomic Publishing Co., Inc., 851 New Holland Ave., Box 3535, Lancaster, PA 17604. TEL 717-291-5609. FAX 717-295-4538. *1811*

ADVANCES IN VEGETATION SCIENCE.
Kluwer Academic Publishers, Postbus 17, 3300 AA Dordrecht, Netherlands. TEL 31-78-6392392. FAX 31-78-6392254. *690*

ADVANCES IN VETERINARY DERMATOLOGY.
Elsevier Science Ltd., Books Division, P.O. Box 800, Kidlington, Oxford OX5 1DX, England. TEL 44-1865-843000. FAX 44-1865-843010. *7263*

ADVANCES IN VETERINARY SCIENCE AND COMPARATIVE MEDICINE.
Academic Press, Inc., 525 B St., Ste. 1900, San Diego, CA 92101-4495. TEL 619-231-0926. FAX 619-699-6715. *7264*

ADVANCES IN VIRAL ONCOLOGY.
Lippincott - Raven Publishers, 227 E. Washington Sq., Philadelphia, PA 19106. TEL 215-238-4200. FAX 215-238-4227. *4969*

ADVANCES IN VIRUS RESEARCH.
Academic Press, Inc., 525 B St., Ste. 1900, San Diego, CA 92101-4495. TEL 619-231-0926. FAX 619-699-6715. *779*

ADVANCES IN WATER RESOURCES.
Elsevier Science Ltd., P.O. Box 800, Kidlington, Oxford OX5 1DX, England. TEL 44-1865-843000. FAX 44-1865-843010. *7286*

ADVANCES IN WORLD AQUACULTURE.
World Aquaculture Society, 143 J M Parker Coliseum, Louisiana State University, Baton Rouge, LA 70803. TEL 504-388-3137. FAX 504-388-3493. *2399*

ADVANCES IN WOUND CARE.
Springhouse Corporation, 1111 Bethlehem Pike, Box 908, Springhouse, PA 19477. TEL 215-646-8700. *4874*

ADVANCES IN X-RAY ANALYSIS.
Plenum Publishing Corp., 233 Spring St., New York, NY 10013-1578. TEL 212-620-8000. FAX 212-463-0742. *5184*

ADVENTURE WEST.
Adventure Media, Inc., Box 3210, Incline Village, NV 89450-3210. TEL 702-832-3700. FAX 702-832-3775. *7183*

ADVERSE DRUG REACTION BULLETIN.
Chapman & Hall, Journals Department 2-6 Boundary Row, London SE1 8HN, England. TEL 44-171-8650066. FAX 44-171-5229623. *5645*

ADVERTISING LAW ANTHOLOGY.
International Library Law Book Publishers, Inc., 4301 N. Fairfax Dr., Ste. 875, Arlington, VA 22203. TEL 703-528-1000. FAX 703-528-6060. *3906*

ADVOCATE (BETHESDA).
Autism Society of America, 7910 Woodmont Ave., Ste. 650, Bethesda, MD 20814-3015. TEL 301-657-0881. FAX 301-657-0869. *2580*

THE ADVOCATE (BOISE).
Idaho State Bar, 525 Jefferson St., Box 895, Boise, ID 83701. TEL 208-334-4500. FAX 208-334-4515. *3906*

ADVOCATE (PRATTSVILLE).
P K A Publications, 301A Rolling Hills Park, Prattsville, NY 12468. TEL 518-299-3103. *4371*

AEROBIOLOGIA.
Elsevier Science Ireland Ltd., P.O. Box 85, Limerick, Ireland. TEL 353-61-471944. FAX 353-61-472144. *584*

AERONAUTICAL MANUFACTURING TECHNOLOGY.
Beijing Hangkong Gongyi Yanjiusuo, P.O. Box 863, Beijing 100024, People's Republic of China. TEL 5761731. FAX 5762306. *53*

AERONAUTICAL SATELLITE NEWS.
Inmarsat, 99 City Rd., London EC1Y 1AX, England. TEL 0171-728-1449. FAX 0171-728-1344. *53*

AEROSOL SCIENCE AND TECHNOLOGY.
Elsevier Science Inc., Box 945, New York, NY 10159-0945. TEL 212-633-3730. FAX 212-633-3680. *1738*

REFEREED SERIALS

AEROSPACE CHINA.
Hangtian Gongye Zong Gongsi, Xinxi Yanjiu-suo, P.O. Box 1408, 1 Binhe Lu, Hepingli, Beijing 100013, People's Republic of China. TEL 86-10-6837-2847. FAX 86-10-6422-7606. *53*

AEROSPACE JAPAN WEEKLY.
Ikaros Publications Ltd., 3-2 Kagurazaka, Shinjuku-ku, Tokyo 162, Japan. TEL 81-3-3267-2832. FAX 81-3-3267-2787. *54*

AEROSPACE SCIENCE AND TECHNOLOGY.
Gauthier-Villars, 5 rue Laromiguiere, 75005 Paris, France. TEL 33-1-40466200. FAX 33-1-40466201. *54*

AESTHETIC PLASTIC SURGERY.
Springer-Verlag, Medical Journals, 175 Fifth Ave., New York, NY 10010. TEL 212-460-1500. FAX 212-473-6272. *5134*

AESTHETIC SURGERY JOURNAL.
Mosby - Year Book, Inc., 11830 Westline Industrial Dr., St. Louis, MO 63146-3318. TEL 314-872-8370. FAX 314-432-1380. *5134*

AETHIOPICA.
Harrassowitz Verlag, 65174 Wiesbaden, Germany. TEL 49-611-530555. FAX 49-611-530559. *3523*

AFAQ IQTISADIYYAH.
Federation of U A E Chambers of Commerce and Industry, P.O. Box 3014, Abu Dhabi, United Arab Emirates. TEL 971-2-214144. FAX 971-2-339210. *1176*

AFGHANISTAN STUDIES JOURNAL.
Center for Afghanistan Studies, University of Nebraska at Omaha, Omaha, NE 68182-0006. TEL 402-554-2901. FAX 402-554-3242. *3531*

AFINIDAD.
Instituto Quimico de Sarria, Asociacion de Quimicos, Via Augusta 390, 08017 Barcelona, Spain. TEL 34-3-2804276. FAX 34-3-2804276. *1738*

AFRICA.
Istituto Italo-Africano, Via Ulisse Aldrovandi 16, 00197 Rome, Italy. TEL 39-6-3221297. FAX 39-6-3225348. *3523*

AFRICA (EDINBURGH).
Edinburgh University Press, 22 George Sq., Edinburgh EH8 9LF, Scotland. TEL 44-131-650-6207. FAX 44-131-662-0053. *3523*

AFRICA MEDIA REVIEW.
African Council for Communication Education, P.O. Box 47495, Nairobi, Kenya. TEL 254-2-227043. FAX 254-2-216135. *1981*

AFRICA TODAY.
Lynne Rienner Publishers, 1800 30th St., Ste. 314, Boulder, CO 80301. TEL 303-444-6684. FAX 303-444-0824. *5889*

AFRICAN ARCHAEOLOGICAL REVIEW.
Plenum Publishing Corp., 233 Spring St., New York, NY 10013-1578. TEL 212-620-8000. FAX 212-463-0742. *346*

AFRICAN CROP SCIENCE JOURNAL.
African Crop Science Society, Faculty of Agriculture and Forestry, Makerere University, P.O. Box 7062, Kampala, Uganda. TEL 256-41-540464. FAX 256-41-531641. *211*

AFRICAN DEVELOPMENT REVIEW.
African Development Bank, B.P. 1387, Abidjan 01, Ivory Coast. *1353*

AFRICAN JOURNAL OF ECOLOGY.
Blackwell Science Ltd., Osney Mead, Oxford OX2 OEL, England. TEL 44-1865-206206. FAX 44-1865-721205. *2222*

AFRICAN JOURNAL OF HEALTH SCIENCES.
African Forum for Health Sciences, P.O. Box 54840, Nairobi, Kenya. TEL 254-2-722541. FAX 254-2-720030. *4633*

AFRICAN JOURNAL OF LIBRARY, ARCHIVES AND INFORMATION SCIENCE.
Archlib & Information Services Ltd., P.O. Box 20492, Ibadan, Oyo State, Nigeria. TEL 267-355-2629. *4157*

AFRICAN JOURNAL OF MEDICINE & MEDICAL SCIENCES.
Spectrum Books Ltd., College of Medicine, University College Hospital, Ibadan, Oyo State, Nigeria. TEL 234-02-2410088. *4633*

AFRICAN LIVESTOCK RESEARCH.
International Livestock Centre for Africa, P.O. Box 5689, Addis Ababa, Ethiopia. *267*

AFRICAN STUDIES QUARTERLY.
University of Florida, Center for African Studies, 427 Grinter Hall, Box 115560, Gainesville, FL 32611-5560. TEL 352-392-2183. FAX 352-392-2435. *6601*

AFRICAN STUDIES REVIEW.
African Studies Association, Credit Union Bldg., Emory University, Atlanta, GA 30322. TEL 404-329-6410. *2994*

AFRICAN VIOLET MAGAZINE.
African Violet Society of America, Inc., 2375 North, Beaumont, TX 77702-1722. TEL 409-839-4725. FAX 409-839-4329. *3179*

AFRICAN WILDLIFE.
Wildlife and Environment Society of South Africa, P.O. Box 394, Howick 3290, South Africa. TEL 27-332-303911. FAX 27-332-304576. *2222*

AFRICAN WOMAN.
Akina Mama wa Afrika, 4 Wild Ct., London WC2B 5AU, England. TEL 44-171-405-0678. FAX 44-171-831-3947. *7312*

AFRICAN YEARBOOK OF INTERNATIONAL LAW.
Martinus Nijhoff Publishers, Human Rights and International Law Postbus 163, 3300 AD Dordrecht, Netherlands. TEL 31-78-334911. FAX 31-78-334254. *4104*

AFRICHE.
Societa delle Missioni Africane, Via Borghero 4, 16148 Genova, Italy. TEL 39-10-3733657. FAX 39-10-3733664. *3524*

AFRO-AMERICANS IN NEW YORK LIFE AND HISTORY.
Afro-American Historical Association of the Niagara Frontier, Box 63, Buffalo, NY 14207. TEL 716-878-4078. *2994*

AFRO-HISPANIC REVIEW.
University of Missouri at Columbia, Romance Languages Department, c/o Dr. Edward Mullen, 143, Arts & Sciences, Columbia, MO 65211. TEL 573-882-2030. FAX 573-884-8171. *2994*

AGAIN.
Conciliar Press, 10090 A Hwy. 9, Box 76, Ben Lomond, CA 95005-0076. TEL 408-336-5118. FAX 408-336-8882. *6391*

AGAINST THE CURRENT.
Center for Changes, 7012 Michigan Ave., Detroit, MI 48210. TEL 313-841-0161. FAX 313-841-8884. *5889*

AGAINST THE GRAIN.
Katina & Bruce Strauch, Eds. & Pubs., Citadel Sta., 171 Moultrier St., Charleston, SC 29409. TEL 803-723-3536. FAX 803-723-3536. *4157*

AGE.
American Aging Association, 2129 Providence Ave., Chester, PA 19013. TEL 610-874-7550. FAX 610-876-7715. *3430*

AGE AND AGEING.
Oxford University Press, Academic Division, Great Clarendon St., Oxford OX2 6DP, England. TEL 44-1865-267907. FAX 44-1865-267485. *3430*

AGENDA ACADEMICA.
Universidad Central de Venezuela, Vicerrectorado Academico, Av. Neveri, Centro los Chaguaramos, Piso 10, Apdo. Postal 47149, 1041-A Caracas, Venezuela. TEL 58-2-6628961. FAX 58-2-6627455. *2531*

AGENT DE VIAJES AL DIA.
Pepperdine Enterprises, 1367 Tadsworth Terr., Heathrow, FL 32746. TEL 407-333-3393. FAX 407-333-3533. *7183*

AGGIORNAMENTI DI TERAPIA OFTALMOLOGICA.
Farmigea S.p.A., Via Carmignani, 2, 56127 Pisa, Italy. TEL 39-50-544000. FAX 39-50-544304. *4989*

AGGRESSION AND VIOLENT BEHAVIOR.
Elsevier Science Ltd., Pergamon, P.O. Box 800, Kidlington, Oxford OX5 1DX, England. TEL 44-1865-843000. FAX 44-1865-843010. *6091*

AGGRESSIVE BEHAVIOR.
John Wiley & Sons, Inc., Journals, 605 Third Ave., New York, NY 10158. TEL 212-850-6645. FAX 212-850-6021. *6091*

AGHAMTAO.
Ugnayang Pang-Aghamtao, Inc., Rm. 208, Philippine Social Science Center, Commonwealth Ave., Diliman, Quezon City, Philippines. TEL 922-9621. *306*

AGING (NEW YORK).
Lippincott - Raven Publishers, 227 E. Washington Sq., Philadelphia, PA 19106. TEL 215-238-4200. FAX 215-238-4227. *3431*

AGING AMERICA.
Demko Publishing, 21946 Pine Trace, Boca Raton, FL 33428. TEL 407-482-6271. *3431*

AGING & MENTAL HEALTH.
Carfax Publishing Co., P.O. Box 25, Abingdon, Oxon OX14 3UE, England. TEL 44-1235-401000. FAX 44-1235-401550. *3431*

AGING ARKANSAS.
Arkansas Aging Foundation, Inc., 706 S. Pulaski St., Little Rock, AR 72201. TEL 501-376-6083. FAX 501-376-6084. *3431*

THE AGING MALE.
Parthenon Publishing Group, Casterton Hall, Carnforth, Lancs LA6 2LA, England. TEL 44-15242-72084. FAX 44-15242-71587. *5173*

AGREKON (ENGLISH EDITION).
Landbou-Ekonomie Vereniging van Suid-Afrika, Posbus 12986, Hatfield 0028, South Africa. TEL 27-12-4203248. FAX 27-12-3422713. *187*

AGRI DERGISI.
Turk Algoloji Derneginin, Istanbul Tip Fakultesi, Agri Merkezi, Capa Klinikleri, 34390 Istanbul, Turkey. TEL 90-212-6350135. FAX 90-212-6310541. *5050*

AGRI-PRACTICE.
Veterinary Practice Publishing Co., Box 6050, Mission Viejo, CA 92690. *7264*

AGRIBIOLOGICAL RESEARCH.
V D L U F A Verlag, Bismarckstr. 41A, 64293 Darmstadt, Germany. TEL 49-61-5126485. FAX 49-61-51293370. *89*

AGRIBUSINESS (NEW YORK).
John Wiley & Sons, Inc., Journals, 605 Third Ave., New York, NY 10158-6012. TEL 212-850-6645. FAX 212-850-6021. *187*

AGRICULTURAL AND BIOLOGICAL RESEARCH.
Young Environmentalist Association, 64 Khurshed Bagh, Lucknow 226 004, India. TEL 91-522-226091. *90*

AGRICULTURAL AND FOOD SCIENCE IN FINLAND.
Agricultural Research Centre of Finland, Editorial Office, FIN-31600 Jokioinen, Finland. FAX 358-3-418-83-39. *90*

AGRICULTURAL AND FOREST METEOROLOGY.
Elsevier Science B.V., P.O. Box 211, 1000 AE Amsterdam, Netherlands. TEL 31-20-4853911. FAX 31-20-4853598. *5226*

AGRICULTURAL ECONOMICS.
Elsevier Science B.V., P.O. Box 211, 1000 AE Amsterdam, Netherlands. TEL 31-20-4853911. FAX 31-20-4853598. *187*

AGRICULTURAL ENGINEERING AUSTRALIA.
Society for Engineering in Agriculture, Institution of Engineers, 11 National Circuit, Barton, A.C.T. 2600, Australia. TEL 61-6-2706555. FAX 61-6-2731488. *90*

AGRICULTURAL ENGINEERING JOURNAL.
Asian Association for Agricultural Engineering, c/o Division of Agricultural and Food Engineering, Asian Institute of Technology, G.P.O. Box 2754, Bangkok 10501, Thailand. TEL 66-2-524-5478. FAX 66-2-524-6200. *90*

AGRICULTURAL FINANCE REVIEW.
Cornell University, Department of Agricultural Resource and Managerial Economics, 357 Warren Hall, Ithaca, NY 14853-7801. TEL 607-255-4534. FAX 607-255-1589. *188*

AGRICULTURAL FINANCIAL STATISTICS.
Statistics Canada, Circulation Management, Jean Talon Bldg., 2-C12, Tunney's Pasture, Ottawa, ON K1A 0T6, Canada. TEL 613-951-7277. FAX 613-951-1584. *167*

AGRICULTURAL HISTORY.
University of California Press, Journals Division, 2120 Berkeley Way, No. 5812, Berkeley, CA 94720-5812. TEL 510-643-7154. FAX 510-642-9917. *91*

AGRICULTURAL SYSTEMS.
Elsevier Science Ltd., P.O. Box 800, Kidlington, Oxford OX5 1DX, England. TEL 44-1865-843000. FAX 44-1865-843010. *92*

AGRICULTURAL WATER MANAGEMENT.
Elsevier Science B.V., P.O. Box 211, 1000 AE Amsterdam, Netherlands. TEL 31-20-4853911. FAX 31-20-4853598. *212*

AGRICULTURE AND HUMAN VALUES.
Kluwer Academic Publishers, Postbus 17, 3300 AA Dordrecht, Netherlands. TEL 31-78-6392392. FAX 31-78-6392254. *92*

AGRICULTURE, ECOSYSTEMS AND ENVIRONMENT.
Elsevier Science B.V., P.O. Box 211, 1000 AE Amsterdam, Netherlands. TEL 31-20-4853911. FAX 31-20-4853598. *93*

AGRICULTURE ET DEVELOPPEMENT.
C I R A D - C A, B.P. 5035, 34032 Montpellier Cedex, France. TEL 67-61-59-18. FAX 67-61-59-21. *93*

AGRO AMBIENTE.
Iacico s.r.l., Via A. Poliziano 80, 00184 Rome, Italy. TEL 39-6-4873183. FAX 39-6-4873144. *93*

AGRO FOOD INDUSTRY HI-TECH.
Teknoscienze s.r.l., Via Aurelio Saffi 23, 20123 Milan, Italy. TEL 39-2-4818118. FAX 39-2-4818070. *93*

AGRO SUR.
Universidad Austral de Chile, Facultad de Ciencias Agrarias, Casilla 567, Valdivia, Chile. TEL 56-63-221660. FAX 56-63-221460. *94*

AGROBOREALIS.
University of Alaska at Fairbanks, Agricultural and Forestry Experiment Station, Fairbanks, AK 99775. TEL 907-474-7653. *94*

AGROCHIMICA.
Gruppo Agrochimica, Via S. Michele degli Scalzi 2, 56124 Pisa, Italy. TEL 39-50-571557. FAX 39-50-598614. *94*

AGROCIENCIA.
Colegio de Postgraduados, Instituto de Estudios, Investigaciones y Servicio Agripefor Chapingo S.C., Cerro del Vigilante 166, Col. Romero de Terrenos, 04310 Mexico DF, Mexico. TEL 915-5-541304. *94*

AGROFORESTRY SYSTEMS.
Kluwer Academic Publishers, Postbus 17, 3300 AA Dordrecht, Netherlands. TEL 31-78-6392392. FAX 31-78-6392254. *94*

AGRONOMIE.
Editions Scientifiques et Medicales Elsevier, 141 rue de Javel, 75747 Paris, France. TEL 33-1-45589022. FAX 33-1-45589421. *212*

AICHI MEDICAL UNIVERSITY ASSOCIATION. JOURNAL.
Aichi Medical University Association, 21, Yazakokarimata, Nagakutecho, Aichi-gun, Aichi-ken 480-11, Japan. TEL 81-561-62-3311. FAX 81-561-62-3348. *4634*

AIDA PARKER NEWSLETTER.
Aida Parker Newsletter Pty. Ltd., P.O. Box 91059, Auckland Park 2006, Johannesburg, South Africa. TEL 27-11-726-6856. FAX 27-11-726-5537. *5889*

AIDS.
Thomson Science, 2-6 Boundary Row, London SE1 8HN, England. TEL 44-171-865-0198. FAX 44-171-928-7876. *4830*

AIDS ALERT.
American Health Consultants, Inc., 3525 Piedmont Rd., N.E., Bldg. 6, Ste. 400, Atlanta, GA 30305. FAX 800-284-3291. *4830*

AIDS & BEHAVIOR.
Plenum Publishing Corp., 233 Spring St., New York, NY 10013-1578. TEL 212-620-8000. FAX 212-463-0742. *4790*

AIDS & PUBLIC POLICY JOURNAL.
University Publishing Group, Inc., 107 E. Church St., Frederick, MD 21701. *4830*

AIDS CARE.
Carfax Publishing Co., P.O. Box 25, Abingdon, Oxon. OX14 3UE, England. TEL 44-1235-401000. FAX 44-1235-401550. *4830*

AIDS EDUCATION AND PREVENTION.
Guilford Publications, Inc., 72 Spring St., 4th Fl., New York, NY 10012. TEL 212-431-9800. FAX 212-966-6708. *4831*

AIDS INFORMATION EXCHANGE.
U.S. Conference of Mayors, Office of Public Affairs, 1620 Eye St., N.W., Washington, DC 20006. TEL 202-293-7330. FAX 202-293-2352. *4831*

AIDS PATIENT CARE AND S T DS.
Mary Ann Liebert, Inc. Publishers, 2 Madison Ave., Larchmont, NY 10538. TEL 914-834-3100. FAX 914-834-3688. *4831*

AIDS PREVENTION AND MENTAL HEALTH.
Plenum Publishing Corp., 233 Spring St., New York, NY 10013-1578. TEL 212-620-8000. FAX 212-463-0742. *4831*

AIDS RESEARCH AND HUMAN RETROVIRUSES.
Mary Ann Liebert, Inc. Publishers, 2 Madison Ave., Larchmont, NY 10538. TEL 914-834-3100. FAX 914-384-3688. *4831*

AINM.
Ulster Place-Name Society, Department of Celtic, Queen's University of Belfast, Belfast BT7 1NN, N. Ireland. TEL 245133. *4238*

AIR FORCE JOURNAL OF LOGISTICS.
U.S. Air Force, Logistics Management Agency, Gunter Annex, Maxwell A.F.B., AL 36114-3236. TEL 334-416-4087. FAX 334-596-4638. *5257*

AIR MEDICAL JOURNAL.
Mosby - Year Book, Inc., 11830 Westline Industrial Dr., St. Louis, MO 63146-3318. TEL 314-872-8370. FAX 314-432-1380. *4634*

AIR POWER HISTORY.
Air Force Historical Foundation, 110 Luke Ave., Ste. 405, Bolling AFB, DC 20332-5113. TEL 202-767-5088. FAX 202-767-5527. *55*

AIR QUALITY MONOGRAPHS.
Elsevier Science B.V., Books Division, P.O. Box 211, 1000 AE Amsterdam, Netherlands. TEL 31-20-4853911. FAX 31-20-4853705. *2965*

AIR TRAFFIC CONTROL QUARTERLY.
John Wiley & Sons, Inc., Journals, 605 Third Ave., New York, NY 10158-0012. TEL 212-850-6645. FAX 212-850-6021. *7062*

AIRPORT MAGAZINE.
American Association of Airport Executives, 4212 King St., Alexandria, VA 22302. TEL 703-824-0504. FAX 703-820-1395. *7064*

AIRPOWER JOURNAL.
U.S. Air Force, Air University, 401 Chennault Circle, Maxwell Air Force Base, AL 36112-6428. TEL 334-953-5322. FAX 334-953-6739. *5257*

AKADEMIA ROLNICZA W SZCZECINIE. INFORMATORY.
Akademia Rolnicza w Szczecinie, Dzial Wydawnictw, Ul. Doktora Judyma 22, 71-460 Szczecin, Poland. TEL 48-91-541639. FAX 48-91-541642. *96*

AKADEMIA ROLNICZA W SZCZECINIE. ROZPRAWY.
Akademia Rolnicza w Szczecinie, Dzial Wydawnictw, Ul. Doktora Judyma 22, 71-460 Szczecin, Poland. TEL 48-91-54169. FAX 48-91-541642. *96*

AKADEMIA ROLNICZA W SZCZECINIE. ZESZYTY NAUKOWE. NAUKI SPOLECZNE I EKONOMICZNE.
Akademia Rolnicza w Szczecinie, Dzial Wydawnictw, Ul. Doktora Judyma 22, 71-460 Szczecin, Poland. TEL 48-91-541639. FAX 48-91-541642. *6601*

AKADEMIA ROLNICZA W SZCZECINIE. ZESZYTY NAUKOWE. ROLNICTWO.
Akademia Rolnicza w Szczecinie, Dzial Wydawnictw, Ul. Doktora Judyma 22, 71-460 Szczecin, Poland. TEL 48-91-541639. FAX 48-91-541642. *213*

AKADEMIA ROLNICZA W SZCZECINIE. ZESZYTY NAUKOWE. RYBACTWO MORSKIE I TECHNOLOGIA ZYWNOSCI.
Akademia Rolnicza w Szczecinie, Dzial Wydawnictw, Ul. Doktora Judyma 22, 71-460 Szczecin, Poland. TEL 48-91-541639. FAX 48-91-541642. *3060*

AKADEMIA ROLNICZA W SZCZECINIE. ZESZYTY NAUKOWE. ZOOTECHNIKA.
Akademia Rolnicza w Szczecinie, Dzial Wydawnictw, Ul. Doktora Judyma 22, 71-460 Szczecin, Poland. TEL 48-91-541639. FAX 48-91-541642. *267*

AKCENTY.
Kosciol Adwentystow Dnia Siodmego, Rada Okregu Warszawskiego, 1 Maja 39-208, 05-807 Podkowa Lesna, k-Warszawy, Poland. TEL 48-22-7589214. FAX 48-22-278619. *6412*

AKITA IGAKU.
Akita Daigaku, Igakubu, 1-1-1 Hondo, Akita 010, Japan. FAX 81-188-33-1740. *4634*

AL RAFIDAYN - JAHRBUCH ZU GESCHICHTE UND KULTUR DES MODERNEN IRAQ.
Ergon Verlag, Grombuehlstr. 7, 97080 Wuerzburg, Germany. TEL 49-931-280084. FAX 49-931-282872. *3653*

ALABAMA COUNSELING ASSOCIATION. JOURNAL.
Alabama Counseling Association, c/o Dr. Ervin L. Wood, Sta. 36, UWA, Livingston, AL 35470. TEL 205-652-9661. FAX 205-652-4065. *5503*

ALABAMA GENEALOGICAL SOCIETY MAGAZINE.
Alabama Genealogical Society, Samford University, Box 2296, 800 Lakeshore Dr., Birmingham, AL 35229. *3211*

ALABAMA GEOLOGICAL SOCIETY. GUIDEBOOK FOR THE ANNUAL FIELD TRIP.
Alabama Geological Society, Box 866184, Tuscaloosa, AL 35486-0055. TEL 205-349-2852. *2330*

ALABAMA REVIEW.
University of Alabama Press, Box 870380, Tuscaloosa, AL 35487-0380. TEL 205-348-5180. FAX 205-348-9201. *3615*

AL-AKADEMIYYAH AL-ARABIYYAH LIL-ELOUM WA AL-TEHNOLOGIA WA AL-NAQL AL-BAHRI. MJALLAHT.
Arab Academy for Science & Technology & Maritime Transport, P.O. Box 1029, Alexandria, Egypt. TEL 203-5862325. FAX 203-5801937. *6510*

ALALUZ.
University of California, Riverside, Department of Spanish and Portuguese, Riverside, CA 92502. TEL 909-788-9009. FAX 909-787-9422. *4372*

ALASKA. DIVISION OF GEOLOGICAL AND GEOPHYSICAL SURVEYS. GEOLOGIC - PROFESSIONAL REPORT.
Department of Natural Resources, Division of Geological and Geophysical Surveys, 794 University Ave., Ste.200, Fairbanks, AK 99709-3645. TEL 907-474-7147. FAX 907-479-4779. *2330*

ALASKA. DIVISION OF GEOLOGICAL AND GEOPHYSICAL SURVEYS. INFORMATION CIRCULAR.
Department of Natural Resources, Division of Geological and Geophysical Surveys, 794 University Ave. Ste. 200, Fairbanks, AK 99709-3645. TEL 907-474-7147. FAX 907-479-4779. *2330*

ALASKA. DIVISION OF GEOLOGICAL AND GEOPHYSICAL SURVEYS. REPORT OF INVESTIGATIONS.
Department of Natural Resources, Division of Geological and Geophysical Surveys, 794 University Ave., Ste. 200, Fairbanks, AK 99709-3645. TEL 907-474-7147. FAX 907-479-4779. *2330*

ALASKA. DIVISION OF GEOLOGICAL AND GEOPHYSICAL SURVEYS. SPECIAL REPORT.
Department of Natural Resources, Division of Geological and Geophysical Surveys, 794 University Ave. Ste. 200, Fairbanks, AK 99709-3645. TEL 907-474-7147. FAX 907-479-4779. *2330*

ALASKA FISHERY RESEARCH BULLETIN.
Department of Fish and Game, Commercial Fisheries Management and Development Division, Box 25526, Juneau, AK 99802-5526. TEL 907-465-4210. FAX 907-465-2604. *3060*

ALASKA MEDICINE.
Alaska State Medical Association, American Society for Circumpolar Health, 4107 Laurel St., Anchorage, AK 99508. TEL 907-562-2662. FAX 907-561-2063. *4634*

ALBANY LAW REVIEW.
Albany Law School, 80 New Scotland Ave., Albany, NY 12208. TEL 518-445-2372. FAX 518-472-5857. *3908*

ALBATROZ.
Association Albatroz, BP 404, 75969 Paris Cedex 20, France. *4372*

ALBERTA HISTORY.
Historical Society of Alberta, 95 Holmwood Ave., N.W., Calgary, AB T2K 2G7, Canada. TEL 403-261-3662. FAX 403-289-8144. *3615*

ALBERTA LAW REVIEW.
University of Alberta, Faculty of Law, Edmonton, AB T6G 2H5, Canada. TEL 403-492-5559. FAX 403-492-4924. *3908*

ALCES.
Lakehead University Bookstore, 855 Oliver Rd., Thunder Bay, ON P7B 5E1, Canada. TEL 807-343-8528. FAX 807-346-7796. *824*

ALCOHOL (NEW YORK).
Elsevier Science Inc., Box 945, New York, NY 10159-0945. TEL 212-633-3730. FAX 212-633-3680. *2298*

ALCOHOL & ALCOHOLISM.
Oxford University Press, Academic Division, Great Clarendon St., Oxford OX2 6DP, England. TEL 44-1865-267907. FAX 44-1865-267485. *2298*

ALCOHOL HEALTH & RESEARCH WORLD.
U.S. National Institute on Alcohol Abuse and Alcoholism, 6000 Executive Blvd., Bethesda, MD 20892-7003. TEL 301-443-3860. FAX 301-480-1726. *2298*

ALCOHOLISM: CLINICAL AND EXPERIMENTAL RESEARCH.
Williams & Wilkins, 351 W. Camden St., Baltimore, MD 21201-2436. TEL 410-528-4068. FAX 410-528-4452. *2298*

ALCOHOLISM TREATMENT QUARTERLY.
Haworth Press, Inc., 10 Alice St., Binghamton, NY 13904. TEL 607-722-5857. FAX 607-722-6362. *2298*

ALCUIN.
Alcuin Club, 11 Abbey St., Chester, Ches. CH1 2JF, England. TEL 44-1244-347811. FAX 44-1244-347823. *6319*

ALERGIA.
Sociedad Mexicana de Alergia e Inmunologia, A.C., Fuente Emperador 6, 53950 Huixquilucan, Edo. de Mexico, Mexico. TEL 52-5-2511844. FAX 52-5-2513975. *4790*

ALERT DIVER.
Divers Alert Network, 3100 Tower Blvd., Ste. 1300, Durham, NC 27707-2563. TEL 919-684-2948. FAX 919-490-6630. *6748*

ALEXANDRIA JOURNAL OF AGRICULTURAL RESEARCH.
University of Alexandria, Faculty of Agriculture, Alexandria, Egypt. FAX 20-3-5972780. *97*

ALEXANDRIA SCIENCE EXCHANGE.
Prof. Dr. A.M. Balba Group for Soil and Water Research, College of Agriculture, University of Alexandria, El-Shatby, Alexandria 21545. TEL 03-5975405. FAX 03-5954684. *6511*

ALEXANDRIE.
Polska Akademia Nauk, Zaklad Archeologii Srodziemnomorskiej, Palac Kultury i Nauki, p. 2105, 00-901 Warsaw, Poland. TEL 48-22-6248593. FAX 48-22-6207651. *347*

ALGEBRA AND LOGIC.
Plenum Publishing Corp., Consultants Bureau, 233 Spring St., New York, NY 10013-1578. TEL 212-620-8468. FAX 212-463-0742. *4558*

ALGEBRA, LOGIC AND APPLICATIONS.
Gordon and Breach - Harwood Academic, Amsteldisk 166, 1st Fl., 1079 LH Amsterdam, Netherlands. *4558*

ALGONQUIAN CONFERENCE. PAPERS.
Algonquian Conference, Department of Linguistics, University of Manitoba, Winnipeg, MB R3T 2N2, Canada. TEL 204-474-9596. *306*

ALGORITHMICA.
Springer-Verlag, Science Journals, 175 Fifth Ave., New York, NY 10010. TEL 212-460-1500. FAX 212-473-6272. *2072*

ALIMENTARY PHARMACOLOGY AND THERAPEUTICS.
Blackwell Science Ltd., Osney Mead, Oxford OX2 OEL, England. TEL 44-1865-206206. FAX 44-1865-721205. *4907*

ALISO.
Rancho Santa Ana Botanic Garden, 1500 N. College Ave., Claremont, CA 91711. TEL 909-625-8767. FAX 909-626-7670. *691*

ALIVE.
Canadian Health Reform Products Ltd., 7436 Fraser Park Dr., Burnaby, BC V5J 5B9, Canada. TEL 604-435-1919. FAX 604-435-4888. *5778*

THE ALKALOIDS.
Academic Press, Inc., 525 B St., Ste. 1900, San Diego, CA 92101-4495. TEL 619-231-0926. FAX 619-699-6715. *1811*

ALLEGRO.
Associated Musicians of Greater New York, AFM, Local 802, 322 W. 48th St., 5th Fl., New York, NY 10036. TEL 212-245-4802. FAX 212-245-6255. *3886*

ALLELOPATHY JOURNAL.
International Allelopathy Foundation, 10-67, Haryana Agricultural University, Hisar 125 004, India. TEL 91-1662-78083. FAX 91-1662-34952. *691*

ALLEMAGNE D'AUJOURD'HUI.
Association pour la Connaissance de l'Allemagne d'Aujourd'hui, 8 rue Faraday, 75017 Paris, France. TEL 33-1-42274155. *3282*

ALLERGOLOGY INTERNATIONAL.
Blackwell Science Pty Ltd, P.O. Box 378, Carlton South, Vic. 3053, Australia. TEL 61-3-93470300. FAX 61-3-93493016. *4790*

ALLERGY.
Munksgaard International Publishers Ltd., 35 Noerre Soegade, P.O. Box 2148, DK-1016 Copenhagen K, Denmark. TEL 45-33-127030. FAX 45-33-129387. *4791*

ALLERTONIA.
National Tropical Botanical Garden, Box 340, Lawai, Kauai, HI 96765. TEL 808-332-7324. FAX 808-332-9765. *691*

ALLIONIA.
Universita degli Studi di Torino, Dipartimento di Biologia Vegetale, Viale P.A. Mattioli 25, 10125 Turin, Italy. TEL 39-11-6699884. FAX 39-11-655839. *691*

ALLURE.
Target s.r.l., Via Bondi 23, 2, 40138 Bologna, Italy. TEL 39-51-342426. FAX 39-51-345554. *509*

ALPE ADRIA MICROBIOLOGY JOURNAL.
Biomedia s.r.l., Via C. Farini 70, 21059 Milan, Italy. TEL 39-2-69001316. FAX 39-2-69001311. *779*

ALTA HOTELERIA INTERNACIONAL.
Alta Hoteleria, S.A. de C.V., Cataluna No. 19, Insurgentes Sur, Mixcoac, 03920 Mexico, D.F., Mexico. TEL 52-5-6112109. FAX 52-5-6114584. *3722*

ALTBABYLONISCHE BRIEFE IM UMSCHRIFT UND UEBERSETZUNG.
E.J. Brill, P.O. Box 9000, 2300 PA Leiden, Netherlands. TEL 31-71-5353500. FAX 31-71-5317532. *5520*

ALTERNATE ROUTES.
c/o Department of Sociology-Anthropology, Carleton University, Ottawa, ON K1S 5B6, Canada. TEL 613-520-2582. FAX 613-520-4062. *6602*

ALTERNATIVE HEALTH PRACTITIONER.
Springer Publishing Company, 536 Broadway, New York, NY 10012-3955. TEL 212-431-4370. FAX 212-941-7842. *294*

ALTERNATIVE THERAPIES IN CLINICAL PRACTICE.
Prime National Corp., 470 Boston Post Rd., Weston, MA 02193. TEL 617-899-2702. FAX 617-899-4900. *294*

ALTERNATIVE THERAPIES IN HEALTH AND MEDICINE.
American Association of Critical Care Nurses, 101 Columbia, Aliso Viejo, CA 92656. TEL 714-362-2000. *294*

ALTERNATIVE TRAVEL DIRECTORY.
Transitions Abroad Publishing, 18 Hulst Rd., Box 1300, Amherst, MA 01004-1300. TEL 413-256-3414. FAX 413-256-0373. *7183*

ALTERNATIVES (BOULDER).
Lynne Rienner Publishers, 1800 30th St., Ste. 314, Boulder, CO 80301-1032. TEL 303-444-6684. FAX 303-444-0824. *6004*

ALTERNATIVES JOURNAL.
University of Waterloo, Faculty of Environmental Studies, Waterloo, ON N2L 3G1, Canada. TEL 519-888-4567. FAX 519-746-0292. *2905*

ALTERNATIVES TO LABORATORY ANIMALS: A T L A
Fund for the Replacement of Animals in Medical Experiments, Russell & Burch House, 96-98 N. Sherwood St., Nottingham NG1 4EE, England. TEL 44-115-958-4740. FAX 44-115-950-3570. *4894*

ALUMNI COMPANION.
University of New Hampshire, Alumni Association, Elliott Alumni Center, 9 Edgewood Rd., Durham, NH 03824. TEL 603-862-2040. FAX 603-862-4126. *1939*

ALUMNUS - THE CITY COLLEGE OF NEW YORK.
City College of New York, Alumni Association, Box 177, New York, NY 10027. TEL 212-234-3000. FAX 212-368-6576. *1939*

ALYTES.
International Society for the Study and Conservation of Amphibians, c/o Laboratoire des Reptiles et Amphibians, Museum National d'Histoire Naturelle, 25 rue Cuvier, 75005 Paris, France. *825*

ALZHEIMER DISEASE AND ASSOCIATED DISORDERS.
Lippincott - Raven Publishers, 227 E. Washington Sq., Philadelphia, PA 19106. TEL 215-238-4200. FAX 215-238-4227. *5050*

ALZHEIMER'S DISEASE REVIEW.
University of Kentucky, Sanders - Brown Center on Aging, Lexington, KY 40536-0230. TEL 606-257-6461. FAX 606-323-2866. *5050*

AM ERKER.
Verlag Am Erker, Dahlweg 64, 48153 Muenster, Germany. TEL 49-251-799580. FAX 49-251-799580. *4372*

AMATEUR GOLF.
Fore Golf Publications Ltd., 129A High St., Dovercourt, Harwich, Essex CO12 3AX, England. TEL 01255-507526. FAX 01255-508483. *6798*

AMATEUR MUSICIAN.
Canadian Amateur Musicians (CAMMAC), 1751 Richardson, Ste. 2509, Montreal, PQ H3K 1G6, Canada. TEL 514-932-8755. FAX 514-932-9811. *5371*

AMBIO.
Royal Swedish Academy of Sciences, P.O. Box 50005, S-104 05 Stockholm, Sweden. TEL 46-8-673-95-51. FAX 46-8-166251. *2906*

AMBIT.
17 Priory Gardens, London N.6, England. TEL 44-181-340-3566. *4372*

AMBIX.
Black Bear Press Ltd., Kings Hedges Rd., Cambridge CB4 2PQ, England. TEL 44-1223-424571. FAX 44-1223-426877. *1738*

AMBULATORY SURGERY.
Elsevier Science B.V., P.O. Box 211, 1000 AE Amsterdam, Netherlands. TEL 31-20-4853757. FAX 31-20-4853432. *5134*

AMEGHINIANA.
Asociacion Paleontologica Argentina, Maipu 645, Piso 1, 1006 Buenos Aires, Argentina. TEL 54-1-3267463. FAX 54-1-3267463. *5557*

AMERASIA JOURNAL.
University of California at Los Angeles, Asian American Studies Center, 3230 Campbell Hall, Box 951546, Los Angeles, CA 90095-1546. TEL 310-825-2968. FAX 310-206-9844. *6700*

AMERICAN ACADEMY OF CHILD AND ADOLESCENT PSYCHIATRY. JOURNAL.
Williams & Wilkins, 351 W. Camden St., Baltimore, MD 21201-2436. TEL 410-528-4068. FAX 410-528-4452. *5050*

AMERICAN ACADEMY OF DERMATOLOGY. JOURNAL.
Mosby - Year Book, Inc., 11830 Westline Industrial Dr., St. Louis, MO 63146-3318. TEL 314-872-8370. FAX 314-432-1380. *4874*

AMERICAN ACADEMY OF NURSE PRACTITIONERS. JOURNAL.
Slack, Inc., 6900 Grove Rd., Thorofare, NJ 08086-9447. TEL 609-848-1000. FAX 609-853-5991. *4928*

AMERICAN ACADEMY OF ORTHOPAEDIC SURGEONS. JOURNAL.
American Academy of Orthopaedic Surgeons, 6300 N. River Rd., Rosemont, IL 60018. TEL 847-384-4130. FAX 847-823-8033. *5004*

AMERICAN ACADEMY OF PHYSICIAN ASSISTANTS. JOURNAL.
Medical Economics Publishing Co., Inc., 5 Paragon Dr., Montvale, NJ 07645. TEL 201-358-7200. FAX 201-573-1045. *4635*

AMERICAN ACADEMY OF PSYCHOANALYSIS. JOURNAL.
Guilford Publications, Inc., 72 Spring St., 4th Fl., New York, NY 10012. TEL 212-431-9800. FAX 212-966-6708. *6091*

AMERICAN ANIMAL HOSPITAL ASSOCIATION. JOURNAL.
American Animal Hospital Association, Box 150899, Denver, CO 80215-0899. TEL 303-986-2800. FAX 303-986-1700. *7264*

AMERICAN ANNALS OF THE DEAF.
Convention of American Instructors of the Deaf, KDES, PAS-6, 800 Florida Ave., N.E., Washington, DC 20002. TEL 202-651-5340. FAX 202-651-5708. *3460*

AMERICAN ANTHROPOLOGIST.
American Anthropological Association, 4350 N. Fairfax Dr., Ste. 640, Arlington, VA 22203-1621. TEL 703-528-1902. *306*

AMERICAN ANTHROPOLOGIST. SPECIAL PUBLICATION.
American Anthropological Association, 4350 N. Fairfax Dr., Ste. 640, Arlington, VA 22203-1621. TEL 703-538-1902. *306*

AMERICAN ANTIQUITY.
Society for American Archaeology, 900 Second St., N.W., No. 12, Washington, DC 20002-3557. TEL 202-789-8200. FAX 202-789-0284. *347*

AMERICAN ARCHAEOLOGY.
Archaeological Conservancy, 5301 Central Ave., N.E., Ste. 1218, Albuquerque, NM 87108-1517. TEL 505-266-1540. FAX 505-266-0311. *347*

AMERICAN ART.
Smithsonian Institution, National Museum of American Art, 601 Indiana Ave., Ste. 200, Washington, DC 20004. TEL 202-357-1812. *420*

AMERICAN ASSOCIATION FOR CANCER RESEARCH. PROCEEDINGS OF THE ANNUAL MEETING.
American Association for Cancer Research, Public Ledger Bldg., 150 S. Independence Mall West, Ste. 816, Philadelphia, PA 19106. TEL 215-440-9300. FAX 215-440-9354. *4970*

AMERICAN ASSOCIATION FOR MEDICAL TRANSCRIPTION. JOURNAL.
American Association for Medical Transcription, Box 576187, Modesto, CA 95357. TEL 209-551-0883. FAX 209-551-9317. *4635*

AMERICAN ASSOCIATION OF EQUINE PRACTITIONERS. PROCEEDINGS OF THE ANNUAL CONVENTION.
American Association of Equine Practitioners, 4075 Iron Works Pike, Lexington, KY 40511-8434. TEL 606-233-0147. FAX 606-233-1968. *7264*

AMERICAN ASSOCIATION OF GYNECOLOGIC LAPAROSCOPISTS. JOURNAL.
American Association of Gynecologic Laparoscopists, 13021 E. Florence Ave., Santa Fe Springs, CA 90670-4505. TEL 310-946-8774. FAX 310-946-9204. *4952*

AMERICAN ASSOCIATION OF OCCUPATIONAL HEALTH NURSES JOURNAL.
Slack, Inc., 6900 Grove Rd., Thorofare, NJ 08086-9447. TEL 609-848-1000. FAX 609-853-5991. *4928*

AMERICAN ASSOCIATION OF PETROLEUM GEOLOGISTS. MEMOIR.
American Association of Petroleum Geologists, Box 979, Tulsa, OK 74101. TEL 918-584-2555. *2330*

AMERICAN ASSOCIATION OF STRATIGRAPHIC PALYNOLOGISTS. CONTRIBUTIONS SERIES.
American Association of Stratigraphic Palynologists Foundation, c/o Vaughn M. Bryant, Jr., Palynology Laboratory, Anthropology Bldg., Texas A & M University, College Station, TX 77843-4352. TEL 409-845-5242. FAX 409-845-4070. *5557*

AMERICAN ASSOCIATION OF STRATIGRAPHIC PALYNOLOGISTS. NEWSLETTER.
American Association of Stratigraphic Palynologists Foundation, c/o Vaughn M. Bryant, Jr., Palynology Laboratory, Texas A & M Univ., College Station, TX 77843-4352. TEL 409-845-5242. FAX 409-845-4070. *2330*

AMERICAN ASSOCIATION OF VARIABLE STAR OBSERVERS. JOURNAL.
American Association of Variable Star Observers, 25 Birch St., Cambridge, MA 02138. TEL 617-354-0484. *488*

AMERICAN BENEDICTINE REVIEW.
American Benedictine Review, Inc., Assumption Abbey, Box A, Richardton, ND 58652. TEL 701-974-3315. FAX 701-974-3317. *6449*

THE AMERICAN BIOLOGY TEACHER.
National Association of Biology Teachers, Inc., 11250 Roger Bacon Dr., Ste. 19, Reston, VA 22090. TEL 703-471-1134. FAX 703-435-5582. *585*

AMERICAN BOARD OF FAMILY PRACTICE. JOURNAL.
American Board of Family Practice, 2228 Young Dr., Lexington, KY 40505. TEL 206-685-3993. FAX 206-543-8911. *4635*

AMERICAN BOOK REVIEW.
Writers Review, Inc., c/o Unit for Contemporary Literature, Campus Box 4241, Illinois State University, Normal, IL 61790-4241. TEL 309-438-3026. FAX 309-438-3523. *4322*

AMERICAN BOTTOM ARCHAEOLOGY.
University of Illinois Press, 1325 S. Oak St., Champaign, IL 61820. TEL 217-333-0950. FAX 217-244-8082. *347*

AMERICAN BUSINESS LAW JOURNAL.
Academy of Legal Studies in Business, c/o Daniel J. Herron, Dept. of Finance, 120 Upham Hall, Miami University, Oxford, OH 45056. TEL 513-529-2945. FAX 513-529-6992. *4072*

AMERICAN BUSINESS REVIEW.
University of New Haven, School of Business, West Haven, CT 06516. *931*

AMERICAN CATHOLIC HISTORICAL SOCIETY OF PHILADELPHIA. RECORDS.
American Catholic Historical Society of Philadelphia, Box 84, Philadelphia, PA 19105-0084. TEL 215-925-5752. *6449*

AMERICAN CERAMIC SOCIETY. JOURNAL.
American Ceramic Society, 735 Ceramic Pl., Westerville, OH 43081. TEL 614-794-5890. FAX 614-794-5854. *1725*

AMERICAN CHIROPRACTIC ASSOCIATION. JOURNAL.
American Chiropractic Association, Inc., 8229 Maryland Ave., St. Louis, MO 63105. TEL 314-862-7800. FAX 314-721-5171. *4826*

AMERICAN COLLEGE OF CARDIOLOGY. JOURNAL.
Elsevier Science Inc., Box 945, New York, NY 10159-0945. TEL 212-633-3730. FAX 212-633-3680. *4808*

AMERICAN COLLEGE OF DENTISTS. JOURNAL.
American College of Dentists, 839 Quince Orchard Blvd., Gaithersburg, MD 20878. TEL 301-977-3223. FAX 301-977-3330. *4849*

AMERICAN COLLEGE OF LABORATORY ANIMAL MEDICINE SERIES.
Academic Press, Inc., 525 B St., Ste. 1900, San Diego, CA 92101-4495. TEL 619-231-6616. FAX 619-699-6715. *4894*

AMERICAN COLLEGE OF NUTRITION. JOURNAL.
American College of Nutrition, c/o Hospital for Joint Diseases, 301 E. 17th St., New York, NY 10003. TEL 718-283-7906. FAX 718-283-7005. *5468*

AMERICAN COLLEGE OF SURGEONS. JOURNAL.
American College of Surgeons, Publishing Department, 54 E. Erie St., Chicago, IL 60611-2798. TEL 312-787-9282. FAX 312-440-7026. *5134*

AMERICAN DENTAL ASSOCIATION. JOURNAL.
American Dental Association, 211 E. Chicago Ave., Chicago, IL 60611. TEL 312-440-2500. FAX 312-440-3538. *4850*

AMERICAN DIALECT SOCIETY. PUBLICATIONS.
University of Alabama Press, Box 870380, Tuscaloosa, AL 35487-0380. TEL 205-348-5180. FAX 205-348-9201. *4239*

AMERICAN DIETETIC ASSOCIATION. JOURNAL.
American Dietetic Association, 216 W. Jackson Blvd., Ste. 800, Chicago, IL 60606-6995. TEL 312-899-0040. FAX 312-899-1757. *5469*

AMERICAN ECONOMIST.
Omicron Delta Epsilon Fraternity, c/o Michael Szenberg, Ed., Graduate School of Business, Dept. of Economics, Pace University, New York, NY 10038. TEL 212-346-1921. FAX 212-346-1573. *1220*

AMERICAN EDUCATIONAL RESEARCH JOURNAL.
American Educational Research Association, 1230 17th St., N.W., Washington, DC 20036-3078. TEL 202-223-9485. FAX 202-775-1824. *2420*

AMERICAN FAMILY PHYSICIAN.
American Academy of Family Physicians, 8880 Ward Pkwy., Kansas City, MO 64114. TEL 816-333-9700. FAX 816-333-0303. *4635*

AMERICAN FAMILY THERAPY ACADEMY NEWSLETTER.
American Family Therapy Academy, Inc., 2020 Pennsylvania Ave., N.W., Ste. 273, Washington, DC 20006. TEL 202-994-2776. FAX 202-994-2775. *6091*

AMERICAN FERN JOURNAL.
American Fern Society, Inc., c/o Dr. David B. Lellinger, 326 West St., N.W., Vienna, VA 22180-4151. *691*

AMERICAN FISHERIES SOCIETY. TRANSACTIONS.
American Fisheries Society, 5410 Grosvenor Ln., Ste. 110, Bethesda, MD 20814-2199. TEL 301-897-8616. FAX 301-897-8096. *3060*

AMERICAN FOREIGN POLICY LIBRARY.
Harvard University Press, 79 Garden St., Cambridge, MA 02138. TEL 617-495-2600. FAX 617-495-5898. *6004*

AMERICAN FRIENDS OF LAFAYETTE. GAZETTE.
American Friends of Lafayette, Skillman Library, Lafayette College, Easton, PA 18042-1797. TEL 610-250-5161. FAX 610-252-0370. *3615*

AMERICAN GENEALOGIST.
David L. Greene, Ed. & Pub., Box 398, Demorest, GA 30535-0398. TEL 706-865-6440. *3211*

AMERICAN GEOPHYSICAL UNION. GEOPHYSICAL MONOGRAPHS BOOK SERIES.
American Geophysical Union, 2000 Florida Ave., N.W., Washington, DC 20009. TEL 202-462-6900. *2378*

AMERICAN GERIATRICS SOCIETY. JOURNAL.
Williams & Wilkins, 351 W. Camden St., Baltimore, MD 21201-2436. TEL 410-528-4068. FAX 410-528-4452. *3432*

AMERICAN GROUP PSYCHOTHERAPY MONOGRAPH SERIES.
International Universities Press, Inc., 59 Boston Post Rd., Box 1524, Madison, CT 06443-1524. TEL 203-245-4000. FAX 203-245-0775. *6091*

AMERICAN HARP JOURNAL.
American Harp Society, Inc., c/o Jane Weidensaul, Ed., 1374 Academy Ln., Teaneck, NJ 07666. TEL 201-836-8909. FAX 201-836-5272. *5371*

AMERICAN HAWKWATCHER.
Wildlife Information Center, Inc., Box 198, Slatington, PA 18080-0198. TEL 610-760-8889. *799*

AMERICAN HEART ASSOCIATION. SUPPLEMENTS.
American Heart Association, 7272 Greenville Ave., Dallas, TX 75231-4596. TEL 214-706-1310. FAX 214-691-2704. *4809*

AMERICAN HEART JOURNAL.
Mosby - Year Book, Inc., 11830 Westline Industrial Dr., St. Louis, MO 63146-3318. TEL 314-872-8370. FAX 314-432-1380. *4809*

AMERICAN HISTORICAL REVIEW.
American Historical Association, 400 A St., S.E., Washington, DC 20003-3889. TEL 202-544-2422. FAX 202-544-8307. *3487*

AMERICAN IMAGO.
Johns Hopkins University Press, Journals Publishing Division, 2715 N. Charles St., Baltimore, MD 21218. TEL 410-516-6980. FAX 410-516-6968. *5051*

AMERICAN INDIAN ART MAGAZINE.
American Indian Art, Inc., 7314 E. Osborn Dr., Scottsdale, AZ 85251. TEL 602-994-5445. *421*

AMERICAN INDIAN CULTURE AND RESEARCH JOURNAL.
University of California at Los Angeles, American Indian Studies Center, Box 951548, Campbell Hall, Los Angeles, CA 90095-1548. TEL 310-825-7315. FAX 310-206-7060. *2996*

AMERICAN INDIAN REPORT.
Falmouth Institute, Inc., 3702 Pender Dr., Ste. 300, Fairfax, VA 22030-6066. TEL 703-641-9100. FAX 703-641-1558. *2996*

AMERICAN INDUSTRIAL HYGIENE ASSOCIATION JOURNAL.
American Industrial Hygiene Association, 2700 Prosperity Ave., Ste. 250, Fairfax, VA 22031-4307. TEL 703-849-8888. FAX 703-207-3561. *5485*

AMERICAN INSTITUTE FOR CONSERVATION OF HISTORIC & ARTISTIC WORKS. JOURNAL.
American Institute for Conservation of Historic and Artistic Works, 1717 K St., N.W., Ste. 301, Washington, DC 20006. TEL 202-452-9545. FAX 202-452-9328. *421*

AMERICAN JOURNAL OF ACUPUNCTURE.
1840 41st Ave., Ste. 102, Box 610, Capitola, CA 95010. TEL 408-475-1700. FAX 408-475-1439. *294*

AMERICAN JOURNAL OF ALTERNATIVE AGRICULTURE.
Henry A. Wallace Institute for Alternative Agriculture, Inc., 9200 Edmonston Rd., Ste. 117, Greenbelt, MD 20770-1551. TEL 301-441-8777. FAX 301-220-0164. *98*

AMERICAN JOURNAL OF ALZHEIMER'S DISEASE.
Prime National Publishing Corp., 470 Boston Post Rd., Weston, MA 02193. TEL 617-899-2702. FAX 617-899-4900. *5051*

AMERICAN JOURNAL OF ANCIENT HISTORY.
Robinson Hall, Harvard University, Cambridge, MA 02138. TEL 617-495-2545. FAX 617-496-3425. *3488*

AMERICAN JOURNAL OF ART THERAPY.
Vermont College of Norwich University, Montpelier, VT 05602. TEL 802-828-8540. FAX 802-828-8585. *2580*

AMERICAN JOURNAL OF BOTANY.
Botanical Society of America, Inc. (Columbus), Business Office, 1735 Neil Ave., Columbus, OH 43210. TEL 614-292-3519. *691*

AMERICAN JOURNAL OF CARDIAC IMAGING.
W.B. Saunders Co., Curtis Center, 3rd Fl., Independence Sq. W., Philadelphia, PA 19106-3399. TEL 215-238-7800. FAX 215-238-6445. *4809*

AMERICAN JOURNAL OF CARDIOLOGY.
Excerpta Medica, Inc., 105 Raider Blvd., Belle Mead, NJ 08502. TEL 908-874-8550. FAX 908-874-8419. *4809*

AMERICAN JOURNAL OF CARDIOVASCULAR PATHOLOGY.
Field & Wood, Medical Periodicals, Inc., Box 975, Blue Bell, PA 19422. TEL 610-828-4010. FAX 215-482-0226. *4809*

AMERICAN JOURNAL OF CLINICAL NUTRITION.
American Society for Clinical Nutrition, Inc., 9650 Rockville Pike, Rm. 2310, Bethesda, MD 20814-3998. TEL 301-530-7024. FAX 301-530-7001. *5469*

AMERICAN JOURNAL OF CLINICAL ONCOLOGY.
Lippincott - Raven Publishers, 227 E. Washington Sq., Philadelphia, PA 19106. TEL 215-238-4200. FAX 215-238-4227. *4970*

AMERICAN JOURNAL OF CLINICAL PATHOLOGY.
American Society of Clinical Pathologists, 2100 W. Harrison St., Chicago, IL 60612. FAX 312-738-0101. *4636*

AMERICAN JOURNAL OF CLINICAL RESEARCH.
Brookwood Medical Publications, Orchard House, Brookwood, Surrey GU24 0AT, England. TEL 44-1483-797975. FAX 44-1483-797915. *4894*

AMERICAN JOURNAL OF COMMUNITY PSYCHOLOGY.
Plenum Publishing Corp., 233 Spring St., New York, NY 10013-1578. TEL 212-620-8000. FAX 212-463-0742. *6700*

AMERICAN JOURNAL OF CONTACT DERMATITIS.
W.B. Saunders Co., Curtis Center, 3rd Fl., Independence Sq. W., Philadelphia, PA 19106-3399. TEL 215-238-7800. FAX 215-238-6445. *4874*

AMERICAN JOURNAL OF CRITICAL CARE.
American Association of Critical Care Nurses, 101 Columbia, Aliso Viejo, CA 92656. TEL 714-362-2000. FAX 714-362-2020. *4928*

AMERICAN JOURNAL OF DANCE THERAPY.
Human Sciences Press, Inc., 233 Spring St., New York, NY 10013-1578. TEL 212-620-8000. FAX 212-463-0742. *2290*

AMERICAN JOURNAL OF DENTISTRY.
Mosher & Linder, Inc., 9859 IH 10 W., Ste. 107-489, San Antonio, TX 78230. TEL 210-493-9660. *4850*

AMERICAN JOURNAL OF DERMATOPATHOLOGY.
Lippincott - Raven Publishers, 227 E. Washington Sq., Philadelphia, PA 19106. TEL 215-238-4200. FAX 215-238-4227. *4636*

AMERICAN JOURNAL OF DISTANCE EDUCATION.
Pennsylvania State University, College of Education, 403 S. Allen St., Ste. 206, University Park, PA 16801-5202. TEL 814-863-3764. FAX 814-865-5878. *2507*

AMERICAN JOURNAL OF DRUG AND ALCOHOL ABUSE.
Marcel Dekker Journals, 270 Madison Ave., New York, NY 10016. TEL 212-696-9000. FAX 212-685-4540. *2299*

AMERICAN JOURNAL OF EDUCATION.
University of Chicago Press, Journals Division, Box 37005, Chicago, IL 60637. TEL 773-753-3347. FAX 773-753-0811. *2421*

AMERICAN JOURNAL OF ELECTRONEURODIAGNOSTIC TECHNOLOGY.
American Society of Electroneurodiagnostic Technologists, Inc., Executive Office, 204 W. Seventh, Carroll, IA 51401. TEL 712-792-2978. FAX 712-792-6962. *5051*

AMERICAN JOURNAL OF EMERGENCY MEDICINE.
W.B. Saunders Co., Curtis Center, 3rd Fl., Independence Sq. W., Philadelphia, PA 19106-3399. TEL 215-238-7800. FAX 215-238-6445. *5004*

AMERICAN JOURNAL OF ENOLOGY AND VITICULTURE.
American Society for Enology and Viticulture, Box 1855, Davis, CA 95617. TEL 916-753-3142. FAX 916-753-3318. *514*

AMERICAN JOURNAL OF EPIDEMIOLOGY.
Johns Hopkins University, School of Hygiene and Public Health, Candler Bldg., Ste. 840, 111 Market Place, Baltimore, MD 21202-6709. TEL 410-223-1600. FAX 410-223-1620. *4636*

AMERICAN JOURNAL OF FAMILY LAW.
John Wiley & Sons, Inc., Journals, 605 Third Ave., New York, NY 10158. TEL 212-850-6645. FAX 212-850-6021. *4099*

AMERICAN JOURNAL OF FORENSIC MEDICINE AND PATHOLOGY.
Lippincott - Raven Publishers, 227 E. Washington Sq., Philadelphia, PA 19106. TEL 215-238-4200. FAX 215-238-4227. *4903*

AMERICAN JOURNAL OF FORENSIC PSYCHIATRY.
American College of Forensic Psychiatry, Box 5870, Balboa Island, CA 92662. TEL 714-831-0236. FAX 714-673-7710. *4903*

AMERICAN JOURNAL OF FORENSIC PSYCHOLOGY.
American College of Forensic Psychiatry, Box 5870, Balboa Island, CA 92662. TEL 714-831-0236. FAX 714-637-7710. *6092*

AMERICAN JOURNAL OF GASTROENTEROLOGY.
Williams & Wilkins, 351 W. Camden St., Baltimore, MD 21201. TEL 410-528-4068. FAX 410-528-4452. *4907*

AMERICAN JOURNAL OF GERIATRIC CARDIOLOGY.
LeJacq Communications, Inc., 777 W. Putnam Ave., Greenwich, CT 06830-5014. TEL 203-531-0450. FAX 203-531-0533. *4809*

AMERICAN JOURNAL OF GERIATRIC PSYCHIATRY.
American Psychiatric Press, Inc., Journals Division, 1400 K St., N.W., Ste. 1101, Washington, DC 20005. TEL 202-682-6240. FAX 202-682-6341. *3432*

AMERICAN JOURNAL OF GERMANIC LINGUISTICS AND LITERATURES.
Society for Germanic Philology, c/o Robert B. Howell, Sec.-Treas., Dept. of German, 818 Van Hise Hall, University of Wisconsin, 1220 Linden Dr., Madison, WI 53706. TEL 608-262-2192. FAX 608-262-7949. *4239*

AMERICAN JOURNAL OF HEALTH BEHAVIOR.
P N G Publications, Box 4593, Star City, WV 26504-4593. TEL 304-293-4699. FAX 304-293-4693. *5778*

AMERICAN JOURNAL OF HEALTH - SYSTEM PHARMACY.
American Society of Health - System Pharmacists, 7272 Wisconsin Ave., Bethesda, MD 20814. TEL 301-657-3000. FAX 301-657-1258. *5646*

AMERICAN JOURNAL OF HEMATOLOGY.
John Wiley & Sons, Inc., Journals, 605 Third Ave., New York, NY 10158. TEL 212-850-6645. FAX 212-850-6021. *4916*

THE AMERICAN JOURNAL OF HOSPICE & PALLIATIVE CARE.
Prime National Publishing Corp., 470 Boston Post Rd., Weston, MA 02193. TEL 617-899-2702. *3432*

AMERICAN JOURNAL OF HUMAN BIOLOGY.
John Wiley & Sons, Inc., Journals, 605 Third Ave., New York, NY 10158. TEL 212-850-6645. FAX 212-850-6021. *585*

AMERICAN JOURNAL OF HUMAN GENETICS.
University of Chicago Press, Journals Division, Box 37005, Chicago, IL 60637. TEL 773-753-3347. FAX 773-753-0811. *763*

AMERICAN JOURNAL OF HYPERTENSION.
Elsevier Science Inc., Box 945, New York, NY 10159-0945. TEL 212-633-3730. FAX 212-633-3680. *4809*

AMERICAN JOURNAL OF INDUSTRIAL MEDICINE.
John Wiley & Sons, Inc., Journals, 605 Third Ave., New York, NY 10158. TEL 212-850-6645. FAX 212-850-6021. *5485*

AMERICAN JOURNAL OF INFECTION CONTROL.
Mosby - Year Book, Inc., 11830 Westline Industrial Dr., St. Louis, MO 63146-3318. TEL 314-872-8370. FAX 314-432-1380-3318. *4832*

AMERICAN JOURNAL OF ISLAMIC SOCIAL SCIENCES.
Association of Muslim Social Scientists, 555 Grove St., Box 669, Herndon, VA 22070. TEL 703-471-1133. FAX 703-471-3922. *6395*

AMERICAN JOURNAL OF KIDNEY DISEASES.
W.B. Saunders Co., Curtis Center, 3rd Fl., Independence Sq. W., Philadelphia, PA 19106-3399. TEL 215-238-7800. FAX 215-238-6445. *5158*

AMERICAN JOURNAL OF KNEE SURGERY.
Slack, Inc., 6900 Grove Rd., Thorofare, NJ 08086-9447. TEL 609-848-1000. FAX 609-853-5991. *5135*

AMERICAN JOURNAL OF LAW & MEDICINE.
American Society of Law, Medicine & Ethics, 765 Commonwealth Ave., Ste. 1634, Boston, MA 02215. TEL 617-262-4990. FAX 617-437-7596. *3909*

AMERICAN JOURNAL OF MATHEMATICAL AND MANAGEMENT SCIENCES.
American Sciences Press, Inc., 20 Cross Rd., Syracuse, NY 13224-2144. *4559*

AMERICAN JOURNAL OF MEDICAL GENETICS.
John Wiley & Sons, Inc., Journals, 605 Third Ave., New York, NY 10158. TEL 212-850-6645. FAX 212-850-6021. *763*

AMERICAN JOURNAL OF MEDICAL QUALITY.
Williams & Wilkins, 351 W. Camden St., Baltimore, MD 21201-2436. TEL 410-528-4068. FAX 410-528-4452. *1465*

THE AMERICAN JOURNAL OF MEDICINE.
Excerpta Medica, Inc., 105 Raider Blvd., Belle Mead, NJ 08502. TEL 908-874-8550. FAX 908-874-8419. *4636*

AMERICAN JOURNAL OF NEPHROLOGY.
S. Karger AG, Allschwilerstr. 10, P.O. Box, CH-4009 Basel, Switzerland. TEL 41-61-3061111. FAX 41-61-3061234. *5159*

AMERICAN JOURNAL OF NURSING.
Lippincott - Raven Publishers, 227 E. Washington Sq., Philadelphia, PA 19106. TEL 215-238-4200. FAX 215-238-4227. *4928*

AMERICAN JOURNAL OF OBSTETRICS AND GYNECOLOGY.
Mosby - Year Book, Inc., 11830 Westline Industrial Dr., St. Louis, MO 63146-3318. TEL 314-872-8370. FAX 314-432-1380. *4952*

AMERICAN JOURNAL OF OCCUPATIONAL THERAPY.
American Occupational Therapy Association, Inc., Box 31220, Bethesda, MD 20824-1220. TEL 301-652-2682. FAX 301-652-7711. *5485*

AMERICAN JOURNAL OF OPHTHALMOLOGY.
Ophthalmic Publishing Co., 77 W. Wacker Dr., Ste. 660, Chicago, IL 60601-1632. TEL 312-629-1690. FAX 312-629-1744. *4989*

AMERICAN JOURNAL OF ORTHODONTICS AND DENTOFACIAL ORTHOPEDICS.
Mosby - Year Book, Inc., 11830 Westline Industrial Dr., St. Louis, MO 63146-3318. TEL 314-872-8370. FAX 314-432-1380. *4850*

THE AMERICAN JOURNAL OF ORTHOPEDICS.
Quadrant HealthCom, 105 Raider Blvd., Belle Mead, NJ 08502-1510. TEL 908-874-0707. FAX 908-874-5611. *5004*

AMERICAN JOURNAL OF ORTHOPSYCHIATRY.
American Orthopsychiatric Association, Inc., 330 Seventh Ave., 18th Fl., New York, NY 10001. TEL 212-564-5930. FAX 212-564-6180. *6092*

AMERICAN JOURNAL OF OTOLARYNGOLOGY.
W.B. Saunders Co., Curtis Center, 3rd Fl., Independence Sq. W., Philadelphia, PA 19106-3399. TEL 215-238-7800. FAX 215-238-6445. *5019*

AMERICAN JOURNAL OF PASTORAL COUNSELING.
Haworth Press, Inc., 10 Alice St., Binghamton, NY 13904. TEL 607-722-5857. FAX 607-722-6362. *6319*

AMERICAN JOURNAL OF PATHOLOGY.
American Society for Investigative Pathology, 9650 Rockville Pike, Bethesda, MD 20814. TEL 301-571-0107. FAX 301-571-0108. *4636*

AMERICAN JOURNAL OF PERINATOLOGY.
Thieme, 381 Park Ave. S., Ste. 1501, New York, NY 10016. TEL 212-683-5088. FAX 212-779-9020. *4952*

AMERICAN JOURNAL OF PHARMACEUTICAL EDUCATION.
American Association of Colleges of Pharmacy, 1426 Prince St., Alexandria, VA 22314-2815. TEL 703-739-2330. *5646*

AMERICAN JOURNAL OF PHYSICAL ANTHROPOLOGY.
John Wiley & Sons, Inc., Journals, 605 Third Ave., New York, NY 10158. TEL 212-850-6645. FAX 212-850-6021. *307*

AMERICAN JOURNAL OF PHYSICAL MEDICINE AND REHABILITATION.
Williams & Wilkins, 351 W. Camden St., Baltimore, MD 21201-2436. TEL 410-528-4068. FAX 410-528-4452. *5041*

AMERICAN JOURNAL OF PHYSICS.
American Association of Physics Teachers, One Physics Ellipse, College Park, MD 20740-3845. TEL 301-209-3333. FAX 301-209-0845. *5796*

AMERICAN JOURNAL OF PHYSIOLOGY.
American Physiological Society, 9650 Rockville Pike, Bethesda, MD 20814. TEL 301-530-7164. FAX 301-571-3813. *811*

AMERICAN JOURNAL OF PHYSIOLOGY: CELL PHYSIOLOGY.
American Physiological Society, 9650 Rockville Pike, Bethesda, MD 20814. TEL 301-530-7164. FAX 301-571-8313. *735*

AMERICAN JOURNAL OF PHYSIOLOGY: ENDOCRINOLOGY AND METABOLISM.
American Physiological Society, 9650 Rockville Pike, Bethesda, MD 20814. TEL 301-530-7071. FAX 301-571-8313. *811*

AMERICAN JOURNAL OF PHYSIOLOGY: GASTROINTESTINAL AND LIVER PHYSIOLOGY.
American Physiological Society, 9650 Rockville Pike, Bethesda, MD 20814. TEL 301-530-7164. FAX 301-571-8313. *812*

AMERICAN JOURNAL OF PHYSIOLOGY: HEART AND CIRCULATORY PHYSIOLOGY.
American Physiological Society, 9650 Rockville Pike, Bethesda, MD 20814. TEL 301-530-7164. FAX 301-571-8313. *812*

AMERICAN JOURNAL OF PHYSIOLOGY: LUNG CELLULAR AND MOLECULAR PHYSIOLOGY.
American Physiological Society, 9650 Rockville Pike, Bethesda, MD 20814. TEL 301-530-7164. FAX 301-571-8313. *812*

AMERICAN JOURNAL OF PHYSIOLOGY: REGULATORY, INTEGRATIVE AND COMPARATIVE PHYSIOLOGY.
American Physiological Society, 9650 Rockville Pike, Bethesda, MD 20814. TEL 301-530-7164. FAX 301-571-3813. *812*

AMERICAN JOURNAL OF PHYSIOLOGY: RENAL, FLUID AND ELECTROLYTE PHYSIOLOGY.
American Physiological Society, 9650 Rockville Pike, Bethesda, MD 20814. TEL 301-530-7164. FAX 301-571-3813. *812*

AMERICAN JOURNAL OF PREVENTIVE MEDICINE.
Elsevier Science Inc., Box 945, New York, NY 10159-0945. TEL 212-633-3730. FAX 212-633-3680. *4636*

AMERICAN JOURNAL OF PRIMATOLOGY.
John Wiley & Sons, Inc., Journals, 605 Third Ave., New York, NY 10158. TEL 212-850-6645. FAX 212-850-6021. *825*

AMERICAN JOURNAL OF PSYCHIATRY.
American Psychiatric Press, Inc., Journal Division, 1400 K St., N.W., Ste. 1101, Washington, DC 20005. TEL 202-682-6020. FAX 202-682-6016. *5051*

AMERICAN JOURNAL OF PSYCHOANALYSIS.
Human Sciences Press, Inc., 233 Spring St., New York, NY 10013. TEL 212-620-8000. FAX 212-463-0742. *6092*

AMERICAN JOURNAL OF PSYCHOLOGY.
University of Illinois Press, 1325 S. Oak St., Champaign, IL 61820. TEL 217-333-0950. FAX 217-244-8082. *6092*

AMERICAN JOURNAL OF PSYCHOTHERAPY.
Association for the Advancement of Psychotherapy, Belfer Education Center, 1300 Morris Park Ave., Rm. 402, Bronx, NY 10461-1602. TEL 718-430-3503. FAX 718-430-8907. *5051*

AMERICAN JOURNAL OF PUBLIC HEALTH.
American Public Health Association, 1015 15th St., N.W., Washington, DC 20005. TEL 202-789-5600. *6228*

AMERICAN JOURNAL OF REPRODUCTIVE IMMUNOLOGY.
Munksgaard International Publishers Ltd., P.O. Box 2148, DK-1016 Copenhagen K, Denmark. TEL 45-33-127030. FAX 45-33-129387. *4791*

AMERICAN JOURNAL OF RESPIRATORY AND CRITICAL CARE MEDICINE.
American Lung Association, 1740 Broadway, New York, NY 10019-4374. TEL 212-315-8700. *5117*

REFEREED SERIALS

AMERICAN JOURNAL OF SCIENCE.
American Journal of Science, Box 6666, Yale Sta., New Haven, CT 06511-8130. TEL 203-432-3131. FAX 203-432-5668. *2310*

AMERICAN JOURNAL OF SOCIOLOGY.
University of Chicago Press, Journals Division, Box 37005, Chicago, IL 60637. TEL 773-753-3347. FAX 773-753-0811. *6700*

AMERICAN JOURNAL OF SPORTS MEDICINE.
American Orthopaedic Society for Sports Medicine, 230 Calvary St., Waltham, MA 02154. TEL 617-736-0707. FAX 617-736-0607. *5128*

AMERICAN JOURNAL OF SURGERY.
Excerpta Medica, Inc., 105 Raider Blvd., Belle Mead, NJ 08502. TEL 908-874-8550. FAX 908-874-8419. *5135*

AMERICAN JOURNAL OF SURGICAL PATHOLOGY.
Lippincott - Raven Publishers, 227 E. Washington Sq., Philadelphia, PA 19106. TEL 215-238-4200. FAX 215-238-4227. *4636*

AMERICAN JOURNAL OF THE MEDICAL SCIENCES.
Lippincott - Raven Publishers, 227 E. Washington Sq., Philadelphia, PA 19106. TEL 215-238-4200. FAX 215-238-4227. *4636*

AMERICAN JOURNAL OF THERAPEUTICS.
Chapman & Hall, Journals Department 2-6 Boundary Row, London SE1 8HN, England. TEL 44-171-8560066. FAX 44-171-5229623. *4637*

AMERICAN JOURNAL OF THERAPY.
McMahon Publishing Co., 83 Peaceable St., West Redding, CT 06896. TEL 203-544-9343. *4637*

AMERICAN JOURNAL OF VETERINARY RESEARCH.
American Veterinary Medical Association, 1931 N. Meacham Rd., Ste. 100, Schaumburg, IL 60173-4360. TEL 847-925-8070. FAX 847-925-1329. *7264*

AMERICAN JOURNALISM.
American Journalism Historians Association, Univ. of Georgia, Grady College of Journalism, Athens, GA 30602. TEL 706-542-5033. FAX 706-542-4785. *3868*

AMERICAN LEATHER CHEMISTS ASSOCIATION. JOURNAL.
American Leather Chemists Association, Campus Sta., Box 210014, Cincinnati, OH 45221. TEL 513-556-1197. *4144*

AMERICAN LITERATURE.
Duke University Press, Box 90660, Durham, NC 27708-0660. TEL 919-687-3600. FAX 919-688-4574. *4373*

AMERICAN MALACOLOGICAL BULLETIN.
American Malacological Union, Inc., c/o Dr. Ronald Toll, Biology Department, Wesleyan College, Macon, GA 31297. TEL 912-474-7057. FAX 912-477-7572. *825*

AMERICAN MATHEMATICAL SOCIETY. ABSTRACTS OF PAPERS PRESENTED.
American Mathematical Society, Box 6248, Providence, RI 02940-6248. TEL 401-455-4000. FAX 401-331-3842. *4617*

AMERICAN MATHEMATICAL SOCIETY. BULLETIN. NEW SERIES.
American Mathematical Society, Box 6248, Providence, RI 02940-6248. TEL 401-455-4000. FAX 401-331-3842. *4559*

AMERICAN MATHEMATICAL SOCIETY. C B M S REGIONAL CONFERENCE SERIES IN MATHEMATICS.
American Mathematical Society, Box 6248, Providence, RI 02940-6248. TEL 401-455-4000. FAX 401-331-3842. *4559*

AMERICAN MATHEMATICAL SOCIETY. COLLOQUIUM PUBLICATIONS.
American Mathematical Society, Box 6248, Providence, RI 02940-6248. TEL 401-455-4000. FAX 401-331-3842. *4559*

AMERICAN MATHEMATICAL SOCIETY. JOURNAL.
American Mathematical Society, Box 6248, Providence, RI 02940-6248. TEL 401-455-4000. FAX 401-331-3842. *4559*

AMERICAN MATHEMATICAL SOCIETY. MEMOIRS.
American Mathematical Society, Box 6248, Providence, RI 02940-6248. TEL 401-455-4000. FAX 401-331-3842. *4559*

AMERICAN MATHEMATICAL SOCIETY. NOTICES.
American Mathematical Society, Box 6248, Providence, RI 02940-6248. TEL 401-455-4000. FAX 401-331-3842. *4559*

AMERICAN MATHEMATICAL SOCIETY. PROCEEDINGS.
American Mathematical Society, Box 6248, Providence, RI 02940-6248. TEL 401-455-4000. FAX 401-331-3842. *4559*

AMERICAN MATHEMATICAL SOCIETY. PROCEEDINGS OF SYMPOSIA IN APPLIED MATHEMATICS.
American Mathematical Society, Box 6248, Providence, RI 02940-6248. TEL 401-455-4000. FAX 401-331-3842. *4559*

AMERICAN MATHEMATICAL SOCIETY. PROCEEDINGS OF SYMPOSIA IN PURE MATHEMATICS.
American Mathematical Society, Box 6248, Providence, RI 02940-6248. TEL 401-455-4000. FAX 401-331-3842. *4559*

AMERICAN MATHEMATICAL SOCIETY. TRANSACTIONS.
American Mathematical Society, Box 6248, Providence, RI 02940-6248. TEL 401-455-4000. FAX 401-331-3842. *4559*

AMERICAN MEDICAL INFORMATICS ASSOCIATION. JOURNAL.
Hanley & Belfus, Inc., 210 S. 13th St., Philadelphia, PA 19107. TEL 215-546-7293. FAX 215-790-9330. *4845*

AMERICAN MEDICAL WOMEN'S ASSOCIATION. JOURNAL.
American Medical Women's Association, Inc., 801 N. Fairfax St., Ste. 400, Alexandria, VA 22314. TEL 212-387-3864. FAX 212-387-3897. *4637*

AMERICAN METEOROLOGICAL SOCIETY. BULLETIN.
American Meteorological Society, 45 Beacon St., Boston, MA 02108-3693. TEL 617-227-2425. FAX 618-742-8718. *5226*

AMERICAN METEOROLOGICAL SOCIETY. HISTORICAL MONOGRAPH SERIES.
American Meteorological Society, 45 Beacon St., Boston, MA 02108-3693. TEL 617-227-2425. FAX 617-742-8718. *5226*

AMERICAN METEOROLOGICAL SOCIETY. METEOROLOGICAL MONOGRAPHS.
American Meteorological Society, 45 Beacon St., Boston, MA 02108-3693. TEL 617-227-2425. FAX 617-742-8718. *5226*

AMERICAN MIDLAND NATURALIST.
University of Notre Dame, Department of Biological Sciences, Box 369, Notre Dame, IN 46556. TEL 219-631-7481. FAX 219-631-7413. *6511*

AMERICAN MINERALOGIST.
Mineralogical Society of America, 1015 Eighteenth St., N.W., Ste. 601, Washington, DC 20036-5274. TEL 202-775-4344. FAX 202-775-0018. *5294*

AMERICAN MONASTIC NEWSLETTER.
American Benedictine Academy, Mount St. Scholastica, 801 South 8th, Atchison, KS 66002. TEL 913-367-6110. FAX 913-367-3866. *6449*

AMERICAN MOSQUITO CONTROL ASSOCIATION. JOURNAL.
American Mosquito Control Association, Box 5416, Lake Charles, LA 70606. TEL 318-474-2723. FAX 318-478-9434. *746*

AMERICAN MUSEUM NOVITATES.
American Museum of Natural History, Central Park W. at 79th St., New York, NY 10024-5192. TEL 212-769-5545. FAX 212-769-5009. *825*

AMERICAN MUSEUM OF NATURAL HISTORY. ANTHROPOLOGICAL PAPERS.
American Museum of Natural History, Central Park W. at 79th St., New York, NY 10024-5192. TEL 212-769-5545. FAX 212-769-5009. *307*

AMERICAN MUSIC.
University of Illinois Press, 1325 S. Oak St., Champaign, IL 61820. TEL 217-333-0950. FAX 217-244-8082. *5371*

AMERICAN MUSICAL INSTRUMENT SOCIETY. JOURNAL.
American Musical Instrument Society, c/o Albert R. Rice, 6114 Corbin Ave., Tarzana, CA 91356-1011. TEL 818-776-9446. *5372*

AMERICAN MUSICOLOGICAL SOCIETY. JOURNAL.
University of Chicago Press, Journals Division, Box 37005, Chicago, IL 60637. TEL 773-753-8038. FAX 773-753-0811. *5372*

THE AMERICAN NATURALIST.
University of Chicago Press, Journals Division, Box 37005, Chicago, IL 60637. TEL 773-753-3347. FAX 773-753-0811. *585*

AMERICAN NEPTUNE.
Peabody Essex Museum of Salem, East India Sq., Salem, MA 01970-3783. TEL 508-745-1876, 508-745-1876 ext. 3172. FAX 508-744-6776. *3616*

AMERICAN NUCLEAR SOCIETY TRANSACTIONS.
American Nuclear Society, 555 N. Kensington Ave., La Grange Park, IL 60526. TEL 708-352-6611. FAX 708-352-0499. *2693*

AMERICAN OIL CHEMISTS' SOCIETY. JOURNAL.
A O C S Press, 1608 Broadmoor Dr., Box 3489, Champaign, IL 61821-0489. TEL 217-359-2344. FAX 217-351-8091. *1812*

AMERICAN OPTOMETRIC ASSOCIATION. JOURNAL.
American Optometric Association, 243 N. Lindbergh Blvd., St. Louis, MO 63141. TEL 314-991-4100. FAX 314-991-4101. *4989*

AMERICAN ORTHOPTIC JOURNAL.
University of Wisconsin Press, Journal Division, 114 N. Murray St., Madison, WI 53715. TEL 608-262-4952. FAX 608-262-7560. *4989*

AMERICAN OTOLOGICAL SOCIETY. TRANSACTIONS.
American Otological Society, c/o Dr. A. Julianna Gulya, 1558 N. Colonial Terr., Arlington, VA 22209. TEL 703-528-3436. FAX 202-784-1312. *5019*

AMERICAN PERIODICALS.
University of North Texas Press, Journals Division, Box 5096, UNT Sta., Denton, TX 76203-5096. TEL 817-565-2134. FAX 817-369-8770. *4373*

AMERICAN PHARMACEUTICAL ASSOCIATION. JOURNAL.
American Pharmaceutical Association, 2215 Constitution Ave., N.W., Washington, DC 20037. TEL 202-628-4410. *5646*

AMERICAN PODIATRIC MEDICAL ASSOCIATION. JOURNAL.
American Podiatric Medical Association, 9312 Old Georgetown Rd., Bethesda, MD 20814-1698. TEL 301-571-9200. FAX 301-530-2752. *5004*

AMERICAN POLITICAL SCIENCE REVIEW.
American Political Science Association, 1527 New Hampshire Ave., N.W., Washington, DC 20036. TEL 202-483-2512. FAX 202-483-2657. *5891*

AMERICAN POTATO JOURNAL.
Potato Association of America, 157 Park St., Ste. 23, Bangor, ME 04401. TEL 207-942-9732. FAX 207-942-9733. *213*

AMERICAN PROFESSIONAL CONSTRUCTOR.
American Institute of Constructors, 466 94th Ave., N., St. Petersburg, FL 33702-2522. TEL 813-578-0317. FAX 813-578-9982. *861*

THE AMERICAN PROSPECT.
American Prospect, Inc., Box 383080, Cambridge, MA 02238-3080. TEL 617-547-2950. FAX 617-547-3896. *5891*

AMERICAN PSYCHIATRIC NURSES ASSOCIATION. JOURNAL.
Mosby - Year Book, Inc., 11830 Westline Industrial Dr., St. Louis, MO 63146-3318. TEL 314-872-8370. FAX 314-872-9164. *4928*

AMERICAN PSYCHOANALYTIC ASSOCIATION. JOURNAL.
Analytic Press, Inc., 101 West St., Hillsdale, NJ 07642. TEL 201-358-9477. FAX 201-358-0621. *6092*

AMERICAN PSYCHOANALYTIC ASSOCIATION. JOURNAL. MONOGRAPH.
International Universities Press, Inc., 59 Boston Post Rd., Box 1524, Madison, CT 06443-1524. TEL 203-245-4000. FAX 203-245-0775. *6092*

AMERICAN PSYCHOANALYTIC ASSOCIATION. WORKSHOP SERIES.
International Universities Press, Inc., 59 Boston Post Rd., Box 1524, Madison, CT 06443-1524. TEL 203-245-4000. FAX 203-245-0775. *6092*

AMERICAN PSYCHOLOGIST.
American Psychological Association, 750 First St., N.E., Washington, DC 20002-4242. TEL 202-336-5600. FAX 202-336-5568. *6092*

AMERICAN PSYCHOPATHOLOGICAL ASSOCIATION SERIES.
Lippincott - Raven Publishers, 227 E. Washington sq., Philadelphia, PA 19106. TEL 215-238-4200. FAX 215-238-4227. *5051*

AMERICAN READING FORUM. YEARBOOK.
American Reading Forum, c/o Dept. of Elementary Education, Utah State University, Logan, UT 84322-2805. TEL 801-797-0399. FAX 801-797-0372. *2421*

AMERICAN RESEARCH CENTER IN EGYPT. REPORTS.
Eisenbrauns, Box 275, Winona Lake, IN 46590. TEL 219-269-2011. FAX 219-269-6788. *347*

AMERICAN REVIEW.
Japanese Association for American Studies, University of Tokyo, Center for American Studies, 8-1, 3-chome, Komaba, Meguro-ku, Tokyo 153, Japan. TEL 03-5454-6163. *3616*

AMERICAN ROMANIAN ACADEMY OF ARTS AND SCIENCES. JOURNAL.
A R A Publications, Department of French and Italian, University of California, Sproul Hall, Davis, CA 95616. TEL 916-758-7720. *2531*

AMERICAN SECONDARY EDUCATION.
c/o John K. Bailey, Ed., Rm. 101 Kates Center, Ashland University, Ashland, OH 44805. TEL 419-289-5377. FAX 419-289-5097. *2421*

AMERICAN SOCIETY FOR INFORMATION SCIENCE. JOURNAL.
John Wiley & Sons, Inc., Journals, 605 Third Ave., New York, NY 10158. TEL 212-850-6645. FAX 212-850-6021. *4158*

AMERICAN SOCIETY FOR MASS SPECTROMETRY. JOURNAL.
Elsevier Science Inc., Box 945, New York, NY 10159-0945. TEL 212-633-3730. FAX 212-633-3680. *5858*

AMERICAN SOCIETY FOR TESTING AND MATERIALS. DATA SERIES PUBLICATIONS.
American Society for Testing and Materials, 100 Barr Harbor Dr., W. Conshohocken, PA 19428-2959. TEL 610-832-9500. FAX 610-832-9555. *2851*

AMERICAN SOCIETY FOR TESTING AND MATERIALS. FIVE-YEAR INDEX TO A S T M TECHNICAL PAPERS AND REPORTS.
American Society for Testing and Materials, 100 Barr Harbor Dr., W. Conshohocken, PA 19428-2959. TEL 610-832-9500. FAX 610-832-9555. *2851*

AMERICAN SOCIETY FOR TESTING AND MATERIALS. SPECIAL TECHNICAL PUBLICATIONS.
American Society for Testing and Materials, 100 Barr Harbor Dr., W. Conshohocken, PA 19428-2959. TEL 610-832-9500. FAX 610-832-9555. *2851*

AMERICAN SOCIETY OF BREWING CHEMISTS. JOURNAL.
American Society of Brewing Chemists, 3340 Pilot Knob Rd., St. Paul, MN 55121-2097. TEL 612-454-7250. FAX 612-454-0766. *514*

AMERICAN SOCIETY OF ECHOCARDIOGRAPHY. JOURNAL.
Mosby - Year Book, Inc., 11830 Westline Industrial Dr., St. Louis, MO 63146-3318. TEL 314-872-8370. FAX 314-432-1380. *4809*

AMERICAN SOCIETY OF FARM MANAGERS AND RURAL APPRAISERS. JOURNAL.
American Society of Farm Managers and Rural Appraisers, 950 S. Cherry St., Ste. 508, Denver, CO 80222. TEL 303-758-3513. FAX 303-758-0190. *98*

AMERICAN SOCIETY OF HYPERTENSION. SYMPOSIUM SERIES.
Lippincott - Raven Publishers, 227 E. Washington Sq., Philadelphia, PA 19106. TEL 215-238-4200. FAX 215-238-4227. *4809*

AMERICAN SOCIETY OF MAMMALOGISTS. SPECIAL PUBLICATIONS.
American Society of Mammalogists, c/o Dr. H. Duane Smith, Sec.-Treas., Monte L. Bean Life Science Museum, Brigham Young University, Provo, UT 84602. TEL 801-378-2492. *825*

AMERICAN SOCIETY OF NEPHROLOGY. JOURNAL.
Williams & Wilkins, 351 W. Camden St., Baltimore, MD 21201-2436. TEL 410-528-4068. FAX 410-528-4452. *5159*

THE AMERICAN SOCIOLOGIST.
Transaction Publishers, Transaction Periodicals Consortium, Department 3092, Rutgers University, New Brunswick, NJ 08903. TEL 908-445-2280. FAX 908-445-3138. *6701*

AMERICAN SPEECH.
University of Alabama Press, Box 870380, Tuscaloosa, AL 35487-0380. TEL 205-348-5180. FAX 205-348-9201. *4239*

AMERICAN STRING TEACHER.
American String Teachers Association, 468 Rebecca St., Morgantown, WV 26505-2249. TEL 412-243-2834. FAX 412-243-9211. *5372*

AMERICAN STUDIES.
University of Kansas at Lawrence, American Studies Department, 2120 Wescoe Hall, Lawrence, KS 66045-2117. TEL 913-864-4878. FAX 913-864-5742. *6602*

AMERICAN SURGEON.
Southeastern Surgical Congress, 141 W. Wienca Rd., No. 3100, Atlanta, GA 30342. TEL 404-255-4549. FAX 404-255-5442. *5135*

AMERICAN SUZUKI JOURNAL.
Suzuki Association of the Americas, Box 17310, Boulder, CO 80308-7310. TEL 303-444-0948. FAX 303-444-0984. *5372*

AMERICAN TAXATION ASSOCIATION. JOURNAL.
American Accouriting Association, 5717 Bessie Dr., Sarasota, FL 34233. TEL 941-921-7747. FAX 941-923-4093. *1599*

AMERICAN UNIVERSITY STUDIES. SERIES 8. PSYCHOLOGY.
Peter Lang Publishing, Inc., 275 Seventh Ave., 28th Fl., New York, NY 10001. TEL 212-647-7700. FAX 212-647-7707. *6092*

AMERICAN VETERINARY MEDICAL ASSOCIATION. JOURNAL.
American Veterinary Medical Association, 1931 N. Meacham Rd., Ste. 100, Schaumburg, IL 60173-4360. TEL 847-925-8070. FAX 847-925-1329. *7265*

AMERICAN WATER RESOURCES ASSOCIATION. JOURNAL.
American Water Resources Association, 950 Herndon Pkwy., Ste. 300, Herndon, VA 22170-5531. TEL 703-904-1225. FAX 703-904-1228. *7287*

AMERICAN WATER WORKS ASSOCIATION. JOURNAL.
American Water Works Association, 6666 W. Quincy Ave., Denver, CO 80235. TEL 303-794-7711. FAX 303-794-7310. *7287*

AMERICAN ZOOLOGIST.
Society for Integrative and Comparative Biology, 401 N. Michigan Ave., Box 809278, Chicago, IL 60611-9278. TEL 312-527-6697. FAX 312-245-1085. *825*

THE AMERICAS.
Academy of American Franciscan History, 1712 Euclid Ave., Berkeley, CA 94709-1208. TEL 510-843-4803. *3616*

AMETHYST REVIEW.
23 Riverside Ave., Truro, NS B2N 4G2, Canada. TEL 902-895-1345. *4502*

AMPHIBIA REPTILIA.
E.J. Brill, P.O. Box 9000, 2300 PA Leiden, Netherlands. TEL 31-71-5353500. FAX 31-71-5317532. *825*

AMSTERDAM MONOGRAPHS IN AMERICAN STUDIES.
Editions Rodopi B.V., Keizersgracht 302-304, 1016 EX Amsterdam, Netherlands. TEL 31-20-6227507. FAX 31-20-6380948. *3772*

AMTSBLATT DES LANDKREISES HOF.
Landratsamt Hof, Schaumbergstr. 14, 95032 Hof, Germany. TEL 49-9281-57-0. FAX 49-9281-58340. *6163*

AMYLOID.
Parthenon Publishing Group, Casterton Hall, Carnforth, Lancs. LA6 2LA, England. TEL 44-152-427-2084. FAX 44-152-427-1587. *5124*

ANAEROBE.
Academic Press Ltd., 24-28 Oval Rd., London NW1 7DX, England. TEL 44-171-482-2893. FAX 44-171-267-0362. *779*

ANAIS BRASILEIROS DE DERMATOLOGIA.
Sociedade Brasileira de Dermatologia, Caixa Postal 389, 20001-970 Rio de Janeiro, Brazil. TEL 55-21-2534767. FAX 55-21-2536747. *4874*

ANALECTA BOLLANDIANA.
Societe des Bollandistes, 24 bd. Saint-Michel, B-1040 Brussels, Belgium. TEL 32-2-7393338. *6320*

ANALECTA HUSSERLIANA.
Kluwer Academic Publishers, Postbus 17, 3300 AA Dordrecht, Netherlands. TEL 31-78-6392392. FAX 31-78-6392254. *5717*

ANALECTA TOR.
Editrice Franciscanum, Via dei Fori Imperiali 1, 00186 Rome, Italy. TEL 39-6-6991540. FAX 39-6-6784970. *6450*

ANALES DE FISICA.
Real Sociedad Espanola de Fisica, Facultad de Fisica y Quimica, Ciudad Universitaria, 28040 Madrid, Spain. TEL 34-1-3944359. FAX 34-1-5433879. *5796*

ANALES DE QUIMICA.
Springer-Verlag Iberica, S.A., Provenca, 388, 1a planta, 08025 Barcelona, Spain. TEL 39-3-4570227. FAX 39-3-4571502. *1739*

ANALES GALDOSIANOS.
International Association of Galdos Scholars, Queen's University, Department of Spanish & Italian, Kingston, ON K7L 3N6, Canada. TEL 613-545-2112. FAX 613-545-6496. *4374*

ANALES OTORRINOLARINGOLOGICOS IBERO-AMERICANOS.
C. Balmes, 24 pral. 1a, 08007 Barcelona, Spain. TEL 34-33173646. FAX 34-3-3173766. *5019*

ANALGESIA.
Cognizant Communication Corporation, 3 Hartsdale Rd., Elmsford, NY 10523-3701. TEL 914-592-7720. FAX 914-592-8981. *4803*

ANALISIS POLITICO.
Universidad Nacional de Colombia, Instituto de Estudios Politicos y Relaciones Internacionales, Apdo. Aereo 14490, Edificio Manuel Ancizar, Of. 3031, Bogota, Colombia. TEL 57-1-3681579. FAX 57-1-3687471. *5891*

REFEREED SERIALS

ANALOG INTEGRATED CIRCUITS AND SIGNAL PROCESSING.
Kluwer Academic Publishers Boston, Box 358, Accord Sta., Hingham, MA 02018-0358. TEL 617-871-6600. FAX 617-871-6528. *2178*

ANALUSIS.
Editions Scientifiques et Medicales Elsevier, 141 rue de Javel, 75747 Paris, France. TEL 33-1-45589022. FAX 33-1-45589421. *1787*

ANALYSE.
Nederlandse Vereniging van BioMedische Laboratoriummedewerkers, Wilhelminapark 52, 3581 NM Utrecht, Netherlands. TEL 31-30-2522881. FAX 31-30-2541814. *4894*

THE ANALYST.
The Royal Society of Chemistry, Thomas Graham House, Science Park, Milton Rd., Cambridge CB4 4WF, England. TEL 44-1223-420066. FAX 44-1223-423429. *1787*

ANALYTICA CHIMICA ACTA.
Elsevier Science B.V., P.O. Box 211, 1000 AE Amsterdam, Netherlands. TEL 31-20-4853911. FAX 31-20-4853598. *1788*

ANALYTICAL & ENUMERATIVE BIBLIOGRAPHY.
Bibliographical Society of Northern Illinois, c/o Department of English, Northern Illinois University, DeKalb, IL 60115. TEL 815-753-6634. FAX 815-753-0606. *532*

ANALYTICAL AND QUANTITATIVE CYTOLOGY AND HISTOLOGY.
Science Printers and Publishers, Inc., 8342 Olive Blvd., St. Louis, MO 63132. TEL 314-991-4440. FAX 314-991-4654. *736*

ANALYTICAL BIOCHEMISTRY.
Academic Press, Inc., Journal Division, 525 B. St., Ste. 1900, San Diego, CA 92101-4495. TEL 619-230-1840. FAX 619-699-6800. *650*

ANALYTICAL CELLULAR PATHOLOGY.
I O S Press, Van Diemenstraat 94, 1013 CN Amsterdam, Netherlands. TEL 31-20-6382189. FAX 31-20-6203419. *736*

ANALYTICAL CHEMISTRY SYMPOSIA SERIES.
Elsevier Science B.V., Books Division, P.O. Box 211, 1000 AE Amsterdam, Netherlands. TEL 31-20-4853911. FAX 31-20-4853705. *1788*

ANALYTICAL COMMUNICATIONS.
The Royal Society of Chemistry, Thomas Graham House, Science Park, Milton Rd., Cambridge CB4 4WF, England. TEL 44-1223-420066. FAX 44-1223-423429. *1788*

ANALYTICAL LETTERS.
Marcel Dekker Journals, 270 Madison Ave., New York, NY 10016. TEL 212-696-9000. FAX 212-685-4540. *1788*

ANALYTICAL PROFILES OF DRUG SUBSTANCES.
Academic Press, Inc., 525 B St., Ste. 1900, San Diego, CA 92101-4495. TEL 619-231-0926. FAX 609-699-6715. *5646*

ANALYTICAL SPECTROSCOPY LIBRARY.
Elsevier Science B.V., Books Division, P.O. Box 211, 1000 AE Amsterdam, Netherlands. TEL 31-20-4853911. FAX 31-20-4853705. *1789*

ANALYTISCHE PSYCHOLOGIE.
S. Karger AG, Allschwilerstr. 10, P.O. Box, CH-4009 Basel, Switzerland. TEL 41-61-3061111. FAX 41-61-3061234. *6093*

ANANDA BICHITRA.
Dainik Bangla Bhaban, 1 Rajuk Avenue, Dhaka 100, Bangladesh. TEL 880-2-955-2086. FAX 880-2-955-2940. *3253*

ANARCHIST STUDIES.
White Horse Press, 10 High St., Knapwell, Cambridge CB3 8NR, England. TEL 44-1954-267527. FAX 44-1954-267527. *5891*

THE ANATOMICAL RECORD.
John Wiley & Sons, Inc., Journals, 605 Third Ave., New York, NY 10158. TEL 212-850-6645. FAX 212-850-6021. *585*

ANATOMICAL SOCIETY OF INDIA. JOURNAL.
Anatomical Society of India, Department of Anatomy, M.L.B. Medical College, Jhansi 284128 (U.P.), India. TEL 0517-442032. *585*

ANCESTORING.
Augusta Genealogical Society, Inc., Box 3743, Augusta, GA 30914-3743. TEL 706-738-2241. *3211*

ANCIENT CIVILIZATIONS FROM SCYTHIA TO SIBERIA.
E.J. Brill, P.O. Box 9000, 2300 PA Leiden, Netherlands. TEL 31-71-5353500. FAX 31-71-5317532. *3531*

ANCIENT HISTORY.
Macquarie Ancient History Association, School of History, Philosophy and Politics, North Ryde, N.S.W. 2109, Australia. TEL 61-2-98508859. FAX 61-2-98508892. *3488*

ANCIENT MESOAMERICA.
Cambridge University Press, Edinburgh Bldg., Shaftesbury Rd., Cambridge CB2 2RU, England. TEL 44-1223-312393. FAX 44-1223-315052. *3616*

ANCIENT T L.
Laboratoire de Physique Copusculaire, 63177 Aubiere Cedex, France. TEL 33-4-73407289. FAX 33-4-73264598. *347*

ANCIENT WORLD.
Ares Publishers, Inc., 7406 N. Sheridan Rd., Chicago, IL 60626-2012. TEL 773-743-1405. FAX 773-743-0657. *3488*

ANDEAN PAST.
Cornell University, Latin American Studies Program, Ithaca, NY 14853. TEL 607-255-2245. FAX 607-255-8919. *348*

ANDREWS UNIVERSITY SEMINARY STUDIES.
Andrews University Press, Berrien Springs, MI 49104. TEL 616-471-6023. FAX 616-471-6202. *6320*

ANESTESIA EN MEXICO.
Obsidiana Editores, S.A., Czda. de Tlalpan 2365, Col. Ciudad Jardin, 04370 Mexico DF, Mexico. TEL 6899133. *4803*

ANESTEZIOLOGIE A NEODKLADNA PECE.
Nakladatelske Stredisko C L S J.E. Purkyne, Sokolska 31, 120 26 Prague 2, Czech Republic. TEL 420-2-24911420. FAX 420-2-24911420. *4803*

ANESTHESIA AND ANALGESIA.
Williams & Wilkins, 351 W. Camden St., Baltimore, MD 21201-2436. TEL 410-528-4068. FAX 410-528-4452. *4803*

ANESTHESIOLOGY.
Lippincott - Raven Publishers, 227 E. Washington Sq., Philadelphia, PA 19106. TEL 215-238-4200. FAX 215-238-4227. *4804*

ANGELAKI.
44 Abbey Rd., Oxford OX2 OAE, England. TEL 44-1865-793891. *5717*

ANGIOLOGY.
Westminster Publications, Inc., 708 Glen Cove Ave., Glen Head, NY 11545. TEL 516-759-0025. FAX 516-759-5524. *4810*

ANGLICAN ADVANCE.
Episcopal Diocese of Chicago, 65 E. Huron St., Chicago, IL 60611. TEL 312-751-4200. FAX 312-787-4534. *6412*

ANGLICAN THEOLOGICAL REVIEW.
Anglican Theological Review, Inc., 600 Haven St., Evanston, IL 60201. TEL 708-864-6024. FAX 708-328-9624. *6320*

ANGLO-CATALAN SOCIETY. OCCASIONAL PUBLICATIONS.
Anglo-Catalan Society, c/o Dr. Alan Yates, Ed., Department of Hispanic Studies, University of Sheffield, Sheffield S10 TN, England. TEL 44-114-222-4402. FAX 44-114-273-9826. *3547*

ANGLO-NORMAN TEXT SOCIETY. OCCASIONAL PUBLICATIONS SERIES.
Anglo-Norman Text Society, Birkbeck College, London WC1E 7HX, England. *3548*

ANGLOPHONIA - CALIBAN.
Presses Universitaires du Mirail-Toulouse, 56 rue du Taur, 31000 Toulouse, France. TEL 33-5-61225831. FAX 33-5-61218420. *4375*

ANGLOPHONIA - SIGMA.
Presses Universitaires du Mirail-Toulouse, 56 rue du Taur, 31000 Toulouse, France. TEL 33-5-61225831. FAX 33-5-61218420. *4240*

ANGOLITE.
Louisiana State Penitentiary, Angola, LA 70712. TEL 504-655-4411. *2261*

ANGORA GOAT & MOHAIR JOURNAL.
S.A. Mohair Grower's Association, P.O. Box 50, Jansenville 6265, South Africa. TEL 27-24-4932-140. *268*

ANIMAL BIOTECHNOLOGY.
Marcel Dekker Journals, 270 Madison Ave., New York, NY 10016. TEL 212-696-9000. FAX 212-685-4540. *677*

ANIMAL FEED SCIENCE AND TECHNOLOGY.
Elsevier Science B.V., P.O. Box 211, 1000 AE Amsterdam, Netherlands. TEL 31-20-4853911. FAX 31-20-4853598. *260*

ANIMAL FEEDING AND NUTRITION.
Academic Press, Inc., 525 B St., Ste. 1900, San Diego, CA 92101-4495. TEL 619-231-6616. FAX 619-699-6715. *7265*

ANIMAL GENETICS.
Blackwell Science Ltd., Osney Mead, Oxford OX2 OEL, England. TEL 44-1865-206206. FAX 44-1865-721205. *763*

ANIMAL KEEPERS' FORUM.
American Association of Zoo Keepers, Inc., 635 S.W. Gage Blvd., Topeka, KS 66606-2066. TEL 913-273-1980. FAX 913-273-1980. *826*

ANIMAL LEARNING & BEHAVIOR.
Psychonomic Society, Inc., 1710 Fortview Rd., Austin, TX 78704. TEL 512-462-2442. *6093*

ANIMAL PRODUCTION IN AUSTRALIA.
A.S.A.P. Publications, c/o Mrs. Lyn Yates, A.B.R.I., University of New England, Armidale, N.S.W. 2351, Australia. TEL 61-67-733773. FAX 61-67-733773. *268*

ANIMAL REPRODUCTION SCIENCE.
Elsevier Science B.V., P.O. Box 211, 1000 AE Amsterdam, Netherlands. TEL 31-20-4853911. FAX 31-20-4853598. *268*

ANIMAL SCIENCE.
Durrant Periodicals, Winton Lea, Pencaitland, E. Lothian EH34 5AY, Scotland. TEL 01875-340354. FAX 01875-340354. *269*

ANIMALS' AGENDA.
Animal Rights Network, Inc., Box 25881, Baltimore, MD 21224. TEL 410-675-4566. FAX 410-675-0066. *301*

ANIMALS' VOICE.
Ontario S P C A, 16640 Yonge St., Newmarket, ON L3Y 4V8, Canada. TEL 905-898-7122. FAX 905-853-8643. *301*

ANIMATION JOURNAL.
A J Press, 2011 Kingsboro Circle, Tustin, CA 92780-6733. TEL 714-544-6255. FAX 714-997-6700. *5323*

ANIMATRIX.
University of California at Los Angeles, Department of Film and Television, 405 Hilgard Ave., Los Angeles, CA 90024. TEL 310-825-5829. FAX 310-825-3383. *5323*

ANKA.
13 rue Santeuil, 75231 Paris Cedex 05, France. TEL 45-35-31-15. FAX 44-08-89-79. *4375*

ANNALES ACADEMIAE SCIENTIARUM FENNICAE. GEOLOGICA-GEOGRAPHICA.
Suomalainen Tiedeakatemia, Mariankatu 5, FIN-00170 Helsinki, Finland. *2330*

ANNALES ACADEMIAE SCIENTIARUM FENNICAE. MATHEMATICA.
Suomalainen Tiedeakatemia, Mariankatu 5, FIN-00170 Helsinki, Finland. *4560*

ANNALES DE BIOCHIMIE CLINIQUE DU QUEBEC.
Marc Letellier, Ed. & Pub., c/o Marc Letellier, Ed., Dept. de Biochimie Clinique, C H U S, Sherbrooke, PQ J1H 5N4, Canada. TEL 819-563-5555. FAX 819-820-6425. *4894*

ANNALES DE BIOLOGIE CLINIQUE.
John Libbey Eurotext, 127 av. de la Republique, 92120 Montrouge, France. TEL 33-1-46730660. FAX 33-1-40840999. *586*

ANNALES DE DROIT DE LOUVAIN.
Bruylant, 67 rue de la Regence, 1000 Brussels, Belgium. TEL 32-2-5129845. FAX 32-2-5117202. *4105*

ANNALES DE MEDECINE VETERINAIRE.
Imprimerie Bietlot, 20 Bd. de Colonster, B42, B-4000 Sart Tilman, Liege, Belgium. TEL 32-41-664020. FAX 32-41-662935. *7265*

ANNALES DE READAPTATION ET DE MEDECINE PHYSIQUE.
Editions Scientifiques et Medicales Elsevier, 141 rue de Javel, 75747 Paris, France. TEL 33-1-45589026. FAX 33-1-45589421. *5041*

ANNALES DE ZOOTECHNIE.
Editions Scientifiques et Medicales Elsevier, 141 rue de Javel, 75747 Paris, France. TEL 33-1-45589022. FAX 33-1-45589421. *826*

ANNALES DES SCIENCES FORESTIERES.
Editions Scientifiques et Medicales Elsevier, 141 rue de Javel, 75747 Paris, France. TEL 33-1-45589022. FAX 33-1-45589421. *3147*

ANNALES DES TELECOMMUNICATIONS.
Presses Polytechniques et Universitaires Romandes, EPFL - Ecublens, CH-1015 Lausanne, Switzerland. TEL 021-6934140. FAX 021-6934027. *1981*

ANNALES FRANCAISES D'ANESTHESIE ET DE REANIMATION.
Editions Scientifiques et Medicales Elsevier, 141 rue de Javel, 75747 Paris, France. TEL 33-1-45589026. FAX 33-1-45589421. *4804*

ANNALES GEOPHYSICAE.
Springer-Verlag, Heidelberger Platz 3, 14197 Berlin, Germany. TEL 49-30-82787-0. FAX 49-30-82787448. *2378*

ANNALES POLONICI MATHEMATICI.
Polska Akademia Nauk, Instytut Matematyczny, Dzial Wydawnictw, Ul. Sniadeckich 8, P.O. Box 137, 00-950 Warsaw, Poland. *4560*

ANNALI D'ITALIANISTICA.
Annali d'Italianistica, Inc., 141 Dey Hall, CB 3170, University of North Carolina, Chapel Hill, NC 27599-3170. TEL 919-962-2062. FAX 919-962-5457. *4375*

ANNALI DI MICROBIOLOGIA ED ENZIMOLOGIA.
Universita degli Studi di Milano, Dipartimento di Scienze e Tecnologie Alimentari e Microbiologiche, Via G. Celoria 2, 20133 Milan, Italy. TEL 39-2-23673444. FAX 39-2-70630829. *780*

ANNALS OF AIR AND SPACE LAW.
McGill University, Centre for Research of Air and Space Law, 3661 Peel St., Montreal, PQ H3A 1X1, Canada. TEL 514-398-5095. FAX 514-398-8197. *57*

ANNALS OF ALLERGY, ASTHMA, & IMMUNOLOGY.
American College of Allergy, Asthma, & Immunology, 85 W. Algonquin Rd., Ste. 550, Arlington Heights, IL 60005-4425. TEL 703-821-5461. *4791*

ANNALS OF BEHAVIORAL SCIENCE AND MEDICAL EDUCATION.
Association for the Behavioral Sciences & Medical Education, 3900 E. Camelback Rd., Ste. 200, Phoenix, AZ 85018. TEL 602-912-5317. FAX 602-957-4828. *6603*

ANNALS OF BIOMEDICAL ENGINEERING.
Blackwell Science Inc., 350 Main St., Malden, MA 02148. TEL 617-876-7000. FAX 617-388-8255. *4638*

ANNALS OF CHILD DEVELOPMENT.
Jessica Kingsley Publishers, 116 Pentonville Rd., London N1 9JB, England. TEL 44-171-833-2307. FAX 44-171-837-2917. *6093*

ANNALS OF CLINICAL BIOCHEMISTRY.
Royal Society of Medicine Press Ltd., 1 Wimpole St., London W1M 8AE, England. TEL 44-171-290-2900. FAX 44-171-290-2929. *650*

ANNALS OF CLINICAL PSYCHIATRY.
Plenum Publishing Corp., 233 Spring St., New York, NY 10013-1578. TEL 212-620-8000. FAX 212-463-0742. *5052*

ANNALS OF COMBINATORICS.
Springer-Verlag Singapore, No. 04-01, Cencon I, One Tannery Rd., Singapore 347719, Singapore. TEL 65-8420112. FAX 65-8420107. *4560*

ANNALS OF DISCRETE MATHEMATICS.
Elsevier Science B.V., Books Division, P.O. Box 211, 1000 AE Amsterdam, Netherlands. TEL 31-20-4853911. FAX 31-20-4853705. *4560*

ANNALS OF DYSLEXIA.
Orton Dyslexia Society, 8600 LaSalle Rd., Ste. 382, Baltimore, MD 21286-2044. TEL 410-296-0232. *2580*

ANNALS OF EMERGENCY MEDICINE.
Mosby - Year Book, Inc., 11830 Westline Industrial Dr., St. Louis, MO 63146-3318. TEL 314-872-8370. FAX 314-432-1380. *5004*

ANNALS OF EPIDEMIOLOGY.
Elsevier Science Inc., Box 945, New York, NY 10159-0945. TEL 212-633-3730. FAX 212-633-3680. *6228*

ANNALS OF EXPERIMENTAL AND CLINICAL MEDICINE.
Graffham Press Ltd., 6 York Pl., Edinburgh EH1 3EP, Scotland. TEL 0131-556-7887. FAX 0131-556-1129. *4894*

ANNALS OF GLOBAL ANALYSIS AND GEOMETRY.
Kluwer Academic Publishers, Postbus 17, 3300 AA Dordrecht, Netherlands. TEL 31-78-6392392. FAX 31-78-6392254. *4560*

ANNALS OF HEALTH LAW.
Loyola University Chicago, School of Law, One E. Pearson St., Chicago, IL 60611. TEL 312-915-6304. FAX 312-915-7201. *3910*

ANNALS OF HUMAN BIOLOGY.
Taylor & Francis Ltd., 1 Gunpowder Sq., London EC4A 3DE, England. TEL 44-171-583-0490. FAX 44-171-583-0585. *586*

ANNALS OF INTERNAL MEDICINE.
American College of Physicians, Independence Mall W., Sixth St. at Race, Philadelphia, PA 19106-1572. TEL 215-351-2400. FAX 215-351-2799. *4924*

ANNALS OF MEDICAL SCIENCES.
Cukurova Universitesi, Tip Fakultesi, Yayin ve Dokumentasyon Kurulu, Balcali, 01330 Adana, Turkey. TEL 90-322-3386060. *4638*

ANNALS OF MEDICINE.
Blackwell Science Ltd., Osney Mead, Oxford OX2 0EL, England. TEL 44-1865-206206. FAX 44-1865-721205. *4894*

ANNALS OF NEUROLOGY.
Lippincott - Raven Publishers, 227 E. Washington Sq., Philadelphia, PA 19106. TEL 215-238-4200. FAX 215-238-4227. *5052*

ANNALS OF NONINVASIVE ELECTROCARDIOLOGY.
Futura Publishing Co., Inc., 135 Bedford Rd., Armonk, NY 10504-0418. TEL 914-273-1014. FAX 914-273-1016. *4810*

ANNALS OF NUCLEAR ENERGY.
Elsevier Science Ltd., Pergamon, P.O. Box 800, Kidlington, Oxford OX5 1DX, England. TEL 44-1865-843000. FAX 44-1865-843010. *2693*

ANNALS OF NUMERICAL MATHEMATICS.
Baltzer Science Publishers B.V., P.O. Box 221, 1400 AE Bussum, Netherlands. TEL 31-20-6370061. FAX 31-20-6323651. *4561*

ANNALS OF NUTRITION AND METABOLISM.
S. Karger AG, Allschwilerstr. 10, P.O. Box, CH-4009 Basel, Switzerland. TEL 41-61-3061111. FAX 41-61-3061234. *5469*

ANNALS OF OCCUPATIONAL HYGIENE.
Elsevier Science Ltd., Pergamon, P.O. Box 800, Kidlington, Oxford OX5 1DX, England. TEL 44-1865-843000. FAX 44-1865-843010. *5486*

ANNALS OF ONCOLOGY.
Kluwer Academic Publishers, Postbus 17, 3300 AA Dordrecht, Netherlands. TEL 31-78-6392392. FAX 31-78-6392254. *4970*

ANNALS OF OPHTHALMOLOGY - GLAUCOMA.
American Society of Contemporary Medicine, Surgery, and Ophthalmology, 4711 Golf Rd., Ste. 408, Skokie, IL 60076-1242. TEL 847-568-1500. FAX 847-568-1527. *4990*

ANNALS OF OTOLOGY, RHINOLOGY AND LARYNGOLOGY.
Annals Publishing Co., 4507 Laclede Ave., St. Louis, MO 63108. TEL 314-367-4987. FAX 314-367-4988. *5020*

THE ANNALS OF PHARMACOTHERAPY.
Harvey Whitney Books Company, Box 42696, Cincinnati, OH 45242. TEL 513-793-3555. FAX 513-793-3600. *5647*

ANNALS OF PHYSICS.
Academic Press, Inc., Journal Division, 525 B St., Ste. 1900, San Diego, CA 92101-4495. TEL 619-230-1840. FAX 619-699-6800. *5796*

ANNALS OF PLASTIC SURGERY.
Lippincott - Raven Publishers, 227 E. Washington Sq., Philadelphia, PA 19106. TEL 215-238-4200. FAX 215-238-4227. *5135*

ANNALS OF PROBABILITY.
Institute of Mathematical Statistics, Business Office, 3401 Investment Blvd., Ste. 7, Hayward, CA 94545-3819. TEL 510-783-8141. FAX 510-783-4131. *4561*

ANNALS OF PURE AND APPLIED LOGIC.
North-Holland, P.O. Box 211, 1000 AE Amsterdam, Netherlands. TEL 31-20-4853911. FAX 31-20-4853598. *4561*

ANNALS OF SAUDI MEDICINE.
King Faisal Specialist Hospital and Research Centre, P.O. Box 3354, Riyadh 11211, Saudi Arabia. TEL 966-1-4647272. FAX 966-1-4427237. *4638*

ANNALS OF SOFTWARE ENGINEERING.
Baltzer Science Publishers B.V., P.O. Box 221, 1400 AE Bussum, Netherlands. TEL 31-20-6370061. FAX 31-20-6323651. *2209*

ANNALS OF SURGERY.
Lippincott - Raven Publishers, 227 E. Washington Sq., Philadelphia, PA 19106. TEL 215-238-4200. FAX 215-238-4227. *5135*

ANNALS OF SURGICAL ONCOLOGY.
Lippincott - Raven Publishers, 227 E. Washington Sq., Philadelphia, PA 19106. TEL 215-238-4200. *5136*

ANNALS OF THE RHEUMATIC DISEASES.
B M J Publishing Group, B.M.A. House, Tavistock Sq., London WC1H 9JR, England. TEL 44-171-383-6270. FAX 44-171-383-6402. *5124*

ANNALS OF THEORETICAL PSYCHOLOGY.
Plenum Publishing Corp., 233 Spring St., New York, NY 10013-1578. TEL 212-670-8000. FAX 212-463-0742. *6093*

REFEREED SERIALS

ANNALS OF THORACIC SURGERY.
Elsevier Science Inc., Box 945, New York, NY 10159-0945. TEL 212-633-3730. FAX 212-633-3680. *5136*

ANNALS OF TOURISM RESEARCH.
Elsevier Science Ltd., Pergamon, P.O. Box 800, Kidlington, Oxford OX5 1DX, England. TEL 44-1865-843000. FAX 44-1865-843010. *7184*

ANNALS OF TROPICAL PAEDIATRICS.
Carfax Publishing Co., P.O. Box 25, Abingdon, Oxon. OX14 3UE, England. TEL 44-1235-401000. FAX 44-1235-401550. *5027*

ANNALS OF TROPICAL RESEARCH.
Visayas State College of Agriculture, Baybay, Leyte 6521-A, Philippines. TEL 53-335-2617. *98*

ANNUAL ALLERTON CONFERENCE ON COMMUNICATION, CONTROL AND COMPUTING.
University of Illinois at Urbana-Champaign, Coordinated Science Laboratory, 1308 W. Main St., Urbana, IL 61801-2306. TEL 217-333-0282. FAX 217-244-1653. *2808*

ANNUAL BIBLIOGRAPHY OF THE HISTORY OF THE PRINTED BOOK AND LIBRARY.
Kluwer Academic Publishers, Postbus 17, 3300 AA Dordrecht, Netherlands. TEL 31-78-6392392. FAX 31-78-6392254. *6087*

ANNUAL EDITIONS: AGING.
Dushkin Publishing Group, Sluice Dock, Guilford, CT 06437-9989. TEL 203-453-4351. FAX 203-453-6000. *3432*

ANNUAL EDITIONS: AMERICAN GOVERNMENT.
Dushkin Publishing Group, Sluice Dock, Guilford, CT 06437-9989. TEL 203-453-4351. FAX 203-453-6000. *5892*

ANNUAL EDITIONS: AMERICAN HISTORY.
Dushkin Publishing Group, Sluice Dock, Guilford, CT 06437-9989. TEL 203-453-4351. FAX 203-453-6000. *3617*

ANNUAL EDITIONS: ANTHROPOLOGY.
Dushkin Publishing Group, Sluice Dock, Guilford, CT 06437-9989. TEL 203-453-4351. FAX 203-453-6000. *307*

ANNUAL EDITIONS: BUSINESS ETHICS.
Dushkin Publishing Group, Sluice Dock, Guilford, CT 06437-9989. TEL 203-453-4351. FAX 203-543-6000. *932*

ANNUAL EDITIONS: CANADIAN POLITICS.
Dushkin Publishing Group, Sluice Dock, Guilford, CT 06437-9989. TEL 203-453-4351. FAX 203-453-6000. *5892*

ANNUAL EDITIONS: COMPARATIVE POLITICS.
Dushkin Publishing Group, Sluice Dock, Guilford, CT 06437-9989. TEL 203-453-4351. FAX 203-453-6000. *5892*

ANNUAL EDITIONS: CRIMINAL JUSTICE.
Dushkin Publishing Group, Sluice Dock, Guilford, CT 06437-9989. TEL 203-453-4351. FAX 203-453-6000. *2261*

ANNUAL EDITIONS: DEVELOPING THIRD WORLD.
Dushkin Publishing Group, Sluice Dock, Guilford, CT 06437-9989. TEL 203-453-4351. FAX 203-453-6000. *3394*

ANNUAL EDITIONS: EARLY CHILDHOOD EDUCATION.
Dushkin Publishing Group, Sluice Dock, Guilford, CT 06437-9989. TEL 203-453-4351. FAX 203-453-6000. *2421*

ANNUAL EDITIONS: ECONOMICS.
Dushkin Publishing Group, Sluice Dock, Guilford, CT 06437-9989. TEL 203-453-4351. FAX 203-453-6000. *932*

ANNUAL EDITIONS: EDUCATING EXCEPTIONAL CHILDREN.
Dushkin Publishing Group, Sluice Dock, Guilford, CT 06437-9989. TEL 203-453-4351. FAX 203-453-6000. *2581*

ANNUAL EDITIONS: EDUCATION.
Dushkin Publishing Group, Sluice Dock, Guilford, CT 06437-9989. TEL 203-453-4351. FAX 203-453-6000. *2421*

ANNUAL EDITIONS: EDUCATIONAL PSYCHOLOGY.
Dushkin Publishing Group, Sluice Dock, Guilford, CT 06437-9989. TEL 203-453-4351. FAX 203-453-6000. *6093*

ANNUAL EDITIONS: ENVIRONMENT.
Dushkin Publishing Group, Sluice Dock, Guilford, CT 06437-9989. TEL 203-453-4351. FAX 203-453-6000. *2906*

ANNUAL EDITIONS: GEOGRAPHY.
Dushkin Publishing Group, Sluice Dock, Guilford, CT 06437-9989. TEL 203-453-4351. FAX 203-453-6000. *3394*

ANNUAL EDITIONS: GLOBAL ISSUES.
Dushkin Publishing Group, Sluice Dock, Guilford, CT 06437-9989. TEL 203-453-4351. FAX 203-453-6000. *3394*

ANNUAL EDITIONS: HEALTH.
Dushkin Publishing Group, Sluice Dock, Guilford, CT 06437-9989. TEL 203-453-4351. FAX 203-453-6000. *5778*

ANNUAL EDITIONS: HUMAN DEVELOPMENT.
Dushkin Publishing Group, Sluice Dock, Guilford, CT 06437-9989. TEL 203-453-4351. FAX 203-453-6000. *812*

ANNUAL EDITIONS: HUMAN RESOURCES.
Dushkin Publishing Group, Sluice Dock, Guilford, CT 06437-9989. TEL 203-453-4351. FAX 203-453-6000. *6701*

ANNUAL EDITIONS: HUMAN SEXUALITY.
Dushkin Publishing Group, Sluice Dock, Guilford, CT 06437-9989. TEL 203-453-4351. FAX 203-453-6000. *586*

ANNUAL EDITIONS: INTERNATIONAL BUSINESS.
Dushkin Publishing Group, Sluice Dock, Guilford, CT 06437-9989. TEL 203-453-4351. FAX 203-453-6000. *1314*

ANNUAL EDITIONS: MACROECONOMICS.
Dushkin Publishing Group, Sluice Dock, Guilford, CT 06437-9989. TEL 203-453-4351. FAX 203-453-6000. *1459*

ANNUAL EDITIONS: MANAGEMENT.
Dushkin Publishing Group, Sluice Dock, Guilford, CT 06437-9989. TEL 203-453-4351. FAX 203-453-6000. *1465*

ANNUAL EDITIONS: MARKETING.
Dushkin Publishing Group, Sluice Dock, Guilford, CT 06437-9989. TEL 203-453-4351. FAX 203-453-6000. *1515*

ANNUAL EDITIONS: MARRIAGE AND FAMILY.
Dushkin Publishing Group, Sluice Dock, Guilford, CT 06437-9989. TEL 203-453-4351. FAX 203-453-6000. *4624*

ANNUAL EDITIONS: MICROECONOMICS.
Dushkin Publishing Group, Sluice Dock, Guilford, CT 06437-9989. TEL 203-453-4351. FAX 203-453-6000. *1296*

ANNUAL EDITIONS: MONEY AND BANKING.
Dushkin Publishing Group, Sluice Dock, Guilford, CT 06437-9989. TEL 203-453-4351. FAX 203-453-6000. *1103*

ANNUAL EDITIONS: NUTRITION.
Dushkin Publishing Group, Sluice Dock, Guilford, CT 06437-9989. TEL 203-453-4351. FAX 203-453-6000. *5469*

ANNUAL EDITIONS: PERSONAL GROWTH AND BEHAVIOR.
Dushkin Publishing Group, Sluice Dock, Guilford, CT 06437-9989. TEL 203-453-4351. FAX 203-453-6000. *6093*

ANNUAL EDITIONS: PSYCHOLOGY.
Dushkin Publishing Group, Sluice Dock, Guilford, CT 06437-9989. TEL 203-453-4351. FAX 203-453-6000. *6093*

ANNUAL EDITIONS: PUBLIC ADMINISTRATION.
Dushkin Publishing Group, Sluice Dock, Guilford, CT 06437-9989. TEL 203-453-4351. FAX 203-453-6000. *6163*

ANNUAL EDITIONS: RACE & ETHNIC RELATIONS.
Dushkin Publishing Group, Sluice Dock, Guilford, CT 06437-9989. TEL 203-453-4351. FAX 203-453-6000. *6701*

ANNUAL EDITIONS: SOCIAL PROBLEMS.
Dushkin Publishing Group, Sluice Dock, Guilford, CT 06437-9989. TEL 203-453-4351. FAX 203-453-6000. *6654*

ANNUAL EDITIONS: SOCIOLOGY.
Dushkin Publishing Group, Sluice Dock, Guilford, CT 06437-9989. TEL 203-453-4351. FAX 203-453-6000. *6701*

ANNUAL EDITIONS: STATE & LOCAL GOVERNMENT.
Dushkin Publishing Group, Sluice Dock, Guilford, CT 06437-9989. TEL 203-453-4351. FAX 203-453-6000. *6164*

ANNUAL EDITIONS: URBAN SOCIETY.
Dushkin Publishing Group, Sluice Dock, Guilford, CT 06437-9989. TEL 203-453-4351. FAX 203-453-6000. *6701*

ANNUAL EDITIONS: VIOLENCE AND TERRORISM.
Dushkin Publishing Group, Sluice Dock, Guilford, CT 06437-9989. TEL 203-453-4351. FAX 203-453-6000. *2261*

ANNUAL EDITIONS: WESTERN CIVILIZATION.
Dushkin Publishing Group, Sluice Dock, Guilford, CT 06437-9989. TEL 203-453-4351. FAX 203-453-6000. *3488*

ANNUAL EDITIONS: WORLD HISTORY.
Dushkin Publishing Group, Sluice Dock, Guilford, CT 06437-9989. TEL 203-453-4351. FAX 203-453-6000. *3488*

ANNUAL EDITIONS: WORLD POLITICS.
Dushkin Publishing Group, Sluice Dock, Guilford, CT 06437-9989. TEL 203-453-4351. FAX 203-453-6000. *6004*

ANNUAL OF ARMENIAN LINGUISTICS.
c/o John A.C. Greppin, Ed., Cleveland State University, Cleveland, OH 44115. TEL 216-687-3967. FAX 216-687-9214. *4240*

ANNUAL PROGRESS IN CHILD PSYCHIATRY AND CHILD DEVELOPMENT.
Brunner - Mazel, Inc., 19 Union Sq. W., New York, NY 10003. TEL 212-924-3344. FAX 212-242-6339. *5052*

ANNUAL REPORTS IN MEDICINAL CHEMISTRY.
Academic Press, Inc., 525 B St., Ste. 1900, San Diego, CA 92101-4495. TEL 619-231-0926. FAX 619-699-6715. *5647*

ANNUAL REPORTS IN ORGANIC SYNTHESIS.
Academic Press, Inc., 525 B St., Ste. 1900, San Diego, CA 92101-4495. TEL 619-231-0926. FAX 619-699-6715. *1825*

ANNUAL REPORTS ON N M R SPECTROSCOPY.
Academic Press, Inc., 525 B St., Ste. 1900, San Diego, CA 92101-4495. TEL 619-231-0926. FAX 619-699-6715. *5859*

ANNUAL REVIEW IN AUTOMATIC PROGRAMMING.
Elsevier Science Ltd., Pergamon, P.O. Box 800, Kidlington, Oxford OX5 1DX, England. TEL 44-1865-843000. FAX 44-1865-843010. *2142*

ANNUAL REVIEW OF BIOPHYSICS AND BIOMOLECULAR STRUCTURE.
Annual Reviews Inc., 4139 El Camino Way, Box 10139, Palo Alto, CA 94303-0139. TEL 650-493-4400. FAX 650-424-0910. *673*

ANNUAL REVIEW OF FISH DISEASES.
Elsevier Science Ltd., Pergamon, P.O. Box 800, Kidlington, Oxford OX5 1DX, England. TEL 44-1865-843000. FAX 44-1865-843010. *826*

ANNUAL REVIEW OF HEALTH SOCIAL SCIENCES.
University of New South Wales, School of Health Services Management, Sydney 2052, Australia. TEL 61-2-3852592. FAX 61-2-3851036. *6654*

ANNUAL REVIEW OF INFORMATION SCIENCE AND TECHNOLOGY.
Information Today, Inc., 143 Old Marlton Pike, Medford, NJ 08055. TEL 609-654-6266. FAX 609-654-4309. *4158*

ANNUAL REVIEW OF WOMEN IN WORLD RELIGIONS.
State University of New York Press, State University Plaza, Albany, NY 12246. TEL 518-472-5000. FAX 518-472-5038. *7340*

ANNUAL SIMULATION SYMPOSIUM. PROCEEDINGS.
Society for Computer Simulation, Box 17900, San Diego, CA 92177. TEL 619-277-3888. FAX 619-277-3930. *2151*

ANOTHER CHICAGO MAGAZINE.
Left Field Press, 3709 N. Kenmore, Chicago, IL 60613. FAX 773-248-7665. *4375*

ANTARCTIC.
New Zealand Antarctic Society, Box 404, Christchurch, New Zealand. TEL 64-3-3650344. FAX 64-3-3654255. *3395*

ANTARCTIC SCIENCE.
Blackwell Science Ltd., Osney Mead, Oxford OX2 0EL, England. TEL 44-1865-206206. FAX 44-1865-721205. *586*

ANTHROPOLOGIAI KOZLEMENYEK.
Magyar Biologiai Tarsasag, c/o Eotvos Lorand University, Dept. Anthropology, Puskin u. 3, 1088 Budapest, Hungary. TEL 36-1-2667857. *307*

ANTHROPOLOGICA.
Wilfrid Laurier University Press, 75 University Ave. W., Waterloo, ON N2L 3C5, Canada. TEL 519-884-0710. FAX 519-725-1399. *307*

ANTHROPOLOGICA.
Pontificia Universidad Catolica del Peru, Fondo Editorial, Apdo. 1761, Lima 32, Peru. TEL 51-14-626390. FAX 51-14-611785. *308*

ANTHROPOLOGICAL FORUM.
University of Western Australia, Department of Anthropology, Nedlands, W.A. 6007, Australia. TEL 61-9-3802851. FAX 61-9-3801062. *308*

ANTHROPOLOGICAL LINGUISTICS.
Indiana University, Anthropology Department, Student Services Bldg. Rm. 130, Bloomington, IN 47405. TEL 812-855-4123. FAX 812-855-7529. *4240*

ANTHROPOLOGIE ET SOCIETES.
Universite Laval, Department d'Anthropologie, Ste.-Foy, PQ G1K 7P4, Canada. TEL 418-656-3027. FAX 418-656-3284. *308*

ANTHROPOLOGY AND ARCHEOLOGY OF EURASIA.
M.E. Sharpe, Inc., 80 Business Park Dr., Armonk, NY 10504. TEL 914-273-1800. FAX 914-273-2106. *308*

ANTHROPOLOGY OF CONSCIOUSNESS.
American Anthropological Association, Society for the Anthropology of Consciousness, 4350 N. Fairfax Dr., Ste. 640, Arlington, VA 22203-1621. TEL 703-528-1902. *309*

ANTHROPOLOGY U C L A.
University of California at Los Angeles, Department of Anthropology, 405 Hilgard Ave., Los Angeles, CA 90024. TEL 310-825-2055. *309*

ANTHROZOOS.
Delta Society, 289 Perimeter Rd. E., Renton, WA 98055-1329. TEL 206-226-7357. FAX 206-235-1076. *309*

ANTI.
60 Dimocharous St., 115 21 Athens, Greece. TEL 30-1-723-2713. FAX 30-1-722-6107. *5892*

ANTI-CANCER DRUGS.
Rapid Science Publishers, The Old Malthouse, Paradise St., Oxford OX1 1LD, England. TEL 44-1865-790447. FAX 44-1865-244012. *4970*

ANTI-SLAVERY REPORTER.
Anti-Slavery International, The Stableyard, Broomgrove Rd., London SW9 9TL, England. TEL 44-171-924-9555. FAX 44-171-738-4110. *5988*

ANTIBIOTICS AND CHEMOTHERAPY.
S. Karger AG, Allschwilerstr. 10, P.O. Box, CH-4009 Basel, Switzerland. TEL 41-61-3061111. FAX 41-61-3061234. *5647*

ANTICANCER RESEARCH.
John G. Delinassios, Ed. & Pub, Km. 1, Kapandritiou-Kalamou, P.O. Box 22, 190 14 Kapandriti, Attiki, Greece. TEL 30-295-53389. FAX 30-295-53389. *4970*

ANTICHTHON.
Australian Society for Classical Studies, c/o Prof. G.R. Stanton, Ed., Dept. of Classics and Ancient History, University of New England, Armidale, N.S.W. 2351, Australia. FAX 61-67-73-3122. *1899*

ANTIETAM REVIEW.
Washington County Arts Council, 7 W. Franklin St., Hagerstown, MD 21740. TEL 301-791-3132. FAX 301-791-3132. *4376*

ANTIMICROBIAL AGENTS AND CHEMOTHERAPY.
American Society for Microbiology, 1325 Massachusetts Ave., N.W., Washington, DC 20005. TEL 202-737-3600. *780*

ANTIMICROBIAL AGENTS ANNUAL.
Elsevier Science B.V., Books Division, P.O. Box 211, 1000 AE Amsterdam, Netherlands. TEL 31-20-4853911. FAX 31-20-4853705. *780*

ANTIMICROBICS AND INFECTIOUS DISEASES NEWSLETTER.
Elsevier Science Inc., Box 945, New York, NY 10159-0945. TEL 212-633-3730. FAX 212-633-3680. *4832*

ANTITRUST LAW JOURNAL.
American Bar Association, Antitrust Law Section, 750 N. Lake Shore Dr., Chicago, IL 60611. TEL 312-988-5606. *4073*

ANTIVIRAL RESEARCH.
Elsevier Science B.V., P.O. Box 211, 1000 AE Amsterdam, Netherlands. TEL 31-20-4853911. FAX 31-20-4853598. *780*

ANTONIANUM.
Edizioni Antonianum, Via Merulana 124, 00185 Rome, Italy. TEL 39-6-70373462. FAX 39-6-70373605. *6450*

ANTONIE VAN LEEUWENHOEK.
Kluwer Academic Publishers, Postbus 17, 3300 AA Dordrecht, Netherlands. TEL 31-78-6392392. FAX 31-78-6392254. *780*

ANTROPOLOGIA PORTUGUESA.
Universidade de Coimbra, Museu e Laboratorio Antropologico, 3000 Coimbra, Portugal. TEL 351-39-23491. FAX 351-39-23491. *310*

ANTROPOLOGISKA STUDIER.
Antropologfoereningen vid Stockholms Universitet, Socialantropologiska Institutionen, S-106 91 Stockholm, Sweden. TEL 46-8-16-33-71. FAX 46-8-15-88-94. *310*

ANUARIO DE ESTUDIOS INDIGENAS.
Instituto de Estudios Indigenas, Dr. Felipe Flores 14, San Cristobal de las Casas, 29200 Chiapas, Mexico. FAX 83534. *310*

ANUARIO DE LETRAS.
Universidad Nacional Autonoma de Mexico, Instituto de Investigaciones Filologicas, Circuito Mario de la Cueva, Zona Cultural, Ciudad Universitaria, 04510 Mexico, D.F., Mexico. TEL 52-5-6652903. FAX 52-5-6657874. *4376*

ANUARIO ESTATISTICO DOS TRANSPORTES.
Empresa Brasileira de Planejamento de Transportes, G E I P O T, SAN Quadra 3 Blocos N-O, 70040-920 Brasilia DF, Brazil. FAX 061-224-8642. *7023*

ANXIETY.
John Wiley & Sons, Inc., Journals, 605 Third Ave., New York, NY 10158. TEL 212-850-6645. FAX 212-850-6021. *6094*

ANXIETY, STRESS AND COPING.
Gordon and Breach - Harwood Academic, Amsteldisk 166, 1st Fl., 1079 LH Amsterdam, Netherlands. *6094*

APHASIOLOGY.
Taylor & Francis Ltd., 1 Gunpowder Sq., London EC4A 3DE, England. TEL 44-171-583-0490. FAX 44-171-583-0585. *5052*

APIDOLOGIE.
Editions Scientifiques et Medicales Elsevier, 141 rue de Javel, 75747 Paris, France. TEL 33-1-45589022. *747*

APOPTOSIS (LONDON).
Rapid Science Publishers, 2-6 Boundary Row, London SE1 8HN, England. TEL 44-171-865-0198. FAX 44-171-410-6600. *736*

APORTES.
Asociacion de Administradores Gubernamentales, Av. Pte. Roque Saenza Pena 511, 7o, Of. 714, 1035 Buenos Aires C.F., Argentina. TEL 54-1-3439001. *6164*

APOSTROPHE.
Mr. Pillow's Press, 41 Canute Rd., Faversham, Kent ME13 8SH, England. TEL 44-1795-536185. *4503*

APOTHECARY.
Health Care Marketing Services, H C M S Inc., Box AP, Los Altos, CA 94023-0179. TEL 415-941-3955. FAX 415-941-2303. *5647*

APOTHEEKMANAGEMENT.
Mediselect B.V., Postbus 28091, 3828 ZH Hoogland, Netherlands. TEL 31-33-4808020. FAX 31-33-4805881. *5647*

APPALACHIAN JOURNAL.
Appalachian State University, Center for Appalachian Studies, Belk Library, Boone, NC 28608. TEL 704-262-4072. FAX 704-262-2553. *3617*

APPELTJES VAN HET MEETJESLAND.
Heemkundig Genootschap van het Meetjesland, Gentstraat 13, B-9971 Kaprijke (Lembeke), Belgium. TEL 091-3772854. *3548*

APPLICABLE ANALYSIS.
Gordon and Breach - Harwood Academic, Amsteldisk 166, 1st Fl., 1079 LH Amsterdam, Netherlands. *4561*

APPLICATIONES MATHEMATICAE.
Polska Akademia Nauk, Instytut Matematyczny, Dzial Wydawnictw, Ul. Sniadeckich 8, P.O. Box 137, 00-950 Warsaw, Poland. TEL 48-22-6282471. FAX 48-22-6293997. *4561*

APPLICATIONS OF FIBONACCI NUMBERS.
Kluwer Academic Publishers, Postbus 17, 3300 AA Dordrecht, Netherlands. TEL 31-78-6392392. FAX 31-78-6392254. *4561*

APPLIED ACOUSTICS.
Elsevier Science Ltd., P.O. Box 800, Kidlington, Oxford OX5 1DX, England. TEL 44-1865-843000. FAX 44-1865-843010. *5871*

APPLIED AND ENVIRONMENTAL MICROBIOLOGY.
American Society for Microbiology, 1325 Massachusetts Ave., N.W., Washington, DC 20005. TEL 202-737-3600. *780*

APPLIED ANIMAL BEHAVIOUR SCIENCE.
Elsevier Science B.V., P.O. Box 211, 1000 AE Amsterdam, Netherlands. TEL 31-20-4853911. FAX 31-20-4853598. *827*

APPLIED ARTIFICIAL INTELLIGENCE.
Taylor & Francis Inc., 1900 Frost Rd., Ste. 101, Bristol, PA 19007-1598. TEL 215-785-5800. FAX 215-785-5515. *2097*

APPLIED BIOCHEMISTRY AND BIOTECHNOLOGY.
Humana Press Inc., 999 Riverview Dr., Ste. 208, Totowa, NJ 07512-1165. TEL 201-256-1699. FAX 201-256-8341. *650*

APPLIED BIOCHEMISTRY AND MICROBIOLOGY.
Maik Nauka - Interperiodica, Mezhdunarodnyi Otdel, Ul. Profsoyuznaya, 90, 117864 Moscow, Russia. TEL 7-095-3360066. FAX 7-095-3360066. *650*

APPLIED CARDIOPULMONARY PATHOPHYSIOLOGY.
Kluwer Academic Publishers, Postbus 17, 3300 AA Dordrecht, Netherlands. TEL 31-78-6392392. FAX 31-78-6392254. *812*

APPLIED CATALYSIS A: GENERAL.
Elsevier Science B.V., P.O. Box 211, 1000 AE Amsterdam, Netherlands. TEL 31-20-4853911. FAX 31-20-4853598. *2755*

APPLIED CATALYSIS B: ENVIRONMENTAL.
Elsevier Science B.V., P.O. Box 211, 1000 AE Amsterdam, Netherlands. TEL 31-20-4853911. FAX 31-20-4853598. *2755*

APPLIED CATEGORICAL STRUCTURES.
Kluwer Academic Publishers, Postbus 17, 3300 AA Dordrecht, Netherlands. TEL 31-78-6392392. FAX 31-78-6392254. *4618*

APPLIED CLAY SCIENCE.
Elsevier Science B.V., P.O. Box 211, 1000 AE Amsterdam, Netherlands. TEL 31-20-4853911. FAX 31-20-4853598. *2331*

APPLIED COGNITIVE PSYCHOLOGY.
John Wiley & Sons Ltd., Journals, Baffins Ln., Chichester, W. Sussex PO19 1UD, England. TEL 44-1243-779777. FAX 44-1243-843232. *6094*

APPLIED COMPOSITE MATERIALS.
Kluwer Academic Publishers, Postbus 17, 3300 AA Dordrecht, Netherlands. TEL 31-78-6392392. FAX 31-78-6392254. *2855*

APPLIED COMPUTATIONAL ELECTROMAGNETICS SOCIETY JOURNAL.
Applied Computational Electromagnetics Society, Inc., c/o Prof. Richard W. Adler, Naval Postgraduate School, Code EC-AB, 833 Dyer Rd., Rm. 437, Monterey, CA 93943. TEL 408-646-1111. FAX 408-649-0300. *5838*

APPLIED COMPUTATIONAL ELECTROMAGNETICS SOCIETY NEWSLETTER.
Applied Computational Electromagnetics Society, Inc., c/o Prof. Richard W. Adler, Naval Postgraduate School, Code EC-AB, 833 Dyer Rd., Rm. 437, CA 93943. TEL 408-646-1111. FAX 408-649-0300. *5838*

APPLIED ECONOMICS.
Routledge, 11 New Fetter Ln., London EC4P 4EE, England. TEL 44-171-583-9855. FAX 44-171-842-2298. *933*

APPLIED ECONOMICS LETTERS.
Routledge, 11 New Fetter Ln., London EC4P 4EE, England. TEL 44-171-583-9855. FAX 44-171-842-2298. *933*

APPLIED ENERGY.
Elsevier Science Ltd., P.O. Box 800, Kidlington, Oxford OX5 1DX, England. TEL 44-1865-843000. FAX 44-1865-843010. *2660*

APPLIED ENGINEERING IN AGRICULTURE.
American Society of Agricultural Engineers, 2950 Niles Rd., St. Joseph, MI 49085-9659. TEL 616-429-0300. FAX 616-429-3852. *99*

APPLIED ENTOMOLOGY AND PHYTOPATHOLOGY.
Plant Pests and Diseases Research Institute, P.O. Box 1454, Tehran 19395, Iran. TEL 98-21-2403012. *747*

APPLIED ERGONOMICS.
Elsevier Science Ltd., P.O. Box 800, Kidlington, Oxford OX5 1DX, England. TEL 44-1865-843000. FAX 44-1865-843010. *2710*

APPLIED FINANCIAL ECONOMICS.
Routledge, 11 New Fetter Ln., London EC4P 4EE, England. TEL 44-171-583-9855. FAX 44-171-842-2298. *1221*

APPLIED GEOCHEMISTRY.
Elsevier Science Ltd., Pergamon, P.O. Box 800, Kidlington, Oxford OX5 1DX, England. TEL 44-1865-843000. FAX 44-1865-843010. *2331*

APPLIED GEOGRAPHY.
Elsevier Science Ltd., Pergamon, P.O. Box 800, Kidlington, Oxford OX5 1DX, England. TEL 44-1865-843000. FAX 44-1865-843010. *3395*

APPLIED H.R.M. RESEARCH.
Society of I-O Graduates, Department of Psychology, Radford University, Radford, VA 24142. TEL 540-831-5513. *6094*

APPLIED INTELLIGENCE.
Kluwer Academic Publishers Boston, Box 358, Accord Sta., Hingham, MA 02018-0358. TEL 617-871-6600. FAX 617-871-6528. *2097*

APPLIED LANGUAGE LEARNING.
Defense Language Institute, Foreign Language Center, AP-AY, Presidio, Monterey, CA 93944-5006. TEL 408-242-5638. FAX 408-242-7214. *4241*

APPLIED MATHEMATICAL FINANCE.
Thomson Professional, 2-6 Boundary Row, London SE1 8HN, England. TEL 44-171-8650066. FAX 44-171-5229623. *4562*

APPLIED MATHEMATICAL MODELLING.
Elsevier Science Inc., Box 945, New York, NY 10159-0945. TEL 212-633-3730. FAX 212-633-3680. *4619*

APPLIED MATHEMATICS.
Gordon and Breach - Harwood Academic, Amsteldisk 166, 1st Fl., 1079 LH Amsterdam, Netherlands. *4562*

APPLIED MATHEMATICS AND COMPUTATION.
Elsevier Science Inc., Box 945, New York, NY 10159-0945. TEL 212-633-3730. FAX 212-633-3680. *4562*

APPLIED MATHEMATICS AND MECHANICS.
Academic Press, Inc., 525 B St., Ste. 1900, San Diego, CA 92101-4495. TEL 619-231-0926. FAX 619-699-6715. *4562*

APPLIED MATHEMATICS AND OPTIMIZATION.
Springer-Verlag, Science Journals, 175 Fifth Ave., New York, NY 10010. TEL 212-460-1500. FAX 212-473-6272. *4562*

APPLIED MATHEMATICS LETTERS.
Elsevier Science Ltd., Pergamon, P.O. Box 800, Kidlington, Oxford OX5 1DX, England. TEL 44-1865-843000. FAX 44-1865-843010. *4562*

APPLIED MEASUREMENT IN EDUCATION.
Lawrence Erlbaum Associates, Inc., 10 Industrial Dr., Mahwah, NJ 07430-2262. TEL 201-236-9500. FAX 201-236-0072. *2421*

APPLIED MECHANICS REVIEWS.
American Society of Mechanical Engineers, 22 Law Dr., Fairfield, NJ 07007-2900. TEL 973-882-1167. FAX 973-882-1717. *2747*

APPLIED NEUROPSYCHOLOGY.
Lawrence Erlbaum Associates, Inc., 10 Industrial Ave., Mahwah, NJ 07430-2262. TEL 201-236-9500. FAX 201-236-0072. *5052*

APPLIED NUMERICAL MATHEMATICS.
North-Holland, P.O. Box 211, 1000 AE Amsterdam, Netherlands. TEL 31-20-4853911. FAX 31-20-4853598. *4619*

APPLIED OCEAN RESEARCH.
Elsevier Science Ltd., P.O. Box 800, Kidlington, Oxford OX5 1DX, England. TEL 44-1865-843000. FAX 44-1865-843010. *2399*

APPLIED OPTICS.
Optical Society of America, Inc., 2010 Massachusetts Ave., N.W., Washington, DC 20036-1023. TEL 202-223-8130. FAX 202-223-1096. *5859*

APPLIED PSYCHOLINGUISTICS AND COMMUNICATION DISORDERS.
Plenum Publishing Corp., 233 Spring St., New York, NY 10013-1578. TEL 212-620-8000. FAX 212-463-0742. *4241*

APPLIED PSYCHOLOGICAL MEASUREMENT.
Sage Publications, Inc., 2455 Teller Rd., Thousand Oaks, CA 91320. TEL 805-449-0721. FAX 805-499-0871. *6094*

APPLIED PSYCHOLOGY.
Taylor & Francis Ltd., Psychology Press, 1 Gunpowder Sq., London EC4A 3DE, England. TEL 44-171-5830490. FAX 44-171-5830585. *6094*

APPLIED PSYCHOPHYSIOLOGY AND BIOFEEDBACK.
Plenum Publishing Corp., 233 Spring St., New York, NY 10013-1578. TEL 212-620-8000. FAX 212-463-0742. *6094*

APPLIED RADIATION AND ISOTOPES.
Elsevier Science Ltd., Pergamon, P.O. Box 800, Kidlington, Oxford OX5 1DX. TEL 44-1865-843000. FAX 44-1865-843010. *5850*

APPLIED RADIOLOGY.
1301 W. Park Ave., Ocean, NJ 07712-3151. TEL 908-695-0600. FAX 908-695-9501. *5103*

APPLIED SEMIOTICS.
University of Toronto, Department of French, 50 St. Joseph St., Toronto, ON M4S 1J4, Canada. *4241*

APPLIED SOIL ECOLOGY.
Elsevier Science B.V., P.O. Box 211, 1000 AE Amsterdam, Netherlands. TEL 31-20-4853911. FAX 31-20-4853598. *213*

APPLIED SOLAR ENERGY.
Allerton Press, Inc., 150 Fifth Ave., New York, NY 10011. TEL 212-924-3950. FAX 212-463-9684. *2705*

APPLIED SPECTROSCOPY.
Society for Applied Spectroscopy, 201B Broadway St., Frederick, MD 21701. TEL 301-694-8122. FAX 301-694-6860. *5859*

APPLIED SPECTROSCOPY REVIEWS.
Marcel Dekker Journals, 270 Madison Ave., New York, NY 10016. TEL 212-696-9000. FAX 212-685-4540. *5859*

APPLIED STOCHASTIC MODELS AND DATA ANALYSIS.
John Wiley & Sons Ltd., Journals, Baffins Ln., Chichester, W. Sussex PO19 1UD, England. TEL 44-1243-779777. FAX 44-1243-775878. *4562*

APPLIED SUPERCONDUCTIVITY.
Elsevier Science Ltd., Pergamon, P.O. Box 800, Kidlington, Oxford OX5 1DX, England. TEL 44-1865-843000. FAX 44-1865-843010. *2809*

APPLIED SURFACE SCIENCE.
North-Holland, P.O. Box 211, 1000 AE Amsterdam, Netherlands. TEL 31-20-4853911. FAX 31-20-4853598. *5186*

APPLIED THERMAL ENGINEERING.
Elsevier Science Ltd., Pergamon, P.O. Box 800, Kidlington, Oxford OX5 1DX, England. TEL 44-1865-843000. FAX 44-1865-843010. *5839*

APPLIED VIROLOGY RESEARCH.
Plenum Publishing Corp., 233 Spring St., New York, NY 10013-1578. TEL 212-620-8000. FAX 212-463-0742. *781*

APPRAISAL JOURNAL.
Appraisal Institute, 875 N. Michigan Ave., Ste. 2400, Chicago, IL 60611-1980. TEL 312-335-4100. FAX 312-353-4400. *6294*

APPRENTISSAGE ET SOCIALISATION.
Universite du Quebec a Hull, C.P. 1250, succ. B, Hull, PQ J8X 3X7, Canada. TEL 819-595-4475. FAX 819-595-4476. *2581*

APPROPRIATE TECHNOLOGY.
Intermediate Technology Publications Ltd., 103-105 Southampton Row, London WC1B 4HH, England. TEL 44-171-436-9761. FAX 44-171-436-2013. *189*

APPROXIMATION THEORY AND ITS APPLICATIONS.
Baltzer Science Publishers B.V., P.O. Box 221, 1400 AE Bussum, Netherlands. TEL 31-20-6370061. FAX 31-20-6323654. *4562*

APUNTES.
Universidad Catolica de Chile, Escuela de Teatro, Jaime Guzman Errazuriz 3300, Santiago, Chile. TEL 56-2-2744041. FAX 56-2-2232577. *7001*

APUNTES DE INGENIERIA.
Pontificia Universidad Catolica de Chile, Escuela de Ingenieria, Casilla 306, Correo 22, Santiago, Chile. TEL 562-552-2375. FAX 562-552-4054. *2710*

AQUA.
Blackwell Science Ltd., Osney Mead, Oxford OX2 0EL, England. TEL 44-1865-206206. FAX 44-1865-721205. *7287*

AQUACULTURAL ENGINEERING.
Elsevier Science Ltd., P.O. Box 800, Kidlington, Oxford OX5 1DX, England. TEL 44-1865-843000. FAX 44-1865-843010. *3060*

AQUACULTURE.
Elsevier Science B.V., P.O. Box 211, 1000 AE Amsterdam, Netherlands. TEL 31-20-4853911. FAX 31-20-4853598. *3061*

AQUACULTURE INTERNATIONAL.
Thomson Science, 2-6 Boundary Row, London SE1 8HN, England. TEL 44-171-8650066. FAX 44-171-8659623. *3061*

AQUACULTURE IRELAND.
P.O. Box 12, B.I.M. Bldg., Crofton Rd., Dun Laoghaire, Co. Dublin, Ireland. TEL 01-2841544. FAX 01-2841123. *3061*

AQUACULTURE NUTRITION.
Blackwell Science Ltd., Osney Mead, Oxford OX2 0EL, England. TEL 44-1865-206206. FAX 44-1865-721205. *3061*

AQUACULTURE RESEARCH.
Blackwell Science Ltd., Osney Mead, Oxford OX2 0EL, England. TEL 44-1865-206206. FAX 44-1865-721205. *3061*

AQUARIUM SCIENCES AND CONSERVATION.
Thomson Science, 2-6 Boundary Row, London SE1 8HN, England. TEL 44-171-865-0066. FAX 44-171-5229623. *3061*

AQUATIC BOTANY.
Elsevier Science B.V., P.O. Box 211, 1000 AE Amsterdam, Netherlands. TEL 31-20-4853911. FAX 31-20-4853598. *692*

AQUATIC CONSERVATION: MARINE AND FRESHWATER ECOSYSTEMS.
John Wiley & Sons Ltd., Journals, Baffins Ln., Chichester, W. Sussex PO19 1UD, England. TEL 44-1243-779777. FAX 44-1243-775878. *2222*

AQUATIC GEOCHEMISTRY.
Kluwer Academic Publishers, Postbus 17, 3300 AA Dordrecht, Netherlands. TEL 31-78-6392392. FAX 31-78-6392254. *2310*

AQUATIC MAMMALS.
European Association for Aquatic Mammals, Hawaii Institute of Marine Biology, Box 1106, Kailua, HI 96734. TEL 808-236-4001. FAX 808-247-5831. *827*

AQUATIC PLANT STUDIES.
Elsevier Science B.V., Books Division, P.O. Box 211, 1000 AE Amsterdam, Netherlands. TEL 31-20-4853911. FAX 31-20-4853705. *692*

AQUATIC TOXICOLOGY.
Elsevier Science B.V., P.O. Box 211, 1000 AE Amsterdam, Netherlands. TEL 31-20-4853911. FAX 31-20-4853598. *2974*

AQUILO. SERIE BOTANICA.
Societas Amicorum Naturae Ouluensis, Department of Botany, University of Oulu, Linnanmaa, FIN-90570 Oulu, Finland. TEL 358-8-553-1546. FAX 358-981-553-1500. *692*

AQUINIAN.
Saint Thomas University, Student Union Bldg., Rm. 32, Fredericton, NB E3B 5G3, Canada, Canada. TEL 506-460-0300. FAX 506-453-4538. *1939*

ARABIAN ARCHAEOLOGY AND EPIGRAPHY.
Munksgaard International Publishers Ltd., 35 Noerre Soegade, P.O. Box 2148, DK-1016 Copenhagen K, Denmark. TEL 45-33-127370. FAX 45-33-129387. *348*

ARABIAN JOURNAL FOR SCIENCE AND ENGINEERING.
King Fahd University of Petroleum and Minerals, P.O. Box 5033, Dhahran 31231, Saudi Arabia. FAX 966-3-860-5458. *2710*

ARABICA.
E.J. Brill, P.O. Box 9000, 2300 PA Leiden, Netherlands. TEL 31-71-5353500. FAX 31-71-5317532. *5520*

ARACHNE.
Arachne, Inc., 2363 Page Rd., Kennedy, NY 14747. *4503*

ARBEITEN ZUR GESCHICHTE DES ANTIKEN JUDENTUMS UND DES URCHRISTENTUMS.
E.J. Brill, P.O. Box 9000, 2300 PA Leiden, Netherlands. TEL 31-71-5353500. FAX 31-71-5317532. *6402*

ARBEJDERHISTORIE.
Selskabet til Forskning i Arbejderbevaegelsens Historie, Noerrebrogade 66 D, Ed.Bd., Denmark. TEL 45-35-361522. FAX 45-35-363222. *1418*

ARBEJDSMILJOE.
Arbejdsmiljoefondet, Vermundsgade 38, 2100 Copenhagen, Denmark. TEL 45-39-16-05-00. FAX 45-39-16-05-80. *5486*

ARBETARHISTORIA.
Arbetarroerelsens Arkiv och Bibliotek, P.O. Box 1124, S-111 81 Stockholm, Sweden. TEL 46-8-45-46-517. FAX 46-8-21-55-60. *3886*

ARCADE.
Ecrits des Forges, c/o Diffusion Collective Radisson, 1497 Laviolette, C.P. 335, Trois-Rivieres, PQ G9A 5G4, Canada. TEL 819-379-9813. FAX 819-376-0774. *4503*

ARCHAEOASTRONOMY.
Center for Archaeoastronomy, Box X, College Park, MD 20740-1024. TEL 301-864-6637. *349*

ARCHAEOASTRONOMY.
Science History Publications Ltd., 16 Rutherford Rd., Cambridge CB2 2HH, England. TEL 44-1223-565532. FAX 44-1223-565532. *488*

ARCHAEOLOGIA.
Society of Antiquaries of London, Burlington House, London W1V 0HS, England. FAX 44-171-287-6967. *349*

ARCHAEOLOGIA JAPONICA.
Japanese Archaeological Association, 5-15-5 Hirai, Edogawa-ku, Tokyo J-132, Japan. TEL 81-3-3618-6608. FAX 81-3-3618-6625. *349*

ARCHAEOLOGICAL EXPLORATION OF SARDIS. MONOGRAPHS.
Harvard University Art Museums, Sardis Exploration Office, 7 Sumner Rd., Cambridge, MA 02138. TEL 617-495-3940. *349*

ARCHAEOLOGICAL JOURNAL.
Royal Archaeological Institute, c/o Society of Antiquaries, Burlington House, Picadilly, London W1V 0HS, England. *349*

ARCHAEOLOGICAL PROSPECTION.
John Wiley & Sons Ltd., Journals, Baffins Ln., Chichester, W. Sussex PO19 1UD, England. TEL 44-1243-779777. FAX 44-1243-775878. *349*

ARCHAEOLOGY.
Archaeological Institute of America, 135 William St., New York, NY 10038. TEL 212-732-5154. FAX 212-732-5707. *351*

ARCHEOGRAFO TRIESTINO.
Societa di Minerva, c/o Biblioteca Civica "Attilio Hortis", Piazza Attilio Hortis 4, 34123 Trieste, Italy. TEL 39-40-301214. *352*

ARCHEOLOGICAL SOCIETY OF VIRGINIA. QUARTERLY BULLETIN.
A S V Press, Box 70395, Richmond, VA 23255-0395. TEL 804-273-9291. FAX 804-273-0885. *352*

ARCHEOLOGIE IN LIMBURG.
Limburgs Geschied- en Oudheidkundig Genootschap, Sectie Archeologie, Postbus 83, 6200 AB Maastricht, Netherlands. TEL 31-43-3212586. FAX 31-43-3218572. *352*

ARCHIMAGE.
University of Wisconsin at Milwaukee, School of Architecture and Urban Planning, Box 413, Milwaukee, WI 53201. TEL 414-229-4014. *393*

ARCHITETTURA CRONACHE E STORIA.
Via Nomentana 150, 00162 Rome, Italy. TEL 39-6-86320684. FAX 39-6-8603662. *396*

ARCHITRONIC.
Kent State University, School of Architecture and Environmental Design, Kent, OH 44242-0001. TEL 330-672-2869. FAX 330-672-3809. *396*

ARCHIVAL ISSUES.
Midwest Archives Conference, c/o Becky Haglund Tousey, Kraft Inc., Archives Dept., 6350 Kirk St., Morton Grove, IL 60053. *3489*

ARCHIVES AND MUSEUM INFORMATICS.
Kluwer Academic Publishers, Postbus 17, 3300 AA Dordrecht, Netherlands. TEL 31-78-6392392. FAX 31-78-6392254. *4229*

ARCHIVES BELGES DE SANTE PUBLIQUE.
Archives de Medecine Sociale et d'Hygiene, Cite Administrative de l'Etat, Quartier Esplanade, No.6, 1010 Brussels, Belgium. TEL 32-2-6425029. FAX 32-2-6425410. *6228*

ARCHIVES DES MALADIES DU COEUR ET DES VAISSEAUX.
Editions J.B. Bailliere, 46 rue La Boetie, 75379 Paris Cedex 08, France. TEL 33-1-49536900. FAX 33-1-45631016. *4810*

ARCHIVES DES MALADIES DU COEUR ET DES VAISSEAUX - PRATIQUE.
Editions J.B. Bailliere, 46 rue La Boetie, 75379 Paris Cedex 08, France. TEL 33-1-49536900. FAX 33-1-45631016. *4810*

ARCHIVES DES SCIENCES ET COMPTE RENDU DES SEANCES DE LA SOCIETE DE PHYSIQUE ET D'HISTOIRE NATURELLE DE GENEVE.
Societe de Physique et d'Histoire Naturelle de Geneve, Museum d'Histoire Naturelle, Case Postale 6434, CH-1211 Geneva 6, Switzerland. TEL 41-22-4186321. FAX 41-22-4186301. *6512*

ARCHIVES ET BIBLIOTHEQUES DE BELGIQUE.
Archives et Bibliotheques de Belgique a.s.b.l., Boulevard de l'Empereur 4, B-1000 Brussels, Belgium. *3549*

ARCHIVES INTERNATIONALES D'HISTOIRE DES IDEES.
Kluwer Academic Publishers, Postbus 17, 3300 AA Dordrecht, Netherlands. TEL 31-78-6392392. FAX 31-78-6392254. *5718*

ARCHIVES ITALIENNES DE BIOLOGIE.
Universita degli Studi di Pisa, Rettorato, Lungarno A. Pacinotti 43, Pisa, Italy. TEL 39-50-920111. FAX 39-50-40834. *5052*

ARCHIVES OF ANDROLOGY.
Taylor & Francis Inc., 1900 Frost Rd., Ste. 101, Bristol, PA 19007-1598. TEL 215-785-5800. FAX 215-785-5515. *4639*

ARCHIVES OF ASIAN ART.
Asia Society, 725 Park Ave., New York, NY 10021-5088. TEL 212-517-8315. FAX 212-288-6400. *422*

ARCHIVES OF BIOCHEMISTRY AND BIOPHYSICS.
Academic Press, Inc., Journal Division, 525 B St., Ste. 1900, San Diego, CA 92101-4495. TEL 619-230-1840. FAX 619-699-6800. *651*

ARCHIVES OF CLINICAL NEUROPSYCHOLOGY.
Elsevier Science Ltd., Pergamon, P.O. Box 800, Kidlington, Oxford OX5 1DX, England. TEL 44-1865-843000. FAX 44-1865-843010. *5052*

ARCHIVES OF DERMATOLOGY.
American Medical Association, 515 N. State St., Chicago, IL 60610. TEL 312-464-5000. FAX 617-667-4948. *4875*

ARCHIVES OF DISEASE IN CHILDHOOD.
B M J Publishing Group, B.M.A. House, Tavistock Sq., London WC1H 9JR, England. TEL 44-171-383-6270. FAX 44-171-383-6402. *5027*

ARCHIVES OF DISEASE IN CHILDHOOD. FETAL AND NEONATAL EDITION.
B M J Publishing Group, B.M.A. House, Tavistock Sq., London WC1H 9JR, England. TEL 44-171-387-4499. FAX 44-171-383-6661. *4953*

REFEREED SERIALS

ARCHIVES OF ENVIRONMENTAL HEALTH.
Heldref Publications, 1319 Eighteenth St., N.W., Washington, DC 20036-1802. TEL 202-296-6267. FAX 202-296-5149. *4640*

ARCHIVES OF FAMILY MEDICINE.
American Medical Association, 515 N. State St., Chicago, IL 60610. TEL 312-464-5000. FAX 312-464-5831. *4640*

ARCHIVES OF GENERAL PSYCHIATRY.
American Medical Association, 515 N. State St., Chicago, IL 60610. TEL 312-464-5000. FAX 312-464-5831. *5052*

ARCHIVES OF GERONTOLOGY AND GERIATRICS.
Elsevier Science Ireland Ltd., P.O. Box 85, Limerick, Ireland. TEL 353-61-471944. FAX 353-61-472144. *3432*

ARCHIVES OF GERONTOLOGY AND GERIATRICS. SUPPLEMENT.
Elsevier Science Ireland Ltd., P.O. Box 85, Limerick, Ireland. TEL 353-61-471944. FAX 353-61-472144. *3432*

ARCHIVES OF GYNECOLOGY AND OBSTETRICS.
Springer-Verlag, Heidelberger Platz 3, 14197 Berlin, Germany. TEL 49-30-82787-0. FAX 49-30-82787448. *4953*

ARCHIVES OF HYDROENGINEERING AND ENVIRONMENTAL MECHANICS.
Polska Akademia Nauk, Instytut Budownictwa Wodnego, Ul. Koscierska 7, 80-952 Gdansk-Oliwa, Poland. TEL 48-58-522011. FAX 48-58-524211. *7288*

ARCHIVES OF INSECT BIOCHEMISTRY AND PHYSIOLOGY.
John Wiley & Sons, Inc., Journals, 605 Third Ave., New York, NY 10158. TEL 212-850-6645. FAX 212-850-6021. *747*

ARCHIVES OF INTERNAL MEDICINE.
American Medical Association, 515 N. State St., Chicago, IL 60610. TEL 312-464-5000. FAX 312-464-5831. *4924*

ARCHIVES OF MEDICAL RESEARCH.
Instituto Mexicano del Seguro Social, Oficina de Bibliotecas y Divulgacion, Apdo. 73-032, 06720 Mexico D.F., Mexico. TEL 52-5-7611503. *4640*

ARCHIVES OF NATURAL HISTORY.
Society for the History of Natural History, c/o The Natural History Museum, Cromwell Rd., London SW7 5BD, England. *6512*

ARCHIVES OF NEUROLOGY.
American Medical Association, 515 N. State St., Chicago, IL 60610. TEL 312-464-5000. FAX 312-464-5831. *5053*

ARCHIVES OF OPHTHALMOLOGY.
American Medical Association, 515 N. State St., Chicago, IL 60610. TEL 312-464-5000. FAX 312-464-5831. *4990*

ARCHIVES OF ORAL BIOLOGY.
Elsevier Science Ltd., Pergamon, P.O. Box 800, Kidlington, Oxford OX5 1DX, England. TEL 44-1865-843000. FAX 44-1865-843010. *4850*

ARCHIVES OF OTOLARYNGOLOGY - HEAD & NECK SURGERY.
American Medical Association, 515 N. State St., Chicago, IL 60610. TEL 312-464-5000. FAX 312-464-5831. *5020*

ARCHIVES OF PATHOLOGY & LABORATORY MEDICINE.
College of American Pathologists, 325 Waukegan Rd., Northfield, IL 60093-2750. TEL 847-832-7000. FAX 847-832-8150. *4640*

ARCHIVES OF PEDIATRICS & ADOLESCENT MEDICINE.
American Medical Association, 515 N. State St., Chicago, IL 60610. TEL 312-464-5000. FAX 312-464-4181. *5028*

ARCHIVES OF PHARMACAL RESEARCH.
Pharmaceutical Society of Korea, 1489-3 Suhcho-3-dong, Suhcho-gu, Seoul 137-073, S. Korea. TEL 02-584-3257. FAX 02-521-1781. *5648*

ARCHIVES OF PHYSICAL MEDICINE AND REHABILITATION.
W.B. Saunders Co., Curtis Center, 3rd Fl., Independence Sq. W., Philadelphia, PA 19106-3399. TEL 215-238-7800. FAX 215-238-6445. *5042*

ARCHIVES OF PHYSIOLOGY AND BIOCHEMISTRY.
Swets & Zeitlinger bv, P.O. Box 825, 2160 SZ Lisse, Netherlands. TEL 31-252-435111. FAX 31-252-415888. *813*

ARCHIVES OF PSYCHIATRIC NURSING.
W.B. Saunders Co., Curtis Center, 3rd Fl., Independence Sq. W., Philadelphia, PA 19106-3399. TEL 215-238-7800. FAX 215-238-6445. *4929*

ARCHIVES OF S T D - HIV RESEARCH.
Reproductive Health Center, 78 Surfsong Rd., Kiawah Island, SC 29455. TEL 803-768-5556. FAX 803-768-6494. *4833*

ARCHIVES OF SEXUAL BEHAVIOR.
Plenum Publishing Corp., 233 Spring St., New York, NY 10013-1578. TEL 212-620-8000. FAX 212-463-0742. *4640*

ARCHIVES OF SOVIET SCIENCE SERIES: PHYSICAL SCIENCES SECTION.
Gordon and Breach - Harwood Academic, Amsteldisk 166, 1st Fl., 1079 LH Amsterdam, Netherlands. *5850*

ARCHIVES OF SUICIDE RESEARCH.
Kluwer Academic Publishers, Postbus 17, 3300 AA Dordrecht, Netherlands. TEL 31-78-6392392. FAX 31-78-6392254. *6095*

ARCHIVES OF SURGERY.
American Medical Association, 515 N. State St., Chicago, IL 60610. TEL 312-464-5000. FAX 312-464-5831. *5136*

ARCHIVIO GEOBOTANICO.
Universita di Pavia, Dipartimento di Ecologia del Territorio, Via S. Epifanio 14, 27100 Pavia, Italy. TEL 39-382-23069. FAX 39-382-34240. *693*

ARCHIVIO TRENTINO.
Museo Storico in Trento, Trento Castello Buon Consiglio, Via Bernardo Clesio 3, 38100 Trento, Italy. TEL 39-461-230482. FAX 39-461-237418. *3549*

ARCHIVO DE FILOLOGIA ARAGONESA.
Institucion Fernando el Catolico, Plaza de Espana 2, 50071 Zaragoza, Spain. TEL 34-976-288878. FAX 34-976-288869. *4242*

ARCHIVO ESPANOL DE ARTE.
Consejo Superior de Investigaciones Cientificas (C.S.I.C.), Centro de Estudios Historicos, Vitruvio 8, 28006 Madrid, Spain. TEL 34-1-5612833. FAX 34-1-5629634. *423*

ARCHIVOS DE MEDICINA VETERINARIA.
Universidad Austral de Chile, Facultad de Ciencias Veterinarias, Casilla 567, Valdivia, Chile. TEL 56-63-221690. FAX 56-63-221480. *7266*

ARCHIVOS DE ZOOTECNIA.
Instituto de Zootecnia, Facultad de Veterinaria, Avda. de Medina Azahara, 9, 14005 Cordoba, Spain. TEL 34-57-218743. FAX 34-57-218666. *269*

ARCHIVOS ESPANOLES DE UROLOGIA.
Iniestares, S.A., C. San Gregorio 8, 3o Pta. 4, 28004 Madrid, Spain. TEL 34-1-3196001. FAX 34-1-3197768. *5159*

ARCHIWUM MEDYCYNY SADOWEJ I KRIMINOLOGII.
Polskie Towarzystwo Medycyny Sadowej i Kryminologii, Ul. Grzegorzecka 16, 31-531 Krakow, Poland. TEL 48-12-211113. *4903*

ARCHIWUM MINERALOGICZNE.
Polska Akademia Nauk, Instytut Nauk Geologicznych, Ul. Zwirki Wigury 93, 02-089 Warsaw, Poland. TEL 48-22-221065. FAX 48-22-221065. *2331*

ARCHIWUM NAUKI O MATERIALACH.
Wydawnictwo Uniwersytetu Slaskiego, Ul. Bankowa 12B, 40-007 Katowice, Poland. TEL 48-32-596929. *2856*

ARCTIC.
Arctic Institute of North America, University of Calgary, MLT 11th Fl., 2500 University Dr. N.W., Calgary, AB T2N 1N4, Canada. TEL 403-220-7518. FAX 403-282-4609. *6512*

ARCTIC AND ALPINE RESEARCH.
University of Colorado, Institute of Arctic and Alpine Research, Campus Box 450, Boulder, CO 80309-0450. TEL 303-492-3765. FAX 303-492-6388. *6513*

ARCTIC ANTHROPOLOGY.
University of Wisconsin Press, Journal Division, 114 N. Murray St., Madison, WI 53715. TEL 608-262-4952. FAX 608-262-7560. *310*

ARCTIC RESEARCH OF THE UNITED STATES.
National Science Foundation, Office of Polar Programs, 4201 Wilson Blvd., Arlington, VA 22230. TEL 703-306-1029. FAX 703-306-0648. *6513*

ARENA MAGAZINE.
Arena Printing and Publications Pty. Ltd., P.O. Box 18, N. Carlton, Vic. 3054, Australia. TEL 61-3-416-0232. FAX 61-3-415-1301. *5892*

ARETE.
Pontificia Universidad Catolica del Peru, Fondo Editorial, Apdo. 1761, Lima 32, Peru. TEL 51-14-626390. FAX 5114-611785. *3772*

ARGENTINA. MUSEO PROVINCIAL DE CIENCIAS NATURALES. COMUNICACIONES.
Ministerio de Educacion y Cultura, Museo Provincial de Ciencias Naturales, Primera Junta 2859, 3000 Santa Fe, Argentina. TEL 54-42-523843. FAX 54-42-523843. *587*

ARGONAUTA.
Associazione Malacologica Internazionale, Casella Postale 322, 00126 Acilia (Rome), Italy. TEL 39-6-5259331. *827*

ARGUMENTATION.
Kluwer Academic Publishers, Postbus 17, 3300 AA Dordrecht, Netherlands. TEL 31-78-6392392. FAX 31-78-6392254. *5718*

ARGUS (BLOOMINGTON).
Illinois Wesleyan University, Box 2900, Bloomington, IL 61702. TEL 309-556-3036. *1940*

ARI.
Springer-Verlag, Heidelberger Platz 3, 14197 Berlin, Germany. TEL 49-30-82787-0. FAX 49-30-82787448. *2331*

ARID SOIL RESEARCH AND REHABILITATION.
Taylor & Francis Ltd., 1 Gunpowder Sq., London EC4A 3DE, England. TEL 44-171-583-0490. FAX 44-171-583-0585. *214*

ARIEL.
University of Sindh, Department of English, Jamshoro, Sindh, Pakistan. TEL 92-221-771681. *4377*

ARIEL (ENGLISH EDITION).
Youval Tal Ltd., P.O. Box 2160, Jerusalem 91021, Israel. FAX 972-2-5380626. *3772*

ARIZONA ARCHAEOLOGIST.
Arizona Archaeological Society, Inc., Box 9665, Phoenix, AZ 85068. TEL 602-488-9589. *353*

ARIZONA ENGLISH BULLETIN.
Arizona English Teachers Association, 525 College of Education, University of Arizona, Tucson, AZ 85721. TEL 520-621-1311. *4242*

ARIZONA GEOLOGICAL SOCIETY DIGEST.
Arizona Geological Society, Box 40952, Tucson, AZ 85717. *2331*

ARIZONA-NEVADA ACADEMY OF SCIENCE. JOURNAL.
Arizona-Nevada Academy of Science, c/o Donald J. Pinkava, Ed., Dept. of Botany, Arizona State University, Tempe, AZ 85287-1601. TEL 602-965-3179. FAX 602-965-1473. *6513*

ARIZONA WILDLIFE VIEWS.
Game and Fish Department, 2221 W. Greenway Rd., Phoenix, AZ 85023. TEL 602-942-3000. *2222*

ARKANSAS. AGRICULTURAL EXPERIMENT STATION. RESEARCH BULLETIN.
Agricultural Experiment Station, Agricultural Publications, 110 Agriculture Bldg., 1 University of Arkansas, Division of Agriculture, Fayetteville, AR 72701-1201. TEL 501-575-5647. FAX 501-575-7531. *169*

ARKANSAS ACADEMY OF SCIENCE. PROCEEDINGS.
Arkansas Academy of Science, Div. of Math & Sciences, Univ. of Arkansas at Monticello, Monticello, AR 71656. TEL 501-460-1265. FAX 501-460-1316. *6513*

ARKANSAS BUSINESS AND ECONOMIC REVIEW.
University of Arkansas, College of Business Administration, Fayetteville, AR 72701. TEL 501-575-4151. FAX 501-575-7687. *933*

ARKANSAS HISTORICAL QUARTERLY.
Arkansas Historical Association, University of Arkansas, Department of History, Old Main 416, Fayetteville, AR 72701. TEL 501-575-5884. FAX 501-575-2642. *3618*

ARKANSAS LAW REVIEW.
University of Arkansas, School of Law, Waterman Hall, Fayetteville, AR 72701. TEL 501-575-5610. FAX 501-575-2053. *3913*

ARKANSAS MEDICAL SOCIETY. JOURNAL.
Arkansas Medical Society, Box 55088, Little Rock, AR 72215-5088. TEL 501-224-8967. FAX 501-224-6489. *4640*

ARKANSAS PHILOLOGICAL ASSOCIATION. PUBLICATIONS.
Arkansas Philological Association, University of Central Arkansas, Conway, AR 72035. TEL 501-450-5118. FAX 201-450-5208. *4242*

ARKANSAS QUARTERLY.
Epiphany Publications, Inc., Box 628, Guymon, OK 73942. *4323*

ARMED FORCES AND SOCIETY.
Transaction Publishers, Transaction Periodicals Consortium, Department 3092, Rutgers University, New Brunswick, NJ 08903. TEL 908-445-2280. FAX 908-445-3138. *5258*

ARMEE ET DEFENSE.
Editions de l'Aulne, 27 rue du Dessous des Berges, 75013 Paris, France. TEL 33-1-45822100. FAX 33-1-45820067. *5259*

ARMY LOGISTICIAN.
U.S. Army Logistics Management College, Ft. Lee, VA 23801-1705. TEL 804-756-4761. FAX 804-765-4463. *5259*

ARMY MEDICAL SERVICES MAGAZINE.
R A M C Historical Museum, Keogh Barracks, Ash Vale, Aldershot, Hants. GU12 5RQ, England. TEL 44-1252-340212. FAX 44-1252-340224. *5260*

ARNAZELLA.
3000 Landerholm Circle, S.E., Bellevue, WA 98007. TEL 206-641-4032. *4377*

ARNOLDIA.
Harvard University, Arnold Arboretum, 125 Arbor Way, Jamaica Plain, MA 02130-2795. TEL 617-524-1718. FAX 617-524-1418. *3208*

AROIDEANA.
Allen Press, Inc., Box 43-1853, S. Miami, FL 33143. TEL 305-271-3767. *3182*

ARQUIVO BRASILEIRO DE MEDICINA VETERINARIA E ZOOTECNIA.
Universidade Federal de Minas Gerais, Escola de Veterinaria, Av. Antonio Carlos, 6627, C.P. 567, 30161-970 Belo Horizonte, Minas Gerais, Brazil. TEL 55-31-4418364. FAX 55-31-4412996. *7266*

ARQUIVOS DE BIOLOGIA E TECNOLOGIA.
Instituto de Tecnologia do Parana, Rua Prof. Algacyr Munhoz Mader, 3775, 81350-010 Curitiba PR, Brazil. TEL 55-41-33463141. FAX 55-41-2476788. *587*

ARQUIVOS DE GASTROENTEROLOGIA.
Instituto Brasileiro de Estudos e Pesquisas de Gastroenterologia, Rua Dr. Seng 320, 01331-020 Sao Paulo SP, Brazil. TEL 55-11-2882119. FAX 55-11-2892768. *4908*

ARQUIVOS DE NEURO-PSIQUIATRIA.
Associacao Arquivos Neuro-Psiquiatria Dr. Oswaldo Lange, Caixa Postal 8877, 01065-970 Sao Paulo, SP, Brazil. TEL 55-11-2879726. FAX 55-11-2898879. *5053*

ARQUIVOS DE SAUDE MENTAL DO ESTADO DE SAO PAULO.
Biblioteca do Hospital de Juqueri, Franco da Rocha E.F.S.J., CEP 07780-000 Sao Paulo, Brazil. TEL 55-11-432-5111. FAX 55-11-432-5444. *5053*

ARS COMBINATORIA.
Charles Babbage Research Centre, P.O. Box 272, St. Norbert Postal Stn., Winnipeg, MB R3V 1L6, Canada. TEL 204-772-2612. *4563*

ARS DECORATIVA.
Iparmuveszeti Muzeum, Hopp Ferenc Keletazsiai Muveszeti Muzeum, Ulloi ut 33-37, 1091 Budapest 9, Hungary. TEL 36-1-2175222. FAX 36-1-2175838. *5350*

ARS HUNGARICA.
Magyar Tudomanyos Akademia, Muveszettorteneti Kutato Intezete, Uri u. 49, 1014 Budapest, Hungary. TEL 36-1-1759011. FAX 36-1-1561849. *423*

ARS LYRICA: JOURNAL OF LYRICA.
Lyrica Society for Word-Music Relations, 90 Church St., Guilford, CT 06437. TEL 203-453-1503. FAX 860-832-2522. *5373*

ARS ORIENTALIS.
Department of History of Art, Tappan Hall, University of Michigan, Ann Arbor, MI 48109-1357. TEL 313-647-3307. FAX 313-763-8976. *5521*

ART BUSINESS NEWS.
Advanstar Communications, Inc., 7500 Old Oak Blvd., Cleveland, OH 44130. TEL 216-826-2839. FAX 216-891-2726. *424*

ART CALENDAR.
Box 199, Upper Fairmount, MD 21867. TEL 410-651-9150. FAX 410-657-5313. *424*

ART CRITICISM.
State University of New York at Stony Brook, Stony Brook, NY 11794. TEL 516-632-7260. *424*

ART DOCUMENTATION.
Art Libraries Society of North America, 4101 Lake Boone Trl., Ste. 201, Raleigh, NC 27607-7506. TEL 919-787-5181. FAX 919-787-4916. *4160*

L'ART DU CINEMA.
Association Cinema Art Nouveau, 11 passage St. Pierre-Amelot, 75011 Paris, France. TEL 33-1-43555269. *5323*

ART LAW & ACCOUNTING REPORTER.
Texas Accountants & Lawyers for the Arts, 1540 Sul Ross, Houston, TX 77006. TEL 713-526-4876. FAX 731-526-1299. *3913*

ART NEXUS.
Arte en Colombia Ltda., Apdo. Aereo 90193, Bogota D.E., Colombia. TEL 571-2625178. FAX 571-4136335. *426*

ART PRICE INDEX INTERNATIONAL.
Sound View Press, 170 Boston Post Rd., Madison, CT 06443. TEL 203-245-2246. FAX 203-245-5116. *6087*

ART REFERENCE SERVICES QUARTERLY.
Haworth Press, Inc., 10 Alice St., Binghamton, NY 13904-1580. TEL 607-722-5857. FAX 607-722-6362. *426*

DE ARTE.
Unisa Press, Periodicals, P.O. Box 392, Pretoria 0001, South Africa. TEL 27-12-4293111. FAX 27-12-4293221. *427*

ARTEFACT.
Archaeological and Anthropological Society of Victoria, G.P.O. 328C, Melbourne, Vic. 3001, Australia. TEL 61-3-95230549. *353*

ARTERIOSCLEROSIS, THROMBOSIS AND VASCULAR BIOLOGY.
American Heart Association, 7272 Greenville Ave., Dallas, TX 75231-4596. TEL 214-706-1310. FAX 214-691-6342. *4810*

ARTERY.
Artery Publishing, 13998 West Ave., E., Fulton, MI 49052. *4810*

ARTES DE MEXICO.
Artes de Mexico y del Mundo S.A., Plaza Rio de Janeiro 52, Col. Roma, 06700 Mexico, D.F., Mexico. TEL 52-5-2083205. FAX 52-5-5255925. *427*

ARTHA-VIKAS.
Sardar Patel University, Department of Economics, Vallabh Vidyanagar, Gujarat 388 120, India. FAX 91-2692-35238. *1579*

ARTHRITIS AND RHEUMATISM.
Lippincott - Raven Publishers, 227 E. Washington Sq., Philadelphia, PA 19106. TEL 215-238-4200. FAX 215-238-4227. *5124*

ARTHRITIS CARE AND RESEARCH.
Arthritis Health Professions Association, 1314 Spring St., N.W., Atlanta, GA 30309. TEL 404-872-7100. *5124*

ARTHROPOD MANAGEMENT TESTS.
Entomological Society of America, 9301 Annapolis Rd., Lanham, MD 20706. TEL 301-731-4535. FAX 301-731-4538. *747*

ARTHROPODS OF FLORIDA AND NEIGHBORING LAND AREAS.
Department of Agriculture and Consumer Services, Division of Plant Industry, 1911 S.W. 34th St., Box 147100, Gainesville, FL 32614-7100. TEL 904-372-3505. FAX 904-955-2301. *747*

ARTHROSCOPY.
W.B. Saunders Co., Curtis Center, 3rd Fl., Independence Sq. W., Philadelphia, PA 19106-3399. TEL 215-238-7800. FAX 215-238-6445. *5004*

ARTICULATOR.
North Central Ohio Dental Society, 1604 E. Perkins Ave., Ste. 209, Sandusky, OH 44870. TEL 419-621-8830. FAX 419-447-2054. *4851*

ARTIFICIAL CELLS, BLOOD SUBSTITUTES, AND IMMOBILIZATION BIOTECHNOLOGY.
Marcel Dekker Journals, 270 Madison Ave., New York, NY 10016. TEL 212-696-9000. FAX 212-685-4540. *4895*

ARTIFICIAL INTELLIGENCE.
North-Holland, P.O. Box 211, 1000 AE Amsterdam, Netherlands. TEL 31-20-4853911. FAX 31-20-4853598. *2098*

ARTIFICIAL INTELLIGENCE AND LAW.
Kluwer Academic Publishers, Postbus 17, 3300 AA Dordrecht, Netherlands. TEL 31-78-6392392. FAX 31-78-6392254. *3913*

ARTIFICIAL INTELLIGENCE COMMUNICATIONS.
I O S Press, Van Diemenstraat 94, 1013 CN Amsterdam, Netherlands. TEL 31-20-6382189. FAX 31-20-6203419. *2098*

ARTIFICIAL INTELLIGENCE IN ENGINEERING.
Elsevier Science Ltd., P.O. Box 800, Kidlington, Oxford OX5 1DX, England. TEL 44-1865-843000. FAX 44-1865-843010. *2098*

ARTIFICIAL INTELLIGENCE IN MEDICINE.
Elsevier Science B.V., P.O. Box 211, 1000 AE Amsterdam, Netherlands. TEL 31-20-4853911. FAX 31-20-4853598. *4845*

ARTIFICIAL INTELLIGENCE REVIEW.
Kluwer Academic Publishers, Postbus 17, 3300 AA Dordrecht, Netherlands. TEL 31-78-6392392. FAX 31-78-6392254. *2098*

ARTIFICIAL ORGANS.
Blackwell Science Inc., 350 Main St., Malden, MA 02148. TEL 617-876-7000. FAX 617-388-8255. *4895*

REFEREED SERIALS

ARTIFICIAL ORGANS TODAY.
V S P, P.O. Box 346, 3700 AH Zeist, Netherlands. TEL 31-30-6925790. FAX 31-30-6932081. *4641*

ARTIFICIAL SATELLITES.
Polska Akademia Nauk, Centrum Badan Kosmicznych, Ul. Bartycka 18 a, 00-716 Warsaw, Poland. TEL 48-22-403766. FAX 48-39-121273. *2378*

ARTIST'S BOOK YEARBOOK.
Magpie Press, 1 Hermitage Cottage, Clamp Hill, Stanmore, Mddx. HA7 3JW, England. FAX 44-181-954-0670. *428*

ARTS BEAT.
Hamilton & Region Arts Council, 2 King St. W., Hamilton, ON L8P 1A1, Canada. TEL 905-529-9485. FAX 905-529-0238. *429*

ARTS EDUCATION POLICY REVIEW.
Heldref Publications, 1319 Eighteenth St., N.W., Washington, DC 20036-1802. TEL 202-296-6267. FAX 202-296-5149. *429*

THE ARTS IN PSYCHOTHERAPY.
Elsevier Science Ltd., Pergamon, P.O. Box 800, Kidlington, Oxford OX5 1DX, England. TEL 44-1865-843000. FAX 44-1865-843010. *6095*

ARTSFOCUS.
Colorado Springs Fine Arts Center, 30 W. Dale St., Colorado Springs, CO 80903. TEL 719-634-5581. *5351*

ASCENT (KOOTENAY BAY).
Yasodhara Ashram Society, Box 9, Kootenay Bay, BC V0B 1X0, Canada. TEL 604-227-9224. FAX 604-227-9494. *5455*

ASEMKA.
University of Cape Coast, c/o Department of French, Cape Coast, Ghana. TEL 233-2441-9. *4377*

ASIA INSTITUTE. BULLETIN.
Bulletin of the Asia Institute, 3287 Bradway Blvd., Bloomfield Hills, MI 48301. TEL 810-647-7917. FAX 810-647-9223. *5521*

ASIA LIFE SCIENCES.
Rushing Water Publishers Ltd., No. 81 Diamond Jubileeville, Masaya, Bay, Laguna 4033, Philippines. TEL 9-63-49-3368. FAX 9-63-49-2721. *587*

ASIA - PACIFIC BUSINESS REVIEW.
Frank Cass, Newbury House, 890-900 Eastern Ave., Newbury Park, Ilford, Essex 1G2 7HH, England. TEL 44-181-599-8866. FAX 44-181-599-0984. *933*

ASIA - PACIFIC DEFENSE FORUM.
U.S. Pacific Command (USCINCPAC), Box 64013, Camp H.M. Smith, HI 96861-4013. TEL 808-477-0760. FAX 808-477-1471. *5260*

ASIA PACIFIC DISABILITY REHABILITATION JOURNAL.
Actionaid - India, Disability Division, J-124, Ushas Apartments, 16th Main, 4th Block, Jayanagar, Bangalore 560 011, India. TEL 91-80-6633762. FAX 91-80-6638045. *6655*

ASIA PACIFIC JOURNAL OF HUMAN RESOURCES.
Australian Human Resources Institute, c/o Business Manager, P.O. Box 461, Mulgrave North, Vic. 3170, Australia. TEL 61-3-93444072. FAX 61-3-93444293. *1562*

ASIA - PACIFIC JOURNAL OF OPHTHALMOLOGY.
Singapore National Eye Centre, 11 Third Hospital Ave., Singapore 0316, Singapore. TEL 65-227-7255. FAX 65-323-1903. *4990*

ASIA PACIFIC JOURNAL OF SOCIAL WORK.
Times Academic Press, Times Centre, One New Industrial Rd., Singapore 536196, Singapore. TEL 65-284-8844. FAX 65-288-9254. *6655*

ASIA - PACIFIC JOURNAL OF TEACHER EDUCATION.
Carfax Publishing Co., P.O. Box 25, Abingdon, Oxon. OX14 3UE, England. TEL 44-1235-401000. FAX 44-1235-401550. *2594*

ASIA PACIFIC LAW REVIEW.
Pearson Professional (Hong Kong) Limited, Ste. 1808, Asian House, 1 Hennessy Rd., Wanchai, Hong Kong, People's Republic of China. TEL 852-2863-2659. FAX 852-2520-6954. *3913*

ASIA-PACIFIC MAGAZINE.
Australian National University, Research School of Pacific & Asian Studies, G.O.P Box 192, Canberra A.C.T. 2601, Australia. TEL 61-6-2494160. *6603*

ASIA - PACIFIC POPULATION RESEARCH ABSTRACTS.
East - West Center, 1601 East-West Rd., Honolulu, HI 96848. TEL 808-944-7482. FAX 808-944-7490. *6060*

ASIA - PACIFIC POPULATION RESEARCH REPORTS.
East - West Center, 1601 East-West Rd., Honolulu, HI 96848. TEL 808-944-7482. FAX 808-944-7490. *6046*

ASIA-PACIFIC VIEWPOINT.
Blackwell Publishers Ltd., 108 Cowley Rd., Oxford OX4 1JF, England. TEL 44-1865-791100. FAX 44-1865-791347. *1354*

ASIAN AFFAIRS: AN AMERICAN REVIEW.
Heldref Publications, 1319 18th St., N.W., Washington, DC 20036-1802. TEL 202-296-6267. FAX 202-296-5149. *6005*

ASIAN AND PACIFIC DEVELOPMENT CENTRE NEWSLETTER.
Asian and Pacific Development Centre, P.O. Box 12224, 50770 Kuala Lumpur, Malaysia. TEL 03-2548088. FAX 03-2550316. *1222*

ASIAN AND PACIFIC MIGRATION JOURNAL.
Scalabrini Migration Center, P.O. Box 10541, Broadway Centrum, Aurora Blvd., 1113 Quezon City, Philippines. TEL 63-2-724-3512. FAX 63-2-721-4296. *6046*

ASIAN AND PACIFIC WOMEN'S RESOURCE AND ACTION SERIES.
Asian and Pacific Development Centre, P.O. Box 12224, 50770 Kuala Lumpur, Malaysia. TEL 03-2548088. FAX 03-2550316. *7313*

ASIAN ART AND CULTURE.
Oxford University Press, Journals, 2001 Evans Rd., Cary, NC 27513. TEL 919-677-0977. FAX 919-677-1714. *5521*

ASIAN - AUSTRALASIAN JOURNAL OF ANIMAL SCIENCES.
Asian - Australasian Association of Animal Production Societies, c/o Dept. of Animal Science & Technology, College of Agriculture & Life Sciences, Seoul National University, Suweon 441-744, S. Korea. TEL 82-331-292-0898. FAX 82-331-294-6543. *269*

ASIAN GEOGRAPHER.
University of Hong Kong, Department of Geography & Geology, Pokfulam Rd., Hong Kong, People's Republic of China. TEL 852-2859-2837. FAX 852-2559-8994. *3395*

ASIAN JOURNAL OF PLANT SCIENCE.
Ranjana Malvey, Pub., 6-4-361 26A Anjarieya Swamy Colony, Bholakpur, Secunderabad 500 380, India. *693*

ASIAN JOURNAL OF POLITICAL SCIENCE.
Times Academic Press, One New Industry Rd., Singapore 536196, Singapore. TEL 65-284-8844. FAX 65-288-9254. *5893*

ASIAN JOURNAL OF SURGERY.
Asian Surgical Association, Queen Mary Hospital, Hong Kong, People's Republic of China. TEL 852-2855-4621. FAX 852-2855-9950. *5136*

ASIAN LIBRARIES.
M C B University Pres Ltd., 60-62 Toller Ln., Bradford, W. Yorks BD8 9BY, England. TEL 44-1274-777700. FAX 44-1274-785200. *4160*

ASIAN PERSPECTIVES.
University of Hawaii Press, Journals Department, 2840 Kolowalu St., Honolulu, HI 96822. TEL 808-956-8833. FAX 808-988-6052. *354*

ASIAN PHILOSOPHY.
Carfax Publishing Co., P.O. Box 25, Abingdon, Oxon. OX14 3UE, England. TEL 44-1235-401000. FAX 44-1235-401550. *5719*

ASIAN STUDIES REVIEW.
Asian Studies Association of Australia, c/o Mr. Leon Comber, Monash Asia Institute, Monash University, Clayton, Vic. 3168, Australia. TEL 61-3-99054993. FAX 61-3-99055370. *3531*

ASIAN SURVEY.
University of California Press, Journals Division, 2120 Berkeley Way, No. 5812, Berkeley, CA 94720-5812. TEL 510-643-7154. FAX 510-642-9917. *5893*

ASIAN THEATRE JOURNAL.
University of Hawaii Press, Journals Department, 2840 Kolowalu St., Honolulu, HI 96822. TEL 808-956-8833. FAX 808-988-6052. *7002*

ASIAN YEARBOOK OF INTERNATIONAL LAW.
Martinus Nijhoff Publishers, Human Rights and International Law Postbus 163, 3300 AD Dordrecht, Netherlands. TEL 31-78-334911. FAX 31-78-334254. *4105*

ASOCIACION DE DEMOGRAFIA HISTORICA. BOLETIN.
Asociacion de Demografia Historica, Centre d'Estudis Demografics, Edifici E2, Universitat Autonoma de Barcelona, 08193 Bellaterra, Spain. TEL 34-3-5813060. FAX 34-3-5813061. *6046*

ASOCIACION ESPANOLA DE ENTOMOLOGIA. BOLETIN.
Asociacion Espanola de Entomologia, Fac. de Ciencias Biologicas, Univ. de Valencia, 46100 Burjasot, Spain. TEL 34-6-3864680. *747*

ASPECTS OF HOMOGENEOUS CATALYSIS: A SERIES OF ADVANCES.
Kluwer Academic Publishers, Postbus 17, 3300 AA Dordrecht, Netherlands. TEL 31-78-6392392. FAX 31-78-6392254. *1812*

ASSAPH. SECTION C. STUDIES IN THE THEATRE.
Tel Aviv University, Faculty of Visual and Performing Arts, Department of Theatre Arts, Ramat Aviv, Tel Aviv 69978, Israel. FAX 972-3-6409482. *7002*

ASSEMBLAGE.
University of Sheffield, Research School of Archaeology, 2 Mappin St., Sheffield S1 4DT, England. TEL 44-114-222-5102. FAX 44-114-272-7347. *354*

ASSEMBLY (WEST POINT).
U.S. Military Academy, Association of Graduates, Herbert Hall, West Point, NY 10996-1607. TEL 914-446-5751. FAX 914-446-6988. *2531*

ASSESSMENT & EVALUATION IN HIGHER EDUCATION.
Carfax Publishing Co., P.O. Box 25, Abingdon, Oxon. OX14 3UE, England. TEL 44-1235-401000. FAX 44-1235-401550. *2532*

ASSESSMENT IN EDUCATION: PRINCIPLES, POLICY AND PRACTICE.
Carfax Publishing Co., P.O. Box 25, Abingdon, Oxon. OX14 3UE, England. TEL 44-1235-401000. FAX 44-1235-401550. *2422*

ASSESSMENT JOURNAL.
International Association of Assessing Officers, 130 E. Randolph, Ste. 850, Chicago, IL 60601. TEL 312-819-6110. *6294*

ASSIA.
Shaare Zadek Medical Center, Falk Schlesinger Institute for Medical Halachic Research, P.O. Box 3235, Jerusalem 91031, Israel. TEL 972-2-6555266. FAX 972-2-6523295. *4642*

ASSIA - JEWISH MEDICAL ETHICS.
Shaare Zadek Medical Center, Falk Schlesinger Institute for Medical Halachic Research, P.O. Box 3235, Jerusalem 91031, Israel. TEL 972-2-6555266. FAX 972-2-6523295. *4642*

ASSICURAZIONI.
Istituto Nazionale delle Assicurazioni, S.p.A., Via Sallustiana 51, 00187 Rome, Italy. TEL 39-6-47888736. FAX 39-6-47224595. *3808*

ASSISTED REPRODUCTIVE TECHNOLOGY - ANDROLOGY.
Reproductive Health Center, 78 Surfsong Rd., Kiawah Island, SC 29455. TEL 803-768-5556. FAX 803-768-6494. *4642*

ASSIUT VETERINARY MEDICAL JOURNAL.
Assiut University, Faculty of Veterinary Medicine, Assiut, Egypt. FAX 088-333938. *7266*

ASSOCIACAO BRASILEIRA DE PSIQUIATRIA E ASOCIACION PSIQUIATRICA DE LA AMERICA LATINA. REVISTA.
Associacao Brasileira de Psiquiatria, Rua Borges Lagoa, 394, 04038-000 Sao Paulo SP, Brazil. TEL 55-11-549-6699. FAX 55-11-570-6210. *5053*

ASSOCIATION DES AMIS D'ALFRED DE VIGNY. BULLETIN.
Association des Amis d'Alfred de Vigny, 6 av. Constant-Coquelin, 75007 Paris, France. TEL 33-1-42731286. *4378*

ASSOCIATION FOR GERONTOLOGY IN HIGHER EDUCATION. BRIEF BIBLIOGRAPHY.
Association for Gerontology in Higher Education, 1001 Connecticut Ave., N.W., Ste. 410, Washington, DC 20036-5504. TEL 202-429-9277. *3448*

ASSOCIATION FOR GLOBAL STRATEGIC INFORMATION. JOURNAL.
Infonortics, Ltd., 15 Market Place, Tetbury, Gloucestershire GLB 8DD, England. TEL 44-1666-505772. FAX 44-1666-505-774. *1174*

ASSOCIATION FOR PRESERVATION TECHNOLOGY INTERNATIONAL. BULLETIN.
Association for Preservation Technology International, Box 3511, Williamsburg, VA 23187-3511. TEL 703-373-1621. FAX 888-723-4242. *397*

ASSOCIATION FOR QUALITY IN HEALTHCARE. JOURNAL.
Association for Quality in Healthcare, 47 Southgate St., Winchester, Hants. SO23 9EH, England. TEL 44-196-287-7700. FAX 44-196-287-7701. *4642*

ASSOCIATION FOR RESEARCH IN NERVOUS AND MENTAL DISEASE. RESEARCH PUBLICATIONS.
Lippincott - Raven Publishers, 227 E. Washington Sq., Philadelphia, PA 19105. TEL 215-238-4200. FAX 215-238-4227. *5053*

ASSOCIATION INTERNATIONALE D'ETUDES DU SUD-EST EUROPEEN. BULLETIN.
International Association of South-East European Studies, 47, Chaussee Kiseleff, 71268 Bucharest 2, Rumania. TEL 401-2225409. FAX 401-2233063. *3550*

ASSOCIATION OF AMERICAN PHYSICIANS. PROCEEDINGS.
Blackwell Science Inc., 350 Main St., Malden, MA 02148. TEL 617-876-7000. FAX 617-388-8255. *4642*

ASSOCIATION OF ASPHALT PAVING TECHNOLOGISTS. PROCEEDINGS.
Association of Asphalt Paving Technologists, 400 Selbay Ave., Ste. I, St. Paul, MN 55102. TEL 612-293-9188. FAX 612-293-9193. *2777*

ASSOCIATION OF NURSES IN AIDS CARE. JOURNAL.
Sage Publicatons, Inc., 2455 Teller Rd., Thousand Oaks, CA 91320. TEL 805-499-0721. FAX 805-499-0871. *4833*

ASSOCIATION OF PAEDIATRIC CHARTERED PHYSIOTHERAPISTS. JOURNAL.
Association of Paediatric Chartered Physiotherapists, 14 Bedford Row, London WC1R 4ED, England. TEL 44-171-242-1941. FAX 44-171-831-4509. *5042*

ASSOCIATION OF PHYSICIANS OF INDIA. JOURNAL.
Association of Physicians of India, Laud Mansion, 3rd Fl., 21 M. Karve Rd., Mumbai 400 004, India. TEL 91-22-382-9348. FAX 91-22-305-1093. *4643*

ASSOCIATION OF RUSSIAN - AMERICAN SCHOLARS IN THE U S A. TRANSACTIONS.
Association of Russian - American Scholars in the U S A, Inc., Box 180035, Richmond Hill, NY 11418-0035. TEL 518-785-6780. FAX 518-388-6462. *2998*

ASSOCIATION OF TEACHERS OF JAPANESE. JOURNAL.
Association of Teachers of Japanese, c/o Patricia Wetzel, Foreign Languages & Literatures, Portland State Univ., Portland, OR 97207. TEL 503-725-5277. FAX 503-725-5276. *4243*

ASSOCIAZIONE ROMANA DI ENTOMOLOGIA. BOLLETTINO.
Associazione Romana di Entomologia, c/o Museo Civico di Zoologia, Via Ulisse Aldrovandi, 18, 00197 Rome, Italy. *747*

ASTERISQUE.
Societe Mathematique de France, Institut Henri Poincare, 11 rue Pierre et Marie Curie, 75231 Paris Cedex 05, France. TEL 33-1-40469096. FAX 33-1-40469096. *4563*

ASTROLOGIE HEUTE.
Astrodata AG, Chilenholzstr. 8, CH-8907 Wettswil, Switzerland. TEL 41-1-4921515. FAX 41-1-4935135. *485*

THE ASTRONOMER.
16 Westminster Close, Basingstoke, Hants. RG22 4PP, England. TEL 44-1256-471074. FAX 44-1256-471074. *489*

ASTRONOMICAL AND ASTROPHYSICAL TRANSACTIONS.
Gordon and Breach - Harwood Academic, Amsteldisk 166, 1st Fl., 1079 LH Amsterdam, Netherlands. *489*

ASTRONOMICAL JOURNAL.
American Institute of Physics, One Physics Ellipse, College Park, MD 20740-3843. TEL 301-209-3000. *489*

ASTRONOMICAL SOCIETY OF AUSTRALIA. PUBLICATIONS.
C.S.I.R.O. Publishing, 150 Oxford St., Collingwood, Vic. 3066, Australia. TEL 61-3-96627500. FAX 61-3-96627611. *489*

ASTRONOMICAL SOCIETY OF INDIA. BULLETIN.
Astronomical Society of India, Indian Institute of Astrophysics, Koramangala, Bangalore 560 034, India. TEL 91-80-5530672. FAX 91-80-5534043. *489*

ASTRONOMICAL SOCIETY OF SOUTHERN AFRICA. MONTHLY NOTES.
Astronomical Society of Southern Africa, P.O. Box 9, Observatory 7935, South Africa. TEL 27-21-5315250. FAX 27-21-473639. *490*

ASTRONOMY & GEOPHYSICS.
I O P Publishing Ltd., Dirac House, Temple Back, Bristol BS1 6BE, England. TEL 44-117-929-7481. FAX 44-117-929-4318. *491*

ASTROPARTICLE PHYSICS.
North-Holland, P.O. Box 211, 1000 AE Amsterdam, Netherlands. TEL 31-20-4853911. FAX 31-20-4853598. *491*

THE ASTROPHYSICAL JOURNAL.
University of Chicago Press, Journals Division, Box 37005, Chicago, IL 60637. TEL 773-753-3347. FAX 773-753-0811. *491*

ASTROPHYSICAL JOURNAL. SUPPLEMENT SERIES.
University of Chicago Press, Journals Division, 37005, Chicago, IL 60637. TEL 773-753-3347. FAX 773-753-0811. *491*

ASTROPHYSICAL LETTERS AND COMMUNICATIONS.
Gordon and Breach - Harwood Academic, Amsteldisk 166, 1st Fl., 1079 LH Amsterdam, Netherlands. *492*

ASTROPHYSICS.
Plenum Publishing Corp., Consultants Bureau, 233 Spring St., New York, NY 10013-1578. TEL 212-620-8468. FAX 212-463-0742. *492*

ASTROPHYSICS AND SPACE PHYSICS REVIEWS.
Gordon and Breach - Harwood Academic, Amsteldisk 166, 1st Fl., 1079 LH Amsterdam, Netherlands. *492*

ASTROPHYSICS AND SPACE SCIENCE.
Kluwer Academic Publishers, Postbus 17, 3300 AA Dordrecht, Netherlands. TEL 31-78-6392392. FAX 31-78-6392254. *492*

ASTROPHYSICS AND SPACE SCIENCE LIBRARY.
Kluwer Academic Publishers, Postbus 17, 3300 AA Dordrecht, Netherlands. TEL 31-78-6392392. FAX 31-78-6392254. *492*

ASYMPTOTIC ANALYSIS.
I O S Press, Van Diemenstraat 94, 1013 CN Amsterdam, Netherlands. TEL 31-20-6382189. FAX 31-20-6203419. *4563*

ATENCION MEDICA.
Intersistemas S.A. de C.V., Aguiar y Seijas 75, Lomas de Chapultepec, 11000 Mexico D.F., Mexico. TEL 52-5-540-0798. FAX 52-5-540-3764. *4643*

ATHEROSCLEROSIS.
Elsevier Science Ireland Ltd., P.O. Box 85, Limerick, Ireland. TEL 353-61-471944. FAX 353-61-472144. *4811*

ATHEROSCLEROSIS REVIEWS.
Lippincott - Raven Publishers, 227 E. Washington Sq., Philadelphia, PA 19106. TEL 215-238-4200. FAX 215-238-4227. *4811*

ATHLERAMA.
Federation Francaise d'Athletisme, 33 bd. Pierre de Coubertin, 75013 Paris, France. TEL 33-1-53-80-70-19. FAX 33-1-45-81-40-54. *6749*

ATHLETES IN ACTION.
Box 588, Lebanon, OH 45036-0588. TEL 513-933-2421. FAX 513-933-2424. *6749*

ATLANTA HISTORY.
Atlanta Historical Society, Inc., 130 West Paces Ferry Rd., Atlanta, GA 30305-1366. TEL 404-814-4000. FAX 404-814-4186. *3618*

ATLANTIC GEOLOGY.
Atlantic Geoscience Society, c/o Acadia Centre for Estuarine Research, Box 115, Acadia University, Wolfville, NS B0P 1X0, Canada. TEL 902-585-1340. FAX 902-585-1074. *2332*

ATLANTIDA.
Universidad Simon Bolivar, Division de Sociales y Humanidades, Valle de Sartenejas, Caracas, Venezuela. TEL 58-2-9063422. FAX 58-2-9063402. *6604*

ATLANTIDE REPORT. SCIENTIFIC RESULTS OF THE DANISH EXPEDITION TO THE COASTS OF TROPICAL WEST AFRICA.
Apollo Books Aps., Kirkeby Sand 19, DK-5771 Stenstrup, Denmark. TEL 45-62-26-37-37. FAX 45-62-26-37-80. *2907*

ATLANTIS.
Mount Saint Vincent University, Institute for the Study of Women, 166 Bedford Hwy., Halifax, NS B3M 2J6, Canada. TEL 902-457-6319. FAX 902-443-1352. *7341*

ATLETISMO ESPANOL.
Real Federacion Espanola de Atletismo, C. Miguel Angel, 16, 28010 Madrid, Spain. TEL 34-1-3103677. FAX 34-1-3085912. *6861*

ATMOSPHERE - OCEAN.
Canadian Meteorological and Oceanographic Society, Ste. 112, McDonald Bldg., 150 Louis Pasteur, Ottawa, ON K1N 6N5, Canada. TEL 613-562-5616. FAX 613-562-5615. *5227*

ATMOSPHERIC AND OCEANOGRAPHIC SCIENCES LIBRARY.
Kluwer Academic Publishers, Postbus 17, 3300 AA Dordrecht, Netherlands. TEL 31-78-6392392. FAX 31-78-6392254. *2310*

ATMOSPHERIC ENVIRONMENT.
Elsevier Science Ltd., Pergamon, P.O. Box 800, Kidlington, Oxford OX5 1DX, England. TEL 44-1865-843000. FAX 44-1865-843010. *2965*

ATMOSPHERIC RESEARCH.
Elsevier Science B.V., P.O. Box 211, 1000 AE Amsterdam, Netherlands. TEL 31-20-4853911. FAX 31-20-4853598. *5227*

ATOMIC DATA AND NUCLEAR DATA TABLES.
Academic Press, Inc., Journal Division, 525 B. St., Ste. 1900, San Diego, CA 92101-4495. TEL 619-230-1840. FAX 619-699-6800. *5850*

ATOMIC ENERGY.
Plenum Publishing Corp., Consultants Bureau, 233 Spring St., New York, NY 10013-1578. TEL 212-620-8468. FAX 212-463-0742. *2694*

ATOMIC ENERGY LEVELS AND GROTRIAN DIAGRAMS.
Elsevier Science B.V., Books Division, P.O. Box 211, 1000 AE Amsterdam, Netherlands. TEL 31-20-4853911. FAX 31-20-4853705. *5850*

ATOMIC SPECTROSCOPY.
Perkin - Elmer Corp., 761 Main Ave., Norwalk, CT 06859-0219. TEL 203-761-2532. FAX 203-761-2892. *1789*

ATOMIZATION AND SPRAYS.
Begell House Inc., 79 Madison Ave., Ste. 1205, New York, NY 10016-7892. TEL 212-725-1999. FAX 212-213-8368. *2756*

AUCKLAND INSTITUTE AND MUSEUM. RECORDS.
Auckland Institute and Museum, Private Bag 92018, Auckland 1, New Zealand. FAX 64-9-3799-956. *5351*

AUDIO-DIGEST ANESTHESIOLOGY.
Audio-Digest Foundation, 1577 E. Chevy Chase Dr., Glendale, CA 91206. TEL 213-245-8505. FAX 818-240-7379. *4804*

AUDIO-DIGEST EMERGENCY MEDICINE.
Audio-Digest Foundation, 1577 E. Chevy Chase Dr., Glendale, CA 91206. TEL 213-245-8505. FAX 818-240-7379. *5004*

AUDIO-DIGEST FAMILY PRACTICE.
Audio-Digest Foundation, 1577 E. Chevy Chase Dr., Glendale, CA 91206. TEL 213-245-8505. FAX 818-240-7379. *4643*

AUDIO-DIGEST GASTROENTEROLOGY.
Audio-Digest Foundation, 1577 E. Chevy Chase Dr., Glendale, CA 91206. TEL 213-245-8505. FAX 818-240-7379. *4908*

AUDIO-DIGEST GENERAL SURGERY.
Audio-Digest Foundation, 1577 E. Chevy Chase Dr., Glendale, CA 91206. TEL 213-245-8505. FAX 818-240-7379. *5136*

AUDIO-DIGEST INTERNAL MEDICINE.
Audio-Digest Foundation, 1577 E. Chevy Chase Dr., Glendale, CA 91206. TEL 213-245-8505. FAX 818-240-7379. *4924*

AUDIO-DIGEST OBSTETRICS - GYNECOLOGY.
Audio-Digest Foundation, 1577 E. Chevy Chase Dr., Glendale, CA 91206. TEL 213-245-8505. FAX 818-240-7379. *4953*

AUDIO-DIGEST OPHTHALMOLOGY.
Audio-Digest Foundation, 1577 E. Chevy Chase Dr., Glendale, CA 91206. TEL 213-245-8505. FAX 818-240-7379. *4990*

AUDIO-DIGEST ORTHOPAEDICS.
Audio-Digest Foundation, 1577 E. Chevy Chase Dr., Glendale, CA 91206. TEL 213-245-8505. FAX 818-240-7379. *5005*

AUDIO-DIGEST OTOLARYNGOLOGY - HEAD AND NECK SURGERY.
Audio-Digest Foundation, 1577 E. Chevy Chase Dr., Glendale, CA 91206. TEL 213-245-8505. FAX 818-240-7379. *5020*

AUDIO-DIGEST PEDIATRICS.
Audio-Digest Foundation, 1577 E. Chevy Chase Dr., Glendale, CA 91206. TEL 213-245-8505. FAX 818-240-7379. *5028*

AUDIO-DIGEST PSYCHIATRY.
Audio-Digest Foundation, 1577 E. Chevy Chase Dr., Glendale, CA 91206. TEL 213-245-8505. FAX 818-240-7379. *5053*

AUDIO-DIGEST UROLOGY.
Audio-Digest Foundation, 1577 E. Chevy Chase Dr., Glendale, CA 91206. TEL 213-245-8505. FAX 818-240-7379. *5159*

AUDIO ENGINEERING SOCIETY. JOURNAL.
Audio Engineering Society, 60 E. 42nd St., New York, NY 10165. TEL 212-661-8528. FAX 212-661-7829. *6742*

AUDIO JOURNAL OF ONCOLOGY.
Chapman & Hall, Journals Department 2-6 Boundary Row, London SE1 8HN, England. TEL 44-171-8650066. FAX 44-171-5229623. *4971*

AUDIOLOGY AND NEURO-OTOLOGY.
S. Karger AG, Allschwilerstr. 10, P.O. Box, CH-4009 Basel, Switzerland. TEL 41-61-3061111. FAX 41-61-3061234. *5020*

AUDIT.
Cork Publishing Ltd., 19 Rutland St., Cork, Ireland. TEL 353-21-313855. FAX 353-21-313496. *1083*

AUDITING.
American Accounting Association, 5717 Bessie Dr., Sarasota, FL 34233. TEL 941-921-7747. FAX 941-923-4093. *1083*

AUDITORY NEUROSCIENCE.
Gordon and Breach - Harwood Academic, Amsteldisk 166, 1st. Fl., 1079 LH Amsterdam, Netherlands. *5053*

AUGUSTINIAN STUDIES.
Villanova University, Augustinian Studies, Tolentine Hall, Villanova, PA 19085. TEL 610-519-7903. FAX 610-519-6697. *6451*

AUK.
American Ornithologists' Union, c/o Frederick Sheldon, Museum of Natural History, 119 Foster Hall, Louisiana State University, Baton Rouge, LA 70803. TEL 504-388-2855. *799*

AUSTIN - HEALEY MAGAZINE.
Austin - Healey Club, Pacific Centre, Box 6197, San Jose, CA 95150. TEL 408-541-9608. FAX 408-541-9320. *7082*

AUSTRA-LINK.
Al-Anon Family Groups (Australia) Pty. Ltd., G.P.O. Box 1002 H, Melbourne, Vic. 3001, Australia. TEL 61-3-96298327. *2299*

AUSTRALASIAN CERAMIC SOCIETY. JOURNAL.
Australasian Ceramic Society, c/o ANSTO, PMBI, Menai, N.S.W. 2234, Australia. TEL 61-2-7173477. FAX 61-2-5439205. *1725*

AUSTRALASIAN DRAMA STUDIES.
University of Queensland, c/o Department of English, Brisbane, Qld. 4072, Australia. TEL 61-7-33652501. FAX 61-7-3652799. *7002*

AUSTRALASIAN GAY AND LESBIAN LAW JOURNAL.
Federation Press Pty. Ltd., P.O. Box 45, Annandale, N.S.W. 2038, Australia. *3914*

AUSTRALASIAN JOURNAL OF COMBINATORICS.
Centre for Combinatorics, Dept. of Mathematics, Univ. of Queensland, Qld. 4072, Australia. TEL 61-7-33653279. FAX 61-7-33651477. *4563*

AUSTRALASIAN JOURNAL OF EMERGENCY CARE.
Ambulance Employees Australia, 117-131 Capel St., North Melbourne, Vic. 3051, Australia. TEL 61-3-92357668. FAX 61-3-92357680. *5005*

AUSTRALASIAN JOURNAL OF PHILOSOPHY.
Oxford University Press, Academic Division, Great Clarendon St., Oxford OX2 6DP, England. TEL 44-1865-267907. FAX 44-1865-267485. *5719*

AUSTRALASIAN JOURNAL OF REGIONAL STUDIES.
Regional Science Association, Australian and New Zealand Section, c/o Linda Pink, University of New England, P.O. Box U271, Armidale, N.S.W. 2351, Australia. TEL 61-67-714838. *1222*

AUSTRALASIAN PHYSICAL & ENGINEERING SCIENCES IN MEDICINE.
Australasian College of Physical Scientists and Engineers in Medicine, Physics Dept., Queensland University of Technololy, G.P.O. Box 2434, Brisbane, Qld. 4001, Australia. TEL 61-7-38642591. FAX 61-7-38641521. *4895*

AUSTRALASIAN PLANT PATHOLOGY.
J & B Desktop Publishing Pty. Ltd., 32 Range St., Toowoomba, Qld. 4350, Australia. TEL 61-76-325654. FAX 61-76-325685. *693*

AUSTRALASIAN PUBLIC LIBRARIES AND INFORMATION SERVICES.
Auslib Press, P.O. Box 622, Blackwood, S.A. 5051, Australia. TEL 61-8-2784363. FAX 61-8-2704000. *4161*

AUSTRALASIAN SOCIETY FOR HISTORICAL ARCHAEOLOGY. NEWSLETTER.
Australasian Society for Historical Archaeology, Box 220 Holme Bldg., University of Sydney, Sydney, N.S.W. 2001, Australia. TEL 61-2-3512763. FAX 61-2-3514889. *354*

AUSTRALASIAN STUDIES IN HISTORY AND PHILOSOPHY OF SCIENCE.
Kluwer Academic Publishers, Postbus 17, 3300 AA Dordrecht, Netherlands. TEL 31-78-6392392. FAX 31-78-6392254. *6514*

AUSTRALIA - JAPAN ECONOMIC INSTITUTE. ECONOMIC BULLETIN.
Australia - Japan Economic Institute, Level 11, The Chifley Tower, Chifley Sq., Sydney, N.S.W. 2000, Australia. TEL 61-2-92338533. FAX 61-2-92338503. *935*

AUSTRALIAN ACCOUNTING REVIEW.
Australian Society of Certified Practising Accountants, 170 Queen St., Melbourne, Vic. 3000, Australia. TEL 61-3-96069606. FAX 61-3-96708901. *1084*

AUSTRALIAN AND NEW ZEALAND JOURNAL OF OBSTETRICS AND GYNECOLOGY.
Royal Australian College of Obstetricians & Gynecologists, 254 Albert St., Melbourne, Vic. 3002, Australia. TEL 61-3-94175427. FAX 61-3-94175406. *4953*

AUSTRALIAN AND NEW ZEALAND JOURNAL OF PUBLIC HEALTH.
Public Health Association of Australia, P.O. Box 319, Curtin, A.C.T. 2605, Australia. TEL 61-6-2852373. FAX 61-6-2825438. *6229*

AUSTRALIAN AND NEW ZEALAND WINE INDUSTRY JOURNAL.
Winetitles, P.O. Box 1140, Marleston, S.A. 5033, Australia. TEL 61-8-82346055. FAX 61-8-82346050. *514*

AUSTRALIAN ART EDUCATION.
Australian Institute of Art Education, c/o Lee Emery, Ed., University of Melbourne, Faculty of Education, Parkville, Vic. 3052, Australia. TEL 61-3-344-8386. FAX 61-3-349-4290. *431*

AUSTRALIAN BALLET NEWS.
Australian Ballet Foundation, 2 Kavanagh St., Southbank, Vic. 3006, Australia. TEL 61-3-96848600. FAX 61-3-96867081. *2290*

AUSTRALIAN BIRDWATCHER.
Bird Observers Club of Australia, P.O. Box 185, Nunawading, Vic. 3131, Australia. TEL 61-3-98775342. FAX 61-3-98944048. *799*

AUSTRALIAN BUREAU OF AGRICULTURAL AND RESOURCE ECONOMICS. AUSTRALIAN FISHERIES SURVEYS REPORT.
Australian Bureau of Agricultural and Resource Economics, G.P.O. Box 1563, Canberra, A.C.T. 2601, Australia. TEL 61-6-272-2211. FAX 61-6-272-3330. *3082*

AUSTRALIAN COMPANY SECRETARY.
Chartered Institute of Company Secretaries in Australia Ltd., G.P.O. Box 1594, Sydney, N.S.W. 2001, Australia. TEL 61-2-223-5744. FAX 61-2-232-7174. *1466*

AUSTRALIAN CRITICAL CARE.
Confederation of Australian Critical Care Nurses Inc., P.O. Box 605, Hornsby, N.S.W. 2077, Australia. TEL 61-2-7435686. FAX 61-2-7435686. *4929*

AUSTRALIAN CULTURAL HISTORY.
Deakin University, Faculty of Arts, Geelong, Vic. 3217, Australia. TEL 61-52-272695. FAX 61-52-272427. *3542*

AUSTRALIAN DISABILITY REVIEW.
Australian Council for Health, Physical Education and Recreation, 214 Port Rd., Hindmarsh, S.A. 5007, Australia. TEL 61-8-83403388. FAX 61-8-83403399. *3453*

AUSTRALIAN ECONOMIC REVIEW.
Blackwell Publishers Ltd., 108 Cowley Rd., Oxford OX4 1JF, England. TEL 44-1865-791100. FAX 44-1865-791347. *935*

AUSTRALIAN ENTOMOLOGIST.
Entomological Society of Queensland, P.O. Box 537, Indooroopilly, Qld. 4068, Australia. *747*

THE AUSTRALIAN FEMINIST LAW JOURNAL.
Australian Feminist Law Foundation Inc., P.O. Box 4337, M.U. Parkville, Victoria 3052, Australia. *7341*

AUSTRALIAN FEMINIST STUDIES.
Carfax Publishing Co., P.O. Box 25, Abingdon, Oxon. OX14 3UE, England. TEL 44-1235-401000. FAX 44-1235-401550. *7341*

AUSTRALIAN FOLKLORE.
Australian Folklore Association, c/o Prof. J.S. Ryan, Ed., Dept. of English & Communication Studies, University of New England, Armidale, N.S.W. 2351, Australia. TEL 61-2-67732601. FAX 61-2-67732623. *3084*

AUSTRALIAN FORESTRY.
Institute of Foresters of Australia, Inc., P.O. Box 2, Yarralumla, A.C.T. 2600, Australia. TEL 61-6-2813992. FAX 61-6-2814693. *3147*

AUSTRALIAN GEMMOLOGIST.
Gemmological Association of Australia, P.O. Box 477, Albany Creek, Brisbane, Qld.4035, Australia. TEL 61-7-32646854. FAX 61-7-32646854. *3862*

AUSTRALIAN HEALTH REVIEW.
Australian Healthcare Association, P.O. Box 54, Deakin West, A.C.T. 2600, Australia. *3703*

AUSTRALIAN HUMANITIES REVIEW.
Australian Vice-Chancellors' Committee, 66 Old Station Rd., Lower Snug, Tas. 7054, Australia. TEL 61-3-62679209. FAX 61-3-62679209. *3773*

AUSTRALIAN JOURNAL OF DAIRY TECHNOLOGY.
Dairy Industry Association of Australia, P.O. Box 8000, Glen Iris, Vic. 3146, Australia, Australia. FAX 61-3-92526555. *252*

AUSTRALIAN JOURNAL OF EDUCATIONAL TECHNOLOGY.
A J E T Publications Ltd., P.O. Box 772, Belconnen, A.C.T. 2616, Australia. TEL 61-6-2532399. FAX 61-6-2532172. *2595*

AUSTRALIAN JOURNAL OF FRENCH STUDIES.
Monash University, Department of Romance Languages, Clayton, Vic. 3168, Australia. TEL 61-3-99052217. FAX 61-3-99052137. *4378*

AUSTRALIAN JOURNAL OF HOSPITAL PHARMACY.
Society of Hospital Pharmacists of Australia, Level 11, 114 Albert Rd., S. Melbourne, Vic. 3205, Australia. TEL 61-3-96906733. FAX 61-3-96967634. *5649*

AUSTRALIAN JOURNAL OF LABOUR ECONOMICS.
Centre for Labour Market Research, Curtin University of Technology, Bentley West, W.A. 6102, Australia. TEL 61-9-3512871. FAX 61-9-3512872. *1419*

AUSTRALIAN JOURNAL OF LAW AND SOCIETY.
School of Law, Macquarie University, N.S.W. 2109, Australia. TEL 61-2-98507685. FAX 61-2-98507686. *3915*

AUSTRALIAN JOURNAL OF LEARNING DISABILITIES.
Australian Resource Educators Association Inc., 4 Canterbury Rd., Toorak, Vic. 3142, Australia. TEL 61-3-98262929. FAX 61-3-98262696. *2581*

AUSTRALIAN JOURNAL OF LINGUISTICS.
Australian Linguistic Society, c/o D. Absalom, English Language Centre, University of Newcastle, N.S.W. 2308, Australia. TEL 61-49-613922. FAX 61-49-615476. *4243*

AUSTRALIAN JOURNAL OF MEDICAL HERBALISM.
National Herbalists Association of Australia, Ste. 305, 3 Smail St., Broadway, N.S.W. 2007, Australia. TEL 61-2-92116437. FAX 61-2-92116452. *295*

AUSTRALIAN JOURNAL OF PHYSIOTHERAPY.
Australian Physiotherapy Association, P.o. Box 6465, Melbourne, Vic. 3004, Australia. TEL 61-3-95349400. FAX 61-3-95349199. *5042*

AUSTRALIAN JOURNAL OF SCIENCE AND MEDICINE IN SPORT.
Sports Medicine Australia, P.O. Box 897, Belconnen, A.C.T. 2616, Australia. TEL 61-6-2516944. FAX 61-6-2531489. *5129*

AUSTRALIAN JOURNAL OF SOIL AND WATER CONSERVATION.
c/o Geoff Cunningham, 9 The Crest, Killara, N.S.W. 2071, Australia. TEL 61-2-94161995. FAX 61-2-94166626. *214*

AUSTRALIAN JOURNAL OF TEACHER EDUCATION.
Social Science Press, P.O. Box 89, Wentworth Falls, N.S.W. 2782, Australia. *2533*

AUSTRALIAN JOURNAL ON AGEING.
Council on the Ageing (Australia), Level 2, 3 Bowen Crescent, Melbourne, Vic. 3004, Australia. TEL 61-3-98202655. *3433*

AUSTRALIAN JOURNAL ON VOLUNTEERING.
Volunteer Centre of South Australia Inc., 155 Pirie St., Adelaide, S.A. 5000, Australia. TEL 61-8-82320199. FAX 61-8-82325161. *6655*

AUSTRALIAN JOURNALISM REVIEW.
Journalism Education Association, c/o School of Communication, Charles Sturt University - Mitchell, Bathurts, N.S.W. 2795, Australia. TEL 61-2-63384524. FAX 61-2-63384409. *3869*

AUSTRALIAN LAW LIBRARIAN.
Australian Law Librarian, c/o Barbara Coat, Ed., Australian Securities Commission (S.A.), G.P.O. Box 9827, Adelaide, S.A. 5001, Australia. TEL 61-8-2028414. FAX 61-8-2028410. *4162*

AUSTRALIAN MAMMALOGY.
Australian Mammal Society Inc., c/o Dr. Graham Ross, Ed., Australian Biological Resources Study (Fauna), G.P.O. Box 636, Canberra, A.C.T. 2601, Australia. TEL 06-250-9435. FAX 06-250-9448. *828*

AUSTRALIAN MATHEMATICS TEACHER.
Australian Association of Mathematics Teachers Inc., G.P.O. Box 1729, Adelaide, S.A. 5001, Australia. TEL 61-8-3630288. FAX 61-8-3629288. *4564*

AUSTRALIAN NATIONAL UNIVERSITY. NATIONAL CENTRE FOR DEVELOPMENT STUDIES. PACIFIC ECONOMIC BULLETIN.
Australian National University, National Centre for Development Studies, Canberra, A.C.T. 0200, Australia. TEL 61-6-2494705. FAX 61-6-2572886. *1222*

AUSTRALIAN ORTHODONTIC JOURNAL.
Australian Society of Orthodontists, 28 Bramble St., Bendigo, Vic. 3550, Australia. TEL 61-3-54430877. FAX 61-3-54410693. *4851*

AUSTRALIAN PARKS & RECREATION.
Royal Australian Institute of Parks & Recreation, Bldg. E, National Exhibition Centre, Flemington Rd., Lyneham, A.C.T. 2602, Australia. TEL 61-06-241-4371. FAX 61-06-241-5817. *2223*

AUSTRALIAN PHARMACIST.
Pharmaceutical Society of Australia, P.O. Box 21, Curtin, A.C.T. 2605, Australia. TEL 61-6-2811366. FAX 61-6-2852869. *5649*

AUSTRALIAN POPULATION ASSOCIATION. JOURNAL.
Australian Population Association, P.O. Box 38, Lyneham, A.C.T. 2602, Australia. TEL 61-6-2494308. FAX 61-6-2493031. *6047*

AUSTRALIAN POULTRY SCIENCE SYMPOSIUM.
University of Sydney, Poultry Research Foundation, Sydney, N.S.W. 2006, Australia. TEL 61-46-550277. FAX 61-46-551331. *270*

AUSTRALIAN PRESCRIBER.
Commonwealth Department of Health and Family Services, P.O. Box 100, Woden, A.C.T. 2606, Australia. TEL 61-6-289-7038. *5649*

AUSTRALIAN PRIMATOLOGY.
Australasian Primate Society, P.O. Box 500, One Tree Hill, S.A. 5114, Australia. TEL 61-8-82807670. *828*

AUSTRALIAN PSYCHOLOGIST.
Australian Psychological Society, c/o Dr. Christina Lee, Department of Psychology, University of Newcastle, Newcastle, N.S.W. 2308, Australia. *6096*

AUSTRALIAN QUARTERLY.
Australian Institute of Political Science, Box 145, Balmain, N.S.W. 2041, Australia. TEL 61-2-98105642. FAX 61-2-98102406. *5894*

AUSTRALIAN SHORT STORIES.
Pascoe Publishing Pty. Ltd., P.O. Box 42, Apolo Bay, Vic. 3233, Australia. TEL 61-52-379227. FAX 61-52-376559. *4378*

AUSTRALIAN SOCIAL WORK.
Australian Association of Social Workers, P.O. Box 4956, Kingsotn, A.C.T. 2604, Australia. TEL 61-6-2730199. FAX 61-62735020. *6655*

AUSTRALIAN SOCIETY OF ENDODONTOLOGY. NEWSLETTER.
Australian Society of Endodontology Inc., 11th Fl., 20 Collins St., Melbourne, Vic. 3000, Australia. TEL 61-3-96504209. FAX 61-3-96504850. *4851*

AUSTRALIAN STRING TEACHER.
Australian String Teachers Association, 60 Ridgway Dr., Flagstaff Hill, S.A. 5159, Australia. TEL 61-8-2702145. *5374*

AUSTRALIAN STUDIES.
Frank Cass, Newbury House, 890-900 Eastern Ave., Newbury Park, Ilford, Essex IG2 7HH, England. TEL 44-181-5998866. FAX 44-181-5990984. *3542*

AUSTRALIAN TAX FORUM.
Taxation Institute of Australia, 7th Fl., 64 Castlereagh St., Sydney, N.S.W. 2000, Australia. TEL 61-2-92323422. FAX 61-2-92216953. *1600*

AUSTRALIAN TOXIC NETWORK NEWS.
Toxic Chemical Committee, Total Environment Centre, 1-88 Cumberland St., Sydney, N.S.W. 2000, Australia. TEL 61-2-92478476. FAX 61-2-92471178. *2975*

AUSTRALIAN WINE RESEARCH INSTITUTE TECHNICAL REVIEW.
Australian Wine Research Institute, P.O. Box 197, Glen Osmond, S.A. 5064, Australia. TEL 61-8-83036600. FAX 61-8-83036601. *515*

AUSTRALIAN YEARBOOK OF INTERNATIONAL LAW.
Centre for International and Public Law, Faculty of Law, Australian National University, Canberra, A.C.T. 0200. TEL 61-6-2490454. FAX 61-6-2490150. *4106*

AUSTRIAN REVIEW OF INTERNATIONAL AND EUROPEAN LAW.
Kluwer Law International, Postbus 85889, 2508 CN The Hague, Netherlands. TEL 31-70-3081500. FAX 31-70-3081515. *4106*

AUTO-BIOGRAPHY.
British Sociological Association Study Group on Auto-Biography, c/o Michael Erben, University of Southampton, School of Education, Southampton SO17 1BJ, England. TEL 44-161-275-2496. FAX 44-1703-593939. *571*

AUTOIMMUNITY.
Gordon and Breach - Harwood Academic, Amsteldisk 166, 1st Fl., 1079 LH Amsterdam, Netherlands. *4792*

AUTOMATED REASONING SERIES.
Kluwer Academic Publishers, Postbus 17, 3300 AA Dordrecht, Netherlands. TEL 31-78-6392392. FAX 31-78-6392254. *2098*

AUTOMATED SOFTWARE ENGINEERING.
Kluwer Academic Publishers, Postbus 17, 3300 AA Dordrecht, Netherlands. TEL 31-78-6392392. FAX 31-78-6392254. *2099*

AUTOMATICA.
Elsevier Science Ltd., Pergamon, P.O. Box 800, Kidlington, Oxford OX5 1DX, England. TEL 44-1865-843000. FAX 44-1865-843010. *2106*

AUTOMATION AND REMOTE CONTROL.
Plenum Publishing Corp., Consultants Bureau, 233 Spring St., New York, NY 10013-1578. TEL 212-620-8468. FAX 212-463-0742. *2106*

AUTOMATION IN CONSTRUCTION.
Elsevier Science B.V., P.O. Box 211, 1000 AE Amsterdam, Netherlands. TEL 31-20-4853911. FAX 31-20-4853598. *2106*

AUTOMATIZACE.
Automatizace s.r.o., Technicka 4, 160 00 Prague 6, Czech Republic. TEL 420-2-24352009. FAX 420-2-24355614. *2106*

AUTOMEDICA.
Gordon and Breach - Harwood Academic, Amsteldisk 166, 1st Fl., 1079 LH Amsterdam, Netherlands. *4845*

AUTOMOTIVE MANAGEMENT.
1 Oxted Chambers, 185-187 Station Rd. E., Oxted, Surrey RH8 0QE, England. TEL 44-1883-732000. FAX 44-1883-730933. *7088*

AUTONOMIC NERVOUS SYSTEM.
Gordon and Breach - Harwood Academic, Amsteldisk 166, 1st Fl., 1079 LH Amsterdam, Netherlands. *813*

AUTONOMOUS ROBOTS.
Kluwer Academic Publishers, Postbus 17, 3300 AA Dordrecht, Netherlands. TEL 31-78-6392392. FAX 31-78-6392254. *2206*

AUTO4WORLD.COM.
Superior Products Corp., Box 11312, Fort Lauderdale, FL 33339. TEL 954-567-1144. FAX 954-564-5105. *7090*

AVANCES EN ALIMENTACION Y MEJORA ANIMAL.
Juan Vigon 3, 2o D., 28003 Madrid, Spain. *270*

AVANTE.
Canadian Association for Health, Physical Education, Recreation and Dance, Place R. Tait McKenzie, 1600 James Naismith Dr., Gloucester, ON K1B 5N4, Canada. TEL 613-748-5622. FAX 613-748-5737. *5778*

AVIAN DISEASES.
American Association of Avian Pathologists, Inc., University of Pennsylvania, New Bolton Center, Kennett Sq., PA 19348-1692. TEL 610-444-4282. FAX 610-444-5387. *7266*

AVIAN PATHOLOGY.
Carfax Publishing Co., P.O. Box 25, Abingdon, Oxon. OX14 3UE, England. TEL 44-1235-401000. FAX 44-1235-401550. *7267*

AVIATION SECURITY INTERNATIONAL.
Halldale Publishing & Media Ltd., 84 Alexandra Rd., Farnborough, Hants GU14 6DD, England. TEL 44-1252-517974. FAX 44-1252-512714. *7065*

AVIATION, SPACE, AND ENVIRONMENTAL MEDICINE.
Aerospace Medical Association, 320 S. Henry St., Alexandria, VA 22314-3579. TEL 703-739-2240. FAX 703-739-9652. *4644*

AVICULTURAL JOURNAL.
Avicultural Advancement Council of Canada, P.O. Box 5126, Sta. B, Victoria, B.C. V8R 6N4, Canada. TEL 604-477-9982. FAX 604-477-9935. *800*

AVIS 81.
Speciallaererforeningen af 1981, Aabenraa 5, 4, DK-1124 Copenhagen K, Denmark. TEL 45-33-14-50-65. FAX 45-33-91-50-01. *2581*

AVOCETTA.
Centro Italiano Studi Ornitologici, c/o Dipartimento di Biologia Animale, Via Accademia Albertina 17, 10123 Turin, Italy. TEL 39-11-8122374. FAX 39-11-8124561. *828*

AVTOMATIKA I VYCHISLITEL'NAYA TEKHNIKA.
Latvian Academy of Sciences, Institute of Electronic and Computer Science, Dzerbenes iela, 14, Riga LV-1006, Latvia. TEL 371-2-554500. FAX 371-8828211. *2107*

AXIOS.
Axios Newsletter, Inc., 30-32 Macaw Ave., Belmopan, Belize. TEL 501-8-23284. FAX 501-8-23633. *6391*

AYLESFORD CARMELITE NEWSLETTER.
Lay Carmelite Office, 8501 Bailey Road, Darien, IL 60561. TEL 630-969-5050. FAX 630-969-5536. *6452*

B & K SPORTS MAGAZINE.
B & K Sports Magazine AB, P.O. Box 3417, S-103 68 Stockholm, Sweden. TEL 46-8-34-77-00. FAX 46-8-34-63-33. *5779*

B & P A.
Murray State University, College of Business and Public Affairs, Murray, KY 42071. TEL 502-762-4188. FAX 502-762-3482. *935*

B B A - BIOENERGETICS.
Elsevier Science B.V., P.O. Box 211, 1000 AE Amsterdam, Netherlands. TEL 31-20-4853911. FAX 31-20-4853598. *694*

B B A - BIOMEMBRANES.
Elsevier Science B.V., P.O. Box 211, 1000 AE Amsterdam, Netherlands. TEL 31-20-4853911. FAX 31-20-4853598. *736*

B B A - GENE STRUCTURE AND EXPRESSION.
Elsevier Science B.V., P.O. Box 211, 1000 AE Amsterdam, Netherlands. TEL 31-20-4853911. FAX 31-20-4853598. *764*

B B A - GENERAL SUBJECTS.
Elsevier Science B.V., P.O. Box 211, 1000 AE Amsterdam, Netherlands. TEL 31-20-4853911. FAX 31-20-4853598. *651*

B B A - LIPIDS & LIPID METABOLISM.
Elsevier Science B.V., P.O. Box 211, 1000 AE Amsterdam, Netherlands. TEL 31-20-4853911. FAX 31-20-4853598. *651*

B B A - MOLECULAR BASIS OF DISEASE.
Elsevier Science B.V., P.O. Box 211, 1000 AE Amsterdam, Netherlands. TEL 31-20-4853911. FAX 31-20-4853598. *4644*

B B A - MOLECULAR CELL RESEARCH.
Elsevier Science B.V., P.O. Box 211, 1000 AE Amsterdam, Netherlands. TEL 31-20-4853911. FAX 31-20-4853598. *736*

B B A - PROTEIN STRUCTURE AND MOLECULAR ENZYMOLOGY.
Elsevier Science B.V., P.O. Box 211, 1000 AE Amsterdam, Netherlands. TEL 31-20-4853911. FAX 31-20-4853598. *651*

B B A - REVIEWS ON BIOMEMBRANES.
Elsevier Science B.V., P.O. Box 211, 1000 AE Amsterdam, Netherlands. TEL 31-20-4853911. FAX 31-20-4853598. *736*

B B A - REVIEWS ON CANCER.
Elsevier Science B.V., P.O. Box 211, 1000 AE Amsterdam, Netherlands. TEL 31-20-4853911. FAX 31-20-4853598. *4971*

B C - BOLETIM CINEMATOGRAFICO.
Rua Candido des Reis 114-3o, 2780 Oeiras, Portugal. TEL 351-1-4420701. FAX 351-1-4429781. *5324*

B C JOURNAL OF SPECIAL EDUCATION.
Special Education Association, 100-550 W. Sixth Ave., Vancouver, BC V5Z 4P2, Canada. TEL 604-871-2283. FAX 604-871-2291. *2581*

B.C. NATURALIST.
Federation of British Columbia Naturalists, 321-1367 West Broadway, Vancouver, BC V6H 4A9, Canada. TEL 604-737-3057. FAX 604-738-7175. *6514*

B C VOICE.
British Columbia Voice of Women, P.O. Box 235, Nanaimo, BC V9R 5K9, Canada. *7313*

B F Z - INFO.
Berufsfoerderungszentrum Essen e.V., Altenessenerstr. 80-84, 45326 Essen, Germany. TEL 49-201-3204271. FAX 49-201-3204276. *5504*

B I C C GROUP WORLD.
B I C C plc, Devonshire House, Mayfair Pl., London W1X 5FH, England. TEL 44-171-629-6622. FAX 44-171-409-0070. *2777*

B J A: INTERNATIONAL JOURNAL OF ANAESTHESIA.
B M J Publishing Group, B.M.A. House, Tavistock Sq., London WC1H 9JR, England. TEL 0171-387-4499. FAX 0171-383-6662. *4804*

B M A NEWS REVIEW.
B M J Publishing Group, B.M.A. House, Tavistock Sq., London WC1H 9JP, England. TEL 44-171-783-6122. FAX 44-171-383-6566. *4644*

B M J.
B M J Publishing Group, B.M.A. House, Tavistock Sq., London WC1H 9JR, England. TEL 44-171-387-4499. FAX 44-171-383-6661. *4644*

B S L BULLETIN.
Bank of Sierra Leone, Research Department, Siaka Stevens St., P.O. Box 30, Freetown, Sierra Leone. TEL 232-22-226501. FAX 232-22-224767. *1223*

B T A SOLUTIONS.
Business Technology Association, 12411 Wornall Rd., Kansas City, MO 64145-1166. TEL 816-941-3100. FAX 816-941-8034. *1554*

B T TECHNOLOGY JOURNAL.
Thomson Science, 2-6 Boundary Row, London SE1 8HN, England. TEL 44-171-8650066. FAX 44-171-5229623. *1982*

B W P JOURNAL.
Oxford University Press, Academic Division, Great Clarendon St., Oxford OX2 6DP, England. TEL 44-1865-267907. FAX 44-1865-267485. *800*

BABEL.
Australian Federation of Modern Languages Teachers Associations, 2 Rubida Grove, Aldgate, S.A. 5154, Australia. TEL 61-8-82704455. FAX 61-8-83705819. *2595*

BABY CONNECTION NEWS JOURNAL.
Parent Education Center for Infant Development, Drawer 3350, San Antonio, TX 78265-3350. *1838*

BACH PERSPECTIVES.
University of Nebraska Press, 312 N. 14th St., Box 880484, Lincoln, NE 68588-0484. TEL 402-472-3581. FAX 402-472-0308. *5375*

BACK TO GODHEAD.
Box 255, Sandy Ridge, NC 27046. TEL 904-462-7794. FAX 904-462-7893. *6393*

BACKHOME.
Box 70, Hendersonville, NC 28793. TEL 704-696-3838. FAX 704-696-0700. *3369*

THE BAFFLER.
Box 378293, Chicago, IL 60637. TEL 773-493-0413. *4324*

BAHA'I STUDIES.
Association for Baha'i Studies, 34 Copernicus St., Ottawa, ON K1N 7K4, Canada. TEL 613-233-1903. *6487*

BAHA'I STUDIES REVIEW.
Association for Baha'i Studies, 27 Rutland Gate, London SW7 1PD, England. TEL 44-171-584-2566. FAX 44-171-584-9402. *6487*

BAHA'I VIZIER.
Stichting Baha'i Literatuur, Riouwstraat 27, 2585 GR The Hague, Netherlands. TEL 31-70-3554017. *6487*

BAILEYA.
L. H. Bailey Hortorium, Cornell University, Ithaca, NY 14853. TEL 607-255-2131. FAX 607-255-7979. *694*

BAILLIERE'S CLINICAL ANAESTHESIOLOGY.
Bailliere Tindall - W.B. Saunders Co. Ltd., 24-28 Oval Rd., London NW1 7DX, England. TEL 44-171-485-4752. FAX 44-171-267-4466. *4804*

BAILLIERE'S CLINICAL ENDOCRINOLOGY AND METABOLISM.
Bailliere Tindall - W.B. Saunders Co. Ltd., 24-28 Oval Rd., London NW1 7DX, England. TEL 44-171-485-4752. FAX 44-171-267-4466. *4882*

BAILLIERE'S CLINICAL GASTROENTEROLOGY.
Bailliere Tindall - W.B. Saunders Co. Ltd., 24-28 Oval Rd., London NW1 7DX, England. TEL 44-171-485-4752. FAX 44-171-267-4466. *4908*

BAILLIERE'S CLINICAL HAEMATOLOGY.
Bailliere Tindall - W.B. Saunders Co. Ltd., 24-28 Oval Rd., London NW1 7DX, England. TEL 44-171-485-4752. FAX 44-171-267-4466. *4916*

BAILLIERE'S CLINICAL INFECTIOUS DISEASES.
Bailliere Tindall - W.B. Saunders Co. Ltd., 24-28 Oval Rd., London NW1 7DX, England. TEL 44-171-485-4752. FAX 44-171-267-4466. *4833*

BAILLIERE'S CLINICAL OBSTETRICS AND GYNAECOLOGY.
Bailliere Tindall - W.B. Saunders Co. Ltd., 24-28 Oval Rd., London NW1 7DX, England. TEL 44-171-485-4752. FAX 44-171-267-4466. *4953*

BAILLIERE'S CLINICAL PAEDIATRICS.
Bailliere Tindall - W.B. Saunders Co. Ltd., 24-28 Oval Rd., London NW1 7DX, England. TEL 44-171-485-4752. FAX 44-171-267-4466. *5028*

BAILLIERE'S CLINICAL PSYCHIATRY.
Bailliere Tindall - W.B. Saunders Co. Ltd., 24-28 Oval Rd., London NW1 7DX, England. TEL 44-171-485-4752. FAX 44-171-267-4466. *5054*

BAILLIERE'S CLINICAL RHEUMATOLOGY.
Bailliere Tindall - W.B. Saunders Co. Ltd., 24-28 Oval Rd., London NW1 7DX, England. TEL 44-171-485-4752. FAX 44-171-267-4466. *5124*

BAILLIERE'S HANDBOOK OF FIRST AID.
Bailliere Tindall - W.B. Saunders Co. Ltd., 24-28 Oval Rd., London NW1 7DX, England. TEL -171-485-4752. FAX 0171-267-4466. *4645*

BAILY'S HUNTING DIRECTORY.
Pearson Publishing, Chesterton Mill, French's Rd., Cambridge CB4 3NP, England. TEL 44-1223-350555. FAX 44-1223-356484. *1654*

BAIYI KEJI.
Zhongguo Baiyi Fangzhi Yanjiuhui, No. 693, Moganshan Lu, Hangzhou, Zhejiang 310011, People's Republic of China. TEL 86-571-8071061. FAX 86-571-5151540. *748*

BALKAN FORUM.
N I P Nova Makedonija, Ul. Mito Hadzivasilev bb, P.O. Box 556, Skopje, Macedonia. TEL 38-91-23-81-79. *5894*

BALLENA PRESS ANTHROPOLOGICAL PAPERS.
Ballena Press, 823 Valparaiso Ave., Menlo Park, CA 94025. TEL 415-323-9261. FAX 415-883-4280. *311*

BALUNGAN.
American Gamelan Institute, Box 1052, Lebanon, NH 03766-4052. TEL 603-448-8837. *5375*

BANACH CENTER PUBLICATIONS.
Polska Akademia Nauk, Instytut Matematyczny, Dzial Wydawnictw, Ul. Sniadeckich 8, P.O. Box 137, 00-950 Warsaw, Poland. TEL 48-22-6282471. FAX 48-22-6293997. *4564*

BANBER HAYASTANI ARKHIVNERI.
Arkhivnoe Upravlenie pri Sovete Ministrov Armenii, Ul. Rachiia Kochara 5, Erevan 375033, Armenia. TEL 7-885-225355. *3552*

BANDAOTI XUEBAO.
Science Press, Marketing and Sales Department, 16 Donghuangchenggen North St., Beijing 100717, People's Republic of China. TEL 4010642. FAX 4019810. *2625*

BANGLADESH JOURNAL OF FOREST SCIENCE.
Bangladesh Forest Research Institute, Chittagong 4000, Bangladesh. TEL 880-31-681586. FAX 880-31-681566. *3147*

BANGLADESH JOURNAL OF ZOOLOGY.
Zoological Society of Bangladesh, c/o Dept. of Zoology, University of Dhaka, Dhaka 1000, Bangladesh. TEL 880-2-868333. FAX 880-2-865583. *828*

BANK DIRECTOR.
Bank Director, Box 3468, Brentwood, TN 37024. TEL 615-371-0406. FAX 615-371-0899. *1108*

BANK OF VALLETTA REVIEW.
Bank of Valletta, Zachary St., Valletta VLT 04, Malta. TEL 356-313134. FAX 356-313139. *936*

BANKING LAW ANTHOLOGY.
International Library Law Book Publishers, Inc., 4301 N. Fairfax Rd., Ste. 875, Arlington, VA 22203. TEL 703-528-1000. FAX 703-528-6060. *3918*

BANKING LAW JOURNAL.
Warren, Gorham & Lamont, One Penn Plaza, New York, NY 10119. TEL 212-971-5000. FAX 212-971-5113. *1112*

BANNER (GRAND RAPIDS).
C R C Publications, 2850 Kalamazoo Ave. S.E., Grand Rapids, MI 49560. TEL 561-224-0725. FAX 561-224-0834. *6414*

BAO PO.
Wuhan Gongye Daxue, Bao Po Bianjibu, 14 Luoshi Lu, Wuchang, Wuhan, Hubei 430070, People's Republic of China. *2756*

BAPTIST QUARTERLY.
Baptist Historical Society, 28 Dowthorpe Hill, Earls Barton, Northampton NN6 0PB, England. TEL 44-1604-811170. FAX 44-1604-811170. *6415*

BARIATRICIAN.
American Society of Bariatric Physicians, 5600 S. Quebec, Ste. 109A, Englewood, CO 80111-2208. TEL 303-770-2526. *5470*

BARRON FAMILY NEWSLETTER.
Family Heritage Publications, 1886 Rice Blvd., Fairborn, OH 45324-3158. TEL 513-372-2744. *3213*

BARTONIA.
Philadelphia Botanical Club, c/o Academy of Natural Sciences of Philadelphia, 1900 Benjamin Franklin Pkwy., Philadelphia, PA 19103. TEL 215-299-1000. *694*

BARTS JOURNAL.
Queen Mary and Westfield College, External Relations Department, Mile End Rd., London E1 4NS, England. TEL 44-171-415-3732. FAX 44-171-975-5556. *3704*

BASEBALL QUARTERLY REVIEWS.
H O K Enterprises, Box 9343, Schenectady, NY 12309. TEL 518-399-7890. *6799*

BASIC AND APPLIED SOCIAL PSYCHOLOGY.
Lawrence Erlbaum Associates, Inc., 10 Industrial Dr., Mahwah, NJ 07430-2262. TEL 201-236-9500. FAX 201-236-0072. *6096*

BASIC AND CLINICAL CARDIOLOGY SERIES.
Marcel Dekker, Inc., 270 Madison Ave., New York, NY 10016. TEL 212-696-9000. FAX 212-685-4540. *4811*

BASIC & CLINICAL ENDOCRINOLOGY.
Marcel Dekker, Inc., 270 Madison Ave., New York, NY 10016. TEL 212-696-9000. FAX 212-685-4540. *4882*

BASIC LEGAL DOCUMENTS ON REGIONAL ENVIRONMENTAL COOPERATION.
Martinus Nijhoff Publishers, Human Rights and International Law Postbus 163, 3300 AD Dordrecht, Netherlands. TEL 31-78-334911. FAX 31-78-334254. *4106*

BASIC LIFE SCIENCES.
Plenum Publishing Corp., 233 Spring St., New York, NY 10013-1578. TEL 212-620-8000. FAX 212-463-0742. *588*

BASIN RESEARCH.
Blackwell Science Ltd., Osney Mead, Oxford OX2 0EL, England. TEL 44-1865-206206. FAX 44-1865-721205. *2310*

BASIS: CHRISTENE SCHOOL.
Christelijk Onderwijzersverbond, Koningsstraat 203, 1210 Brussels, Belgium. TEL 32-2-2274111. FAX 32-2-2194761. *2424*

BATERIA.
Hardenbergstr. 31, 90768 Fuerth, Germany. *4325*

DER BAYERISCHE INTERNIST.
Juergen Hartmann Verlag GmbH, Seefeld 18, 91093 Hessdorf-Klebheim, Germany. TEL 49-9135-7123-0. FAX 49-9135-712340. *4645*

BAYLOR LARIAT.
Baylor University, Lariat, Box 97353, Waco, TX 76798. TEL 817-755-1711. FAX 817-755-1714. *1941*

BEAD FORUM.
Society of Bead Researchers, 1600 Liverpool Ct., Ottawa, ON K1A 0M5, Canada. TEL 613-990-4814. FAX 613-952-1756. *354*

BEADS.
Society of Bead Researchers, 1600 Liverpool Ct., Ottawa, ON K1A 0M5, Canada. TEL 613-990-4814. FAX 613-952-1756. *311*

BEAGLE.
Museum & Art Gallery of the Northern Territory, P.O. Box 4646, Darwin, N.T. 0801, Australia. TEL 61-8-89998201. FAX 61-8--89998289. *5351*

BEAM MODIFICATION OF MATERIALS.
Elsevier Science B.V., Books Division, P.O. Box 211, 1000 AE Amsterdam, Netherlands. TEL 31-20-4853911. FAX 31-20-4853705. *5859*

BEAUFORTIA.
Universiteit van Amsterdam, Instituut voor Systematisch en Populatie Biologie (Zoologisch Museum), P.O. Box 94766, 1090 GT Amsterdam, Netherlands. TEL 31-20-5256901. FAX 31-20-5255402. *828*

BEAUTY INC.
Beauty & Barber Supply Institute, Inc., 11811 N. Tatum Blvd., Ste. 1085, Phoeniz, AZ 85028-1625. TEL 602-404-1800. FAX 602-404-8900. *504*

BEBIDAS MEXICANAS.
Alfa Editores Tecnicos S.A., Libertad No. 107-402, 03660 Mexico DF, Mexico. TEL 525-579-3333. FAX 525-532-9504. *515*

BEE WORLD.
International Bee Research Association, 18 North Rd., Cardiff CF1 3DY, Wales. TEL 44-1222-372409. FAX 44-1222-665522. *101*

BEEKEEPING.
Devon Beekeepers Association, c/o Brian Gant, Ed., Leaf Orchard, Grange Rd., Buckfast, Devon TQ11 0EH, England. TEL 44-1364-642233. FAX 44-1364-342233. *102*

BEEKEEPING & DEVELOPMENT.
Bees for Development, Troy, Monmouth, Gwent NP5 4AB, Wales. TEL 44-1600-713648. FAX 44-1600-716167. *102*

BE'EMMET.
Beit Berl College, Yemima Center for Study and Teaching of Children's Literature, Beit Berl, Doar Beit Berl 44905, Israel. TEL 972-5-7476400. FAX 972-9-7454104. *4380*

BEER-SHEVA.
Ben Gurion University of the Negev Press, P.O. Box 653, Beersheva, Israel. FAX 972-7-6472913. *355*

BEETHOVEN FORUM.
University of Nebraska Press, 312 N. 14th St., Box 880484, Lincoln, NE 68588-0484. TEL 402-472-3581. FAX 402-472-6214. *5376*

THE BEHAVIOR ANALYST.
Association for Behavior Analysis, 213 West Hall, Western Michigan University, Kalamazoo, MI 49008-5052. TEL 616-387-8341. FAX 616-387-8354. *6096*

BEHAVIOR AND PHILOSOPHY.
Cambridge Center for Behavioral Studies, 336 Baker Ave., Concord, MA 01742-2107. TEL 617-491-9020. FAX 617-491-1072. *6096*

BEHAVIOR AND SOCIAL ISSUES.
Cambridge Center for Behavioral Studies, 336 Baker Ave., Concord, MA 01742-2107. TEL 617-491-9020. FAX 617-491-1072. *6096*

BEHAVIOR GENETICS.
Plenum Publishing Corp., 233 Spring St., New York, NY 10013-1578. TEL 212-620-8000. FAX 212-463-0742. *764*

BEHAVIOR RESEARCH METHODS, INSTRUMENTS, AND COMPUTERS.
Psychonomic Society, Inc., 1710 Fortview Rd., Austin, TX 78704. TEL 512-462-2442. *6096*

BEHAVIOR THERAPY.
Association for Advancement of Behavior Therapy, 305 Seventh Ave., Ste. 16A, New York, NY 10001. *6096*

BEHAVIORAL & SOCIAL SCIENCES LIBRARIAN.
Haworth Press, Inc., 10 Alice St., Binghamton, NY 13904. TEL 607-722-5857. FAX 607-722-6362. *4163*

BEHAVIORAL BRAIN RESEARCH.
Elsevier Science B.V., P.O. Box 211, 1000 AE Amsterdam, Netherlands. TEL 31-20-4853911. FAX 31-20-4853598. *5054*

BEHAVIORAL ECOLOGY.
Oxford University Press, Journals, 2001 Evans Rd., Cary, NC 27513. TEL 919-677-0977. FAX 919-677-1714. *588*

BEHAVIORAL INTERVENTIONS.
John Wiley & Sons Ltd., Journals, Baffins Ln., Chichester, W. Sussex PO19 1UD, England. TEL 44-1243-779777. FAX 44-1243-775878. *5054*

BEHAVIORAL MEDICINE.
Heldref Publications, 1319 Eighteenth St., N.W., Washington, DC 20036-1802. TEL 202-396-6267. FAX 202-296-5149. *6097*

BEHAVIORAL NEUROSCIENCE.
American Psychological Association, 750 First St., N.E., Washington, DC 20002-4242. TEL 202-336-5600. FAX 202-336-5568. *6097*

BEHAVIOUR.
E.J. Brill, P.O. Box 9000, 2300 PA Leiden, Netherlands. TEL 31-71-5353500. FAX 31-71-5317532. *828*

BEHAVIOUR AND INFORMATION TECHNOLOGY.
Taylor & Francis Ltd., 1 Gunpowder Sq., London EC4A 3DE, England. TEL 44-171-583-0490. FAX 44-171-583-0585. *6097*

BEHAVIOUR RESEARCH AND THERAPY.
Elsevier Science Ltd., Pergamon, P.O. Box 800, Kidlington, Oxford OX5 1DX, England. TEL 44-1865-843000. FAX 44-1865-843010. *6097*

BEHAVIOURAL PROCESSES.
Elsevier Science B.V., P.O. Box 211, 1000 AE Amsterdam, Netherlands. TEL 31-20-4853911. FAX 31-20-4853598. *5054*

BEIERSDORF JOURNAL.
Beiersdorf AG, Unnastr. 48, 20253 Hamburg, Germany. FAX 49-40-5696143. *1579*

BEIFANG YUANYI.
Beifang Yuanyi Bianjibu, Yifayuan, Haping Lu, Harbin, Heilongjiang 150069, People's Republic of China. TEL 86-451-6674276. FAX 86-451-666-2358. *3182*

BEIJING YIKE DAXUE XUEBAO.
Beijing Yike Daxue, Xueyuan Lu, Beijing 100083, People's Republic of China. TEL 861-2091551. FAX 861-2015681. *4645*

BEITRAEGE ZUR INFUSIONSTHERAPIE UND TRANSFUSIONSMEDIZIN.
S. Karger AG, Allschwilerstr. 10, P.O. Box, CH-4009 Basel, Switzerland. TEL 41-61-3061111. FAX 41-61-3061234. *4645*

BEITRAEGE ZUR NAMENFORSCHUNG.
Universitaetsverlag C. Winter Heidelberg GmbH, Hans-Bunte-Str. 18, 69123 Heidelberg, Germany. TEL 49-6221-770260. FAX 49-6221-770269. *4244*

BEITRAEGE ZUR PALAEONTOLOGIE.
Institut fuer Palaeontologie, Althanstr. 14, A-1090 Vienna, Austria. TEL 43-1-313369724. FAX 43-1-31336784. *5557*

BEITRAEGE ZUR RHEINKUNDE.
Rhein-Museum e.V., Charlottenstr. 53a, 56077 Koblenz-Ehrenbreitstein, Germany. TEL 49-261-703450. FAX 49-261-703450. *3552*

BEITRAEGE ZUR UROLOGIE.
S. Karger AG, Allschwilerstr. 10, P.O. Box, CH-4009 Basel, Switzerland. TEL 41-61-3061111. FAX 41-61-3061234. *5159*

BELGIAN JOURNAL OF BOTANY.
Societe Royale de Botanique de Belgique, Chaussee de Wavre 1850, B-1160 Brussels, Belgium. TEL 32-2-2693905. FAX 32-2-2701567. *694*

BELGIAN MATHEMATICAL SOCOCIETY - SIMON STEVIN. BULLETIN.
Belgian Mathematical Society, c/o Prof. Jules Leroy, Sec., Campus Plaine, C.P. 218-01, Bd. du Triomphe, 1050 Brussels, Belgium. TEL 32-2-6505845. FAX 32-2-6505867. *4564*

BELGISCHE FRUITREVUE.
Prov. Pomologische Vereniging Van Oost-Vlaanderen v.z.w., c/o M. Albert Vereecken, Ed., Boonstraat 12, 9220 Hamme, Belgium. TEL 32-52-477485. FAX 32-52-481193. *3182*

BELL LABS TECHNICAL JOURNAL.
Lucent Technologies, 600 Mountain Ave., Rm. 3C-412, Box 636, Murray Hill, NJ 07974-0636. TEL 908-582-4834. FAX 908-582-4430. *2032*

BELOIT POETRY JOURNAL.
Beloit Poetry Journal Foundation, Inc., Box 154, R.F.D. 2, Ellsworth, ME 04605. TEL 207-667-5598. *4503*

BELOIT POETRY JOURNAL. CHAPBOOK.
Beloit Poetry Journal Foundation, Inc., Box 154, R.F.D. 2, Ellsworth, ME 04605. TEL 207-667-5598. *4504*

BELTSVILLE SYMPOSIA IN AGRICULTURAL RESEARCH.
Kluwer Academic Publishers, Postbus 17, 3300 AA Dordrecht, Netherlands. TEL 31-78-6392392. FAX 31-78-6392254. *102*

BENJAMINS TRANSLATION LIBRARY.
John Benjamins Publishing Co., Amsteldijk 44, P.O. Box 75577, 1070 AN Amsterdam, Netherlands. TEL 31-20-6738156. FAX 31-20-6792956. *4244*

BERCEO.
Instituto de Estudios Riojanos, C. Muro de la Mata, 8 principal, 26071 Logrono, Spain. TEL 34-41-262064. FAX 34-41-246667. *3773*

BEREAVEMENT CARE.
Cruse - Bereavement Care, 126 Sheen Rd., Richmond, Surrey TW9 1UR, England. TEL 0181-940-4818. FAX 0181-940-7638. *6656*

BERGEY'S MANUAL OF DETERMINATIVE BACTERIOLOGY.
Williams and Wilkins, Book Division 351 W. Camden St., Baltimore, MD 21201. TEL 410-528-4000. FAX 410-528-4312. *781*

BERICHTE NATURWISSENSCHAFTLICH - MEDIZINISCHEN VEREINS IN INNSBRUCK.
Naturwissenschaftlich - Medizinischer Verein in Innsbruck, Technikerstr. 25, A-6020 Innsbruck, Austria. TEL 43-512-5076142. FAX 43-512-2185358. *588*

BERKELEY JOURNAL OF EMPLOYMENT AND LABOR LAW.
University of California Press, Journals Division, 2120 Berkeley Way, No. 5812, Berkeley, CA 94720-5812. TEL 510-643-7154. FAX 510-642-9917. *1421*

BERKELEY JOURNAL OF INTERNATIONAL LAW.
University of California Press, Journals Division, 2120 Berkeley Way, No. 5812, Berkeley, CA 94720-5812. TEL 510-643-7154. FAX 510-642-9917. *4106*

BERKELEY PLANNING JOURNAL.
University of California at Berkeley, Department of City and Regional Planning, Graduate Students, Wurster Hall, Rm. 228, Berkeley, CA 94720. TEL 415-642-3256. FAX 510-643-9576. *3741*

BERKELEY TECHNOLOGY LAW JOURNAL.
University of California Press, Journals Division, 2120 Berkeley Way, No. 5812, Berkeley, CA 94720-5812. TEL 510-643-7154. FAX 510-642-9917. *3919*

BERKELEY WOMEN'S LAW JOURNAL.
University of California Press, Journals Division, 2120 Berkeley Way, No. 5812, Berkeley, CA 94720-5812. TEL 510-643-7154. FAX 510-642-9917. *3919*

BERKSHIRE ARCHAEOLOGICAL JOURNAL.
Berkshire Archaeological Society, 28 Holmes Rd., Reading, Berks, England. *355*

BERNHARD-HARMS-VORLESUNGEN.
Institut fuer Weltwirtschaft, Duesternbrooker Weg 120, 24105 Kiel, Germany. TEL 49-431-8814305. FAX 49-431-8814520. *1226*

BERNOULLI.
Thomson Science, 2-6 Boundary Row, London SE1 8HN, England. TEL 44-171-8650066. FAX 44-171-5229623. *4564*

BERYTUS ARCHEOLOGICAL STUDIES.
American University of Beirut, Faculty of Arts and Sciences, A U B Post Hall 106, Beirut, Lebanon. FAX 873-1450231. *355*

BEST BOOK CATALOG IN THE WORLD.
Loompanics Unlimited, Box 1197, Port Townsend, WA 98368. TEL 360-385-5087. FAX 360-385-7785. *533*

BEST OF LONG RANGE PLANNING.
Elsevier Science Ltd., Books Division, P.O. Box 800, Kidlington, Oxford OX5 1DK. TEL 44-1865-843000. FAX 44-1865-843010. *1466*

BEST READ GUIDE.
Box 1958, 77 Finlay Rd., Orleans, MA 02653. TEL 508-240-1212. FAX 508-240-2912. *7188*

BEST'S LOSS CONTROL ENGINEERING MANUAL.
A.M. Best Co., Ambest Rd., Oldwick, NJ 08858. TEL 908-439-2200. FAX 908-439-3296. *3809*

BEST'S UNDERWRITING NEWSLETTER.
A.M. Best Co., Ambest Rd., Oldwick, NJ 08858. TEL 908-439-2200. FAX 908-439-3296. *3810*

BESTUURSDINAMIKA.
Suider-Afrika Instituut vir Bestuurswetenskaplikes, c/o Dept. Ondernemingsbestuur, Privaatsak X1, Matieland 7602, South Africa. TEL 27-21-8082222. FAX 27-21-8082226. *1466*

BESTUURSFORUM.
C D A - bestuurdersvereniging, P.O. Box 30453, 2500 GL The Hague, Netherlands. TEL 31-70-3424890. FAX 31-70-3643417. *6165*

BESTUURSKUNDE.
Vuga Uitgeverij B.V., Postbus 16400, 2500 BK The Hague, Netherlands. TEL 31-70-3614011. FAX 31-70-3632338. *6165*

BETTER ROADS.
Gras Industries Inc., Box 558, Park Ridge, IL 60068. TEL 312-693-7710. FAX 847-696-3445. *2778*

BEYOND WORDS.
Wycliffe Bible Translators Australia, Graham Rd., Kangaroo Ground, Vic. 3097, Australia. TEL 61-3-97122777. FAX 61-3-97122799. *6323*

BHANDARKAR ORIENTAL RESEARCH INSTITUTE. ANNALS.
Bhandarkar Oriental Research Institute, Deccan Gymkhana, Pune 411 004, India. TEL 91-212-356932. *5522*

BIBLE TODAY.
Liturgical Press, St. John's Abbey, Collegeville, MN 56321-7500. TEL 320-363-2213. FAX 800-445-5899. *6323*

BIBLICAL INTERPRETATION.
E.J. Brill, P.O. Box 9000, 2300 PA Leiden, Netherlands. TEL 31-71-5353500. FAX 31-71-5317532. *6324*

BIBLICAL INTERPRETATION SERIES.
E.J. Brill, P.O. Box 9000, 2300 PA Leiden, Netherlands. TEL 31-71-5353500. FAX 31-71-5317532. *6324*

BIBLICAL THEOLOGY BULLETIN.
Biblical Theology Bulletin, Inc., Box 1038, S. Orange, NJ 07079. TEL 201-761-9770. FAX 201-325-7136. *6324*

BIBLIOGRAPHICAL SOCIETY OF AUSTRALIA AND NEW ZEALAND. BULLETIN.
Bibliographical Society of Australia & New Zealand, c/o State Library of Victoria, 328 Swanston St., Melbourne, Vic. 3000, Australia. TEL 61-3-96699032. FAX 61-3-96699012. *6263*

BIBLIOGRAPHICAL SOCIETY OF CANADA. PAPERS.
Bibliographical Society of Canada, P.O. Box 575, Sta. "P", Toronto, ON M5S 2T1, Canada. *537*

BIBLION.
Greenwood Press, Inc., 88 Post Rd. W., Box 5007, Westport, CT 06881. TEL 203-226-3571. FAX 203-222-1502. *4163*

BIBLIOTECA ITALIANA.
University of California Press, 2120 Berkeley Way, Berkeley, CA 94720. TEL 510-642-4247. FAX 510-643-7127. *4381*

BIBLIOTHECA HERTZIANA. ROEMISCHES JAHRBUCH.
Bibliotheca Hertziana, Via Gregoriana 28, 00187 Rome, Italy. TEL 39-6-69993258. FAX 39-6-69993333. *432*

BIBLIOTHECA NUTRITIO ET DIETA.
S. Karger AG, Allschwilerstr. 10, P.O. Box, CH-4009 Basel, Switzerland. TEL 41-61-3061111. FAX 41-61-3061234. *5470*

BIBLIOTHECA PSYCHIATRICA.
S. Karger AG, Allschwilerstr. 10, P.O. Box, CH-4009 Basel, Switzerland. TEL 41-61-3061111. FAX 41-61-3061234. *5054*

BIBLIOTHECA SACRA.
Dallas Theological Seminary, 3909 Swiss Ave., Dallas, TX 75204. TEL 214-824-3094. FAX 214-841-3532. *6416*

BIG SKY MAC E - ZINE.
B - Smug, Big - Sky Mac User Group, Box 80553, Billings, MT 59108. *2195*

BIJEN.
Bijen, Postbus 198, 6720 AD Bennekom, Netherlands. TEL 31-317-422422. FAX 31-317-424180. *103*

BILINGUAL RESEARCH JOURNAL.
National Association for Bilingual Education, 1220 L. St., N.W., Ste. 605, Washington, DC 20005. *2425*

BILINGUAL REVIEW.
Bilingual Review Press, Hispanic Research Center, Arizona State University, Tempe, AZ 85287-2702. TEL 602-965-3867. FAX 602-965-8309. *4245*

BILLY JAMES HARGIS' CHRISTIAN CRUSADE.
Church of Christian Crusade, Box 977, Tulsa, OK 74102. TEL 417-451-4234. FAX 501-438-6054. *6325*

BINARY: COMPUTING IN MICROBIOLOGY.
Academic Press Ltd., 24-28 Oval Rd., London NW1 7DX, England. TEL 44-171-267-4466. FAX 44-171-482-2293. *781*

BINGDUXUE ZAZHI.
Science Press, Marketing and Sales Department, 16 Donghuangchenggen North St., Beijing 100717, People's Republic of China. TEL 4010642. FAX 4019810. *781*

BINOCULAR VISION & STRABISMUS QUARTERLY.
Binoculus Publishing, Box 3727, Summit Haus, 740 Piney Acres Cir., Dillon, CO 80435-3727. TEL 970-262-0753. FAX 970-262-0753. *4990*

BIO.
A B E S, Av. Beira-Mar, 216-13 andar, 20021-060 Rio de Janeiro, RJ, Brazil. TEL 55-21-2103221. FAX 55-21-2626838. *2778*

BIO-MEDICAL MATERIALS AND ENGINEERING.
I O S Press, Van Diemenstraat 94, 1013 CN Amsterdam, Netherlands. TEL 31-20-6382189. FAX 31-20-6203419. *646*

BIOACTIVE MOLECULES.
Elsevier Science B.V., Books Division, P.O. Box 211, 1000 AE Amsterdam, Netherlands. TEL 31-20-4853911. FAX 31-20-4853705. *589*

BIOCATALYSIS AND BIOTRANSFORMATION.
Gordon and Breach - Harwood Academic, Amsteldisk 166, 1st Fl., 1079 LH Amsterdam, Netherlands. *678*

BIOCELL.
Centro Regional de Investigaciones Cientificas y Tecnologicas, Casilla de Correo 131, 5500 Mendoza, Argentina. TEL 54-61-205020 ext. 2670. FAX 54-61-380232. *796*

BIOCHEMICAL AND BIOPHYSICAL RESEARCH COMMUNICATIONS.
Academic Press, Inc., Journal Division, 525 B St., Ste. 1900, San Diego, CA 92101-4495. TEL 619-230-1840. FAX 619-699-6800. *652*

BIOCHEMICAL AND MOLECULAR MEDICINE.
Academic Press, Inc., Journal Division, 525 B. St., Ste. 1900, San Diego, CA 92101-4495. TEL 619-230-1840. FAX 619-699-6800. *652*

BIOCHEMICAL EDUCATION.
Elsevier Science Ltd., Pergamon, P.O. Box 800, Kidlington, Oxford OX5 1DX, England. TEL 44-1865-843000. FAX 44-1865-843010. *652*

BIOCHEMICAL GENETICS.
Plenum Publishing Corp., 233 Spring St., New York, NY 10013-1578. TEL 212-620-8000. FAX 212-463-0742. *652*

BIOCHEMICAL JOURNAL.
Portland Press Ltd., 59 Portland Pl., London W1N 3AJ, England. TEL 44-171-580-5530. FAX 44-171-323-1136. *652*

BIOCHEMICAL PHARMACOLOGY.
Elsevier Science Inc., Box 945, New York, NY 10159-0945. TEL 212-633-3730. FAX 212-633-3680. *5650*

BIOCHEMICAL SOCIETY SYMPOSIUM.
Portland Press Ltd., 59 Portland Pl., London W1N 3AJ, England. TEL 44-171-580-5530. FAX 44-171-323-1136. *652*

BIOCHEMICAL SOCIETY TRANSACTIONS.
Portland Press Ltd., 59 Portland Pl., London W1N 3AJ, England. TEL 44-171-580-5530. FAX 44-171-323-1136. *653*

BIOCHEMICAL SYSTEMATICS AND ECOLOGY.
Elsevier Science Ltd., Pergamon, P.O. Box 800, Kidlington, Oxford OX5 1DX, England. TEL 44-1865-843000. FAX 44-1865-843010. *653*

BIOCHEMISTRY (MOSCOW).
Maik Nauka - Interperiodica, Mezhdunarodnyi Otdel, Ul. Profsoyuznaya, 90, 117864 Moscow, Russia. TEL 7-095-3360060. FAX 212-463-0742. *653*

BIOCHEMISTRY AND CELL BIOLOGY.
National Research Council of Canada, Research Journals, Ottawa, ON K1A 0R6, Canada. TEL 613-993-9084. FAX 613-952-7656. *653*

BIOCHEMISTRY & MOLECULAR BIOLOGY OF FISHES.
Elsevier Science B.V., Books Division, P.O. Box 211, 1000 AE Amsterdam, Netherlands. TEL 31-20-4853911. FAX 31-20-4853705. *829*

BIOCHEMISTRY OF THE ELEMENTS.
Plenum Publishing Corp., 233 Spring St., New York, NY 10013-1578. TEL 212-620-8000. FAX 212-463-0742. *653*

BIOCHEMISTRY: SERIES OF MONOGRAPHS.
John Wiley & Sons, Inc., Journals, 605 Third Ave., New York, NY 10158-0012. TEL 212-850-6000. *654*

BIOCHIMICA ET BIOPHYSICA ACTA.
Elsevier Science B.V., P.O. Box 211, 1000 AE Amsterdam, Netherlands. TEL 31-20-4853911. FAX 31-20-4853598. *654*

BIOCHIMIE.
Editions Scientifiques et Medicales Elsevier, 141 rue de Javel, 75747 Paris, France. TEL 33-1-45589022. FAX 33-1-45589421. *654*

BIOCONTROL.
Centro Internacional para el Control Biologico de Plagas y Patogenos, Apdo. 18-1057, Lima 18, Peru. TEL 51-14-792291. FAX 51-14-792291. *781*

BIOCONTROL SCIENCE AND TECHNOLOGY.
Carfax Publishing Co., P.O. Box 25, Abingdon, Oxon. OX14 3UE, England. TEL 44-1235-401000. FAX 44-1235-401550. *216*

BIOCYCLE.
J G Press, Inc., 419 State Ave., Emmaus, PA 18049. TEL 610-967-4135. *2983*

BIODEGRADATION.
Kluwer Academic Publishers, Postbus 17, 3300 AA Dordrecht, Netherlands. TEL 31-78-6392392. FAX 31-78-6392254. *2983*

BIODIVERSITY AND CONSERVATION.
Chapman & Hall, Journals Department 2-6 Boundary Row, London SE1 8HN, England. TEL 44-171-8650066. FAX 44-171-5229623. *2224*

BIODRUGS.
Adis International Limited, Private Bag 65901, Mairangi Bay, Auckland 10, New Zealand. TEL 64-9-479-8100. FAX 215-741-5251. *5650*

BIOELECTROCHEMISTRY AND BIOENERGETICS.
Elsevier Science S.A., P.O. Box 564, CH-1001 Lausanne 1, Switzerland. TEL 41-21-3207381. FAX 41-21-3235444. *654*

BIOELECTROMAGNETICS.
John Wiley & Sons, Inc., Journals, 605 Third Ave., New York, NY 10158. TEL 212-850-6645. FAX 212-850-6021. *673*

BIOETHICS YEARBOOK.
Kluwer Academic Publishers, Postbus 17, 3300 AA Dordrecht, Netherlands. TEL 31-78-6392392. FAX 31-78-6392254. *6325*

BIOFACTORS.
I O S Press, Van Diemenstraat 94, 1013 CN Amsterdam, Netherlands. TEL 31-20-6382189. FAX 31-20-6203419. *654*

BIOFOULING.
Gordon and Breach - Harwood Academic, Amsteldisk 166, 1st Fl., 1079 LH Amsterdam, Netherlands. *2975*

BIOGENIC AMINES.
V S P, P.O. Box 346, 3700 AH Zeist, Netherlands. TEL 31-30-6925790. FAX 31-30-6932081. *654*

BIOGEOCHEMISTRY.
Kluwer Academic Publishers, Postbus 17, 3300 AA Dordrecht, Netherlands. TEL 31-78-6392392. FAX 31-78-6392254. *654*

BIOGRAPHY (HONOLULU).
University of Hawaii Press, Journals Department, 2840 Kolowalu St., Honolulu, HI 96822. TEL 808-956-8833. FAX 808-988-6052. *571*

BIOLOGIA ACUATICA.
Instituto de Limnologia, Casilla de Correo 712, 1900 La Plata, Argentina. TEL 54-1-2375864. FAX 54-1-2377799. *590*

BIOLOGIA OGGI.
Associazione Nazionale Laureati in Scienze Biologiche, Via Guglielmo degli Ubertini, 64, 00176 Rome, Italy. TEL 39-6-21707494. *590*

REFEREED SERIALS

BIOLOGIA PLANTARUM.
Kluwer Academic Publishers, Postbus 17, 3300 AA Dordrecht, Netherlands. TEL 31-78-6392392. FAX 31-78-6392254. *695*

BIOLOGICAL BULLETIN.
Science Press, Marketing and Sales Department, 16 Donghuangchenggen North St., Beijing 100717, People's Republic of China. TEL 4010642. FAX 4012180. *590*

BIOLOGICAL BULLETIN.
Marine Biological Laboratory, Woods Hole, MA 02543. TEL 508-289-7428. FAX 508-457-1924. *590*

BIOLOGICAL CONSERVATION.
Elsevier Science Ltd., P.O. Box 800, Kidlington, Oxford OX5 1DX, England. TEL 44-1865-843000. FAX 44-1865-843010. *2224*

BIOLOGICAL MAGNETIC RESONANCE.
Plenum Publishing Corp., 233 Spring St., New York, NY 10013-1578. TEL 212-620-8000. FAX 212-463-0742. *5798*

BIOLOGICAL PSYCHIATRY.
Elsevier Science Inc., Box 945, New York, NY 10159-0945. TEL 212-633-3730. FAX 212-633-3680. *5055*

BIOLOGICAL PSYCHOLOGY.
North-Holland, P.O. Box 211, 1000 AE Amsterdam, Netherlands. TEL 31-20-4853911. FAX 31-20-4853598. *6098*

BIOLOGICAL REGULATION & DEVELOPMENT.
Plenum Publishing Corp., 233 Spring St., New York, NY 10013-1578. TEL 212-620-8000. FAX 212-463-0742. *655*

BIOLOGICAL RESEARCH.
Sociedad de Biologia de Chile, Casilla 16164, Santiago 9, Chile. TEL 56-2-6862850. FAX 56-2-2225515. *590*

BIOLOGICAL SCIENCE REPORT.
U.S. National Biological Service, Information Transfer Center, 1201 Oak Ridge Dr., Ste. 200, Ft. Collins, CO 80525-5589. TEL 970-226-9401. FAX 970-226-9455. *591*

BIOLOGICAL SCIENCES REVIEW.
Philip Allan Publishers Ltd., Market Pl., Deddington, Oxon. OX15 0SE, England. TEL 44-1869-338652. FAX 44-1869-338803. *591*

BIOLOGICAL SIGNALS.
S. Karger AG, Allschwilerstr. 10, P.O. Box, CH-4009 Basel, Switzerland. TEL 41-61-3061111. FAX 41-61-3061234. *655*

BIOLOGICAL SOCIETY OF WASHINGTON. PROCEEDINGS.
Biological Society of Washington, National Museum of Natural History, Smithsonian Institution, Washington, DC 20560. TEL 202-786-2550. *591*

BIOLOGICAL TRACE ELEMENT RESEARCH.
Humana Press Inc., 999 Riverview Dr., Ste. 208, Totowa, NJ 07512. TEL 973-256-1699. FAX 973-256-8341. *655*

BIOLOGICHESKIE MEMBRANY.
Biologicheskie Membrany, Vavilova ul., 34, komn.335, 117990 Moscow, Russia. TEL 7-095-1359886. FAX 7-095-1359886. *673*

BIOLOGISCHE MEDIZIN.
Aurelia Verlag GmbH, Dr.-Reckeweg-Str. 2-4, 76532 Baden-Baden, Germany. TEL 49-7221-50102. FAX 49-7221-501420. *4826*

BIOLOGY AND PHILOSOPHY.
Kluwer Academic Publishers, Postbus 17, 3300 AA Dordrecht, Netherlands. TEL 31-78-6392392. FAX 31-78-6392254. *592*

BIOLOGY OF REPRODUCTION.
Society for the Study of Reproduction, 1603 Monroe St., Madison, WI 53711-2021. TEL 608-256-2777. FAX 608-256-4610. *764*

BIOLOGY OF THE CELL.
Editions Scientifiques et Medicales Elsevier, 141 rue de Javel, 75747 Paris, France. TEL 33-1-45589022. FAX 33-1-45589421. *737*

BIOLOGY OF THE NEONATE.
S. Karger AG, Allschwilerstr. 10, P.O. Box, CH-4009 Basel, Switzerland. TEL 41-61-3061111. FAX 41-61-3061234. *4953*

BIOMASS & BIOENERGY.
Elsevier Science Ltd., Pergamon, P.O. Box 800, Kidlington, Oxford OX5 1DX, England. TEL 44-1865-843000. FAX 44-1865-843010. *2661*

BIOMATERIALS.
Elsevier Science Ltd., P.O. Box 800, Kidlington, Oxford OX5 1DX, England. TEL 44-1865-843000. FAX 44-1865-843010. *4646*

BIOMEDICAL AND CLINICAL ASPECTS OF COENZYME Q.
Elsevier Science B.V., Books Division, P.O. Box 211, 1000 AE Amsterdam, Netherlands. TEL 31-20-4853911. FAX 31-20-4853705. *813*

BIOMEDICAL AND ENVIRONMENTAL SCIENCES.
Zhongguo Yufang Yixue Kexueyuan, 27 Nanwei Rd., Beijing 100050, People's Republic of China. TEL 86-10-6317-3957. FAX 86-10-6317-0892. *4646*

BIOMEDICAL ENGINEERING.
Plenum Publishing Corp., Consultants Bureau, 233 Spring St., New York, NY 10013-1578. TEL 212-620-8468. FAX 212-463-0742. *4647*

BIOMEDICAL ENGINEERING AND COMPUTATION SERIES.
Gordon and Breach - Harwood Academic, Amsteldisk 166, 1st Fl., 1079 LH Amsterdam, Netherlands. *646*

BIOMEDICAL INSTRUMENTATION & TECHNOLOGY.
Hanley & Belfus, Inc., 210 S. 13th St., Philadelphia, PA 19107. TEL 215-546-7293. FAX 215-790-9330. *4647*

BIOMEDICAL MARKET NEWSLETTER.
David G. Anast, Ed.& Pub., 3237 Idaho Pl., Costa Mesa, CA 92626-2207. TEL 714-434-9500. FAX 714-434-9755. *1517*

BIOMEDICAL PEPTIDES, PROTEINS & NUCLEIC ACIDS.
Mayflower Worldwide Ltd., P.O. Box 13, Kingswinford, W. Midlands DY6 0HQ, England. TEL 44-1384-279324. FAX 44-1384-294463. *655*

BIOMEDICAL SCIENCES INSTRUMENTATION.
Instrument Society of America, 67 Alexander Dr., Box 12277, Research Triangle Park, NC 27709. TEL 919-549-8411. FAX 919-549-8288. *4647*

BIOMEDICINE AND PHARMACOTHERAPY.
Editions Scientifiques et medicales Elsevier, 141 rue de Javel, 75747 Paris, France. TEL 33-1-45589026. FAX 33-1-45589421. *4647*

BIOMEMBRANES.
Plenum Publishing Corp., 233 Spring St., New York, NY 10013-1578. TEL 212-620-8000. FAX 212-463-0742. *737*

BIOMETRICS.
International Biometric Society, 808 17th St., N.W., Ste. 200, Washington, DC 20006-3910. TEL 202-223-9669. FAX 202-223-9569. *6901*

BIOMIMETICS.
Plenum Publishing Corp., 233 Spring St., New York, NY 10013-1578. TEL 212-620-8000. FAX 212-463-0742. *646*

BIOORGANIC & MEDICINAL CHEMISTRY LETTERS.
Elsevier Science Ltd., Pergamon, P.O. Box 800, Kidlington, Oxford OX5 1DX, England. TEL 44-1865-843000. FAX 44-1865-843010. *1812*

BIOORGANIC CHEMISTRY.
Academic Press, Inc., Journal Division, 525 B St., Ste. 1900, San Diego, CA 92101-4495. TEL 619-230-1840. FAX 619-699-6800. *1812*

BIOPHYSICAL CHEMISTRY.
Elsevier Science B.V., P.O. Box 211, 1000 AE Amsterdam, Netherlands. TEL 31-20-4853911. FAX 31-20-4853598. *674*

BIOPHYSICAL JOURNAL.
Biophysical Society, 9650 Rockville Pike, Bethesda, MD 20814-3998. TEL 301-571-8338. FAX 301-530-7133. *674*

BIOPHYSICAL SOCIETY. ANNUAL MEETING. ABSTRACTS.
Biophysical Society, 9650 Rockville Pike, Bethesda, MD 20814-3998. TEL 301-571-8338. FAX 301-530-7133. *636*

BIOPHYSICS.
Elsevier Science Ltd., Pergamon, P.O. Box 800, Kidlington, Oxford OX5 1DX, England. TEL 44-1865-843000. FAX 44-1865-843010. *674*

BIOPOLYMERS.
John Wiley & Sons, Inc., Journals, 605 Third Ave., New York, NY 10158. TEL 212-692-6645. FAX 212-850-6021. *1812*

BIOPROCESS TECHNOLOGY SERIES.
Marcel Dekker, Inc., 270 Madison Ave., New York, NY 10016. TEL 212-696-9000. FAX 212-685-4540. *592*

BIOPSY INTERPRETATION SERIES.
Lippincott - Raven Publishers, 227 E. Washington Sq., Philadelphia, PA 19106. TEL 215-238-4200. FAX 215-238-4227. *4648*

BIORESOURCE TECHNOLOGY.
Elsevier Science Ltd., P.O. Box 800, Kidlington, Oxford OX5 1DX, England. TEL 44-1865-843000. FAX 44-1865-843010. *678*

BIORHEOLOGY.
Elsevier Science Ltd., Pergamon, P.O. Box 800, Kidlington, Oxford OX5 1DX, England. TEL 44-1865-843000. FAX 44-1865-843010. *674*

BIOSAFETY.
Science Reviews Ltd., P.O. Box 81, Northwood, Middlesex HA6 3DY, England. TEL 44-1923-823586. FAX 44-1923-825006. *592*

BIOSCIENCE.
American Institute of Biological Sciences, 1444 Eye St., N.W., Ste. 200, Washington, DC 20005. TEL 202-628-1500. FAX 202-628-1509. *593*

BIOSCIENCE, BIOTECHNOLOGY, AND BIOCHEMISTRY.
Japan Society for Bioscience, Biotechnology, and Agrochemistry, 2-4-16 Yayoi, Bunkyo-ku, Tokyo 113, Japan. TEL 03-3811-8789. FAX 81-3-3815-1920. *593*

BIOSCIENCE REPORTS.
Plenum Publishing Corp., 233 Spring St., New York, NY 10013-1578. TEL 212-620-8000. FAX 212-463-0742. *737*

BIOSENSORS AND BIOELECTRONICS.
Elsevier Science Ltd., P.O. Box 800, Kidlington, Oxford OX5 1DX, England. TEL 44-1865-843000. FAX 44-1865-843010. *679*

BIOSEPARATION.
Kluwer Academic Publishers, Postbus 17, 3300 AA Dordrecht, Netherlands. TEL 31-78-6392392. FAX 31-78-6392254. *679*

BIOSPECTROSCOPY.
John Wiley & Sons, Inc., Journals, 605 Third Ave., New York, NY 10158. TEL 212-850-6645. FAX 212-850-6021. *1789*

BIOSYNTHETIC PRODUCTS FOR CANCER CHEMOTHERAPY.
Elsevier Science B.V., Books Division, P.O. Box 211, 1000 AE Amsterdam, Netherlands. TEL 31-20-4853911. FAX 31-20-4853705. *4971*

BIOSYSTEMS.
Elsevier Science Ireland Ltd., P.O. Box 85, Limerick, Ireland. TEL 353-61-471944. FAX 353-61-472144. *593*

BIOTECHNIC AND HISTOCHEMISTRY.
Williams & Wilkins, 351 W. Camden St., Baltimore, MD 21201. TEL 410-528-4068. FAX 410-528-4452-2436. *796*

BIOTECHNOLOGY ADVANCES.
Elsevier Science Inc., Box 945, New York, NY 10159-0945. TEL 212-633-3730. FAX 212-633-3680. *679*

BIOTECHNOLOGY AND APPLIED BIOCHEMISTRY.
Portland Press Ltd., 59 Portland Pl., London W1N 3AJ, England. TEL 44-171-580-5530. FAX 44-171-323-1136. *679*

BIOTECHNOLOGY AND BIOENGINEERING.
John Wiley & Sons, Inc., Journals, 605 Third Ave., New York, NY 10158-0012. TEL 212-850-6645. FAX 212-850-6021. *680*

BIOTECHNOLOGY ANNUAL REVIEW.
Elsevier Science B.V., P.O. Box 211, 1000 AE Amsterdam, Netherlands. TEL 31-20-4853911. FAX 31-20-4853705. *680*

BIOTECHNOLOGY EDUCATION.
Helix Publishing, 1 Howard Ct., 94-96 Blackheath Hill, Greenwich, London SE10 8AF, England. *680*

BIOTECHNOLOGY LETTERS.
Chapman & Hall, Journals Department 2-6 Boundary Row, London SE1 8HN, England. TEL 44-171-8560066. FAX 44-171-5229623. *680*

BIOTECHNOLOGY PROGRESS.
American Institute of Chemical Engineers, 345 E. 47th St., New York, DC 20036. TEL 212-705-8100. FAX 212-705-8400. *680*

BIOTECHNOLOGY TECHNIQUES.
Chapman & Hall, Journals Department 2-6 Boundary Row, London SE1 8HN, England. TEL 44-171-8560066. FAX 44-171-5229323. *681*

BIOTHERAPY.
Kluwer Academic Publishers, Postbus 17, 3300 AA Dordrecht, Netherlands. TEL 31-78-6392392. FAX 31-78-6392254. *681*

BIOTHERAPY.
Cancer and Chemotherapy Publishers, Inc., Russhu Bldg., 2-2-3 Nihonbashi, Tokyo 103, Japan. TEL 81-3-3278-0052. FAX 81-3-3281-0435. *681*

BIOTROPICA.
Association for Tropical Biology, Inc., c/o Dr. Julie S. Denslow, Exec. Dir., Dept. of Plant Biology, Louisiana State University, Baton Rouge, LA 70803. TEL 504-388-8411. FAX 504-388-8459. *593*

BIRD STUDY.
British Trust for Ornithology, The Nunnery, Nunnery Pl., Thetford, Norwich IP24 2PU, England. *800*

BIRMINGHAM POETRY REVIEW.
English Department, University of Alabama, Birmingham, AL 35294. TEL 205-934-8573. FAX 205-975-8125. *4504*

BISON WORLD.
National Bison Association, 4701 Marion St., Ste. 100, Denver, CO 80216. TEL 303-292-2833. FAX 303-292-2564. *270*

BITON LEMORIM LE'ARAVIT.
Institute for Arabic Studies, Givat Haviva, M.P. Menasche 37 850, Israel. TEL 972-6-373336. FAX 972-6-373335. *4245*

BIULETYN NUMIZMATYCZNY.
Polskie Towarzystwo Numizmatyczne, Ul. Jezuicka 6, P.O. Box 2, 00-958 Warsaw, Poland. TEL 48-22-313928. FAX 48-22-313928. *5463*

BLACK EXCELLENCE.
N A F E O Excellence, Lovejoy Bldg., 400 12th St., N.E., Washington, DC 20002. TEL 202-543-9111. *1864*

BLACK ICE.
University of Colorado, English Department, Box 494, Boulder, CO 80309. TEL 303-492-8938. *4381*

BLACK MUSIC RESEARCH JOURNAL.
Center for Black Music Research, Columbia College Chicago, 600 S. Michigan Ave., Chicago, IL 60605. TEL 312-663-1600. FAX 312-663-9019. *5377*

BLACK TRAVELER MAGAZINE.
A & E Publishing, Inc., 11631 Victory Blvd., Ste. 201, N. Hollywood, CA 91606. TEL 818-753-9198. FAX 818-753-8405. *7188*

BLAKES REPORT ON INTELLECTUAL PROPERTY.
Blake, Cassels & Graydon, Box 25, Commerce Court West, Toronto, Ont. M5L 1A9, Canada. TEL 416-863-5840. FAX 416-863-2653. *3920*

BLIKI.
Natturufraedistofnun Islands, Hlemmur 3, P.O. Box 5320, 125 Reykjavik, Iceland. TEL 354-562-9822. FAX 354-562-0815. *801*

BLOOD.
W.B. Saunders Co., Curtis Center, 3rd Fl., Independence Sq. W., Philadelphia, PA 19106-3399. TEL 215-238-7800. FAX 215-238-6445. *4916*

BLOOD CELLS, MOLECULES, AND DISEASES.
Academic Press, Inc., Journal Division, 525 B St., Ste. 1900, San Diego, CA 92101. TEL 619-230-1840. FAX 619-699-6800. *4916*

BLOOD PRESSURE MONITORING.
Thomson Science, 2-6 Boundary Row, London SE1 8HN, England. TEL 44-171-865-0198. FAX 44-171-410-6600. *4811*

BLOOD PURIFICATION.
S. Karger AG, Allschwilerstr. 10, P.O. Box, CH-4009 Basel, Switzerland. TEL 41-61-3061111. FAX 41-61-3061234. *4917*

BLOOD THERAPY JOURNAL INTERNATIONAL.
Institute of Haematology, 11, 6-B Pusa Road, New Delhi 110 005, India. TEL 91-11-2246228. FAX 91-11-2247189. *4917*

BLOODSONGS.
Bambada Press, P.O. Box 7530, St. Kilda Rd., Melbourne, Vic. 3004, Australia. TEL 61-3-95762919. *4529*

BLUE BOOK OF CANADIAN BUSINESS.
International Press Publications Inc., 90 Nolan Ct., Ste. 21, Markham, ON L3R 4L9, Canada. TEL 905-946-9588. FAX 905-946-9590. *1226*

BLUMEA.
Rijksherbarium - Hortus Botanicus, Publications Department, P.O. Box 9514, 2300 RA Leiden, Netherlands. *695*

BLUMEA. SUPPLEMENT.
Rijksherbarium - Hortus Botanicus, Publications Department, P.O. Box 9514, 2300 RA Leiden, Netherlands. *695*

BOCHUMER PHILOSOPHISCHES JAHRBUCH FUER ANTIKE UND MITTELALTER.
John Benjamins Publishing Co., Amsteldijk 44, P.O. Box 75577, 1070 AN Amsterdam, Netherlands. TEL 31-20-6762325. FAX 31-20-6792956. *5720*

BODY CONTOURING SURGERY.
Field & Wood, Medical Periodicals, Inc., Box 975, Blue Bell, PA 19422. TEL 610-828-4010. FAX 215-482-0226. *5137*

BOGAZICI JOURNAL: REVIEW OF SOCIAL, ECONOMIC AND ADMINISTRATIVE STUDIES.
Bogazici Universitesi, Bebek, 80815 Istanbul, Turkey. TEL 90-212-2631500. FAX 90-212-2651479. *6605*

BOGTRYKKERNE - DISTRIKTSBLADENE.
Dansk Bogtrykker- og Presseforening, City Vest, P.O. Box 1559, DK-8220 Brabrand, Denmark. *6075*

BOHUSLAEN.
Bohuslaens Museum, P.O. Box 40, S-451 19 Uddevalla, Sweden. *3554*

BOIS ET FORETS DES TROPIQUES.
C I R A D - Foret, B.P. 5035, 34032 Montpellier Cedex 1, France. TEL 33-4-67745800. *3148*

BOLETIN ACEPRENSA.
Aceprensa, S.A., Nunez de Balboa, 125, 28006 Madrid, Spain. TEL 341-5628712. FAX 341-563-1243. *3774*

BOLETIN CHILENO DE PARASITOLOGIA.
Universidad de Chile, Departamento de Parasitologia, Casilla No. 9183, Santiago, Chile. TEL 56-2-6786252 ext. 5340. FAX 56-2-6786252. *4833*

BOLETIN DE FILOLOGIA.
Universidad de Chile, Departamento de Linguistica, Casilla 10136, Correo Central, Santiago, Chile. TEL 56-2-6787027. FAX 56-2-2716823. *4245*

BOLETIN INDUSTRIAL.
Editorial Nova, S.A. de C.V., Goldsmith 37-401, Col. Polanco, 11550 Mexico, D.F., Mexico. TEL 52-5-2806080. FAX 52-5-2803194. *1580*

BOLI YU TANGCI.
Zhongguo Qinggong Zonghui, Boli Tangci Yanjiusuo, No.6, Lane 365, Xinhua Lu, Shanghai 200052, People's Republic of China. TEL 2403230. *1726*

BOLLETTARIO.
Associazione Culturale "Le Avanguardie", Corso Camalchiaro 26-A, 41100 Modena, Italy. TEL 39-59-211791. *4382*

BOLLETTINO DEI CHIMICI IGIENISTI.
Societa Editoriale Farmaceutica s.r.l., Via Ausonio 12, 20123 Milan, Italy. TEL 39-2-89404545. FAX 39-2-89401168. *2756*

BOLLETTINO DEL LAVORO E DEI TRIBUTI.
Casa Editrice Edis s.r.l., Via S. Franca 60, 29100 Piacenza, Italy. TEL 39-523-325684. FAX 39-523-336782. *3921*

BOLLETTINO DI PSICOLOGIA APPLICATA.
Organizzazioni Speciali, Via fra Paolo Sarpi 7-A, 50136 Florence, Italy. TEL 39-55-672580. FAX 39-55-669446. *6098*

BOLLETTINO DI ZOOLOGIA AGRARIA E DI BACHICOLTURA.
Universita degli Studi di Milano, Istituto di Entomologia Agraria, Via Celoria 2, 20133 Milan, Italy. TEL 39-2-2362880. FAX 39-2-26680320. *748*

BOLLETTINO MALACOLOGICO.
Societa Italiana di Malacologia, c/o Acquario Civico, Viale Gadio 2, 20121 Milan, Italy. FAX 39-2-468563. *829*

BOND LAW REVIEW.
Bond University, Law School, Robina, Qld. 4211, Australia. TEL 61-7-55951060. FAX 61-7-55952246. *3921*

BONDINGS.
New Ways Ministry, 4012 29th St., Mt. Rainier, MD 20712. TEL 301-277-5674. FAX 301-864-6948. *3692*

BONE.
Elsevier Science Inc., Box 945, New York, NY 10159-0945. TEL 212-633-3730. FAX 212-633-3680. *5005*

THE BONE AND MINERAL RESEARCH ANNUAL.
Elsevier Science B.V., Books Division, P.O. Box 211, 1000 AE Amsterdam, Netherlands. TEL 31-20-4853911. FAX 31-20-4853705. *5005*

THE BOOK TRADE IN CANADA.
Key Publishers Co. Ltd., Quill & Quire, 70 The Esplanade, Ste. 210, Toronto, ON M5E 1R2, Canada. TEL 416-360-0044. FAX 416-955-0794. *6264*

BOOKBIRD.
Box 807, Highland Park, IL 60035-0807. TEL 317-494-0400. FAX 317-496-1700. *1865*

BOOKS IN LIBRARY AND INFORMATION SCIENCE SERIES.
Marcel Dekker, Inc., 270 Madison Ave., New York, NY 10016. TEL 212-696-9000. FAX 212-685-4540. *4224*

BOOKS IN SOILS PLANTS AND THE ENVIRONMENT SERIES.
Marcel Dekker, Inc., 270 Madison Ave., New York, NY 10016. TEL 212-696-9000. FAX 212-685-4540. *216*

BOPUXUE ZAZHI.
Zhongguo Kexueyuan, Wuhan Wuli Yanjiusuo, P.O. Box 71010, Xiaohongshan, Wuchang-qu, Wuhan, Hubei 430071, People's Republic of China. TEL 86-27-786-7791. FAX 86-27-788-5291. *5859*

BORDER HEALTH.
Pan American Health Organization, El Paso Field Office, 6006 N. Mesa, Ste. 600, El Paso, TX 79912. TEL 915-581-6645. FAX 915-833-4768. *6229*

BORDER STATES.
American Studies Association, Kentucky-Tennessee Chapter, c/o Michael Dunne, Sarah Howell, Eds., Department of English, Middle Tennessee State University, Murfreesboro, TN 37132. TEL 615-898-2649. *3619*

BORDERLINES: STUDIES IN AMERICAN CULTURE.
University of Wales Press, 6 Gwennyth St., Cathays, Cardiff CF2 4YD, Wales. TEL 44-1222-231919. FAX 44-1222-230908. *4382*

BOREAL ENVIRONMENT RESEARCH.
Finnish Environment Institute, P.O. Box 140, FIN-00251 Helsinki, Finland. TEL 358-0-1929-220. FAX 358-0-192902354. *2966*

BOSO NO KONCHU.
Chibaken Konchu Danwakai, c/o Mr. Yasutoshi Matsui, 3-102, 427-5 Nedo, Kashiwa-shi, Chiba-ken 277, Japan. *748*

BOSTON STUDIES IN APPLIED ECONOMICS.
Kluwer Academic Publishers, Postbus 17, 3300 AA Dordrecht, Netherlands. TEL 31-78-6392392. FAX 31-78-6392254. *1297*

BOSTON STUDIES IN THE PHILOSOPHY OF SCIENCE.
Kluwer Academic Publishers, Postbus 17, 3300 AA Dordrecht, Netherlands. TEL 31-78-6392392. FAX 31-78-6392254. *6516*

BOTANICA COMPLUTENSIS.
Universidad Complutense de Madrid, Servicio de Publicaciones, Ciudad Universitaria, 28040 Madrid, 28040 Madrid, Spain. TEL 34-1-3944402. FAX 34-1-3945034. *696*

BOTANICA MACARONESICA.
Jardin Botanico Canario Viera y Clavijo, Apartado de Correo 14 de Tarifa Alta s-n, 35017 Las Palmas de Gran Canaria, Spain. TEL 34-28-353604. FAX 34-28-352250. *696*

THE BOTANICAL REVIEW.
New York Botanical Garden, Scientific Publications Department, Bronx, NY 10458-5126. TEL 718-817-8721. FAX 718-817-8842. *696*

BOUILLABAISSE.
Alpha Beat Press, 31 Waterloo St., New Hope, PA 18938. TEL 215-862-0299. *4325*

BOUNDARY HISTORICAL SOCIETY. REPORT.
Boundary Historical Society, Box 580, Grand Forks, BC V0H 1H0, Canada. TEL 250-442-3283. *3619*

BOUNDARY-LAYER METEOROLOGY.
Kluwer Academic Publishers, Postbus 17, 3300 AA Dordrecht, Netherlands. TEL 31-78-6392392. FAX 31-78-6392254. *5228*

BOUNDARY 2.
Duke University Press, Box 90660, Durham, NC 27708-0660. TEL 919-687-3600. FAX 919-688-4574. *4383*

BRADLEYA.
British Cactus & Succulent Society, 71 Lakes Ln., Newport Pagnell, Bucks. MK16 8HT, England. TEL 44-1908-611650. *697*

BRAHMS STUDIES.
University of Nebraska Press, 312 N. 14th St., Box 880484, Lincoln, NE 68588-0484. TEL 402-472-3581. FAX 402-472-6213. *5378*

BRAIN AND COGNITION.
Academic Press, Inc., Journal Division, 525 B St., Ste. 1900, San Diego, CA 92101-4495. TEL 619-230-1840. FAX 619-699-6800. *6098*

BRAIN AND DEVELOPMENT.
Elsevier Science B.V., P.O. Box 211, 1000 AE Amsterdam, Netherlands. TEL 31-20-4853911. FAX 31-20-4853598. *5055*

BRAIN AND LANGUAGE.
Academic Press, Inc., Journal Division, 525 B St., Ste. 1900, San Diego, CA 92101-4495. TEL 619-230-1840. FAX 619-699-6800. *6098*

BRAIN, BEHAVIOR AND EVOLUTION.
S. Karger AG, Allschwilerstr. 10, P.O. Box, CH-4009 Basel, Switzerland. TEL 41-61-3061111. FAX 41-61-3061234. *5055*

BRAIN, BEHAVIOR, AND IMMUNITY.
Academic Press, Inc., Journal Division, 525 B St., Ste. 1900, San Diego, CA 92101-4495. TEL 619-230-1840. FAX 619-699-6800. *4792*

BRAIN INJURY.
Taylor & Francis Ltd., 1 Gunpowder Sq., London EC4A 3DE, England. TEL 44-171-583-0490. FAX 44-171-583-0585. *5055*

BRAIN RESEARCH BULLETIN.
Elsevier Science Inc., Box 945, New York, NY 10159-0945. TEL 212-633-3730. FAX 212-633-3680. *5056*

BRAIN TOPOGRAPHY.
Human Sciences Press, Inc., 233 Spring St., New York, NY 10013-1578. TEL 212-620-8000. FAX 212-463-0742. *5056*

BRANCHING OUT FROM ST. CLAIR COUNTY, ILLINOIS.
Marissa Historical and Genealogical Society, Box 47, Marissa, IL 62257. TEL 618-295-3337. *3214*

BRAND.
Kulturfoereningen Brand, P.O. Box 15015, S-104 65 Stockholm, Sweden. TEL 46-8-85-34-69. *4326*

BRASIL - BRAZIL.
Brown University, Department of Portuguese and Brazilian Studies, Box O, Providence, RI 02912. TEL 401-863-3042. FAX 401-863-7261. *4326*

BRAVO.
Bravo Editions, c/o John Edwin Cowen, Pub., 1081 Trafalgar St., Teaneck, NJ 07666. TEL 201-836-5922. *4504*

BRAZIL. SERVICO NACIONAL DE APRENDIZAGEM COMERCIAL. BOLETIM TECNICO.
Servico Nacional de Aprendizagem Comercial, Rua Dona Mariana, 48, 7 andar, Botafogo, 22280 Rio de Janeiro RJ, Brazil. TEL 55-21-5375898. FAX 55-21-2860645. *2425*

BRAZIL BUSINESS BRIEF.
Brazilian Chamber of Commerce, 32 Green St., London W1Y 3FD, England. TEL 44-171-499-0186. FAX 44-171-493-4621. *7188*

BRAZILIAN JOURNAL OF EPILEPSY AND CLINICAL NEUROPHYSIOLOGY.
Liga Brasileira de Epilepsia, Av. Ipiranga 6690, Sala 322, 90610-000 Porto Alegre RS, Brazil. TEL 55-51-3394936. FAX 55-51-3394936. *5056*

BRAZILIAN JOURNAL OF GENETICS.
Sociedade Brasileira de Genetica, R. Cap. Adelmio Norberto da Silva 736, 14025-670 Ribeirao Preto SP, Brazil. TEL 55-16-6218540. FAX 55-16-6201251. *764*

BRAZILIAN JOURNAL OF PHYSICS.
Sociedade Brasileira de Fisica, Universidade de Sao Paulo, Instituto de Fisica, Rua do Mateo, Travessa R 187, 05508-900 Sao Paulo SP, Brazil. TEL 81-271-0111. FAX 081-2710359. *5798*

BREAD OF LIFE.
C.C.S.O. Bread of Life Renewal Centre, P.O. Box 395, Hamilton, ON L8N 3H8, Canada. TEL 416-529-4496. FAX 416-529-5373. *6453*

BREAST CANCER.
Field & Wood, Medical Periodicals, Inc., Box 975, Blue Bell, PA 19422. TEL 610-828-4010. FAX 215-482-0226. *4971*

BREAST CANCER RESEARCH AND TREATMENT.
Kluwer Academic Publishers Boston, Box 358, Accord Sta., Hingham, MA 02018-0358. TEL 617-871-6600. FAX 617-871-6528. *4971*

BREASTFEEDING REVIEW.
Nursing Mothers' Association of Australia, P.O. Box 231, Nunawading, Vic. 3131, Australia. TEL 61-3-98775011. FAX 61-3-9894-3270. *5470*

BREEDING SCIENCE.
Japanese Society of Breeding, c/o Faculty of Agriculture, University of Tokyo, Bunkyo-ku, Tokyo 113, Japan. TEL 03-3812-2111. FAX 03-3815-5851. *764*

BRETAGNE ECONOMIQUE.
Edition Bretagne Economique, 1 rue du General Guillaudot, 35044 Rennes Cedex, France. TEL 33-2-99254137. FAX 33-2-99633528. *1180*

BREWING TECHNIQUES.
New Wine Press, Inc., 1127 Lincoln St., Eugene, OR 97401. TEL 541-687-2993. FAX 541-687-8534. *518*

A BRIEF RELATION.
Historic St. Mary's City Foundation, Inc., Box 24, St. Mary's City, MD 20686. TEL 301-862-0990. FAX 301-862-0968. *3619*

BRIG.
Stirling University Students' Association, Stirling FK9 4LA, Scotland. TEL 44-1786-467166. FAX 44-1786-467190. *1942*

BRILL'S INDOLOGICAL LIBRARY.
E.J. Brill, P.O. Box 9000, 2300 PA Leiden, Netherlands. TEL 31-71-5353500. FAX 31-71-5317532. *5523*

BRILL'S JAPANESE STUDIES LIBRARY.
E.J. Brill, P.O. Box 9000, 2300 PA Leiden, Netherlands. TEL 31-71-5353500. FAX 31-71-5317532. *5523*

BRILL'S SERIES IN JEWISH STUDIES.
E.J. Brill, P.O. Box 9000, 2300 PA Leiden, Netherlands. TEL 31-71-5353500. FAX 31-71-5317532. *6402*

BRILL'S STUDIES IN EPISTEMOLOGY, PSYCHOLOGY AND PSYCHIATRY.
E.J. Brill, P.O. Box 9000, 2300 PA Leiden, Netherlands. TEL 31-71-5353500. FAX 31-71-5317532. *5720*

BRILL'S STUDIES IN INTELLECTUAL HISTORY.
E.J. Brill, P.O. Box 9000, 2300 PA Leiden, Netherlands. TEL 31-71-5353500. FAX 31-71-5317532. *3774*

BRIMLEYANA.
North Carolina State Museum of Natural Sciences, 102 N. Salisbury St., Box 29555, Raleigh, NC 27626-0555. TEL 919-733-7450. *829*

BRITANNIA.
Society for the Promotion of Roman Studies, Senate House, Malet House, London WC1E 7HU, England. TEL 44-171-323-9583. FAX 44-171-323-9584. *3555*

BRITISH ACTUARIAL JOURNAL.
Institute of Actuaries, Staple Inn Hall, High Holborn, London WC1E 7QJ, England. TEL 44-171-242-0106. FAX 44-171-405-2482. *3810*

BRITISH ARACHNOLOGICAL SOCIETY. BULLETIN.
British Arachnological Society, c/o Dr. P. Merrett, Ed., 6 Hillcrest, Swanage, Dorset BH19 2HS, England. *829*

BRITISH ARCHAEOLOGICAL ASSOCIATION. JOURNAL.
W.S. Maney & Son Ltd., Hudson Rd., Leeds LS9 7DL, England. TEL 01532-497481. FAX 01532-486983. *356*

BRITISH ASSOCIATION OF TEACHERS OF THE DEAF. JOURNAL.
British Association of Teachers of the Deaf, 41 The Orchard, Leven, N. Humberside HU17 5QA, England. TEL 44-1964-544243. *3461*

BRITISH ASTRONOMICAL ASSOCIATION. HANDBOOK.
British Astronomical Association, Burlington House, Piccadilly, London W1V 9AG, England. TEL 44-171-734-4145. *492*

BRITISH BIRDS.
British Birds Ltd., Fountains, Park Ln., Blunham, Bedford MK44 3NJ, England. TEL 01767-640467. FAX 01767-640025. *801*

BRITISH COLUMBIA. MINISTRY OF AGRICULTURE, FISHERIES AND FOOD. ANNUAL STATISTICS (YEAR).
Ministry of Agriculture, Fisheries and Food, Public Affairs Branch, Windsor Court, 808 Douglas St., Victoria, BC V8W 2Z7, Canada. TEL 604-387-7169. FAX 604-387-9105. *171*

BRITISH COLUMBIA GEOGRAPHICAL SERIES: OCCASIONAL PAPERS IN GEOGRAPHY.
University of British Columbia, Geography Department, 1984 West Mall, Rm. 217, Vancouver, BC V6T 1Z2, Canada. TEL 604-822-0859. FAX 604-822-6150. *3397*

BRITISH COLUMBIA HISTORICAL NEWS.
British Columbia Historical Federation, P.O. Box 5254, Sta. B, Victoria, BC V8R 6N4, Canada. TEL 250-422-3594. FAX 250-422-3244. *3619*

BRITISH COLUMBIA MEDICAL JOURNAL.
British Columbia Medical Association, 115-1665 W. Broadway, Vancouver, BC V6J 5A4, Canada. TEL 604-736-5551. FAX 604-733-7317. *4648*

BRITISH DENTAL JOURNAL.
Stockton Press, Houndmills, Basingstoke, Hants RG21 6XS, England. TEL 44-171-843-4833. *4852*

BRITISH EDUCATIONAL RESEARCH JOURNAL.
Carfax Publishing Co., P.O. Box 25, Abingdon, Oxon. OX14 3UE, England. TEL 44-1235-400100. FAX 44-1235-401550. *2425*

BRITISH ELECTIONS & PARTIES YEARBOOK.
Frank Cass, Newbury House, 890-900 Eastern Ave., Newbury Park, Ilford, Essex IG2 7HH, England. TEL 44-181-599-8866. FAX 44-181-599-0984. *5895*

BRITISH HOMOEOPATHIC JOURNAL.
Faculty of Homoeopathy, 2 Powis Pl., Great Ormond St., London WC1N 3HT, England. TEL 44-171-837-9469. FAX 44-171-278-7900. *4826*

BRITISH JOURNAL FOR THE HISTORY OF PHILOSOPHY.
Routledge, 11 New Fetter Ln., London EC4P 4EE, England. TEL 44-1264-342755. FAX 44-1264-343005. *5720*

BRITISH JOURNAL FOR THE HISTORY OF SCIENCE.
Cambridge University Press, Edinburgh Bldg., Shaftesbury Rd., Cambridge CB2 2RU, England. TEL 44-1223-312393. FAX 44-1223-315052. *6516*

THE BRITISH JOURNAL FOR THE PHILOSOPHY OF SCIENCE.
Oxford University Press, Academic Division, Great Clarendon St., Oxford OX2 6DP, England. TEL 44-1865-267907. FAX 44-1865-267485. *6516*

THE BRITISH JOURNAL OF AESTHETICS.
Oxford University Press, Academic Division, Great Clarendon St., Oxford OX2 6DP, England. TEL 44-1865-267907. FAX 44-1865-267485. *5720*

BRITISH JOURNAL OF AUDIOLOGY.
Whurr Publishers Ltd., 19b Compton Terrace, London N1 2UN, England. TEL 44-171-359-5979. FAX 44-171-226-5290. *3461*

BRITISH JOURNAL OF BIOMEDICAL SCIENCE.
Royal Society of Medicine Press Ltd., 1 Wimpole St., London W1M 8AE, England. TEL 44-171-290-2900. FAX 44-171-290-2929. *4895*

BRITISH JOURNAL OF CANADIAN STUDIES.
British Association for Canadian Studies, 21 George Sq., Edinburgh EH8 9LD, Scotland. TEL 44-131-662-1117. FAX 44-131-662-1118. *6605*

BRITISH JOURNAL OF CLINICAL PHARMACOLOGY.
Blackwell Science Ltd., Osney Mead, Oxford OX2 OEL, England. TEL 44-1865-206206. FAX 44-1865-721205. *5650*

BRITISH JOURNAL OF CLINICAL PSYCHOLOGY.
British Psychological Society, St. Andrew's House, 48 Princess Rd. E., Leicester LE1 7DR, England. TEL 44-116-254-9568. FAX 44-116-247-0787. *6099*

BRITISH JOURNAL OF CLINICAL RESEARCH.
Brookwood Medical Publications, Orchard House, Brookwood, Surrey GU24 0AT, England. TEL 44-1483-797975. FAX 44-1483-797915. *4649*

BRITISH JOURNAL OF CURRICULUM & ASSESSMENT.
Hodder & Stoughton Educational, Charles Knight, Pub., 338 Euston Rd., London NW1 3BH, England. TEL 44-171-873-6239. FAX 44-171-873-6299. *2596*

BRITISH JOURNAL OF DERMATOLOGY.
Blackwell Science Ltd., Osney Mead, Oxford OX2 OEL, England. TEL 44-1865-206206. FAX 44-1865-721205. *4875*

BRITISH JOURNAL OF DEVELOPMENTAL DISABILITIES.
S E F A (Publications) Ltd., The Globe, 4 Great William St., Stratford-upon-Avon CV37 6RY, England. *2581*

BRITISH JOURNAL OF DEVELOPMENTAL PSYCHOLOGY.
British Psychological Society, St. Andrew's House, 48 Princess Rd. E., Leicester LE1 7DR, England. TEL 44-116-254-9568. FAX 44-116-247-0787. *6099*

BRITISH JOURNAL OF EDUCATIONAL PSYCHOLOGY.
British Psychological Society, St. Andrew's House, 48 Princess Rd. E., Leicester LE1 7DR, England. TEL 44-116-254-9568. FAX 44-116-247-0787. *6099*

BRITISH JOURNAL OF EDUCATIONAL STUDIES.
Blackwell Publishers Ltd., 108 Cowley Rd., Oxford OX4 1JF, England. TEL 44-1865-791100. FAX 44-1865-791347. *2426*

BRITISH JOURNAL OF EDUCATIONAL TECHNOLOGY.
Blackwell Publishers Ltd., 108 Cowley Rd., Oxford OX4 1FH, England. TEL 44-1865-244083. FAX 44-1865-381381. *2596*

BRITISH JOURNAL OF ETHNOMUSICOLOGY.
British Forum for Ethnomusicology, c/o Centre of Music Studies, School of Oriental and African Studies, Thornhaugh St., London WC1H 0XG, England. FAX 44-171-436-3844. *5379*

BRITISH JOURNAL OF GUIDANCE AND COUNSELLING.
Carfax Publishing Co., P.O. Box 25, Abingdon, Oxon OX14 3UE, England. TEL 44-1235-401000. FAX 44-1235-401550. *5505*

BRITISH JOURNAL OF HAEMATOLOGY.
Blackwell Science Ltd., Osney Mead, Oxford OX2 OEL, England. TEL 44-1865-206206. FAX 44-1865-721205. *4917*

BRITISH JOURNAL OF HEALTH PSYCHOLOGY.
British Psychological Society, St. Andrew's House, 48 Princess Rd. E., Leicester LE1 7DR, England. TEL 44-116-254-9568. FAX 44-116-247-0787. *6099*

BRITISH JOURNAL OF INDUSTRIAL RELATIONS.
Blackwell Publishers Ltd., 108 Cowley Rd., Oxford OX4 1JF, England. TEL 44-1865-791100. FAX 44-1865-791347. *1421*

BRITISH JOURNAL OF MANAGEMENT.
Blackwell Publishers Ltd., 108 Cowley Rd., Oxford OX4 1JF, England. TEL 44-1865-791100. FAX 44-1865-791347. *1467*

BRITISH JOURNAL OF MATHEMATICAL AND STATISTICAL PSYCHOLOGY.
British Psychological Society, St. Andrew's House, 48 Princess Rd. E., Leicester LE1 7DR, England. TEL 44-116-254-9568. FAX 44-116-247-0787. *6099*

BRITISH JOURNAL OF MEDICAL ECONOMICS.
Brookwood Medical Publications, Orchard House, Brookwood, Surrey GU24 0AT, England. TEL 44-1483-797975. FAX 44-1483-797915. *4649*

BRITISH JOURNAL OF MEDICAL PSYCHOLOGY.
British Psychological Society, St. Andrew's House, 48 Princess Rd. E., Leicester LE1 7DR, England. TEL 44-116-254-9568. FAX 44-116-247-0787. *6099*

BRITISH JOURNAL OF NEUROSURGERY.
Carfax Publishing Co., P.O. Box 25, Abingdon, Oxon. OX14 3UE, England. TEL 44-1235-401000. FAX 44-1235-401550. *5137*

BRITISH JOURNAL OF OBSTETRICS & GYNAECOLOGY.
Blackwell Science Ltd., Osney Mead, Oxford OX2 OEL, England. TEL 44-1865-206206. FAX 44-1865-721205. *4954*

BRITISH JOURNAL OF OCCUPATIONAL THERAPY.
College of Occupational Therapists Ltd., 6-8 Marshalsea Rd., Southwark, London SE1 1HL, England. TEL 44-171-357-6480. FAX 44-171-378-8095. *4649*

BRITISH JOURNAL OF OPHTHALMOLOGY.
B M J Publishing Group, B.M.A. House, Tavistock Sq., London WC1H 9JR, England. TEL 44-171-383-6270. FAX 44-171-383-6402. *4991*

BRITISH JOURNAL OF PHYSICAL EDUCATION. RESEARCH SUPPLEMENT.
Physical Education Association of the United Kingdom, Ste. 5, 10 Churchill Sq., Kings Hill, W. Malling, Kent ME19 4DU, England. TEL 44-1732-875888. FAX 44-1732-875777. *2596*

BRITISH JOURNAL OF PHYTOTHERAPY.
School of Phytotherapy, Bucksteep Manor, Bodle St. Green, Near Hailsham, E. Sussex BN27 4RJ, England. TEL 44-1323-833812. FAX 44-1323-833869. *295*

BRITISH JOURNAL OF PSYCHIATRY.
Royal College of Psychiatrists, 17 Belgrave Sq., London SW1X 8PG, England. TEL 44-171-235-8857. FAX 44-171-245-1231. *5056*

BRITISH JOURNAL OF PSYCHOLOGY.
British Psychological Society, St. Andrew's House, 48 Princess Rd. E., Leicester LE1 7DR, England. TEL 44-166-254-9568. FAX 44-166-247-0787. *6100*

BRITISH JOURNAL OF RELIGIOUS EDUCATION.
Christian Education Movement, Royal Bldgs., Victoria St., Derby DE1 1GW, England. TEL 44-1332-296655. FAX 44-1332-343253. *6325*

BRITISH JOURNAL OF RHEUMATOLOGY.
Oxford University Press, Academic Division, Great Clarendon St., Oxford OX2 6DP, England. TEL 44-1865-267907. FAX 44-1865-267485. *5125*

BRITISH JOURNAL OF SOCIAL PSYCHOLOGY.
British Psychological Society, St. Andrew's House, 48 Princess Rd. E., Leicester LE1 7DR, England. TEL 44-116-2549568. FAX 44-116-2470787. *6100*

BRITISH JOURNAL OF SOCIOLOGY OF EDUCATION.
Carfax Publishing Co., P.O. Box 25, Abingdon, Oxon. OX14 3UE, England. TEL 44-1235-401000. FAX 44-1235-401550. *2426*

BRITISH JOURNAL OF SPORTS MEDICINE.
B M J Publishing Group, B.M.A. House, Tavistock Sq., London WC1H 9JR, England. TEL 44-171-383-6270. FAX 44-171-383-6402. *5129*

BRITISH JOURNAL OF SURGERY.
Blackwell Science Ltd., Osney Mead, Oxford OX2 OEL, England. TEL 44-1865-206206. FAX 44-1865-721205. *5137*

BRITISH JOURNAL OF THEATRE NURSING.
National Association of Theatre Nurses, 22 Mount Parade, Harrogate HG1 1BX, England. TEL 44-1423-508079. FAX 44-1423-531613. *4929*

BRITISH JOURNAL OF UROLOGY.
Blackwell Science Ltd., Osney Mead, Oxford OX2 OEL, England. TEL 44-1865-206206. FAX 44-1865-721205. *5159*

BRITISH POULTRY SCIENCE.
Carfax Publishing Co., P.O. Box 25, Abingdon, Oxon. OX14 3UE, England. TEL 44-1235-401000. FAX 44-1235-401550. *271*

BRITISH PSYCHOLOGICAL SOCIETY. EDUCATION SECTION. REVIEW.
British Psychological Society, St. Andrew's House, 48 Princess Rd. E., Leicester LE1 7DR, England. TEL 44-116-254-9568. FAX 44-116-247-0787. *2426*

BRITISH SCHOOL AT ATHENS. ANNUAL.
British School at Athens, 31-34 Gordon Sq., London WC1H 0PY, England. TEL 44-171-387-8029. FAX 44-171-383-0781. *356*

BRITISH VETERINARY JOURNAL.
Bailliere Tindall - W.B. Saunders Co. Ltd., 24-28 Oval Rd., London NW1 7DX, England. TEL 44-171-485-4752. FAX 44-171-267-4466. *7267*

BRITTONIA.
New York Botanical Garden, Scientific Publications Department, Bronx, NY 10458-5126. TEL 718-871-8721. FAX 718-817-8842. *697*

BROMATOLOGIA I CHEMIA TOKSYKOLOGICZNA.
Polskie Towarzystwo Farmaceutyczne, Ul. Dluga 16, 00-238 Warsaw, Poland. TEL 48-22-8310241. FAX 48-22-8310243. *5651*

BROMELIAD SOCIETY. JOURNAL.
Bromeliad Society, Inc., 720 Millertown Rd., Auburn, CA 95603. TEL 916-885-0201. *697*

BRONCHIAL MUCOLOGY SERIES.
Lippincott - Raven Publishers, 227 E. Washington Sq., Philadelphia, PA 19106. TEL 215-238-4200. FAX 215-238-4227. *5117*

BROOKHAVEN SYMPOSIA IN BIOLOGY.
Plenum Publishing Corp., 233 Spring St., New York, NY 10013-1578. TEL 212-620-8000. FAX 212-463-0742. *594*

BROOKLYN REVIEW.
City University of New York, Brooklyn College, Department of English, Brooklyn, NY 11210. TEL 718-596-6885. *4505*

BROWN BOVERI SYMPOSIA. PROCEEDINGS.
Plenum Publishing Corp., 233 Spring St., New York, NY 10013-1578. TEL 212-620-8000. FAX 212-463-0742. *2810*

BRUNSWICKAN.
University of New Brunswick, Student Union, P.O. Box 4400, Fredericton, NB E3B 5A3, Canada. TEL 506-453-4983. FAX 506-458-4958. *1943*

BRYN MAWR CLASSICAL REVIEW.
Bryn Mawr Commentaries, Inc., Bryn Mawr College, Thomas Library, Bryn Mawr, PA 19010. TEL 610-526-5384. FAX 610-526-7475. *1901*

BRYN MAWR MEDIEVAL REVIEW.
Bryn Mawr Commentaries, Inc., Bryn Mawr College, Thomas Library, Bryn Mawr, PA 19010. TEL 215-526-5384. FAX 610-526-7475. *3555*

BRYN MAWR REVIEWS.
Bryn Mawr Commentaries, Inc., Bryn Mawr College, Thomas Library, Bryn Mawr, PA 19010. TEL 610-526-5384. FAX 610-526-7475. *3555*

BRYOLOGIST.
American Bryological & Lichenological Society, c/o Robert J. Thomas, Sec.-Treas., Department of Biology, Bates College, Lewiston, ME 04240. TEL 207-786-6105. FAX 207-786-6035. *697*

BUDAPEST STUDIES IN ARABIC.
Eotvos Lorand University, Chair for Arabic Studies, Muzeum kit. 4-b, 1088 Budapest, Hungary. *4246*

BUDDHIST - CHRISTIAN STUDIES.
University of Hawaii Press, Journals Department, 2840 Kolowalu St., Honolulu, HI 96822. TEL 808-956-8833. FAX 808-988-6052. *6388*

BUENA VISTA TODAY.
Buena Vista University, 610 W. Fourth St., Storm Lake, IA 50588. TEL 712-749-2120. FAX 712-749-1459. *1943*

BUILDING ACOUSTICS.
Multi-Science Publishing Co. Ltd., 107 High St., Brentwood, Essex CM14 4RX, England. TEL 44-1277-224632. FAX 44-1277-223453. *5872*

BUILDING AND ENVIRONMENT.
Elsevier Science Ltd., Pergamon, P.O. Box 800, Kidlington, Oxford OX5 1DX, England. TEL 44-1865-843000. FAX 44-1865-843010. *869*

BUILDING RESEARCH AND INFORMATION.
Thomson Professional, 2-6 Boundary Row, London SE1 8HN, England. TEL 44-171-8650066. FAX 44-171-5229623. *871*

BULGARIAN JOURNAL OF PLANT PHYSIOLOGY.
Publishing House of the Bulgarian Academy of Sciences, Acad. G. Bonchev St., Bldg. 6, 1113 Sofia, Bulgaria. *3184*

BULLAN.
Hertford College, Oxford OX1 3BW, England. TEL 44-1865-58236. *3555*

BULLDADA.
Box 80204, Indianapolis, IN 46280-0204. TEL 317-875-7149. *4326*

BULLETIN DE LA COMMUNICATION PARLEE.
Institut de la Communication Parlee, Universite Stendhal, B.P. 25 X, 38040 Grenoble Cedex, France. TEL 33-76-57-47-10. FAX 33-76-57-48-26. *4246*

BULLETIN DES SOCIETES CHIMIQUES BELGES.
Comite van Beheer van het Bulletin v.z.w., Krijgslaan 281, S-12, B-9000 Ghent, Belgium. TEL 32-9-2644831. FAX 32-9-2644992. *1740*

BULLETIN DU CANCER.
Editions Scientifiques et Medicales Elsevier, 141 rue de Javel, 75747 Paris, France. TEL 33-1-45589026. FAX 33-1-45589421. *4971*

BULLETIN DU CANCER - RADIOTHERAPIE.
Editions Scientifiques et Medicales Elsevier, 141 rue de Javel, 75747 Paris, France. TEL 33-1-45589026. FAX 33-1-45589421. *4972*

BULLETIN FOR BIBLICAL RESEARCH.
Institute for Biblical Research, Box 275, Winona Lake, IN 46590-0275. TEL 219-269-2011. FAX 219-269-6788. *6326*

BULLETIN OF BEEF CATTLE SCIENCE.
Sakura Print, c/o Department of Animal Science, College of Agriculture, Kyoto University, Kyoto 606, Japan. TEL 81-75-753-6054. FAX 81-75-753-6344. *272*

BULLETIN OF CONCERNED ASIAN SCHOLARS.
Bulletin of Concerned Asian Scholars, Inc., 464 19th St., Oakland, CA 94612-2297. TEL 510-451-1742. FAX 510-835-3017. *6007*

BULLETIN OF ECONOMIC RESEARCH.
Blackwell Publishers Ltd., 108 Cowley Rd., Oxford OX4 1JF, England. TEL 44-1865-791100. FAX 44-1865-791347. *938*

BULLETIN OF ELECTROCHEMISTRY.
Central Electrochemical Research Institute, c/o Scientific Distribution Service, 5-A, Bhagat-kj-kothi Box No. 33, Jodhpur, Rajasthan 342 001, India. FAX 91-291-49093. *1804*

BULLETIN OF ENVIRONMENTAL CONTAMINATION AND TOXICOLOGY.
Springer-Verlag, Life Science Journals, 175 Fifth Ave., New York, NY 10010. TEL 212-460-1500. FAX 212-473-6272. *2975*

BULLETIN OF EXPERIMENTAL BIOLOGY AND MEDICINE.
Plenum Publishing Corp., Consultants Bureau, 233 Spring St., New York, NY 10013-1578. TEL 212-620-8468. FAX 212-463-0742. *594*

BULLETIN OF FRANCOPHONE AFRICA.
University of Westminster, Francophone Africa Research Centre, School of Languages, 9-18 Euston Centre, London NW1 3ET, England. TEL 44-171-911-5000. FAX 44-171-911-5001. *3247*

THE BULLETIN OF HISTORICAL RESEARCH IN MUSICAL EDUCATION.
University of Kansas, M E M T Division, 311 Baily Hall, Lawrence, KS 66045-2344. TEL 913-864-4784. FAX 913-864-5076. *5379*

BULLETIN OF INFORMATICS AND CYBERNETICS.
Tokei Kagaku Kenkyukai, c/o Kyushu University 33, 10-1, Hakozaki 6-chome, Higashi-ku, Fukuoka 812, Japan. TEL 81-92-642-2697. FAX 81-92-642-2698. *4565*

BULLETIN OF JUDAEO-GREEK STUDIES.
University of Cambridge, Faculty of Oriental Studies, Sidgwick Ave., Cambridge CB3 9DA, England. FAX 44-1223-332582. *6403*

BULLETIN OF LATIN AMERICAN RESEARCH.
Elsevier Science Ltd., Pergamon, P.O. Box 800, Kidlington, Oxford OX5 1DX, England. TEL 44-1865-843000. FAX 44-1865-843010. *6605*

BULLETIN OF MARINE SCIENCE.
Rosenstiel School of Marine and Atmospheric Science, 4600 Rickenbacker Causeway, Miami, FL 33149. TEL 305-361-4190. *2400*

BULLETIN OF MATHEMATICAL BIOLOGY.
Elsevier Science Inc., Box 945, New York, NY 10159-0945. TEL 212-633-3730. FAX 212-633-3680. *594*

THE BULLETIN OF SCIENCE, TECHNOLOGY & SOCIETY.
S T S Press, 102 Materials Research Laboratory, Pennsylvania State University, University Park, PA 16802. TEL 814-865-1137. FAX 814-863-7040. *6517*

THE BULLETIN OF SYMBOLIC LOGIC.
Association for Symbolic Logic, Department of Mathematics, University of Illinois at Urbana-Champaign, 1409 W. Green St., Urbana, IL 61801. TEL 217-244-7902. FAX 217-333-9576. *4565*

BULLETIN OF THE CANTIGUEIROS.
Society of the Cantigueiros de Santa Maria, Department of Romance Languages - ML 377, University of Cincinnati, Cincinnati, OH 45221. TEL 513-556-1836. FAX 513-556-2577. *6326*

BULLETIN OF THE COMEDIANTES.
University of California at Riverside, Department of Spanish & Portuguese, Riverside, CA 92521-0222. TEL 909-787-5007. FAX 909-787-2294. *4384*

BULLETIN OF ZOOLOGICAL NOMENCLATURE.
International Commission on Zoological Nomenclature, c/o Natural History Museum, Cromwell Rd., London. TEL 44-171-938-9387. *830*

BULLETIN SUBTERRANEA BRITANNICA.
Subterranea Britannica, 96A Brighton Rd., S. Croydon, Surrey CR2 6AD, England. TEL 44-1737-823456. FAX 44-181-654-8507. *356*

BULLETINS OF AMERICAN PALEONTOLOGY.
Paleontological Research Institution, 1259 Trumansburg Rd., Ithaca, NY 14850-1398. TEL 607-273-6623. FAX 607-273-6620. *5558*

BULLETTINO STORICO EMPOLESE.
Associazione Turistica Pro-Empoli (ATPE), Via G. Del Papa, 50053 Empoli, Italy. TEL 39-571-76115. *3555*

BUNYAN STUDIES.
Open University, Faculty of Arts, Parsifal College, 527 Finchley Rd., London NW3 7BG, England. TEL 44-171-794-0575. FAX 44-171-433-6196. *4384*

BURIED HISTORY.
Australian Institute of Archaeology, Level 2, Centreway Arcade, 259 Collins St., Melbourne, Vic. 3000, Australia. TEL 61-3-96503477. FAX 61-3-96542774. *356*

BURLINGTON MAGAZINE.
Burlington Magazine Publications Ltd., 14-16 Duke's Rd., London WC1H 9AD, England. TEL 44-171-388-1228. FAX 44-171-388-1230. *433*

BURNS.
Elsevier Science Ltd., P.O. Box 800, Kidlington, Oxford OX5 1DX, England. TEL 44-1865-843000. FAX 44-1865-843010. *5005*

BUSINESS & ECONOMIC REPORT & KANSAS ECONOMIC INDICATORS.
Wichita State University, W. Frank Barton School of Business, Wichita, KS 67260-0121. TEL 316-978-3225. FAX 316-978-3950. *1227*

BUSINESS & PROFESSIONAL ETHICS JOURNAL.
Box 15017, Gainesville, FL 32604. TEL 904-392-2084. FAX 904-392-5577. *5720*

BUSINESS AND SOCIETY.
Sage Publications, Inc., 2455 Teller Rd., Thousand Oaks, CA 91320. TEL 805-499-0721. FAX 805-499-0871. *939*

BUSINESS & THE CONTEMPORARY WORLD.
John Wiley & Sons, Inc., 605 Third Ave., New York, NY 10158. TEL 212-850-6645. FAX 212-850-6021. *1317*

BUSINESS ESPIONAGE REPORT.
Business Espionage Controls & Countermeasures Association (BECCA), Box 55582, Seattle, WA 98155-0582. TEL 206-364-4672. FAX 206-367-3316. *1317*

BUSINESS ETHICS.
Blackwell Publishers Ltd., 108 Cowley Rd., Oxford OX4 1JF, England. TEL 44-1865-791100. FAX 44-1865-791347. *940*

BUSINESS FORUM (LOS ANGELES).
California State University, Los Angeles, School of Business & Economics, 5151 State University Dr., Los Angeles, CA 90032-8120. TEL 213-343-2806. FAX 213-343-5263. *941*

BUSINESS, GROWTH & PROFITABILITY.
Henry Stewart Publications, Russell House, 28-30 Little Russell St., London WC1A 2HN, England. TEL 44-171-404-3040. FAX 44-171-404-2081. *1640*

BUSINESS HISTORY.
Frank Cass, Newbury House, 890-900 Eastern Ave., Newbury Park, Ilford, Essex 1G2 7HH, England. TEL 44-181-599-8866. FAX 44-181-599-0984. *941*

BUSINESS LIBRARY REVIEW.
Gordon and Breach - Harwood Academic, Amsteldisk 166, 1st Fl., 1079 LH Amsterdam, Netherlands. *1117*

BUSINESS STUDIES ON THE U.S.S.R.
Gordon and Breach - Harwood Academic, Amsteldisk 166, 1st Fl., 1079 LH Amsterdam, Netherlands. *1318*

BUSINESS TRAVELLER.
Perry Publications (Holdings) PLC, Compass House, 22 Redan Pl., London W2 4SZ, England. TEL 44-171-229-7799. FAX 44-171-229-9441. *7189*

BUSINESS VALUATION REVIEW.
American Society of Appraisers, Business Valuation Committee, Box 101923, Denver, CO 80250. TEL 303-758-6148. *1117*

BUSSEI KENKYU.
Bussei Kenkyu Kankokai, c/o Kyoto Daigaku Yukawa Kinenkan, Kitashirakawa Oiwake-cho, Sakyo-ku, Kyoto 606, Japan. TEL 81-75-753-7051. FAX 81-75-722-6339. *5798*

BUTSURI KYOIKU.
Physics Education Society of Japan, P.O. Box 29, Koishikawa Yubbinkyoku, Tokyo 112, Japan. TEL 81-3-3942-0875. *5798*

BUTSURIGAKUSHI.
Butsurigakushi Kenkyukai, c/o Tomohiro Hyodo, Faculty of Business Administration, Ritsumeikan University, 56-1 Toji-in Kitamachi, Kita-ku, Kyoto 603-77, Japan. TEL 81-75-465-1111. FAX 81-75-465-7883. *5798*

BYLINE.
Box 130596, Edmond, OK 73013. TEL 405-348-5591. *3870*

BYOIN, CHIIKI SEISHIN IGAKU.
Byoin, Chiiki Seishin Igakkai, National Center for Neurology & Psychiatry, 1-1, Ogawa Higashicho 4-chome, Kodaira-shi, Tokyo 187, Japan. TEL 81-423-41-2711. FAX 423-44-6745. *5057*

BYZANTINA AUSTRALIENSIA.
Australian Association for Byzantine Studies, University of Sydney, Department of Modern Greek, Sydney, N.S.W. 2006, Australia. TEL 61-2-3513658. FAX 61-2-3513543. *3556*

BYZANTINA NEERLANDICA.
E.J. Brill, P.O. Box 9000, 2300 PA Leiden, Netherlands. TEL 31-71-5353500. FAX 31-71-5317532. *3556*

BYZANTINE AND MODERN GREEK STUDIES.
c/o Prof. Anthony Bryer, Centre for Byzantine, Ottoman and Modern Greek Studies, University of Birmingham, P.O. Box 363, Edgbaston, Birmingham B15 2TT, England. TEL 44-121-414-5775. FAX 44-121-414-3595. *3556*

BYZANTINOSLAVICA.
John Benjamins Publishing Co., Amsteldijk 44, P.O. Box 75577, 1070 AN Amsterdam, Netherlands. TEL 31-20-6738156. FAX 31-20-6792956. *5523*

C A - A CANCER JOURNAL FOR CLINICIANS.
Lippincott - Raven Publishers, 227 E. Washington Sq., Philadelphia, PA 19106. TEL 215-238-4200. *4972*

C A E D H H JOURNAL.
University of Alberta, Department of Educational Psychology, 6-102 Education North, Edmonton, AB T6G 2G5, Canada. TEL 403-492-4204. FAX 403-492-0390. *3461*

C A L I C O JOURNAL.
Computer Assisted Language & Instruction Consortium, 014 Language Bldg., Box 90267, Duke University, Durham, NC 27708-0267. TEL 919-660-3180. FAX 919-660-3183. *2515*

C A L M SCIENCE.
Department of Conservation and Land Management, Locked Bag 104, Bentley Delivery Centre, W.A. 6893, Australia. TEL 61-9-334-0333. FAX 61-9-334-8296. *2225*

C A S JOURNAL.
Catgut Acoustical Society, c/o Carleen M. Hutchins, Sec., 112 Essex Ave., Montclair, NJ 07042. TEL 973-744-4029. FAX 973-744-9197. *5379*

C A T M O G.
Environmental Publications, c/o R.A. Cullington, School of Environmental Sciences, University of East Anglia, Norwich NR4 7TJ, England. TEL 44-1603-592560. FAX 44-1603-507719. *3397*

C A U T BULLETIN.
Canadian Association of University Teachers, 2675 Queensview Dr., Ottawa, ON K2B 8K2, Canada. TEL 613-820-2270. FAX 613-820-2417. *2534*

C B A RECORD.
Chicago Bar Association, 321 S. Plymouth Ct., Chicago, IL 60604-3997. TEL 312-554-2000. FAX 312-554-2054. *3924*

C B M S - N S F REGIONAL CONFERENCE SERIES IN APPLIED MATHEMATICS.
Society for Industrial and Applied Mathematics, 3600 University City Science Center, Philadelphia, PA 19104-2688. TEL 215-382-9800. FAX 215-386-7999. *4565*

C C L.
Canadian Children's Press, University of Guelph, Department of English, Guelph, ON N1G 2W1, Canada. TEL 519-824-4120. FAX 519-837-1315. *6266*

C E A CRITIC.
College English Association, c/o Bege K. Bowers and Julia M. Gergits, Eds., Dept. of English, Youngstown State University, Youngstown, OH 44555. TEL 330-742-3414. FAX 330-742-2304. *4384*

C E D E J EGYPTE - MONDE ARABE.
Centre d'Etudes et de Documentation Economique, Juridique et Sociale, 14 Sharia Gameyet al-Nisr, Mohandessin, Cairo, Egypt. TEL 3611932. FAX 3493518. *5896*

C E M S BUSINESS REVIEW.
Kluwer Academic Publishers Boston, Box 358, Accord Sta., Hingham, MA 02018-0358. TEL 617-871-6600. FAX 617-871-6528. *1469*

C E P S PAPERS.
Centre for European Policy Studies, Place du Congres 1, B-1000 Brussels, Belgium. TEL 32-2-2293911. FAX 32-2-2194151. *6007*

C E P S WORKING DOCUMENTS.
Centre for European Policy Studies, Place du Congres 1, B-1000 Brussels, Belgium. TEL 32-2-2293911. FAX 32-2-2194151. *6007*

C E U PRIVATIZATION REPORTS.
Central European University Press, Nador u. 9, 1051 Budapest, Hungary. TEL 36-1-1762333. FAX 36-1-1762778. *1297*

C H R I A NEWS.
Committee for Health Rights in the Americas, 474 Valencia St., Ste. 120, San Francisco, CA 94103-3415. TEL 415-431-7760. FAX 415-431-7768. *1355*

C I M A QUESTIONS AND SUGGESTED ANSWERS.
Chartered Institute of Management Accountants, 63 Portland Pl., London W1N 4AB, England. TEL 44-171-917-9229. FAX 44-171-323-1487. *1085*

C I M BULLETIN.
Canadian Institute of Mining, Metallurgy & Petroleum, Xerox Tower, 3400 de Maisonneuve Blvd. W., Ste. 1210, Montreal, PQ H3Z 3B8, Canada. TEL 514-939-2710. FAX 514-939-2714. *5296*

C I R M.
Centro Internazionale Radio-Medico, Via Architettura 41, 00144 Rome, Italy. TEL 39-6-5923331. FAX 39-6-5923333. *4650*

C I R V I BOLLETTINO.
Centro Interuniversitario di Ricerche sul Viaggio in Italia, Str. Rivigliasco 6, 10024 Moncalieri, Italy. TEL 39-11-6407488. FAX 39-11-6407488. *7190*

C I S NEWS.
Chemical Information Systems, Inc., 810 Glen Eagles Ct., Ste. 300, Baltimore, MD 21286-2203. TEL 410-321-8440. FAX 410-296-0712. *1799*

C L A O JOURNAL.
Kellner-McCaffery Associates, Inc., 150 Fifth Ave., New York, NY 10011. TEL 212-741-0280. *4991*

C M A J.
Canadian Medical Association, P.O. Box 8650, Ottawa, ON K1G 0G8, Canada. TEL 613-731-9331. FAX 613-523-0937. *4650*

C N L.
Colonial Newsletter American Numismatic Society, Broadway & 155th St., New York, NY 10032-7598. TEL 212-234-3130. FAX 212-234-3381. *5463*

C N S DRUG REVIEWS.
Neva Press, Inc., Box 347, Branford, CT 06405. TEL 203-272-5338. FAX 203-272-5338. *5651*

C N S DRUGS.
Adis International Limited, Private Bag 65901, Mairangi Bay, Auckland 10, New Zealand. TEL 64-9-479-8100. FAX 64-9-479-8145. *5651*

C N S: THE JOURNAL FOR ADVANCED NURSING PRACTICE.
Williams & Wilkins, 351 W. Camden St., Baltimore, MD 21201-2436. TEL 410-528-4000. FAX 410-528-4312. *4930*

C O O L DOCTOR - COMPUTING ONLINE DOCTOR.
Kissware Works!, *2074*

C O R E.
Carfax Publishing Co., P.O. Box 25, Abingdon, Oxon. OX14 3UE, England. TEL 44-1235-401000. FAX 44-1235-401550. *2426*

C O R O S CHRONICLE.
Collectors of Religion on Stamps, c/o Dr. Allan Hauck, Box 165, Somers, WI 53171-0165. TEL 414-552-8740. *5705*

REFEREED SERIALS

C O S P A R INFORMATION BULLETIN.
Elsevier Science Ltd., Pergamon, P.O. Box 800, Kidlington, Oxford OX5 1DX, England. TEL 44-1865-843000. FAX 44-1865-843010. *60*

C.S.I.R.O. LAND AND WATER. POSITION PAPERS.
C.S.I.R.O. Land and Water, G.P.O. Box 1666, Canberra, A.C.T. 2601, Australia. FAX 61-6-2465800. *2393*

C.S.I.R.O. LAND AND WATER. SCIENTIFIC REPORT.
C.S.I.R.O. Land and Water, G.P.O. Box 1666, Canberra, A.C.T. 2601, Australia. FAX 61-6-2465800. *2393*

C T L R.
Sweet & Maxwell, Mill St., Oxford OX2 0JU, England. TEL 44-1865-249248. FAX 44-1865-792301. *1983*

C THEORY.
Concordia University, 1455 de Maisonneuve West, Montreal, PQ H3G 1M8, Canada. TEL 514-282-9298. *5897*

C U N Y FORUM.
City University of New York, Ph.D. Program in Linguistics, Graduate Center, 33 W. 42nd St., New York, NY 10036-8099. TEL 212-642-2154. FAX 212-642-2595. *4247*

C W I MONOGRAPHS.
Elsevier Science B.V., Books Division, P.O. Box 211, 1000 AE Amsterdam, Netherlands. TEL 31-20-4853911. *4619*

CABLE TALK.
Straightline Publishing Ltd., 29 Main St., Bothwell, Glasgow G71 8RD, Scotland. TEL 44-1698-853000. FAX 44-1698-854208. *2810*

CABO.
Historical Society of Cape Town, c/o Etaine Eberhard, Ed., P.O. Box 157, Newlands 7725, South Africa. TEL 27-12-6864939. FAX 27-12-6866404. *3525*

CACTACEAS Y SUCULENTAS MEXICANAS.
Sociedad Mexicana de Cactologia, A.C., 2da. de Juarez, No. 42, Colonia San Alvaro, 02090 Mexico, D.F., Mexico. TEL 3411796. *698*

CADERNOS DO PATRIMONIO CULTURAL.
Secretaria Municipal de Cultura, Departamento Geral do Patrimonio Cultural, Rua Afonso Cavalcanti, 455, sala 207, 20211-110 Cidade Nova, Rio de Janeiro RJ, Brazil. TEL 55-21-2734095. FAX 55-21-5032158. *6606*

CADUCEUS.
S I U School of Medicine, Department of the Medical Humanities, The Pearson Museum, Box 19230, Springfield, IL 62794-9230. FAX 217-782-9132. *5352*

CAESARAUGUSTA.
Institucion Fernando el Catolico, Plaza de Espana 2, 50071 Zaragoza, Spain. TEL 34-976-288878. FAX 34-976-288869. *357*

CAHIER TECHNIQUE DU BIOLOGISTE.
Centre National des Biologistes, 80, Av. du Maine, 75014 Paris, France. TEL 43-22-97-70. FAX 43-21-73-12. *594*

LES CAHIERS D'OTO-RHINOLARYNGOLOGIE, DE CHIRUGIE CERVICO-FACIALE ET D'AUDIOPHONOLOGIE.
Editions la Simarre, Z.I. No. 2 - rue Joseph-Cugnot, 37300 Joue-les-Tours, France. TEL 33-2-47535366. FAX 33-2-47674505. *5020*

CAHIERS DE BIOLOGIE MARINE.
Station Biologique de Roscoff, B.P. 74, 29682 Roscoff Cedex, France. TEL 33-2-98292302. FAX 33-2-98292324. *594*

CAHIERS DE DROIT EUROPEEN.
Bruylant, 67 rue de la Regence, 1000 Brussels, Belgium. TEL 32-2-5129845. FAX 32-2-5117202. *4107*

CAHIERS DE L'IROISE.
Societe d'Etudes de Brest et du Leon, Rue des Archives, 29200 Brest, France. *3556*

CAHIERS DE LINGUISTIQUE ASIE ORIENTALE.
Centre de Recherches Linguistiques sur l'Asie Orientale, 54 bd. Raspail, 75006 Paris, France. TEL 33-1-49542435. FAX 33-1-49542671. *4247*

CAHIERS DE MEDECINE DU TRAVAIL.
Association Professionnelle Belge des Medecins du Travail, Ave. de Venus 14, 1410 Waterloo, Belgium. TEL 32-2-3547775. FAX 32-2-3510451. *5488*

CAHIERS ELISABETHAINS.
Universite de Montpellier (Universite Paul Valery), Centre d'Etudes et de Recherches Elisabethaines, B.P. 5043, Route de Mende, 34032 Montpellier, France. TEL 33-467-142406. FAX 33-467-142332. *3557*

CAHIERS HENRI BOSCO.
Amitie Henri Bosco, Palais Aurore, 33 bd. Tzarewitch, 06000 Nice, France. *4495*

CAHIERS HOSPITALIERS.
Berger - Levrault, 5 rue Auguste-Comte, 75006 Paris, France. TEL 33-1-40467030. FAX 33-1-44071525. *3705*

CAHIERS LINGUISTIQUES D'OTTAWA.
University of Ottawa, Department of Linguistics, 70 Laurier St., Ottawa, ON K1N 6N5, Canada. TEL 613-564-4207. FAX 613-564-9067. *4247*

CAHIERS PEDAGOGIQUES.
Cercle de Recherche et d'Action Pedagogiques (CRAP), 10 rue Chevreul, 75011 Paris, France. TEL 33-1-43482230. FAX 33-1-43485321. *2426*

CAHIERS SOCIALE GESCHIEDENIS.
Uitgeverij Verloren, Larenseweg 123, 1221 CL Hilversum, Netherlands. TEL 31-35-6859856. FAX 31-35-6836557. *3557*

CAKE AND COCKHORSE.
Banbury Historical Society, Banbury Museum, 8 Horsefair, Banbury, Oxon. OX16 0AA, England. TEL 01295-259855. *3557*

CAKELELE: MALUKU RESEARCH JOURNAL.
University of Hawaii, Center for Southeast Asian Studies, 1890 East-West Rd., Moore 416, Honolulu, HI 96822. TEL 808-956-2688. FAX 808-956-2688. *6606*

CALCIFIED TISSUE INTERNATIONAL.
Springer-Verlag, Medical Journals, 175 Fifth Ave., New York, NY 10010. TEL 212-460-1500. FAX 212-473-6272. *4883*

CALCUTTA HISTORICAL JOURNAL.
K.P. Bagchi & Company, 286 B.B. Ganpuli St., Calcutta 700 012, India. TEL 91-33-26-7474. FAX 91-33-2482973. *3532*

CALIFORNIA ACADEMY OF SCIENCES. ACADEMY NEWSLETTER.
California Academy of Sciences, Golden Gate Park, San Francisco, CA 94118. TEL 415-750-7142. *5352*

CALIFORNIA ACADEMY OF SCIENCES. MEMOIRS.
California Academy of Sciences, Golden Gate Park, San Francisco, CA 94118. TEL 415-750-7243. *594*

CALIFORNIA ACADEMY OF SCIENCES. PROCEEDINGS.
California Academy of Sciences, Golden Gate Park, San Francisco, CA 94118. TEL 415-750-7243. *594*

CALIFORNIA CHIROPRACTIC ASSOCIATION JOURNAL.
California Chiropractic Association, 7801 Folsom Blvd., Ste. 375, Sacramento, CA 95826. TEL 916-387-0177. FAX 916-387-6222. *4826*

CALIFORNIA COOPERATIVE OCEANIC FISHERIES INVESTIGATIONS REPORTS.
California Cooperative Oceanic Fisheries Investigations, Scripps Institution of Oceanography, University of California, La Jolla, CA 92093-0227. TEL 619-534-4236. FAX 619-534-6500. *3063*

CALIFORNIA FAMILY PHYSICIAN.
California Academy of Family Physicians, 114 Sansome St., Ste. 1305, San Francisco, CA 94104-3824. TEL 415-394-9121. FAX 415-394-9119. *4650*

CALIFORNIA HISTORY (SAN FRANCISCO).
California Historical Society, 678 Mission St., San Francisco, CA 94105. TEL 415-357-1848. *3620*

CALIFORNIA INSECT SURVEY. BULLETIN.
University of California Press, 2120 Berkeley Way, Berkeley, CA 94720. TEL 510-642-4247. FAX 510-643-7127. *748*

CALIFORNIA LAW REVIEW.
University of California Press, Journals Division, 2120 Berkeley Way, No. 5812, Berkeley, CA 94720-5812. TEL 510-643-7154. FAX 510-642-9917. *3926*

CALIFORNIA MANAGEMENT REVIEW.
University of California at Berkeley, S549 Haas School of Business, Ste. 1900, Berkeley, CA 94720-1900. TEL 510-642-7159. FAX 510-642-1318. *1469*

CALIFORNIA NATURAL HISTORY GUIDES.
University of California Press, 2120 Berkeley Way, Berkeley, CA 94720. TEL 510-642-4247. FAX 510-643-7127. *595*

CALIFORNIA READER.
California Reading Association, 3186 Airway Ave., Ste. D, Costa Mesa, CA 92626-4650. TEL 714-880-5605. FAX 714-435-0269. *2597*

CALIFORNIA SCHOOLS.
California School Board Association, 3100 Beacon Blvd., Box 1660, W. Sacramento, CA 95819. TEL 916-371-4691. FAX 916-371-3407. *2427*

CALIFORNIA SERIES ON SOCIAL CHOICE & POLITICAL ECONOMY.
University of California Press, 2120 Berkeley Way, Berkeley, CA 94720. TEL 510-643-7127. FAX 510-643-7127. *5897*

CALIFORNIA STUDIES IN THE HISTORY OF ART.
University of California Press, 2120 Berkeley Way, Berkeley, CA 94720. TEL 510-642-4247. FAX 510-643-7127. *433*

CALIFORNIA STUDIES IN THE HISTORY OF SCIENCE.
University of California Press, 2120 Berkeley Way, Berkeley, CA 94720. TEL 510-642-4247. FAX 510-643-7127. *6517*

CALIFORNIA STUDIES IN 19TH CENTURY MUSIC.
University of California Press, 2120 Berkeley Way, Berkeley, CA 94720. TEL 510-642-4247. FAX 510-643-7127. *5380*

CALIFORNIA VETERINARIAN.
California Veterinary Medical Association, 5231 Madison Ave., Sacramento, CA 95841. TEL 916-344-4985. FAX 916-344-6147. *7267*

CALLIOPE (BRISTOL).
Roger Williams University, Creative Writing Program, Bristol, RI 02809. TEL 401-254-3217. FAX 401-254-3286. *4505*

CALPHAD.
Elsevier Science Ltd., Pergamon, P.O. Box 800, Kidlington, Oxford OX5 1DX, England. TEL 44-1865-843000. FAX 44-1865-843010. *1799*

CALVIN THEOLOGICAL JOURNAL.
Calvin Theological Seminary, 3233 Burton St. S.E., Grand Rapids, MI 49546. TEL 616-957-6010. FAX 616-957-8621. *6416*

CALYX.
Calyx, Inc., Box B, Corvallis, OR 97339. TEL 541-753-9384. FAX 541-753-0515. *433*

CAMBRIDGE ANTIQUARIAN SOCIETY. PROCEEDINGS.
Cambridge Antiquarian Society, Museum of Archaeology and Anthropology, c/o Dr. D. Banham, 45 Malcolm Pl., King St., Cambridge, England. FAX 01223-333503. *3557*

CAMBRIDGE ARCHAEOLOGICAL JOURNAL.
Cambridge University Press, Edinburgh Bldg., Shaftesbury Rd., Cambridge CB2 2RU, England. TEL 44-1223-312393. FAX 44-1223-315052. *357*

CAMBRIDGE JOURNAL OF EDUCATION.
Carfax Publishing Co., P.O. Box 25, Abingdon, Oxon. OX14 3UE, England. TEL 44-1235-401000. FAX 44-1235-401550. *2534*

CAMBRIDGE LECTURE NOTES IN PHYSICS.
University of Cambridge, Press Syndicate, The Pitt Bldg., Trumpington St., Cambridge CB2 1RP, England. TEL 44-1223-315052. *5798*

CAMDEN HISTORY REVIEW.
Camden History Society, c/o Local Studies and Archive Centre, Holborn Library, 32-38 Theobalds Rd., London WCIX 8PA, England. TEL 44-171-794-1735. FAX 44-171-794-6695. *3557*

CAMPI IMMAGINABILI.
Rubbettino Editore, Viale dei Pini 10, 88049 Soveria Mannelli (CA), Italy. TEL 39-968-662034. *3774*

CAMPUS TIMES (ROCHESTER).
University of Rochester, Students Association, Wilson Commons 102, CPU 277086, Rochester, NY 14627-7086. TEL 716-275-5943. FAX 716-256-3664. *1944*

CANADA. CANADIAN WILDLIFE FEDERATION. PUBLICATION LIST.
Malcolm Publishing Inc., 11 450 Albert-Hudon Blvd., Montreal N., PQ H1G 3J9, Canada. TEL 514-327-4464. FAX 514-327-7592. *2225*

CANADA: THE STATE OF THE FEDERATION.
Institute of Intergovernmental Relations, Queen's University, Kingston, ON K7L 3N6, Canada. TEL 603-545-2080. FAX 603-545-6868. *5898*

CANADIAN ADMINISTRATOR.
University of Alberta, Department of Educational Policy Studies, Edmonton, AB T6G 2H1, Canada. TEL 403-492-7625. FAX 403-492-2024. *2497*

CANADIAN AGRICULTURAL ENGINEERING.
Canadian Society of Agricultural Engineering, Box 381, R P O University, Saskatoon, SK S7N 4J8, Canada. TEL 306-966-5335. FAX 306-966-5334. *205*

CANADIAN - AMERICAN PUBLIC POLICY.
Canadian - American Center, 154 College Ave., Orono, ME 04473-1591. TEL 207-581-4220. FAX 207-581-4223. *6007*

CANADIAN ASSOCIATION OF RADIOLOGISTS. JOURNAL.
Canadian Medical Association, P.O. Box 8650, Ottawa, ON K1G 0G8, Canada. TEL 613-731-9331. FAX 613-523-0937. *5103*

CANADIAN BOOKSELLER.
Canadian Booksellers Association, 301 Donlands Ave., Toronto, ON M4J 3R8, Canada. TEL 416-467-7883. FAX 416-467-7886. *6267*

CANADIAN BULLETIN OF MEDICAL HISTORY.
Wilfrid Laurier University Press, 75 University Ave. W., Waterloo, ON N2L 3C5, Canada. TEL 519-884-0710. FAX 519-725-1399. *4651*

CANADIAN CATHOLIC HISTORICAL STUDIES.
Canadian Catholic Historical Association, c/o Secretary General, 1155 Yonge St., Toronto, ON M4T 1W2, Canada. TEL 416-934-0606. FAX 416-934-3444. *6453*

CANADIAN CHIROPRACTIC ASSOCIATION. JOURNAL.
Canadian Chiropractic Association, 1396 Eglinton Ave. W., Toronto, ON M6C 2E4, Canada. TEL 416-781-5656. FAX 416-781-7344. *4826*

CANADIAN CHURCH HISTORICAL SOCIETY JOURNAL.
Canadian Church Historical Society, c/o Archives, Anglican Church of Canada, 600 Jarvis St., Toronto, ON M4Y 2J6, Canada. TEL 416-924-9192. FAX 416-968-7983. *6327*

CANADIAN DENTAL ASSOCIATION. JOURNAL.
Canadian Dental Association, 1815 Alta Vista Dr., Ottawa, ON K1G 3Y6, Canada. TEL 613-523-1770. FAX 613-523-7736. *4852*

CANADIAN DENTAL HYGIENISTS ASSOCIATION. PROBE.
Canadian Dental Hygienists Association, 96 Centrepointe Dr., Nepean, ON K2G 6B1, Canada. TEL 613-224-5515. FAX 613-224-7283. *4852*

CANADIAN DIETETIC ASSOCIATION. JOURNAL.
Dietitians of Canada, 480 University Ave., Ste. 604, Toronto, ON M5G 1V2, Canada. TEL 416-596-0857. FAX 416-596-0603. *5471*

CANADIAN EMERGENCY NEWS.
Pendragon Publishing Ltd., Box 68010, 7750 Ranchview Dr., N.W., Calgary, AB T3G 3N8, Canada. TEL 403-547-5748. FAX 403-547-5749. *5005*

CANADIAN ENTOMOLOGIST.
Entomological Society of Canada, 393 Winston Ave., Ottawa, ON K2A 1Y8, Canada. TEL 613-725-2619. FAX 613-725-9349. *748*

CANADIAN ETHNIC STUDIES.
Canadian Ethnic Studies Association, Research Centre for Canadian Ethnic Studies, University of Calgary, 2500 University Dr., N.W., Calgary, AB T2N 1N4, Canada. TEL 403-220-7257. FAX 403-284-5467. *3003*

CANADIAN FAMILY PHYSICIAN.
College of Family Physicians of Canada, 2630 Skymark Ave., Mississauga, ON L4W 5A4, Canada. TEL 905-629-0900. FAX 905-629-0893. *4651*

CANADIAN FOLKLORE.
Folklore Studies Association of Canada, c/o Universite Laval, Cite Universitaire, Quebec, PQ G1K 7P4, Canada. TEL 418-656-7200. FAX 418-656-2019. *3085*

CANADIAN GEMMOLOGIST.
Canadian Gemmological Association, 1767 Avenue Rd., North York, ON M5M 3Y8, Canada. TEL 416-785-0962. FAX 416-785-9043. *3863*

THE CANADIAN GEOGRAPHER.
Canadian Association of Geographers, Burnside Hall, McGill University, 805 Sherbrooke St. W., Montreal, PQ H3A 2K6, Canada. TEL 514-398-4946. *3398*

CANADIAN GEOGRAPHIC.
Canadian Geographical Enterprises, 39 McArthur Ave., Vanier, ON K1L 8L7, Canada. TEL 613-745-4629. FAX 613-744-0947. *3259*

CANADIAN GEOTECHNICAL JOURNAL.
National Research Council of Canada, Research Journals, Ottawa, ON K1A 0R6, Canada. TEL 613-993-9084. FAX 613-952-7656. *2311*

CANADIAN ISSUES.
Association for Canadian Studies, P.O. Box 8888, Sta. Centre Ville, Montreal, PQ H3C 3P8, Canada. TEL 514-987-7784. FAX 514-987-8210. *3774*

CANADIAN JEWISH STUDIES.
Association for Canadian Jewish Studies, c/o Dept. of Religion, Concordia U., 1455 de Maisonneuve Blvd. W., Montreal, PQ H3G 1M8, Canada. TEL 514-848-2066. FAX 514-848-4541. *3003*

CANADIAN JOURNAL FOR THE STUDY OF ADULT EDUCATION.
Canadian Association for the Study of Adult Education, OISE-UT, 252 Bloor St. W., Office 3-345, Toronto, ON M5S 1V6, Canada. *2508*

CANADIAN JOURNAL OF ADMINISTRATIVE SCIENCES.
Administrative Sciences Association of Canada, Faculty of Commerce and Administration, Concordia University, 1455 de Maisonneuve Blvd. W., Montreal, QC H3G 1M8, Canada. TEL 514-848-2719. FAX 514-848-2839. *946*

CANADIAN JOURNAL OF ANAESTHESIA.
Canadian Anaesthetists' Society, 1 Eglinton Ave., E., Ste. 208, Toronto, ON M4P 3A1, Canada. TEL 416-480-0602. FAX 416-480-0320. *4805*

CANADIAN JOURNAL OF ANIMAL SCIENCE.
Agricultural Institute of Canada, 141 Laurier Ave., W. Ste. 1112, Ottawa, ON K1P 5J3, Canada. TEL 613-232-9459. FAX 613-594-5190. *273*

CANADIAN JOURNAL OF APPLIED PHYSIOLOGY.
Human Kinetics Publishers, Inc., Box 5076, Champaign, IL 61825-5076. TEL 217-351-5076. FAX 217-351-2674. *6755*

CANADIAN JOURNAL OF ARCHAEOLOGY.
Canadian Archaeological Association, c/o Bjorn Simonsen, Secy.-Treas., 352 Viaduct Ave. W., R.R. 3, Victoria, BC V8X 3X1, Canada. TEL 604-479-1147. FAX 604-381-3890. *357*

CANADIAN JOURNAL OF BOTANY.
National Research Council of Canada, Research Journals, Ottawa, ON K1A 0R6, Canada. TEL 613-993-9084. FAX 613-952-7656. *698*

CANADIAN JOURNAL OF CARDIOLOGY.
Pulsus Group Inc., 2902 S. Sheridan Way, Oakville, ON L6J 7L6, Canada. TEL 905-829-4770. FAX 905-829-4799. *4811*

CANADIAN JOURNAL OF CARDIOVASCULAR NURSING.
Canadian Council of Cardiovascular Nurses, 160 George St., Ste. 200, Ottawa, ON K1N 9M2, Canada. TEL 613-241-4361. FAX 416-241-3278. *4930*

CANADIAN JOURNAL OF CHEMISTRY.
National Research Council of Canada, Research Journals, Ottawa, ON K1A 0R6, Canada. TEL 613-993-9084. FAX 613-952-7656. *1741*

CANADIAN JOURNAL OF CIVIL ENGINEERING.
National Research Council of Canada, Research Journals, Ottawa, ON K1A 0R6, Canada. TEL 613-993-9084. FAX 613-952-7656. *2779*

CANADIAN JOURNAL OF COMMUNICATION.
Wilfrid Laurier University Press, 75 University Ave. W., Waterloo, ON N2L 3C5, Canada. TEL 519-884-0710. FAX 519-725-1399. *2047*

CANADIAN JOURNAL OF DERMATOLOGY.
Rodar Publishing Inc., 8102 Trans Canada Hwy., St. Laurent, PQ H4S 1Z4, Canada. TEL 514-333-5350. *4875*

CANADIAN JOURNAL OF DIABETES CARE.
Canadian Diabetes Association, 15 Toronto St., Ste. 800, Toronto, ON M5C 2E3, Canada. TEL 416-363-3373. FAX 416-363-3393. *4883*

CANADIAN JOURNAL OF EARTH SCIENCES.
National Research Council of Canada, Research Journals, Ottawa, ON K1A 0R6, Canada. TEL 613-993-9084. FAX 613-952-7656. *2311*

CANADIAN JOURNAL OF EDUCATIONAL COMMUNICATION.
Association for Media and Technology in Education in Canada (AMTEC), 3 - 1750 The Queensway, Ste. 1318, Etobicoke, ON M9C 5H5, Canada. *2597*

CANADIAN JOURNAL OF ELECTRICAL AND COMPUTER ENGINEERING.
Institute of Electrical and Electronic Engineers Canada, Laval University, Department of Electrical and Computer Engineering, Quebec, PQ G1K 7P4, Canada. TEL 418-656-2984. FAX 418-656-3159. *2811*

CANADIAN JOURNAL OF FILM STUDIES.
McGill University, Graduate Program in Communications, 3465 Peel St., Montreal, PQ H3A 1W7, Canada. TEL 514-398-4935. FAX 514-398-4934. *5325*

CANADIAN JOURNAL OF FISHERIES AND AQUATIC SCIENCES.
National Research Council of Canada, Research Journals, Ottawa, ON K1A 0R6, Canada. TEL 613-993-9084. FAX 613-952-7656. *3063*

CANADIAN JOURNAL OF FOREST RESEARCH.
National Research Council of Canada, Research Journals, Ottawa, ON K1A 0R6, Canada. TEL 613-993-9084. FAX 613-952-7656. *3149*

CANADIAN JOURNAL OF GASTROENTEROLOGY.
Pulsus Group Inc., 2902 S. Sheridan Way, Oakville, ON L6J 7L6, Canada. TEL 905-829-4770. FAX 905-829-4799. *4908*

CANADIAN JOURNAL OF HIGHER EDUCATION.
Canadian Society for the Study of Higher Education, c/o Centre for Higher Education Research and Development, University of Manitoba, 220 Sinnott Bldg., 70 Dysart Rd., Winnipeg, MB R3T 2N2, Canada. TEL 204-474-6211. FAX 204-275-0831. *2535*

CANADIAN JOURNAL OF HISTORY.
University of Saskatchewan, 707 Arts Bldg., 9 Campus Dr., Saskatoon, SK S7N 5A5, Canada. TEL 306-966-5794. FAX 306-966-5852. *3491*

CANADIAN JOURNAL OF HOSPITAL PHARMACY.
Canadian Society of Hospital Pharmacists, 1145 Hunt Club Rd., Ste. 350, Ottawa, ON K1V 0Y3, Canada. TEL 613-736-9733. FAX 613-736-5660. *5651*

CANADIAN JOURNAL OF HUMAN SEXUALITY.
Sex Information and Education Council of Canada, 850 Coxwell Ave., East York, ON M4C 5R1, Canada. TEL 416-466-5304. FAX 416-778-0785. *6101*

CANADIAN JOURNAL OF INFECTION CONTROL.
Pulsus Group Inc., 2902 S. Sheridan Way, Oakville, ON L6J 7L6, Canada. TEL 905-829-4770. FAX 905-829-4799. *4833*

CANADIAN JOURNAL OF INFECTIOUS DISEASES.
Pulsus Group Inc., 2902 S. Sheridan Way, Oakville, ON L6J 7L6, Canada. TEL 905-829-4770. FAX 905-829-4799. *4834*

THE CANADIAN JOURNAL OF IRISH STUDIES.
Canadian Association for Irish Studies, c/o Memorial University of Newfoundland, Dept. of English, St. John, NF A1C 5S7, Canada. TEL 709-737-8275. FAX 709-737-4528. *3774*

CANADIAN JOURNAL OF LINGUISTICS.
Canadian Linguistic Association, c/o Dept. de Linguistique, UQAM, C.P. 8888, Succ. Centre-Ville, Montreal, PQ H3C 3P8, Canada. TEL 514-987-3000. FAX 514-987-4652. *4248*

CANADIAN JOURNAL OF MARKETING RESEARCH.
Professional Marketing Research Society, 2175 Sheppard Ave. E., Ste. 110, Willowdale, ON M2J 1W8, Canada. TEL 416-493-4080. *1520*

CANADIAN JOURNAL OF MICROBIOLOGY.
National Research Council of Canada, Research Journals, Ottawa, ON K1A 0R6, Canada. TEL 613-993-9084. FAX 613-952-7656. *782*

CANADIAN JOURNAL OF NATIVE EDUCATION.
University of Alberta, Educational Policy Studies, 7th Fl. Education North, Edmonton, AB T6G 2G5, Canada. TEL 403-465-3480. FAX 403-492-2024. *2427*

CANADIAN JOURNAL OF NETHERLANDIC STUDIES.
Canadian Association for the Advancement of Netherlandic Studies, Department of French, University of Windsor, Windsor, ON N9B 3P4, Canada. TEL 519-253-4232. FAX 519-971-3648. *4386*

CANADIAN JOURNAL OF NEUROLOGICAL SCIENCES.
Canadian Journal of Neurological Sciences, Inc., P.O. Box 4220, Sta. C, Calgary, AB T2T 5N1, Canada. TEL 403-229-9575. FAX 403-229-1661. *5057*

THE CANADIAN JOURNAL OF NURSING RESEARCH.
McGill University, School of Nursing, 3506 University St., Montreal, PQ H3A 2A7, Canada. TEL 514-398-4160. FAX 514-398-8455. *4930*

CANADIAN JOURNAL OF OCCUPATIONAL THERAPY.
Canadian Association of Occupational Therapists, CTTC Ste. 3400, 1125 Colonel By-drive, Ottawa, ON K1S 5R1, Canada. TEL 613-523-2268. FAX 613-523-2552. *5042*

CANADIAN JOURNAL OF OPHTHALMOLOGY.
Canadian Ophthalmological Society, 1525 Carling Ave., Ottawa, ON K1Z 8R9, Canada. TEL 613-729-6779. FAX 613-729-7209. *4991*

CANADIAN JOURNAL OF PEDIATRICS.
Rodar Publishing Inc., 8102 Trans Canada Hwy., St. Laurent, PQ H4S 1Z4, Canada. TEL 514-333-5350. FAX 514-457-2679. *5029*

CANADIAN JOURNAL OF PHILOSOPHY.
University of Calgary Press, 2500 University Dr. N.W., Calgary, AB T2N 1N4, Canada. TEL 403-220-7578. FAX 403-282-0085. *5721*

CANADIAN JOURNAL OF PHYSICS.
National Research Council of Canada, Research Journals, Ottawa, ON K1A 0R6, Canada. TEL 613-993-9084. FAX 613-952-7656. *5799*

CANADIAN JOURNAL OF PHYSIOLOGY AND PHARMACOLOGY.
National Research Council of Canada, Research Journals, Ottawa, ON K1A 0R6, Canada. TEL 613-993-9084. FAX 613-952-7656. *814*

CANADIAN JOURNAL OF PLANT SCIENCE.
Agricultural Institute of Canada, 141 Laurier Ave. W., Ste. 1112, Ottawa, ON K1P 5J3, Canada. TEL 613-232-9459. FAX 613-594-5190. *698*

CANADIAN JOURNAL OF POLITICAL SCIENCE.
Wilfrid Laurier University Press, 75 University Ave. W., Waterloo, ON N2L 3C5, Canada. TEL 519-884-0710. FAX 519-725-1399. *5898*

CANADIAN JOURNAL OF PROGRAM EVALUATION.
University of Calgary Press, 2500 University Dr. N.W., Calgary, AB T2N 1N4, Canada. TEL 403-220-7578. FAX 403-282-0085. *6167*

CANADIAN JOURNAL OF PSYCHIATRY.
Canadian Psychiatric Association, 237 Argyle Ave., Ste. 200, Ottawa, ON K2P 1B8, Canada. TEL 613-234-2815. FAX 613-234-9857. *5057*

CANADIAN JOURNAL OF PSYCHOANALYSIS.
Canadian Psychoanalytic Society, 7000 Cote des Neiges, Montreal, PQ H3S 2C1, Canada. TEL 514-738-6105. FAX 514-738-6393. *5057*

CANADIAN JOURNAL OF PUBLIC HEALTH.
Canadian Public Health Association, 1565 Carling Ave., Ste. 400, Ottawa, ON K1Z 8R1, Canada. TEL 613-725-3769. FAX 613-725-9826. *6230*

CANADIAN JOURNAL OF REGIONAL SCIENCE.
University of New Brunswick, Department of Economics, P.O. Box 4400, Fredericton, NB E3B 5A3, Canada. TEL 506-447-3206. FAX 506-453-4514. *1297*

CANADIAN JOURNAL OF RESPIRATORY THERAPY.
Canadian Medical Association, 1867 Alta Vista Dr., P.O. Box 8650, Ottawa, ON K1G 0G8, Canada. TEL 613-731-9331. FAX 613-523-0937. *5118*

THE CANADIAN JOURNAL OF RURAL MEDICINE.
Canadian Medical Association, P.O. Box 8650, Ottawa, ON K1G 0G8, Canada. TEL 613-731-9331. FAX 613-523-0937. *4651*

CANADIAN JOURNAL OF SOCIOLOGY.
University of Toronto Press, Journals Department, 5201 Dufferin St., Downsview, ON M3H 5T8, Canada. TEL 416-667-7710. FAX 416-667-7881. *6704*

CANADIAN JOURNAL OF SOIL SCIENCE.
Agricultural Institute of Canada, 141 Laurier Ave. W., Ste 1112, Ottawa, ON K1P 5J3, Canada. TEL 613-232-9459. FAX 613-594-5190. *218*

CANADIAN JOURNAL OF UNIVERSITY CONTINUING EDUCATION.
Canadian Association for University Continuing Education, c/o Beverly Stevenson, Coordinator, 600 - 350 Albert St., Ottawa, ON K1R 1B1, Canada. TEL 613-563-1236. FAX 613-563-9745. *2535*

CANADIAN JOURNAL OF VETERINARY RESEARCH.
Canadian Veterinary Medical Association, 339 Booth St., Ottawa, ON K1R 7K1, Canada. TEL 613-236-1162. FAX 613-236-9681. *7268*

CANADIAN JOURNAL OF ZOOLOGY.
National Research Council of Canada, Research Journals, Ottawa, ON K1A 0R6, Canada. TEL 613-993-9084. FAX 613-952-7656. *830*

CANADIAN JOURNAL ON AGING.
Canadian Association on Gerontology, MacKinnon Bldg., Rm. 039, University of Guelph, Guelph, ON N1G 2W1, Canada. TEL 519-824-4121. FAX 519-837-9953. *3433*

CANADIAN LEADER.
Canyouth Publications Ltd., Box 5112, Station F, Ottawa, ON K2C 3H4, Canada. TEL 613-224-5131. FAX 613-224-5982. *1840*

CANADIAN LITERATURE.
University of British Columbia, No. 167, 1855 West Mall, Vancouver, BC V6T 1Z2, Canada. TEL 604-822-2780. FAX 604-822-5504. *4386*

CANADIAN MARITIME BIBLIOGRAPHY.
Memorial University of Newfoundland, Maritime Studies Research Unit, St. John's, NF A1C 5S7, Canada. TEL 709-737-8424. FAX 709-737-4569. *7050*

CANADIAN MATHEMATICAL SOCIETY. CONFERENCE PROCEEDINGS.
American Mathematical Society, Box 6248, Providence, RI 02940-6248. TEL 401-455-4000. FAX 401-331-3842. *4566*

CANADIAN METALLURGICAL QUARTERLY.
Elsevier Science Ltd., Pergamon, P.O. Box 800, Kidlington, Oxford OX5 1DX, England. TEL 44-1865-843000. FAX 44-1865-843010. *5187*

CANADIAN MODERN LANGUAGE REVIEW.
University of Toronto Press, Journals Department, 5201 Dufferin St., North York, ON M3H 5T8, Canada. TEL 416-667-7710. FAX 416-667-7881. *4248*

CANADIAN MUSIC EDUCATOR.
Canadian Music Educators Association, Faculty of Education, Memorial University of Newfoundland, St. John's, NF A1B 3X8, Canada. TEL 709-737-7603. FAX 709-737-2345. *5381*

CANADIAN ONCOLOGY NURSING JOURNAL.
Pappin Communications, The Victoria Centre, 84 Isabella St., Pembroke, ON K8A 5S5, Canada. TEL 613-735-0952. FAX 613-735-7983. *4930*

CANADIAN ORAL HISTORY ASSOCIATION. FORUM.
Canadian Oral History Association, P.O. Box 2064, Stn. "D", Ottawa, ON K1P 5W3, Canada. TEL 613-996-6996. FAX 613-995-6575. *3620*

CANADIAN PHARMACEUTICAL JOURNAL.
Keith Healthcare Communications, 21 Concourse Gate, No. 13, Nepean, ON K2E 7S4, Canada. TEL 613-727-1364. FAX 613-727-3757. *5651*

CANADIAN POETRY.
c/o Department of English, University of Western Ontario, London, ON N6A 3K7, Canada. TEL 519-661-3403. *4505*

CANADIAN PROPERTY MANAGEMENT.
MediaEdge Communications Inc., 5255 Yonge St., Ste. 1000, North York, ON M2N 6P4, Canada. TEL 416-512-8186. FAX 416-512-8344. *6297*

CANADIAN PUBLIC POLICY.
University of Toronto Press, Journals Department, 5201 Dufferin St., Downsview, ON M3H 5T8, Canada. TEL 416-667-7710. FAX 416-667-7881. *1229*

CANADIAN RAILWAY MODELLER.
28103-1453 Henderson Hwy., Winnipeg, MB R2G 4E9, Canada. TEL 204-668-0168. FAX 204-668-0168. *3664*

CANADIAN RESPIRATORY JOURNAL.
Pulsus Group Inc., 2902 S. Sheridan Way, Oakville, ON L6J 7L6, Canada. TEL 905-829-4770. FAX 905-829-4799. *5118*

CANADIAN REVIEW OF AMERICAN STUDIES.
University of Calgary Press, 2500 University Dr. N.W., Calgary, AB T2N 1N4, Canada. TEL 403-220-7578. FAX 403-282-0085. *3621*

CANADIAN REVIEW OF ART EDUCATION RESEARCH AND ISSUES.
Canadian Society for Education Through Art, 675 Samuel de Champlain, Boucherville, PQ J4B 6C4, Canada. TEL 514-655-2435. FAX 514-655-4379. *2427*

THE CANADIAN REVIEW OF SOCIOLOGY AND ANTHROPOLOGY.
Canadian Sociology and Anthropology Association, Concordia University, 1455 bd. de Maisonneuve Ouest, Montreal, PQ H3G 1M8, Canada. TEL 514-848-8780. FAX 514-848-4539. *6704*

CANADIAN REVIEW OF STUDIES IN NATIONALISM.
Canadian Review of Studies in Nationalism, Inc., c/o University of Prince Edward Island, Charlottetown, PE C1A 4P3, Canada. TEL 902-566-0527. FAX 902-628-4323. *3491*

CANADIAN SOCIAL WORK REVIEW.
Wilfred Laurier University Press, 75 University Ave. W., Waterloo, ON N2L 3C5, Canada. TEL 519-884-0710. FAX 519-725-1399. *6657*

CANADIAN SOCIETY FOR COMPUTATIONAL STUDIES OF INTELLIGENCE. PROCEEDINGS OF THE BIENNIAL CONFERENCE.
Morgan Kaufmann Publishers, Inc., 340 Pine St., 6th Fl., San Francisco, CA 94104-3205. TEL 415-392-2665. FAX 415-982-2665. *2099*

CANADIAN SOCIETY FOR MECHANICAL ENGINEERING. TRANSACTIONS.
Canadian Society for Mechanical Engineering, McGill University, Rm. 454 Thomas Workman Engineering Bldg., 817 Sherbrooke St. W., Montreal, PQ H3A 2K6, Canada. TEL 514-398-6311. FAX 514-398-4476. *2881*

CANADIAN STUDIES UPDATE.
Association for Canadian Studies in the U S, 1311 F. Street N.W., Ste. 920, Washington, DC 20004-1105. TEL 202-393-2580. FAX 202-393-2582. *2535*

CANADIAN VETERINARY JOURNAL.
Canadian Veterinary Medical Association, 339 Booth St., Ottawa, ON K1R 7K1, Canada. TEL 613-236-1162. FAX 613-236-9681. *7268*

CANADIAN WATER RESOURCES JOURNAL.
Canadian Water Resources Association, Membership Service Office, P.O. Box 1329, Cambridge, ON N1R 7G6, Canada. TEL 519-888-1211. FAX 579-746-2031. *7289*

CANBERRA ANTHROPOLOGY.
Australian National University, Research School of Pacific and Asian Studies, Canberra, A.C.T. 0200, Australia. TEL 61-6-2490769. FAX 61-6-2494896. *312*

CANBERRA CYCLIST.
Pedal Power A.C.T., Inc., G.P.O. Box 581, Canberra, A.C.T. 2601, Australia. TEL 06-248-7995. FAX 06-207-3199. *6825*

CANBERRA PAPERS ON STRATEGY AND DEFENSE.
Strategic and Defence Studies Centre, Australian National University, Canberra, A.C.T. 0200, Australia. TEL 61-6-2438537. FAX 61-6-2480816. *5262*

CANCER.
John Wiley & Sons, Inc., Journals, 605 Third Ave., New York, NY 10158. TEL 212-850-6645. FAX 212-850-6021. *4972*

CANCER AND METASTASIS REVIEWS.
Kluwer Academic Publishers Boston, Box 358, Accord Sta., Hingham, MA 02018-0358. TEL 617-871-6600. FAX 617-871-6528. *4972*

CANCER BIOCHEMISTRY BIOPHYSICS.
Gordon and Breach - Harwood Academic, Amsteldisk 166, 1st Fl., 1079 LH Amsterdam, Netherlands. *4972*

CANCER BIOTHERAPY & RADIOPHARMACEUTICALS.
Mary Ann Liebert, Inc. Publishers, 2 Madison Ave., Larchmont, NY 10538. TEL 914-834-3100. FAX 914-834-3688. *4972*

CANCER CHEMOTHERAPY AND BIOLOGICAL RESPONSE MODIFIERS.
Elsevier Science B.V., Regional Sales Office, P.O. Box 211, 1000 AE Amsterdam, Netherlands. TEL 31-20-4853957. FAX 31-20-4853432. *4972*

CANCER CONTROL.
Moffitt Cancer Center, 12902 Magnolia Dr., Tampa, FL 33612. TEL 813-632-1349. FAX 813-632-1380. *4973*

CANCER DETECTION AND PREVENTION.
Blackwell Science Inc., 350 Main St., Malden, MA 02148. TEL 617-876-7000. FAX 617-388-8255. *4973*

CANCER EPIDEMIOLOGY, BIOMARKERS & PREVENTION.
American Association for Cancer Research, Public Ledger Bldg., 150 S. Independence Mall West, Ste. 816, Philadelphia, PA 19106-3483. TEL 215-440-9300. FAX 215-440-9354. *4973*

CANCER FORUM.
Australian Cancer Society, Inc., G.P.O. Box 4708, Sydney, N.S.W. 2000, Australia. FAX 61-2-93564558. *4973*

CANCER GENE THERAPY.
Appleton & Lange, Journal Division Box 120041, Stamford, CT 06912-0041. TEL 203-406-4500. *4973*

CANCER GENETICS & CYTOGENETICS.
Elsevier Science Inc., Box 945, New York, NY 10159-0945. TEL 212-633-3730. FAX 212-633-3680. *4973*

CANCER INVESTIGATION.
Marcel Dekker Journals, 270 Madison Ave., New York, NY 10016. TEL 212-696-9000. FAX 212-685-4540. *4973*

THE CANCER JOURNAL FROM SCIENTIFIC AMERICAN.
Scientific American, Inc., 415 Madison Ave., New York, NY 10017-1111. TEL 212-754-0550. FAX 212-980-3062. *4974*

CANCER LETTERS.
Elsevier Science Ireland Ltd., P.O. Box 85, Limerick, Ireland. TEL 353-61-471944. FAX 353-61-472144. *4974*

CANCER MOLECULAR BIOLOGY.
Ain Shams Medical Faculty, Oncology Diagnostic Unit, Abbassia, Cairo, Egypt. TEL 20-2-2858940. FAX 20-2-2859928. *4974*

CANCER NURSING.
Lippincott - Raven Publishers, 227 E. Washington Sq., Philadelphia, PA 19106. TEL 215-238-4200. FAX 215-238-4227. *4930*

CANCER PRACTICE.
Lippincott - Raven Publishers, 227 E. Washington Square, Philadelphia, PA 19106. TEL 215-238-4200. FAX 215-238-4227. *4974*

CANCER PREVENTION INTERNATIONAL.
Cognizant Communication Corporation, 3 Hartsdale Rd., Elmsford, NY 10523-3701. TEL 914-592-7720. FAX 914-592-8981. *4974*

CANCER RESEARCH.
American Association for Cancer Research, Public Ledger Bldg., 150 S. Independence Mall West, Ste. 816, Philadelphia, PA 19106. TEL 215-440-9300. FAX 215-440-9354. *4974*

CANCER TOPICS.
Eurocommunica Publications, 4 Bersted Mews, Bersted St., Bognor Regis, W. Sussex PO22 9RR, England. TEL 01234-823180. FAX 01234-823180. *4974*

CANCER TOPICS ABSTRACTS SERVICE.
Eurocommunica Publications, 4 Bersted Mews, Bersted St., Bognor Regis, W. Sussex PO22 9RR, England. TEL 01243-823180. FAX 01243-823180. *4766*

CANCER TREATMENT AND RESEARCH.
Kluwer Academic Publishers, Postbus 17, 3300 AA Dordrecht, Netherlands. TEL 31-78-6392392. FAX 31-78-6392254. *4975*

CANINE PRACTICE.
Veterinary Practice Publishing Co., Box 6050, Mission Viejo, CA 92690. *7268*

CANSANG TONGBAO.
Zhejiang Cansang Xuehui, Huajiachi, Hangzhou, Zhejiang 310029, People's Republic of China. TEL 86-571-6041733. FAX 86-571-6049815. *107*

CAPSICUM & EGGPLANT NEWSLETTER.
Universita di Torino, Plant Breeding and Seed Production, Via P. Giuria 15, 10126 Turin, Italy. TEL 39-11-657300. FAX 39-11-6502754. *3185*

CARBOHYDRATE LETTERS.
Gordon and Breach - Harwood Academic, Amsteldisk 166, 1st Fl., 1079 LH Amsterdam, Netherlands. *656*

CARBOHYDRATE POLYMERS.
Elsevier Science Ltd., P.O. Box 800, Kidlington, Oxford OX5 1DX, England. TEL 44-1865-843000. FAX 44-1865-843010. *1813*

CARBOHYDRATE RESEARCH.
Elsevier Science Ltd., P.O. Box 800, Kidlington, Oxford OX5 1DX, England. TEL 44-1865-843000. FAX 44-1865-843010. *1813*

CARBON.
Elsevier Science Ltd., Pergamon, P.O. Box 800, Kidlington, Oxford OX5 1DX, England. TEL 44-1865-843000. FAX 44-1865-843010. *1813*

CARBONATES AND EVAPORITES.
Northeastern Science Foundation, Inc., 15 Third St., Box 746, Troy, NY 12181-0746. TEL 518-273-3247. FAX 518-273-3249. *2334*

CARCINOGENESIS.
Lippincott - Raven Publishers, 227 E. Washington Sq., Philadelphia, PA 19106. TEL 215-238-4200. FAX 215-238-4227. *4975*

CARD TALK.
American Business Card Club, Box 460297, Aurora, CO 80046-0297. TEL 303-690-6496. *33*

CARDIFF BUSINESS SCHOOL. DISCUSSION PAPER SERIES IN FINANCIAL AND BANKING ECONOMICS.
Cardiff Business School, University of Wales, Aberconway Bldg., Colum Dr., Cardiff CF1 3EU, Wales. TEL 44-1222-874417. FAX 44-1222-874419. *1119*

LA CARDIOLOGIA NELLA PRATICA CLINICA.
Springer-Verlag Italia Srl, Via Podgora 4, 20122 Milan, Italy. TEL 39-2-55194656. FAX 39-2-55193360. *4812*

CARDIOLOGY.
S. Karger AG, Allschwilerstr. 10, P.O. Box, CH-4009 Basel, Switzerland. TEL 41-61-3061111. FAX 41-61-3061234. *4812*

CARDIOLOGY IN THE ELDERLY.
Rapid Science Publishers, 2-6 Boundary Row, London SE1 8HN, England. TEL 44-171-865-0198. FAX 44-171-410-6600. *4812*

CARDIOLOGY REVIEW.
M R A Publications, Inc., 2 Greenwich Office Park, Greenwich, CT 06831-5154. TEL 203-629-3550. FAX 203-629-2536. *4812*

CARDIOLOGY UPDATE.
Elsevier Science Inc., Box 945, New York, NY 10159-0945. TEL 212-633-3730. FAX 212-633-3680. *4812*

CARDIOVASCULAR AND INTERVENTIONAL RADIOLOGY.
Springer-Verlag, Medical Journals, 175 Fifth Ave., New York, NY 10010. TEL 212-460-1500. FAX 212-473-6272. *5104*

CARDIOVASCULAR CASES.
Erasmus Publishing B.V., Verzamelgebouw Rotterdam-Zuid, Strevelsweg 700-314, 3083 AS Rottersam, Netherlands. TEL 31-10-4815222. FAX 31-10-4815250. *4812*

CARDIOVASCULAR DRUG REVIEWS.
Neva Press Inc., Box 347, Branford, CT 06405. TEL 203-272-5338. FAX 203-272-5338. *5652*

CARDIOVASCULAR DRUGS AND THERAPY.
Kluwer Academic Publishers Boston, Box 358, Accord Sta., Hingham, MA 02018-0358. TEL 617-871-6300. FAX 617-871-6528. *4813*

CARDIOVASCULAR PATHOBIOLOGY.
Woodland Publications, Inc., 69 Murray St., New York, NY 10007. TEL 212-566-4294. FAX 212-406-6496. *4813*

CARDIOVASCULAR PATHOLOGY.
Elsevier Science Inc., Box 945, New York, NY 10159-0945. TEL 212-633-3730. FAX 212-633-3680. *4813*

CARDIOVASCULAR RESEARCH.
Elsevier Science B.V., P.O. Box 211, 1000 AE Amsterdam, Netherlands. TEL 31-20-4853911. FAX 31-20-4853598. *4813*

CARDIOVASCULAR REVIEWS & REPORTS.
LeJacq Communications, Inc., 777 W. Putnam Ave., Greenwich, CT 06830-5014. TEL 203-531-0450. FAX 203-531-0533. *4813*

CARDIOVASCULAR SURGERY.
American Heart Association, 7272 Greenville Ave., Dallas, TX 75231-4596. TEL 214-706-1310. FAX 214-691-6342. *4813*

CARDIOVASCULAR SURGERY.
Elsevier Science Ltd., P.O. Box 800, Kidlington, Oxford OX5 1DX, England. TEL 44-1865-843000. FAX 44-1865-843010. *4813*

CARDOZO STUDIES IN LAW AND LITERATURE.
Jacob Burns Institute for Advanced Legal Studies, Cardoza School of Law, Yeshiva University, 55 Fifth Ave., New York, NY 10003. TEL 212-790-0370. FAX 212-790-0345. *3929*

CARE OF THE CRITICALLY ILL.
Stockton Press, Houndmills, Basingstoke, Hants RG21 6XS, England. TEL 44-1256-329242. FAX 44-1256-328339. *5005*

CAREERS & COLLEGES.
E.M. Guild, Inc., 989 Ave. of the Americas, 6th Fl., New York, NY 10018. TEL 212-563-4688. FAX 212-967-2531. *5506*

CARIB-LATIN ENERGY CONSULTANT.
Carib-Latin Energy Consultants Ltd., P.O. Box 3074, St. James P.O., Trinidad & Tobago, W.I. TEL 809-637-9038. FAX 809-637-9038. *2661*

CARIBBEAN GEOGRAPHY.
Jamaican Geographical Society, c/o Geogrpahy Dept., University of the West Indies, Kingston 7, Jamaica, W.I. TEL 809-927-2129. FAX 809-977-6029. *3398*

CARIBBEAN JOURNAL OF SCIENCE.
University of Puerto Rico, College of Arts and Science, Box 5000, Mayaguez, PR 00681-5000. TEL 787-265-3809. FAX 787-265-1225. *595*

CARIBBEAN LAW REVIEW.
University of the West Indies, Cave Hill Campus, St. Michael, Barbados, W.I. TEL 246-425-1310. FAX 246-424-1788. *3929*

CARIBBEAN STUDIES (NEW YORK).
Gordon and Breach - Harwood Academic, Amsteldisk 166, 1st Fl., 1079 LH Amsterdam, Netherlands. *3621*

THE CARIBBEAN WRITER.
University of the Virgin Islands, RR 2, Box 10,000, Kingshill, St. Croix, VI 00850. TEL 809-692-4152. FAX 809-692-4026. *4387*

CARIES RESEARCH.
S. Karger AG, Allschwilerstr. 10, P.O. Box CH-4009 Basel, Switzerland. TEL 41-61-3061111. FAX 41-61-3061234. *4852*

CARL NEWELL JACKSON LECTURES.
Harvard University Press, 79 Garden St., Cambridge, MA 02138. TEL 617-495-2600. FAX 617-495-5898. *3085*

CARLETON GERMANIC PAPERS.
Carleton University, Department of Modern Languages, 1125 Colonel By Drive, Ottawa, ON K1S 5B6, Canada. TEL 613-520-2116. FAX 613-520-2564. *4387*

CARNEGIE-ROCHESTER CONFERENCE SERIES ON PUBLIC POLICY.
North-Holland, P.O. Box 211, 1000 AE Amsterdam, Netherlands. TEL 31-20-4853911. FAX 31-20-4853598. *947*

THE CAROLINA QUARTERLY.
University of North Carolina at Chapel Hill, Greenlaw Hall CB 3520, Chapel Hill, NC 27599-3520. TEL 919-962-0244. *4387*

CARTA DEL PERU.
Embajada del Peru en Bolivia, Avda. 6 de Agosto 2190, La Paz, Bolivia. TEL 5912-376773. FAX 5912-367640. *6008*

THE CARTOGRAPHIC JOURNAL.
British Cartographic Society, Centre for Remote Sensing and Mapping Science, Department of Geography, University of Aberdeen, Elphinstone Rd., Aberdeen AB24 3UF, Scotland. TEL 44-1224-272324. FAX 44-1224-272331. *3429*

CARTOGRAPHIC PERSPECTIVES.
North American Cartographic Information Society, Box 399, Milwaukee, WI 53201. FAX 414-229-3621. *3398*

CARTOGRAPHY.
Mapping Sciences Institute Australia, G.P.O. Box 6836, E. Perth, W.A. 6892, Australia. TEL 61-9-3517566. FAX 61-9-3512703. *3398*

CASA DE LAS AMERICAS.
3ra y G, Vedado, Habana 10400, Cuba. TEL 537-323587. FAX 537-334554. *4387*

CASOPIS LEKARU CESKYCH.
Nakladatelske Stredisko C L S J.E. Purkyne, Sokolska 31, 120 26 Prague 2, Czech Republic. TEL 420-2-24911420. FAX 420-2-24911420. *4651*

CASTANEA.
Southern Appalachian Botanical Society, Department of Biology, University of North Carolina at Charlotte, Charlotte, NC 28223. TEL 704-547-4065. FAX 704-547-3128. *699*

CASUALTY ACTUARIAL SOCIETY. PROCEEDINGS.
Casualty Actuarial Society, 11009 N. Glebe Rd., Ste. 600, Arlington, VA 22201. TEL 703-276-3100. FAX 703-276-3108. *3838*

CAT WORLD.
Cat World Ltd., Avalon Court, Star Rd., Partridge Green, W. Sussex RH13 8RY. *5635*

CAT WORLD ANNUAL.
Cat World Ltd., Avalon Court, Star Rd., Partridge Green, W. Sussex RH13 8RY. TEL 44-1403-711511. FAX 44-1403-711521. *5635*

CATALOGING & CLASSIFICATION QUARTERLY.
Haworth Press, Inc., 10 Alice St., Binghamton, NY 13904. TEL 607-722-5857. FAX 607-722-6362. *4169*

CATALOGUE OF PALAEARCTIC DIPTERA.
Elsevier Science B.V., Books Division, P.O. Box 211, 1000 AE Amsterdam, Netherlands. TEL 31-20-4853911. FAX 31-20-4853705. *748*

CATALYSIS BY METAL COMPLEXES.
Kluwer Academic Publishers, Postbus 17, 3300 AA Dordrecht, Netherlands. TEL 31-78-6392392. FAX 31-78-6392254. *1813*

CATALYSIS REVIEWS: SCIENCE AND ENGINEERING.
Marcel Dekker Journals, 270 Madison Ave., New York, NY 10016. TEL 212-696-9000. FAX 212-685-4540. *1826*

CATALYSIS TODAY.
Elsevier Science B.V., P.O. Box 211, 1000 AE Amsterdam, Netherlands. TEL 31-20-4853911. FAX 31-20-4853598. *2756*

CATALYST (MELBOURNE).
Royal Melbourne Institute of Technology, Student Union, P.O. Box 12387, A'Beckett St., Melbourne, Vic. 8006, Australia. TEL 61-3-96602884. FAX 61-3-96603705. *1944*

THE CATALYST (WESTMINSTER).
National Council on Community Services & Continuing Education, c/o Sue Hartman, Professional Development Program, Front Range Community College, 3645 W. 112th Ave., Westminster, CO 80030. *2508*

CATENA.
Elsevier Science B.V., P.O. Box 211, 1000 AE Amsterdam, Netherlands. TEL 31-20-4853911. FAX 31-20-4853598. *2334*

CATHEDRA.
Yad Izhak Ben-Zvi, P.O. Box 7660, Jerusalem 91076, Israel. TEL 972-2-5637268. FAX 972-2-5638310. *3655*

CATHETERIZATION AND CARDIOVASCULAR DIAGNOSIS.
John Wiley & Sons, Inc., Journals, 605 Third Ave., New York, NY 10158. TEL 212-850-6645. FAX 212-850-6021. *4813*

CATHOLIC LIBRARY WORLD.
Catholic Library Association, 9009 Carter, Allen Park, MI 48101. TEL 313-388-7429. *4169*

CATHOLIC NEAR EAST MAGAZINE.
Catholic Near East Welfare Association, 1011 First Ave., New York, NY 10022-4195. TEL 212-826-1480. FAX 212-826-8979. *6456*

CATHOLIC WORKMAN.
Box 47, New Prague, MN 56071. TEL 612-758-2229. FAX 612-758-6221. *6457*

CATNAP.
Narcolepsy Association (U.K.), 1 Brook St., Stoke-on-Trent ST4 1JN, England. TEL 44-1782-416417. FAX 44-1782-416417. *5057*

CAUDA PAVONIS.
Washington State University, Department of English, Pullman, WA 99164. TEL 509-335-3023. FAX 509-335-2582. *4387*

CAUSE - EFFECT MAGAZINE.
C A U S E, 4830 Pearl E. Cir., Ste. 302E, Boulder, CO 80301. TEL 303-449-4430. FAX 303-440-0461. *2515*

CEIBA.
Escuela Agricola Panamericana, Adpo. 93, Tegucigalpa D.C., Honduras. TEL 504-76-6140. FAX 504-76-6242. *107*

CELEBRITY ACCESS: THE DIRECTORY (YEAR).
Celebrity Access Publications, 20 Sunnyside Ave., Ste. A241, Mill Valley, CA 94941. TEL 415-389-8133. *5325*

CELEHIS.
Universidad Nacional de Mar del Plata, Centro de Letras Hispanoamericanas, Funes 3250, 7600 Mar del Plata, Argentina. TEL 54-3423-513906. *4387*

CELESTIAL MECHANICS AND DYNAMICAL ASTRONOMY.
Kluwer Academic Publishers, Postbus 17, 3300 AA Dordrecht, Netherlands. TEL 31-78-6392392. FAX 31-78-6392254. *492*

CELESTINESCA.
Michigan State University, Department of Romance Languages, E. Lansing, MI 48824. TEL 517-355-8350. FAX 517-432-3844. *4388*

CELL.
Cell Press, 1050 Massachusetts Ave., Cambridge, MA 02138. TEL 617-661-7060. *737*

CELL AND CHROMOSOME RESEARCH JOURNAL.
University of Calcutta, Centre of Advanced Studies in Botany, 35 Ballygunge Circular Rd., Calcutta 700 019, India. TEL 91-33-4754772. *737*

CELL BIOCHEMISTRY AND BIOPHYSICS.
Humana Press Inc., 999 Riverview Dr., Ste. 208, Totowa, NJ 07512. TEL 973-256-1699. FAX 973-256-8341. *737*

CELL BIOLOGY AND TOXICOLOGY.
Kluwer Academic Publishers, Postbus 17, 3300 AA Dordrecht, Netherlands. TEL 31-78-6392392. FAX 31-78-6392254. *2975*

CELL GROWTH & DIFFERENTIATION.
American Association for Cancer Research, Public Ledger Bldg., 150 S. Independence Mall West, Ste. 816, Philadelphia, PA 19106. TEL 215-440-9300. FAX 215-440-9354. *4975*

CELL MEMBRANES, METHODS AND REVIEWS.
Plenum Publishing Corp., 233 Spring St., New York, NY 10013-1578. TEL 212-620-8000. FAX 212-463-0742. *595*

CELL MOTILITY AND THE CYTOSKELETON.
John Wiley & Sons, Inc., Journals, 605 Third Ave., New York, NY 10158. TEL 212-850-6645. FAX 212-850-6021. *738*

CELL PROLIFERATION.
Blackwell Science Ltd., Osney Mead, Oxford OX2 OEL, England. TEL 44-1865-206206. FAX 44-1865-721205. *738*

CELL RESEARCH.
Science Press, Marketing and Sales Department, 16 Donghuangchenggen North St., Beijing 100717, People's Republic of China. TEL 4010642. FAX 4019810. *595*

CELL TRANSPLANTATION.
Elsevier Science Inc., Box 945, New York, NY 10159-0945. TEL 212-633-3730. FAX 212-633-3680. *738*

CELL VISION.
Eaton Publishing Co., 154 E. Central St., Natick, MA 01760. TEL 508-655-8282. FAX 508-655-9910. *595*

CELLS AND MATERIALS.
Scanning Microscopy International, Inc., 1034 Alabam Dr., Elk Grove Village, IL 60007-2920. TEL 708-529-6677. FAX 708-980-6698. *4652*

CELLULAR AND MOLECULAR BIOLOGY.
C M B Association, 1 av. du Pave Neuf, 93160 Noisy-le-Grand, France. TEL 33-1-45923719. FAX 33-1-43042030. *596*

CELLULAR AND MOLECULAR LIFE SCIENCES.
Birkhaeuser Verlag, P.O. Box 133, CH-4010 Basel, Switzerland. TEL 41-61-2050730. FAX 41-61-2050791. *596*

CELLULAR & MOLECULAR NEUROBIOLOGY.
Plenum Publishing Corp., 233 Spring St., New York, NY 10013-1578. TEL 212-620-8000. FAX 212-463-0742. *5057*

CELLULAR IMMUNOLOGY.
Academic Press, Inc., Journal Division, 525 B St., Ste. 1900, San Diego, CA 92101-4495. TEL 619-230-1840. FAX 619-699-6800. *4792*

CELLULAR NEUROBIOLOGY.
Academic Press, Inc., 525 B St., Ste. 1900, San Diego, CA 92101-4495. TEL 619-231-0926. FAX 619-699-6715. *739*

CELLULAR PHYSIOLOGY AND BIOCHEMISTRY.
S. Karger AG, Allschwilerstr. 10, P.O. Box, CH-4009 Basel, Switzerland. TEL 41-61-3061111. FAX 41-61-3061234. *656*

CELLULAR POLYMERS.
Rapra Technology Ltd., Shawbury, Shrewsbury, Shrops. SY4 4NR, England. TEL 44-1939-250383. FAX 44-1939-251118. *5876*

CELLULAR SIGNALLING.
Elsevier Science Inc., Box 945, New York, NY 10159-0945. TEL 212-633-3730. FAX 212-633-3680. *739*

CELLULOSE.
Thomson Science, 2-6 Boundary Row, London SE1 8HN, England. TEL 44-171-8650066. FAX 44-171-5229623. *699*

CEMENT AND CONCRETE COMPOSITES.
Elsevier Science Ltd., P.O. Box 800, Kidlington, Oxford OX5 1DX, England. TEL 44-1865-843000. FAX 44-1865-843010. *875*

CEMENT AND CONCRETE RESEARCH.
Elsevier Science Ltd., Pergamon, P.O. Box 800, Kidlington, Oxford OX5 1DX, England. TEL 44-1865-843000. FAX 44-1865-843010. *875*

CEMENTO.
Instituto del Cemento Portland Argentino, San Martin 1137, Buenos Aires, Argentina. TEL 54-1-3123040. FAX 54-1-3121700. *875*

CENTAURUS.
Munksgaard International Publishers Ltd., 35 Noerre Soegade, P.O. Box 2148, DK-1016 Copenhagen K, Denmark. TEL 45-33-127030. FAX 45-33-129387. *6518*

CENTENNIAL REVIEW.
Michigan State University, College of Arts & Letters, 312 Linton Hall, E. Lansing, MI 48824-1044. TEL 517-355-1905. FAX 517-336-1858. *3775*

CENTER FOCUS.
Center of Concern, 3700 13th St., N.E., Washington, DC 20017. TEL 202-635-2757. FAX 202-832-9494. *6704*

CENTER FOR CHILDREN'S BOOKS. BULLETIN.
University of Illinois Press, 1325 S. Oak St., Champaign, IL 61820. TEL 217-244-0324. FAX 217-333-5603. *543*

CENTO.
Centre College, Box 745, Danville, KY 40422. TEL 606-238-5533. FAX 606-236-7925. *1944*

CENTRAL ASIA MONITOR.
Institute for Democratic Development, R.R. 2, Box 6880, Fair Haven, VT 05743. TEL 802-537-4361. FAX 802-537-4362. *5899*

CENTRAL ASIAN SURVEY.
Carfax Publishing Co., P.O. Box 25, Abingdon, Oxon. OX14 3UE, England. TEL 44-1235-401000. FAX 44-1235-401550. *5899*

CENTRAL-EUROPEAN JOURNAL OF IMMUNOLOGY.
Polskie Towarzystwo Immunologiczne, c/o Samodzielna Pracownia Immunologii, Centrum Zdrowia Dziecka, Al. Dzieci Polskich 20, 07-736 Warsaw, Poland. TEL 48-22-157156. FAX 48-22-157159. *4792*

CENTRAL EUROPEAN JOURNAL OF PUBLIC HEALTH.
Nakladatelske Stredisko C L S J.E. Purkyne, Sokolska 31, 120 26 Prague 2, Czech Republic. TEL 420-2-24911420. FAX 420-2-24911420. *6230*

CENTRAL STATES ARCHAEOLOGICAL JOURNAL.
Central States Archaeological Societies, Inc., 646 Knierim Pl., Kirkwood, MO 63122. TEL 314-821-7675. *358*

CENTRAL STATES CONFERENCE ON THE TEACHING OF FOREIGN LANGUAGES. EDUCATION SERIES.
National Textbook Co., 4255 W. Touhy Ave., Lincolnwood, IL 60646. TEL 847-679-5500. FAX 847-679-2494. *4248*

CENTRE CULTUREL CALOUSTE GULBENKIAN. ACTES DES COLLOQUES.
Centre Culturel Calouste Gulbenkian, Fondation Calouste Gulbenkian (Lisbonne), 51 av. d'lena, 75116 Paris, France. TEL 33-1-53239393. FAX 33-1-53239399. *3775*

CENTRE D'ETUDES DE L'ASIE DE L'EST. CAHIERS.
Universite de Montreal, Faculte des Arts et des Sciences, C.P. 6128, Succ. A, Montreal, PQ H3C 3J7, Canada. TEL 514-343-5970. FAX 514-343-7716. *5524*

CENTRE FOR EUROPEAN POLICY STUDIES. FINANCIAL MARKETS UNIT. RESEARCH REPORT.
Centre for European Policy Studies, Place du Congres 1, B-1000 Brussels, Belgium. TEL 32-2-2293911. FAX 32-2-2194151. *1120*

CENTRE FOR MEDICINES RESEARCH WORKSHOP.
Kluwer Academic Publishers, Postbus 17, 3300 AA Dordrecht, Netherlands. TEL 31-78-6392392. FAX 31-78-6392254. *5652*

CENTRO DE INVESTIGACIONES HISTORICAS Y ESTETICAS. BOLETIN.
Universidad Central de Venezuela, Facultad de Arquitectura y Urbanismo, Caracas, Venezuela. FAX 58-2-7526718. *399*

CENTRO DE INVESTIGACIONES PENALES Y CRIMINOLOGICAS. REVISTA.
Universidad de los Andes, Centro de Investigaciones Penales y Criminologicas, Apdo. 730, Merida 5101, Venezuela. FAX 58-74-402055. *2263*

CENTRO NAVAL. BOLETIN.
Centro Naval Argentina, Florida 826, 1St, 1005 Buenos Aires, Argentina. TEL 54-1-311-0041. FAX 54-1-311-0123. *5263*

CERAMICA PER L'ARCHITETTURA.
Gruppo Editoriale Faenza Editrice S.p.A., Via Pier. de Crescenzi, 44, Faenza, Italy. TEL 39-546-663488. FAX 39-546-660440. *1727*

CERAMICS INTERNATIONAL.
Elsevier Science Ltd., P.O. Box 800, Kidlington, Oxford OX5 1DX, England. TEL 44-1865-843000. FAX 44-1865-843010. *1727*

CEREBRAL CORTEX.
Oxford University Press, Journals, 2001 Evans Rd., Cary, NC 27513. TEL 919-677-0977. FAX 919-677-1714. *5057*

CEREBROVASCULAR DISEASES.
S. Karger AG, Allschwilerstr. 10, P.O. Box, CH-4009 Basel, Switzerland. TEL 41-61-3061111. FAX 41-61-3061234. *5058*

CERVANTES.
Cervantes Society of America, Pomona College, Claremont, CA 91711. TEL 909-621-8937. FAX 909-621-8065. *4388*

CERVANTES SOCIETY OF AMERICA. BULLETIN.
Cervantes Society of America (Emporia), Emporia State University, Division of Foreign Languages, Emporia, KS 66801-5087. TEL 316-341-5519. FAX 316-341-5681. *4388*

CESKA A SLOVENSKA FARMACIE.
Nakladatelske Stredisko C L S J.E. Purkyne, Sokolska 31, 120 26 Prague 2, Czech Republic. TEL 420-2-24911420. FAX 420-2-24911420. *5652*

CESKA A SLOVENSKA GASTROENTEROLOGIE.
Nakladatelske Stredisko C L S J.E. Purkyne, Sokolska 31, 120 26 Prague 2, Czech Republic. TEL 420-2-24911420. FAX 420-2-24911420. *4908*

CESKA A SLOVENSKA NEUROLOGIE A NEUROCHIRURGIE.
Nakladatelske Stredisko C L S J.E. Purkyne, Sokolska 31, 120 26 Prague 2, Czech Republic. TEL 420-2-24911420. *5058*

CESKA A SLOVENSKA OFTALMOLOGIE.
Nakladatelske Stredisko C L S J.E. Purkyne, Sokolska 31, 120 26 Prague 2, Czech Republic. TEL 420-2-24911420. FAX 420-2-24911420. *4991*

CESKA A SLOVENSKA PSYCHIATRIE.
Nakladatelske Stredisko C L S J.E. Purkyne, Sokolska 31, 120 26 Prague 2, Czech Republic. TEL 420-2-24911420. FAX 420-2-24911420. *5058*

CESKA GYNEKOLOGIE.
Nakladatelske Stredisko C L S J.E. Purkyne, Sokolska 31, 120 26 Prague 2, Czech Republic. TEL 420-2-24911420. FAX 420-2-24911420. *4954*

CESKA RADIOLOGIE.
Nakladatelske Stredisko C L S J.E. Purkyne, Sokolska 31, 120 26 Prague 2, Czech Republic. TEL 420-2-24911420. FAX 420-2-24911420. *5104*

CESKA REUMATOLOGIE.
Nakladatelske Stredisko C L S J.E. Purkyne, Sokolska 31, 120 26 Prague 2, Czech Republic. TEL 420-2-24922420. FAX 420-2-24922420. *5125*

CESKA STOMATOLOGIE.
Nakladatelske Stredisko C L S J.E. Purkyne, Sokolska 31, 120 26 Prague 2, Czech Republic. TEL 420-2-24911420. FAX 420-2-24911420. *4852*

CESKO-SLOVENSKA DERMATOLOGIE.
Nakladatelske Stredisko C L S J.E. Purkyne, Sokolska 31, 120 26 Prague 2, Czech Republic. TEL 420-2-24911420. FAX 420-2-24911420. *4876*

CESKO-SLOVENSKA PATOLOGIE A SOUDNI LEKARSTVI.
Nakladatelske Stredisko C L S J.E. Purkyne, Sokolska 31, 120 26 Prague 2, Czech Republic. TEL 420-2-42911420. FAX 420-2-24911420. *4652*

CESKO-SLOVENSKA PEDIATRIE.
Nakladatelske Stredisko C L S J.E. Purkyne, Sokolska 31, 120 26 Prague 2, Czech Republic. TEL 420-2-24911420. FAX 420-2-24911420. *5029*

CESKOSLOVENSKA FYZIOLOGIE.
Nakladatelske Stredisko C L S J.E. Purkyne, Sokolska 31, 120 26 Prague 2, Czech Republic. TEL 420-2-24911420. FAX 420-2-24911420. *814*

CEYLON JOURNAL OF MEDICAL SCIENCE.
University of Colombo, Faculty of Medicine, Kynsey Rd., Colombo 8, Sri Lanka. TEL 01-583043. FAX 01-586432. *4652*

CEYLON MEDICAL JOURNAL.
Sri Lanka Medical Association, Wijerama House, 6 Wijerama Mawatha, Colombo 7, Sri Lanka. TEL 941-693324. FAX 941-698802. *4652*

THE CHALLENGE.
Pakistan Anti-Tuberculosis Association, Block No. 55, Rm. 8, Pakistan Secretariat, Karachi, Pakistan. TEL 92-21-5688011. *5118*

CHALLENGE (ARMONK).
M.E. Sharpe, Inc., 80 Business Park Dr., Armonk, NY 10504. TEL 914-273-1800. FAX 914-273-2106. *947*

CHALLENGE (ATLANTA).
Morehouse Research Institute, 830 Westview Dr., S.W., Atlanta, GA 30314. *3004*

THE CHALLENGE (BANNING).
Cancer Federation, Box 1298, Banning, CA 92220-0009. TEL 909-849-4325. FAX 909-849-0156. *4975*

CHAMPLAIN SOCIETY, TORONTO. REPORT.
Champlain Society, P.O. Box 60, 260 Adelaide St. E., Toronto, ON M5A 1N1, Canada. TEL 416-482-9635. FAX 416-482-9341. *3491*

CHANCE.
Springer-Verlag, Science Journals, 175 Fifth Ave., New York, NY 10010. TEL 212-460-1612. FAX 212-473-6272. *6905*

CHANGE (WASHINGTON).
Heldref Publications, 1319 18th St., N.W., Washington, DC 20036-1802. TEL 202-296-6267. FAX 202-296-5149. *2535*

CHANGES.
John Wiley & Sons Ltd., Journals, Baffins Ln., Chichester, W. Sussex PO19 1UD, England. TEL 44-1243-779777. FAX 44-1243-775878. *6659*

CHANGJIANG KEXUEYUAN YUANBAO.
Changjiang Kexueyuan, Jiu Wan Fang, Zhao Jia Tiao, Wuhan, Hubei 430010, People's Republic of China. TEL 86-27-2829904. FAX 86-27-2829726. *2871*

CHAOS.
American Institute of Physics, One Physics Ellipse, College Park, MD 20740-3843. TEL 301-209-3000. *5799*

CHAOS, SOLITONS AND FRACTALS.
Elsevier Science Ltd., Pergamon, P.O. Box 800, Kidlington, Oxford OX5 1DX, England. TEL 44-1865-843000. FAX 44-1865-843010. *4566*

CHARITY.
Centurion Press Ltd., 48 George St., London W1R 5RF, England. TEL 44-171-487-4284. FAX 44-171-487-3022. *6659*

CHARLES ELIOT NORTON LECTURES.
Harvard University Press, 79 Garden St., Cambridge, MA 02138. TEL 617-495-2600. FAX 617-495-5898. *3775*

CHARLES LAMB BULLETIN.
Charles Lamb Society, c/o Duncan Wu, Ed., Department of English Literature, University of Glasgow, Glasgow G12 8QQ, Scotland. TEL 44-141-339-8855. FAX 44-141-330-4601. *4388*

CHARLES REDD MONOGRAPHS IN WESTERN HISTORY.
Signature Books, 564 W. 400 North, Salt Lake City, UT 84116. TEL 801-531-1483. FAX 801-531-1488. *3491*

CHARLES S. PEIRCE SOCIETY. TRANSACTIONS.
Charles S. Peirce Society, State University of New York at Buffalo, c/o Peter H. Hare, Dept. of Philosophy, 607 Baldy Hall, Buffalo, NY 14260-1010. TEL 716-645-2444 ext.774. FAX 716-645-6139. *5721*

THE CHARLESTON REPORT.
Charleston Group, 164 Market St., Ste. 213, Charleston, SC 29401. TEL 813-937-2974. FAX 813-937-1370. *4170*

CHARTERED ACCOUNTANTS JOURNAL OF NEW ZEALAND.
Institute of Chartered Accountants, Cigna House, 40 Mercer St., Wellington, New Zealand. TEL 64-4-4747842. FAX 64-4-4998033. *1087*

CHARTERED INSTITUTION OF WATER AND ENVIRONMENTAL MANAGEMENT. JOURNAL.
Lavenham Press Ltd., Water St., Lavenham, Suffolk CO10 9RN, England. TEL 44-1787-247436. FAX 44-1787-248267. *7289*

CHARTERED INSURANCE INSTITUTE. SOCIETY OF FELLOWS. JOURNAL.
Chartered Insurance Institute, Society of Fellows, 20 Aldermanbury, London EC2V 7HY, England. TEL 44-181-898-8464. FAX 44-171-726-0131. *3812*

CHARTIST.
Chartist Publications, 18 Southcote Rd., London N19 5BJ, England. TEL 44-171-254-8601. *5900*

CHASTNAYA SHKOLA.
Izdatel'stvo Chastnaya Shkola, Katykova Marshala ul., 15 - 1, 123181 Moscow, Russia. TEL 7-095-4995295. FAX 7-095-4995295. *2428*

CHAUCER REVIEW.
Pennsylvania State University Press, USB 1, Ste. C, University Park, PA 16802-1003. TEL 814-865-1327. FAX 814-863-1408. *4389*

CHELONIAN CONSERVATION BIOLOGY.
International Union for Conservation of Nature and Natural Resources, Rue Mauverney 28, CH-1196 Gland, Switzerland. TEL 41-22-9990001. FAX 41-22-9990002. *2226*

CHEMECA - AUSTRALASIAN CONFERENCE ON CHEMICAL ENGINEERING. PROCEEDINGS.
Institution of Chemical Engineers in Australia, P.O. Box 542, Collaroy, N.S.W. 2097, Australia. TEL 61-2-982-7245. FAX 61-2-982-1065. *2757*

CHEMIA ANALITYCZNA.
Instytut Chemii Fizycznej, Ul. Kasprzaka 44-52, 01-224 Warsaw, Poland. TEL 48-22-222393. FAX 48-22-225996. *1789*

CHEMICAL ANALYSIS.
John Wiley & Sons, Inc., 605 Third Ave., New York, NY 10158-0012. TEL 212-850-6000. FAX 212-850-6088. *1789*

CHEMICAL AND PETROLEUM ENGINEERING.
Plenum Publishing Corp., Consultants Bureau, 233 Spring St., New York, NY 10013-1578. TEL 212-620-8468. FAX 212-463-0742. *2757*

CHEMICAL COMMUNICATIONS.
The Royal Society of Chemistry, Thomas Graham House, Science Park, Milton Rd., Cambridge CB4 4WF, England. TEL 44-1223-420066. FAX 44-1223-423429. *1742*

CHEMICAL EDUCATOR.
Springer-Verlag, 175 Fifth Ave., New York, NY 10010. TEL 212-460-1500. FAX 212-473-6272. *1742*

THE CHEMICAL ENGINEER.
Institution of Chemical Engineers, George E. Davis Bldg., 165-189 Railway Terr., Rugby, Warks. CV21 3HQ, England. TEL 44-1788-578214. FAX 44-1788-547262. *2757*

CHEMICAL ENGINEERING.
McGraw-Hill Companies, 1221 Ave. of the Americas, New York, NY 10020. TEL 212-512-2197. *2757*

CHEMICAL ENGINEERING AND PROCESSING.
Elsevier Science S.A., P.O. Box 564, CH-1001 Lausanne 1, Switzerland. TEL 41-21-3207381. FAX 41-21-3235444. *2757*

CHEMICAL ENGINEERING: CONCEPTS AND REVIEWS.
Gordon and Breach - Harwood Academic, Amsteldisk 166, 1st Fl., 1079 LH Amsterdam, Netherlands. *2758*

CHEMICAL ENGINEERING EDUCATION.
American Society for Engineering Education, Chemical Engineering Division, 227 Chemical Engineering Bldg., Box 116005, Gainesville, FL 32611-6005. TEL 352-392-0857. FAX 352-392-9513. *2758*

CHEMICAL ENGINEERING JOURNAL AND BIOCHEMICAL ENGINEERING JOURNAL.
Elsevier Science S.A., P.O. Box 564, CH-1001 Lausanne 1, Switzerland. TEL 41-21-3207381. FAX 41-21-3235444. *2758*

CHEMICAL ENGINEERING MONOGRAPHS.
Elsevier Science B.V., Books Division, P.O. Box 211, 1000 AE Amsterdam, Netherlands. TEL 31-20-4853911. FAX 31-20-4853705. *2758*

CHEMICAL ENGINEERING RESEARCH & DESIGN.
Institution of Chemical Engineers, George E. Davis Bldg., 165-189 Railway Terr., Rugby, Warks. CV21 3HQ, England. TEL 44-1788-578214. FAX 44-1788-560833. *2759*

CHEMICAL ENGINEERING SCIENCE.
Elsevier Science Ltd., Pergamon, P.O. Box 800, Kidlington, Oxford OX5 1GDX, England. TEL 44-1865-843000. FAX 44-1865-843010. *2759*

CHEMICAL GEOLOGY.
Elsevier Science B.V., P.O. Box 211, 1000 AE Amsterdam, Netherlands. TEL 31-20-4853911. FAX 31-20-4853598. *2312*

CHEMICAL HEALTH AND SAFETY.
American Chemical Society, Division of Chemical Health and Safety, 1155 16th St., N.W., Washington, DC 20036. TEL 202-872-4600. FAX 202-872-4403. *2975*

CHEMICAL IMMUNOLOGY.
S. Karger AG, Allschwilerstr. 10, P.O. Box, CH-4009 Basel, Switzerland. TEL 41-61-3061111. FAX 41-61-3061234. *4792*

THE CHEMICAL INTELLIGENCER.
Springer-Verlag, Life Science Journals, 175 Fifth Ave., New York, NY 10010. TEL 212-460-1500. FAX 212-473-6272. *1742*

CHEMICAL PHYSICS.
North-Holland, P.O. Box 211, 1000 AE Amsterdam, Netherlands. TEL 31-20-4853911. FAX 31-20-4853598. *1826*

CHEMICAL PHYSICS LETTERS.
North-Holland, P.O. Box 211, 1000 AE Amsterdam, Netherlands. TEL 31-20-4853911. FAX 31-20-4853598. *1826*

CHEMICAL PHYSICS OF SOLID SURFACES.
Elsevier Science B.V., Books Division, P.O. Box 211, 1000 AE Amsterdam, Netherlands. TEL 31-20-4853911. FAX 31-20-4853705. *1826*

CHEMICAL PHYSICS REPORTS.
Gordon and Breach - Harwood Academic, Amsteldisk 166, 1st Fl., 1079 LH Amsterdam, Netherlands. *5799*

CHEMICAL RESEARCH IN TOXICOLOGY.
American Chemical Society, 1155 16th St., N.W., Washington, DC 20036. TEL 800-333-9511. FAX 614-447-3671. *2975*

CHEMICAL SOCIETY OF ETHIOPIA. BULLETIN.
Chemical Society of Ethiopia, P.O. Box 32934, Addis Ababa, Ethiopia. TEL 251-1-121201. FAX 251-1-551244. *1743*

CHEMICAL THERMODYNAMICS.
Elsevier Science B.V., Books Division, P.O. Box 211, 1000 AE Amsterdam, Netherlands. TEL 31-20-4853911. FAX 31-20-4853705. *5799*

CHEMICAL VAPOR DEPOSITION.
V C H Verlagsesellschaft mbH, Postfach 101161, 69451 Weinheim, Germany. TEL 49-6201-606147. FAX 49-6201-606117. *1801*

CHEMICALLY MODIFIED SURFACES.
Gordon and Breach - Harwood Academic, Amsteldisk 166, 1st Fl., 1079 LH Amsterdam, Netherlands. *1827*

CHEMICALS IN AGRICULTURE.
Elsevier Science B.V., Books Division, P.O. Box 211, 1000 AE Amsterdam, Netherlands. TEL 31-20-4853911. FAX 31-20-4853705. *218*

CHEMICKY PRUMYSL.
Enonomia, a.s., Na Florenci 3, 115 43 Prague 1, Czech Republic. TEL 421-2-2823845. *1744*

CHEMICO-BIOLOGICAL INTERACTIONS.
Elsevier Science Ireland Ltd., P.O. Box 85, Limerick, Ireland. TEL 353-61-471944. FAX 353-61-472144. *2975*

CHEMIST.
American Institute of Chemists, Inc., 501 Wythe St., Alexandria, VA 22314. TEL 703-836-2090. FAX 703-836-2091. *1744*

CHEMISTRY AND BIOCHEMISTRY OF AMINO ACIDS, PEPTIDES, AND PROTEINS.
Marcel Dekker, Inc., 270 Madison Ave., New York, NY 10016. TEL 212-696-9000. FAX 212-685-4540. *656*

CHEMISTRY & BIOLOGY.
Current Biology Ltd., 400 Market St., Ste. 700, Philadelphia, PA 19106. FAX 215-574-2270. *681*

CHEMISTRY AND ECOLOGY.
Gordon and Breach - Harwood Academic, Amsteldisk 166, 1st Fl., 1079 LH Amsterdam, Netherlands. *1744*

CHEMISTRY AND PHYSICS OF CARBON: A SERIES OF ADVANCES.
Marcel Dekker, Inc., 270 Madison Ave., New York, NY 10016. TEL 212-696-9000. FAX 212-685-4540. *1814*

CHEMISTRY AND PHYSICS OF LIPIDS.
Elsevier Science Ireland Ltd., P.O. Box 85, Limerick, Ireland. TEL 353-61-471944. FAX 353-61-472144. *656*

CHEMISTRY AND TECHNOLOGY OF FUELS AND OILS.
Plenum Publishing Corp., Consultants Bureau, 233 Spring St., New York, NY 10013-1578. TEL 212-762-8468. FAX 212-463-0742. *5598*

CHEMISTRY OF FUNCTIONAL GROUPS.
John Wiley & Sons, Inc., 605 Third Ave., New York, NY 10158. TEL 212-850-6000. FAX 212-850-6088. *1745*

CHEMISTRY OF HETEROCYCLIC COMPOUNDS (NEW YORK, 1951).
John Wiley & Sons, Inc., 605 Third Ave., New York, NY 10158. TEL 212-850-6000. FAX 212-850-6088. *1814*

CHEMISTRY OF HETEROCYCLIC COMPOUNDS (NEW YORK, 1965).
Plenum Publishing Corp., Consultants Bureau, 233 Spring St., New York, NY 10013-1578. TEL 212-620-8468. FAX 212-463-0742. *1814*

CHEMISTRY OF NATURAL COMPOUNDS.
Plenum Publishing Corp., Consultants Bureau, 233 Spring St., New York, NY 10013-1578. TEL 212-620-8468. FAX 212-463-0742. *1814*

CHEMISTRY REVIEWS.
Gordon and Breach - Harwood Academic, Amsteldisk 166, 1st Fl., 1079 LH Amsterdam, Netherlands. *1745*

CHEMISTS AND CHEMISTRY.
Kluwer Academic Publishers, Postbus 17, 3300 AA Dordrecht, Netherlands. TEL 31-78-6392392. FAX 31-78-6392254. *1745*

CHEMOMETRICS AND INTELLIGENT LABORATORY SYSTEMS.
Elsevier Science B.V., P.O. Box 211, 1000 AE Amsterdam, Netherlands. TEL 31-20-4853911. FAX 31-20-4853598. *1799*

CHEMOSPHERE.
Elsevier Science Ltd., Pergamon, P.O. Box 800, Kidlington, Oxford OX5 1DX, England. TEL 44-1865-843000. FAX 44-1865-843010. *2976*

CHEMOTHERAPY.
S. Karger AG, Allschwilerstr. 10, P.O. Box, CH-4009 Basel, Switzerland. TEL 41-61-3061111. FAX 41-61-3061234. *5652*

CHEMUNG HISTORICAL JOURNAL.
Chemung County Historical Society, 415 E. Water St., Elmira, NY 14901. TEL 607-734-4167. FAX 607-734-1565. *3621*

CHENGSHI JINRONG LUNTAN.
Chengshi Jinrong Luntan Bianjibu, 15 Cuiwei Rd., Haidian, Beijing 100036, People's Republic of China. TEL 86-10-8185253. FAX 86-10-8217853. *1121*

CHENJI XUEBAO.
Science Press, Marketing and Sales Department, 16 Donghuangchenggen North St., Beijing 100717, People's Republic of China. TEL 4010642. FAX 4019810. *2334*

CHESHIRE AND WIRRAL BIRD REPORT.
Cheshire - Wirral Ornithological Society, 113 Nantwich Rd., Middlewich, Ches. CW10 9 HD, England. *802*

CHEST.
American College of Chest Physicians, 3300 Dundee Rd., Northbrook, IL 60062. TEL 847-498-1400. FAX 847-498-5460. *5118*

CHETHAM SOCIETY PUBLICATIONS - REMAINS, HISTORICAL AND LITERARY, CONNECTED WITH THE PALATINE COUNTIES OF LANCASTER AND CHESTER.
Carnegie Publishing Ltd., 18 Maynard St., Preston, Lancs. PR2 2AL, England. TEL 01772-881246. FAX 01772-881442. *3559*

CHIBA IGAKU ZASSHI.
Chiba Igakkai, c/o Chiba Daigaku Igakubu, 1-8-1, Inohana, Chuo-ku, Chiba-shi 260, Japan. TEL 81-43-222-7171. FAX 81-43-226-2005. *4653*

CHICAGO ARTISTS' NEWS.
Chicago Artists' Coalition, 11 E. Hubbard St., 7th Fl., Chicago, IL 60611. TEL 312-670-2060. FAX 312-670-2521. *435*

CHICAGO GUIDES TO WRITING, EDITING, AND PUBLISHING.
University of Chicago Press, 5801 S. Ellis Ave., Chicago, IL 60637. TEL 773-702-7899. *6267*

CHICAGO HISTORY OF AMERICAN CIVILIZATION.
University of Chicago Press, 5801 S. Ellis Ave., Chicago, IL 60637. TEL 773-702-7899. *3622*

CHICAGO HISTORY OF AMERICAN RELIGION.
University of Chicago Press, 5801 S. Ellis Ave., Chicago, IL 60637. TEL 773-702-7899. *6328*

CHICAGO JOURNAL OF THEORETICAL COMPUTER SCIENCE.
M I T Press, 5 Cambridge Center, Cambridge, MA 02142-1493. TEL 617-253-2889. FAX 617-577-1545. *2074*

CHICAGO LECTURES IN MATHEMATICS.
University of Chicago Press, 5801 S. Ellis Ave., Chicago, IL 60637. TEL 773-702-7899. *4566*

CHICAGO LECTURES IN PHYSICS.
University of Chicago Press, 5801 S. Ellis Ave., Chicago, IL 60637. TEL 773-702-7899. *5799*

CHICAGO LINGUISTIC SOCIETY. PAPERS FROM THE REGIONAL MEETINGS.
Chicago Linguistic Society, University of Chicago, Classics 314A, 1050 E. 59th St., Chicago, IL 60637. TEL 773-702-8529. *4249*

CHICAGO MEDICINE.
Chicago Medical Society, 515 N. Dearborn, Chicago, IL 60610. TEL 312-670-2550. FAX 312-670-3646. *4653*

CHICAGO STUDIES IN THE HISTORY OF JUDAISM.
University of Chicago Press, 5801 S. Ellis Ave., Chicago, IL 60637. TEL 773-702-7899. *6403*

CHIEFTAIN.
Black Hawk College, Quad Cities Campus, 6600 34th Ave., Moline, IL 61265. FAX 309-792-5976. *1945*

CHIKEI.
Nihon Chikeigaku Rengo, Kyoto Daigaku Bosai Kenkyujo, Chikei Dojo Saigai Kenkyu Bumon, Gokanosho, Uji-shi, Kyoto 611, Japan. TEL 81-774-32-6041. FAX 81-774-32-4115. *2335*

CHILD ABUSE & NEGLECT.
Elsevier Science Ltd., Pergamon, P.O. Box 800, Kidlington, Oxford OX5 1DX, England. TEL 44-1865-843000. FAX 44-1865-843010. *1840*

CHILD AND ADOLESCENT SOCIAL WORK JOURNAL.
Human Sciences Press, Inc., 233 Spring St., New York, NY 10013-1578. TEL 212-620-8000. FAX 212-463-0742. *6704*

CHILD & FAMILY BEHAVIOR THERAPY.
Haworth Press, Inc., 10 Alice St., Binghamton, NY 13904. TEL 607-722-5857. FAX 607-722-6362. *6101*

CHILD AND YOUTH CARE FORUM.
Human Sciences Press, Inc., 233 Spring St., New York, NY 10013-1578. TEL 212-620-8000. FAX 212-463-0742. *1840*

CHILD & YOUTH SERVICES.
Haworth Press, Inc., 10 Alice St., Binghamton, NY 13904. TEL 607-722-5857. FAX 607-722-6362. *6659*

CHILD CARE FOCUS.
Manitoba Child Care Association, 364 McGregor St., Winnipeg, MB R2W 4X3, Canada. TEL 204-586-8587. FAX 204-589-5613. *1841*

CHILD: CARE, HEALTH AND DEVELOPMENT.
Blackwell Science Ltd., Osney Mead, Oxford OX2 0EL, England. TEL 44-1865-206206. FAX 44-1865-721205. *5029*

CHILD DEVELOPMENT.
University of Chicago Press, Journals Division, Box 37005, Chicago, IL 60637. TEL 773-753-3347. FAX 773-753-0811. *1841*

CHILD DEVELOPMENT ABSTRACTS AND BIBLIOGRAPHY.
University of Chicago Press, Journals Division, 5720 S. Woodlawn Ave., Chicago, IL 60637. TEL 773-753-3347. FAX 773-753-0811. *1861*

CHILD MALTREATMENT.
Sage Publications, Inc., 2455 Teller Rd., Thousand Oaks, CA 91320. TEL 805-499-0721. FAX 805-499-0871. *1841*

CHILD NEUROPSYCHOLOGY.
Swets & Zeitlinger bv, P.O. Box 825, 2160 SZ Lisse, Netherlands. TEL 31-252-435111. FAX 31-252-415888. *6101*

CHILD NURTURANCE.
Plenum Publishing Corp., 233 Spring St., New York, NY 10013-1578. TEL 212-620-8000. FAX 212-463-0742. *1841*

CHILD PSYCHIATRY AND HUMAN DEVELOPMENT.
Human Sciences Press, Inc., 233 Spring St., New York, NY 10013-1578. TEL 212-620-8000. FAX 212-463-0742. *5058*

CHILD PSYCHOLOGY AND PSYCHIATRY REVIEW.
Cambridge University Press, Edinburgh Bldg., Shaftesbury Rd., Cambridge CB2 2RU, England. TEL 44-1223-312393. FAX 44-1223-315052. *6102*

REFEREED SERIALS

CHILD STUDY JOURNAL.
State University of New York at Buffalo, Behavioral and Humanistic Studies, Bacon Hall 306, 1300 Elmwood Ave., Buffalo, NY 14222-1095. TEL 716-878-5302. FAX 716-878-5833. *2428*

CHILDHOOD.
Sage Publications Ltd., 6 Bonhill St., London EC2A 4PU, England. TEL 44-171-374-0645. FAX 44-171-374-8741. *1841*

CHILDMINDING.
Scottish Childminding Association, Rm. 7, Stirling Business Centre, Wellgreen, Stirling FK8 2DZ, Scotland. TEL 44-1786-445377. FAX 44-1786-449062. *1841*

CHILDREN AND YOUTH SERVICES REVIEW.
Elsevier Science Ltd., Pergamon, P.O. Box 800, Kidlington, Oxford OX5 1DX, England. TEL 44-1865-843000. FAX 44-1865-843010. *1842*

CHILDREN'S BOOK AND PLAY REVIEW.
Brigham Young University, Harold B. Lee Library, 5042-J HBLL, Provo, UT 84602. TEL 801-378-6685. FAX 801-378-6708. *1866*

CHILDREN'S BOOK INSIDER.
Children's Book Insider, Box 1030, Fairplay, CO 80440-1030. TEL 719-836-0394. *6267*

CHILDREN'S ENVIRONMENTS.
Chapman & Hall, Journals Department 2-6 Boundary Row, London SE1 8HN, England. TEL 44-171-8650066. FAX 44-171-5229623. *6102*

CHILDREN'S HOSPITAL QUARTERLY.
Human Sciences Press, Inc., 233 Spring St., New York, NY 10013. TEL 212-620-8000. FAX 212-463-0742. *5029*

CHILDREN'S LANGUAGE.
Lawrence Erlbaum Associates, Inc., 10 Industrial Dr., Mahwah, NJ 07430-2262. TEL 201-236-9500. FAX 201-236-0072. *4249*

CHILDREN'S LEGAL RIGHTS JOURNAL.
William S. Hein & Co., Inc., 1285 Main St., Buffalo, NY 14209. TEL 716-882-2600. FAX 716-883-8100. *4100*

CHILDREN'S LITERATURE IN EDUCATION.
Human Sciences Press, Inc., 233 Spring St., New York, NY 10013. TEL 212-620-8000. FAX 212-463-0742. *1842*

CHILDREN'S SOCIAL & ECONOMICS EDUCATION.
Multilingual Matters Ltd., Frankfurt Lodge, Clevedon Hall, Victoria Rd., Clevedon BS21 7SJ, England. TEL 44-1275-876519. FAX 44-1275-343096. *2428*

CHILDRIGHT.
Children's Legal Centre Ltd., University of Essex, Wivenhoe Park, Colchester, Essex CO4 3SQ. TEL 44-1206-872477. FAX 44-1206-873428. *1843*

CHILD'S NERVOUS SYSTEM.
Springer-Verlag, Heidelberger Platz 3, 14197 Berlin, Germany. TEL 49-30-82787-0. FAX 49-30-82787448. *5058*

CHILTON'S REVIEW OF OPTOMETRY.
Chilton Co., Chilton Way, Radnor, PA 19089. TEL 610-964-4370. *4991*

CHIMICA ACTA TURCICA.
Istanbul Universitesi, Muhendislik Fakultesi Dekanligi, 34850 Avcilar - Istanbul, Turkey. TEL 90-212-5911998. FAX 90-212-5911997. *1746*

CHIMICA OGGI.
Teknoscienze s.r.l., Via Aurelio Saffi, 23, 20123 Milan, Italy. TEL 39-2-4818118. FAX 39-2-4818070. *1746*

CHINA BUSINESS REVIEW.
United States - China Business Council, 1818 N St., N.W., Ste. 200, Washington, DC 20036-2406. TEL 202-429-0340. FAX 202-833-9027. *1319*

CHINA CENTER OF ADVANCED SCIENCE AND TECHNOLOGY SERIES.
Gordon and Breach - Harwood Academic, Amsteldisk 166, 1st Fl., 1079 LH Amsterdam, Netherlands. *6519*

CHINA INFORMATION.
Rijksuniversiteit te Leiden, Sinologisch Instituut, Postbus 9515, 2300 RA Leiden, Netherlands. TEL 31-71-5272516. FAX 31-71-5272615. *5524*

THE CHINA JOURNAL.
Contemporary China Centre, Australian National University, Research School of Pacific and Asian Studies, Canberra, A.C.T. 0200, Australia. TEL 06-249-4150. FAX 06-257-3642. *5524*

CHINA OCEAN ENGINEERING.
China Ocean Press, International Cooperation Department, Haimao Dalou, 1 Fuxingmenwai Dajie, Beijing 100860, People's Republic of China. TEL 8032211. FAX 8033515. *2713*

THE CHINA POST.
China Post, No.8, Fu Shun St., Taipei, Taiwan 104, Republic of China. TEL 886-2-596-9971. FAX 886-2-595-7962. *3365*

CHINA REPORT.
Sage Publications India Pvt. Ltd., P.O. Box 4215, New Delhi 110 048. TEL 91-11-644-4958. FAX 91-11-647-2426. *6009*

CHINA STEEL TECHNICAL REPORT.
China Steel Corporation, Technology Division, No. 1 Chungkang Rd., Lin Hai Industrial District, Hsiaokang, Kaohsiung, Taiwan, Republic of China. TEL 886-7-8021111. FAX 886-7-7-8022432. *5188*

CHINESE ASTRONOMY AND ASTROPHYSICS.
Elsevier Science Ltd., Pergamon, P.O. Box 800, Kidlington, Oxford OX5 1DX, England. TEL 44-1865-843000. FAX 44-1865-843010. *493*

CHINESE CHEMICAL LETTERS.
Chinese Chemical Society, P.O. Box 2709, Beijing 100080, People's Republic of China. TEL 86-10-6256-8157. FAX 86-10-6256-8157. *1746*

CHINESE ECONOMIC STUDIES.
M.E. Sharpe, Inc., 80 Business Park Dr., Armonk, NY 10504. TEL 914-273-1800. FAX 914-273-2106. *948*

CHINESE EDUCATION AND SOCIETY.
M.E. Sharpe, Inc., 80 Business Park Dr., Armonk, NY 10504. TEL 914-273-1800. FAX 914-273-2106. *2428*

CHINESE ENVIRONMENTAL SCIENCE.
Chinese Society for Environmental Sciences, No.115, Xizhimennei Nanxiaojie, Beijing 100035, People's Republic of China. TEL 86-1-6066498. FAX 86-1-6020031. *2910*

CHINESE GEOGRAPHICAL SCIENCE.
Science Press, Marketing and Sales Department, 16 Donghuangchenggen North St., Beijing 100717, People's Republic of China. TEL 4010642. FAX 4019810. *2335*

CHINESE JOURNAL OF ACOUSTICS.
Science Press, Marketing and Sales Department, 16 Donghuangchenggen North St., Beijing 100717, People's Republic of China. TEL 4010642. FAX 4019810. *5872*

CHINESE JOURNAL OF ADMINISTRATION.
National Chengchi University, Center for Public and Business Administration Education, 187 Chin Hua St., Taipei, Taiwan, Republic of China. TEL 886-2-3940690. FAX 886-2-3975219. *1470*

CHINESE JOURNAL OF ATMOSPHERIC SCIENCES.
Allerton Press, Inc., 150 Fifth Ave., New York, NY 10011. TEL 212-924-3950. FAX 212-463-9684. *5228*

CHINESE JOURNAL OF BIOTECHNOLOGY.
Allerton Press, Inc., 150 Fifth Ave., New York, NY 10011. TEL 212-924-3950. FAX 212-463-9684. *682*

CHINESE JOURNAL OF BOTANY.
Science Press, Marketing and Sales Department, 16 Donghuangchenggen North St., Beijing 100717, People's Republic of China. TEL 4010642. FAX 4019810. *699*

CHINESE JOURNAL OF CANCER RESEARCH.
Beijing Institute for Cancer Research, Da-Hong-Luo-Chang Street, Western District, Beijing, People's Republic of China. TEL 861-603-1122. FAX 861-602-3658. *4975*

CHINESE JOURNAL OF CHEMISTRY.
Science Press, Marketing and Sales Department, 16 Donghuangchenggen North St., Beijing 100717, People's Republic of China. TEL 4010642. FAX 4019810. *1746*

CHINESE JOURNAL OF GEOCHEMISTRY.
Science Press, Marketing and Sales Department, 16 Donghuangchenggen North St., Beijing 100717, People's Republic of China. TEL 4010642. FAX 4019810. *2335*

CHINESE JOURNAL OF GEOPHYSICS.
Allerton Press, Inc., 150 Fifth Ave., New York, NY 10011. TEL 212-924-3950. FAX 212-463-9684. *2379*

CHINESE JOURNAL OF LASERS.
Science Press, Marketing and Sales Department, 16 Donghuangchenggen North St., Beijing 100717, People's Republic of China. *5859*

CHINESE JOURNAL OF MECHANICAL ENGINEERING.
China Machine Press, 1 Nanjie, Baiwanzhuang, Beijing 100037, People's Republic of China. TEL 86-10-6832-6677. FAX 86-10-6832-6337. *2881*

CHINESE JOURNAL OF MICROBIOLOGY AND IMMUNOLOGY.
Chinese Society of Microbiology, National Taiwan University, College of Medicine, Jen-Ai Rd., Taipei, Taiwan, Republic of China. *782*

CHINESE JOURNAL OF OCEANOLOGY AND LIMNOLOGY.
Science Press, Marketing and Sales Department, 16 Donghuangchenggen North St., Beijing 100717, People's Republic of China. TEL 4010642. FAX 4019810. *2400*

CHINESE JOURNAL OF PHYSIOLOGICAL SCIENCES.
Science Press, Marketing and Sales Department, 16 Donghuangchenggen North St., Beijing 100717, People's Republic of China. TEL 4010642. FAX 4019810. *814*

CHINESE JOURNAL OF POLYMER SCIENCE.
Science Press, Marketing and Sales Department, 16 Donghuangchenggen North St., Beijing 100717, People's Republic of China. TEL 86-10-4010642. FAX 86-10-4019810. *1814*

CHINESE JOURNAL OF PSYCHOLOGY.
Chinese Psychological Association, c/o Department of Psychology, National Taiwan University, Taipei 10764, Taiwan, Republic of China. FAX 886-2-3629909. *6102*

CHINESE LAW AND GOVERNMENT.
M.E. Sharpe, Inc., 80 Business Park Dr., Armonk, NY 10504. TEL 914-273-1800. FAX 914-273-2106. *3930*

CHINESE LITERATURE: ESSAYS, ARTICLES, REVIEWS.
c/o Dept. of Comparative Literature, Ballantine Hall Rm. 402, Indiana University, Bloomington, IN 47405. TEL 812-855-7070. *4389*

CHINESE MEDICAL JOURNAL.
Chinese Medical Association, P.O. Box 2258, 42 Dongsi Xidajie, Beijing 100710, People's Republic of China. TEL 5133311. *4653*

CHINESE MEDICAL SCIENCES JOURNAL.
Chinese Academy of Medical Sciences (CAMS), 9 Dong Dan San Tiao, Beijing 100730, People's Republic of China. TEL 5133074. FAX 5124876. *4653*

CHINESE MUSIC.
Chinese Music Society of North America, One Heritage Plaza, Box 5275, Woodridge, IL 60517-0275. TEL 630-910-1551. FAX 630-910-1561. *5382*

CHINESE PHYSICS LETTERS.
Allerton Press, Inc., 150 Fifth Ave., New York, NY 10011. TEL 212-924-3950. FAX 212-463-9684. *5799*

CHINESE SCIENCE BULLETIN.
Science Press, Marketing and Sales Department, 16 Donghuangchenggen Beijie, Beijing, People's Republic of China. TEL 4010642. FAX 4019810. *6519*

CHINESE SOCIOLOGY AND ANTHROPOLOGY.
M.E. Sharpe, Inc., 80 Business Park Dr., Armonk, NY 10504. TEL 914-273-1800. FAX 914-273-2106. *6704*

CHINESE STUDIES IN HISTORY.
M.E. Sharpe, Inc., 80 Business Park Dr., Armonk, NY 10504. TEL 914-273-1800. FAX 914-273-2106. *3491*

CHINESE STUDIES IN PHILOSOPHY.
M.E. Sharpe, Inc., 80 Business Park Dr., Armonk, NY 10504. TEL 914-273-1800. FAX 914-273-2106. *5721*

CHINOPERL PAPERS.
Conference on Chinese Oral and Performing Literature, c/o Bell Yung, Music Department, University of Pittsburgh, Pittsburgh, PA 15260. TEL 412-624-4061. FAX 412-624-4186. *5524*

CHIRALITY.
John Wiley & Sons, Inc., Journals, 605 Third Ave., New York, NY 10158. TEL 212-850-6645. FAX 212-850-6021. *782*

CHIRON REVIEW.
Chiron Review Press, 522 E. South Ave., St. John, KS 67576-2212. TEL 316-549-3933. *4505*

CHIROPODY REVIEW.
Institute of Chiropodists, 27 Wright St., Southport, Merseyside PR9 0TL, England. TEL 44-1704-546141. FAX 44-1704-500477. *5138*

CHIROPRACTIC HISTORY.
Association for the History of Chiropractic, 1000 Brady St., Davenport, IA 52803. TEL 319-326-9894. FAX 319-326-9897. *4826*

CHIROPRACTIC JOURNAL OF AUSTRALIA.
Chiropractors' Association of Australia, P.O. Box 748, Wagga Wagga, N.S.W. 2650, Australia. TEL 61-69-213238. FAX 61-69-262556. *4826*

CHIROPRACTIC RESEARCH JOURNAL.
Life College, School of Chiropractic, 1269 Barclay Circle, Marietta, GA 30060. TEL 770-426-2636. FAX 770-425-5496. *4827*

CHIROPRACTIC TECHNIQUE.
Williams & Wilkins, 351 W. Camden St., Baltimore, MD 21201-2436. TEL 410-528-4068. FAX 410-528-4452. *4827*

CHIRURGIA.
Edizioni Minerva Medica, Corso Bramante 83-85, 10126 Turin, Italy. TEL 39-11-678282. FAX 39-11-674502. *5138*

CHIRURGIA DEL PIEDE.
Edizioni Minerva Medica, Corso Bramante 83-85, Turin 10126, Italy. TEL 39-11-678282. FAX 39-11-674502. *5138*

CHIRURGIA TRIVENETA.
Ospedale Civile Maggiore, I Divisione Chirurgia Generale, Piazzale Stefani 1, 37126 Verona, Italy. TEL 045-8072410. FAX 045-8072057. *5138*

CHIRURGIE.
Masson - Periodiques, 120 bd. St. Germain, 75006 Paris, France. TEL 33-1-40466200. FAX 33-1-40466201. *5138*

CHIRURGISCHE GASTROENTEROLOGIE.
S. Karger AG, Allschwilerstr. 10, P.O. Box, CH-4009 Basel, Switzerland. TEL 41-61-3061111. FAX 41-61-3061234. *4908*

CHOICE (MIDDLETOWN).
Choice, 100 Riverview Ctr., Middletown, CT 06457. TEL 203-347-6933. FAX 203-346-8586. *6289*

CHONGQING HUANJING KEXUE.
Chongqing Huanjing Kexue Xuehui, 212 Renmin Lu, Chongqing, Sichuan 630015, People's Republic of China. TEL 86-811-3868871. FAX 86-811-3850021. *2910*

CHOONPA IGAKU.
Nihon Choonpa Igakkai, Hongo 3-23-1, Crosevia Hongo 3F, Bunkyo-ku, Tokyo 113, Japan. TEL 81-3-3813-5540. FAX 81-3-3816-7644. *5104*

CHORAL JOURNAL.
American Choral Directors Association, Box 6310, Lawton, OK 73506-0310. TEL 405-355-8161. FAX 405-248-1465. *5382*

CHOREOGRAPHY AND DANCE.
Gordon and Breach - Harwood Academic, Amsteldisk 166, 1st Fl., 1079 LH Amsterdam, Netherlands. *2291*

CHREODS.
c/o Manchester Metropolitan University, School of Education, 799 Wilmslow Rd., Didsbury, Manchester M20 2RR, England. *2428*

HET CHRISTELIJK OOSTEN.
Instituut voor Oosters Christendom te Nijmegen, Erasmusplein 1, 6525 HT Nijmegen, Netherlands. TEL 31-24-3615603. FAX 31-24-3611802. *6328*

CHRISTIAN BIOETHICS.
Swets & Zeitlinger bv, P.O. Box 825, 2160 SZ Lisse, Netherlands. TEL 31-252-435111. FAX 31-252-415888. *4653*

CHRISTIAN MEDICAL COLLEGE VELLORE ALUMNI JOURNAL.
Christian Medical College, Alumni Association, Vellore 632 002, Tamil Nadu, India. TEL 91-416-22603. FAX 91-416-32788. *4653*

CHRISTIAN MONTHLY.
Apostolic Lutheran Book Concern, Box 2126, Battle Ground, WA 98604-2126. TEL 360-687-4416. *6418*

CHRISTIAN OBSERVER.
Christian Observer, Inc., 9400 Fairview Ave., Manassas, VA 20110-5802. TEL 703-335-2844. FAX 703-368-4817. *6418*

CHRISTIAN SCHOLAR'S REVIEW.
c/o Calvin College, Grand Rapids, MI 49546. *6329*

CHRISTIAN WEEK.
Fellowship for Print Witness Inc., Box 725, Winnipeg, MB R3C 2K3, Canada. TEL 204-982-2060. FAX 204-947-5632. *6418*

CHRISTIANITY AND LITERATURE.
Conference on Christianity and Literature, State University of West Georgia, Carrollton, GA 30118-2200. TEL 206-836-6512. FAX 770-830-2334. *4327*

CHROMATOGRAPHIA.
Elsevier Science Ltd., Pergamon, P.O. Box 800, Kidlington, Oxford OX5 1DX, Germany. TEL 44-1865-843000. FAX 44-1865-843010. *1789*

CHROMATOGRAPHIC SCIENCE SERIES.
Marcel Dekker, Inc., 270 Madison Ave., New York, NY 10016. TEL 212-696-9000. FAX 212-685-4540. *1790*

CHROMATOGRAPHY ABSTRACTS.
The Royal Society of Chemistry, Thomas Graham House, Science Park, Milton Rd., Cambridge CB4 4WF, England. TEL 44-1223-420066. FAX 44-1223-423429. *1782*

CHROMOSOME RESEARCH.
Rapid Science Publishers, The Old Malthouse, Paradise St., Oxford OX1 1LD, England. TEL 44-1865-790447. FAX 44-1865-244012. *765*

CHRONICA DERMATOLOGICA.
Istituto Dermopatico dell'Immacolata, Via Monti di Creta, 104, 00167 Rome, Italy. FAX 39-6-66464437. *4876*

CHRONOBIOLOGY INTERNATIONAL.
Marcel Dekker Journals, 270 Madison Ave., New York, NY 10016. TEL 212-696-9000. FAX 212-685-4540. *596*

CHUBAN FAXING YANJIU.
China Book Publishing House, No. A-7, Xirongxian Hutong, Xicheng-qu, Beijing 100031, People's Republic of China. TEL 010-6059539. *6268*

CHUGOKU SHIKOKU NO NOGYO KISHO.
Nihon Nogyo Kisho Gakkai, Chugoku Shikoku Shibu, c/o Research Institute for Bioresources, Okayama University, Kurashiki 710, Japan. TEL 086-434-1239. FAX 086-421-0699. *5228*

CHUNG-WAI LITERARY MONTHLY.
c/o Department of Foreign Languages, National Taiwan University, Roosevelt Rd. Sec. 4, Taipei 106, Taiwan, Republic of China. TEL 886-2-3630231. FAX 886-2-3639395. *4390*

CHURCH.
National Pastoral Life Center, 18 Bleecker St., New York, NY 10012-2404. TEL 212-431-7825. FAX 212-274-9786. *6458*

CHURCH ADVOCATE.
Churches of God, General Conference, Box 926, Findlay, OH 45839. TEL 419-424-1961. FAX 419-424-3433. *6330*

CHURCH HISTORY.
American Society of Church History, Box 8517, Red Bank, NJ 07701-8517. *6330*

CHURCH PULPIT YEAR BOOK (YEAR).
Chansitor Publications Ltd., St. Mary's Works, St. Mary's Plain, Norwich, Norfolk NR3 3BH, England. TEL 44-1603-616563. FAX 44-1603-624483. *6330*

CH4 ENERGIA METANO.
Ventus S.n.c., Largo Regio Parco 11, 10152 Turin, Italy. TEL 39-11-4345965. FAX 39-11-4472990. *5598*

CICLOS.
Instituto de Investigaciones de Historia Economia y Social, Fac. de Ciencias Economicas (UBA), Av. Cordoba 2122, 2o piso, 1120 Buenos Aires, Argentina. TEL 54-1-3732075. FAX 54-1-8016819. *3622*

CIEL ET TERRE.
Societe Royale Belge d'Astronomie, de Meteorologie et de Physique du Globe, 3 av. Circulaire, 1180 Brussels, Belgium. TEL 32-2-3730253. FAX 32-2-374-9822. *493*

CIENCIA AGRONOMICA.
Universidade Federal do Ceara, Centro de Ciencias Agrarias, Av. Mister Hull, Caixa Postal 12168, 60355 Fortaleza, Ceara, Brazil. TEL 55-85-243-9668. FAX 55-85-243-9513. *108*

CIENCIA DEL SUELO.
Asociacion Argentina de la Ciencia del Suelo, J. Ramirez de Velasco 847, 1414 Buenos Aires, Argentina. TEL 54-1-7718968. *218*

CIENCIA RURAL.
Universidade Federal de Santa Maria, Centro de Ciencias Rurais, Campus Universitario, 97119-900 Santa Maria, Rio Grande do Sul, Brazil. TEL 55-55-226-2698. *108*

CIENCIAS.
Universidad Nacional Autonoma de Mexico, Facultad de Ciencias, Cub. 319, 320 and 321, Circuito Exterior, Ciudad Universitaria, 04510 Mexico, D.F., Mexico. TEL 52-5-6224935. FAX 52-5-6160326. *6520*

CIENCIAS MARINAS.
Universidad Autonoma de Baja California, Instituto de Investigaciones Oceanologicas, Apdo. Postal 423, Ensenada, Baja California, Mexico. TEL 52-66-61745451. FAX 52-66-61745303. *2400*

CINCINNATI CLASSICAL STUDIES. NEW SERIES.
E.J. Brill, P.O. Box 9000, 2300 PA Leiden, Netherlands. TEL 31-71-5353500. FAX 31-71-5317532. *1901*

CINEMA JOURNAL.
University of Texas Press, Journals Division, Box 7819, Austin, TX 78713. TEL 512-471-4531. FAX 512-320-0668. *5327*

CINESIOLOGIE.
Syndicat National des Medecins du Sport, 1 rue d'Alsace, 49100 Angers, France. TEL 33-1-41883535. FAX 33-1-41881355. *4766*

CINOPSIS.
Rue M. Poedts, 10, 1160 Brussels, Belgium.
TEL 32-32206620321. *5328*

CIRCULATION (DALLAS).
American Heart Association, 7272 Greenville Ave., Dallas, TX 75231-4596. TEL 214-706-1310. FAX 214-691-6342. *4814*

CIRCULATION RESEARCH.
American Heart Association, 7272 Greenville Ave., Dallas, TX 75231-4596. TEL 214-706-1310. FAX 214-691-6342. *4814*

CIRENCESTER EXCAVATIONS.
Cotswold Archaeological Trust, Cirencester Excavation Committee, Corinium Museum, Park St., Cirencester, Glos. GL7 2BX, England. TEL 01285-643625. FAX 01285-644641. *358*

CISTERCIAN STUDIES QUARTERLY.
Order of the Cistercians of the Strict Observance, U S Region, Santa Rita Abbey, HC 1, Box 929, Sonoita, AZ 85637-9705. TEL 520-455-5595. FAX 520-455-5770. *6330*

CITIES.
Elsevier Science Ltd., Pergamon, P.O. Box 800, Kidlington, Oxford OX5 1DX, England. TEL 44-1865-843000. FAX 44-1865-843010. *6212*

CIUDAD Y TERRITORIO: ESTUDIOS TERRITORIALES.
Ministerio de Fomento, Direccion General para la Vivienda, la Arquitectura, y el Urbanismo, Paseo de la Castellana, 67, 28071 Madrid, Spain. TEL 34-1-5975883. FAX 34-1-5975884. *6212*

CIUDADES.
Red Nacional de Investigacion Urbana, Av. Maximino Avila Camacho 208, 72000 Puebla, Pue., Mexico. TEL 52-22-462832. FAX 52-22-324506. *6212*

CIVIL AVIATION MEDICAL ASSOCIATION. BULLETIN.
Civil Aviation Medical Association, Box 23864, Oklahoma City, OK 73123-2864. TEL 405-840-0199. FAX 405-848-1053. *4654*

CIVIL ENGINEERING.
South African Institution of Civil Engineers, P.O. Box 93495, Yeoville 2143, South Africa. TEL 27-11-648-1184. FAX 27-11-648-7427. *2779*

CIVIL ENGINEERING (NEW YORK).
American Society of Civil Engineers, 345 E. 47th St., New York, NY 10017-2398. TEL 212-705-7288. FAX 212-980-4681. *2779*

CIVIL ENGINEERING PRACTICE.
Boston Society of Civil Engineers Section, Engineering Center, 1 Walnut St., Boston, MA 02108. TEL 617-227-5551. *2780*

CIVIL ENGINEERING SURVEYOR.
Surco Ltd., 26 Market St., Altrincham, Cheshire WA14 1PF, England. TEL 44-161-928-8074. FAX 44-161-929-4434. *2780*

CIVIL LIBERTY.
New South Wales Council for Civil Liberties, P.O. Box 201, Glebe, N.S.W. 2037, Australia. TEL 61-2-96607582. FAX 41-2-95664162. *5989*

CIVIL RIGHTS MONITOR.
Leadership Conference on Education Fund, 1629 K St., Ste. 1010, Washington, DC 20006. TEL 202-466-3434. *4059*

CIVILTA BRESCIANA.
Fondazione Civilta Bresciana, Vicolo San Giuseppe 5, 25100 Brescia, Italy. TEL 39-30-3757267. FAX 39-30-3774365. *3775*

CLARINET.
International Clarinet Association, College of Music, University of North Texas, Denton, TX 76203. TEL 817-565-4096. FAX 817-565-2002. *5384*

CLASS: CLASSIFICATION LITERATURE AUTOMATED SEARCH SERVICE.
Classification Society of North America, c/o William H.E. Day, P.O. Box 17, Port Midland, NS B0W 2V0, Canada. TEL 902-649-2996. *4566*

CLASSICAL ANTIQUITY.
University of California Press, Journals Division, 2120 Berkeley Way, No. 5812, Berkeley, CA 94720-5812. TEL 510-643-7154. FAX 510-642-9917. *1901*

CLASSICAL BULLETIN.
Bolchazy - Carducci Publishers, Inc., 1000 Brown St., Unit 101, Wauconda, IL 60084. TEL 847-526-4344. FAX 847-526-2867. *1901*

CLASSICAL PHILOLOGY.
University of Chicago Press, Journals Division, Box 37005, Chicago, IL 60637. TEL 773-753-3347. FAX 773-753-0811. *1902*

CLASSICAL WORLD.
Duquesne University, Department of Classics, Pittsburgh, PA 15282-1704. TEL 412-396-6450. FAX 412-396-5197. *1902*

THE CLASSICIST.
Transaction Publishers, Transaction Periodicals Consortium, Department 3092, Rutgers University, New Brunswick, NJ 08903. TEL 908-445-2280. FAX 908-445-3138. *400*

CLASSICS IN THE HISTORY AND PHILOSOPHY OF SCIENCE.
Gordon and Breach - Harwood Academic, Amsteldisk 166, 1st Fl., 1079 LH Amsterdam, Netherlands. *6520*

CLASSICS IN URBAN HISTORY.
University of California Press, 2120 Berkeley Way, Berkeley, CA 94720. TEL 510-642-4247. FAX 510-643-7127. *3743*

CLASSICS IRELAND.
Classical Association of Ireland, Department of Classics, University College, Dublin 4, Ireland. *4328*

CLASSICS OF SOVIET MATHEMATICS.
Gordon and Breach - Harwood Academic, Amsteldisk 166, 1st Fl., 1079 LH Amsterdam, Netherlands. *4566*

CLASSICUM.
Classical Association of New South Wales, c/o H. Tarrant, Ed., Dept. of Classics, University of Newcastle, N.S.W. 2308, Australia. FAX 61-49-21-6947. *1902*

CLAYS AND CLAY MINERALS.
Clay Minerals Society, Box 4416, Boulder, CO 80306. TEL 303-444-6405. *5298*

THE CLEARING HOUSE.
Heldref Publications, 1319 Eighteenth St., N.W., Washington, DC 20036-1802. TEL 202-296-6267. FAX 202-296-5149. *2429*

CLEFT PALATE - CRANIOFACIAL JOURNAL.
Decker Periodicals, P.O. Box 620, LCD 1, Hamilton, ON L8N 3K7, Canada. TEL 905-522-7017. FAX 905-522-7839. *5139*

CLEVELAND CLINIC JOURNAL OF MEDICINE.
Cleveland Clinic Educational Foundation, 9500 Euclid Ave., EE37, Cleveland, OH 44195. TEL 216-444-2667. FAX 216-444-9385. *4654*

CLIMACTERIC.
Parthenon Publishing Group, Casterton Hall, Carnforth, Lancs LA6 2LA, England. TEL 44-15242-72084. FAX 44-15242-71587. *7308*

CLIMATIC CHANGE.
Kluwer Academic Publishers, Postbus 17, 3300 AA Dordrecht, Netherlands. TEL 31-78-6392392. FAX 31-78-6392254. *5229*

CLINICA CHIMICA ACTA.
Elsevier Science B.V., P.O. Box 211, 1000 AE Amsterdam, Netherlands. TEL 31-20-4853911. FAX 31-20-4853598. *4654*

CLINICAL ANATOMY.
John Wiley & Sons, Inc., Journals, 605 Third Ave., New York, NY 10158. TEL 212-850-6645. FAX 212-850-6021. *4654*

CLINICAL AND BIOCHEMICAL ANALYSIS.
Marcel Dekker, Inc., 270 Madison Ave., New York, NY 10016. TEL 212-696-9000. FAX 212-685-4540. *656*

CLINICAL AND DIAGNOSTIC LABORATORY IMMUNOLOGY.
American Society for Microbiology, 1325 Massachusetts Ave., N.W., Washington, DC 20005. TEL 202-942-9319. FAX 202-942-9346. *4792*

CLINICAL AND DIAGNOSTIC VIROLOGY.
Elsevier Science B.V., P.O. Box 211, 1000 AE Amsterdam, Netherlands. TEL 31-20-4853911. FAX 31-20-4853598. *4834*

CLINICAL AND EXPERIMENTAL ALLERGY.
Blackwell Science Ltd., Osney Mead, Oxford OX2 OEL, England. TEL 44-1865-206206. FAX 44-1865-721205. *4792*

CLINICAL AND EXPERIMENTAL DERMATOLOGY.
Blackwell Science Ltd., Osney Mead, Oxford OX2 OEL, England. TEL 44-1865-206206. FAX 44-1865-721205. *4876*

CLINICAL AND EXPERIMENTAL HYPERTENSION.
Marcel Dekker Journals, 270 Madison Ave., New York, NY 10016. TEL 212-696-9000. FAX 212-685-4540. *4814*

CLINICAL AND EXPERIMENTAL IMMUNOLOGY.
Blackwell Science Ltd., Osney Mead, Oxford OX2 OEL, England. TEL 44-1865-206206. FAX 44-1865-721205. *4793*

CLINICAL AND EXPERIMENTAL OBSTETRICS AND GYNECOLOGY.
S O G Canada, Inc., 4900 Cote St. Luc, Apt. 212, Montreal, PQ H3W 2H3, Canada. TEL 514-489-3242. FAX 514-485-4513. *4955*

CLINICAL AND INVESTIGATIVE MEDICINE.
Canadian Medical Association, 1867 Alta Vista Dr., Ottawa, ON K1G 3Y6, Canada. TEL 613-731-9331. FAX 613-523-0937. *4654*

CLINICAL AND LABORATORY HAEMATOLOGY.
Blackwell Science Ltd., Osney Mead, Oxford OX2 OEL, England. TEL 44-1865-206206. FAX 44-1865-721205. *4917*

CLINICAL ASPECTS OF BIOMEDICINE.
Elsevier Science B.V., Books Division, P.O. Box 211, 1000 AE Amsterdam, Netherlands. TEL 31-20-4853911. FAX 31-20-4853705. *4655*

CLINICAL BIOCHEMISTRY.
Elsevier Science Inc., Box 945, New York, NY 10159-0945. TEL 212-633-3730. FAX 212-633-3680. *657*

CLINICAL BIOMECHANICS.
Elsevier Science Ltd., Pergamon, P.O. Box 800, Kidlington, Oxford OX5 1DX, England. TEL 44-1865-843000. FAX 44-1865-843010. *4827*

CLINICAL BULLETIN OF MYOFASCIAL THERAPY.
Haworth Press, Inc., 10 Alice St., Binghamton, NY 13904. TEL 607-722-5857. FAX 607-722-6362. *4655*

CLINICAL CANCER RESEARCH.
American Association for Cancer Research, Public Ledger Bldg., 150 S. Independence Mall West, Ste. 816, Philadelphia, PA 19106. TEL 215-440-9300. FAX 215-440-9354. *4976*

CLINICAL CARDIOLOGY (MAHWAH).
Clinical Cardiology Publishing Company, Inc., Box 832, Mahwah, NJ 07430-0832. TEL 201-818-1010. FAX 201-818-0086. *4814*

CLINICAL CHEMISTRY.
American Association for Clinical Chemistry, Inc., 2101 L St. N.W., Ste. 202, Washington, DC 20037-1526. TEL 800-892-1400. FAX 202-887-5093. *4655*

CLINICAL CHEMISTRY AND ENZYMOLOGY COMMUNICATIONS.
Gordon and Breach - Harwood Academic, Amsteldisk 166, 1st Fl., 1079 LH Amsterdam, Netherlands. *657*

CLINICAL DIABETES.
American Diabetes Association, 1660 Duke St., Alexandria, VA 22314. TEL 703-549-1500. FAX 703-836-7439. *4883*

CLINICAL DRUG INVESTIGATION.
Adis International Limited, Private Bag 65901, Mairangi Bay, Auckland 10, New Zealand. TEL 64-9-479-8100. FAX 64-9-479-8145. *5653*

CLINICAL DYSMORPHOLOGY.
Chapman & Hall, Journals Department 2-6 Boundary Row, London SE1 8HN, England. TEL 44-171-8650066. FAX 44-171-5229623. *814*

CLINICAL ELECTROENCEPHALOGRAPHY.
American Medical Electroencephalographic Association, 850 Elm Grove Rd., Ste. 11, Elm Grove, WI 53122. TEL 414-797-7800. *5058*

CLINICAL ENDOCRINOLOGY.
Blackwell Science Ltd., Osney Mead, Oxford OX2 OEL, England. TEL 44-1865-206206. FAX 44-1865-721205. *4883*

CLINICAL ENGINEERING SERIES.
Academic Press, Inc., 525 B St., Ste. 1900, San Diego, CA 92101-4495. TEL 619-231-0926. FAX 619-699-6715. *4655*

CLINICAL EYE AND VISION CARE.
Elsevier Science Ireland Ltd., P.O. Box 85, Limerick, Ireland. TEL 353-61-471944. FAX 353-61-472144. *4991*

CLINICAL GENETICS.
Munksgaard International Publishers Ltd., 35 Noerre Soegade, P.O. Box 2148, DK-1016 Copenhagen K, Denmark. TEL 45-33-127030. FAX 45-33-129387. *765*

CLINICAL GERONTOLOGIST.
Haworth Press, Inc., 10 Alice St., Binghamton, NY 13904. TEL 607-722-5857. FAX 607-722-6362. *3434*

CLINICAL HEMORHEOLOGY.
I O S Press, Van Diemenstraat 94, 1013 CN Amsterdam, Netherlands. TEL 31-20-6382189. FAX 31-20-6203419. *4917*

CLINICAL IMAGING.
Elsevier Science Inc., Box 945, New York, NY 10159-0945. TEL 212-633-3730. FAX 212-633-3680. *5104*

CLINICAL IMMUNOLOGY NEWSLETTER.
Elsevier Science Inc., Box 945, New York, NY 10159-0945. TEL 212-633-3730. FAX 212-633-3680. *4793*

CLINICAL INFANT REPORTS. MONOGRAPH.
International Universities Press, Inc., 59 Boston Post Rd., Box 1524, Madison, CT 06443-1524. TEL 203-245-4000. FAX 203-245-0775. *5029*

CLINICAL INFECTIOUS DISEASES.
University of Chicago Press, Journals Division, Box 37005, Chicago, IL 60637. TEL 773-753-3347. FAX 773-753-0811. *4834*

CLINICAL JOURNAL OF PAIN.
Lippincott - Raven Publishers, 227 E. Washington Sq., Philadelphia, PA 19106. TEL 215-238-4200. FAX 215-238-4227. *5058*

CLINICAL JOURNAL OF SPORT MEDICINE.
Lippincott - Raven Publishers, 227 E. Washington Sq., Philadelphia, PA 19106. TEL 215-238-4200. FAX 215-238-4227. *5129*

CLINICAL KINESIOLOGY.
American Kinesiotherapy Association, c/o Dr. John Drowatzky, Ed., University of Toledo, Dept. of Health Promotion & Human Performance, 2801 W. Bancroft, Toledo, OH 43606. TEL 419-530-2743. FAX 419-530-4759. *5042*

CLINICAL LABORATORY.
Clinical Laboratory Publications, Im Breitspiel 15, 69126 Heidelberg, Germany. TEL 49-6221-3432133. FAX 49-6221-300291. *4883*

CLINICAL LABORATORY MANAGEMENT REVIEW.
Williams & Wilkins, 351 W, Camden St., Baltimore, MD 21201-2436. TEL 410-528-4068. FAX 410-528-4452. *4896*

CLINICAL LABORATORY METHODS AND TECHNIQUES.
Field & Wood, Medical Periodicals, Inc., Box 975, Blue Bell, PA 19422. TEL 610-828-4010. FAX 610-482-0226. *4896*

CLINICAL LABORATORY PRODUCT COMPARISON SYSTEM.
E C R I, 5200 Butler Pike, Plymouth Meeting, PA 19462. TEL 610-825-6000. FAX 610-834-1275. *4896*

CLINICAL LINGUISTICS & PHONETICS.
Taylor & Francis Ltd., 1 Gunpowder Sq., London EC4A 3DE, England. TEL 44-171-583-0490. FAX 44-171-583-0585. *5058*

CLINICAL MEDICAL ETHICS.
Kluwer Academic Publishers, Postbus 17, 3300 AA Dordrecht, Netherlands. TEL 31-78-6392392. FAX 31-78-6392254. *4655*

CLINICAL NEUROLOGY AND NEUROSURGERY.
Elsevier Science B.V., P.O. Box 211, 1000 AE Amsterdam, Netherlands. TEL 31-20-4853911. FAX 31-20-4853598. *5059*

CLINICAL NEUROPHARMACOLOGY.
Lippincott - Raven Publishers, 227 E. Washington Sq., Philadelphia, PA 19106. TEL 215-238-4200. FAX 215-238-4227. *5653*

CLINICAL NEUROPHYSIOLOGY UPDATES.
Elsevier Science B.V., Books Division, P.O. Box 211, 1000 AE Amsterdam, Netherlands. TEL 31-20-4853911. FAX 31-20-4853705. *5059*

CLINICAL NEUROSCIENCE.
John Wiley & Sons, Inc., Journals, 605 Third Ave., New York, NY 10158. TEL 212-850-6645. FAX 212-850-6021. *5059*

CLINICAL NUCLEAR MEDICINE.
Lippincott - Raven Publishers, 227 E. Washington Sq., Philadelphia, PA 19106. TEL 215-238-4200. FAX 215-238-4227. *5104*

CLINICAL NURSING RESEARCH.
Sage Publications, Inc., 2455 Teller Rd., Thousand Oaks, CA 91320. TEL 805-499-0721. FAX 805-499-0871. *4931*

CLINICAL OBSTETRICS AND GYNECOLOGY.
Lippincott - Raven Publishers, 227 E. Washington Sq., Philadelphia, PA 19106. TEL 215-238-4200. FAX 215-238-4227. *4955*

CLINICAL ONCOLOGY ALERT.
American Health Consultants, Inc., 3525 Piedmont Rd., N.E., Bldg. 6, Ste. 400, Atlanta, GA 30305. TEL 404-262-7436. *4976*

CLINICAL ORAL IMPLANTS RESEARCH.
Munksgaard International Publishers Ltd., 35 Noerre Soegade, P.O. Box 2148, DK-1016 Copenhagen K, Denmark. TEL 45-33-127030. FAX 45-33-129387. *4853*

CLINICAL ORAL INVESTIGATIONS.
Springer-Verlag, Heidelberger Platz 3, 14197 Berlin, Germany. TEL 49-30-82787-0. FAX 49-30-82787448. *4853*

CLINICAL ORTHOPAEDIC SOCIETY. JOURNAL.
John Wiley & Sons, Inc., Journals, 605 Third Ave., New York, NY 10158. TEL 212-850-6645. FAX 212-850-6021. *5006*

CLINICAL ORTHOPAEDICS AND RELATED RESEARCH.
Lippincott - Raven Publishers, 227 E. Washington Sq., Philadelphia, PA 19106. TEL 215-238-4200. FAX 215-238-4227. *5006*

CLINICAL OTOLARYNGOLOGY AND ALLIED SCIENCES.
Blackwell Science Ltd., Osney Mead, Oxford OX2 OEL, England. TEL 44-1865-206206. FAX 44-1865-721205. *5021*

CLINICAL PEDIATRICS.
Westminster Publications, Inc., 708 Glen Cove Ave., Glen Head, NY 11545. TEL 516-759-0025. FAX 516-759-5524. *5029*

CLINICAL PEDIATRICS SERIES.
Marcel Dekker, Inc., 270 Madison Ave., New York, NY 10016. TEL 212-696-9000. FAX 212-685-4540. *5029*

CLINICAL PERFORMANCE AND QUALITY HEALTH CARE.
Slack, Inc., 6900 Grove Rd., Thorofare, NJ 08086-9447. TEL 609-848-1000. FAX 609-853-5991. *4655*

CLINICAL PHARMACOKINETICS.
Adis International Limited, Private Bag 65901, Mairangi Bay, Auckland 10, New Zealand. TEL 64-9-479-8100. FAX 64-9-479-8145. *5653*

CLINICAL PHARMACOLOGY & THERAPEUTICS.
Mosby - Year Book, Inc., 11830 Westline Industrial Dr., St. Louis, MO 63146-3318. TEL 314-872-8370. FAX 314-432-1380. *5653*

CLINICAL PHYSIOLOGY.
Blackwell Science Ltd., Osney Mead, Oxford OX2 OEL, England. TEL 44-1865-206206. FAX 44-1865-721205. *4655*

CLINICAL PRACTICE OF GYNECOLOGY.
Elsevier Science Inc., Box 945, New York, NY 10159-0945. TEL 212-633-3730. FAX 212-633-3680. *4955*

THE CLINICAL PSYCHOLOGIST.
American Psychological Association, Division of Clinical Psychology, Box 1082, Niwot, CO 80544-1082. TEL 405-721-2792. *6102*

CLINICAL PSYCHOLOGY & PSYCHOTHERAPY.
John Wiley & Sons Ltd., Journals, Baffins Ln., Chichester, W. Sussex PO19 1UD, England. TEL 44-1243-779777. FAX 44-1243-775878. *6102*

CLINICAL PSYCHOLOGY REVIEW.
Elsevier Science Ltd., Pergamon, P.O. Box 800, Kidlington, Oxford OX5 1DX, England. TEL 44-1865-843000. FAX 44-1865-843010. *6102*

CLINICAL PSYCHOLOGY: SCIENCE AND PRACTICE.
Oxford University Press, Journals, 2001 Evans Rd., Cary, NC 27513. TEL 919-677-0977. FAX 919-677-1714. *6102*

CLINICAL RADIOLOGY.
Blackwell Science Ltd., Osney Mead, Oxford OX2 OEL, England. TEL 44-1865-206206. FAX 44-1865-721205. *5104*

CLINICAL RESEARCH AND REGULATORY AFFAIRS.
Marcel Dekker Journals, 270 Madison Ave., New York, NY 10016. TEL 212-696-9000. FAX 212-685-4540. *5653*

CLINICAL REVIEWS IN ALLERGY & IMMUNOLOGY.
Humana Press Inc., 999 Riverview Dr., Ste. 208, Totowa, NJ 07512. TEL 973-256-1699. FAX 973-256-8341. *4793*

CLINICAL SCIENCE.
Portland Press Ltd., 59 Portland Pl., London W1N 3AJ, England. TEL 44-171-580-5530. FAX 44-171-323-1136. *4656*

CLINICAL SOCIAL WORK JOURNAL.
Human Sciences Press, Inc., 233 Spring St., New York, NY 10013-1578. TEL 212-620-8000. FAX 212-463-0742. *6660*

CLINICAL SOCIOLOGY: RESEARCH AND PRACTICE.
Plenum Publishing Corp., 233 Spring St., New York, NY 10013-1578. TEL 212-620-8000. FAX 212-463-0742. *6608*

CLINICAL SOCIOLOGY REVIEW.
Sociological Practice Association, c/o Richard T. Bedea, Anne Arundel Community College, 101 College Pkwy., MD 21012-1895. TEL 410-541-2835. *6705*

CLINICAL SUPERVISOR.
Haworth Press, Inc., 10 Alice St., Binghamton, NY 13904. TEL 607-722-5857. FAX 607-722-6362. *6660*

CLINICAL SURVEYS IN ENDOCRINOLOGY.
Plenum Publishing Corp., 233 Spring St., New York, NY 10013-1578. TEL 212-620-8000. FAX 212-463-0742. *4883*

CLINICAL THERAPEUTICS.
Excerpta Medica, 105 Raider Blvd., Belle Mead, NJ 08502-1510. TEL 908-874-8550. FAX 908-874-3250. *4656*

CLINICAL TRANSPLANTATION.
Munksgaard International Publishers Ltd., 35 Noerre Soegade, P.O. Box 2148, DK-1016 Copenhagen K, Denmark. TEL 45-33-127030. FAX 45-33-129387. *5139*

CLINICIAN REVIEWS.
Clinicians Publishing Group, 4 Brighton Rd., Clifton, NJ 07012. TEL 201-916-1000. FAX 201-916-0021. *4656*

CLINICIAN'S RESEARCH DIGEST.
American Psychological Association, 750 First St., N.E., Washington, DC 20002-4242. TEL 202-336-5600. FAX 202-336-5568. *6102*

CLINICS IN DERMATOLOGY.
Elsevier Science Inc., Box 945, New York, NY 10159-0945. TEL 212-633-3730. FAX 212-633-3680. *4876*

CLIO (FORT WAYNE).
Indiana University, English Department, 2101 Coliseum Blvd. E., Fort Wayne, IN 46805. TEL 219-481-6753. FAX 219-481-6985. *3492*

CLIONET.
James Cook University of North Queensland, Department of History and Politics, Townsville, Qld. 4811, Australia. TEL 61-77-814170. FAX 61-77-814487. *3492*

CLOSED-END FUND DIGEST.
Madent Publishing, Inc., 1224 Coast Village Circle, Ste. 11, Santa Barbara, CA 93108. TEL 805-565-5651. *1380*

CLOTHING & TEXTILES RESEARCH JOURNAL.
International Textile and Apparel Association, Box 1360, Monument, CO 80132. TEL 719-488-3716. *1914*

CLYDESDALE STUD BOOK.
Clydesdale Society of Great Britain and Ireland, 3 Grosvenor Gardens, Edinburgh EH12 5JU, Scotland. TEL 44-1764-664925. *6850*

COACHING DIGEST.
American Baseball Coaches Association, 108 S. University Ave., Ste. 3, Mt. Pleasant, MI 48858-2327. TEL 517-775-3300. FAX 517-775-3600. *6801*

COAL PREPARATION.
Gordon and Breach - Harwood Academic, Amsteldisk 166, 1st Fl., 1079 LH Amsterdam, Netherlands. *5298*

COAL SCIENCE AND TECHNOLOGY.
Elsevier Science B.V., Books Division, P.O. Box 211, 1000 AE Amsterdam, Netherlands. TEL 31-20-4853911. FAX 31-20-4853705. *5298*

COASTAL ENGINEERING.
Elsevier Science B.V., P.O. Box 211, 1000 AE Amsterdam, Netherlands. TEL 31-20-4853911. FAX 31-20-4853598. *2780*

COASTAL MANAGEMENT.
Taylor & Francis Inc., 1900 Frost Rd., Ste. 101, Bristol, PA 19007. TEL 215-785-5800. FAX 215-785-5515. *2401*

COASTAL RESEARCH.
Florida State University, Geology Department, Tallahassee, FL 32306-3026. TEL 904-644-5860. FAX 904-644-4214. *2401*

COCUK SAGLIGI VE HASTALIKLARI DERGISI.
Turkish and International Children's Center, P.O. Box 66, Samanpazari, 06240 Ankara, Turkey. TEL 90-312-3242326. FAX 90-312-3112253. *5030*

COELACANTH.
Border Historical Society, c/o East London Museum, P.O. Box 11021, Southernwood 5213, South Africa. TEL 27-431-22623. *3525*

COGITO.
Carfax Publishing Co., P.O. Box 25, Abingdon, Oxon. OX14 3UE, England. TEL 44-1235-401000. FAX 44-1235-401550. *5721*

COGNITION.
Elsevier Science B.V., P.O. Box 211, 1000 AE Amsterdam, Netherlands. TEL 31-20-4853911. FAX 31-20-4853598. *6103*

COGNITION AND EMOTION.
Taylor & Francis Ltd., Psychology Press, 1 Gunpowder Sq., London EC4A 3DE, England. TEL 44-171-5830490. FAX 44-171-5830585. *6103*

COGNITION AND INSTRUCTION.
Lawrence Erlbaum Associates, Inc., 10 Industrial Dr., Mahwah, NJ 07430-2262. TEL 201-236-9500. FAX 201-236-0072. *6103*

COGNITION AND LANGUAGE.
Plenum Publishing Corp., 233 Spring St., New York, NY 10013-1578. TEL 212-620-8000. FAX 212-463-0742. *4249*

COGNITIVA.
Fundacion Infancia y Aprendizaje, Ctra. de Canillas 138, 16C, 28043 Madrid, Spain. TEL 34-1-3883874. FAX 34-1-3003527. *6103*

COGNITIVE AND BEHAVIORAL PRACTICE.
Association for Advancement of Behavior Therapy, 305 Seventh Ave., Ste. 16A, New York, NY 10001-6008. TEL 212-647-1890. FAX 212-647-1865. *6103*

COGNITIVE BRAIN RESEARCH.
Elsevier Science B.V., P.O. Box 211, 1000 AE Amsterdam, Netherlands. TEL 31-20-4853911. FAX 31-20-4853598. *5059*

COGNITIVE LINGUISTICS.
Walter de Gruyter und Co., Mouton de Gruyter, Genthiner Str. 13, 10785 Berlin, Germany. TEL 49-30-26005-0. FAX 49-30-26005-251. *4249*

COGNITIVE NEUROPSYCHOLOGY.
Taylor & Francis Ltd., Psychology Press, 1 Gunpowder Sq., London EC4A 3DE, England. TEL 44-171-5830490. FAX 44-171-5830585. *5059*

COGNITIVE PSYCHOLOGY.
Academic Press, Inc., Journal Division, 525 B St., Ste. 1900, San Diego, CA 92101-4495. TEL 619-230-1840. FAX 619-699-6800. *6103*

COGNITIVE SCIENCE SERIES (CAMBRIDGE).
Harvard University Press, 79 Garden St., Cambridge, MA 02138. TEL 617-495-2600. FAX 617-495-5898. *6103*

COGNITIVE SCIENCE SERIES: TECHNICAL MONOGRAPHS AND EDITED COLLECTIONS.
Lawrence Erlbaum Associates, Inc., 10 Industrial Dr., Mahwah, NJ 07430-2262. TEL 201-236-9500. FAX 201-236-0072. *6103*

COGNITIVE THERAPY AND RESEARCH.
Plenum Publishing Corp., 233 Spring St., New York, NY 10013-1578. TEL 212-620-8000. FAX 212-463-0742. *6103*

COHESION AND STRUCTURE.
Elsevier Science B.V., Books Division, P.O. Box 211, 1000 AE Amsterdam, Netherlands. TEL 31-20-4853911. FAX 31-20-4853705. *5799*

COLD FUSION.
Wayne Green Inc., 70 Rte. 202 N., Peterborough, NH 03458. TEL 603-924-0058. FAX 603-924-8613. *2695*

COLD REGIONS SCIENCE AND TECHNOLOGY.
Elsevier Science B.V., P.O. Box 211, 1000 AE Amsterdam, Netherlands. TEL 31-20-4853911. FAX 31-20-4853598. *6956*

COLEGIO BRASILEIRO DE CIRURGIOES. REVISTA.
Colegio Brasileiro de Cirurgioes, R. Visconde de Silva, 52, 3o andar, 22271-090 Rio de Janeiro, RJ, Brazil. TEL 55-21-5379164. FAX 55-21-2862595. *5139*

COLEOPTERISTS BULLETIN.
Coleopterists Society, c/o Terry N. Seeno, 3294 Meadowview Rd., Sacramento, CA 95832-1448. TEL 916-262-1160. FAX 916-262-1190. *749*

COLLABORATIVE COMPUTING.
Chapman & Hall, Journals Department 2-6 Boundary Row, London SE1 8HN, England. TEL 44-171-8650066. FAX 44-171-5229623. *2131*

COLLECTANEA MATHEMATICA.
Universidad de Barcelona, Gran Via de les Corts Catalanes 585, 08071 Barcelona, Spain. FAX 34-3-4021637. *4566*

COLLECTION AGENCY REPORT.
First Detroit Corp., Box 5025, Warren, MI 48090-5025. TEL 810-573-0045. FAX 810-573-9219. *1121*

COLLECTION MANAGEMENT.
Haworth Press, Inc., 10 Alice St., Binghamton, NY 13904. TEL 607-722-5857. FAX 607-722-6362. *4171*

COLLECTIONS (COLUMBIA).
Columbia Museum of Art, 1112 Bull St., Columbia, SC 29201. TEL 803-799-2810. FAX 803-343-2219. *5353*

COLLECTORS CLUB PHILATELIST.
Collectors Club, Inc., 22 E. 35th St., New York, NY 10016-0559. TEL 313-665-7166. FAX 313-665-5816. *5705*

COLLEGE & UNDERGRADUATE LIBRARIES.
Haworth Press, Inc., 10 Alice St., Binghamton, NY 13904. TEL 800-342-9678. FAX 607-722-6362. *4171*

COLLEGE E S L.
City University of New York, Office of Academic Affairs, Instructional Resource Center, 535 E. 80th St., New York, NY 10021. TEL 212-794-5444. *4249*

COLLEGE LITERATURE.
West Chester University, 554 New Main, West Chester, PA 19383. TEL 610-436-2901. FAX 610-436-3150. *4391*

COLLEGE MATHEMATICS JOURNAL.
Mathematical Association of America, 1529 18th St. N.W., Washington, DC 20036. TEL 202-387-5200. *4566*

COLLEGE MUSIC SYMPOSIUM.
College Music Society, 202 W. Spruce St., Missoula, MT 59802. TEL 406-721-9616. FAX 406-721-9419. *5384*

COLLEGE OF PHYSICIANS AND SURGEONS PAKISTAN. JOURNAL.
College of Physicians and Surgeons Pakistan, Seventh Central St., Defence Housing Authority, Karachi 75500, Pakistan. TEL 92-21-5892801. FAX 92-21-5887513. *4656*

COLLEGE QUARTERLY.
A C A A T O, P.O. Box 362, Thornhill, ON L3T 4A2, Canada. TEL 905-764-1246. *2536*

COLLEGE STUDENT AFFAIRS JOURNAL.
Southern Association for College Student Affairs, c/o Diane L. Cooper, Ed., University of Georgia, 402 Aderhold Hall, Athens, GA 30602-7142. TEL 706-542-1812. FAX 706-542-4130. *1946*

COLLEGE TEACHING.
Heldref Publications, 1319 Eighteenth St., N.W., Washington, DC 20036-1802. TEL 202-296-6267. FAX 202-296-5149. *2537*

COLLOIDS AND SURFACES A: PHYSICOCHEMICAL AND ENGINEERING ASPECTS.
Elsevier Science B.V., P.O. Box 211, 1000 AE Amsterdam, Netherlands. TEL 31-20-4853911. FAX 31-20-4853598. *1827*

COLLOIDS AND SURFACES B: BIOINTERFACES.
Elsevier Science B.V., P.O. Box 211, 1000 AE Amsterdam, Netherlands. TEL 31-20-4853911. FAX 31-20-4853598. *1827*

COLLOQUIA MATHEMATICA SOCIETATIS JANOS BOLYAI.
Elsevier Science B.V., Books Division, P.O. Box 211, 1000 AE Amsterdam, Netherlands. TEL 31-20-4853911. FAX 31-20-4853705. *4567*

COLLOQUIUM MATHEMATICUM.
Polska Akademia Nauk, Instytut Matematyczny, Dzial Wydawnictw, Ul. Sniadeckich 8, P.O. Box 8, 00-950 Warsaw, Poland. TEL 48-22-6282471. FAX 48-22-6293997. *4567*

COLLOQUIUM ON THE HISTORY OF LANDSCAPE ARCHITECTURE. PAPERS.
Dumbarton Oaks, Research Library and Collection, 1703 32nd St., N.W., Washington, DC 20007. TEL 202-339-6431. *400*

COLLOQUY (MILFORD).
Frequency Marketing Inc., Box 3920, Milford, OH 45150-3920. TEL 513-248-9184. FAX 513-248-9084. *1521*

COLOMBIA: CIENCIA Y TECNOLOGIA.
Colciencias, Transversal 9a No. 133-28, P.O. Box 051580, Bogota, Colombia. TEL 2169800. FAX 6251788. *6520*

COLONIAL LATIN AMERICAN HISTORICAL REVIEW.
Spanish Colonial Research Center, Zimmerman Library, University of New Mexico, Albuquerque, NM 87131. TEL 505-277-1370. FAX 505-277-4603. *3623*

COLONIAL WATERBIRDS.
Colonial Waterbird Society, Oakland University, Rochester, MI 48309. TEL 810-370-3222. *802*

COLOR RESEARCH AND APPLICATION.
John Wiley & Sons, Inc., Journals, 605 Third Ave., New York, NY 10158. TEL 212-850-6645. FAX 212-850-6021. *2762*

COLORADO DENTAL ASSOCIATION. JOURNAL.
Colorado Dental Association, 3690 S. Yosemite, Ste. 100, Denver, CO 80237-1808. TEL 303-740-6900. FAX 303-740-7989. *4853*

COLORADO MEDICINE.
Colorado Medical Society, 7800 E. Dorado Pl., Englewood, CO 80111. TEL 303-779-5455. FAX 303-771-8657. *4657*

COLORADO PROSPECTOR.
Alan J. Kania, Ed. & Pub., Box 623, Parker, CO 80134-0623. TEL 303-841-0101. *3623*

COLTELLI, CHE PASSIONE!
Phenix Editions, Casella Postale 519, 20101 Milan, Italy. TEL 39-2-48402857. FAX 39-2-48402857. *3665*

COLUMBIA (NEW YORK, 1977).
Columbia University, School of the Arts, 415 Dodge Hall, Columbia University, New York, NY 10027. TEL 212-854-4216. *4328*

COLUMBIA BIOLOGICAL SERIES.
Columbia University Press, 562 W. 113th St., New York, NY 10025. TEL 212-666-1000. *596*

THE COLUMBIA JOURNAL OF EUROPEAN LAW.
Juris Publishing, Inc., Executive Park, One Odell Plaza, Yonkers, NY 10701. TEL 914-375-3400. FAX 914-375-6047. *4108*

COLUMBIA REVIEW.
Columbia University, Columbia Review, 101 Ferris Booth Hall, New York, NY 10027. TEL 212-854-3611. *4391*

COLUMBIA SERIES IN MOLECULAR BIOLOGY.
Columbia University Press, 562 W. 113th St., New York, NY 10025. TEL 212-666-1000. *597*

COLUMBIA STUDIES IN THE CLASSICAL TRADITION.
E.J. Brill, P.O. Box 9000, 2300 PA Leiden, Netherlands. TEL 31-71-5353500. FAX 31-71-5317532. *1902*

COMBINATORIAL CHEMISTRY & HIGH THROUGHPUT SCREENING.
Bentham Science Publishers, 7436 S.W. 117 Ave., Box 130, Miami, FL 33183. FAX 305-596-5120. *1746*

COMBUSTION AND FLAME.
Elsevier Science Inc., Box 945, New York, NY 10159-0945. TEL 212-633-3730. FAX 212-633-3680. *2713*

COMBUSTION, EXPLOSION, AND SHOCK WAVES.
Plenum Publishing Corp., Consultants Bureau, 233 Spring St., New York, NY 10013-1578. TEL 212-620-8468. FAX 212-463-0742. *2762*

COMBUSTION SCIENCE AND TECHNOLOGY.
Gordon and Breach - Harwood Academic, Amsteldisk 166, 1st Fl., 1079 LH Amsterdam, Netherlands. *1827*

COMBUSTION THEORY AND MODELLING.
I O P Publishing Ltd., Dirac House, Temple Back, Bristol BS1 6BE, England. TEL 44-117-9297481. FAX 44-117-9294318. *5840*

COMITATUS.
University of California at Los Angeles, Center for Medieval and Renaissance Studies, 212 Royce Hall, 405 Hilgard Ave., Los Angeles, CA 90024-1485. TEL 310-825-1880. FAX 310-825-0655. *4391*

COMMAND.
Officers' Christian Fellowship of the United States of America, Box 1177, Englewood, CO 80150-1177. TEL 303-761-1984. FAX 303-761-6226. *5263*

COMMENTATIONES MATHEMATICAE UNIVERSITATIS CAROLINAE.
Universita Karlova, Matematicko-Fizikalni Fakulta, Sokolovska 83, 18600 Prague 8, Czech Republic. TEL 42-2-21913202. FAX 42-2-2323394. *4567*

COMMENTS ON ASTROPHYSICS.
Gordon and Breach - Harwood Academic, Amsteldisk 166, 1st Fl., 1079 LH Amsterdam, Netherlands. *493*

COMMERCIAL INVESTMENT REAL ESTATE JOURNAL.
Commercial Investment Real Estate Institute, 430 N. Michigan Ave., Ste. 600, Chicago, IL 60611-4092. TEL 312-321-4470. FAX 312-321-4530. *6298*

COMMERCIAL LAW PRACTITIONER.
Round Hall Sweet & Maxwell, Brehorn House, 4 Upper Ormond Quay, Dublin 7, Ireland. TEL 353-1-8730101. FAX 353-1-8720078. *4077*

COMMON MARKET LAW REVIEW.
Kluwer Law International, Postbus 85889, 2508 CN The Hague, Netherlands. TEL 31-70-3081500. FAX 31-70-3081515. *4109*

COMMON SENSE.
Edinburgh Conference of Socialist Economists, c/o Werner Bonefeld, Ed., Dept. of Politics, University of York, Heslington, York YO1 4DD. *1298*

COMMONWEALTH NOVEL IN ENGLISH.
B S C Center for International Understanding, Bluefield St. College, Humanities, Bluefield, WV 24701-2198. TEL 304-325-7747. FAX 304-327-4036. *4391*

COMMUNICARE.
Southern African Communication Association, Department of Communication, Rand Afrikaans University, P.O. Box 524, Auckland Park 2006, South Africa. TEL 27-11-4892139. FAX 27-11-4892426. *1984*

COMMUNICATIO.
Unisa Press, Periodicals, P.O. Box 392, Pretoria 0001, South Africa. TEL 27-12-4296565. FAX 27-12-4293346. *1984*

COMMUNICATION & COGNITION.
Communication and Cognition, Blandijnberg 2, 9000 Ghent, Belgium. TEL 32-9-2643952. FAX 32-9-2644197. *1985*

COMMUNICATION AND THE HUMAN CONDITION.
Gordon & Breach - Harwood Academic, Amsteldisk 166, 1st Fl., 1079 LH Amsterdam, Netherlands. *4392*

COMMUNICATION EDUCATION.
Speech Communication Association, 5105 Backlick Rd., Bldg. E., Annandale, VA 22003. TEL 703-750-0533. FAX 703-914-9471. *2598*

COMMUNICATION RESEARCH TRENDS.
Centre for the Study of Communication and Culture, Xavier Hall 325, St. Louis University, Box 59607, St. Louis, MO 63156-0907. TEL 314-977-7290. FAX 314-977-7296. *1985*

THE COMMUNICATION REVIEW.
Gordon and Breach - Harwood Academic, Amsteldisk 166, 1st Fl., 1079 LH Amsterdam, Netherlands. *1985*

COMMUNICATION STUDIES.
Boylor Universitg, Waco, TX 76798. TEL 405-332-8000. FAX 405-332-1623. *1985*

COMMUNICATION THEORY.
Guilford Publications, Inc., 72 Spring St., 4th Fl., New York, NY 10012. TEL 212-431-9800. FAX 212-966-6708. *4250*

COMMUNICATIONS IN ALGEBRA.
Marcel Dekker Journals, 270 Madison Ave., New York, NY 10016. TEL 212-696-9000. FAX 212-685-4540. *4567*

COMMUNICATIONS IN ANALYSIS AND GEOMETRY.
International Press, Box 2872, Cambridge, MA 02238-2872. TEL 617-491-0329. FAX 617-495-2180. *4567*

COMMUNICATIONS IN NUMERICAL METHODS IN ENGINEERING.
John Wiley & Sons Ltd., Journals, Baffins Ln., Chichester, W. Sussex PO19 1UD, England. TEL 44-1243-779777. FAX 44-1243-775878. *4567*

COMMUNICATIONS IN PARTIAL DIFFERENTIAL EQUATIONS.
Marcel Dekker Journals, 270 Madison Ave., New York, NY 10016. TEL 212-696-9000. FAX 212-685-4540. *4567*

COMMUNICATIONS IN SCIENCE AND DEVELOPMENT RESEARCH.
Prof. Dr. A.M. Balba Group for Soil and Water Research, College of Agriculture, University of Alexandria, El-Shatby, Alexandria 21545. TEL 03-5975405. FAX 03-5954684. *6520*

COMMUNICATIONS IN SOIL SCIENCE AND PLANT ANALYSIS.
Marcel Dekker Journals, 270 Madison Ave., New York, NY 10016. TEL 212-696-9000. FAX 212-685-4540. *220*

COMMUNICATIONS IN STATISTICS. PART A: THEORY AND METHODS.
Marcel Dekker Journals, 270 Madison Ave., New York, NY 10016. TEL 212-696-9000. FAX 212-685-4540. *6907*

COMMUNICATIONS IN STATISTICS. PART B: SIMULATION AND COMPUTATION.
Marcel Dekker Journals, 270 Madison Ave., New York, NY 10016. TEL 212-696-9000. FAX 212-685-4540. *6907*

COMMUNICATIONS IN THEORETICAL PHYSICS.
Baltzer Science Publishers B.V., P.O. Box 221, 1400 AE Bussum, Netherlands. TEL 31-20-6370061. FAX 31-20-6323651. *5800*

COMMUNICATIONS OF C O L I P S.
Chinese and Oriental Languages Information Processing Society, c/o Dept. of Information Systems & Computer Science, National University of Singapore, Kent Ridge, Singapore 0511, Singapore. TEL 65-772-2782. FAX 65-779-4580. *4319*

COMMUNICATIONS ON PURE AND APPLIED MATHEMATICS.
John Wiley & Sons, Inc., Journals, 605 Third Ave., New York, NY 10158. TEL 212-850-6645. FAX 212-850-6021. *4567*

THE COMMUNICATOR (ALBANY).
New York State Public Employees Federation, 1168-70 Troy-Schenectady Rd., Box 12414, Albany, NY 12212-2414. TEL 518-785-1900. FAX 518-785-1814. *1423*

COMMUNIO.
Communio, Inc., 487 Michigan Ave., N.E., Washington, DC 20017. TEL 202-526-0251. FAX 202-526-1934. *6459*

COMMUNIQUE (COLUMBUS, 1967).
Business Professionals of America, 5454 Cleveland Ave., Columbus, OH 43231-4021. TEL 614-895-7277. FAX 614-895-1165. *1556*

COMMUNIST AND POST-COMMUNIST STUDIES.
Elsevier Science Ltd., Pergamon, P.O. Box 800, Kidlington, Oxford OX5 1DX, England. TEL 44-1865-843000. FAX 44-1865-843010. *5901*

COMMUNIST ECONOMIES AND ECONOMIC TRANSFORMATION.
Carfax Publishing Co., P.O. Box 25, Abingdon, Oxon. OX14 3UE, England. TEL 44-1235-401000. FAX 44-1235-401550. *1298*

COMMUNITY ALTERNATIVES.
Human Service Associates, Inc., 336 N. Robert St., Ste. 1520, St. Paul, MN 55101. TEL 612-224-8967. FAX 612-224-6057. *6608*

COMMUNITY & JUNIOR COLLEGE LIBRARIES.
Haworth Press, Inc., 10 Alice St., Binghamton, NY 13904. TEL 607-722-5857. FAX 607-722-6362. *4172*

COMMUNITY CARE MARKET NEWS.
Laing & Buisson, Lymehouse Studios, 38 Georgiana St., London NW1 OEB, England. TEL 44-171-284-1268. FAX 44-171-267-8269. *6231*

COMMUNITY COLLEGE JOURNAL OF RESEARCH AND PRACTICE.
Taylor & Francis Inc., 1900 Frost Rd., Ste. 101, Bristol, PA 19007-1598. TEL 215-785-5800. FAX 215-785-5515. *2508*

COMMUNITY COLLEGE REVIEW.
North Carolina State University, Department of Adult and Community College Education, Box 7801, Raleigh, NC 27695-7801. TEL 919-515-6248. FAX 919-515-4039. *2537*

COMMUNITY DENTISTRY AND ORAL EPIDEMIOLOGY.
Munksgaard International Publishers Ltd., 35 Noerre Soegade, P.O. Box 2148, DK-1016 Copenhagen K, Denmark. TEL 45-33-127030. FAX 45-33-129387. *4853*

COMMUNITY EDUCATION JOURNAL.
National Community Education Association, 3929 Old Lee Hwy., Ste. 91-A, Fairfax, VA 22030-2401. TEL 703-359-8973. FAX 703-359-0972. *2429*

COMMUNITY LEADER BRIEFINGS.
City Leaders Institute, 3045 Thayen Pl., Boise, ID 83709-3953. TEL 208-887-6326. FAX 208-887-6015. *6213*

COMMUNITY MENTAL HEALTH JOURNAL.
Human Sciences Press, Inc., 233 Spring St., New York, NY 10013-1578. TEL 212-620-8000. FAX 212-463-0742. *6661*

COMPAR-A-ISON.
Verlag Peter Lang AG, Jupiterstr. 15, CH-3000 Bern 15, Switzerland. TEL 41-31-9402121. FAX 41-31-9402131. *4392*

THE COMPARATIST.
Southern Comparative Literature Association, Comparatist, c/o Marcel Cornis-Pope, Ed., Department of English, Virginia Commonwealth University, Richmond, VA 23284-2005. TEL 804-828-4530. FAX 804-828-2171. *4392*

COMPARATIVE BIOCHEMISTRY AND PHYSIOLOGY. PART A: COMPARATIVE PHYSIOLOGY.
Elsevier Science Inc., Box 945, New York, NY 10159-0945. TEL 212-633-3730. FAX 212-633-3680. *657*

COMPARATIVE BIOCHEMISTRY AND PHYSIOLOGY. PART B: COMPARATIVE BIOCHEMISTRY.
Elsevier Science Inc., Box 945, New York, NY 10159-0945. TEL 212-633-3730. FAX 212-633-3680. *657*

COMPARATIVE BIOCHEMISTRY AND PHYSIOLOGY. PART C: COMPARATIVE PHARMACOLOGY & TOXICOLOGY.
Elsevier Science Inc., Box 945, New York, NY 10159-0945. TEL 212-989-5800. FAX 212-633-3990. *657*

COMPARATIVE CIVILIZATIONS REVIEW.
International Society for the Comparative Study of Civilizations, Dept. of History & Political Science, University of Missouri - Rolla, Rolla, MO 65401. TEL 314-341-4815. FAX 314-341-6127. *6608*

COMPARATIVE DRAMA.
Western Michigan University, Department of English, Kalamazoo, MI 49008-3851. TEL 616-387-2576. FAX 616-387-8750. *4392*

COMPARATIVE ECONOMIC STUDIES.
Association for Comparative Economic Studies, c/o Robert Stuart, Ed., Department of Economics, Rutgers University, New Brunswick, NJ 08903-5055. TEL 908-932-7368. FAX 908-932-7416. *1298*

COMPARATIVE EDUCATION.
Carfax Publishing Co., P.O. Box 25, Abingdon, Oxon. OX14 3UE, England. TEL 44-1235-401000. FAX 44-1235-401550. *2430*

COMPARATIVE EDUCATION REVIEW.
University of Chicago Press, Journals Division, Box 37005, Chicago, IL 60637. TEL 773-702-3347. FAX 773-753-0811. *2430*

COMPARATIVE HAEMATOLOGY INTERNATIONAL.
Springer-Verlag London Ltd., Sweetapple House, Catteshall Rd., Godalming, Surrey GU7 3DJ, England. TEL 44-1483-418800. FAX 44-1483-415144. *4917*

COMPARATIVE IMMUNOLOGY, MICROBIOLOGY AND INFECTIOUS DISEASES.
Elsevier Science Ltd., Pergamon, P.O. Box 800, Kidlington, Oxford OX5 1DX, England. TEL 44-1865-843000. FAX 44-1865-843010. *782*

COMPARATIVE LAW YEARBOOK.
Martinus Nijhoff Publishers, Human Rights and International Law Postbus 163, 3300 AD Dordrecht, Netherlands. TEL 31-78-334911. FAX 31-78-334254. *4109*

COMPARATIVE LITERATURE.
University of Oregon, Comparative Literature, 1223 Friendly Hall, Eugene, OR 97403-1233. TEL 503-346-4022. FAX 503-346-4030. *4392*

COMPARATIVE LITERATURE STUDIES.
Pennsylvania State University Press, USB 1, Ste. C, University Park, PA 16802-1003. TEL 814-865-1327. FAX 814-863-1408. *4392*

COMPARATIVE POLITICS.
City University of New York, Political Science Program, 33 W. 42nd St., New York, NY 10036. TEL 212-642-2377. *5902*

COMPARATIVE STRATEGY.
Taylor & Francis Inc., 1900 Frost Rd., Ste. 101, Bristol, PA 19007. TEL 215-785-5800. FAX 215-785-5515. *5902*

COMPARATIVE STUDIES IN RELIGION & SOCIETY.
University of California Press, 2120 Berkeley Way, Berkeley, CA 94720. TEL 510-642-4247. FAX 510-643-7127. *6331*

COMPARATIVE STUDIES OF HEALTH SYSTEMS & MEDICAL CARE.
University of California Press, 2120 Berkeley Way, Berkeley, CA 94720. TEL 510-642-4247. FAX 510-643-7127. *4657*

COMPARATIVE STUDIES ON MUSLIM SOCIETIES.
University of California Press, 2120 Berkeley Way, Berkeley, CA 94720. TEL 510-642-4247. FAX 510-643-7127. *6396*

COMPARATIVE URBAN AND COMMUNITY RESEARCH.
Transaction Publishers, Transaction Periodicals Consortium, Department 3092, Rutgers University, New Brunswick, NJ 08903. TEL 908-445-2280. FAX 908-445-3138. *3744*

COMPARE.
Carfax Publishing Co., P.O. Box 25, Abingdon, Oxon. OX14 3UE, England. TEL 44-1235-401000. FAX 44-1235-401550. *2430*

COMPASS (NORMAN).
Society of Sigma Gamma Epsilon, c/o Charles J. Mankin, University of Oklahoma, 100 E. Boyd St., Rm. N-131, Norman, OK 73019. TEL 405-325-3031. FAX 405-325-7069. *2312*

COMPENDIUM OF CONTINUING EDUCATION IN DENTISTRY.
Dental Learning Systems Co., Inc., P.O. Box 505, Jamesburg, NJ 08831-0505. TEL 908-656-1143. FAX 908-656-1146. *4853*

COMPETITION REFRESHER.
Competition Refresher Pvt. Ltd., 2767 Bright House, Darya Ganj, New Delhi 110 002, India. TEL 91-11-3282227. FAX 91-11-3269227. *949*

COMPETITIVE INTELLIGENCE REVIEW.
John Wiley & Sons, Inc., Journals, 605 Third Ave., New York, NY 10158. TEL 212-850-6645. FAX 212-850-6021. *1470*

COMPETITIVENESS REVIEW.
American Society for Competitiveness, Box 1658, Indiana, PA 15705. TEL 412-357-5759. FAX 412-357-5743. *1320*

COMPLEX VARIABLES: THEORY AND APPLICATION.
Gordon and Breach - Harwood Academic, Amsteldisk 166, 1st Fl., 1079 LH Amsterdam, Netherlands. *4567*

COMPLEXITY (NEW YORK).
John Wiley & Sons, Inc., Journals, 605 Third Ave., New York, NY 10158. TEL 212-850-6645. FAX 212-850-6021. *4568*

COMPLEXITY INTERNATIONAL.
c/o School of Information Techonology, Charles Sturt University, Panorama Ave., Bathurst, N.S.W. 2795, Australia. TEL 61-63-384272. FAX 61-63-384649. *2154*

COMPOSITE INTERFACES.
V S P, P.O. Box 346, 3700 AH Zeist, Netherlands. TEL 31-30-6925790. FAX 31-30-6932081. *5800*

COMPOSITE MATERIALS SERIES.
Elsevier Science B.V., Books Division, P.O. Box 211, 1000 AE Amsterdam, Netherlands. TEL 31-20-4853911. FAX 31-20-4853705. *2856*

COMPOSITE STRUCTURES.
Elsevier Science Ltd., P.O. Box 800, Kidlington, Oxford OX5 1DX, England. TEL 44-1865-843000. FAX 44-1865-843010. *2780*

COMPOSITES PART A: APPLIED SCIENCE AND MANUFACTURING.
Elsevier Science Ltd., Pergamon, P.O. Box 800, Kidlington, Oxford OX5 1DX, England. TEL 44-1865-843000. FAX 44-1865-843010. *2856*

COMPOSITES PART B: ENGINEERING.
Elsevier Science Ltd., Pergamon, P.O. Box 800, Kidlington, Oxford OX5 1DX, England. TEL 44-1865-843000. FAX 44-1865-843010. *2714*

COMPOSITES SCIENCE AND TECHNOLOGY.
Elsevier Science Ltd., P.O. Box 800, Kidlington, Oxford OX5 1DX, England. TEL 44-1865-843000. FAX 44-1865-843010. *6957*

COMPOSITIO MATHEMATICA.
Kluwer Academic Publishers, Postbus 17, 3300 AA Dordrecht, Netherlands. TEL 31-78-6392392. FAX 31-78-6392254. *4568*

COMPOSITION STUDIES - FRESHMAN ENGLISH NEWS.
DePaul University, English Department, Chicago, IL 60614. TEL 773-325-7211. FAX 773-325-7303. *2599*

COMPOST SCIENCE & UTILIZATION.
J G Press, Inc., 419 State Ave., Emmaus, PA 18049. TEL 610-967-4135. *2983*

COMPREHENSIVE ANALYTICAL CHEMISTRY.
Elsevier Science B.V., Books Division, P.O. Box 211, 1000 AE Amsterdam, Netherlands. TEL 31-20-4853911. FAX 31-20-4853705. *1790*

COMPREHENSIVE BIOCHEMISTRY.
Elsevier Science B.V., Books Division, P.O. Box 211, 1000 AE Amsterdam, Netherlands. TEL 31-20-4853911. FAX 31-20-4853705. *657*

COMPREHENSIVE CHEMICAL KINETICS.
Elsevier Science B.V., Books Division, P.O. Box 211, 1000 AE Amsterdam, Netherlands. TEL 31-20-4853911. FAX 31-20-4853705. *1827*

COMPREHENSIVE ENDOCRINOLOGY.
Lippincott - Raven Publishers, 227 E. Washington Sq., Philadelphia, PA 19106. TEL 215-238-4200. FAX 215-238-4227. *4883*

COMPREHENSIVE IMMUNOLOGY.
Plenum Publishing Corp., 233 Spring St., New York, NY 10013-1578. TEL 212-620-8000. FAX 212-463-0742. *4793*

COMPREHENSIVE PSYCHIATRY.
W.B. Saunders Co., Curtis Center, 3rd Fl., Independence Sq. W., Philadelphia, PA 19106-3399. TEL 215-238-7800. FAX 215-238-6445. *5059*

COMPREHENSIVE PSYCHOTHERAPY.
Gordon & Breach - Harwood Academic, Amsteldisk 166, 1st Fl., 1079 LH Amsterdam, Netherlands. *6104*

COMPREHENSIVE THERAPY.
American Society of Contemporary Medicine, Surgery, and Ophthalmology, 4711 Golf Rd., Ste. 408, Skokie, IL 60076. TEL 847-568-1500. FAX 847-568-1527. *4657*

COMPUTATIONAL ACOUSTICS.
Elsevier Science B.V., Books Division, P.O. Box 211, 1000 AE Amsterdam, Netherlands. TEL 31-20-4853911. FAX 31-20-4853705. *5838*

COMPUTATIONAL & MATHEMATICAL ORGANIZATION THEORY.
Kluwer Academic Publishers Boston, Box 358, Accord Sta., Hingham, MA 02018-0358. TEL 617-871-6600. FAX 617-871-6528. *4619*

COMPUTATIONAL AND THEORETICAL POLYMER SCIENCE.
Elsevier Science Ltd., The Boulevard, Langford Lane, Kidlington, Oxford OX5 1GB, England. TEL 44-1865-843000. FAX 44-1865-843010. *5887*

COMPUTATIONAL ECONOMICS.
Kluwer Academic Publishers, Postbus 17, 3300 AA Dordrecht, Netherlands. TEL 31-78-6392392. FAX 31-78-6392254. *1199*

COMPUTATIONAL GEOMETRY.
North-Holland, P.O. Box 211, 1000 AE Amsterdam, Netherlands. TEL 31-20-4853911. FAX 31-20-4853598. *4619*

COMPUTATIONAL GEOSCIENCES.
Baltzer Science Publishers B.V., P.O. Box 221, 1400 AE Bussum, Netherlands. TEL 31-20-6370061. FAX 31-20-6323651. *2328*

COMPUTATIONAL IMAGING AND VISION.
Kluwer Academic Publishers, Postbus 17, 3300 AA Dordrecht, Netherlands. TEL 31-78-6392392. FAX 31-78-6392254. *2120*

COMPUTATIONAL INTELLIGENCE.
Elsevier Science B.V., P.O. Box 211, 1000 AE Amsterdam, Netherlands. TEL 31-20-4853911. FAX 31-20-4853598. *2099*

COMPUTATIONAL LINGUISTICS.
M I T Press, 5 Cambridge Center, Cambridge, MA 02142. TEL 617-253-2889. FAX 617-577-1545. *4320*

COMPUTATIONAL MATERIALS SCIENCE.
Elsevier Science B.V., P.O. Box 211, 1000 AE Amsterdam, Netherlands. TEL 31-20-4853911. FAX 31-20-4853598. *2857*

COMPUTATIONAL MATHEMATICS AND APPLICATIONS.
Academic Press, Inc., 525 B St., Ste. 1900, San Diego, CA 92101-4495. TEL 619-231-0926. FAX 619-699-6715. *2160*

COMPUTATIONAL MATHEMATICS AND MATHEMATICAL PHYSICS.
Elsevier Science Ltd., Pergamon, P.O. Box 800, Kidlington, Oxford OX5 1DX, England. TEL 44-1865-843000. FAX 44-1865-843010. *4568*

COMPUTATIONAL MATHEMATICS AND MODELING.
Plenum Publishing Corp., Consultants Bureau, 233 Spring St., New York, NY 10013-1578. TEL 212-620-8000. FAX 212-463-0742. *4620*

COMPUTATIONAL OPTIMIZATION AND APPLICATIONS.
Kluwer Academic Publishers Boston, Box 358, Accord Sta., Hingham, MA 02018-0358. TEL 617-871-6600. FAX 617-871-6528. *4620*

COMPUTATIONAL STATISTICS.
Physica-Verlag GmbH und Co., Postfach 105280, 69042 Heidelberg, Germany. TEL 49-6221-487492. FAX 49-6221-487177. *6907*

COMPUTATIONAL STATISTICS AND DATA ANALYSIS.
North-Holland, P.O. Box 211, 1000 AE Amsterdam, Netherlands. TEL 31-20-4853911. FAX 31-20-4853598. *4620*

COMPUTE - ED. *2430*

COMPUTER-AIDED CHEMICAL ENGINEERING.
Elsevier Science B.V., Books Division, P.O. Box 211, 1000 AE Amsterdam, Netherlands. TEL 31-20-4853911. FAX 31-20-4853705. *2802*

COMPUTER-AIDED DESIGN.
Elsevier Science Ltd., P.O. Box 800, Kidlington, Oxford OX5 1DX, England. TEL 44-1865-843000. FAX 44-1865-843010. *2120*

COMPUTER-AIDED DESIGN OF ELECTRONIC CIRCUITS.
Elsevier Science B.V., Books Division, P.O. Box 211, 1000 AE Amsterdam, Netherlands. TEL 31-20-4853911. FAX 31-20-4853705. *2802*

COMPUTER-AIDED GEOMETRIC DESIGN.
North-Holland, P.O. Box 211, 1000 AE Amsterdam, Netherlands. TEL 31-20-4853911. FAX 31-20-4853598. *2121*

COMPUTER APPLICATIONS IN ENGINEERING EDUCATION.
John Wiley & Sons, Inc., Journals, 605 Third Ave., New York, NY 10158. TEL 212-850-6645. FAX 212-850-6021. *2802*

COMPUTER AUDIT UPDATE.
Elsevier Science Ltd., P.O. Box 800, Kidlington, Oxford OX5 1DX, England. TEL 44-1865-843000. FAX 44-1865-843010. *2148*

COMPUTER COMMUNICATIONS.
Elsevier Science B.V., P.O. Box 211, 1000 AE Amsterdam, Netherlands. TEL 31-20-4853911. FAX 31-20-4853598. *2168*

COMPUTER DESIGN AND ARCHITECTURE SERIES.
Elsevier Science Inc., Box 945, New York, NY 10159-0945. TEL 212-633-3730. FAX 212-633-3680. *2113*

COMPUTER EDUCATION.
Staffordshire University, Computer Education Group, c/o CEG Treasurer, Beaconside, Stafford ST18 0AD, England. TEL 44-115-9280253. *2515*

COMPUTER GRAPHICS FORUM.
Blackwell Publishers Ltd., 108 Cowley Rd., Oxford OX4 1JF, England. TEL 44-1865-791100. FAX 44-1865-791347. *2121*

COMPUTER-INTEGRATED MANUFACTURING SYSTEMS.
Elsevier Science Ltd., P.O. Box 800, Kidlington, Oxford OX5 1DX, England. TEL 44-1865-843000. FAX 44-1865-843010. *2803*

COMPUTER LANGUAGES.
Elsevier Science Ltd., Pergamon, P.O. Box 800, Kidlington, Oxford OX5 1DX, England. TEL 44-1865-843000. FAX 44-1865-843010. *2142*

COMPUTER LAW & SECURITY REPORT.
Elsevier Science Ltd., P.O. Box 800, Kidlington, Oxford OX5 1DX, England. TEL 44-1865-843000. FAX 44-1865-843010. *2149*

COMPUTER METHODS AND PROGRAMS IN BIOMEDICINE.
Elsevier Science Ireland Ltd., P.O. Box 85, Limerick, Ireland. TEL 353-61-471944. FAX 353-61-472144. *4845*

COMPUTER METHODS IN APPLIED MECHANICS AND ENGINEERING.
Elsevier Science S.A., P.O. Box 564, CH-1001 Lausanne 1, Switzerland. TEL 41-21-3207381. FAX 41-21-3235444. *2803*

COMPUTER METHODS IN THE GEOSCIENCES.
Elsevier Science Ltd., Books Division, P.O. Box 800, Kidlington, Oxford OX5 1DK, England. TEL 44-1865-843000. FAX 44-1865-843010. *6593*

COMPUTER MUSIC JOURNAL.
M I T Press, 5 Cambridge Center, Cambridge, MA 02142. TEL 617-253-2889. FAX 617-577-1545. *5449*

COMPUTER NETWORKS AND I S D N SYSTEMS.
North-Holland, P.O. Box 211, 1000 AE Amsterdam, Netherlands. TEL 31-20-4853911. FAX 31-20-4853598. *2131*

COMPUTER PHYSICS COMMUNICATIONS.
North-Holland, P.O. Box 211, 1000 AE Amsterdam, Netherlands. TEL 31-20-4853911. FAX 31-20-4853598. *5838*

COMPUTER STANDARDS AND INTERFACES.
Elsevier Science B.V., P.O. Box 211, 1000 AE Amsterdam, Netherlands. TEL 31-20-4853911. FAX 31-20-4853598. *2077*

COMPUTER STUDIES: COMPUTERS IN EDUCATION.
Dushkin Publishing Group, Sluice Dock, Guilford, CT 06437-9989. TEL 203-453-4351. FAX 203-453-6000. *2515*

COMPUTER SUPPORTED COOPERATIVE WORK.
Kluwer Academic Publishers, Postbus 17, 3300 AA Dordrecht, Netherlands. TEL 31-78-6392392. FAX 31-78-6392254. *6608*

COMPUTERIZED MEDICAL IMAGING AND GRAPHICS.
Elsevier Science Ltd., Pergamon, P.O. Box 800, Kidlington, Oxford OX5 1DX, England. TEL 44-1865-843000. FAX 44-1865-843010. *4845*

COMPUTERS AND ARTIFICIAL INTELLIGENCE.
Slovenska Akademia Vied, Ustav Pocitacovych Systemov, Dubravska cesta 9, 842 37 Bratislava, Slovakia. TEL 421-7-374703. FAX 421-7-371004. *2099*

COMPUTERS AND BIOMEDICAL RESEARCH.
Academic Press, Inc., Journal Division, 525 B. St., Ste. 1900, San Diego, CA 92101-4495. TEL 619-230-1840. FAX 619-699-6800. *4846*

COMPUTERS & CHEMICAL ENGINEERING.
Elsevier Science Ltd., Pergamon, P.O. Box 800, Kidlington, Oxford OX5 1DX, England. TEL 44-1865-843000. FAX 44-1865-843010. *1799*

COMPUTERS & CHEMISTRY.
Elsevier Science Ltd., Pergamon, P.O. Box 800, Kidlington, Oxford OX5 1DX, England. TEL 44-1865-843000. FAX 44-1865-843010. *1799*

COMPUTERS & EDUCATION.
Elsevier Science Ltd., Pergamon, P.O. Box 800, Kidlington, Oxford OX5 1DX, England. TEL 44-1865-843000. FAX 44-1865-843010. *2515*

COMPUTERS & ELECTRICAL ENGINEERING.
Elsevier Science Ltd., Pergamon, P.O. Box 800, Kidlington, Oxford OX5 1DX, England. TEL 44-1865-843000. FAX 44-1865-843010. *2803*

COMPUTERS AND ELECTRONICS IN AGRICULTURE.
Elsevier Science B.V., P.O. Box 211, 1000 AE Amsterdam, Netherlands. TEL 31-20-4853911. FAX 31-20-4853598. *210*

COMPUTERS & FLUIDS.
Elsevier Science Ltd., Pergamon, P.O. Box 800, Kidlington, Oxford OX5 1DX, England. TEL 44-1865-843000. FAX 44-1865-843010. *2803*

COMPUTERS & GEOSCIENCES.
Elsevier Science Ltd., Pergamon, P.O. Box 800, Kidlington, Oxford OX5 1DX, England. TEL 44-1865-843000. FAX 44-1865-843010. *2328*

COMPUTERS AND GEOTECHNICS.
Elsevier Science Ltd., P.O. Box 800, Kidlington, Oxford OX5 1DX, England. TEL 44-1865-843000. FAX 44-1865-843010. *2803*

COMPUTERS & GRAPHICS.
Elsevier Science Ltd., Pergamon, P.O. Box 800, Kidlington, Oxford OX5 1DX, England. TEL 44-1865-843000. FAX 44-1865-843010. *2121*

REFEREED SERIALS

COMPUTERS & INDUSTRIAL ENGINEERING.
Elsevier Science Ltd., Pergamon, P.O. Box 800, Kidlington, Oxford OX5 1DX, England. TEL 44-1865-843000. FAX 44-1865-843010. *2803*

COMPUTERS & MATHEMATICS WITH APPLICATIONS.
Elsevier Science Ltd., Pergamon, P.O. Box 800, Kidlington, Oxford OX5 1DX, England. TEL 44-1865-843000. FAX 44-1865-843010. *4620*

COMPUTERS & OPERATIONS RESEARCH.
Elsevier Science Ltd., Pergamon, P.O. Box 800, Kidlington, Oxford OX5 1DX, England. TEL 44-1865-843000. FAX 44-1865-843010. *2078*

COMPUTERS & SECURITY.
Elsevier Science Ltd., P.O. Box 800, Kidlington, Oxford OX5 1DX, England. TEL 44-1865-843000. FAX 44-1865-843010. *2149*

COMPUTERS & STRUCTURES.
Elsevier Science Ltd., Pergamon, P.O. Box 800, Kidlington, Oxford OX5 1DX, England. TEL 44-1865-843000. FAX 44-1865-843010. *2804*

COMPUTERS AND THE HISTORY OF ART.
Gordon and Breach - Harwood Academic, Amsteldisk 166, 1st Fl., 1079 LH Amsterdam, Netherlands. *477*

COMPUTERS AND THE HUMANITIES.
Kluwer Academic Publishers, Postbus 17, 3300 AA Dordrecht, Netherlands. TEL 31-78-6392392. FAX 31-78-6392254. *3800*

COMPUTERS, ENVIRONMENT AND URBAN SYSTEMS.
Elsevier Science Ltd., Pergamon, P.O. Box 800, Kidlington, Oxford OX5 1DX, England. TEL 44-1865-843000. FAX 44-1865-843010. *2964*

COMPUTERS IN BIOLOGY AND MEDICINE.
Elsevier Science Ltd., Pergamon, P.O. Box 800, Kidlington, Oxford OX5 1DX, England. TEL 44-1865-843000. FAX 44-1865-843010. *735*

COMPUTERS IN EDUCATION JOURNAL.
American Society for Engineering Education, Computers in Education Division, Box 68, Port Royal Sq., Port Royal, VA 22535. TEL 804-742-5611. FAX 804-742-5030. *2516*

COMPUTERS IN HUMAN BEHAVIOR.
Elsevier Science Ltd., Pergamon, P.O. Box 800, Kidlington, Oxford OX5 1DX, England. TEL 44-1865-843000. FAX 44-1865-843010. *6741*

COMPUTERS IN HUMAN SERVICES.
Haworth Press, Inc., 10 Alice St., Binghamton, NY 13904. TEL 607-722-5857. FAX 607-722-6362. *6741*

COMPUTERS IN INDUSTRY.
North-Holland, P.O. Box 211, 1000 AE Amsterdam, Netherlands. TEL 31-20-4853911. FAX 31-20-4853598. *1199*

COMPUTERS IN MUSIC RESEARCH.
Wisconsin Center for Music Technology, School of Music, University of Wisconsin, Madison, WI 53706. TEL 608-263-1900. *5449*

COMPUTERS IN PHYSICS.
American Association of Physics, One Physics Ellipse, College Park, MD 20740-3843. TEL 301-209-3000. *5838*

COMPUTERS IN THE SCHOOLS.
Haworth Press, Inc., 10 Alice St., Binghamton, NY 13904. TEL 607-722-5857. FAX 607-722-6362. *2516*

COMPUTERWORLD HONG KONG.
I D G Communications (HK) Ltd., Mount Parker House, Ste. 1011-15, 1111 King's Rd., Quarry Bay, Hong Kong, People's Republic of China. TEL 852-2861-3238. FAX 852-2861-0953. *2127*

COMPUTING IN BIOMEDICINE.
Elsevier Science B.V., Books Division, P.O. Box 211, 1000 AE Amsterdam, Netherlands. TEL 31-20-4853911. FAX 31-20-4853705. *4846*

COMPUTING SYSTEMS.
M I T Press, 55 Hayward St., Cambridge, MA 02142-1399. TEL 617-253-2889. FAX 617-258-6779. *2142*

CONCEPTS AND TRANSFORMATION.
John Benjamins Publishing Co., Amsteldijk 44, P.O. Box 75577, 1070 AN Amsterdam, Netherlands. TEL 31-20-6762325. FAX 31-20-6792956. *1564*

CONCEPTS IN MAGNETIC RESONANCE.
John Wiley & Sons, Inc., Journals, 605 Third Ave., New York, NY 10158-0012. TEL 212-850-6347. FAX 212-850-6021. *5104*

CONCERNS (NEW YORK).
Women's Caucus for the Modern Languages, College of Staten Island, City University of New York, Staten Island, NY 10314. TEL 718-982-2315. FAX 718-982-2316. *7342*

LA CONCHIGLIA.
Conchiglia, Via C. Federici 1, 00147 Rome, Italy. TEL 39-6-5110192. FAX 39-6-5110192. *830*

CONCISE.
Airworthy Publications International Ltd., Bassfield South, Manchester Rd., Walmersley, Bury, Lancs. BL9 5LY, England. TEL 44-1706-828811. FAX 44-1706-828300. *62*

CONCORD.
Lutherans Concerned North America, Box 10461, Fort Dearborn Sta., Chicago, IL 60610. *3693*

CONCORDIA JOURNAL.
Ovid Bell Press, Inc., 801 Demun, Clayton, MO 63105. TEL 314-505-7000. FAX 314-505-7001. *6331*

CONCORDIA TORCH.
Concordia Mutual Life Association, 3041 Woodcreek Dr., Downers Grove, IL 60515. TEL 708-971-8000. FAX 708-971-9332. *3813*

CONCRETE IN AUSTRALIA.
Engineers Australia Pty. Ltd., 2 Ernest St., P.O. Box 588, Crows Nest, N.S.W. 2065, Australia. TEL 61-2-94381533. FAX 61-2-9438-5934. *877*

CONCURRENCY: PRACTICE AND EXPERIENCE.
John Wiley & Sons Ltd., Journals, Baffins Ln., Chichester, W. Sussex PO19 1UD, England. TEL 44-1243-779777. FAX 44-1243-775878. *2142*

CONCURRENT ENGINEERING: RESEARCH AND APPLICATIONS.
Technomic Publishing Co., Inc., 851 New Holland Ave., Box 3535, Lancaster, PA 17604. TEL 717-291-5609. FAX 717-295-45638. *2115*

CONCURRENT SYSTEMS ENGINEERING SERIES.
I O S Press, Van Diemenstraat 94, 1013 CN Amsterdam, Netherlands. TEL 31-20-6382189. FAX 31-20-6203419. *2115*

CONDENSED MATTER NEWS.
Gordon and Breach - Harwood Academic, Amsteldisk 166, 1st Fl., 1079 LH Amsterdam, Netherlands. *2812*

CONDENSED MATTER THEORIES.
Plenum Publishing Corp., 233 Spring St., New York, NY 10013-1578. TEL 212-620-8000. FAX 212-463-0742. *5800*

THE CONDUCTOR.
National Association of Brass Band Conductors, Marrey, 7 Carr View Rd., Hepworth, Huddersfield HD7 7HN, England. TEL 44-1484-683793. FAX 44-1484-608512. *5385*

CONFECTIONERY PRODUCTION.
Specialised Publications Ltd., 5 Grove Rd., Surbiton, Surrey KT6 4BT, England. TEL 44-181-390-0222. FAX 44-181-390-0126. *3136*

CONFERENCE ON REMOTE SYSTEMS TECHNOLOGY. PROCEEDINGS.
American Nuclear Society, 555 N. Kensington Ave., La Grange Park, IL 60525. TEL 708-352-6611. FAX 708-352-0499. *2206*

CONFIDENTIAL A-I-R LETTER.
Air Incident Research, Box 4745, East Lansing, MI 48826. TEL 517-336-9375. FAX 517-336-9375. *2264*

CONFLUENCIA.
University Press of Colorado, Box 849, Niwot, CO 80544. TEL 303-530-5337. FAX 303-530-5306. *3006*

CONFORMAL GEOMETRY AND DYNAMICS.
American Mathematical Society, Box 6248, Providence, RI 02940-6248. TEL 401-455-4000. FAX 401-331-3842. *4568*

CONFRONTATION.
Long Island University, C.W. Post College, Dept. of English, Greenvale, NY 11548. TEL 516-299-2391. FAX 516-299-2735. *4393*

CONGENITAL ANOMALIES.
Nihon Senten Ijo Gakkai, Dept. of Anatomy and Developmental Biology, Faculty of Medicine, Kyoto University, Kyoto 606-01, Japan. TEL 81-75-753-4670. FAX 81-75-751-7529. *4657*

CONGESTIVE HEART FAILURE.
LeJacq Communications, Inc., 777 W. Putnam Ave., Greenwich, CT 06830. TEL 203-531-0450. FAX 203-531-0533. *4814*

CONGRESSUS NUMERANTIUM.
Utilitas Mathematica Publishing Inc., Box 7, University Centre, University of Manitoba, Winnipeg, MB R3T 2N2, Canada. TEL 204-474-8675. *4568*

CONNECTICUT ACADEMY OF ARTS AND SCIENCES. TRANSACTIONS.
Connecticut Academy of Arts and Sciences, Box 208211, New Haven, CT 06520-8211. TEL 203-432-3113. FAX 203-432-5712. *3776*

CONNECTICUT SUPPLEMENT.
Commission on Official Legal Publications, Office of Production and Distribution, 111 Phoenix Ave., Enfield, CT 06082. TEL 203-741-3027. FAX 203-745-2178. *3934*

CONNECTICUT WARBLER.
Connecticut Ornithological Association, Inc., 314 Unquowa Rd., Fairfield, CT 06430-5018. TEL 203-259-2623. *802*

CONNECTION SCIENCE.
Carfax Publishing Co., P.O. Box 25, Abingdon, Oxon. OX14 3UE, England. TEL 44-1235-401000. FAX 44-1235-401550. *2099*

CONNECTIVE TISSUE RESEARCH.
Gordon and Breach - Harwood Academic, Amsteldisk 166, 1st Fl., 1079 LH Amsterdam, Netherlands. *739*

THE CONRADIAN.
Editions Rodopi B.V., Keizersgracht 302-304, 1016 EX Amsterdam, Netherlands. TEL 31-20-6227507. FAX 31-20-6380948. *4393*

CONSCIOUSNESS AND COGNITION.
Academic Press, Inc., Journal Division, 525 B St., Ste. 1900, San Diego, CA 92101-4495. TEL 619-230-1840. FAX 619-699-6800. *6104*

CONSCIOUSNESS AND SELF-REGULATION: ADVANCES IN RESEARCH AND THEORY.
Plenum Publishing Corp., 233 Spring St., New York, NY 10013-1578. TEL 212-620-8000. FAX 212-463-0742. *6104*

CONSERVATION AND MANAGEMENT OF ARCHAEOLOGICAL SITES.
James & James (Science Publishers) Ltd., 35-37 William Rd., London NW1 3ER, England. TEL 44-171-387-8558. FAX 44-171-387-8998. *359*

CONSERVATION ECOLOGY. *2227*

CONSERVATIVE JUDAISM.
Rabbinical Assembly, 3080 Broadway, New York, NY 10027. TEL 212-678-8060. FAX 212-749-9166. *6403*

CONSERVER.
British Trust for Conservation Volunteers, 36 St. Mary's St., Wallingford, Oxon. OX10 0EU, England. TEL 44-1491-839766. FAX 44-1491-839646. *2227*

CONSORTIUM ON REVOLUTIONARY EUROPE. SELECTED PAPERS.
Consortium on Revolutionary Europe, c/o Dr. Kyle Eidahl, Secy.-Treas., 6611 Crooked Creek Rd., Tallahassee, FL 32311. *3560*

CONSPECTUS FLORAE ORIENTALIS.
Israel Academy of Sciences and Humanities, 43 Jabotinski St., P.O. Box 4040, Jerusalem 91040, Israel. TEL 972-2-636211. FAX 972-2-666059. *699*

CONSTELLATIONS.
Blackwell Publishers Ltd., 108 Cowley Rd., Oxford OX4 1JF, England. TEL 44-1865-791100. FAX 44-1865-791347. *5903*

CONSTITUTIONAL POLITICAL ECONOMY.
Kluwer Academic Publishers Boston, Box 358, Accord Sta., Hingham, MA 02018-0358. TEL 617-871-6600. FAX 617-871-6528. *4069*

CONSTRUCTION AND BUILDING MATERIALS.
Elsevier Science Ltd., P.O. Box 800, Kidlington, Oxford OX5 1DX, England. TEL 44-1865-310366. FAX 44-1865-310898. *879*

CONSTRUCTION MANAGEMENT AND ECONOMICS.
Thomson Professional, 2-6 Boundary Row, London SE1 8HN, England. TEL 44-171-8650066. FAX 44-171-5229623. *881*

CONSTRUCTIVE APPROXIMATION.
Springer-Verlag, Science Journals, 175 Fifth Ave., New York, NY 10010. TEL 212-460-1500. FAX 212-473-6272. *4568*

CONSULTANT (GREENWICH).
Cliggott Publishing Co., 55 Holly Hill Ln., Box 4010, Greenwich, CT 06831. TEL 203-661-0600. *4657*

CONSULTING PSYCHOLOGY JOURNAL: PRACTICE AND RESEARCH.
American Psychological Association, 750 First St., N.E., Washington, DC 20002-4242. TEL 202-336-5600. FAX 202-336-5568. *6104*

CONSUMER CURRENTS.
Consumers International, Regional Office for Asia and Pacific, P.O. Box 1045, 10830 Penang, Malaysia. TEL 60-4-229-1296. FAX 60-4-228-6506. *2253*

CONSUMER INTERESTS ANNUAL.
American Council on Consumer Interests, c/o Anita Metzen, Exec. Dir., 240 Stanley Hall, University of Missouri, Columbia, MO 65211. TEL 573-882-3817. FAX 573-884-6571. *2253*

CONTACT (ALDERSHOT).
Officers' Christian Union, Havelock House, Barrack Rd., Aldershot GU11 3NP, England. TEL 44-1252-311221. FAX 44-1252-311222. *6332*

CONTACT DERMATITIS.
Munksgaard International Publishers Ltd., 35 Noerre Soegade, P.O. Box 2148, DK-1016 Copenhagen K, Denmark. TEL 45-33-127030. FAX 45-33-129387. *4876*

CONTACT LENS & ANTERIOR EYE.
Stockton Press, Houndmills, Basingstoke, Hants. RG21 6XS, England. *4991*

CONTEMPORARY ACCOUNTING RESEARCH.
Canadian Academic Accounting Association, 223 Scurfield Hall, Faculty of Management, University of Calgary, Calgary, AB T2N 1N4, Canada. TEL 403-220-8517. FAX 403-282-0095. *1088*

CONTEMPORARY ANALYSES IN EDUCATION.
Taylor & Francis Ltd., Rankine Rd., Basingstoke, Hants. RF24 0PR, England. *2430*

CONTEMPORARY BRITISH HISTORY.
Frank Cass, Newbury House, 890-900 Eastern Ave., Newbury Park, Ilford, Essex IG2 7HH, England. TEL 44-181-599-8866. FAX 44-181-599-0984. *3560*

CONTEMPORARY CONCEPTS IN PHYSICS.
Gordon and Breach - Harwood Academic, Amsteldisk 166, 1st Fl., 1079 LH Amsterdam, Netherlands. *5800*

CONTEMPORARY ECONOMIC POLICY.
Western Economic Association International, 7400 Center Ave., Ste. 109, Huntington Beach, CA 92647-3039. TEL 714-898-3222. *950*

CONTEMPORARY EDUCATION.
Indiana State University, School of Education, Statesman Towers, Rm. 1005, Terre Haute, IN 47809. TEL 812-237-2925. FAX 812-237-4348. *2430*

CONTEMPORARY ENDOCRINOLOGY.
Plenum Publishing Corp., 233 Spring St., New York, NY 10013-1578. TEL 212-620-8000. FAX 212-463-0742. *4883*

CONTEMPORARY FAMILY THERAPY.
Human Sciences Press, Inc., 233 Spring St., New York, NY 10013-1578. TEL 212-620-8000. FAX 212-463-0742. *6104*

CONTEMPORARY FRENCH CIVILIZATION.
Montana State University, Department of Modern Languages, Bozeman, MT 59717. TEL 406-994-6447. FAX 406-994-2893. *3560*

CONTEMPORARY GERIATRIC MEDICINE.
Plenum Publishing Corp., 233 Spring St., New York, NY 10013-1578. TEL 212-620-8000. FAX 212-463-0742. *3434*

CONTEMPORARY GERONTOLOGY.
Springer Publishing Company, 536 Broadway, New York, NY 10012-3955. TEL 212-431-4370. FAX 212-941-7842. *3434*

CONTEMPORARY HEMATOLOGY - ONCOLOGY.
Plenum Publishing Corp., 233 Spring St., New York, NY 10013-1578. TEL 212-620-8000. FAX 212-463-0742611. *4918*

CONTEMPORARY HYPNOSIS.
Whurr Publishers Ltd., 19b Compton Terrace, London N1 2UN, England. TEL 44-171-359-5979. FAX 44-171-226-5290. *4923*

CONTEMPORARY INTERNAL MEDICINE.
Appleton & Lange, Box 120041, Stamford, CT 06912-0041. TEL 203-406-4500. FAX 203-406-4603. *4924*

CONTEMPORARY ISSUES IN GENETICS AND EVOLUTION.
Kluwer Academic Publishers, Postbus 17, 3300 AA Dordrecht, Netherlands. TEL 31-78-6392392. FAX 31-78-6392254. *765*

CONTEMPORARY ISSUES IN RISK ANALYSIS.
Plenum Publishing Corp., 233 Spring St., New York, NY 10013-1578. TEL 212-620-8000. FAX 212-463-0742. *6231*

CONTEMPORARY JEWRY.
Association for Social Scientific Study of Jewry, Box 5302, Connecticut College, New London, CT 06320. TEL 860-439-2241. FAX 860-439-5478. *3006*

CONTEMPORARY MATHEMATICS.
American Mathematical Society, Box 6248, Providence, RI 02940-6248. TEL 401-455-4000. FAX 401-331-3842. *4568*

CONTEMPORARY METABOLISM.
Plenum Publishing Corp., 233 Spring St., New York, NY 10013-1578. TEL 212-620-8000. FAX 212-463-0742. *4883*

CONTEMPORARY MUSIC REVIEW.
Gordon and Breach - Harwood Academic, Amsteldisk 166, 1st Fl., 1079 LH Amsterdam, Netherlands. *5385*

CONTEMPORARY MUSIC STUDIES.
Gordon and Breach - Harwood Academic, Amsteldisk 166, 1st Fl., 1079 LH Amsterdam, Netherlands. *5385*

CONTEMPORARY NEPHROLOGY.
Plenum Publishing Corp., 233 Spring St., New York, NY 10013-1578. TEL 212-620-8000. FAX 212-463-0742. *5160*

CONTEMPORARY NEUROLOGY SERIES.
F.A. Davis Company, 1915 Arch St., Philadelphia, PA 19103. FAX 215-568-5065. *5060*

CONTEMPORARY NURSE.
Churchill Livingstone, 95 Coventry St., P.O. Box 1338, S. Melbourne, Vic. 3205, Australia. TEL 61-3-96970787. FAX 61-3-96965205. *4931*

CONTEMPORARY OB-GYN.
Medical Economics, 5 Paragon Dr., Montvale, NJ 07645. FAX 201-358-7260. *4955*

THE CONTEMPORARY PACIFIC.
University of Hawaii Press, Journals Department, 2840 Kolowalu St., Honolulu, HI 96822. TEL 808-956-8833. FAX 808-988-6052. *3250*

CONTEMPORARY PHILOSOPHY.
Kluwer Academic Publishers, Postbus 17, 3300 AA Dordrecht, Netherlands. TEL 31-78-6392392. FAX 31-78-6392254. *5722*

CONTEMPORARY PHYSICS.
Taylor & Francis Ltd., 1 Gunpowder Sq., London EC4A 3DE, England. TEL 44-171-583-0490. FAX 44-171-583-0585. *5800*

CONTEMPORARY PSYCHOANALYSIS.
William Alanson White Psychoanalytic Institute, 20 W. 74th St., New York, NY 10023. TEL 212-873-0725. FAX 212-362-6967. *6105*

CONTEMPORARY PSYCHOLOGY.
American Psychological Association, 750 First St., N.E., Washington, DC 20002-4242. TEL 202-336-5600. FAX 202-336-5568. *6105*

CONTEMPORARY REVIEWS IN OBSTETRICS AND GYNAECOLOGY.
Parthenon Publishing Group, Casterton Hall, Carnforth, Lancs. LA6 2LA, England. TEL 44-152-427-2084. FAX 44-152-427-1587. *4955*

CONTEMPORARY SECURITY POLICY.
Frank Cass, Newbury House, 890-900 Eastern Ave., Newbury Park, Ilford, Essex IG2 7HH, England. TEL 44-181-599-8866. FAX 44-181-599-0984. *6009*

CONTEMPORARY SOCIAL PSYCHOLOGY.
Society for the Advancement of Social Psychology, Department of Psychology, Mercer University, 1400 Coleman Ave., Macon, GA 31207-0001. TEL 912-752-2972. FAX 912-752-2956. *6105*

CONTEMPORARY SOUTH ASIA.
Carfax Publishing Co., P.O. Box 25, Abingdon, Oxon. OX14 3UE, England. TEL 44-1238-401000. FAX 44-1235-401550. *5903*

CONTEMPORARY SURGERY.
Bobit Publishing Company, 2512 Artesia Blvd., Redondo Beach, CA 90278-3210. TEL 310-376-8788. FAX 310-376-9043. *5139*

CONTEMPORARY THEATRE REVIEW.
Gordon and Breach - Harwood Academic, Amsteldisk 166, 1st Fl., 1079 LH Amsterdam, Netherlands. *7004*

CONTEMPORARY THEATRE STUDIES.
Gordon and Breach - Harwood Academic, Amsteldisk 166, 1st Fl., 1079 LH Amsterdam, Netherlands. *7004*

CONTEMPORARY TOPICS IN IMMUNOBIOLOGY.
Plenum Publishing Corp., 233 Spring St., New York, NY 10013-1578. TEL 212-620-8000. FAX 212-463-0742. *4793*

CONTEMPORARY TOPICS IN INFORMATION TRANSFER.
Elsevier Science B.V., Books Division, P.O. Box 211, 1000 AE Amsterdam, Netherlands. TEL 31-20-4853911. FAX 31-20-4853705. *2181*

CONTEMPORARY TOPICS IN MOLECULAR IMMUNOLOGY.
Plenum Publishing Corp., 233 Spring St., New York, NY 10013-1578. TEL 212-620-8047. FAX 212-463-0742. *4793*

CONTEMPORARY TOPICS IN PURE AND APPLIED CONDENSED MATTER SCIENCE.
Gordon and Breach - Harwood Academic, Amsteldisk 166, 1st Fl., 1079 LH Amsterdam, Netherlands. *5800*

REFEREED SERIALS

CONTEMPORARY WALES.
University of Wales Press, 6 Gwennyth St., Cathays, Cardiff CF2 4YD, Wales. TEL 44-1222-231919. FAX 44-1222-230908. *6609*

CONTEXT SOUTH.
Context South Foundation, c/o David Breeden, Ed., Box 4504, 2100 Memorial Blvd., Kerrville, TX 78028-5611. TEL 501-972-6095. *4506*

CONTEXTS OF LEARNING.
Swets & Zeitlinger bv, P.O. Box 825, 2160 SZ Lisse, Netherlands. TEL 31-252-435111. FAX 31-252-415888. *2430*

CONTINENTAL SHELF RESEARCH.
Elsevier Science Ltd., Pergamon, P.O. Box 800, Kidlington, Oxford OX5 1DX, England. TEL 44-1865-843000. FAX 44-1865-843010. *2401*

CONTINUUM.
Edith Cowan University, 2 Bradford St., Mount Lawley, W.A. 6050, Australia. TEL 61-9-3706219. FAX 61-9-3706668. *5328*

CONTINUUM (CHICAGO).
American Hospital Association, 1 N. Franklin, Chicago, IL 60606. TEL 312-445-3616. FAX 312-445-3708. *3706*

CONTRACEPTION.
Elsevier Science Inc., Box 945, New York, NY 10159-0945. TEL 712-633-3730. FAX 212-633-3680. *856*

CONTRACEPTIVE TECHNOLOGY UPDATE.
American Health Consultants, Inc., 3525 Piedmont Rd., N.E., Bldg. 6, Ste. 400, Atlanta, GA 30305. TEL 404-262-7436. FAX 800-284-3291. *856*

CONTRIBUTIONS FROM THE NEW YORK BOTANICAL GARDEN.
New York Botanical Garden, Scientific Publications Department, Bronx, NY 10458-5126. TEL 718-817-8721. FAX 718-817-8842. *699*

CONTRIBUTIONS IN MARINE SCIENCE - MONOGRAPHIC SERIES.
University of Texas at Austin, Marine Science Institute, 750 Channelview Dr., Port Aransas, TX 78373. TEL 512-749-6723. FAX 512-749-6725. *597*

CONTRIBUTIONS IN SCIENCE.
Natural History Museum of Los Angeles County, 900 Exposition Blvd., Los Angeles, CA 90007. TEL 213-744-3330. FAX 213-742-0730. *6520*

CONTRIBUTIONS ON ENTOMOLOGY, INTERNATIONAL.
Associated Publishers, Box 140103, Gainesville, FL 32614-0103. TEL 352-371-4071. FAX 352-371-4071. *749*

CONTRIBUTIONS TO BIBLICAL EXEGESIS AND THEOLOGY.
Kok Pharos Publishing House, Postbus 5016, 8260 GA Kampen, Netherlands. TEL 31-38-3392555. FAX 31-38-3328912. *6332*

CONTRIBUTIONS TO ECONOMIC ANALYSIS.
Elsevier Science B.V., Books Division, P.O. Box 211, 1000 AE Amsterdam, Netherlands. TEL 31-20-4853911. FAX 31-20-4853705. *1298*

CONTRIBUTIONS TO EPIDEMIOLOGY AND BIOSTATISTICS.
S. Karger AG, Allschwilerstr. 10, P.O. Box, CH-4009 Basel, Switzerland. TEL 41-61-3061111. FAX 41-61-3061234. *6231*

CONTRIBUTIONS TO GYNECOLOGY AND OBSTETRICS.
S. Karger AG, Allschwilerstr. 10, P.O. Box, CH-4009 Basel, Switzerland. TEL 41-61-3061111. FAX 41-61-3061234. *4955*

CONTRIBUTIONS TO MICROBIOLOGY.
S. Karger AG, Allschwilerstr. 10, P.O. Box, CH-4009 Basel, Switzerland. TEL 41-61-3061111. FAX 41-61-3061234. *4793*

CONTRIBUTIONS TO MINERALOGY AND PETROLOGY.
Springer-Verlag, Heidelberger Platz 3, 14197 Berlin, Germany. TEL 49-30-82787-0. FAX 49-30-82787448. *2336*

CONTRIBUTIONS TO MUSIC EDUCATION.
Ohio Music Education Association, Hugh A. Glauser School of Music, Kent State University, Kent, OH 44242-0001. TEL 330-672-2397. *5386*

CONTRIBUTIONS TO NEPALESE STUDIES.
Tribhuvan University, Research Centre for Nepal and Asian Studies, Kirtipur, Nepal. TEL 977-1-231740. FAX 977-1-227184. *3532*

CONTRIBUTIONS TO NEPHROLOGY.
S. Karger AG, Allschwilerstr. 10, P.O. Box, CH-4009 Basel, Switzerland. TEL 41-61-3061111. FAX 41-61-3061234. *5160*

CONTRIBUTIONS TO ONCOLOGY.
S. Karger AG, Allschwilerstr. 10, CH-4009 Basel, Switzerland. TEL 41-61-3061111. FAX 41-61-3061234. *4976*

CONTRIBUTIONS TO PHENOMENOLOGY.
Kluwer Academic Publishers, Postbus 17, 3300 AA Dordrecht, Netherlands. TEL 31-78-6392392. FAX 31-78-6392254. *5722*

CONTRIBUTIONS TO THE HISTORY OF LABOR AND SOCIETY.
E.J. Brill, P.O. Box 9000, 2300 PA Leiden, Netherlands. TEL 31-71-5353500. FAX 31-71-5317532. *3888*

CONTRIBUTIONS TO THE SOCIOLOGY OF JEWISH LANGUAGES.
E.J. Brill, P.O. Box 9000, 2300 PA Leiden, Netherlands. TEL 31-71-5353500. FAX 31-71-5317532. *4250*

CONTRIBUTIONS TO ZOOLOGY.
Universiteit van Amsterdam, Commissie voor de Artis Bibliotheek, Plantage Middenlaan 45A, 1018 DC Amsterdam, Netherlands. *831*

CONTROL.
Institute of Operations Management, University of Warwick Science Park, Sir William Lyons Rd., Coventry, Warks. CV4 7EZ, England. TEL 44-1203-692266. FAX 44-1203-692305. *1471*

CONTROL AND COMPUTERS.
International Association of Science and Technology for Development, 4500 16th Ave., N.W., Ste. 80, Calgary, AB T3B 0M6, Canada. TEL 403-288-1195. FAX 403-247-6851. *2108*

CONTROL AND CYBERNETICS.
Polish Academy of Sciences, Systems Research Institute, Ul. Newelska 6, 01-447 Warsaw, Poland. TEL 48-22-364103. FAX 48-22-372772. *2160*

CONTROL ENGINEERING PRACTICE.
Elsevier Science Ltd., Pergamon, P.O. Box 800, Kidlington, Oxford OX5 1DX, England. TEL 44-1865-843000. FAX 44-1865-843010. *2804*

CONTROLLED CLINICAL TRIALS.
Elsevier Science Inc., Box 945, New York, NY 10159-0945. TEL 212-633-3730. FAX 212-633-3680. *4896*

CONTROLLED RELEASE SERIES.
Elsevier Science B.V., Books Division, P.O. Box 211, 1000 AE Amsterdam, Netherlands. TEL 31-20-4853911. FAX 31-20-4853705. *1814*

CONTROVERSIES IN CLINICAL OPHTHALMOLOGY.
Field & Wood, Medical Periodicals, Inc., Box 975, Blue Bell, PA 19422. TEL 610-828-4010. FAX 610-482-0226. *4992*

CONVERGENCE.
International Council for Adult Education, 720 Bathurst St., Ste. 500, Toronto, ON M5S 2R4, Canada. TEL 416-588-1211. FAX 416-588-5725. *2508*

COOPERATION AND CONFLICT.
Sage Publications Ltd., 6 Bonhill St., London EC2A 4PU, England. TEL 44-171-374-0645. FAX 44-171-374-8741. *6010*

COOPERATIVES ET DEVELOPPEMENT.
Centre Interuniversitaire de Recherche d'Information et d'Enseignement sur les Cooperatives, 5255 av. Decelles, Montreal, PQ H3T 1V6, Canada. TEL 514-340-6016. FAX 514-340-6995. *1205*

COORDINATION CHEMISTRY REVIEWS.
Elsevier Science S.A., P.O. Box 564, CH-1001 Lausanne 1, Switzerland. TEL 41-21-3207381. FAX 41-21-3235444. *1747*

COPEIA.
American Society of Ichthyologists and Herpetologists, c/o Dean A. Hendrickson, Sec., A S I H - Texas Natural History Collection, University of Texas - R4000, Austin, TX 78712-1100. TEL 512-471-0998. FAX 512-471-8775. *831*

COR ET VASA.
Praha Publishing Ltd., Anglicka 19, 120 00 Prague 2, Czech Republic. TEL 42-2-66312615. FAX 42-2-24247568. *4814*

CORAX.
Zum Brook 16, 24238 Bauersdorf, Germany. TEL 49-4384-1537. *802*

CORELLA.
Australian Bird Study Association, P.O. Box A313, S. Sydney, N.S.W. 1235, Australia. TEL 61-2-92318166. FAX 61-2-92517231. *802*

LE CORMORAN.
Groupe Ornithologique Normand, Universite de Caen, 14032 Caen Cedex, France. TEL 31 43 52 56. FAX 31-93-27-07. *802*

CORNEA.
Lippincott - Raven Publishers, 227 E. Washington Sq., Philadelphia, PA 19106. TEL 215-238-4200. FAX 215-238-4227. *4992*

CORNELL BIENNIAL ELECTRICAL ENGINEERING CONFERENCE.
Cornell University, School of Electrical Engineering, Phillips Hall, Ithaca, NY 14853. *2812*

CORNELL DAILY SUN.
Cornell Daily Sun, Inc., 119 S. Cayuga St., Ithaca, NY 14850. TEL 607-273-3606. FAX 607-273-0746. *1947*

CORNELL EAST ASIA SERIES.
Cornell University, East Asia Program, 140 Uris Hall, Ithaca, NY 14853-7601. TEL 607-255-6222. FAX 607-255-1388. *5525*

THE CORNELL HOTEL & RESTAURANT ADMINISTRATION QUARTERLY.
Elsevier Science Inc., Box 945, New York, NY 10159-0945. TEL 212-633-3730. FAX 212-633-3680. *3724*

CORNELL LINGUISTIC CONTRIBUTIONS.
E.J. Brill, P.O. Box 9000, 2300 PA Leiden, Netherlands. TEL 31-71-5353500. FAX 31-71-5317532. *4250*

CORNELL MODERN INDONESIA PROJECT PUBLICATIONS.
Cornell University, Cornell Modern Indonesia Project, 640 Stewart Ave., Ithaca, NY 14850. TEL 607-255-4359. FAX 607-277-1904. *5525*

CORNELL PHONETICS LABORATORY. WORKING PAPERS.
C L C Publications, Cornell University, Department of Linguistics, 227 Morill Hall, Ithaca, NY 14853. TEL 607-255-1105. FAX 607-255-2044. *4250*

CORNELL WORKING PAPERS IN LINGUISTICS.
C L C Publications, Cornell University, Department of Linguistics, 227 Morill Hall, Ithaca, NY 14853-4701. TEL 607-255-1105. FAX 607-255-2044. *4250*

CORNISH ARCHAEOLOGY.
Cornwall Archaeological Society, c/o Royal Institution of Cornwall, River St., Truro, Cornwall, England. *359*

CORONARY ARTERY DISEASE.
Thomson Science, 2-6 Boundary Row, London SE1 8HN, England. TEL 44-171-410-6600. FAX 44-171-865-0198. *4767*

CORPORATE AND BUSINESS LAW JOURNAL.
Adelaide Law Review Association, c/o Department of Law, University of Adelaide, Adelaide, S.A. 5005, Australia. TEL 61-8-303-4440. FAX 61-8-303-4344. *4078*

CORPORATE GOVERNANCE.
Blackwell Publishers Ltd., 108 Cowley Rd., Oxford OX4 1JF, England. TEL 44-1865-791100. FAX 44-1865-791347. *951*

CORPORATE REPUTATION REVIEW.
Henry Stewart Publications, Russell House, 28-30 Little Russell St., London WC1A 2HN, England. TEL 44-171-404-3040. *1471*

CORRECTIVE AND SOCIAL PSYCHIATRY AND JOURNAL OF BEHAVIORAL TECHNOLOGY METHODS AND THERAPY.
Martin Psychiatric Research Foundation, Box 3365, Fairfield, CA 94533-0587. FAX 7078640910. *6105*

CORRELATION.
Astrological Association of Great Britain, 396 Caledonian Rd., London N1 1DN, England. TEL 44-171-700-3746. FAX 44-171-700-6479. *486*

IL CORRIERE DEI CIECHI.
Unione Italiana Ciechi, Via Borgognona 38, 00187 Rome, Italy. TEL 39-6-69988375. FAX 39-6-6786815. *3469*

CORROSION.
N A C E International, Box 218340, Houston, TX 77218. TEL 713-492-0535. FAX 713-492-8254. *2881*

CORROSION ABSTRACTS.
N A C E International, Box 218340, Houston, TX 77218. TEL 713-492-0535. FAX 713-492-8254. *2748*

CORROSION MANAGEMENT.
Impact Company Publications, Media House, 55 Old Rd., Leighton Buzzard, Beds. LU7 7RB, England. TEL 44-1525-370013. FAX 44-1525-382487. *2857*

CORROSION SCIENCE.
Elsevier Science Ltd., Pergamon, P.O. Box 800, Kidlington, Oxford OX5 1DX, England. TEL 44-1865-843000. FAX 44-1865-843010. *5189*

COSMETIC SCIENCE AND TECHNOLOGY SERIES.
Marcel Dekker, Inc., 270 Madison Ave., New York, NY 10016. TEL 212-696-9000. FAX 212-685-4540. *4658*

COSMIC RESEARCH.
Maik Nauka - Interperiodica, Mezhdunarodnyi Otdel, Ul. Profsoyuznaya 90, Moscow 117864, Russia. TEL 7-95-3360066. FAX 7-95-3660666. *62*

COSMOS.
Cosmos Club, 2121 Massachusetts Ave., N.W., Washington, DC 20008. TEL 202-387-7783. FAX 202-234-6817. *6609*

COSTA RICA. ARCHIVO NACIONAL. REVISTA.
Archivo Nacional, Apartado 10217, 1000 San Jose, Costa Rica. TEL 506-2347925. FAX 506-2347312. *3492*

COUNCIL FOR RESEARCH IN MUSIC EDUCATION. BULLETIN.
University of Illinois at Urbana-Champaign, School of Music, 1114 W. Nevada, Urbana, IL 61801. TEL 217-333-1027. FAX 217-244-4585. *5386*

COUNCIL ON UNDERGRADUATE RESEARCH QUARTERLY.
Council on Undergraduate Research, University of North Carolina, Asheville, NC 28804. TEL 704-251-6006. FAX 704-251-6002. *2538*

COUNSELLING.
British Association for Counselling, 1 Regent Pl., Rugby, Warks. CV21 2PJ, England. TEL 01788-550899. FAX 01788-562189. *6105*

COUNSELLING PSYCHOLOGY QUARTERLY.
Carfax Publishing Co., P.O. Box 25, Abingdon, Oxon. OX14 3UE, England. TEL 44-1235-401000. FAX 44-1235-401550. *6105*

THE COUNSELOR (ARLINGTON).
National Association of Alcoholism and Drug Abuse Counselors, 1911 Fort Myer Dr., Ste. 900, Arlington, VA 22209-1603. TEL 703-741-7686. FAX 703-741-7648. *2300*

COUNSELOR PREPARATION (YEARS).
Accelerated Development, 1900 Frost Rd., Ste. 101, Bristol, PA 19007-1598. TEL 215-785-5800. FAX 215-785-5515. *2431*

COUNTERPOISE.
American Library Association, Social Responsibilities Round Table, 1716 S.W. Williston Rd., Gainesville, FL 32608-4049. TEL 352-335-2200. *4329*

COUNTRY STYLE HOMES, PLANS AND DESIGNS.
HomeStyle Publishing and Marketing Co., 213 E. 4th St., St. Paul, MN 55101. TEL 612-602-5000. FAX 612-602-5001. *400*

COUNTY COMPASS.
National Organization of Black County Officials, 440 First St., N.W., Ste. 500, Washington, DC 20001. TEL 202-347-6953. FAX 202-393-6596. *3007*

COUNTY PROGRESS.
Zachry Associates, 709 N. 2nd St., Abilene, TX 79601. TEL 915-673-4822. FAX 915-677-2631. *6170*

COUP D'OEIL OPHTALMOLOGIQUE.
Editions et Regarde Attentivement, 68 bd. des Poilus, 44300 Nantes, France. TEL 40-68-96-06. FAX 40-68-98-76. *4992*

THE COURIER (BROCKTON).
Courier Publishing Co. (Brockton), Box 1878, Brockton, MA 02403. TEL 508-587-0975. *3666*

COVERED WAGON.
Shasta Historical Society, Box 990277, Redding, CA 96099-0277. TEL 916-243-3720. *3624*

COWBOY ARTISTS OF AMERICA NEWSLETTER.
Cowboy Artists of America Museum, 1550 Bandera Hwy., Box 1716, Kerrville, TX 78029. TEL 210-896-2553. FAX 210-896-2556. *5353*

THE COWRY NEW SERIES.
Jiri Zidek, Ed. & Pub., Box 95, Socorro, NM 87801. *831*

CRANIO: JOURNAL OF CRANIOMANDIBULAR PRACTICE.
Chroma Inc., Box 8887, Chatanooga, TN 37414. TEL 800-624-4141. FAX 615-490-0791. *4658*

CRAZYHORSE.
Crazyhorse Association, Department of English, University of Arkansas at Little Rock, 2801 S. University, Little Rock, AR 72204. TEL 501-569-3161. *4394*

CREATION - EVOLUTION.
National Center for Science Education, Box 9477, Berkeley, CA 94709-0477. TEL 510-526-1674. FAX 510-526-1675. *6521*

CREATION RESEARCH SOCIETY QUARTERLY.
Creation Research Society, Box 8263, St. Joseph, MO 64508-8263. *6521*

CREATIVE NONFICTION.
5501 Walnut St., Ste. 202, Pittsburgh, PA 15232. TEL 412-688-0304. FAX 412-683-9173. *4394*

CREATIVE NURSING.
Creative Nursing Management, Inc., Box 8286, Minneapolis, MN 55408. TEL 612-823-0637. FAX 612-339-2065. *4932*

CREATIVE REAL ESTATE MAGAZINE.
Professional Publishers, Inc., Drawer L, Rancho Santa Fe, CA 92067. TEL 619-756-1441. FAX 619-756-1111. *6299*

CREATIVITY AND INNOVATION MANAGEMENT.
Blackwell Publishers Ltd., 108 Cowley Rd., Oxford OX4 1JF, England. TEL 44-1865-791100. FAX 44-1865-791347. *952*

CREDIT CONTROL.
House of Words Ltd., 7 Greding Walk, Hutton, Brentwood, Essex CM13 2UF, England. TEL 44-1277-225402. FAX 44-1277-201554. *1125*

CRIME AND JUSTICE.
University of Chicago Press, Journals Division, 5720 S. Woodlawn Ave., Chicago, IL 60637. TEL 773-702-7600. FAX 773-702-0172. *2264*

CRIME LABORATORY DIGEST.
U.S. Federal Bureau of Investigation Laboratory, FSRTC, F B I Academy, Quantico, VA 22135. TEL 703-640-1531. *4903*

CRIME, LAW AND SOCIAL CHANGE.
Kluwer Academic Publishers, Postbus 17, 3300 AA Dordrecht, Netherlands. TEL 31-78-6392392. FAX 31-78-6392254. *2265*

CRIMINAL BEHAVIOUR AND MENTAL HEALTH.
Whurr Publishers Ltd., 19b Compton Terrace, London N1 2UN, England. TEL 44-171-359-5979. FAX 44-171-226-5290. *5060*

CRIMINAL JUSTICE (CHICAGO).
A B A Press, 750 N. Lake Shore Dr., Chicago, IL 60611-4497. TEL 312-988-6076. FAX 312-988-6281. *4088*

CRIMINAL JUSTICE ETHICS.
Institute for Criminal Justice Ethics, John Jay College of Criminal Justice, City University of New-York, 899 Tenth Ave., New-York, NY 10019. TEL 212-237-8033. FAX 212-237-8901. *5722*

CRIMINAL LAW BULLETIN.
Warren, Gorham & Lamont, 395 Hudson St., New York, NY 10014. TEL 212-367-6486. FAX 212-367-6718. *4089*

CRIMINAL LAW FORUM.
Rutgers University, School of Law, Camden, 5th & Penn Streets, Camden, NJ 08102. TEL 609-757-6352. FAX 609-757-6487. *4089*

CRIMSON.
Vampire Guild, 82 Rip Croft, Portland, Dorset DT5 2EE, England. TEL 44-1305-822826. *4530*

CRITICA HISPANICA.
Department of Modern Language, Duquesne University, Pittsburgh, PA 15282. TEL 412-396-6415. FAX 412-396-4894. *4394*

CRITICA JURIDICA.
Universidad Nacional Autonoma de Mexico, Instituto de Investigaciones Juridicas, Departamento de Publicaciones, Circuito Mario de la Cueva, Zona Cultural, Ciudad Universitaria, 04510 Mexico, D.F., Mexico. TEL 52-5-6651911. FAX 52-5-6652193. *3936*

CRITICAL ARTS.
Centre for Cultural and Media Studies, University of Natal, King George V Ave., Durban 4001, South Africa. TEL 27-31-2602505. FAX 27-31-2601519. *1987*

CRITICAL CARE MEDICINE.
Williams & Wilkins, 351 W. Camden St., Baltimore, MD 21201-2436. TEL 410-528-4068. FAX 410-528-4452. *4658*

CRITICAL CARE NURSE.
American Association of Critical Care Nurses, 101 Columbia, Aliso Viejo, CA 92656. TEL 714-362-2000. *4932*

CRITICAL CRIMINOLOGY.
Collective Press, 185-9040 Blundell Rd., Ste. 361, Richmond, BC V6Y 1K3, Canada. TEL 604-869-8270. FAX 604-869-7620. *2283*

CRITICAL INQUIRY.
University of Chicago Press, Journals Division, Box 37005, Chicago, IL 60637. TEL 773-753-3347. FAX 773-753-0811. *4330*

CRITICAL ISSUES IN DEVELOPMENTAL & BEHAVIORAL PEDIATRICS.
Plenum Publishing Corp., 233 Spring St., New York, NY 10013-1578. TEL 212-620-8000. FAX 212-463-0742. *6106*

CRITICAL MATRIX.
Princeton University, Program in Women's Studies, 113 Dickinson Hall, Princeton University, Princeton, NJ 08544-1017. TEL 609-258-5430. FAX 609-258-1833. *7342*

CRITICAL PERSPECTIVES ON ACCOUNTING.
Academic Press Ltd., 24-28 Oval Rd., London NW1 7DX, England. TEL 44-171-267-4466. FAX 44-171-482-2293. *1089*

CRITICAL QUARTERLY.
Blackwell Publishers Ltd., 108 Cowley Rd., Oxford OX4 1JF, England. TEL 44-1865-791100. FAX 44-1865-791347. *4394*

CRITICAL REVIEW.
Critical Review Foundation, Inc., Box 1254, Danbury, CT 06813-1254. TEL 203-794-1312. FAX 203-794-1007. *4330*

CRITICAL REVIEW.
James Cook University, P.O. Box 6811, Cairns, Qld. 4870, Australia. TEL 61-70-421051. FAX 61-70-421290. *4394*

CRITICAL REVIEW OF BOOKS IN RELIGION.
Scholars Press, Box 15399, Atlanta, GA 30333-0399. TEL 404-727-2320. FAX 404-727-2345. *6332*

CRITICAL REVIEWS IN ANALYTICAL CHEMISTRY.
C R C Press, Inc., 2000 Corporate Blvd., N.W., Boca Raton, FL 33431. TEL 561-994-0555. FAX 561-998-9784. *1790*

CRITICAL REVIEWS IN BIOCHEMISTRY AND MOLECULAR BIOLOGY.
C R C Press, Inc., 2000 Corporate Blvd., N.W., Boca Raton, FL 33431. TEL 561-994-0555. FAX 561-998-9784. *658*

CRITICAL REVIEWS IN BIOMEDICAL ENGINEERING.
Begell House Inc., 79 Madison Ave., Ste. 1205, New York, NY 10016-7892. TEL 212-725-1999. FAX 212-213-8368. *647*

CRITICAL REVIEWS IN BIOTECHNOLOGY.
C R C Press, Inc., 2000 Corporate Blvd., N.W., Boca Raton, FL 33431. TEL 561-994-0555. FAX 561-998-9784. *682*

CRITICAL REVIEWS IN CLINICAL LABORATORY SCIENCES.
C R C Press, Inc., 2000 Corporate Blvd., N.W., Boca Raton, FL 33431. TEL 561-994-0555. FAX 561-998-9784. *4658*

CRITICAL REVIEWS IN DIAGNOSTIC IMAGING.
C R C Press, Inc., 2000 Corporate Blvd., N.W., Boca Raton, FL 33431. TEL 561-994-0555. FAX 561-998-9784. *5105*

CRITICAL REVIEWS IN ENVIRONMENTAL SCIENCE & TECHNOLOGY.
C R C Press, Inc., 2000 Corporate Blvd., N.W., Boca Raton, FL 33431. TEL 561-994-0555. FAX 561-998-9784. *2967*

CRITICAL REVIEWS IN FISHERIES SCIENCE.
C R C Press, Inc., 2000 Corporate Blvd., N.W., Boca Raton, FL 33431. TEL 561-994-0555. FAX 561-998-9784. *3064*

CRITICAL REVIEWS IN FOOD SCIENCE AND NUTRITION.
C R C Press, Inc., 2000 Corporate Blvd., N.W., Boca Raton, FL 33431. TEL 561-994-0555. FAX 561-998-9784. *3101*

CRITICAL REVIEWS IN IMMUNOLOGY.
Begell House Inc., 79 Madison Ave., Ste. 1205, New York, NY 10016-7892. TEL 212-213-8368. FAX 212-725-1999. *4793*

CRITICAL REVIEWS IN MICROBIOLOGY.
C R C Press, Inc., 2000 Corporate Blvd., N.W., Boca Raton, FL 33431. TEL 561-994-0555. FAX 561-998-9784. *782*

CRITICAL REVIEWS IN ONCOLOGY - HEMATOLOGY.
Elsevier Science Ireland Ltd., P.O. Box 85, Limerick, Ireland. TEL 353-61-471944. FAX 353-61-472144. *4976*

CRITICAL REVIEWS IN PLANT SCIENCES.
C R C Press, Inc., 2000 Corporate Blvd., N.W., Boca Raton, FL 33431. TEL 561-994-0555. FAX 561-998-9784. *220*

CRITICAL REVIEWS IN SOLID STATE & MATERIALS SCIENCES.
C R C Press, Inc., 2000 Corporate Blvd., N.W., Boca Raton, FL 33431. TEL 561-994-0555. FAX 561-998-9784. *5800*

CRITICAL REVIEWS IN TOXICOLOGY.
C R C Press, Inc., 2000 Corporate Blvd., N.W., Boca Raton, FL 33431. TEL 561-994-0555. FAX 561-998-9784. *2976*

CRITICAL STUDIES.
Editions Rodopi B.V., Keizersgracht 302-304, 1016 EX Amsterdam, Netherlands. TEL 31-20-6227507. FAX 31-20-6380948. *4394*

CRITICAL STUDIES IN MASS COMMUNICATION.
Speech Communication Association, 5105 Backlick Rd., Bldg. E., Annandale, VA 22003. TEL 703-750-0533. FAX 703-914-9471. *1987*

CRITIQUE OF ANTHROPOLOGY.
Sage Publications Ltd., 6 Bonhill St., London EC2A 4PU, England. TEL 44-171-374-0645. FAX 44-171-374-8741. *313*

CRITIQUE: STUDIES IN MODERN FICTION.
Heldref Publications, 1319 Eighteenth St., N.W., Washington, DC 20036-1802. TEL 202-296-6267. FAX 202-296-5149. *4395*

CROATIAN MEDICAL JOURNAL.
Pabst Science Publishers, Am Eichengrund 28, 49525 Lengerich, Germany. TEL 49-5484-308. FAX 49-5484-550. *4658*

CRONE CHRONICLES.
Crone Corp., Box 81, Kelly, WY 83011-0081. TEL 307-733-5409. FAX 307-733-8639. *7316*

CROP PROTECTION.
Elsevier Science Ltd., P.O. Box 800, Kidlington, Oxford OX5 1DX, England. TEL 44-1865-843000. FAX 44-1865-843010. *2762*

CROSS-CULTURAL RESEARCH.
Sage Publications, Inc., 2455 Teller Rd., Thousand Oaks, CA 91320. TEL 805-499-0721. FAX 805-499-0871. *6609*

CROSSROADS: AN INTERDISCIPLINARY JOURNAL OF SOUTHEAST ASIAN STUDIES.
Southeast Asia Publications, Northern Illinois University, Center for Southeast Asian Studies, DeKalb, IL 60115. TEL 815-753-1981. FAX 815-753-1651. *3533*

CRUCIFERAE NEWSLETTER.
European Association for Research on Plant Breeding, INRA - Station d'Amelioration des Plantes, B.P. 29, 35650 Le Rheu, France. TEL 99-28-51-00. FAX 99-28-51-20. *110*

CRUSADER (SELINSGROVE).
Susquehanna University, Campus Activities, Box 22, Selinsgrove, PA 17870. TEL 717-372-4298. FAX 717-372-2757. *1948*

CRUSTACEANA.
E.J. Brill, P.O. Box 9000, 2300 PA Leiden, Netherlands. TEL 31-71-5353500. FAX 31-71-5317532. *831*

CRUSTACEANA. SUPPLEMENTS.
E.J. Brill, P.O. Box 9000, 2300 PA Leiden, Netherlands. TEL 31-71-5353500. FAX 31-71-5317532. *831*

CRYO - LETTERS.
7 Wootton Way, Cambridge CB3 9LX, England. TEL 44-1223-504309. FAX 44-1223-504309. *815*

CRYOBIOLOGY.
Academic Press, Inc., Journal Division, 525 B St., Ste. 1900, San Diego, CA 92101-4495. TEL 619-230-1840. FAX 619-699-6800. *674*

CRYOGENICS.
Elsevier Science Ltd., P.O. Box 800, Kidlington, Oxford OX5 1DX, England. TEL 44-1865-843000. FAX 44-1865-843010. *5840*

CRYSTALLOGRAPHY REVIEWS.
Gordon and Breach - Harwood Academic, Amsteldisk 166, 1st Fl., 1079 LH Amsterdam, Netherlands. *1801*

CUADERNOS AMERICANOS.
Universidad Nacional Autonoma de Mexico, Centro Coordinador y Difusor de Estudios Latinoamericanos, Torre I de Humanidades, Piso 2, Ciudad Universitaria, 04510 Mexico, D.F. TEL 52-5-6271902. FAX 52-5-6162515. *4395*

CUADERNOS DE ARAGON.
Institucion Fernando el Catolico, Plaza de Espana 2, 50071 Zaragoza, Spain. TEL 34-976-288878. FAX 34-976-288869. *3561*

CUADERNOS DE BIOESTADISTICA Y SUS APLICACIONES INFORMATICAS.
Universidad de Zaragoza, Facultad de Medicina, Domingo Miral, s-n, 50009 Zaragoza, Spain. TEL 34-76-761703. FAX 34-76-761704. *638*

CUADERNOS DE ECONOMIA.
Pontificia Universidad Catolica de Chile, Instituto de Economia, Casilla 76, Correo 17, Santiago, Chile. TEL 56-2-6864314. FAX 56-2-5521310. *952*

CUADERNOS DE GEOGRAFIA.
Universidad de Valencia, Facultad de Geografia e Historia, Apdo. 22060, 46080 Valencia, Spain. TEL 34-6-3864237. FAX 34-6-3864234. *3399*

CUADERNOS DE GEOLOGIA IBERICA.
Universidad Complutense, Servicio de Publicaciones, Calle Isaac Peral s-n, Ciudad Universitaria, 28040 Madrid, Spain. TEL 34-1-3946934. FAX 34-1-3946954. *2336*

CUADERNOS EUROPEOS DE DEUSTO.
Universidad de Deusto, Instituto de Estudios Europeos, Avda. de las Universidades, 24, 48080 Bilbao, Spain. TEL 34-4-4139012. FAX 34-4-4139284. *3776*

CUBA. MINISTERIO DE LA INDUSTRIA LIGERA. REVISTA CIENCIA Y TECNICA.
Ministerio de la Industria Ligera, Empedrado 302, esq. a Aguiar, Havana 10100, Cuba. TEL 357-60-3111. *6521*

CUIHUA XUEBAO.
Science Press, Marketing and Sales Department, 16 Donghuangchenggen North St., Beijing 100717, People's Republic of China. TEL 4010642. FAX 4019810. *1807*

CULTIVOS TROPICALES.
Instituto Nacional de Ciencias Agricolas, Gaveta Postal No. 1, San Jose de las Lajas, Havana 32700, Cuba. TEL 537-64-63290. FAX 537-64-63867. *221*

CULTURA Y EDUCACION.
Fundacion Infancia y Aprendizaje, Crta. de Canillas, 138, 28043 Madrid, Spain. TEL 34-1-3883874. FAX 34-1-3003527. *4251*

CULTURAL DIVERSITY AND MENTAL HEALTH.
John Wiley & Sons, Inc., Journals, 605 Third Ave., New York, NY 10158. TEL 212-850-6645. FAX 212-850-6021. *6707*

CULTURAL DYNAMICS.
Sage Publications Ltd., 6 Bonhill St., London EC2A 4PU, England. TEL 44-171-374-0645. FAX 44-171-374-8741. *5723*

CULTURAL PERSPECTIVES ON THE AMERICAN SOUTH.
Gordon and Breach - Harwood Academic, Amsteldisk 166, 1st Fl., 1079 LH Amsterdam, Netherlands. *3624*

CULTURAL TRENDS.
Carfax Publishing Co., P.O. Box 25, Abingdon, Oxon. OX14 3UE, England. TEL 44-1235-401000. FAX 44-1235-401550. *437*

CULTURE, ILLNESS AND HEALING.
Kluwer Academic Publishers, Postbus 17, 3300 AA Dordrecht, Netherlands. TEL 31-78-6392392. FAX 31-78-6392254. *314*

CULTURE, MEDICINE AND PSYCHIATRY.
Kluwer Academic Publishers, Postbus 17, 3300 AA Dordrecht, Netherlands. TEL 31-78-6392392. FAX 31-78-6392254. *314*

CULTURES, BELIEFS, AND TRADITIONS.
E.J. Brill, P.O. Box 9000, 2300 PA Leiden, Netherlands. TEL 31-71-5353500. FAX 31-71-5317532. *6333*

CUORE.
Casa Editrice Scientifica Internazionale Periodici s.a.s., Via Cremona 19, 00161 Rome, Italy. TEL 39-6-44290783. FAX 39-6-44241-598. *4815*

CURIO.
Curio Magazine, Inc., 81 Pondfield Rd., Ste. 264, Bronxville, NY 10708. TEL 914-961-8649. FAX 914-779-4033. *4331*

CURRENT (KENOSHA).
Carthage College, Kenosha, WI 53141. TEL 414-551-6150. *1948*

CURRENT (PACIFIC GROVE).
National Marine Education Association, Box 51215, Pacific Grove, CA 93950. TEL 408-648-4841. FAX 408-648-7960. *597*

CURRENT (WASHINGTON, 1960).
Heldref Publications, 1319 18th St., N.W., Washington, DC 20036-1802. TEL 202-296-6267. FAX 202-296-5149. *2431*

CURRENT AGRICULTURAL RESEARCH.
Association of Agricultural Scientists, College of Agriculture Bldg., O.U.A.T., Bhubaneswar 751003, India. *111*

CURRENT ANTHROPOLOGY.
University of Chicago Press, Journals Division, Box 37005, Chicago, IL 60637. TEL 773-753-3347. FAX 773-753-0811. *314*

CURRENT AWARENESS PROFILE ON QUANTUM CHEMISTRY.
Indiana University, QCPE, Creative Arts 181, Bloomington, IN 47405. TEL 812-855-4784. FAX 812-855-5539. *1747*

CURRENT BIOLOGY.
Current Biology Ltd., 800 Market St., Ste. 700, Philadelphia, PA 19106. TEL 800-552-5866. FAX 215-574-2270. *639*

CURRENT CLINICAL PRACTICE.
Elsevier Science B.V., Books Division, P.O. Box 211, 1000 AE Amsterdam, Netherlands. TEL 31-20-4853911. FAX 31-20-4853705. *4659*

CURRENT ENDOCRINOLOGY.
Elsevier Science B.V., Books Division, P.O. Box 211, 1000 AE Amsterdam, Netherlands. TEL 31-20-4853911. FAX 31-20-4853705. *4883*

CURRENT HISTOPATHOLOGY.
Kluwer Academic Publishers, Postbus 17, 3300 AA Dordrecht, Netherlands. TEL 31-78-6392392. FAX 31-78-6392254. *4924*

CURRENT ISSUES IN CRIMINAL JUSTICE.
University of Sydney, Institute of Criminology, Faculty of Law, 173-175 Phillip St., Sydney, N.S.W. 2000, Australia. TEL 61-2-93510239. FAX 61-2-93510200. *2266*

CURRENT ISSUES IN MIDDLE LEVEL EDUCATION.
State University of West Georgia, College of Education, Carrollton, GA 30118. TEL 770-836-6560. FAX 770-836-4643. *2431*

CURRENT ISSUES IN PRODUCTION ECOLOGY.
Kluwer Academic Publishers, Postbus 17, 3300 AA Dordrecht, Netherlands. TEL 31-78-6392392. FAX 31-78-6392254. *6957*

CURRENT MAMMALOGY.
Plenum Publishing Corp., 233 Spring St., New York, NY 10013-1578. TEL 212-620-8000. FAX 212-463-0742. *831*

CURRENT MANAGEMENT OF PAIN.
Kluwer Academic Publishers, Postbus 17, 3300 AA Dordrecht, Netherlands. TEL 31-78-6392392. FAX 31-78-6392254. *5060*

CURRENT MEDICAL RESEARCH AND OPINION.
Librapharm Ltd., Gemini House, 162 Craven Rd., Newbury, Berks RG14 5NR, England. TEL 44-1635-522651. FAX 44-1635-522651. *4659*

CURRENT MEDICINAL CHEMISTRY.
Bentham Science Publishers, 7436 S.W. 117 Ave., Box 130, Miami, FL 33183. FAX 305-596-5120. *1747*

CURRENT MICROBIOLOGY.
Springer-Verlag, Life Science Journals, 175 Fifth Ave., New York, NY 10010. TEL 212-460-1500. FAX 212-473-6272. *782*

CURRENT ONCOLOGY (TORONTO).
Multimed Inc., 1120 Finch Ave. W., Ste. 601, Toronto, ON M3J 3H7, Canada. TEL 416-650-0610. FAX 416-650-0639. *4976*

CURRENT ORGANIC CHEMISTRY.
Bentham Science Publishers, 7436 S.W. 117 Ave., Box 130, Miami, FL 33183. FAX 305-596-5120. *1814*

CURRENT ORNITHOLOGY.
Plenum Publishing Corp., 233 Spring St., New York, NY 10013-1578. TEL 212-620-8000. FAX 212-463-0742. *802*

CURRENT PHARMACEUTICAL DESIGN.
Bentham Science Publishers, 7436 S.W. 117 Ave., Box 130, Miami, FL 33183. FAX 305-596-5120. *5654*

CURRENT PHYSICS - SOURCES AND COMMENTS.
Elsevier Science B.V., Books Division, P.O. Box 211, 1000 AE Amsterdam, Netherlands. TEL 31-20-4853911. FAX 31-20-4853705. *5800*

CURRENT PLANT SCIENCE AND BIOTECHNOLOGY IN AGRICULTURE.
Kluwer Academic Publishers, Postbus 17, 3300 AA Dordrecht, Netherlands. TEL 31-78-6392392. FAX 31-78-6392254. *682*

CURRENT PROBLEMS IN DERMATOLOGY.
S. Karger AG, Allschwilerstr. 10, P.O. Box, CH-4009 Basel, Switzerland. TEL 41-61-3061111. FAX 41-61-3061234. *4876*

CURRENT PROBLEMS IN PHARMACOVIGILANCE.
Department of Health, Medicines Control Agency, Market Towers, Rm. 1023, 1 Nine Elms Ln., London SW8 5NQ, England. TEL 0171-273-0254. FAX 44-171-273-0269. *6231*

CURRENT PSYCHOLOGY (NEW BRUNSWICK).
Transaction Publishers, Transaction Periodicals Consortium, Department 3092, Rutgers University, New Brunswick, NJ 08903. TEL 908-445-2280. FAX 908-445-3138. *6106*

CURRENT RESEARCH IN THE PLEISTOCENE.
Oregon State University, Center for the Study of First Americans, Weniger 355, Corvalis, OR 97331-6510. TEL 541-737-4595. *359*

CURRENT STATUS OF CLINICAL CARDIOLOGY.
Kluwer Academic Publishers, Postbus 17, 3300 AA Dordrecht, Netherlands. TEL 31-78-6392392. FAX 31-78-6392254. *4815*

CURRENT STUDIES IN HEMATOLOGY AND BLOOD TRANSFUSION.
S. Karger AG, Allschwilerstr. 10, P.O. Box, CH-4009 Basel, Switzerland. TEL 41-61-3061111. FAX 41-61-3061234. *4918*

CURRENT STUDIES IN LIBRARIANSHIP.
Clarion University, Department of Library Science, Clarion, PA 16214. TEL 814-226-2343. FAX 814-226-1862. *4173*

CURRENT SURGERY.
Williams & Wilkins, 351 W. Camden St., Baltimore, MD 21201-2436. TEL 410-528-4068. FAX 410-528-4452. *5140*

CURRENT THERAPEUTIC RESEARCH.
Excerpta Medica, Inc., 105 Raider Blvd., Belle Mead, NJ 08502-1510. TEL 908-874-8550. FAX 908-874-3250. *4659*

CURRENT TOPICS IN BIOENERGETICS.
Academic Press, Inc., 525 B St., Ste. 1900, San Diego, CA 92101-4495. TEL 619-231-0926. FAX 619-699-6715. *674*

CURRENT TOPICS IN CARDIOLOGY.
Elsevier Science B.V., Books Division, P.O. Box 211, 1000 AE Amsterdam, Netherlands. TEL 31-20-4853911. FAX 31-20-4853705. *4815*

CURRENT TOPICS IN CELLULAR REGULATION.
Academic Press, Inc., 525 B St., Ste. 1900, San Diego, CA 92101-4495. TEL 619-231-0926. FAX 619-699-6715. *597*

CURRENT TOPICS IN CHINESE SCIENCE. SECTION A: PHYSICS.
Gordon and Breach - Harwood Academic, Amsteldisk 166, 1st Fl., 1079 LH Amsterdam, Netherlands. *5800*

CURRENT TOPICS IN CHINESE SCIENCE. SECTION B: CHEMISTRY.
Gordon and Breach - Harwood Academic, Amsteldisk 166, 1st Fl., 1079 LH Amsterdam, Netherlands. *1747*

CURRENT TOPICS IN CHINESE SCIENCE. SECTION C: MATHEMATICS.
Gordon and Breach - Harwood Academic, Amsteldisk 166, 1st Fl., 1079 LH Amsterdam, Netherlands. *4569*

CURRENT TOPICS IN CHINESE SCIENCE. SECTION D: BIOLOGY.
Gordon and Breach - Harwood Academic, Amsteldisk 166, 1st Fl., 1079 LH Amsterdam, Netherlands. *597*

CURRENT TOPICS IN CHINESE SCIENCE. SECTION E: ASTRONOMY.
Gordon and Breach - Harwood Academic, Amsteldisk 166, 1st Fl., 1079 LH Amsterdam, Netherlands. *493*

CURRENT TOPICS IN CHINESE SCIENCE. SECTION F: EARTH SCIENCE.
Gordon & Breach Science Publishers, c/o International Publishers Distributor, P.O. Box 3054, Langhorne, PA 19047-3054. TEL 215-750-2642. FAX 215-750-6343. *2312*

CURRENT TOPICS IN CHINESE SCIENCE. SECTION G: MEDICAL SCIENCE.
Gordon and Breach - Harwood Academic, Amsteldisk 166, 1st Fl., 1079 LH Amsterdam, Netherlands. *4659*

CURRENT TOPICS IN DEVELOPMENTAL BIOLOGY.
Academic Press, Inc., 525 B St., Ste. 1900, San Diego, CA 92101-4495. TEL 619-231-0926. FAX 619-699-6715. *597*

CURRENT TOPICS IN ENVIRONMENTAL AND TOXICOLOGICAL CHEMISTRY.
Gordon and Breach - Harwood Academic, Amsteldisk 166, 1st Fl., 1079 LH Amsterdam, Netherlands. *2976*

CURRENT TOPICS IN GENERAL THORACIC SURGERY.
Elsevier Science B.V., Books Division, P.O. Box 211, 1000 AE Amsterdam, Netherlands. TEL 31-20-4853911. FAX 31-20-4853705. *5140*

CURRENT TOPICS IN MATERIALS SCIENCE.
Elsevier Science B.V., Books Division, P.O. Box 211, 1000 AE Amsterdam, Netherlands. TEL 31-20-4853911. FAX 31-20-4853705. *5801*

CURRENT TOPICS IN MEMBRANES AND TRANSPORT.
Academic Press, Inc., 525 B St., Ste. 1900, San Diego, CA 92101-4495. TEL 619-231-0926. FAX 619-699-6715. *739*

CURRENT TOPICS IN NUTRITION AND DISEASE.
John Wiley & Sons, Inc., Journals, 605 Third Ave., New York, NY 10158. TEL 212-475-7700. *5471*

CURRENT TOPICS IN OBSTETRICS & GYNAECOLOGY.
Elsevier Science B.V., Books Division, P.O. Box 211, 1000 AE Amsterdam, Netherlands. TEL 31-20-4853911. FAX 31-20-4853705. *4956*

CURRENT TOPICS IN PULMONARY PHARMACOLOGY AND TOXICOLOGY.
Elsevier Science B.V., Books Division, P.O. Box 211, 1000 AE Amsterdam, Netherlands. TEL 31-20-4853911. FAX 31-20-4853705. *5655*

REFEREED SERIALS

CURRENT TOPICS IN REMOTE SENSING.
Gordon and Breach - Harwood Academic, Amsteldisk 166, 1st Fl., 1079 LH Amsterdam, Netherlands. *3399*

CURRENT TOPICS IN VETERINARY MEDICINE AND ANIMAL SCIENCE.
Kluwer Academic Publishers, Postbus 17, 3300 AA Dordrecht, Netherlands. TEL 31-78-6392392. FAX 31-78-6392254. *7268*

CURRENTS IN EMERGENCY CARDIAC CARE.
American Heart Association, Citizen CPR Foundation, 7272 Greenville Ave., Dallas, TX 75231-4596. TEL 214-706-1310. FAX 214-373-3461. *4815*

CURRICULUM AND TEACHING.
James Nicholas Publishers, P.O. Box 244, Albert Park, Vic. 3206, Australia. TEL 61-3-696-5545. FAX 61-3-699-2040. *2599*

CURRICULUM INQUIRY.
Blackwell Publishers, 238 Main St., Cambridge, MA 02142. TEL 617-547-7110. FAX 617-547-0789. *2599*

CURRICULUM STUDIES.
Triangle Journals Ltd., P.O. Box 65, Wallingford, Oxon. OX10 OYG, England. TEL 44-1491-838013. FAX 44-1491-834968. *2600*

CURSUS.
Universite de Montreal, Ecole de Bibliotheconomie et des Sciences de l'Information, C.P. 6128, succ. Centre Ville, Montreal PQ H3C 3J7, Canada. *4173*

CURTIN UNIVERSITY. SCHOOL OF ENVIRONMENTAL BIOLOGY. BULLETIN.
Curtin University, School of Environmental Biology, Bentley, W.A., Australia. TEL 61-9-3517964. FAX 61-9-3512495. *597*

CURTIS'S BOTANICAL MAGAZINE.
Blackwell Publishers Ltd., 108 Cowley Rd., Oxford OX4 1JF, England. TEL 44-1865-791100. FAX 44-1865-791347. *3186*

CUSTOMER SERVICE.
International Customer Service Association, 401 N. Michigan Ave., Chicago, IL 60611-4267. TEL 312-321-6800. FAX 312-321-6869. *952*

CUTBANK.
University of Montana, Department of English, Missoula, MT 59812. TEL 406-243-6156. *4507*

CUTIS.
Quadrant HealthCom, 105 Raider Blvd., Belle Mead, NJ 08502-1510. TEL 908-874-0707. FAX 908-874-5611. *4876*

CYBERNETICS AND SYSTEMS (BRISTOL).
Taylor & Francis Inc., 1900 Frost Rd., Ste. 101, Bristol, PA 19007-1598. TEL 215-785-5800. FAX 215-785-5515. *2161*

CYBERNETICS AND SYSTEMS (NEW YORK).
Gordon and Breach - Harwood Academic, Amsteldisk 166, 1st Fl., 1079 LH Amsterdam, Netherlands. *2161*

CYBERNETICS AND SYSTEMS ANALYSIS.
Plenum Publishing Corp., Consultants Bureau, 233 Spring St., New York, NY 10013-1578. TEL 212-620-8468. FAX 212-463-0742. *2161*

CYBIUM.
Societe Francaise d'Ichtyologie, 43 rue Cuvier, 75231 Paris Cedex 05, France. TEL 33-1-40793749. FAX 33-1-40793771. *3064*

CYTOGENETICS AND CELL GENETICS.
S. Karger AG, Allschwilerstr. 10, P.O. Box, CH-4009 Basel, Switzerland. TEL 41-61-3061111. FAX 41-61-3061234. *765*

CYTOKINE AND GROWTH FACTOR REVIEWS.
Elsevier Science Ltd., Pergamon, P.O. Box 800, Kidlington, Oxford OX5 1DX, England. TEL 44-1865-843000. FAX 44-1865-843010. *658*

CYTOKINES.
S. Karger AG, Allschwilerstr. 10, P.O. Box, CH-4009 Basel, Switzerland. TEL 41-61-3061111. FAX 41-61-3061234. *783*

CYTOKINES, CELLULAR AND MOLECULAR THERAPY.
Martin Dunitz Ltd., 7-9 Pratt St., Camden, London NW1 OAE, England. TEL 44-171-4822202. FAX 44-171-2670159. *4794*

CYTOMETRY (NEW YORK).
John Wiley & Sons, Inc., Journals, 605 Third Ave., New York, NY 10158. TEL 212-850-6645. FAX 212-850-6021. *739*

CYTOPATHOLOGY.
Blackwell Science Ltd., Osney Mead, Oxford OX2 OEL, England. TEL 44-1865-206206. FAX 44-1865-721205. *739*

CYTOTECHNOLOGY.
Kluwer Academic Publishers, Postbus 17, 3300 AA Dordrecht, Netherlands. TEL 31-78-6392392. FAX 31-78-6392254. *739*

CZECHOSLOVAK JOURNAL OF PHYSICS.
Plenum Publishing Corp., 233 Spring St., New York, NY 10013-1578. TEL 212-620-8000. FAX 212-463-0742. *5801*

CZECHOSLOVAK MATHEMATICAL JOURNAL.
Plenum Publishing Corp., 233 Spring St., New York, NY 10013-1578. TEL 212-620-8000. FAX 212-463-0742. *4569*

D C A M M REPORT.
Danish Center for Applied Mathematics and Mechanics, Department of Solid Mechanics, Technical University of Denmark, Lyngby, Denmark. *4569*

D M REVIEW.
Powell Publishing, Inc., 617 S. 94th St., West Allis, WI 52314-1222. TEL 414-771-7687. FAX 414-771-8058. *2165*

D N A AND CELL BIOLOGY.
Mary Ann Liebert, Inc. Publishers, 2 Madison Ave., Larchmont, NY 10538. TEL 914-834-3100. FAX 914-834-3688. *658*

D N A SEQUENCE.
Gordon and Breach - Harwood Academic, Amsteldisk 166, 1st Fl., 1079 LH Amsterdam, Netherlands. *766*

D S P & MULTIMEDIA TECHNOLOGY.
Golden Gate Enterprises, Inc., Box 1603, Los Altos, CA 94023. TEL 415-969-6920. FAX 415-969-0222. *2628*

D W P S.
Aston Business School, 11th Fl., S. Wing, Aston University, Aston Triangle, Birmingham B4 7ET, England. *1472*

DADI GOUZAO YU CHENGKUANGXUE.
Science Press, Marketing and Sales Department, 16 Donghuangchenggen North St., Beijing 100717, People's Republic of China. TEL 4010642. FAX 4019810. *2336*

DAILY MISSISSIPPIAN.
Farley Hall, University, MS 38677. TEL 601-232-7118. FAX 601-232-5703. *1948*

DAIMON.
Universidad de Murcia, Servicio de Publicaciones, Santo Cristo 1, 30080 Murcia, Spain. TEL 34-68-363012. FAX 34-68-363414. *5723*

DAIRY, FOOD AND ENVIRONMENTAL SANITATION.
International Association of Milk, Food and Environmental Sanitarians, Inc., 6200 Aurora Ave., Ste. 200 W, Des Moines, IA 50322. TEL 515-276-3344. FAX 515-276-8655. *6231*

DAIRY STATISTICS.
Livestock Improvement Corporation Ltd., Cnr. Ruakura & Morrinsville Rds., Private Bag 3016, Hamilton, New Zealand. TEL 64-7-8560700. FAX 64-7-8562429. *173*

DALHOUSIE UNIVERSITY. SCHOOL OF LIBRARY AND INFORMATION STUDIES. OCCASIONAL PAPERS.
Dalhousie University, School of Library and Information Studies, Halifax, NS B3H 3J5, Canada. TEL 902-494-3656. FAX 902-494-2451. *4173*

DALTON TRANSACTIONS.
The Royal Society of Chemistry, Thomas Graham House, Science Park, Milton Rd., Cambridge CB4 4WF, England. TEL 44-1223-420066. FAX 44-1223-423623. *1807*

DANA-REPORT.
Scandinavian Science Press Ltd., Universiteitsparken 15, 1260 Copenhagen, Denmark. *2401*

DANCE CRITICS ASSOCIATION. NEWSLETTER.
Dance Critics Association, Box 1882, Old Chelsea Sta., New York, NY 10011. TEL 212-343-3584. *2292*

DANCE INTERNATIONAL.
Vancouver Ballet Society, 1415 Barclay St., Vancouver, BC V6G 1J6, Canada. TEL 604-681-1525. FAX 604-681-7732. *2292*

DANDELION ARTS MAGAZINE.
Fern Publications, Casa Alba, 24 Frosty Hollow, E. Hunsbury, Northants. NN4 OSY, England. TEL 44-1604-701730. FAX 44-1604-701730. *4507*

DANG'AN YU JIANSHE.
Jiangsu Sheng Dang'an Ju, Jiangsu Sheng Dang'an Xuehui, 1 Qingdao Lu, Nanjing, Jiangsu 210008, People's Republic of China. TEL 86-25-3301449. *4173*

DANGDAI WAIGUO WENXUE.
Nanjing Daxue, Waiguo Wenxue Yanjiusuo, Hankou Lu, Nanjing 210093, People's Republic of China. TEL 86-25-6637551. FAX 86-25-3325737. *4396*

DANSTIDNINGEN.
Danstidningen i Stockholm Ekonomisk Foerening, P.O. Box 9237, Bergsundsgatan 6, S-102 73 Stockholm, Sweden. TEL 46-8-658-38-18. FAX 46-8-669-01-11. *2293*

DANTE STUDIES.
State University of New York Press, State University Plaza, Albany, NY 12246. TEL 518-472-5000. FAX 518-472-5038. *4396*

DAQI KEXUE.
Science Press, Marketing and Sales Department, 16 Donghuangchenggen North St., Beijing 100717, People's Republic of China. TEL 4010642. FAX 4019810. *5229*

DARGONZINE.
Dargon Project, *4530*

DARWINIANA.
Instituto de Botanica Darwinion, Labarden y del Campo, Casilla de Correo 22, San Isidro 1642, Buenos Aires, Argentina. TEL 742-8534. FAX 541-747-4748. *700*

DATA & KNOWLEDGE ENGINEERING.
North-Holland, P.O. Box 211, 1000 AE Amsterdam, Netherlands. TEL 31-20-4853911. FAX 31-20-4853598. *2080*

DATA HANDLING IN SCIENCE AND TECHNOLOGY.
Elsevier Science B.V., Books Division, P.O. Box 211, 1000 AE Amsterdam, Netherlands. TEL 31-20-4853911. FAX 31-20-4853705. *2165*

DATA SECURITY LETTER.
Trusted Information Systems, Inc., 3060 Rte. 97, Glenwood, MD 21738. TEL 301-854-6889. FAX 301-854-5363. *2149*

DAUGAVA.
Daugava Ltd., Balasta Dambis 3, 1081 Riga, Latvia. TEL 7-132-465-996. *4331*

DAUGHTERS OF THE AMERICAN REVOLUTION MAGAZINE.
National Society of the Daughters of the American Revolution, 1776 D St., N.W., Washington, DC 20006. TEL 202-879-3286. FAX 202-879-3283. *3624*

DAXUE HUAXUE.
Zhongguo Huaxue Xuehui, Daxue Huaxue Bianjibu, Beijing University, Chemistry Bldg., Haidian-qu, Beijing 100871, People's Republic of China. TEL 861-6275-1721. FAX 861-6275-4096. *1747*

DAYLILY JOURNAL.
American Hemerocallis Society, Inc., 2630 Campbell St., Kansas City, MO 64108-2732. TEL 816-227-3384. *3186*

DAZIRAN TANSUO.
Sichuan Kexue Jishu Chubanshe, 3, Yandao Jie, Chengdu, Sichuan 610012, People's Republic of China. TEL 86-28-666-4688. *6521*

DE MONTFORT UNIVERSITY. LEICESTER BUSINESS SCHOOL. OCCASIONAL PAPER.
De Montfort University, Leicester Business School, Scraptcroft, Leicester LE7 9SU, England. TEL 0116-257-7780. FAX 0116-257-7795. *953*

DE REBUS.
Association of Law Societies, P.O. Box 36626, Menlo Park 0102, South Africa. TEL 27-12-3621729. FAX 27-12-3620969. *3938*

DEAD OF NIGHT.
Dead of Night Publications, 916 Shaker Rd., Ste. 228, Longmeadow, MA 01106-2416. *4530*

DEAD SEA DISCOVERIES.
E.J. Brill, P.O. Box 9000, 2300 PA Leiden, Netherlands. TEL 31-71-5353500. FAX 31-71-5317532. *6333*

DEANOTATIONS.
11919 Moss Point Lane, Reston, VA 20194. TEL 703-471-7907. *4507*

DEATH STUDIES.
Taylor & Francis Inc., 1900 Frost Rd., Ste. 101, Bristol, PA 19007-1598. TEL 215-785-5800. FAX 215-785-5515. *6107*

DEBATES EN SOCIOLOGIA.
Pontificia Universidad Catolica del Peru, Fondo Editorial, Apdo. 1761, Lima 32, Peru. TEL 51-14-626390. FAX 51-14-611785. *6707*

DEBATTE.
Carfax Publishing Co., P.O. Box 25, Abingdon, Oxon OX14 3UE, England. TEL 44-1235-401000. FAX 44-1235-401550. *3561*

DECISION.
Postfach 651180, 22371 Hamburg, Germany. FAX 49-40-5604523. *4396*

DECISION SUPPORT SYSTEMS.
North-Holland, P.O. Box 211, 1000 AE Amsterdam, Netherlands. TEL 31-20-4853911. FAX 31-20-4853598. *1473*

DEEP-SEA RESEARCH. PART 1: OCEANOGRAPHIC RESEARCH PAPERS.
Elsevier Science Ltd., Pergamon, P.O. Box 800, Kidlington, Oxford OX5 1DX, England. TEL 44-1865-843000. FAX 44-1865-843010. *2401*

DEEP-SEA RESEARCH. PART 2: TOPICAL STUDIES IN OCEANOGRAPHY.
Elsevier Science Ltd., Pergamon, P.O. Box 800, Kidlington, Oxford OX5 1DX, England. TEL 44-1865-843000. FAX 44-1865-843010. *2402*

DEEP SOUTH GENEALOGICAL QUARTERLY.
Mobile Genealogical Society, Box 6224, Mobile, AL 36660. TEL 334-626-6573. *3219*

DEFENCE SCIENCE JOURNAL.
Defence Scientific Information & Documentation Centre (DESIDOC), Metcalfe House, New Delhi 110 054, India. TEL 011-239975. FAX 011-2919151. *5265*

DEFENSE TRANSPORTATION JOURNAL.
National Defense Transportation Association, 50 South Pickett St., No. 220, Alexandria, VA 22304-3008. TEL 703-751-5011. FAX 703-823-8761. *7026*

DEIR EL-BAHARI.
Polska Akademia Nauk, Zaklad Archeologii Srodziemnomorskiej, Palac Kultury i Nauki, p. 2105, 00-901 Warsaw, Poland. TEL 48-22-6248593. FAX 48-22-6207651. *360*

DEL CONDOMINIUM LIFE.
Del Property Management Inc., 4800 Dufferin St., Downsview, ON M3H 5S9, Canada. TEL 416-736-2552. FAX 416-661-8923. *3844*

DELAWARE HISTORY.
Historical Society of Delaware, 505 Market St., Wilmington, DE 19801. TEL 302-655-7161. FAX 302-655-7844. *3624*

DELAWARE JOURNAL OF CORPORATE LAW.
Widener University, School of Law, Box 7286, Wilmington, DE 19803. TEL 302-477-2145. FAX 302-477-2042. *4079*

DELAWARE MEDICAL JOURNAL.
Medical Society of Delaware, 1925 Lovering Ave., Wilmington, DE 19806-2147. TEL 302-658-7596. FAX 302-658-9669. *4660*

DELAWARE VALLEY RAIL PASSENGER.
Delaware Valley Association of Railroad Passengers, Box 7505, Philadelphia, PA 19010-7505. TEL 215-673-6445. FAX 215-885-7448. *7125*

DELOS.
Harold P. Hanson, Ed. & Pub., 215 Williamson Hall, Gainesville, FL 32611. TEL 352-377-1560. FAX 352-392-0542. *4397*

DELTA BUSINESS REVIEW.
Northeast Louisiana University, Center for Business & Economic Research, Monroe, LA 71209-0101. TEL 318-342-1215. FAX 318-342-1209. *953*

DELTA KAPPA GAMMA BULLETIN.
Delta Kappa Gamma Society International, Box 1589, Austin, TX 78767-1589. TEL 512-478-5748. FAX 512-478-3961. *2538*

DELTA RESEARCH MONOGRAPH.
Massey University, Education Faculty, Palmerston N., New Zealand. FAX 64-6-35505635. *2432*

DELTION BIBLIKON MELETON.
Artos Zoes Publications, 28 Bouboulinas Str., 2nd fl., Athens 106 82, Greece. TEL 30-1-8824-547. *6334*

DEMENTIA AND GERIATRIC COGNITIVE DISORDERS.
S. Karger AG, Allschwilerstr. 10, P.O. Box, CH-4009 Basel, Switzerland. TEL 41-61-3061111. FAX 41-61-3061234. *5061*

DEMOCRACY AND EDUCATION.
Institute for Democracy in Education, Ohio University, College of Education, 313 McCracken Hall, Athens, OH 45701-2979. TEL 614-593-4531. FAX 614-593-0177. *2432*

DEMOCRACY & NATURE.
Aigis Publications, 1449 W. Littleton Blvd., Ste. 200, Littleton, CO 80120. TEL 303-730-6232. FAX 303-798-6568. *2912*

DEMOCRATIZATION.
Frank Cass, Newbury House, 890-900 Eastern Ave., Newbury Park, Ilford, Essex IG2 7HH, England. TEL 44-181-599-8866. FAX 44-181-599-0984. *6011*

DEMOGRAPHIC MONOGRAPHS.
Gordon and Breach - Harwood Academic, Amsteldisk 166, 1st Fl., 1079 LH Amsterdam, Netherlands. *6048*

DEMONSTRATIO MATHEMATICA.
Politechnika Warszawska, Instytut Matematyki, c/o Biblioteka Glowna, Pl. Politechniki 1, 00-661 Warsaw, Poland. TEL 48-22-6607355. *4569*

DEMOS (AMSTERDAM).
Gordon and Breach - Harwood Academic, Amsteldisk 166, 1st Fl., 1079 LH Amsterdam, Netherlands. *3008*

DEN GAMLE BY.
DK-8000 Aarhus C, Denmark. TEL 45-86-12-31-88. FAX 45-86-76-06-87. *5354*

DENRYOKU TO KISHO.
Denryoku Kisho Renrakukai, Nihon Kisho Kyokai, Nanbu Bldg., 2-7 Nishiki-cho, Kanda, Chiyoda-ku, Tokyo 101, Japan. TEL 81-3-3295-1521. FAX 81-3-3295-7835. *5229*

DENTAL COMPUTER NEWSLETTER.
Andent, Inc., 1000 North Ave., Waukegan, IL 60085. TEL 847-223-5077. *4846*

DENTAL HEALTH.
British Dental Hygienists' Association, St. Luke, Maywood, Portsmouth Rd., Camberley, Surrey GU15 1LH, England. TEL 44-1276-677156. FAX 44-1276-671072. *4854*

DENTAL LAB MANAGEMENT TODAY.
Dental Lab Publications, Inc., 731 Main St., No. A2, Monroe, CT 06468. TEL 203-459-2888. FAX 203-459-2889. *4854*

DENTAL MATERIALS.
Academy of Dental Materials, 3302 Gaston Ave., Dallas, TX 75246. TEL 214-828-8378. FAX 214-874-4503. *4855*

DENTAL REVIEW.
MediMedia Asia, 1501 Tung Sun Commercial Centre, 194-200 Lockhart Rd., Wanchai, Hong Kong, People's Republic of China. TEL 852-2511-0765. FAX 852-2507-3817. *4855*

DENTALHYGIENE.
Swiss Dental Hygienists' Association, Oberstadt 8, CH-6204 Sempach-Stadt, Switzerland. TEL 41-41-4627065. FAX 41-41-4627061. *4856*

DENTISTRY TODAY.
Dentistry Today, Inc., 26 Park St., Montclair, NJ 07042. TEL 201-783-3190. FAX 201-783-6835. *4856*

DENTOMAXILLOFACIAL RADIOLOGY.
Stockton Press, Houndmills, Basingstoke, Hants. RG21 6XS, England. TEL 44-1286-351898. FAX 44-1286-328339. *5105*

THE DEPARTMENT CHAIR.
Anker Publishing Company, Inc., 176 Ballville Rd., Box 249, Bolton, MA 01740-0249. TEL 508-779-6190. FAX 508-779-6366. *2570*

DEPRESSION.
John Wiley & Sons, Inc., Journals, 605 Third Ave., New York, NY 10158. TEL 212-850-6645. FAX 212-850-6021. *6107*

DEPRESSION AND ANXIETY.
John Wiley & Sons, Inc., 605 Third Ave., New York, NY 10158. TEL 212-850-6645. *6107*

DEPRESSION AND STRESS.
International Universities Press, Inc., 59 Boston Post Rd., Box 1524, Madison, CT 06443-1524. TEL 203-245-4000. FAX 203-245-0775. *6107*

DERBYSHIRE ARCHAEOLOGICAL JOURNAL.
Derbyshire Archaeological Society, 12 Longbow Close, Stretton, Burton-on-Trent, Derbys. DE13 0XY, England. TEL 01283-530218. *360*

DERECHO.
Pontificia Universidad Catolica del Peru, Fondo Editorial, Apdo. 1761, Lima 32, Peru. TEL 51-14-626390. FAX 5114-611785. *3939*

DERIVATIVES USE, TRADING & REGULATION.
Henry Stewart Publications, Russell House, 28-30 Little Russell St., London WC1A 2HN, England. TEL 44-171-404-3040. FAX 44-171-404-2081. *1382*

DERMATOLOGIA.
Obsidiana Editores, S.A., Czda. de Tlalpan 2365, Col. Ciudad Jardin, 04370 Mexico DF, Mexico. TEL 6899133. *4877*

DERMATOLOGIC SURGERY.
Elsevier Science Inc., Box 945, New York, NY 10159-0945. TEL 212-633-3730. FAX 212-633-3680. *5140*

DERMATOLOGY.
S. Karger AG, Allschwilerstr. 10, P.O. Box, CH-4009 Basel, Switzerland. TEL 41-61-3061111. FAX 41-61-3061234. *4877*

DERMATOLOGY (NEW YORK).
Marcel Dekker, Inc., 270 Madison Ave., New York, NY 10016. TEL 212-696-9000. FAX 212-685-4540. *4877*

DERMATOLOGY NURSING.
Jannetti Publications, Inc., East Holly Ave., Box 56, Pitman, NJ 08071-0056. TEL 609-256-2300. FAX 609-589-7463. *4877*

DESALINATION.
Elsevier Science B.V., P.O. Box 211, 1000 AE Amsterdam, Netherlands. TEL 31-20-4853911. FAX 31-20-4853598. *7290*

DESARROLLO TECNOLOGICO.
Universidad Nacional Autonoma de Mexico, Instituto de Investigaciones en Matematicas Aplicadas y en Sistemas, Apdo. Postal 20-726, Del. V.A. Obregon, 01000 Mexico D.F., Mexico. TEL 622-35-62. FAX 550-00-47. *6957*

DESERT BIGHORN COUNCIL. TRANSACTIONS.
Desert Bighorn Council, c/o Bighorn Institute, 51000 Highway 74, Palm Desert, CA 92260. TEL 702-646-3401. *2228*

DESERT PLANTS.
2120 E. Allen Rd., Tucson, AZ 85719. TEL 520-318-7046. FAX 520-621-1296. *700*

DESIGN AUTOMATION FOR EMBEDDED SYSTEMS.
Kluwer Academic Publishers, Postbus 17, 3300 AA Dordrecht, Netherlands. TEL 31-78-6392392. FAX 31-78-6392254. *2154*

DESIGN DK.
Dansk Design Center, H.C. Andersens Boulevard 18, DK-1553 Copenhagen V, Denmark. TEL 45-33-14-66-88. FAX 45-33-32-00-48. *6957*

DESIGN ISSUES.
M I T Press, 5 Cambridge Center, Cambridge, MA 02142. TEL 617-235-2889. FAX 617-577-1545. *438*

DESIGN NEWS.
Cahners Publishing Company (Newton), Division of Reed Elsevier Inc., 275 Washington St., Newton, MA 02158-1630. TEL 617-558-4762. FAX 617-558-4677. *6957*

DESIGN STUDIES.
Elsevier Science Ltd., P.O. Box 800, Kidlington, Oxford OX5 1DX, England. TEL 44-1865-843000. FAX 44-1865-843010. *402*

DESIGNS, CODES AND CRYPTOGRAPHY.
Kluwer Law International, Postbus 85889, 2508 CN The Hague, Netherlands. TEL 31-70-3081500. FAX 31-70-3081515. *4569*

DESTINATION CALGARY AND AREA.
Calgary Convention & Visitors Bureau, 237 Eighth Ave., S.E., Ste. 200, Calgary, AB T2G 0K8, Canada. TEL 403-750-8510. FAX 403-262-3809. *7195*

DETEKTIV-KURIER.
Zentralstelle fuer die Ausbildung im Detektivgewerbe, Zur Boeckelt 20, 47608 Geldern, Germany. TEL 49-2831-1095. FAX 49-2831-1097. *2286*

DEUS LOCI.
James A. Brigham, Ed. & Pub., c/o Department of English, Okanagan University College, Kelowna, B.C. V1Y 4X8, Canada. TEL 604-762-5445. *4397*

DEUTSCHER RAT FUER LANDESPFLEGE. SCHRIFTENREIHE.
Deutscher Rat fuer Landespflege, Konstantinstr. 110, 53179 Bonn, Germany. TEL 0228-331097. FAX 0228-334727. *2912*

DEVELOPER.
Kwazulu Finance and Investment Corporation Ltd., P.O. Box 2801, Durban 4000, South Africa. TEL 27-31-9078612. FAX 27-31-9073292. *1128*

DEVELOPMENT AND CHANGE.
Blackwell Publishers Ltd., 108 Cowley Rd., Oxford OX4 1JF, England. TEL 44-1865-791100. FAX 44-1865-791347. *1357*

DEVELOPMENT DISABILITIES BULLETIN.
University of Alberta, Developmental Disabilities Centre, 6-123D Education North, Edmonton, AB T6G 2H1, Canada. TEL 403-492-4505. FAX 403-492-1318. *5061*

DEVELOPMENT, GENES AND EVOLUTION.
Springer-Verlag, Heidelberger Platz 3, 14197 Berlin, Germany. TEL 49-30-82787-0. FAX 49-30-82787448. *598*

DEVELOPMENT, GROWTH AND DIFFERENTIATION.
Blackwell Science Pty Ltd, P.O. Box 378, Carlton South, Vic. 3053, Australia. TEL 61-3-93470300. FAX 61-3-93493016. *598*

DEVELOPMENT IN PRACTICE.
Oxfam, 274 Banbury Rd., Oxford OX2 7DZ, England. TEL 44-1865-311311. FAX 44-1865-313925. *1357*

DEVELOPMENT POLICY REVIEW.
Blackwell Publishers Ltd., 108 Cowley Rd., Oxford OX4 1JF, England. TEL 44-1865-791100. FAX 44-1865-791347. *1358*

DEVELOPMENTAL AND COMPARATIVE IMMUNOLOGY.
Elsevier Science Ltd., Pergamon, P.O. Box 800, Kidlington, Oxford OX5 1DX, England. TEL 44-1865-843000. FAX 44-1865-843010. *4794*

DEVELOPMENTAL BIOLOGY.
Academic Press, Inc., Journal Division, 525 B St., Ste. 1900, San Diego, CA 92101-4495. TEL 619-230-1840. FAX 619-699-6800. *598*

DEVELOPMENTAL BRAIN DYSFUNCTION.
S. Karger AG, Allschwilerstr. 10, P.O. Box, CH-4009 Basel, Switzerland. TEL 41-61-3061111. FAX 41-61-3061234. *5061*

DEVELOPMENTAL DYNAMICS.
John Wiley & Sons, Inc., Journals, 605 Third Ave., New York, NY 10158. TEL 212-850-6645. FAX 212-850-6021. *598*

DEVELOPMENTAL GENETICS.
John Wiley & Sons, Inc., Journals, 605 Third Ave., New York, NY 10158. TEL 212-850-6645. FAX 212-850-6021. *766*

DEVELOPMENTAL IMMUNOLOGY.
Gordon and Breach - Harwood Academic, Amsteldisk 166, 1st Fl., 1079 LH Amsterdam, Netherlands. *4794*

DEVELOPMENTAL MEDICINE AND CHILD NEUROLOGY.
Mac Keith Press, High Holborn House, 52-54 High Holborn, London WC1V 6RL, England. TEL 44-171-405-5355. FAX 44-171-405-5365. *5030*

DEVELOPMENTAL NEUROPSYCHOLOGY.
Lawrence Erlbaum Associates, Inc., 10 Industrial Dr., Mahwah, NJ 07430-2262. TEL 201-236-9500. FAX 201-236-0072. *6107*

DEVELOPMENTAL NEUROSCIENCE.
S. Karger AG, Allschwilerstr. 10, P.O. Box, CH-4009 Basel, Switzerland. TEL 41-61-3061111. FAX 41-61-3061234. *5061*

DEVELOPMENTAL PSYCHOBIOLOGY.
John Wiley & Sons, Inc., Journals, 605 Third Ave, New York, NY 10158-0012. TEL 212-850-6645. FAX 212-850-6021. *598*

DEVELOPMENTAL PSYCHOLOGY.
American Psychological Association, 750 First St., N.E., Washington, DC 20002-4242. TEL 202-336-5600. FAX 202-336-5568. *6107*

DEVELOPMENTAL REVIEW.
Academic Press, Inc., Journal Division, 525 B St., Ste. 1900, San Diego, CA 92101-4495. TEL 619-230-1840. FAX 619-699-6800. *6107*

DEVELOPMENTS IN AGRICULTURAL AND MANAGED FOREST ECOLOGY.
Elsevier Science B.V., Books Division, P.O. Box 211, 1000 AE Amsterdam, Netherlands. TEL 31-20-4853911. FAX 31-20-4853705. *3150*

DEVELOPMENTS IN AGRICULTURAL ECONOMICS.
Elsevier Science B.V., Books Division, P.O. Box 211, 1000 AE Amsterdam, Netherlands. TEL 31-20-4853911. FAX 31-20-4853705. *191*

DEVELOPMENTS IN AGRICULTURAL ENGINEERING.
Elsevier Science B.V., Books Division, P.O. Box 211, 1000 AE Amsterdam, Netherlands. TEL 31-20-4853911. FAX 31-20-4853705. *221*

DEVELOPMENTS IN ANIMAL AND VETERINARY SCIENCES.
Elsevier Science B.V., Books Division, P.O. Box 211, 1000 AE Amsterdam, Netherlands. TEL 31-20-4853911. FAX 31-20-4853705. *7269*

DEVELOPMENTS IN AQUACULTURE AND FISHERIES SCIENCE.
Elsevier Science B.V., Books Division, P.O. Box 211, 1000 AE Amsterdam, Netherlands. TEL 31-20-4853911. FAX 31-20-4853705. *832*

DEVELOPMENTS IN ATMOSPHERIC SCIENCE.
Elsevier Science B.V., Books Division, P.O. Box 211, 1000 AE Amsterdam, Netherlands. TEL 31-20-4853911. FAX 31-20-4853705. *5230*

DEVELOPMENTS IN BIOCHEMISTRY.
Elsevier Science B.V., Books Division, P.O. Box 211, 1000 AE Amsterdam, Netherlands. TEL 31-20-4853911. FAX 31-20-4853705. *658*

DEVELOPMENTS IN BIOENERGETICS AND BIOMEMBRANES.
Elsevier Science B.V., Books Division, P.O. Box 211, 1000 AE Amsterdam, Netherlands. TEL 31-20-4853911. FAX 31-20-4853705. *647*

DEVELOPMENTS IN BIOGEOCHEMISTRY.
Kluwer Academic Publishers, Postbus 17, 3300 AA Dordrecht, Netherlands. TEL 31-78-6392392. FAX 31-78-6392254. *2313*

DEVELOPMENTS IN BIOLOGICAL STANDARDIZATION.
S. Karger AG, Allschwilerstr. 10, P.O. Box, CH-4009 Basel, Switzerland. TEL 41-61-3061111. FAX 41-61-3061234. *5250*

DEVELOPMENTS IN BIOMECHANICS.
Kluwer Academic Publishers, Postbus 17, 3300 AA Dordrecht, Netherlands. TEL 31-78-6392392. FAX 31-78-6392254. *815*

DEVELOPMENTS IN BUSINESS SIMULATION & EXPERIENTIAL EXERCISES.
Oklahoma State University, Stillwater, College of Business Administration, Stillwater, OK 74078. TEL 405-744-8647. FAX 405-744-5180. *2151*

DEVELOPMENTS IN CANCER RESEARCH.
Elsevier Science B.V., Books Division, P.O. Box 211, 1000 AE Amsterdam, Netherlands. TEL 31-20-4853911. FAX 31-20-4853705. *4977*

DEVELOPMENTS IN CARDIOVASCULAR MEDICINE.
Kluwer Academic Publishers, Postbus 17, 3300 AA Dordrecht, Netherlands. TEL 31-78-6392392. FAX 31-78-6392254. *4815*

DEVELOPMENTS IN CIVIL AND FOUNDATION ENGINEERING.
Kluwer Academic Publishers, Postbus 17, 3300 AA Dordrecht, Netherlands. TEL 31-78-6392392. FAX 31-78-6392254. *2781*

DEVELOPMENTS IN CIVIL ENGINEERING.
Elsevier Science B.V., Books Division, P.O. Box 211, 1000 AE Amsterdam, Netherlands. TEL 31-20-4853911. FAX 31-20-4853705. *2782*

DEVELOPMENTS IN CLINICAL BIOCHEMISTRY.
Kluwer Academic Publishers, Postbus 17, 3300 AA Dordrecht, Netherlands. TEL 31-78-6392392. FAX 31-78-6392254. *658*

DEVELOPMENTS IN CRITICAL CARE MEDICINE AND ANESTHESIOLOGY.
Kluwer Academic Publishers, Postbus 17, 3300 AA Dordrecht, Netherlands. TEL 31-78-6392392. FAX 31-78-6392254. *4805*

DEVELOPMENTS IN CROP SCIENCE.
Elsevier Science B.V., Books Division, P.O. Box 211, 1000 AE Amsterdam, Netherlands. TEL 31-20-4853911. FAX 31-20-4853705. *222*

DEVELOPMENTS IN EARTH SURFACE PROCESSES.
Elsevier Science B.V., Books Division, P.O. Box 211, 1000 AE Amsterdam, Netherlands. TEL 31-20-4853911. FAX 31-20-4853705. *2337*

DEVELOPMENTS IN ECONOMIC GEOLOGY.
Elsevier Science B.V., Books Division, P.O. Box 211, 1000 AE Amsterdam, Netherlands. TEL 31-20-4853911. FAX 31-20-4853705. *2337*

DEVELOPMENTS IN ENDOCRINOLOGY (AMSTERDAM).
Elsevier Science B.V., Books Division, P.O. Box 211, 1000 AE Amsterdam, Netherlands. TEL 31-20-4853911. FAX 31-20-4853705. *4883*

DEVELOPMENTS IN ENVIRONMENTAL BIOLOGY OF FISHES.
Kluwer Academic Publishers, Postbus 17, 3300 AA Dordrecht, Netherlands. TEL 31-78-6392392. FAX 31-78-6392254. *832*

DEVELOPMENTS IN ENVIRONMENTAL ECONOMICS.
Elsevier Science B.V., Books Division, P.O. Box 211, 1000 AE Amsterdam, Netherlands. TEL 31-20-4853911. FAX 31-20-4853705. *2912*

DEVELOPMENTS IN ENVIRONMENTAL MODELLING.
Elsevier Science B.V., Books Division, P.O. Box 211, 1000 AE Amsterdam, Netherlands. TEL 31-20-4853911. FAX 31-20-4853705. *2964*

DEVELOPMENTS IN FOOD PRESERVATION.
Elsevier Science Ltd., Books Division, P.O. Box 800, Kidlington, Oxford OX5 1DX, England. TEL 44-1865-843000. FAX 44-1865-843010. *3101*

DEVELOPMENTS IN FOOD PROTEINS.
Elsevier Science Ltd., Books Division, P.O. Box 800, Kidlington, Oxford OX5 1DX, England. TEL 44-1865-843000. FAX 44-1865-843010. *3101*

DEVELOPMENTS IN FOOD SCIENCE.
Elsevier Science B.V., Books Division, P.O. Box 211, 1000 AE Amsterdam, Netherlands. TEL 31-20-4853911. FAX 31-20-4853705. *1815*

DEVELOPMENTS IN GASTROENTEROLOGY.
Kluwer Academic Publishers, Postbus 17, 3300 AA Dordrecht, Netherlands. TEL 31-78-6392392. FAX 31-78-6392254. *4908*

DEVELOPMENTS IN GEOCHEMISTRY.
Elsevier Science B.V., Books Division, P.O. Box 211, 1000 AE Amsterdam, Netherlands. TEL 31-20-4853911. FAX 31-20-4853705. *2337*

DEVELOPMENTS IN GEOMATHEMATICS.
Elsevier Science B.V., Books Division, P.O. Box 211, 1000 AE Amsterdam, Netherlands. TEL 31-20-4853911. FAX 31-20-4853705. *2380*

DEVELOPMENTS IN GEOTECHNICAL ENGINEERING.
Elsevier Science B.V., Books Division, P.O. Box 211, 1000 AE Amsterdam, Netherlands. TEL 31-20-4853911. FAX 31-20-4853705. *2782*

DEVELOPMENTS IN GEOTECTONICS.
Elsevier Science B.V., Books Division, P.O. Box 211, 1000 AE Amsterdam, Netherlands. TEL 31-20-4853911. FAX 31-20-4853705. *2337*

DEVELOPMENTS IN HEMATOLOGY AND IMMUNOLOGY.
Kluwer Academic Publishers, Postbus 17, 3300 AA Dordrecht, Netherlands. TEL 31-78-6392392. FAX 31-78-6392254. *4918*

DEVELOPMENTS IN HYDROBIOLOGY.
Kluwer Academic Publishers, Postbus 17, 3300 AA Dordrecht, Netherlands. TEL 31-78-6392392. FAX 31-78-6392254. *598*

DEVELOPMENTS IN IMMUNOLOGY.
Elsevier Science B.V., Books Division, P.O. Box 211, 1000 AE Amsterdam, Netherlands. TEL 31-20-4853911. FAX 31-20-4853705. *4794*

DEVELOPMENTS IN INDUSTRIAL MICROBIOLOGY SERIES.
Elsevier Science B.V., Books Division, P.O. Box 211, 1000 AE Amsterdam, Netherlands. TEL 31-20-4853911. FAX 31-20-4853705. *783*

DEVELOPMENTS IN INTERNATIONAL LAW.
Martinus Nijhoff Publishers, Human Rights and International Law Postbus 163, 3300 AD Dordrecht, Netherlands. TEL 31-78-334911. FAX 31-78-334254. *4111*

DEVELOPMENTS IN LANDSCAPE MANAGEMENT AND URBAN PLANNING.
Elsevier Science B.V., Books Division, P.O. Box 211, 1000 AE Amsterdam, Netherlands. TEL 31-20-4853911. FAX 31-20-4853705. *3745*

DEVELOPMENTS IN MARINE BIOLOGY.
Elsevier Science B.V., Books Division, P.O. Box 211, 1000 AE Amsterdam, Netherlands. TEL 31-20-4853911. FAX 31-20-4853705. *2402*

DEVELOPMENTS IN MARINE TECHNOLOGY.
Elsevier Science B.V., Books Division, P.O. Box 211, 1000 AE Amsterdam, Netherlands. TEL 31-20-4853911. FAX 31-20-4853705. *2882*

DEVELOPMENTS IN MEDICAL VIROLOGY.
Kluwer Academic Publishers, Postbus 17, 3300 AA Dordrecht, Netherlands. TEL 31-78-6392392. FAX 31-78-6392254. *4834*

DEVELOPMENTS IN MINERAL PROCESSING.
Elsevier Science B.V., Books Division, P.O. Box 211, 1000 AE Amsterdam, Netherlands. TEL 31-20-4853911. FAX 31-20-4853705. *2337*

DEVELOPMENTS IN MOLECULAR AND CELLULAR BIOCHEMISTRY.
Kluwer Academic Publishers, Postbus 17, 3300 AA Dordrecht, Netherlands. TEL 31-78-6392392. FAX 31-78-6392254. *658*

DEVELOPMENTS IN MOLECULAR VIROLOGY.
Kluwer Academic Publishers, Postbus 17, 3300 AA Dordrecht, Netherlands. TEL 31-78-6392392. FAX 31-78-6392254. *783*

DEVELOPMENTS IN NANOTECHNOLOGY.
Gordon and Breach - Harwood Academic, Amsteldisk 166, 1st Fl., 1079 LH Amsterdam, Netherlands. *5801*

DEVELOPMENTS IN NEPHROLOGY.
Kluwer Academic Publishers, Postbus 17, 3300 AA Dordrecht, Netherlands. TEL 31-78-6392392. FAX 31-78-6392254. *5160*

DEVELOPMENTS IN NEUROSCIENCE.
Elsevier Science B.V., Books Division, P.O. Box 211, 1000 AE Amsterdam, Netherlands. TEL 31-20-4853911. FAX 31-20-4853705. *5061*

DEVELOPMENTS IN NUCLEAR MEDICINE.
Kluwer Academic Publishers, Postbus 17, 3300 AA Dordrecht, Netherlands. TEL 31-78-6392392. FAX 31-78-6392254. *5105*

DEVELOPMENTS IN ONCOLOGY.
Kluwer Academic Publishers, Postbus 17, 3300 AA Dordrecht, Netherlands. TEL 31-78-6392392. FAX 31-78-6392254. *4977*

DEVELOPMENTS IN OPHTHALMOLOGY.
S. Karger AG, Allschwilerstr. 10, P.O. Box, CH-4009 Basel, Switzerland. TEL 41-61-3061111. FAX 41-61-3061234. *4992*

DEVELOPMENTS IN ORIENTED POLYMERS.
Elsevier Science Ltd., Books Division, P.O. Box 800, Kidlington, Oxford OX5 1DX, England. TEL 44-1865-843000. FAX 44-1865-843010. *1815*

DEVELOPMENTS IN PALAEONTOLOGY AND STRATIGRAPHY.
Elsevier Science B.V., Books Division, P.O. Box 211, 1000 AE Amsterdam, Netherlands. TEL 31-20-4853911. FAX 31-20-4853705. *5558*

DEVELOPMENTS IN PETROLEUM ENGINEERING.
Elsevier Science Ltd., Books Division, P.O. Box 800, Kidlington, Oxford OX5 1DX, England. TEL 44-1865-843000. FAX 44-1865-843010. *5599*

DEVELOPMENTS IN PETROLEUM SCIENCE.
Elsevier Science B.V., Books Division, P.O. Box 211, 1000 AE Amsterdam, Netherlands. TEL 31-20-4853911. FAX 31-20-4853705. *5599*

DEVELOPMENTS IN PETROLOGY.
Elsevier Science B.V., Books Division, P.O. Box 211, 1000 AE Amsterdam, Netherlands. TEL 31-20-4853911. FAX 31-20-4853705. *2337*

DEVELOPMENTS IN PHARMACOLOGY.
Kluwer Academic Publishers, Postbus 17, 3300 AA Dordrecht, Netherlands. TEL 31-78-6392392. FAX 31-78-6392254. *5655*

DEVELOPMENTS IN PLANT AND SOIL SCIENCES.
Kluwer Academic Publishers, Postbus 17, 3300 AA Dordrecht, Netherlands. TEL 31-78-6392392. FAX 31-78-6392254. *222*

DEVELOPMENTS IN PLANT BREEDING.
Kluwer Academic Publishers, Postbus 17, 3300 AA Dordrecht, Netherlands. TEL 31-78-6392392. FAX 31-78-6392254. *700*

DEVELOPMENTS IN PLANT GENETICS AND BREEDING.
Elsevier Science B.V., Books Division, P.O. Box 211, 1000 AE Amsterdam, Netherlands. TEL 31-20-4853911. FAX 31-20-4853705. *766*

DEVELOPMENTS IN PLANT PATHOLOGY.
Kluwer Academic Publishers, Postbus 17, 3300 AA Dordrecht, Netherlands. TEL 31-78-6392392. FAX 31-78-6392254. *701*

DEVELOPMENTS IN PRECAMBRIAN GEOLOGY.
Elsevier Science B.V., Books Division, P.O. Box 211, 1000 AE Amsterdam, Netherlands. TEL 31-20-4853911. FAX 31-20-4853705. *2337*

DEVELOPMENTS IN PSYCHIATRY.
Elsevier Science B.V., Books Division, P.O. Box 211, 1000 AE Amsterdam, Netherlands. TEL 31-20-4853911. FAX 31-20-4853705. *5061*

DEVELOPMENTS IN RUBBER TECHNOLOGY.
Elsevier Science Ltd., Books Division, P.O. Box 800, Kidlington, Oxford OX5 1DX, England. TEL 44-1865-843000. FAX 44-1865-843010. *6501*

DEVELOPMENTS IN SEDIMENTOLOGY.
Elsevier Science B.V., Books Division, P.O. Box 211, 1000 AE Amsterdam, Netherlands. TEL 31-20-4853911. FAX 31-20-4853705. *2337*

DEVELOPMENTS IN SOIL SCIENCE.
Elsevier Science B.V., Books Division, P.O. Box 211, 1000 AE Amsterdam, Netherlands. TEL 31-20-4853911. FAX 31-20-4853705. *222*

DEVELOPMENTS IN SOLID EARTH GEOPHYSICS.
Elsevier Science B.V., Books Division, P.O. Box 211, 1000 AE Amsterdam, Netherlands. TEL 31-20-4853911. FAX 31-20-4853705. *2380*

DEVELOPMENTS IN STRUCTURAL GEOLOGY.
Elsevier Science B.V., Books Division, P.O. Box 211, 1000 AE Amsterdam, Netherlands. TEL 31-20-4853911. FAX 31-20-4853705. *2337*

DEVELOPMENTS IN SURGERY.
Kluwer Academic Publishers, Postbus 17, 3300 AA Dordrecht, Netherlands. TEL 31-78-6392392. FAX 31-78-6392254. *5140*

DEVELOPMENTS IN TOXICOLOGY AND ENVIRONMENTAL SCIENCE.
Elsevier Science B.V., Books Division, P.O. Box 211, 1000 AE Amsterdam, Netherlands. TEL 31-20-4853911. FAX 31-20-4853705. *2976*

DEVELOPMENTS IN TRANSPORT STUDIES.
Kluwer Academic Publishers, Postbus 17, 3300 AA Dordrecht, Netherlands. TEL 31-78-6392392. FAX 31-78-6392254. *7027*

DEVELOPMENTS IN VETERINARY MEDICINE.
Kluwer Academic Publishers, Postbus 17, 3300 AA Dordrecht, Netherlands. TEL 31-78-6392392. FAX 31-78-6392254. *7269*

DEVELOPMENTS IN VOLCANOLOGY.
Elsevier Science B.V., Books Division, P.O. Box 211, 1000 AE Amsterdam, Netherlands. TEL 31-20-4853911. FAX 31-20-4853705. *2380*

DEVELOPMENTS IN WATER SCIENCE.
Elsevier Science B.V., Books Division, P.O. Box 211, 1000 AE Amsterdam, Netherlands. TEL 31-20-4853911. FAX 31-20-4853705. *7290*

DEVIANT BEHAVIOR.
Taylor & Francis Inc., 1900 Frost Rd., Ste. 101, Bristol, PA 19007-1598. TEL 215-785-5800. FAX 215-785-5515. *6707*

DEVON HISTORIAN.
Devon History Society, c/o Devon & Exeter Institution, 7 The Close, Exeter, Devon EX1 1EZ, England. *3562*

REFEREED SERIALS

DEVONSHIRE ASSOCIATION FOR THE ADVANCEMENT OF SCIENCE, LITERATURE AND ART. REPORT AND TRANSACTIONS.
Devonshire Association, 7 Cathedral Close, Exeter, Devon EX1 1EZ, England. TEL 44-1392-52461. FAX 44-1392-52461. *438*

DIABETES.
Finnish Diabetes Association, Kirjoniementie 15, 33680 Tampere, Finland. TEL 358-3-28-60-111. FAX 358-3-3600-462. *4884*

DIABETES.
American Diabetes Association, 1660 Duke St., Alexandria, VA 22314. TEL 703-549-1500. FAX 703-836-7439. *4884*

DIABETES ANNUAL.
Elsevier Science B.V., Regional Sales Office, P.O. Box 211, 1000 AE Amsterdam, Netherlands. TEL 31-20-4853757. FAX 31-20-4853432. *4884*

DIABETES CARE.
American Diabetes Association, 1660 Duke St., Alexandria, VA 22314. TEL 703-549-1500. FAX 703-836-7439. *4884*

DIABETES - METABOLISM REVIEWS.
John Wiley & Sons Ltd., Journals, Baffins Ln., Chichester, W. Sussex PO19 1UD, England. TEL 44-1243-779777. FAX 44-1243-775878. *4885*

DIABETES PREVENTION AND THERAPY.
John Wiley & Sons Ltd., Journals, Baffins Ln., Chichester, W. Sussex PO19 1UD, England. TEL 44-1243-779777. FAX 44-1243-775878. *4885*

DIABETES RESEARCH AND CLINICAL PRACTICE.
Elsevier Science Ireland Ltd., P.O. Box 85, Limerick, Ireland. TEL 353-61-471944. FAX 353-61-472144. *4885*

DIABETES SELF-MANAGEMENT.
R.A. Rapaport Publishing, Inc., 150 W. 22nd St., New York, NY 10011. TEL 212-989-0200. FAX 212-989-4786. *4885*

DIABETES SPECTRUM.
American Diabetes Association, 1660 Duke St., Alexandria, VA 22314. TEL 703-549-1500. FAX 703-836-7439. *4885*

DIABETIC MEDICINE.
John Wiley & Sons Ltd., Journals, Baffins Ln., Chichester, W. Sussex PO19 1UD, England. TEL 44-1243-779777. FAX 44-1243-775878. *4885*

THE DIABETIC TRAVELER.
Box 8223 - RW, Stamford, CT 06905. TEL 203-327-5832. *4886*

DIABLO DESCENDENTS NEWSLETTER.
Contra Costa County Genealogical Society, Box 910, Concord, CA 94522-0910. *3219*

DIAGNOSTIC AND THERAPEUTIC ENDOSCOPY.
Gordon and Breach - Harwood Academic, Amsteldisk 166, 1st Fl., 1079 LH Amsterdam, Netherlands. *4896*

DIAGNOSTIC CYTOPATHOLOGY.
John Wiley & Sons, Inc., Journals, 605 Third Ave., New York, NY 10158. TEL 212-850-6645. FAX 212-850-6021. *740*

DIAGNOSTIC IMAGING & RADIOLOGY PRODUCT COMPARISON SYSTEM.
E C R I, 5200 Butler Pike, Plymouth Meeting, PA 19462. TEL 610-825-6000. FAX 610-834-1275. *5105*

DIAGNOSTIC MICROBIOLOGY AND INFECTIOUS DISEASE.
Elsevier Science Inc., Box 945, New York, NY 10159-0945. TEL 212-633-3730. FAX 212-633-3680. *783*

DIAGNOSTIC MOLECULAR PATHOLOGY.
Lippincott - Raven Publishers, 227 E. Washington Sq., Philadelphia, PA 19106. TEL 215-238-4200. FAX 215-238-4227. *4661*

DIALECTICAL ANTHROPOLOGY.
Kluwer Academic Publishers, Postbus 17, 3300 AA Dordrecht, Netherlands. TEL 31-78-6392392. FAX 31-78-6392254. *314*

DIALOGAS.
Poliilogas, Antakalnio 31, 2055 Vilnius, Lithuania. TEL 370-2-748943. FAX 370-2-748943. *2432*

DIALOGOS.
Frank Cass, Newbury House, 890-900 Eastern Ave., Newbury Park, Ilford, Essex IG2 7HH, England. TEL 44-181-599-8866. FAX 44-181-599-0984. *1902*

DIALOGOS.
Universidad de Puerto Rico, Departamento de Filosofia, Box 21572, San Juan, PR 00931. TEL 787-764-0000 ext. 2072. FAX 787-764-5899. *5723*

DIALOGUE (MILWAUKEE).
Phi Sigma Tau, Dept. of Philosophy, Marquette University, Milwaukee, WI 53233. TEL 414-288-6857. *5723*

DIALOGUE (WATERLOO).
Wilfrid Laurier University Press, 75 University Ave. W., Waterloo, ON N2L 3C5, Canada. TEL 519-884-0710. FAX 519-725-1399. *5724*

DIALOGUE & ALLIANCE.
International Religious Foundation, Inc. (IRF), 4 W. 43rd St., New York, NY 10036. TEL 212-869-6023. FAX 212-869-6424. *6334*

DIALYSE JOURNAL.
Pabst Science Publishers, Am Eichengrund 28, 49525 Lengerich, Germany. TEL 49-5484-308. FAX 49-5484-550. *5160*

DIALYSIS & TRANSPLANTATION.
Creative Age Publications, Inc., 7628 Densmore Ave., Van Nuys, CA 91406-2042. TEL 818-782-7328. FAX 818-782-7450. *5160*

DIAMOND AND RELATED MATERIALS.
Elsevier Science S.A., P.O. Box 564, CH-1001 Lausanne 1, Switzerland. TEL 41-21-3207381. FAX 41-21-3235444. *1801*

DIAMOND FILMS AND TECHNOLOGY.
M Y U, Scientific Publishing Division, 2-32-3 Sendagi, Bunkyo-ku, Tokyo 113, Japan. TEL 81-3-3821-2930. FAX 81-3-3827-8547. *2882*

DIAN HUAXUE.
Chinese Chemical Society, P.O. Box 2709, Beijing 100080, People's Republic of China. TEL 86-10-62568157. FAX 86-10-62568157. *1804*

DIANZI KEXUE XUEKAN.
Science Press, Marketing and Sales Department, 16 Donghuangchenggen North St., Beijing 100717, People's Republic of China. TEL 4010642. FAX 4019810. *2628*

DIASPORA: A JOURNAL OF TRANSNATIONAL STUDIES.
University of Toronto Press, Journals Department, 5201 Duffering St., Toronto, ON M3H 5T8, Canada. TEL 416-667-7710. FAX 416-667-7881. *6610*

DIATRIBE.
University of Southampton, Centre for Language & Cultural Theory, Highfield, Southampton SO17 1BJ, England. TEL 44-1703-593406. FAX 44-1703-593987. *3777*

DICENGXUE ZAZHI.
Science Press, Marketing and Sales Department, 16 Donghuangchenggen North St., Beijing 100717, People's Republic of China. TEL 4010642. FAX 4019810. *2337*

DIER - EN - ARTS.
Transmondial B.V., Waalreseweg 17, 5554 HA Valkenswaard, Netherlands. TEL 31-40-2030535. FAX 31-40-2030535. *7269*

DIFFERENTIAL AND INTEGRAL EQUATIONS.
Khayyam Publishing Company, Inc., Box 429, Athens, OH 45701. TEL 614-592-6136. FAX 614-592-1252. *4569*

DIFFERENTIAL EQUATIONS.
Plenum Publishing Corp., Consultants Bureau, 233 Spring St., New York, NY 10013-1578. TEL 212-620-8468. FAX 212-463-0742. *4569*

DIFFERENTIAL EQUATIONS AND DYNAMICAL SYSTEMS.
Research Square Publications, Plot No.20, H. No.13-481, Alakapuri, Saroornagar Post, Hyderabad 500 035, India. TEL 91-40-879023. *4569*

DIFFERENTIAL GEOMETRY AND ITS APPLICATIONS.
North-Holland, P.O. Box 211, 1000 AE Amsterdam, Netherlands. TEL 31-20-4853911. FAX 31-20-4853598. *4570*

DIGEST OF MIDDLE EAST STUDIES.
University of Wisconsin at Milwaukee, Milwaukee School of Library and Information Science, Box 413, Milwaukee, WI 53201. TEL 414-229-4707. FAX 414-229-4848. *5526*

DIGESTION.
S. Karger AG, Allschwilerstr. 10, P.O. Box, CH-4009 Basel, Switzerland. TEL 41-61-3061111. FAX 41-61-3061234. *4909*

DIGESTIVE DISEASES.
S. Karger AG, Allschwilerstr. 10, P.O. Box, CH-4009 Basel, Switzerland. TEL 41-61-3061111. FAX 41-61-3061234. *4909*

DIGESTIVE DISEASES AND SCIENCES.
Plenum Publishing Corp., 233 Spring St., New York, NY 10013-1578. TEL 212-620-8000. FAX 212-463-0742. *4909*

DIGESTIVE SURGERY.
S. Karger AG, Allschwilerstr. 10, P.O. Box, CH-4009 Basel, Switzerland. TEL 41-61-3061111. FAX 41-61-3061234. *5140*

DIGITAL TECHNICAL JOURNAL.
Digital Equipment Corporation, Ak02-3-B3, 50 Nagog Park, Acton, MA 01720-9843. TEL 508-264-7549. FAX 508-264-7493. *2115*

DILI JIAOYU.
Dili Jiaoyu Bianjibu, 12 Tianchen Lu, Shapingba, Chongqing, Sichuan 630047, People's Republic of China. TEL 86-811-531-1155. FAX 86-811-531-0333. *3400*

DILI KEXUE.
Science Press, Marketing and Sales Department, 16 Donghuangchenggen North St., Beijing 100717, People's Republic of China. TEL 4010642. FAX 4019810. *3400*

DILI XUEBAO.
Science Press, Marketing and Sales Department, 16 Donghuangchenggen Beijing, Beijing 100707, People's Republic of China. TEL 4010642. FAX 4012180. *3400*

DILI YANJIU.
Science Press, Marketing and Sales Department, 16 Donghuangchenggen North St., Beijing 100717, People's Republic of China. TEL 4010642. FAX 4019810. *3400*

DIME NOVEL ROUND-UP.
J. Randolph Cox, Ed. & Pub., P.O. Box 226, Dundas, MN 55019-0226. TEL 507-645-5711. FAX 507-646-3734. *6269*

DIMENSIONS OF CRITICAL CARE NURSING.
Hall Johnson Communications, Inc., 9737 W. Ohio Ave., Lakewood, CO 80226. TEL 303-988-0056. *4932*

DIMENSIONS OF EARLY CHILDHOOD.
Southern Early Childhood Association, Box 55930, Little Rock, AR 72215-5930. TEL 501-663-0353. FAX 501-663-2114. *1844*

DINE ISRAEL.
Tel Aviv University, Faculty of Law, Ramat Aviv, Tel Aviv 69978, Israel. *3940*

DIONYSOS.
Seattle University, Addiction Studies Program, Broadway and Madison, Seattle, WA 98122-4490. TEL 206-296-5350. FAX 206-296-5997. *2300*

DIOTIMA.
Evanghelos A. Moutsopoulos, Ed. & Pub., 40 Ypsilantou St., 115 21 Athens, Greece. TEL 30-1-725-1212. FAX 30-1-722-7322. *5724*

DIPLOMACY & STATECRAFT.
Frank Cass, Newbury House, 890-900 Eastern Ave., Newbury Park, Ilford, Essex 1G2 7HH, England. TEL 44-181-599-8866. FAX 44-181-599-0984. *3493*

DIPLOMATIC HISTORY.
Blackwell Publishers, 238 Main St., Cambridge, MA 02142. TEL 617-547-7110. FAX 617-547-0789. *3493*

DIQIU HUAXUE.
Science Press, Marketing and Sales Department, 16 Donghuangchenggen North St., Beijing 100717, People's Republic of China. TEL 4010642. FAX 4019810. *2337*

DIQIU WULI XUEBAO.
Science Press, Marketing and Sales Department, 16 Donghuangchenggen North St., Beijing 100717, People's Republic of China. TEL 4010642. FAX 4019810. *2380*

DIRASAT. ADMINISTRATIVE SCIENCES.
University of Jordan, Deanship of Academic Research, Amman, Jordan. TEL 962-6-843555. FAX 962-6-840263. *1473*

DIRASAT. AGRICULTURAL SCIENCES.
University of Jordan, Deanship of Academic Research, Amman, Jordan. TEL 962-6-843555. FAX 962-6-840263. *112*

DIRASAT. EDUCATIONAL SCIENCES.
University of Jordan, Deanship of Academic Research, Amman, Jordan. TEL 962-6-843555. FAX 962-6-840263. *2433*

DIRASAT. HUMAN AND SOCIAL SCIENCES.
University of Jordan, Deanship of Academic Research, Amman, Jordan. TEL 962-6-843555. FAX 962-6-840263. *3777*

DIRASAT. NATURAL AND ENGINEERING SCIENCES.
University of Jordan, Deanship of Academic Research, Amman, Jordan. TEL 962-6-843555. FAX 962-6-840263. *6522*

DIRASAT. SHARI'A AND LAW SCIENCES.
University of Jordan, Deanship of Academic Research, Amman, Jordan. TEL 962-843555. FAX 962-6-840263. *3940*

DIRASAT ARABIYAT.
Dar at-Tali'at, P.O. Box 111813, Beirut, Lebanon. TEL 961-1-314659. FAX 961-1-309470. *5921*

DIRECTIONS.
University of South Pacific, Institute of Education, P.O. Box 1168, Suva, Fiji. TEL 679-313900. FAX 679-302409. *2433*

DIRECTIONS.
New Zealand Automobile Association, 342 Lambton Quay, P.O. Box 1, Wellington, New Zealand. TEL 64-4-4738738. FAX 64-4-4712080. *3339*

DIRECTIONS IN MENTAL HEALTH COUNSELING.
Hatherleigh Company Ltd., 1114 First Ave., Ste. 500, New York, NY 10021-8325. TEL 212-355-0882. FAX 212-308-7930. *6108*

DIRECTIONS IN PSYCHIATRY.
Hatherleigh Company Ltd., 1114 First Ave., Ste. 500, New York, NY 10021-8325. TEL 212-355-0882. FAX 212-308-7930. *5062*

DIRECTORY OF PHILIPPINE GARMENT & TEXTILE EXPORTERS.
Garments and Textile Export Board, Market Development Division, P.O. Box 1771 MCC - New Solid Bldg., 357 Gil J. Puyat Ave. Ext., Makati, Metro Manila, Philippines. TEL 632-8904651. FAX 632-8904653. *1914*

DIRECTORY OF PRODUCTS AND SERVICES FOR THE VACUUM INDUSTRY.
Association of Vacuum Equipment Manufacturers, 440 Live Oak Loop, Albuquerque, NM 87122. TEL 505-856-6924. FAX 505-856-6716. *1670*

DISABILITY AND REHABILITATION.
Taylor & Francis Ltd., 1 Gunpowder Sq., London EC4A 3DE, England. TEL 44-171-583-0490. FAX 44-171-583-0585. *3453*

DISABILITY & SOCIETY.
Carfax Publishing Co., P.O. Box 25, Abingdon, Oxon. OX14 3UE, England. TEL 44-1235-401000. FAX 44-1235-401550. *3466*

DISABILITY, PREGNANCY & PARENTHOOD INTERNATIONAL.
D P P I, 1 Chiswick Staithe, London W4 3TP, England. TEL 44-181-994-0896. FAX 44-181-994-1135. *3454*

DISASTERS.
Blackwell Publishers Ltd., 108 Cowley Rd., Oxford OX4 1JF, England. TEL 44-1865-791100. FAX 44-1865-791347. *1358*

DISCLOSURE (LEXINGTON).
University of Kentucky, Committee on Social Theory, c/o Dept. of Philosophy, University of Kentucky, Lexington, KY 40506-0027. TEL 606-257-6035. FAX 606-257-2931. *6610*

DISCOURSE.
Carfax Publishing Co., P.O. Box 25, Abingdon, Oxon. OX14 3UE, England. TEL 44-1235-401000. FAX 44-1235-401550. *2571*

DISCOURSE & SOCIETY.
Sage Publications Ltd., 6 Bonhill St., London EC2A 4PU, England. TEL 44-171-374-0645. FAX 44-171-374-8741. *6108*

DISCOVERIES IN PHARMACOLOGY.
Elsevier Science B.V., Books Division, P.O. Box 211, 1000 AE Amsterdam, Netherlands. TEL 31-20-4853911. FAX 31-20-4853705. *5656*

DISCOVERY.
Vancouver Natural History Society, Box 3021, Vancouver, BC V6B 3X5, Canada. TEL 604-737-3074. FAX 604-433-8100. *6523*

DISCOVERY (NEW HAVEN).
Peabody Museum of Natural History, Yale University, 170 Whitney Ave., Box 208118, New Haven, CT 06520-8118. TEL 203-432-3786. FAX 203-432-9816. *6523*

DISCOVERY AND INNOVATION.
Academy Science Publishers, P.O. Box 14798, Nairobi, Kenya. TEL 254-2-884401. FAX 254-2-884406. *658*

DISCOVERY Y M C A.
Y M C A of the U S A, 101 W. Wacker Dr., Chicago, IL 60606-1718. TEL 312-977-0031. FAX 312-977-9063. *6663*

DISCRETE & COMPUTATIONAL GEOMETRY.
Springer-Verlag, Science Journals, 175 Fifth Ave., New York, NY 10010. TEL 212-460-1500. FAX 212-473-6272. *4570*

DISCRETE AND CONTINUOUS DYNAMICAL SYSTEMS.
Department of Mathematics, Southwest Missouri State University, Springfield, MO 65804. TEL 417-836-5377. FAX 417-886-0559. *4570*

DISCRETE APPLIED MATHEMATICS.
North-Holland, P.O. Box 211, 1000 AE Amsterdam, Netherlands. TEL 31-20-4853911. FAX 31-20-4853598. *4570*

DISCRETE EVENT DYNAMIC SYSTEMS: THEORY AND APPLICATIONS.
Kluwer Academic Publishers Boston, Box 358, Accord Sta., Hingham, MA 02018-0358. TEL 617-871-6600. FAX 617-871-6528. *2151*

DISCRETE MATHEMATICS.
North-Holland, P.O. Box 211, 1000 AE Amsterdam, Netherlands. TEL 31-20-4853911. FAX 31-20-4853598. *4570*

DISCRETE MATHEMATICS AND APPLICATIONS.
V S P, P.O. Box 346, 3700 AH Zeist, Netherlands. TEL 31-30-6925790. FAX 31-30-6932081. *4570*

DISCUSSION PAPER IN ECONOMICS AND ECONOMETRICS.
University of Nottingham, Department of Economics, University Park, Nottingham NG7 2RD, England. TEL 44-115-9515480. FAX 44-115-9514159. *954*

DISEASE MARKERS.
I O S Press, Van Diemenstraat 94, 1013 CN Amsterdam, Netherlands. TEL 31-20-6382189. FAX 31-20-6204319. *4977*

DISEASES OF THE COLON AND RECTUM.
Williams & Wilkins, 351 W. Camden St., Baltimore, MD 21201-2436. TEL 410-528-4000. FAX 410-528-4312. *5141*

DISIJI YANJIU.
Science Press, Marketing and Sales Department, 16 Donghuangchenggen North St., Beijing 100717, People's Republic of China. TEL 4010642. FAX 4019810. *2338*

DISLOCATIONS IN SOLIDS.
Elsevier Science B.V., Books Division, P.O. Box 211, 1000 AE Amsterdam, Netherlands. TEL 31-20-4853911. FAX 31-20-4853705. *5801*

DISPLAYS.
Elsevier Science B.V., P.O. Box 211, 1000 AE Amsterdam, Netherlands. TEL 31-20-4853911. FAX 31-20-4853598. *2122*

DISSERTATIONES MATHEMATICAE.
Polska Akademia Nauk, Instytut Matematyczny, Dzial Wydawnictw, Ul. Sniadeckich 8, P.O. Box 137, 00-950 Warsaw, Poland. TEL 48-22-6282471. FAX 48-22-6293997. *4570*

DISSOCIATION.
International Society for the Study of Dissociation, 4700 W. Lake Ave., Glenview, IL 60025. *6108*

DISTRIBUTED AND PARALLEL DATABASES.
Kluwer Academic Publishers Boston, Box 358, Accord Sta., Hingham, MA 02018-0358. TEL 617-871-6600. FAX 617-871-6528. *2166*

DIVERSITY FACTOR.
P.O. Box 3188, Teaneck, NJ 07666. TEL 201-833-0011. FAX 201-833-4184. *1564*

DIWEN WULI XUEBAO.
Science Press, Marketing and Sales Department, 16 Donghuangchenggen North St., Beijing 100717, People's Republic of China. TEL 4010642. FAX 4019810. *5840*

DIZHEN DIZHI.
Guojia Dizhen-ju, Dizhi Yanjiusuo, Qijia Huozi, Deshengmenwai, Beijing 100029, People's Republic of China. TEL 86-1-2023377. FAX 86-1-2028617. *2380*

DIZHEN GONGCHENG YU GONGCHENG ZHENDONG.
Science Press, Marketing and Sales Department, 16 Donghuangchenggen North St., Beijing 100717, People's Republic of China. TEL 4010642. FAX 4019810. *2380*

DIZHEN XUEBAO.
Science Press, Marketing and Sales Department, 16 Donghuangchenggen North St., Beijing 100717, People's Republic of China. TEL 4010642. FAX 4019810. *2380*

DIZHI KEXUE.
Science Press, Marketing and Sales Department, 16 Donghuangchenggen North St., Beijing 100717, People's Republic of China. TEL 4010642. FAX 4019810. *2338*

DIZHI XUEBAO.
Science Press, Marketing and Sales Department, 16 Donghuangchenggen North St., Beijing 100717, People's Republic of China. TEL 4010642. FAX 4019810. *2338*

DMITROVSKII VESTNIK.
Dmitrovskii Vestnik, Moskovskaya ul., 5, block 5, 141800 Dmitrov - Moscow, Russia. TEL 7-095-58733487. FAX 7-09622-74504. *3352*

DOCUMENT WORLD.
Chappell House, The Green, Datchet, Berkshire SL3 9EH, England. TEL 44-1753-592100. FAX 44-1753-592101. *4231*

DOCUMENTA.
Documentatiecentrum voor Dramatische Kunst v.z.w., Rozier 44, 9000 Gent, Belgium. TEL 32-9-2643696. FAX 32-9-2644184. *7005*

DOCUMENTA ET MONUMENTA ORIENTIS ANTIQUI.
E.J. Brill, P.O. Box 9000, 2300 PA Leiden, Netherlands. TEL 31-71-5353500. FAX 31-71-5317532. *3655*

DOCUMENTA MATHEMATICA.
Deutsche Mathematiker Vereinigung, Postfach 100131, 33501 Bielefeld, Germany. *4570*

DOCUMENTA OPHTHALMOLOGICA.
Kluwer Academic Publishers, Postbus 17, 3300 AA Dordrecht, Netherlands. TEL 31-78-6392392. FAX 31-78-6392254. *4992*

DOCUMENTA OPHTHALMOLOGICA PROCEEDINGS SERIES.
Kluwer Academic Publishers, Postbus 17, 3300 AA Dordrecht, Netherlands. TEL 31-78-6392392. FAX 31-78-6392254. *4993*

DOCUMENTACAO DE ESTUDOS EM LINGUISTICA TEORICA E APLICADA.
Editora da Pontificia Universidade Catolica de Sao Paulo, Departamento de Linguistica, Rua Monte Alegre, 984, 05014-001 Sao Paulo SP, Brazil. TEL 55-11-629598. FAX 55-11-624920. *4253*

DOCUMENTOS DE ARQUITECTURA NACIONAL Y AMERICANA.
Instituto Argentino de Investigaciones de Historia de la Arquitectura y del Urbanismo, Casilla de Correo 120, Sucursal 48B, 1448 Buenos Aires, Argentina. FAX 54-1-8119249. *402*

DOKKYO JOURNAL OF MEDICAL SCIENCES.
Dokkyo University School of Medicine, Dokkyo Medical Society, Mibu, Tochigi 321-02, Japan. TEL 81-282-86-1111. FAX 81-282-86-5678. *4662*

DOKLADY BIOCHEMISTRY.
Maik Nauka - Interperiodica, Mezhdunarodnyi Otdel, Ul. Profsoyuznaya, 90, 117864 Moscow, Russia. TEL 7-095-3360066. FAX 7-095-3360666. *658*

DOKLADY BIOLOGICAL SCIENCES.
Maik Nauka - Interperiodica, Mezhdunarodnyi Otdel, Ul. Profsoyuznaya, 90, 117864 Moscow, Russia. TEL 7-095-3360066. FAX 7-095-3360666. *599*

DOKLADY BIOPHYSICS.
Maik Nauka - Interperiodica, Mezhdunarodnyi Otdel, Ul. Profsoyuznaya, 90, 117864 Moscow, Russia. TEL 7-095-3360066. FAX 7-095-3360666. *674*

DOKLADY BOTANICAL SCIENCES.
Maik Nauka - Interperiodica, Mezhdunarodnyi Otdel, Ul. Profsoyuznaya, 90, 117864 Moscow, Russia. TEL 7-095-3360066. FAX 7-095-3360666. *701*

DOKLADY CHEMICAL TECHNOLOGY.
Maik Nauka - Interperiodica, Mezhdunarodnyi Otdel, Ul. Profsoyuznaya, 90, 117864 Moscow, Russia. TEL 7-095-3360066. FAX 7-095-3360666. *2762*

DOKLADY CHEMISTRY.
Maik Nauka - Interperiodica, Mezhdunarodnyi Otdel, Ul. Profsoyuznaya, 90, 117864 Moscow, Russia. TEL 7-095-3360066. FAX 7-095-23360666. *1748*

DOKLADY PHYSICAL CHEMISTRY.
Maik Nauka - Interperiodica, Mezhdunarodnyi Otdel, Ul. Profsoyuznaya, 90, 117864 Moscow, Russia. TEL 7-095-3360066. FAX 7-095-3360666. *1827*

DOMESTIC ANIMAL ENDOCRINOLOGY.
Elsevier Science Inc., Box 945, New York, NY 10159-0945. TEL 212-633-3730. FAX 212-633-3680. *7269*

DONANA (ACTA VERTEBRATA).
Estacion Biologica de Donana, Avda. Maria Luisa, s-n, Pabellon Peru, 41013 Seville, Spain. TEL 34-54-232340. FAX 34-54-621125. *832*

DONGNAN DAXUE XUEBAO.
Dongnan Daxue, 2 Sipailou, Nanjing, Jiangsu 210018, People's Republic of China. TEL 86-25-3792627. FAX 86-25-7712719. *6523*

DONGWU FENLEI XUEBAO.
Science Press, Marketing and Sales Department, 16 Donghuangchenggen North St., Beijing 100717, People's Republic of China. TEL 4010642. FAX 4019810. *832*

DONGWU XUEBAO.
Science Press, Marketing and Sales Department, 16 Donghuangchenggen North St., Beijing 100717, People's Republic of China. TEL 4010642. FAX 4019810. *832*

DONGWUXUE ZAZHI.
Science Press, Marketing and Sales Department, 16 Donghuangchenggen Beijie, Beijing 100707, People's Republic of China. TEL 4010642. FAX 4012180. *832*

DOOMED TO OBSCURITY.
Box 2257, Philadelphia, PA 19103. *4398*

DOORS AND HARDWARE.
Door and Hardware Institute, 14170 Newbrook Dr., Chantilly, VA 20151. TEL 703-222-2010. FAX 703-222-2410. *927*

DOSHISHA DAIGAKU RIKOGAKU KENKYU HOKOKU.
Doshisha University, Science and Engineering Research Institute, Tanabe-cho, Tsuzukigun, Kyoto 610-03, Japan. FAX 774-65-6804. *2715*

DOVETAIL (KALAMAZOO).
Dovetail Publishing, P.O. Box 19945, Kalamazoo, MI 49019-0945. TEL 616-342-2900. FAX 616-342-1012. *6335*

DOWN SYNDROME NEWS.
National Down Syndrome Congress, 1605 Chantilly Dr., NE, Ste 250, Atlanta, GA 30324-3269. TEL 404-633-1555. FAX 404-633-2817. *5062*

DOWN SYNDROME: RESEARCH AND PRACTICE.
University of Portsmouth, Sarah Duffen Centre, Belmont St., Southsea, Hants PO5 1NA, England. TEL 44-1705-824261. FAX 44-1705-824265. *5062*

DR. H.S. GOUR VISHWAVIDYALAYA, SAGAR BOTANICAL SOCIETY. BULLETIN.
Dr. H.S. Gour Vishwavidyalaya, Sagar Botanical Society, Department of Botany, Gour Nagar, Sagar 470 003, Madhya Pradesh, India. TEL 91-7582-25452. FAX 91-7582-23236. *701*

DRACHENMAGAZIN.
Drachenverlags GmbH, Postfach 201863, 20208 Hamburg, Germany. TEL 49-40-4395667. FAX 49-40-4395377. *3666*

DRAKE LAW REVIEW.
Drake University, Law School, Cartwright Hall, Des Moines, IA 50311. TEL 515-271-2930. FAX 515-271-4926. *3942*

DREAM NETWORK.
1337 Powerhouse Ln., Ste. 22, Moab, UT 84532. TEL 801-259-5936. FAX 801-259-5936. *5456*

DREAM SWITCHBOARD.
Dream Switchboard, Box 8032, Hicksville, NY 11802-8032. TEL 516-796-9455. FAX 516-731-2395. *2433*

DREAM TIME.
Association for the Study of Dreams, Box 1600, Vienna, VA 22183. TEL 703-242-8888. FAX 510-527-7929. *6108*

DREAMING.
Human Sciences Press, Inc., 233 Spring St., New York, NY 10013. TEL 212-620-8000. FAX 212-463-0742. *815*

DREAMS AND DRAGONS. *4399*

DRUG ABUSE.
Swedish Council for Information on Alcohol and other Drugs (CAN), Documentation Center, P.O. Box 27302, S-102 54 Stockholm, Sweden. FAX 46-8-661-64-84. *2300*

DRUG AND ALCOHOL DEPENDENCE.
Elsevier Science Ireland Ltd., P.O. Box 85, Limerick, Ireland. TEL 353-61-471944. FAX 353-61-472144. *2300*

DRUG AND ALCOHOL REVIEW.
Carfax Publishing Co., P.O. Box 25, Abingdon, Oxon. OX14 3UE, England. TEL 44-1235-401000. FAX 44-1235-401550. *2300*

DRUG AND CHEMICAL TOXICOLOGY.
Marcel Dekker Journals, 270 Madison Ave., New York, NY 10016. TEL 212-696-9000. FAX 212-685-4540. *5656*

DRUG AND CHEMICAL TOXICOLOGY SERIES.
Marcel Dekker, Inc., 270 Madison Ave., New York, NY 10016. TEL 212-696-9000. FAX 212-685-4540. *5656*

DRUG DELIVERY.
Taylor & Francis Inc., 1900 Frost Rd., Ste. 101, Bristol, PA 19007-1598. TEL 215-785-5800. FAX 215-785-5515. *5656*

DRUG DESIGN AND DISCOVERY.
Gordon and Breach - Harwood Academic, Amsteldisk 166, 1st Fl., 1079 LH Amsterdam, Netherlands. *5656*

DRUG DEVELOPMENT AND INDUSTRIAL PHARMACY.
Marcel Dekker Journals, 270 Madison Ave., New York, NY 10016. TEL 212-696-9000. FAX 212-685-4540. *5657*

DRUG DEVELOPMENT RESEARCH.
John Wiley & Sons, Inc., Journals, 605 Third Ave., New York, NY 10158. TEL 212-850-6645. FAX 212-850-6021. *5657*

DRUG DISCOVERY TODAY.
Elsevier Science Ltd., P.O. Box 800, Kidlington, Oxford OX2 1DX, England. TEL 44-1865-843000. FAX 44-1865-843010. *5657*

DRUG INDUCED DISORDERS.
Elsevier Science B.V., Books Division, P.O. Box 211, 1000 AE Amsterdam, Netherlands. TEL 31-20-4853911. FAX 31-20-4853705. *5657*

DRUG INFORMATION JOURNAL.
Drug Information Association, Box 3113, Maple Glen, PA 19002. TEL 215-628-2288. FAX 215-641-1229. *5657*

DRUG METABOLISM AND DISPOSITION.
Williams & Wilkins, 351 W. Camden St., Baltimore, MD 21201. TEL 410-528-4068. FAX 410-528-4452. *5657*

DRUG METABOLISM REVIEWS.
Marcel Dekker Journals, 270 Madison Ave., New York, NY 10016. TEL 212-696-9000. FAX 212-685-4540. *4663*

DRUG SAFETY.
Adis International Limited, Private Bag 65901, Mairangi Bay, Auckland 10, New Zealand. TEL 64-9-479-8100. FAX 64-9-479-8145. *5658*

DRUGS.
Adis International Limited, Private Bag 65901, Mairangi Bay, Auckland 10, New Zealand. TEL 64-9-479-8100. FAX 64-9-479-8145. *5658*

DRUGS & AGING.
Adis International Limited, Private Bag 65901, Mairangi Bay, Auckland 10, New Zealand. TEL 64-9-479-8100. FAX 64-9-479-8145. *5658*

DRUGS & SOCIETY.
Haworth Press, Inc., 10 Alice St., Binghamton, NY 13904. TEL 607-722-5857. FAX 607-722-6362. *2301*

DRUGS AND THE PHARMACEUTICAL SCIENCES.
Marcel Dekker, Inc., 270 Madison Ave., New York, NY 10016. TEL 212-696-9000. FAX 212-685-4540. *5658*

DRUGS & THERAPY PERSPECTIVES.
Adis International Limited, Private Bag 65901, Mairangi Bay, Auckland 10, New Zealand. TEL 64-9-479-8100. FAX 64-9-479-8145. *5658*

DRUGS: EDUCATION, PREVENTION & POLICY.
Carfax Publishing Co., P.O. Box 25, Abingdon, Oxon. OX14 3UE, England. TEL 44-1235-401000. FAX 44-1235-401550. *2301*

DRYING TECHNOLOGY.
Marcel Dekker Journals, 270 Madison Ave., New York, NY 10016. TEL 212-696-9000. FAX 212-685-4540. *1827*

DUBLIN SEMINAR FOR NEW ENGLAND FOLKLIFE. ANNUAL PROCEEDINGS.
Boston University, Scholarly Publications, 985 Commonwealth Ave., Boston, MA 02215. TEL 617-353-4106. *3086*

DUCA POST.
Duca Community Credit Union Ltd., Box 1100, Willowdale, ON M2N 5W5, Canada. TEL 416-223-8502. FAX 416-223-2575. *1128*

DUKE MATHEMATICAL JOURNAL.
Duke University Press, Box 90660, Durham, NC 27708-0660. TEL 919-687-3600. FAX 919-688-4574. *4570*

DUMERILIA.
A A L R A M, c/o Alain Dubois, 25 rue Cuvier, 75005 Paris, France. TEL 33-1-40793487. *832*

DUNIA WANITA.
Jalan Brigjen, Katamso No. 1, Medan 20151, Indonesia. TEL 62-550858. FAX 62-510025. *7317*

DUODECIMAL BULLETIN.
Dozenal Society of America, c/o Math Department, Nassau Community College, Garden City, NY 11530. TEL 516-669-0273. *4571*

DUQUESNE STUDIES. LANGUAGE AND LITERATURE SERIES.
Duquesne University Press, 600 Forbes Ave., Pittsburgh, PA 15282. TEL 412-396-6610. FAX 412-396-5984. *4253*

DURBAN MUSEUM NOVITATES.
Durban Natural Science Museum, P.O. Box 4085, Durban 4000, South Africa. TEL 27-31-3006211. FAX 27-31-3006302. *832*

DUTCH BIRDING.
Stichting Dutch Birding Association, Postbus 75611, 1070 AP Amsterdam, Netherlands. TEL 31-23-5378024. FAX 31-23-5376749. *802*

DYES AND PIGMENTS.
Elsevier Science Ltd., P.O. Box 800, Kidlington, Oxford OX5 1DX, England. TEL 44-1865-843000. FAX 44-1865-843010. *1748*

DYMAT JOURNAL.
Editions de Physique, B.P. 112, Z.I. de Courteboeuf, 7 av. du Hoggar, 91944 Les Ulis Cedex, France. TEL 69-07-36-88. FAX 69-28-84-91. *2857*

DYNA.
Universidad Nacional de Colombia, Facultad Nacional de Minas, Apdo. Aereo 1027, Medellin, Colombia. TEL 57-2344503. FAX 57-2341002. *2715*

DYNA.
Asociacion Nacional de Ingenieros Industriales de Espana, Alameda de Mazarredo, 69, Apdo. 646, 48009 Bilbao, Spain. TEL 34-4-423-7566. FAX 34-4-4234461. *2715*

DYNAMIC ECONOMICS: THEORY AND APPLICATIONS (SERIES).
Elsevier Science B.V., Books Division, P.O. Box 211, 1000 AE Amsterdam, Netherlands. TEL 31-20-4853911. FAX 31-20-4853705. *955*

DYNAMIC NUTRITION RESEARCH.
S. Karger AG, Allschwilerstr. 10, P.O. Box, CH-4009 Basel, Switzerland. TEL 41-61-3061111. FAX 41-61-3061234. *5471*

DYNAMICAL PROPERTIES OF SOLIDS.
Elsevier Science B.V., Books Division, P.O. Box 211, 1000 AE Amsterdam, Netherlands. TEL 31-20-4853911. FAX 31-20-4853705. *5844*

DYNAMICS AND CONTROL.
Kluwer Academic Publishers Boston, Box 358, Accord Sta., Hingham, MA 02018-0358. TEL 617-871-6600. FAX 617-871-6528. *2154*

DYNAMICS AND STABILITY OF SYSTEMS.
Carfax Publishing Co., P.O. Box 25, Abingdon, Oxon. OX14 3UE, England. TEL 44-1235-401000. FAX 44-1235-41550. *2081*

DYNAMICS OF ATMOSPHERES AND OCEANS.
Elsevier Science B.V., P.O. Box 211, 1000 AE Amsterdam, Netherlands. TEL 31-20-4853911. FAX 31-20-4853598. *5230*

DYSLEXIA.
John Wiley & Sons Ltd., Journals, Baffins Ln., Chichester, W. Sussex PO19 1UD, England. TEL 44-1243-779777. FAX 44-1243-775878. *5062*

DYSPHAGIA.
Springer-Verlag, Medical Journals, 175 Fifth Ave., New York, NY 10010. TEL 212-460-1500. FAX 212-473-6272. *5021*

E A A EXPERIMENTER.
Experimental Aircraft Association, Inc., Box 3086, Oshkosh, WI 54903-3086. TEL 414-426-4800. FAX 414-426-4828. *63*

E A I E NEWSLETTER.
European Association for International Education, Van Diemenstraat 344, 1013 CR Amsterdam, Netherlands. TEL 31-20-6252727. FAX 31-20-6209406. *2564*

E A JOURNAL.
National Association of Enrolled Agents, 200 Orchard Ridge Dr., Ste. 302, Gaithersburg, MD 20878-1978. TEL 301-212-9608. FAX 301-990-1611. *1607*

E A R.
University of Edinburgh, Department of Architecture, 20 Chambers St., Edinburgh EH1 1JZ, Scotland. FAX 0131-650-8019. *402*

E A R SE L ADVANCES IN REMOTE SENSING YEARBOOK.
European Association of Remote Sensing Laboratories, 2 av. Rapp, 75340 Paris Cedex 07, France. TEL 33-1-45567360. FAX 33-1-45567361. *2313*

E B U TECHNICAL REVIEW.
European Broadcasting Union, Case postale 67, CH-1218 Grand-Saconnex, Switzerland. TEL 41-22-7172111. FAX 41-22-7172200. *1988*

E D I LAW REVIEW.
Kluwer Law International, Postbus 85889, 2508 CN The Hague, Netherlands. TEL 31-70-3081500. FAX 31-70-3081515. *2169*

E D T N A - E R C A JOURNAL.
European Dialysis and Transplant Nurses Association, European Renal Care Association, P.O. Box 3052, CH-6002 Luzern, Switzerland. *5160*

E E: EVALUATION ENGINEERING.
Nelson Publishing Co., 2504 N. Tamiami Trail, Nokomis, FL 34275-3476. TEL 813-966-9521. FAX 813-966-2590. *2630*

E H E NEWS.
Exceptional Human Experience Network, 414 Rockledge Rd., New Bern, NC 28562-9553. TEL 919-636-8734. FAX 919-636-8371. *5456*

E H P.
Medicultura International B.V., P.O. Box 108, 3958 ZV Amerongen, Netherlands. TEL 31-343-452941. FAX 31-343-451144. *5659*

E H P SUPPLEMENTS.
U.S. Department of Health and Human Services, National Institute of Environmental Health Sciences, Box 12233, Research Triangle Park, NC 27709. TEL 919-541-3406. FAX 919-541-0273. *2913*

E LAW.
Murdoch University, School of Law, Perth, W.A. 6150, Australia. FAX 61-9-3106671. *3943*

E P A NEWSLETTER.
European Photochemistry Association, Stiftstr. 34-36, 45470 Muelheim, Germany. TEL 49-208-30643672. FAX 49-208-30643951. *1827*

E P E JOURNAL.
E P E Association, Secretariat S R B E, Av. de la Plaine 2, 1050 Brussels, Belgium. TEL 32-2-6292819. FAX 32-2-6293620. *2630*

E P P O BULLETIN.
Blackwell Science Ltd., Osney Mead, Oxford OX2 0EL, England. TEL 44-1865-206206. FAX 44-1865-721205. *222*

E P S I G NEWS.
Electronic Publishing Special Interest Group, c/o GCARI, 100 Daingerfield Rd., Alexandria, VA 22314. TEL 703-519-8184. FAX 703-548-2867. *6270*

E P S L ONLINE.
Elsevier Science B.V., P.O. Box 211, 1000 AE Amsterdam, Netherlands. TEL 31-20-4853911. FAX 31-20-4853705. *2313*

E S C W A POPULATION BULLETIN.
United Nations Publications, Sales and Marketing Section, Room DC2-0853, New York, NY 10017. TEL 212-963-8302. FAX 212-963-3489. *6049*

E U R E G.
Akademie fuer Raumforschung und Landesplanung, Hohenzollernstr. 11, 30161 Hannover, Germany. TEL 49-511-3484231. FAX 49-511-3484241. *1252*

THE EAR.
Irvine Valley College, School of Humanities, 5500 Irvine Center Dr., Irvine, CA 92620. TEL 714-451-5341. *4399*

EAR AND HEARING.
Williams & Wilkins, 351 W. Camden St., Baltimore, MD 21201-2436. TEL 410-528-4068. FAX 410-528-4452. *5021*

EAR, NOSE AND THROAT JOURNAL.
Medquest Communications, Inc., 629 Euclid Ave., Ste. 500, Cleveland, OH 44114-3003. TEL 216-522-9700. FAX 216-522-9707. *5021*

EARLY AMERICAN LITERATURE.
University of North Carolina Press, Box 2288, Chapel Hill, NC 27515-2288. TEL 919-966-3561. FAX 800-272-6817. *4400*

EARLY CHILD DEVELOPMENT AND CARE.
Gordon and Breach - Harwood Academic, Amsteldisk 166, 1st Fl., 1079 LH Amsterdam, Netherlands. *1844*

EARLY CHILDHOOD EDUCATION JOURNAL.
Human Sciences Press, Inc., 233 Spring St., New York, NY 10013-1578. TEL 212-620-8000. FAX 212-463-0742. *2434*

EARLY DEVELOPMENT AND PARENTING.
John Wiley & Sons Ltd., Journals, Baffins Ln., Chichester, W. Sussex PO19 1UD, England. TEL 44-1243-779777. FAX 44-1243-775878. *6108*

EARLY HUMAN DEVELOPMENT.
Elsevier Science Ireland Ltd., P.O. Box 85, Limerick, Ireland. TEL 353-61-471944. FAX 353-61-472144. *4956*

EARLY KEYBOARD JOURNAL.
Southeastern Historical Keyboard Society, Box 32022, Charlotte, NC 28232-2022. TEL 704-334-3468. FAX 704-334-3468. *5390*

EARLY PREGNANCY BIOLOGY & MEDICINE.
Society for the Investigation of Early Pregnancy, 1697 Lark Ln., Cherry Hill. TEL 609-429-2699. FAX 609-429-7414. *4956*

EARLY SCIENCE AND MEDICINE.
E.J. Brill, P.O. Box 9000, 2300 PA Leiden, Netherlands. TEL 31-71-5353500. FAX 31-71-5317532. *4663*

EARLY THEATRE.
McMaster University, English Department, 150 Charles St. W., Toronto, ON M5S 1K9, Canada. TEL 905-585-4504. FAX 905-585-4594. *7005*

EARTH AND PLANETARY SCIENCE LETTERS.
Elsevier Science B.V., P.O. Box 211, 1000 AE Amsterdam, Netherlands. TEL 31-20-4853911. FAX 31-20-4853598. *2313*

EARTH FIRST!
Box 1415, Eugene, OR 97440-1415. TEL 541-741-9191. FAX 541-741-9192. *2228*

REFEREED SERIALS

EARTH, MOON AND PLANETS.
Kluwer Academic Publishers, Postbus 17, 3300 AA Dordrecht, Netherlands. TEL 31-78-6392392. FAX 31-78-6392254. *494*

EARTH OBSERVATION AND REMOTE SENSING.
Gordon and Breach - Harwood Academic, Amsteldisk 166, 1st Fl., 1079 LH Amsterdam, Netherlands. *2716*

EARTH SCIENCE REVIEWS.
Elsevier Science B.V., P.O. Box 211, 1000 AE Amsterdam, Netherlands. TEL 31-20-4853911. FAX 31-20-4853598. *2314*

EARTH SURFACE PROCESSES AND LANDFORMS.
John Wiley & Sons Ltd., Journals, Baffins Ln., Chichester, W. Sussex PO19 1UD, England. TEL 44-1243-779777. FAX 44-1243-775878. *2338*

EARTHQUAKES AND VOLCANOES.
U.S. Geological Survey, 12201 Sunrise Valley Dr., Reston, VA 22092. TEL 202-648-4000. *2381*

EARTHSONG.
Heard Museum, 22 E. Monte Vista Rd., Phoenix, AZ 85004-1480. TEL 602-252-8840. FAX 602-252-9757. *5354*

EAST AFRICAN AGRICULTURAL AND FORESTRY JOURNAL.
Kenya Agricultural Research Institute, P.O. Box 30148, Nairobi, Kenya. TEL 254-2-444144. *113*

THE EAST AFRICAN MEDICAL JOURNAL.
Kenya Medical Association House, Chyulu Rd., P.O. Box 41632, Nairobi, Kenya. TEL 254-2-712010. FAX 254-2-724617. *4663*

EAST AND CENTRAL AFRICAN JOURNAL OF SURGERY.
Association of Surgeons of East Africa, P.O. Box 320159, Woodlands, Lusaka, Zambia. TEL 260-1-230710. FAX 260-1-250753. *5141*

EAST ANGLIAN ARCHAEOLOGY. REPORT.
Norfolk Field Archaeology Division, Union House, Gressenhall, Dereham, Norfolk NR20 4DR, England. TEL 44-1362-860528. FAX 44-1362-860951. *361*

EAST ASIAN HISTORY.
Australian National University, Division of Pacific and Asian History, Canberra, A.C.T. 0200, Australia. TEL 61-6-2493141. FAX 61-6-2495525. *3533*

EAST EUROPEAN MEDICAL JOURNAL.
Edit Dan Publishing Co., P.O. Box 209, 600 Iasi 1, Rumania. TEL 40-98-135778. FAX 40-98-117607. *4663*

EAST EUROPEAN POLITICS & SOCIETIES.
University of California Press, Journals Division, 2120 Berkeley Way, No. 5812, Berkeley, CA 94720-5812. TEL 510-643-7154. FAX 510-642-9917. *5922*

EAST LOTHIAN LIFE.
P J Design, 2 Beveridge Row, Belhaven, Dunbar, E. Lothian EH42 1TP, Scotland. TEL 44-1368-863593. FAX 44-1368-863593. *3296*

EAST TEXAS HISTORICAL JOURNAL.
East Texas Historical Association, Box 6223, SFA Sta., Nacogdoches, TX 75962. TEL 405-468-2407. FAX 409-468-2190. *3625*

EAST - WEST CENTER OCCASIONAL PAPERS: POPULATION SERIES.
East - West Center, 1601 East-West Rd., Honolulu, HI 96848. TEL 808-944-7482. FAX 808-944-7490. *6049*

EAST-WEST JOURNAL OF NUMERICAL MATHEMATICS.
V S P, P.O. Box 346, 3700 AH Zeist, Netherlands. TEL 31-30-6925790. FAX 31-30-6932081. *4620*

EAST-WEST PERSPECTIVES.
Kluwer Academic Publishers, Postbus 17, 3300 AA Dordrecht, Netherlands. TEL 31-78-6392392. FAX 31-78-6392254. *6012*

EASTERN AFRICA SOCIAL SCIENCE RESEARCH REVIEW.
Organization for Social Science Research in Eastern Africa, P.O. Box 31971, Addis Ababa, Ethiopia. TEL 251-1-119705. FAX 251-1-551399. *6611*

EASTERN ART REPORT.
Eastern Art Publishing Group, P.O. Box 13666, London SW14 8WF, England. TEL 44-181-392-1122. FAX 44-181-392-1422. *439*

EASTERN BUDDHIST.
Eastern Buddhist Society, Otani University, Koyama, Kita-ku, Kyoto 603, Japan. TEL 81-75-431-4390. FAX 81-75-431-4390. *6388*

EASTERN CHALLENGE.
International Missions, Inc., Box 14866, Reading, PA 19612-4866. TEL 610-375-0300. FAX 610-375-6862. *6422*

EASTERN ECONOMIC JOURNAL.
Eastern Economic Association, Iona College, New Rochelle, NY 10801. TEL 610-559-8050. FAX 610-250-8961. *955*

EASTERN EUROPEAN ECONOMICS.
M.E. Sharpe, Inc., 80 Business Park Dr., Armonk, NY 10504. TEL 914-273-1800. FAX 914-273-2106. *955*

EASTERN NEWS.
Box 1061, Stn. B, Mississauga, ON L4Y 2E0, Canada. TEL 905-858-7525. FAX 905-858-7951. *3009*

EASTERN PHARMACIST.
507 Ashok Bhawan, 93, Nehru Place, New Delhi 110 019, India. TEL 91-11-6433315. *5659*

EATING DISORDERS.
Brunner - Mazel, Inc., 19 Union Sq. W., New York, NY 10003. TEL 212-924-3344. FAX 212-242-6339. *6108*

ECCLESIASTICAL LAW JOURNAL.
Ecclesiastical Law Society, 1 The Sanctuary, Westminster, London SW1P 3JT, England. TEL 44-171-222-5381. *6335*

ECHOCARDIOGRAPHY.
Futura Publishing Company, Inc., 135 Bedford Rd., Box 418, Armonk, NY 10504. TEL 914-273-1014. FAX 914-273-1015. *4816*

ECHOCARDIOGRAPHY JOURNAL OF CARDIAC ULTRASOUND. *4816*

ECHOES.
Echoes of Service, 1 Widcombe Cresc., Bath, Avon BA2 6AQ, England. TEL 44-1225-310893. FAX 44-1225-480134. *6422*

ECHOS DU MONDE CLASSIQUE.
University of Calgary Press, 2500 University Dr. N.W., Calgary, AB T2N 1N4, Canada. TEL 403-220-7578. FAX 403-282-0085. *1903*

ECO DEL MANTE.
Guerrero 701 Ote., 89800 Mante, Tamaulipas, Mexico. TEL 55-123-20040. FAX 55-123-22420. *3335*

ECOGRAPHY.
Munksgaard International Publishers Ltd., 35 Noerre Soegade, P.O. Box 2148, DK-1016 Copenhagen K, Denmark. TEL 45-33-127030. FAX 45-33-129387. *2915*

ECOLOGIA EN BOLIVIA.
Instituto de Ecologia, Casilla 10077, La Paz, Bolivia. TEL 591-2-792582. FAX 591-2-797511. *599*

ECOLOGICAL APPLICATIONS.
Ecological Society of America, 2010 Massachusetts Ave., N.W., Ste. 400, Washington, DC 20036. TEL 202-833-8773. FAX 202-833-8775. *2915*

ECOLOGICAL ECONOMICS.
Elsevier Science B.V., P.O. Box 211, 1000 AE Amsterdam, Netherlands. TEL 31-20-4853911. FAX 31-20-4853598. *2915*

ECOLOGICAL ENGINEERING.
Elsevier Science B.V., P.O. Box 211, 1000 AE Amsterdam, Netherlands. TEL 31-20-4853911. FAX 31-20-4853598. *2915*

ECOLOGICAL ENTOMOLOGY.
Blackwell Science Ltd., Osney Mead, Oxford OX2 0EL, England. TEL 44-1865-206206. FAX 44-1865-721205. *749*

ECOLOGICAL MODELLING.
Elsevier Science B.V., P.O. Box 211, 1000 AE Amsterdam, Netherlands. TEL 31-20-4853911. FAX 31-20-4853598. *2964*

ECOLOGICAL MONOGRAPHS.
Ecological Society of America, 2010 Massachusetts Ave., N.W., Ste. 400, Washington, DC 20036. TEL 202-833-8773. FAX 202-833-8775. *2915*

ECOLOGICAL PSYCHOLOGY.
Lawrence Erlbaum Associates, Inc., 10 Industrial Dr., Mahwah, NJ 07430-2262. TEL 201-236-9500. FAX 201-236-0072. *6109*

ECOLOGY.
Ecological Society of America, 2010 Massachusetts Ave., N.W., Ste. 400, Washington, DC 20036. TEL 202-833-8773. FAX 202-833-8775. *2916*

ECOLOGY & ENVIRONMENT.
Kluwer Academic Publishers, Postbus 17, 3300 AA Dordrecht, Netherlands. TEL 31-78-6392392. FAX 31-78-6392254. *2916*

ECOLOGY, ECONOMY & ENVIRONMENT.
Kluwer Academic Publishers, Postbus 17, 3300 AA Dordrecht, Netherlands. TEL 31-78-6392392. FAX 31-78-6392254. *2916*

ECOLOGY LAW QUARTERLY.
University of California Press, Journals Division, 2120 Berkeley Way, No. 5812, Berkeley, CA 94720-5812. TEL 510-643-7154. FAX 510-642-9917. *3943*

ECOLOGY OF FOOD AND NUTRITION.
Gordon and Breach - Harwood Academic, Amsteldisk 166, 1st Fl., 1079 LH Amsterdam, Netherlands. *5472*

ECOLOGY OF FRESHWATER FISH.
Munksgaard International Publishers Ltd., 35 Noerre Soegade, P.O. Box 2148, DK-1016 Copenhagen K, Denmark. TEL 45-33-127030. FAX 45-33-129387. *833*

ECONOMETRICA.
Blackwell Publishers Ltd., 108 Cowley Rd., Oxford OX4 1JF, England. TEL 44-1865-791100. FAX 44-1865-791347. *956*

ECONOMIA.
Pontificia Universidad Catolica del Peru, Fondo Editorial, Apdo. 1761, Lima 32, Peru. TEL 51-14-626390. FAX 5114-611785. *956*

ECONOMIA CAFETERA.
Federacion Nacional de Cafeteros de Colombia, Calle 73 No. 8-13, piso 10 B, Bogota D.E., Colombia. TEL 57-1-3451088. FAX 57-1-2171021. *192*

ECONOMIA E SOCIOLOGIA.
Instituto Superior Economico e Social, Rua Vasco da Gama 15, 7000 Evora, Portugal. TEL 23327. *1253*

ECONOMIA EM REVISTA.
Universidade Estadual de Maringa, Departamento de Economia, Av. Colombo 5790, 87020-900 Maringa PR, Brazil. TEL 55-442614305. FAX 55-442232676. *956*

ECONOMIC AFFAIRS.
Blackwell Publishers Ltd., 108 Cowley Rd., Oxford OX4 1JF, England. TEL 44-1865-791100. FAX 44-1865-791347. *957*

ECONOMIC & FINANCIAL COMPUTING.
European Economics and Financial Centre, Publications Department, P.O. Box 2498, London W2 4LE, England. TEL 0171-229-0402. FAX 0171-221-5118. *1200*

ECONOMIC & FINANCIAL MODELLING.
European Economics and Financial Centre, Publications Department, P.O. Box 2498, London W2 4LE, England. TEL 44-171-229-0402. FAX 44-171-221-5118. *1200*

ECONOMIC & FINANCIAL REVIEW.
European Economics and Financial Centre, P.O. Box 2498, London W2 4LE, England. TEL 0171-229-0402. FAX 0171-221-5118. *957*

ECONOMIC AND INDUSTRIAL DEMOCRACY.
Sage Publications Ltd., 6 Bonhill St., London EC2A 4PU, England. TEL 44-171-374-0645. FAX 44-171-374-8741. *5923*

ECONOMIC AND POLITICAL WEEKLY.
Sameeksha Trust, Hitkari House, 284, Shahid Bhagatsingh Rd., Mumbai 400 038, India. TEL 91-22-2676072. FAX 91-22-269-6072. *957*

ECONOMIC BOTANY.
New York Botanical Garden, Scientific Publications Department, Bronx, NY 10458-5126. TEL 718-817-8721. FAX 718-817-8842. *701*

ECONOMIC DESIGN.
North-Holland, P.O. Box 211, 1000 AE Amsterdam, Netherlands. TEL 31-20-4853911. FAX 31-20-4853598. *1302*

ECONOMIC DEVELOPMENT AND CULTURAL CHANGE.
University of Chicago Press, Journals Division, Box 37005, Chicago, IL 60637. TEL 773-753-3347. FAX 773-753-0811. *1358*

ECONOMIC HISTORY REVIEW.
Blackwell Publishers Ltd., 108 Cowley Rd., Oxford OX4 1JF, England. TEL 44-1865-791100. FAX 44-1865-791347. *1302*

ECONOMIC INQUIRY.
Western Economic Association International, 7400 Center Ave., Ste. 109, Huntington Beach, CA 92647. TEL 714-898-3222. *958*

ECONOMIC JOURNAL.
Blackwell Publishers Ltd., 108 Cowley Rd., Oxford OX4 1JF, England. TEL 44-1865-791100. FAX 44-1865-791347. *958*

ECONOMIC MICROBIOLOGY.
Academic Press, Inc., 525 B St., Ste. 1900, San Diego, CA 92101-4495. TEL 619-231-0926. FAX 619-699-6715. *783*

ECONOMIC MODELLING.
North-Holland, P.O. Box 211, 1000 AE Amsterdam, Netherlands. TEL 31-20-4853757. FAX 31-20-4853432. *1302*

ECONOMIC OUTLOOK.
Pakistan Press International, Press Centre, Shahrah-e-Kamal Ataturk, Karachi, Pakistan. TEL 92-21-2635751. FAX 92-21-2631125. *1254*

ECONOMIC OUTLOOK.
Blackwell Publishers Ltd., 108 Cowley Rd., Oxford OX4 1JF, England. TEL 44-1865-791100. FAX 44-1865-791347. *1254*

ECONOMIC POLICY.
Blackwell Publishers Ltd., 108 Cowley Rd., Oxford OX4 1JF, England. TEL 44-1865-791100. FAX 44-1865-791347. *958*

ECONOMIC RECORD.
Economic Society of Australia, c/o R.A. Williams, Ed., Dept. of Economics, Melbourne University, Melbourne, Vic. 3052, Australia. TEL 61-3-93447426. FAX 61-3-93446899. *958*

ECONOMIC REVIEW OF AGRICULTURE.
Ministry of Agriculture, Development Planning Division, P.O. Box 30028, Nairobi, Kenya. TEL 254-2-718870. *192*

ECONOMIC SYSTEMS.
Physica-Verlag GmbH und Co., Postfach 105280, 69042 Heidelberg, Germany. TEL 49-6221-487492. FAX 49-6221-487177. *1322*

ECONOMIC SYSTEMS RESEARCH.
Carfax Publishing Co., P.O. Box 25, Abingdon, Oxon. OX14 3UE, England. TEL 44-1235-401000. FAX 44-1235-401550. *1302*

ECONOMICA.
Blackwell Publishers Ltd., 108 Cowley Rd., Oxford OX4 1JF, England. TEL 44-1865-791100. FAX 44-1865-791347. *959*

ECONOMICS & POLITICS.
Blackwell Publishers Ltd., 108 Cowley Rd., Oxford OX4 1JF, England. TEL 44-1865-791100. FAX 44-1865-791347. *1302*

ECONOMICS LETTERS.
Elsevier Science S.A., P.O. Box 564, CH-1001 Lausanne 1, Switzerland. TEL 41-21-3207381. FAX 41-21-3235444. *1302*

ECONOMICS OF EDUCATION REVIEW.
Elsevier Science Ltd., Pergamon, P.O. Box 800, Kidlington, Oxford OX5 1DX, England. TEL 44-1865-843000. FAX 44-1865-843010. *2571*

ECONOMICS OF INNOVATION AND NEW TECHNOLOGY.
Gordon and Breach - Harwood Academic, Amsteldisk 166, 1st Fl., 1079 LH Amsterdam, Netherlands. *6958*

ECONOMICS OF PLANNING.
Kluwer Academic Publishers, Postbus 17, 3300 AA Dordrecht, Netherlands. TEL 31-78-6392392. FAX 31-78-6392254. *1255*

ECONOMICS OF SCIENCE, TECHNOLOGY AND INNOVATION.
Kluwer Academic Publishers, Postbus 17, 3300 AA Dordrecht, Netherlands. TEL 31-78-6392392. FAX 31-78-6392254. *6958*

ECONOMIE ET SOCIALISME.
Centre d'Etudes et de Recherches Aziz Belal, B.P. 6330, Rabat, Morocco. TEL 77-62-17. FAX 77-38-89. *1255*

ECONOMIE RURALE.
Societe Francaise d'Economie Rurale, 16 rue Claude Bernard, 75231 Paris Cedex 05, France. TEL 33-1-47074786. FAX 33-1-44081842. *192*

DE ECONOMIST.
Kluwer Academic Publishers, Postbus 17, 3300 AA Dordrecht, Netherlands. TEL 31-78-6392392. FAX 31-78-6392254. *959*

ECONOMY & ENVIRONMENT.
Kluwer Academic Publishers, Postbus 17, 3300 AA Dordrecht, Netherlands. TEL 31-78-6392392. FAX 31-78-6392254. *2916*

ECOSYSTEMS OF THE WORLD.
Elsevier Science B.V., Books Division, P.O. Box 211, 1000 AE Amsterdam, Netherlands. TEL 31-20-4853911. FAX 31-20-4853705. *2916*

ECOTOXICOLOGY.
Chapman & Hall, Journals Department 2-6 Boundary Row, London SE1 8HN, England. TEL 44-171-8650066. FAX 44-171-5229623. *2976*

ECOTOXICOLOGY AND ENVIRONMENTAL SAFETY.
Academic Press, Inc., Journal Division, 525 B St., Ste. 1900, San Diego, CA 92101-4495. TEL 619-250-1840. FAX 619-699-6800. *2977*

ECQUID NOVI.
Institute for Communication Research, Potchefstroom University, Potchefstroom 2520, South Africa. TEL 27-148-2991648. FAX 27-148-2991651. *3872*

ECUADOR DEBATE.
Centro Andino de Accion Popular, Apdo. Postal 17-15-173-B, Quito, Ecuador. TEL 593-2-523262. FAX 593-2-568452. *5923*

ECUMENE.
Arnold, 338 Euston Rd., London NW1 3BH, England. TEL 44-171-873-6000. FAX 44-171-873-6325. *2916*

EDINBURGH REVIEW.
Edinburgh University Press, 22 George Sq., Edinburgh EH8 9LF, Scotland. TEL 44-131-650-6207. FAX 44-131-662-0053. *4332*

EDMUNDITE.
Society of St. Edmund, P.O. Box 399, Mystic, CT 06355-0399. TEL 203-536-7540. *6462*

EDUBBA.
University of Sydney, Department of Ancient History, Sydney, N.S.W. 2006, Australia. TEL 61-2-93512156. FAX 61-2-93517760. *3494*

EDUCACAO E SOCIEDADE.
Centro de Estudos de Educacao e Sociedade, Caixa Postal 6022, 13083-790 Campinas SP, Brazil. TEL 55-19-2391598. *2435*

EDUCACION.
Pontificia Universidad Catolica del Peru, Fondo Editorial, Apdo. 1761, Lima 32, Peru. TEL 51-14-626390. FAX 51-14-611785. *2435*

EDUCACION (HAVANA).
Editorial Pueblo y Educacion, Av. 3ra A No. 4601, entre 46 y 60, Playa, Havana 11300, Cuba. TEL 537-236192. FAX 537-330844. *2435*

EDUCACION SUPERIOR Y SOCIEDAD.
UNESCO (Venezuela), Centro Regional para Educacion Superior en America Latina y el Caribe, Apdo. Postal 68394, Caracas 1062 A, Venezuela. FAX 58-2-2612129. *2540*

EDUCACION Y CIENCIAS HUMANAS.
Universidad Simon Rodriguez, Decanato de Postgrado, Calle 5 entre 7ma. y 8va. Transversal, Edif. El Caney, La Urbina, Caracas, Venezuela. TEL 58-2-2422622. FAX 58-2-2436346. *2435*

EDUCATION AND AGEING.
Triangle Journals Ltd., P.O. Box 65, Wallingford, Oxon. OX10 0YG, England. TEL 44-1491-838013. FAX 44-1491-834968. *2509*

EDUCATION AND HEALTH.
Schools Health Education Unit, University of Exeter, School of Education, Heavitree Rd., Exeter EX1 2LU, England. TEL 44-1392-264722. FAX 44-1392-264761. *2571*

EDUCATION AND SOCIETY.
James Nicholas Publishers, P.O. Box 244, Albert Park, Vic. 3206, Australia. TEL 03-696-5545. FAX 613-699-2040. *2436*

EDUCATION AND SOCIETY IN THE MIDDLE AGES AND RENAISSANCE.
E.J. Brill, P.O. Box 9000, 2300 PA Leiden, Netherlands. TEL 31-71-5353500. FAX 31-71-5317532. *3563*

EDUCATION AND TREATMENT OF CHILDREN.
Pressley Ridge Schools, 530 Marshall Ave., Pittsburgh, PA 15214. TEL 412-321-6995. FAX 412-321-5313. *2600*

EDUCATION ECONOMICS.
Carfax Publishing Co., P.O. Box 25, Abingdon, Oxon. OX14 3UE, England. TEL 44-1235-401000. FAX 44-1235-401550. *2571*

EDUCATION ET FRANCOPHONIE.
Association Canadienne d'Education de Langue Francaise, 268 rue Marie-de-l'Incarnation, Quebec, PQ G1N 3G4, Canada. TEL 418-681-4661. FAX 418-681-3389. *2437*

EDUCATION FOR LIBRARY AND INFORMATION SERVICES: AUSTRALIA.
Australian Library and Information Association, P.O. Box E441, Queen Victoria Terrace, A.C.T. 2600, Australia. TEL 61-6-285-1877. FAX 61-6-282-2249. *4176*

EDUCATION IN RUSSIA, THE INDEPENDENT STATES AND EASTERN EUROPE.
Study Group on Education in Russia, the Independent States and Eastern Europe, c/o Department of Modern Languages, University of Bradford, Bradford, W. Yorks BD7 1DP, England. TEL 44-1274-541901. *2437*

EDUCATION INTERNATIONAL QUARTERLY MAGAZINE.
Education International, Bd. E. Jacqmain 155, 8th Fl., 1210 Brussels, Belgium. TEL 32-2-2240611. FAX 32-2-2240606. *2437*

EDUCATION LIBRARIES.
Special Library Association, Education Division, Concordia University, Education Department, 1455 de Maisonneuve W., Montreal, PQ H3G 1M8, Canada. TEL 514-848-2543. FAX 514-848-3492. *4176*

EDUCATION MARKETING.
Heist, The Coach House, 184 Ohey Rd., Leeds LS16 5LW, England. TEL 44-113-226-5858. FAX 44-113-226-7878. *2571*

REFEREED SERIALS

EDUCATION POLICY ANALYSIS ARCHIVES.
Arizona State University, College of Education, Box 872411, Tempe, AZ 85287-2411. TEL 602-965-2692. *2438*

EDUCATION RESEARCH AND PERSPECTIVES.
University of Western Australia, Department of Education, Nedlands, W.A. 6009, Australia. TEL 61-9-3802385. FAX 61-9-3801052. *2540*

EDUCATION TODAY.
Pitman Publishing, 128 Long Acre, London WC2E 9AN, England. TEL 44-171-447-2000. FAX 44-171-240-5771. *2438*

EDUCATION 3-13.
Pitman Publishing, 128 Long Acre, London WC2E 9AN, England. TEL 44-171-447-2000. FAX 44-171-240-5771. *2438*

EDUCATIONAL ACTION RESEARCH.
Triangle Journals Ltd., P.O. Box 65, Wallingford, Oxon. OX10 0YG, England. TEL 44-1491-838013. FAX 44-1491-834968. *2600*

EDUCATIONAL ADMINISTRATION QUARTERLY.
Corwin Press, Inc., 2455 Teller Rd., Thousand Oaks, CA 91320. TEL 805-499-0721. FAX 805-499-0871. *2571*

EDUCATIONAL & CHILD PSYCHOLOGY.
British Psychological Society, Division of Educational and Child Psychology, St. Andrew's House, 48 Princess Rd. E., Leicester LE1 7DR, England. *6109*

EDUCATIONAL AND PSYCHOLOGICAL MEASUREMENT.
Sage Publications Inc., 2455 Teller Rd., Thousand Oaks, CA 91320. TEL 805-499-0721. FAX 805-499-0871. *6109*

EDUCATIONAL CONSIDERATIONS.
Kansas State University, College of Education, Bluemont Hall 313, Manhattan, KS 66506. TEL 913-532-5543. FAX 913-532-7304. *2438*

EDUCATIONAL EVALUATION & POLICY ANALYSIS.
American Educational Research Association, 1230 17th St., N.W., Washington, DC 20036-3078. TEL 202-223-9485. FAX 202-775-1824. *2439*

EDUCATIONAL FORUM.
Kappa Delta Pi International Honor Society in Education, Box A, West Lafayette, IN 47906-0576. TEL 765-743-1705. FAX 765-743-2202. *2540*

EDUCATIONAL GERONTOLOGY.
Taylor & Francis Inc., 1900 Frost Rd., Ste. 101, Bristol, PA 19007-1598. TEL 215-785-5800. FAX 215-785-5515. *2509*

EDUCATIONAL MANAGEMENT & ADMINISTRATION.
Sage Publications Ltd., 6 Bonhill St., London EC2A 4PU, England. TEL 44-171-374-9645. FAX 44-171-374-8741. *2571*

EDUCATIONAL MEASUREMENT: ISSUES AND PRACTICE.
National Council on Measurement in Education, 1230 17th St. N.W., Washington, DC 20036-3078. TEL 202-223-9313. FAX 202-775-1824. *2439*

EDUCATIONAL PHILOSOPHY AND THEORY.
Philosophy of Education Society of Australasia, c/o Prof. Jim Walker, Ed., Faculty of Education, UWS Nepean, P.O. Box 10, Kingwood, N.S.W. 2747, Australia. TEL 61-47-360214. FAX 61-47-360400. *2439*

EDUCATIONAL PLANNING.
International Society for Educational Planning, School of Education, University of South Dakota, 414 East Clark St., Vermillion, SD 57069. TEL 605-677-5454. *2439*

EDUCATIONAL POLICY.
Corwin Press, Inc., 2455 Teller Rd., Thousand Oaks, CA 91320. TEL 805-499-0721. FAX 805-499-0871. *2439*

EDUCATIONAL PRACTICE AND THEORY.
James Nicholas Publishers, P.O. Box 244, Albert Park, Vic. 3206, Australia. TEL 61-3-696-5545. FAX 613-699-2040. *2439*

EDUCATIONAL PSYCHOLOGIST.
Lawrence Erlbaum Associates, Inc., 10 Industrial Dr., Mahwah, NJ 07430-2262. TEL 201-236-9500. FAX 201-236-0072. *6109*

EDUCATIONAL PSYCHOLOGY.
Carfax Publishing Co., P.O. Box 25, Abingdon, Oxon. OX14 3UE, England. TEL 44-1235-401000. FAX 44-1235-401550. *6109*

EDUCATIONAL PSYCHOLOGY IN PRACTICE.
Pitman Publishing, 128 Long Acre, London WC2E 9AN, England. TEL 44-171-447-2000. FAX 44-171-240-5771. *6109*

EDUCATIONAL PSYCHOLOGY REVIEW.
Plenum Publishing Corp., 233 Spring St., New York, NY 10013-1578. TEL 212-620-8000. FAX 212-463-0742. *2439*

EDUCATIONAL RESEARCH AND EVALUATION.
Swets & Zeitlinger bv, P.O. Box 825, 2160 SZ Lisse, Netherlands. TEL 31-252-435111. FAX 31-252-415888. *2440*

EDUCATIONAL RESEARCH QUARTERLY.
113 Greenbriar Dr., W. Monroe, LA 71291. TEL 318-274-2355. *2440*

EDUCATIONAL RESEARCHER.
American Educational Research Association, 1230 17th St. N.W., Washington, DC 20036-3078. TEL 202-223-9485. FAX 202-775-1824. *2440*

EDUCATIONAL REVIEW.
Carfax Publishing Co., P.O. Box 25, Abingdon, Oxon. OX14 3UE, England. TEL 44-1235-401000. FAX 44-1235-401550. *2440*

EDUCATIONAL REVIEW PUBLICATIONS. HEADLINE SERIES.
Educational Review Publications, University of Birmingham, School of Education, Edgbaston, Birmingham B15 2TT, England. *2601*

EDUCATIONAL STUDIES.
Carfax Publishing Co., P.O. Box 25, Abingdon, Oxon. OX14 3UE, England. TEL 44-1235-401000. FAX 44-1235-401550. *2440*

EDUCATIONAL STUDIES IN MATHEMATICS.
Kluwer Academic Publishers, Postbus 17, 3300 AA Dordrecht, Netherlands. TEL 31-78-6392392. FAX 31-78-6392254. *4571*

EDUCATIONAL TECHNOLOGY RESEARCH & DEVELOPMENT.
Association for Educational Communications and Technology, 1025 Vermont Ave. N.W., Ste. 820, Washington, DC 20005-3516. TEL 202-347-7834. FAX 202-347-7839. *2601*

EDUQUER & FORMER.
Institut Superieur de Pedagogie de la Region de Bruxelles - Capitale, Bd. de Waterloo 100-103, 1000 Brussels, Belgium. TEL 32-2-5428351. FAX 32-2-5428390. *2441*

EFFECTIVE MANAGEMENT SERIES.
Blackwell Publishers Ltd., 108 Cowley Rd., Oxford OX4 1JF, England. TEL 44-1865-791100. FAX 44-1865-791347. *1475*

EGYPTIAN JOURNAL OF DAIRY SCIENCE.
Egyptian Society of Dairy Science, National Research Centre, Sharia Tahrir, Dokki, Cairo, Egypt. TEL 20-2-701211. FAX 20-2-700931. *254*

EHIMEKEN KENSETSU KENKYUJO KENKYUJOHO.
Ehimeken Kensetsu Kenkyujo, 440, Higashiishii-machi, Mtsuyama-shi, Ehime-ken 790, Japan. TEL 81-89-956-0292. FAX 81-89-956-0293. *2783*

EIDOLON.
Eidolon Publications, P.O. Box 225, North Perth, WA 6006, Australia. TEL 61-8-92729850. *4530*

EIDOS.
University of Waterloo, Philosophy Graduate Student Association, Dept. of Philosophy, Waterloo, ON N2L 3G1, Canada. TEL 519-885-1211. *5724*

EIDOS: STUDIES IN CLASSICAL KINDS.
University of California Press, 2120 Berkeley Way, Berkeley, CA 94720. TEL 510-642-4247. FAX 510-643-7127. *1903*

EIGHTEENTH-CENTURY STUDIES.
Johns Hopkins University Press, Journals Publishing Division, 2715 N. Charles St., Baltimore, MD 21218-4319. TEL 410-516-6987. FAX 410-516-6968. *3494*

THE EINSTEIN QUARTERLY.
Springer-Verlag, Medical Journals, 175 Fifth Ave., New York, NY 10010. TEL 212-460-1500. FAX 212-473-6272. *599*

EIRENE.
John Benjamins Publishing Co., Amsteldijk 44, P.O. Box 75577, 1070 AN Amsterdam, Netherlands. TEL 31-20-6738156. FAX 31-20-6792956. *1903*

EKO I MY.
Agencja Wydawnicza Eko-Medium, Ul. Dembowskiego 25-71, 71-535 Szczecin, Poland. TEL 48-91-553101. FAX 48-91-553101. *2917*

EKONOMIA.
Cyprus Economic Society, P.O. Box 8724, Nicosia, Cyprus. *1303*

EKONOMIKA I ORGANIZACJA PRZEDSIEBIORSTWA.
Instytut Organizacji i Zarzadzania w Przemysle, Ul. Zelazna 87, 00-879 Warsaw, Poland. TEL 48-22-6546061. FAX 48-22-6204360. *1475*

EKONOMIKA SEL'SKOGO KHOZYAISTVA ROSSII.
AgriPress, Sadovaya-Spasskaya, 18, 107807 Moscow, Russia. TEL 7-095-2071662. *192*

EKONOMIKA UKRAINY.
Vidavnitstvo Presa Ukrainy, Peremogy pr., 50, 252047 Kiev 47, Ukraine. TEL 38-44-4418214. FAX 38-44-2908663. *1303*

EKONOMISTA.
Polskie Towarzystwo Ekonomiczne, Ul. Nowy Swiat 49, 00-242 Warsaw, Poland. TEL 48-22-275031. FAX 48-22-279904. *960*

EKSPRESS - ZAKON.
Izdatel'stvo I N F R A - M, Dmitrovskoe shosse, 107, 127247 Moscow, Russia. TEL 7-095-4855779. FAX 7-095-4855318. *1607*

ELECTORAL STUDIES.
Elsevier Science Ltd., Pergamon, P.O. Box 800, Kidlington, Oxford OX5 1DX, England. TEL 44-1865-843000. FAX 44-1865-843010. *5924*

ELECTRIC MACHINES AND POWER SYSTEMS.
Taylor & Francis Inc., 1900 Frost Rd., Ste. 101, Bristol, PA 19007-1598. TEL 215-785-5800. FAX 215-785-5515. *2817*

ELECTRIC POWER SYSTEMS RESEARCH.
Elsevier Science S.A., P.O. Box 564, CH-1001 Lausanne 1, Switzerland. TEL 41-21-3207381. FAX 41-21-3235444. *2817*

ELECTRICAL TECHNOLOGY.
Elsevier Science Ltd., Pergamon, P.O. Box 800, Kidlington, Oxford OX5 1DX, England. TEL 44-1865-843000. FAX 44-1865-843010. *2819*

ELECTRICIDADE.
Empresa Editorial Electrotecnica Edel, Ltda., Rua de Dona Estefania 48, 3 Esq, 1000 Lisbon, Portugal. TEL 351-1-528608. FAX 351-1-3561640. *2819*

ELECTRO- AND MAGNETOBIOLOGY.
Marcel Dekker Journals, 270 Madison Ave., New York, NY 10016. TEL 212-696-9000. FAX 212-685-4540. *674*

ELECTRO-TECHNOLOGY.
Society of Electronic Engineers, Box 9324, LRDE, DRDO Complex, CV Raman Nagar, Bangalore 560 093, India. TEL 91-80-5242035. FAX 91-80-5242916. *2820*

ELECTROANALYTICAL CHEMISTRY: A SERIES OF ADVANCES.
Marcel Dekker, Inc., 270 Madison Ave., New York, NY 10016. TEL 212-696-9000. FAX 212-685-4540. *1790*

ELECTROCHEMICAL SCIENCE AND TECHNOLOGY OF POLYMERS.
Elsevier Science Ltd., Books Division, P.O. Box 800, Kidlington, Oxford OX5 1DX, England. TEL 44-1865-843000. FAX 44-1865-843010. *1804*

ELECTROCHIMICA ACTA.
Elsevier Science Ltd., Pergamon, P.O. Box 800, Kidlington, Oxford OX5 1DX, England. TEL 44-1865-843000. FAX 44-1865-843010. *1805*

ELECTROCOMPONENT SCIENCE MONOGRAPHS.
Gordon and Breach - Harwood Academic, Amsteldisk 166, 1st Fl., 1079 LH Amsterdam, Netherlands. *2820*

ELECTROENCEPHALOGRAPHY AND CLINICAL NEUROPHYSIOLOGY INCLUDING EVOKED POTENTIALS AND ELECTROMYOGRAPHY AND MOTOR CONTROL.
Elsevier Science Ireland Ltd., P.O. Box 85, Limerick, Ireland. TEL 353-61-471944. FAX 353-61-472144. *5062*

ELECTROENCEPHALOGRAPHY AND CLINICAL NEUROPHYSIOLOGY. SUPPLEMENTS.
Elsevier Science B.V., Books Division, P.O. Box 211, 1000 AE Amsterdam, Netherlands. TEL 31-20-4853911. FAX 31-20-4853705. *5062*

ELECTROMAGNETIC WAVES.
Elsevier Science B.V., Books Division, P.O. Box 211, 1000 AE Amsterdam, Netherlands. TEL 31-20-4853911. FAX 31-20-4853705. *5801*

ELECTROMAGNETICS.
Taylor & Francis Inc., 1900 Frost Rd., Ste. 101, Bristol, PA 19007-1598. TEL 215-758-5800. FAX 215-758-5515. *2820*

ELECTROMECHANICAL BENCH REFERENCE.
Barks Publications, Inc., 400 N. Michigan Ave., Chicago, IL 60611-4198. TEL 312-321-9440. FAX 312-321-1288. *2820*

ELECTROMYOGRAPHY AND MOTOR CONTROL.
Elsevier Science Ireland Ltd., P.O. Box 85, Limerick, Ireland. TEL 353-61-471944. FAX 353-61-472144. *5062*

ELECTRON MICROSCOPY IN BIOLOGY AND MEDICINE.
Kluwer Academic Publishers, Postbus 17, 3300 AA Dordrecht, Netherlands. TEL 31-78-6392392. FAX 31-78-6392254. *796*

ELECTRONIC ANTIQUITY.
University of Tasmania, Department of Classics, Hobart, Tasmania 7001, Australia. TEL 61-02-202-294. FAX 61-02-202-288. *1903*

ELECTRONIC GREEN JOURNAL.
University of Idaho Library, University of Idaho Library, Moscow, ID 83844. TEL 208-885-6631. FAX 208-885-6817. *2917*

ELECTRONIC JOURNAL OF DIFFERENTIAL EQUATIONS.
Southwest Texas State University, Department of Mathematics, San Marcos, TX 78666-4616. TEL 512-245-2551. *4571*

ELECTRONIC JOURNAL OF GEOTECHNICAL ENGINEERING. *2783*

THE ELECTRONIC JOURNAL OF RADICAL ORGANISATION THEORY. *6611*

ELECTRONIC JOURNAL OF SOCIOLOGY.
University of Alberta, Department of Sociology, Edmonton, AB T6G 2H4, Canada. *6708*

ELECTRONIC JOURNAL OF STRATEGIC INFORMATION SYSTEMS.
University of Sheffield, Information Studies Department, 211 Portobello St., Regents Court, Rm. 315, Sheffield S10 2UH, England. TEL 44-742-768555. FAX 44-742-780300. *2181*

THE ELECTRONIC JOURNAL ON VIRTUAL CULTURE. TEL 330-273-5932. *2132*

ELECTRONIC PRODUCTION.
Inside Communications Ltd., 9 White Lion St., London N1, England. TEL 44-171-837-8727. *2633*

ELECTRONIC RECRUITING NEWS.
Internet Business Network, 346 Starling Rd., Mill Valley, CA 94941. TEL 415-380-8244. FAX 415-383-8676. *1564*

ELECTRONICS COOLING.
Flomerics Ltd., c/o Livewire Public Relations, 13 Uxbridge Rd., Kingston upon Thames, Surrey KT1 2LH. TEL 44-181-547-3418. FAX 44-181-547-3419. *2634*

ELECTRONICS LETTERS.
I.E.E., Michael Faraday House, Six Hills Way, Stevenage, Herts. SG1 2AY, England. TEL 44-1438-313311. FAX 44-1438-742840. *2634*

ELECTRONICS LETTERS ONLINE.
I.E.E., Michael Faraday House, Six Hills Way, Stevenage, Herts. SG1 2AY, England. TEL 44-1438-313311. FAX 44-1438-742840. *2634*

ELEKTRONIKK BRANSJEN.
Elektronikk Forbundet, Brynsengvn. 2, P.O. Box 6322, Etterstad, N-0604 Oslo, Norway. TEL 47-22-72-21-40. FAX 47-22-72-21-21. *2636*

ELEKTRONNOE MODELIROVANIE.
Akademiya Nauk Ukrainy, Institut Problem Modelyuvannya v Energetytsi, Ul. Generala Naumova, 15, 252680 Kiev, Ukraine. TEL 38-44-4441466. FAX 38-44-4440586. *2151*

ELEKTROTECHNICKY CASOPIS.
Slovenska Akademia Vied, Elektrotechnicky Ustav, Ilkovicova 3, 812 19 Bratislava, Slovakia. TEL 420-7-351646. FAX 420-7-720415. *2822*

THE ELEMENTARY SCHOOL JOURNAL.
University of Chicago Press, Journals Division, Box 37005, Chicago, IL 60637. TEL 773-753-3347. FAX 773-753-0811. *2441*

ELEVATORI.
Volpe Editore, Via di Vittorio 21A, 20060 Vignate, Italy. TEL 39-2-95360416. FAX 39-2-95360418. *7027*

ELEVENTH MUSE.
Poetry West, Box 2413, Colorado Springs, CO 80901. TEL 719-578-5909. *4508*

THE ELIZABETHAN REVIEW.
84-35 62 Dr., Ste. T-41, Mioole Village, NY 11379. TEL 718-458-5675. FAX 718-457-6602. *3564*

ELLEN GLASGOW NEWSLETTER.
Ellen Glasgow Society, c/o Prof. Catherine Rainwater, School of Humanities, St. Edwards University, 3001 S. Congress Ave., Austin, TX 78704-6489. TEL 512-837-6579. *4401*

ELSEVIER HANDLING AND PROCESSING OF SOLIDS SERIES.
Elsevier Science Ltd., Books Division, P.O. Box 800, Kidlington, Oxford OX5 1DX, England. TEL 44-1865-843000. FAX 44-1865-843010. *2871*

ELSEVIER OCEANOGRAPHY SERIES.
Elsevier Science B.V., Books Division, P.O. Box 211, 1000 AE Amsterdam, Netherlands. TEL 31-20-4853911. FAX 31-20-4853705. *2402*

ELSEVIER SERIES IN FORENSIC AND POLICE SCIENCE.
Elsevier Science B.V., Books Division, P.O. Box 211, 1000 AE Amsterdam, Netherlands. TEL 31-20-4853911. FAX 31-20-4853705. *4904*

ELSEVIER SERIES IN PRACTICAL ASPECTS OF CRIMINAL & FORENSIC INVESTIGATION.
Elsevier Science B.V., Books Division, P.O. Box 211, 1000 AE Amsterdam, Netherlands. TEL 31-20-4853911. FAX 31-20-4853705. *4904*

EM ABERTO.
Instituto Nacional de Estudos e Pesquisas Educacionais, Sgas Q.607 Bl.50 - L2 Sul, 70200-670 Brasilia, DF, Brazil. TEL 55-61-2442612. FAX 55-61-2444712. *2441*

EMBLEMATA.
Institucion Fernando el Catolico, Plaza de Espana 2, 50071 Zaragoza, Spain. TEL 34-976-288878. FAX 34-976-288869. *3220*

EMERGENCY AND OFFICE PEDIATRICS.
Mary Ann Liebert, Inc. Publishers, 2 Madison Ave., Larchmont, NY 10538. TEL 914-834-3100. FAX 914-834-3688. *5030*

EMERGENCY LIBRARIAN.
Ken Haycock & Associates, Inc., 101-1001 W. Broadway, Ste. 343, Vancouver, BC V6H 4E4, Canada. TEL 604-925-0266. FAX 604-925-0566. *4177*

EMERGENCY MEDICAL SERVICES.
Summer Communications Inc., Attn.: Barbara Feiner, 7626 Densmore Ave., Van Nuys, CA 91406. TEL 818-786-4367. FAX 818-786-9246. *5006*

EMERGENCY PRODUCT BUYER.
C M E Communications, Inc., 20854 Dalton Rd., P.O. Box 507, Sutton W., ON L0E 1L0, Canada. TEL 416-722-9839. FAX 416-722-9687. *5141*

EMERGENCY RADIOLOGY.
Williams & Wilkins, 351 W. Camden St., Baltimore, MD 21201-2436. TEL 410-528-4068. FAX 410-528-4452. *5105*

EMERGING DRUGS.
Ashley Publications Ltd., First Fl., The Library, 1 Shepherds Hill, Highgate, London N6 5QJ, England. TEL 44-181-347-5030. FAX 44-181-347-5040. *5659*

EMERGING INFECTIOUS DISEASES.
U.S. National Center for Infectious Diseases, 1600 Clifton Rd., Mailstop C-12, Atlanta, GA 30333. TEL 404-639-3967. FAX 404-639-3039. *6232*

EMERGING THERAPEUTIC TARGETS.
Ashley Publications Ltd., First Fl., The Library, 1 Shepards Hill, Highgate, London N6 5QJ, England. TEL 44-181-347-5030. FAX 44-181-347-5040. *5659*

EMIRATES JOURNAL FOR ENGINEERING RESEARCH.
United Arab Emirates University, Faculty of Engineering, P.O. Box 17555, Al-Ain, United Arab Emirates. TEL 971-3-637833. FAX 971-3-632382. *2716*

EMIRATES MEDICAL JOURNAL.
Emirates Medical Association, P.O. Box 6600, Dubai, United Arab Emirates. TEL 971-4-377377. FAX 971-4-344082. *4664*

EMOTIONS AND BEHAVIOR. MONOGRAPH.
International Universities Press, Inc., 59 Boston Post Rd., Box 1524, Madison, CT 06443-1524. TEL 203-245-4000. FAX 203-245-0775. *5062*

EMPATHY.
Gay and Lesbian Advocacy Research Project, Inc., Box 5085, Columbia, SC 29250. TEL 803-791-1607. *3693*

EMPIRE STATE MASON.
Grand Lodge Free and Accepted Masons of the State of New York, Committee on Publications, 37 Oliver St., Lockport, NY 14094-4615. TEL 716-434-4946. FAX 716-434-4946. *1931*

EMPIRICAL ECONOMICS.
Physica-Verlag GmbH und Co., Postfach 105280, 69042 Heidelberg, Germany. TEL 49-6221-487492. FAX 49-6221-487177. *960*

EMPIRICAL SOFTWARE ENGINEERING.
Kluwer Academic Publishers Boston, Box 358, Accord Sta., Hingham, MA 02018-0358. TEL 617-871-6600. FAX 617-871-6528. *2211*

EMPLOYEE ASSISTANCE QUARTERLY.
Haworth Press, Inc., 10 Alice St., Binghamton, NY 13904. TEL 607-722-5857. FAX 607-722-6362. *1565*

EMPLOYEE RESPONSIBILITIES AND RIGHTS JOURNAL.
Plenum Publishing Corp., 233 Spring St., New York, NY 10013-1578. TEL 212-620-8000. FAX 212-463-0742. *1427*

EMPLOYMENT TESTING.
University Publications of America, 4520 East-West Hwy., Ste. 800, Bethesda, MD 20814-3389. TEL 301-657-3200. FAX 301-657-3203. *3945*

REFEREED SERIALS

EMPRESA BRASILEIRA DE PESQUISA AGROPECUARIA. CENTRO NACIONAL DE PESQUISA DE FLORESTAS. DOCUMENTOS.
Empresa Brasileira de Pesquisa Agropecuaria, Centro Nacional de Pesquisa de Florestas, Caixa Postal 319, 83411-000 Colombo, Brazil. TEL 55-41-7661313. FAX 55-41-7661692. *3150*

ENCAPSULATOR.
Monash Medical Centre, Pharmacy Department, 246 Clayton Rd., Clayton, Vic. 3168, Australia. TEL 61-3-95502596. FAX 61-3-95502595. *5659*

ENCOUNTER: EDUCATION FOR MEANING AND SOCIAL JUSTICE.
Psychology Press, Inc., c/o Charles S. Jakiela, Pub., Box 328, Brandon, VT 05733-0328. TEL 802-247-8312. FAX 802-247-8312. *2441*

ENCOUNTERS.
Islamic Foundation, Markfield Dawah Centre, Ratby Lane, Markfield, Leicester LE6 0RN, England. TEL 01530-244944. FAX 01530-244946. *6336*

ENCUENTRO.
Universidad Centroamericana, Apdo. 69, 70352 Managua, Nicaragua. TEL 505-2-670352. FAX 505-2-670106. *6611*

ENCYCLIA.
Utah Academy of Sciences, Arts, and Letters, c/o Thomas F. Rogers, Ed., 4089A JKHB, Brigham Young University, Provo, UT 84602. TEL 801-378-3385. FAX 802-378-4649. *6524*

ENDEAVOUR.
Elsevier Science Ltd., Pergamon, P.O. Box 800, Kidlington, Oxford OX5 1DX, England. TEL 44-1865-843000. FAX 44-1865-843010. *6524*

ENDOCRINE JOURNAL.
Japan Endocrine Society, Department of Veterinary Physiology, Veterinary Medical Science, University of Tokyo, 1-1-1 Yayoi Bunkyo-ku, Tokyo 113, Japan. FAX 011-81-3-815-4266. *4886*

ENDOCRINE PATHOLOGY.
Humana Press Inc., 999 Riverview Dr., Ste. 208, Totowa, NJ 07512. TEL 973-256-1699. FAX 973-256-8341. *4886*

ENDOCRINE RESEARCH.
Marcel Dekker Journals, 270 Madison Ave., New York, NY 10016. TEL 212-696-9000. FAX 212-685-4540. *4886*

ENDOCRINE SOCIETY OF AUSTRALIA. PROCEEDINGS.
Endocrine Society of Australia, Ewen Downie Metabolic Unit, Alfred Hospital, Commercial Rd., Prahran, Vic. 3181, Australia. TEL 61-3-92763453. FAX 61-3-92763782. *4887*

THE ENDOCRINOLOGIST.
Williams & Wilkins, 351 W. Camden St., Baltimore, MD 21201-2436. TEL 410-528-4068. FAX 410-528-4452. *4887*

ENDOCRINOLOGY.
Endocrine Society, 4350 East West Hwy., Ste. 500, Bethesda, MD 20814-4410. TEL 301-941-0200. FAX 301-941-0259. *4887*

ENDOCRINOLOGY AND METABOLISM.
Bailliere Tindall - W.B. Saunders Co. Ltd., 24-28 Oval Rd., London NW1 7DX, England. TEL 44-171-485-4752. FAX 44-171-267-4466. *4887*

ENDOCRINOLOGY AND METABOLISM. SUPPLEMENT.
Bailliere Tindall - W.B. Saunders Co. Ltd., 24-28 Oval Rd., London NW1 7DX, England. TEL 44-171-485-4752. FAX 44-171-267-4466. *4887*

ENDOCURIETHERAPY - HYPERTHERMIA ONCOLOGY.
Endocurietherapy Research Foundation, 2801 Atlantic Ave., Long Beach, CA 90801. TEL 310-933-2929. FAX 310-933-0301. *4977*

ENDODONTICS & DENTAL TRAUMATOLOGY.
Munksgaard International Publishers Ltd., 35 Noerre Soegade, P.O. Box 2148, DK-1016 Copenhagen K, Denmark. TEL 45-33-127030. FAX 45-33-129387. *4856*

ENDOSURGERY.
Edizioni Minerva Medica, Corso Bramante 83-85, 10126 Turin, Italy. TEL 39-11-678282. FAX 39-11-674502. *5141*

ENERGIA AMBIENTE E INNOVAZIONE.
Ente per le Nuove Tecnologie, l'Energie e l'Ambiente, Lungotevere Thaon di Revel 76, 00196 Rome, Italy. TEL 39-6-36272401. FAX 39-6-36272299. *2664*

ENERGY.
Elsevier Science Ltd., Pergamon, P.O. Box 800, Kidlington, Oxford OX5 1DX, England. TEL 44-1865-843000. FAX 44-1865-843010. *2664*

ENERGY AND BUILDINGS.
Elsevier Science S.A., P.O. Box 564, CH-1001 Lausanne 1, Switzerland. TEL 41-21-3207381. FAX 41-21-3235444. *2665*

ENERGY AND ENGINEERING SCIENCE.
Gordon and Breach - Harwood Academic, Amsteldisk 166, 1st Fl., 1079 LH Amsterdam, Netherlands. *2665*

ENERGY & ENVIRONMENT.
Multi-Science Publishing Co. Ltd., 107 High St., Brentwood, Essex CM14 4RX, England. TEL 44-1277-224632. FAX 44-1277-223453. *2665*

ENERGY CONVERSION AND MANAGEMENT.
Elsevier Science Ltd., Pergamon, P.O. Box 800, Kidlington, Oxford OX5 1DX, England. TEL 44-1865-843000. FAX 44-1865-843010. *2666*

ENERGY ECONOMICS.
North-Holland, P.O. Box 211, 1000 AE Amsterdam, Netherlands. TEL 31-20-4853757. FAX 31-20-4853432. *2666*

ENERGY IN THE NEWS.
New York Mercantile Exchange, Corporate Communications Department, One North End Ave., World Financial Center, New York, NY 10282-1101. TEL 212-299-2777. FAX 212-301-4700. *1211*

ENERGY IN WORLD AGRICULTURE.
Elsevier Science B.V., Books Division, P.O. Box 211, 1000 AE Amsterdam, Netherlands. TEL 31-20-4853911. FAX 31-20-4853705. *2667*

ENERGY JOURNAL.
International Association for Energy Economics, 28790 Chagrin Blvd., Ste. 210, Cleveland, OH 44122. TEL 216-464-5365. FAX 216-464-2737. *2667*

ENERGY POLICY.
Elsevier Science Ltd., P.O. Box 800, Kidlington, Oxford OX5 1DX, England. TEL 44-1865-843000. FAX 44-1865-843010. *2667*

ENERGY RESEARCH.
Elsevier Science B.V., Books Division, P.O. Box 211, 1000 AE Amsterdam, Netherlands. TEL 31-20-4853911. FAX 31-20-4853705. *2668*

ENERGY SOURCES.
Taylor & Francis Inc., 1900 Frost Rd., Ste. 101, Bristol, PA 19007-1598. TEL 215-785-5800. FAX 215-785-5515. *2668*

ENERGY STUDIES REVIEW.
McMaster University, Institute for Energy Studies, Hamilton, ON L8S 4M4, Canada. TEL 905-525-9140. FAX 905-777-8344. *2668*

ENFERMEDADES INFECCIOSAS Y MICROBIOLOGIA.
Obsidiana Editores, S.A., Czda. de Tlalpan 2365, Col. Ciudad Jardin, 04370 Mexico DF, Mexico. TEL 6899133. *4834*

ENGENHARIA AGRICOLA.
Brazilian Agricultural Engineering Society, Departamento de Engenharia Rural - UNESP, Faculdade de Ciencias Agrarias e Veterinarias, Rodovia Carlos Tonnani, km 5, 14870-000 Jaboticabal SP, Brazil. TEL 55-16-3233341. *113*

ENGINEER.
Association of Professional Engineers of Nova Scotia, 1355 Barrington St., Box 129, Halifax, NS B3J 2M4, Canada. TEL 902-429-2250. FAX 902-423-9769. *2716*

ENGINEER - I.M.E. NEWS.
Institution of Mechanical Engineers (India), Janmabhoomi Chambers, 3rd Fl., 29 W. Hirachand Marg, Ballard Estate, Mumbai 400 038, India. TEL 91-22-2692885. FAX 91-22-2614815. *2883*

ENGINEERING ANALYSIS WITH BOUNDARY ELEMENTS.
Elsevier Science Ltd., P.O. Box 800, Kidlington, Oxford OX5 1DX, England. TEL 44-1865-843000. FAX 44-1865-843010. *2883*

ENGINEERING APPLICATIONS OF ARTIFICIAL INTELLIGENCE.
Elsevier Science Ltd., Pergamon, P.O. Box 800, Kidlington, Oxford OX5 1DX, England. TEL 44-1865-843000. FAX 44-1865-843010. *2099*

ENGINEERING APPLICATIONS OF SYSTEMS RELIABILITY AND RISK ANALYSIS.
Kluwer Academic Publishers, Postbus 17, 3300 AA Dordrecht, Netherlands. TEL 31-78-6392392. FAX 31-78-6392254. *2115*

ENGINEERING CONSTRUCTION AND ARCHITECTURAL MANAGEMENT.
Blackwell Science Ltd., Osney Mead, Oxford OX2 0EL, England. TEL 44-1865-206206. FAX 44-1865-721205. *892*

ENGINEERING DESIGN & AUTOMATION.
John Wiley & Sons, Inc., Journals, 605 Third Ave., New York, NY 10158. TEL 212-850-6645. FAX 212-850-6021. *2206*

ENGINEERING DESIGN GRAPHICS JOURNAL.
American Society for Engineering Education, Engineering Design Graphics Division, c/o Mary A. Sadowski, Ed., 1419 Knoy Hall, Purdue University, W. Lafayette, IN 47907-1419. TEL 317-494-8206. FAX 317-494-9267. *6959*

ENGINEERING FAILURE ANALYSIS.
Elsevier Science Ltd., Pergamon, P.O. Box 800, Kidlington, Oxford OX5 1DX, England. TEL 44-1865-843000. FAX 44-1865-843010. *2857*

ENGINEERING FRACTURE MECHANICS.
Elsevier Science Ltd., Pergamon, P.O. Box 800, Kidlington, Oxford OX5 1DX, England. TEL 44-1865-843000. FAX 44-1865-843010. *2858*

ENGINEERING GEOLOGY.
Elsevier Science B.V., P.O. Box 211, 1000 AE Amsterdam, Netherlands. TEL 31-20-4853911. FAX 31-20-4853598. *2784*

ENGINEERING OPTIMIZATION.
Gordon and Breach - Harwood Academic, Amsteldisk 166, 1st Fl., 1079 LH Amsterdam, Netherlands. *2718*

ENGINEERING SCIENCE AND EDUCATION JOURNAL.
Institution of Electrical Engineers, Michael Faraday House, Six Hills Way, Stevenage, Herts. SG1 2AY, England. TEL 44-1438-313311. FAX 44-1438-742792. *2823*

ENGINEERING SCIENCE AND TECHNOLOGY.
University of Malaya, Lembah Pantai, 59100 Kuala Lumpur, Malaysia. FAX 603-755-3466. *2718*

ENGINEERING SIMULATION.
Gordon and Breach - Harwood Academic, Amsteldisk 166, 1st Fl., 1079 LH Amsterdam, Netherlands. *2637*

ENGINEERING STRUCTURES.
Elsevier Science Ltd., P.O. Box 800, Kidlington, Oxford OX5 1DX, England. TEL 44-1865-843000. FAX 44-1865-843010. *2784*

ENGLERA.
Botanischer Garten und Botanisches Museum Berlin-Dahlem, Koenigin-Luise-Str. 6-8, 14191 Berlin, Germany. TEL 49-30-83006194. FAX 49-30-83006186. *702*

ENGLISH.
The English Association, University of Leicester, University Rd., Leicester LE1 7RH, England. TEL 44-116-252-3982. FAX 44-116-252-2301. *4401*

ENGLISH & MEDIA MAGAZINE.
English & Media Centre, 136 Chalton St., London NW1 1RX, England. *4401*

ENGLISH FOR SPECIFIC PURPOSES.
Elsevier Science Ltd., Pergamon, P.O. Box 800, Kidlington, Oxford OX5 1DX, England. TEL 44-1865-843000. FAX 44-1865-843010. *4254*

ENGLISH IN AUSTRALIA.
Australian Association for the Teaching of English, P.O. Box 3203, Norwood, S.A. 5067, Australia. TEL 61-8-3322845. FAX 61-8-3330394. *4254*

ENGLISH IN EDUCATION.
National Association for the Teaching of English, Broadfield Business Centre, 50 Broadfield Rd., Sheffield S8 0XJ, England. TEL 44-1142-555419. FAX 44-1142-555296. *2602*

ENGLISH LANGUAGE AND LINGUISTICS.
Cambridge University Press, Edinburgh Bldg., Shaftesbury Rd., Cambridge CB2 2RU, England. TEL 44-1223-312393. FAX 44-1223-315052. *4254*

ENGLISH LANGUAGE NOTES.
University of Colorado, English Language Notes, CB 226, Boulder, CO 80309. TEL 303-492-7176. FAX 303-492-3521. *4401*

ENGLISH LITERATURE IN TRANSITION, 1880-1920.
Robert Langenfeld, Ed. & Pub., Department of English, University of North Carolina, Greensboro, NC 27412-5001. TEL 910-334-5446. FAX 910-334-3281. *4401*

ENGLISH MONARCHS SERIES.
University of California Press, 2120 Berkeley Way, Berkeley, CA 94720. TEL 510-642-4247. FAX 510-643-7127. *3564*

ENGLISH PLACE-NAME SOCIETY JOURNAL.
English Place-Name Society, University of Nottingham, Department of English, Nottingham NG7 2RD, England. TEL 44-1159-515919. FAX 44-1159-515924. *3401*

ENGLISH QUARTERLY.
Canadian Council of Teachers of English, 340 Education, University of Manitoba, Winnipeg, MB R3T 2N2, Canada. TEL 204-474-8564. FAX 204-275-5962. *2602*

ENGLISH STUDIES.
Swets & Zeitlinger bv, P.O. Box 825, 2160 SZ Lisse, Netherlands. TEL 31-252-435111. FAX 31-252-415888. *4254*

ENGLISH STUDIES IN AFRICA.
University of the Witwatersrand, Department of English, Wits 2050, South Africa. FAX 27-11-4037309. *3778*

ENGLISH STUDIES IN CANADA.
Association of Canadian College and University Teachers of English, Department of English, Carleton University, 1125 Colonel By Dr., Ottawa, ON K1S 5B6, Canada. TEL 613-788-2600. FAX 613-788-3544. *4401*

ENTERPRISE SYSTEMS JOURNAL.
Cardinal Business Media, Inc., 12225 Greenville Ave., Ste. 700, Dallas, TX 75243-9338. TEL 972-669-9000. FAX 972-669-9909. *2174*

ENTOMOLOGIA EXPERIMENTALIS ET APPLICATA.
Kluwer Academic Publishers, Postbus 17, 3300 AA Dordrecht, Netherlands. TEL 31-78-6392392. FAX 31-78-6392254. *750*

ENTOMOLOGICA FENNICA.
Entomologica Fennica ry, c/o Institute of Zoology, P.O. Box 17, FIN-00014 University of Helsinki, Finland. FAX 358-0-635017. *750*

ENTOMOLOGICAL NEWS.
American Entomological Society, Academy of Natural Sciences, 1900 Benjamin Franklin Pkwy., Philadelphia, PA 19103-1195. TEL 215-561-3978. FAX 215-299-1028. *750*

ENTOMOLOGICAL REVIEW.
Maika Nauka - Interperiodica, Ul. Profsoyuznaya, 90, 117864 Moscow, Russia. *750*

ENTOMOLOGICAL SOCIETY OF AMERICA. ANNALS.
Entomological Society of America, 9301 Annapolis Rd., Lanham, MD 20706. TEL 301-731-4535. FAX 301-731-4538. *750*

ENTOMOLOGICAL SOCIETY OF BRITISH COLUMBIA. JOURNAL.
Entomological Society of British Columbia, c/o R.G. Bennett, Ministry of Forests, Seed Pest Management, 7380 Puckle Rd., Saanichton, BC V8M 1W4, Canada. TEL 604-652-6593. FAX 604-652-4204. *750*

ENTOMOLOGICAL SOCIETY OF CANADA. MEMOIRS.
Entomological Society of Canada, 393 Winston Ave., Ottawa, ON K2A 1Y8, Canada. TEL 613-725-2619. FAX 613-725-9349. *750*

ENTOMOLOGICAL SOCIETY OF MANITOBA. PROCEEDINGS.
Entomological Society of Manitoba, Inc., 195 Dafoe Rd., Winnipeg, MB R3T 2M9, Canada. TEL 204-945-8444. *751*

ENTOMOLOGICAL SOCIETY OF ONTARIO. PROCEEDINGS.
Entomological Society of Ontario, Queen's University, Dept. of Biology, Kingston, ON K7L 3N6, Canada. TEL 613-545-6136. FAX 613-545-6617. *751*

ENTOMOLOGICAL SOCIETY OF WASHINGTON. MEMOIRS.
Entomological Society of Washington, c/o Dept. of Entomology, Smithsonian Institution NHB 168, Washington, DC 20560. *751*

ENTOMOLOGICAL SOCIETY OF WASHINGTON. PROCEEDINGS.
Entomological Society of Washington, c/o Dept. of Entomology, Smithsonian Institution NHB 168, Washington, DC 20560. *751*

ENTOMOLOGISK TIDSKRIFT.
Sveriges Entomologiska Foerening, Uppsala Universitet, Genetiska Institutionen, Programmet i Naturvaardsbiologi, Box 7003, S-750 07 Uppsala, Sweden. TEL 46-90-18-65-26. *751*

ENTOMONOGRAPH.
E.J. Brill, P.O. Box 9000, 2300 PA Leiden, Netherlands. TEL 31-71-5353500. FAX 31-71-5317532. *752*

ENTOURAGE.
Roeher Institute, Kinsmen Bldg., York University, 4700 Keele St., North York, ON M3J 1P3, Canada. TEL 416-661-9611. FAX 416-661-5701. *3454*

ENTREPRENEUR (IRVINE).
Entrepreneur Media, Inc., 2392 Morse Ave., Irvine, CA 92614. TEL 714-261-2325. FAX 714-755-4211. *1642*

ENTREPRENEURSHIP & REGIONAL DEVELOPMENT.
Taylor & Francis Ltd., Rankine Rd., Basingstoke, Hants. RG24 8PR, England. TEL 44-1256-840366. FAX 44-1256-479438. *961*

ENTREPRENEURSHIP, INNOVATION AND CHANGE.
Plenum Publishing Corp., 233 Spring St., New York, NY 10013-1578. TEL 212-620-8000. FAX 212-463-0742. *1475*

ENVIRONMENT.
Heldref Publications, 1319 Eighteenth St., N.W., Washington, DC 20036-1802. TEL 202-296-6267. FAX 202-296-5149. *2918*

ENVIRONMENT & ASSESSMENT.
Kluwer Academic Publishers, Postbus 17, 3300 AA Dordrecht, Netherlands. TEL 31-78-6392392. FAX 31-78-6392254. *2918*

ENVIRONMENT AND DEVELOPMENT ECONOMICS.
Cambridge University Press, Edinburgh Bldg., Shaftesbury Rd., Cambridge CB2 2RU, England. TEL 44-1223-312393. FAX 44-1223-315052. *2918*

ENVIRONMENT AND HISTORY.
White Horse Press, 10 High St., Knapwell, Cambridge CB3 8NR, England. TEL 44-1954-267527. FAX 44-1954-267527. *3564*

ENVIRONMENT & MANAGEMENT.
Kluwer Academic Publishers, Postbus 17, 3300 AA Dordrecht, Netherlands. TEL 31-78-6392392. FAX 31-78-6392254. *2918*

ENVIRONMENT AND PLANNING A.
Pion Ltd., 207 Brondesbury Park, London NW2 5JN, England. TEL 44-181-459-0066. FAX 44-181-451-6454. *3746*

ENVIRONMENT AND PLANNING B: PLANNING & DESIGN.
Pion Ltd., 207 Brondesbury Park, London NW2 5JN, England. TEL 44-181-459-0066. FAX 44-181-451-6454. *3746*

ENVIRONMENT AND PLANNING C: GOVERNMENT & POLICY.
Pion Ltd., 207 Brondesbury Park, London NW2 5JN, England. TEL 44-181-459-0066. FAX 44-181-451-6454. *6173*

ENVIRONMENT AND PLANNING D: SOCIETY & SPACE.
Pion Ltd., 207 Brondesbury Park, London NW2 5JN, England. TEL 44-181-459-0066. FAX 44-181-451-6454. *3746*

ENVIRONMENT AND URBANIZATION.
International Institute for Environment and Development (IIED), 3 Endsleigh St., London WC1H 0DD, England. TEL 44-171-388-2117. FAX 44-171-388-2826. *2918*

ENVIRONMENT BULLETIN.
Department of the Environment, Customs House, Dublin 1, Ireland. TEL 353-1-6793377. *2967*

ENVIRONMENT INTERNATIONAL.
Elsevier Science Ltd., Pergamon, P.O. Box 800, Kidlington, Oxford OX5 1DX, England. TEL 44-1865-843000. FAX 44-1865-843010. *2919*

ENVIRONMENT SOUTH AUSTRALIA.
Conservation Council of South Australia, Conservation Centre, 120 Wakefield St., Adelaide, S.A. 5000, Australia. TEL 61-8-82235155. FAX 61-8-82324782. *2919*

ENVIRONMENTAL AND ECOLOGICAL STATISTICS.
Thomson Science, 2-6 Boundary Row, London SE1 8HN, England. TEL 44-171-8650066. FAX 44-171-5229623. *2961*

ENVIRONMENTAL AND ENGINEERING GEOSCIENCE.
Association of Engineering Geologists, 323 Boston Post Rd., Ste. 2D, Box 132, Sudbury, MA 01776. TEL 508-443-4639. *2338*

ENVIRONMENTAL AND EXPERIMENTAL BOTANY.
Elsevier Science Ltd., Pergamon, P.O. Box 800, Kidlington, Oxford OX5 1DX, England. TEL 44-1865-843000. FAX 44-1865-843010. *702*

ENVIRONMENTAL AND MOLECULAR MUTAGENESIS.
John Wiley & Sons, Inc., Journals, 605 Third Ave., New York, NY 10158. TEL 212-850-6645. FAX 212-850-6021. *766*

ENVIRONMENTAL AND RESOURCE ECONOMICS.
Kluwer Academic Publishers, Postbus 17, 3300 AA Dordrecht, Netherlands. TEL 31-78-6392392. FAX 31-78-6392254. *2920*

ENVIRONMENTAL BIOLOGY OF FISHES.
Kluwer Academic Publishers, Postbus 17, 3300 AA Dordrecht, Netherlands. TEL 31-78-6392392. FAX 31-78-6392254. *833*

ENVIRONMENTAL CARCINOGENESIS & ECOTOXICOLOGY REVIEWS.
Marcel Dekker Journals, 270 Madison Ave., New York, NY 10016. TEL 212-696-9000. FAX 212-685-4540. *2977*

ENVIRONMENTAL CONSERVATION.
Cambridge University Press, Edinburgh Bldg., Shaftesbury Rd., Cambridge CB2 2RU, England. TEL 44-1223-312393. FAX 44-1223-315052. *2921*

ENVIRONMENTAL EDUCATION AND INFORMATION.
University of Salford, Department of Environmental Resources, Allerton Bldg., Salford M5 4WT, England. TEL 44-161-745-5000. FAX 44-161-745-5999. *2921*

ENVIRONMENTAL EDUCATION RESEARCH.
Carfax Publishing Co., P.O. Box 25, Abingdon, Oxon. OX14 3UE, England. TEL 44-1235-401000. FAX 44-1235-401550. *2602*

REFEREED SERIALS

ENVIRONMENTAL ENTOMOLOGY.
Entomological Society of America, 9301 Annapolis Rd., Lanham, MD 20706. TEL 301-731-4535. FAX 301-731-4538. *752*

ENVIRONMENTAL ETHICS.
Environmental Philosophy, Inc., Center for Environmental Philosophy, University of North Texas, Box 13496, Denton, TX 76203-6496. TEL 817-565-2727. FAX 817-565-4448. *5725*

ENVIRONMENTAL FLUID MECHANICS.
Kluwer Academic Publishers, Postbus 17, 3300 AA Dordrecht, Netherlands. TEL 31-78-6392392. FAX 31-78-6392254. *2314*

ENVIRONMENTAL GEOCHEMISTRY AND HEALTH.
Chapman & Hall, Journals Department 2-6 Boundary Row, London SE1 8HN, England. TEL 44-171-8560066. FAX 44-171-5229623. *2922*

ENVIRONMENTAL HEALTH PERSPECTIVES.
U.S. Department of Health and Human Services, National Institute of Environmental Health Sciences, Box 12233, Research Triangle Park, NC 27709. TEL 919-541-3406. FAX 919-541-0273. *2922*

ENVIRONMENTAL HEALTH REVIEW.
D2 C3 Enterprises, W.R.P.S. Box 75264, White Rock, BC V4A 9N4, Canada. TEL 604-543-0904. *6232*

ENVIRONMENTAL HISTORY.
Forest History Society, 701 Vickers Ave., Durham, NC 27701-3147. TEL 919-682-9319. *3494*

ENVIRONMENTAL LAW ANTHOLOGY.
International Library Law Book Publishers, Inc., 4301 N. Fairfax Dr., Ste. 875, Arlington, VA 22203. TEL 703-528-1000. FAX 703-528-6060. *3946*

ENVIRONMENTAL MANAGEMENT (NEW YORK).
Springer-Verlag, Life Science Journals, 175 Fifth Ave., New York, NY 10010. TEL 212-460-1500. FAX 212-473-6272. *2923*

ENVIRONMENTAL MEDICINE.
Nagoya Daigaku, Kankyo Igaku Kenkyujo, Furo-cho, Chikusa-ku, Nagoya 464-01, Japan. TEL 81-52-789-3873. FAX 81-52-789-3876. *4664*

ENVIRONMENTAL MODELING & ASSESSMENT.
Baltzer Science Publishers B.V., P.O. Box 221, 1400 AE Bussum, Netherlands. TEL 31-20-6370061. FAX 31-20-6323651. *2964*

ENVIRONMENTAL MODELING SERIES.
Computational Mechanics Publications, Ashurst Lodge, Ashurst, Southampton, Hants. SO40 7AA, England. TEL 44-1703-293223. FAX 44-1703-792853. *2964*

ENVIRONMENTAL MODELLING & SOFTWARE.
Elsevier Science Ltd., P.O. Box 800, Kidlington, Oxford OX5 1DX, England. TEL 44-1865-843000. FAX 44-1865-843010. *2964*

ENVIRONMENTAL MONITORING AND ASSESSMENT.
Kluwer Academic Publishers, Postbus 17, 3300 AA Dordrecht, Netherlands. TEL 31-78-6392392. FAX 31-78-6392254. *2923*

ENVIRONMENTAL POLITICS.
Frank Cass, Newbury House, 890-900 Eastern Ave., Newbury Park, Ilford, Essex IG2 7HH, England. TEL 44-181-599-8866. FAX 44-181-599-0984. *6012*

ENVIRONMENTAL POLLUTION.
Elsevier Science Ltd., P.O. Box 800, Kidlington, Oxford OX5 1DX, England. TEL 44-1865-843000. FAX 44-1865-843010. *2967*

ENVIRONMENTAL PROFESSIONAL.
Blackwell Science Inc., 350 Main St., Malden, MA 02148. TEL 617-876-7000. FAX 617-388-8255. *2924*

ENVIRONMENTAL PROTECTION.
Stevens Publishing Corporation, 3700 J.H. Kultgen Frwy., Waco, TX 76706. TEL 817-776-9000. FAX 817-776-9018. *2924*

ENVIRONMENTAL PROTECTION BULLETIN.
Institution of Chemical Engineers, 165-189 Railway Terr., Rugby, Warks. CV21 3HQ, England. TEL 44-1788-578214. FAX 44-1788-560833. *2763*

ENVIRONMENTAL RADIATION SURVEILLANCE IN WASHINGTON STATE. ANNUAL REPORT.
Department of Health, Division of Radiation Protection, Box 47827, Olympia, WA 98504-7827. TEL 206-586-3306. FAX 206-753-1496. *2924*

ENVIRONMENTAL RESEARCH.
Academic Press, Inc., Journal Division, 525 B St., Ste. 1900, San Diego, CA 92101-4495. TEL 619-230-1840. FAX 619-699-6800. *2925*

ENVIRONMENTAL REVIEWS.
National Research Council of Canada, Research Journals, Ottawa, ON K1A 0R6, Canada. TEL 613-993-9084. FAX 613-952-7656. *2925*

ENVIRONMENTAL SCIENCE AND TECHNOLOGY.
Kluwer Academic Publishers, Postbus 17, 3300 AA Dordrecht, Netherlands. TEL 31-78-6392392. FAX 31-78-6392254. *2925*

ENVIRONMENTAL SCIENCE RESEARCH.
Plenum Publishing Corp., 233 Spring St., New York, NY 10013-1578. TEL 212-620-8000. FAX 212-463-0742. *2925*

ENVIRONMENTAL SCIENCES.
M Y U, Scientific Publishing Division, 2-32-3 Sendagi, Bunkyo-ku, Tokyo 113, Japan. *2925*

ENVIRONMENTAL TECHNOLOGY.
Hunter Publishing Limited Partnership, 2101 S. Arlington Heights Rd., Ste. 150, Arlington Heights, IL 60005. TEL 847-427-9512. FAX 847-427-2097. *2926*

ENVIRONMENTAL TOPICS.
Gordon and Breach - Harwood Academic, Amsteldisk 166, 1st Fl., 1079 LH Amsterdam, Netherlands. *2926*

ENVIRONMENTAL TOXICOLOGY AND CHEMISTRY.
Society of Environmental Toxicology and Chemistry, 1010 N. 12th St., Pensacola, FL 32501-3370. TEL 904-469-1500. FAX 904-469-9778. *2977*

ENVIRONMENTAL TOXICOLOGY AND PHARMACOLOGY.
Elsevier Science B.V., P.O. Box 211, 1000 AE Amsterdam, Netherlands. TEL 31-20-4853911. FAX 31-20-4853598. *2977*

ENVIRONMENTAL TOXICOLOGY AND WATER QUALITY.
John Wiley & Sons, Inc., Journals, 605 Third Ave., New York, NY 10158-0012. TEL 212-850-6645. FAX 212-850-6021. *2977*

ENVIRONMENTAL VALUES.
White Horse Press, 10 High St., Knapwell, Cambridge CB3 8NR, England. TEL 44-1954-267527. FAX 44-1954-267527. *2926*

THE ENVIRONMENTALIST.
Chapman & Hall, Journals Department 2-6 Boundary Row, London SE1 8HN, England. TEL 44-171-8560066. FAX 44-171-5229623. *2926*

ENVIRONMENTS.
University of Waterloo, Faculty of Environmental Studies, Waterloo, ON N2L 3G1, Canada. TEL 519-888-4567. FAX 519-746-2031. *2926*

ENVIRONMETRICS.
John Wiley & Sons Ltd., Journals, Baffins Ln., Chichester, W. Sussex PO19 1UD, England. TEL 44-1243-779777. FAX 44-1243-775878. *2926*

ENZYME AND MICROBIAL TECHNOLOGY.
Elsevier Science Inc., Box 945, New York, NY 10159-0945. TEL 212-633-3730. FAX 212-633-3680. *682*

ENZYME ENGINEERING.
New York Academy of Sciences, 2 E. 63rd St., New York, NY 10021. TEL 212-838-0230. *659*

EOS.
American Geophysical Union, 2000 Florida Ave. N.W., Washington, DC 20009. TEL 202-462-6900. FAX 202-328-0566. *2381*

EOS.
Uniwersytet im. Adama Mickiewicza, Instytut Filologii Klasycznej, Al. Niepodleglosci 4, 61-874 Poznan, Poland. TEL 48-61-521191. FAX 48-61-536536. *4255*

EPIDEMIOLOGICAL NEWS BULLETIN.
Committee on Epidemic Diseases, Quarantine & Epidemiology Dept., 40 Scotts Rd., Environment Bldg., Singapore 228231, Singapore. TEL 65-732-9758. FAX 65-734-8287. *4835*

EPIDEMIOLOGIE, MIKROBIOLOGIE, IMUNOLOGIE.
Nakladatelske Stredisko C L S J.E. Purkyne, Sokolska 31, 120 26 Prague 2, Czech Republic. TEL 420-2-24911420. FAX 420-2-24911420. *783*

EPILEPSIA.
Lippincott - Raven Publishers, 227 E. Washington Sq., Philadelphia, PA 19106. TEL 215-238-4200. FAX 215-238-4227. *5063*

EPILEPSY RESEARCH.
Elsevier Science B.V., P.O. Box 211, 1000 AE Amsterdam, Netherlands. TEL 31-20-4853911. FAX 31-20-4853598. *5063*

EPILEPSY RESEARCH SUPPLEMENTS.
Elsevier Science B.V., Books Division, P.O. Box 211, 1000 AE Amsterdam, Netherlands. TEL 31-20-4853911. FAX 31-20-4853705. *5063*

EPISODES (NOTTINGHAM).
International Union of Geological Sciences, c/o British Geological Survey, Keyworth, Nottingham NG12 5GG, England. TEL 44-1602-363100. FAX 44-1602-363474. *2339*

EPISTEME.
Kluwer Academic Publishers, Postbus 17, 3300 AA Dordrecht, Netherlands. TEL 31-78-6392392. FAX 31-78-6392254. *6525*

EPITOANYAG.
Szilikatipari Tudomanyos Egyesulet, Fo utca 68, 1027 Budapest, Hungary. TEL 36-1-2019360. *893*

EQUINE ATHLETE.
Veterinary Practice Publishing Co., Box 6050, Mission Viejo, CA 92690. *7269*

EQUINE PRACTICE.
Veterinary Practice Publishing Co., Box 6050, Mission Viejo, CA 92690. *7269*

EQUIVALENCIAS.
Fundacion Fernando Rielo, Jorge Juan 102, 2nd B, 28009 Madrid, Spain. TEL 575-4091. *4508*

ERASMUS OF ROTTERDAM SOCIETY YEARBOOK.
Erasmus of Rotterdam Society, 1015 Patterson Office Tower, Lexington, KY 40506-0027. TEL 606-257-5710. FAX 606-257-3743. *5725*

ERDESZETI LAPOK.
Orszagos Erdeszeti Egyesulet, Fo utca 68, 1027 Budapest, Hungary. TEL 36-1-2016293. FAX 36-1-2017737. *3150*

ERGONOMIA.
Polska Akademia Nauk, Komitet Ergonomii, Ul. Sw. Jana 28, 31-118 Krakow, Poland. FAX 48-12-222791. *6525*

ERGONOMICS.
Taylor & Francis Ltd., 1 Gunpowder Sq., London EC4A 3DE, England. TEL 44-171-583-0490. FAX 44-171-583-0585. *2719*

ERGONOMICS ABSTRACTS.
Taylor & Francis Ltd., 1 Gunpowder Sq., London EC4A 3DE, England. TEL 44-171-583-0490. FAX 44-171-583-0585. *2749*

ERGONOMICS IN DESIGN.
Human Factors and Ergonomics Society, Box 1369, Santa Monica, CA 90406-1369. TEL 310-394-1811. FAX 310-394-2410. *2719*

ERKENNTNIS.
Kluwer Academic Publishers, Postbus 17, 3300 AA Dordrecht, Netherlands. TEL 31-78-6392392. FAX 31-78-6392254. *5725*

ERNEST BLOCH LECTURES.
University of California Press, 2120 Berkeley Way, Berkeley, CA 94720. TEL 510-642-4247. FAX 510-643-7127. *2540*

ERYTHROPOIESIS.
Adis International Ltd., Chowley Oak Ln., Tattenhall, Chester, Ches. CH3 9GA, England. TEL 44-1829-771155. FAX 44-1829-770330. *4918*

ERZIEHERBRIEF.
Arbeitsgemeinschaft Sudetendeutscher Lehrer und Erzieher e.V., Hochstr. 8, 81669 Munich, Germany. TEL 49-89-480003-28. *6012*

ESCRITOS.
Universidad Central de Venezuela, Facultad de Humanidades y Educacion, P.O. Box 47.687, 1041-A Caracas, Vezenuela. TEL 58-2-694926. FAX 58-2-6052862. *440*

ESCUELA NACIONAL DE INTELIGENCIA. REVISTA.
Escuela Nacional de Inteligencia, C. Libertad 1235, 1012 Buenos Aires, Argentina. TEL 54-1-812-4930. FAX 54-1-812-9230. *5267*

ESPACIO ABIERTO.
Universidad del Zulia, Consejo de Desarrollo Cientifico y Humanistico, Av. Universidad (Calle 60) 25-266, Sector Grano de Oro, Maracaibo, Venezuela. TEL 58-61-515131. FAX 58-61-528934. *6708*

ESPACIO Y DESARROLLO.
Pontificia Universidad Catolica del Peru, Fondo Editorial, Apdo. 1761, Lima 32, Peru. TEL 51-14-626390. FAX 5114-611785. *3778*

ESPRIT CREATEUR.
University of Kentucky, 1015 Patterson, Lexington, KY 40506-0001. TEL 606-257-7557. FAX 606-257-3743. *4402*

ESSAYS IN ARTS AND SCIENCES.
University of New Haven, School of Arts and Sciences, West Haven, CT 06516. TEL 203-932-7371. FAX 203-932-1469. *440*

ESSAYS IN BIOCHEMISTRY.
Portland Press Ltd., 59 Portland Pl., London W1N 3AJ, England. TEL 44-171-580-5530. FAX 44-171-323-1136. *659*

ESSAYS IN ECONOMIC AND BUSINESS HISTORY.
Ohio State University, Department of History, 106 Dulles Hall, 230 W. 17th Ave., OH 43210-1367. TEL 614-292-2674. FAX 614-292-2282. *1303*

ESSAYS IN HISTORY.
University of Virginia, Corcoran Department of History, Charlottesville, VA 22903. TEL 804-924-7146. *3494*

ESSAYS IN THEATRE.
University of Guelph, Department of Drama, Guelph, ON N1G 2W1, Canada. TEL 519-824-4120. FAX 519-824-0560. *7006*

ESTACION EXPERIMENTAL DE AULA DEI. ANALES.
Estacion Experimental de Aula Dei, Apdo. de Correos 202, C. Montanana 177, 50081 Zaragoza, Spain. TEL 34-76-576511. FAX 34-76-575620. *222*

ESTATE PLANNING (NEW YORK).
Warren, Gorham & Lamont, One Penn Plaza, New York, NY 10119. TEL 212-971-5000. FAX 212-971-5113. *4096*

ESTHETIC DENTISTRY UPDATE.
Health Care Advancements Inc., c/o Dr. Lenin, 10 New Plant Ct., Owings Mills, MD 21117-3514. *4857*

ESTRENO.
350 N. Burrowes Bldg., University Park, PA 16802. TEL 814-238-0270. FAX 814-863-7944. *7006*

ESTUARIES.
Estuarine Research Federation, 490 Chippingwood Dr., No. 2, Port Republic, MD 20676-2140. TEL 318-475-5443. FAX 318-475-5675. *600*

ESTUDIOS DE ECONOMIA.
Universidad de Chile, Facultad de Ciencias Economicas y Administrativas, Av. Ranacagua 257, Santiago, Chile. FAX 562-634-7342. *961*

ESTUDIOS DE FILOSOFIA.
Universidad de Antioquia, Instituto de Filosofia, Apdo. Aereo 1226, Medellin, Colombia. TEL 57-4-2105680. FAX 57-4-2638282. *5725*

ESTUDIOS DE LINGUISTICA APPLICADA.
Universidad Nacional Autonoma de Mexico, Centro de Ensenanza de Lenguas Extranjeras, Circuito Interior, Ciudad Universitaria, 04510 Mexico, D.F., Mexico. TEL 52-5-6220678. FAX 52-5-5503008. *4255*

ESTUDIOS DE PSICOLOGIA.
Fundacion Infancia y Aprendizaje, Ctr. de Canillas 138, 2o 16C, 28043 Madrid, Spain. TEL 34-1-3883874. FAX 34-1-3003527. *6110*

ESTUDIOS DEL TRABAJO.
Asociacion Argentina de Especialistas en Estudios del Trabajo, Araoz 2838, 1425 Buenos Aires, Argentina. TEL 54-1-8044949. FAX 54-1-8045856. *1429*

ESTUDIOS GEOLOGICOS.
Consejo Superior de Investigaciones Cientificas (C.S.I.C.), Bitruvio 8, 28006 Madrid, Spain. TEL 34-1-5612833. FAX 34-1-5629634. *2314*

ESTUDIOS INTERDISCIPLINARIOS DE AMERICA LATINA Y EL CARIBE.
University of Tel Aviv, Aranne School of History, Ramat Aviv 69978, Israel. FAX 972-3-6409457. *3778*

ESTUDIOS INTERNACIONALES.
Universidad de Chile, Instituto de Estudios Internacionales, Condell 249, Casilla 14187, Suc. 21, Santiago 9, Chile. TEL 56-2-2745377. FAX 56-2-2740155. *6013*

ESTUDIOS JALISCIENSES.
Colegio de Jalisco, 5 de Mayo 321, 45100 Zapopan, Jal., Mexico. TEL 633-2196. FAX 633-2154. *3778*

ESTUDIOS OCEANOLOGICOS.
Universidad de Antofagasta, Facultad de Recursos del Mar, Casilla 170, Antofagasta, Chile. FAX 56-55-247542. *2402*

ESTUDIOS SOBRE LAS CULTURAS CONTEMPORANEAS.
Universidad de Colima, Centro Universitario de Investigaciones Sociales, Av. 25 de Julio 965, 28045 Colima, Col., Mexico. TEL 52-331-41133. FAX 52-331-30397. *3778*

ESTUDOS AFRO-ASIATICOS.
Sociedade Brasileira de Instrucao, Centro de Estudos Afro-Asiaticos, Rua da Assembleia, 10 Conj. 501, 20011-000 Rio de Janeiro, Brazil. TEL 55-21-5312636. FAX 55-21-5312155. *6612*

ETCH A SKETCH CLUB. NEWSLETTER.
Ohio Art Company, Etch a Sketch Club, 1 Toy St., Box 111, Bryan, OH 43506. TEL 419-636-3141. FAX 419-636-7614. *1871*

ETHEL BROWNING'S TOXICITY AND METABOLISM OF INDUSTRIAL SOLVENTS.
Elsevier Science B.V., Books Division, P.O. Box 211, 1000 AE Amsterdam, Netherlands. TEL 31-20-4853911. FAX 31-20-4853705. *2977*

ETHICS (CHICAGO).
University of Chicago Press, Journals Division, Box 37005, Chicago, IL 60637. TEL 773-753-3347. FAX 773-753-0811. *5726*

ETHICS & BEHAVIOR.
Lawrence Erlbaum Associates, Inc., 10 Industrial Dr., Mahwah, NJ 07430-2262. TEL 201-236-9500. FAX 201-236-0072. *6110*

ETHICS & INTERNATIONAL AFFAIRS (JOURNAL).
Carnegie Council on Ethics and International Affairs, c/o Matthew Mattern, Ed., Merrill House, 170 E. 64th St., New York, NY 10021-7478. TEL 212-838-4120. FAX 212-752-2432. *6013*

ETHICS AND MEDICS.
Pope John XXIII Medical-Moral Research and Education Center, 186 Forbes Rd., Braintree, MA 02184. TEL 617-848-6965. FAX 617-849-1309. *5726*

ETHICS AND THE ENVIRONMENT.
J A I Press Inc., 55 Old Post Rd., No. 2, Box 1678, Greenwich, CT 06830-1678. TEL 203-661-7602. FAX 203-661-0792. *5726*

THE ETHIOPIAN JOURNAL OF HEALTH DEVELOPMENT.
Ethiopian Public Health Association, P.O. Box 32812, Addis Ababa, Ethiopia. TEL 251-1-518999. FAX 251-1-517701. *6233*

ETHIOPIAN REVIEW.
P.O. Box 98499, Atlanta, CA 30359. TEL 404-325-8411. FAX 404-325-8411. *6612*

ETHNIC HISTORY OF CHICAGO.
University of Illinois Press, 1325 S. Oak St., Champaign, IL 61820. TEL 217-333-0950. FAX 217-244-8082. *3010*

ETHNIC STUDIES REPORT.
International Centre for Ethnic Studies, 554-1 Peradeniya Rd., Kandy, Sri Lanka. TEL 08-234892. FAX 08-234892. *3010*

ETHNICITY & DISEASE.
International Society on Hypertension in Blacks, 2045 Manchester St., N.E., Atlanta, GA 30324-4110. TEL 404-875-6263. FAX 404-875-6334. *4665*

ETHNOBOTANY.
Deep Publications, A-3-27A DDA Flats, Paschim Vihar, New Delhi 110063, India. TEL 91-11-5579514. FAX 91-11-5437621. *702*

ETHNOHISTORY.
Duke University Press, Box 90660, Durham, NC 27708-0660. TEL 919-687-3600. FAX 919-688-4574. *315*

ETHNOLOGY.
University of Pittsburgh, Department of Anthropology, Pittsburgh, PA 15260. TEL 412-648-7503. FAX 412-648-7535. *315*

ETHNOMUSICOLOGY.
Society for Ethnomusicology, Morrison Hall Rm. 005, Indiana University, Bloomington, IN 47405-2501. TEL 217-333-3057. FAX 217-244-8082. *5391*

ETHNOMUSICOLOGY ONLINE. *5391*

ETHNOS.
Folkens Museum Etnografiska, P.O. Box 27140, 102 52 Stockholm, Sweden. FAX 46-8-666-50-70. *315*

ETNOLOSKA TRIBINA.
Institut za Etnologiju i Folkloristiku, Ul. Kralja Zvonimira 17, 41000 Zagreb, Croatia. TEL 385-41-440880. *316*

ETOLOGIA.
Sociedad Espanola de Etologia, c/o Museu de Zoologia, Apdo. 593, 08080 Barcelona, Spain. TEL 34-3-3196912. FAX 34-3-3104999. *833*

ETRUSCAN STUDIES.
Wayne State University Press, 4809 Woodward Ave., Detroit, MI 48201-1309. TEL 313-577-6120. FAX 313-577-6131. *1903*

ETTORE MAJORANA INTERNATIONAL SCIENCE SERIES. PHYSICAL SCIENCES.
Plenum Publishing Corp., 233 Spring St., New York, NY 10013-1578. TEL 212-620-8000. FAX 212-463-0742. *6525*

LES ETUDES CLASSIQUES.
Facultes Notre-Dame de la Paix, Faculte de Philosophie et Lettres, Rue de Bruxelles, 61, B-5000 Namur, Belgium. TEL 32-81-724189. FAX 32-81-724203. *1903*

ETUDES FRANCOPHONES.
University of Southwestern Louisiana, Conseil International d'Etudes Francophones, Box 43331, Lafayette, LA 70504-3331. TEL 318-482-6811. FAX 318-482-5446. *3011*

ETUDES MONGOLES ET SIBERIENNES.
Laboratoire d'Ethnologie et de Sociologie Comparative, Universite de Paris X, 200 av. de la Republique, 92001 Nanterre, France. TEL 33-2-40977522. FAX 33-2-40977117. *316*

ETUDES SUR LE JUDAISME MEDIEVAL.
E.J. Brill, P.O. Box 9000, 2300 PA Leiden, Netherlands. TEL 31-71-5353500. FAX 31-71-5317532. *6404*

EUPHYTICA.
Kluwer Academic Publishers, Postbus 17, 3300 AA Dordrecht, Netherlands. TEL 31-78-6392392. FAX 31-78-6392254. *223*

EURESIS - CAHIERS ROUMAINS D'ETUDES LITTERAIRES.
Editura Univers, Piata Presei Libere 1, 79739 Bucharest, Rumania. TEL 40-1-2226629. FAX 40-1-2225652. *4404*

EURO COURSES. ADVANCED SCIENTIFIC TECHNIQUES.
Kluwer Academic Publishers, Postbus 17, 3300 AA Dordrecht, Netherlands. TEL 31-78-6392392. FAX 31-78-6392254. *6959*

EURO COURSES. CHEMICAL AND ENVIRONMENTAL SCIENCES.
Kluwer Academic Publishers, Postbus 17, 3300 AA Dordrecht, Netherlands. TEL 31-78-6392392. FAX 31-78-6392254. *2927*

EURO COURSES. COMPUTER AND INFORMATION SCIENCE.
Kluwer Academic Publishers, Postbus 17, 3300 AA Dordrecht, Netherlands. TEL 31-78-6392392. FAX 31-78-6392254. *2081*

EURO COURSES. ENVIRONMENTAL IMPACT ASSESSMENT.
Kluwer Academic Publishers, Postbus 17, 3300 AA Dordrecht, Netherlands. TEL 31-78-6392392. FAX 31-78-6392254. *2927*

EURO COURSES. ENVIRONMENTAL MANAGEMENT.
Kluwer Academic Publishers, Postbus 17, 3300 AA Dordrecht, Netherlands. TEL 31-78-6392392. FAX 31-78-6392254. *2927*

EURO COURSES. HEALTH PHYSICS AND RADIATION PROTECTION.
Kluwer Academic Publishers, Postbus 17, 3300 AA Dordrecht, Netherlands. TEL 31-78-6392392. FAX 31-78-6392254. *2696*

EURO COURSES. NUCLEAR SCIENCE AND TECHNOLOGY.
Kluwer Academic Publishers, Postbus 17, 3300 AA Dordrecht, Netherlands. TEL 31-78-6392392. FAX 31-78-6392254. *2696*

EURO COURSES. RELIABILITY AND RISK ANALYSIS.
Kluwer Academic Publishers, Postbus 17, 3300 AA Dordrecht, Netherlands. TEL 31-78-6392392. FAX 31-78-6392254. *6959*

EURO COURSES. REMOTE SENSING.
Kluwer Academic Publishers, Postbus 17, 3300 AA Dordrecht, Netherlands. TEL 31-78-6392392. FAX 31-78-6392254. *6959*

EURO COURSES. TECHNOLOGICAL INNOVATION.
Kluwer Academic Publishers, Postbus 17, 3300 AA Dordrecht, Netherlands. TEL 31-78-6392392. FAX 31-78-6392254. *6959*

EURO-LATIN AMERICAN RELATIONS.
Kluwer Academic Publishers, Postbus 17, 3300 AA Dordrecht, Netherlands. TEL 31-78-6392392. FAX 31-78-6392254. *6013*

EUROBIOLOGISTE.
Centre National des Biologistes, 80 av. du Maine, 75014 Paris, France. TEL 33-1-43229770. FAX 33-1-43217312. *600*

EUROLINK AGE BULLETIN.
Eurolink Age, 1268 London Rd., London SW16 4ER, England. TEL 44-181-679-8000. FAX 44-181-679-6727. *3435*

EUROPA MEDICOPHYSICA.
Edizioni Minerva Medica, Corso Bramante 83-85, 10126 Turin, Italy. TEL 39-11-678282. FAX 39-11-674502. *5043*

EUROPE - ASIA STUDIES.
Carfax Publishing Co., P.O. Box 25, Abingdon, Oxon. OX14 3UE, England. TEL 44-1235-401000. FAX 44-1235-401550. *962*

EUROPE IN THE MIDDLE AGES.
Elsevier Science B.V., Books Division, P.O. Box 211, 1000 AE Amsterdam, Netherlands. TEL 31-20-4853911. FAX 31-20-4853705. *3565*

EUROPEAN ACADEMY OF DERMATOLOGY AND VENEREOLOGY. JOURNAL.
Elsevier Science B.V., P.O. Box 211, 1000 AE Amsterdam, Netherlands. TEL 31-20-4853911. FAX 31-20-4853598. *4878*

EUROPEAN ACADEMY OF DERMATOLOGY AND VENEREOLOGY. JOURNAL. SUPPLEMENT.
Elsevier Science B.V., Books Division, P.O. Box 211, 1000 AE Amsterdam, Netherlands. TEL 31-20-4853911. FAX 31-20-4853705. *4878*

THE EUROPEAN ACCOUNTING REVIEW.
Thomson Professional, 2-6 Boundary Row, London SE1 8HN, England. TEL 44-171-865-0066. FAX 44-171-522-9621. *1089*

EUROPEAN APPLIED RESEARCH REPORTS: NUCLEAR SCIENCE AND TECHNOLOGY SECTION.
Gordon and Breach - Harwood Academic, Amsteldisk 166, 1st Fl., 1079 LH Amsterdam, Netherlands. *5851*

EUROPEAN APPLIED RESEARCH REPORTS SPECIAL TOPICS SERIES.
Gordon and Breach - Harwood Academic, Amsteldisk 166, 1st Fl., 1079 LH Amsterdam, Netherlands. *5851*

EUROPEAN BREWERY CONVENTION. PROCEEDINGS OF THE INTERNATIONAL CONGRESS.
I R L Press Ltd., Walton St., Oxford OX2 6 DP, England. TEL 44-1865-56767. FAX 44-1865-56646. *520*

THE EUROPEAN BUSINESS JOURNAL.
Whurr Publishers Ltd., 19b Compton Terrace, London N1 2UN, England. TEL 44-171-359-5979. FAX 44-171-226-5290. *962*

EUROPEAN CANCER NEWS.
Kluwer Academic Publishers, Postbus 17, 3300 AA Dordrecht, Netherlands. TEL 31-78-6392392. FAX 31-78-6392254. *4977*

EUROPEAN CERAMIC SOCIETY. JOURNAL.
Elsevier Science Ltd., P.O. Box 800, Kidlington, Oxford OX5 1DX, England. TEL 44-1865-843000. FAX 44-1865-843010. *1728*

EUROPEAN CHILD & ADOLESCENT PSYCHIATRY.
Dr. Dietrich Steinkopff Verlag, Saalbaustr. 12, 64283 Darmstadt. TEL 49-6151-1745-0. FAX 49-6151-174510. *5063*

EUROPEAN COMMUNICATION POLICY RESEARCH SERIES.
I O S Press, Van Diemenstraat 94, 1013 CN Amsterdam, Netherlands. TEL 31-20-6382189. FAX 31-20-6203419. *1989*

EUROPEAN COMMUNITIES ENVIRONMENTAL POLICY SERIES.
Martinus Nijhoff Publishers, Human Rights and International Law Postbus 17, 3300 AA Dordrecht, Netherlands. TEL 31-78-334911. FAX 31-78-334254. *2927*

EUROPEAN COMMUNITY SHIPOWNERS' ASSOCIATIONS. ANNUAL REPORT.
European Community Shipowners' Associations, 45 rue Ducale, 1000 Brussels, Belgium. TEL 32-2-5113949. FAX 32-2-5118092. *7149*

EUROPEAN CONVENTION ON HUMAN RIGHTS. YEARBOOK.
Martinus Nijhoff Publishers, Human Rights and International Law Postbus 163, 3300 AD Dordrecht, Netherlands. TEL 31-78-334911. FAX 31-78-334254. *5990*

EUROPEAN EARLY CHILDHOOD EDUCATION RESEARCH JOURNAL.
Amber Publishing, Worcester College of Higher Education, Henwick Grove, Worcester WR2 6AJ, England. TEL 44-1905-855068. FAX 44-1905-855068. *2442*

EUROPEAN EATING DISORDERS REVIEW.
John Wiley & Sons Ltd., Journals, Baffins Ln., Chichester, W. Sussex PO19 1UD, England. TEL 44-1243-779777. FAX 44-1243-775878. *6110*

EUROPEAN ECONOMIC PERSPECTIVES.
Centre for Economic Policy Research, 25-28 Old Burlington St., London W1X 1LB, England. TEL 44-171-878-2900. FAX 44-171-878-2999. *1303*

EUROPEAN ECONOMIC REVIEW.
North-Holland, P.O. Box 211, 1000 AE Amsterdam, Netherlands. TEL 31-20-4853911. FAX 31-20-4853598. *962*

EUROPEAN EDUCATION.
M.E. Sharpe, Inc., 80 Business Park Dr., Armonk, NY 10504. TEL 914-273-1800. FAX 914-273-2106. *2442*

EUROPEAN ENVIRONMENTAL LAW REVIEW.
Kluwer Law International, Postbus 85889, 2508 CN The Hague, Netherlands. TEL 31-70-3081500. FAX 31-70-3081515. *3948*

EUROPEAN FINANCE REVIEW.
Kluwer Academic Publishers Boston, Box 358, Accord Sta., Hingham, MA 02018-0358. TEL 617-871-6600. FAX 617-871-6528. *1130*

EUROPEAN FINANCIAL MANAGEMENT.
Blackwell Publishers Ltd., 108 Cowley Rd., Oxford OX4 1JF, England. TEL 44-1865-791100. FAX 44-1865-791347. *1130*

EUROPEAN FINANCIAL SERVICES LAW.
Kluwer Law International, Postbus 85889, 2508 CN The Hague, Netherlands. TEL 31-70-30815003. FAX 31-70-3081515. *1131*

EUROPEAN FOREIGN AFFAIRS REVIEW.
Kluwer Law International, Postbus 85889, 2508 CN The Hague, Netherlands. TEL 31-70-3081500. FAX 31-70-3081515. *6013*

EUROPEAN HISTORY QUARTERLY.
Sage Publications Ltd., 6 Bonhill St., London EC2A 4PU, England. TEL 44-171-374-0645. FAX 44-171-374-8741. *3565*

EUROPEAN JOURNAL OF AGRICULTURAL EDUCATION AND EXTENSION.
P.O. Box 194, 6700 AD Wageningen, Netherlands. TEL 31-317-484018. FAX 31-317-485123. *114*

EUROPEAN JOURNAL OF ANAESTHESIOLOGY.
Blackwell Science Ltd., Osney Mead, Oxford OX2 0EL, England. TEL 44-1865-206206. FAX 44-1865-721205. *4805*

EUROPEAN JOURNAL OF CANCER.
Elsevier Science Ltd., Pergamon, P.O. Box 800, Kidlington, Oxford OX5 1DX, England. TEL 44-1865-843000. FAX 44-1865-843010. *4977*

EUROPEAN JOURNAL OF CANCER. PART B: ORAL ONCOLOGY.
Elsevier Science Ltd., Pergamon, P.O. Box 800, Kidlington, Oxford OX5 1DX, England. TEL 44-1865-843000. FAX 44-1865-843010. *4977*

EUROPEAN JOURNAL OF CANCER CARE (ENGLISH EDITION).
Blackwell Science Ltd., Osney Mead, Oxford OX2 0EL, England. TEL 44-1865-206206. FAX 44-1865-721205. *4978*

EUROPEAN JOURNAL OF CARDIO-THORACIC SURGERY.
Elsevier Science B.V., P.O. Box 211, 1000 AE Amsterdam, Netherlands. TEL 31-20-4853757. FAX 31-20-4853432. *4816*

EUROPEAN JOURNAL OF CHIROPRACTIC.
European Chiropractors' Union, c/o Simon Leyson, Ed., 16 Uplands Crescent, Swansea SA2 0PB, Wales. TEL 44-1792-476644. FAX 44-1639-639649. *4827*

EUROPEAN JOURNAL OF CLINICAL INVESTIGATION.
Blackwell Science Ltd., Osney Mead, Oxford OX2 0EL, England. TEL 44-1865-206206. FAX 44-1865-721205. *4665*

EUROPEAN JOURNAL OF CLINICAL MICROBIOLOGY & INFECTIOUS DISEASES.
M M V Medizin Verlag, Neumarkter Str. 18, 81673 Munich, Germany. TEL 49-89-43189-0. FAX 49-89-43189633. *783*

EUROPEAN JOURNAL OF CLINICAL RESEARCH.
Brookwood Medical Publications, Orchard House, Brookwood, Surrey GU24 0AT, England. TEL 44-1483-797975. FAX 44-1483-797915. *4665*

EUROPEAN JOURNAL OF COGNITIVE PSYCHOLOGY.
Taylor & Francis Ltd., Psychology Press, 1 Gunpowder Sq., London EC4A 3DE, England. TEL 44-171-5830490. FAX 44-171-5830585. *6110*

EUROPEAN JOURNAL OF COMMUNICATION.
Sage Publications Ltd., 6 Bonhill St., London EC2A 4PU, England. TEL 44-171-374-0645. FAX 44-171-374-8741. *1989*

EUROPEAN JOURNAL OF CONTRACEPTION AND REPRODUCTIVE HEALTH CARE.
Parthenon Publishing Group, Casterton Hall, Carnforth, Lancs LA6 2LA, England. TEL 44-15242-72084. FAX 44-15242-71587. *856*

THE EUROPEAN JOURNAL OF DEVELOPMENT RESEARCH.
Frank Cass, Newbury House, 890-900 Eastern Ave., Newbury Park, Ilford, Essex IG2 7HH, England. TEL 44-181-599-8666. FAX 44-181-599-0984. *1359*

EUROPEAN JOURNAL OF DISORDERS OF COMMUNICATION.
Whurr Publishers Ltd., 19b Compton Terrace, London N1 2UN, England. TEL 44-171-359-5979. FAX 44-171-226-5290. *2583*

EUROPEAN JOURNAL OF EDUCATION.
Carfax Publishing Co., P.O. Box 25, Abingdon, Oxon. OX14 3UE, England. TEL 44-1235-401000. FAX 44-1235-401550. *2442*

EUROPEAN JOURNAL OF EMERGENCY MEDICINE.
Chapman & Hall, Journals Department 2-6 Boundary Row, London SE1 8HN, England. TEL 44-171-8650066. FAX 44-171-5229623. *5007*

EUROPEAN JOURNAL OF ENDOCRINOLOGY.
Journal of Endocrinology Ltd., 17-18 The Courtyard, Woodlands, Bradley Stoke, Bristol BS12 4NQ, England. TEL 44-1454-616046. FAX 44-1454-616071. *4887*

EUROPEAN JOURNAL OF ENGINEERING EDUCATION.
Carfax Publishing Co., P.O. Box 25, Abingdon, Oxon. OX14 3UE, England. TEL 44-1235-401000. FAX 44-1235-401550. *2719*

EUROPEAN JOURNAL OF ENGLISH STUDIES.
Swets & Zeitlinger bv, P.O. Box 825, 2160 SZ Lisse, Netherlands. TEL 31-252-435111. FAX 31-252-415888. *4404*

EUROPEAN JOURNAL OF ENTOMOLOGY.
Academy of Sciences of the Czech Republic, Institute of Entomology, Branisovska 31, 37005 Ceske Budejovice, Czech Republic. TEL 420-38-817213. FAX 420-38-43624. *752*

EUROPEAN JOURNAL OF EPIDEMIOLOGY.
Kluwer Academic Publishers, Postbus 17, 3300 AA Dordrecht, Netherlands. TEL 31-78-6392392. FAX 31-78-6392254. *4665*

THE EUROPEAN JOURNAL OF FINANCE.
Thomson Professional, 2-6 Boundary Row, London SE1 8HN, England. TEL 44-171-8650066. FAX 44-171-5229623. *1131*

EUROPEAN JOURNAL OF FOREST PATHOLOGY.
Blackwell Wissenschaft, Kurfuerstendamm 57, 10707 Berlin, Germany. TEL 49-30-32790634. FAX 49-30-32790610. *3150*

EUROPEAN JOURNAL OF GASTROENTEROLOGY AND HEPATOLOGY.
Rapid Science Publishers, 2-6 Boundary Row, London SE1 8HN, England. TEL 44-171-865-0198. FAX 44-171-410-6600. *4909*

THE EUROPEAN JOURNAL OF GENERAL PRACTICE.
Mediselect B.V., Postbus 28091, 3828 ZH Hoogland, Netherlands. TEL 31-33-4808020. FAX 31-33-4805881. *4665*

EUROPEAN JOURNAL OF GENETICS IN SOCIETY.
European Bioethical Research, 191 Leith Walk, Edinburgh EH6 8NX, Scotland. TEL 44-131-554-8869. FAX 44-131-1236-451299. *5726*

EUROPEAN JOURNAL OF GYNECOLOGICAL ONCOLOGY.
S O G Canada, Inc., 4900 Cote St. Luc, Apt. 212, Montreal, PQ H3W 2H3, Canada. TEL 514-489-3242, 39-49-8758644. FAX 514-485-4513. *4978*

EUROPEAN JOURNAL OF HAEMATOLOGY.
Munksgaard International Publishers Ltd., 35 Noerre Soegade, P.O. Box 2148, DK-1016 Copenhagen K, Denmark. TEL 45-33-127030. FAX 45-33-129387. *4918*

EUROPEAN JOURNAL OF HAEMATOLOGY. SUPPLEMENTUM.
Munksgaard International Publishers Ltd., P.O. Box 2148, DK-1016 Copenhagen K, Denmark. TEL 45-33-127030. FAX 45-33-129387. *4918*

EUROPEAN JOURNAL OF HEALTH LAW.
Kluwer Law International, Postbus 85889, 2508 CN The Hague, Netherlands. TEL 31-70-3081500. FAX 31-70-3081515. *4666*

EUROPEAN JOURNAL OF HERBAL MEDICINE.
National Institute of Medical Herbalists, 56 Longbrook St., Exeter EX4 6AH, England. TEL 44-181-340-2900. FAX 44-181-341-7425. *5660*

EUROPEAN JOURNAL OF HUMAN GENETICS.
Stockton Press, Houndmills, Basingstoke, Hants RG21 6XS, England. TEL 44-1256-351898. FAX 44-1256-328339. *766*

EUROPEAN JOURNAL OF IMMUNOGENETICS.
Blackwell Science Ltd., Osney Mead, Oxford OX2 0EL, England. TEL 44-1865-206206. FAX 44-1865-721205. *766*

EUROPEAN JOURNAL OF INTERNATIONAL RELATIONS.
Sage Publications Ltd., 6 Bonhill St., London EC2A 4PU, England. TEL 44-171-374-0645. FAX 44-171-374-8741. *6014*

EUROPEAN JOURNAL OF LAW AND ECONOMICS.
Kluwer Academic Publishers Boston, Box 358, Accord St., Hingham, MA 02018-0358. TEL 617-871-6600. FAX 617-871-6528. *962*

EUROPEAN JOURNAL OF MECHANICAL AND ENVIRONMENTAL ENGINEERING.
Societe Belge des Mecaniciens, 21 rue des Drapiers, B-1050 Brussels, Belgium. TEL 32-2-5118286. *2883*

EUROPEAN JOURNAL OF MEDICINAL CHEMISTRY.
Editions Scientifiques et Medicales Elsevier, 141 rue de Javel, 75747 Paris, France. TEL 33-1-45589022. FAX 33-1-45589421. *659*

EUROPEAN JOURNAL OF MINERALOGY.
E. Schweizerbart'sche Verlagsbuchhandlung, Johannesstr. 3A, 70176 Stuttgart, Germany. TEL 49-711-625001. FAX 49-711-625005. *5300*

EUROPEAN JOURNAL OF NEUROLOGY.
Rapid Science Publishers, 2-6 Boundary Row, London SE1 8HN, England. TEL 44-171-865-0198. FAX 44-171-410-6600. *5063*

EUROPEAN JOURNAL OF OBSTETRICS & GYNECOLOGY AND REPRODUCTIVE BIOLOGY.
Elsevier Science Ireland Ltd., P.O. Box 85, Limerick, Ireland. TEL 353-61-471944. FAX 353-61-472144. *4956*

EUROPEAN JOURNAL OF OPERATIONAL RESEARCH.
North-Holland, P.O. Box 211, 1000 AE Amsterdam, Netherlands. TEL 31-20-4853911. FAX 31-20-4853598. *1476*

EUROPEAN JOURNAL OF ORAL SCIENCES.
Munksgaard International Publishers Ltd., 35 Noerre Soegade, P.O. Box 2148, DK-1016 Copenhagen K, Denmark. TEL 45-33-127030. FAX 45-33-129387. *4857*

EUROPEAN JOURNAL OF PARAPSYCHOLOGY.
Koestler Chair of Parapsychology, Dept. of Psychology, Univ. of Edinburgh, 7 George Sq., Edinburgh EH8 9JZ, Scotland. TEL 44-131-650-3348. FAX 44-131-650-3461. *5575*

EUROPEAN JOURNAL OF PARENTERAL SCIENCES.
Euromed Communications, The Old Surgery, Liphook Rd., Haslemere, Surrey, England. TEL 44-428-656665. FAX 44-428-656643. *5660*

EUROPEAN JOURNAL OF PHARMACEUTICAL SCIENCES.
Elsevier Science B.V., P.O. Box 211, 1000 AE Amsterdam, Netherlands. TEL 31-20-4853911. FAX 31-20-4853598. *5660*

EUROPEAN JOURNAL OF PHARMACOLOGY.
Elsevier Science B.V., P.O. Box 211, 1000 AE Amsterdam, Netherlands. TEL 31-20-4853911. FAX 31-20-4853598. *5660*

EUROPEAN JOURNAL OF PHARMACOLOGY. MOLECULAR PHARMACOLOGY SECTION.
Elsevier Science B.V., P.O. Box 211, 1000 AE Amsterdam, Netherlands. TEL 31-20-4853911. FAX 31-20-4853598. *5661*

EUROPEAN JOURNAL OF PHILOSOPHY.
Blackwell Publishers Ltd., 108 Cowley Rd., Oxford OX4 1JF, England. TEL 44-1865-791100. FAX 44-1865-791347. *5726*

EUROPEAN JOURNAL OF PLANT PATHOLOGY.
Kluwer Academic Publishers, Postbus 17, 3300 AA Dordrecht, Netherlands. TEL 31-78-6392392. FAX 31-78-6392254. *702*

EUROPEAN JOURNAL OF POLITICAL ECONOMY.
North-Holland, P.O. Box 211, 1000 AE Amsterdam, Netherlands. TEL 31-20-4853911. FAX 31-20-4853598. *1460*

EUROPEAN JOURNAL OF POLITICAL RESEARCH.
Kluwer Academic Publishers, Postbus 17, 3300 AA Dordrecht, Netherlands. TEL 31-78-6392392. FAX 31-78-6392254. *5925*

EUROPEAN JOURNAL OF POPULATION.
Kluwer Academic Publishers, Postbus 17, 3300 AA Dordrecht, Netherlands. TEL 31-78-6392392. *6065*

EUROPEAN JOURNAL OF PSYCHIATRY.
University of Zaragoza, P.O. Box 6029, Avda. S. Juan Bosco 15, 50009 Zaragoza. TEL 34-976-597818. FAX 34-976-559795. *5064*

EUROPEAN JOURNAL OF PSYCHOLOGY OF EDUCATION.
Instituto Superior de Psicologia Aplicada, Rua Jardim do Tabaco, 44, 1100 Lisbon, Portugal. TEL 351-1-8863184. FAX 351-1-8860954. *2443*

EUROPEAN JOURNAL OF PURCHASING AND SUPPLY MANAGEMENT.
Elsevier Science Ltd., Pergamon, P.O. Box 800, Kidlington, Oxford OX5 1DX, England. TEL 44-1865-843000. FAX 44-1865-843010. *1526*

EUROPEAN JOURNAL OF RADIOLOGY.
Elsevier Science Ireland Ltd., P.O. Box 85, Limerick, Ireland. TEL 353-61-471944. FAX 353-61-472144. *5106*

EUROPEAN JOURNAL OF SOCIAL PSYCHOLOGY.
John Wiley & Sons Ltd., Journals, Baffins Ln., Chichester, W. Sussex PO19 1UD, England. TEL 44-1243-779777. FAX 44-1243-775878. *6111*

EUROPEAN JOURNAL OF SOIL SCIENCE.
Blackwell Science Ltd., Osney Mead, Oxford OX2 0EL, England. TEL 44-1865-206206. FAX 44-1865-721205. *223*

EUROPEAN JOURNAL OF TEACHER EDUCATION.
Carfax Publishing Co., P.O. Box 25, Abingdon, Oxon. OX14 3UE, England. TEL 44-1235-401000. FAX 44-1235-401550. *2443*

EUROPEAN JOURNAL OF ULTRASOUND.
Elsevier Science Ireland Ltd., P.O. Box 85, Limerick, Ireland. TEL 353-61-471944. FAX 353-61-472144. *5106*

EUROPEAN JUDAISM.
Berghahn Books Inc., 165 Taber Ave., Providence, RI 02906. TEL 401-861-9330. FAX 401-521-0046. *6404*

THE EUROPEAN LEGACY.
M I T Press, 5 Cambridge Center, Cambridge, MA 02142. TEL 617-253-2889. FAX 617-577-1545. *5726*

EUROPEAN MANAGEMENT JOURNAL.
Elsevier Science Ltd., Pergamon, P.O. Box 800, Kidlington, Oxford OX5 1DX, England. TEL 44-1865-843000. FAX 44-1865-843010. *1476*

EUROPEAN MASS SPECTROSCOPY.
I M Publications, 6 Charlton Mill, Charlton, Chichester, W. Sussex PO18 0HY, England. TEL 44-1243-811334. FAX 44-1243-811711. *1790*

EUROPEAN MATERIALS RESEARCH SOCIETY. MONOGRAPHS.
Elsevier Science B.V., Books Division, P.O. Box 211, 1000 AE Amsterdam, Netherlands. TEL 31-20-4853911. FAX 31-20-4853705. *2858*

EUROPEAN MATERIALS RESEARCH SOCIETY. SYMPOSIA PROCEEDINGS.
Elsevier Science B.V., Books Division, P.O. Box 211, 1000 AE Amsterdam, Netherlands. TEL 31-20-4853911. FAX 31-20-4853705. *2858*

EUROPEAN NEUROLOGY.
S. Karger AG, Allschwilerstr. 10, P.O. Box, CH-4009 Basel, Switzerland. TEL 41-61-3061111. FAX 41-61-3061234. *5064*

EUROPEAN NEUROPSYCHOPHARMACOLOGY.
Elsevier Science B.V., P.O. Box 211, 1000 AE Amsterdam, Netherlands. TEL 31-20-4853911. FAX 31-20-4853598. *5064*

EUROPEAN NURSE.
Arnold, 338 Euston Rd., London NW1 3BH, England. TEL 44-171-873-6000. FAX 44-171-873-6325. *4932*

EUROPEAN ORGANIZATION FOR RESEARCH ON TREATMENT OF CANCER. MONOGRAPH SERIES.
Lippincott - Raven Publishers, 227 E. Washington Sq., Philadelphia, PA 19106. TEL 215-238-4200. FAX 215-238-4227. *4978*

EUROPEAN PHYSICAL EDUCATION REVIEW.
Studies in Education, Driffield Rd., Nafferton, Driffield, E. Yorks YO25 0JL, England. TEL 44-1377-254231. FAX 44-1377-256861. *2602*

EUROPEAN PLANNING STUDIES.
Carfax Publishing Co., P.O. Box 25, Abingdon, Oxon. OX14 3UE, England. TEL 44-1235-401000. FAX 44-1235-401550. *3747*

EUROPEAN POLYMER JOURNAL.
Elsevier Science Ltd., Pergamon, P.O. Box 800, Kidlington, Oxford OX5 1DX, England. TEL 44-1865-843000. FAX 44-1865-843010. *1815*

EUROPEAN PSYCHIATRY.
Editions Scientifiques et Medicales Elsevier, 141 rue de Javel, 75747 Paris, France. TEL 33-1-45589026. FAX 33-1-45589421. *5064*

EUROPEAN PSYCHOLOGIST.
Hogrefe & Huber Publishers, Box 2487, Kirkland, WA 98083. TEL 206-820-1500. FAX 206-823-8324. *6111*

EUROPEAN PUBLIC LAW.
Kluwer Law International, Postbus 85889, 2508 CN The Hague, Netherlands. TEL 31-70-3081500. FAX 31-70-3081515. *4113*

EUROPEAN RESEARCH IN REGIONAL SCIENCE.
Pion Ltd., 207 Brondesbury Park, London NW2 5JN, England. TEL 44-181-459-0066. FAX 44-181-451-6454. *3747*

EUROPEAN RESEARCH LIBRARY COOPERATION.
Ligue des Bibliotheques Europeenes de Recherche (LIBER), LIBER Secretariat, Kongelige Bibliotek, P.O. Box 2149, DK-1016 Copenhagen K, Denmark. TEL 45-33-93-62-22. FAX 45-33-91-95-96. *4177*

THE EUROPEAN RESPIRATORY JOURNAL.
Munksgaard International Publishers Ltd., 35 Noerre Soegade, P.O. Box 2148, DK-1016 Copenhagen K, Denmark. TEL 45-33-127030. FAX 45-33-129387. *5118*

EUROPEAN RESPIRATORY REVIEW.
Munksgaard International Publishers Ltd., 35 Noerre Soegade, P.O. Box 2148, DK-2148 Copenhagen K, Denmark. TEL 45-33-127030. FAX 45-33-129387. *5119*

EUROPEAN REVIEW.
Cambridge University Press, Edinburgh Bldg., Shaftesbury Rd., Cambridge CB2 2RU, England. TEL 44-1223-312393. FAX 44-1223-315052. *6525*

EUROPEAN REVIEW OF ECONOMIC HISTORY.
Cambridge University Press, Edinburgh Bldg., Shaftesbury Rd., Cambridge CB2 2RU, England. TEL 44-1223-312393. FAX 44-1223-315052. *1304*

EUROPEAN REVIEW OF HISTORY.
Carfax Publishing Co., P.O. Box 25, Abingdon, Oxon. OX14 3UE, England. TEL 44-1235-401000. FAX 44-1235-401550. *3565*

EUROPEAN REVIEW OF PRIVATE LAW.
Kluwer Law International, Postbus 85889, 2508 CN The Hague, Netherlands. TEL 31-70-3081500. FAX 31-70-3081515. *4113*

EUROPEAN REVIEW OF SOCIAL PSYCHOLOGY.
John Wiley & Sons Ltd., Journals, Baffins Ln., Chichester, W. Sussex PO19 1UD, England. TEL 44-1243-779777. FAX 44-1243-775878. *6111*

EUROPEAN SECURITY.
Frank Cass, Newbury House, 890-900 Eastern Ave., Newbury Park, Ilford, Essex 1G2 7HH, England. TEL 44-181-599-8866. FAX 44-181-599-0984. *6014*

EUROPEAN SOCIOLOGICAL REVIEW.
Oxford University Press, Academic Division, Great Clarendon St., Oxford OX2 6DP, England. TEL 44-1865-267907. FAX 44-1865-267485. *6709*

EUROPEAN SPINE JOURNAL.
Springer-Verlag, Heidelberger Platz 3, 14197 Berlin, Germany. TEL 49-30-82787-0. FAX 49-30-82787448. *5142*

EUROPEAN STUDIES IN LAW.
Elsevier Science B.V., Books Division, P.O. Box 211, 1000 AE Amsterdam, Netherlands. TEL 31-20-4853911. FAX 31-20-4853705. *3948*

EUROPEAN STUDIES IN PHILOSOPHY OF MEDICINE.
Kluwer Academic Publishers, Postbus 17, 3300 AA Dordrecht, Netherlands. TEL 31-78-6392392. FAX 31-78-6392254. *4666*

EUROPEAN STUDIES JOURNAL.
University of Northern Iowa, Department of Modern Languages, Cedar Falls, IA 50614-0504. TEL 319-273-6048. FAX 319-273-2921. *3565*

EUROPEAN STUDIES ON MULTILINGUALISM.
Swets & Zeitlinger bv, P.O. Box 825, 2160 SZ Lisse, Netherlands. TEL 31-252-435111. FAX 31-252-415888. *4256*

EUROPEAN SURGICAL RESEARCH.
S. Karger AG, Allschwilerstr. 10, P.O. Box, CH-4009 Basel, Switzerland. TEL 41-61-3061111. FAX 41-61-3061234. *5142*

EUROPEAN UROLOGY.
S. Karger AG, Allschwilerstr. 10, P.O. Box, CH-4009 Basel, Switzerland. TEL 41-61-3061111. FAX 41-61-3061234. *5161*

EUROPEAN WATER POLLUTION CONTROL.
Elsevier Science B.V., P.O. Box 211, 1000 AE Amsterdam, Netherlands. TEL 31-20-4853911. FAX 31-20-4853598. *2968*

EVALUATION AND PROGRAM PLANNING.
Elsevier Science Ltd., Pergamon, P.O. Box 800, Kidlington, Oxford OX5 1DX, England. TEL 44-1865-843000. FAX 44-1865-843010. *6613*

EVELYN WAUGH NEWSLETTER AND STUDIES.
Evelyn Waugh Society, Nassau Community College, State University of New York, Department of English, Garden City, NY 11530. TEL 516-572-7792. *4404*

THE EVERGREEN CHRONICLES.
Box 8939, Minneapolis, MN 55408-0939. TEL 612-823-6638. *4404*

EVOKED POTENTIALS.
Elsevier Science Ireland Ltd., P.O. Box 85, Limerick, Ireland. TEL 353-61-471944. FAX 353-61-472144. *5064*

EVOLUTION.
Allen Press, Inc., 1041 New Hampshire Ave., Box 1897, Lawrence, KS 66044-8897. FAX 913-843-1274. *767*

EVOLUTION OF COMMUNICATION.
John Benjamins Publishing Co., Amsteldijk 44, P.O. Box 75577, 1070 AN Amsterdam, Netherlands. TEL 31-20-6762325. FAX 31-20-6792956. *4256*

EVOLUTIONARY ANTHROPOLOGY.
John Wiley & Sons, Inc., Journals, 605 Third Ave., New York, NY 10158-0012. TEL 212-850-6000. FAX 212-850-6088. *316*

EVOLUTIONARY BIOLOGY.
Plenum Publishing Corp., 233 Spring St., New York, NY 10013-1578. TEL 212-620-8000. FAX 212-463-0742. *767*

EVOLUTIONARY COMPUTATION.
M I T Press, 5 Cambridge Center, Cambridge, MA 02142. TEL 617-253-2889. FAX 617-577-1545. *735*

EVOLUTIONARY ECOLOGY.
Chapman & Hall, Journals Department 2-6 Boundary Row, London SE1 8HN, England. TEL 44-171-8650066. FAX 44-171-5229623. *2927*

EVOLUTIONARY MONOGRAPHS.
University of Chicago, Department of Ecology and Evolution, 1101 E. 57th St., Chicago, IL 60637. TEL 312-702-9475. *600*

EVOLUTIONARY THEORY.
University of Chicago, Department of Ecology and Evolution, 1101 E. 57th St., Chicago, IL 60637. TEL 312-702-9475. *601*

THE EXAMINER (RALEIGH).
Society of Financial Examiners, 4101 Lake Boone Trail, No. 201, Raleigh, NC 27607. TEL 919-787-5181. FAX 919-787-4961. *1089*

EXCAVACIONES ARQUEOLOGICAS EN ESPANA.
Instituto del Patrimonio Historico Espanol, C. El Greco, 4, Ciudad Universitaria, 28040 Madrid, Spain. *362*

EXCEPTIONAL CHILDREN.
Council for Exceptional Children, 1920 Association Dr., Reston, VA 22091. TEL 703-620-3660. FAX 703-264-9494. *1845*

EXCEPTIONAL HUMAN EXPERIENCE.
Exceptional Human Experience Network, 414 Rockledge Rd., New Bern, NC 28562. TEL 919-636-8734. FAX 919-636-8371. *5457*

EXCEPTIONALITY EDUCATION CANADA.
University of Prince Edward Island, c/o Vianne Timmons, Dean of Education, 550 University Ave., Charlottetown, PE C1A 4P3, Canada. *2584*

EXCHANGE.
E.J. Brill, P.O. Box 9000, 2300 PA Leiden, Netherlands. TEL 31-71-5353500. FAX 31-71-5317532. *6338*

EXECUTIVE COMPUTING.
Association of Computer Users, 1250 45th St., Ste. 200, Emeryville, CA 94608-2924. TEL 510-596-9300. *1200*

EXECUTIVE ENGINEER.
Institution of Incorporated Executive Engineers, Wix Hill House, W. Horsley, Surrey KT24 6DZ, England. TEL 44-1483-222383. FAX 44-1483-211109. *2720*

EXECUTIVE HOUSEKEEPING TODAY.
International Executive Housekeepers Association, 1001 Eastwind Dr., Ste. 301, Westerville, OH 43081. TEL 614-895-7166. FAX 614-895-1248. *5489*

EXECUTIVE INTELLIGENCE REVIEW.
E I R News Service, Box 17390, Washington, DC 20041. TEL 202-544-7022. FAX 703-771-3099. *5925*

EXECUTIVE SYSTEMS INTERNATIONAL.
Business Intelligence Publishing, 25 Prospect Rd., Southborough, Tunbridge Wells, Kent TN4 OEL, England. TEL 01892-517340. FAX 01892-517476. *1200*

EXEMPLARIA.
Pegasus Press, University of North Carolina, Asheville, NC 28804. TEL 704-232-5143. FAX 704-232-5146. *4404*

EXIT.
Ecrits des Forges, c/o Diffusion Collective Radisson, 1497 Laviolette, C.P. 335, Trois-Rivieres, PQ G9A 5G4, Canada. TEL 819-379-9813. FAX 819-376-0774. *4508*

EXLIBRISKUNST UND GRAPHIK. JAHRBUCH.
Deutsche Exlibris-Gesellschaft e.V., Am Loewentor 46, 56075 Koblenz, Germany. TEL 49-261-57885. FAX 49-261-57885. *440*

EXPEDITION.
University of Pennsylvania Museum, 33rd & Spruce Sts., Philadelphia, PA 19104-6324. TEL 215-898-0023. FAX 215-898-0657. *316*

EXPERIMENT.
Institute of Modern Russian Culture, Box 4353, University of Southern California, Los Angeles, CA 90089-4353. TEL 213-740-2735. FAX 213-740-8550. *3011*

EXPERIMENTAL & APPLIED ACAROLOGY.
Thomson Science, 2-6 Boundary Row, London SE1 8HN, England. TEL 44-171-8560066. FAX 44-171-5229623. *601*

EXPERIMENTAL AND CLINICAL IMMUNOGENETICS.
S. Karger AG, Allschwilerstr. 10, P.O. Box, CH-4009 Basel, Switzerland. TEL 41-61-3061111. FAX 41-61-3061234. *767*

EXPERIMENTAL AND MOLECULAR MEDICINE.
Korean Society of Medical Biochemistry and Molecular Biology, No. 12 KOFST, 635-4 Yeoksam-dong, Kangnam-gu, Seoul 135-703, S. Korea. TEL 82-2-565-1621. FAX 82-2-565-1622. *660*

EXPERIMENTAL AND MOLECULAR PATHOLOGY.
Academic Press, Inc., Journal Division, 525 B St., Ste. 1900, San Diego, CA 92101-4495. TEL 619-230-1840. FAX 619-699-6800. *4666*

EXPERIMENTAL ASTRONOMY.
Kluwer Academic Publishers, Postbus 17, 3300 AA Dordrecht, Netherlands. TEL 31-78-6392392. FAX 31-78-6392254. *494*

EXPERIMENTAL BIOLOGY ONLINE.
Springer-Verlag, Heidelberger Platz 3, 14197 Berlin, Germany. TEL 49-30-82787-0. FAX 49-30-82787448. *601*

EXPERIMENTAL CELL RESEARCH.
Academic Press, Inc., Journal Division, 525 B St., Ste. 1900, San Diego, CA 92101-4495. TEL 619-230-1840. FAX 619-699-6800. *740*

EXPERIMENTAL DERMATOLOGY.
Munksgaard International Publishers Ltd., 35 Noerre Soegade, P.O. Box 2148, DK-1016 Copenhagen K, Denmark. TEL 45-33-127030. FAX 45-33-129387. *4878*

EXPERIMENTAL EYE RESEARCH.
Academic Press Ltd., 24-28 Oval Rd., London NW1 7DX, England. TEL 44-171-267-4466. FAX 44-171-482-2293. *4993*

EXPERIMENTAL GERONTOLOGY.
Elsevier Science Inc., Box 945, New York, NY 10159-0945. TEL 212-633-3730. FAX 212-633-3680. *3435*

EXPERIMENTAL HEAT TRANSFER.
Taylor & Francis Inc., 1900 Frost Rd., Ste. 101, Bristol, PA 19007-1598. TEL 215-785-5800. FAX 215-785-5515. *5840*

EXPERIMENTAL LUNG RESEARCH.
Taylor & Francis Inc., 1900 Frost Rd., Ste. 101, Bristol, PA 19007-1598. TEL 215-785-5800. FAX 215-785-5515. *5119*

EXPERIMENTAL MATHEMATICS.
A K Peters, Ltd., 289 Linden St., Wellesley, MA 02181-5910. TEL 617-235-2210. FAX 617-235-2404. *4572*

EXPERIMENTAL MECHANICS.
Sage Publications, Inc., Sage Science Press, 2455 Teller Rd., Thousand Oaks, CA 91320. TEL 805-499-0721. FAX 805-499-0871. *2858*

EXPERIMENTAL METHODS IN THE PHYSICAL SCIENCES.
Academic Press, Inc., 525 B St., Ste. 1900, San Diego, CA 92101-4495. TEL 619-231-0926. FAX 619-699-6715. *5802*

EXPERIMENTAL NEPHROLOGY.
S. Karger AG, Allschwilerstr. 10, P.O. Box, CH-4009 Basel, Switzerland. TEL 41-61-3061111. FAX 41-61-3061235. *5161*

EXPERIMENTAL NEUROLOGY.
Academic Press, Inc., Journal Division, 525 B St., Ste. 1900, San Diego, CA 92101-4495. TEL 619-230-1840. FAX 619-699-6800. *5065*

EXPERIMENTAL PARASITOLOGY.
Academic Press, Inc., Journal Division, 525 B St., Ste. 1900, San Diego, CA 92101-4495. TEL 619-230-1840. FAX 619-699-6800. *4835*

EXPERIMENTAL TECHNIQUES.
Society for Experimental Mechanics, 7 School St., Bethel, CT 06801. TEL 203-790-6373. FAX 203-790-4472. *2858*

EXPERIMENTAL THERMAL AND FLUID SCIENCE.
Elsevier Science Inc., Box 945, New York, NY 10159-0945. TEL 212-633-3730. FAX 212-633-3680. *2720*

EXPERIMENTAL VIROLOGY.
Academic Press, Inc., 525 B St., Ste. 1900, San Diego, CA 92101-4495. TEL 619-231-0926. FAX 619-699-6715. *783*

EXPERT OPINION IN INVESTIGATIONAL DRUGS.
Ashley Publications Ltd., First Fl., The Library, 1 Shepherds Hill, Highgate, London N6 5QJ, England. TEL 44-181-347-5030. FAX 44-181-347-5040. *5661*

EXPERT OPINION ON THERAPEUTIC PATENTS.
Ashley Publications Ltd., First Fl., The Library, 1 Shepherds Hill, Highgate, London N6 5QJ, England. TEL 44-181-347-5030. FAX 44-181-347-5040. *5661*

EXPERT SYSTEMS WITH APPLICATIONS.
Elsevier Science Ltd., Pergamon, P.O. Box 800, Kidlington, Oxford OX5 1DX, England. TEL 44-1865-843000. FAX 44-1865-843010. *2155*

EXPLICACION DE TEXTOS LITERARIOS.
California State University, Sacramento, Department of Foreign Languages, 6000 J St., Sacramento, CA 95819-6087. TEL 916-454-6011. FAX 916-278-5502. *4405*

THE EXPLICATOR.
Heldref Publications, 1319 Eighteenth St., N.W., Washington, DC 20036-1802. TEL 202-296-6267. FAX 202-296-5149. *4405*

EXPLORATION & MINING GEOLOGY.
Elsevier Science Ltd., Pergamon, P.O. Box 800, Kidlington, Oxford OX5 1DX, England. TEL 44-1865-843000. FAX 44-1865-843010. *2339*

EXPLORATIONS (JUNEAU).
University of Alaska Southeast, English Department, 11120 Glacier Hwy., Juneau, AK 99801-8761. TEL 907-465-6418. FAX 907-465-6406. *4405*

EXPLORATIONS IN ETHNIC STUDIES.
National Association for Ethnic Studies, Inc., Dept. of English, Arizona State University, Tempe, AZ 85287-0302. TEL 602-965-2197. FAX 602-965-3451. *3011*

EXPLORATIONS IN RENAISSANCE CULTURE.
Southwest Missouri State University, Department of English, Springfield, MO 65804. TEL 417-836-5107. FAX 417-836-4226. *3778*

EXPLORER (LAKE WORTH).
Atlantic Coast District Dental Association, 5700 Lake Worth Rd., Ste. 206, Lake Worth, FL 33463. TEL 561-968-7714. FAX 561-968-4834. *4857*

EXPLORING THE ROMAN WORLD.
University of California Press, 2120 Berkeley Way, Berkeley, CA 94720. TEL 510-642-4247. FAX 510-643-7127. *1903*

EXPO.
Hill-stiftelsen, Box 1030, S-114 79 Stockholm, Sweden. TEL 46-8-429-89-49. FAX 46-8-429-89-59. *5925*

EXPOSURE (DALLAS).
Society for Photographic Education, Box 222116, Dallas, TX 75222-2116. TEL 817-272-2845. FAX 817-272-2846. *5764*

EXQUISITE CORPSE.
Illinois State University, Campus Box 4241, Normal, IL 61790-4241. *4333*

EXTRACTA MATHEMATICAE.
Universidad de Extremadura, Departamento de Matematicas, Avda. Elvas, s-n, 06071 Badajoz, Spain. FAX 34-24-272911. *4572*

EXTRAPOLATION.
Kent State University Press, Box 5190, 307 Lowry Hall, Kent, OH 44242-0001. TEL 330-672-7913. FAX 330-672-3104. *4531*

EXTREMOPHILES.
Springer-Verlag Tokyo, 3-13, Hongo 3-chome, Bunkyo-ku, Tokyo 113, Japan. TEL 81-3-38120331. FAX 81-3-38120719. *682*

EYE.
B M J Publishing Group, B M A House, Tavistock Sqr., London WC1H QJR, England. *4993*

EYE ON IMPROVEMENT.
Institute for Healthcare Improvement, Box 38100, Cleveland, OH 44138-0100. TEL 216-235-8580. FAX 216-235-2714. *3707*

EYE SCIENCE.
Sun Yat-sen University of Medical Sciences, Zhongshan Ophthalmic Center, 54 Xianlie Rd., Guangzhou, Guangdong 510060, People's Republic of China. *4993*

EYEOPENER.
Rye Eye Publishing Inc, 380 Victoria, Rm. A-54, Toronto, ON M5B 1W7, Canada. TEL 416-595-1490. FAX 416-595-1374. *1951*

F A M - FIRE AND MATERIALS.
John Wiley & Sons Ltd., Journals, Baffins Ln., Chichester, W. Sussex PO19 1UD, England. TEL 44-1243-779777. FAX 44-1243-775878. *1828*

F A R M S REVIEW OF BOOKS.
Foundation for Ancient Research and Mormon Studies, Box 7113, University Sta., Provo, UT 84602. TEL 801-378-3295. FAX 801-373-5342. *6490*

F A S E B JOURNAL.
Federation of American Societies for Experimental Biology, 9650 Rockville Pike, Bethesda, MD 20814. TEL 301-530-7100. FAX 301-571-1855. *601*

F A T E IN REVIEW.
Foundations in Art Theory and Education, Art Department FAA 216, Eastern Illinois Univ., Charleston, IL 61920. TEL 808-956-5250. FAX 808-956-9043. *440*

9800 REFEREED SERIALS

F E E M SERIES ON ECONOMICS, ENERGY AND ENVIRONMENT.
Kluwer Academic Publishers, Postbus 17, 3300 AA Dordrecht, Netherlands. TEL 31-78-6392392. FAX 31-78-6392254. *2669*

F E M S. IMMUNOLOGY AND MEDICAL MICROBIOLOGY.
Elsevier Science B.V., P.O. Box 211, 1000 AE Amsterdam, Netherlands. TEL 31-20-4853911. FAX 31-20-4853598. *784*

F E M S. MICROBIOLOGY.
Elsevier Science B.V., P.O. Box 211, 1000 AE Amsterdam, Netherlands. TEL 31-20-4853911. FAX 31-20-4853598. *784*

F E M S. MICROBIOLOGY ECOLOGY.
Elsevier Science B.V., P.O. Box 211, 1000 AE Amsterdam, Netherlands. TEL 31-20-4853911. FAX 31-20-4853598. *784*

F E M S. MICROBIOLOGY LETTERS.
Elsevier Science B.V., P.O. Box 211, 1000 AE Amsterdam, Netherlands. TEL 31-20-4853911. FAX 31-20-4853598. *784*

F E M S. MICROBIOLOGY REVIEWS.
Elsevier Science B.V., P.O. Box 211, 1000 AE Amsterdam, Netherlands. TEL 31-20-4853911. FAX 31-20-4853598. *784*

F E M S SYMPOSIUM.
Plenum Publishing Corp., 233 Spring St., New York, NY 10013-1578. TEL 212-620-8000. FAX 212-463-0742. *784*

F F COMMUNICATIONS.
Suomalainen Tiedeakatemia, Mariankatu 5, FIN-00170 Helsinki, Finland. *3086*

F M R A NEWS.
American Society of Farm Managers and Rural Appraisers, 950 S. Cherry St., Ste. 508, Denver, CO 80222-2664. TEL 303-758-3513. FAX 303-758-0190. *193*

F P R D I JOURNAL.
Forest Products Research and Development Institute, College, Laguna 4031, Philippines. TEL 63-94-2360. FAX 63-94-3630. *3171*

F R I BULLETIN.
Forest Research Institute, Private Bag 3020, Rotorua, New Zealand. TEL 64-7-3475899. *3150*

LE FABLIER.
Societe des Amis de Jean de la Fontaine, B.P. 284, 02400 Chateau-Thierry, France, France. *4405*

FACIES.
Universitaet Erlangen - Nuernberg, Institut fuer Palaeontologie, Loewenichstr. 28, 91054 Erlangen, Germany. TEL 49-9131-852622. FAX 49-9131-852690. *2314*

FACTS.
African Oxygen Ltd., Box 5404, Johannesburg 2000, South Africa. TEL 27-11-490-0400. FAX 27-11-493-8828. *2720*

FAILURE & LESSONS LEARNED IN INFORMATION TECHNOLOGY MANAGEMENT.
Cognizant Communication Corporation, 3 Hartsdale Rd., Elmsford, NY 10523. TEL 914-592-7720. FAX 914-592-8981. *2181*

FALK SYMPOSIUM.
Kluwer Academic Publishers, Postbus 17, 3300 AA Dordrecht, Netherlands. TEL 31-78-6392392. FAX 31-78-6392254. *4666*

FALMER.
University of Sussex Society, Alumni Office, Sussex House, Falmer, Brighton BN1 9RH, England. TEL 44-1273-678258. FAX 44-1273-678335. *1952*

FAMILIA CRISTIANA.
Ediciones Paulinas, S.A., Apdo. 69-766, 04460 Coyoacan, Mexico D.F., Mexico. TEL 525-5491454. FAX 525-6709392. *6463*

FAMILIES IN SOCIETY.
Families International, Inc., 11700 W. Lake Park Dr., Milwaukee, WI 53224. TEL 414-359-1040. FAX 414-359-1074. *6665*

FAMILY BUSINESS REVIEW.
Family Firm Institute, 12 Harris St., Brookline, MA 02146. TEL 617-738-1591. *1642*

FAMILY ECONOMICS AND NUTRITION REVIEW.
U.S. Department of Agriculture, Center for Nutrition Policy and Promotion, 1120 20th St., N.W., Ste. 200, North Lobby, Washington, DC 20036. TEL 202-606-4816. FAX 202-208-2321. *3684*

FAMILY MEDIATION.
National Family Mediation, 9 Tavistock Pl., London WC1H 9SN, England. TEL 44-171-383-5993. FAX 44-171-383-5994. *6665*

FAMILY MEDICAL PRACTICE ON-LINE.
Priory Lodge Education Ltd., *4667*

FAMILY PLANNING PERSPECTIVES.
Alan Guttmacher Institute, 120 Wall St., New York, NY 10005. TEL 212-248-1111. FAX 212-248-1951. *4956*

FAMILY PRACTICE RECERTIFICATION.
M R A Publications, Inc., 2 Greenwich Office Park, Greenwich, CT 06831-5154. TEL 203-629-3550. FAX 203-629-2536. *4667*

FAMILY RESEARCH REPORT.
Family Research Institute, Inc., Box 62640, Colorado Springs, CO 80962. TEL 303-681-3113. FAX 303-681-3427. *3693*

FAMILY RESOURCE COALITION REPORT.
Family Resource Coalition, 200 S. Michigan Ave., 16th Fl., Chicago, IL 60604-2404. TEL 312-341-0900. FAX 312-341-9361. *6665*

FAMILY SYSTEMS.
Georgetown Family Center, 4400 MacArthur Blvd., N.W., Ste. 102, Washington, DC 20007. TEL 202-965-0730. FAX 202-337-6801. *5065*

FAMILY VIOLENCE & SEXUAL ASSAULT BULLETIN.
Family Violence & Sexual Assualt Institute, 1121 E., S.E. Loop 323 Ste. 130, Tyler, TX 75701-9660. TEL 903-534-5100. FAX 903-534-5454. *6665*

FANTASY COMMENTATOR.
A. Langley Searles, Ed. & Pub., 48 Highland Circle, Bronxville, NY 10708-5909. TEL 914-961-6799. FAX 914-961-6847. *4531*

FAR EAST JOURNAL OF MATHEMATICAL SCIENCES.
Pushpa Publishing House, VIJAYA NIWAS, 198, Mumfordganj, Allahabad 211 002, India. TEL 91-532-642078. FAX 91-532-642078. *4572*

FARADAY DISCUSSIONS.
The Royal Society of Chemistry, Thomas Graham House, Science Park, Milton Rd., Cambridge CB4 4WF, England. TEL 44-1223-420066. FAX 44-1223-423429. *1828*

FARADAY TRANSACTIONS.
The Royal Society of Chemistry, Thomas Graham House, Science Park, Milton Rd., Cambridge CB4 4WF, England. TEL 44-1223-420066. FAX 44-1223-423623. *1828*

FARAVID.
Pohjois-Suomen Historiallinen Yhdistys, Oulun Yliopisto, Historian Laitos, Postilokero 111, FIN-90571 Oulu, Finland. FAX 358-81-5533315. *3566*

FARM GATE.
North Waterloo Publishing, 15 King St., Elmira, ON N3B 2R1, Canada. TEL 519-669-5155. FAX 519-669-5928. *116*

FARM TIMES, INCORPORATED.
Farm Times, 504 Sixth St., Rupert, ID 83350. TEL 208-436-1111. FAX 208-436-9455. *116*

FARMING WALES.
National Farmer's Union, 24 Tawe Business Village, Phoenix Way, Swansea Enterprise Park, Llansamlet, Swansea SA7 9LB, Wales. TEL 44-1792-774848. FAX 44-1792-774758. *118*

FARZANEH.
Bano Publications, P.O. Box 19575-165, Tehran, Iran. TEL 98-21-2055157. *7342*

FAT TUESDAY.
Fat Tuesday Productions, 560 Manada Gap Rd., Grantville, PA 17028. TEL 717-469-7159. *4405*

FATIGUE & FRACTURE OF ENGINEERING MATERIALS AND STRUCTURES.
Structural Integrity Research Institute, University of Sheffield, Sheffield S1 3JD, England. TEL 44-114-222-7719. FAX 44-114-275-3671. *2720*

FAUNA ENTOMOLOGICA SCANDINAVICA.
E.J. Brill, P.O. Box 9000, 2300 PA Leiden, Netherlands. TEL 31-71-5353500. FAX 31-71-5317532. *752*

FAUNA NORVEGICA SERIES A. NORWEGIAN FAUNA EXCEPT ENTOMOLOGY AND ORNITHOLOGY.
Norsk Institutt for Naturforskning (NINA), c/o Kjetil Bevanger, Tungasletta 2, N-7005 Trondheim, Norway. TEL 47-73-58-05-00. FAX 47-73-91-54-33. *833*

FAUNA PALAESTINA.
Israel Academy of Sciences and Humanities, 43 Jabotinsky St., P.O. Box 4040, 91040 Jerusalem, Israel. TEL 972-2-636211. FAX 972-2-666059. *834*

FAUNA SLODKOWODNA POLSKI.
Wydawnictwo Naukowe P W N, Ul. Miodowa 10, 00-251 Warsaw, Poland. TEL 48-22-260207. FAX 48-22-6954288. *834*

FAUX TITRE.
Editions Rodopi B.V., Keizersgracht 302-304, 1016 EX Amsterdam, Netherlands. TEL 31-20-6227507. FAX 31-20-6380948. *4405*

FEDERAL BENEFITS FOR VETERANS AND DEPENDENTS.
U.S. Department of Veterans Affairs, Office of Public Affairs, 810 Vermont Ave., Washington, DC 20420. *3815*

FEDERAL INFORMATION PROCESSING STANDARDS PUBLICATION.
U.S. National Institute of Standards and Technology, Gaithersburg, MD 20899. TEL 301-975-3058. *5250*

FEDERAL RESERVE BANK OF MINNEAPOLIS. QUARTERLY REVIEW.
Federal Reserve Bank of Minneapolis, Minneapolis, MN 55480-0291. TEL 612-240-6455. FAX 612-204-5515. *1133*

FEDERAL SENTENCING REPORTER.
University of California Press, Journals Division, 2120 Berkeley Way, No. 5812, Berkeley, CA 94720-5812. TEL 510-643-7154. FAX 510-642-9917. *2267*

FELINE PRACTICE.
Veterinary Practice Publishing Co., Box 6050, Mission Viejo, CA 92690. *7270*

FELLOWSHIP.
Fellowship of Reconciliation, 521 N. Broadway, Box 271, Nyack, NY 10960. TEL 914-358-4601. FAX 914-358-4924. *5926*

FEMALE PATIENT: PRACTICAL OB-GYN MEDICINE.
Quadrant HealthCom, 105 Raider Blvd., Belle Mead, NJ 08502-1510. TEL 908-874-0707. FAX 908-874-5611. *4957*

FEMINA.
Edipresse Publications SA, Av. de la Gare 33, CH-1001 Lausanne, Switzerland. TEL 41-21-3494848. FAX 41-21-3494859. *7319*

FEMINARIA.
C.C. 402, 1000 Buenos Aires, Argentina. TEL 54-1-5683029. *7342*

FEMINISM & PSYCHOLOGY.
Sage Publications Ltd., 6 Bonhill St., London EC2A 4PU, England. TEL 44-171-374-0645. FAX 44-171-374-8741. *6112*

FEMINIST LEGAL STUDIES.
Deborah Charles Publications, 173 Mather Ave., Liverpool L18 6JZ, England. TEL 44-151-724-2500. FAX 44-151-729-0371. *3950*

FEMME MIRROR.
Tri Ess, Box 194, Tulane, CA 93275. TEL 209-688-9246. *3693*

FEN-X.
Esperanto Nederland, c/o Hans Bakker, Ed., Kastelenstraat 231, 1082 EG Amsterdam, Netherlands. TEL 31-20-6421853. FAX 31-20-6421853. *4257*

FENGJING MINGSHENG.
Hangzhou Yuanlin Wenwu Guanliju, 12 Jiangyuan Nong, Xiaoying Xiang, Hangzhou, Zhejiang 310003, People's Republic of China. TEL 86-571-711944. FAX 86-571-7027890. *7199*

FERN GAZETTE.
British Pteridological Society, c/o Botany Department, Natural History Museum, Cromwell Rd., London SW7 5BD, England. TEL 44-171-938-9497. *703*

FERNSTROM FOUNDATION SERIES.
Elsevier Science B.V., Books Division, P.O. Box 211, 1000 AE Amsterdam, Netherlands. TEL 31-20-4853911. FAX 31-20-4853705. *4668*

FERROELECTRICITY AND RELATED PHENOMENA.
Gordon and Breach - Harwood Academic, Amsteldisk 166, 1st Fl., 1079 LH Amsterdam, Netherlands. *2824*

FERROELECTRICS.
Gordon and Breach - Harwood Academic, Amsteldisk 166, 1st Fl., 1079 LH Amsterdam, Netherlands. *5802*

FERROELECTRICS LETTERS.
Gordon and Breach - Harwood Academic, Amsteldisk 166, 1st Fl., 1079 LH Amsterdam, Netherlands. *2824*

FERTILITY AND STERILITY.
American Society for Reproductive Medicine, 1209 Montgomery Hwy., Birmingham, AL 35216-2809. TEL 205-978-5000. FAX 205-978-5005. *4957*

FERTILIZER SCIENCE AND TECHNOLOGY SERIES.
Marcel Dekker, Inc., 270 Madison Ave., New York, NY 10016. TEL 212-696-9000. FAX 212-658-4540. *224*

FESTIVAL MANAGEMENT & EVENT TOURISM.
Cognizant Communication Corporation, 3 Hartsdale Rd., Elmsford, NY 10523-3701. TEL 914-592-7720. FAX 914-592-8981. *7200*

FETAL AND MATERNAL MEDICINE REVIEW.
Cambridge University Press, Edinburgh Bldg., Shaftesbury Rd., Cambridge CB2 2RU, England. TEL 44-1223-312393. FAX 44-1223-315052. *4957*

FETAL DIAGNOSIS AND THERAPY.
S. Karger AG, Allschwilerstr. 10, P.O. Box, CH-4009 Basel, Switzerland. TEL 41-61-3061111. FAX 41-61-3061234. *4957*

FIBER AND INTEGRATED OPTICS.
Taylor & Francis Inc., 1900 Frost Rd., Ste. 101, Bristol, PA 19007. TEL 215-785-5800. FAX 215-785-5515. *5860*

THE FIBONACCI QUARTERLY.
Fibonacci Association, c/o South Dakota State University, Computer Science Dept., Box 2201, Brookings, SD 57007-1596. TEL 605-688-5719. FAX 605-688-5878. *4572*

FIBRE CHEMISTRY.
Plenum Publishing Corp., Consultants Bureau, 233 Spring St., New York, NY 10013-1578. TEL 212-620-8468. FAX 212-463-0742. *6986*

FICHTE-STUDIEN.
Editions Rodopi B.V., Keizersgracht 302-304, 1016 EX Amsterdam, Netherlands. TEL 31-20-6227507. FAX 31-20-6380948. *5727*

FIDES ET HISTORIA.
Conference on Faith and History, c/o Richard V. Pierard, Dept. of History, Indiana State University, Terre Haute, IN 47809. TEL 812-232-2707. *3495*

FIELD.
Oberlin College, Rice Hall, Oberlin, OH 44074. TEL 216-775-8408. FAX 216-775-8124. *4508*

FIELD CROPS RESEARCH.
Elsevier Science B.V., P.O. Box 211, 1000 AE Amsterdam, Netherlands. TEL 31-20-4853911. FAX 31-20-4853598. *224*

FIELD GUIDE TO FOSSILS.
Palaeontological Association, c/o J.M. Hilton, Department of Earth Sciences, University of Wales, Cardiff CF1 3YE, Wales. TEL 44-1222-874830. FAX 44-1222-874326. *5558*

FIELD STUDIES.
Field Studies Council, Central Services, Preston Montford, Montford Bridge, Shrewsbury, Shrops. SY4 1HW, England. TEL 01743-850674. FAX 01743-850178. *2928*

FIELDIANA: ANTHROPOLOGY.
Field Museum Press, Roosevelt Rd. at Lake Shore Dr., Chicago, IL 60605-2498. TEL 312-922-9410. FAX 312-427-7269. *317*

FIELDIANA: BOTANY.
Field Museum Press, Roosevelt Rd. at Lake Shore Dr., Chicago, IL 60605-2498. TEL 312-922-9410. FAX 312-427-7269. *703*

FIELDIANA: GEOLOGY.
Field Museum Press, Roosevelt Rd. at Lake Shore Dr., Chicago, IL 60605-2498. TEL 312-922-9410. FAX 312-427-7269. *2339*

FIELDIANA: ZOOLOGY.
Field Museum Press, Roosevelt Rd. at Lake Shore Dr., Chicago, IL 60605-2498. TEL 312-922-9410. FAX 312-427-7269. *834*

FILM HISTORIA.
Universidad de Barcelona, Departamento de Historia Contemporanea, P.O. Box 12109, 08080 Barcelona, Spain. TEL 34-3-4420391. *5332*

FILM HISTORY.
John Libbey & Company Pty. Ltd., 15-17 Young St., Sydney, N.S.W. 2000, Australia. TEL 61-2-9251-4099. FAX 61-2-9251-4428. *5332*

FILM QUARTERLY.
University of California Press, Journals Division, 2120 Berkeley Way, No. 5812, Berkeley, CA 94720-5812. TEL 510-643-7154. FAX 510-642-9917. *5333*

FILOLOGIA ANTICA E MODERNA.
Universita degli Studi della Calabria, Dipartimento di Filologia, 87036 Arcavacata di Rende (Cosenza), Italy. TEL 39-984-493128. FAX 39-984-493163. *4406*

FILOSOFISKE STUDIER.
University of Copenhagen, Department of Education, Philosophy and Rhetoric, Njalsgade 80, DK-2300 Copenhagen S, Denmark. TEL 45-35-32-88-69. FAX 45-35-32-88-50. *5727*

FILTRATION & SEPARATION.
Elsevier Science Ltd., P.O. Box 800, Kidlington, Oxford OX5 1DX, England. TEL 44-1865-843000. FAX 44-1865-843010. *2764*

FINANCE AND STOCHASTICS.
Springer-Verlag, Heidelberger Platz 3, 14197 Berlin, Germany. TEL 49-30-82787-0. FAX 49-30-82787448. *1133*

FINANCE INDIA.
Indian Institute of Finance, P.O. Box 8486, Ashok Vihar, Delhi 110 052, India. TEL 91-11-7125791. FAX 91-11-7454128. *1134*

FINANCIAL ACCOUNTABILITY & MANAGEMENT.
Blackwell Publishers Ltd., 108 Cowley Rd., Oxford OX4 1JF, England. TEL 44-1865-791100. FAX 44-1865-791347. *1609*

FINANCIAL AND MONETARY POLICY STUDIES.
Kluwer Academic Publishers, Postbus 17, 3300 AA Dordrecht, Netherlands. TEL 31-78-6392392. FAX 31-78-6392254. *1134*

FINANCIAL COUNSELING AND PLANNING.
Association for Financial Counseling and Planning Education, c/o Sherman Hanna, Ed., Consumer and Textile Sciences Dept., Ohio State University, 1787 Neil Ave., Columbus, OH 43210-1295. TEL 614-292-4584. FAX 614-292-7536. *1134*

FINANCIAL ENGINEERING AND THE JAPANESE MARKETS.
Kluwer Academic Publishers, Postbus 17, 3300 AA Dordrecht, Netherlands. TEL 31-78-6392392. FAX 31-78-6392254. *1175*

FINANCIAL EXECUTIVE.
Financial Executives Institute, 10 Madison Ave., Box 1938, Morristown, NJ 07962-1938. TEL 201-898-4621. FAX 201-267-4031. *1478*

FINANCIAL HISTORY REVIEW.
Cambridge University Press, The Edinburgh Bldg., Shaftesbury Rd., Cambridge CB2 2RU, England. TEL 44-1223-312393. FAX 44-1223-315052. *1134*

FINANCIAL MANAGEMENT.
Financial Management Association, University of South Florida, College of Business, Tampa, FL 33620. TEL 813-974-2084. FAX 813-974-3318. *1478*

FINANCIAL PRACTICE AND EDUCATION.
Financial Management Association, Univ. of South Florida, College of Bus. Admin. 3331, Tampa, FL 33620. TEL 813-974-2084. FAX 813-974-3318. *1135*

FINANCIAL REVIEW (STATESBORO).
Eastern Finance Association, c/o Univ. of Tennessee, 426 Stokley Management Ctr., Knoxville, TN 37996-0540. TEL 423-974-1713. FAX 423-974-1716. *1135*

FINANCIER: ANALYSES OF CAPITAL AND MONEY MARKET TRANSACTIONS.
Financier, Inc., 220 Locust St., Apt. 3-E, Philadelphia, PA 19106-3928. TEL 215-829-1354. FAX 215-829-1376. *1136*

FINANCING AGRICULTURE.
Agricultural Finance Corporation Ltd., Dhanraj Mahal, 1st Fl., Chatrapati Shivaji Maharaj Marg, Mumbai 400 001, India. TEL 91-22-202-8924. FAX 91-22-202-966. *118*

FINANSOVYE BUKHALTERSKIE KONSYL'TATSII.
Myasnitskaya ul., 44-1, 101000 Moscow, Russia. TEL 7-095-9249271. FAX 7-095-9212214. *1090*

FINANZA MARKETING E PRODUZIONE.
E G E A s.p.a., Via Sarfatti 25, 20136 Milan, Italy. TEL 39-2-58363726. FAX 39-2-58363793. *1478*

FINITE ELEMENTS IN ANALYSIS AND DESIGN.
North-Holland, P.O. Box 211, 1000 AE Amsterdam, Netherlands. TEL 31-20-4853911. FAX 31-20-4853598. *2805*

FINITE FIELDS AND THEIR APPLICATIONS.
Academic Press, Inc., Journal Division, 525 B St., Ste. 1900, San Diego, CA 92101-4495. TEL 619-230-1840. FAX 619-688-6800. *4572*

FIRE AUSTRALIA.
Fire Protection Association Australia, P.O. Box 456, Canberwell, Vic. 3124, Australia. TEL 61-3-98822800. *3054*

FIRE SAFETY JOURNAL.
Elsevier Science Ltd., P.O. Box 800, Kidlington, Oxford OX5 1DX, England. TEL 44-1865-843000. FAX 44-1865-843010. *3055*

FIRE TECHNOLOGY.
National Fire Protection Association, 1 Batterymarch Park, Quincy, MA 02269. TEL 617-984-7562. FAX 617-984-7010. *3055*

FIREWEED.
Fireweed Inc., P.O. Box 279, Stn. B, Toronto, ON M5T 2W2, Canada. TEL 416-504-1339. *7320*

FIRST BREAK.
Blackwell Science Ltd., Osney Mead, Oxford OX2 0EL, England. TEL 44-1865-206206. FAX 44-1865-721205. *2381*

REFEREED SERIALS

FIRST MAGAZINE.
First Magazine Ltd., 77 Oxford St., London W1R 1RB, England. TEL 44-171-287-0561. FAX 44-171-287-1437. *1478*

FIRST MONDAY.
Munksgaard International Publishers Ltd., Noerre Soegade 35, P.O. Box 2148, DK-1016 Copenhagen, Denmark. TEL 45-33-127030. *2133*

FIRUDO BAIOROJISUTO.
Gunma Yagai Seibutsu Gakkai, c/o Mr. S. Saito, Gunma Pref. Women's University, 1395 Kaminote, Tamamuramachi, Sawa-gun, Gunma-ken 370-11, Japan. TEL 0270-65-8511. FAX 0270-65-9538. *601*

FISCAL STUDIES.
Institute of Fiscal Studies, 7 Ridgmount St., London WC1E 7AE, England. TEL 44-171-636-3784. FAX 44-171-323-4780. *1610*

FISH AND SHELLFISH IMMUNOLOGY.
Academic Press Ltd., 24-28 Oval Rd., London NW1 7DX, England. TEL 44-171-267-4466. FAX 44-171-482-2293. *601*

FISHERIES.
American Fisheries Society, 5410 Grosvenor Ln., Ste. 110, Bethesda, MD 20814-2199. TEL 301-897-8616. FAX 301-897-8096. *3066*

FISHERIES OCEANOGRAPHY.
Blackwell Science Ltd., Osney Mead, Oxford OX2 0EL, England. TEL 44-1865-206206. FAX 44-1865-721205. *3066*

FISHERIES RESEARCH.
Elsevier Science B.V., P.O. Box 211, 1000 AE Amsterdam, Netherlands. TEL 31-20-4853911. FAX 31-20-4853598. *3066*

FISHERY BULLETIN.
U.S. National Marine Fisheries Service, Scientific Publications Office, 7600 Sandpoint Way, N.E., Bin C15700, Seattle, WA 98115. TEL 206-526-6107. FAX 206-526-6426. *3067*

FISHERY TECHNOLOGY.
Society of Fisheries Technologists (India), Matsyapuri P.O., Cochin 682029, India. TEL 91-484-666845. FAX 91-484-668212. *3067*

FISICA DE LA TIERRA.
Universidad Complutense de Madrid, Calle Isaac Peral s-n, Ciudad Universitaria, 28040 Madrid, Spain. TEL 34-1-3946934. FAX 34-1-3946954. *2381*

FITOPATOLOGIA.
Asociacion Latinoamericana de Fitopatologia, Apdo. 1558, Lima 100, Peru. FAX 51-1-4351570. *703*

FITOSOCIOLOGIA.
Societa Italiana di Fitosociologia, Via Scopoli 22-24, 27100 Pavia, Italy. FAX 39-382-34240. *703*

FITOSSANIDADE.
Fitossanitaristas do Ceara, Rua Livreiro Edesio, 612-401, 60135-620 Fortaleza, Ceara, Brazil. TEL 55-85-2571242. FAX 55-85-2438442. *703*

FIVE POINTS.
Georgia State University, Department of English, University Plaza, Atlanta, GA 30303-3083. TEL 404-651-2900. FAX 404-651-1710. *4406*

FIZBIN MAGIC MAGAZINE.
John Fleischer, Ed. & Pub., 119 Nashua Rd., Gronton, MA 01450. *3667*

FIZIK TEDAVI REHABILITASYON DERGISI.
Turkiye Fiziksel Tip ve Rehabilitasyon Dernegi, Capa, 34390 Istanbul, Turkey. TEL 90-212-6330505. FAX 90-212-6328464. *5043*

FLAGSCAN.
Canadian Flag Association, 50 Heathfield Dr., Scarborough, ON M1M 3B1, Canada. TEL 416-267-9618. FAX 416-267-9618. *3222*

FLANNERY O'CONNOR BULLETIN.
Georgia College, Department of English and Speech, Box 44, Milledgeville, GA 31061. TEL 912-453-4581. *4406*

FLETCHER FORUM OF WORLD AFFAIRS.
Fletcher School of Law and Diplomacy, Tufts University, Medford, MA 02155. TEL 617-623-3610. FAX 617-627-3979. *6014*

FLINDERS JOURNAL OF HISTORY AND POLITICS.
Flinders University of South Australia, History and Politics Departments, Politics Dept., P.O. Box 2100, Adelaide, S.A. 5001, Australia. TEL 61-8-82012432. FAX 61-8-82015111. *3542*

FLORA MALESIANA. SERIES 1: SPERMATOPHYTA.
Rijksherbarium - Hortus Botanicus, Publications Department, P.O. Box 9514, 2300 RA Leiden, Netherlands. *704*

FLORA MALESIANA. SERIES 2: PTERIDOPHYTA.
Rijksherbarium - Hortus Botanicus, Publications Department, P.O. Box 9514, 2300 RA Leiden, Netherlands. *704*

FLORA MALESIANA BULLETIN.
Rijksherbarium - Hortus Botanicus, Publications Department, P.O. Box 9514, 2300 RA Leiden, Netherlands. *704*

FLORA NEOTROPICA.
New York Botanical Garden, Scientific Publications Department, Bronx, NY 10458-5126. TEL 718-817-8721. FAX 718-817-8842. *704*

FLORA OF ECUADOR.
Nordic Publications in Botany, Gothersgade 130, DK-1123 Copenhagen K, Denmark. *704*

FLORA OG FAUNA.
Botanical Museum, Copenhagen University, Gothersgade 130, DK-1123 Copenhagen K, Denmark. TEL 45-89-42-27-58. FAX 45-86-12-51-75. *6526*

FLORA PALAESTINA.
Israel Academy of Sciences and Humanities, 43 Jabotinsky St., P.O. Box 4040, Jerusalem 91040, Israel. *704*

FLORA POLSKI: GRZYBY.
Polska Akademia Nauk, Instytut Botaniki im. W. Szafera, Ul. Lubicz 46, 31-512 Krakow, Poland. TEL 48-12-215144. FAX 48-12-219790. *704*

FLORESTA.
Fundacao de Pesquisas Florestais do Parana, Caixa Postal 4088, 82501-970 Curitiba, PR, Brazil. TEL 55-41-352-2443. FAX 55-41-253-2332. *3151*

FLORIDA ANTHROPOLOGIST.
Florida Anthropological Society, Inc., Box 82255, Tampa, FL 33682-2255. TEL 813-821-7600. FAX 813-822-2368. *317*

FLORIDA COMMUNICATION JOURNAL.
Florida Communication Association, School of Communication, University of Central Florida, Orlando, FL 32816-1344. TEL 407-823-5958. FAX 407-823-6360. *1990*

FLORIDA EDUCATIONAL RESEARCH COUNCIL. RESEARCH BULLETIN.
Florida Educational Research Council, Inc., Box 506, Sanibel, FL 33957. TEL 813-472-4397. *2444*

FLORIDA ENTOMOLOGIST.
Florida Entomological Society, c/o R.M. Baranowski, Ed., 18905 S.W. 280 St., Homestead, FL 33031. TEL 813-324-5502. FAX 904-374-5852. *753*

FLORIDA FAMILY PHYSICIAN.
Journalistic, Inc., c/o FAFP, 1627 Rogero Rd., Jacksonville, FL 32211-4866. TEL 919-489-1916. FAX 919-489-4767. *4668*

FLORIDA FIELD NATURALIST.
Florida Ornithological Society, Florida State Museum, University of Florida, Gainesville, FL 32611. TEL 352-376-6481. *803*

FLORIDA GEOGRAPHER.
Florida State University, Department of Geography, Tallahassee, 2, FL 32306-2050. TEL 850-644-1706. FAX 850-644-5913. *3402*

FLORIDA JOURNAL OF ANTHROPOLOGY.
University of Florida, Department of Anthropology, 1350 GPA, Gainesville, FL 32611. TEL 904-392-2031. FAX 904-392-6929. *317*

FLORIDA LIBRARIES.
Florida Library Association, 1133 W. Morse Blvd., No. 201, Winter Park, FL 32789-3788. TEL 407-647-8839. FAX 407-629-2502. *4178*

FLORIDA MEDICAL ASSOCIATION. JOURNAL.
Florida Medical Association, Inc., Box 10269, Tallahassee, FL 32302-2269. TEL 904-356-1571. FAX 904-353-1247. *4668*

FLORIDA MUSIC DIRECTOR.
Florida Music Educators Association, c/o Vicki Miazga, Man. Ed., 207 Office Plaza Dr., Tallahassee, FL 32301. TEL 904-878-6844. FAX 904-942-1793. *5393*

FLORIDA READING QUARTERLY.
Florida Reading Association, c/o Dept. of Learning & Curriculum, Box 117048, Univ. of Florida, Gainesville, FL 32611-7044. TEL 352-392-9191. FAX 352-392-9193. *2444*

FLORIDA SCIENTIST.
Florida Academy of Sciences, Inc., c/o Orlando Science Center, 777 E. Princeton St., Orlando, FL 32803. TEL 407-514-2079. *6526*

FLORIDA STATE UNIVERSITY RESEARCH IN REVIEW.
Florida State University, Office of Graduate Studies and Research, 109 HMB R-23, Tallahassee, FL 32306. TEL 904-644-8634. *6526*

FLOW MEASUREMENT AND INSTRUMENTATION.
Elsevier Science Ltd., P.O. Box 800, Kidlington, Oxford OX5 1DX, England. TEL 44-1865-843000. FAX 44-1865-843010. *3801*

FLOW, TURBULENCE AND COMBUSTION.
Kluwer Academic Publishers, Postbus 17, 3300 AA Dordrecht, Netherlands. TEL 31-78-6392392. FAX 31-78-6392254. *6526*

FLUID DYNAMICS.
Plenum Publishing Corp., Consultants Bureau, 233 Spring St., New York, NY 10013-1578. TEL 212-620-8468. FAX 212-463-0742. *5844*

FLUID DYNAMICS RESEARCH.
North-Holland, P.O. Box 211, 1000 AE Amsterdam, Netherlands. TEL 31-20-4853911. FAX 31-20-4853598. *2871*

FLUID MECHANICS AND ITS APPLICATIONS.
Kluwer Academic Publishers, Postbus 17, 3300 AA Dordrecht, Netherlands. TEL 31-78-6392392. FAX 31-78-6392254. *5845*

FLUID MECHANICS OF ASTROPHYSICS AND GEOPHYSICS.
Gordon and Breach - Harwood Academic, Amsteldisk 166, 1st Fl., 1079 LH Amsterdam, Netherlands. *5845*

FLUID PHASE EQUILIBRIA.
Elsevier Science B.V., P.O. Box 211, 1000 AE Amsterdam, Netherlands. TEL 31-20-4853911. FAX 31-20-4853598. *1828*

FLUID POWER JOURNAL.
Innovative Designs and Publishing, 4544 Pheasant Run, Bethlehem, PA 18017-9512. TEL 610-694-0650. FAX 610-694-0611. *2872*

FLUORIDE.
International Society for Fluoride Research, 81 A Landscape Rd., Mount Eden, Auckland, New Zealand. TEL 64-9-6307114. *4779*

FLYING HORSE.
Flying Horse, Box 445, Marblehead, MA 01945. *4509*

FOCUS (GAITHERSBURG).
Life Technologies, Inc., Box 6482, Rockville, MD 20849-6482. TEL 301-840-8000. *767*

FOCUS (WESTFIELD).
Westfield State College, Public Affairs Office, Western Ave., Westfield, MA 01086. TEL 413-572-5208. FAX 413-572-4843. *1952*

FOCUS ON AUTISM AND OTHER DEVELOPMENTAL DISABILITIES.
Pro-Ed Inc., 8700 Shoal Creek Blvd., Austin, TX 78757-6897. TEL 512-451-3246. FAX 512-451-8542. *5065*

FOCUS ON N A R I.
National Association of the Remodeling Industry, 4900 Seminary Rd., Ste. 320, Alexandria, VA 22311-1811. TEL 703-575-1121. *894*

FOCUS: SOCIAL AND PREVENTIVE MEDICINE.
Community Health Services Association, 455 2nd Ave. N., Saskatoon, SK S7K 2C2, Canada. TEL 306-652-0300. FAX 306-664-4120. *6234*

FOLDING AND DESIGN.
Current Biology Ltd., 400 Market St., Ste. 700, Philadelphia, PA 19106-2514. TEL 800-427-1796, 215-574-2225. *660*

FOLIA BIOLOGICA.
Polska Akademia Nauk, Instytut Systematyki i Ewolucji Zwierzat, Ul. Slawkowska 17, 31-016 Krakow, Poland. TEL 48-12-227006. FAX 48-12-224294. *602*

FOLIA BIOTHEORETICA.
Kluwer Academic Publishers, Postbus 17, 3300 AA Dordrecht, Netherlands. TEL 31-78-6392392. FAX 31-78-6392254. *602*

FOLIA ENTOMOLOGICA MEXICANA.
Sociedad Mexicana de Entomologia, A.C., Consejo Editorial Folia Entomologica Mexicana, Apdo. Postal 63, 91000 Xalapa, Veracruz, Mexico. TEL 52-28-421800. FAX 52-28-187809. *753*

FOLIA FORESTALIA.
Metsantutkimuslaitos, Unioninkatu 40 A, FIN-00170 Helsinki, Finland. TEL 358-0-857051. FAX 358-0-625308. *3151*

FOLIA GEOBOTANICA ET PHYTOTAXONOMICA.
Czechoslovak Academy of Sciences, Botanical Institute, P.O. Box 25187, S-750 25 Uppsala, Sweden. TEL 46-18-320662. FAX 46-18-321368. *705*

FOLIA HISTOCHEMICA ET CYTOBIOLOGICA.
Polskie Towarzystwo Histochemikow i Cytochemikow, c/o P.O. Box 843, 30-960 Krakow 1, Poland. TEL 48-12-227027. FAX 48-12-227027. *740*

FOLIA HORTICULTURAE.
Polskie Towarzystwo Nauk Ogrodniczych, Al. 29 Listopada 54, 31-425 Krakow, Poland. FAX 48-12-111322. *705*

FOLIA MORPHOLOGICA.
Polskie Towarzystwo Anatomiczne, c/o Akademia Medyczna w Poznaniu, Zaklad Anatomii, Ul. Swiecickiego 6, 60-781 Poznan, Poland. TEL 48-61-699181. FAX 48-61-658985. *602*

FOLIA NEUROPATHOLOGICA.
Stowarzyszenie Neuropatologow Polskish, Ul. Dworkowa 3, 00-784 Warsaw, Poland. TEL 48-22-496793. FAX 48-22-496973. *5065*

FOLIA OPHTHALMOLOGICA JAPONICA.
Association of Folia Ophthalmologica Japonica, 302-3-6 Mihogaoka, Ibaraki 567, Japan. TEL 81-726-23-7878. FAX 81-726-23-6060. *4993*

FOLIA PARASITOLOGICA.
Academy of Sciences of the Czech Republic, Parasitological Institute, Branisovska 31, 37005 Ceske Budejovice, Czech Republic. TEL 0042-38-41158. *4835*

FOLIA PHARMACOLOGICA JAPONICA.
Japanese Pharmacological Society, Editorial Office, Kantohya Bldg., Gokomachi-Ebisugawa, Nakagyo-ku, Kyoto 604, Japan. TEL 81-75-252-4641. FAX 81-75-252-4618. *5663*

FOLIA PHONIATRICA ET LOGOPAEDICA.
S. Karger AG, Allschwilerstr. 10, P.O. Box, CH-4009 Basel, Switzerland. TEL 41-61-3061111. FAX 41-61-3061234. *5021*

FOLIA PRIMATOLOGICA.
S. Karger AG, Allschwilerstr. 10, P.O. Box, CH-4009 Basel, Switzerland. TEL 41-61-3061111. FAX 41-61-3061234. *834*

FOLIA ZOOLOGICA.
Academy of Sciences of the Czech Republic, Institute of Landscape Ecology, Kvetna 8, 60365 Brno, Czech Republic. TEL 42-5-43211346. *834*

FOLK ART MESSENGER.
Folk Art Society of America, Box 17041, Richmond, VA 23226. TEL 804-285-4532. FAX 804-285-4532. *441*

FOLK-LORE.
Association Quebecoise des Loisirs Folkloriques, 4545 ave. Pierre Coubertin, C.P. 1000, Sta. M, Montreal, PQ H1V 3R2, Canada. TEL 514-252-3022. FAX 514-251-8038. *3086*

FOLKLORE & SOCIETY.
University of Illinois Press, 1325 S. Oak St., Champaign, IL 61820. TEL 217-333-0950. FAX 217-244-8082. *3087*

FOLKLORE FORUM.
Folklore Publications Group, Inc., 504 N. Fess, Bloomington, IN 47405. TEL 812-855-1027. *3087*

FOLKTALES OF THE WORLD.
University of Chicago Press, 5801 S. Ellis Ave., Chicago, IL 60637. TEL 773-702-7899. *3087*

FONDAZIONE LUIGI MICHELETTI. ANNALI.
Fondazione Luigi Micheletti, Via Cairoli, 9, 25122 Brescia, Italy. TEL 39-30-48578. FAX 39-30-45203. *3566*

FONORAMA.
Fonopress, Ul. Jozefitow 3-12, 30-039 Krakow, Poland. TEL 48-12-335735. FAX 48-12-336007. *5394*

FONTANUS.
McGill University Libraries, McLennan Library Bldg., 3459 McTavish St., Montreal, PQ H3A 1Y1, Canada. TEL 514-398-4740. FAX 514-398-7356. *3778*

FONTES ARTIS MUSICAE.
International Association of Music Libraries, Archives and Documentation Centres (U.S.), c/o Susan T. Sommer, Editor in Chief, New York Public Library for the Performing Arts, New York, NY 10023-7498. TEL 212-870-1620. FAX 212-870-1704. *5447*

FOOD ADDITIVES AND CONTAMINANTS.
Taylor & Francis Ltd., 1 Gunpowder Sq., London EC4A 3DE, England. TEL 44-171-583-0490. FAX 44-171-583-0585. *5663*

FOOD AND AGRICULTURAL IMMUNOLOGY.
Carfax Publishing Co., P.O. Box 25, Abingdon, Oxon. OX14 3UE, England. TEL 44-1235-401000. FAX 44-1235-401550. *602*

FOOD AND BIOPRODUCTS PROCESSING.
Institution of Chemical Engineers, George E. Davis Bldg., 165-189 Railway Terr., Rugby, Warks. CV21 3HQ, England. TEL 44-1788-78214. FAX 44-1788-578214. *683*

FOOD AND CHEMICAL TOXICOLOGY.
Elsevier Science Ltd., Pergamon, P.O. Box 800, Kidlington, Oxford OX5 1DX, England. TEL 44-1865-843000. FAX 44-1865-843010. *2978*

FOOD AND FOODWAYS.
Gordon and Breach - Harwood Academic, Amsteldisk 166, 1st Fl., 1079 LH Amsterdam, Netherlands. *5473*

FOOD AND NUTRITION BULLETIN.
United Nations University Press, 53-70, Jingumae 5-chome, Shibuya-ku, Tokyo 150, Japan. TEL 03-3499-2811. FAX 03-3499-2828. *5473*

FOOD AND NUTRITION IN HISTORY AND ANTHROPOLOGY.
Gordon and Breach - Harwood Academic, Amsteldisk 166, 1st Fl., 1079 LH Amsterdam, Netherlands. *317*

FOOD AUSTRALIA.
Australian Institute of Food Science and Technology, Inc., P.O. Box 1493, North Sydney, N.S.W. 2059, Australia. TEL 61-2-99594499. FAX 61-299544327. *3105*

FOOD BIOTECHNOLOGY.
Marcel Dekker Journals, 270 Madison Ave., New York, NY 10016. TEL 212-969-9000. FAX 212-685-4540. *683*

FOOD CHEMISTRY.
Elsevier Science Ltd., P.O. Box 800, Kidlington, Oxford OX5 1DX, England. TEL 44-1865-843000. FAX 44-1865-843010. *1749*

FOOD CONTROL.
Elsevier Science Ltd., P.O. Box 800, Kidlington, Oxford OX5 1DX, England. TEL 44-1865-843000. FAX 44-1865-843010. *3105*

FOOD EQUALS LOVE.
God's Love We Deliver, 166 Ave. of the Americas, New York, NY 10013-1207. TEL 212-294-8100. FAX 212-294-8101. *6666*

FOOD HYGIENIC SOCIETY OF JAPAN. JOURNAL.
Food Hygienic Society of Japan, 2-6-1 Jingumae, Shibuya-ku, Tokyo 150, Japan. FAX 03-3470-2933. *6234*

FOOD POLICY.
Elsevier Science Ltd., Pergamon, P.O. Box 800, Kidlington, Oxford OX5 1DX, England. TEL 44-1865-843000. FAX 44-1865-843010. *193*

FOOD PRODUCT DESIGN.
Weeks Publishing Co., 3400 Dundee Rd., Ste. 100, Northbrook, IL 60062-2333. TEL 847-559-0385. FAX 847-559-0389. *3107*

FOOD QUALITY AND PREFERENCE.
Elsevier Science Ltd., P.O. Box 800, Kidlington, Oxford OX5 1DX, England. TEL 44-1865-843000. FAX 44-1865-843010. *3108*

FOOD RESEARCH INTERNATIONAL.
Elsevier Science Ltd., P.O. Box 800, Kidlington, Oxford OX5 1DX, England. TEL 44-1865-843000. FAX 44-1865-843010. *3108*

FOOD SCIENCE AND TECHNOLOGY SERIES.
Marcel Dekker, Inc., 270 Madison Ave., New York, NY 10016. TEL 212-696-9000. FAX 212-685-4540. *3108*

FOOD STRUCTURE.
Scanning Microscopy International, Inc., Box 66507, AMF O'Hare, Chicago, IL 60666-0507. TEL 312-529-6677. FAX 312-980-6698. *5473*

FOOD TECHNOLOGIST.
New Zealand Institute of Food Science and Technology, P.O. Box 35-187, Browns Bay, Auckland, New Zealand. TEL 64-4-2378426. FAX 64-9-2378426. *3109*

THE FOOT.
Churchill Livingstone, Robert Stevenson House, 1-3 Baxter's Pl., Leith Walk, Edinburgh EH1 3AF, Scotland. TEL 44-131-556-2424. FAX 44-131-535-1704. *5007*

FOOT AND ANKLE CLINICS.
W.B. Saunders Co., Curtis Center, 3rd Fl., Independence Sq. W., Philadelphia, PA 19106-3399. TEL 215-238-7800. FAX 212-238-6445. *5007*

FOOT & ANKLE INTERNATIONAL.
Williams & Wilkins, 351 W. Camden St., Baltimore, MD 21201-2436. TEL 410-528-4068. FAX 410-528-4452. *5007*

FOOT AND ANKLE SURGERY.
Blackwell Science Ltd. (Paris), c/o Aileen Boyd-Squires, Pub., 224 bd. Saint-Germain, 75007 Paris, France. TEL 33-1-45496525. FAX 33-1-45491245. *5142*

FOR THE RECORD (VALLEY FORGE).
Great Valley Publishing, Box 2224, Valley Forge, PA 19482. TEL 610-917-9300. FAX 610-917-9186. *4668*

FOR YOUR INFORMATION (NEW YORK).
New York Foundation for the Arts, 155 Ave. of the Americas, New York, NY 10013. TEL 212-366-6900. FAX 212-366-1778. *441*

FORDHAM INTELLECTUAL PROPERTY, MEDIA & ENTERTAINMENT LAW JOURNAL.
Lincoln Center, 140 W. 62nd St., New York, NY 10023. TEL 212-636-6948. FAX 212-636-6582. *3953*

REFEREED SERIALS

FOREIGN LANGUAGE ANNALS.
American Council on the Teaching of Foreign Languages, Inc., 6 Executive Plaza, Yonkers, NY 10701-6801. TEL 914-963-8830. FAX 914-963-1275. *4258*

FORENSIC SCIENCE INTERNATIONAL.
Elsevier Science Ireland Ltd., P.O. Box 85, Limerick, Ireland. TEL 353-61-471944. FAX 353-61-472144. *4904*

FORENSISCHE PSYCHIATRIE UND PSYCHOTHERAPIE.
Pabst Science Publishers, Am Eichengrund 28, 49525 Lengerich, Germany. TEL 49-5484-308. FAX 49-5484-550. *6112*

FOREST & LANDSCAPE RESEARCH.
Danish Forest and Landscape Research Institute, Hoersholm Kongevej 11, DK-2970 Hoersholm, Denmark. TEL 45-45-76-32-00. FAX 45-45-76-32-33. *3151*

FOREST ECOLOGY AND MANAGEMENT.
Elsevier Science B.V., P.O. Box 211, 1000 AE Amsterdam, Netherlands. TEL 31-20-4853911. FAX 31-20-4853598. *3151*

FOREST GENETICS RESEARCH INSTITUTE. RESEARCH REPORT.
Forest Genetics Research Institute, P.O. Box 24, Suwon, Kyonggi-do 441-350, S. Korea. TEL 0331-290-1114. FAX 0331-292-4458. *3151*

FOREST SCIENCE.
Society of American Foresters, 5400 Grosvenor Ln., Bethesda, MD 20814. TEL 301-897-8720. FAX 301-897-3690. *3152*

FORESTS & PEOPLE.
Louisiana Forestry Association, Drawer 5067, Alexandria, LA 71307. TEL 318-443-2558. *3153*

FORMA.
Society for Science on Form, Japan, Tokyo University of Agriculture & Technology, Dept. of Mechanical System Engineering, 24-16 Nakamachi 2-chome, Koganei-shi, Tokyo 184, Japan. TEL 81-423-88-7224. FAX 81-423-85-7203. *4573*

FORMAL LINGUISTICS SERIES.
Kluwer Academic Publishers, Postbus 17, 3300 AA Dordrecht, Netherlands. TEL 31-78-6392392. FAX 31-78-6392254. *4258*

FORMAL METHODS IN SYSTEM DESIGN.
Kluwer Academic Publishers Boston, Box 358, Accord Sta., Hingham, MA 02018-0358. TEL 617-871-6600. FAX 617-871-6528. *2155*

FORMULARY.
Advanstar Communications, Inc., 7500 Old Oak Blvd., Cleveland, OH 44130. TEL 216-826-2839. FAX 216-891-2726. *5663*

FORO HISPANICO.
Editions Rodopi B.V., Keizersgracht 302-304, 1016 EX Amsterdam, Netherlands. TEL 31-20-6227507. FAX 31-20-6380948. *4407*

FORT.
Fortress Study Group, c/o Athanassios Migos, Ed., Nearchos, 9 Rock Park, Rock Ferry, Wirral L42 1PJ, England. TEL 44-151-644-0761. FAX 44-151-707-2953. *5268*

FORT HARE PAPERS.
Fort Hare University Press, Private Bag X1314, Alice 5700, South Africa. TEL 27-404-22011. FAX 27-404-31255. *6526*

FORTSCHRITTE IN DER GEOLOGIE VON RHEINLAND UND WESTFALEN.
Geologisches Landesamt Nordrhein-Westfalen, Postfach 1080, 47710 Krefeld, Germany. TEL 49-2151-8971. FAX 49-2151-897505. *2340*

FORUM (SANTA ROSA).
Polebridge Press, 2120 Bluebell Dr., Box 6144, Santa Rosa, CA 95406. TEL 707-523-1323. FAX 707-523-1350. *6339*

FORUM FOR APPLIED RESEARCH AND PUBLIC POLICY.
University of Tennessee at Knoxville, Energy, Environment and Resources Center, Conference Center Bldg., Ste. 311, Knoxville, TN 37996-4134. TEL 423-974-4251. FAX 423-974-8491. *2928*

FORUM FOR DEVELOPMENT STUDIES.
Norsk Utenrikspolitisk Institutt, P.O. Box 8159, Dep., N-0033 Oslo, Norway. TEL 47-22-17-70-50. FAX 47-22-17-70-15. *6015*

FORUM FOR READING.
University of Pittsburgh, School of Education, 5T01 Forbes Quadrangle, Pittsburgh, PA 15260. *2603*

FORUM FOR SOCIAL ECONOMICS.
Association for Social Economics, Department of Economics, Saint Louis University, 3674 Lindell Blvd., St. Louis, MO 63108. TEL 314-977-3814. FAX 314-977-3897. *1304*

FORUM ITALICUM.
State University of New York at Stony Brook, Center for Italian Studies, Stony Brook, NY 11794-3359. TEL 516-632-7444. *4407*

FORUM OF EDUCATION.
Sydney University, Faculty of Education, Sydney, N.S.W. 2066, Australia. TEL 61-2-3514799. FAX 61-2-3514580. *2541*

FORUM: TRENDS IN EXPERIMENTAL AND CLINICAL MEDICINE.
Scuola Internazionale di Oncologia e Medicina Sperimentale, Piazza della Vittoria 15-1, 16121 Genova, Italy. TEL 39-10-5458611. FAX 39-10-541761. *4897*

FOSSILIEN.
Goldschneck Verlag, Postfach 1265, 71399 Korb, Germany. TEL 49-7151-660119. FAX 49-7151-660778. *5558*

FOTO KURIER.
Agencja Reklamowo-Wydawnicza Foto Kurier, Ul. Wislicka 4-17, 02-114 Warsaw, Poland. TEL 48-22-232757. FAX 48-22-232757. *5764*

FOUNDATION.
Science Fiction Foundation, University of Reading, Department of History, Faculty of Letters and Social Sciences, Whiteknights, Reading RG6 6AA, England. TEL 44-1734-318145. *4531*

FOUNDATIONS.
British Evangelical Council, Evershed Hse., Alma Rd., St. Albans, Herts. AL1 3AR, England. TEL 44-1727-855655. FAX 44-1727-855-655. *6339*

FOUNDATIONS OF NEUROLOGICAL SURGERY.
Kluwer Academic Publishers, Postbus 17, 3300 AA Dordrecht, Netherlands. TEL 31-78-6392392. FAX 31-78-6392254. *5065*

FOUNDATIONS OF NEUROLOGY.
Kluwer Academic Publishers, Postbus 17, 3300 AA Dordrecht, Netherlands. TEL 31-78-6392392. FAX 31-78-6392254. *5065*

FOUNDATIONS OF NEUROPSYCHOLOGY.
Kluwer Academic Publishers, Postbus 17, 3300 AA Dordrecht, Netherlands. TEL 31-78-6392392. FAX 31-78-6392254. *5066*

FOUNDATIONS OF PHYSICS.
Plenum Publishing Corp., 233 Spring St., New York, NY 10013-1578. TEL 212-620-8000. FAX 212-463-0742. *5804*

FOUNDATIONS OF PHYSICS LETTERS.
Plenum Publishing Corp., 233 Spring St., New York, NY 10013-1578. TEL 212-620-8000. FAX 212-463-0742. *5804*

FOUNDATIONS OF SCIENCE.
Kluwer Academic Publishers, Postbus 17, 3300 AA Dordrecht, Netherlands. TEL 31-78-6392392. FAX 31-78-6392254. *6527*

FOUR SEASONS (BERKELEY).
East Bay Regional Park District, Tilden Regional Park, Botanic Garden, Berkeley, CA 94708-2396. TEL 510-841-8732. FAX 510-848-6025. *705*

FRA FYSIKKENS VERDEN.
Norsk Fysisk Selskap, P.O. Box 1048 Blindern, N-0316 Oslo, Norway. TEL 47-22-85-64-28. FAX 47-22-85-64-22. *5804*

FRACASTORO.
Azienda Ospitaliera Verona, Ple. Stefani 1, Verona, Italy. TEL 39-45-8072370. FAX 39-45-8072042. *4669*

FRACTAL TRANSLIGHT NEWSLETTER.
B M F T G, 15825 Sunnyside Ave., Morgan Hill, CA 95037. TEL 408-779-1025. *4573*

FRAGMENTA FLORISTICA ET GEOBOTANICA.
Polska Akademia Nauk, Instytut Botaniki im. W. Szafera, Ul. Lubicz 46, 31-512 Krakow, Poland. TEL 48-12-215144. FAX 48-12-219790. *705*

FRAGMENTA FLORISTICA ET GEOBOTANICA. SERIES POLONICA.
Polska Akademia Nauk, Instytut Botaniki im. W. Szafera, Ul. Lubicz 46, 31-512 Krakow, Poland. TEL 48-12-215144. FAX 48-12-219790. *705*

FRAMES ARCHITETTURA DEI SERRAMENTI.
Gruppo Editoriale Faenza Editrice S.p.A., Via Pier. de Crescenzi, 44, 48018 Faenza RA, Italy. TEL 39-546-663488. FAX 39-546-660440. *894*

FRANCE JAPON ECO.
Chambre de Commerce et d'Industrie Francaise du Japon, IIDA Bldg., 5-5, Rokubancho, Chiyoda-ku, Tokyo 102, Japan. TEL 81-3-3288-9621. FAX 81-3288-9558. *1187*

FRANCHISE INTERNATIONAL.
Franchise Development Services Ltd., Castle House, Castle Meadow, Norwich, Norfolk NR2 1PJ, England. TEL 44-1603-620301. FAX 44-1603-630174. *1527*

FRANCHISE NEWS.
Consultants America Corporation, 3820 Premier Ave., Memphis, TN 38118. TEL 901-368-3333. FAX 901-368-1144. *1527*

FRANKLIN INSTITUTE. JOURNAL.
Elsevier Science Ltd., Pergamon, P.O. Box 800, Kidlington, Oxford OX5 1DX, England. TEL 44-1865-843000. FAX 44-1865-843010. *5804*

FREE FOCUS.
Wagner Press, Box 7415, New York, NY 10116-7415. *4509*

FREE INQUIRY.
Council for Secular Humanism, Box 664, Buffalo, NY 14226. TEL 716-636-1425. FAX 716-636-1733. *5728*

FREE INQUIRY IN CREATIVE SOCIOLOGY.
Oklahoma State University, Sociology Department, 006 Classroom Bldg., Stillwater, OK 74078-4062. TEL 405-744-6126. FAX 405-744-5780. *6710*

FREE RADICAL BIOLOGY & MEDICINE.
Elsevier Science Inc., Box 945, New York, NY 10159-0945. TEL 212-633-3730. FAX 212-633-3680. *602*

FREE RADICAL RESEARCH.
Gordon and Breach - Harwood Academic, Amsteldisk 166, 1st Fl., 1079 LH Amsterdam, Netherlands. *660*

FRENCH FORUM.
French Forum Publishers Inc., Box 130, Nicholasville, KY 40340. TEL 606-885-1446. FAX 606-257-3743. *4335*

FRENCH LITERATURE SERIES.
University of South Carolina, Department of French & Classics, Columbia, SC 29208. TEL 803-777-4881. FAX 803-777-0454. *4495*

FRESH INK.
Naugatuck Valley Community-Technical College, Student Senate, c/o Gloria D. Pond, Advisor, 750 Chase Pkwy., Waterbury, CT 06708. TEL 203-596-8603. *4408*

FRESHWATER.
Marine Museum Great Lakes - Kingston, 55 Ontario St., Kingston, ON K7L 2Y2, Canada. TEL 613-542-2261. FAX 613-542-0043. *7150*

FRESHWATER BIOLOGY.
Blackwell Science Ltd., Osney Mead, Oxford OX2 0EL, England. TEL 44-1865-206206. FAX 44-1865-721205. *602*

IL FRIULI MEDICO.
Tipografia Editrice A. Pellegrini, Via della Vigna 24-A, 33100 Udine, Italy. TEL 39-432-559400. FAX 39-432-559420. *4669*

FRONESIS.
Ediluz, Apdo. 526, Maracaibo 4011, Venezuela. TEL 58-61-424788. FAX 58-61-423913. *5728*

FRONTIERS: A JOURNAL OF WOMEN STUDIES.
Washington State University Press, Box 645910, Pullman, WA 99164-5910. TEL 509-335-3518. FAX 509-335-8568. *7343*

FRONTIERS IN APPLIED MATHEMATICS.
Society for Industrial and Applied Mathematics, 3600 University City Science Center, Philadelphia, PA 19104-2688. TEL 215-382-9800. FAX 215-386-7999. *4573*

FRONTIERS IN DIABETES.
S. Karger AG, Allschwilerstr. 10, P.O. Box, CH-4009 Basel, Switzerland. TEL 41-61-3061111. FAX 41-61-3061234. *4888*

FRONTIERS IN HEADACHE RESEARCH.
Lippincott - Raven Publishers, 227 E. Washington sq., Philadelphia, PA 19106. TEL 215-238-4200. FAX 215-238-4227. *4669*

FRONTIERS IN METABOLISM.
Portland Press Ltd., 59 Portland Pl., London W1N 3AJ, England. TEL 44-171-580-5530. FAX 44-171-323-1136. *660*

FRONTIERS IN NEUROBIOLOGY.
Portland Press Ltd., 59 Portland Pl., London W1N 3AJ, England. TEL 44-171-580-5530. FAX 44-171-323-1136. *816*

FRONTIERS IN NEUROENDOCRINOLOGY.
Academic Press, Inc., Journal Division, 528 B. St., Ste. 1900, San Diego, CA 92101-4495. TEL 619-230-1840. FAX 619-699-6800. *4888*

FRONTIERS OF GASTROINTESTINAL RESEARCH.
S. Karger AG, Allschwilerstr. 10, P.O. Box, CH-4009 Basel, Switzerland. TEL 41-61-3061111. FAX 41-61-3061234. *4909*

FRONTIERS OF HORMONE RESEARCH.
S. Karger AG, Allschwilerstr. 10, P.O. Box, CH-4009 Basel, Switzerland. TEL 41-61-3061111. FAX 41-61-3061234. *4888*

FRONTIERS OF RADIATION THERAPY AND ONCOLOGY.
S. Karger AG, Allschwilerstr. 10, P.O. Box, CH-4009 Basel, Switzerland. TEL 41-61-3061111. FAX 41-61-3061234. *5106*

FRUIT VARIETIES JOURNAL.
American Pomological Society, c/o Dr. Robert M. Crassweller, Bus. Mgr., 103 Tyson Bldg., University Park, PA 16802. TEL 814-863-6163. FAX 814-863-6139. *3188*

FRUITS.
Editions Scientifiques et Medicales Elsevier, 141 rue de Javel, 75747 Paris Cedex 15, France. TEL 33-1-45589022. FAX 33-1-45589421. *3188*

FU JEN STUDIES.
Fu Jen University, College of Foreign Languages & Literatures, 24205 Hsinchuang, Taipei, Taiwan, Republic of China. TEL 886-2-903-1111. FAX 886-2-902-1327. *4408*

FUEL.
Elsevier Science Ltd., P.O. Box 800, Kidlington, Oxford OX5 1DX, England. TEL 44-1865-843000. FAX 44-1865-843010. *5601*

FUEL AND ENERGY ABSTRACTS.
Elsevier Science Ltd, P.O. Box 800, Kidlington, Oxford OX5 1DX, England. TEL 44-1865-843000. FAX 44-1865-843010. *5629*

FUEL PROCESSING TECHNOLOGY.
Elsevier Science B.V., P.O. Box 211, 1000 AE Amsterdam, Netherlands. TEL 31-20-4853911. FAX 31-20-4853598. *5601*

FUGUE.
University of Idaho, English Department, Brink Hall, Rm. 200, Moscow, ID 83844-1102. *4408*

FUJIAN JIANZHU.
Fujian Tumu Jianzhu Xuehui, 240 Beida Rd., Fuzhou, Fujian 350001, People's Republic of China. TEL 86-591-7855358. *404*

FUKUYAMA DAIGAKU FUZOKU NAIKAI SEIBUTSU SHIGEN KENKYUJO HOKOKU.
Fukuyama Daigaku, Fuzoku Naikai Seibutsu Shigen Kenkyujo, Ohamacho, Innoshima-shi, Hiroshima-ken 722-21, Japan. TEL 81-849-36-2111. FAX 81-849-36-2023. *2403*

FULLERENE SCIENCE AND TECHNOLOGY.
Marcel Dekker, Inc., 270 Madison Ave., New York, NY 10016. TEL 212-696-9000. FAX 212-685-4540. *1828*

FUNCTION.
Monash University, Department of Mathematics, Wellington Road, Clayton, Vic. 3168, Australia. TEL 61-3-99032723. FAX 61-3-99032227. *4573*

FUNCTIONAL ANALYSIS AND ITS APPLICATIONS.
Plenum Publishing Corp., Consultants Bureau, 233 Spring St., New York, NY 10013-1578. TEL 212-620-8468. FAX 212-463-0742. *4573*

FUNCTIONAL ECOLOGY.
Blackwell Science Ltd., Osney Mead, Oxford OX2 0EL, England. TEL 44-1865-206206. FAX 44-1865-721205. *2231*

FUNDAMENTA INFORMATICAE.
I O S Press, Van Diemenstraat 94, 1013 CN Amsterdam, Netherlands. TEL 31-20-6382189. FAX 31-20-6203419. *4620*

FUNDAMENTA MATHEMATICAE.
Polska Akademia Nauk, Instytut Matematyczny, Dzial Wydawnictw, Ul. Sniadeckich 8, P.O. Box 137, 00-950 Warsaw, Poland. TEL 48-22-6282471. FAX 48-22-6293997. *4573*

FUNDAMENTAL AND APPLIED TOXICOLOGY.
Academic Press, Inc., Journal Division, 525 B St., Ste. 1900, San Diego, CA 92101-4495. TEL 619-230-1840. FAX 619-699-6800. *2978*

FUNDAMENTAL AND CLINICAL PHARMACOLOGY.
Editions Scientifiques et Medicales Elsevier, 141 rue de Javel, 75747 Paris, France. TEL 33-1-45589026. FAX 33-1-45589421. *5663*

FUNDAMENTAL ASPECTS OF POLLUTION CONTROL AND ENVIRONMENTAL SCIENCE.
Elsevier Science B.V., Books Division, P.O. Box 211, 1000 AE Amsterdam, Netherlands. TEL 31-20-4853911. FAX 31-20-4853705. *2968*

FUNDAMENTAL ISSUES IN ARCHAEOLOGY.
Plenum Publishing Corp., 233 Spring St., New York, NY 10013-1578. TEL 212-620-8000. FAX 212-463-0742. *363*

FUNDAMENTAL MATERIALS RESEARCH.
Plenum Publishing Corp., 233 Spring St., New York, NY 10013-1578. TEL 212-620-8000. FAX 212-463-0742. *2858*

FUNDAMENTAL STUDIES IN COMPUTER SCIENCE.
Elsevier Science B.V., Books Division, P.O. Box 211, 1000 AE Amsterdam, Netherlands. TEL 31-20-4853911. FAX 31-20-4853705. *2081*

FUNDAMENTAL STUDIES IN ENGINEERING.
Elsevier Science B.V., Books Division, P.O. Box 211, 1000 AE Amsterdam, Netherlands. TEL 31-20-4853911. FAX 31-20-4853705. *2720*

FUNDAMENTAL THEORIES OF PHYSICS.
Kluwer Academic Publishers, Postbus 17, 3300 AA Dordrecht, Netherlands. TEL 31-78-6392392. FAX 31-78-6392254. *5804*

FUNDAMENTALS OF COSMIC PHYSICS.
Gordon and Breach - Harwood Academic, Amsteldisk 166, 1st Fl., 1079 LH Amsterdam, Netherlands. *494*

FUNDAMENTALS OF PURE AND APPLIED ECONOMICS SERIES.
Gordon and Breach - Harwood Academic, Amsteldisk 166, 1st Fl., 1079 LH Amsterdam, Netherlands. *1304*

FUNGAL GENETICS AND BIOLOGY.
Academic Press, Inc., Journal Division, 525 B St., Ste. 1900, San Diego, CA 92101-4495. TEL 619-230-1840. FAX 619-699-6800. *705*

FUNNY TIMES.
Susan Wolpert & Raymond Lesser, Eds. & Pubs., Box 18530, Cleveland Heights, OH 44118. TEL 216-371-8600. FAX 216-371-8696. *4335*

FURONG.
Hunan Wenyi Chubanshe, 67, Yinpen Nanlu, Changsha, Hunan 410006, People's Republic of China. TEL 86-731-8882460. FAX 86-731-8883393. *4408*

FUSE MAGAZINE.
Arton's Publishing, 401 Richmond St. W., Ste. 454, Toronto, ON M5V 3A8, Canada. TEL 416-340-8026. FAX 416-340-0494. *3261*

FUSION ENGINEERING AND DESIGN.
Elsevier Science S.A., P.O. Box 564, CH-1001 Lausanne 1, Switzerland. TEL 41-21-3207381. FAX 41-21-3235444. *2884*

FUSION TECHNOLOGY.
American Nuclear Society, 555 N. Kensington Ave., La Grange Park, IL 60525. TEL 708-352-6611. *2696*

FUTURA.
Go Creative Group, Via Tortona 14, 20144 Milan, Italy. TEL 39-2-58106415. FAX 39-2-58106428. *2108*

FUTURES.
Elsevier Science Ltd., Pergamon, P.O. Box 800, Kidlington, Oxford OX5 1DX, England. TEL 44-1865-843000. FAX 44-1865-843010. *1261*

FUTURICS.
Minnesota Futurists, 365 Summit Ave., St. Paul, MN 55102. TEL 612-290-2846. FAX 612-290-2847. *6711*

FUZZY SETS AND SYSTEMS.
North-Holland, P.O. Box 211, 1000 AE Amsterdam, Netherlands. TEL 31-20-4853911. FAX 31-20-4853598. *4574*

G A L - BULLETIN.
Gesellschaft fuer Angewandte Linguistik e.V., Universitaet Wuppertal, 42097 Wuppertal, Germany. TEL 49-202-4392254. FAX 49-202-4392254. *4259*

G A N P A C BRIEF.
German-American National Public Affairs Committee, Box 11124, Pensacola, FL 32524-1124. FAX 904-478-4993. *3012*

G F F.
Swedish Science Press, P.O. Box 118, S-751 04 Uppsala, Sweden. TEL 46-18-36-55-66. FAX 46-18-36-52-77. *2340*

G F W C OF MINNESOTA NEWS.
General Federation of Women's Clubs of Minnesota, Inc., 5701 Normandale Rd., Ste. 345, Minneapolis, MN 55424. TEL 612-920-2057. *1932*

G I S ASIA - PACIFIC.
Pearson Professional, 159 Telok Ayer St., Singapore 068614, Singapore. TEL 65-6-257-2519. FAX 65-6-357-2518. *3429*

G S F MENSCH UND UMWELT SPEZIAL.
G S F - Forschungszentrum fuer Umwelt und Gesundheit, Ingolstaedter Landstr. 1, 85764 Oberschleissheim, Germany. TEL 49-89-3187-2711. FAX 49-89-3187-3324. *2929*

G W U M C. DEPARTMENT OF BIOCHEMISTRY. ANNUAL SPRING SYMPOSIA SERIES.
Plenum Publishing Corp., 233 Spring St., New York, NY 10013-1578. TEL 212-620-8000. FAX 212-463-0742. *660*

REFEREED SERIALS

GACETA LABORAL.
Universidad del Zulia, Facultad de Ciencias Juridicas, Av. 16A, Ciudad Universitaria, Dr. Antonio Borjas Romero, Nucleo Humanistico, Apdo. Postal 740, Maracaibo, Venezuela. TEL 61-596685. FAX 58-61-536069. *3954*

GACETA MEDICA.
Laboratorios Chalver de Colombia Ltda., Av. 68 No. 40-21 Sur, Bogota, Colombia. TEL 571-7100477. FAX 571-2303573. *4670*

GACETA RURAL.
Gestora Editorial Rural, S.L., Avda. de Ramon y Cajal 5, 28016 Madrid, Spain. TEL 34-1-3440462. FAX 34-1-3440463. *120*

GAEA.
Association for Women Geoscientists, 4779 126th St., N., White Bear Lake, MN 55110-5910. TEL 612-426-3316. FAX 612-426-5449. *2314*

GAIT AND POSTURE.
Elsevier Science B.V., P.O. Box 211, 1000 AE Amsterdam, Netherlands. TEL 31-20-4853911. FAX 31-20-4853598. *4670*

GALAXIA.
Asociacion Argentina de Quimicos y Coloristas Textiles, Bulnes 1425, 1176 Buenos Aires, Argentina. TEL 54-1-963-0394. *6987*

GALILEAN ELECTRODYNAMICS.
Space Time Analyses, Ltd., 141 Rhinecliff St., Arlington, MA 02174. TEL 617-643-3155. FAX 617-646-8114. *5804*

GALLOWAY PRESS.
Galloway Press, 647 Fouth St., Berthoud, CO 80513. TEL 970-532-0797. FAX 970-532-0797. *276*

GAMMA.
Nederlandse Vereniging van Radiologisch Laboranten, P.O. Box 19207, 3501 DE Utrecht, Netherlands. TEL 31-30-2318842. FAX 31-30-2321362. *5106*

GANGUANG CAILIAO.
Huagong Bu, Ganguang Cailiao Xinxi Zhan, c/o Zhongguo Lekai Jiaopian Gongsi, Jianshe Rd., Baoding, Hebei 071054, People's Republic of China. TEL 86-312-3033279. FAX 86-312-3026296. *1749*

GANGUANG KEXUE YU GUANGHUAXUE.
Science Press, Marketing and Sales Department, 16 Donghuangchenggen North St., Beijing 100717, People's Republic of China. TEL 4010642. FAX 4019810. *5766*

GANN MONOGRAPHS ON CANCER RESEARCH.
Gakkai Shuppan Senta, 2-10, Hongo 6-chome, Bunkyo-ku, Tokyo 113, Japan. *4978*

GANSU SHEHUI KEXUE.
Gansu Sheng Shehui Kexueyuan, Shi Li Dian, Lanzhou, Gansu 730070, People's Republic of China. TEL 86-931-7668021. *6615*

GAOFENZI XUEBAO.
Science Press, Marketing and Sales Department, 16 Donghuangchenggen North St., Beijing 100717, People's Republic of China. TEL 4010642. FAX 4019810. *1828*

GAONENG WULI YU HE WULI.
Science Press, Marketing and Sales Department, 16 Donghuangchenggen North St., Beijing 100717, People's Republic of China. TEL 4010642. FAX 4109810. *5851*

THE GARDEN DESIGN JOURNAL.
Society of Garden Designers, 6 Borough Rd., Kingston-upon-Thames, Surrey KT2 6BD, England. TEL 44-181-974-9483. *3189*

GARDEN PATH.
Ohio Association of Garden Clubs, c/o Faye Collins, 11158 SR 139, Minford, OH 45653-8718. TEL 614-820-8402. *3189*

GARDENS' BULLETIN, SINGAPORE.
National Parks Board, Singapore Botanic Gardens, Cluny Rd., Singapore 1025, Singapore. TEL 4741165. FAX 4754295. *705*

GARTEN MAGAZIN FUER ALLE.
Oesterreichische Gartenbaugesellschaft, Parkring 12, A-1010 Vienna, Austria. TEL 43-1-5128416. FAX 43-1-5128416. *3190*

GAS.
Stichting Tijdschrift Openbare Gasvoorziening, Postbus 220, 7300 AE Apeldoorn, Netherlands. TEL 31-55-5393217. FAX 31-55-5393228. *5602*

GAS AKTUELL.
Messer Griesheim GmbH, 47793 Krefeld, Germany. TEL 49-2151-379434. FAX 49-2151-379116. *2764*

GAS INDUSTRIES MAGAZINE.
Gas Industries Inc., Box 558, Park Ridge, IL 60068. TEL 312-693-3682. FAX 847-696-3445. *5602*

GASSHO.
Dharmanet International, Box 4951, Berkeley, CA 94704-4951. TEL 510-620-0936. *6389*

GASTROENTEROLOGY.
W.B. Saunders Co., Curtis Center, 3rd Fl., Independence Sq. W., Philadelphia, PA 19106-3399. TEL 215-238-7800. FAX 215-238-6445. *4910*

GASTROENTEROLOGY AND ENDOSCOPY NEWS.
McMahon Group, 148 W. 24th St., New York, NY 10011. TEL 212-620-4600. FAX 212-620-5928. *4910*

GASTROENTEROLOGY & HEPATOLOGY SERIES.
Marcel Dekker, Inc., 270 Madison Ave., New York, NY 10016. TEL 212-696-9000. FAX 212-685-4540. *4910*

GASTROINTESTINAL ENDOSCOPY.
Mosby - Year Book, Inc., 11830 Westline Industrial Dr., St. Louis, MO 63146-3318. TEL 314-872-8370. FAX 314-432-1380. *4910*

GAY AND LESBIAN MEDICAL ASSOCIATION. JOURNAL.
Plenum Publishing Corp., 233 Spring St., New York, NY 10013-1578. TEL 212-620-8000. FAX 212-463-0742. *4670*

GAZELLA. ANNUAL REPORT AND SCIENTIFIC ARTICLES.
Zoologicka Zahrada v Praze, U Trojskeho Zamku 3-120, 171 00 Prague 7, Czech Republic. TEL 420-2-6880480. FAX 420-2-6890369. *835*

GAZETA LEKARSKA.
Naczelna Izba Lekarska w Warszawie, Ul. Grojecka 65A, 02-094 Warsaw, Poland. TEL 48-22-6250121. FAX 48-22-6296333. *4670*

GAZETA NIEDZIELNA.
Veritas Foundation Publication Centre, 63 Jeddo Rd., London WI2 9EE, England. TEL 44-181-749-4957. FAX 44-181-749-4965. *3348*

GAZETTE.
Sage Publications Ltd., 6 Bonhill St., London EC2A 4PU, England. TEL 44-171-374-0645. FAX 44-171-374-8741. *3873*

GAZI MEDICAL JOURNAL.
Gazi Universitesi, Tip Fakultesi Dekanligi, 06500 Besevler, Ankara, Turkey. TEL 90-312-2141000. FAX 90-312-2124647. *4671*

GAZI UNIVERSITESI ECZACILIK FAKULTESI DERGISI.
Gazi Universitesi, Eczacilik Fakultesi, 06330 Etiler - Ankara, Turkey. TEL 90-312-2227225. FAX 90-312-2235018. *5663*

GEFAHRSTOFFE - REINHALTUNG DER LUFT.
Springer V D I Verlag, Heinrichstr. 24, 40239 Duesseldorf, Germany. TEL 49-221-6103-0. FAX 49-221-6103414. *2968*

GEKKAN CHIIKI IGAKU.
Chiiki Iryo Shinko Kyokai, Hibiya-dai Bldg., 13F., 1-2-2 Uchisaiwai-cho, Chiyoda-ku, Tokyo 100, Japan. TEL 81-3-3580-8471. FAX 81-3-3580-8472. *4671*

GEKKAN GASORIN STUTANDO.
Gekkan Gasorin Sutandosha, 3-2-3 Shinbashi, Minato-ku, Tokyo 105, Japan. TEL 81-3-3502-5941. FAX 81-3-3502-5940. *5603*

GELDERS ERFGOED.
Stichting Gelders Oudheidkundig Contact, Postbus 4040, 7200 BA Zutphen, Netherlands. TEL 31-575-511826. FAX 31-575-543223. *3568*

GELFAND MATHEMATICAL SEMINARS.
Birkhauser Boston, 675 Massachusetts Ave., Cambridge, MA 02139. TEL 617-876-2333. FAX 617-876-1272. *4574*

GEMS OF GENEALOGY.
Bay Area Genealogical Society, Inc., c/o Lisa Youngblood, Box 283, Green Bay, WI 54305-0283. TEL 414-494-9286. *3223*

GENDER AND DEVELOPMENT DIRECTORY. AUSTRALIA.
Australian Development Studies Network, National Centre for Development Studies, Australian National University, Canberra, A.C.T. 0200, Australia. TEL 61-6-2492466. FAX 61-6-2572886. *7344*

GENDER AND EDUCATION.
Carfax Publishing Co., P.O. Box 25, Abingdon, Oxon. OX14 3UE, England. TEL 44-1235-401000. FAX 44-1235-401550. *2445*

GENDER AND HISTORY.
Blackwell Publishers Ltd., 108 Cowley Rd., Oxford OX4 1JF, England. TEL 44-1865-791100. FAX 44-1865-791347. *3495*

GENDER & PSYCHOANALYSIS.
International Universities Press, Inc., 59 Boston Post Rd., Box 1524, Madison, CT 06443-1524. TEL 203-245-4000. FAX 203-245-0775. *6113*

GENDER, PLACE AND CULTURE.
Carfax Publishing Co., P.O. Box 25, Abingdon, Oxon. OX14 3UE, England. TEL 44-1235-401000. FAX 44-1235-401550. *7344*

GENDER, WORK AND ORGANIZATION.
Blackwell Publishers Ltd., 108 Cowley Rd., Oxford OX4 1JF, England. TEL 44-1865-791100. FAX 44-1865-791347. *1479*

GENE.
Elsevier Science B.V., P.O. Box 211, 1000 AE Amsterdam, Netherlands. TEL 31-20-4853911. FAX 31-20-4853598. *767*

GENE AMPLIFICATION AND ANALYSIS SERIES.
Elsevier Science B.V., Books Division, P.O. Box 211, 1000 AE Amsterdam, Netherlands. TEL 31-20-4853911. FAX 31-20-4853705. *767*

GENE THERAPY (BASINGSTOKE).
Stockton Press, Houndmills, Basingstoke, Hants RG21 6XS, England. TEL 44-1256-302622. FAX 44-1256-810526. *4671*

GENEALOGIST.
Picton Press, Box 1111, Canden, ME 04843. *3224*

GENEESMIDDELENBULLETIN.
Stichting Geneesmiddelenbulletin, Lomanlaan 85, 3526 XC Utrecht, Netherlands. TEL 31-30-2802660. *5664*

GENERAL AND COMPARATIVE ENDOCRINOLOGY.
Academic Press, Inc., Journal Division, 525 B St., Ste. 1900, San Diego, CA 92101-4495. TEL 619-230-1840. FAX 619-699-6800. *4888*

GENERAL DENTISTRY.
Academy of General Dentistry, 211 E. Chicago Ave., Ste. 1200, Chicago, IL 60611. TEL 312-440-4300. FAX 312-440-0559. *4858*

GENERAL HISTORY OF AFRICA.
UNESCO Publishing, 7 place de Fontenoy, 75352 Paris 07 SP, France. TEL 33-1-45684300. FAX 33-1-45685741. *3526*

GENERAL HOSPITAL PSYCHIATRY.
Elsevier Science Inc., Box 945, New York, NY 10159-0945. TEL 212-633-3730. FAX 212-633-3680. *5066*

GENERAL MOTORS SYMPOSIA SERIES.
Plenum Publishing Corp., 233 Spring St., New York, NY 10013-1578. TEL 212-620-8000. FAX 212-463-0742. *7100*

GENERAL PHARMACOLOGY.
Elsevier Science Inc., Box 945, New York, NY 10159-0945. TEL 212-633-3730. FAX 212-633-3680. *5664*

GENERAL RELATIVITY AND GRAVITATION.
Plenum Publishing Corp., 233 Spring St., New York, NY 10013-1578. TEL 212-620-8000. FAX 212-463-0742. *5804*

GENES & DEVELOPMENT.
Cold Spring Harbor Laboratory Press, Publications Department, Box 100, Cold Spring Harbor, NY 11724. TEL 800-843-4388. FAX 516-349-1946. *767*

GENES & GENETIC SYSTEMS.
Genetics Society of Japan, c/o National Institute of Genetics, 1111 Yata, Mishima-shi, Shizuoka-ken 411, Japan. TEL 81-849-36-2111. FAX 81-849-36-2024. *768*

GENES, CHROMOSOMES & CANCER.
John Wiley & Sons, Inc., Journals, 605 Third Ave., New York, NY 10158. TEL 212-850-6645. FAX 212-850-6021. *768*

GENES TO CELLS.
Blackwell Science Ltd., Osney Mead, Oxford OX2 0EL, England. TEL 44-1865-206206. FAX 44-1865-721205. *785*

GENESIS OF BEHAVIOR.
Plenum Publishing Corp., 233 Spring St., New York, NY 10013-1578. TEL 212-620-8000. FAX 212-463-0742. *5066*

GENETIC ANALYSIS, BIOMOLECULAR ENGINEERING.
Elsevier Science B.V., P.O. Box 211, 1000 AE Amsterdam, Netherlands. TEL 31-20-4853911. FAX 31-20-4853598. *683*

GENETIC DISORDER.
Box 151362, San Diego, CA 92175. *4336*

THE GENETIC ENGINEER AND BIOTECHNOLOGIST.
Carfax Publishing Co., P.O. Box 25, Abingdon, Oxon. OX14 3UE, England. TEL 44-1235-401000. FAX 44-1235-401550. *647*

GENETIC ENGINEERING.
Plenum Publishing Corp., 233 Spring St., New York, NY 10013-1578. TEL 212-620-8000. FAX 212-463-0742. *768*

GENETIC ENGINEERING AND BIOTECHNOLOGY YEARBOOK.
Elsevier Science B.V., Books Division, P.O. Box 211, 1000 AE Amsterdam, Netherlands. TEL 31-20-4853911. FAX 31-20-4853705. *768*

GENETIC EPIDEMIOLOGY.
John Wiley & Sons, Inc., Journals, 605 Third Ave., New York, NY 10158. TEL 212-850-6645. FAX 212-850-6021. *768*

GENETIC EPISTEMOLOGIST.
Jean Piaget Society, Department of Psychology, Franklin and arshall College, Box 3003, Lancaster, PA 17604. *6113*

GENETIC RESOURCES AND CROP EVOLUTION.
Kluwer Academic Publishers, Postbus 17, 3300 AA Dordrecht, Netherlands. TEL 31-78-6392392. FAX 31-78-6392254. *706*

GENETIC, SOCIAL, AND GENERAL PSYCHOLOGY MONOGRAPHS.
Heldref Publications, 1319 Eighteenth St., N.W., Washington, DC 20036-1802. TEL 202-296-6267. FAX 202-296-5149. *6113*

GENETICA.
Kluwer Academic Publishers, Postbus 17, 3300 AA Dordrecht, Netherlands. TEL 31-78-6392392. FAX 31-78-6392254. *768*

GENETICS.
Genetics Society of America, 9650 Rockville Pike, Bethesda, MD 20814. TEL 301-571-1825. FAX 301-530-7001. *769*

GENETICS, SELECTION, EVOLUTION.
Editions Scientifiques et Medicales Elsevier, 141 rue de Javel, 75747 Paris, France. TEL 33-1-45589022. FAX 33-1-45589421. *769*

GENEVA PAPERS ON RISK AND INSURANCE THEORY.
Kluwer Academic Publishers Boston, Box 358, Accord Sta., Hingham, MA 02018-0358. TEL 617-871-6600. FAX 617-871-6528. *3817*

GENEWATCH.
Council for Responsible Genetics (CRG), 5 Upland Rd., Ste. 3, Cambridge, MA 02140-2717. TEL 617-868-0870. FAX 617-491-5344. *769*

GENGO TO KYOIKU NO KENKYU.
Saitama Daigaku Kyoiku Gakubu, Kyoiku Gakubu, Takenaga Laboratory, 255, Shimo Okubo, Urawa-shi 338, Japan. TEL 048-858-3175. FAX 048-858-3690. *2603*

GENOME.
National Research Council of Canada, Research Journals, Ottawa, ON K1A 0R6, Canada. TEL 613-993-9084. FAX 613-952-7656. *769*

GENOME RESEARCH.
Cold Spring Harbor Laboratory Press, Publications Department, Box 100, Cold Spring Harbor, NY 11724. TEL 516-367-8492. FAX 516-367-8334. *785*

GENOMICS.
Academic Press, Inc., Journal Division, 525 B St., Ste. 1900, San Diego, CA 92101-4495. TEL 619-230-1840. FAX 619-699-6800. *770*

GENTES.
Lega Missionaria Studenti, Via M. Massimo, 7, 00144 Rome, Italy. TEL 39-6-5439628. FAX 39-6-5910803. *6340*

THE GENTLE SURVIVALIST.
Laura Martin-Buhler Co., Box 4004, St. George, UT 84770. *5457*

GEOARCHAEOLOGY.
John Wiley & Sons, Inc., Journals, 605 Third Ave., New York, NY 10158-0012. TEL 212-850-6645. FAX 212-850-6021. *364*

GEOBIOS.
Universite Claude Bernard Lyon I, Sciences de la Terre, Bldg. 402, 43 bd. du 11 Novembre, 69622 Villeurbanne, France. TEL 33-4-72431631. FAX 33-4-72448428. *5559*

GEOBOTANY.
Kluwer Academic Publishers, Postbus 17, 3300 AA Dordrecht, Netherlands. TEL 31-78-6392392. FAX 31-78-6392254. *2341*

GEOCHIMICA ET COSMOCHIMICA ACTA.
Elsevier Science Ltd., Pergamon, P.O. Box 800, Kidlington, Oxford OX5 1DX, England. TEL 44-1865-843000. FAX 44-1865-843010. *2341*

GEODERMA.
Elsevier Science B.V., P.O. Box 211, 1000 AE Amsterdam, Netherlands. TEL 31-20-4853911. FAX 31-20-4853598. *226*

GEOFISICA INTERNACIONAL.
Universidad Nacional Autonoma de Mexico, Instituto de Geofisica, Circuito Exterior, Ciudad Universitaria, Mexico 20, D.F., Mexico. TEL 52-5-622-4113. FAX 52-5-550-2486. *2381*

GEOFORUM.
Elsevier Science Ltd., Pergamon, P.O. Box 800, Kidlington, Oxford OX5 1DX, England. TEL 44-1865-843000. FAX 44-1865-843010. *3403*

GEOGRAFIA FISICA E DINAMICA QUATERNARIA.
Comitato Glaciologico Italiano, Via Accademia delle Scienze N. 5, 10123 Turin, Italy. TEL 39-50-847233237. FAX 39-50-500932. *2341*

GEOGRAFIA NELLE SCUOLE.
Associazione Italiana Insegnanti di Geografia, Via Tigor 22, 34124 Trieste, Italy. TEL 040-6763615. FAX 040-6763647. *3403*

GEOGRAFICKY CASOPIS.
Slovenska Akademia Vied, Geograficky Ustav, Stefanikova 49, 814 73 Bratislava, Slovakia. TEL 421-7-495587. FAX 421-7-491340. *3404*

GEOGRAPHICAL ANALYSIS.
Ohio State University Press, 1070 Carmack Rd., Columbus, OH 43210. TEL 614-292-6930. FAX 614-292-2065. *3405*

GEOGRAPHICAL BULLETIN.
Gamma Theta Upsilon, c/o C. Nicholas Raphael, Ed., Department of Geography and Geology, Eastern Michigan University, Ypsilanti, MI 48197. TEL 313-487-1480. FAX 313-487-6979. *3405*

GEOGRAPHICAL JOURNAL OF ZIMBABWE.
Geographical Association of Zimbabwe, c/o University of Zimbabwe, Dept. of Geography, P.O. Box MP 167, Mt. Pleasant, Harare, Zimbabwe. TEL 263-4-303211. FAX 263-4-335249. *3405*

GEOGRAPHICAL REVIEW OF INDIA.
Geographical Society of India, c/o Calcutta University, Geography Department, 35 Ballygunge Circular Rd., Calcutta 700 019, India. TEL 91-33-475-3681. *3405*

GEOGRAPHY TEACHERS ASSOCIATION OF NEW SOUTH WALES. GEOGRAPHY BULLETIN.
Geography Teachers Association of New South Wales, P.O. Box 602, Gladesville, N.S.W. 2111, Australia. TEL 61-2-817-3647. FAX 61-2-817-4592. *3407*

GEOINFORMATICA.
Kluwer Academic Publishers Boston, Box 358, Accord Sta., Hingham, MA 02018-0358. TEL 617-871-6600. FAX 617-871-6528. *2329*

GEOJOURNAL.
Kluwer Academic Publishers, Postbus 17, 3300 AA Dordrecht, Netherlands. TEL 31-78-6392392. FAX 31-78-6392254. *3407*

GEOJOURNAL LIBRARY.
Kluwer Academic Publishers, Postbus 17, 3300 AA Dordrecht, Netherlands. TEL 31-78-6392392. FAX 31-78-6392254. *2341*

GEOLINGUISTICS.
American Society of Geolinguistics, 485 Brooklawn Ave., Fairfield, CT 06432-1805. TEL 203-333-8920. *4259*

GEOLOGI.
Danmarks og Groenlands Geologiske Undersoegelse, Thoravej 8, DK-2400 Copenhagen NV, Denmark. *2342*

GEOLOGIA SUDETICA.
Polska Akademia Nauk, Instytut Nauk Geologicznych, Ul. Zwirki i Wigury 93, 02-089 Warsaw, Poland. TEL 48-22-221065. FAX 48-22-221065. *2342*

GEOLOGICA CARPATHICA - CLAYS.
Vydavatel'stvo S A P, s.r.o., P.O. Box 57, Nam. Slobody 6, 810 05 Bratislava, Slovakia. TEL 42-7-211729. *2342*

GEOLOGICA ULTRAIECTINA.
Universiteit Utrecht, Faculteit Aardwetenschappen, Budapestlaan 4, 3584 CD Utrecht, Netherlands. TEL 31-30-2534994. FAX 31-30-2535030. *2342*

GEOLOGICAL SOCIETY OF AMERICA. BULLETIN.
Geological Society of America, 3300 Penrose Pl., Box 9140, Boulder, CO 80301. TEL 303-447-2020. FAX 303-447-1133. *2343*

GEOLOGICAL SOCIETY OF AMERICA. SPECIAL PAPERS.
Geological Society of America, 3300 Penrose Pl., Box 9140, Boulder, CO 80301. TEL 303-447-2020. FAX 303-447-1133. *2343*

GEOLOGICAL SOCIETY OF INDIA. JOURNAL.
Geological Society of India, Post Box 1922, Gavipuran, Bangalore 560 019, India. TEL 91-80-6613352. *2344*

GEOLOGICKA SLUZBA SLOVENSKEJ REPUBLIKY. GEOLOGICKE PRACE. SPRAVY.
Geologicka Sluzba Slovenskej Republiky, Mlynska Dolina 1, 817 04 Bratislava, Slovakia. TEL 421-7-3705111. FAX 421-7-371940. *2345*

GEOLOGIE EN MIJNBOUW.
Kluwer Academic Publishers, Postbus 17, 3300 AA Dordrecht, Netherlands. TEL 31-78-6392392. FAX 31-78-6392254. *2345*

GEOLOGY (BOULDER).
Geological Society of America, 3300 Penrose Pl., Box 9140, Boulder, CO 80301. TEL 303-447-2020. FAX 303-447-1133. *2347*

GEOLOGY OF GREENLAND SURVEY BULLETIN.
Danmarks og Groenlands Geologiske Undersoegelse, Thoravej 8, DK-2400 Copenhagen NV, Denmark. TEL 45-31-10-66-00. FAX 45-31-19-68-68. *2347*

GEOLOGY OF THE PACIFIC OCEAN.
Gordon and Breach - Harwood Academic, Amsteldisk 166, 1st Fl., 1079 LH Amsterdam, Netherlands. *2347*

GEOLOGY REVIEWS.
Gordon and Breach - Harwood Academic, Amsteldisk 166, 1st Fl., 1079 LH Amsterdam, Netherlands. *2347*

GEOLOGY TODAY.
Blackwell Science Ltd., Osney Mead, Oxford OX2 OEL, England. TEL 44-1865-206206. FAX 44-1865-721205. *2347*

GEOMAGNETISM AND AERONOMY.
American Geophysical Union, 2000 Florida Ave., N.W., Washington, DC 20009. TEL 202-462-6900. FAX 202-328-0566. *2382*

GEOMATICA.
Canadian Institute of Geomatics, Box 5378, Sta. F, Ottawa, ON K2C 3J1, Canada. TEL 613-224-9851. FAX 613-224-9577. *3407*

GEOMETRIAE DEDICATA.
Kluwer Academic Publishers, Postbus 17, 3300 AA Dordrecht, Netherlands. TEL 31-78-6392392. FAX 31-78-6392254. *4574*

GEOMICROBIOLOGY JOURNAL.
Taylor & Francis Inc., 1900 Frost Rd., Ste. 101, Bristol, PA 19007-1598. TEL 215-785-5800. FAX 215-785-5515. *785*

GEOMORPHOLOGY.
Elsevier Science B.V., P.O. Box 211, 1000 AE Amsterdam, Netherlands. TEL 31-20-4853911. FAX 31-20-4853598. *2347*

GEOPHYSICAL AND ASTROPHYSICAL FLUID DYNAMICS.
Gordon and Breach - Harwood Academic, Amsteldisk 166, 1st Fl., 1079 LH Amsterdam, Netherlands. *2382*

GEOPHYSICAL JOURNAL.
Gordon and Breach - Harwood Academic, Amsteldisk 166, 1st Fl., 1079 LH Amsterdam, Netherlands. *2382*

GEOPHYSICAL JOURNAL INTERNATIONAL.
Blackwell Science Ltd., Osney Mead, Oxford OX2 OEL, England. TEL 44-1865-206206. FAX 44-1865-721205. *2382*

GEOPHYSICAL PROSPECTING.
Blackwell Science Ltd., Osney Mead, Oxford OX2 OEL, England. TEL 44-1865-206206. FAX 44-1865-721205. *2382*

GEOPHYSICAL RESEARCH LETTERS.
American Geophysical Union, 2000 Florida Ave., N.W., Washington, DC 20009. TEL 202-462-6900. FAX 202-328-0566. *2382*

GEOPHYSICS.
Society of Exploration Geophysicists, Box 702740, Tulsa, OK 74170-2740. TEL 918-493-3516. *2383*

GEOPHYSICS AND ASTROPHYSICS MONOGRAPHS.
Kluwer Academic Publishers, Postbus 17, 3300 AA Dordrecht, Netherlands. TEL 31-78-6392392. FAX 31-78-6392254. *494*

GEOPHYTOLOGY.
Palaeobotanical Society, 53 University Rd., Lucknow 7, India. TEL 91-522-74291. FAX 91-522-374528. *5559*

GEOPOLITICS AND INTERNATIONAL BOUNDARIES.
Frank Cass, Newbury House, 890-900 Eastern Ave., Newbury Park, Ilford, Essex IG2 7HH, England. TEL 44-181-5990984. FAX 44-181-5998866. *6016*

GEORGE ELIOT - GEORGE HENRY LEWES STUDIES.
Dr. W. Baker, Ed. & Pub., Department of English, Northern Illinois University, Dekalb, IL 60115. TEL 815-753-1857. FAX 815-753-2003. *4336*

GEORGE HERBERT JOURNAL.
c/o Sidney Gottlieb, Ed., English Department, Sacred Heart University, 5151 Park Ave., Fairfield, CT 06432. TEL 203-371-7810. *4509*

GEORGETOWN REVIEW.
Milkbone Publishing, Box 6309, Southern Sta., Hattiesburg, MS 39406-6309. TEL 601-583-6940. FAX 601-583-6940. *4409*

GEORGIA ANCHORAGE.
Georgia Ports Authority, Box 2406, Savannah, GA 31402. TEL 912-964-3811. FAX 912-964-3921. *7151*

GEORGIA GENEALOGICAL MAGAZINE.
LaBruce M.S. Lucas, Ed. & Pub., Box 1267, Greenville, SC 29602-1267. TEL 864-233-2346. FAX 864-233-2349. *3224*

GEORGIA JOURNAL OF SCIENCE.
Georgia Academy of Science, c/o John Aliff, Ed., DeKalb College, Gwinnett Campus, 5155 Sugarloaf Pkwy., Lawrenceville, GA 30243. *6528*

GEORGIA LIBRARIAN.
Georgia Library Association, 1438 W. Peachtree St., N.W., Atlanta, GA 30309-2955. *4179*

GEORGIA MUSIC NEWS.
Georgia Music Educators Association, c/o Mary Leglar, Ed., University of Georgia School of Music, Athens, GA 30602. TEL 706-542-2763. FAX 706-542-2773. *5395*

GEORGIAN MATHEMATICAL JOURNAL.
Plenum Publishing Corp., 233 Spring St., New York, NY 10013-1578. TEL 212-620-8000. FAX 212-463-0742. *4574*

GEOSCIENCE INFORMATION SOCIETY. PROCEEDINGS.
Geoscience Information Society, c/o American Geological Institute, 4220 King St., Alexandria, VA 22302. *2315*

GEOTECHNICAL AND GEOLOGICAL ENGINEERING.
Thomson Science, 2-6 Boundary Row, London SE1 8HN, England. TEL 44-171-8650066. FAX 44-171-522-9623. *5301*

GEOTECHNICAL TESTING JOURNAL.
American Society for Testing and Materials, 100 Barr Harbor Dr., W. Conshohocken, PA 19428-2959. TEL 610-832-9500. FAX 610-832-9555. *2785*

GEOTECHNIK.
Verlag Glueckauf GmbH, Postfach 185620, 45206 Essen, Germany. TEL 49-2054-924122. FAX 49-2054-924129. *2721*

GEOTECHNIQUE.
Thomas Telford Services Ltd., Thomas Telford House, 1 Heron Quay, London E14 4JD, England. TEL 44-171-987-6999. FAX 44-171-538-9620. *2785*

GEOTEXTILES AND GEOMEMBRANES.
Elsevier Science Ltd., P.O. Box 800, Kidlington, Oxford OX5 1DX, England. TEL 44-1865-843000. FAX 44-1865-843010. *740*

GEOTHERMAL SCIENCE AND TECHNOLOGY.
Gordon and Breach - Harwood Academic, Amsteldisk 166, 1st Fl., 1079 LH Amsterdam, Netherlands. *2348*

GEOTHERMICS.
Elsevier Science Ltd., Pergamon, P.O. Box 800, Kidlington, Oxford OX5 1DX, England. TEL 44-1865-843000. FAX 44-1865-843010. *2315*

GEREFORMEERD THEOLOGISCH TIJDSCHRIFT.
Uitgeversmaatschappij J.H. Kok B.V., Postbus 130, 8260 AC Kampen, Netherlands. TEL 31-38-3392555. FAX 31-38-3327331. *6426*

GERIATRIC NEPHROLOGY AND UROLOGY.
Kluwer Academic Publishers, Postbus 17, 3300 AA Dordrecht, Netherlands. TEL 31-78-6392392. FAX 31-78-6392254. *5161*

GERIATRICS.
Advanstar Communications, Inc., 7500 Old Oak Blvd., Cleveland, OH 44130. TEL 216-826-2839. FAX 216-891-2726. *3436*

GERMAN COMMENTS.
Markt 81, 53757 St. Augustin, Germany. TEL 49-2241-246592. FAX 49-2241-246610. *3285*

GERMAN HISTORY.
Arnold, 338 Euston Rd., London NW1 3BH, England. TEL 44-171-873-6000. FAX 44-171-873-6325. *3568*

GERMAN LIFE.
Zeitgeist Publishing, 1 Corporate Dr., Grantsville, MD 21536. TEL 301-895-3859. FAX 301-895-5029. *3285*

GERMAN LIFE AND LETTERS.
Blackwell Publishers Ltd., 108 Cowley Rd., Oxford OX4 1JF, England. TEL 44-1865-791100. FAX 44-1865-791347. *4409*

GERMAN POLITICS.
Frank Cass, Newbury House, 890-900 Eastern Ave., Newbury Park, Ilford, Essex, England. TEL 44-181-599-8866. FAX 44-181-599-0984. *6016*

GERMAN POLITICS & SOCIETY.
University of California at Berkeley, Center for German and European Studies - International and Area Studies, 247 Moses Hall, Berkeley, CA 94720-2324. TEL 510-642-4065. FAX 510-643-7062. *5929*

GERMAN QUARTERLY.
American Association of Teachers of German, Inc., 112 Haddontowne Ct., Ste. 104, Cherry Hill, NJ 08034. TEL 609-795-5553. FAX 609-795-9398. *4260*

GERMANIC NOTES AND REVIEWS.
Department of Modern and Classical Languages, Bemidji State University, Bemidji, MN 56601. TEL 218-751-6265. FAX 218-751-2958. *4260*

GERMANIC REVIEW.
Heldref Publications, 1319 Eighteenth St., N.W., Washington, DC 20036-1802. TEL 202-296-6267. FAX 202-296-5149. *4260*

GERMANO-SLAVICA.
University of Waterloo, Department of Germanic and Slavic Languages and Literature, Waterloo, ON N2L 3G1, Canada. TEL 519-885-1211. FAX 519-746-5243. *4409*

GERMANTOWN CRIER.
Germantown Historical Society, 5501 Germantown Ave., Philadelphia, PA 19144-2291. TEL 215-844-0514. FAX 215-844-2831. *3627*

GERODONTOLOGY.
F D I World Dental Press Ltd., 7 Carlisle St., London W1V 5RG, England. TEL 0171-935-7852. FAX 0171-486-0183. *4858*

THE GERONTOLOGIST.
Gerontological Society of America, 1275 K St., N.W., Ste. 350, Washington, DC 20005-4006. TEL 202-842-1275. FAX 202-842-1150. *3436*

GERONTOLOGY.
S. Karger AG, Allschwilerstr. 10, P.O. Box, CH-4009 Basel, Switzerland. TEL 41-61-3061111. FAX 41-61-3061234. *3436*

GERONTOLOGY & GERIATRICS EDUCATION.
Haworth Press, Inc., 10 Alice St., Binghamton, NY 13904. TEL 607-722-5857. FAX 607-722-6362. *3436*

GESELLSCHAFT FUER NIEDERSAECHSISCHE KIRCHENGESCHICHTE. JAHRBUCH.
Buchdruckerei Rihn, Industriestr. 16, 32819 Blomberg, Germany. *3569*

GESHER.
World Jewish Congress, P.O. Box 4293, Jerusalem 91042, Israel. TEL 972-2-635262. FAX 972-2-635544. *3013*

GHANA JOURNAL OF AGRICULTURAL SCIENCE.
National Science and Technology Press, P.O. Box M.32, Accra, Ghana. *120*

GHANA JOURNAL OF SCIENCE.
National Science and Technology Press, Box M. 32, Accra, Ghana. TEL 233-21-777651. FAX 223-21-777355. *6528*

GIFTED CHILD QUARTERLY.
National Association for Gifted Children, 1707 L St., N.W., Ste. 550, Washington, DC 20036-4201. TEL 202-785-4268. *1846*

GIFU PREFECTURAL FISHERIES EXPERIMENTAL STATION. REPORT.
Gifu Prefectural Fisheries Experimental Station, 2605, Hane, Hagiwara-cho, Mashita-gun, Gifu 509-25, Japan. TEL 0576-52-3111. FAX 0576-52-4354. *3068*

GIFUKEN SHOKUBUTSU KENKYUKAISHI.
Gifuken Shokubutsu Kenkyukai, Gifu Daigaku Kyoikugakubu, Seibutsugaku Kyoshitsu Shokubutsu, Bunrui Kenkyushitsu, Yanagido, Gifu-shi, Gifu-ken 501-11, Japan. TEL 058-293-2258. FAX 058-293-2207. *706*

GIGAJOULE.
Sasol Heating Fuels, P.O. Box 4211, Randburg 2125, South Africa. TEL 27-11-889-7600. *2670*

GINECOLOGIA CLINICA E ONCOLOGICA.
Tipografia Editrice La Garangola, Via Montona 6, 35137 Padua, Italy. TEL 39-49-8750550. FAX 39-49-8751743. *4957*

GIORNALE ITALIANO DI CHIRURGIA VASCOLARE.
Edizioni Minerva Medica, Corso Bramante 83-85, 10126 Turin, Italy. TEL 011-678282. FAX 39-11-674502. *5142*

GISTER EN VANDAG.
South African Society for History Teaching, c/o P.H. Kapp, Ed., P.O. Box 6341, Uniedal 7612, South Africa. TEL 27-21-8082186. FAX 27-21-8084336. *3495*

GLACIAL GEOLOGY AND GEOMORPHOLOGY.
John Wiley & Sons Ltd., Journals, Baffins Ln., Chichester, W. Sussex PO19 1UD, England. TEL 44-1243-779777. FAX 44-1243-843232. *2315*

GLACIOLOGY AND QUATERNARY GEOLOGY.
Kluwer Academic Publishers, Postbus 17, 3300 AA Dordrecht, Netherlands. TEL 31-78-6392392. FAX 31-78-6392254. *2348*

GLAD TIDINGS.
Women's Missionary Society, 50 Wynford Dr., North York, ON M3C 1J7, Canada. TEL 416-441-1111. FAX 416-441-2825. *6426*

GLASGOW INTRODUCTORY GUIDES TO FRENCH LITERATURE.
University of Glasgow, French and German Publications, Modern Languages Bldg., Glasgow G12 8QL, Scotland. TEL 44-141-330-4599. FAX 44-141-330-4234. *4410*

GLASGOW NATURALIST.
Glasgow Natural History Society, c/o Dr. J.R. Downie, Ed., Graham Kerr (Zoology) Bldg., University of Glasgow, Glasgow G12 8QQ, Scotland. TEL 44-141-330-5157. FAX 44-141-330-5971. *603*

GLASRA.
National Botanic Gardens, Glasnevin, Dublin 9, Ireland. TEL 353-1-8374388. FAX 353-1-8360080. *706*

GLASS AND CERAMICS.
Plenum Publishing Corp., Consultants Bureau, 233 Spring St., New York, NY 10013-1578. TEL 212-620-8468. FAX 212-463-0742. *1729*

GLASS PHYSICS AND CHEMISTRY.
Maik Nauka - Interperiodica, Mezhdunarodnyi Otdel, Ul. Profsoyuznaya, 90, 117864 Moscow, Russia. TEL 7-095-3360066. FAX 7-095-3360666. *1730*

GLASS SCIENCE AND TECHNOLOGY.
Deutsche Glastechnische Gesellschaft e.V., Mendelssohnstr. 75-77, 60325 Frankfurt a.M., Germany. TEL 49-69-975861-0. FAX 49-69-97586199. *1730*

GLASS SCIENCE AND TECHNOLOGY.
Elsevier Science B.V., Books Division, P.O. Box 211, 1000 AE Amsterdam, Netherlands. TEL 31-20-4853911. FAX 31-20-4853705. *1730*

GLEAMS.
Glaucoma Research Foundation, 490 Post, Ste. 830, San Francisco, CA 94102. TEL 415-986-3162. FAX 415-986-3763. *4993*

GLIA.
John Wiley & Sons, Inc., Journals, 605 Third Ave., New York, NY 10158. TEL 212-850-6645. FAX 212-850-6021. *5066*

GLOBAL AND PLANETARY CHANGE.
Elsevier Science B.V., P.O. Box 211, 1000 AE Amsterdam, Netherlands. TEL 31-20-4853911. FAX 31-20-4853598. *2349*

GLOBAL ATMOSPHERE AND OCEAN SYSTEM.
Gordon and Breach - Harwood Academic, Amsteldisk 166, 1st Fl., 1079 LH Amsterdam, Netherlands. *2403*

GLOBAL BIOGEOCHEMICAL CYCLES.
American Geophysical Union, 2000 Florida Ave., N.W., Washington, DC 20009. TEL 202-462-6900. FAX 202-328-0566. *6528*

GLOBAL BUSINESS AND FINANCE REVIEW.
Indiana State University, School of Business, Terre Haute, IN 47809. TEL 912-237-2117. FAX 812-237-8563. *1327*

GLOBAL CHANGE BIOLOGY.
Blackwell Science Ltd., Osney Mead, Oxford OX2 0EL, England. TEL 44-1865-206206. FAX 44-1865-721205. *603*

GLOBAL CHURCH GROWTH.
Church Growth Center, 1230 US Hwy. 6, Box 145, Corunna, IN 46730. TEL 219-281-2452. FAX 219-281-2167. *6491*

GLOBAL GOVERNANCE.
Lynne Rienner Publishers, 1800 30th St., Ste. 314, Boulder, CO 80301. TEL 303-444-6684. FAX 303-444-0824. *6016*

GLOBAL REAL ESTATE NEWS.
International Real Estate Institute, 8383 E. Evans Rd., Scottsdale, AZ 85260. TEL 602-998-8267. FAX 602-998-8022. *6301*

GLOBAL RISK ASSESSMENTS.
Global Risk Assessments, Inc., 3638 University Ave., Ste. 215, Riverside, CA 92501. TEL 909-788-0672. FAX 909-788-0672. *1328*

GLOBULUS.
Polygon Verlag, Am Aschweg 57, 85114 Buxheim, Germany. TEL 49-8458-8281. FAX 49-8458-4746. *6528*

GLOS NALECZOWA.
Towarzystwo Przyjaciol Naleczowa, Palac Malachowskich, Muzeum Boleslawa Prusa, Poland. TEL 48-71-114552. *4336*

GLYCOCONJUGATE JOURNAL.
Chapman & Hall, Journals Department 2-6 Boundary Row, London SE1 8HN, England. TEL 44-171-8650066. FAX 44-171-5229623. *660*

GNOSIS.
Concordia University, Philosophy Department, 1455 de Maisonneuve Blvd. W., Montreal, PQ H3G 1M8, Canada. TEL 514-848-2500. *5728*

GO.
Interserve, 325 Kennington Rd., London SE11 4QH, England. TEL 44-171-735-8227. FAX 44-171-587-5362. *6426*

GOLD COAST NEWS.
Charles Hesser & Co., Box 3637, Miami Beach, FL 33140. TEL 305-674-9746. FAX 305-674-1939. *3374*

GOLDEN ROOTS OF THE MOTHER LODE.
Tuolumne County Genealogical Society, Box 3956, Sonora, CA 95370. TEL 209-532-1317. *3225*

GOLF NEWS.
Golf News, s.r.l., Via Scarlatti, 30, 20124 Milan, Italy. TEL 39-2-6692299. FAX 39-2-6692306. *6807*

GONGCHENG RE-WULI XUEBAO.
Science Press, Marketing and Sales Department, 16 Donghuangchenggen North St., Beijing 100717, People's Republic of China. TEL 4010642. FAX 4012180. *5840*

GONGNENG GAOFENZI XUEBAO.
Gongneng Gaofenzi Xuebao Bianjibu, 130 Meilong Rd., Shanghai 200237, People's Republic of China. TEL 86-21-6413-2666. FAX 86-21-6477-7138. *2764*

GONGYE JIANZHU.
Yejin-bu, Jianzhu Yanjiu Zongyuan, 33 Xitucheng Lu, Haidian-qu, Beijing 100088, People's Republic of China. TEL 86-10-6222-5599. FAX 86-10-6222-5938. *895*

GOOD CLINICAL PRACTICE JOURNAL.
Brookwood Medical Publications, Orchard House, Brookwood, Surrey GU24 0AT, England. TEL 44-1483-797975. FAX 44-1483-797915. *4672*

GOOD TIDINGS.
Good Tidings Press, P.O. Box 8895, Sta. A, 57 Thorburn Rd., St. John's, NF A1B 3T2, Canada. TEL 709-753-6314. FAX 709-753-4945. *6341*

GORTANIA.
Comune di Udine, Museo Friulano di Storia Naturale, Via Grazzano 1, 33100 Udine, Italy. TEL 39-432-510221. FAX 39-432-271578. *2316*

THE GOSPEL HERALD AND SUNDAY SCHOOL TIMES.
Union Gospel Press, Box 6059, Cleveland, OH 44101. TEL 216-749-2100. FAX 216-459-1337. *6341*

GOVERNMENT ACCOUNTANTS JOURNAL.
Association of Government Accountants, 2200 Mount Vernon Ave., Alexandria, VA 22301-1314. TEL 703-684-6931. FAX 703-548-9367. *1090*

GOVERNMENT AND OPPOSITION.
London School of Economics and Political Science, Houghton St., London WC2, England. TEL 44-171-405-5991. FAX 44-171-405-5991. *5929*

GOVERNMENT INFORMATION QUARTERLY.
J A I Press Inc., 55 Old Post Rd., No. 2, Box 1678, Greenwich, CT 06830-1678. TEL 203-661-7602. FAX 203-661-0792. *4180*

GRACE AND TRUTH.
St. Joseph's Theological Institute, Private Bag 6004, Hilton 3245, South Africa. TEL 27-331-433293. FAX 27-331-431232. *6464*

GRADIVA.
c/o S. Morandina, Man. Ed., Department of French and Italian, State University of New York at Stony Brook, Stony Brook, NY 11794-3359. TEL 516-632-7448. FAX 516-632-9612. *4410*

GRADUATE WOMEN.
Australian Federation of University Women, A.F.U.W. Federal Council, Dymocks Bldg., 428 George St., Sydney, N.S.W. 2000, Australia. TEL 61-2-2351335. FAX 61-2-2351335. *7321*

GRAELLSIA.
Museo Nacional de Ciencias Naturales, Jose Gutierrez Abascal 2, 28006 Madrid, Spain. TEL 34-1-4111328. FAX 34-1-5645078. *835*

GRAIL: AN ECUMENICAL JOURNAL.
Novalis, St. Paul University, 223 Main St., Ottawa, ON K1S 1C4, Canada. TEL 613-236-1393. FAX 613-782-3004. *6341*

GRAND TIMES.
Grand Times Publishing, Inc., 403 Village Dr., El Cerrito, CA 94530-3355. TEL 510-527-4337. *3437*

GRANTHALAYA VIJNANA.
P. Kaula Endowment for Library and Information Science, C-239 Indira Nagar, Lucknow 226 016, India. *4180*

GRAPHICS INTERFACE. PROCEEDINGS - COMPTES RENDUS.
Canadian Information Processing Society, 430 King St., W., Ste. 106, Toronto, ON M5V 1L5, Canada. TEL 416-593-4040. FAX 416-593-5184. *2133*

GRASS AND FORAGE SCIENCE.
Blackwell Science Ltd., Osney Mead, Oxford OX2 0EL, England. TEL 44-1865-206206. FAX 44-1865-721205. *121*

GRASSLANDS REVIEW.
Box 626, Berea, OH 44017. *4410*

GRAVESIANA.
Nene College, Department of English, Northampton, England. TEL 44-1869-242341. FAX 44-1604-791114. *4411*

THE GREAT CIRCLE.
Australian Association for Maritime History, c/o G.R. Henning, Ed., Dept. of Economic History, University of New England, Armidale, N.S.W. 2351, Australia. TEL 61-67-732702. FAX 61-67-73-3596. *3495*

GREAT LAKES ENTOMOLOGIST.
Michigan Entomological Society, c/o Dept. of Entomology, Michigan State Univ., East Lansing, MI 48824. TEL 517-321-2192. *753*

GREAT LAKES FISHERY COMMISSION. SPECIAL PUBLICATION.
Great Lakes Fishery Commission, 2100 Commonwealth Blvd., Ste. 209, Ann Arbor, MI 48105-1563. TEL 313-662-3209. FAX 313-741-2010. *3069*

GREAT LAKES FISHERY COMMISSION (UNITED STATES AND CANADA) TECHNICAL REPORT SERIES.
Great Lakes Fishery Commission, 2100 Commonwealth Blvd., Ste. 209, Ann Arbor, MI 48105-1563. TEL 313-662-3209. FAX 313-741-2010. *3069*

GREAT LAKES GEOGRAPHER.
University of Western Ontario, Department of Geography, London, ON N6A 3K7, Canada. TEL 519-661-3423. FAX 519-661-3750. *3408*

GREAT PLAINS QUARTERLY.
University of Nebraska at Lincoln, Center for Great Plains Studies, 1214 Oldfather Hall, Lincoln, NE 68588-0313. TEL 402-472-6058. FAX 402-472-0463. *3628*

GREATER HOUSTON DENTAL SOCIETY. JOURNAL.
Greater Houston Dental Society, One Greenway Plaza, Ste. 110, Houston, TX 77046. TEL 713-961-4337. FAX 713-961-3617. *4858*

GREEK ORTHODOX THEOLOGICAL REVIEW.
Holy Cross Orthodox Press, 50 Goddard Ave., Brookline, MA 02146. TEL 617-731-3500. FAX 617-566-9075. *6391*

GREENER MANAGEMENT INTERNATIONAL.
Greenleaf Publishing, 8-10 Broomhall Rd., Sheffield S10 2DR, England. TEL 44-114-266-3789. FAX 44-114-267-9403. *2931*

GREENPEACE QUARTERLY.
Greenpeace, National Office, 1436 U St., N.W., Washington, DC 20009. TEL 202-462-1177. FAX 202-462-4507. *2231*

GREGORIOS O PALAMAS.
Metropolis Thessalonikes, P.O. Box 10335, Thessaloniki, Greece. FAX 30-31-230-722. *3569*

GRIFFITHIANA.
Cineteca del Friuli, Via Osoppo 26, 33014 Gemona, Italy. TEL 39-432-980458. FAX 39-432-970542. *5335*

GRIST ON-LINE.
17 W. 64th St. Apt. 2-E, New York, NY 10023-6710. TEL 212-787-2861. *4510*

GROSS REPORT.
John E. Gross, Ed. & Pub., 355 New York Ave., Huntington, NY 11743. TEL 516-271-9457. *1044*

GROUND WATER.
Ground Water Publishing Co., 601 Dempsey Rd., Westerville, OH 43081-8978. TEL 614-337-8229. *2393*

GROUND WATER MONITORING & REMEDIATION.
Ground Water Publishing Co., 601 Dempsey Rd., Westerville, OH 43081-8978. TEL 614-337-8229. *2393*

GROUP DECISION AND NEGOTIATION.
Kluwer Academic Publishers, Postbus 17, 3300 AA Dordrecht, Netherlands. TEL 31-78-6392392. FAX 31-78-6392254. *1479*

GROUPE D'ETUDE DES RYTHMES BIOLOGIQUES. BULLETIN.
Groupe d'Etude des Rythmes Biologiques, c/o Institut de Physiologie, Universite Louis Pasteur, 4 rue Kirschleger, 67085 Strasbourg Cedex, France. TEL 33-3-88358768. FAX 33-3-88243334. *603*

GROWTH AND CHANGE.
Blackwell Publishers, 238 Main St., Cambridge, MA 02141. TEL 617-547-7110. FAX 617-547-0789. *1585*

GROWTH, DEVELOPMENT & AGING.
Growth Publishing Co., Inc., Box 42, Bar Harbor, ME 04609-0042. TEL 207-288-3533. FAX 207-288-6079. *603*

GROWTH FACTORS.
Gordon and Breach - Harwood Academic, Amsteldisk 166, 1st Fl., 1079 LH Amsterdam, Netherlands. *816*

GROWTH REGULATION.
Churchill Livingstone, Robert Stevenson House, 1-3 Baxter's Pl., Leith Walk, Edinburgh EH1 3AF, Scotland. TEL 44-131-556-2424. FAX 44-131-535-1704. *4888*

GRUNDLAGENSTUDIEN AUS KYBERNETIK UND GEISTESWISSENSCHAFT.
Akademia Libroservo - IfK Paderborn, Kleinenberger Weg 16, 33100 Paderborn, Germany. TEL 49-5251-64200. FAX 49-5251-1633533. *2161*

GRUNDTVIG STUDIER.
Grundtvig-Selskabet af 8. September 1947, c/o Kirkeligt Samfund, Vartorv, Farvergade 27, DK-1463 Copenhagen K, Denmark. TEL 45-33-13-76-70. *6427*

GUANG TONGXIN JISHU.
Guilin Institute of Optical Communications, P.O. Box 5, Guilin, Guangxi 541004, People's Republic of China. TEL 0773-5813838. FAX 0773-5812724. *1991*

GUANGDIAN GONGCHENG.
Guangdian Gongcheng Bianjibu, P.O. Box 350 (29), Shuangliu, Chengdu, Sichuan 610209, People's Republic of China. TEL 86-28-5180032. FAX 86-28-582190. *2825*

GUANGDONG MINZU XUEYUAN XUEBAO.
Guangdong Minzu Xueyuan, Shipai, Guangzhou, Guangdong 510633, People's Republic of China. TEL 86-20-8551-5722. FAX 86-20-8551-5901. *6615*

GUANGPUXUE YU GUANGPU FENXI.
Beijing University Press, Haidian-qu, Beijing 100871, People's Republic of China. TEL 86-10-2182998. FAX 86-10-2181051. *5860*

GUELPH ALUMNUS.
University of Guelph, Communications and Public Affairs, Guelph, ON N1G 2W1, Canada. TEL 519-824-4120. FAX 519-824-7962. *1954*

GUIDANCE & COUNSELLING.
University of Toronto, Guidance Centre, 712 Gordon Baker Rd., Toronto, ON M2H 3R7, Canada. TEL 416-502-1262. FAX 416-502-1101. *2446*

GUIDE TO EATING ONTARIO SPORT FISH.
Ministry of Environment and Energy, Communications Branch, 125 Resources Rd., Etobicoke, ON M9P 3V6, Canada. TEL 416-235-6220. FAX 416-235-6235. *3069*

GUILD NEWS.
Graphic Artists Guild, 11 W. 20th St., 8th Fl., New York, NY 10011-3704. TEL 212-463-7730. FAX 212-463-8779. *444*

GUINEA PIG ZERO.
Box 42531, Philadelphia, PA 19101. *5664*

GUISUANYAN XUEBAO.
Chinese Ceramic Society, Guojia Jiancaiju Nei (Inside National Bureau of Bldg. Materials), Baiwanzhuang, Beijing 100831, People's Republic of China. TEL 861-8311144. FAX 861-8313364. *1807*

GUJIZHUI DONGWU XUEBAO.
Science Press, Marketing and Sales Department, 16 Donghuangchenggen North St., Beijing 100717, People's Republic of China. TEL 4010642. FAX 4019810. *5559*

GULDEN PASSER.
Vereeniging der Antwerpsche Bibliophielen, Museum Plantin-Moretus, Vrijdagmarkt 22-23, 2000 Antwerp, Belgium. TEL 32-3-2330294. FAX 32-3-2262516. *6272*

GULF OF MEXICO SCIENCE.
Dauphin Island Sea Lab, c/o Dauphin Island Sea Lab, Box 369-370, Dauphin Island, AL 36528. TEL 334-460-6351. FAX 334-460-7357. *2403*

GULF RESEARCH REPORTS.
Gulf Coast Research Laboratory, P.O. Box 7000, Ocean Springs, MS 39566-7000. TEL 601-872-4200. FAX 601-872-4204. *2403*

GULHANE ASKERI TIP AKADEMISI BULTEN.
Gulhane Askeri Tip Akademisi, 06018 Etlik - Ankara, Turkey. TEL 90-312-3231072. FAX 90-312-3234923. *4673*

GUNNERIA.
Norges Teknisk-Naturvitenskapelige Universitet, Vitenskapmuseet, N-7004 Trondheim, Norway. TEL 47-73-59-21-45. FAX 47-73-59-22-23. *364*

GUO MORUO XUEKAN.
Guo Moruo Xuekan Qikanshe, Dafo Si Nei, Leshan, Sichuan 614003, People's Republic of China. TEL 86-833-2139721. *574*

GUOJI GUANGBO DIANSHI JISHU.
Guangbo Yingshi Bu, Keji Xinxi Yanjiusuo, P.O. Box 2116, Beijing 100866, People's Republic of China. TEL 86-10-6092081. FAX 86-10-6092040. *1991*

GUOSHU KEXUE.
Zhongguo Nongye Kexueyuan, Zhengzhou Guoshu Yanjiusuo, Nanjiao, Zhengzhou, Henan 450004, People's Republic of China. TEL 86-371-633-5771. FAX 86-371-633-5740. *3192*

GUSHENGWU XUEBAO.
Science Press, Marketing and Sales Department, 16 Donghuangchenggen North St., Beijing 100717, People's Republic of China. TEL 4010642. FAX 4019810. *5559*

GUT.
B M J Publishing Group, B.M.A. House, Tavistock Sq., London WC1H 9JR, England. TEL 44-171-387-4499. FAX 44-171-383-6661. *4911*

GUTI DIANZIXUE YANJIU YU JINZHAN.
Nanjing Dianzi Qijian Yanjiusuo, 524 Zhongshan Donglu, P.O. Box 1601, Nanjing, Jiangsu 210016, People's Republic of China. TEL 86-25-4611855. FAX 86-25-4617126. *2638*

GYNAECOLOGICAL ENDOSCOPY.
Blackwell Science Ltd., Osney Mead, Oxford OX2 0EL, England. TEL 44-1865-206206. FAX 44-1865-721205. *4958*

GYNAEKOLOGISCH - GEBURTSHILFLICHE RUNDSCHAU.
S. Karger AG, Allschwilerstr. 10, P.O. Box, CH-4009 Basel, Switzerland. TEL 41-61-3061111. FAX 41-61-3061234. *4958*

GYNECOLOGIC AND OBSTETRIC INVESTIGATION.
S. Karger AG, Allschwilerstr. 10, P.O. Box, CH-4009 Basel, Switzerland. TEL 41-61-3061111. FAX 41-61-3061234. *4958*

GYNECOLOGIC ENDOSCOPY.
Elsevier Science B.V., Books Division, P.O. Box 211, 1000 AE Amsterdam, Netherlands. TEL 31-20-4853911. FAX 31-20-4853705. *4958*

GYNECOLOGIC ONCOLOGY.
Academic Press, Inc., Journal Division, 525 B St., Ste. 1900, San Diego, CA 92101-4495. TEL 619-230-1840. FAX 619-699-6800. *4958*

GYNECOLOGICAL ENDOCRINOLOGY.
Parthenon Publishing Group, Casterton Hall, Carnforth, Lancs. LA6 2LA, England. TEL 44-152-427-2084. FAX 44-152-427-1587. *4888*

GYNECOLOGIE INTERNATIONALE.
Presence et Communication Medicales, 11 rue de Rome, 75008 Paris, France. TEL 44-70-75-00. FAX 44-70-75-09. *4959*

GYOBYO KENKYU.
Japanese Society of Fish Pathology, c/o Dept. of Fisheries, Faculty of Agriculture, University of Tokyo, Yayoi 1-1-1, Bunkyo-ku, Tokyo 113, Japan. TEL 81-3-3812-2111. FAX 81-3-3813-2776. *835*

GYPSY LORE SOCIETY. JOURNAL.
Gypsy Lore Society, 5607 Greenleaf Rd., Cheverly, MD 20785. TEL 301-341-1261. FAX 301-341-1261. *317*

H A L - P C USER JOURNAL.
Houston Area League of P C Users, Inc., 2200 Post Oak Blvd., Ste. 512, Houston, TX 77056-4706. TEL 713-963-4155. FAX 713-623-4251. *2196*

H C I LETTERS.
Springer-Verlag London Ltd., Sweetapple House, Cattashall Rd., Godalming, Surrey GU7 3DJ, England. TEL 44-1483-418822. FAX 44-1483-415151. *2082*

H E C FORUM.
Kluwer Academic Publishers, Postbus 17, 3300 AA Dordrecht, Netherlands. TEL 31-78-6392392. FAX 31-78-6392254. *3708*

H L Q THREE RIVERS RESOURCE GUIDE FOR HOLISTIC LIVING.
H L Q Associates, Box 86054, Pittsburgh, PA 15221-0054. TEL 412-242-9355. *296*

H M O PRACTICE.
H M O Group, 900 Guaranty Bldg., Buffalo, NY 14202. TEL 716-857-6361. FAX 716-847-0047. *4673*

H P B SURGERY.
Gordon and Breach - Harwood Academic, Amsteldisk 166, 1st Fl., 1079 LH Amsterdam, Netherlands. *5143*

HABERSHAM REVIEW.
Piedmont College, Box 10, Demorest, GA 30535. TEL 706-778-3000. FAX 706-776-2811. *4412*

HABITAT INTERNATIONAL.
Elsevier Science Ltd., Pergamon, P.O. Box 800, Kidlington, Oxford OX5 1DX, England. TEL 44-1865-843000. FAX 44-1865-843010. *2931*

HACETTEPE BULLETIN OF NATURAL SCIENCES AND ENGINEERING.
Hacettepe Universitesi, Fen Fakultesi, 06532 Beytepe, Ankara, Turkey. FAX 90-4-2352531. *6529*

HACETTEPE DIS HEKIMLIGI FAKULTESI DERGISI.
Hacettepe Universitesi, Dis Hekimligi Fakultesi, Yayin Kurulu Sekreterligi, 06100 Sihhiye - Ankara, Turkey. TEL 90-312-3116461. FAX 90-312-3091138. *4858*

HACETTEPE FEN VE MUHENDISLIK BILIMLERI DERGISI. SERI A: BIYOLOJI.
Hacettepe Universitesi, Fen Fakultesi, 06532 Beytepe, Ankara, Turkey. FAX 90-312-2352531. *603*

HAEMATOLOGIA.
V S P, P.O. Box 346, 3700 AH Zeist, Netherlands. TEL 31-30-6925790. FAX 31-30-6932081. *4918*

HAEMOPHILIA.
Blackwell Science Ltd., Osney Mead, Oxford OX2 OEL, England. TEL 44-1865-206206. FAX 44-1865-721205. *4919*

HAEMOSTASIS.
S. Karger AG, Allschwilerstr. 10, P.O. Box, CH-4009 Basel, Switzerland. TEL 41-61-3061111. FAX 41-61-3061234. *4919*

HAGIOGRAPHICA.
N.V. Brepols, Steenweg op Tielen 68, 2300 Turnhout, Belgium. TEL 32-14-402500. FAX 32-14-428919. *6464*

HAGUE YEARBOOK OF INTERNATIONAL LAW.
Kluwer Academic Publishers, Postbus 17, 3300 AA Dordrecht, Netherlands. TEL 31-78-6392392. FAX 31-78-6392254. *4114*

HAGUE-ZAGREB ESSAYS.
Kluwer Academic Publishers, Postbus 17, 3300 AA Dordrecht, Netherlands. TEL 31-78-6392392. FAX 31-78-6392254. *4114*

HAIKIBUTSU GAKKAISHI.
Japan Society of Waste Management Experts, 2F 13-11 Shiba 5-chome, Minato-ku, Tokyo 108, Japan. TEL 81-3-3769-5099. FAX 81-3-3769-1492. *2985*

HAIYANG XUEBAO.
China Ocean Press, International Cooperation Department, Haimao Dalou, 1 Fuxingmenwai Dajie, Beijing 100860, People's Republic of China. TEL 8032211. FAX 8033515. *2404*

HAIYANG YU HUZHAO.
Science Press, Marketing and Sales Department, 16 Donghuangchenggen Beijie, Beijing 100707, People's Republic of China. TEL 4010642. FAX 4019810. *2404*

HALCYON.
Nevada Humanities Committee, Box 8029, Reno, NV 89507. TEL 702-784-6755. FAX 702-784-6266. *3779*

HALKBILIMI.
Has Der Folk Arts Association, P.O. Box 199, Lefkosa - Kibris, Mersin 10, Turkey. TEL 90-392-2283146. FAX 90-392-2284125. *3087*

HAMBURGISCHES ZOOLOGISCHES MUSEUM UND INSTITUT. MITTEILUNGEN.
Universitaet Hamburg, Zoologisches Institut, Martin-Luther-King-Platz 3, 20146 Hamburg, Germany. TEL 49-4123-3960. FAX 49-4123-3937. *835*

HAMLET STUDIES.
R.W. Desai Publishing Company Ltd., Rangoon Villa, 1-10 W. Patel Nagar, New Delhi 110 008, India. TEL 91-11-574-7399. *4412*

HAMPSHIRE STUDIES (YEAR).
Hampshire Field Club, c/o A.C. King, King Alfred's College, Winchester SO22 4NR, England. TEL 44-1962-841515. *365*

HANDAI KAGAKU NETSUGAKU REPOTO.
Osaka Daigaku, Rigakubu, 1-1, Machikaneyamacho, Toyonaka-shi, Osaka 560, Japan. TEL 81-6-850-5523. FAX 81-6-850-5526. *1829*

HANDBOOK OF ANXIETY.
Elsevier Science B.V., Books Division, P.O. Box 211, 1000 AE Amsterdam, Netherlands. TEL 31-20-4853911. FAX 31-20-4853705. *6114*

HANDBOOK OF AROMA RESEARCH.
Kluwer Academic Publishers, Postbus 17, 3300 AA Dordrecht, Netherlands. TEL 31-78-6392392. FAX 31-78-6392254. *3111*

HANDBOOK OF BEHAVIORAL NEUROBIOLOGY.
Plenum Publishing Corp., 233 Spring St., New York, NY 10013-1578. TEL 212-620-8000. FAX 212-463-0742. *5067*

HANDBOOK OF CHEMICAL NEUROANATOMY.
Elsevier Science B.V., Books Division, P.O. Box 211, 1000 AE Amsterdam, Netherlands. TEL 31-20-4853911. FAX 31-20-4853705. *5067*

HANDBOOK OF CLINICAL NEUROLOGY.
Elsevier Science B.V., Books Division, P.O. Box 211, 1000 AE Amsterdam, Netherlands. TEL 31-20-4853911. FAX 31-20-4853705. *5067*

HANDBOOK OF COMPOSITES.
Elsevier Science B.V., Books Division, P.O. Box 211, 1000 AE Amsterdam, Netherlands. TEL 31-20-4853911. FAX 31-20-4853705. *1829*

HANDBOOK OF ELECTROENCEPHALOGRAPHY AND CLINICAL NEUROPHYSIOLOGY.
Elsevier Science B.V., Books Division, P.O. Box 211, 1000 AE Amsterdam, Netherlands. TEL 31-20-4853911. FAX 31-20-4853705. *5067*

HANDBOOK OF ENDOTOXIN.
Elsevier Science B.V., Books Division, P.O. Box 211, 1000 AE Amsterdam, Netherlands. TEL 31-20-4853911. FAX 31-20-4853705. *5664*

HANDBOOK OF ENVIRONMENTAL ISOTOPE GEOCHEMISTRY.
Elsevier Science B.V., Books Division, P.O. Box 211, 1000 AE Amsterdam, Netherlands. TEL 31-20-4853911. FAX 31-20-4853705. *2316*

HANDBOOK OF EXPLORATION GEOCHEMISTRY.
Elsevier Science B.V., Books Division, P.O. Box 211, 1000 AE Amsterdam, Netherlands. TEL 31-20-4853911. FAX 31-20-4853705. *2350*

HANDBOOK OF HYPERTENSION.
Elsevier Science B.V., Regional Sales Office, P.O. Box 211, 1000 AE Amsterdam, Netherlands. TEL 31-20-4853757. FAX 31-20-4853432. *4674*

HANDBOOK OF INFLAMMATION.
Elsevier Science B.V., Books Division, P.O. Box 211, 1000 AE Amsterdam, Netherlands. TEL 31-20-4853911. FAX 31-20-4853705. *4674*

HANDBOOK OF LIPID RESEARCH.
Plenum Publishing Corp., 233 Spring St., New York, NY 10013-1578. TEL 212-620-8000. FAX 212-463-0742. *1816*

HANDBOOK OF NATURAL PRODUCTS DATA.
Elsevier Science B.V., Books Division, P.O. Box 211, 1000 AE Amsterdam, Netherlands. TEL 31-20-4853911. FAX 31-20-4853705. *1750*

HANDBOOK OF NATURAL TOXINS.
Marcel Dekker, Inc., 270 Madison Ave., New York, NY 10016. TEL 212-696-9000. FAX 212-685-4540. *4674*

HANDBOOK OF NEUROPSYCHOLOGY.
Elsevier Science B.V., Books Division, P.O. Box 211, 1000 AE Amsterdam, Netherlands. TEL 31-20-4853911. FAX 31-20-4853705. *5067*

HANDBOOK OF NUMERICAL ANALYSIS.
Elsevier Science B.V., Books Division, P.O. Box 211, 1000 AE Amsterdam, Netherlands. TEL 31-20-4853911. FAX 31-20-4853705. *4575*

HANDBOOK OF PAPER SCIENCE.
Elsevier Science B.V., Books Division, P.O. Box 211, 1000 AE Amsterdam, Netherlands. TEL 31-20-4853911. FAX 31-20-4853705. *5567*

HANDBOOK OF PHYSIOLOGY.
American Physiological Society, 9650 Rockville Pike, Bethesda, MD 20814. TEL 301-530-7164. FAX 301-571-8313. *816*

HANDBOOK OF PLASMA PHYSICS.
Elsevier Science B.V., Books Division, P.O. Box 211, 1000 AE Amsterdam, Netherlands. TEL 31-20-4853911. FAX 31-20-4853705. *5804*

HANDBOOK OF POWDER TECHNOLOGY.
Elsevier Science B.V., Books Division, P.O. Box 211, 1000 AE Amsterdam, Netherlands. TEL 31-20-4853911. FAX 31-20-4853705. *2786*

HANDBOOK OF PSYCHOLOGY AND HEALTH SERIES.
Lawrence Erlbaum Associates, Inc., 10 Industrial Dr., Mahwah, NJ 07430-2262. TEL 201-236-9500. FAX 201-236-0072. *6114*

HANDBOOK OF SCHIZOPHRENIA.
Elsevier Science B.V., Books Division, P.O. Box 211, 1000 AE Amsterdam, Netherlands. TEL 31-20-4853911. FAX 31-20-4853705. *5067*

HANDBOOK OF SEMICONDUCTORS.
Elsevier Science B.V., Books Division, P.O. Box 211, 1000 AE Amsterdam, Netherlands. TEL 31-20-4853911. FAX 31-20-4853705. *2638*

HANDBOOK OF SOIL MECHANICS.
Elsevier Science B.V., Books Division, P.O. Box 211, 1000 AE Amsterdam, Netherlands. TEL 31-20-4853911. FAX 31-20-4853705. *2316*

HANDBOOK OF STRATA-BOUND AND STRATIFORM ORE DEPOSITS.
Elsevier Science B.V., Books Division, P.O. Box 211, 1000 AE Amsterdam, Netherlands. TEL 31-20-4853911. FAX 31-20-4853705. *2350*

HANDBOOK OF THE SPINAL CORD.
Marcel Dekker, Inc., 270 Madison Ave., New York, NY 10016. TEL 212-696-9000. FAX 212-685-4540. *4674*

HANDBOOK ON FERROMAGNETIC MATERIALS.
Elsevier Science B.V., Books Division, P.O. Box 211, 1000 AE Amsterdam, Netherlands. TEL 31-20-4853911. FAX 31-20-4853705. *5193*

HANDBOOK ON SYNCHROTRON RADIATION.
Elsevier Science B.V., Books Division, P.O. Box 211, 1000 AE Amsterdam, Netherlands. TEL 31-20-4853911. FAX 31-20-4853705. *3801*

HANDBOOK ON THE PHYSICS AND CHEMISTRY OF RARE EARTHS.
Elsevier Science B.V., Books Division, P.O. Box 211, 1000 AE Amsterdam, Netherlands. TEL 31-20-4853911. FAX 31-20-4853705. *5805*

HANDBOOK ON THE PHYSICS AND CHEMISTRY OF THE ACTINIDES.
Elsevier Science B.V., Books Division, P.O. Box 211, 1000 AE Amsterdam, Netherlands. TEL 31-20-4853911. FAX 31-20-4853705. *5805*

HANDBOOKS IN ECONOMICS.
Elsevier Science B.V., Books Division, P.O. Box 211, 1000 AE Amsterdam, Netherlands. TEL 31-20-4853911. FAX 31-20-4853705. *1304*

HANDBOOKS IN OPERATIONS RESEARCH AND MANAGEMENT SCIENCE.
Elsevier Science B.V., Books Division, P.O. Box 211, 1000 AE Amsterdam, Netherlands. TEL 31-20-4853911. FAX 31-20-4853705. *2082*

HANDBUCH DER ORIENTALISTIK.
E.J. Brill, P.O. Box 9000, 2300 PA Leiden, Netherlands. TEL 31-71-5353500. FAX 31-71-5317532. *5527*

HANDBUCH DER ORIENTALISTIK. 1. ABTEILUNG. DER NAHE UND DER MITTLERE OSTEN.
E.J. Brill, P.O. Box 9000, 2300 PA Leiden, Netherlands. TEL 31-71-5353500. FAX 31-71-5317532. *5527*

HANDBUCH DER ORIENTALISTIK. 2. ABTEILUNG. INDIEN.
E.J. Brill, P.O. Box 9000, 2300 PA Leiden, Netherlands. TEL 31-71-5353500. FAX 31-71-5317532. *5527*

HANDBUCH DER ORIENTALISTIK. 3. ABTEILUNG. INDONESIEN, MALAYSIA UND DIE PHILIPPINEN.
E.J. Brill, P.O. Box 9000, 2300 PA Leiden, Netherlands. TEL 31-71-5353500. FAX 31-71-5317532. *5527*

HANDBUCH DER ORIENTALISTIK. 4. ABTEILUNG. CHINA.
E.J. Brill, P.O. Box 9000, 2300 PA Leiden, Netherlands. TEL 31-71-5353500. FAX 31-71-5317532. *5527*

HANDBUCH DER ORIENTALISTIK. 5. ABTEILUNG. JAPAN.
E.J. Brill, P.O. Box 9000, 2300 PA Leiden, Netherlands. TEL 31-71-5353500. FAX 31-71-5317532. *5528*

HANDBUCH DER ORIENTALISTIK. 8. ABTEILUNG. HANDBOOK OF URALIC STUDIES.
E.J. Brill, P.O. Box 9000, 2300 PA Leiden, Netherlands. TEL 31-71-5353500. FAX 31-71-5317532. *5528*

HANDS ON LANGUAGE.
Pacific Northwest Council for Languages, c/o Foreign Languages & Literatures, Oregon State Univ., 210 Kidder Hall, Corvallis, OR 97331-4603. TEL 541-737-3945. FAX 541-737-3563. *2447*

HARE KRISHNA WORLD.
International Society for Krishna Consciousness, Box 238, Alachua, FL 32616. TEL 904-462-5054. FAX 904-462-5056. *6491*

HARROWSMITH COUNTRY LIFE.
Malcolm Publishing, 11450 Blvd. Albert Houdon, Montreal North, PQ, H1G 3J9, Canada. TEL 514-327-4464. FAX 514-327-7592. *3192*

HART BULLETIN.
Misset, P.O. Box 1110, 3600 BC Maarssen, Netherlands. TEL 31-346-558222. FAX 31-346-554287. *4816*

HARVARD AIDS INSTITUTE SERIES ON GENE REGULATION OF HUMAN RETROVIRUSES.
Lippincott - Raven Publishers, 227 E. Washington Sq., Philadelphia, PA 19106. TEL 215-238-4200. FAX 215-238-4227. *770*

HARVARD ARMENIAN TEXTS AND STUDIES.
Harvard University Press, 79 Garden St., Cambridge, MA 02138. TEL 617-495-2600. FAX 617-495-5898. *3655*

HARVARD BOOKS IN BIOPHYSICS.
Harvard University Press, 79 Garden St., Cambridge, MA 02138. TEL 617-495-2600. FAX 617-495-5898. *675*

HARVARD EAST ASIAN SERIES.
Harvard University Press, 79 Garden St., Cambridge, MA 02138. TEL 617-495-2600. FAX 617-495-5898. *3533*

HARVARD ECONOMIC STUDIES.
Harvard University Press, 79 Garden St., Cambridge, MA 02138. TEL 617-495-2600. FAX 617-495-5898. *968*

HARVARD HISTORICAL MONOGRAPHS.
Harvard University Press, 79 Garden St., Cambridge, MA 02138. TEL 617-495-2600. FAX 617-495-5898. *3496*

HARVARD HISTORICAL STUDIES.
Harvard University Press, 79 Garden St., Cambridge, MA 02138. TEL 617-495-2600. FAX 617-495-5898. *3496*

THE HARVARD JOURNAL OF WORLD AFFAIRS.
Harvard University, John F. Kennedy School of Government, 273 Taubman Bldg., 79 John F. Kennedy St., Cambridge, MA 02138. TEL 617-496-0517. FAX 617-496-9027. *6017*

HARVARD LAW RECORD.
Harvard Law Record Corporation, Harvard Law School, Cambridge, MA 02138. TEL 617-495-4418. FAX 617-495-8457. *3958*

HARVARD PAPERS IN BOTANY.
Harvard University Herbaria, 22 Divinity Ave., Cambridge, MA 02138. TEL 617-495-2360. FAX 617-495-9484. *707*

HARVARD PUBLICATIONS IN MUSIC.
Harvard University, Department of Music, Music Bldg. G6, Cambridge, MA 02138. TEL 617-495-2791. FAX 617-496-8081. *5397*

HARVARD REVIEW OF PSYCHIATRY.
Mosby, Journal Subscription Services 11830 Westline Industrial Dr., St. Louis, MO 63146-3318. TEL 314-453-4351. FAX 314-432-1158. *5067*

HARVARD STUDIES IN BUSINESS HISTORY.
Harvard University Press, 79 Garden St., Cambridge, MA 02138. TEL 617-495-2600. FAX 617-495-5898. *1304*

HARVARD STUDIES IN CLASSICAL PHILOLOGY.
Harvard University, Department of the Classics, Boylston 320, Cambridge, MA 02138. TEL 617-496-6720. FAX 617-495-4027. *4261*

HARVARD STUDIES IN COMPARATIVE LITERATURE.
Harvard University Press, 79 Garden St., Cambridge, MA 02138. TEL 617-495-2600. FAX 617-495-5898. *4412*

HARVARD STUDIES IN URBAN HISTORY.
Harvard University Press, 79 Garden St., Cambridge, MA 02138. TEL 617-495-2600. FAX 617-495-5898. *3748*

HARVARD UKRAINIAN STUDIES.
Harvard University, Ukrainian Research Institute, 1583 Massachusetts Ave., Cambridge, MA 02138. TEL 617-495-4243. FAX 617-495-8097. *3570*

HARVARD UNIVERSITY. RUSSIAN RESEARCH CENTER. STUDIES.
Harvard University Press, 79 Garden St., Cambridge, MA 02138. TEL 617-495-2600. FAX 617-495-5898. *3570*

HARVARD - YENCHING INSTITUTE. STUDIES.
Harvard University Press, 79 Garden St., Cambridge, MA 02138. TEL 617-495-2600. FAX 617-495-5898. *3534*

DER HAUTARZT.
Springer-Verlag, Heidelberger Platz 3, 14197 Berlin, Germany. TEL 49-30-82787-0. FAX 49-30-82787448. *4878*

HAVSFISKELABORATORIET. MEDDELANDE.
National Board of Fisheries, Institute of Marine Research, Box 4, 453 21 Lysekil, Sweden. TEL 46-523-18700. FAX 46-523-13977. *3069*

HAWAII INSTITUTE OF MARINE BIOLOGY. TECHNICAL REPORTS.
Hawaii Institute of Marine Biology, Box 1346, Kaneohe, HI 96744. TEL 808-237-7401. FAX 808-247-6634. *603*

HAWAII MEDICAL JOURNAL.
Hawaii Medical Association, 1360 S. Beretania St., 2nd Fl., Honolulu, HI 96814. TEL 808-536-7702. FAX 808-528-2376. *4675*

HAWAII PACIFIC REVIEW.
Hawaii Pacific University, 1060 Bishop St., Honolulu, HI 96813. TEL 808-544-0214. *4412*

HAWAIIAN ENTOMOLOGICAL SOCIETY. PROCEEDINGS.
Hawaiian Entomological Society, c/o Entomology Dept., Bishop Museum, 1525 Bernice St., Honolulu, HI 96817. TEL 808-956-7076. FAX 808-956-2428. *753*

HAYDN SOCIETY JOURNAL.
Haydn Society, University of Lancaster, Music Department, Bailrigg, Lancaster LA1 4YW, England. TEL 44-1524-593777. FAX 44-1524-847298. *5397*

HE JISHU.
Science Press, Marketing and Sales Department, 16 Donghuangchenggen North St., Beijing 100717, People's Republic of China. TEL 86-1-4010642. FAX 86-1-4019810. *2697*

HEAD & NECK.
John Wiley & Sons, Inc., Journals, 605 Third Ave., New York, NY 10158. TEL 212-692-6645. FAX 212-850-6021. *5143*

HEADACHE QUARTERLY.
H Q, 467 W. Demming Pl., Ste 500, Chicago, IL 60614. TEL 773-388-6376. *4779*

HEALTH AFFAIRS.
Project Hope, 7500 Old Georgetown Rd., No. 600, Bethesda, MD 20814-6133. TEL 301-656-7401. FAX 301-654-2845. *6235*

HEALTH & ENVIRONMENT DIGEST.
Freshwater Foundation, 2500 Shadywood Rd., Navarre, MN 55331. TEL 612-471-9773. FAX 612-471-7685. *2931*

HEALTH AND HOMOEOPATHY.
Homeopathic Society, Two Powis Pl., Great Ormond St., London WC1N 3HT, England. TEL 44-171-837-9469. FAX 44-171-278-8860. *4827*

HEALTH & PLACE.
Elsevier Science Ltd., Pergamon, P.O. Box 800, Kidlington, Oxford OX5 1DX, England. TEL 44-1865-843000. FAX 44-1865-843010. *3408*

HEALTH AND SOCIAL CARE IN THE COMMUNITY.
Blackwell Science Ltd., Osney Mead, Oxford OX2 0EL, England. TEL 44-1865-206206. FAX 44-1865-721205. *6236*

HEALTH AND STRESS.
American Institute of Stress, 124 Park Ave., Yonkers, NY 10703. TEL 914-963-1200. FAX 914-965-6267. *4675*

HEALTH CARE ANALYSIS.
John Wiley & Sons Ltd., Journals, Baffins Ln., Chichester, W. Sussex PO19 1UD, England. TEL 44-1243-779777. FAX 44-1243-775878. *4675*

HEALTH CARE RISK REPORT.
Eclipse Group Ltd., 18-20 Highbury Pl., London N5 1QP, England. TEL 44-171-354-5858. FAX 44-171-354-8106. *3709*

HEALTH COMMUNICATION.
Lawrence Erlbaum Associates, Inc., 10 Industrial Dr., Mahwah, NJ 07430-2262. TEL 201-236-9500. FAX 201-236-0072. *6236*

HEALTH DEVICES.
E C R I, 5200 Butler Pike, Plymouth Meeting, PA 19462. TEL 610-825-6000. FAX 610-834-1275. *4676*

HEALTH DEVICES ALERTS.
E C R I, 5200 Butler Pike, Plymouth Meeting, PA 19462. TEL 610-825-6000. FAX 610-834-1275. *4779*

HEALTH DEVICES INSPECTION & PREVENTIVE MAINTENANCE SYSTEM.
E C R I, 5200 Butler Pike, Plymouth Meeting, PA 19462. TEL 610-825-6000. FAX 610-834-1275. *4676*

HEALTH DEVICES SOURCEBOOK.
E C R I, 5200 Butler Pike, Plymouth Meeting, PA 19462. TEL 610-825-6000. FAX 610-834-1275. *4676*

HEALTH ECONOMICS.
John Wiley & Sons Ltd., Journals, Baffins Ln., Chichester, W. Sussex PO19 1UD, England. TEL 44-1243-779777. FAX 44-1243-775878. *4676*

HEALTH EDUCATION & BEHAVIOR.
Sage Publications, Inc., 2455 Teller Rd., Thousand Oaks, CA 91320. TEL 805-499-0721. FAX 805-499-0871. *4676*

HEALTH EDUCATION RESEARCH.
Oxford University Press, Academic Division, Great Clarendon St., Oxford OX2 6DP, England. TEL 44-1865-267907. FAX 44-1865-267485. *6668*

HEALTH INFORMATION MANAGEMENT.
Australasian Medical Publishing Co., Private Bag 901, N. Sydney, N.S.W. 2059, Australia. TEL 61-2-99548666. FAX 61-2-99567644. *4676*

HEALTH JOURNAL.
Madison Publishing, 263 Summer St., Boston, MA 02210. TEL 617-428-4600. FAX 617-428-4626. *5783*

HEALTH LAW JOURNAL.
Health Law Institute, 457 Law Centre, University of Alberta, Edmonton, AB T6G 2H5, Canada. TEL 403-492-8343. FAX 403-492-9575. *3959*

HEALTH MARKETING QUARTERLY.
Haworth Press, Inc., 10 Alice St., Binghamton, NY 13904. TEL 607-722-5857. FAX 607-722-6362. *6237*

HEALTH MATRIX: JOURNAL OF LAW-MEDICINE.
Case Western Reserve University, School of Law, 11075 East Blvd., Cleveland, OH 44106-7148. TEL 216-368-3304. FAX 216-368-3310. *3959*

HEALTH PHYSICS.
Williams & Wilkins, 351 W. Camden St., Baltimore, MD 21201-2436. TEL 410-528-4068. FAX 410-528-4452. *4677*

HEALTH POLICY.
Elsevier Science Ireland Ltd., P.O. Box 85, Limerick, Ireland. TEL 353-61-471944. FAX 353-61-472144. *6237*

HEALTH POLICY MONOGRAPHS.
Elsevier Science B.V., Books Division, P.O. Box 211, 1000 AE Amsterdam, Netherlands. TEL 31-20-4853911. FAX 31-20-4853705. *6237*

HEALTH PROGRESS.
Catholic Health Association of the United States, 4455 Woodson Rd., St. Louis, MO 63134-3797. TEL 314-427-2500. FAX 314-427-0029. *3709*

HEALTH PROMOTION INTERNATIONAL.
Oxford University Press, Academic Division, Great Clarendon St., Oxford OX2 6DP, England. TEL 44-1865-267907. FAX 44-1865-267485. *6237*

HEALTH PSYCHOLOGY.
American Psychological Association, 750 First St., N.E., Washington, DC 20002-4242. TEL 202-336-5600. FAX 202-336-5568. *6114*

HEALTH SERVICES RESEARCH.
Health Administration Press, 1 North Franklin St., Ste. 1700, Chicago, IL 60606-3491. TEL 312-424-2800. FAX 312-424-0014. *3709*

HEALTH, SOCIETY AND CULTURE.
Gordon and Breach - Harwood Academic, Amsteldisk 166, 1st Fl., 1079 LH Amsterdam, Netherlands. *6712*

HEALTH TECHNOLOGY MANAGEMENT.
E C R I, 5200 Butler Pike, Plymouth Meeting, PA 19462. TEL 610-825-6000. FAX 610-834-1275. *4677*

HEALTH TECHNOLOGY TRENDS.
E C R I, 5200 Butler Pike, Plymouth Meeting, PA 19462. TEL 610-825-6000. FAX 610-834-1275. *4677*

HEALTH VISITOR.
Professional & Scientific Publications, BMA House, Tavistock Sq., London WC1H 9JR, England. TEL 0171-383-6640. FAX 0171-383-6662. *4933*

HEALTHCARE ENVIRONMENTAL MANAGEMENT SYSTEM.
E C R I, 5200 Butler Pike, Plymouth Meeting, PA 19462. TEL 610-825-6000. FAX 610-834-1275. *4678*

HEALTHCARE HAZARDOUS MATERIALS MANAGEMENT.
E C R I, 5200 Butler Pike, Plymouth Meeting, PA 19462. TEL 610-834-1275. FAX 610-834-1275. *4678*

HEALTHCARE MANAGEMENT FORUM.
Canadian College of Health Service Executives, 350 Sparks St., Ste. 402, Ottawa, ON K1R 7S8, Canada. TEL 613-235-7218. FAX 613-235-5451. *3710*

HEALTHCARE MARKET NEWS.
Laing & Buisson, Lymehouse Studios, 38 Georgiana St., London NW1 0EB, England. TEL 44-171-284-1268. FAX 44-171-267-8269. *3710*

HEALTHINFORM.
Infolink, Box 306, 31 Albany Post Rd., Montrose, NY 10548. TEL 914-736-1565. FAX 914-736-3806. *296*

HEARING RESEARCH.
Elsevier Science B.V., P.O. Box 211, 1000 AE Amsterdam, Netherlands. TEL 31-20-4853911. FAX 31-20-4853598. *5022*

HEART.
B M J Publishing Group, B.M.A. House, Tavistock Sq., London WC1H 9JR, England. TEL 0171-383-6270. FAX 0171-383-6402. *4817*

HEART & LUNG.
Mosby - Year Book, Inc., 11830 Westline Industrial Dr., St. Louis, MO 63146-3318. TEL 314-872-8370. FAX 314-432-1380. *4933*

HEART FAILURE REVIEWS.
Kluwer Academic Publishers Boston, Box 358, Accord Sta., Hingham, MA 02018-0358. TEL 617-871-6600. FAX 617-871-6528. *4817*

HEAT ENGINEERING.
Foster Wheeler Corp., Perryville Corporate Park, Clinton, NJ 08809-4000. TEL 908-730-4000. FAX 908-730-5315. *2721*

HEAT TRANSFER ENGINEERING.
Taylor & Francis Inc., 1900 Frost Rd., Ste. 101, Bristol, PA 19007-1598. TEL 215-785-5800. FAX 215-785-5515. *2764*

HEATHER NOTES.
Northeast Heather Society, Box 101, Highland View, Alstead, NH 03602-0101. TEL 603-835-6165. *3193*

HEAVY VEHICLE SYSTEMS.
Inderscience Enterprises Ltd., World Trade Centre Bldg., 110 Ave. Lousis Casai, Case Postale 306, CH-1215 Geneva-Aeroport, Switzerland. FAX 41-22-7910885. *7029*

HEBBEL - MENSCH UND DICHTER IM WERK.
Friedrich-Hebbel-Gesellschaft, Frauengasse 14, A-1170 Vienna, Austria. TEL 43-1-4893432. *4412*

HEBEI ZHONGYI.
Hebei Yixue Kexueyuan, Qingbao Yanjiusuo, 241 Qingyuan St., Shijiazhuang, Hebei 050021, People's Republic of China. TEL 86-311-5812687. FAX 86-311-5809161. *296*

HEBREW STUDIES.
National Association of Professors of Hebrew, 1346 Van Hise Hall, 1220 Linden Dr., University of Wisconsin-Madison, Madison, WI 53706. TEL 608-262-3204. FAX 608-262-9417. *4261*

HECATE.
Hecate Press, c/o English Dept., Univ. of Queensland, St. Lucia, Qld. 4067, Australia. TEL 61-7-33653146. FAX 61-7-33652799. *7344*

HEELAL.
Vereniging voor Sterrenkunde v.z.w., Brieversweg 147, 8310 Brugge, Belgium. TEL 32-50-358872. FAX 32-50-355007. *494*

HEEMKRING OKEGEM. MEDEDELINGEN.
Heemkring Okegem, Idevoordelaan 27, 9400 Ninove-Okegem, Belgium. *3570*

HEGEL SOCIETY OF AMERICA. PROCEEDINGS.
State University of New York Press, State University Plaza, Albany, NY 12246. TEL 518-472-5000. FAX 518-472-5038. *5728*

HEIMEN.
Landslaget for Lokalhistorie, Historisk Institutt, N-7055 Dragvoll, Norway. TEL 47-73-59-64-33. FAX 47-73-59-64-41. *3571*

HELLENIC JOURNAL OF CARDIOLOGY.
Hellenic Cardiological Society, 6 Potamianou, 115 28 Athens, Greece. TEL 30-1-722-1633. FAX 30-1-722-6139. *4817*

HELLENIC JOURNAL OF GASTROENTEROLOGY.
Beta Medical Publishers Ltd., Adrianiou 3, 115 25 Athens, Greece. TEL 30-1-7232-302. FAX 30-1-7232-302. *4911*

HELLENIKA.
Foereningen Svenska Atheninstitutets Vanner, P.O. Box 14124, S-104 41 Stockholm, Sweden. TEL 46-8-663-21-02. *1904*

HELLENISTIC CULTURE & SOCIETY.
University of California Press, 2120 Berkeley Way, Berkeley, CA 94720. TEL 510-642-4247. FAX 510-643-7127. *1904*

HELMINTHOLOGIA.
Slovak Academy of Sciences, Parasitological Institute, Hlinkova 3, 04001 Kosice, Slovakia. TEL 42-95-6331411. FAX 42-95-3631414. *836*

THE HELPER.
Herpes Resource Center, Box 13827, Research Triangle Park, NC 27709. TEL 919-361-8488. FAX 919-361-8425. *4836*

HEMATOLOGIE.
John Libbey Eurotext, 127 av. de la Republique, 92120 Montrouge, France. TEL 33-1-46730660. FAX 33-1-40840999. *4919*

HEMATOLOGY.
Gordon and Breach - Harwood Academic, Amsteldisk 166, 1st Fl., 1079 LH Amsterdam, Netherlands. *4919*

HEMATOLOGY - ONCOLOGY CLINICS OF NORTH AMERICA.
W.B. Saunders Co., Curtis Center, 3rd Fl., Independence Sq. W., Philadelphia, PA 19106-3399. TEL 215-238-7800. FAX 215-238-6445. *4978*

HEMATOLOGY SERIES.
Marcel Dekker, Inc., 270 Madison Ave., New York, NY 10016. TEL 212-696-9000. FAX 212-658-4540. *4919*

HEMATOPATHOLOGY AND MOLECULAR HEMATOLOGY.
Marcel Dekker Journals, 270 Madison Ave., New York, NY 10016. TEL 212-696-9000. FAX 212-685-4540. *4919*

THE HEMINGWAY REVIEW.
University of Idaho Press, c/o Susan F. Beegel, Ed., 180 Polpis Rd., Nantucket, MA 02554. TEL 508-325-7157. *4413*

HEMOGLOBIN.
Marcel Dekker Journals, 270 Madison Ave., New York, NY 10016. TEL 212-696-9000. FAX 212-685-4540. *4919*

HEPATOLOGY.
W.B. Saunders Co., Curtis Center, 3rd Fl., Independence Sq. W., Philadelphia, PA 19106-3399. TEL 215-238-7800. FAX 215-238-6445. *4911*

HEPATOLOGY RESEARCH.
Elsevier Science Ireland Ltd., P.O. Box 85, Limerick, Ireland. TEL 353-61-471944. FAX 353-61-472144. *4911*

HERALD OF LIBRARY SCIENCE.
P. Kaula Endowment for Library and Information Science, C-239 Indira Nagar, Lucknow 226 016, India. *4181*

HEREDITY.
Blackwell Science Ltd., Osney Mead, Oxford OX2 0EL, England. TEL 44-1865-206206. FAX 44-1865-721205. *770*

HERITAGE (LAWRENCEVILLE).
Gwinnett Historical Society, Inc., Box 261, Lawrenceville, GA 30246. TEL 770-822-5174. *3629*

HERITAGE CANADA.
Heritage Canada, 412 MacLaren, Ottawa, ON K2P 0M8, Canada. TEL 613-237-1066. FAX 613-237-5987. *405*

HERPETOLOGICAL REVIEW.
Society for the Study of Amphibians and Reptiles, c/o Robert Aldridge, St Louis Univ., Dept. of Biology, 3507 Laclede Ave., St. Louis, MO 63103-2010. *836*

HERVORMDE TEOLOGIESE STUDIES.
Universiteit van Pretoria, Fakulteit Teologie, Afdeling A, Pretoria 0002, South Africa. TEL 27-12-4203156. FAX 27-12-420-2887. *6343*

HESPERIA.
American School of Classical Studies at Athens, 6-8 Charlton St., Princeton, NJ 08540-5232. TEL 609-683-0800. FAX 609-924-0578. *365*

HESPERIS - TAMUDA.
Universite Mohammed V, Faculte des Lettres et des Sciences Humaines, B.P. 1040, Rabat, Morocco. TEL 212-7-773308. FAX 212-7-772068. *5528*

HETEROCERA SUMATRANA.
Heterocera Sumatrana Society e.V., Kreuzburgerstr. 6, 37085 Goettingen, Germany. TEL 49-551-76786. *753*

HETEROCYCLES.
Japan Institute of Heterocyclic Chemistry, 1-1-7-804 Motoakasaka, Minato-ku, Tokyo 107, Japan. TEL 81-3-3404-5019. FAX 81-3-3497-9370. *1816*

HETEROGENEOUS CHEMISTRY REVIEWS.
John Wiley & Sons, Inc., Journals, 605 Third Ave., New York, NY 10158-0012. TEL 212-850-6645. FAX 212-850-6021. *1750*

HEYTHROP JOURNAL.
Blackwell Publishers Ltd., 108 Cowley Rd., Oxford OX4 1JF, England. TEL 44-1865-791100. FAX 44-1865-791347. *6343*

HIGH ENERGY CHEMISTRY.
Maik Nauka - Interperiodica, Mezhdunarodnyi Otdel, Ul. Prosoyuznaya, 90, 117864 Moscow, Russia. TEL 7-095-3360066. FAX 7-095-3360066. *1829*

HIGH PLAINS LITERARY REVIEW.
High Plains Literary Review, Inc., 180 Adams St., Ste. 250, Denver, CO 80206. TEL 303-320-6828. FAX 303-320-0463. *4413*

HIGH PRESSURE RESEARCH.
Gordon and Breach - Harwood Academic, Amsteldisk 166, 1st Fl., 1079 LH Amsterdam, Netherlands. *5845*

HIGH SCHOOL JOURNAL.
University of North Carolina Press, Box 2288, Chapel Hill, NC 27515-2288. TEL 919-966-3561. FAX 800-272-6817. *2448*

HIGH TEMPERATURE.
Maik Nauka - Interperiodica, Mezhdunarodnyi Otdel, Ul. Profsoyuznaya, 90, 117864 Moscow, Russia. TEL 7-095-231-2164. FAX 7-095-233-5590. *5841*

HIGH TEMPERATURE AND MATERIALS SCIENCE.
Humana Press Inc., 999 Riverview Dr., Ste. 208, Totowa, NJ 07512. TEL 973-256-1699. FAX 973-256-8341. *1829*

HIGH TEMPERATURES - HIGH PRESSURES.
Pion Ltd., 207 Brondesbury Park, London NW2 5JN, England. TEL 44-181-459-0069. FAX 44-181-451-6454. *5841*

HIGHER EDUCATION.
Kluwer Academic Publishers, Postbus 17, 3300 AA Dordrecht, Netherlands. TEL 31-78-6392392. FAX 31-78-6392254. *2543*

HIGHER EDUCATION QUARTERLY.
Blackwell Publishers Ltd., 108 Cowley Rd., Oxford OX4 1JF, England. TEL 44-1865-791100. FAX 44-1865-791347. *2544*

HIGHER EDUCATION RESEARCH AND DEVELOPMENT.
Carfax Publishing Co., P.O. Box 25, Abingdon, Oxon OX14 3UE, England. *2448*

HIGHER EDUCATION REVIEW.
Tyrrell Burgess Associates Ltd., 34 Sandilands, Croydon CR0 5DB, England. TEL 44-181-656-1770. *2544*

HIGHLIGHTS OF AGRICULTURAL RESEARCH.
Alabama Agricultural Experiment Station, 2 Comer Hall, Auburn University, AL 36849. TEL 334-844-4877. FAX 334-844-5892. *122*

HIGHWAYS AND TRANSPORTATION.
Institution of Highways and Transportation, 6 Endsleigh St., London WC1H 0DZ, England. TEL 44-171-387-2525. FAX 44-171-387-2808. *2786*

HIKOBIA.
Hikobia Botanical Club, c/o Laboratory of Plant Taxonomy & Ecology, Dept. of Biological Science, Faculty of Science, Hiroshima University, 5-1, Kagamiyama 1-chome, Higashi-hiroshima-shi 739, Japan. TEL 81-824-24-7451. FAX 81-824-24-0734. *707*

HIMACHAL JOURNAL OF AGRICULTURAL RESEARCH.
H.P. Agriculture University, Himachal Pradesh Krishi Vishvavidyalaya, Palampur 176 062, Himachal Pradesh, India. TEL 91-189-30406. FAX 91-1894-30511. *123*

HIMAL SOUTH ASIA.
Himal Inc. Pvt. Ltd., G.P.O. Box 7251, Kathmandu, Nepal. TEL 977-1-523845. FAX 977-1-521013. *5931*

HIMALAYAN JOURNAL.
Himalayan Club, P.O. Box 1905, Mumbai 400 001, India. TEL 91-22-495-0772. FAX 91-22-496-8804. *6871*

HIMALAYAN JOURNAL OF ENVIRONMENT AND ZOOLOGY.
Indian Academy of Environmental Sciences, c/o Dept. of Zoology, Gurukula Kangri University, Hardwar 249404, India. TEL 91-133-425793. *2931*

HIMALAYAN PLANT JOURNAL.
Primulaceae Books, P.O. Box No. 6, Kalimpong-Darjeeling 734 301, West Bengal, India. TEL 91-3552-55673. FAX 91-3552-55673. *3193*

HINDU - CHRISTIAN STUDIES BULLETIN.
Centre for Studies in Religion and Society, University of Victoria, P.O. Box 3045, Victoria, BC V8W 3P4, Canada. TEL 250-721-6325. FAX 250-721-6234. *6394*

HINDUSTAN (MUMBAI).
Bombay Printers Ltd., 19-21, Ambalal Doshi Marg, Fort, Mumbai 400 001, India. TEL 91-22-2653014. FAX 91-22-2832504. *3311*

THE HIPPOCAMPUS.
John Wiley & Sons, Inc., Journals, 605 Third Ave., New York, NY 10158. TEL 212-850-6645. FAX 202-850-6021. *4678*

HIRAM POETRY REVIEW.
Hiram College, English Department, Box 162, Hiram, OH 44234. TEL 330-569-5330. FAX 330-569-5449. *4510*

HIROSHIMA JOURNAL OF MATHEMATICS EDUCATION.
Hiroshima University, Department of Mathematics Education, 1-1-2 Kagamiyama Higashi Hiroshima, Hiroshima 739, Japan. *4575*

HIROSHIMA SHUDO DAIGAKU RINSHO SHINRIGAKU KENKYU.
Hiroshima Shudo Daigaku, Shinrigaku Kyoshitsu, 1717, Otsuka, Numatacho, Asaminami-ku, Hiroshima-shi 731-31, Japan. TEL 81-82-830-1139. FAX 81-82-848-6633. *6114*

HISPAMERICA.
c/o Saul Sosnowski, Ed. & Pub., 5 Pueblo Ct., Gaithersburg, MD 20878-2067. TEL 301-948-3494. *4413*

HISPANIA.
American Association of Teachers of Spanish and Portuguese, Inc., University of Northern Colorado, 210 Butler-Hancock Hall, Greeley, CO 80639. TEL 920-351-1090. FAX 970-351-1095. *4262*

HISPANIC AMERICAN HISTORICAL REVIEW.
Duke University Press, Box 90660, Durham, NC 27708-0660. TEL 919-687-3600. FAX 919-688-4574. *3629*

HISPANIC JOURNAL.
Indiana University of Pennsylvania, Department of Spanish and Classical Languages, 462 Sutton Hall, Indiana, PA 15705. TEL 412-357-7528. FAX 412-357-2514. *3015*

THE HISTOCHEMICAL JOURNAL.
Chapman & Hall, Journals Department 2-6 Boundary Row, London SE1 8HN, England. TEL 44-171-8650066. FAX 44-171-5229623. *740*

HISTOIRE DES SCIENCES ET DES TECHNIQUES.
Gordon and Breach - Harwood Academic, Amsteldisk 166, 1st Fl., 1079 LH Amsterdam, Netherlands. *6530*

HISTOIRE EPISTEMOLOGIE LANGAGE.
Societe d'Histoire et d'Epistemologie des Sciences du Langage, Universite de Paris 7, Tour Centrale, 9e Etage, 2 place Jussieu, 75221 Paris Cedex 05, France. TEL 33-1-44275688. *4262*

HISTOIRE SOCIALE.
University of Toronto Press, Journals Department, 5201 Dufferin St., Downsview, ON M3H 5T8, Canada. TEL 416-667-7710. FAX 416-667-7881. *3496*

HISTOPATHOLOGY.
Blackwell Science Ltd., Osney Mead, Oxford OX2 0EL, England. TEL 44-1865-206206. FAX 44-1865-721205. *4979*

HISTORIA.
Historical Association of South Africa, Department of History & Cultural History, University of Pretoria, Pretoria 0002, South Africa. TEL 27-12-4202323. FAX 27-12-4202656. *3497*

HISTORIA.
Foundation Historia, Uri u. 53, 1014 Budapest I, Hungary. TEL 36-1-1560457. *3571*

HISTORIA, ANTROPOLOGIA Y FUENTES ORALES.
Asociacion Historia y Fuente Oral, Sta. Llucia, 1, 08002 Barcelona, Spain. TEL 34-3-3181195. FAX 34-3-3178327. *3497*

HISTORIA, CIENCIAS, SAUDE - MANGUINHOS.
Fundacao Oswaldo Cruz, Avda. Brasil 4365, 21045-360 Rio de Janeiro RJ, Brazil. TEL 55-21-2809241. FAX 55-21-5984437. *3497*

HISTORIA MATHEMATICA.
Academic Press, Inc., Journal Division, 525 B St., Ste. 1900, San Diego, CA 92101-4495. TEL 619-230-1840. FAX 619-699-6800. *4575*

HISTORIA MEDICINAE VETERINARIAE.
Historia Medicinae Veterinariae, Soendergade 39, 4130 Viby Sjaelland, Denmark. *7270*

THE HISTORIAN (EAST LANSING).
Michigan State University Press, Manly Miles Bldg., Ste. 25, 1405 S. Harrison Rd., East Lansing, MI 48823-5202. TEL 517-432-9543. FAX 517-336-2611. *3497*

HISTORIC BRASS SOCIETY JOURNAL.
Historic Brass Society, Inc., 148 W. 23rd St., No. 2A, New York, NY 10011. TEL 212-627-3820. FAX 212-627-3820. *5398*

HISTORIC BRASS SOCIETY NEWSLETTER.
Historic Brass Society, Inc., 148 West 23rd St., No. 2A, New York, NY 10011. TEL 212-627-3820. FAX 212-627-3820. *5398*

HISTORIC MADISON.
Historic Madison, Inc. of Wisconsin, Box 2721, Madison, WI 53701-2721. TEL 608-238-5050. *3630*

HISTORIC SOCIETY OF LANCASHIRE AND CHESHIRE. TRANSACTIONS.
Historic Society of Lancashire and Cheshire, c/o Department of History, Manchester University, Manchester M13 9PL, England. *3572*

HISTORICA.
Pontificia Universidad Catolica del Peru, Fondo Editorial, Apdo. 1761, Lima 32, Peru. TEL 51-14-626390. FAX 51-14-611785. *3630*

HISTORICAL ARCHAEOLOGY.
Society for Historical Archaeology, Box 30446, Tucson, AZ 85751. TEL 520-886-8006. FAX 520-886-0182. *365*

HISTORICAL BIOLOGY.
Gordon and Breach - Harwood Academic, Amsteldisk 166, 1st Fl., 1079 LH Amsterdam, Netherlands. *5559*

HISTORICAL FOOTNOTES (STONINGTON).
Stonington Historical Society, Box 103, Stonington, CT 06378. TEL 860-535-1131. *3630*

HISTORICAL JOURNAL OF FILM, RADIO AND TELEVISION.
Carfax Publishing Co., P.O. Box 25, Abingdon, Oxon. OX14 3UE, England. TEL 44-1235-401000. FAX 44-1235-401550. *3498*

HISTORICAL METALLURGY.
Historical Metallurgy Society Ltd., Rock House, Bowens Hill, Coleford, Glos. GL16 8DH, England. TEL 44-1594-833778. *5193*

HISTORICAL METHODS.
Heldref Publications, 1319 Eighteenth St., N.W., Washington, DC 20036-1802. TEL 202-296-6267. FAX 202-296-5149. *3498*

HISTORICAL NEW HAMPSHIRE.
New Hampshire Historical Society, 30 Park St., Concord, NH 03301. TEL 603-225-3381. FAX 603-224-0463. *3630*

HISTORICAL REFLECTIONS.
Alfred University, Division of Human Studies, Kanakadea Hall, Alfred, NY 14802. TEL 607-871-2217. *3498*

HISTORICAL RESEARCH.
Blackwell Publishers Ltd., 108 Cowley Rd., Oxford OX4 1JF, England. TEL 44-1865-791100. FAX 44-1865-791347. *3498*

HISTORICAL REVIEW OF BERKS COUNTY.
Historical Society of Berks County, 940 Centre Ave., Reading, PA 19601. TEL 215-375-4375. FAX 610-375-4376. *3630*

HISTORICAL STUDIES IN EDUCATION.
Canadian Association of History of Education, University of British Columbia, Faculty of Education, 2125 Main Mall, Vancouver, BC V6T 1Z4, Canada. TEL 604-822-5353. FAX 604-822-4244. *2448*

HISTORICAL STUDIES IN THE PHYSICAL AND BIOLOGICAL SCIENCES.
University of California Press, Journals Division, 2120 Berkeley Way, No. 5812, Berkeley, CA 94720-5812. TEL 510-643-7154. FAX 510-642-9917. *6530*

HISTORISK TIDSKRIFT.
Svenska Historiska Foereningen, P.O.Box 5405, S-114 84 Stockholm, Sweden. TEL 08-783-2502. FAX 08-7832515. *3573*

HISTORISK TIDSSKRIFT.
Danske Historiske Forening, Institut for Historie, Njalsgade 102, Tr. 15, DK-2300 Copenhagen S, Denmark. TEL 45-35-32-82-44. FAX 45-35-32-82-41. *3573*

HISTORY.
Blackwell Publishers Ltd., 108 Cowley Rd., Oxford OX4 1JF, England. TEL 44-1865-791100. *3499*

HISTORY AND ANTHROPOLOGY.
Gordon and Breach - Harwood Academic, Amsteldisk 166, 1st Fl., 1079 LH Amsterdam, Netherlands. *318*

HISTORY AND COMPUTING (EDINBURGH).
Edinburgh University Press, 22 George Sq., Edinburgh EH8 9LF, Scotland. TEL 44-131-650-6207. FAX 44-131-662-0053. *2082*

HISTORY AND PHILOSOPHY OF LOGIC.
Taylor & Francis Ltd., 1 Gunpowder Sq., London EC4A 3DE, England. TEL 44-171-583-0490. FAX 44-171-583-0585. *5729*

HISTORY AND PHILOSOPHY OF THE LIFE SCIENCES.
Taylor & Francis Ltd., 1 Gunpowder Sq., London EC4A 3DE, England. TEL 44-171-583-0490. FAX 44-171-583-0585. *604*

HISTORY AND TECHNOLOGY.
Gordon and Breach - Harwood Academic, Amsteldisk 166, 1st Fl., 1079 LH Amsterdam, Netherlands. *3499*

HISTORY AND THEORY.
Blackwell Publishers, 238 Main St., Cambridge, MA 02142. TEL 617-547-7110. FAX 617-547-0789. *3499*

HISTORY COMPUTER REVIEW.
Pittsburg State University, History Department, Russ Hall 308, Pittsburg, KS 66762. TEL 316-235-4312. FAX 316-232-7515. *2516*

HISTORY IN AFRICA.
African Studies Association, Credit Union Bldg., Emory University, Atlanta, GA 30322. TEL 404-329-6410. FAX 404-324-6433. *3526*

HISTORY OF BIBLICAL INTERPRETATION SERIES.
E.J. Brill, P.O. Box 9000, 2300 PA Leiden, Netherlands. TEL 31-71-5353500. FAX 31-71-5317532. *6343*

HISTORY OF EDUCATION.
Taylor & Francis Ltd., Rankine Rd., Basingstoke, Hants. RG24 8PR, England. TEL 44-1256-840366. FAX 44-1256-479438. *2448*

HISTORY OF EDUCATION QUARTERLY.
Indiana University, School of Education, Bloomington, IN 47405. FAX 812-856-8440. *2448*

HISTORY OF EDUCATION REVIEW.
Australian and New Zealand Education Society, c/o Christine Brown Business Manager, School of Education, James Cook Univ. of N. Queensland, Twnsville, Qld. 4811, Australia. FAX 077251690. *2448*

HISTORY OF EUROPEAN IDEAS.
Elsevier Science Ltd., Pergamon, P.O. Box 800, Kidlington, Oxford OX5 1DX, England. TEL 44-1865-843000. FAX 44-1865-843010. *5729*

HISTORY OF HIGHER EDUCATION ANNUAL.
Pennsylvania State University, Higher Education Program, 403 S. Allen St., Ste. 115, University Park, PA 16801-5202. TEL 814-863-2690. FAX 814-865-0543. *2544*

HISTORY OF MATHEMATICS.
American Mathematical Society, Box 6248, Providence, RI 02940-6248. TEL 401-455-4000. FAX 401-331-3842. *4575*

HISTORY OF PHOTOGRAPHY.
Taylor & Francis Ltd., Rankine Rd., Basingstoke, Hants. RG24 8PR, England. TEL 44-1256-840366. FAX 44-1256-479438. *5766*

HISTORY OF POLITICAL ECONOMY.
Duke University Press, Box 90660, Durham, NC 27708-0660. TEL 919-687-3600. FAX 919-688-4574. *1305*

HISTORY OF POLITICAL THOUGHT.
Imprint Academic, P.O. Box 1, Thorverton, Exeter, Devon EX5 5YX, England. TEL 44-1392-841600. FAX 44-1392-841478. *5931*

HISTORY OF RELIGIONS.
University of Chicago Press, Journals Division, Box 37005, Chicago, IL 60637. TEL 773-753-3347. FAX 773-753-0811. *6343*

HISTORY OF SCIENCE.
Science History Publications Ltd., 16 Rutherford Rd., Cambridge CB2 2HH, England. TEL 44-1223-565532. FAX 44-1223-565532. *6531*

HISTORY OF THE HUMAN SCIENCES.
Sage Publications Ltd., 6 Bonhill St., London EC2A 4PU, England. TEL 44-171-374-0645. FAX 44-171-374-8741. *6616*

HISTORY: REVIEWS OF NEW BOOKS.
Heldref Publications, 1319 Eighteenth St., N.W., Washington, DC 20036-1802. TEL 202-296-6267. FAX 202-296-5149. *3499*

HITCHCOCK ANNUAL.
Hitchcock Annual Corporation, Box 2568, New London, NH 03257. TEL 614-427-3156. *5335*

HIV AND AIDS CURRENT TRENDS.
Mediscript Ltd., 1 Mountview Ct., 310 Friern Barnet Ln., London N20 OLD, England. TEL 44-181-446-8898. FAX 44-181-446-9194. *4836*

HOBART PAPERBACKS.
Institute of Economic Affairs, 2 Lord North St., London SW1P 3LB, England. TEL 44-171-799-3745. FAX 44-171-799-2137. *1305*

HOBART PAPERS.
Institute of Economic Affairs, 2 Lord North St., London SW1P 3LB, England. TEL 44-171-799-3745. FAX 44-171-799-2137. *968*

HOEHNEA.
Instituto de Botanica, Caixa Postal 4005, 01061-970 Sao Paulo, SP, Brazil. TEL 55-11-55846300. FAX 55-11-5773678. *707*

HOKKAIDO JOURNAL OF MEDICAL SCIENCE.
Hokkaido Medical Society, Hokkaido Daigaku Igakubu, Nishi 7-chome, Kita 15-jo, Kita-ku, Sapporo-shi, Hokkaido 060, Japan. TEL 81-11-706-5007. FAX 81-11-706-7866. *4679*

HOKKAIDO UNIVERSITY. FACULTY OF SCIENCE. JOURNAL. SERIES 4: GEOLOGY AND MINERALOGY.
Hokkaido University, Faculty of Science, Nishi-8-chome, Kita-10-jo, Kita-ku, Sapporo 060, Japan. TEL 011-706-3225. FAX 011-716-0394. *2350*

HOKURIKU GEKA GAKKAI ZASSHI.
Hokuriku Geka Gakkai, Kanazawa Daigaku Igakubu Daiichi Gekagaku Kyoshitsu, 13-1, Takaramachi, Kanazawa-shi, Ishikawa-ken 920, Japan. FAX 81-762-22-6833. *5143*

HOLARCTIC LEPIDOPTERA.
Association for Tropical Lepidoptera, Box 141210, Gainsville, FL 32614-1210. *753*

HOLISTIC LIFE.
New York Institute for Holistic Life, Box 302, Bronx, NY 10458. TEL 718-364-2202. FAX 718-364-2202. *296*

HOLOCAUST AND GENOCIDE STUDIES.
Oxford University Press, Journals, 2001 Evans Rd., Cary, NC 27513. TEL 919-677-0977. FAX 919-677-1714. *3573*

HOLOCAUST STUDIES SERIES.
Kluwer Academic Publishers, Postbus 17, 3300 AA Dordrecht, Netherlands. TEL 31-78-6392392. FAX 31-78-6392254. *3574*

HOLSTEIN FRIESIAN JOURNAL.
Holstein Friesian Society of Great Britain & Ireland, Scotsbridge House, Rickmansworth, Herts. WD3 3BB, England. TEL 44-1923-494600. FAX 44-1923-770003. *255*

HOME AND COUNTRY.
National Federation of Women's Institutes, 104 New Kings Rd., Fulham, London SW6 4LY, England. TEL 44-171-731-5777. FAX 44-171-736-4061. *7322*

HOME ECONOMICS INSTITUTE OF AUSTRALIA. JOURNAL.
Home Economics Institute of Australia Inc., Q U T, Kelvin Grove Campus, Locked Bag No. 2, Red Hill, Qld., 4059, Australia. TEL 61-7-864-3522. FAX 61-7-864-3369. *3685*

HOME ECONOMIST JOURNAL.
Institute of Home Economics, 21 Portland Pl., London WIN 3AF, England. TEL 44-171-436-5677. *3685*

HOME ENERGY.
Energy Auditor and Retrofitter, Inc., 2124 Kittredge St., No. 95, Berkeley, CA 94704. TEL 510-524-5405. *2670*

HOME HEALTH CARE SERVICES QUARTERLY.
Haworth Press, Inc., 10 Alice St., Binghamton, NY 13904. TEL 607-722-5857. FAX 607-722-6362. *3711*

HOME SCHOOL MARKET GUIDE.
Bluestocking Press, Dept. U, Box 1014, Placerville, CA 95667. TEL 916-621-1123. FAX 642-9222. *2449*

HOME SCHOOL RESEARCHER.
National Home Education Research Institute, Box 13939, Salem, OR 97309. TEL 503-364-1490. FAX 503-364-2827. *2449*

HOMELIFE.
Society of St. Paul, Inc., MCPO Box 1722, 1299 Makati, Metro Manila, Philippines. FAX 632-890-7131. *3347*

HOMEOSTASIS.
Collegium Internationale Activitatis Nervosae Superioris, c/o Institute of Hygiene and Epidemiology, Srobarova 48, 10042 Prague 10, Czech Republic. *5068*

HOMES AND COTTAGES.
In-Home Show Ltd., 6557 Mississauga Rd., No. D, Mississauga, ON L5N 1A6, Canada. TEL 905-567-1440. FAX 905-567-1442. *896*

HOMES & LIVING.
H B M Publishing, 33 Brisbane St., E. Perth, W.A. 6000, Australia. TEL 09-228-9334. FAX 09-227-8337. *896*

HONG KONG MEDICAL JOURNAL.
Hong Kong Academy of Medicine, 9th Fl., Multicentre Block A, Pamela Youde Nethersole Eastern Hospital, 3 Lok Man Rd., Chaiwan, Hong Kong, People's Republic of China. TEL 852-2515-5799. FAX 852-2505-3194. *4680*

HONG KONG PSYCHOLOGICAL SOCIETY. BULLETIN.
Hong Kong Psychological Society Ltd., c/o Department of Education Studies, Hong Kong Baptist University, Kowloon Tong, Hong Kong, People's Republic of China. FAX 852-2339-7894. *6115*

HONGWAI YU JIGUANG GONGCHENG.
Hangtian Gongye Zong Gongsi, Tianjin Jinhang Jishu Wuli Yanjiusuo, P.O. Box 225-32, Tianjin 300192, People's Republic of China. TEL 86-22-23363000. FAX 86-22-23363423. *68*

HONYU DOBUTSU SHIKEN BUNKAKAI KAIHO.
Nihon Kankyo Hen'igen Gakkai, Honyu Dobutsu Shiken Bunkakai, Shokuhin Yakuhin Anzen Senta Hadano Kenkyujo, 729-5 Ochiai, Hadano-shi, Kanagawa-ken 257, Japan. *770*

HOOFDZAKEN.
Nederlandse Vereniging van Migrainepatienten, Termijen 99, 1852 TG Heiloo, Netherlands. TEL 31-72-5333994. FAX 31-72-5333994. *5068*

THE HOOK.
Tailhook Association, 9696 Businesspark Ave., San Diego, CA 92131-1643. TEL 619-689-9227. FAX 619-578-8839. *5270*

HOPSCOTCH.
Bluffton News Printing and Publishing Co., Box 164, 103 N. Main St., Bluffton, OH 45817-0164. TEL 419-358-4610. FAX 419-358-5027. *1874*

HORIZONS.
Haifa University, Department of Geography, Mount Carmel, Haifa 31905, Israel. FAX 972-4-246814. *3408*

HORIZONS (VILLANOVA).
Wilfrid Laurier University Press, 75 University Ave. W., Waterloo, ON N2L 3C5, Canada. TEL 519-884-0710. FAX 519-725-1399. *6465*

HORIZONTES.
Universidad Catolica de Puerto Rico, 2250 Ave. Las Americas, Ste. 510, Ponce, PR 00731-6382. TEL 787-841-2000 ext. 1050. *3780*

HORMONE RESEARCH.
S. Karger AG, Allschwilerstr. 10, P.O. Box, CH-4009 Basel, Switzerland. TEL 41-61-3061111. FAX 41-61-3061234. *4889*

HORMONES AND BEHAVIOR.
Academic Press, Inc., Journal Division, 525 B St., Ste. 1900, San Diego, CA 92101-4495. TEL 619-230-1840. FAX 619-699-6800. *4889*

HOROLOGICAL TIMES.
American Watchmakers Institute, 701 Enterprise Dr., Harrison, OH 45030-1696. TEL 513-367-9802. FAX 513-367-1414. *3864*

THE HORTICULTURIST.
Institute of Horticulture, 14-15 Belgrave Sq., London SW1X 8PS, England. TEL 44-171-245-6943. *3194*

HOSHASEN SEIBUTSU KENKYU.
Hoshasen Seibutsu Kenkyukai, c/o Research Reactor Institute, Kyoto University, Kumatori-cho, Sennan-gun, Osaka 590-04, Japan. TEL 81-724-51-2628. FAX 81-724-51-2628. *675*

HOSPICE JOURNAL.
Haworth Press, Inc., 10 Alice St., Binghamton, NY 13904. TEL 607-722-5857. FAX 607-722-6362. *3711*

EL HOSPITAL (CINCINNATI).
Salud Publications International Inc., 2724 Erie Ave., Ste. B, Cincinnati, OH 45208-2125. TEL 513-533-5470. FAX 513-533-5474. *4680*

HOSPITAL DE NINOS. REVISTA.
Asociacion Medica del Hospital de Ninos, Gallo 1330, 1425 Buenos Aires, Argentina. TEL 54-1-9614609. FAX 54-1-9614609. *5031*

HOSPITAL MEDICINE.
Quadrant HealthCom, 105 Raider Blvd., Belle Mead, NJ 08502-1510. TEL 908-874-0707. FAX 908-874-5611. *4680*

HOSPITAL PHYSICIAN.
Turner White Communications, Inc., 125 Strafford Ave., Ste. 220, Wayne, PA 19087-3391. TEL 610-975-4541. FAX 610-975-4564. *4680*

HOSPITAL PRACTICE.
McGraw-Hill Companies (Minneapolis), 4530 W. 77th St., Minneapolis, MN 55435. TEL 612-835-3222. FAX 612-835-3460. *4680*

HOSPITAL PRODUCT COMPARISON SYSTEM.
E C R I, 5200 Butler Pike, Plymouth Meeting, PA 19462. TEL 610-825-6000. FAX 610-834-1275. *3713*

HOSPITAL RISK CONTROL.
E C R I, 5200 Butler Pike, Plymouth Meeting, PA 19462. TEL 610-825-6000. FAX 610-834-1275. *3713*

HOSPITAL TOPICS.
Heldref Publications, 1319 Eighteenth St., N.W., Washington, DC 20036. TEL 202-296-6267. FAX 202-296-5149. *3714*

HOTEL EXCLUSIV.
Am Wingertsberg 24, 76857 Waldhambach, Germany. TEL 49-6346-6431. FAX 49-6346-6518. *3728*

LES HOUCHES SUMMER SCHOOL PROCEEDINGS.
Elsevier Science B.V., Books Division, P.O. Box 211, 1000 AE Amsterdam, Netherlands. TEL 31-20-4853911. FAX 31-20-4853705. *5805*

HOUSE EAR INSTITUTE. REVIEW.
House Ear Institute, 2100 W. Third St., 5th Fl., Los Angeles, CA 90057. TEL 213-484-2642. FAX 213-483-8789. *5022*

HOUSING POLICY DEBATE.
Federal National Mortgage Association, 3900 Wisconsin Ave., N.W., Washington, DC 20016-2899. TEL 202-752-4422. FAX 202-752-4933. *3749*

HOUSING STUDIES.
Carfax Publishing Co., P.O. Box 25, Abingdon, Oxon. OX14 3UE, England. TEL 44-1235-401000. FAX 44-1235-401550. *3749*

HOUSTON JOURNAL OF MATHEMATICS.
University of Houston, Department of Mathematics, Houston, TX 77204-3476. TEL 713-743-3475. FAX 713-743-3505. *4575*

HOUSTON REVIEW: HISTORY AND CULTURE OF THE GULF COAST.
Houston Metropolitan Research Center, Houston Public Library, 500 McKinney, Houston, TX 77002. TEL 713-247-1661. *3630*

HUAN BOHAI JINGJI LIAOWANG.
Huan Bohai Diqu Jingji Xinxi Xiehui, 39 Youyi Lu, Hexi Qu, Tianjin 300201, People's Republic of China. TEL 86-22-813-1745. FAX 86-22-835-4270. *969*

HUANG ZHONG.
Wuhan Yiyue Xueyuan, No. 255, Jiefang Lu, Wuchang, Wuhan, Hubei 430060, People's Republic of China. TEL 86-27-8066354. *5398*

HUANJING HUAXUE.
Science Press, Marketing and Sales Department, 16 Donghuangchenggen North St., Beijing 100717, People's Republic of China. TEL 4010642. FAX 4012180. *1751*

HUANJING KEXUE.
Science Press, Marketing and Sales Department, 16 Donghuangchenggen North St., Beijing 100717, People's Republic of China. TEL 4010642. FAX 4019810. *2932*

HUANJING KEXUE XUEBAO.
Science Press, Marketing and Sales Department, 16 Donghuangchenggen North St., Beijing 100717, People's Republic of China. TEL 4010642. FAX 4019810. *2932*

HUANJING YAOGAN.
Science Press, Marketing and Sales Department, 16 Donghuangchenggen North St., Beijing 100717, People's Republic of China. TEL 4010642. FAX 4019810. *3408*

HUAXUE XUEBAO.
Science Press, Marketing and Sales Department, 16 Donghuangchenggen North St., Beijing 100717, People's Republic of China. TEL 4010642. FAX 4019810. *1751*

HUBBUB.
5344 S.E. 38th, Portland, OR 97202. TEL 503-775-0370. *4511*

HUDEBNI VEDA.
Ceska Akademie Ved, Ustav pro Hudebni Vedu, Puskinovo nam. 9, 160 00 Prague 6, Czech Republic. TEL 420-2-24311212. FAX 420-2-3121740. *5399*

HUDSON REVIEW.
Hudson Review, Inc., 684 Park Ave., New York, NY 10021. TEL 212-650-0020. *4338*

HUEBNER SERIES IN RISK AND INSURANCE.
Kluwer Academic Publishers, Postbus 17, 3300 AA Dordrecht, Netherlands. TEL 31-78-6392392. FAX 31-78-6392254. *3818*

HUISARTS EN WETENSCHAP.
Bohn Stafleu van Loghum B.V., Postbus 246, 3990 GA Houten, Netherlands. TEL 31-3403-95711. FAX 31-3403-50903. *4680*

HUMAN ANTIBODIES.
Forefront Publishing Group, 5 River Rd., Ste. 113, Wilton, CT 06897-4069. TEL 203-834-0631. FAX 203-834-0940. *4794*

HUMAN BEHAVIOR AND ENVIRONMENT.
Plenum Publishing Corp., 233 Spring St., New York, NY 10013-1578. TEL 212-620-8000. FAX 212-463-0742. *6115*

HUMAN BIOLOGY (DETROIT).
Wayne State University Press, 4809 Woodward Ave., Detroit, MI 48201-1309. TEL 313-577-6120. FAX 313-577-6131. *604*

HUMAN BRAIN MAPPING.
John Wiley & Sons, Inc., Journals, 605 Third Ave., New York, NY 10158. TEL 212-850-6645. FAX 212-850-6021. *5068*

HUMAN - COMPUTER INTERACTION (MAHWAH).
Lawrence Erlbaum Associates, Inc., 10 Industrial Dr., Mahwah, NJ 07430-2262. TEL 201-236-9500. FAX 201-236-0072. *2082*

HUMAN DEVELOPMENT.
S. Karger AG, Allschwilerstr. 10, P.O. Box, CH-4009 Basel, Switzerland. TEL 41-61-3061111. FAX 41-61-3061234. *816*

HUMAN DEVELOPMENT (SILVER SPRINGS).
Jesuit Educational Center for Human Development, 8901 New Hampshire Ave., Silver Springs, MA 20903-3898. TEL 301-422-5500. FAX 301-422-5519. *6115*

HUMAN ECOLOGY (NEW YORK).
Plenum Publishing Corp., 233 Spring St., New York, NY 10013-1578. TEL 212-620-8000. FAX 212-463-0742. *318*

HUMAN FACTORS.
Human Factors and Ergonomics Society, Box 1369, Santa Monica, CA 90406-1369. TEL 310-394-1811. FAX 310-394-2410. *2722*

HUMAN FACTORS AND ERGONOMICS SOCIETY ANNUAL MEETING. PROCEEDINGS.
Human Factors and Ergonomics Society, Box 1369, Santa Monica, CA 90406-1369. TEL 310-394-1811. FAX 310-394-2410. *2722*

HUMAN FACTORS IN ERGONOMICS AND MANUFACTURING.
John Wiley & Sons, Inc., Journals, 605 Third Ave., New York, NY 10158. TEL 212-850-6645. FAX 212-850-6021. *2876*

HUMAN FACTORS IN INFORMATION TECHNOLOGY.
Elsevier Science B.V., Books Division, P.O. Box 211, 1000 AE Amsterdam, Netherlands. TEL 31-20-4853911. FAX 31-20-4853705. *2182*

HUMAN GEOGRAPHY.
Human Geographical Society of Japan, Kinkichiho-Hatsumei Center, 14 Yoshida Kawara-cho, Sakyo-ku, Kyoto 606, Japan. TEL 81-75-751-7687. FAX 81-75-751-7687. *3409*

HUMAN HEREDITY.
S. Karger AG, Allschwilerstr. 10, P.O. Box, CH-4009 Basel, Switzerland. TEL 41-61-3061111. FAX 41-61-3061234. *771*

HUMAN IMMUNOLOGY.
Elsevier Science Inc., Box 945, New York, NY 10159-0945. TEL 212-633-3730. FAX 212-633-3680. *4794*

HUMAN MOVEMENT SCIENCE.
North-Holland, P.O. Box 211, 1000 AE Amsterdam, Netherlands. TEL 31-20-4853911. FAX 31-20-4853598. *4681*

HUMAN MUTATION.
John Wiley & Sons, Inc., Journals, 605 Third Ave., New York, NY 10158-0012. TEL 212-850-6645. FAX 212-850-6021. *771*

HUMAN NUTRITION.
Plenum Publishing Corp., 233 Spring St., New York, NY 10013-1578. TEL 212-620-8468. FAX 212-463-0742. *5474*

HUMAN ORGANIZATION.
Society for Applied Anthropology, Box 24083, Oklahoma City, OK 73124-0084. TEL 405-843-5113. *318*

HUMAN PARASITIC DISEASES.
Elsevier Science B.V., Books Division, P.O. Box 211, 1000 AE Amsterdam, Netherlands. TEL 31-20-4853911. FAX 31-20-4853705. *4836*

HUMAN PATHOLOGY.
W.B. Saunders Co., Curtis Center, 3rd Fl., Independence Sq. W., Philadelphia, PA 19106-3399. TEL 215-238-7800. FAX 215-238-6445. *4681*

HUMAN PERFORMANCE.
Lawrence Erlbaum Associates, Inc., 10 Industrial Dr., Mahwah, NJ 07430-2262. TEL 201-236-9500. FAX 201-236-0072. *6115*

HUMAN PHYSIOLOGY.
Maik Nauka - Interperiodica, Mezhdunarodnyi Otdel, Ul. Profsoyuznaya, 90, 117864 Moscow, Russia. TEL 7-095-3360066. FAX 7-095-3360066. *816*

HUMAN PSYCHOPHARMACOLOGY: CLINICAL AND EXPERIMENTAL.
John Wiley & Sons Ltd., Journals, Baffins Ln., Chichester, W. Sussex PO19 1UD, England. TEL 44-1243-779777. FAX 44-1243-775878. *5068*

HUMAN RELATIONS.
Plenum Publishing Corp., 233 Spring St., New York, NY 10013-1578. TEL 212-260-8000. FAX 212-463-0742. *6617*

HUMAN RESOURCE DEVELOPMENT QUARTERLY.
Jossey-Bass Inc., Publishers, 350 Sansome St., 5th Fl., San Francisco, CA 94104. FAX 800-605-2665. *1567*

HUMAN RIGHTS IN DEVELOPING COUNTRIES YEARBOOK.
Kluwer Law International, Postbus 85889, 2508 CN The Hague, Netherlands. TEL 31-70-3081500. FAX 31-70-3081515. *5992*

HUMAN RIGHTS LAW AND PRACTICE.
Brooker's Limited, Level 1 - Telecom Networks House, 68-86 Jervois Quay, Wellington, New Zealand. TEL 64-4-4998178. FAX 64-4-4998173. *4070*

HUMAN STUDIES.
Kluwer Academic Publishers, Postbus 17, 3300 AA Dordrecht, Netherlands. TEL 31-78-6392392. FAX 31-78-6392254. *5729*

HUMAN SYSTEMS.
University of Leeds, Department of Psychology, Leeds Family Therapy & Research Centre, Leeds LS2 9JT, England. TEL 44-113-2335728. FAX 44-113-2335700. *6115*

HUMANE HEALTH CARE INTERNATIONAL.
Multimed, 1120 Finch Ave. W., Ste. 601, Downsville, ON M3J 3H7, Canada. TEL 416-650-0610. FAX 416-650-6039. *4681*

HUMANIST IN CANADA.
Canadian Humanist Publications, P.O. Box 3769, Station C, Ottawa, ON K1Y 4J8, Canada. TEL 613-749-8929. FAX 613-749-8929. *5729*

THE HUMANISTIC PSYCHOLOGIST.
American Psychological Association, Division of Humanistic Psychology, Psychology Dept., University of West Georgia, Carrollton, GA 30118. TEL 770-836-4578. FAX 770-836-6791. *6115*

HUMANITIES COLLECTIONS.
Haworth Press, Inc., 10 Alice St., Binghamton, NY 13904-1580. TEL 607-722-5857. FAX 607-722-6362. *4181*

HUME PAPERS ON PUBLIC POLICY.
Edinburgh University Press, 22 George Sq., Edinburgh EH8 9LF, Scotland. TEL 44-131-650-6207. FAX 44-131-662-0053. *6178*

HUME STUDIES.
Hume Society, 338 Orson Spencer Hall, University of Utah, Salt Lake City, UT 84112. TEL 801-581-8161. FAX 801-585-5195. *5730*

HUNAN JIAOYU XUEYUAN XUEBAO.
Hunan Jiaoyu Xueyuan, Xuebao Bianjibu, Zuojialong, Changsha, Hunan 410012, People's Republic of China. TEL 86-731-8825923. *2544*

HURRICANE ALICE.
Hurricane Alice Foundation, Rhode Island College, Dept. of English, Providence, RI 02908. TEL 401-456-8377. FAX 401-456-8379. *7323*

HUSSERL STUDIES.
Kluwer Academic Publishers, Postbus 17, 3300 AA Dordrecht, Netherlands. TEL 31-78-6392392. FAX 31-78-6392254. *5730*

HUSSERLIANA.
Kluwer Academic Publishers, Postbus 17, 3300 AA Dordrecht, Netherlands. TEL 31-78-6392392. FAX 31-78-6392254. *5730*

HYBRIDOMA.
Mary Ann Liebert, Inc. Publishers, 2 Madison Ave., Larchmont, NY 10538. TEL 914-834-3100. FAX 914-834-3688. *661*

HYDRO INTERNATIONAL.
G I T C bv, Nieuwedijk 43, 8531 HK Lemmer, Netherlands. TEL 31-514-56-18-54. FAX 31-514-56-38-98. *2692*

HYDRO REVIEW.
H C I Publications, 410 Archibald St., Kansas City, MO 64111-3046. TEL 816-931-1311. FAX 816-931-2015. *2692*

HYDROBIOLOGIA.
Kluwer Academic Publishers, Postbus 17, 3300 AA Dordrecht, Netherlands. TEL 31-78-6392392. FAX 31-78-6392254. *604*

HYDROCARBON TECHNOLOGY INTERNATIONAL.
Sterling Publications Ltd., 86-88 Edgware Rd., London W2 2YW, England. TEL 44-171-915-9600. FAX 44-171-915-9619. *5605*

HYDROGEN TODAY.
American Hydrogen Association, 216 S. Clark Dr., Ste. 103, Tempe, AZ 85281. TEL 602-921-0433. FAX 602-967-6601. *2693*

HYDROGEOLOGY JOURNAL.
Verlag Heinz Heise GmbH und Co. KG, Helstorferstr. 7, 30625 Hannover, Germany. TEL 49-511-5352-0. FAX 49-511-5352-294. *2394*

HYDROLOGICAL PROCESSES: AN INTERNATIONAL JOURNAL.
John Wiley & Sons Ltd., Journals, Baffins Ln., Chichester, W. Sussex PO19 1UD, England. TEL 44-1243-779777. FAX 44-1243-775878. *2394*

HYDROLOGICAL SCIENCE AND TECHNOLOGY.
American Institute of Hydrology, 2499 Rice St., Ste. 135, St. Paul, MN 55113-3724. TEL 612-484-8169. FAX 612-484-8357. *7294*

HYDROLOGICAL SCIENCES JOURNAL.
I A H S Press, Institute of Hydrology, Wallingford, Oxfordshire OX10 8BB, England. TEL 44-1491-692442. FAX 44-1491-692448. *2394*

HYDROMETALLURGY.
Elsevier Science B.V., P.O. Box 211, 1000 AE Amsterdam, Netherlands. TEL 31-20-4853911. FAX 31-20-4853598. *5193*

HYDROTECHNICAL CONSTRUCTION.
Plenum Publishing Corp., Consultants Bureau, 233 Spring St., New York, NY 10013-1578. TEL 212-620-8000. FAX 212-463-0742. *2786*

HYGIENA.
Nakladatelske Stredisko C L S J.E. Purkyne, Sokolska 31, 120 26 Prague 2, Czech Republic. TEL 420-2-24911420. FAX 420-2-24911420. *5784*

HYGIENE & MEDIZIN - INFECTION CONTROL AND HEALTHCARE.
M H P Verlag GmbH, Ostring 13, 65205 Wiesbaden, Germany. TEL 49-6122-7709131. FAX 49-6122-76331. *4681*

HYMN SOCIETY OF GREAT BRITAIN AND IRELAND. BULLETIN.
Hymn Society of Great Britain and Ireland, c/o Rev. Michael Garland, St. Nicholas Rectory, Curdworth, Sutton Coldfield, W. Midlands B76 9ES, England. TEL 44-1675-470384. *5399*

HYMNOLOGISKE MEDDELELSER.
Salmehistorisk Selskab, Koebenhavns Universitet, Institut for Kirkehistorie, Koebmagergade 44-46, DK-1150 Copenhagen K, Denmark. TEL 45-35-32-36-23. FAX 45-35-36-32. *6428*

HYPATIA.
Indiana University Press, 601 N. Morton St., Bloomington, IN 47404. TEL 812-855-9449. FAX 812-855-8507. *7344*

HYPERTENSION.
American Heart Association, 7272 Greenville Ave., Dallas, TX 75231-4596. TEL 214-706-1310. FAX 214-691-6342. *4818*

HYPERTENSION IN PREGNANCY.
Marcel Dekker Journals, 270 Madison Ave., New York, NY 10016. TEL 212-696-9000. FAX 212-685-4540. *4818*

I A B M C P NEWSLETTER.
International Academy of Behavioral Medicine, Counseling and Psychotherapy, 13140 Coit Rd., Ste. 307, Dallas, TX 75240. TEL 972-437-3370. FAX 972-437-1190. *6115*

I B M JOURNAL OF RESEARCH AND DEVELOPMENT.
International Business Machines Corp., Box 218, Yorktown Heights, NY 10598. TEL 914-945-3836. *2083*

I B M SYSTEMS JOURNAL.
International Business Machines, Box 218, Yorktown Heights, NY 10598. TEL 914-945-3836. *2155*

I C A S A NEWS.
International Consortium for Agricultural Systems Applications (ICASA), 2500 Dole St., Krauss 22, Honolulu, HI 96822. TEL 808-956-8858. FAX 808-956-3421. *227*

I C A S E - L A R C INTERDISCIPLINARY SERIES IN SCIENCE.
Kluwer Academic Publishers, Postbus 17, 3300 AA Dordrecht, Netherlands. TEL 31-78-6392392. FAX 31-78-6392254. *6531*

I C L SYSTEMS JOURNAL.
International Computers Ltd., Lovelace Rd., Bracknell, Berks. RG12 4SN, England, England. TEL 44-1344-472000. FAX 44-1344-472700. *2083*

I C U M S A METHODS BOOK.
I C U M S A Publications, c/o British Sugar Technical Centre, Norwich Research Park, Colney, Norwich NR4 7UB, England. TEL 44-1493-751678. FAX 44-1493-751807. *3112*

I D N.
Systems Design Ltd., 5-9 Gresson St., Shop C, Wanchai, Hong Kong, People's Republic of China. TEL 852-2528-5744. FAX 852-2529-1296. *2170*

I D U G SOLUTIONS JOURNAL.
Design Liberte, 5048 W. Coyle Ave., Skokie, IL 60077. TEL 847-677-9326. *2212*

I E E E DESIGN & TEST OF COMPUTERS.
I E E E Computer Society, 10662 Los Vaqueros Circle, Box 3014, Los Alamitos, CA 90720-1264. TEL 714-821-8380. *2115*

I E E E JOURNAL OF TECHNOLOGY COMPUTER AIDED DESIGN.
Institute of Electrical and Electronics Engineers, Inc., 345 E. 47th St., New York, NY 10017-2394. *2123*

I E E PROCEEDINGS - CIRCUITS, DEVICES AND SYSTEMS.
I.E.E., Michael Faraday House, Six Hills Way, Stevenage, Herts. SG1 2AY, England. TEL 44-1438-313311. FAX 44-1438-742840. *2832*

I E T E JOURNAL OF RESEARCH.
Institution of Electronics and Telecommunication Engineers, 2, Institutional Area, Lodi Rd., New Delhi 110 003, India. TEL 91-11-4631850. FAX 91-11-463-1810. *1992*

I F A C WORKSHOP SERIES.
Elsevier Science Ltd., Books Division, P.O. Box 800, Kidlington, Oxford OX2 1DX, England. TEL 44-1865-843000. FAX 44-1865-843010. *2885*

I G B P GLOBAL CHANGE REPORT.
Royal Swedish Academy of Sciences, International Geosphere-Biosphere Programme, P.O. Box 50005, S-104 05 Stockholm, Sweden. TEL 46-8-16-64-48. FAX 46-8-16-64-05. *2350*

I G C C NEWSLETTER.
Institute on Global Conflict and Cooperation, University of California, 9500 Gilman Dr., La Jolla, CA 92093-0518. TEL 619-534-1979. FAX 619-534-7655. *6017*

I G C C POLICY BRIEFS.
Institute on Global Conflict and Cooperation, University of California, 9500 Gilman Dr., La Jolla, CA 92093-0518. TEL 619-534-1979. FAX 619-534-7655. *6018*

I G C C POLICY PAPERS.
Institute on Global Conflict and Cooperation, University of California, 9500 Gilman Dr., La Jolla, CA 92093-0518. TEL 619-534-1979. FAX 619-534-7655. *6018*

I G P L LOGIC JOURNAL.
Oxford University Press, Academic Division, Great Clarendon St., Oxford OX2 6DP, England. TEL 44-1865-267907. FAX 44-1865-267485. *5730*

I H R I M - LINK.
International Association for Human Resource Information Management, 14643 Dallas Parkway, No. 525, Dallas, TX 75240. TEL 972-661-3727. FAX 972-386-8180. *1568*

I I E TRANSACTIONS.
Thomson Science, 2-6 Boundary Row, London SE1 8HN, England. TEL 44-171-8560066. FAX 44-171-5229623. *2876*

I L A R JOURNAL.
Institute of Laboratory Animal Resources, 2101 Constitution Ave., N.W., Washington, DC 20418. TEL 202-334-2590. FAX 202-334-1687. *4897*

I L S A JOURNAL OF INTERNATIONAL AND COMPARATIVE LAW.
International Law Students Association, Tillar House, 2223 Massachusetts Ave., N.W., Washington, DC 20008. TEL 305-423-5325. FAX 305-423-5327. *4115*

I P O ANNUAL PROGRESS REPORT.
I P O, Centrum voor Onderzoek naar Mens - Systeem Interactie, P.O. Box 513, 5600 MB Eindhoven, Netherlands. TEL 31-40-2435200. FAX 31-40-2431930. *4262*

I R B REVISTA.
Instituto de Resseguros do Brasil, Secretaria Geral da Presidencia, Av. Marechal Camara 171-8, Rio de Janeiro, Brazil. TEL 55-21-2720317. FAX 55-21-2406261. *3818*

I S A TRANSACTIONS.
Elsevier Science B.V., P.O. Box 211, 1000 AE Amsterdam, Netherlands. TEL 31-20-4853911. FAX 31-20-4853598. *2723*

I S L A: A JOURNAL OF MICRONESIAN STUDIES.
University of Guam Press, UOG Station, Mangilao, Guam 96923. TEL 671-735-2171. FAX 617-734-3676. *6617*

I S P R S JOURNAL OF PHOTOGRAMMETRY AND REMOTE SENSING.
Elsevier Science B.V., P.O. Box 211, 1000 AE Amsterdam, Netherlands. TEL 31-20-4853911. FAX 31-20-4853598. *3409*

I S T C TODAY.
Iron and Steel Trades Confederation, Swinton House, 324 Gray's Inn Rd., London WC1X 8DD, England. TEL 44-171-837-6691. FAX 44-171-278-8378. *3891*

I T C JOURNAL.
International Institute for Aerospace Survey and Earth Sciences, P.O. Box 6, 7500 AA Enschede, Netherlands. TEL 31-53-4874382. FAX 31-53-4874400. *3409*

I T E A PRODUCCION ANIMAL.
Asociacion Interprofesional para el Desarrollo Agrario, Montanana 177, Apdo. 727, 50080 Zaragoza, Spain. TEL 34-76-576311. FAX 34-76-575501. *277*

I T E A PRODUCCION VEGETAL.
Asociacion Interprofesional para el Desarrollo Agrario, Montanana 177, Apdo. 727, 50080 Zaragoza, Spain. TEL 34-76-576311. FAX 34-76-575501. *227*

I T G JOURNAL.
International Trumpet Guild, Drawer 2025, Columbia, SC 29202. *5399*

I T L REVIEW OF APPLIED LINGUISTICS.
Katholieke Universiteit Leuven, Instituut Toegepaste Linguistiek, Blijde Inkomstraat 21, P.O. Box 33, 3000 Leuven, Belgium. TEL 32-16-325030. FAX 32-16-324767. *4263*

I T TRAINING.
51 High St., Ruislip, Middx. HA4 7BG, England. TEL 0895-622112. FAX 0895-621582. *1569*

I U P STRESS AND HEALTH SERIES.
International Universities Press, Inc., 59 Boston Post Rd., Box 1524, Madison, CT 06443-1524. TEL 203-245-4000. FAX 203-245-0775. *5068*

IBARAKI DAIGAKU KYOIKUGAKUBU KIYO. SHIZEN KAGAKU.
Ibaraki Daigaku, Kyoikugakubu, 1-1, Bunkyo 2-chome, Mito-shi, Ibaraki-ken 310, Japan. TEL 81-29-228-8282. FAX 81-29-228-8329. *6532*

IBERIAN STUDIES.
University of Keele, Centre for Iberian Studies, Keele, Staffs. ST5 5BG, England. TEL 44-1782-621111. FAX 44-1782-613847. *6617*

IBERO-AMERICANA PRAGENSIA.
Vydavatelstvi Karolinum, Ovocny trh 5, 116 36 Prague 1, Czech Republic. TEL 42-2-24491265. FAX 42-2-24212041. *3631*

IBEROAMERICANA.
Universidad Sofia, Instituto Iberoamericano, 7-1 Kioicho, Chiyoda-ku, Tokyo, Japan. TEL 81-3-3238-3530. FAX 81-3-3238-3229. *6618*

ICARUS (SAN DIEGO).
Academic Press, Inc., Journal Division, 525 B St., Ste. 1900, San Diego, CA 92101-4495. TEL 619-230-1840. FAX 619-699-6800. *495*

ICHNOS.
Gordon and Breach - Harwood Academic, Amsteldisk 166, 1st Fl., 1079 LH Amsterdam, Netherlands. *5559*

ICON.
Frank Cass, Newbury House, 890-900 Eastern Ave., Newbury Park, Ilford, Essex IG2 7HH, England. TEL 44-181-5998866. FAX 44-181-5990984. *6962*

ICONOGRAPHY OF RELIGIONS.
E.J. Brill, P.O. Box 9000, 2300 PA Leiden, Netherlands. TEL 31-71-5353500. FAX 31-71-5317532. *445*

ICONOGRAPHY OF RELIGIONS. SECTION 2, NEW ZEALAND.
E.J. Brill, P.O. Box 9000, 2300 PA Leiden, Netherlands. TEL 31-71-5353500. FAX 31-71-5317532. *445*

ICONOGRAPHY OF RELIGIONS. SECTION 5, AUSTRALIA.
E.J. Brill, P.O. Box 9000, 2300 PA Leiden, Netherlands. TEL 31-71-5353500. FAX 31-71-5317532. *445*

ICONOGRAPHY OF RELIGIONS. SECTION 7, AFRICA.
E.J. Brill, P.O. Box 9000, 2300 PA Leiden, Netherlands. TEL 31-71-5353500. FAX 31-71-5317532. *445*

ICONOGRAPHY OF RELIGIONS. SECTION 8, ARCTIC PEOPLES.
E.J. Brill, P.O. Box 9000, 2300 PA Leiden, Netherlands. TEL 31-71-5353500. FAX 31-71-5317532. *445*

ICONOGRAPHY OF RELIGIONS. SECTION 9, SOUTH AMERICA.
E.J. Brill, P.O. Box 9000, 2300 PA Leiden, Netherlands. TEL 31-71-5353500. FAX 31-71-5317532. *445*

ICONOGRAPHY OF RELIGIONS. SECTION 10, NORTH AMERICA.
E.J. Brill, P.O. Box 9000, 2300 PA Leiden, Netherlands. TEL 31-71-5353500. FAX 31-71-5317532. *445*

ICONOGRAPHY OF RELIGIONS. SECTION 11, ANCIENT AMERICA.
E.J. Brill, P.O. Box 9000, 2300 PA Leiden, Netherlands. TEL 31-71-5353500. FAX 31-71-5317532. *446*

ICONOGRAPHY OF RELIGIONS. SECTION 12, EAST AND CENTRAL ASIA.
E.J. Brill, P.O. Box 9000, 2300 PA Leiden, Netherlands. TEL 31-71-5353500. FAX 31-71-5317532. *446*

ICONOGRAPHY OF RELIGIONS. SECTION 13, INDIAN RELIGIONS.
E.J. Brill, P.O. Box 9000, 2300 PA Leiden, Netherlands. TEL 31-71-5353500. FAX 31-71-5317532. *446*

ICONOGRAPHY OF RELIGIONS. SECTION 14, IRAN.
E.J. Brill, P.O. Box 9000, 2300 PA Leiden, Netherlands. TEL 31-71-5353500. FAX 31-71-5317532. *446*

ICONOGRAPHY OF RELIGIONS. SECTION 15, MESOPOTAMIA AND THE NEAR EAST.
E.J. Brill, P.O. Box 9000, 2300 PA Leiden, Netherlands. TEL 31-71-5353500. FAX 31-71-5317532. *446*

ICONOGRAPHY OF RELIGIONS. SECTION 16, EGYPT.
E.J. Brill, P.O. Box 9000, 2300 PA Leiden, Netherlands. TEL 31-71-5353500. FAX 31-71-5317532. *446*

ICONOGRAPHY OF RELIGIONS. SECTION 17, GREECE AND ROME.
E.J. Brill, P.O. Box 9000, 2300 PA Leiden, Netherlands. TEL 31-71-5353500. FAX 31-71-5317532. *446*

ICONOGRAPHY OF RELIGIONS. SECTION 19, ANCIENT EUROPE.
E.J. Brill, P.O. Box 9000, 2300 PA Leiden, Netherlands. TEL 31-71-5353500. FAX 31-71-5317532. *446*

ICONOGRAPHY OF RELIGIONS. SECTION 20, MANICHAEISM.
E.J. Brill, P.O. Box 9000, 2300 PA Leiden, Netherlands. TEL 31-71-5353500. FAX 31-71-5317532. *446*

ICONOGRAPHY OF RELIGIONS. SECTION 21, MANDAEISM.
E.J. Brill, P.O. Box 9000, 2300 PA Leiden, Netherlands. TEL 31-71-5353500. FAX 31-71-5317532. *446*

ICONOGRAPHY OF RELIGIONS. SECTION 22, ISLAM.
E.J. Brill, P.O. Box 9000, 2300 PA Leiden, Netherlands. TEL 31-71-5353500. FAX 31-71-5317532. *446*

ICONOGRAPHY OF RELIGIONS. SECTION 23, JUDAISM.
E.J. Brill, P.O. Box 9000, 2300 PA Leiden, Netherlands. TEL 31-71-5353500. FAX 31-71-5317532. *446*

ICONOGRAPHY OF RELIGIONS. SECTION 24, CHRISTIANITY.
E.J. Brill, P.O. Box 9000, 2300 PA Leiden, Netherlands. TEL 31-71-5353500. FAX 31-71-5317532. *446*

ICONOGRAPHY OF RELIGIONS. SUPPLEMENTS.
E.J. Brill, P.O. Box 9000, 2300 PA Leiden, Netherlands. TEL 31-71-5353500. FAX 31-71-5317532. *446*

IDAHO ACADEMY OF SCIENCE. JOURNAL.
Idaho Academy of Science, c/o Phil Anderson, Exec. Dir., 909 Lucille Ave., Pocatello, ID 83201-2542. TEL 208-526-3395. *6532*

IDAHO BUREAU OF LAND MANAGEMENT TECHNICAL BULLETIN.
U.S. Bureau of Land Management, Idaho State Office, 1387 S. Vinnell Way, Boise, ID 83709. TEL 208-373-3827. FAX 208-373-3805. *2232*

IDAHO CURRENTS.
Department of Water Resources, Box 83720, Boise, ID 83720-0098. TEL 208-327-7982. FAX 208-327-7866. *2671*

IDAHO YESTERDAYS.
Idaho State Historical Society, 450 N. Fourth St., Boise, ID 83702. TEL 208-334-3428. FAX 208-334-3198. *3631*

IDEAS Y VALORES.
Universidad Nacional de Colombia, Departamento de Filosofia, Apdo. 14490, Ciudad Universitaria, Bogota, Colombia. TEL 57-1-2220463. *5730*

IDENTITIES.
Gordon and Breach - Harwood Academic, Amsteldijk 166, 1st Fl., 1079 LH Amsterdam, Netherlands. *3016*

IDESIA.
Universidad de Tarapaca, Instituto de Agronomia, Casilla 6-D, Arica, Chile. TEL 56-58-224157. FAX 56-58-226737. *124*

IDOJARAS.
Hungarian Meteorological Service, P.O. Box 39, 1675 Budapest, Hungary. TEL 36-1-2907387. FAX 36-1-2907387. *5234*

IHERINGIA. SERIE ZOOLOGIA.
Fundacao Zoobotanica do Rio Grande do Sul, Museu de Ciencias Naturais, Caixa Postal 1188, 90690-000 Porto Alegre, RS, Brazil. TEL 55-51-336151. FAX 55-51-361778. *837*

ILLIANA NEWS.
Jewish Federation, Inc. - Northwest Indiana, 2939 Jewett St., Highland, IN 46322. TEL 219-972-2250. FAX 219-972-4779. *3017*

ILLINOIS. NATURAL HISTORY SURVEY. BIOLOGICAL NOTES.
Department of Natural Resources, Natural History Survey, Natural Resources Bldg., 607 E. Peabody Dr., Champaign, IL 61820. TEL 217-244-2115. FAX 217-333-4949. *605*

ILLINOIS. NATURAL HISTORY SURVEY. BULLETIN.
Department of Natural Resources, Natural History Survey Division, Natural Resources Bldg., 607 E. Peabody Dr., Champaign, IL 61820. TEL 217-244-2115. FAX 217-333-4949. *605*

ILLINOIS. STATE MUSEUM. INVENTORY OF THE COLLECTIONS.
Illinois State Museum, Springfield, IL 62706. TEL 217-782-7386. FAX 217-782-1254. *5356*

ILLINOIS. STATE MUSEUM. POPULAR SCIENCE SERIES.
Illinois State Museum, Springfield, IL 62706. TEL 217-782-7386. FAX 217-782-1254. *6532*

ILLINOIS. STATE MUSEUM. SCIENTIFIC PAPERS SERIES.
Illinois State Museum, Springfield, IL 62706. TEL 217-782-7386. FAX 217-782-1254. *6532*

ILLINOIS BIOLOGICAL MONOGRAPHS.
University of Illinois Press, 1325 S. Oak St., Champaign, IL 61820. TEL 217-333-0950. FAX 217-244-8082. *605*

ILLINOIS ENGLISH BULLETIN.
University of Illinois at Urbana-Champaign, English Department, 608 Wright St., Urbana, IL 61801. TEL 217-333-1006. FAX 217-333-4321. *2605*

ILLINOIS GEOGRAPHICAL SOCIETY. BULLETIN.
Illinois Geographical Society, c/o Michael Sublett, Illinois State University, Campus Box 4400, Normal, IL 61790-4400. TEL 309-438-7649. FAX 309-438-5310. *3409*

ILLINOIS HISTORICAL JOURNAL.
Illinois Historic Preservation Agency, Old State Capitol, Springfield, IL 62701. TEL 217-782-4836. *3631*

ILLINOIS JOURNAL OF MATHEMATICS.
University of Illinois Press, 1325 S. Oak St., Champaign, IL 61820. TEL 217-333-0950. FAX 217-244-8082. *4576*

ILLINOIS MEDIEVAL MONOGRAPH SERIES.
University of Illinois Press, 1325 S. Oak St., Champaign, IL 61820. TEL 217-333-0950. FAX 217-244-8082. *3574*

ILLINOIS MUSIC EDUCATOR.
Illinois Music Educators Association, c/o Dr. Don Davis, Ed., 72 Marchelle, Springfield, IL 62702. TEL 217-787-6323. FAX 217-787-3610. *5399*

ILLINOIS SCHOOL RESEARCH AND DEVELOPMENT.
Illinois Association for Supervision and Curriculum Development, College of Education 5300, Illinois State University, Normal, IL 61790-5300. TEL 309-438-8294. FAX 309-438-3813. *2605*

ILLINOIS SPEECH AND THEATRE ASSOCIATION. JOURNAL.
Illinois Speech and Theatre Association, Bradley University, Dept. of Communication, IL 61625. TEL 309-677-2364. FAX 309-677-2330. *1993*

ILLINOIS STATE ACADEMY OF SCIENCE. TRANSACTIONS.
Illinois State Academy of Sciences, Illinois State Museum, Springfield, IL 62706. TEL 217-782-6436. FAX 217-782-1254. *6532*

ILLINOIS STEWARD.
Illinois Stewardship Committee, W503 Turner Hall, 1102 S. Goodwin Ave., Urbana, IL 61801. TEL 217-333-2778. FAX 217-244-3219. *2233*

ILLINOIS STUDIES IN ANTHROPOLOGY.
University of Illinois Press, 1325 S. Oak St., Champaign, IL 61820. TEL 217-333-0950. FAX 217-244-8082. *319*

ILLUSTRATED CASE REPORTS IN GASTROENTEROLOGY.
Chapman & Hall, Journals Department 2-6 Boundary Row, London SE1 8HN, England. TEL 44-171-8650066. FAX 44-171-5229323. *4911*

AL-ILM.
University of Durban - Westville, Center for Research in Islamic Studies, Private Bag X54001, Durban 4000, South Africa. TEL 27-31-2044173. FAX 27-31-2044160. *6397*

ILTALEHTI.
Kustannusosakeyhtio Italehti, P.O. Box 372, FIN-00101 Helsinki, Finland. TEL 358-9-50-77-21. FAX 358-9-17-73-13. *3278*

IMAGE & TEXT.
University of Pretoria, Faculty of Arts: Visual Art & Art History, Pretoria 0002, South Africa. TEL 27-12-4202286. FAX 27-12-4203686. *447*

IMAGE AND VISION COMPUTING.
Elsevier Science B.V., P.O. Box 211, 1000 AE Amsterdam, Netherlands. TEL 31-20-4853911. FAX 31-20-4853598. *2123*

IMAGE: JOURNAL OF NURSING SCHOLARSHIP.
Sigma Theta Tau International Honor Society of Nursing, 550 W. North St., Indianapolis, IN 46202. TEL 317-634-8171. FAX 317-634-8188. *4934*

IMAGE PROCESSING.
European Technology Publishing, Preston Barn, Preston Ln., Ramsbury, Malborough, Wilts. SN8 2HF, England. TEL 44-1632-520788. FAX 44-1672-520789. *5861*

REFEREED SERIALS

IMAGE TECHNOLOGY.
British Kinematograph Sound and Television Society, G3-71 Victoria House, Vernon Pl., London WC1B 4DA, England. TEL 44-171-242-8400. FAX 44-171-405-3560. *5336*

IMAGINATION, COGNITION AND PERSONALITY.
Baywood Publishing Co., Inc., 26 Austin Ave., Box 337, Amityville, NY 11701. TEL 516-691-1270. FAX 516-691-1770. *6116*

IMAGING ABSTRACTS.
Pira International, Randalls Rd., Leatherhead, Surrey KT22 7RU, England. TEL 44-1372-802050. FAX 44-1372-802239. *5777*

IMAGING DECISIONS M R I.
Blackwell Wissenschaft, Kurfuerstendamm 57, 10707 Berlin, Germany. TEL 49-30-32790635. FAX 49-30-32790610. *5107*

IMAGING SCIENCE JOURNAL.
The Barn, Whitehall, Near Middle Marwood, Barnstaple, N. Devon EX31 4EQ, England. TEL 44-1271-72482. FAX 44-1271-24716. *5767*

IMAGO MUNDI.
Imago Mundi Ltd., c/o the Map Library, The British Library, Great Russell St., London WC1B 3DG, England. *3409*

IMMIGRANTS AND MINORITIES.
Frank Cass, Newbury House, 890-900 Eastern Ave., Newbury Park, Ilford, Essex IG2 7HH, England. TEL 44-181-599-8866. FAX 44-181-599-0984. *3500*

IMMIGRATION AND NATIONALITY LAW REVIEW.
William S. Hein & Co., Inc., 1285 Main St., Buffalo, NY 14209. TEL 716-882-2600. FAX 800-882-7571. *4115*

IMMIGRATION NEWSLETTER.
National Lawyers Guild (Boston), National Immigration Project, 14 Beacon St., Ste. 506, Boston, MA 02108. TEL 617-227-9727. FAX 617-227-5495. *4115*

IMMUNITY.
Cell Press, 1050 Massachusetts Ave., Cambridge, MA 02138. TEL 617-661-7060. FAX 617-661-7061. *4794*

THE IMMUNOASSAY KIT DIRECTORY. SERIES A: CLINICAL CHEMISTRY.
Kluwer Academic Publishers, Postbus 17, 3300 AA Dordrecht, Netherlands. TEL 31-78-6392392. FAX 31-78-6392254. *4795*

IMMUNOLOGIC RESEARCH.
Humana Press Inc., 999 Riverview Dr., Ste. 208, Totowa, NJ 07512-1165. TEL 973-256-1699. FAX 973-256-8341. *4795*

IMMUNOLOGICAL INVESTIGATIONS.
Marcel Dekker Journals, 270 Madison Ave., New York, NY 10016. TEL 212-696-9000. FAX 212-685-4540. *4795*

IMMUNOLOGICAL REVIEWS.
Munksgaard International Publishers Ltd., 35 Noerre Soegade, P.O. Box 2148, DK-1016 Copenhagen K, Denmark. TEL 45-33-127030. FAX 45-33-129387. *4795*

IMMUNOLOGY.
Blackwell Science Ltd., Osney Mead, Oxford OX2 0EL, England. TEL 44-1865-206206. FAX 44-1865-721205. *4795*

IMMUNOLOGY AND MEDICINE.
Kluwer Academic Publishers, Postbus 17, 3300 AA Dordrecht, Netherlands. TEL 31-78-6392392. FAX 31-78-6392254. *4796*

IMMUNOLOGY LETTERS.
Elsevier Science B.V., P.O. Box 211, 1000 AE Amsterdam, Netherlands. TEL 31-20-4853911. FAX 31-20-4853598. *4796*

IMMUNOLOGY SERIES.
Marcel Dekker, Inc., 270 Madison Ave., New York, NY 10016. TEL 212-696-9000. FAX 212-685-4540. *4796*

IMMUNOLOGY TODAY (REFERENCE EDITION).
Elsevier Science Ltd., P.O. Box 800, Kidlington, Oxford OX5 1DX, England. TEL 44-1865-843000. FAX 44-1865-843010. *4796*

IMMUNOPHARMACOLOGY.
Elsevier Science B.V., P.O. Box 211, 1000 AE Amsterdam, Netherlands. TEL 31-20-4853911. FAX 31-20-4853598. *4796*

IMMUNOPHARMACOLOGY AND IMMUNOTOXICOLOGY.
Marcel Dekker Journals, 270 Madison Ave., New York, NY 10016. TEL 212-696-9000. FAX 212-685-4540. *5666*

IMMUNOTECHNOLOGY.
Elsevier Science B.V., P.O. Box 211, 1000 AE Amsterdam, Netherlands. TEL 31-20-4853911. FAX 31-20-4853598. *4796*

IMPACT (NORTH YORK).
Seneca College, Student Federation Council, 1750 Finch Ave. E., North York, ON M2J 2X5, Canada. TEL 416-491-5050. FAX 416-756-2765. *1956*

IMPACT ASSESSMENT.
International Association for Impact Assessment, Box 5256, Fargo, ND 58105. TEL 701-231-1006. FAX 701-231-1007. *6962*

IMPIANTI SPORT.
Edizioni Publipam s.r.l., Torre 10, S. Felice, 20090 Segrate (MI), Italy. TEL 39-2-7530009. FAX 39-2-7533027. *4149*

IMPLANT DENTISTRY.
Williams & Wilkins, 351 W. Camden St., Baltimore, MD 21201-2436. TEL 410-528-4068. FAX 410-528-4452. *4859*

IMPRESSIONS (DALLAS).
Miller Freeman Inc. (Dallas), 13760 Noel Rd., Ste. 500, Dallas, TX 75240. TEL 214-239-3060. FAX 214-419-7825. *1924*

IN DIE SKRIFLIG.
Buro vir Wetenskaplike Tydskrifte, Private Bag X6001, Potchefstroom 2520, South Africa. TEL 27-148-2991769. FAX 27-148-2991562. *6428*

IN GEARDAGUM.
Society for New Language Study, Box 10596, Denver, CO 80210-9998. TEL 303-871-6115. FAX 303-871-4432. *4263*

IN OTHER WORDS.
Wycliffe Bible Translators, Inc., Box 2727, Huntington Beach, CA 92647. TEL 714-969-4600. FAX 714-969-4661. *6344*

IN SESSION: PSYCHOTHERAPY IN PRACTICE.
John Wiley & Sons, Inc., Journals, 605 Third Ave., New York, NY 10158. TEL 212-850-6645. FAX 212-850-6021. *6116*

IN SITU.
Marcel Dekker Journals, 270 Madison Ave., New York, NY 10016. TEL 212-696-9000. FAX 212-685-4540. *2723*

IN TOUCH (LONDON, ONTARIO).
University of Western Ontario, Information Technology Services, Natural Sciences Centre, London, ON N6A 3K7, Canada. TEL 519-661-2151. FAX 519-661-3486. *2084*

IN VITRO CELLULAR & DEVELOPMENTAL BIOLOGY - ANIMAL.
Society for In Vitro Biology, 9315 Largo Dr. W. Ste. 255, Largo, MD 20774. TEL 301-324-5054. FAX 301-324-5057. *785*

IN VITRO CELLULAR & DEVELOPMENTAL BIOLOGY - PLANT.
Society for In Vitro Biology, 9315 Largo Dr. W. Ste. 255, Largo, MD 20774. TEL 301-324-5054. FAX 301-324-5057. *786*

IN VITRO REPORT.
Society for In Vitro Biology, 9315 Largo Dr. W., Ste. 255, Largo, MD 20774. TEL 301-324-5054. FAX 301-324-5057. *786*

IN VIVO.
John D. Delinassios, Ed. & Pub., Km. 1, Kapandritiou-Kalamou, P.O. Box 22, 190 14 Kapandriti, Attiki, Greece. TEL 30-295-53359. FAX 30-295-52945. *4898*

INDAGATIONES MATHEMATICAE.
North-Holland, P.O. Box 211, 1000 AE Amsterdam, Netherlands. TEL 31-20-4853911. FAX 31-20-4853598. *4576*

INDEX OF ARTICLES ON JEWISH STUDIES.
Jewish National and University Library, P.O. Box 34165, Jerusalem 91341, Israel. TEL 972-2-585039. FAX 972-2-511771. *3052*

INDIAN ACADEMY OF MATHEMATICS. JOURNAL.
Indian Academy of Mathematics, 15 Kaushaliya Puri, Chitawad Rd., Indore 452001, India. TEL 91-731-400464. FAX 91-731-401389. *4576*

INDIAN CERAMIC SOCIETY. TRANSACTIONS.
Indian Ceramic Society, c/o Central Glass and Ceramic Research Institute, Calcutta 700 032, India. TEL 91-33-473-3496. FAX 91-33-473-0957. *1731*

INDIAN CHEMICAL ENGINEER.
Indian Institute of Chemical Engineers, P.O. Box 17001, Raja S C Mullick Rd., Calcutta 700 032, India. TEL 9133-473-4670. *2765*

INDIAN CHEMICAL SOCIETY. JOURNAL.
Indian Chemical Society, 92 Acharya Prafulla Chandra Rd., Calcutta 700009, India. TEL 91-33-350-3478. *1751*

INDIAN DEFENCE REVIEW.
Lancer Publishers & Distributors, 56 Gautam Nagar, New Delhi 110 049, India. TEL 91-11-655652. FAX 91-11-6862077. *5270*

INDIAN ECONOMIC AND SOCIAL HISTORY REVIEW.
Sage Publications India Pvt. Ltd., P.O. Box 4215, New Delhi 110 048, India. TEL 91-11-644-4958. FAX 91-11-647-2426. *6618*

INDIAN ECONOMIC JOURNAL.
Indian Economic Association, c/o Dynaram Electronics & Computers, No. 20, 1st Fl., South Cross Rd., Bosavanagadi, Bangalore 560004, India. TEL 91-80-602822. FAX 91-80-6600440. *971*

INDIAN FERN JOURNAL.
Indian Fern Society, Punjabi University, Department of Botany, Patiala 147 002, India. TEL 91-175-822250. *708*

INDIAN GEOGRAPHICAL JOURNAL.
Indian Geographical Society, c/o Dept. of Geography, University of Madras, Chepauk, Madras 600 005, India. TEL 91-44-568778. FAX 91-44-566693. *3409*

INDIAN GEOLOGISTS' ASSOCIATION. BI-ANNUAL BULLETIN.
Indian Geologists' Association, c/o N. Kochhar, Secretary, Department of Geology, Panjab University, Chandigarh 160 014, India. TEL 91-172-541-740. FAX 91-172-541-409. *2351*

INDIAN JOURNAL OF AGRICULTURAL MARKETING.
Indian Society of Agricultural Marketing, F-5 Utkarsh Anurag Apts., Agrasen Marg, Giripeth, Nagpur 440 010, India. TEL 91-712-558-767. FAX 91-712-548-236. *124*

INDIAN JOURNAL OF ANIMAL NUTRITION.
Animal Nutrition Society of India, National Dairy Research Institute, Karnal 132 001 (Haryana), India. TEL 91-21832. *278*

INDIAN JOURNAL OF COLO-PROCTOLOGY.
Association of Colon and Rectal Surgeons of India, Surgeon, Tata Memorial Hospital, Parel, Bombay 400 012, India. TEL 91-22-413-7316. *4912*

INDIAN JOURNAL OF COMPARATIVE ANIMAL PHYSIOLOGY.
Indian Society for Comparative Animal Physiologists, Dept. of Zoology, Sri Venkateswara University, Tirupati 517502, India. TEL 91-8574-24166. FAX 91-8574-24111. *837*

INDIAN JOURNAL OF DENTAL RESEARCH.
Indian Society for Dental Research, c/o Dept. of Oral Medicine & Radiology, KMC-College of Dental Surgery, Mangalore 575 001, India. TEL 91-824-428716. FAX 91-824-428183. *4859*

INDIAN JOURNAL OF EARTH SCIENCES.
Indian Society of Earth Sciences, Department of Geology, Presidency College, Calcutta 700 073, India. TEL 91-33-241-1908. *2316*

INDIAN JOURNAL OF ECOLOGY.
Indian Ecological Society, Punjab Agricultural University, Ludhiana 141004, Punjab, India. TEL 91-161-401960. FAX 91-161-400945. *2933*

INDIAN JOURNAL OF ECONOMICS.
University of Allahabad, Department of Economics and Commerce, Allahabad 211 002, Uttar Pradesh, India. FAX 91-532-609857. *971*

INDIAN JOURNAL OF FINANCE AND RESEARCH.
Indian Financial Management Association, 116-D Pocket IV, Mayur Vihar, New Delhi 110 091, India. TEL 2250164. *1145*

INDIAN JOURNAL OF FISHERIES.
Central Marine Fisheries Research Institute, P.B. No. 1603, Dr. Salim Ali Rd., Cochin 682 014, Kerala, India. TEL 91-489-394867. *3070*

INDIAN JOURNAL OF GASTROENTEROLOGY.
Indian Society of Gastroenterology, 23, Bombay Mutual Terrace, 534 Sandhurst Bridge, Mumbai 400 007, India. TEL 91-22-3613344. FAX 91-22-4143435. *4912*

INDIAN JOURNAL OF GENDER STUDIES.
Sage Publications India Pvt. Ltd., P.O. Box 4215, New Delhi 110 048, India. TEL 91-11-6444958. FAX 91-11-6472426. *7344*

INDIAN JOURNAL OF HETEROCYCLIC CHEMISTRY.
C-85, Sector B, Aliganj Scheme, Lucknow 226 024, India. TEL 91-22-323421. *1752*

INDIAN JOURNAL OF HOSPITAL PHARMACY.
Indian Hospital Pharmacists' Association, R-566 New Rajinder Nagar, New Delhi 110 060, India. TEL 91-11-5754344. *5666*

INDIAN JOURNAL OF INDUSTRIAL RELATIONS.
Shri Ram Centre for Industrial Relations & Human Resources, 4E-16 Jhandewalan Extention, New Delhi 110 055, India. TEL 91-11-7519064. FAX 91-11-7526036. *1434*

INDIAN JOURNAL OF MALARIOLOGY.
Indian Council of Medical Research, Malaria Research Center, 22, Sham Nath Marg, Delhi 110 054, India. TEL 91-11-2528455. FAX 91-11-7234234. *4836*

INDIAN JOURNAL OF MEDICAL RESEARCH. SECTION A: INFECTIOUS DISEASES.
Indian Council of Medical Research, Division of Publication & Information, P.O. Box 4911, Ansari Nagar, New Delhi 110 029, India. TEL 91-11-6963980. FAX 91-11-6868662. *4683*

INDIAN JOURNAL OF NATURAL RUBBER RESEARCH.
Rubber Research Institute of India, Kottayam 686 009, Kerala, India. TEL 91-481-578316. FAX 91-481-578317. *6502*

INDIAN JOURNAL OF NUTRITION AND DIETETICS.
Avinashilingam Institute for Home Science and Higher Education for Women, c/o Rajammal P. Devadas, Ed., Coimbatore 641 043, India. TEL 40241. *5474*

INDIAN JOURNAL OF PHARMACOLOGY.
Indian Pharmacological Society, Department of Pharmacology, Jipmer, Pondicherry 605 006, India. TEL 91-413-36380. FAX 91-413-38132. *5666*

INDIAN JOURNAL OF PHYSIOLOGY AND PHARMACOLOGY.
Association of Physiologists and Pharmacologists of India, Department of Physiology, All India Institute of Medical Sciences, Ansari Nagar, New Delhi 110 029, India. *816*

INDIAN JOURNAL OF PLASTIC SURGERY.
Association of Plastic Surgeons of India, Ganga Hospital, Swarnambika Layout, Coimbatore 641 009, India. TEL 91-422-235051. FAX 91-422-235608. *5143*

INDIAN JOURNAL OF POLITICS.
Aligarh Muslim University, Aligarh 202001, Uttar Pradesh, India. TEL 91-571-401720. FAX 91-671-401617. *5933*

INDIAN JOURNAL OF PSYCHIATRY.
Indian Psychiatric Society, K.G.'s Medical College, B-8, Sector A, Mahanagar, Lucknow 226 006, India. TEL 91-522-371481. FAX 91-522-0266025. *5068*

INDIAN JOURNAL OF REGIONAL SCIENCE.
Regional Science Association, India, CK-134 Salt Lake City, Sect. II, Calcutta 700 091, India. TEL 91-33-3583927. *6618*

INDIAN JOURNAL OF RURAL TECHNOLOGY.
Department of Rural Development, Council for Advancement of People's Action and Rural Technology (CAPART), D-58 Pankha Rd., New Delhi 110058, India. TEL 91-11-464-7954. FAX 91-11-464-8607. *6962*

INDIAN JOURNAL OF TRAINING & DEVELOPMENT.
Indian Society for Training & Development, B-41, Institutional Area, Behind Qutab Hotel, New Delhi 110 016, India. TEL 91-11-6867710. FAX 91-11-6867607. *1569*

INDIAN JOURNAL OF TUBERCULOSIS.
Tuberculosis Association of India, 3 Red Cross Rd., New Delhi 110 001, India. TEL 91-11-3711303. *5119*

INDIAN ODONATOLOGY.
International Odonatological Society, D-f, Saraswati Nagar, Jodhpur 342 005, India. TEL 91-291-40766. *754*

INDIAN POTATO ASSOCIATION. JOURNAL.
Indian Potato Association, Central Potato Research Institute, Simla 171 001, India. TEL 0177-72182. FAX 0177-5016. *228*

INDIAN PSYCHOLOGICAL ABSTRACTS AND REVIEWS.
Sage Publications India Pvt. Ltd., P.O. Box 4215, New Delhi 110 048, India. TEL 91-11-644-4958. FAX 91-11-647-2426. *6160*

INDIAN SCIENCE CRUISER.
Institute of Science, Education and Culture, 42-B Syed Amir Ali Ave., Calcutta 700 017, India. TEL 91-33-247-7985. *6533*

INDIAN THOUGHT.
E.J. Brill, P.O. Box 9000, 2300 PA Leiden, Netherlands. TEL 31-71-5353500. FAX 31-71-5317532. *5731*

INDIAN VACUUM SOCIETY. BULLETIN.
Indian Vacuum Society, c/o Technical Physics & Prototype Engineering Division, Bhabha Atomic Research Centre, Mumbai 400 085, India. TEL 91-22-556-3060. FAX 91-22-556-0750. *5806*

INDIANA ACADEMY OF SCIENCE. PROCEEDINGS.
Indiana Academy of Science, 140 N. Senate Ave., Indianapolis, IN 46204. TEL 317-232-3686. *6533*

INDIANA CENTER ON GLOBAL CHANGE AND WORLD PEACE. OCCASIONAL PAPER SERIES.
Indiana Center on Global Change and World Peace, Indiana University, 201 N. Indiana Ave., Bloomington, IN 47405-3603. TEL 812-855-8859. FAX 812-855-3209. *2933*

INDIANA DENTAL ASSOCIATION. JOURNAL.
Indiana Dental Association, Box 2467, Indianapolis, IN 46206-2467. TEL 317-634-2610. FAX 317-634-2612. *4859*

INDIANA MUSICATOR.
Indiana Music Educators Association, Ball State University, School of Music, Muncie, IN 47306. TEL 765-285-5496. FAX 765-285-1139. *5400*

INDIANA UNIVERSITY MATHEMATICS JOURNAL.
Indiana University, Department of Mathematics, Rawles Hall 115, Bloomington, IN 47405. TEL 812-855-2252. FAX 812-855-0046. *4577*

INDIGENOUS KNOWLEDGE AND DEVELOPMENT MONITOR.
Centre for International Research and Advisory Networks (CIRAN), P.O. Box 29777, 2502 LT The Hague, Netherlands. TEL 31-70-4260324. FAX 31-70-4260329. *1362*

INDIGENOUS WOMAN.
Indigenous Women's Network, Box 174, Lake Elmo, MN 55042. *6713*

INDO-BRITISH REVIEW.
Indo-British Historical Society, Sinai, 21 Rajaram Mehta Ave., Nelson Rd., Madras 600 029, India. TEL 91-44-4802404. *3534*

INDO-IRANIAN JOURNAL.
Kluwer Academic Publishers, Postbus 17, 3300 AA Dordrecht, Netherlands. TEL 31-78-6392392. FAX 31-78-6392254. *5528*

INDO-PACIFIC FISHES.
Bishop Museum Press, 1525 Bernice St., Box 19000-A, Honolulu, HI 96817. TEL 808-848-4135. *837*

INDOLOGICA TAURINENSIA.
Association Internationale pour les Etudes Sanskrites, c/o C E S M E O, Via Cavour 17, 10123 Turin, Italy. TEL 33-1-44-27-10-98. *5528*

INDONESIA HUMAN RIGHTS CAMPAIGN. OCCASIONAL REPORTS.
Indonesia Human Rights Campaign, 111 Northwood Rd., Thornton Heath, Surrey CR7 8HW, England. TEL 44-181-771-2904. FAX 44-181-653-0322. *5993*

INDOOR AIR.
Munksgaard International Publishers Ltd., 35 Noerre Soegade, P.O. Box 2148, DK-1016 Copenhagen K, Denmark. TEL 45-33-127030. FAX 45-33-129387. *6239*

INDOOR AND BUILT ENVIRONMENT.
S. Karger AG, Allschwilerstr. 10, P.O. Box, CH-4009 Basel, Switzerland. TEL 41-61-3061111. FAX 41-61-3061234. *4797*

INDUSTRIA ALIMENTARIA.
Alfa Editores Tecnicos S.A., Libertad No. 107-402, 03660 Mexico DF, Mexico. TEL 525-579-3333. FAX 525-532-9504. *3113*

INDUSTRIAL AND LABOR RELATIONS REVIEW.
Cornell University, New York State School of Industrial and Labor Relations, Ithaca, NY 14853-3901. TEL 607-255-2732. FAX 607-255-8016. *1435*

INDUSTRIAL AUTOMATION JOURNAL.
Singapore Industrial Automation Association, 151 Chin Swee Rd., No. 03-13 Manhattan House, Singapore 169876, Singapore. TEL 65-734-6911. FAX 65-235-5721. *2109*

INDUSTRIAL CHEMISTRY LIBRARY.
Elsevier Science B.V., Books Division, P.O. Box 211, 1000 AE Amsterdam, Netherlands. TEL 31-20-4853911. FAX 31-20-4853705. *1752*

INDUSTRIAL CROPS AND PRODUCTS.
Elsevier Science B.V., P.O. Box 211, 1000 AE Amsterdam, Netherlands. TEL 31-20-4853911. FAX 31-20-4853598. *228*

INDUSTRIAL ECONOMIST.
S-15 Industrial Estate, Guindy, Chennai 600 032, India. TEL 91-44-234-2248. FAX 91-44-234-9382. *1586*

INDUSTRIAL HEALTH.
National Institute of Industrial Health, 21-1 Nagao 6-chome, Tama-ku, Kawasaki-shi, Kanagawa-ken 214, Japan. TEL 81-044-865-6111. FAX 81-044-865-6116. *5491*

INDUSTRIAL LABORATORY.
Plenum Publishing Corp., Consultants Bureau, 233 Spring St., New York, NY 10013-1578. TEL 212-620-8468. FAX 212-463-0742. *6962*

INDUSTRIAL MARKETING MANAGEMENT.
Elsevier Science Inc., Box 945, New York, NY 10159-0945. TEL 212-633-3730. FAX 212-633-3680. *1530*

INDUSTRIAL MATHEMATICS.
Industrial Mathematics Society, Box 159, Roseville, MI 48066. TEL 810-771-0403. *4577*

INDUSTRIAL NATION.
Moon Mystique, 3420 N. Halsted, Chicago, IL 60657-2513. TEL 773-665-9016. FAX 773-665-9116. *5400*

INDUSTRIAL RELATIONS JOURNAL.
Blackwell Publishers Ltd., 108 Cowley Rd., Oxford OX4 1JF, England. TEL 44-1865-791100. FAX 44-1865-791347. *1435*

INDUSTRIAL SAFETY SERIES.
Elsevier Science B.V., Books Division, P.O. Box 211, 1000 AE Amsterdam, Netherlands. TEL 31-20-4853911. FAX 31-20-4853705. *5492*

INDUSTRIAL SELLING.
Institute of Industrial Selling, c/o European Marketing Association, 18 St. Peters Steps, Brixham, Devon, England. *1530*

INDUSTRIE MANAGEMENT.
G I T O Verlag, Kellenzeile 50A, 13437 Berlin, Germany. TEL 49-30-31425118. FAX 49-30-4148270. *2084*

INDUSTRIELLE BEZIEHUNGEN.
Rainer Hampp Verlag, Meringerzellerstr. 16, 86415 Mering, Germany. TEL 49-8233-4783. FAX 49-8233-30755. *1436*

INDUSTRY AND HIGHER EDUCATION.
Coleridge House, 4-5 Coleridge Gardens, London NW6 3QH, England. TEL 44-171-372-2600. FAX 44-171-372-2253. *2545*

INDUSTRY OF FREE CHINA.
Publishing Committee of Industry of Free China, 9th Fl., No. 87 Nanking E. Rd., Sec. 2, Taipei, Taiwan 10408, Republic of China. TEL 886-2-522-5404. FAX 886-2-562-2950. *971*

INFANCIA Y APRENDIZAJE.
Fundacion Infancia y Aprendizaje, Crta. de Canillas, 138, 28043 Madrid, Spain. TEL 34-1-3883874. FAX 34-1-3003527. *6116*

INFANT BEHAVIOR AND DEVELOPMENT.
Ablex Publishing Corporation, Box 5297, Greenwich, CT 06831-0504. TEL 203-661-7602. FAX 203-661-0792. *6116*

INFANT MENTAL HEALTH JOURNAL.
John Wiley & Sons, Inc., Journals, 605 Third Ave., New York, NY 10158-0012. TEL 212-850-6645. FAX 212-850-6021. *5031*

INFANT - TODDLER INTERVENTION.
Singular Publishing Group, Inc., 401 W. A St., Ste. 325, San Diego, CA 92101-7901. FAX 800-774-8398. *5032*

INFECTIEZIEKTEN BULLETIN.
Rijksinstituut voor Volksgezondheid en Milieu, Postbus 1, 3720 BA Bilthoven, Netherlands. TEL 31-30-2743551. FAX 31-30-2744409. *4836*

INFECTION AND IMMUNITY.
American Society for Microbiology, 1325 Massachusetts Ave., N.W., Washington, DC 20005. TEL 202-737-3600. *4797*

INFECTION CONTROL & HOSPITAL EPIDEMIOLOGY.
Slack, Inc., 6900 Grove Rd., Thorofare, NJ 08086-9447. TEL 609-848-1000. FAX 609-853-5991. *4836*

INFECTION CONTROL & STERILIZATION TECHNOLOGY.
Mayworm Associates, Inc., 507 N. Milwaukee Ave., Libertyville, IL 60048. TEL 847-680-7878. FAX 847-680-8180. *4837*

INFECTIOUS DISEASES IN OBSTETRICS AND GYNECOLOGY.
John Wiley & Sons, Inc., Journals, 605 Third Ave., New York, NY 10158. TEL 212-850-6645. FAX 212-850-6021. *4959*

INFEKTOLOGIIA.
Natsionalen Tsentar po Zarasni i Parasitni Bolesti, Bul. Yanko Sakazov 26, 1504 Sofia, Bulgaria. TEL 395-2-4347399. FAX 359-2-442260. *4837*

INFERTILITY.
c/o Dr. Louis A. Mucelli, Ed., 614 2nd Ave., Ste. H, New York, NY 10016. TEL 212-684-4242. FAX 212-684-4290. *4959*

INFIRMIERE DU QUEBEC.
Ordre des Infirmieres et Infirmiers du Quebec, 4200 Dorchester Blvd. W., Montreal, PQ H3Z 1V4, Canada. TEL 514-935-2501. FAX 514-935-2055. *4934*

INFLAMMATION.
Plenum Publishing Corp., 233 Spring St., New York, NY 10013-1578. TEL 212-620-8000. FAX 212-463-0742. *4683*

INFLAMMATION AND DRUG THERAPY SERIES.
Kluwer Academic Publishers, Postbus 17, 3300 AA Dordrecht, Netherlands. TEL 31-78-6392392. FAX 31-78-6392254. *5667*

INFLAMMATORY BOWEL DISEASES.
Lippincott - Raven Publishers, 227 E. Washington Sq., Philadelphia, PA 19106. TEL 215-238-4200. *4912*

INFLAMMOPHARMACOLOGY.
Kluwer Academic Publishers, Postbus 17, 3300 AA Dordrecht, Netherlands. TEL 31-78-6392392. FAX 31-78-6392254. *5667*

INFO-SOURDS JOURNAL.
Federation Francophone des Sourds de Belgique, 32 rue Capronnier, 1030 Brussels, Belgium. FAX 32-2-2452363. *3463*

INFORMACION SEMANAL DE COMERCIO EXTERIOR.
Canalejas 30, entlo. 2o, 08028 Barcelona, Spain. TEL 34-3-4226199. FAX 34-3-4211858. *1330*

INFORMAL LOGIC.
Department of Philosophy, University of Windsor, Windsor, ON N9B 3P4, Canada. TEL 519-253-4232. FAX 519-973-7050. *5731*

INFORMATICA Y AUTOMATICA.
Asociacion Espanola de Informatica y Automatica, Hortaleza, 104, 28004 Madrid, Spain. TEL 34-1-3192565. FAX 34-1-3083028. *2109*

INFORMATION AND MANAGEMENT.
North-Holland, P.O. Box 211, 1000 AE Amsterdam, Netherlands. TEL 31-20-4853911. FAX 31-20-4853598. *2166*

INFORMATION AND SOFTWARE TECHNOLOGY.
Elsevier Science B.V., P.O. Box 211, 1000 AE Amsterdam, Netherlands. TEL 31-20-4853911. FAX 31-20-4853598. *2175*

INFORMATION AND SYSTEMS ENGINEERING.
I O S Press, Van Diemenstraat 94, 1013 CN Amsterdam, Netherlands. TEL 31-20-6382189. FAX 31-20-6203419. *2834*

INFORMATION BULLETIN ON VARIABLE STARS.
Hungarian Academy of Sciences, Konkoly Observatory, Box 67, 1525 Budapest, Hungary. *495*

INFORMATION ECONOMICS AND POLICY.
North-Holland, P.O. Box 211, 1000 AE Amsterdam, Netherlands. TEL 31-20-4853911. FAX 31-20-4853598. *1994*

INFORMATION EXCHANGE.
National Sudden Infant Death Syndrome Resource Center, 2070 Chain Bridge Rd., Ste. 450, Vienna, VA 22182-2536. TEL 703-821-8955. FAX 703-821-2098. *5032*

INFORMATION INFRASTRUCTURE AND POLICY.
I O S Press, Van Diemenstraat 94, 1013 CN Amsterdam, Netherlands. TEL 31-20-6382189. FAX 31-20-6203419. *2183*

INFORMATION LAW SERIES.
Kluwer Law International, Postbus 85889, 2508 CN The Hague, Netherlands. TEL 31-70-3081500. FAX 31-70-3081515. *3963*

INFORMATION NETWORK AND DATA COMMUNICATION.
Elsevier Science B.V., Books Division, P.O. Box 211, 1000 AE Amsterdam, Netherlands. TEL 31-20-4853911. FAX 31-20-4853705. *2134*

INFORMATION PROCESSING & MANAGEMENT.
Elsevier Science Ltd., Pergamon, P.O. Box 800, Kidlington, Oxford OX5 1DX, England. TEL 44-1865-843000. FAX 44-1865-843010. *4184*

INFORMATION PROCESSING LETTERS.
North-Holland, P.O. Box 211, 1000 AE Amsterdam, Netherlands. TEL 31-20-4853911. FAX 31-20-4853598. *2175*

INFORMATION PROCESSING SOCIETY OF JAPAN. TRANSACTIONS.
Information Processing Society of Japan, 7th Fl., Shibaura-Maekawa Bldg., 3-16-20, Shibaura, Minato-ku, Tokyo 108, Japan. TEL 81-3-5484-3535. FAX 81-3-5484-3534. *2175*

INFORMATION RESOURCES MANAGEMENT JOURNAL.
Idea Group Publishing, 1331 E. Chocolate Ave., Hershey, PA 17033-1117. TEL 717-541-9150. FAX 717-541-9159. *1482*

INFORMATION SERVICES & USE.
I O S Press, Van Diemenstraat 94, 1013 CN Amsterdam, Netherlands. TEL 31-20-6382189. FAX 31-20-6203419. *2183*

THE INFORMATION SOCIETY.
Taylor & Francis Inc., 1900 Frost Rd., Ste. 101, Bristol, PA 19007-1598. TEL 215-785-5800. FAX 215-785-5515. *2183*

INFORMATION SYSTEMS.
Elsevier Science Ltd., Pergamon, P.O. Box 800, Kidlington, Oxford OX5 1DX, England. TEL 44-1865-843000. FAX 44-1865-843010. *4232*

INFORMATION SYSTEMS JOURNAL.
Blackwell Science Ltd., Osney Mead, Oxford OX2 0EL, England. TEL 44-1865-206206. FAX 44-1865-721205. *2183*

INFORMATION TECHNOLOGY AND LIBRARIES.
American Library Association, 50 E. Huron St, Chicago, IL 60611-2795. TEL 312-944-6780. FAX 312-440-9374. *4185*

INFORMATION TECHNOLOGY AND PUBLIC POLICY.
Parliamentary Information Technology Committee, W. Heaton, Old Hillside Rd., Winchester, Hants SO22 5LN, England. TEL 44-1962-868900. *4185*

INFORMATION TECHNOLOGY AND THE LAW.
Kluwer Law International, Postbus 85889, 2508 CN The Hague, Netherlands. TEL 31-70-3081500. FAX 31-70-3081515. *4053*

INFORMATION TECHNOLOGY, EDUCATION AND SOCIETY.
James Nicholas Publishers, P.O. Box 244, Alberst Park, Vic. 3206, Australia. TEL 61-3-6965545. FAX 61-3-6992040. *2183*

INFORMATION TECHNOLOGY FOR DEVELOPMENT.
I O S Press, Van Diemenstraat 94, 1013 CN Amsterdam, Netherlands. TEL 31-20-6382189. FAX 31-20-6203419. *1362*

INFORMATION TECHNOLOGY REPORT.
U.S. National Biological Service, Information Transfer Center, c/o Managing Editor, 1201 Oak Ridge Dr., Ste. 200, Ft. Collins, CO 80525-5589. TEL 970-226-9401. FAX 970-226-9455. *735*

INFORMATION TECHNOLOGY REVIEW.
Primedia Publishing (Pty) Ltd., P.O. Box 784698, Sandton 2146, South Africa. TEL 27-11-8843857. FAX 27-11-8844677. *2084*

INFORMATORE DI VETERINARIA E ZOOTECNIA.
Organizzazione Editoriale Medico Farmaceutica, Via Edolo 42, 20125 Milan, Italy. TEL 39-2-675051. FAX 39-2-67505223. *7271*

INFORMAZIONI SUI FARMACI.
Farmacie Comunali Riunite di Reggio Emilia, Servizio Informazione e Documentazione Scientifica, Via Doberdo 9, 42100 Reggio Emilia, Italy. TEL 39-522-543450. FAX 39-522-550146. *5667*

INFRARED PHYSICS AND TECHNOLOGY.
Elsevier Science B.V., P.O. Box 211, 1000 AE Amsterdam, Netherlands. TEL 31-20-4853911. FAX 31-20-4853598. *5861*

INFUSIONSTHERAPIE UND TRANSFUSIONSMEDIZIN.
S. Karger AG, Allschwilerstr. 10, P.O. Box, CH-4009 Basel, Switzerland. TEL 41-61-3061111. FAX 41-61-3061234. *4920*

INGEGNERIA ALIMENTARE - CONSERVE ANIMALI.
G M Editoriale s.a.s., Via Ausonio 4, 20123 Milan, Italy. TEL 39-2-8372347. FAX 39-2-89401494. *3113*

INGENIERIA HIDRAULICA EN MEXICO.
Instituto Mexicano de Tecnologia del Agua, Apdo. Postal No. 202, C.P. 65500, CIVAC, Morelos, Mexico. TEL 52-73-194000 ext. 532. FAX 52-73-194341. *7295*

INHALATION TOXICOLOGY.
Taylor & Francis Inc., 1900 Frost Rd., Ste. 101, Bristol, PA 19007-1598. TEL 215-785-5800. FAX 215-785-5515. *2978*

INITIATIVES.
National Association for Women in Education, 1325 18th St., N.W., No. 210, Washington, DC 20036-6511. TEL 202-659-9330. FAX 202-457-0946. *2573*

INJURY.
Elsevier Science Ltd., P.O. Box 800, Kidlington, Oxford OX5 1DX, England. TEL 44-1865-843000. FAX 44-1865-843010. *5008*

INJURY PREVENTION.
B M J Publishing Group, B.M.A. House, Tavistock Sq., London WC1H 9JR, England. TEL 44-171-383-9270. FAX 44-171-383-6402. *5032*

INNER VOICE.
Forest Service Employees for Environmental Ethics, Box 11615, Eugene, OR 97440. TEL 541-484-2692. FAX 541-484-3004. *3155*

INNER VOICES.
Inner Voices, Box 4500, No. 219, Bloomington, IN 47402. TEL 812-596-4927. *4416*

INNOVACION Y CIENCIA.
Asociacion Colombiana para el Avance de la Ciencia, Carrera 50 No. 27-70, Edif. C. Torres, Apdo. Aereo 92581, Santafe de Bogota, Colombia. TEL 57-1-2217348. FAX 57-1-2216950. *6533*

INNOVANT.
Sentrum vir Mensilike Ontwikkeling in Psigososiele Konteks - SEMKO, Department of Psychology, University of Pretoria, Lynnwood Rd., Brooklyn 0181, South Africa. TEL 27-12-4203430. FAX 27-12-4202404. *6117*

INNOVATION (ABINGDON).
Carfax Publishing Co., P.O. Box 25, Abingdon, Oxon. OX14 3UE, England. TEL 44-1235-401000. FAX 44-1235-401550. *6618*

INNOVATIVE HIGHER EDUCATION.
Human Sciences Press, Inc., 233 Spring St., New York, NY 10013-1578. TEL 212-620-8000. FAX 212-463-0742. *2545*

INORGANIC MATERIALS.
Maik Nauk - Interperiodica, Mezhdunarodnyi Otdel, Ul. Profsoyuznaya, 90, 117864 Moscow, Russia. TEL 7-095-3360066. FAX 7-095-3360666. *1807*

INORGANIC SYNTHESES SERIES.
John Wiley & Sons, Inc., Journals, 605 Third Ave., New York, NY 10158-0012. TEL 212-850-6645. *1829*

INORGANICA CHIMICA ACTA.
Elsevier Science S.A., P.O. Box 564, CH-1001 Lausanne 1, Switzerland. TEL 41-21-3207381. FAX 41-21-3235444. *1808*

INQUIRY (ROCHESTER).
Finger Lakes Blue Cross and Blue Shield, Box 25399, Rochester, NY 14625. TEL 716-264-9122. FAX 716-264-9122. *4684*

INSECT BIOCHEMISTRY AND MOLECULAR BIOLOGY.
Elsevier Science Ltd., Pergamon, P.O. Box 800, Kidlington, Oxford OX5 1DX, England. TEL 44-1865-843000. FAX 44-1865-843010. *754*

INSECT MOLECULAR BIOLOGY.
Blackwell Science Ltd., Osney Mead, Oxford OX2 0EL, England. TEL 44-1865-206206. FAX 44-1865-721205. *754*

INSECTA MUNDI.
Center for Systematic Entomology, Box 140429, Gainesville, FL 32614. *754*

INSECTS OF VIRGINIA.
Virginia Museum of Natural History, 1001 Douglas Ave., VA 24112. TEL 540-666-8629. *754*

INSIDE ARTS.
Association of Performing Arts Presenters, 1112 16th St., N.W., Ste. 400, Washington, DC 20036. TEL 202-833-2787. FAX 202-833-1543. *7007*

INSIDE THE VATICAN.
Urbi et Orbi Communications, 3050 Gap Knob Rd., New Hope, KY 40052. TEL 502-325-3061. FAX 502-325-3091. *6465*

INSIGHT.
Mosby - Year Book, Inc., 11830 Westline Industrial Dr., St. Louis, MO 63146-3318. TEL 314-872-8370. FAX 314-432-1380. *4994*

INSIGHT (NORTHAMPTON).
British Institute of Non-Destructive Testing, 1 Spencer Parade, Northampton NN1 5AA, England. TEL 44-1604-30124. FAX 44-1604-231489. *5194*

INSTITUT DE LA COMMUNICATION PARLEE. RAPPORT DE RECHERCHE.
Institut de la Communication Parlee, Universite Stendhal, B.P. 25 X, 38040 Grenoble Cedex 9, France. TEL 76-82-43-37. FAX 76-82-43-35. *4263*

INSTITUT FOURIER. ANNALES.
Association des Annales de l'Institut Fourier, B.P. 74, 38402 Saint-Martin-d'Heres Cedex, France. FAX 33-4-76514478. *4577*

INSTITUT FUER ALLGEMEINE BOTANIK UND BOTANISCHER GARTEN. MITTEILUNGEN.
Universitaet Hamburg, Institut fuer Allgemeine Botanik und Botanischer Garten, Ohnhorststr. 18, 22609 Hamburg, Germany. FAX 49-40-82282254. *709*

INSTITUT FUER WELTWIRTSCHAFT. ANNUAL REPORT.
Institut fuer Weltwirtschaft, Duesternbrooker Weg 120, 24105 Kiel, Germany. TEL 49-431-8814305. FAX 49-431-8814527. *1265*

INSTITUT PASTEUR. ANNALES. ACTUALITES.
Editions Scientifiques et Medicales Elsevier, 141 rue de Javel, 75747 Paris, France. TEL 33-1-45589022. FAX 33-1-45589421. *786*

INSTITUT PASTEUR. BULLETIN.
Editions Scientifiques et Medicales Elsevier, 141 rue de Javel, 75747 Paris, France. TEL 33-1-45589022. FAX 33-1-45589421. *4837*

INSTITUT ROYAL DU PATRIMOINE ARTISTIQUE. BULLETIN.
Institut Royal du Patrimoine Artistique, 1 Parc du Cinquantenaire, 1000 Brussels, Belgium. TEL 32-2-7396711. FAX 32-2-7320105. *447*

INSTITUTE OF ECONOMIC AFFAIRS. OCCASIONAL PAPERS.
Institute of Economic Affairs, 2 Lord North St., London SW1P 3LB, England. TEL 44-171-799-3745. FAX 44-171-799-2137. *972*

INSTITUTE OF ECONOMIC AFFAIRS. RESEARCH MONOGRAPHS.
Institute of Economic Affairs, 2 Lord North St., London SW1P 3LB, England. TEL 44-171-799-3745. FAX 44-171-799-2137. *972*

INSTITUTE OF ENVIRONMENTAL SCIENCES. JOURNAL.
Institute of Environmental Sciences, 940 E. Northwest Hwy., Mt. Prospect, IL 60056. TEL 708-255-1561. FAX 708-255-1699. *2934*

INSTITUTE OF HEALTH EDUCATION. JOURNAL.
Institute of Health Education, University Dental Hospital, Higher Cambridge St., Manchester M15 6FH, England. TEL 44-161-275-6610. FAX 44-161-275-6610. *2451*

INSTITUTE OF MATHEMATICAL GEOGRAPHY. MONOGRAPH SERIES.
Institute of Mathematical Geography, 2790 Briarcliff, Ann Arbor, MI 48105-1429. TEL 313-761-1231. *4577*

INSTITUTE OF MEASUREMENT AND CONTROL. TRANSACTIONS.
Institute of Measurement and Control, 87 Gower St., London WC1E 6AA, England. TEL 44-171-387-4949. FAX 44-171-388-8431. *3802*

INSTITUTE OF MEDICINE OF CHICAGO. PROCEEDINGS.
Institute of Medicine of Chicago, 332 S. Michigan Ave., Chicago, IL 60604-4022. TEL 312-663-0040. FAX 312-663-9058. *4684*

INSTITUTE OF METAL FINISHING. TRANSACTIONS.
Institute of Metal Finishing, Exeter House, 48 Holloway Head, Birmingham B1 1NQ, England. TEL 44-121-622-7387. FAX 44-121-666-6316. *5194*

INSTITUTE OF ROMANCE STUDIES. JOURNAL.
Institute of Romance Studies, Publications Office, Senate House, Malet St., London WC1E 7HU, England. TEL 44-171-636-8000. FAX 44-171-436-4533. *4264*

INSTITUTE OF STATISTICAL MATHEMATICS. ANNALS.
Kluwer Academic Publishers, Postbus 17, 3300 AA Dordrecht, Netherlands. TEL 31-78-6392392. FAX 31-78-6392254. *4578*

INSTITUTION OF CHEMISTS (INDIA). JOURNAL.
Institution of Chemists (India), 11-4, Dr. Biresh Guha Road, Calcutta 700 017, India. TEL 91-33-240-3832. *1752*

INSTITUTION OF CIVIL ENGINEERS. PROCEEDINGS. CIVIL ENGINEERING.
Thomas Telford Services Ltd., Thomas Telford House, 1 Heron Quay, London E14 4JD, England. TEL 44-171-987-6999. FAX 44-171-538-9620. *2787*

INSTITUTION OF CIVIL ENGINEERS. PROCEEDINGS. GEOTECHNICAL ENGINEERING.
Thomas Telford Services Ltd., Thomas Telford House, 1 Heron Quay, London E14 4JD, England. TEL 44-171-987-6999. FAX 44-171-538-9620. *2787*

INSTITUTION OF CIVIL ENGINEERS. PROCEEDINGS. MUNICIPAL ENGINEER.
Thomas Telford Services Ltd., Thomas Telford House, 1 Heron Quay, London E14 4JD, England. TEL 44-171-987-6999. FAX 44-171-538-9620. *2787*

INSTITUTION OF CIVIL ENGINEERS. PROCEEDINGS. STRUCTURES AND BUILDINGS.
Thomas Telford Services Ltd., Thomas Telford House, 1 Heron Quay, London E14 4JD, England. TEL 44-171-987-6999. FAX 44-171-538-9620. *2787*

INSTITUTION OF CIVIL ENGINEERS. PROCEEDINGS. TRANSPORT.
Thomas Telford Services Ltd., Thomas Telford House, 1 Heron Quay, London E14 4JD, England. TEL 44-171-987-6999. FAX 44-171-538-9620. *2787*

INSTITUTION OF CIVIL ENGINEERS. PROCEEDINGS. WATER, MARITIME AND ENERGY.
Thomas Telford Services Ltd., Thomas Telford House, 1 Heron Quay, London E14 4JD, England. TEL 44-171-987-6999. FAX 44-171-538-9620. *2788*

INSTITUTION OF ENGINEERS (INDIA). AEROSPACE ENGINEERING DIVISION. JOURNAL.
Institution of Engineers (India), 8 Gokhale Rd., Calcutta 700 020, India. TEL 91-33-2238334. FAX 91-33-2238345. *69*

INSTITUTION OF ENGINEERS (INDIA). AGRICULTURAL ENGINEERING DIVISION. JOURNAL.
Institution of Engineers (India), 8 Gokhale Rd., Calcutta 700 020, India. TEL 91-33-2238334. FAX 91-33-2238345. *229*

INSTITUTION OF ENGINEERS (INDIA). CHEMICAL ENGINEERING DIVISION. JOURNAL.
Institution of Engineers (India), 8 Gokhale Rd., Calcutta 700 020, India. TEL 91-33-2238334. FAX 91-33-2238345. *2766*

INSTITUTION OF ENGINEERS (INDIA). CIVIL ENGINEERING DIVISION. JOURNAL.
Institution of Engineers (India), 8 Gokhale Rd., Calcutta 700 020, India. TEL 91-33-2238334. FAX 91-33-2238345. *2788*

INSTITUTION OF ENGINEERS (INDIA). COMPUTER ENGINEERING DIVISION. JOURNAL.
Institution of Engineers (India), 8 Gokhale Rd., Calcutta 700 020, India. TEL 91-33-2238334. FAX 91-33-2238345. *2115*

INSTITUTION OF ENGINEERS (INDIA). ELECTRICAL ENGINEERING DIVISION. JOURNAL.
Institution of Engineers (India), 8 Gokhale Rd., Calcutta 700 020, India. TEL 91-33-2238334. FAX 91-33-2238345. *2834*

INSTITUTION OF ENGINEERS (INDIA). ELECTRONICS AND TELECOMMUNICATION ENGINEERING DIVISION. JOURNAL.
Institution of Engineers (India), 8 Gokhale Rd., Calcutta 700 020, India. TEL 91-33-2238334. FAX 91-33-2238345. *2642*

INSTITUTION OF ENGINEERS (INDIA). ENVIRONMENTAL ENGINEERING DIVISION. JOURNAL.
Institution of Engineers (India), 8 Gokhale Rd., Calcutta 700 020, India. TEL 91-33-2238334. FAX 91-33-2238345. *2934*

INSTITUTION OF ENGINEERS (INDIA). HINDI SECTION. JOURNAL.
Institution of Engineers (India), 8 Gokhale Rd., Calcutta 700 020, India. TEL 91-33-2238334. FAX 91-33-2238345. *2724*

INSTITUTION OF ENGINEERS (INDIA). INTERDISCIPLINARY PANELS JOURNAL.
Institution of Engineers (India), 8 Gokhale Rd., Calcutta 700 020, India. TEL 91-33-2238334. FAX 91-33-2238345. *2724*

INSTITUTION OF ENGINEERS (INDIA). MARINE ENGINEERING DIVISION. JOURNAL.
Institution of Engineers (India), 8 Gokhale Rd., Calcutta 700 020, India. TEL 91-33-2238334. FAX 91-33-2238345. *2872*

INSTITUTION OF ENGINEERS (INDIA). MECHANICAL ENGINEERING DIVISION. JOURNAL.
Institution of Engineers (India), 8 Gokhale Rd., Calcutta 700 020, India. TEL 91-33-2238334. FAX 91-33-2238345. *2885*

INSTITUTION OF ENGINEERS (INDIA). METALLURGY & MATERIAL SCIENCE DIVISION. JOURNAL.
Institution of Engineers (India), 8 Gokhale Rd., Calcutta 700 020, India. TEL 91-33-2238334. FAX 91-33-2238345. *5194*

INSTITUTION OF ENGINEERS (INDIA). MINING ENGINEERING DIVISION. JOURNAL.
Institution of Engineers (India), 8 Gokhale Rd., Calcutta 700 020, India. TEL 91-33-2238334. FAX 91-33-2238345. *5303*

INSTITUTION OF ENGINEERS (INDIA). TEXTILE ENGINEERING DIVISION. JOURNAL.
Institution of Engineers (India), 8 Gokhale Rd., Calcutta 700 020, India. TEL 91-33-2238334. FAX 91-33-2238335. *6989*

INSTITUTION OF MECHANICAL ENGINEERS. PROCEEDINGS. PART J: JOURNAL OF ENGINEERING TRIBOLOGY.
Mechanical Engineering Publications Ltd., Northgate Ave., Bury St. Edmunds, Suffolk IP32 6BW, England. TEL 44-1284-763277. FAX 44-1284-704006. *2886*

INSTITUTION OF PROFESSIONAL ENGINEERS NEW ZEALAND. CIVIL ENGINEERING SECTION. TRANSACTIONS.
Institution of Professional Engineers New Zealand, Civil Engineering Section, 101 Molesworth St., P.O. Box 12-241, Wellington, New Zealand. TEL 64-4-473-9444. FAX 64-4-473-2324. *2788*

INSTITUTION OF PROFESSIONAL ENGINEERS NEW ZEALAND. ELECTRICAL, MECHANICAL AND CHEMICAL ENGINEERING SECTION. TRANSACTIONS.
Institution of Professional Engineers New Zealand, Electrical, Mechanical and Chemical Engineering Section, 101 Molesworth St., P.O. Box 12-241, Wellington, New Zealand. TEL 64-4-473-9444. FAX 64-4-473-2324. *2834*

INSTITUTION OF PROFESSIONAL ENGINEERS NEW ZEALAND. GENERAL ENGINEERING SECTION. TRANSACTIONS.
Institution of Professional Engineers New Zealand, General Engineering Section, 101 Molesworth St., P.O. Box 12-241, Wellington, New Zealand. TEL 64-4-473-9444. FAX 64-4-473-9324. *2725*

INSTITUTO ADOLFO LUTZ. REVISTA.
Instituto Adolfo Lutz, Av. Dr. Arnaldo 355, C.P. 7027, 01246-902 Sao Paulo SP, Brazil. TEL 55-11-8510111. FAX 55-11-8533505. *786*

INSTITUTO BARRAQUER. ANALES.
Instituto Barraquer, Laforja 88, Barcelona, Spain. TEL 34-3-2006311. FAX 343-2099977. *4994*

INSTITUTO DE INVESTIGACION TEXTIL Y DE COOPERACION INDUSTRIAL. BOLETIN INTEXTER.
Instituto de Investigacion Textil y de Cooperacion Industrial, Colon 15, 08222 Terrassa, Spain. TEL 34-3-7398277. FAX 34-3-7398272. *6989*

INSTITUTO DE INVESTIGACIONES LITERARIAS. ANUARIO.
Fondo Editorial Tropykos, Calle El Escorial, Edif. Luxor 7 Fl., Las Acacias, Caracas, Venezuela. TEL 58-02-6930565. FAX 58-02-624926. *4416*

INSTITUTO DE LA PATAGONIA. ANALES. CIENCIAS SOCIALES.
Universidad de Magallanes, Instituto de la Patagonia, Casilla de Correo 113-D, Punta Arenas, Magallanes, Chile. TEL 56-61-212913. FAX 56-61-212973. *3632*

INSTITUTO NACIONAL DE CANCEROLOGIA. REVISTA.
Instituto Nacional de Cancerologia, Ave. San Fernando 22, Col. Tlalpan, 14000 Mexico, D.F., Mexico. TEL 52-5-6551437. FAX 52-5-5733627. *4979*

INSTITUTO NACIONAL DE ENFERMEDADES RESPIRATORIAS. REVISTA.
Instituto Nacional de Enfermedades Respiratorias, Clz. Tlalpan 4502, Col. Seccion XVI, 14082 Mexico DF, Mexico. TEL 52-5-6663187. FAX 52-5-6663187. *5119*

INSTITUTO NACIONAL DE MEDICINA LEGAL DE COLOMBIA. REVISTA.
Instituto Nacional de Medicina Legal y Ciencias Forenses, Division de Desarrollo Tecnologico y Normalizacion, Calle 7A, No. 12-61, Bogota, DC, Colombia. TEL 571-2-339883. FAX 571-2-338534. *4904*

INSTITUTO POLITECNICO NACIONAL. ESCUELA NACIONAL DE CIENCIAS BIOLOGICAS. ANALES.
Instituto Politecnico Nacional, Escuela Nacional de Ciencias Biologicas, Carpio y Plan de Ayala, Col. Santo Tomas, Apdo. Postal 42-186, 11340, Mexico, D.F., Mexico. FAX 52-5-3963503. *606*

INSTITUTO PORTUGUES DE INVESTIGACAO MARITIMA. BOLETIM.
Instituto Portugues de Investigacao Maritima, Divisao de Informacao e Documentacao, Avenida de Brasilia, 1400 Lisbon, Portugal. *2405*

INSTITUTO RIVA-AGUERO. BOLETIN.
Pontificia Universidad Catolica del Peru, Fondo Editorial, Apdo. 1761, Lima 32, Peru. TEL 51-14-277678. FAX 51-14-260531. *3781*

INSTITUTUL DE STUDII SI PROIECTARI ENERGETICE. BULETINUL.
Institutul de Studii si Proiectari Energetice, Bd. Lacul Tei nr. 1, Sector 2, 72301 Bucharest 30, Rumania. TEL 401-2107080. FAX 401-2103620. *2671*

INSTRUCTIONAL SCIENCE.
Kluwer Academic Publishers, Postbus 17, 3300 AA Dordrecht, Netherlands. TEL 31-78-6392392. FAX 31-78-6392254. *2605*

INSTRUCTIONAL STRATEGIES: AN APPLIED RESEARCH SERIES.
Delta Pi Epsilon Graduate Business Education Society, National Office, Box 4340, Little Rock, AR 72214. TEL 501-562-1233. FAX 501-562-1293. *2606*

INSTRUMENTATION, CONTROLS, AND AUTOMATION IN THE POWER INDUSTRY.
Instrument Society of America, 67 Alexander Dr., Box 12277, Research Triangle Park, NC 27709. TEL 919-549-8411. FAX 919-549-8288. *3802*

INSTRUMENTATION FOR THE PROCESS INDUSTRIES.
Instrument Society of America, 67 Alexander Dr., Box 12277, Research Triangle Park, NC 27709. TEL 919-549-8411. FAX 919-549-8288. *3802*

INSTRUMENTATION SCIENCE & TECHNOLOGY.
Marcel Dekker Journals, 270 Madison Ave., New York, NY 10016. TEL 212-696-9000. FAX 212-685-4540. *1791*

INSTRUMENTS AND EXPERIMENTAL TECHNIQUES.
Maik Nauka - Interperiodica, Mezhdunarodnyi Otdel, Ul. Profsoyuznaya, 90, 117864 Moscow, RU. TEL 7-095-3360066. FAX 7-095-3360666. *3802*

INSTYTUT AUTOMATYKI SYSTEMOW ENERGETYCZNYCH. PRACE.
Instytut Automatyki Systemow Energetycznych, Wystawowa 1, 51-618 Wroclaw, Poland. TEL 48-71-3484221. FAX 48-71-482183. *2834*

INSTYTUT LACZNOSCI. PRACE.
Instytut Lacznosci, Ul. Szachowa 1, 04-894 Warsaw, Poland. TEL 48-22-128450. FAX 48-22-129969. *1994*

INSTYTUT MEDYCYNY MORSKIEJ I TROPIKALNEJ W GDYNI. BULETIN.
Instytut Medycyny Morskiej i Tropikalnej w Gdyni, Ul. Powstania Styczniowego 9B, 81-519 Gdynia-Radlowo, Poland. TEL 48-58-223011. FAX 48-58-223354. *4838*

INSTYTUT METALURGII ZELAZA. PRACE.
Instytut Metalurgii Zelaza, Ul. K. Miarki 12, 44-100 Gliwice, Poland. TEL 48-32-314051. FAX 48-32-313594. *5194*

INSTYTUT TECHNOLOGII DREWNA. PRACE.
Instytut Technologii Drewna, Ul. Winiarska 1, 60-654 Poznan, Poland. TEL 48-61-224081. FAX 48-61-224372. *925*

INSURANCE BROKER.
National Insurance Brokers Association, 2 Jocelyn Ct., Doncaster East, Vic. 3109, Australia. TEL 61-3-98407671. FAX 61-3-98486908. *3819*

INSURANCE INSTITUTE OF CANADA. PERSPECTIVES.
Insurance Institute of Canada, 18 King St. E., 6th Fl., Toronto, ON M5C 1C4, Canada. TEL 416-362-8586. FAX 416-362-1126. *3820*

INSURANCE LAW ANTHOLOGY.
International Library Law Book Publishers, Inc., 4301 N. Fairfax Dr., Ste 875, Arlington, VA 22203. TEL 703-528-1000. FAX 703-528-6060. *3820*

INSURANCE: MATHEMATICS & ECONOMICS.
North-Holland, P.O. Box 211, 1000 AE Amsterdam, Netherlands. TEL 31-20-4853911. FAX 31-20-4853598. *3820*

INSURANCE SERIES.
Elsevier Science B.V., Books Division, P.O. Box 211, 1000 AE Amsterdam, Netherlands. TEL 31-20-4853911. FAX 31-20-4853705. *3821*

INTEGRAL.
Eastman School of Music, 26 Gibbs St., Rochester, NY 14604. TEL 716-274-1000. FAX 716-274-1088. *5401*

INTEGRATED COMPUTER-AIDED ENGINEERING.
John Wiley & Sons, Inc., Journals, 605 Third Ave., New York, NY 10158. TEL 212-850-6645. FAX 212-850-6021. *2115*

INTEGRATED FERROELECTRICS.
Gordon and Breach - Harwood Academic, Amsteldisk 166, 1st Fl., 1079 LH Amsterdam, Netherlands. *2835*

INTEGRATED PEST MANAGEMENT REVIEWS.
Thomson Science, 2-6 Boundary Row, London SE1 8HN, England. TEL 44-171-8650066. FAX 44-171-5229623. *229*

INTEGRATION.
Elsevier Science B.V., P.O. Box 211, 1000 AE Amsterdam, Netherlands. TEL 31-20-4853911. FAX 31-20-4853598. *2179*

INTEGRATIVE PSYCHIATRY.
Academia Medicina Psychiatria, Box 157, Tarrytown, NY 10591. *5069*

INTELLECTUAL PROPERTY LAW (NEW YORK).
Gordon and Breach - Harwood Academic, Amsteldisk 166, 1st Fl., 1079 LH Amsterdam, Netherlands. *5585*

INTELLIGENCE (NORWOOD).
Ablex Publishing Corporation, Box 5297, Greenwich, CT 06831-0504. TEL 203-661-7602. FAX 203-661-0792. *6117*

INTELLIGENCE AND NATIONAL SECURITY.
Frank Cass, Newbury House, 890-900 Eastern Ave., Newbury Park, Ilford, Essex IG2 7HH, England. TEL 44-181-599-8866. FAX 44-181-599-0984. *6019*

INTELLIGENT DATA ANALYSIS.
Elsevier Science Inc., Box 945, New York, NY 10159-0945. TEL 212-633-3730. FAX 212-633-3990. *2100*

INTENSIV.
Georg Thieme Verlag, Ruedigerstr. 14, 70469 Stuttgart, Germany. TEL 0711-8931443. FAX 0711-8931258. *4684*

INTENSIVE CARE WORLD.
King & Wirth Publishing Co. Ltd., 14 Temple Fortune Ln., London NW11 7UD, England. TEL 44-181-455-0760. FAX 44-181-201-8955. *4685*

INTERACTING WITH COMPUTERS.
Elsevier Science B.V., P.O. Box 211, 1000 AE Amsterdam, Netherlands. TEL 31-20-4853911. FAX 31-20-4853598. *2084*

INTER-AMERICAN TROPICAL TUNA COMMISSION. BULLETIN.
Inter-American Tropical Tuna Commission, c/o Scripps Institution of Oceanography, 8604 La Jolla Shores Dr., La Jolla, CA 92037-1508. TEL 619-546-7100. FAX 619-546-7133. *3071*

INTERCHANGE.
Kluwer Academic Publishers, Postbus 17, 3300 AA Dordrecht, Netherlands. TEL 31-78-6392392. FAX 31-78-6392254. *2451*

INTERCULTURAL COMMUNICATION STUDIES.
Institute for Cross-Cultural Research, Trinity University, No. 418, 715 Stadium Dr., San Antonio, TX 78212-7200. TEL 210-736-7369. FAX 210-736-7578. *6714*

INTERDISCIPLINARY CONTRIBUTIONS TO ARCHAEOLOGY.
Plenum Publishing Corp., 233 Spring St., New York, NY 10013-1578. TEL 212-620-8000. FAX 212-463-0742. *367*

INTERDISCIPLINARY TOPICS IN GERONTOLOGY.
S. Karger AG, Allschwilerstr. 10, CH-4009 Basel, Switzerland. TEL 41-61-3061111. FAX 41-61-3061234. *3437*

INTERFACE: BRADFORD STUDIES IN LANGUAGE, CULTURE AND SOCIETY.
University of Bradford, Department of Modern Languages, Bradford, W. Yorks. BD7 1DP, England. TEL 44-1274-733466. FAX 44-1274-385590. *4416*

INTERFACE SCIENCE.
Kluwer Academic Publishers Boston, Box 358, Accord Sta., Hingham, MA 02018-0358. TEL 617-871-6600. FAX 617-871-6528. *1829*

INTERFACES: LINGUISTICS, PSYCHOLOGY AND HEALTH THERAPEUTICS.
Providence College Press, Providence, RI 02918. *4264*

INTERMETALLICS.
Elsevier Science Ltd., P.O. Box 800, Kidlington, Oxford OX5 1DX, England. TEL 44-1865-843000. FAX 44-1865-843010. *5194*

INTERMOUNTAIN JOURNAL OF SCIENCES.
Montana Academy of Sciences, Box 3014, Bozeman, MT 59772-3014. *6534*

INTERNATIONAL ACADEMY FOR BIOMEDICAL AND DRUG RESEARCH.
S. Karger AG, Allschwilerstr. 10, P.O. Box, CH-4009 Basel, Switzerland. TEL 41-61-3061111. FAX 41-61-3061234. *5667*

INTERNATIONAL ADVANCES IN NONDESTRUCTIVE TESTING.
Gordon and Breach - Harwood Academic, Amsteldisk 166, 1st Fl., 1079 LH Amsterdam, Netherlands. *2859*

INTERNATIONAL AGROPHYSICS.
Polska Akademia Nauk, Instytut Agrofizyki, Ul. Doswiadczalna 4, P.O. Box 121, 20-236 Lublin, Poland. TEL 48-81-7445061. FAX 48-81-7445067. *229*

INTERNATIONAL ANGIOLOGY.
Edizioni Minerva Medica, Corso Bramante 83-85, 10126 Turin, Italy. TEL 39-11-678282. FAX 39-11-674502. *4818*

INTERNATIONAL ANNALS OF ADOLESCENT PSYCHIATRY.
University of Chicago Press, Journals Division, Box 37005, Chicago, IL 60637. TEL 773-753-3347. FAX 773-753-0811. *5069*

INTERNATIONAL ANTIVIRAL NEWS.
MediTech Media Ltd., 125 High Holborn, London WC1V 6QA, England. TEL 44-171-404-7151. FAX 44-171-404-6946. *4797*

INTERNATIONAL APPLIED MECHANICS.
Plenum Publishing Corp., Consultants Bureau, 233 Spring St., New York, NY 10013-1578. TEL 212-620-8468. FAX 212-463-0742. *2859*

INTERNATIONAL ARCHIVES OF ALLERGY AND IMMUNOLOGY.
S. Karger AG, Allschwilerstr. 10, P.O. Box, CH-4009 Basel, Switzerland. TEL 41-61-3061111. FAX 41-61-3061234. *4797*

INTERNATIONAL ASSOCIATION FOR HUMAN RESOURCE INFORMATION MANAGEMENT. CONFERENCE HIGHLIGHTS.
International Association for Human Resource Information Management, 14643 Dallas Parkway, No. 525, Dallas, TX 75240. TEL 972-661-3727. FAX 972-386-8180. *1569*

INTERNATIONAL ASSOCIATION OF ENGINEERING GEOLOGY. BULLETIN.
A I G I, Laboratoire Central des Ponts et Chaussees, 58 bd. Lefebvre, 75732 Paris Cedex 15, France. FAX 40-43-54-98. *2352*

INTERNATIONAL ASSOCIATION OF PHYSICIANS IN AIDS CARE. JOURNAL.
Medical Publications Corporation, 225 Washington St., Ste. 2200, Chicago, IL 60606. TEL 312-755-1227. FAX 312-755-1252. *4838*

INTERNATIONAL ASSOCIATION OF ZOO EDUCATORS. JOURNAL.
International Association of Zoo Educators, c/o Melbourne Zoo Education Service, P.O. Box 74, Parkville, Vic. 3052, Australia. TEL 61-3-92859355. FAX 61-3-92859340. *2233*

INTERNATIONAL ASTRONOMICAL UNION. GENERAL ASSEMBLY. HIGHLIGHTS.
Kluwer Academic Publishers, Postbus 17, 3300 AA Dordrecht, Netherlands. TEL 31-78-6392392. FAX 31-78-6392254. *495*

INTERNATIONAL ASTRONOMICAL UNION. PROCEEDINGS OF SYMPOSIA.
Kluwer Academic Publishers, Postbus 17, 3300 AA Dordrecht, Netherlands. TEL 31-78-6392392. FAX 31-78-6392254. *496*

INTERNATIONAL ASTRONOMICAL UNION. TRANSACTIONS.
Kluwer Academic Publishers, Postbus 17, 3300 AA Dordrecht, Netherlands. TEL 31-78-6392392. FAX 31-78-6392254. *496*

INTERNATIONAL BIODETERIORATION & BIODEGRADATION.
Elsevier Science Ltd., P.O. Box 800, Kidlington, Oxford OX5 1DX, England. TEL 44-1865-843000. FAX 44-1865-843010. *683*

INTERNATIONAL BIODETERIORATION SYMPOSIUM. PROCEEDINGS.
Elsevier Science Ltd., Books Division, P.O. Box 800, Kidlington, Oxford OX5 1DX, England. TEL 44-1865-843000. FAX 44-1865-843010. *683*

INTERNATIONAL BUSINESS REVIEW.
Elsevier Science Ltd., Pergamon, P.O. Box 800, Kidlington, Oxford OX5 1DX, England. TEL 44-1865-843000. FAX 44-1865-843010. *973*

INTERNATIONAL CATALOGUING AND BIBLIOGRAPHIC CONTROL.
International Federation of Library Associations, UBCIM Programme, c/o Deutsche Bibliothek, Adickesallee 1, 60322 Frankfurt a.M., Germany. TEL 49-69-15251140. FAX 49-69-15251142. *4186*

INTERNATIONAL CHRISTIAN UNIVERSITY. LANGUAGE RESEARCH BULLETIN.
International Christian University, Division of Languages, 3-10-2 Osawa, Mitaka, Tokyo 181, Japan. TEL 0422-33-3214. FAX 0412-33-9887. *4264*

INTERNATIONAL COMET QUARTERLY.
International Comet Quarterly, Smithsonian Astrophysical Observatory, M.S.18, 60 Garden St., Cambridge, MA 02138. TEL 617-495-7440. *496*

INTERNATIONAL COMMISSION ON RADIOLOGICAL PROTECTION. ANNALS.
Elsevier Science Ltd., Pergamon, P.O. Box 800, Kidlington, Oxford OX5 1DX, England. TEL 44-1865-843000. FAX 44-1865-843010. *5107*

INTERNATIONAL COMMUNICATIONS IN HEAT AND MASS TRANSFER.
Elsevier Science Ltd., Pergamon, P.O. Box 800, Kidlington, Oxford OX5 1DX, England. TEL 44-1865-843000. FAX 44-1865-843010. *2886*

INTERNATIONAL CONFERENCE ON BASEMENT TECTONICS. PROCEEDINGS.
Kluwer Academic Publishers, Postbus 17, 3300 AA Dordrecht, Netherlands. TEL 31-78-6392392. FAX 31-78-6392254. *2317*

INTERNATIONAL CONFERENCE ON COMPUTER COMMUNICATIONS. (PROCEEDINGS).
Elsevier Science Inc., Box 945, New York, NY 10159-0945. TEL 212-633-3730. FAX 212-633-3680. *2170*

INTERNATIONAL CONFERENCE ON VERY LARGE DATA BASES. PROCEEDINGS.
Morgan Kaufmann Publishers, Inc., 340 Pine St., 6th Fl., San Francisco, CA 94104-3205. TEL 415-392-2665, FAX 415-982-2665. *2167*

INTERNATIONAL CONGRESS FOR STEREOLOGY. PROCEEDINGS.
International Society for Stereology, c/o Dr. Aurora Astudillo, Sec.-Treas., Tatiana, Univ. de Oviedo, Ed. Quimicas, Julian Claveria s-n, 33006 Oviedo, Spain. TEL 34-85-103658. *2859*

INTERNATIONAL CONGRESS OF OPHTHALMOLOGY. ABSTRACTS.
International Federation of Ophthalmological Societies, c/o Dr. Bruce E. Spivey, Northwestern Healthcare Network, 980 N. Michigan Ave., Ste. 1500, Chicago, IL 60611. *4994*

INTERNATIONAL CONGRESS ON COMBUSTION ENGINES. PROCEEDINGS.
International Council on Combustion Engines, c/o V D M A e.V., Lyoner Strasse 18, 60528 Frankfurt, Germany. TEL 49-69-6603-1567. FAX 49-69-6603-1566. *2887*

INTERNATIONAL CONGRESS SERIES.
Elsevier Science B.V., P.O. Box 211, 1000 AE Amsterdam, Netherlands. TEL 31-20-4853757. FAX 31-20-4853432. *6534*

INTERNATIONAL CONTACT LENS CLINIC.
Elsevier Science Inc., Box 945, New York, NY 10159-0945. TEL 212-633-3730. FAX 212-633-3680. *4994*

INTERNATIONAL CRISIS BEHAVIOR.
University of California Press, 2120 Berkeley Way, Berkeley, CA 94720. TEL 510-642-4247. FAX 510-643-7127. *6020*

INTERNATIONAL CRYOGENICS MONOGRAPH SERIES.
Plenum Publishing Corp., 233 Spring St., New York, NY 10013-1578. TEL 212-620-8000. FAX 212-463-0742. *5841*

INTERNATIONAL DAIRY JOURNAL.
Elsevier Science Ltd., P.O. Box 800, Kidlington, Oxford OX5 1DX, England. TEL 44-1865-843000. FAX 44-1865-843010. *255*

INTERNATIONAL DEFENCE NEWSLETTER.
I T X Publishing, P.O. Box 28, Twickenham, Mddx. TW1 1EH, England. TEL 44-181-8927471. FAX 44-181-7442704. *5271*

INTERNATIONAL DENTAL JOURNAL.
F D I World Dental Press Ltd., 7 Carlisle St., London W1V 5RG, England. TEL 0171-935-7852. FAX 0171-486-0183. *4859*

INTERNATIONAL DIRECTORY OF DISTINGUISHED LEADERSHIP.
American Biographical Institute, Inc., Governing Board of Editors, 5126 Bur Oak Circle, Box 31226, Raleigh, NC 27622. TEL 919-781-8710. FAX 919-781-8712. *574*

INTERNATIONAL DIRECTORY OF PRIMATOLOGY.
University of Wisconsin Press, 114 N. Murray St., Madison, WI 53715-1299. TEL 608-262-8782. FAX 608-262-7560. *837*

INTERNATIONAL ECONOMIC DEVELOPMENT LAW.
Kluwer Law International, Postbus 85889, 2508 CN The Hague, Netherlands. TEL 31-70-3081500. FAX 31-70-3081515. *4117*

INTERNATIONAL ECONOMIC JOURNAL.
Department of International Economics, College of Social Sciences, Seoul University, Seoul 151-742, S. Korea. TEL 82-2-880-6394. FAX 82-2-876-0357. *1266*

INTERNATIONAL ECONOMIC REVIEW.
University of Pennsylvania, Department of Economics, 3718 Locust Walk, University of Pennsylvania, Philadelphia, PA 19104-6297. TEL 215-898-5841. FAX 215-573-2072. *973*

INTERNATIONAL EDUCATION.
University of Tennessee at Knoxville, College of Education, 212 Claxton, Knoxville, TN 37996-3400. TEL 423-974-5252. FAX 423-974-8718. *2565*

INTERNATIONAL EMERGENCY MANAGEMENT AND ENGINEERING CONFERENCE. PROCEEDINGS.
Society for Computer Simulation, Box 17900, San Diego, CA 92177. TEL 619-277-3888. FAX 609-277-3930. *2152*

INTERNATIONAL ENDODONTIC JOURNAL.
Blackwell Science Ltd., Osney Mead, Oxford OX2 OEL, England. TEL 01865-206206. FAX 01865-721205. *4860*

INTERNATIONAL ENVIRONMENTAL LAW AND POLICY.
Kluwer Academic Publishers, Postbus 17, 3300 AA Dordrecht, Netherlands. TEL 31-78-6392392. FAX 31-78-6392254. *2935*

THE INTERNATIONAL EXECUTIVE.
John Wiley & Sons, Inc., Journals, 605 Third Ave., New York, NY 10158. TEL 212-850-6645. FAX 212-850-6021. *1331*

INTERNATIONAL FAMILY PLANNING PERSPECTIVES.
Alan Guttmacher Institute, 120 Wall St., New York, NY 10005. TEL 212-248-1111. FAX 212-248-1951. *4960*

INTERNATIONAL FEDERATION FOR INFORMATION AND DOCUMENTATION. PROCEEDINGS OF CONGRESS.
Elsevier Science B.V., Books Division, P.O. Box 211, 1000 AE Amsterdam, Netherlands. TEL 31-20-4853911. FAX 31-20-4853705. *4186*

INTERNATIONAL FIBER SCIENCE AND TECHNOLOGY SERIES.
Marcel Dekker, Inc., 270 Madison Ave., New York, NY 10016. TEL 212-696-9000. FAX 212-685-4540. *1816*

INTERNATIONAL FICTION REVIEW.
University of New Brunswick, Department of German, Russian, Fredericton, NB E3B 5A3, Canada. TEL 506-453-4636. FAX 506-453-4659. *4417*

INTERNATIONAL GAS TURBINE INSTITUTE TECHNOLOGY REPORT. LAND, SEA & AIR.
International Gas Turbine Institute, 5801 Peachtree Dunwoody Rd., N.E., Ste. 100, Atlanta, GA 30342-1503. TEL 404-847-0072. FAX 404-847-0151. *4545*

THE INTERNATIONAL INFORMATION AND LIBRARY REVIEW.
Academic Press Ltd., 24-28 Oval Rd., London NW1 7DX, England. TEL 44-171-482-2293. FAX 44-171-482-2293. *4186*

INTERNATIONAL INFORMATION, COMMUNICATION AND EDUCATION.
P. Kaula Endowment for Library and Information Science, C-239, Indira Nagar, Lucknow 226 016, India. *4186*

INTERNATIONAL INSTRUMENTATION SYMPOSIUM.
Instrument Society of America, 67 Alexander Dr., Box 12277, Research Triangle Park, NC 27709. TEL 919-549-8411. FAX 919-549-8288. *70*

INTERNATIONAL INTERACTIONS.
Gordon and Breach - Harwood Academic, Amsteldisk 166, 1st Fl., 1079 LH Amsterdam, Netherlands. *6020*

INTERNATIONAL JOINT CONFERENCE ON ARTIFICIAL INTELLIGENCE. PROCEEDINGS.
Morgan Kaufmann Publishers, Inc., 340 Pine St., 6th Fl., San Francisco, CA 94104. TEL 415-392-2665. FAX 415-982-2665. *2101*

INTERNATIONAL JOURNAL.
Canadian Institute of International Affairs, 5 Devonshire Pl., Toronto, ON M5S 2C8, Canada. TEL 416-979-1851. FAX 416-979-8575. *6020*

INTERNATIONAL JOURNAL FOR CONSUMER SAFETY.
Aeolus Press, Postbus 740, 4116 ZJ Buren, Netherlands. TEL 31-344-572055. FAX 31-344-572562. *2256*

INTERNATIONAL JOURNAL FOR HOUSING SCIENCE AND ITS APPLICATIONS.
Ural and Associates, Inc., Box 340525, Coral Gables, FL 33134. TEL 305-446-9462. FAX 305-461-0921. *3750*

INTERNATIONAL JOURNAL FOR JOINING OF MATERIALS.
J O M Institute, D T U - Helsingoer, Rasmus Knudsens Vej 50, DK-3000 Helsingoer, Denmark. TEL 45-49-21-66-22. FAX 45-49-21-33-24. *5222*

INTERNATIONAL JOURNAL FOR MICROCIRCUITS AND ELECTRONIC PACKAGING.
International Microelectronics and Packaging Society, 1850 Centennial Park Dr., Ste. 105, Reston, VA 22091-1517. TEL 703-758-1060. FAX 703-758-1066. *2643*

INTERNATIONAL JOURNAL FOR NUMERICAL AND ANALYTICAL METHODS IN GEOMECHANICS.
John Wiley & Sons Ltd., Journals, Baffins Ln., Chichester, W. Sussex PO19 1UD, England. TEL 44-1243-779777. FAX 44-1243-775878. *2788*

INTERNATIONAL JOURNAL FOR PARASITOLOGY.
Elsevier Science Ltd., Pergamon, P.O. Box 800, Kidlington, Oxford OX5 1DX, England. TEL 44-1865-843000. FAX 44-1865-843010. *4838*

INTERNATIONAL JOURNAL FOR PHILOSOPHY OF RELIGION.
Kluwer Academic Publishers, Postbus 17, 3300 AA Dordrecht, Netherlands. TEL 31-78-6392392. FAX 31-78-6392254. *6345*

INTERNATIONAL JOURNAL FOR QUALITY IN HEALTH CARE.
Elsevier Science Ltd., Pergamon, P.O. Box 800, Kidlington, Oxford OX5 1DX, England. TEL 44-1865-843000. FAX 44-1865-843010. *4685*

INTERNATIONAL JOURNAL FOR THE ADVANCEMENT OF COUNSELLING.
Kluwer Academic Publishers, Postbus 17, 3300 AA Dordrecht, Netherlands. TEL 31-78-6392392. FAX 31-78-6392254. *2451*

INTERNATIONAL JOURNAL FOR THE PSYCHOLOGY OF RELIGION.
Lawrence Erlbaum Associates, Inc., 10 Industrial Dr., Mahwah, NJ 07430-2262. TEL 201-236-9500. FAX 201-236-0072. *6345*

INTERNATIONAL JOURNAL FOR THE SEMIOTICS OF LAW.
Deborah Charles Publications, 173 Mather Ave., Liverpool L18 6JZ, England. TEL 44-151-724-2500. FAX 44-151-729-0371. *3964*

INTERNATIONAL JOURNAL OF ACAROLOGY.
Indira Publishing House, Box 250456, West Bloomfield, MI 48325-0456. TEL 810-661-2529. FAX 810-661-4066. *755*

INTERNATIONAL JOURNAL OF ADAPTIVE CONTROL AND SIGNAL PROCESSING.
John Wiley & Sons Ltd., Journals, Baffins Ln., Chichester, W. Sussex PO19 1UD, England. TEL 44-1243-779777. FAX 44-1243-775878. *2835*

INTERNATIONAL JOURNAL OF ADHESION AND ADHESIVES.
Elsevier Science Ltd., P.O. Box 800, Kidlington, Oxford OX5 1DX, England. TEL 44-1865-843000. FAX 44-1865-843010. *5878*

INTERNATIONAL JOURNAL OF ADOLESCENCE AND YOUTH.
A B Academic Publishers, P.O. Box 42, Bicester, Oxon. OX6 7NW, England. TEL 44-1869-320949. *1847*

INTERNATIONAL JOURNAL OF ADULT ORTHODONTICS AND ORTHOGNATHIC SURGERY.
Quintessence Publishing Co., Inc., 551 Kimberly Dr., Carol Stream, IL 60188-1881. TEL 630-682-3223. FAX 630-682-3288. *4860*

INTERNATIONAL JOURNAL OF ADVANCED MANUFACTURING TECHNOLOGY.
Springer-Verlag London Ltd., Sweetapple House, Catteshall Rd., Godalming, Surrey GU7 3DJ, England. TEL 44-1483-418800. FAX 44-1483-415144. *2887*

INTERNATIONAL JOURNAL OF ADVERTISING.
Blackwell Publishers Ltd., 108 Cowley Rd., Oxford OX4 1JF, England. TEL 44-1865-791100. FAX 44-1865-791347. *37*

INTERNATIONAL JOURNAL OF AGING & HUMAN DEVELOPMENT.
Baywood Publishing Co., Inc., 26 Austin Ave., Box 337, Amityville, NY 11701. TEL 516-691-1270. FAX 516-691-1770. *3437*

INTERNATIONAL JOURNAL OF AMERICAN LINGUISTICS.
University of Chicago Press, Journals Division, Box 37005, Chicago, IL 60637. TEL 773-753-3347. FAX 773-753-0811. *4264*

INTERNATIONAL JOURNAL OF ANDROLOGY.
Blackwell Science Ltd., Osney Mead, Oxford OX2 0EL, England. TEL 44-1865-206206. FAX 44-1865-721205. *5161*

INTERNATIONAL JOURNAL OF ANGIOLOGY.
Springer-Verlag, Medical Journals, 175 Fifth Ave., New York, NY 10010. TEL 212-460-1500. FAX 212-473-6272. *4818*

INTERNATIONAL JOURNAL OF ANIMAL SCIENCES.
Nitasha Publications, 921, Sector 14, Sonepat, 131001 Haryana, India. TEL 91-1662-32703. *279*

INTERNATIONAL JOURNAL OF ANTIMICROBIAL AGENTS.
Elsevier Science B.V., P.O. Box 211, 1000 AE Amsterdam, Netherlands. TEL 31-20-4853911. FAX 31-20-4853598. *786*

INTERNATIONAL JOURNAL OF APPLIED ELECTROMAGNETICS AND MECHANICS.
I O S Press, Van Diemenstraat 94, 1013 CN Amsterdam, Netherlands. TEL 31-20-6382189. FAX 31-20-6203419. *2835*

INTERNATIONAL JOURNAL OF APPROXIMATE REASONING.
Elsevier Science Inc., Box 945, New York, NY 10159-0945. TEL 212-633-3730. FAX 212-633-3680. *2101*

INTERNATIONAL JOURNAL OF ARTS MEDICINE.
I J A M, M M B Music, Inc., Contemporary Arts Bldg., 3526 Washington Ave., St. Louis, MO 63103-1019. TEL 314-531-9635. FAX 314-531-8384. *4685*

INTERNATIONAL JOURNAL OF AVIATION PSYCHOLOGY.
Lawrence Erlbaum Associates, Inc., 10 Industrial Dr., Mahwah, NJ 07430-2262. TEL 201-236-9500. FAX 201-236-0072. *70*

INTERNATIONAL JOURNAL OF BEHAVIORAL DEVELOPMENT.
Taylor & Francis Ltd., Psychology Press, 1 Gunpowder Sq., London EC4A 3DE, England. TEL 44-171-5830490. FAX 44-171-5830585. *6118*

INTERNATIONAL JOURNAL OF BIO-MEDICAL COMPUTING.
Elsevier Science Ireland Ltd., P.O. Box 85, Limerick, Ireland. TEL 353-61-471944. FAX 353-61-472144. *4847*

INTERNATIONAL JOURNAL OF BIOCHEMISTRY & CELL BIOLOGY.
Elsevier Science Ltd., Pergamon, P.O. Box 800, Kidlington, Oxford OX5 1DX, England. TEL 44-1865-843000. FAX 44-1865-843010. *661*

INTERNATIONAL JOURNAL OF BIOLOGICAL MACROMOLECULES.
Elsevier Science B.V., P.O. Box 211, 1000 AE Amsterdam, Netherlands. TEL 31-20-4853911. FAX 31-20-4853598. *661*

INTERNATIONAL JOURNAL OF BIOSOCIAL AND MEDICAL RESEARCH.
Life Sciences Press, Box 1174, Tacoma, WA 98401-1174. TEL 206-922-0442. FAX 206-922-0479. *5475*

INTERNATIONAL JOURNAL OF BOUNDARY ELEMENT METHODS AND COMMUNICATIONS.
Computational Mechanics Publications, Ashurst Lodge, Ashurst, Southampton, Hants. SO40 7AA. TEL 44-1703-293223. FAX 44-1703-292853. *2726*

INTERNATIONAL JOURNAL OF BUSINESS.
Premier Publishing, Inc., Box 27647, Fresno, CA 93729-7647. TEL 209-434-2886. FAX 209-434-2886. *973*

INTERNATIONAL JOURNAL OF BUSINESS, ECONOMY & INDUSTRY STUDIES.
P.O. Box 98029, S. Common Post, 2150 Burnhamthorpe Rd., Mississauga, ON L5L 3A0, Canada. FAX 416-277-2875. *973*

INTERNATIONAL JOURNAL OF CANADIAN STUDIES.
International Council for Canadian Studies, 325 Dalhousie, S-800, Ottawa, ON K1N 7G2, Canada. TEL 613-789-7834. FAX 613-789-7830. *6714*

INTERNATIONAL JOURNAL OF CANCER.
John Wiley & Sons, Inc., Journals, 605 Third Ave., New York, NY 10158. TEL 212-850-6645. FAX 212-850-6021. *4979*

INTERNATIONAL JOURNAL OF CARDIAC IMAGING.
Kluwer Academic Publishers, Postbus 17, 3300 AA Dordrecht, Netherlands. TEL 31-78-6392392. FAX 31-78-6392254. *4818*

INTERNATIONAL JOURNAL OF CARDIOLOGY.
Elsevier Science Ireland Ltd., P.O. Box 85, Limerick, Ireland. TEL 353-61-471944. FAX 353-61-472144. *4818*

INTERNATIONAL JOURNAL OF CHEMICAL KINETICS.
John Wiley & Sons, Inc., Journals, 605 Third Ave., New York, NY 10158. TEL 212-850-6645. FAX 212-850-6021. *1829*

INTERNATIONAL JOURNAL OF CHILDBIRTH EDUCATION.
International Childbirth Education Association, Box 20048, Minneapolis, MN 55420-0048. TEL 612-854-8660. FAX 612-854-8772. *4960*

INTERNATIONAL JOURNAL OF CHILDREN & ADOLESCENTS.
P.O. Box 98029, S. Common Post, 2150 Burnhamthorpe Rd., Mississauga, ON L5L 3A0, Canada. FAX 416-277-2875. *1847*

THE INTERNATIONAL JOURNAL OF CHILDREN'S RIGHTS.
Kluwer Law International, Postbus 85889, 2508 CN The Hague, Netherlands. TEL 31-70-3081500. FAX 31-70-3081515. *5993*

INTERNATIONAL JOURNAL OF CIRCUMPOLAR HEALTH.
Institute for Arctic Medicine, Aapistie 1, FIN-90220 Oulu, Finland. TEL 358-8-537-6201. FAX 358-8-537-6203. *4686*

INTERNATIONAL JOURNAL OF CLINICAL MONITORING AND COMPUTING.
Kluwer Academic Publishers, Postbus 17, 3300 AA Dordrecht, Netherlands. TEL 31-78-6392392. FAX 31-78-6392254. *4805*

INTERNATIONAL JOURNAL OF CLINICAL ONCOLOGY.
Churchill Livingstone Japan, Churchill Bldg., 2-8-16 Yutenji, Meguro-ku, Tokyo 153, Japan. TEL 81-3-5721-0442. FAX 81-3-5721-0445. *4980*

INTERNATIONAL JOURNAL OF CLINICAL PRACTICE.
Medicom International Ltd., Churston House, Portsmouth Rd., Esher, Surrey KT10 9AD, England. TEL 44-1372-471671. FAX 44-1372-471672. *4686*

INTERNATIONAL JOURNAL OF CLINICAL PRACTICE. SYMPOSIUM SUPPLEMENT.
Medicom International Ltd., Churston House, Portsmouth Rd., Esher, Surrey KT10 9AD, England. TEL 44-1372-471671. FAX 44-1372-471672. *4686*

INTERNATIONAL JOURNAL OF COAL GEOLOGY.
Elsevier Science B.V., P.O. Box 211, 1000 AE Amsterdam, Netherlands. TEL 31-20-4853911. FAX 31-20-4853598. *2352*

INTERNATIONAL JOURNAL OF COMMERCE AND MANAGEMENT.
Indiana University of Pennsylvania, International Academy of Business Disciplines, Indiana, PA 15705. TEL 412-357-5759. FAX 412-357-5743. *1483*

INTERNATIONAL JOURNAL OF COMMUNICATION SYSTEMS.
John Wiley & Sons Ltd., Journals, Baffins Ln., Chichester, W. Sussex PO19 1UD, England. TEL 44-1243-779777. FAX 44-1243-775878. *2835*

THE INTERNATIONAL JOURNAL OF COMPARATIVE LABOUR LAW AND INDUSTRIAL RELATIONS.
Kluwer Law International, Postbus 85889, 2508 CN The Hague, Netherlands. TEL 31-70-3081500. FAX 31-70-3081515. *3964*

INTERNATIONAL JOURNAL OF COMPARATIVE SOCIOLOGY.
E.J. Brill, P.O. Box 9000, 2300 PA Leiden, Netherlands. TEL 31-71-5353500. FAX 31-71-5317532. *6714*

INTERNATIONAL JOURNAL OF COMPUTER ALGEBRA IN MATHEMATICS EDUCATION.
Research Information Ltd., 222 Maylands Ave., Hemel Hempstead, Herts. HP2 7TD, England. TEL 44-1442-213222. FAX 44-1442-259395. *2114*

INTERNATIONAL JOURNAL OF COMPUTER APPLICATIONS IN TECHNOLOGY.
Inderscience Enterprises Ltd., World Trade Centre Bldg., 110 Ave. Louis Casai, Case Postale 306, CH-1215 Geneva-Aeroport, Switzerland. FAX 41-22-7910885. *2213*

INTERNATIONAL JOURNAL OF COMPUTER INTEGRATED MANUFACTURING.
Taylor & Francis Ltd., 1 Gunpowder Sq., London EC4A 3DE, England. TEL 44-171-583-0490. FAX 44-171-583-0585. *1202*

INTERNATIONAL JOURNAL OF COMPUTER MATHEMATICS.
Gordon and Breach - Harwood Academic, Amsteldisk 166, 1st Fl., 1079 LH Amsterdam, Netherlands. *4621*

INTERNATIONAL JOURNAL OF COMPUTER SYSTEMS SCIENCE AND ENGINEERING.
C R L Publishing Ltd., P.O. Box 31, Market Harborough, Leics. LE16 9RQ, England. TEL 44-8158-525382. FAX 44-1858-525635. *2156*

INTERNATIONAL JOURNAL OF COMPUTERS FOR MATHEMATICAL LEARNING.
Kluwer Academic Publishers, Postbus 17, 3300 AA Dordrecht, Netherlands. TEL 31-78-6392392. FAX 31-78-6392254. *4621*

INTERNATIONAL JOURNAL OF CONTEMPORARY HOSPITALITY MANAGEMENT.
M C B University Press Ltd., 60-62 Toller Ln., Bradford, W. Yorks BD8 9BY, England. TEL 44-1274-777700. FAX 44-1274-785200. *3730*

INTERNATIONAL JOURNAL OF CONTROL.
Taylor & Francis Ltd., 1 Gunpowder Sq., London EC4A 3DE, England. TEL 44-171-583-0490. FAX 44-171-583-0585. *2726*

INTERNATIONAL JOURNAL OF COSMETIC SCIENCE.
Thomson Science, 2-6 Boundary Row, London SE1 8HN, England. TEL 44-171-8650066. FAX 44-171-5229623. *511*

INTERNATIONAL JOURNAL OF CRASHWORTHINESS.
Woodhead Publishing Ltd., Abington Hall, Abington, Cambridge CB1 6AH, England. TEL 44-1223-891358. FAX 44-1223-893694. *7030*

INTERNATIONAL JOURNAL OF DAMAGE MECHANICS.
Technomic Publishing Co., Inc., 851 New Holland Ave., Box 3535, Lancaster, PA 17604. TEL 717-291-5609. FAX 717-295-4538. *2887*

INTERNATIONAL JOURNAL OF DERMATOLOGY.
Blackwell Science Ltd., Osney Mead, Oxford OX2 0EL, England. TEL 44-1865-206206. FAX 44-1865-721205. *4879*

INTERNATIONAL JOURNAL OF DEVELOPMENTAL BIOLOGY.
U B C Press, Casilla 1397, 48080 Bilbao, Spain. TEL 34-4-4648800 ext. 2153. FAX 34-4-4648966. *606*

INTERNATIONAL JOURNAL OF DEVELOPMENTAL NEUROSCIENCE.
Elsevier Science Ltd., Pergamon, P.O. Box 800, Kidlington, Oxford OX5 1DX, England. TEL 44-1865-843000. FAX 44-1865-843010. *5069*

REFEREED SERIALS

INTERNATIONAL JOURNAL OF DISCRIMINATION AND THE LAW.
A B Academic Publishers, P.O. Box 42, Bicester, Oxon. OX6 7NW, England. TEL 44-1869-320949. *5994*

INTERNATIONAL JOURNAL OF DRUG POLICY.
Whurr Publishers Ltd., 19b Compton Terrace, London N1 2UN, England. TEL 44-171-359-5979. FAX 44-171-226-5290. *2302*

INTERNATIONAL JOURNAL OF EATING DISORDERS.
John Wiley & Sons, Inc., Journals, 605 Third Ave., New York, NY 10158. TEL 212-850-6645. FAX 212-850-6021. *5475*

INTERNATIONAL JOURNAL OF ECOLOGY AND ENVIRONMENTAL SCIENCES.
International Scientific Publications, 50-B Pocket C, Sidhartha Extension, New Delhi 110 014, India. TEL 91-11-6912169. *2935*

INTERNATIONAL JOURNAL OF EDUCATIONAL DEVELOPMENT.
Elsevier Science Ltd., Pergamon, P.O. Box 800, Kidlington, Oxford OX5 1DX, England. TEL 44-1865-843000. FAX 44-1865-843010. *2452*

INTERNATIONAL JOURNAL OF EDUCATIONAL REFORM.
Technomic Publishing Co., Inc., 851 New Holland Ave., Box 3535, Lancaster, PA 17604. TEL 717-291-5609. FAX 717-295-4538. *2452*

INTERNATIONAL JOURNAL OF EDUCATIONAL RESEARCH.
Elsevier Science Ltd., Pergamon, P.O. Box 800, Kidlington, Oxford OX5 1DX, England. TEL 44-1865-843000. FAX 44-1865-843010. *2565*

INTERNATIONAL JOURNAL OF EDUCATIONAL TELECOMMUNICATIONS.
Association for the Advancement of Computing in Education, Box 2966, Charlottesville, VA 22902. TEL 804-973-3987. FAX 804-978-7449. *2517*

INTERNATIONAL JOURNAL OF EDUCOLOGY.
Educology Research Associates, P.O. Box 216, Terrigal, N.S.W. 2260, Australia. TEL 61-43-653120. FAX 61-43-652871. *2510*

INTERNATIONAL JOURNAL OF ELECTRICAL POWER & ENERGY SYSTEMS.
Elsevier Science Ltd., P.O. Box 800, Kidlington, Oxford OX5 1DX, England. TEL 44-1865-843000. FAX 44-1865-843010. *2836*

INTERNATIONAL JOURNAL OF ELECTRONIC COMMERCE.
M.E. Sharpe, Inc., 80 Business Park Dr., Armonk, NY 10504. TEL 914-273-1800. FAX 914-273-2106. *1202*

INTERNATIONAL JOURNAL OF ELECTRONICS.
Taylor & Francis Ltd., 1 Gunpowder Sq., London EC4A 3DE, England. TEL 44-171-583-0490. FAX 44-171-583-0585. *2643*

INTERNATIONAL JOURNAL OF ENERGY RESEARCH.
John Wiley & Sons Ltd., Journals, Baffins Ln., Chichester, W. Sussex PO19 1UD, England. TEL 44-1243-779777. FAX 44-1243-775878. *2672*

INTERNATIONAL JOURNAL OF ENGINEERING EDUCATION.
Tempus Publications, Berliner Tor 21, 20099 Hamburg, Germany. TEL 49-40-24883014. FAX 49-40-24882847. *2726*

INTERNATIONAL JOURNAL OF ENGINEERING SCIENCE.
Elsevier Science Ltd., Pergamon, P.O. Box 800, Kidlington, Oxford OX5 1DX, England. TEL 44-1865-843000. FAX 44-1865-843010. *2726*

INTERNATIONAL JOURNAL OF ENVIRONMENT AND POLLUTION.
Inderscience Enterprises Ltd., World Trade Centre Bldg., 110 Ave. Louis Casai, Case Postale 309, CH-1215 Geneva-Aeroport, Switzerland. FAX 41-22-7910885. *2969*

INTERNATIONAL JOURNAL OF ENVIRONMENTAL ANALYTICAL CHEMISTRY.
Gordon and Breach - Harwood Academic, Amsteldisk 166, 1st Fl., 1079 LH Amsterdam, Netherlands. *1791*

INTERNATIONAL JOURNAL OF ENVIRONMENTAL & BIODIVERSITY AWARENESS.
P.O. Box 98029, S. Common Post, 2150 Burnhamthorpe Rd., Mississagua, ON L5L 3A0, Canada. FAX 416-277-2875. *684*

INTERNATIONAL JOURNAL OF ENVIRONMENTAL STUDIES. SECTIONS A & B.
Gordon and Breach - Harwood Academic, Amsteldisk 166, 1st Fl., 1079 LH Amsterdam, Netherlands. *2935*

INTERNATIONAL JOURNAL OF EXPERIMENTAL PATHOLOGY.
Blackwell Science Ltd., Osney Mead, Oxford OX2 0EL, England. TEL 44-1865-206206. FAX 44-1865-721205. *4686*

INTERNATIONAL JOURNAL OF FATIGUE.
Elsevier Science Ltd., P.O. Box 800, Kidlington, Oxford OX5 1DX, England. TEL 44-1865-843000. FAX 44-1865-843000. *2859*

INTERNATIONAL JOURNAL OF FERTILITY AND WOMEN'S MEDICINE.
M S P (Medical Science Publishing) International, Inc., 405 Main St., Port Washington, NY 11050. TEL 516-944-7340. FAX 516-944-8663. *4686*

INTERNATIONAL JOURNAL OF FINANCE.
206 Rabbit Run Dr., Cherry Hill, NJ 08003-1427. TEL 609-424-2262. FAX 609-424-6007. *1147*

INTERNATIONAL JOURNAL OF FLEXIBLE MANUFACTURING SYSTEMS.
Kluwer Academic Publishers Boston, Box 358, Accord Sta., Hingham, MA 02018-0358. TEL 617-871-6600. FAX 617-871-6528. *2860*

INTERNATIONAL JOURNAL OF FLUID DYNAMICS.
Monash University, Department of Mechanical Engineering, Clayton 3168, Australia. TEL 61-3-99059624. FAX 61-3-99059639. *5845*

INTERNATIONAL JOURNAL OF FOOD MICROBIOLOGY.
Elsevier Science B.V., P.O. Box 211, 1000 AE Amsterdam, Netherlands. TEL 31-20-4853911. FAX 31-20-4853598. *787*

INTERNATIONAL JOURNAL OF FOOD SCIENCE AND TECHNOLOGY.
Blackwell Science Ltd., Osney Mead, Oxford OX2 0EL, England. TEL 44-1865-206206. FAX 44-1865-721205. *3114*

INTERNATIONAL JOURNAL OF FORECASTING.
North-Holland, P.O. Box 211, 1000 AE Amsterdam, Netherlands. TEL 31-20-4853911. FAX 31-20-4853598. *1266*

INTERNATIONAL JOURNAL OF FORENSIC DOCUMENT EXAMINERS.
Shunderson Communications, P.O. Box 42057, Ottawa, ON K1K 4L8, Canada. TEL 613-830-4750. FAX 613-830-9654. *2269*

INTERNATIONAL JOURNAL OF FRACTURE.
Kluwer Academic Publishers, Postbus 17, 3300 AA Dordrecht, Netherlands. TEL 31-78-6392392. FAX 31-78-6392254. *2860*

INTERNATIONAL JOURNAL OF GENERAL SYSTEMS.
Gordon and Breach - Harwood Academic, Amsteldisk 166, 1st Fl., 1079 LH Amsterdam, Netherlands. *2156*

INTERNATIONAL JOURNAL OF GEOGRAPHICAL INFORMATION SCIENCE.
Taylor & Francis Ltd., 1 Gunpowder Sq., London EC4A 3DE, England. TEL 44-171-583-0490. FAX 44-171-583-0585. *3429*

INTERNATIONAL JOURNAL OF GLOBAL ENERGY ISSUES.
Inderscience Enterprises Ltd., World Trade Centre Bldg., 110 Ave. Louis Casai, Case Postale 306, CH-1215 Geneva-Aeroport, Switzerland. FAX 41-22-7910885. *2672*

INTERNATIONAL JOURNAL OF GROUP PSYCHOTHERAPY.
Guilford Publications, Inc., 72 Spring St., 4th Fl., New York, NY 10012. TEL 212-431-9800. FAX 212-966-6708. *6118*

INTERNATIONAL JOURNAL OF GROUP TENSIONS.
Human Sciences Press, Inc., 233 Spring St., New York, NY 10013-1578. TEL 212-620-8000. FAX 212-463-0742. *6118*

INTERNATIONAL JOURNAL OF GYNECOLOGICAL PATHOLOGY.
Lippincott - Raven Publishers, 227 E. Washington Sq., Philadelphia, PA 19106. TEL 215-238-4200. *4960*

INTERNATIONAL JOURNAL OF GYNECOLOGY AND OBSTETRICS.
Elsevier Science Ireland Ltd., P.O. Box 85, Limerick, Ireland. TEL 353-61-471944. FAX 353-61-472144. *4960*

INTERNATIONAL JOURNAL OF HEALTH PLANNING AND MANAGEMENT.
John Wiley & Sons Ltd., Journals, Baffins Ln., Chichester, W. Sussex PO19 1UD, England. TEL 44-1243-779777. FAX 44-1243-775878. *6671*

INTERNATIONAL JOURNAL OF HEALTH SERVICES.
Baywood Publishing Co., Inc., 26 Austin Ave., Box 337, Amityville, NY 11701. TEL 516-691-1270. FAX 516-691-1770. *6240*

INTERNATIONAL JOURNAL OF HEAT AND FLUID FLOW.
Elsevier Science Inc., Box 945, New York, NY 10159-0945. TEL 212-633-3730. FAX 212-633-3680. *5841*

INTERNATIONAL JOURNAL OF HEAT AND MASS TRANSFER.
Elsevier Science Ltd., Pergamon, P.O. Box 800, Kidlington, Oxford OX5 1DX, England. TEL 44-1865-843000. FAX 44-1865-843010. *2887*

INTERNATIONAL JOURNAL OF HEMATOLOGY.
Elsevier Science Ireland Ltd., P.O. Box 85, Limerick, Ireland. TEL 353-61-471944. FAX 353-61-472144. *4920*

INTERNATIONAL JOURNAL OF HERITAGE STUDIES.
Intellect, Earl Richards Rd. N., Exeter, Devon EX2 6AS. TEL 44-1392-475101. FAX 44-1392-475110. *3501*

INTERNATIONAL JOURNAL OF HISTORICAL ARCHAEOLOGY.
Plenum Publishing Corp., 233 Spring St., New York, NY 10013-1578. TEL 212-620-8000. FAX 212-463-0742. *367*

INTERNATIONAL JOURNAL OF HOSPITALITY MANAGEMENT.
Elsevier Science Ltd., Pergamon, P.O. Box 800, Kidlington, Oxford OX5 1DX, England. TEL 44-1865-843000. FAX 44-1865-843010. *3730*

INTERNATIONAL JOURNAL OF HUMAN RESOURCES MANAGEMENT.
Thomson Professional, 2-6 Boundary Row, London SE1 8HN, England. TEL 44-171-865-0066. FAX 44-171-522-9621. *1569*

THE INTERNATIONAL JOURNAL OF HUMAN RIGHTS.
Frank Cass, Newbury House, 890-900 Eastern Ave., Newbury Park, Ilford, Essex IG2 7HH, England. TEL 44-181-5998866. FAX 44-181-5990984. *5994*

THE INTERNATIONAL JOURNAL OF HUMANITIES AND PEACE.
Vasant V. Merchant, Ed. & Pub., IJHP Journal, 1436 Evergreen Drive, Flagstaff, AZ 86001. TEL 520-774-4793. FAX 520-774-4793. *3781*

INTERNATIONAL JOURNAL OF HYDROGEN ENERGY.
Elsevier Science Ltd., Pergamon, P.O. Box 800, Kidlington, Oxford OX5 1DX, England. TEL 44-1865-843000. FAX 44-1865-843010. *2672*

INTERNATIONAL JOURNAL OF HYPERTHERMIA.
Taylor & Francis Ltd., 1 Gunpowder Sq., London EC4A 3DE, England. TEL 44-171-583-0490. FAX 44-171-583-0585. *4980*

INTERNATIONAL JOURNAL OF IBERIAN STUDIES.
Intellect, Earl Richards Rd. N., Exeter, Devon EX2 6AS, England. TEL 44-1392-475110. FAX 44-1392-475110. *3575*

INTERNATIONAL JOURNAL OF IMAGING SYSTEMS AND TECHNOLOGY.
John Wiley & Sons, Inc., Journals, 605 Third Ave., New York, NY 10158-0012. TEL 212-850-6645. FAX 212-850-6021. *5807*

INTERNATIONAL JOURNAL OF IMMUNOPATHOLOGY AND PHARMACOLOGY.
Biomedical Research Press, s.a.s., c/o Universita di Chieti, Depto. di Immunologia, Via dei Vestini, Chieti, Italy. TEL 39-871-355293. FAX 39-871-561635. *4797*

INTERNATIONAL JOURNAL OF IMMUNOPHARMACOLOGY.
Elsevier Science Ltd., Pergamon, P.O. Box 800, Kidlington, Oxford OX5 1DX, England. TEL 44-1865-843000. FAX 44-1865-843010. *5668*

INTERNATIONAL JOURNAL OF IMPACT ENGINEERING.
Elsevier Science Ltd., Pergamon, P.O. Box 800, Kidlington, Oxford OX5 1DX, England. TEL 44-1865-843000. FAX 44-1865-843010. *2726*

INTERNATIONAL JOURNAL OF INCLUSIVE EDUCATION.
Taylor & Francis Ltd., 1 Gunpowder Sq., London EC4A 3DE, England. TEL 44-171-5830490. FAX 44-171-5830585. *2452*

INTERNATIONAL JOURNAL OF INDUSTRIAL ERGONOMICS.
Elsevier Science B.V., P.O. Box 211, 1000 AE Amsterdam, Netherlands. TEL 31-20-4853911. FAX 31-20-4853598. *2726*

INTERNATIONAL JOURNAL OF INDUSTRIAL ORGANIZATION.
North-Holland, P.O. Box 211, 1000 AE Amsterdam, Netherlands. TEL 31-20-4853911. FAX 31-20-4853598. *1484*

INTERNATIONAL JOURNAL OF INFORMATION MANAGEMENT.
Elsevier Science Ltd., Pergamon, P.O. Box 800, Kidlington, Oxford OX5 1DX, England. TEL 44-1865-843000. FAX 44-1865-843010. *2184*

INTERNATIONAL JOURNAL OF INFRARED AND MILLIMETER WAVES.
Plenum Publishing Corp., 233 Spring St., New York, NY 10013-1578. TEL 212-620-8000. FAX 212-463-0742. *5862*

INTERNATIONAL JOURNAL OF INSECT MORPHOLOGY AND EMBRYOLOGY.
Elsevier Science Ltd., Pergamon, P.O. Box 800, Kidlington, Oxford OX5 1DX, England. TEL 44-1865-843000. FAX 44-1865-843010. *755*

INTERNATIONAL JOURNAL OF INSTRUCTIONAL MEDIA.
Westwood Press, Inc., 23 E. 22nd St., 4th Fl., New York, NY 10010. TEL 212-420-8008. FAX 212-353-8291. *2606*

INTERNATIONAL JOURNAL OF INTELLIGENT SYSTEMS.
John Wiley & Sons, Inc., Journals, 605 Third Ave., New York, NY 10158. TEL 212-570-6645. FAX 212-850-6021. *2101*

INTERNATIONAL JOURNAL OF INTELLIGENT SYSTEMS IN ACCOUNTING, FINANCE & MANAGEMENT.
John Wiley & Sons Ltd., Journals, Baffins Ln., Chichester, W. Sussex PO19 1UD, England. TEL 44-1243-779777. FAX 44-1243-775878. *1202*

INTERNATIONAL JOURNAL OF INTENSIVE CARE.
Greycoat Publishing, 1 Harley St., London W1N 1DA, England. TEL 44-171-637-1828. FAX 44-171-637-3020. *4686*

INTERNATIONAL JOURNAL OF INTERCULTURAL RELATIONS.
Elsevier Science Ltd., Pergamon, P.O. Box 800, Kidlington, Oxford OX5 1DX, England. TEL 44-1865-843000. FAX 44-1865-843010. *6714*

INTERNATIONAL JOURNAL OF ISLAMIC STUDIES.
P.O. Box 98029, S. Common Post, 2150 Burnhamthorpe Rd., Mississagua, ON L5L 3A0, Canada. FAX 416-277-2875. *5529*

INTERNATIONAL JOURNAL OF LAW AND PSYCHIATRY.
Elsevier Science Ltd., Pergamon, P.O. Box 800, Kidlington, Oxford OX5 1DX, England. TEL 44-1865-843000. FAX 44-1865-843010. *3965*

INTERNATIONAL JOURNAL OF LEPROSY AND OTHER MYCOBACTERIAL DISEASES.
International Leprosy Association, One ALM Way, Greenville, SC 29601. TEL 864-271-7040. FAX 864-271-7062. *4838*

INTERNATIONAL JOURNAL OF LIFELONG EDUCATION.
Taylor & Francis Ltd., Rankine Rd., Basingstoke, Hants. RG24 8PR, England. TEL 44-1256-840366. FAX 44-1256-479438. *2510*

INTERNATIONAL JOURNAL OF LOGISTICS MANAGEMENT.
International Logistics Research Institute, Inc., Box 2166, Pt. Vedra Beach, FL 32004-2166. TEL 904-880-8653. FAX 904-880-8654. *1484*

INTERNATIONAL JOURNAL OF MACHINE TOOLS & MANUFACTURE.
Elsevier Science Ltd., Pergamon, P.O. Box 800, Kidlington, Oxford OX5 1DX, England. TEL 44-1865-843000. FAX 44-1865-843010. *2877*

INTERNATIONAL JOURNAL OF MANAGEMENT.
P.O. Box 982, Poole, Dorset BH12 5YF, England. *1484*

INTERNATIONAL JOURNAL OF MANUFACTURING SYSTEM DESIGN.
World Scientific Publishing Co. Pte. Ltd., Farrer Rd., P.O. Box 128, Singapore 9128, Singapore. TEL 65-3825663. FAX 65-3825919. *2110*

INTERNATIONAL JOURNAL OF MARINE AND COASTAL LAW.
Kluwer Law International, Postbus 85889, 2508 CN The Hague, Netherlands. TEL 31-70-3081500. FAX 31-70-3081515. *4142*

INTERNATIONAL JOURNAL OF MARITIME HISTORY.
Maritime Economic History Association, c/o Memorial University of Newfoundland, Maritime Studies Research Unit, St. John's, NF A1C 5S7, Canada. TEL 709-737-8424. FAX 709-737-8427. *7153*

INTERNATIONAL JOURNAL OF MASS SPECTROMETRY AND ION PROCESSES.
Elsevier Science B.V., P.O. Box 211, 1000 AE Amsterdam, Netherlands. TEL 31-20-4853911. FAX 31-20-4853598. *5862*

INTERNATIONAL JOURNAL OF MATERIALS & PRODUCT TECHNOLOGY.
Inderscience Enterprises Ltd., World Trade Centre Bldg., 110 Ave. Louis Casai, Case Postale 306, CH-1215 Geneva-Aeroport, Switzerland. FAX 41-22-7910885. *2860*

INTERNATIONAL JOURNAL OF MATHEMATICAL AND STATISTICAL SCIENCES.
Thesaurus Editoria de Brasilia, Sig Quadra 08, Lotte 2356, 70610-400 Brasilia, D.F., Brazil, FL 33132. TEL 55-61-3443738. FAX 55-61-3442353. *4578*

INTERNATIONAL JOURNAL OF MATHEMATICAL EDUCATION IN SCIENCE AND TECHNOLOGY.
Taylor & Francis Ltd., Rankine Rd., Basingstoke, Hants. RG24 8PR, England. TEL 44-1256-840366. FAX 44-1256-47943. *4578*

INTERNATIONAL JOURNAL OF MECHANICAL SCIENCES.
Elsevier Science Ltd., Pergamon, P.O. Box 800, Kidlington, Oxford OX5 1DX, England. TEL 44-1865-843000. FAX 44-1865-843010. *2860*

INTERNATIONAL JOURNAL OF MENTAL HEALTH.
M.E. Sharpe, Inc., 80 Business Park Dr., Armonk, NY 10504. TEL 914-273-1800. FAX 913-273-2106. *6118*

INTERNATIONAL JOURNAL OF MICROGRAPHICS & OPTICAL TECHNOLOGY.
Research Information Ltd., 222 Maylands Ave., Hemel Hempstead, Herts. HP2 7TD, England. TEL 44-1442-213222. FAX 44-1442-259395. *4232*

INTERNATIONAL JOURNAL OF MICROWAVE AND MILLIMETER-WAVE COMPUTER AIDED ENGINEERING.
John Wiley & Sons, Inc., Journals, 605 Third Ave., New York, NY 10158. TEL 212-692-6645. FAX 212-850-6021. *2805*

INTERNATIONAL JOURNAL OF MINERAL PROCESSING.
Elsevier Science B.V., P.O. Box 211, 1000 AE Amsterdam, Netherlands. TEL 31-20-4853911. FAX 31-20-4853598. *5303*

INTERNATIONAL JOURNAL OF MULTIPHASE FLOW.
Elsevier Science Ltd., Pergamon, P.O. Box 800, Kidlington, Oxford OX5 1DX, England. TEL 44-1865-843000. FAX 44-1865-843010. *2887*

INTERNATIONAL JOURNAL OF NETWORK MANAGEMENT.
John Wiley & Sons Ltd., Journals, Baffins Ln., Chichester, W. Sussex PO19 1UD, England. TEL 44-1243-779777. FAX 44-1243-775878. *1994*

INTERNATIONAL JOURNAL OF NEURORADIOLOGY.
Lippincott - Raven Publishers, 227 E. Washington Sq., Philadelphia, PA 19106. TEL 215-238-4200. FAX 215-238-4227. *5107*

INTERNATIONAL JOURNAL OF NEUROSCIENCE.
Gordon and Breach - Harwood Academic, Amsteldisk 166, 1st Fl., 1079 LH Amsterdam, Netherlands. *5069*

INTERNATIONAL JOURNAL OF NON-LINEAR MECHANICS.
Elsevier Science Ltd., Pergamon, P.O. Box 800, Kidlington, Oxford OX5 1DX, England. TEL 44-1865-843000. FAX 44-1865-843010. *2860*

INTERNATIONAL JOURNAL OF NONVIOLENCE.
Nonviolence International, Box 39127, Friendship Sta., N.W., 4530 Cathedral Ave., N.W., Washington, DC 20016. TEL 202-244-0951. FAX 202-244-6396. *6714*

INTERNATIONAL JOURNAL OF NURSING STUDIES.
Elsevier Science Ltd., Pergamon, P.O. Box 800, Kidlington, Oxford OX5 1DX, England. TEL 44-1865-843000. FAX 44-1865-843010. *4935*

INTERNATIONAL JOURNAL OF OBESITY.
Stockton Press, Houndmills, Basingstoke, Hants RG21 2XS, England. TEL 44-1256-329242. FAX 44-1256-328339. *5475*

INTERNATIONAL JOURNAL OF OBSTETRIC ANESTHESIA.
Churchill Livingstone, Robert Stevenson House, 1-3 Baxter's Pl., Leith Walk, Edinburgh EH1 3AF, Scotland. TEL 44-131-556-2424. FAX 44-131-535-1704. *4960*

INTERNATIONAL JOURNAL OF OCCUPATIONAL AND ENVIRONMENTAL HEALTH.
Hanley and Belfus, Inc., 210 S. 13th St., Philadelphia, PA 19107. TEL 215-546-4995. FAX 215-790-9330. *5492*

INTERNATIONAL JOURNAL OF OCCUPATIONAL MEDICINE AND ENVIRONMENTAL HEALTH.
Instytut Medycyny Pracy im. Jerzego Nofera, Ul. Sw. Teresy 8, P.O. Box 199, 90-950 Lodz, Poland. TEL 48-42-314718. FAX 48-42-348331. *5492*

INTERNATIONAL JOURNAL OF OCCUPATIONAL MEDICINE, IMMUNOLOGY AND TOXICOLOGY.
Princeton Scientific Publishing Co., Inc., Box 2155, Princeton, NJ 08543. TEL 609-683-4750. FAX 609-683-0838. *5492*

INTERNATIONAL JOURNAL OF OFFENDER THERAPY AND COMPARATIVE CRIMINOLOGY.
Sage Publications, Inc., 2455 Teller Rd., Thousand Oaks, CA 91320. TEL 805-499-0721. FAX 805-499-0871. *2269*

INTERNATIONAL JOURNAL OF OFFSHORE AND POLAR ENGINEERING.
International Society of Offshore and Polar Engineers, Box 1107, Golden, CO 80402-1107. TEL 303-420-8114. FAX 303-420-3760. *2887*

INTERNATIONAL JOURNAL OF ONCOLOGY.
Demetrios A. Spandidos, Ed. & Pub., Editorial Office, 1, S. Merkouri St., Athens 116 35, Greece. TEL 30-1-722-6469. FAX 30-1-752-3866. *4980*

INTERNATIONAL JOURNAL OF OPERATIONS AND QUANTITATIVE MANAGEMENT.
Indiana University Northwest, Division of Business and Economics, 3400 Broadway, Gary, IN 46408-1197. TEL 219-980-6500. *1484*

INTERNATIONAL JOURNAL OF OPTOELECTRONICS.
Taylor & Francis Ltd., 1 Gunpowder Sq., London EC4A 3DE, England. TEL 44-171-583-0490. FAX 44-171-583-0585. *5862*

INTERNATIONAL JOURNAL OF ORAL & MAXILLOFACIAL IMPLANTS.
Quintessence Publishing Co., Inc., 551 Kimberly Dr., Carol Stream, IL 60188-1881. TEL 630-682-3223. FAX 630-682-3288. *4860*

INTERNATIONAL JOURNAL OF ORAL & MAXILLOFACIAL SURGERY.
Munksgaard International Publishers Ltd., 35 Noerre Soegade, P.O. Box 2148, DK-1016 Copenhagen K, Denmark. TEL 45-33-127030. FAX 45-33-129387. *4860*

INTERNATIONAL JOURNAL OF OSTEOARCHAEOLOGY.
John Wiley & Sons Ltd., Journals, Baffins Ln., Chichester, W. Sussex PO19 1UD, England. TEL 44-1243-779777. FAX 44-1243-775878. *320*

INTERNATIONAL JOURNAL OF PAEDIATRIC DENTISTRY.
Blackwell Science Ltd., Osney Mead, Oxford OX2 0EL, England. TEL 44-1865-206206. FAX 44-1865-721205. *4860*

INTERNATIONAL JOURNAL OF PANCREATOLOGY.
Humana Press Inc., 999 Riverview Dr., Ste. 208, Totowa, NJ 07512. TEL 973-256-1699. FAX 973-256-8341. *4889*

INTERNATIONAL JOURNAL OF PARALLEL PROGRAMMING.
Plenum Publishing Corp., 233 Spring St., New York, NY 10013-1578. TEL 212-620-8000. FAX 212-463-0742. *2144*

INTERNATIONAL JOURNAL OF PATTERN RECOGNITION AND ARTIFICIAL INTELLIGENCE.
World Scientific Publishing Co. Pte. Ltd., Farrer Rd., P.O. Box 128, Singapore 9128, Singapore. TEL 65-3825663. FAX 65-3825919. *2123*

INTERNATIONAL JOURNAL OF PEDIATRIC OTORHINOLARYNGOLOGY.
Elsevier Science Ireland Ltd., P.O. Box 85, Limerick, Ireland. TEL 353-61-471944. FAX 353-61-472144. *5022*

INTERNATIONAL JOURNAL OF PERIODONTICS & RESTORATIVE DENTISTRY.
Quintessence Publishing Co., Inc., 551 Kimberly Dr., Carol Stream, IL 60188-1881. TEL 630-682-3223. FAX 630-682-3288. *4860*

INTERNATIONAL JOURNAL OF PEST MANAGEMENT.
Taylor & Francis Ltd., 1 Gunpowder Sq., London EC4A 3DE, England. TEL 44-171-583-0490. FAX 44-171-583-0585. *230*

INTERNATIONAL JOURNAL OF PHARMACEUTICS.
Elsevier Science B.V., P.O. Box 211, 1000 AE Amsterdam, Netherlands. TEL 31-20-4853911. FAX 31-20-4853598. *5668*

INTERNATIONAL JOURNAL OF PLANT SCIENCES.
University of Chicago Press, Journals Division, Box 37005, Chicago, IL 60637. TEL 773-753-3347. FAX 773-753-0811. *709*

INTERNATIONAL JOURNAL OF PLASTICITY.
Elsevier Science Ltd., Pergamon, P.O. Box 800, Kidlington, Oxford OX5 1DX, England. TEL 44-1865-843000. FAX 44-1865-843010. *2860*

INTERNATIONAL JOURNAL OF POETRY & POETS.
P.O. Box 98029, S. Common Post, 2150 Burnhamthorpe Rd., Mississagua, ON L5L 3A0, Canada. FAX 416-277-2875. *4511*

INTERNATIONAL JOURNAL OF POLICE NEGOTIATIONS AND CRISIS MANAGEMENT.
Society of Police and Criminal Psychology, c/o Dr. Wayman Mullins, Managing Editor, Southwest Texas State University, Hines Academy Center, Rm. 120, TX 75367-0292. TEL 512-245-2174. FAX 512-245-8063. *2269*

INTERNATIONAL JOURNAL OF POLITICAL ECONOMY.
M.E. Sharpe, Inc., 80 Business Park Dr., Armonk, NY 10504. TEL 914-273-1800. FAX 914-273-2106. *5934*

INTERNATIONAL JOURNAL OF POLITICS, CULTURE, AND SOCIETY.
Human Sciences Press, Inc., 233 Spring St., New York, NY 10013. TEL 212-620-8000. FAX 212-463-0742. *6020*

INTERNATIONAL JOURNAL OF POLYMERIC MATERIALS.
Gordon and Breach - Harwood Academic, Amsteldisk 166, 1st Fl., 1079 LH Amsterdam, Netherlands. *2766*

INTERNATIONAL JOURNAL OF POPULATION GEOGRAPHY.
John Wiley & Sons Ltd., Journals, Baffins Ln., Chichester, W. Sussex PO19 1UD, England. TEL 44-1243-779777. FAX 44-1243-775878. *6052*

INTERNATIONAL JOURNAL OF POWDER METALLURGY.
A P M I International, 105 College Rd. E., Princeton, NJ 08540. TEL 609-452-7700. FAX 609-987-8523. *5195*

INTERNATIONAL JOURNAL OF PRESSURE VESSELS AND PIPING.
Elsevier Science Ltd., P.O. Box 800, Kidlington, Oxford OX5 1DX, England. TEL 44-1865-843000. FAX 44-1865-843010. *2888*

INTERNATIONAL JOURNAL OF PRIMATOLOGY.
Plenum Publishing Corp., 233 Spring St., New York, NY 10013-1578. TEL 212-620-8000. FAX 212-463-0742. *837*

INTERNATIONAL JOURNAL OF PRODUCTION ECONOMICS.
Elsevier Science B.V., P.O. Box 211, 1000 AE Amsterdam, Netherlands. TEL 31-20-4853911. FAX 31-20-4853598. *2877*

INTERNATIONAL JOURNAL OF PROJECT MANAGEMENT.
Elsevier Science Ltd., Pergamon, P.O. Box 800, Kidlington, Oxford OX5 1DX, England. TEL 44-1865-843000. FAX 44-1865-843010. *1202*

INTERNATIONAL JOURNAL OF PROSTHODONTICS.
Quintessence Publishing Co., Inc., 551 Kimberly Dr., Carol Stream, IL 60188-1881. TEL 630-682-3223. FAX 630-682-3288. *4860*

INTERNATIONAL JOURNAL OF PSYCHIATRIC NURSING RESEARCH.
University of Southampton, School of Nursing and Midwifery, South Academic Block, Southampton General Hospital, Southampton, Hants. SO16 6YD, England. TEL 44-1703-796549. FAX 44-1703-796922. *5070*

INTERNATIONAL JOURNAL OF PSYCHIATRY IN MEDICINE.
Baywood Publishing Co., Inc., 26 Austin Ave., Box 337, Amityville, NY 11701. TEL 516-691-1270. FAX 516-691-1770. *5070*

INTERNATIONAL JOURNAL OF PSYCHO-ANALYSIS.
Institute of Psychoanalysis, 63 New Cavendish St., London W1M 7RD, England. TEL 0171-323-5312. FAX 0171-580-4952. *6118*

INTERNATIONAL JOURNAL OF PSYCHOPHYSIOLOGY.
Elsevier Science B.V., P.O. Box 211, 1000 AE Amsterdam, Netherlands. TEL 31-20-4853911. FAX 31-20-4853598. *6119*

INTERNATIONAL JOURNAL OF PUNJAB STUDIES.
Sage Publications India Pvt. Ltd., Box 4215, New Delhi 110 048, India. TEL 91-11-644-4958. FAX 91-11-647-2426. *6620*

INTERNATIONAL JOURNAL OF QUALITATIVE STUDIES IN EDUCATION.
Taylor & Francis Ltd., Rankine Rd., Basingstoke, Hants RG24 8PR, England. TEL 44-1256-840366. FAX 44-1256-479438. *2452*

INTERNATIONAL JOURNAL OF QUANTUM CHEMISTRY.
John Wiley & Sons, Inc., Journals, 605 Third Ave., New York, NY 10158. TEL 212-850-6645. FAX 212-850-6021. *1753*

INTERNATIONAL JOURNAL OF RADIATION BIOLOGY.
Taylor & Francis Ltd., 1 Gunpowder Sq., London EC4A 3DE, England. TEL 44-171-583-0490. FAX 44-171-583-0585. *4980*

INTERNATIONAL JOURNAL OF RADIATION: ONCOLOGY - BIOLOGY - PHYSICS.
Elsevier Science Inc., Box 945, New York, NY 10159-0945. TEL 212-633-3730. FAX 212-633-3680. *5107*

INTERNATIONAL JOURNAL OF RADIOACTIVE MATERIALS TRANSPORT.
Nuclear Technology Publishing, P.O. Box 7, Ashford, Kent TN23 1YW, England. TEL 44-1233-641683. FAX 44-1233-610021. *7030*

INTERNATIONAL JOURNAL OF REFRACTORY METALS AND HARD MATERIALS.
Elsevier Science Ltd., P.O. Box 800, Kidlington, Oxford OX5 1DX, England. TEL 44-1865-843000. FAX 44-1865-843010. *5195*

INTERNATIONAL JOURNAL OF REFRIGERATION.
Elsevier Science Ltd., P.O. Box 800, Kidlington, Oxford OX5 1DX, England. TEL 44-1865-843000. FAX 44-1865-843010. *3481*

INTERNATIONAL JOURNAL OF REHABILITATION AND HEALTH.
Plenum Publishing Corp., 233 Spring St., New York, NY 10013-1578. TEL 212-620-8000. FAX 212-463-0742. *3455*

INTERNATIONAL JOURNAL OF REHABILITATION RESEARCH.
Thomson Science, 2-6 Boundary Row, London SE1 8HN, England. TEL 44-171-865-0198. FAX 44-171-410-6600. *3455*

INTERNATIONAL JOURNAL OF RELIABILITY, QUALITY & SAFETY ENGINEERING.
World Scientific Publishing Co. Pte. Ltd., Farrer Rd., P.O. Box 128, Singapore 9128, Singapore. TEL 65-3825663. FAX 65-3825919. *2727*

INTERNATIONAL JOURNAL OF REMOTE SENSING.
Taylor & Francis Ltd., 1 Gunpowder Sq., London EC4A 3DE, England. TEL 44-171-583-0490. FAX 44-171-583-0585. *2317*

INTERNATIONAL JOURNAL OF RESEARCH IN MARKETING.
North-Holland, P.O. Box 211, 1000 AE Amsterdam, Netherlands. TEL 31-20-4853911. FAX 31-20-4853598. *1531*

INTERNATIONAL JOURNAL OF RISK AND SAFETY IN MEDICINE.
I O S Press, Van Diemenstraat 94, 1013 CN Amsterdam, Netherlands. TEL 31-20-6382189. FAX 31-20-6203419. *4687*

INTERNATIONAL JOURNAL OF ROBOTICS RESEARCH.
M I T Press, 5 Cambridge Center, Cambridge, MA 02142. TEL 617-253-2889. FAX 617-577-1545. *2207*

INTERNATIONAL JOURNAL OF ROCK MECHANICS & MINING SCIENCES.
Elsevier Science Ltd., Pergamon, P.O. Box 800, Kidlington, Oxford OX5 1DX, England. TEL 44-1865-843000. FAX 44-1865-843010. *5303*

INTERNATIONAL JOURNAL OF RURAL STUDIES.
International Task Force for the Rural Poor, Amarpurkashi Rural Polytechnic, P.O. Bilari 202411, District Moradabad (U.P.), India. TEL 91-5926-41267. *6715*

INTERNATIONAL JOURNAL OF S T D & AIDS.
Royal Society of Medicine Press Ltd., 1 Wimpole St., London W1M 8AE, England. TEL 44-171-290-2900. FAX 44-171-290-2929. *4838*

INTERNATIONAL JOURNAL OF SALT LAKE RESEARCH.
Kluwer Academic Publishers, Postbus 17, 3300 AA Dordrecht, Netherlands. TEL 31-78-6392392. FAX 31-78-6392254. *7295*

INTERNATIONAL JOURNAL OF SCIENCE EDUCATION.
Taylor & Francis Ltd., 1 Gunpowder Sq., London EC4A 3DE, England. TEL 44-171-583-0490. FAX 44-171-583-0585. *2452*

INTERNATIONAL JOURNAL OF SCIENTIFIC AMERICA & MIDDLE EAST STUDIES.
P.O. Box 98029, S. Common Post, 2150 Burnhamthorpe Rd., Mississagua, ON L5L 3A0, Canada. FAX 416-277-2875. *5529*

INTERNATIONAL JOURNAL OF SELECTION AND ASSESSMENT.
Blackwell Publishers Ltd., 108 Cowley Rd., Oxford OX4 1JF, England. TEL 44-1865-791100. FAX 44-1865-791347. *1569*

INTERNATIONAL JOURNAL OF SLAVIC LINGUISTICS AND POETICS.
Slavica Publishers, Inc., Box 14388, Columbus, OH 43214. TEL 614-268-4002. FAX 614-268-0106. *4265*

INTERNATIONAL JOURNAL OF SOCIAL EDUCATION.
Ball State University, Department of History, Muncie, IN 47306-0480. TEL 317-285-8704. *6620*

INTERNATIONAL JOURNAL OF SOCIAL SCIENCES.
P.O. Box 98029, S. Common Post, 2150 Burnhamthorpe Rd., Mississagua, ON L5L 3A0, Canada. FAX 416-277-2875. *6620*

INTERNATIONAL JOURNAL OF SOCIOLOGY.
M.E. Sharpe, Inc., 80 Business Park Dr., Armonk, NY 10504. TEL 914-273-1800. FAX 914-273-2106. *6715*

INTERNATIONAL JOURNAL OF SOLAR ENERGY.
Gordon and Breach - Harwood Academic, Amsteldisk 166, 1st Fl., 1079 LH Amsterdam, Netherlands. *2706*

INTERNATIONAL JOURNAL OF SOLIDS AND STRUCTURES.
Elsevier Science Ltd., Pergamon, P.O. Box 800, Kidlington, Oxford OX5 1DX, England. TEL 44-1865-843000. FAX 44-1865-843010. *5845*

INTERNATIONAL JOURNAL OF SPACE STRUCTURES.
Multi-Science Publishing Co. Ltd., 107 High St., Brentwood, Essex CM14 4RX, England. TEL 44-1277-224632. FAX 44-1277-223453. *899*

INTERNATIONAL JOURNAL OF SPEECH TECHNOLOGY.
Kluwer Academic Publishers, Postbus 17, 3300 AA Dordrecht, Netherlands. TEL 31-78-6392392. FAX 31-78-6392254. *4320*

INTERNATIONAL JOURNAL OF SPORT NUTRITION.
Human Kinetics Publishers, Inc., Box 5076, Champaign, IL 61825-5076. TEL 217-351-5076. FAX 217-351-2674. *5475*

INTERNATIONAL JOURNAL OF SPORTS, TOURISM & PHYSICAL EDUCATION.
P.O. Box 98029, S. Common Post, 2150 Burnhamthorpe Rd., Mississagua, ON L5L 3A0, Canada. FAX 416-277-2875. *5785*

INTERNATIONAL JOURNAL OF STRESS MANAGEMENT.
Human Sciences Press, Inc., 233 Spring St., New York, NY 10013. TEL 212-620-8000. FAX 212-463-0742. *4687*

INTERNATIONAL JOURNAL OF STRUCTURES.
Nem Chand & Bros., Civil Lines, Roorkee 247667, India. TEL 91-1332-72258. FAX 91-1332-73258. *2789*

INTERNATIONAL JOURNAL OF SUPERCOMPUTER APPLICATIONS AND HIGH-PERFORMANCE COMPUTING.
Sage Publications, Inc., Sage Science Press, 2455 Teller Rd., Thousand Oaks, CA 91320. TEL 805-499-0721. FAX 805-499-0871. *2214*

INTERNATIONAL JOURNAL OF SURGICAL PATHOLOGY.
Westminster Publications, Inc., 708 Glen Cove Ave., Glen Head, NY 11545. TEL 516-759-0025. FAX 516-759-5524. *5143*

INTERNATIONAL JOURNAL OF SUSTAINABLE DEVELOPMENT AND WORLD ECOLOGY.
Parthenon Publishing Group, Casterton Hall, Carnforth, Lancs. LA6 2LA, England. TEL 44-152-427-2084. FAX 44-152-427-1587. *2935*

INTERNATIONAL JOURNAL OF SYSTEMATIC BACTERIOLOGY.
American Society for Microbiology, 1325 Massachusetts Ave., N.W., Washington, DC 20005. TEL 202-737-3600. *787*

INTERNATIONAL JOURNAL OF SYSTEMS SCIENCE.
Taylor & Francis Ltd., 1 Gunpowder Sq., London EC4A 3DE, England. TEL 44-171-583-0490. FAX 44-171-583-0585. *2727*

THE INTERNATIONAL JOURNAL OF TECHNICAL COOPERATION.
Frank Cass, Newbury House, 890-900 Eastern Ave., Newbury Park, Ilford, Essex IG2 7HH, England. TEL 44-181-559-8866. FAX 44-181-599-0984. *1363*

INTERNATIONAL JOURNAL OF TECHNOLOGY ADVANCES.
P.O. Box 98029, S. Common Post, 2150 Burnhamthorpe Rd., Mississagua, ON L5L 3A0, Canada. FAX 416-277-2875. *6963*

INTERNATIONAL JOURNAL OF TECHNOLOGY AND DESIGN EDUCATION.
Kluwer Academic Publishers, Postbus 17, 3300 AA Dordrecht, Netherlands. TEL 31-78-6392392. FAX 31-78-6392254. *2606*

INTERNATIONAL JOURNAL OF THE CLASSICAL TRADITION.
Transaction Publishers, Transaction Periodicals Consortium, Department 3092, Rutgers University, New Brunswick, NJ 08903. TEL 908-445-2280. FAX 908-445-3138. *1904*

INTERNATIONAL JOURNAL OF THE ECONOMICS OF BUSINESS.
Carfax Publishing Co., P.O. Box 25, Abingdon, Oxon. OX14 3UE, England. TEL 44-1235-401000. FAX 44-1235-401550. *973*

THE INTERNATIONAL JOURNAL OF THE HISTORY OF SPORT.
Frank Cass, Newbury House, 890-900 Eastern Ave., Newbury Park, Ilford, Essex IG2 7HH, England. TEL 44-181-599-8866. FAX 44-181-599-0984. *3501*

INTERNATIONAL JOURNAL OF THE LEGAL PROFESSION.
Carfax Publishing Co., P.O. Box 25, Abingdon, Oxon. OX14 3UE, England. TEL 44-1235-401000. FAX 44-1235-401550. *3965*

INTERNATIONAL JOURNAL OF THEORETICAL PHYSICS.
Plenum Publishing Corp., 233 Spring St., New York, NY 10013-1578. TEL 212-620-8000. FAX 212-463-0742. *5807*

INTERNATIONAL JOURNAL OF THERMOPHYSICS.
Plenum Publishing Corp., 233 Spring St., New York, NY 10013-1578. TEL 212-620-8000. FAX 212-463-0742. *5841*

INTERNATIONAL JOURNAL OF THYMOLOGY.
Thymus Medizinischer Fachbuchverlag, Rudolf-Huch-Str. 14, 38667 Bad Harzburg, Germany. TEL 49-5322-960532. FAX 49-5322-3017. *4889*

INTERNATIONAL JOURNAL OF TOXICOLOGY.
Taylor & Francis Ltd., 1 Gunpowder Sq., London EC4A 3DE, England. TEL 44-171-583-0490. FAX 44-171-583-0585. *2978*

INTERNATIONAL JOURNAL OF TRAINING & DEVELOPMENT.
Blackwell Publishers Ltd., 108 Cowley Rd., Oxford OX4 1JF, England. TEL 44-1865-791100. FAX 44-1865-791347. *1569*

INTERNATIONAL JOURNAL OF TRANSPERSONAL STUDIES.
Bolda-Lok Publishing and Educational Enterprises, P.O. Box 5513, Stafford Heights, Qld. 4053, Australia. TEL 61-7-33592547. FAX 61-7-33592547. *6119*

INTERNATIONAL JOURNAL OF TRAUMA NURSING.
Mosby - Year Book, Inc., 11830 Westline Industrial Dr., St.Louis, MO 63146. TEL 314-872-8370. FAX 314-872-9164. *4935*

INTERNATIONAL JOURNAL OF TUBERCULOSIS AND LUNG DISEASE.
International Union Against Tuberculosis and Lung Disease (IUATLD), 68 bd. Saint-Michel, 75006 Paris, France. TEL 33-1-44320360. FAX 33-1-43299087. *5119*

INTERNATIONAL JOURNAL OF UNIVERSITY ADULT EDUCATION.
International Congress of University Adult Education, c/o John F. Morris, Sec. Treas., Dept. of Extension and Summer Session, Univ. of New Brunswick, Box 4400, Fredericton, NB E3B 5A3, Canada. TEL 506-453-4646. FAX 506-453-3572. *2511*

INTERNATIONAL JOURNAL OF URBAN AND REGIONAL RESEARCH.
Blackwell Publishers Ltd., 108 Cowley Rd., Oxford OX4 1JF, England. TEL 44-1865-791100. FAX 44-1865-791347. *3750*

INTERNATIONAL JOURNAL OF UROLOGY.
Churchill Livingstone Japan, Churchill Bldg., 2-8-16 Yutenji, Meguro-ku, Tokyo 153, Japan. TEL 81-3-5721-0442. FAX 81-3-5721-0445. *5161*

INTERNATIONAL JOURNAL OF VALUE-BASED MANAGEMENT.
Kluwer Academic Publishers Boston, Box 358, Accord Sta., Hingham, MA 02018-0358. TEL 617-871-6600. FAX 617-871-6528. *1485*

INTERNATIONAL JOURNAL OF VEHICLE DESIGN.
Inderscience Enterprises Ltd., World Trade Centre Bldg., 110 Ave. Louis Casai, Case Postale 306, CH-1215 Geneva-Aeroport, Switzerland. FAX 41-22-7910885. *7031*

INTERNATIONAL JOURNAL OF VISUAL COMPUTING.
Intellect, Earl Richards Rd. N., Exeter, Devon EX2 6AS, England. TEL 44-1392-475110. FAX 44-1392-475110. *477*

INTERNATIONAL JOURNAL OF VOCATIONAL EDUCATION AND TRAINING.
International Vocational Education and Training Association, Box 1636, Grand Rapids, MI 49501-1636. TEL 614-847-9550. FAX 614-847-9844. *2565*

INTERNATIONAL JOURNAL OF WATER JET TECHNOLOGY.
International Society of Water Jet Technology, Box 46039, 2339 Ogilvie Rd., Gloucester, ON K1J 9M7, Canada. TEL 613-993-2731. FAX 613-952-1395. *2873*

INTERNATIONAL JOURNAL OF WATER RESOURCES DEVELOPMENT.
Carfax Publishing Co., P.O. Box 25, Abingdon, Oxon. OX14 3UE, England. TEL 44-1235-401000. FAX 44-1235-401550. *7295*

INTERNATIONAL JOURNAL OF WEIGHT ENGINEERING.
Society of Allied Weight Engineers, Inc., 5530 Aztec Dr., La Mesa, CA 91942-2110. TEL 619-465-1367. FAX 619-465-2561. *70*

INTERNATIONAL JOURNAL OF WIRELESS INFORMATION NETWORKS.
Plenum Publishing Corp., 233 Spring St., New York, NY 10013-1578. TEL 212-620-8000. FAX 212-463-0742. *1994*

INTERNATIONAL JOURNAL ON DIGITAL LIBRARIES.
Springer-Verlag, Heidelberger Platz 3, 14197 Berlin, Germany. TEL 49-30-82787-0. FAX 49-30-82787448. *4233*

THE INTERNATIONAL JOURNAL ON HYDROPOWER & DAMS.
Aqua-Media International Ltd., Westmead House, Westmead Rd., Sutton, Surrey SM1 4JH, England. TEL 44-181-643-4727. FAX 44-181-643-8200. *2693*

INTERNATIONAL JOURNAL ON MINORITY AND GROUP RIGHTS.
Kluwer Law International, Postbus 85889, 2508 CN The Hague, Netherlands. TEL 31-70-3081500. FAX 31-70-3081515. *5994*

INTERNATIONAL LABOR AND WORKING CLASS HISTORY.
Cambridge University Press, Edinburgh Bldg., Shaftesbury Rd., Cambridge CB2 2RU, England. TEL 44-1223-312393. FAX 44-1223-315052. *1437*

INTERNATIONAL LABOUR LAW REPORTS.
Kluwer Academic Publishers, Postbus 17, 3300 AA Dordrecht, Netherlands. TEL 31-78-6392392. FAX 31-78-6392254. *3965*

INTERNATIONAL LAW IN ASIAN PERSPECTIVE.
Martinus Nijhoff Publishers, Human Rights and International Law Postbus 163, 3300 AD Dordrecht, Netherlands. TEL 31-78-334911. FAX 31-78-334254. *4118*

INTERNATIONAL LAW IN JAPANESE PERSPECTIVE.
Martinus Nijhoff Publishers, Human Rights and International Law Postbus 163, 3300 AD Dordrecht, Netherlands. TEL 31-78-334911. FAX 31-78-334254. *4118*

INTERNATIONAL LAW PRACTICUM.
New York State Bar Association, International Law and Practice Section, 1 Elk St., Albany, NY 12207-1096. TFl. 518-463-3200. FAX 518-463-8844. *4119*

INTERNATIONAL LAWYER.
American Bar Association, International Law and Practice Section, 740 15th St., N.W., Washington, DC 20005. TEL 202-662-1673. FAX 202-662-1669. *4119*

INTERNATIONAL LECTURE SERIES IN COMPUTER SCIENCE.
Academic Press, Inc., 525 B St., Ste. 1900, San Diego, CA 92101-4495. TEL 619-231-0926. FAX 619-699-6715. *2085*

INTERNATIONAL MASS MEDIA COMMUNICATIONS REVIEW.
Inter-Com Publications, Box 1156, Anacortes, WA 98221. TEL 360-293-0732. FAX 360-293-8919. *1994*

INTERNATIONAL MEDICAL JOURNAL.
Japan International Cultural Exchange Foundation, 2-15-5-207 Shoto, Shibuya-ku, Tokyo 150, Japan. TEL 81-3-3424-9090. FAX 81-3-3424-9119. *4687*

INTERNATIONAL MIGRATION REVIEW.
Center for Migration Studies, 209 Flagg Pl., Staten Island, NY 10304-1199. TEL 718-351-8800. FAX 718-667-4598. *6052*

INTERNATIONAL NEGOTIATION REVIEW.
Kluwer Law International, Postbus 85889, 2508 CN The Hague, Netherlands. TEL 31-70-3081500. FAX 31-78-3081515. *4119*

INTERNATIONAL NEUROPSYCHOLOGICAL SOCIETY. JOURNAL.
Cambridge University Press, Edinburgh Bldg., Shaftesbury Rd., Cambridge CB2 2RU, England. TEL 44-1223-312393. FAX 44-1223-315052. *5070*

INTERNATIONAL OPHTHALMOLOGY.
Kluwer Academic Publishers, Postbus 17, 3300 AA Dordrecht, Netherlands. TEL 31-78-6392392. FAX 31-78-6392254. *4994*

INTERNATIONAL ORGANIZATION.
M I T Press, 5 Cambridge Center, Cambridge, MA 02142. TEL 617-253-2889. FAX 617-577-1545. *6020*

INTERNATIONAL ORGANIZATION AND THE EVOLUTION OF WORLD SOCIETY.
Kluwer Academic Publishers, Postbus 17, 3300 AA Dordrecht, Netherlands. TEL 31-78-6392392. FAX 31-78-6392254. *4119*

INTERNATIONAL ORGANIZATIONS AND THE LAW OF THE SEA (YEAR).
Kluwer Academic Publishers, Postbus 17, 3300 AA Dordrecht, Netherlands. TEL 31-78-6392392. FAX 31-78-6392254. *4142*

INTERNATIONAL PEACEKEEPING.
Frank Cass, Newbury House, 890-900 Eastern Ave., Newbury Park, Ilford, Essex 1G2 7HH, England. TEL 44-181-599-8866. FAX 44-181-599-0984. *6020*

INTERNATIONAL PEACEKEEPING.
Kluwer Law International, Postbus 85889, 2508 CN The Hague, Netherlands. TEL 31-70-3081500. FAX 31-70-3081515. *6021*

INTERNATIONAL PHARMACY JOURNAL.
International Pharmaceutical Federation, Andries Bickerweg 5, 2517 JP The Hague, Netherlands. TEL 31-70-3631925. FAX 31-70-3633914. *5668*

INTERNATIONAL PHILOSOPHICAL QUARTERLY.
Foundation for International Philosophical Exchange, Fordham University, Bronx, NY 10458. TEL 718-817-4776. FAX 718-817-4785. *5732*

INTERNATIONAL PLAY JOURNAL.
Chapman & Hall, Journals Department 2-6 Boundary Row, London SE1 8HN, England. TEL 44-171-8650066. FAX 44-171-5229623. *6119*

INTERNATIONAL POETRY.
International Writers and Artists Association, Bluffton College, Bluffton, OH 45817. TEL 419-358-3418. FAX 419-358-3323. *4511*

INTERNATIONAL POLITICAL SCIENCE REVIEW.
Sage Publications Ltd., 6 Bonhill St., London EC2A 4PU, England. TEL 44-171-374-0645. FAX 44-171-374-8741. *6021*

INTERNATIONAL POLITICS.
Kluwer Law International, Postbus 85889, 2508 CN The Hague, Netherlands. TEL 31-70-3081500. FAX 31-70-3081515. *6620*

INTERNATIONAL PSYCHOGERIATRICS.
Springer Publishing Company, 536 Broadway, New York, NY 10012-3955. TEL 212-431-4370. FAX 212-941-7842. *5070*

INTERNATIONAL PUBLIC RELATIONS REVIEW.
International Public Relations Association, Ste. 1007, South Tower, 175 Bloor St. E., Toronto ON M4W 3R8. TEL 416-968-7311. FAX 416-968-6281. *38*

INTERNATIONAL QUARTERLY OF COMMUNITY HEALTH EDUCATION.
Baywood Publishing Co., Inc., 26 Austin Ave., Box 337, Amityville, NY 11701. TEL 516-691-1270. FAX 516-691-1770. *6240*

INTERNATIONAL REGIONAL SCIENCE REVIEW.
West Virginaia University, Regional Research Institute, Morgantown, WV 26506-6825. TEL 304-293-8542. FAX 304-293-6699. *6620*

INTERNATIONAL RESEARCH IN GEOGRAPHICAL AND ENVIRONMENTAL EDUCATION.
Multilingual Matters Ltd., Frankfurt Lodge, Clevedon Hall, Victoria Rd., Clevedon BS21 7SJ, England. TEL 44-1275-876519. FAX 44-1275-343096. *3410*

INTERNATIONAL REVIEW OF ADMINISTRATIVE SCIENCES.
Sage Publications Ltd., 6 Bonhill St., London EC2A 4PU, England. TEL 44-171-374-0645. FAX 44-171-374-8741. *6180*

INTERNATIONAL REVIEW OF CHILD NEUROLOGY SERIES.
Lippincott - Raven Publishers, 227 E. Washington Sq., Philadelphia, PA 19106. TEL 215-238-4200. FAX 215-238-4227. *5070*

INTERNATIONAL REVIEW OF CHINESE LINGUISTICS.
John Benjamins Publishing Co., Amsteldijk 44, P.O. Box 75577, 1070 AN Amsterdam, Netherlands. TEL 31-20-6762325. FAX 31-20-6792956. *4265*

INTERNATIONAL REVIEW OF CYTOLOGY.
Academic Press, Inc., 525 B St., Ste. 1900, San Diego, CA 92101-4495. TEL 619-231-0926. FAX 619-699-6715. *741*

INTERNATIONAL REVIEW OF ECONOMICS AND FINANCE.
J A I Press Inc., 55 Old Post Rd., No. 2, Box 1678, Greenwich, CT 06830-1678. TEL 203-661-7602. FAX 203-661-0792. *1266*

INTERNATIONAL REVIEW OF EDUCATION.
UNESCO Institute for Education, Feldbrunnenstrasse 58, 2000 Hamburg 13, Germany. TEL 49-40-4480410. FAX 49-40-4107723. *2452*

INTERNATIONAL REVIEW OF EXPERIMENTAL PATHOLOGY.
Academic Press, Inc., 525 B St., Ste. 1900, San Diego, CA 92101-4495. TEL 619-231-0926. FAX 619-699-6715. *4687*

INTERNATIONAL REVIEW OF FINANCIAL ANALYSIS.
J A I Press Inc., 55 Old Post Rd., No. 2, Box 1678, Greenwich, CT 06830-1678. TEL 203-661-7602. FAX 203-661-0792. *1148*

INTERNATIONAL REVIEW OF INDUSTRIAL AND ORGANIZATIONAL PSYCHOLOGY.
John Wiley & Sons Ltd., Journals, Baffins Ln., Chichester, W. Sussex PO19 1UD, England. TEL 44-1243-779777. FAX 44-1243-775878. *6119*

INTERNATIONAL REVIEW OF LAW AND ECONOMICS.
Elsevier Science Inc., Box 945, New York, NY 10159-0945. TEL 212-633-3730. FAX 212-633-3680. *3965*

INTERNATIONAL REVIEW OF LAW, COMPUTERS & TECHNOLOGY.
Carfax Publishing Co., P.O. Box 25, Abingdon, Oxon. OX14 3UE, England. TEL 44-1235-401000. FAX 44-1235-401550. *4068*

INTERNATIONAL REVIEW OF NEUROBIOLOGY.
Academic Press, Inc., 525 B St., Ste. 1900, San Diego, CA 92101-4495. TEL 619-231-0926. FAX 619-699-6715. *5070*

INTERNATIONAL REVIEW OF PROFESSIONAL ISSUES IN SELECTION AND ASSESSMENT.
John Wiley & Sons Ltd., Journals, Baffins Ln., Chichester, W. Sussex PO19 1UD, England. TEL 44-1243-779777. FAX 44-1243-843232. *1485*

INTERNATIONAL REVIEW OF PSYCHIATRY.
Carfax Publishing Co., P.O. Box 25, Abingdon, Oxon. OX14 3UE, England. TEL 44-1235-401000. FAX 44-1235-401550. *5070*

INTERNATIONAL REVIEW OF RESEARCH IN MENTAL RETARDATION.
Academic Press, Inc., 525 B St., Ste. 1900, San Diego, CA 92101-4495. TEL 619-231-0926. FAX 619-699-6715. *5070*

INTERNATIONAL REVIEW OF RETAIL, DISTRIBUTION AND CONSUMER RESEARCH.
Thomson Professional, 2-6 Boundary Row, London SE1 8HN, England. TEL 44-171-865-0066. FAX 44-171-522-9621. *1531*

INTERNATIONAL REVIEW OF SOCIAL HISTORY.
Cambridge University Press, Edinburgh Bldg., Shaftesbury Rd., Cambridge CB2 2RU, England. TEL 44-1223-312393. FAX 44-1223-315052. *3501*

INTERNATIONAL REVIEW OF SOCIOLOGY.
Carfax Publishing Co., P.O. Box 25, Abingdon, Oxon. OX14 3UE, England. TEL 44-1235-401000. FAX 44-1235-401550. *6715*

INTERNATIONAL REVIEWS IN PHYSICAL CHEMISTRY.
Taylor & Francis Ltd., 1 Gunpowder Sq., London EC4A 3DE, England. TEL 44-171-583-0490. FAX 44-171-583-0585. *1829*

INTERNATIONAL REVIEWS OF IMMUNOLOGY.
Gordon and Breach - Harwood Academic, Amsteldisk 166, 1st Fl., 1079 LH Amsterdam, Netherlands. *4797*

INTERNATIONAL SATELLITE SYMPOSIUM ON ACUTE RENAL FAILURE. PROCEEDINGS.
International Society of Nephrology, Commission on Acute Renal Failure, Hippokration General Hospital, 50 Papanastasiou St., 543 42 Thessaloniki, Greece. TEL 30-31-835955. FAX 30-31-861111. *5162*

INTERNATIONAL SCHOOL OF PHYSICS "ENRICO FERMI". PROCEEDINGS.
I O S Press, Van Diemenstraat 94, 1013 CN Amsterdam, Netherlands. TEL 31-20-6382189. FAX 31-20-6203419. *5807*

INTERNATIONAL SECURITY.
M I T Press, 5 Cambridge Center, Cambridge, MA 02142. TEL 617-253-2889. FAX 617-577-1545. *6021*

INTERNATIONAL SERIES IN ECONOMIC MODELING.
Kluwer Academic Publishers, Postbus 17, 3300 AA Dordrecht, Netherlands. TEL 31-78-6392392. FAX 31-78-6392254. *1202*

INTERNATIONAL SERIES IN INTELLIGENT TECHNOLOGIES.
Kluwer Academic Publishers, Postbus 17, 3300 AA Dordrecht, Netherlands. TEL 31-78-6392392. FAX 31-78-6392254. *2101*

INTERNATIONAL SERIES IN QUANTITATIVE MARKETING.
Kluwer Academic Publishers, Postbus 17, 3300 AA Dordrecht, Netherlands. TEL 31-78-6392392. FAX 31-78-6392254. *1531*

INTERNATIONAL SERIES IN SOCIAL WELFARE.
Kluwer Academic Publishers, Postbus 17, 3300 AA Dordrecht, Netherlands. TEL 31-78-6392392. FAX 31-78-6392254. *6671*

INTERNATIONAL SERIES OF MONOGRAPHS ON CHEMISTRY.
Oxford University Press, Walton St., Oxford OX2 6DP, England. TEL 44-1865-56767. FAX 44-1865-56646. *1753*

INTERNATIONAL SERIES OF MONOGRAPHS ON PHYSICS.
Oxford University Press, Walton St., Oxford OX2 6DP, England. TEL 44-1865-56767. FAX 44-1865-56646. *5807*

INTERNATIONAL SMALL BUSINESS JOURNAL.
Woodcock Publications Ltd., P.O. Box 1, Macclesfield, Cheshire SK10 4YQ, England. TEL 44-1625-528516. FAX 44-1625-532644. *1644*

INTERNATIONAL SOCIAL SCIENCE JOURNAL.
Blackwell Publishers Ltd., 108 Cowley Road, Oxford OX4 1JF, England. TEL 44-1865-791100. FAX 44-1865-791347. *6620*

INTERNATIONAL SOCIAL WORK.
Sage Publications Ltd., 6 Bonhill St., London EC2A 4PU, England. TEL 44-171-374-0645. FAX 44-171-374-8741. *6671*

INTERNATIONAL SOCIETY FOR RESPIRATORY PROTECTION. JOURNAL.
International Society for Respiratory Protection, Fission Energy and System Safety Program,Hazards Control Dept., Lawrence Livermore National Laboratory, Box 808, L-379, Livermore, CA 94550. TEL 510-422-5215. FAX 510-422-5176. *5119*

INTERNATIONAL SOCIETY FOR TERRAIN-VEHICLE SYSTEMS. PROCEEDINGS OF INTERNATIONAL CONFERENCE.
International Society for Terrain-Vehicle Systems, c/o Dr. Ronald A. Liston, USACRREL, 72 Lyme Rd., Hanover, NH 03755-1290. TEL 603-646-4362. *2789*

INTERNATIONAL SOCIETY OF CITRICULTURE. PROCEEDINGS.
International Society of Citriculture, c/o Dir. Charlie Coggins, Department of Botany and Plant Sciences, University of California, Riverside, CA 92521-0124. TEL 909-787-4412. FAX 909-787-4437. *127*

INTERNATIONAL SOCIETY ON OPTICS WITHIN LIFE SCIENCES. SERIES (PROCEEDINGS).
Elsevier Science B.V., Books Division, P.O. Box 211, 1000 AE Amsterdam, Netherlands. TEL 31-20-4853911. FAX 31-20-4853705. *606*

INTERNATIONAL SOCIOLOGY.
Sage Publications Ltd., 6 Bonhill St., London EC2A 4PU, England. TEL 44-171-374-0645. FAX 44-171-374-8741. *6715*

INTERNATIONAL STRAITS OF THE WORLD.
Kluwer Academic Publishers, Postbus 17, 3300 AA Dordrecht, Netherlands. TEL 31-78-6392392. FAX 31-78-6392254. *6021*

INTERNATIONAL STUDIES.
Sage Publications India Pvt. Ltd., P.O. Box 4215, New Delhi 110 048, India. TEL 91-11-644-4958. FAX 91-11-647-2426. *6021*

INTERNATIONAL STUDIES IN ECONOMICS AND ECONOMETRICS.
Kluwer Academic Publishers, Postbus 17, 3300 AA Dordrecht, Netherlands. TEL 31-78-6392392. FAX 31-78-6392254. *974*

INTERNATIONAL STUDIES IN EDUCATIONAL ACHIEVEMENT.
Elsevier Science Ltd., Pergamon, P.O. Box 800, Kidlington, Oxford OX5 1DX, England. TEL 44-1865-843000. FAX 44-1865-843010. *2453*

INTERNATIONAL STUDIES IN GLOBAL CHANGE.
Gordon and Breach - Harwood Academic, Amsteldisk 166, 1st Fl., 1079 LH Amsterdam, Netherlands. *1485*

INTERNATIONAL STUDIES IN HUMAN RIGHTS.
Kluwer Academic Publishers, Postbus 17, 3300 AA Dordrecht, Netherlands. TEL 31-78-6392392. FAX 31-78-6392254. *5994*

INTERNATIONAL STUDIES IN SOCIOLOGY AND SOCIAL ANTHROPOLOGY.
E.J. Brill, P.O. Box 9000, 2300 PA Leiden, Netherlands. TEL 31-71-5353500. FAX 31-71-5317532. *6715*

INTERNATIONAL STUDIES IN SOCIOLOGY OF EDUCATION.
Triangle Journals Ltd., P.O. Box 65, Wallingford, Oxon. OX10 0YG, England. TEL 44-1491-838013. FAX 44-1491-834968. *2606*

INTERNATIONAL STUDIES IN THE PHILOSOPHY OF SCIENCE.
Carfax Publishing Co., P.O. Box 25, Abingdon, Oxon. OX14 3UE, England. TEL 44-1235-401000. FAX 44-1235-401550. *5732*

INTERNATIONAL STUDIES IN THE SERVICE ECONOMY.
Kluwer Academic Publishers, Postbus 17, 3300 AA Dordrecht, Netherlands. TEL 31-78-6392392. FAX 31-78-6392254. *1588*

INTERNATIONAL STUDIES OF MANAGEMENT AND ORGANIZATION.
M.E. Sharpe, Inc., 80 Business Park Dr., Armonk, NY 10504. TEL 914-273-1800. FAX 914-273-2106. *1485*

INTERNATIONAL STUDIES ON TERRORISM.
Kluwer Academic Publishers, Postbus 17, 3300 AA Dordrecht, Netherlands. TEL 31-78-6392392. FAX 31-78-6392254. *6021*

INTERNATIONAL STUDIES QUARTERLY.
Blackwell Publishers, 238 Main St., Cambridge, MA 02142. TEL 617-547-7110. FAX 617-547-0789. *6021*

INTERNATIONAL SURGERY.
Edizioni Minerva Medica, Corso Bramante 83-85, 10126 Turin, Italy. TEL 39-11-678282. FAX 39-11-674502. *5144*

INTERNATIONAL SYMPOSIUM ON ATOMIC, MOLECULAR AND SOLID-STATE THEORY, COLLISION PHENOMENA AND COMPUTATIONAL METHODS. PROCEEDINGS.
John Wiley & Sons, Inc., 605 Third Ave., New York, NY 10158. TEL 212-850-6000. *1753*

INTERNATIONAL SYMPOSIUM ON QUANTUM BIOLOGY AND QUANTUM PHARMACOLOGY. PROCEEDINGS.
John Wiley & Sons, Inc., 605 Third Ave., New York, NY 10158. TEL 212-850-6000. FAX 212-850-6088. *606*

INTERNATIONAL TAX AND PUBLIC FINANCE.
Kluwer Academic Publishers Boston, Box 358, Accord Sta., Hingham, MA 02018-0358. TEL 617-871-6600. FAX 617-871-6528. *1615*

INTERNATIONAL TELEMETERING CONFERENCE.
Instrument Society of America, 67 Alexander Dr., Box 12277, Research Triangle Park, NC 27709. TEL 919-549-8411. FAX 919-549-8288. *1995*

INTERNATIONAL TINNITUS JOURNAL.
State University of New York, Health Science Center at Brooklyn, Box 1239, 450 Clarkson Ave., Brooklyn, NY 11203. TEL 718-773-0888. FAX 718-465-3669. *5022*

THE INTERNATIONAL TRADE JOURNAL.
Taylor & Francis Inc., 1900 Frost Rd., Bristol, PA 19007-1598. TEL 215-785-5800. FAX 215-785-5515. *1332*

INTERNATIONAL TRADE LAW AND REGULATION.
Sweet & Maxwell, Mill St., Oxford OX2 OJU, England. TEL 44-1865-249248. FAX 44-1865-792301. *4120*

INTERNATIONAL TRANSACTIONS IN OPERATIONAL RESEARCH.
Elsevier Science Ltd., Pergamon, P.O. Box 800, Kidlington, Oxford OX5 1DX, England. TEL 44-1865-843000. FAX 44-1865-843010. *2085*

INTERNATIONAL UROGYNECOLOGY JOURNAL.
Springer-Verlag London Ltd., Sweetapple House, Catteshall Rd., Godalming, Surrey GU7 3DJ, England. TEL 44-1483-418800. FAX 44-1483-415144. *4960*

INTERNATIONAL UROLOGY AND NEPHROLOGY.
Akademiai Kiado Rt., P.O. Box 245, H-1519 Budapest, Hungary. TEL 36-1-2043976. FAX 36-1-2045600. *5162*

INTERNATIONAL VISUAL LITERACY ASSOCIATION. ANNUAL CONFERENCE READINGS.
International Visual Literacy Association (Spokane), c/o Barbara I. Clark, Gonzaga University, E. 502 Boone AD 25, Spokane, WA 99258-0001. *2606*

INTERNATIONAL WESTERN GEOGRAPHICAL SERIES.
University of Victoria, Department of Geography, Victoria, BC V8W 3P5, Canada. TEL 604-721-7327. FAX 604-721-6216. *3410*

INTERNATIONAL WHALING COMMISSION. REPORT. SPECIAL ISSUE.
International Whaling Commission, Red House, Station Rd., Histon, Cambs. CB4 4NP, England. TEL 01223-233971. FAX 01223-232876. *3071*

INTERNATIONAL WOLF.
International Wolf Center, 5930 Brooklyn Blvd., Minneapolis, MN 55429. TEL 612-560-7374. FAX 612-569-7368. *2234*

INTERNATIONAL WORKSHOP ON H D T V. PROCEEDINGS.
Elsevier Science B.V., Books Division, P.O. Box 211, 1000 AE Amsterdam, Netherlands. TEL 31-20-4853911. FAX 31-20-4853705. *2016*

INTERNATIONAL YEARBOOK OF RURAL PLANNING.
Elsevier Science Ltd., Books Division, P.O. Box 800, Kidlington, Oxford OX5 1DX, England. TEL 44-1865-843000. FAX 44-1865-843010. *3750*

INTERNATIONALE STIFTUNG MOZARTEUM. MITTEILUNGEN.
Internationale Stiftung Mozarteum, Schwarzstr. 26, Postfach 34, A-5024 Salzburg, Austria. TEL 43-662-88940-10. FAX 43-662-882418. *5402*

INTERNET ARCHAEOLOGY.
Council for British Archaeology, Internet Archaeology Office, Dept. of Archaeology, University of York, The King's Manor, York YO1 2EP, England. TEL 44-1904-433955. FAX 44-1904-433939. *367*

INTERNET JOURNAL OF LANGUAGE, CULTURE AND SOCIETY. *4265*

INTERNET REFERENCE SERVICES QUARTERLY.
Haworth Press, Inc., 10 Alice St., Binghamton, NY 13904. TEL 607-722-5857. FAX 607-722-6362. *2135*

L'INTERNISTA.
P C A Publishing, Via Clerici 12, 20032 Brusuglio di Corman (MI), Italy. TEL 39-2-66300802. FAX 39-2-6151239. *4925*

INTERPRETATION (FLUSHING).
Interpretation, Inc., Queens College, Flushing, NY 11367-1597. TEL 718-997-5542. FAX 718-997-5565. *5935*

INTERPRETING.
John Benjamins Publishing Co., Amsteldijk 44, P.O. Box 75577, 1070 AN Amsterdam, Netherlands. TEL 31-20-6762325. FAX 31-20-6792956. *4265*

REFEREED SERIALS

INTERPRETING THE PAST.
University of California Press, 2120 Berkeley Way, Berkeley, CA 94720. TEL 510-642-4247. FAX 510-643-7127. *367*

INTERSCIENCE CONFERENCE ON ANTIMICROBIAL AGENTS AND CHEMOTHERAPY. PROGRAM AND ABSTRACTS.
American Society for Microbiology, 1325 Massachusetts Ave., N.W., Washington, DC 20005-4171. TEL 202-737-3600. *787*

INTER-STATE HIGH WAY.
Whole Health, Inc., Denali Center, HC89, Box 451, Willow, AK 99688-9705. TEL 907-495-6853. *5458*

INTERVENTION IN SCHOOL AND CLINIC.
Pro-Ed Inc., 8700 Shoal Creek Blvd., Austin, TX 78757-6897. TEL 512-451-3246. FAX 512-451-8542. *2585*

INTERVENTIONAL CARDIOLOGY.
Kluwer Academic Publishers, Postbus 17, 3300 AA Dordrecht, Netherlands. TEL 31-78-6392392. FAX 31-78-6392254. *4819*

INTERVIROLOGY.
S. Karger AG, Allschwilerstr. 10, P.O. Box, CH-4009 Basel, Switzerland. TEL 41-61-3061111. FAX 41-61-3061234. *787*

INTI.
Inti Publications, Box 20657, Cranston, RI 02920. TEL 401-865-2690. FAX 401-865-1264. *4417*

INVASION AND METASTASIS.
S. Karger AG, Allschwilerstr. 10, P.O. Box, CH-4009 Basel, Switzerland. TEL 41-61-3061111. FAX 41-61-3061234. *741*

INVENTIONES MATHEMATICAE.
Springer-Verlag, Heidelberger Platz 3, 14197 Berlin, Germany. TEL 49-30-82787-0. FAX 49-30-82787448. *4579*

INVERTEBRATE BIOLOGY.
Allen Press, Inc., 1041 New Hampshire Ave., Box 1897, Lawrence, KS 66044. TEL 913-843-1234. *838*

INVERTEBRATE NEUROSCIENCE.
Sheffield Academic Press Ltd., Mansion House, 19 Kingfield Rd., Sheffield S11 9AS, England. TEL 44-114-255-4433. FAX 44-114-255-4626. *755*

INVESTIGACION BIBLIOTECOLOGICA.
Universidad Nacional Autonoma de Mexico, Centro Universitario de Investigaciones Bibliotecologicas, Torre II de Humanidades, pisos 12 y 13, Ciudad Universitaria, 04510 Mexico, D.F., Mexico. TEL 52-5-6230352. FAX 52-5-5507461. *4187*

INVESTIGACION CLINICA.
Universidad del Zulia, Instituto de Investigaciones Clinicas, Apdo. Postal 1151, Maracaibo, Venezuela. TEL 5861-523844. FAX 58-61-916053. *4687*

INVESTIGATIONAL NEW DRUGS.
Kluwer Academic Publishers Boston, Box 358, Accord Sta., Hingham, MA 02018-0358. TEL 617-871-6600. FAX 617-871-6528. *5668*

INVESTIGATIVE OPHTHALMOLOGY & VISUAL SCIENCE.
Lippincott - Raven Publishers, 227 E. Washington Sq., Philadelphia, PA 19106. TEL 215-238-4200. FAX 215-238-4227. *4994*

INVESTIGATIVE RADIOLOGY.
Lippincott - Raven Publishers, 227 E. Washington Sq., Philadelphia, PA 19106. TEL 215-238-4200. FAX 215-28-4227. *5108*

INVESTING IN KWAZULU NATAL.
KwaNatal Marketing Initiative, P.O. Box 1105, Durban 4000, South Africa. TEL 27-31-9078700. FAX 27-31-9075685. *1390*

THE INVESTMENT REPORTER.
Share Holder Communication Systems, 4600 Campus Dr., Ste. 205, Newport Beach, CA 92660-1801. TEL 714-724-0444. *1391*

INVITATION.
Islamic Information Center of America, Box 4052, Des Plaines, IL 60016. TEL 847-541-8141. FAX 847-824-8436. *6397*

ION EXCHANGE AND SOLVENT EXTRACTION.
Marcel Dekker, Inc., 270 Madison Ave., New York, NY 10016. TEL 212-696-9000. FAX 212-685-4540. *1829*

IOWA ACADEMY OF SCIENCE. JOURNAL.
Allen Press, 175 Baker Hall, University of Northern Iowa, Cedar Falls, IA 50614. TEL 319-273-2021. *6535*

IOWA ARCHITECT.
Mauck & Associates, 516 3d St., Ste. 200, Des Moines, IA 50309-1702. TEL 515-243-4010. FAX 515-243-6011. *406*

IOWA ENGLISH BULLETIN.
Iowa Council of Teachers of English Language Arts, 130 Baker Hall, English Dept., University of Northern Iowa, Cedar Falls, IA 50614. TEL 319-273-2729. FAX 319-273-5807. *4265*

IOWA JOURNAL OF COMMUNICATION.
Iowa Communication Association, c/o Marvin D. Jensen, Dept. of Communication Studies, University of Northern Iowa, Cedar Falls, IA 50614. TEL 319-273-2593. FAX 319-273-2731. *1995*

THE IOWA ORTHOPAEDIC JOURNAL.
University of Iowa, Department of Orthopaedics, Iowa City, IA 52242. *5008*

IOWA P T A BULLETIN.
Iowa Congress of Parents and Teachers, 610 Merle Hay Towers, Des Moines, IA 50310. *2453*

IOWA STATE UNIVERSITY VETERINARIAN.
Iowa State University, College of Veterinary Medicine, Ames, IA 50011. TEL 515-294-0867. *7272*

IQBAL REVIEW.
Iqbal Academy Pakistan, Aiwan-e-Iqbal Complex, 6th Fl., Khayaban-e-Iqbal Rd., Lahore, Pakistan. TEL 92-42-6314510. FAX 92-42-6314496. *5732*

IRAN.
British Institute of Persian Studies, c/o British Academy, 20-21 Cornwall Terrace, London NW1 4QP, England. TEL 44-171-920-0823. *3656*

IRAN AGRICULTURAL RESEARCH.
Shiraz University, College of Agriculture, Shiraz, Iran. TEL 98-71-28193. FAX 98-71-28193. *127*

IRANIAN JOURNAL OF CHEMISTRY AND CHEMICAL ENGINEERING (INTERNATIONAL ENGLISH EDITION).
Jihad Danishgahi, P.O. Box 14155-4364, Tehran, Iran. TEL 98-21-6497572. FAX 98-21-6400730. *1753*

IRANIAN JOURNAL OF PLANT PATHOLOGY.
Iranian Phytopathological Society, Box 19395-1454, Teheran, Iran. TEL 98-21-2400645. FAX 98-21-2400645. *709*

IRANIAN JOURNAL OF SCIENCE AND TECHNOLOGY.
Shiraz University, School of Engineering, Shiraz, Iran. TEL 98-71-672060. FAX 98-71-672060. *6535*

IRANIAN MATHEMATICAL SOCIETY. BULLETIN.
Iranian Mathematical Society, P.O. Box 13145-418, Teheran, Iran. FAX 98-21-8847275. *4579*

IRANIAN STUDIES.
Society for Iranian Studies, c/o Princeton Univ. Library, 1 Washington Rd., Princeton, NJ 08544-2098. TEL 609-258-1308. FAX 609-258-0441. *5529*

IRANICA ANTIQUA.
Editions Peeters s.p.r.l., Bondgenotenlaan 153, 3000 Leuven, Belgium. TEL 32-16-235170. FAX 32-16-228500. *367*

IRIS: A JOURNAL ABOUT WOMEN.
University of Virginia, Women's Center, Box 323 HSC, University of Virginia, Charlottesville, VA 22908. TEL 804-924-4500. *7324*

IRISH ARTS REVIEW YEARBOOK.
State Apartments, Dublin Castle, Dublin 2, Ireland. TEL 353-1-679-3503. FAX 353-1-679-3503. *448*

THE IRISH ASTRONOMICAL JOURNAL.
Armagh Observatory, College Hill, Armagh BT61 9DG, N. Ireland. TEL 44-1861-522928. FAX 44-1861-527174. *496*

IRISH BIBLICAL STUDIES.
Irish Biblical Studies, 26 College Green, Belfast BT7 1JT, Northern Ireland. TEL 44-1232-325374. FAX 44-1232-316839. *6346*

IRISH BIRDS.
Irish Wildbird Conservancy, Ruttledge House, 8 Longford Pl., Monkstown, Co. Dublin, Ireland. TEL 353-1-2804322. FAX 353-1-2844407. *804*

IRISH CATHOLIC DIRECTORY.
Veritas Book Co. Ltd., Veritas House, 7-8 Lower Abbey St., Dublin, Ireland. *6465*

IRISH COLLEGES OF PHYSICIANS AND SURGEONS. JOURNAL.
Royal College of Surgeons in Ireland, Mercer Library, Mercer St. Lower, Dublin 2, Ireland. TEL 353-1-4780674. FAX 353-1-4022457. *4688*

IRISH ECONOMIC AND SOCIAL HISTORY.
Economic and Social History Society of Ireland, History Department, University College, Belfield, Dublin 4, Ireland. TEL 0353-17068376. FAX 0353-12837022. *3575*

IRISH GEOGRAPHY.
Geographical Society of Ireland, Department of Geography, University College Dublin, Befield, Dublin 4, Ireland. TEL 353-1-7068484. FAX 353-1-2695597. *3411*

IRISH IN BRITAIN DIRECTORY.
Brent Irish Advisory Service, Premier House, 313 Kilburn Lane, London W9 3EG, England. TEL 44-181-968-6914. FAX 44-181-960-5636. *3019*

IRISH JOURNAL OF PSYCHOLOGICAL MEDICINE.
MedMedia Ltd., Media House, 99 Upper George's St., Dun Laoghaire, Co. Dublin, Ireland. TEL 353-1-2803967. FAX 353-1-2807076. *5070*

IRISH JOURNAL OF PSYCHOLOGY.
Psychological Society of Ireland, c/o Queen's University, School of Psychology, Belfast BT7 1NN, N. Ireland. TEL 44-1232-245133. FAX 44-1232-664144. *6119*

IRISH JOURNAL OF SOCIOLOGY.
Sociological Association of Ireland, Department of Political Science and Sociology, University College Galway, Galway, Ireland. TEL 091-24411. *6715*

IRISH MARKETING REVIEW.
Mercury Publications Ltd., 37 Main St., Donnybrook, Dublin 4, Ireland. TEL 353-1-2602171. FAX 353-1-2696705. *1532*

THE IRISH NATURALISTS' JOURNAL.
Irish Naturalists' Journal Ltd., School of Biology and Biochemistry, Queen's University, Belfast BT7 1NN, N. Ireland. TEL 44-1232-335793. FAX 44-1232-236505. *6535*

IRON GAME HISTORY.
University of Texas at Austin, McLean Sport History Fellowship, Rm. 217, Gregory Gymnasium, Austin, TX 78712. TEL 512-447-3635. FAX 512-443-0381. *6809*

IRRIGATION AND DRAINAGE SYSTEMS.
Kluwer Academic Publishers, Postbus 17, 3300 AA Dordrecht, Netherlands. TEL 31-78-6392392. FAX 31-78-6392254. *207*

ISELYA.
X Club, Department of Biological Science, Nicholls State University, Thibodaux, LA 70310. *709*

ISIS.
University of Chicago Press, Journals Division, Box 37005, Chicago, IL 60637. TEL 773-753-3347. FAX 773-753-0811. *6535*

AL-ISLAAM.
Ahmadiyya Moslim Missie Holland, Oostduinlaan 79, 2596 JJ The Hague, Netherlands. TEL 31-70-3245902. FAX 31-70-3242881. *6397*

ISLAM AND CHRISTIAN - MUSLIM RELATIONS.
Carfax Publishing Co., P.O. Box 25, Abingdon, Oxon. OX14 3UE, England. TEL 44-1235-401000. FAX 44-1235-401550. *6397*

ISLAMIC ACADEMY OF SCIENCES. JOURNAL.
Anadolu Health and Research Foundation, Mithatpasa Caddesi 66-5, Kizilay, 06420 Ankara, Turkey. TEL 90-312-4250319. FAX 90-312-4259487. *6535*

ISLAMIC HISTORY AND CIVILIZATION.
E.J. Brill, P.O. Box 9000, 2300 PA Leiden, Netherlands. TEL 31-71-5353500. FAX 31-71-5317532. *6397*

ISLAMIC LAW & SOCIETY.
E.J. Brill, P.O. Box 9000, 2300 PA Leiden, Netherlands. TEL 31-71-5353500. FAX 31-71-5317532. *6397*

ISLAMIC PHILOSOPHY, THEOLOGY AND SCIENCE.
E.J. Brill, P.O. Box 9000, 2300 PA Leiden, Netherlands. TEL 31-71-5353500. FAX 31-71-5317532. *6398*

THE ISLAND ARC.
Blackwell Science Pty Ltd, P.O. Box 378, Carlton South, Vic. 3053, Australia. TEL 61-3-93470300. FAX 61-3-93493016. *2352*

ISLAND MAGAZINE.
Prince Edward Island Museum and Heritage Foundation, 2 Kent St., Charlottetown, PE C1A 1M6, Canada. TEL 902-368-6604. FAX 902-368-6608. *3632*

ISLAND PARENT MAGAZINE.
Island Parent Group Enterprises Ltd., 941 Kings Rd., Victoria, BC V8T 1W7, Canada. TEL 604-388-6905. FAX 604-388-4391. *2256*

ISOLATION AND PURIFICATION.
Gordon and Breach - Harwood Academic, Amsteldisk 166, 1st Fl., 1079 LH Amsterdam, Netherlands. *1791*

ISOTOPES IN ORGANIC CHEMISTRY.
Elsevier Science B.V., Books Division, P.O. Box 211, 1000 AE Amsterdam, Netherlands. TEL 31-20-4853911. FAX 31-20-4853705. *1816*

ISOTOPES IN THE PHYSICAL AND BIOMEDICAL SCIENCES.
Elsevier Science B.V., Books Division, P.O. Box 211, 1000 AE Amsterdam, Netherlands. TEL 31-20-4853911. FAX 31-20-4853705. *1753*

ISPRA COURSES ON ENERGY SYSTEMS AND TECHNOLOGY.
Kluwer Academic Publishers, Postbus 17, 3300 AA Dordrecht, Netherlands. TEL 31-78-6392392. FAX 31-78-6392254. *2698*

ISPRA COURSES ON NUCLEAR ENGINEERING AND TECHNOLOGY SERIES.
Gordon and Breach - Harwood Academic, Amsteldisk 166, 1st Fl., 1079 LH Amsterdam, Netherlands. *2698*

ISRAEL AFFAIRS.
Frank Cass, 890-900 Eastern Ave., Newbury Park, Ilford, Essex IG2 7HH, England. TEL 44-181-599-8866. FAX 44-181-599-0984. *6022*

ISRAEL ANNUAL CONFERENCE ON AEROSPACE SCIENCES. PROCEEDINGS.
Technion - Israel Institute of Technology, Faculty of Aerospace Engineering, Technion City, Haifa 32000, Israel. TEL 972-4-8292260. FAX 972-4-8231848. *71*

ISRAEL JOURNAL OF CHEMISTRY.
Laser Pages Publishing (1992) Ltd., P.O. Box 50257, Jerusalem 91502, Israel. TEL 972-2-370699. FAX 972-2-370625. *1753*

ISRAEL JOURNAL OF EARTH SCIENCES.
Laser Pages Publishing (1992) Ltd., P.O. Box 50257, Jerusalem 91502, Israel. TEL 972-2-370699. FAX 972-2-370625. *2317*

ISRAEL JOURNAL OF ENTOMOLOGY.
Entomological Society of Israel, P.O. Box 6, Bet Dagan 50200, Israel. TEL 972-3-9683520. FAX 972-3-9604180. *755*

ISRAEL JOURNAL OF MEDICAL SCIENCES.
Israel Journal of Medical Sciences, 2 Etzel St., French Hill, Jerusalem 97853, Israel. TEL 972-2-817727. FAX 972-2-815722. *4688*

ISRAEL JOURNAL OF OBSTETRICS & GYNECOLOGY.
Menachem Horowitz Publishing, 22 Shlomzion Hamalca St., Tel Aviv 62276, Israel. TEL 972-3-6048676. FAX 972-3-6049422. *4960*

ISRAEL JOURNAL OF PLANT SCIENCES.
Laser Pages Publishing (1992) Ltd., P.O. Box 52507, Jerusalem 91502, Israel. TEL 972-2-370699. FAX 972-2-370625. *709*

ISRAEL JOURNAL OF ZOOLOGY.
Laser Pages Publishing (1992) Ltd., P.O. Box 50257, Jerusalem 91502, Israel. TEL 972-2-370699. FAX 972-2-370625. *838*

ISRAEL ORIENTAL STUDIES.
E.J. Brill, P.O. Box 9000, 2300 PA Leiden, Netherlands. TEL 31-71-5353500. FAX 31-71-5317532. *5530*

ISRAEL SOCIAL SCIENCE RESEARCH.
Hubert H. Humphrey Institute for Social Research, Ben-Gurion University of the Negev, P.O. Box 653, Beer-Sheva 84105, Israel. TEL 972-7-6461112. FAX 972-7-6472938. *6620*

ISRAEL STUDIES IN MUSICOLOGY.
Israel Musicology Society, P.O. Box 503, Jerusalem, Israel. *5402*

ISRAELI JOURNAL OF AQUACULTURE - BAMIDGEH.
c/o Department of Animal Sciences, Faculty of Agriculture, Hebrew University of Jerusalem, P.O. Box 12, Rehovot 76100, Israel. TEL 972-8-9481302. FAX 972-8-9465763. *3071*

ISSUES IN ACCOUNTING EDUCATION.
American Accounting Association, 5717 Bessie Dr., Sarasota, FL 33583-2399. TEL 941-921-7747. FAX 941-923-4093. *1092*

ISSUES IN APPLIED LINGUISTICS.
University of California at Los Angeles, Department of TESL and Applied Linguistics, 3300 Rolfe Hall, Box 951531, Los Angeles, CA 90095-1531. TEL 310-825-4631. FAX 310-206-4118. *4265*

ISSUES IN BUSINESS ETHICS.
Kluwer Academic Publishers, Postbus 17, 3300 AA Dordrecht, Netherlands. TEL 31-78-6392392. FAX 31-78-6392254. *5732*

ISSUES IN CHILD ABUSE ACCUSATIONS.
Institute for Psychological Therapies, 13200 Cannon City Blvd., Northfield, MN 55057. TEL 507-645-8881. FAX 507-645-8883. *1848*

ISSUES IN COMPREHENSIVE PEDIATRIC NURSING.
Taylor & Francis Inc., 1900 Frost Rd., Ste. 101, Bristol, PA 19007-1598. TEL 215-785-5800. FAX 215-785-5515. *4935*

ISSUES IN CRIMINOLOGICAL AND LEGAL PSYCHOLOGY.
British Psychological Society, Division of Criminological and Legal Psychology, St. Andrew's House, 48 Princess Rd. E., Leicester LE1 7DR, England. TEL 44-116-254-9568. FAX 44-116-247-0787. *6119*

ISSUES IN INTEGRATIVE STUDIES.
Association for Integrative Studies, c/o Prof. William H. Newell, Exec. Dir., School of Interdisciplinary Studies, Miami University, Oxford, OH 45056. TEL 513-529-2213. FAX 513-529-5849. *2453*

ISSUES IN LAW AND MEDICINE.
National Legal Center for the Medically Dependent and Disabled, Inc., Box 1586, Terre Haute, IN 47808-1586. TEL 812-232-0103. *4688*

ISSUES IN MENTAL HEALTH NURSING.
Taylor & Francis Inc., 1900 Frost Rd., Ste. 101, Bristol, PA 19007-1598. TEL 215-785-5800. FAX 215-785-5515. *4935*

ISSUES IN SOCIAL WORK EDUCATION.
Association of Teachers in Social Work Education, Department of Sociological Studies, University of Sheffield, Sheffield S10 2TN, England. TEL 44-114-276-8555. FAX 44-114-276-8125. *6671*

ISSUES IN WRITING.
University of Wisconsin at Stevens Point, Department of English, Stevens Point, WI 54481. TEL 715-346-4477. FAX 715-346-4215. *3874*

ISTITUTO ITALIANO DEGLI ATTUARI. GIORNALE.
Istituto Italiano degli Attuari, Via del Corea 3, 00186 Rome, Italy. TEL 39-6-3226051. FAX 39-6-326056. *3822*

ISTITUTO ITALIANO DI NAVIGAZIONE. ATTI.
Istituto Italiano di Navigazione, Via Prisciano, 42, 00136 Rome, Italy. TEL 39-6-35452841. FAX 39-6-35452841. *71*

ISTITUTO ITALIANO DI NUMISMATICA. ANNALI.
Istituto Italiano di Numismatica, Palazzo Barberini, Via Quattro Fontane 13, 00195 Rome, Italy. TEL 39-6-4743603. FAX 39-6-4743603. *5465*

ISTITUTO RICERCHE PESCA MARITTIMA. QUADERNI.
Istituto Ricerche sulla Pesca Marittima, Molo Mandracchio, 60100 Ancona, Italy. TEL 39-71-5314. FAX 39-71-55313. *3071*

ISTITUTO SPERIMENTALE TALASSOGRAFICO DI TRIESTE. PUBBLICAZIONE.
Consiglio Nazionale delle Ricerche, Istituto Sperimentale Talassografico di Trieste, Viale Romolo Gessi, 2, 34123 Trieste, Italy. TEL 39-40-305312. FAX 39-40-308941. *2406*

ISTITUTO STORICO ITALIANO PER IL MEDIO EVO E ARCHIVIO MURATORIANO. BULLETTINO.
Istituto Storico Italiano per il Medio Evo, Palazzo Borromini, Piazza dell'Orologio 4, 00186 Rome, Italy. FAX 39-6-6877059. *3576*

ISTITUTO SUPERIORE DELLE POSTE E DELLE TELECOMUNICAZIONI. NOTE RECENSIONI NOTIZIE.
Istituto Superiore delle Poste e delle Telecomunicazioni, Viale Europa 190, 00144 Rome, Italy. TEL 39-6-59584370. FAX 39-6-5410904. *1995*

ISTMICA.
Universidad Nacional, Facultad de Filosofia y Letras, Apdo. 86, 3000 Heredia, Costa Rica. TEL 506-237-6363 ext. 429. *3782*

ISTMO.
Centros Culturales de Mexico, A.C., Goya 73-303, 03910 Mexico D.F., Mexico. TEL 52-5-5632557. FAX 52-5-5636435. *3335*

ITALIAN AMERICANA.
University of Rhode Island, College of Continuing Education, 80 Washington St., Providence, RI 02903-1803. TEL 401-277-5306. FAX 401-227-5100. *3019*

ITALIAN JOURNAL OF INTELLECTIVE IMPAIRMENT.
GISSTIMMAI Editore, Via Liberta 21, 61039 S. Costanza, Italy. TEL 39-721-950234. *5070*

ITALIAN JOURNAL OF MINERAL & ELECTROLYTE METABOLISM.
Edizioni Minerva Medica, Corso Bramante 83-85, 10126 Turin, Italy. TEL 39-11-678282. FAX 39-11-674502. *4689*

ITALIAN QUARTERLY.
Rutgers University, Department of Italian, 84 College Ave., New Brunswick, NJ 08903. TEL 908-932-7031. *4418*

ITALIAN STUDIES IN LAW.
Kluwer Academic Publishers, Postbus 17, 3300 AA Dordrecht, Netherlands. TEL 31-78-6392392. FAX 31-78-6392254. *3966*

ITALY ITALY.
Italy Italy Corp. s.r.l., Via Michele Mercati 51, 00197 Rome, Italy. TEL 39-6-3221150. FAX 39-6-3223869. *7213*

ITINERA GEOBOTANICA.
Universidad de Leon, Secretariado de Publicaciones, Campus de Verganza, s-n, 24007 Leon, Spain. TEL 34-87-291558. FAX 34-87-291558. *709*

IURIS SCRIPTA HISTORICA.
Koninklijke Academie voor Wetenschappen, Letteren en Schone Kunsten van Belgie, 1 Hertogsstraat, B-1000 Brussels, Belgium. *3966*

REFEREED SERIALS

IYAKUHIN KENKYU.
Nihon Koteisho Kyokai, 12-15, Shibuya 2-chome, Shibuya-ku, Tokyo 150, Japan. TEL 81-3-3400-5634. FAX 81-3-3400-3158. *4689*

IYO DENSHI TO SEITAI KOGAKU.
Gakkaishi Kanko Senta, 4-16, Yayoi 2-chome, Bunkyo-ku, Tokyo 113, Japan. *4689*

J A M A: THE JOURNAL OF THE AMERICAN MEDICAL ASSOCIATION.
American Medical Association, 515 N. State St., Chicago, IL 60610. TEL 312-464-5000. FAX 312-464-4184. *4689*

J A O A: JOURNAL OF THE AMERICAN OSTEOPATHIC ASSOCIATION.
American Osteopathic Association, 142 E. Ontario St., Chicago, IL 60611. TEL 312-280-5800. FAX 312-280-5893. *4828*

J A R D - JOURNAL OF AGE RELATED DISORDERS.
Medical Media C C, P.O. Box 581, 1620 Kempton Park, South Africa. TEL 27-11-9756439. FAX 27-11-9702532. *3438*

J A S T.
American Studies Association of Turkey, c/o Dr. Irem Balkir, Dept. of English, Bilkent Universitesi, 06553 Ankara, Turkey. FAX 90-312-2664934. *3632*

J C C CIRCLE.
Jewish Community Centers Association of North America, 15 E. 26th St., New York, NY 10010-1579. TEL 212-532-4949. FAX 212-481-4174. *3019*

J E I.
Association for Evolutionary Economics, 1101 McClung Tower, University of Tennessee, Knoxville, TN 37996-0411. TEL 615-974-1689. FAX 615-974-3915. *1305*

J E T: JOURNAL OF EDUCATIONAL THOUGHT.
University of Calgary, Faculty of Education, Rm. 1002, Education Tower, Calgary, AB T2N 1N4, Canada. TEL 403-220-5629. FAX 403-284-4162. *2453*

J G R: JOURNAL OF GEOPHYSICAL RESEARCH.
American Geophysical Union, 2000 Florida Ave., N.W., Washington, DC 20009. TEL 202-462-6900. FAX 202-328-0566. *5236*

J G R: JOURNAL OF GEOPHYSICAL RESEARCH: OCEANS.
American Geophysical Union, 2000 Florida Ave., N.W., Washington, DC 20009. TEL 202-462-6900. FAX 202-328-0566. *2384*

J G R: JOURNAL OF GEOPHYSICAL RESEARCH: SOLID EARTH.
American Geophysical Union, 2000 Florida Ave., N.W., Washington, DC 20009. TEL 202-462-6900. FAX 202-328-0566. *2384*

J I S S I: INTERNATIONAL JOURNAL OF SCIENTOMETRICS AND INFORMETRICS.
Brzark Information Systems (P) Ltd., 112 Humayun Pur, Safdarjung Enclave, New Delhi 110 029, India. TEL 91-11-688-2366. FAX 91-33-551-2180. *4187*

J L B SMITH INSTITUTE OF ICHTHYOLOGY. ICHTHYOLOGICAL BULLETIN.
J L B Smith Institute of Ichthyology, Private Bag 1015, Grahamstown 6140, South Africa. TEL 27-461-311002. FAX 27-461-22403. *838*

J L B SMITH INSTITUTE OF ICHTHYOLOGY. SPECIAL PUBLICATION.
J L B Smith Institute of Ichthyology, Private Bag 1015, Grahamstown 6140, South Africa. TEL 27-461-27124. FAX 27-461-22403. *838*

J M N R.
E.J. Gossett Publishing, Inc, 7145 S. Maplewood Ave., Chicago, IL 60629-2045. TEL 312-476-5978. FAX 312-476-3259. *4935*

J P S.
Polynesian Society, Inc., c/o Maori Dept., University of Auckland, Auckland, New Zealand. *320*

THE J. PAUL GETTY MUSEUM JOURNAL.
J. Paul Getty Museum, 17985 Pacific Coast Highway, Malibu, CA 90265. TEL 310-459-7611. FAX 310-454-8156. *5356*

J R A - THE SUPPLEMENTARY SERIES.
95 Peleg Rd. Rd., Portsmouth, RI 02871. TEL 401-683-1955. FAX 401-683-1975. *368*

J S A E REVIEW.
Elsevier Science B.V., P.O. Box 211, 1000 AE Amsterdam, Netherlands. TEL 31-20-4853911. FAX 31-20-4853598. *7103*

J U F NEWS.
Jewish United Fund - Jewish Federation of Metropolitan Chicago, One S. Franklin St., Rm. 701, Chicago, IL 60606. TEL 312-357-4848. FAX 312-855-2470. *6671*

JACKSONVILLE MEDICINE.
Duval County Medical Society, 515 Lomax St., Jacksonville, FL 32204. TEL 904-355-6561. FAX 904-353-5848. *4689*

JAHRBUCH FUER ANTISEMITISMUSFORSCHUNG.
Campus Verlag, Heerstr. 149, 60488 Frankfurt a.M., Germany. TEL 49-69-97651610. FAX 49-69-97651678. *6621*

JAMAICAN JOURNAL OF SCIENCE AND TECHNOLOGY.
Scientific Research Council, P.O. Box 350, Kingston 6, Jamaica, W.I. TEL 876-927-1771. FAX 876-927-5347. *6536*

JAMANA.
B.P. 2043, Bamako, Mali. TEL 22-62-89. FAX 22-76-39. *3247*

JAMES JOYCE QUARTERLY.
Academic Publications (Tulsa), 600 S. College Ave., Tulsa, OK 74104. TEL 918-631-2501. FAX 918-584-0623. *4419*

JAPAN. FORESTRY AND FOREST PRODUCTS RESEARCH INSTITUTE. BULLETIN.
Forestry and Forest Products Research Institute, P.O. Box 16, Tsukuba Norin Kenkyu Danchi-nai, Ibaraki 305, Japan. TEL 81-298-73-3211. FAX 81-298-74-8507. *3156*

JAPAN AND THE WORLD ECONOMY.
North-Holland, P.O. Box 211, 1000 AE Amsterdam, Netherlands. TEL 31-20-4853911. FAX 31-20-4853598. *1306*

JAPAN ORTHODONTIC SOCIETY. JOURNAL.
Japan Orthodontic Society, c/o Oral health Association of Japan, 1-44-2 Komagome, Toshima-ku, Tokyo 170, Japan. TEL 81-3-3947-8891. FAX 81-3-3947-8341. *4860*

JAPAN PETROLEUM AND ENERGY TRENDS.
Japan Petroleum and Energy Consultants, Ltd., P.O. Box 1185, Tokyo Central, Tokyo 100-91, Japan. TEL 81-4-573-1931. FAX 81-4-7573-1934. *5607*

JAPAN PETROLEUM INSTITUTE. JOURNAL.
Japan Petroleum Institute, COSMO Hirakawa-cho Bldg., 1-3-14 Hirakawa-cho, Chiyoda-ku, Tokyo 102, Japan. TEL 81-3-3221-7301. FAX 81-3-3221-8175. *5607*

JAPAN SOCIETY OF LIBRARY SCIENCE. ANNALS.
Japan Society of Library Science, c/o Office of Library and Information Science, Faculty of Sociology, Tokyo University, 28-20 Hakusan 5-chome, Bunkyo-ku, Tokyo 112, Japan. TEL 81-3-3945-7444. *4187*

JAPANESE ECONOMIC REVIEW.
Blackwell Publishers Ltd., 108 Cowley Rd., Oxford OX4 1JF, England. TEL 44-1865-791100. FAX 44-1865-791347. *974*

JAPANESE ECONOMIC STUDIES.
M.E. Sharpe, Inc., 80 Business Park Dr., Armonk, NY 10504. TEL 914-273-1800. FAX 914-273-2106. *974*

JAPANESE JOURNAL OF CHEMOTHERAPY.
Nihon Kagaku Ryoho Gakkai, 2-20-8 Kamiosaki, Shinagawa-ku, Tokyo 141, Japan. TEL 81-3-3493-7129. FAX 81-3-5434-0843. *5669*

JAPANESE JOURNAL OF MEDICAL SCIENCE AND BIOLOGY.
National Institute of Health, 23-1, Toyama 1-chome, Shinjuku-ku, Tokyo 162, Japan. *4690*

JAPANESE JOURNAL OF OPHTHALMOLOGY.
University of Tokyo, School of Medicine, Department of Ophthalmology, 7-3-1 Hongo, Bunkyo-ku, Tokyo 113, Japan. TEL 81-3-3815-5411. FAX 81-3-3817-0798. *4995*

JAPANESE JOURNAL OF PHARMACOLOGY.
Japanese Pharmacological Society, Editorial Office, Kantohya Bld., Gokomachi-Ebisugawa, Nakagyo-ku, Kyoto 604, Japan. TEL 81-75-252-4641. FAX 81-75-252-4618. *5669*

JAPANESE JOURNAL OF PHYCOLOGY (JAPANESE EDITION).
Japanese Society of Phycology, c/o Division of Biological Sciences, Graduate School of Science, Hokkaido University, Sapporo 060, Japan. TEL 81-11-706-2745. FAX 81-11-746-1512. *710*

JAPANESE JOURNAL OF PHYSICAL FITNESS AND SPORTS MEDICINE.
Japanese Society of Physical Fitness and Sports Medicine, 3-25-8 Nishi-Shibashi, Minato-ku, Tokyo 105, Japan. *5785*

JAPANESE JOURNAL OF PHYSIOLOGY.
Center for Academic Publications Japan, 2-4-16 Yayoi, Bunkyo-ku, Tokyo 113, Japan. TEL 03-3817-5821. FAX 03-3817-5830. *817*

JAPANESE SOCIETY FOR STUDY OF BONE AND JOINT INFECTIONS. JOURNAL.
Nihon Kotsu Kansetsu Kansensho Kenkyukai, University of Tukuba, Dept. of Orthopaedic Surgery, 1-1-1 Tennoudai, Tsukuba-shi, Ibaraki 305, Japan. TEL 81-298-53-3219. FAX 81-298-53-3214. *5009*

JAPANESE SOCIETY OF COMPUTATIONAL STATISTICS. JOURNAL.
Japanese Society of Computational Statistics, University of Tsukuba, Institute of Policy and Planning Sciences, 1-1-1 Tennodai, Tsukuba, Ibaraki 305, Japan. TEL 0298-53-5008. FAX 0298-55-3849. *6921*

JAPANESE SOCIETY OF SUGAR BEET TECHNOLOGISTS. PROCEEDINGS.
Sugar Crop Development Fund, Upland Agriculture Research Center, Hokkaido National Agricultural Experiment Sta., Shinsei, Memuro, Hokkaido 082, Japan. TEL 81-155-62-2721. FAX 81-155-61-2127. *231*

JAPANOPHILE.
Japanophile, Box 223, Okemos, MI 48805-0223. TEL 517-669-2109. *5530*

JARDIN BOTANICO DE MADRID. ANALES.
Consejo Superior de Investigaciones Cientificas, Vitruvio 8, 28006 Madrid, Spain. TEL 34-1-4203017. FAX 34-1-4200157. *710*

JASLOK HOSPITAL & RESEARCH CENTRE. BULLETIN.
Jaslok Hospital & Research Centre, 15 Dr. G. Deshmukh Marg, Mumbai 400 026, India. TEL 91-22-4933333. FAX 91-22-4950508. *4690*

JAVA REPORT.
Sigs Publications, Inc., 71 W. 23rd St., 3rd Fl., New York, NY 10010-4102. TEL 212-274-0640. FAX 212-274-0646. *2144*

JAWETZ, MELNICK & ADELBERG'S MEDICAL MICROBIOLOGY.
Appleton & Lange, Box 120041, Stamford, CT 06912-0041. TEL 203-406-4500. *787*

JEFFERSONIANA.
Virginia Museum of Natural History, 1001 Douglas Ave., Martinsville, VA 24112. TEL 540-666-8656. FAX 540-632-6487. *6536*

JERSEY AT HOME.
Royal Jersey Agricultural and Horticultural Society, Springfield, St. Helier, Jersey JE2 4LF, Channel Islands. TEL 44-1534-866555. FAX 44-1534-865619. *256*

JERUSALEM SYMPOSIA ON QUANTUM CHEMISTRY AND BIOCHEMISTRY.
Kluwer Academic Publishers, Postbus 17, 3300 AA Dordrecht, Netherlands. TEL 31-78-6392392. FAX 31-78-6392254. *1830*

JEWISH AFFAIRS.
South African Jewish Board of Deputies, P.O. Box 87557, Houghton 2041, South Africa. TEL 27-11-4861434. FAX 27-11-6464940. *3020*

JEWISH BIBLE QUARTERLY.
Jewish Bible Association, P.O. Box 29002, Jerusalem, Israel. TEL 972-2-6759144. FAX 972-2-6759144. *6347*

JEWISH CURRENTS.
Association for Promotion of Jewish Secularism, Inc., 22 E. 17th St., Rm. 601, New York, NY 10003. TEL 212-924-5740. FAX 212-924-5740. *3020*

JEWISH JURISPRUDENCE SERIES.
Gordon and Breach - Harwood Academic, Amsteldisk 166, 1st Fl., 1079 LH Amsterdam, Netherlands. *3967*

JEWISH LAW ANNUAL.
Gordon and Breach - Harwood Academic, Amsteldisk 166, 1st Fl., 1079 LH Amsterdam, Netherlands. *3967*

JEWISH LAW IN CONTEXT.
Gordon and Breach - Harwood Academic, Amsteldisk 166, 1st Fl., 1079 LH Amsterdam, Netherlands. *3967*

JEWISH PRESS (BROOKLYN).
Jewish Press, Inc., c/o Sholom Klass, Ed. & Pub., 338 Third Ave., Brooklyn, NY 11215. TEL 718-330-1100. FAX 718-935-1215. *3021*

JEWISH REPORTER.
Jewish Federation of Las Vegas, 3909 S. Maryland Pkwy., Ste. 400, Las Vegas, NV 89119-7520. TEL 702-732-0556. FAX 702-732-3228. *3022*

JEWISH STAR (EDISON).
Jewish Federation of Greater Middlesex County, 230 Old Bridge Turnpike, South River, NJ 08882-2053. TEL 732-432-7711. FAX 732-432-0292. *3022*

THE JEWISH VOICE (PROVIDENCE).
Jewish Federation of Rhode Island, 130 Sessions St., Providence, RI 02906. TEL 401-421-4111. FAX 401-331-7961. *3022*

JIANGSU CHUANBO.
Jiangsu Sheng Chuanbo Sheji Yanjiusuo, 37 Zhengdong Road, Zhenjiang, Jiangsu 212003, People's Republic of China. TEL 86-511-4422493. FAX 86-511-4424389. *7154*

JIANGSU NONGYE XUEBAO.
Jiangsu Sheng Nongye Kexueyuan, Xiaolingwei, Nanjing, Jiangsu 210014, People's Republic of China. TEL 86-25-4390285. *129*

JIAOYU YANJIU.
Jiaoyu Yanjiu Zazhishe, 46, Beisanhuan Zhonglu, Beijing 100088, People's Republic of China. TEL 86-10-6201-1873. FAX 86-10-6203-3132. *2454*

JINGJI GUANLI WENZHAI.
Jingji Guanli Wenzhai Bianjibu, No. 11, Rendinghu Beixiang, Huangshi Dajie, Beijing 100011, People's Republic of China. TEL 86-10-6201-5945. FAX 86-10-6204-9117. *1485*

JINKO KOKYU.
Nihon Kokyurhyohou Igakkai, Fukushima Kenritsu Ika Daigaku Masuikagaku Kyoshitsu, 1, Hikarigaoka, Fukushima-shi, Fukushima-ken 960-12, Japan. TEL 81-245-48-0828. FAX 81-245-48-0828. *5119*

JINSHU KEXUE YU GONGYI.
Harbin Gongye Daxue, 166, Dazhi Jie, Harbin, Heilongjiang 150001, People's Republic of China. TEL 86-451-3621000. FAX 86-451-321048. *5197*

JINSHU XUEBAO.
Science Press, Marketing and Sales Department, 16 Donghuangchenggen North St., Beijing 100707, People's Republic of China. TEL 4010642. FAX 4012180. *5197*

JIOSINSETIKKUSU SHINPOJUMU HAPPYO RONBUNSHU.
Kokusai Jiosinsetikkusu Gakkai, Nihon Shibu, Doshitsu Kogakkai, 2-23, Kanda Awaji-cho, Chiyoda-ku, Tokyo 101, Japan. TEL 81-3-3251-7661. FAX 81-3-3251-6688. *2353*

JISHU KAIFA YU YINJIN.
Fujiansheng Keji Xinxi Yanjiusuo, 11 Hudong Lu, Fuzhou, Fujian 350003, People's Republic of China. TEL 86-591-7850828. FAX 86-591-7856468. *6964*

JISUAN JIEGOU LIXUE JIQI YINGYONG.
Dalian Ligong Daxue, P.O. Box 320, Dalian, Liaoning 116023, People's Republic of China. TEL 86-411-4708405. FAX 86-411-4671009. *2889*

JISUAN SHUXUE.
Science Press, Marketing and Sales Department, 16 Donghuangchenggen North St., Beijing 100717, People's Republic of China. TEL 4010642. FAX 4019810. *4579*

JISUANJI XUEBAO.
Science Press, Marketing and Sales Department, 16 Donghuangchenggen North St., Beijing 100717, People's Republic of China. TEL 86-10-4010630. FAX 86-10-4012180. *2221*

JISUANJI YANJIU YU FAZHAN.
Science Press, Marketing and Sales Department, 16 Donghuangchenggen North St., Beijing 100717, People's Republic of China. TEL 86-1-4010642. FAX 86-1-4019810. *2116*

JISUANJI YU YINGYONG HUAXUE.
Science Press, Marketing and Sales Department, 16 Donghuangchenggen North St., Beijing 100717, People's Republic of China. TEL 4010642. FAX 4019810. *1800*

JOB PRATIQUE MAGAZINE.
23 rue des Appenins, 75017 Paris, France. TEL 33-1-42285900. FAX 33-1-42282458. *5511*

JOGGING - LE GRANDE CORSA.
Publimaster s.r.l., Via Winckelmann 2, 20146 Milan, Italy. TEL 39-2-424191. FAX 39-2-47710278. *6766*

JOHN CLARE SOCIETY JOURNAL.
John Clare Society, Nottingham Trent University, Clifton Ln., Nottingham NG11 6GB, England. TEL 44-115-941-8418. FAX 44-115-948-6632. *4420*

JOHN DONNE JOURNAL: STUDIES IN THE AGE OF DONNE.
North Carolina State University, Department of English, Box 8105, Raleigh, NC 27695-8105. TEL 919-515-4148. FAX 919-515-1836. *4420*

JOHN RYLANDS UNIVERSITY LIBRARY OF MANCHESTER. BULLETIN.
John Rylands University Library, Manchester M13 9PP, England. TEL 44-161-275-3757. FAX 44-161-273-7488. *3782*

JOHNS HOPKINS A P L TECHNICAL DIGEST.
Johns Hopkins University, Applied Physics Laboratory, Johns Hopkins Rd., Laurel, MD 20723. TEL 301-953-5625. FAX 301-953-1093. *5808*

JOHO SHORI.
Information Processing Society of Japan, 7th Fl., Shibaura-Maekawa Bldg., 3-16-20, Shibaura, Minato-ku, Tokyo 108, Japan. TEL 81-3-5484-3535. FAX 81-3-5484-3534. *2176*

JOINT CENTER FOR URBAN STUDIES. PUBLICATIONS.
Harvard University Press, 79 Garden St., Cambridge, MA 02138. TEL 617-495-2600. FAX 617-495-5898. *3750*

JONG HOLLAND.
Stichting Jong Holland, Postbus 90418, 2509 LK The Hague, Netherlands. TEL 31-70-3852415. FAX 31-70-3852415. *449*

JORDEMODERN.
Svenska Barnmorskefoerbundet, Ostermalmsg. 19, 114 26 Stockholm, Sweden. TEL 46-8-10-70-98. FAX 46-8-24-49-46. *4961*

JOSHI EIYO DAIGAKU KIYO.
Joshi Eiyo Daigaku, 24-3, Komagome 3-chome, Toshima-ku, Tokyo 170, Japan. *5475*

JOURNAL ASIATIQUE.
Editions Peeters s.p.r.l., Bondgenotenlaan 153, 3000 Leuven, Belgium. TEL 32-16-235170. FAX 32-16-228500. *5530*

JOURNAL DE CHIMIE PHYSIQUE ET DE PHYSICO-CHIMIE BIOLOGIQUE.
Editions Scientifiques et Medicales Elsevier, 141 rue de Javel, 75747 Paris, France. TEL 33-1-45589022. FAX 33-1-45589421. *1830*

JOURNAL DE PEDIATRIE ET DE PUERICULTURE.
Editions Scientifiques et Medicales Elsevier, 141 rue de Javel, 75747 Paris, France. TEL 33-1-45589026. FAX 33-1-45589421. *4691*

JOURNAL DES TRIBUNAUX.
Larcier, Rue des Minimes 39, 1000 Brussels, Belgium. TEL 32-2-5480711. FAX 32-2-5139009. *3968*

JOURNAL FOR CONTEMPORARY HISTORY.
University of the Orange Free State, Institute for Contemporary History, P.O. Box 2320, Bloemfontein 9300, South Africa. TEL 27-51-4012250. FAX 27-51-4473416. *6023*

JOURNAL FOR EAST EUROPEAN MANAGEMENT STUDIES.
Rainer Hampp Verlag, Meringerzellerstr. 16, 86415 Mering, Germany. TEL 49-8233-4783. FAX 49-8233-30755. *1486*

JOURNAL FOR GENERAL PHILOSOPHY OF SCIENCE.
Kluwer Academic Publishers, Postbus 17, 3300 AA Dordrecht, Netherlands. TEL 31-78-6392392. FAX 31-78-6392254. *6537*

JOURNAL FOR RESEARCH IN MATHEMATICS EDUCATION.
National Council of Teachers of Mathematics, 1906 Association Dr., Reston, VA 22091. TEL 703-620-9840. FAX 703-476-2970. *4580*

JOURNAL FOR STUDIES IN ECONOMICS AND ECONOMETRICS.
University of Stellenbosch, Bureau for Economic Research, Private Bag 5050, University, Stellenbosch 7599, South Africa. TEL 27-21-8872810. FAX 27-21-8899225. *1306*

JOURNAL FOR THE EDUCATION OF THE GIFTED.
Prufrock Press, Box 8813, Waco, TX 76714. FAX 800-240-0333. *2585*

JOURNAL FOR THE HISTORY OF ASTRONOMY.
Science History Publications Ltd., 16 Rutherford Rd., Cambridge CB2 2HH, England. TEL 44-1223-565532. FAX 44-1223-565532. *496*

JOURNAL FOR THE PROFESSIONAL COUNSELOR.
New York Counseling Association, Box 12636, Albany, NY 12212-2636. TEL 518-235-2026. *2454*

JOURNAL FOR THE SCIENTIFIC STUDY OF RELIGION.
Society for the Scientific Study of Religion, c/o Ralph Hood, Department of Psychology, University of Tennessee, Chattanooga, TN 37403. TEL 423-755-4262. *6347*

JOURNAL FOR THE STUDY OF JUDAISM. SUPPLEMENT.
E.J. Brill, P.O. Box 9000, 2300 PA Leiden, Netherlands. TEL 31-71-5353500. FAX 31-71-5317532. *6406*

JOURNAL FOR THE STUDY OF JUDAISM IN THE PERSIAN, HELLENISTIC AND ROMAN PERIOD.
E.J. Brill, P.O. Box 9000, 2300 PA Leiden, Netherlands. TEL 31-71-5353500. FAX 31-71-5317532. *6406*

JOURNAL FOR THE STUDY OF RELIGION.
Association for the Study of Religion in Southern Africa, c/o Dept. of Religious Studies, University of Natal, Pietermaritzburg 3201, South Africa. TEL 27-331-2605571. *6347*

JOURNAL FOR THE THEORY OF SOCIAL BEHAVIOUR.
Blackwell Publishers Ltd., 108 Cowley Rd, Oxford OX4 1JF, England. TEL 44-1865-791100. FAX 44-1865-791347. *6120*

JOURNAL FOR VOCATIONAL SPECIAL NEEDS EDUCATION.
National Association of Vocational Education Special Needs Personnel, 624 Aderhold Hall, University of Georgia, Athens, GA 30602-7162. TEL 706-542-4461. FAX 706-542-4054. *2585*

JOURNAL FOR WEAVERS, SPINNERS & DYERS.
Association of Guilds of Weavers, Spinners & Dyers, 33 Fennel Gardens, Lymington SO41 9FS, England. TEL 44-1590-670625. *6990*

JOURNAL FUER ANAESTHESIE UND INTENSIVBEHANDLUNG.
Pabst Science Publishers, Am Eichengrund 28, 49525 Lengerich, Germany. TEL 49-5484-308. FAX 49-5484-550. *4805*

JOURNAL FUER BETRIEBSWIRTSCHAFT.
Linde Verlag Wien GmbH, Scheydgasse 24, A-1210 Vienna, Austria. TEL 43-1-313364692. FAX 43-1-31336712. *1486*

JOURNAL FUER DAS NEPHROLOGISCHE TEAM.
Pabst Science Publishers, Am Eichengrund 28, 49525 Lengerich, Germany. TEL 49-5484-308. FAX 49-5484-550. *5162*

JOURNAL FUER ORNITHOLOGIE.
Blackwell Wissenschaft, Kurfuerstendamm 57, 10707 Berlin, Germany. TEL 49-30-327906-0. FAX 49-30-32790610. *804*

JOURNAL INTERNATIONAL MEDICAL SCIENCES ACADEMY.
International Medical Sciences Academy, National Medical Library Bldg., Ansari Nagar, Ring Rd., New Delhi 110 029, India. TEL 91-11-696-4660. *4691*

JOURNAL OF ABDOMINAL SURGERY.
American Society of Abdominal Surgeons, 675 Main St., Melrose, MA 02176. TEL 617-665-6102. *5144*

JOURNAL OF ABNORMAL CHILD PSYCHOLOGY.
Plenum Publishing Corp., 233 Spring St., New York, NY 10013-1578. TEL 212-620-8000. FAX 212-463-0742. *6120*

JOURNAL OF ABNORMAL PSYCHOLOGY.
American Psychological Association, 750 First St., N.E., Washington, DC 20002-4242. TEL 202-336-5600. FAX 202-336-5568. *6120*

THE JOURNAL OF ACADEMIC LIBRARIANSHIP.
J A I Press Inc., 55 Old Post Rd., No. 2, Box 1678, Greenwich, CT 06830-1678. TEL 203-661-7602. FAX 203-661-0792. *4187*

JOURNAL OF ACAROLOGY.
Acarological Society of India, University of Agricultural Sciences, Entomology Division, G.K.V.K., Bangalore 560 065, India. TEL 91-80-330153. *756*

JOURNAL OF ACCIDENT AND EMERGENCY MEDICINE.
B M J Publishing Group, B.M.A. House, Tavistock Sq., London WC1H 9JR, England. TEL 44-171-383-6270. FAX 44-171-383-6402. *5144*

JOURNAL OF ACCOUNTANCY.
American Institute of Certified Public Accountants, Harborside Financial Ctr., 201 Plaza Three, Jersey City, NJ 07311-9801. TEL 201-938-3796. FAX 201-329-1112. *1092*

JOURNAL OF ACCOUNTING AND ECONOMICS.
North-Holland, P.O. Box 211, 1000 AE Amsterdam, Netherlands. TEL 31-20-4853911. FAX 31-20-4853598. *1092*

JOURNAL OF ACCOUNTING AND PUBLIC POLICY.
Elsevier Science Inc., Box 945, New York, NY 10159-0945. TEL 212-633-3730. FAX 212-633-3680. *1092*

JOURNAL OF ACCOUNTING EDUCATION.
Elsevier Science Ltd., Pergamon, P.O. Box 800, Kidlington, Oxford OX5 1DX, England. TEL 44-1865-843000. FAX 44-1865-843010. *1092*

JOURNAL OF ACCOUNTING LITERATURE.
University of Florida, Accounting Research Center, Fisher School of Accounting-267 BUS, College of Business Administration, Gainsville, FL 32611. TEL 904-392-0155. *1093*

JOURNAL OF ACQUIRED IMMUNE DEFICIENCY SYNDROMES AND HUMAN RETROVIROLOGY.
Lippincott - Raven Publishers, 227 E. Washington Sq., Philadelphia, PA 19106. TEL 215-238-4200. FAX 215-238-4227. *4838*

JOURNAL OF ACTUARIAL PRACTICE.
Absalom Press, Inc., Box 22098, Lincoln, NE 68542-2098. TEL 402-421-8149. FAX 402-421-8149. *3822*

JOURNAL OF ADDICTIONS NURSING.
Mary Ann Liebert, Inc. Publishers, 2 Madison Ave., Larchmont, NY 10538. TEL 914-834-3100. FAX 914-834-3688. *4936*

JOURNAL OF ADDICTIVE DISEASES.
Haworth Press, Inc., 10 Alice St., Binghamton, NY 13904. TEL 607-722-5857. FAX 607-722-6362. *2302*

JOURNAL OF ADHESION.
Gordon and Breach - Harwood Academic, Amsteldisk 166, 1st Fl., 1079 LH Amsterdam, Netherlands. *5809*

JOURNAL OF ADHESION SCIENCE AND TECHNOLOGY.
V S P, P.O. Box 346, 3700 AH Zeist, Netherlands. TEL 31-30-6925790. FAX 31-30-6932081. *5878*

JOURNAL OF ADOLESCENT AND ADULT LITERACY.
International Reading Association, Inc., 800 Barksdale Rd., Box 8139, Newark, DE 19714-8139. TEL 302-731-1600. FAX 302-731-1057. *2454*

JOURNAL OF ADOLESCENT HEALTH.
Elsevier Science Inc., Box 945, New York, NY 10159-0945. TEL 212-633-3730. FAX 212-633-3680. *4691*

JOURNAL OF ADOLESCENT RESEARCH.
Sage Publications, Inc., 2455 Teller Rd., Thousand Oaks, CA 91320. TEL 805-499-0721. FAX 805-499-0871. *1848*

JOURNAL OF ADULT DEVELOPMENT.
Plenum Publishing Corp., 233 Spring St., New York, NY 10013-1578. TEL 212-620-8468. FAX 212-463-0742. *6121*

JOURNAL OF ADVANCED MATERIALS.
Intercontact Science, Leninskii Prospekt 49, 117911 Moscow, Russia. TEL 095-135-62-97. FAX 095-135-86-80. *2861*

JOURNAL OF ADVANCED NURSING.
Blackwell Science Ltd., Osney Mead, Oxford OX2 0EL, England. TEL 44-1865-206206. FAX 44-1865-721205. *4936*

JOURNAL OF ADVANCED TRANSPORTATION.
Institute for Transportation, Inc., 305-4625 Varsity Drive N.W., Ste. 68, Calgary, AL T3A 0Z9, Canada. TEL 403-286-9429. FAX 403-286-9638. *7031*

JOURNAL OF ADVANCEMENT IN MEDICINE.
Human Sciences Press, Inc., 233 Spring St., New York, NY 10013-1578. TEL 212-620-8000. FAX 212-807-1047. *4691*

JOURNAL OF AEROSOL SCIENCE.
Elsevier Science Ltd., Pergamon, P.O. Box 800, Kidlington, Oxford OX5 1DX, England. TEL 44-1865-843000. FAX 44-1865-843010. *5545*

JOURNAL OF AEROSPACE ENGINEERING.
American Society of Civil Engineers, 345 E. 47th St., New York, NY 10017-2398. TEL 212-705-7288. FAX 212-980-4681. *2789*

JOURNAL OF AESTHETIC EDUCATION.
University of Illinois Press, 1325 S. Oak St., Champaign, IL 61820. TEL 217-333-0950. FAX 217-244-8082. *2454*

JOURNAL OF AFFECTIVE DISORDERS.
Elsevier Science B.V., P.O. Box 211, 1000 AE Amsterdam, Netherlands. TEL 31-20-4853911. FAX 31-20-4853598. *5071*

JOURNAL OF AFRICAN AMERICAN MEN.
Transaction Publishers, Transaction Periodicals Consortium, Department 3092, Rutgers University, New Brunswick, NJ 08903. TEL 908-445-2280. FAX 908-445-3138. *5183*

JOURNAL OF AFRICAN EARTH SCIENCES (AND THE MIDDLE EAST).
Elsevier Science Ltd., Pergamon, P.O. Box 800, Kidlington, Oxford OX5 1DX, England. TEL 44-1865-843000. FAX 44-1865-843010. *2353*

JOURNAL OF AFRICAN STUDIES.
Japan Association of Africanists, c/o Dogura & Co. Ltd., 1-8 Nishihanaikecho, Koyama, Kita-ku, Kyoto 603, Japan. TEL 075-451-4844. FAX 075-441-0436. *3527*

JOURNAL OF AFRICAN TRAVEL WRITING.
University of North Carolina, Institute of African American Research, Box 346, Chapel Hill, NC 27514. *7214*

JOURNAL OF AFRO-LATIN AMERICAN STUDIES AND LITERATURES.
c/o Dept. of Modern Languages & Literatures, Howard University, 2400 Sixth St., N.W. - Locke Hall, Washington, DC 20059. TEL 202-806-6758. *3782*

JOURNAL OF AGING AND ETHNICITY.
Springer Publishing Company, 536 Broadway, New York, NY 10012-3955. TEL 212-431-4370. FAX 212-941-7842. *3438*

JOURNAL OF AGING AND HEALTH.
Sage Publications, Inc., 2455 Teller Rd., Thousand Oaks, CA 91320. TEL 805-499-0721. FAX 805-499-0871. *3438*

JOURNAL OF AGING & IDENTITY.
Human Sciences Press, Inc., 233 Spring St., New York, NY 10013-1578. TEL 212-620-8000. FAX 212-463-0742. *3438*

JOURNAL OF AGING & SOCIAL POLICY.
Haworth Press, Inc., 10 Alice St., Binghamton, NY 13904. TEL 607-722-5857. FAX 607-722-6362. *3438*

JOURNAL OF AGRICULTURAL AND ENVIRONMENTAL ETHICS.
Kluwer Academic Publishers, Postbus 17, 3300 AA Dordrecht, Netherlands. TEL 31-78-6392392. FAX 31-78-6392254. *5733*

JOURNAL OF AGRICULTURAL AND FOOD CHEMISTRY.
American Chemical Society, 1155 16th St., N.W., Washington, DC 20036. TEL 800-333-9511. FAX 614-447-3671. *231*

JOURNAL OF AGRICULTURAL & FOOD INFORMATION.
Haworth Press, Inc., 10 Alice St., Binghamton, NY 13904. TEL 607-722-5857. FAX 607-722-6362. *129*

JOURNAL OF AGRICULTURAL & RESOURCE ECONOMICS.
Western Agricultural Economics Association, Utah State Univ., Economics Dept., Logan, UT 84322-3530. TEL 801-797-2294. FAX 801-797-2701. *196*

JOURNAL OF AGRICULTURAL ENTOMOLOGY.
South Carolina Entomological Society, Inc., Box 582, Clemson, SC 29633. TEL 864-944-8401. FAX 864-656-5065. *756*

JOURNAL OF AGRICULTURAL SAFETY AND HEALTH.
American Society of Agricultural Engineers, 2950 Niles Rd., St. Joseph, MI 49085-9659. TEL 616-429-0300. FAX 616-429-3852. *129*

JOURNAL OF AGROMEDICINE.
Haworth Press, Inc., 10 Alice St., Binghamton, NY 13904. TEL 607-722-5857. FAX 607-722-6362. *5493*

JOURNAL OF AIR TRANSPORT MANAGEMENT.
Elsevier Science Ltd., Pergamon, P.O. Box 800, Kidlington, Oxford OX5 1DX, England. TEL 44-1865-843000. FAX 44-1865-843010. *1486*

JOURNAL OF AIRCRAFT.
American Institute of Aeronautics and Astronautics, Inc., 1801 Alexander Dr., Ste. 500, Reston, VA 20191. TEL 703-264-7500. *72*

JOURNAL OF ALCOHOL AND DRUG EDUCATION.
American Alcohol and Drug Information Foundation (Lansing), c/o M I C A P, Box 10212, Lansing, MI 48901. TEL 517-484-2636. FAX 517-484-0444. *2302*

JOURNAL OF ALGEBRA.
Academic Press, Inc., Journal Division, 525 B St., Ste. 1900, San Diego, CA 92101-4495. TEL 619-230-1840. FAX 619-699-6800. *4580*

JOURNAL OF ALGEBRAIC COMBINATORICS.
Kluwer Academic Publishers Boston, Box 358, Accord Sta., Hingham, MA 02018-0358. TEL 617-871-6600. FAX 617-871-6528. *4580*

THE JOURNAL OF ALGERIAN STUDIES.
Frank Cass, Newbury House, 890-900 Eastern Ave., Newbury Park, Ilford, Essex IG2 7HH, England. TEL 44-181-5998866. FAX 44-181-5990984. *3656*

JOURNAL OF ALGORITHMS.
Academic Press, Inc., Journal Division, 525 B St., Ste. 1900, San Diego, CA 92101-4495. TEL 619-230-1840. FAX 619-699-6800. *4621*

THE JOURNAL OF ALLERGY AND CLINICAL IMMUNOLOGY.
Mosby - Year Book, Inc., 11830 Westline Industrial Dr., St. Louis, MO 63146-3318. TEL 314-872-8370. FAX 314-872-9164. *4798*

JOURNAL OF ALLIED HEALTH.
University of Illinois at Chicago, College of Associated Health Professions (M-C 518), 808 S. Wood St., Chicago, IL 60612. TEL 312-413-0197. FAX 312-413-0086. *6241*

JOURNAL OF ALLOYS AND COMPOUNDS.
Elsevier Science S.A., P.O. Box 564, CH-1001 Lausanne 1, Switzerland. TEL 41-21-3207381. FAX 41-21-3235444. *5197*

JOURNAL OF AMBULATORY CARE MARKETING.
Haworth Press, Inc., 10 Alice St., Binghamton, NY 13904. TEL 607-722-5857. FAX 607-722-1424. *5009*

JOURNAL OF AMERICAN COLLEGE HEALTH.
Heldref Publications, 1319 Eighteenth St., N.W., Washington, DC 20036-1802. TEL 202-296-6267. FAX 202-296-5149. *5785*

JOURNAL OF AMERICAN CULTURE.
Popular Press, Bowling Green State University, Bowling Green, OH 43403. TEL 419-372-2981. *3782*

JOURNAL OF AMERICAN DRAMA AND THEATRE.
C A S T A, City University of New York, Graduate School, 33 W. 42nd St., New York, NY 10036. TEL 212-642-2231. FAX 212-642-2221. *7008*

JOURNAL OF AMERICAN INDIAN EDUCATION.
Arizona State University, Center for Indian Education, College of Education, Box 871311, Tempe, AZ 85287-1311. TEL 602-965-6292. FAX 602-965-8115. *3023*

JOURNAL OF ANALYTIC SOCIAL WORK.
Haworth Press, Inc., 10 Alice St., Binghamton, NY 13904. TEL 607-722-5857. FAX 607-722-6362. *6672*

JOURNAL OF ANALYTICAL AND APPLIED PYROLYSIS.
Elsevier Science B.V., P.O. Box 211, 1000 AE Amsterdam, Netherlands. TEL 31-20-4853911. FAX 31-20-4853598. *1754*

JOURNAL OF ANALYTICAL ATOMIC SPECTROMETRY.
The Royal Society of Chemistry, Thomas Graham House, Science Park, Milton Rd., Cambridge CB4 4WF, England. TEL 44-1223-420066. FAX 44-1223-423429. *1792*

JOURNAL OF ANALYTICAL CHEMISTRY.
Maik Nauka - Interperiodica, Mezhdunarodnyi Otdel, Ul. Profsoyuznaya, 90, 117864 Moscow, Russia. TEL 7-095-33600664. FAX 7-095-3360666. *1792*

JOURNAL OF ANALYTICAL TOXICOLOGY.
Preston Publications, Inc., 7800 Merrimac Ave., Box 48312, Niles, IL 60714. TEL 847-965-0566. FAX 847-965-7639. *2979*

JOURNAL OF ANDROLOGY.
American Society of Andrology, c/o Dept. of Urology Research, Guggenheim 1711, Mayo Clinic, 200 First St., S.W., Rochester, MN 55905. TEL 507-284-2423. FAX 507-284-2384. *4691*

JOURNAL OF ANIMAL AND FEED SCIENCES.
Polska Akademia Nauk, Instytut Fizjologii i Zywienia Zwierzat im. Jana Kielanowskiego, 00-110 Jablonna, Poland, Poland. TEL 48-22-7824175. FAX 48-22-7742038. *279*

JOURNAL OF ANIMAL ECOLOGY.
Blackwell Science Ltd., Osney Mead, Oxford OX2 0EL, England. TEL 44-1865-206206. FAX 44-1865-721205. *607*

JOURNAL OF ANIMAL SCIENCE.
American Society of Animal Science, 1111 N. Dunlap Ave., Savoy, IL 61874. TEL 217-356-3182. FAX 217-398-4119. *280*

JOURNAL OF ANIMAL SCIENCE. SUPPLEMENT. BIENNIAL SYMPOSIUM ON ANIMAL REPRODUCTION.
American Society of Animal Science, 1111 N. Dunlap Ave., Savoy, IL 61874. TEL 217-356-3192. FAX 217-398-4119. *280*

JOURNAL OF ANTHROPOLOGICAL ARCHAEOLOGY.
Academic Press, Inc., Journal Division, 525 B St., Ste. 1900, San Diego, CA 92101-4495. TEL 619-230-1840. FAX 619-699-6859. *321*

JOURNAL OF ANTHROPOLOGICAL RESEARCH.
University of New Mexico, Department of Anthropology, Albuquerque, NM 87131. TEL 505-277-4544. FAX 505-277-0874. *321*

JOURNAL OF ANXIETY DISORDERS.
Elsevier Science Ltd., Pergamon, P.O. Box 800, Kidlington, Oxford OX5 1DX, England. TEL 44-1865-843000. FAX 44-1865-843010. *6121*

JOURNAL OF APHIDOLOGY.
Aphidological Society, India, Aphid Biocontrol Laboratory, Department of Zoology, University of Gorakhpur, Gorakhpur 273 009, U.P., India. TEL 91-551-333944. FAX 91-551-336797. *231*

JOURNAL OF APICULTURAL RESEARCH.
International Bee Research Association, 18 North Rd., Cardiff CF1 3DY, Wales. TEL 44-1222-372409. FAX 44-1222-665522. *130*

JOURNAL OF APPALACHIAN STUDIES.
West Virginia University, Regional Research Institute, Box 6825, Morgantown, WV 26506. TEL 304-293-8541. FAX 304-293-6699. *6621*

JOURNAL OF APPLIED AGRICULTURAL ECONOMICS.
Southern Agricultural Economics Association, c/o Phil Kenkel, Department of Agricultural Economics, Oklahoma State University, Stillwater, OK 74078-0505. TEL 405-794-6157. FAX 405-794-8210. *196*

JOURNAL OF APPLIED ANIMAL RESEARCH.
Garuda Scientific Publications, 151 Janakpuri, P.O. Box 6, Izatnagar 243 122, India. TEL 91-581-479723. FAX 91-581-450147. *839*

JOURNAL OF APPLIED ANIMAL WELFARE SCIENCE.
American Society for the Prevention of Cruelty to Animals, 424 E. 92nd St., New York, NY 10128. *303*

JOURNAL OF APPLIED AQUACULTURE.
Haworth Press, Inc., Food Products Press, 10 Alice St., Binghamton, NY 13904. TEL 607-722-5857. FAX 607-722-6362. *3072*

JOURNAL OF APPLIED BEHAVIOR ANALYSIS.
Society for the Experimental Analysis of Behavior, Inc. (Lawrence), c/o Department of Human Development, University of Kansas, Lawrence, KS 66045. TEL 913-843-0008. *6121*

JOURNAL OF APPLIED BIOBEHAVIORAL RESEARCH.
Bellwether Publishing, Ltd., 8640 Guilford Rd., Ste. 200, Columbia, MD 21046. TEL 410-290-3870. FAX 410-290-8726. *6121*

JOURNAL OF APPLIED BIOMECHANICS.
Human Kinetics Publishers, Inc., Box 5076, Champaign, IL 61825-5076. TEL 217-351-5076. FAX 217-351-2674. *5130*

JOURNAL OF APPLIED BUSINESS RESEARCH.
Western Academic Press, Box 620760, Littleton, CO 80162. TEL 303-904-4750. FAX 303-978-0413. *975*

JOURNAL OF APPLIED COMMUNICATION RESEARCH.
Speech Communication Association, 5105 Backlick Rd., Bldg. E, Annandale, VA 22003. TEL 703-750-0533. FAX 703-914-9471. *1995*

JOURNAL OF APPLIED COMMUNICATIONS.
Agricultural Communicators in Education, Box 35, Evinston, FL 32633. TEL 352-392-9588. FAX 352-392-8583. *130*

JOURNAL OF APPLIED CORPORATE FINANCE.
Stern Stewart Management Services, Inc., 40 W. 57th St., New York, NY 10019-4001. TEL 212-261-0600. FAX 212-581-6420. *1149*

JOURNAL OF APPLIED CRYSTALLOGRAPHY.
Munksgaard International Publishers Ltd., 35 Noerre Soegade, P.O. Box 2148, DK-1016 Copenhagen K, Denmark. TEL 45-33-127030. FAX 45-33-129387. *1802*

JOURNAL OF APPLIED DEVELOPMENTAL PSYCHOLOGY.
Ablex Publishing Corporation, Box 5297, Greenwich, CT 06831-0504. TEL 203-661-7602. FAX 203-661-0792. *6121*

JOURNAL OF APPLIED ECOLOGY.
Blackwell Science Ltd., Osney Mead, Oxford OX2 0EL, England. TEL 44-1865-206206. FAX 44-1865-721205. *607*

JOURNAL OF APPLIED ELECTROCHEMISTRY.
Thomson Science, 2-6 Boundary Row, London SE1 8HN, England. TEL 44-171-8650066. FAX 44-171-5229623. *1805*

JOURNAL OF APPLIED FIRE SCIENCE.
Baywood Publishing Co., Inc., 26 Austin Ave., Box 337, Amityville, NY 11701. TEL 516-691-1270. FAX 516-691-1770. *3056*

JOURNAL OF APPLIED GENETICS.
Polska Akademia Nauk, Instytut Genetyki Roslin, Strzeszynska 34, 60-479 Poznan, Poland. TEL 48-61-233511. FAX 48-61-233671. *771*

JOURNAL OF APPLIED GEOPHYSICS.
Elsevier Science B.V., P.O. Box 211, 1000 AE Amsterdam, Netherlands. TEL 31-20-4853911. FAX 31-20-4853598. *2385*

JOURNAL OF APPLIED GERONTOLOGY.
Sage Publications, Inc., 2455 Teller Rd., Thousand Oaks, CA 91320. TEL 805-499-0721. FAX 805-499-0871. *3438*

JOURNAL OF APPLIED MANAGEMENT STUDIES.
Carfax Publishing Co., P.O. Box 25, Abingdon, Oxon. OX14 3UE, England. TEL 44-1235-401000. FAX 44-1235-401550. *1486*

JOURNAL OF APPLIED MATHEMATICS AND MECHANICS.
Elsevier Science Ltd., Pergamon, P.O. Box 800, Kidlington, Oxford OX5 1GB, England. TEL 44-1865-843000. FAX 44-1865-843010. *2861*

JOURNAL OF APPLIED MECHANICS AND TECHNICAL PHYSICS.
Plenum Publishing Corp., Consultants Bureau, 233 Spring St., New York, NY 10013-1578. TEL 212-620-8468. FAX 212-463-0742. *2861*

JOURNAL OF APPLIED METEOROLOGY.
American Meteorological Society, 45 Beacon St., Boston, MA 02108-3693. TEL 617-227-2425. FAX 617-742-8718. *5236*

JOURNAL OF APPLIED MICROBIOLOGY.
Blackwell Science Ltd., Osney Mead, Oxford OX2 0EL, England. TEL 44-1865-206206. FAX 44-1865-721205. *787*

JOURNAL OF APPLIED NUTRITION.
International Academy of Nutrition and Preventive Medicine, Box 18433, Asheville, NC 28814-0433. TEL 704-258-3243. *5476*

JOURNAL OF APPLIED PHYCOLOGY.
Kluwer Academic Publishers, Postbus 17, 3300 AA Dordrecht, Netherlands. TEL 31-78-6392392. FAX 31-78-6392254. *710*

JOURNAL OF APPLIED PHYSIOLOGY.
American Physiological Society, 9650 Rockville Pike, Bethesda, MD 20814. TEL 301-530-7164. FAX 301-571-8313. *817*

JOURNAL OF APPLIED POLYMER SCIENCE. SYMPOSIA.
John Wiley & Sons, Inc., 605 Third Ave., New York, NY 10158. TEL 212-692-6000. FAX 212-850-6088. *2767*

JOURNAL OF APPLIED PROBABILITY.
Applied Probability Trust, School of Mathematics, University of Sheffield, Sheffield S3 7RH, England. TEL 44-114-222-3920. FAX 44-114-272-9782. *4580*

JOURNAL OF APPLIED PSYCHOLOGY.
American Psychological Association, 750 First St., N.E., Washington, DC 20002-4242. TEL 202-336-5600. FAX 202-336-5568. *6121*

JOURNAL OF APPLIED RECREATION RESEARCH.
Wilfrid Laurier University Press, 75 University Ave. W., Waterloo, ON N2L 3C5, Canada. TEL 519-884-0710. FAX 519-725-1399. *4149*

JOURNAL OF APPLIED SCIENCE IN SOUTHERN AFRICA.
University of Zimbabwe Publications, P.O. Box MP 203, Mt. Pleasant, Harare, Zimbabwe. TEL 263-4-303211. FAX 263-4-333407. *6537*

JOURNAL OF APPLIED SOCIAL PSYCHOLOGY.
V.H. Winston & Son, Inc., c/o Bellwether Publishing, Ltd., 8640 Guilford Rd., Ste. 200, Columbia, MD 21046. TEL 410-290-3870. FAX 410-290-8726. *6121*

JOURNAL OF APPLIED SOCIAL SCIENCES.
Springer Publishing Company, 536 Broadway, New York, NY 10012. TEL 212-431-4370. FAX 212-941-7842. *6672*

JOURNAL OF APPLIED SPECTROSCOPY.
Plenum Publishing Corp., Consultants Bureau, 233 Spring St., New York, NY 10013-1578. TEL 212-620-8468. FAX 212-463-0742. *5862*

JOURNAL OF APPLIED SPORT PSYCHOLOGY.
Association for the Advancement of Applied Sport Psychology, c/o Faculty of Kinesiology, University of Western Ontario, London, ON N6A 3K7, Canada. TEL 519-661-4118. FAX 519-661-2008. *5130*

JOURNAL OF APPLIED STATISTICS.
Carfax Publishing Co., P.O. Box 25, Abingdon, Oxon. OX14 3UE, England. TEL 44-1235-401000. FAX 44-1235-401550. *6921*

JOURNAL OF APPROXIMATION THEORY.
Academic Press, Inc., Journal Division, 525 B St., Ste. 1900, San Diego, CA 92101-4495. TEL 619-230-1840. FAX 619-699-6800. *4580*

JOURNAL OF AQUACULTURE IN THE TROPICS.
Oxford & I.B.H. Publishing Co. Pvt. Ltd., 66 Janpath, New Delhi 110 001, India. FAX 91-11-3322639. *3072*

JOURNAL OF AQUARICULTURE AND AQUATIC SCIENCES.
The Written Word, 7601 E. Forest Lake Dr., N.W., Parkville, MO 64152. TEL 816-842-5936. FAX 816-474-5597. *608*

JOURNAL OF AQUATIC ANIMAL HEALTH.
American Fisheries Society, 5410 Grosvenor Ln., Ste. 110, Bethesda, MD 20814-2199. TEL 301-897-8616. FAX 301-897-8096. *3072*

JOURNAL OF AQUATIC ECOSYSTEM HEALTH.
Kluwer Academic Publishers, Postbus 17, 3300 AA Dordrecht, Netherlands. TEL 31-78-6392392. FAX 31-78-6392254. *2936*

JOURNAL OF AQUATIC FOOD PRODUCT TECHNOLOGY.
Haworth Press, Inc., Food Products Press, 10 Alice St., Binghamton, NY 13904-1580. TEL 800-342-9676. FAX 607-722-6362. *3115*

JOURNAL OF AQUATIC PLANT MANAGEMENT.
Aquatic Plant Management Society, Inc., Box 121086, Clermont, FL 34712-1086. TEL 202-547-5437. FAX 202-547-5645. *710*

JOURNAL OF ARABIC LITERATURE.
E.J. Brill, P.O. Box 9000, 2300 PA Leiden, Netherlands. TEL 31-71-5353500. FAX 31-71-5317532. *4420*

JOURNAL OF ARACHNOLOGY.
American Arachnological Society, c/o Norman I. Platnick, Secretary, American Museum of Natural History, Central Park W. at 79th St., New York, NY 10024. TEL 212-769-5612. FAX 212-769-5277. *756*

JOURNAL OF ARCHAEOLOGICAL METHOD AND THEORY.
Plenum Publishing Corp., 233 Spring St., New York, NY 10013-1578. TEL 212-620-8000. FAX 212-463-0742. *368*

JOURNAL OF ARCHAEOLOGICAL RESEARCH.
Plenum Publishing Corp., 233 Spring St., New York, NY 10013-1578. TEL 212-620-8000. FAX 212-463-0742. *368*

JOURNAL OF ARCHITECTURAL AND PLANNING RESEARCH.
Locke Science Publishing Company, Inc., 117 West Harrison Bldg., Ste. 640-L221, Chicago, IL 60605. *407*

JOURNAL OF ARCHITECTURAL CONSERVATION.
Donhead Publishing Ltd., 28 Southdean Gardens, Wimbledon, London SW19 6NU, England. TEL 44-181-789-0138. FAX 44-181-789-9114. *407*

JOURNAL OF ARCHITECTURAL EDUCATION.
M I T Press, 5 Cambridge Center, Cambridge, MA 02142. TEL 617-253-2889. FAX 617-577-1545. *407*

JOURNAL OF ARCHITECTURAL ENGINEERING.
American Society of Civil Engineers, Architectural Engineering Division, 345 E. 47th St., New York, NY 10007-0335. TEL 212-705-7000. *407*

THE JOURNAL OF ARCHITECTURE.
Thomson Professional, 2-6 Boundary Row, London SE1 8HN, England. TEL 44-171-8650066. FAX 44-171-5229623. *407*

JOURNAL OF ART AND DESIGN EDUCATION.
Blackwell Publishers Ltd., 108 Cowley Rd., Oxford OX4 1DF, England. TEL 44-1865-791100. FAX 44-1865-791347. *2607*

JOURNAL OF ARTHROPLASTY.
Churchill Livingstone, 650 Ave. of the Americas, New York, NY 10011. TEL 212-206-5040. FAX 212-727-7808. *5009*

JOURNAL OF ARTIFICIAL INTELLIGENCE IN EDUCATION.
Association for the Advancement of Computing in Education, Box 2966, Charlottesville, VA 22902-2966. TEL 804-973-3987. FAX 804-978-7449. *2517*

JOURNAL OF ARTS MANAGEMENT, LAW, AND SOCIETY.
Heldref Publications, 1319 18th St., N.W., Washington, DC 20036-1802. TEL 202-296-6267. FAX 202-296-5149. *3968*

JOURNAL OF ASIA - PACIFIC BUSINESS.
Haworth Press, Inc., 10 Alice St., Binghamton, NY 13904. TEL 607-722-5857. FAX 607-722-6362. *1339*

JOURNAL OF ASIAN AND AFRICAN STUDIES.
E.J. Brill, P.O. Box 9000, 2300 PA Leiden, Netherlands. TEL 31-71-5353500. FAX 31-71-5317532. *6716*

JOURNAL OF ASIAN BUSINESS.
Association for Asian Studies, 130 Lane Hall, Ann Arbor, MI 48109-1290. TEL 313-763-4508. FAX 313-747-2083. *1267*

JOURNAL OF ASIAN MARTIAL ARTS.
Via Media Publishing Co., 821 W. 24th St., Erie, PA 16502. TEL 814-455-9517. FAX 814-838-7811. *5530*

JOURNAL OF ASIAN PACIFIC COMMUNICATION.
St. John's University, Institute of E S L, Jamaica, NY 11439. TEL 718-990-1929. FAX 201-967-9829. *1995*

JOURNAL OF ASSISTED REPRODUCTION AND GENETICS.
Plenum Publishing Corp., 233 Spring St., New York, NY 10013-1578. TEL 212-620-8000. FAX 212-463-0742. *4961*

JOURNAL OF ASTHMA (NEW YORK).
Marcel Dekker Journals, 270 Madison Ave., New York, NY 10016. TEL 212-685-4540. *5119*

JOURNAL OF ATHLETIC TRAINING.
National Athletic Trainers Association, Inc., 2952 N. Stemmons Fwy., Dallas, TX 75247. TEL 800-879-6282. FAX 214-637-2206. *5130*

JOURNAL OF ATMOSPHERIC AND OCEANIC TECHNOLOGY.
American Meteorological Society, 45 Beacon St., Boston, MA 02108-3693. TEL 617-227-2425. FAX 617-742-8718. *5236*

JOURNAL OF ATMOSPHERIC AND SOLAR - TERRESTRIAL PHYSICS.
Elsevier Science Ltd., Pergamon, P.O. Box 800, Kidlington, Oxford OX5 1DX, England. TEL 44-1865-843000. FAX 44-1865-843010. *2385*

JOURNAL OF ATMOSPHERIC CHEMISTRY.
Kluwer Academic Publishers, Postbus 17, 3300 AA Dordrecht, Netherlands. TEL 31-78-6392392. FAX 31-78-6392254. *1754*

JOURNAL OF AUDIO VISUAL MEDIA IN MEDICINE.
Carfax Publishing Co., P.O. Box 25, Abingdon, Oxon OX14 3UE, England. TEL 44-1235-401000. FAX 44-1235-401550. *4692*

JOURNAL OF AUDIOLOGICAL MEDICINE.
Whurr Publishers Ltd., 19b Compton Terrace, London N1 2UN, England. TEL 44-171-359-5979. FAX 44-171-226-5290. *5022*

JOURNAL OF AUSTRALASIAN GRAPHICS IMAGERY.
Curtin University of Technology, School of Computing, Hayman Rd., Bentley, W.A. 6102, Australia. TEL 619-351-7680. *2124*

JOURNAL OF AUSTRALIAN POLITICAL ECONOMY.
Australian Political Economy Movement, P.O. Box 76, Wentworth Bldg., University of Sydney, N.S.W. 2006. TEL 61-2-93516617. *1267*

JOURNAL OF AUTISM AND DEVELOPMENTAL DISORDERS.
Plenum Publishing Corp., 233 Spring St., New York, NY 10013-1578. TEL 212-620-8000. FAX 212-463-0742. *5071*

JOURNAL OF AUTOMATED REASONING.
Kluwer Academic Publishers, Postbus 17, 3300 AA Dordrecht, Netherlands. TEL 31-78-6392392. FAX 31-78-6392254. *2102*

JOURNAL OF AUTOMATIC CHEMISTRY.
Taylor & Francis Ltd., 1 Gunpowder Sq., London EC4A 3DE, England. TEL 44-171-583-0490. FAX 44-171-583-0585. *6594*

JOURNAL OF AUTONOMIC PHARMACOLOGY.
Blackwell Science Ltd., Osney Mead, Oxford OX2 0EL, England. TEL 44-1865-206206. FAX 44-1865-721205. *5670*

JOURNAL OF AVIAN BIOLOGY.
Munksgaard International Publishers Ltd., 35 Noerre Soegade, P.O. Box 2148, DK-1016 Copenhagen K, Denmark. TEL 45-33-127030. FAX 45-33-129387. *805*

JOURNAL OF AVIAN MEDICINE AND SURGERY.
Association of Avian Veterinarians, Box 210732, Bedford, TX 76095. TEL 817-428-7900. FAX 817-485-4800. *7272*

JOURNAL OF BACTERIOLOGY.
American Society for Microbiology, 1325 Massachusetts Ave., N.W., Washington, DC 20005. TEL 202-737-3600. *787*

JOURNAL OF BAHA'I STUDIES.
Association for Baha'i Studies, 34 Copernicus St., Ottawa, ON K1N 7K4, Canada. TEL 613-233-1903. FAX 613-233-3644. *6492*

JOURNAL OF BANKING AND FINANCE.
North-Holland, P.O. Box 211, 1000 AE Amsterdam, Netherlands. TEL 31-20-4853911. FAX 31-20-4853598. *1149*

JOURNAL OF BASIC WRITING.
City University of New York, Office of Academic Affairs, Instructional Resource Center, 535 E. 80th St., New York, NY 10021. TEL 212-794-5779. FAX 212-794-5706. *2546*

JOURNAL OF BECKETT STUDIES.
Florida State University, Department of English, Tallahassee, FL 32306. TEL 904-664-6038. FAX 904-644-0811. *4420*

JOURNAL OF BEHAVIOR THERAPY AND EXPERIMENTAL PSYCHIATRY.
Elsevier Science Ltd., Pergamon, P.O. Box 800, Kidlington, Oxford OX5 1DX, England. TEL 44-1865-843000. FAX 44-1865-843010. *5071*

JOURNAL OF BEHAVIORAL EDUCATION.
Human Sciences Press, Inc., 233 Spring St., New York, NY 10013. TEL 212-620-8000. FAX 212-463-0742. *6122*

JOURNAL OF BEHAVIORAL MEDICINE.
Plenum Publishing Corp., 233 Spring St., New York, NY 10013-1578. TEL 212-620-8000. FAX 212-463-0742. *5071*

JOURNAL OF BEHAVIORAL OPTOMETRY.
Optometric Extension Program, 1921 Carnegie Ave., Ste. 3L, Santa Ana, CA 92705-5510. TEL 714-250-8070. FAX 714-250-8157. *4995*

JOURNAL OF BIBLICAL ETHICS IN MEDICINE.
Biblical Medical Ethics, Inc., Box 13231, Florence, SC 29504. TEL 803-665-6853. *4692*

JOURNAL OF BIG BEND STUDIES.
Sul Ross State University, Center for Big Bend Studies, Box C-71, Alpine, TX 79832. TEL 915-837-8179. FAX 915-837-8381. *3633*

JOURNAL OF BIOACTIVE AND COMPATIBLE POLYMERS.
Technomic Publishing Co., Inc., 851 New Holland Ave., Box 3535, Lancaster, PA 17604. TEL 717-291-5609. FAX 717-295-4538. *662*

JOURNAL OF BIOCHEMICAL AND BIOPHYSICAL METHODS.
Elsevier Science B.V., P.O. Box 211, 1000 AE Amsterdam, Netherlands. TEL 31-20-4853911. FAX 31-20-4853598. *662*

JOURNAL OF BIOENERGETICS AND BIOMEMBRANES.
Plenum Publishing Corp., 233 Spring St., New York, NY 10013-1578. TEL 212-620-8000. FAX 212-463-0742. *662*

JOURNAL OF BIOGEOGRAPHY.
Blackwell Science Ltd., Osney Mead, Oxford OX2 0EL, England. TEL 44-1865-206206. FAX 44-1865-721205. *3411*

JOURNAL OF BIOLOGICAL CHEMISTRY.
American Society for Biochemistry and Molecular Biology, Inc., Box 630591, Baltimore, MD 21263. *662*

JOURNAL OF BIOLOGICAL EDUCATION.
Institute of Biology, 20-22 Queensberry Pl., London SW7 2DZ, England. TEL 44-171-581-8333. FAX 44-171-823-9409. *608*

JOURNAL OF BIOLOGICAL PHOTOGRAPHY.
Biological Photographic Association, Inc., 1819 Peachtree St., N.E., Ste. 620, Atlanta, GA 30309-1849. TEL 404-351-6300. FAX 404-351-3348. *608*

JOURNAL OF BIOLOGICAL PHYSICS.
European Physical Society, 34 rue Marc Seguin, B.P. 2136, 68060 Mulhouse Cedex, France. TEL 33-3-89329440. FAX 33-3-89329449. *675*

JOURNAL OF BIOLOGICAL RHYTHMS.
Sage Publications, Inc., Sage Science Press, 2455 Teller Rd., Thousand Oaks, CA 91320. TEL 805-499-0721. FAX 805-499-0871. *5071*

JOURNAL OF BIOMATERIALS APPLICATIONS.
Technomic Publishing Co., Inc., 851 New Holland Ave., Box 3535, Lancaster, PA 17604. TEL 717-291-5609. FAX 717-295-4538. *5878*

JOURNAL OF BIOMATERIALS SCIENCE. POLYMER EDITION.
V S P, P.O. Box 346, 3700 AH Zeist, Netherlands. TEL 31-30-6925790. FAX 31-30-6932081. *684*

JOURNAL OF BIOMECHANICAL ENGINEERING.
American Society of Mechanical Engineers, 22 Law Dr., Fairfield, NJ 07007-2900. TEL 973-882-1167. FAX 973-882-1717. *4692*

JOURNAL OF BIOMECHANICS.
Elsevier Science Ltd., Pergamon, P.O. Box 800, Kidlington, Oxford OX5 1DX, England. TEL 44-1865-843000. FAX 44-1865-843010. *4692*

JOURNAL OF BIOMEDICAL MATERIALS RESEARCH.
John Wiley & Sons, Inc., Journals, 605 Third Ave., New York, NY 10158. TEL 212-850-6645. FAX 212-850-6021. *684*

JOURNAL OF BIOMEDICAL OPTICS.
International Society for Optical Engineering (SPIE), Box 10, Bellington, WA 98227. TEL 360-676-3290. FAX 360-647-1445. *5862*

JOURNAL OF BIOMEDICAL SCIENCE.
S. Karger AG, Allschwilerstr. 10, P.O. Box, CH-4009 Basel, Switzerland. TEL 41-61-3061111. FAX 41-61-3061234. *4692*

JOURNAL OF BIOPHARMACEUTICAL STATISTICS.
Marcel Dekker Journals, 270 Madison Ave., New York, NY 10016. TEL 212-696-9000. FAX 212-685-4540. *5701*

JOURNAL OF BIOSOCIAL SCIENCE.
Cambridge University Press, Edinburgh Bldg., Shaftesbury Rd., Cambridge CB2 2RU, England. TEL 44-1223-312393. FAX 44-1223-315052. *772*

JOURNAL OF BIOTECHNOLOGY.
Elsevier Science B.V., P.O. Box 211, 1000 AE Amsterdam, Netherlands. TEL 31-20-4853911. FAX 31-20-4853598. *684*

JOURNAL OF BIOTECHNOLOGY IN HEALTHCARE.
Henry Stewart Publications, Russell House, 28-30 Little Russell St., London WC1A 2HN, England. TEL 44-171-404-3040. FAX 44-171-486-7083. *684*

JOURNAL OF BONE AND JOINT SURGERY: AMERICAN VOLUME.
Journal of Bone and Joint Surgery, Inc., 20 Pickering St., Needham, MA 02192-3157. TEL 617-449-9738. *5009*

JOURNAL OF BONE AND JOINT SURGERY: BRITISH VOLUME.
British Editorial Society of Bone and Joint Surgery, 22 Buckingham St., London WC2N 6ET, England. TEL 0171-782-0010. FAX 0171-782-0995. *5009*

JOURNAL OF BRITISH STUDIES.
University of Chicago Press, Journals Division, Box 37005, Chicago, IL 60637. TEL 773-753-3347. FAX 773-753-0811. *3577*

JOURNAL OF BRONCHOLOGY.
Lippincott - Raven Publishers, 227 E. Washington Sq., Philadelphia, PA 19106. TEL 215-238-4200. FAX 215-238-4227. *5120*

JOURNAL OF BRYOLOGY.
W.S. Maney & Son Ltd., Hudson Rd., Leeds LS9 7DL, England. TEL 01532-497481. FAX 01532-486983. *710*

JOURNAL OF BUDDHIST ETHICS.
University of London, Goldsmiths, London SE14, England. TEL 44-171-919-7497. FAX 44-171-919-7398. *6389*

JOURNAL OF BURMA STUDIES.
Southeast Asia Publications, Northern Illinois University, Center for Southeast Asia Studies, DeKalb, IL 60115. TEL 815-753-1981. FAX 815-753-1651. *3535*

JOURNAL OF BURN CARE & REHABILITATION.
Mosby - Year Book, Inc., 11830 Westline Industrial Dr., St. Louis, MO 63146-3318. TEL 314-872-8370. FAX 314-432-1380. *4692*

THE JOURNAL OF BUSINESS (CHICAGO).
University of Chicago Press, Journals Division, Box 37005, Chicago, IL 60637. TEL 773-753-3347. FAX 773-753-0811. *975*

JOURNAL OF BUSINESS AND ECONOMIC PERSPECTIVES.
University of Tennessee at Martin, School of Business Administration, 113 Business Administration Bldg., Martin, TN 38238-5015. TEL 901-587-7226. FAX 901-587-7241. *975*

JOURNAL OF BUSINESS AND ECONOMIC STUDIES.
Salem State College, 352 Lafayette, Salem, MA 01970. TEL 508-741-6664. FAX 508-741-6027. *975*

JOURNAL OF BUSINESS & FINANCE LIBRARIANSHIP.
Haworth Press, Inc., 10 Alice St., Binghamton, NY 13904. TEL 607-722-5857. FAX 607-722-6362. *4188*

JOURNAL OF BUSINESS & PSYCHOLOGY.
Human Sciences Press, Inc., 233 Spring St., New York, NY 10013-1578. TEL 212-620-8000. FAX 212-463-0742. *6122*

JOURNAL OF BUSINESS ETHICS.
Kluwer Academic Publishers, Postbus 17, 3300 AA Dordrecht, Netherlands. TEL 31-78-6392392. FAX 31-78-6392254. *976*

JOURNAL OF BUSINESS FINANCE & ACCOUNTING.
Blackwell Publishers Ltd., 108 Cowley Rd., Oxford OX4 1JF, England. TEL 44-1865-791100. FAX 44-1865-791347. *1093*

JOURNAL OF BUSINESS FORECASTING METHODS AND SYSTEMS.
Graceway Publishing Co., Box 670159, Flushing, NY 11367-0159. TEL 718-463-3914. FAX 718-544-9086. *976*

JOURNAL OF BUSINESS IN DEVELOPING NATIONS.
North Carolina Central University, School of Business, JBND, Durham, NC 27707. *1363*

JOURNAL OF BUSINESS RESEARCH.
Elsevier Science Inc., Box 945, New York, NY 10159-0945. TEL 212-633-3730. FAX 212-633-3680. *1486*

JOURNAL OF BUSINESS-TO-BUSINESS MARKETING.
Haworth Press, Inc., 10 Alice St., Binghamton, NY 13904. TEL 607-722-5857. FAX 607-722-6362. *1532*

JOURNAL OF BUSINESS VENTURING.
Elsevier Science Inc., Box 945, New York, NY 10159-0945. TEL 212-633-3730. FAX 212-633-3680. *976*

JOURNAL OF CALIFORNIA AND GREAT BASIN ANTHROPOLOGY.
California State University, Bakersfield, Department of Sociology - Anthropology, 9001 Stockdale Hwy., Bakersfield, CA 93311. TEL 805-664-3153. *321*

JOURNAL OF CALIFORNIA LAW ENFORCEMENT.
California Peace Officers Association, 1455 Response Rd., Ste. 190, Sacramento, CA 95815. TEL 916-923-1825. FAX 916-263-6090. *2270*

JOURNAL OF CANADIAN ART HISTORY.
Concordia University, 1455 boul. de Maisonneuve Ouest, S-VA 432, Montreal, PQ H3G 1M8, Canada. TEL 514-848-4699. FAX 514-848-8627. *449*

REFEREED SERIALS

JOURNAL OF CANADIAN PETROLEUM TECHNOLOGY.
Canadian Institute of Mining, Metallurgy and Petroleum, Petroleum Society, 101 6 Ave., S.W., Ste. 320, Calgary, AB T2P 3P4, Canada. TEL 403-237-5112. FAX 403-262-4792. *5607*

JOURNAL OF CANADIAN POETRY.
Borealis Press Limited, 9 Ashburn Dr., Nepean, ON K2E 6N4, Canada. TEL 613-224-6837. FAX 613-829-7783. *4511*

JOURNAL OF CANCER EDUCATION.
Hanley & Belfus, Inc., 210 S. 13th St., Philadelphia, PA 19107. TEL 215-546-7293. FAX 215-790-9330. *4981*

JOURNAL OF CANCER RESEARCH AND CLINICAL ONCOLOGY.
Springer-Verlag, Heidelberger Platz 3, 14197 Berlin, Germany. TEL 49-30-82787-0. FAX 49-30-82787448. *4981*

JOURNAL OF CARBOHYDRATE CHEMISTRY.
Marcel Dekker Journals, 270 Madison Ave., New York, NY 10016. TEL 212-696-9000. FAX 212-685-4540. *1754*

JOURNAL OF CARDIAC FAILURE.
Churchill Livingstone, 650 Ave. of the Americas, New York, NY 10011. TEL 212-206-5040. FAX 212-727-7808. *4819*

JOURNAL OF CARDIAC SURGERY.
Futura Publishing Company, Inc., 135 Bedford Rd., Box 418, Armonk, NY 10504-0418. TEL 914-273-1014. FAX 914-273-1015. *4819*

JOURNAL OF CARDIOPULMONARY REHABILITATION.
Lippincott - Raven Publishers, 227 E. Washington Sq., Philadelphia, PA 19106. TEL 215-238-4200. FAX 215-238-4227. *4819*

JOURNAL OF CARDIOTHORACIC AND VASCULAR ANESTHESIA.
W.B. Saunders Co., The Curtis Center, 3rd Fl., Independence Sq. W., Philadelphia, PA 19106-3399. TEL 215-238-7800. FAX 215-238-6445. *4820*

JOURNAL OF CARDIOVASCULAR DIAGNOSIS AND PROCEDURES.
Mary Ann Liebert, Inc. Publishers, 2 Madison Ave., Larchmont, NY 10538. TEL 914-834-3100. FAX 914-834-3688. *4820*

JOURNAL OF CARDIOVASCULAR ELECTROPHYSIOLOGY.
Futura Publishing Company, Inc., 135 Bedford Rd., Box 418, Armonk, NY 10504-0418. TEL 914-273-1014. FAX 914-273-1015. *4820*

JOURNAL OF CARDIOVASCULAR PHARMACOLOGY.
Lippincott - Raven Publishers, 227 E. Washington Sq., Philadelphia, PA 19106. TEL 215-238-4200. FAX 215-238-4227. *5670*

JOURNAL OF CARDIOVASCULAR RISK.
Thomson Science, 2-6 Boundary Row, London SE1 8HN, England. TEL 44-171-865-0198. FAX 44-171-410-6600. *4820*

THE JOURNAL OF CARDIOVASCULAR SURGERY.
Edizioni Minerva Medica, Corso Bramante 83-85, 10126 Turin, Italy. TEL 39-11-678282. FAX 39-11-674502. *4820*

JOURNAL OF CAREER ASSESSMENT.
Psychological Assessment Resources, Inc., 16204 N. Florida Ave., Lutz, FL 33549. TEL 813-968-3003. FAX 813-968-2598. *6122*

JOURNAL OF CAREER DEVELOPMENT.
Human Sciences Press, Inc., 233 Spring St., New York, NY 10013-1578. TEL 212-620-8000. FAX 212-463-0742. *5512*

JOURNAL OF CASE MANAGEMENT.
Springer Publishing Company, 536 Broadway, New York, NY 10012-3955. TEL 212-431-4370. FAX 212-941-7842. *4692*

JOURNAL OF CATALYSIS.
Academic Press, Inc., Journal Division, 525 B St., Ste. 1900, San Diego, CA 92101-4495. TEL 619-230-1840. FAX 619-699-6800. *1830*

JOURNAL OF CATARACT AND REFRACTIVE SURGERY.
American Society of Cataract and Refractive Surgery, 4000 Legato Rd., Ste. 850, Fairfax, VA 22033-4003. TEL 703-591-2220. FAX 703-591-0614. *4995*

JOURNAL OF CELL BIOLOGY.
Rockefeller University Press, 1114 First Ave., 4th Fl., New York, NY 10021. TEL 212-327-8572. FAX 212-327-7944. *741*

JOURNAL OF CELLULAR BIOCHEMISTRY.
John Wiley & Sons, Inc., Journals, 605 Third Ave., New York, NY 10158. TEL 212-850-6645. FAX 212-850-6021. *663*

JOURNAL OF CELLULAR BIOCHEMISTRY. SUPPLEMENT.
John Wiley & Sons, Inc., Journals, 605 Third Ave., New York, NY 10158. TEL 212-850-6645. FAX 212-850-6021. *741*

JOURNAL OF CELLULAR PATHOLOGY.
Oxford University Press, Academic Division, Great Clarendon St., Oxford OX2 6DP, England. TEL 44-1865-267907. FAX 44-1865-267485. *741*

JOURNAL OF CELLULAR PHYSIOLOGY.
John Wiley & Sons, Inc., Journals, 605 Third Ave., New York, NY 10158. TEL 212-850-6645. FAX 212-850-6021. *817*

JOURNAL OF CELLULAR PLASTICS.
Technomic Publishing Co., Inc., 851 New Holland Ave., Box 3535, Lancaster, PA 17604. TEL 717-291-5609. FAX 717-295-4538. *5879*

JOURNAL OF CEREBRAL BLOOD FLOW AND METABOLISM.
Lippincott - Raven Publishers, 227 E. Washington Sq., Philadelphia, PA 19106. TEL 215-238-4200. FAX 215-238-4227. *5072*

JOURNAL OF CHEMICAL CRYSTALLOGRAPHY.
Plenum Publishing Corp., 233 Spring St., New York, NY 10013-1578. TEL 212-620-8000. FAX 212-463-0742. *1802*

JOURNAL OF CHEMICAL DEPENDENCY TREATMENT.
Haworth Press, Inc., 10 Alice St., Binghamton, NY 13904. TEL 607-722-5857. FAX 607-722-6362. *2302*

JOURNAL OF CHEMICAL ECOLOGY.
Plenum Publishing Corp., 233 Spring St., New York, NY 10013-1578. TEL 212-620-8000. FAX 212-463-0742. *2936*

JOURNAL OF CHEMICAL EDUCATION.
American Chemical Society, c/o Dept. of Chemistry, Montana State University, Bozeman, MT 59717-0340. TEL 406-994-5393. FAX 406-994-5407. *1754*

JOURNAL OF CHEMICAL EDUCATION: SOFTWARE. SERIES B.
American Chemical Society, Division of Chemical Education, Inc., c/o Dept. of Chemistry, Univ. of Wisconsin at Madison, 1101 University Ave., Madison, WI 53706-1396. TEL 608-262-5753. FAX 608-265-8094. *2517*

JOURNAL OF CHEMICAL EDUCATION: SOFTWARE. SERIES C.
American Chemical Society, Division of Chemical Education, Inc., c/o Dept. of Chemistry, Univ. of Wisconsin at Madison, 1101 University Ave., Madison, WI 53706-1396. TEL 608-262-5163. FAX 608-265-8094. *2517*

JOURNAL OF CHEMICAL EDUCATION: SOFTWARE. SERIES D.
American Chemical Society, Division of Chemical Education, Inc., c/o Dept. of Chemistry, Univ. of Wisconisn at Madison, 1101 University Ave., Madison, WI 53706-1396. TEL 608-262-5153. FAX 608-265-8094. *2517*

JOURNAL OF CHEMICAL EDUCATION: SOFTWARE. SPECIAL ISSUE SERIES.
American Chemical Society, Division of Chemical Education, Inc., c/o Dept. of Chemistry, Univ. of Wisconsin at Madison, 1101 University Ave., Madison, WI 53706-1396. TEL 608-262-5153. FAX 608-265-8094. *2517*

JOURNAL OF CHEMICAL INFORMATION AND COMPUTER SCIENCES.
American Chemical Society, 1155 16th St. N.W., Washington, DC 20036. TEL 800-333-9511. FAX 614-447-3671. *1800*

JOURNAL OF CHEMICAL NEUROANATOMY.
Elsevier Science B.V., P.O. Box 211, 1000 AE Amsterdam, Netherlands. TEL 31-20-4853911. FAX 31-20-4853598. *5072*

JOURNAL OF CHEMICAL PHYSICS.
American Institute of Physics, One Physics Ellipse, College park, MD 20740-3843. TEL 301-209-3000. FAX 516-349-9704. *5809*

JOURNAL OF CHEMICAL RESEARCH.
The Royal Society of Chemistry, Thomas Graham House, Science Park, Milton Rd., Cambridge CB4 4WF, England. TEL 44-1223-420066. FAX 44-1223-423429. *1755*

JOURNAL OF CHEMICAL TECHNOLOGY AND BIOTECHNOLOGY.
John Wiley & Sons Ltd., Journals, Baffins Ln., Chichester, W. Sussex PO19 1UD, England. TEL 44-1243-779777. FAX 44-1243-775878. *684*

JOURNAL OF CHEMICAL VAPOR DEPOSITION.
Technomic Publishing Co., Inc., 851 New Holland Ave., Box 3535, Lancaster, PA 17604. TEL 717-291-5609. FAX 717-295-4538. *1802*

JOURNAL OF CHEMOMETRICS.
John Wiley & Sons Ltd., Journals, Baffins Ln., Chichester, W. Sussex PO19 1UD, England. TEL 44-1243-779777. FAX 44-1243-775878. *1792*

JOURNAL OF CHEMOTHERAPY.
E I F T srl, Via XX Settembre 102, 50129 Florence, Italy. TEL 39-55-486147. FAX 39-55-474426. *4981*

JOURNAL OF CHILD AND ADOLESCENT GROUP THERAPY.
Human Sciences Press, Inc., 233 Spring St., New York, NY 10013. TEL 212-620-8000. FAX 212-463-0742. *5072*

JOURNAL OF CHILD AND ADOLESCENT PSYCHIATRIC NURSING.
Nursecom, Inc., 1211 Locust St., Philadelphia, PA 19107. TEL 215-545-7222. FAX 215-545-1807. *4936*

JOURNAL OF CHILD & ADOLESCENT SUBSTANCE ABUSE.
Haworth Press, Inc., 10 Alice St., Binghamton, NY 13904. TEL 607-722-5857. FAX 607-722-6362. *2302*

JOURNAL OF CHILD AND FAMILY STUDIES.
Human Sciences Press, Inc., 233 Spring St., New York, NY 10013-1578. TEL 212-620-8000. FAX 212-463-0742. *6122*

JOURNAL OF CHILD NEUROLOGY.
Decker Periodicals, P.O. Box 620, LCD 1, Hamilton, ON L8N 3K7, Canada. TEL 905-522-7017. FAX 905-522-7839. *5072*

JOURNAL OF CHILD PSYCHOLOGY & PSYCHIATRY & ALLIED DISCIPLINES.
Cambridge University Press, Edinburgh Bldg., Shaftesbury Rd., Cambridge CB2 2RU, England. TEL 44-1223-312393. FAX 44-1223-315052. *6122*

JOURNAL OF CHILD SEXUAL ABUSE.
Haworth Press, Inc., 10 Alice St., Binghamton, NY 13904. TEL 607-722-5857. FAX 607-722-6362. *6672*

JOURNAL OF CHILDREN'S LITERATURE.
Children's Literature Assembly, c/o Marjorie R. Hancock, 2037 Plymouth Rd., Manhattan, KS 66503. TEL 913-532-5917. *1848*

JOURNAL OF CHINESE LINGUISTICS.
Project on Linguistic Analysis, 2222 Piedmont Ave., Berkeley, CA 94720. TEL 510-642-5937. FAX 510-841-7205. *4267*

JOURNAL OF CHINESE LINGUISTICS MONOGRAPH SERIES.
Project on Linguistic Analysis, 2222 Piedmont Ave., Berkeley, CA 94720. TEL 510-642-5937. FAX 510-841-7205. *4267*

JOURNAL OF CHINESE PHARMACEUTICAL SCIENCES.
Chinese Pharmaceutical Association, Beijing Medical University, School of Pharmaceutical Sciences, Beijing 100083, People's Republic of China. TEL 86-10-6209-1713. FAX 86-10-6201-5584. *5670*

JOURNAL OF CHINESE RELIGIONS.
Society for the Study of Chinese Religions, c/o Linda Penkower, Treas., Department of Religious Studies, 2604 CL, University of Pittsburgh, Pittsburgh, PA 15260. TEL 412-624-2277. FAX 412-624-5994. *6492*

JOURNAL OF CHRISTIAN EDUCATION.
Australian Christian Forum on Education Inc., P.O. Box 139, Lidcombe, N.S.W. 2141, Australia. TEL 61-2-97642084. FAX 61-2-97462710. *6348*

JOURNAL OF CHROMATOGRAPHY.
Elsevier Science B.V., P.O. Box 211, 1000 AE Amsterdam, Netherlands. TEL 31-20-4853911. FAX 31-20-4853598. *1792*

JOURNAL OF CHROMATOGRAPHY - BIOMEDICAL APPLICATIONS.
Elsevier Science B.V., P.O. Box 211, 1000 AE Amsterdam, Netherlands. TEL 31-20-4853911. FAX 31-20-4853598. *1755*

JOURNAL OF CHROMATOGRAPHY LIBRARY.
Elsevier Science B.V., Books Division, P.O. Box 211, 1000 AE Amsterdam, Netherlands. TEL 31-20-4853911. FAX 31-20-4853705. *1792*

JOURNAL OF CHRONIC FATIGUE SYNDROME.
Haworth Press, Inc., 10 Alice St., Binghamton, NY 13904. FAX 607-722-6362. *4692*

JOURNAL OF CIRCUITS, SYSTEMS AND COMPUTERS.
World Scientific Publishing Co. Pte. Ltd., Farrer Rd., P.O. Box 128, Singapore 9128, Singapore. TEL 65-3825663. FAX 65-3825919. *2728*

JOURNAL OF CITRICULTURE.
Haworth Press, Inc., 10 Alice St., Binghamton, NY 13094. TEL 607-722-5857. FAX 607-722-6362. *231*

JOURNAL OF CLASSIFICATION.
Springer-Verlag, Science Journals, 175 Fifth Ave., New York, NY 10010. TEL 212-460-1500. FAX 212-473-6272. *4581*

JOURNAL OF CLEANER PRODUCTION.
Elsevier Science Ltd., P.O. Box 800, Kidlington, Oxford OX5 1DX, England. TEL 44-1865-843000. FAX 44-1865-843010. *2877*

JOURNAL OF CLIMATE.
American Meteorological Society, 45 Beacon St., Boston, MA 02108-3693. TEL 617-227-2425. FAX 617-742-8718. *5236*

JOURNAL OF CLINICAL ANESTHESIA.
Elsevier Science Inc., Box 945, New York, NY 10159-0945. TEL 212-633-3730. FAX 212-633-3680. *4806*

JOURNAL OF CLINICAL APHERESIS.
John Wiley & Sons, Inc., Journals, 605 Third Ave., New York, NY 10158. TEL 212-850-6645. FAX 212-850-6021. *5162*

JOURNAL OF CLINICAL CHILD PSYCHOLOGY.
Lawrence Erlbaum Associates, Inc., 10 Industrial Dr., Mahwah, NJ 07430-2262. TEL 201-236-9500. FAX 201-236-0072. *6122*

JOURNAL OF CLINICAL ENDOCRINOLOGY AND METABOLISM.
Endocrine Society, 4350 East West Hwy., Ste. 500, Bethesda, MD 20814-4410. TEL 301-941-0200. FAX 301-941-0259. *4889*

JOURNAL OF CLINICAL ENGINEERING.
Lippincott - Raven Publishers, 227 E. Washington Sq., Philadelphia, PA 19106-3780. TEL 215-238-4200. *648*

JOURNAL OF CLINICAL EPIDEMIOLOGY.
Elsevier Science Inc., Box 945, New York, NY 10159-0945. TEL 212-633-3730. FAX 212-633-3680. *4693*

JOURNAL OF CLINICAL ETHICS.
The Journal of Clinical Ethics, Inc., 107 E. Church St., Frederick, MD 21701. TEL 301-694-8561. *4693*

JOURNAL OF CLINICAL GASTROENTEROLOGY.
Lippincott - Raven Publishers, 227 E. Washington Sq., Philadelphia, PA 19106. TEL 215-238-4200. FAX 215-238-4227. *4912*

JOURNAL OF CLINICAL GEROPSYCHOLOGY.
Plenum Publishing Corp., 233 Spring St., New York, NY 10013-1578. TEL 212-620-8000. FAX 212-463-0742. *3438*

JOURNAL OF CLINICAL IMMUNOLOGY.
Plenum Publishing Corp., 233 Spring St., New York, NY 10013-1578. TEL 212-620-8000. FAX 212-463-0742. *4798*

JOURNAL OF CLINICAL INVESTIGATION.
Rockefeller University Press, 11114 First Ave., New York, NY 10021. TEL 212-327-8572. FAX 212-327-7944. *4693*

JOURNAL OF CLINICAL LABORATORY ANALYSIS.
John Wiley & Sons, Inc., Journals, 605 Third Ave., New York, NY 10158. TEL 212-850-6645. FAX 212-850-6021. *4898*

JOURNAL OF CLINICAL LIGAND ASSAY.
Kellner-McCaffery Associates, Inc., 150 Fifth Ave., Ste. 840, New York, NY 10011. TEL 212-741-0280. *4798*

JOURNAL OF CLINICAL MICROBIOLOGY.
American Society for Microbiology, 1325 Massachusetts Ave., N.W., Washington, DC 20005. TEL 202-737-3600. *788*

JOURNAL OF CLINICAL MONITORING.
Kluwer Academic Publishers, Postbus 17, 3300 AA Dordrecht. TEL 31-78-6392392. FAX 31-78-6392254. *4693*

JOURNAL OF CLINICAL NEUROPHYSIOLOGY.
Lippincott - Raven Publishers, 227 E. Washington Sq., Philadelphia, PA 19106. TEL 215-238-4200. *5072*

JOURNAL OF CLINICAL NURSING.
Blackwell Science Ltd., Osney Mead, Oxford OX3 0EL, England. TEL 44-1865-206206. FAX 44-1865-721205. *4936*

JOURNAL OF CLINICAL ONCOLOGY.
W.B. Saunders Co., Curtis Center, 3rd Fl., Independence Sq. W., Philadelphia, PA 19106-3399. TEL 215-238-7800. FAX 215-238-6445. *4981*

JOURNAL OF CLINICAL ORTHODONTICS.
J C O Inc., 1828 Pearl St., Boulder, CO 80302. FAX 303-443-9356. *4861*

JOURNAL OF CLINICAL OUTCOMES MANAGEMENT.
Turner White Communications, Inc., 125 Strafford Ave., Ste. 220, Wayne, PA 19087-3391. TEL 610-975-4541. FAX 610-975-4564. *4693*

JOURNAL OF CLINICAL PATHOLOGY.
B M J Publishing Group, B.M.A. House, Tavistock Sq., London WC1H 9JR, England. TEL 44-171-383-6270. FAX 44-171-383-6402. *4693*

JOURNAL OF CLINICAL PEDIATRIC DENTISTRY.
Tufts University, School of Dental Medicine, Dept. of Pediatric Dentistry, 1 Kneeland St., Boston, MA 02111. TEL 617-956-6902. FAX 205-995-1588. *4861*

JOURNAL OF CLINICAL PERIODONTOLOGY.
Munksgaard International Publishers Ltd., 35 Noerre Soegade, P.O. Box 2148, DK-1016 Copenhagen K, Denmark. TEL 45-33-127030. FAX 45-33-129387. *4861*

JOURNAL OF CLINICAL PHARMACOLOGY.
Lippincott - Raven Publishers, 227 E. Washington Sq., Philadelphia, PA 19106. TEL 215-238-4200. *5670*

JOURNAL OF CLINICAL PHARMACY AND THERAPEUTICS.
Blackwell Science Ltd., Osney Mead, Oxford OX2 0EL, England. TEL 44-1865-206206. FAX 44-1865-721205. *5670*

JOURNAL OF CLINICAL PSYCHIATRY.
Physicians Postgraduate Press, Inc., Box 752870, Memphis, TN 38175-2870. TEL 901-682-1001. FAX 901-682-6992. *5072*

JOURNAL OF CLINICAL PSYCHOANALYSIS.
International Universities Press, Inc., 59 Boston Post Rd., Box 1524, Madison, CT 06443-1524. TEL 203-245-4000. FAX 203-245-0775. *6122*

JOURNAL OF CLINICAL PSYCHOLOGY.
John Wiley & Sons, Inc., Journals, 605 Third Ave., New York, NY 10158-0012. TEL 212-850-6645. FAX 212-850-6021. *6122*

JOURNAL OF CLINICAL PSYCHOLOGY IN MEDICAL SETTINGS.
Plenum Publishing Corp., 233 Spring St., New York, NY 10013-1578. TEL 212-620-8000. FAX 212-463-0742. *6123*

JOURNAL OF CLINICAL PSYCHOPHARMACOLOGY.
Williams & Wilkins, 351 W. Camden St., Baltimore, MD 21201-2436. TEL 410-528-4068. FAX 410-528-4452. *5670*

JOURNAL OF CLINICAL ULTRASOUND.
John Wiley & Sons, Inc., Journals, 605 Third Ave., New York, NY 10158. TEL 212-850-6645. FAX 212-850-6021. *5108*

JOURNAL OF CLUSTER SCIENCE.
Plenum Publishing Corp., 233 Spring St., New York, NY 10013-1578. TEL 212-620-8000. FAX 212-463-0742. *1755*

JOURNAL OF COASTAL CONSERVATION.
Opulus Press AB, P.O. Box 25137, S-750 25 Uppsala, Sweden. TEL 46-18-32-06-62. FAX 46-18-32-13-68. *2406*

JOURNAL OF COASTAL RESEARCH.
Coastal Education & Research Foundation, Box 21087, Royal Palm Beach, FL 33421-0187. TEL 561-753-7557. FAX 561-753-7558. *2406*

JOURNAL OF COATED FABRICS.
Technomic Publishing Co., Inc., 851 New Holland Ave., Box 3535, Lancaster, PA 17604. TEL 717-291-5609. FAX 717-295-4538. *6990*

JOURNAL OF COGNITIVE NEUROSCIENCE.
M I T Press, 5 Cabridge Center, Cambridge, MA 02142. TEL 617-253-2889. FAX 617-577-1545. *5073*

JOURNAL OF COGNITIVE PSYCHOTHERAPY.
Springer Publishing Company, 536 Broadway, New York, NY 10012-3955. TEL 212-431-4370. FAX 212-941-7842. *6123*

JOURNAL OF COLD REGIONS ENGINEERING.
American Society of Civil Engineers, 345 E. 47th St., New York, NY 10017-2398. TEL 212-705-7288. FAX 212-980-4681. *2790*

JOURNAL OF COLLEGE & UNIVERSITY FOODSERVICE.
Haworth Press, Inc., Food Products Press, 10 Alice St., Binghamton, NY 13904. TEL 607-722-5857. FAX 607-722-6362. *3115*

JOURNAL OF COLLEGE AND UNIVERSITY STUDENT HOUSING.
Association of College and University Housing Officers' International, 364 West Lane Ave., Ste. C, Columbus, OH 43201-1062. TEL 614-292-0099. FAX 614-292-3205. *2546*

JOURNAL OF COLLEGE STUDENT DEVELOPMENT.
American College Personnel Association, One Dupont Circle, Ste. 300, Washington, DC 20036-1110. TEL 202-835-2272. FAX 202-296-3286. *6123*

JOURNAL OF COLLEGE STUDENT PSYCHOTHERAPY.
Haworth Press, Inc., 10 Alice St., Binghamton, NY 13904. TEL 607-722-5857. FAX 607-722-6362. *6123*

JOURNAL OF COLLOID AND INTERFACE SCIENCE.
Academic Press, Inc., Journal Division, 525 B St., Ste. 1900, San Diego, CA 92101-4495. TEL 619-230-1840. FAX 619-699-6800. *1830*

JOURNAL OF COMBINATORIAL DESIGNS.
John Wiley & Sons, Inc., Journals, 605 Third Ave., New York, NY 10158. TEL 212-850-6645. FAX 212-850-6021. *4581*

JOURNAL OF COMBINATORIAL MATHEMATICS AND COMBINATORIAL COMPUTING.
Charles Babbage Research Centre, P.O. Box 272, St. Norbert Postal Stn., Winnipeg, MB R3V 1L6, Canada. TEL 204-772-2612. *4581*

JOURNAL OF COMBINATORIAL OPTIMIZATION.
Kluwer Academic Publishers, Postbus 17, 3300 AA Dordrecht, Netherlands. TEL 31-78-6392392. FAX 31-78-6392254. *4621*

JOURNAL OF COMBINATORIAL THEORY. SERIES A.
Academic Press, Inc., Journal Division, 525 B St., Ste. 1900, San Diego, CA 92101-4495. TEL 619-230-1840. FAX 619-699-6800. *4581*

JOURNAL OF COMBINATORIAL THEORY. SERIES B.
Academic Press, Inc., Journal Division, 525 B St., Ste. 1900, San Diego, CA 92101-4490. TEL 619-230-1840. FAX 619-699-6800. *4581*

JOURNAL OF COMMON MARKET STUDIES.
Blackwell Publishers Ltd., 108 Cowley Rd., Oxford OX4 1JF, England. TEL 44-1865-791100. FAX 44-1865-791347. *5936*

THE JOURNAL OF COMMONWEALTH & COMPARATIVE POLITICS.
Frank Cass, Newbury House, 890-900 Eastern Ave., Newbury Park, Ilford, Essex IG2 7HH, England. TEL 44-181-599-8866. FAX 44-181-599-0984. *6023*

JOURNAL OF COMMUNICATION.
Oxford University Press, Journals, 2001 Evans Rd., Cary, NC 27513. TEL 919-677-0977. FAX 919-677-1714. *1996*

JOURNAL OF COMMUNICATION DISORDERS.
Elsevier Science Inc., Box 945, New York, NY 10159-0945. TEL 212-633-3730. FAX 212-633-3990. *6123*

JOURNAL OF COMMUNICATION MANAGEMENT.
Henry Stewart Publications, Russell House, 28-30 Little Russell St., London WC1A 2HN, England. TEL 44-171-404-3040. FAX 44-171-404-2081. *1487*

THE JOURNAL OF COMMUNIST STUDIES AND TRANSITION POLITICS.
Frank Cass, Newbury House, 890-900 Eastern Ave., Newbury Park, Ilford, Essex IG2 7HH, England. TEL 44-181-599-8866. FAX 44-181-599-0984. *6023*

JOURNAL OF COMMUNITY AND APPLIED SOCIAL PSYCHOLOGY.
John Wiley & Sons Ltd., Journals, Baffins Ln., Chichester, W. Sussex PO19 1UD, England. TEL 44-1243-779777. FAX 44-1243-775878. *6123*

JOURNAL OF COMMUNITY HEALTH.
Human Sciences Press, Inc., 233 Spring St., New York, NY 10013-1578. TEL 212-620-8000. FAX 212-463-0742. *4693*

JOURNAL OF COMMUNITY HEALTH NURSING.
Lawrence Erlbaum Associates, Inc., 10 Industrial Dr., Mahwah, NJ 07430-2262. TEL 201-236-9500. FAX 201-236-0072. *4936*

JOURNAL OF COMMUNITY NURSING.
P T M Publishers Ltd., 282 High St., Sutton, Surrey SM1 1PQ, England. TEL 44-181-642-0162. FAX 44-181-643-2275. *4936*

JOURNAL OF COMMUNITY PSYCHOLOGY.
John Wiley & Sons, Inc., Journals, 605 Third Ave., New York, NY 10158-0012. TEL 212-850-6645. FAX 212-850-6021. *6123*

JOURNAL OF COMPARATIVE FAMILY STUDIES.
University of Calgary, Department of Sociology, 2500 University Dr. N.W., Calgary, AB T2N 1N4, Canada. TEL 403-220-7317. FAX 403-282-9298. *6716*

THE JOURNAL OF COMPARATIVE GERMAN LINGUISTICS.
Kluwer Academic Publishers, Postbus 17, 3300 AA Dordrecht, Netherlands. TEL 31-78-6392392. FAX 31-78-6392254. *4267*

JOURNAL OF COMPARATIVE LITERATURE AND AESTHETICS.
Vishvanatha Kaviraja Institute of Comparative Literature and Aesthetics, B8 Sambalpur University, Jyotivihar 768 019, Orissa, India. TEL 91-663-430314. *4420*

THE JOURNAL OF COMPARATIVE NEUROLOGY.
John Wiley & Sons, Inc., Journals, 605 Third Ave., New York, NY 10158. TEL 212-850-6645. FAX 212-850-6021. *5073*

JOURNAL OF COMPARATIVE PHYSICAL AND EDUCATION SPORT.
Verlag Karl Hofmann, Postfach 1360, 73603 Schorndorf, Germany. TEL 49-7181-402127. FAX 49-7181-402111. *6766*

JOURNAL OF COMPARATIVE PSYCHOLOGY.
American Psychological Association, 750 First St., N.E., Washington, DC 20002-4242. TEL 202-336-5600. FAX 202-336-5568. *6123*

JOURNAL OF COMPARATIVE RELIGION.
Universal Publications (a division of S T C), P.O. Box 7305, Ottawa, ON K1L 8E4, Canada. TEL 613-831-1052. FAX 613-831-8452. *6348*

JOURNAL OF COMPARATIVE SOCIOLOGY AND ETHICS.
Universal Publications, P.O. Box 7305, Ottawa, ON K1L 8E4, Canada. TEL 613-831-1052. FAX 613-831-8452. *6716*

JOURNAL OF COMPLEXITY.
Academic Press, Inc., Journal Division, 525 B St., Ste. 1900, San Diego, CA 92101-4495. TEL 619-230-1840. FAX 619-699-6800. *4621*

JOURNAL OF COMPOSITE MATERIALS.
Technomic Publishing Co., Inc., 851 New Holland Ave., Box 3535, Lancaster, PA 17604. TEL 717-291-5609. FAX 717-295-4538. *2861*

JOURNAL OF COMPOSITES TECHNOLOGY AND RESEARCH.
American Society for Testing and Materials, 100 Barr Harbor Dr., W. Conshohocken, PA 19428-2959. TEL 610-832-9500. FAX 610-832-9555. *2889*

JOURNAL OF COMPUTATIONAL AND APPLIED MATHEMATICS.
North-Holland, P.O. Box 211, 1000 AE Amsterdam, Netherlands. TEL 31-20-4853911. FAX 31-20-4853598. *4581*

JOURNAL OF COMPUTATIONAL BIOLOGY.
Mary Ann Liebert, Inc. Publishers, 2 Madison Ave., Larchmont, NY 10538. TEL 914-834-3100. FAX 914-834-3688. *608*

JOURNAL OF COMPUTATIONAL CHEMISTRY.
John Wiley & Sons, Inc., Journals, 605 Third Ave., New York, NY 10158. TEL 212-850-6645. FAX 212-850-6021. *1755*

JOURNAL OF COMPUTATIONAL MATHEMATICS.
Science Press, Marketing and Sales Department, 16 Donghuangchenggen North St., Beijing 100717, People's Republic of China. TEL 4010642. FAX 4019810. *4581*

JOURNAL OF COMPUTATIONAL NEUROSCIENCE.
Kluwer Academic Publishers, Postbus 17, 3300 AA Dordrecht, Netherlands. TEL 31-78-6392392. FAX 31-78-6392254. *5073*

JOURNAL OF COMPUTATIONAL PHYSICS.
Academic Press, Inc., Journal Division, 525 B St., Ste. 1900, San Diego, CA 92101-4495. TEL 619-230-1840. FAX 619-699-6800. *5838*

JOURNAL OF COMPUTER - AIDED MATERIALS DESIGN.
E S C O M Science Publishers BV, P.O. Box 214, 2300 AE Leiden, Netherlands. TEL 31-71-127052. FAX 31-71-121772. *1800*

JOURNAL OF COMPUTER AND SYSTEM SCIENCES.
Academic Press, Inc., Journal Division, 525 B St., Ste. 1900, San Diego, CA 92101-4495. TEL 619-230-1840. FAX 619-699-6800. *2085*

JOURNAL OF COMPUTER ASSISTED LEARNING.
Blackwell Science Ltd., Osney Mead, Oxford OX2 0EL, England. TEL 44-1865-206206. FAX 44-1865-721205. *2114*

JOURNAL OF COMPUTER-ASSISTED MICROSCOPY.
Plenum Publishing Corp., 233 Spring St., New York, NY 10013-1578. TEL 212-620-8000. FAX 212-463-0742. *2152*

JOURNAL OF COMPUTER ASSISTED TOMOGRAPHY.
Lippincott - Raven Publishers, 227 E. Washington Sq., Philadelphia, PA 19106. TEL 215-238-4200. FAX 215-238-4227. *5108*

JOURNAL OF COMPUTER INFORMATION SYSTEMS.
International Association for Computer Information Systems, 217 College of Business, Oklahoma State University, Stillwater, OK 74078. TEL 405-744-8632. FAX 405-744-5180. *2156*

JOURNAL OF COMPUTER SCIENCE AND TECHNOLOGY.
Science Press, Marketing and Sales Department, 16 Donghuangchenggen North St., Beijing 100717, People's Republic of China. TEL 4010642. FAX 4019810. *2221*

JOURNAL OF COMPUTERS IN MATHEMATICS AND SCIENCE TEACHING.
Association for the Advancement of Computing in Education, Box 2966, Charlottesville, VA 22902-2966. TEL 804-973-3987. FAX 804-978-7449. *4621*

JOURNAL OF COMPUTING IN CHILDHOOD EDUCATION.
Association for the Advancement of Computing in Education, Box 2966, Charlottesville, VA 22902-2966. TEL 804-973-3987. FAX 804-978-7449. *2517*

JOURNAL OF COMPUTING IN HIGHER EDUCATION.
Norris Publishers, Box 2593, Amherst, MA 01004-2593. TEL 413-545-4232. FAX 413-545-3203. *2517*

JOURNAL OF COMPUTING IN TEACHER EDUCATION.
International Society for Technology in Education, 1787 Agate St., Eugene, OR 97403-1923. TEL 541-346-4414. *2518*

JOURNAL OF CONFEDERATE HISTORY.
Southern Heritage Press, 4035 Emerald Dr., Murfreesboro, TN 37130. *5273*

JOURNAL OF CONFLICT STUDIES.
University of New Brunswick, Centre for Conflict Studies, P.O. Box 4400, Fredericton, NB E3B 5A3, Canada. TEL 506-453-4587. FAX 506-453-4599. *4341*

JOURNAL OF CONSCIOUSNESS STUDIES.
Imprint Academic, P.O. Box 1, Thorverton, Exeter, Devon EX5 5YX, England. TEL 44-1392-841600. FAX 44-1392-841478. *6124*

JOURNAL OF CONSTRUCTIONAL STEEL RESEARCH.
Elsevier Science Ltd., P.O. Box 800, Kidlington, Oxford OX5 1DX, England. TEL 44-1865-843000. FAX 44-1865-843010. *2790*

JOURNAL OF CONSTRUCTIVIST PSYCHOLOGY.
Taylor & Francis Inc., 1900 Frost Rd., Ste. 101, Bristol, PA 19007-1598. TEL 215-785-5800. FAX 215-785-5515. *6124*

JOURNAL OF CONSULTING AND CLINICAL PSYCHOLOGY.
American Psychological Association, 750 First St., N.E., Washington, DC 20002-4242. TEL 202-336-5600. FAX 202-336-5568. *6124*

JOURNAL OF CONSUMER AFFAIRS.
American Council on Consumer Interests, 240 Stanley Hall, University of Missouri, Columbia, MO 65211. TEL 573-882-3817. FAX 573-884-6571. *2256*

JOURNAL OF CONSUMER POLICY.
Kluwer Academic Publishers, Postbus 17, 3300 AA Dordrecht, Netherlands. TEL 31-78-6392392. FAX 31-78-6392254. *2256*

JOURNAL OF CONSUMER PSYCHOLOGY.
Lawrence Erlbaum Associates, Inc., 10 Industrial Dr., Mahwah, NJ 07430-2262. TEL 201-236-9500. FAX 201-236-0072. *38*

JOURNAL OF CONSUMER RESEARCH.
University of Chicago Press, Journals Division, Box 37005, Chicago, IL 60637. TEL 773-753-3347. FAX 773-753-0811. *1532*

JOURNAL OF CONSUMER STUDIES & HOME ECONOMICS.
Blackwell Science Ltd., Osney Mead, Oxford OX2 0EL, England. TEL 01865-206206. FAX 01865-721205. *2256*

JOURNAL OF CONTAMINANT HYDROLOGY.
Elsevier Science B.V., P.O. Box 211, 1000 AE Amsterdam, Netherlands. TEL 31-20-4853911. FAX 31-20-4853598. *2969*

JOURNAL OF CONTEMPLATIVE PSYCHOTHERAPY.
Naropa Institute, 2130 Arapahoe Ave., Boulder, CO 80302. TEL 303-444-0202. *6124*

JOURNAL OF CONTEMPORARY HEALTH LAW AND POLICY.
Catholic University of America, Columbus School of Law, Washington, DC 20064. TEL 202-319-5732. FAX 202-319-4313. *4694*

JOURNAL OF CONTEMPORARY HISTORY.
Sage Publications Ltd., 6 Bonhill St., London EC2A 4PU, England. TEL 44-171-374-0645. FAX 44-171-374-8741. *3502*

JOURNAL OF CONTEMPORARY NEUROLOGY.
M I T Press, 5 Cambridge Center, Cambridge, MA 02142. TEL 617-253-2889. FAX 617-577-1545. *5073*

JOURNAL OF CONTEMPORARY PSYCHOTHERAPY.
Human Sciences Press, Inc., 233 Spring St., New York, NY 10013-1578. TEL 212-620-8000. FAX 212-463-0742. *6124*

JOURNAL OF CONTEMPORARY RELIGION.
Carfax Publishing Co., P.O. Box 25, Abingdon, Oxon. OX14 3UE, England. TEL 44-1235-401000. FAX 44-1235-401550. *6348*

JOURNAL OF CONTINGENCIES AND CRISIS MANAGEMENT.
Blackwell Publishers Ltd., 108 Cowley Rd., Oxford OX4 1JF, England. TEL 44-1865-791100. FAX 44-1865-791347. *1487*

JOURNAL OF CONTINUING EDUCATION IN NURSING.
Slack, Inc., 6900 Grove Rd., Thorofare, NJ 08086-9447. TEL 609-848-1000. FAX 609-853-5991. *4936*

JOURNAL OF CONTINUING EDUCATION IN THE HEALTH PROFESSIONS.
Decker Periodicals, P.O. Box 620, LCD 1, Hamilton, ON L8N 3K7, Canada. TEL 905-522-7017. FAX 905-522-7839. *4694*

JOURNAL OF CONTINUING HIGHER EDUCATION.
Association for Continuing Higher Education (University Park), 506 Keller Bldg., University Park, PA 16802. TEL 814-863-7752. FAX 814-863-2765. *2511*

JOURNAL OF CONTROLLED RELEASE.
Elsevier Science B.V., P.O. Box 211, 1000 AE Amsterdam, Netherlands. TEL 31-20-4853911. FAX 31-20-4853598. *5671*

JOURNAL OF COORDINATION CHEMISTRY.
Gordon and Breach - Harwood Academic, Amsteldisk 166, 1st Fl., 1079 LH Amsterdam, Netherlands. *1755*

JOURNAL OF CORPORATE FINANCE.
North-Holland, P.O. Box 211, 1000 AE Amsterdam, Netherlands. TEL 31-20-4853911. FAX 31-20-4853598. *1149*

JOURNAL OF CORRECTIONAL HEALTH CARE.
National Commission on Correctional Health Care, 2105 N. Southport, Ste. 200, Chicago, IL 60614-4017. TEL 773-528-0818. FAX 773-528-4915. *4694*

JOURNAL OF COST ANALYSIS.
Society of Cost Estimating and Analysis, 101 S. Whiting St., Ste. 201, Alexandria, VA 22304. TEL 703-751-8069. FAX 703-461-7328. *1093*

JOURNAL OF COUNSELING PSYCHOLOGY.
American Psychological Association, 750 First St., N.E., Washington, DC 20002-4242. TEL 202-336-5600. FAX 202-336-5568. *6124*

JOURNAL OF COUPLES THERAPY.
Haworth Press, Inc., 10 Alice St., Binghamton, NY 13904. TEL 607-722-5857. FAX 607-722-6362. *6124*

JOURNAL OF CRANIO-MAXILLOFACIAL TRAUMA.
Montage Media Corp., 1000 Wyckoff Ave., Mahwah, NJ 07430. TEL 201-236-0700. FAX 201-236-1339. *5144*

JOURNAL OF CRANIOFACIAL GENETICS AND DEVELOPMENTAL BIOLOGY.
Munksgaard International Publishers Ltd., P.O. Box 2148, DK-1016 Copenhagen K, Denmark. TEL 45-33-127030. FAX 45-33-129387. *772*

JOURNAL OF CRANIOFACIAL SURGERY.
Lippincott - Raven Publishers, 227 E. Washington Sq., Philadelphia, PA 19106. TEL 215-238-4200. FAX 215-238-4227. *5144*

JOURNAL OF CRIMINAL JUSTICE.
Elsevier Science Ltd., Pergamon, P.O. Box 800, Kidlington, Oxford, OX5 1DX, England. TEL 44-1865-843000. FAX 44-1865-843010. *4092*

JOURNAL OF CRIMINAL JUSTICE AND POPULAR CULTURE.
State University of New York at Albany, School of Criminal Justice, 135 Western Ave., Albany, NY 12222. TEL 518-442-5210. *4092*

JOURNAL OF CRITICAL CARE.
W.B. Saunders Co., Curtis Center, 3rd Fl., Independence Sq. W., Philadelphia, PA 19106-3399. TEL 215-238-7800. FAX 215-238-6445. *5010*

THE JOURNAL OF CRITICAL ILLNESS.
Cliggott Publishing Co., 55 Holly Hill Lane, Box 4010, Greenwich, CT 06831. TEL 203-661-0600. *4694*

JOURNAL OF CROSS-CULTURAL GERONTOLOGY.
Kluwer Academic Publishers, Postbus 17, 3300 AA Dordrecht, Netherlands. TEL 31-78-6392392. FAX 31-78-6392254. *3439*

JOURNAL OF CRUSTACEAN BIOLOGY.
Crustacean Society, 810 E. 10th St., Box 1897, Lawrence, KS 66044. TEL 913-843-1221. FAX 913-843-1274. *839*

JOURNAL OF CRYPTOLOGY.
Springer-Verlag, Science Journals, 175 Fifth Ave., New York, NY 10010. TEL 212-460-1500. FAX 212-474-6272. *4582*

JOURNAL OF CRYSTAL GROWTH.
North-Holland, P.O. Box 211, 1000 AE Amsterdam, Netherlands. TEL 31-20-4853911. FAX 31-20-4853598. *1802*

JOURNAL OF CULTURAL DIVERSITY.
Tucker Publications, Inc., Box 580, Lisle, IL 60532. TEL 630-969-3809. FAX 630-969-3895. *4936*

JOURNAL OF CULTURAL ECONOMICS.
Kluwer Academic Publishers, Postbus 17, 3300 AA Dordrecht, Netherlands. TEL 31-78-6392392. FAX 31-78-6392254. *1306*

JOURNAL OF CURRICULUM STUDIES.
Taylor & Francis Ltd., Rankine Rd., Basingstoke, Hants. RG24 8PR, England. TEL 44-1256-840366. FAX 44-1256-479438. *2607*

JOURNAL OF CUSTOMER SERVICE IN MARKETING & MANAGEMENT.
Haworth Press, Inc., 10 Alice St., Binghamton, NY 13904. TEL 607-722-5857. FAX 607-722-6362. *976*

JOURNAL OF CUTANEOUS PATHOLOGY.
Munksgaard International Publishers Ltd., 35 Noerre Soegade, P.O. Box 2148, DK-1016 Copenhagen K, Denmark. TEL 45-33-127030. FAX 45-33-129387. *4879*

JOURNAL OF CYTOLOGY AND GENETICS.
Society of Cytologists and Geneticists, Department of Botany, Bangalore University, Bangalore 560 056, India. TEL 91-81-3355036. *772*

JOURNAL OF DAIRY SCIENCE.
American Dairy Science Association, 1111 N. Dunlap Ave., Savoy, IL 61874. TEL 217-356-3182. FAX 217-398-4119. *256*

THE JOURNAL OF DATA MINING AND KNOWLEDGE DISCOVERY.
Kluwer Academic Publishers Boston, Box 358, Accord Sta., Hingham, MA 02018-0358. TEL 617-871-6600. FAX 617-871-6528. *2184*

JOURNAL OF DATABASE MANAGEMENT.
Idea Group Publishing, 1331 E. Chocolate Ave., Hershey, PA 17033-1751. TEL 717-541-9150. FAX 717-541-9159. *2167*

THE JOURNAL OF DATABASE MARKETING.
Henry Stewart Publications, Russell House, 28-30 Little Russell St., London WC1A 2HN, England. TEL 44-171-404-3040. FAX 44-171-404-2081. *1202*

THE JOURNAL OF DEAF STUDIES AND DEAF EDUCATION.
Oxford University Press, Journals, 2001 Evans Rd., Cary, NC 27513. TEL 919-677-0977. FAX 919-677-1714. *3463*

THE JOURNAL OF DEMENTIA CARE.
Hawker Publications, 140 Battersea Park Rd., London SW11 4NB, England. TEL 44-171-720-2108. FAX 44-171-498-3023. *5073*

JOURNAL OF DENTAL HYGIENE.
American Dental Hygienists' Association, 444 N. Michigan Ave., Ste. 3400, Chicago, IL 60611. TEL 312-440-8900. FAX 312-440-8929. *4861*

JOURNAL OF DENTAL RESEARCH.
American Association for Dental Research, 1619 Duke St., Alexandria, VA 22314-3406. TEL 703-548-0066. FAX 703-548-1883. *4861*

JOURNAL OF DENTISTRY.
Elsevier Science Ltd., P.O. Box 800, Kidlington, Oxford OX5 1DX, England. TEL 44-1865-843000. FAX 44-1865-843010. *4861*

JOURNAL OF DENTISTRY FOR CHILDREN.
American Society of Dentistry for Children, 875 N. Michigan Ave., Ste. 4040, Chicago, IL 60611-1901. TEL 312-943-1244. FAX 312-943-5341. *4861*

JOURNAL OF DERMATOLOGICAL SCIENCE.
Elsevier Science Ireland Ltd., P.O. Box 85, Limerick, Ireland. TEL 353-61-471944. FAX 353-61-472144. *4879*

JOURNAL OF DERMATOLOGICAL TREATMENT.
Martin Dunitz Ltd., 7-9 Pratt St., Camden, London NW1 0AE, England. TEL 44-171-4822202. FAX 44-171-2670159. *4879*

JOURNAL OF DESIGN & MANUFACTURING.
Chapman & Hall, Journals Department 2-6 Boundary Row, London SE1 8HN, England. TEL 44-171-8650066. FAX 44-171-5229623. *2889*

JOURNAL OF DEVELOPING AREAS.
Western Illinois University, Morgan Hall 232, Macomb, IL 61455. TEL 309-298-1108. FAX 309-298-2865. *1363*

JOURNAL OF DEVELOPING SOCIETIES.
E.J. Brill, P.O. Box 9000, 2300 PA Leiden, Netherlands. TEL 31-71-5353500. FAX 31-71-5317532. *6622*

JOURNAL OF DEVELOPMENT ECONOMICS.
North-Holland, P.O. Box 211, 1000 AE Amsterdam, Netherlands. TEL 31-20-4853911. FAX 31-20-4853598. *1363*

THE JOURNAL OF DEVELOPMENT STUDIES.
Frank Cass, Newbury House, 890-900 Eastern Ave., Newbury Park, Ilford, Essex IG2 7HH, England. TEL 44-181-599-8866. FAX 44-181-599-0984. *1364*

JOURNAL OF DEVELOPMENTAL AND BEHAVIORAL PEDIATRICS.
Williams & Wilkins, 351 W. Camden St., Baltimore, MD 21201-2436. TEL 410-528-4068. FAX 410-528-4452. *5032*

JOURNAL OF DEVELOPMENTAL AND PHYSICAL DISABILITIES.
Plenum Publishing Corp., 233 Spring St., New York, NY 10013-1578. TEL 212-620-8000. FAX 212-463-0742. *3455*

JOURNAL OF DEVELOPMENTAL EDUCATION.
Appalachian State University, National Center for Developmental Education, Boone, NC 28608. TEL 704-262-2876. FAX 704-262-2128. *2546*

JOURNAL OF DHARMA.
Dharmaram College, Centre for the Study of World Religions, Bangalore 560 029, India. TEL 81-80-5536866. FAX 81-80-5536046. *6348*

JOURNAL OF DIABETES AND ITS COMPLICATIONS.
Elsevier Science Inc., Box 945, New York, NY 10159-0945. TEL 212-633-3730. FAX 212-633-3680. *4890*

JOURNAL OF DIAGNOSTIC MEDICAL SONOGRAPHY.
Lippincott - Raven Publishers, 227 E. Washington Sq., Philadelphia, PA 19106. TEL 215-238-4200. FAX 215-238-4227. *5108*

JOURNAL OF DIARRHOEAL DISEASES RESEARCH.
International Centre for Diarrhoeal Disease Research, Bangladesh, G.P.O. Box 128, Dhaka 1000, Bangladesh. TEL 880-2-871751. FAX 880-2-883116. *4781*

JOURNAL OF DIFFERENTIAL EQUATIONS.
Academic Press, Inc., Journal Division, 525 B St., Ste. 1900, San Diego, CA 92101-4495. TEL 619-230-1840. FAX 619-699-6800. *4582*

JOURNAL OF DIGITAL IMAGING.
W.B. Saunders Co., The Curtis Center, 3rd Fl., Independence Sq. W., Philadelphia, PA 19106-3399. TEL 215-238-7800. FAX 215-238-6445. *5109*

JOURNAL OF DISABILITY POLICY STUDIES.
University of Arkansas, Department of Rehabilitation Education and Research, 346 N. West Ave., Fayetteville, AR 72701. TEL 501-575-3656. FAX 501-575-3253. *3455*

JOURNAL OF DISPERSION SCIENCE AND TECHNOLOGY.
Marcel Dekker Journals, 270 Madison Ave., New York, NY 10016. TEL 212-696-9000. FAX 212-685-4540. *1830*

JOURNAL OF DISTANCE EDUCATION.
Canadian Association for Distance Education, One Stewart St., Ste. 205, Ottawa, ON K1N 6H7, Canada. FAX 613-230-2746. *2607*

JOURNAL OF DIVORCE & REMARRIAGE.
Haworth Press, Inc., 10 Alice St., Binghamton, NY 13904. TEL 607-722-5857. FAX 607-722-6362. *4626*

JOURNAL OF DOCUMENTATION.
Aslib, Association for Information Management, Publications Department, Information House, 20-24 Old St., London EC1V 9AP, England. TEL 44-171-253-4488. FAX 44-171-430-0514. *4188*

JOURNAL OF DRUG EDUCATION.
Baywood Publishing Co., Inc., 26 Austin Ave., Box 337, Amityville, NY 11701. TEL 516-691-1270. FAX 516-691-1770. *2302*

JOURNAL OF DRUG ISSUES.
Journal of Drug Issues Inc., Box 4021, Leon Sta., Tallahassee, FL 32315. TEL 904-668-6669. *2303*

JOURNAL OF DYNAMIC SYSTEMS, MEASUREMENT AND CONTROL.
American Society of Mechanical Engineers, 22 Law Dr., Fairfield, NJ 07007-2900. TEL 873-882-1167. FAX 973-882-1717. *2861*

JOURNAL OF DYNAMICAL AND CONTROL SYSTEMS.
Plenum Publishing Corp., 233 Spring St., New York, NY 10013-1578. TEL 212-620-8000. FAX 212-463-0742. *2877*

JOURNAL OF DYNAMICS AND DIFFERENTIAL EQUATIONS.
Plenum Publishing Corp., 233 Spring St., New York, NY 10013-1578. TEL 212-620-8000. FAX 212-463-0742. *4582*

THE JOURNAL OF E C T.
Lippincott - Raven Publishers, 227 E. Washington Sq., Philadelphia, PA 19106. TEL 215-238-4200. FAX 215-238-4227. *5073*

JOURNAL OF EARLY ADOLESCENCE.
Sage Publications, Inc., 2455 Teller Rd., Thousand Oaks, CA 91320. TEL 805-499-0721. FAX 805-499-0871. *1849*

JOURNAL OF EARLY CHRISTIAN STUDIES.
Johns Hopkins University Press, Journals Publishing Division, 2715 N. Charles St., Ste. 750, Baltimore, MD 21218-4319. TEL 410-516-6987. FAX 410-516-6968. *6348*

JOURNAL OF EARLY MODERN HISTORY.
E.J. Brill, P.O. Box 9000, 2300 PA Leiden, Netherlands. TEL 31-71-5353566. FAX 31-71-5317532. *3502*

JOURNAL OF EARLY SOUTHERN DECORATIVE ARTS.
Museum of Early Southern Decorative Arts, P.O. Box 10310, Winston-Salem, NC 27108-0310. TEL 910-721-7360. FAX 910-721-7367. *341*

JOURNAL OF EARTHQUAKE ENGINEERING.
World Scientific Publishing Co. Pte. Ltd., Farrer Rd., P.O. Box 128, Singapore 9128, Singapore. TEL 65-3825663. FAX 65-3825919. *2790*

JOURNAL OF EAST AFRICAN NATURAL HISTORY.
East Africa Natural History Society, P.O. Box 44486, Nairobi, Kenya. TEL 254-2-749957. FAX 254-2-741049. *608*

JOURNAL OF EAST ASIAN AFFAIRS.
Research Institute for International Affairs, SI. Kangnam, P.O. Box 1838, Seoul 135-618, S. Korea. TEL 82-2-565-3557. FAX 82-2-565-3558. *6023*

JOURNAL OF EAST ASIAN LINGUISTICS.
Kluwer Academic Publishers, Postbus 17, 3300 AA Dordrecht, Netherlands. TEL 31-78-6392392. FAX 31-78-6392254. *4267*

JOURNAL OF EAST - WEST BUSINESS.
Haworth Press, Inc., 10 Alice St., Binghamton, NY 13904. TEL 607-722-5857. FAX 607-722-6362. *1306*

JOURNAL OF EASTERN AFRICAN RESEARCH & DEVELOPMENT.
Gideon S. Were Press, P.O. Box 10622, Nairobi, Kenya. TEL 254-2-331135. FAX 254-2-331135. *3527*

JOURNAL OF ECOBIOLOGY.
Palani Paramount Publications, 69D, Anna Nagar, Palani 624 602, India. TEL 91-4545-42332. FAX 91-4545-42199. *608*

JOURNAL OF ECOLOGY.
Blackwell Science Ltd., Osney Mead, Oxford OX2 0EL, England. TEL 44-1865-206206. FAX 44-1865-721205. *608*

JOURNAL OF ECONOMETRICS.
Elsevier Science S.A., P.O. Box 564, CH-1001 Lausanne 1, Switzerland. TEL 41-21-3207381. FAX 41-21-3235444. *1306*

JOURNAL OF ECONOMIC BEHAVIOR & ORGANIZATION.
North-Holland, P.O. Box 211, 1000 AE Amsterdam, Netherlands. TEL 31-20-4853911. FAX 31-20-4853598. *976*

JOURNAL OF ECONOMIC DYNAMICS AND CONTROL.
North-Holland, P.O. Box 211, 1000 AE Amsterdam, Netherlands. TEL 31-20-4853911. FAX 31-20-4853598. *1307*

THE JOURNAL OF ECONOMIC EDUCATION.
Heldref Publications, 1319 18th St., N.W., Washington, DC 20036-1802. TEL 202-296-6267. FAX 202-296-5149. *976*

JOURNAL OF ECONOMIC ENTOMOLOGY.
Entomological Society of America, 9301 Annapolis Rd., Lanham, MD 20706. TEL 301-731-4535. FAX 301-731-4538. *756*

JOURNAL OF ECONOMIC GROWTH.
Kluwer Academic Publishers Boston, Box 358, Accord Sta., Hingham, MA 02018-0358. TEL 617-871-6600. FAX 617-871-6528. *1307*

JOURNAL OF ECONOMIC INTEGRATION.
Sejong University, Institute for International Economics, Seongdong-ku, Seoul 143-747, S. Korea. TEL 81-2-460-0338. FAX 82-2-460-0338. *976*

JOURNAL OF ECONOMIC METHODOLOGY.
Routledge, 11 New Fetter Ln., London EC4P 4EE, England. TEL 44-171-583-9855. FAX 44-171-842-2298. *977*

JOURNAL OF ECONOMIC PSYCHOLOGY.
North-Holland, P.O. Box 211, 1000 AE Amsterdam, Netherlands. TEL 31-20-4853911. FAX 31-20-4853598. *1533*

JOURNAL OF ECONOMIC SURVEYS.
Blackwell Publishers Ltd., 108 Cowley Rd., Oxford OX4 1JF, England. TEL 44-1865-791100. FAX 44-1865-791347. *977*

JOURNAL OF ECONOMICS AND BUSINESS.
Elsevier Science Inc., Box 945, New York, NY 10159-0945. TEL 212-633-3730. FAX 212-633-3680. *977*

JOURNAL OF ECONOMICS AND FINANCE.
University of Southern Mississippi, Southern Sta., Box 5076, Hattiesburg, MS 39406-5076. TEL 601-266-4691. FAX 601-266-5992. *977*

JOURNAL OF ECONOMICS & MANAGEMENT STRATEGY.
M I T Press, 5 Cambridge Center, Cambridge, MA 02142. TEL 617-253-2889. FAX 617-577-1545. *1307*

JOURNAL OF ECOTOXICOLOGY & ENVIRONMENTAL MONITORING.
Palani Paramount Publications, 69D, Anna Nagar, Palani 624 602, India. TEL 91-4545-42332. FAX 91-4545-42199. *2979*

JOURNAL OF ECUMENICAL STUDIES.
Temple University, 022-38, 1114 W. Berks St., Rm. 511, Philadelphia, PA 19122-6090. TEL 215-204-7714. FAX 215-204-4569. *6348*

JOURNAL OF EDUCATION AND PSYCHOLOGY.
Sardar Patel University, Department of Education, Vallabh Vidyanagar, Pin 388 120, India. TEL 91-2792-30379. *2455*

JOURNAL OF EDUCATION FINANCE.
A S B O International, 11461 N. Shore Dr., Reston, VA 20190. TEL 703-478-0405. FAX 703-478-0205. *2573*

JOURNAL OF EDUCATION FOR BUSINESS.
Heldref Publications, 1319 18th St., N.W., Washington, DC 20036-1802. TEL 202-296-6267. FAX 202-296-5149. *977*

JOURNAL OF EDUCATION FOR LIBRARY AND INFORMATION SCIENCE.
Association for Library and Information Science Education, Box 7640, Arlington, VA 22207. *4188*

JOURNAL OF EDUCATION FOR STUDENTS PLACED AT RISK.
Lawrence Erlbaum Associates, Inc., 10 Industrial Ave., Mahwah, NJ 07430-2262. TEL 201-236-9500. FAX 201-236-0072. *2607*

JOURNAL OF EDUCATION FOR TEACHING.
Carfax Publishing Co., P.O. Box 25, Abingdon, Oxon. OX14 3UE, England. TEL 44-1235-401000. FAX 44-1235-401550. *2546*

JOURNAL OF EDUCATION POLICY.
Taylor & Francis Ltd., Rankine Rd., Basingstoke, Hants RG24 8PR, England. TEL 44-1256-840366. FAX 44-1256-479438. *2573*

JOURNAL OF EDUCATIONAL AND BEHAVIORAL STATISTICS.
American Educational Research Association, 1230 17th St., N.W., Washington, DC 20036-3078. TEL 202-223-9485. FAX 202-775-1824. *2501*

JOURNAL OF EDUCATIONAL AND PSYCHOLOGICAL CONSULTATION.
Lawrence Erlbaum Associates, Inc., 10 Industrial Dr., Mahwah, NJ 07430-2262. TEL 201-236-9500. FAX 201-236-0072. *2455*

JOURNAL OF EDUCATIONAL COMPUTING RESEARCH.
Baywood Publishing Co., Inc., 26 Austin Ave., Box 337, Amityville, NY 11701. TEL 516-691-1270. FAX 516-691-1770. *2518*

JOURNAL OF EDUCATIONAL MEASUREMENT.
National Council on Measurement in Education, 1230 17th St., N.W., Washington, DC 20036-3078. TEL 202-223-9318. FAX 202-775-1824. *2455*

JOURNAL OF EDUCATIONAL MEDIA.
Carfax Publishing Co., P.O. Box 25, Abingdon, Oxon. OX14 3UE, England. TEL 44-1235-401000. FAX 44-1235-401550. *2052*

JOURNAL OF EDUCATIONAL MULTIMEDIA AND HYPERMEDIA.
Association for the Advancement of Computing in Education, Box 2966, Charlottesville, VA 22902-2966. TEL 804-973-3987. FAX 804-973-3987. *2518*

JOURNAL OF EDUCATIONAL PLANNING AND ADMINISTRATION.
National Institute of Educational Planning and Administration, 17-B, Sri Aurobindo Marg, New Delhi 110 016, India. TEL 91-11-66-1938. FAX 91-11-685-3041. *2574*

JOURNAL OF EDUCATIONAL PSYCHOLOGY.
American Psychological Association, 750 First St., N.E., Washington, DC 20002-4242. TEL 202-336-5600. FAX 202-336-5568. *6125*

JOURNAL OF EDUCATIONAL RELATIONS.
Educational Communication Center, Box 657, 1830 Walnut St., Camp Hill, PA 17011. TEL 717-761-6620. *1996*

THE JOURNAL OF EDUCATIONAL RESEARCH.
Heldref Publications, 1319 18th St., N.W., Washington, DC 20036-1802. TEL 202-296-6267. FAX 202-296-5149. *2455*

JOURNAL OF EDUCATIONAL TECHNOLOGY SYSTEMS.
Baywood Publishing Co., Inc., 26 Austin Ave., Box 337, Amityville, NY 11701. TEL 516-691-1270. FAX 516-691-1770. *2518*

JOURNAL OF EGYPTIAN ARCHAEOLOGY.
Egypt Exploration Society, 3 Doughty Mews, London WC1N 2PG, England. TEL 44-171-242-1880. FAX 44-171-404-6118. *368*

JOURNAL OF ELASTICITY.
Kluwer Academic Publishers, Postbus 17, 3300 AA Dordrecht, Netherlands. TEL 31-78-6392392. FAX 31-78-6392254. *2862*

JOURNAL OF ELASTOMERS AND PLASTICS.
Technomic Publishing Co. Inc., 851 New Holland Ave., Box 3535, Lancaster, PA 17604. TEL 717-291-5609. FAX 717-295-4538. *5879*

JOURNAL OF ELDER ABUSE & NEGLECT.
Haworth Press, Inc., 10 Alice St., Binghamton, NY 13904. TEL 607-722-5857. FAX 607-722-6362. *3439*

JOURNAL OF ELECTROANALYTICAL CHEMISTRY.
Elsevier Science S.A., P.O. Box 564, CH-1001 Lausanne 1, Switzerland. TEL 41-21-3207381. FAX 41-21-3235444. *1792*

JOURNAL OF ELECTROCARDIOLOGY.
Churchill Livingstone, 650 Ave. of the Americas, New York, NY 10011. TEL 212-206-5040. FAX 212-727-7808. *4820*

JOURNAL OF ELECTROCERAMICS.
Kluwer Academic Publishers Boston, Box 358, Accord Sta., Hingham, MA 02018-0358. TEL 617-871-6600. FAX 617-871-6528. *2862*

JOURNAL OF ELECTROMAGNETIC WAVES AND APPLICATIONS.
V S P, P.O. Box 346, 3700 AH Zeist, Netherlands. TEL 31-30-6925790. FAX 31-30-6932081. *5809*

JOURNAL OF ELECTROMYOGRAPHY AND KINESIOLOGY.
Elsevier Science Ltd., P.O. BOx 800, Kidlington, Oxford OX2 8DP, England. TEL 44-1865-843000. FAX 44-1865-843010. *675*

JOURNAL OF ELECTRON SPECTROSCOPY AND RELATED PHENOMENA.
Elsevier Science B.V., P.O. Box 211, 1000 AE Amsterdam, Netherlands. TEL 31-20-4853911. FAX 31-20-4853598. *5862*

JOURNAL OF ELECTRONIC PACKAGING.
American Society of Mechanical Engineers, 22 Law Dr., Fairfield, NJ 07007-2900. TEL 973-882-1167. FAX 973-882-1717. *2644*

JOURNAL OF ELECTRONIC TESTING.
Kluwer Academic Publishers Boston, Box 358, Accord Sta., Hingham, MA 02018-0358. TEL 617-871-6600. FAX 617-871-6528. *2837*

JOURNAL OF ELECTRONICS (CHINA).
Science Press, Marketing and Sales Department, 16 Donghuangchenggen North St., Beijing 100717, People's Republic of China. TEL 4010642. FAX 4019810. *2644*

JOURNAL OF ELECTRONICS MANUFACTURING.
World Scientific Publishing Co. Pte. Ltd., Farrer Rd., P.O. Box 128, Singapore 9128, Singapore. TEL 65-3825663. FAX 65-3825919. *2644*

JOURNAL OF ELECTROPHYSIOLOGICAL TECHNOLOGY.
Electrophysiological Technologists' Association, c/o E.E.G. Department, St. Bartholomew's Hospital, W. Smithfield, London EC1A 7BE, England. TEL 44-171-601-8859. FAX 44-171-601-7875. *817*

JOURNAL OF ELECTROSTATICS.
Elsevier Science B.V., P.O. Box 211, 1000 AE Amsterdam, Netherlands. TEL 31-20-4853911. FAX 31-20-4853598. *2837*

JOURNAL OF ELECTROTOPOGRAPHY.
Electrotopograph Corporation, Box 98, Eldred, PA 16731. TEL 814-225-3296. *5809*

JOURNAL OF EMERGENCY MEDICINE.
Elsevier Science Inc., Box 945, New York, NY 10159-0945. TEL 212-633-3730. FAX 212-633-3680. *5010*

JOURNAL OF EMERGING MARKETS.
Center for Global Education, St. John's University, 8000 Utopia Pkwy., Jamaica, New York, NY 11439. TEL 718-990-1951. FAX 718-380-8934. *1149*

JOURNAL OF EMOTIONAL AND BEHAVIORAL DISORDERS.
Pro-Ed Inc., 8700 Shoal Creek Blvd., Austin, TX 78757-6897. TEL 512-451-3246. FAX 512-451-8542. *5073*

JOURNAL OF EMPIRICAL FINANCE.
North-Holland, P.O. Box 211, 1000 AE Amsterdam, Netherlands. TEL 31-20-4853911. FAX 31-20-4853598. *1149*

JOURNAL OF EMPIRICAL GENERALISATIONS IN MARKETING SCIENCE.
University of South Australia, North Terrace, Marketing Science Centre, Adelaide, S.A. 5001, Australia. TEL 61-8-3020715. FAX 61-8-3020442. *1533*

JOURNAL OF EMPLOYEE OWNERSHIP LAW AND FINANCE.
National Center for Employee Ownership, Inc., 1201 Martin Luther King Jr. Way, Oakland, CA 94612. TEL 510-272-9461. FAX 510-272-9510. *3969*

JOURNAL OF END USER COMPUTING.
Idea Group Publishing, 1331 E. Chocolate Ave., Hershey, PA 17033-1117. TEL 717-541-9150. FAX 717-541-9159. *2189*

THE JOURNAL OF ENDODONTICS.
Williams & Wilkins, 351 W. Camden St., Baltimore, MD 21201-2436. TEL 410-528-4068. FAX 410-528-4452. *4861*

JOURNAL OF ENDOUROLOGY.
Mary Ann Liebert, Inc. Publishers, 2 Madison Ave., Larchmont, NY 10538. TEL 914-834-3100. FAX 914-834-3688. *5162*

JOURNAL OF ENDOVASCULAR SURGERY.
Futura Publishing Company, Inc., 135 Bedford Rd., Box 418, Armonk, NY 10504-0418. TEL 914-273-1014. FAX 914-273-1015. *5145*

JOURNAL OF ENERGY AND NATURAL RESOURCES LAW.
Kluwer Law International, Postbus 85889, 2508 CN The Hague, Netherlands. TEL 31-70-3081500. FAX 31-70-3081515. *3969*

JOURNAL OF ENERGY, HEAT AND MASS TRANSFER.
Regional Centre for Energy, Heat and Mass Transfer for Asia and the Pacific, Madras 60036, India. TEL 91-44-235-1365. FAX 91-44-235-3094. *2673*

JOURNAL OF ENERGY IN SOUTHERN AFRICA.
Energy Research Institute, Information Service, P.O. Box 207, Plumstead 7801, South Africa. TEL 27-21-705-0120. FAX 27-21-705-6266. *2673*

JOURNAL OF ENERGY RESOURCES TECHNOLOGY.
American Society of Mechanical Engineers, 22 Law Dr., Fairfield, NJ 07007-2900. TEL 973-882-1167. FAX 973-882-1717. *2673*

JOURNAL OF ENGINEERING AND TECHNOLOGY MANAGEMENT.
Elsevier Science B.V., P.O. Box 211, 1000 AE Amsterdam, Netherlands. TEL 31-20-4853911. FAX 31-20-4853598. *1487*

JOURNAL OF ENGINEERING DESIGN.
Carfax Publishing Co., P.O. Box 25, Abingdon, Oxon. OX14 3UE, England. TEL 44-1235-401000. FAX 44-1235-401550. *2728*

JOURNAL OF ENGINEERING MATERIALS AND TECHNOLOGY.
American Society of Mechanical Engineers, 22 Law Dr., Fairfield, NJ 07007-2900. TEL 973-882-1167. FAX 973-882-1717. *2862*

JOURNAL OF ENGINEERING MATHEMATICS.
Kluwer Academic Publishers, Postbus 17, 3300 AA Dordrecht, Netherlands. TEL 31-78-6392392. FAX 31-78-6392254. *2728*

JOURNAL OF ENGINEERING MECHANICS.
American Society of Civil Engineers, 345 E. 47th St., New York, NY 10017-2398. TEL 212-705-7288. FAX 212-980-4681. *2790*

JOURNAL OF ENGINEERING TECHNOLOGY.
American Society for Engineering Education, Engineering Technology Division, c/o Cecil A. Harrison, Ed., Univ. of Southern Mississippi, Box 5137, Hattiesburg, MS 39406-5137. TEL 601-266-5628. FAX 601-266-5717. *2728*

JOURNAL OF ENGLISH AND GERMANIC PHILOLOGY.
University of Illinois Press, 1325 S. Oak St., Champaign, IL 61820. TEL 217-333-0950. FAX 217-244-8082. *4267*

JOURNAL OF ENTOMOLOGICAL SCIENCE.
Georgia Entomological Society, Inc., c/o G. David Buntin, Department of Entomology, Georgia Experiment Station, Griffin, GA 30223-1797. TEL 404-228-7288. FAX 404-228-7287. *756*

JOURNAL OF ENTREPRENEURSHIP.
Sage Publications India Pvt. Ltd., P.O. Box 4215, New Delhi 110 048, India. TEL 91-11-644-4958. FAX 91-11-647-2426. *1487*

REFEREED SERIALS

JOURNAL OF ENVIRONMENTAL BIOLOGY.
711, Civil Lines (South), Muzaffarnagar 251 001, India. TEL 91-131-405306. *2937*

THE JOURNAL OF ENVIRONMENTAL EDUCATION.
Heldref Publications, 1319 Eighteenth St., N.W., Washington, DC 20036-1802. TEL 202-296-6267. *2937*

JOURNAL OF ENVIRONMENTAL ENGINEERING.
American Society of Civil Engineers, 345 E. 47th St., New York, NY 10017-2398. TEL 212-705-7288. FAX 212-980-4681. *2937*

JOURNAL OF ENVIRONMENTAL HEALTH.
National Environmental Health Association, 720 S. Colorado Blvd., S. Tower, Ste. 970, Denver, CO 80246. TEL 303-756-9090. FAX 303-691-9490. *2937*

JOURNAL OF ENVIRONMENTAL HORTICULTURE.
Horticultural Research Institute, 1250 I St., N.W., Ste. 500, Washington, DC 20005. TEL 202-789-2900. FAX 202-789-1893. *3196*

JOURNAL OF ENVIRONMENTAL PATHOLOGY, TOXICOLOGY AND ONCOLOGY.
Begell House Inc., 79 Madison Ave., Ste. 1205, New York, NY 10016-7892. TEL 212-725-1999. FAX 212-213-8368. *2979*

JOURNAL OF ENVIRONMENTAL PLANNING AND MANAGEMENT.
Carfax Publishing Co., P.O. Box 25, Abingdon, Oxon. OX14 3UE, England. TEL 44-1235-401000. FAX 44-1235-401550. *3751*

JOURNAL OF ENVIRONMENTAL POLYMER DEGRADATION.
Plenum Publishing Corp., 233 Spring St., New York, NY 10013-1578. TEL 212-620-8000. FAX 212-463-0742. *663*

JOURNAL OF ENVIRONMENTAL QUALITY.
American Society of Agronomy, Inc., 677 S. Segoe Rd., Madison, WI 53711. TEL 608-273-8080. FAX 608-273-2021. *2937*

JOURNAL OF ENVIRONMENTAL RADIOACTIVITY.
Elsevier Science Ltd., P.O. Box 800, Kidlington, Oxford OX5 1DX, England. TEL 44-1865-843000. FAX 44-1865-843010. *2938*

JOURNAL OF ENVIRONMENTAL SCIENCE AND HEALTH. PART A: ENVIRONMENTAL SCIENCE AND ENGINEERING AND TOXICOLOGY.
Marcel Dekker Journals, 270 Madison Ave., New York, NY 10016. TEL 212-696-9000. FAX 212-685-4540. *2979*

JOURNAL OF ENVIRONMENTAL SCIENCE AND HEALTH. PART B: PESTICIDES, FOOD CONTAMINANTS, AND AGRICULTURAL WASTES.
Marcel Dekker Journals, 270 Madison Ave., New York, NY 10016. TEL 212-696-9000. FAX 212-685-4540. *2938*

JOURNAL OF ENVIRONMENTAL SYSTEMS.
Baywood Publishing Co., Inc., 26 Austin Ave., Box 337, Amityville, NY 11701. TEL 516-691-1270. FAX 516-691-1770. *2938*

JOURNAL OF ENZYME INHIBITION.
Gordon and Breach - Harwood Academic, Amsteldisk 166, 1st Fl., 1079 LH Amsterdam, Netherlands. *663*

JOURNAL OF EPIDEMIOLOGY & COMMUNITY HEALTH.
B M J Publishing Group, B.M.A. House, Tavistock Sq., London WC1H 9JR, England. TEL 44-171-383-6270. FAX 44-171-383-6402. *4694*

JOURNAL OF EPILEPSY.
Elsevier Science inc., Box 945, New York, NY 10159-0945. TEL 212-633-3730. FAX 212-633-3680. *5073*

THE JOURNAL OF ETHICS.
Kluwer Academic Publishers, Postbus 17, 3300 AA Dordrecht, Netherlands. TEL 31-78-6392392. FAX 31-78-6392254. *5733*

JOURNAL OF ETHICS, LAW, AND AGING.
Springer Publishing Company, 536 Broadway, New York, NY 10012-3955. TEL 212-431-4370. FAX 212-941-7842. *3439*

JOURNAL OF ETHNOBIOLOGY.
Society of Ethnobiology, c/o Gayle Fritz, Anthropology - CB1114, Washington University, St. Louis, MO 63130-4899. TEL 314-935-8588. FAX 314-935-8535. *609*

JOURNAL OF ETHNOPHARMACOLOGY.
Elsevier Science Ireland Ltd., P.O. Box 85, Limerick, Ireland. TEL 353-61-471944. FAX 353-61-472144. *5671*

THE JOURNAL OF EUKARYOTIC MICROBIOLOGY.
Allen Press, Inc., 1041 New Hampshire Ave., Box 1897, Lawrence, KS 66044. TEL 913-843-1221. FAX 913-843-1274. *839*

JOURNAL OF EUROMARKETING.
Haworth Press, Inc., 10 Alice St., Binghamton, NY 13904. TEL 607-722-5857. FAX 607-722-6362. *1533*

JOURNAL OF EUROMED PHARMACY.
University of Malta, Department of Pharmacy, Msida, Malta. TEL 356-343764. FAX 356-340427. *5671*

JOURNAL OF EUROPEAN SOCIAL POLICY.
Sage Publications Ltd., 6 Bonhill St., London EC2A 4PU, England. TEL 44-171-374-0645. FAX 44-171-374-8741. *6023*

JOURNAL OF EVOLUTIONARY BIOCHEMISTRY AND PHYSIOLOGY.
Maik Nauka - Interperiodica, Mezhdunarodnyi Otdel, Ul. Profsoyuznaya, 90, 117864 Moscow, Russia. TEL 7-095-3360066. FAX 7-095-3360066. *663*

JOURNAL OF EXPERIMENTAL & THEORETICAL ARTIFICIAL INTELLIGENCE.
Taylor & Francis Ltd., 1 Gunpowder Sq., London EC4A 3DE, England. TEL 44-171-583-0490. FAX 44-171-583-0585. *2102*

JOURNAL OF EXPERIMENTAL BIOLOGY.
Company of Biologists Ltd., Bidder Bldg., 140 Cowley Rd., Cambridge CB4 4DL, England. TEL 44-1223-426164. FAX 44-1223-423353. *609*

JOURNAL OF EXPERIMENTAL CHILD PSYCHOLOGY.
Academic Press, Inc., Journal Division, 525 B St., Ste. 1900, San Diego, CA 92101-4495. TEL 619-230-1840. FAX 619-699-6800. *6125*

JOURNAL OF EXPERIMENTAL EDUCATION.
Heldref Publications, 1319 18th St., N.W., Washington, DC 20036-1802. TEL 202-296-6267. FAX 202-296-5149. *2608*

JOURNAL OF EXPERIMENTAL MARINE BIOLOGY AND ECOLOGY.
Elsevier Science B.V., P.O. Box 211, 1000 AE Amsterdam, Netherlands. TEL 31-20-4853911. FAX 31-20-4853598. *609*

JOURNAL OF EXPERIMENTAL MEDICINE.
Rockefeller University Press, 1114 First Ave., New York, NY 10021. TEL 212-327-8572. FAX 212-327-7944. *4898*

JOURNAL OF EXPERIMENTAL PSYCHOLOGY: ANIMAL BEHAVIOR PROCESSES.
American Psychological Association, 750 First St., N.E., Washington, DC 20002-4242. TEL 202-336-5600. FAX 202-336-5568. *6125*

JOURNAL OF EXPERIMENTAL PSYCHOLOGY: APPLIED.
American Psychological Association, 750 First St., N.E., Washington, DC 20002-4242. TEL 202-336-5600. FAX 202-336-5568. *6125*

JOURNAL OF EXPERIMENTAL PSYCHOLOGY: GENERAL.
American Psychological Association, 750 First St., N.E., Washington, DC 20002-4242. TEL 202-336-5600. FAX 202-336-5568. *6125*

JOURNAL OF EXPERIMENTAL PSYCHOLOGY: HUMAN PERCEPTION AND PERFORMANCE.
American Psychological Association, 750 First St., N.E., Washington, DC 20002-4242. TEL 202-336-5600. FAX 202-336-5568. *6126*

JOURNAL OF EXPERIMENTAL PSYCHOLOGY: LEARNING, MEMORY, AND COGNITION.
American Psychological Association, 750 First St., N.E., Washington, DC 20002-4242. TEL 202-336-5600. FAX 202-336-5568. *6126*

JOURNAL OF EXPERIMENTAL SOCIAL PSYCHOLOGY.
Academic Press, Inc., Journal Division, 525 B St., Ste. 1900, San Diego, CA 92101-4495. TEL 619-230-1840. FAX 619-699-6800. *6126*

JOURNAL OF EXPERIMENTAL THERAPEUTICS AND ONCOLOGY.
Rapid Science Publishers, 2-6 Boundary Row, London SE1 8HN, England. TEL 44-171-865-0198. FAX 44-171-410-6600. *4981*

JOURNAL OF EXPERIMENTAL ZOOLOGY.
John Wiley & Sons, Inc., Journals, 605 Third Ave., New York, NY 10158. TEL 212-850-6645. FAX 212-850-6021. *839*

JOURNAL OF EXPERIMENTAL ZOOLOGY. SUPPLEMENT.
John Wiley & Sons, Inc., Journals, 605 Third Ave., New York, NY 10158-0012. TEL 212-850-6645. FAX 212-850-6021. *839*

JOURNAL OF EXPOSURE ANALYSIS AND ENVIRONMENTAL EPIDEMIOLOGY.
Princeton Scientific Publishing Co., Inc., Box 2155, Princeton, NJ 08543. TEL 609-683-4750. FAX 609-683-0838. *2938*

JOURNAL OF EXTENSION (ASCII EDITION).
Journal of Extension, Inc., c/o Virginia Tech, Blacksburg, VA 24061-0452. TEL 541-686-2697. *2456*

JOURNAL OF EYE TRAUMA.
Slack, Inc., 6900 Grove Rd., Thorofare, NJ 08086-9447. TEL 609-848-1000. FAX 609-853-5991. *4995*

JOURNAL OF FAMILY AND CONSUMER SCIENCES.
American Association of Family and Consumer Sciences, 1555 King St., Alexandria, VA 22314. TEL 703-706-4600. FAX 703-706-4663. *3686*

JOURNAL OF FAMILY AND ECONOMIC ISSUES.
Human Sciences Press, Inc., 233 Spring St., New York, NY 10013-1578. TEL 212-620-8000. FAX 212-463-0742. *6126*

JOURNAL OF FAMILY LIFE.
72 Philip St., Albany, NY 12202. TEL 518-432-1578. FAX 518-462-6836. *6716*

JOURNAL OF FAMILY NURSING.
Sage Publications, Inc., 2455 Teller Rd., Thousand Oaks, CA 91320. TEL 805-499-0721. FAX 805-499-0871. *4937*

JOURNAL OF FAMILY PRACTICE.
Appleton & Lange, Journal Division Box 120041, Stamford, CT 06912-0041. TEL 203-406-4500. *4694*

JOURNAL OF FAMILY PSYCHOTHERAPY.
Haworth Press, Inc., 10 Alice St., Binghamton, NY 13904. TEL 607-722-5857. FAX 607-722-6362. *6126*

JOURNAL OF FAMILY SOCIAL WORK.
Haworth Press, Inc., 10 Alice St., Binghamton, NY 13904. TEL 607-722-5857. FAX 607-722-6362. *6673*

JOURNAL OF FAMILY STUDIES.
La Trobe University Press, Bundoora, Vic. 3085, Australia. TEL 61-3-94791746. FAX 61-3-94791783. *4626*

JOURNAL OF FAMILY THERAPY.
Blackwell Publishers Ltd., 108 Cowley Rd., Oxford OX4 1JF, England. TEL 44-1865-791100. FAX 44-1865-791347. *5073*

JOURNAL OF FAMILY VIOLENCE.
Plenum Publishing Corp., 233 Spring St., New York, NY 10013-1578. TEL 212-620-8000. FAX 212-463-0742. *2270*

JOURNAL OF FASHION MARKETING AND MANAGEMENT.
Henry Stewart Publications, Russell House, 28-30 Little Russell St., London WC1A 2HN, England. TEL 44-171-404-3040. FAX 44-171-404-2081. *1533*

JOURNAL OF FEMINIST FAMILY THERAPY.
Haworth Press, Inc., 10 Alice St., Binghamton, NY 13904. TEL 607-722-5857. FAX 607-722-6362. *7345*

JOURNAL OF FERMENTATION AND BIOENGINEERING.
Society of Fermentation and Bioengineering, Japan, c/o Osaka Daigaku Kogakubu, 2-1 Yamadaoka, Suita-shi, Osaka-fu 565, Japan. TEL 81-6-877-5111. FAX 81-6-879-2034. *648*

JOURNAL OF FIELD ARCHAEOLOGY.
Boston University, Journal of Field Archaeology, 675 Commonwealth Ave., Boston, MA 02215. TEL 617-353-2357. FAX 617-353-6800. *369*

JOURNAL OF FILM AND VIDEO.
University Film and Video Association (Atlanta), c/o California State University, Broadcast - ommunications, 5151 State University Dr., Los Angeles, CA 90032. TEL 213-343-4206. *5337*

JOURNAL OF FINANCIAL AND QUANTITATIVE ANALYSIS.
University of Washington, Graduate School of Business Administration, 326 Lewis Hall, Box 353200, Seattle, WA 98195. FAX 206-543-6872. *1150*

JOURNAL OF FINANCIAL ECONOMICS.
Elsevier Science S.A., P.O. Box 564, CH-1001 Lausanne 1, Switzerland. TEL 41-21-3207381. FAX 41-21-3235444. *977*

JOURNAL OF FINANCIAL INTERMEDIATION.
Academic Press, Inc., Journal Division, 525 B St., Ste. 1900, San Diego, CA 92101-4495. TEL 619-230-1840. FAX 619-699-6800. *1307*

JOURNAL OF FINANCIAL MANAGEMENT AND ANALYSIS.
Om Sai Ram Centre for Financial Management Research, 15 Prakash Co-operative Housing Society, Relief Rd., Santacruz (W.), Mumbai 400 054, India. TEL 91-22-6121715. *1150*

JOURNAL OF FINANCIAL PLANNING.
Institute of Certified Financial Planners, 3801 E. Florida Ave., No. 708, Denver, CO 80210-2571. TEL 303-759-4900. FAX 303-759-0749. *1392*

JOURNAL OF FINANCIAL PLANNING TODAY.
New Directions Publications, Inc., Box 6097, W. Palm Beach, FL 33405. TEL 407-434-0100. FAX 407-641-4801. *1150*

JOURNAL OF FINANCIAL REGULATION AND COMPLIANCE.
Henry Stewart Publications, Russell House, 28-30 Little Russell St., London WC1A 2HN, England. TEL 44-171-404-3040. FAX 44-171-404-2081. *1150*

JOURNAL OF FINANCIAL SERVICES RESEARCH.
Kluwer Academic Publishers Boston, Box 358, Accord Sta., Hingham, MA 02018-0358. TEL 617-871-6300. FAX 617-871-6528. *1150*

JOURNAL OF FIRE SCIENCES.
Technomic Publishing Co., Inc., 851 New Holland Ave., Box 3535, Lancaster, PA 17604. TEL 717-291-5609. FAX 717-295-4538. *3056*

JOURNAL OF FISH DISEASES.
Blackwell Science Ltd., Osney Mead, Oxford OX2 0EL, England. TEL 44-1865-206206. FAX 44-1865-721205. *3072*

JOURNAL OF FLOW VISUALIZATION AND IMAGE PROCESSING.
Begell House Inc., 79 Madison Ave., Ste. 1205, New York, NY 10016-7892. TEL 212-725-1999. FAX 212-213-8368. *2890*

JOURNAL OF FLUENCY DISORDERS.
Elsevier Science Inc., Box 945, New York, NY 10159-0945. TEL 212-633-3730. FAX 212-633-3680. *6126*

JOURNAL OF FLUIDS ENGINEERING.
American Society of Mechanical Engineers, 22 Law Dr., Fairfield, NJ 07007-2900. TEL 973-882-1167. FAX 973-882-1717. *2873*

JOURNAL OF FLUORESCENCE.
Plenum Publishing Corp., 233 Spring St., New York, NY 10013-1578. TEL 212-620-8000. FAX 212-463-0742. *1808*

JOURNAL OF FLUORINE CHEMISTRY.
Elsevier Science S.A., P.O. Box 564, CH-1001 Lausanne 1, Switzerland. TEL 41-21-3207381. FAX 41-21-3235444. *1808*

JOURNAL OF FOLKLORE RESEARCH.
Indiana University, Folklore Institute, 504 North Fess, Bloomington, IN 47405. TEL 812-855-8049. FAX 812-855-4008. *3088*

JOURNAL OF FOOD ENGINEERING.
Elsevier Science Ltd., P.O. Box 800, Kidlington, Oxford OX5 1DX, England. TEL 44-1865-843000. FAX 44-1865-843010. *3116*

JOURNAL OF FOOD PRODUCTS MARKETING.
Haworth Press, Inc., 10 Alice St., Binghamton, NY 13904. TEL 607-722-5857. FAX 607-722-6362. *3116*

JOURNAL OF FOOD PROTECTION.
International Association of Milk, Food and Environmental Sanitarians, Inc., 6200 Aurora Ave., Ste. 200 W, Des Moines, IA 50322. TEL 515-276-3344. FAX 515-276-8655. *6241*

JOURNAL OF FOOD SCIENCE AND TECHNOLOGY.
Association of Food Scientists and Technologists (India), Central Executive Committee, CFTRI Campus, Mysore 570 013, India. TEL 28157. FAX 521747. *3116*

JOURNAL OF FOOT AND ANKLE SURGERY.
Data Trace Publishing Company, 110 West Rd., Ste. 227, Baltimore, MD 21204. TEL 410-494-4994. FAX 410-528-0515. *5145*

JOURNAL OF FORAMINIFERAL RESEARCH.
Cushman Foundation for Foraminiferal Research, Invertebrate Paleontology, Museum of Comparative Zoology, Harvard University, Cambridge, MA 02138. *5559*

JOURNAL OF FORECASTING.
John Wiley & Sons Ltd., Journals, Baffins Ln., Chichester, W. Sussex PO19 1UD, England. TEL 44-1243-779777. FAX 44-1243-775878. *1487*

JOURNAL OF FORENSIC ECONOMICS.
National Association of Forensic Economics, Box 30067, Kansas City, MO 64112. TEL 816-235-2833. FAX 816-235-5263. *1307*

JOURNAL OF FORENSIC IDENTIFICATION.
International Association for Identification, Box 2423-0247, Alameda, CA 94501-2423. TEL 510-865-2174. FAX 510-865-2167. *4905*

JOURNAL OF FORENSIC MEDICINE.
Ministry of Justice, Institute of Forensic Sciences, 1347 West Guangfu Rd., Shanghai 200063, People's Republic of China. TEL 021-2440148. FAX 021-2442691. *4905*

JOURNAL OF FORENSIC SCIENCES.
American Society for Testing and Materials, 100 Barr Harbor Dr., W. Conshohocken, PA 19428-2959. TEL 610-832-9500. FAX 610-832-9555. *4905*

JOURNAL OF FOREST ECONOMICS.
Sveriges Landbruksuniversitet (SLU), Department of Forest Economics, S-901 83 Umeaa, Sweden. TEL 46-90-786-62-71. FAX 46-90-786-60-73. *3156*

JOURNAL OF FORESTRY.
Society of American Foresters, 5400 Grosvenor Ln., Bethesda, MD 20814. TEL 301-897-8720. FAX 301-897-3690. *3156*

JOURNAL OF FRESHWATER ECOLOGY.
Oikos Publishers, Inc., Box 2558, La Crosse, WI 54602-2558. TEL 608-526-9577. FAX 608-526-9477. *2395*

JOURNAL OF FUNCTIONAL ANALYSIS.
Academic Press, Inc., Journal Division, 525 B St., Ste. 1900, San Diego, CA 92101-4495. TEL 619-230-1840. FAX 619-699-6800. *4582*

JOURNAL OF FUNCTIONAL AND LOGIC PROGRAMMING.
M I T Press, 5 Cambridge Center, Cambridge, MA 02142. TEL 617-253-2889. FAX 617-577-1545. *2144*

JOURNAL OF FUSION ENERGY.
Plenum Publishing Corp., 233 Spring St., New York, NY 10013-1578. TEL 212-620-8000. FAX 212-463-0742. *2699*

JOURNAL OF GAMBLING STUDIES.
Human Sciences Press, Inc., 233 Spring St., New York, NY 10013-1578. TEL 212-620-8000. FAX 212-463-0742. *5073*

JOURNAL OF GASTROINTESTINAL SURGERY.
Quality Medical Publishing, Inc., 11970 Borman Dr., Ste. 222, St. Louis, MO 63146. TEL 314-878-7808. FAX 314-878-9937. *5145*

JOURNAL OF GAY & LESBIAN PSYCHOTHERAPY.
Haworth Press, Inc., 10 Alice St., Binghamton, NY 13904. TEL 607-722-5857. FAX 607-722-6362. *6126*

JOURNAL OF GAY & LESBIAN SOCIAL SERVICES.
Haworth Press, Inc., 10 Alice St., Binghamton, NY 13904. TEL 607-722-5857. FAX 607-722-6362. *6673*

JOURNAL OF GAY, LESBIAN & BISEXUAL IDENTITY.
Human Sciences Press, Inc., 233 Spring St., New York, NY 10013-1578. TEL 212-620-8000. FAX 212-643-0742. *3696*

THE JOURNAL OF GEMMOLOGY.
Gemmological Association and Gem Testing Laboratory of Great Britain, 27 Greville St., London EC1N 8SU, England. TEL 44-171-404-3334. FAX 44-171-404-8843. *3865*

JOURNAL OF GENDER, CULTURE, AND HEALTH.
Plenum Publishing Corp., 233 Spring St., New York, NY 10013-1578. TEL 212-620-8000. FAX 212-463-0742. *4694*

JOURNAL OF GENDER STUDIES.
Carfax Publishing Co., P.O. Box 25, Abingdon, Oxon. OX14 3UE, England. TEL 44-1235-401000. FAX 44-1235-401550. *7345*

JOURNAL OF GENERAL EDUCATION.
Pennsylvania State University Press, USB 1, Ste. C, University Park, PA 16802-1003. TEL 814-865-1327. FAX 814-863-1408. *2456*

JOURNAL OF GENERAL INTERNAL MEDICINE.
Blackwell Science Inc., 350 Main St., Malden, MA 02148. TEL 617-876-7000. FAX 617-388-8255. *4925*

JOURNAL OF GENERAL PHYSIOLOGY.
Rockefeller University Press, 1114 First Ave., New York, NY 10021. TEL 212-327-8572. FAX 212-327-7944. *817*

THE JOURNAL OF GENERAL PSYCHOLOGY.
Heldref Publications, 1319 Eighteenth St., N.W., Washington, DC 20036. TEL 202-296-6267. FAX 202-296-5149. *6126*

JOURNAL OF GENETIC COUNSELING.
Human Sciences Press, Inc., 233 Spring St., New York, NY 10013-1578. TEL 212-620-8432. FAX 212-463-0742. *6127*

THE JOURNAL OF GENETIC PSYCHOLOGY.
Heldref Publications, 1319 Eighteenth St., N.W., Washington, DC 20036-1802. TEL 202-296-6267. FAX 202-296-5149. *6127*

JOURNAL OF GENETICS & BREEDING.
Istituto Sperimentale per la Cerealicoltura, Via Cassia, 176, 00191 Rome, Italy. TEL 39-6-3295705. FAX 39-6-36306022. *130*

JOURNAL OF GEOCHEMICAL EXPLORATION.
Elsevier Science B.V., P.O. Box 211, 1000 AE Amsterdam, Netherlands. TEL 31-20-4853911. FAX 31-20-4853598. *2317*

JOURNAL OF GEODYNAMICS.
Elsevier Science Ltd., Pergamon, P.O. Box 800, Kidlington, Oxford OX5 1DX, England. TEL 44-1865-843000. FAX 44-1865-843010. *2385*

JOURNAL OF GEOGRAPHIC INFORMATION AND DECISION ANALYSIS.
Geographic Information and Decision Analysis Research Group, Dept. of Geography, University of Western Ontario, London, ON N6A 5C2, Canada. *3411*

JOURNAL OF GEOGRAPHICAL SCIENCE.
National Taiwan University, Department of Geography, National Taiwan University, Taipei, Taiwan, Republic of China. TEL 886-2-3629908. FAX 886-2-3622911. *3411*

JOURNAL OF GEOGRAPHY IN HIGHER EDUCATION.
Carfax Publishing Co., P.O. Box 25, Abingdon, Oxon. OX14 3UE, England. TEL 44-1235-401000. FAX 44-1245-401550. *3411*

JOURNAL OF GEOLOGY.
University of Chicago Press, Journals Division, Box 37005, Chicago, IL 60637. TEL 773-753-3347. FAX 773-753-0811. *2353*

JOURNAL OF GEOMETRIC ANALYSIS.
Mathematica Josephina, Inc., Box 1146, Washington University, One Brookings Dr., St. Louis, MO 63130-4899. TEL 401-455-4000. FAX 401-331-3848. *4582*

JOURNAL OF GEOMETRY AND PHYSICS.
North-Holland, P.O. Box 211, 1000 AE Amsterdam, Netherlands. TEL 31-20-4853911. FAX 31-20-4853598. *4582*

JOURNAL OF GEOSCIENCE EDUCATION.
National Association of Geoscience Teachers, Inc., Box 5443, Bellingham, WA 98227-5443. TEL 360-650-3587. FAX 360-650-7302. *2353*

JOURNAL OF GEOSCIENCES.
Osaka City University, Department of Geosciences, Faculty of Science, 3-3-138 Sugimoto, Sumiyoshi-ku, Osaka 558, Japan. TEL 81-6-605-2587. FAX 81-6-605-2522. *2317*

JOURNAL OF GEOTECHNICAL ENGINEERING.
American Society of Civil Engineers, 345 E. 47th St., New York, NY 10017-2398. TEL 212-705-7288. FAX 212-980-4681. *2790*

JOURNAL OF GERIATRIC DERMATOLOGY.
Health Management Publications, Inc., 950 W Valley Rd., Ste. 2800, Wayne, PA 19087. TEL 215-337-4466. FAX 215-337-0890. *3439*

JOURNAL OF GERIATRIC DRUG THERAPY.
Haworth Press, Inc., 10 Alice St., Binghamton, NY 13904. TEL 607-722-5857. FAX 607-722-6362. *5671*

JOURNAL OF GERIATRIC PSYCHIATRY.
International Universities Press, Inc., 59 Boston Post Rd., Box 1524, Madison, CT 06443-1524. TEL 203-245-4000. FAX 203-245-0775. *5074*

JOURNAL OF GERONTOLOGICAL NURSING.
Slack, Inc., 6900 Grove Rd., Thorofare, NJ 08086-9447. TEL 609-848-1000. FAX 609-853-5991. *3439*

JOURNAL OF GERONTOLOGICAL SOCIAL WORK.
Haworth Press, Inc., 10 Alice St., Binghamton, NY 13904. TEL 607-722-5857. FAX 607-722-6362. *3439*

JOURNAL OF GLAUCOMA.
Lippincott - Raven Publishers, 227 E. Washington Sq., Philadelphia, PA 19106. TEL 215-238-4200. *4995*

JOURNAL OF GLOBAL BUSINESS.
Association for Global Business, Box 1381, Harrisonburg, VA 22801. TEL 540-433-7403. FAX 540-433-7403. *978*

JOURNAL OF GLOBAL MARKETING.
Haworth Press, Inc., 10 Alice St., Binghamton, NY 13904. TEL 607-722-9678. FAX 607-722-6362. *1533*

JOURNAL OF GLOBAL OPTIMIZATION.
Kluwer Academic Publishers, Postbus 17, 3300 AA Dordrecht, Netherlands. TEL 31-78-6392392. FAX 31-78-6392254. *6594*

JOURNAL OF GOVERNMENT INFORMATION.
Elsevier Science Ltd., Pergamon, P.O. Box 800, Kidlington, Oxford OX5 1DX, England. TEL 44-1865-843000. FAX 44-1865-843010. *6180*

JOURNAL OF GRAPH THEORY.
John Wiley & Sons, Inc., Journals, 605 Third Ave., New York, NY 10158. TEL 212-850-6645. FAX 212-850-6021. *4582*

JOURNAL OF GRAPHICS TOOLS.
A K Peters, Ltd., 289 Linden St., Wellesley, MA 02181. TEL 617-235-2210. FAX 617-235-2404. *2124*

JOURNAL OF GREAT LAKES RESEARCH.
International Association for Great Lakes Research, 2200 Bonisteel Blvd., Ann Arbor, MI 48109-2099. TEL 312-325-7422. FAX 312-325-7421. *2938*

JOURNAL OF GROUP PSYCHOTHERAPY, PSYCHODRAMA & SOCIOMETRY.
Heldref Publications, 1319 Eighteenth St., N.W., Washington, DC 20036-1802. TEL 202-296-6267. FAX 202-296-5149. *6127*

JOURNAL OF GUIDANCE, CONTROL, AND DYNAMICS.
American Institute of Aeronautics and Astronautics, Inc., 1801 Alexander Dr., Ste. 500, Reston, VA 20191. TEL 703-264-7500. *72*

JOURNAL OF GYNECOLOGIC SURGERY.
Mary Ann Liebert, Inc. Publishers, 2 Madison Ave., Larchmont, NY 10538. TEL 914-834-3100. FAX 914-834-3688. *4961*

JOURNAL OF GYNECOLOGIC TECHNIQUES.
Churchill Livingstone, 650 Ave. of the Americas, New York, NY 10011. TEL 212-206-5040. FAX 212-727-7808. *4961*

JOURNAL OF HAND SURGERY: AMERICAN VOLUME.
Churchill Livingstone, 650 Ave. of the Americas, New York, NY 10011. TEL 212-206-5040. FAX 212-727-7808. *5145*

JOURNAL OF HAND THERAPY.
Hanley & Belfus, Inc., 210 S. 13th St., Philadelphia, PA 19107. TEL 215-546-7293. FAX 215-790-9330. *5043*

JOURNAL OF HAZARDOUS MATERIALS.
Elsevier Science B.V., P.O. Box 211, 1000 AE Amsterdam, Netherlands. TEL 31-20-4853911. FAX 31-20-4853598. *2986*

JOURNAL OF HEAD TRAUMA REHABILITATION.
Aspen Publishers, Inc., 200 Orchard Ridge Dr., Gaithersburg, MD 20878. FAX 301-417-7550. *5010*

JOURNAL OF HEALTH AND HUMAN SERVICES ADMINISTRATION.
Southern Public Administration Education Foundation, Pennsylvania State University at Harrisburg, Division of Public Affairs, Middletown, PA 17057. TEL 717-948-6363. FAX 717-540-1383. *3715*

JOURNAL OF HEALTH AND SOCIAL BEHAVIOR.
American Sociological Association, 1722 N St., N.W., Washington, DC 20036. TEL 202-833-3410. FAX 202-785-0146. *6717*

JOURNAL OF HEALTH & SOCIAL POLICY.
Haworth Press, Inc., 10 Alice St., Binghamton, NY 13904. TEL 607-722-5857. FAX 607-722-6362. *6673*

JOURNAL OF HEALTH CARE CHAPLAINCY.
Haworth Press, Inc., 10 Alice St., Binghamton, NY 13904. TEL 607-722-5857. FAX 607-722-6362. *5786*

JOURNAL OF HEALTH CARE FOR THE POOR AND UNDERSERVED.
Sage Publications, Inc., 2455 Teller Rd., Thousand Oaks, CA 91320. TEL 805-499-0721. FAX 805-499-0721. *4695*

JOURNAL OF HEALTH COMMUNICATION.
Taylor & Francis Inc., 1900 Frost Rd., Ste. 101, Bristol, PA 19007-1598. TEL 215-785-5800. FAX 215-785-5515. *4695*

JOURNAL OF HEALTH ECONOMICS.
North-Holland, P.O. Box 211, 1000 AE Amsterdam, Netherlands. TEL 31-20-4853911. FAX 31-20-4853598. *6241*

JOURNAL OF HEALTH EDUCATION.
American Alliance for Health, Physical Education, Recreation, and Dance, 1900 Association Dr., Reston, VA 22091. TEL 703-476-3400. FAX 703-476-9527. *2608*

JOURNAL OF HEALTH POLITICS, POLICY AND LAW.
Duke University Press, Box 90660, Durham, NC 27708-0660. TEL 919-687-3600. FAX 919-687-4574. *4695*

JOURNAL OF HEALTH SERVICES MANAGEMENT RESEARCH.
Financial Times Healthcare, Technology Centre, St. Andrews, Fife KY16 9EA, Scotland. TEL 44-1334-447660. FAX 44-1334-477180. *4695*

JOURNAL OF HEALTHCARE RESOURCE MANAGEMENT.
Mayworm Associates, Inc., 507 N. Milwaukee Ave., Libertyville, IL 60048-2018. TEL 847-680-7878. FAX 847-680-8180. *3715*

JOURNAL OF HEALTHCARE RISK MANAGEMENT.
American Hospital Association, One North Franklin, Chicago, IL 60606. TEL 312-422-3989. FAX 312-422-4580. *3715*

THE JOURNAL OF HEART AND LUNG TRANSPLANTATION.
Mosby - Year Book, Inc., 11830 Westline Industrial Dr., St. Louis, MO 63146-3318. TEL 314-872-8370. FAX 314-432-1380. *5145*

JOURNAL OF HEART VALVE DISEASE.
I C R Publishers Ltd., 9 West End Ct., West End Ave., Pinner, Middx. HA5 1BP, England. TEL 44-1923-836873. *4820*

JOURNAL OF HEAT TRANSFER.
American Society of Mechanical Engineers, 22 Law Dr., Fairfield, NJ 07007-2900. TEL 973-882-1167. FAX 973-882-1717. *2890*

JOURNAL OF HELLENIC STUDIES.
Society for the Promotion of Hellenic Studies, Senate House, London WC1E 7HU, England. TEL 44-171-232-9590. FAX 44-171-232-9591. *1905*

JOURNAL OF HELMINTHOLOGY.
CAB International, Wallingford, Oxon OX10 8DE, England. TEL 44-1491-832111. FAX 44-1491-826090. *4839*

JOURNAL OF HEMATOTHERAPY.
Mary Ann Liebert, Inc. Publishers, 2 Madison Ave., Larchmont, NY 10538. TEL 914-834-3100. FAX 914-834-3688. *4920*

JOURNAL OF HEPATOLOGY.
Munksgaard International Publishers Ltd., 35 Noerre Soegade, P.O. Box 2148, DK-1016 Copenhagen K, Denmark. TEL 45-33-127030. FAX 45-33-129387. *4913*

JOURNAL OF HERBS, SPICES & MEDICINAL PLANTS.
Haworth Press, Inc., 10 Alice St., Binghamton, NY 13904. TEL 607-722-5857. FAX 607-722-6362. *3196*

JOURNAL OF HEREDITY.
Oxford University Press, Journals, 2001 Evans Rd., Cary, NC 27513. TEL 919-677-0977. FAX 919-677-1714. *772*

JOURNAL OF HERPETOLOGY.
Society for the Study of Amphibians and Reptiles, c/o Robert Aldridge, St. Louis Univ., Dept. of Biology, 3507 Laclede Ave., St. Louis, KS 67601-0626. *840*

JOURNAL OF HETEROCYCLIC CHEMISTRY.
HeteroCorporation, Box 993, Odessa, FL 33556-0993. *1816*

JOURNAL OF HEURISTICS.
Kluwer Academic Publishers Boston, Box 358, Accord Sta., Hingham, MA 02018-0358. TEL 617-871-6600. FAX 617-871-6528. *5733*

JOURNAL OF HIGH SPEED NETWORKS.
I O S Press, Van Diemenstraat 94, 1013 CN Amsterdam, Netherlands. TEL 31-20-6382189. FAX 31-20-6203419. *2136*

THE JOURNAL OF HIGHER CRITICISM.
Institute for Higher Critical Studies, Drew University Theological School, 36 Madison Ave., Madison, NJ 07940. TEL 201-408-3000. *6348*

JOURNAL OF HIGHER EDUCATION.
Ohio State University Press, 1070 Carmack Rd., Columbus, OH 43210. TEL 614-292-6930. FAX 614-292-2065. *2547*

JOURNAL OF HISTOCHEMISTRY AND CYTOCHEMISTRY.
Histochemical Society, Box 85630, Seattle, WA 98145-1630. TEL 212-362-1801. FAX 212-874-8313. *741*

JOURNAL OF HISTORICAL SOCIOLOGY.
Blackwell Publishers Ltd., 108 Cowley Rd., Oxford OX4 1JF, England. TEL 44-1865-791100. FAX 44-1865-791347. *6717*

JOURNAL OF HISTORICAL STUDIES.
Historical Science Society of Japan, Seika Bldg., 2 Kanda Jimbo-cho 2-chome, Chiyoda-ku, Tokyo 101, Japan. TEL 81-3-3261-4985. FAX 81-3-3261-4993. *3521*

JOURNAL OF HISTOTECHNOLOGY.
National Society for Histotechnology, 4201 Northview Dr., Ste. 502, Bowie, MD 20716-1073. TEL 301-262-6221. FAX 301-262-9188. *742*

JOURNAL OF HIV - AIDS PREVENTION & EDUCATION FOR ADOLESCENTS & CHILDREN.
Haworth Press, Inc., 10 Alice St., Binghamton, NY 13904. TEL 607-722-5857. FAX 607-722-6362. *4839*

THE JOURNAL OF HOLOCAUST EDUCATION.
Frank Cass, Newbury House, 890-900 Eastern Ave., Newbury Park, Ilford, Essex IG2 7HH, England. TEL 44-181-599-8866. FAX 44-181-599-0984. *3578*

JOURNAL OF HOMOSEXUALITY.
Haworth Press, Inc., 10 Alice St., Binghamton, NY 13904. TEL 607-722-5857. FAX 607-722-6362. *3696*

JOURNAL OF HOSPITAL MARKETING.
Haworth Press, Inc., 10 Alice St., Binghamton, NY 13904. TEL 607-722-5857. FAX 607-722-6362. *1533*

JOURNAL OF HOSPITALITY & LEISURE MARKETING.
Haworth Press, Inc., 10 Alice St., Binghamton, NY 13904. TEL 607-722-5857. FAX 607-722-6362. *3730*

JOURNAL OF HOUSING FOR THE ELDERLY.
Haworth Press, Inc., 10 Alice St., Binghamton, NY 13904. TEL 607-722-5857. FAX 607-722-6362. *3439*

JOURNAL OF HOUSING RESEARCH.
Federal National Mortgage Association, 3900 Wisconsin Ave., N.W., Washington, DC 20016-2899. TEL 202-752-4422. FAX 202-752-4933. *3751*

JOURNAL OF HUMAN ECOLOGY.
Kamla-Raj Enterprises, 2273 Gali Bari Paharwali, Chawri Bazar, Delhi 110 006, India. TEL 91-11-725-7803. *2938*

JOURNAL OF HUMAN NUTRITION AND DIETETICS.
Blackwell Science Ltd., Osney Mead, Oxford OX2 0EL, England. TEL 44-1865-206206. FAX 44-1865-721205. *5476*

JOURNAL OF HUMAN VALUES.
Sage Publications India Pvt. Ltd., P.O. Box 4215, New Delhi 110 048, India. TEL 91-11-644-4958. FAX 91-11-647-2426. *5733*

JOURNAL OF HUMAN VIROLOGY.
Lippincott - Raven Publishers, 227 E. Washington Sq., Philadelphia, PA 19106-3780. TEL 215-238-4200. FAX 215-238-4227. *4839*

JOURNAL OF HYDRAULIC ENGINEERING (NEW YORK).
American Society of Civil Engineers, 345 E. 47th St., New York, NY 10017-2398. TEL 212-705-7288. FAX 212-980-4681. *2791*

JOURNAL OF HYDRODYNAMICS.
China Ocean Press, International Cooperation Department, Haimao Dalou, 1 Fuxingmenwai Dajie, Beijing 100860, People's Republic of China. TEL 8032211. FAX 8033515. *5809*

JOURNAL OF HYDROLOGY.
Elsevier Science B.V., P.O. Box 211, 1000 AE Amsterdam, Netherlands. TEL 31-20-4853911. FAX 31-20-4853598. *2395*

JOURNAL OF HYDROLOGY. NEW ZEALAND.
New Zealand Hydrological Society, P.O. Box 12-300, Wellington, New Zealand. TEL 64-3-3256701. FAX 64-3-3252418. *2396*

JOURNAL OF HYPERTENSION.
Thomson Science, 2-6 Boundary Row, London SE1 8HN, England. TEL 44-171-865-0198. FAX 44-171-410-6600. *4820*

JOURNAL OF IMAGE GUIDED SURGERY.
John Wiley & Sons, Inc., Journals, 605 Third Ave., New York, NY 10158-0012. TEL 212-850-6645. FAX 212-850-6021. *5145*

THE JOURNAL OF IMAGING SCIENCE AND TECHNOLOGY.
Society for Imaging Science and Technology, 7003 Kilworth Ln., Springfield, VA 22151. TEL 703-642-9090. FAX 703-642-9094. *5768*

JOURNAL OF IMMUNOASSAY.
Marcel Dekker Journals, 270 Madison Ave., New York, NY 10016. TEL 212-696-9000. FAX 212-685-4540. *5671*

JOURNAL OF IMMUNOLOGICAL METHODS.
Elsevier Science B.V., P.O. Box 211, 1000 AE Amsterdam, Netherlands. TEL 31-20-4853911. FAX 31-20-4853598. *4798*

JOURNAL OF IMMUNOLOGY.
American Association of Immunologists, 9650 Rockville Pike, Bethesda, MD 20814. TEL 301-530-7197. FAX 301-571-1813. *4798*

JOURNAL OF IMMUNOTHERAPY WITH EMPHASIS ON TUMOR IMMUNOLOGY.
Lippincott - Raven Publishers, 227 E. Washington Sq., Philadelphia, PA 19106. TEL 215-238-4200. FAX 215-238-4227. *4798*

THE JOURNAL OF IMPERIAL AND COMMONWEALTH HISTORY.
Frank Cass, Newbury House, 890-900 Eastern Ave., Newbury Park, Ilford, Essex IG2 7HH, England. TEL 44-181-599-8866. FAX 44-181-599-0984. *3502*

JOURNAL OF IN-SERVICE EDUCATION.
Triangle Journals Ltd., P.O. Box 65, Wallingford, Oxon. OX10 0YG, England. TEL 44-1491-838013. FAX 44-1491-834968. *2608*

JOURNAL OF INCLUSION PHENOMENA AND MOLECULAR RECOGNITION IN CHEMISTRY.
Kluwer Academic Publishers, Postbus 17, 3300 AA Dordrecht, Netherlands. TEL 31-78-6392392. FAX 31-78-6392254. *1830*

JOURNAL OF INDIAN PHILOSOPHY.
Kluwer Academic Publishers, Postbus 17, 3300 AA Dordrecht, Netherlands. TEL 31-78-6392392. FAX 31-78-6392254. *5733*

JOURNAL OF INDIGENOUS STUDIES.
Gabriel Dumont Institute of Native Studies and Applied Research, 505 - 23rd St., E., Saskatoon, SK S7K 4K7, Canada. TEL 306-934-4941. FAX 306-934-4941. *321*

JOURNAL OF INDIVIDUAL EMPLOYMENT RIGHTS.
Baywood Publishing Co., Inc., 26 Austin Ave., Box 337, Amityville, NY 11701. TEL 516-691-1270. FAX 516-691-1770. *1439*

JOURNAL OF INDO-EUROPEAN STUDIES.
Institute for the Study of Man, 1133 13th St., N.W., No. C-2, Washington, DC 20005. TEL 202-371-2700. FAX 202-371-1523. *6622*

JOURNAL OF INDUSTRIAL ECONOMICS.
Blackwell Publishers Ltd., 108 Cowley Rd., Oxford OX4 1JF, England. TEL 44-1865-791100. FAX 44-1865-791347. *978*

JOURNAL OF INDUSTRIAL MICROBIOLOGY AND BIOTECHNOLOGY.
Stockton Press, Houndmills, Basingstoke, Hants. RG21 6XS, England. TEL 44-1256-351898. FAX 44-1256-328339. *685*

JOURNAL OF INDUSTRIAL RELATIONS.
Industrial Relations Society of Australia, c/o Braham Dabscheck, Ed., School of Industrial Relations and Organisational Behaviour, Univ. of N.S.W., Sydney, N.S.W. 2052, Australia. TEL 61-2-93852148. FAX 61-2-96628531. *1439*

JOURNAL OF INDUSTRIAL RELATIONS.
Universal Publications, P.O. Box 7305, Ottawa, ON K1L 8E4, Canada. TEL 613-831-1052. FAX 613-831-8452. *1439*

JOURNAL OF INDUSTRIAL TECHNOLOGY.
National Association of Industrial Technology, 3300 Washtenaw Ave., Ste. 220, Ann Arbor, MI 48104-4200. TEL 313-677-0720. FAX 313-677-2407. *6964*

JOURNAL OF INFECTION AND CHEMOTHERAPY.
Churchill Livingstone Japan, Churchill Bldg., 2-8-16 Yutenji, Meguro-ku, Tokyo 153, Japan. TEL 81-3-5721-0442. FAX 81-5721-0415. *5671*

JOURNAL OF INFECTIOUS DISEASE PHARMACOTHERAPY.
Haworth Press, Inc., Pharmaceutical Products Press, 10 Alice St., Binghamton, NY 13904. TEL 607-722-5857. FAX 607-722-6362. *5671*

JOURNAL OF INFECTIOUS DISEASES.
University of Chicago Press, Journals Division, Box 37005, Chicago, IL 60637. TEL 773-753-3347. FAX 773-753-0811. *4839*

JOURNAL OF INFLAMMATION.
John Wiley & Sons, Inc., Journals, 605 Third Ave., New York, NY 10158. TEL 212-850-6645. FAX 212-850-6021. *4821*

JOURNAL OF INFORMATION & OPTIMIZATION SCIENCES.
Analytic Publishing Co., F-23 Model Town-I, Delhi-110009, India. TEL 91-11-7129726. FAX 91-11-7459024. *4583*

JOURNAL OF INFORMATION, LAW AND TECHNOLOGY.
University of Strathclyde, Centre for Law, Computers and Technology, 173 Cathedral St., Glasgow G4 0RQ, Scotland. TEL 44-141-552-4400. FAX 44-141-553-1546. *3969*

JOURNAL OF INFORMATION SCIENCE - PRINCIPLES AND PRACTICE.
Bowker - Saur Ltd., A member of the Reed Elsevier plc group, Maypole House, Maypole Rd., E. Grinstead, W. Sussex RH19 1HU, England. TEL 44-1342-330100. FAX 44-1342-330192. *4188*

JOURNAL OF INFORMATION TECHNOLOGY.
Thomson Professional, 2-6 Boundary Row, London SE1 8HN, England. TEL 44-171-8650066. FAX 44-171-5229623. *4188*

JOURNAL OF INFORMATION TECHNOLOGY FOR TEACHER EDUCATION.
Triangle Journals Ltd., P.O. Box 65, Wallingford, Oxon. OX10 0YG, England. TEL 44-1491-838013. FAX 44-1491-834968. *2608*

JOURNAL OF INFRASTRUCTURE SYSTEMS.
American Society of Civil Engineers, 345 E. 47th St., New York, NY 10017-2398. TEL 212-705-7000. *2791*

JOURNAL OF INHERITED METABOLIC DISEASE.
Kluwer Academic Publishers, Postbus 17, 3300 AA Dordrecht, Netherlands. TEL 31-78-6392392. FAX 31-78-6392254. *5033*

REFEREED SERIALS

JOURNAL OF INORGANIC AND ORGANOMETALLIC POLYMERS.
Plenum Publishing Corp., 233 Spring St., New York, NY 10013-1578. TEL 212-620-8000. FAX 212-463-0742. *1816*

JOURNAL OF INORGANIC BIOCHEMISTRY.
Elsevier Science Inc., Box 945, New York, NY 10159-0945. TEL 212-633-3730. FAX 212-633-3680. *663*

JOURNAL OF INSECT BEHAVIOR.
Plenum Publishing Corp., 233 Spring St., New York, NY 10013-1578. TEL 212-620-8000. FAX 212-463-0742. *756*

JOURNAL OF INSECT PHYSIOLOGY.
Elsevier Science Ltd., Pergamon, P.O. Box 800, Kidlington, Oxford OX5 1DX, England. TEL 44-1865-843000. FAX 44-1865-843010. *756*

JOURNAL OF INSURANCE REGULATION.
National Association of Insurance Commissioners, 120 W. 12th St., Kansas City, MO 64105. TEL 816-374-7259. *3822*

JOURNAL OF INTELLECTUAL DISABILITY RESEARCH.
Blackwell Science Ltd., Osney Mead, Oxford OX2 OEL, England. TEL 44-1865-206206. FAX 44-1865-721205. *5074*

JOURNAL OF INTELLIGENT AND FUZZY SYSTEMS.
John Wiley & Sons, Inc., Journals, 605 Third Ave., New York, NY 10158. TEL 212-850-6645. FAX 212-850-6021. *4583*

JOURNAL OF INTELLIGENT AND ROBOTIC SYSTEMS.
Kluwer Academic Publishers, Postbus 17, 3300 AA Dordrecht, Netherlands. TEL 31-78-6392392. FAX 31-78-6392254. *2102*

JOURNAL OF INTELLIGENT INFORMATION SYSTEMS.
Kluwer Academic Publishers Boston, Box 358, Accord Sta., Hingham, MA 02018-0358. TEL 617-871-6600. FAX 617-871-6528. *2102*

JOURNAL OF INTELLIGENT MANUFACTURING.
Thomson Science, 2-6 Boundary Row, London SE1 8HN, England. TEL 44-171-8650066. FAX 44-171-5229624. *2110*

JOURNAL OF INTELLIGENT MATERIAL SYSTEMS AND STUCTURES.
Technomic Publishing Co., Inc., 851 New Holland Ave., Box 3535, Lancaster, PA 17604. TEL 717-291-5609. FAX 717-295-4538. *6537*

JOURNAL OF INTENSIVE CARE MEDICINE.
Blackwell Science Inc., 350 Main St., Malden, MA 02148. TEL 617-876-7000. FAX 617-388-8255. *4695*

JOURNAL OF INTERACTIVE LEARNING RESEARCH.
Association for the Advancement of Computing in Education, Box 2966, Charlottesville, VA 22902. TEL 804-973-3987. FAX 804-978-7449. *2518*

JOURNAL OF INTERACTIVE MARKETING.
John Wiley & Sons, Inc., Journals, 605 Third Ave., New York, NY 10158. TEL 212-850-6645. FAX 212-850-6021. *1533*

JOURNAL OF INTERAMERICAN STUDIES AND WORLD AFFAIRS.
University of Miami, North - South Center Press, Box 248205, Coral Gables, FL 33124-3027. TEL 305-284-8914. FAX 305-284-5083. *6023*

JOURNAL OF INTERDISCIPLINARY HISTORY.
M I T Press, 5 Cambridge Center, Cambridge, MA 02142. TEL 617-253-2889. FAX 617-577-1545. *3502*

JOURNAL OF INTERDISCIPLINARY STUDIES.
Institute for Interdisciplinary Research, 2828 Third St., Ste. 11, Santa Monica, CA 90405-4150. TEL 310-396-0517. *3783*

JOURNAL OF INTERFERON & CYTOKINE RESEARCH.
Mary Ann Liebert, Inc. Publishers, 2 Madison Ave., Larchmont, NY 10538. TEL 914-834-3100. FAX 914-834-3688. *4798*

JOURNAL OF INTERIOR DESIGN.
Interior Design Educators Council, Inc., c/o Denise Guerin, University of Minnesota, 240 McNeal Hall, 1985 Buford Ave., St. Paul, MN 55108. TEL 612-626-1257. FAX 612-624-2750. *3847*

JOURNAL OF INTERLIBRARY LOAN, DOCUMENT DELIVERY & INFORMATION SUPPLY.
Haworth Press, Inc., 10 Alice St., Binghamton, NY 13904. TEL 607-722-5857. FAX 607-722-6362. *4188*

JOURNAL OF INTERNAL MEDICINE.
Blackwell Science Ltd., Osney Mead, Oxford OX2 OEL, England. TEL 44-1865-206206. FAX 44-1865-721205. *4926*

JOURNAL OF INTERNATIONAL ARBITRATION.
Kluwer Law International, Postbus 85889, 2508 CN The Hague, Netherlands. TEL 31-70-3081500. FAX 31-70-3081515. *4120*

JOURNAL OF INTERNATIONAL BUSINESS STUDIES.
University of Western Ontario, Western Business School, London, ON N6A 3K7, Canada. TEL 519-661-4031. FAX 519-661-3700. *978*

JOURNAL OF INTERNATIONAL CONSUMER MARKETING.
Haworth Press, Inc., 10 Alice St., Binghamton, NY 13904. TEL 607-722-5857. FAX 607-722-6362. *1533*

JOURNAL OF INTERNATIONAL DEVELOPMENT.
John Wiley & Sons Ltd., Journals, Baffins Ln., Chichester, W. Sussex PO19 1UD, England. TEL 44-1243-779777. FAX 44-1243-775878. *6622*

JOURNAL OF INTERNATIONAL ECONOMICS.
North-Holland, P.O. Box 211, 1000 AE Amsterdam, Netherlands. TEL 31-20-4853911. FAX 31-20-4853598. *978*

JOURNAL OF INTERNATIONAL EDUCATION.
U K C O S A - The Council for International Education, 9-17 St. Albans Pl., London N1 0NX, England. TEL 44-171-226-3762. FAX 44-171-226-3373. *2565*

JOURNAL OF INTERNATIONAL FINANCIAL MANAGEMENT AND ACCOUNTING.
Blackwell Publishers Ltd., 108 Cowley Rd., Oxford OX4 1JF, England. TEL 44-1865-791100. *1150*

JOURNAL OF INTERNATIONAL FINANCIAL MARKETS, INSTITUTIONS & MONEY.
Elsevier Science Ltd., Pergamon, P.O. Box 800, Kidlington, Oxford OX5 1DX. TEL 44-1865-843000. FAX 44-1865-843010. *1150*

JOURNAL OF INTERNATIONAL FOOD & AGRIBUSINESS MARKETING.
Haworth Press, Inc., 10 Alice St., Binghamton, NY 13904. TEL 607-722-5857. FAX 607-722-1424. *196*

JOURNAL OF INTERNATIONAL HOSPITALITY, LEISURE AND TOURISM MANAGEMENT.
Haworth Press, Inc., Food Products Press, 10 Alice St., Binghamton, NY 13904. TEL 607-722-5857. FAX 607-722-6362. *3731*

JOURNAL OF INTERNATIONAL HUMAN RESOURCE MANAGEMENT.
Universal Publications, P.O. Box 7305, Ottawa, ON K1L 8E4, Canada. TEL 613-831-1052. FAX 613-831-8452. *1570*

JOURNAL OF INTERNATIONAL INFORMATION MANAGEMENT.
International Information Management Association, Department of Information and Decision Sciences, California State University, San Bernardino, CA 92407. TEL 909-880-5786. FAX 909-880-5994. *1488*

JOURNAL OF INTERNATIONAL MANAGEMENT.
John Wiley & Sons, Inc., Journals, 605 Third Ave., New York, NY 10158. TEL 212-850-6645. FAX 212-820-6021. *1488*

JOURNAL OF INTERNATIONAL MARKETING.
Michigan State University Press, Manly Miles Bldg., Ste. 25, 1405 S. Harrison Rd., East Lansing, MI 48823-5202. TEL 517-355-9543. FAX 517-432-2611. *1533*

JOURNAL OF INTERNATIONAL MEDICAL RESEARCH.
Cambridge Medical Publications Ltd., Wicker House, High St., Worthing, W. Sussex BN11 1DJ, England. TEL 01903-205884. FAX 01903-234862. *4695*

JOURNAL OF INTERNATIONAL MONEY AND FINANCE.
Elsevier Science Ltd., Pergamon, P.O. Box 800, Kidlington, Oxford OX5 1DX, England. TEL 44-1865-843000. FAX 44-1865-843010. *1150*

JOURNAL OF INTERNATIONAL SELLING & SALES MANAGEMENT.
European Marketing Association, 18 St. Peters Steps, Brixham, Devon, England. *1534*

JOURNAL OF INTERNATIONAL STUDIES.
Sophia University, Institute of International Relations, 7-1 Kioi-cho, Chiyoda-ku, Tokyo 102, Japan. TEL 81-3-3238-3561. FAX 81-3-3238-3592. *6024*

JOURNAL OF INTERPROFESSIONAL CARE.
Carfax Publishing Co., P.O. Box 25, Abingdon, Oxon. OX14 3UE, England. TEL 44-1235-401000. FAX 44-1235-401550. *4695*

JOURNAL OF INTERVENTIONAL CARDIAC ELECTROPHYSIOLOGY.
Kluwer Academic Publishers, Postbus 17, 3300 AA Dordrecht, Netherlands. TEL 31-78-6392392. FAX 31-78-6392254. *4821*

JOURNAL OF INTERVENTIONAL CARDIOLOGY.
Futura Publishing Company, Inc., 135 Bedford Rd., Box 418, Armonk, NY 10504-0418. TEL 914-273-1014. FAX 914-273-1015. *4821*

JOURNAL OF INTRAVENOUS NURSING.
Lippincott - Raven Publishers, 227 E. Washington Sq., Philadelphia, PA 19106. TEL 215-238-4200. FAX 215-238-4227. *4937*

JOURNAL OF INVASIVE CARDIOLOGY.
Health Management Publications, Inc., 950 W Valley Rd., Ste. 2800, Wayne, PA 19087. TEL 215-337-4466. FAX 215-337-0890. *4821*

JOURNAL OF INVERSE AND ILL-POSED PROBLEMS.
V S P, P.O. Box 346, 3700 AH Zeist, Netherlands. TEL 31-30-6925790. FAX 31-30-6932081. *4583*

JOURNAL OF INVERTEBRATE PATHOLOGY.
Academic Press, Inc., Journal Division, 525 B St., Ste. 1900, San Diego, CA 92101-4495. TEL 619-230-1840. FAX 619-699-6800. *756*

JOURNAL OF INVESTIGATIVE DERMATOLOGY.
Blackwell Science Inc., 350 Main St., Malden, MA 02148. TEL 617-876-7000. FAX 617-388-8255. *4879*

JOURNAL OF INVESTIGATIVE MEDICINE.
Slack, Inc., 6900 Grove Rd., Thorofare, NJ 08086-9447. TEL 609-848-1000. FAX 609-853-5991. *4905*

JOURNAL OF INVESTIGATIVE SURGERY.
Taylor & Francis Inc., 1900 Frost Rd., Ste. 101, Bristol, PA 19007. TEL 215-785-5800. FAX 215-785-5515. *5145*

JOURNAL OF INVITATIONAL THEORY AND PRACTICE.
International Alliance for Invitational Education, School of Education, University of North Carolina at Greensboro, Greensboro, NC 27412-5001. TEL 919-334-3431. FAX 919-334-5060. *2456*

JOURNAL OF IRRIGATION AND DRAINAGE.
American Society of Civil Engineers, 345 E. 47th St., New York, NY 10017-2398. TEL 212-705-7288. FAX 212-980-4681. *2791*

THE JOURNAL OF ISRAELI HISTORY.
Frank Cass, Newbury House, 890-900 Eastern Ave., Newbury Park, Ilford, Essex 1G2 7HH, England. TEL 44-181-599-8866. FAX 44-181-599-0984. *3656*

JOURNAL OF JAPANESE STUDIES.
Society for Japanese Studies, University of Washington, Box 353650, Seattle, WA 98195-3650. TEL 206-543-9302. FAX 206-685-0668. *5531*

JOURNAL OF JEWISH COMMUNAL SERVICE.
Jewish Communal Service Association, 3084 State Hwy. 27, Ste. 9, Kendall Park, NJ 08824-1657. TEL 908-821-1871. FAX 908-821-5335. *6673*

JOURNAL OF JEWISH THOUGHT AND PHILOSOPHY.
Gordon and Breach - Harwood Academic, Amsteldisk 166, 1st Fl., 1079 LH Amsterdam, Netherlands. *6406*

JOURNAL OF KNOT THEORY AND ITS RAMIFICATIONS.
World Scientific Publishing Co. Pte. Ltd., Farrer Rd., P.O. Box 128, Singapore 9128, Singapore. TEL 65-3826553. FAX 65-3825919. *4583*

JOURNAL OF LABELLED COMPOUNDS AND RADIOPHARMACEUTICALS.
John Wiley & Sons Ltd., Journals, Baffins Ln., Chichester, W. Sussex PO19 1UD, England. TEL 44-1243-779777. FAX 44-1243-775878. *1793*

JOURNAL OF LABOR ECONOMICS.
University of Chicago Press, Journals Division, Box 37005, Chicago, IL 60637. TEL 773-753-3347. FAX 773-753-0811. *1439*

JOURNAL OF LABOR RESEARCH.
George Mason University, Department of Economics, MSN 3G4, 4400 University Dr., Fairfax, VA 22030-4444. TEL 703-993-1155. FAX 703-993-1133. *1439*

THE JOURNAL OF LABORATORY AND CLINICAL MEDICINE.
Mosby - Year Book, Inc., 11830 Westline Industrial Dr., St. Louis, MO 63146. TEL 314-872-8370. FAX 314-432-1380. *4898*

JOURNAL OF LANGUAGE FOR INTERNATIONAL BUSINESS.
American Graduate School of International Management, Modern Language Department, 15249 N. 59th Ave., Glendale, AZ 85306-6012. TEL 602-978-7290. FAX 602-439-1435. *4268*

JOURNAL OF LASER APPLICATIONS.
Chapman & Hall, Journals Department 2-6 Boundary Row, London SE1 8HN, England. TEL 44-171-8650066. FAX 44-171-5229623. *5863*

JOURNAL OF LATIN AMERICAN AFFAIRS.
Box 3762, Washington, DC 20007. *3633*

JOURNAL OF LATIN AMERICAN LORE.
University of California at Los Angeles, Latin American Center, 10342 Bunche Hall, Box 951447, Los Angeles, CA 90095-1447. TEL 310-825-6634. FAX 310-206-6859. *3088*

JOURNAL OF LAW AND ECONOMICS.
University of Chicago Press, Journals Division, Box 37005, Chicago, IL 60637. TEL 773-753-3347. FAX 773-753-0811. *3969*

JOURNAL OF LAW AND RELIGION.
Hamline University School of Law, Journal of Law and Religion, 1536 Hewitt Ave., St. Paul, MN 55104. TEL 612-523-2082. FAX 612-523-2236. *3969*

JOURNAL OF LAW AND SOCIAL WORK.
Wilfrid Laurier University Press, 75 University Ave. W., Waterloo, ON N2L 3C5, Canada. TEL 519-884-0710. FAX 519-725-1399. *3969*

JOURNAL OF LAW, ECONOMICS, AND ORGANIZATION.
Oxford University Press, Journals, 2001 Evans Rd., Cary, NC 27513. TEL 919-677-0977. FAX 919-677-1714. *3970*

THE JOURNAL OF LAW, MEDICINE & ETHICS.
American Society of Law, Medicine & Ethics, 765 Commonwealth Ave., Ste. 1634, Boston, MA 02215. TEL 617-262-4990. FAX 617-437-7596. *3970*

JOURNAL OF LEADERSHIP STUDIES.
Baker College, Center for Graduate Studies, 1050 W. Bristol Rd., Flint, MI 48507. TEL 810-766-4105. FAX 810-766-4399. *1488*

JOURNAL OF LEARNING DISABILITIES.
Pro-Ed Inc., 8700 Shoal Creek Blvd., Austin, TX 78757-6897. TEL 512-451-3246. FAX 512-451-8542. *2586*

JOURNAL OF LEGAL ECONOMICS.
American Academy of Economic and Financial Experts, University of North Alabama, Box 5077, Florence, AL 35632. TEL 205-760-4144. FAX 205-760-4170. *1308*

THE JOURNAL OF LEGAL HISTORY.
Frank Cass, Newbury House, 890-900 Eastern Ave., Newbury Park, Ilford, Essex IG2 7HH, England. TEL 44-181-599-8866. FAX 44-181-599-0984. *3502*

THE JOURNAL OF LEGAL MEDICINE.
Taylor & Francis Inc., 1900 Frost Rd., Ste. 101, Bristol, PA 19007-1598. TEL 215-785-5800. FAX 215-785-5515. *4696*

JOURNAL OF LEGAL STUDIES.
University of Chicago Press, Journals Division, Box 37005, Chicago, IL 60637. TEL 773-753-3347. FAX 773-753-0811. *3970*

JOURNAL OF LEGISLATION.
University of Notre Dame, Notre Dame Law School, Notre Dame, IN 46556. TEL 219-631-5918. *3970*

THE JOURNAL OF LEGISLATIVE STUDIES.
Frank Cass, 890-900 Eastern Ave., Newbury Park, Ilford, Essex IG2 7HH, England. TEL 44-181-599-8866. FAX 44-181-599-0984. *6024*

JOURNAL OF LESBIAN STUDIES.
Haworth Press, Inc., 10 Alice St., Binghamton, NY 13904. TEL 607-722-5857. FAX 607-722-6362. *3696*

JOURNAL OF LIBRARY ADMINISTRATION.
Haworth Press, Inc., 10 Alice St., Binghamton, NY 13904. TEL 607-722-5857. FAX 607-722-6362. *4189*

JOURNAL OF LIE THEORY.
Heldermann Verlag, Langer Graben 13d, 32657 Lemgo, Germany. TEL 49-5261-10226. FAX 49-5261-15264. *4583*

JOURNAL OF LIGHTWAVE TECHNOLOGY.
Institute of Electrical and Electronics Engineers, Inc., 345 E. 47th St., New York, NY 10017-2394. TEL 732-981-0060. FAX 732-981-9667. *5863*

JOURNAL OF LIMITED LIABILITY COMPANIES.
Warren, Gorham & Lamont, One Penn Plaza, New York, NY 10119-4098. TEL 212-971-5423. FAX 212-971-5113. *1617*

JOURNAL OF LIPID MEDIATORS AND CELL SIGNALING.
Elsevier Science B.V., P.O. Box 211, 1000 AE Amsterdam, Netherlands. TEL 31-20-4853911. FAX 31-20-4853598. *663*

JOURNAL OF LIPID RESEARCH.
Federation of American Societies for Experimental Biology, 9650 Rockville Pike, Bethesda, MD 20814. TEL 301-530-7100. FAX 301-571-1855. *663*

JOURNAL OF LIPOSOME RESEARCH.
Marcel Dekker Journals, 270 Madison Ave., New York, NY 10016. TEL 212-696-9000. FAX 212-685-4540. *5672*

JOURNAL OF LIQUID CHROMATOGRAPHY & RELATED TECHNOLOGIES.
Marcel Dekker Journals, 270 Madison Ave., New York, NY 10016. TEL 212-696-9000. FAX 212-685-4540. *1755*

JOURNAL OF LITERARY STUDIES.
University of South Africa, Department of Literary Theory, P.O. Box 392, Pretoria 0001, South Africa. TEL 27-12-4296058. FAX 27-12-4293221. *4421*

JOURNAL OF LOGIC, LANGUAGE AND INFORMATION.
Kluwer Academic Publishers, Postbus 17, 3300 AA Dordrecht, Netherlands. TEL 31-78-6392392. FAX 31-78-6392254. *4268*

JOURNAL OF LOGIC PROGRAMMING.
Elsevier Science Inc., Box 945, New York, NY 10159-0945. TEL 212-633-3730. FAX 212-633-3680. *2144*

JOURNAL OF LONG TERM HOME HEALTH CARE.
Springer Publishing Company, 536 Broadway, New York, NY 10012-3955. TEL 212-431-4370. FAX 212-941-7842. *3716*

JOURNAL OF LOSS PREVENTION IN THE PROCESS INDUSTRIES.
Elsevier Science Ltd., P.O. Box 800, Kidlington, Oxford OX5 1DX, England. TEL 44-1865-843000. FAX 44-1865-843010. *2767*

JOURNAL OF LOW FREQUENCY NOISE & VIBRATION.
Multi-Science Publishing Co. Ltd., 107 High St., Brentwood, Essex CM14 4RX, England. TEL 44-1277-224632. FAX 44-1277-223453. *5873*

JOURNAL OF LOW TEMPERATURE PHYSICS.
Plenum Publishing Corp., 233 Spring St., New York, NY 10013-1578. TEL 212-620-8000. FAX 212-463-0742. *5841*

JOURNAL OF LUMINESCENCE.
North-Holland, P.O. Box 211, 1000 AE Amsterdam, Netherlands. TEL 31-20-4853911. FAX 31-20-4853598. *5863*

JOURNAL OF M U D RESEARCH. *6622*

JOURNAL OF MACROMOLECULAR SCIENCE: PART A - PURE AND APPLIED CHEMISTRY.
Marcel Dekker Journals, 270 Madison Ave., New York, NY 10016. TEL 212-696-9000. FAX 212-685-4540. *1816*

JOURNAL OF MACROMOLECULAR SCIENCE: PART B - PHYSICS.
Marcel Dekker Journals, 270 Madison Ave., New York, NY 10016. TEL 212-696-9000. FAX 212-685-4540. *5810*

JOURNAL OF MACROMOLECULAR SCIENCE: PART C - REVIEWS IN MACROMOLECULAR CHEMISTRY AND PHYSICS.
Marcel Dekker Journals, 270 Madison Ave., New York, NY 10016. TEL 212-696-9000. FAX 212-685-4540. *1816*

JOURNAL OF MAGNETIC RESONANCE.
Academic Press, Inc., Journal Division, 525 B St., Ste. 1900, San Diego, CA 92101-4495. TEL 619-230-1840. FAX 619-699-6800. *5810*

JOURNAL OF MAGNETIC RESONANCE IMAGING.
Williams & Wilkins, 351 W. Camden St., Baltimore, MD 21201-2436. TEL 410-528-4068. FAX 410-528-4452. *5109*

JOURNAL OF MAGNETISM AND MAGNETIC MATERIALS.
European Physical Society, 34 rue Marc Seguin, B.P. 2136, 68060 Mulhouse Cedex, France. TEL 33-3-89329440. FAX 33-3-89329449. *5810*

JOURNAL OF MAGNETOHYDRODYNAMICS AND PLASMA RESEARCH.
Nova Science Publishers, Inc., 6080 Jericho Tpke., Ste. 207, Commack, NY 11725-2808. TEL 516-499-3103. FAX 516-499-3146. *5841*

JOURNAL OF MAHARASHTRA AGRICULTURAL UNIVERSITIES.
Poona Agricultural College, Poona 411 005, India. TEL 327033. *130*

JOURNAL OF MAINTENANCE IN THE ADDICTIONS.
Haworth Press, Inc., 10 Alice St., Binghamton, NY 13904. TEL 607-722-5857. FAX 607-722-6362. *2303*

JOURNAL OF MALTESE STUDIES.
University of Malta, Faculty of Arts, Msida, Malta. TEL 356-336451. FAX 356-336450. *3578*

JOURNAL OF MAMMALIAN EVOLUTION.
Plenum Publishing Corp., 233 Spring St., New York, NY 10013-1578. TEL 212-620-8000. FAX 212-807-1047. *840*

JOURNAL OF MAMMALOGY.
American Society of Mammalogists, c/o Dr. H. Duane Smith, Sec.-Treas., Monte L. Bean Life Science Museum, Brigham Young University, Provo, UT 84602. TEL 801-378-2492. *840*

JOURNAL OF MAMMARY GLAND BIOLOGY AND NEOPLASIA.
Plenum Publishing Corp., 233 Spring St., New York, NY 10013-1578. TEL 212-620-8000. FAX 212-463-0742. *4961*

JOURNAL OF MANAGEMENT & GOVERNANCE.
Kluwer Academic Publishers Boston, Box 358, Accord Sta., Hingham, MA 02018-0358. TEL 617-871-6600. FAX 617-871-6528. *1488*

JOURNAL OF MANAGEMENT CONSULTING.
858 Longview Rd., Burlingame, CA 94010-6974. TEL 415-342-1954. FAX 415-344-5005. *1488*

JOURNAL OF MANAGEMENT INFORMATION SYSTEMS.
M.E. Sharpe, Inc., 80 Business Park Dr., Armonk, NY 10504. TEL 914-273-1800. FAX 914-273-2106. *2184*

JOURNAL OF MANAGEMENT STUDIES.
University of Ghana, School of Administration, P.O. Box 78, Legon, Ghana. TEL 233-21-500592. FAX 233-21-500024. *1488*

JOURNAL OF MANAGEMENT STUDIES.
Blackwell Publishers Ltd., 108 Cowley Rd., Oxford OX4 1JF, England. TEL 44-1865-791100. FAX 44-1865-791347. *1488*

JOURNAL OF MANAGERIAL ISSUES.
Pittsburg State University, Department of Economics, Finance & Banking, 1701 S. Broadway, Pittsburg, KS 66762-7533. TEL 316-235-4547. FAX 316-235-4578. *1489*

JOURNAL OF MANIPULATIVE AND PHYSIOLOGICAL THERAPEUTICS.
Williams & Wilkins, 351 W. Camden St., Baltimore, MD 21201-2436. TEL 410-528-4068. FAX 410-528-4452. *4828*

JOURNAL OF MANUFACTURING SYSTEMS.
Elsevier Science Ltd., P.O. Box 800, Kidlington, Oxford OX5 1DX, England. TEL 44-1865-843000. FAX 44-1865-843010. *2156*

JOURNAL OF MARINE AND ATMOSPHERIC RESEARCH.
Cochin University of Science and Technology, School of Marine Sciences, Fine Arts Ave., Cochin 682 016, India. *2406*

JOURNAL OF MARINE BIOTECHNOLOGY.
Springer-Verlag, Life Science Journals, 175 Fifth Ave., New York, NY 10010. TEL 212-460-1500. FAX 212-473-6272. *685*

JOURNAL OF MARINE RESEARCH.
Sears Foundation for Marine Research, Kline Geology Laboratory, Yale University, Box 208109, New Haven, CT 06520-8109. TEL 203-432-3154. *2406*

JOURNAL OF MARINE SYSTEMS.
Elsevier Science B.V., P.O. Box 211, 1000 AE Amsterdam, Netherlands. TEL 31-20-4853911. FAX 31-20-4853598. *2407*

JOURNAL OF MARKET - FOCUSED MANAGEMENT.
Kluwer Academic Publishers Boston, Box 358, Accord Sta., Hingham, MA 02018-0358. TEL 617-871-6600. FAX 617-871-6528. *1489*

JOURNAL OF MARKETING CHANNELS.
Haworth Press, Inc., 10 Alice St., Binghamton, NY 13904. TEL 607-722-5857. FAX 607-722-6362. *1534*

JOURNAL OF MARKETING COMMUNICATIONS.
Thomson Professional, 2-6 Boundary Row, London SE1 8HN, England. TEL 44-171-8650066. FAX 44-171-5229623. *1534*

JOURNAL OF MARKETING FOR HIGHER EDUCATION.
Haworth Press, Inc., 10 Alice St., Binghamton, NY 13904. TEL 607-722-5857. FAX 607-722-6362. *1534*

JOURNAL OF MASS MEDIA ETHICS.
Lawrence Erlbaum Associates, Inc., 10 Industrial Dr., Mahwah, NJ 07430-2262. TEL 201-236-9500. FAX 201-236-0072. *1996*

JOURNAL OF MASS SPECTROMETRY.
John Wiley & Sons Ltd., Journals, Baffins Ln., Chichester, W. Sussex PO19 1UD, England. TEL 44-1243-779777. FAX 44-1243-775878. *1793*

JOURNAL OF MATERIALS ENGINEERING AND PERFORMANCE.
A S M International, Materials Division, Materials Park, OH 44073-0022. TEL 216-338-5151. FAX 216-338-4634. *2862*

JOURNAL OF MATERIALS IN CIVIL ENGINEERING: PROPERTIES, APPLICATIONS, DURABILITY.
American Society of Civil Engineers, 345 E. 47th St., New York, NY 10017-2398. TEL 212-705-7288. FAX 212-980-4681. *2791*

JOURNAL OF MATERIALS PROCESSING AND MANUFACTURING SCIENCE.
Technomic Publishing Co., Inc., 851 New Holland Ave., Box 3535, Lancaster, PA 17604. TEL 717-291-5609. FAX 717-295-4538. *6964*

JOURNAL OF MATERIALS PROCESSING TECHNOLOGY.
Elsevier Science S.A., P.O. Box 564, CH-1001 Lausanne 1, Switzerland. TEL 41-21-3207381. FAX 41-21-3235444. *2890*

JOURNAL OF MATERIALS SCIENCE.
Thomson Science, 2-6 Boundary Row, London SE1 8HN, England. TEL 44-171-8650066. FAX 44-171-5229623. *2862*

JOURNAL OF MATERIALS SCIENCE & TECHNOLOGY.
Chinese Society for Metals (Shenyang), 72 Wenhua Rd., Shenyang 110015, People's Republic of China. TEL 86-24-384-3531. FAX 86-24-389-1320. *5197*

JOURNAL OF MATERIALS SCIENCE LETTERS.
Chapman & Hall, Journals Department 2-6 Boundary Row, London SE1 8HN, England. TEL 44-171-8650066. FAX 44-171-5229623. *2862*

JOURNAL OF MATERIALS SCIENCE: MATERIALS IN ELECTRONICS.
Thomson Science, 2-6 Boundary Row, London SE1 8HN, England. TEL 44-171-8650066. FAX 44-171-5229623. *2863*

JOURNAL OF MATERIALS SCIENCE: MATERIALS IN MEDICINE.
Thomson Science, 2-6 Boundary Row, London SE1 8HN, England. TEL 44-171-8650066. FAX 44-171-5229623. *2863*

JOURNAL OF MATERIALS SYNTHESIS AND PROCESSING.
Plenum Publishing Corp., 233 Spring St., New York, NY 10013-1578. TEL 212-620-8000. FAX 212-463-0172. *2863*

JOURNAL OF MATERNAL - FETAL INVESTIGATION.
Springer-Verlag, Medical Journals, 175 Fifth Ave., New York, NY 10010. TEL 212-460-1500. FAX 212-473-6272. *4961*

THE JOURNAL OF MATERNAL - FETAL MEDICINE.
John Wiley & Sons, Inc., Journals, 605 Third Ave., New York, NY 10158-0012. TEL 212-850-6645. FAX 212-850-6021. *4961*

JOURNAL OF MATHEMATICAL ANALYSIS AND APPLICATIONS.
Academic Press, Inc., Journal Division, 525 B St., Ste. 1900, San Diego, CA 92101-4495. TEL 619-230-1840. FAX 619-699-6800. *4583*

JOURNAL OF MATHEMATICAL BEHAVIOR.
Ablex Publishing Corporation, Box 5297, Greenwich, CT 06831-0504. TEL 203-661-7602. FAX 203-661-0792. *4583*

JOURNAL OF MATHEMATICAL BIOLOGY.
Springer-Verlag, Heidelberger Platz 3, 14197 Berlin, Germany. TEL 49-30-82787-0. FAX 49-30-82787448. *609*

JOURNAL OF MATHEMATICAL ECONOMICS.
Elsevier Science S.A., P.O. Box 564, CH-1001 Lausanne 1, Switzerland. TEL 41-21-3207381. FAX 41-21-3235444. *1308*

JOURNAL OF MATHEMATICAL IMAGING AND VISION.
Kluwer Academic Publishers Boston, Box 358, Accord Sta., Hingham, MA 02018-0358. TEL 617-871-6600. FAX 617-871-6528. *4621*

JOURNAL OF MATHEMATICAL PHYSICS.
American Institute of Physics, One Physics Ellipse, College Park, MD 20740-3843. TEL 301-209-3000. *5810*

JOURNAL OF MATHEMATICAL PSYCHOLOGY.
Academic Press, Inc., Journal Division, 525 B St., Ste. 1900, San Diego, CA 92101-4495. TEL 619-230-1840. FAX 619-699-6800. *6128*

JOURNAL OF MATHEMATICAL SCIENCES.
Plenum Publishing Corp., Consultants Bureau, 233 Spring St., New York, NY 10013-1578. TEL 212-620-8468. FAX 212-463-0742. *4583*

JOURNAL OF MATHEMATICAL SOCIOLOGY.
Gordon and Breach - Harwood Academic, Amsteldisk 166, 1st Fl., 1079 LH Amsterdam, Netherlands. *6717*

JOURNAL OF MAYAN LINGUISTICS.
Geoscience Publications, Box 16010, Baton Rouge, LA 70893-6010. TEL 504-388-6245. FAX 504-388-4420. *4268*

JOURNAL OF MECHANICAL DESIGN.
American Society of Mechanical Engineers, 22 Law Dr., Fairfield, NJ 07007-2900. TEL 973-882-1167. FAX 973-882-1717. *2890*

JOURNAL OF MEDIA ECONOMICS.
Lawrence Erlbaum Associates, Inc., 10 Industrial Dr., Mahwah, NJ 07430-2262. TEL 201-236-9500. FAX 201-236-0072. *1996*

JOURNAL OF MEDICAL & VETERINARY MYCOLOGY.
Blackwell Science Ltd., Osney Mead, Oxford OX2 OEL, England. TEL 44-1865-206206. FAX 44-1865-721205. *4839*

JOURNAL OF MEDICAL AND VETERINARY MYCOLOGY. SUPPLEMENT.
Blackwell Science Ltd., Osney Mead, Oxford OX2 OEL, England. TEL 44-1865-206206. FAX 44-1865-721205. *4839*

JOURNAL OF MEDICAL BIOGRAPHY.
Royal Society of Medicine Press Ltd., 1 Wimpole St., London W1M 8AE, England. TEL 44-171-290-2900. FAX 44-171-290-2929. *575*

JOURNAL OF MEDICAL ENGINEERING & TECHNOLOGY.
Taylor & Francis Ltd., 1 Gunpowder Sq., London EC4A 3DE, England. TEL 44-171-583-0490. FAX 44-171-583-0585. *4696*

JOURNAL OF MEDICAL ENTOMOLOGY.
Entomological Society of America, 9301 Annapolis Rd., Lanham, MD 20706. TEL 301-731-4535. FAX 301-731-4538. *4696*

JOURNAL OF MEDICAL ETHICS.
B M J Publishing Group, B.M.A. House, Tavistock Sq., London WC1H 9JR, England. TEL 44-171-383-6270. FAX 44-171-383-6402. *4696*

JOURNAL OF MEDICAL GENETICS.
B M J Publishing Group, B.M.A. House, Tavistock Sq., London WC1H 9JR, England. TEL 44-171-383-6270. FAX 44-171-383-6402. *772*

JOURNAL OF MEDICAL HUMANITIES.
Human Sciences Press, Inc., 233 Spring St., New York, NY 10013-1578. TEL 212-620-8000. FAX 212-463-0742. *4696*

JOURNAL OF MEDICAL MICROBIOLOGY.
Thomson Science, 2-6 Boundary Row, London SE1 8HN, England. TEL 44-171-8650066. FAX 44-171-5229623. *4696*

JOURNAL OF MEDICAL PRIMATOLOGY.
Munksgaard International Publishers Ltd., P.O. Box 2148, DK-1016 Copenhagen K, Denmark. TEL 45-33-127030. FAX 45-33-129387. *840*

JOURNAL OF MEDICAL SCREENING.
B M J Publishing Group, B.M.A. House, Tavistock Sq., London WC1H 9JR, England. TEL 44-171-383-6270. FAX 44-171-383-6402. *4840*

JOURNAL OF MEDICAL SPEECH - LANGUAGE PATHOLOGY.
Singular Publishing Group, Inc., 401 W. A ST., Ste. 325, San Diego, CA 92101-7901. TEL 800-521-8545. FAX 800-774-8398. *5022*

JOURNAL OF MEDICAL SYSTEMS.
Plenum Publishing Corp., 233 Spring St., New York, NY 10013-1578. TEL 212-620-8000. FAX 212-463-0742. *4847*

JOURNAL OF MEDICAL VIROLOGY.
John Wiley & Sons, Inc., Journals, 605 Third Ave., New York, NY 10158. TEL 212-850-6645. FAX 212-850-6021. *4697*

JOURNAL OF MEDICINAL CHEMISTRY.
American Chemical Society, 1155 16th St., N.W., Washington, DC 20036. TEL 800-333-9511. FAX 614-447-3671. *5672*

JOURNAL OF MEDICINE.
P J D Publications Ltd., Box 966, Westbury, NY 11590. TEL 516-626-0650. FAX 516-626-5546. *4697*

THE JOURNAL OF MEDICINE AND PHILOSOPHY.
Kluwer Academic Publishers, Postbus 17, 3300 AA Dordrecht, Netherlands. TEL 31-78-6392392. FAX 31-78-6392254. *4697*

JOURNAL OF MEDIEVAL AND EARLY MODERN STUDIES.
Duke University Press, Box 90660, Durham, NC 27708-0660. TEL 919-687-3600. FAX 919-688-4574. *3783*

JOURNAL OF MEDIEVAL HISTORY.
Elsevier Science B.V., P.O. Box 211, 1000 AE Amsterdam, Netherlands. TEL 31-20-4853911. FAX 31-20-4853598. *3578*

JOURNAL OF MEDIEVAL LATIN.
N.V. Brepols, Steenweg op Tielen 68, 2300 Turnhout, Belgium. TEL 32-14-402500. FAX 32-14-428919. *4268*

JOURNAL OF MEDITERRANEAN STUDIES.
Malta University Services Ltd., Msida MSD 06, Malta. TEL 356-343572. *3783*

JOURNAL OF MEMBRANE BIOLOGY.
Springer-Verlag, Life Science Journals, 175 Fifth Ave., New York, NY 10010. TEL 212-460-1500. FAX 212-473-6272. *742*

JOURNAL OF MEMBRANE SCIENCE.
Elsevier Science B.V., P.O. Box 211, 1000 AE Amsterdam, Netherlands. TEL 31-20-4853911. FAX 31-20-4853598. *1831*

JOURNAL OF MENNONITE STUDIES.
University of Winnipeg, Winnipeg, MB R3B 2E9, Canada. TEL 204-786-9391. FAX 204-774-4134. *6429*

JOURNAL OF MEN'S STUDIES.
Men's Studies Press, P.O. Box 32, Harriman, TN 37748-0032. *5183*

JOURNAL OF MENTAL HEALTH.
Carfax Publishing Co., P.O. Box 25, Abingdon, Oxon. OX14 3UE, England. TEL 44-1235-401000. FAX 44-1235-401550. *5074*

JOURNAL OF MENTAL HEALTH ADMINISTRATION.
Sage Publications, Inc., 2455 Teller Rd., Thousand Oaks, CA 91320. TEL 805-499-0721. FAX 805-499-0871. *6241*

JOURNAL OF MENTAL HEALTH AND AGING.
Springer Publishing Company, 536 Broadway, New York, NY 10012-3955. TEL 212-431-4370. FAX 212-941-7842. *3439*

JOURNAL OF METAMORPHIC GEOLOGY.
Blackwell Science Inc., 350 Main St., Malden, MA 02148. TEL 617-876-7000. FAX 617-388-8255. *2353*

JOURNAL OF METEOROLOGY.
Artetech Publishing Co., 54 Frome Rd., Bradford-on-Avon BA15 1LD, England. TEL 44-1225-862482. FAX 44-1225-865601. *5236*

JOURNAL OF MICROBIOLOGICAL METHODS.
Elsevier Science B.V., P.O. Box 211, 1000 AE Amsterdam, Netherlands. TEL 31-20-4853911. FAX 31-20-4853598. *788*

JOURNAL OF MICROCOLUMN SEPARATIONS.
John Wiley & Sons, Inc., Journals, 605 Third Ave., New York, NY 10158-0012. TEL 212-850-6645. FAX 212-850-6021. *1793*

JOURNAL OF MICROELECTRONIC SYSTEMS INTEGRATION.
Plenum Publishing Corp., 233 Spring St., New York, NY 10013-1578. TEL 212-620-8000. FAX 212-463-0742. *2837*

JOURNAL OF MICROENCAPSULATION.
Taylor & Francis Ltd., 1 Gunpowder Sq., London EC4A 3DE, England. TEL 44-171-583-0490. FAX 44-171-583-0585. *5672*

JOURNAL OF MICROSCOPY.
Blackwell Science Ltd., Osney Mead, Oxford OX2 0EL, England. TEL 44-1865-206206. FAX 44-1865-721205. *797*

JOURNAL OF MICROSCOPY RESEARCH AND TECHNIQUE.
John Wiley & Sons, Inc., Journals, 605 Third Ave., New York, NY 10158. TEL 212-850-6645. FAX 212-850-6021. *797*

JOURNAL OF MICROWAVE POWER AND ELECTROMAGNETIC ENERGY.
International Microwave Power Institute, 10210 Leatherleaf Ct., Manassas, VA 20111-4245. TEL 703-257-1415. *2837*

JOURNAL OF MILITARY HISTORY.
Society for Military History, c/o George C. Marshall Library, Virginia Military Institute, Lexington, VA 24450. TEL 540-464-7468. FAX 540-464-5229. *5274*

JOURNAL OF MIND AND BEHAVIOR.
Institute of Mind & Behavior, Box 522, Village Sta., New York, NY 10014. TEL 212-595-4853. *6128*

JOURNAL OF MINERAL POLICY, BUSINESS AND ENVIRONMENT - RAW MATERIALS REPORT.
Raavarugruppen Ekonomisk Foerening, P.O. Box 44062, S-100 73 Stockholm, Sweden. TEL 46-8-744-00-65. FAX 46-8-7440066. *1364*

JOURNAL OF MINING AND GEOLOGY.
Nigerian Mining and Geosciences Society, University of Ibadan, Department of Geology, Ibadan, Oyo State, Nigeria. TEL 234-2-8101100. *5304*

JOURNAL OF MINING SCIENCE.
Plenum Publishing Corp., Consultants Bureau, 233 Spring St., New York, NY 10013-1578. TEL 212-620-8468. FAX 212-463-0742. *5305*

JOURNAL OF MINISTRY IN ADDICTION & RECOVERY.
Haworth Press, Inc., 10 Alice St., Binghamton, NY 13904. TEL 607-722-5857. FAX 607-722-6362. *6349*

JOURNAL OF MINISTRY MARKETING & MANAGEMENT.
Haworth Press, Inc., 10 Alice St., Binghamton, NY 13904. TEL 607-722-5857. FAX 607-722-6362. *6349*

JOURNAL OF MODERN HISTORY.
University of Chicago Press, Journals Division, Box 37005, Chicago, IL 60637. TEL 773-753-3347. FAX 773-753-0811. *3502*

JOURNAL OF MODERN OPTICS.
Taylor & Francis Ltd., 1 Gunpowder Sq., London EC4A 3DE, England. TEL 44-171-583-0490. FAX 44-171-583-0585. *5863*

JOURNAL OF MOLECULAR CATALYSIS A: CHEMICAL.
Elsevier Science B.V., P.O. Box 211, 1000 AE Amsterdam, Netherlands. TEL 31-20-4853911. FAX 31-20-4853598. *1831*

JOURNAL OF MOLECULAR CATALYSIS B: ENZYMATIC.
Elsevier Science B.V., P.O. Box 211, 1000 AE Amsterdam, Netherlands. TEL 31-20-4853911. FAX 31-20-4853598. *1831*

JOURNAL OF MOLECULAR EVOLUTION.
Springer-Verlag, Life Science Journals, 175 Fifth Ave., New York, NY 10010. TEL 212-460-1500. FAX 212-473-6272. *772*

JOURNAL OF MOLECULAR GRAPHICS.
Elsevier Science Inc., Box 945, New York, NY 10159-0945. TEL 212-633-3730. FAX 212-633-3680. *2124*

JOURNAL OF MOLECULAR LIQUIDS.
Elsevier Science B.V., P.O. Box 211, 1000 AE Amsterdam, Netherlands. TEL 31-20-4853911. FAX 31-20-4853598. *1831*

JOURNAL OF MOLECULAR NEUROSCIENCE.
Humana Press Inc., 999 Riverview Dr., Ste. 208, Totowa, NJ 07512. TEL 973-256-1699. FAX 973-256-8341. *5074*

JOURNAL OF MOLECULAR RECOGNITION.
John Wiley & Sons Ltd., Journals, Baffins Ln., Chichester, W. Sussex PO19 1UD, England. TEL 44-1243-779777. FAX 44-1243-775878. *664*

JOURNAL OF MOLECULAR SPECTROSCOPY.
Academic Press, Inc., Journal Division, 525 B St., Ste. 1900, San Diego, CA 92101-4495. TEL 619-230-1840. FAX 619-699-6800. *5863*

JOURNAL OF MOLECULAR STRUCTURE.
Elsevier Science B.V., P.O. Box 211, 1000 AE Amsterdam, Netherlands. TEL 31-20-4853911. FAX 31-20-4853598. *1756*

JOURNAL OF MOLECULAR STRUCTURE: THEOCHEM.
Elsevier Science B.V., P.O. Box 211, 1000 AE Amsterdam, Netherlands. TEL 31-20-4853911. FAX 31-20-4853598. *1756*

JOURNAL OF MONETARY ECONOMICS.
North-Holland, P.O. Box 211, 1000 AE Amsterdam, Netherlands. TEL 31-20-4853911. FAX 31-20-4853598. *1151*

JOURNAL OF MONEY, CREDIT & BANKING.
Ohio State University Press, 1070 Carmack Rd., Columbus, OH 43210. TEL 614-292-6930. FAX 614-292-2065. *1151*

JOURNAL OF MORAL EDUCATION.
Carfax Publishing Co., P.O. Box 25, Abingdon, Oxon. OX14 3UE, England. TEL 44-1235-401000. FAX 44-1235-401550. *5733*

JOURNAL OF MORPHOLOGY.
John Wiley & Sons, Inc., Journals, 605 Third Ave., New York, NY 10158. TEL 212-850-6645. FAX 212-850-6021. *609*

JOURNAL OF MOTOR BEHAVIOR.
Heldref Publications, 1319 Eighteenth St., N.W., Washington, DC 20036-1802. TEL 202-296-6267. FAX 202-296-5149. *6128*

JOURNAL OF MULTICULTURAL NURSING AND HEALTH.
Riley Publications, Inc., Box 889, Chautauqua Institution, Chautauqua, NY 14722. TEL 716-357-2479. FAX 716-357-2479. *4937*

JOURNAL OF MULTICULTURAL SOCIAL WORK.
Haworth Press, Inc., 10 Alice St., Binghamton, NY 13904. TEL 607-722-5857. FAX 607-722-1424. *6717*

JOURNAL OF MULTINATIONAL FINANCIAL MANAGEMENT.
North-Holland, P.O. Box 211, 1000 AE Amsterdam, Netherlands. TEL 31-20-4853757. FAX 31-20-4853432. *1489*

JOURNAL OF MULTISTATE TAXATION.
Warren, Gorham & Lamont, One Penn Plaza, New York, NY 10119. TEL 212-971-5000. FAX 212-971-5113. *1617*

JOURNAL OF MULTIVARIATE ANALYSIS.
Academic Press, Inc., Journal Division, 525 B St., Ste. 1900, San Diego, CA 92101-4495. TEL 619-230-1840. FAX 619-699-6800. *4584*

JOURNAL OF MUSCLE RESEARCH AND CELL MOTILITY.
Chapman & Hall, Journals Department 2-6 Boundary Row, London SE1 8HN, England. TEL 44-171-8650066. FAX 44-171-5229623. *4697*

JOURNAL OF MUSCLE SHOALS HISTORY.
Tennessee Valley Historical Society, Box 149, Sheffield, AL 35660. TEL 205-381-2298. *3633*

THE JOURNAL OF MUSCULOSKELETAL MEDICINE.
Cliggott Publishing Co., 55 Holly Hill Ln., Box 4010, Greenwich, CT 06831. TEL 203-661-0600. *5010*

JOURNAL OF MUSCULOSKELETAL PAIN.
Haworth Press, Inc., 10 Alice St., Binghamton, NY 13904. TEL 607-722-5857. FAX 607-722-6362. *5010*

JOURNAL OF MUSCULOSKELETAL RESEARCH.
World Scientific Publishing Co. Pte. Ltd., Farrer Rd., P.O. Box 128, Singapore 9128, Singapore. TEL 65-382-5663. FAX 65-382-5919. *5010*

JOURNAL OF MUSIC THEORY.
Yale University, School of Music, Box 208310, New Haven, CT 06520. TEL 203-432-2985. FAX 203-432-2983. *5404*

JOURNAL OF MUSIC THEORY PEDAGOGY.
University of Oklahoma, School of Music, Parrington Oval, Norman, OK 73019. TEL 405-325-2081. *5404*

JOURNAL OF MUSIC THERAPY.
National Association for Music Therapy, Inc., 8455 Colesville Rd, Ste. 1000, Silver Spring, MD 20910-3392. TEL 301-589-3300. FAX 301-589-5175. *5404*

JOURNAL OF MUSICOLOGICAL RESEARCH.
Gordon and Breach - Harwood Academic, Amsteldisk 166, 1st Fl., 1079 LH Amsterdam, Netherlands. *5404*

JOURNAL OF MUSICOLOGY.
University of California Press, Journals Division, 2120 Berkeley Way, No. 5812, Berkeley, CA 94720-5812. TEL 510-643-7154. FAX 510-642-9917. *5405*

JOURNAL OF MYCOPATHOLOGICAL RESEARCH.
Indian Mycological Society, Department of Botany, University of Calcutta, 35 B.C. Rd., Calcutta 700 019, India. TEL 91-33-551-4189. FAX 91-33-475-3681. *711*

JOURNAL OF NATAL AND ZULU HISTORY.
University of Natal, Department of History, King George V Ave., Durban 4001, South Africa. TEL 27-31-2602620. FAX 27-31-2602621. *3527*

JOURNAL OF NATURAL GEOMETRY.
University of London, Mathematical Research Unit, Birbeck College, 7-15 Gresse St., London W1P 1PA, England. TEL 44-171-580-7710. FAX 44-171-631-6270. *4584*

JOURNAL OF NATURAL HISTORY.
Taylor & Francis Ltd., 1 Gunpowder Sq., London EC4A 3DE, England. TEL 44-171-583-0490. FAX 44-171-583-0585. *609*

JOURNAL OF NATURAL PRODUCTS.
American Society of Pharmacognosy, Dept. L-0011, Columbus, OH 43268-0011. TEL 614-447-3776. FAX 614-447-3671. *5672*

JOURNAL OF NATURAL RESOURCES AND LIFE SCIENCES EDUCATION.
American Society of Agronomy, Inc., 677 S. Segoe Rd., Madison, WI 53711. TEL 608-273-8080. FAX 608-273-2021. *232*

JOURNAL OF NATURAL TOXINS.
Alaken, Inc., 305 W. Magnolia St., Ste. 196, Ft. Collins, CO 80521. TEL 970-223-5348. FAX 970-226-8655. *5672*

JOURNAL OF NEAR-DEATH STUDIES.
Human Sciences Press, Inc., 233 Spring St., New York, NY 10013-1578. TEL 212-620-8000. FAX 212-463-0742. *6128*

JOURNAL OF NEAR EASTERN STUDIES.
University of Chicago Press, Journals Division, Box 37005, Chicago, IL 60637. TEL 773-753-3347. FAX 773-753-0811. *369*

JOURNAL OF NEAR INFRARED SPECTROSCOPY.
N I R Publications, 6 Charlton Mill, Charlton, Chichester, W. Sussex PO18 0HY, England. TEL 44-1243-811334. FAX 44-1243-811711. *1793*

JOURNAL OF NEGRO EDUCATION.
Howard University Press, Marketing Department, 2600 Sixth St., N.W., Washington, DC 20059. TEL 202-806-8120. FAX 202-806-8434. *2456*

JOURNAL OF NEGRO HISTORY.
Association for the Study of Afro-American Life and History, Inc., c/o Alton Hornsby, Jr., Ed., Dept. of History, Morehouse College, Atlanta, GA 30314. TEL 404-215-2620. FAX 404-215-2715. *3024*

JOURNAL OF NEMATOLOGY.
Society of Nematologists, c/o Dr. M. McClure, 3012 Skyview Dr., Lakeland, FL 33801-7072. TEL 815-665-4481. FAX 815-665-1297. *840*

JOURNAL OF NERVOUS AND MENTAL DISEASE.
Williams & Wilkins, 351 W. Camden St., Baltimore, MD 21201-2436. TEL 410-528-4068. FAX 410-528-4452. *5074*

JOURNAL OF NETWORK AND SYSTEMS MANAGEMENT.
Plenum Publishing Corp., 233 Spring St., New York, NY 10013-1578. TEL 212-620-8000. FAX 212-463-0742. *2156*

JOURNAL OF NEURO-AIDS.
Haworth Press, Inc., 10 Alice St., Binghamton, NY 13904. TEL 607-722-5857. FAX 609-722-6362. *5075*

JOURNAL OF NEURO-ONCOLOGY.
Kluwer Academic Publishers Boston, Box 358, Accord Sta., Hingham, MA 02018-0358. TEL 617-871-6600. FAX 617-871-6528. *4981*

JOURNAL OF NEURO-OPHTHALMOLOGY.
Lippincott - Raven Publishers, 227 E. Washington Sq., Philadelphia, PA 19106. TEL 215-238-4200. FAX 215-238-4227. *4995*

JOURNAL OF NEUROBIOLOGY.
John Wiley & Sons, Inc., Journals, 605 Third Ave., New York, NY 10158. TEL 212-850-6645. FAX 212-850-6021. *818*

JOURNAL OF NEUROCHEMISTRY.
Lippincott - Raven Publishers, 227 E. Washington Sq., Philadelphia, PA 19106. TEL 215-238-4200. FAX 215-238-4227. *664*

JOURNAL OF NEUROCYTOLOGY.
Chapman & Hall, Journals Department 2-6 Boundary Row, London SE1 8HN, England. TEL 44-171-8650066. FAX 44-171-5229623. *742*

JOURNAL OF NEUROENDOCRINOLOGY.
Blackwell Science Ltd., Osney Mead, Oxford OX2 0EL, England. TEL 44-1865-206206. FAX 44-1865-721205. *5075*

JOURNAL OF NEUROGENETICS.
Gordon and Breach - Harwood Academic, Amsteldisk 166, 1st Fl., 1079 LH Amsterdam, Netherlands. *5075*

JOURNAL OF NEUROIMAGING.
Lippincott - Raven Publishers, 227 E. Washington Sq., Philadelphia, PA 19106. TEL 215-238-4200. FAX 215-238-4227. *5075*

JOURNAL OF NEUROIMMUNOLOGY.
Elsevier Science B.V., P.O. Box 211, 1000 AE Amsterdam, Netherlands. TEL 31-20-4853911. FAX 31-20-4853598. *5075*

JOURNAL OF NEUROLINGUISTICS.
Elsevier Science Ltd., Pergamon, P.O. Box 800, Kidlington, Oxford OX5 1DX, England. TEL 44-1865-843000. FAX 44-1865-843010. *5075*

JOURNAL OF NEUROLOGY, NEUROSURGERY AND PSYCHIATRY.
B M J Publishing Group, B.M.A. House, Tavistock Sq., London WC1H 9JR, England. TEL 44-171-383-6270. FAX 44-171-383-6402. *5075*

JOURNAL OF NEUROPATHOLOGY AND EXPERIMENTAL NEUROLOGY.
American Association of Neuropathologists, Inc., Box 1897, Lawrence, KS 66044-8897. TEL 608-265-4414. *5076*

JOURNAL OF NEUROPHYSIOLOGY.
American Physiological Society, 9650 Rockville Pike, Bethesda, MD 20814. TEL 301-530-7164. FAX 301-571-3813. *818*

JOURNAL OF NEUROPSYCHIATRY AND CLINICAL NEUROSCIENCES.
American Psychiatric Press, Inc., Journals Division, 1400 K St. N.W., Ste., 1101, Washington, DC 20005. TEL 202-682-6240. FAX 202-682-6341. *5076*

JOURNAL OF NEUROSCIENCE.
Society for Neuroscience, 11 Dupont Cir., N.W., Ste. 500, Washington, DC 20036. TEL 202-462-6688. FAX 202-462-1547. *5076*

JOURNAL OF NEUROSCIENCE METHODS.
Elsevier Science B.V., P.O. Box 211, 1000 AE Amsterdam, Netherlands. TEL 31-20-4853911. FAX 31-20-4853598. *5076*

JOURNAL OF NEUROSCIENCE NURSING.
American Association of Neuroscience Nurses, 224 N. Des Plaines, Ste. 601, Chicago, IL 60661. TEL 312-993-0043. FAX 312-993-0962. *4937*

JOURNAL OF NEUROSCIENCE RESEARCH.
John Wiley & Sons, Inc., Journals, 605 Third Ave., New York, NY 10158. TEL 212-850-6645. FAX 212-850-6021. *5076*

JOURNAL OF NEUROSURGERY.
American Association of Neurological Surgeons, 1224 W. Main St., Ste. 450, Charlottesville, VA 22903. TEL 804-924-5503. FAX 804-924-2702. *5076*

JOURNAL OF NEUROSURGICAL ANESTHESIOLOGY.
Lippincott - Raven Publishers, 227 E. Washington Sq., Philadelphia, PA 19106. TEL 215-238-4200. FAX 215-238-4227. *4806*

JOURNAL OF NEUROSURGICAL SCIENCES.
Edizioni Minerva Medica, Corso Bramante 83-85, 10126 Turin, Italy. TEL 39-11-678282. FAX 39-11-674502. *5146*

JOURNAL OF NEUROVASCULAR DISEASE.
Prime National Publishing Corp., 470 Boston Post Rd., Weston, MA 02193. TEL 617-899-2702. *5076*

JOURNAL OF NEW ENERGY.
Fusion Information Center, Inc., Box 58639, Salt Lake City, UT 84158-0639. TEL 801-583-6232. FAX 801-583-2963. *2673*

JOURNAL OF NEW ZEALAND LITERATURE.
University of Otago, Department of English, P.O. Box 56, Dunedin, New Zealand. TEL 64-3-4798636. FAX 64-3-4798558. *4421*

JOURNAL OF NON-CRYSTALLINE SOLIDS.
North-Holland, P.O. Box 211, 1000 AE Amsterdam, Netherlands. TEL 31-20-4853911. FAX 31-20-4853598. *5810*

JOURNAL OF NON-NEWTONIAN FLUID MECHANICS.
Elsevier Science B.V., P.O. Box 211, 1000 AE Amsterdam, Netherlands. TEL 31-20-4853911. FAX 31-20-4853598. *5846*

JOURNAL OF NONDESTRUCTIVE EVALUATION.
Plenum Publishing Corp., 233 Spring St., New York, NY 10013-1578. TEL 212-620-8000. FAX 212-463-0742. *2863*

JOURNAL OF NONLINEAR SCIENCE.
Springer-Verlag, Science Journals, 175 Fifth Ave., New York, NY 10010. TEL 212-460-1500. FAX 212-473-6272. *5810*

JOURNAL OF NONPROFIT & PUBLIC SECTOR MARKETING.
Haworth Press, Inc., 10 Alice St., Binghamton, NY 13904. TEL 607-722-5857. FAX 607-722-6362. *1535*

JOURNAL OF NONPROFIT AND VOLUNTARY SECTOR MARKETING.
Henry Stewart Publications, Russell House, 28-30 Little Russell St., London WC1A 2HN, England. TEL 44-171-404-3040. FAX 44-171-404-2081. *1535*

JOURNAL OF NONVERBAL BEHAVIOR.
Human Sciences Press, Inc., 233 Spring St., New York, NY 10013-1578. TEL 212-620-8000. FAX 212-463-0742. *6128*

THE JOURNAL OF NORTH AFRICAN STUDIES.
Frank Cass, Newbury House, 890-900 Eastern Ave., Newbury Park, Ilford, Essex IG2 7HH, England. TEL 44-181-5998866. FAX 44-181-5990984. *3527*

JOURNAL OF NORTHERN LUZON.
Saint Mary's University, Nueva Vizcaya 3700, Philippines. TEL 321-2221. FAX 321-2117. *6717*

JOURNAL OF NORTHWEST SEMITIC LANGUAGES.
University of Stellenbosch, Department of Ancient Near Eastern Studies, University, 7600 Stellenbosch, South Africa. TEL 27-21-808-3203. FAX 27-21-8084336. *4268*

JOURNAL OF NUCLEAR CARDIOLOGY.
Mosby - Year Book, Inc., 11830 Westline Industrial Dr., St. Louis, MO 63146-3318. TEL 314-872-8370. FAX 314-432-1380. *5109*

JOURNAL OF NUCLEAR MATERIALS.
North-Holland, P.O. Box 211, 1000 AE Amsterdam, Netherlands. TEL 31-20-4853911. FAX 31-20-4853598. *5853*

JOURNAL OF NUCLEAR MATERIALS MANAGEMENT.
Institute of Nuclear Materials Management, Inc., 60 Revere Dr., Ste. 500, Northbrook, IL 60062-1563. TEL 847-480-9573. FAX 847-480-9282. *2699*

JOURNAL OF NUCLEAR MEDICINE.
Society of Nuclear Medicine, 1850 Samuel Morse Dr., Reston, VA 22090-5316. TEL 703-708-9000. FAX 703-708-9015. *5109*

JOURNAL OF NUCLEAR MEDICINE TECHNOLOGY.
Society of Nuclear Medicine, 1850 Samuel Morse Dr., Reston, VA 22090-5316. TEL 703-708-9000. FAX 703-708-9015. *5109*

JOURNAL OF NUMBER THEORY.
Academic Press, Inc., Journal Division, 525 B St., Ste. 1900, San Diego, CA 92101-4495. TEL 619-230-1840. FAX 619-699-6800. *4584*

JOURNAL OF NURSE - MIDWIFERY.
Elsevier Science Inc., Box 945, New York, NY 10159-0945. TEL 212-633-3730. FAX 212-633-3680. *4962*

JOURNAL OF NURSING LAW.
K R M Information Services, Inc., 200 Spring St., Eau Claire, WI 54703. TEL 715-833-5208. FAX 715-836-0031. *4937*

JOURNAL OF NURSING MANAGEMENT.
Blackwell Science Ltd., Osney Mead, Oxford OX2 0EL, England. TEL 44-1865-206206. FAX 44-1865-721205. *4937*

JOURNAL OF NURSING MEASUREMENT.
Springer Publishing Company, 526 Broadway, New York, NY 10012-3955. TEL 212-431-4370. FAX 212-941-7842. *4938*

JOURNAL OF NUTRACEUTICALS, FUNCTIONAL & MEDICAL FOODS.
Haworth Press, Inc., 10 Alice St., Binghamton, NY 13904. TEL 607-722-5857. FAX 607-722-6362. *5672*

JOURNAL OF NUTRITION.
American Institute of Nutrition, 9650 Rockville Pike, Bethesda, MD 20814. TEL 301-530-7027. FAX 301-571-1892. *5476*

JOURNAL OF NUTRITION FOR THE ELDERLY.
Haworth Press, Inc., 10 Alice St., Binghamton, NY 13904. TEL 607-722-5857. FAX 607-722-6362. *3439*

JOURNAL OF NUTRITION IN RECIPE & MENU DEVELOPMENT.
Haworth Press, Inc., 10 Alice St., Binghamton, NY 13904. TEL 607-722-5857. FAX 607-722-6362. *5476*

JOURNAL OF NUTRITIONAL & ENVIRONMENTAL MEDICINE.
Carfax Publishing Co., P.O. Box 25, Abingdon, Oxon. OX14 3UE, England. TEL 44-1235-401000. FAX 44-1235-401550. *5476*

JOURNAL OF NUTRITIONAL IMMUNOLOGY.
Haworth Press, Inc., 10 Alice St., Binghamton, NY 13904. TEL 607-722-5857. FAX 607-722-6362. *4799*

JOURNAL OF OBJECT - ORIENTED PROGRAMMING.
Sigs Publications, Inc., 71 W. 23rd St., New York, NY 10010-4102. TEL 212-242-7447. FAX 212-242-7574. *2144*

JOURNAL OF OBSTETRICS AND GYNAECOLOGY.
Carfax Publishing Co., P.O. Box 25, Abingdon, Oxon. OX14 3UE, England. TEL 44-1235-401000. FAX 44-1235-401550. *4962*

JOURNAL OF OCCUPATIONAL AND ENVIRONMENTAL MEDICINE.
Williams & Wilkins, 351 W. Camden St., Baltimore, MD 21201-2436. TEL 410-528-4068. FAX 410-528-4452. *4697*

JOURNAL OF OCCUPATIONAL AND ORGANIZATIONAL PSYCHOLOGY.
British Psychological Society, St. Andrew's House, 48 Princess Rd. E., Leicester LE1 7DR, England. TEL 44-116-254-9568. FAX 44-116-247-0787. *6128*

JOURNAL OF OCCUPATIONAL HEALTH AND SAFETY: AUSTRALIA AND NEW ZEALAND.
C C H Australia Ltd., P.O. Box 230, North Ryde, N.S.W. 2113, Australia. TEL 61-1-300300224. FAX 61-2-300306224. *5493*

JOURNAL OF OCCUPATIONAL HEALTH PSYCHOLOGY.
American Psychological Association, 750 First St., N.E., Washington, DC 20002-4242. TEL 202-336-5600. FAX 202-336-5568. *5493*

JOURNAL OF OCCUPATIONAL REHABILITATION.
Plenum Publishing Corp., 233 Spring St., New York, NY 10013-1578. TEL 212-620-8000. FAX 212-463-0742. *5493*

JOURNAL OF OCCUPATIONAL SCIENCE.
c/o University of South Australia, N. Terrace, Adelaide, S.A. 5000, Australia. TEL 61-8-83022484. FAX 61-8-83022645. *6717*

JOURNAL OF OCEANOGRAPHY.
Oceanographical Society of Japan, 6-14, Minamidai 1-chome, Nakano-ku, Tokyo 164, Japan. TEL 81-3-3377-3951. FAX 81-3-3378-9419. *2407*

JOURNAL OF OCULAR PHARMACOLOGY AND THERAPEUTICS.
Mary Ann Liebert, Inc. Publishers, 2 Madison Ave., Larchmont, NY 10538. TEL 914-834-3100. FAX 914-834-3688. *4995*

JOURNAL OF OFFENDER REHABILITATION.
Haworth Press, Inc., 10 Alice St., Binghamton, NY 13904. TEL 607-722-5857. FAX 607-722-6362. *2271*

JOURNAL OF OFFSHORE MECHANICS AND ARCTIC ENGINEERING.
American Society of Mechanical Engineers, 22 Law Dr., Fairfield, NJ 07007-2900. TEL 973-882-1167. FAX 973-882-1717. *2890*

JOURNAL OF ONCOLOGY PHARMACY PRACTICE.
Appleton & Lange, Journal Division, Box 120041, Stamford, CT 06912-0041. TEL 203-406-4500. FAX 203-406-4603. *5672*

THE JOURNAL OF ONE-DAY SURGERY.
Newton Mann Ltd., Stretton Rd., Tansley, Matlock, Derbyshire DE4 5GE, England. TEL 44-1629-583941. FAX 4401629-580479. *5146*

JOURNAL OF OPERATIONS MANAGEMENT.
Elsevier Science B.V., P.O. Box 211, 1000 AE Amsterdam, Netherlands. TEL 31-20-4853911. FAX 31-20-4853598. *2877*

JOURNAL OF OPTIMIZATION THEORY AND APPLICATIONS.
Plenum Publishing Corp., 233 Spring St., New York, NY 10013-1578. TEL 212-620-8000. FAX 212-463-0742. *4584*

JOURNAL OF ORAL AND MAXILLOFACIAL SURGERY.
W.B. Saunders Co., Curtis Center, 3rd Fl., Independence Sq. W., Philadelphia, PA 19106-3399. TEL 215-238-7800. FAX 215-238-6445. *4862*

JOURNAL OF ORAL PATHOLOGY & MEDICINE.
Munksgaard International Publishers Ltd., 35 Noerre Soegade, P.O. Box 2148, DK-1016 Copenhagen K, Denmark. TEL 45-33-127030. FAX 45-33-129387. *4862*

JOURNAL OF ORAL REHABILITATION.
Blackwell Science Ltd., Osney Mead, Oxford OX2 0EL, England. TEL 44-1865-206206. FAX 44-1865-721205. *4862*

JOURNAL OF ORGANIC CHEMISTRY (WASHINGTON)
American Chemical Society, 1155 16th St., N.W., Washington, DC 20036. TEL 800-333-9511. FAX 614-447-3671. *1817*

JOURNAL OF ORGANIZATIONAL BEHAVIOR MANAGEMENT.
Haworth Press, Inc., 10 Alice St., Binghamton, NY 13904. TEL 607-722-5857. FAX 607-722-6362. *6128*

JOURNAL OF ORGANIZATIONAL BEHAVIOUR.
John Wiley & Sons Ltd., Journals, Baffins Ln., Chichester, W. Sussex PO19 1UD, England. TEL 44-1243-779777. FAX 44-1243-775878. *6129*

JOURNAL OF ORGANOMETALLIC CHEMISTRY.
Elsevier Science S.A., P.O. Box 564, CH-1001 Lausanne 1, Switzerland. TEL 41-21-3207381. FAX 41-21-3235444. *1817*

JOURNAL OF ORGANOMETALLIC CHEMISTRY LIBRARY.
Elsevier Science B.V., Books Division, P.O. Box 211, 1000 AE Amsterdam, Netherlands. TEL 31-20-4853911. FAX 31-20-4853705. *1756*

JOURNAL OF ORGONOMY.
Orgonomic Publications, Box 490, Princeton, NJ 08542. TEL 908-821-1144. FAX 908-821-0174. *5076*

JOURNAL OF OROFACIAL PAIN.
Quintessence Publishing Co., Inc., 551 Kimberly Dr., Carol Stream, IL 60188-1881. TEL 630-682-3223. FAX 630-682-3288. *4862*

JOURNAL OF ORTHOPAEDIC AND SPORTS PHYSICAL THERAPY.
Williams & Wilkins, 351 W. Camden St., Baltimore, MD 21201-2436. TEL 410-528-4068. FAX 410-528-4452. *5130*

JOURNAL OF ORTHOPAEDIC RESEARCH.
Journal of Bone and Joint Surgery, Inc., 20 Pickering St., Needham, MA 02192-3145. TEL 617-734-2835. *5010*

JOURNAL OF ORTHOPAEDIC TECHNIQUES.
Stockton Press, Houndmills, Basingstoke, Hants. RG21 6XS, England. TEL 44-1256-351898. FAX 44-1256-328339. *5011*

JOURNAL OF OTOLARYNGOLOGY OF JAPAN.
Oto-Rhino-Laryngological Society of Japan, c/o Chateau Takanawa, 23-14, 3-chome, Minato-ku, Tokyo 108, Japan. TEL 81-3-3443-3085. FAX 81-3-3443-3037. *5023*

JOURNAL OF PACIFIC HISTORY.
Journal of Pacific History Inc., c/o Research School of Pacific Studies, Australian National Univ., Canberra, A.C.T. 0200, Australia. FAX 61-6-249-5525. *3543*

JOURNAL OF PAEDIATRICS AND CHILD HEALTH.
Blackwell Science Pty Ltd, P.O. Box 378, Carlton South, Vic. 3053, Australia. TEL 61-3-93470300. FAX 61-3-93493016. *5033*

JOURNAL OF PAIN AND SYMPTOM MANAGEMENT.
Elsevier Science Inc., Box 945, New York, NY 10159-0945. TEL 212-633-3730. FAX 212-633-3680. *4806*

JOURNAL OF PALEOLIMNOLOGY.
Kluwer Academic Publishers, Postbus 17, 3300 AA Dordrecht, Netherlands. TEL 31-78-6392392. FAX 31-78-6392254. *5559*

JOURNAL OF PALEONTOLOGY.
Paleontological Society, Business Office, Box 1897, Lawrence, KS 66044-8897. TEL 913-843-1221. *5560*

JOURNAL OF PALESTINE STUDIES.
University of California Press, Journals Division, 2120 Berkeley Way, No. 5812, Berkeley, CA 94720-5812. TEL 510-643-7154. FAX 510-642-9917. *3657*

JOURNAL OF PARALLEL AND DISTRIBUTED COMPUTING.
Academic Press, Inc., Journal Division, 525 B St., Ste. 1900, San Diego, CA 92101-4495. TEL 619-230-1840. FAX 619-699-6800. *2086*

JOURNAL OF PARAPSYCHOLOGY.
Parapsychology Press, 402 N. Buchanan Blvd., Durham, NC 27701-1728. TEL 919-688-8241. FAX 919-683-4338. *5576*

JOURNAL OF PARENTERAL AND ENTERAL NUTRITION.
American Society for Parenteral and Enteral Nutrition, 8630 Fenton St., Ste. 412, Silver Spring, MD 20910-3805. TEL 301-587-6315. FAX 301-587-3323. *5477*

JOURNAL OF PEACE RESEARCH.
Sage Publications Ltd., 6 Bonhill St., London EC2A 4PU, England. TEL 44-171-374-0645. FAX 44-171-374-8741. *6024*

THE JOURNAL OF PEASANT STUDIES.
Frank Cass, Newbury House, 890-900 Eastern Ave., Newbury Park, Ilford, Essex 1G2 7HH, England. TEL 44-181-599-8866. FAX 44-181-599-0984. *6717*

JOURNAL OF PEDIATRIC GASTROENTEROLOGY AND NUTRITION.
Lippincott - Raven Publishers, 227 E. Washington Sq., Philadelphia, PA 19106. TEL 215-238-4200. FAX 215-238-4227. *4913*

JOURNAL OF PEDIATRIC HEALTH CARE.
Mosby - Year Book, Inc., 11830 Westline Industrial Dr., St. Louis, MO 63146-3318. TEL 314-872-8370. FAX 314-432-1380. *5033*

JOURNAL OF PEDIATRIC HEMATOLOGY - ONCOLOGY.
Lippincott - Raven Publishers, 227 E. Washington Sq., Philadelphia, PA 19106. TEL 215-238-4200. FAX 215-2384227. *4981*

JOURNAL OF PEDIATRIC NURSING.
W.B. Saunders Co., Curtis Center, 3rd Fl., Independence Sq. W., Philadelphia, PA 19106-3399. TEL 215-238-7800. FAX 215-238-6445. *4938*

JOURNAL OF PEDIATRIC ONCOLOGY NURSING.
W.B. Saunders Co., The Curtis Center, 3rd Fl., Independence Sq. W., Philadelphia, PA 19106-3399. TEL 215-238-7800. FAX 215-238-6445. *4981*

JOURNAL OF PEDIATRIC OPHTHALMOLOGY AND STRABISMUS.
Slack, Inc., 6900 Grove Rd., Thorofare, NJ 08086-9447. TEL 609-848-1000. FAX 609-853-5991. *4996*

JOURNAL OF PEDIATRIC ORTHOPAEDICS.
Lippincott - Raven Publishers, 227 E. Washington Sq., Philadelphia, PA 19106. TEL 215-238-4200. FAX 215-238-4227. *5011*

JOURNAL OF PEDIATRIC ORTHOPAEDICS, PART B.
Lippincott - Raven Publishers, 227 E. Washington Sq., Philadelphia, PA 19106. TEL 215-238-4200. FAX 215-238-4227. *5011*

JOURNAL OF PEDIATRIC PSYCHOLOGY.
Oxford University Press, Academic Division, Great Clarendon St., Oxford OX2 6DP, England. TEL 44-1865-267907. FAX 44-1865-267485. *6129*

JOURNAL OF PEDIATRIC SURGERY.
W.B. Saunders Co., Curtis Center, Independence Sq. W., Philadelphia, PA 19106-3399. TEL 215-238-7800. FAX 215-238-6445. *5146*

THE JOURNAL OF PEDIATRICS.
Mosby - Year Book, Inc., 11830 Westline Industrial Dr., St. Louis, MO 63146-3318. TEL 314-872-8370. FAX 314-432-1380. *5033*

JOURNAL OF PELVIC SURGERY.
Lippincott - Raven Publishers, 227 E. Washington Sq., Philadelphia, PA 19106. TEL 215-238-4200. FAX 215-238-4227. *5146*

JOURNAL OF PEPTIDE RESEARCH.
Munksgaard International Publishers Ltd., 35 Noerre Soegade, P.O. Box 2148, DK-1016 Copenhagen K, Denmark. TEL 45-33-127030. FAX 45-33-129387. *664*

JOURNAL OF PEPTIDE SCIENCE.
John Wiley & Sons Ltd., Journals, Baffins Ln., Chichester, W. Sussex PO19 1UD, England. TEL 44-1243-779777. FAX 44-1243-775878. *664*

JOURNAL OF PERIANESTHESIA NURSING.
W.B. Saunders Co., Curtis Center, 3rd Fl., Independence Sq., Philadelphia, PA 19106-3399. TEL 215-238-7800. FAX 215-238-6445. *4938*

JOURNAL OF PERINATOLOGY.
Mosby - Year Book, Inc., 11830 Westline Industrial Dr., St. Louis, MO 63146-3318. TEL 314-872-8370. FAX 314-432-1380. *4962*

JOURNAL OF PERIODONTAL RESEARCH.
Munksgaard International Publishers Ltd., 35 Noerre Soegade, P.O. Box 2148, DK-1016 Copenhagen K, Denmark. TEL 45-33-127030. FAX 45-33-129387. *4862*

JOURNAL OF PERIODONTOLOGY.
American Academy of Periodontology, 737 N. Michigan, Ste. 800, Chicago, IL 60611. TEL 312-573-3220. FAX 312-573-3225. *4862*

JOURNAL OF PERSONAL SELLING AND SALES MANAGEMENT.
C T C Press, Box 1826, Clemson, SC 29631. TEL 800-844-2443. FAX 864-859-7002. *1535*

JOURNAL OF PERSONALITY.
Duke University Press, Box 90660, Durham, NC 27708-0660. TEL 919-687-3600. FAX 919-688-4574. *6129*

JOURNAL OF PERSONALITY AND SOCIAL PSYCHOLOGY.
American Psychological Association, 750 First St., N.E., Washington, DC 20002-4242. TEL 202-336-5600. FAX 202-336-5568. *6129*

JOURNAL OF PERSONALITY ASSESSMENT.
Lawrence Erlbaum Associates, Inc., 10 Industrial Dr., Mahwah, NJ 07430-2262. TEL 201-236-9500. FAX 201-236-0072. *6129*

JOURNAL OF PERSONALITY DISORDERS.
Guilford Publications, Inc., 72 Spring St., 4th Fl., New York, NY 10012. TEL 212-431-9800. FAX 212-966-6708. *6129*

JOURNAL OF PERSONNEL EVALUATION IN EDUCATION.
Kluwer Academic Publishers Boston, Box 358, Accord Sta., Hingham, MA 02018-0358. TEL 617-871-6600. FAX 617-871-6528. *2456*

JOURNAL OF PESTICIDE SCIENCE (INTERNATIONAL EDITION).
Pesticide Science Society of Japan, c/o Tamagawa University, Machida-shi, Tokyo, Japan. *2767*

JOURNAL OF PETROLEUM GEOLOGY.
Scientific Press Ltd., P.O. Box 21, Beaconsfield, Bucks. HP9 1NS, England. TEL 44-1494-675139. FAX 44-1494-670155. *5608*

JOURNAL OF PETROLEUM SCIENCE AND ENGINEERING.
Elsevier Science B.V., P.O. Box 211, 1000 AE Amsterdam, Netherlands. TEL 31-20-4853911. FAX 31-20-4853598. *5608*

JOURNAL OF PHARMACEUTICAL AND BIOMEDICAL ANALYSIS.
Elsevier Science B.V., P.O. Box 211, 1000 AE Amsterdam, Netherlands. TEL 31-20-4853911. FAX 31-20-4853598. *5672*

JOURNAL OF PHARMACEUTICAL CARE IN PAIN & SYMPTOM CONTROL.
Haworth Press, Inc., 10 Alice St., Binghamton, NY 13904. TEL 607-722-5857. FAX 607-722-6362. *5672*

JOURNAL OF PHARMACEUTICAL MARKETING AND MANAGEMENT.
Haworth Press, Inc., 10 Alice St., Binghamton, NY 13904. TEL 607-722-5857. FAX 607-722-6362. *5673*

JOURNAL OF PHARMACEUTICAL MEDICINE.
Chapman & Hall, 2-6 Boundary Row, London SE1 8HN, England. TEL 44-171-8650066. FAX 44-171-5229623. *5673*

JOURNAL OF PHARMACEUTICAL SCIENCES.
American Pharmaceutical Association, 2215 Constitution Ave., N.W., Washington, DC 20037. TEL 202-628-4410. FAX 202-638-3783. *5673*

JOURNAL OF PHARMACOEPIDEMIOLOGY.
Haworth Press, Inc., 10 Alice St., Binghamton, NY 13904. TEL 607-722-5857. FAX 607-722-6362. *5673*

JOURNAL OF PHARMACOKINETICS AND BIOPHARMACEUTICS.
Plenum Publishing Corp., 233 Spring St., New York, NY 10013-1578. TEL 212-620-8000. FAX 212-463-0742. *5673*

JOURNAL OF PHARMACOLOGICAL AND TOXICOLOGICAL METHODS.
Elsevier Science Inc., Box 945, New York, NY 10159-0945. TEL 212-633-3730. FAX 212-633-3680. *2979*

JOURNAL OF PHARMACOLOGY AND EXPERIMENTAL THERAPEUTICS.
Williams & Wilkins, 351 W. Camden St., Baltimore, MD 21201-2436. TEL 410-528-4068. FAX 410-528-4452. *5673*

JOURNAL OF PHARMACY TEACHING.
Haworth Press, Inc., 10 Alice St., Binghamton, NY 13904. TEL 607-722-5857. FAX 607-722-6362. *5673*

JOURNAL OF PHARMACY TECHNOLOGY.
Harvey Whitney Books Company, Box 42696, Cincinnati, OH 45242. TEL 513-793-3555. FAX 513-793-3600. *5673*

JOURNAL OF PHASE EQUILIBRIA.
A S M International, Materials Information, Materials Park, OH 44073-0002. TEL 216-338-5151. FAX 216-338-4634. *5197*

JOURNAL OF PHILIPPINE DEVELOPMENT.
Philippine Institute for Development Studies, NEDA sa Makati Bldg., 3rd Fl., Rm. 304, 106 Amorsolo St., Legaspi Village, Makati 1229, Metro Manila, Philippines. TEL 632-893-5705. FAX 632-8161091. *1617*

JOURNAL OF PHILOSOPHICAL LOGIC.
Kluwer Academic Publishers, Postbus 17, 3300 AA Dordrecht, Netherlands. TEL 31-78-6392392. FAX 31-78-6392254. *5734*

JOURNAL OF PHILOSOPHICAL RESEARCH.
Bowling Green State University, Philosophy Documentation Center, Bowling Green, OH 43403-0189. TEL 419-372-2419. FAX 419-372-6987. *5734*

JOURNAL OF PHILOSOPHY OF EDUCATION.
Blackwell Publishers Ltd., 108 Cowley Rd., Oxford OX4 1JF, England. TEL 44-1865-791100. FAX 44-1865-791347. *5734*

JOURNAL OF PHOTOCHEMISTRY AND PHOTOBIOLOGY, A: CHEMISTRY.
Elsevier Science S.A., P.O. Box 564, CH-1001 Lausanne 1, Switzerland. TEL 41-21-3207381. FAX 41-21-3235444. *1831*

JOURNAL OF PHOTOCHEMISTRY AND PHOTOBIOLOGY, B: BIOLOGY.
Elsevier Science S.A., P.O. Box 564, CH-1001 Lausanne 1, Switzerland. TEL 41-21-3207381. FAX 41-21-3235444. *664*

JOURNAL OF PHYCOLOGY.
Allen Press, Inc., 1041 New Hampshire St., Box 1897, Lawrence, KS 66044. TEL 913-843-1221. FAX 913-843-1274. *711*

JOURNAL OF PHYSICAL AND CHEMICAL REFERENCE DATA.
American Institute of Physics, One Physics Ellipse, College Park, MD 20740-3843. TEL 301-209-3000. *1756*

JOURNAL OF PHYSICAL CHEMISTRY.
American Chemical Society, 1155 16th St., N.W., Washington, DC 20036. TEL 800-333-9511. FAX 614-447-3671. *1831*

JOURNAL OF PHYSICAL OCEANOGRAPHY.
American Meteorological Society, 45 Beacon St., Boston, MA 02108-3693. TEL 617-227-2425. FAX 617-742-8718. *2407*

JOURNAL OF PHYSICAL ORGANIC CHEMISTRY.
John Wiley & Sons Ltd., Journals, Baffins Ln., Chichester, W. Sussex PO19 1UD, England. TEL 44-1243-779777. FAX 44-1243-775878. *1832*

THE JOURNAL OF PHYSICS AND CHEMISTRY OF SOLIDS.
Elsevier Science Ltd., Pergamon, P.O. Box 800, Kidlington, Oxford OX5 1DX, England. TEL 44-1865-843000. FAX 44-1865-843010. *5811*

JOURNAL OF PHYSICS OF THE EARTH.
Center for Academic Publications Japan, 2-4-16 Yayoi, Bunkyo-ku, Tokyo 113, Japan. TEL 81-3-3817-5821. FAX 81-3-5817-5820. *2385*

JOURNAL OF PHYSIOLOGY.
Cambridge University Press, Edinburgh Bldg., Shaftesbury Rd., Cambridge CB2 2RU, England. TEL 44-1223-312393. FAX 44-1223-315052. *818*

JOURNAL OF PHYSIOLOGY (PARIS).
Editions Scientifiques et Medicales Elsevier, 141 rue de Javel, 75747 Paris, France. TEL 33-1-45589022. FAX 33-1-45589421. *818*

JOURNAL OF PHYSIOLOGY AND PHARMACOLOGY.
Polskie Towarzystwo Fizjologiczne, Ul. Grzegorzecka 16, 31-531 Krakow, Poland. TEL 48-12-211006. FAX 48-12-211578. *818*

JOURNAL OF PINEAL RESEARCH.
Munksgaard International Publishers Ltd., P.O. Box 2148, DK-1016 Copenhagen K, Denmark. TEL 45-33-127030. FAX 45-33-129387. *5076*

JOURNAL OF PLANNING EDUCATION AND RESEARCH.
Association of Collegiate Schools of Planning, College of Urban and Public Affairs, University of New Orleans, New Orleans, LA 70148. TEL 504-280-7106. FAX 504-280-6272. *3751*

JOURNAL OF PLANNING LITERATURE.
Sage Publications, Inc., 2455 Teller Rd., Thousand Oaks, CA 91320. TEL 805-499-0721. FAX 805-499-0871. *3751*

JOURNAL OF PLANT BIOCHEMISTRY AND BIOTECHNOLOGY.
Society for Plant Biochemistry and Biotechnology, Division of Biochemistry, Indian Agricultural Research Institute, New Delhi 110 012, India. TEL 91-11-5750932. FAX 91-11-5750932. *664*

JOURNAL OF PLANT GROWTH REGULATION.
Springer-Verlag, Life Science Journals, 175 Fifth Ave., New York, NY 10010. TEL 212-460-1500. FAX 212-473-6272. *711*

JOURNAL OF PLANT NUTRITION.
Marcel Dekker Journals, 270 Madison Ave., New York, NY 10016. TEL 212-696-9000. FAX 212-685-4540. *711*

JOURNAL OF PLANT PATHOLOGY.
University of Pisa, Via del Borghetto 80, 56124 Pisa, Italy. TEL 39-50-571556. FAX 39-50-543564. *711*

JOURNAL OF PLANT RESEARCH.
Botanical Society of Japan, Toshin Bldg., Hongo 2-27-2, Bunkyo-ku, Tokyo 113, Japan. TEL 81-3-3814-5675. FAX 81-3-3814-5352. *712*

JOURNAL OF PLANTATION CROPS.
Indian Society for Plantation Crops, Central Plantation Crops Research Institute, Kasaragod - 671 124, Kerala, India. TEL 91-499-530894. FAX 91-499-530322. *232*

JOURNAL OF PLASTIC FILM AND SHEETING.
Technomic Publishing Co., Inc., 851 New Holland Ave., Box 3535, Lancaster, PA 07604. TEL 717-291-5609. FAX 717-295-4538. *5879*

JOURNAL OF POETRY THERAPY.
Human Sciences Press, Inc., 233 Spring St., New York, NY 10013-1578. TEL 212-620-8000. FAX 212-463-0742. *4512*

JOURNAL OF POLICE AND CRIMINAL PSYCHOLOGY.
Society of Police and Criminal Psychology, c/o Wayman C. Mullins, Managing Ed., Southwest Texas State University, Hines Academy Center, Rm. 120, San Marcos, TX 78666. TEL 512-245-2174. FAX 512-245-8063. *2271*

JOURNAL OF POLICY ANALYSIS AND MANAGEMENT.
John Wiley & Sons, Inc., Journals, 605 Third Ave., New York, NY 10158. TEL 212-850-6645. FAX 212-850-6021. *6181*

JOURNAL OF POLICY HISTORY.
Pennsylvania State University Press, USB 1, Ste. C, University Park, PA 16802-1003. TEL 814-865-1327. FAX 814-863-1408. *3503*

JOURNAL OF POLICY MODELING.
Elsevier Science Inc., Box 945, New York, NY 10159-0945. TEL 212-633-3730. FAX 212-633-3680. *5937*

JOURNAL OF POLITICAL AND MILITARY SOCIOLOGY.
J P M S, c/o Dept. of Sociology, Northern Illinois University, DeKalb, IL 60115. TEL 815-753-6433. FAX 815-753-6302. *6717*

JOURNAL OF POLITICAL ECONOMY.
University of Chicago Press, Journals Division, Box 37005, Chicago, IL 60637. TEL 773-753-3347. FAX 773-753-0811. *978*

JOURNAL OF POLITICAL PHILOSOPHY.
Blackwell Publishers Ltd., 108 Cowley Rd., Oxford OX4 1JF, England. TEL 44-1865-791100. FAX 44-1865-791347. *5734*

JOURNAL OF POLITICAL SCIENCE.
College of Charleston, Department of Political Science, Charleston, SC 29424. TEL 803-953-5724. FAX 803-656-0258. *5937*

JOURNAL OF POLITICAL SCIENCE.
Government College, Department of Political Science, Lahore, Pakistan. *5937*

JOURNAL OF POLYMER MATERIALS.
Oxford & I.B.H. Publishing Co. Pvt. Ltd., 66 Janpath, New Delhi 110 001, India. FAX 91-11-3322639. *1817*

JOURNAL OF POLYMER SCIENCE. PART A: POLYMER CHEMISTRY.
John Wiley & Sons, Inc., Journals, 605 Third Ave., New York, NY 10158. TEL 212-850-6645. FAX 212-850-6021. *1817*

JOURNAL OF POLYMER SCIENCE. PART B: POLYMER PHYSICS.
John Wiley & Sons, Inc., Journals, 605 Third Ave., New York, NY 10158. TEL 212-850-6645. FAX 212-850-6021. *1817*

JOURNAL OF POLYMER SCIENCE. SYMPOSIA PROCEEDINGS.
John Wiley & Sons, Inc., Journals, 605 Third Ave., New York, NY 10158-0012. TEL 212-850-6000. FAX 212-850-6088. *1817*

JOURNAL OF POPULAR CULTURE.
Popular Press, Bowling Green State University, Bowling Green, OH 43403. TEL 419-372-7866. *4421*

JOURNAL OF POPULAR FILM AND TELEVISION.
Heldref Publications, 1319 Eighteenth St., N.W., Washington, DC 20036-1802. TEL 202-296-6267. FAX 202-296-5149. *5337*

JOURNAL OF POPULATION.
University of Indonesia, Faculty of Economics, Gedung A Lt. 2-3, Kampus UI, Depok 16424, Indonesia. TEL 62-21-787-2911. FAX 62-21-787-2909. *6053*

JOURNAL OF POPULATION STUDIES.
National Taiwan University, Population Studies Center, Taipei, Taiwan, Republic of China. TEL 886-2-3630231. FAX 886-2-3630197. *6053*

JOURNAL OF POROUS MATERIALS.
Kluwer Academic Publishers, Postbus 17, 3300 AA Dordrecht, Netherlands. TEL 31-78-6392392. FAX 31-78-6392254. *2863*

JOURNAL OF PORPHYRINS AND PHTHALOCYANINES.
John Wiley & Sons Ltd., Journals, Baffins Ln., Chichester, W. Sussex PO19 1UD, England. TEL 44-1243-779777. FAX 44-1243-775878. *1756*

JOURNAL OF POST KEYNESIAN ECONOMICS.
M.E. Sharpe, Inc., 80 Business Park Dr., Armonk, NY 10504. TEL 914-273-1800. FAX 914-273-2106. *1308*

JOURNAL OF POTASSIUM RESEARCH.
Potash Research Institute of India, Sector 19, Dundahera, Gurgaon 122 001 (Haryana), India. TEL 0124-340185. *5197*

JOURNAL OF POWER SOURCES.
Elsevier Science S.A., P.O. Box 564, CH-1001 Lausanne 1, Switzerland. TEL 41-21-3207381. FAX 41-21-3235444. *2837*

JOURNAL OF PRACTICAL APPROACHES TO DEVELOPMENTAL HANDICAP.
University of Calgary, Rehabilitation Studies, c/o Rehabilitation Studies, Education Tower 4th Fl., University of Calgary, 2500 University Dr., N.W., Calgary, AB T2N 1N4, Canada. TEL 403-220-7429. FAX 403-284-5569. *2586*

JOURNAL OF PRACTICAL HYGIENE.
Montage Media Corp., 1000 Wyckoff Ave., Mahwah, NJ 07430. TEL 201-236-0700. FAX 201-236-1339. *4862*

JOURNAL OF PRACTICAL NURSING.
National Association for Practical Nurse Education and Service, Inc., 1400 Spring St., Ste. 330, Silver Spring, MD 20910. TEL 301-588-2491. FAX 301-588-2839. *4938*

JOURNAL OF PRAGMATICS.
North-Holland, P.O. Box 211, 1000 AE Amsterdam, Netherlands. TEL 31-20-4853911. FAX 31-20-4853598. *4269*

JOURNAL OF PRE-RAPHAELITE STUDIES.
Stong College, York University, Toronto, ON M3J 1P3, Canada. TEL 416-736-5166. *4421*

JOURNAL OF PRECISION TEACHING AND CELERATION.
Standard Celeration Society, Center for Individualized Instruction, Jacksonville State University, Jacksonville, AL 36265. TEL 205-782-5570. FAX 205-782-5573. *2456*

JOURNAL OF PREVENTION AND INTERVENTION IN THE COMMUNITY.
Haworth Press, Inc., 10 Alice St., Binghamton, NY 13904. TEL 607-722-5857. FAX 607-722-6362. *6161*

JOURNAL OF PRIMARY PREVENTION.
Human Sciences Press, Inc., 233 Spring St., New York, NY 10013-1578. TEL 212-620-8000. FAX 212-463-0742. *6129*

JOURNAL OF PROCESS CONTROL.
Elsevier Science Ltd., P.O. Box 800, Kidlington, Oxford OX5 1DX, England. TEL 44-1865-843000. FAX 44-1865-843010. *2176*

JOURNAL OF PRODUCT INNOVATION MANAGEMENT.
Elsevier Science Inc., Box 945, New York, NY 10159-0945. TEL 212-633-3730. FAX 212-633-3680. *1588*

JOURNAL OF PRODUCTIVITY ANALYSIS.
Kluwer Academic Publishers Boston, Box 358, Accord Sta., Hingham, MA 02018-0358. TEL 617-871-6600. FAX 617-871-6528. *1489*

JOURNAL OF PRODUCTS AND TOXICS LIABILITY.
Elsevier Science Ltd., Pergamon, P.O. Box 800, Kidlington, Oxford OX5 1DX, England. TEL 44-1865-843000. FAX 44-1865-843010. *3971*

JOURNAL OF PROFESSIONAL ISSUES IN ENGINEERING AND PRACTICE.
American Society of Civil Engineers, 345 E. 47th St., New York, NY 10017-2398. TEL 212-705-7288. FAX 212-980-4681. *2791*

JOURNAL OF PROFESSIONAL SERVICES MARKETING.
Haworth Press, Inc., 10 Alice St., Binghamton, NY 13904. TEL 607-722-5857. FAX 607-722-6362. *1535*

JOURNAL OF PROGRAMMING LANGUAGES.
Chapman & Hall, Journals Department 2-6 Boundary Row, London SE1 8HN, England. TEL 44-171-8650066. FAX 44-171-5229623. *2144*

JOURNAL OF PROGRESSIVE HUMAN SERVICES.
Haworth Press, Inc., 10 Alice St., Binghamton, NY 13904. TEL 607-722-5857. FAX 607-722-6362. *6673*

JOURNAL OF PROMOTION MANAGEMENT.
Haworth Press, Inc., 10 Alice St., Binghamton, NY 13904. TEL 607-722-5857. FAX 607-722-6362. *38*

JOURNAL OF PROPERTY RESEARCH.
Thomson Professional, 2-6 Boundary Row, London SE1 8HN, England. TEL 44-171-865-0066. FAX 44-171-522-9621. *3751*

JOURNAL OF PROPULSION AND POWER.
American Institute of Aeronautics and Astronautics, Inc., 1801 Alexander Dr., Ste. 500, Reston, VA 20191. TEL 703-264-7500. *72*

THE JOURNAL OF PROSTHETIC DENTISTRY.
Mosby - Year Book, Inc., 11830 Westline Industrial Dr., St. Louis, MO 63146-3318. TEL 314-872-8370. FAX 314-432-1380. *4862*

JOURNAL OF PROSTHETICS AND ORTHOTICS.
American Academy of Orthotists and Prosthetists, 1650 King St., Ste. 500, Alexandria, VA 22314. TEL 703-836-7116. FAX 703-836-0838. *5011*

JOURNAL OF PROSTHODONTICS.
W.B. Saunders Co., Curtis Center, 3rd Fl., Independence Sq. W., Philadelphia, PA 19106-3399. TEL 215-238-7800. FAX 215-238-6445. *4862*

JOURNAL OF PROTEIN CHEMISTRY.
Plenum Publishing Corp., 233 Spring St., New York, NY 10013-1578. TEL 212-620-8000. FAX 212-463-0742. *1817*

JOURNAL OF PSYCHIATRIC AND MENTAL HEALTH NURSING.
Blackwell Science Ltd., Osney Mead, Oxford OX2 0EL, England. TEL 44-1865-206206. FAX 44-1865-721205. *5077*

JOURNAL OF PSYCHIATRIC RESEARCH.
Elsevier Science Ltd., Pergamon, P.O. Box 800, Kidlington, Oxford OX5 1DX, England. TEL 44-1865-843000. FAX 44-1865-843010. *5077*

JOURNAL OF PSYCHOACTIVE DRUGS.
Haight-Ashbury Publications, 612 Clayton St., San Francisco, CA 94117. TEL 415-565-1904. FAX 415-864-6162. *2303*

JOURNAL OF PSYCHOEDUCATIONAL ASSESSMENT.
Psychoeducational Corporation, 505 22nd St., Knoxville, TN 37916. TEL 423-546-9651. FAX 423-974-2135. *6130*

JOURNAL OF PSYCHOHISTORY.
Association for Psychohistory, Inc., 140 Riverside Dr., New York, NY 10024-2605. TEL 212-799-2294. FAX 212-799-2294. *6130*

JOURNAL OF PSYCHOLINGUISTIC RESEARCH.
Plenum Publishing Corp., 233 Spring St., New York, NY 10013-1578. TEL 212-620-8000. FAX 212-463-0742. *4269*

JOURNAL OF PSYCHOLOGICAL TYPE.
Dr. Thomas G. Carskadon, Ed. & Pub., c/o Department of Psychology, Mississippi State Univ., Box 6161, Mississippi State, MS 39762. TEL 601-325-7655. FAX 601-325-7212. *6130*

JOURNAL OF PSYCHOLOGY AND CHRISTIANITY.
Christian Association for Psychological Studies, Inc., c/o Robert R. King, Jr., Box 310400, New Braunfels, TX 78131-0400. TEL 210-629-2277. FAX 210-629-2342. *6130*

JOURNAL OF PSYCHOLOGY & HUMAN SEXUALITY.
Haworth Press, Inc., 10 Alice St., Binghamton, NY 13904. TEL 607-722-5857. FAX 607-722-6362. *6130*

JOURNAL OF PSYCHOLOGY AND JUDAISM.
Human Sciences Press, Inc., 233 Spring St., New York, NY 10013-1578. TEL 212-620-8000. FAX 212-463-0742. *6130*

JOURNAL OF PSYCHOLOGY: INTERDISCIPLINARY & APPLIED.
Heldref Publications, 1319 Eighteenth St., N.W., Washington, DC 20036-1802. TEL 202-296-6267. FAX 202-296-5149. *6130*

JOURNAL OF PSYCHOPATHOLOGY AND BEHAVIORAL ASSESSMENT.
Plenum Publishing Corp., 233 Spring St., New York, NY 10013-1578. TEL 212-620-8000. FAX 212-463-0742. *6130*

JOURNAL OF PSYCHOSOCIAL ONCOLOGY.
Haworth Press, Inc., 10 Alice St., Binghamton, NY 13904. TEL 607-722-5857. FAX 607-722-6362. *4982*

JOURNAL OF PSYCHOSOMATIC OBSTETRICS AND GYNAECOLOGY.
Parthenon Publishing Group, Casterton Hall, Casterton, Carnforth, Lancs. LA6 2LA, England. TEL 44-152-427-2084. FAX 44-152-427-1587. *4962*

JOURNAL OF PSYCHOSOMATIC RESEARCH.
Elsevier Science Inc., Box 945, New York, NY 10159-0945. TEL 212-633-3730. FAX 212-633-3680. *5077*

JOURNAL OF PSYCHOTHERAPY INTEGRATION.
Plenum Publishing Corp., 233 Spring St., New York, NY 10013-1578. TEL 212-620-8000. FAX 212-463-0742. *5077*

JOURNAL OF PUBLIC ADMINISTRATION RESEARCH AND THEORY.
Transaction Publishers, Transaction Periodicals Consortium, Department 3092, Rutgers University, New Brunswick, NJ 08903. TEL 908-445-2280. FAX 908-445-3138. *6181*

JOURNAL OF PUBLIC HEALTH MANAGEMENT AND PRACTICE.
Aspen Publishers, Inc., 200 Orchard Ridge Dr., Gaithersburg, MD 20873. FAX 301-417-7550. *6242*

JOURNAL OF PUBLIC HEALTH POLICY.
Journal of Public Health Policy, Inc., 208 Meadowood Dr., South Burlington, VT 05403. TEL 802-658-0136. FAX 802-862-4011. *6242*

JOURNAL OF PUBLIC RELATIONS RESEARCH.
Lawrence Erlbaum Associates, Inc., 10 Industrial Dr., Mahwah, NJ 07430-2262. TEL 201-236-9500. FAX 201-236-0072. *38*

JOURNAL OF PURE AND APPLIED ALGEBRA.
North-Holland, P.O. Box 211, 1000 AE Amsterdam, Netherlands. TEL 31-20-4853911. FAX 31-20-4853598. *4584*

JOURNAL OF PURE AND APPLIED ULTRASONICS.
Ultrasonics Society of India, c/o Ultrasonic Section, National Physical Laboratory, Hillside Rd., New Delhi 110 012, India. TEL 91-11-5781736. FAX 91-11-5752678. *5873*

JOURNAL OF QUALITY MANAGEMENT.
J A I Press Inc., 55 Old Post Rd., No. 2, Box 1678, Greenwich, CT 06830-1678. TEL 203-661-7602. FAX 203-661-0792. *1489*

JOURNAL OF QUANTITATIVE ANTHROPOLOGY.
Kluwer Academic Publishers, Postbus 17, 3300 AA Dordrecht, Netherlands. TEL 31-78-6392392. FAX 31-78-6392254. *321*

JOURNAL OF QUANTITATIVE CRIMINOLOGY.
Plenum Publishing Corp., 233 Spring St., New York, NY 10013-1578. TEL 212-620-8000. FAX 212-463-0742. *2271*

JOURNAL OF QUANTITATIVE SPECTROSCOPY AND RADIATIVE TRANSFER.
Elsevier Science Ltd., Pergamon, P.O. Box 800, Kidlington, Oxford OX5 1DX, England. TEL 44-1865-843000. FAX 44-1865-843010. *5864*

JOURNAL OF QUATERNARY SCIENCE.
John Wiley & Sons Ltd., Journals, Baffins Ln., Chichester, W. Sussex PO19 1UD, England. TEL 44-1243-779777. FAX 44-1243-775878. *2354*

JOURNAL OF QUESTIONED DOCUMENT EXAMINATION.
Independent Association of Questioned Document Examiners, Inc., 10809 S. Sandusky, Tulsa, OK 74137-6834. TEL 918-299-9663. *2271*

JOURNAL OF RADIATION CURING.
Technology Marketing Corporation, One Technology Plaza, Norwalk, CT 06854. TEL 203-852-6800. FAX 203-853-2845. *1756*

JOURNAL OF RADIOANALYTICAL AND NUCLEAR CHEMISTRY. ARTICLES.
Akademiai Kiado Rt., P.O. Box 245, H-1519 Budapest, Hungary. TEL 36-1-2043976. FAX 36-1-2043973. *1793*

JOURNAL OF RADIOANALYTICAL AND NUCLEAR CHEMISTRY. LETTERS.
Akademiai Kiado Rt., P.O. Box 245, H-1519 Budapest, Hungary. TEL 36-1-2043976. FAX 36-1-2043973. *1793*

JOURNAL OF RAMAN SPECTROSCOPY.
John Wiley & Sons Ltd., Journals, Baffins Ln., Chichester, W. Sussex PO19 1UD, England. TEL 44-1243-779777. FAX 44-1243-775878. *1793*

JOURNAL OF RANGE MANAGEMENT.
Society for Range Management, 1839 York St., Denver, CO 80206-1213. TEL 303-355-7070. *609*

JOURNAL OF RAPTOR RESEARCH.
Raptor Research Foundation, Inc., c/o O S N A, Box 1897, 810 E. 10th St., Lawrence, KS 66044-8897. TEL 612-437-4359. FAX 612-438-2908. *805*

JOURNAL OF RATIONAL-EMOTIVE AND COGNITIVE-BEHAVIOR THERAPY.
Human Sciences Press, Inc., 233 Spring St., New York, NY 10013-1578. TEL 212-620-8000. FAX 212-463-0742. *6131*

JOURNAL OF REAL ESTATE FINANCE AND ECONOMICS.
Kluwer Academic Publishers Boston, Box 358, Accord Sta., Hingham, MA 02018-0358. TEL 617-871-6600. FAX 617-871-6528. *6304*

JOURNAL OF REAL ESTATE LITERATURE.
Kluwer Academic Publishers Boston, Box 358, Accord Sta., Hingham, MA 02018-0358. TEL 617-871-6300. FAX 617-871-6528. *6304*

JOURNAL OF REAL ESTATE PORTFOLIO MANAGEMENT.
American Real Estate Society, c/o James R. Webb, Cleveland State University, Dept. of Finance, College of Business, University Center, Rm. 592A, Cleveland, OH 44115. TEL 216-687-4732. FAX 216-687-9354. *6304*

JOURNAL OF REAL ESTATE RESEARCH.
American Real Estate Society, c/o James R. Webb, Cleveland State University, Dept. of Finance, College of Business, University Center, Rm. 592A, Cleveland, OH 44115. TEL 216-687-4732. FAX 216-687-9354. *6304*

JOURNAL OF RECEPTOR AND SIGNAL TRANSDUCTION RESEARCH.
Marcel Dekker Journals, 270 Madison Ave., New York, NY 10016. TEL 212-696-9000. *610*

JOURNAL OF REFRACTIVE SURGERY.
Slack, Inc., 6900 Grove Rd., Thorofare, NJ 08086-9447. TEL 609-848-1000. FAX 609-853-5991. *5146*

JOURNAL OF REGRESSION THERAPY.
Association for Past-Life Research and Therapies, Inc., Box 20151, Riverside, CA 92516-0151. TEL 909-784-1570. FAX 909-789-8440. *6131*

JOURNAL OF REGULATORY ECONOMICS.
Kluwer Academic Publishers Boston, Box 358, Accord Sta., Hingham, MA 02018-0358. TEL 617-871-6600. FAX 617-871-6528. *1308*

JOURNAL OF REHABILITATION.
National Rehabilitation Association, 633 S. Washington St., Alexandria, VA 22314-4109. TEL 703-836-0850. FAX 703-836-0848. *5044*

JOURNAL OF REHABILITATION ADMINISTRATION.
Journal of Rehabilitation Administration, Inc., c/o Fred McFarlane, Man.Ed., Box 19891, San Diego, CA 92159. TEL 619-594-6115. FAX 619-594-4208. *1489*

JOURNAL OF REINFORCED PLASTICS & COMPOSITES.
Technomic Publishing Co., Inc., 851 New Holland Ave., Box 3535, Lancaster, PA 17604. TEL 717-291-5609. FAX 717-295-4538. *2863*

THE JOURNAL OF RELIGION.
University of Chicago Press, Journals Division, Box 37005, Chicago, IL 60637. TEL 773-753-3347. FAX 773-753-0811. *6349*

JOURNAL OF RELIGION AND HEALTH.
Human Sciences Press, Inc., 233 Spring St., New York, NY 10013-1578. TEL 212-620-8000. FAX 212-463-0742. *6349*

JOURNAL OF RELIGION IN AFRICA.
E.J. Brill, P.O. Box 9000, 2300 PA Leiden, Netherlands. TEL 31-71-5353500. FAX 31-71-5317532. *6349*

JOURNAL OF RELIGION IN DISABILITY & REHABILITATION.
Haworth Press, Inc., 10 Alice St., Binghamton, NY 13904. TEL 607-722-5857. FAX 607-722-6362. *6349*

JOURNAL OF RELIGIOUS & THEOLOGICAL INFORMATION.
Haworth Press, Inc., 10 Alice St., Binghamton, NY 13904. TEL 607-722-5857. FAX 607-722-6362. *6349*

JOURNAL OF RELIGIOUS GERONTOLOGY.
Haworth Press, Inc., 10 Alice St., Binghamton, NY 13904. TEL 607-722-5857. FAX 607-722-6362. *3440*

JOURNAL OF RELIGIOUS HISTORY.
Blackwell Publishers Ltd., 108 Cowley Rd., Oxford, OX4 1JF, England. TEL 44-1865-791100. FAX 44-1865-791347. *6350*

JOURNAL OF RELIGIOUS THOUGHT.
Howard University Press, 1240 Randolph St., N.E., Washington, DC 20017. TEL 202-806-0785. FAX 202-806-0502. *6350*

JOURNAL OF RENAL NUTRITION.
W.B. Saunders Co., Curtis Center, 3rd Fl., Independence Sq. W., Philadelphia, PA 19106-3399. TEL 215-238-7800. FAX 215-238-6445. *5477*

JOURNAL OF REPRODUCTION AND DEVELOPMENT.
Japanese Society of Animal Reproduction, c/o Dept. of Veterinary Physiology, University of Tokyo, 1-1-1 Yayoi, Bunkyo-ku, Tokyo 113, Japan. TEL 81-3-3812-2111. FAX 81-3-3815-4266. *818*

JOURNAL OF REPRODUCTION AND FERTILITY.
Journals of Reproduction & Fertility Ltd., 22 Newmarket Rd., Cambridge CB5 8DT, England. TEL 44-1223-351809. FAX 44-1223-359754. *664*

JOURNAL OF REPRODUCTIVE AND INFANT PSYCHOLOGY.
Carfax Publishing Co., P.O. Box 25, Abingdon, Oxon. OX14 3UE, England. TEL 44-1235-401000. FAX 44-1235-401550. *6131*

JOURNAL OF REPRODUCTIVE IMMUNOLOGY.
Elsevier Science Ireland Ltd., P.O. Box 85, Limerick, Ireland. TEL 353-61-471944. FAX 353-61-472144. *4799*

JOURNAL OF REPRODUCTIVE MEDICINE.
Journal of Reproductive Medicine, Inc., 8342 Olive Blvd., St. Louis, MO 63132. TEL 314-991-4440. FAX 314-991-4654. *4962*

JOURNAL OF RESEARCH AND DEVELOPMENT IN EDUCATION.
University of Georgia, College of Education, 427 Tucker Hall, Athens, GA 30602. TEL 404-542-1154. *2457*

JOURNAL OF RESEARCH IN MUSIC EDUCATION.
Music Educators National Conference, 1806 Robert Fulton Dr., Reston, VA 20191-4348. TEL 703-860-4000. FAX 703-860-4826. *5405*

JOURNAL OF RESEARCH IN PERSONALITY.
Academic Press, Inc., Journal Division, 525 B St., Ste. 1900, San Diego, CA 92101-4495. TEL 619-230-1840. FAX 619-699-6800. *6131*

JOURNAL OF RESEARCH IN PHARMACEUTICAL ECONOMICS.
Haworth Press, Inc., 10 Alice St., Binghamton, NY 13904. TEL 607-722-5857. FAX 607-722-6362. *5674*

JOURNAL OF RESEARCH IN READING.
Blackwell Publishers Ltd., 108 Cowley Rd., Oxford OX4 1JF, England. TEL 44-1865-791100. FAX 44-1865-791347. *2457*

JOURNAL OF RESEARCH IN SCIENCE TEACHING.
John Wiley & Sons, Inc., Journals, 605 Third Ave., New York, NY 10158. TEL 212-850-6645. FAX 212-850-6021. *6538*

JOURNAL OF RESEARCH ON ADOLESCENCE.
Lawrence Erlbaum Associates, Inc., 10 Industrial Dr., Mahwah, NJ 07430-2262. TEL 201-236-9500. FAX 201-236-0072. *1849*

THE JOURNAL OF RESPIRATORY DISEASES.
Cliggott Publishing Co., 55 Holly Hill Ln., Box 4010, Greenwich, CT 06831. TEL 203-661-0600. *5120*

JOURNAL OF RESTAURANT & FOODSERVICE MARKETING.
Haworth Press, Inc., 10 Alice St., Binghamton, NY 13904. TEL 607-722-5857. FAX 607-722-6362. *3731*

JOURNAL OF RETAILING AND CONSUMER SERVICES.
Elsevier Science Ltd., Pergamon, P.O. Box 800, Kidlington, Oxford OX2 8DP, England. TEL 44-1865-843000. FAX 44-1865-843010. *1535*

JOURNAL OF RHEOLOGY.
American Institute of Physics, One Physics Ellipse, College Park, MD 20740-3843. TEL 301-209-3000. *5846*

JOURNAL OF RISK AND UNCERTAINTY.
Kluwer Academic Publishers Boston, Box 358, Accord Sta., Hingham, MA 02018-0358. TEL 617-871-6600. FAX 617-871-6528. *6131*

JOURNAL OF ROBOTIC SYSTEMS.
John Wiley & Sons, Inc., Journals, 605 Third Ave., New York, NY 10158. TEL 212-692-6645. FAX 212-850-6021. *2207*

JOURNAL OF RURAL HEALTH.
National Rural Health Association, 1 W. Armour Blvd., Ste. 301, Kansas City, MO 64111. TEL 816-756-3140. FAX 816-756-3144. *4698*

JOURNAL OF RURAL MANAGEMENT AND HUMAN RESOURCES.
Agricultural Manpower Society, University of Reading, Earley Gate, P.O. Box 236, Reading, Berks. RG6 2AT, England. TEL 44-1568-613175. *130*

JOURNAL OF RURAL STUDIES.
Elsevier Science Ltd., Pergamon, P.O. Box 800, Kidlington, Oxford OX5 1DX, England. TEL 44-1865-843000. FAX 44-1865-843010. *6718*

JOURNAL OF RUSSIAN AND EAST EUROPEAN PSYCHOLOGY.
M.E. Sharpe, Inc., 80 Business Park Dr., Armonk, NY 10504. TEL 914-273-1800. FAX 914-273-2106. *6131*

JOURNAL OF RUSSIAN LASER RESEARCH.
Plenum Publishing Corp., Consultants Bureau, 233 Spring St., New York, NY 10013-1578. TEL 212-620-8468. FAX 212-463-0742. *2729*

JOURNAL OF SAFETY RESEARCH.
Elsevier Science Ltd., Pergamon, P.O. Box 800, Kidlington, Oxford OX5 1DX, England. TEL 44-1865-843000. FAX 44-1865-843010. *5493*

JOURNAL OF SAN DIEGO HISTORY.
San Diego Historical Society, Box 81825, San Diego, CA 92138. TEL 619-232-6203. FAX 619-232-6297. *3633*

JOURNAL OF SCHOOL HEALTH.
American School Health Association, Box 708, Kent, OH 44240. TEL 216-678-1601. FAX 216-678-4526. *6242*

JOURNAL OF SCHOOL LEADERSHIP.
Technomic Publishing Co., Inc., 851 New Holland Ave., Box 3535, Lancaster, PA 17604. TEL 717-291-5609. FAX 717-295-4538. *2574*

JOURNAL OF SCHOOL PSYCHOLOGY.
Elsevier Science Ltd., Pergamon, P.O. Box 800, England. TEL 44-1865-843000. FAX 44-1865-843010. *6131*

JOURNAL OF SCIENCE (INTERNATIONAL EDITION).
University of Tehran Press Co., P.O. Box 14155-6455, Tehran, Iran. TEL 98-21-6113305. FAX 98-21-6405141. *6538*

JOURNAL OF SCIENCE (NATIONAL EDITION).
University of Teheran Press Co., P.O. Box 14155-6455, Teheran, Iran. TEL 98-21-6113305. FAX 98-21-6405141. *6538*

JOURNAL OF SCIENCE EDUCATION AND TECHNOLOGY.
Plenum Publishing Corp., 233 Spring St., New York, NY 10013-1578. TEL 212-620-8000. FAX 212-463-0742. *2457*

JOURNAL OF SCIENCE TEACHER EDUCATION.
Kluwer Academic Publishers, Postbus 17, 3300 AA Dordrecht, Netherlands. TEL 31-78-6392392. FAX 31-78-6392254. *2457*

JOURNAL OF SCIENCES, ISLAMIC REPUBLIC OF IRAN.
National Center for Scientific Research, 1188 Enghelab Ave., P.O. Box 13145-478, Tehran, Iran. TEL 98-21-6462778. FAX 98-21-6468180. *6538*

JOURNAL OF SCIENTIFIC COMPUTING.
Plenum Publishing Corp., 233 Spring St., New York, NY 10013-1578. TEL 212-620-8000. FAX 212-463-0742. *6594*

JOURNAL OF SCIENTIFIC EXPLORATION.
Society for Scientific Exploration, Box 5848, Stanford University, Stanford, CA 94309-5848. TEL 415-593-8581. FAX 415-595-4466. *6538*

REFEREED SERIALS

JOURNAL OF SEA RESEARCH.
Elsevier Science B.V., Earth Science Department, P.O. Box 1930, 1000 BX Amsterdam, Netherlands. *2407*

JOURNAL OF SECONDARY GIFTED EDUCATION.
Prufrock Press, Box 8813, Waco, TX 76714-8813. FAX 800-240-0333. *2586*

JOURNAL OF SECURITY ADMINISTRATION.
B L S S, Inc., Box 164509, Miami, FL 33116-4509. TEL 305-254-7006. FAX 305-254-9662. *2287*

JOURNAL OF SEDIMENTARY RESEARCH. SECTION A: SEDIMENTARY PETROLOGY AND PROCESSES.
S E P M, 1731 E. 71st St., Tulsa, OK 74136-5108. TEL 918-493-3361. FAX 918-493-2093. *2317*

JOURNAL OF SEISMOLOGY.
Kluwer Academic Publishers, Postbus 17, 3300 AA Dordrecht, Netherlands. TEL 31-78-6392392. FAX 31-78-6392254. *2385*

JOURNAL OF SERICULTURAL SCIENCE OF JAPAN.
Japanese Society of Sericultural Science, National Institute of Sericultural and Entomological Science, 1-2 Owashi, Tsukuba-shi, Ibaraki-ken 305, Japan. TEL 0298-38-6056. FAX 0298-38-6028. *757*

JOURNAL OF SEROTONIN RESEARCH.
Euroscience Press, P.O. Box 3405, London N1 0NZ, England. TEL 44-171-601-8138. FAX 44-171-601-7969. *664*

JOURNAL OF SEX EDUCATION AND THERAPY.
American Association of Sex Educators, Counselors and Therapists, Box 238, Mount Vernon, IA 52314. TEL 319-895-8407. FAX 319-895-6203. *5786*

JOURNAL OF SEX RESEARCH.
Society for the Scientific Study of Sexuality, Box 208, Mt. Vernon, IA 52314. TEL 319-895-8407. FAX 319-895-6203. *6131*

JOURNAL OF SHELLFISH RESEARCH.
National Shellfisheries Association, Inc., Natural Science Division, Southampton College, Southampton, NY 11968. TEL 516-287-8407. FAX 516-287-8419. *840*

JOURNAL OF SHOULDER AND ELBOW SURGERY.
Mosby - Year Book, Inc., 11830 Westline Industrial Dr., St. Louis, MO 63146-3318. TEL 314-872-8370. FAX 314-432-1380. *5146*

JOURNAL OF SINGING.
Singular Publishing Group, Inc., 401 W. A St., Ste. 325, San Diego, CA 92101-7961. FAX 800-774-8398. *5405*

JOURNAL OF SLAVIC LINGUISTICS.
Dept. of Slavic Languages, IU, Ballantine 502, Bloomington, IN 47405. TEL 812-855-2829. FAX 812-855-2107. *4269*

THE JOURNAL OF SLAVIC MILITARY STUDIES.
Frank Cass, Newbury House, 890-900 Eastern Ave., Newbury Park, Ilford, Essex IG2 7HH, England. TEL 44-181-599-8866. FAX 44-181-599-0984. *5274*

JOURNAL OF SLEEP RESEARCH.
Blackwell Science Ltd., Osney Mead, Oxford OX2 0EL, England. TEL 44-1865-206206. FAX 44-1865-721205. *4698*

JOURNAL OF SMALL ANIMAL PRACTICE.
British Veterinary Association Publications, 7 Mansfield St., London W1M 0AT, England. TEL 44-171-636-6541. FAX 44-171-637-0620. *7273*

JOURNAL OF SMALL BUSINESS STRATEGY.
Small Business Institute Directors' Association, Wittenberg University, Box 720, Springfield, OH 45501. *1644*

JOURNAL OF SMALL FRUIT & VITICULTURE.
Haworth Press, Inc., 10 Alice St., Binghamton, NY 13904. TEL 607-722-5857. FAX 607-722-6362. *232*

JOURNAL OF SOCIAL AND CLINICAL PSYCHOLOGY.
Guilford Publications, Inc., 72 Spring St., 4th Fl., New York, NY 10012. TEL 212-431-9800. FAX 212-966-6708. *6132*

JOURNAL OF SOCIAL AND PERSONAL RELATIONSHIPS.
Sage Publications Ltd., 6 Bonhill St., London EC2A 4PU, England. TEL 44-171-374-0645. FAX 44-171-374-8741. *6132*

JOURNAL OF SOCIAL BEHAVIOR AND PERSONALITY.
Select Press, Box 37, Corte Madera, CA 94976-0037. TEL 415-924-1612. FAX 415-924-7179. *6132*

JOURNAL OF SOCIAL DEVELOPMENT IN AFRICA.
School of Social Work, Private Bag 66022, Kopje, Harare, Zimbabwe. TEL 263-4-751815. FAX 263-4-751903. *6674*

JOURNAL OF SOCIAL DISTRESS AND THE HOMELESS.
Human Sciences Press, Inc., 233 Spring St., New York, NY 10013. TEL 212-620-8000. FAX 212-463-0742. *6674*

JOURNAL OF SOCIAL ISSUES.
Blackwell Publishers, 238 Main St., Cambridge, MA 02142. TEL 617-547-7110. FAX 617-547-0789. *6132*

THE JOURNAL OF SOCIAL PSYCHOLOGY.
Heldref Publications, 1319 Eighteenth St., N.W., Washington, DC 20036-1802. TEL 202-296-6267. FAX 202-296-5149. *6132*

JOURNAL OF SOCIAL SCIENCES (NEW DELHI).
Sambalpur University, Department of Anthropology, Sambalpur 768 019, Orissa, India. TEL 91-663-400426. FAX 91-663-430158. *6623*

JOURNAL OF SOCIAL SERVICE RESEARCH.
Haworth Press, Inc., 10 Alice St., Binghamton, NY 13904. TEL 607-722-5857. FAX 607-722-6362. *6674*

JOURNAL OF SOCIAL WORK EDUCATION.
Council on Social Work Education, 1600 Duke St., Alexandria, VA 22314-3421. TEL 703-683-8080. FAX 703-683-8099. *6674*

JOURNAL OF SOCIAL WORK PRACTICE.
Carfax Publishing Co., P.O. Box 25, Abingdon, Oxon. OX14 3UE, England. TEL 44-1235-401000. FAX 44-1235-401550. *6674*

JOURNAL OF SOCIOLOGY AND SOCIAL WELFARE.
Western Michigan University, School of Social Work, c/o Fritz MacDonald, Managing Ed., Kalamazoo, MI 49008-5034. TEL 616-387-3198. FAX 616-387-3217. *6718*

JOURNAL OF SOFTWARE MAINTENANCE: RESEARCH AND PRACTICE.
John Wiley & Sons Ltd., Journals, Baffins Ln., Chichester, W. Sussex PO19 1UD, England. TEL 44-1243-779777. FAX 44-1243-775878. *2214*

JOURNAL OF SOFTWARE TESTING, VERIFICATION AND RELIABILITY.
John Wiley & Sons Ltd., Journals, Baffins Ln., Chichester, W. Sussex PO19 1UD, England. TEL 44-1243-779777. FAX 44-1243-843232. *2214*

JOURNAL OF SOIL AND WATER CONSERVATION.
Soil and Water Conservation Society, 7515 N.E. Ankeny Rd., Ankeny, IA 50021. TEL 515-289-2331. FAX 515-289-1227. *232*

JOURNAL OF SOIL AND WATER CONSERVATION IN INDIA.
Soil Conservation Society of India, B-19 Paryat Apts., Pilampura, 4 Outer Ring Rd., New Delhi 110034, India. TEL 91-11-5743811. *2234*

JOURNAL OF SOIL BIOLOGY AND ECOLOGY.
Indian Society of Soil Biology and Ecology, University of Agricultural Sciences, Department of Entomology, Hebbal, Bangalore 560 024, India. TEL 91-80-3330153. FAX 91-80-3330277. *610*

JOURNAL OF SOIL CONTAMINATION.
C R C Press, Inc., 2000 Corporate Blvd., N.W., Boca Raton, FL 33431. TEL 561-994-0555. FAX 561-998-9784. *2969*

JOURNAL OF SOL-GEL SCIENCE AND TECHNOLOGY.
Kluwer Academic Publishers, Postbus 17, 3300 AA Dordrecht, Netherlands. TEL 31-78-6392392. FAX 31-78-6392254. *2863*

JOURNAL OF SOLAR ENERGY ENGINEERING.
American Society of Mechanical Engineers, 22 Law Dr., Fairfield, NJ 07007-2900. TEL 973-882-1167. FAX 973-882-1717. *2706*

JOURNAL OF SOLID STATE CHEMISTRY.
Academic Press, Inc., Journal Division, 525 B St., Ste. 1900, San Diego, CA 92101-4495. TEL 619-230-1840. FAX 619-699-6800. *1832*

JOURNAL OF SOLID WASTE TECHNOLOGY AND MANAGEMENT.
Widener University, c/o Dept. of Civil Engineering, 1 University Place, 1 University Pl., Chester, PA 19013-5792. TEL 610-499-4042. FAX 610-499-4059. *2939*

JOURNAL OF SOLUTION CHEMISTRY.
Plenum Publishing Corp., 233 Spring St., New York, NY 10013-1578. TEL 212-620-8000. FAX 212-463-0742. *1832*

JOURNAL OF SOUTH AMERICAN EARTH SCIENCES.
Elsevier Science Ltd., Pergamon, P.O. Box 800, Kidlington, Oxford OX5 1DX, England. TEL 44-1865-843000. FAX 44-1865-843010. *2318*

JOURNAL OF SOUTH-EAST ASIAN EARTH SCIENCES.
Elsevier Science Ltd., Pergamon, P.O. Box 800, Kidlington, Oxford OX5 1DX, England. TEL 44-1865-843000. FAX 44-1865-843010. *2354*

JOURNAL OF SOUTHERN AFRICAN STUDIES.
Carfax Publishing Co., P.O. Box 25, Abingdon, Oxon. OX14 3UE, England. TEL 44-1235-401000. FAX 44-1235-401550. *6623*

JOURNAL OF SOUTHERN HISTORY.
Southern Historical Association, Rice University, 6100 Main St., Houston, TX 77005-1892. TEL 713-527-3069. FAX 713-285-5207. *3633*

JOURNAL OF SOUTHWEST GEORGIA HISTORY.
Thronateeska Heritage Center, 100 Roosevelt Ave., Albany, GA 31701. TEL 912-432-6955. FAX 912-432-6955. *3633*

JOURNAL OF SPACECRAFT AND ROCKETS.
American Institute of Aeronautics and Astronautics, Inc., 1801 Alexander Dr., Ste. 500, Reston, VA 20191. TEL 703-264-7500. *72*

THE JOURNAL OF SPECIAL EDUCATION.
Pro-Ed Inc., 8700 Shoal Creek Blvd., Austin, TX 78757-6897. TEL 512-451-3246. FAX 512-451-8542. *2586*

JOURNAL OF SPECIAL EDUCATION TECHNOLOGY.
Council for Exceptional Children, Technology and Media Division, c/o Herbert Rieth, Ed., University of Texas at Austin, Department of Special Education, Sanchez Bldg. No. 306, Austin, TX 78712-1290. TEL 512-471-4161. FAX 512-471-4061. *2586*

JOURNAL OF SPECULATIVE PHILOSOPHY.
Pennsylvania State University Press, USB 1, Ste. C, University Park, PA 16802-1003. TEL 814-865-1327. FAX 814-863-1408. *5734*

JOURNAL OF SPEECH - LANGUAGE PATHOLOGY AND AUDIOLOGY.
Canadian Association of Speech - Language Pathologists and Audiologists, 2006 - 130 Albert St., Ottawa, ON K1P 5G4, Canada. TEL 613-567-9968. FAX 613-567-2859. *2586*

JOURNAL OF SPICES AND AROMATIC CROPS.
Indian Society for Spices, c/o Indian Institute of Spices Research, P.O. Box 1701, Marikunnu P.O., Calicut 673 012, Kerala, India. TEL 91-495-370294. FAX 91-495-370294. *232*

JOURNAL OF SPINAL CORD MEDICINE.
American Paraplegia Society, 75-20 Astoria Blvd., Jackson Heights, NY 11370-1177. TEL 718-803-3782. FAX 718-803-0414. *5044*

JOURNAL OF SPINAL DISORDERS.
Lippincott - Raven Publishers, 227 E. Washington Sq., Philadelphia, PA 19106. TEL 215-238-4200. FAX 215-238-4227. *5011*

JOURNAL OF SPIRITUAL BODYWORK.
Spiritual Massage healing Ministry, 6907 Sherman St., Philadelphia, PA 19119. TEL 215-842-0265. FAX 215-842-0265. *297*

JOURNAL OF SPORT AND EXERCISE PSYCHOLOGY.
Human Kinetics Publishers, Inc., Box 5076, Champaign, IL 61825-5076. TEL 217-351-5076. FAX 217-351-2674. *6132*

JOURNAL OF SPORT BEHAVIOR.
University of South Alabama, Department of Health, Physical Education and Leisure Studies, Mobile, AL 36688. TEL 334-460-7131. FAX 334-460-7252. *6767*

JOURNAL OF SPORT MANAGEMENT.
Human Kinetics Publishers, Inc., Box 5076, Champaign, IL 61825-5076. TEL 217-351-5076. FAX 217-351-2674. *6767*

JOURNAL OF SPORT REHABILITATION.
Human Kinetics Publishers, Inc., Box 5076, Champaign, IL 61825-5076. TEL 217-351-5076. FAX 217-351-2674. *5130*

JOURNAL OF SPORTS CHIROPRACTIC AND REHABILITATION.
Williams & Wilkins, 351 W. Camden St., Baltimore, MD 21201-2436. TEL 410-528-4068. FAX 410-528-4452. *4828*

THE JOURNAL OF SPORTS MEDICINE AND PHYSICAL FITNESS.
Edizioni Minerva Medica, Corso Bramante 83-85, 10126 Turin, Italy. TEL 39-11-678282. FAX 39-11-674502. *5130*

JOURNAL OF SPORTS SCIENCES.
Thomson Professional, 2-6 Boundary Row, London SE1 8HN, England. TEL 44-171-865-0066. FAX 44-171-522-9623. *6767*

JOURNAL OF STATISTICAL COMPUTATION AND SIMULATION.
Gordon and Breach - Harwood Academic, Amsteldisk 166, 1st Fl., 1079 LH Amsterdam, Netherlands. *2152*

JOURNAL OF STATISTICAL PHYSICS.
Plenum Publishing Corp., 233 Spring St., New York, NY 10013-1578. TEL 212-620-8000. FAX 212-463-0742. *5811*

JOURNAL OF STATISTICAL PLANNING AND INFERENCE.
North-Holland, P.O. Box 211, 1000 AE Amsterdam, Netherlands. TEL 31-20-4853911. FAX 31-20-4853598. *6921*

JOURNAL OF STEROID BIOCHEMISTRY AND MOLECULAR BIOLOGY.
Elsevier Science Ltd., Pergamon, P.O. Box 800, Kidlington, Oxford OX5 1DX, England. TEL 44-1865-843000. FAX 44-1865-843010. *665*

JOURNAL OF STORED PRODUCTS RESEARCH.
Elsevier Science Ltd., Pergamon, P.O. Box 800, Kidlington, Oxford OX5 1DX, England. TEL 44-1865-843000. FAX 44-1865-843010. *232*

JOURNAL OF STRATEGIC INFORMATION SYSTEMS.
Elsevier Science B.V., P.O. Box 211, 1000 AE Amsterdam, Netherlands. TEL 31-20-4853911. FAX 31-20-4853598. *2150*

JOURNAL OF STRATEGIC MARKETING.
Thomson Professional, 2-6 Boundary Row, London SE1 8HN, England. TEL 44-171-8650066. FAX 44-171-5229623. *1535*

THE JOURNAL OF STRATEGIC STUDIES.
Frank Cass, Newbury House, 890-900 Eastern Ave., Newbury Park, Ilford, Essex IG2 7HH, England. TEL 44-181-599-8866. FAX 44-181-599-0984. *6024*

JOURNAL OF STRENGTH AND CONDITIONING RESEARCH.
Human Kinetics Publishers, Inc., Box 5076, Champaign, IL 61825-5076. TEL 217-351-5076. FAX 217-351-2674. *5130*

JOURNAL OF STRUCTURAL BIOLOGY.
Academic Press, Inc., Journal Division, 525 B St., Ste. 1900, San Diego, CA 92101-4495. TEL 619-230-1840. FAX 619-699-6859. *610*

JOURNAL OF STRUCTURAL CHEMISTRY.
Plenum Publishing Corp., Consultants Bureau, 233 Spring St., New York, NY 10013-1578. TEL 212-620-8468. FAX 212-463-0742. *1756*

JOURNAL OF STRUCTURAL GEOLOGY.
Elsevier Science Ltd., Pergamon, P.O. Box 800, Kidlington, Oxford OX5 1DX, England. TEL 44-1865-843000. FAX 44-1865-843010. *2354*

JOURNAL OF STRUCTURAL LEARNING.
Gordon and Breach - Harwood Academic, Amsteldisk 166, 1st Fl., 1079 LH Amsterdam, Netherlands. *6132*

JOURNAL OF STUDIES ON ALCOHOL. SUPPLEMENT.
Alcohol Research Documentation, Inc., Box 969, Piscataway, NJ 08855. TEL 732-445-3510. FAX 732-445-3500. *2303*

JOURNAL OF SUBSTANCE ABUSE TREATMENT.
Elsevier Science Inc., Box 945, New York, NY 10159-0945. TEL 212-633-3730. FAX 212-633-3680. *2303*

JOURNAL OF SUBSTANCE MISUSE.
Churchill Livingstone, Robert Stevenson House, 1-3 Baxter's Pl., Leith Walk, Edinburgh EH1 3AF, Scotland. TEL 44-131-556-2424. FAX 44-131-535-1704. *2303*

JOURNAL OF SUDDEN INFANT DEATH SYNDROME AND INFANT MORTALITY.
Plenum Publishing Corp., 233 Spring St., New York, NY 10013-1578. TEL 212-620-8000. FAX 212-463-0742. *5033*

JOURNAL OF SUPERCOMPUTING.
Kluwer Academic Publishers Boston, Box 358, Accord Sta., Hingham, MA 02018-0358. TEL 617-871-6300. FAX 617-871-6528. *2086*

JOURNAL OF SUPERCONDUCTIVITY.
Plenum Publishing Corp., 233 Spring St., New York, NY 10013-1578. TEL 212-620-8000. FAX 212-463-0742. *5811*

JOURNAL OF SUPERCRITICAL FLUIDS.
Elsevier Science B.V., P.O. Box 211, 1000 AE Amsterdam, Netherlands. TEL 31-20-4853911. FAX 31-20-4853598. *1794*

JOURNAL OF SUPREME COURT HISTORY.
Supreme Court Historical Society, 111 Second St., N.E., Washington, DC 20002. TEL 202-543-0400. FAX 202-547-7730. *4133*

JOURNAL OF SURGICAL ONCOLOGY.
John Wiley & Sons, Inc., Journals, 605 Third Ave., New York, NY 10158. TEL 212-850-6645. FAX 212-850-6021. *5146*

JOURNAL OF SURGICAL PATHOLOGY.
Chapman & Hall, Journals Department 2-6 Boundary Row, London SE1 8HN, England. TEL 44-171-8650066. FAX 44-171-5229623. *4698*

JOURNAL OF SURGICAL RESEARCH.
Academic Press, Inc., Journal Division, 525 B St., Ste. 1900, San Diego, CA 92101-4495. TEL 619-230-1840. FAX 619-699-6800. *5147*

JOURNAL OF SURVEYING ENGINEERING.
American Society of Civil Engineers, 345 E. 47th St., New York, NY 10017-2398. TEL 212-705-7288. FAX 212-980-4681. *2791*

JOURNAL OF SUSTAINABLE AGRICULTURE.
Haworth Press, Inc., 10 Alice St., Binghamton, NY 13904. TEL 607-722-5857. FAX 607-722-6362. *2234*

JOURNAL OF SUSTAINABLE FORESTRY.
Haworth Press, Inc., 10 Alice St., Binghamton, NY 13904. TEL 607-722-5857. FAX 607-722-6362. *3157*

JOURNAL OF SWIMMING RESEARCH.
American Swimming Coaches Association, 2101 N. Andrews Ave., No.107, Fort Lauderdale, FL 33311. FAX 954-563-9813. *6767*

JOURNAL OF SYNCHROTRON RADIATION.
Munksgaard International Publishers Ltd., 35 Noerre Soegade, P.O. Box 1248, DK-1016 Copenhagen K, Denmark. TEL 45-33-127030. FAX 45-33-129387. *5853*

JOURNAL OF SYNTHETIC LUBRICATION.
Leaf Coppin Publishing Co., P.O. Box 111, Deal, Kent CT14 6SX, England. TEL 44-1304-360241. FAX 44-1304-360241. *5608*

JOURNAL OF SYSTEMS AND SOFTWARE.
Elsevier Science Inc., Box 945, New York, NY 10159-0945. TEL 212-633-3730. FAX 212-633-3680. *2214*

JOURNAL OF SYSTEMS ARCHITECTURE.
North-Holland, P.O. Box 211, 1000 AE Amsterdam, Netherlands. TEL 31-20-4853911. FAX 31-20-4853598. *2189*

JOURNAL OF SYSTEMS ENGINEERING.
Springer-Verlag London Ltd., Sweetapple House, Catteshall Rd., Godalming, Surrey GU7 3DJ, England. TEL 44-1483-418800. FAX 44-1483-415144. *2877*

JOURNAL OF SYSTEMS ENGINEERING AND ELECTRONICS.
Science Press, Marketing and Sales Department, 16 Donghuangchenggen North St., Beijing 100717, People's Republic of China. TEL 4010642. FAX 4019810. *72*

JOURNAL OF SYSTEMS INTEGRATION.
Kluwer Academic Publishers Boston, Box 358, Accord Sta., Hingham, MA 02018-0358. TEL 617-871-6600. FAX 617-871-6528. *2156*

JOURNAL OF TAIWAN MUSEUM.
Taiwan Provincial Museum, 2 Siangyang Rd., Taipei, Taiwan 100, Republic of China. TEL 886-2-397-9396. FAX 886-2-397-9514. *5356*

JOURNAL OF TARGETING, MEASUREMENT AND ANALYSIS.
Henry Stewart Publications, Russell House, 28-30 Little Russell St., London WC1A 2HN, England. TEL 44-171-404-3040. FAX 44-171-486-2081. *1589*

THE JOURNAL OF TAXATION.
Warren, Gorham & Lamont, One Penn Plaza, New York, NY 10119. TEL 212-971-5185. FAX 212-971-5113. *1618*

JOURNAL OF TEACHER EDUCATION.
Corwin Press, Inc., 2455 Teller Rd., Thousand Oaks, CA 91320. TEL 805-499-0721. FAX 805-499-0871. *2547*

JOURNAL OF TEACHING IN INTERNATIONAL BUSINESS.
Haworth Press, Inc., 10 Alice St., Binghamton, NY 13904. TEL 607-722-5857. FAX 607-722-6362. *2457*

JOURNAL OF TEACHING IN PHYSICAL EDUCATION.
Human Kinetics Publishers, Inc., Box 5076, Champaign, IL 61825-5076. TEL 217-351-5076. FAX 217-351-2674. *2608*

JOURNAL OF TEACHING IN SOCIAL WORK.
Haworth Press, Inc., 10 Alice St., Binghamton, NY 13904. TEL 607-722-5857. FAX 607-722-6362. *2608*

JOURNAL OF TECHNICAL WRITING AND COMMUNICATION.
Baywood Publishing Co., Inc., 26 Austin Ave., Box 337, Amityville, NY 11701. TEL 516-691-1270. FAX 516-691-1770. *2457*

JOURNAL OF TECHNOLOGY AND TEACHER EDUCATION.
Association for the Advancement of Computing in Education, Box 2966, Charlottesville, VA 22901-2966. TEL 804-973-3987. FAX 804-978-7449. *2518*

JOURNAL OF TECHNOLOGY EDUCATION.
Virginia Polytechnic Institute, Technology Education Program, c/o Mark Sanders, Ed., 144 Smyth Hall, Blacksburg, VA 24061-0432. FAX 703-231-4188. *6964*

JOURNAL OF TECHNOLOGY STUDIES.
Epsilon Pi Tau, c/o Jerry Streichler, Ed., Bowling Green State University, Bowling Green, OH 43403-0305. *6964*

JOURNAL OF TECHNOLOGY TRANSFER.
Technology Transfer Society, 435 N. Michigan Ave., Chicago, IL 60611-4001. *6964*

REFEREED SERIALS

JOURNAL OF TERRAMECHANICS.
Elsevier Science Ltd., Pergamon, P.O. Box 800, Kidlington, Oxford OX5 1DX, England. TEL 44-1865-843000. FAX 44-1865-843010. *7032*

JOURNAL OF TESTING AND EVALUATION.
American Society for Testing and Materials, 100 Barr Harbor Dr., W. Conshohocken, PA 19428-2959. TEL 610-832-9500. FAX 610-832-9555. *2864*

JOURNAL OF THE ATMOSPHERIC SCIENCES.
American Meteorological Society, 45 Beacon St., Boston, MA 02108-3693. TEL 617-227-2425. FAX 617-742-8718. *5237*

JOURNAL OF THE AUSTRALIAN WAR MEMORIAL.
Australian War Memorial, G.P.O. Box 345, Canberra, A.C.T. 2601, Australia. TEL 61-6-2434345. FAX 61-6-2434325. *5274*

JOURNAL OF THE AUTONOMIC NERVOUS SYSTEM.
Elsevier Science B.V., P.O. Box 211, 1000 AE Amsterdam, Netherlands. TEL 31-20-4853911. FAX 31-20-4853598. *5077*

JOURNAL OF THE ECONOMIC AND SOCIAL HISTORY OF THE ORIENT.
E.J. Brill, P.O. Box 9000, 2300 PA Leiden, Netherlands. TEL 31-71-5353500. FAX 31-71-5317532. *3657*

JOURNAL OF THE FANTASTIC IN THE ARTS.
International Association for the Fantastic in the Arts, c/o Jade Seas Publishing, 2084 Hidden Lake Dr., Apt. B, Stow, OH 44224-5328. TEL 216-688-2818. *4532*

JOURNAL OF THE FRESHMAN YEAR EXPERIENCE.
University of South Carolina, National Center for the Study of the Freshman Year Experience, 1728 College St., Columbia, SC 29208. TEL 803-777-6029. FAX 803-777-4699. *2547*

JOURNAL OF THE GULF AND ARABIAN PENINSULA STUDIES.
University of Kuwait, P.O. Box 17073, Al-Khaldiah 72451, Kuwait. TEL 965-4816807. FAX 965-4814295. *3657*

JOURNAL OF THE HISTORY OF BIOLOGY.
Kluwer Academic Publishers, Postbus 17, 3300 AA Dordrecht, Netherlands. TEL 31-78-6392392. FAX 31-78-6392254. *610*

JOURNAL OF THE HISTORY OF DENTISTRY.
American Academy of the History of Dentistry, c/o Aletha Kowitz, 100 S. Vail Ave., Arlington Heights, IL 60005-1866. TEL 847-670-7561. *4863*

JOURNAL OF THE HISTORY OF MEDICINE AND ALLIED SCIENCES.
Oxford University Press, Academic Division, Great Clarendon St., Oxford OX2 6DP, England. TEL 44-1865-267907. FAX 44-1865-267485. *4698*

JOURNAL OF THE HISTORY OF SEXUALITY.
University of Chicago Press, Journals Division, Box 37005, Chicago, IL 60637. TEL 773-753-3347. FAX 773-753-0811. *6718*

JOURNAL OF THE HISTORY OF THE BEHAVIORAL SCIENCES.
John Wiley & Sons, Inc., Journals, 605 Third Ave., New York, NY 10158-0012. TEL 212-850-6645. FAX 212-850-6021. *6133*

JOURNAL OF THE HISTORY OF THE NEUROSCIENCES.
Swets & Zeitlinger bv, P.O. Box 825, 2160 SZ Lisse, Netherlands. TEL 31-252-435111. FAX 31-252-415888. *5078*

JOURNAL OF THE LEARNING SCIENCES.
Lawrence Erlbaum Associates, Inc., 10 Industrial Dr., Mahwah, NJ 07430-2262. TEL 201-236-9500. FAX 201-236-0072. *2457*

JOURNAL OF THE MECHANICS AND PHYSICS OF SOLIDS.
Elsevier Science Ltd., Pergamon, P.O. Box 800, Kidlington, Oxford OX5 1DX, England. TEL 44-1865-843000. FAX 44-1865-843010. *5846*

JOURNAL OF THE NEUROLOGICAL SCIENCES.
Elsevier Science B.V., P.O. Box 211, 1000 AE Amsterdam, Netherlands. TEL 31-20-4853911. FAX 31-20-4853598. *5078*

JOURNAL OF THE NEUROMUSCULOSKELETAL SYSTEM.
Data Trace Publishing Company, 110 West Rd., Ste. 227, Baltimore, MD 21204-2316. TEL 410-494-4994. FAX 410-494-0515. *5078*

JOURNAL OF THE PERIPHERAL NERVOUS SYSTEM.
Woodland Publications, Inc., 69 Murray St., New York, NY 10007. TEL 212-566-4294. *5078*

JOURNAL OF THE PHILOSOPHY OF SPORT.
Human Kinetics Publishers, Inc., Box 5076, Champaign, IL 61825-5076. TEL 217-351-5076. FAX 217-351-2674. *6767*

JOURNAL OF THE ROYAL ASIATIC SOCIETY.
Cambridge University Press, Edinburgh Bldg., Shaftesbury Rd., Cambridge CB2 2RU, England. TEL 44-1223-312393. FAX 44-1223-315052. *5531*

JOURNAL OF THE SCIENCE OF FOOD AND AGRICULTURE.
John Wiley & Sons Ltd., Journals, Baffins Ln., Chichester, W. Sussex PO19 1UD, England. TEL 44-1243-779777. FAX 44-1243-775878. *130*

JOURNAL OF THE THIRD WORLD SPECTRUM.
Box 44843, Washington, DC 20026-4843. TEL 202-806-7649. *6623*

JOURNAL OF THE WEST.
Journal of the West, Inc., 1531 Yuma, Box 1009, Manhattan, KS 66505-1009. TEL 913-539-1888. FAX 913-539-2233. *3634*

JOURNAL OF THEOLOGY FOR SOUTHERN AFRICA.
c/o University of Cape Town, Department of Religious Studies, 7700 Rondebosch, South Africa. TEL 27-21-650-3457. FAX 27-21-689-7575. *6350*

JOURNAL OF THEORETICAL POLITICS.
Sage Publications Ltd., 6 Bonhill St., London EC2A 4PU, England. TEL 44-171-374-0645. FAX 44-171-374-8741. *5938*

JOURNAL OF THEORETICAL PROBABILITY.
Plenum Publishing Corp., 233 Spring St., New York, NY 10013-1578. TEL 212-620-8000. FAX 212-463-0742. *4584*

JOURNAL OF THEORY CONSTRUCTION AND TESTING.
Tucker Publications, Inc., Box 580, Lisle, IL 60532. TEL 630-969-3809. FAX 630-969-3895. *4938*

JOURNAL OF THERAPEUTIC HORTICULTURE.
American Horticultural Therapy Association, 362A Christopher Ave., Gaithersburg, MD 20879-3660. TEL 301-948-3010. FAX 301-869-2397. *3196*

JOURNAL OF THERMAL ANALYSIS.
Akademiai Kiado Rt., P.O. Box 245, H-1519 Budapest, Hungary. TEL 36-1-2043976. FAX 36-1-2045600. *1832*

JOURNAL OF THERMAL INSULATION AND BUILDING ENVELOPES.
Technomic Publishing Co., Inc., 851 New Holland Ave., Box 3535, Lancaster, PA 17604. TEL 717-291-5609. FAX 717-295-4538. *2729*

JOURNAL OF THERMAL SCIENCE.
Science Press, Marketing and Sales Department, 16 Donghuangchengen North St., Beijing 100717, People's Republic of China. TEL 4010642. FAX 4019810. *5842*

JOURNAL OF THERMAL SPRAY TECHNOLOGY.
A S M International, Materials Information, Materials Park, OH 44073-0002. TEL 216-338-5151. FAX 216-338-4634. *5842*

JOURNAL OF THERMAL STRESSES.
Taylor & Francis Inc., 1900 Frost Rd., Ste. 101, Bristol, PA 19007-1598. TEL 215-785-5800. FAX 215-785-5515. *2890*

JOURNAL OF THERMOPHYSICS AND HEAT TRANSFER.
American Institute of Aeronautics and Astronautics, Inc., 1801 Alexander Dr., Ste. 500, Reston, VA 20191. TEL 703-264-7500. *5812*

JOURNAL OF THERMOPLASTIC COMPOSITE MATERIALS.
Technomic Publishing Co., Inc., 851 New Holland Ave., Box 3535, Lancaster, PA 17604. TEL 717-291-5609. FAX 717-295-4538. *5879*

JOURNAL OF THIRD WORLD STUDIES.
Association of Third World Studies, Inc., Box 1232, Americus, GA 31709. TEL 912-924-8287. FAX 912-931-2270. *3503*

THE JOURNAL OF THORACIC AND CARDIOVASCULAR SURGERY.
Mosby - Year Book, Inc., 11830 Westline Industrial Dr., St. Louis, MO 63146-3318. TEL 314-872-8370. FAX 314-432-1380. *5147*

JOURNAL OF THORACIC IMAGING.
Lippincott - Raven Publishers, 276 E. Washington Sq., Philadelphia, PA 19106. TEL 215-238-4200. FAX 215-238-4227. *5109*

JOURNAL OF THROMBOSIS AND THROMBOLYSIS.
Kluwer Academic Publishers, Postbus 17, 3300 AA Dordrecht, Netherlands. TEL 31-78-6392392. FAX 31-78-6392254. *4821*

JOURNAL OF TIME SERIES ANALYSIS.
Blackwell Publishers Ltd., 108 Cowley Rd., Oxford OX4 1JF, England. TEL 44-1865-791100. FAX 44-1865-791347. *6922*

JOURNAL OF TISSUE VIABILITY.
Tissue Viability Society, c/o Wessex Rehabilitation Association, Salisbury District Hospital, Salisbury, Wilts. SP2 8BJ, England. TEL 44-1722-336262. FAX 44-1722-325904. *4879*

THE JOURNAL OF TOURISM STUDIES.
James Cook University of North Queensland, Department of Tourism, Townsville, Qld. 4811, Australia. TEL 61-77-815133. FAX 61-77-251116. *7214*

JOURNAL OF TOXICOLOGY. CLINICAL TOXICOLOGY.
Marcel Dekker Journals, 270 Madison Ave., New York, NY 10016. TEL 212-696-9000. FAX 212-685-4540. *2303*

JOURNAL OF TOXICOLOGY. CUTANEOUS AND OCULAR TOXICOLOGY.
Marcel Dekker Journals, 270 Madison Ave., New York, NY 10016. TEL 212-696-9000. FAX 212-685-4540. *5674*

JOURNAL OF TOXICOLOGY. TOXIN REVIEWS.
Marcel Dekker Journals, 270 Madison Ave., New York, NY 10016. TEL 212-696-9000. FAX 212-685-4540. *5674*

JOURNAL OF TOXICOLOGY AND ENVIRONMENTAL HEALTH. PART A.
Taylor & Francis Inc., 1900 Frost Rd., Ste. 101, Bristol, PA 19007-1598. FAX 215-785-5515. *2979*

JOURNAL OF TRACE AND MICROPROBE TECHNIQUES.
Marcel Dekker Journals, 270 Madison Ave., New York, NY 10016. TEL 212-696-9000. FAX 212-685-4540. *1794*

THE JOURNAL OF TRACE ELEMENTS IN EXPERIMENTAL MEDICINE.
John Wiley & Sons, Inc., Journals, 605 Third Ave., New York, NY 10158. TEL 212-850-6645. FAX 212-850-6021. *4899*

JOURNAL OF TRACE ELEMENTS IN MEDICINE AND BIOLOGY.
Gustav Fischer Verlag, Villengang 2, 07745 Jena, Germany. TEL 49-3641-626430. FAX 49-3641-626421. *610*

JOURNAL OF TRADITIONAL MEDICINES.
Chuo Insatsu Co., 1-4-5, Shimookui, Toyama 930-01, Japan. TEL 0764-32-6572. *5674*

JOURNAL OF TRAFFIC MEDICINE.
International Association for Accident and Traffic Medicine, c/o Dir. Erdal Cila, MD, IAATM Office, Kizilirmak Cad. 53-5, 06640-Kocatpe, Ankara, Turkey. TEL 90-312-285-0202. FAX 90-312-287-2390. *5011*

JOURNAL OF TRANSCULTURAL NURSING.
Transcultural Nursing Society, 601 N. Wenona, Bay City, MI 48706. TEL 517-684-7381. FAX 517-684-1248. *4939*

JOURNAL OF TRANSNATIONAL MANAGEMENT DEVELOPMENT.
Haworth Press, Inc., 10 Alice St., Binghamton, NY 13904. TEL 607-722-5857. FAX 607-722-6362. *1339*

JOURNAL OF TRANSPLANT COORDINATION.
American Association of Critical Care Nurses, 101 Columbia, Aliso Viejo, CA 92656. TEL 714-362-2000. FAX 714-362-2020. *5147*

JOURNAL OF TRANSPORT ECONOMICS AND POLICY.
University of Bath, Claverton Down, Bath BA2 7AY, England. TEL 44-1225-826302. FAX 44-1225-826767. *7032*

JOURNAL OF TRANSPORT GEOGRAPHY.
Elsevier Science Ltd., Pergamon, P.O. Box 800, Kidlington, Oxford OX5 1DX, England. TEL 44-1865-843000. FAX 44-1865-843010. *3412*

JOURNAL OF TRANSPORTATION ENGINEERING.
American Society of Civil Engineers, 345 E. 47th St., New York, NY 10017-2398. TEL 212-705-7288. FAX 212-980-4681. *7032*

JOURNAL OF TRAUMA - INJURY, INFECTION AND CRITICAL CARE.
Williams & Wilkins, 351 W. Camden St., Baltimore, MD 21201-2436. TEL 410-528-4068. FAX 410-528-4452. *5011*

JOURNAL OF TRAUMATIC STRESS.
Plenum Publishing Corp., 233 Spring St., New York, NY 10013-1578. TEL 212-620-8000. FAX 212-463-0742. *6133*

JOURNAL OF TRAVEL & TOURISM MARKETING.
Haworth Press, Inc., 10 Alice St., Binghamton, NY 13904. TEL 607-722-5857. FAX 607-722-6362. *7214*

JOURNAL OF TREE FRUIT PRODUCTION.
Haworth Press, Inc., 10 Alice St., Binghamton, NY 13904. TEL 607-722-5857. FAX 607-722-6362. *233*

JOURNAL OF TRIBOLOGY.
American Society of Mechanical Engineers, 22 Law Dr., Fairfield, NJ 07007-2900. TEL 973-882-1167. FAX 973-882-1717. *5608*

JOURNAL OF TROPICAL AGRICULTURE.
Kerala Agricultural University, College of Horticulture, Vellanikkara 680 654, Trichur, Kerala, India. TEL 91-487-21822. FAX 91-487-399019. *130*

JOURNAL OF TROPICAL AGRICULTURE AND FOOD SCIENCE.
Malaysian Agricultural Research & Development Institute, P.O. Box 12301, General Post Office, 50774 Kuala Lumpur, Malaysia. TEL 03-9437236. FAX 03-9482216. *130*

JOURNAL OF TROPICAL FOREST PRODUCTS.
Forest Research Institute Malaysia, Kepong, 52109 Kuala Lumpur, Malaysia. *3157*

JOURNAL OF TROPICAL FOREST SCIENCE.
Forest Research Institute Malaysia, Kepong, 52109 Kuala Lumpur, Malaysia. *3157*

JOURNAL OF TROPICAL MEDICINE.
Royal Society of Tropical Medicine & Hygiene, Egyptian Branch, Tager Bldg., 1 Ozoris St., Garden City, Cairo, Egypt. TEL 3541857. *4840*

JOURNAL OF TROPICAL METEOROLOGY.
Guangzhou Redai Haiyang Qixiang Yanjiusuo, No. 6, Fujin Rd., Dongshan District, Guangzhou, Guangdong 510080, People's Republic of China. TEL 86-20-8777-6918. FAX 86-20-8777-3952. *5237*

JOURNAL OF TURBOMACHINERY.
American Society of Mechanical Engineers, 22 Law Dr., Fairfield, NJ 07007-2900. TEL 973-882-1167. FAX 973-882-1717. *2890*

JOURNAL OF TURFGRASS MANAGEMENT.
Haworth Press, Inc., Food Products Press, 10 Alice St., Binghamton, NY 13904. TEL 607-722-5857. FAX 607-722-6362. *233*

JOURNAL OF UKRAINIAN STUDIES.
Canadian Institute of Ukrainian Studies, 352 Athabasca Hall, University of Alberta, Edmonton, AB T6G 2E8, Canada. TEL 403-492-2972. FAX 403-492-4967. *4421*

JOURNAL OF ULTRASOUND IN MEDICINE.
American Institute for Ultrasound in Medicine, 14750 Sweitzer Ln., Ste. 100, Laurel, MD 20707-5906. TEL 301-498-4100. FAX 301-498-4450. *5109*

JOURNAL OF UNDERGRADUATE MATHEMATICS.
Guilford College, Department of Mathematics, Greensboro, NC 27410. *4584*

JOURNAL OF UNDERGRADUATE RESEARCH IN PHYSICS.
Guilford College, Department of Physics, Guilford, NC 27410. TEL 910-316-2279. FAX 910-316-2951. *5812*

JOURNAL OF UNITARIAN UNIVERSALIST HISTORY.
Unitarian Universalist Historical Society, c/o Conrad Wright, Harvard Divinity School, Andover Hall, Cambridge, MA 02138. TEL 617-536-1608. FAX 617-859-0074. *6493*

JOURNAL OF UROGENITAL PATHOLOGY.
Field & Wood, Medical Periodicals, Inc., Box 975, Blue Bell, PA 19422. TEL 610-828-4010. FAX 215-482-0226. *5162*

JOURNAL OF UROLOGIC PATHOLOGY.
Humana Press Inc., 999 Riverview Dr., Ste. 208, Totowa, NJ 07512. TEL 973-256-1699. FAX 973-256-8341. *5162*

JOURNAL OF UROLOGY.
Williams & Wilkins, 351 W. Camden St., Baltimore, MD 21201-2436. TEL 410-528-4068. FAX 410-528-4452. *5163*

JOURNAL OF V L S I SIGNAL PROCESSING.
Kluwer Academic Publishers Boston, Box 358, Accord Sta., Hingham, MA 02018-0358. TEL 617-871-6600. FAX 617-871-6528. *2170*

JOURNAL OF VACATION MARKETING.
Henry Stewart Publications, Russell House, 28-30 Little Russell St., London WC1A 2HN, England. TEL 44-171-404-3040. FAX 44-171-404-2081. *7214*

JOURNAL OF VACUUM SCIENCE AND TECHNOLOGY. PART A. VACUUM, SURFACES AND FILMS.
American Institute of Physics, One Physics Ellipse, College Park, MD 20740-3843. TEL 301-209-3000. *5812*

JOURNAL OF VACUUM SCIENCE AND TECHNOLOGY. PART B. MICROELECTRONICS AND NANOMETER STRUCTURES.
American Institute of Physics, One Physics Ellipse, College Park, MD 20740-3843. TEL 301-209-3000. *5812*

THE JOURNAL OF VALUE INQUIRY.
Kluwer Academic Publishers, Postbus 17, 3300 AA Dordrecht, Netherlands. TEL 31-78-6392392. FAX 31-78-6392254. *5734*

JOURNAL OF VASCULAR AND INTERVENTIONAL RADIOLOGY.
Lippincott - Raven Publishers, 227 E. Washington Sq., Philadelphia, PA 19106. TEL 215-238-4200. FAX 215-238-4227. *5109*

JOURNAL OF VASCULAR NURSING.
Mosby - Year Book, Inc., 11830 Westline Industrial Dr., St. Louis, MO 63146-3318. TEL 314-872-8370. FAX 314-432-1380. *4939*

JOURNAL OF VASCULAR RESEARCH.
S. Karger AG, Allschwilerstr. 10, P.O. Box, CH-4009 Basel, Switzerland. TEL 41-61-3061111. FAX 41-61-3061234. *665*

JOURNAL OF VASCULAR SURGERY.
Mosby - Year Book, Inc., 11830 Westline Industrial Dr., St. Louis, MO 63146-3318. TEL 314-872-8370. FAX 314-432-1380. *5147*

JOURNAL OF VASCULAR TECHNOLOGY.
Society of Vascular Technology, 4601 Presidents Dr., Ste. 260, Lanham, MD 20706-4365. TEL 301-459-7550. FAX 301-459-5651. *4821*

JOURNAL OF VECTOR ECOLOGY.
Society for Vector Ecology, Box 87, Santa Ana, CA 92702. TEL 714-971-2421. FAX 714-971-3940. *757*

JOURNAL OF VEGETABLE CROP PRODUCTION.
Haworth Press, Inc., 10 Alice St., Binghamton, NY 13904. TEL 607-722-5857. FAX 607-722-6362. *233*

JOURNAL OF VEGETATION SCIENCE.
Opulus Press AB, P.O. Box 25137, S-750 25 Uppsala, Sweden. TEL 46-18-32-06-62. FAX 46-18-32-13-68. *712*

JOURNAL OF VENOMOUS ANIMALS AND TOXINS.
Universidade Estadual Paulista, Centro de Estudos de Venenos e Animais Peconhentos, Caixa Postal 577, 18618-000 Botucatu SP, Brazil. TEL 55-14-8212121. FAX 55-14-8213963. *5674*

JOURNAL OF VERTEBRATE PALEONTOLOGY.
Society of Vertebrate Paleontology, W. 436 Nebraska Hall, University of Nebraska, Lincoln, NE 68588-0542. TEL 402-472-4604. FAX 402-472-8949. *5560*

JOURNAL OF VESTIBULAR RESEARCH: EQUILIBRIUM AND ORIENTATION.
Elsevier Science Inc., Box 945, New York, NY 10159-0945. TEL 212-633-3730. FAX 212-633-3680. *818*

JOURNAL OF VETERINARY ALLERGY AND CLINICAL IMMUNOLOGY.
Veterinary Practice Publishing Co., Box 6050, Mission Viejo, CA 92690. *7273*

JOURNAL OF VETERINARY DIAGNOSTIC INVESTIGATION.
American Association of Veterinary Laboratory Diagnosticians, c/o H.S. Gosser, Sec.-Treas., Box 6023, Columbia, MO 65205. TEL 314-882-6811. FAX 314-882-1411. *7273*

JOURNAL OF VETERINARY EMERGENCY AND CRITICAL CARE.
V.E.C.C.S. Administration Office, 8015 Broadway, Ste., 216, San Antonio, TX 78209. TEL 210-826-1488. *7273*

JOURNAL OF VETERINARY INTERNAL MEDICINE.
W.B. Saunders Co., Curtis Center, 3rd Fl., Independence Sq. W., Philadelphia, PA 19106-3399. TEL 215-238-7800. FAX 215-238-6445. *7273*

JOURNAL OF VETERINARY PHARMACOLOGY AND THERAPEUTICS.
Blackwell Science Ltd., Osney Mead, Oxford OX2 OEL, England. TEL 44-1865-206206. FAX 44-1865-721205. *5674*

JOURNAL OF VIBRATION AND ACOUSTICS.
American Society of Mechanical Engineers, 22 Law Dr., Fairfield, NJ 07007-2900. TEL 973-882-1167. FAX 973-882-1717. *2891*

JOURNAL OF VIBRATION AND CONTROL.
Sage Publications, Inc., Sage Science Press, 2455 Teller Rd., Thousand Oaks, CA 91320. TEL 805-499-0721. FAX 805-499-0871. *5873*

JOURNAL OF VIETNAMESE STUDIES.
Australian Association of Vietnamese Studies, G.P.O. Box 2918DD, Mwlvouenw, Vic. 3001, Australia. TEL 61-3-93539363. FAX 61-3-93502484. *5531*

JOURNAL OF VINYL & ADDITIVE TECHNOLOGY.
Society of Plastics Engineers, Inc., 14 Fairfield Dr., Box 0403, Brookfield, CT 06804-0403. TEL 203-775-0471. FAX 203-775-8490. *5879*

JOURNAL OF VIRAL HEPATITIS.
Blackwell Science Ltd., Osney Mead, Oxford OX2 OEL, England. TEL 44-1865-206206. FAX 44-1865-721205. *4913*

JOURNAL OF VIROLOGICAL METHODS.
Elsevier Science B.V., P.O. Box 211, 1000 AE Amsterdam, Netherlands. TEL 31-20-4853911. FAX 31-20-4853598. *788*

JOURNAL OF VISUAL COMMUNICATION AND IMAGE REPRESENTATION.
Academic Press, Inc., Journal Division, 525 B St., Ste. 1900, San Diego, CA 92101-4495. TEL 619-230-1840. FAX 619-699-6800. *2124*

JOURNAL OF VISUAL IMPAIRMENT & BLINDNESS.
American Foundation for the Blind, Inc., 11 Penn Plaza, Ste. 300, New York, NY 10001-2018. TEL 212-502-7652. FAX 212-502-7774. *3471*

THE JOURNAL OF VISUALIZATION AND COMPUTER ANIMATION.
John Wiley & Sons Ltd., Journals, Baffins Ln., Chichester, W. Sussex PO19 1UD, England. TEL 44-1243-779777. FAX 44-1243-775878. *2124*

JOURNAL OF VOCATIONAL EDUCATION AND TRAINING.
Triangle Journals Ltd., P.O. Box 65, Wallingford, Oxon. OX10 0YG, England. TEL 44-1491-838013. FAX 44-1491-834968. *2511*

JOURNAL OF VOCATIONAL EDUCATION RESEARCH.
American Vocational Education Research Association, c/o Natalie Wysong, Center on Education & Work, 964 Educational Sciences Bldg., 1025 W. Johnson, Madison, WI 53706. TEL 608-262-8415. FAX 608-262-9197. *2609*

JOURNAL OF VOCATIONAL REHABILITATION.
Elsevier Science Ireland Ltd., P.O. Box 85, Limerick, Ireland. TEL 353-61-472144. FAX 353-61-472144. *5493*

JOURNAL OF VOICE.
Lippincott - Raven Publishers, 227 E. Washington Sq., Philadelphia, PA 19106. TEL 215-238-4200. *5023*

JOURNAL OF VOLCANOLOGY AND GEOTHERMAL RESEARCH.
Elsevier Science B.V., P.O. Box 211, 1000 AE Amsterdam, Netherlands. TEL 31-20-4853911. FAX 31-20-4853598. *2386*

JOURNAL OF VOLUNTEER ADMINISTRATION.
Association for Volunteer Administration, 10565 Lee Hwy., Ste. 104, Fairfax, VA 22030-3135. TEL 703-352-6222. FAX 703-352-6767. *6674*

JOURNAL OF W O C N.
Mosby - Year Book, Inc., 11830 Westline Industrial Dr., St. Louis, MO 63146-3318. TEL 314-872-8370. FAX 314-432-1380. *5147*

JOURNAL OF WASTE MANAGEMENT & RESOURCE RECOVERY.
E P P Publications, 52 Kings Rd., Richmond, Surrey TW10 6EP, England. TEL 44-181-948-7165. FAX 44-181-747-9663. *2986*

JOURNAL OF WATER RESOURCES PLANNING AND MANAGEMENT.
American Society of Civil Engineers, 345 E. 47th St., New York, NY 10017-2398. TEL 212-705-7288. FAX 212-980-4681. *2792*

JOURNAL OF WEATHER MODIFICATION.
Weather Modification Association, Box 26926, Fresno, CA 93729-6926. TEL 209-434-3486. FAX 209-434-3486. *5237*

JOURNAL OF WELSH RELIGIOUS HISTORY.
Welsh Religious Historical Society, c/o Rev. Roger L. Brown, Welshpool Vicarage, Powys SY21 7DT, Wales. TEL 44-1938-553164. *6429*

JOURNAL OF WILDLIFE DISEASES.
Wildlife Disease Association, Inc., Box 1897, Lawrence, KS 66044-8897. TEL 913-843-1221. FAX 913-843-1221. *7274*

JOURNAL OF WILDLIFE MANAGEMENT.
Wildlife Society, 5410 Grosvenor Ln., Bethesda, MD 20814. TEL 301-897-9770. FAX 301-530-2471. *2234*

JOURNAL OF WILDLIFE REHABILITATION.
International Wildlife Rehabilitation Council, 4437 Central Pl., Ste. B4, Suisun, CA 94585-1669. TEL 707-864-1761. FAX 707-864-3106. *610*

JOURNAL OF WIND ENGINEERING AND INDUSTRIAL AERODYNAMICS.
Elsevier Science B.V., P.O. Box 211, 1000 AE Amsterdam, Netherlands. TEL 31-20-4853911. FAX 31-20-4853598. *2891*

JOURNAL OF WINE RESEARCH.
Carfax Publishing Co., P.O Box 25, Abingdon, Oxon. OX14 3UE, England. TEL 44-1235-401000. FAX 44-1235-401550. *233*

JOURNAL OF WOMEN AND AGING.
Haworth Press, Inc., 10 Alice St., Binghamton, NY 13904. TEL 607-722-5857. FAX 607-722-6362. *7345*

JOURNAL OF WOMEN AND MINORITIES IN SCIENCE AND ENGINEERING.
Begell House Inc., 79 Madison Ave., Ste. 1205, New York, NY 10016-7892. TEL 212-725-1999. FAX 212-213-8368. *2729*

JOURNAL OF WOMEN'S HEALTH.
Mary Ann Liebert, Inc. Publishers, 2 Madison Ave., Larchmont, NY 10538. TEL 914-834-3100. FAX 914-834-3688. *7309*

JOURNAL OF WOMEN'S IMAGING.
Lippincott - Raven Publishers, 227 E. Washington Sq., Philadelphia, PA 19106-3780. TEL 215-238-4200. FAX 215-238-4227. *5110*

JOURNAL OF WOOD CHEMISTRY AND TECHNOLOGY.
Marcel Dekker Journals, 270 Madison Ave., New York, NY 10016. TEL 212-696-9000. FAX 212-685-4540. *1756*

JOURNAL OF WORLD HISTORY.
University of Hawaii Press, Journals Department, 2840 Kolowalu St., Honolulu, HI 96822. TEL 808-956-8833. FAX 808-988-6052. *3503*

JOURNAL OF WORLD PREHISTORY.
Plenum Publishing Corp., 233 Spring St., New York, NY 10013-1578. TEL 212-620-8000. FAX 212-463-0742. *369*

JOURNAL OF WORLD TRADE.
Kluwer Law International, Postbus 85889, 2508 CN The Hague, Netherlands. TEL 31-70-3081500. FAX 31-70-3081515. *4121*

JOURNAL OF WOUND CARE.
Macmillan Magazines Ltd., Porters South, 4-6 Crinan St., London N1 9XW, England. TEL 44-171-833-6000. FAX 44-171-843-4640. *5011*

JOURNAL OF X-RAY SCIENCE AND TECHNOLOGY.
Academic Press, Inc., Journal Division, 525 B St., Ste. 1900, San Diego, CA 92101-4495. TEL 619-230-1840. FAX 619-699-6800. *5812*

JOURNAL OF YOUTH AND ADOLESCENCE.
Plenum Publishing Corp., 233 Spring St., New York, NY 10013-1578. TEL 212-620-8000. FAX 212-463-0742. *1849*

JOURNAL OF ZOO AND WILDLIFE MEDICINE.
American Association of Zoo Veterinarians, 3400 Girard Ave., Philadelphia, PA 19104-1196. TEL 215-387-9094. FAX 215-387-2165. *7274*

JOURNAL ON EXCELLENCE IN COLLEGE TEACHING.
Miami University, O A S T, Oxford, OH 45056. TEL 513-529-6648. *2547*

JOURNALISM HISTORY.
Greenspun School of Communication, University of Nevada, Las Vegas, NV 89154-5007. TEL 702-895-3964. FAX 702-895-4805. *3875*

JUDAICA LIBRARIANSHIP.
Association of Jewish Libraries, 15 E. 26th St., Rm. 1034, New York, NY 10010-1579. TEL 212-678-8092. FAX 212-678-8998. *4189*

JUDARNA I F.D. SOVJET.
Svenska Kommitten foer Judarna i f.d. Sovjet, P.O. Box 5053, S-102 42 Stockholm, Sweden. TEL 46-8-664-53-38. FAX 46-8-664-05-91. *5994*

THE JUDGES.
Martinus Nijhoff Publishers, Human Rights and International Law Postbus 163, 3300 AH Dordrecht, Netherlands. TEL 31-78-334911. FAX 31-78-334254. *4121*

JUDICATURE.
American Judicature Society, 180 N. Michigan Ave., Ste. 600, Chicago, IL 60601-7401. *4133*

THE JUDICIAL REVIEW.
Judicial Commission of New South Wales, Level 5, 201 George St., Sydney, N.S.W. 2000, Australia. TEL 61-2-92994421. FAX 61-2-92903194. *4133*

JUMP CUT.
Jump Cut Associates, Box 865, Berkeley, CA 94701. TEL 607-257-2245. *5337*

JUNTENDO MEDICAL JOURNAL.
Juntendo Medical Society, 2-1-1 Hongo, Bunkyo-ku, Tokyo 113, Japan. FAX 91-3-3814-9100. *4699*

JURIST.
Catholic University of America, Department of Canon Law, Washington, DC 20064. TEL 202-319-5439. FAX 202-319-5439. *3972*

JUST POLICY.
Victorian Council of Social Service, 5th Fl., 130 Lt. Collins St., Melbourne, Vic. 3000, Australia. TEL 61-3-96545649. FAX 61-96545749. *6674*

JUSUR.
University of California at Los Angeles, Von Grunebaum Center for Near Eastern Studies, 10286 Bunche Hall, Los Angeles, CA 90095. TEL 310-825-1181. *3657*

JUVENILE AND FAMILY COURT JOURNAL.
National Council of Juvenile and Family Court Judges, Box 8970, Reno, NV 89507. TEL 702-784-6012. FAX 702-784-1084. *4102*

K - THEORY.
Kluwer Academic Publishers, Postbus 17, 3300 AA Dordrecht, Netherlands. TEL 31-78-6392392. FAX 31-78-6392254. *4584*

THE KABBALIST.
International Order of Kabbalists, 25 Circle Gardens, Merton Park, London SW19 3JX, England. TEL 44-181-542-3611. *5576*

KAFKA SOCIETY OF AMERICA. JOURNAL.
Temple University, Department of Germanic and Slavic Languages and Literatures, AB 529, Philadelphia, PA 19122. TEL 215-787-8282. FAX 215-204-7752. *4422*

KAI TIAKI: NURSING NEW ZEALAND.
New Zealand Nurses' Organisation, P.O. Box 2128, Wellington, New Zealand. TEL 64-4-385-0847. FAX 64-4-382-9993. *4939*

KAIYO CHOSA GIJUTSU.
Kaiyo Chosa Gijutsu Gakkai, Nihon Suiro Kyokai, 3-1, Tsukiji 5-chome, Chuo-ku, Tokyo 104, Japan. TEL 81-3-3545-6255. FAX 81-3-3545-6255. *2407*

KALAMAZOO COLLEGE QUARTERLY.
Kalamazoo College, 1200 Academy St., Kalamazoo, MI 49006-3295. TEL 616-377-7304. FAX 616-337-7305. *1958*

KALLIOPE.
Florida Community College, Kalliope Writers' Collective, 3939 Roosevelt Blvd., Jacksonville, FL 32205. TEL 904-381-3511. *4422*

KANAGAWA-KEN SEISHIN IGAKKAISHI.
Kanagawa Association of Psychiatry, c/o Department of Psychiatry, Yokohama City University School of Medicine, 3-9, Fukuura, Kanagawa-ku, Yokohama 236, Japan. TEL 81-45-787-2667. FAX 81-45-783-2540. *5078*

KANARA CHAMBER OF COMMERCE & INDUSTRY JOURNAL.
Kanara Chamber of Commerce & Industry, Box 116, Bunder, Mangalore 575 001, India. TEL 420128. *1191*

KANAZAWA DAIGAKU IRYOU GIJUTSU TANKI DAIGAKUBU SAGYO RYOHOGAKKA SOTSUGYO KENKYU RONBUNSHU.
Kanazawa Daigaku, Iryo Gijutsu Tanki Daigakubu, 11-80, Kodatsuno 5-chome, Kanazawa-shi, Ishikawa-ken 920, Japan. TEL 81-762-22-2211. FAX 81-762-34-4375. *4699*

KANSAS BIOLOGY TEACHER.
Emporia State University Press, 1200 Commercial, Emporia, KS 66801-5087. TEL 316-341-5614. *611*

KANSAS ENTOMOLOGICAL SOCIETY. JOURNAL.
Kansas Entomological Society, Box 1897, Lawrence, KS 66044-8897. TEL 913-843-1221. FAX 913-843-1274. *757*

KANSAS MEDICINE.
Kansas Medical Society, 623 S.W. 10th Ave., Topeka, KS 66612. TEL 913-235-2383. FAX 913-235-5114. *4699*

KAOGU.
Science Press, Marketing and Sales Department, 16 Donghuangchenggen North St., Beijing 100717, People's Republic of China. TEL 4010642. FAX 4019810. *370*

KAOGU XUEBAO.
Science Press, Marketing and Sales Department, 16 Donghuangchenggen North St., Beijing 100717, People's Republic of China. TEL 4010642. FAX 4019810. *370*

KAPPA DELTA PI RECORD.
Kappa Delta Pi Publications, P.O. Box A, 1601 West State Street, West Lafayette, IN 47906-0576. TEL 765-743-1705. FAX 765-743-2202. *2609*

KARLSRUHER PAEDAGOGISCHE BEITRAEGE.
Paedagogischer Hochschule Karlsruhe, Bismarckstr. 10, 76133 Karlsruhe, Germany. TEL 49-721-9254014. FAX 49-721-9254000. *2609*

AL-KARMIL.
Haifa University, Institute of Middle Eastern Studies, Ha-Carmel, Haifa 31999, Israel. *4423*

KAROLINSKA INSTITUTE NOBEL CONFERENCE SERIES.
Lippincott - Raven Publishers, 227 E. Washington Sq., Philadelphia, PA 19106. TEL 215-238-4200. FAX 215-238-4227. *4699*

KARSTENIA.
Finnish Mycological Society, P.O. Box 7; FIN-00014 University of Helsinki, Finland. TEL 358-9-708-4784. FAX 358-9-708-4830. *712*

KARTHAGO.
Universite de Paris IV (Paris-Sorbonne), Centre d'Etudes Archeologiques de la Mediterranee, c/o Institut d'Art, 3 rue Michelet, 75006, France. TEL 33-1-40463217. *370*

KATACHI NO KAGAKKAIHO.
Katachi no Kagakkai, Tokyo University of Agriculture & Technology, Dept. of Mechanical System Engineering, 24-16 Nakamachi 2-chome, Koganei-shi, Tokyo 184, Japan. TEL 81-423-67-5607. FAX 81-423-67-5607. *611*

KATTJOURNALEN.
Sveriges Kattklubbars Riksfoerbund (SVERAK), Johannlundsg. 3, S-502 35 Boraas, Sweden. TEL 46-33-10-15-65. FAX 46-33-10-08-99. *5639*

KAVYA BHARATI.
American College, Scilet, P.O. Box 63, Madurai 625 002, Tamil Nadu, India. *4512*

KEATS - SHELLEY JOURNAL.
Keats - Shelley Association of America, Inc., Rm. 226 New York Public Library, 5th Ave. & 42nd St., New York, NY 10018-2788. TEL 212-764-0655. FAX 212-259-2467. *4512*

KECHENG - JIAOCAI - JIAOFA.
Renmin Jiaoyu Chubanshe, 55, Shatan Houjie, Beijing 100009, People's Republic of China. TEL 86-1-4035745. FAX 86-1-4010370. *2609*

KEEP ON TRUCKIN' NEWS.
Mid-West Truckers Association, Inc., 2727 N. Dirksen Parkway, Springfield, IL 62702. TEL 217-525-0310. FAX 217-525-0342. *7175*

KEIO JOURNAL OF MEDICINE.
Keio Gijuku Daigaku, Igakubu, 35 Shinano-machi, Shinjuku-ku, Tokyo 160, Japan. TEL 81-3-3353-1211. FAX 81-3-5379-6059. *4700*

KEIRAKU CHIRYO.
Keiraku Chiryo Gakkai, 14-9, Jinan 1-chome, Shibuya-ku, Tokyo 150, Japan. TEL 81-3-3461-2426. FAX 81-3-3770-1675. *291*

KEIRYO KOKUGO GAKU.
Keiryo Kokugo Gakkai, c/o Tokyo Joshi Daigaku, Zenpukuji 2-6-1, Suginami-ku, Tokyo 167, Japan. TEL 81-3-3395-1211. *4270*

KEIZAI KAGAKU.
Nagoya Daigaku, Keizaigakubu, Furo-cho, Chikusa-ku, Nagoya 464-01, Japan. TEL 81-52-789-2360. FAX 81-52-789-4924. *979*

KEJI GUANLI YANJIU.
Science & Technology Management Research Periodicals House, No. 100, Xianlie Zhonglu, Guangzhou, Guangdong 510070, People's Republic of China. TEL 86-20-8766-8145. FAX 86-20-8777-5791. *6539*

KELSEY REVIEW.
Mercer County Community College, 1200 Old Trenton Rd., Trenton, NJ 08690. TEL 609-586-4800. FAX 609-586-2318. *4423*

KENKALUSIKKA.
Suomen Kenkakauppiaiden Liitto r.y., Fredrikinkatu 67 E 42, FIN-00100 Helsinki 10, Finland. TEL 358-0-409-932. FAX 358-0-409-563. *6595*

KENTUCKY ACADEMY OF SCIENCE. TRANSACTIONS.
Kentucky Academy of Science, c/o J.G. Rodriguez, Exec. Sec., Box 4484, Lexington, KY 40544-4484. TEL 606-257-4902. *6540*

KENTUCKY ENGLISH BULLETIN.
Kentucky Council of Teachers of English - Language Arts, Western Kentucky University, Dept. of English, Bowling Green, KY 42101. TEL 502-745-3043. FAX 502-745-2533. *4270*

KENTUCKY MEDICAL ASSOCIATION. JOURNAL.
Kentucky Medical Association, 4965 US Highway 42, 2000, Louisville, KY 40222-6372. TEL 502-426-6200. FAX 502-426-6877. *4700*

KENTUCKY REVIEW.
University of Kentucky, Library Associates, Lexington, KY 40506-0039. TEL 606-257-3801. FAX 606-257-1563. *3783*

KENTUCKY SCHOOL DIRECTORY.
Department of Education, Office of Communication Services, 1908 Capital Plaza Tower, 500 Mero St., 19th Fl., Frankfort, KY 40601. TEL 502-564-3421. *2525*

KENYA. MINISTRY OF FOREIGN AFFAIRS. DIRECTORY OF DIPLOMATIC CORPS & INTERNATIONAL ORGANIZATIONS.
Ministry of Foreign Affairs., Protocol Department, Nairobi, Kenya. TEL 254-2-334433. FAX 254-2-335494. *5938*

KERKHISTORISCHE BIJDRAGEN.
E.J. Brill, P.O. Box 9000, 2300 PA Leiden, Netherlands. TEL 31-71-5353500. FAX 31-71-5317532. *6351*

KERN INSTITUTE, LEIDEN. MEMOIRS.
E.J. Brill, P.O. Box 9000, 2300 PA Leiden, Netherlands. TEL 31-71-5353500. FAX 31-71-5317532. *5531*

KESKI-SUOMI.
Keski-Suomen Museo, P.O. Box 634, 40101 Jyvaskyla, Finland. TEL 358-14-624910. FAX 358-14-624933. *3579*

KETTENWIRK-PRAXIS.
Karl Mayer GmbH, Postfach 1120, 63166 Obertshausen, Germany. TEL 49-6104-402-0. FAX 49-6104-43574. *6990*

KEXUE TONGBAO.
Science Press, Marketing and Sales Department, 16 Donghuangchenggen North St., Beijing 100717, People's Republic of China. TEL 4010642. FAX 4019810. *6540*

KEYS TO THE FAUNA OF THE U S S R.
E.J. Brill, P.O. Box 9000, 2300 PA Leiden, Netherlands. TEL 31-71-5353500. FAX 31-71-5317532. *841*

THE KIDNEY (NEW YORK, 1968).
National Kidney Foundation, 30 East 33rd St., New York, NY 10016. TEL 212-889-2210. *5163*

KIDNEY (NEW YORK, 1992).
Springer-Verlag, Medical Journals, 175 Fifth Ave., New York, NY 10010. TEL 212-460-1500. FAX 212-473-6272. *4781*

KIDNEY AND BLOOD PRESSURE RESEARCH.
S. Karger AG, Allschwilerstr. 10, P.O. Box, CH-4009 Basel, Switzerland. TEL 41-61-3061111. FAX 41-61-3061234. *5163*

KIDNEY DISEASES.
Marcel Dekker, Inc., 270 Madison Ave., New York, NY 10016. TEL 212-696-9000. FAX 212-685-4540. *5163*

KIDS WORLD MAGAZINE.
M2 Communications, 93 Lombard Ave., Ste. 108, Winnipeg, MB R3B 3B1, Canada. TEL 204-985-8160. FAX 204-943-8991. *1876*

KIDSAFE.
Child Accident Prevention Foundation of Australia, 123 Queen St., 10th Fl., Melbourne, Vic. 3000, Australia. TEL 61-3-6701319. FAX 61-3-6707616. *1849*

KIELER ARBEITSPAPIERE.
Institut fuer Weltwirtschaft, Duesternbrooker Weg 120, 24105 Kiel, Germany. TEL 49-431-8814305. FAX 49-431-8814527. *1268*

KIELER BIBLIOGRAPHIEN ZU AKTUELLEN OEKONOMISCHEN THEMEN.
Institut fuer Weltwirtschaft, Duesternbrooker Weg 120, 24105 Kiel, Germany. TEL 49-431-8814305. FAX 49-431-8814527. *1053*

KIELER DISKUSSIONSBEITRAEGE.
Institut fuer Weltwirtschaft, Duesternbrooker Weg 120, 24105 Kiel, Germany. TEL 49-431-8814305. FAX 49-431-8814527. *1268*

KIELER KURZBERICHTE.
Institut fuer Weltwirtschaft, Duesternbrooker Weg 120, 24105 Kiel, Germany. TEL 49-431-8814305. FAX 49-431-8814527. *1268*

KIELER VORTRAEGE.
Institut fuer Weltwirtschaft, Duesternbrooker Weg 120, 24105 Kiel, Germany. TEL 49-431-8814305. FAX 49-431-8814527. *1268*

KIERKEGAARDIANA.
C.A. Reitzels Forlag, Noerregade 20, DK-1165 Copenhagen K, Denmark. *5735*

KIMIKA.
Kapisanan ng mga Kimiko sa Pilipinas, PFC Office, NSRI Bldg., U.P. Diliman, Quezon City, Philippines. TEL 632-97-57-74. FAX 632-928-68-68. *1758*

KINEMA.
University of Waterloo, Department of Fine Arts and Film Studies, Waterloo, ON N2L 3G1, Canada. TEL 519-885-1211. FAX 519-746-4982. *5338*

KINETICS AND CATALYSIS.
Maik Nauka - Interperiodica, Mezhdunarodnyi Otdel, Ul. Profsoyuznaya, 90, 117864 Moscow, Russia. TEL 7-095-3360066. FAX 7-095-3360666. *1832*

KINETOSCOPIO.
Centro Colombo Americano, Carrera 45, No. 53-24, Apdo. Aereo 8734, Medellin, Colombia. TEL 574-513-4444. FAX 574-513-2666. *5338*

KING SAUD UNIVERSITY. JOURNAL. ADMINISTRATIVE SCIENCES.
King Saud University, University Libraries, P.O. Box 22480, Riyadh 11495, Saudi Arabia. TEL 966-1-4676148. FAX 966-1-4676162. *980*

KING SAUD UNIVERSITY. JOURNAL. AGRICULTURAL SCIENCES.
King Saud University, University Libraries, P.O. Box 22480, Riyadh 11495, Saudi Arabia. TEL 966-1-4676148. FAX 966-1-4676162. *132*

KING SAUD UNIVERSITY. JOURNAL. ARCHITECTURE AND PLANNING.
King Saud University, University Libraries, P.O. Box 22480, Riyadh 11495, Saudi Arabia. TEL 966-1-4676148. FAX 966-1-4676162. *3752*

KING SAUD UNIVERSITY. JOURNAL. ARTS.
King Saud University, University Libraries, P.O. Box 22480, Riyadh 11495, Saudi Arabia. TEL 966-1-4676148. FAX 966-1-4676162. *450*

KING SAUD UNIVERSITY. JOURNAL. COMPUTER AND INFORMATION SCIENCES.
King Saud University, University Libraries, P.O. Box 22480, Riyadh 11495, Saudi Arabia. TEL 966-1-4676148. FAX 966-1-4676162. *2086*

KING SAUD UNIVERSITY. JOURNAL. EDUCATIONAL SCIENCES AND ISLAMIC STUDIES.
King Saud University, University Libraries, P.O. Box 22480, Riyadh 11495, Saudi Arabia. TEL 966-1-4676148. FAX 966-1-4676162. *6398*

KING SAUD UNIVERSITY. JOURNAL. ENGINEERING SCIENCES.
King Saud University, University Libraries, P.O. Box 22480, Riyadh 11495, Saudi Arabia. TEL 966-1-4676148. FAX 966-1-4676162. *2729*

KING SAUD UNIVERSITY. JOURNAL. SCIENCE.
King Saud University, University Libraries, P.O Box 22480, Riyadh 11495, Saudi Arabia. TEL 966-1-4676148. FAX 966-1-4676162. *6541*

KING'S COLLEGE LAW JOURNAL.
King's College London, School of Law, Strand, London WC2R 2LS, England. TEL 44-171-836-5454. FAX 44-171-873-2465. *3973*

KINOSCHRIFTEN.
Synema - Gesellschaft fuer Film und Medien, Neubaugasse 36-1-1-1, A-1070 Vienna, Austria. TEL 43-1-5233797. FAX 43-1-5233797. *5338*

KISHO RIYO KENKYU.
Kisho Riyo Kenkyukai, Kyushu Daigaku Nogakubu Nogyo Kishogaku Kyoshitsu, 10-1, Hakozaki 6-chome, Higashi-ku, Fukuoka-shi, Fukuoka-ken 812, Japan. TEL 81-92-641-1101. FAX 81-92-641-2928. *5237*

KITAKANTO MEDICAL JOURNAL.
Kitakanto Medical Society, c/o Gumma University, School of Medicine, 3-39-22 Showa-machi, Maebashi-shi 371, Japan. TEL 81-272-20-7111. *4700*

KITANO HOSPITAL JOURNAL OF MEDICINE.
Tazuke Kofukai Foundation, Medical Research Institute, 13-3 Kamiyama-cho, Kita-ku, Osaka 530, Japan. TEL 81-6-312-1221. FAX 81-6-361-0588. *4700*

THE KIWI.
New Zealand Society of Great Britain, 24 Irwin Rd., Guildford, Surrey GU2 5PP, England. TEL 44-1483-567185. *5708*

KLINICKA BIOCHEMIE A METABOLISMUS.
Nakladatelske Stredisko C L S J.E. Purkyne, Sokolska 31, 120 26 Prague 2, Czech Republic. TEL 420-2-24911420. FAX 420-2-24911420. *665*

KLUWER INTERNATIONAL SERIES IN ENGINEERING AND COMPUTER SCIENCE.
Kluwer Academic Publishers, Postbus 17, 3300 AA Dordrecht, Netherlands. TEL 31-78-6392392. FAX 31-78-6392254. *2086*

THE KLUWER INTERNATIONAL SERIES IN SOFTWARE ENGINEERING.
Kluwer Academic Publishers, Postbus 17, 3300 AA Dordrecht, Netherlands. TEL 31-78-6392392. FAX 31-78-6392254. *2214*

KLUWER NIJHOFF STUDIES IN HUMAN ISSUES.
Kluwer Academic Publishers, Postbus 17, 3300 AA Dordrecht, Netherlands. TEL 31-78-6392392. FAX 31-78-6392254. *6719*

KLUWER TEXTS IN THE MATHEMATICAL SCIENCES.
Kluwer Academic Publishers, Postbus 17, 3300 AA Dordrecht, Netherlands. TEL 31-78-6392392. FAX 31-78-6392254. *4585*

THE KNEE.
Elsevier Science B.V., P.O. Box 211, 1000 AE Amsterdam, Netherlands. TEL 31-20-4853757. FAX 31-20-4853432. *819*

KNOWLEDGE AND PROCESS MANAGEMENT.
John Wiley & Sons Ltd., Journals, Baffins Ln., Chichester, W. Sussex PO19 1UD, England. TEL 44-1243-779777. FAX 44-1243-843232. *1490*

KNOWLEDGE-BASED SYSTEMS.
Elsevier Science B.V., P.O. Box 211, 1000 AE Amsterdam, Netherlands. TEL 31-20-4853911. FAX 31-20-4853598. *2102*

KNOWLEDGE ORGANIZATION.
Ergon Verlag, Grombuehlstr. 7, 97080 Wuerzburg, Germany. TEL 49-931-280084. FAX 49-931-282872. *4190*

KOBE WOMEN'S UNIVERSITY. FACULTY OF HOME ECONOMICS. BULLETIN.
Kobe Women's University, Faculty of Home Economics, Aoyama, Suma-ku, Kobe-shi 654, Japan. TEL 81-78-731-4416. FAX 81-78-732-5161. *3686*

KOBIETA I BIZNES.
Szkola Glowna Handlowa, Kolegium Gospodarki Swiatowej, Al. Niepodleglosci 162, 02-554 Warsaw, Poland. TEL 48-22-495084. FAX 48-22-495084. *1644*

KOCHI UNIVERSITY. MARINE SCIENCES AND FISHERIES. BULLETIN.
Kochi University, Usa Marine Biological Institute, Usa-cho, Tosa, Kochi 781-11, Japan. TEL 0888-56-0422. FAX 0888-56-0425. *2408*

KODAI MATHEMATICAL JOURNAL.
Tokyo Kogyo Daigaku, 12-1 Ookayama 2-chome, Meguro-ku, Tokyo 152, Japan. TEL 81-3-5734-2220. FAX 81-3-5734-2738. *4585*

KODALY ENVOY.
Organization of American Kodaly Educators, 1457 S. 23rd St., Fargo, ND 58103-3708. TEL 701-235-0366. FAX 701-241-7051. *5406*

KODO RYOHO KENKYU.
Nihon Kodo Ryoho Gakkai, c/o Masahiko Sugiyama, Sec.-Gen., Institute of Special Education, University of Tsukuba, 1-1-1 Tennoudai Tsukuba, Ibaraki 305, Japan. TEL 81-298-53-6719. FAX 81-298-53-6719. *6133*

KOEDOE.
National Parks Board, P.O. Box 787, Pretoria 0001, South Africa. TEL 27-12-343-9770. FAX 27-12-343-2832. *2235*

KOERS.
Buro vir Wetenskaplike Tydskrifte, Private Bag X6001, Potchefstroom 2520, South Africa. TEL 27-148-2991769. FAX 27-148-2991562. *6351*

KOKU IGAKU JIKKENTAI HOKOKU.
Japan Air Self Defense Force, Aeromedical Laboratory, 2-10, Sakae-cho 1-chome, Tachikawa-shi, Tokyo, Japan. TEL 0245-24-4131. *4701*

KOLA.
Black Writers' Guild, C.P. 1602, Place Bonaventure, Montreal, PQ H5A 1H6, Canada. TEL 514-737-4629. FAX 514-737-4629. *4423*

KOLEKCJONER LOMZYNSKI.
Polskie Towarzystwo Numizmatyczne, Oddzial w Lomzy, Ul. Krzywe Kolo 1, 18-400 Lomza, Poland. TEL 162937. *341*

KON POLSKI.
Kon Polski Sp. z o.o., Zlota 63a m.6, 00-819 Warsaw, Poland. TEL 48-22-209817. FAX 48-22-243628. *6853*

KONGELIGE NORSKE VIDENSKABERS SELSKAB. SKRIFTER.
Kongelige Norske Videnskabers Selskab, Erling Skakkes gt. 47 b, N-7013 Trondheim, Norway. TEL 47-73-59-21-57. FAX 47-73-59-58-95. *6541*

KONGJIAN KEXUE XUEBAO.
Science Press, Marketing and Sales Department, 16 Donghuangchenggen North St., Beijing 100717, People's Republic of China. TEL 4010642. FAX 4019810. *73*

KONGQI DONGLIXUE XUEBAO.
Zhongguo Kongqi Dongli Yanjiu yu Fazhan Zhongxin, P.O. Box 211, Mianyang, Sichuan 621000, People's Republic of China. TEL 86-816-2364034. *5846*

KONINKLIJK NEDERLANDS GEOLOGISCH MIJNBOUWKUNDIG GENOOTSCHAP. VERHANDELINGEN.
Kluwer Academic Publishers, Postbus 17, 3300 AA Dordrecht, Netherlands. TEL 31-78-6392392. FAX 31-78-6392254. *2355*

KONINKLIJKE NEDERLANDSE AKADEMIE VAN WETENSCHAPPEN. AFDELING LETTERKUNDE. VERHANDELINGEN. NIEUWE REEKS.
Elsevier Science B.V., Books Division, P.O. Box 211, 1000 AE Amsterdam, Netherlands. TEL 31-20-4853911. FAX 31-20-4853705. *3784*

KONINKLIJKE NEDERLANDSE AKADEMIE VAN WETENSCHAPPEN. AFDELING NATUURKUNDE. VERHANDELINGEN. TWEEDE REEKS.
Elsevier Science B.V., Books Division, P.O. Box 211, 1000 AE Amsterdam, Netherlands. TEL 31-20-4853911. FAX 31-20-4853705. *6542*

DIE KONSENTRASIEKAMP-GEDENKREEKS.
Oorlogsmuseum van die Boererepublieke, Posbus 704, Bloemfontein 9300, South Africa. TEL 27-51-470079. FAX 27-51-471322. *3527*

KOREAN INSTITUTE OF METALS AND MATERIALS. JOURNAL.
Korean Institute of Metals and Materials, Rm. 605, Keoyang Bldg., 51-8 Susong-dong, Chong Ro-ku, Seoul 110-140, S. Korea. TEL 02-734-0595. FAX 02-734-0596. *5198*

KOREAN JOURNAL OF BREEDING.
Korean Breeding Society, College of Agriculture and Life Sciences, Seoul National University, Suwon 441-744, S. Korea. TEL 0331-290-6641. FAX 0331-292-4560. *280*

KOREAN JOURNAL OF PARASITOLOGY.
Korean Society for Parasitology, c/o Dept. of Parasitology, College of Medicine, Seoul National University, Seoul 110 799, S. Korea. TEL 82-2-740-8348. FAX 82-2-765-6142. *4840*

KOREAN JOURNAL OF PHARMACOLOGY.
Society of Pharmacology, c/o Dept. of Pharmacology, College of Medicine, 28 Yunkun-dong, Chongro-ku, Seoul 110, S. Korea. TEL 02-361-5210. FAX 02-745-7996. *5675*

KOREAN SOCIETY FOR CLINICAL PHARMACOLOGY AND THERAPEUTICS. JOURNAL.
Korean Society for Clinical Pharmacology and Therapeutics, c/o Seoul National University College of Medicine, Department of Neuropsychiatry, 28 Yongon-dong, Chongno-gu, Seoul 110-744, S. Korea. TEL 740-8286. FAX 745-7996. *5675*

KOREAN SOCIETY OF OCEANOGRAPHY. JOURNAL.
Hangug Haeyang Haghoe, c/o Dept. of Oceanography, Seoul National University, Seoul 151-742, S. Korea. TEL 82-2-872-5032. FAX 82-2-872-0311. *2408*

KOREAN STUDIES.
University of Hawaii Press, Journals Department, 2840 Kolowalu St., Honolulu, HI 96822. TEL 808-956-8833. FAX 808-988-6052. *5532*

KOREANSK JOURNAL.
Swedish-Korean Society, Box 3259, S-103 65 Stockholm 3, Sweden. TEL 46-8-759-59-75. *6024*

KORROZIOS FIGYELO.
V E K O R Ltd., Wartha V. u. 1, Bldg. M, 8200 Veszprem, Hungary. TEL 36-88-328514. FAX 36-88-328514. *5553*

KOSMON VOICE.
Universal Faithists of Kosmon, Box 654, McCook, NE 69001. TEL 308-345-6369. *6493*

KOSMOS.
International Society for Astrological Research, Inc., Box 38613, Los Angeles, CA 90038-0613. TEL 805-525-0461. FAX 805-525-0461. *486*

KOSMOS.
Polskie Towarzystwo Przyrodnikow im. Kopernika, Ul. Pawinskiego 5a, 02-106 Warsaw, Poland. TEL 48-22-6584729. *611*

KOTAIGUN SEITAI GAKKAI KAIHO.
Kotaigun Seitai Gakkai, Ogawa Higashi Iru, Shimodachuri Dori, Kamigayo-ku, Kyoto 602, Japan. TEL 81-298-53-6858. FAX 81-298-53-6614. *6053*

KRED.
University of Kent Students' Union, Mandela Bldg., University of Kent, Canterbury, Kent CT2 7NW, England. TEL 01227-765224. FAX 01227-464625. *1958*

KREFELD IMMIGRANTS AND THEIR DESCENDANTS.
Links Genealogy Publications, 7677 Abaline Way, Sacramento, CA 95823. TEL 916-428-2245. FAX 916-428-2245. *3230*

KRIEGSGRAEBERFUERSORGE.
Volksbund Deutsche Kriegsgraeberfuersorge e.V., Werner-Hilpert-Str. 2, 34112 Kassel, Germany. TEL 49-561-7009-0. FAX 49-561-7009221. *5274*

KRONOS.
University of the Western Cape, Institute for Historical Research, Private Bag X17, Bellville 7530, South Africa. TEL 27-21-9592616. FAX 27-21-9593178. *3527*

KUMAMOTO IGAKKAI ZASSHI.
Kumamoto Igakkai, c/o Kumamoto Daigaku Igakubu, 2-1, Honjo 2-chome, Kumamoto-shi, Kumamoto-ken 860, Japan. TEL 81-96-373-5122. FAX 81-96-373-5123. *4701*

KUNCHONG XUEBAO.
Science Press, Marketing and Sales Department, 16 Donghuangchenggen North St., Beijing 100717, People's Republic of China. TEL 4010642. FAX 4019810. *757*

KURENAI: JAPANESE EMBROIDERY JOURNAL.
Embroidery Research Press Inc., 10800 Alpharetta Hwy., Ste. 208 G-4, Roswell, Roswell, GA 30076. TEL 770-390-0617. FAX 770-512-7837. *5452*

KURUME MEDICAL JOURNAL.
Kurume University School of Medicine, 67 Asahi-machi, Kurume 830, Japan. TEL 81-942-35-3311. FAX 81-942-32-1665. *4701*

KUWAIT INTERNATIONAL JOURNAL OF CREATIVE ACHIEVEMENTS.
P.O. Box 98029, S. Common Post, 2150 Burnhamthorpe Rd., Mississauga, ON L5L 3A0, Canada. FAX 416-277-2875. *6542*

KYORIN IGAKKAI ZASSHI.
Kyorin Medical Society, Kyorin University, 20-2, 6-chome, Shinkawa, Mitaka-shi, Tokyo 181, Japan. TEL 81-422-47-5511. FAX 81-422-40-7281. *4702*

KYOSANSHUGISHA.
Kaihohsha, 525-3, Waseda Tsurumaki-cho, Shinjuku-ku, Tokyo 162, Japan. TEL 81-3-3207-1261. FAX 81-3-5273-2351. *5939*

KYOTO JOURNAL.
Heian Bunka Center, 35 Minamigosho-machi, Okazaki, Sakyo-ku, Kyoto 606, Japan. TEL 81-75-761-1433. FAX 81-75-751-1196. *5532*

KYOTO PREFECTURAL UNIVERSITY OF MEDICINE. MEDICAL SOCIETY. JOURNAL.
Kyoto Prefectural University of Medicine, Kyoto Foundations for the Promotion of Medical Science, Hirokoji, Kawara-machi, Kamigyo-ku, Kyoto 602, Japan. TEL 81-75-212-5466. FAX 81-75-212-5467. *4702*

KYOTO UNIVERSITY. BIOLOGICAL LABORATORY. CONTRIBUTIONS.
Kyoto University, Faculty of General Education, Yoshida Nihonmatsucho, Sakyo-ku, Kyoto 606, Japan. TEL 81-75-753-6849. FAX 81-75-753-6864. *611*

KYUSHU UNIVERSITY. DEPARTMENT OF EARTH AND PLANETARY SCIENCES. SCIENCE REPORTS.
Kyushu University 33, Department of Earth and Planetary Sciences, 6-10-1 Hakozaki, Higashi-ku, Fukuoka 812-81, Japan. TEL 81-92-642-2696. FAX 81-92-642-2684. *2355*

L A D O C.
Latin American Documentation, Apdo. 18-0964, Lima 18, Peru. TEL 51-14-475210. FAX 51-14-454681. *6352*

L A S A FORUM.
Latin American Studies Association, William Pitt Union, 9th Fl., University of Pittsburgh, Pittsburgh, PA 15260. TEL 412-648-7929. FAX 412-624-7145. *6624*

L E BEACON.
L.E. Support Group, 8039 Nova Court, N. Charleston, SC 29420. TEL 803-764-1769. *5126*

L E R S MONOGRAPH SERIES.
Raven Publishers, 227 E. Washington Sq., Philadelphia, PA 19106. TEL 215-238-4200. FAX 215-238-4235. *4702*

L I N Q.
James Cook University of North Queensland, Department of English, Townsville, Qld. 4811, Australia. TEL 61-77-815097. FAX 61-77-815655. *4424*

L I S P AND SYMBOLIC COMPUTATION.
Kluwer Academic Publishers Boston, Box 358, Accord Sta., Hingham, MA 02018-0358. TEL 617-871-6600. FAX 617-871-6528. *2124*

L I T: LITERATURE INTERPRETATION THEORY.
Gordon and Breach - Harwood Academic, Amsteldisk 166, 1st Fl., 1079 LH Amsterdam, Netherlands. *4424*

L R I BULLETIN.
Lonergan Research Institute, 10 St. Mary St., Ste. 500, Toronto, ON M4Y 1P9, Canada. TEL 416-922-8374. *5735*

LAB ANIMAL.
Nature Publishing Co., 345 Park Ave. S., 10th Fl., New York, NY 10012-2467. *4899*

LABMEDICA INTERNATIONAL.
Globetech Publishing, 8 Cannon Rd., Wilton, CT 06897. TEL 203-762-3432. FAX 203-762-8640. *4899*

LABOR HISTORY.
Tamiment Institute, Ben Josephson Library, New York University, Bobst Library, 10th Fl., 70 Washington Sq. S., New York, NY 10012. TEL 212-737-2715. FAX 212-741-6790. *1440*

LABORATORIUMS MEDIZIN.
Blackwell Wissenschaft, Kurfuerstendamm 57, 10707 Berlin, Germany. TEL 49-30-32790624. FAX 49-30-32790610. *4899*

LABORATORY ANIMAL SCIENCE.
American Association for Laboratory Animal Science, 70 Timber Creek Dr., Ste. 5, Cordova, TN 38018. TEL 901-754-8620. *4900*

LABORATORY ANIMALS.
Royal Society of Medicine Press Ltd., 1 Wimpole St., London W1M 8AE, England. TEL 44-171-290-2900. FAX 44-171-290-2929. *4900*

LABORATORY AUTOMATION AND INFORMATION MANAGEMENT.
Elsevier Science B.V., P.O. Box 211, 1000 AE Amsterdam, Netherlands. TEL 31-20-4853911. FAX 31-20-4853598. *6594*

LABORATORY INVESTIGATION.
Williams & Wilkins, 351 W. Camden St., Baltimore, MD 21201-2436. TEL 410-528-4068. FAX 410-528-4452. *4900*

LABORATORY MEDICINE.
American Society of Clinical Pathologists, 2100 W. Harrison St., Chicago, IL 60612. FAX 312-738-0101. *4900*

LABORATORY ROBOTICS AND AUTOMATION.
John Wiley & Sons, Inc., Journals, 605 Third Ave., New York, NY 10158-0012. TEL 212-850-6645. FAX 212-850-6021. *2110*

LABORATORY TECHNIQUES IN BIOCHEMISTRY AND MOLECULAR BIOLOGY.
Elsevier Science B.V., Books Division, P.O. Box 211, 1000 AE Amsterdam, Netherlands. TEL 31-20-4853911. FAX 31-20-4853705. *665*

LABOR'S HERITAGE.
George Meany Center for Labor Studies, 10000 New Hampshire Ave., Silver Spring, MD 20903. TEL 301-431-5457. FAX 301-431-0385. *1441*

LABOUR.
Canadian Committee on Labour History, Department of History, Memorial University of Newfoundland, St. John's, NF A1C 5S7, Canada. TEL 709-737-2144. FAX 709-737-4342. *1442*

LABOUR.
Blackwell Publishers Ltd., 108 Cowley Rd., Oxford OX4 1JF, England. TEL 44-1865-791100. FAX 44-1865-791347. *1442*

LABOUR & INDUSTRY.
Centre for Workplace Culture Change, P.O. Box 581, Market St., Melbourne, Vic. 8007, Australia. TEL 61-3-96421269. FAX 61-3-96421326. *1442*

LABOUR, CAPITAL AND SOCIETY.
McGill University, Centre for Developing Area Studies, 3715 Peel St., Montreal, PQ H3A 1X1, Canada. TEL 514-398-3508. FAX 514-398-8432. *6650*

LABOUR ECONOMICS.
North-Holland, P.O. Box 211, 1000 AE Amsterdam, Netherlands. TEL 31-20-4853911. FAX 31-20-4853598. *1442*

LABOUR FOCUS ON EASTERN EUROPE.
Labor Focus on Eastern Europe, 30 Bridge St., Oxford OX2 0BA, England. TEL 44-1865-723207. *1442*

LABOUR HISTORY.
Australian Society for the Study of Labour History, Institute Bldg. H03, Faculty of Economics, University of Sydney, N.S.W. 2006, Australia. TEL 61-2-93513786. FAX 61-2-93514729. *1442*

LABOUR HISTORY REVIEW.
Edinburgh University Press, 22 George Sq., Edinburgh EH8 9LF, Scotland. TEL 44-131-650-6207. FAX 44-131-662-0053. *1442*

LACANIAN STUDIES.
Ellie Ragland, Ed. & Pub., 502 W. Rockcreek Dr., Colombia, MO 65203. TEL 573-884-6212. FAX 314-882-5785. *6134*

LACERTA.
Nederlandse Vereniging voor Herpetologie en Terrariumkunde, c/o P.D. Gorseman, Prins Hendrikstraat 55, 3331 XR Zwijndrecht, Netherlands. TEL 31-78-6123908. FAX 31-78-6121550. *841*

LACIO DROM.
Centro Studi Zingari, Via dei Barbieri 22, 00186 Rome, Italy. TEL 39-6-6833181. FAX 39-6-6868760. *3025*

LACKAWANNA JURIST.
Lackawanna Bar Association, 205 1 Pyramid Center, Corner Spruce and Wyoming Aves., Scranton, PA 18503. TEL 717-969-9161. FAX 717-969-9150. *3975*

LACTEOS Y CARNICOS MEXICANOS.
Alfa Editores Tecnicos S.A., Libertad No. 107-402, 03660 Mexico DF, Mexico. TEL 525-579-3333. FAX 525-5329504. *3118*

LACTIC ACID BACTERIA.
Elsevier Science Ltd., Books Division, P.O. Box 800, Kidlington, Oxford OX5 1DX, England. TEL 44-1865-843000. FAX 44-1865-843010. *789*

LAEGEMIDDELKATALOGET.
Laegemiddelkataloget, Stroedamvej 50 B, DK-2100 Copenhagen Oe, Denmark. TEL 45-39-27-44-88. FAX 45-39-27-59-10. *5676*

LE LAIT.
Editions Scientifiques et Medicales Elsevier, 141 rue de Javel, 75747 Paris, France. TEL 33-1-45589022. FAX 33-1-45589421. *256*

LAKE BIWA STUDY MONOGRAPHS.
Lake Biwa Research Institute, 1-10, Uchide-hama, Otsu-shi, Shiga-ken 520, Japan. TEL 81-775-26-4800. FAX 81-775-26-4803. *2396*

LAKES AND RESERVOIRS: RESEARCH AND MANAGEMENT.
Blackwell Science Pty Ltd., P.O. Box 378, Carlton South, Vic. 3053, Australia. TEL 61-3-93470300. FAX 61-3-93493016. *7296*

LAKOKRASOCHNYE MATERIALY I IKH PRIMENENIE.
Journal LKM Ltd., Myussjata Sq., D.I. Mendeleev PCHTU, 125047 Moscow, Russia. TEL 7-095-9789779. FAX 7-095-9879779. *5553*

LAMAR JOURNAL OF THE HUMANITIES.
Lamar University, Department of English and Foreign Languages, Box 10023, Beaumont, TX 77710. TEL 409-880-8558. *3784*

LAMMERGEYER.
Natal Parks Board, P.O. Box 662, Pietermaritzburg 3200, South Africa. TEL 27-331-471961. FAX 27-331-471037. *2235*

LANCASTER WORKING PAPERS IN POLITICAL ECONOMY. POLITICAL ECONOMY OF LOCAL GOVERNANCE SERIES.
Lancaster University, Department of Sociology, Lancaster LA1 4YL, England. TEL 44-1524-594178. FAX 44-1524-594256. *1308*

THE LANCET.
The Lancet Ltd., 42 Bedford Sq., London WC1B 3SL, England. TEL 44-171-4364981. FAX 44-171-4367570. *4702*

THE LANCET (NORTH AMERICAN EDITION).
The Lancet Ltd., 655 Ave. of the Americas, New York, NY 10011. TEL 212-633-3800. FAX 212-633-3850. *4702*

LAND & WATER.
Land and Water, Inc., Box 1197, Ft. Dodge, IA 50501. TEL 515-576-3191. FAX 515-576-2606. *2235*

LAND AND WATER LAW REVIEW.
University of Wyoming, College of Law, Box 3035, Laramie, WY 82071-3035. TEL 307-766-2329. FAX 307-766-6417. *3975*

LAND CONTAMINATION & RECLAMATION.
E P P Publications, 52 Kings Rd., Richmond, Surrey, TW10 6EP, England. TEL 44-181-948-7165. FAX 44-181-747-9663. *2970*

LAND DEGRADATION AND DEVELOPMENT.
John Wiley & Sons Ltd., Journals, Baffins Ln., Chichester, W. Sussex PO19 1UD, England. TEL 44-1243-779777. FAX 44-1243-775878. *2318*

LAND INFO.
Department of Land Affairs, Directorate: Communication Services, Private Bag X833, Pretoria 0001, South Africa. TEL 27-12-3128323. FAX 27-12-3233693. *6182*

LAND USE POLICY.
Elsevier Science Ltd., Pergamon, P.O. Box 800, Kidlington, Oxford OX5 1DX, England. TEL 44-1865-843000. FAX 44-1865-843010. *3752*

LANDSCAPE ECOLOGY.
Kluwer Academic Publishers, Postbus 17, 3300 AA Dordrecht, Netherlands. TEL 31-78-6392392. FAX 31-78-6392254. *2940*

LANDSCAPE HISTORY.
Society for Landscape Studies, 91 Oakfield Rd., Selly Park, Birmingham B29 7HL, England. TEL 44-121-472-4253. *3504*

LANDSCAPE ISSUES.
Department of Countryside and Landscape, Cheltenham and Gloucester College of Higher Education, Francis Close Hall, Swindon Rd., Cheltenham, England. TEL 44-1242-532930. FAX 44-1242-532997. *408*

LANDSCAPE RESEARCH.
Carfax Publishing Co., P.O. Box 24, Abingdon, Oxon OX14 3UE, England. TEL 44-1235-401000. FAX 44-1235-401550. *408*

LANDSCHAFTSVERBAND WESTFALEN-LIPPE. MITTEILUNGEN DES LANDESJUGENDAMTES.
Landschaftsverband Westfalen-Lippe, Landesjugendamt, 48133 Muenster, Germany. TEL 49-251-591-3641. FAX 49-251-591-275. *6675*

LANDSCHAP.
Werkgemeenschap Landschapsecologisch Onderzoek (WLO), Postbus 23, 6700 AA Wageningen, Netherlands. TEL 31-317-477986. FAX 31-317-424988. *2940*

LANDWARDS.
Institution of Agricultural Engineers, West End Rd., Silsoe, Beds. MK45 4DU, England. TEL 44-1525-861096. FAX 44-1525-861660. *133*

LANGUAGE ACQUISITION.
Lawrence Erlbaum Associates, Inc., 10 Industrial Dr., Mahwah, NJ 07430-2262. TEL 201-236-9500. FAX 201-236-0072. *4271*

LANGUAGE AND COGNITIVE PROCESSES.
Taylor & Francis Ltd., Psychology Press, 1 Gunpowder Sq., London EC4A 3DE, England. TEL 44-171-5830490. FAX 44-171-5830585. *4272*

LANGUAGE & COMMUNICATION.
Elsevier Science Ltd., Pergamon, P.O. Box 800, Kidlington, Oxford OX5 1DX, England. TEL 44-1865-843000. FAX 44-1865-843010. *4272*

LANGUAGE AND LITERATURE.
Institute for Cross-Cultural Research, Trinity University, No. 418, 715 Stadium Dr., San Antonio, TX 78212-7200. TEL 210-736-7369. FAX 210-736-7578. *4272*

LANGUAGE, CULTURE AND CURRICULUM.
Multilingual Matters Ltd., Frankfurt Lodge, Clevedon Hall, Victoria Rd., Clevedon BS21 7SJ, England. TEL 44-1275-876519. FAX 44-1275-343096. *4272*

LANGUAGE IN SOCIETY.
Cambridge University Press, Edinburgh Bldg., Shaftesbury Rd., Cambridge CB2 2RU, England. TEL 44-1223-312393. FAX 44-1223-315052. *4273*

LANGUAGE INTERNATIONAL.
John Benjamins Publishing Co., Amsteldijk 44, P.O. Box 75577, 1070 AN Amsterdam, Netherlands. TEL 31-20-6738156. FAX 31-20-6792956. *4273*

LANGUAGE LEARNING AND TECHNOLOGY.
University of Hawaii, National Foreign Language Resource Center, East-West Rd., Bldg. 1, Rm. 6-A, Honolulu, HI 96822. TEL 808-956-9424. *4320*

LANGUAGE OF DANCE.
Gordon and Breach - Harwood Academic, Amsteldisk 166, 1st Fl., 1079 LH Amsterdam, Netherlands. *2294*

LANGUAGE QUARTERLY.
University of South Florida, College of Arts & Sciences, 4202 E. Fowler Ave., CPR 107, Tampa, FL 33620-5550. TEL 813-974-5618. FAX 813-974-5618. *4273*

LANGUAGE RESEARCH.
Soeul National University, San 56-1, Sinlim-dong, Kwanak-ku, Seoul 151-742, S. Korea. TEL 82-2-880-5485. FAX 82-2-871-6907. *4273*

LANGUAGE SCIENCES.
Elsevier Science Ltd., Pergamon, P.O. Box 800, Kidlington, Oxford OX5 1DX, England. TEL 44-1865-843000. FAX 44-1865-843010. *4273*

LANGUAGES OF DESIGN.
Penrose Press, Box 470925, San Francisco, CA 94147. *477*

LANNAN SERIES.
University of California Press, 2120 Berkeley Way, Berkeley, CA 94720. TEL 510-642-4247. FAX 510-643-7127. *4424*

LAPIS.
Christian Weise Verlag GmbH, Orleansstr. 69, 81667 Munich, Germany. TEL 49-89-4802933. FAX 49-89-6886160. *2355*

LARYNGOSCOPE.
Lippincott - Raven Publishers, 227 E. Washington Sq., Philadelphia, PA 19106-3780. TEL 215-238-4200. FAX 215-238-4227. *5023*

LASER CHEMISTRY.
Gordon and Breach - Harwood Academic, Amsteldisk 166, 1st Fl., 1079 LH Amsterdam, Netherlands. *5864*

LASER HANDBOOK.
Elsevier Science B.V., Books Division, P.O. Box 211, 1000 AE Amsterdam, Netherlands. TEL 31-20-4853911. FAX 31-20-4853705. *5864*

LASER SCIENCE AND TECHNOLOGY.
Gordon and Breach - Harwood Academic, Amsteldisk 166, 1st Fl., 1079 LH Amsterdam, Netherlands. *5864*

LASER THERAPY.
International Laser Therapy Association, c/o 14-18 Iwaicho, Tochigi City, Tochigi 328, Japan. TEL 81-282-24-0313. FAX 81-282-22-5019. *4702*

LASERS & OPTRONICS.
Gordon Publications, Part of Cahners Publishing Company, Division of Reed Elsevier Inc., 301 Gibraltar Dr., Box 650, Morris Plains, NJ 07950-0650. TEL 973-292-5100 ext.317. FAX 973-292-0783. *5865*

LASERS IN ENGINEERING.
Gordon and Breach - Harwood Academic, Amsteldisk 166, 1st Fl., 1079 LH Amsterdam, Netherlands. *5865*

LASERS IN SURGERY AND MEDICINE.
John Wiley & Sons, Inc., Journals, 605 Third Ave., New York, NY 10158. TEL 212-850-6645. FAX 212-850-6021. *5148*

LASERS IN THE LIFE SCIENCES.
Gordon and Breach - Harwood Academic, Amsteldisk 166, 1st Fl., 1079 LH Amsterdam, Netherlands. *5865*

LATE IMPERIAL CHINA.
Johns Hopkins University Press, Journals Publishing Division, 2715 N. Charles St., Baltimore, MD 21218-4319. TEL 410-516-6987. FAX 410-516-6968. *3536*

LATIN AMERICAN ANTIQUITY.
Society for American Archaeology, 900 Second St., N.W., No. 12, Washington, DC 20002-3557. TEL 202-789-8200. FAX 202-789-0284. *371*

LATIN AMERICAN INDIAN LITERATURES JOURNAL.
Penn State University, McKeesport, University Dr., McKeesport, PA 15132-7698. TEL 412-675-9466. FAX 412-675-9043. *4425*

LATIN AMERICAN LITERATURE AND CULTURE.
University of California Press, 2120 Berkeley Way, Berkeley, CA 94720. TEL 510-642-4247. FAX 510-643-7127. *3635*

LATIN AMERICAN THEATRE REVIEW.
University of Kansas, Center of Latin American Studies, 107 Lippincott Hall, Lawrence, KS 66045. TEL 913-864-3851. FAX 913-864-4298. *7008*

LATINO REVIEW OF BOOKS.
State University of New York at Albany, Center for Latino, Latin American, and Caribbean Studies (CELAC), SS-247, Albany, NY 12222. TEL 518-442-4590. FAX 519-442-4790. *6624*

LATINO STUDIES JOURNAL.
Long Island University, 720 Northern Blvd., Hoxie Hall 205, Brookville, NY 11548-1300. TEL 516-299-2458. FAX 516-299-4287. *6025*

LATVIJAS FIZIKAS UN TEHNISKO ZINATNU ZURNALS.
Latvijas Zinatnu Akademijas, Fizikalas Energetikas Instituts, Aizkraukles iela, 21, 1006 Riga, Latvia. TEL 371-7552011. FAX 371-7820339. *5813*

LAUREL REVIEW (MARYVILLE).
GreenTower Press, c/o William Trowbridge, Dept. of English, Northwest Missouri State University, Maryville, MO 64468. TEL 816-562-1265. *4425*

LAVAL THEOLOGIQUE ET PHILOSOPHIQUE.
Universite Laval, Faculte de Philosophie, Cite Universitaire, Quebec, PQ G1K 7P4, Canada. TEL 418-656-2131. FAX 418-656-7267. *5735*

LAW AND CRITIQUE.
Deborah Charles Publications, 173 Mather Ave., Liverpool L18 6JZ, England. TEL 0151-724-2500. FAX 0151-729-0371. *3976*

LAW AND HISTORY REVIEW.
University of Illinois Press, 1325 S. Oak St., Champaign, IL 61820. TEL 217-244-0950. FAX 217-244-8082. *3976*

LAW AND HUMAN BEHAVIOR.
Plenum Publishing Corp., 233 Spring St., New York, NY 10013-1578. TEL 212-620-8000. FAX 212-463-0742. *3976*

LAW AND PHILOSOPHY.
Kluwer Academic Publishers, Postbus 17, 3300 AA Dordrecht, Netherlands. TEL 31-78-6392392. FAX 31-78-6392254. *3976*

LAW AND PHILOSOPHY LIBRARY.
Kluwer Academic Publishers, Postbus 17, 3300 AA Dordrecht, Netherlands. TEL 31-78-6392392. FAX 31-78-6392254. *3976*

LAW AND SOCIAL INQUIRY.
University of Chicago Press, Journals Division, Box 37005, Chicago, IL 60637. TEL 773-753-3347. FAX 773-753-0811. *3976*

LAW & SOCIETY REVIEW.
Law and Society Association, Hampshire House, Box 33615, University of Massachusetts, Amherst, MA 01003-3615. TEL 413-545-4617. FAX 413-545-1640. *3977*

LAW IN EASTERN EUROPE.
Martinus Nijhoff Publishers, Human Rights and International Law, Postbus 163, 3300 AD Dordrecht, Netherlands. TEL 31-78-334228. FAX 31-78-334254. *4121*

LAW, SOCIETY AND POLICY.
Plenum Publishing Corp., 233 Spring St., New York, NY 10013-1578. TEL 212-620-8000. FAX 212-463-0742. *3978*

LAW SOCIETY OF SOUTH AUSTRALIA. BULLETIN.
Law Society of South Australia, 124 Waymouth St., Adelaide, S.A. 5000, Australia. TEL 61-8-82290222. FAX 61-8-82311929. *3978*

LEAD BELLY LETTER.
Lead Belly Society, Box 6679, Ithaca, NY 14851. TEL 607-273-6615. FAX 607-844-4810. *5407*

LEADER MAGAZINE.
Active Parenting Publishers, 810 Franklin Court, Ste. B, Marietta, GA 30067-8943. TEL 770-429-0565. FAX 770-429-0334. *1850*

LEADERSHIP MEDICA.
Ce.S.I.L. srl, Via Olmetto 5, 20123 Milan, Italy. TEL 39-2-878397. FAX 39-2-866576. *4703*

LEAFLET (LEXINGTON).
New England Association of Teachers of English, Box 291, Chemmsford, MA 01824-0291. TEL 617-646-2575. *4274*

LEARNING AND INSTRUCTION.
Elsevier Science Ltd., Pergamon, P.O. Box 800, Kidlington, Oxford OX5 1DX, England. TEL 44-1865-843000. FAX 44-1865-843010. *2460*

LEARNING & MEMORY.
Cold Spring Harbor Laboratory Press, Publications Department, Box 100, Cold Spring Harbor, NY 11724. TEL 516-367-8492. FAX 516-349-1946. *5078*

LEARNING DISABILITY QUARTERLY.
C L D, Box 40303, Overland Park, KS 66204. TEL 913-492-8755. *2587*

LEATHERS.
Council for Leather Exports, 53 Sydenhams Rd., Periamet, Madras 600 003, India. TEL 91-44-589098. FAX 91-44-588713. *4146*

LECTURA Y VIDA.
International Reading Association, Inc., 800 Barksdale Rd., Box 8139, Newark, DE 19714-8139. TEL 302-731-1600. FAX 302-731-1057. *4274*

LECTURES IN ECONOMICS: THEORY, INSTITUTIONS, POLICY.
Elsevier Science B.V., Books Division, P.O. Box 211, 1000 AE Amsterdam, Netherlands. TEL 31-20-4853911. FAX 31-20-4853705. *1308*

LEDELSE I DAG.
Ledernes Hovedorganisation, Vermlandsgade 63, DK-2300 Copenhagen S, Denmark. TEL 45-31-57-56-22. FAX 45-31-57-90-22. *1491*

THE LEECH.
University of the Witwatersrand Medical School, 7 York Rd., Parktown 2193, South Africa. TEL 27-11-6472451. FAX 27-11-6434318. *4703*

LEESGOED.
N B L C Uitgeverij, P.O. Box 43300, 2504 AH The Hague, Netherlands. TEL 31-70-3090335. FAX 31-70-3090200. *2460*

LEFT HISTORY.
Left History Press, York University, Dept. of History, 4700 Keele St., North York, ON M3J 1P3, Canada. TEL 416-736-5123. FAX 416-736-5836. *3635*

LEGACY (UNIVERSITY PARK).
Pennsylvania State University Press, USB 1, Ste. C, University Park, PA 16802-1003. TEL 814-865-1327. FAX 814-863-1408. *4425*

LEGAL ABACUS.
Institute of Legal Cashiers and Administrators, 146-148 Eltham Hill, 2nd Fl., Eltham, London SE9 5DX, England. TEL 44-181-294-2887. FAX 44-181-859-1682. *3980*

LEGAL AND CRIMINOLOGICAL PSYCHOLOGY.
British Psychological Society, St. Andrew's House, 48 Princess Rd. E., Leicester LE1 7DR, England. TEL 44-116-254-9568. FAX 44-116-2470787. *6134*

LEGAL ASPECTS OF INTERNATIONAL ORGANIZATION.
Kluwer Law International, Postbus 85889, 2508 CN The Hague, Netherlands. TEL 31-70-3081500. FAX 31-70-3081515. *4121*

LEGAL REFERENCE SERVICES QUARTERLY.
Haworth Press, Inc., 10 Alice St., Binghamton, NY 13904. TEL 607-722-5857. FAX 607-722-6362. *4192*

LEGAL STUDIES FORUM.
American Legal Studies Association, c/o Law, Policy and Society Program, 341 Cushing Hall, Northeastern University, Boston, MA 02114. TEL 617-437-5211. FAX 617-437-4691. *3982*

LEGAL THEORY.
Cambridge University Press, Edinburgh Bldg., Shaftesbury Rd., Cambridge CB2 2RU, England. TEL 44-1223-312393. FAX 44-1223-315052. *3982*

LEGISLATIVE STUDIES QUARTERLY.
University of Iowa, Comparative Legislative Research Center, 334 Schaeffer Hall, Iowa City, IA 52242. TEL 319-335-2361. FAX 319-335-3211. *5940*

LEGON JOURNAL OF THE HUMANITIES.
Black Mask Ltd., P.O. Box 69, Legon, Ghana. TEL 233-21-775178. FAX 233-21-667701. *3785*

LEIBNIZ SOCIETY REVIEW.
Ohio State University, Philosophy Department, 1680 University Dr., Mansfield, OH 44906-1599. TEL 419-755-4354. FAX 419-755-4367. *5735*

LEICESTERSHIRE ARCHAEOLOGICAL AND HISTORICAL SOCIETY. TRANSACTIONS.
Leicestershire Archaeological and Historical Society, The Guildhall, Guildhall Lane, Leicester LE1 5FQ, England. *371*

LEIDEN JOURNAL OF INTERNATIONAL LAW.
Kluwer Law International, Postbus 85889, 2508 CN The Hague, Netherlands. TEL 31-70-3081500. FAX 31-70-3081515. *4121*

LEIDSE JURIDISCHE REEKS.
E.J. Brill, P.O. Box 9000, 2300 PA Leiden, Netherlands. TEL 31-71-5353500. FAX 31-71-5317532. *3983*

LEIDSE ROMANISTISCHE REEKS.
E.J. Brill, P.O. Box 9000, 2300 PA Leiden, Netherlands. TEL 31-71-5353500. FAX 31-71-5317532. *4274*

DE LEIEGOUW.
Vereniging voor Geschied- Taal- en Volkskundig Onderzoek in het Kortrijkse, Keizer Karelstraat 83, 8000 Brugge, Belgium. TEL 32-50-317366. *3580*

LEISURE SCIENCES.
Taylor & Francis Inc., 1900 Frost Rd., Ste. 101, Bristol, PA 19007. TEL 215-785-5800. FAX 215-785-5515. *4150*

LEISURE STUDIES.
Thomson Professional, 2-6 Boundary Row, London SE1 8HN, England. TEL 171-8650066. FAX 171-5229623. *4150*

LEJEUNIA.
Botanical Society in Liege, Universite de Liege, Departement de Botanique, Sart Tilman, B-4000 Liege, Belgium. TEL 32-4-3663850. FAX 32-4-3663840. *713*

LENGUAJE.
Universidad del Valle, Escuela de Ciencias del Lenguaje y Literatura, Apdo. Aereo 25360, Cali, Colombia. TEL 5792-3330494. FAX 5792-3398497. *4274*

LENOX AVENUE: A JOURNAL OF INTERARTISTIC INQUIRY.
Center for Black Music Research, Columbia College, 600 S. Michigan Ave., Chicago, IL 60605. TEL 312-663-1600. FAX 312-663-9019. *5407*

LEONARDO: ART SCIENCE AND TECHNOLOGY.
M I T Press, 5 Cambridge Center, Cambridge, MA 02142. TEL 617-253-2889. FAX 617-577-1545. *452*

LEONARDO MUSIC JOURNAL.
M I T Press, 5 Cambridge Center, Cambridge, MA 02142. TEL 617-253-2889. FAX 617-577-1545. *5407*

LETRAS DE DEUSTO.
Universidad de Deusto, Facultad de la Filosofia y Letras, Departamento de Publicaciones, Apdo. 1, 48080 Bilbao, Spain. TEL 34-4-4453100. FAX 34-4-445-8916. *3785*

LET'S LIVE.
Franklin Publications, 320 N. Larchmont Blvd., 3rd Fl., Box 74908, Los Angeles, CA 90004. TEL 213-469-3901. FAX 213-469-9597. *5786*

LETTERS IN APPLIED MICROBIOLOGY.
Blackwell Science Ltd., Osney Mead, Oxford OX2 0EL, England. TEL 44-1865-206206. FAX 44-1865-721205. *789*

LETTERS IN MATHEMATICAL PHYSICS.
Kluwer Academic Publishers, Postbus 17, 3300 AA Dordrecht, Netherlands. TEL 31-78-6392392. FAX 31-78-6392254. *5813*

LETTRE AUX AMIS DU MONDE.
Editions Quart Monde, 15 rue Maitre Albert, 75005 Paris, France. TEL 33-1-46334977. FAX 33-1-43296448. *6675*

LA LETTRE DE TAPORI.
Editions Quart Monde, 15 rue Maitre Albert, 75005 Paris, France. TEL 33-1-46334977. FAX 33-1-43296448. *1878*

LES LETTRES ROMANES.
Faculte de Philosophie et Lettres, Place Blaise Pascal 1, B-1348 Louvain-la-Neuve, Belgium. TEL 32-10-474921. FAX 32-10-472579. *4426*

LEUKEMIA.
Stockton Press, Houndmills, Basingstoke, Hants RG21 2XS, England. TEL 44-1256-329242. FAX 44-1256-328339. *4920*

LEUKEMIA AND LYMPHOMA.
Gordon and Breach - Harwood Academic, Amsteldisk 166, 1st Fl., 1079 LH Amsterdam, Netherlands. *4921*

LEUKEMIA RESEARCH.
Elsevier Science Ltd., Pergamon, P.O. Box 800, Kidlington, Oxford OX5 1DX, England. TEL 44-1865-843000. FAX 44-1865-843010. *4921*

LEVANT.
British School of Archaeology in Jerusalem, c/o British Academy, 20-21 Cornwall Terrace, London NW1 4QP, England. *371*

LEVANT MORGENLAND.
Action Chretienne en Orient, 7 rue du General Offenstein, 67100 Strasbourg, France. TEL 33-3-88391155. FAX 33-3-88402798. *6353*

LEVELTARI KOZLEMENYEK.
Magyar Orszagos Leveltar, Becsi Kapu ter 2-4, 1014 Budapest, Hungary. TEL 36-1-565-811. *3504*

LEVEN EN LATEN LEVEN.
Nederlandse Vegetariersbond, Larenseweg 26, 1221 CM Hilversum, Netherlands. TEL 31-35-6834796. FAX 31-35-6836152. *5477*

LEXINGTON THEOLOGICAL QUARTERLY.
Lexington Theological Seminary, 631 S. Limestone St., Lexington, KY 40508. FAX 606-281-6042. *6353*

LEXIS.
Pontificia Universidad Catolica del Peru, Fondo Editorial, Apdo. 1761, Lima 32, Peru. TEL 51-14-626390. FAX 51-14-611785. *4275*

LIANGSHI WENTI YANJIU.
Sichuan Liangshi Jingji Xuehui, 67 Dajie, Chengdu, Sichuan 610012, People's Republic of China. TEL 86-28-6671208. FAX 86-28-6661969. *3118*

LIBERIAN STUDIES JOURNAL.
Liberian Studies Association, c/o Dr. Arnold Odio, Albany State University, 504 College Dr., P.O. Box 31222, Albany, GA 31705-2791. TEL 912-430-4833. *6624*

LIBERTAS MATHEMATICA.
A R A Publications (Arlington), Department of Mathematics, University of Texas, Box 19408, Arlington, TX 76019. TEL 817-272-5765. FAX 817-272-5802. *4586*

LIBRARIES & CULTURE.
University of Texas Press, Journals Division, Box 7819, Austin, TX 78713. TEL 512-471-3821. FAX 512-320-0668. *4192*

LIBRARY ACQUISITIONS: PRACTICE AND THEORY.
Elsevier Science Ltd., Pergamon, P.O. Box 800, Kidlington, Oxford OX5 1DX, England. TEL 44-1865-843000. FAX 44-1865-843010. *4193*

LIBRARY & ARCHIVAL SECURITY.
Haworth Press, Inc., 10 Alice St., Binghamton, NY 13904. TEL 607-722-5857. FAX 607-722-6362. *4193*

LIBRARY AND INFORMATION SCIENCE.
Mita Society for Library and Information Science, c/o Keio University, 2-15-45 Mita, Minato-ku, Tokyo 108, Japan. TEL 03-3453-3920. FAX 03-3798-7480. *4193*

LIBRARY ASSOCIATION OF CHINA. NEWSLETTER.
Library Association of China, c/o National Central Library, 20 Chung Shan S. Rd., Taipei, Taiwan 10040, Republic of China. FAX 02-382-0747. *4194*

LIBRARY HI TECH JOURNAL.
Pierian Press, Box 1808, Ann Arbor, MI 48106. TEL 313-434-5530. FAX 313-434-6409. *4233*

LIBRARY HISTORY.
Library Association, Library History Group, 7 Ridgmount St., London WC1E 7AE, England. *4194*

LIBRARY MOSAICS.
Yenor, Inc., P.O. Box 5171, Culver City, CA 90231. TEL 310-645-4998. *4195*

LIBRARY OF ANTHROPOLOGY.
Gordon & Breach Science Publishers, c/o International Publishers Distributor, P.O. Box 3054, Langhorne, PA 19047-3054. TEL 215-750-2642. FAX 215-750-6343. *322*

LIBRARY OF PEASANT STUDIES.
Frank Cass, Newbury House, 890-900 Eastern Ave., Newbury Park, Ilford, Essex IG2 7HH, England. TEL 44-181-599-8866. FAX 44-181-599-0984. *3026*

THE LIBRARY QUARTERLY.
University of Chicago Press, Journals Division, Box 37005, Chicago, IL 60637. TEL 773-753-3347. FAX 773-753-0811. *4195*

LIBRES: LIBRARY AND INFORMATION SCIENCE RESEARCH ELECTRONIC JOURNAL.
Dept. of Information Studies, Curtin University of Technology, G.P.O. Box U1987, Perth, WA 6845, Australia. TEL 61-9-3517217. FAX 61-9-3513152. *4196*

LIBRI.
K.G. Saur Verlag KG, A member of the Reed Elsevier plc group, Ortlerstr. 8, 81373 Munich, Germany. TEL 49-89-76902-0. FAX 49-89-76902150. *4196*

LICHENS.
Centro de Investigacion y Reproduccion de Especies Silvestres, Apartado Posta 397, Merida 5101, Venezuela. TEL 58-74-712939. FAX 58-74-712939. *713*

THE LICKING RIVER REVIEW.
Northern Kentucky University, Department of Literature and Language, 500 Landrum Academic Center, Highland Heights, KY 41099. TEL 606-572-6636. FAX 606-572-5566. *4426*

LIER EN BOOG.
Postbus 1718, 1000 BS Amsterdam, Netherlands. FAX 31-20-6221787. *452*

LIETUVIU KALBOTYROS KLAUSIMAI.
Lietuviu Kalbos Institutas, Antakalnio 6, 2055 Vilnius, Lithuania. TEL 370-2-2-226573. FAX 370-2-226573. *4275*

LIETUVOS FIZIKOS ZHURNALAS.
Leidykla Fisica, A. Gostauto 11, 2600 Vilnius, Lithuania. TEL 370-2-619-402. FAX 370-2-618-464. *5813*

LIFE CHEMISTRY REPORTS.
Gordon and Breach - Harwood Academic, Amsteldisk 166, 1st Fl., 1079 LH Amsterdam, Netherlands. *1759*

LIFE SCIENCES.
Elsevier Science Inc., Box 945, New York, NY 10159-0945. TEL 212-633-3730. FAX 212-633-3680. *6543*

LIFE SUPPORT AND BIOSPHERE SCIENCE.
Cognizant Communication Corporation, 3 Hartsdale Rd., Elmsford, NY 10523-3701. TEL 914-592-7720. FAX 914-592-8981. *612*

LIFELINES (TORONTO).
Toronto Vegetarian Association, 736 Bathurst St., Toronto, ON M5S 2R4, Canada. TEL 416-533-3897. *5477*

LIFELONG LEARNING IN EUROPE.
K V S Foundation, c/o LLinE, Museokatu 18 A 2, FIN-00100 Helsinki, Finland. TEL 358-9-549-18-855. FAX 358-9-549-18-811. *2511*

LIFETIME DATA ANALYSIS.
Kluwer Academic Publishers, Postbus 17, 3300 AA Dordrecht, Netherlands. TEL 31-78-6392392. FAX 31-78-6392254. *6923*

LIGHT OF CONSCIOUSNESS.
Truth Consciousness at Desert Ashram., 3403 W. Sweetwater Dr., Tucson, AZ 85745-9301. TEL 520-743-8821. FAX 520-743-3394. *5458*

LIGHT OF LIFE.
Christian Digest Society of India, 21 YMCA Rd., Mumbai 400 008, India. TEL 91-22-3076941. FAX 91-22-3076941. *6353*

LIGHTWORKS.
Lightworks Magazine, Inc., Box 1202, Birmingham, MI 48012-1202. TEL 248-626-8026. FAX 248-737-0046. *452*

LIGUE POUR L'ADAPTATION DU DIMINUE PHYSIQUE AU TRAVAIL. CAHIERS.
Ligue pour l'Adaptation du Diminue Physique au Travail, 102 rue des Poissonniers, 75018 Paris, France. TEL 33-1-53418000. FAX 33-1-53418010. *2587*

LIMBA SI LITERATURA.
Societatea de Stiinte Filologice din Romania, Bd. Schitul Magureanu nr.1, Bucharest, cod 79664, sector 5, Rumania. TEL 40-1-615-1792. *4275*

LIMEN.
Kaos Theatre, *7008*

LIMNETICA.
Asociacion Espanola de Limnologia, Museo Nacional de Ciencias Naturales, C. Jose Gutierrez Abascal, 2, 28006 Madrid, Spain. TEL 91 4649881. FAX 91 3974168. *2396*

LIMNOLOGY AND OCEANOGRAPHY.
American Society of Limnology and Oceanography, Inc., School of Oceanography, WB-10, University of Washington, Seattle, WA 98195. TEL 206-543-0952. FAX 206-543-8655. *2396*

LINCOLN LABORATORY JOURNAL.
Massachusetts Institute of Technology, Lincoln Laboratory, 244 Wood St., Lexington, MA 02173-9108. TEL 617-981-2342. *2645*

LINEAR ALGEBRA AND ITS APPLICATIONS.
Elsevier Science Inc., Box 945, New York, NY 10159-0945. TEL 212-633-3730. FAX 212-633-3680. *4586*

LINEAR AND MULTILINEAR ALGEBRA.
Gordon and Breach - Harwood Academic, Amsteldisk 166, 1st Fl., 1079 LH Amsterdam, Netherlands. *4586*

LINGUA.
North-Holland, P.O. Box 211, 1000 AE Amsterdam, Netherlands. TEL 31-20-4853911. FAX 31-20-4853598. *4275*

LINGUISTIC ANALYSIS.
c/o David Willingham, Man. Ed., Box 2418, Vashon, WA 98070. TEL 206-567-4373. FAX 206-567-5711. *4276*

LINGUISTIC BIBLIOGRAPHY.
Kluwer Academic Publishers, Postbus 17, 3300 AA Dordrecht, Netherlands. TEL 31-78-6392392. FAX 31-78-6392254. *4318*

LINGUISTIC CALCULATION.
Kluwer Academic Publishers, Postbus 17, 3300 AA Dordrecht, Netherlands. TEL 31-78-6392392. FAX 31-78-6392254. *4276*

LINGUISTIC INQUIRY.
M I T Press, 5 Cambridge Center, Cambridge, MA 02142. TEL 617-253-2889. FAX 617-577-1545. *4276*

LINGUISTIC TYPOLOGY.
Walter de Gruyter und Co., Mouton de Gruyter, Genthiner Str. 13, 10785 Berlin, Germany. TEL 49-30-260050. FAX 49-30-26005222. *4276*

LINGUISTICA SILESIANA.
Polska Akademia Nauk, Oddzial w Katowicach, Ul. Graniczna 32, 40-018 Katowice, Poland. *4277*

LINGUISTICS ABSTRACTS.
Blackwell Publishers Ltd., 108 Cowley Rd., Oxford OX4 1JF, England. TEL 44-1865-791100. FAX 44-1865-791347. *4319*

LINGUISTICS AND PHILOSOPHY.
Kluwer Academic Publishers, Postbus 17, 3300 AA Dordrecht, Netherlands. TEL 31-78-6392392. FAX 31-78-6392254. *4277*

LINGUISTICS OF THE TIBETO - BURMAN AREA.
University of California at Berkeley, Department of Linguistics, 2337 Dwinelle Hall, Berkeley, CA 94720. TEL 510-643-9910. FAX 510-643-9911. *4277*

LINKS.
Southern Links Magazine Publishing Associates, 1040 William Hilton Pkwy., Ste. 200, Hilton Head Island, SC 29938. TEL 803-842-6200. FAX 803-842-6233. *6810*

LINNEAN SOCIETY OF NEW SOUTH WALES. PROCEEDINGS.
Southwood Press Pty. Ltd., P.O. Box 457, Milsons Point, N.S.W. 2061, Australia. TEL 61-2-99290253. *781*

LINNEANA BELGICA.
c/o R. Leestmans, Ed., Krabbosstraat 179, 1653 Beersel Dworp, Belgium. TEL 32-2-3803979. *758*

LINYE KEXUE.
Science Press, Marketing and Sales Department, 16 Donghuangchenggen North St., Beijing 100717, People's Republic of China. TEL 4010642. FAX 4019810. *3158*

THE LION AND THE UNICORN.
Johns Hopkins University Press, Journals Publishing Division, 2715 N. Charles St., Baltimore, MD 21218. TEL 410-516-6987. FAX 410-516-6968. *4427*

LIPID TECHNOLOGY NEWSLETTER.
P.J. Barnes & Associates, P.O. Box 345, High Wycombe HP10 9HL, England. *665*

LIPIDS.
A O C S Press, 1608 Broadmoor Dr., Box 3489, Champaign, IL 61821-0489. TEL 217-359-2344. FAX 217-351-8091. *665*

LIPPINCOTT-RAVEN PRESS SERIES IN PHYSIOLOGY.
Lippincott - Raven Publishers, 227 E. Washington Sq., Philadelphia, PA 19106. TEL 215-238-4200. FAX 215-238-4227. *819*

LIQUID CRYSTALS.
Taylor & Francis Ltd., 1 Gunpowder Sq., London EC4A 3DE, England. TEL 44-171-583-0490. FAX 44-171-583-0585. *1802*

LIQUID CRYSTALS TODAY.
Taylor & Francis Inc., 1900 Frost Rd., Ste. 101, Bristol, PA 19007-1598. TEL 215-785-5800. FAX 215-785-5515. *1802*

LISHI DANG'AN.
Historical Archives Magazine House, Palace Museum inside Xihuamen, Beijing 100031, People's Republic of China. TEL 86-10-6309-7399. FAX 86-10-6309-6489. *3536*

LISZT SAECULUM.
International Liszt Centre, Synaalsvaegen 5, S-161 49 Bromma, Sweden. TEL 46-8-25-17-16. FAX 46-8-25-17-36. *5408*

LITERACY LINK.
Australian Council For Adult Literacy, G.P.O. Box 2283, Canberra, A.C.T. 2601, Australia. *2511*

LITERARY CRITERION.
c/o English Dept., Bangalore University, Jnana Bharathi, Bangalore 560 056, India. TEL 91-80-3355299. *4343*

LITERARY REVIEW.
Fairleigh Dickinson University, Literary Review, 285 Madison Ave., Madison, NJ 07940. TEL 201-443-8564. *4428*

LITERATOR.
Buro vir Wetenskaplike Tydskrifte, Private Bag X6001, Potchefstroom 2520, South Africa. TEL 27-148-2991769. FAX 27-148-2991562. *4278*

LITERATURA MEXICANA.
Universidad Nacional Autonoma de Mexico, Instituto de Investigaciones Filologicas, Circuito Mario de la Cueva, Zona Cultural, Ciudad Universitaria, 04510 Mexico, D.F., Mexico. TEL 52-5-6227493. FAX 52-5-6657874. *4428*

LITERATURE AND AESTHETICS.
Sydney Society of Literature and Aesthetics, c/o Dept. of English, University of Sydney, Sydney, N.S.W. 2006, Australia. TEL 61-2-93512349. FAX 61-2-93512434. *4429*

LITERATURE AND BELIEF.
Brigham Young University, College of Humanities, Center, Study of Christian Values in Literature, 3076F Jesse Knight Bldg., Provo, UT 84604-9989. TEL 801-378-3073. FAX 801-378-4720. *6353*

LITERATURE - FILM QUARTERLY.
Salisbury State University, Salisbury, MD 21801. TEL 410-543-6446. FAX 410-543-6068. *5339*

LITHOLOGY AND MINERAL RESOURCES.
Maik Nauka - Interperiodica, Mezhdunarodnyi Otdel, Ul. Profsoyuznaya, 90, 117864 Moscow, Russia. TEL 7-095-3360066. FAX 7-095-3360666. *2355*

LITHOS.
Elsevier Science B.V., P.O. Box 211, 1000 AE Amsterdam, Netherlands. TEL 31-20-4853911. FAX 31-20-4853598. *2356*

LITHUANIAN MATHEMATICAL JOURNAL.
Plenum Publishing Corp., Consultants Bureau, 233 Spring St., New York, NY 10013-1578. TEL 212-620-8468. FAX 212-463-0742. *4586*

LITHUANIAN PAPERS.
Tasmanian University, Lithuanian Studies Society, P.O. Box 777, Sandy Bay, Tas. 7005, Australia. TEL 61-3-62252505. *3026*

LITURGY NEWS.
Archdiocese of Brisbane, Liturgical Commission, G.P.O. Box 282, Brisbane, Qld. 4001, Australia. TEL 61-7-32243329. FAX 61-7-32211705. *6468*

LIUTI LIXUE SHIYAN YU CELIANG.
Zhongguo Kongqi Dongli Yanjiu yu Fazhan Zhongxin, P.O. Box 211, Mianyang, Sichuan 621000, People's Republic of China. TEL 86-816-2364034. *5846*

LIVER.
Munksgaard International Publishers Ltd., 35 Noerre Soegade, P.O. Box 2148, DK-1016 Copenhagen K, Denmark. TEL 45-33-127030. FAX 45-33-129387. *4913*

LIVER TRANSPLANTATION AND SURGERY.
W.B. Saunders Co., Curtis Center, 3rd Fl., Independence Sq., W., Philadelphia, PA 19106-3399. TEL 215-238-7800. FAX 215-238-3445. *4913*

LIVERPOOL LAW REVIEW.
Deborah Charles Publications, 173 Mather Ave., Liverpool L18 6JZ, England. TEL 44-151-724-2500. FAX 44-151-729-0371. *3984*

LIVERPOOL STUDIES IN LANGUAGE AND DISCOURSE.
University of Liverpool, Department of English Language and Literature, Modern Languages Bldg., P.O. Box 147, Liverpool L69 3BX, England. TEL 44-151-794-2705. FAX 44-151-794-2730. *4278*

LIVESTOCK PRODUCTION SCIENCE.
Elsevier Science B.V., P.O. Box 211, 1000 AE Amsterdam, Netherlands. TEL 31-20-4853911. FAX 31-20-4853598. *281*

LIVING (GROTTOES).
Shalom Foundation, Inc., Rte. 2, Box 656, Grottoes, VA 24441. TEL 540-249-3177. FAX 540-249-3177. *6719*

LIVING WORLD.
International Life Services, Inc., 2606 1-2 W. 8th St., Los Angeles, CA 90057. TEL 213-382-2156. FAX 213-382-4203. *6676*

LIVRUSTKAMMAREN.
Kungliga Livrustkammaren, Kungliga Slottet, Slottsbacken 3, S-111 30 Stockholm, Sweden. TEL 46-8-666-44-68. FAX 46-8-666-44-68. *5357*

LIXUE JINZHAN.
Zhongguo Kexueyuan, Lixue Yanjiusuo, 15 Zhongguancun Lu, Beijing 100080, People's Republic of China. TEL 2554108. FAX 86-1-2561284. *5846*

LIXUE XUEBAO.
Science Press, Marketing and Sales Department, 16 Donghuangchenggen North St., Beijing 100717, People's Republic of China. TEL 4010642. FAX 4019810. *5846*

LIXUE YU SHIJIAN.
Science Press, Marketing and Sales Department, 16 Donghuangchenggen North St., Beijing 100717, People's Republic of China. TEL 4010642. FAX 4019810. *2892*

LOCAL ECONOMY.
Pitman Publishing, 128 Long Acre, London WC2E 9AN, England. TEL 44-171-447-2000. FAX 44-171-240-5771. *982*

LOCAL GOVERNMENT POLICY MAKING.
Pitman Publishing, 128 Long Acre, London WC2E 9AN, England. TEL 44-171-447-2000. FAX 44-171-240-5771. *6218*

LOCAL GOVERNMENT STUDIES.
Frank Cass, Newbury House, 890-900 Eastern Ave., Newbury Park, Ilford, Essex IG2 7HH, England. TEL 44-181-599-8866. FAX 44-181-599-0984. *6219*

LOCAL POPULATION STUDIES.
University of Essex, Department of History, LPS General Office, Colchester CO4 3SQ, England. TEL 44-1206-872190. *6053*

LOCATION SCIENCE.
Elsevier Science Ltd., Pergamon, P.O. Box 800, Kidlington, Oxford OX5 1DX, England. TEL 44-1865-843000. FAX 44-1865-843010. *6134*

LOEB CLASSICAL LIBRARY.
Harvard University Press, 79 Garden St., Cambridge, MA 02138. TEL 617-495-2600. FAX 617-495-5898. *4430*

LOG OF MYSTIC SEAPORT.
Mystic Seaport Museum, Inc., Mystic, CT 06355-0990. TEL 203-572-5347. FAX 203-572-5326. *5358*

LOGISTICA MANAGEMENT.
Edizioni Ritman s.r.l., Via Varesina 76, 20156 Milan, Italy. TEL 39-2-38008859. FAX 39-2-38008828. *1491*

LOGOS.
Whurr Publishers Ltd., 19b Compton Terrace, London N1 2UN, England. TEL 44-171-359-5979. FAX 44-171-226-5290. *6277*

LONDON GERMAN STUDIES.
University of London, Institute of Germanic Studies, 29 Russell Sq., London WC1B 5DP, England. TEL 44-171-580-2711. FAX 44-171-436-3497. *4430*

LONDON JOURNAL.
London Journal Trust, c/o Centre for Metropolitan History, Senate House, Rm. 351, Malet St., London WC1E 7HU, England. TEL 44-171-636-0272. FAX 44-171-436-2183. *3581*

LONDON MATHEMATICAL SOCIETY. BULLETIN.
London Mathematical Society, Burlington House, Picadilly, London W1V ONL, England. TEL 44-171-437-5377. FAX 44-171-439-4629. *4586*

LONDON MATHEMATICAL SOCIETY. JOURNAL.
Cambridge University Press, Edinburgh House, Shaftesbury Rd., Cambridge CB2 2RU, England. TEL 44-1223-312393. FAX 44-1223-315052. *4586*

LONDON MATHEMATICAL SOCIETY. MONOGRAPHS.
Academic Press, Inc., 525 B St., Ste. 1900, San Diego, CA 92101-4495. TEL 619-231-0926. FAX 619-699-6715. *4587*

LONG ISLAND HISTORICAL JOURNAL.
State University of New York at Stony Brook, Department of History, Stony Brook, NY 11794-4348. TEL 516-632-7500. FAX 516-632-7367. *3635*

LONG ISLAND POSTAL HISTORIAN.
Long Island Postal History Society, 144 Hamilton Ave., Clifton, NJ 07011. TEL 201-772-1413. *2019*

LONG RANGE PLANNING.
Elsevier Science Ltd., Pergamon, P.O. Box 800, Kidlington, Oxford OX5 1DX, England. TEL 44-1865-843000. FAX 44-1865-843010. *1492*

LONGITUDINAL RESEARCH IN THE BEHAVIORAL, SOCIAL AND MEDICAL SCIENCES.
Kluwer Academic Publishers, Postbus 17, 3300 AA Dordrecht, Netherlands. TEL 31-78-6392392. FAX 31-78-6392254. *6625*

THE LONSDALE.
Vagabond Press, VIP Meguro 802, 4-1-16 Shimo-Meguro, Meguro-ku, Tokyo 153, Japan. TEL 81-3-5721-9979. FAX 81-3-5721-9979. *4513*

LOOP TRANSFORMATIONS FOR RESTRUCTURING COMPILERS.
Kluwer Academic Publishers, Postbus 17, 3300 AA Dordrecht, Netherlands. TEL 31-78-6392392. FAX 31-78-6392254. *2116*

LORIS.
Wildlife & Nature Protection Society of Sri Lanka, Chaitiya Rd., Fort, Colombo 1, Sri Lanka. TEL 25248. FAX 941-580721. *2236*

LOS ALAMOS SERIES IN BASIC AND APPLIED SCIENCES.
University of California Press, 2120 Berkeley Way, Berkeley, CA 94720. TEL 510-642-4247. FAX 510-643-7127. *6543*

LOS ANGELES.
11100 Santa Monica Blvd., 7th Fl., Los Angeles, CA 90025. TEL 310-477-1181. *3377*

LOS ANGELES LAWYER.
Los Angeles County Bar Association, Box 55020, Los Angeles, CA 90055. TEL 213-896-6503. FAX 213-623-2348. *3984*

LOSINKA.
Losinka, Letchika Babushkina ul., 1, 129344 Moscow, Russia. *6219*

LOSS, GRIEF & CARE.
Haworth Press, Inc., 10 Alice St., Binghamton, NY 13904. TEL 607-722-5857. FAX 607-722-6362. *6134*

LOSS PREVENTION BULLETIN.
Institution of Chemical Engineers, George E. Davis Bldg., 165-189 Railway Terr., Rugby, Warks. CV21 3HQ, England. TEL 44-1788-578214. FAX 44-1788-560833. *2768*

LOUISIANA ACADEMY OF SCIENCES. PROCEEDINGS.
Louisiana Academy of Sciences, c/o Ms. Ella Edwards, Archivist, Centenary College, Ruston, LA 71272. *6544*

LOUISIANA AGRICULTURE.
Louisiana State University, Agricultural Center, Box 25100, Baton Rouge, LA 70894-5100. TEL 504-388-2263. FAX 504-388-4524. *134*

LOUISIANA ENGLISH JOURNAL.
Louisiana Council of Teachers of English, Louisiana State University at Eunice, Box 1129, Eunice, LA 70535. TEL 318-457-7311. FAX 318-546-6620. *4279*

LOUISIANA LAW REVIEW.
Louisiana State University, Law Center, Baton Rouge, LA 70803. TEL 504-388-1683. FAX 504-388-1685. *3985*

LOUISIANA LITERATURE.
Southeastern Louisiana University, English Department, SLU-792, Hammond, LA 70402. TEL 504-549-5022. FAX 504-549-5021. *4431*

LOUISIANA STATE MEDICAL SOCIETY. JOURNAL.
Journal of the Louisiana State Medical Society, Inc., 3501 N. Causeway Blvd., Ste. 800, Metairie, LA 70002-3625. TEL 504-832-9815. FAX 504-833-7685. *4703*

LOUISVILLE MEDICINE.
Jefferson County Medical Society, 101 W. Chestnut, Louisville, KY 40202-1805. TEL 502-589-2001. FAX 502-581-9022. *3825*

LOUVAIN STUDIES.
Katholieke Universiteit Leuven, Faculteit Godgeleerdheid, St. Michielsstraat 2, B-3000 Leuven, Belgium. TEL 32-16-283894. FAX 32-16-283858. *6353*

LOVE AND RAGE.
Box 853, New York, NY 10009-0853. TEL 718-834-9077. *5942*

LOW INTENSITY CONFLICT & LAW ENFORCEMENT.
Frank Cass, Newbury House, 890-900 Eastern Ave., Newbury Park, Ilford, Essex IG2 7HH, England. TEL 44-181-599-8866. FAX 44-181-599-0984. *6025*

LOWER EXTREMITY.
Churchill Livingstone, 650 Ave. of the Americas, New York, NY 10011. TEL 212-206-5040. FAX 212-727-7808. *4704*

LOYOLA JOURNAL OF SOCIAL SCIENCES.
Loyola College of Social Sciences, Thiruvananthapuram 695 017, India. TEL 91-471-445097. *6625*

LUBELSKIE WIADOMOSCI NUMIZMATYCZNE.
Polskie Towarzystwo Numizmatyczne, Oddzial w Lublinie, c/o Prof. Dr. Edward Soczewinski, Ul. Staszica 6, 20-081 Lublin, Poland. TEL 48-81-5320413. FAX 48-81-5328903. *5465*

LUBRICATION ENGINEERING.
Society of Tribologists and Lubrication Engineers, 840 Busse Hwy., Park Ridge, IL 60068-2376. TEL 847-825-5536. FAX 847-825-1456. *2892*

LUBRICATION SCIENCE.
Leaf Coppin Publishing Co., P.O. Box 111, Deal, Kent CT14 6SX, England. TEL 44-1304-360241. FAX 44-1304-360241. *5609*

LUCIANO MANARA.
Associazione Nazionale Bersaglieri, Via V. Monti 59, 20145 Milan, Italy. TEL 39-2-48010925. *3582*

LUCKNOW LIBRARIAN.
Uttar Pradesh Library Association, Lucknow Branch, U.P. Library Association, P.O. Box 446, Lucknow 226 001, India. TEL 91-522-211547. FAX 91-522-228227. *4196*

LUNG.
Springer-Verlag, Medical Journals, 175 Fifth Ave., New York, NY 10010. TEL 212-460-1500. FAX 212-473-6272. *5120*

LUNG BIOLOGY IN HEALTH AND DISEASE.
Marcel Dekker, Inc., 270 Madison Ave., New York, NY 10016. TEL 212-696-9000. FAX 212-685-4540. *5120*

LUNG CANCER.
Elsevier Science Ireland Ltd., P.O. Box 85, Limerick, Ireland. TEL 353-61-471944. FAX 353-61-472144. *4982*

LUSITANIA SACRA.
Universidade Catolica Portuguesa, Centro de Estudos de Historia Religiosa, Palma de Cima, 1600 Lisbon, Portugal. TEL 351-1-7214130. FAX 351-1-7270256. *6354*

LUTHERAN WOMAN'S QUARTERLY.
Lutheran Church - Missouri Synod, Lutheran Women's Missionary League, 3558 S. Jefferson Ave., St. Louis, MO 63118-3910. TEL 314-268-1531. *6432*

LUTHERSK BARNTIDNING.
Missionssaellskapet Bibeltrogna Vaenner, P.O. Box 6160, S-102 33 Stockholm, Sweden. TEL 46-8-33-25-23. FAX 46-8-34-58-18. *6433*

LUTRA.
Bureau V Z Z, Emmalaan 41, 3581 HP Utrecht, Netherlands. TEL 31-30-2544642. *841*

LUZO - BRAZILIAN REVIEW.
University of Wisconsin Press, Journal Division, 114 N. Murray St., Madison, WI 53715. TEL 608-262-4952. FAX 608-262-7560. *4344*

LYMPHOLOGY.
International Society of Lymphology, c/o Dr. Charles L. Witte, Ed., Dept. of Surgery - Trauma, Arizona Health Sciences Center, Box 245063, Tucson, AZ 85724-5063. TEL 520-626-6118. FAX 520-626-0822. *4890*

LYNX.
A H A Books, Box 1250, Gualala, CA 95445-0767. TEL 707-882-2226. *4513*

LYON PHARMACEUTIQUE.
Editions Scientifiques et Medicales Elsevier, 141 rue de Javel, 75747 Paris, France. TEL 33-1-45589026. FAX 33-1-45589421. *5676*

LYSOSOMES IN BIOLOGY AND PATHOLOGY.
Elsevier Science B.V., Books Division, P.O. Box 211, 1000 AE Amsterdam, Netherlands. TEL 31-20-4853911. FAX 31-20-4853705. *612*

LYTS FRISIA.
Jongfryske Mienskip, Julianalaan 26, 9801 BP Zuidhorn, Netherlands. TEL 31-594-502829. *4344*

M A R D I REPORT.
Malaysian Agricultural Research & Development Institute, P.O. Box 12301, General Post Office, 50774 Kuala Lumpur, Malaysia. TEL 03-9437236. FAX 03-9482216. *135*

M COMPUTING.
M Technology Association, 1738 Elton Rd., Ste. 205, Silver Spring, MD 20903. TEL 301-431-4070. FAX 301-431-0017. *2145*

M.D. COMPUTING (NEW YORK).
Springer-Verlag, Medical Journals, 175 Fifth Ave., New York, NY 10010. TEL 212-460-1500. FAX 212-473-4262. *4847*

M E L A NOTES.
Middle East Librarians Association, c/o Mary St. Germain, Secy., Cataloging, Suzallo Library, U. of WA, Box 352900, Seattle, WA 98195-2900. TEL 206-543-1828. FAX 206-685-8049. *4197*

M E L U S.
Society for the Study of the Multi-Ethnic Literature of the United States, 272 Bartlett Hall, Department of English, University of Massachusetts, Amherst, MA 01003. TEL 413-545-3166. FAX 413-545-3880. *4431*

M G V.
Nederlands Centrum Geestelijke Volksgezondheid, Postbus 5103, 3502 JC Utrecht, Netherlands. TEL 31-2154-82211. *5079*

M I M S IRELAND.
Medical Publications (Ireland) Ltd., 15 Harcourt St., Dublin 2, Ireland. TEL 353-1-4757461. FAX 353-1-757467. *4704*

M R S INTERNET JOURNAL OF NITRIDE SEMICONDUCTOR RESEARCH.
Materials Research Society, 9800 McKnight Rd., Pittsburg, PA 15237. TEL 412-307-3003. FAX 412-307-3000. *2864*

M S L A JOURNAL.
Manitoba School Library Association, c/o Manitoba Teachers' Society, 191 Harcourt St., Winnipeg, Man. R3J 3H2, Canada. TEL 204-888-7961. *2610*

M UND A REPORT.
M und A Verlag fuer Messen, Ausstellungen und Kongresse GmbH, Postfach 101528, 60015 Frankfurt a.M., Germany. TEL 49-69-759502. FAX 49-69-75951280. *39*

MCCALLUM OBSERVER.
Box 313, Lansing, IL 60438-0313. TEL 708-895-0736. *575*

MACCOM. *2198*

MACEDONIAN TRIBUNE.
Macedonian Patriotic Organization of the U S and Canada, 124 W. Wayne, Fort Wayne, IN 46802-2505. TEL 219-422-5900. FAX 219-422-1348. *1934*

MCGILL LAW JOURNAL.
McGill Law Journal, Chancellor Day Hall, 3644 Peel St., Montreal, PQ H3A 1W9, Canada. TEL 514-874-9038. FAX 514-874-0679. *3985*

MCGOLDRICK'S CANADIAN CUSTOMS GUIDE "HARMONIZED SYSTEM".
McMullin Publishers Ltd., 417 St. Pierre, Montreal, PQ H2Y 2M4, Canada. TEL 514-849-1424. FAX 514-849-9809. *1340*

THE MCGUFFEY WRITER & ILLUSTRATOR.
McGuffey Foundation School, 5128 Westgate Dr., Oxford, OH 45056. TEL 513-523-7742. FAX 513-523-5565. *1879*

THE MACGUFFIN.
Schoolcraft College, English Department, Schoolcraft College, 18600 Haggerty Rd., Livonia, MI 48152. TEL 313-462-4400. FAX 313-462-4558. *4431*

MACH.
Mach, P.O. Box 5002, S-161 05 Bromma, Sweden. TEL 46008-17-88-50. FAX 46-08-17-88-55. *74*

MACHETE.
Machete Press, Box 605, Cooper Sq. Sta., New York, NY 10276. TEL 718-237-1471. *4431*

MACHINE DYNAMICS PROBLEMS.
Wydawnictwo M E T, c/o Mieczyslaw Pekalak, Ul. Piekalkiewicza 5 m.6, 00-710 Warsaw, Poland. TEL 48-22-490195. FAX 48-22-490306. *2892*

MACHINE INTELLIGENCE AND PATTERN RECOGNITION.
Elsevier Science B.V., Books Division, P.O. Box 211, 1000 AE Amsterdam, Netherlands. TEL 31-20-4853911. FAX 31-20-4853705. *2103*

MACHINE LEARNING.
Kluwer Academic Publishers Boston, Box 358, Accord Sta., Hingham, MA 02018-0358. TEL 617-871-6300. FAX 617-871-6528. *2086*

MACHINE LEARNING ONLINE.
Kluwer Academic Publishers Boston, Box 358, Accord Sta., Hingham, MA 02018-0358. TEL 617-871-6600. FAX 617-871-6528. *2087*

MACHINE TRANSLATION.
Kluwer Academic Publishers, Postbus 17, 3300 AA Dordrecht, Netherlands. TEL 31-78-6392392. FAX 31-78-6392254. *4320*

MCILVAINEA.
North American Mycological Association, 3556 Oakwood, Ann Arbor, MI 48104-5213. TEL 313-971-2552. *713*

MACROMOLECULES.
American Chemical Society, 1155 16th St., N.W., Washington, DC 20036. TEL 800-333-9511. FAX 614-447-3671. *1818*

MADISON REVIEW (TALLAHASSEE).
James Madison Institute for Public Policy, P.O. Box 13894, Tallahassee, FL 32317-3894. TEL 904-386-3131. FAX 904-386-1807. *5942*

MADRAS AGRICULTURAL JOURNAL.
Madras Agricultural Students' Union, Tamil Nadu Agricultural University Campus, Coimbatore 641 003, India. *135*

MADRE.
Madre, Inc., 121 W. 27th St., Rm. 301, New York, NY 10001. *7326*

MAGAZINE OF ALBEMARLE COUNTY HISTORY.
Albemarle County Historical Society, Publications Committee, 200 Second St., N.E., Charlottesville, VA 22902. TEL 804-296-1492. FAX 804-296-4576. *3636*

MAGAZINE OF CONCRETE RESEARCH.
Thomas Telford Services Ltd., Thomas Telford House, 1 Heron Quay, London E14 4JD, England. TEL 44-171-987-6999. FAX 44-171-538-9620. *902*

MAGNES NEWS.
Judah L. Magnes Museum, 2911 Russell St., Berkeley, CA 94705. TEL 510-549-6950. FAX 510-849-3673. *5358*

MAGNETIC AND ELECTRICAL SEPARATION.
Gordon and Breach - Harwood Academic, Amsteldisk 166, 1st Fl., 1079 LH Amsterdam, Netherlands. *5814*

MAGNETIC RESONANCE IMAGING.
Elsevier Science Inc., Box 945, New York, NY 10159-0945. TEL 212-633-3730. FAX 212-633-3680. *5110*

MAGNETIC RESONANCE IN CHEMISTRY.
John Wiley & Sons Ltd., Journals, Baffins Ln., Chichester, W. Sussex PO19 1UD, England. TEL 44-1243-779777. FAX 44-1243-775878. *1832*

MAGNETIC RESONANCE IN MEDICINE.
Williams & Wilkins, 351 W. Camden St., Baltimore, MD 21201-2436. TEL 410-528-4068. FAX 410-528-4452. *5111*

MAGNETIC RESONANCE MATERIALS IN PHYSICS, BIOLOGY AND MEDICINE.
Chapman & Hall, Journals Department 2-6 Boundary Row, London SE1 8HN, England. TEL 44-171-8560066. FAX 44-171-5229623. *5853*

MAGNETIC RESONANCE REVIEW.
Gordon and Breach - Harwood Academic, Amsteldisk 166, 1st Fl., 1079 LH Amsterdam, Netherlands. *5814*

MAGNETOHYDRODYNAMICS.
Plenum Publishing Corp., Consultants Bureau, 233 Spring St., New York, NY 10013-1578. TEL 212-620-8468. FAX 212-463-0742. *2839*

MAGNETS IN YOUR FUTURE.
A Z Printing Co., 4000 Highway 62, Ste. 102, Hardy, AR 72542-9550. TEL 870-856-3877. FAX 870-856-3840. *2839*

MAGYAR EGYHAZTORTENETI VAZLATOK.
M E T E M - International Society of Toronto for Hungarian Church History, Regis College, 15 St. Mary St., Toronto, ON M4Y 2R5, Canada. TEL 416-922-2476. FAX 416-225-3814. *3582*

MAGYAR NYELVOR.
Magyar Tudomanyos Akademia, Magyar Nyelvi Bizottsaga, Piarista Koz 1, 1052 Budapest, Hungary. TEL 36-1-2670966. *4279*

MAGYAR PEDAGOGIA.
Jozsef Attila Tudomanyegyetem, Department of Education, Petofi sgt. 30-34, 6722 Szeged, Hungary. TEL 36-62-321034. *2461*

MAI PIAC.
Magyar Szakkkiado Kft, Pozsonyi ut 54, 1133 Budapest, Hungary. TEL 36-1-3443235. FAX 36-1-3443237. *1695*

MAILOUT.
Mailout Trust, Kirklees Media Centre, 7 Northumberland St., Huddersfield HD1 1RL, England. TEL 44-1484-469009. FAX 44-1484-469009. *453*

LA MAIN.
Blackwell Science Ltd. (Paris), Arnette S.A., 224 bd. Saint-Germain, 75007 Paris, France. TEL 33-1-45496525. FAX 33-1-45491245. *5148*

MAINE HISTORY.
Maine Historical Society, 485 Congress St., Portland, ME 04101. TEL 207-744-1822. FAX 207-775-4301. *3636*

MAINE IN PRINT.
Maine Writers & Publishers Alliance, 12 Pleasant St., Brunswick, ME 04011-1513. *4432*

MAJALAH U S U.
University of North Sumatra, Jl. Dr. Mansur, Kampus USU, Medan 20155, Indonesia. TEL 62-61-524033. FAX 62-61-520822. *2548*

MAJALLAT AL-ALUM AL-INSANNYAH AL-ILEJTIMAEYAH.
Jami'at al-Imarat al-Arabiyyah al-Muttahidah, Kulliyyat al-Aadaab, P.O. Box 17771, Al-Ain, United Arab Emirates. TEL 971-3-678007. FAX 971-3-671612. *3785*

MAJALLAT AL-IMARAT LIL-'ULUM AL-ZIRA'IYYAH.
United Arab Emirates University, Faculty of Agriculture, P.O. Box 17555, Al-Ain, United Arab Emirates. TEL 971-3-635647. FAX 971-3-632384. *135*

MAJALLAT AL-SHARI'AH WAL-QANUN.
United Arab Emirates University, Faculty of Law and Islamic Jurisprudence, P.O. Box 15551, Al-Ain, United Arab Emirates. TEL 643998. FAX 660655. *3986*

MAJALLAT AL-WAHDAH AL-IQTISADIYYAH AL-ARABIYYAH.
Majlis al-Wahdah al-Iqtisadiyyah al-Arabiyyah, Al-Amanah al-Aamah, P.O. Box 925100, Amman, Jordan. TEL 664329. *1308*

MAJOR HEALTH ISSUES.
Elsevier Science B.V., Books Division, P.O. Box 211, 1000 AE Amsterdam, Netherlands. TEL 31-20-4853911. FAX 31-20-4853705. *6243*

MARJORIE KINNAN RAWLINGS JOURNAL OF FLORIDA LITERATURE.
Illinois State University, Department of English, Normal, IL 61790-4240. TEL 309-438-5776. FAX 309-438-5414. *4432*

MAKING SENSE OF SCIENCE.
Portland Press Ltd., 59 Portland Pl., London W1N 3AJ, England. TEL 44-171-580-5530. FAX 44-171-323-1136. *1879*

MALAYSIAN APPLIED BIOLOGY JOURNAL.
Malaysian Society of Applied Biology, c/o Faculty of Science, Universiti Kebangsaan Malaysia, 43600 UKM, Bangi, Selangor, Malaysia. *135*

MALAYSIAN JOURNAL OF SCIENCE SERIES A: LIFE SCIENCES.
University of Malaya, Lembah Pantai, 59100 Kuala Lumpur, Malaysia. TEL 565000. *613*

MALTA NATIONAL BIBLIOGRAPHY.
National Library of Malta, 36 Old Treasury St., Valletta, Malta. TEL 356-236585. FAX 356-235992. *556*

MAMMAL REVIEW.
Blackwell Science Ltd., Osney Mead, Oxford OX2 0EL, England. TEL 44-1865-206206. FAX 44-1865-721205. *842*

MAMMALIA.
Museum National d'Histoire Naturelle, Mammiferes et Oiseaux, 55 rue Buffon, 75005 Paris, France. TEL 33-1-40793069. FAX 33-1-40793063. *842*

MAMMALIAN GENOME.
Springer-Verlag, Life Science Journals, 175 Fifth Ave., New York, NY 10010. TEL 212-460-1500. FAX 212-473-6272. *773*

MAMMALIAN SPECIES.
American Society of Mammalogists, c/o Dr. H. Duane Smith, Sec.-Treas., Monte L. Bean Life Science Museum, Brigham Young University, Provo, UT 84602. TEL 801-378-2492. *842*

MAN AND WORLD.
Kluwer Academic Publishers, Postbus 17, 3300 AA Dordrecht, Netherlands. TEL 31-78-6392392. FAX 31-78-6392254. *5736*

MAN MAGNUM.
South Africa Man Pty. Ltd., P.O. Box 35204, Northway 4065, South Africa. TEL 27-31-526551. FAX 27-31-5628389. *6874*

MANA.
Universidade Federal dc Rio de Janeiro, Departamento de Antropologia, Quinta da Boa Vista s-n, Sao Cristovao, 20940-040 Rio de Janeiro RJ, Brazil. TEL 55-21-5689642. FAX 55-21-2546695. *323*

MANAGEMENT AND AVOIDANCE OF COMPLICATIONS IN EYELID SURGERY.
Field & Wood, Medical Periodicals, Inc., Box 975, Blue Bell, PA 19422. TEL 610-828-4010. FAX 215-482-0226. *5148*

MANAGEMENT DEVELOPMENT.
Bangladesh Management Development Centre, Mirpur Rd., Dhaka 7, Bangladesh. TEL 802-817405-7. FAX 802-814304. *1493*

MANAGEMENT IN EDUCATION.
Pitman Publishing, 128 Long Acre, London WC2E 9AN, England. TEL 44-171-447-2000. FAX 44-171-240-5771. *1493*

MANAGERIAL AND DECISION ECONOMICS.
John Wiley & Sons Ltd., Journals, Baffins Ln., Chichester, W. Sussex PO19 1UD, England. TEL 44-1243-779777. FAX 44-1243-775878. *1495*

MANAGERSEMINARE.
ManagerSeminare Gerhard May Verlags GmbH, Endenicherstr. 282, 53121 Bonn, Germany. TEL 49-228-97791-0. FAX 49-228-616164. *1495*

MANCHESTER SCHOOL OF ECONOMIC AND SOCIAL STUDIES.
Blackwell Publishers Ltd., 108 Cowley Rd., Oxford OX4 1JF, England. TEL 44-1865-791100. FAX 44-1865-791347. *1309*

THE MANEATER.
University of Missouri at Columbia, A038 Brady Commons, Columbia, MO 65211. TEL 314-882-8500. FAX 314-882-5550. *1960*

MANKIND QUARTERLY.
Scott - Townsend Publishers, Box 34070, N.W., Washington, DC 20043. TEL 202-371-2700. FAX 202-371-1523. *323*

MANOA.
University of Hawaii Press, Journals Department, 2840 Kolowalu St., Honolulu, HI 96822. TEL 808-956-8833. FAX 808-988-6052. *4433*

MANSOURA JOURNAL OF PHARMACEUTICAL SCIENCES.
University of Mansoura, Faculty of Pharmacy, University P.O. 35516, Mansoura, Egypt. *5677*

MANUAL THERAPY.
Churchill Livingstone, Robert Stevenson House, 1-3 Baxter's Pl., Leith Walk, Edinburgh EH1 3AF, Scotland. TEL 44-131-556-2424. FAX 44-131-535-1704. *5044*

MANUFACTURING RESEARCH AND TECHNOLOGY.
Elsevier Science B.V., Books Division, P.O. Box 211, 1000 AE Amsterdam, Netherlands. TEL 31-20-4853911. FAX 31-20-4853705. *1590*

MANUFACTURING REVIEW.
American Society of Mechanical Engineers, 22 Law Dr., Fairfield, NJ 07007-2300. TEL 201-882-1170. FAX 201-882-5155. *6966*

MANYU YANJIU.
Heilongjiang Manyu Yanjiusuo, 74 Qingbin Rd., Nangang, Harbin, Heilongjiang 150080, People's Republic of China. TEL 6303931. *5532*

MARCOLIAN.
Marietta College, Box A-20, Marietta, OH 45750-4000. TEL 614-376-4937. FAX 614-376-4810. *1960*

MARINE AND FRESHWATER BEHAVIOUR AND PHYSIOLOGY.
Gordon and Breach - Harwood Academic, Amsteldisk 166, 1st Fl., 1079 LH Amsterdam, Netherlands. *613*

MARINE AND PETROLEUM GEOLOGY.
Elsevier Science Ltd., P.O. Box 800, Kidlington, Oxford OX5 1DX, England. TEL 44-1865-843000. FAX 44-1865-843010. *2356*

MARINE BIOLOGICAL ASSOCIATION OF THE UNITED KINGDOM. JOURNAL.
Cambridge University Press, Edinburgh Bldg., Shaftesbury Rd., Cambridge CB2 2RU, England. TEL 44-1223-312393. FAX 44-1223-315052. *613*

MARINE BIOLOGICAL ASSOCIATION OF THE UNITED KINGDOM. OCCASIONAL PUBLICATIONS.
Marine Biological Association of the United Kingdom, Citadel Hill, Plymouth PL1 2PB, England. TEL 44-1752-633334. FAX 44-1752-633102. *613*

MARINE BOARD OF HOBART. ANNUAL REPORT.
Marine Board of Hobart, Franklin Wharf, Tas. 7000, Australia. TEL 61-03-62351000. FAX 61-03-62310692. *7157*

MARINE CHEMISTRY.
Elsevier Science B.V., P.O. Box 211, 1000 AE Amsterdam, Netherlands. TEL 31-20-4853911. FAX 31-20-4853598. *2318*

MARINE ENVIRONMENTAL RESEARCH.
Elsevier Science Ltd., P.O. Box 800, Kidlington, Oxford OX5 1DX, England. TEL 44-1865-843000. FAX 44-1865-843010. *2970*

MARINE FISHERIES REVIEW.
U.S. National Marine Fisheries Service, Scientific Publications Office, 7600 Sandpoint Way, N.E., Bin C15700, Seattle, WA 98115. TEL 206-526-6107. FAX 206-526-6426. *3073*

MARINE GEODESY.
Taylor & Francis Inc., 1900 Frost Rd., Ste. 101, Bristol, PA 19007. TEL 215-785-5800. FAX 215-785-5515. *3413*

MARINE GEOLOGY.
Elsevier Science B.V., P.O. Box 211, 1000 AE Amsterdam, Netherlands. TEL 31-20-4853911. FAX 31-20-4853598. *2409*

MARINE GEOPHYSICAL RESEARCHES.
Kluwer Academic Publishers, Postbus 17, 3300 AA Dordrecht, Netherlands. TEL 31-78-6392392. FAX 31-78-6392254. *2409*

MARINE GEORESOURCES AND GEOTECHNOLOGY.
Taylor & Francis Inc., 1900 Frost Rd., Ste. 101, Bristol, PA 19007. TEL 215-785-5800. FAX 215-785-5515. *2409*

MARINE MICROPALEONTOLOGY.
Elsevier Science B.V., P.O. Box 211, 1000 AE Amsterdam, Netherlands. TEL 31-20-4853911. FAX 31-20-4853598. *5560*

MARINE ORNITHOLOGY.
African Seabird Group, P.O. Box 34113, Rhodes Gift 7707, South Africa. TEL 27-21-6503294. FAX 27-21-6503295. *805*

MARINE POLICY.
Elsevier Science Ltd., Pergamon, P.O. Box 800, Kidlington, Oxford OX5 1DX, England. TEL 44-1865-843000. FAX 44-1865-843010. *2410*

MARINE POLLUTION BULLETIN.
Elsevier Science Ltd., Pergamon, P.O. Box 800, Kidlington, Oxford OX5 1DX, England. TEL 44-1865-843000. FAX 44-1865-843010. *2970*

MARINE STRUCTURES.
Elsevier Science Ltd., P.O. Box 800, Kidlington, Oxford OX5 1DX, England. TEL 44-1865-843000. FAX 44-1865-843010. *2892*

MARINE TECHNOLOGY AND S N A M E NEWS.
Society of Naval Architects and Marine Engineers, 601 Pavonia Ave., Jersey City, NJ 07306-2907. TEL 201-798-4800. FAX 201-798-4975. *7157*

MARINE TECHNOLOGY SOCIETY JOURNAL.
Marine Technology Society, Inc., 1828 L St., N.W., Ste. 906, Washington, DC 20036-5104. TEL 202-775-5966. FAX 202-429-9417. *2410*

MARINEBLAD.
Koninklijke Vereniging van Marine-Officieren, Wassenaarseweg 2b, 2596 CH The Hague, Netherlands. TEL 31-70-3839504. FAX 31-70-3835911. *5275*

MARINER'S MIRROR.
Society for Nautical Research, Department of History, University of Exeter, Devon, England. TEL 44-1392-264324. FAX 44-1392-264377. *3505*

MARITIME BRIEFING.
International Boundaries Research Unit, University of Durham, Mountjoy Research Centre, Ste. 3P, Durham DH1 3UR, England. TEL 44-191-374-7701. FAX 44-191-374-7702. *4142*

MARITIME COMMAND TRIDENT.
Trident Military Newspaper Ltd., P.O. Box 3308 S., Halifax, NS B3J 3J1, Canada. TEL 902-427-4235. FAX 902-427-4238. *5275*

MARITIME POLICY AND MANAGEMENT.
Taylor & Francis Ltd., 1 Gunpowder Sq., London EC4A 3DE, England. TEL 44-171-583-0490. FAX 44-171-583-0585. *7158*

MARKET.
Canalejas 30, entlo. 2o, 08028 Barcelona, Spain. TEL 34-3-4226289. FAX 34-3-4211858. *1341*

MARKETING AND RESEARCH TODAY.
European Society for Opinion and Marketing Research, J.J. Viottastraat 29, 1071 JP Amsterdam, Netherlands. TEL 31-20-664-2141. FAX 31-20-664-2922. *1539*

MARKETING LETTERS.
Kluwer Academic Publishers Boston, Box 358, Accord Sta., Hingham, MA 02018-0358. TEL 617-871-6600. FAX 617-871-6528. *1539*

MARKETING RESEARCH.
American Marketing Association, 250 S. Wacker Dr., Ste. 200, Chicago, IL 60606. TEL 312-648-0536. FAX 312-993-7542. *1540*

MARKETPLACE MAGAZINE.
A D D Inc., 211 N. Lynndale Dr., Ste. 8, Appleton, WI 54913-1897. TEL 414-735-5969. FAX 414-735-5970. *984*

MARMARA UNIVERSITY. FACULTY OF DENTISTRY. JOURNAL.
Marmara University, Faculty of Dentistry, Buyukciftlik Sok. No. 6, 80200 Nisantasi - Istanbul, Turkey. TEL 90-212-2483127. FAX 90-212-2465247. *4863*

MARO POLYMER NOTES.
Maro Communications, Box 37019, Tucson, AZ 85740-7019. TEL 602-322-5739. *5887*

MARRIAGE & FAMILY REVIEW.
Haworth Press, Inc., 10 Alice St., Binghamton, NY 13904. TEL 607-722-5857. FAX 607-722-6362. *6720*

MARTIN CLASSICAL LECTURES.
Princeton University Press, 41 William St., Princeton, NJ 08540. TEL 609-258-4900. FAX 609-258-6305. *1905*

MARTYRDOM AND RESISTANCE.
American Society for Yad Vashem, 500 Fifth Ave., New York, NY 10110-1699. TEL 212-220-4304. FAX 212-220-4308. *3027*

LE MARXISME AUJOURD'HUI.
Federation des Cercles "le Marxisme Aujourd'hui", B.P. 9012, 64050 Pau Cedex 9, France. TEL 33-4-76623799. FAX 33-1-76250854. *5943*

MARYKNOLL MAGAZINE.
Maryknoll Fathers and Brothers, Box 308, Maryknoll, NY 10545-0308. TEL 914-941-7590. FAX 914-945-0670. *6470*

MARYLAND BIRDLIFE.
Maryland Ornithological Society, Inc., Patuxent Wildlife Research, Laurel, MD 20708-4015. TEL 301-497-5641. FAX 301-497-5624. *806*

MARYLAND ENGLISH JOURNAL.
Maryland Council of Teachers of English Language Arts, Frostburg State University, Dept. of English, Frostburg, MD 21532. TEL 301-687-4221. FAX 301-687-4495. *2610*

MARYLAND HISTORIAN.
University of Maryland, Department of History, College Park, MD 20742. TEL 301-405-4331. *3505*

MARYLAND MEDICAL JOURNAL.
Medical and Chirurgical Faculty of Maryland, 1211 Cathedral St., Baltimore, MD 21201. TEL 410-539-0872. FAX 410-547-0915. *4705*

MARYLAND POETRY REVIEW.
Maryland State Poetry and Literary Society, Drawer H, Catonsville, MD 21228. TEL 410-747-0594. *4514*

MARYLAND STATE DENTAL ASSOCIATION. JOURNAL.
Maryland State Dental Association, 6450 Dobbin Rd., Columbia Business Center, Columbia, MD 21045-4744. TEL 410-964-2880. FAX 410-964-0583. *4863*

MASHABEI EINOSH.
Eush Ltd., P.O. Box 3202, Herzliya 46104, Israel. TEL 972-8-9500882. FAX 972-9-9582785. *1571*

MASHHAD UNIVERSITY. FACULTY OF LETTERS AND HUMANITIES. JOURNAL.
Mashhad University, Faculty of Letters and Humanities, Mashhad 91384, Iran. TEL 98-51-831026. FAX 98-51-816556. *4433*

MASONRY SOCIETY JOURNAL.
Masonry Society, 3970 Broadway St., Ste. 201-D, Boulder, CO 80304-1135. TEL 303-939-9700. FAX 303-541-9215. *903*

MASS SPECTROMETRY REVIEWS.
John Wiley & Sons, Inc., Journals, 605 Third Ave., New York, NY 10158. TEL 212-850-6645. FAX 212-850-6021. *5865*

MASSACHUSETTS BEVERAGE BUSINESS.
New Beverage Publications, Inc., Box 932, Boston, MA 02117-0932. TEL 617-423-7200. FAX 617-482-7163. *524*

MASSACHUSETTS INSTITUTE OF TECHNOLOGY. FLIGHT TRANSPORTATION LABORATORY. F T L REPORTS AND MEMORANDA.
Massachusetts Institute of Technology, Department of Aeronautics and Astronautics, Rm. 33-412, Cambridge, MA 02139. TEL 617-253-2424. *74*

MASSACHUSETTS INSTITUTE OF TECHNOLOGY. RESEARCH LABORATORY OF ELECTRONICS. R L E PROGRESS REPORT.
Massachusetts Institute of Technology, Research Laboratory of Electronics, Cambridge, MA 02139. TEL 617-253-2566. FAX 617-258-7864. *2839*

MASSAGE MAGAZINE.
1315 W. Mallon Ave, Spokane, WA 99201-2038. TEL 509-324-8117. FAX 509-324-8606. *5787*

MASSAGE THERAPY JOURNAL.
American Massage Therapy Association, 820 Davis St., Ste. 100, Evanston, IL 60201-4444. TEL 708-864-0123. FAX 708-864-1178. *5787*

MASSUA.
Massua - Center for Holocaust Studies, Kibbutz Tel Yitzhak, Doar Tel Yitzhak 45805, Israel. TEL 972-9-89699997. FAX 972-9-8997410. *3027*

MASTER, MATE & PILOT.
International Organization of Masters, Mates & Pilots, 700 Maritime Blvd., Linthicum Heights, MD 21090. TEL 410-850-8700. FAX 410-850-0973. *3894*

MASTER'S THESES IN THE PURE AND APPLIED SCIENCES.
Plenum Publishing Corp., 233 Spring St., New York, NY 10013-1578. TEL 212-620-8000. FAX 212-463-0742. *6591*

MATCH.
Universitaet Bayreuth, Lehrstuhl II fuer Mathematik, 95540 Bayreuth, Germany. TEL 49-921-553387. FAX 49-921-553385. *1759*

MATCH NEWS.
Match International Centre, 1102-200 Elgin St., Ottawa, ON K2P 1L5, Canada. TEL 613-238-1312. FAX 613-238-6867. *7326*

MATEKON.
M.E. Sharpe, Inc., 80 Business Park Dr., Armonk, NY 10504. TEL 914-273-1800. FAX 914-273-2106. *984*

MATEMATICA APLICADA E COMPUTACIONAL.
Birkhauser Boston, 675 Massachusetts Ave., Cambridge, MA 02139. TEL 617-876-2333. FAX 617-876-1272. *4622*

MATEMATICA E LA SUA DIDATTICA.
Pitagora Editrice, Via del Legatore 3, 40138 Bologna, Italy. TEL 39-51-530003. FAX 39-51-535301. *4587*

MATEMATYKA (WROCLAW).
Wydawnictwa Szkolne i Pedagogiczne (Wroclaw), Ul. Dawida 1a, 50-527 Wroclaw, Poland. TEL 48-71-677028. *4588*

MATERIAL HISTORY REVIEW.
National Museum of Science and Technology, Box 9724, Sta. T, Ottawa, ON K1G 5A3, Canada. TEL 613-990-7529. FAX 613-990-3635. *3505*

MATERIALS AND CORROSION.
Wiley - V C H, Postfach 101161, 69451 Weinheim, Germany. TEL 49-6201-606147. FAX 49-6201-606117. *5200*

MATERIALS & MANUFACTURING PROCESSES.
Marcel Dekker Journals, 270 Madison Ave., New York, NY 10016. TEL 212-696-9000. FAX 212-685-4540. *2893*

MATERIALS AND STRUCTURES.
International Union of Testing and Research Laboratories for Materials and Structures (RILEM), Pavillon des Jardins 61, Av. du President Wilson, 94235 Cachan Cedex, France. *903*

MATERIALS CHARACTERIZATION.
Elsevier Science Inc., Box 945, New York, NY 10159-0945. TEL 212-633-3730. FAX 212-633-3680. *5200*

MATERIALS CHEMISTRY AND PHYSICS.
Elsevier Science S.A., P.O. Box 564, CH-1001 Lausanne 1, Switzerland. TEL 41-21-3207381. FAX 41-21-3235444. *2865*

MATERIALS EVALUATION.
American Society for Nondestructive Testing, 1711 Arlingate Lane, Box 28518, Columbus, OH 43228-0158. TEL 614-274-6003. FAX 614-274-6899. *2865*

MATERIALS LETTERS.
North-Holland, P.O. Box 211, 1000 AE Amsterdam, Netherlands. TEL 31-20-4853911. FAX 31-20-4853598. *5814*

MATERIALS PROCESSING: THEORY AND PRACTICES.
Elsevier Science B.V., Books Division, P.O. Box 211, 1000 AE Amsterdam, Netherlands. TEL 31-20-4853911. FAX 31-20-4853705. *5814*

MATERIALS RESEARCH BULLETIN.
Elsevier Science Ltd., Pergamon, P.O. Box 800, Kidlington, Oxford OX5 1DX, England. TEL 44-1865-843000. FAX 44-1865-843010. *1802*

MATERIALS RESEARCH SOCIETY OF JAPAN. TRANSACTIONS.
Elsevier Science B.V., Books Division, P.O. Box 211, 1000 AE Amsterdam, Netherlands. TEL 31-20-4853911. FAX 31-20-4853705. *2865*

MATERIALS SCIENCE.
Plenum Publishing Corp., Consultants Bureau, 233 Spring St., New York, NY 10013-1578. TEL 212-620-8468. FAX 212-463-0742. *2866*

MATERIALS SCIENCE AND ENGINEERING A: STRUCTURAL MATERIALS: PROPERTIES, MICROSTRUCTURES AND PROCESSING.
Elsevier Science S.A., P.O. Box 564, CH-1001 Lausanne 1, Switzerland. TEL 41-21-3207381. FAX 41-21-3235444. *2866*

MATERIALS SCIENCE AND ENGINEERING B: SOLID-STATE MATERIALS FOR ADVANCED TECHNOLOGY.
Elsevier Science S.A., P.O. Box 564, CH-1001 Lausanne 1, Switzerland. TEL 41-21-3207381. FAX 41-21-3235444. *2866*

MATERIALS SCIENCE AND ENGINEERING R: REPORTS.
Elsevier Science S.A., P.O. Box 564, CH-1001 Lausanne 1, Switzerland. TEL 41-21-3207381. FAX 41-21-3235444. *2866*

MATERIALS SCIENCE AND TECHNOLOGY.
Centro de Investigacion y Produccion de Materiales, Apdo. Postal 397, Merida 5101, Venezuela. TEL 58-74-712939. *2866*

MATERIALS SCIENCE MONOGRAPHS.
Elsevier Science B.V., Books Division, P.O. Box 211, 1000 AE Amsterdam, Netherlands. TEL 31-20-4853911. FAX 31-20-4853705. *2731*

MATERIALS SCIENCE OF MINERALS AND ROCKS.
Kluwer Academic Publishers, Postbus 17, 3300 AA Dordrecht, Netherlands. TEL 31-78-6392392. FAX 31-78-6392254. *2357*

MATERIALS SCIENCE RESEARCH.
Plenum Publishing Corp., 233 Spring St., New York, NY 10013-1578. TEL 212-620-8000. FAX 212-463-0742. *2866*

MATERIALS SCIENCE RESEARCH INTERNATIONAL.
Chapman & Hall, Journals Department 2-6 Boundary Row, London SE1 8HN, England. TEL 44-171-8650066. FAX 44-171-5229623. *2867*

MATERIALS TECHNOLOGY.
Elsevier Science Inc., Box 945, New York, NY 10159-0945. TEL 212-633-3730. FAX 212-633-3680. *5201*

MATERIALY GLYATSIOLOGICHESKIKH ISSLEDOVANII.
Rossiiskaya Akademiya Nauk, Institut Geografii, Staromonetnyi St. 29, Moscow 109017, Russia. TEL 7-095-2388610. FAX 7-095-2302090. *2386*

MATERIALY ZACHODNIO-POMORSKIE.
Muzeum Narodowe, Szczecin, Staromlynska 27, 70-561 Szczecin, Poland. TEL 48-91-335066. FAX 48-91-347894. *5358*

MATERNAL AND CHILD HEALTH JOURNAL.
Plenum Publishing Corp., 233 Spring St., New York, NY 10013-1578. TEL 212-620-8000. FAX 212-463-0742. *4963*

MATHEMATICA JAPONICA.
Nihon Suri Kagaku Kyokai, Shin Sakai-Higashi Bldg., 2-1-18 Minami-Hanadaguchi, Sakai-shi, Osaka-fu 590, Japan. FAX 81-722-22-7987. *4588*

MATHEMATICA SLOVACA.
Slovenska Akademia Vied, Matematicky Ustav, Stefanikova 49, 814 73 Bratislava, Slovakia. FAX 421-7-397316. *4588*

MATHEMATICAL AND COMPUTER MODELLING.
Elsevier Science Ltd., Pergamon, P.O. Box 800, Kidlington, Oxford OX5 1DX, England. TEL 44-1865-843000. FAX 44-1865-843010. *4589*

MATHEMATICAL BIOSCIENCES.
Elsevier Science Inc., Box 945, New York, NY 10159-0945. TEL 212-633-3730. FAX 212-633-3680. *4589*

MATHEMATICAL CONCEPTS AND METHODS IN SCIENCE AND ENGINEERING.
Plenum Publishing Corp., 233 Spring St., New York, NY 10013-1578. TEL 212-620-8000. FAX 212-463-0742. *4589*

MATHEMATICAL ENGINEERING IN INDUSTRY.
V S P, P.O. Box 346, 3700 AH Zeist, Netherlands. TEL 31-30-6925790. FAX 31-30-6932081. *4589*

MATHEMATICAL GEOLOGY.
Plenum Publishing Corp., 233 Spring St., New York, NY 10013-1578. TEL 212-620-8000. FAX 212-463-0742. *2357*

THE MATHEMATICAL INTELLIGENCER.
Springer-Verlag, Science Journals, 175 Fifth Ave., New York, NY 10010. TEL 212-460-1500. FAX 212-473-6272. *4589*

MATHEMATICAL METHODS IN THE APPLIED SCIENCES.
John Wiley & Sons Ltd., Journals, Baffins Ln., Chichester, W. Sussex PO19 1UD, England. TEL 44-1243-779777. FAX 44-1243-775878. *4589*

MATHEMATICAL METHODS OF OPERATIONS RESEARCH.
Physica-Verlag GmbH und Co., Postfach 105280, 69042 Heidelberg, Germany. TEL 49-6221-487492. FAX 49-6221-487177. *4622*

MATHEMATICAL MODELING AND COMPUTATIONAL EXPERIMENT.
John Wiley & Sons, Inc., Journals, 605 Third Ave., New York, NY 10158. TEL 212-850-6645. FAX 212-850-6021. *4622*

MATHEMATICAL MODELLING OF SYSTEMS.
Swets & Zeitlinger bv, P.O. Box 825, 2160 SZ Lisse, Netherlands. TEL 31-252-435111. FAX 31-252-415888. *4622*

MATHEMATICAL PHYSICS, ANALYSIS AND GEOMETRY.
Kluwer Academic Publishers, Postbus 17, 3300 AA Dordrecht, Netherlands. TEL 31-78-6392392. FAX 31-78-6392254. *5814*

MATHEMATICAL PHYSICS AND APPLIED MATHEMATICS.
Kluwer Academic Publishers, Postbus 17, 3300 AA Dordrecht, Netherlands. TEL 31-78-6392392. FAX 31-78-6392254. *4590*

MATHEMATICAL PHYSICS STUDIES.
Kluwer Academic Publishers, Postbus 17, 3300 AA Dordrecht, Netherlands. TEL 31-78-6392392. FAX 31-78-6392254. *5815*

MATHEMATICAL POPULATION STUDIES.
Gordon and Breach - Harwood Academic, Amsteldisk 166, 1st Fl., 1079 LH Amsterdam, Netherlands. *6054*

MATHEMATICAL PROGRAMMING.
North-Holland, P.O. Box 211, 1000 AE Amsterdam, Netherlands. TEL 31-20-4853911. FAX 31-20-4853598. *4622*

MATHEMATICAL REPORTS.
Gordon and Breach - Harwood Academic, Amsteldisk 166, 1st Fl., 1079 LH Amsterdam, Netherlands. *4590*

MATHEMATICAL REVIEWS.
American Mathematical Society, Box 6248, Providence, RI 02940-6248. TEL 401-455-4000. FAX 401-331-3842. *4617*

THE MATHEMATICAL SCIENTIST.
Applied Probability Trust, School of Mathematics, University of Sheffield, Sheffield S3 7RH, England. TEL 44-114-222-3920. FAX 44-114-272-9782. *4590*

MATHEMATICAL SOCIAL SCIENCES.
North-Holland, P.O. Box 211, 1000 AE Amsterdam, Netherlands. TEL 31-20-4853911. FAX 31-20-4853598. *4590*

MATHEMATICAL SPECTRUM.
Applied Probability Trust, School of Mathematics, University of Sheffield, Sheffield S3 7RH, England. TEL 44-114-222-3920. FAX 44-114-272-9782. *4590*

MATHEMATICAL SURVEYS & MONOGRAPHS.
American Mathematical Society, Box 6248, Providence, RI 02940-6248. TEL 401-455-4000. FAX 401-331-3842. *4591*

MATHEMATICS AND COMPUTER EDUCATION.
M A T Y C Journal, Inc., Box 158, Old Bethpage, NY 11804. TEL 516-822-5475. *4622*

MATHEMATICS AND COMPUTERS IN SIMULATION.
North-Holland, P.O. Box 211, 1000 AE Amsterdam, Netherlands. TEL 31-20-4853911. FAX 31-20-4853598. *2152*

MATHEMATICS AND ITS APPLICATIONS.
Gordon and Breach - Harwood Academic, Amsteldisk 166, 1st Fl., 1079 LH Amsterdam, Netherlands. *4591*

MATHEMATICS AND ITS APPLICATIONS.
Kluwer Academic Publishers, Postbus 17, 3300 AA Dordrecht, Netherlands. TEL 31-78-6392392. FAX 31-78-6392254. *4591*

MATHEMATICS AND ITS APPLICATIONS: CHINESE SERIES.
Kluwer Academic Publishers, Postbus 17, 3300 AA Dordrecht, Netherlands. TEL 31-78-6392392. FAX 31-78-6392254. *4591*

MATHEMATICS AND ITS APPLICATIONS: EAST EUROPEAN SERIES.
Kluwer Academic Publishers, Postbus 17, 3300 AA Dordrecht, Netherlands. TEL 31-78-6392392. FAX 31-78-6392254. *4591*

MATHEMATICS AND ITS APPLICATIONS: JAPANESE SERIES.
Kluwer Academic Publishers, Postbus 17, 3300 AA Dordrecht, Netherlands. TEL 31-78-6392392. FAX 31-78-6392254. *4591*

MATHEMATICS AND ITS APPLICATIONS: SOVIET SERIES.
Kluwer Academic Publishers, Postbus 17, 3300 AA Dordrecht, Netherlands. TEL 31-78-6392392. FAX 31-78-6392254. *4591*

MATHEMATICS AND MATHEMATICAL PHYSICS REVIEW.
Gordon and Breach - Harwood Academic, Amsteldisk 166, 1st Fl., 1079 LH Amsterdam, Netherlands. *5815*

MATHEMATICS AND MECHANICS OF SOLIDS.
Sage Publications, Inc., Sage Science Press, 2455 Teller Rd., Thousand Oaks, CA 91320. TEL 805-499-0721. FAX 805-499-0871. *5815*

MATHEMATICS CONTESTS.
Australian Mathematics Trust, P.O. Box 1, Belconnen, A.C.T. 2616, Australia. TEL 61-6-2015137. FAX 61-6-2015135. *4591*

MATHEMATICS EDUCATION LIBRARY.
Kluwer Academic Publishers, Postbus 17, 3300 AA Dordrecht, Netherlands. TEL 31-78-6392392. FAX 31-78-6392254. *2462*

MATHEMATICS EDUCATION RESEARCH JOURNAL.
Mathematics Education Research Group of Australasia, c/o Dr. M. Mitchelmore, School of Education, Macquarie University, North Ryde, N.S.W. 2109, Australia. TEL 61-2-985086545. FAX 61-2-98508674. *2610*

MATHEMATICS IN SCHOOL.
Pitman Publishing, 128 Long Acre, London WC2E 9AN, England. TEL 44-171-447-2000. FAX 44-171-240-5771. *4591*

MATHEMATICS IN SCIENCE AND ENGINEERING.
Academic Press, Inc., 525 B St., Ste. 1900, San Diego, CA 92101-4495. TEL 619-231-0926. FAX 619-699-6715. *4591*

MATHEMATICS OF COMPUTATION.
American Mathematical Society, Box 6248, Providence, RI 02940-6248. TEL 401-455-4000. *4591*

MATHEMATICS OF OPERATIONS RESEARCH.
Institute for Operations Research and the Management Sciences, 901 Elkridge Landing Rd., Ste. 400, Linthicum, MD 21090-2909. TEL 410-850-0300. *2087*

MATHEMATICS TEACHER.
National Council of Teachers of Mathematics, 1906 Association Dr., Reston, VA 22091. TEL 703-620-9840. FAX 703-476-2970. *4592*

MATHEMATICS TEACHING IN THE MIDDLE SCHOOL.
National Council of Teachers of Mathematics, 1906 Association Dr., Reston, VA 22091-1593. TEL 703-620-9840. FAX 703-476-2970. *4592*

MATHEMATISCHE GESELLSCHAFT IN HAMBURG. MITTEILUNGEN.
Mathematische Gesellschaft in Hamburg, Bundesstr. 55, 20146 Hamburg, Germany. TEL 49-40-41235138. FAX 49-40-41235190. *4592*

MATHESIS.
Grupo Editorial Iberoamerica, S.A. de C.V., Nebraska 199, Col. Napoles, 03810 Mexico, D.F., Mexico. TEL 52-5-5230640. FAX 52-5-5431173. *4593*

MATHWARE AND SOFT COMPUTING.
Universitat Politecnica de Catalunya, E T S d'Arquitectura de Barcelona, Seccio de Matematiques i Informacion, Diagonal 649, 08028 Barcelona, Spain. FAX 34-3-4016367. *4623*

MATI.
Standards Institution of Israel, 42 Chaim Levanon St., Tel Aviv 69977, Israel. TEL 972-3-6465154. FAX 972-3-6419683. *5252*

MATTOID.
Deakin University, Deakin Literary Society, Vic. 3217, Australia. FAX 61-3-52272495. *4434*

MATURITAS.
Elsevier Science Ireland Ltd., P.O. Box 85, Limerick, Ireland. TEL 353-61-471944. FAX 353-61-472144. *3441*

THE MAUI WINDSURFING REPORT.
Box 1202, Kula, HI 96790. *6874*

MAYDICA.
Istituto Sperimentale per la Cerealicoltura, Sezione di Bergamo, Via Stezzano 24, 24126 Bergamo, Italy. TEL 39-35-313132. FAX 39-35-316054. *235*

MAYFLOWER QUARTERLY.
General Society of Mayflower Descendants, Box 3297, Plymouth, MA 02361. *3232*

MAYNOOTH OCCASIONAL PAPERS.
St. Patrick's College, Department of Geography, Maynooth, Co. Kildare, Ireland. TEL 01-6285222. FAX 01-6289063. *3413*

MAYO CLINIC PROCEEDINGS.
Dowden Publishing Company, 110 Summit Ave., Montvale, NJ 07645. TEL 201-782-5735. FAX 201-391-2778. *4706*

MAZOWIECKIE STUDIA HUMANISTYCZNE.
Mazowiecka Wyzsza Szkola Humanistyczno-Pedagogiczna, Ul. 3 Maja 7, 99-400 Lowicz, Poland. TEL 48-46-374392. FAX 48-46-374392. *3785*

MEADOWLARK.
Illinois Ornithological Society, Box 1971, Evanston, IL 60204-1971. *806*

MEASUREMENT.
Elsevier Science B.V., P.O. Box 211, 1000 AE Amsterdam, Netherlands. TEL 31-20-4853911. FAX 31-20-4853598. *5252*

MEASUREMENT TECHNIQUES.
Plenum Publishing Corp., Consultants Bureau, 233 Spring St., New York, NY 10013-1578. TEL 212-620-8468. FAX 212-463-0742. *5252*

MEASUREMENTS AND CONTROL.
Measurements & Data Corp., 2994 W. Liberty Ave., Pittsburgh, PA 15216. TEL 412-343-9666. *3804*

MEAT SCIENCE.
Elsevier Science Ltd., P.O. Box 800, Kidlington, Oxford OX5 1DX, England. TEL 44-1865-843000. FAX 44-1865-843010. *3120*

MECCANICA.
Kluwer Academic Publishers, Postbus 17, 3300 AA Dordrecht, Netherlands. TEL 31-78-6392392. FAX 31-78-6392254. *5847*

MECHANICAL ENGINEERING.
American Society of Mechanical Engineers, 22 Law Dr., Fairfield, NJ 07007-2900. TEL 973-882-1167. FAX 973-882-1717. *2893*

MECHANICAL ENGINEERING SERIES.
Marcel Dekker, Inc., 270 Madison Ave., New York, NY 10016. TEL 212-696-9000. FAX 212-658-4540. *2893*

MECHANICS AND MATHEMATICAL METHODS - SERIES OF HANDBOOKS.
Elsevier Science B.V., Books Division, P.O. Box 211, 1000 AE Amsterdam, Netherlands. TEL 31-20-4853911. FAX 31-20-4853705. *4593*

MECHANICS AND PHYSICS OF DISCRETE SYSTEMS.
Elsevier Science B.V., Books Division, P.O. Box 211, 1000 AE Amsterdam, Netherlands. TEL 31-20-4853911. FAX 31-20-4853705. *2893*

MECHANICS OF COHESIVE FRICTIONAL MATERIALS.
John Wiley & Sons Ltd., Journals, Baffins Ln., Chichester, W. Sussex PO19 1UD, England. TEL 44-1243-779777. FAX 44-1243-775878. *2867*

MECHANICS OF COMPOSITE MATERIALS.
Plenum Publishing Corp., Consultants Bureau, 233 Spring St., New York, NY 10013-1578. TEL 212-620-8468. FAX 212-463-0742. *2768*

MECHANICS OF COMPOSITE MATERIALS AND STRUCTURES.
Taylor & Francis Ltd., 1 Gunpowder Sq., London EC4A 3DE, England. TEL 44-171-583-0490. FAX 44-171-583-0585. *2867*

MECHANICS OF MATERIALS.
North-Holland, P.O. Box 211, 1000 AE Amsterdam, Netherlands. TEL 31-20-4853911. FAX 31-20-4853598. *2867*

MECHANICS OF STRUCTURES AND MACHINES.
Marcel Dekker Journals, 270 Madison Ave., New York, NY 10016. TEL 212-696-9000. FAX 212-685-4540. *2893*

MECHANICS OF TIME DEPENDENT MATERIALS.
Kluwer Academic Publishers, Postbus 17, 3300 AA Dordrecht, Netherlands. TEL 31-78-6392392. FAX 31-78-6392254. *5847*

MECHANICS RESEARCH COMMUNICATIONS.
Elsevier Science Ltd., Pergamon, P.O. Box 800, Kidlington, Oxford OX5 1DX, England. TEL 44-1865-843000. FAX 44-1865-843010. *2867*

MECHANIKA TEORETYCZNA I STOSOWANA.
Polskie Towarzystwo Mechaniki Teoretycznej i Stosowanej, Palac Kultury, p.309, 00-901 Warsaw, Poland. *2867*

MECHANISM AND MACHINE THEORY.
Elsevier Science Ltd., Pergamon, P.O. Box 800, Kidlington, Oxford OX5 1DX, England. TEL 44-1865-843000. FAX 44-1865-843010. *2894*

MECHANISMS OF AGEING AND DEVELOPMENT.
Elsevier Science Ireland Ltd., P.O. Box 85, Limerick, Ireland. TEL 353-61-471944. FAX 353-61-472144. *3441*

MECHANISMS OF DEVELOPMENT.
Elsevier Science Ireland Ltd., P.O. Box 85, Limerick, Ireland. TEL 353-61-471944. FAX 353-61-472144. *742*

MECHANISMS OF INORGANIC AND ORGANOMETALLIC REACTIONS.
Plenum Publishing Corp., 233 Spring St., New York, NY 10013-1578. TEL 212-620-8000. FAX 212-463-0742. *1808*

MECHATRONICS.
Elsevier Science Ltd., Pergamon, P.O. Box 800, Kidlington, Oxford OX5 1DX, England. TEL 44-1865-843000. FAX 44-1865-843010. *2894*

THE MEDAL.
British Art Medal Trust, c/o Philip Attwood, Ed., Department of Coins and Medals, British Museum, London WC1B 3DG, England. TEL 44-171-323-8260. FAX 44-171-323-8171. *5465*

LE MEDECIN DU QUEBEC.
Federation des Medecins Omnipraticiens du Quebec, 1440 rue St.Catherine Ouest, Ste. 1000, Montreal, PQ H3G 1R8, Canada. TEL 514-878-1911. FAX 514-878-4455. *4706*

MEDECINE - BIOLOGIE - ENVIRONNEMENT.
European Institute of Ecology and Cancer, c/o Lega Contro i Tumori, Piazza Botta 10, 27100 Pavia, Italy. TEL 39-382-506333. FAX 39-382-303673. *4982*

MEDECINE ET CHIRURGIE DIGESTIVES.
B.C. Diffusion, 116 av. des Champs-Elysees, 75008 Paris, France. TEL 33-1-44218026. FAX 33-1-44218299. *4913*

MEDECINE ET ENFANCE, ADOLESCENCE.
Edition et Communication Medicales, 23 rue Saint-Ferdinand, 75017 Paris, France. TEL 45-74-44-65. FAX 40-55-94-13. *5034*

MEDECINE NUCLEAIRE.
Editions Scientifiques et Medicales Elsevier, 141 rue de Javel, 75747 Paris, France. TEL 33-1-45589068. FAX 33-1-45589421. *5111*

MEDECINE THERAPEUTIQUE.
John Libbey Eurotext, 127 av. de la Republique, 92120 Montrouge, France. TEL 33-1-46730660. FAX 33-1-40840999. *4706*

MEDIA.
Media & Marketing Ltd., 1002 McDonald's Bldg., 46-54 Yee Wo Street, Causeway Bay, Hong Kong, People's Republic of China. TEL 852-2577-2628. FAX 852-2576-9171. *40*

MEDIA CULTURE & SOCIETY.
Sage Publications Ltd., 6 Bonhill St., London EC2A 4PU, England. TEL 44-171-374-0645. FAX 44-171-374-8741. *2053*

MEDIAPLUSNEWS.
Diade s.r.l., Via Ausonio 5, 20123 Milan, Italy. TEL 39-2-8372407. FAX 39-2-58100311. *6966*

MEDIATION QUARTERLY.
Jossey-Bass Inc., Publishers, 350 Sansome St., 5th Fl., San Francisco, CA 94104. FAX 800-605-2665. *6135*

MEDICAL AND PEDIATRIC ONCOLOGY.
John Wiley & Sons, Inc., Journals, 605 Third Ave., New York, NY 10158. TEL 212-850-6645. FAX 212-850-6021. *4982*

MEDICAL AND PEDIATRIC ONCOLOGY. SUPPLEMENT.
John Wiley & Sons, Inc., Journals, 605 Third Ave., New York, NY 10158. TEL 212-850-6645. FAX 212-850-6021. *4982*

MEDICAL & SURGICAL DERMATOLOGY.
Springer-Verlag, Medical Journals, 175 Fifth Ave., New York, NY 10010. TEL 212-460-1500. FAX 212-473-6272. *4782*

MEDICAL ANTHROPOLOGY.
Gordon and Breach - Harwood Academic, Amsteldisk 166, 1st Fl., 1079 LH Amsterdam, Netherlands. *323*

MEDICAL ARTIFICIAL INTELLIGENCE.
Elsevier Science B.V., Books Division, P.O. Box 211, 1000 AE Amsterdam, Netherlands. TEL 31-20-4853911. FAX 31-20-4853705. *2103*

MEDICAL CARE.
Lippincott - Raven Publishers, 227 E. Washington Sq., Philadelphia, PA 19106. TEL 215-238-4200. FAX 215-238-4227. *4707*

MEDICAL CARE RESEARCH AND REVIEW.
Sage Publications, Inc., 2455 Teller Rd., Thousand Oaks, CA 91320. TEL 805-499-0721. FAX 805-499-0871. *6257*

MEDICAL DECISION MAKING.
Hanley & Belfus, Inc., 210 S. 13th St., Philadelphia, PA 19107. TEL 215-546-7293. FAX 215-790-9330. *4707*

MEDICAL DOSIMETRY.
Elsevier Science Inc., Box 945, New York, NY 10159-0945. TEL 212-633-3730. FAX 212-633-3680. *5111*

MEDICAL EDUCATION.
Blackwell Science Ltd., Osney Mead, Oxford OX2 0EL, England. TEL 44-1865-206206. FAX 44-1865-721205. *4708*

MEDICAL EDUCATION ONLINE. *4708*

MEDICAL ENGINEERING AND PHYSICS.
Elsevier Science Ltd., P.O. Box 800, Kidlington, Oxford OX5 1DX, England. TEL 44-1865-843000. FAX 44-1865-843010. *4708*

MEDICAL GRAND ROUNDS.
University of Texas, Southwestern Medical Center, 5323 Harry Hines Blvd., Dallas, TX 75235-9030. TEL 214-648-2635. FAX 214-648-9100. *4708*

MEDICAL HISTORY.
Professional & Scientific Publications, BMA House, Tavistock Sq., London WC1H 9JR, England. TEL 0171-383-6640. FAX 0171-383-6662. *4708*

MEDICAL IMAGE ANALYSIS.
Oxford University Press, Academic Division, Great Clarendon St., Oxford OX2 6DP, England. TEL 44-1865-267907. FAX 44-1865-267485. *5111*

MEDICAL IMAGING TECHNOLOGY.
Digital Press, Inc., Texico Bldg., 9-7 Higashi-Ikebukuro, Toshima-ku, Tokyo 170, Japan. TEL 81-298-58-7116. FAX 81-3-3971-6703. *5111*

MEDICAL INFORMATICS.
Taylor & Francis Ltd., 1 Gunpowder Sq., London EC4A 3DE, England. TEL 44-171-583-0490. FAX 44-171-583-0585. *4847*

MEDICAL JOURNAL ARMED FORCES INDIA.
Armed Forces Medical College, Pune 411 040, Maharashtra, India. TEL 91-212-673290. FAX 91-212-679539. *4709*

MEDICAL JOURNAL OF AUSTRALIA.
Australasian Medical Publishing Co., Private Bag 901, N. Sydney, N.S.W. 2059, Australia. TEL 61-2-99548666. FAX 61-2-99567644. *4709*

MEDICAL LAW INTERNATIONAL.
A B Academic Publishers, P.O. Box 42, Bicester, Oxon. OX6 7NW, England. TEL 44-1869-320949. *3989*

MEDICAL LETTER ON DRUGS AND THERAPEUTICS (ENGLISH EDITION).
Medical Letter, Inc., 1000 Main St., New Rochelle, NY 10801. TEL 914-235-0500. FAX 914-632-1733. *5677*

MEDICAL LIBRARY ASSOCIATION. BULLETIN.
Medical Library Association, 6 N. Michigan Ave., Ste. 300, Chicago, IL 60602-4805. TEL 312-419-9094. FAX 312-419-8905. *4709*

MEDICAL MISSION NEWS.
Catholic Medical Mission Board, Inc., 10 W. 17th St., New York, NY 10011. TEL 212-242-7757. FAX 212-807-9161. *6470*

MEDICAL ONCOLOGY.
Chapman & Hall, Journals Department 2-6 Boundary Row, London SE1 8HN, England. TEL 44-171-8560066. FAX 44-171-5229623. *4983*

MEDICAL PHYSICS.
American Institute of Physics, One Physics Ellipse, College Park, MD 20740-3843. TEL 301-209-3000. *4710*

MEDICAL PRINCIPLES AND PRACTICE.
S. Karger AG, Allschwilerstr. 10, P.O. Box, CH-4009 Basel, Switzerland. TEL 41-61-3061111. FAX 41-61-3061234. *4710*

MEDICAL PROBLEMS OF PERFORMING ARTISTS.
Hanley & Belfus, Inc., 210 S. 13th St., Philadelphia, PA 19107. TEL 215-546-7293. FAX 215-790-9330. *4710*

MEDICAL PROGRESS THROUGH TECHNOLOGY.
Kluwer Academic Publishers, Postbus 17, 3300 AA Dordrecht, Netherlands. TEL 31-78-6392392. FAX 31-78-6392254. *685*

MEDICAL REFERENCE SERVICES QUARTERLY.
Haworth Press, Inc., 10 Alice St., Binghamton, NY 13904. TEL 607-722-5857. FAX 607-722-6362. *4198*

MEDICAL SCIENCE RESEARCH.
Chapman & Hall, Journals Department 2-6 Boundary Row, London SE1 8HN, England. TEL 44-171-8560066. FAX 44-171-5229623. *4711*

MEDICAL SCIENCE SYMPOSIA SERIES.
Kluwer Academic Publishers, Postbus 17, 3300 AA Dordrecht, Netherlands. TEL 31-78-6392392. FAX 31-78-6392254. *4711*

MEDICAL TEACHER.
Carfax Publishing Co., P.O. Box 25, Abingdon, Oxon. OX14 3UE, England. TEL 44-1235-401000. FAX 44-1235-401550. *4711*

MEDICAMUNDI.
Philips Medical Systems International B.V., P.O. Box 10000, 5680 DA Best, Netherlands. TEL 31-40-2763856. FAX 31-40-2762019. *5111*

MEDICINA.
Fundacion Revista Medicina, Donato Alvarez 3150, 1427 Buenos Aires, Argentina. TEL 541-5236619. FAX 541-5236619. *4712*

MEDICINA.
Universidade de Sao Paulo, Faculdade de Medicina de Ribeirao Preto, Campus Universitario, Av. Bandeirantes, 3900, 14049 Ribeirao Preto, SP, Brazil. FAX 55-16-6331144. *4712*

MEDICINA DELLO SPORT.
Edizioni Minerva Medica, Corso Bramante 83-85, 10126 Turin, Italy. TEL 39-11-678282. FAX 39-11-674502. *5131*

MEDICINA INTERNA.
Obsidiana Editores, S.A., Czda. de Tlalpan 2365, Col. Ciudad Jardin, 04370 Mexico DF, Mexico. TEL 6899133. *4926*

MEDICINA, PSICHE E ADOLESCENZA.
Centro Italiano Studi di Psicologia Medica, Viale Romagna 51, 20133 Milan, Italy. TEL 39-2-2666880. FAX 39-2-2361226. *5079*

MEDICINA TORACICA.
Masson S.p.A., Divisione Periodici, Via Flli. Bressan 2, 20126 Milan, Italy. TEL 39-2-270741. FAX 39-2-27074210. *5120*

MEDICINA VETERINARIA.
Pulso Ediciones S.A., Rambla del Celler, 117-119, 08190 Sant Cugat del Valles (Barcelona), Spain. TEL 34-3-5896264. *7275*

MEDICINAL CHEMISTRY RESEARCH.
Birkhaeuser, 675 Massachusetts Ave., Cambridge, MA 02139-3309. FAX 201-348-4505. *4712*

MEDICINAL RESEARCH REVIEWS.
John Wiley & Sons, Inc., Journals, 605 Third Ave., New York, NY 10158. TEL 212-850-6645. FAX 212-850-6021. *5677*

MEDICINAL RESEARCH SERIES.
Marcel Dekker, Inc., 270 Madison Ave., New York, NY 10016. TEL 212-696-9000. FAX 212-658-4540. *4712*

MEDICINE (BALTIMORE).
Williams & Wilkins, 351 W. Camden St., Baltimore, MD 21201-2436. TEL 410-528-4068. FAX 410-528-4452. *4713*

MEDICINE AND LAW.
Yozmot Heiliger (1989) Ltd., 3 Yohanan Hasandlar St., P.O. Box 56055, Tel Aviv 61560, Israel. TEL 972-3-5284851. FAX 972-3-5285397. *3989*

MEDICINE AND SCIENCE IN SPORTS AND EXERCISE.
American College of Sports Medicine, Box 1440, Indianapolis, IN 46206-1440. TEL 317-637-9200. FAX 317-634-7817. *5131*

MEDICINE AND SOCIETY.
University of California Press, 2120 Berkeley Way, Berkeley, CA 94720. TEL 510-642-4247. FAX 510-643-7127. *5079*

MEDICINE AND SPORT SCIENCE.
S. Karger AG, Allschwilerstr. 10, P.O. Box, CH-4009 Basel, Switzerland. TEL 41-61-3061111. FAX 41-61-3061234. *5131*

MEDICINE AUSTRALIA.
N R D G P, 186 Molesworth St., Lismore, N.S.W. 2480, Australia. *4713*

MEDICINE, CONFLICT AND SURVIVAL.
Frank Cass, Newbury House, 890-900 Eastern Ave., Newbury Park, Ilford, Essex 1G2 7HH, England. TEL 44-181-599-8866. FAX 44-181-599-0984. *4713*

MEDICINE ON THE MIDWAY.
University of Chicago Hospitals, Office of Public Affairs, 5841 S. Maryland Ave., Mail Code 6063, Chicago, IL 60637. TEL 312-702-7322. FAX 312-702-3171. *1960*

MEDICINE, SCIENCE AND THE LAW.
Chiltern Publishing, 34 Aylesbury End, Beaconsfield, Bucks HP9 1LW, England. TEL 44-1494-678914. FAX 44-1494-678914. *4906*

MEDICINSKI RAZGLEDI.
Univerza v Ljubljani, Medicinska Fakulteta, Korytkova 2, 61105 Ljubljana, Slovenia. TEL 442-356. *4713*

MEDIEVAL AND RENAISSANCE AUTHORS.
E.J. Brill, P.O. Box 9000, 2300 PA Leiden, Netherlands. TEL 31-71-5353500. FAX 31-71-5317532. *4434*

MEDIEVAL AND RENAISSANCE AUTHORS AND TEXTS.
E.J. Brill, P.O. Box 9000, 2300 PA Leiden, Netherlands. TEL 31-71-5353500. FAX 31-71-5317532. *3583*

MEDIEVAL AND RENAISSANCE TEXTS.
E.J. Brill, P.O. Box 9000, 2300 PA Leiden, Netherlands. TEL 31-71-5353500. FAX 31-71-5317532. *3583*

MEDIEVAL ARCHAEOLOGY.
Society for Medieval Archaeology, Department of Archaeology, University of York, York YO1 1JZ, England. TEL 44-1904-636731. FAX 44-1904-433433. *373*

MEDIEVAL ENCOUNTERS.
E.J. Brill, P.O. Box 9000, 2300 PA Leiden, Netherlands. TEL 31-71-5353500. FAX 31-71-5317532. *3505*

MEDIEVAL ENGLISH THEATRE.
Medieval English Theatre, c/o Dept. of English, University of Lancaster, Lancaster LA1 4YT, England. TEL 44-1524-65201. FAX 44-1524-843085. *7009*

MEDIEVAL IBERIAN PENINSULA.
E.J. Brill, P.O. Box 9000, 2300 PA Leiden, Netherlands. TEL 31-71-5353500. FAX 31-71-5317532. *3583*

MEDIEVAL LIFE.
Medieval Life Publications, Rectory End, Gilling E., York YO6 4JQ, England. TEL 44-1439-788410. *3583*

THE MEDIEVAL MEDITERRANEAN.
E.J. Brill, P.O. Box 9000, 2300 PA Leiden, Netherlands. TEL 31-71-5353500. FAX 31-71-5317532. *3505*

MEDIEVAL PHILOSOPHY AND THEOLOGY.
Cambridge University Press, Edinburgh Bldg., Shaftesbury Rd., Cambridge CB2 2RU, England. TEL 44-1223-312393. FAX 44-1223-315052. *5737*

MEDIFILE.
T P S Drug Information Centre, P.O. Box 31238, Braamfontein 2017, South Africa. FAX 27-11-3393819. *5678*

MEDIPHORS.
Mediphors Inc., Box 327, Bloomsburg, PA 17815. *4434*

MEDITATOR'S NEWSLETTER.
Sacred Orchard Corporation, Box 298, Harriman, NY 10926-0298. TEL 914-783-3849. *6354*

MEDITERRANEAN HISTORICAL REVIEW.
Frank Cass, Newbury House, 890-900 Eastern Ave., Newbury Park, Ilford, Essex 1G2 7HH, England. TEL 44-181-599-8866. FAX 44-181-599-0984. *3658*

MEDITERRANEAN JOURNAL OF EDUCATIONAL STUDIES.
University of Malta, Faculty of Education, Msida MSD 06, Malta. TEL 356-32902936. FAX 356-336450. *2462*

MEDITERRANEAN QUARTERLY.
Duke University Press, Box 90660, Durham, NC 27708-0660. TEL 919-687-3600. FAX 919-688-4574. *6026*

MEDITSINA TRUDA I PROMYSHLENNAYA EKOLOGIYA.
Institut Meditsiny Truda, Prospekt Budennogo, 31, 105275 Moscow, Russia. TEL 7-095-3661110. FAX 7-095-3660583. *5494*

MEDIUM AEVUM.
Society for the Study of Mediaeval Languages and Literature, c/o Dr. D.G. Pattison, Hon. Treas., Magdalen College, Oxford OX1 4AU, England. TEL 44-1865-276087. *4434*

MEDSURG NURSING.
Jannetti Publications, Inc., East Holly Ave., Box 56, Pitman, NJ 08071-0056. TEL 609-256-2300. FAX 609-589-7463. *5148*

MEETINGS AND CONVENTIONS ASIA PACIFIC.
Venture Asia Publishing, 10 Craig Rd., Singapore 089670, Singapore. TEL 65-223-2911. FAX 65-223-0811. *5171*

MEGADRILOGICA.
Oligochaetology Laboratory, Sir Sandford Fleming College, P.O. Box 8000, Lindsay, ON K9V 5E6, Canada. TEL 705-324-9144. FAX 705-878-9312. *842*

MEGAMOT.
Henrietta Szold Institute, 9 Columbia St., Kiryat Menachem, Jerusalem 96583, Israel. FAX 2-437698. *6720*

MEIGUO YANJIU.
Zhongguo Shehui Kexueyuan, Meiguo Yanjiusuo, No. 3, Zhangzizhong Rd., Beijing 100007, People's Republic of China. TEL 86-10-400-0071. *6625*

MEIKAI UNIVERSITY DENTAL JOURNAL.
Meikai University, School of Dentistry, 1-1 Keyakidai, Sakado, Saitama 350-02, Japan. TEL 81-492-85-5511. FAX 81-492-87-6657. *4864*

MEIYUAN.
Lu Xun Meishu Xueyuan, 19 Sanhao Jie, Heping Qu, Shenyang, Liaoning 110003, People's Republic of China. TEL 3920125. FAX 390334. *454*

MELANGES DE SCIENCE RELIGIEUSE.
Institut Catholique de Lille, 60 bd. Vauban, B.P. 109, 59016 Lille Cedex, France. TEL 33-3-20134089. FAX 33-3-20134090. *6470*

MELBOURNE JOURNAL OF POLITICS.
University of Melbourne, Political Science Department, Parkville, Vic. 3052, Australia. TEL 61-3-3446571. *5944*

MELBOURNE UNIVERSITY LAW REVIEW.
University of Melbourne, Law School, Parkville 3052, Vic., Australia. TEL 61-3-93446593. FAX 61-3-93478087. *3989*

MELITA THEOLOGICA SUPPLEMENTARY SERIES.
Theology Students' Association, University of Malta, Msida MSD 04, Malta. TEL 356-333998. *6355*

MELLIAND TEXTILBERICHTE.
Melliand Textilberichte GmbH, Mainzer Landstr. 251, 60326 Frankfurt a.M., Germany. TEL 49-69-75951651. FAX 49-69-75951650. *6991*

MELVILLE SOCIETY EXTRACTS.
Melville Society, c/o Dennis Berthold, Department of English, Texas A&M University, College Station, TX 77843-4227. TEL 409-845-8317. FAX 409-862-2292. *4434*

MEMBRANE AND CELL BIOLOGY.
Gordon and Breach - Harwood Academic, Amsteldisk 166, 1st Fl., 1079 LH Amsterdam, Netherlands. *742*

MEMBRANE SCIENCE AND TECHNOLOGY SERIES.
Elsevier Science B.V., Books Division, P.O. Box 211, 1000 AE Amsterdam, Netherlands. TEL 31-20-4853911. FAX 31-20-4853705. *742*

MEMISA MEDISCH.
Memisa Medicus Mundi, Eendrachtsweg 48, 3012 LD Rotterdam, Netherlands. FAX 31-10-4047319. *4715*

MEMOIRS ON ENTOMOLOGY, INTERNATIONAL.
Associated Publishers, Box 140103, Gainesville, FL 32614-0103. TEL 352-371-4071. FAX 352-371-4071. *758*

MEMORIAL UNIVERSITY OF NEWFOUNDLAND. OCCASIONAL PAPERS IN BIOLOGY.
Memorial University of Newfoundland, Department of Biology, St. John's, NF A1C 5S7, Canada. TEL 709-737-7498. FAX 709-737-3018. *614*

MEMORIE DI SCIENZE GEOLOGICHE.
Universita di Padova, Dipartimento di Geologia, Paleontologia e Geofisica, Via Giotto 1, 35137 Padua, Italy. TEL 39-49-8272056. FAX 39-49-8272070. *2357*

MEMORY AND COGNITION.
Psychonomic Society, Inc., 1710 Fortview Rd., Austin, TX 78704. TEL 512-462-2442. *6135*

MENDELEEV COMMUNICATIONS.
Turpion - Moscow Ltd., 47 Leninsky prospekt, 117913 Moscow, Russia. TEL 7-95-1356417. FAX 7-95-1358860. *1760*

MENNINGER CLINIC. BULLETIN.
Menninger Foundation, Box 829, Topeka, KS 66601-0829. TEL 913-273-7500. FAX 913-273-8625. *5079*

MENNONITISCHE GESCHICHTSBLAETTER.
Mennonitischer Geschichtsverein, Weierhof, 67295 Bolanden, Germany. *6433*

MENOPAUSE.
Lippincott - Raven Publishers, 227 E. Washington Sq., Philadelphia, PA 19106. TEL 215-238-4200. FAX 215-238-4227. *4963*

MENTAL HEALTH NURSING JOURNAL.
Community Psychiatric Nurses Association, 50 Southwark St., London SE1 1UN, England. TEL 44-171-717-4000. FAX 44-171-717-4030. *5080*

MENTAL MEASUREMENTS YEARBOOK.
Buros Institute of Mental Measurements, 135 Bancroft, University of Nebraska-Lincoln, Lincoln, NE 68588-0348. TEL 402-472-6203. FAX 402-472-6207. *6136*

MENTAL RETARDATION AND DEVELOPMENTAL DISABILITIES (NEW YORK, 1970).
Plenum Publishing Corp., 233 Spring St., New York, NY 10013-1578. TEL 212-620-8000. FAX 212-463-0742. *5080*

MENTAL RETARDATION AND DEVELOPMENTAL DISABILITIES (NEW YORK, 1995).
John Wiley & Sons, Inc., Journals, 605 Third Ave., New York, NY 10158. TEL 212-850-6645. FAX 212-850-6021. *5080*

MERCER BULLETIN.
William M. Mercer Limited, B C E Place, 161 Bay St., P.O. Box 501, Toronto, ON M5J 2S5. TEL 416-868-2892. FAX 416-868-7555. *3826*

MERIDIAN.
American Library Association, Map and Geography Round Table, 50 E. Huron St., Chicago, IL 60611-2795. TEL 312-944-6780. FAX 312-440-9374. *4198*

MERIDIONALE.
Largo Randazzo, 89048 Siderno (RC), Italy. TEL 39-964-381698. FAX 39-964-381085. *3327*

MERRILL - PALMER QUARTERLY.
Wayne State University Press, Leonard N. Simons Bldg., 4809 Woodward Ave., Detroit, MI 48201-1309. TEL 313-577-6120. FAX 313-577-6131. *6136*

LE MESSAGE DE L'AHMADIYYAT.
Ahmadiyya Muslim Association, P.O. Box 6, Rose Hill, Mauritius. TEL 230-464-1747. FAX 230-454-2223. *6399*

MESSAGE OF THE TEACHER.
Ministry of Education, Educational Publications Division, P.O. Box 1646, Amman, Jordan. TEL 607331. FAX 666019. *2549*

METABOLIC ASPECTS OF CARDIOVASCULAR DISEASE.
Elsevier Science B.V., Books Division, P.O. Box 211, 1000 AE Amsterdam, Netherlands. TEL 31-20-4853911. FAX 31-20-4853705. *4821*

METABOLIC BRAIN DISEASE.
Plenum Publishing Corp., 233 Spring St., New York, NY 10013-1578. TEL 212-620-8000. FAX 212-463-0742. *4716*

METABOLIC, PEDIATRIC AND SYSTEMIC OPHTHALMOLOGY.
Opto Education Corp, 105 E. 90th St., New York, NY 10128. TEL 212-427-1246. *4996*

METABOLISM: CLINICAL AND EXPERIMENTAL.
W.B. Saunders Co., Curtis Center, 3rd Fl., Independence Sq. W., Philadelphia, PA 19106-3399. TEL 215-238-7800. FAX 215-238-6445. *4890*

METAL FINISHING.
Elsevier Science Inc., Box 945, New York, NY 10159-0945. TEL 212-633-3730. FAX 212-633-3680. *5202*

METAL IONS IN BIOLOGICAL SYSTEMS.
Marcel Dekker, Inc., 270 Madison Ave., New York, NY 10016. TEL 212-696-9000. FAX 212-658-4540. *1808*

METAL PHYSICS AND ADVANCED TECHNOLOGIES.
Gordon and Breach - Harwood Academic, Amsteldisk 166, 1st Fl., 1079 LH Amsterdam, Netherlands. *5202*

METAL SCIENCE AND HEAT TREATMENT.
Plenum Publishing Corp., Consultants Bureau, 233 Spring St., New York, NY 10013-1578. TEL 212-620-8468. FAX 212-463-0742. *5202*

METALLIZED PLASTICS.
Plenum Publishing Corp., 233 Spring St., New York, NY 10013-1578. TEL 212-620-8000. FAX 212-863-0742. *1806*

METALLURGICAL AND MATERIALS TRANSACTIONS A - PHYSICAL METALLURGY AND MATERIALS SCIENCE.
A S M International, Materials Information, Materials Park, OH 44073-0002. TEL 216-338-5151. FAX 216-338-4634. *5203*

METALLURGICAL AND MATERIALS TRANSACTIONS B - PROCESS METALLURGY AND MATERIALS PROCESSING SCIENCE.
A S M International, Materials Information, Materials Park, OH 44073-0002. TEL 216-338-5151. FAX 216-338-4634. *5203*

METALLURGIST.
Plenum Publishing Corp., Consultants Bureau, 233 Spring St., New York, NY 10013-1578. TEL 212-620-8468. FAX 212-463-0742. *5203*

METAPHILOSOPHY.
Blackwell Publishers Ltd., 108 Cowley Rd., Oxford OX4 1JF, England. TEL 44-1865-791100. FAX 44-1865-791347. *5737*

METAPHOR AND SYMBOLIC ACTIVITY.
Lawrence Erlbaum Associates, Inc., 10 Industrial Dr., Mahwah, NJ 07430-2262. TEL 201-236-9500. FAX 201-236-0072. *4281*

METEORITICS AND PLANETARY SCIENCE.
Meteoritical Society, c/o Hazel Sears, Business Editor, Department of Chemistry and Biochemistry, University of Arkansas, Fayetteville, AR 72701. TEL 501-575-7625. FAX 501-575-7778. *497*

METEOROLOGICAL AND GEOASTROPHYSICAL ABSTRACTS.
American Meteorological Society, c/o Inforonics, Inc., 550 Newtown Rd., Littleton, MA 01460. TEL 508-486-8976. FAX 508-486-0027. *5248*

METHOD: JOURNAL OF LONERGAN STUDIES.
Lonergan Institute at Boston College, Bapst Library, Boston College, Chestnut Hill, MA 02167-3806. TEL 617-552-8095. *5737*

METHODS: A COMPANION TO METHODS IN ENZYMOLOGY.
Academic Press, Inc., Journal Division, 525 B St., Ste. 1900, San Diego, CA 92101-4495. TEL 619-230-1840. FAX 619-699-6800. *666*

METHODS AND PHENOMENA.
Elsevier Science B.V., Books Division, P.O. Box 211, 1000 AE Amsterdam, Netherlands. TEL 31-20-4853911. FAX 31-20-4853705. *6545*

METHODS IN CELL BIOLOGY.
Academic Press, Inc., 525 B St., Ste. 1900, San Diego, CA 92101-4495. TEL 619-231-0926. FAX 619-699-6715. *742*

METHODS IN CELL SCIENCE.
Kluwer Academic Publishers, Postbus 17, 3300 AA Dordrecht, Netherlands. TEL 31-78-6392392. FAX 31-78-6392254. *789*

METHODS IN COMPUTATIONAL CHEMISTRY.
Plenum Publishing Corp., 233 Spring St., New York, NY 10013-1578. TEL 212-620-8000. FAX 212-463-0742. *1800*

METHODS IN ENZYMOLOGY.
Academic Press, Inc., 525 B St., Ste. 1900, San Diego, CA 92101-4495. TEL 619-231-0926. FAX 619-699-6715. *666*

METHODS IN GEOCHEMISTRY AND GEOPHYSICS.
Elsevier Science B.V., Books Division, P.O. Box 211, 1000 AE Amsterdam, Netherlands. TEL 31-20-4853911. FAX 31-20-4853705. *2319*

METHODS IN MICROANALYSIS.
Gordon and Breach - Harwood Academic, Amsteldisk 166, 1st Fl., 1079 LH Amsterdam, Netherlands. *797*

METHODS IN MOLECULAR AND CELLULAR BIOLOGY.
John Wiley & Sons, Inc., Journals, 605 Third Ave., New York, NY 10158. TEL 212-850-6645. FAX 212-850-6021. *742*

METHODS IN PHYSIOLOGY SERIES.
American Physiological Society, 9650 Rockville Pike, Bethesda. TEL 301-530-7164. FAX 301-571-8313. *819*

METHODS OF BIOCHEMICAL ANALYSIS.
John Wiley & Sons, Inc., 605 Third Ave., New York, NY 10158-0012. TEL 212-850-6000. *666*

METHODS OF FUNCTIONAL ANALYSIS AND TOPOLOGY.
T B I M C Scientific Publishers, P.O. Box 119, 253156 Kiev, Ukraine. FAX 380-44-5138407. *4593*

METHODS OF SURFACE CHARACTERIZATION.
Plenum Publishing Corp., 233 Spring St., New York, NY 10013-1578. TEL 212-620-8000. FAX 212-463-0742. *1806*

METMENYS.
A M & M Publications, 306 55th Place, Downers Grove, IL 60516. TEL 630-852-3887. *4434*

METRIKA.
Physica-Verlag GmbH und Co., Postfach 105280, 69042 Heidelberg, Germany. TEL 49-6221-487492. FAX 49-6221-487177. *6926*

METROECONOMICA.
Blackwell Publishers Ltd., 108 Cowley Rd., Oxford OX4 1JF, England. TEL 44-1865-791100. FAX 44-1865-791347. *985*

METRON.
Universita degli Studi di Roma, Facolta di Scienze Statistiche Demografiche ed Attuariali, Dipartimento di Statistica, Probabilita e Stat. Applicate, Piazzale Aldo Moro 5, 00185 Rome, Italy. TEL 39-6-4958308. FAX 39-6-4959241. *6926*

METROPOLITAN MUSEUM JOURNAL.
Metropolitan Museum of Art, 1000 Fifth Ave., New York, NY 10028. TEL 212-879-5500. FAX 212-472-8725. *5358*

METROPOLITAN TORONTO POLICE ASSOCIATION. NEWS & VIEWS.
Metropolitan Toronto Police Association, 180 Yorkland Blvd., North York, ON M2J 1R5, Canada. TEL 416-491-4301. FAX 416-494-4948. *2273*

MEXICAN STUDIES.
University of California Press, Journals Division, 2120 Berkeley Way, No. 5812, Berkeley, CA 94720-5812. TEL 510-643-7154. FAX 510-642-9917. *3785*

MEYER'S DIRECTORY OF GENEALOGICAL SOCIETIES IN THE U S A & CANADA.
Libra - Pipe Creek Publications, 5179 Perry Rd., Pipe Creek, Mt. Airy, MD 21771. TEL 410-875-2824. FAX 410-875-0180. *3232*

MEYLER'S SIDE EFFECTS OF DRUGS.
Elsevier Science B.V., Books Division, P.O. Box 211, 1000 AE Amsterdam, Netherlands. TEL 31-20-4853911. FAX 31-20-4853705. *5678*

MIAMI MEDICINE.
Dade County Medical Association, 1501 N.W. North River Dr., Miami, FL 33125. TEL 305-324-8717. FAX 305-325-1316. *4716*

MIAMIAN.
Miami University, University Relations Division, Oxford, OH 45056. TEL 513-529-7592. FAX 513-529-1950. *1961*

MICHIGAN ACADEMICIAN.
Michigan Academy of Science, Arts and Letters, 400 Fourth St., Ann Arbor, MI 48109-4816. TEL 313-936-2938. FAX 313-763-6927. *6545*

MICHIGAN ASSOCIATION OF SPEECH COMMUNICATION JOURNAL.
Michigan Association of Speech Communication, Eastern Michigan University, Communication & Theater Arts Dept., Ypsilanti, MI 48197. TEL 517-577-8727. *2587*

MICHIGAN BOTANIST.
Michigan Botanical Club, Inc., University of Michigan Herbarium, 2001 N. University Bldg., 1205 N. University Ave., Ann Arbor, MI 48109-1057. TEL 313-764-2407. *714*

MICHIGAN HISTORICAL REVIEW (MT. PLEASANT).
Clarke Historical Library, Central Michigan University, Mt. Pleasant, MI 48859. TEL 517-774-6567. FAX 517-774-4499. *3637*

MICHIGAN MONOGRAPHS IN CHINESE STUDIES.
University of Michigan, Center for Chinese Studies, 104 Lane Hall, Ann Arbor, MI 48109-1290. TEL 313-998-7181. FAX 313-936-2948. *3536*

MICHIGAN PHARMACIST.
Michigan Pharmacists Association, 815 N. Washington Ave., Lansing, MI 48906. TEL 517-484-1466. FAX 517-484-4893. *5678*

MICHIGAN READING JOURNAL.
Michigan Reading Association, c/o Robert L. Smith, 5241 Plainfield, N.E., Ste. 1, Grand Rapids, MI 49505. TEL 313-698-2098. *2463*

MICHIGAN STATE UNIVERSITY. AGRICULTURAL ECONOMICS REPORT.
Michigan State University, Department of Agricultural Economics, Reference Rm., East Lansing, MI 48824-1039. TEL 517-355-6650. FAX 517-432-1800. *198*

MICHIGAN STATE UNIVERSITY. DETROIT COLLEGE OF LAW. LAW REVIEW.
Michigan State University, Detroit College of Law, 130 E. Elizabeth St., Detroit, MI 48201. TEL 313-226-0151. FAX 313-965-5097. *3990*

MICHIGAN STATE UNIVERSITY. MUSEUM PUBLICATIONS. ANTHROPOLOGICAL SERIES.
Michigan State University, Museum, East Lansing, MI 48824. TEL 517-355-2370. *323*

MICHIGAN WATER ENVIRONMENT MATTERS.
Michigan Water Environment Association, P.O. Box 82410, Rochester, MI 48308-2410. TEL 810-375-0548. FAX 810-375-0522. *7297*

MICHKAR CHAKLAEI BEYISRAEL.
Agricultural Research Organization, Volcani Center, P.O. Box 6, Bet Dagan 50250, Israel. TEL 972-3-9683215. FAX 972-3-993998. *136*

MICHMANIM.
Reuben and Edith Hecht Museum, Haifa University, Mt. Carmel, Haifa 31905, Israel. TEL 972-4-8257773. FAX 972-4-8240724. *373*

MICROBIAL & COMPARATIVE GENOMICS.
Mary Ann Liebert, Inc. Publishers, 2 Madison Ave., Larchmont, NY 10538. TEL 914-834-3100. FAX 914-834-3688. *773*

MICROBIAL DRUG RESISTANCE: MECHANISM, EPIDEMIOLOGY, AND DISEASE.
Mary Ann Liebert, Inc. Publishers, 2 Madison Ave., Larchmont, NY 10538. TEL 914-834-3100. FAX 914-834-3688. *789*

MICROBIAL ECOLOGY.
Springer-Verlag, Life Science Journals, 175 Fifth Ave., New York, NY 10010. TEL 212-460-1500. FAX 212-473-6272. *789*

MICROBIOLOGY.
Maik Nauka - Interperiodica, Mezhdunarodnyi Otdel, Ul. Profsoyuznaya, 90, 117864 Moscow, Russia. TEL 7-095-3360066. FAX 7-095-3360666. *790*

MICROBIOLOGY AND IMMUNOLOGY.
Center for Academic Publications Japan, 2-4-16 Yayoi, Bunkyo-ku, Tokyo 113, Japan. TEL 81-3-3817-5821. FAX 81-3-3817-5820. *790*

MICROBIOLOGY AND MOLECULAR BIOLOGY REVIEWS.
American Society for Microbiology, 1325 Massachusetts Ave., N.W., Washington, DC 20005. TEL 202-737-3600. *790*

MICROBIOLOGY EUROPE.
V C H Verlagsgesellschaft mbH, Postfach 101161, 69451 Weinheim, Germany. TEL 49-6201-606147. FAX 49-6201-606117. *790*

MICROBIOLOGY SERIES.
Marcel Dekker, Inc., 270 Madison Ave., New York, NY 10016. TEL 212-889-9595. FAX 212-658-4540. *790*

MICROCHEMICAL JOURNAL.
Academic Press, Inc., Journal Division, 525 B St., Ste. 1900, San Diego, CA 92101-4495. TEL 619-230-1840. FAX 619-699-6800. *797*

MICROCIRCULATION.
Chapman & Hall, 2-6 Boundary Row, London SE1 8HN, England. TEL 44-171-8650066. FAX 44-171-5229623. *4716*

MICROCIRCULATION, ENDOTHELIUM AND LYMPHATICS.
B M A Publications, Box 562, 31 Willows Rd., Ayer, MA 01432-0562. TEL 212-270-2194. *4921*

MICROCIRCULATION REVIEWS.
Kluwer Academic Publishers, Postbus 17, 3300 AA Dordrecht, Netherlands. TEL 31-78-6392392. FAX 31-78-6392254. *819*

MICROCOMPUTERS IN CIVIL ENGINEERING.
Blackwell Publishers, 238 Main St., Cambridge, MA 02142. TEL 617-547-7110. FAX 617-547-0789. *2806*

MICROELECTRONIC ENGINEERING.
North-Holland, P.O. Box 211, 1000 AE Amsterdam, Netherlands. TEL 31-20-4853911. FAX 31-20-4853598. *2646*

MICROELECTRONICS AND RELIABILITY.
Elsevier Science Ltd., Pergamon, P.O. Box 800, Kidlington, Oxford OX5 1DX, England. TEL 44-1865-843000. FAX 44-1865-843010. *2646*

MICROELECTRONICS JOURNAL.
Elsevier Science Ltd., P.O. Box 800, Kidlington, Oxford OX5 1DX, England. TEL 44-1865-843000. FAX 44-1865-843010. *2646*

MICRON.
Elsevier Science Ltd., Pergamon, P.O. Box 800, Kidlington, Oxford OX5 1DX, England. TEL 44-1865-843000. FAX 44-1865-843010. *797*

MICRONESICA.
University of Guam Press, UOG Station, Mangilao, Guam 96923. TEL 671-735-2787. FAX 671-734-1299. *323*

MICROPALEONTOLOGY.
American Museum of Natural History, Central Park W. at 79th St., New York, NY 10024-5192. TEL 212-769-5656. FAX 212-769-5653. *5560*

MICROPOROUS MATERIALS.
Elsevier Science B.V., P.O. Box 211, 1000 AE Amsterdam, Netherlands. TEL 31-20-4853911. FAX 31-20-4853598. *1833*

MICROPROCESSOR - BASED AND INTELLIGENT SYSTEMS ENGINEERING.
Kluwer Academic Publishers, Postbus 17, 3300 AA Dordrecht, Netherlands. TEL 31-78-6392392. FAX 31-78-6392254. *2732*

MICROPROCESSOR REPORT.
874 Gravenstein Hwy. So., Ste.14, Sebastopol, CA 95472. TEL 707-824-4004. FAX 707-823-0504. *2191*

MICROPROCESSORS & MICROSYSTEMS.
Elsevier Science B.V., P.O. Box 211, 1000 AE Amsterdam, Netherlands. TEL 31-20-4853911. FAX 31-20-4853598. *2191*

MICROSCOPE.
McCrone Research Institute, 2820 S. Michigan Ave., Chicago, IL 60616-3292. TEL 312-842-7100. FAX 312-842-1078. *797*

MICROSCOPICAL SOCIETY OF CANADA. BULLETIN.
Microscopical Society of Canada, c/o F. Leggett, 2918 13th Ave. S., Lethbridge, AB T1K 0T2, Canada. TEL 403-327-4342. FAX 403-382-3156. *797*

MICROSCOPY AND MICROANALYSIS.
Springer-Verlag, 175 Fifth Ave., New York, NY 10060. TEL 212-460-1500. FAX 212-533-5977. *3804*

MICROSURGERY.
John Wiley & Sons, Inc., Journals, 605 Third Ave., New York, NY 10158. TEL 212-850-6645. FAX 212-850-6021. *5148*

MICROSYSTEM TECHNOLOGIES.
Springer-Verlag, Heidelberger Platz 3, 14197 Berlin, Germany. TEL 49-30-82787-0. FAX 49-30-82787448. *2116*

MICROVASCULAR RESEARCH.
Academic Press, Inc., Journal Division, 525 B St., Ste. 1900, San Diego, CA 92101-4495. TEL 619-230-1840. FAX 619-699-6800. *4822*

MICROWAVE & OPTICAL TECHNOLOGY LETTERS.
John Wiley & Sons, Inc., Journals, 605 Third Ave., New York, NY 10158. TEL 212-850-6645. FAX 212-850-6021. *5865*

MICROWAVE JOURNAL (INTERNATIONAL EDITION).
Horizon - House - Publications, Inc., 685 Canton St., Norwood, MA 02062. TEL 617-769-9750. FAX 617-762-9230. *2840*

MID-AMERICA (CHICAGO).
Loyola University of Chicago, Department of History, 6525 Sheridan Rd., Chicago, IL 60626. TEL 312-508-2230. *3637*

MID-AMERICA FOLKLORE.
Mid-America Folklore Society, c/o Lyon College, Batesville, AR 72501. TEL 501-793-9813. FAX 501-698-4346. *3089*

MID-AMERICAN JOURNAL OF BUSINESS.
Ball State University, Bureau of Business Research, Muncie, IN 47306. TEL 317-285-5926. FAX 317-285-8024. *985*

MID-AMERICAN REVIEW.
Bowling Green State University, Department of English, Bowling Green State University, Bowling Green, OH 43403. TEL 419-372-2725. *4346*

MIDDLE EAST COMMERCIAL LAW REVIEW.
Sweet & Maxwell, Mill St., Oxford OX2 0JU, England. TEL 44-1865-249248. FAX 44-1865-792301. *4122*

MIDDLE EAST FORUM.
Institute of Middle East Studies "Al Mamun" (IMSAM), c/o Prof. John Karkazis, Ed., Smirnis 1, 15772 Zografou, Greece. TEL 30-1-6123631. FAX 30-1-6123631. *6026*

MIDDLE EAST REPORT.
Middle East Research & Information Project, 1500 Massachusetts Ave., N.W., Ste. 119, Washington, DC 20005. TEL 202-223-3677. FAX 202-223-3604. *3658*

MIDDLE EASTERN STUDIES.
Frank Cass, Newbury House, 890-900 Eastern Ave., Newbury Park, Ilford, Essex 1G2 7HH, England. TEL 44-181-599-8836. FAX 44-181-599-0984. *3658*

MIDDLE SCHOOL JOURNAL.
National Middle School Association, 2600 Corporate Exchange Dr., Ste. 370, Columbus, OH 43231. TEL 614-895-4730. FAX 614-895-4750. *2611*

MIDDLE STATES COUNCIL FOR THE SOCIAL STUDIES. JOURNAL.
Middle States Council for the Social Studies, Rider College, 2083 Lawrenceville Rd., Lawrenceville, NJ 08648-3099. TEL 609-896-5068. *6626*

MIDLAND CATHOLIC HISTORY.
Midland Catholic History Society, c/o Vincent Burke, 16 Brandhall Ct., Wolverhampton Rd., Warley, W. Midlands B68 8DE, England. *6470*

MIDLAND HISTORY.
University of Birmingham, School of History, Edgbaston, Birmingham B15 2TT, England. TEL 44-121-414-5761. *3584*

MIDLAND REVIEW.
Oklahoma State University, English Department, Morrill Hall, Stillwater, OK 74078. TEL 405-744-9474. *4435*

MIDWEST HISTORY OF EDUCATION SOCIETY. JOURNAL.
Midwest History of Education Society, University of Dayton, Dayton, OH 45469-0525. TEL 513-229-3328. *2463*

MIDWEST QUARTERLY.
Pittsburg State University, Midwest Quarterly, Pittsburg, KS 66762. TEL 316-235-4317. FAX 316-232-7515. *3786*

MIDWESTERNER.
Big Shoulders Publishing Company, 343 S. Dearborn St., Ste. 610, Chicago, IL 60604-3807. TEL 312-913-9610. FAX 312-913-9639. *3379*

MIDWIVES.
Nursing Notes Ltd., 120 High Rd., E. Finchley, London N2 8AG, England. TEL 44-181-442-0801. FAX 44-181-442-0623. *4963*

MIGRATORI ALATI.
R G F di Realini Gianfranco e C. s.a.s., Via Cascine, 4, 21027 Ispra (VA), Italy. TEL 0332-781057. *806*

MIKROBIYOLOJI BULTENI.
Ankara Microbiology Society, Hacettepe University Faculty of Medicine, Dept. of Microbiology, 06100 Ankara, Turkey. TEL 90-312-3114752. FAX 90-312-3115250. *790*

MILITARY ADVOCATE.
Judge Advocates Association, 1815 H St. N.W., Ste. 408, Washington, DC 20006-3697. TEL 202-628-0979. FAX 202-775-0295. *4143*

MILITARY CHAPLAIN.
Military Chaplains Association of the United States of America, Box 42660, Washington, DC 20015-0660. TEL 717-642-6792. FAX 717-642-6792. *5276*

MILITARY HISTORY OF THE WEST.
University of North Texas, Department of History, Box 310650, Denton, TX 76203-0650. TEL 940-565-2288. FAX 940-369-8838. *3637*

MILITARY MEDICINE.
Association of Military Surgeons of the U S, 9320 Old Georgetown Rd., Bethesda, MD 20814. TEL 301-897-8800. FAX 301-530-5446. *4716*

MILITARY OPERATIONS RESEARCH.
Gordon and Breach - Harwood Academic, Asteldisk 166, 1st Fl., 1079 LH Amsterdam, Netherlands. *5277*

MILITARY PSYCHOLOGY.
Lawrence Erlbaum Associates, Inc., 10 Industrial Dr., Mahwah, NJ 07430-2262. TEL 201-236-9500. FAX 201-236-0072. *6136*

MILITARY SCIENCE INDEX.
Royal Military College of Science Library, Shrivenham, Swindon, Wiltshire SN6 8LA, England. TEL 44-1793-785484. FAX 44-1793-785555. *5292*

MILJOE EKO.
A M T Hedberg Foerlag AB, Byvaegen 54, S-133 34 Saltsjoebaden, Sweden. TEL 46-8-748-00-10. FAX 56-8-748-02-98. *2942*

MILLENNIUM.
Millennium Publishing Group, Houghton St., London WC2A 2AE, England. TEL 44-171-955-7929. FAX 44-171-955-7438. *6027*

MILLTOWN STUDIES.
Milltown Institute of Theology & Philosophy, Milltown Park, Dublin 6, Ireland. TEL 353-1-2698802. FAX 353-1-2692528. *6355*

MINAMI-KYUSHU DAIGAKU ENGEIGAKUBU KENKYU HOKOKU. JINBUN SHAKAI KAGAKUKEI.
Minami-Kyushu Daigaku, Engeigakubu, Hibarigaoka, Takanabe-cho, Koyu-gun, Miyazaki-ken 884, Japan. TEL 81-983-23-0793. FAX 81-983-22-3444. *6626*

MINAMI-KYUSHU DAIGAKU ENGEIGAKUBU KENKYU HOKOKU. SHIZEN KAGAKUKEI.
Minami-Kyushu Daigaku, Engeigakubu, Hibarigaoka, Takanabe-cho, Koyu-gun, Miyazaki-ken 884, Japan. TEL 81-983-23-0793. FAX 81-983-22-3444. *3198*

MINAMI TAIHEIYO KENKYU.
Kagoshima University, Research Center for the South Pacific, 1-21-24, Korimoto, Kagoshima 890, Japan. TEL 81-99-285-7394. FAX 81-99-256-9358. *6545*

MIND & LANGUAGE.
Blackwell Publishers Ltd., 108 Cowley Rd., Oxford OX4 1JF, England. TEL 44-1865-791100. FAX 44-1865-791347. *5738*

MIND YOUR OWN BUSINESS.
Market Place Publishing Ltd., 106 Church Rd., London SE19 2UB, England. TEL 44-181-771-3614. FAX 44-181-771-4592. *1558*

MINDANAO ART & CULTURE.
Mindanao State University, Mamitua Saber Research Center, P.O. Box 5594, Iligan City 9200, Philippines. *3089*

MINDANAO STATE UNIVERSITY. U R C PROFESSIONAL PAPERS.
Mindanao State University, Mamitua Saber Research Center, P.O. Box 5594, Iligan City 9200, Philippines. *6545*

MINDS AND MACHINES.
Kluwer Academic Publishers, Postbus 17, 3300 AA Dordrecht, Netherlands. TEL 31-78-6392392. FAX 31-78-6392254. *2103*

MINERAL AND ELECTROLYTE METABOLISM.
S. Karger AG, Allschwilerstr. 10, P.O. Box, CH-4009 Basel, Switzerland. TEL 41-61-3061111. FAX 41-61-3061234. *4716*

MINERAL INDUSTRY SURVEY.
Geology and Mines Commission, Upper Brickdam, P.O. Box 1028, Georgetown, Guyana. FAX 592-2-53047. *5307*

MINERAL PROCESSING AND EXTRACTIVE METALLURGY REVIEW.
Gordon and Breach - Harwood Academic, Amsteldisk 166, 1st Fl., 1079 LH Amsterdam, Netherlands. *5204*

MINERAL RESOURCES ENGINEERING.
World Scientific Publishing Co. Pte. Ltd., Farrer Rd., P.O. Box 128, Singapore 9128, Singapore. TEL 65-3825663. FAX 65-3825919. *5307*

MINERALES.
Instituto de Ingenieros de Minas de Chile, Casilla 14668, Correo 21, Santiago, Chile. TEL 56-2-6953849. FAX 56-2-6972351. *5307*

THE MINERALOGICAL RECORD.
Mineralogical Record, Inc., 4631 Paseo Tubutama, Tucson, AZ 85740. FAX 520-544-0815. *3671*

MINERALS AND METALLURGICAL PROCESSING.
Society for Mining, Metallurgy and Exploration, Box 625002, Littleton, CO 80162-5002. TEL 303-973-9550. FAX 303-973-3845. *5308*

MINERALS ENGINEERING.
Elsevier Science Ltd., Pergamon, P.O. Box 800, Kidlington, Oxford OX5 1DX, England. TEL 44-1865-843000. FAX 44-1865-843010. *5308*

MINERALS RESEARCH LABORATORY NEWSLETTER.
North Carolina State University, Minerals Research Laboratory, 180 Coxe Ave., Asheville, NC 28801. TEL 704-251-6155. *5308*

MINERVA.
Royal Institution of South Wales, Swansea Museum, Victoria Rd., Swansea SA1 1SN, Wales. TEL 44-1792-653763. *3584*

MINERVA ANESTESIOLOGICA.
Edizioni Minerva Medica, Corso Bramante 83-85, 10126 Turin, Italy. TEL 39-11-678282. FAX 39-11-674502. *4806*

MINERVA BIOTECNOLOGICA.
Edizioni Minerva Medica, Corso Bramante 83-85, 10126 Turin, Italy. TEL 39-11-678282. FAX 39-11-674502. *685*

MINERVA CARDIOANGIOLOGICA.
Edizioni Minerva Medica, Corso Bramante 83-85, 10126 Turin, Italy. TEL 39-11-678282. FAX 39-11-674502. *4822*

MINERVA CHIRURGICA.
Edizioni Minerva Medica, Corso Bramante 83-85, 10126 Turin, Italy. TEL 39-11-678282. FAX 39-11-674502. *5148*

MINERVA ENDOCRINOLOGICA.
Edizioni Minerva Medica, Corso Bramante 83-85, 10126 Turin, Italy. TEL 39-11-678282. FAX 39-11-674502. *4890*

MINERVA GASTROENTEROLOGICA E DIETOLOGICA.
Edizioni Minerva Medica, Corso Bramante 83-85, 10126 Turin, Italy. TEL 39-11-678282. FAX 39-11-674502. *4913*

MINERVA GINECOLOGICA.
Edizioni Minerva Medica, Corso Bramante 83-85, 10126 Turin, Italy. TEL 39-11-678282. FAX 39-11-674502. *4963*

MINERVA MEDICA.
Edizioni Minerva Medica, Corso Bramante 83-85, 10126 Turin, Italy. TEL 39-11-678282. FAX 39-11-674502. *4926*

MINERVA ORTOGNATODONTICA.
Edizioni Minerva Medica, Corso Bramante 83-85, 10126 Turin, Italy. TEL 39-11-678282. FAX 39-11-674502. *4864*

MINERVA PEDIATRICA.
Edizioni Minerva Medica, Corso Bramante 83-85, 10126 Turin, Italy. TEL 39-11-678282. FAX 39-11-674502. *5034*

MINERVA PNEUMOLOGICA.
Edizioni Minerva Medica, Corso Bramante 83-85, 10126 Turin, Italy. TEL 39-11-678282. FAX 39-11-674502. *5120*

MINERVA PSICHIATRICA.
Edizioni Minerva Medica, Corso Bramante 83-85, 10126 Turin, Italy. TEL 39-11-678282. FAX 39-11-674502. *5080*

MINERVA STOMATOLOGICA.
Edizioni Minerva Medica, Corso Bramante 83-85, 10126 Turin, Italy. TEL 39-11-678282. FAX 39-11-674502. *4864*

MINERVA UROLOGICA E NEFROLOGICA.
Edizioni Minerva Medica, Corso Bramante 83-85, 10126 Turin, Italy. TEL 39-11-678282. FAX 39-11-674502. *5163*

MING PAO DAILY NEWS.
Ming Pao Newspaper Canada Ltd., 1355 Huntingwood Dr., Scarborough, ON M1S 3J1, Canada. TEL 416-321-0088. FAX 416-321-6339. *3028*

MINIATURE COLLECTOR.
Scott Publications, 30595 Eight Mile Rd., Livonia, MI 48152-1798. TEL 810-477-6650. FAX 810-477-6795. *3671*

MINIMALLY INVASIVE THERAPY AND ALLIED TECHNOLOGIES.
Blackwell Science Ltd., Osney Mead, Oxford OX2 0EL, England. TEL 44-1865-206206. FAX 44-1865-721205. *4716*

MINING ENGINEERING.
Society for Mining, Metallurgy and Exploration, Box 625002, Littleton, CO 80162-5002. TEL 303-973-9550. FAX 303-973-3845. *5309*

REFEREED SERIALS

MINING R & D NEWS.
C S I R, Division of Mining Technology, P.O. Box 91230, Auckland Park 2006, South Africa. *5310*

MINNESOTA ACADEMY OF SCIENCE. JOURNAL.
Minnesota Academy of Science, 408 St. Peter St., Ste. 410, St. Paul, MN 55102-1119. TEL 612-227-6361. *6545*

MINNESOTA LITERATURE.
1 Nord Circle, St. Paul, MN 55127. TEL 612-483-3904. *4435*

MINNESOTA STUDIES IN THE PHILOSOPHY OF SCIENCE.
University of Minnesota Press, 111 Third Ave. S., Ste. 290, Minneapolis, MN 55401-2520. TEL 773-568-1550. FAX 773-660-2235. *5738*

MINOTAURO.
Gruppo Autonomo di Psicologia Analitica, Via della Consulta 50, 00184 Rome, Italy. TEL 39-6-4885304. FAX 39-6-36303643. *6136*

MINZU.
Minzu Zazhishe, 18 Wenshuyuan Jie, Chengdu, Sichuan 610017, People's Republic of China. TEL 86-28-6610665. FAX 86-28-6742119. *3029*

MIR KAMNYA.
Plus Ltd. Publishing, P.O. Box 162, 103050 Moscow, Russia. TEL 7-95-2033574. FAX 7-95-2926511. *5310*

MIRROR NEWS.
Henry Ford Community College, Student Center, Rm. C-4K, 5101 Evergreen, Dearborn, MI 48128. TEL 313-845-9639. FAX 313-845-9876. *1961*

MISCEL.LANIA ZOOLOGICA.
Museu de Zoologia, Attn: Dr. Anna Omedes, Ed., Apdo. de Correus 593, 08080 Barcelona, Spain. TEL 34-3-3196912. FAX 34-3-3104999. *842*

MISSISSIPPI COLLEGE LAW REVIEW.
Mississippi College Law Review, 151 E. Griffith St., Jackson, MS 39201. TEL 601-925-7167. FAX 601-925-7113. *3990*

MISSISSIPPI GEOLOGY.
Department of Environmental Quality, Office of Geology, Box 20307, Jackson, MS 39289. TEL 601-961-5500. FAX 601-961-5521. *2358*

MISSISSIPPI KITE.
Mississippi Ornithological Society, Box Z, Mississippi State, MS 39762. *806*

MISSISSIPPI REVIEW.
University of Southern Mississippi, Center for Writers, Box 5144, Southern Sta., Hattiesburg, MS 39406. TEL 601-266-4321. FAX 601-266-5757. *4436*

MISSISSIPPI STATE MEDICAL ASSOCIATION. JOURNAL.
Mississippi State Medical Association, 735 Riverside Dr., Box 5229, Jackson, MS 39296-5229. TEL 601-354-5433. *4717*

MISSOURI. DIVISION OF GEOLOGICAL SURVEY AND WATER RESOURCES. ENGINEERING GEOLOGY SERIES.
Department of Natural Resources, Division of Geology and Land Survey, Box 250, Rolla, MO 65401. TEL 314-368-2125. *2794*

MISSOURI. DIVISION OF HIGHWAY SAFETY (YEAR). HIGHWAY SAFETY PLAN.
Division of Highway Safety, Box 104808, Jefferson City, MO 65110-4808. TEL 314-751-4161. FAX 314-634-5977. *7139*

MISSOURI ACADEMY OF SCIENCE. TRANSACTIONS.
Missouri Academy of Science, Ophelia Parrish 113B, 100 E. Normal St., Kirksville, MO 63501-4221. TEL 816-785-4635. FAX 816-785-4045. *6546*

MISSOURI JOURNAL OF RESEARCH IN MUSIC EDUCATION.
Missouri Music Educators Association, c/o Martin J. Bergee, 140 Fine Arts. Missouri University, Columbia, MO 65211. TEL 417-887-5252. FAX 314-882-5071. *5410*

MISYJNE DROGI.
Misjonarze Oblaci Maryi Niepokalanej, Ul. Ostatnia 14, 60-102 Poznan, Poland. TEL 48-61-306517. FAX 48-61-305513. *6471*

MITIGATION AND ADAPTATION STRATEGIES FOR GLOBAL CHANGE.
Kluwer Academic Publishers, Postbus 17, 3300 AA Dordrecht, Netherlands. TEL 31-78-6392392. FAX 31-78-6392254. *2942*

MITTELLATEINISCHE STUDIEN UND TEXTE.
E.J. Brill, P.O. Box 9000, 2300 PA Leiden, Netherlands. TEL 31-71-5353500. FAX 31-71-5317532. *3585*

HAMIZRAH HEHADASH.
Magnes Press, Hebrew University, Jerusalem, P.O. Box 7695, Jerusalem 91076, Israel. TEL 972-2-5660341. FAX 972-2-5633370. *5533*

MNEMOSYNE.
E.J. Brill, P.O. Box 9000, 2300 PA Leiden, Netherlands. TEL 31-71-5353500. FAX 31-71-5317532. *1906*

MNEMOSYNE. SUPPLEMENTS.
E.J. Brill, P.O. Box 9000, 2300 PA Leiden, Netherlands. TEL 31-71-5353500. FAX 31-71-5317532. *1906*

MOBILE NETWORKS & APPLICATIONS.
Baltzer Science Publishers B.V., P.O. Box 221, 1400 AE Bussum, Netherlands. TEL 31-20-6370061. FAX 31-20-6323651. *2137*

MODELISM INTERNATIONAL.
Piata Presei Libere 1, 71341 Bucharest, Rumania. TEL 40-1-6170101. FAX 40-1-2102204. *3673*

MODELLING, MEASUREMENT AND CONTROL.
A M S E Press, 16 av. de Grange Blanche, 69160 Tassin-la-Demi-Lune, France. TEL 33-4-78343604. FAX 33-4-78345417. *4623*

MODELLING, MEASUREMENT & CONTROL. A: GENERAL PHYSICS, ELECTRONICS, ELECTRICAL ENGINEERING.
A M S E Press, 16 av. de Grange Blanche, 69160 Tassin-la-Demi-Lune, France. TEL 33-4-78343604. FAX 33-4-78345417. *4623*

MODELLING, MEASUREMENT & CONTROL. B: SOLID & FLUID MECHANICS & THERMICS, MECHANICAL SYSTEMS.
A M S E Press, 16 av. de Grange Blanche, 69160 Tassin-la-Demi-Lune, France. TEL 33-4-78343604. FAX 33-4-78345417. *4623*

MODELLING, MEASUREMENT & CONTROL. C: ENERGETICS, CHEMISTRY, EARTH, ENVIRONMENTAL & BIOMEDICAL PROBLEMS.
A M S E Press, 16 av. de Grange Blanche, 69160 Tassin-la-Demi-Lune, France. TEL 33-4-78343604. FAX 33-4-78345417. *4623*

MODELLING, MEASUREMENT & CONTROL. D: MANUFACTURING, MANAGEMENT, HUMAN AND SOCIO-ECONOMIC PROBLEMS.
A M S E Press, 16 av. de Grange Blanche, 69160 Tassin-la-Demi-Lune, France. TEL 33-4-78343604. FAX 33-4-78345417. *4623*

MODELS OF SCIENTIFIC THOUGHT.
Gordon and Breach - Harwood Academic, Amsteldisk 166, 1st Fl., 1079 LH Amsterdam, Netherlands. *4281*

MODERN AGING RESEARCH.
John Wiley & Sons, Inc., Journals, 605 Third Ave., New York, NY 10158. TEL 212-475-7700. *3442*

MODERN ANALYTICAL CHEMISTRY.
Plenum Publishing Corp., 233 Spring St., New York, NY 10013-1578. TEL 212-620-8000. FAX 212-463-0742. *1794*

MODERN APPROACHES IN GEOPHYSICS.
Kluwer Academic Publishers, Postbus 17, 3300 AA Dordrecht, Netherlands. TEL 31-78-6392392. FAX 31-78-6392254. *2387*

MODERN ASPECTS OF ELECTROCHEMISTRY.
Plenum Publishing Corp., 233 Spring St., New York, NY 10013-1578. TEL 212-620-8000. FAX 212-463-0742. *1806*

MODERN AUSTRIAN LITERATURE.
International Arthur Schnitzler Research Association, c/o Donald G. Daviau, Ed., Department of Literatures and Languages, University of California, Riverside, CA 92521. TEL 909-787-5007. FAX 909-787-2160. *4436*

MODERN BIOLOGY SERIES.
Holt, Rinehart and Winston, Inc., c/o Harcourt Brace Jovanovich, 6277 Sea Harbor Dr., Orlando, FL 32887. TEL 407-345-2500. *614*

MODERN FICTION STUDIES.
Johns Hopkins University Press, Journals Publishing Division, 2715 N. Charles St., Baltimore, MD 21218-4319. TEL 410-516-6987. FAX 410-516-6968. *4436*

MODERN GEOLOGY.
Gordon and Breach - Harwood Academic, Amsteldisk 166, 1st Fl., 1079 LH Amsterdam, Netherlands. *2358*

MODERN GREEK SOCIETY: A SOCIAL SCIENCE NEWSLETTER.
Modern Greek Society, Box 9411, Providence, RI 02940-9411. TEL 401-274-2397. FAX 401-456-8679. *3585*

MODERN GREEK STUDIES ASSOCIATION BULLETIN.
Modern Greek Studies Association, Box 1826, New Haven, CT 06508. TEL 203-392-5668. FAX 203-392-5670. *3585*

MODERN INORGANIC CHEMISTRY.
Plenum Publishing Corp., 233 Spring St., New York, NY 10013-1578. TEL 212-620-8000. FAX 212-463-0742. *1808*

MODERN LANGUAGE JOURNAL.
University of Wisconsin Press, Journal Division, 114 N. Murray St., Madison, WI 53715. TEL 608-262-4925. FAX 608-262-7560. *4281*

MODERN LOGIC.
Modern Logic Publishing, c/o Sha'n Stefani, 224 E. 205h St., 1C, Covington, KY 41014. TEL 515-292-8990. *4593*

MODERN MEDICINE.
Advanstar Communications, Inc., 7500 Old Oak Blvd., Cleveland, OH 44130. TEL 216-826-2839. FAX 216-891-2726. *4717*

MODERN METHODS IN PHARMACOLOGY.
John Wiley & Sons, Inc., Journals, 605 Third Ave., New York, NY 10158. TEL 212-475-7700. *5679*

MODERN MONOGRAPHS IN ANALYTICAL CHEMISTRY.
Marcel Dekker, Inc., 270 Madison Ave., New York, NY 10016. TEL 212-696-9000. FAX 212-658-4540. *1794*

MODERN NEURORADIOLOGY SERIES.
Lippincott - Raven Publishers, 227 E. Washington Sq., Philadelphia, PA 19106. TEL 215-238-4200. FAX 215-238-4227. *5111*

MODERN ORTHODOX SAINTS.
Institute for Byzantine and Modern Greek Studies, 115 Gilbert Rd., Belmont, MA 02178. TEL 617-484-6595. *6392*

MODERN PATHOLOGY.
Williams & Wilkins, 351 W. Camden St., Baltimore, MD 21201-2436. TEL 410-528-4068. FAX 410-528-4452. *4717*

MODERN PHILOLOGY.
University of Chicago Press, Journals Division, 5720 S. Woodlawn Ave., Chicago, IL 60637. TEL 773-753-3347. FAX 773-753-0811. *4282*

MODERN POETRY IN TRANSLATION.
King's College London, School of Humanities, Strand, London WC2R 2LS, England. TEL 44-171-873-2360. FAX 44-171-873-2415. *4514*

MODERN PROBLEMS IN CONDENSED MATTER SCIENCES.
Elsevier Science B.V., Books Division, P.O. Box 211, 1000 AE Amsterdam, Netherlands. TEL 31-20-4853911. FAX 31-20-4853705. *5815*

MODERN PROBLEMS OF PHARMACOPSYCHIATRY.
S. Karger AG, Allschwilerstr. 10, P.O. Box, CH-4009 Basel, Switzerland. TEL 41-61-3061111. FAX 41-61-3061234. *5080*

MODERN PSYCHOANALYSIS.
Center for Modern Psychoanalytic Studies, 16 W. 10th St., New York, NY 10011. TEL 212-260-7050. FAX 212-260-7052. *6136*

MODERN SCHOOLMAN.
Saint Louis University, 221 N. Grand, St. Louis, MO 63103. TEL 314-977-3149. *5738*

MODERN THEOLOGY.
Blackwell Publishers Ltd., 108 Cowley Rd., Oxford OX4 1JF, England. TEL 44-1865-791100. FAX 44-1865-791347. *6356*

MODERN THEORETICAL CHEMISTRY.
Plenum Publishing Corp., 233 Spring St., New York, NY 10013-1578. TEL 212-620-8000. FAX 212-463-0742. *1760*

MODERNISM - MODERNITY.
Johns Hopkins University Press, Journals Publishing Division, 2715 N. Charles St., Baltimore, MD 21218. TEL 410-516-6987. FAX 410-516-6968. *3506*

MOLECULAR AND BIOCHEMICAL PARASITOLOGY.
Elsevier Science B.V., P.O. Box 211, 1000 AE Amsterdam, Netherlands. TEL 31-20-4853911. FAX 31-20-4853598. *666*

MOLECULAR AND CELLULAR BIOCHEMISTRY.
Kluwer Academic Publishers Boston, Box 358, Accord Sta., Hingham, MA 02018-0358. TEL 617-871-6600. FAX 617-871-6528. *666*

MOLECULAR AND CELLULAR BIOLOGY.
American Society for Microbiology, 1325 Massachusetts Ave., N.W., Washington, DC 20005. TEL 202-737-3600. *791*

MOLECULAR AND CELLULAR ENDOCRINOLOGY.
Elsevier Science Ireland Ltd., P.O. Box 85, Limerick, Ireland. TEL 353-61-471944. FAX 353-61-472144. *4891*

MOLECULAR AND CELLULAR NEUROSCIENCES.
Academic Press, Inc., Journal Division, 525 B St., Ste. 1900, San Diego, CA 92101-4495. TEL 619-230-1840. FAX 619-699-6800. *5080*

MOLECULAR AND CHEMICAL NEUROPATHOLOGY.
Humana Press Inc., 999 Riverview Dr., Ste. 208, Totowa, NJ 07512. TEL 973-256-1699. FAX 973-256-8341. *5080*

MOLECULAR ASPECTS OF CELLULAR REGULATION.
Elsevier Science B.V., Books Division, P.O. Box 211, 1000 AE Amsterdam, Netherlands. TEL 31-20-4853911. FAX 31-20-4853705. *743*

MOLECULAR ASPECTS OF MEDICINE.
Elsevier Science Ltd., Pergamon, P.O. Box 800, Kidlington, Oxford OX5 1DX, England. TEL 44-1865-843000. FAX 44-1865-843010. *4717*

MOLECULAR BIOLOGY (NEW YORK).
Maik Nauka - Interperiodica, Ul. Profsoyuznaya 90, Moscow 117864, Russia. TEL 7-095-3360066. FAX 7-095-3360666. *666*

MOLECULAR BIOLOGY AND EVOLUTION.
University of Chicago Press, Journals Division, 5702 S. Woodlawn Ave., Chicago, IL 60637. TEL 773-753-3347. FAX 773-753-0811. *614*

MOLECULAR BIOLOGY OF THE CELL.
American Society for Cell Biology, 9650 Rockville Pike, Bethesda, MD 20814-3992. TEL 301-530-7153. FAX 301-571-7139. *743*

MOLECULAR BIOLOGY REPORTS.
Kluwer Academic Publishers, Postbus 17, 3300 AA Dordrecht, Netherlands. TEL 31-78-6392392. FAX 31-78-6392254. *666*

MOLECULAR BIOTECHNOLOGY.
Humana Press, Inc., 999 Riverview Dr., Ste. 208, Totowa, NJ 07512-1165. TEL 973-256-1699. FAX 973-256-8341. *685*

MOLECULAR BREEDING.
Kluwer Academic Publishers, Postbus 17, 3300 AA Dordrecht, Netherlands. TEL 31-78-6392392. FAX 31-78-6392254. *714*

MOLECULAR CARCINOGENESIS.
John Wiley & Sons, Inc., Journals, 605 Third Ave., New York, NY 10158. TEL 212-850-6645. FAX 212-850-6021. *4983*

MOLECULAR CRYSTALS AND LIQUID CRYSTALS SCIENCE AND TECHNOLOGY. SECTION A: MOLECULAR CRYSTALS AND LIQUID CRYSTALS.
Gordon and Breach - Harwood Academic, Amsteldisk 166, 1st Fl., 1079 LH Amsterdam, Netherlands. *1803*

MOLECULAR CRYSTALS AND LIQUID CRYSTALS SCIENCE AND TECHNOLOGY. SECTION B: NONLINEAR OPTICS.
Gordon and Breach - Harwood Academic, Amsteldisk 166, 1st Fl., 1079 LH Amsterdam, Netherlands. *5866*

MOLECULAR CRYSTALS AND LIQUID CRYSTALS SCIENCE AND TECHNOLOGY. SECTION C: MOLECULAR MATERIALS.
Gordon and Breach - Harwood Academic, Amsteldisk 166, 1st Fl., 1079 LH Amsterdam, Netherlands. *1803*

MOLECULAR CRYSTALS AND LIQUID CRYSTALS SCIENCE AND TECHNOLOGY. SECTION D: DISPLAY AND IMAGING.
Gordon and Breach - Harwood Academic, Amsteldisk 166, 1st Fl., 1079 LH Amsterdam, Netherlands. *5866*

MOLECULAR DIAGNOSIS.
Churchill Livingstone, 650 Ave. of the Americas, New York, NY 10010. TEL 212-206-5000. FAX 212-206-7808. *4717*

MOLECULAR ECOLOGY.
Blackwell Science Ltd., Osney Mead, Oxford OX2 0EL. TEL 44-1865-206206. FAX 44-1865-721205. *791*

MOLECULAR ENDOCRINOLOGY.
Endocrine Society, 4350 East West Hwy., Ste. 500, Bethesda, MD 20814-4410. TEL 301-941-0200. FAX 301-941-0259. *4891*

MOLECULAR ENGINEERING.
Kluwer Academic Publishers, Postbus 17, 3300 AA Dordrecht, Netherlands. TEL 31-78-6392392. FAX 31-78-6392254. *2769*

MOLECULAR GENETICS, MICROBIOLOGY AND VIROLOGY.
Allerton Press, Inc., 150 Fifth Ave., New York, NY 10011. TEL 212-924-3950. FAX 212-463-9684. *773*

MOLECULAR IMMUNOLOGY.
Elsevier Science Ltd., Pergamon, P.O. Box 800, Kidlington, Oxford OX5 1DX, England. TEL 44-1865-843000. FAX 44-1865-843010. *667*

MOLECULAR MEDICINE.
Springer-Verlag, Medical Journals, 175 Fifth Ave., New York, NY 10010. TEL 212-460-1500. FAX 212-473-6272. *4717*

MOLECULAR MEMBRANE BIOLOGY.
Taylor & Francis Ltd., 1 Gunpowder Sq., London EC4A 3DE, England. TEL 44-171-583-0490. FAX 44-171-583-0585. *667*

MOLECULAR MICROBIOLOGY.
Blackwell Science Ltd., Osney Mead, Oxford OX2 0EL, England. TEL 44-1865-206206. FAX 44-1865-721205. *791*

MOLECULAR NEUROBIOLOGY.
Humana Press Inc., 999 Riverview Dr., Ste. 208, Totowa, NJ 07512. TEL 973-256-1699. FAX 973-256-8341. *5081*

MOLECULAR PATHOLOGY.
B M J Publishing Group, B.M.A. House, Tavistock Sq., London WC1H 9JR, England. TEL 44-171-387-4499. FAX 44-171-383-6661. *4901*

MOLECULAR PHARMACOLOGY.
Williams & Wilkins, 351 W. Camden St., Baltimore, MD 21201-2436. TEL 410-528-4068. FAX 410-528-4452. *5679*

MOLECULAR PHYLOGENETICS AND EVOLUTION.
Academic Press, Inc., Journal Division, 525 B St., Ste. 1900, San Diego, CA 92101-4495. TEL 619-230-1840. FAX 619-699-6800. *773*

MOLECULAR PHYSICS.
Taylor & Francis Ltd., 1 Gunpowder Sq., London EC4A 3DE, England. TEL 44-171-583-0490. FAX 44-171-583-0585. *1833*

MOLECULAR REPRODUCTION AND DEVELOPMENT.
John Wiley & Sons, Inc., Journals, 605 Third Ave., New York, NY 10158. TEL 212-850-6645. FAX 212-850-6021. *791*

MOLECULAR SIMULATION.
Gordon and Breach - Harwood Academic, Amsteldisk 166, 1st Fl., 1079 LH Amsterdam, Netherlands. *1760*

MOLECULAR STRUCTURES AND DIMENSIONS.
Kluwer Academic Publishers, Postbus 17, 3300 AA Dordrecht, Netherlands. TEL 31-78-6392392. FAX 31-78-6392254. *1803*

MOLLUSCAN RESEARCH.
Malacological Society of Australasia, Division of Invertebrate Zoology, Australian Museum, 6 College St., Sydney, N.S.W. 2000, Australia. TEL 61-2-3206275. FAX 61-2-3206050. *843*

MOLOCHNAYA PROMYSHLENNOST'
Sadovaya-Spasskaya , 18, 107807 Moscow, Russia. TEL 7-95-2072050. FAX 7-95-2072870. *257*

MOLOCHNO-M'YASNE SKOTARSTVO.
Akademiya Nauk Ukrainy, Institut Tvarinnitstva, P-v Kulinichi, 312120 Kharkov, Ukraine. TEL 38-572-953181. FAX 38-572-953066. *257*

MONALDI ARCHIVES FOR CHEST DISEASE.
PI-ME Tipografia Editrice s.r.l., Viale Sardegna 64, 27100 Pavia, Italy. TEL 39-322-88847111. FAX 39-322830294. *5121*

MONASH UNIVERSITY LAW REVIEW.
Monash University, Faculty of Law, Wellington Rd., Clayton, Vic. 3168, Australia. TEL 03-9053374. FAX 61-3-9055305. *3991*

MONDE ALPIN ET RHODANIEN.
Centre Alpin et Rhodanien d'Ethnologie, Musee Dauphinois, 30 rue Maurice Gignoux, 38031 Grenoble Cedex, France. TEL 33-4-76851913. FAX 33-4-76876022. *323*

MONDE LIBERTAIRE.
Federation Anarchiste, 145 rue Amelot, 75011 Paris, France. TEL 48-05-34-08. FAX 49-29-98-59. *5945*

MONETARY AND ECONOMIC REVIEW.
F A M C Inc., 3500 J F K Pkwy., Fort Collins, CO 80525. TEL 970-223-4962. FAX 970-223-4996. *985*

MONIST.
Hegeler Institute, Box 600, La Salle, IL 61301. TEL 815-223-2520. FAX 815-223-4486. *5738*

MONO GEO GRAPHY.
Haifa University, Department of Geography, Mount Carmel, Haifa 31905, Israel. FAX 972-4-246814. *3414*

MONOGRAPH OF LIVING CHITONS (MOLLUSCA: POLYPLACOPHORA).
E.J. Brill, P.O. Box 9000, 2300 PA Leiden, Netherlands. TEL 31-71-5353500. FAX 31-71-5317532. *843*

MONOGRAPH SERIES ON SCHIZOPHRENIA.
International Universities Press, Inc., 59 Boston Post Rd., Box 1524, Madison, CT 06443-1524. TEL 203-245-4000. FAX 203-245-0775. *5081*

MONOGRAPHIAE BIOLOGICAE.
Kluwer Academic Publishers, Postbus 17, 3300 AA Dordrecht, Netherlands. TEL 31-78-6392392. FAX 31-78-6392254. *614*

MONOGRAPHS AND THEORETICAL STUDIES IN SOCIOLOGY AND ANTHROPOLOGY IN HONOUR OF NELS ANDERSON.
E.J. Brill, P.O. Box 9000, 2300 PA Leiden, Netherlands. TEL 31-71-5353500. FAX 31-71-5317532. *6720*

MONOGRAPHS IN ALLERGY.
S. Karger AG, Allschwilerstr. 10, P.O. Box, CH-4009 Basel, Switzerland. TEL 41-61-3061111. FAX 41-61-3061234. *4799*

MONOGRAPHS IN ANAESTHESIOLOGY.
Elsevier Science B.V., Regional Sales Oggice, P.O. Box 211, 1000 AE Amsterdam, Netherlands. TEL 31-20-4853757. FAX 31-20-4853432. *4806*

MONOGRAPHS IN CLINICAL CYTOLOGY.
S. Karger AG, Allschwilerstr. 10, P.O. Box, CH-4009 Basel, Switzerland. TEL 41-61-3061111. FAX 41-61-3061234. *4718*

MONOGRAPHS IN CLINICAL NEUROSCIENCE.
S. Karger AG, Allschwilerstr. 10, P.O. Box, CH-4009 Basel, Switzerland. TEL 41-61-3061111. FAX 41-61-3061234. *5081*

MONOGRAPHS IN CONTEMPORARY MATHEMATICS.
Plenum Publishing Corp., Consultants Bureau, 233 Spring St., New York, NY 10013-1578. TEL 212-620-8000. FAX 212-463-0742. *4593*

MONOGRAPHS IN CRYOGENICS.
Oxford University Press, Walton St., Oxford OX2 6DP, England. TEL 44-1865-56767. FAX 44-1865-56646. *2732*

MONOGRAPHS IN ELECTROANALYTICAL CHEMISTRY AND ELECTROCHEMISTRY SERIES.
Marcel Dekker, Inc., 270 Madison Ave., New York, NY 10016. TEL 212-696-9000. FAX 212-658-4540. *1806*

MONOGRAPHS IN EPIDEMIOLOGY AND BIOSTATISTICS.
Oxford University Press, Walton St., Oxford OX2 6DP, England. TEL 44-1865-56767. FAX 44-1865-56646. *6244*

MONOGRAPHS IN HUMAN GENETICS.
S. Karger AG, Allschwilerstr. 10, P.O. Box, CH-4009 Basel, Switzerland. TEL 41-61-3061111. FAX 41-61-3061234. *774*

MONOGRAPHS IN INTERNATIONAL STUDIES: AFRICA SERIES.
Ohio University Press, Scott Quadrangle, Athens, OH 45701. TEL 614-593-1159. *3528*

MONOGRAPHS IN INTERNATIONAL STUDIES: LATIN AMERICA SERIES.
Ohio University Press, Scott Quadrangle, Athens, OH 45701. TEL 614-593-1159. *3638*

MONOGRAPHS IN INTERNATIONAL STUDIES: SOUTHEAST ASIA SERIES.
Ohio University Press, Scott Quadrangle, Athens, OH 45701. TEL 614-593-1159. *3537*

MONOGRAPHS IN NEUROSCIENCE.
Gordon and Breach - Harwood Academic, Amsteldisk 166, 1st Fl., 1079 LH Amsterdam, Netherlands. *5081*

MONOGRAPHS IN OPHTHALMOLOGY.
Kluwer Academic Publishers, Postbus 17, 3300 AA Dordrecht, Netherlands. TEL 31-78-6392392. FAX 31-78-6392254. *4996*

MONOGRAPHS IN ORAL SCIENCE.
S. Karger AG, Allschwilerstr. 10, P.O. Box, CH-4009 Basel, Switzerland. TEL 41-61-3061111. FAX 41-61-3061234. *4864*

MONOGRAPHS IN PHYSICAL MEASUREMENT.
Academic Press, Inc., 525 B St., Ste. 1900, San Diego, CA 92101-4495. TEL 619-231-0926. FAX 619-699-6715. *2732*

MONOGRAPHS IN PRIMATOLOGY.
John Wiley & Sons, Inc., Journals, 605 Third Ave., New York, NY 10158. *843*

MONOGRAPHS IN PSYCHOBIOLOGY.
Gordon and Breach - Harwood Academic, Amsteldisk 166, 1st Fl., 1079 LH Amsterdam, Netherlands. *6136*

MONOGRAPHS IN VIROLOGY.
S. Karger AG, Allschwilerstr. 10, P.O. Box, CH-4009 Basel, Switzerland. TEL 41-61-3061111. FAX 41-61-3061234. *791*

MONOGRAPHS ON ASTRONOMICAL SUBJECTS.
Oxford University Press, Walton St., Oxford OX2 6DP, England. TEL 44-1865-56767. FAX 44-1865-56646. *498*

MONOGRAPHS ON NUMERICAL ANALYSIS.
Oxford University Press, Walton St., Oxford OX2 6DP, England. TEL 44-1865-56767. FAX 44-1865-56646. *4593*

MONOGRAPHS ON PHYSICAL BIOCHEMISTRY.
Oxford University Press, Walton St., Oxford OX2 6DP, England. TEL 44-1865-56767. FAX 44-1865-56646. *667*

MONOGRAPHS ON SCIENCE, TECHNOLOGY, AND SOCIETY.
Oxford University Press, Walton St., Oxford OX2 6DP, England. TEL 44-1865-56767. FAX 44-1865-56646. *6967*

MONOGRAPHS ON SOIL AND RESOURCES SURVEY.
Oxford University Press, Walton St., Oxford OX2 6DP, England. TEL 44-1865-56767. FAX 44-1865-56646. *235*

MONOGRAPHS ON THE PHYSICS AND CHEMISTRY OF MATERIALS.
Oxford University Press, Walton St., Oxford OX2 6DP, England. TEL 44-1865-56767. FAX 44-1865-56646. *5815*

MONTANAN.
University of Montana, Office of News and Publications, Missoula, MT 59812. TEL 406-243-2522. FAX 406-243-4520. *1962*

MONTE CARLO METHODS AND APPLICATIONS.
V S P, P.O. Box 346, 3700 AH Zeist, Netherlands. TEL 31-30-6925790. FAX 31-30-6932081. *4623*

MONTREAL CAMPUS.
Editions Montreal Camping Inc., C.P. 8888, Succ. Centre-Ville, Montreal, PQ H3C 3P8, Canada. TEL 514-987-7018. FAX 514-987-8210. *1962*

MONTRES MAGAZINE.
Montaigne Publications, 69 rue de la Tour, Paris, France. TEL 33-143-054646. FAX 33-143-054647. *3866*

MONUMENTA GRAECA ET ROMANA.
E.J. Brill, P.O. Box 9000, 2300 PA Leiden, Netherlands. TEL 31-71-5353500. FAX 31-71-5317532. *409*

MONUMENTA NIPPONICA.
Sophia University, 7-1 Kioi-cho, Chiyoda-ku, Tokyo 102, Japan. TEL 81-3-3238-3544. FAX 81-3-3238-5056. *5533*

MONUMENTS OF RENAISSANCE MUSIC.
University of Chicago Press, 5801 S. Ellis Ave., Chicago, IL 60637. TEL 773-702-7899. *5411*

MOOREANA.
Townsville City Council, P.O. Box 1268, Townsville, Qld. 4810, Australia. TEL 61-77-220455. FAX 61-77-253290. *714*

MOREANA.
Moreana Publications, B.P. 808, 49008 Angers Cedex 01, France. TEL 33-41-87-19-32. FAX 33-41-88-74-42. *3585*

MOROCCO.
Frank Cass, Newbury House, 890-900 Eastern Ave., Newbury Park, Ilford, Essex IG2 7HH, England. TEL 44-181-5998866. FAX 44-181-5990984. *3658*

MORRIS COUNTY FAMILY.
Kids Monthly Publications, Inc., Box 159, Westfield, NJ 07091. TEL 908-232-2913. *1851*

MOSAIC.
Soleil Publishing Inc., Box 847, Welland, ON L3B 5Y5, Canada. TEL 905-788-2674. *4282*

MOSAIC (WINNIPEG, 1967).
University of Manitoba, 208 Tier Bldg., Winnipeg, MB R3T 2N2, Canada. TEL 204-474-9763. FAX 204-261-9086. *4437*

MOSCOW PHYSICAL SOCIETY. JOURNAL.
Allerton Press, Inc., 150 Fifth Ave., New York, NY 10011. TEL 212-924-3950. FAX 212-463-9684. *5815*

MOSENODI.
Botswana Educational Research Association, University of Botswana, Private Bag 0022, Gaborone, Botswana. TEL 267-351151. FAX 267-356591. *2463*

MOST.
Kluwer Academic Publishers, Postbus 17, 3300 AA Dordrecht, Netherlands. TEL 31-78-6392392. FAX 31-78-6392254. *1309*

MOTHER EARTH INTERNATIONAL JOURNAL.
Uniting the World Press, Inc., c/o National Poetry Association, 934 Brannan St., 2nd Fl., San Francisco, CA 94103. TEL 415-552-9261. FAX 415-552-9271. *4347*

MOTIVATION AND EMOTION.
Plenum Publishing Corp., 233 Spring St., New York, NY 10013-1578. TEL 212-620-8000. FAX 212-463-0742. *6136*

MOTOR CONTROL.
Human Kinetics Publishers, Inc., Box 5076, Champaign, IL 61825-5076. TEL 217-351-5076. FAX 217-351-1549. *5044*

MOUNT OLIVE REVIEW.
Mt. Olive College Press, 634 Henderson St., Mt. Olive, NC 28365. TEL 919-658-2502. FAX 919-658-7160. *4437*

MOUNT SINAI JOURNAL OF MEDICINE.
Mount Sinai Hospital, Committee on Medical Education and Publications, 50 E. 98th St., Box 1094, New York, NY 10029. TEL 212-241-6108. FAX 212-722-6386. *4718*

MOUNTAIN PLAINS JOURNAL OF ADULT EDUCATION.
Mountain Plains Adult Education Association, Journal, Boise Graduate Center, University of Idaho, 800 Park Blvd., Ste. 200, Boise, ID 83712. TEL 208-334-2999. FAX 208-364-4035. *2512*

MOUNTAIN RESEARCH AND DEVELOPMENT.
University of California Press, Journals Division, 2120 Berkeley Way, No. 5812, Berkeley, CA 94720-5812. TEL 510-643-7154. FAX 510-642-9917. *2319*

MOUNTAIN XPRESS.
Mountain Xpress, Inc., Box 144, Asheville, NC 28802. TEL 704-251-1333. FAX 704-251-1311. *3379*

MOVEMENT DISORDERS.
Lippincott - Raven Publishers, 227 Washington Sq., Philadelphia, PA 19106. TEL 215-238-4200. FAX 215-238-4227. *5081*

MOVEMENT THEATRE QUARTERLY.
National Movement Theatre Association, Box 1437, Portsmouth, NH 03802-1437. TEL 603-436-6660. *7009*

MOVIE.
c/o Ian Cameron, Ed. & Pub., P.O. Box 1, Moffat, Dumfriesshire DG10 9SU, Scotland. TEL 44-1683-220808. FAX 44-1683-220012. *5340*

MOVING OUT.
Moving Out Collective, Box 21249, Detroit, MI 48221. TEL 313-267-6596. FAX 313-267-6596. *7328*

MOYO.
Ministry of Health, P.O. Box 30377, Lilongwe 3, Malawi. TEL 265-783-044. FAX 265-783-109. *3333*

MUELLERIA.
National Herbarium of Victoria, Birdwood Ave., South Yarra, Vic. 3141, Australia. TEL 61-3-92522300. FAX 61-3-92522350. *714*

MUENCHENER JAHRBUCH DER BILDENDEN KUNST.
Staatliche Kunstsammlungen Bayerns, Prinzregentenstr. 3, 80538 Munich, Germany. TEL 49-89-211241. FAX 49-89-21124201. *456*

MUHENDIS VE MAKINA.
Chamber of Mechanical Engineers, Sumer Sokak, 36-1-A Demirtepe, 06440 Ankara, Turkey. TEL 90-4-2313159. FAX 90-4-2313165. *2894*

MULTIBODY SYSTEM DYNAMICS.
Kluwer Academic Publishers, Postbus 17, 3300 AA Dordrecht, Netherlands. TEL 31-78-6392392. FAX 31-78-6392254. *5847*

MULTIDIMENSIONAL SYSTEMS AND SIGNAL PROCESSING.
Kluwer Academic Publishers Boston, Box 358, Accord Sta., Hingham, MA 02018-0358. TEL 617-871-6600. FAX 617-871-6528. *2157*

MULTIMEDIA TOOLS AND APPLICATIONS.
Kluwer Academic Publishers, Postbus 17, 3300 AA Dordrecht, Netherlands. TEL 31-78-6392392. FAX 31-78-6392254. *2216*

MULTINATIONAL BUSINESS REVIEW.
University of Detroit Mercy, College of Business Administration, Box 19900, Detroit, MI 48219-0900. TEL 313-993-1264. FAX 313-993-1052. *1342*

MULTINATIONAL EMPLOYER.
P.O. Box 149, Farnham, Surrey GU9 8YH, England. TEL 44-1252-726416. FAX 44-1252-713730. *986*

MULTIPHASE SCIENCE AND TECHNOLOGY.
Begell House Inc., 79 Madison Ave., Ste. 1205, New York, NY 10016-7892. TEL 212-725-1999. FAX 212-213-8368. *2732*

MULTIVARIATE BEHAVIORAL RESEARCH.
Lawrence Erlbaum Associates, Inc., 10 Industrial Dr., Mahwah, NJ 07430-2262. TEL 201-236-9500. FAX 201-236-0072. *6136*

MUNDO ELECTRONICO.
Cetisa - Boixareu S.A., Concepcion Arenal 5, 08027 Barcelona, Spain. TEL 34-3-3527061. FAX 34-3-3492350. *2647*

MUQARNAS.
E.J. Brill, P.O. Box 9000, 2300 PA Leiden, Netherlands. TEL 31-71-5353500. FAX 31-71-5317532. *456*

MUQARNAS, SUPPLEMENTS.
E.J. Brill, P.O. Box 9000, 2300 PA Leiden, Netherlands. TEL 31-71-5353500. FAX 31-71-5317532. *456*

MUSCLE & NERVE.
John Wiley & Sons, Inc., Journals, 605 Third Ave., New York, NY 10158. TEL 212-850-6645. FAX 212-850-6021. *4718*

MUSCULO-SKELETAL MANAGEMENT.
Blackwell Science Ltd., Osney Mead, Oxford OX2 0EL, England. TEL 44-1865-206206. FAX 44-1865-721205. *5012*

MUSEE NATIONAL DE VARSOVIE. BULLETIN.
Muzeum Narodowe w Warszawie, Al. Jerozolimskie 3, 00-495 Warsaw, Poland. TEL 48-2-6211031. FAX 48-2-6228559. *5359*

MUSEES.
Societe des Musees Quebecois, C.P. 8888, Succ. Centre-Ville, UQAM, Montreal, PQ H3C 3P8, Canada. TEL 514-987-3264. FAX 514-987-3379. *5359*

MUSEO CIVICO DI STORIA NATURALE DI VENEZIA. BOLLETTINO.
Museo Civico di Storia Naturale di Venezia, Fontego dei Turchi, S. Croce 1730, 30135 Venice, Italy. TEL 39-41-721852. FAX 39-41-5242592. *615*

MUSEO DE HISTORIA NATURAL DE VALPARAISO. ANALES.
Museo de Historia Natural de Valparaiso, Condell 1546, Casilla 3208 Correo 3, Valparaiso, Chile. TEL 56-32-257441. FAX 56-32-220846. *6546*

MUSEU DE ARQUEOLOGIA E ETNOLOGIA. REVISTA.
Universidade de Sao Paulo, Museu de Arqueologia e Etnologia, Av. Prof. Almeida Prado, 1466, Cidade Universitaria, 05508-900 Sao Paulo SP, Brazil. TEL 55-11-8184978. FAX 55-11-8185042. *374*

MUSEU DE ZOOLOGIA. TREBALLS.
Museu de Zoologia, Attn: Dr. Anna Omedes, Ed., Apdo. 593, 08080 Barcelona, Spain. TEL 34-3-3196912. FAX 34-3-3104999. *843*

MUSEUM INTERNACIONAL.
UNESCO Publishing, 7 place de Fontenoy, 75352 Paris 07 SP, France. TEL 33-1-45684300. FAX 33-1-45685741. *5360*

MUSEUM INTERNATIONAL.
Blackwell Publishers Ltd., 108 Cowley Road, Oxford OX4 1JF, England. TEL 44-1865-791100. FAX 44-1865-791347. *5360*

MUSEUM INTERNATIONAL (FRENCH EDITION).
UNESCO Publishing, 7 place de Fontenoy, 75352 Paris 07 SP, France. TEL 33-1-45684300. FAX 33-1-45685741. *5360*

MUSEUM MANAGEMENT AND CURATORSHIP.
Elsevier Science Ltd., Pergamon, P.O. Box 800, Kidlington, Oxford OX5 1DX, England. TEL 44-1865-843000. FAX 44-1865-843010. *5360*

MUSEUM NOTES (PROVIDENCE).
Rhode Island School of Design, Museum of Art, 224 Benefit St., Providence, RI 02903-2723. TEL 401-454-6500. FAX 401-454-6556. *5361*

MUSEUM PRACTICE.
Museums Association, 42 Clerkenwell Close, London EC1R 0PA, England. TEL 44-171-250-1834. FAX 44-171-250-1929. *5361*

MUSHROOM NEWS.
American Mushroom Institute, One Massachusetts Ave., N.W., Ste. 800, Washington, DC 20001-1401. TEL 202-842-4344. FAX 202-408-7763. *235*

MUSIC ANALYSIS.
Blackwell Publishers Ltd., 108 Cowley Rd., Oxford OX4 1JF, England. TEL 44-1865-791100. FAX 44-1865-791347. *5411*

MUSIC IN AMERICAN LIFE.
University of Illinois Press, 1325 S. Oak St., Champaign, IL 61820. TEL 217-333-0950. FAX 217-244-8082. *5412*

MUSIC PERCEPTION.
University of California Press, Journals Division, 2120 Berkeley Way, No. 5812, Berkeley, CA 94720-5812. TEL 510-643-7154. FAX 510-642-9917. *5413*

MUSIC REFERENCE SERVICES QUARTERLY.
Haworth Press, Inc., 10 Alice St., Binghamton, NY 13904. TEL 607-722-5857. FAX 607-722-6362. *4200*

MUSIC RESEARCH.
Music Research Institute, Osaka College of Music, 1-1-4 Meishinguchi, Toyonaka, Osaka 561, Japan. TEL 81-6-865-0545. FAX 81-6-866-8490. *5414*

MUSIC THEORY SPECTRUM.
University of California Press, Journals Division, 2120 Berkeley Way, No. 5812, Berkeley, CA 94720-5812. TEL 510-643-7154. FAX 510-642-9917. *5414*

MUSIC THERAPY PERSPECTIVES.
National Association for Music Therapy, Inc., 8455 Colesville Rd., Ste. 1000, Silver Spring, MD 20910-3392. TEL 301-589-3300. FAX 301-589-5175. *5414*

MUSICK.
Vancouver Society for Early Music, 1254 W. Seventh Ave., Vancouver, BC V6H 1B6, Canada. TEL 604-732-1610. FAX 604-732-1602. *5416*

MUSICOLOGY.
Gordon and Breach - Harwood Academic, Amsteldisk 166, 1st Fl., 1079 LH Amsterdam, Netherlands. *5416*

MUSICUS.
Unisa Press, Periodicals, P.O. Box 392, Pretoria 0001, South Africa. TEL 27-12-4292953. FAX 27-12-4293221. *5416*

MUSIIKKI.
Suomen Musiikkitieteellinen Seura, P.O. Box 35, FIN-00014 Helsinki, Finland. FAX 358-9-1917955. *5416*

MUSLIM EDUCATION QUARTERLY.
The Islamic Academy, 23 Metcalfe Rd., Cambridge CB4 2DB, England. TEL 44-1223-350976. FAX 44-1223-350976. *6399*

THE MUSLIM NEWS.
Visitcrest Ltd., P.O. Box 380, Harrow, Mddx. HA2 6LL, England. TEL 44-171-831-0428. FAX 44-171-831-0830. *6399*

MU'TAH LIL-BUHUTH WAL-DIRASAT. AL-SILSILAH A: AL-'ULUM AL-INSANIYYAH WAL-IJTIMA'IYYAH.
Mu'tah University, Deanship of Academic Research and Graduate Studies, P.O. Box 7, Mu'tah, Jordan. FAX 962-6-654061. *3786*

MU'TAH LIL-BUHUTH WAL-DIRASAT. AL-SILSILAH B: AL-'ULUM AL-TABI'IYYAH WAL-TATBIQIYYAH.
Mu'tah University, Deanship of Academic Research and Graduate Studies, P.O. Box 7, Mu'tah, Jordan. FAX 962-2-654061. *6546*

MUTATION RESEARCH.
Elsevier Science B.V., P.O. Box 211, 1000 AE Amsterdam, Netherlands. TEL 31-20-4853911. FAX 31-20-4853598. *774*

MUTATION RESEARCH - D N A REPAIR.
Elsevier Science B.V., P.O. Box 211, 1000 AE Amsterdam, Netherlands. TEL 31-20-4853911. FAX 31-20-4853598. *774*

MUTATION RESEARCH - FUNDAMENTAL AND MOLECULAR MECHANISMS OF MUTAGENESIS.
Elsevier Science B.V., P.O. Box 211, 1000 AE Amsterdam, Netherlands. TEL 31-20-4853911. FAX 31-20-4853598. *774*

MUTATION RESEARCH - GENETIC TOXICOLOGY AND ENVIRONMENTAL MUTAGENESIS.
Elsevier Science B.V., P.O. Box 211, 1000 AE Amsterdam, Netherlands. TEL 31-20-4853911. FAX 31-20-4853598. *774*

MUTATION RESEARCH LETTERS.
Elsevier Science B.V., P.O. Box 211, 1000 AE Amsterdam, Netherlands. TEL 31-20-4853911. FAX 31-20-4853598. *775*

MUTATION RESEARCH - MUTATION RESEARCH GENOMICS.
Elsevier Science B.V., P.O. Box 211, 1000 AE Amsterdam, Netherlands. TEL 31-20-4853757. FAX 31-20-4853432. *775*

MUTATION RESEARCH - REVIEWS IN GENETIC TOXICOLOGY.
Elsevier Science B.V., P.O. Box 211, 1000 AE Amsterdam, Netherlands. TEL 31-20-4853911. FAX 31-20-4853598. *775*

MUZEUM ZIEMI. PRACE.
Polska Akademia Nauk, Muzeum Ziemi, Al. Na Skarpie 20-26, 00-488 Warsaw, Poland. TEL 48-22-6298061. FAX 48-22-6297497. *2359*

MUZZLE BLASTS.
National Muzzle Loading Rifle Association, Box 67, Friendship, IN 47021. TEL 812-667-5131. FAX 812-667-5137. *6875*

MYCETEAE.
Centro de Investigacion y Reproduccion de Especies Silvestres, Apartado Postal 397, Merida 5101, Venezuela. TEL 58-74-712939. FAX 58-74-712939. *715*

MYCOLOGIA.
New York Botanical Garden, Scientific Publications Department, Bronx, NY 10458-5126. TEL 718-817-8721. FAX 718-817-8842. *715*

MYCOLOGY SERIES.
Marcel Dekker, Inc., 270 Madison Ave., New York, NY 10016. TEL 212-696-9000. FAX 212-658-4540. *715*

MYCOPATHOLOGIA.
Kluwer Academic Publishers, Postbus 17, 3300 AA Dordrecht, Netherlands. TEL 31-78-6392392. FAX 31-78-6392254. *791*

MYCOTAXON.
Mycotaxon Ltd., Box 264, Ithaca, NY 14851. TEL 607-273-4357. FAX 607-273-4357. *716*

N A C T A JOURNAL.
National Association of Colleges and Teachers of Agriculture, 608 W. Vermont, Urbana, IL 61801. TEL 217-344-5738. *137*

N A C W P I JOURNAL.
Simpson Publishing Co., c/o Richard K. Weerts, Ed., Division of Fine Arts, Truman State University, Kirksville, MO 63501. TEL 816-785-4442. FAX 816-785-7463. *5418*

N A F T A LAW AND POLICY SERIES.
Martinus Nijhoff Publishers, Human Rights and International Law Postbus 163, 3300 AD Dordrecht, Netherlands. FAX 31-78-392254. *4122*

N A I E C NEWSLETTER.
National Association for Industry - Education Cooperation, 235 Hendricks Blvd., Buffalo, NY 14226-3304. TEL 716-837-7047. FAX 716-834-7047. *1497*

N A R I REMODELER'S JOURNAL.
National Association of the Remodeling Industry, 4900 Deminary Rd., Ste. 320, Alexandria, VA 22311-1811. TEL 703-575-1100. FAX 703-575-1121. *905*

N A T O ADVANCED SCIENCE INSTITUTES SERIES. PARTNERSHIP SUB-SERIES 4: SCIENCE AND TECHNOLOGY POLICY.
Kluwer Academic Publishers, Postbus 17, 3300 AA Dordrecht, Netherlands. TEL 31-78-6392392. FAX 31-78-6392254. *6547*

N A T O ADVANCED SCIENCE INSTITUTES SERIES A: LIFE SCIENCES.
Plenum Publishing Corp., 233 Spring St., New York, NY 10013-1578. TEL 212-620-8000. FAX 212-463-0742. *615*

N A T O ADVANCED SCIENCE INSTITUTES SERIES B: PHYSICS.
Plenum Publishing Corp., 233 Spring St., New York, NY 10013-1578. TEL 212-620-8000. FAX 212-463-0742. *5815*

N A T O ADVANCED SCIENCE INSTITUTES SERIES C: MATHEMATICAL AND PHYSICAL SCIENCES.
Kluwer Academic Publishers, Postbus 17, 3300 AA Dordrecht, Netherlands. TEL 31-78-6392392. FAX 31-78-6392254. *4594*

N A T O ADVANCED SCIENCE INSTITUTES SERIES D: BEHAVIOURAL AND SOCIAL SCIENCES.
Kluwer Academic Publishers, Postbus 17, 3300 AA Dordrecht, Netherlands. TEL 31-78-6392392. FAX 31-78-6392254. *6137*

N A T O ADVANCED SCIENCE INSTITUTES SERIES E: APPLIED SCIENCES.
Kluwer Academic Publishers, Postbus 17, 3300 AA Dordrecht, Netherlands. TEL 31-78-6392392. FAX 31-78-6392254. *6967*

N A T O ADVANCED SCIENCE INSTITUTES SERIES F: COMPUTER AND SYSTEMS SCIENCES.
Springer-Verlag, Heidelberger Platz 3, 14197 Berlin, Germany. TEL 49-30-8207-0. FAX 49-30-8214091. *2157*

N A T O ADVANCED SCIENCE INSTITUTES SERIES G: ECOLOGICAL SCIENCES.
Kluwer Academic Publishers, Postbus 17, 3300 AA Dordrecht, Netherlands. TEL 31-78-6392392. FAX 31-78-6392254. *2943*

N A T O ADVANCED SCIENCE INSTITUTES SERIES H: CELL BIOLOGY.
Kluwer Academic Publishers, Postbus 17, 3300 AA Dordrecht, Netherlands. TEL 31-78-6392392. FAX 31-78-6392254. *743*

N A T O CHALLENGES OF MODERN SOCIETY.
Plenum Publishing Corp., 233 Spring St., New York, NY 10013-1578. TEL 212-620-8000. FAX 212-463-0742. *2943*

N.B. NATURALIST.
New Brunswick Federation of Naturalists, 277 Douglas Ave., Saint John, NB E2K 1E5, Canada. TEL 506-887-2091. *6547*

N C J W JOURNAL.
National Council of Jewish Women, 53 W. 23rd St., New York, NY 10010. TEL 212-645-4048. FAX 212-645-7466. *7328*

N D T & E INTERNATIONAL.
Elsevier Science Ltd., Pergamon, P.O. Box 800, Kidlington, Oxford OX5 1DX, England. TEL 44-1865-843000. FAX 44-1865-843010. *2868*

N E M L A ITALIAN STUDIES.
Prof. Umberto C. Mariani, Ed. & Pub., Rutgers Univ., Dept. of Italian, 84 College Ave., New Brunswick, NJ 08903. TEL 908-932-7536. FAX 908-932-1686. *4438*

N E T A WORLD.
InterNational Electrical Testing Association, 106 Stone St., Box 687, Morrison, CO 80465. TEL 303-697-8441. FAX 303-697-8431. *2841*

N I M H A N S JOURNAL.
National Institute of Mental Health & Neuro Sciences, Bangalore 560 029, India. TEL 91-80-664-2121. FAX 91-80-663-1830. *5081*

N I P R SYMPOSIUM ON ANTARCTIC GEOSCIENCES. PROCEEDINGS.
National Institute of Polar Research, Library, 9-10, Kaga 1-chome, Itabashi-ku, Tokyo 173, Japan. TEL 81-3-3962-2214. FAX 81-3-3962-2225. *2359*

N I P R SYMPOSIUM ON ANTARCTIC METEORITES. PROCEEDINGS.
National Institute of Polar Research, Library, 9-10, Kaga 1-chome, Itabashi-ku, Tokyo 173, Japan. TEL 81-3-3962-2214. FAX 81-3-3962-2225. *2359*

N I P R SYMPOSIUM ON POLAR BIOLOGY. PROCEEDINGS.
National Institute of Polar Research, Library, 9-10, Kaga 1-chome, Itabashi-ku, Tokyo 173, Japan. TEL 81-3-3962-2214. FAX 81-3-3962-2225. *615*

N I P R SYMPOSIUM ON POLAR METEOROLOGY AND GLACIOLOGY. PROCEEDINGS.
National Institute of Polar Research, Library, 9-10, Kaga 1-chome, Itabashi-ku, Tokyo 173, Japan. TEL 81-3-3962-2214. FAX 81-3-3962-2225. *2359*

N I P R SYMPOSIUM ON UPPER ATMOSPHERE PHYSICS. PROCEEDINGS.
National Institute of Polar Research, Library, 9-10, Kaga 1-chome, Itabashi-ku, Tokyo 173, Japan. TEL 81-3-3962-2214. FAX 81-3-3962-2225. *5816*

N I S T BUILDING SCIENCE SERIES.
U.S. National Institute of Standards and Technology, Gaithersburg, MD 20899. TEL 301-975-3058. *905*

N I S T HANDBOOK.
U.S. National Institute of Standards and Technology, Gaithersburg, MD 20899. TEL 301-975-3058. *5253*

N I S T MONOGRAPH.
U.S. National Institute of Standards and Technology, Gaithersburg, MD 20899. TEL 301-975-3058. *5253*

N I S T SPECIAL PUBLICATION.
U.S. National Institute of Standards and Technology, Gaithersburg, MD 20899. TEL 301-975-3058. *5253*

N I S T TECHNICAL NOTES.
U.S. National Institute of Standards and Technology, Gaithersburg, MD 20899. TEL 301-975-3058. *5253*

N J A O P S JOURNAL.
New Jersey Association of Osteopathic Physicians and Surgeons, 1 Distribution Way, Monmouth Jct., NJ 08852-3001. TEL 908-940-9000. FAX 908-940-8899. *4828*

N L P WORLD.
Les 3 Chasseurs, CH-1413 Orzens, Switzerland. TEL 41-21-8877721. FAX 41-21-8877976. *6137*

N M C D.
Medikal Press s.r.l., Vioa Luigi Zoja 30, 20153 Milan, Italy. TEL 39-2-48202740. FAX 39-2-48201219. *5478*

N M R IN BIOMEDICINE.
John Wiley & Sons Ltd., Journals, Baffins Ln., Chichester, W. Sussex PO19 1UD, England. TEL 44-1243-779777. FAX 44-1243-775878. *5111*

N S R D S - N B S: NATIONAL STANDARD REFERENCE DATA SERIES.
U.S. National Institute of Standards and Technology, Gaithersburg, MD 20899. TEL 301-975-3058. *5253*

N Y U PHYSICIAN.
New York University School of Medicine, 550 First Ave., New York, NY 10016. FAX 212-263-8425. *1962*

N Z FAMILY PHYSICIAN.
Royal New Zealand College of General Practitioners, c/o Dr. T. Turnbull, Ed., 62 Park Rd., Katikati, New Zealand. TEL 64-7-54904112. FAX 64-7-5491222. *4719*

NA SZLAKU.
Oficyna Wydawnicza Sudety, Rynek - Ratusz 11-12, 50-106 Wroclaw, Poland. TEL 48-71-3438669. FAX 48-71-3436746. *7223*

NAG HAMMADI AND MANICHAEAN STUDIES.
E.J. Brill, P.O. Box 9000, 2300 PA Leiden, Netherlands. TEL 31-71-5353500. FAX 31-71-5317532. *6357*

NAGOYA MEDICAL JOURNAL.
Nagoya-shiritsu Daigaku, Igakubu, Kawasumi 1, Mizuho-cho, Mizuho-ku, Nagoya 467, Japan. TEL 81-52-853-8159. FAX 81-52-851-4166. *4719*

NAGOYA SHIRITSU DAIGAKU IGAKKAI ZASSHI.
Nagoya-shiritsu Daigaku, Igakkai, 1 Kawasumi, Mizuho-cho, Mizuho-ku, Nagoya-shi, Aichi-ken 467, Japan. TEL 81-52-853-8084. FAX 81-52-842-0863. *4719*

THE NAIROBI LAW MONTHLY.
Kaibi Ltd., P.O. Box 53234, Nairobi, Kenya. TEL 254-2-330480. *3993*

NAMENKUNDLICHE INFORMATIONEN.
Universitaet Leipzig, Abteilung Deutsch-Slavische Namenforschung, Augustusplatz 9, 04109 Leipzig, Germany. TEL 49-341-9737464. FAX 49-341-9737499. *4283*

NAMES.
American Name Society, c/o Wayne H. Finke, Department of Modern Languages, Baruch College, Box G-1224, 17 Lexington Ave., New York, NY 10010-5526. TEL 212-387-1570. FAX 212-387-1591. *4283*

NANFANG WENXUE.
Guilin Shi Wenlian, No. 41 Rongcheng Rd., Guilin, Guangxi 541001, People's Republic of China. TEL 886-773-2830772. FAX 886-773-2824578. *4438*

NANJING DAXUE XUEBAO (ZIRAN KEXUE BAN).
Nanjing Daxue Chubanshe, Hankou Lu, Nanjing, Jiangsu 210008, People's Republic of China. TEL 86-25-6634651. FAX 86-25-3302728. *6548*

NANJING TIEDAO YIXUEYUAN XUEBAO.
Nanjing Tiedao Yixueyuan, 87 Dingjiaqiao, Nanjing, Jiangsu 210009, People's Republic of China. TEL 301509. FAX 3317073. *4719*

NANKYOKU SHIRYO.
National Institute of Polar Research, Library, 9-10, Kaga 1-chome, Itabashi-ku, Tokyo 173, Japan. TEL 81-3-3962-2214. FAX 81-3-3962-2225. *3414*

NANOBIOLOGY.
Gordon and Breach - Harwood Academic, Amsteldisk 166, 1st Fl., 1079 LH Amsterdam, Netherlands. *791*

NANOSTRUCTURED MATERIALS.
Elsevier Science Ltd., Pergamon, P.O. Box 800, Kidlington, Oxford OX5 1DX, England. TEL 44-1865-843000. FAX 44-1865-843010. *2868*

NANOTECHNOLOGY.
I O P Publishing Ltd., Dirac House, Temple Back, Bristol BS1 6BE, England. TEL 44-117-929-7481. FAX 44-117-929-4318. *5816*

NAPRSTKOVO MUZEUM ASIJSKYCH, AFRICKYCH A AMERICKYCH KULTUR. ANNALS.
Naprstkovo Muzeum Asijskych, Africkych a Americkych Kultur, Betlemske nam. 1, 110 00 Prague 1, Czech Republic. TEL 42-2-24214537. FAX 42-2-24226488. *325*

NARA IGAKU ZASSHI.
Nara Igakkai, Nara Medical University, Kashihara 634, Nara, Japan. TEL 81-7442-2-3051. FAX 81-7442-5-7308. *4719*

NARRATIVE.
Ohio State University Press, 1070 Carmack Rd., Columbus, OH 43210. TEL 614-292-6930. FAX 614-292-2065. *4438*

NARRATIVE INQUIRY.
John Benjamins Publishing Co., Amsteldijk 44, P.O. Box 75577, 1070 AN Amsterdam, Netherlands. TEL 31-20-6738156. FAX 31-20-6792956. *4438*

NASIONALE MUSEUM, BLOEMFONTEIN. NAVORSINGE.
Nasionale Museum, Bloemfontein, P.O. Box 266, Bloemfontein 9300, South Africa. TEL 27-51-4479609. FAX 27-51-4476273. *6548*

NASSARRE.
Institucion Fernando el Catolico, Plaza de Espana 2, 50071 Zaragoza, Spain. TEL 34-976-288878. FAX 34-976-288869. *5419*

NASSAU COUNTY DENTAL SOCIETY. NEWSLETTER.
Nassau County Dental Society Headquarters, 377 Oak St., No. 205, Garden City, NY 11530-6543. TEL 516-764-9620. FAX 516-227-1114. *4864*

NASSAU REVIEW.
Nassau Community College, State University of New York, Department of English, Garden City, NY 11530. TEL 516-572-7792. *4438*

NASSAUISCHE ANNALEN.
Verein fuer Nassauische Altertumskunde und Geschichtsforschung e.V., Mosbacher Str. 55, 65187 Wiesbaden, Germany. TEL 49-611-881-0. FAX 49-611-881145. *3586*

NATAL MUSEUM. ANNALS.
Natal Museum, Private Bag 9070, Pietermaritzburg 3200, South Africa. TEL 27-331-451404. FAX 27-331-450561. *844*

NATAL MUSEUM JOURNAL OF HUMANITIES.
Natal Museum, Private Bag 9070, Pietermaritzburg 3200, South Africa. TEL 27-331-451404. FAX 27-331-450561. *374*

NATHANIEL HAWTHORNE REVIEW.
Nathaniel Hawthorne Society, Dept. of English, Duquesne University, Pittsburgh, PA 15282. TEL 412-396-5165. FAX 412-396-5197. *4438*

NATIONAL (OTTAWA, 1974).
Maclean-Hunter Ltd., Business Publications Division, 777 Bay St., 5th Fl., Toronto, ON M5W 1A7, Canada. TEL 416-593-3162. *3993*

NATIONAL ACADEMY OF SCIENCES OF THE UNITED STATES OF AMERICA. PROCEEDINGS.
National Academy of Sciences, Proceedings Office, 2101 Constitution Ave., N.W., Washington, DC 20418. TEL 202-625-4725. FAX 202-625-4747. *6548*

NATIONAL ASSOCIATION OF CONSERVATION DISTRICTS. TUESDAY LETTER.
National Association of Conservation Districts, Box 855, League City, TX 77574-0855. TEL 713-332-3402. FAX 713-332-5259. *2237*

NATIONAL BOTANIC GARDENS. OCCASIONAL PAPERS.
National Botanic Gardens, Glasnevin, Dublin 9, Ireland. TEL 353-1-8374388. FAX 353-18360080. *716*

NATIONAL BOTANIC RESEARCH INSTITUTE, LUCKNOW. PROGRESS REPORT.
National Botanical Research Institute, Lucknow, Lucknow 226001, India. TEL 91-522-282849. FAX 91-522-282849. *716*

NATIONAL BOTANICAL INSTITUTE. REVIEW.
National Botanical Institute (Claremont), Private Bag X7, Claremont 7735, South Africa. TEL 27-21-762-1166. FAX 27-21-762-3229. *716*

NATIONAL CANCER INSTITUTE. JOURNAL.
Oxford University Press, Academic Division, Great Clarendon St., Oxford OX2 6DP, England. TEL 44-1865-267907. FAX 44-1865-267485. *4983*

NATIONAL CANCER INSTITUTE. JOURNAL. MONOGRAPHS.
U.S. National Cancer Institute, R. A. Bloch International Cancer Information Center, Bldg. 82, Rm. 227, Bethesda, MD 20814. TEL 301-496-4907. *4983*

NATIONAL CENTER FOR SCIENCE EDUCATION. REPORTS.
National Center for Science Education, Box 8880, Madison, WI 53708-8880. TEL 608-259-2926. FAX 608-258-2415. *6549*

NATIONAL CONFERENCE ON WEIGHTS AND MEASURES. REPORT.
U.S. National Institute of Standards and Technology, Gaithersburg, MD 20899. TEL 301-975-3058. *5253*

NATIONAL CONTRACT MANAGEMENT JOURNAL.
National Contract Management Association, 1912 Woodford Rd., Vienna, VA 22182-3728. *1497*

NATIONAL FORENSIC JOURNAL.
National Forensic Association, Robinson Hall, Washington & Lee University, Lexington, VA 24450-0303. TEL 540-463-8812. *1999*

NATIONAL FORUM OF APPLIED EDUCATIONAL RESEARCH JOURNAL.
National Forum Journals, 4000 Locke Ln. Ste. 9, Lake Charles, LA 70605-2244. TEL 318-477-0008. *2465*

NATIONAL FORUM OF EDUCATION ADMINISTRATION AND SUPERVISION JOURNAL.
National Forum Journals, 4000 Locke Ln., Ste. 9, Lake Charles, LA 70605-2244. TEL 318-477-0008. *2575*

NATIONAL FORUM OF INSTRUCTIONAL TECHNOLOGY JOURNAL.
National Forum Journals, 4000 Locke Ln., Ste. 9, Lake Charles, LA 70605-2244. TEL 318-477-0008. *2519*

NATIONAL FORUM OF SPECIAL EDUCATION JOURNAL.
National Forum Journals, 4000 Locke Ln., Ste. 9, Lake Charles, LA 70605-2244. TEL 318-477-0008. *2588*

NATIONAL FORUM TEACHER EDUCATION JOURNAL.
National Forum Journals, 4000 Locke Ln., Ste. 9, Lake Charles, LA 70605-2244. TEL 318-477-0008. *2465*

NATIONAL GENEALOGICAL SOCIETY QUARTERLY.
National Genealogical Society, Box 870212, University of Alabama, Tuscaloosa, AL 35487-0212. TEL 703-525-0050. FAX 205-752-5979. *3233*

NATIONAL GEOGRAPHICAL JOURNAL OF INDIA.
National Geographical Society of India, Banaras Hindu University, Department of Geography, Varanasi 221005, Uttar Pradesh, India. TEL 91-542-310291. FAX 91-542-312059. *3415*

NATIONAL INSTITUTE OF MATERIALS AND CHEMICAL RESEARCH. JOURNAL.
National Institute of Materials and Chemical Research, Ibaraki 305, Japan. TEL 81-298-54-4410. FAX 81-298-54-4422. *1760*

NATIONAL INSTITUTE OF POLAR RESEARCH. MEMOIRS. SPECIAL ISSUE.
National Institute of Polar Research, Library, 9-10, Kaga 1-chome, Itabashi-ku, Tokyo 173, Japan. TEL 81-3-3962-2214. FAX 81-3-3962-2225. *2319*

NATIONAL INSTITUTE OF STANDARDS AND TECHNOLOGY. JOURNAL OF RESEARCH.
U.S. National Institute of Standards and Technology, U.S. Department of Commerce, Gaithersburg, MD 20899. TEL 301-975-3058. *5253*

NATIONAL INSTITUTE OF WATER AND ATMOSPHERIC RESEARCH. BIODIVERSITY MEMOIRS.
National Institute of Water and Atmospheric Research Ltd., P.O. Box 14-901, Kilbirnie, Wellington, New Zealand. TEL 64-4-3860388. FAX 64-4-3862153. *2410*

NATIONAL MEDICAL ASSOCIATION. JOURNAL.
Slack, Inc., 6900 Grove Rd., Thorofare, NJ 08086-9447. TEL 609-848-1000. FAX 609-853-5991. *4720*

NATIONAL MEDICAL JOURNAL OF INDIA.
All India Institute of Medical Sciences, New Delhi 110 029, India. TEL 91-11-6863002. FAX 91-11-6862663. *4720*

NATIONAL RESEARCH COUNCIL OF THAILAND. JOURNAL.
National Research Council of Thailand, 196 Phahonyothin Rd., Chatuchak, Bangkok 10900, Thailand. TEL 66-2-579-2690. FAX 66-2-561-3049. *6549*

NATIONAL SECURITY REVIEW.
National Defense College of the Philippines, Logcom Area, Camp Aguinaldo, Quezon City, Philippines. *5946*

NATIONAL TAIWAN UNIVERSITY. COLLEGE OF MEDICINE. MEMOIRS.
National Taiwan University, College of Medicine, No. 1 Jen-Ai Rd. Sec. 1, Taipei, Taiwan, Republic of China. TEL 02-3970800. *4720*

NATIONAL TECHNICAL REPORT.
Matsushita Electric Industrial Co., Ltd., 3-1-1 Yakumonaka-machi, Moriguchi-shi, Osaka 570, Japan. FAX 91-6-906-0177. *2841*

NATIONALISM & ETHNIC POLITICS.
Frank Cass, 890-900 Eastern Ave., Newbury Park, Ilford, Essex IG2 7HH, England. TEL 44-181-599-8866. FAX 44-181-599-0984. *6028*

NATIONALITIES PAPERS.
Carfax Publishing Co., P.O. Box 25, Agingdon, Oxon. OX14 3UE, England. TEL 44-1235-401000. FAX 44-1235-401550. *6627*

NATIONS AND NATIONALISM.
Cambridge University Press, Edinburgh Bldg., Shaftesbury Rd., Cambridge CB2 2RU, England. TEL 44-1223-312393. FAX 44-1223-315052. *5947*

NATIVE PEOPLES.
Media Concepts Group, Inc., 5333 N. Seventh St., Ste. C-224, Phoenix, AZ 85014. TEL 602-252-2236. FAX 602-265-3113. *3031*

NATIVE STUDIES REVIEW.
University of Saskatchewan, Native Studies Department, 104 McLean Hall, 106 Wiggins Rd., Saskatoon, SK S7N 5E6, Canada. TEL 306-966-6208. FAX 306-966-6242. *3031*

NATURAL AREAS JOURNAL.
Natural Areas Association, Box 900, Chesterfield, MO 63006-0900. TEL 314-878-7850. FAX 314-878-3410. *2943*

NATURAL HAZARDS.
Kluwer Academic Publishers, Postbus 17, 3300 AA Dordrecht, Netherlands. TEL 31-78-6392392. FAX 31-78-6392254. *2319*

NATURAL HISTORY.
American Museum of Natural History, Central Park W. at 79th St., New York, NY 10024-5192. TEL 212-769-5500. FAX 212-769-5511. *6550*

NATURAL HISTORY MUSEUM AND INSTITUTE, CHIBA. BULLETIN. HUMANITIES.
Natural History Museum and Institute, Chiba, 955-2 Aoba-cho, Chuo-ku, Chiba 260, Japan. TEL 81-43-265-3111. FAX 81-43-266-2481. *3537*

NATURAL HISTORY MUSEUM AND INSTITUTE, CHIBA. JOURNAL.
Natural History Museum and Institute, Chiba, 955-2 Aoba-cho, Chuo-ku, Chiba 260, Japan. TEL 81-43-265-3111. FAX 81-43-266-2481. *6550*

NATURAL HISTORY MUSEUM AND INSTITUTE, CHIBA. JOURNAL. SPECIAL ISSUE.
Natural History Museum and Institute, Chiba, 955-2 Aoba-cho, Chuo-ku, Chiba 260, Japan. TEL 81-43-265-3111. FAX 81-43-266-2481. *616*

NATURAL HISTORY MUSEUM OF LOS ANGELES COUNTY. SCIENCE SERIES.
Natural History Museum of Los Angeles County, 900 Exposition Blvd., Los Angeles, CA 90007. TEL 213-744-3330. FAX 213-742-0730. *6550*

NATURAL HISTORY RESEARCH.
Natural History Museum and Institute, Chiba, 955-2 Aoba-cho, Chuo-ku, Chiba 260, Japan. TEL 81-43-265-3111. FAX 81-43-266-2481. *6550*

NATURAL HISTORY RESEARCH. SPECIAL ISSUE.
Natural History Museum and Institute, Chiba, 955-2 Aoba-cho, Chuo-ku, Chiba 260, Japan. TEL 81-43-265-3111. FAX 81-43-266-2481. *616*

NATURAL HISTORY SOCIETY OF NORTHUMBRIA. TRANSACTIONS.
Natural History Society of Northumbria, Hancock Museum, Newcastle upon Tyne NE2 4PT, England. TEL 44-191-232-6386. *6550*

NATURAL IMMUNITY.
S. Karger AG, Allschwilerstr. 10, P.O. Box, CH-4009 Basel, Switzerland. TEL 41-61-3061111. FAX 41-61-3061234. *791*

NATURAL LANGUAGE AND LINGUISTIC THEORY.
Kluwer Academic Publishers, Postbus 17, 3300 AA Dordrecht, Netherlands. TEL 31-78-6392392. FAX 31-78-6392254. *4284*

NATURAL LANGUAGE ENGINEERING.
Cambridge University Press, Edinburgh Bldg., Shaftesbury Rd., Cambridge CB22RU, England. TEL 44-1223-312393. FAX 44-1223-315052. *2145*

NATURAL LANGUAGE SEMANTICS.
Kluwer Academic Publishers, Postbus 17, 3300 AA Dordrecht, Netherlands. TEL 31-78-6392392. FAX 31-78-6392254. *4284*

NATURAL RESOURCE MANAGEMENT AND POLICY.
Kluwer Academic Publishers, Postbus 17, 3300 AA Dordrecht, Netherlands. TEL 31-78-6392392. FAX 31-78-6392254. *2238*

NATURAL RESOURCES FORUM.
Elsevier Science Ltd., Pergamon, P.O. Box 800, Kidlington, Oxford OX5 1DX, England. TEL 44-1865-843000. FAX 44-1865-843010. *3415*

NATURAL RESOURCES MANAGEMENT AND POLICY.
Kluwer Academic Publishers, Postbus 17, 3300 AA Dordrecht, Netherlands. TEL 31-78-6392392. FAX 31-78-6392254. *2944*

NATURAL TOXINS.
John Wiley & Sons, Inc., Journals, 605 Third Ave., New York, NY 10158. TEL 212-692-6445. FAX 212-850-6021. *1795*

NATURE.
Macmillan Magazines Ltd., 4 Porters South, Crinan St., London N1 9XW, England. TEL 44-171-8334000. FAX 44-171-8434640. *6550*

NATURE BIOTECHNOLOGY.
Nature Publishing Co., 345 Park Ave. S., 10th Fl., New York, NY 10010-1707. TEL 212-726-9200. FAX 212-696-9006. *686*

NATURE IN AVON.
Bristol Naturalists' Society, City Museum, Bristol BS8 1RL, England. *6551*

NATURE MEDICINE.
Macmillan Magazines Ltd., Porters South, Crinan St., London N1 9SQ, England. TEL 44-171-8434962. FAX 44-171-8434998. *4720*

NATURE STRUCTURAL BIOLOGY.
MacMillan Magazines Ltd., 1234 National Press Bldg., Washington, DC 20045. TEL 202-626-2513. FAX 202-628-1609. *616*

NAUTILUS (SANIBEL ISLAND).
Bailey-Matthews Shell Museum, Box 1580, Sanibel Island, FL 33957. TEL 941-395-2233. FAX 941-395-6706. *844*

NAVAL ENGINEERS JOURNAL.
American Society of Naval Engineers, Inc., 1452 Duke St., Alexandria, VA 22314. TEL 703-836-6727. FAX 703-836-7491. *2733*

NAVAL RESEARCH LOGISTICS: AN INTERNATIONAL JOURNAL.
John Wiley & Sons, Inc., Journals, 605 Third Ave., New York, NY 10158. TEL 212-850-6645. FAX 212-850-6021. *5293*

NAVIGATION NEWSLETTER.
Australian Institute of Navigation, Box 2250 G.P.O, Sydney, N.S.W. Australia. TEL 61-2-92646413. FAX 61-2-92671682. *7035*

NAVIONEERS.
American Navion Society, 225 N. 5th St., Ste. 301, Grand Junction, CO 81501. TEL 970-243-8513. *75*

NAVY CHAPLAIN.
U.S. Navy, Bureau of Naval Personnel, Washington, DC 20370. TEL 804-444-7665. FAX 804-445-1006. *5279*

NAZAN STUDIES IN RELIGION & CULTURE.
University of California Press, 2120 Berkeley Way, Berkeley, CA 94720. TEL 510-642-4247. FAX 510-643-7127. *5739*

NEA PAPHOS.
Polska Akademia Nauk, Zaklad Archeologii Srodziemnomorskiej, Palac Kultury i Nauki, p. 2105, 00-901 Warsaw, Poland. TEL 48-22-6248593. FAX 48-22-6207651. *374*

NEBRASKA ACADEMY OF SCIENCES. TRANSACTIONS.
Nebraska Academy of Sciences, 302 Morrill Hall, 14th & U Sts., Lincoln, NE 68588-0339. FAX 402-472-8899. *6552*

THE NEBRASKA LAWYER MAGAZINE.
Nebraska State Bar Association, 635 S. 14th St., Box 81809, Lincoln, NE 68501-1809. TEL 402-475-7091. FAX 402-475-7098. *3995*

NEBRASKA MUSIC EDUCATOR.
Nebraska Music Educators Association, Box 83046, Lincoln, NE 68501-3046. TEL 402-435-6913. FAX 402-474-3250. *5419*

NEDERDUITSE GEREFORMEERDE TEOLOGIESE TYDSKRIF.
Nederduitse Gereformeerde Kerk Uitgewers, P.O. Box 4539, Cape Town, South Africa. TEL 27-21-215540. FAX 27-21-4191865. *6435*

NEDERLANDS ARCHIEF VOOR KERKGESCHIEDENIS.
E.J. Brill, P.O. Box 9000, 2300 PA Leiden, Netherlands. TEL 31-71-5353500. FAX 31-71-5317532. *6357*

NEDERLANDS TIJDSCHRIFT VOOR DE ZORG AAN VERSTANDELIJK GEHANDICAPTEN.
Bisschop Bekkers Instituut - B B I, Postbus 415, 3500 AK Utrecht, Netherlands. TEL 31-30-2333504. FAX 31-30-2340026. *3456*

NEDERLANDS TIJDSCHRIFT VOOR MEDISCHE MICROBIOLOGIE.
Misset, P.O. Box 1110, 3600 BC Maarssen, Netherlands. TEL 31-346-558222. FAX 31-546-554287. *792*

NEDERLANDS TIJDSCHRIFT VOOR UROLOGIE.
Misset, P.O. Box 1110, 3600 BC Maarssen, Netherlands. TEL 31-346-558222. FAX 31-346-554287. *5163*

NEDERLANDSE CHEMISCHE INDUSTRIE.
Vereniging van de Nederlandse Chemische Industrie, Postbus 443, 2260 AK Leidschendam, Netherlands. TEL 31-70-3378787. FAX 31-70-3208438. *2769*

NEDERLANDSE OUDHEDEN.
Rijksdienst voor het Oudheidkundig Bodemonderzoek te Amersfoort, Kerkstraat 1, 3811 CV Amersfoort, Netherlands. TEL 31-33-4634233. FAX 31-33-4653235. *375*

NEEDLE'S EYE.
Union Special Corp., 1 Union Special Plaza, Huntley, IL 60142. TEL 847-669-4334. FAX 847-669-3534. *1917*

NEGOTIATION JOURNAL.
Plenum Publishing Corp., 233 Spring St., New York, NY 10013-1578. TEL 212-620-8000. FAX 212-463-0742. *6028*

NEGRO EDUCATIONAL REVIEW.
Negro Educational Review, Inc., Box 70425, Florida A & M University, Tallahassee, FL 32307. TEL 904-599-8446. FAX 904-561-2100. *2466*

NEMATOLOGIA BRASILEIRA.
Sociedade Brasileira de Nematologia, Secao de Nematologia, Caixa Postal 28, 13020-902 Campinas SP, Brazil. TEL 55-192-415188. FAX 55-192-314943. *845*

NEMATOLOGIA MEDITERRANEA.
Istituto di Nematologia Agraria, Via G. Amendola, 165-A, 70126 Bari, Italy. TEL 39-80-5484186. FAX 39-80-5484165. *236*

NEMATOLOGICA.
E.J. Brill, P.O. Box 9000, 2300 PA Leiden, Netherlands. TEL 31-71-5353500. FAX 31-71-5317532. *845*

NEMOURIA.
Delaware Museum of Natural History, Box 3937, Wilmington, DE 19807-0937. TEL 302-658-9111. FAX 302-658-2610. *845*

NENSHO NO KAGAKU TO GIJUTSU.
Saiensu Komyunikeshonzu Intanashonaru, 3-14-9 Okubo, Shinjuku-ku, Tokyo 169, Japan. TEL 81-3-3208-2325. FAX 81-3-3204-7303. *1833*

NEOMETAPHYSICAL DIGEST.
Society of Metaphysicians Ltd., Archers' Ct., Stonestile Ln., The Ridge, Hastings, E. Sussex TN35 4PG, England. TEL 44-1424-751577. FAX 44-1424-722387. *5577*

NEONATAL INTENSIVE CARE.
Goldstein and Associates Publishing, Inc., 1150 Yale St., Ste. 12, Santa Monica, CA 90403-4738. TEL 213-828-1309. *4963*

NEONATAL NETWORK.
Neonatal Network, 1304 Southpoint Blvd., Ste. 280, Petaluma, CA 94954-6859. TEL 707-762-2646. FAX 707-762-0791. *4941*

NEOPHILOLOGUS.
Kluwer Academic Publishers, Postbus 17, 3300 AA Dordrecht, Netherlands. TEL 31-78-6392392. FAX 31-78-6392254. *4439*

NEOTESTAMENTICA.
New Testament Society of South Africa, c/o Department of New Testament, University of the Orange Free State, P.O. Box 339, Bloemfontein 9300, South Africa. TEL 27-51-4012667. FAX 27-51-489203. *6357*

NEPAL MEDICAL ASSOCIATION. JOURNAL.
Nepal Medical Association, Siddhi Sadan, Exhibition Road, G.P.O. Box 189, Kathmandu, Nepal. *4721*

NEPHROLOGY NEWS & ISSUES.
Nephrology News & Issues, Inc., 15150 N. Hayden Rd., Ste. 101, Scottsdale, AZ 85260-2514. TEL 602-443-4635. FAX 602-443-4528. *5164*

NEPHRON.
S. Karger AG, Allschwilerstr. 10, P.O. Box, CH-4009 Basel, Switzerland. TEL 41-61-3061111. FAX 41-61-3061234. *5164*

NEPTUNO.
Sindicato dos Capitaes Oficiais Pilotos Comissarios e Radiotecnicos da Marinha Mercante, Pc. D. Luis 9 1o D., Lisbon, Portugal. TEL 351-1-3960433. FAX 351-1-3961099. *7159*

NESTLE NUTRITION SERIES.
Lippincott - Raven Publishers, 227 E. Washington Sq., Philadelphia, PA 19106. TEL 215-238-4200. FAX 215-238-4227. *5478*

NETHERLANDS INSTITUTE OF ARCHAEOLOGY AND ARABIC STUDIES IN CAIRO. PUBLICATIONS.
E.J. Brill, P.O. Box 9000, 2300 PA Leiden, Netherlands. TEL 31-71-5353500. FAX 31-71-5317532. *375*

NETHERLANDS INTERNATIONAL LAW REVIEW.
Kluwer Law International, Postbus 85889, 2508 CN The Hague, Netherlands. TEL 31-70-3081500. FAX 31-70-3081515. *4123*

NETHERLANDS JOURNAL OF MEDICINE.
Elsevier Science B.V., P.O. Box 211, 1000 AE Amsterdam, Netherlands. TEL 31-20-4853911. FAX 31-20-4853598. *4926*

NETHERLANDS JOURNAL OF ZOOLOGY.
E.J. Brill, P.O. Box 9000, 2300 PA Leiden, Netherlands. TEL 31-71-5353500. FAX 31-71-5317532. *845*

NETHERLANDS QUARTERLY OF HUMAN RIGHTS.
Kluwer Law International, Postbus 85889, 2508 CN The Hague, Netherlands. TEL 31-70-3081500. FAX 31-70-3081515. *4123*

NETHERLANDS YEARBOOK OF INTERNATIONAL LAW.
Martinus Nijhoff Publishers, Human Rights and International Law Postbus 163, 3300 AD Dordrecht, Netherlands. TEL 31-78-334267. FAX 31-78-334254. *4123*

NETSU BUSSEI.
Nihon Netsu Bussei Gakkai, Dept. of Mechanical Engineering, Nagaoka University of Technology, 1603-1 Kamitomioka-cho, Nagaoka-shi, Niigata-ken 940, Japan. TEL 81-258-46-6000. FAX 81-258-46-6972. *5842*

NETWORKING.
Adelaide Institute, Learn Network, P.O. Box 1872, Adelaide, S.A. 5001, Australia. TEL 61-8-82078438. FAX 61-8-82078434. *4202*

NETWORKS.
John Wiley & Sons, Inc., Journals, 605 Third Ave., New York, NY 10158. TEL 212-850-6645. FAX 212-850-6021. *4623*

NEUMOLOGIA Y CIRUGIA DE TORAX.
Obsidiana Editores, S.A., Czda. de Tlalpan 2365, Col. Ciudad Jardin, 04370 Mexico DF, Mexico. TEL 6899133. *5148*

NEURAL COMPUTATION.
M I T Press, 5 Cambridge Center, Cambridge, MA 02142. TEL 617-253-2889. FAX 617-577-1545. *2103*

NEURAL NETWORK WORLD.
V S P, P.O. Box 346, 3700 AH Zeist, Netherlands. TEL 31-30-6925790. FAX 31-30-6932081. *2103*

NEURAL NETWORKS.
Elsevier Science Ltd., Pergamon, P.O. Box 800, Kidlington, Oxford OX5 1DX, England. TEL 44-1865-843000. FAX 44-1865-843010. *2103*

NEURO-OPHTHALMOLOGY.
Aeolus Press, Postbus 740, 4116 ZJ Buren, Netherlands. TEL 31-344-572055. FAX 31-344-572562. *5082*

NEUROBIOLOGIA.
Sociedade Editora da Revista Neurobiologia, Caixa Postal 651, 50001-970 Recife PE, Brazil. TEL 55-81-268-5495. FAX 39-55-81-2224359. *5082*

NEUROBIOLOGY OF AGING.
Elsevier Science Inc., Box 945, New York, NY 10159-0945. TEL 212-633-3730. FAX 212-633-3680. *819*

NEUROBIOLOGY OF DISEASE.
Academic Press, Inc., Journal Division, 525 B St., Ste. 1900, San Diego, CA 92101-4495. TEL 619-230-1840. FAX 619-699-6800. *5082*

NEUROBIOLOGY OF LEARNING AND MEMORY.
Academic Press, Inc., Journal Division, 525 B. St., Ste. 1900, San Diego, CA 92101-4495. TEL 619-230-1840. FAX 619-699-6800. *5082*

NEUROCHEMICAL RESEARCH.
Plenum Publishing Corp., 233 Spring St., New York, NY 10013-1578. TEL 212-620-8000. FAX 212-463-0742. *5083*

NEUROCHEMISTRY INTERNATIONAL.
Elsevier Science Ltd., Pergamon, P.O. Box 800, Kidlington, Oxford OX5 1DX, England. TEL 44-1865-843000. FAX 44-1865-843010. *5083*

NEUROCOMPUTING.
North-Holland, P.O. Box 211, 1000 AE Amsterdam, Netherlands. TEL 31-20-4853911. FAX 31-20-4853598. *2103*

NEUROENDOCRINE PERSPECTIVES.
Springer-Verlag, 175 Fifth Ave., New York, NY 10010. TEL 212-460-1500. FAX 212-473-6272. *5083*

NEUROENDOCRINOLOGY.
S. Karger AG, Allschwilerstr. 10, P.O. Box, CH-4009 Basel, Switzerland. TEL 41-61-3061111. FAX 41-61-3061234. *4891*

NEUROEPIDEMIOLOGY.
S. Karger AG, Allschwilerstr. 10, P.O. Box, CH-4009 Basel, Switzerland. TEL 41-61-3061111. FAX 41-61-3061234. *5083*

NEUROGASTROENTEROLOGY AND MOTILITY.
Blackwell Science Ltd., Osney Mead, Oxford OX2 0EL, England. TEL 44-1865-206206. FAX 44-1865-721205. *4913*

NEUROGENETICS.
Springer-Verlag, Heidelberger Platz 3, 14197 Berlin, Germany. TEL 49-30-8207-0. FAX 49-30-8214091. *5083*

NEUROIMAGE.
Academic Press, Inc., Journal Division, 525 B St., Ste. 1900, San Diego, CA 92101-4495. TEL 619-230-1840. FAX 619-699-6800. *5083*

NEUROIMMUNOMODULATION.
S. Karger AG, Allschwilerstr. 10, P.O. Box, CH-4009 Basel, Switzerland. TEL 41-61-3061111. FAX 41-61-3061234. *4800*

NEUROLOGIA CROATICA.
University Hospital, Department of Neurology, Kispaticeva 12, 41000 Zagreb, Croatia. TEL 385-41-222706. *5083*

NEUROLOGIA MEDICO-CHIRURGICA.
SciMed Publications, c/o Sumitomo Seimei, Akasaka Bldg., 3-3-3, Akasaka, Minato-ku, Tokyo 107, Japan. FAX 81-3-3812-8092. *5083*

NEUROLOGICAL RESEARCH.
Forefront Publishing Group, 5 River Rd., Ste. 113, Wilton, CT 06897-4069. TEL 203-834-0631. FAX 203-834-0940. *5084*

NEUROLOGY.
Lippincott - Raven Publishers, 227 E. Washington Sq., Philadelphia, PA 19106. TEL 215-238-4200. FAX 215-238-4227. *5084*

NEUROLOGY REVIEWS.
Partners in Medical Communication, 4 Brighton Rd., Clifton, NJ 07012. TEL 201-913-1000. FAX 201-916-0021. *5084*

NEUROMUSCULAR DISORDERS.
Elsevier Science Ltd., Pergamon, P.O. Box 800, Kidlington, Oxford OX5 1DX, England. TEL 44-1865-843000. FAX 44-1865-843010. *5084*

NEUROPATHOLOGY AND APPLIED NEUROBIOLOGY.
Blackwell Science Ltd., Osney Mead, Oxford OX2 0EL, England. TEL 44-1865-206206. FAX 44-1865-721205. *5084*

NEUROPHARMACOLOGY.
Elsevier Science Ltd., Pergamon, P.O. Box 800, Kidlington, Oxford OX5 1DX, England. TEL 44-1865-843000. FAX 44-1865-843010. *5680*

NEUROPHYSIOLOGIE CLINIQUE.
Editions Scientifiques et Medicales Elsevier, 141 rue de Javel, 75747 Paris, France. TEL 33-1-45589026. FAX 33-1-45589421. *5084*

NEUROPHYSIOLOGY.
Plenum Publishing Corp., Consultants Bureau, 233 Spring St., New York, NY 10013-1578. TEL 212-620-8468. FAX 212-463-0742. *5085*

NEUROPROTECTION.
I O S Press, Van Diemenstraat 94, 1013 CN Amsterdam, Netherlands. TEL 31-20-6382189. FAX 31-20-6203419. *5085*

NEUROPSYCHIATRY, NEUROPSYCHOLOGY AND BEHAVIORAL NEUROLOGY.
Lippincott - Raven Publishers, 227 E. Washington Sq., Philadelphia, PA 19106. TEL 215-238-4200. FAX 215-238-4227. *5085*

NEUROPSYCHOBIOLOGY.
S. Karger AG, Allschwilerstr. 10, P.O. Box, CH-4009 Basel, Switzerland. TEL 41-61-3061111. FAX 41-61-3061234. *5085*

NEUROPSYCHOLOGIA.
Elsevier Science Ltd., Pergamon, P.O. Box 800, Kidlington, Oxford OX5 1DX, England. TEL 44-1865-843000. FAX 44-1865-843010. *5085*

NEUROPSYCHOLOGY.
American Psychological Association, 750 First St., N.E., Washington, DC 20002-4242. TEL 202-336-5600. FAX 202-336-5568. *5085*

NEUROPSYCHOLOGY AND COGNITION.
Kluwer Academic Publishers, Postbus 17, 3300 AA Dordrecht, Netherlands. TEL 31-78-6392392. FAX 31-78-6392254. *5085*

NEUROPSYCHOLOGY, DEVELOPMENT AND COGNITION. SECTION A: JOURNAL OF CLINICAL AND EXPERIMENTAL NEUROPSYCHOLOGY.
Swets & Zeitlinger bv, P.O. Box 825, 2160 SZ Lisse, Netherlands. TEL 31-252-435111. FAX 31-252-415888. *6137*

NEUROPSYCHOLOGY, DEVELOPMENT AND COGNITION. SECTION B: AGING, NEUROPSYCHOLOGY AND COGNITION.
Swets & Zeitlinger bv, P.O. Box 825, 2160 SZ Lisse, Netherlands. TEL 31-252-435111. FAX 31-252-415888. *6137*

NEUROPSYCHOLOGY REVIEW.
Plenum Publishing Corp., 233 Spring St., New York, NY 10013-1578. TEL 212-620-8000. FAX 212-463-0742. *5085*

NEUROPSYCHOPHARMACOLOGY.
Elsevier Science Inc., Box 945, New York, NY 10159-0945. TEL 212-633-3730. FAX 212-633-3680. *5086*

NEUROREHABILITATION.
Elsevier Science Ireland Ltd., P.O. Box 85, Limerick, Ireland. FAX 353-61-472144. *5086*

NEUROSCIENCE.
Elsevier Science Ltd., Pergamon, P.O. Box 800, Kidlington, Oxford OX5 1DX, England. TEL 44-1865-843000. FAX 44-1865-843010. *5086*

NEUROSCIENCE AND BEHAVIORAL PHYSIOLOGY.
Plenum Publishing Corp., Consultants Bureau, 233 Spring St., New York, NY 10013-1578. TEL 212-620-8468. FAX 212-463-0742. *5086*

NEUROSCIENCE AND BIOBEHAVIORAL REVIEWS.
Elsevier Science Ltd., Pergamon, P.O. Box 800, Kidlington, Oxford OX5 1DX, England. TEL 44-1865-843000. FAX 44-1865-843010. *5086*

NEUROSCIENCE LETTERS.
Elsevier Science Ireland Ltd., P.O. Box 85, Limerick, Ireland. TEL 353-61-471944. FAX 353-61-472144. *5086*

NEUROSCIENCE RESEARCH.
Elsevier Science Ireland Ltd., P.O. Box 85, Limerick, Ireland. TEL 353-61-471944. FAX 353-61-472144. *5086*

NEUROSCIENCE RESEARCH COMMUNICATIONS.
John Wiley & Sons Ltd., Journals, Baffins Ln., Chichester, W. Sussex PO19 1UD, England. TEL 44-1243-779777. FAX 44-1243-775878. *5087*

NEUROSURGERY (BALTIMORE).
Williams & Wilkins, 351 W. Camden St., Baltimore, MD 21201-2436. TEL 410-528-4068. FAX 410-528-4452. *5087*

NEUROSURGERY QUARTERLY.
Lippincott - Raven Publishers, 227 E. Washington Sq., Philadelphia, PA 19106. TEL 215-238-4200. FAX 215-238-4227. *5149*

NEUROTOXICOLOGY AND TERATOLOGY.
Elsevier Science Inc., Box 945, New York, NY 10159-0945. TEL 212-633-3730. FAX 212-633-3680. *5087*

NEUROUROLOGY AND URODYNAMICS.
John Wiley & Sons, Inc., Journals, 605 Third Ave., New York, NY 10158. TEL 212-850-6645. FAX 212-850-6021. *5164*

NEUTRON NEWS.
Gordon and Breach - Harwood Academic, Amsteldisk 166, 1st Fl., 1079 LH Amsterdam, Netherlands. *5854*

NEVADA. BUREAU OF MINES AND GEOLOGY. BULLETIN.
Bureau of Mines and Geology, Publications Sales, Mail Stop 178, University of Nevada at Reno, Reno, NV 89557-0088. TEL 702-784-6691. FAX 702-784-1709. *2360*

NEVADA. BUREAU OF MINES AND GEOLOGY. EDUCATIONAL SERIES.
Bureau of Mines and Geology, Publication Sales, Mail Stop 178, University of Nevada at Reno, Reno, NV 89557-0088. TEL 702-784-6691. FAX 702-784-1709. *2360*

NEVADA. BUREAU OF MINES AND GEOLOGY. LISTS.
Bureau of Mines and Geology, Publication Sales, Mail Stop 178, University of Nevada at Reno, Reno, NV 89557-0088. TEL 702-784-6691. FAX 702-184-1709. *2360*

NEVADA. BUREAU OF MINES AND GEOLOGY. OPEN-FILE REPORT.
Bureau of Mines and Geology, Publications Sales, Mail Stop 178, University of Nevada at Reno, Reno, NV 89557-0088. TEL 702-784-6691. FAX 702-784-1709. *2360*

NEVADA. BUREAU OF MINES AND GEOLOGY. PAMPHLET.
Bureau of Mines and Geology, Publications Sales, Mail Stop 178, University of Nevada at Reno, Reno, NV 89557-0088. TEL 702-784-6691. FAX 702-784-1709. *2360*

NEVADA. BUREAU OF MINES AND GEOLOGY. REPORT.
Bureau of Mines and Geology, Publications Sales, Mail Stop 178, University of Nevada at Reno, Reno, NV 89557-0088. TEL 702-784-6691. FAX 702-784-1709. *2360*

NEVADA. BUREAU OF MINES AND GEOLOGY. SPECIAL PUBLICATIONS.
Bureau of Mines and Geology, Publications Sales, Mail Stop 178, University of Nevada at Reno, Reno, NV 89557-0088. TEL 702-784-6691. FAX 702-784-1709. *2360*

NEVADA GEOLOGY.
Bureau of Mines and Geology, Publication Sales, Mail Stop 178, University of Nevada at Reno, Reno, NV 89557-0088. TEL 702-784-6691. FAX 702-784-1709. *2360*

NEVADA LAWYER.
State Bar of Nevada, 1325 Airmotive Way, Ste. 140, Reno, NV 89502-3239. TEL 702-329-4100. FAX 702-329-0522. *3996*

NEVADA MINERAL INDUSTRY (YEAR).
Bureau of Mines and Geology, Publications Sales, Mail Stop 178, University of Nevada at Reno, Reno, NV 89557-0088. TEL 702-784-6691. FAX 702-784-1709. *2360*

THE NEW ADVOCATE.
Christopher - Gordon Publishers, Inc., 480 Washington St., Norwood, MA 02062. TEL 617-762-5577. *4439*

NEW AGE SOURCEBOOK.
Reference Press International, Box 812726, Boca Raton, FL 33481-2726. TEL 561-994-3499. FAX 561-994-3699. *5459*

NEW ARCADIAN JOURNAL.
New Arcadian Press, 13 Graham Grove, Burley, Leeds LS4 2NF, England. TEL 44-113-2304608. FAX 44-1274-753236. *410*

NEW ASTRONOMY.
Elsevier Science B.V., P.O. Box 211, 1000 AE Amsterdam, Netherlands. TEL 31-20-4853911. FAX 31-20-4853705. *498*

NEW BEGINNINGS (FRANKLIN PARK).
La Leche League International, Inc, 1400 N. Meacham Rd., P.O. Box 4079, Schaumburg, IL 60168-4079. TEL 708-445-7730, 847-519-7730. FAX 708-455-0125. *1852*

THE NEW BOOKBINDER.
Designer Bookbinders Publications Ltd., 1 chemin du Canal, 65700 Labatut-Riviere, France. TEL 33-5-62963257. FAX 33-5-62963257. *6278*

NEW CANADIAN.
Japan Communications Inc., 524 Front St. W., 2nd Fl., Toronto, ON M5V 1B8, Canada. TEL 416-593-6118. FAX 416-593-1871. *3032*

NEW CHURCH LIFE.
General Church of the New Jerusalem, Box 277, Bryn Athyn, PA 19009. TEL 215-947-4200. FAX 215-938-2616. *6495*

NEW CITY (LONDON).
Mariapolis Ltd. Focolare Movement, 57 Twyford Ave., London W3 9PZ, England. TEL 44-181-993-6944. FAX 44-181-993-6944. *6358*

NEW CLINICAL APPLICATIONS. DERMATOLOGY.
Kluwer Academic Publishers, Postbus 17, 3300 AA Dordrecht, Netherlands. TEL 31-78-6392392. FAX 31-78-6392254. *5164*

NEW CLINICAL APPLICATIONS. GASTROENTEROLOGY.
Kluwer Academic Publishers, Postbus 17, 3300 AA Dordrecht, Netherlands. TEL 31-78-6392392. FAX 31-78-6392254. *4914*

NEW CLINICAL APPLICATIONS. NEPHROLOGY.
Kluwer Academic Publishers, Postbus 17, 3300 AA Dordrecht, Netherlands. TEL 31-78-6392392. FAX 31-78-6392254. *5164*

NEW CLINICAL APPLICATIONS. PAEDIATRICS.
Kluwer Academic Publishers, Postbus 17, 3300 AA Dordrecht, Netherlands. TEL 31-78-6392392. FAX 31-78-6392254. *5034*

NEW CLINICAL APPLICATIONS. RADIOLOGY.
Kluwer Academic Publishers, Postbus 17, 3300 AA Dordrecht, Netherlands. TEL 31-78-6392392. FAX 31-78-6392254. *5112*

NEW COMPREHENSIVE BIOCHEMISTRY.
Elsevier Science B.V., Books Division, P.O. Box 211, 1000 AE Amsterdam, Netherlands. TEL 31-20-4853911. FAX 31-20-4853705. *667*

NEW CONTREE.
University of the North West, Department of History, Private Bag X2046, Mmabatho 2735, South Africa. TEL 27-140-892194. FAX 27-140-25771. *3528*

NEW DELTA REVIEW.
English Department, Louisiana State University, Baton Rouge, LA 70803-5001. TEL 504-388-4079. FAX 504-388-4129. *4440*

NEW DIRECTIONS IN CULTURAL ANALYSIS.
University of California Press, 2120 Berkeley Way, Berkeley, CA 94720. TEL 510-642-4247. FAX 510-643-7127. *3786*

NEW ENGLAND CLASSICAL NEWSLETTER & JOURNAL.
Classical Association of New England, Greek and Roman Studies, Fairfield University, Fairfield, CT 06430. TEL 203-254-4000. *1906*

NEW ENGLAND JOURNAL OF HISTORY.
New England History Teachers Association, Home Office, Bentley College, Waltham, MA 02254. TEL 617-444-3181. *3639*

NEW ENGLAND JOURNAL OF MEDICINE.
Massachusetts Medical Society, 10 Shattuck St., Boston, MA 02115. TEL 617-734-9800. FAX 617-893-8103. *4721*

NEW ENGLAND JOURNAL OF OPTOMETRY.
New England Council of Optometrists, 101 Tremont St., Boston, MA 02108. TEL 617-542-1233. FAX 617-542-4574. *4996*

NEW ENGLAND PROGRESS.
178 Forbes Rd., Ste. 218, Braintree, MA 01701. TEL 617-843-3800. FAX 617-843-1178. *3482*

NEW ENGLAND QUARTERLY.
New England Quarterly, Inc., Meserve Hall, 2nd Fl., Northeastern University, Boston, MA 02115. TEL 617-373-2734. FAX 617-373-2661. *4440*

NEW ENGLAND READING ASSOCIATION. JOURNAL.
New England Reading Association, Box 322, Moody, ME 04054-0322. TEL 207-641-2085. *2466*

NEW ENGLAND THEATRE JOURNAL.
New England Theatre Conference, c/o Department of Theatre, Northeastern University, 360 Huntington Ave., Boston, MA 02115. TEL 617-424-9275. FAX 617-424-1057. *7010*

NEW EQUITABLE LIFE TAX GUIDE.
Blackwell Publishers Ltd., 108 Cowley Rd., Oxford OX4 1JF, England. TEL 44-1865-791100. FAX 44-1865-791347. *1621*

NEW ERA IN EDUCATION.
World Education Fellowship, University of Hertfordshire, Wall Hall, Aldenham, Watford, Herts. WD2 8AT, England. TEL 44-1707-285677. FAX 44-1707-285616. *2466*

NEW FARMER AND GROWER.
Soil Association, 86 Colston St., Bristol, Avon BS1 5BB, England. TEL 44-117-929-9666. FAX 44-117-925-2504. *139*

NEW FORESTS.
Kluwer Academic Publishers, Postbus 17, 3300 AA Dordrecht, Netherlands. TEL 31-78-6392392. FAX 31-78-6392254. *3158*

NEW FORMATIONS.
Lawrence & Wishart Ltd., 99a Wallis Rd., London E9 5LN, England. TEL 44-181-533-2506. FAX 44-181-533-7369. *4348*

NEW GERMAN REVIEW.
University of California at Los Angeles, Department of Germanic Languages, 302 Royce Hall, Los Angeles, CA 90034. TEL 310-825-3955. FAX 310-825-7954. *4440*

NEW GLASS REVIEW.
Efekt, Co. Ltd., Ciklova 3, 128 00 Prague 2, Czech Republic. TEL 42-2-6926207. *1732*

NEW HAMPSHIRE. AGRICULTURAL EXPERIMENT STATION, DURHAM. RESEARCH REPORTS.
University of New Hampshire, Agricultural Experiment Station, Durham, NH 03824. TEL 603-862-1234. *139*

NEW HAVEN STUDIES IN INTERNATIONAL LAW AND WORLD PUBLIC ORDER.
Kluwer Academic Publishers, Postbus 17, 3300 AA Dordrecht, Netherlands. TEL 31-78-6392392. FAX 31-78-6392254. *4123*

THE NEW HISTORICISM: STUDIES IN CULTURAL POETICS.
University of California Press, 2120 Berkeley Way, Berkeley, CA 94720. TEL 510-642-4247. FAX 510-643-7127. *4440*

NEW HORIZONS (WILLOW GROVE).
Orthodox Presbyterian Church, Committee on Christian Education, P.O. Box P, Willow Grove, PA 19090-0920. TEL 215-830-0900. FAX 215-830-0350. *6435*

NEW HORIZONS IN EDUCATION.
World Education Fellowship (Australia), 21 Ridgway Dr., Flagstaff Hill, S.A. 5159, Australia. TEL 61-8-82703541. FAX 61-8-82967932. *2467*

NEW HORIZONS IN THERAPEUTICS: SMITH, KLINE & FRENCH LABORATORIES RESEARCH SYMPOSIA SERIES.
Plenum Publishing Corp., 233 Spring St., New York, NY 10013-1578. TEL 212-620-8000. FAX 212-463-0742. *4721*

NEW IDEAS IN PSYCHOLOGY.
Elsevier Science Ltd., Pergamon, P.O. Box 800, Kidlington, Oxford OX5 1DX, England. TEL 44-1865-843000. FAX 44-1865-843010. *6138*

NEW JERSEY ACADEMY OF SCIENCE. BULLETIN.
New Jersey Academy of Science, Beck Hall, Rm. 216, Livingston Campus, Rutgers University, Piscataway, NJ 08854. TEL 908-463-0511. *6553*

NEW JERSEY LAW JOURNAL.
American Lawyer Media, L.P. (Newark), 238 Mulberry St., Box 20081, Newark, NJ 07101-6081. TEL 201-642-0075. FAX 201-642-0920. *3996*

NEW JERSEY MEDICINE.
Medical Society of New Jersey, 2 Princess Rd., Trenton, NJ 08648. TEL 609-393-7196. FAX 609-393-3759. *4721*

NEW JERSEY WASTEWATER TREATMENT TRUST. ANNUAL REPORT.
New Jersey Wastewater Treatment Trust, CN 440, Trenton, NJ 08625. TEL 609-219-8600. FAX 609-219-8620. *2987*

NEW LAUREL REVIEW.
Smoke Bend Publishing, 828 Lesseps St., New Orleans, LA 70117. TEL 504-947-6001. *4440*

NEW LITERATURES REVIEW.
University of Wollongong, Department of English, Northfields Ave., Wollongong, N.S.W. 2522, Australia. TEL 61-42-213677. FAX 61-42-214471. *4440*

NEW MEXICO GEOLOGICAL SOCIETY. GUIDEBOOK, FIELD CONFERENCE.
New Mexico Geological Society, Inc., Campus Station, Socorro, NM 87801. TEL 505-835-5410. *2360*

NEW NOVEL REVIEW.
Elmira College, Humanities Department, Elmira, NY 14901. TEL 607-735-1898. FAX 607-735-1758. *4440*

NEW OBSERVATIONS.
New Observations Ltd., 611 Broadway, No. 701, New York, NY 10012. TEL 212-677-8561. *457*

NEW ORLEANS REVIEW.
Loyola University, Box 195, New Orleans, LA 70118. TEL 504-865-2295. FAX 504-865-2294. *4440*

THE NEW PLANTSMAN.
Royal Horticultural Society, 80 Vincent Sq., London SW1P 2PE, England. TEL 44-171-834-4333. FAX 44-171-630-6060. *3200*

NEW POLITICAL ECONOMY.
Carfax Publishing Co., P.O. Box 25, Abingdon, Oxon OX14 3UE, England. TEL 44-1235-401000. FAX 44-1235-401550. *1309*

NEW POLITICAL SCIENCE.
Caucus for a New Political Science, c/o John C. Berg, Treas., Department of Government, Suffolk University, Boston, MA 02108-2770. TEL 617-573-8126. FAX 617-367-4623. *5948*

NEW SYNTHESE HISTORICAL LIBRARY.
Kluwer Academic Publishers, Postbus 17, 3300 AA Dordrecht, Netherlands. TEL 31-78-6392392. FAX 31-78-6392254. *5739*

NEW TECHNOLOGY IN THE HUMAN SERVICES.
Computers in Teaching Initiative, Centre for Human Service Technology, University of Southampton, Department of Social Work Studies, Southampton, Hants. SO17-1BJ, England. TEL 44-1703-593536. FAX 44-1703-592779. *6741*

NEW TECHNOLOGY, WORK & EMPLOYMENT.
Blackwell Publishers Ltd., 108 Cowley Rd., Oxford OX4 1JF, England. TEL 44-1865-791100. FAX 44-1865-791347. *1447*

NEW TESTAMENT TOOLS AND STUDIES.
E.J. Brill, P.O. Box 9000, 2300 PA Leiden, Netherlands. TEL 31-71-5353500. FAX 31-71-5317532. *6358*

NEW TRENDS IN LIPID MEDIATORS RESEARCH.
S. Karger AG, Allschwilerstr. 10, P.O. Box, CH-4009 Basel, Switzerland. TEL 41-61-3061111. FAX 41-61-3061234. *5680*

NEW YORK ACADEMY OF SCIENCES. ANNALS.
New York Academy of Sciences, 2 E. 63rd St., New York, NY 10021. TEL 212-838-0230. *6553*

NEW YORK ACADEMY OF SCIENCES. TRANSACTIONS.
New York Academy of Sciences, 2 E. 63rd St., New York, NY 10021. *6553*

NEW YORK BOTANICAL GARDEN. MEMOIRS.
New York Botanical Garden, Scientific Publications Department, Bronx, NY 10458-5126. TEL 718-817-8721. FAX 718-817-8842. *717*

NEW YORK ECONOMIC REVIEW.
New York State Economic Association, c/o William O'Dea, Ed., Dept. of Economics and Business, SUNY-Oneonta, Oneonta, NY 13820. TEL 607-436-2127. FAX 607-436-2107. *1273*

NEW YORK ENTOMOLOGICAL SOCIETY. JOURNAL.
New York Entomological Society, c/o American Museum of Natural History, Central Park West at 79th St., New York, NY 10024-5192. TEL 212-769-5613. FAX 212-769-5277. *758*

NEW YORK FOLKLORE.
New York Folklore Society, Box 130, Newfield, NY 14867. TEL 607-273-9137. FAX 607-273-3620. *3090*

NEW YORK GENEALOGICAL AND BIOGRAPHICAL RECORD.
New York Genealogical and Biographical Society, 122 E. 58th St., New York, NY 10022-1939. TEL 212-755-8532. FAX 212-754-4218. *3234*

NEW YORK HEALTH SCIENCES JOURNAL.
New York Medical College, Graduate School of Health Sciences, Valhalla, NY 10595. TEL 914-993-4531. FAX 914-993-4292. *4722*

NEW YORK INTERNATIONAL LAW REVIEW.
New York State Bar Association, International Law and Practice Section, 1 Elk St., Albany, NY 12207-1096. TEL 518-463-3200. FAX 518-463-8844. *4123*

THE NEW YORK JOURNAL OF MATHEMATICS.
State University of New York at Albany, *4594*

NEW YORK PSYCHOANALYTIC INSTITUTE. KRIS STUDY GROUP. MONOGRAPHS.
International Universities Press, Inc., 59 Boston Post Rd., Box 1524, Madison, CT 06443-1524. TEL 203-245-4000. FAX 203-245-0775. *6138*

NEW YORK REVIEW OF SCIENCE FICTION.
Dragon Press, Box 78, Pleasantville, NY 10570. TEL 914-769-5545. *4534*

NEW YORK STATE CONSERVATIONIST.
Department of Environmental Conservation, 50 Wolf Rd., Albany, NY 12233. TEL 518-457-5547. FAX 518-457-0858. *2239*

NEW YORK STATE NURSES ASSOCIATION. JOURNAL.
New York State Nurses Association, 46 Cornell Rd., Latham, NY 12110-1403. TEL 518-782-9400. FAX 518-782-9533. *4941*

NEW YORK UNIVERSITY JOURNAL OF INTERNATIONAL LAW AND POLITICS.
New York University, Law Publications, 110 W. Third St., New York, NY 10012. TEL 212-998-6520. FAX 212-995-4032. *4123*

NEW ZEALAND BUSINESS LAW QUARTERLY.
Brooker's Limited, Level 1 - Telecom Networks House, 68-86 Jervois Quay, Wellington, New Zealand. TEL 64-4-4998178. FAX 64-4-4998173. *4084*

NEW ZEALAND DAIRY EXPORTER.
New Zealand Dairy Exporter Ltd., P.O. Box 299, Wellington, New Zealand. TEL 64-4-990300. FAX 64-4-4990330. *258*

NEW ZEALAND ECONOMIC PAPERS.
New Zealand Association of Economists, P.O. Box 568, Wellington, New Zealand. TEL 64-3-4798655. FAX 64-3-4798174. *988*

NEW ZEALAND JOURNAL OF AGRICULTURAL RESEARCH.
S I R Publishing, P.O. Box 399, Wellington, New Zealand. TEL 64-4-472-7421. FAX 64-4-473-1841. *139*

NEW ZEALAND JOURNAL OF BOTANY.
S I R Publishing, P.O. Box 399, Wellington, New Zealand. TEL 64-4-472-7421. FAX 64-4-473-1841. *717*

NEW ZEALAND JOURNAL OF CROP AND HORTICULTURAL SCIENCE.
S I R Publishing, P.O. Box 399, Wellington, New Zealand. TEL 64-4-472-7421. FAX 64-4-473-1841. *139*

NEW ZEALAND JOURNAL OF ECOLOGY.
New Zealand Ecological Society, Inc., P.O. Box 25-178, Christchurch, New Zealand. TEL 64-3-3256701. FAX 64-3-3252418. *617*

NEW ZEALAND JOURNAL OF FORESTRY SCIENCE.
Forest Research Institute, Private Bag 3020, Rotorua, New Zealand. TEL 64-7-3475889. FAX 64-7-347-9380. *3159*

NEW ZEALAND JOURNAL OF FRENCH STUDIES.
Massey University, Department of European Languages, Private Bag 11-222, Palmerston North, New Zealand. TEL 64-6-3505237. FAX 64-6-3505633. *4441*

NEW ZEALAND JOURNAL OF GEOLOGY AND GEOPHYSICS.
S I R Publishing, P.O. Box 399, Wellington, New Zealand. TEL 64-4-472-7421. FAX 64-4-473-1841. *2361*

NEW ZEALAND JOURNAL OF MARINE AND FRESHWATER RESEARCH.
S I R Publishing, P.O. Box 399, Wellington, New Zealand. TEL 64-4-472-7421. FAX 64-4-473-1841. *2411*

NEW ZEALAND JOURNAL OF SPORTS MEDICINE.
Sports Medicine New Zealand, 96 Anzac Ave., P.O. Box 6398, Dunedin, New Zealand. TEL 64-3-4777887. FAX 64-3-4777882. *5131*

NEW ZEALAND JOURNAL OF TAXATION LAW AND POLICY.
Brooker's Limited, Level 1 - Telecom Networks House, 68-86 Jervois Quay, Wellington, New Zealand. TEL 64-4-4998178. FAX 64-4-4998173. *1622*

NEW ZEALAND JOURNAL OF ZOOLOGY.
S I R Publishing, P.O. Box 399, Wellington, New Zealand. TEL 64-4-472-7421. FAX 64-4-473-1841. *845*

NEW ZEALAND KIWIFRUIT.
Kiwifruit New Zealand, P.O. Box 9906, Auckland, New Zealand. TEL 64-9-3677500. FAX 64-9-3670220. *236*

NEW ZEALAND LAW REVIEW.
Legal Research Foundation, University of Auckland, Private Bag, Auckland, New Zealand. TEL 64-9-3099540. FAX 64-9-3737473. *3999*

NEW ZEALAND NATURAL SCIENCES.
University of Canterbury, Zoology Department, Private Bag 4800, Christchurch 1, New Zealand. TEL 64-3-364-2860. FAX 64-3-364-2024. *617*

NEW ZEALAND SLAVONIC JOURNAL.
Victoria University of Wellington, School of European Languages, P.O. Box 600, Wellington, New Zealand. TEL 64-4-471-5322. FAX 64-4-496-5419. *3787*

REFEREED SERIALS

NEW ZEALAND SOCIETY OF PERIODONTOLOGY. JOURNAL.
New Zealand Society of Periodontology, P.O. Box 647, Dunedin, New Zealand. TEL 64-3-4797-108. FAX 64-3-4790-673. *4865*

NEW ZEALAND STATISTICIAN.
New Zealand Statistical Association (Inc.), P.O. Box 1731, Wellington, New Zealand. TEL 64-6-350-4265. FAX 64-6-350-5611. *6928*

NEW ZEALAND VETERINARY JOURNAL.
New Zealand Veterinary Association, P.O. Box 27-499, Wellington, New Zealand. TEL 64-4-471-0484. FAX 64-4-471-0494. *7275*

A NEWBERRY NEWSLETTER.
Newberry Library, 60 W. Walton St., Chicago, IL 60610. TEL 312-255-3548. *4203*

NEWFOUNDLAND. DEPARTMENT OF MINES AND ENERGY. GEOLOGICAL SURVEY BRANCH. ORE HORIZONS.
Department of Mines and Energy, P.O. Box 8700, St. John's, NF A1B 4J6, Canada. TEL 709-729-3159. FAX 709-729-3493. *5311*

NEWFOUNDLAND. DEPARTMENT OF NATURAL RESOURCES. GEOLOGICAL SURVEY. CURRENT RESEARCH.
Department of Mines and Energy, Geological Survey, P.O. Box 8700, St. John's, NF A1B 4J6, Canada. TEL 709-729-3159. FAX 709-729-3493. *5311*

NEWFOUNDLAND STUDIES.
Memorial University of Newfoundland, Department of English, St. John's, NF A1C 5S7, Canada. TEL 709-737-2144. FAX 709-737-4342. *3264*

NEWPORT REVIEW.
Words in Motion Publishing, 484 Broadway, Newport, RI 02840. TEL 401-847-7978. FAX 401-847-7978. *4441*

NEWPORT TRAVELER.
Traveler Publications, Inc., 172 Bellevue Ave., Ste. 319, Newport, RI 02840. TEL 401-847-0089. FAX 401-847-5267. *7224*

THE NEWS.
Beauronne, 24650 Chancelade, France. TEL 33-5-53081773. FAX 33-5-53081773. *3280*

NEWS FROM APROVECHO.
Aprovecho Institute, 80574 Hazelton Rd., Cottage Grove, OR 97424. TEL 541-942-8198. FAX 541-942-0302. *2566*

NEWS IN PHYSIOLOGICAL SCIENCES.
American Physiological Society, 9650 Rockville Pike, Bethesda, MD 20814. TEL 301-530-7164. FAX 301-571-3813. *819*

NEWS TIBET.
Office of Tibet, 241 E. 32nd St., New York, NY 10016. TEL 212-213-5010. FAX 212-779-9245. *3033*

NEWS - 400.
Duke Communications International, 221 E. 29th St., Ste. 242, Loveland, CO 80538. TEL 970-663-4700. FAX 970-663-3285. *2180*

NEXUS (HAMILTON).
c/o Department of Anthropology, McMaster University, Hamilton, ON L8S 4L9, Canada. TEL 416-525-9140. *325*

NEXUS NEW TIMES.
Nexus Magazine Pty Ltd., P.O. Box 30, Mapleton, Qld. 4650, Australia. TEL 61-7-5442-9280. FAX 61-7-5442-9381. *5577*

NIANGJIU KEJI.
Niangjiu Keji Zazhishe, 45 Shachong Zhonglu, Guiyang, Guizhou 550002, People's Republic of China. TEL 86-851-5796163. *525*

NICARAGUA UPDATE.
Nicaragua Solidarity Campaign, 129 Seven Sisters Rd., London N7 7QG, England. TEL 44-171-272-9619. FAX 44-171-272-5476. *5948*

NICOLAUS. STUDI STORICI.
Comunita dei Padri Domenicani della Basilica Pontificia di S. Nicola, Centro Studi Nicolaiani, Largo Abate Elia, 15, 70122 Bari, Italy. TEL 39-80-5237247. *3587*

NIELS BOHR - COLLECTED WORKS.
Elsevier Science B.V., Books Division, P.O. Box 211, 1000 AE Amsterdam, Netherlands. TEL 31-20-4853911. FAX 31-20-4853705. *5816*

NIGERIA ENGINEER.
Nigerian Society of Engineers, Editorial Committee, National Engineering Centre, 1 Engineering Close, P.O. Box 72667, Victoria Island, Lagos State, Nigeria. TEL 234-1-2617349. FAX 234-1-2617315. *2734*

NIGERIA SOCIETY OF PHYSIOTHERAPY. JOURNAL.
Nigeria Society of Physiotherapy, Department of Physiotherapy, College of Medicine, University of Lagos, Idi-Araba, Lagos, Nigeria. FAX 234-1-837630. *5045*

NIGERIAN FIELD.
Nigerian Field Society, P.O. Box 30385, Secretariat Post Office, Ibadan, Oyo State, Nigeria. TEL 234-22-8102138. *6554*

NIGERIAN JOURNAL OF PALMS AND OIL SEEDS.
Nigerian Institute for Oil Palm Research, P.M.B. 1030, Benin City, Bendel State, Nigeria. TEL 234-52-440130. FAX 234-52-440150. *717*

NIGHTSUN.
Frostburg State University, Department of English, Frostburg, MD 21532. TEL 301-687-4221. FAX 301-687-4495. *4441*

NIHON BENTOSU GAKKAISHI.
Nihon Bentosu Gakkai, Ocean Research Institute, University of Tokyo, Minami-Dai, Nakano-ku, Tokyo 164, Japan. TEL 81-3-5351-6469. FAX 81-3-3375-6716. *617*

NIHON CONTACT LENS GAKKAISHI.
Japan Contact Lens Society, Nihon Ganka Kiyo Kai, 302 Yamamoto Bldg., 3-6 Mihogaoka, Ibaraki 567, Japan. TEL 81-726-23-7878. FAX 81-726-23-6060. *4997*

NIHON GAISHO GAKKAI ZASSHI.
Nihon Gaisho Gakkai, Teikyo Daigaku Kyumei Kyukyu Senta, 11-1, Kaga 2-chome, Itabashi-ku, Tokyo 173, Japan. TEL 81-3-3964-1211. FAX 81-3-5375-0854. *5012*

NIHON HIKAKU NAIBUNPI GAKKAI NYUSU.
Nihon Hikaku Naibunpi Gakkai, Tokyo Daigaku Rigakubu Dobutsugaku Kyoshitsu, 3-1, Hongo 7-chome, Bunkyo-ku, Tokyo 113, Japan. TEL 81-3-5351-6467. FAX 81-3-5351-6463. *4891*

NIHON IDEN GAKKAI TAIKAI PUROGURAMU YOKOSHU.
Nihon Iden Gakkai, Kokuritsu Idengaku Kenkyujo, 111 Yata, Mishima-shi, Shizuoka-ken 411, Japan. *642*

NIHON KIJI MIZUTORI KYOKAISHI.
Nihon Kiji Mizutori Kyokai, 17-11 Kuwazu 3-chome, Higashisumiyoshi-ku, Osaka 546, Japan. FAX 81-06-719-2616. *806*

NIHON ONKYO GAKKAISHI.
Nihon Onkyo Gakkai, 7-7, Yoyogi 2-chome, Shibuya-ku, Tokyo 151, Japan. TEL 81-3-3379-1200. FAX 81-3-3379-1456. *5873*

NIHON OYO DOBUTSU KONCHU GAKKAI CHUGOKU SHIBU KAIHO.
Nihon Oyo Dobutsu Konchu Gakkai, Chugoku Shibu, Chugoku Nogyo Shikenjo, 12-1, Nishifukatsucho 6-chome, Fukuyama-shi, Hiroshima-ken 721, Japan. TEL 81-0849-23-4100. FAX 81-0849-24-7893. *759*

NIHON RINSHO EIYO GAKKAI ZASSHI.
Nihon Rinsho Eiyo Gakkai, c/o Nihon Gakkai Jimu Senta, 16-9 Honkomagome 5-chome, Bunkyo-ku, Tokyo 113, Japan. TEL 81-3-5814-5801. *5478*

NIHON SANFUJINKA SHINSEIJI KETSUEKI GAKKAISHI.
Japanese Society of Obstetrical, Gynecological and Neonatal Hematology, Hamamatsu University, School of Medicine, Department of Obstetrics and Gynecology, 3600 Handa-cho, Hamamatsu 431-31, Japan. TEL 81-53-435-2309. FAX 81-53-435-2308. *4964*

NIHON SEIKEI GEKA CHOONPA KENKYUKAI KAISHI.
Nihon Seikei Geka Choonpa Kenkyukai, Osaka Ika Daigaku Seikei Gekagaku Kyoshitsu, 2-7, Daigakumachi, Takatsuki-shi, Osaka 569, Japan. *5012*

NIHON SEKIGAISEN GAKKAISHI.
Nihon Sekigaisen Gakkai, Nihon Gakkai Jimu Senta, 16-9, Honkomagome 5-chome, Bunkyo-ku, Tokyo 113, Japan. TEL 03-5814-5801. FAX 03-5814-5820. *5842*

NIHON SHIKA MASUI GAKKAI ZASSHI.
Nihon Shika Masui Gakkai, Osaka University, 1-8 Yamadaoka, Suita, 565 Osaka, Japan. TEL 81-3-3947-8891. FAX 81-3-3947-8341. *4806*

NIHON UNIVERSITY. JOURNAL OF ORAL SCIENCE.
Nihon University, School of Dentistry at Matsudo, 870-1 Sakaecho, Nishi-2, Matsudo-shi, Chiba-ken 271, Japan. TEL 81-47-368-6111. FAX 81-47-364-6295. *4865*

NIHONKAI MATHEMATICAL JOURNAL.
Niigata Daigaku, Rigakubu, c/o Dept. of mathematics, 8050, Igarashi 2, Niigata, 951-21, Japan. *4594*

NIHONKAIKU SUISAN KENKYUJO KENKYU HOKOKU.
Japan Sea National Fisheries Research Institute, 5939-22, Suido-cho 1-chome, Niigata-shi, Niigata 951, Japan. TEL 81-25-228-0451. FAX 81-25-224-0950. *3074*

NIJHOFF INTERNATIONAL PHILOSOPHY SERIES.
Kluwer Academic Publishers, Postbus 17, 3300 AA Dordrecht, Netherlands. TEL 31-78-6392392. FAX 31-78-6392254. *5739*

NIJHOFF LAW SPECIALS.
Kluwer Academic Publishers, Postbus 17, 3300 AA Dordrecht, Netherlands. TEL 31-78-6392392. FAX 31-78-6392254. *4000*

NIMBUS.
Societa Meteorologica Subalpina, V. Gioberti 88, 10128 Turin, Italy. TEL 39-11-591145. FAX 39-11-5683190. *5240*

NINETEENTH-CENTURY CONTEXTS.
Gordon and Breach - Harwood Academic, Amsteldisk 166, 1st Fl., 1079 LH Amsterdam, Netherlands. *4441*

NINETEENTH CENTURY FRENCH STUDIES.
State University of New York, College at Fredonia, Department of Foreign Languages, Fredonia, NY 14063. TEL 716-673-3387. FAX 716-673-1627. *4441*

NINETEENTH-CENTURY LITERATURE (BERKELEY).
University of California Press, Journals Division, 2120 Berkeley Way, No. 5812, Berkeley, CA 94720-5812. TEL 510-643-7154. FAX 510-642-9917. *4442*

19TH-CENTURY MUSIC.
University of California Press, Journals Division, 2120 Berkeley Way, No. 5812, Berkeley, CA 94720-5812. TEL 510-643-7154. FAX 510-642-9917. *5420*

NINETEENTH-CENTURY STUDIES.
Franklin & Marshall College, Department of English, Box 3003, Lancaster, PA 17604-3003. TEL 717-291-3899. FAX 803-953-7084. *4442*

NIPPON GANKA GAKKAI ZASSHI.
Nippon Ganka Gakkai, 2-4-11-402 Sarugaku-cho, Chiyoda-ku, Tokyo 101, Japan. TEL 81-3-3295-2360. FAX 81-3-3293-9384. *4997*

NIPPON MEDICAL SCHOOL. JOURNAL.
Nippon Medical School, Medical Association, 1-1-5 Sendagi, Bunkyo-ku, Tokyo 113, Japan. TEL 81-3-3822-2131. FAX 81-3-3822-3759. *4722*

NIPPON SUISAN GAKKAISHI (JAPANESE EDITION).
Japanese Society of Scientific Fisheries, c/o Tokyo University of Fisheries, 4-5-7, Konan, Minato-ku, Tokyo 108, Japan. TEL 81-3-3471-2165. FAX 81-3-3471-2054. *3074*

NIPPONDENSO TECHNICAL DISCLOSURE. JOURNAL.
Nippondenso Co., Ltd., 1-1, Showa-cho, Kariya-shi, Aichi-ken 448, Japan. FAX 566-25-4554. *2895*

NOISE & VIBRATION BULLETIN.
Multi-Science Publishing Co. Ltd., 107 High St., Brentwood, Essex CM14 4RX, England. TEL 44-1277-224632. FAX 44-1277-223453. *2962*

NOISE & VIBRATION IN INDUSTRY.
Multi-Science Publishing Co. Ltd., 107 High St., Brentwood, Essex CM14 4RX, England. TEL 44-1277-224632. FAX 44-1277-223453. *5873*

NOISE CONTROL ENGINEERING JOURNAL.
Institute of Noise Control Engineering, Department of Mechanical Engineering, Auburn University, Auburn, AL 36849-5341. TEL 205-844-3306. FAX 205-844-3307. *2895*

NOMINA.
Society for Name Studies in Britain and Ireland, c/o Dr. Mary Higham, 22 Peel Park Ave., Clitheroe, Lancashire BB7 1ET, England. TEL 44-1200-423771. *4284*

NOMINA AFRICANA.
Names Society of Southern Africa, c/o Dr. Lucie A. Moeller, Sec.-Treas., Names Research Institute, P.O. Box 26582, Gezina 0031, South Africa. TEL 27-12-3022164. FAX 27-12-3265362. *4284*

NONDESTRUCTIVE TESTING AND EVALUATION.
Gordon and Breach - Harwood Academic, Amsteldisk 166, 1st Fl., 1079 LH Amsterdam, Netherlands. *2868*

NONDESTRUCTIVE TESTING MONOGRAMS AND TRACTS.
Gordon and Breach - Harwood Academic, Amsteldisk 166, 1st Fl., 1079 LH Amsterdam, Netherlands. *2868*

NONGYE HUANJING BAOHU.
Zhongguo Nongye Shengtai Huanjing Baohu Xiehui, 31 Kangfu Lu, Nankai Qu, Tianjin 300191, People's Republic of China. TEL 361247. *2945*

NONGYE JISHU JINGJI.
Zhongguo Nongye Jishu Jingji Yanjiuhui, 30 Baishiqiao Lu, Beijing 100081, People's Republic of China. TEL 86-10-6217-6213. FAX 86-10-6218-7545. *199*

NONGYE JIXIE XUEBAO.
Zhongguo Nongye Jixie Xuehui, 1 Bei Shatan, Dewai, Beijing 100083, People's Republic of China. TEL 86-10-6201-7131. FAX 86-10-6204-3686. *208*

NONLINEAR ANALYSIS.
Elsevier Science Ltd., Pergamon, P.O. Box 800, Kidlington, Oxford OX5 1DX, England. TEL 44-1865-843000. FAX 44-1865-843010. *2734*

NONLINEAR DYNAMICS.
Kluwer Academic Publishers, Postbus 17, 3300 AA Dordrecht, Netherlands. TEL 31-78-6392392. FAX 31-78-6392254. *2895*

NONLINEAR DYNAMICS, PSYCHOLOGY, AND LIFE SCIENCES.
Human Sciences Press, Inc., 233 Spring St., New York, NY 10013-1578. TEL 212-620-8000. FAX 212-463-0742. *6138*

NONPARAMETRIC STATISTICS.
Gordon and Breach - Harwood Academic, Amsteldisk 166, 1st Fl., 1079 LH Amsterdam, Netherlands. *6929*

NONPROFIT AND VOLUNTARY SECTOR QUARTERLY.
Sage Publications, Inc., 2455 Teller Rd., Thousand Oaks, CA 91320. TEL 805-499-0721. FAX 805-499-0871. *6679*

NONPROFIT MANAGEMENT AND LEADERSHIP.
Jossey-Bass Inc., Publishers, 350 Sansome St., 5th Fl., San Francisco, CA 94104. TEL 800-605-2665. *1498*

THE NONPROLIFERATION REVIEW.
Monterey Institute of International Studies, Center for Nonproliferation Studies, 425 Van Buren St., Monterey, CA 93940. TEL 408-647-6575. FAX 408-647-6522. *6029*

NONRENEWABLE RESOURCES.
Plenum Publishing Corp., 233 Spring St., New York, NY 10013-1578. TEL 212-620-8000. FAX 212-463-0742. *5311*

NORDIC HYDROLOGY.
Nordic Association of Hydrology, c/o ISVA, Technical University of Denmark, Bldg. 115, DK-2800 Lyngby, Denmark. TEL 45-45-25-14-50. FAX 45-45-93-28-60. *2396*

NORDIC JOURNAL OF BOTANY.
Nordic Publications in Botany, The Secretary, Gothersgade 130, DK-1123 Copenhagen K, Denmark. *717*

NORDIC JOURNAL OF COMPUTING.
University of Helsinki, Department of Computer Science, P.O. Box 26, FIN-00014 University of Helsinki, Finland. TEL 358-9-70851. FAX 358-9-70844441. *2088*

NORDIC JOURNAL OF INTERNATIONAL LAW.
Kluwer Law International, Postbus 85889, 2508 CN The Hague, Netherlands. TEL 31-70-3081500. FAX 31-70-3081515. *4123*

NORDISK PSYKOLOGI.
Hans Reitzels Forlag, P.O. Box 1072, DK-1008 Copenhagen K, Denmark. TEL 45-33-14-04-51. FAX 45-33-15-51-55. *6138*

NORDISK TIDSKRIFT FOR VETENSKAP, KONST OCH INDUSTRI.
Letterstedtska Foereningen Nordisk Tidskrift, P.O. Box 34037, S-100 26 Stockholm, Sweden. TEL 08-6567570. FAX 08-6567570. *4349*

NOR'EASTER (DULUTH).
Lake Superior Marine Museum Association, Box 177, Duluth, MN 55802. TEL 218-727-2497. FAX 218-720-5270. *3639*

NORMALIZACJA.
Wydawnictwa Normalizacyjne "Alfa", Ul. Elektoralna 2, 00-139 Warsaw, Poland. TEL 48-22-200241. *2734*

NOROESTE DE MEXICO.
Centro I N A H Sonora, Apdo. Postal 1664, 83080 Hermosillo, Sonora, Mexico. TEL 52-62-131234. FAX 52-62-172580. *325*

NOROIS.
97 av. du Recteur Pineau, 86022 Poitiers Cedex, France. TEL 33-5-49454150. FAX 33-5-49453239. *3415*

NOROPSIKIYATRI ARSIVI.
Turk Noropsikiyatri Dernegi, Istanbul Universitesi, Istanbul Tip Fakultesi, 34390 Topkapi - Istanbul, Turkey. FAX 90-212-6312400. *5088*

NORSK POLARINSTITUTT. SKRIFTER.
Norsk Polarinstitutt, Middelthuns gate 29, P.O. Box 5072 Majorstua, N-0301 Oslo, Norway. TEL 47-22-95-95-12. FAX 47-22-95-95-02. *2361*

NORSK VETERINAERTIDSSKRIFT.
Norske Veterinaerforening, General Birchs Gate 16, N-0454 Oslo, Norway. TEL 47-22-59-16-50. FAX 47-22-69-04-50. *7275*

NORSKE TANNLEGEFORENINGS TIDENDE.
Norske Tannlegeforening, P.O. Box 3063 Elisenberg, 0207 Oslo, Norway. TEL 47-22-54-74-00. FAX 47-22-55-11-09. *4865*

NORTE.
Frente de Afirmacion Hispanista A.C., Lago Como 201, 11320 Mexico DF, Mexico. TEL 525-5963328. FAX 525-5962426. *4442*

NORTH AMERICAN ARCHAEOLOGIST.
Baywood Publishing Co., Inc., 26 Austin Ave., Box 337, Amityville, NY 11701. TEL 516-691-1270. FAX 516-691-1770. *375*

NORTH AMERICAN BENTHOLOGICAL SOCIETY. JOURNAL.
North American Benthological Society, c/o Lynda Corkum, Sec., Dept. of Biological Sciences, University of Windsor, Windsor, ON N9B 3PA, Canada. TEL 519-253-4232. FAX 519-971-3609. *846*

NORTH AMERICAN BIRD BANDER.
35 Logan Hill Rd., Candor, NY 13743. *806*

NORTH AMERICAN FAUNA.
U.S. National Biological Service, Information Transfer Center, c/o Managing Editor, 1201 Oak Ridge Dr., Ste. 200, CO 80525-5589. TEL 970-226-9401. FAX 970-226-9455. *846*

NORTH AMERICAN FLORA.
New York Botanical Garden, Scientific Publications Department, Bronx, NY 10458-5126. TEL 718-817-8721. FAX 718-817-8842. *717*

NORTH AMERICAN JOURNAL OF FISHERIES MANAGEMENT.
American Fisheries Society, 5410 Grosvenor Ln., Ste. 110, Bethesda, MD 20814-2199. TEL 301-897-8616. FAX 301-897-8096. *3075*

NORTH AMERICAN MINING.
Mining Media, Inc., 100 W. Grove St., Ste. 240, Reno, NV 89509-4027. TEL 702-827-1115. FAX 702-827-1292. *5312*

NORTH AMERICAN MISSIONS.
Association of North American Missions, 3859 Nottingham Dr., Sarasota, FL 34235. TEL 941-955-8529. FAX 941-951-0805. *6435*

NORTH ATLANTIC REVIEW.
North Eagle Corp. of N.Y., 15 Arbutus Ln., Stony Brook, NY 11790-1408. TEL 516-751-7886. FAX 516-689-8266. *4442*

NORTH CAROLINA ENGLISH TEACHER.
North Carolina English Teachers Association, c/o Chris Gould, Ed., English Department, Univ. of North Carolina at Wilmington, Wilmington, NC 28403. TEL 910-962-3268. FAX 910-962-7166. *4285*

NORTH CAROLINA HISTORICAL REVIEW.
North Carolina Division of Archives and History, Historical Publications Section, 109 E. Jones St., Raleigh, NC 27601-2807. TEL 919-733-7442. FAX 919-733-1439. *3639*

NORTH CAROLINA INSIGHT.
North Carolina Center for Public Policy Research, Inc., Box 430, Raleigh, NC 27602. TEL 919-832-2839. FAX 919-832-2847. *5949*

NORTH CAROLINA NATURALIST.
Friends of the North Carolina State Museum of Natural Sciences, Box 27655, Raleigh, NC 27626. TEL 919-733-7450. FAX 919-733-1573. *5363*

NORTH COAST REVIEW.
Poetry Harbor, Box 103, Duluth, MN 55801-0103. TEL 218-728-3728. *4515*

NORTH COUNTRY NATURALIST.
North County Institute for Natural Philosophy, Inc., RD No. 3, Emery Rd. Box 53, Mexico, NY 13114. TEL 315-963-4854. *6554*

NORTH DAKOTA ACADEMY OF SCIENCE. PROCEEDINGS.
North Dakota Academy of Science, Box 7081, Grand Forks, ND 58202-7081. TEL 701-231-8697. *6555*

NORTH DAKOTA HISTORY.
State Historical Society of North Dakota, North Dakota Heritage Center, Bismarck, ND 58505. TEL 701-328-2799. FAX 701-328-3710. *3640*

NORTH-HOLLAND DELTA SERIES.
Elsevier Science B.V., Books Division, P.O. Box 211, 1000 AE Amsterdam, Netherlands. TEL 31-20-4853911. FAX 31-20-4853705. *5817*

NORTH-HOLLAND LINGUISTIC SERIES.
Elsevier Science B.V., Books Division, P.O. Box 211, 1000 AE Amsterdam, Netherlands. TEL 31-20-4853911. FAX 31-20-4853705. *4285*

NORTH-HOLLAND MATHEMATICAL LIBRARY.
Elsevier Science B.V., Books Division, P.O. Box 211, 1000 AE Amsterdam, Netherlands. TEL 31-20-4853911. FAX 31-20-4853705. *4595*

NORTH-HOLLAND MATHEMATICS STUDIES.
Elsevier Science B.V., Books Division, P.O. Box 211, 1000 AE Amsterdam, Netherlands. TEL 31-20-4853911. FAX 31-20-4853705. *4595*

NORTH-HOLLAND PERSONAL LIBRARY.
Elsevier Science B.V., Books Division, P.O. Box 211, 1000 AE Amsterdam, Netherlands. TEL 31-20-4853911. FAX 31-20-4853705. *5817*

NORTH-HOLLAND SERIES IN APPLIED MATHEMATICS AND MECHANICS.
Elsevier Science B.V., Books Division, P.O. Box 211, 1000 AE Amsterdam, Netherlands. TEL 31-20-4853911. FAX 31-20-4853705. *4595*

NORTH-HOLLAND SERIES IN STATISTICS AND PROBABILITY.
Elsevier Science B.V., Books Division, P.O. Box 211, 1000 AE Amsterdam, Netherlands. TEL 31-20-4853911. FAX 31-20-4853705. *4595*

NORTH-HOLLAND SERIES IN SYSTEM SCIENCE AND ENGINEERING.
Elsevier Science B.V., Books Division, P.O. Box 211, 1000 AE Amsterdam, Netherlands. TEL 31-20-4853911. FAX 31-20-4853705. *2806*

NORTH-HOLLAND STUDIES IN TELECOMMUNICATION.
Elsevier Science B.V., Books Division, P.O. Box 211, 1000 AE Amsterdam, Netherlands. TEL 31-20-4853911. FAX 31-20-4853705. *2000*

NORTH-HOLLAND SYSTEMS AND CONTROL SERIES.
Elsevier Science B.V., Books Division, P.O. Box 211, 1000 AE Amsterdam, Netherlands. TEL 31-20-4853911. FAX 31-20-4853705. *2157*

THE NORTH STONE REVIEW.
D Station, Box 14098, Minneapolis, MN 55414. TEL 612-721-8011. *4442*

NORTH WIND.
George MacDonald Society, The Library, King's College, Strand, London WC2R 2LS, England. TEL 44-1342-823859. *4350*

NORTHEAST ANTHROPOLOGY.
State University of New York at Albany, c/o Department of Anthropology, Social Science Bldg. 263, Albany, NY 12222. TEL 518-442-4721. FAX 518-442-5710. *325*

NORTH EAST LABOUR HISTORY BULLETIN.
North East Labour History Society, University of Northumbria, Dept. of English and History, Lipman Bldg., Newcastle Upon Tyne NE1 8ST, England. TEL 44-191-227-3738. FAX 44-191-227-4572. *1448*

NORTH EAST LINGUISTIC SOCIETY. PROCEEDINGS.
North East Linguistic Society, c/o Graduate Linguistic Student Association, Department of Linguistics, University of Massachusetts, Amherst, MA 01003. TEL 413-545-6838. FAX 413-545-2992. *4285*

NORTH EASTERN DOCTORS CALLING.
Indian Medical Association, I.M.A. House, Indraprastha Marg, New Delhi 110 002, India. *4723*

NORTHEASTERN NEVADA HISTORICAL SOCIETY QUARTERLY.
Northeastern Nevada Historical Society, 1515 Idaho St., Elko, NV 89801. TEL 702-738-3418. FAX 702-778-9318. *3640*

NORTHERN CONTOURS.
Plumas County Arts Commission, Box 618, Quincy, CA 95971. TEL 916-283-3402. *4350*

NORTHERN ECONOMIC REVIEW.
University of Northumbria, Northern Economic Research Unit, 6 N. East St., Newcastle upon Tyne NE1 8ST, England. TEL 44-191-227-4609. FAX 44-191-227-4608. *3754*

NORTHERN ILLINOIS UNIVERSITY. CENTER FOR SOUTHEAST ASIAN STUDIES. OCCASIONAL PAPERS SERIES.
Southeast Asia Publications, Center for Southeast Asian Studies, DeKalb, IL 60115. TEL 815-753-1981. FAX 815-753-1651. *3537*

NORTHERN ILLINOIS UNIVERSITY. CENTER FOR SOUTHEAST ASIAN STUDIES. SPECIAL REPORT SERIES.
Southeast Asia Publications, Northern Illinois University, Center for Southeast Asian Studies, DeKalb, IL 60115. TEL 815-753-1981. FAX 815-753-1651. *3537*

NORTHERN JOURNAL OF APPLIED FORESTRY.
Society of American Foresters, 5400 Grosvenor Ln., Bethesda, MD 20814. TEL 301-897-8720. FAX 301-897-3690. *3159*

NORTHERN MARINER.
Memorial University of Newfoundland, Maritime Research Studies Unit, St. John's, NF A1C 5S7, Canada. TEL 709-737-8424. FAX 709-737-4569. *3506*

NORTHERN MOSAIC.
Thunder Bay Multicultural Association, 17 N. Court St., Thunder Bay, ON P7A 4T4, Canada. TEL 807-345-0551. FAX 807-345-0173. *3033*

NORTHERN NEW ENGLAND REVIEW.
Franklin Pierce College, Box 60, Rindge, NH 03461. TEL 603-899-4089. FAX 603-899-6448. *4442*

NORTHERN REVIEW.
Yukon College, P.O. Box 2799, Whitehorse, YT Y1A 5K4, Canada. TEL 403-668-8773. FAX 403-668-8828. *3787*

NORTHERN SCOTLAND.
University of Aberdeen, Centre for Scottish Studies, Old Brewery, King's College, Old Aberdeen AB9 2UB, Scotland. TEL 01224-272203. FAX 01224-487048. *3588*

NORTHWEST ANTHROPOLOGICAL RESEARCH NOTES.
University of Idaho, Laboratory of Anthropology, Moscow, ID 83844-1111. TEL 208-885-6123. FAX 208-885-2034. *325*

NORTHWEST FOLKLORE.
c/o Scandinavian Dept., 318 Raitt Hall, DL20, University of Washington, Seattle, WA 98195. TEL 206-543-6884. FAX 206-685-9173. *3090*

THE NORTH WEST GEOGRAPHER.
Manchester Geographical Society, Department of Geography, University of Manchester, Manchester M13 9PL, England. TEL 44-161-275-3635. FAX 44-161-273-4407. *3416*

NORTHWEST LITERARY FORUM.
Irvington St. Press, Inc., 3439 N.E. Sandy Blvd., No. 143, Portland, OR 97232. *4350*

NORTHWEST OHIO QUARTERLY.
Maumee Valley Historical Society, University of Toledo, Department of History, Toledo, OH 43606. TEL 419-530-2209. FAX 419-530-4539. *3640*

NORTHWEST SCIENCE.
Washington State University Press, Pullman, WA 99164-5910. TEL 509-335-3518. FAX 509-335-8568. *6555*

NORTHWESTERN NATURALIST.
Allen Press, 1041 New Hampshire Ave., Box 1897, Lawrence, KS 66044. TEL 913-843-0629. FAX 913-843-1274. *846*

NORTHWESTERN UNIVERSITY. ROBERT H. LURIE CANCER CENTER. JOURNAL.
Northwestern University, Robert H. Lurie Cancer Center, Olson Pavilion 8250, 303 E. Chicago Ave., Chicago, IL 60611. TEL 312-908-6346. FAX 312-908-1372. *4983*

NOS OISEAUX.
Societe Romande pour l'Etude et la Protection des Oiseaux, c/o Musee d'histoire naturelle, CH-2300 La Chaux-de-Fonds, Switzerland. TEL 41-22-7359982. FAX 41-22-7359982. *806*

NOTA LEPIDOPTEROLOGICA.
Apollo Books Aps, Kirkeby Sand 19, DK-5771 Stenstrup, Denmark. TEL 45-62-26-37-37. FAX 45-62-26-37-80. *759*

NOTARIUS INTERNATIONAL.
Kluwer Law International, Postbus 85889, 2508 CN The Hague, Netherlands. TEL 31-70-3081500. FAX 31-70-3081515. *4123*

NOTATKI ORNITOLOGICZNE.
Polskie Towarzystwo Zoologiczne, Ul. Sienkiewicza 21, 50-335 Wroclaw, Poland. TEL 48-71-225041. FAX 48-71-222817. *806*

NOTES ON NUMERICAL FLUID MECHANICS.
Friedr. Vieweg und Sohn Verlagsgesellschaft mbH, Postfach 5829, 65048 Wiesbaden, Germany. TEL 49-611-7878357. FAX 49-611-7878420. *2873*

NOTICIARIO DE HISTORIA AGRARIA.
Universidad de Murcia, Facultad de Ciencias Economicas y Empresariales, C. Ronda de Levante, 10, 30008 Murcia, Spain. TEL 34-968-761770. FAX 34-968-363831. *141*

NOTICIARIO ECONOMICO - M B.
Canalejas 30, entlo. 2o, 08028 Barcelona, Spain. TEL 34-3-4226199. FAX 34-3-4211858. *989*

NOTORNIS.
Ornithological Society of New Zealand Inc., P.O. Box 12-397, Wellington, New Zealand. TEL 64-6-3546540. FAX 64-6-3546731. *806*

NOTRE DAME JOURNAL.
Notre Dame University, 9600 Cotabato City, Philippines. TEL 63-64-421-4312. FAX 63-64-421-4312. *2468*

NOTRE DAME TECHNICAL REVIEW.
University of Notre Dame, Engineering Department, 218 Cushing Mall, Notre Dame, IN 46556. TEL 219-283-3524. FAX 219-239-8007. *2734*

NOTTINGHAM FRENCH STUDIES.
Nottingham University Press, Nottingham NG7 2RD, England. TEL 44-115-951-5872. FAX 44-115-951-4998. *4443*

NOUVELLE REVUE D'ONOMASTIQUE.
Societe Francaise d'Onomastique, 87 rue Vielle-du-Temple, 75003 Paris, France. *4285*

NOUVELLES QUESTIONS FEMINISTES.
Nouvelles Questions Feministes - I R E S C O, c/o Christine Delphy, Ed., 59-61 rue Pouchet, 75017 Paris, France. TEL 33-01-40-26-74-98. FAX 33-01-40-26-74-98. *7330*

NOVA ET VETERIS IURIS GENTIUM. SERIES A: MODERN INTERNATIONAL LAW.
Martinus Nijhoff Publishers, Human Rights and International Law Postbus 163, 3300 AD Dordrecht, Netherlands. TEL 31-78-334911. FAX 31-78-334254. *4123*

NOVA SCOTIAN INSTITUTE OF SCIENCE. PROCEEDINGS.
Nova Scotian Institute of Science, Science Services, Killam Library, Dalhousie University, Halifax, NS B3H 4H8, Canada. TEL 902-494-2384. FAX 902-494-2062. *6555*

NOVOE VREMYA.
Novoe Vremya, Pl. Pushkina, Moscow 103782 GSP, Russia. TEL 229-88-72. FAX 095-200-4223. *6030*

NOVON.
Missouri Botanical Garden, Scientific Publications, c/o Amy McPherson, Box 299, St. Louis, MO 63166-0299. TEL 314-577-9534. FAX 314-577-9594. *718*

NOVUM TESTAMENTUM.
E.J. Brill, P.O. Box 9000, 2300 PA Leiden, Netherlands. TEL 31-71-5353500. FAX 31-71-5317532. *6359*

NOVUM TESTAMENTUM. SUPPLEMENTS.
E.J. Brill, P.O. Box 9000, 2300 PA Leiden, Netherlands. TEL 31-71-5353500. FAX 31-71-5317532. *6359*

NUBIA.
Polska Akademia Nauk, Zaklad Archeologii Srodziemnomorskiej, Palac Kultury i Nauki, p. 2105, 00-901 Warsaw, Poland. TEL 48-22-6248593. FAX 48-22-6207651. *376*

NUCLEAR ENERGY.
Thomas Telford Services Ltd., Thomas Telford House, 1 Heron Quay, London E14 4JD, England. TEL 44-171-987-6999. FAX 44-171-538-9620. *2700*

NUCLEAR ENGINEERING AND DESIGN.
Elsevier Science S.A., P.O. Box 546, CH-1001 Lausanne 1, Switzerland. TEL 41-21-3207381. FAX 41-21-3235444. *2868*

NUCLEAR INSTRUMENTS & METHODS IN PHYSICS RESEARCH. SECTION A. ACCELERATORS, SPECTROMETERS, DETECTORS, AND ASSOCIATED EQUIPMENT.
North-Holland, P.O. Box 211, 1000 AE Amsterdam, Netherlands. TEL 31-20-4853911. FAX 31-20-4853598. *5854*

NUCLEAR INSTRUMENTS & METHODS IN PHYSICS RESEARCH. SECTION B. BEAM INTERACTIONS WITH MATERIALS AND ATOMS.
North-Holland, P.O. Box 211, 1000 AE Amsterdam, Netherlands. TEL 31-20-4853911. FAX 31-20-4853598. *5854*

NUCLEAR MEDICINE AND BIOLOGY.
Elsevier Science Inc., Box 945, New York, NY 10159-0945. TEL 212-633-3730. FAX 212-633-3680. *5112*

NUCLEAR MEDICINE ANNUAL.
Lippincott - Raven Publishers, 227 E. Washington Sq., Philadelphia, PA 19106. TEL 215-238-4200. FAX 215-238-4227. *5112*

NUCLEAR MEDICINE COMMUNICATIONS.
Chapman & Hall, Journals Department 2-6 Boundary Row, London SE1 8HN, England. TEL 44-171-8650066. FAX 44-171-522-9623. *5112*

NUCLEAR PHYSICS NEWS.
Gordon and Breach - Harwood Academic, Amsteldisk 166, 1st Fl., 1079 LH Amsterdam, Netherlands. *5854*

NUCLEAR PHYSICS, SECTION A.
North-Holland, P.O. Box 211, 1000 AE Amsterdam, Netherlands. TEL 31-20-4853911. FAX 31-20-4853598. *5854*

NUCLEAR PHYSICS, SECTION B.
North-Holland, P.O. Box 211, 1000 AE Amsterdam, Netherlands. TEL 31-20-4853911. FAX 31-20-4853598. *5854*

NUCLEAR PHYSICS, SECTION B, PROCEEDINGS SUPPLEMENTS.
North-Holland, P.O. Box 211, 1000 AE Amsterdam, Netherlands. TEL 31-20-4853911. FAX 31-20-4853598. *5855*

NUCLEAR SCIENCE AND ENGINEERING.
American Nuclear Society, 555 N. Kensington Ave., La Grange Park, IL 60525. TEL 708-352-6611. *2702*

NUCLEAR SCIENCE AND TECHNIQUES.
Science Press, Marketing and Sales Department, 16 Donghuangchenggen North St., Beijing 100717, People's Republic of China. TEL 86-10-6401-0642. FAX 86-10-6401-9810. *5855*

NUCLEAR SCIENCE APPLICATIONS - SECTION B: IN DEPTH REVIEWS.
Gordon and Breach - Harwood Academic, Amsteldisk 166, 1st Fl., 1079 LH Amsterdam, Netherlands. *5855*

NUCLEAR SCIENCE RESEARCH CONFERENCE SERIES.
Gordon and Breach - Harwood Academic, Amsteldisk 166, 1st Fl., 1079 LH Amsterdam, Netherlands. *5855*

NUCLEOTECNICA.
Comision Chilena de Energia Nuclear, Amunategui 95, Casilla 188-D, Santiago, Chile. TEL 56-2-6990070. FAX 56-2-6994548. *2702*

NUCLEUS.
University of Calcutta, Department of Botany, 35 Ballygunj Circular Rd., Calcutta 19, West Bengal, India. TEL 91-33-440-5802. FAX 91-33-478-7603. *743*

NUEVO TEXTO CRITICO.
Stanford University, Department of Spanish and Portuguese, Stanford, CA 94305-2014. TEL 415-725-0112. FAX 415-723-0482. *4443*

NUKLEONIKA.
Polska Akademia Nauk, Instytut Chemii i Techniki Jadrowej, Ul. Dorodna 16, 03-195 Warsaw, Poland. TEL 48-22-110656. FAX 48-22-111532. *2702*

NUMBER ONE.
Volunteer State Community College, Humanities Division, 1480 Nashville Pike, Gallatin, TN 37066. TEL 615-452-8600. *4516*

NUMEN.
E.J. Brill, P.O. Box 9000, 2300 PA Leiden, Netherlands. TEL 31-71-5353500. FAX 31-71-5317532. *6359*

NUMEN SUPPLEMENTS.
E.J. Brill, P.O. Box 9000, 2300 PA Leiden, Netherlands. TEL 31-71-5353500. FAX 31-71-5317532. *6359*

NUMERICAL FUNCTIONAL ANALYSIS AND OPTIMIZATION.
Marcel Dekker Journals, 270 Madison Ave., New York, NY 10016. TEL 212-696-9000. FAX 212-685-4540. *4596*

NUMERICAL HEAT TRANSFER PART A: APPLICATIONS.
Taylor & Francis Inc., 1900 Frost Rd., Ste. 101, Bristol, PA 19007-1598. TEL 215-785-5800. FAX 215-785-5515. *2896*

NUMERICAL HEAT TRANSFER PART B: FUNDAMENTALS.
Taylor & Francis Inc., 1900 Frost Rd., Ste. 101, Bristol, PA 19007-1598. TEL 215-785-5800. FAX 215-785-5515. *2896*

NUMERICAL LINEAR ALGEBRA.
John Wiley & Sons Ltd., Journals, Baffins Ln., Chichester, W. Sussex PO19 1UD, England. TEL 44-1243-779777. FAX 44-1243-775878. *4596*

NUMERICAL METHODS FOR PARTIAL DIFFERENTIAL EQUATIONS: AN INTERNATIONAL JOURNAL.
John Wiley & Sons, Inc., Journals, 605 Third Ave., New York, NY 10158. TEL 212-850-6645. FAX 212-850-6021. *4596*

NUMISMATICA E ANTICHITA CLASSICHE.
Amici dei Quaderni Ticinesi di Numismatica e Antichita Classiche, Secretariat, C.P. 3157, CH-6901 Lugano, Switzerland. TEL 41-91-6061606. *5466*

NUOVE LETTERE.
Istituto Italiano di Cultura di Napoli, Via Bernardo Cavallino 89, 80131 Naples, Italy. TEL 39-81-5461662. FAX 39-81-5461662. *4443*

NUOVO DIRITTO.
Via Antonio Labriola, 64, 00136 Rome, Italy. TEL 39-6-39736327. FAX 39-6-85351547. *4001*

THE NURSE PRACTITIONER.
Springhouse Corporation, 1111 Bethlehem Pike, Box 908, Springhouse, PA 19477. TEL 215-646-8700. *4942*

NURSE PRACTITIONERS' PRESCRIBING REFERENCE.
Prescribing Reference, Inc., 53 Park Pl., Ste. 1010, New York, NY 10007. TEL 212-766-7200. FAX 212-732-2360. *5681*

NURSE RESEARCHER.
R C N Publishing Co., Viking House, 17-19 Peterborough Rd., Harrow, Middlesex HA1 2AX, England. TEL 44-181-423-1066. FAX 44-181-423-3867. *4942*

THE NURSE, THE PATIENT AND THE LAW.
Cox Publications, Box 20316, Billings, MT 59104-0316. TEL 406-256-2248. FAX 406-256-7550. *4942*

NURSE TO NURSE.
Registered Nurses Association of Nova Scotia, 120 Eileen Stubbs Ave., Ste. 104, Dartmouth, NS B3B 1Y1, Canada. TEL 902-468-9744. FAX 902-468-9510. *4942*

NURSING AND HEALTH SCIENCE EDUCATION.
James Nicholas Publishers, P.O. Box 244, Albert Park, Vic. 3206, Australia. TEL 61-3-6965545. FAX 61-3-6992040. *4943*

NURSING CONNECTIONS.
Washington Hospital Center, Division of Nursing, 110 Irving St., N.W., Washington, DC 20010. TEL 202-877-3048. FAX 202-877-8082. *4943*

NURSING DIAGNOSIS.
Nursecom, Inc., 1211 Locust St., Philadelphia, PA 19107. TEL 215-545-7222. FAX 215-545-8107. *4943*

NURSING ECONOMICS.
Jannetti Publications, Inc., East Holly Ave., Box 56, Pitman, NJ 08071-0056. TEL 609-256-2300. FAX 609-589-7463. *4943*

NURSING ETHICS.
Arnold, 338 Euston Rd., London NW1 3BH, England. TEL 44-171-873-6000. FAX 44-171-873-6325. *4943*

NURSING FORUM.
Nursecom Inc., 1211 Locust St., Philadelphia, PA 19107. TEL 215-545-7222. FAX 215-545-8107. *4943*

NURSING INQUIRY.
Blackwell Science Pty Ltd, P.O. Box 378, Carlton South, Vic. 3053, Australia. TEL 61-3-93470300. FAX 61-3-93493016. *4944*

NURSING JOURNAL OF INDIA.
Trained Nurses Association of India, L-17 Green Park, New Delhi 110016, India. TEL 91-11-666665. FAX 91-11-6858304. *4944*

NURSING LEADERSHIP FORUM.
Springer Publishing Company, 536 Broadway, New York, NY 10012-3955. TEL 212-431-4370. FAX 212-941-7842. *4944*

NURSING MANAGEMENT.
Springhouse Corporation, 1111 Bethlehem Pike, Box 908, Springhouse, PA 19477. TEL 215-646-8700. *4944*

NURSING MANAGEMENT.
R C N Publishing Co., Viking House, 17-19 Peterborough Rd., Harrow-on-the-Hill, Middlesex HA1 2AX, England. TEL 44-181-423-1066. FAX 44-181-423-3867. *4944*

NURSING NEWS.
Democratic Nursing Organisation of South Africa, P.O. Box 1280, Pretoria 0001, South Africa. TEL 27-12-3432315. FAX 27-12-3440750. *4944*

NURSING NEWS (CONCORD).
New Hampshire Nurses' Association, 48 West St., Concord, NH 03301. TEL 603-225-3783. FAX 603-228-6672. *4944*

NURSING SCIENCE QUARTERLY.
Chestnut House Publications, Box 22492, Pittsburgh, PA 15222. TEL 412-391-8585. FAX 412-391-8458. *4945*

NUTRICIA SYMPOSIA.
Kluwer Academic Publishers, Postbus 17, 3300 AA Dordrecht, Netherlands. TEL 31-78-6392392. FAX 31-78-6392254. *5478*

NUTRIENT CYCLING IN AGROECOSYSTEMS.
Kluwer Academic Publishers, Postbus 17, 3300 AA Dordrecht, Netherlands. TEL 31-78-6392392. FAX 31-78-6392254. *236*

NUTRITION.
Elsevier Science Inc., Box 945, New York, NY 10159-0945. TEL 212-633-3730. FAX 212-633-3680. *5479*

NUTRITION AND CANCER.
Lawrence Erlbaum Associates, Inc., 10 Industrial Dr., Mahwah, NJ 07430-2262. TEL 201-236-9500. FAX 201-236-0072. *4984*

NUTRITION AND THE BRAIN.
Lippincott - Raven Publishers, 227 E. Washington Sq., Philadelphia, PA 19106. TEL 215-238-4200. FAX 215-238-4227. *5479*

NUTRITION IN CLINICAL PRACTICE.
American Society for Parenteral and Enteral Nutrition, 8630 Fenton St., Ste. 412, Silver Spring, MD 20910. TEL 301-587-6315. FAX 301-587-3323. *5479*

NUTRITION RESEARCH.
Elsevier Science Inc., Box 945, New York, NY 10159-0945. TEL 212-633-3730. FAX 212-633-3680. *5480*

NUTTALL ORNITHOLOGICAL CLUB. PUBLICATIONS.
Nuttall Ornithological Club, c/o Museum of Comparative Zoology, Harvard University, Cambridge, MA 02138. TEL 617-495-2471. *807*

NY KULTUR.
Stiftelsen Ny Kultur, Sjoemannsgatan 15 B, S-413 15 Goeteborg, Sweden. TEL 46-31-14-83-71. FAX 46-31-14-83-71. *5459*

O C L.
John Libbey Eurotext, 127 av. de la République, 92120 Montrouge, France. TEL 33-1-46730660. FAX 33-1-40840999. *1819*

O D T U GELISME DERGISI.
Orta Dogu Teknik Universitesi, Iktisadi ve Idari Bilimler Fakultesi, Department of Economics, Balgat 06531 Ankara, Turkey. TEL 90-312-2102006. FAX 90-312-2101244. *1309*

O E C T A REPORTER.
Ontario English Catholic Teachers Association, 65 St. Clair Ave. E., Toronto, ON M4T 2Y8, Canada. TEL 416-925-2493. FAX 416-925-7764. *2468*

THE O E M REPORT.
O E M Health Information Inc., 8 West St., Beverly Farms, MA 01915. TEL 508-921-7300. FAX 508-921-0304. *5495*

O I E REVUE SCIENTIFIQUE ET TECHNIQUE.
Office International des Epizooties, 12 rue de Prony, 75017 Paris, France. TEL 33-1-44151888. FAX 33-1-42670987. *7275*

O N A NEWS.
Ontario Nurses' Association, 85 Grenville St., Ste. 600, Toronto, ON M5S 3A2, Canada. TEL 416-964-8833. FAX 416-964-8864. *4945*

O N S NURSING SCAN IN ONCOLOGY.
Nursecom, Inc., 1211 Locust St., Philadelphia, PA 19107. TEL 215-545-7222. FAX 215-545-8107. *4784*

O O H N A JOURNAL.
Ontario Occupational Health Nurses Association, Ste. 605, 302 The East Mall, Etobicoke, ON M9B 6C7, Canada. TEL 416-239-6462. FAX 416-239-5462. *4945*

O P A L.
Ontario Puppetry Association, c/o 62-6770 Glen Erin, Mississauga ON L5N 2L1, Canada. TEL 416-861-0202. *7010*

O P E C REVIEW.
Blackwell Publishers Ltd., 108 Cowley Rd., Oxford OX4 1JF, England. TEL 44-1865-791100. FAX 44-1865-791347. *5613*

O R L.
S. Karger AG, Allschwilerstr. 10, P.O. Box, CH-4009 Basel, Switzerland. TEL 41-61-3061111. FAX 41-61-3061234. *5023*

O R L - HEAD AND NECK NURSING.
Health Information Publications, Inc., 1719 Rte. 10, Ste. 220, Parsippany, NJ 07054. TEL 201-267-8938. FAX 201-664-3771. *5024*

O R TESOL JOURNAL.
Portland State University, Applied Linguistics Department, Portland, OR 97207. TEL 503-725-4088. FAX 503-725-4882. *4286*

THE O S L A CONNECTION.
Ontario Association of Speech - Language Pathologists and Audiologists, 410 Jarvis St., Toronto, ON M4Y 2G6, Canada. TEL 416-920-3676. FAX 416-920-6214. *2588*

O S M T ADVOCATE.
Ontario Society of Medical Technologists, 234 Eglinton Ave. E., Ste. 402, Toronto, ON M4P 1K5, Canada. *4901*

O S - 2 COMPUTING! MAGAZINE. *2145*

OBESITY RESEARCH.
North American Association for the Study of Obesity, c/o Pennington Biomedical Research Center, 6400 Perkins Rd., Baton Rouge, LA 70808. TEL 504-763-0934. *4723*

OBJECT.
Centre for Contemporary Craft, Level 4, 88 George St., The Rocks, Sydney, N.S.W. 2000, Australia. TEL 61-2-92479126. FAX 61-2-92472641. *482*

OBJECT-ORIENTED SYSTEMS.
Chapman & Hall, Journals Department 2-6 Boundary Row, London SE1 8HN, England. TEL 44-171-8650066. FAX 44-171-5229623. *2145*

OBSERVATOIRE DE STRASBOURG. CENTRE DE DONNEES ASTRONOMIQUES DE STRASBOURG. INFORMATION BULLETIN.
Observatoire de Strasbourg, 11 rue de l'Universite, 67000 Strasbourg, France. TEL 33-3-88150720. FAX 33-3-88150760. *498*

OBSERVATORY.
c/o Dr. D.J. Stickland, Ed., Space and Astrophysics Div., Rutherford Appleton Laboratory, Chilton, Didcot, Oxon OX11 0QX, England. FAX 44-1235-445848. *499*

OBSERVER (NOTRE DAME).
University of Notre Dame - Saint Mary's College, 314 LaFortune Student Center, Box Q, Notre Dame, IN 46556. TEL 219-631-7471. FAX 219-631-6927. *1964*

OBSIDIAN II: BLACK LITERATURE IN REVIEW.
North Carolina State University, English Department, Box 8105, Raleigh, NC 27695-8105. TEL 919-515-6053. FAX 919-515-6071. *4444*

OBSTETRIC ANESTHESIA DIGEST.
Lippincott - Raven Publishers, 227 E. Washington Sq., Philadelphia, PA 19106. TEL 215-238-4200. FAX 215-238-4227. *4807*

OBSTETRICS AND GYNECOLOGY.
Elsevier Science Inc., Box 945, New York, NY 10159-0945. TEL 212-633-3730. FAX 212-633-3680. *4965*

OBSTETRICS AND GYNECOLOGY CLINICS OF NORTH AMERICA.
W.B. Saunders Co., Curtis Center, 3rd Fl., Independence Sq. W., Philadelphia, PA 19106-3399. TEL 215-238-7800. FAX 215-238-6445. *4965*

OCCASIONAL PAPERS IN ANTHROPOLOGY.
Pennsylvania State University, Department of Anthropology, 409 Carpenter Bldg., University Park, PA 16802. TEL 814-865-2509. FAX 814-863-1474. *326*

OCCASIONAL PAPERS IN EDUCATION AND INTERDISCIPLINARY STUDIES.
University of Southampton, School of Education, Southampton SO9 5NH, England. TEL 44-1703-592414. FAX 44-1703-593939. *2551*

OCCASIONAL PAPERS IN ENTOMOLOGY.
Department of Food and Agriculture, Division of Plant Industry, 1220 N St., Sacramento, CA 95814. TEL 916-445-5421. *759*

OCCASIONAL PAPERS ON ISLANDS AND SMALL STATES.
Foundation for International Studies, Islands and Small States Institute, St. Paul's St., Valletta VLT 07, Malta. TEL 356-230551. FAX 356-230551. *6030*

OCCUPATIONAL AND ENVIRONMENTAL MEDICINE.
B M J Publishing Group, B.M.A. House, Tavistock Sq., London WC1H 9JR, England. TEL 44-171-383-6270. FAX 44-171-383-6402. *5495*

OCCUPATIONAL ERGONOMICS.
Chapman & Hall, Journals Department 2-6 Boundary Row, London SE1 8HN, England. TEL 44-171-8650066. FAX 44-171-5229623. *5495*

OCCUPATIONAL HEALTH.
Reed Business Information, Quadrant House., Quadrant, Sutton, Surrey SM2 5AS, England. *4945*

OCCUPATIONAL HEALTH & SAFETY.
Stevens Publishing Corporation, 3700 J.H. Kultgen Frwy., Waco, TX 76706. TEL 817-776-9000. FAX 817-776-9018. *5496*

OCCUPATIONAL MEDICINE.
Rapid Science Publishers, 2-6 Boundary Row, London SE1 8HN, England. TEL 44-171-865-0198. FAX 44-171-410-6600. *5496*

OCCUPATIONAL MEDICINE (PHILADELPHIA).
Hanley & Belfus, Inc., 210 S. 13th St., Philadelphia, PA 19107. TEL 215-546-7293. FAX 215-790-9330. *5496*

OCCUPATIONAL PROGRAMS IN CALIFORNIA PUBLIC COMMUNITY COLLEGES.
Leo A. Meyer Associates, Inc., 23850 Clawiter Rd., Ste. 1, Hayward, CA 94545. TEL 510-785-1091. FAX 510-785-1099. *2525*

OCCUPATIONAL SAFETY AND HEALTH SERIES (NEW YORK).
Marcel Dekker, Inc., 270 Madison Ave., New York, NY 10016. TEL 212-696-9000. FAX 212-658-4540. *6246*

OCCUPATIONAL THERAPY IN HEALTH CARE.
Haworth Press, Inc., 10 Alice St., Binghamton, NY 13904. TEL 607-722-5857. FAX 607-722-6362. *4723*

OCCUPATIONAL THERAPY IN MENTAL HEALTH.
Haworth Press, Inc., 10 Alice St., Binghamton, NY 13904. TEL 607-722-5857. FAX 607-722-6362. *5088*

OCCUPATIONAL THERAPY INTERNATIONAL.
Whurr Publishers Ltd., 19b Compton Terrace, London N1 2UN, England. TEL 44-171-359-5979. FAX 44-171-226-5290. *5497*

OCCUPATIONAL THERAPY JOURNAL OF RESEARCH.
Slack, Inc., 6900 Grove Rd., Thorofare, NJ 08086-9447. TEL 609-848-1000. FAX 609-853-5991. *4724*

OCEAN & COASTAL MANAGEMENT.
Elsevier Science Ltd., P.O. Box 800, Kidlington, Oxford OX5 1DX, England. TEL 44-1865-843000. FAX 44-1865-843010. *2411*

OCEAN DEVELOPMENT AND INTERNATIONAL LAW.
Taylor & Francis Inc., 1900 Frost Rd., Ste. 101, Bristol, PA 19007-1598. TEL 215-785-5800. FAX 215-785-5515. *2411*

OCEAN DRILLING PROGRAM. SCIENTIFIC RESULTS. PROCEEDINGS. SCIENTIFIC RESULTS.
Texas A&M University, Ocean Drilling Program, 1000 Discovery Dr., College Station, TX 77845-9547. TEL 409-845-2016. FAX 409-845-4857. *2411*

OCEAN ENGINEERING.
Elsevier Science Ltd., Pergamon, P.O. Box 800, Kidlington, Oxford OX5 1DX, England. TEL 44-1865-843000. FAX 44-1865-843010. *2412*

OCEAN YEARBOOK.
University of Chicago Press, Journals Division, 5720 S. Woodlawn Ave., Chicago, IL 60637. TEL 773-702-7600. FAX 773-702-0172. *2412*

OCEANIC LINGUISTICS.
University of Hawaii Press, Journals Department, 2840 Kolowalu St., Honolulu, HI 96822. TEL 808-956-8833. FAX 808-988-6052. *4286*

OCEANOGRAPHIC LITERATURE REVIEW.
Elsevier Science Ltd., Pergamon, P.O. Box 800, Kidlington, Oxford OX5 1DX, England. TEL 44-1865-843000. FAX 44-1865-843010. *2326*

OCEANOGRAPHIC RESEARCH INSTITUTE. INVESTIGATIONAL REPORT.
Oceanographic Research Institute, P.O. Box 10712, Marine Parade, Durban 4056, South Africa. TEL 27-31-373536. FAX 27-31-372132. *846*

OCEANOGRAPHIC SCIENCES LIBRARY.
Kluwer Academic Publishers, Postbus 17, 3300 AA Dordrecht, Netherlands. TEL 31-78-6392392. FAX 31-78-6392254. *2412*

OCEANOGRAPHY.
Oceanography Society, 4052 Timber Ridge Dr., Virginia Beach, VA 23455. TEL 804-464-0131. FAX 804-683-5550. *2412*

OCEANS. CONFERENCE RECORD.
Institute of Electrical and Electronics Engineers, Inc., 345 E. 47th St., New York, NY 10017-2394. TEL 732-981-0060. FAX 732-981-9667. *2735*

OCULAR IMMUNOLOGY AND INFLAMMATION.
Aeolus Press, Postbus 740, 4116 ZJ Buren, Netherlands. TEL 31-344-572055. FAX 31-344-572562. *4997*

OCULAR INFECTIOUS DISEASES.
Field & Wood, Medical Periodicals, Inc., Box 975, Blue Bell, PA 19422. TEL 610-828-4010. FAX 215-482-0226. *4997*

ODONTOLOGO.
Asociacion Odontologica Panamena, Apdo. 6777, Zona 5, Panama, Panama. TEL 507-269-1603. FAX 507-269-3749. *4866*

OEKOLOGIE UND LANDBAU.
Stiftung Oekologie und Landbau, Postfach 1516, 67089 Bad Duerkheim, Germany. TEL 49-6322-66002. FAX 49-6322-989701. *142*

OEKOLOGIEPOLITIK.
Oekologisch - Demokratische Partei, Bundesgeschaeftsstelle, Marienstr. 41, 40210 Duesseldorf, Germany. TEL 49-211-134375. FAX 49-211-134376. *2240*

OESTERREICHISCHE GEOGRAPHISCHE GESELLSCHAFT. MITTEILUNGEN.
Oesterreichische Geographische Gesellschaft, Karl-Schweighofer-Gasse 3, A-1070 Vienna, Austria. TEL 43-1-5237974. FAX 43-1-5237974. *3416*

OESTERREICHISCHE GEOLOGISCHE GESELLSCHAFT. MITTEILUNGEN.
Oesterreichische Geologische Gesellschaft, c/o Geological Survey of Austria, Rasumofskygasse 23, Postfach 127, A-1031 Vienna, Austria. TEL 01-712567443. FAX 01-712567456. *2362*

OFF OUR BACKS.
Off Our Backs, Inc., 2337B 18th St., N.W., Washington, DC 20009-2003. TEL 202-234-8072. *7346*

OFFENE SYSTEME.
Springer-Verlag, Heidelberger Platz 3, 14197 Berlin, Germany. TEL 49-30-82787-0. FAX 49-30-82787448. *2216*

OFFICE SYSTEMS RESEARCH JOURNAL.
Office Systems Research Association, University of Nebraska, 529A Nebraska Hall, Lincoln, NE 68588-0515. TEL 402-472-3647. FAX 402-472-5907. *2088*

OFFICERS CALL.
National Officers Association, Box 4975, Reston, VA 20195-1464. TEL 703-438-3060. FAX 703-438-3072. *5280*

OFFSHORE.
Global Group Ltd., P.O. Box CB13039, Nassau, Bahamas. *1159*

OFFSHORE INVESTMENT.
European Magazine Services Ltd., 62 Brompton Rd., Knightsbridge, London SW3 1BW, England. TEL 44-171-225-0550. FAX 44-171-584-1093. *1159*

OH CALCUTTA.
Aditi Nath Roy, Ed. & Pub., CB-168, Sector 1, Salt Lake, Calcutta 700 064, India. TEL 91-33-374502. *3316*

OHIO AGRICULTURAL RESEARCH AND DEVELOPMENT CENTER, WOOSTER. RESEARCH BULLETIN.
Ohio State University, Ohio Agricultural Research and Development Center, Wooster, 1680 Madison Ave., Wooster, OH 44691-4096. TEL 330-263-3777. *142*

OHIO AGRICULTURAL RESEARCH AND DEVELOPMENT CENTER, WOOSTER. RESEARCH CIRCULAR.
Ohio State University, Ohio Agricultural Research and Development Center, Wooster, 1680 Madison Ave., Wooster, OH 44691-4096. TEL 330-263-3777. *142*

OHIO BIOLOGICAL SURVEY. BULLETIN. NEW SERIES.
Ohio Biological Survey, 1315 Kinnear Rd., Columbus, OH 43212. TEL 614-292-9645. FAX 614-688-4322. *618*

OHIO BIOLOGICAL SURVEY. MISCELLANEOUS CONTRIBUTIONS.
Ohio Biological Survey, 1315 Kinnear Rd., Columbus, OH 43212. TEL 614-292-9645. FAX 614-688-4322. *618*

THE OHIO JOURNAL OF SCIENCE.
Ohio Academy of Science, 1500 W. Third Ave., Ste. 223, Columbus, OH 43212. TEL 614-488-2228. *6556*

OHIO LAWYER.
Ohio State Bar Association, Box 16562, Columbus, OH 43216-6562. TEL 614-487-2050. FAX 614-487-1008. *4003*

OHIO NURSES REVIEW.
Ohio Nurses Association, 4000 E. Main St., Columbus, OH 43213-2983. TEL 614-237-5414. FAX 614-237-6074. *4945*

OHIO READING TEACHER.
International Reading Association, Inc., Ohio Council, 401 McGuffey Hall, Miami University, Oxford, OH 45056. TEL 513-529-6451. *2469*

OHIO STATE UNIVERSITY. BYRD POLAR RESEARCH CENTER. CONTRIBUTION SERIES.
Ohio State University, Byrd Polar Research Center, 1090 Carmack Rd., Columbus, OH 43210-1002. TEL 614-292-6715. *6556*

OHIO STATE UNIVERSITY. COLLEGE OF MEDICINE. JOURNAL.
Ohio State University, College of Medicine, 370 W. 9th Ave., Columbus, OH 43210-1238. TEL 614-292-5671. FAX 614-292-1544. *4724*

OHIO UNIVERSITY PRESS. EASTERN AFRICA SERIES.
Ohio University Press, Scott Quadrangle, Athens, OH 45701. TEL 614-593-1159. *3528*

OHIO UNIVERSITY PRESS. SERIES IN CONTINENTAL THOUGHT.
Ohio University Press, Scott Quadrangle, Athens, OH 45701. TEL 614-593-1159. *5740*

OIKOS.
Munksgaard International Publishers Ltd., 35 Noerre Soegade, P.O. Box 2148, DK-1016 Copenhagen K, Denmark. TEL 45-33-127030. FAX 45-33-129387. *2946*

OIL AND ENERGY TRENDS.
Blackwell Publishers Ltd., 108 Cowley Rd., Oxford OX4 1JF, England. TEL 44-1865-791110. FAX 44-1865-791347. *2675*

OIL AND ENERGY TRENDS: ANNUAL STATISTICAL REVIEW.
Blackwell Publishers Ltd., 108 Cowley Rd., Oxford OX4 1JF, England. TEL 44-1865-791100. FAX 44-1865-791347. *2685*

OIL SHALE.
Estonian Academy of Sciences, Institute of Chemistry, Akadeemia 15, 0026 Tallinn, Estonia. TEL 3722-537084. FAX 3722-536371. *5312*

OILFIELD REVIEW.
Oilfield Review Services, Long Barn, New Russia Hall, Chester Rd., Tattenhall CH3 9AH, England. *5616*

OKAJIMA'S FOLIA ANATOMICA JAPONICA.
Okajima Foria Anatomica Yaponika Henshubu, c/o Keio University, School of Medicine, Dept. of Anatomy, 35, Shinano-machi, Shinjuku-ku, Tokyo 160, Japan. TEL 81-3-3353-1211. FAX 81-3-5379-1977. *618*

OKINAWA SEIBUTSU GAKKAISHI.
Okinawa Seibutsu Gakkai, Ryukyu Daigaku Rigakubu, 1, Senbaru, Nishiharacho, Nakagami-gun, Okinawa-ken 903-01, Japan. FAX 81-98-895-5376. *618*

OKINAWA TOSHO KENKYU.
Ryukyu Daigaku, Rigakubu Seibutsugakka, 1, Senbaru, Nishiharacho, Nakagami-gun, Okinawa-ken 903-01, Japan. TEL 81-98-895-8541. FAX 81-98-895-5376. *2320*

OKLAHOMA ACADEMY OF SCIENCE. PROCEEDINGS.
Oklahoma Academy of Science, c/o Edward N. Nelson, Exec. Sec.-Treas., Box 701915, Tulsa, OK 74170-1915. TEL 914-495-6944. FAX 918-495-6033. *6556*

OKLAHOMA BAR JOURNAL.
Oklahoma Bar Association, c/o Carol A. Manning, Dir. of Public Information, Box 53036, Oklahoma City, OK 73152. TEL 405-524-2365. FAX 405-524-1115. *4003*

OKLAHOMA DENTAL ASSOCIATION JOURNAL.
Oklahoma Dental Association, c/o Suzie J. Weir, 629 W. I-44 Service Rd., Oklahoma City, OK 73118-6098. TEL 405-848-8873. FAX 405-848-8875. *4866*

OKLAHOMA GEOLOGICAL SURVEY. CIRCULAR.
Oklahoma Geological Survey, 100 E. Boyd, Rm. N-131, Norman, OK 73019. TEL 405-325-3031. FAX 405-325-7069. *2362*

OKLAHOMA GEOLOGICAL SURVEY. SPECIAL PUBLICATION SERIES.
Oklahoma Geological Survey, 100 E. Boyd, Rm. N-131, Norman, OK 73019. TEL 405-325-3031. FAX 405-325-7069. *2363*

OKLAHOMA GEOLOGY NOTES.
Oklahoma Geological Survey, 100 E. Boyd, Rm N-131, Norman, OK 73019. TEL 405-325-3031. FAX 405-325-7069. *2363*

OLD CROW REVIEW.
F K B Press, Box 403, Easthampton, MA 01027-0403. *4516*

OLD RED KIMONO.
Floyd College, Humanities Division, Box 1864, Rome, GA 30162. TEL 706-295-6312. FAX 706-295-6610. *4445*

OLD TESTAMENT ESSAYS.
Old Testament Society of South Africa, Department of Ancient Languages, University of Pretoria, 0002 Pretoria, South Africa. TEL 27-12-4202685. *6360*

OLD YORK ROAD HISTORICAL SOCIETY BULLETIN.
Old York Road Historical Society, c/o Jenkintown Library, York and Vista Rds., Jenkintown, PA 19046. TEL 215-884-0593. *3641*

OLIFANT.
University of Virginia, Department of French, Charlottesville, VA 22903. TEL 804-924-4627. *4516*

OLTRE ...
Edizioni Il Borghetto, Borgo Buio 11, 53045 Montepulciano (SI), Italy. TEL 39-578-757535. *4534*

OLYMPIKA.
International Centre for Olympic Studies, Thames Hall, University of Western Ontario, London, ON N6A 3K7, Canada. TEL 519-661-4113. FAX 519-661-4148. *6774*

OMEGA.
Elsevier Science Ltd., Pergamon, P.O. Box 800, Kidlington, Oxford OX5 1DX, England. TEL 44-1865-843000. FAX 44-1865-843010. *1499*

OMEGA: JOURNAL OF DEATH AND DYING.
Baywood Publishing Co., Inc., 26 Austin Ave., Box 337, Amityville, NY 11701. TEL 516-691-1270. FAX 516-691-1770. *6138*

9900 REFEREED SERIALS

OMETECA.
Ometeca Institute, Box 38, New Brunswick, NJ 08903-0038. TEL 908-435-0152. FAX 908-932-6916. *3787*

OMNI.
Omni International, Ltd., 277 Park Ave., 4th Fl., New York, NY 10172. TEL 212-702-6000. FAX 212-702-6282. *6556*

ON-CALL.
University of Queensland, Centre for Language Teaching and Research, Brisbane, Qld. 4072, Australia. TEL 61-7-3656897. FAX 61-7-3657077. *4321*

ON SPEC.
Copper Pig Collective, Box 4727, Edmonton, AB T6E 5G6, Canada. TEL 403-413-2015. FAX 403-413-0215. *4534*

ON - STAGE STUDIES.
University of Colorado, Department of Theatre & Dance, Box 261, Boulder, CO 80309-0261. TEL 303-492-7355. FAX 303-492-7722. *7010*

ON THE LEVEL.
Family Planning N.S.W., 328-336 Liverpool Rd., Ashfield, N.S.W. 2131, Australia. TEL 61-2-716-6099. *6721*

ON THE MOVE.
Citigate Publishing, 52 St. John St., London EC2M 4DT, England. TEL 44-171-490-8079. FAX 44-171-490-8088. *7036*

ONCOLOGIA.
Sociedad de Lucha contra el Cancer, Av. Pedro J. Menendez Gilbert, P.O. Box 5255 o 3626, Guayaquil, Ecuador. TEL 593-4-281744. FAX 593-4-287151. *4984*

THE ONCOLOGIST.
AlphaMed Press, Inc., One Prestige Pl., Ste. 290, Miamisburg, OH 45342-3758. TEL 937-291-2355. FAX 937-291-4229. *4984*

ONCOLOGY.
S. Karger AG, Allschwilerstr. 10, P.O. Box, CH-4009 Basel, Switzerland. TEL 41-61-3061111. FAX 41-61-3061234. *4984*

ONCOLOGY NURSING FORUM.
Oncology Nursing Press, Inc., 501 Holiday Dr., Pittsburgh, PA 15220-2749. TEL 412-921-7373. FAX 412-921-2131. *4945*

ONCOLOGY REPORTS.
Demetrios A. Spandidos, Ed. & Pub., Editorial Office, 1, S. Merkouri St., Athens 116 35, Greece. TEL 30-1-722-6469. FAX 30-1-752-3866. *4984*

ONCOLOGY RESEARCH.
Cognizant Communication Corporation, 3 Hartsdale Rd., Elmsford, NY 10523-3701. TEL 914-592-7720. FAX 914-592-8981. *4985*

ONCOLOGY TIMES.
Lippincott - Raven Publishers, 227 E. Washington Sq., Philadelphia, PA 19106. TEL 215-238-4200. FAX 215-238-4227. *4985*

ONDERSTEPOORT JOURNAL OF VETERINARY RESEARCH.
Agricultural Research Council, Onderstepoort Veterinary Institute, Private Bag X5, Onderstepoort 0110, South Africa. TEL 27-12-5299101. FAX 27-12-5299318. *7276*

ONDOKUZ MAYIS UNIVERSITESI TIP DERGISI.
Ondokuz Mayis Universitesi, Tip Fakultesi Dekanligi, Kurupelit, 55139 Samsun, Turkey. TEL 90-362-4576070. FAX 90-362-4576041. *4724*

ONION RIVER REVIEW.
Box 7345, York, PA 17404-0345. *4351*

ONKOLOGIE.
S. Karger AG, Allschwilerstr. 10, P.O. Box, CH-4009 Basel, Switzerland. TEL 41-61-3061111. FAX 41-61-3061234. *4985*

THE ONLINE JOURNAL OF CURRENT CLINICAL TRIALS.
Chapman & Hall, Journals Department 2-6 Boundary Row, London SE1 8HN, England. TEL 44-171-8650066. FAX 44-171-5229623. *4724*

ONLINE JOURNAL OF KNOWLEDGE SYNTHESIS FOR NURSING.
Sigma Theta Tau International Honor Society of Nursing, 550 W. North St., Indianapolis, IN 46202. TEL 317-634-8171. FAX 317-634-8188. *4945*

ONOMA.
International Centre of Onomastics, Blijde-Inkomststraat 21, P.O. Box 33, 3000 Leuven, Belgium. FAX 32-16-325025. *4286*

ONOMASTICA CANADIANA.
Canadian Society for the Study of Names, c/o Wolfgang Ahrens, Dept. of Languages, Literatures and Linguistics, York University, North York, ON M3J 1P3, Canada. TEL 416-736-5016. FAX 416-736-5483. *4286*

ONS GEESTELIJK ERF.
Editions Peeters s.p.r.l., Bondgenotenlaan 153, 3000 Leuven, Belgium. TEL 32-16-235170. FAX 32-16-228500. *6360*

ONTARIO. MINISTRY OF NATURAL RESOURCES. FOREST RESEARCH INFORMATION PAPER.
Ministry of Natural Resources, Ontario Forest Research Institute, P.O. Box 969 - 1235 Queen St. E., Sault Ste. Marie, ON P6A 5N5, Canada. TEL 705-946-2981. FAX 705-946-2030. *3159*

ONTARIO ARCHAEOLOGY.
Ontario Archaeological Society, 126 Willowdale Ave., North York, ON M2N 4Y2, Canada. *376*

ONTARIO BIRDS.
Ontario Field Ornithologists, P.O. Box 62014 Postal Outlet, Burlington, ON L7R 4K2, Canada. *807*

ONTARIO MATHEMATICS GAZETTE.
Ontario Association for Mathematics Education, 112 Peter St. N., Orillia, ON L3V 4Z2, Canada. TEL 705-327-1441. *4596*

ONTARIO MUSEUM ANNUAL.
Ontario Museum Association, George Brown House, 50 Baldwin St., Toronto, ON M5T 1L4, Canada. TEL 416-348-8672. FAX 416-348-0438. *5364*

OPCION.
Universidad del Zulia, Facultad Experimental de Ciencias, Apdo. 15.197, 4005-A Las Delicias Maracaibo, Venezuela. TEL 58-61-519793. FAX 58-61-5153900. *6628*

OPEN.
c/o C. Van Schendel, Keizersgracht 802III, 1017 ED Amsterdam, Netherlands. TEL 31-20-6224322. FAX 31-20-6384860. *4205*

OPEN ECONOMIES REVIEW.
Kluwer Academic Publishers, Postbus 17, 3300 AA Dordrecht, Netherlands. TEL 31-78-6392392. FAX 31-78-6392254. *1309*

OPEN HOUSE INTERNATIONAL.
Open House International Association, c/o NBS Services, Mansion House Chambers, The Close, Newcastle-upon-Tyne NE1 3RE, England. TEL 44-191-2329594. FAX 44-191-2325714. *3755*

OPEN ROAD.
Hachette Filipacchi Magazines, Inc. (Newport Beach), 1499 Monrovia Ave., Newport Beach, CA 92663. TEL 714-720-5300. FAX 714-631-2757. *7112*

OPEN SYSTEMS & INFORMATION DYNAMICS.
Kluwer Academic Publishers, Postbus 17, 3300 AA Dordrecht, Netherlands. TEL 31-78-6392392. FAX 31-78-6392254. *2184*

OPENBAAR BESTUUR.
Samsom H.D. Tjeenk Willink B.V., Postbus 316, 2400 AH Alphen aan den Rijn, Netherlands. TEL 31-1720-66822. FAX 31-1720-66639. *6187*

OPERA BOTANICA.
Nordic Publications in Botany, The Secretary, Gothersgade 130, DK-1123 Copenhagen K, Denmark. *718*

OPERA JOURNAL.
National Opera Association, Inc., Department of Music, University of Nevada - Las Vegas, 4505 Maryland Pkwy., Las Vegas, NV 89154-5025. TEL 702-895-1665. FAX 702-895-4194. *5422*

OPERA QUARTERLY.
Duke University Press, Box 90660, Durham, NC 27708-0660. TEL 919-687-3600. FAX 919-688-4571. *5422*

OPERATING ROOM RISK MANAGEMENT.
E C R I, 5200 Butler Pike, Plymouth Meeting, PA 19462. TEL 610-825-6000. FAX 610-834-1275. *5150*

OPERATIONS RESEARCH.
Institute for Operations Research and the Management Sciences, 901 Elkridge Landing Rd., Ste. 400, Linthicum, MD 21090-2909. TEL 410-850-0300. FAX 410-684-2963. *2088*

OPERATIONS RESEARCH COMPUTER SCIENCE INTERFACE.
Kluwer Academic Publishers, Postbus 17, 3300 AA Dordrecht, Netherlands. TEL 31-78-6392392. FAX 31-78-6392254. *2088*

OPERATIONS RESEARCH LETTERS.
North-Holland, P.O. Box 211, 1000 AE Amsterdam, Netherlands. TEL 31-20-4853911. FAX 31-20-4853598. *6556*

OPERATIVE DENTISTRY.
University of Washington, School of Dentistry, Box 357457, Seattle, WA 98195-7457. TEL 206-543-5913. FAX 206-543-7783. *4866*

OPERATIVE TECHNIQUES IN ORTHOPAEDICS.
W.B. Saunders Co., Curtis Center, 3rd Fl., Independence Sq. W., Philadelphia, PA 19106-3399. TEL 215-238-7862. FAX 215-238-6445. *5013*

OPERATIVE TECHNIQUES IN OTOLARYNGOLOGY - HEAD AND NECK SURGERY.
W.B. Saunders Co., Curtis Center, 3rd Fl., Independence Sq. W., Philadelphia, PA 19106-3399. TEL 215-238-7800. *5024*

OPERATIVE TECHNIQUES IN PLASTIC AND RECONSTRUCTIVE SURGERY.
W.B. Saunders Co., Curtis Center, 3rd Fl., Independence Sq. W., Philadelphia, PA 19106-3399. TEL 215-238-7800. FAX 215-238-6445. *5150*

OPHTHALMIC AND PHYSIOLOGICAL OPTICS.
Elsevier Science Ltd., P.O. Box 800, Kidlington, Oxford OX5 1DX, England. TEL 44-1865-843000. FAX 44-1865-843010. *4998*

OPHTHALMIC EPIDEMIOLOGY.
Aeolus Press, Postbus 740, 4116 ZJ Buren, Netherlands. TEL 31-344-572055. FAX 31-344-572562. *4998*

OPHTHALMIC GENETICS.
Aeolus Press, Postbus 740, 4116 ZJ Buren, Netherlands. TEL 31-344-572055. FAX 31-344-572562. *4998*

OPHTHALMIC PLASTIC AND RECONSTRUCTIVE SURGERY.
Lippincott - Raven Publishers, 227 E. Washington Sq., Philadelphia, PA 19106. TEL 215-238-4200. FAX 215-238-4227. *4998*

OPHTHALMIC RESEARCH.
S. Karger AG, Allschwilerstr. 10, P.O. Box, CH-4009 Basel, Switzerland. TEL 41-61-3061111. FAX 41-61-3061234. *4998*

OPHTHALMOLOGICA.
S. Karger AG, Allschwilerstr. 10, P.O. Box, CH-4009 Basel, Switzerland. TEL 41-61-3061111. FAX 41-61-3061234. *4998*

OPHTHALMOLOGY.
Lippincott - Raven Publishers, 227 E. Washington Sq., Philadelphia, PA 19106. TEL 215-238-4200. FAX 215-238-4227. *4999*

OPPORTUNISTIC PATHOGENS.
Elsevier Science B.V., P.O. Box 211, 1000 AE Amsterdam, Netherlands. TEL 31-20-4853911. FAX 31-20-4853598. *4841*

OPTICAL AND QUANTUM ELECTRONICS.
Thomson Science, 2-6 Boundary Row, London SE1 8HN, England. TEL 44-171-8650066. FAX 44-171-5229623. *2648*

OPTICAL ENGINEERING.
International Society for Optical Engineering (SPIE), Box 10, 1000 20th St., Bellingham, WA 98227-0010. TEL 360-676-3290. FAX 360-647-1445. *5866*

OPTICAL FIBER TECHNOLOGY.
Academic Press, Inc., Journal Division, 525 B St., Ste. 1900, San Diego, CA 92101-4495. TEL 619-699-6715. FAX 619-231-6616. *5867*

OPTICAL MATERIALS.
North-Holland, P.O. Box 211, 1000 AE Amsterdam, Netherlands. TEL 31-20-4853911. FAX 31-20-4853598. *5867*

OPTICAL PHYSICS AND ENGINEERING.
Plenum Publishing Corp., 233 Spring St., New York, NY 10013-1578. TEL 212-620-8000. FAX 212-463-0742. *5867*

OPTICAL SOCIETY OF AMERICA. JOURNAL PART A.
Optical Society of America, Inc., 2010 Massachusetts Ave., N.W., Washington, DC 20036-1023. TEL 202-223-8130. FAX 202-223-1096. *5867*

OPTICAL SOCIETY OF AMERICA. JOURNAL PART B.
Optical Society of America, Inc., 2010 Massachusetts Ave., N.W., Washington, DC 20036-1023. TEL 202-223-8130. FAX 202-223-1096. *5867*

OPTICAL WAVE SCIENCES AND TECHNOLOGY.
Elsevier Science B.V., Books Division, P.O. Box 211, 1000 AE Amsterdam, Netherlands. TEL 31-20-4853911. FAX 31-20-4853705. *5867*

OPTICS AND LASER TECHNOLOGY.
Elsevier Science Ltd., P.O. Box 800, Kidlington, Oxford OX5 1DX, England. TEL 44-1865-843000. FAX 44-1865-843010. *5867*

OPTICS AND LASERS IN ENGINEERING.
Elsevier Science Ltd., P.O. Box 800, Kidlington, Oxford OX5 1DX, England. TEL 44-1865-843000. FAX 44-1865-843010. *5867*

OPTICS AND SPECTROSCOPY.
Optical Society of America, Inc., 2010 Massachusetts Ave., N.W., Washington, DC 20036-1023. TEL 202-223-8130. FAX 202-223-1096. *5868*

OPTICS COMMUNICATIONS.
North-Holland, P.O. Box 211, 1000 AE Amsterdam, Netherlands. TEL 31-20-4853911. FAX 31-20-4853598. *5868*

OPTICS LETTERS.
Optical Society of America, Inc., 2010 Massachusetts Ave., N.W., Washington, DC 20036-1023. TEL 202-223-8130. FAX 202-223-1096. *5868*

OPTIMA.
Anglo American & De Beers of South Africa, P.O. Box 61587, Marshalltown 2107, South Africa. TEL 27-11-638-5189. FAX 27-11-638-3771. *5312*

OPTIMAL CONTROL APPLICATIONS AND METHODS.
John Wiley & Sons Ltd., Journals, Baffins Ln., Chichester, W. Sussex PO19 1UD, England. TEL 44-1243-779777. FAX 44-1243-775878. *2111*

OPTOMETRY AND VISION SCIENCE.
Williams & Wilkins, 351 W. Camden St., Baltimore, MD 21201-2436. TEL 410-528-4068. FAX 410-528-4452. *4999*

OPUSCULA ZOOLOGICA FLUMINENSIA.
Flumserberg Scientific Publishers, Casa d'Uors, Postfach 34, CH-8896 Flumserberg, Switzerland. TEL 081-332214. *846*

B'OR HA'TORAH.
Shamir, Association of Religious Professionals from the Former Soviet Union in Israel, 6 David Yellin St., P.O. Box 5749, Jerusalem, Israel. TEL 972-2-385702. FAX 972-2-5385118. *6407*

ORAL HISTORY.
University of Essex, Department of Sociology, Wivenhoe Park, Colchester CO4 3SQ, England. TEL 44-1206-873333. FAX 44-1206-873410. *3589*

ORAL MICROBIOLOGY AND IMMUNOLOGY.
Munksgaard International Publishers Ltd., 35 Noerre Soegade, P.O. Box 2148, DK-1016 Copenhagen K, Denmark. TEL 45-33-127030. FAX 45-33-129387. *792*

ORAL SURGERY, ORAL MEDICINE, ORAL PATHOLOGY, ORAL RADIOLOGY, AND ENDODONTICS.
Mosby - Year Book, Inc., 11830 Westline Industrial Dr., St. Louis, MO 63146-3318. TEL 314-872-8370. FAX 314-432-1380. *4866*

ORAL TRADITION.
Slavica Publishers, Inc., Box 14388, Columbus, OH 43214. TEL 614-268-4002. FAX 614-268-0106. *3090*

ORALPROPHYLAXE.
Carl Hanser Verlag, Kolbergerstr. 22, 81679 Munich, Germany. TEL 49-89-99830603. FAX 49-89-99830623. *4866*

THE ORATORY.
St. Joseph's Oratory, 3800 Queen Mary Rd., Montreal, PQ H3V 1H6, Canada. TEL 514-733-8211. FAX 514-733-9735. *6474*

ORBIS LITTERARUM.
Munksgaard International Publishers Ltd., 35 Noerre Soegade, P.O. Box 2148, DK-1016 Copenhagen K, Denmark. TEL 45-33-127030. FAX 45-33-129387. *4445*

ORBIS MUSICAE.
Tel Aviv University, Department of Musicology, Ramat Aviv 69978, Israel. TEL 972-3-6408332. FAX 972-3-6407358. *5423*

ORBIT.
Aeolus Press, Postbus 740, 4116 ZJ Buren, Netherlands. TEL 31-344-572055. FAX 31-344-572562. *5000*

ORCHADIAN.
Australasian Native Orchid Society, G.P.O. Box 978, Sydney, N.S.W. 1043, Australia. *3201*

THE ORCHARD.
United Jewish Appeal, Rabbinic Cabinet, 99 Park Ave., Ste. 300, New York, NY 10016. TEL 212-880-1418. FAX 212-867-1074. *6408*

ORCHID DIGEST.
Orchid Digest Corporation, c/o Robert Schuler, Executive Director, Box 1216, Redlands, CA 92373-0402. *3201*

ORDER.
Kluwer Academic Publishers, Postbus 17, 3300 AA Dordrecht, Netherlands. TEL 31-78-6392392. FAX 31-78-6392254. *4596*

ORE GEOLOGY REVIEWS.
Elsevier Science B.V., P.O. Box 211, 1000 AE Amsterdam, Netherlands. TEL 31-20-4853911. FAX 31-20-4853598. *2363*

OREGON GEOLOGY.
Department of Geology and Mineral Industries, 800 N.E. Oregon St., No. 28, Ste. 965, Portland, OR 97232-2109. TEL 503-731-4100. FAX 503-731-4066. *2363*

OREGON STATE UNIVERSITY. FOREST RESEARCH LABORATORY. RESEARCH CONTRIBUTION.
Oregon State University, Forest Research Laboratory, Corvallis, OR 97331. TEL 541-737-4271. *3159*

ORFF ECHO.
American Orff-Schulwerk Association, 3105 Lincoln Blvd., Cleveland, OH 44118-2035. TEL 216-321-7573. FAX 216-321-19461. *5423*

ORGANIC CHEMISTRY.
Academic Press, Inc., 525 B St., Ste. 1900, San Diego, CA 92101-4495. TEL 619-231-0926. FAX 619-699-6715. *1819*

ORGANIC ELECTRONIC SPECTRAL DATA.
John Wiley & Sons, Inc., 605 Third Ave., New York, NY 10158. TEL 212-850-6000. FAX 212-850-6088. *1795*

ORGANIC GEOCHEMISTRY.
Elsevier Science Ltd., Pergamon, P.O. Box 800, Kidlington, Oxford OX5 1DX, England. TEL 44-1865-843000. FAX 44-1865-843010. *1819*

ORGANIC PHOTOCHEMISTRY: A SERIES OF ADVANCES.
Marcel Dekker, Inc., 270 Madison Ave., New York, NY 10016. TEL 212-696-9000. FAX 212-685-4540. *1819*

ORGANIC PREPARATIONS AND PROCEDURES INTERNATIONAL.
Organic Preparations and Procedures, Inc., Box 9, Newton Highlands, MA 02161. *1819*

ORGANIC REACTION MECHANISMS. ANNUAL SURVEY.
John Wiley & Sons, Inc., 605 Third Ave., New York, NY 10158. TEL 212-850-6000. FAX 212-860-6088. *1820*

ORGANIC REACTIONS.
John Wiley & Sons, Inc., 605 Third Ave., New York, NY 10158. TEL 212-850-6000. FAX 212-850-6088. *1820*

ORGANIC SYNTHESES.
John Wiley & Sons, Inc., 605 Third Ave., New York, NY 10158. TEL 212-850-6000. FAX 212-850-6088. *1820*

ORGANISTS' REVIEW.
Marcus Knight, 6 Homefield Close, Chelmsford, Essex CM1 2HE, England. TEL 44-1245-259120. *5423*

ORGANIZATION & ENVIRONMENT.
Sage Publications, Inc., 2455 Teller Rd., Thousand Oaks, CA 91320. TEL 805-499-0721. FAX 805-499-0871. *5497*

ORGANIZATION DEVELOPMENT JOURNAL.
Organization Development Institute (Cleveland), 781 Beta Dr., Ste. K, Cleveland, OH 44143. TEL 216-461-4333. FAX 216-729-9319. *1499*

ORGANIZING.
St. Joseph's University Press, 5600 City Ave., Philadelphia, PA 19131-1395. TEL 215-878-4253. FAX 215-879-3148. *6680*

ORGANOMETALLICS.
American Chemical Society, 1155 16th St., N.W., Washington, DC 20036. TEL 800-333-9511. FAX 614-447-3671. *1820*

ORIENS.
E.J. Brill, P.O. Box 9000, 2300 PA Leiden, Netherlands. TEL 31-71-5353500. FAX 31-71-5317532. *5534*

ORIENTAL INSECTS.
Associated Publishers, Box 140103, Gainesville, FL 32614-0103. TEL 352-371-4071. FAX 352-371-4071. *759*

ORIENTAL NOTES AND STUDIES.
Magnes Press, Hebrew University, Jerusalem, P.O. Box 7695, Jerusalem 91076, Israel. TEL 972-2-5660341. FAX 972-2-5633370. *3659*

ORIENTAL SOCIETY OF AUSTRALIA. JOURNAL.
Oriental Society of Australia, University of Sydney, School of Asian Studies, Sydney, N.S.W. 2006, Australia. TEL 61-2-93516759. FAX 61-2-93512319. *5535*

ORIENTALIA LOVANIENSIA ANALECTA.
Editions Peeters s.p.r.l., Bondgenotenlaan 153, 3000 Leuven, Belgium. TEL 32-16-235170. FAX 32-16-228500. *5535*

ORIENTALIA RHENO-TRAIECTINA.
E.J. Brill, P.O. Box 9000, 2300 PA Leiden, Netherlands. TEL 31-71-5353500. FAX 31-71-5317532. *5535*

ORIENTATION SCOLAIRE ET PROFESSIONNELLE.
Institut National d'Etude du Travail et d'Orientation Professionnelle, 41 rue Gay Lussac, 75005 Paris, France. TEL 33-1-44107848. FAX 33-1-44107911. *6139*

ORIGINS.
Calvin College Archives, 3207 Burton S.E., Grand Rapids, MI 49546. TEL 616-957-6313. FAX 616-957-6470. *6436*

ORIGINS OF LIFE AND EVOLUTION OF THE BIOSPHERE.
Kluwer Academic Publishers, Postbus 17, 3300 AA Dordrecht, Netherlands. TEL 31-78-6392392. FAX 31-78-6392254. *619*

ORION.
Operations Research Society of South Africa, P.O. Box 850, Groenkloof 0027, South Africa. *2088*

ORIS MEDICINA.
Diade s.r.l., Via Ausonio 5, 20123 Milan, Italy. TEL 39-2-8372407. FAX 39-2-58100311. *4725*

ORNIS FENNICA.
Finnish Ornithological Society, University of Helsinki, Department of Ecology and Systematics, Division of Population Biology, P.O. Box 17, SF-00014 Helsinki, Finland. TEL 358-81-5531214. FAX 358-81-5531227. *807*

ORNIS HUNGARICA.
Hungarian Ornithological and Nature Conservation Society, Kolto u. 21, 1121 Budapest, Hungary. *807*

L'OROPTERO.
In-tersezioni, Piazza della Liberta 17, 50059 Vinci (Fi), Italy. TEL 39-571-567923. FAX 39-571-56520. *5000*

ORTHODOX WORD.
St. Herman of Alaska Brotherhood, Box 70, Platina, CA 96076. TEL 916-352-4430. *6392*

ORTHOPAEDIC NURSING JOURNAL.
Jannetti Publications, Inc., East Holly Ave., Box 56, Pitman, NJ 08071-0056. TEL 609-256-2300. FAX 609-589-7463. *4945*

ORTHOPAEDICS TODAY INTERNATIONAL EDITION.
Slack, Inc., 6900 Grove Rd., Thorofare, NJ 08086-9447. TEL 609-848-1000. FAX 609-853-5991. *5013*

ORTHOPEDIC CLINICS OF NORTH AMERICA.
W.B. Saunders Co., Curtis Center, 3rd Fl., Independence Sq. W., Philadelphia, PA 19106-3399. TEL 215-238-7800. FAX 215-238-6445. *5014*

ORTHOPEDICS.
Slack, Inc., 6900 Grove Rd., Thorofare, NJ 08086-9447. TEL 609-848-1000. FAX 609-853-5991. *5014*

ORTNAMNSSAELLSKAPETS I UPPSALA AARSSKRIFT.
Ortnamnssaellskapet i Uppsala, P.O. Box 135, 751 04 Uppsala, Sweden. TEL 46-18-65-21-72. FAX 46-18-65-21-65. *4287*

ORVOSI HETILAP.
Springer Hungarica Kiado Ltd., 36 Csanyi Laszlo St., 1043 Budapest, Hungary. TEL 36-1-3709074. FAX 36-1-3909075. *4725*

ORVOSTORTENETI KOZLEMENYEK.
Semmelweis Orvostorteneti Muzeum, Konyvtar es Leveltar, Torok u. 12, 1023 Budapest, Hungary. TEL 36-1-2125421. FAX 36-1-1753936. *4725*

ORYX.
Blackwell Science Ltd., Osney Mead, Oxford OX2 0EL, England. TEL 44-1865-206206. FAX 44-1865-721205. *2241*

OSAKA CITY UNIVERSITY. FACULTY OF ENGINEERING. MEMOIRS.
Osaka City University, Faculty of Engineering, 3-138 Sugimoto 3-chome, Sumiyoshi-ku, Osaka 558, Japan. *2735*

OSAKA TOSEKI KENKYUKAI KAISHI.
Osaka Toseki Kenkyukai, Osaka Shiritsu Daigaku Igakubu Hinyokika Kyoshitsu, 5-7, Asahimachi 1-chome, Abeno-ku, Osaka 545, Japan. TEL 81-6-645-2166. FAX 81-6-647-4426. *5164*

OSHO TIMES INTERNATIONAL.
Tao Publishing (Pvt.) Ltd., 50 Koregaon Park, Poona 411 001, Maharashtra, India. TEL 91-212-628561. FAX 91-212-624181. *6394*

OSIRIS (CHICAGO).
University of Chicago Press, Journals Division, Box 37005, Chicago, IL 60637. TEL 773-753-3347. FAX 773-753-0811. *6557*

OSIRIS (DEERFIELD).
Box 297, Deerfield, MA 01342. TEL 413-774-4027. FAX 413-772-1100. *4516*

OSMANIA PAPERS IN LINGUISTICS.
Osmania University, Department of Linguistics, Hyderabad 500 007, Andhra Pradesh, India. TEL 868951. *4287*

OSNABRUECKER NATURWISSENSCHAFTLICHE MITTEILUNGEN.
Naturwissenschaftlicher Verein Osnabrueck, Am Schoelerberg 8, 49082 Osnabrueck, Germany. TEL 49-541-5600332. FAX 49-541-5600337. *6557*

OSO.
Stichting Instituut ter Bevordering van de Surinamistiek, Koperslagershoek 13, 3981 SB Bunnik, Netherlands. TEL 31-30-6567543. FAX 31-30-2534666. *326*

OSTEOPATHIC PROGRESS.
American Osteopathic Healthcare Association, 5550 Frienship Blvd., Ste. 300, Chevy Chase, MD 20815-7201. TEL 202-686-1700. FAX 202-686-7615. *3718*

OSTEOPOROSIS REPORT.
National Osteoporosis Foundation, 1150 17th St., N.W., Ste. 500, Washington, DC 20036. TEL 202-223-2226. FAX 202-223-2237. *4725*

OTECHESTVENNAYA GEOLOGIYA.
Ts N I G R I, Varshavskoe Shosse, 129B, 113545 Moscow, Russia. TEL 7-095-3152847. FAX 7-095-3152701. *2363*

OTHER REALITIES.
Undena Publications, Box 97, Malibu, CA 90265. TEL 805-746-5870. FAX 805-746-2728. *326*

OTHER VOICES.
Other Voices, Inc., University of Illinois at Chicago, Department of English MC 162, 601 S. Morgan St., Chicago, IL 60607-7120. TEL 312-413-2209. *4445*

OTOLARYNGOLOGY - HEAD AND NECK SURGERY.
Mosby - Year Book, Inc., 11830 Westline Industrial Dr., St. Louis, MO 63146-3318. TEL 314-872-8370. FAX 314-432-1380. *5024*

THE OTOLARYNGOLOGY JOURNAL CLUB JOURNAL.
Lippincott - Raven Publishers, 227 E. Washington Sq., Philadelphia, PA 19106. TEL 215-238-4200. FAX 215-238-4227. *4784*

OTORINOLARINGOLOGIA.
Edizioni Minerva Medica, Corso Bramante 83-85, 10126 Turin, Italy. TEL 39-11-678282. FAX 39-11-674502. *5024*

OTORINOLARYNGOLOGIE A FONIATRIE.
Nakladatelske Stredisko C L S J.E. Purkyne, Sokolska 31, 120 26 Prague 2, Czech Republic. TEL 420-2-24911420. FAX 420-2-24911420. *5024*

OTTAWA LAW REVIEW.
University of Ottawa, Faculty of Law, 57 rue Louis Pasteur, Ottawa, ON K1N 6N5, Canada, Canada. TEL 613-562-5800. FAX 613-562-5124. *4005*

THE OTTOMAN EMPIRE AND ITS HERITAGE.
E.J. Brill, P.O. Box 9000, 2300 PA Leiden, Netherlands. TEL 31-71-5353500. FAX 31-71-5317532. *3659*

OUDTESTAMENTISCHE STUDIEN.
E.J. Brill, P.O. Box 9000, 2300 PA Leiden, Netherlands. TEL 31-71-5353500. FAX 31-71-5317532. *6360*

OUGHTRED SOCIETY. JOURNAL.
Oughtred Society, 2160 Middlefield Rd., Palo Alto, CA 94301. TEL 415-324-1821. *4597*

OUR PAPER.
Grain Dealers Mutual Insurance Co., 1752 N. Meridian St., Box 1747, Indianapolis, IN 46206. TEL 317-923-2453. *3829*

OUT IN THE MOUNTAINS.
Box 177, Burlington, VT 05402. *3699*

OUTLOOK ON AGRICULTURE.
CAB International, Wallingford, Oxon. OX10 8DE, England. TEL 44-1491-832111. FAX 44-1491-826090. *143*

OVULATION METHOD RESEARCH AND REFERENCE CENTRE OF AUSTRALIA. BULLETIN.
Ovulation Method Research and Reference Centre of Australia, Billings Family Life Centre, 27 Alexandra Parade, N. Fitzroy, Melbourne, Vic. 3068, Australia. TEL 61-3-94811722. FAX 61-3-94824208. *858*

OWL OF MINERVA.
Hegel Society of America, Philosophy Documentation Center, Bowling Green State University, Bowling Green, OH 43403-0189. TEL 773-508-3477. *5740*

OXFORD BULLETIN OF ECONOMICS AND STATISTICS.
Blackwell Publishers Ltd., 108 Cowley Rd., Oxford OX4 1JF, England. TEL 44-1865-791100. FAX 44-1865-791347. *990*

OXFORD DEVELOPMENT STUDIES.
Carfax Publishing Co., P.O. Box 25, Abingdon, Oxon. OX14 3UE, England. TEL 44-1235-401000. FAX 44-1235-401550. *1366*

OXFORD JOURNAL OF ARCHAEOLOGY.
Blackwell Publishers Ltd., 108 Cowley Rd., Oxford OX4 1JF, England. TEL 44-1865-791100. FAX 44-1865-791347. *376*

OXFORD LITERARY REVIEW.
Department of English Studies, University of Durham, Elvet Riverside, New Elvet, Durham DH1 3JT, England. TEL 44-191-374-2730. FAX 44-191-374-7471. *4446*

OXFORD MATHEMATICAL MONOGRAPHS.
Oxford University Press, Walton St., Oxford OX2 6DP, England. TEL 44-1865-56767. FAX 44-1865-56646. *4597*

OXFORD MONOGRAPHS ON BIOGEOGRAPHY.
Oxford University Press, Walton St., Oxford OX2 6UP, England. TEL 44-1865-56767. FAX 44-1865-56646. *619*

OXFORD MONOGRAPHS ON GEOLOGY AND GEOPHYSICS.
Oxford University Press, Walton St., Oxford OX2 6DP, England. TEL 44-1865-56767. FAX 44-1865-56646. *2363*

OXFORD MONOGRAPHS ON MEDICAL GENETICS.
Oxford University Press, Walton St., Oxford OX2 6DP, England. TEL 44-1865-56767. FAX 44-1865-56646. *4726*

OXFORD MONOGRAPHS ON METEOROLOGY AND PHYSICAL OCEANOGRAPHY.
Oxford University Press, Walton St., Oxford OX2 6DP, England. TEL 44-1865-56767. FAX 44-1865-56646. *5241*

OXFORD NEUROLOGICAL MONOGRAPHS.
Oxford University Press, Walton St., Oxford OX2 6DP, England. TEL 44-1865-56767. FAX 44-1865-56646. *5088*

OXFORD REVIEW OF EDUCATION.
Carfax Publishing Co., P.O. Box 25, Abingdon, Oxon. OX14 3UE, England. TEL 44-1235-401000. FAX 44-1235-401550. *2470*

OXFORD REVIEWS OF REPRODUCTIVE BIOLOGY.
Oxford University Press, Oxford Journals, Walton St., Oxford OX2 6DP, England. TEL 44-1865-56767. FAX 44-1865-56646. *846*

OXFORD STUDIES IN ANCIENT PHILOSOPHY.
Oxford University Press, Walton St., Oxford OX2 6DP, England. TEL 44-1865-56767. FAX 44-1865-56646. *5740*

OXFORD STUDIES IN COMPARATIVE EDUCATION.
Triangle Journals Ltd., P.O. Box 65, Wallingford, Oxon. OX10 0YG, England. TEL 44-1491-838013. FAX 44-1491-834968. *2470*

OXIDATION OF METALS.
Plenum Publishing Corp., 233 Spring St., New York, NY 10013-1578. TEL 212-620-8000. FAX 212-463-0742. *1833*

OYEN ECHO.
109 6 Ave. E., P.O. Box 420, Oyen, AB T0J 2J0, Canada. TEL 403-664-3622. FAX 403-664-3622. *3264*

OYO TOKEIGAKU.
Oyo Tokei Gakkai, Dept. of Administration Engineering, Keio University, 14-1, Hiyoshi 3-chome, Kohoku-ku, Yokohama-shi, Kanagawa-ken 223, Japan. FAX 81-45-562-4442. *6931*

OYO YAKURI.
Oyo Yakuri Kenkyukai, C.P.O. Box 180, Sendai 980-91, Japan. TEL 81-22-267-3810. FAX 81-22-222-0515. *5682*

OZ CLARK'S WINE GUIDE (YEAR).
Websters Wine Guide Ltd., Axe & Bottle Ct., 70 Newcomen St., London SE1 1YT, England. TEL 44-171-407-5956. FAX 44-171-407-6437. *526*

OZONE: SCIENCE AND ENGINEERING.
Lewis Publishers, Inc., Journals Department, 2000 Corporate Blvd., N.W., Boca Raton, FL 33431. TEL 407-994-0555. FAX 407-997-0949. *2769*

P A C E.
Futura Publishing Company, Inc., 135 Bedford Rd., Box 418, Armonk, NY 10504-0418. TEL 914-273-1014. FAX 914-973-1015. *4822*

P & T.
Quadrant HealthCom, 105 Raider Blvd., Belle Mead, NJ 08052-1510. TEL 908-874-0707. FAX 908-874-5611. *5682*

P - FORM.
Randolph Street Gallery, 756 N. Milwaukee Ave., Chicago, IL 60622. TEL 312-666-7737. FAX 312-666-8986. *459*

P I D S RESEARCH PAPER SERIES.
Philippine Institute for Development Studies, NEDA sa Makati Bldg., 3rd Fl., Rm. 304, 106 Amorsolo St., Legaspi Village, Makati 1229, Metro Manila, Philippines. TEL 632-8935705. FAX 632-8161091. *1366*

P L I WARWICK JOURNAL OF PHILOSOPHY.
University of Warwick, Department of Philosophy, Coventry CV4 7AL, England. TEL 44-1203-523421. FAX 44-1203-523019. *5740*

P S A JOURNAL.
Photographic Society of America, Inc., 3000 United Founders Blvd., No. 103, Oklahoma City, OK 73112-3940. TEL 405-843-1437. FAX 405-843-1438. *5769*

P S: POLITICAL SCIENCE & POLITICS.
American Political Science Association, 1527 New Hampshire Ave., N.W., Washington, DC 20036. TEL 202-483-2512. FAX 202-483-2657. *5953*

PACIFIC BASIN FINANCE JOURNAL.
North-Holland, P.O. Box 211, 1000 AE Amsterdam, Netherlands. TEL 31-20-4853911. FAX 31-20-4853598. *1160*

PACIFIC COAST PHILOLOGY.
Pacific Ancient and Modern Language Association, c/o Cyndia Clegg, Ed., Dept. of Humanities, Pepperdine University, Malibu, CA 90263-4225. TEL 310-456-4435. *4446*

PACIFIC CONSERVATION BIOLOGY.
Surrey Beatty & Sons, 43 Rickard Rd., Chipping Norton, N.S.W. 2170, Australia. TEL 61-2-96023888. FAX 61-2-982112553. *2241*

PACIFIC HISTORICAL REVIEW.
University of California Press, Journals Division, 2120 Berkeley Way, No. 5812, Berkeley, CA 94720-5812. TEL 510-643-7154. FAX 510-642-9917. *3642*

PACIFIC JOURNAL OF MATHEMATICS.
International Press, Pacific Journal of Mathematics, Mathematics Department, University of California, Los Angeles, CA 90095-1555. TEL 310-825-1148. FAX 310-206-6673. *4597*

PACIFIC NORTHWEST QUARTERLY.
University of Washington, 4045 Brooklyn Ave., N.E., Seattle, WA 98105-6261. TEL 206-543-2992. *3642*

PACIFIC NORTHWESTERNER.
Westerners, Spokane Corral, N. 13415 Peninsula Dr., Newman Lake, WA 99025. TEL 509-928-9540. *3642*

PACIFIC PHILOSOPHICAL QUARTERLY.
Blackwell Publishers Ltd., 108 Cowley Rd., Oxford OX4 1JF, England. TEL 44-1865-791100. FAX 44-1865-791347. *5741*

PACIFIC SCIENCE.
University of Hawaii Press, Journals Department, 2840 Kolowalu St., Honolulu, HI 96822. TEL 808-956-8833. FAX 808-988-6052. *6558*

PACIFIC SCIENCE ASSOCIATION. INFORMATION BULLETIN.
Pacific Science Association, Box 17801, Honolulu, HI 96817. TEL 808-848-4139. FAX 808-847-8252. *6558*

PACIFIC SEABIRDS.
Pacific Seabird Group, 4505 University Way, N.E., Box 179, Seattle, WA 98105. *807*

PACIFIC SOCIETY. JOURNAL.
Pacific Society, 4-15-29-3F, Mita, Minato-ku, Tokyo 108, Japan. TEL 81-3-5442-2706. FAX 81-3-5442-2716. *326*

PACIFIC STUDIES.
Institute for Polynesian Studies, Brigham Young University - Hawaii, Box 1829, Laie, HI 96762. TEL 808-293-3667. FAX 808-293-3645. *6628*

PACIFIC TOURISM REVIEW.
Cognizant Communication Corporation, 3 Hartsdale Rd., Elmsford, NY 10523. TEL 914-592-7720. FAX 914-592-8981. *7227*

PAEDAGOGICA HISTORICA.
Universiteit Gent, H. Dunantlaan 1, 9000 Ghent, Belgium. TEL 32-9-2240224. FAX 32-9-2259311. *2470*

PAEDIATRIC & PERINATAL EPIDEMIOLOGY.
Blackwell Science Ltd., Osney Mead, Oxford OX2 0EL, England. TEL 44-1865-206206. FAX 44-1865-721205. *5035*

PAEDIATRIC NURSING.
R C N Publishing Co., Viking House, 17-19 Peterborough Rd., Harrow-on-the-Hill, Middlesex HA1 2AX, England. TEL 44-181-423-1066. FAX 44-181-423-3867. *4945*

PAEDIATRICS AND CHILD HEALTH.
Canadian Paediatric Society, 2204 Walkley Rd., Ste. 100, Ottawa, ON K1G 4G8, Canada. TEL 613-526-9397. FAX 613-526-3332. *5035*

PAIDEUSIS.
Canadian Philosophy of Education Society, c/o Prof. Don Cochrane, Managing Ed., University of Saskatchewan, Dept. of Educational Foundations, Saskatoon, SK S7N 0W0, Canada. FAX 306-966-7020. *5741*

PAIN.
Elsevier Science B.V., P.O. Box 211, 1000 AE Amsterdam, Netherlands. TEL 31-20-4853911. FAX 31-20-4853598. *5089*

PAIN AND HEADACHE.
S. Karger AG, Allschwilerstr. 10, P.O. Box, CH-4009 Basel, Switzerland. TEL 41-61-3061111. FAX 41-61-3061234. *5089*

THE PAIN CLINIC.
V S P, P.O. Box 346, 3700 AH Zeist, Netherlands. TEL 31-30-6925790. FAX 31-30-6932081. *4807*

PAIN DIGEST.
Springer-Verlag, Medical Journals, 175 Fifth Ave., New York, NY 10010. TEL 212-460-1575. FAX 212-473-6272. *4807*

PAIN FORUM.
Churchill Livingstone, 650 Ave. of the Americas, New York, NY 10011. TEL 212-206-5040. FAX 212-206-7808. *5089*

PAIN RESEARCH AND CLINICAL MANAGEMENT.
Elsevier Science B.V., Books Division, P.O. Box 211, 1000 AE Amsterdam, Netherlands. TEL 31-20-4853911. FAX 31-20-4853705. *4726*

PAINT TITLES.
Paint Research Association, 8 Waldegreave Rd., Teddington, Middlesex TW118LD, England. TEL 44-181-977-4427. FAX 44-181-943-4705. *5556*

PAKISTAN CONGRESS OF ZOOLOGY. PROCEEDINGS.
Zoological Society of Pakistan, c/o Department of Zoology, University of the Punjab, New Campus, Lahore, Pakistan. TEL 92-42-5868376. *846*

PAKISTAN HORIZON.
Pakistan Institute of International Affairs, P.O. Box 1447, Aiwan-i-Sadar Rd., Karachi 74200, Pakistan. TEL 92-21-5682891. FAX 92-21-5686069. *6031*

PAKISTAN JOURNAL OF APPLIED ECONOMICS.
University of Karachi, Applied Economics Research Centre, P.O. Box 8403, Karachi 75270, Pakistan. TEL 92-21-474749. FAX 92-21-4969729. *1281*

PAKISTAN JOURNAL OF BOTANY.
Pakistan Botanical Society, Dept. of Botany, University of Karachi, Karachi 75270, Pakistan. TEL 92-21-447867. FAX 92-21-466896. *718*

PAKISTAN JOURNAL OF HYDROCARBON RESEARCH.
Hydrocarbon Development Institute of Pakistan, 230 Nizamuddin Rd. F 7-4, P.O. Box 1308, Islamabad, Pakistan. TEL 92-51-823690. FAX 92-51-828773. *5617*

PAKISTAN JOURNAL OF NEMATOLOGY.
Pakistan Society of Nematologists, National Nematological Research Centre, University of Karachi, Karachi 75270, Pakistan. FAX 92-21-4963373. *846*

PAKISTAN JOURNAL OF PHARMACEUTICAL SCIENCES.
University of Karachi, Faculty of Pharmacy, Karachi 75270, Pakistan. *5682*

PAKISTAN JOURNAL OF ZOOLOGY.
Zoological Society of Pakistan, c/o Department of Zoology, University of the Punjab, New Campus, Lahore, Pakistan. TEL 92-42-5868376. *846*

PAKISTAN VETERINARY JOURNAL.
University of Agriculture, Faculty of Veterinary Science, Faisalabad 38040, Pakistan. TEL 92-41-624607. FAX 92-41-610200. *7276*

PAKN TREGER.
National Yiddish Book Center, 48 Woodbridge St., South Hadley, MA 01075. TEL 413-535-1303. FAX 413-535-1007. *4447*

PAKPHYTON.
Agriculturalists, Breeders and Botanists' Club of Pakistan, Department of Botany, University of the Punjab, Quaid-e-Azam Campus, Lahore 54590, Pakistan. TEL 92-42-5869939. FAX 92-42-5868313. *719*

PALAEOGEOGRAPHY, PALAEOCLIMATOLOGY, PALAEOECOLOGY.
Elsevier Science B.V., P.O. Box 211, 1000 AE Amsterdam, Netherlands. TEL 31-20-4853911. FAX 31-20-4853598. *5561*

PALAEONTOGRAPHICA AMERICANA.
Paleontological Research Institution, 1259 Trumansburg Rd., Ithaca, NY 14850. TEL 607-273-6623. FAX 607-273-6620. *5561*

PALAEONTOLOGIA AFRICANA.
University of the Witwatersrand, Johannesburg, Bernard Price Institute for Palaeontological Research, Wits 2050, South Africa. TEL 27-11-7162870. FAX 27-11-4031423. *5561*

PALAEONTOLOGIA CATHAYANA.
Science Press, Marketing and Sales Department, 16 Donghuangchenggen North St., Beijing 100717, People's Republic of China. TEL 4010642. FAX 4012180. *5561*

PALAEONTOLOGY.
Blackwell Publishers Ltd., 108 Cowley Rd., Oxford OX4 1JF, England. TEL 44-1865-791100. FAX 44-1865-791347. *5562*

PALAESTRA.
Challenge Publications, Ltd., Circulation Department, Box 508, 1948 Riverview Dr., Macomb, IL 61455-0508. TEL 309-833-1902. FAX 309-833-1902. *3457*

PALAIOS.
S E P M, 1731 E. 71st. St., Tulsa, OK 74136-5108. TEL 918-493-3361. FAX 918-493-2093. *5562*

PALEOBIOLOGY.
Paleontological Society, Business Office, Box 1897, Lawrence, KS 66044-8897. TEL 913-843-1221. *5562*

PALEOBIOS.
University of California at Berkeley, Museum of Paleontology, Berkeley, CA 94720. TEL 510-642-1821. FAX 510-642-1822. *5562*

PALEOCEANOGRAPHY.
American Geophysical Union, 2000 Florida Ave., N.W., Washington, DC 20009. TEL 202-462-6900. FAX 202-328-0566. *6558*

PALEONTOLOGICAL JOURNAL.
Maik Nauka - Interperiodica, Mezhdunarodnyi Otdel, Ul. Profsoyuznaya, 90, 117864 Moscow, Russia. *5562*

PALESTINE YEARBOOK OF INTERNATIONAL LAW.
Al-Shaybani Society of International Law, P.O. Box 4247, 1702 Nicosia, Cyprus. TEL 357-2-429396. FAX 357-2-312104. *4124*

PALLIATIVE CARE TODAY.
C C T Healthcare Communications Ltd., 50-52 Union St., London SE1 1TD, England. TEL 0171-407-9731. FAX 0171-407-7083. *4985*

PALMYRE.
Polska Akademia Nauk, Zaklad Archeologii Srodziemnomorskiej, Palac Kultury i Nauki, p. 2105, 00-901 Warsaw, Poland. TEL 48-22-6248593. FAX 48-22-6207651. *377*

PALYNOLOGY.
American Association of Stratigraphic Palynologists Foundation, c/o Vaughn M. Bryant, Jr., Palynology Laboratory, Anthropology Bldg., Texas A & M University, College Station, TX 77843-4352. TEL 409-845-5242. FAX 409-845-4070. *5562*

PAN AMERICAN JOURNAL OF ORGAN REPLACEMENT THERAPIES.
Field & Wood, Medical Periodicals, Inc., Box 975, Blue Bell, PA 19422. TEL 610-828-4010. FAX 215-482-0226. *5164*

PAN-PACIFIC ENTOMOLOGIST.
Pacific Coast Entomological Society, c/o California Academy of Sciences, Golden Gate Park, San Francisco, CA 94118-4599. TEL 415-750-7227. FAX 415-750-7228. *759*

PANCREAS.
Lippincott - Raven Publishers, 227 E. Washington Sq., Philadelphia, PA 19106. TEL 215-238-4200. FAX 215-238-4227. *4891*

PANGOLIN PAPERS.
Turtle Press, Box 241, Nordland, WA 98358. TEL 360-385-3626. *4352*

PANJAB PAST AND PRESENT.
Punjabi University, Department of Punjab Historical Studies, Patiala 147 002, Punjab, India. TEL 822161-65. *3538*

PANMINERVA MEDICA.
Edizioni Minerva Medica, Corso Bramante 83-85, 10126 Turin, Italy. TEL 39-11-678282. FAX 39-11-674502. *4726*

PAPERS IN COMPARATIVE STUDIES.
Ohio State University, Division of Comparative Studies in the Humanities, 308 Dulles Hall, 230 W. 17th Ave., Columbus, OH 43210-1311. TEL 614-292-2559. FAX 614-292-6707. *4447*

PAPERS IN REGIONAL SCIENCE.
Regional Science Association International, 1-3 Observatory, 901 S. Mathews, Univ. of Illinois, Urbana, IL 61801-3681. TEL 217-333-8904. FAX 217-244-1785. *6629*

PAPERS ON LANGUAGE AND LITERATURE.
Southern Illinois University at Edwardsville, Edwardsville, IL 62026. TEL 618-692-2119. FAX 618-692-3509. *4447*

PAPYROLOGICA LUGDUNO-BATAVA.
E.J. Brill, P.O. Box 9000, 2300 PA Leiden, Netherlands. TEL 31-71-5353500. FAX 31-71-5317532. *4448*

PARA.DOXA.
Delta Productions, Box 2237, Vashon, WA 98070. TEL 206-567-4373. *4448*

PARADOXIST LITERARY MOVEMENT.
Paradoxist Literary Association, 2456 S. Rose Peak Dr., Tucson, AZ 85710-6122. TEL 520-886-7413. *4448*

PARAGRAPH.
Edinburgh University Press, 22 George Sq., Edinburgh EH8 9LF, Scotland. TEL 44-131-650-6207. FAX 44-131-662-0053. *4448*

PARALLEL AND DISTRIBUTED SIMULATION WORKSHOP. PROCEEDINGS.
Society for Computer Simulation, Box 17900, San Diego, CA 92177. TEL 619 277 3888. FAX 619 277-3930. *2152*

PARALLEL COMPUTING.
North-Holland, P.O. Box 211, 1000 AE Amsterdam, Netherlands. TEL 31-20-4853911. FAX 31-20-4853598. *2158*

PARAMETERS (CARLISLE BARRACKS).
U.S. Army War College, Carlisle Barracks, PA 17013-6050. TEL 717-245-4943. FAX 717-245-4721. *5281*

PARASITE.
Princeps Editions, 64 av. Charles de Gaulle, 92130 Issy-les-Moulineaux, France. TEL 33-1-46382414. FAX 33-1-40957215. *4841*

PARASITE IMMUNOLOGY.
Blackwell Science Ltd., Osney Mead, Oxford OX2 0EL, England. TEL 44-1865-206206. FAX 44-1865-721205. *4841*

PARASITOLOGIA AL DIA.
Sociedad Chilena de Parasitologia, Casilla 50470, Santiago 1, Chile. FAX 56-2-5416840. *792*

PARASITOLOGY TODAY.
Elsevier Science Ltd., P.O. Box 800, Kidlington, Oxford OX5 1DX, England. TEL 44-1865-843000. FAX 44-1865-843010. *4842*

PARASITOLOGY TODAY (REFERENCE EDITION).
Elsevier Science Ltd., P.O. Box 800, Kidlington, Oxford OX5 1DX, England. TEL 44-1865-843000. FAX 44-1865-843010. *4842*

PARCHMENT.
90 Charlton Blvd., Willowdale, ON M2M 1B9, Canada. TEL 416-221-2088. FAX 416-979-5273. *4448*

PARDES.
Editions Le Cerf, 24 bd. Saint-Michel, 75006 Paris, France. *6408*

PARENTESI.
Associazione Culturale Parentesi, S.S. 114 Pal Iles, 98125 Messina, Italy. TEL 39-90-692568. FAX 39-90-692568. *3327*

PARERGON.
Australian and New Zealand Association for Medieval and Renaissance Studies, University of Sydney, Department of English, Sydney, N.S.W. 2006, Australia. FAX 02-692-2434. *4448*

PARIS TRANSCONTINENTAL.
Institut du Monde Anglophone, TEL 33-1-69018635. *4448*

PARISH AND COMMUNITY LIBRARIES NEWS.
Catholic Library Association, Parish Section, Box 16321, St. Paul, MN 55116. FAX 612-690-2131. *4206*

PARK-NICOLLET INSTITUTE FOR RESEARCH AND EDUCATION BULLETIN.
Park Nicollet Medical Center, 5000 W. 39th St, Minneapolis, MN 55416. TEL 612-993-3123. *4727*

PARKINSONISM AND RELATED DISORDERS.
Elsevier Science Ltd., P.O. Box 800, Kidlington, Oxford OX5 1DX, England. TEL 44-1865-843000. FAX 44-1865-843010. *5089*

PARLIAMENTARY HISTORY.
Edinburgh University Press, 22 George Sq., Edinburgh EH8 9LF, Scotland. TEL 44-131-650-6207. FAX 44-131-662-0053. *3507*

PARNASSOS.
Parnassos Literary Society, 8 St. George Karytsis Sq., 105 61 Athens, Greece. TEL 30-1-322-1917. FAX 30-1-324-9398. *3787*

PARTICLE ACCELERATORS.
Gordon and Breach - Harwood Academic, Amsteldisk 166, 1st Fl., 1079 LH Amsterdam, Netherlands. *5855*

PARTICLE WORLD.
Gordon and Breach - Harwood Academic, Amsteldisk 166, 1st Fl., 1079 LH Amsterdam, Netherlands. *5817*

PARTICULATE SCIENCE AND TECHNOLOGY.
Taylor & Francis Inc., 1900 Frost Rd., Ste. 101, Bristol, PA 19007-1598. TEL 215-785-5800. FAX 215-785-5515. *2769*

PARTISAN REVIEW.
Partisan Review, Inc., 236 Bay State Rd., Boston, MA 02215. TEL 617-353-4260. FAX 617-353-7444. *4352*

PARTS & PEOPLE.
Automotive Counseling & Publishing Co., Inc., 837 Sherman St., Ste. 2B, Denver, CO 80203-2913. TEL 303-860-0545. FAX 303-860-0532. *7113*

PASSAGES NORTH.
c/o Northern Michigan Univ., 1401 Presque Isle Ave., Marquette, MI 49855. TEL 906-227-1203. *4448*

PAST IMPERFECT.
University of Alberta, History Graduate Students Association, c/o History Dept., 2-28 Tory Bldg., Edmonton, AB T6G 2H4, Canada. TEL 403-492-4568. FAX 403-492-9125. *3508*

PASTORAL CARE IN EDUCATION.
Blackwell Publishers Ltd., 108 Cowley Rd., Oxford OX4 1JF, England. TEL 44-1865-791100. FAX 44-1865-791347. *2471*

PASTORAL PSYCHOLOGY.
Human Sciences Press, Inc., 233 Spring St., New York, NY 10013-1578. TEL 212-620-8000. FAX 212-463-0742. *6139*

PATHOBIOLOGY.
S. Karger AG, Allschwilerstr. 10, P.O. Box, CH-4009 Basel, Switzerland. TEL 41-61-3061111. FAX 41-61-3061234. *4727*

PATHOLOGY INTERNATIONAL.
Blackwell Science Pty Ltd, P.O. Box 378, Carlton South, Vic. 3053, Australia. TEL 61-3-347-0300. FAX 61-3-347-5001. *4727*

PATHOLOGY: STATE OF THE ART REVIEWS.
Hanley & Belfus, Inc., 210 S. 13th St., Philadelphia, PA 19107. TEL 215-546-7293. FAX 215-790-9330. *4727*

PATHOPHYSIOLOGY.
Elsevier Science B.V., P.O. Box 211, 1000 AE Amsterdam, Netherlands. TEL 31-20-4853911. FAX 31-20-4853598. *820*

PATIENT EDUCATION AND COUNSELING.
Elsevier Science Ireland Ltd., P.O. Box 85, Limerick, Ireland. TEL 353-61-471944. FAX 353-61-472144. *6246*

PATOLOGIA.
Obsidiana Editores, S.A., Czda. de Tlalpan 2365, Col. Ciudad Jardin, 04370 Mexico DF, Mexico. TEL 6899133. *619*

PATOLOGO CLINICO.
A I P A C Service s.r.l., Via Luigi Ungarelli 23, 00162 Rome, Italy. TEL 39-6-8600007. FAX 39-6-8600042. *4728*

PATRISTICA ET MEDIAEVALIA.
Universidad de Buenos Aires, Centro de Estudios de Filosofia Medieval, Puan 480, 4o piso, 1406 Buenos Aires, Argentina. FAX 54-1-4320121. *3508*

PATTERN RECOGNITION.
Elsevier Science Ltd., Pergamon, P.O. Box 800, Kidlington, Oxford OX5 1DX, England. TEL 44-1865-843000. FAX 44-1865-843010. *2125*

PATTERN RECOGNITION AND IMAGE ANALYSIS.
Maik Nauka - Interperiodica, Mezhdunarodnyi Otdel, Ul. Profsoyuznaya, 90, 117864 Moscow, Russia. TEL 7-095-3360066. FAX 7-095-3360666. *4597*

PATTERN RECOGNITION LETTERS.
North-Holland, P.O. Box 211, 1000 AE Amsterdam, Netherlands. TEL 31-20-4853911. FAX 31-20-4853598. *2125*

PATTERNS OF PREJUDICE.
Sage Publications Ltd., 6 Bonhill St., London EC2A 4PU, England. TEL 44-171-374-0645. FAX 44-171-374-8741. *5997*

PAUL ANTHONY BRICK LECTURES.
University of Missouri Press, 2910 LeMone Blvd., Columbia, MO 65202. TEL 314-882-7641. FAX 314-884-4498. *5741*

PAWA EREKUTORONIKUSU KENKYUKAI RONBUNSHI.
Pawa Erekutoronikusu Kenkyukai, c/o Center for Academic Societies Japan, Osaka, 14th Fl., Senri Life Science Center Bldg., 1-4-2 Shinsenrihigashi-machi, Toyonaka 565, Japan. TEL 81-6-879-7982. FAX 81-6-879-7984. *2648*

PAYS LORRAIN.
Societe d'Archeologie Lorraine, Palais Ducal, 64 Grande Rue, 54000 Nancy, France. TEL 33-3-83321874. FAX 33-3-83379915. *3591*

PEABODY JOURNAL OF EDUCATION.
Lawrence Erlbaum Associates, Inc., 10 Industrial Dr., Mahwah, NJ 07430-2262. TEL 201-236-9500. FAX 201-236-0072. *2471*

PEACEKEEPING & INTERNATIONAL RELATIONS.
Canadian PeaceKeeping Press, Pearson Peacekeeping Centre Cornwallis Park, P.O. Box 100, Clementsport, NS B0S 1E0, Canada. TEL 902-638-8611. FAX 902-638-8576. *6032*

PEACHTREE MAGAZINE.
C S Publishers, Inc., 120 Interstate N. Pkwy. E., Ste. 445, Atlanta, GA 30339. TEL 770-956-1207. FAX 770-988-8972. *3382*

PE'AMIM.
Ben Zvi Institute for the Study of Jewish Communities in the East, P.O. Box 7560, Jerusalem 91076, Israel. TEL 972-2-5639204. FAX 972-2-5638310. *3659*

PEDAGOGIEKJOERNAAL.
University of Pretoria, Faculty of Education, Pretoria 0002, South Africa. TEL 27-12-4202272. FAX 27-12-3422914. *2471*

PEDAGOGISCH TIJDSCHRIFT.
Institute of Psychology, Tiensestraat 102, B-3000 Leuven, Belgium. TEL 32-16-326102. FAX 32-16-326000. *2471*

PEDIATRIA POLSKA.
Wydawnictwo Medyczne Urban i Partner, Ul. Marii Sklodowskiej-Curie 55-61, 50-950 Wroclaw, Poland. TEL 48-71-225497. FAX 48-71-224391. *5036*

PEDIATRIC ALLERGY AND IMMUNOLOGY.
Munksgaard International Publishers Ltd., 35 Noerre Soegade, P.O. Box 2148, DK-1016 Copenhagen K, Denmark. TEL 45-33-127030. FAX 45-33-129387. *5036*

PEDIATRIC ALLERGY AND IMMUNOLOGY. SUPPLEMENTUM.
Munksgaard International Publishers Ltd., 35 Norre Soegade, P.O. Box 2148, DK-1016 Copenhagen, Denmark. TEL 45-33-127030. FAX 45-33-129387. *5036*

PEDIATRIC AND ADOLESCENT MEDICINE.
S. Karger AG, Allschwilerstr. 10, P.O. Box, CH-4009 Basel, Switzerland. TEL 41-61-3061111. FAX 41-61-3061234. *5036*

PEDIATRIC CARDIOLOGY.
Springer-Verlag, Medical Journals, 175 Fifth Ave., New York, NY 10010. TEL 212-460-1500. FAX 212-473-6272. *4822*

PEDIATRIC DENTISTRY.
American Academy of Pediatric Dentistry, 211 E. Chicago Ave., Ste. 700, Chicago, IL 60611-2616. TEL 312-337-2169. FAX 312-337-6329. *4867*

PEDIATRIC DERMATOLOGY.
Blackwell Science Inc., 350 Main St., Malden, MA 02148. TEL 617-876-7000. FAX 617-388-8255. *4880*

PEDIATRIC EMERGENCY & CRITICAL CARE.
Riverpress, Inc., Box 23, Jersey City, NJ 07303-0023. TEL 201-434-5073. FAX 201-434-7230. *4786*

PEDIATRIC EMERGENCY CARE.
Williams & Wilkins, 351 W. Camden St., Baltimore, MD 21201-2436. TEL 410-528-4068. FAX 410-528-4452. *5037*

PEDIATRIC EXERCISE SCIENCE.
Human Kinetics Publishers, Inc., Box 5076, Champaign, IL 61825-5076. TEL 217-351-5076. FAX 217-351-2674. *5037*

PEDIATRIC HEMATOLOGY & ONCOLOGY.
Taylor & Francis Inc., 1900 Frost Rd., Ste. 101, Bristol, PA 19007-1598. TEL 215-785-5800. FAX 215-785-5515. *5037*

PEDIATRIC HEMATOLOGY - ONCOLOGY SERIES.
Lippincott - Raven Publishers, 227 E. Washington Sq., Philadelphia, PA 19106. TEL 215-238-4200. FAX 215-238-4227. *4985*

THE PEDIATRIC INFECTIOUS DISEASE JOURNAL.
Williams & Wilkins, 351 W. Camden St., Baltimore, MD 21201-2436. TEL 410-528-4068. FAX 410-528-4452. *5037*

PEDIATRIC NEUROLOGY.
Elsevier Science Inc., Box 945, New York, NY 10159-0945. TEL 212-633-3730. FAX 212-633-3680. *5037*

PEDIATRIC NEUROSURGERY.
S. Karger AG, Allschwilerstr. 10, P.O. Box, CH-4009 Basel, Switzerland. TEL 41-61-3061111. FAX 41-61-3061234. *5089*

PEDIATRIC NURSING.
Jannetti Publications, Inc., East Holly Ave., Box 56, Pitman, NJ 08071-0056. TEL 609-256-2300. FAX 609-589-7463. *4946*

PEDIATRIC PATHOLOGY & LABORATORY MEDICINE.
Taylor & Francis Inc., 1900 Frost Rd., Ste. 101, Bristol, PA 19007-1598. TEL 215-785-5800. FAX 215-785-5515. *5037*

PEDIATRIC PHYSICAL THERAPY.
Williams & Wilkins, 351 W. Camden St., Baltimore, MD 21201-2436. TEL 410-528-4068. FAX 410-528-4452. *5038*

PEDIATRIC PRIMARY CARE.
Riverpress, Inc., Box 23, Jersey City, NJ 07303-0023. TEL 201-434-5073. FAX 201-434-7230. *4786*

PEDIATRIC PULMONOLOGY.
John Wiley & Sons, Inc., Journals, 605 Third Ave., New York, NY 10158. TEL 212-850-6645. FAX 212-850-6021. *5038*

PEDIATRIC RESEARCH.
Williams & Wilkins, 351 W. Camden St., Baltimore, MD 21201-2436. TEL 410-528-4068. FAX 410-528-4452. *5038*

PEDIATRIC REVIEWS AND COMMUNICATIONS.
Gordon and Breach - Harwood Academic, Amsteldisk 166, 1st Fl., 1079 LH Amsterdam, Netherlands. *5038*

PEDIATRIC SURGERY UPDATE.
Box 10426, Caparra Heights Sta., San Juan, PR 00922-0426. *5150*

PEDIATRICS IN REVIEW.
American Academy of Pediatrics, 141 Northwest Point Blvd., Box 927, Elk Grove Village, IL 60009-0927. TEL 847-228-5005. FAX 847-228-5097. *5038*

PEDOLOGIST.
Japanese Society of Pedology, c/o National Institute of Agro-Environmental Sciences, 3-1-1 Kannondai, Tsukuba, Ibaraki 305, Japan. TEL 81-298-38-8275. FAX 81-298-38-8199. *238*

PEDOSPHERE.
Science Press, Marketing and Sales Department, 16 Donghuangchenggen North St., Beijing 100717, People's Republic of China. TEL 4010642. FAX 4019810. *2320*

PENN SOUNDS.
Composer Services Inc., 345 S. 19th St., Philadelphia, PA 19103. TEL 215-985-0963. FAX 215-985-0736. *5424*

PENNSYLVANIA ACADEMY OF SCIENCE. JOURNAL.
Pennsylvania Academy of Science, c/o Dr. S.K. Majumdar, Ed., Dept. of Biology, Lafayette College, Easton, PA 18042. TEL 610-250-5464. FAX 610-250-6557. *6559*

PENNSYLVANIA DENTAL JOURNAL.
Pennsylvania Dental Association, Box 3341, Harrisburg, PA 17105. TEL 717-234-5941. FAX 717-232-7169. *4867*

PENNSYLVANIA ECONOMIC REVIEW.
Pennsylvania Economic Association, Economics Dept., Millersville University, Box 1002, Millersville, PA 17551. TEL 717-872-3561. FAX 717-871-2326. *991*

PENNSYLVANIA FOLKLIFE.
Pennsylvania Folklife Society, Box 92, Collegeville, PA 19426. TEL 215-489-4111. *3642*

PENNSYLVANIA GENEALOGICAL MAGAZINE.
Genealogical Society of Pennsylvania, 1305 Locust St., Philadelphia, PA 19107. TEL 215-545-0391. FAX 215-545-0936. *3237*

PENNSYLVANIA GEOGRAPHER.
University of Pittsburgh at Johnstown, Department of Geography, Johnstown, PA 15904. TEL 814-269-2994. FAX 814-269-7255. *3416*

PENNSYLVANIA HISTORY.
Pennsylvania Historical Association, Weaver Bldg., Penn State University, State College, PA 16802. TEL 814-865-1367. *3642*

PENNSYLVANIA MAGAZINE OF HISTORY AND BIOGRAPHY.
Historical Society of Pennsylvania, 1300 Locust St., Philadelphia, PA 19107. TEL 215-732-6200. FAX 215-732-2680. *3642*

PENNSYLVANIA OSTEOPATHIC MEDICAL ASSOCIATION. JOURNAL.
Pennsylvania Osteopathic Medical Association, 1330 Eisenhower Blvd., Harrisburg, PA 17111. TEL 717-939-9318. FAX 717-939-7255. *4728*

PENSAMIENTO CONSTITUCIONAL.
Pontificia Universidad Catolica del Peru, Fondo Editorial, Apdo. 1761, Lima 32, Peru. TEL 51-14-626390. FAX 51-14-611785. *5954*

THE PENTAGON.
Kappa Mu Epsilon, c/o Larry Scott, Bus. Manager, Div. of Mathematics & Computer Science, Emporia State University, Emporia, KS 66801. TEL 316-341-5638. FAX 316-341-6055. *4597*

PEOPLE DYNAMICS.
Institute of Personnel Management, P.O. Box 31390, Braamfontein 2017, South Africa. TEL 27-11-4824970. FAX 27-11-4825542. *1572*

PEOPLE SEARCHING NEWS.
Adoption Education Resources, Box 100444, Palm Bay, FL 32910-0444. TEL 407-768-2222. FAX 407-728-7999. *6681*

PEPPERDINE LAW REVIEW.
Pepperdine University, School of Law, 24255 Pacific Coast Hwy., Malibu, CA 90263-4694. TEL 310-456-4694. FAX 310-317-7283. *4007*

PEPPER'N SALT.
Standard Schnauzer Club of America, 1884 W. Lake Storey Rd., Galesburg, IL 61401. TEL 309-344-1140. *5640*

PEPTIDES.
Elsevier Science Inc., Box 945, New York, NY 10159-0945. TEL 212-633-3730. FAX 212-633-3680. *668*

PERCEPTION.
Pion Ltd., 207 Brondesbury Park, London NW2 5JN, England. TEL 44-181-459-0066. FAX 44-181-451-6454. *6139*

PERCEPTION & PSYCHOPHYSICS.
Psychonomic Society, Inc., 1710 Fortview Rd., Austin, TX 78704. TEL 512-462-2442. *6139*

PERCEPTUAL AND MOTOR SKILLS.
Dr. C.H. Ammons & Dr. R.B. Ammons, Eds. & Pubs., Box 9229, Missoula, MT 59807. TEL 406-728-1710. *6139*

PERFORMANCE EVALUATION.
North-Holland, P.O. Box 211, 1000 AE Amsterdam, Netherlands. TEL 31-20-4853911. FAX 31-20-4853598. *2089*

PERGAMON UNIFIED ENGINEERING SERIES.
Elsevier Science Ltd., Books Division, P.O. Box 800, Kidlington, Oxford OX3 0BW, England. TEL 44-1865-843000. FAX 44-1865-843010. *2736*

PERIODICA ISLAMICA.
31 Jalan Riong, 59100 Kuala Lumpur, Malaysia. TEL 60-3-282-5286. FAX 60-3-282-8489. *6400*

PERIODICA MATHEMATICA HUNGARICA.
Kluwer Academic Publishers, Postbus 17, 3300 AA Dordrecht, Netherlands. TEL 31-78-6392392. FAX 31-78-6392254. *4597*

PERIODICA POLYTECHNICA. CHEMICAL ENGINEERING.
Budapesti Muszaki Egyetem, Periodica Polytechnica, 1521 Budapest, Hungary. TEL 36-1-4631469. FAX 36-1-4632141. *2770*

PERIODICA POLYTECHNICA. CIVIL ENGINEERING.
Budapesti Muszaki Egyetem, Periodica Polytechnica, 1521 Budapest, Hungary. TEL 36-1-4631469. FAX 36-1-4632141. *2795*

PERIODICA POLYTECHNICA. ELECTRICAL ENGINEERING.
Budapesti Muszaki Egyetem, Periodica Polytechnica, 1521 Budapest, Hungary. TEL 36-1-4631469. FAX 36-1-4632141. *2842*

PERIODICA POLYTECHNICA. MECHANICAL ENGINEERING.
Budapesti Muszaki Egyetem, Periodica Polytechnica, 1521 Budapest, Hungary. TEL 36-1-4631469. FAX 36-1-4632141. *2896*

PERIODICA POLYTECHNICA. SOCIAL AND MANAGEMENT SCIENCES.
Budapesti Muszaki Egyetem, Periodica Polytechnica, 1521 Budapest, Hungary. TEL 36-1-4631469. FAX 36-1-4632141. *3788*

PERIODICA POLYTECHNICA. TRANSPORT ENGINEERING.
Budapesti Muszaki Egyetem, Periodica Polytechnica, 1521 Budapest, Hungary. TEL 36-1-4631469. FAX 36-1-4632141. *7036*

PERIODONTOLOGY.
Australian Society of Periodontology, Dept. of Dentistry, University of Queensland, Brisbane, Qld. 4000, Australia. TEL 61-7-365-8055. FAX 61-7-365-8199. *4867*

PERIODONTOLOGY 2000.
Munksgaard International Publishers Ltd., 35 Noerre Soegade, P.O. Box 2148, DK-1016 Copenhagen K, Denmark. TEL 45-33-127030. FAX 45-33-129387. *4867*

PERITO AGRARIO.
IACICO s.r.l., Via A. Poliziano 80, 00184 Rome, Italy. TEL 39-6-4873183. FAX 39-6-4873144. *145*

PERMAFROST AND PERIGLACIAL PROCESSES.
John Wiley & Sons Ltd., Journals, Baffins Ln., Chichester, W. Sussex PO19 1UD, England. TEL 44-1243-779777. FAX 44-1243-775878. *2364*

PERSIMMON HILL.
National Cowboy Hall of Fame and Western Heritage Center, 1700 N.E. 63rd St., Oklahoma City, OK 73111. TEL 405-478-2250. FAX 405-478-4714. *3643*

PERSONAL RELATIONSHIPS.
Cambridge University Press, The Edinburgh Bldg., Shaftesbury Rd., Cambridge CB2 2RU, England. TEL 44-1223-312393. FAX 44-1223-315052. *6161*

PERSONALITY AND INDIVIDUAL DIFFERENCES.
Elsevier Science Ltd., Pergamon, P.O. Box 800, Kidlington, Oxford OX5 1DX, England. TEL 44-1865-843000. FAX 44-1865-843010. *6140*

PERSONALITY, PSYCHOPATHOLOGY AND PSYCHOTHERAPY.
Academic Press, Inc., 525 B St., Ste. 1900, San Diego, CA 92101-4495. TEL 619-231-0926. FAX 619-699-6715. *6140*

PERSONNEL POLICIES IN EUROPE.
P-E International plc, Park House, Wick Rd., Egham, Surrey TW20 0HW, England. TEL 44-1784-434411. FAX 44-1784-476369. *1573*

PERSONNEL PSYCHOLOGY.
Personnel Psychology, Inc., 745 Haskins Rd., Ste. A, Bowling Green, OH 43402-1600. TEL 419-352-1562. FAX 419-352-2645. *6140*

PERSONNEL, TRAINING AND EDUCATION.
Library Association, Personnel, Training and Education Group, 14 Aireville Ave., Bradford BD9 4ET, England. FAX 01274-594685. *4206*

PERSOONIA.
Rijksherbarium - Hortus Botanicus, Publications Department, P.O. Box 9514, 2300 RA Leiden, Netherlands. *719*

PERSPECTIVAS EM CIENCIA DA INFORMACAO.
Universidade Federal de Minas Gerais, Escola de Biblioteconomia, Caixa Postal 1606, 30161-970 Belo Horizonte MG, Brazil. TEL 55-31-4995227. FAX 55-31-4995200. *4206*

PERSPECTIVE.
Institute for Christian Studies, 229 College St., Toronto, ON M5T 1R4, Canada. TEL 416-979-2331. FAX 416-979-2332. *5741*

PERSPECTIVE OF PHYSICS.
Gordon and Breach - Harwood Academic, Amsteldisk 166, 1st Fl., 1079 LH Amsterdam, Netherlands. *5817*

PERSPECTIVES (COLUMBUS).
Association for General and Liberal Studies, Ohio Dominican College, 1216 Sunbury Rd., Columbus, OH 43219-2099. TEL 614-251-4663. FAX 614-252-0776. *2472*

PERSPECTIVES (TORONTO).
Gerontological Nursing Association, P.O. Box 368, Station "K", Toronto, ON M4P 2G7, Canada. TEL 416-767-4454. FAX 416-591-6812. *3443*

PERSPECTIVES IN ARTIFICIAL INTELLIGENCE.
Academic Press, Inc., 525 B St., Ste. 1900, San Diego, CA 92101-4495. TEL 619-231-6616. FAX 619-699-6715. *2104*

PERSPECTIVES IN BIOLOGY AND MEDICINE.
University of Chicago Press, Journals Division, Box 37005, Chicago, IL 60637. TEL 773-753-3347. FAX 773-753-0811. *4728*

PERSPECTIVES IN BIOMECHANICS.
Gordon and Breach - Harwood Academic, Amsteldisk 166, 1st Fl., 1079 LH Amsterdam, Netherlands. *619*

PERSPECTIVES IN COMPUTING.
Academic Press, Inc., 525 B St., Ste. 1900, San Diego, CA 92101-4495. TEL 619-231-6616. FAX 619-699-6715. *2089*

PERSPECTIVES IN CONDENSED MATTER PHYSICS.
Kluwer Academic Publishers, Postbus 17, 3300 AA Dordrecht, Netherlands. TEL 31-78-6392392. FAX 31-78-6392254. *5817*

PERSPECTIVES IN DRUG DISCOVERY AND DESIGN.
E S C O M Science Publishers BV, P.O. Box 214, 2300 AE Leiden, Netherlands. TEL 31-71-127052. FAX 31-71-121772. *5683*

PERSPECTIVES IN EDUCATION AND DEAFNESS.
Gallaudet University, Pre-College Programs, KDES PAS-6, 800 Florida Ave., N.E., Washington, DC 20002-3695. TEL 202-651-5340. FAX 202-651-5708. *2588*

PERSPECTIVES IN ENERGY.
Turpion - Moscow Ltd., 47 Leninsky pr Park, Moscow 117913, Russia. TEL 7-95-1356417. FAX 7-95-1358860. *2675*

PERSPECTIVES IN ETHOLOGY.
Plenum Publishing Corp., 233 Spring St., New York, NY 10013-1578. TEL 212-620-8000. FAX 212-463-0742. *847*

PERSPECTIVES IN HUMAN BIOLOGY.
Centre for Human Biology, Dept. of Anatomy & Human Biology, Univ. of Western Australia, Nedlands, W.A. 6907, Australia. TEL 61-9-3803491. FAX 61-9-3801051. *619*

PERSPECTIVES IN HYPERTENSION SERIES.
Lippincott - Raven Publishers, 227 E. Washington Sq., Philadelphia, PA 19106. TEL 215-238-4200. FAX 215-238-4227. *4822*

PERSPECTIVES IN IMMUNOLOGY.
Academic Press, Inc., 525 B St., Ste. 1900, San Diego, CA 92101-4495. TEL 619-231-0926. FAX 619-699-6715. *4800*

PERSPECTIVES IN LAW AND PSYCHOLOGY.
Plenum Publishing Corp., 233 Spring St., New York, NY 10013-1578. TEL 212-620-8000. FAX 212-463-0742. *4008*

PERSPECTIVES IN MATHEMATICS.
Academic Press, Inc., 525 B St., Ste. 1900, San Diego, CA 92101-4495. TEL 619-231-6616. FAX 619-699-6715. *4597*

PERSPECTIVES IN MEDICAL VIROLOGY.
Elsevier Science B.V., Books Division, P.O. Box 211, 1000 AE Amsterdam, Netherlands. TEL 31-20-4853911. FAX 31-20-4853705. *792*

PERSPECTIVES IN MEXICAN AMERICAN STUDIES.
University of Arizona, Mexican American Studies & Research Center, Douglass Bldg., Rm. 315, Tucson, AZ 85721. TEL 520-621-7551. FAX 602-621-7966. *3036*

PERSPECTIVES IN NEUROLINGUISTICS, NEUROPSYCHOLOGY, AND PSYCHOLINGUISTICS.
Academic Press, Inc., 525 B St., Ste. 1900, San Diego, CA 92101-4495. TEL 619-231-6616. FAX 619-699-6715. *5089*

PERSPECTIVES IN PEDIATRIC PATHOLOGY.
S. Karger AG, Allschwilerstr. 10, P.O. Box, CH-4009 Basel, Switzerland. TEL 41-61-3061111. FAX 41-61-3061234. *5039*

PERSPECTIVES IN PHYSICS.
Academic Press, Inc., 525 B St., Ste. 1900, San Diego, CA 92101-4495. TEL 619-231-6616. FAX 619-699-6715. *5817*

PERSPECTIVES IN PSYCHIATRIC CARE.
Nursecom Inc., 1211 Locust St., Philadelphia, PA 19107. TEL 215-545-7222. FAX 215-545-8107. *4946*

PERSPECTIVES IN PSYCHOTHERAPY.
Gordon and Breach - Harwood Academic, Amsteldisk 166, 1st Fl., 1079 LH Amsterdam, Netherlands. *6140*

PERSPECTIVES IN RELIGIOUS STUDIES.
National Association of Baptist Professors of Religion, c/o Dr. Rollin Armour, Ed., Department of Christianity, Mercer University, Macon, GA 31207. TEL 912-752-2759. FAX 912-752-2384. *6437*

PERSPECTIVES IN VERTEBRATE SCIENCE.
Kluwer Academic Publishers, Postbus 17, 3300 AA Dordrecht, Netherlands. TEL 31-78-6392392. FAX 31-78-6392254. *847*

PERSPECTIVES OF NEW MUSIC.
Perspectives of New Music, Inc., University of Washington, Music, Box 353450, Seattle, WA 98195-3450. TEL 206-543-0196. FAX 206-543-9285. *5425*

PERSPECTIVES ON MEDICAL RESEARCH.
Medical Research Modernization Committee, Box 2751, New York, NY 10163. TEL 216-832-3904. FAX 216-283-6702. *4901*

PERSPECTIVES ON POLITICAL SCIENCE.
Heldref Publications, 1319 18th St, N.W., Washington, DC 20036-1802. TEL 202-296-6267. FAX 202-296-5149. *5955*

PERSPECTIVES ON SCIENCE: HISTORICAL, PHILOSOPHICAL, SOCIAL.
University of Chicago Press, Journals Division, Box 37005, Chicago, IL 60637. TEL 773-702-7600. FAX 773-753-0811. *6559*

PERSPECTIVES ON SOUTHERN AFRICA.
University of California Press, 2120 Berkeley Way, Berkeley, CA 94720. TEL 510-642-4247. FAX 510-643-7127. *5955*

PERTANIKA JOURNAL OF SCIENCE AND TECHNOLOGY.
Universiti Pertanian Malaysia Press, Serdang, Selangor, Malaysia. TEL 03-9433740. FAX 03-9433404. *6559*

PERTANIKA JOURNAL OF SOCIAL SCIENCE AND HUMANITIES.
Universiti Pertanian Malaysia Press, Serdang, Selangor, Malaysia. TEL 03-9433740. FAX 03-9433404. *6629*

PERTANIKA JOURNAL OF TROPICAL AGRICULTURAL SCIENCE.
Universiti Pertanian Malaysia Press, Serdang, Selangor, Malaysia. FAX 03-9483745. *145*

PERU REPORT'S GUIDE TO TOP PEOPLE IN PERU.
Peru Reporting E.I.R.L., Francisco Grana 319, Magdalena, Lima 17, Peru. TEL 5114-617416. FAX 5114-634466. *576*

PESARO CITTA E CONTA.
Societa Pesarese di Studi Storici, Via Abbati 30, Casella 9, 61100 Pesaro, Italy. TEL 39-721-34411. *3591*

PESHITTA INSTITUTE, LEIDEN. MONOGRAPHS.
E.J. Brill, P.O. Box 9000, 2300 PA Leiden, Netherlands. TEL 31-71-5353500. FAX 31-71-5317532. *6408*

PESQUISA E PLANEJAMENTO ECONOMICO.
Instituto de Pesquisa Economica Aplicada, Av. Presidente Antonio Carlos, 51, 13 andar, 20020-010 Rio de Janeiro, RJ, Brazil. TEL 55-21-2205533. FAX 55-21-2401920. *1593*

PEST CONTROL.
Advanstar Communications, Inc., 7500 Old Oak Blvd., Cleveland, OH 44130. TEL 216-243-8100. FAX 216-891-2675. *238*

PESTICIDE BIOCHEMISTRY AND PHYSIOLOGY.
Academic Press, Inc., Journal Division, 525 B St., Ste. 1900, San Diego, CA 92101-4495. TEL 619-230-1840. FAX 619-699-6800. *238*

PESTICIDE SCIENCE.
John Wiley & Sons Ltd., Journals, Baffins Ln., Chichester, W. Sussex PO19 1UD, England. TEL 44-1243-779777. FAX 44-1243-775878. *239*

PESTICIDE USAGE SURVEY REPORTS ON AGRICULTURE AND HORTICULTURE.
M A F F Publications, London SE99 7TP, England. TEL 44-1645-556000. *239*

PETROLE ET TECHNIQUES.
Association Francaise des Techniciens et des Professionels du Petrole (A F T P), 92038 Paris la Defense, France. TEL 33-1-47-17-67-32. FAX 33-1-47-17-67-44. *5617*

PETROLEUM CHEMISTRY.
Elsevier Science Ltd., Pergamon, P.O. Box 800, Kidlington, Oxford OX5 1DX, England. TEL 44-1865-843000. FAX 44-1865-843010. *5618*

PETROLEUM ENGINEERING AND DEVELOPMENT STUDIES.
Kluwer Academic Publishers, Postbus 17, 3300 AA Dordrecht, Netherlands. TEL 31-78-6392392. FAX 31-78-6392254. *5618*

PETROLEUM GEOLOGY OF TAIWAN.
Chinese Petroleum Corporation, 83 Chung Hwa Rd., Sec.1, Taipei, Taiwan 100, Republic of China. TEL 886-2-361-0221. FAX 886-2-331-7473. *5618*

PETROLEUM SCIENCE AND TECHNOLOGY.
Marcel Dekker, Inc., 270 Madison Ave., New York, NY 10016. TEL 212-696-9000. FAX 212-685-4540. *2736*

PETROLOGY AND STRUCTURAL GEOLOGY.
Kluwer Academic Publishers, Postbus 17, 3300 AA Dordrecht, Netherlands. TEL 31-78-6392392. FAX 31-78-6392254. *2364*

PHAENOMENOLOGICA.
Kluwer Academic Publishers, Postbus 17, 3300 AA Dordrecht, Netherlands. TEL 31-78-6392392. FAX 31-78-6392254. *5741*

PHARMA SELECTA.
Stichting Pharma Selecta, Postbus 122, 8430 Oosterwolde, Netherlands. TEL 31-597-646812. FAX 31-597-645174. *5683*

PHARMACEUTICA ACTA HELVETIAE.
Elsevier Science B.V., P.O. Box 211, 1000 AE Amsterdam, Netherlands. TEL 31-20-4853911. FAX 31-20-4853598. *5684*

PHARMACEUTICAL CHEMISTRY JOURNAL.
Plenum Publishing Corp., Consultants Bureau, 233 Spring St., New York, NY 10013-1578. TEL 212-620-8468. FAX 212-463-0742. *5684*

PHARMACEUTICAL DEVELOPMENT AND TECHNOLOGY.
Marcel Dekker Journals, 270 Madison Ave., New York, NY 10016. TEL 212-696-9000. FAX 212-685-4540. *5684*

PHARMACEUTICAL MEDICINE (LONDON).
Chapman & Hall, Journals Department 2-6 Boundary Row, London SE1 8HN, England. TEL 0171-865-0066. FAX 0171-522-9623. *5685*

PHARMACEUTICAL RESEARCH.
Plenum Publishing Corp., 233 Spring St., New York, NY 10013-1578. TEL 212-620-8000. FAX 212-463-0742. *5685*

PHARMACEUTICAL SOCIETY OF KOREA. JOURNAL.
Pharmaceutical Society of Korea, 1489-3 Suhcho-3-dong, Suhcho-gu, Seoul 137-073, S. Korea. TEL 02-584-3257. FAX 02-521-1781. *5685*

PHARMACEUTICAL TECHNOLOGY.
Advanstar Communications, Inc., 7500 Old Oak Blvd., Cleveland, OH 44130. TEL 216-826-2839. FAX 216-891-2726. *5685*

PHARMACEUTICAL TECHNOLOGY EUROPE - BIOPHARM.
Advanstar Communications, Advanstar House, Park West, Sealand Rd., Chester CH1 4RN, England. TEL 44-1244-378888. FAX 44-1244-370512. *5685*

PHARMACIST'S LETTER.
Therapeutic Research Center, 2453 Grand Canal Blvd., Ste. A, Box 8190, Stockton, CA 95208. TEL 209-472-2240. FAX 209-472-2249. *5686*

PHARMACOCHEMISTRY LIBRARY.
Elsevier Science B.V., Books Division, P.O. Box 211, 1000 AE Amsterdam, Netherlands. TEL 31-20-4853911. FAX 31-20-4853705. *5686*

PHARMACOECONOMICS.
Adis International Limited, Private Bag 65901, Mairangi Bay, Auckland 10, New Zealand. TEL 64-9-479-8100. FAX 64-9-479-8145. *5686*

PHARMACOEPIDEMIOLOGY AND DRUG SAFETY.
John Wiley & Sons Ltd., Journals, Baffins Ln., Chichester, W. Sussex PO19 1UD, England. TEL 44-1243-779777. FAX 44-1243-775878. *5686*

PHARMACOGENETICS.
Chapman & Hall, Journals Department 2-6 Boundary Row, London SE1 8HN, England. TEL 44-171-8650066. FAX 44-171-5229623. *775*

PHARMACOLOGICAL REVIEWS.
Williams & Wilkins, 351 W. Camden St., Baltimore, MD 21201-2436. TEL 410-528-4068. FAX 410-528-4452. *5687*

PHARMACOLOGY.
S. Karger AG, Allschwilerstr. 10, P.O. Box, CH-4009 Basel, Switzerland. TEL 41-61-3061111. FAX 41-61-3061234. *5687*

PHARMACOLOGY AND THE SKIN.
S. Karger AG, Allschwilerstr. 10, P.O. Box, CH-4009 Basel, Switzerland. TEL 41-61-3061111. FAX 41-61-3061234. *4880*

PHARMACOLOGY AND THERAPEUTICS.
Elsevier Science Inc., Box 945, New York, NY 10159-0945. TEL 212-633-3730. FAX 212-633-3680. *5687*

PHARMACOLOGY & TOXICOLOGY.
Munksgaard International Publishers Ltd., 35 Noerre Soegade, P.O. Box 2148, DK-1016 Copenhagen K, Denmark. TEL 45-33-127030. FAX 45-33-129387. *5687*

PHARMACOLOGY & TOXICOLOGY. SUPPLEMENTUM.
Munksgaard International Publishers Ltd., 35 Noerre Soegade, P.O. Box 2148, DK-1016 Copenhagen K, Denmark. TEL 45-33-127030. FAX 45-33-129387. *5687*

PHARMACOLOGY, BIOCHEMISTRY AND BEHAVIOR.
Elsevier Science Inc., Box 945, New York, NY 10159-0945. TEL 212-633-3730. FAX 212-633-3680. *668*

PHARMACOTHERAPY.
Pharmacotherapy Publications, Inc., New England Medical Center - Box 806, 750 Washington St., Boston, MA 02111. TEL 617-636-5390. FAX 617-636-5318. *5688*

PHARMACY CADENCE.
P E N S Pharmacy Editorial & News Services, Inc., Box 6565, Athens, GA 30604. TEL 706-613-0100. FAX 706-613-0200. *5688*

DIE PHARMAZIE.
Govi Pharmazeutischer Verlag GmbH, Ginnheimerstr. 26, 65760 Eschborn, Germany. TEL 49-6196-928262. FAX 49-6196-928203. *5689*

PHAROS (MENLO PARK).
Alpha Omega Alpha Honor Medical Society, 525 Middlefield Rd., Ste. 130, Menlo Park, CA 94025. TEL 415-329-0291. FAX 415-329-1618. *4729*

PHASE TRANSITION PHENOMENA.
Elsevier Science B.V., Books Division, P.O. Box 211, 1000 AE Amsterdam, Netherlands. TEL 31-20-4853911. FAX 31-20-4853705. *5817*

PHASE TRANSITIONS.
Gordon and Breach - Harwood Academic, Amsteldisk 166, 1st Fl., 1079 LH Amsterdam, Netherlands. *5817*

PHI SIGMA IOTA FORUM.
Phi Sigma Iota Honor Society, Department of Foreign Languages, University of Nevada, Las Vegas, NV 89154. FAX 504-769-7105. *4288*

PHILADELPHIA MEDICINE.
Philadelphia County Medical Society, 2100 Spring Garden St., Philadelphia, PA 19130. TEL 215-563-5343. FAX 215-563-3627. *4729*

THE PHILIPPINE ENTOMOLOGIST.
Philippine Association of Entomologists, c/o Department of Entomology, University of the Philippines at Los Banos, College, Laguna 4031, Philippines. TEL 49-536-236-2351. FAX 49-536-3527. *759*

PHILIPPINE JOURNAL OF VETERINARY MEDICINE.
University of the Philippines Los Banos, College of Veterinary Medicine, Los Banos, Laguna 4031, Philippines. TEL 94-536-2730. FAX 94-536-2727. *7276*

PHILIPPINE QUARTERLY OF CULTURE AND SOCIETY.
San Carlos Publications, P.O. Box 182, 6000 Cebu City, Philippines. FAX 6332-54341. *3788*

PHILIPPINE STUDIES.
Ateneo de Manila University Press, P.O. Box 154, 1099 Manila, Philippines. TEL 632-9244495. FAX 632-9207215. *3788*

PHILIPS JOURNAL OF RESEARCH.
Elsevier Science Ltd., P.O. Box 800, Kidlington, Oxford OX5 1DX, England. TEL 44-1865-843000. FAX 44-1865-843010. *2736*

PHILOSOPHIA ANTIQUA.
E.J. Brill, P.O. Box 9000, 2300 PA Leiden, Netherlands. TEL 31-71-5353500. FAX 31-71-5317532. *5742*

PHILOSOPHIA MATHEMATICA.
Wilfrid Laurier University Press, 75 University Ave. W., Waterloo, ON N2L 3C5, Canada. TEL 519-884-0710. FAX 519-725-1399. *5742*

PHILOSOPHIA PATRUM.
E.J. Brill, P.O. Box 9000, 2300 PA Leiden, Netherlands. TEL 31-71-5353500. FAX 31-71-5317532. *6362*

PHILOSOPHIA PERENNIS.
Society for Aristotelian Sudies, c/o Robert Augros, Treas., Box 1643, St. Anselm College, 100 St. Anselm Dr., Manchester, NH 03102. TEL 603-641-7065. *5742*

PHILOSOPHICAL INQUIRY.
D.Z. Andriopoulos, Ed. & Pub., P.O. Box 3825, Central Post Office, Athens 10210, Greece. TEL 301-802-2949. *5743*

PHILOSOPHICAL INVESTIGATIONS.
Blackwell Publishers Ltd., 108 Cowley Rd., Oxford OX4 1JF, England. TEL 44-1865-791100. FAX 44-1865-791347. *5743*

PHILOSOPHICAL MAGAZINE A: PHYSICS OF CONDENSED MATTER, DEFECTS AND MECHANICAL PROPERTIES.
Taylor & Francis Ltd., 1 Gunpowder Sq., London EC4A 3DE, England. TEL 44-171-583-0490. FAX 44-171-583-0585. *5818*

PHILOSOPHICAL MAGAZINE LETTERS.
Taylor & Francis Ltd., 1 Gunpowder Sq., London EC4A 3DE, England. TEL 44-171-583-0490. FAX 44-171-583-0585. *5818*

PHILOSOPHICAL PAPERS.
c/o Dept. of Philosophy, University of the Witwatersrand, P.O. Wits, Johannesburg 2050, South Africa. TEL 716-2757. FAX 403-1174. *5743*

PHILOSOPHICAL PROBLEMS TODAY.
Kluwer Academic Publishers, Postbus 17, 3300 AA Dordrecht, Netherlands. TEL 31-78-6392392. FAX 31-78-6392254. *5743*

PHILOSOPHICAL PSYCHOLOGY.
Carfax Publishing Co., P.O. Box 25, Abingdon, Oxon. OX14 3UE, England. TEL 44-1235-401000. FAX 44-1235-401550. *6140*

PHILOSOPHICAL QUARTERLY.
Blackwell Publishers Ltd., 108 Cowley Rd., Oxford OX4 1JF, England. TEL 44-1865-791100. FAX 44-1865-791347. *5743*

PHILOSOPHICAL REVIEW.
Cornell University, Sage School of Philosophy, 327 Goldwin Smith Hall, Ithaca, NY 14853. TEL 607-255-6817. FAX 607-255-8177. *5743*

PHILOSOPHICAL STUDIES.
Kluwer Academic Publishers, Postbus 17, 3300 AA Dordrecht, Netherlands. TEL 31-78-6392392. FAX 31-78-6392254. *5743*

PHILOSOPHICAL STUDIES SERIES.
Kluwer Academic Publishers, Postbus 17, 3300 AA Dordrecht, Netherlands. TEL 31-78-6392392. FAX 31-78-6392254. *5743*

PHILOSOPHY AND EDUCATION.
Kluwer Academic Publishers, Postbus 17, 3300 AA Dordrecht, Netherlands. TEL 31-78-6392392. FAX 31-78-6392254. *5744*

PHILOSOPHY AND MEDICINE.
Kluwer Academic Publishers, Postbus 17, 3300 AA Dordrecht, Netherlands. TEL 31-78-6392392. FAX 31-78-6392254. *5744*

PHILOSOPHY AND PHENOMENOLOGICAL RESEARCH.
International Phenomenological Society, Brown University, Box 1947, Providence, RI 02912. TEL 401-863-3215. FAX 401-863-2719. *5744*

PHILOSOPHY AND RELIGION.
E.J. Brill, P.O. Box 9000, 2300 PA Leiden, Netherlands. TEL 31-71-5353500. FAX 31-71-5317532. *5744*

PHILOSOPHY AND RHETORIC.
Pennsylvania State University Press, USB 1, Ste. C, University Park, PA 16802-1003. TEL 814-865-1327. FAX 814-863-1408. *5744*

PHILOSOPHY & SOCIAL ACTION.
Committee of Concerned Indian Philosophers for Social Action, M-120 Greater Kailash 1, New Delhi 110 048, India. TEL 91-11-641-5365. FAX 91-11-647-4646. *6629*

PHILOSOPHY & SOCIAL CRITICISM.
Sage Publications Ltd., 6 Bonhill St., London EC2A 4PU, England. TEL 44-171-374-0645. FAX 44-171-374-8741. *3788*

PHILOSOPHY AND TECHNOLOGY.
Kluwer Academic Publishers, Postbus 17, 3300 AA Dordrecht, Netherlands. TEL 31-78-6392392. FAX 31-78-6392254. *6970*

PHILOSOPHY EAST AND WEST.
University of Hawaii Press, Journals Department, 2840 Kolowalu St., Honolulu, HI 96822. TEL 808-956-8833. FAX 808-988-6052. *5745*

PHILOSOPHY OF HISTORY AND CULTURE.
E.J. Brill, P.O. Box 9000, 2300 PA Leiden, Netherlands. TEL 31-71-5353500. FAX 31-71-5317532. *5745*

PHILOSOPHY OF MUSIC EDUCATION REVIEW.
Indiana University, School of Music, Music Education Department, Bloomington, IN 47405. TEL 812-855-2051. FAX 812-855-4936. *5425*

PHILOSOPHY OF SCIENCE.
University of Chicago Press, Journals Division, Box 37005, Chicago, IL 60637. TEL 773-753-3347. FAX 773-753-0811. *6559*

PHILOSOPHY, PSYCHIATRY & PSYCHOLOGY.
Johns Hopkins University Press, Journals Publishing Division, 2715 N. Charles St., Baltimore, MD 21218. TEL 410-516-6987. FAX 410-516-6968. *5745*

PHILOTELIA.
Hellenic Philotelic Society, 57 Akademias St., 106 79 Athens, Greece. TEL 30-1-3621-971. FAX 30-1-9422-157. *5711*

PHOENIX FICTION.
University of Chicago Press, 5801 S. Ellis Ave., Chicago, IL 60637. TEL 773-702-7899. *4449*

PHOENIX POETS.
University of Chicago Press, 5801 S. Ellis Ave., Chicago, IL 60637. TEL 773-702-7899. *4517*

PHONETICA.
S. Karger AG, Allschwilerstr. 10, P.O. Box, CH-4009 Basel, Switzerland. TEL 41-61-3061111. FAX 41-61-3061234. *4288*

PHONOSCOPE.
Singular Publishing Group, 401 W. "A" St., Ste. 325, San Diego, CA 92101. TEL 619-238-6777. FAX 619-238-6789. *5025*

PHOSPHORUS, SULPHUR AND SILICON AND THE RELATED ELEMENTS.
Gordon and Breach - Harwood Academic, Amsteldisk 166, 1st Fl., 1079 LH Amsterdam, Netherlands. *1809*

PHOTO ELECTRONIC IMAGING.
Professional Photographers of America, 57 Forsyth St., N.W., Ste. 1600, Atlanta, GA 30303. TEL 404-522-8600. FAX 404-614-6405. *5770*

PHOTOCHEMICAL & PHOTOBIOLOGICAL REVIEWS.
Plenum Publishing Corp., 233 Spring St., New York, NY 10013-1578. TEL 212-620-8000. FAX 212-463-0742. *1762*

PHOTOCHEMISTRY.
C R C Press, Inc., TEL 561-994-0555. FAX 561-998-9784. *1833*

PHOTOCHEMISTRY AND PHOTOBIOLOGY.
American Society for Photobiology, BioTech Park, Ste. 9, 1021 15th St., Augusta, GA 30901. TEL 706-721-2601. FAX 706-721-3048. *1762*

PHOTODERMATOLOGY, PHOTOIMMUNOLOGY & PHOTOMEDICINE.
Munksgaard International Publishers Ltd., 35 Noerre Soegade, P.O. Box 2148, DK-1016 Copenhagen K, Denmark. TEL 45-33-127030. FAX 45-33-129387. *4880*

PHOTOGRAMMETRIC RECORD.
Photogrammetric Society, Department of Photogrammetry & Surveying, University College London, Gower St., London WC1E 6BT, England. TEL 44-171-387-7050. FAX 44-171-380-0453. *3417*

PHOTOSYNTHESIS BIBLIOGRAPHY.
c/o Zdanek Sestak, Ed., Czech Academy of Sciences, Institute of Experimental Botany, Na Karlovce 1A, 160 00 Prague 6, Czech Republic. TEL 420-2-3111032. FAX 420-2-24310113. *644*

PHOTOSYNTHESIS RESEARCH.
Kluwer Academic Publishers, Postbus 17, 3300 AA Dordrecht, Netherlands. TEL 31-78-6392392. FAX 31-78-6392254. *668*

PHOTOSYNTHETICA.
Kluwer Academic Publishers, Postbus 17, 3300 AA Dordrecht, Netherlands. TEL 31-78-6392392. FAX 31-78-6392254. *719*

PHOTOVISION.
Arte y Proyectos Editoriales, S.L., Apdo. 164, 41710 Utrera (Seville), Spain. TEL 95-486-28-95. *5773*

PHUKET MARINE BIOLOGICAL CENTER. RESEARCH BULLETIN.
Phuket Marine Biological Center, P.O. Box 60, Phuket 83000, Thailand. TEL 076-391128. FAX 076-391127. *619*

PHYCOLOGIA.
International Phycological Society, Box 1897, Lawrence, KS 66044-8897. TEL 913-843-1221. FAX 913-843-1274. *719*

PHYCOLOGICAL RESEARCH.
Blackwell Science Pty Ltd, P.O. Box 378, Carlton South, Vic. 3053, Australia. TEL 61-3-93470300. FAX 61-3-93493016. *719*

PHYSICA A - STATISTICAL AND THEORETICAL PHYSICS.
European Physical Society, 34 rue Marc Seguin, B.P. 2136, 68060 Mulhouse Cedex, France. TEL 33-3-89329440. FAX 33-3-89329449. *5818*

PHYSICA B - PHYSICS OF CONDENSED MATTER.
European Physical Society, 34 rue Marc Seguin, B.P. 2136, 68060 Mulhouse Cedex, France. TEL 33-3-89329440. FAX 33-1-89329449. *5818*

PHYSICA C - SUPERCONDUCTIVITY.
European Physical Society, 34 rue Marc Seguin, B.P. 2136, 68060 Mulhouse Cedex, France. TEL 33-3-89329440. FAX 33-3-89329449. *5818*

PHYSICA D - NONLINEAR PHENOMENA.
European Physical Society, 34 rue Marc Seguin, B.P. 2136, 68060 Mulhouse Cedex, France. TEL 33-3-89329440. FAX 33-3-89329449. *5818*

PHYSICAL ACOUSTICS: PRINCIPLES AND METHODS.
Academic Press, Inc., 525 B St., Ste. 1900, San Diego, CA 92101-4495. TEL 619-231-0926. FAX 619-699-6715. *5873*

PHYSICAL & OCCUPATIONAL THERAPY IN GERIATRICS.
Haworth Press, Inc., 10 Alice St., Binghamton, NY 13904. TEL 607-722-5857. FAX 607-722-6362. *3443*

PHYSICAL & OCCUPATIONAL THERAPY IN PEDIATRICS.
Haworth Press, Inc., 10 Alice St., Binghamton, NY 13904. TEL 607-722-5857. FAX 607-722-6362. *5039*

PHYSICAL EDUCATION AND SPORT.
Wingate Institute, Wingate Post 42902, Israel. TEL 972-9-8639480. FAX 972-9-8639482. *2473*

PHYSICAL GEOGRAPHY.
V.H. Winston & Son, Inc., c/o Bellwether Publishing, Ltd., 8640 Guilford Rd., Ste. 200, Columbia, MD 21046. TEL 410-290-3870. FAX 410-290-8726. *2320*

PHYSICAL MEDICINE & REHABILITATION.
Hanley & Belfus, Inc., 210 S. 13th St., Philadelphia, PA 19107. TEL 215-546-7293. FAX 215-790-9330. *5045*

PHYSICAL REVIEW A.
American Physical Society, One Physics Ellipse, College Park, MD 20740-3844. TEL 301-209-3202. *5819*

PHYSICAL REVIEW B (CONDENSED MATTER).
American Physical Society, One Physics Ellipse, College Park, MD 20740-3844. TEL 301-209-3202. *5819*

PHYSICAL REVIEW C (NUCLEAR PHYSICS).
American Physical Society, One Physics Ellipse, College Park, MD 20740-3843. TEL 301-209-3000. *5856*

PHYSICAL REVIEW ABSTRACTS.
American Physical Society, One Physics Ellipse, College Park, MD 20740-3844. TEL 301-209-3202. *5836*

PHYSICAL REVIEW LETTERS.
American Physical Society, One Physics Ellipse, College Park, MD 20740-3844. TEL 301-209-3202. *5819*

PHYSICAL SCIENCES DATA.
Elsevier Science B.V., Books Division, P.O. Box 211, 1000 AE Amsterdam, Netherlands. TEL 31-20-4853911. FAX 31-20-4853705. *5819*

PHYSICAL THERAPY.
American Physical Therapy Association, 1111 N. Fairfax St., Alexandria, VA 22314-1488. TEL 703-684-2782. FAX 703-706-3169. *5045*

PHYSICIAN ASSISTANT (SPRINGHOUSE).
Springhouse Corporation, 1111 Bethlehem Pike, Box 908, Springhouse, PA 19477. TEL 215-646-8700. *4729*

PHYSICIAN ASSISTANTS' PRESCRIBING REFERENCE.
Prescribing Reference, Inc., 53 Park Pl., Ste. 1010, New York, NY 10007. TEL 212-766-7200. FAX 212-732-2360. *5690*

PHYSICIAN EXECUTIVE.
American College of Physician Executives, Two Urban Centre, Ste. 200, 4890 W. Kennedy Blvd., Tampa, FL 33609. TEL 813-287-2000. FAX 813-287-8993. *3718*

PHYSICS: A SERIES OF MONOGRAPHS & TRACTS.
Gordon and Breach - Harwood Academic, Amsteldisk 166, 1st Fl., 1079 LH Amsterdam, Netherlands. *5819*

PHYSICS AND CHEMISTRY OF LIQUIDS.
Gordon and Breach - Harwood Academic, Amsteldisk 166, 1st Fl., 1079 LH Amsterdam, Netherlands. *5847*

PHYSICS AND CHEMISTRY OF MATERIALS WITH LOW-DIMENSIONAL STRUCTURES.
Kluwer Academic Publishers, Postbus 17, 3300 AA Dordrecht, Netherlands. TEL 31-78-6392392. FAX 31-78-6392254. *5847*

PHYSICS AND CHEMISTRY OF THE EARTH.
Elsevier Science Ltd., Pergamon, P.O. Box 800, Kidlington, Oxford OX5 1DX, England. TEL 44-1865-843000. FAX 44-1865-843010. *2320*

PHYSICS EDUCATION.
I O P Publishing Ltd., Dirac House, Temple Back, Bristol BS1 6BE, England. TEL 44-117-929-7481. FAX 44-117-929-4318. *5820*

PHYSICS ESSAYS.
c/o Alft, Inc., 189 Deveault St., Unit 7, Hull, PQ J8Z 1S7, Canada. FAX 819-770-3862. *5820*

PHYSICS IN CANADA.
Canadian Association of Physicists, 150 Louis Pasteur Ave., Ste. 112, Ottawa, ON K1N 6N5, Canada. TEL 613-562-5614. FAX 613-562-5615. *5820*

PHYSICS LETTERS. SECTION A: GENERAL, ATOMIC AND SOLID STATE PHYSICS.
North-Holland, P.O. Box 211, 1000 AE Amsterdam, Netherlands. TEL 31-20-4853911. FAX 31-20-4853598. *5856*

PHYSICS LETTERS. SECTION B: NUCLEAR, ELEMENTARY PARTICLE AND HIGH-ENERGY PHYSICS.
North-Holland, P.O. Box 211, 1000 AE Amsterdam, Netherlands. TEL 31-20-4853911. FAX 31-20-4853598. *5856*

PHYSICS OF FLUIDS.
American Institute of Physics, One Physics Ellipse, College Park, MD 20740-3843. TEL 301-209-3000. *5820*

PHYSICS OF METALS AND METALLOGRAPHY.
Maik Nauka - Interperiodica, Mezhdunarodnyi Otdel, Ul. Profsoyuznaya, 90, 117864 Moscow, Russia. TEL 7-095-3360066. FAX 7-095-3360666. *5206*

PHYSICS OF PARTICLES AND NUCLEI.
American Institute of Physics, One Physics Ellipse, College Park, MD 20740-3843. TEL 301-209-3000. *5856*

PHYSICS OF PLASMAS.
American Institute of Physics, One Physics Ellipse, College Park, MD 20740-3843. TEL 301-209-3000. *5820*

PHYSICS OF THE EARTH AND PLANETARY INTERIORS.
Elsevier Science B.V., P.O. Box 211, 1000 AE Amsterdam, Netherlands. TEL 31-20-4853911. FAX 31-20-4853598. *2387*

PHYSICS OF THIN FILMS: ADVANCES IN RESEARCH AND DEVELOPMENT.
Academic Press, Inc., 525 B St., Ste. 1900, San Diego, CA 92101-4495. TEL 619-231-0926. FAX 619-699-6715. *5820*

PHYSICS REPORTS.
North-Holland, P.O. Box 211, 1000 AE Amsterdam, Netherlands. TEL 31-20-4853911. FAX 31-20-4853598. *5821*

PHYSICS REPORTS REPRINTS BOOK SERIES.
Elsevier Science B.V., Books Division, P.O. Box 211, 1000 AE Amsterdam, Netherlands. TEL 31-20-4853911. FAX 31-20-4853705. *5821*

PHYSICS REVIEWS.
Gordon and Breach - Harwood Academic, Amsteldisk 166, 1st Fl., 1079 LH Amsterdam, Netherlands. *5821*

PHYSICS TODAY.
American Institute of Physics, One Physics Ellipse, College Park, MD 20740-3843. TEL 301-209-3037. *5821*

PHYSICS - USPEKHI.
Turpion - Moscow Ltd., 47 Leninsky prospekt, 117913 Moscow, Russia. TEL 7-95-1356417. FAX 7-95-1358860. *5821*

PHYSIOLOGIA PLANTARUM.
Munksgaard International Publishers Ltd., 35 Noerre Soegade, P.O. Box 2148, DK-1016 Copenhagen K, Denmark. TEL 45-33-127030. FAX 45-33-129387. *719*

PHYSIOLOGICAL CHEMISTRY AND PHYSICS AND MEDICAL N M R.
Pacific Press, Box 1452 Melville, NY 11747. TEL 516-694-2929. FAX 516-249-3734. *676*

PHYSIOLOGICAL ENTOMOLOGY.
Blackwell Science Ltd., Osney Mead, Oxford OX2 0EL, England. TEL 44-1865-206206. FAX 44-1865-721205. *759*

PHYSIOLOGICAL REVIEWS.
American Physiological Society, 9650 Rockville Pike, Bethesda, MD 20814. TEL 301-530-7164. FAX 301-571-8313. *820*

PHYSIOLOGICAL ZOOLOGY.
University of Chicago Press, Journals Division, Box 37005, Chicago, IL 60637. TEL 773-753-3347. FAX 773-753-0811. *847*

PHYSIOLOGIST.
American Physiological Society, 9650 Rockville Pike, Bethesda, MD 20814. TEL 301-530-7164. FAX 301-571-8313. *820*

PHYSIOLOGY AND BEHAVIOR.
Elsevier Science Inc., Box 945, New York, NY 10159-0945. TEL 212-633-3730. FAX 212-633-3680. *820*

PHYSIOTHERAPY.
Chartered Society of Physiotherapy, 14 Bedford Row, London WC1R 4ED, England. TEL 44-171-306-6662. FAX 44-171-306-6667. *5046*

PHYSIOTHERAPY RESEARCH INTERNATIONAL.
Whurr Publishers Ltd., 19b Compton Terrace, London N1 2UN, England. TEL 44-171-359-5979. FAX 44-171-226-5290. *5046*

PHYSIOTHERAPY THEORY AND PRACTICE.
Taylor & Francis Ltd., Psychology Press, 1 Gunpowder Sq., London EC4A 3DE, England. TEL 44-171-5830490. FAX 44-171-5830585. *5046*

PHYSIS.
Asociacion Argentina de Ciencias Naturales, Museo Argentino de Ciencias Naturales "Bernardino Rivadavia", Avenida Angel Gallardo 470, 1405 Buenos Aires, Argentina. TEL 54-1-9828370. FAX 54-1-9824494. *847*

PHYTOCHEMICAL ANALYSIS.
John Wiley & Sons Ltd., Journals, Baffins Ln., Chichester, W. Sussex PO19 1UD, England. TEL 44-1243-779777. FAX 44-1243-775878. *720*

PHYTOCHEMISTRY.
Elsevier Science Ltd., Pergamon, P.O. Box 800, Kidlington, Oxford OX5 1DX, England. TEL 44-1865-843000. FAX 44-1865-843010. *720*

PHYTOLOGIA.
c/o Michael J. Warnock, Ed., 185 Westridge Dr., Huntsville, TX 77340. TEL 409-295-5410. FAX 409-291-0009. *720*

PHYTOMA ESPANA.
Agropubli S.L., Blasco Ibanlez 24, 2a, 46010 Valencia, Spain. TEL 6-393-39-49. FAX 6-360-57-79. *239*

PHYTOPARASITICA: ISRAEL JOURNAL OF PLANT PROTECTION SCIENCES.
Priel Publishers, P.O. Box 2385, Rehovot 76123, Israel. TEL 972-8-9365757. FAX 972-8-9365858. *239*

PHYTOPATHOLOGIA POLONICA.
Polskie Towarzystwo Fitopatologiczne, Ul. Wojska Polskiego 71 c, 60-625 Poznan, Poland. TEL 48-61-487713. FAX 48-61-487145. *720*

REFEREED SERIALS

PHYTOPATHOLOGY.
A P S Press, 3340 Pilot Knob Rd., St. Paul, MN 55121-2097. TEL 612-454-7250. FAX 612-454-0766. *721*

PHYTOPROTECTION.
Societe de Protection des Plantes du Quebec, 430 bvd. Gouin, St-Jean-sur-Richelieu, PQ J3B 3E6, Canada. TEL 514-346-4494. FAX 514-346-7740. *239*

PHYTOTHERAPY RESEARCH.
John Wiley & Sons Ltd., Journals, Baffins Ln., Chichester, W. Sussex PO19 1UD, England. TEL 44-1243-779777. FAX 44-1243-775878. *721*

PI MU EPSILON JOURNAL.
Pi Mu Epsilon, c/o Joan Weiss, Fairfield University, Dept. of Mathematics and Computer Science, Fairfield, CT 06430-5195. TEL 203-254-4000 ext.2516. FAX 203-254-4126. *4597*

PICTISH ARTS SOCIETY JOURNAL.
Pictish Arts Society, 27 George Sq., Edinburgh EH8 9LD, Scotland. *3591*

PICTURA NOVA.
N.V. Brepols, Steenweg op Tielen 68, 2300 Turnhout, Belgium. TEL 32-14-402500. FAX 32-14-428919. *460*

PIECEWORK.
Interweave Press, Inc., 201 E. Fourth St., Loveland, CO 80537. TEL 970-669-7672. FAX 970-667-8317. *5453*

PIG IRON.
Pig Iron Press, Box 237, Youngstown, OH 44501. TEL 330-747-6932. *4450*

THE PIG JOURNAL.
Grove International, Southview, E. Tytherton, Chippenhham, Wilts. SN15 41X, England. TEL 44-1249-740380. FAX 44-1380-859222. *7276*

PIGMENT CELL.
S. Karger AG, Allschwilerstr. 10, P.O. Box, CH-4009 Basel, Switzerland. TEL 41-61-3061111. FAX 41-61-3061234. *776*

PIGMENT CELL RESEARCH.
Munksgaard International Publishers Ltd., P.O. Box 2148, DK-1016 Copenhagen K, Denmark. TEL 45-33-127030. FAX 45-33-129387. *743*

PING PONG.
Henry Miller Memorial Library, Highway One, Big Sur, CA 93920. TEL 408-667-2574. FAX 408-667-2574. *4450*

PINTER REVIEW: ANNUAL ESSAYS.
University of Tampa, Box 11F, Tampa, FL 33606. *7011*

PIONEER.
Regional Synod of Canada Inc., Reformed Church in America, R.R. 4, Cambridge, ON N1R 5S5, Canada. TEL 519-622-1777. FAX 519-622-1993. *6437*

PIONEER BRANCHES.
Northeast Washington Genealogical Society, c/o Colville Public Library, 195 S. Oak St., Colville, WA 99114. TEL 509-935-6336. *3237*

PITTSBURGH SERIES IN PHILOSOPHY & HISTORY OF SCIENCE.
University of California Press, 2120 Berkeley Way, Berkeley, CA 94720. TEL 510-642-4247. FAX 510-643-7127. *5745*

PLAINS ANTHROPOLOGIST.
Plains Anthropological Society, c/o Lawrence Tomsyck, 410 Wedgewood Dr., Lincoln, NE 68510. TEL 402-488-3813. *327*

PLAN.
Foereningen foer Samhaellsplanering, Regional Planering, KTH, S-100 44 Stockholm, Sweden. TEL 46-8-790-79-38. FAX 46-8-790-67-61. *3755*

PLAN AMSTERDAM.
Dienst Ruimtelijke Ordening Amsterdam, Voorlichting D R O, Wibautstraat 3, 1091 GH Amsterdam, Netherlands. TEL 31-20-5961645. FAX 31-20-5961307. *3755*

PLANETARY AND SPACE SCIENCE.
Elsevier Science Ltd., Pergamon, P.O. Box 800, Kidlington, Oxford OX5 1DX, England. TEL 44-1865-843000. FAX 44-1865-843010. *499*

PLANKTON BIOLOGY AND ECOLOGY.
Plankton Society of Japan, c/o Laboratory of Aquatic Ecology, Faculty of Agriculture, Tohoku University, 1-1 Amamiya-machi, Tsutsumi-dori, Aoba-ku, Sendai 981, Japan. TEL 81-22-717-8734. FAX 81-22-717-8734. *620*

PLANNING IN LONDON.
Land Research Unit Ltd., The Studio, Crown Reach, 149a Grosvenor Rd., London SW1V 3JY, England. TEL 44-171-834-9471. FAX 44-171-834-9470. *3756*

PLANNING PERSPECTIVES.
Thomson Professional, 2-6 Boundary Row, London SE1 8HN, England. TEL 44-171-8650066. FAX 44-171-5229623. *3508*

PLANNING PRACTICE AND RESEARCH.
Carfax Publishing Co., P.O. Box 25, Abingdon, Oxon. OX14 3UE, England. TEL 44-1235-401000. FAX 44-1235-401550. *3756*

PLANT AND SOIL.
Kluwer Academic Publishers, Postbus 17, 3300 AA Dordrecht, Netherlands. TEL 31-78-6392392. FAX 31-78-6392254. *721*

PLANT CELL.
American Society of Plant Physiologists, 15501 Monona Dr., Rockville, MD 20855. TEL 301-251-0560. FAX 301-279-2996. *722*

PLANT, CELL AND ENVIRONMENT.
Blackwell Science Ltd., Osney Mead, Oxford OX2 OEL, England. TEL 44-1865-206206. FAX 44-1865-721205. *620*

PLANT CELL, TISSUE AND ORGAN CULTURE.
Kluwer Academic Publishers, Postbus 17, 3300 AA Dordrecht, Netherlands. TEL 31-78-6392392. FAX 31-78-6392254. *743*

PLANT DISEASE.
A P S Press, 3340 Pilot Knob Rd., St. Paul, MN 55121-2097. TEL 612-454-7250. FAX 612-454-0766. *240*

PLANT ECOLOGY.
Kluwer Academic Publishers, Postbus 17, 3300 AA Dordrecht, Netherlands. TEL 31-78-6392392. FAX 31-78-6392254. *722*

PLANT FOODS FOR HUMAN NUTRITION.
Kluwer Academic Publishers, Postbus 17, 3300 AA Dordrecht, Netherlands. TEL 31-78-6392392. FAX 31-78-6392254. *5481*

PLANT GROWTH REGULATION.
Kluwer Academic Publishers, Postbus 17, 3300 AA Dordrecht, Netherlands. TEL 31-78-6392392. FAX 31-78-6392254. *722*

THE PLANT JOURNAL FOR CELL AND MOLECULAR BIOLOGY.
Blackwell Science Ltd., Osney Mead, Oxford OX2 OEL, England. TEL 44-1865-206206. FAX 44-1865-721205. *722*

PLANT MOLECULAR BIOLOGY.
Kluwer Academic Publishers, Postbus 17, 3300 AA Dordrecht, Netherlands. TEL 31-78-6392392. FAX 31-78-6392254. *620*

PLANT PATHOLOGY.
Blackwell Science Ltd., Osney Mead, Oxford OX2 OEL, England. TEL 44-1865-206206. FAX 44-1865-721205. *722*

PLANT PHYSIOLOGY.
American Society of Plant Physiologists, 15501 Monona Dr., Rockville, MD 20855. TEL 301-251-0560. FAX 301-279-2996. *723*

PLANT PROTECTION QUARTERLY.
R.G. & F.J. Richardson, Ed. & Pub., P.O. Box 42, Meredith, Vic. 3333, Australia. TEL 61-3-52861533. FAX 61-3-52861533. *240*

PLANT SCIENCE.
Elsevier Science Ireland Ltd., P.O. Box 85, Limerick, Ireland. TEL 353-61-471944. FAX 353-61-472144. *723*

PLANT SPECIES BIOLOGY.
Society for the Study of Species Biology, c/o Kyoto Daigaku Rigakubu, Shokubutsugaku Kyoshitsu, Oiwakecho, Kitashirakawa, Sakyo-ku, Kyoto 606, Japan. TEL 81-75-753-4131. FAX 81-75-753-4145. *723*

PLANT TISSUE CULTURE.
Bangladesh Association for Plant Tissue Culture, University of Dhaka, Department of Botany, Dhaka-1000, Bangladesh. TEL 880-2-506378. FAX 880-2-865583. *723*

PLANT VARIETIES AND SEEDS.
National Institute of Agricultural Botany, Huntingdon Rd., Cambridge CB3 OLE, England. TEL 44-1223-276381. FAX 44-1223-277602. *240*

THE PLANTAGENET CONNECTION.
Heliotrope Communications, Box 1401, Arvada, CO 80001. TEL 303-657-2723. *3591*

PLANTER.
Incorporated Society of Planters, P.O. Box 10262, 50708 Kuala Lumpur, Malaysia. TEL 60-3-242-5561. FAX 60-3-242-6898. *146*

PLASMA CHEMISTRY & PLASMA PROCESSING.
Plenum Publishing Corp., 233 Spring St., New York, NY 10013-1578. TEL 212-620-8000. FAX 212-463-0742. *2770*

PLASMA DEVICES AND OPERATIONS.
Gordon and Breach - Harwood Academic, Amsteldisk 166, 1st Fl., 1079 LH Amsterdam, Netherlands. *5822*

PLASMA PHYSICS AND CONTROLLED FUSION.
I O P Publishing Ltd., Dirac House, Temple Back, Bristol BS1 6BE, England. TEL 44-117-929-7481. FAX 44-117-929-4318. *5822*

PLASMA SOURCES SCIENCE AND TECHNOLOGY.
I O P Publishing Ltd., Dirac House, Temple Back, Bristol BS1 6BE, England. TEL 44-117-929-7481. FAX 44-117-929-4318. *5822*

PLASMA TECHNOLOGY.
Elsevier Science B.V., Books Division, P.O. Box 211, 1000 AE Amsterdam, Netherlands. TEL 31-20-4853911. FAX 31-20-4853705. *5822*

PLASMAS AND POLYMERS.
Plenum Publishing Corp., 233 Spring St., New York, NY 10013-1578. TEL 212-620-8000. FAX 212-463-0742. *1820*

PLASMID.
Academic Press, Inc., Journal Division, 525 B St., Ste. 1900, San Diego, CA 92101-4495. TEL 619-230-1840. FAX 619-699-6800. *620*

PLASTIC AND RECONSTRUCTIVE SURGERY.
Williams & Wilkins, 351 W. Camden St., Baltimore, MD 21201-2436. TEL 410-528-4068. FAX 410-528-4452. *5151*

PLASTICS ENGINEERING SERIES.
Marcel Dekker, Inc., 270 Madison Ave., New York, NY 10016. TEL 212-696-9000. FAX 212-685-4540. *5882*

PLASTICS IN BUILDING CONSTRUCTION.
Technomic Publishing Co., Inc., 851 New Holland Ave., Box 3535, Lancaster, PA 17604. TEL 717-291-5609. FAX 717-295-45388. *908*

PLASTICS NEWS.
All India Plastics Manufacturers Association, A-52, Street No. 1, M.I.D.C., Marol, Andheri (East), Mumbai 400 093, India. TEL 91-22-8217324. FAX 91-22-8216390. *5883*

PLASTICS, RUBBER & COMPOSITES PROCESSING AND APPLICATIONS.
Institute of Materials, 1 Carlton House Terr., London SW1Y 5DB, England. TEL 44-171-839-4071. FAX 44-171-839-2078. *5883*

PLASTICULTURE.
Comite International des Plastiques en Agriculture, 65 rue de Prony, 75854 Paris Cedex 17, France. TEL 33-1-44011649. FAX 33-1-44011655. *5884*

PLAYTIMES.
Playgroup Association of Queensland, 396 Milton Rd., Auchenflower, Qld. 4066, Australia. TEL 61-7-3718253. FAX 61-7-8700569. *1854*

PLEIN SOLEIL.
Association Diabete Quebec Inc., 5635 rue Sherbrooke E., Montreal, PQ H1N 1A2, Canada. TEL 514-259-3422. FAX 514-259-9286. *4891*

THE PLOUGH.
Plough Publishing House, Spring Valley Bruderhof, R.D. 2, Box 446, Farmington, PA 15437. TEL 412-329-1100. FAX 412-329-0914. *6437*

POD WIATR.
Agencja Wydawniczo-Reklamowa M T, Ul. Zmudzka 5-29, 85-028 Bydgoszcz, Poland. TEL 48-52-421546. FAX 48-52-421546. *1883*

POET.
World Poetry Society Intercontinental, c/o Dr. Krishna Srinivas, Ed., 118 Raja St., Madras 600 042, India. TEL 91-44-2350186. *4518*

POETCRIT.
Poetcrit, c/o D.C. Chambial, Ed., Maranda 176 102, India. TEL 91-1894-31407. *4518*

POETICA.
Shubun International Co., Ltd., 12-7, 4-chome Komagome, Toshima-ku, Tokyo 170, Japan. TEL 81-3-3915-0800. FAX 81-3-3915-8290. *4289*

POETICS.
North-Holland, P.O. Box 211, 1000 AE Amsterdam, Netherlands. TEL 31-20-4853911. FAX 31-20-4853598. *4451*

POETICS TODAY.
Duke University Press, Box 90660, Durham, NC 27708-0660. TEL 919-687-3600. FAX 919-688-4574. *4353*

POETRIX.
Western Women Writers, P.O. Box 479, Footscray, Vic. 3011, Australia. TEL 61-3-93141082. FAX 61-3-93141082. *4519*

POETRY.
Poetry Publications, Jasnal, 2nd Fl., Old Christian St., Berhampur 760 001, India. *4519*

POETRY MOTEL.
1911 E. First St., Duluth, MN 55812-1723. *4519*

POETRY: U S A QUARTERLY.
National Poetry Association, Inc., 934 Brannan St., 2nf Fl., San Francisco, CA 94103. TEL 415-552-9261. FAX 415-552-9271. *4520*

POKROF.
Aktie en Ontmoeting Oosterse Kerken, Dr. Nuijensstraat 4, 5014 RL Tilburg, Netherlands. TEL 31-13-5368985. FAX 31-13-5439510. *6392*

POKROKY MATEMATIKY, FYZIKY A ASTRONOMIE.
Jednota Ceskych Matematiku a Fyziku, Zitna 25, 117 10 Prague 1, Czech Republic. TEL 420-2-24213973. FAX 420-2-24227633. *6559*

POLAR RESEARCH.
Norwegian Polar Institute, Middelthuns gate 29, P.O. Box 5072 Majorstua, N-0301 Oslo, Norway. TEL 47-22-95-95-00. FAX 47-22-95-95-01. *6559*

POLARFORSCHUNG.
Deutsche Gesellschaft fuer Polarforschung e.V., c/o Alfred-Wegener-Institut fuer Polar- und Meeresforschung, Postfach 120161, 27515 Bremerhaven, Germany. TEL 49-471-4831200. FAX 49-471-4831149. *2320*

POLEN.
Includes original papers on palynology and aerobiology., Avda. de San Alberto Magno s-n, 14004 Cordoba, Spain. TEL 57-218599. FAX 57-218598. *724*

POLESTAR.
42 St. Peter's Court, Rock Ferry, Merseyside L42 1PF, England. TEL 44-151-645-7185. FAX 44-151-645-7185. *2473*

POLICING AND SOCIETY.
Gordon and Breach - Harwood Academic, Amsteldisk 166, 1st Fl., 1079 LH Amsterdam, Netherlands. *2276*

POLICY.
Centre for Independent Studies, Box 92, St. Leonards, N.S.W. 2065, Australia. TEL 61-2-94384377. FAX 61-2-94397310. *992*

POLICY ANALYSIS RESEARCH UNIT. DISCUSSION PAPER.
Glasgow Caledonian University, Policy Analysis Research Unit, Cowcaddens Rd., Glasgow G4 0BA, Scotland. TEL 0141-331-3319. FAX 0141-331-3293. *6188*

POLICY AND POLITICS.
The Policy Press, Rodney Lodge, Grange Rd., Bristol, Avon BS8 4EA, England. TEL 44-117-9741117. FAX 44-117-9737308. *3756*

POLICY FORUM.
University of Illinois at Urbana-Champaign, Institute of Government and Public Affairs, 1007 W. Nevada St., Urbana, IL 61801. TEL 217-333-3340. FAX 217-244-4817. *6188*

POLICY SCIENCES.
Kluwer Academic Publishers, Postbus 17, 3300 AA Dordrecht, Netherlands. TEL 31-78-6392392. FAX 31-78-6392254. *5956*

POLIMERY W MEDYCYNIE.
Akademia Medyczna we Wroclawiu, Zaklad Chirurgii Eksperymentalnej i Badania Biomaterialow, Ul. Poniatowskiego 2, 50-326 Wroclaw, Poland. TEL 48-71-226310. FAX 48-71-215729. *1820*

POLISH ACADEMY OF SCIENCES. BULLETIN. BIOLOGICAL SCIENCES.
Polska Akademia Nauk, Centrum Upowszechniania Nauki, Palac Kultury i Nauki, Pietro XXIII, pok.23-10, 00-901 Warsaw, Poland. *620*

POLISH ACADEMY OF SCIENCES. BULLETIN. CHEMISTRY.
Polska Akademia Nauk, Centrum Upowszechniania Nauki, Palac Kultury i Nauki, Pietro XXIII, pok.23-10, 00-901 Warsaw, Poland. *1762*

POLISH ACADEMY OF SCIENCES. BULLETIN. MATHEMATICS.
Polska Akademia Nauk, Centrum Upowszechniania Nauki, Palac Kultury i Nauki, Pietro XXIII, pok.23-10, 00-901 Warsaw, Poland. *4597*

POLISH ACADEMY OF SCIENCES. BULLETIN. TECHNICAL SCIENCES.
Polska Akademia Nauk, Centrum Upowszechniania Nauki, Palac Kultury i Nauki, Pietro XXIII, pok.23-10, 00-901 Warsaw, Poland. *6970*

POLISH BOTANICAL STUDIES.
Polska Akademia Nauk, Instytut Botaniki im. W. Szafera, Ul. Lubicz 46, 31-512 Krakow, Poland. TEL 48-12-215144. FAX 48-12-219790. *724*

POLISH BOTANICAL STUDIES. GUIDEBOOK SERIES.
Polska Akademia Nauk, Instytut Botaniki im. W. Szafera, Ul. Lubicz 46, 31-512 Krakow, Poland. TEL 48-12-215144. FAX 48-12-219790. *724*

POLISH JOURNAL OF FOOD AND NUTRITION SCIENCES.
Polska Akademia Nauk, Instytut Rozrodu Zwierzat i Badan Zywnosci, Ul. J. Tuwima 10, 10-718 Olsztyn-Kortowo, Poland. TEL 48-89-5237670. FAX 48-89-5237824. *3123*

POLISH JOURNAL OF PATHOLOGY.
Polskie Towarzystwo Patologow, Ul. Grzegorzecka 16, 31-531 Krakow, Poland. TEL 48-12-211564. FAX 48-12-215210. *4787*

POLISH LIBRARIES TODAY.
Biblioteka Narodowa, Zespol Redakcji Czasopism, Al. Niepodleglosci 213, 00-973 Warsaw, Poland. TEL 48-22-6082252. FAX 48-22-255251. *4206*

POLISH MUSIC HISTORY SERIES.
Friends of Polish Music, University of Southern California, School of Music, Los Angeles, CA 90089-0851. TEL 213-877-1906. FAX 818-509-8435. *5426*

POLISH REVIEW.
Polish Institute of Arts and Sciences of America, Inc., 208 E. 30th St., New York, NY 10016. TEL 212-686-4164. FAX 212-545-1130. *3349*

POLITICAL AND ECONOMIC REVIEW.
University of Limerick, Limerick, Ireland. TEL 353-61-202670. FAX 353-61-202572. *5957*

POLITICAL BEHAVIOR.
Plenum Publishing Corp., 233 Spring St., New York, NY 10013-1578. TEL 212-620-8000. FAX 212-463-0742. *5957*

POLITICAL CHRONICLE.
Florida Political Science Association, St. Leo College, Institute of Political Science, Box 2127, Saint Leo, FL 33574. *5957*

POLITICAL COMMUNICATION.
Taylor & Francis Inc., 1900 Frost Rd., Ste. 101, Bristol, PA 19007. TEL 215-785-5800. FAX 215-785-5515. *5957*

POLITICAL CROSSROADS.
James Nicholas Publishers, P.O. Box 244, Albert Park, Vic. 3206, Australia. TEL 61-3-6965545. FAX 61-3-6992040. *5957*

POLITICAL GEOGRAPHY.
Elsevier Science Ltd., Pergamon, P.O. Box 800, Kidlington, Oxford OX5 1DX, England. TEL 44-1865-843000. FAX 44-1865-843010. *5957*

POLITICAL PSYCHOLOGY.
Blackwell Publishers, 238 Main St., Cambridge, MA 02142. TEL 617-547-7110. FAX 617-547-0789. *5957*

POLITICAL QUARTERLY.
Blackwell Publishers Ltd., 108 Cowley Rd., Oxford OX4 1JF, England. TEL 44-1865-791100. FAX 44-1865-791347. *5958*

POLITICAL RESEARCH QUARTERLY.
University of Utah, 252 Orson Spencer Hall, Salt Lake City, UT 84112. *5958*

POLITICAL SCIENCE QUARTERLY.
Academy of Political Science, 475 Riverside Dr., Ste. 1274, New York, NY 10115-1274. TEL 212-870-2500. FAX 212-870-2202. *5958*

POLITICAL STUDIES.
Blackwell Publishers Ltd., 108 Cowley Rd., Oxford OX4 1JF, England. TEL 44-1865-791100. FAX 44-1865-791347. *5958*

POLITICAL THEORY NEWSLETTER.
Australian National University, Research School of Social Sciences, Canberra, A.C.T. 0200, Australia. TEL 61-6-2492120. FAX 61-6-2493051. *5958*

POLITICKA EKONOMIE.
Vysoka Skola Ekonomicka, Nam. W. Churchilla 4, 130 67 Prague 3, Czech Republic. TEL 42-2-24095819. FAX 42-2-24220675. *992*

POLITICS.
Blackwell Publishers Ltd., 108 Cowley Rd., Oxford OX4 1JF, England. TEL 44-1865-791100. FAX 44-1865-791347. *5959*

POLITICS AND SOCIETY.
Sage Publications, Inc., 2455 Teller Rd., Thousand Oaks, CA 91320. TEL 805-499-0721. FAX 805-499-0871. *5959*

POLITICS AND THE LIFE SCIENCES.
Beech Tree Publishing, 10 Watford Close, Guildford, Surrey GU1 2EP, England. TEL 44-1483-567497. FAX 44-1483-567497. *4731*

POLITIK UND GESELLSCHAFT. WUERZBURGER UNIVERSITAETSSCHRIFTEN.
Ergon Verlag, Grombuehlstr. 7, 97080 Wuerzburg, Germany. TEL 49-931-280084. FAX 49-931-282872. *5959*

POLITIKON.
Staatkundige Vereniging van Suid Afrika, P.O. Box 1041, Florida 1710, South Africa. FAX 27-11-7825500. *5959*

POLITIQUE AFRICAINE.
Editions Karthala, 22-24 Bd. Arago, 75013 Paris, France. TEL 33-1-43311559. FAX 33-1-45352705. *5959*

POLITYKA.
Spoldzielnia Pracy "Polityka", Miedziana 11, 00-835 Warsaw, Poland. TEL 48-22-635-3491. FAX 48-22-635-1797. *3349*

POLLUTION ATMOSPHERIQUE.
Association pour la Prevention de la Pollution Atmospherique, 58 rue du Rocher, 75008 Paris, France. TEL 33-1-42936930. FAX 33-1-42934199. *2971*

POLSKI PRZEGLAD CHIRURGICZNY.
Fundacja Polski Przeglad Chirurgiczny, Ul. Nowiniarska 1 m 28, 00-235 Warsaw, Poland. FAX 48-22-6354531. *5151*

POLSKIE PISMO ENTOMOLOGICZNE.
Polskie Towarzystwo Entomologiczne, Ul. Sienkiewicza 21, 50-335 Wroclaw, Poland. TEL 48-71-225041. *759*

POLSKIE TOWARZYSTWO JEZYKOZNAWCZE. BIULETYN.
Wydawnictwo Energia, sp. z o.o., Ul. Szturmowa 1, 02-678 Warsaw, Poland. TEL 48-22-470053. *4289*

POLYCYCLIC AROMATIC COMPOUNDS.
Gordon and Breach - Harwood Academic, Amsteldisk 166, 1st Fl., 1079 LH Amsterdam, Netherlands. *1821*

POLYHEDRON.
Elsevier Science Ltd., Pergamon, P.O. Box 800, Kidlington, Oxford OX5 1DX, England. TEL 44-1865-843000. FAX 44-1865-843010. *1809*

POLYMER.
Elsevier Science Ltd., Part of the Reed Elsevier group, Langford Ln., Kidlington, Oxford OX5 3DR, England. TEL 44-1865-843000. FAX 44-1865-843010. *1821*

POLYMER BLENDS, ALLOYS AND INTERPENETRATING POLYMER NETWORKS ABSTRACTS.
Technomic Publishing Co., Inc., 851 New Holland Ave., Box 3535, Lancaster, PA 17604. TEL 717-291-5609. FAX 717-295-4538. *1785*

POLYMER CONTENTS.
Elsevier Science Ltd., P.O. Box 800, Kidlington, Oxford OX5 1DX, England. TEL 44-1865-843000. FAX 44-1865-843010. *2751*

POLYMER DEGRADATION AND STABILITY.
Elsevier Science Ltd., P.O. Box 800, Kidlington, Oxford OX5 1DX, England. TEL 44-1865-843000. FAX 44-1865-843010. *1821*

POLYMER ENGINEERING AND SCIENCE.
Society of Plastics Engineers, Inc., 14 Fairfield Dr., Box 403, Brookfield, CT 06804-0403. TEL 203-775-0471. FAX 203-775-8490. *2771*

POLYMER GELS AND NETWORKS.
Elsevier Science Ltd., P.O. Box 800, Kidlington, Oxford OX5 1DX, England. TEL 44-1865-843000. FAX 44-1865-843010. *2771*

POLYMER INTERNATIONAL.
John Wiley & Sons Ltd., Journals, Baffins Ln., Chichester, W. Sussex PO19 1UD, England. TEL 44-1243-779777. FAX 44-1243-775878. *5884*

POLYMER MONOGRAPHS.
Gordon and Breach - Harwood Academic, Amsteldisk 166, 1st Fl., 1079 LH Amsterdam, Netherlands. *1821*

POLYMER NEWS.
Gordon and Breach - Harwood Academic, Amsteldisk 166, 1st Fl., 1079 LH Amsterdam, Netherlands. *1821*

POLYMER-PLASTICS TECHNOLOGY AND ENGINEERING.
Marcel Dekker Journals, 270 Madison Ave., New York, NY 10016. TEL 212-696-9000. FAX 212-685-4540. *1821*

POLYMER REACTION ENGINEERING.
Marcel Dekker, Inc., 270 Madison Ave., New York, NY 10016. TEL 212-696-9000. FAX 212-685-4540. *2771*

POLYMER SCIENCE.
Maik Nauka - Interperiodica, Mezhdunarodnyi Otdel, Ul. Profsoyuznaya, 90, 117864 Moscow, Russia. TEL 7-095-3360066. FAX 7-095-3360666. *1821*

POLYMER SCIENCE AND TECHNOLOGY.
Plenum Publishing Corp., 233 Spring St., New York, NY 10013-1578. TEL 212-620-8000. FAX 212-463-0742. *1821*

POLYMER SCIENCE LIBRARY.
Elsevier Science B.V., Books Division, P.O. Box 211, 1000 AE Amsterdam, Netherlands. TEL 31-20-4853911. FAX 31-20-4853705. *1763*

POLYMER TESTING.
Elsevier Science Ltd., P.O. Box 800, Kidlington, OX5 1DX, England. TEL 44-1865-843000. FAX 44-1865-843010. *5884*

POLYMER THERAPEUTICS.
I O S Press, Van Diemenstraat 94, 1013 CN Amsterdam, Netherlands. TEL 31-20-6382189. FAX 31-20-6203419. *5690*

POLYMER YEARBOOK.
Gordon and Breach - Harwood Academic, Amsteldisk 166, 1st Fl., 1079 LH Amsterdam, Netherlands. *1763*

POLYMERIC MATERIALS SCIENCE AND ENGINEERING.
American Chemical Society, Division of Polymeric Materials Science & Engineering, 1155 16th St., N.W., Washington, DC 20036. *1822*

POLYMERS AND POLYMER COMPOSITES.
Rapra Technology Ltd., Shawbury, Shrewsbury, Shrops. SY4 4NR, England. TEL 44-1939-250383. FAX 44-1939-251118. *5885*

POLYTECHNICAL UNIVERSITY OF BUCHAREST. SCIENTIFIC BULLETIN. SERIES A: APPLIED MATHEMATICS AND PHYSICS.
Universitatea Politehnica Bucuresti, Biblioteca Centrala, Splaiul Independentei 313, 77206 Bucharest 16, Rumania. TEL 40-1-6317185. FAX 40-1-3120188. *4598*

POME NEWS.
Home Orchard Society, Box 230192, Tigard, OR 97281-0192. TEL 503-293-1468. *3202*

POMPEBLEDEN.
Stichting Algemiene Fryske Underrjocht Kommisje, P.B. 53, 8900 AB Leeuwarden, Netherlands. TEL 31-58-2138045. FAX 31-58-2159475. *4289*

POPULAR CULTURE IN LIBRARIES.
Haworth Press, Inc., 10 Alice St., Binghamton, NY 13904. TEL 607-722-5857. FAX 607-722-6362. *4206*

POPULATION AND ENVIRONMENT.
Human Sciences Press, Inc., 233 Spring St., New York, NY 10013-1578. TEL 212-620-8000. FAX 212-463-0742. *6141*

POPULATION RESEARCH AND POLICY REVIEW.
Kluwer Academic Publishers, Postbus 17, 3300 AA Dordrecht, Netherlands. TEL 31-78-6392392. FAX 31-78-6392254. *6056*

PORTICUS.
University of Rochester, Memorial Art Gallery, 500 University Ave., Rochester, NY 14607. TEL 716-473-7720. FAX 716-473-6266. *5364*

PORTLAND PRESS PROCEEDINGS.
Portland Press Ltd., 59 Portland Pl., London W1N 3AJ, England. TEL 44-171-580-5530. FAX 44-171-323-1136. *4901*

PORTLAND PRESS RESEARCH MONOGRAPH.
Portland Press Ltd., 59 Portland Pl., London W1N 3AJ, England. TEL 44-171-580-5530. FAX 44-171-323-1136. *669*

PORTUGUESE STUDIES REVIEW.
International Conference Group on Portugal, Univ. of New Hampshire, Dept. of History, HSCC 408, Durham, NH 03824. TEL 603-862-3018. FAX 603-868-6935. *3788*

POSITIVE OUTLOOK.
AIDS Training, Information & Counselling Centre (ATICC), 42 Havelock Rd., Pietermaritzburg 3201, South Africa. TEL 27-331-942111. FAX 27-331-423245. *4842*

POSITIVITY.
Kluwer Academic Publishers, Postbus 17, 3300 AA Dordrecht, Netherlands. TEL 31-78-6392392. FAX 31-78-6392254. *4598*

POST-MEDIEVAL ARCHAEOLOGY.
Society for Post-Medieval Archaeology, c/o Dr. Paul Courtney, 20 Lytton Rd., Leicester LE2 1WJ, England. TEL 44-1533-707999. *378*

POST SCRIPT (COMMERCE).
Post Script, Inc., Department of Literature and Languages, Texas A & M University, Commerce, TX 75429. TEL 903-886-5260. FAX 903-886-5980. *3788*

POSTEPY ASTRONOMII.
Polskie Towarzystwo Astronomiczne, Ul. Bartycka 18, 00-716 Warsaw, Poland. TEL 48-22-410041. FAX 48-22-410046. *499*

POSTEPY BIOLOGII KOMORKI.
Fundacja Postepu Biologii Komorki, Ul. Marymoncka 99, 01-813 Warsaw, Poland. TEL 48-22-340344. FAX 48-22-370470. *743*

POSTGRADUATE MEDICINE.
McGraw-Hill Companies (Minneapolis), 4530 W. 77th St., Minneapolis, 609-426-7070, MN 55435. TEL 609-426-7070. FAX 612-835-3460. *4732*

POSTHARVEST BIOLOGY AND TECHNOLOGY.
Elsevier Science B.V., P.O. Box 211, 1000 AE Amsterdam, Netherlands. TEL 31-20-4853911. FAX 31-20-4853598. *686*

POSTHORN.
Scandinavian Collectors Club, 2316 Lakeview Dr., Fergus Falls, MN 56537-3903. TEL 218-739-3260. *5712*

POTENTIAL ANALYSIS.
Kluwer Academic Publishers, Postbus 17, 3300 AA Dordrecht, Netherlands. TEL 31-78-6392392. FAX 31-78-6392254. *4598*

POTPOURRI.
Potpourri Publications, Box 8278, Prairie Village, KS 66208. TEL 913-642-1503. FAX 913-642-3128. *4354*

POULTRY AND AVIAN BIOLOGY REVIEWS.
Science and Technology Letters, P.O. Box 81, Northwood, Middlesex HA6 3DY, England. TEL 44-1923-823586. FAX 44-1923-825066. *285*

POULTRY SCIENCE SYMPOSIUM SERIES.
Carfax Publishing Co., P.O. Box 25, Abingdon, Oxon. OX14 3UE, England. TEL 44-1235-401000. FAX 44-1235-401550. *286*

POVIJESNI PRILOZI.
Institut za Suvremenu Povijest, Opaticka 10, 41000 Zagreb, Croatia. *3508*

POWDER TECHNOLOGY.
Elsevier Science S.A., P.O. Box 564, CH-1001 Lausanne 1, Switzerland. TEL 41-21-3207381. FAX 41-21-3235444. *2771*

POWER (NEW YORK).
McGraw-Hill Companies, 1221 Ave. of the Americas, New York, NY 10020. TEL 212-512-2000. *2898*

POWER INTERNATIONAL.
Lincoln Publications, 28 Centre Point House, St. Giles High St., London WC2H 8LW, England. TEL 44-171-240-5562. FAX 44-171-497-2811. *2676*

POWYS NOTES.
Powys Society of North America, 205 E. 10th St., New York, NY 10003. *4452*

POWYS REVIEW.
c/o Belinda Humfrey, Ed., Department of English, University of Wales, Lampeter, Dyfed SA48 7ED, Wales. TEL 44-1570-424764. FAX 44-1570-423634. *4452*

POZNAN STUDIES IN THE PHILOSOPHY OF THE SCIENCES AND THE HUMANITIES.
Editions Rodopi B.V., Keizersgracht 302-304, 1016 EX Amsterdam, Netherlands. TEL 31-20-6227507. FAX 31-20-6380948. *5745*

PRACHYA PRATIBHA.
Birla Institute of Art and Music, Prachya Niketan, Birla Museum, P.O. Vallabh Bhavan, Bhopal 462004, India. TEL 0755-551388. *5536*

PRACOVNI LEKARSTVI.
Nakladatelske Stredisko C L S J.E. Purkyne, Sokolska 31, 120 26 Prague 2, Czech Republic. TEL 420-2-24911420. FAX 420-2-24911420. *4732*

PRACTICAL DIABETOLOGY.
R.A. Rapaport Publishing, Inc., 150 W. 22nd St., New York, NY 10011. TEL 212-989-0200. FAX 212-989-4786. *4891*

PRACTICAL GASTROENTEROLOGY.
Shugar Publishing, 12 Moniebogue Lane, Westhampton Beach, NY 11978. *4914*

PRACTICAL METHODS IN ELECTRON MICROSCOPY.
Elsevier Science B.V., Books Division, P.O. Box 211, 1000 AE Amsterdam, Netherlands. TEL 31-20-4853911. FAX 31-20-4853705. *798*

THE PRACTICAL REAL ESTATE LAWYER.
American Law Institute - American Bar Association, Committee on Continuing Professional Education, 4025 Chestnut St., Philadelphia, PA 19104. TEL 215-243-1604. FAX 215-243-1664. *4009*

PRACTICAL SPECTROSCOPY SERIES.
Marcel Dekker, Inc., 270 Madison Ave., New York, NY 10016. TEL 212-696-9000. FAX 212-685-4540. *1795*

PRACTITIONER'S HANDBOOKS ON THE WORLD COURT.
Kluwer Law International, Postbus 85889, 2508 CN The Hague, Netherlands. TEL 31-70-3081500. FAX 31-70-3081515. *4124*

PRAESENTATIONSHAEFTE.
Danske Sprog- og Litteraturselskab, Frederiksholms Kanal 18 A, DK-1220 Copenhagen K, Denmark. TEL 45-33-13-06-60. FAX 45-33-14-06-08. *4452*

PRAGMATICS & COGNITION.
John Benjamins Publishing Co., Amsteldijk 44, P.O. Box 75577, 1070 AN Amsterdam, Netherlands. TEL 31-20-6738156. FAX 31-20-6792956. *4321*

PRAGUE CONFERENCE ON INFORMATION THEORY, STATISTICAL DECISION FUNCTIONS, RANDOM PROCESSES. TRANSACTIONS.
Kluwer Academic Publishers, Postbus 17, 3300 AA Dordrecht, Netherlands. TEL 31-78-6392392. FAX 31-78-6392254. *2185*

PRAGUE ECONOMIC PAPERS.
Vysoka Skola Ekonomicka, Nam. W. Churchilla 4, 130 67 Prague 3, Czech Republic. TEL 42-2-24095819. FAX 42-2-24220657. *992*

PRAIRIE FORUM.
Canadian Plains Research Center, University of Regina, Regina, SK S4S 0A2, Canada. TEL 306-585-4795. FAX 306-585-4699. *2947*

PRAIRIE NATURALIST.
Noth Dakota Natural Science Society, Division of Biological Sciences, Box 4050, Emporia State University, Emporia, KS 66801. TEL 316-341-5612. *621*

PRAJNAN (PUNE).
National Institute of Bank Management, NIBM Post Office, Kondhwe Khurd, Pune 411 048, India. TEL 91-212-673080. FAX 91-212-674478. *1161*

PRAKTICKE ZUBNI LEKARSTVI.
Nakladatelske Stredisko C L S J.E. Purkyne, Sokolska 31, 120 26 Prague 2, Czech Republic. TEL 420-2-24911420. FAX 420-2-24911420. *4868*

PRAKTICKY LEKAR.
Nakladatelske Stredisko C L S J.E. Purkyne, Sokolska 31, 120 26 Prague 2, Czech Republic. TEL 420-2-24911420. FAX 420-2-24911420. *4732*

PRAXISREPORT PSYCHOLOGISCHE THERAPIEN UND PSYCHOTHERAPIEN.
Psychomedia Verlags GmbH, Postfach 465, 12214 Berlin, Germany. TEL 49-30-4927200. FAX 49-30-7749176. *6141*

PRE- AND PERI-NATAL PSYCHOLOGY JOURNAL.
Human Sciences Press, Inc., 233 Spring St., New York, NY 10013-1578. TEL 212-620-8000. FAX 212-463-0742. *4965*

PRE-VUE ENTERTAINMENT MAGAZINE.
National Pre-Vue Network, 7825 Fay Ave., La Jolla, CA 92037. TEL 619-456-5577. FAX 619-542-0114. *5342*

PRECAMBRIAN RESEARCH.
Elsevier Science B.V., P.O. Box 211, 1000 AE Amsterdam, Netherlands. TEL 31-20-4853911. FAX 31-20-4853598. *2364*

PRECISION ENGINEERING.
Elsevier Science Inc., Box 945, New York, NY 10159-0945. TEL 212-633-3730. FAX 212-633-3680. *2737*

PREHISTORIC SOCIETY, LONDON. PROCEEDINGS.
Prehistoric Society, Institute of Archaeology, 31-34 Gordon Sq., London WC1H 0PY, England. *378*

PREHOSPITAL EMERGENCY CARE.
Hanley & Belfus, Inc., 210 S. 13th St., Philadelphia, PA 19107. TEL 215-546-7293. FAX 215-790-9330. *5015*

PRENATAL AND NEONATAL MEDICINE.
Parthenon Publishing Group, Casterton Hall, Carnforth, Lancs. LA6 2LA, England. TEL 44-152-427-2084. FAX 44-152-427-1587. *4966*

PRENATAL DIAGNOSIS.
John Wiley & Sons Ltd., Journals, Baffins Ln., Chichester, W. Sussex PO19 1UD, England. TEL 44-1243-779777. FAX 44-1243-775878. *4966*

PRENSA DEL RIOJA.
Chile 9, 1o, 26005 Logrono, Spain. TEL 34-41-221968. FAX 34-41-223110. *526*

PREPARATIVE BIOCHEMISTRY AND BIOTECHNOLOGY.
Marcel Dekker Journals, 270 Madison Ave., New York, NY 10016. TEL 212-696-9000. FAX 212-685-4540. *669*

PREPUBLICATIONS.
Universite d'Aarhus, Institut d'Etudes Romanes, Niels Juels gade 84, DK-8200 Aarhus N, Denmark. TEL 45-89-42-19-39. FAX 45-86-16-38-61. *4290*

PRESBYTERIAN NEWSLETTER.
Presbyterian Communication Department, B.P. 19, Buea, Cameroon. TEL 237-32-22-77. FAX 237-32-23-13. *6438*

PRESBYTERIAN SUN.
Synod of the Sun, 920 S. I-35 E., Denton, TX 76205-7898. *6438*

PRESCRIBER.
A & M Publishing Ltd., Alexandra House, First Fl., 1-5 Alexandra Terr., Guildford, Surrey GU1 3DA, England. TEL 44-1483-34888. FAX 44-1483-33316. *5690*

PRESCRIBER'S LETTER.
Therapeutic Research Center, 2453 Grand Canal Blvd., Ste. A, Box 8190, Stockton, CA 95208. TEL 209-472-2240. FAX 209-472-2249. *5690*

PRESCRIBING REFERENCE FOR OBSTETRICIANS AND GYNECOLOGISTS.
Prescribing Reference, Inc., 53 Park Pl., Ste. 1010, New York, NY 10007. TEL 212-766-7200. FAX 212-732-2360. *5690*

PRESCRIBING REFERENCE FOR PEDIATRICIANS.
Prescribing Reference, Inc., 53 Park Pl., Ste. 1010, New York, NY 10007. TEL 212-766-7200. FAX 212-732-2360. *5690*

PRESCRIRE INTERNATIONAL.
Association Mieux Prescrire, B.P. 459, 75527 Paris Cedex 11, France. TEL 33-1-47009445. FAX 33-1-48078732. *5691*

PRESIDENTIAL STUDIES QUARTERLY.
Center for the Study of the Presidency, 208 E. 75th St., New York, NY 10021. TEL 212-249-1200. FAX 212-628-9503. *5961*

LA PRESSE MEDICALE.
Masson - Periodiques, 120 bd. St. Germain, 75006 Paris, France. TEL 33-1-40466200. FAX 33-1-40466201. *4732*

PREVENTING SCHOOL FAILURE.
Heldref Publications, 1319 Eighteenth St., N.W., Washington, DC 20036-1802. TEL 202-296-6267. FAX 202-296-5149. *2588*

PREVENTIVE MEDICINE.
Academic Press, Inc., Journal Division, 525 B St., Ste. 1900, San Diego, CA 92101-4495. TEL 619-230-1840. FAX 619-699-6800. *4733*

PREVENTIVE VETERINARY MEDICINE.
Elsevier Science B.V., P.O. Box 211, 1000 AE Amsterdam, Netherlands. TEL 31-20-4853911. FAX 31-20-4853598. *7277*

PREVIEWS OF HEAT AND MASS TRANSFER.
Rumford Publishing Co., Inc., Box 5370, Chicago, IL 60680. *2752*

PRIMARY CARDIOLOGY.
P W Communications, Inc., 400 Plaza Dr., Secaucus, NJ 07094. TEL 201-865-7500. *4823*

PRIMARY CARE UPDATE FOR OB - GYNS.
Elsevier Science Inc., Box 945, New York, NY 10159-0945. TEL 212-633-3730. FAX 212-633-3680. *4966*

PRIMARY FILE.
Primary File Publishing, 61 Gray's Inn Rd., London WC1X 8TZ, England. TEL 44-171-404-2776. FAX 44-171-404-2766. *2615*

PRIMARY SCIENCE REVIEW.
Association for Science Education., College Ln., Hatfield, Herts. AL10 9AA, England. TEL 44-1707-267411. FAX 44-1707-266532. *6560*

PRIMARY SENSORY NEURON.
V S P, P.O. Box 346, 3700 AH Zeist, Netherlands. TEL 31-30-6925790. FAX 31-30-6932081. *5090*

PRIMARY SOURCES & ORIGINAL WORKS.
Haworth Press, Inc., 10 Alice St., Binghamton, NY 13904. TEL 607-722-5857. FAX 607-722-6362. *4207*

PRIMARY SOURCES IN PHENOMENOLOGY.
Kluwer Academic Publishers, Postbus 17, 3300 AA Dordrecht, Netherlands. TEL 31-78-6392392. FAX 31-78-6392254. *5746*

PRIMUS.
U.S. Military Academy, Department of Mathematics, West Point, NY 10996-9902. TEL 914-938-3200. FAX 914-938-2409. *4598*

PRINCETON HISTORY.
Historical Society of Princeton, 158 Nassau St., Princeton, NJ 08542. TEL 609-921-6748. *3643*

PRINCETON MATHEMATICAL SERIES.
Princeton University Press, 41 William St., Princeton, NJ 08540. TEL 609-258-4900. FAX 609-258-6305. *4598*

THE PRINCETON PAPERS.
Markus Wiener Publishers, Inc., 114 Jefferson Rd., Princeton, NJ 08540. TEL 609-921-1141. FAX 609-921-1140. *3659*

PRINCETON SERIES IN PHYSICS.
Princeton University Press, 41 William St., Princeton, NJ 08540. TEL 609-258-4900. FAX 609-258-6305. *5823*

PRINCETON UNIVERSITY LIBRARY CHRONICLE.
Princeton University Library, 1 Washington Rd., Princeton, NJ 08544. TEL 609-258-3184. FAX 609-258-4105. *3789*

PRINCIPIA CYBERNETICA NEWSLETTER.
Principia Cybernetica Project, c/o Free University of Brussels, Pleinlaan 2, 1050 Brussels, Belgium. TEL 32-2-6412525. FAX 32-2-6412489. *2163*

PRISM (NEW BRIGHTON).
Prism Publishers, 3000 Fifth St. N.W., New Brighton, MN 55112. TEL 612-633-4311. FAX 612-633-4315. *6363*

PRISM INTERNATIONAL.
University of British Columbia, Creative Writing Department, E462-1866 Main Mall, Vancouver, BC V6T 1Z1, Canada. TEL 604-822-2514. FAX 604-822-3616. *4452*

THE PRISON JOURNAL.
Sage Publications, Inc., 2455 Teller Rd., Thousand Oaks, CA 91320. TEL 805-499-0721. FAX 805-499-0871. *2277*

PRO MATHEMATICA.
Pontificia Universidad Catolica del Peru, Fondo Editorial, Apdo. 1761, Lima 23, Peru. TEL 51-14-626390. FAX 5114-611785. *4598*

PRO NATURA.
Schweizerischer Bund fuer Naturschutz, Postfach, CH-4020 Basel, Switzerland. TEL 41-61-3179191. FAX 41-61-3179266. *6560*

PROBABILISTIC ENGINEERING MECHANICS.
Elsevier Science Ltd., P.O. Box 800, Kidlington, Oxford OX5 1DX, England. TEL 44-1865-843000. FAX 44-1865-843010. *2898*

PROBABILITY AND MATHEMATICAL STATISTICS.
Academic Press, Inc., 525 B St., Ste. 1900, San Diego, CA 92101-4495. TEL 619-231-0926. FAX 619-699-6715. *4598*

PROBLEME DER AEGYPTOLOGIE.
E.J. Brill, P.O. Box 9000, 2300 PA Leiden, Netherlands. TEL 31-71-5353500. FAX 31-71-5317532. *5536*

PROBLEMS IN GENERAL SURGERY.
Lippincott - Raven Publishers, 227 E. Washington Sq., Philadelphia, PA 19106. TEL 215-238-4200. *5151*

PROBLEMS IN PRIVATE INTERNATIONAL LAW.
Elsevier Science B.V., Books Division, P.O. Box 211, 1000 AE Amsterdam, Netherlands. TEL 31-20-4853911. FAX 31-20-4853705. *4124*

PROBLEMS OF DESERT DEVELOPMENT.
Allerton Press, Inc., 150 Fifth Ave., New York, NY 10011. TEL 212-924-3950. FAX 212-463-9684. *2948*

PROBLEMS OF ECONOMIC TRANSITION.
M.E. Sharpe, Inc., 80 Business Park Dr., Armonk, NY 10504. TEL 914-273-1800. FAX 914-273-2106. *993*

PROBLEMS OF INDUSTRIAL PSYCHIATRIC MEDICINE SERIES.
Human Sciences Press, Inc., 233 Spring St., New York, NY 10013-1578. TEL 212-620-8000. FAX 212-463-0742. *6141*

PROBLEMS OF INFORMATION TRANSMISSION.
Plenum Publishing Corp., Consultants Bureau, 233 Spring St., New York, NY 10013-1578. TEL 212-620-8468. FAX 212-463-0742. *2171*

PROBLEMS OF POST-COMMUNISM.
M.E. Sharpe, Inc., 80 Business Park Dr., Armonk, NY 10504. TEL 914-273-1800. FAX 914-273-2106. *5961*

PROBLEMY PROJEKTOWE PRZEMYSLU I BUDOWNICTWA.
Przedsiebiorstwo Inzynierskie "Biprohut", Sp. z o.o., Ul. Dubois 16, 44-100 Gliwice, Poland. TEL 48-32-316011. FAX 48-32-312435. *5207*

PROBLEMY ROZWOJU BUDOWNICTWA.
Instytut Gospodarki Mieszkaniowej, Ul. Filtrowa 1, 00-925 Warsaw 58, Poland. FAX 48-22-250683. *909*

PROCESS BIOCHEMISTRY.
Elsevier Science Ltd., P.O. Box 800, Kidlington, Oxford OX5 1DX, England. TEL 44-1865-843000. FAX 44-1865-843010. *686*

PROCESS CONTROL AND QUALITY.
Elsevier Science B.V., P.O. Box 211, 1000 AE Amsterdam, Netherlands. TEL 31-20-4853911. FAX 31-20-4853598. *5254*

PROCESS MEASUREMENT & CONTROL.
Elsevier Science B.V., Books Division, P.O. Box 211, 1000 AE Amsterdam, Netherlands. TEL 31-20-4853911. FAX 31-20-4853705. *2772*

PROCESS METALLURGY.
Elsevier Science B.V., Books Division, P.O. Box 211, 1000 AE Amsterdam, Netherlands. TEL 31-20-4853911. FAX 31-20-4853705. *5207*

PROCESS SAFETY AND ENVIRONMENTAL PROTECTION.
Institution of Chemical Engineers, George E. Davis Bldg., 165-189 Railway Terr., Rugby, Warks. CV21 3HQ, England. TEL 44-1788-578214. FAX 44-1788-578214. *2772*

PROCESS SIMULATION & MODELING.
Elsevier Science B.V., Books Division, P.O. Box 211, 1000 AE Amsterdam, Netherlands. TEL 31-20-4853911. FAX 31-20-4853705. *2152*

PROCESS TECHNOLOGY PROCEEDINGS.
Elsevier Science B.V., Books Division, P.O. Box 211, 1000 AE Amsterdam, Netherlands. TEL 31-20-4853911. FAX 31-20-4853705. *2878*

PRODUCTION AND OPERATIONS MANAGEMENT.
Production and Operations Management Society, c/o Dr. Sushil K. Gupta, PC-543, Florida International University, Miami, FL 33199. TEL 410-837-4976. FAX 410-837-5675. *1502*

PRODUCTION PLANNING & CONTROL.
Taylor & Francis Ltd., Rankine Rd., Basingstoke, Hants. RG24 8PR, England. TEL 44-1256-840366. FAX 44-1256-479438. *2806*

PROEFTUIN NIEUWS.
Binnenweg 6, 2860 Sint-Ka telijine-Waver, Belgium. TEL 32-15-552771. FAX 32-15-553061. *241*

PROFESSIONAL EDUCATOR.
Auburn University, College of Education, 3084 Haley Ctr., Auburn, AL 36849-5218. TEL 334-844-5979. FAX 334-844-5785. *2615*

PROFESSIONAL ETHICS.
Box 15017, Gainesville, FL 32604. TEL 904-392-2084. FAX 904-392-5575. *5746*

PROFESSIONAL FLORAL DESIGNER.
American Floral Services, 3737 N.W. 34th St., Oklahoma City, OK 73112. TEL 405-440-6226. FAX 405-943-1337. *3210*

THE PROFESSIONAL MANAGER.
Institute of Management Foundation, 2 Savoy Ct., 3rd. Fl., Strand, London WC2R OEZ, England. TEL 44-171-497-0580. FAX 44-171-497-0463. *1502*

PROFESSIONAL PRINTER.
Institute of Printing, 8 Lonsdale Gardens, Tunbridge Wells, Kent TN1 1NU, England. TEL 44-1892-538118. FAX 44-1892-518028. *6084*

PROFESSIONAL PSYCHOLOGY: RESEARCH AND PRACTICE.
American Psychological Association, 750 First St., N.E., Washington, DC 20002-4242. TEL 202-336-5600. FAX 202-336-5568. *6141*

PROFESSIONAL SPEAKER.
National Speakers Association, 1500 S. Priest Dr., Tempe, AZ 85281-6203. TEL 602-968-2552. FAX 602-968-0911. *4290*

PROFILE OF THE WORLDWIDE SEMICONDUCTOR INDUSTRY.
Elsevier Science Ltd., Books Division, P.O. Box 800, Kidlington, Oxford OX5 1DX, England. TEL 44-1865-843000. FAX 44-1865-843010. *2649*

PROFILES.
Kluwer Academic Publishers, Postbus 17, 3300 AA Dordrecht, Netherlands. TEL 31-78-6392392. FAX 31-78-6392254. *5746*

PROGRAM.
Aslib, Association for Information Management, Publications Department, Information House, 20-24 Old St., London EC1V 9AP, England. TEL 44-171-253-4488. FAX 44-171-430-0514. *4234*

PROGRAMMING AND COMPUTER SOFTWARE.
Maik Nauka - Interperiodica, Mezhdunarodnyi Otdel, Ul. Profsoyuznaya, 90, 117864 Moscow, Russia. TEL 7-095-3360666. FAX 7-095-3360666. *2145*

PROGRES EN UROLOGIE.
Progres en Urologie S.A.R.L., 7 bd. Flandrin, 75116 Paris, France. TEL 33-1-45033196. FAX 33-1-45047289. *5165*

PROGRESS AND TOPICS IN CYTOGENETICS.
John Wiley & Sons, Inc., Journals, 605 Third Ave., New York, NY 10158. TEL 212-475-7700. *776*

PROGRESS IN AEROSPACE SCIENCES.
Elsevier Science Ltd., Pergamon, P.O. Box 800, Kidlington, Oxford OX5 1DX, England. TEL 44-1865-843000. FAX 44-1865-843010. *76*

PROGRESS IN AIDS PATHOLOGY.
Field & Wood, Medical Periodicals, Inc., Box 975, Blue Bell, PA 19422. TEL 610-828-4010. FAX 215-482-0226. *4842*

PROGRESS IN APPLIED MICROCIRCULATION.
S. Karger AG, Allschwilerstr. 10, P.O. Box, CH-4009 Basel, Switzerland. TEL 41-61-3061111. FAX 41-61-3061234. *4823*

PROGRESS IN BASIC AND CLINICAL PHARMACOLOGY.
S. Karger AG, Allschwilerstr. 10, P.O. Box, CH-4009 Basel, Switzerland. TEL 41-61-3061111. FAX 41-61-3061234. *5691*

PROGRESS IN BIOCHEMICAL PHARMACOLOGY.
S. Karger AG, Allschwilerstr. 10, P.O. Box, CH-4009 Basel, Switzerland. TEL 41-61-3061111. FAX 41-61-3061234. *5691*

PROGRESS IN BIOMEDICAL ENGINEERING.
Elsevier Science B.V., Books Division, P.O. Box 211, 1000 AE Amsterdam, Netherlands. TEL 31-20-4853911. FAX 31-20-4853705. *648*

PROGRESS IN BIOPHYSICS & MOLECULAR BIOLOGY.
Elsevier Science Ltd., Pergamon, P.O. Box 800, Kidlington, Oxford OX5 1DX, England. TEL 44-1865-843000. FAX 44-1865-843010. *676*

PROGRESS IN BIOTECHNOLOGY.
Elsevier Science B.V., Books Division, P.O. Box 211, 1000 AE Amsterdam, Netherlands. TEL 31-20-4853911. FAX 31-20-4853705. *687*

PROGRESS IN BRAIN RESEARCH.
Elsevier Science B.V., Books Division, P.O. Box 211, 1000 AE Amsterdam, Netherlands. TEL 31-20-4853911. FAX 31-20-4853705. *5090*

PROGRESS IN CANCER RESEARCH AND THERAPY.
Lippincott - Raven Publishers, 227 E. Washington Sq., Philadelphia, PA 19106. TEL 215-238-4200. FAX 215-238-4227. *4986*

PROGRESS IN CARDIOVASCULAR DISEASES.
W.B. Saunders Co., Curtis Center, 3rd Fl., Independence Sq. W., Philadelphia, PA 19106-3399. TEL 215-238-7800. FAX 215-238-6445. *4823*

PROGRESS IN CARDIOVASCULAR NURSING.
Medquest Communications, Inc., 629 Euclid Ave., Ste. 500, Cleveland, OH 44114-3003. TEL 216-522-9700. FAX 216-522-9707. *4823*

PROGRESS IN CELL RESEARCH.
Elsevier Science B.V., Books Division, P.O. Box 211, 1000 AE Amsterdam, Netherlands. TEL 31-20-4853911. FAX 31-20-4853705. *744*

PROGRESS IN CLINICAL AND BIOLOGICAL RESEARCH.
John Wiley & Sons, Inc., Journals, 605 Third Ave., New York, NY 10158. TEL 212-475-7700. *4733*

PROGRESS IN CRYSTAL GROWTH AND CHARACTERIZATION OF MATERIALS.
Elsevier Science Ltd., Pergamon, P.O. Box 800, Kidlington, Oxford OX5 1DX, England. TEL 44-1865-843000. FAX 44-1865-843010. *1803*

PROGRESS IN ENDOCRINE RESEARCH AND THERAPY.
Lippincott - Raven Publishers, 227 E. Washington Sq., Philadelphia, PA 19106. TEL 215-238-4200. FAX 215-238-4227. *4892*

PROGRESS IN ENERGY AND COMBUSTION SCIENCE.
Elsevier Science Ltd., Pergamon, P.O. Box 800, Kidlington, Oxford OX5 1DX, England. TEL 44-1865-843000. FAX 44-1865-843010. *2676*

PROGRESS IN EXPERIMENTAL TUMOR RESEARCH.
S. Karger AG, Allschwilerstr. 10, P.O. Box, CH-4009 Basel, Switzerland. TEL 41-61-3061111. FAX 41-61-3061234. *4986*

PROGRESS IN FILTRATION AND SEPARATION.
Elsevier Science B.V., Books Division, P.O. Box 211, 1000 AE Amsterdam, Netherlands. TEL 31-20-4853911. FAX 31-20-4853705. *1763*

PROGRESS IN HORMONE BIOCHEMISTRY.
Kluwer Academic Publishers, Postbus 17, 3300 AA Dordrecht, Netherlands. TEL 31-78-6392392. FAX 31-78-6392254. *669*

PROGRESS IN INDUSTRIAL MICROBIOLOGY.
Elsevier Science B.V., Books Division, P.O. Box 211, 1000 AE Amsterdam, Netherlands. TEL 31-20-4853911. FAX 31-20-4853705. *793*

PROGRESS IN INORGANIC CHEMISTRY.
John Wiley & Sons, Inc., 605 Third Ave., New York, NY 10158. TEL 212-850-6000. FAX 212-850-6088. *1809*

PROGRESS IN LIPID RESEARCH.
Elsevier Science Ltd., Pergamon, P.O. Box 800, Kidlington, Oxford OX5 1DX, England. TEL 44-1865-843000. FAX 44-1865-843010. *1822*

PROGRESS IN LIVER DISEASE.
W.B. Saunders Co., Curtis Center, 3rd Fl., PA 19106-3399. TEL 215-238-7800. FAX 215-238-6445. *4914*

PROGRESS IN LOW TEMPERATURE PHYSICS.
Elsevier Science B.V., Books Division, P.O. Box 211, 1000 AE Amsterdam, Netherlands. TEL 31-20-4853911. FAX 31-20-4853705. *5842*

PROGRESS IN MATERIALS SCIENCE.
Elsevier Science Ltd., Pergamon, P.O. Box 800, Kidlington, Oxford OX5 1DX, England. TEL 44-1865-843000. FAX 44-1865-843010. *2869*

PROGRESS IN MEDICAL VIROLOGY.
S. Karger AG, Allschwilerstr. 10, P.O. Box, CH-4009 Basel, Switzerland. TEL 41-61-3061111. FAX 41-61-3061234. *4842*

PROGRESS IN MEDICINAL CHEMISTRY.
Elsevier Science B.V., Books Division, P.O. Box 211, 1000 AE Amsterdam, Netherlands. TEL 31-20-4853911. FAX 31-20-4853705. *1763*

PROGRESS IN MOLECULAR AND SUBCELLULAR BIOLOGY.
Springer-Verlag, 175 Fifth Ave., New York, NY 10010. TEL 212-460-1500. FAX 212-473-6272. *744*

PROGRESS IN MUTATION RESEARCH.
Elsevier Science B.V., Books Division, P.O. Box 211, 1000 AE Amsterdam, Netherlands. TEL 31-20-4853911. FAX 31-20-4853705. *776*

PROGRESS IN NEURO-PSYCHOPHARMACOLOGY AND BIOLOGICAL PSYCHIATRY.
Elsevier Science Inc., Box 945, New York, NY 10159-0945. TEL 212-633-3730. FAX 212-633-3680. *5691*

PROGRESS IN NEUROBIOLOGY.
Elsevier Science Ltd., Pergamon, P.O. Box 800, Kidlington, Oxford OX5 1DX, England. TEL 44-1865-843000. FAX 44-1865-843010. *821*

PROGRESS IN NEUROLOGICAL SURGERY.
S. Karger AG, Allschwilerstr. 10, P.O. Box, CH-4009 Basel, Switzerland. TEL 41-61-3061111. FAX 41-61-3061234. *5090*

PROGRESS IN NEUROPATHOLOGY.
Lippincott - Raven Publishers, 227 E. Washington Sq., Philadelphia, PA 19106. TEL 215-238-4200. FAX 215-238-4227. *5090*

PROGRESS IN NUCLEAR ENERGY.
Elsevier Science Ltd., Pergamon, P.O. Box 800, Kidlington, Oxford OX5 1DX, England. TEL 44-1865-843000. FAX 44-1865-843010. *2703*

PROGRESS IN NUCLEAR MAGNETIC RESONANCE SPECTROSCOPY.
Elsevier Science B.V., P.O. Box 211, 1000 AE Amsterdam, Netherlands. TEL 31-20-4853911. FAX 31-20-4853598. *1795*

PROGRESS IN NUCLEIC ACID RESEARCH AND MOLECULAR BIOLOGY.
Academic Press, Inc., 525 B St., Ste. 1900, San Diego, CA 92101-4495. TEL 619-231-0926. FAX 619-699-6715. *621*

PROGRESS IN OBESITY RESEARCH (YEAR).
John Libbey & Co. Ltd., 13 Smiths Yard, Summerley St., London SW18 4HR, England. TEL 44-181-947-2777. FAX 44-181-947-2664. *4733*

PROGRESS IN OCEANOGRAPHY.
Elsevier Science Ltd., Pergamon, P.O. Box 800, Kidlington, Oxford OX5 1DX, England. TEL 44-1865-843000. FAX 44-1865-843010. *2413*

PROGRESS IN OPTICS.
Elsevier Science B.V., Books Division, P.O. Box 211, 1000 AE Amsterdam, Netherlands. TEL 31-20-4853911. FAX 31-20-4853705. *5869*

PROGRESS IN ORGANIC COATINGS.
Elsevier Science S.A., P.O. Box 564, CH-1001 Lausanne 1, Switzerland. TEL 41-21-3207381. FAX 41-21-3235444. *5555*

PROGRESS IN PAPER RECYCLING.
Doshi & Associates Inc., Box 2771, Appleton, WI 54913-2771. TEL 414-832-9101. FAX 414-832-0870. *5571*

PROGRESS IN PARTICLE AND NUCLEAR PHYSICS.
Elsevier Science Ltd., Pergamon, P.O. Box 800, Kidlington, Oxford OX5 1DX, England. TEL 44-1865-843000. FAX 44-1865-843010. *5856*

PROGRESS IN PEDIATRIC CARDIOLOGY.
Elsevier Science Ireland Ltd., P.O. Box 85, Limerick, Ireland. TEL 353-31-471944. FAX 353-61-472144. *4823*

PROGRESS IN PHOTOVOLTAICS.
John Wiley & Sons, Inc., Journals, Baffins Ln., Chichester, W. Sussex PO19 1UD, England. TEL 44-1243-779777. FAX 44-1243-775878. *2676*

PROGRESS IN PHYCOLOGICAL RESEARCH.
Elsevier Science B.V., Books Division, P.O. Box 211, 1000 AE Amsterdam, Netherlands. TEL 31-20-4853911. FAX 31-20-4853705. *724*

PROGRESS IN PHYSICAL ORGANIC CHEMISTRY.
John Wiley & Sons, Inc., 605 Third Ave., New York, NY 10158. TEL 212-850-6000. FAX 212-850-6088. *1833*

PROGRESS IN PLANNING.
Elsevier Science Ltd., Pergamon, P.O. Box 800, Kidlington, Oxford OX5 1DX, England. TEL 44-1865-843000. FAX 44-1865-843010. *3757*

PROGRESS IN POLYMER SCIENCE.
Elsevier Science Ltd., Pergamon, P.O. Box 800, Kidlington, Oxford OX5 1DX, England. TEL 44-1865-843000. FAX 44-1865-843010. *1822*

PROGRESS IN PSYCHOBIOLOGY AND PHYSIOLOGICAL PSYCHOLOGY.
Academic Press, Inc., 525 B St., Ste. 1900, San Diego, CA 92101-4495. TEL 619-231-0926. FAX 619-699-6715. *6141*

PROGRESS IN QUANTUM ELECTRONICS.
Elsevier Science Ltd., Pergamon, P.O. Box 800, Kidlington, Oxford OX5 1DX, England. TEL 44-1865-843000. FAX 44-1865-843010. *2649*

PROGRESS IN REACTION KINETICS.
Elsevier Science Ltd., Pergamon, P.O. Box 800, Kidlington, Oxford OX5 1DX, England. TEL 44-1865-843000. FAX 44-1865-843010. *1833*

PROGRESS IN REPRODUCTIVE BIOLOGY AND MEDICINE.
S. Karger AG, Allschwilerstr. 10, P.O. Box, CH-4009 Basel, Switzerland. TEL 41-61-3061111. FAX 41-61-3061234. *4947*

PROGRESS IN RESPIRATORY RESEARCH.
S. Karger AG, Allschwilerstr. 10, P.O. Box, CH-4009 Basel, Switzerland. TEL 41-61-3061111. FAX 41-61-3061234. *5121*

PROGRESS IN RETINAL AND EYE RESEARCH.
Elsevier Science Ltd., Pergamon, P.O. Box 800, Kidlington, Oxford OX5 1DX, England. TEL 44-1865-843000. FAX 44-1865-843010. *5000*

PROGRESS IN RUBBER AND PLASTICS TECHNOLOGY.
R A P R A Technology Ltd., Shawbury, Shrewsbury, Shrops. SY4 4NR, England. TEL 44-1939-250383. FAX 44-1939-251118. *6503*

PROGRESS IN SOLID STATE CHEMISTRY.
Elsevier Science Ltd., Pergamon, P.O. Box 800, Kidlington, Oxford OX5 1DX, England. TEL 44-1865-843000. FAX 44-1865-843010. *1834*

PROGRESS IN SURFACE SCIENCE.
Elsevier Science Ltd., Pergamon, P.O. Box 800, Kidlington, Oxford OX5 1DX, England. TEL 44-1865-843000. FAX 44-1865-843010. *5823*

PROGRESS IN SURGERY.
S. Karger AG, Allschwilerstr. 10, P.O. Box, CH-4009 Basel, Switzerland. TEL 41-61-3061111. FAX 41-61-3061234. *5151*

PROGRESS IN SURGICAL PATHOLOGY.
Field & Wood, Medical Periodicals, Inc., Box 975, Blue Bell, PA 19422. TEL 610-828-4010. FAX 215-482-0226. *4733*

PROGRESS IN THEORETICAL ORGANIC CHEMISTRY.
Elsevier Science B.V., Books Division, P.O. Box 211, 1000 AE Amsterdam, Netherlands. TEL 31-20-4853911. FAX 31-20-4853705. *1822*

PROGRESS IN VETERINARY NEUROLOGY.
Veterinary Practice Publishing Co., Box 6050, Mission Viejo, CA 92690. *7277*

PROGRESSIVE FISH-CULTURIST.
American Fisheries Society, 5410 Grosvenor Lane, Ste. 110, Bethesda, MD 20814-2199. TEL 301-897-8616. FAX 301-897-8096. *3076*

PROJECT APPRAISAL.
Beech Tree Publishing, 10 Watford Close, Guildford, Surrey GU1 2EP, England. TEL 44-1483-567497. FAX 44-1483-567497. *1403*

PROJECT MANAGEMENT JOURNAL.
Project Management Institute, Publications Division, Attn: Shirley Parker, 40 Colonial Sq., Sylva, NC 28779. TEL 704-586-3715. FAX 704-586-4020. *1502*

PROJECTS IN METAL.
Village Press, Inc., 2779 Aero Park Dr., Traverse City, MI 49686. TEL 616-946-3712. FAX 616-946-3289. *4551*

PROMAX INTERNATIONAL.
Promotion & Marketing Executives in the Electronic Media, 2029 Century Pk. E., Ste. 555, Los Angeles, CA 90067-2906. TEL 310-788-7600. FAX 310-788-7616. *2057*

PROMETHEUS.
Carfax Publishing Co., Abingdon, Oxon. OX14 3UE, England. TEL 44-1235-401000. FAX 44-1235-401550. *2001*

PROMOCION COMERCIAL EUROPEA.
Canalejas 30, entlo. 2o, 08028 Barcelona, Spain. TEL 34-3-4226289. FAX 34-3-4211858. *1345*

REFEREED SERIALS

PROPOSTE E RICERCHE.
Universita degli Studi di Ancona, Camerino, Chieti, Macerata, Perugia, San Marino, Museo di Storia della Mezzadria, Piazzale delle Grazie, 60019 Senigallia AN, Italy. TEL 39-71-7923127. FAX 39-71-7927684. *3592*

PROSE POEM.
Providence College, English Department, Providence, RI 02918. TEL 401-865-2292. FAX 401-865-2057. *4521*

PROSE STUDIES.
Frank Cass, Newbury House, 890-900 Eastern Ave., Newbury Park, Ilford, Essex IG2 7HH, England. TEL 44-181-599-8666. FAX 44-181-599-0984. *4453*

PROSECUTOR.
National District Attorneys Association, 99 Canal Center Plaza, Ste. 510, Alexandria, VA 22314. TEL 703-549-9222. *4011*

PROSPECT.
National Centre for English Language Teaching and Research, Macquarie University, New South Wales 2109, Australia. TEL 61-2-98507673. FAX 61-2-98507849. *2513*

PROSPETTIVE SOCIALI E SANITARIE.
Istituto per la Ricerca Sociale, Via XX Settembre 24, 20123 Milan, Italy. TEL 39-2-46764276. FAX 39-2-46764227. *6682*

PROSTAGLANDINS.
Elsevier Science Inc., Box 945, New York, NY 10159-0945. TEL 212-633-3730. FAX 212-633-3680. *4892*

PROSTAGLANDINS, LEUKOTRIENES AND CANCER.
Kluwer Academic Publishers, Postbus 17, 3300 AA Dordrecht, Netherlands. TEL 31-78-6392392. FAX 31-78-6392254. *4986*

THE PROSTATE.
John Wiley & Sons, Inc., Journals, 605 Third Ave., New York, NY 10158. TEL 212-850-6645. FAX 212-850-6021. *4734*

PROSTHETICS AND ORTHOTICS INTERNATIONAL.
International Society for Prosthetics and Orthotics, Borgervaenget 5, DK-2100 Copenhagen OE, Denmark. TEL 45-31-20-72-60. FAX 45-31-18-16-69. *5015*

PROTECTING CHILDREN.
American Humane Association, Children's Division, 63 Inverness Dr. E., Englewood, CO 80112-5117. TEL 303-792-9900. FAX 303-792-5333. *6682*

PROTECTION OF METALS.
Maik Nauka - Interperiodica, Mezhdunarodnyi Otdel, Ul. Profsoyuznaya 90, Moscow 117864, Russia. TEL 7-095-231-2164. FAX 7-095-233-5590. *5207*

PROTEE.
Protee, 555 bd. de l'Universite, Chicoutimi, PQ, Canada. TEL 418-545-5011. FAX 418-545-5012. *3789*

PROTEIN AND PEPTIDE LETTERS.
Bentham Science Publishers, 7436 S.W. 117 Ave., Box 130, Miami, FL 33183. FAX 305-596-5120. *669*

PROTEIN ENGINEERING.
Oxford University Press, Academic Division, Great Clarendon St., Oxford OX2 6DP, England. TEL 44-1865-267907. FAX 44-1865-267485. *669*

PROTEIN EXPRESSION AND PURIFICATION.
Academic Press, Inc., Journal Division, 525 B St., Ste. 1900, San Diego, CA 92101-4495. TEL 619-230-1840. FAX 619-699-6800. *670*

PROTEIN SCIENCE.
Cambridge University Press, Edinburgh Bldg., Shaftesbury Rd., Cambridge CB2 2RU, England. TEL 44-1223-312393. FAX 44-1223-315052. *670*

PROTEINS: STRUCTURE, FUNCTION, AND GENETICS.
John Wiley & Sons, Inc., Journals, 605 Third Ave., New York, NY 10158. TEL 212-850-6645. FAX 212-850-6021. *670*

PROTEUS.
Shippensburg University, Shippensburg, PA 17257. TEL 717-532-1206. FAX 717-532-1253. *3383*

PROTOONER.
Protooner, Box 2270, Daly City, CA 94017-2270. TEL 415-755-4827. FAX 415-755-3005. *462*

PROVENANCE.
Society of Georgia Archivists, Box 80631, Athens, GA 30608. TEL 706-542-7123. *3644*

PROYECCIONES.
Universidad Catolica del Norte, Departamento de Matematicas, Avda. Angamos 0610, Casilla 1280, Antofagasta, Chile. TEL 241148. FAX 241724. *4599*

PRUDENTIA.
University of Auckland, Department of Classic and Ancient History, Attn: Dr. T.C. Gilmour, Private Bag, Auckland, New Zealand. TEL 3737-999. FAX 3732-878. *3509*

PRZEGLAD ANTROPOLOGICZNY.
Polskie Towarzystwo Antropologiczne, Ul. Marymoncka 34, 01-813 Warsaw, Poland. *327*

PRZEGLAD POWSZECHNY.
Officyna Wydawnicza Przegladu Powszechnego, Ul. Rakowiecka 61, 02-532 Warsaw, Poland. TEL 48-22-489131. FAX 48-22-489499. *4355*

PSEUDEPIGRAPHA VETERIS TESTAMENTI GRAECE.
E.J. Brill, P.O. Box 9000, 2300 PA Leiden, Netherlands. TEL 31-71-5353500. FAX 31-71-5317532. *6363*

PSICHIATRIA E PSICOTERAPIA ANALITICA.
Via Trionfale 11224, 00135 Rome, Italy. TEL 39-6-8072063. *5091*

PSICOLOGIA: TEORIA E PESQUISA.
Universidade de Brasilia, Instituto de Psicologia, Campus Universitario, 70910-900 Brasilia DF, Brazil. TEL 55-61-2746455. FAX 55-61-2736378. *6142*

PSICOLOGICA.
Universitat de Valencia, Departamento de Metodologia, Psicobiologia e Psicologia Social, Avda. Blasco Ibanez 21, 46010 Valencia, Spain. TEL 39-6-3864420 ext. 6264. FAX 39-6-3864668. *6142*

PSICOTHEMA: REVISTA DE PSICOLOGIA.
Universidad de Oviedo, Facultad de Psicologia, C. San Francisco 3, 33003 Oviedo, Spain. TEL 34-85-104486. FAX 34-85-104488. *6142*

PSIQUIATRIA PUBLICA.
Jarpyo Editores, S.A., Antonio Lopez Aguado 4, 28029 Madrid, Spain. TEL 34-1-3144338. FAX 34-1-3144499. *5091*

PSYCHE.
Cambridge Entomological Club, 26 Oxford St., Cambridge, MA 02138. TEL 617-495-2464. FAX 617-495-5667. *760*

PSYCHE.
M I T Press, 55 Hayward St., Cambridge, MA 02142. TEL 617-253-2889. FAX 617-258-67796. *6143*

PSYCHIATRIA POLSKA.
Polskie Towarzystwo Psychiatryczne, Ul. Lenartowicza 14, 31-138 Krakow, Poland. TEL 48-12-331203. FAX 48-12-334067. *5091*

PSYCHIATRIC BULLETIN.
Royal College of Psychiatrists, 17 Belgrave Sq., London SW1X 8PG, England. TEL 44-171-235-8857. FAX 44-171-245-1231. *5091*

PSYCHIATRIC GENETICS.
Rapid Science Publishers, The Old Malthouse, Paradise St., Oxford OX1 1LD, England. TEL 44-1865-790447. FAX 44-1865-244012. *776*

PSYCHIATRIC QUARTERLY.
Human Sciences Press, Inc., 233 Spring St., New York, NY 10013-1578. TEL 212-620-8000. FAX 212-463-0742. *5092*

PSYCHIATRIC REHABILITATION JOURNAL.
Boston University, 930 Commonwealth Ave., Boston, MA 02215. TEL 617-353-3549. FAX 617-353-9209. *6143*

PSYCHIATRIC SERVICES.
American Psychiatric Press, Inc., Journals Division, 1400 K St., N.W., Ste.1101, Washington, DC 20005. TEL 202-682-6070. FAX 202-682-6189. *5092*

PSYCHIATRIC TIMES.
C M E Inc., 2801 McGraw Ave., Irvine, CA 92614-5835. TEL 714-250-1008. FAX 714-250-0045. *5092*

PSYCHIATRY.
Guilford Publications, Inc., 72 Spring St., 4th Fl., New York, NY 10012. TEL 212-431-9800. FAX 212-966-6708. *5092*

PSYCHIATRY ON-LINE. *5093*

PSYCHIATRY PSYCHOLOGY AND LAW.
Australian Academic Press Pty. Ltd., 32 Jeays St., Bowen Hills, Qld. 4006, Australia. TEL 61-7-32571176. FAX 61-7-32525908. *5093*

PSYCHIATRY RESEARCH.
Elsevier Science Ireland Ltd., P.O. Box 85, Limerick, Ireland. TEL 353-61-471944. FAX 353-61-472144. *5093*

PSYCHIATRY RESEARCH: NEUROIMAGING SECTION.
Elsevier Science Ireland Ltd., P.O. Box 85, Limerick, Ireland. TEL 353-61-471944. FAX 353-61-472144. *5093*

PSYCHIC STUDIES.
Gordon and Breach - Harwood Academic, Amsteldisk 166, 1st Fl., 1079 LH Amsterdam, Netherlands. *5577*

PSYCHO-ONCOLOGY.
John Wiley & Sons Ltd., Journals, Baffins Ln., Chichester, W. Sussex PO19 1UD, England. TEL 44-1243-779777. FAX 44-1243-775878. *4986*

PSYCHOANALYSIS AND CONTEMPORARY THOUGHT.
International Universities Press, Inc., 59 Boston Post Rd., Box 1524, Madison, CT 06443-1524. TEL 203-245-4000. FAX 203-245-0775. *5093*

PSYCHOANALYTIC PSYCHOLOGY.
Lawrence Erlbaum Associates, Inc., 10 Industrial Dr., Mahwah, NJ 07430-2262. TEL 201-236-9500. FAX 201-236-0072. *6143*

PSYCHOANALYTIC REVIEW.
Guilford Publications, Inc., 72 Spring St., 4th Fl., New York, NY 10012. TEL 212-431-9800. FAX 212-966-6708. *6143*

PSYCHOBIOLOGY.
Psychonomic Society, Inc., 1710 Fortview Rd., Austin, TX 78704. TEL 512-462-2442. *6144*

PSYCHOLOGICA BELGICA.
Societe Belge de Psychologie, Tiensestraat 102, 3000 Leuven, Belgium. TEL 32-16-326013. FAX 32-16-326000. *6144*

PSYCHOLOGICAL ASSESSMENT.
American Psychological Association, 750 First St., N.E., Washington, DC 20002-4242. TEL 202-336-5600. FAX 202-336-5568. *6144*

PSYCHOLOGICAL BULLETIN.
American Psychological Association, 750 First St., N.E., Washington, DC 20002-4242. TEL 202-336-5600. FAX 202-336-5568. *6144*

PSYCHOLOGICAL INQUIRY.
Lawrence Erlbaum Associates, Inc., 10 Industrial Dr., Mahwah, NJ 07430-2262. TEL 201-236-9500. FAX 201-236-0072. *6144*

PSYCHOLOGICAL ISSUES.
International Universities Press, Inc., 59 Boston Post Rd., Box 1524, Madison, CT 06443-1524. TEL 203-245-4000. FAX 203-245-0775. *6144*

THE PSYCHOLOGICAL RECORD.
Kenyon College, Gambier, OH 43022-9623. TEL 614-427-5377. FAX 614-427-4950. *6145*

PSYCHOLOGICAL REPORTS.
Dr. C.H. Ammons & Dr. R.B. Ammons, Eds. & Pubs., Box 9229, Missoula, MT 59807. *6145*

PSYCHOLOGICAL RESEARCH BULLETIN.
Lund University, Department of Psychology, Paradisgatan 5 P, 223 50 Lund, Sweden. TEL 46-46-2228770. FAX 46-46-2224209. *6145*

PSYCHOLOGICAL REVIEW.
American Psychological Association, 750 First St., N.E., Washington, DC 20002-4242. TEL 202-336-5600. FAX 202-336-5568. *6145*

PSYCHOLOGISCHE BEITRAEGE.
Pabst Science Publishers, Am Eichengrund 28, 49525 Lengerich, Germany. TEL 35-5484-308. FAX 35-5484-550. *6146*

THE PSYCHOLOGIST.
British Psychological Society, St. Andrew's House, 48 Princess Rd. E., Leicester LE1 7DR, England. TEL 44-166-254-9568. FAX 44-166-247-0787. *6146*

PSYCHOLOGY.
Institute for Leadership and Organization Effectiveness, 1409 Mt. Ayre, Bowling Green, KY 42101. FAX 614-292-7999. *6146*

PSYCHOLOGY AND DEVELOPING SOCIETIES.
Sage Publications India Pvt. Ltd., P.O. Box 4215, New Delhi 110 048, India. TEL 91-11-744-4958. FAX 91-11-647-2426. *6146*

PSYCHOLOGY & HEALTH.
Gordon and Breach - Harwood Academic, Amsteldisk 166, 1st Fl., 1079 LH Amsterdam, Netherlands. *6146*

PSYCHOLOGY & MARKETING.
John Wiley & Sons, Inc., Journals, 605 Third Ave., New York, NY 10158. TEL 212-850-6645. FAX 212-850-6021. *6146*

PSYCHOLOGY BULLETIN.
Psychology Resource Centre, Private Bag X17, Bellville 7535, South Africa. TEL 27-21-959-2283. FAX 27-21-959-3515. *6147*

PSYCHOLOGY, CRIME AND LAW.
Gordon and Breach - Harwood Academic, Amsteldisk 166, 1st Fl., 1079 LH Amsterdam, Netherlands. *6147*

PSYCHOLOGY GRADUATE STUDENT JOURNAL.
c/o School of Psychology, University of Ottawa, 145 Jean Jacques Lussier, Ottawa ON K1N 6N5, Canada. *6147*

PSYCHOLOGY, HEALTH & MEDICINE.
Carfax Publishing Co., P.O. Box 25, Abingdon, Oxon. OX14 3UE, England. TEL 44-1235-401000. FAX 44-1235-401550. *6147*

PSYCHOLOGY IN THE SCHOOLS.
John Wiley & Sons, Inc., Journals, 605 Third Ave., New York, NY 10158-0012. TEL 212-850-6645. FAX 212-850-6021. *6147*

PSYCHOLOGY OF ADDICTIVE BEHAVIORS.
American Psychological Association, 750 First St., N.E., Washington, DC 20002-4242. TEL 202-336-5600. FAX 202-336-5568. *2305*

PSYCHOLOGY OF MUSIC.
Society for Research in Psychology of Music and Music Education, Department of Psychology, The University, Leicester LE1 7RH, England. TEL 44-116-2522155. FAX 44-116-2522067. *5427*

PSYCHOLOGY OF WOMEN QUARTERLY.
Cambridge University Press, Edinburgh Bldg., Shaftesbury Rd., Cambridge CB2 2RU, England. TEL 44-1223-312393. FAX 44-1223-315052. *6147*

PSYCHOLOGY, PUBLIC POLICY, AND LAW.
American Psychological Association, 750 First St., N.E., Washington, DC 20002-4242. TEL 202-336-5600. FAX 202-336-5568. *6147*

PSYCHOLOGY TODAY.
Sussex Publishers Inc., 49 E. 21st St., 11th Fl., New York, NY 10010. TEL 212-260-7210. FAX 212-260-7445. *6147*

PSYCHOMUSICOLOGY.
Florida State University, Center for Music Research, 214 KMU, Tallahassee, FL 32306-2098. TEL 904-644-5786. FAX 904-644-6100. *5427*

PSYCHONEUROENDOCRINOLOGY.
Elsevier Science Ltd., Pergamon, P.O. Box 800, Kidlington, Oxford OX5 1DX, England. TEL 44-1865-843000. FAX 44-1865-843010. *5094*

PSYCHONOMIC BULLETIN & REVIEW.
Psychonomic Society, Inc., 1710 Fortview Rd., Austin, TX 78704. TEL 512-462-2442. FAX 512-462-1101. *6148*

PSYCHOPATHOLOGY.
S. Karger AG, Allschwilerstr. 10, P.O. Box, CH-4009 Basel, Switzerland. TEL 41-61-3061111. FAX 41-61-3061234. *5094*

PSYCHOPHARMACOLOGY.
Elsevier Science B.V., Books Division, P.O. Box 211, 1000 AE Amsterdam, Netherlands. TEL 31-20-4853911. FAX 31-20-4853705. *5691*

PSYCHOPHYSIOLOGY.
Cambridge University Press, Edinburgh Bldg., Shaftesbury Rd., Cambridge CB2 2RU, England. TEL 44-1223-312393. FAX 44-1223-315052. *4734*

PSYCHOPOETICA.
Psychopoetica Publications, University of Hull, Dept. of Psychology, Hull HU6 7RX, England. TEL 44-1482-465581. FAX 44-1482-465599. *4521*

PSYCHOSOMATIC MEDICINE.
Williams & Wilkins, 351 W. Camden St., Baltimore, MD 21201-2436. TEL 410-528-4068. FAX 410-528-4452. *5094*

PSYCHOSOMATICS.
American Psychiatric Press, Inc., Journals Division, 1400 K St., N.W., Ste. 1101, Washington, DC 20005. TEL 202-682-6240. FAX 202-682-6341. *5094*

PSYCHOTHERAPY.
American Psychological Association, Division of Psychotherapy, 2665 S. Bayshore Dr., Ste. 406, Coconut Grove, FL 33133. TEL 305-854-0848. FAX 305-856-8202. *5094*

PSYCHOTHERAPY AND PSYCHOSOMATICS.
S. Karger AG, Allschwilerstr. 10, P.O. Box, CH-4009 Basel, Switzerland. TEL 41-61-3061111. FAX 41-61-3061234. *5094*

PSYCHOTHERAPY IN PRIVATE PRACTICE.
Haworth Press, Inc., 10 Alice St., Binghamton, NY 13904. TEL 607-722-5857. FAX 607-722-6362. *6148*

THE PSYCHOTHERAPY PATIENT.
Haworth Press, Inc., 10 Alice St., Binghamton, NY 13904. TEL 607-722-5857. FAX 607-722-6362. *6148*

PSYCHOTHERAPY RESEARCH.
Guilford Publications, Inc., 72 Spring St., 4th Fl., New York, NY 10012. TEL 212-431-9800. FAX 212-966-6708. *6148*

PSYCOLOQUY.
c/o Cognitive Sciences Centre, Dept. of Psychology, Univ. of Southampton, Highfield, Southampton SO17 1BJ, England. *6148*

PTERIDOLOGIA.
American Fern Society, Inc., c/o Dr. David B. Lellinger, 326 West St., N.W., Vienna, VA 22180-4151. *724*

PUBLIC ADMINISTRATION.
Blackwell Publishers Ltd., 108 Cowley Rd., Oxford OX4 1JF, England. TEL 44-1865-791100. FAX 44-1865-791347. *6189*

PUBLIC ADMINISTRATION AND DEVELOPMENT.
John Wiley & Sons Ltd., Journals, Baffins Ln., Chichester, W. Sussex PO19 1UD, England. TEL 44-1243-779777. FAX 44-1243-775878. *1366*

PUBLIC ADMINISTRATION QUARTERLY.
Southern Public Administration Education Foundation, c/o Dr. Jack Rabin, Pennsylvania State University at Harrisburg, Division of Public Affairs, Middletown, PA 17057. TEL 717-948-6363. FAX 717-540-1383. *6189*

PUBLIC & ACCESS SERVICES QUARTERLY.
Haworth Press, Inc., 10 Alice St., Binghamton, NY 13904. TEL 607-722-5857. FAX 607-722-6362. *4207*

PUBLIC CHOICE.
Kluwer Academic Publishers, Postbus 17, 3300 AA Dordrecht, Netherlands. TEL 31-78-6392392. FAX 31-78-6392254. *993*

PUBLIC CULTURE.
Duke University Press, Brightleaf Sq., 905 W. Main St., Ste. 18-B, Box 90660, Durham, NC 27708. TEL 919-687-3653. FAX 919-688-4574. *4355*

PUBLIC FINANCE.
Foundation Journal Public Finance, Goethestr. 13, 61462 Koenigstein, Germany. TEL 49-6174-23370. *6190*

PUBLIC HEALTH REVIEWS.
Technosdar Ltd., P.O. Box 31684, Tel Aviv 61316, Israel. TEL 972-3-5607418. FAX 972-3-5604932. *6248*

THE PUBLIC HISTORIAN.
University of California Press, Journals Division, 2120 Berkeley Way, No. 5812, Berkeley, CA 94720-5812. TEL 510-643-7154. FAX 510-642-9917. *3509*

PUBLIC LIBRARY JOURNAL.
Library Association, Public Library Group, 7 Ridgmount St., London WC1E 7AE, England. TEL 44-1563-526401. FAX 44-1563-529661. *4207*

PUBLIC LIBRARY QUARTERLY.
Haworth Press, Inc., 10 Alice St., Binghamton, NY 13904. TEL 607-722-5857. FAX 607-722-6362. *4207*

THE PUBLIC MANAGER.
Bureaucrat, Inc., 12007 Titian Way, Potomac, MD 20854. TEL 301-279-9445. FAX 301-251-5872. *6190*

PUBLIC MONEY AND MANAGEMENT.
Blackwell Publishers Ltd., 108 Cowley Rd., Oxford OX4 1JF, England. TEL 44-1865-791100. FAX 44-1865-791347. *6190*

PUBLIC OPINION QUARTERLY.
University of Chicago Press, Journals Division, Box 37005, Chicago, IL 60637. TEL 773-753-3347. FAX 773-753-0811. *5962*

PUBLIC POLICY ISSUES IN RESOURCE MANAGEMENT.
University of Washington Press, Box 50096, Seattle, WA 98105. TEL 206-543-4050. *1594*

PUBLIC PRODUCTIVITY AND MANAGEMENT REVIEW.
Sage Publications, Inc., 2455 Teller Rd., Thousand Oaks, CA 91320. TEL 805-499-0721. FAX 805-499-0871. *6190*

PUBLIC TREASURER.
L G C Communications, 33-39 Bowling Green Ln., London EC1R 0DA, England. TEL 44-171-505-8400. FAX 44-171-837-2725. *1625*

PUBLIC UTILITIES LAW ANTHOLOGY.
International Library Law Book Publishers, Inc., 4301 N. Fairfax Rd., Ste. 875, Arlington, VA 22203. TEL 703-528-1000. FAX 703-528-6060. *4011*

PUBLICACIONS MATEMATIQUES.
Universitat Autonoma de Barcelona, Departament de Matematiques, Apartat Postal 53, 08193 Bellterra (Barcelona), Spain. TEL 34-3-5811304. FAX 34-3-5812790. *4599*

PUBLICATIONS ON OCEAN DEVELOPMENT.
Kluwer Academic Publishers, Postbus 17, 3300 AA Dordrecht, Netherlands. TEL 31-78-6392392. FAX 31-78-6392254. *2413*

REFEREED SERIALS

PUBLISHING TECHNOLOGY REVIEW.
Pira International, Randalls Rd., Leatherhead, Surrey KT22 7RU, England. TEL 44-1372-802050. FAX 44-1372-802239. *6282*

PUDDING MAGAZINE.
Pudding House Publications, c/o Pudding House Writers Resource Center, 60 N. Main St., Johnstown, OH 43031. TEL 614-967-6060. *4521*

PUFF.
Odsgard Reklame - Marketing ApS, Hovedvejen 182, DK-2600 Glostrup, Denmark. TEL 45-43-45-34-91. FAX 45-43-43-13-28. *909*

PULA.
National Institute of Development Research and Documentation, University of Botswana, Private Bag 0022, Gaborone, Botswana. TEL 267-356364. FAX 267-357573. *6033*

PULMONARY PERSPECTIVES.
American College of Chest Physicians, 3300 Dundee Rd., Northbrook, IL 60062. TEL 847-498-1400. FAX 847-498-5460. *5121*

PULMONARY REVIEWS.
Partners in Medical Communication, 4 Brighton Rd., Clifton, NJ 07012. TEL 201-916-1000. FAX 201-916-0021. *5121*

PULPIT HELPS.
Advancing the Ministries of the Gospel International, 6815 Shallowford Rd., Chattanooga, TN 37421-1755. FAX 423-894-6863. *6363*

PUNJAB UNIVERSITY JOURNAL OF ZOOLOGY.
University of the Punjab, Department of Zoology, Quaid-e-Azam Campus, Lahore 54590, Pakistan. TEL 92-42-5864028. *848*

PUNTO DE VISTA.
Casilla de Correo 39, Sucursal 49 (B), Buenos Aires, Argentina. TEL 541-381-7229. *3249*

PURABHILEKH - PURATATVA.
Directorate of Archives, Archaeology and Museum, Rua de Ourem, Panaji-Goa 403 001, India. TEL 226692. *3538*

PURE AND APPLIED MATHEMATICS.
Academic Press, Inc., 525 B St., Ste. 1900, San Diego, CA 92101-4495. TEL 619-231-0926. FAX 619-699-6715. *4599*

PURE AND APPLIED MATHEMATICS: A WILEY INTERSCIENCE SERIES OF TEXTS, MONOGRAPHS AND TRACTS.
John Wiley & Sons, Inc., 605 Third Ave., New York, NY 10158-0012. TEL 212-850-6418. *4599*

PURE AND APPLIED MATHEMATICS SERIES.
Marcel Dekker, Inc., 270 Madison Ave., New York, NY 10016. TEL 212-696-9000. FAX 212-685-4540. *4599*

PURE FACTS.
Feingold Association of the United States, Box 6550, Alexandria, VA 22306. TEL 703-768-3287. *5094*

PUSH AND PULL.
Keighley & Worth Valley Railway, Haworth Sta., Keighley, W. Yorks. BD22 8NJ, England. TEL 44-1535-645214. FAX 44-1535-647317. *7130*

PUSHCART PRIZE: BEST OF THE SMALL PRESSES.
Pushcart Press, Box 380, Wainscott, NY 11975. TEL 516-324-9300. *4453*

PUTISHTA.
Ministerstvo na Transporta, Glavno Upravlenie na Putishchata, 3, Macedonia Bvrd., 1606 Sofia, Bulgaria. TEL 359-2-521354. FAX 359-2-9806151. *7140*

PUTTERIDGE BURY MANAGEMENT REVIEW.
University of Luton, Putteridge Bury, Hitchin Rd., Luton, Beds. LU2 8LE, England. TEL 01582-482555. FAX 01582-482689. *1503*

PYNCHON NOTES.
c/o Bernard Duyfhuizen, Man. Ed., English Dept., Univ. of Wisconsin, Eau Claire, WI 54702-4004. TEL 715-836-3165. FAX 715-836-2380. *4453*

THE PYROTECHNIC LITERATURE SERIES.
Pyrotechnic Journal, Inc., 1775 Blair Rd., Whitewater, CO 81527-9513. TEL 970-245-0692. FAX 970-245-0692. *2773*

THE PYROTECHNIC REFERENCE SERIES.
Pyrotechnic Journal, Inc., 1775 Blair Rd., Whitewater, CO 81527-9513. TEL 970-245-0692. FAX 970-245-0692. *2773*

PYROTECHNICA.
Pyrotechnica Publications, 2302 Tower Dr., Austin, TX 78703. TEL 512-476-4062. FAX 512-476-4062. *2773*

Q J I.
Louisiana State University, Shreveport, 1 University Pl., Shreveport, LA 71115-2399. TEL 318-797-5235. FAX 318-797-5122. *5962*

QIANGJIGUANG YU LIZISHU.
Qiang Jiguang yu Lizishu Journal Agency, P.O. Box 511-5, Chengdu, Sichuan 610003, People's Republic of China. TEL 86-816-2485754. FAX 86-816-2271175. *2703*

QINGNIAN WENXUEJIA.
Qiqiha'er Shi Wenlian, Tiyuchang Nan 2 Men, Hecheng, Qiqiha'er, Heilongjiang 161005, People's Republic of China. TEL 86-452-2472248. *4454*

QIXIANG XUEBAO.
China Meteorological Press, 46 Baishiqiao Rd., West Suburb, Beijing 100081, People's Republic of China. TEL 86-10-6217-6428. FAX 86-10-6217-5925. *5241*

QUADERNI DI COOPERAZIONE SANITARIA.
Amici di Raoul Follereau, Via Borselli 4, 40135 Bologna, Italy. TEL 39-51-433402. FAX 39-51-434046. *4842*

QUADERNI FRIULANI DI ARCHEOLOGIA.
Societa Friulana di Archeologia, c/o Civici Musei, 33100 Castello di Udine, Italy. TEL 39-432-26560. *378*

QUADRANT.
Christian Research, Vision Bldg., 4 Footscray Rd., Eltham, London SE9 2TZ, England. TEL 44-181-294-1989. FAX 44-181-294-0014. *6387*

QUAERENDO.
E.J. Brill, P.O. Box 9000, 2300 PA Leiden, Netherlands. TEL 31-71-5353500. FAX 31-71-5317532. *6282*

QUAKER HISTORY.
Friends Historical Association, Haverford College Library, Haverford, PA 19041. TEL 610-896-1161. FAX 610-896-1102. *6496*

QUALITATIVE INQUIRY.
Sage Publications, Inc., 2455 Teller Rd., Thousand Oaks, CA 91320. TEL 805-499-0721. FAX 805-499-0871. *6631*

QUALITATIVE SOCIOLOGY.
Human Sciences Press, Inc., 233 Spring St., New York, NY 10013-1578. TEL 212-620-8000. FAX 212-463-0742. *6723*

QUALITIQUE.
Editions Labeau, 9 rue Albert Einstein, 77420 Champs-sur-Marne, France. TEL 33-1-64682193. FAX 33-1-64687904. *994*

QUALITY AND QUANTITY.
Kluwer Academic Publishers, Postbus 17, 3300 AA Dordrecht, Netherlands. TEL 31-78-6392392. FAX 31-78-6392254. *6723*

QUALITY AND RELIABILITY ENGINEERING INTERNATIONAL.
John Wiley & Sons Ltd., Journals, Baffins Ln., Chichester, W. Sussex PO19 1UD, England. TEL 44-1243-779777. FAX 44-1243-775878. *2844*

QUALITY ENGINEERING.
Marcel Dekker Journals, 270 Madison Ave., New York, NY 10016. TEL 212-696-9000. FAX 212-685-4540. *2738*

QUALITY IN HEALTH CARE.
B M J Publishing Group, B.M.A. House, Tavistock Sq., London WC1H 9JR, England. TEL 44-171-383-6270. FAX 44-171-383-6402. *4735*

THE QUALITY MAGAZINE.
Quality Society of Australasia, P.O. Box 742, Crows Nest, N.S.W. 2065, Australia. TEL 61-2-99019938. FAX 61-2-99014677. *1503*

QUALITY OF LIFE NEWSLETTER.
M A P I Research Institute, 27 rue de la Villette, 69003 Lyon, France. TEL 33-4-72136667. FAX 33-4-72136668. *4735*

QUALITY PROGRESS.
American Society for Quality Control, 611 E. Wisconsin Ave., Box 3005, Milwaukee, WI 53201-3005. TEL 414-272-8575. FAX 414-272-1734. *2738*

QUANTITATIVE GEOLOGY AND GEOSTATISTICS.
Kluwer Academic Publishers, Postbus 17, 3300 AA Dordrecht, Netherlands. TEL 31-78-6392392. FAX 31-78-6392254. *2365*

QUANTUM (NEW YORK).
Springer-Verlag, Science Journals, 175 Fifth Ave., New York, NY 10010. TEL 212-460-1500. FAX 212-473-6272. *6561*

QUANTUM ELECTRONICS.
Turpion - Moscow Ltd., 47 Leninsky prospekt, 11793 Moscow, Russia. TEL 7-95-1356417. FAX 7-95-1358860. *2844*

QUARTERLY ACCOUNT.
Money Advice Association, Gresham House, 1st Fl., 24 Holborn Viaduct, London EC1A 2BN, England. TEL 44-171-236-3566. *994*

QUARTERLY JOURNAL OF ADMINISTRATION.
Obafemi Awolowo University Press Ltd., Periodicals Department, University P.O. Box 1044, Ile-Ife, Osun State, Nigeria. TEL 234-36-230290-9. FAX 234-2-8101963. *6191*

QUARTERLY JOURNAL OF BUSINESS AND ECONOMICS.
University of Nebraska at Lincoln, College of Business Administration, CBA Bldg., Lincoln, NE 68588-0407. TEL 402-472-3309. FAX 402-472-9777. *994*

QUARTERLY JOURNAL OF EXPERIMENTAL PSYCHOLOGY. SECTION A: HUMAN EXPERIMENTAL PSYCHOLOGY.
Taylor & Francis Ltd., Psychology Press, 1 Gunpowder Sq., London EC4A 3DE, England. TEL 44-171-5830490. FAX 44-171-5830585. *6149*

QUARTERLY JOURNAL OF EXPERIMENTAL PSYCHOLOGY. SECTION B: COMPARATIVE AND PHYSIOLOGICAL PSYCHOLOGY.
Taylor & Francis Ltd., Psychology Press, 1 Gunpowder Sq., London EC4A 3DE, England. TEL 44-171-5830490. FAX 44-171-5830585. *6149*

THE QUARTERLY JOURNAL OF MUSIC TEACHING AND LEARNING.
University of Northern Colorado, School of Music, 123 Frazier Hall, Greeley, CO 80639. TEL 970-351-2254. FAX 970-351-1923. *5428*

THE QUARTERLY JOURNAL OF NUCLEAR MEDICINE.
Edizioni Minerva Medica, Corso Bramante 83-85, 10126 Turin, Italy. TEL 39-11-678282. FAX 39-11-674502. *5113*

THE QUARTERLY JOURNAL OF SPEECH.
Speech Communication Association, 5105 Backlick Rd., Bldg. E., Annandale, VA 22003. TEL 703-750-0533. FAX 703-914-9471. *2475*

QUARTERLY OF APPLIED MATHEMATICS.
Brown University, Department of Mathamatics, 182 George St., Providence, RI 02940. *4600*

QUARTERLY REVIEW OF BIOLOGY.
University of Chicago Press, Journals Division, 5720 S. Woodlawn Ave., Chicago, IL 60637. TEL 773-753-3347. FAX 773-753-0811. *621*

QUARTERLY REVIEW OF FILM AND VIDEO.
Gordon and Breach - Harwood Academic, Amsteldisk 166, 1st Fl., 1079 LH Amsterdam, Netherlands. *5343*

QUARTERLY REVIEW OF LITERATURE POETRY SERIES.
26 Haslet Ave., Princeton, NJ 08540. TEL 609-921-6976. FAX 609-258-2230. *4521*

QUARTERLY REVIEW OF WINES.
Q R W, Inc., 24 Garfield Ave., Winchester, MA 01890. TEL 617-729-7132. FAX 617-721-0572. *526*

QUARTERLY WEST.
University of Utah, Quarterly West, 317 Olpin Union, Salt Lake City, UT 84112. TEL 801-581-3938. *4454*

QUATERNARIO.
Associazione Italiana per lo Studio del Quaternario, c/o Dr. Ravazzi, Dipto. Scienze Terra, Piazza Cittadella 4, 24129 Bergamo, Italy. TEL 39-35-248051. *2321*

QUATERNARY INTERNATIONAL.
Elsevier Science Ltd., Pergamon, P.O. Box 800, Kidlington, Oxford OX5 1DX, England. TEL 44-1865-843000. FAX 44-1865-843010. *2365*

QUATERNARY RESEARCH.
Academic Press, Inc., Journal Division, 525 B St., Ste. 1900, San Diego, CA 92101-4495. TEL 619-230-1840. FAX 619-699-6800. *2365*

QUATERNARY SCIENCE REVIEWS.
Elsevier Science Ltd., Pergamon, P.O. Box 800, Kidlington, Oxford OX5 1DX, England. TEL 44-1865-843000. FAX 44-1865-843010. *2365*

QUEBEC STUDIES.
American Council for Quebec Studies, c/o Robert Schwartzwald, Ed., French and Italian Dept., Univ. of Massachusetts, Amherst, MA 01003. TEL 413-545-6704. FAX 413-545-4778. *4454*

QUEEN CITY HERITAGE.
Cincinnati Historical Society, The Museum Center, Cincinnati Union Terminal, 1301 Western Ave., Cincinnati, OH 45203-1129. TEL 513-287-7058. FAX 513-287-7095. *3644*

QUEEN'S LAW JOURNAL.
Queen's University, Faculty of Law, Kingston, ON K7M 1B5, Canada. TEL 613-545-2246. FAX 613-545-6509. *4012*

QUEEN'S QUARTERLY.
Queen's Quarterly, Queen's University, Kingston, ON K7L 3N6, Canada. TEL 613-545-2667. FAX 613-545-6822. *3265*

QUEENSLAND UNIVERSITY OF TECHNOLOGY LAW JOURNAL.
Queensland University of Technology, Faculty of Law, George St., Brisbane, Qld. 4001, Australia. TEL 61-7-8642707. FAX 61-7-38644253. *4012*

QUEPO.
Sociedad Peruana de Cactus y Suculentas, Apdo. 3215, Lima 100, Peru. TEL 51-1-4792360. FAX 51-1-4762102. *724*

QUERY.
Saskatchewan Teachers' Federation, Saskatchewan Reading Council, 24 Thorn Crescent, Moose Jaw, SK S6J 1J1, Canada. TEL 306-694-5999. FAX 306-692-4990. *2475*

QUEST.
Quest, P.O. Box 9114, 9703 LC Groningen, Netherlands. TEL 31-50-3637509. FAX 31-50-3637100. *5746*

QUEST (CHAMPAIGN).
Human Kinetics Publishers, Inc., Box 5076, Champaign, IL 61825-5076. TEL 217-351-5076. FAX 217-351-2674. *2616*

QUEST (GRAND RAPIDS).
CSPACE Press, Box 9331, Grand Rapids, MI 49509-0331. TEL 616-452-5500. FAX 616-452-5538. *77*

QUESTIIO.
Institut d'Estadistica de Catalunya, Via Laietana 58, 08003 Barcelona, Spain. TEL 34-3-4121730. FAX 34-3-4123145. *6933*

QUESTIONS AND ANSWERS IN GENERAL TOPOLOGY.
Symposium of General Topology, Uzumasa Higashiga-Oka-13-2, Neyagawa-shi, Osaka 572, Japan. *4600*

QUFO.
Societas Upsaliensis, Institute of Earth Science, Quaternary Geology, Norbyvaegen 18 B, S-752 36 Uppsala, Sweden. TEL 46-18-18-25-00. FAX 46-18-18-25-91. *2366*

QUI PARLE.
University of California at Berkeley, Doreen B. Townsend Center for the Humanities, 460 Stephens Hall, Berkeley, CA 94720. TEL 510-643-9670. FAX 510-643-5284. *3789*

QUINCY BUSINESS NEWS.
John R. Graham, Inc., 40 Oval Rd., Ste. 2, Quincy, MA 02170-3813. TEL 617-328-0069. FAX 617-471-1504. *994*

QUINTESSENCE INTERNATIONAL.
Quintessence Publishing Co., Inc., 551 Kimberly Dr., Carol Stream, IL 60188-1881. TEL 630-682-3223. FAX 630-682-3288. *4869*

QUIPU.
Sociedad Latinoamericana de Historia de las Ciencias y la Tecnologia, Apdo. Postal 21-873, CP 04000 Mexico, DF, Mexico. TEL 525-6221864. FAX 525-6596406. *6561*

R A I R O RECHERCHE OPERATIONNELLE - OPERATIONS RESEARCH.
Gauthier - Villars, 5 rue Laromiguiere, 75005 Paris, France. TEL 33-1-40466200. FAX 33-1-40466201. *2163*

R A P R A ABSTRACTS.
Rapra Technology Ltd., Shawbury, Shrewsbury, Shrops. SY4 4NR, England. TEL 44-1939-250383. FAX 44-1939-251118. *6506*

R & D MANAGEMENT.
Blackwell Publishers Ltd., 108 Cowley Rd., Oxford OX4 1JF, England. TEL 44-1865-791100. FAX 44-1865-791347. *1503*

R B M - REVUE EUROPEENNE DE TECHNOLOGIE BIOMEDICALE.
Editions Scientifiques et Medicales Elsevier, 141 rue de Javel, 75747 Paris, France. TEL 33-1-45589067. FAX 33-1-45589421. *687*

R I F NEWSLETTER.
Reading Is Fundamental, Inc., Smithsonian Institution, 600 Maryland Ave., S.W., Rm. 600, Washington, DC 20024-2569. TEL 202-287-3220. FAX 202-287-3196. *2475*

R N A.
Cambridge University Press, Edinburgh Bldg., Shaftesbury Rd., Cambridge CB2 2RU, England. TEL 44-1223-312393. FAX 44-1223-315052. *670*

R Q.
American Library Association, 50 E. Huron St., Chicago, IL 60611-2795. TEL 312-944-6780. FAX 312-440-9374. *4208*

R S G.
Uitgeverij Isidoro B.V., Scheltuslaan 53, 2273 DM Voorburg, Netherlands. TEL 31-70-3864430. FAX 31-70-3862372. *6777*

R S R.
Pierian Press, Box 1808, Ann Arbor, MI 48106. TEL 313-434-5530. FAX 313-434-6409. *4208*

R S - S I.
Universite Laval, Cite universite, Departement des litteratures, Quebec, PQ G1K 7P4, Canada. TEL 418-565-2131. FAX 418-656-2991. *4292*

R S V P: THE DIRECTORY OF ILLUSTRATION AND DESIGN.
253 Washington Ave., Box 050314, Brooklyn, NY 11205-0314. TEL 718-857-9267. FAX 718-783-2376. *1708*

RACE, SEX & CLASS.
City University of New York, Queens College, Michael Harrington Center, 65-30 Kissena Blvd., Flushing, NY 11367-1597. *5183*

RACHUNKOWOSC.
Rachunkowosc Sp. z o.o., Ul. Tamka 18, lokal 29, 00-349 Warsaw, Poland. TEL 48-22-265621. FAX 48-22-265621. *1097*

RACING & FOOTBALL OUTLOOK.
Outlook Press Ltd., Kemp House, 152-160 City Rd., London EC1N 2NP, England. TEL 44-171-490-1212. FAX 44-171-608-3299. *6777*

RADDLE MOON.
Raddle Moon Press, 2239 Stephens St., Vancouver, BC V6K 3W5, Canada. TEL 604-736-9769. FAX 604-873-3713. *4455*

RADIATION EFFECTS AND DEFECTS IN SOLIDS.
Gordon and Breach - Harwood Academic, Amsteldisk 166, 1st Fl., 1079 LH Amsterdam, Netherlands. *5857*

RADIATION MEASUREMENTS.
Elsevier Science Ltd., Pergamon, P.O. Box 800, Kidlington, Oxford OX5 1DX, England. TEL 44-1865-843000. FAX 44-1865-843010. *5857*

RADIATION PHYSICS AND CHEMISTRY.
Elsevier Science Ltd., Pergamon, The Boulevard, Langford Ln., Kidlington, Oxford OX5 1GB, England. TEL 44-1865-843000. FAX 44-1865-843010. *5857*

RADIATION PROTECTION DOSIMETRY.
Nuclear Technology Publishing, P.O. Box 7, Ashford, Kent TN23 1JW, England. TEL 44-1233-641683. FAX 44-1233-610021. *5857*

RADIATION PROTECTION MANAGEMENT.
R S A Publications, 19 Pendleton Dr., Box 19, Hebron, CT 06248. TEL 203-228-0824. FAX 203-228-4402. *5498*

RADIATION RESEARCH.
Carden Jennings Publishing Co., Ltd., 1224 W. Main St., Ste. 200, Charlottesville, VA 22903-2858. TEL 804-979-4913. *5857*

RADIATION THERAPIST.
American Society of Radiologic Technologists, 15000 Central Ave., S.E., Albuquerque, NM 87123. TEL 505-298-4500. FAX 505-298-5063. *5113*

RADICAL AMERICA.
Alternative Education Project, Inc., 237A Holland St., Somerville, MA 02144-2402. TEL 617-628-6585. FAX 617-628-6585. *5963*

RADICAL PHILOSOPHY.
Radical Philosophy Ltd., c/o Jean Grimshaw, North View, Dundry Ln., Dundry, Bristol BS18 8JG, England. TEL 44-117-064-2986. *5746*

RADICAL TEACHER.
Boston Women's Teachers' Group, Box 383316, Cambridge, MA 02238-3316. *2476*

RADIO CLUB OF AMERICA. PROCEEDINGS.
Radio Club of America, Inc., c/o Gerri Hopkins, 3 Caro St., Red Bank, NJ 07701. TEL 732-842-5070. FAX 732-219-1938. *2027*

RADIO RIVISTA.
Ediradio, Via Scarlatti 31, 20124 Milan, Italy. TEL 2-6692894. FAX 2-66714809. *2028*

RADIO SCIENCE.
American Geophysical Union, 2000 Florida Ave., N.W., Washington, DC 20009. TEL 202-462-6900. FAX 202-328-0566. *2388*

RADIOACTIVE WASTE MANAGEMENT AND ENVIRONMENTAL RESTORATION.
Gordon and Breach - Harwood Academic, Amsteldisk 166, 1st Fl., 1079 LH Amsterdam, Netherlands. *2988*

RADIOACTIVE WASTE MANAGEMENT HANDBOOK.
Gordon and Breach - Harwood Academic, Amsteldisk 166, 1st Fl., 1079 LH Amsterdam, Netherlands. *2988*

RADIOACTIVE WASTE MANAGEMENT SERIES.
Gordon and Breach - Harwood Academic, Amsteldisk 166, 1st Fl., 1079 LH Amsterdam, Netherlands. *2988*

RADIOCARBON.
University of Arizona, Department of Geosciences, 4717 E. Ft. Lowell Rd., Tucson, AZ 85712. TEL 520-881-0857. FAX 520-881-0554. *6561*

RADIOCHEMISTRY.
Maik Nauka - Interperiodica, Mezhdunarodnyi Otdel, Ul. Profsoyuznaya, 90, 117864 Moscow, Russia. TEL 7-095-3360066. FAX 7-095-3360666. *1834*

RADIOLOGIA BRASILEIRA.
Colegio Brasileiro de Radiologia, Departamento da Associacao Medica Brasileira, Av. Paulista, 491, 13a andar, 01311-909 Sao Paulo, Brazil. TEL 55-11-285-4022. *5114*

RADIOLOGIA MEDICA.
Edizioni Minerva Medica, Corso Bramante 83-85, 10126 Turin, Italy. TEL 39-11-678282. FAX 39-11-674502. *5114*

RADIOLOGIC TECHNOLOGY.
American Society of Radiologic Technologists, 15000 Central Ave. S.E., Albuquerque, NM 87123-3917. TEL 505-298-4500. FAX 505-298-5063. *5114*

RADIOLOGY ONCOLOGY INVESTIGATIONS.
John Wiley & Sons, Inc., Journals, 605 Third Ave., New York, NY 10158. TEL 212-850-6645. FAX 212-850-6021. *4986*

RADIONIC JOURNAL.
Radionic Association Ltd., Baerlein House, Goose Green, Deddington, Banbury, Oxon OX15 0SZ, England. TEL 44-1869-338852. FAX 44-1869-338852. *4735*

RADIONUCLIDES IN NEPHROUROLOGY.
Field & Wood, Medical Periodicals, Inc., Box 975, Blue Bell, PA 19422. TEL 610-828-4010. FAX 215-482-0226. *5114*

RADIOPHARMACY AND RADIOPHARMACOLOGY YEARBOOK SERIES.
Gordon and Breach - Harwood Academic, Amsteldisk 166, 1st Fl., 1079 LH Amsterdam, Netherlands. *5692*

RADIOPHYSICS AND QUANTUM ELECTRONICS.
Plenum Publishing Corp., Consultants Bureau, 233 Spring St., New York, NY 10013-1578. TEL 212-620-8468. FAX 212-463-0742. *2650*

RADIOTHERAPY AND ONCOLOGY.
Elsevier Science Ireland Ltd., P.O. Box 85, Limerick, Ireland. TEL 353-61-471944. FAX 353-61-472144. *5114*

RAFT.
c/o John A.C. Greppin, Cleveland State University, Cleveland, OH 44115. TEL 216-687-3967. FAX 216-687-9214. *4521*

RAGGED EDGE.
Advocado Press, Box 145, Louisville, KY 40201. TEL 502-459-5343. FAX 502-899-9562. *3457*

RAILWATCH.
Railway Development Society, 4 Christchurch Sq., London E9 7HU, England. TEL 44-181-985-8548. FAX 44-181-985-8212. *7131*

RAILWAY AND CANAL HISTORICAL SOCIETY JOURNAL.
Railway and Canal Historical Society, Fron Fawnog, Hafod Rd., Gwernymynydd Mold, Clwyd CH75JE, Wales. *7131*

RAILWAYS AFRICA.
Rail-Link C C, P.O. Box 4794, 2125 Randburg, Transvaal, South Africa. TEL 27-11-463-4330. FAX 27-11-463-4224. *7132*

THE RAMANUJAN JOURNAL.
Kluwer Academic Publishers, Postbus 17, 3300 AH Dordrecht, Netherlands. TEL 31-78-6392392. FAX 31-78-6392254. *4600*

RAMBUNCTIOUS REVIEW.
Rambunctious Press, Inc., 1221 W. Pratt Blvd., Chicago, IL 60626. *4455*

RAMUS.
Aureal Publications, P.O. Box 49, Bendigo North, Vic. 3550, Australia. FAX 61-3-54447970. *1907*

RAND JOURNAL OF ECONOMICS.
Rand Corporation, 1700 Main St., Box 2138, Santa Monica, CA 90407-2138. TEL 310-393-0411. FAX 310-393-4818. *995*

RANDOM MATERIALS AND PROCESSES.
Elsevier Science B.V., Books Division, P.O. Box 211, 1000 AE Amsterdam, Netherlands. TEL 31-20-4853911. FAX 31-20-4853705. *5823*

RANDOM OPERATORS AND STOCHASTIC EQUATIONS.
V S P, P.O. Box 346, 3700 AH Zeist, Netherlands. TEL 31-30-6925790. FAX 31-30-6932081. *4600*

RANDOM STRUCTURES & ALGORITHMS.
John Wiley & Sons, Inc., Journals, 605 Third Ave., New York, NY 10158. TEL 212-850-6645. FAX 212-850-6021. *4600*

RANGIFER.
Nordisk Organ for Reinforskning (NOR), c/o NVH, Institute of Arctic Veterinary Medicine, N-9005 Tromsoe, Norway. TEL 47-77-68-43-10. FAX 47-77-68-44-11. *848*

RANLIAO HUAXUE XUEBAO.
Science Press, Marketing and Sales Department, 16 Donghuangchenggen North St., Beijing 100717, People's Republic of China. TEL 4010642. FAX 4019810. *2773*

THE RAOUL WALLENBERG INSTITUTE HUMAN RIGHTS STUDIES.
Kluwer Law International, Postbus 85889, 2508 CN The Hague, Netherlands. TEL 31-78-3381500. FAX 31-70-3051515. *5998*

RAPA NUI JOURNAL.
Easter Island Foundation, Box 6774, Los Osos, CA 93412-6774. TEL 805-528-6279. FAX 805-534-9301. *327*

RAPID COMMUNICATIONS IN MASS SPECTROMETRY.
John Wiley & Sons Ltd., Journals, Baffins Ln., Chichester, W. Sussex PO19 1UD, England. TEL 44-1243-779777. FAX 44-1243-775878. *5869*

RARA VOLUMINA.
Maria Pacini Fazzi Editore, Piazza S. Romano 16, Casella Postale 173, 55100 Lucca, Italy. TEL 39-583-55530. FAX 39-583-418245. *6282*

RARE COIN REVIEW.
Bowers and Merena Galleries, Inc., Box 1224, Wolfeboro, NH 03894. TEL 603-596-5095. FAX 603-569-5319. *5467*

RARE EARTH BULLETIN.
Multi-Science Publishing Co. Ltd., 107 High St., Brentwood, Essex CM14 4RX, England. TEL 44-1277-224632. FAX 44-1277-223453. *5208*

RARE METALS.
Zhongguo Youse Jinshu Xuehui, 2 Xinjiekouwai Dajie, Beijing 100088, People's Republic of China. TEL 86-10-6201-4488. FAX 86-10-6201-5019. *5208*

RASSEGNA MEDICO-CHIRURGICA.
Mess, Viale Mellusi 134, 82100 Benevento, Italy. TEL 39-824-311311. *4735*

RATIO.
Blackwell Publishers Ltd., 108 Cowley Rd., Oxford OX4 1JF, England. TEL 44-1865-791100. FAX 44-1865-791347. *5747*

RAVEN: A JOURNAL OF VEXILLOLOGY.
North American Vexillological Association, 1977 N. Olden Ave. Ext., Ste. 225, Trenton, NJ 08618-2193. *3238*

RAVEN CHRONICLES.
Raven Chronicles, Box 95918, University Sta., Seattle, WA 98145. TEL 206-328-1676. FAX 206-543-0501. *4356*

LA RAZA LAW JOURNAL.
University of California Press, Journals Division, 2120 Berkeley Way, No. 5812, Berkeley, CA 94720-5812. TEL 510-643-7154. FAX 510-642-9917. *4013*

RAZON ESPANOLA.
Fundacion Balmes, Paseo Santa Maria de la Cabeza 59, 4o D., 28045 Madrid, Spain. TEL 34-1-4744689. *5747*

RE: A L.
Stephen F. Austin State University, School of Liberal Arts, Box 13007, SFA Sta., Nacogdoches, TX 75962. TEL 409-468-2059. *3789*

REACTION KINETICS AND CATALYSIS LETTERS.
Akademiai Kiado Rt., P.O. Box 245, H-1519 Budapest, Hundary. TEL 36-1-20439761. FAX 36-1-2043973. *1834*

REACTIVE AND FUNCTIONAL POLYMERS.
Elsevier Science B.V., P.O. Box 211, 1000 AE Amsterdam, Netherlands. TEL 31-20-4853911. FAX 31-20-4853598. *2773*

REACTIVITY AND STRUCTURE: CONCEPTS OF ORGANIC CHEMISTRY.
Springer-Verlag, 175 Fifth Ave., New York, NY 10010. TEL 212-460-1500. FAX 212-473-6272. *1822*

READER (SYRACUSE).
Literacy Volunteers of America, Inc., 635 James St., Syracuse, NY 13203-2241. TEL 315-472-0001. FAX 315-472-0002. *2513*

READING.
Blackwell Publishers Ltd., 108 Cowley Rd., Oxford OX4 1JF, England. TEL 44-1865-791100. FAX 44-1865-791347. *2476*

READING AND WRITING.
Kluwer Academic Publishers, Postbus 17, 3300 AA Dordrecht, Netherlands. TEL 31-78-6392392. FAX 31-78-6392254. *4292*

READING AND WRITING QUARTERLY: OVERCOMING LEARNING DIFFICULTIES.
Taylor & Francis Inc., 1900 Frost Rd., Ste. 101, Bristol, PA 19007-1598. TEL 215-785-5800. FAX 215-785-5515. *2589*

READING IN POLITICAL ECONOMY.
Institute of Economic Affairs, 2 Lord North St., London SW1P 3LB, England. TEL 44-171-799-3745. FAX 44-171-799-2137. *995*

THE READING PROFESSOR.
International Reading Association, Special Interest Group: Professors of Reading Teacher Educators, c/o Dr. Lawrence M. Kenney, Ed., College of Education, Winther Hall 2035, University of Wisconsin, Whitewater, Whitewater, WI 53190. TEL 414-472-4677. FAX 414-472-5716. *2553*

READING PSYCHOLOGY.
Taylor & Francis Inc., 1900 Frost Rd., Ste. 101, Bristol, PA 19007-1598. TEL 215-785-5800. FAX 215-785-5515. *2616*

READING RESEARCH AND INSTRUCTION.
College Reading Association, c/o Dr. Gary L. Shaffer, 83 Sharon St., Harrisonburg, VA 22801-2715. TEL 540-434-2951. FAX 540-434-2951. *2616*

READING RESEARCH QUARTERLY.
International Reading Association, Inc., 800 Barksdale Rd., Box 8139, Newark, DE 19714-8139. TEL 302-731-1600. FAX 302-731-1057. *2476*

READING TEACHER.
International Reading Association, Inc., 800 Barksdale Rd., Box 8139, Newark, DE 19714-8139. TEL 302-731-1600. FAX 302-731-1057. *2616*

READING THE PAST.
University of California Press, 2120 Berkeley Way, Berkeley, CA 94720. TEL 510-642-4247. FAX 510-643-7127. *4292*

REAL ACADEMIA DE FARMACIA. ANALES.
Real Academia de Farmacia, Calle de Farmacia 11, 28004 Madrid, Spain. TEL 915-31-03-07. FAX 91-531-03-06. *5692*

REAL ACADEMIA GALEGA DE CIENCIAS. REVISTA.
Real Academia Galega de Ciencias, Rua do Franco 2, 15702 Santiago de Compostela, Spain. TEL 91-582049. FAX 91-582049. *6562*

REAL ESTATE ECONOMICS.
American Real Estate and Urban Economics Association, Indiana University, School of Business, Ste. 461, 1309 East Tenth St., Bloomington, IN 47405. *6310*

REAL ESTATE LAW JOURNAL.
Warren, Gorham & Lamont, One Penn Plaza, New York, NY 10119. TEL 212-971-5000. FAX 212-971-5113. *4013*

REAL ESTATE RESEARCH ISSUES.
Kluwer Academic Publishers, Postbus 17, 3300 AA Dordrecht, Netherlands. TEL 31-78-6392392. FAX 31-78-6392254. *6311*

REAL ESTATE REVIEW.
Warren, Gorham & Lamont, One Penn Plaza, New York, NY 10119. TEL 212-971-5000. FAX 212-971-5240. *6311*

REAL ESTATE TAX DIGEST.
Matthew Bender & Co., Inc., 2 Park Ave., New York, NY 10016. TEL 212-448-2000. *6311*

REAL-TIME SAFETY CRITICAL SYSTEMS.
Elsevier Science B.V., P.O. Box 211, 1000 AE Amsterdam, Netherlands. TEL 31-20-4853911. FAX 31-20-4853598. *2158*

REAL-TIME SYSTEMS.
Kluwer Academic Publishers Boston, Box 358, Accord Sta., Hingham, MA 02018-0358. TEL 617-871-6600. FAX 617-871-6528. *2158*

RECALL.
C T I Modern Languages, The University of Hull, School of European Languages & Cultures, Cottingham Rd., Hull HU6 7RX, England. TEL 44-1482-466373. FAX 44-1482-473816. *4321*

RECENT ADVANCES IN EPILEPSY.
Churchill Livingstone, Robert Stevenson House, 1-3 Baxter's Pl., Leith Walk, Edinburgh EH1 3AF, Scotland. TEL 44-131-556-2424. FAX 44-131-459-1177. *5095*

RECENT DEVELOPMENTS IN ALCOHOLISM.
Plenum Publishing Corp., 233 Spring St., New York, NY 10013-1578. TEL 212-620-8000. FAX 212-463-0742. *2305*

RECENT ECONOMIC THOUGHT.
Kluwer Academic Publishers, Postbus 17, 3300 AA Dordrecht, Netherlands. TEL 31-78-6392392. FAX 31-78-6392254. *1310*

RECENT PROGRESS IN HORMONE RESEARCH. PROCEEDINGS OF THE LAURENTIAN HORMONE CONFERENCE.
Academic Press, Inc., 525 B St., Ste. 1900, San Diego, CA 92101-4495. TEL 619-231-0926. FAX 619-699-6715. *4892*

RECEPTORS AND SIGNAL TRANSDUCTION.
Humana Press Inc., 999 Riverview Dr., Ste. 208, Totowa, NJ 07512. TEL 973-256-1699. FAX 973-256-8341. *670*

RECHERCHES FEMINISTES.
Universite Laval, Groupe de Recherche Multidisciplinaire Feministe, 3e etage, 2336 Chemin Ste-Foy, Quebec, Que. G1K 7P4, Canada. TEL 418-656-2131. FAX 418-656-3266. *7346*

RECHERCHES SOCIOGRAPHIQUES.
Universite Laval, Departement de Sociologie, Cite Universitaire, Quebec, PQ G1K 7P4, Canada. TEL 418-656-3544. FAX 418-656-7390. *6724*

RECLAIMING CHILDREN AND YOUTH.
Pro-Ed Inc., 8700 Shoal Creek Blvd., Austin, TX 78757-6897. TEL 512-451-3246. FAX 512-451-8542. *6149*

RECONSTRUCTION SURGERY AND TRAUMATOLOGY.
S. Karger AG, Allschwilerstr. 10, P.O. Box, CH-4009 Basel, Switzerland. TEL 41-61-3061111. FAX 41-61-3061234. *5152*

RECORD (NORWOOD).
Factory Mutual Engineering Corp., 1151 Boston-Providence Turnpike, Norwood, MA 02062. TEL 617-255-4657. FAX 617-255-4672. *3058*

THE RECORD (WEST PERTH).
587 Newcastle St., W. Perth, W.A. 6005, Australia. TEL 61-9-2277080. FAX 61-9-2277087. *6477*

RECORDER (NEW YORK).
American Irish Historical Society, 991 Fifth Ave., New York, NY 10028. TEL 212-288-2263. FAX 212-628-7927. *3038*

RECORDS OF NORTH QUEENSLAND HISTORY.
James Cook University, Department of History and Politics, Townsville, Qld. 4811, Australia. TEL 61-77-814170. FAX 61-77-814487. *3544*

RED CROSS, RED CRESCENT.
International Federation of Red Cross and Red Crescent Societies, P.O. Box 372, CH-1211 Geneva 19, Switzerland. TEL 41-22-7304222. FAX 41-22-7530395. *6683*

REDAI HAIYANG.
Science Press, Marketing and Sales Department, 16 Donghuangchenggen North St., Beijing 100717, People's Republic of China. TEL 4010642. FAX 4019810. *2414*

REDAI QIXIANG XUEBAO.
Guangzhou Redai Haiyang Qixiang Yanjiusuo, No. 6, Fujin Rd., Dongshan District, Guangzhou, Guangdong 510080, People's Republic of China. TEL 86-20-8777-6918. FAX 86-20-87773952. *5241*

REDOUBT.
University of Canberra, c/o Ron Miller, Ed., P.O. Box 1, Belconnen, A.C.T. 2614, Australia. TEL 61-6-2012945. FAX 61-6-2015300. *4356*

REFERATEDIENST ZUR LITERATURWISSENSCHAFT.
Geisteswissenschaftliche Zentren Berlin e.V., Zentrum fuer Literaturforschung, Jaegerstr. 10-11, 10117 Berlin, Germany. TEL 49-30-20192169. FAX 49-30-20192154. *4456*

REFERENCE LIBRARIAN.
Haworth Press, Inc., 10 Alice St., Binghamton, NY 13904. TEL 607-722-5857. FAX 607-722-6362. *4209*

REFERENCES EN GYNECOLOGIE OBSTETRIQUE.
Editions Mellet, 25 av. de Trudaine, 75009 Paris, France. TEL 33-1-42821562. *4966*

REFLECTIONS: NARRATIVES OF PROFESSIONAL HELPING.
University Press, California State University at Long Beach, c/o Dept. of Social Work, Long Beach, CA 90840-0902. TEL 562-985-4626. FAX 562-985-5514. *6683*

REFLECTIONS ON HIGHER EDUCATION.
Higher Education Foundation, Westminster College, Oxford OX2 9AT, England. TEL 44-1865-247644. FAX 44-1865-251847. *2554*

REFORMED WORSHIP.
C R C Publications, Education, Worship and Evangelism Department, 2850 Kalamazoo S.E., Grand Rapids, MI 49560. FAX 561-246-0834. *6439*

REFRACTORIES AND INDUSTRIAL CERAMICS.
Plenum Publishing Corp., Consultants Bureau, 233 Spring St., New York, NY 10013-1578. TEL 212-620-8468. FAX 212-463-0742. *1732*

REGENT ONLINE JOURNAL OF COMMUNICATION.
Regent University, College of Communication and the Arts, School of Communication Studies, Virginia Beach, VA 23464-9800. TEL 804-523-7943. FAX 804-424-7051. *5343*

REGIONAL AND FEDERAL STUDIES.
Frank Cass, Newbury House, 890-900 Eastern Ave., Newbury Park, Ilford, Essex IG2 7HH, England. TEL 44-181-599-8866. FAX 44-181-599-0984. *6034*

REGIONAL DEVELOPMENT STUDIES.
United Nations Centre for Regional Development, Nagono 1-47-1, Nakamura-ku, Nagoya 450, Japan. TEL 052-561-9377. FAX 052-561-9375. *1367*

THE REGIONAL REVIEW.
Yorkshire and Humberside Regional Research Observatory, University of Leeds, School of Geography, Leeds LS2 9JT, England. TEL 44-113-233-3336. FAX 44-113-233-3308. *6562*

REGIONAL SCIENCE & URBAN ECONOMICS.
North-Holland, P.O. Box 211, 1000 AE Amsterdam, Netherlands. TEL 31-20-4853911. FAX 31-20-4853598. *3757*

REGIONAL STUDIES.
Carfax Publishing Co., P.O. Box 25, Abingdon, Oxon. OX14 3UE, England. TEL 44-1235-401000. FAX 44-1235-401550. *3758*

THE REGIONALIST.
Institute of Community and Area Development, University of Georgia, 1234 S. Lumpkin St., Athens, GA 30602-3552. TEL 706-542-3350. FAX 706-542-6189. *6192*

REGULATED RIVERS: RESEARCH AND MANAGEMENT.
John Wiley & Sons Ltd., Journals, Baffins Ln., Chichester, W. Sussex PO19 1UD, England. TEL 44-1243-779777. FAX 44-1243-775878. *7299*

REGULATORY PEPTIDES.
Elsevier Science B.V., P.O. Box 211, 1000 AE Amsterdam, Netherlands. TEL 31-20-4853911. FAX 31-20-4853598. *1822*

REGULATORY TOXICOLOGY AND PHARMACOLOGY.
Academic Press, Inc., Journal Division, 525 B St., Ste. 1900, San Diego, CA 92101-4495. TEL 619-230-1840. FAX 619-699-6800. *2980*

REHAB & COMMUNITY CARE MANAGEMENT.
B C S Communications Ltd., 101 Thorncliffe Park Dr., Toronto, ON M4H 1M2, Canada. TEL 416-421-7944. FAX 416-421-0966. *5046*

REHABILITACE A FYZIKALNI LEKARSTVI.
Nakladatelske Stredisko C L S J.E. Purkyne, Sokolska 31, 120 26 Prague 2, Czech Republic. TEL 420-2-24911420. FAX 420-2-24911420. *5126*

REHABILITACIA.
F. Liecreh, Cervenova 34, 811 03 Bratislava, Slovakia. TEL 42-7-5314700. FAX 42-7-5314700. *4736*

REHABILITATION EDUCATION.
Elliott & Fitzpatrick, Inc., 1135 Cedar Shoals Dr., Athens, GA 30605. TEL 706-548-8161. FAX 706-546-8417. *2589*

REHABILITATION PSYCHOLOGY.
Springer Publishing Company, 536 Broadway, New York, NY 10012-3955. TEL 212-431-4370. FAX 212-941-7842. *6149*

REIMPRESSION.
Gordon and Breach - Harwood Academic, Amsteldisk 166, 1st Fl., 1079 LH Amsterdam, Netherlands. *4456*

REJYONAL ANESTEZI BULTEN.
Rejyonal Anestezi Dernegi, c/o Dr. Serdar Erdine, Ed., Istanbul Tip Fakultesi, Agri Merkezi, Capa Klinikleri, 34390 Istanbul, Turkey. TEL 90-212-6350135. FAX 90-212-6310541. *4807*

RELACIONES.
Editorial Periodica S.R.L., Avda. Luis A. de Herrera, 1042, Ap. 708, 11300 Montevideo, Uruguay. TEL 598-2-621108. FAX 598-2-621108. *6149*

RELIABILITY ASSESSMENT.
North American Electric Reliability Council, Princeton Forrestal Village, 116-290 Village Blvd., Princeton, NJ 08540-5731. TEL 609-452-8060. *2691*

RELIABILITY ENGINEERING AND SYSTEM SAFETY.
Elsevier Science Ltd., P.O. Box 800, Kidlington, Oxford OX5 1DX, England. TEL 44-1865-843000. FAX 44-1865-843010. *2738*

RELIABLE COMPUTING.
Kluwer Academic Publishers, Postbus 17, 3300 AA Dordrecht, Netherlands. TEL 31-78-6392392. FAX 31-78-6392254. *2116*

RELIGION.
Academic Press Ltd., 24-28 Oval Rd., London NW1 7DX, England. TEL 44-171-267-4466. FAX 44-171-482-2293. *6365*

RELIGION AND AMERICAN CULTURE.
Indiana University Press, Journal Division, 601 N. Morton St., Bloomington, IN 47404. TEL 812-855-9449. FAX 812-855-8507. *6365*

RELIGION AND LITERATURE.
University of Notre Dame, Department of English, Notre Dame, IN 46556. TEL 219-239-5725. FAX 219-631-8609. *4456*

RELIGION & PUBLIC EDUCATION.
Webster University, 470 E. Lockwood, Webster Groves, MO 63119. TEL 314-968-7135. *2476*

RELIGION AND PUBLIC LIFE.
Transaction Publishers, Transaction Periodicals Consortium, Department 3092, Rutgers University, New Brunswick, NJ 08903. TEL 908-445-2280. FAX 908-445-3138. *6365*

RELIGION & THEOLOGY.
Unisa Press, Periodicals, P.O. Box 392, Pretoria 0001, South Africa. TEL 27-12-4292953. FAX 27-12-4293221. *6365*

RELIGION FOR PEACE.
World Conference on Religion and Peace, International Division, 777 United Nations Plaza, New York, NY 10017. TEL 212-687-2163. FAX 212-983-0566. *6365*

RELIGION, STATE AND SOCIETY: THE KESTON JOURNAL.
Carfax Publishing Co., P.O. Box 25, Abingdon, Oxon. OX14 3UE, England. TEL 44-1235-401000. FAX 44-1235-401550. *6366*

RELIGIONS IN THE GRAECO-ROMAN WORLD.
E.J. Brill, P.O. Box 9000, 2300 PA Leiden, Netherlands. TEL 31-71-5353500. FAX 31-71-5317532. *6366*

REMEDIAL AND SPECIAL EDUCATION.
Pro-Ed Inc., 8700 Shoal Creek Blvd., Austin, TX 78757-6897. TEL 512-451-3246. FAX 512-451-8542. *2589*

REMOTE SENSING OF EARTH RESOURCES AND ENVIRONMENT.
Kluwer Academic Publishers, Postbus 17, 3300 AA Dordrecht, Netherlands. TEL 31-78-6392392. FAX 31-78-6392254. *2321*

REMOTE SENSING OF ENVIRONMENT.
Elsevier Science Inc., Box 945, New York, NY 10159-0945. TEL 212-633-3730. FAX 212-633-3680. *3419*

REMOTE SENSING REVIEWS.
Gordon and Breach - Harwood Academic, Amsteldisk 166, 1st Fl., 1079 LH Amsterdam, Netherlands. *2738*

RENAISSANCE (CAMBRIDGE).
National Certified Nursing Assistant Association, 1 Kendall Sq., Bldg. 200, Ste. 2200, Cambridge, MA 02139. *4948*

RENAISSANCE AND REFORMATION.
University of Guelph, Department of French Studies, Guelph, ON N1G 2W1, Canada. TEL 519-824-4120. FAX 519-763-9572. *4456*

RENAL FAILURE.
Marcel Dekker Journals, 270 Madison Ave., New York, NY 10016. TEL 212-696-9000. FAX 212-685-4540. *5165*

RENASCENCE.
Marquette University Renascence, Brooks Hall, Box 1881, Milwaukee, WI 53201-1881. TEL 414-288-6725. *4456*

RENDITIONS.
Chinese University of Hong Kong, Research Centre for Translation, Shatin, New Territories, Hong Kong, People's Republic of China. TEL 852-26097407. FAX 852-26035149. *5536*

RENEWABLE ENERGY.
Elsevier Science Ltd., Pergamon, P.O. Box 800, Kidlington, Oxford OX5 1DX, England. TEL 44-1865-843000. FAX 44-1865-843010. *2677*

RENEWABLE RESOURCES JOURNAL.
Renewable Natural Resources Foundation, 5430 Grosvenor Ln., Bethesda, MD 20814. TEL 301-493-9101. FAX 301-493-6148. *2949*

RENEWAL NEWS.
Presbyterian Renewal Publications, Box 429, Black Mountain, NC 28711-0429. TEL 704-669-7373. FAX 704-669-4880. *6440*

RENLEIXUE XUEBAO.
Science Press, Marketing and Sales Department, 16 Donghuangchenggen North St., Beijing 100717, People's Republic of China. TEL 86-10-4010642. FAX 86-10-4019810. *327*

RENWEN JI SHEHUI KEXUE JIKAN.
Academia Sinica, Sun Yat-Sen Institute for Social Sciences and Philosophy, Nankang, Taipei, Taiwan 11529, Republic of China. TEL 886-2-782-1693. FAX 886-2-785-4160. *5747*

REPORT ON OBJECT ANALYSIS AND DESIGN.
Sigs Publications, Inc., 71 W. 23rd St., New York, NY 10010-4102. TEL 212-242-7447. FAX 212-242-7574. *2145*

REPORT PSYCHOLOGIE.
Deutscher Psychologen Verlag GmbH, Heilsbachstr. 22, 53123 Bonn, Germany. TEL 49-228-98731-0. FAX 49-228-9873170. *6149*

REPORTS ON MATHEMATICAL PHYSICS.
Elsevier Science Ltd., Pergamon, P.O. Box 800, Kidlington, Oxford OX5 1DX, England. TEL 44-1865-843000. FAX 44-1865-843010. *5823*

REPORTS ON PROGRESS IN PHYSICS.
I O P Publishing Ltd., Dirac House, Temple Back, Bristol BS1 6BE, England. TEL 44-117-929-7481. FAX 44-117-929-4318. *5824*

REPORTS ON RESEARCH ASSISTED BY THE PETROLEUM RESEARCH FUND.
American Chemical Society, 1155 16th St., N.W., Washington, DC 20036. TEL 202-872-4600. FAX 202-872-4615. *5621*

REPRESENTATION: JOURNAL OF REPRESENTATIVE DEMOCRACY.
The Arthur McDougall Fund, 6 Chancel St., London SE1 0UU, England. TEL 44-171-620-1080. FAX 44-171-928-4366. *5964*

REPRESENTATIONS.
University of California Press, Journals Division, 2120 Berkeley Way, No. 5812, Berkeley, CA 94720-5812. TEL 510-643-7154. FAX 510-642-9917. *3790*

REPRESENTATIVE RESEARCH IN SOCIAL PSYCHOLOGY.
University of North Carolina at Chapel Hill, Department of Psychology, Davie Hall, Campus Box 3270, Chapel Hill, NC 27599-3270. TEL 919-962-7636. FAX 919-962-2537. *6150*

REPRESENTING CHILDREN.
Independent Representation for Children in Need (I R C H I N), 1 Downham Rd. S., Heswall, Wirral, Merseyside L60 5RG, England. TEL 44-151-342-7852. FAX 44-151-342-7852. *6683*

REPRODUCTION BULLETIN.
Andrews Paper & Chemical Co., Inc., 1 Channel Dr., Box 509, Port Washington, NY 11050. TEL 516-767-2800. FAX 516-767-1632. *6085*

REPRODUCTION, NUTRITION, DEVELOPMENT.
Editions Scientifiques et Medicales Elsevier, 141 rue de Javel, 75747 Paris, France. TEL 33-1-45589022. FAX 33-1-45589421. *622*

REPRODUCTIVE TOXICOLOGY.
Elsevier Science Inc., Box 945, New York, NY 10159-0945. TEL 212-633-3730. FAX 212-633-3680. *2980*

REPUBLIC OF CHINA. NATIONAL SCIENCE COUNCIL. PROCEEDINGS. PART B: LIFE SCIENCES.
National Science Council, 106 Ho-Ping E. Rd., Sec. 2, Taipei, Taiwan 106, Republic of China. TEL 2-737-7594. FAX 2-737-7248. *4737*

REQUIREMENTS FOR CERTIFICATION OF TEACHERS, COUNSELORS, LIBRARIANS, ADMINISTRATORS FOR ELEMENTARY SCHOOLS, SECONDARY SCHOOLS, JUNIOR COLLEGES.
University of Chicago Press, 5801 S. Ellis Ave., Chicago, IL 60637. TEL 773-702-7899. *2577*

RES PUBLICA.
Deborah Charles Publications, 173 Mather Ave., Liverpool L18 6JZ, England. TEL 44-151-724-2500. FAX 44-151-729-0371. *5747*

RESEARCH ADVANCES IN ALCOHOL & DRUG PROBLEMS.
Plenum Publishing Corp., 233 Spring St., New York, NY 10013-1578. TEL 212-620-8000. FAX 212-463-0742. *2305*

RESEARCH AND CLINICAL CENTER FOR CHILD DEVELOPMENT. ANNUAL REPORT.
Hokkaido University, Research and Clinical Center for Child Development, Nishi 7-chome, Kita 11-jo, Kita-ku, Sapporo-shi 060, Japan. TEL 81-11-706-2607. FAX 81-11-706-4946. *1855*

RESEARCH & DEVELOPMENT.
Cahners Publishing Company (Des Plaines), Division of Reed Elsevier Inc., 1350 E. Touhy Ave., Box 5080, Des Plaines, IL 60018-5080. TEL 847-390-2343. FAX 847-390-2618. *6971*

RESEARCH AND TEACHING IN DEVELOPMENTAL EDUCATION.
New York College Learning Skills Association, Finger Lakes Community College, 4355 Lake Shore Dr., Canandaigua, NY 14424. TEL 716-394-3500. FAX 716-394-5005. *2477*

RESEARCH COMMUNICATIONS IN ALCOHOL & SUBSTANCES OF ABUSE.
P J D Publications Ltd., Box 966, Westbury, NY 11590. TEL 516-626-0650. FAX 516-626-5546. *5692*

RESEARCH COMMUNICATIONS IN MOLECULAR PATHOLOGY AND PHARMACOLOGY.
P J D Publications Ltd., Box 966, Westbury, NY 11590. TEL 516-626-0650. *4737*

RESEARCH COMMUNICATIONS IN PSYCHOLOGY, PSYCHIATRY AND BEHAVIOR.
P J D Publications Ltd., Box 966, Westbury, NY 11590. TEL 516-626-0650. FAX 516-626-5546. *6150*

RESEARCH EVALUATION.
Beech Tree Publishing, 10 Watford Close, Guildford, Surrey GU1 2EP, England. TEL 44-1483-567497. FAX 44-1483-567497. *6562*

RESEARCH GROUP FOR EUROPEAN MIGRATION PROBLEMS. PUBLICATIONS.
Kluwer Academic Publishers, Postbus 17, 3300 AA Dordrecht, Netherlands. TEL 31-78-6392392. FAX 31-78-6392254. *6057*

RESEARCH IN DEVELOPMENTAL DISABILITIES.
Elsevier Science Ltd., Pergamon, P.O. Box 800, Kidlington, Oxford OX5 1DX, England. TEL 44-1865-843000. FAX 44-1865-843010. *5095*

RESEARCH IN EXPERIMENTAL MEDICINE.
Springer-Verlag, Heidelberger Platz 3, 14197 Berlin, Germany. TEL 49-30-82787-0. FAX 49-30-82787448. *4902*

RESEARCH IN HIGHER EDUCATION.
Human Sciences Press, Inc., 233 Spring St., New York, NY 10013. TEL 212-620-8000. FAX 212-463-0742. *2577*

RESEARCH IN IMMUNOLOGY.
Editions Scientifiques et Medicales Elsevier, 141 rue de Javel, 75747 Paris, France. TEL 33-1-45589022. FAX 33-1-45589421. *4800*

RESEARCH IN MICROBIOLOGY.
Editions Scientifiques et Medicales Elsevier, 141 rue de Javel, 75747 Paris, France. TEL 33-1-45589022. FAX 33-1-45589421. *793*

RESEARCH IN MIDDLE LEVEL EDUCATION QUARTERLY.
National Middle School Association, 2600 Corporate Exchange Dr., Ste. 370, Columbus, OH 43231. TEL 614-895-4730. FAX 614-895-4750. *2616*

RESEARCH IN NONDESTRUCTIVE EVALUATION.
Springer-Verlag, Science Journals, 175 Fifth Ave., New York, NY 10010. TEL 212-460-1500. FAX 212-473-6272. *2739*

RESEARCH IN NURSING & HEALTH.
John Wiley & Sons, Inc., Journals, 605 Third Ave., New York, NY 10158. TEL 212-850-6645. FAX 212-850-6021. *4948*

RESEARCH IN PHILOSOPHY AND TECHNOLOGY.
J A I Press Inc., 55 Old Post Rd., No. 2, Box 1678, Greenwich, CT 06830-1678. TEL 203-661-7602. FAX 203-661-0792. *5747*

RESEARCH IN POST-COMPULSORY EDUCATION.
Triangle Journals Ltd., P.O. Box 65, Wallingford, Oxon. OX10 0YG, England. TEL 44-1491-838013. FAX 44-1491-834968. *2554*

RESEARCH IN SCIENCE & TECHNOLOGICAL EDUCATION.
Carfax Publishing Co., P.O. Box 25, Abingdon, Oxon. OX14 3UE, England. TEL 44-1235-401000. FAX 44-1235-401550. *2477*

RESEARCH IN SCIENCE EDUCATION.
Australasian Science Education Research Association, c/o C.J. McRobbie, Ed., Center for Mathematics & Science Education, Queensland University of Technology, Victoria Park Rd., Kelvin Grove, Brisbane, Qld. 4059, Australia. TEL 61-7-38643333. *2616*

RESEARCH IN THE SOCIAL SCIENTIFIC STUDY OF RELIGION.
J A I Press Inc., 55 Old Post Rd., No. 2, Box 1678, Greenwich, CT 06830-1678. TEL 203-661-7602. FAX 203-661-0792. *6367*

RESEARCH IN VIROLOGY.
Editions Scientifiques et Medicales Elsevier, 141 rue de Javel, 75747 Paris, France. TEL 33-1-45589022. FAX 33-1-45589421. *4843*

RESEARCH IN YORUBA: LANGUAGE & LITERATURE.
Technicians of the Sacred, c/o Lawrence O. Adewole, Editor, Department of African Language and Literature, Obafemi Awolowo University, Ile-Ilfe, Osun State, Nigeria. *4292*

RESEARCH METHODS IN NEUROCHEMISTRY.
Plenum Publishing Corp., 233 Spring St., New York, NY 10013-1578. TEL 212-620-8000. FAX 212-463-0742. *670*

RESEARCH MONOGRAPHS IN CELL AND TISSUE PHYSIOLOGY.
Elsevier Science B.V., Books Division, P.O. Box 211, 1000 AE Amsterdam, Netherlands. TEL 31-20-4853911. FAX 31-20-4853705. *4737*

RESEARCH MONOGRAPHS IN IMMUNOLOGY.
Elsevier Science B.V., Books Division, P.O. Box 211, 1000 AE Amsterdam, Netherlands. TEL 31-20-4853911. FAX 31-20-4853705. *4800*

RESEARCH NOTES IN ARTIFICIAL INTELLIGENCE.
Morgan Kaufmann Publishers, Inc., 340 Pine St., 6th Fl., San Francisco, CA 94104-3205. TEL 415-392-2665. FAX 415-982-2665. *2104*

RESEARCH NOTES IN MATHEMATICS.
John Wiley & Sons, Inc., Journals, 605 Third Ave., New York, NY 10158-0012. TEL 212-850-6000. FAX 212-850-6088. *4601*

RESEARCH ON CHEMICAL INTERMEDIATES.
V S P, P.O. Box 346, 3700 AH Zeist, Netherlands. TEL 31-30-6925790. FAX 31-30-6932081. *1764*

RESEARCH ON TECHNOLOGICAL INNOVATION, MANAGEMENT AND POLICY.
J A I Press Inc., 55 Old Post Rd., No. 2, Box 1678, Greenwich, CT 06830-1678. TEL 203-661-7602. FAX 203-661-0792. *6972*

RESEARCH PAPERS IN GEOGRAPHY AND ENVIRONMENTAL SCIENCE.
University of Newcastle, Department of Geography and Environmental Science, Newcastle, N.S.W. 2308, Australia. TEL 61-49-215095. FAX 61-49-215877. *3419*

RESEARCH PAPERS IN MANAGEMENT STUDIES.
University of Cambridge, Judge Institute of Management Studies, Trumpington St., Cambridge CB2 1AG, England. TEL 44-1223-339700. FAX 44-1223-339701. *1575*

RESEARCH POLICY.
North-Holland, P.O. Box 211, 1000 AE Amsterdam, Netherlands. TEL 31-20-4853911. FAX 31-20-4853598. *6562*

RESEARCH STRATEGIES.
J A I Press Inc., 55 Old Post Rd., No. 2, Box 1678, Greenwich, CT 06830-1678. TEL 203-661-7602. FAX 203-661-0792. *4209*

RESEARCHES ON POPULATION ECOLOGY.
Kotaigun Seitai Gakkai, Ogawa Higashi Iru, Shimodachuri Dori, Kamigyo-ku, Kyoto 602, Japan. TEL 81-298-53-4760. FAX 81-298-53-6614. *6057*

RESIDENTIAL TREATMENT FOR CHILDREN & YOUTH.
Haworth Press, Inc., 10 Alice St., Binghamton, NY 13904. TEL 607-722-5857. FAX 607-722-6362. *1855*

RESIDENTS' PRESCRIBING REFERENCE.
Prescribing Reference, Inc., 5 Park Pl., Ste. 1010, New York, NY 10007. TEL 212-766-7200. FAX 212-732-2360. *5692*

RESOURCE AND ENERGY ECONOMICS.
North-Holland, P.O. Box 211, 1000 AE Amsterdam, Netherlands. TEL 31-20-4853911. FAX 31-20-4853598. *2678*

RESOURCE MANAGEMENT AND OPTIMIZATION.
Gordon and Breach - Harwood Academic, Amsteldisk 166, 1st Fl., 1079 LH Amsterdam, Netherlands. *2243*

RESOURCE SHARING & INFORMATION NETWORKS.
Haworth Press, Inc., 10 Alice St., Binghamton, NY 13904. TEL 607-722-5857. FAX 607-722-6362. *4209*

RESOURCES (NASHVILLE).
F I S I - Madison Financial, Box 40726, Nashville, TN 37204. TEL 615-371-2658. *2258*

RESOURCES, CONSERVATION AND RECYCLING.
Elsevier Science B.V., P.O. Box 211, 1000 AE Amsterdam, Netherlands. TEL 31-20-4853911. FAX 31-20-4853598. *2990*

RESOURCES FOR AMERICAN LITERARY STUDY.
Pennsylvania State University Press, USB 1, Ste. C, University Park, PA 16802-1003. TEL 814-865-1327. FAX 814-863-1408. *4457*

RESOURCES POLICY.
Elsevier Science Ltd., Pergamon, P.O. Box 945, Kidlington, Oxford OX5 1DX, England. TEL 44-1865-843000. FAX 44-1865-843010. *2678*

RESPIRATION.
S. Karger AG, Allschwilerstr. 10, P.O. Box, CH-4009 Basel, Switzerland. TEL 41-61-3061111. FAX 41-61-3061234. *5122*

RESPIRATION PHYSIOLOGY.
Elsevier Science B.V., P.O. Box 211, 1000 AE Amsterdam, Netherlands. TEL 31-20-4853911. FAX 31-20-4853598. *821*

RESPONSE (FAIRFAX).
National Association for Search and Rescue, 4500 Southgate Pl., Ste. 100, Chantilly, VA 22021-1714. TEL 703-352-1349. FAX 703-352-0309. *5015*

RESTAURATOR.
K.G. Saur Verlag KG, A member of the Reed Elsevier plc group, Ortlerstr. 8, 81373 Munich, Germany. TEL 49-89-76902-0. FAX 49-89-76902150. *4210*

RESTORATION & EIGHTEENTH CENTURY THEATRE RESEARCH.
Loyola University of Chicago, Department of English, 6525 N. Sheridan Rd., Chicago, IL 60626. FAX 312-508-8696. *4457*

RESTORATION AND MANAGEMENT NOTES.
University of Wisconsin Press, Journal Division, 114 N. Murray St., Madison, WI 53715. TEL 608-262-4952. FAX 608-262-7560. *2243*

RESTORATION QUARTERLY.
Restoration Quarterly Corporation, ACU Station, Box 8227, Abilene, TX 79699. TEL 915-674-3781. FAX 915-674-3776. *6367*

RESTORATION: STUDIES IN ENGLISH LITERARY CULTURE, 1660-1700.
Tennessee Technological University, Department of the College of Arts and Sciences, Cookeville, TN 38505. TEL 931-372-3119. FAX 931-372-6142. *4457*

RESTORATIVE NEUROLOGY AND NEUROSCIENCE.
Elsevier Science Ireland Ltd., P.O. Box 85, Limerick, Ireland. TEL 353-61-471944. FAX 353-61-472144. *5095*

RESTORICA.
Simon van der Stel Foundation, P.O. Box 12293, Centrahil 6006, South Africa. TEL 27-41-562849. FAX 27-41-562849. *414*

RESUSCITATION.
Elsevier Science Ireland Ltd., P.O. Box 85, Limerick, Ireland. TEL 353-61-471944. FAX 353-61-472144. *5122*

RETAIL SYSTEMS ALERT.
Ardea Research Corp., 77 Oak St., Ste. 201, Box 332, Newton Upper Falls, MA 02164. TEL 617-527-8102. FAX 617-527-8102. *2177*

RETHINKING SCHOOLS.
Rethinking Schools Limited, 1001 E. Keefe Ave., Milwaukee, WI 53212. TEL 414-694-9646. FAX 414-964-7220. *2477*

RETINA.
Lippincott - Raven Publishers, 227 E. Washington Sq., Philadelphia, PA 19106. TEL 215-238-4200. FAX 215-238-4227. *5000*

REUMATISMO.
Societa Italiana di Reumatologia (S.I.R.), C.so Plebisciti 9, 20129 Milano, Italy. TEL 39-2-7382330. FAX 39-2-7385763. *5126*

REUMATOLOGIA.
Instytut Reumatologiczny, Ul. Spartanska 1, 02-637 Warsaw, Poland. TEL 48-22-444241. FAX 48-22-449522. *5127*

REUSE - RECYCLE.
Technomic Publishing Co. Inc., 851 New Holland Ave., Box 3535, Lancaster, PA 17604. TEL 717-291-5609. FAX 717-295-4538. *2990*

REVEIL MISSIONNAIRE.
Missionnaires de la Consolata, 2505 W. bd. Gouin, Montreal, PQ H3M 1B5, Canada. TEL 514-334-1910. FAX 514-332-1940. *6367*

REVIEW (BINGHAMTON).
Fernand Braudel Center for the Study of Economies, Historical Systems, and Civilizations, Box 6000, Binghamton University, Binghamton, NY 13902-6000. TEL 607-777-4924. FAX 607-777-4315. *1310*

REVIEW (WASHINGTON).
Heldref Publications, 1319 Eighteenth St., N.W., Washington, DC 20036-1802. TEL 202-296-6267. *3473*

REVIEW FOR RELIGIOUS.
Jesuits of the Missouri Province, 3601 Lindell Blvd., St. Louis, MO 63108. TEL 314-977-7363. FAX 314-977-7362. *6477*

REVIEW OF ACCOUNTING INFORMATION SYSTEMS.
Western Academic Press, Box 620760, Littleton, CO 80162. TEL 303-904-4750. FAX 303-978-0413. *1097*

REFEREED SERIALS

REVIEW OF ACCOUNTING STUDIES.
Kluwer Academic Publishers Boston, Box 358, Accord Sta., Hingham, MA 02018-0358. TEL 617-871-6600. FAX 617-871-6528. *1097*

REVIEW OF AFRICAN POLITICAL ECONOMY.
Carfax Publishing Co., P.O. Box 25, Abingdon, Oxon. OX14 3UE, England. TEL 44-1235-401000. FAX 44-1235-401550. *6034*

REVIEW OF AGRICULTURAL ECONOMICS.
American Agricultural Economics Association, 1110 Buckeye Ave., Ames, IA 50010-8063. TEL 515-233-3234. FAX 515-233-3101. *201*

THE REVIEW OF ARCHAEOLOGY.
Review of Archaeology, Inc., 10 Liberty St., Salem, MA 01970. TEL 508-745-1876. FAX 508-745-8303. *379*

REVIEW OF AUSTRIAN ECONOMICS.
Kluwer Academic Publishers Boston, Box 358, Accord Sta., Hingham, MA 02018-0358. TEL 617-871-6600. FAX 617-871-6528. *1310*

REVIEW OF BUSINESS.
St. John's University, College of Business Administration, Bent Hall, 8000 Utopia Pkwy., Jamaica, NY 11439. TEL 718-990-6768. FAX 718-990-1868. *996*

REVIEW OF CENTRAL AND EAST EUROPEAN LAW.
Kluwer Law International, Postbus 85889, 2508 CN The Hague, Netherlands. TEL 31-70-3081500. FAX 31-70-3081515. *4016*

REVIEW OF CONSTITUTIONAL STUDIES.
Centre for Constitutional Studies, Rm. 459, Law Centre, University of Alberta, Edmonton, AB T6G 2H5, Canada. TEL 403-492-5681. FAX 403-492-9959. *4071*

THE REVIEW OF CONTEMPORARY FICTION.
Review of Contemporary Fiction, Inc., 4241 Illinois State University, Normal, IL 61790-4241. TEL 309-438-7555. FAX 309-437-7422. *4457*

REVIEW OF DERIVATIVES RESEARCH.
Kluwer Academic Publishers Boston, Box 358, Accord Sta., Hingham, MA 02018-0358. TEL 617-871-6600. FAX 617-871-6528. *1164*

THE REVIEW OF ECONOMICS AND STATISTICS.
M I T Press, 5 Cambridge Center, Cambridge, MA 02142-1399. TEL 617-577-1545. FAX 617-577-1545. *996*

THE REVIEW OF EDUCATION - PEDAGOGY - CULTURAL STUDIES.
Gordon and Breach - Harwood Academic, Amsteldisk 166, 1st Fl., 1079 LH Amsterdam, Netherlands. *2503*

REVIEW OF EDUCATIONAL RESEARCH.
American Educational Research Association, 1230 17th St., N.W., Washington, DC 20036-3078. TEL 202-223-9485. FAX 202-775-1824. *2478*

REVIEW OF EMPLOYMENT TOPICS.
Labour Relations Agency, Windsor House, 9-15 Bedford St., Belfast BT2 7NU, N. Ireland. TEL 44-1232-321442. FAX 44-1232-330827. *1452*

REVIEW OF EXISTENTIAL PSYCHOLOGY AND PSYCHIATRY.
Humanities Press, 165 First Ave., Atlantic Highlands, NJ 07716-1289. TEL 908-872-1441. FAX 908-872-0717. *6150*

REVIEW OF FINANCIAL ECONOMICS.
J A I Press Inc., 55 Old Post Rd., No. 2, Box 1678, Greenwich, CT 06830-1678. TEL 203-661-7602. FAX 203-661-0792. *996*

REVIEW OF FINANCIAL MARKETS.
John Wiley & Sons (Asia) Pte. Ltd., 2 Clementi Loop 02-01, Jin Xing Distripark, Singapore 129809, Singapore. TEL 65-4632400. FAX 65-4634605. *1164*

THE REVIEW OF FINANCIAL STUDIES.
Oxford University Press, Journals, 2001 Evans Rd., Cary, NC 27513. TEL 919-677-0977. FAX 919-677-1714. *1164*

REVIEW OF INCOME AND WEALTH.
International Association for Research in Income and Wealth, New York University, Dept. of Economics, 269 Mercer St., Rm. 700, New York, NY 10003. TEL 212-998-8917. FAX 212-366-5067. *1461*

REVIEW OF INDUSTRIAL ORGANIZATION.
Kluwer Academic Publishers, Postbus 17, 3300 AA Dordrecht, Netherlands. TEL 31-78-6392392. FAX 31-78-6392254. *1310*

REVIEW OF INFORMATION SCIENCE.
University Association for Information Science, *4210*

REVIEW OF INTERNATIONAL ECONOMICS.
Blackwell Publishers Ltd., 108 Cowley Rd., Oxford OX4 1JF, England. TEL 44-1865-791100. FAX 44-1865-791347. *996*

REVIEW OF ISLAMIC ECONOMICS.
Islamic Foundation, Markfield Dawah Centre, Ratby Lane, Markfield, Leicester LE67 9RN, England. TEL 01530-244944. FAX 01530-244946. *1286*

REVIEW OF LAW & SOCIAL CHANGE.
New York University, Review of Law & Social Change, 110 W. Third St., New York, NY 10012. TEL 212-998-6370. FAX 212-995-4032. *4016*

REVIEW OF OPHTHALMOLOGY.
Chilton Co., 201 King of Prussia Rd., Radnor, PA 19089. TEL 610-964-4370. FAX 610-964-2959. *5000*

REVIEW OF PALAEOBOTANY AND PALYNOLOGY.
Elsevier Science B.V., P.O. Box 211, 1000 AE Amsterdam, Netherlands. TEL 31-20-4853911. FAX 31-20-4853598. *5563*

THE REVIEW OF POLICY ISSUES.
Sheffield Hallam University, Unit 7, Sheffield Science Park, Howard St., Sheffield S1 2LX, England. TEL 44-114-2534462. FAX 44-114-2534467. *997*

REVIEW OF QUANTITATIVE FINANCE AND ACCOUNTING.
Kluwer Academic Publishers Boston, Box 358, Accord Sta., Hingham, MA 02018-0358. FAX 617-871-6528. *1097*

REVIEW OF REGIONAL STUDIES.
Southern Regional Science Association, 505A Stokely Management Center, The University of Tennessee, Knoxville, TN 37996-0550. TEL 615-974-3303. FAX 615-974-4601. *3758*

REVIEW OF RESEARCH IN EDUCATION.
American Educational Research Association, 1230 17th St., N.W., Washington, DC 20036-3078. TEL 202-223-9485. FAX 202-775-1824. *2616*

REVIEW OF SCIENTIFIC INSTRUMENTS.
American Institute of Physics, One Physics Ellipse, College Park, MD 20740-3843. TEL 301-209-3000. *3805*

REVIEW OF SCOTTISH CULTURE.
Tuckwell Press, The Mill House, Phantassie, E. Linton, E. Lothian EH40 3DG, Scotland. TEL 44-1620-860164. *3039*

REVIEW OF SOCIAL ECONOMY.
Routledge, 11 New Fetter Ln., London EC4P 4EE, England. TEL 44-171-583-9855. FAX 44-171-842-2298. *997*

REVIEWS IN ANTHROPOLOGY.
Gordon and Breach - Harwood Academic, Amsteldisk 166, 1st Fl., 1079 LH Amsterdam, Netherlands. *328*

REVIEWS IN CLINICAL AND EXPERIMENTAL HAEMATOLOGY.
Martin Dunitz Ltd., 7-9 Pratt St., Camden, London NW1 0AE, England. TEL 44-171-482-2202. *4921*

REVIEWS IN CONTEMPORARY PHARMACOTHERAPY.
Marius Press, P.O. Box 15, Carnforth LA6 1HW, England. TEL 44-1524-733027. FAX 44-1524-736659. *5692*

REVIEWS IN ENGINEERING GEOLOGY.
Geological Society of America, 3300 Penrose Pl., Box 9140, Boulder, CO 80301. TEL 303-447-2020. FAX 303-447-1133. *2796*

REVIEWS IN FISH BIOLOGY AND FISHERIES.
Thomson Science, 2-6 Boundary Row, London SE1 8HN, England. TEL 44-171-8650066. FAX 44-171-5229623. *848*

REVIEWS IN MEDICAL MICROBIOLOGY.
Thomson Science, 2-6 Boundary Row, London SE1 8HN, England. TEL 44-171-865-0198. FAX 44-171-928-7876. *793*

REVIEWS IN MEDICAL VIROLOGY.
John Wiley & Sons Ltd., Journals, Baffins Ln., Chichester, W. Sussex PO19 1UD, England. TEL 44-1243-779777. FAX 44-1243-775878. *793*

REVIEWS IN PARTICULATE MATERIALS.
Metal Powder Industries Federation, 105 College Rd. E., Princeton, NJ 08540. TEL 609-987-8523. FAX 609-987-8523. *5208*

REVIEWS IN PERINATAL MEDICINE.
Lippincott - Raven Publishers, 227 E. Washington Sq., Philadelphia, PA 19106. TEL 215-238-4200. FAX 215-238-4227. *4967*

REVIEWS IN TOXICOLOGY.
I O S Press, Van Diemenstraat 94, 1013 CN Amsterdam, Netherlands. TEL 31-20-6382189. FAX 31-20-6203419. *2980*

REVIEWS OF GEOPHYSICS.
American Geophysical Union, 2000 Florida Ave., N.W., Washington, DC 20009. TEL 202-462-6900. FAX 202-328-0566. *2388*

REVIEWS OF HEMATOLOGY.
P J D Publications Ltd., Box 966, Westbury, NY 11590. TEL 516-626-0650. FAX 516-626-5546. *4921*

REVIEWS OF MODERN PHYSICS.
American Physical Society, One Physics Ellipse, College Park, MD 20740-3844. TEL 301-209-3202. *5824*

REVIEWS OF OCULOMOTOR RESEARCH.
Elsevier Science B.V., Books Division, P.O. Box 211, 1000 AE Amsterdam, Netherlands. TEL 31-20-4853911. FAX 31-20-4853705. *5001*

REVIEWS OF PHYSIOLOGY, BIOCHEMISTRY AND PHARMACOLOGY.
Springer-Verlag, 175 Fifth Ave., New York, NY 10010. TEL 212-460-1500. FAX 212-473-6272. *821*

REVIEWS OF PLASMA PHYSICS.
Plenum Publishing Corp., Consultants Bureau, 233 Spring St., New York, NY 10013-1578. TEL 212-620-8000. FAX 212-463-0742. *5824*

REVIEWS OF REPRODUCTION.
Journals of Reproduction & Fertility Ltd., 22 Newmarket Rd., Cambridge CB5 8DT, England. TEL 44-1223-351809. FAX 44-1223-359754. *622*

REVIEWS ON HETEROATOM CHEMISTRY.
M Y U, Scientific Publishing Division, 2-32-3 Sendagi, Bunkyo-ku, Tokyo 113, Japan. TEL 81-3-3821-2930. FAX 81-3-3827-8547. *1764*

REVISION: A JOURNAL OF CONSCIOUSNESS AND TRANSFORMATION.
Heldref Publications, 1319 Eighteenth St., N.W., Washington, DC 20036-1802. TEL 202-296-6267. FAX 202-296-5149. *5460*

REVISTA A M R I G S.
Associacao Medica do Rio Grande do Sul, Av. Ipiranga, 5311, 90620 Porto Alegre RS, Brazil. TEL 55-51-3392899. FAX 55-51-3392998. *4737*

REVISTA ARGENTINA DE MICROBIOLOGIA.
Asociacion Argentina de Microbiologia, Bulnes 44, P.B. B, 1176 Buenos Aires, Argentina. TEL 54-1-9584888. FAX 54-1-9824888. *793*

REVISTA BRASILEIRA DE BOTANICA.
Sociedade Botanica de Sao Paulo, Caixa Postal 11491, 05422-970 Sao Paulo, SP, Brazil. TEL 55-11-55846300. FAX 55-11-5773678. *725*

REVISTA BRASILEIRA DE CIENCIAS SOCIAIS.
Associacao Nacional de Pos-Graduacao e Pesquisa em Ciencias Sociais, Ave. Prof. Luciano Gaulberto 315, Sala 116, Butanta - Cidade Universitaria, 05508-900 Sao Paulo, Brazil. TEL 55-11-8184664. FAX 55-11-8185043. *6632*

REVISTA BRASILEIRA DE ENTOMOLOGIA.
Sociedade Brasileira de Entomologia, Caixa Postal 9063, 01065-970 Sao Paulo SP, Brazil. TEL 55-11-274-3455 ext. 260. FAX 55-11-2743690. *760*

REVISTA BRASILEIRA DE ESTUDOS PEDAGOGICOS.
Instituto Nacional de Estudos e Pesquisas Educacionais, Sgas Q.607 Bl.50 - L2 Sul, 70200-670 Brasilia DF, Brazil. TEL 55-61-2442612. FAX 55-61-2444712. *2478*

REVISTA BRASILEIRA DE FISIOLOGIA VEGETAL.
Sociedade Brasileira de Fisiologia Vegetal, Cx. Postal 0281, 70359-9700 Brasilis DF, Brazil. FAX 55-61-556744. *725*

REVISTA BRASILEIRA DE INFORMACAO BIBLIOGRAFICA EM CIENCIAS SOCIAIS.
Associacao Nacional de Pos-Graduacao e Pesquisa em Ciencias Sociais, Ave. Prof. Luciano Gualberto 315, Sala 116, Butanta - Cidade Universitaria, 05508-900 Sao Paulo, Brazil. TEL 55-11-8184664. FAX 55-11-8185043. *6650*

REVISTA BRASILEIRA DE OTO-RINO-LARINGOLOGIA.
Sociedade Brasileira de Otorrinolaringologia, Rua Visconde de Piraja 330, Grupo 510, 22410 Rio de Janeiro RJ, Brazil. TEL 55-21-2870893. FAX 55-21-2870893. *5025*

REVISTA BRASILEIRA DE PESQUISAS MEDICAS E BIOLOGICAS.
Associacao Brasilira de Divulgacao Cientifica, c/o Eduardo Moacyr Krieger, Faculdade de Medicina de Ribeirao Preto, Campus de Ribeirao Preto, 14049-900 Ribeirao Preto SP, Brazil. TEL 55-16-633-3825. *4737*

REVISTA BRASILEIRA DE SAUDE ESCOLAR.
Associacao Brasileira de Saude Escolar, Prof. Rubiao Meira 61, Praca 02, Ciudade Universitaria, 05508-900 Sao Paulo SP, Brazil. *6249*

REVISTA CENTROAMERICANA DE ADMINISTRACION PUBLICA.
Instituto Centroamericano de Administracion Publica, Apdo. 10025, 1000 San Jose, Costa Rica. TEL 506-234-1011. FAX 506-225-2049. *6192*

REVISTA CERES.
Universidade Federal de Vicosa, 36570-000 Vicosa, Minas Gerais, Brazil. TEL 55-31-8992136. FAX 55-31-8992205. *148*

REVISTA CHILENA DE HISTORIA Y GEOGRAFIA.
Sociedad Chilena de Historia y Geografia, Londres 65, Casilla 1386, Santiago, Chile. TEL 56-2-6382489. *3645*

REVISTA CHILENA DE LITERATURA.
Universidad de Chile, Facultad de Filosofia y Humanidades, Casilla 10136, Santiago, Chile. TEL 56-2-6787022. FAX 56-2-2716823. *4458*

REVISTA COLOMBIANA DE MATEMATICAS.
Sociedad Colombiana de Matematicas, Apdo. Aereo No. 2521, Bogota, Colombia. FAX 2686465. *4601*

REVISTA CUBANA DE CIENCIA AGRICOLA.
Instituto de Ciencia Animal, Tulipan No. 1011 e-47 y Loma, Nuevo Vedado, Havana, Cuba. TEL 537-99180. FAX 537-335382. *148*

REVISTA DE AGRICULTURA.
Caixa Postal 60, 13400-970 Piracicaba, Sao Paulo, Brazil. TEL 0194-22-3604. *148*

REVISTA DE ANTROPOLOGIA.
Universidade de Sao Paulo, Faculdade de Filosofia, Letras e Ciencias Humanas, C.P. 8105, 01065-970 Sao Paulo SP, Brazil. TEL 55-11-8183726. FAX 55-11-8183163. *328*

REVISTA DE BIOLOGIA MARINA Y OCEANOGRAFIA.
Universidad de Valparaiso, Instituto de Oceanologia, Casilla 13-D, Vina del Mar, Chile. TEL 56-32-832702. FAX 56-32-833214. *623*

REVISTA DE CRITICA LITERARIA LATINOAMERICANA.
Latinoamericana Editores, 4319 Dwinelle Hall, University of California, Department of Spanish and Portuguese, Berkeley, CA 94720-2590. TEL 510-883-9443. FAX 510-883-9443. *4458*

REVISTA DE DERECHO CIVIL ARAGONES.
Institucion Fernando el Catolico, Plaza de Espana 2, 50071 Zaragoza, Spain. TEL 34-976-288878. FAX 34-976-288869. *4066*

REVISTA DE ECOLOGIA LATINOAMERICANA.
Centro de Investigacion y Reproduccion de Especies Silvestres, Apdo. Postal 397, Merida 5101, Venezuela. TEL 58-74-712939. *623*

REVISTA DE ECONOMIA POLITICA.
Centro de Economia Politica, Avda. Jorge Joao Saad 104, 05618-000 Sao Paulo, SP, Brazil. TEL 55-11-8443196. FAX 55-11-8446137. *5965*

REVISTA DE ESTUDIOS COLOMBIANOS.
Association of North American Colombianists, c/o James Alstrum, Secy., Illinois State U., Dept. of For. Lang., Normal, IL 61761. TEL 309-438-7620. FAX 309-438-8038. *3645*

REVISTA DE ESTUDIOS HISPANICOS.
University of Puerto Rico, Seminario de Estudios Hispanicos "Federico de Onis", P.O. Box 21787, San Juan, PR 00931-1787. TEL 787-764-0000 ext. 3673. FAX 787-763-5899. *3790*

REVISTA DE ESTUDIOS REGIONALES.
Universidad Nacional de Cuyo, Facultad de Filosofia y Letras, Centro Universitario, Parque Gral. San Martin, CC 345, 5500 Mendoza, Argentina. TEL 54-61-253010. FAX 54-61-380457. *6633*

REVISTA DE ESTUDOS IBERO-AMERICANOS.
Pontificia Universidade Catolica do Rio Grande do Sul, Pos-Graduacao em Historia da Cultura, Avda. Ipiranga 6681, Caixa Postal 1429, 90619-900 Porto Alegre RS, Brazil. *3039*

REVISTA DE FILOSOFIA.
Universidad del Zulia, Centro de Estudios Filosoficos, Edif. Viyaluz, Av. 4 esq. Calle 74, 8o piso, Maracaibo, Zulia, Venezuela. TEL 58-61-596840. *5748*

REVISTA DE GASTROENTEROLOGIA DE MEXICO.
Obsidiana Editores, S.A., Czda. de Tlalpan 2365, Col. Ciudad Jardin, 04370 Mexico DF, Mexico. TEL 6899133. *4914*

REVISTA DE GASTROENTEROLOGIA DEL PERU.
Sociedad de Gastroenterologia del Peru, Casilla Postal 14, 0028 Lima, Peru. TEL 51-1-4492467. FAX 51-1-4729055. *4914*

REVISTA DE HISTORIA JERONIMO ZURITA.
Institucion Fernando el Catolico, Plaza de Espana 2, 50071 Zaragoza, Spain. TEL 34-976-288878. FAX 34-976-288869. *3595*

REVISTA DE INVESTIGACION CLINICA.
Instituto Nacional de la Nutricion "Salvador Zubiran", Av. San Fernando y Viaducto Tlalpan, Mexico 22, D.F., Mexico. TEL 915-573-1200. FAX 915-655-1076. *4738*

REVISTA DE INVESTIGACION Y DESARROLLO PESQUERO.
Instituto Nacional de Investigacion y Desarrollo Pesquero, Casilla de Correo 175, 7600 Mar del Plata, Argentina. TEL 54-23-860963. FAX 54-23-861830. *3077*

REVISTA DE MARINA.
Armada de Chile, Casilla 220, Valparaiso, Chile. TEL 56-32-281222. FAX 56-32-281223. *5283*

REVISTA DE MEDICINA LEGALA.
Societatea de Medicina Legala din Romania, Sos. Vitan-Birzesti 9, 75669 Bucharest, Rumania. TEL 40-1-6343890. FAX 40-1-3210260. *4906*

REVISTA DE MEDICINA SI FARMACIE.
Universitatea de Medicina si Farmacie din Targu Mures, Str. Gh. Marinescu Nr. 38, 4300 Targu-Mures, Rumania. TEL 40-65-213127. FAX 40-65-210407. *4738*

REVISTA DE MICROBIOLOGIA.
Sociedade Brasileira de Microbiologia, c/o Luiz Rachid Trabulsi, Ed., Depto. de Microbiologia, Instituto de Ciencias Biomedicas USP, Av. Prof. Lineu Prestes, 1374, 05508-900 Sao Paulo, SP, Brazil. TEL 55-11-8139647. FAX 55-11-81396747. *793*

REVISTA DE PSICOLOGIA.
Pontificia Universidad Catolica del Peru, Fondo Editorial, Apdo. 1761, Lima 32, Peru. TEL 51-14-626390. FAX 51-14-611785. *6150*

REVISTA DE PSICOLOGIA SOCIAL.
Fundacion Infancia y Aprendizaje, Ctra. de Canillas 138, 16 C, 28043 Madrid, Spain. TEL 34-1-3883874. FAX 34-1-3003527. *6150*

REVISTA DE QUIMICA.
Pontificia Universidad Catolica del Peru, Fondo Editorial, Apdo. 1761, Lima 32, Peru. TEL 51-14-626390. FAX 5114-611785. *1765*

REVISTA DE SAUDE PUBLICA.
Universidade de Sao Paulo, Faculdade de Saude Publica, Av. Dr. Arnaldo 715, 01246-904 Sao Paulo, Brazil. TEL 55-11-2809163. *6249*

REVISTA ESPANOLA DE ANTROPOLOGIA BIOLOGICA.
Sociedad Espanola de Antropologia Biologica, Fac. de Biologia, Dpto. Biologia Animal I, Univ. Complutense, 28040 Madrid, Spain. TEL 34-1-3944936. FAX 34-1-3944947. *328*

REVISTA ESPANOLA DE ECONOMIA AGRARIA.
Ministerio de Agricultura, Pesca y Alimentacion, Centro de Publicaciones, Paseo de la Infanta Isabel 1, 28071 Madrid, Spain. TEL 34-1-3475551. FAX 34-1-3475722. *201*

REVISTA ESPANOLA DE FISICA.
Real Sociedad Espanola de Fisica, Fac. de Fisica, Univ. Complutense, Ciudad Universitaria, 28040 Madrid, Spain. TEL 34-1-3944359. FAX 34-1-5433879. *5824*

REVISTA FORESTAL CENTROAMERICANA.
Centro Agronomico Tropical de Investigacion y Ensenanza, Area de Comunicacion e Informatica, CATIE 7170, Turrialba, Costa Rica. TEL 506-556-6784. FAX 506-556-6282. *3161*

REVISTA IBEROAMERICANA DE MICOLOGIA.
Asociacion Espanola de Micologia, Depto. Inmunologia, Microbiologia y Parasitologia, Universidad del Pais Vasco, Apartado 699, 48080 Bilbao, Spain. TEL 34-4-4648800 ext. 2745. FAX 34-4-4649266. *4739*

REVISTA MATEMATICA IBEROAMERICANA.
Real Sociedad Matematica Espanola, c/o Departamento de Matematicas, Universidad Autonoma de Madrid, 28049 Madrid, Spain. TEL 34-1-397-4930. FAX 34-1-397-4889. *4601*

REVISTA MEDICA DE CHILE.
Sociedad Medica de Santiago, Casilla 168, Correo 55, Santiago 9, Chile. TEL 56-2-2748985. FAX 56-2-3651724. *4739*

REVISTA MEXICANA DE ASTRONOMIA Y ASTROFISICA.
Universidad Nacional Autonoma de Mexico, Instituto de Astronomia, Apdo. Postal 70-264, 04510 Mexico DF, Mexico. TEL 52-5-6223900. FAX 52-5-616-0653. *500*

REVISTA MEXICANA DE FISICA.
Sociedad Mexicana de Fisica, A.C., Apdo. 70-348, Coyoacan, 04511 Mexico, D.F., Mexico. TEL 525-622-4848. *5824*

REVISTA MEXICANA DE FITOPATOLOGIA.
Sociedad Mexicana de Fitopatologia, Apdo. Postal 128-F., Ciudad Universitaria, 66450 San Nicolas de los Garza, NL, Mexico. TEL 52-8-3766320. *242*

REVISTA MEXICANA DE OFTALMOLOGIA.
Sociedad Mexicana de Oftalmologia, Boston, No. 99, Col. Noche Buena, 03720 Mexico D.F., Mexico. *5001*

REVISTA MEXICANA DE SOCIOLOGIA.
Universidad Nacional Autonoma de Mexico, Instituto de Investigaciones Sociales, Circuito Mario de la Cueva, Ciudad Universitaria, 04510 Mexico, D.F., Mexico. TEL 52-5-666-4616. FAX 52-5-6652443. *6725*

REVISTA MINELOR.
Directia Generala Strategia Industriei Miniere si Geologiei, Calea Victoriei 220, Sector 1, 71104 Bucharest, Rumania. TEL 40-1-6505020. *5314*

REVISTA MUSICAL CHILENA.
Universidad de Chile, Facultad de Artes, Compania 1264, Casilla 2100, Santiago, Chile. TEL 56-2-6781337. FAX 56-2-6711435. *5430*

REVISTA PADURILOR.
R.A. Romsilva, Bd. Magheru nr.31, etaj. 1, sector 1, 70162 Bucharest, Rumania. TEL 40-1-6592020. FAX 40-1-2228428. *3161*

REVISTA PAULISTA DE MEDICINA.
Associacao Paulista de Medicina, Av. Brigadeiro Luiz Antonio, 278, andar 8, 01318 Sao Paulo SP, Brazil. TEL 55-11-2323141 ext. 242. FAX 55-11-6077979. *4739*

REVISTA PORTUGUESA DE ESTOMATOLOGIA E CIRURGIA MAXILO FACIAL.
Sociedade Portuguesa de Estomatologia e Medicina Dentaria, Av. Rainha D. Amelia 36, 1600 Lisbon, Portugal. TEL 351-1-7593948. *4869*

REVISTA TECNOLOGICA.
Ministerio de Industria Basica, Calle San Jose 857, CP 10300, Havana, Cuba. TEL 537-702540. FAX 537-335345. *6972*

REVISTA TIEMPO Y ESPACIO.
Universidad del Bio-Bio, Departamento de Historia, Geografia y Ciencias Sociales, Casilla 447, Chillan, Chile. TEL 56-42-214417. FAX 56-42-214417. *3510*

REVISTA UNIMAR.
Universidade Estadual de Maringa, Av. Colombo, 3690, 87020-900 Maringa PR, Brazil. TEL 55-442-224378. FAX 55-442-232676. *2554*

REVISTA VENEZOLANA DE GERENCIA.
Universidad del Zulia, Vicerrectorado Academico, Edificio del Rectorado, Apdo. Postal 15401, Ave. Guajira con Calle 66, Maracaibo, Estado Zulia, Venezuela. TEL 58-61-528397. FAX 58-61-528397. *1505*

REVIVER.
Alcoholics Anonymous Central Service Office, 127 Edwin St., Croydon, N.S.W. 2132, Australia. TEL 61-2-97991199. FAX 61-2-9716754. *2305*

REVMATOLOGIIA.
Tsentar za Informatsiia po Meditsina, 1, Sv. Georgi Sofiiski St., 1431 Sofia, Bulgaria. TEL 359-2-522342. FAX 359-2-522393. *5127*

REVOLUTION: THE JOURNAL OF NURSE EMPOWERMENT.
A.D. Von Publishers, Inc., 56 McArthur Ave., Staten Island, NY 10312. FAX 718-317-0858. *4948*

REVOLUTIONARY RUSSIA.
Frank Cass, Newbury House, 890-900 Eastern Ave., Newbury Park, Ilford, Essex 1G2 7HH, England. TEL 44-181-599-8866. FAX 44-181-599-0984. *3595*

REVUE AGRICOLE ET SUCRIERE DE MAURICE.
Societe de Technologie Agricole et Sucriere de l'Ile Maurice, c/o M.S.I.R.I., Reduit, Mauritius. TEL 230-4541061. FAX 230-4541971. *242*

REVUE ANDRE MALRAUX REVIEW.
c/o Karen Levy, John Roweiser, Eds., University of Tennessee, Dept. of Romance and Asian Languages, 601 McClung Tower, Knoxville, TN 36996-0460. TEL 423-974-2311. FAX 423-974-2313. *4458*

REVUE ARACHNOLOGIQUE.
J.C. Ledoux, Ed. & Pub., 43 rue Paul Bert, 30390 Aramon, France. *848*

REVUE BELGE D'HISTOIRE CONTEMPORAINE.
Jan Dhondt Foundation v.z.w., Blandijnberg 2, 9000 Ghent, Belgium. TEL 32-9-2644007. FAX 32-9-2644189. *3510*

REVUE BELGE DE SECURITE SOCIALE.
Ministere des Affaires Sociales, de la Sante Publique et del'Environnement, Service des Publications, Rue de la Vierge Noire 3C, 1000 Brussels, Belgium. TEL 32-2-5098019. *6684*

REVUE D'HISTOIRE DE L'AMERIQUE FRANCAISE.
Institut d'Histoire de l'Amerique Francaise, 261 Avenue Bloomfield, Montreal, PQ H2V 3R6, Canada. TEL 514-278-2232. FAX 514-271-6369. *3645*

REVUE D'HISTOIRE DU THEATRE.
Societe d'Histoire du Theatre, 98 Bd. Kellermann, 75013 Paris, France. TEL 33-1-45884655. FAX 33-1-45898763. *7012*

REVUE D'INTEGRATION EUROPEENNE.
Canadian Council for European Affairs, c/o Department of Political Studies, University of Saskatchewan, Saskatoon, SK S7N 0W0, Canada. TEL 306-966-5231. FAX 306-966-5250. *6035*

REVUE DE BIO-MATHEMATIQUE.
Editions Europeennes, 11 bis Ave. de la Providence, 92160 Antony, France. *4601*

REVUE DE DROIT COMMERCIAL BELGE.
Kluwer Rechtswetenschappen Belgie, Santvoortbeeklaan 21-25, 2100 Antwerp, Belgium. FAX 32-3-3600467. *4018*

REVUE DE LA CERAMIQUE ET DU VERRE.
61 rue Marconi, B.P. 3, 62880 Vendin-le-Vieil, France. TEL 33-3-21794444. FAX 33-3-21794445. *1733*

REVUE DE MATHEMATIQUES SPECIALES.
Librairie Vuibert, 20 rue Berbier du Mets, 75647 Paris cedex 13, France. TEL 33-1-44084900. FAX 33-1-44084959. *4601*

REVUE DE METALLURGIE.
Revue de Metallurgie, 11-13 cours Valmy, 92070 La Defense Cedex, France. TEL 33-1-41020380. FAX 33-1-41020388. *5209*

REVUE DE MICROPALEONTOLOGIE.
Maison de la Geologie, B.P. 11705, 75224 Paris Cedex 05, France. *5563*

REVUE DE QUMRAN.
J. Gabalda et Cie, 18 rue P.et M. Curie, 75005 Paris, France. *6368*

REVUE DES COLLECTIVITES LOCALES ET L'EQUIPEMENT.
Publications Periodique Professionnelles, 31 rue du General Delestraint, 75016 Paris, France. TEL 33-1-53845353. FAX 33-1-53845351. *6223*

REVUE DES ETUDES GEORGIENNES ET CAUCASIENNES.
Editions Peeters s.p.r.l., Bondgenotenlaan 153, 3000 Leuven, Belgium. TEL 32-16-235170. FAX 32-16-228500. *3595*

REVUE DES QUESTIONS SCIENTIFIQUES.
Societe Scientifique de Bruxelles, Rue de Bruxelles 61, B-5000 Namur, Belgium. TEL 32-81-724464. FAX 32-81-724502. *6563*

REVUE EUROPEENE DE PSYCHOLOGIE APPLIQUEE.
Swets & Zeitlinger bv, P.O. Box 825, 2160 SZ Lisse, Netherlands. TEL 31-252-435111. FAX 31-252-415888. *6151*

REVUE EUROPEENNE DES MIGRATIONS INTERNATIONALES.
Association pour l'Etude des Migrations Internationales, 99 av. du Recteur-Pineau, 86022 Poitiers Cedex, France. TEL 33-5-49454656. FAX 33-5-49454645. *6058*

REVUE FRANCAISE D'ACUPUNCTURE.
Association Francaise d'Acupuncture, Tour CIT, 3 rue de l'Arrivee, 75749 Paris Cedex 15, France. TEL 33-1-43202626. FAX 33-1-43205446. *298*

REVUE FRANCAISE D'AQUARIOLOGIE, HERPETOLOGIE.
Musee de Zoologie, 34 rue Sainte-Catherine, 54000 Nancy, France. *848*

REVUE FRANCAISE D'ETUDES AMERICAINES.
Editions Belin, 8 rue Ferou, 75278 Paris Cedex 06, France. TEL 33-1-46342142. FAX 33-1-43251829. *6725*

REVUE GENERALE DE THERMIQUE.
Editions Scientifiques et Medicales Elsevier, 141 rue de Javel, 75747 Paris, France. TEL 33-1-45589000. FAX 33-1-45-589419. *5842*

REVUE GENERALE DES ROUTES ET DES AERODROMES.
9 rue Magellan, 75008 Paris, France. TEL 33-1-40738003. FAX 33-1-49520180. *7140*

REVUE HELLENIQUE DE DROIT INTERNATIONAL.
Hellenic Institute of International and Foreign Law, 73 Solonos St., 10679 Athens, Greece. TEL 30-1-3615-646. FAX 30-1-3619-777. *4125*

REVUE INDEPENDANTE.
Syndicat des Journalistes et Ecrivains, 206-208, rue Edouard-Branly, 93100 Montreuil-sous-Bois, France. TEL 33-3-88150720. FAX 33-3-88150760. *4357*

REVUE INTERDISCIPLINAIRE D'ETUDES JURIDIQUES.
Facultes Universitaires de Saint Louis, Seminaire Interdisciplinaire d'Etudes Juridiques, Boulevard du Jardin Botanique, 43, 1000 Brussels, Belgium. TEL 32-2-2117894. FAX 32-2-2117997. *4018*

REVUE INTERNATIONALE DE POLICE CRIMINELLE.
International Criminal Police Organization (Interpol), Secretariat General, 200 quai Charles de Gaulle, 69006 Lyon, France. TEL 33-4-72447000. FAX 33-4-72447163. *2279*

REVUE MEDICALE DE BRUXELLES.
Association des Medecins Anciens Etudiants de l'Universite Libre de Bruxelles (A.M.U.B.), Route de Lennik 808, Bte. 612, 1070 Brussels, Belgium. TEL 32-2-555-6062. FAX 32-2-555-6117. *4739*

REVUE MEDICALE DE LIEGE.
Institut de Medecine, 13 rue Alex Bouvy, 4020 Liege, Belgium. TEL 32-41-437572. FAX 32-41-437572. *4739*

REVUE QUART MONDE.
Editions Quart Monde, 15 rue Maitre Albert, 75005 Paris, France. TEL 33-1-46334977. FAX 33-1-43296448. *6684*

REVUE ROMANE.
Munksgaard International Publishers Ltd., 35 Noerre Soegade, P.O. Box 2148, DK-1016 Copenhagen K, Denmark. TEL 45-33-127030. FAX 45-33-129387. *4294*

REVUE SVETOVEJ LITERATURY.
Slovak Society of Literary Translations, Laurinska 2, 815 08 Bratislava, Slovakia. TEL 42-7-5334016. FAX 42-7-5331294. *4357*

RHEEDEA.
Indian Association for Angiosperm Taxonomy, c/o University of Calicut, Department of Botany, Calicut, India. *725*

RHETORIC REVIEW.
University of Arizona, Department of English, Rhetoric Review, Tucson, AZ 85721. TEL 602-621-3371. FAX 602-621-7397. *2554*

RHETORIC SOCIETY QUARTERLY.
Rhetoric Society of America, c/o Department of English, Pennsylvania State University, University Park, PA 16802-6200. TEL 814-863-9585. FAX 814-863-7285. *4459*

RHETORICA.
University of California Press, Journals Division, 2120 Berkeley Way, No. 5812, Berkeley, CA 94720-5812. TEL 510-643-7154. FAX 510-642-9917. *4294*

RHEUMATOLOGY.
S. Karger AG, Allschwilerstr. 10, P.O. Box, CH-4009 Basel, Switzerland. TEL 41-61-3061111. FAX 41-61-3061234. *5127*

RHINOLOGY.
International Rhinologic Society, c/o Journal Rhinology, Postbus 85500, 3508 GA Utrecht, Netherlands. TEL 31-30-2506645. FAX 31-30-2541922. *5025*

THE RHODODENDRON.
Australian Rhododendron Society, P.O. Box 21, Olinda, Vic. 3788, Australia. TEL 61-3-98441558. *3204*

RHODORA.
New England Botanical Club, Inc., 22 Divinity Ave., Cambridge, MA 02138. TEL 603-862-3222. FAX 603-862-4757. *726*

RIHABIRITESHON IGAKU.
Japanese Association of Rehabilitation Medicine, 1-1-17 Komone, Itabashi-ku, Tokyo, Japan. TEL 81-3-5966-2031. FAX 81-3-5966-2033. *5047*

RIJKSINSTITUUT VOOR OORLOGSDOCUMENTATIE. MONOGRAFIEEN.
Kluwer Academic Publishers, Postbus 17, 3300 AA Dordrecht, Netherlands. TEL 31-78-6392392. FAX 31-78-6392254. *3596*

RIJKSMUSEUM VAN OUDHEDEN, LEIDEN. OUDHEIDKUNDIGE MEDEDELINGEN.
Rijksmuseum van Oudheden, Postbus 11114, 2301 EC Leiden, Netherlands. TEL 31-71-5163163. FAX 31-71-5149941. *380*

RIKUSUI SEIBUTSUGAKUHO.
Nara Rikusui Seibutsu Kenkyukai, c/o Nara Joshi Daigaku Rigakubu, Seibutsugaku Kyoshitsu, Kitauoyanish-machi, Nara-shi, Nara-ken 630, Japan. TEL 0742-20-3424. *623*

RIO BRAVO.
University of Texas - Pan American, Center for International Studies, LA 102, Edinburg, TX 78539. TEL 210-381-3572. FAX 210-316-7012. *6035*

RIRON TO HOHO.
Japanese Association for Mathematical Sociology, Osaka University, Faculty of Human Sciences, 1-2, Yamadaoka, Suita 565, Japan. TEL 81-6-879-8068. FAX 81-6-879-8068. *6726*

RISK ANALYSIS.
Plenum Publishing Corp., 233 Spring St., New York, NY 10013-1578. TEL 212-620-8000. FAX 212-463-0742. *4601*

RISK, DECISION AND POLICY.
Thomson Professional, 2-6 Boundary Row, London SE1 8HN, England. TEL 44-171-8650066. FAX 44-171-5229623. *1505*

RISK: HEALTH, SAFETY & ENVIRONMENT.
Franklin Pierce Law Center, 2 White St., Concord, NH 03301. TEL 603-228-1541. FAX 603-224-3342. *6249*

RIVAON HA-YISRAELI L'MISIM.
State Revenue Administration, Custom Sq., 32 Agron St., Jerusalem, Israel. TEL 972-2-6703201. FAX 972-2-6258602. *1626*

RIVEON LEBANKAUT.
Association of Banks in Israel, P.O. Box 2258, Tel Aviv 61021, Israel. TEL 972-3-5609019. FAX 972-3-5660317. *1165*

RIVER STYX.
Big River Association, 3207 Washington Ave., St. Louis, MO 63103-1218. TEL 314-533-4541. *4357*

RIVERS.
S E L & Associates, 408 Arikaree Peak Dr., Livermore, CO 80536-9391. *7299*

RIVISTA.
British-Italian Society, 21-22 Grosvenor St., London W1X 9FE, England. TEL 44-171-495-5536. *6035*

RIVISTA DI NEURORADIOLOGIA.
Edizioni del Cantauro, Via del Pratello 8, 40122 Bologna, Italy. TEL 39-337-532604. *5115*

RIVISTA DI PEDIATRIA PREVENTIVA E SOCIALE.
Edizioni Minerva Medica, Corso Bramante 83-85, 10126 Turin, Italy. TEL 39-11-678282. FAX 39-11-674502. *5040*

RIVISTA DI STORIA DELL'AGRICOLTURA.
Accademia dei Georgofili, Logge Uffizi Corti, 50122 Florence, Italy. TEL 39-55-212114. FAX 39-55-2302754. *149*

RIVISTA ITALIANA DI ANALISI TRANSAZIONALE E METODOLOGIE PSICOTERAPEUTICHE.
Societa Italiana di Metodologie Psicoterapeutiche e Analisi Transazionale, Via F. Nicolai 70, 00136 Rome, Italy. TEL 39-6-35344043. FAX 39-6-35402495. *6151*

RIVISTA ITALIANA DI PALEONTOLOGIA E STRATIGRAFIA.
Universita degli Studi di Milano, Dipartimento di Scienze della Terra, Via Mangiagalli 34, 20133 Milan, Italy. TEL 39-2-23698232. FAX 39-2-70638261. *5563*

RIVISTA ITALIANA ESSENZE, PROFUMI, PIANTE OFFICINALI, AROMI, SAPONI, AEROSOL, COSMETICI.
Istituto Tetrahedron, Via Capitani di Mozzo, 12, 24030 Mozzo (BG), Italy. TEL 39-35-468511. FAX 39-35-463803. *512*

RIVISTA MARITTIMA.
Stato Maggiore della Marina, Via Romeo Romei 5, 00136 Rome, Italy. FAX 39-6-36804304. *5284*

ROBINSON JEFFERS NEWSLETTER.
California State University, Department of English, 1250 Bellflower Blvd., Long Beach, CA 90840. TEL 310-985-4235. FAX 310-985-2369. *4522*

ROBOTICS AND AUTONOMOUS SYSTEMS.
North-Holland, P.O. Box 211, 1000 AE Amsterdam, Netherlands. TEL 31-20-4853911. FAX 31-20-4853598. *2207*

ROBOTICS AND COMPUTER-INTEGRATED MANUFACTURING.
Elsevier Science Ltd., Pergamon, P.O. Box 800, Kidlington, Oxford OX5 1DX, England. TEL 44-1865-843000. FAX 44-1865-843010. *2208*

ROCHESTER STUDIES IN ECONOMICS AND POLICY ISSUES.
Kluwer Academic Publishers, Postbus 17, 3300 AA Dordrecht, Netherlands. TEL 31-78-6392392. FAX 31-78-6392254. *1311*

ROCK ART RESEARCH.
Archaeological Publications, P.O. Box 216, Caulfield South, Vic. 3162, Australia. TEL 61-3-95230549. FAX 61-3-95230549. *328*

ROCK GARDEN.
Scottish Rock Garden Club, 43 Rubislaw Park Crescent, Aberdeen AB1 8BT, Scotland. TEL 44-1224-314533. *3204*

ROCKET LITERARY QUARTERLY.
Rocket Press, Box 730, Greenport, NY 11944-0730. *4460*

ROCKFORD REVIEW.
Rockford Writers' Guild, Box 858, Rockford, IL 61105. *4460*

ROCKS AND MINERALS.
Heldref Publications, 1319 Eighteenth St., N.W., Washington, DC 20036-1802. TEL 202-296-6267. FAX 202-296-5149. *5315*

ROCKY MOUNTAIN JOURNAL OF MATHEMATICS.
Rocky Mountain Mathematics Consortium, Arizona State University, Department of Mathematics, Tempe, AZ 85287. TEL 602-965-3788. *4602*

ROCKY MOUNTAIN MEDIEVAL AND RENAISSANCE ASSOCIATION. JOURNAL.
Rocky Mountain Medieval and Renaissance Association, c/o Susan Aronstein, Treasurer, Department of English, University of Wyoming, Laramie, WY 82071. TEL 307-766-2373. *3596*

ROCKY MOUNTAIN REVIEW OF LANGUAGE AND LITERATURE.
Rocky Mountain Modern Language Association, Department of English, Boise State University, Boise, ID 83725. TEL 208-385-1233. FAX 208-385-4373. *4460*

ROCZNIK BIBLIOTEKI NARODOWEJ.
Biblioteka Narodowa, Zespol Redakcji Czasopism, Al. Niepodleglosci 213, 00-973 Warsaw, Poland. TEL 48-22-6082252. FAX 48-22-255251. *4210*

ROCZNIK SADECKI.
Racznik Sadecki, Ul. Jagiellonska 30, 33-300 Nowy Sacz, Poland. TEL 48-18-437003. *3597*

RODD'S CHEMISTRY OF CARBON COMPOUNDS.
Elsevier Science B.V., Books Division, P.O. Box 211, 1000 AE Amsterdam, Netherlands. TEL 31-20-4853911. FAX 31-20-4853705. *1823*

RODD'S CHEMISTRY OF CARBON COMPOUNDS. SUPPLEMENTS TO THE SECOND EDITION.
Elsevier Science B.V., Books Division, P.O. Box 211, 1000 AE Amsterdam, Netherlands. TEL 31-20-4853911. FAX 31-20-4853705. *1823*

ROEPER REVIEW.
Roeper School, Box 329, Bloomfield Hills, MI 48303. TEL 810-642-1500. FAX 810-642-1500. *2479*

ROLLER COASTER!
American Coaster Enthusiasts, Box 352, Penfield, NY 14526. TEL 716-381-1012. FAX 716-381-1012. *7232*

ROMANCE PHILOLOGY.
University of California Press, Journals Division, 2120 Berkeley Way, No. 5812, Berkeley, CA 94720-5812. TEL 510-643-7154. FAX 510-642-9117. *4295*

ROMANCE STUDIES.
University of Wales Swansea, School of European Languages, c/o D.F. Connon, School of European Languages, Singleton Park, Swansea, W. Glamorgan SA2 8PP, England. TEL 44-1792-295967. *4460*

ROMANCE WRITERS' REPORT.
Romance Writers of America, Inc., R W A Headquarters, 13700 Veterans Memorial Pkwy., Ste. 315, Houston, TX 77014-1023. TEL 281-440-6885. FAX 281-440-7510. *4499*

ROMANIAN CIVILIZATION.
Center for Romanian Studies, Oficiul Postal I, Casuta Postala 108, 6600 Iasi, Rumania. TEL 40-32-210274. *3597*

ROMANIAN JOURNAL OF METEOROLOGY.
National Institute of Meteorology and Hydrology, 97 Bucuresti-Ploiesti Hwy., 71581 Bucharest, Rumania. TEL 40-1-6793240. FAX 40-1-3129843. *5242*

ROMANIAN JOURNAL OF PETROLOGY.
Institutul Geologic al Romaniei, Str. Caransebes Nr. 1, 78344 Bucharest, Rumania. TEL 40-1-6656625. FAX 40-1-3128444. *2367*

ROMANIAN JOURNAL OF PHYSICS.
Editura Academiei Romane, Calea 13 Septiembre 13, 76117 Bucharest, Rumania. TEL 40-1-6807040. *5825*

ROMANIAN PHYSICAL SOCIETY. NATIONAL CONFERENCE FOR PHYSICS. ABSTRACTS.
Institutul de Fizica Atomica, P.O. Box MG-6, Bucharest-Magurele, Rumania. TEL 40-1-6807040. FAX 40-1-6122247. *5857*

ROMANICA GANDENSIA.
Blandijnberg 2, 9000 Gent, Belgium. TEL 32-9-2644045. FAX 32-9-2644174. *4295*

ROMATOLOJI VE TIBBI REHABILITASYON DERGISI.
Turk Tibbi Rehabilitasyon Kurumu Dernegi, Hacettepe Universitesi, Tip Fakultesi, 06100 Hacettepe - Ankara, Turkey. TEL 90-312-309-4142. FAX 90-312-3105769. *5128*

ROSSICA OLOMUCENSIA.
Universita Palackeho, Filozoficka Fakulta, Krizkovskeho 10, 771 47 Olomouc, Czech Republic. TEL 42-28-5508371. FAX 42-28-26476. *4295*

ROSSICA SOCIETY OF RUSSIAN PHILATELY JOURNAL.
Rossica Society of Russian Philately, Inc., c/o Kennedy Wilson, Ed., Box 357, South Thomaston, ME 04858-0357. *5712*

THE ROUND TABLE.
Carfax Publishing Co., P.O. Box 25, Abingdon, Oxon. OX14 3UE, England. TEL 44-1235-401000. FAX 44-1235-401550. *6035*

ROYAL ASTRONOMICAL SOCIETY. MONTHLY NOTICES.
Blackwell Science Ltd., Osney Mead, Oxford OX2 0EL, England. TEL 44-1865-206206. FAX 44-1865-721205. *500*

REFEREED SERIALS

ROYAL CALEDONIAN CURLING CLUB. ANNUAL.
Royal Caledonian Curling Club, Cairnie House, Ave. K, Ingliston Showground, Newbridge, Midlothian EH28 2NB, Scotland. TEL 44-131-333-3003. FAX 44-131-333-3323. *6779*

ROYAL COLLEGE OF PHYSICIANS AND SURGEONS OF CANADA. ANNALS.
Royal College of Physicians & Surgeons of Canada, 774 Echo Dr., Ottawa, ON K1S 5N8, Canada. TEL 613-730-6200. FAX 613-730-8830. *4741*

ROYAL COLLEGE OF PHYSICIANS OF EDINBURGH. PROCEEDINGS.
Royal College of Physicians of Edinburgh, 9 Queen St., Edinburgh EH2 1JQ, Scotland. TEL 0131-225-7324. FAX 0131-220-3939. *4741*

ROYAL COLLEGE OF PHYSICIANS OF LONDON. JOURNAL.
Royal College of Physicians, 11 St. Andrews Pl., Regents Park, London NW1 4LE, England. TEL 44-171-935-1174. FAX 44-171-487-5218. *4741*

ROYAL COLLEGE OF SURGEONS OF EDINBURGH. JOURNAL.
Blackwell Science Ltd., Osney Mead, Oxford OX2 0EL, England. TEL 44-1865-206206. FAX 44-1865-721205. *5152*

ROYAL INSTITUTE OF PHILOSOPHY CONFERENCE.
Kluwer Academic Publishers, Postbus 17, 3300 AA Dordrecht, Netherlands. TEL 31-78-6392392. FAX 31-78-6392254. *5749*

ROYAL MUSICAL ASSOCIATION. R.M.A. RESEARCH CHRONICLE.
Royal Musical Association, c/o Jonathan Stock, Department of Music, University of Durham, Palace Green, Durham DH1 3RL, England. FAX 44-191-374-3219. *5432*

ROYAL NAVAL MEDICAL SERVICE. JOURNAL.
Institute of Naval Medicine, Alverstoke, Gosport, Hants. PO12 2DL, England. TEL 44-1705-768110. FAX 44-1705-504823. *4741*

ROYAL NETHERLANDS ACADEMY OF SCIENCES. PROCEEDINGS.
North-Holland, P.O. Box 211, 1000 AE Amsterdam, Netherlands. TEL 31-20-4853911. FAX 31-20-4853598. *6563*

ROYAL SOCIETY OF CANADA. TRANSACTIONS.
University of Toronto Press, 10 St. Mary St., Ste. 700, Toronto, ON M4Y 2W8, Canada. TEL 416-978-2239. FAX 416-978-4738. *6564*

ROYAL SOCIETY OF CHEMISTRY. JOURNAL: PERKIN TRANSACTIONS 1.
The Royal Society of Chemistry, Thomas Graham House, Science Park, Milton Rd., Cambridge CB4 4WF, England. TEL 44-1223-420066. FAX 44-1223-423429. *1823*

ROYAL SOCIETY OF CHEMISTRY. JOURNAL: PERKIN TRANSACTIONS 2.
The Royal Society of Chemistry, Thomas Graham House, Science Park, Milton Rd., Cambridge CB4 4WF, England. TEL 44-1223-420066. FAX 44-1223-423429. *1834*

ROYAL SOCIETY OF EDINBURGH. PROCEEDINGS. SECTION A (MATHEMATICS).
Royal Society of Edinburgh, 22 George St., Edinburgh EH2 2PQ, Scotland. TEL 44-131-225-6057. FAX 44-131-220-6889. *4602*

ROYAL SOCIETY OF EDINBURGH. TRANSACTIONS. (EARTH SCIENCES).
Royal Society of Edinburgh, 22 George St., Edinburgh EH2 2PQ, Scotland. TEL 44-131-225-6057. FAX 44-131-220-6889. *2321*

ROYAL SOCIETY OF HEALTH JOURNAL.
Royal Society of Health, R S H House, 38A St., George's Dr., London SW1V 4BH, England. TEL 44-171-630-0121. FAX 44-171-976-6847. *6684*

ROYAL SOCIETY OF LONDON. NOTES AND RECORDS.
Royal Society of London, 6 Carlton House Terrace, London SW1Y 5AG, England. TEL 44-171-839-5561. FAX 44-171-976-1837. *6564*

ROYAL SOCIETY OF LONDON. PHILOSOPHICAL TRANSACTIONS. SERIES A. MATHEMATICAL, PHYSICAL AND ENGINEERING SCIENCES.
Royal Society of London, 6 Carlton House Terrace, London SW1Y 5AG, England. TEL 44-171-839-5561. FAX 44-171-976-1837. *5825*

ROYAL SOCIETY OF LONDON. PHILOSOPHICAL TRANSACTIONS. SERIES B. BIOLOGICAL SCIENCES.
Royal Society of London, 6 Carlton House Terrace, London SW1Y 5AG, England. TEL 44-171-839-5561. FAX 44-171-976-1837. *624*

ROYAL SOCIETY OF LONDON. PROCEEDINGS. SERIES A. MATHEMATICAL, PHYSICAL AND ENGINEERING SCIENCES.
Royal Society of London, 6 Carlton House Terrace, London SW1Y 5AG, England. TEL 44-171-839-5561. FAX 44-171-976-1837. *4602*

ROYAL SOCIETY OF LONDON. PROCEEDINGS. SERIES B. BIOLOGICAL SCIENCES.
Royal Society of London, 6 Carlton House Terrace, London SW1Y 5AG, England. TEL 44-171-839-5561. FAX 44-171-976-1837. *624*

ROYAL SOCIETY OF MEDICINE. JOURNAL.
Royal Society of Medicine Press Ltd., 1 Wimpole St., London W1M 8AF, England. TEL 44-171-290-2900. FAX 44-171-290-2929. *4741*

ROYAL SOCIETY OF NEW SOUTH WALES. JOURNAL AND PROCEEDINGS.
Royal Society of New South Wales, P.O. Box 1525, Macquarie Centre, N.S.W. 2113, Australia. TEL 61-2-98874448. FAX 61-2-98874448. *6564*

ROYAL SOCIETY OF NEW ZEALAND. JOURNAL.
S I R Publishing, P.O. Box 399, Wellington, New Zealand. TEL 64-4-472-7421. FAX 64-4-473-1841. *6564*

ROYAL SOCIETY OF QUEENSLAND. PROCEEDINGS.
Royal Society of Queensland, P.O. Box 21, St. Lucia, Queensland 4067, Australia. TEL 61-7-38641325. *6564*

ROYAL SOCIETY OF SOUTH AFRICA. TRANSACTIONS.
Royal Society of South Africa, P.D. Hahn Building, P.O. Box 594, Cape Town 8000, South Africa. TEL 27-21-650-2543. FAX 27-21-650-2710. *6564*

ROYAL SOCIETY OF SOUTH AUSTRALIA. TRANSACTIONS.
Royal Society of South Australia Inc., S.A. Museum, North Terrace, Adelaide, S.A. 5000, Australia. TEL 61-8-223-5360. *6564*

ROYAL SOCIETY OF TASMANIA, HOBART. PAPERS AND PROCEEDINGS.
Royal Society of Tasmania, Box 1166M, Hobart, Tas. 7001, Australia. TEL 61-362-350777. FAX 61-362-347139. *6564*

ROYAL SOCIETY OF TROPICAL MEDICINE AND HYGIENE. TRANSACTIONS.
Royal Society of Tropical Medicine and Hygiene, Manson House, 26 Portland Pl., London W1N 4EY, England. TEL 44-171-580-2127. FAX 44-171-436-1389. *4843*

ROYAL SOCIETY OF WESTERN AUSTRALIA. JOURNAL.
Royal Society of Western Australia, Inc., c/o Western Australian Museum, Perth, W.A. 6000, Australia. TEL 61-9-3802235. FAX 61-9-3801029. *6564*

ROYAL STATISTICAL SOCIETY. JOURNAL. SERIES A: STATISTICS IN SOCIETY.
Blackwell Publishers Ltd., 108 Cowley Road, Oxford OX4 1JF, England. TEL 44-1865-791100. FAX 44-1865-791347. *6934*

ROYAL STATISTICAL SOCIETY. JOURNAL. SERIES B: METHODOLOGICAL.
Blackwell Publishers Ltd., 108 Cowley Road, Oxford OX4 1JF, England. TEL 44-1865-791100. FAX 44-1865-791347. *6935*

ROYAL STATISTICAL SOCIETY. JOURNAL. SERIES C: APPLIED STATISTICS.
Blackwell Publishers Ltd., 108 Cowley Rd., Oxford OX4 1JF, England. TEL 44-1865-791100. FAX 44-1865-791347. *6935*

ROZHLEDY V CHIRURGII.
Nakladatelske Stredisko C L S J.E. Purkyne, Sokolska 31, 120 26 Prague 2, Czech Republic. TEL 420-2-24911420. FAX 420-2-24911420. *5152*

ROZPRAWY HYDROTECHNICZNE.
Polska Akademia Nauk, Instytut Budownictwa Wodnego, Ul. Koscierska 7, 80-952 Gdansk-Oliwa, Poland. TEL 48-58-522011. FAX 48-58-524211. *7299*

RUAH.
Power of Poetry, c/o Dominican School of Philosophy & Theology, 2401 Ridge Rd., Berkeley, CA 94709. TEL 510-849-2030. FAX 510-849-1372. *4522*

RUANJIAN XUEBAO.
Ruanjian Xuebao Bianjibu, P.O. Box 8718, Beijing 100080, People's Republic of China. TEL 86-10-6256-2563. FAX 86-10-6256-3916. *2217*

RUBBER NEWS.
Polymer Publications, 41-1191, Adarsh Nagar, Prabhadevi, Mumbai 400 023, India. TEL 91-22-437-3813. FAX 91-22-430-0696. *6504*

RUBBERSTAMPMADNESS.
Rubberstampmadness, Inc., 408 S.W. Monroe, Ste. 210, Corvallis, OR 97330. TEL 541-752-0075. FAX 541-752-5475. *483*

RUCH FILOZOFICZNY.
Polskie Towarzystwo Filozoficzne, c/o Uniwersytet Mikolaja Kopernika, Instytut Filozofii, Ul. Podmurna 74, 87-100 Torun, Poland. TEL 48-56-21157. FAX 48-56-21157. *5749*

RUDARSKO-METALURSKI ZBORNIK.
Univerza v Ljubljani, Fakulteta za Naravoslovje in Tehnologijo, Askerceva 20, P.O. Box 594, 61001 Ljubljana, Slovenia. TEL 386-61-1254121. FAX 386-61-1258114. *5315*

RUDY I METALLY.
Ts N I G R I, Varshavskoe Shosse, 129B, 113545 Moscow, Russia. TEL 7-095-3152847. FAX 7-095-3152701. *5315*

RUECKERT STUDIEN.
Ergon Verlag, Grombuehlstr. 7, 97080 Wuerzburg, Germany. TEL 49-931-280084. FAX 49-931-282872. *4461*

RUNA.
Universidad de Buenos Aires, Facultad de Filosofia y Letras, Museo Etnografico Juan B. Ambrosetti, Moreno 350, 1091 Buenos Aires, Argentina. TEL 54-1-331-7788. *329*

RUNNING & FITNEWS.
American Running and Fitness Association, 4405 East-West Hwy., Ste. 405, Bethesda, MD 20814. TEL 301-913-9517. FAX 301-913-9520. *5789*

RUPAMBARA.
22B Pratapaditya Rd., Calcutta 26, India. TEL 91-33-466-4269. *4461*

RURAL DESIGN AND BUILDING.
Rural Design and Building Association, Harper Adams, Newport, Shropshire TF10 8NB, England. TEL 44-1952-814555. FAX 44-1952-814777. *209*

RURAL ROOTS.
Prince Albert Daily Herald, 30-10th St., P.O. Box 550, Prince Albert, SK S6V 5R9, Canada. TEL 306-764-4276. FAX 306-763-3331. *150*

RUSSELL REVIEW.
Russell Review Partnership, P.O. Box 179, Russell, New Zealand. TEL 64-9-4037431. FAX 64-9-4038009. *3544*

RUSSIA AND HER NEIGHBORS.
Highgate Road Social Science Research Station, Inc., 32 Highgate Rd., Berkeley, CA 94707. TEL 510-525-3248. FAX 510-525-3313. *329*

RUSSIAN ACADEMY OF SCIENCE. IZVESTIYA. MATHEMATICS.
Turpion - Moscow Ltd., 47 Leninsky prospekt, 117913 Moscow, Russia. TEL 7-95-1356417. FAX 7-95-1358860. *4602*

RUSSIAN ACADEMY OF SCIENCE. LEBEDEV PHYSICS INSTITUTE. PROCEEDINGS.
Nova Science Publishers, Inc., 6080 Jericho Tpke., Ste. 207, Commack, NY 11725-2808. TEL 516-499-3103. *5870*

RUSSIAN ACADEMY OF SCIENCES. BIOLOGY BULLETIN.
Maik Nauka - Interperiodica, Mezhdunarodnyi Otdel, Ul. Prosoyuznaya, 90, 117864 Moscow, Russia. TEL 7-095-3360066. FAX 7-095-3360066. *624*

RUSSIAN ACADEMY OF SCIENCES. COLLOID JOURNAL.
Maik Nauka - Interperiodica, Mezhdunarodnyi Otdel, Ul. Profsoyuznaya, 90, 117864 Moscow, Russia. TEL 7-095-3360066. FAX 7-095-3360066. *1834*

RUSSIAN ACADEMY OF SCIENCES. INSTITUTE OF GENERAL PHYSICS. PROCEEDINGS.
Nova Science Publishers, Inc., 6080 Jericho Tpke. Ste. 207, Commack, NY 11725-2808. TEL 516-499-3103. *5825*

RUSSIAN ACADEMY OF SCIENCES. MATHEMATICAL NOTES.
Plenum Publishing Corp., Consultants Bureau, 233 Spring St., New York, NY 10013-1578. TEL 212-620-8468. FAX 212-463-0742. *4602*

RUSSIAN ACADEMY OF SCIENCES. SBORNIK. MATHEMATICS.
Turpion - Moscow Ltd., 47 Leninsky prospekt, 117913 Moscow, Russia. TEL 7-95-1356417. FAX 7-95-1358860. *4602*

RUSSIAN AND EAST EUROPEAN FINANCE AND TRADE.
M.E. Sharpe, Inc., 80 Business Park Dr., Armonk, NY 10504. TEL 914-273-1800. FAX 914-273-2106. *1346*

RUSSIAN CHEMICAL BULLETIN.
Plenum Publishing Corp., Consultants Bureau, 233 Spring St., New York, NY 10013-1578. TEL 212-620-8468. FAX 212-463-0742. *1765*

RUSSIAN CHEMICAL REVIEWS.
Turpion - Moscow Ltd., 47 Leninsky prospekt, 117913 Moscow, Russia. TEL 7-95-1356417. FAX 7-95-1358860. *1766*

RUSSIAN ECONOMIC TRENDS.
Whurr Publishers Ltd., 19b Compton Terr., London N1 2UN, England. TEL 44-171-359-5979. FAX 44-171-226-5290. *1287*

RUSSIAN EDUCATION AND SOCIETY.
M.E. Sharpe, Inc., 80 Business Park Dr., Armonk, NY 10504. TEL 914-273-1800. FAX 914-273-2106. *2479*

RUSSIAN JOURNAL OF APPLIED CHEMISTRY.
Maik Nauka - Interperiodica, Mezhdunarodnyi Otdel, Ul. Profsoyuznaya, 90, 117864 Moscow, Russia. TEL 7-095-3360066. FAX 7-095-3360066. *2773*

RUSSIAN JOURNAL OF BIOORGANIC CHEMISTRY.
Maik Nauka - Interperiodica, Mezhdunarodnyi Otdel, Ul. Profsoyuznaya, 90, 117864 Moscow, Russia. TEL 7-095-3360066. FAX 7-095-3360066. *1823*

RUSSIAN JOURNAL OF COMPUTATIONAL MECHANICS.
John Wiley & Sons, Inc., Journals, 605 Third Ave., New York, NY 10158. TEL 212-850-6645. FAX 212-850-6021. *5848*

RUSSIAN JOURNAL OF COORDINATION CHEMISTRY.
Maik Nauka - Interperiodica, Mezhdunarodnyi Otdel, Ul. Profsoyuznaya, 90, 117864 Moscow, Russia. TEL 7-095-3360066. FAX 7-095-3360066. *1766*

RUSSIAN JOURNAL OF DEVELOPMENTAL BIOLOGY.
Maik Nauka - Interperiodica, Mezhdunarodnyi Otdel, Ul. Profsoyuznaya, 90, 117864 Moscow, Russia. TEL 7-095-3360066. FAX 7-095-3360066. *776*

RUSSIAN JOURNAL OF ECOLOGY.
Maik Nauka - Interperiodica, Mezhdunarodnyi Otdel, Ul. Profsoyuznaya, 90, 117864 Moscow, Russia. TEL 7-95-3360066. FAX 7-95-3360066. *2950*

RUSSIAN JOURNAL OF ELECTROCHEMISTRY.
Maik Nauka - Interperiodica, Mezhdunarodnyi Otdel, Ul. Profsoyuznaya, 90, 117864 Moscow, Russia. TEL 7-095-3360066. FAX 7-095-3360066. *1806*

RUSSIAN JOURNAL OF GENERAL CHEMISTRY.
Maik Nauka - Interperiodica, Mezhdunarodnyi Otdel, Ul. Profsoyuznaya, 90, 17864 Moscow, Russia. TEL 7-095-3360066. FAX 7-095-3360066. *1766*

RUSSIAN JOURNAL OF GENETICS.
Maik Nauka - Interperiodica, Mezhdunarodnyi Otdel, Ul. Profsoyuznaya, 90, 117864 Moscow, Russia. TEL 7-095-3360066. FAX 7-095-3360066. *776*

RUSSIAN JOURNAL OF MARINE BIOLOGY.
Maik Nauka - Interperiodica, Mezhdunarodnyi Otdel, Ul. Profsoyuznaya, 90, 117864 Moscow, Russia. TEL 7-095-3360066. FAX 7-095-3360066. *624*

RUSSIAN JOURNAL OF MATHEMATICAL PHYSICS.
John Wiley & Sons, Inc., Journals, 605 Third Ave., New York, NY 10158. TEL 212-850-6645. FAX 212-850-6021. *5825*

RUSSIAN JOURNAL OF NONDESTRUCTIVE TESTING.
Plenum Publishing Corp., Consultants Bureau, 233 Spring St., New York, NY 10013-1578. TEL 212-620-8468. FAX 212-463-0742. *1766*

RUSSIAN JOURNAL OF NUMERICAL ANALYSIS AND MATHEMATICAL MODELLING.
V S P, P.O. Box 346, 3700 AH Zeist, Netherlands. TEL 31-30-6925790. FAX 31-30-6932081. *4602*

RUSSIAN JOURNAL OF ORGANIC CHEMISTRY.
Maik Nauka - Interperiodica, Mezhdunarodnyi Otdel, Ul. Profsoyuznaya, 90, 117864 Moscow, Russia. TEL 7-095-3360066. FAX 7-095-3360066. *1823*

RUSSIAN JOURNAL OF PLANT PHYSIOLOGY.
Maik Nauka - Interperiodica, Mezhdunarodnyi Otdel, Ul. Profsoyuznaya, 90, 117864 Moscow, Russia. TEL 7-095-3360066. FAX 7-095-3360066. *726*

RUSSIAN LINGUISTICS.
Kluwer Academic Publishers, Postbus 17, 3300 AA Dordrecht, Netherlands. TEL 31-78-6392392. FAX 31-78-6392254. *4295*

RUSSIAN LITERATURE.
North-Holland, P.O. Box 211, 1000 AE Amsterdam, Netherlands. TEL 31-20-4853911. FAX 31-20-4853598. *4461*

RUSSIAN MICROELECTRONICS.
Maik Nauk - Interperiodica, Mezhdunarodnyi Otdel, Ul. Profsoyuznaya, 90, 117864 Moscow, Russia. TEL 7-095-33600664. FAX 7-095-3360066. *2651*

RUSSIAN PHYSICS JOURNAL.
Plenum Publishing Corp., Consultants Bureau, 233 Spring St., New York, NY 10013-1578. TEL 212-620-8468. FAX 212-463-0742. *5825*

RUSSIAN POLITICS AND LAW.
M.E. Sharpe, Inc., 80 Business Park Dr., Armonk, NY 10504. TEL 914-273-1800. FAX 914-273-2106. *4020*

RUSSIAN POLITICS AND SOCIETY.
James Nicholas Publishers, P.O. Box 244, Albert Park, Vic. 3206, Australia. TEL 61-3-6965545. FAX 61-3-6992040. *6035*

RUSSIAN SERIES ON SOCIAL HISTORY.
Kluwer Academic Publishers, Postbus 17, 3300 AA Dordrecht, Netherlands. TEL 31-78-6392392. FAX 31-78-6392254. *3598*

RUSSIAN SOCIAL SCIENCE REVIEW.
M.E. Sharpe, Inc., 80 Business Park Dr., Armonk, NY 10504. TEL 914-273-1800. FAX 914-273-2106. *5967*

RUSSIAN STUDIES IN HISTORY.
M.E. Sharpe, Inc., 80 Business Park Dr., Armonk, NY 10504. TEL 914-273-1800. FAX 914-273-2106. *3511*

RUSSIAN STUDIES IN LITERATURE.
M.E. Sharpe, Inc., 80 Business Park Dr., Armonk, NY 10504. TEL 914-273-1800. FAX 914-273-2106. *4461*

RUSSIAN STUDIES IN PHILOSOPHY.
M.E. Sharpe, Inc., 80 Business Park Dr., Armonk, NY 10504. TEL 914-273-1800. FAX 914-273-2106. *5750*

RUSSKOE VOZROZHDENIE.
St. Seraphim Foundation, 887 Stockton Rd., Valley Cottage, NY 10989. TEL 914-268-5548. FAX 914-267-4818. *6393*

S A F E SYMPOSIUM PROCEEDINGS.
S A F E Association, 107 Music City Circle, Ste. 112, Nashville, TN 37214. TEL 615-902-0056. FAX 615-902-0077. *77*

S A Q: THE SOUTH ATLANTIC QUARTERLY.
Duke University Press, Box 90660, Durham, NC 27708-0660. TEL 919-687-3600. FAX 919-688-4574. *4357*

S A W E NEWSLETTER.
Society of Allied Weight Engineers, Inc., 5530 Aztec Dr., La Mesa, CA 91942-2110. TEL 619-465-1367. FAX 619-465-2561. *77*

S B A N E ENTERPRISE.
Smaller Business Association of New England, 204 Second Ave., Waltham, MA 02154. TEL 617-890-9070. FAX 617-890-4567. *1646*

S C I PSYCHOSOCIAL PROCESS.
American Association of Spinal Cord Injury Psychologists and Social Workers, 75-20 Astoria Blvd., Jackson Heights, NY 11370-1177. TEL 718-803-3782. FAX 718-803-0414. *6151*

S D A D NEWS.
Communication Service for the Deaf, 102 N. Krohn Pl., Sioux Falls, SD 57103. TEL 605-367-5760. FAX 605-367-5958. *3465*

S E C O L A S ANNALS.
Southeastern Council on Latin American Studies, L.B. 8106, Georgia Southern University, Statesboro, GA 30460. TEL 912-681-5929. FAX 912-681-0824. *3646*

S E R EN EL 2000.
Hipolito Yrigoyen 1994, 2do. 4, 1089 Buenos Aires, Argentina. TEL 54-1-9510712. *5284*

S I A M - A M S PROCEEDINGS.
American Mathematical Society, Box 6248, Providence, RI 02940-6248. TEL 401-455-4000. FAX 401-331-3842. *4603*

S I A M JOURNAL ON APPLIED MATHEMATICS.
Society for Industrial and Applied Mathematics, 3600 University City Science Center, Philadelphia, PA 19104-2688. TEL 215-382-9800. FAX 215-386-7999. *4603*

S I A M JOURNAL ON COMPUTING.
Society for Industrial and Applied Mathematics, 3600 University City Science Center, Philadelphia, PA 19104-2688. TEL 215-382-9800. FAX 215-386-7999. *4624*

S I A M JOURNAL ON CONTROL AND OPTIMIZATION.
Society for Industrial and Applied Mathematics, 3600 University City Science Center, Philadelphia, PA 19104-2688. TEL 215-382-9800. FAX 215-386-7999. *4603*

S I A M JOURNAL ON DISCRETE MATHEMATICS.
Society for Industrial and Applied Mathematics, 3600 University City Science Center, Philadelphia, PA 19104-2688. TEL 215-382-9800. FAX 215-386-7998. *4603*

S I A M JOURNAL ON MATHEMATICAL ANALYSIS.
Society for Industrial and Applied Mathematics, 3600 University City Science Center, Philadelphia, PA 19104-2688. TEL 215-382-9800. FAX 215-386-7999. *4603*

S I A M JOURNAL ON MATRIX ANALYSIS AND APPLICATIONS.
Society for Industrial and Applied Mathematics, 3600 University City Science Center, Philadelphia, PA 19104-2688. TEL 215-382-9800. FAX 215-386-7999. *4603*

S I A M JOURNAL ON NUMERICAL ANALYSIS.
Society for Industrial and Applied Mathematics, 3600 University City Science Center, Philadelphia, PA 19104-2688. TEL 215-382-9800. FAX 215-386-7999. *4603*

S I A M JOURNAL ON OPTIMIZATION.
Society for Industrial and Applied Mathematics, 3600 University City Science Center, Philadelphia, PA 19104-2688. TEL 215-382-9800. FAX 215-386-7999. *4603*

S I A M JOURNAL ON SCIENTIFIC COMPUTING.
Society for Industrial and Applied Mathematics, 3600 University City Science Center, Philadelphia, PA 19104-2688. TEL 215-382-9800. FAX 215-386-7999. *4604*

S I A M NEWS.
Society for Industrial and Applied Mathematics, 3600 University City Science Center, Philadelphia, PA 19104-2688. TEL 215-382-9800. FAX 215-386-7999. *4604*

S I A M REVIEW.
Society for Industrial and Applied Mathematics, 3600 University City Science Center, Philadelphia, PA 19104-2688. TEL 215-382-9800. FAX 215-386-7999. *4604*

S I A - SURFACE AND INTERFACE ANALYSIS.
John Wiley & Sons Ltd., Journals, Baffins Ln., Chichester, W. Sussex PO19 1UD, England. TEL 44-1243-779777. FAX 44-1243-775878. *2773*

S I D A - E T S.
Obsidiana Editores, S.A., Czda. de Tlalpan 2365, Col. Ciudad Jardin, 04370 Mexico DF, Mexico. TEL 6899133. *4843*

S I E C C A N NEWSLETTER.
Sex Information and Education Council of Canada, 850 Coxwell Ave., East York, ON M4C 5R1, Canada. TEL 416-446-5304. FAX 416-778-0785. *5789*

S L D.
New Paradigm Press, 3636 Taliuna Ave., Apt. 127, Knoxville, TN 37919-7816. TEL 423-588-8878. *4462*

S M P T E JOURNAL.
Society of Motion Picture and Television Engineers, 595 W. Hartsdale Ave., White Plains, NY 10607-1824. TEL 914-761-1100. FAX 914-761-3115. *5343*

S P E DRILLING & COMPLETION.
Society of Petroleum Engineers, Inc., Box 833836, Richardson, TX 75083-3836. TEL 972-952-9393. FAX 972-952-9435. *5621*

S P E FORMATION EVALUATION.
Society of Petroleum Engineers, Inc., Box 833836, Richardson, TX 75083-3836. TEL 972-952-9393. FAX 972-952-9435. *5621*

S P E PRODUCTION & FACILITIES.
Society of Petroleum Engineers, Inc., Box 833836, Richardson, TX 75083-3836. TEL 972-952-9393. FAX 972-952-9435. *5621*

S P E RESERVOIR ENGINEERING.
Society of Petroleum Engineers, Inc., Box 833836, Richardson, TX 75083-3836. TEL 972-952-9393. FAX 972-952-9435. *5621*

S R A T E JOURNAL.
Southeastern Regional Association of Teacher Educators, c/o W.S. Hopkins, Department of Curriculum and Instruction, College of Education, University of South Alabama, Mobile, AL 36688-0002. TEL 205-380-2895. *2479*

S S A JOURNAL.
Cognizant Communication Corporation, 3 Hartsdale Rd., Elmsford, NY 10523-3701. TEL 914-592-7720. FAX 914-592-8981. *5498*

S S C R JOURNAL.
Scottish Society for Conservation and Restoration, The Glasite Meeting House, 33 Barony St., Edinburgh EH3 6NX, Scotland. TEL 44-131-556-8417. FAX 44-131-557-5977. *464*

S T A R.
U.S. National Aeronautics and Space Administration, Scientific and Technical Information Office, 800 Elkridge Landing Rd., Linthicum Heights, MD 21090-2934. *84*

S T O P PRESS.
Society to Overcome Pollution (Stop) Inc., 651 Notre Dame St. W., Ste. 130, Montreal, PQ, H3C 1H92, Canada. TEL 514-393-9559. FAX 514-393-9588. *2972*

SADO MARINE BIOLOGICAL STATION. REPORT.
Niigata Daigaku, Rigakubu Fuzoku Sado Rinkai Jikkenjo, 2-8050 Igarashi, Niigata 950-21, Japan. TEL 0259-75-2012. FAX 0259-75-2012. *624*

SAFE & VAULT TECHNOLOGY.
Safe & Vault Technicians Association, 3003 Live Oak St., Dallas, TX 75204-6189. TEL 214-827-7233. FAX 214-827-1810. *2288*

THE SAFETY & HEALTH PRACTITIONER.
Paramount Publishing Ltd., 17-21 Shenley Rd., Borehamwood, Herts. WD6 1RT, England. TEL 44-181-207-5599. FAX 44-181-207-2598. *6250*

SAFETY RESOURCES.
Gulf Atlantic Communications Corporation, Inc., Box 407000, Ft. Lauderdale, FL 33340-7000. TEL 954-489-4070. FAX 954-489-4079. *5499*

SAFETY SCIENCE.
Elsevier Science B.V., P.O. Box 211, 1000 AE Amsterdam, Netherlands. TEL 31-20-4853911. FAX 31-20-4853598. *5499*

SAGAMORE ARMY MATERIALS RESEARCH CONFERENCE. PROCEEDINGS.
Plenum Publishing Corp., 233 Spring St., New York, NY 10013-1578. TEL 212-620-8000. FAX 212-463-0742. *5284*

SAGE SERIES IN WRITTEN COMMUNICATION.
Sage Publications, Inc., 2455 Teller Rd., Thousand Oaks, CA 91320. TEL 805-499-0721. FAX 805-499-0871. *2002*

SAGGI.
Masson S.p.A., Divisione Periodici, Via Flli. Bressan 2, 20126 Milan, Italy. TEL 39-2-270741. FAX 39-2-27074210. *5097*

SAGYOSEN.
Nihon Sagyosen Kyokai, 9-7, Yaesu 2-chome, Chuo-ku, Tokyo 104, Japan. TEL 81-3-3271-5618. FAX 81-3-3281-2975. *7163*

LE SAHARIEN.
Rahla, 116 rue Damremont, 75018 Paris, France. TEL 33-1-44920503. FAX 33-1-44920503. *3248*

ST. CATHERINE'S CONFERENCE REPORT.
King George VI and Queen Elizabeth Foundation of St. Catharine's, Cumberland Lodge, The Great Park, Windsor, Berkshire SL4 2HP, England. TEL 44-1784-432316. FAX 44-1784-438507. *6685*

ST. JOHN'S JOURNAL OF MEDICINE.
St. John's Medical College, Alumni Association, c/o Dr. S.V. Srikishna, Gen. Sec., Robert Koch Bhavan, 1st Fl., St. John's Medical College, Bangalore 560 034, India. TEL 565435. *4742*

ST. JOHN'S REVIEW.
St. John's College, Annapolis, MD 21404. TEL 410-263-2371. FAX 410-263-4828. *2555*

ST. LOUIS METROPOLITAN MEDICINE.
St. Louis Medical Service Bureau, 3839 Lindell Blvd., St. Louis, MO 63108. TEL 314-371-5225. FAX 314-533-8601. *4742*

SAKKELET.
Nemzeti Sport Kft., c/o Andras Ozsvath, Ed., Falk Miksa u.10, 1005 Budapest 5, Hungary. TEL 36-1-1312790. FAX 36-1-1319738. *6780*

SALAMANDER.
Salamander, Inc., 48 Ackers Ave., Brookline, MA 02146. TEL 617-232-4647. *4358*

SALMAGUNDI.
Skidmore College, Saratoga Springs, NY 12866. TEL 518-581-5186. FAX 518-580-5188. *3791*

SALUD MENTAL.
Editorial Laser S.A. de C.V., Lago Alberto 442-7, Col. Anahuac, Deleg. Miguel Hidalgo, 11320 Mexico DF, Mexico. TEL 52-5-2600250. FAX 52-5-2600048. *5097*

SALUD PUBLICA DE MEXICO.
Instituto Nacional de Salud Publica, Secretaria de Salud, Av. Universidad, 665, Planta Baja, Col. Santa Maria Ahuacatitlad, 62508 Cuernavaca, Morelos, Mexico. TEL 52-73-110111. FAX 52-73-175745. *6250*

SALUT.
South African National Defence Force, Private Bag X158, Pretoria 0001, South Africa. TEL 27-12-3556339. FAX 27-12-3556401. *5284*

SAN DIEGO SOCIETY OF NATURAL HISTORY. PROCEEDINGS.
San Diego Society of Natural History, San Diego Natural History Museum Library, Box 1390, San Diego, CA 92112. TEL 619-232-3821. FAX 619-232-0248. *6565*

SAN JOAQUIN AGRICULTURAL LAW REVIEW.
San Joaquin College of Law, 901 5th St., Clovis, CA 93612-1312. *4021*

SANANJALKA.
Suomen Kielen Seura, Fennicum, Henrikinkatu 3, 20500 Turku, Finland. FAX 358-2-3335282. *4296*

SANDLAPPER.
Sandlapper Society, Inc., Box 1108, Lexington, SC 29071. TEL 803-359-9954. FAX 803-957-8226. *3384*

SANDMUTOPIAN GUARDIAN.
A S W G T Inc., Utopian Network, Box 1146, New York, NY 10156. TEL 516-842-1711. FAX 516-842-7518. *5181*

SANS LAISSE.
Editions Cynofil, BP 28, 15 rue Reclosiere, 39160 Saint-Amour, France. TEL 33-3-84443073. FAX 33-3-84488033. *5642*

SANTE MENTALE AU QUEBEC.
Revue Sante Mentale au Quebec, C.P. 548, Succ. Place d'Armes, Montreal, PQ H2Y 3H3, Canada. TEL 514-523-0607. FAX 514-523-0797. *6152*

SAPIENZA.
Editrice Domenicana Italiana, Via Luigi Palmieri, 19, 80133 Naples, Italy. TEL 39-81-459003. FAX 39-81-5526670. *5750*

SARCOMA.
Carfax Publishing Co., P.O. Box 25, Abingdon, Oxon OX14 3UE, England. TEL 44-1235-401000. FAX 44-1235-401550. *4987*

SARSIA.
University of Bergen, Department of Fisheries and Marine Biology, Bergen High Technology Center, N-5020 Bergen, Norway. TEL 47-55-584400. FAX 47-55-584450. *625*

SARTRE STUDIES INTERNATIONAL.
Berghahn Books Inc., 165 Taber Ave., Providence, RI 02906. TEL 401-861-9330. FAX 401-521-0046. *5750*

SASKATCHEWAN HISTORY.
Saskatchewan Archives Board, Murray Building, Universiy of Saskatchewan, 3 Campus Dr., Saskatoon, SK S7N 5A4, Canada. TEL 306-933-8326. FAX 306-933-7305. *3646*

SASKATCHEWAN LAW REVIEW.
University of Saskatchewan, College of Law, 15 Campus Dr., Saskatoon, SK S7N 5A6, Canada. TEL 306-966-5869. FAX 306-966-5900. *4022*

SASKATCHEWAN MEDICAL JOURNAL.
University of Saskatchewan, Division of Continuing Medical Education, Box 60001, RPO University, Saskatoon, SK S7N 4J8, Canada. TEL 306-966-7787. FAX 306-966-7673. *4742*

SATHER CLASSICAL LECTURES.
University of California Press, 2120 Berkeley Way, Berkeley, CA 94720. TEL 510-642-4247. FAX 510-643-7127. *1907*

SAUDI HEART JOURNAL.
King Abdul Aziz University Hospital, P.O. Box 6615, Jeddah 21452, Saudi Arabia. TEL 966-2-6697043. FAX 966-2-6697043. *4823*

SAUDI JOURNAL OF KIDNEY DISEASES AND TRANSPLANTATION.
Saudi Center for Organ Transplantation, Publication Office, P.O. Box 27049, Riyadh 11417, Saudi Arabia. TEL 966-1-4765500. FAX 966-1-4783988. *5165*

SAUDI MEDICAL JOURNAL.
Saudi Arabian Armed Forces Ministry of Defence and Aviation, Medical Services Department, P.O. Box 7897, Riyadh 11159, Saudi Arabia. TEL 966-1-4777714. FAX 966-1-4777194. *4742*

SAURIA.
Terrariengemeinschaft Berlin e.V., Planetenstr. 45, 12057 Berlin, Germany. TEL 49-30-6847140. *849*

SAUSSUREA.
Societe Botanique de Geneve, Case Postale 60, CH-1292 Chambesy-GE, Switzerland. TEL 41-22-4185100. FAX 41-22-4185101. *726*

SAUTI YA VITA.
Salvation Army, P.O. Box 40575, Nairobi, Kenya. TEL 254-2-227541. FAX 254-2-335538. *6497*

SAVANNAH JEWISH NEWS.
Savannah Jewish Federation, 5111 Abercorn St., Box 23527, Savannah, GA 31403. TEL 912-355-8111. *3041*

SAYBROOK REVIEW.
Saybrook Institute, Graduate School and Research Center, 450 Pacific, 3rd. Fl., San Francisco, CA 94133. TEL 415-433-9200. FAX 415-433-9271. *6152*

SCANDIA.
Scandia Foundation, University of Lund, P.O. Box 2074, S-220 02 Lund, Sweden. TEL 46-46-222-00-00. FAX 46-46-222-42-07. *3511*

SCANDINAVIA NOW ONLINE.
Elfwendahl & Co., Runebergsgatan 6, SE-114 29 Stockholm, Sweden. TEL 46-8-678-32-30. FAX 46-8-611-23-58. *1000*

SCANDINAVIAN - CANADIAN STUDIES.
Association for the Advancement of Scandinavian Studies in Canada, Department of Languages, Literatures and Linguistics, York University, North York, ON M3J 1P3, Canada. TEL 416-736-5016. FAX 416-736-5483. *4463*

SCANDINAVIAN CONFERENCE ON ARTIFICIAL INTELLIGENCE.
I O S Press, Van Diemenstraat 94, 1013 CN Amsterdam, Netherlands. TEL 31-20-6382189. FAX 31-20-6203419. *2104*

SCANDINAVIAN JOURNAL OF CLINICAL & LABORATORY INVESTIGATION.
Scandinavian University Press, P.O. Box 2959 Toeyen, N-0608 Oslo, Norway. TEL 47-22-57-54-00. FAX 47-22-57-53-53. *4902*

SCANDINAVIAN JOURNAL OF DEVELOPMENT ALTERNATIVES AND AREA STUDIES.
Bethany Books, Sweden, P.O. Box 7444, S-103 91 Stockholm, Sweden. TEL 46-8-580-196-87. *6634*

SCANDINAVIAN JOURNAL OF ECONOMICS.
Blackwell Publishers Ltd., 108 Cowley Rd., Oxford OX4 1JF, England. TEL 44-1865-791100. FAX 44-1165-791347. *1000*

SCANDINAVIAN JOURNAL OF EDUCATIONAL RESEARCH.
Carfax Publishing Co., P.O. Box 25, Abingdon, Oxon. OX14 3UE, England. TEL 44-1235-401000. FAX 44-1235-401550. *2480*

SCANDINAVIAN JOURNAL OF IMMUNOLOGY.
Blackwell Science Ltd., Osney Mead, Oxford OX2 0EL, England. TEL 44-1865-206206. FAX 44-1865-721205. *4800*

SCANDINAVIAN JOURNAL OF MANAGEMENT.
Elsevier Science Ltd., Pergamon, P.O. Box 800, Kidlington, Oxford OX5 1DX, England. TEL 44-1865-843000. FAX 44-1865-843010. *1506*

SCANDINAVIAN JOURNAL OF MEDICINE & SCIENCE IN SPORTS.
Munksgaard International Publishers Ltd., P.O. Box 2148, DK-1016 Copenhagen K, Denmark. TEL 45-33-127030. FAX 45-33-129387. *5131*

SCANDINAVIAN JOURNAL OF METALLURGY.
Munksgaard International Publishers Ltd., 35 Noerre Soegade, P.O. Box 2148, DK-1016 Copenhagen K, Denmark. TEL 45-33-127030. FAX 45-33-129387. *5209*

SCANDINAVIAN JOURNAL OF OCCUPATIONAL THERAPY.
Scandinavian University Press, P.O. Box 2959 Toeyen, N-0608 Oslo, Norway. TEL 47-22-57-54-00. FAX 47-22-57-53-53. *4742*

SCANDINAVIAN JOURNAL OF SOCIAL WELFARE.
Munksgaard International Publishers Ltd., 35 Noerre Soegade, P.O. Box 2148, DK-1016 Copenhagen K, Denmark. TEL 45-33-127030. FAX 45-33-129387. *6685*

SCANDINAVIAN JOURNAL OF STATISTICS.
Blackwell Publishers Ltd., 108 Cowley Rd., Oxford OX4 1JF, England. TEL 44-1865-791100. FAX 44-1865-791347. *6935*

THE SCANDINAVIAN PSYCHOANALYTIC REVIEW.
Munksgaard International Publishers Ltd., 35 Noerre Soegade, P.O. Box 2148, DK-1016 Copenhagen K, Denmark. TEL 45-33-127030. FAX 45-33-129387. *5097*

SCANDINAVIAN STUDIES (PROVO).
Society for the Advancement of Scandinavian Study, c/o Steven P. Sondrup, Ed., Department of Comparative Literature, Brigham Young University, Provo, UT 84602-6118. TEL 801-378-2579. FAX 801-378-4649. *4463*

SCANDO-SLAVICA.
Munksgaard International Publishers Ltd., 35 Noerre Soegade, P.O. Box 2148, DK-1016 Copenhagen K, Denmark. TEL 45-33-127030. FAX 45-33-129387. *4297*

SCANNING MICROSCOPY.
Scanning Microscopy International, Inc., Box 66507, AMF O'Hare, Chicago, IL 60666-0507. TEL 708-529-6677. FAX 708-980-6698. *798*

SCARP.
University of Wollongong, Faculty of Creative Arts, Northfields Ave., Wollongong, N.S.W. 2522, Australia. TEL 61-42-213867. FAX 61-42-213301. *4522*

SCHIZOPHRENIA BULLETIN.
U.S. Public Health Service, National Institute of Mental Health, 5600 Fishers Ln., Rockville, MD 20857. TEL 301-443-9772. FAX 301-443-7895. *5097*

SCHIZOPHRENIA RESEARCH.
Elsevier Science B.V., P.O. Box 211, 1000 AE Amsterdam, Netherlands. TEL 31-20-4853911. FAX 31-20-4853598. *5097*

SCHOLARLY INQUIRY FOR NURSING PRACTICE.
Springer Publishing Company, 536 Broadway, New York, NY 10012-3955. TEL 212-431-4370. FAX 212-941-7842. *4948*

SCHOLASTIC MAGAZINE.
University of Notre Dame, La Fortune Center, Notre Dame, 303 LaFortune Student Center, IN 46556-5635. TEL 219-239-7569. FAX 219-63-9648. *1970*

SCHOLIA.
University of Natal (Durban), Department of Classics, Durban 4041, South Africa. TEL 27-31-2602312. FAX 27-31-2602698. *1907*

SCHOOL ARTS.
Davis Publications, Inc. (Worcester), 50 Portland St., Printers Bldg., Worcester, MA 01608. TEL 508-754-7201. FAX 508-753-3834. *2618*

SCHOOL EFFECTIVENESS AND SCHOOL IMPROVEMENT.
Swets & Zeitlinger bv, P.O. Box 825, 2160 SZ Lisse, Netherlands. TEL 31-252-435111. FAX 31-252-415888. *2480*

SCHOOL FOOD SERVICE RESEARCH REVIEW.
American School Food Service Association, 1600 Duke St., 7th Fl., Alexandria, VA 22314-3436. TEL 703-739-3900. FAX 703-739-3915. *3126*

SCHOOL HEALTH ALERT.
Box 150127, Nashville, TN 37215-0127. TEL 615-255-3609. FAX 615-255-6956. *4948*

SCHOOL LEADERSHIP & MANAGEMENT.
Carfax Publishing Co., P.O. Box 25, Abingdon, Oxon OX14 3UE, England. TEL 44-1235-401000. FAX 44-1235-401550. *2578*

SCHOOL LIBRARIES IN CANADA.
Canadian School Library Association, 602-200 Elgin St., Ottawa, Ont. K2P 1L5, Canada. TEL 613-232-9625. FAX 613-563-9895. *4212*

SCHOOL OF INTERNATIONAL STUDIES. PUBLICATIONS ON ASIA.
University of Washington Press, Box 50096, Seattle, WA 98105. TEL 206-543-4050. *3538*

SCHOOL OF INTERNATIONAL STUDIES. PUBLICATIONS ON RUSSIA AND EASTERN EUROPE.
University of Washington Press, Box 50096, Seattle, WA 98105. TEL 206-543-4050. *5967*

SCHOOL PSYCHOLOGY INTERNATIONAL.
Sage Publications Ltd., 6 Bonhill St., London EC2A 4PU, England. TEL 44-171-374-0645. FAX 44-171-374-8741. *2618*

SCHOOL PSYCHOLOGY QUARTERLY.
Guilford Publications, Inc., 72 Spring St., 4th Fl., New York, NY 10012. TEL 212-431-9800. FAX 212-966-6708. *6152*

SCHOOL PSYCHOLOGY REVIEW.
National Association of School Psychologists, 4340 East West Hwy., Ste. 402, Bethesda, MD 20814-4411. TEL 301-657-0270. FAX 301-657-3127. *6152*

SCHOOL SCIENCE AND MATHEMATICS.
School Science and Mathematics Association, Weniger Hall 237, Oregon State University, Cornwallis, OR 97331-6508. TEL 541-737-1818. FAX 541-737-1817. *2481*

SCHOOL SOCIAL WORK JOURNAL.
Illinois Association of School Social Workers, Box 634, Algonquin, IL 60102. TEL 847-676-3365. FAX 847-831-5100. *2590*

SCHULINTERN.
Ministerium fuer Kultus, Jugend und Sport, Schlossplatz 4, 70173 Stuttgart, Germany. TEL 49-711-2792613. FAX 49-711-2792838. *2618*

SCHUYLER COUNTY HISTORICAL SOCIETY. JOURNAL.
Schuyler County Historical Society, Gray Brick Museum, Montour Falls, NY 14865. TEL 607-535-9741. *3646*

SCHWEIZER HEBAMME.
Schweizer Hebammenverband, Flurstr. 26, CH-3000 Bern 22, Switzerland. TEL 41-31-3313520. *4948*

SCHWEIZER STRAHLER.
Schweizer Vereinigung der Strahler, Mineralien- und Fossiliensammler, Sekretariat SVSMF, CH-1595 Faoug, Switzerland. TEL 41-26-6722628. FAX 41-26-6722628. *5315*

DER SCHWEIZER TREUHAENDER.
Treuhand-Kammer, Postfach 892, CH-8025 Zurich, Switzerland. TEL 41-1-2677575. FAX 41-1-2677555. *1098*

SCIENCE.
American Association for the Advancement of Science, 1200 New York Ave., N.W., Washington, DC 20005. TEL 202-326-6417. *6566*

SCIENCE ACTIVITIES.
Heldref Publications, 1319 Eighteenth St., N.W., Washington, DC 20036-1802. TEL 202-296-6267. FAX 202-296-5149. *2481*

REFEREED SERIALS

SCIENCE & EDUCATION.
Kluwer Academic Publishers, Postbus 17, 3300 AA Dordrecht, Netherlands. TEL 31-78-6392392. FAX 31-78-6392254. *6566*

SCIENCE AND ENGINEERING ETHICS.
Opragen Publications, P.O. Box 54, Guildford, Surrey GU1 2YF, England. TEL 44-1483-560074. FAX 44-1483-560074. *6567*

SCIENCE AND GLOBAL SECURITY.
Gordon and Breach - Harwood Academic, Amsteldisk 166, 1st Fl., 1079 LH Amsterdam, Netherlands. *6567*

SCIENCE AND GLOBAL SECURITY MONOGRAPH SERIES.
Gordon and Breach - Harwood Academic, Amsteldisk 166, 1st Fl., 1079 LH Amsterdam, Netherlands. *6036*

SCIENCE AND ITS CONCEPTUAL FOUNDATIONS.
University of Chicago Press, 5801 S. Ellis Ave., Chicago, IL 60637. TEL 773-702-7899. *6567*

SCIENCE AND PHILOSOPHY.
Kluwer Academic Publishers, Postbus 17, 3300 AA Dordrecht, Netherlands. TEL 31-78-6392392. FAX 31-78-6392254. *6567*

SCIENCE AND PRACTICE OF SURGERY SERIES.
Marcel Dekker, Inc., 270 Madison Ave., New York, NY 10016. TEL 212-696-9000. FAX 212-685-4540. *5153*

SCIENCE AND PUBLIC POLICY.
Beech Tree Publishing, 10 Watford Close, Guildford, Surrey GU1 2EP, England. TEL 44-1483-567497. FAX 44-1483-567497. *6567*

SCIENCE & SOCIETY.
Guilford Publications, Inc., 72 Spring St., 4th Fl., New York, NY 10012. TEL 212-431-9800. FAX 212-966-6708. *5968*

SCIENCE & TECHNOLOGY LIBRARIES.
Haworth Press, Inc., 10 Alice St., Binghamton, NY 13904. TEL 607-722-5857. FAX 607-722-6362. *4213*

SCIENCE AS CULTURE.
Process Press, 26 Freegrove Rd., London L7 9RQ, England. TEL 44-171-609-0507. FAX 44-171-609-4837. *6567*

SCIENCE COMMUNICATION.
Sage Publications, Inc., 2455 Teller Rd., Thousand Oaks, CA 91320. TEL 805-499-0721. FAX 805-499-0871. *2003*

SCIENCE EDUCATION.
John Wiley & Sons, Inc., Journals, 605 Third Ave., New York, NY 10158. TEL 212-850-6645. FAX 212-850-6021. *6568*

SCIENCE ET COMPORTEMENT.
Association Scientifique pour la Modification du Comportement, 309 rue Godin, Repentigny, PQ J6A 5Z8, Canada. TEL 514-253-8200. FAX 514-585-9935. *6152*

SCIENCE ET SPORTS.
Editions Scientifiques et Medicales Elsevier, 141 rue de Javel, 75747 Paris, France. TEL 33-1-45589026. FAX 33-1-45589421. *5132*

SCIENCE FICTION.
University of Western Australia, Department of English, c/o Dr. Van Ikin, Ed., Nedlands, W.A. 6907, Australia. TEL 61-9-380-2280. FAX 61-9-380-1030. *4536*

SCIENCE-FICTION STUDIES.
S F - T H, Inc., c/o Prof. Arthur B. Evans, Ed., DePauw University, Greencastle, IN 46135-0037. TEL 765-658-4758. FAX 765-658-4856. *4536*

SCIENCE IN CHINA. SERIES A: MATHEMATICS, PHYSICS, ASTRONOMY.
Gordon and Breach - Harwood Academic, Amsteldisk 166, 1st Fl., 1079 LH Amsterdam, Netherlands. *4604*

SCIENCE IN CHINA. SERIES B: CHEMISTRY.
Gordon and Breach - Harwood Academic, Amsteldisk 166, 1st Fl., 1079 LH Amsterdam, Netherlands. *1766*

SCIENCE IN NEW GUINEA.
University of Papua New Guinea, Faculty of Science, P.O. Box 320, University, Papua New Guinea. FAX 260-369. *6568*

SCIENCE OF ADVANCED MATERIAL AND PROCESS ENGINEERING SERIES.
Society for the Advancement of Material and Process Engineering, Box 2459, Covina, CA 91722. TEL 818-331-0616. FAX 818-332-8929. *2869*

SCIENCE OF COMPUTER PROGRAMMING.
North-Holland, P.O. Box 211, 1000 AE Amsterdam, Netherlands. TEL 31-20-4853911. FAX 31-20-4853598. *2145*

THE SCIENCE OF THE TOTAL ENVIRONMENT.
Elsevier Science B.V., P.O. Box 211, 1000 AE Amsterdam, Netherlands. TEL 31-20-4853911. FAX 31-20-4853598. *2951*

SCIENCE PROGRESS.
Science Reviews Ltd., P.O. Box 81, Northwood, Middlesex HA6 3DY, England. TEL 44-1923-823586. FAX 44-1923-825066. *6569*

SCIENCE, TECHNOLOGY & DEVELOPMENT.
Frank Cass, Newbury House, 890-900 Eastern Ave., Newbury Park, Ilford, Essex 1G2 7HH, England. TEL 44-181-599-8866. FAX 44-181-599-0984. *1368*

SCIENCE, TECHNOLOGY & SOCIETY.
Sage Publications India Pvt. Ltd., P.O. Box 4215, New Delhi 110 048, India. TEL 91-11-6444958. FAX 91-11-6472426. *6570*

SCIENCELAND.
Komat Inc., 501 Fifth Ave., Ste. 2108, New York, NY 10017. TEL 212-490-2180. FAX 212-490-2187. *1886*

THE SCIENCES.
New York Academy of Sciences, 2 E. 63rd St., New York, NY 10021. *6570*

SCIENCES DE LA SOCIETE.
Presses Universitaires du Mirail, 56, rue du Taur, 31000 Toulouse, France. TEL 33-5-612258311. FAX 33-5-61218420. *6634*

SCIENCES OF SOIL.
Kurfurstenstr. 13, 54295 Trier, Germany. TEL 49-651-47163. FAX 49-651-47163. *243*

SCIENTIA. SERIES A: MATHEMATICAL SCIENCES.
Universidad Tecnica Federico Santa Maria, Casilla 110-V, Valparaiso, Chile. TEL 0056-32-626364. FAX 0056-32-660504. *4605*

SCIENTIA FORESTALIS.
Universidade de Sao Paulo, Instituto de Pesquisas e Estudos Florestais, Escola Superior de Agricultura "Luiz de Queiroz", Caixa Postal 530, 13400-970 Piracicaba SP, Brazil. TEL 55-19-4336155. FAX 55-19-4336081. *3161*

SCIENTIA GEOLOGICA SINICA.
Science Press, Marketing and Sales Department, 16 Donghuangchenggen North St., Beijing 100717, People's Republic of China. *2368*

SCIENTIA HORTICULTURAE.
Elsevier Science B.V., P.O. Box 211, 1000 AE Amsterdam, Netherlands. TEL 31-20-4853911. FAX 31-20-4853598. *3204*

SCIENTIA IRANICA.
Sharif University of Technology, P.O. Box 11365-8639, Tehran, Iran. TEL 98-21-6005419. FAX 98-21-6012983. *6570*

SCIENTIA MARINA.
International Centre for Coastal Resources Research, Carrer Gran Capita s-n, Campus Nord, UPC, Modul D1, 08034 Barcelona, Spain. TEL 34-3-2806400. FAX 34-3-2806019. *2414*

SCIENTIA PAEDAGOGICA EXPERIMENTALIS.
State University Ghent, Labo Pedagogiek, Blandijnberg 2, B-9000 Gent, Belgium. TEL 32-9-2643952. FAX 32-9-2646498. *2481*

SCIENTIFIC AMERICAN.
Scientific American, Inc., 415 Madison Ave., New York, NY 10017-1111. TEL 212-754-0550. FAX 212-754-1138. *6570*

SCIENTIFIC AMERICAN MEDICINE.
Scientific American, Inc., 415 Madison Ave., New York, NY 10017-1111. TEL 212-754-0550. FAX 212-754-1138. *4743*

SCIENTIFIC AND APPLIED PHOTOGRAPHY.
Gordon and Breach - Harwood Academic, Amsteldisk 166, 1st Fl., 1079 LH Amsterdam, Netherlands. *5774*

SCIENTIFIC PROGRAMMING: TOOLS & TECHNIQUES.
John Wiley & Sons, Inc., Journals, 605 Third Ave., New York, NY 10158. TEL 212-850-6645. FAX 212-850-6021. *2217*

SCIENTIFIC REPORTS OF CETACEAN RESEARCH.
Institute of Cetacean Research, Tokyo Suisan Bldg., 4-18 Toyomi-cho, Chuo-ku, Tokyo 104, Japan. TEL 81-3-3536-6521. FAX 81-3-3536-6522. *849*

SCIENTOMETRICS.
Akademiai Kiado Rt., P.O. Box 245, H-1519 Budapest, Hungary. TEL 36-1-2043976. FAX 36-1-3043973. *6571*

SCOPUS.
East Africa Natural History Society, Ornithological Sub-Committee, P.O. Box 15194, Nairobi, Kenya. TEL 254-2-891419. *808*

SCOTIA.
Old Dominion University, Department of History, Arts and Letters Building, Norfolk, VA 23529. TEL 757-683-3949. FAX 757-683-5644. *3599*

SCOTLANDS.
Edinburgh University Press, 22 George Sq., Edinburgh EH8 9LF, Scotland. TEL 44-131-650-6207. FAX 44-131-662-0053. *3041*

SCOTTISH AFFAIRS.
Unit for the Study of Government in Scotland, 31 Buccleuch Pl., Edinburgh EH8 9JT, Scotland. TEL 0131-650-4197. FAX 0131-668-3263. *5968*

SCOTTISH BIRDS.
Scottish Ornithologists Club, 21 Regent Terrace, Edinburgh EH7 5BT, Scotland. TEL 44-131-556-6042. *808*

SCOTTISH CHURCH HISTORY SOCIETY. RECORDS.
Scottish Church History Society, 1 Denham Green Terrace, Edinburgh EH5 3PG, Scotland. TEL 44-131-552-4059. FAX 44-131-552-4059. *6370*

SCOTTISH ECONOMIC AND SOCIAL HISTORY.
22 George Sq., Edinburgh EH8 9LF, Scotland. TEL 44-131-650-4223. FAX 44-131-662-0053. *6634*

SCOTTISH FORESTRY.
Royal Scottish Forestry Society, The Stables, Dalkeith Country Park, Dalkeith, Midlothian EH22 2NA, Scotland. TEL 44-131-660-9480. FAX 44-131-660-9490. *3162*

SCOTTISH HISTORICAL REVIEW.
Edinburgh University Press, 22 George Sq., Edinburgh EH8 9LF, Scotland. TEL 44-131-650-6207. FAX 44-131-662-0053. *3512*

SCOTTISH JOURNAL OF ADULT AND CONTINUING EDUCATION.
Scottish Community Education Council, Marketing and Public Affairs Unit, Rosebery House, 9 Haymarket Terrace, Edinburgh EH12 5EZ, Scotland. TEL 44-131-313-2488. FAX 44-131-313-6800. *2513*

SCOTTISH JOURNAL OF POLITICAL ECONOMY.
Blackwell Publishers Ltd., 108 Cowley Rd., Oxford OX4 1JF, England. TEL 44-1865-791100. FAX 44-1865-791347. *1000*

SCOTTISH JOURNAL OF RELIGIOUS STUDIES.
University of Stirling, Department of Religious Studies, Stirling FK9 4LA, Scotland. TEL 44-1786-467565. FAX 44-1786-451335. *6370*

SCOTTISH LAW & PRACTICE QUARTERLY.
T & T Clark Ltd., 59 George St., Edinburgh EH2 2LQ, England. TEL 44-131-225-4703. FAX 44-131-220-4260. *4023*

SCOTTISH PLANNING AND ENVIRONMENTAL LAW.
Planning Exchange, Tontine House, 8 Gordon St., Glasgow G1 3PL, Scotland. TEL 44-141-248-8541. FAX 44-141-248-8277. *4023*

SCOTTISH WILDLIFE.
Scottish Wildlife Trust, Cramond House, Kirk Cramond, Cramond Glebe Rd., Edinburgh EH4 6NS, Scotland. TEL 44-131-312-7765. FAX 44-131-312-8705. *2244*

SCREAM FACTORY.
Deadline Press, Box 2808, Apache Junction, AZ 85217. TEL 408-353-4450. *4536*

THE SCRIBE.
University of Bridgeport, Student Center, 244 University Ave., Bridgeport, CT 06601. TEL 203-576-4382. FAX 203-576-4485. *1970*

SCRIPPS INSTITUTION OF OCEANOGRAPHY. BULLETIN.
University of California Press, 2120 Berkeley Way, Berkeley, CA 94720. TEL 510-642-4247. FAX 510-643-7127. *2414*

SCRIPTA MATERIALIA.
Elsevier Science Ltd., Pergamon, P.O. Box 800, Kidlington, Oxford OX5 1DX, England. TEL 44-1865-843000. FAX 44-1865-843010. *5210*

SCRIPTURA.
University of Stellenbosch, Department of Religion, 7602 Matieland, South Africa. TEL 27-21-8082117. FAX 27-21-8082031. *6441*

SEA CHEST.
Puget Sound Maritime Historical Society, Box 433, Bremerton, WA 98337. *7164*

SEA TECHNOLOGY.
Compass Publications, Inc. (Arlington), Ste. 1000, 1117 N. 19th St., Arlington, VA 22209. TEL 703-524-3136. FAX 703-841-0852. *2740*

SEABIRD.
Seabird Group, c/o R.S.P.B., The Lodge, Sandy, Beds. SG19 2DL, England. *808*

SEABY'S STANDARD CATALOGUE OF BRITISH COINS.
Spink & Son Ltd., 5 King St., St. James's, London SW1Y 6QS. TEL 44-171-930-7888. FAX 44-171-839-4853. *5467*

SEATTLE UNIVERSITY LAW REVIEW.
Seattle University, School of Law, 950 Broadway Plaza, Tacoma, WA 98402. TEL 206-591-2995. FAX 206-591-6313. *4023*

SECEUR.
Young Europeans for Security, Postbus 84, 3500 AB Utrecht, Netherlands. TEL 31-30-2538218. FAX 31-30-2537012. *6036*

SECURE COMPUTING.
West Coast Publishing Ltd., William Knox House, Britannic Way, Llandarcy, Swansea SA10 6EL, Wales. TEL 44-1792-324000. FAX 44-1792-324001. *2150*

SECURITIES REGULATION LAW JOURNAL.
Warren, Gorham & Lamont, One Penn Plaza, New York, NY 10119. TEL 212-971-5000. FAX 212-971-5113. *1406*

SECURITY AFFAIRS.
Jewish Institute for National Security Affairs, 1717 K St., N.W., Ste. 800, Washington, DC 20006. TEL 202-833-0020. FAX 202-296-6452. *6036*

SECURITY DIALOGUE.
Sage Publications Ltd., 6 Bonhill St., London EC2A 4PU, England. TEL 44-171-374-0645. FAX 44-171-374-8741. *5968*

SECURITY JOURNAL.
Elsevier Science Ireland Ltd., P.O. Box 85, Limerick, Ireland. TEL 353-61-471944. FAX 353-61-472144. *2288*

SECURITY STUDIES.
Frank Cass, Newbury House, 890-900 Eastern Ave., Newbury Park, Ilford, Essex 1G2 7HH, England. TEL 44-181-599-8866. FAX 44-181-599-0984. *6036*

SEDIMENTARY BASINS OF THE WORLD.
Elsevier Science B.V., Books Division, P.O. Box 211, 1000 AE Amsterdam, Netherlands. TEL 31-20-4853911. FAX 31-20-4853705. *2322*

SEDIMENTARY GEOLOGY.
Elsevier Science B.V., P.O. Box 211, 1000 AE Amsterdam, Netherlands. TEL 31-20-4853911. FAX 31-20-4853598. *2368*

SEDIMENTOLOGY.
Blackwell Science Ltd., Osney Mead, Oxford OX2 0EL, England. TEL 44-1865-206206. FAX 44-1865-721205. *2368*

SEDIMENTOLOGY AND PETROLEUM GEOLOGY.
Kluwer Academic Publishers, Postbus 17, 3300 AA Dordrecht, Netherlands. TEL 31-78-6392392. FAX 31-78-6392254. *5622*

SEED TECHNOLOGY.
Association of Official Seed Analysts, Inc., Box 81152, Lincoln, NE 68501-1152. TEL 402-476-3852. *152*

SEEMEILE.
Seemeile Verlag, Zelglistr. 20, CH-8634 Hombrechtikon, Switzerland. TEL 41-55-2444387. FAX 41-55-2444317. *6844*

SEI MARIANNA IKA DAIGAKU KIYO.
St. Marianna University School of Medicine, 2-16-1 Sugao Miyamae-ku, Kawasaki-shi 216, Japan. TEL 81-44-977-8111. FAX 81-44-977-9835. *2527*

SEIBUTSU BUTSURI.
Nihon Seibutsu Butsuri Gakkai, Realize Inc., 4-1-4 Hongo, Bunkyo-ku, Tokyo 133, Japan. TEL 81-3-3815-8511. FAX 81-3-3815-8529. *676*

SEIBUTSU KANKYO CHOSETSU.
Nihon Seibutsu Kankyo Chosetsu Gakkai, Tokyo Daigaku Nogakubu, Nogyo Gokkaka Kankyo Chosetsu Kogaku Kenkyushitsu, 1-1 Yayoi 1-chome, Bunkyo-ku, Tokyo 113. TEL 81-3-3812-2111. FAX 81-3-3813-2437. *625*

SEIBUTSU KYOIKU.
Nihon Seibutsu Kyoiku Gakkai, Tokyo Gakugei Daigaku Seibutsugaku Kyoshitsu, 1-1 Nukui Kitamachi 4-chome, Koganei-shi, Tokyo 184, Japan. *625*

SEISMOLOGICAL RESEARCH LETTERS.
Seismological Society of America, 201 Plaza Professional Bldg., El Cerrito, CA 94530-4003. TEL 510-525-5474. FAX 510-525-7204. *2389*

SEISMOLOGICAL SOCIETY OF AMERICA. BULLETIN.
Seismological Society of America, 201 Plaza Professional Bldg., El Cerrito, CA 94530. TEL 510-525-5474. FAX 510-525-7204. *2389*

SEITENWECHSEL.
Georg August Universitaet - Goettingen, Zentrale Einrichtung fuer den Allgemeinen Hochschulsport, Sprangerweg 2, 37075 Goettingen, Germany. *6781*

SEIYOSHIGAKU.
Japanese Society of Western History, Osaka University, Faculty of Letters, 1-5 Machikaneyama-cho, Toyonaka-shi 560, Japan. TEL 81-6-850-5104. FAX 81-6-850-5105. *3599*

SEIZURE.
W.B. Saunders Co. Ltd., 24-28 Oval Rd., London NW1 7DX, England. TEL 44-171-267-4466. FAX 44-171-482-2293. *5098*

SELECTA (CORVALLIS).
Pacific Northwest Council for Languages, c/o Foreign Languages & Literatures, Oregon State Univ., 210 Kidder Hall, Corvallis, OR 97331-4603. TEL 541-737-3945. FAX 541-737-3563. *4297*

SELECTED REPORTS IN ETHNOMUSICOLOGY.
University of California at Los Angeles, Department of Ethnomusicology and Systematic Musicology, Box 951657, Los Angeles, CA 90095-1657. TEL 213-825-5947. FAX 213-206-4738. *5434*

SELECTED TABLES IN MATHEMATICAL STATISTICS.
American Mathematical Society, Box 6248, Providence, RI 02940-6248. TEL 401-455-4000. FAX 401-331-3842. *4605*

SELECTED TOPICS IN MASS SPECTROMETRY.
Plenum Publishing Corp., 233 Spring St., New York, NY 10013-1578. TEL 212-620-8000. FAX 212-463-0742. *1795*

SELECTED TOPICS IN SOLID STATE PHYSICS.
Elsevier Science B.V., Books Division, P.O. Box 211, 1000 AE Amsterdam, Netherlands. TEL 31-20-4853911. FAX 31-20-4853705. *5826*

SELECTED TOPICS IN SUPERCONDUCTIVITY.
Plenum Publishing Corp., 233 Spring St., New York, NY 10013-1578. TEL 212-620-8000. FAX 212-463-0742. *5826*

SELECTION AND DEVELOPMENT REVIEW.
British Psychological Society, St Andrew's House, 48 Princess Rd. E., Leicester LE1 7DR, England. TEL 44-166-254-9568. FAX 44-166-247-0787. *1506*

SEL'SKOKHOZYAISTVENNAYA LITERATURA.
Rossiiskaya Akademiya Sel'skokhozyaistvennykh Nauk, Tsentral'naya Nauchnaya Sel'skokhozyaistvennaya Biblioteka, Orlikov per. 3, 107804 Moscow, Russia. TEL 7-095-2078972. FAX 7-095-2075662. *182*

SEMIGROUP FORUM.
Springer-Verlag, Science Journals, 175 Fifth Ave., New York, NY 10010. TEL 212-460-1500. FAX 212-473-6272. *4605*

SEMINARIO DE ARTE ARAGONES.
Institucion Fernando el Catolico, Plaza de Espana 2, 50071 Zaragoza, Spain. TEL 34-976-288878. FAX 34-976-288869. *465*

SEMINARS IN ARTHRITIS & RHEUMATISM.
W.B. Saunders Co., Curtis Center, 3rd Fl., Independence Sq. W., Philadelphia, PA 19106-3399. TEL 215-238-7800. FAX 215-238-6445. *5128*

SEMINARS IN CELL AND DEVELOPMENTAL BIOLOGY.
Academic Press Ltd., 24-28 Oval Rd., London NW1 7DX, England. TEL 44-171-267-4466. FAX 44-171-482-2293. *744*

SEMINARS IN DIALYSIS.
Blackwell Science Inc., 350 Main St., Malden, MA 02148. TEL 617-876-7000. FAX 617-388-8255. *5165*

SEMINARS IN NEUROLOGICAL SURGERY.
Lippincott - Raven Publishers, 227 E. Washington Sq., Philadelphia, PA 19106. TEL 215-238-4200. FAX 215-238-4227. *5153*

SEMINARS IN SURGICAL ONCOLOGY.
John Wiley & Sons, Inc., Journals, 605 Third Ave., New York, NY 10158. TEL 212-850-6645. FAX 212-850-6021. *4987*

SEMINARS IN VETERINARY MEDICINE AND SURGERY: SMALL ANIMAL.
W.B. Saunders Co., Curtis Center, 3rd Fl., Independence Sq. W., Philadelphia, PA 19106-3399. TEL 215-238-7800. FAX 215-238-6445. *7278*

SEMIOTIC REVIEW OF BOOKS.
Victoria University, 73 Queen's Park Crescent E., Toronto, ON M5S 1K7, Canada. TEL 416-585-4456. FAX 416-585-4584. *3791*

SEMITIC STUDY SERIES.
E.J. Brill, P.O. Box 9000, 2300 PA Leiden, Netherlands. TEL 31-71-5353500. FAX 31-71-5317532. *4298*

SENAS.
Canalejas 30, entlo. 2o, 08028 Barcelona, Spain. TEL 34-3-4226289. FAX 34-3-4211858. *1000*

REFEREED SERIALS

THE SENIOR MESSENGER.
City of Vancouver, Box 1995, Vancouver, WA 98668. TEL 360-696-8016. FAX 360-696-8942. *3445*

SENSORS.
Helmers Publishing, Inc., 174 Concord St., Box 874, Peterborough, NH 03458-0874. TEL 603-924-9631. FAX 603-924-2076. *3805*

SENSORS AND ACTUATORS: A PHYSICAL.
Elsevier Science S.A., P.O. Box 564, CH-1001 Lausanne 1, Switzerland. TEL 41-21-3207381. FAX 41-21-3235444. *5839*

SENSORS AND ACTUATORS: B CHEMICAL.
Elsevier Science S.A., P.O. Box 564, CH-1001 Lausanne 1, Switzerland. TEL 41-21-3207381. FAX 41-21-3235444. *1806*

SENSORS AND MATERIALS.
M Y U, Scientific Publishing Division, 2-32-3 Sendagi, Bunkyo-ku, Tokyo 113, Japan. TEL 81-3-3821-2930. FAX 81-3-3827-8547. *5826*

SENSORY SYSTEMS.
Plenum Publishing Corp., Consultants Bureau, 233 Spring St., New York, NY 10013-1578. TEL 212-620-8468. FAX 212-463-0742. *6153*

SEPARATION AND PURIFICATION METHODS.
Marcel Dekker Journals, 270 Madison Ave., New York, NY 10016. TEL 212-696-9000. FAX 212-685-4540. *1795*

SEPARATION & PURIFICATION TECHNOLOGY.
Elsevier Science Ltd., P.O. Box 800, Kidlington, Oxford OX5 1DX, England. TEL 44-1865-843000. FAX 44-1865-843010. *2774*

SEPARATION SCIENCE AND TECHNOLOGY.
Marcel Dekker Journals, 270 Madison Ave., New York, NY 10016. TEL 212-696-9000. FAX 212-685-4540. *1795*

SEPIA.
Kawabata Press, Knill Cross House, Knill Cross, Millbrook, Torpoint, Cornwall, England. *4523*

SEPSIS.
Kluwer Academic Publishers Boston, Box 358, Accord Sta., Hingham, MA 02018-0358. TEL 617-871-6600. FAX 617-871-6528. *4843*

SERIALS LIBRARIAN.
Haworth Press, Inc., 10 Alice St., Binghamton, NY 13904. TEL 607-722-5857. FAX 607-722-6362. *4213*

SERIALS REVIEW.
J A I Press Inc., 55 Old Post Rd., No. 2, Box 1678, Greenwich, CT 06830-1678. TEL 203-661-7602. FAX 203-661-0792. *4214*

SERIE D'ECRITURE.
Burning Deck, 71 Elmgrove Ave., Providence, RI 02906. TEL 401-351-0015. *4523*

SERIE MEMORIA VIVA DA EDUCACAO BRASILEIRA.
Instituto Nacional de Estudos e Pesquisas Educacionais, Sgas Q.607 Bl.50 - L2 Sul, 70200-670 Brasilia DF, Brazil. TEL 55-61-2442612. FAX 55-61-2444712. *2482*

SERIES ENTOMOLOGICA.
Kluwer Academic Publishers, Postbus 17, 3300 AA Dordrecht, Netherlands. TEL 31-78-6392392. FAX 31-78-6392254. *760*

SERIES IN DEATH EDUCATION, AGING, AND HEALTH CARE.
Taylor & Francis Inc., 1900 Frost Rd., Ste. 101, Bristol, PA 19007-1598. TEL 215-785-5800. FAX 215-785-5515. *6153*

SERIES IN FOOD MATERIAL SCIENCE.
Kluwer Academic Publishers, Postbus 17, 3300 AA Dordrecht, Netherlands. TEL 31-78-6392392. FAX 31-78-6392254. *3127*

SERIES IN INTERNATIONAL BUSINESS AND ECONOMICS.
Elsevier Science Ltd., Books Division, P.O. Box 800, Kidlington, Oxford OX2 1DX, England. TEL 44-1865-843000. FAX 44-1865-8430410. *1288*

SERIES IN RADIOLOGY.
Kluwer Academic Publishers, Postbus 17, 3300 AA Dordrecht, Netherlands. TEL 31-78-6392392. FAX 31-78-6392254. *5115*

SERVAMUS.
S A R P Uitgewers, Postbus 828, Pretoria 0001, South Africa. TEL 27-12-3220557. *2280*

THE SERVICE INDUSTRIES JOURNAL.
Frank Cass, Newbury House, 890-900 Eastern Ave., Newbury Park, Ilford, Essex IG2 7HH, England. TEL 44-181-599-8866. FAX 44-181-599-0984. *1000*

SET-VALUED ANALYSIS.
Kluwer Academic Publishers, Postbus 17, 3300 AA Dordrecht, Netherlands. TEL 31-78-6392392. FAX 31-78-6392254. *4606*

SETGUULCH.
Press Institute of Mongolia, P.O. Box 46-600, Ulaanbaatar, Mongolia. TEL 977-1-313912. FAX 977-1-313912. *3880*

SETO MARINE BIOLOGICAL LABORATORY. PUBLICATIONS.
Kyoto University, Faculty of Science, Seto Marine Biological Laboratory, Shirahama-cho, Nishimuro-gun, Wakayama-ken 649-22, Japan. TEL 81-739-42-3515. FAX 81-739-42-4518. *626*

THE SETTLER.
Bradford County Historical Society, 21 Main St., Towanda, PA 18848. TEL 717-265-2240. *3647*

SETTORE CULTURA E SPETTACOLO. RASSEGNA DI STUDI E DI NOTIZIE.
Settore Cultura e Spettacolo, Civiche Raccolte d'Arte Applicata ed Incisioni, Castello Sforzesco, 20121 Milan, Italy. FAX 39-2-8693071. *465*

SEVASHRAM NEWS.
London Sevashram Sangha, 99A Devonport Rd., Shepherds Bush, London W12 8PB, England. TEL 44-181-723-4257. FAX 44-181-7234257. *4359*

THE SEVENTEENTH CENTURY.
University of Durham, Centre for 17th Century Studies, Palace Green, Durham DH1 3RN, England. TEL 44-191-374-2721. FAX 44-191-374-2716. *4464*

SEVENTEENTH CENTURY FRENCH STUDIES.
Society for Seventeenth-Century French Studies, French Department, The University, Glasgow G12 8QL, Scotland. TEL 44-141-339-8855. FAX 44-141-330-4234. *4464*

SEVENTEENTH - CENTURY NEWS.
Texas A & M University, Department of English, College Station, TX 77843-4227. TEL 409-845-8340. FAX 409-862-2292. *4464*

SEVERNI MORAVA.
Okresni Vlastivedne Muzeum v Sumperku, 787 34 Sumperk, Czech Republic. TEL 420-64-9214070. FAX 420-64-214909. *6572*

SEWANEE MEDIAEVAL STUDIES.
University of the South, Sewanee Mediaeval Colloquium, Office of Communications, 735 University Ave., Sewanee, TN 37383-1000. TEL 615-598-1531. *3599*

SEX OVER FORTY.
D K T International, Inc., Box 1600, Chapel Hill, NC 27515. TEL 919-929-3797. FAX 919-929-3026. *6153*

SEX ROLES.
Plenum Publishing Corp., 233 Spring St., New York, NY 10013-1578. TEL 212-620-8000. FAX 212-463-0742. *6153*

SEXUAL ABUSE.
Plenum Publishing Corp., 233 Spring St., New York, NY 10013-1578. TEL 212-620-8000. FAX 212-463-0742. *6153*

SEXUAL AND MARITAL THERAPY.
Carfax Publishing Co., P.O. Box 25, Abingdon, Oxon. OX14 3UE, England. TEL 44-1235-401000. FAX 44-1235-401550. *6153*

SEXUAL PLANT REPRODUCTION.
Springer-Verlag, Heidelberger Platz 3, 14197 Berlin, Germany. TEL 49-30-82787-0. FAX 49-30-82787448. *727*

SEXUALITY AND DISABILITY.
Human Sciences Press, Inc., 233 Spring St., New York, NY 10013-1578. TEL 212-620-8000. FAX 212-463-0742. *4744*

SEXUALLY TRANSMITTED DISEASES.
Lippincott - Raven Publishers, 227 E. Washington Sq., Philadelphia, PA 19106. TEL 215-238-4200. FAX 215-238-4227. *4881*

SEXUALLY TRANSMITTED INFECTIONS.
B M J Publishing Group, B.M.A. House, Tavistock Sq., London WC1H 9JR, England. TEL 44-171-383-6270. FAX 44-171-383-6402. *4881*

THE SHADOW.
Shadow Press, Box 20298, New York, NY 10009. TEL 212-631-1181. *5968*

SHAKESPEARE BULLETIN.
Lafayette College, English Department, Easton, PA 18042. TEL 610-250-5245. FAX 610-559-4006. *7012*

SHAKESPEARE IN SOUTHERN AFRICA.
Rhodes University, Institute for the Study of English in Africa, P.O. Box 94, Grahamstown 6140, South Africa. TEL 27-461-26093. FAX 27-461-318566. *4464*

SHAMAN.
Molnar & Kelemen Oriental Publishers, P.O. Box 1195, 6701 Szeged, Hungary. TEL 36-1-3310007. FAX 36-1-3025009. *298*

THE SHANDEAN.
The Shandean, P.O. Box 71851, 1008 EB Amsterdam, Netherlands. FAX 31-20-4445405. *4465*

SHANDI YANJIU.
Science Press, Marketing and Sales Department, 16 Donghuangchenggen North Ave., Beijing 100717, People's Republic of China. TEL 4010642. FAX 4019810. *2368*

SHANDONG SHIDA XUEBAO (SHEHUI KEXUE BAN).
Shandong Shifan Daxue, Xuebao Bianjibu, Wenhua Donglu, Jinan, Shandong 250014, People's Republic of China. TEL 86-531-2961064. *6635*

SHANGHAI DANG'AN.
684 Gubei Rd., Shanghai 200335, People's Republic of China. TEL 86-21-62751700. FAX 86-21-62752867. *4214*

SHANGHAI JIAOYU KEYAN.
Shanghai Shi Putong Jiaoyu Kexue Yanjiusuo, 21 Chaling Beilu, Shanghai 200032, People's Republic of China. TEL 86-21-6403-2733. FAX 86-21-6403-2607. *2482*

SHAREPAPER. *2217*

SHAW.
Pennsylvania State University Press, USB 1, Ste. C, University Park, PA 16802-1003. TEL 814-865-1327. FAX 814-863-1408. *4466*

SHEAF.
Sheaf Publishing Society, University of Saskatchewan, 93 Campus Drive, Saskatoon, SK S7N 5B2, Canada. TEL 306-966-8688. FAX 306-966-8699. *1971*

SHENGLI KEXUE JINZHAN.
Zhongguo Shengli Xuehui, 38 Xueyuan Rd., Beijing Medical University, Beijing 100083, People's Republic of China. TEL 861-209-1150. FAX 861-202-9252. *822*

SHENGLI XUEBAO.
Science Press, Marketing and Sales Department, 16 Donghuangchenggen North St., Beijing 100717, People's Republic of China. TEL 4010642. FAX 4019810. *822*

SHENGTAI XUEBAO.
Science Press, Marketing and Sales Department, 16 Donghuangchenggen North St., Beijing 100717, People's Republic of China. TEL 86-1-4010642. FAX 86-1-4019810. *2951*

SHENGTAIXUE ZAZHI.
Zhongguo Shengtaixue Xuehui, 72, Wenhua Lu, Shenyang, Liaoning 110015, People's Republic of China. TEL 86-24-391-6249. FAX 86-24-384-313. *2951*

SHENGWU GONGCHENG XUEBAO.
Science Press, Marketing and Sales Department, 16 Donghuangchenggen North St., Beijing 100717, People's Republic of China. TEL 4010642. FAX 4019810. *687*

SHENGWU HUAXUE YU SHENGWU WULI JINZHAN.
Science Press, Marketing and Sales Department, 16 Donghuangchenggen North St., Beijing 100717, People's Republic of China. TEL 4010642. FAX 4019810. *671*

SHENGWU HUAXUE ZAZHI.
Beijing Yike Daxue, Shengwu Huaxue yu Fenzi Shengwuxue Xi, No. 38, Xueyuan Lu, Beijing 100083, People's Republic of China. TEL 8610-2091416. FAX 8610-2015681. *671*

SHENGXUE XUEBAO.
Science Press, Marketing and Sales Department, 16 Donghuangchenggen North St., Beijing 100717, People's Republic of China. TEL 4010642. FAX 4019810. *5874*

SHENJI LILUN YU SHIJIAN.
Beijing Shenji Yanjiusuo, 69 Xibianmennei Dajie, Beijing 100053, People's Republic of China. TEL 86-10-6303-4849. *1098*

SHENYANG YAOKE DAXUE XUEBAO.
Shenyang Yaoke Daxue, Xuebao Bianjibu, 103 Wenhua Rd., Shenyang, Liaoning 110015, People's Republic of China. TEL 86-24-3843711. FAX 86-24-3891576. *5694*

SHIJIE DIANXIN.
Youdian-bu, Keji Qingbao Zhongxin, 40 Xueyuan Rd., Haidian, Beijing 100083, People's Republic of China. TEL 86-10-6230-1569. FAX 86-10-6230-4077. *2003*

SHILAP.
Sociedad Hispano-Luso-Americana de Lepidopterologia, Apdo. 331, 28080 Madrid, Spain. FAX 34-1-4475609. *760*

SHIN BOEI RONSHU.
Boei Gakkai, Daini-Matsuda Bldg., 7-8-7, Roppongi, Minato-ku, Tokyo 106, Japan. TEL 81-3-3713-2469. FAX 81-3-3713-2723. *5285*

SHINKEI GANKA.
Nihon Shinkei Ganka Gakkai, Kitasato Daigaku Igakubu Ganka, 15-1, Kitasato 1-chome, Sagamihara-shi, Kanagawa-ken 228, Japan. TEL 81-427-78-8464. FAX 81-427-78-2357. *5001*

SHINKO PANTEC GIHO.
Shinko Pantec Co. Ltd., 1-4, 1-chome, Murotani, Nishi-ku, Kobe-shi, Hyogo-ken 651-22, Japan. TEL 81-78-992-6525. FAX 81-78-992-6504. *2899*

SHINKO TEKUNO GIHO.
Shinko Tekuno K.K., 10-26, Wakihamacho 2-chome, Chuo-ku, Kobe-shi, Hyogo-ken 651, Japan. TEL 81-78-393-5001. FAX 81-78-393-5011. *2899*

SHINRIGAKU HYORON.
Kyoto University, Graduate School of Letters, Yoshida Honmachi, Sakyo-ku, Kyoto 606, Japan. FAX 81-75-753-2835. *6153*

SHIPPERS TODAY.
Hong Kong Shippers Council, 31F, Wu Chung House, 213 Queen's Rd. E., Hong Kong, People's Republic of China. TEL 852-2834-0010. FAX 852-2891-9787. *7165*

SHIYONG ZHONGLIU ZAZHI.
Zhejiang Yike Daxue, 157 Yan'an Lu, Hangzhou, Zhejiang 310006, People's Republic of China. TEL 722700. *4987*

SHIYOU HUAGONG.
Ministry of Chemical Industry, Beijing Research Institute of Chemical Industry, P.O. Box 1442, Hepingli, Beijing, People's Republic of China. TEL 86-10-6429-5032. FAX 86-10-6429-5032. *5622*

SHIYOU KANTAN YU KAIFA.
Shiyou Kantan yu Kaifa Bianjibu, No. 20 Xueyuan Lu, P.O. Box 910, Beijing 100083, People's Republic of China. TEL 86-10-6209-7424. FAX 86-10-6209-7181. *5622*

SHIYOU LIANZHI YU HUAGONG.
Shiyou Lianzhi yu Huagong Bianjibu, 18 Xueyuan Rd., Beijing 100083, People's Republic of China. TEL 86-10-2019183. FAX 86-10-2017429. *5622*

SHIYOU ZHUANTAN JISHU.
Shiyou Zhuantan Jishu Bianjibu, 35 Dongfeng Donglu, Dezhou, Shandong 253005, People's Republic of China. TEL 86-534-262-2554. FAX 86-534-262-2468. *5623*

SHOCK.
BioMedical Press, 1021 15th St., Ste. 9, Augusta, GA 30901. TEL 706-722-7511. FAX 706-722-7515. *4745*

SHOCK AND VIBRATION.
John Wiley & Sons, Inc., Journals, 605 Third Ave., New York, NY 10158. TEL 212-850-6645. FAX 212-850-6021. *5874*

SHORT STORY.
University of Texas, Brownsville, Department of English, 80 Ft. Brown, Brownsville, TX 78520. TEL 210-544-8239. *4359*

SHOUDU YIKE DAXUE.
Shoudu Yike Daxue, You'anmenwai, Beijing 100054, People's Republic of China. TEL 86-10-6305-1258. FAX 86-10-6329-1972. *4745*

SHOULEI XUEBAO.
Science Press, Marketing and Sales Department, 16 Donghuangchenggen North St., Beijing 100717, People's Republic of China. TEL 4010642. FAX 4019810. *849*

SHOW ME MISSOURI FARM BUREAU.
Missouri Farm Bureau Federation, Box 658, Jefferson City, MO 65102. TEL 314-893-1400. FAX 573-893-1470. *152*

SHOWBIZ MAGAZINE.
Las Vegas Sun, Inc., Box 4275, Las Vegas, NV 89127. TEL 702-383-7185. FAX 702-383-1089. *7234*

SHRI RAMAKRISHNA JYOT.
Sri Ramakrishna Ashrama, Dr. Yagnik Rd., Rajkot 360 001, India. TEL 91-281-445200. FAX 91-281-52000. *3792*

SHUICHAN KEJI QINGBAO.
Shanghai Shuichan Xuehui, 265 Jiamusi Lu, Shanghai 200433, People's Republic of China. TEL 5483215. FAX 5489502. *3078*

SHUISHENG SHENGWU XUEBAO.
Science Press, Marketing and Sales Department, 16 Donghuangchenggen North St., Beijing 100717, People's Republic of China. TEL 4010642. FAX 4019810. *626*

SHU'UN IJTIMA'IYYAH.
Sociological Association of the U A E, P.O. Box 3745, Sharjah, United Arab Emirates. TEL 971-6-522267. FAX 971-6-548161. *6727*

SHUXUE DE SHIJIAN YU RENSHI.
Science Press, Marketing and Sales Department, 16 Donghuangchenggen North St., Beijing 100717, People's Republic of China. TEL 4010642. FAX 4019810. *4606*

SHUXUE XUEBAO.
Science Press, Marketing and Sales Department, 16 Donghuangchenggen North St., Beijing 100717, People's Republic of China. TEL 4010642. FAX 4019810. *4606*

SHUZHI JISUAN YU JISUANJI YINGYONG.
Science Press, Marketing and Sales Department, 16 Donghuangchenggen North St., Beijing 100717, People's Republic of China. TEL 4010642. FAX 4019810. *6594*

SIBERIAN MATHEMATICAL JOURNAL.
Plenum Publishing Corp., Consultants Bureau, 233 Spring St., New York, NY 10013-1578. TEL 212-620-8468. FAX 212-463-0742. *4606*

SIBOGA EXPEDITION.
E.J. Brill, P.O. Box 9000, 2300 PA Leiden, Netherlands. TEL 31-71-5353500. FAX 31-71-5317532. *626*

SIDA: CONTRIBUTIONS TO BOTANY.
Botanical Research Institute of Texas, Inc., 509 Pecan St., Fort Worth, TX 76102-4060. TEL 817-332-4441. FAX 817-332-4112. *728*

SIDE EFFECTS OF DRUGS ANNUAL.
Elsevier Science B.V., Books Division, P.O. Box 211, 1000 AE Amsterdam, Netherlands. TEL 31-20-4853911. FAX 31-20-4853705. *5694*

SIDEWALKS.
Sidewalks, Box 321, Champlin, MN 55316. TEL 612-421-3512. *4359*

SIDOR HOY INTERNACIONAL.
C.V.G. Siderurgica del Orinoco C.A. (Sidor), Gerencia Corporativa de Asuntos Publicos, Edificio Administrativo 1, Piso 7, Matanzas - Edo. Bolivar, Venezuela. TEL 58-86-907383. FAX 58-86-940796. *5210*

SIGLO XX.
Society of Spanish and Spanish-American Studies, Department of Spanish and Portuguese, University of Colorado, Campus Box 278, Boulder, CO 80309-0278. TEL 303-492-7308. FAX 303-492-3699. *4466*

SIGNAL PROCESSING.
Elsevier Science B.V., P.O. Box 211, 1000 AE Amsterdam, Netherlands. TEL 31-20-4853911. FAX 31-20-4853598. *2146*

SIGNAL PROCESSING: IMAGE COMMUNICATION.
Elsevier Science B.V., P.O. Box 211, 1000 AE Amsterdam, Netherlands. TEL 31-20-4853911. FAX 31-20-4853598. *2171*

SIGNO Y SENA.
Universidad de Buenos Aires, Instituto de Linguistica, 25 de Mayo 221, 1002 Buenos Aires, Argentina. TEL 54-1-3431196. FAX 54-1-343-2733. *4298*

SIGNS: JOURNAL OF WOMEN IN CULTURE AND SOCIETY.
University of Chicago Press, Journals Division, Box 37005, Chicago, IL 60637. TEL 773-753-3347. FAX 773-753-0811. *7347*

SILHOUETTE.
McMaster Students Union, Rm. 406, Hamilton Hall, 1280 Main St. W., Hamilton, ON L8S 4K1, Canada. TEL 905-525-9140. FAX 905-523-0107. *4359*

SILICATES INDUSTRIELS.
Belgian Ceramic Society, 4 ave. Gouverneur Cornez, 7000 Mons, Belgium. TEL 32-65-348000. FAX 32-65-348005. *1733*

SILNICNI OBZOR.
Nakladatelstvi Silnicni Spolecnosti, Novotneho Lavka 5, 116 68 Prague 1, Czech Republic. TEL 42-2-21082388. FAX 42-2-24227836. *7141*

SILVER.
Silver Magazine Inc., Box 9690, Rancho Santa Fe, CA 92067. TEL 619-756-1054. FAX 619-756-9928. *343*

SILVER WINGS.
Poetry on Wings, Inc., Box 1000, Pearblossom, CA 93553-1000. TEL 805-264-3726. *4523*

SIMON'S TOWN HISTORICAL SOCIETY BULLETIN.
Simon's Town Historical Society, P.O. Box 56, Simon's Town 7995, South Africa. *3529*

SIMPLIFIED SPELLING SOCIETY. JOURNAL.
Simplified Spelling Society, 61 Valentine Rd., Birmingham B14 7AJ, England. TEL 44-121-689-2597. FAX 44-121-359-6153. *4298*

SIMULATION (SAN DIEGO).
Society for Computer Simulation, Box 17900, San Diego, CA 92117-7900. TEL 619-277-3888. FAX 619-277-3930. *2152*

SIMULATION PRACTICE AND THEORY.
Elsevier Science B.V., P.O. Box 211, 1000 AE Amsterdam, Netherlands. TEL 31-20-4853911. FAX 31-20-4853598. *2153*

SIMULATION SERIES.
Society for Computer Simulation, Box 17900, San Diego, CA 92177. TEL 619-277-3888. FAX 619-277-3930. *2153*

SINERGIE.
Consorzio Universitario Economia Industriale e Manageriale, Via S. Cristoforo 4, 37129 Verona, Italy. TEL 39-45-597655. FAX 39-45-597550. *1506*

SINET.
Addis Ababa University, Faculty of Science, P.O. Box 31226, Addis Ababa, Ethiopia. TEL 251-1-553177. FAX 251-1-552112. *6573*

SINGAPORE JOURNAL OF TROPICAL GEOGRAPHY.
Blackwell Publishers Ltd., 108 Cowley Rd., Oxford OX4 1JF, England. TEL 44-1865-791100. FAX 44-1865-791347. *3421*

SINGAPORE LITERATURE.
Singapore Literature Society, 122B Sims Ave., Singapore 1438, Singapore. TEL 65-7477134. FAX 65-7428701. *4467*

SINGAPORE NATIONAL INSTITUTE OF CHEMISTRY. BULLETIN.
Singapore National Institute of Chemistry, c/o Department of Chemistry, National University of Singapore, Kent Ridge, Singapore 0511, Singapore. TEL 65-772-2914. FAX 65-779-1691. *1766*

SINGAPORE PAEDIATRIC JOURNAL.
Singapore Paediatric Society, c/o Department of Paediatrics, National University Hospital, Lower Kent Ridge Rd., Singapore 119074, Singapore. TEL 65-7724112. *5040*

SINICA LEIDENSIA.
E.J. Brill, P.O. Box 9000, 2300 PA Leiden, Netherlands. TEL 31-71-5353500. FAX 31-71-5317532. *3538*

SINN UND FORM.
Aufbau-Verlag Berlin und Weimar, Franzoesische Str. 32, 10117 Berlin, Germany. TEL 030-22350. FAX 030-2298637. *4467*

SINO - JAPANESE STUDIES.
University of California at Santa Barbara, History Department, Santa Barbara, CA 93106. TEL 805-893-4065. FAX 805-893-8795. *3539*

SIR THOMAS BROWNE INSTITUTE. PUBLICATIONS. NEW SERIES.
E.J. Brill, P.O. Box 9000, 2300 PA Leiden, Netherlands. TEL 31-71-5353500. FAX 31-71-5317532. *3599*

SISTER NAMIBIA.
Sister Namibia Collective, P.O. Box 40092, Windhoek, Namibia. TEL 264-61-230618. FAX 264-61-236371. *7333*

SITARA TELUGU FILM WEEKLY.
Eenadu Complex, Somajiguda, Hyderabad 500 482, India. TEL 91-40-318181. FAX 91-40-392530. *5345*

SIXTEENTH CENTURY JOURNAL.
Sixteenth Century Journal Publishers, Inc., Truman State University, MC 111L, Kirksville, MO 63501. TEL 816-785-4665. FAX 816-785-4181. *3599*

SJOGREN'S SYNDROME FOUNDATION INC.
Sjogren's Syndrome Foundation Inc., c/o Rita M. May, Exec. Dir., 333 N. Broadway, Ste. 2000, NY 11753-2007. TEL 516-933-6365. FAX 516-933-6368. *4801*

SKEPTIC.
Millenium Press, 2761 N. Marengo Ave., Box 338, Altadena, CA 91001. TEL 818-794-3119. FAX 818-794-1301. *5578*

SKIN PHARMACOLOGY AND APPLIED SKIN PHYSIOLOGY.
S. Karger AG, Allschwilerstr. 10, P.O. Box, CH-4009 Basel, Switzerland. TEL 41-61-3061111. FAX 41-61-30161234. *5694*

SKIN RESEARCH AND TECHNOLOGY.
Munksgaard International Publishers Ltd., 35 Noerre Soegade, P.O. Box 1248, DK-1016 Copenhagen K, Denmark. TEL 45-33-127030. FAX 45-33-129387. *4881*

SKIPPING STONES.
Box 3939, Eugene, OR 97403-0939. TEL 541-342-4956. *1887*

SKYDD & SAEKERHET.
Svenska Stoeldskyddsfoereningen, S-115 87 Stockholm, Sweden. TEL 46-8-783-7450. FAX 46-8-663-9652. *2289*

SKYLARK.
Purdue University Calumet, 2200 169th St., Hammond, IN 46323. TEL 219-989-2262. *4359*

SKYWINGS.
British Hang Gliding and Paragliding Association Ltd., Old Schoolroom, Loughborough Rd., Leicester LE4 5PJ, England. TEL 44-114-267-9227. *6883*

SLANT: A JOURNAL OF POETRY.
University of Central Arkansas, Box 5063, Conway, AR 72035-5000. TEL 501-450-5107. *4523*

SLAVE AND POST-SLAVE SOCIETIES AND CULTURES.
Frank Cass, Newbury House, 890-900 Eastern Ave., Newbury Park, Ilford, Essex 1G2 7HH, England. TEL 44-181-599-8866. FAX 44-181-599-0984. *6727*

SLAVERY & ABOLITION.
Frank Cass, Newbury House, 890-900 Eastern Ave., Newbury Park, Ilford, Essex 1G2 7HH, England. TEL 44-181-599-8866. FAX 44-181-599-0984. *6727*

SLAVICA LUNDENSIA.
Lunds Universitet, Slaviska Institutionen, Finngatan 12, S-223 62 Lund, Sweden. TEL 46-222-88-21. FAX 46-222-88-25. *4299*

SLAVONICA.
University of Manchester, Arts Bldg., Manchester M13 9PL, England. TEL 44-161-275-3138. FAX 44-161-275-3031. *4467*

SLIPSTREAM (NIAGARA FALLS).
Slipstream Publications, Box 2071, Niagara Falls, NY 14301. TEL 716-282-2616. *4523*

SLOAN MANAGEMENT REVIEW.
Massachusetts Institute of Technology, Sloan School of Management, 77 Massachussetts Ave., E53-416, Cambridge, MA 02139. TEL 617-253-7170. FAX 617-258-9739. *1507*

SLOVAK GEOLOGICAL MAGAZINE.
Geologicka Sluzba Slovenskej Republiky, Mlynska Dolina 1, 817 04 Bratislava, Slovakia. TEL 421-7-3705111. FAX 421-7-371940. *2322*

SLOVENSKE DIVADLO.
Slovenska Akademia Vied, Kabinet Divadla a Filmu, Dubravska cesta 9, 813 64 Bratislava, Slovakia. TEL 42-7-377193. FAX 42-7-373567. *7013*

SLOVENSKO ETNOLOSKO DRUSTVO. GLASNIK.
Slovensko Etnolosko Drustvo, Zavetiska 5, 61000 Ljubljana, Slovenia. TEL 386-61-262782. FAX 386-61-1231220. *3600*

SLOVENSKY NARODOPIS.
Slovenska Akademia Vied, Ustav Etnologie, Jakubovo nam. 12, 813 64 Bratislava, Slovakia. TEL 421-7-5334925. FAX 421-7-361312. *3043*

SLUMGULLION.
412 N. Alfred St., Ste. 6, Alexandria, VA 22314. *4468*

SMALL BUSINESS ADVISOR.
Small Business Advisors, Inc., Box 436, Woodmere, NY 11598. TEL 516-374-1387. FAX 516-374-1175. *1646*

SMALL BUSINESS ECONOMICS.
Kluwer Academic Publishers, Postbus 17, 3300 AA Dordrecht, Netherlands. TEL 31-78-6392392. FAX 31-78-6392254. *1647*

SMALL BUSINESS, MARKETING AND SOCIETY.
James Nicholas Publishers, P.O. Box 224, Alber Park, Vic. 3206, Australia. TEL 61-3-6965545. FAX 61-3-6992040. *1647*

SMALL ENTERPRISE DEVELOPMENT.
Intermediate Technology Publications Ltd., 103-105 Southampton Row, London WC1B 4HH, England. TEL 44-171-436-9761. FAX 44-171-436-2013. *1647*

SMALL POND MAGAZINE OF LITERATURE.
Napoleon St. Cyr, Ed. & Pub., Box 664, Stratford, CT 06497. TEL 203-378-4066. *4468*

SMALL RUMINANT RESEARCH.
Elsevier Science B.V., P.O. Box 211, 1000 AE Amsterdam, Netherlands. TEL 31-20-4853911. FAX 31-20-4853598. *289*

SMALL WARS AND INSURGENCIES.
Frank Cass, Newbury House, 890-900 Eastern Ave., Newbury Park, Ilford, Essex 1G2 7HH, England. TEL 44-181-599-8866. FAX 44-181-599-0984. *6036*

SMARANDACHE NOTIONS.
Erhus University Press, 13333 Colossal Cave Rd., Box 722, Vail, AZ 85641. *4606*

SMITH COLLEGE STUDIES IN SOCIAL WORK.
Smith College, School for Social Work, Lilly Hall, Northampton, MA 01063. TEL 413-585-7984. FAX 413-585-7994. *6687*

SMOKE.
Windows Project, 40 Canning St., Liverpool L8 7NP, England. TEL 44-151-709-3688. *4523*

SNAIL'S PACE REVIEW.
Snail's Pace Press, R.R. 2, Darwin Rd., Box 403, Cambridge, NY 12816. TEL 518-677-5208. *4523*

SNAKE NATION REVIEW.
Snake Nation Press, 110 No. 2 W. Force, Valdosta, GA 31602. TEL 912-249-2787. FAX 912-249-8334. *4523*

SNEWS.
Ms. Jay Hensley, Ed. & Pub., Box 98, Wilmore, KY 40390. TEL 606-986-8001. FAX 606-858-4043. *3484*

SOCCER JOURNAL.
National Soccer Coaches Association of America, East Gymnasium, Binghamton University, Binghamton, NY 13902-6000. TEL 607-777-2133. FAX 607-777-4467. *6817*

SOCIAL AND ECONOMIC STUDIES.
University of the West Indies, Institute of Social and Economic Research, Mona Campus, Kingston 7, Jamaica, W.I. TEL 809-927-1020. FAX 809-927-2409. *6636*

SOCIAL & LEGAL STUDIES.
Sage Publications Ltd., 6 Bonhill St., London EC2A 4PU, England. TEL 44-171-374-0645. FAX 44-171-374-8741. *6727*

SOCIAL ANTHROPOLOGY.
Cambridge University Press, Edinburgh Bldg., Shaftesbury Rd., Cambridge CB2 2RU, England. TEL 44-1223-312393. FAX 44-1223-315052. *329*

SOCIAL BEHAVIOR AND PERSONALITY.
Society for Personality Research (Inc.), P.O. Box 1539, Palmerston North, New Zealand. TEL 64-6-355-5736. FAX 64-6-355-5736. *6154*

SOCIAL BIOLOGY.
Society for the Study of Social Biology, Box 2349, Port Angeles, WA 98362. TEL 608-233-1487. *776*

SOCIAL COGNITION.
Guilford Publications, Inc., 72 Spring St., 4th Fl., New York, NY 10012. TEL 212-431-9800. FAX 212-966-6708. *6154*

SOCIAL COMPASS.
Sage Publications Ltd., 6 Bonhill St., London EC2A 4PU, England. TEL 44-171-374-0645. FAX 44-171-374-8741. *6728*

THE SOCIAL CREDITER.
K R P Ltd., P.O. Box 13855, Edinburgh EH15 1YD, Scotland. TEL 44-131-657-4740. *5969*

SOCIAL DEVELOPMENT.
Blackwell Publishers Ltd., 108 Cowley Rd., Oxford OX4 1JF, England. TEL 44-1865-791100. FAX 44-1865-791347. *6728*

SOCIAL DIMENSIONS OF ECONOMICS.
Kluwer Academic Publishers, Postbus 17, 3300 AA Dordrecht, Netherlands. TEL 31-78-6392392. FAX 31-78-6392254. *1311*

SOCIAL, ECONOMIC AND POLITICAL STUDIES OF THE MIDDLE EAST.
E.J. Brill, P.O. Box 9000, 2300 PA Leiden, Netherlands. TEL 31-71-5353500. FAX 31-71-5317532. *3660*

SOCIAL EDUCATION.
National Council for the Social Studies, 3501 Newark St., N.W., Washington, DC 20016. TEL 202-966-7840. *6637*

SOCIAL EPISTEMOLOGY.
Taylor & Francis Ltd., Rankine Rd., Basingstoke, Hants. RG24 8PR, England. TEL 44-1256-840366. FAX 44-1256-479438. *5751*

SOCIAL FORCES.
University of North Carolina Press, Box 2288, Chapel Hill, NC 27515-2288. TEL 919-966-3561. FAX 919-966-3829. *6728*

SOCIAL INDICATORS RESEARCH.
Kluwer Academic Publishers, Postbus 17, 3300 AA Dordrecht, Netherlands. TEL 31-78-6392392. FAX 31-78-6392254. *6728*

SOCIAL JUSTICE.
Global Options, Box 40601, San Francisco, CA 94140. TEL 415-550-1703. *6036*

SOCIAL JUSTICE RESEARCH.
Plenum Publishing Corp., 233 Spring St., New York, NY 10013-1578. TEL 212-620-8000. FAX 212-463-0742. *6728*

SOCIAL NETWORKS.
North-Holland, P.O. Box 211, 1000 AE Amsterdam, Netherlands. TEL 31-20-4853911. FAX 31-20-4853598. *6637*

SOCIAL ORDERS SERIES.
Gordon and Breach - Harwood Academic, Amsteldisk 166, 1st Fl., 1079 LH Amsterdam, Netherlands. *6729*

SOCIAL PATHOLOGY.
Harrow and Heston Publishers, 1830 Western Ave., Albany, NY 12203. TEL 518-456-4894. FAX 518-456-4894. *6729*

SOCIAL POLICY AND ADMINISTRATION.
Blackwell Publishers Ltd., 108 Cowley Rd., Oxford OX4 1JF, England. TEL 44-1865-791100. FAX 44-1865-791347. *6729*

SOCIAL POLITICS.
Oxford University Press, Academic Division, Great Clarendon St., Oxford OX2 6DP, England. TEL 44-1865-267907. FAX 44-1865-267485. *7347*

SOCIAL PROBLEMS.
University of California Press, Journals Division, 2120 Berkeley Way, Berkeley, CA 94720. TEL 510-643-7154. FAX 510-642-9917. *6729*

SOCIAL PSYCHOLOGICAL APPLICATIONS TO SOCIAL ISSUES.
Plenum Publishing Corp., 233 Spring St., New York, NY 10013-1578. TEL 212-620-8000. FAX 212-463-0742. *6154*

SOCIAL PSYCHOLOGY OF EDUCATION.
Kluwer Academic Publishers, Postbus 17, 3300 AA Dordrecht, Netherlands. TEL 31-78-6392392. FAX 31-78-6392254. *2483*

SOCIAL SCIENCE & MEDICINE.
Elsevier Science Ltd., Pergamon, P.O. Box 800, Kidlington, Oxford OX5 1DX, England. TEL 44-1865-843000. FAX 44-1865-843010. *4746*

SOCIAL SCIENCE COMPUTER REVIEW.
Sage Publications, Inc., 2455 Teller Rd., Thousand Oaks, CA 91320. *2519*

SOCIAL SCIENCE HISTORY.
Duke University Press, Box 90660, Durham, NC 27708-0660. TEL 919-687-3600. FAX 919-688-4574. *6637*

SOCIAL SCIENCE INFORMATION.
Sage Publications Ltd., 6 Bonhill St., London EC2A 4PU, England. TEL 44-171-374-0645. FAX 44-171-374-8741. *6637*

SOCIAL SCIENCES IN HEALTH.
Arnold, 338 Euston Rd., London NW1 3BH, England. TEL 44-171-873-6000. FAX 44-171-873-6325. *6251*

SOCIAL SEMIOTICS.
Carfax Publishing Co., P.O. Box 25, Abingdon, Oxon OX14 3UE, England. TEL 44-1235-401000. FAX 44-1235-401550. *5751*

SOCIAL SERVICE REVIEW.
University of Chicago Press, Journals Division, Box 37005, Chicago, IL 60637. TEL 773-753-3347. FAX 773-753-0811. *6688*

THE SOCIAL STUDIES.
Heldref Publications, 1319 Eighteenth St., N.W., Washington, DC 20036-1802. TEL 202-296-6267. FAX 202-296-5149. *2483*

SOCIAL STUDIES OF SCIENCE.
Sage Publications Ltd., 6 Bonhill St., London EC2A 4PU, England. TEL 44-171-374-0645. FAX 44-171-374-8741. *6573*

SOCIAL STUDIES REVIEW.
California Council for Social Studies, 1255 Vista Grande, Millbrae, CA 94030-2213. TEL 415-692-9260. FAX 415-692-4830. *6638*

SOCIAL WORK.
University of Stellenbosch, Department of Social Work, P.O. Box 223, Stellenbosch 7599, South Africa. TEL 27-21-8082069. FAX 27-21-8083765. *6688*

SOCIAL WORK AND CHRISTIANITY.
North American Association of Christians in Social Work, Box 121, Botsford, CT 06404-0121. TEL 203-270-8780. FAX 203-270-8780. *6688*

SOCIAL WORK IN EUROPE.
Russell House Publishing Ltd., 38 Silver St., Lyme Regis, Dorset DT7 3HS, England. TEL 44-1297-443948. FAX 44-1297-443948. *6688*

SOCIAL WORK IN HEALTH CARE.
Haworth Press, Inc., 10 Alice St., Binghamton, NY 13904. TEL 607-722-5857. FAX 607-722-6362. *6689*

SOCIAL WORK WITH GROUPS.
Haworth Press, Inc., 10 Alice St., Binghamton, NY 13904. TEL 607-722-5857. FAX 607-722-6362. *6689*

SOCIAL WORKER.
Myropen Publications Ltd., 383 Parkdale Ave., Ste. 402, Ottawa, ON K1Y 4R4, Canada. TEL 613-729-6668. FAX 613-729-9608. *6689*

SOCIALE WETENSCHAPPEN.
Tilburg University, Faculty of Social Sciences, Postbus 90153, 5000 LE Tilburg, Netherlands. FAX 31-13-4662370. *6638*

SOCIALIST STANDARD.
Socialist Party of Great Britain, 52 Clapham High St., London SW4 7UN, England. TEL 44-171-622-3811. FAX 44-171-720-3665. *5970*

SOCIALIST STUDIES.
Societe for Socialist Studies, University College, No. 448, University of Manitoba, Winnipeg, MB R3T 2M8, Canada. TEL 204-474-9119. FAX 204-261-0021. *5970*

SOCIALIST WORKER.
Socialist Worker Organisation, P.O. Box 18530, Hillbrow 2038, South Africa. TEL 27-11-4845377. FAX 27-11-4845377. *6037*

SOCIEDAD ARGENTINA PARA LA INVESTIGACION DE PRODUCTOS AROMATICOS. ANALES.
Sociedad Argentina para la Investigacion de Productos Aromaticos, Libertad 1079, 2o piso, 1012 Buenos Aires, Argentina. TEL 54-1-383-2360. *728*

SOCIEDAD BOTANICA DE MEXICO. BOLETIN.
Sociedad Botanica de Mexico, A.C., Apdo. Postal 70-385, Del. Coyoacan; Ciudad Universitaria, 04510 Mexico D.F., Mexico. *728*

SOCIEDAD ESPANOLA DE CERAMICA Y VIDRIO. BOLETIN.
Sociedad Espanola de Ceramica y Vidrio, Ctra. Antigua de Valencia, km. 24300, 28500 Arganda del Rey (Madrid), Spain. TEL 34-1-871-18-00. FAX 34-1-870-05-50. *1733*

SOCIEDAD ESPANOLA DE MINERALOGIA. BOLETIN.
Sociedad Espanola de Mineralogia, Alenza 1, 28003 Madrid, Spain. TEL 34-1-4417138. FAX 34-58-243368. *5316*

SOCIEDAD ESPANOLA DE QUIMICA CLINICA. REVISTA.
Ediciones Mayo, S.A., Muntaner, 374-376, 4o, 08006 Barcelona, Spain. TEL 34-3-2090255. FAX 34-3-2020643. *1767*

SOCIEDAD MATEMATICA MEXICANA. BOLETIN.
Sociedad Matematica Mexicana, Apdo. Postal 14-170, 07000 Mexico, D.F., Mexico. TEL 525-747-7103. FAX 525-747-7104. *4606*

SOCIEDAD MICOLOGICA DE MADRID. BOLETIN.
Sociedad Micologica de Madrid, c/o Real Jardin Botanico, Claudio Moyano 1, 28014 Madrid, Spain. FAX 34-1-4200157. *728*

SOCIEDAD QUIMICA DE MEXICO. REVISTA.
Sociedad Quimica de Mexico, Mar del Norte 5, Col. San Alvaro, Deleg. Azcapotzalco, 02090 Mexico, D.F., Mexico. TEL 52-5-3860255. FAX 52-5-3862905. *1767*

SOCIEDADE BRASILEIRA DE HISTORIA DA CIENCIA. BOLETIM.
Sociedade Brasileira de Historia da Ciencia, c/o Centro Simao Mathias de Estudos em Historia da Ciencia, Potificia Universidade Catolica de Sao Paulo, Rua Marques de Paranagua, Predio 1, Sala 2, 01303-050 Sao Paulo, Brazil. TEL 55-11-2561622. FAX 55-11-8225771. *6574*

SOCIEDADE BRASILEIRA DE MATEMATICA. BOLETIM, NOVA SERIE.
Springer-Verlag, 175 Fifth Ave., New York, NY 10010. TEL 212-460-1500. FAX 212-473-6272. *4606*

SOCIEDADE ENTOMOLOGICA DO BRASIL. ANAIS.
Sociedade Entomologica do Brasil, EMBRAPA - CNPSo, Caixa Postal 231, 86001-970 Londrina, Parana, Brazil. TEL 55-43-3204253. FAX 55-43-3204253. *760*

SOCIEDADE PARANAENSE DE MATEMATICA. BOLETIM.
Sociedade Paranaense de Matematica, Caixa Postal 19081, 81531-990 Curitiba, Parana, Brazil. FAX 55-41-2674236. *4606*

SOCIETAS PRO FAUNA ET FLORA FENNICA. MEMORANDA.
Societas pro Fauna et Flora Fennica, P.O. Box 17, FIN-00014 University of Helsinki, Finland. *627*

SOCIETATIS GEOLOGORUM POLONIAE. ANNALES.
Polskie Towarzystwo Geologiczne, Ul. Oleandry 2A, 30-063 Krakow, Poland. FAX 48-12-221609. *2369*

SOCIETE ALGERIENNE DE CHIMIE. JOURNAL.
Societe Algerienne de Chimie, B.P. 109, El Alia, 16111 Bab Ezzouar, Alger, Algeria. *1767*

SOCIETE AMERICAINE DE PHILOSOPHIE DE LANGUE FRANCAISE. BULLETIN.
Societe Americaine de Philosophie de Langue Francaise, c/o Northern Illinois University, 635 Joanne Lane, DeKalb, IL 60115. TEL 815-753-6463. FAX 815-753-6302. *5751*

SOCIETE BELGE D'ETUDES GEOGRAPHIQUES. BULLETIN.
Societe Belge d'Etudes Geographiques, De Croylaan 42, 3001 Heverlee, Belgium. TEL 32-16-322427. FAX 32-6-322980. *3422*

SOCIETE BELGE DE GEOLOGIE. BULLETIN.
Societe Belge de Geologie, 13 rue Jenner, 1000 Brussels, Belgium. TEL 32-2-6270410. FAX 32-2-6477359. *2369*

SOCIETE BELGE DE PHOTOGRAMMETRIE - TELEDETECTION ET CARTOGRAPHIE. BULLETIN TRIMESTRIEL.
Societe Belge de Photogrammetrie-Teledetection et Cartographie, C.A.E.-Tour Finances, Bte. 38, 50 bd. du Jardin Botanique, B-1010 Brussels, Belgium. TEL 32-2-2103575. *3422*

SOCIETE CHIMIQUE DE FRANCE. BULLETIN.
Editions Scientifiques et Medicales Elsevier, 141 rue de Javel, 75747 Paris, France. TEL 33-1-45589022. FAX 33-1-45589421. *1767*

SOCIETE DES AMERICANISTES. JOURNAL.
Societe des Americanistes, Musee de l'Homme, 17 Place du Trocadero, 75116 Paris, France. TEL 33-1-47046311. *330*

SOCIETE DES SCIENCES MEDICALES DU GRAND-DUCHE DE LUXEMBOURG. BULLETIN.
Societe des Sciences Medicales du Grand-Duche de Luxembourg, Centre Hospitalier de Luxembourg, 4 rue Barble, L-1210 Luxembourg, Luxembourg. TEL 352-4411-2024. FAX 352-441209. *4746*

SOCIETE FRANCAISE DE CHIMIE. ANNUAIRE.
Societe Francaise de Chimie, 250 rue St. Jacques, 75005 Paris, France. TEL 33-1-40467160. FAX 33-1-40467161. *1767*

SOCIETE FRANCAISE DE PHOTOGRAMMETRIE ET DE TELEDETECTION. BULLETIN.
Societe Francaise de Photogrammetrie et de Teledetection, B.P. 68, 2 av. Pasteur, 94160 Saint-Mande, France. TEL 33-1-43988073. FAX 33-1-43988541. *3422*

SOCIETE FRANCAISE DU VIDE. PROCEEDINGS.
Societe Francaise du Vide, 19 rue du Renard, 75004 Paris, France. TEL 33-1-53-01-90-30. FAX 33-1-42-78-63-20. *5827*

SOCIETE GEOLOGIQUE DE BELGIQUE. ANNALES.
Societe Geologique de Belgique, Universite de Liege, 7 Place du Vingt-Aout, 4000 Liege, Belgium. TEL 32-4-3665395. FAX 32-4-3665338. *2369*

SOCIETE GEOLOGIQUE DE FRANCE. BULLETIN.
Societe Geologique de France, 77 rue Claude Bernard, 75005 Paris, France. TEL 33-1-43317735. FAX 33-1-45357910. *2369*

SOCIETE GEOLOGIQUE DE FRANCE. MEMOIRES.
Societe Geologique de France, 77 rue Claude-Bernard, 75005 Paris, France. TEL 33-1-43317735. FAX 33-1-45357910. *2369*

SOCIETE GEOLOGIQUE DE NORMANDIE ET DES AMIS DU MUSEUM DU HAVRE. BULLETIN TRIMESTRIEL.
Editions du Museum du Havre, Place du Vieux Marche, 76600 le Havre, France. TEL 33-2-35413728. FAX 33-2-35421240. *2369*

SOCIETE LINNEENNE DE PROVENCE. BULLETIN.
Societe Linneenne de Provence, Lycee Victor Hugo, 3 Bd Desplaces, 13003 Marseille, France. TEL 33-4-91632832. FAX 33-4-91632832. *728*

SOCIETE ROYALE BELGE D'ENTOMOLOGIE. BULLETIN ET ANNALES.
Societe Royal Belge d'Entomologie, 29, Rue Vautier, 1000 Brussels, Belgium. TEL 32-2-6274296. FAX 32-2-6274132. *761*

SOCIETE THEOPHILE GAUTIER. BULLETIN.
University Paul Valery, B.P. 5043, 34032 Montpellier Cedex 1, France. TEL 33-67-56-52-25. FAX 33-67-14-20-52. *4468*

SOCIETE VAUDOISE DES SCIENCES NATURELLES. BULLETIN.
Societe Vaudoise des Sciences Naturelles, Palais de Rumine, CH-1005 Lausanne, Switzerland. TEL 41-21-312-4334. *6574*

SOCIETE ZOOLOGIQUE DE FRANCE. BULLETIN.
Societe Zoologique de France, 195 rue Saint-Jacques, 75005 Paris, France. TEL 33-1-40793110. *849*

SOCIETE ZOOLOGIQUE DE FRANCE. MEMOIRES.
Societe Zoologique de France, 195 rue Saint Jacques, 75005 Paris, France. TEL 33-1-40793110. *850*

SOCIETY.
Transaction Publishers, Transaction Periodicals Consortium, Department 3092, Rutgers University, New Brunswick, NJ 08903. TEL 908-445-2280. FAX 908-445-3138. *6639*

SOCIETY & ANIMALS.
White Horse Press, 10 High St., Knapwell, Cambridge CB3 8NR, England. TEL 44-1954-267527. FAX 44-1954-267527. *304*

SOCIETY AND CULTURE IN EAST-CENTRAL EUROPE.
University of California Press, 2120 Berkeley Way, Berkeley, CA 94720. TEL 510-643-7127. FAX 510-643-7127. *3601*

SOCIETY AND NATURAL RESOURCES.
Taylor & Francis Ltd., 1 Gunpowder Sq., London EC4A 3DE, England. TEL 44-171-583-0490. FAX 44-171-583-0585. *2952*

SOCIETY FOR APPLIED BACTERIOLOGY. SYMPOSIUM SERIES.
Academic Press, Inc., 525 B St., Ste. 1900, San Diego, CA 92101-4495. TEL 619-231-0926. FAX 619-699-6719. *794*

SOCIETY FOR APPLIED BACTERIOLOGY. TECHNICAL SERIES.
Academic Press, Inc., 525 B St., Ste. 1900, San Diego, CA 92101-4495. TEL 619-231-0926. FAX 619-699-6715. *794*

SOCIETY FOR COMPUTER SIMULATION. TRANSACTIONS.
Society for Computer Simulation, Box 17900, San Diego, CA 92177. TEL 619-277-3888. FAX 619-277-3930. *2153*

SOCIETY FOR EXISTENTIAL ANALYSIS. JOURNAL.
Society for Existential Analysis, BM Existential, London WC1N 3XX, England. TEL 44-171-538-0050. FAX 44-171-538-0050. *6154*

SOCIETY FOR EXPERIMENTAL BIOLOGY AND MEDICINE. PROCEEDINGS.
Blackwell Science Inc., 350 Main St., Malden, MA 02148. TEL 617-876-7000. FAX 617-388-8255. *627*

SOCIETY FOR GYNECOLOGIC INVESTIGATION. JOURNAL.
Elsevier Science Inc., Box 945, New York, NY 10159-0945. TEL 212-633-3730. FAX 212-633-3680. *4968*

SOCIETY FOR IN VITRO BIOLOGY. MONOGRAPH SERIES.
Society for In Vitro Biology, 9315 Largo Dr. W., Ste. 255, Largo, MD 20774. TEL 301-324-5054. FAX 301-324-5057. *794*

SOCIETY FOR IN VITRO BIOLOGY. PROCEEDINGS.
Society for In Vitro Biology, 9315 Largo Dr. W., Ste. 255, Largo, MD 20774. TEL 301-324-5054. FAX 301-324-5057. *794*

SOCIETY FOR INFORMATION DISPLAY. SYMPOSIUM DIGEST.
Society for Information Display, 1526 Brookhollow Dr., Ste. 82, Santa Ana, CA 92705-5421. TEL 714-545-1526. FAX 714-545-1547. *2741*

SOCIETY FOR PIRANDELLO STUDIES. YEARBOOK.
Society for Pirandello Studies, School of Languages, University of Kent, Canterbury CT2 7NF, England. FAX 44-1227-475476. *4468*

SOCIETY FOR RESEARCH IN CHILD DEVELOPMENT. MONOGRAPHS.
University of Chicago Press, Journals Division, 7520 S. Woodlawn Ave., Chicago, IL 60637. TEL 773-702-7600. FAX 773-702-0172. *1857*

SOCIETY FOR SPANISH AND PORTUGUESE HISTORICAL STUDIES. BULLETIN.
Society for Spanish and Portuguese Historical Studies, c/o William D. Phillips, Jr., Gen. Sec., History Department, University of Minnesota, Minneapolis, MN 55455. TEL 612-624-2800. FAX 612-624-7096. *3601*

SOCIETY FOR THE SCIENTIFIC STUDY OF RELIGION. MONOGRAPH SERIES.
Society for the Scientific Study of Religion, 1365 Stone Hall, Sociology Dept., Purdue Univ., West Lafayette, IN 47907-1365. TEL 317-494-6286. *6372*

SOCIETY FOR THE STUDY OF ARCHITECTURE IN CANADA. BULLETIN.
Society for the Study of Architecture in Canada, Box 2302, Sta. D, Ottawa, ON K1P 5W5, Canada. *415*

SOCIETY FOR THE STUDY OF HUMAN BIOLOGY. SYMPOSIUM SERIES.
Cambridge University Press, Edinburgh Bldg., Shaftesbury Rd., Cambridge CB2 2RU, England. TEL 44-1223-312393. FAX 44-1223-315052. *822*

SOCIETY OF ARCHIVISTS. JOURNAL.
Carfax Publishing Co., P.O. Box 25, Abingdon, Oxon. OX14 3UE, England. TEL 44-1235-401000. FAX 44-1235-401550. *4214*

SOCIETY OF ARCHIVISTS. NEWSLETTER.
Society of Archivists, Information House, 20-24 Old St., London EC1V 9AP, England. TEL 44-171-253-5087. FAX 44-171-253-3942. *4214*

SOCIETY OF DEPRECIATION PROFESSIONALS. JOURNAL.
Society of Depreciation Professionals, 5505 Connecticut Ave. N.W., No. 280, Washington, DC 20015-2601. TEL 202-362-0680. FAX 202-866-2283. *1099*

SOCIETY OF EXPLORATION GEOPHYSICISTS. SPECIAL PUBLICATIONS (SYMPOSIA) SERIES.
Society of Exploration Geophysicists, Box 702740, Tulsa, OK 74170-2740. TEL 918-493-3516. *2389*

SOCIETY OF LEATHER TECHNOLOGISTS AND CHEMISTS. JOURNAL.
Society of Leather Technologists and Chemists, 1 Edges Court, Moulton, Northampton NN3 7UJ, England. TEL 01604-647318. FAX 01604-35932. *4147*

SOCIETY OF PEDIATRIC NURSES. JOURNAL.
Nursecom, Inc., 1211 Locust St., Philadelphia, PA 19107. TEL 215-545-7222. FAX 215-545-8107. *4949*

SOCIETY OF THE PLASTICS INDUSTRY. POLYURETHANE DIVISION. CONFERENCE PROCEEDINGS.
Technomic Publishing Co., Inc., 851 New Holland Ave., Box 3535, Lancaster, PA 17604. TEL 717-291-5609. FAX 717-295-4538. *5885*

SOCIO-ECONOMIC PLANNING SCIENCES.
Elsevier Science Ltd., Pergamon, P.O. Box 800, Kidlington, Oxford OX5 1DX, England. TEL 44-1865-843000. FAX 44-1865-843010. *6194*

SOCIOBIOLOGY.
California State University, Chico, Department of Biological Sciences, Chico, CA 95926. TEL 916-898-5116. FAX 916-898-4363. *627*

SOCIOLOGIA RURALIS.
Blackwell Publishers Ltd., 108 Cowley Rd., Oxford OX4 1JF, England. TEL 44-1865-791100. FAX 44-1865-791347. *6730*

SOCIOLOGICA.
Universidad Autonoma Metropolitana - Azcapotzalco, Departamento de Sociologia, Av. San Pablo 180, Edif., Piso 3, Azcapotzalco, 02200 Mexico, D.F., Mexico. TEL 52-5-7244339. FAX 52-5-3948093. *6730*

SOCIOLOGICAL FORUM.
Plenum Publishing Corp., 233 Spring St., New York, NY 10013-1578. TEL 212-620-8000. FAX 212-463-0742. *6730*

SOCIOLOGICAL IMAGINATION.
Wisconsin Sociological Association, University of Wisconsin at Whitewater, Department of Sociology, Whitewater, WI 53190. TEL 414-472-1133. FAX 414-472-5238. *6731*

SOCIOLOGICAL PAPERS.
Sociological Institute for Community Studies, Bar-Ilan University, Ramat Gan 52900, Israel. TEL 972-3-5344449. FAX 972-3-6350422. *6731*

SOCIOLOGICAL QUARTERLY.
University of California Press, Journals Division, 2120 Berkeley Way, No. 5812, Berkely, CA 94720-5812. TEL 510-643-7154. FAX 510-642-9917. *6731*

SOCIOLOGICAL RESEARCH.
M.E. Sharpe, Inc., 80 Business Park Dr., Armonk, NY 10504. TEL 914-273-1800. FAX 914-273-2106. *6731*

SOCIOLOGICAL RESEARCH ONLINE.
Sage Publications Ltd., 6 Bonhill St., London EC2A 4PU, England. TEL 44-171-374-0645. FAX 44-171-374-8741. *6731*

SOCIOLOGICAL REVIEW.
Blackwell Publishers Ltd., 108 Cowley Rd., Oxford OX4 1JF, England. TEL 44-1865-791100. FAX 44-1865-791347. *6732*

SOCIOLOGICAL SPECTRUM.
Taylor & Francis Inc., 1900 Frost Rd., Ste. 101, Bristol, PA 19007-1598. TEL 215-785-5800. FAX 215-785-5515. *6732*

SOCIOLOGICAL VIEWPOINTS.
Pennsylvania Sociological Society, c/o University of Scranton, Scranton, PA 18510-4605. TEL 717-941-7425. FAX 717-941-6369. *6732*

SOCIOLOGY OF HEALTH AND ILLNESS.
Blackwell Publishers Ltd., 108 Cowley Rd., Oxford OX4 1JF, England. TEL 44-1865-791100. FAX 44-1865-791347. *6733*

SOCIOLOGY OF SPORT JOURNAL.
Human Kinetics Publishers, Inc., Box 5076, Champaign, IL 61825-5076. TEL 217-351-5076. FAX 217-351-2674. *6733*

SOCIOLOGY OF THE SCIENCES. YEARBOOK.
Kluwer Academic Publishers, Postbus 17, 3300 AA Dordrecht, Netherlands. TEL 31-78-6392392. FAX 31-78-6392254. *6574*

SOCIOLOGY OF THE SCIENCES MONOGRAPHS.
Kluwer Academic Publishers, Postbus 17, 3300 AA Dordrecht, Netherlands. TEL 31-78-6392392. FAX 31-78-6392254. *6733*

SOFIISKI UNIVERSITET. GEOLOGO-GEOGRAFSKI FAKULTET. GEOLOGIIA. GODISHNIK.
Izdatelstvo Sv. Kliment Ohridski, 125 Tsarigradsko Shosse Blvd., Bl.4, 1113 Sofia, Bulgaria. FAX 359-2-703216. *2369*

SOFTWARE - CONCEPTS & TOOLS.
Springer-Verlag, Heidelberger Platz 3, 14197 Berlin, Germany. TEL 49-30-82787-0. FAX 49-30-82787448. *2146*

SOFTWARE DEVELOPMENT MONITOR.
Elsevier Science Ltd., P.O. Box 800, Kidlington, Oxford OX5 1DX, England. TEL 44-1865-843000. FAX 44-1865-843010. *2218*

SOFTWARE FUTURES.
A P T Data Group plc., 12 Sutton Row, 4th Fl., London W1V 5FH, England. TEL 44-171-528-7083. FAX 44-171-439-1105. *2218*

SOFTWARE: PRACTICE & EXPERIENCE.
John Wiley & Sons Ltd., Journals, Baffins Ln., Chichester, W. Sussex PO19 1UD, England. TEL 44-1243-779777. FAX 44-1243-775878. *2218*

SOFTWARE PROCESS IMPROVEMENT AND PRACTICE.
John Wiley & Sons Ltd., Journals, Baffins Ln., Chichester, W. Sussex PO19 1UD, England. TEL 44-1243-779777. FAX 44-1243-775878. *2219*

SOFTWARE QUALITY JOURNAL.
Thomson Science, 2-6 Boundary Row, London SE1 8HN, England. TEL 44-171-8650066. FAX 44-171-5229623. *2219*

SOIL & ENVIRONMENT.
Kluwer Academic Publishers, Postbus 17, 3300 AA Dordrecht, Netherlands. TEL 31-78-6392392. FAX 31-78-6392254. *2952*

SOIL AND TILLAGE RESEARCH.
Elsevier Science B.V., P.O. Box 211, 1000 AE Amsterdam, Netherlands. TEL 31-20-4853911. FAX 31-20-4853598. *153*

SOIL BIOLOGY & BIOCHEMISTRY.
Elsevier Science Ltd., Pergamon, P.O. Box 800, Kidlington, Oxford OX5 1DX, England. TEL 44-1865-843000. FAX 44-1865-843010. *628*

SOIL DYNAMICS AND EARTHQUAKE ENGINEERING.
Elsevier Science Ltd., P.O. Box 800, Kidlington, Oxford OX5 1DX, England. TEL 44-1865-843000. FAX 44-1865-843010. *2389*

SOIL MECHANICS AND FOUNDATION ENGINEERING.
Plenum Publishing Corp., Consultants Bureau, 233 Spring St., New York, NY 10013-1578. TEL 212-620-8468. FAX 212-463-0742. *2797*

SOIL SCIENCE.
Williams & Wilkins, 351 W. Camden St., Baltimore, MD 21201-2436. TEL 410-528-4068. FAX 410-528-4452. *244*

SOIL SCIENCE SOCIETY OF AMERICA. JOURNAL.
Soil Science Society of America, 677 S. Segoe Rd., Madison, WI 53711. TEL 608-273-8080. FAX 608-273-2021. *245*

SOIL TECHNOLOGY.
Elsevier Science B.V., P.O. Box 211, 1000 AE Amsterdam, Netherlands. TEL 31-20-4853911. FAX 31-20-4853598. *245*

SOIL USE AND MANAGEMENT.
CAB International, Wallingford, Oxon. OX10 8DE, England. TEL 01491-832111. FAX 44-1491-826090. *245*

SOLANUS.
University of London, School of Slavonic and East European Studies, The British Library, Great Russell St., London WC1B 3DG, England. TEL 44-171-412-7587. FAX 44-171-412-7554. *4215*

SOLAR ENERGY.
Elsevier Science Ltd., Pergamon, P.O. Box 800, Kidlington, Oxford OX5 1DX, England. TEL 44-1865-843000. FAX 44-1865-843010. *2706*

SOLAR ENERGY MATERIALS AND SOLAR CELLS.
Elsevier Science B.V., P.O. Box 211, 1000 AE Amsterdam, Netherlands. TEL 31-20-4853911. FAX 31-20-4853598. *2706*

SOLAR PHYSICS.
Kluwer Academic Publishers, Postbus 17, 3300 AA Dordrecht, Netherlands. TEL 31-78-6392392. FAX 31-78-6392254. *501*

SOLAR SYSTEM RESEARCH.
Maik Nauka - Interperiodica, Mezhdunarodnyi Otdel, Ul. Profsoyuznaya, 90, 117864 Moscow, Russia. TEL 7-095-3360066. FAX 7-095-3360666. *501*

SOLICITOR'S JOURNAL.
Canadian Bar Association, New Brunswick Branch, 1133 Regent St., Ste. 206, Fredericton, NB E3B 3Z2, Canada. TEL 506-458-8536. FAX 506-451-1421. *4025*

SOLID EARTH SCIENCES LIBRARY.
Kluwer Academic Publishers, Postbus 17, 3300 AA Dordrecht, Netherlands. TEL 31-78-6392392. FAX 31-78-6392254. *2322*

SOLID FUEL CHEMISTRY.
Allerton Press, Inc., 150 Fifth Ave., New York, NY 10011. TEL 212-924-3950. FAX 212-463-9684. *2774*

SOLID MECHANICS AND ITS APPLICATIONS.
Kluwer Academic Publishers, Postbus 17, 3300 AA Dordrecht, Netherlands. TEL 31-78-6392392. FAX 31-78-6392254. *5849*

SOLID STATE COMMUNICATIONS.
Elsevier Science Ltd., Pergamon, P.O. Box 800, Kidlington, Oxford OX5 1DX, England. TEL 44-1865-843000. FAX 44-1865-843010. *5827*

SOLID-STATE ELECTRONICS.
Elsevier Science Ltd., Pergamon, P.O. Box 800, Kidlington, Oxford OX5 1DX, England. TEL 44-1865-843000. FAX 44-1865-843010. *2652*

SOLID STATE IONICS.
North-Holland, P.O. Box 211, 1000 AE Amsterdam, Netherlands. TEL 31-20-4853911. FAX 31-20-4853598. *5827*

SOLID STATE NUCLEAR MAGNETIC RESONANCE.
Elsevier Science B.V., P.O. Box 211, 1000 AE Amsterdam, Netherlands. TEL 31-20-4853911. FAX 31-20-4853598. *1796*

SOLID STATE PHYSICS: ADVANCES IN RESEARCH AND APPLICATIONS.
Academic Press, Inc., 525 B St., Ste. 1900, San Diego, CA 92101-4495. TEL 619-231-0926. FAX 619-699-6715. *5827*

SOLID-STATE SCIENCE AND TECHNOLOGY LIBRARY.
Kluwer Academic Publishers, Postbus 17, 3300 AA Dordrecht, Netherlands. TEL 31-78-6392392. FAX 31-78-6392254. *2652*

SOLID STATE TECHNOLOGY.
PennWell Publishing Co. (Nashua), 10 Tara Blvd., 5th Fl., Nashua, NH 03062-2801. TEL 603-891-0123. FAX 609-891-0597. *2652*

SOLOS E ROCHAS.
Associacao Brasileira de Mecanica dos Solos, I P T, Predio Geotecnica, Cidade Universitaria, Caixa Postal 7141, 01064-970 Sao Paulo, Brazil. TEL 55-11-2687325. FAX 55-11-2687325. *2741*

SOLSTICE: AN ELECTRONIC JOURNAL OF GEOGRAPHY AND MATHEMATICS.
Institute of Mathematical Geography, 2790 Briarcliff, Ann Arbor, MI 48105-1429. TEL 313-761-1231. *4607*

SOLUBILITY DATA SERIES.
Oxford University Press, Oxford Journals, Walton St., Oxford OX2 6DB, England. TEL 44-1865-56767. FAX 44-1865-267985. *1767*

SOLUCIONES AVANZADAS.
Xview, S.A. de C.V., Tuxpan 2, Desp. 603, Col. Roma Sur, 06760 Mexico DF, Mexico. TEL 574-5316. FAX 574-5318. *1203*

SOLVENT EXTRACTION AND ION EXCHANGE.
Marcel Dekker Journals, 270 Madison Ave., New York, NY 10016. TEL 212-696-9000. FAX 212-685-4540. *1796*

SOLVENT EXTRACTION RESEARCH AND DEVELOPMENT, JAPAN.
Japan Association of Solvent Extraction, Dept. of Chemical Science & Technology, Kyushy University, Fukuoka 812-81, Japan. TEL 81-952-288671. FAX 81-952-288591. *1823*

SOMATIC CELL AND MOLECULAR GENETICS.
Plenum Publishing Corp., 233 Spring St., New York, NY 10013-1578. TEL 212-620-8000. FAX 212-463-0742. *776*

SOMATOSENSORY AND MOTOR RESEARCH.
Carfax Publishing Co., P.O. Box 25, Abingdon, Oxon OX14 3UE. TEL 44-1235-401000. FAX 44-1235-401550. *822*

SOMMERFELTIA.
University of Oslo, Botanical Garden and Museum, Trondheimsveien 23B, N-0562 Oslo, Norway. TEL 47-22-85-16-29. FAX 47-22-85-18-35. *728*

SON OF SPAMM! MAGAZINE.
Mass Media, Inc., Box 230699, Portland, OR 97281-0699. *5436*

SONIC ARTS NETWORK JOURNAL.
Sonic Arts Network, London House, 271-273 King St., London W6 9LZ, England. TEL 44-181-741-7422. FAX 44-181-741-7433. *5436*

SONOMA COUNTY PHYSICIAN.
Sonoma County Medical Association, 3033 Cleveland Ave., Santa Rosa, CA 95403. TEL 707-525-4325. FAX 707-525-4289. *4746*

SONOMA MANDALA.
Sonoma State University, English Department, Rohnert Park, CA 94928. TEL 717-664-3902. FAX 707-664-2505. *4469*

SONS OF NORWAY VIKING.
Sons of Norway, 1455 W. Lake St., Minneapolis, MN 55408. TEL 612-827-3611. FAX 612-827-0658. *3043*

SOPHIA.
Society for Philosophy of Religion and Philosophical Theology, Dept. of Philosophy, P.O. Box 4230, Melbourne University, Vic. 3052, Australia. TEL 61-3-93444778. FAX 61-3-93444280. *5751*

SOPHIA.
De La Salle University, Philosophy Department, 2401 Taft Ave., Manila 1004, Philippines. TEL 524-46-11. *5751*

SOSHIKI BAIYO KENKYU.
Nihon Soshiki Baiyo Gakkai, Research Institute for Functional Peptides, 4-3-32 Shimojo-machi, Yamagata-shi, Yamagata-ken 990, Japan. TEL 81-236-46-2525. FAX 81-236-46-2526. *744*

SOURCE (SEATTLE).
Church Council of Greater Seattle, 4759 15 Ave., N.E., 3rd Fl., Seattle, WA 98105-4404. TEL 206-525-1213. FAX 206-525-1218. *6372*

SOURCE: NOTES IN THE HISTORY OF ART.
Ars Brevis Foundation, Inc., 1 E. 87th St., Ste. 8A, New York, NY 10128. TEL 212-369-1667. FAX 212-360-6494. *466*

SOUTH AFRICA. SEA FISHERIES RESEARCH INSTITUTE. INVESTIGATIONAL REPORT.
Sea Fisheries Research Institute, Private Bag X2, Rogge Bay 8012, Cape Town, South Africa. TEL 27-21-4023911. FAX 27-21-252920. *3078*

SOUTH AFRICAN ASSOCIATION FOR MARINE BIOLOGICAL RESEARCH. BULLETIN.
South African Association for Marine Biological Research, P.O. Box 10712, Marine Parade 4056, South Africa. TEL 27-31-373536. FAX 27-31-372132. *628*

SOUTH AFRICAN BANKER.
Institute of Bankers in South Africa, P.O. Box 61420, Marshalltown 2107, South Africa. TEL 27-11-8321371. *1167*

SOUTH AFRICAN COMPUTER JOURNAL.
Computer Society of South Africa, P.O. Box 1714, Halfway House 1685, South Africa. TEL 27-12-420-2504. FAX 27-12-436454. *2090*

SOUTH AFRICAN FAMILY PRACTICE.
South African Academy of Family Practice - Primary Care, P.O. Box 2731, Rivonia 2128, South Africa. TEL 27-11-8076605. FAX 27-11-8076611. *4746*

SOUTH AFRICAN GEOGRAPHICAL JOURNAL.
South African Society of Geographers, c/o Dept. of Environmental & Geographical Science, University of Cape Town, Rondebosch 7700, South Africa. TEL 27-21-6502877. FAX 27-21-6503791. *3422*

SOUTH AFRICAN HISTORICAL JOURNAL.
South African Historical Society, c/o University of South Africa, Department of History, P.O. Box 392, Pretoria 0001, South Africa. TEL 27-12-4296272. FAX 27-12-4293221. *3529*

SOUTH AFRICAN INSTITUTE OF MINING AND METALLURGY. JOURNAL.
South African Institute of Mining and Metallurgy, P.O. Box 61217, Marshalltown 2107, South Africa. TEL 27-11-8341273. FAX 27-11-8385923. *5210*

SOUTH AFRICAN JOURNAL OF AFRICAN LANGUAGES.
Foundation for Education, Science & Technology, P.O. Box 1758, Pretoria 0001, South Africa. TEL 27-12-3226404. FAX 27-12-3207803. *4300*

SOUTH AFRICAN JOURNAL OF ANIMAL SCIENCE.
Foundation for Education, Science & Technology, P.O. Box 1758, Pretoria 0001, South Africa. TEL 27-12-3226404. FAX 27-12-3207803. *289*

SOUTH AFRICAN JOURNAL OF BOTANY.
Foundation for Education, Science & Technology, P.O. Box 1758, Pretoria 0001, South Africa. TEL 27-12-3226404. FAX 27-12-3207803. *728*

SOUTH AFRICAN JOURNAL OF BUSINESS MANAGEMENT.
Foundation for Education, Science & Technology, P.O. Box 1758, Pretoria 0001, South Africa. TEL 27-12-3226404. FAX 27-12-3207803. *1507*

SOUTH AFRICAN JOURNAL OF CHEMISTRY.
Foundation for Education, Science & Technology, P.O. Box 1758, Pretoria 0001, South Africa. TEL 27-12-3226404. FAX 27-12-3207803. *1767*

SOUTH AFRICAN JOURNAL OF COMMUNICATION DISORDERS.
South African Speech - Language - Hearing Association, P.O. Box 600, Wits 2050, South Africa. TEL 27-11-4031892. FAX 27-11-4036689. *5026*

SOUTH AFRICAN JOURNAL OF ECONOMIC HISTORY.
Economic History Society of Southern Africa, University of South Africa, Economics Department, P.O. Box 392, Pretoria 0001. TEL 27-12-4294502. FAX 27-12-4293433. *1311*

SOUTH AFRICAN JOURNAL OF ETHNOLOGY.
Foundation for Education, Science & Technology, P.O. Box 1758, Pretoria 0001, South Africa. TEL 27-12-3226404. FAX 27-12-3207803. *330*

SOUTH AFRICAN JOURNAL OF GEOLOGY.
Foundation for Education, Science & Technology, P.O. Box 1758, Pretoria 0001, South Africa. TEL 27-12-3226404. FAX 27-12-3207803. *2370*

SOUTH AFRICAN JOURNAL OF LABOUR RELATIONS.
University of South Africa, Graduate School of Business Leadership, P.O. Box 392, Pretoria 0001, South Africa. TEL 27-11-6520343. FAX 27-11-6520299. *1453*

SOUTH AFRICAN JOURNAL OF LIBRARY AND INFORMATION SCIENCE.
Foundation for Education, Science & Technology, P.O. Box 1758, Pretoria 0001, South Africa. TEL 27-12-3226404. FAX 27-12-3207803. *4215*

SOUTH AFRICAN JOURNAL OF LINGUISTICS.
Foundation for Education, Science & Technology, P.O. Box 1758, Pretoria 0001, South Africa. TEL 27-12-3226404. FAX 27-12-3207803. *4300*

SOUTH AFRICAN JOURNAL OF MARINE SCIENCE.
Sea Fisheries Research Institute, Private Bag X2, Rogge Bay 8012, Cape Town, South Africa. TEL 27-21-4023911. FAX 27-21-252920. *3079*

SOUTH AFRICAN JOURNAL OF MUSIC THERAPY.
Music Therapy Society of Southern Africa, 2 Shaw Rd., Rondebosch, 7700 Cape Town, South Africa. TEL 27-21-7623523. FAX 27-21-7977575. *5437*

SOUTH AFRICAN JOURNAL OF MUSICOLOGY.
Musicological Society of Southern Africa, University of Natal, Department of Music, Private Bag X10, Dalbridge 4014, South Africa. TEL 27-31-2603053. FAX 27-31-2601048. *5437*

SOUTH AFRICAN JOURNAL OF PHILOSOPHY.
Foundation for Education, Science & Technology, P.O. Box 1758, Pretoria 0001, South Africa. TEL 27-12-3226404. FAX 27-12-3207803. *5752*

SOUTH AFRICAN JOURNAL OF PLANT AND SOIL.
Foundation for Education, Science & Technology, P.O. Box 1758, Pretoria 0001, South Africa. TEL 27-12-3226404. FAX 27-12-3207803. *245*

SOUTH AFRICAN JOURNAL OF PSYCHOLOGY.
Foundation for Education, Science & Technology, P.O. Box 1758, Pretoria 0001, South Africa. TEL 27-12-3226404. FAX 27-12-3207803. *6154*

SOUTH AFRICAN JOURNAL OF SCIENCE.
Foundation for Research Development, P.O. Box 2600, Pretoria 0001, South Africa. TEL 27-12-8414076. FAX 27-12-8042679. *6575*

SOUTH AFRICAN JOURNAL OF ZOOLOGY.
Foundation for Education, Science & Technology, P.O. Box 1758, Pretoria 0001, South Africa. TEL 27-12-3226404. FAX 27-12-3207803. *850*

SOUTH AFRICAN LABOUR BULLETIN.
Umanyano Publications c.c., P.O. Box 3851, Johannesburg 2000, South Africa. TEL 27-11-4871603. FAX 27-11-4871508. *1453*

SOUTH AFRICAN MUSEUM. ANNALS.
South African Museum, P.O. Box 61, Cape Town 8000, South Africa. TEL 27-21-243330. FAX 27-21-246716. *628*

SOUTH AFRICAN MUSIC TEACHER.
South African Society of Music Teachers, P.O. Box 20032, Noordbrug 2522, South Africa. TEL 27-148-299-1699. FAX 27-148-2991707. *5437*

SOUTH AFRICAN PHILATELIST.
Philatelic Federation of Southern Africa, P.O. Box 2789, Cape Town 8000, South Africa. FAX 27-21-238763. *5713*

SOUTH AFRICAN SOCIETY OF PATHOLOGISTS. CONGRESS BROCHURE.
South Africa Society of Pathologists, P.O. Box 2034, Pretoria 0001, South Africa. TEL 27-12-3283600. *5172*

SOUTH AFRICAN VETERINARY ASSOCIATION. SCIENTIFIC JOURNAL.
South African Veterinary Association, P.O. Box 25033, Monument Park, 0105 Pretoria, South Africa. TEL 27-12-3461150. FAX 27-12-3462929. *7279*

SOUTH ASIA: JOURNAL OF SOUTH ASIAN STUDIES.
South Asian Studies Association, c/o Department of History, University of New England, Armidale, N.S.W. 2351, Australia. TEL 61-67-732479. FAX 61-67-733520. *3539*

SOUTH ASIAN ANTHROPOLOGIST.
Sarat Chandra Roy Institute of Anthropological Studies, House No. H 1-98, Harmu Housing Colony, Harmu, Ranchi 834 012, Bihar, India. TEL 91-651-307824. *330*

SOUTH ASIAN REVIEW.
South Asian Literary Association, c/o Univ. of North Florida, Jacksonville, FL 32224. TEL 904-646-2580. *4469*

SOUTH ASIAN SOCIAL SCIENTIST.
South Asian Social Scientists Association, Department of Anthropology, University of Madras, Tamil Nadu, Madras 600 005, India. TEL 568778. *5537*

SOUTH ASIAN SURVEY.
Sage Publications India Pvt. Ltd., P.O. Box 4215, New Delhi 110 048, India. TEL 91-11-644-4958. FAX 91-11-647-2426. *3539*

SOUTH CAROLINA HISTORICAL ASSOCIATION. PROCEEDINGS.
South Carolina Historical Association, USCA History Department, 171 University Pkwy., Aiken, SC 29801. TEL 803-641-3223. *3647*

SOUTH CAROLINA MEDICAL ASSOCIATION. JOURNAL.
South Carolina Medical Association, Box 11188, Columbia, SC 29211. TEL 803-798-6207. FAX 803-772-6783. *4747*

SOUTH CENTRAL REVIEW.
South Central Modern Language Association, Department of English, Texas A & M University, College Station, TX 77843-4227. TEL 409-845-7041. FAX 409-862-2292. *4469*

SOUTH DAKOTA HISTORY.
South Dakota State Historical Society, 900 Governors Dr., Pierre, SD 57501-2217. TEL 605-773-3458. FAX 605-773-6041. *3648*

SOUTH DAKOTA JOURNAL OF MEDICINE.
South Dakota State Medical Association, 1323 S. Minnesota Ave., Sioux Falls, SD 57105. TEL 605-336-1965. FAX 605-336-0270. *4747*

SOUTH DAKOTA MUNICIPALITIES.
South Dakota Municipal League, 214 E. Capitol, Pierre, SD 57501. TEL 605-224-8654. FAX 605-224-8655. *6224*

SOUTH EUROPEAN SOCIETY & POLITICS.
Frank Cass, Newbury House, 890-900 Eastern Ave., Newbury Park, Ilford, Essex IG2 7HH, England. TEL 44-181-899-8866. FAX 44-181-599-0984. *6639*

SOUTH INDIA CHURCHMAN.
Church of South India, c/o Christian Literature Society, Box 501, Park Town, Madras 600003, India. TEL 044-852-1566. *6497*

SOUTHEAST ASIA PAPERS.
University of Hawaii at Manoa, Center for Southeast Asian Studies, c/o Program Coordinator, 1890 East-West Rd., Moore Hall 416, Honolulu, HI 96822. TEL 808-956-2688. FAX 808-956-2682. *5537*

SOUTH EAST ASIA RESEARCH.
Coleridge House, 4-5 Coleridge Gardens, London NW6 3QH, England. TEL 44-171-372-2600. FAX 44-171-372-2253. *5971*

SOUTHEASTERN ARCHAEOLOGY.
Southeastern Archaeological Conference, c/o Southeastern Archaeological Survey, Box 1249, Fayetteville, AR 72702-1249. *383*

SOUTHEASTERN ASSOCIATION OF FISH AND WILDLIFE AGENCIES. PROCEEDINGS.
Southeastern Association of Fish and Wildlife Agencies, c/o Robert M. Brantly, Exec. Sec., 7221 Covey Trace, Tallahassee, FL 32308. TEL 904-893-1204. FAX 904-893-1204. *3079*

SOUTHEASTERN GEOGRAPHER.
Association of American Geographers, Southeastern Division, University of Georgia, Department of Geography, Athens, GA 30602. TEL 706-542-2350. FAX 706-542-2388. *3422*

SOUTHEASTERN GEOLOGY.
Duke University, Box 90233, Durham, NC 27708-0233. TEL 919-684-5321. FAX 919-684-5833. *2371*

SOUTHEASTERN JOURNAL OF MUSIC EDUCATION.
University of Georgia School of Music, c/o Mary Leglar, Ed., 250 River Rd., Athens, GA 30602. TEL 706-542-2763. FAX 706-542-2773. *5437*

SOUTHEASTERN POLITICAL REVIEW.
Georgia Southern University, Department of Political Science, Box 8101, Statesboro, GA 30460-8101. TEL 912-681-5698. FAX 912-764-6466. *5971*

SOUTHERN AFRICA JOURNAL OF MATHEMATICS AND SCIENCE.
University of Botswana, Department of Mathematics and Science Education, Private Bag 0022, Gaborone, Botswana. TEL 267-351151. FAX 267-256591. *4607*

SOUTHERN AFRICAN FIELD ARCHAEOLOGY.
Albany Museum, Somerset St., Grahamstown 6140, South Africa. TEL 27-461-22312. FAX 27-461-22398. *384*

SOUTHERN AFRICAN FORESTRY JOURNAL.
Southern African Institute of Forestry, P.O. Box 1022, Pretoria 0001, South Africa. TEL 27-12-473479. FAX 27-12-473479. *3162*

SOUTHERN AFRICAN JOURNAL OF AQUATIC SCIENCES.
Southern African Society of Aquatic Scientists, c/o F.C. de Moor, Albany Museum, Somerset St., Grahamstown 6140. TEL 27-461-22318. FAX 27-461-22398. *628*

SOUTHERN AFRICAN JOURNAL OF EPIDEMIOLOGY AND INFECTION.
P.O. Box 1038, Johannesburg 2000, South Africa. TEL 27-11-4899021. FAX 27-11-4899022. *4881*

SOUTHERN BUSINESS & ECONOMIC JOURNAL.
Auburn University at Montgomery, School of Business, 7300 University Dr., Montgomery, AL 36117-3596. TEL 334-244-3523. FAX 334-244-3792. *1002*

SOUTHERN CALIFORNIA ACADEMY OF SCIENCES. BULLETIN.
Southern California Academy of Sciences, 1041 New Hampshire Ave., Box 1897, Lawrence, KS 66044-8897. FAX 913-843-1274. *6575*

SOUTHERN CALIFORNIA ANTHOLOGY.
University of Southern California, Master of Professional Writing Program, WPH 404, Los Angeles, CA 90089-4034. TEL 213-740-3252. *4469*

SOUTHERN CALIFORNIA QUARTERLY.
Historical Society of Southern California, 200 East Ave., No. 43, Los Angeles, CA 90031-1399. TEL 213-222-0546. *3648*

SOUTHERN ECONOMIC JOURNAL.
University of North Carolina at Chapel Hill, Southern Economic Association, 300 Hanes Hall, CB 3540, Chapel Hill, NC 27514. TEL 919-966-5261. FAX 919-932-5469. *1002*

SOUTHERN FOLKLORE.
University Press of Kentucky, 663 S. Limestone St., Lexington, KY 40508-4008. TEL 606-257-8439. FAX 606-257-2984. *3092*

SOUTHERN HISTORY.
Southern History Society, c/o R.A.E. Wells, Ed., Department of History, Christ Church College, Canterbury CT1 1QU, England. TEL 44-1227-767700. FAX 01273-643128. *3602*

SOUTHERN HUMANITIES REVIEW.
Auburn University, 9088 Haley Center, Auburn, AL 36849. TEL 334-844-9088. FAX 334-844-9027. *3792*

SOUTHERN ILLINOIS UNIVERSITY LAW JOURNAL.
Southern Illinois University at Carbondale, School of Law, Lesar Law Bldg., Carbondale, IL 62901. TEL 618-453-8721. FAX 618-453-8769. *4026*

SOUTHERN JOURNAL OF APPLIED FORESTRY.
Society of American Foresters, 5400 Grosvenor Ln., Bethesda, MD 20814. TEL 301-897-8720. FAX 301-897-3690. *3163*

SOUTHERN JOURNAL OF OPTOMETRY.
Southern Council of Optometrists, 4661 N. Shallowford Rd., Atlanta, GA 30338. TEL 770-451-8206. FAX 770-451-3156. *5001*

SOUTHERN LITERARY JOURNAL.
University of North Carolina Press, Box 2288, Chapel Hill, NC 27515-2288. TEL 919-966-3561. FAX 800-272-6817. *4469*

SOUTHERN MEDICAL JOURNAL.
Southern Medical Association, 35 Lakeshore Dr., Box 190088, Birmingham, AL 35219-0088. TEL 205-945-1840. FAX 205-945-1548. *4747*

SOUTHERN ORTHOPAEDIC ASSOCIATION. JOURNAL.
Southern Orthopaedic Association, 35 Lake Shore Dr., Box 190088, Birmingham, AL 35219-0088. FAX 205-945-1548. *5016*

SOUTHERN POETRY REVIEW.
Central Piedmont Community College, Charlotte, NC 28235. *4524*

SOUTHERN SOCIAL STUDIES JOURNAL.
Kentucky Council for the Social Studies, Morehead State University, U.P.O 738, Morehead, KY 40351. TEL 606-783-2765. FAX 606-783-2678. *6639*

SOUTHERN STARS.
Royal Astronomical Society of New Zealand (Inc.), P.O. Box 3181, Wellington, New Zealand. TEL 64-4-5276398. FAX 64-4-5276374. *501*

SOUTHERN STUDIES.
Northwestern State University of Louisiana, Southern Studies Institute, Natchitoches, LA 71497. TEL 318-357-5507. FAX 318-357-6153. *6640*

SOUTHWEST JOURNAL OF LINGUISTICS.
University of North Texas and Linguistics Association of the Southwest, University of North Texas, Department of English, Denton, TX 76203-3827. TEL 505-277-7416. FAX 505-277-6355. *4300*

SOUTHWEST JOURNAL OF PURE AND APPLIED MATHEMATICS.
Cameron University, *4607*

SOUTHWEST JOURNAL ON AGING.
Southwest Society on Aging, Oklahoma State University, CHES Rm. 125, Stillwater, OK 74078-6116. TEL 405-744-8280. FAX 405-744-6843. *3446*

SOUTHWEST PHILOSOPHY REVIEW. JOURNAL.
Southwestern Philosophical Society, Department of Philosophy, Wittenberg Univ., Box 720, Springfield, OH 45501-0720. *5752*

SOUTHWESTERN ENTOMOLOGIST.
Southwestern Entomological Society, 17360 Coit Rd., Dallas, TX 75252. TEL 972-952-9222. *761*

SOUTHWESTERN ENTOMOLOGIST. SUPPLEMENT.
Southwestern Entomological Society, 17360 Coit Rd., Dallas, TX 75252. TEL 972-952-9222. *761*

SOUTHWESTERN MASS COMMUNICATION JOURNAL.
Southwest Education Council for Journalism and Mass Communication, P.O. Box 1930, Arkansas State University, State University, AR 72467. *3880*

SOUTHWESTERN NATURALIST.
Southwestern Association of Naturalists, c/o Dr. Paula Williamson, Treas., Biology Department, Southwest Texas State University, 601 University Dr., San Marcos, TX 78666. TEL 512-245-2178. FAX 512-245-8095. *6575*

SOUTHWESTERN STUDIES. MONOGRAPHS.
Texas Western Press, University of Texas at El Paso, El Paso, TX 79968-0633. TEL 915-747-5688. FAX 915-747-7515. *3648*

SOVIET AND POST SOVIET REVIEW.
Charles Schlacks Jr., Publisher, c/o University of California, CMTS, GFS 344, Los Angeles, CA 90089-1694. FAX 213-740-5810. *3602*

SOVIET SCIENTIFIC REVIEWS. SECTION F: PHYSIOLOGY AND GENERAL BIOLOGY REVIEWS.
Gordon and Breach - Harwood Academic, Amsteldisk 166, 1st Fl., 1079 LH Amsterdam, Netherlands. *822*

SOVIET SCIENTIFIC REVIEWS SUPPLEMENT SERIES. SECTION C: PHYSICOCHEMICAL BIOLOGY.
Gordon and Breach - Harwood Academic, Amsteldisk 166, 1st Fl., 1079 LH Amsterdam, Netherlands. *671*

SOVIET STUDIES.
Gordon and Breach - Harwood Academic, Amsteldisk 166, 1st Fl., 1079 LH Amsterdam, Netherlands. *6734*

SOVIETICA. PUBLICATIONS AND MONOGRAPHS.
Kluwer Academic Publishers, Postbus 17, 3300 AA Dordrecht, Netherlands. TEL 31-78-6392392. FAX 31-78-6392254. *3602*

SOW'S EAR POETRY REVIEW.
19535 Pleasant View Dr., Abingdon, VA 24211-6827. TEL 540-628-2651. *4524*

SPACE FORUM.
Gordon and Breach - Harwood Academic, Amsteldisk 166, 1st Fl., 1079 LH Amsterdam, Netherlands. *79*

SPACE POLICY.
Elsevier Science Ltd., P.O. Box 800, Kidlington, Oxford OX5 1DX, England. TEL 44-1865-843000. FAX 44-1865-843010. *79*

SPACE SCIENCE REVIEWS.
Kluwer Academic Publishers, Postbus 17, 3300 AA Dordrecht, Netherlands. TEL 31-78-6392392. FAX 31-78-6392254. *501*

SPACE TECHNOLOGY.
Elsevier Science Ltd., Pergamon, P.O. Box 800, Kidlington, Oxford OX5 1DX, England. TEL 44-1865-843000. FAX 44-1865-843010. *6974*

SPACE TECHNOLOGY LIBRARY.
Kluwer Academic Publishers, Postbus 17, 3300 AA Dordrecht, Netherlands. TEL 31-78-6392392. FAX 31-78-6392254. *80*

REFEREED SERIALS

SPAN.
South Pacific Association for Commonwealth Literature and Language Studies, University of Waikato, Dept. of English, Private Bag 3105, Hamilton, New Zealand. *4470*

SPANISH YEARBOOK OF INTERNATIONAL LAW.
Martinus Nijhoff Publishers, Human Rights and International Law Postbus 163, 3300 AD Dordrecht, Netherlands. TEL 31-78-334911. FAX 31-78-334254. *4126*

SPATIAL VISION.
V S P, P.O. Box 346, 3700 AH Zeist, Netherlands. TEL 31-30-6925790. FAX 31-30-6932081. *4624*

SPECIAL ASPECTS OF EDUCATION.
Gordon and Breach - Harwood Academic, Amsteldisk 166, 1st Fl., 1079 LH Amsterdam, Netherlands. *2484*

SPECIAL CARE IN DENTISTRY.
Federation of Special Care Organizations in Dentistry, 211 East Chicago Ave., Chicago, IL 60611. TEL 312-440-2661. *4871*

SPECIAL SERVICES IN THE SCHOOLS.
Haworth Press, Inc., 10 Alice St., Binghamton, NY 13904. TEL 607-722-5857. FAX 607-722-6362. *2591*

SPECIAL TOPICS IN SUPERCOMPUTING.
Elsevier Science B.V., Books Division, P.O. Box 211, 1000 AE Amsterdam, Netherlands. TEL 31-20-4853911. FAX 31-20-4853705. *2159*

SPECIALIST.
Doctor Publications (Pvt) Ltd., P.O. Box 8766, Raja Ghazanfar Ali Rd., Saddar, Karachi, Pakistan. TEL 92-21-5688791. FAX 92-21-5689860. *4747*

LO SPECIALISTA.
Ansid - Edit s.r.l., Viale Monte Ceneri 58, 20155 Milan, Italy. TEL 39-2-33003971. FAX 39-2-39215800. *7116*

SPECIFIER REPORTS.
Rensselaer Polytechnic Institute, Lighting Research Center, Troy, NY 12180-3590. TEL 518-276-8716. FAX 518-276-2999. *913*

SPECTROCHIMICA ACTA. PART A: MOLECULAR AND BIOMOLECULAR SPECTROSCOPY.
Elsevier Science B.V., P.O. Box 211, 1000 AE Amsterdam, Netherlands. TEL 31-20-4853911. FAX 31-20-4853598. *1796*

SPECTROCHIMICA ACTA. PART B: ATOMIC SPECTROSCOPY.
Elsevier Science B.V., P.O. Box 211, 1000 AE Amsterdam, Netherlands. TEL 31-20-4853911. FAX 31-20-4853598. *1796*

SPECTROSCOPY.
I O S Press, Van Diemenstraat 94, 1013 CN Amsterdam, Netherlands. TEL 31-20-6382189. FAX 31-20-6203419. *671*

SPECTROSCOPY LETTERS.
Marcel Dekker Journals, 270 Madison Ave., New York, NY 10016. TEL 212-696-9000. FAX 212-685-4540. *5870*

SPECTRUM (GREENBELT).
National Association of Black Accountants, 7249A Hanover Pkwy, Greenbelt, MD 20770-3653. TEL 301-474-6222. *1099*

SPECULATIONS IN SCIENCE AND TECHNOLOGY.
Chapman & Hall, Journals Department 2-6 Boundary Row, London SE1 8HN, England. TEL 44-171-8560066. FAX 44-171-5229623. *6576*

SPEECH AND DRAMA.
Society of Teachers of Speech and Drama, 4 Fane Rd., Oxford OX3 OSA, England. TEL 44-1865-728304. *7013*

SPEECH COMMUNICATION.
North-Holland, P.O. Box 211, 1000 AE Amsterdam, Netherlands. TEL 31-20-4853911. FAX 31-20-4853598. *4300*

SPEEDHORSE - RACING REPORT.
Speedhorse, Inc., Box 1000, Norman, OK 73070-1000. TEL 405-573-1050. FAX 405-573-1059. *6856*

SPEKTRUM DER AUGENHEILKUNDE.
Springer-Verlag, Sachsenplatz 4-6, P.O. Box 89, A-1201 Vienna, Austria. TEL 43-1-3302415. FAX 43-1-3302415. *5002*

SPILL SCIENCE & TECHNOLOGY BULLETIN.
Elsevier Science Ltd., Pergamon, P.O. Box 800, Kidlington, Oxford OX5 1DX, England. TEL 44-1865-843000. FAX 44-1865-843010. *2972*

SPILL TECHNOLOGY NEWSLETTER.
Environment Canada, Technology Development and Technical Services Branch, Ottawa, ON K1A 0H3, Canada. TEL 613-990-7297. FAX 613-991-9485. *6576*

SPINAL CORD INJURY LIFE.
National Spinal Cord Injury Association, 8300 Colesville Rd., Silver Spring, MD 20910-3243. *3467*

SPINE (PHILADELPHIA, 1986).
Hanley & Belfus, Inc., 210 S. 13th St., Philadelphia, PA 19107. TEL 215-546-7293. FAX 215-790-9330. *5016*

SPIRAGLI.
Centro Internazionale di Cultura "Lilybaeum", Contrada S. Giuseppe Tafalia 74-B, 91025 Marsala, Italy. TEL 0923-989772. *4360*

SPOON RIVER POETRY REVIEW.
Illinois State University, Unit for Contemporary Literature, Normal, IL 61790-4241. TEL 309-438-7906. *4524*

SPORT HISTORY REVIEW.
Human Kinetics Publishers, Inc., Box 5076, Champaign, IL 61825-5076. *6784*

SPORT MARKETING QUARTERLY.
Fitness Information Technology Inc., Box 4425, University Ave., Morgantown, WV 26504-4425. TEL 304-599-3482. FAX 304-599-3482. *6784*

THE SPORT PSYCHOLOGIST.
Human Kinetics Publishers, Inc., Box 5076, Champaign, IL 61825-5076. TEL 217-351-5076. FAX 217-351-2674. *6154*

SPORT SCIENCE REVIEW.
Human Kinetics Publishers, Inc., Box 5076, Champaign, IL 61825-5076. TEL 217-351-5076. FAX 217-351-3674. *5132*

SPORTPARACHUTIST.
Koninklijke Nederlandse Vereniging voor Luchtvaart, Afdeling Parachutespringen, Jozef Israelsplein 8, 2596 AS The Hague, Netherlands. TEL 31-70-3245457. FAX 31-70-3240230. *6884*

SPORTS AFIELD.
Hearst Corporation, Sports Afield, 250 W. 55th St., New York, NY 10019. TEL 212-649-4000. FAX 212-581-3923. *6884*

THE SPORTS HISTORIAN.
British Society of Sports History, c/o Benny J. Peiser, Ed., Dept. of Human Sciences, Liverpool John Moores Univ., Byrom St., Liverpool L3 3AF, England. TEL 44-151-231-2490. *6787*

SPORTS MEDICINE.
Adis International Limited, Private Bag 65901, Mairangi Bay, Auckland 10, New Zealand. TEL 64-9-479-8100. FAX 64-9-479-8145. *5132*

SPORTS MEDICINE AND ARTHROSCOPY REVIEW.
Lippincott - Raven Publishers, 227 E. Washington Sq., Philadelphia, PA 19106. TEL 215-238-4200. FAX 215-238-4227. *5016*

SPORTS MEDICINE IN PRIMARY CARE.
Phys Ed Fitness Ltd., Box 717, Decatur, GA 30031-0717. TEL 404-377-0300. FAX 404-377-0604. *5133*

SPORTS MEDICINE, TRAINING AND REHABILITATION.
Gordon and Breach - Harwood Academic, Amsteldisk 166, 1st Fl., 1079 LH Amsterdam, Netherlands. *5133*

SPORTS TURF RESEARCH INSTITUTE. JOURNAL.
Sports Turf Research Institute, St. Ives Estate, Bingley, W. Yorkshire BD16 1AU, England. TEL 44-1274-565131. FAX 44-1274-561891. *6787*

SPRAAK OCH STIL.
Adolf Noreen-saellskapet foer Svensk Spraak- och Stilforskning, PO Box 513, S-751 20 Uppsala, Sweden. TEL 46-18-18-12-82. FAX 46-18-18-12-72. *4300*

SPRING JOURNAL.
Box 583, Putnam, CT 06260. TEL 203-974-3428. FAX 203-974-3195. *6155*

SPRINGFIELD PARENT.
Box 4732, Springfield, MO 65808. TEL 417-869-9800. FAX 417-831-5478. *1857*

SPRINGS.
Spring Manufacturers Institute, Inc., 2001 Midwest Rd., Ste. 106, Oak Brook, IL 60521-1335. TEL 630-495-8588. FAX 630-495-8595. *2900*

SPUR.
World Development Movement, 25 Beehive Pl., London SW9 7QR, England. TEL 44-171-737-6215. FAX 44-171-274-8232. *1368*

SRI VENKATESWARA UNIVERSITY. ORIENTAL JOURNAL.
Sri Venkateswara University, Oriental Research Institute, Tirupati 517502, District Chittoor, India. TEL 91-8574-24166. FAX 91-8574-24111. *3539*

SRPSKO BRATSTVO.
1 Secroft Cres., North York, ON M3N 1R5, Canada. TEL 416-769-7181. FAX 416-850-4401. *3044*

STADLER GENETICS SYMPOSIUM. PROCEEDINGS.
Plenum Publishing Corp., 233 Spring St., New York, NY 10013-1578. TEL 212-620-8000. FAX 212-463-0742. *776*

STAFFORDSHIRE ARCHAEOLOGICAL AND HISTORICAL SOCIETY. TRANSACTIONS.
Staffordshire Archaeological and Historical Society, William Salt Library, Eastgate St., Stafford ST16 2LZ, England. *384*

STANDARDS ACTIVITIES OF ORGANIZATIONS IN THE U.S.
U.S. National Institute of Standards and Technology, Gaithersburg, MD 20899. TEL 301-975-3058. *5255*

STANDBY.
Chameleon b.v., Van Breestraat 60, 1071 ZR Amsterdam, Netherlands. TEL 31-20-5740070. FAX 31-20-5740079. *4871*

STANFORD NURSE.
Stanford Health Services, Division of Patient Care Services, Center for Education and Professional Development, 300 Pasteur Dr., Ste. NOB, Stanford, CA 94305. *4949*

STANISLAUS CONNECTIONS.
Modesto Peace - Life Center - Stanislaus Safe Energy Committee, Box 134, Modesto, CA 95353. TEL 209-529-5750. *5972*

STARBURST.
Creative Arts and Science Enterprises, 341 Miller St., Abilene, TX 79605. TEL 915-670-9921. FAX 915-670-0989. *4470*

STARK RAVING SANITY.
1835 Cedar River Dr., Jacksonville, FL 32210-1301. *4471*

STATE FOREST OF NEW SOUTH WALES. FOREST RESEARCH AND DEVELOPMENT DIVISION. RESEARCH PAPERS.
State Forest of New South Wales, Forest Research and Development Division, 121-131 Oratava Ave., W. Pennant Hills, N.S.W. 2125, Australia. TEL 61-2-98720111. FAX 61-2-98716941. *3163*

STATE FORESTS OF NEW SOUTH WALES. FOREST RESEARCH AND DEVELOPMENT DIVISION. FOREST RESOURCES SERIES.
State Forests of New South Wales, Forest Research and Development Division, 121-131 Oratava Ave., W. Pennant Hills, N.S.W. 2125, Australia. TEL 61-2-98720111. FAX 61-2-98716941. *3163*

STATE FORESTS OF NEW SOUTH WALES. FOREST RESEARCH AND DEVELOPMENT DIVISION. TECHNICAL PAPERS.
State Forests of New South Wales, Forest Research and Development Division, 121-131 Oratava Ave., W. Pennant Hills, N.S.W. 2125, Australia. TEL 61-2-98720111. FAX 61-2-98716941. *3163*

STATEMENT (FORT COLLINS).
Colorado Language Arts Society, Colorado State University, English Dept., Eddy Bldg., Fort Collins, CO 80523. TEL 970-491-5264. FAX 970-491-5601. *2619*

STATISTICA NEERLANDICA.
Blackwell Publishers Ltd., 108 Cowley Rd., Oxford OX4 1JF, England. TEL 44-1865-791100. FAX 44-1865-791347. *6942*

STATISTICAL AND SOCIAL INQUIRY SOCIETY OF IRELAND. JOURNAL.
Statistical and Social Inquiry Society of Ireland, c/o Central Statistics Office, Ardee Rd., Rathmines, Dublin 6, Ireland. TEL 353-1-4977144. FAX 353-1-4972360. *6942*

STATISTICAL SCIENCE.
Institute of Mathematical Statistics, 3401 Investment Blvd., Ste. 7, Hayward, CA 94545-3819. TEL 510-783-8141. FAX 510-783-4131. *6943*

THE STATISTICIAN.
Blackwell Publishers Ltd., 108 Cowley Rd., Oxford OX4 1DF, England. TEL 44-1865-791100. FAX 44-1865-791347. *6944*

STATISTICS.
Gordon and Breach - Harwood Academic, Amsteldisk 166, 1st Fl., 1079 LH Amsterdam, Netherlands. *6944*

STATISTICS AND COMPUTING.
Thomson Science, 2-6 Boundary Row, London SE1 8HN, England. TEL 44-171-8650066. FAX 44-171-5229623. *6944*

STATISTICS & PROBABILITY LETTERS.
North-Holland, P.O. Box 211, 1000 AE Amsterdam, Netherlands. TEL 31-20-4853911. FAX 31-20-4853598. *6944*

STATISTICS IN MEDICINE.
John Wiley & Sons Ltd., Journals, Baffins Ln., Chichester, W. Sussex PO19 1UD, England. TEL 44-1243-779777. FAX 44-1243-775878. *4789*

STATUTES AND DECISIONS: THE LAWS OF THE U S S R & ITS SUCCESSOR STATES.
M.E. Sharpe, Inc., 80 Business Park Dr., Armonk, NY 10504. TEL 914-273-1800. FAX 914-273-2106. *4029*

STEAMBOAT BILL.
Steamship Historical Society of America, Inc., 300 Ray Dr., Ste. 4, Providence, RI 02906. *7167*

STEEL INDIA.
Steel Authority of India Ltd., R & D Centre for Iron & Steel, Ranchi 834 002, India. FAX 91-651-300023. *5211*

STEINE SPRECHEN.
Oesterreichische Gesellschaft fuer Denkmal und Ortsbildpflege, Karlsplatz 5, A-1010 Vienna, Austria. TEL 43-1-587-96630. FAX 43-1-5232374. *2245*

STEM CELLS.
AlphaMed Press, Inc., One Prestige Pl., Ste. 290, Miamisburg, OH 45342-3758. TEL 937-291-2355. FAX 937-291-4229. *628*

STEPHEN CRANE STUDIES.
Virginia Polytechnic Institute and State University, Department of English, Blacksburg, VA 24061-0112. TEL 540-231-5932. FAX 540-231-5692. *4524*

STEREO DRIVE.
T W F Publicity, Bolestein 592, 1081 EK Amsterdam, Netherlands. TEL 31-20-6461727. FAX 31-20-6463726. *6746*

STEREOCHEMISTRY OF ORGANOMETALLIC AND INORGANIC COMPOUNDS.
Elsevier Science B.V., Books Division, P.O. Box 211, 1000 AE Amsterdam, Netherlands. TEL 31-20-4853911. FAX 31-20-4853705. *1796*

STEREOTACTIC AND FUNCTIONAL NEUROSURGERY.
S. Karger AG, Allschwilerstr. 10, P.O. Box, CH-4009 Basel, Switzerland. TEL 41-61-3061111. FAX 41-61-3061234. *5154*

STEROIDS.
Elsevier Science Inc., Box 945, New York, NY 10159-0945. TEL 212-633-3730. FAX 212-633-3680. *822*

STEVENS INDICATOR.
Stevens Alumni Association, Castle Point, Hoboken, NJ 07030. TEL 201-216-5161. FAX 201-216-5374. *1972*

STIMME DER WAHRHEIT.
Gemeinde Gottes e.V., Schurwaldstr. 10, 73660 Urbach, Germany. TEL 49-7181-81433. *6443*

STOCHASTIC ANALYSIS AND APPLICATIONS.
Marcel Dekker Journals, 270 Madison Ave., New York, NY 10016. TEL 212-696-9000. FAX 212-685-4540. *4607*

STOCHASTIC PROCESSES AND THEIR APPLICATIONS.
North-Holland, P.O. Box 211, 1000 AE Amsterdam, Netherlands. TEL 31-20-4853911. FAX 31-20-4853598. *4608*

STOCHASTICS AND STOCHASTICS REPORTS.
Gordon and Breach - Harwood Academic, Amsteldisk 166, 1st Fl., 1079 LH Amsterdam, Netherlands. *4608*

STOCHASTICS MONOGRAPHS.
Gordon and Breach - Harwood Academic, Amsteldisk 166, 1st Fl., 1079 LH Amsterdam, Netherlands. *4608*

STOCHASTIK IN DER SCHULE.
Verein zur Foerderung des Schulischen Statistikunterrichts e.V., Kammannstr. 13, 58097 Hagen, Germany. *6946*

STOCKHOLM STUDIES IN POLITICS.
University of Stockholm, Department of Political Science, S-106 91, Stockholm, Sweden. TEL 46-8-16-20-00. FAX 46-8-15-25-29. *5972*

STRABISMUS.
Aeolus Press, Postbus 740, 4116 ZJ Buren, Netherlands. TEL 31-344-572055. FAX 31-344-572562. *5002*

STRATEGIC AND DEFENCE STUDIES CENTRE. WORKING PAPERS.
Strategic and Defence Studies Centre, Australian National University, Canberra, A.C.T. 0200, Australia. TEL 61-6-2438537. FAX 61-6-2480816. *5286*

STRATEGIC CHANGE.
John Wiley & Sons Ltd., Journals, Baffins Ln., Chichester, W. Sussex PO19 1UD, England. TEL 44-1243-779777. FAX 44-1243-775878. *1508*

STRATEGIC MANAGEMENT JOURNAL.
John Wiley & Sons Ltd., Journals, Baffins Ln., Chichester, W. Sussex PO19 1UD, England. TEL 44-1243-779777. FAX 44-1243-775878. *1508*

STRENGTH OF MATERIALS.
Plenum Publishing Corp., Consultants Bureau, 233 Spring St., New York, NY 10013-1578. TEL 212-620-8468. FAX 212-463-0742. *2869*

STRESS AND EMOTION.
Taylor & Francis, 1900 Frost Rd., Ste. 101, Bristol, PA 19007-1598. TEL 215-785-5800. FAX 215-785-5515. *6155*

STRESS MEDICINE.
John Wiley & Sons Ltd., Journals, Baffins Ln., Chichester, W. Sussex PO19 1UD, England. TEL 44-1243-779777. FAX 44-1243-775878. *5099*

STRIAE.
Societas Upsaliensis, Institute of Earth Sciences, Quaternary Geology, Norbyvaegen 18 B, S-752 36 Uppsala, Sweden. TEL 46-18-18-25-00. FAX 46-18-18-25-91. *2371*

STRIJDKREET.
Salvation Army, Spoordreef 10, 1315 GN Almere, Netherlands. TEL 31-36-5398153. FAX 31-36-5398172. *6498*

STRIOLAE.
Societas Upsaliensis, Institute of Earth Sciences, Quaternary Geology, Norbyvaegen 18 B, S-752 36 Uppsala, Sweden. TEL 46-18-18-25-00. FAX 46-18-18-25-91. *2371*

STROKE.
American Heart Association, 7272 Greenville Ave., Dallas, TX 75231-4596. TEL 214-706-1310. FAX 214-691-6342. *4824*

STRUCTURAL CHANGE AND ECONOMIC DYNAMICS.
Elsevier Science B.V., P.O. Box 211, 1000 AE Amsterdam, Netherlands. TEL 31-20-4853911. FAX 31-20-4853598. *1311*

STRUCTURAL CHEMISTRY.
Plenum Publishing Corp., 233 Spring St., New York, NY 10013-1578. FAX 212-463-0742. *1768*

STRUCTURAL DESIGN OF TALL BUILDINGS.
John Wiley & Sons Ltd., Journals, Baffins Ln., Chichester, W. Sussex PO19 1UD, England. TEL 44-1243-779777. FAX 44-1243-775878. *2798*

STRUCTURAL ENGINEER.
Structural Engineers Trading Organisation Ltd., 11 Upper Belgrave St., London SW1X 8BH, England. TEL 44-171-235-4535. FAX 44-171-235-4294. *2798*

STRUCTURAL SAFETY.
Elsevier Science B.V., P.O. Box 211, 1000 AE Amsterdam, Netherlands. TEL 31-20-4853911. FAX 31-20-4853598. *2799*

STRUCTURE.
Current Biology Ltd., 400 Market St., Ste. 700, Philadelphia, PA 19106. FAX 215-574-2270. *628*

STRUCTURE REPORTS. SECTION A: METALS AND INORGANIC COMPOUNDS.
Kluwer Academic Publishers, Postbus 17, 3300 AA Dordrecht, Netherlands. TEL 31-78-6392392. FAX 31-78-6392254. *1803*

THE STUDEBAKER FAMILY.
Studebaker Family National Association, 6555 S. State Rt. 202, Tipp City, OH 45371-9444. TEL 937-667-4451. FAX 937-667-9322. *3242*

STUDI BRESCIANI.
Fondazione Luigi Micheletti, Via Cairoli 9, 25122 Brescia, Italy. TEL 39-30-48578. FAX 39-30-45203. *3604*

STUDI PIEMONTESI.
Centro Studi Piemontesi, Via Octavio Revel 15, 10121 Turin, Italy. TEL 39-11-537486. FAX 39-11-534777. *4472*

STUDIA AD CORPUS HELLENISTICUM NOVI TESTAMENTI.
E.J. Brill, P.O. Box 9000, 2300 PA Leiden, Netherlands. TEL 31-71-5353500. FAX 31-71-5317532. *6373*

STUDIA BIBLICA.
E.J. Brill, P.O. Box 9000, 2300 PA Leiden, Netherlands. TEL 31-71-5353500. FAX 31-71-5317532. *6373*

STUDIA CANONICA.
Saint Paul University, Faculty of Canon Law, 223 Main St., Ottawa, ON K1S 1C4, Canada. TEL 613-751-4024. FAX 613-751-4036. *6373*

STUDIA COPERNICANA - BRILL SERIES.
E.J. Brill, P.O. Box 9000, 2300 PA Leiden, Netherlands. TEL 31-71-5353500. FAX 31-71-5317532. *502*

STUDIA CROATICA.
Instituto Croata Latinoamericano de Cultura, Zapata 234-3E, 1426 Buenos Aires, Argentina. TEL 54-1-771-4954. *3044*

REFEREED SERIALS

STUDIA ET DOCUMENTA AD IURA ORIENTIS ANTIQUI PERTINENTIA.
E.J. Brill, P.O. Box 9000, 2300 PA Leiden, Netherlands. TEL 31-71-5353500. FAX 31-71-5317532. *5538*

STUDIA FORESTALIA SUECICA.
Swedish University of Agricultural Sciences, Research Information Centre, Box 7057, S-750 07 Uppsala, Sweden. TEL 46-18-67-11-17. FAX 46-18-67-35-20. *3163*

STUDIA GEOLOGICA POLONICA.
Polska Akademia Nauk, Instytut Nauk Geologicznych, Al. Zwirki i Wigury 93, 02-089 Warsaw, Poland. TEL 48-22-221065. FAX 48-22-221065. *2371*

STUDIA GEOPHYSICA ET GEODAETICA.
Plenum Publishing Corp., 233 Spring St., New York, NY 10013-1578. TEL 212-620-8000. FAX 212-463-0742. *2390*

STUDIA HISTORICA SEPTENTRIONALIA.
Pohjois-Suomen Historiallinen Yhdistys, Oulun Yliopisto, Historian Laitos, Postilokero 111, FIN-90571 Oulu, Finland. FAX 358-81-553-33-15. *3604*

STUDIA HUMANITATIS.
E.J. Brill, P.O. Box 9000, 2300 PA Leiden, Netherlands. TEL 31-71-5353500. FAX 31-71-5317532. *3604*

STUDIA IMAGOLOGICA.
Editions Rodopi B.V., Keizersgracht 302-304, 1016 EX Amsterdam, Netherlands. TEL 31-20-6227507. FAX 31-20-6380948. *4472*

STUDIA IN VETERIS TESTAMENTI PSEUDEPIGRAPHA.
E.J. Brill, P.O. Box 9000, 2300 PA Leiden, Netherlands. TEL 31-71-5353500. FAX 31-71-5317532. *6373*

STUDIA LINGUISTICA.
Blackwell Publishers Ltd., 108 Cowley Rd., Oxford OX4 1JF, England. TEL 44-1865-791100. FAX 44-1865-791347. *4302*

STUDIA LITURGICA.
Societas Liturgica, Box 597, Notre Dame, IN 46556. *6374*

STUDIA LOGICA.
Kluwer Academic Publishers, Postbus 17, 3300 AA Dordrecht, Netherlands. TEL 31-78-6392392. FAX 31-78-6392254. *5753*

STUDIA MATHEMATICA.
Polska Akademia Nauk, Instytut Matematyczny, Dzial Wydawnictw, Ul. Sniadeckich 8, P.O. Box 137, 00-950 Warsaw, Poland. TEL 48-22-6282471. FAX 48-22-6293997. *4608*

STUDIA MORALIA.
Editiones Academiae Alfonsianae, Via Merulana 31, C.P. 2458, 00100 Rome, Italy. TEL 39-6-49490322. FAX 39-6-4465887. *6374*

STUDIA MUSICOLOGICA NORVEGICA.
Scandinavian University Press, P.O. Box 2959 Toeyen, NO-0608 Oslo, Norway. *5439*

STUDIA NAD DAWNYM WOJSKIEM, BRONIA I BARWA.
Instytut w Tarnowskich Gorach, Ul. Ligonia 7, P.O. Box 112, 42-600 Tarnowskie Gory, Poland. TEL 48-32-1855030. *3605*

STUDIA ORIENTALIA LUNDENSIA.
Lund University Press, P.O. Box 141, S-221 00 Lund, Sweden. TEL 46-46-31-20-00. FAX 46-46-30-53-38. *5538*

STUDIA SEMIOTYCZNE.
Polskie Towarzystwo Semiotyczne, c/o Uniwersytet Warszawski, Wydzial Filozofii, Krakowskie Przedmiescie 3, 00-927 Warsaw, Poland. TEL 48-22-8265418. FAX 48-22-8265734. *4303*

STUDIA SILENSIA.
Abadia de Santo Domingo de Silos, Libreria de la Abadia, 09610 Burgos, Spain. TEL 34-47-390068. FAX 34-47-390033. *6374*

STUDIA Z FILOLOGII POLSKIEJ I SLOWIANSKIEJ.
Polska Akademia Nauk, Instytut Slawisyki, Al. Ujazdowskie 18, m.16, 00-478 Warsaw, Poland. TEL 48-22-6243729. FAX 48-22-6290075. *4303*

STUDIEN UND TEXTE ZUR GEISTESGESCHICHTE DES MITTELALTERS.
E.J. Brill, P.O. Box 9000, 2300 PA Leiden, Netherlands. TEL 31-71-5353500. FAX 31-71-5317532. *5753*

STUDIEN ZUR KINDERPSYCHOANALYSE. JAHRBUCH.
Oesterreichische Studiengesellschaft fuer Kinderpsychoanalyse, Robert-Bosch-Breite 6, 37079 Goettingen, Germany. TEL 49-551-6959-0. FAX 49-551-695917. *6155*

STUDIEN ZUR PROBLEMGESCHICHTE DER ANTIKEN UND MITTELALTERLICHEN PHILOSOPHIE.
E.J. Brill, P.O. Box 9000, 2300 PA Leiden, Netherlands. TEL 31-71-5353500. FAX 31-71-5317532. *5753*

STUDIES AND RESEARCHES IN VETERINARY MEDICINE.
Pasteur National Institute of Veterinary Medicine, 333 Giulesti Rd., 77826 Bucharest 6, Rumania. TEL 40-1-2206920. FAX 40-1-2206915. *7279*

STUDIES IN AMERICAN FICTION.
Northeastern University, Department of English, Boston, MA 02115. TEL 617-437-3687. *4472*

STUDIES IN AMERICAN HUMOR.
American Humor Studies Association (New Haven), c/o Joseph Alvarez, Sec., Box 35009, Central Piedmont Community College, Charlotte, NC 28235-5009. TEL 704-330-4097. FAX 704-330-5930. *4361*

STUDIES IN AMERICAN JEWISH LITERATURE.
Studies in American Jewish Literature, Inc., 117 Burrowes Bldg., University Park, PA 16802. TEL 814-863-3753. FAX 814-863-7285. *3044*

STUDIES IN ANALYTICAL CHEMISTRY.
Elsevier Science B.V., Books Division, P.O. Box 211, 1000 AE Amsterdam, Netherlands. TEL 31-20-4853911. FAX 31-20-4853705. *1797*

STUDIES IN ANCIENT MEDICINE.
E.J. Brill, P.O. Box 9000, 2300 PA Leiden, Netherlands. TEL 31-71-5353500. FAX 31-71-5317532. *4748*

STUDIES IN ANTHROPOLOGY AND HISTORY.
Gordon and Breach - Harwood Academic, Amsteldisk 166, 1st Fl., 1079 LH Amsterdam, Netherlands. *3514*

STUDIES IN APPLIED ELECTROMAGNETICS AND MECHANICS.
I O S Press, Van Diemenstraat 94, 1013 CN Amsterdam, Netherlands. TEL 31-20-6382189. FAX 31-20-6203419. *2846*

STUDIES IN APPLIED MATHEMATICS (CAMBRIDGE).
Blackwell Publishers, 238 Main St., Cambridge, MA 02142. TEL 617-547-7110. *4608*

STUDIES IN APPLIED MECHANICS.
Elsevier Science B.V., Books Division, P.O. Box 211, 1000 AE Amsterdam, Netherlands. TEL 31-20-4853911. FAX 31-20-4853705. *5849*

STUDIES IN ARABIC LITERATURE.
E.J. Brill, P.O. Box 9000, 2300 PA Leiden, Netherlands. TEL 31-71-5353500. FAX 31-71-5317532. *4473*

STUDIES IN ASIAN ART AND ARCHAEOLOGY.
E.J. Brill, P.O. Box 9000, 2300 PA Leiden, Netherlands. TEL 31-71-5353500. FAX 31-71-5317532. *5538*

STUDIES IN ASTRONAUTICS.
Elsevier Science B.V., Books Division, P.O. Box 211, 1000 AE Amsterdam, Netherlands. TEL 31-20-4853911. FAX 31-20-4853705. *80*

STUDIES IN AUSTRIAN ECONOMICS.
Kluwer Academic Publishers, Postbus 17, 3300 AA Dordrecht, Netherlands. TEL 31-78-6392392. FAX 31-78-6392254. *1312*

STUDIES IN AUTOMATION AND CONTROL.
Elsevier Science B.V., Books Division, P.O. Box 211, 1000 AE Amsterdam, Netherlands. TEL 31-20-4853911. FAX 31-20-4853705. *2112*

STUDIES IN AVIAN BIOLOGY.
Cooper Ornithological Society, Inc. (Riverside), Department of Biology, University of California at Riverside, Riverside, CA 92521. FAX 909-787-4286. *809*

STUDIES IN BAYESIAN ECONOMETRICS AND STATISTICS.
Elsevier Science B.V., Books Division, P.O. Box 211, 1000 AE Amsterdam, Netherlands. TEL 31-20-4853911. FAX 31-20-4853705. *1312*

STUDIES IN BILINGUALISM.
John Benjamins Publishing Co., Amsteldijk 44, P.O. Box 75577, 1070 AN Amsterdam, Netherlands. TEL 31-20-6738156. FAX 31-20-6792956. *4304*

STUDIES IN BUSINESS AND SOCIETY.
University of Chicago Press, 5801 S. Ellis Ave., Chicago, IL 60637. TEL 773-702-7899. *1004*

STUDIES IN CENTRAL AND EAST ASIAN RELIGIONS.
Seminar for Buddhist Studies, 11 Hallandsgade, I.TV, 2300 Copenhagen S., Denmark. TEL 45-35-32-25-96. FAX 45-35-32-25-95. *6390*

STUDIES IN CHRISTIAN MISSION.
E.J. Brill, P.O. Box 9000, 2300 PA Leiden, Netherlands. TEL 31-71-5353500. FAX 31-71-5317532. *6374*

STUDIES IN COMPARATIVE ECONOMIC POLICIES.
Elsevier Science B.V., Books Division, P.O. Box 211, 1000 AE Amsterdam, Netherlands. TEL 31-20-4853911. FAX 31-20-4853705. *1312*

STUDIES IN COMPARATIVE LITERATURE.
University of North Carolina Press, Box 2288, Chapel Hill, NC 27515-2288. TEL 919-966-3561. FAX 919-966-3829. *4473*

STUDIES IN COMPUTATIONAL MATHEMATICS.
Elsevier Science B.V., Books Division, P.O. Box 211, 1000 AE Amsterdam, Netherlands. TEL 31-20-4853911. FAX 31-20-4853705. *4608*

STUDIES IN COMPUTER AND COMMUNICATIONS SYSTEMS.
I O S Press, Van Diemenstraat 94, 1013 CN Amsterdam, Netherlands. TEL 31-20-6382189. FAX 31-20-6203419. *2018*

STUDIES IN COMPUTER SCIENCE AND ARTIFICIAL INTELLIGENCE.
Elsevier Science B.V., Books Division, P.O. Box 211, 1000 AE Amsterdam, Netherlands. TEL 31-20-4853911. FAX 31-20-4853705. *2104*

STUDIES IN CONFLICT AND TERRORISM.
Taylor & Francis Inc., 1900 Frost Rd., Ste. 101, Bristol, PA 19007. TEL 215-785-5800. FAX 215-785-5515. *6038*

STUDIES IN CONSERVATION.
International Institute for Conservation of Historic and Artistic Works, 6 Buckingham St., London WC2N 6BA, England. TEL 44-171-839-5975. FAX 44-171-976-1564. *467*

STUDIES IN CONTEMPORARY HISTORY.
Kluwer Academic Publishers, Postbus 17, 3300 AA Dordrecht, Netherlands. TEL 31-78-6392392. FAX 31-78-6392254. *3605*

STUDIES IN CYBERNETICS.
Gordon and Breach - Harwood Academic, Amsteldisk 166, 1st Fl., 1079 LH Amsterdam, Netherlands. *2164*

STUDIES IN DANCE HISTORY.
A Cappella Books, Inc., 106 W. Franklin Ave., 814 N. Franklin St., Chicago, IL 60610-3109. TEL 609-737-6525. FAX 609-737-3787. *2295*

STUDIES IN DEMOGRAPHY.
University of California Press, 2120 Berkeley Way, Berkeley, CA 94720. TEL 510-643-7127. FAX 510-643-7127. *6058*

STUDIES IN DEVELOPMENT AND PLANNING.
Kluwer Academic Publishers, Postbus 17, 3300 AA Dordrecht, Netherlands. TEL 31-78-6392392. FAX 31-78-6392254. *1368*

STUDIES IN DISCOURSE AND GRAMMAR.
John Benjamins Publishing Co., Amsteldijk 44, P.O. Box 75577, 1070 AN Amsterdam, Netherlands. TEL 31-20-6738156. FAX 31-20-6792956. *4304*

STUDIES IN EAST EUROPEAN THOUGHT.
Kluwer Academic Publishers, Postbus 17, 3300 AA Dordrecht, Netherlands. TEL 31-78-6392392. FAX 31-78-6392254. *5973*

STUDIES IN ECONOMIC ORGANIZATION.
Kluwer Academic Publishers, Postbus 17, 3300 AA Dordrecht, Netherlands. TEL 31-78-6392392. FAX 31-78-6392254. *1312*

STUDIES IN ECONOMICS AND FINANCE.
University of North Carolina at Charlotte, Economics Department, Charlotte, NC 28223-0001. TEL 704-547-4130. FAX 704-547-4130. *1312*

STUDIES IN EDUCATIONAL EVALUATION.
Elsevier Science Ltd., Pergamon, P.O. Box 800, Kidlington, Oxford OX5 1DX, England. TEL 44-1865-843000. FAX 44-1865-843010. *2485*

STUDIES IN ELECTRICAL AND ELECTRONIC ENGINEERING.
Elsevier Science B.V., Books Division, P.O. Box 211, 1000 AE Amsterdam, Netherlands. TEL 31-20-4853911. FAX 31-20-4853705. *2847*

STUDIES IN ENGLISH LITERATURE.
English Literary Society of Japan, 501 Kenkyusha Bldg., 9 Surugadai 2-chome, Kanda, Chiyoda-ku, Tokyo 101, Japan. TEL 03-3293-7528. FAX 03-3233-3398. *4473*

STUDIES IN ENVIRONMENTAL SCIENCE.
Elsevier Science B.V., Books Division, P.O. Box 211, 1000 AE Amsterdam, Netherlands. TEL 31-20-4853911. FAX 31-20-4853705. *2953*

STUDIES IN FERTILITY AND STERILITY.
Kluwer Academic Publishers, Postbus 17, 3300 AA Dordrecht, Netherlands. TEL 31-78-6392392. FAX 31-78-6392254. *628*

STUDIES IN GENDER AND CULTURE.
Gordon and Breach - Harwood Academic, Amsteldisk 166, 1st Fl., 1079 LH Amsterdam, Netherlands. *6734*

STUDIES IN GREEK AND ROMAN RELIGION.
E.J. Brill, P.O. Box 9000, 2300 PA Leiden, Netherlands. TEL 31-71-5353500. FAX 31-71-5317532. *6374*

STUDIES IN HIGH ENERGY PHYSICS SERIES.
Gordon and Breach - Harwood Academic, Amsteldisk 166, 1st Fl., 1079 LH Amsterdam, Netherlands. *5828*

STUDIES IN HIGHER EDUCATION.
Carfax Publishing Co., P.O. Box 25, Abingdon, Oxon. OX14 3UE, England. TEL 44-1235-401000. FAX 44-1235-401550. *2556*

STUDIES IN HISTORY (NEW DELHI).
Sage Publications India Pvt. Ltd., P.O. Box 4215, New Delhi 110 048, India. TEL 91-11-644-4958. FAX 91-11-647-2426. *3539*

STUDIES IN HISTORY AND PHILOSOPHY OF SCIENCE.
Elsevier Science Ltd., Pergamon, P.O. Box 800, Kidlington, Oxford OX5 1DX, England. TEL 44-1865-843000. FAX 44-1865-843010. *6577*

STUDIES IN HISTORY AND PHILOSOPHY OF SCIENCE PART B: STUDIES IN HISTORY AND PHILOSOPHY OF MODERN PHYSICS.
Elsevier Science Ltd., Pergamon, P.O. Box 800, Kidlington, Oxford OX5 1DX, England. TEL 44-1865-843000. FAX 44-1865-843010. *5828*

STUDIES IN HISTORY OF GARDENS & LANDSCAPE.
Taylor & Francis Ltd., 1 Gunpowder Sq., London EC4A 3DE, England. TEL 44-171-583-0490. FAX 44-171-583-0585. *3205*

STUDIES IN HISTORY OF MEDICINE AND SCIENCE.
Jamia Hamdard, Hamdard Nagar, New Delhi 110 062, India. TEL 91-11-698-4685. FAX 91-11-698-8874. *4748*

STUDIES IN HOGG AND HIS WORLD.
James Hogg Society, Department of English Studies, University of Stirling, Stirling FK9 4LA, Scotland. *4473*

STUDIES IN HUMAN SOCIETY.
E.J. Brill, P.O. Box 9000, 2300 PA Leiden, Netherlands. TEL 31-71-5353500. FAX 31-71-5317532. *6734*

STUDIES IN INDUSTRIAL ORGANIZATION.
Kluwer Academic Publishers, Postbus 17, 3300 AA Dordrecht, Netherlands. TEL 31-78-6392392. FAX 31-78-6392254. *1312*

STUDIES IN INFECTIOUS DISEASES RESEARCH.
University of Chicago Press, 5801 S. Ellis Ave., Chicago, IL 60637. TEL 773-702-7899. *4844*

STUDIES IN INFORMATICS AND CONTROL.
Research Institute for Informatics, 8-10 Averescu Ave., 71316 Bucharest 1, Rumania. TEL 40-1-2223778. FAX 40-1-3128539. *4234*

STUDIES IN INORGANIC CHEMISTRY.
Elsevier Science B.V., Books Division, P.O. Box 211, 1000 AE Amsterdam, Netherlands. TEL 31-20-4853911. FAX 31-20-4853705. *1809*

STUDIES IN INTERFACE SCIENCE.
Elsevier Science B.V., Books Division, P.O. Box 211, 1000 AE Amsterdam, Netherlands. TEL 31-20-4853911. FAX 31-20-4853705. *5828*

STUDIES IN INTERNATIONAL ECONOMICS.
Elsevier Science B.V., Books Division, P.O. Box 211, 1000 AE Amsterdam, Netherlands. TEL 31-20-4853911. FAX 31-20-4853705. *1004*

STUDIES IN INTERRELIGIOUS DIALOGUE.
Kok Pharos Publishing House, Postbus 5019, 8260 GA Kampen, Netherlands. TEL 31-38-3392565. FAX 31-38-3328912. *6374*

STUDIES IN ISLAMIC LAW & SOCIETY.
E.J. Brill, P.O. Box 9000, 2300 PA Leiden, Netherlands. TEL 31-71-5353500. FAX 31-71-5317532. *6401*

STUDIES IN JUDAISM IN LATE ANTIQUITY.
E.J. Brill, P.O. Box 9000, 2300 PA Leiden, Netherlands. TEL 31-71-5353500. FAX 31-71-5317532. *6409*

STUDIES IN JUDAISM IN MODERN TIMES.
E.J. Brill, P.O. Box 9000, 2300 PA Leiden, Netherlands. TEL 31-71-5353500. FAX 31-71-5317532. *6409*

STUDIES IN LANGUAGE.
John Benjamins Publishing Co., Amsteldijk 44, P.O. Box 75577, 1070 AN Amsterdam, Netherlands. TEL 31-20-6738156. FAX 31-20-6792956. *4304*

STUDIES IN LATIN AMERICAN POPULAR CULTURE.
c/o Charles M. Tatum, College of Humanities, Office of the Dean, Modern Languages Bldg. Rm. 345, University of Arizona, Tucson, AZ 85721. TEL 602-621-1044. FAX 602-621-5594. *6735*

STUDIES IN LEGAL HISTORY.
University of North Carolina Press, Box 2288, Chapel Hill, NC 27515-2288. TEL 919-966-3561. FAX 919-966-3829. *4030*

STUDIES IN LINGUISTICS AND PHILOSOPHY.
Kluwer Academic Publishers, Postbus 17, 3300 AA Dordrecht, Netherlands. TEL 31-78-6392392. FAX 31-78-6392254. *6155*

STUDIES IN LOCATIONAL ANALYSIS.
International Institute of Interdisciplinary Studies in Environmental Management, Locational Decisions & Regional Planning, c/o J. Karkazis, Smirnis 1, 15772 Zografou, Greece. TEL 30-1-6123-631. FAX 30-1-6123-631. *3760*

STUDIES IN LOGIC AND COMPUTATION.
Oxford University Press, Walton St., Oxford OX2 6DP, England. TEL 44-1865-56767. FAX 44-1865-56646. *4608*

STUDIES IN LOGIC AND THE FOUNDATIONS OF MATHEMATICS.
Elsevier Science B.V., Books Division, P.O. Box 211, 1000 AE Amsterdam, Netherlands. TEL 31-20-4853911. FAX 31-20-4853705. *4608*

STUDIES IN MANAGEMENT SCIENCE AND SYSTEMS.
Elsevier Science B.V., Books Division, P.O. Box 211, 1000 AE Amsterdam, Netherlands. TEL 31-20-4853911. FAX 31-20-4853705. *1508*

STUDIES IN MATHEMATICAL AND MANAGERIAL ECONOMICS.
Elsevier Science B.V., Books Division, P.O. Box 211, 1000 AE Amsterdam, Netherlands. TEL 31-20-4853911. FAX 31-20-4853705. *1508*

STUDIES IN MATHEMATICAL PHYSICS.
Elsevier Science B.V., Books Division, P.O. Box 211, 1000 AE Amsterdam, Netherlands. TEL 31-20-4853911. FAX 31-20-4853705. *5828*

STUDIES IN MATHEMATICS (WASHINGTON).
Mathematical Association of America, 1529 Eighteenth St., N.W., Washington, DC 20036. TEL 202-387-5200. *4608*

STUDIES IN MATHEMATICS AND ITS APPLICATIONS.
Elsevier Science B.V., Books Division, P.O. Box 211, 1000 AE Amsterdam, Netherlands. TEL 31-20-4853911. FAX 31-20-4853705. *4609*

STUDIES IN MECHANICAL ENGINEERING.
Elsevier Science B.V., Books Division, P.O. Box 211, 1000 AE Amsterdam, Netherlands. TEL 31-20-4853911. FAX 31-20-4853705. *2900*

STUDIES IN MEDIEVAL AND REFORMATION THOUGHT.
E.J. Brill, P.O. Box 9000, 2300 PA Leiden, Netherlands. TEL 31-71-5353500. FAX 31-71-5317532. *6374*

STUDIES IN MELANESIAN ANTHROPOLOGY.
University of California Press, 2120 Berkeley Way, Berkeley, CA 94720. TEL 510-642-4247. FAX 510-643-7127. *331*

STUDIES IN MODERN THERMODYNAMICS.
Elsevier Science B.V., Books Division, P.O. Box 211, 1000 AE Amsterdam, Netherlands. TEL 31-20-4853911. FAX 31-20-4853705. *1835*

STUDIES IN MONETARY ECONOMICS.
Elsevier Science B.V., Books Division, P.O. Box 211, 1000 AE Amsterdam, Netherlands. TEL 31-20-4853911. FAX 31-20-4853705. *1168*

STUDIES IN NATURAL LANGUAGE AND LINGUISTIC THEORY.
Kluwer Academic Publishers, Postbus 17, 3300 AA Dordrecht, Netherlands. TEL 31-78-6392392. FAX 31-78-6392254. *4304*

STUDIES IN NATURAL PRODUCTS CHEMISTRY.
Elsevier Science B.V., Books Division, P.O. Box 211, 1000 AE Amsterdam, Netherlands. TEL 31-20-4853911. FAX 31-20-4853705. *1768*

STUDIES IN NEW MUSIC RESEARCH.
Swets & Zeitlinger bv, P.O. Box 825, 2160 SZ Lisse, Netherlands. TEL 31-252-435111. FAX 31-252-415888. *2130*

STUDIES IN NONLINEAR DYNAMICS AND ECONOMETRICS.
M I T Press, 5 Cambridge Center, Cambridge, MA 02142-1399. TEL 617-253-2889. FAX 617-258-6779. *4609*

STUDIES IN OPERATIONAL REGIONAL SCIENCE.
Kluwer Academic Publishers, Postbus 17, 3300 AA Dordrecht, Netherlands. TEL 31-78-6392392. FAX 31-78-6392254. *1312*

STUDIES IN OPERATIONS RESEARCH.
Gordon and Breach - Harwood Academic, Amsteldisk 166, 1st Fl., 1079 LH Amsterdam, Netherlands. *2090*

STUDIES IN ORGANIC CHEMISTRY.
Elsevier Science B.V., Books Division, P.O. Box 211, 1000 AE Amsterdam, Netherlands. TEL 31-20-4853911. FAX 31-20-4853705. *1823*

STUDIES IN PHILOLOGY.
University of North Carolina Press, Box 2288, Chapel Hill, NC 27515-2288. TEL 919-966-3561. FAX 800-272-6817. *4305*

STUDIES IN PHILOSOPHY AND EDUCATION.
Kluwer Academic Publishers, Postbus 17, 3300 AA Dordrecht, Netherlands. TEL 31-78-6392392. FAX 31-78-6392254. *2486*

STUDIES IN PHILOSOPHY AND RELIGION.
Kluwer Academic Publishers, Postbus 17, 3300 AA Dordrecht, Netherlands. TEL 31-78-6392392. FAX 31-78-6392254. *5754*

STUDIES IN PHYSICAL AND THEORETICAL CHEMISTRY.
Elsevier Science B.V., Books Division, P.O. Box 211, 1000 AE Amsterdam, Netherlands. TEL 31-20-4853911. FAX 31-20-4853705. *1835*

STUDIES IN PHYSIOLOGY.
Portland Press Ltd., 59 Portland Pl., London W1N 3AJ, England. TEL 44-171-580-5530. FAX 44-171-323-1136. *822*

STUDIES IN PLANT SCIENCE.
Elsevier Science B.V., Books Division, P.O. Box 211, 1000 AE Amsterdam, Netherlands. TEL 31-20-4853911. FAX 31-20-4853705. *729*

STUDIES IN POLITICAL ECONOMY.
Association d'Ecnomie Politique, SR 303, Carleton University, 1125 Colonel By Dr., Ottawa, ON K1S 5B6, Canada. TEL 613-788-2600. *5973*

STUDIES IN POLYMER SCIENCE.
Elsevier Science B.V., Books Division, P.O. Box 211, 1000 AE Amsterdam, Netherlands. TEL 31-20-4853911. FAX 31-20-4853705. *1768*

STUDIES IN POPULAR CULTURE.
Popular Culture Association in the South, c/o Michael Dunne & Sara Lewis Dunne, Eds., Middle Tennessee State University, Department of English, Murfreesboro, TN 37132. *6735*

STUDIES IN PRE-COLUMBIAN ART AND ARCHAEOLOGY.
Dumbarton Oaks, Publications Office, 1703 32nd St., N.W., Washington, DC 20007. TEL 202-339-6431. *385*

STUDIES IN PRODUCTION AND ENGINEERING ECONOMICS.
Elsevier Science B.V., Books Division, P.O. Box 211, 1000 AE Amsterdam, Netherlands. TEL 31-20-4853911. FAX 31-20-4853705. *1004*

STUDIES IN PRODUCTIVITY ANALYSIS.
Kluwer Academic Publishers, Postbus 17, 3300 AA Dordrecht, Netherlands. TEL 31-78-6392392. FAX 31-78-6392254. *1508*

STUDIES IN PROOF THEORY.
Elsevier Science B.V., Books Division, P.O. Box 211, 1000 AE Amsterdam, Netherlands. TEL 31-20-4853911. FAX 31-20-4853705. *4609*

STUDIES IN PUBLIC CHOICE.
Kluwer Academic Publishers, Postbus 17, 3300 AA Dordrecht, Netherlands. TEL 31-78-6392392. FAX 31-78-6392254. *1312*

STUDIES IN REGIONAL AND URBAN PLANNING.
International Institute of Interdisciplinary Studies in Environmental Management, Locational Decisions & Regional Planning, c/o Prof. John Karkazis, Ed., Smirnis 1, 15772 Zografou, Greece. TEL 30-1-6123-631. FAX 30-1-6123-631. *3760*

STUDIES IN REGIONAL SCIENCE AND URBAN ECONOMICS.
Elsevier Science B.V., Books Division, P.O. Box 211, 1000 AE Amsterdam, Netherlands. TEL 31-20-4853911. FAX 31-20-4853705. *1290*

STUDIES IN RISK AND UNCERTAINTY.
Kluwer Academic Publishers, Postbus 17, 3300 AA Dordrecht, Netherlands. TEL 31-78-6392392. FAX 31-78-6392254. *1312*

STUDIES IN SCOTTISH LITERATURE.
G. Ross Roy, Ed.& Pub., c/o English Dept., University of South Carolina, Columbia, SC 29208. TEL 803-767-6601. FAX 803-777-9064. *4474*

STUDIES IN SECOND LANGUAGE ACQUISITION.
Cambridge University Press, Edinburgh Bldg., Shaftesbury Rd., Cambridge CB2 2RU, England. TEL 44-1223-312393. FAX 44-1223-315052. *4305*

STUDIES IN SEMITIC LANGUAGES AND LINGUISTICS.
E.J. Brill, P.O. Box 9000, 2300 PA Leiden, Netherlands. TEL 31-71-5353500. FAX 31-71-5317532. *4305*

STUDIES IN SOCIAL HISTORY.
Kluwer Academic Publishers, Postbus 17, 3300 AA Dordrecht, Netherlands. TEL 31-78-6392392. FAX 31-78-6392254. *6640*

STUDIES IN SOCIAL LIFE.
Kluwer Academic Publishers, Postbus 17, 3300 AA Dordrecht, Netherlands. TEL 31-78-6392392. FAX 31-78-6392254. *6735*

STUDIES IN SPEECH PATHOLOGY AND CLINICAL LINGUISTICS.
John Benjamins Publishing Co., Amsteldijk 44, P.O. Box 75577, 1070 AN Amsterdam, Netherlands. TEL 31-20-6738156. FAX 31-20-6792956. *5099*

STUDIES IN SPELEOLOGY.
William Pengelly Cave Studies Trust Ltd., 107 Andover Rd., Newbury, Berks. RG14 6JH, England. TEL 44-1202-721164. *2371*

STUDIES IN STATISTICAL MECHANICS.
Elsevier Science B.V., Books Division, P.O. Box 211, 1000 AE Amsterdam, Netherlands. TEL 31-20-4853911. FAX 31-20-4853705. *5849*

STUDIES IN SURFACE SCIENCE AND CATALYSIS.
Elsevier Science B.V., Books Division, P.O. Box 211, 1000 AE Amsterdam, Netherlands. TEL 31-20-4853911. FAX 31-20-4853705. *5849*

STUDIES IN TEXTILE AND COSTUME HISTORY.
E.J. Brill, P.O. Box 9000, 2300 PA Leiden, Netherlands. TEL 31-71-5353500. FAX 31-71-5317532. *3514*

STUDIES IN THE AGE OF CHAUCER.
Ohio State University, Department of English, 421 Denney Hall, 164 W. 17th Ave., Columbus, OH 43210. TEL 614-292-2061. FAX 614-292-1599. *4474*

STUDIES IN THE DECORATIVE ARTS.
Bard Graduate Center for Studies in the Decorative Arts, 18 W. 86th St., New York, NY 10024. TEL 212-501-3058. FAX 212-501-3089. *467*

STUDIES IN THE DEVELOPMENT OF MODERN MATHEMATICS.
Gordon and Breach - Harwood Academic, Amsteldisk 166, 1st Fl., 1079 LH Amsterdam, Netherlands. *4609*

STUDIES IN THE GERMANIC LANGUAGES AND LITERATURES.
University of North Carolina Press, Box 2288, Chapel Hill, NC 27515-2288. TEL 919-966-3561. FAX 919-966-3829. *4474*

STUDIES IN THE HISTORY AND PHILOSOPHY OF MATHEMATICS.
Elsevier Science B.V., Books Division, P.O. Box 211, 1000 AE Amsterdam, Netherlands. TEL 31-20-4853911. FAX 31-20-4853705. *4609*

STUDIES IN THE HISTORY OF CHRISTIAN THOUGHT.
E.J. Brill, P.O. Box 9000, 2300 PA Leiden, Netherlands. TEL 31-71-5353500. FAX 31-71-5317532. *6375*

STUDIES IN THE HISTORY OF LEIDEN UNIVERSITY.
E.J. Brill, P.O. Box 9000, 2300 PA Leiden, Netherlands. TEL 31-71-5353500. FAX 31-71-5317532. *3606*

STUDIES IN THE HUMANITIES (INDIANA).
Indiana University of Pennsylvania, English Department, Indiana, PA 15705. TEL 412-357-2322. FAX 412-357-3056. *3973*

STUDIES IN TROPICAL OCEANOGRAPHY.
Office of the Bulletin of Marine Science, 4600 Rickenbacker Causeway, Miami, FL 33149-1098. TEL 305-361-4190. *2415*

STUDIES IN TWENTIETH CENTURY LITERATURE.
Kansas State University, Department of Modern Languages, Eisenhower 104, Manhattan, KS 66506-1003. TEL 913-532-6760. FAX 913-532-7004. *4474*

STUDIES IN U S NATIONAL SECURITY.
Kluwer Academic Publishers, Postbus 17, 3300 AA Dordrecht, Netherlands. TEL 31-78-6392392. FAX 31-78-6392254. *5287*

STUDIES IN VISUAL INFORMATION PROCESSING.
Elsevier Science B.V., Books Division, P.O. Box 211, 1000 AE Amsterdam, Netherlands. TEL 31-20-4853911. FAX 31-20-4853705. *5099*

STUDIES IN WIND ENGINEERING AND INDUSTRIAL ENGINEERING.
Elsevier Science B.V., Books Division, P.O. Box 211, 1000 AE Amsterdam, Netherlands. TEL 31-20-4853911. FAX 31-20-4853705. *2879*

STUDIES OF CLASSICAL INDIA.
Kluwer Academic Publishers, Postbus 17, 3300 AA Dordrecht, Netherlands. TEL 31-78-6392392. FAX 31-78-6392254. *5754*

STUDIES ON CHINA.
University of California Press, 2120 Berkeley Way, Berkeley, CA 94720. TEL 510-642-4247. FAX 510-643-7127. *3539*

STUDIES ON RELIGION IN AFRICA.
E.J. Brill, P.O. Box 9000, 2300 PA Leiden, Netherlands. TEL 31-71-5353500. FAX 31-71-5317532. *6375*

STUDIES ON THE TEXTS OF THE DESERT OF JUDAH.
E.J. Brill, P.O. Box 9000, 2300 PA Leiden, Netherlands. TEL 31-71-5353500. FAX 31-71-5317532. *6410*

STUDII SI ARTICOLE DE ISTORIE.
Societatea de Stiinte Istorice din Romania, Bdul. Republicii 13, 70031 Bucharest, Rumania. TEL 40-1-6131329. FAX 40-1-3210535. *3606*

STUDIME FILOLOGJIKE.
Academia e Shkencave e RPSSH, Instituti i Gjuhesise dhe i Letersise, Rruga N. Frasheri 7, Tirana, Albania. TEL 355-42-3514. FAX 355-42-3514. *4305*

STUDIO.
Havatzeleth Cultural and Educational Institutes of Hashomer Hatzair, P.O. Box 23570, Tel Aviv 61231, Israel. TEL 972-3-2512207. FAX 972-3-2512202. *468*

STUDIO (ALBURY).
Studio, 727 Peel St., Albury, N.S.W. 2640, Australia. TEL 61-6-211135. *4474*

STUDIO MAGAZINE.
E M A P Alpha, 150 rue Gallieni, 92100 Boulogne-Billancourt, France. *5346*

STUDIO ONE.
College of Saint Benedict, St. Joseph, MN 56374. *4524*

STYLE (DEKALB).
Northern Illinois University, Department of English, DeKalb, IL 60115. TEL 815-753-6653. FAX 815-753-0606. *4474*

SUBCELLULAR BIOCHEMISTRY.
Plenum Publishing Corp., 233 Spring St., New York, NY 10013-1578. TEL 212-620-8000. FAX 212-463-0742. *672*

SUBNUCLEAR SERIES.
Plenum Publishing Corp., 233 Spring St., New York, NY 10013-1578. TEL 212-620-8000. FAX 212-463-0742. *5828*

SUBSCRIPTIONS STRATEGY.
P.O. Box 2, Mullion, Helston, Cornwall TR12 7YA, England. TEL 44-1326-240039. FAX 44-1326-240039. *6285*

SUBSIDIA HAGIOGRAPHICA.
Societe des Bollandistes, 24 bd. Saint-Michel, B-1040 Brussels, Belgium. TEL 32-2-7393338. *6481*

SUBSTANCE ABUSE.
Plenum Publishing Corp., 233 Spring St., New York, NY 10013-1578. TEL 212-620-8000. FAX 212-463-0742. *2306*

SUBSTANCE USE AND MISUSE.
Marcel Dekker Journals, 270 Madison Ave., New York, NY 10016. TEL 212-696-9000. FAX 212-685-4540. *2306*

SUBTLE ENERGIES.
International Society for the Study of Subtle Energies and Energy Medicine, 356 Goldco Circle, Golden, CO 80403-1347. TEL 303-278-2228. FAX 303-279-3539. *299*

SUCHT.
Neuland Verlagsgesellschaft mbH, Markt 24-26, 21502 Geesthacht, Germany. TEL 49-4152-81342. FAX 49-4152-81343. *2306*

SUDANIC AFRICA.
University of Bergen, Centre for Middle Eastern and Islamic Studies, Parkv. 22A, N-5007 Bergen, Norway. TEL 47-55-58-27-11. FAX 47-55-58-98-91. *3529*

SUFFOLK INSTITUTE OF ARCHAEOLOGY AND HISTORY. PROCEEDINGS.
Suffolk Institute of Archaeology and History, c/o E.A. Martin, Hon. Secy., Oak Tree Farm, Finborough Rd., Hitcham, Ipswich, Suffolk IP7 7LS, England. TEL 44-1449-741266. *385*

SUFFOLK TRANSNATIONAL LAW REVIEW.
Suffolk University Law School, Suffolk Transnational Law Review, 41 Temple St., Boston, MA 02114-4280. TEL 617-573-8610. *4031*

SUFFOLK UNIVERSITY LAW REVIEW.
Darby Printing Co. (Boston), Beacon Hill, 41 Temple St., Boston, MA 02114-4280. TEL 617-573-8180. FAX 617-723-5847. *4031*

SUGAR SERIES.
Elsevier Science B.V., Books Division, P.O. Box 211, 1000 AE Amsterdam, Netherlands. TEL 31-20-4853911. FAX 31-20-4853705. *3128*

SUI YUAN WEN HSIEN.
Association of Fellow Provincials of Sui Yuan, 101 Fourth St., Chung Yang Rd., Hsin Tien, Taipei Hsien, Taiwan 23127, Republic of China. TEL 886-2-219-6633. *3044*

SUICIDE AND LIFE-THREATENING BEHAVIOR.
Guilford Publications, Inc., 72 Spring St., 4th Fl., New York, NY 10012. TEL 212-431-9800. FAX 212-966-6708. *6156*

SUID-AFRIKAANSE ARGIEFBLAD.
South African Society of Archivists, Private Bag X236, Pretoria 0001, South Africa. TEL 27-12-3235300. FAX 27-12-3235287. *4216*

SUIZIDPROPHYLAXE.
S. Roderer Verlag, Postfach 110506, 93018 Regensburg, Germany. TEL 49-941-795124. FAX 49-941-795198. *5099*

SULFUR LETTERS.
Gordon and Breach - Harwood Academic, Amsteldisk 166, 1st Fl., 1079 LH Amsterdam, Netherlands. *1768*

SULFUR REPORTS.
Gordon and Breach - Harwood Academic, Amsteldisk 166, 1st Fl., 1079 LH Amsterdam, Netherlands. *1768*

SULPHUR IN AGRICULTURE.
Sulphur Institute, 1140 Connecticut Ave., N.W., Ste. 612, Washington, DC 20036. TEL 202-331-9660. FAX 202-293-2940. *155*

SULPHURIC ACID AND INDUSTRY.
Sulphuric Acid Association of Japan, 21-1, 2-chome, Shinbashi, Minato-ku, Tokyo 105, Japan. TEL 81-3-3572-5498. FAX 81-3-3572-5490. *1768*

SUMMA PHYTOPATHOLOGICA.
Grupo Paulista de Fitopatologia, Universidade de Sao Paulo, Rodovia C. Tonanni Km 5, 14870-000 Jaboticabal SP, Brazil. TEL 55-16-3232500. FAX 55-16-3224275. *729*

SUO.
Helsinki University, Department of Forest Ecology, P.O. Box 24, FIN-00014 Helsinki, Finland. FAX 358-9-191-7605. *3163*

SUOMEN ANTROPOLOGI.
Suomen Antropologinen Seura, P.O. Box 13, SF-00014 University of Helsinki, Finland. TEL 358-9-191-7828. FAX 358-9-191-7829. *331*

SUOMEN LAAKARILEHTI.
Suomen Laakariliitto, Makelankatu 2, 00500 Helsinki, Finland. TEL 358-90-393-0795. *4749*

SUPERCOMPUTER.
ASFRA B.V., Voorhaven 33, 1135 BL Edam, Netherlands. TEL 31-2993-72751. FAX 31-2993-72877. *2164*

SUPRAMOLECULAR CHEMISTRY.
Gordon and Breach - Harwood Academic, Amsteldisk 166, 1st Fl., 1079 LH Amsterdam, Netherlands. *1768*

SUPRAMOLECULAR SCIENCE.
Elsevier Science Ltd., P.O. Box 800, Kidlington, Oxford OX2 8DP, England. TEL 44-1865-843000. FAX 44-1865-843010. *5828*

SUPREME COURT ECONOMIC REVIEW.
University of Chicago Press, Journals Division, 5720 S. Woodlawn Ave., Chicago, IL 60637. TEL 773-702-7600. FAX 773-702-0172. *4138*

SUPREME COURT REVIEW.
University of Chicago Press, Journals Division, 5720 S. Woodlawn Ave., Chicago, IL 60637. TEL 773-702-7600. FAX 773-702-0172. *4139*

SURFACE AND COATINGS TECHNOLOGY.
Elsevier Science S.A., P.O. Box 564, CH-1001 Lausanne 1, Switzerland. TEL 41-21-3207381. FAX 41-21-3235444. *1797*

SURFACE AND COLLOID SCIENCE.
Plenum Publishing Corp., 233 Spring St., New York, NY 10013-1578. TEL 212-620-8000. FAX 212-463-0742. *1835*

SURFACE COATINGS.
Elsevier Science Ltd., Books Division, P.O. Box 800, Kidlington, Oxford OX5 1DX, England. TEL 44-1865-843000. FAX 44-1865-843010. *5555*

SURFACE INVESTIGATION: X-RAY, SYNCHROTRON AND NEUTRON TECHNIQUES.
Gordon and Breach - Harwood Academic, Amsteldisk 166, 1st Fl., 1079 LH Amsterdam, Netherlands. *2900*

SURFACE SCIENCE.
North-Holland, P.O. Box 211, 1000 AE Amsterdam, Netherlands. TEL 31-20-4853911. FAX 31-20-4853598. *5828*

SURFACE SCIENCE REPORTS.
North-Holland, P.O. Box 211, 1000 AE Amsterdam, Netherlands. TEL 31-20-4853911. FAX 31-20-4853598. *5829*

SURFACTANT SCIENCE SERIES.
Marcel Dekker, Inc., 270 Madison Ave., New York, NY 10016. TEL 212-696-9000. FAX 212-685-4540. *1768*

SURGERY.
Mosby - Year Book, Inc., 11830 Westline Industrial Dr., St. Louis, MO 63146-3318. TEL 314-872-8370. FAX 314-432-1380. *5154*

SURGICAL ENDOSCOPY.
Springer-Verlag, Medical Journals, 175 Fifth Ave., New York, NY 10010. TEL 212-460-1500. FAX 212-473-6272. *5155*

SURGICAL LAPAROSCOPY AND ENDOSCOPY.
Lippincott - Raven Publishers, 227 E. Washington Sq., Philadelphia, PA 19106. TEL 215-238-4200. FAX 215-238-4227. *5155*

SURGICAL NEUROLOGY.
Elsevier Science Inc., Box 945, New York, NY 10159-0945. TEL 212-633-3730. FAX 212-633-3680. *5155*

SURGICAL PATHOLOGY.
Field & Wood, Medical Periodicals, Inc., Box 975, Blue Bell, PA 19422. TEL 610-828-4010. FAX 215-482-0226. *4749*

SURGICAL PRACTICE NEWS.
McMahon Publishing Co., 83 Peaceable St., West Redding, CT 06896. TEL 203-944-9343. *5155*

SURGICAL RESEARCH COMMUNICATIONS.
Gordon and Breach - Harwood Academic, Amsteldisk 166, 1st Fl., 1079 LH Amsterdam, Netherlands. *5155*

SURGICAL SERVICES MANAGEMENT.
Association of Operating Room Nurses, Inc., c/o Peggy Lehr, 2170 S. Parker Rd., Ste. 300, Denver, CO 80231. TEL 303-755-6304. FAX 303-750-3441. *5155*

SURGICAL UPDATE.
American Association of Oral and Maxillofacial Surgeons, 9700 W. Bryn Mawr Ave., Rosemont, IL 60018. TEL 708-678-6200. FAX 708-678-6286. *4871*

SURVEY OF OPHTHALMOLOGY.
Survey of Ophthalmology, Inc., 7 Kent St., Ste. 4, Brookline, MA 02146. TEL 617-566-2138. FAX 617-566-4019. *4789*

SURVEYS IN GEOPHYSICS.
Kluwer Academic Publishers, Postbus 17, 3300 AA Dordrecht, Netherlands. TEL 31-78-6392392. FAX 31-78-6392254. *2390*

SURVEYS IN HIGH ENERGY PHYSICS.
Gordon and Breach - Harwood Academic, Amsteldisk 166, 1st Fl., 1079 LH Amsterdam, Netherlands. *5829*

SUSSEX RECORD SOCIETY.
Sussex Record Society, Barbican House, Lewes BN7 1YE, England. TEL 44-1243-533911. FAX 44-1243-533959. *3607*

SUZHOU DAXUE XUEBAO (ZHEXUE SHEHUI KEXUE BAN).
Suzhou Daxue, 1 Shizi Jie, Suzhou, Jiangsu 215006, People's Republic of China. TEL 0512-5223614. FAX 0512-5231918. *6641*

SUZUGAMINE JOSHI TANDAI KENKYU SHUHO. SHIZEN KAGAKU.
Suzugamine Joshi Tanki Daigaku, 6-8 Inokuchi 4-chome, Nishi-ku, Hiroshima-shi, Hiroshima-ken 733, Japan. TEL 082-278-1103. FAX 082-277-0301. *6577*

SVENSK FLYGHISTORISK TIDSKRIFT.
Svensk Flyghistorisk Foerening, P.O. Box 10267, S-100 55 Stockholm, Sweden. *80*

SVENSK VETERINAERTIDNING.
Sveriges Veterinaerfoerbund, P.O. Box 12 709, S-112 94 Stockholm, Sweden. TEL 08-654-2480. FAX 08-6517082. *7279*

SVENSKA LINNE-SALLSKAPET AARSSKRIFT.
Linne-Sallskapet, Kungshuset, S-222 22 Lund, Sweden. TEL 46-46-222-75-89. FAX 46-46-222-46-06. *729*

SVETSAREN.
Esab AB, Marketing Communications, P.O. Box 8004, S-402 77 Goeteborg, Sweden. FAX 46-31-509-390. *5224*

SVILUPPO.
Comitato Studi e Ricerche sullo Sviluppo, c/o Dipto. di Scienze Economiche, Universita la Sapienza, Via Nomentana 41, 00161 Rome, Italy. TEL 39-6-8552780. FAX 39-6-8558054. *1312*

SVINEAVL OG PRODUKTION I DANMARK. AARSBERETNING.
Landsudvalget for Svin, Axelborg, Axeltorv 3, DK-1609 Copenhagen V, Denmark. FAX 45-33-11-68-14. *290*

SWAMY BOTANICAL CLUB. JOURNAL.
Swamy Botanical Club, c/o Dr. K.V. Krishnamurthy, Dept. of Plant Sciences, Bharathidasan University, Tiruchirapalli 620 024, India. TEL 0431-60351. FAX 0431-96245. *729*

REFEREED SERIALS

SWEDISH BOOK REVIEW.
Swedish-English Literary Translators Association, University of Wales, Lampeter SA48 7ED, Wales. TEL 44-1570-422351. FAX 44-1570-423782. *6285*

SWISS - AMERICAN HISTORICAL SOCIETY. REVIEW.
Swiss - American Historical Society, c/o Erdmann Schmocker, 6440 N. Bosworth Ave., Chicago, IL 60626. TEL 773-262-8336. *3514*

SWISS SURGERY.
Hans Huber AG, Laenggassstr. 76, CH-3000 Bern 9, Switzerland. TEL 41-31-3004500. FAX 41-31-3004590. *5156*

SYCAMORE REVIEW.
Purdue University, Department of English, W. Lafayette, IN 47907. TEL 765-494-3783. FAX 765-494-3780. *4475*

SYDNEY ORGAN JOURNAL.
Organ Society of Sydney, G.P.O. Box 2348, Sydney, N.S.W. 2001, Australia. TEL 61-43-591551. *5440*

SYMBOLA ET EMBLEMATA.
E.J. Brill, P.O. Box 9000, 2300 PA Leiden, Netherlands. TEL 31-71-5353500. FAX 31-71-5317532. *468*

SYMMETRY: CULTURE AND SCIENCE.
International Society for the Interdisciplinary Study of Symmetry, c/o Symmetrion, P.O. Box 994, 1245 Budapest, Hungary. TEL 36-1-1318326. FAX 36-1-1313161. *6577*

SYMPLOKE.
Ballantine 914, Indiana University, Bloomington, IN 47405. TEL 813-855-7070. FAX 812-885-2688. *3793*

SYMPOSIA FOUNDATION MERIEUX.
Elsevier Science B.V., Books Division, P.O. Box 211, 1000 AE Amsterdam, Netherlands. TEL 31-20-4853911. FAX 31-20-4853705. *4749*

SYMPOSIA MATHEMATICA.
Academic Press, Inc., 525 B St., Ste. 1900, San Diego, CA 92101-4495. TEL 619-231-0926. FAX 619-699-6715. *4610*

SYMPOSIUM.
Heldref Publications, 1319 Eighteenth St., N.W., Washington, DC 20036-1802. TEL 202-296-6267. FAX 202-296-5149. *4476*

SYMPOSIUM (INTERNATIONAL) ON COMBUSTION.
Combustion Institute, 5001 Baum Blvd., Pittsburgh, PA 15213. TEL 412-387-1366. FAX 412-687-0340. *1835*

SYMPOSIUM ON COMPUTER ARITHMETIC. PROCEEDINGS.
I E E E Computer Society Press, 10662 Los Vaqueros Circle, Los Alamitos, CA 90720-1264. TEL 714-821-8380. FAX 714-821-4641. *2164*

SYMPOSIUM ON FUSION ENGINEERING. PROCEEDINGS.
Institute of Electrical and Electronics Engineers, Inc., 345 E. 47th St., New York, NY 10017-2394. TEL 732-981-0060. FAX 732-981-9667. *2704*

SYNAPSE (NEW YORK).
John Wiley & Sons, Inc., Journals, 605 Third Ave., New York, NY 10158. TEL 212-850-6645. FAX 212-850-6021. *5099*

SYNCHROTRON RADIATION NEWS.
Gordon and Breach - Harwood Academic, Amsteldisk 166, 1st Fl., 1079 LH Amsterdam, Netherlands. *5858*

SYNERGY.
A F L Deeson Partnership Ltd., Ewell House, Faversham, Kent ME13 8UP, England. TEL 44-1795-535468. FAX 44-1795-535469. *5116*

SYNOPSES OF THE BRITISH FAUNA.
Backhuys Publishers, P.O. Box 321, 2300 AH Leiden, Netherlands. TEL 31-71-5170208. FAX 31-71-5171856. *850*

SYNTHESE.
Kluwer Academic Publishers, Postbus 17, 3300 AA Dordrecht, Netherlands. TEL 31-78-6392392. FAX 31-78-6392254. *5754*

SYNTHESE LIBRARY.
Kluwer Academic Publishers, Postbus 17, 3300 AA Dordrecht, Netherlands. TEL 31-78-6392392. FAX 31-78-6392254. *5754*

SYNTHESIS (KNOXVILLE).
New Paradigm Press, University of Tennessee, 608 McClung Tower, Knoxville, TN 37919. TEL 423-588-8878. *4476*

SYNTHESIS AND REACTIVITY IN INORGANIC AND METALORGANIC CHEMISTRY.
Marcel Dekker Journals, 270 Madison Ave., New York, NY 10016. TEL 212-696-9000. FAX 212-685-4540. *1835*

SYNTHETIC COMMUNICATIONS.
Marcel Dekker Journals, 270 Madison Ave., New York, NY 10016. TEL 212-696-9000. FAX 212-685-4540. *1824*

SYNTHETIC METALS.
Elsevier Science S.A., P.O. Box 564, CH-1001 Lausanne 1, Switzerland. TEL 41-21-3207381. FAX 41-21-3235444. *2870*

SYNTHETIC METHODS OF ORGANIC CHEMISTRY.
S. Karger AG, Allschwilerstr. 10, P.O. Box, CH-4009 Basel, Switzerland. TEL 41-61-3061111. FAX 41-61-3061234. *1824*

SYRACUSE UNIVERSITY LIBRARY ASSOCIATES COURIER.
Syracuse University Library Associates, 600 Bird Library, Syracuse, NY 13244-2010. TEL 315-443-2130. FAX 315-443-2671. *3793*

SYSTEM.
Elsevier Science Ltd., Pergamon, P.O. Box 800, Kidlington, Oxford OX5 1DX, England. TEL 44-1865-843000. FAX 44-1865-843010. *2619*

SYSTEM DYNAMICS.
System Dynamics Society of India, c/o Dept. of Industrial Engineering & Management, Indian Institute of Technology, Kharagpur 721 302, India. TEL 91-3222-55221. FAX 91-3222-55303. *2741*

SYSTEM DYNAMICS REVIEW.
John Wiley & Sons Ltd., Journals, Baffins Ln., Chichester, W. Sussex PO19 1UD, England. TEL 44-1243-779777. FAX 44-1243-775878. *1509*

SYSTEMATIC BIOLOGY.
Taylor & Francis Inc., 1900 Frost Rd., Ste. 101, Bristol, PA 19007-1598. FAX 215-785-5515. *851*

SYSTEMATIC BOTANY.
American Society of Plant Taxonomists (Laramie), University of Wyoming, Dept. of Botany, Laramie, WY 82071-3165. TEL 307-766-2214. FAX 307-766-2851. *730*

SYSTEMATIC BOTANY MONOGRAPHS.
American Society of Plant Taxonomists (Ann Arbor), University of Michigan Herbarium, N. University Bldg., Ann Arbor, MI 48109-1057. TEL 313-647-2812. FAX 313-763-0369. *730*

SYSTEMATIC ENTOMOLOGY.
Blackwell Science Ltd., Osney Mead, Oxford OX2 0EL, England. TEL 44-1865-206206. FAX 44-1865-721205. *761*

SYSTEMATIC PARASITOLOGY.
Kluwer Academic Publishers, Postbus 17, 3300 AA Dordrecht, Netherlands. TEL 31-78-6392392. FAX 31-78-6392254. *629*

SYSTEMIC PRACTICE AND ACTION RESEARCH.
Plenum Publishing Corp., 233 Spring St., New York, NY 10013-1578. TEL 212-620-8000. FAX 212-463-0742. *1509*

SYSTEMS AND CONTROL LETTERS.
North-Holland, P.O. Box 211, 1000 AE Amsterdam, Netherlands. TEL 31-20-4853911. FAX 31-20-4853598. *2159*

SYSTEMS RESEARCH.
John Wiley & Sons Ltd., Journals, Baffins Ln., Chichester, W. Sussex PO19 1UD, England. TEL 44-1243-779777. FAX 44-1243-775878. *2159*

SYSTEMS RESEARCH IN PHYSIOLOGY.
Gordon and Breach - Harwood Academic, Amsteldisk 166, 1st Fl., 1079 LH Amsterdam, Netherlands. *6156*

SYSTEMS SCIENCE AND MATHEMATICAL SCIENCES.
Science Press, Marketing and Sales Department, 16 Donghuangchenggen North St., Beijing 100717, People's Republic of China. *4610*

THE SYSTEMS THINKER.
Pegasus Communications, Inc., Box 120, Kendal Sq., Cambridge, MA 02142. TEL 617-576-1231. FAX 617-576-3114. *1509*

SZIVARVANY.
Framo Publishing, 561 W. Diversey Pkwy., Chicago, IL 60614. TEL 312-477-1485. FAX 312-477-2698. *3045*

SZKOLA ZAWODOWA.
Szkola Zawodowa, Ul. Smulikowskiego 6-8, 00-389 Warsaw, Poland. TEL 48-22-261011. *2486*

SZKOLY POBOZNE.
Kuria Prowincjalna Zakonu Pijarow, Ul. Pijarska 2, 31-015 Krakow, Poland. *6482*

T A H P E R D JOURNAL.
Texas Association for Health, Physical Education, Recreation and Dance, 6300 La Calma Dr., No. 100, Austin, TX 78752. TEL 512-459-1299. FAX 512-459-1290. *5791*

T A P P I COATING CONFERENCE.
Technical Association of the Pulp and Paper Industry, Inc., Technology Park - Atlanta, Box 105113, Atlanta, GA 30348. TEL 770-446-1400. FAX 770-446-6947. *5572*

T A P P I ENGINEERING CONFERENCE PROCEEDINGS (YEAR).
Technical Association of the Pulp and Paper Industry, Inc., Technology Park - Atlanta, Box 105113, Atlanta, GA 30348. TEL 770-446-1400. FAX 770-446-6947. *2741*

T A P P I FINISHING AND CONVERTING CONFERENCE. PROCEEDINGS (YEAR).
Technical Association of the Pulp and Paper Industry, Inc., Technology Park - Atlanta, Box 105113, Atlanta, GA 30348. TEL 770-446-1400. FAX 770-446-6947. *5572*

T A P P I HOT MELT CONFERENCE (YEAR).
Technical Association of the Pulp and Paper Industry, Inc., Technology Park - Atlanta, Box 105113, Atlanta, GA 30348. TEL 770-446-1400. FAX 770-446-6947. *5572*

T A P P I INTERNATIONAL CORRUGATED CONTAINERS CONFERENCE. PROCEEDINGS.
Technical Association of the Pulp and Paper Industry, Inc., Technology Park - Atlanta, Box 105113, Atlanta, GA 30348. TEL 770-446-1400. FAX 770-446-6947. *5572*

T A P P I INTERNATIONAL ENVIRONMENTAL CONFERENCE. PROCEEDINGS.
Technical Association of the Pulp and Paper Industry, Inc., Technology Park - Atlanta, Box 105113, Atlanta, GA 30348. TEL 770-446-1400. FAX 770-446-6947. *2953*

T A P P I INTERNATIONAL PROCESS & PRODUCT QUALITY CONFERENCE PROCEEDINGS (YEAR).
Technical Association of the Pulp and Paper Industry, Inc., Technology Park - Atlanta, Box 105113, Atlanta, GA 30348. TEL 770-446-1400. FAX 770-446-6947. *5572*

T A P P I JOURNAL.
Technical Association of the Pulp and Paper Industry, Inc., Technology Park - Atlanta, Box 105113, Atlanta, GA 30348. TEL 770-446-1400. FAX 770-446-6947. *5572*

T A P P I NONWOOD PLANT FIBER PULPING PROGRESS REPORT.
Technical Association of the Pulp and Paper Industry, Inc., Technology Park - Atlanta, Box 105113, Atlanta, GA 30348. TEL 770-446-1400. FAX 770-446-6947. *5572*

REFEREED SERIALS

T A P P I NONWOVENS CONFERENCE. PROCEEDINGS (YEAR).
Technical Association of the Pulp and Paper Industry, Inc., Technology Park - Atlanta, Box 105113, Atlanta, GA 30348. TEL 770-446-1400. FAX 770-446-6947. *5572*

T A P P I PAPERMAKERS CONFERENCE.
Technical Association of the Pulp and Paper Industry, Inc., Technology Park - Atlanta, Box 105113, Atlanta, GA 30348. TEL 770-446-1400. FAX 770-446-6947. *5572*

T A P P I POLYMERS, LAMINATIONS & COATINGS CONFERENCE. PROCEEDINGS (YEAR).
Technical Association of the Pulp and Paper Industry, Inc., Technology Park - Atlanta, Box 105113, Atlanta, GA 30348. TEL 770-446-1400. FAX 770-446-6947. *5572*

T A P P I PROCEEDINGS (YEAR).
Technical Association of the Pulp and Paper Industry, Inc., Technology Park - Atlanta, Box 105113, Atlanta, GA 30348. TEL 770-446-1400. FAX 770-446-6947. *5572*

T A P P I PROCESS CONTROL CONFERENCE. PROCEEDINGS (YEAR).
Technical Association of the Pulp and Paper Industry, Inc., Technology Park - Atlanta, Box 105113, Atlanta, GA 30348. TEL 770-446-1400. FAX 770-446-6947. *5572*

T A P P I PULPING CONFERENCE. PROCEEDINGS.
Technical Association of the Pulp and Paper Industry, Inc., Technology Park - Atlanta, Box 105113, Atlanta, GA 30348. TEL 770-446-1400. FAX 770-446-6947. *5572*

T A P P I TEST METHODS.
Technical Association of the Pulp and Paper Industry, Inc., Technology Park - Atlanta, Box 105113, Atlanta, GA 30348. TEL 770-446-1400. FAX 770-446-6947. *5572*

T C.
Box 15399, Atlanta, GA 30333-0399. TEL 404-727-2344. *6376*

T E S O L MATTERS.
Teachers of English to Speakers of Other Languages, 1600 Cameron St., Ste. 300, Alexandria, VA 22314-2751. TEL 703-836-0774. FAX 703-836-7864. *4306*

T H E JOURNAL.
Ed Warnshius Ltd., 150 El Camino Real, Ste. 112, Tustin, CA 92780. TEL 714-730-4011. FAX 714-730-3739. *2519*

T I M S STUDIES IN THE MANAGEMENT SCIENCES.
Elsevier Science B.V., Books Division, P.O. Box 211, 1000 AE Amsterdam, Netherlands. TEL 31-20-4853911. FAX 31-20-4853705. *1204*

T M A JOURNAL.
Treasury Management Association, 7315 Wisconsin Ave., Ste. 600 W., Bethesda, MD 20814. TEL 301-907-2862. FAX 301-907-2864. *1169*

T R C SPECTRAL DATA - INFRARED.
Thermodynamics Research Center, Texas Engineering Experiment Station, Texas A & M University System, College Station, TX 77843-3111. TEL 409-845-4940. FAX 409-847-8590. *1797*

T R C SPECTRAL DATA - ULTRAVIOLET.
Thermodynamics Research Center, Texas Engineering Experiment Station, Texas A & M University System, College Station, TX 77843-3111. TEL 409-845-4940. FAX 409-847-8590. *1797*

T R C SPECTRAL DATA - 13 C NUCLEAR MAGNETIC RESONANCE.
Thermodynamics Research Center, Texas Engineering Experiment Station, Texas A & M University System, College Station, TX 77843-3111. TEL 409-845-4940. FAX 409-847-8590. *1797*

T R C THERMODYNAMIC TABLES - HYDROCARBONS.
Thermodynamics Research Center, Texas Engineering Experiment Station, Texas A & M University System, College Station, TX 77843-3111. TEL 409-845-4940. FAX 409-847-8590. *1835*

T R C THERMODYNAMIC TABLES - NON-HYDROCARBONS.
Thermodynamics Research Center, Texas Engineering Experiment Station, Texas A & M University System, College Station, TX 77843-3111. TEL 409-845-4940. FAX 409-847-8590. *1797*

T R Q.
Tullis Russell Group Ltd., Markinch, Glenrothes, Fife KY7 6PB, Scotland. TEL 44-1592-753311. FAX 44-1592-610371. *3301*

T SQUARED NEWSLETTER.
Technology Transfer Society, 435 N. Michigan Ave., Chicago, IL 60611-4001. *6975*

T W TAGUNGSREGIONEN.
M und A Verlag fuer Messen, Ausstellungen und Kongresse GmbH, Postfach 101528, 60015 Frankfurt a.M., Germany. TEL 49-69-759502. FAX 49-69-75951280. *5172*

TAAL EN TONGVAL.
Seminarie Vlaamse Dialektologie te Gent, Blandijnberg 2, B-9000 Gent, Belgium. TEL 32-9-2644075. FAX 32-9-2644170. *4306*

TAIPEI PICTORIAL.
Taipei City Government, Department of Information, 1, Shih Fu Rd., Taipei, Taiwan, Republic of China. TEL 886-2-728-7551. FAX 886-2-720-5909. *3365*

TAKAHE.
Takahe Collective Trust, P.O. Box 13-335, Christchurch 1, New Zealand. TEL 64-3-3598133. *4476*

TAKAOKA REBYU.
Takaoka Seisakusho, 2-1, Ote-machi 2-chome, Chiyoda-ku, Tokyo 100, Japan. TEL 81-3-3211-1674. FAX 81-3-3270-8067. *2847*

TALANTA.
Elsevier Science B.V., P.O. Box 211, 1000 AE Amsterdam, Netherlands. TEL 31-20-4853911. FAX 31-20-4853598. *1798*

TALISMAN.
Talisman House Publishing, Box 3157, Jersey City, NJ 07303-3157. TEL 201-938-0698. *4525*

TALKING POLITICS.
Politics Association, 64 W. Hill Dr., Dartford, Kent DA1 3EA, England. TEL 44-1322-275145. *5974*

TALLER DE LETRAS.
Pontificia Universidad Catolica de Chile, Instituto de Letras, Jaime Guzman Errazuriz 3300, Campus Oriente U.C., Casilla 6277, Correo 22, Santiago, Chile. TEL 562-274-4041 ext. 5189. FAX 562-2233125. *4476*

TAMAQUA.
Parkland College, Humanities Department, 2400 W. Bradley Ave., Champaign, IL 61821-1899. TEL 217-351-2380. FAX 217-373-3899. *4362*

TAMKANG JOURNAL OF MATHEMATICS.
Tamkang University Press, Tamsui, Taipei, Taiwan 25137, Republic of China. TEL 886-2-621-5656. FAX 886-2-620-2613. *4610*

TAMPA REVIEW.
University of Tampa Press, 401 W. Kennedy Blvd., Tampa, FL 33606-1490. TEL 813-253-3333. FAX 813-258-7593. *4525*

T'ANG STUDIES.
T'ang Studies Society, c/o Prof. Michael R. Drompp, Rhodes College, Department of History, 2000 N. Pkwy., Memphis, TN 38112. TEL 901-726-3655. FAX 901-726-3727. *5538*

TANKUANG GONGCHENG.
Dizhi Kuangchan Bu, Kantan Jishu Yanjiusuo, 26, Baiwanzhuang Lu, Beijing 100037, People's Republic of China. TEL 8311133. *5317*

TANMIAT AL-RAFIDAIN.
Majallat Tanmiat al-Rafidain, P.O. Box 78, Mosul, Iraq. TEL 814433. *6197*

TAOIST RESOURCES.
Indiana University, East Asian Studies Center, Memorial Hall W 207, Indiana University, Bloomington, IN 47405. TEL 812-855-3765. FAX 812-855-7762. *6498*

TAOS MAGAZINE.
Whitney Publishing Co., Inc., Box 1380, Taos, NM 87571. TEL 505-758-5404. *7256*

TAPOL.
Indonesia Human Rights Campaign, 111 Northwood Rd., Thornton Heath, Surrey CR7 8HW, England. TEL 44-181-771-2904. FAX 44-181-653-0322. *5999*

TAPROOT LITERARY REVIEW.
Tikvah Feinstein, Ed. & Pub., Box 204, Ambridge, PA 15003. TEL 412-266-8476. *4476*

AL-TARBIYYAH.
National Commission for Education, Culture and Science, P.O. Box 9865, Doha, Qatar. TEL 861412. FAX 880911. *2486*

TARGET.
John Benjamins Publishing Co., Amsteldijk 44, P.O. Box 75577, 1070 AN Amsterdam, Netherlands. TEL 31-20-6738156. FAX 31-20-6792956. *4306*

TASKS FOR VEGETATION SCIENCE.
Kluwer Academic Publishers, Postbus 17, 3300 AA Dordrecht, Netherlands. TEL 31-78-6392392. FAX 31-78-6392254. *730*

TASMANIA. DEPARTMENT OF PRIMARY INDUSTRY AND FISHERIES. MARINE RESOURCES DIVISION. TECHNICAL REPORT.
Department of Primary Industry and Fisheries, Marine Resources Division, P.O. Box 619F, Hobart, Tas. 7001, Australia. TEL 61-3-6227727. FAX 61-02-278035. *3080*

TASMANIAN MASTER BUILDER.
Master Builders' Association of Tasmania, G.P.O. 992 K, Hobart, Tas. 7001, Australia. TEL 61-03-6232377. FAX 61-03-6234194. *915*

TASMANIAN NATURALIST.
Tasmanian Field Naturalist Club, Inc., G.P.O. Box 68A, Hobart, Tas. 7001, Australia. TEL 61-3-62337870. FAX 61-3-62337594. *629*

TASMANIAN TRAVELWAYS.
Creative Publications Pty., Ltd., 71-75 Paterson St., Launceston, Tas. 7250, Australia. *7237*

TAUBMAN LECTURES IN JEWISH STUDIES.
California University Press, 2120 Berkeley Way, Berkeley, CA 94720. TEL 510-643-7127. FAX 510-643-7127. *6410*

TAWAGOTO.
Hohm Press, Box 4272, Prescott, AZ 86302. TEL 520-778-9189. FAX 520-717-1779. *6498*

AL-TAWHID.
Foundation of Islamic Thought, P.O. Box 37165-111, Qum, Islamic Republic of Iran. TEL 98-251-21588. FAX 98-251-21588. *6401*

TAXATION FOR LAWYERS.
Warren, Gorham & Lamont, One Penn Plaza, New York, NY 10119. TEL 212-971-5000. FAX 212-971-5240. *1634*

TAXATION IN AUSTRALIA (BLUE EDITION).
Taxation Institute of Australia, 7th Fl., 64 Castlereagh St., Sydney, N.S.W. 2000, Australia. TEL 61-2-92323422. FAX 61-2-92216953. *1634*

TAXATION IN AUSTRALIA (RED EDITION).
Taxation Institute of Australia, 7th Fl., 64 Castlereagh St., Sydney, N.S.W. 2000, Australia. TEL 61-2-92323422. FAX 61-2-92216953. *1634*

TAXATION PRACTITIONER.
Chartered Institute of Taxation, 12 Upper Belgrave St., London SW1X 8BB, England. TEL 44-171-235-9381. FAX 44-171-235-2562. *1635*

TAXON.
International Association for Plant Taxonomy, Botanischer Garten & Botanisches Museum, Koenigin-Luise-Str. 6-8, 14191 Berlin, Germany. TEL 49-30-8316010. FAX 49-30-83006218. *730*

TAYLOR.
Taylor University, 500 W. Reade Ave., Upland, IN 46989. TEL 765-998-2751. FAX 765-998-4910. *2557*

TE REO.
Linguistic Society of New Zealand, c/o University of Auckland, English Dept., Private Bag 92019, Auckland 1, New Zealand. TEL 64-9-3737999. FAX 64-9-3737449. *4306*

TEACHER DEVELOPMENT.
Triangle Journals Ltd., P.O. Box 65, Wallingford, Oxon. OX10 0YG, England. TEL 44-1491-838013. FAX 44-1491-834968. *2620*

TEACHER EDUCATION AND PRACTICE.
Texas Association of Colleges of Teacher Education, c/o Lamar University, College of Education and Human Development, Beaumont, TX 77710. *2557*

TEACHER IN ZIMBABWE.
Zimbabwe Publishing House, P.O. Box 350, Harare, Zimbabwe. TEL 263-4-497548. FAX 263-4-497554. *2487*

TEACHING AND LEARNING IN MEDICINE.
Lawrence Erlbaum Associates, Inc., 10 Industrial Dr., Mahwah, NJ 07430-2262. TEL 201-236-9500. FAX 201-236-0072. *4750*

TEACHING AND LEARNING: THE JOURNAL OF NATURAL INQUIRY.
University of North Dakota, Box 7189, Univ. Sta., Grand Forks, ND 58202-7189. TEL 701-777-4421. FAX 701-777-4365. *2620*

TEACHING & TEACHER EDUCATION.
Elsevier Science Ltd., Pergamon, P.O. Box 800, Kidlington, Oxford OX5 1DX, England. TEL 44-1865-843000. FAX 44-1865-843010. *2620*

TEACHING BUSINESS ETHICS.
Kluwer Academic Publishers, Postbus 17, 3300 AA Dordrecht, Netherlands. TEL 31-78-6392392. FAX 31-78-9392254. *5755*

TEACHING CHILDREN MATHEMATICS.
National Council of Teachers of Mathematics, 1906 Association Dr., Reston, VA 22091-1593. TEL 703-620-9840. FAX 703-476-2970. *4610*

TEACHING EARTH SCIENCES.
Institute of Earth Studies, University of Wales, Aberstwyth, Dyfed SY23 3DB, Wales. TEL 44-1970-622639. FAX 44-1970-622659. *2372*

TEACHING EXCEPTIONAL CHILDREN.
Council for Exceptional Children, 1920 Association Dr., Reston, VA 22091. TEL 703-620-3660. FAX 703-264-9494. *2591*

TEACHING HISTORY: A JOURNAL OF METHODS.
Emporia State University, Division of Social Sciences, Box 4032, Emporia, KS 66801. TEL 316-341-5579. FAX 316-341-5143. *2621*

TEACHING OF PSYCHOLOGY.
Lawrence Erlbaum Associates, Inc., 10 Industrial Dr., Mahwah, NJ 07430-2262. TEL 201-236-9500. FAX 201-236-0072. *6156*

TEACHING PROFESSOR.
Magna Publications, Inc., 2718 Dryden Dr., Madison, WI 53704-3006. TEL 608-246-3580. FAX 608-249-0355. *2557*

TEACHING PUBLIC ADMINISTRATION.
Sheffield Business School, Policy Research Centre, Unit 7, Science Park, Howard St., Sheffield S1 2LX, England. TEL 44-114-253-4460. FAX 44-114-253-4467. *2621*

TEACHING SECONDARY PHYSICAL EDUCATION.
Human Kinetics Publishers, Inc., Box 5076, Champaign, IL 61825-5076. TEL 217-351-1549. FAX 217-351-1549. *2621*

TEACHING STATISTICS.
Teaching Statistics Trust, RSS Centre for Statistical Education, University of Nottingham, Nottingham N97 2RD, England. TEL 44-115-951-4911. FAX 44-115-951-4951. *2504*

TECHNICA.
Comite National de la Bijouterie, Horlogerie, Joaillerie, Orfevrerie, Blvd. de Smet de Naeyer 290a, 1090 Brussels, Belgium. TEL 32-2-4282245. FAX 32-2-4283078. *3867*

TECHNICAL ANALYSIS OF STOCKS & COMMODITIES.
Technical Analysis, Inc., 4757 California Ave., S.W., Seattle, WA 98116-4499. TEL 206-938-0570. FAX 206-938-1307. *1411*

TECHNICAL COMMUNICATION QUARTERLY.
University of Minnesota, Rhetoric Department, 201 Haecker Hall, St. Paul, MN 55108. TEL 612-624-9729. FAX 612-624-3167. *2621*

TECHNICAL SERVICES QUARTERLY.
Haworth Press, Inc., 10 Alice St., Binghamton, NY 13904. TEL 607-722-5857. FAX 607-722-6362. *4217*

TECHNIKA POSZUKIWAN GEOLOGICZNYCH, GEOSYNOPTYKA I GEOTERMIA.
Polska Akademia Nauk, Centrum Podstawowych Problemow Gospodarki Surowcami Mineralnymi i Energia, Ul. Jozefa Wybickiego 7, 31-261 Krakow, Poland. TEL 48-12-322435. FAX 48-12-323534. *2372*

TECHNIQUES AND INSTRUMENTATION IN ANALYTICAL CHEMISTRY.
Elsevier Science B.V., Books Division, P.O. Box 211, 1000 AE Amsterdam, Netherlands. TEL 31-20-4853911. FAX 31-20-4853705. *1798*

TECHNIQUES IN ORTHOPAEDICS.
Lippincott - Raven Publishers, 227 Washington Sq., Philadelphia, PA 19106. TEL 215-238-4200. FAX 215-238-4227. *5017*

TECHNIQUES IN THE BEHAVIORAL AND NEURAL SCIENCES.
Elsevier Science B.V., Books Division, P.O. Box 211, 1000 AE Amsterdam, Netherlands. TEL 31-20-4853911. FAX 31-20-4853705. *5099*

TECHNIQUES IN UROLOGY.
Lippincott - Raven Publishers, 227 E. Washington Sq., Philadelphia, PA 19106. TEL 215-238-4200. FAX 215-238-4227. *5165*

TECHNIQUES OF CHEMISTRY.
John Wiley & Sons, Inc., 605 Third Ave., New York, NY 10158. TEL 212-850-6000. FAX 212-850-6088. *1768*

TECHNIQUES OF PHYSICS.
Academic Press, Inc., 525 B St., Ste. 1900, San Diego, CA 92101-4495. TEL 619-231-0926. FAX 619-699-6715. *5829*

TECHNISCHE UNIVERSITEIT EINDHOVEN. FACULTEIT DER WISKUNDE EN INFORMATICA. E U T REPORTS - W S K.
Technische Universiteit Eindhoven, Faculteit der Wiskunden Informatica, Postbus 513, 5600 MB Eindhoven, Netherlands. *4610*

TECHNOLOGICAL FORECASTING AND SOCIAL CHANGE.
Elsevier Science Inc., Box 945, New York, NY 10159-0945. TEL 212-633-3730. FAX 212-633-3680. *6976*

TECHNOLOGY ANALYSIS & STRATEGIC MANAGEMENT.
Carfax Publishing Co., P.O. Box 25, Abingdon, Oxon. OX14 3UE, England. TEL 44-1235-401000. FAX 44-1235-401550. *6977*

TECHNOLOGY AND CULTURE.
University of Chicago Press, Journals Division, Box 37005, Chicago, IL 60637. TEL 773-753-3347. FAX 773-753-0811. *6977*

TECHNOLOGY AND DISABILITY.
Elsevier Science Ireland Ltd., P.O. Box 85, Limerick, Ireland. TEL 353-61-471944. FAX 353-61-472144. *3458*

TECHNOLOGY AND HEALTH CARE.
I O S Press, Van Diemenstraat 94, 1013 CN Amsterdam, Netherlands. TEL 31-20-6382189. FAX 31-20-6203419. *4750*

TECHNOLOGY FOR ALASKAN TRANSPORTATION.
Alaska Transportation Technology Transfer Program, DOT & PF T2 Program, 2301 Peger Rd., Fairbanks, AK 99709-5399. TEL 907-451-5320. FAX 907-451-2313. *7040*

TECHNOLOGY FOR ANESTHESIA.
E C R I, 5200 Butler Pike, Plymouth Meeting, PA 19462. TEL 610-825-6000. FAX 610-834-1275. *4808*

TECHNOLOGY FOR CARDIOLOGY.
E C R I, 5200 Butler Pike, Plymouth Meeting, PA 19462. TEL 610-825-6000. FAX 610-834-1275. *4824*

TECHNOLOGY FOR CRITICAL CARE NURSES.
E C R I, 5200 Butler Pike, Plymouth Meeting, PA 19462. TEL 610-825-6000. FAX 610-834-1274. *4950*

TECHNOLOGY FOR EMERGENCY CARE NURSES.
E C R I, 5200 Butler Pike, Plymouth Meeting, PA 19462. TEL 610-825-6000. FAX 610-834-1275. *4950*

TECHNOLOGY FOR RESPIRATORY THERAPY.
E C R I, 5200 Butler Pike, Plymouth Meeting, PA 19462. TEL 610-825-6000. FAX 610-834-1275. *5123*

TECHNOLOGY IN SOCIETY.
Elsevier Science Ltd., Pergamon, P.O. Box 800, Kidlington, Oxford OX5 1DX, England. TEL 44-1865-843000. FAX 44-1865-843010. *6736*

TECHNOLOGY MANAGEMENT.
Gordon and Breach - Harwood Academic, Amsteldisk 166, 1st Fl., 1079 LH Amsterdam, Netherlands. *6977*

TECHNOLOGY, RISK AND SOCIETY.
Kluwer Academic Publishers, Postbus 17, 3300 AA Dordrecht, Netherlands. TEL 31-78-6392392. FAX 31-78-6392254. *1313*

TECHNOLOGY TRANSFER SOCIETY. INTERNATIONAL SYMPOSIUM PROCEEDINGS.
Technology Transfer Society, 435 N. Michigan Ave., Chicago, IL 60611-4001. TEL 317-738-3908. FAX 317-738-3908. *1509*

TECHNOMETRICS.
American Statistical Association, 1429 Duke St., Alexandria, VA 22314-3415. TEL 703-684-1221. FAX 703-684-2037. *2742*

TECHNOVATION.
Elsevier Science Ltd., P.O. Box 800, Kidlington, Oxford OX5 1DX, England. TEL 44-1865-843000. FAX 44-1865-843010. *6978*

TECHTRENDS.
Association for Educational Communications and Technology, 1025 Vermont Ave., N.W., Ste. 820, Washington, DC 20005-3516. TEL 202-347-7834. FAX 202-347-7839. *2622*

TECNOLOGIA DE ALIMENTOS.
Asociacion de Tecnologos Alimentos de Mexico, Mar del Norte 5, San Alvaro, Atzcapotzalco, 02090 Mexico DF, Mexico. TEL 525-3861368. FAX 525-3861952. *3129*

TECNOLOGIA Y CONSTRUCCION.
Instituto de Desarrollo Experimental de la Construccion, Apdo. Postal 47169, Caracas 1041-A, Venezuela. TEL 58-2-6931269. FAX 58-2-6931183. *915*

TECTONOPHYSICS.
Elsevier Science B.V., P.O. Box 211, 1000 AE Amsterdam, Netherlands. TEL 31-20-4853911. FAX 57-20-4853598. *2391*

TEHUDA.
Weizman Institute of Science, Department of Science Teaching, Rehovot 76100, Israel. TEL 972-8-9342981. FAX 972-8-9344174. *5829*

TEKI HISTORYCZNE.
Polish Historical Society in Great Britain, 20 Princes Gate, London SW7 1QA, England. *3607*

TEKNIK DERGI.
Turkish Chamber of Civil Engineers, Selanik Caddesi 19-1, Kizilay 06650 Ankara, Turkey. TEL 90-312-4337626. FAX 90-312-4170632. *2799*

TELECOMMUNICATION JOURNAL OF AUSTRALIA.
Telecommunication Society of Australia Ltd., P.O. Box 4050, Melbourne, Vic. 3001, Australia. TEL 61-3-96390906. FAX 61-3-96391515. *2005*

TELECOMMUNICATIONS POLICY.
Elsevier Science Ltd., Pergamon, P.O. Box 800, Kidlington, Oxford OX5 1DX, England. TEL 44-1865-843000. FAX 44-1865-843010. *2005*

TELEKTRONIKK.
Telenor AS, P.O. Box 83, N-2007 Kjeller, Norway. TEL 47-63-84-84-00. FAX 47-63-81-00-76. *2006*

TELEMATICS AND INFORMATICS.
Elsevier Science Ltd., Pergamon, P.O. Box 800, Kidlington, Oxford OX5 1DX, England. TEL 44-1865-843000. FAX 44-1865-843010. *2006*

TELEMEDICINE JOURNAL.
Mary Ann Liebert, Inc. Publishers, 2 Madison Ave., Larchmont, NY 10538. TEL 914-834-3100. FAX 914-834-3688. *4848*

TELETRAFFIC SCIENCE AND ENGINEERING.
Elsevier Science B.V., Books Division, P.O. Box 211, 1000 AE Amsterdam, Netherlands. TEL 31-20-4853911. FAX 31-20-4853705. *2018*

TELLUS. SERIES A: DYNAMIC METEOROLOGY AND OCEANOGRAPHY.
Munksgaard International Publishers Ltd., P.O. Box 2148, DK-1016 Copenhagen K, Denmark, Denmark. TEL 45-33-127030. FAX 45-33-129387. *2391*

TELLUS. SERIES B: CHEMICAL AND PHYSICAL METEOROLOGY.
Munksgaard International Publishers Ltd., 35 Noerre Soegade, P.O. Box 2148, DK-1016 Copenhagen K, Denmark. TEL 45-33-127030. FAX 45-33-129387. *2391*

TEMPORARY CULTURE.
Box 43072, Upper Montclair, NJ 07043-0072. *4537*

TEMPUS.
University of Queensland, Anthropology Museum, St. Lucia, Qld. 4072, Australia. TEL 61-7-33652674. FAX 61-7-33654696. *331*

TENNESSEE ACADEMY OF SCIENCE. JOURNAL.
Tennessee Academy of Science, 2001 Craven Ln., Prairie Peninsula, Hixson, TN 37343. TEL 615-251-1573. *6578*

TENNESSEE HISTORICAL QUARTERLY.
Tennessee Historical Society, War Memorial Bldg., Nashville, TN 37243. TEL 615-741-8934. FAX 615-741-8937. *3649*

TENNESSEE NURSE.
Tennessee Nurses Association, 545 Mainstream Dr., Ste. 405, Nashville, TN 37228-1201. TEL 615-254-0350. FAX 615-254-0303. *4950*

TENNESSEE REGISTER.
Diocese of Nashville, 2400 21st Ave. S, Nashville, TN 37212-5302. TEL 615-783-0770. FAX 615-292-8411. *6482*

TENNESSEE TOWN AND CITY.
Tennessee Municipal League, 226 Capitol Blvd., Nashville, TN 37219. TEL 615-255-6416. FAX 615-255-7428. *6225*

TENNESSEE WILDLIFE.
Wildlife Resources Agency, Box 40747, Nashville, TN 37204. TEL 615-781-6504. FAX 615-741-4606. *851*

TENSO.
Societe Guilhem IX, c/o Classical & Modern Languages, University of Louisville, Louisville, KY 40292. TEL 502-852-6686. FAX 502-852-8885. *4477*

TERATOGENESIS, CARCINOGENESIS, AND MUTAGENESIS.
John Wiley & Sons, Inc., Journals, 605 Third Ave., New York, NY 10158. TEL 212-850-6645. FAX 212-850-6021. *4751*

TERATOLOGY.
John Wiley & Sons, Inc., Journals, 605 Third Ave., New York, NY 10158. TEL 212-850-6645. FAX 212-850-6021. *629*

TERMINOLOGY.
John Benjamins Publishing Co., Amsteldijk 44, P.O. Box 75577, 1070 AN Amsterdam, Netherlands. TEL 31-20-6762325. FAX 31-20-6792956. *4307*

TERRA D'ESTE.
Societa Gabinetto di Lettura di Este, Piazza Maggiore n. 12, 35042 Este, Padova, Italy. TEL 39-49-4292301. FAX 39-49-4292301. *3607*

TERRA E SOLE.
IACICO S.r.L., Via A. Poliziano 80, 00184 Rome, Italy. TEL 39-6-4873183. FAX 39-6-4873144. *157*

TERRA NOVA.
Blackwell Science Ltd., Osney Mead, Oxford OX2 0EL, England. TEL 44-1865-206206. FAX 44-1865-721205. *2323*

TERRAE INCOGNITAE.
Society for the History of Discoveries, University of Texas at Arlington, Department of History, Box 19529, Arlington, TX 76019-0529. TEL 817-272-2898. FAX 817-272-2852. *3515*

TERRAIN.
Ministere de la Culture, 65 rue de Richelieu, 75002 Paris, France. TEL 33-1-40158527. FAX 33-1-40158733. *332*

TERRORISM AND POLITICAL VIOLENCE.
Frank Cass, Newbury House, 890-900 Eastern Ave., Newbury Park, Ilford, Essex IG2 7HH, England. TEL 44-181-599-8866. FAX 44-181-599-0984. *6039*

TETRAHEDRON.
Elsevier Science Ltd., Pergamon, P.O. Box 800, Kidlington, Oxford OX5 1DX, England. TEL 44-1865-843000. FAX 44-1865-843010. *1824*

TETRAHEDRON: ASYMMETRY.
Elsevier Science Ltd., Pergamon, P.O. Box 800, Kidlington, Oxford OX5 1DX, England. TEL 44-1865-843000. FAX 44-1865-843010. *1824*

TETRAHEDRON LETTERS.
Elsevier Science Ltd., Pergamon, P.O. Box 800, Kidlington, Oxford OX5 1DX, England. TEL 44-1865-843000. FAX 44-1865-843010. *1824*

TEXAS A & M UNIVERSITY. COLLEGE OF GEOSCIENCES. CONTRIBUTIONS IN OCEANOGRAPHY.
Texas A & M University, Department of Oceanography, College Sta., TX 77843. TEL 409-845-7327. FAX 409-845-6331. *2415*

TEXAS CHILD CARE.
Texas Workforce Commission, Box 162881, 101 E.. 15th St., Rm. 416T, Austin, TX 78716-2881. TEL 512-441-6633. FAX 512-441-6522. *1857*

TEXAS HEART INSTITUTE JOURNAL.
Texas Heart Institute, Publications & Communications, MC 1-194, Box 20345, Houston, TX 77225-0345. TEL 713-794-6630. FAX 713-791-3714. *4824*

TEXAS JOURNAL OF POLITICAL STUDIES.
Angelo State University, Department of Government, San Angelo, TX 76909-0896. TEL 409-294-1462. FAX 409-294-3622. *5974*

TEXAS JOURNAL OF SCIENCE.
Texas Academy of Science, c/o Texas Tech University, The Museum, Box 4499, Lubbock, TX 79409. TEL 806-742-2487. *6578*

TEXAS TALK.
Arc of Texas, 1600 W. 38th St., Austin, TX 78731. TEL 512-454-6694. FAX 512-454-4956. *3458*

TEXAS TECH LAW REVIEW.
Texas Tech University, School of Law, Lubbock, TX 79409-0004. TEL 806-742-3789. FAX 806-742-1629. *4033*

TEXAS WOMAN'S NEWS.
T W N Communications Inc., HCR 5, Box 574-46, Kerrville, TX 78028-9025. TEL 210-257-2567. FAX 210-257-2567. *7334*

TEXT AND PERFORMANCE QUARTERLY.
Speech Communication Association, 5105 Backlick Rd., Bldg. E., Annandale, VA 22003. TEL 703-750-0533. FAX 703-914-9471. *4477*

TEXT TECHNOLOGY.
Wright State University - Lake Campus, 7600 State Rt. 703, Celina, OH 45822-2952. TEL 419-586-0317. FAX 419-586-0368. *3881*

TEXTIEL BEHEER.
Stichting Vakblad Textielreiniging, Postbus 10, 4060 GA Ophmert, Netherlands. FAX 31-34-4651525. *1911*

TEXTILE CHEMIST AND COLORIST.
American Association of Textile Chemists and Colorists, One Davis Dr., Box 12215, Research Triangle Park, NC 27709-2215. TEL 919-549-8141. FAX 919-549-8933. *6995*

TEXTILE MUSEUM JOURNAL.
Textile Museum, 2320 S St., N.W., Washington, DC 20008. TEL 202-667-0441. FAX 202-483-0994. *6996*

TEXTILE RESEARCH JOURNAL.
Textile Research Institute, 601 Prospect Ave., Box 625, Princeton, NJ 08542. TEL 609-924-3150. FAX 609-683-7836. *6997*

TEXTILE SCIENCE AND TECHNOLOGY.
Elsevier Science B.V., Books Division, P.O. Box 211, 1000 AE Amsterdam, Netherlands. TEL 31-20-4853911. FAX 31-20-4853705. *6997*

TEXTO Y ESPECTACULO.
Spanish Literature Publications Co., Inc., Box 707, York, SC 29745. TEL 803-366-9763. *4478*

TEXTS ON COMPUTATIONAL MECHANICS.
Elsevier Science B.V., Books Division, P.O. Box 211, 1000 AE Amsterdam, Netherlands. TEL 31-20-4853911. FAX 31-20-4853705. *2901*

TEXTUAL STUDIES IN CANADA.
University College of the Cariboo, English Department, Box 3010, Kamloops, BC V2C 5N3, Canada. TEL 604-828-5000. FAX 604-828-5086. *4362*

TEXTURE.
Texture Press, 3760 Cedar Ridge Dr., Norman, OK 73072. TEL 405-366-7730. FAX 405-364-3627. *4525*

TEXTURES AND MICROSTRUCTURES.
Gordon and Breach - Harwood Academic, Amsteldisk 166, 1st Fl., 1079 LH Amsterdam, Netherlands. *2372*

THALIA.
Association for the Study of Humor, c/o Jacqueline Tavernier-Courbin, Ed., Dept. of English, University of Ottawa, Ottawa, ON K1N 6N5, Canada. TEL 613-230-9505. FAX 613-565-5786. *4478*

THEATRE ANNUAL.
College of William and Mary, Department of Theatre and Speech, Williamsburg, VA 23187. TEL 804-221-2668. FAX 804-221-1287. *7015*

THEATRE HISTORY STUDIES.
Mid-America Theatre Association, Theatre Program, Central College, Pella, IA 50219. TEL 515-628-5234. FAX 515-628-5316. *7016*

THEATRE STUDIES.
Ohio State University, Theatre Research Institute, 1430 Lincoln Tower, 1800 Cannon Dr., Columbus, OH 43210. TEL 614-292-6614. FAX 614-292-3222. *7016*

THEATRE SURVEY.
American Society for Theatre Research, c/o Gordon Armstrong, Sec., Dept. of Fine Arts Ctr., Univ. of Rhode Island, Kingston, RI 02881-0824. *7016*

REFEREED SERIALS

THEATRE TOPICS.
Johns Hopkins University Press, Journals Publishing Division, 2715 N. Charles St., Baltimore, MD 21218. TEL 410-516-6987. FAX 410-516-6968. *7017*

THEMIS.
Zeta Tau Alpha, International Office, 3450 Founders Rd., Indianapolis, IN 46268. TEL 317-872-0540. FAX 371-876-3948. *1974*

THEOLOGICAL STUDIES.
Theological Studies, Inc., Georgetown University, 37th and O Sts., N.W., Washington, DC 20057. TEL 202-338-0754. FAX 202-687-7679. *6377*

THEOLOGY AND MEDICINE.
Kluwer Academic Publishers, Postbus 17, 3300 AA Dordrecht, Netherlands. TEL 31-78-6392392. FAX 31-78-6392254. *6378*

THEOLOGY & PUBLIC POLICY.
Churches' Center for Theology and Public Policy, 4500 Massachusetts Ave. N.W., Washington, DC 20016-5690. TEL 202-885-8648. *6378*

THEORETICAL AND APPLIED FRACTURE MECHANICS.
Elsevier Science B.V., P.O. Box 211, 1000 AE Amsterdam, Netherlands. TEL 31-20-4853911. FAX 31-20-4853598. *5849*

THEORETICAL AND EXPERIMENTAL BIOLOGY.
Academic Press, Inc., 525 B St., Ste. 1900, San Diego, CA 92101-4495. TEL 619-231-0962. FAX 619-699-6715. *629*

THEORETICAL AND EXPERIMENTAL CHEMISTRY.
Plenum Publishing Corp., Consultants Bureau, 233 Spring St., New York, NY 10013-1578. TEL 212-620-8468. FAX 212-463-0742. *1769*

THEORETICAL AND MATHEMATICAL PHYSICS.
Plenum Publishing Corp., Consultants Bureau, 233 Spring St., New York, NY 10013-1578. TEL 212-620-8468. FAX 212-463-0742. *5830*

THEORETICAL CHEMISTRY.
Academic Press, Inc., 525 B St., Ste. 1900, San Diego, CA 92101-4495. TEL 619-231-0926. FAX 619-699-6715. *1769*

THEORETICAL COMPUTER SCIENCE.
North-Holland, P.O. Box 211, 1000 AE Amsterdam, Netherlands. TEL 31-20-4853911. FAX 31-20-4853598. *2221*

THEORETICAL FOUNDATIONS OF CHEMICAL ENGINEERING.
Maik Nauka - Interperiodica, Mezhdunarodnyi Otdel, Ul. Profsoyuznaya, 90, 117864 Moscow, Russia. TEL 7-095-3360066. FAX 7-095-3360666. *2774*

THEORETICAL MEDICINE.
Kluwer Academic Publishers, Postbus 17, 3300 AA Dordrecht, Netherlands. TEL 31-78-6392392. FAX 31-78-6392254. *4751*

THEORETICAL POPULATION BIOLOGY.
Academic Press, Inc., Journal Division, 525 B St., Ste. 1900, San Diego, CA 92101-4495. TEL 619-230-1840. FAX 619-699-6800. *629*

THEORIA.
Berghahn Books Inc., 165 Taber Ave., Providence, RI 02906. TEL 401-861-9330. FAX 401-521-0046. *3794*

THEORIA.
Centro de Analisis, Logica e Informatica Juridica, Universidad del Pais Vasco, Servicio Editorial, Apdo. 1397, 48080 Bilbao, Spain. TEL 34-43-291725. FAX 34-4-4801314. *5755*

THEORY AND APPLICATIONS OF TRANSPORT IN POROUS MEDIA.
Kluwer Academic Publishers, Postbus 17, 3300 AA Dordrecht, Netherlands. TEL 31-78-6392392. FAX 31-78-6392254. *5830*

THEORY AND APPLICATONS OF CATEGORIES.
Mount Allison University, Department of Mathematics and Science, *4611*

THEORY AND DECISION.
Kluwer Academic Publishers, Postbus 17, 3300 AA Dordrecht, Netherlands. TEL 31-78-6392392. FAX 31-78-6392254. *6642*

THEORY AND DECISION LIBRARY. SERIES A: PHILOSOPHY AND METHODOLOGY OF THE SOCIAL SCIENCES.
Kluwer Academic Publishers, Postbus 17, 3300 AA Dordrecht, Netherlands. TEL 31-78-6392392. FAX 31-78-6392254. *6642*

THEORY AND DECISION LIBRARY. SERIES B: MATHEMATICAL AND STATISTICAL METHODS.
Kluwer Academic Publishers, Postbus 17, 3300 AA Dordrecht, Netherlands. TEL 31-78-6392392. FAX 31-78-6392254. *4611*

THEORY AND DECISION LIBRARY. SERIES C: GAME THEORY, MATHEMATICAL PROGRAMMING AND OPERATIONS RESEARCH.
Kluwer Academic Publishers, Postbus 17, 3300 AA Dordrecht, Netherlands. TEL 31-78-6392392. FAX 31-78-6392254. *4624*

THEORY AND DECISION LIBRARY. SERIES D: SYSTEM THEORY, KNOWLEDGE ENGINEERING AND PROBLEM SOLVING.
Kluwer Academic Publishers, Postbus 17, 3300 AA Dordrecht, Netherlands. TEL 31-78-6392392. FAX 31-78-6392254. *2164*

THEORY & PRACTICE OF OBJECT BASED SYSTEMS.
John Wiley & Sons, Inc., Journals, 605 Third Ave., New York, NY 10158. TEL 212-850-6645. FAX 212-850-6021. *2104*

THEORY & PSYCHOLOGY.
Sage Publications Ltd., 6 Bonhill St., London EC2A 4PU, England. TEL 44-171-374-0645. FAX 44-171-374-8741. *6156*

THEORY AND RESEARCH IN BEHAVIORAL PEDIATRICS.
Plenum Publishing Corp., 233 Spring St., New York, NY 10013-1578. TEL 202-620-8000. FAX 212-463-0742. *6156*

THEORY AND SOCIETY.
Kluwer Academic Publishers, Postbus 17, 3300 AA Dordrecht, Netherlands. TEL 31-78-6392392. FAX 31-78-6392254. *6736*

THEORY, CULTURE & SOCIETY.
Sage Publications Ltd., 6 Bonhill St., London EC2A 4PU, England. TEL 44-171-374-0645. FAX 44-171-374-8741. *6736*

THEORY INTO PRACTICE.
Ohio State University, College of Education, 172 Arps Hall, 1945 N. High St., Columbus, OH 43210-1172. TEL 614-292-3407. FAX 614-688-3942. *2488*

THEORY OF COMPUTING SYSTEMS.
Springer-Verlag, Science Journals, 175 Fifth Ave., New York, NY 10010. TEL 212-460-1500. FAX 212-473-6272. *2221*

THEORY OF PROBABILITY AND ITS APPLICATIONS.
Society for Industrial and Applied Mathematics, 3600 University City Science Center, Philadelphia, PA 19104-2688. TEL 215-382-9800. FAX 215-386-7999. *4611*

THEOSOPHICAL HISTORY.
c/o Department of Religious Studies, California State University, Box 6868, Fullerton, CA 92634-6868. TEL 714-773-3727. FAX 714-693-0142. *3515*

THEOSOPHY IN AUSTRALIA.
Theosophical Society in Australia, 484 Kent St., Sydney, N.S.W. 2000, Australia. TEL 61-2-92647056. FAX 61-2-92645857. *6498*

THERAPEUTIC DRUG MONITORING.
Lippincott - Raven Publishers, 227 E. Washington Sq., Philadelphia, PA 19106. TEL 215-238-4200. FAX 215-238-4227. *5695*

THERAPEUTIC IMMUNOLOGY.
Blackwell Science Ltd., Osney Mead, Oxford OX2 0EL, England. TEL 44-1865-206206. FAX 44-1865-721205. *4801*

THERIOGENOLOGY.
Elsevier Science Inc., Box 945, New York, NY 10159-0945. TEL 212-633-3730. FAX 212-633-3680. *7279*

THERMOCHIMICA ACTA.
Elsevier Science B.V., P.O. Box 211, 1000 AE Amsterdam, Netherlands. TEL 31-20-4853911. FAX 31-20-4853598. *1836*

THERMODYNAMICS AT TEXAS A & M.
Thermodynamics Research Center, Texas Engineering Experiment Station, Texas A & M University System, College Station, TX 77843. TEL 409-845-4940. FAX 409-847-8590. *1836*

THERMOPHYSICAL PROPERTIES.
Nihon Netsu Bussei Gakkai, Nagaoka Gijutsu Kagaku Daigaku, Kikaikei, 1603 Kamitomioka-cho, Nagaoka-shi, Niigata-ken 940-21, Japan. TEL 81-258-46-6000. FAX 81-258-46-6972. *5843*

THETA.
Crewe & Alsager Faculty of M M U, Crewe, Ches. CW1 1DU, England. TEL 44-161-247-5089. FAX 44-161-247-6370. *4611*

THIN FILMS SCIENCE AND TECHNOLOGY.
Elsevier Science B.V., Books Division, P.O. Box 211, 1000 AE Amsterdam, Netherlands. TEL 31-20-4853911. FAX 31-20-4853705. *5830*

THIN SOLID FILMS.
Elsevier Science S.A., P.O. Box 564, CH-1001 Lausanne 1, Switzerland. TEL 41-21-3207381. FAX 41-21-3235444. *5830*

THIN-WALLED STRUCTURES.
Elsevier Science Ltd., P.O. Box 800, Kidlington, Oxford OX5 1DX, England. TEL 44-1865-843000. FAX 44-1865-843010. *2901*

THE THIRD ALTERNATIVE.
T T A Press, 5 Martins Ln., Witcham, Ely, Cambs. CB6 2LB, England. TEL 44-1353-777931. *4537*

THIRD TEXT.
Kala Press, P.O. Box 3509, London NW6 3PJ, England. TEL 44-171-372-0826. *469*

THIRD WORLD LEGAL STUDIES (YEAR).
International Third World Legal Studies Association, c/o Valparaiso University, School of Law, Valparaiso, IN 46383. TEL 219-465-7830. FAX 219-465-7917. *4126*

THIRD WORLD QUARTERLY.
Carfax Publishing Co., P.O. Box 25, Abingdon, Oxon. OX14 3UE, England. TEL 44-1235-401000. FAX 44-1235-401550. *1368*

THIRTIETH DISTRICT DENTAL SOCIETY, FRESNO, CALIFORNIA. BULLETIN.
Fresno-Madera Dental Society, 371 E. Bullard Ave., Ste. 120, Fresno, CA 93710-5217. TEL 209-438-7284. FAX 209-438-7287. *4872*

THOMAS HARDY JOURNAL.
Thomas Hardy Society Ltd., c/o Simon Curtis, Ed., 25 Hawthorn Grove, Heaton Moor, Stockport SK4 4HZ, England. TEL 44-161-4329075. *4478*

THOMAS HARDY YEAR BOOK.
Toucan Press, The White Cottage, Rue de Carteret, Castel, Guernsey, Channel Islands. TEL 44-1481-57017. *4478*

THOMAS WOLFE REVIEW.
Thomas Wolfe Society, c/o Terry Roberts, Ed., Box 636, Chapel Hill, NC 27514. TEL 919-929-1828. *4479*

THOMIST.
Thomist Press, 487 Michigan Ave., N.E., Washington, DC 20017. TEL 202-529-5300. FAX 202-636-4460. *6483*

THOMSON'S CONSTRUCTION AUSTRALIA.
Thomson Business Publishing, 47 Chippen St., Chippendale, N.S.W. 2008, Australia. TEL 02-699-2411. FAX 02-698-3920. *916*

THORAX.
B M J Publishing Group, B.M.A. House, Tavistock Sq., London WC1H 9JR, England. TEL 44-171-383-6270. FAX 44-171-383-6402. *4752*

THOUGHTS FOR ALL SEASONS.
Valley Press, 478 N.E. 56th St., Miami, FL 33137-2621. TEL 305-756-8800. *4479*

THRESHOLDS IN EDUCATION.
Thresholds in Education Foundation, 427 Graham St., Dekalb, IL 60115-3078. TEL 815-753-9357. FAX 815-753-8750. *2488*

THROMBOSIS RESEARCH.
Elsevier Science Ltd., Pergamon, P.O. Box 800, Kidlington, Oxford OX5 1DX, England. TEL 44-1865-843000. FAX 44-1865-843010. *4824*

THUNDER BAY HISTORICAL MUSEUM SOCIETY. PAPERS AND RECORDS.
Thunder Bay Historical Museum Society, 425 Donald St., E., Thunder Bay, ON P7E 5V1, Canada. TEL 807-623-0801. FAX 807-622-6880. *3649*

THYMUS.
Kluwer Academic Publishers, Postbus 17, 3300 AA Dordrecht, Netherlands. TEL 31-78-6392392. FAX 31-78-6392254. *4801*

THYMUS UPDATE.
Gordon and Breach - Harwood Academic, Amsteldisk 166, 1st Fl., 1079 LH Amsterdam, Netherlands. *4801*

TIANJIN DAXUE XUEBAO.
Tianjin Daxue, Qilitai, Nankai Qu, Tianjin 300072, People's Republic of China. TEL 022-3359116. FAX 022-3358706. *6578*

TIANJIN FANGZHI GONGXUEYUAN XUEBAO.
Tianjin Fangzhi Gongxueyuan, 63 Chenglinzhuang Rd., Tianjin 300160, People's Republic of China. TEL 86-22-4344477. FAX 86-22-4344572. *6997*

TIANJIN UNIVERSITY. TRANSACTIONS.
Tianjin Daxue, Qilitai, Nankai Qu, Tianjin 300072, People's Republic of China. TEL 022-3359116. FAX 022-3358706. *6579*

TIANRANQI GONGYE.
Tianranqi Gongye Zazhishe, No.3, Sec. 1, Fuqing Lu, Chengdu, Sichuan 610051, People's Republic of China. TEL 86-28-3324911. FAX 86-28-3358727. *5625*

TIANTI WULI XUEBAO.
Science Press, Marketing and Sales Department, 16 Donghuangchenggen North St., Beijing 100717, People's Republic of China. TEL 4010642. FAX 4019810. *502*

TIANWEN XUEBAO.
Science Press, Marketing and Sales Department, 16 Donghuangchenggen North St., Beijing 100717, People's Republic of China. TEL 4010642. FAX 4019810. *502*

TIANWENXUE JINZHAN.
Science Press, Marketing and Sales Department, 16 Donghuangchenggen North St., Beijing 100717, People's Republic of China. TEL 4010642. FAX 4019810. *502*

TIDSSKRIFT FOR SOEVAESEN.
Soe-Lieutenant-Selskabet, Overgaden oven Vandet 62B, DK-1415 Copenhagen K, Denmark. TEL 45-32-95-99-54. FAX 45-32-95-99-53. *5287*

THE TIE (SCHAUMBURG).
College of Chaplains, Inc., 1701 E. Woodfield Rd., Ste. 311, Schaumburg, IL 60173. FAX 847-240-1015. *6378*

TIEDAO YIXUE.
Nanjing Tiedao Yixueyuan, 87 Dingjiaqiao, Nanjing, Jiangsu 210009, People's Republic of China. TEL 3301508. FAX 3317073. *4752*

TIJDSCHRIFT LANDINRICHTING.
Stichting Tijdschrift Landinrichting, P.O. Box 20021, 3502 LA Utrecht, Netherlands. TEL 31-30-858722. FAX 31-30-858999. *247*

TIJDSCHRIFT VOOR FERTILITEITSONDERZOEK.
Excerpta Medica Medical Communications b.v., P.O. Box 1126, 1000 BC Amsterdam, Netherlands. TEL 31-20-5159457. FAX 31-20-5159407. *4968*

TIJDSCHRIFT VOOR GENEESKUNDE.
Tijdschrift voor Geneeskunde A.S.B.L., De-Pintelaan 185, 9000 Ghent, Belgium. TEL 32-9-2403330. FAX 32-9-2403390. *4752*

TIJDSCHRIFT VOOR INTEGRALE GENEESKUNDE.
Stichting Tijdschrift voor Integrale Geneeskunde, Tooropstraat 181, 6521 NM Nijmegen, Netherlands. TEL 31-80-601688. *299*

TIJDSCHRIFT VOOR MEDISCHE INFORMATICA.
Vereniging voor Medische en Biologische Informatieverwerking, c/o Erasmus University EE2116, Postbus 1738, 3000 DR Rotterdam, Netherlands. FAX 31-10-4362882. *4848*

TIJDSCHRIFT VOOR NUCLEAIRE GENEESKUNDE.
Stichting ter Bevordering van de Nucleaire Geneeskunde, c/o Paula A. Boeijen, Ouderkerkerdijk 37, 1096 CR Amsterdam, Netherlands. TEL 31-20-6657723. FAX 31-20-6636494. *5116*

TIJDSCHRIFT VOOR OUDE MUZIEK.
Organisatie Oude Muziek, Postbus 734, 3500 AS Utrecht, Netherlands. TEL 31-30-2362236. FAX 31-30-2322798. *5441*

TIJDSCHRIFT VOOR RECHTSGESCHIEDENIS.
Kluwer Law International, Postbus 85889, 2508 CN The Hague, Netherlands. TEL 31-70-3081500. FAX 31-70-3081515. *4034*

TIJDSCHRIFT VOOR SEKSUOLOGIE.
Stichting Tijdschrift voor Seksuologie, Postbus 1738, 3000 DR Rotterdam, Netherlands. *4752*

TIJDSCHRIFT VOOR SOCIALE GEZONDHEIDSZORG.
Stichting Journals for Public Health and Science, Admiraal Helfrichlaan 1, 3527 KV Utrecht, Netherlands. TEL 31-30-2913252. FAX 31-30-2913242. *4752*

TIJDSCHRIFT VOOR THEOLOGIE.
Uitgeverij S U N, Postbus 1609, 6501 BP Nijmegen, Netherlands. TEL 31-24-3221700. FAX 31-24-3235493. *6483*

TIME & SOCIETY.
Sage Publications Ltd., 6 Bonhill St., London EC2A 4PU, England. TEL 44-171-374-0645. FAX 44-171-374-8741. *6736*

TIROLER LANDESMUSEUM FERDINANDEUM, INNSBRUCK. VEROEFFENTLICHUNGEN.
Tiroler Landesmuseum Ferdinandeum, Museumstr. 15, A-6020 Innsbruck, Austria. TEL 43-512-59489. FAX 43-512-5948988. *5367*

TISSUE & CELL.
Churchill Livingstone, Robert Stevenson House, 1-3 Baxter's Pl., Leith Walk, Edinburgh EH1 3AF, Scotland. TEL 44-131-556-2424. FAX 44-131-535-1704. *744*

TISSUE ANTIGENS.
Munksgaard International Publishers Ltd., 35 Noerre Soegade, P.O. Box 2148, DK-1016 Copenhagen K, Denmark. TEL 45-33-127030. FAX 45-33-129387. *4752*

TISSUE ENGINEERING.
Mary Ann Liebert, Inc. Publishers, 2 Madison Ave., Larchmont, NY 10538. TEL 914-834-3100. FAX 914-834-3688. *744*

TO MATSAKONI.
c/o John Giannopoulos, 3, Samara Str., Patissia, 11144 Athens, Greece. *6736*

TOBACCO CONTROL.
B M J Publishing Group, B.M.A. House, Tavistock Sq., London WC1H 9JR, England. TEL 44-171-383-6270. FAX 44-171-383-6402. *7021*

TODAY'S C P A.
Texas Society of C P A's, 14860 Montfort Dr., Ste. 150, Dallas, TX 75240-6718. TEL 214-689-6000. FAX 214-689-6046. *1099*

TODAY'S CHRISTIAN DOCTOR.
Christian Medical & Dental Society, 501 Fifth St., King Bldg., 3rd Fl., Bristol, TN 37620. TEL 615-844-1000. FAX 615-844-1005. *4752*

TODAY'S F D A.
Florida Dental Association, 1111 E. Tennessee St., Tallahassee, FL 32308-6914. TEL 850-681-3629. FAX 850-561-0504. *4872*

TODAY'S GROCER.
Florida Grocer Publications, Inc., Box 430760, S. Miami, FL 33243-0760. TEL 305-441-1138. FAX 305-661-6720. *3145*

TODAY'S LIFE SCIENCE.
Reed Business Publishing Pty. Ltd., P.O. Box 5487, W. Chatswood, N.S.W. 2057, Australia. TEL 61-2-699-2411. FAX 61-2-698-3920. *6579*

TOHKAI SEIKEI GEKA GAISHO KENKYU KAISHI.
Tohkai Seikei Geka Gaisho Kenkyukai, Gifu Kenritsu Tajimi Byoin Seikei Geka, 5-161, Maebatacho, Tajimi-shi, Gifu-ken 507, Japan. TEL 81-572-22-5311. FAX 81-572-25-1246. *5017*

TOHKAI SEKITSUI GEKA.
Tohkai Sekitsui Geka Kenkyukai, Gifu Kenritsu Tajimi Byoin, 5-161, Maebatacho, Tajimi-shi, Gifuken 507, Japan. TEL 81-572-22-5311. FAX 81-572-25-1246. *5017*

TOHO UNIVERSITY MEDICAL SOCIETY. JOURNAL.
Toho University Medical Society, c/o Library, School of Medicine, 5-21-16 Omori Nishi, Ota-ku, Tokyo 143, Japan. TEL 81-3762-4151. FAX 81-3764-1642. *4753*

TOHOKU MATHEMATICAL JOURNAL.
Tohoku Daigaku, Suugaku Kyoshitsu, Aramaki aza Aoba, Aoba-ku, Sendai-shi, Miyagi-ken 980-77, Japan. FAX 81-22-217-6400. *4611*

TOHOKU NO NOGYO KISHO.
Nihon Nogyo Kisho Gakkai, Tohoku Shibu, Norin Suisansho Tohoku Nogyo Shikenjo, 4 Akahira, Shimokuriyagawa, Morioka-shi, Iwate-ken 020-01, Japan. TEL 81-196-43-3461. FAX 81-196-41-7794. *5244*

TOKUSHIMA JOURNAL OF EXPERIMENTAL MEDICINE.
Tokushima Daigaku, Igakubu, 18-15 Kuramoto-cho 3-chome, Tokushima-shi, Tokushima-ken 770, Japan. TEL 81-886-33-7081. FAX 81-886-33-7082. *4903*

TOKYO DAIGAKU TEOIN SENTA DAYORI.
Tokyo Daigaku, Teion Senta, 11-16, Yayoi 2-chome, Bunkyo-ku, Tokyo 113, Japan. TEL 81-3-3812-2111. FAX 81-3-3815-8389. *5843*

TOKYO JOSHI IKA DAIGAKU ZASSHI.
Tokyo Joshi Ika Daigaku Gakkai, c/o Library, 8-1 Kawada-cho, Shinjuku-ku, Tokyo 162, Japan. TEL 81-3-3353-8111. *4753*

TOKYO METROPOLITAN UNIVERSITY. BULLETIN OF NATURAL HISTORY.
Tokyo Toritsu Daigaku, Rigakubu, 1-1, Minami-osawa, Hachioji-shi, Tokyo 192-03, Japan. *6579*

TOLEDO MEDICINE.
Academy of Medicine of Toledo and Lucas County, 4428 Secor Rd., Toledo, OH 43623. TEL 419-473-3200. FAX 419-475-6744. *4753*

TONGJI MEDICAL UNIVERSITY. JOURNAL.
Tongji Medical University, c/o Prof. Liu Xunfang, Wuhan, Hubei 430030, People's Republic of China. TEL 01-506-6688. FAX 01-506-3101. *4753*

TOP RAIL.
B L A Group Ltd., 5-8 Hardwick St., London EC1R 4RB, England. TEL 44-171-278-7603. FAX 44-171-278-6246. *7239*

TOPICS (CAMBRIDGE).
E R Consultants, Compass House, 80 Newmarket Rd., Cambridge CB5 8DZ, England. TEL 01223-315944. FAX 01223-322565. *1455*

TOPICS IN CATALYSIS.
Baltzer Science Publishers B.V., P.O. Box 221, 1400 AE Bussum, Netherlands. TEL 31-20-6370061. FAX 31-20-6323651. *1769*

TOPICS IN CHEMICAL ENGINEERING.
Gordon and Breach - Harwood Academic, Amsteldisk 166, 1st Fl., 1079 LH Amsterdam, Netherlands. *2774*

REFEREED SERIALS

TOPICS IN CHEMICAL MUTAGENESIS.
Plenum Publishing Corp., 233 Spring St., New York, NY 10013-1578. TEL 212-620-8000. FAX 212-463-0742. *672*

TOPICS IN CLINICAL CHIROPRACTIC.
Aspen Publishers, Inc., 200 Orchard Ridge Dr., Gaithersburg, MD 20878. FAX 301-417-7550. *4829*

TOPICS IN COMPUTER MATHEMATICS.
Gordon and Breach - Harwood Academic, Amsteldisk 166, 1st Fl., 1079 LH Amsterdam, Netherlands. *4624*

TOPICS IN DISCRETE MATHEMATICS.
Elsevier Science B.V., Books Division, P.O. Box 211, 1000 AE Amsterdam, Netherlands. TEL 31-20-4853911. FAX 31-20-4853705. *4611*

TOPICS IN EARLY CHILDHOOD SPECIAL EDUCATION.
Pro-Ed Inc., 8700 Shoal Creek Blvd., Austin, TX 78757-6897. TEL 512-451-3246. FAX 512-451-8542. *2592*

TOPICS IN ENVIRONMENTAL HEALTH.
Elsevier Science B.V., Books Division, P.O. Box 211, 1000 AE Amsterdam, Netherlands. TEL 31-20-4853911. FAX 31-20-4853705. *630*

TOPICS IN F-ELEMENT CHEMISTRY.
Kluwer Academic Publishers, Postbus 17, 3300 AA Dordrecht, Netherlands. TEL 31-78-6392392. FAX 31-78-6392254. *1810*

TOPICS IN GASTROENTEROLOGY.
Plenum Publishing Corp., 233 Spring St., New York, NY 10013-1578. TEL 212-620-8000. FAX 212-463-0742. *4915*

TOPICS IN GEOBIOLOGY.
Plenum Publishing Corp., 233 Spring St., New York, NY 10013-1578. TEL 212-620-8000. FAX 212-463-0742. *2373*

TOPICS IN INCLUSION SCIENCE.
Kluwer Academic Publishers, Postbus 17, 3300 AA Dordrecht, Netherlands. TEL 31-78-6392392. FAX 31-78-6392254. *1824*

TOPICS IN INORGANIC AND GENERAL CHEMISTRY.
Elsevier Science B.V., Books Division, P.O. Box 211, 1000 AE Amsterdam, Netherlands. TEL 31-20-4853911. FAX 31-20-4853705. *1810*

TOPICS IN MAGNETIC RESONANCE IMAGING.
Lippincott - Raven Publishers, 227 Washington Sq., Philadelphia, PA 19106. TEL 215-238-4200. FAX 215-238-4227. *5116*

TOPICS IN MOLECULAR ORGANIZATION AND ENGINEERING.
Kluwer Academic Publishers, Postbus 17, 3300 AA Dordrecht, Netherlands. TEL 31-78-6392392. FAX 31-78-6392254. *2774*

TOPICS IN MOLECULAR PHARMACOLOGY.
Elsevier Science B.V., Books Division, P.O. Box 211, 1000 AE Amsterdam, Netherlands. TEL 31-20-4853911. FAX 31-20-4853705. *5696*

TOPICS IN NEUROSURGERY.
Kluwer Academic Publishers, Postbus 17, 3300 AA Dordrecht, Netherlands. TEL 31-78-6392392. FAX 31-78-6392254. *5100*

TOPICS IN PHILOSOPHY.
University of California Press, 2120 Berkeley Way, Berkeley, CA 94720. TEL 510-642-4247. FAX 510-643-7127. *5756*

TOPICS IN PHOTOSYNTHESIS.
Elsevier Science B.V., Books Division, P.O. Box 211, 1000 AE Amsterdam, Netherlands. TEL 31-20-4853911. FAX 31-20-4853705. *630*

TOPICS IN RENAL MEDICINE.
Kluwer Academic Publishers, Postbus 17, 3300 AA Dordrecht, Netherlands. TEL 31-78-6392392. FAX 31-78-6392254. *5165*

TOPICS IN SAFETY, RISK, RELIABILITY AND QUALITY.
Kluwer Academic Publishers, Postbus 17, 3300 AA Dordrecht, Netherlands. TEL 31-78-6392392. FAX 31-78-6392254. *5501*

TOPICS IN STEREOCHEMISTRY.
John Wiley & Sons, Inc., 605 Third Ave., New York, NY 10158. TEL 212-850-6000. FAX 212-850-6088. *1769*

TOPICS IN STROKE REHABILITATION.
Aspen Publishers, Inc., 200 Orchard Ridge Dr., Ste. 200, Gaithersburg, MD 20878. *4824*

TOPICS IN THE NEUROSCIENCES.
Kluwer Academic Publishers, Postbus 17, 3300 AA Dordrecht, Netherlands. TEL 31-78-6392392. FAX 31-78-6392254. *5100*

TOPOI.
Kluwer Academic Publishers, Postbus 17, 3300 AA Dordrecht, Netherlands. TEL 31-78-6392392. FAX 31-78-6392254. *5756*

TOPOLOGY.
Elsevier Science Ltd., Pergamon, P.O. Box 800, Kidlington, Oxford OX5 1DX, England. TEL 44-1865-843000. FAX 44-1865-843010. *4611*

TOPOLOGY AND ITS APPLICATIONS.
North-Holland, P.O. Box 211, 1000 AE Amsterdam, Netherlands. TEL 31-20-4853911. FAX 31-20-4853598. *4612*

TOPOLOGY PROCEEDINGS.
Auburn University, Mathematics Department, Auburn, AL 36830-5310. TEL 334-844-6566. FAX 334-884-6555. *4612*

TOPOSCOPE.
Lower Albany Historical Society, Box 155, Bathurst 6166, South Africa. TEL 27-464-42190. *3529*

TOR.
Societas Archaeologica Upsaliensis, Gustavianum, S-753 10 Uppsala, Sweden. TEL 46-18-18-20-76. FAX 46-18-69-62-19. *3608*

THE TORCH (VALPARAISO).
Valparaiso University, 816 Union St., Valparaiso, IN 46383. TEL 219-464-5426. *1974*

TORNIONLAAKSON VUOSIKIRJA.
Tornionlaakson Neuvosto, Vesaisenkatu 4 B, FIN-95400 Tornio, Finland. TEL 358-16-4320448. FAX 358-16-432453. *3608*

TORONTO JOURNAL OF THEOLOGY.
Wilfrid Laurier University Press, 75 University Ave. W., Waterloo, ON N2L 3C5, Canada. TEL 519-884-0710. FAX 519-725-1399. *6378*

TORQUAY NATURAL HISTORY SOCIETY, TRANSACTIONS AND PROCEEDINGS.
Torquay Natural History Society, The Museum, Babbacombe Rd., Torquay TQ1 1HG, England. TEL 44-1803-293975. FAX 44-1803-294186. *6579*

TOTAL QUALITY MANAGEMENT.
Carfax Publishing Co., P.O. Box 25, Abingdon, Oxon. OX14 3UE, England. TEL 44-1235-401000. FAX 44-1235-401550. *1510*

TOUCHSTONE (SPRING).
Touchstone Press, Box 8308, Spring, TX 77387-8308. *4525*

T'OUNG PAO.
E.J. Brill, P.O. Box 9000, 2300 PA Leiden, Netherlands. TEL 31-71-5353500. FAX 31-71-5317532. *5539*

T'OUNG PAO. MONOGRAPHIES.
E.J. Brill, P.O. Box 9000, 2300 PA Leiden, Netherlands. TEL 31-71-5353500. FAX 31-71-5317532. *5539*

TOURISM ANALYSIS.
Cognizant Communication Corporation, 3 Hartsdale Rd., Elmsford, NY 10523. TEL 914-592-7720. FAX 914-592-8981. *7240*

TOURISM ECONOMICS.
Coleridge House, 4-5 Coleridge Gardens, London NW6 3QH, England. TEL 44-171-372-2600. FAX 44-171-372-2253. *7240*

TOURISM MANAGEMENT.
Elsevier Science Ltd., Pergamon, P.O. Box 800, Kidlington, Oxford OX5 1DX, England. TEL 44-1865-843000. FAX 44-1865-843010. *7240*

TOURISTICS.
Western Australian Tourism Commission, G.P.O. Box X2261, Perth, W.A. 6001, Australia. TEL 61-9-2201700. FAX 61-9-2201735. *7241*

TOWARD AN ELECTRONIC PATIENT RECORD.
Medical Records Institute, Box 600770, Newtonville, MA 02160. TEL 617-964-3923. FAX 617-964-3926. *4848*

TOWSON STATE JOURNAL OF INTERNATIONAL AFFAIRS.
Towson State University, Department of Political Science, Baltimore, MD 21204. TEL 410-830-3526. FAX 410-830-2960. *6039*

TOXIC SUBSTANCE MECHANISMS.
Taylor & Francis Inc., 1900 Frost Rd., Ste. 101, Bristol, PA 19007-1598. TEL 215-785-5800. FAX 215-785-5515. *2981*

TOXICOLOGIC PATHOLOGY.
Society of Toxicologic Pathologists, c/o Dr. Carl L. Alden, Ed., G.D. Searle & Co., 4901 Searle Pky., Skokie, IL 60077. TEL 847-982-7379. FAX 847-982-7374. *2981*

TOXICOLOGICAL AND ENVIRONMENTAL CHEMISTRY.
Gordon and Breach - Harwood Academic, Amsteldisk 166, 1st Fl., 1079 LH Amsterdam, Netherlands. *2981*

TOXICOLOGY AND APPLIED PHARMACOLOGY.
Academic Press, Inc., Journal Division, 525 B St., Ste. 1900, San Diego, CA 92101-4495. TEL 619-230-1840. FAX 619-699-6800. *2981*

TOXICOLOGY AND INDUSTRIAL HEALTH.
Princeton Scientific Publishing Co., Inc., Box 2155, Princeton, NJ 08543. TEL 609-683-4750. FAX 609-683-0838. *2982*

TOXICOLOGY IN VITRO.
Elsevier Science Ltd., Pergamon, P.O. Box 800, Kidlington, Oxford OX5 1DX, England. TEL 44-1865-843000. FAX 44-1865-843010. *2982*

TOXICOLOGY LETTERS.
Elsevier Science Ireland Ltd., P.O. Box 85, Limerick, Ireland. TEL 353-61-471944. FAX 353-61-472144. *2982*

TOXICOLOGY METHODS.
Taylor & Francis Inc., 1900 Frost Rd., Ste. 101, Bristol, PA 19007-1598. TEL 215-785-5800. FAX 215-785-5515. *2982*

TOXICON.
Elsevier Science Ltd., Pergamon, P.O. Box 800, Kidlington, Oxford OX5 1DX, England. TEL 44-1865-843000. FAX 44-1865-843010. *5696*

TOYODA KOKI KOKAI GIHO.
Toyoda Koki K.K., Chiteki Zaisanbu, 1-1, Asahi-cho, Kariya-shi, Aichi-ken 448, Japan. TEL 81-566-25-5272. FAX 81-566-25-5489. *2901*

TRACE METALS IN THE ENVIRONMENT.
Elsevier Science B.V., Books Division, P.O. Box 211, 1000 AE Amsterdam, Netherlands. TEL 31-20-4853911. FAX 31-20-4853705. *2982*

TRACE SUBSTANCES IN ENVIRONMENTAL HEALTH.
Science Reviews Ltd., 18 Oaklands Gate, Northwood, Mddx. HA6 3AA, England. TEL 44-1923-823586. FAX 44-1923-825066. *2982*

TRACES OF INDIANA AND MIDWESTERN HISTORY.
Indiana Historical Society, 315 W. Ohio, Indianapolis, IN 46202-3299. TEL 317-232-1878. FAX 317-233-3109. *3649*

TRADITIONAL DWELLINGS AND SETTLEMENTS REVIEW.
International Association for the Study of Traditional Environments, Center for Environmental Design Research, 390 Wurster Hall, Department of Architecture, University of California, Berkeley, CA 94720-1839. TEL 510-642-2896. FAX 510-643-5571. *416*

TRAITEMENT DU SIGNAL.
Groupe de Recherche et d'Etude de Traitement du Signal et des Images (GRETSI), B.P. 46, 38402 Saint-Martin d'Heres, France. TEL 33-4-76826274. FAX 33-4-76826384. *5830*

TRAJECTA.
Postbus 9100, 6500 HA Nijmegen, Netherlands. *6483*

TRAMES.
Teaduste Akadeemia Kirjastus, Estonia pst.7, 0001 Tallinn, Estonia. TEL 372-2-454156. FAX 372-6-466026. *6642*

TRANSAFRICAN JOURNAL OF HISTORY.
Gideon S. Were Press, P.O. Box 10622, Nairobi, Kenya. TEL 254-2-331135. FAX 254-2-331135. *3515*

TRANSCULTURAL PSYCHIATRY.
Sage Publications Ltd., 6 Bonhill St., London EC2A 4PU, England. TEL 44-171-374-0645. FAX 44-171-374-8741. *5100*

TRANSFORMATION OF THE CLASSICAL HERITAGE.
University of California Press, 2120 Berkeley Way, Berkeley, CA 94720. TEL 510-642-4247. FAX 510-613-7127. *1908*

TRANSFUSION MEDICINE.
Blackwell Science Ltd., Osney Mead, Oxford OX2 0EL, England. TEL 44-1865-206206. FAX 44-1865-721205. *4922*

TRANSFUSION SCIENCE.
Elsevier Science Ltd., Pergamon, P.O. Box 800, Kidlington, Oxford OX5 1DX, England. TEL 44-1865-843000. FAX 44-1865-843010. *4922*

TRANSGENIC RESEARCH.
Chapman & Hall, Journals Department 2-6 Boundary Row, London SE1 8HN, England. TEL 44-171-8650066. FAX 44-171-5229623. *777*

TRANSGRESSIONS.
University of Newcastle, Geography Department, Daysh Bldg., Newcastle NE1 7RU, England. TEL 44-191-222-6439. FAX 44-191-222-5421. *3761*

TRANSITION METAL CHEMISTRY.
Thomson Science, 2-6 Boundary Row, London SE1 8HN, England. TEL 44-171-8650066. FAX 44-171-5229623. *5214*

TRANSLATION AND LITERATURE.
Edinburgh University Press, 22 George Sq., Edinburgh EH8 9LF, Scotland. TEL 44-131-650-6207. FAX 44-131-662-0053. *4308*

TRANSLATION REVIEW.
American Literary Translators Association, University of Texas at Dallas, Box 830688, Richardson, TX 75083-0688. TEL 972-883-2093. FAX 972-883-6303. *4308*

TRANSLATIONS OF MATHEMATICAL MONOGRAPHS.
American Mathematical Society, Box 6248, Providence, RI 02940-6248. TEL 401-455-4000. FAX 401-331-3842. *4612*

THE TRANSLATOR.
St. Jerome Publishing, 2 Maple Rd. W., Brooklands, Manchester M23 9HH, England. TEL 44-161-973-9856. FAX 44-161-905-3498. *4308*

TRANSNATIONAL CORPORATIONS AND TRANSBORDER DATA FLOWS.
Elsevier Science B.V., Books Division, P.O. Box 211, 1000 AE Amsterdam, Netherlands. TEL 31-20-4853911. FAX 31-20-4853705. *1204*

TRANSNATIONAL ORGANIZED CRIME.
Frank Cass, 890-900 Eastern Ave., Newbury Park, Ilford, Essex IG2 7HH, England. TEL 44-181-599-8866. FAX 44-181-599-0984. *6039*

TRANSPLANTATION.
Williams & Wilkins, 351 W. Camden St., Baltimore, MD 21201-2436. TEL 410-528-4068. FAX 410-528-4452. *5156*

TRANSPLANTATION PROCEEDINGS.
Elsevier Science Inc., Box 945, New York, NY 10159-0945. TEL 212-633-3730. FAX 212-633-3680. *5156*

TRANSPLANTATION REVIEWS.
W.B. Saunders Co., Curtis Center, 3rd Fl., Independence Sq. W., Philadelphia, PA 19106-3399. TEL 215-238-7800. FAX 215-238-6445. *5156*

TRANSPLANTATIONSMEDIZIN.
Pabst Science Publishers, Am Eichengrund 28, 49525 Lengerich, Germany. TEL 49-5484-308. FAX 49-5484-550. *5156*

TRANSPORT IN POROUS MEDIA.
Kluwer Academic Publishers, Postbus 17, 3300 AA Dordrecht, Netherlands. TEL 31-78-6392392. FAX 31-78-6392254. *1769*

TRANSPORT MANAGEMENT.
Institute of Transport Administration, 32 Palmerston Rd., Southampton SO14 1LL, England. FAX 44-1703-634165. *7042*

TRANSPORT POLICY.
Elsevier Science Ltd., Pergamon, P.O. Box 800, Kidlington, Oxford OX5 1DX, England. TEL 44-1865-843000. FAX 44-1865-843010. *7042*

TRANSPORT PROCESSES IN ENGINEERING.
Elsevier Science B.V., Books Division, P.O. Box 211, 1000 AE Amsterdam, Netherlands. TEL 31-20-4853911. FAX 31-20-4853705. *2902*

TRANSPORT REVIEWS.
Taylor & Francis Ltd., 1 Gunpowder Sq., London EC4A 3DE, England. TEL 44-171-583-0490. FAX 44-171-583-0585. *7042*

TRANSPORT THEORY AND STATISTICAL PHYSICS.
Marcel Dekker Journals, 270 Madison Ave., New York, NY 10016. TEL 212-696-9000. FAX 212-685-4540. *5831*

TRANSPORTATION.
Kluwer Academic Publishers, Postbus 17, 3300 AA Dordrecht, Netherlands. TEL 31-78-6392392. FAX 31-78-6392254. *7043*

TRANSPORTATION PLANNING AND TECHNOLOGY.
Gordon and Breach - Harwood Academic, Amsteldisk 166, 1st Fl., 1079 LH Amsterdam, Netherlands. *7043*

TRANSPORTATION RESEARCH. PART A: POLICY & PRACTICE.
Elsevier Science Ltd., Pergamon, P.O. Box 800, Kidlington, Oxford OX5 1DX, England. TEL 44-1865-843000. FAX 44-1865-843010. *7044*

TRANSPORTATION RESEARCH. PART B: METHODOLOGICAL.
Elsevier Science Ltd., Pergamon, P.O. Box 800, Kidlington, Oxford OX5 1DX, England. TEL 44-1865-843000. FAX 44-1865-843010. *7044*

TRANSPORTATION RESEARCH. PART C: EMERGING TECHNOLOGIES.
Elsevier Science Ltd., Pergamon, P.O. Box 800, Kidlington, Oxford OX5 1DX, England. TEL 44-1865-843000. FAX 44-1865-843010. *7044*

TRANSPORTATION RESEARCH. PART D: TRANSPORT & ENVIRONMENT.
Elsevier Science Ltd., Pergamon, P.O. Box 800, Kidlington, Oxford OX5 1DX, England. TEL 44-1865-843000. FAX 44-1865-843010. *7044*

TRANSPORTATION RESEARCH, ECONOMICS AND POLICY.
Kluwer Academic Publishers, Postbus 17, 3300 AA Dordrecht, Netherlands. TEL 31-78-6392392. FAX 31-78-6392254. *7044*

TRANSPORTATION RESEARCH RECORD.
U.S. National Research Council, Transportation Research Board, 2101 Constitution Ave., N.W., Washington, DC 20418. TEL 202-334-3213. FAX 202-334-2519. *7142*

TRANSPORTATION STUDIES.
Gordon and Breach - Harwood Academic, Amsteldisk 166, 1st Fl., 1079 LH Amsterdam, Netherlands. *7044*

TRANSPORTS URBAINS.
Groupement pour l'Etude des Transports Urbains Modernes, 173 rue Armand Silvestre, 92400 Courbevoie, France. TEL 33-1-43334454. *7045*

TRAPANANDA.
Co-Austral y Chile Futuro, 21 de Mayo, 466, Coyhaique, Chile. *3649*

TRAUMA QUARTERLY.
V S P, P.O. Box 346, 3700 AH Zeist, Netherlands. TEL 31-30-6925790. FAX 31-30-6932081. *5156*

TRAVEL INDUSTRY WORLD YEARBOOK.
Child & Waters, Inc., Box 610, Rye, NY 10580-0811. TEL 914-921-0988. *7256*

TREASURYLOG.
Go Public Relations, Badnerstr. 3-21, A-2500 Baden, Austria. *1170*

TREATISE ON MATERIALS SCIENCE & TECHNOLOGY.
Academic Press, Inc., 525 B St., Ste. 1900, San Diego, CA 92101-4495. TEL 619-231-0926. FAX 619-699-6715. *2870*

TREE PHYSIOLOGY.
Heron Publishing, 202-3994 Shelbourne St., Victoria, BC V8N 3E2, Canada. TEL 250-721-9921. FAX 250-721-9924. *730*

TREE - RING BULLETIN.
Tree - Ring Society, University of Arizona, Tree - Ring Laboratory, Tucson, AZ 85721. TEL 520-621-1608. FAX 520-621-8229. *730*

TREE TRACERS.
Southwest Oklahoma Genealogical Society, Tree Tracers Committee, Box 148, Lawton, OK 73502-1048. FAX 405-248-0243. *3244*

TRENCHLESS TECHNOLOGY.
Trenchless Technology, Inc., 1770 Main St., Box 190, Peninsula, OH 44264. TEL 216-467-7588. FAX 216-468-2289. *2743*

TRENDS IN AMPLIFICATION.
Woodland Publications, Inc., 69 Murray St., New York, NY 10007. TEL 212-566-4294. FAX 212-406-6496. *5026*

TRENDS IN ANALYTICAL CHEMISTRY.
Elsevier Science B.V., P.O. Box 211, 1000 AE Amsterdam, Netherlands. TEL 31-20-4853911. FAX 31-20-4853598. *1798*

TRENDS IN ANALYTICAL CHEMISTRY: REFERENCE EDITION.
Elsevier Science B.V., Books Division, P.O. Box 211, 1000 AE Amsterdam, Netherlands. TEL 31-20-4853911. FAX 31-20-4853705. *1798*

TRENDS IN BIOCHEMICAL SCIENCES.
Elsevier Science Ltd., P.O. Box 800, Kidlington, Oxford OX5 1DX, England. TEL 44-1865-843000. FAX 44-1865-843010. *672*

TRENDS IN BIOCHEMICAL SCIENCES (REFERENCE EDITION).
Elsevier Science Ltd., P.O. Box 800, Kidlington, Oxford OX5 1DX, England. TEL 44-1865-843000. FAX 44-1865-843010. *672*

TRENDS IN BIOTECHNOLOGY.
Elsevier Science Ltd., P.O. Box 800, Kidlington, Oxford OX5 1DX, England. TEL 44-1865-843000. FAX 44-1865-843010. *687*

TRENDS IN BIOTECHNOLOGY (REFERENCE EDITION).
Elsevier Science Ltd., P.O. Box 800, Kidlington, Oxford OX5 1DX, England. TEL 44-1865-843000. FAX 44-1865-843010. *687*

TRENDS IN CARDIOVASCULAR MEDICINE.
Elsevier Science Inc., Box 945, New York, NY 10159-0945. TEL 212-633-3730. FAX 212-633-3680. *4825*

TRENDS IN CELL BIOLOGY.
Elsevier Science Ltd., P.O. Box 800, Kidlington, Oxford OX5 1DX, England. TEL 44-1865-843000. FAX 44-1865-843010. *745*

TRENDS IN CELL BIOLOGY (REFERENCE EDITION).
Elsevier Science Ltd., P.O. Box 800, Kidlington, Oxford OX5 1DX, England. TEL 44-1865-843000. FAX 44-1865-843010. *745*

TRENDS IN ECOLOGY AND EVOLUTION.
Elsevier Science Ltd., P.O. Box 800, Kidlington, Oxford OX5 1DX, England. TEL 44-1865-843000. FAX 44-1865-843010. *630*

REFEREED SERIALS

TRENDS IN ECOLOGY AND EVOLUTION (REFERENCE EDITION).
Elsevier Science Ltd., P.O. Box 800, Kidlington, Oxford OX5 1DX, England. TEL 44-1865-843000. FAX 44-1865-843010. *777*

TRENDS IN ENDOCRINOLOGY AND METABOLISM.
Elsevier Science Inc., Box 945, New York, NY 10159-0945. TEL 212-633-3730. FAX 212-633-3680. *4893*

TRENDS IN FOOD SCIENCE AND TECHNOLOGY.
Elsevier Science Ltd., P.O. Box 800, Kidlington, Oxford OX5 1DX, England. TEL 44-1865-843000. FAX 44-1865-843010. *3129*

TRENDS IN FOOD SCIENCE AND TECHNOLOGY (REFERENCE EDITION).
Elsevier Science Ltd., P.O. Box 800, Kidlington, Oxford OX5 1DX, England. TEL 44-1865-843000. FAX 44-1865-843010. *3130*

TRENDS IN GENETICS.
Elsevier Science Ltd., P.O. Box 800, Kidlington, Oxford OX5 1DX, England. TEL 44-1865-843000. FAX 44-1865-843010. *777*

TRENDS IN GENETICS (REFERENCE EDITION).
Elsevier Science Ltd., P.O. Box 800, Kidlington, Oxford OX5 1DX, England. TEL 44-1865-843000. FAX 44-1865-843010. *777*

TRENDS IN GLYCOSCIENCE AND GLYCOTECHNOLOGY.
F C C A, 3-10-1 Koufudai, Fujishiro-cho, Kitasoma-gun, Ibaraki-ken 300-15, Japan. TEL 81-297-837635. FAX 81-297-837645. *1824*

TRENDS IN MICROBIOLOGY.
Elsevier Science Ltd., P.O. Box 800, Kidlington, Oxford OX5 1DX, England. TEL 44-1865-843000. FAX 44-1865-843010. *794*

TRENDS IN MICROBIOLOGY (REFERENCE EDITION).
Elsevier Science Ltd., P.O. Box 800, Kidlington, Oxford OX5 1DX, England. TEL 44-1865-843000. FAX 44-1865-843010. *794*

TRENDS IN NEUROSCIENCES.
Elsevier Science Ltd., P.O. Box 800, Kidlington, Oxford OX5 1DX, England. TEL 44-1865-843000. FAX 44-1865-843010. *5100*

TRENDS IN NEUROSCIENCES (REFERENCE EDITION).
Elsevier Science Ltd., P.O. Box 800, Kidlington, Oxford OX5 1DX, England. TEL 44-1865-843000. FAX 44-1865-843010. *5100*

TRENDS IN PHARMACOLOGICAL SCIENCES.
Elsevier Science Ltd., P.O. Box 800, Kidlington, Oxford OX5 1DX, England. TEL 44-1865-843000. FAX 44-1865-843010. *5696*

TRENDS IN PHARMACOLOGICAL SCIENCES (REFERENCE EDITION).
Elsevier Science Ltd., P.O. Box 800, Kidlington, Oxford OX5 1DX, England. TEL 44-1865-843000. FAX 44-1865-843010. *5696*

TRENDS IN POLYMER SCIENCE.
Elsevier Science Ltd., P.O. Box 800, Kidlington, Oxford OX5 1DX, England. TEL 44-1865-843000. FAX 44-1865-843010. *2775*

TRENDS IN POLYMER SCIENCE (REFERENCE EDITION).
Elsevier Science Ltd., P.O. Box 800, Kidlington, Oxford OX5 1DX, England. TEL 44-1865-843000. FAX 44-1865-843010. *2775*

TRI-STATE BLUEGRASS ASSOCIATION BAND AND FESTIVAL GUIDE.
Tri-State Bluegrass Association, R.R. 1, Kahoka, MO 63445. TEL 573-853-4344. *5441*

TRIBHUVAN UNIVERSITY. NATURAL HISTORY MUSEUM. JOURNAL.
Tribhuvan University, Natural History Museum, Swoyambhu, Kathmandu, Nepal. *731*

TRIBOLOGY INTERNATIONAL.
Elsevier Science Ltd., P.O. Box 800, Kidlington, Oxford OX5 1DX, England. TEL 44-1865-843000. FAX 44-1865-843010. *2902*

TRIBOLOGY LETTERS.
Baltzer Science Publishers B.V., P.O. Box 221, 1400 AE Bussum, Netherlands. TEL 31-20-6370061. FAX 31-20-6323651. *2870*

TRIBOLOGY SERIES.
Elsevier Science B.V., Books Division, P.O. Box 211, 1000 AE Amsterdam, Netherlands. TEL 31-20-4853911. FAX 31-20-4853705. *2902*

TRIBOLOGY TRANSACTIONS.
Society of Tribologists and Lubrication Engineers, 840 Busse Hwy., Park Ridge, IL 60068-2376. TEL 847-825-5536. FAX 847-825-1456. *2775*

TRIBUNA MEDICA.
Ediciones Lerner Ltda., Calle 8A No.68A-41, Bogota, Colombia. TEL 57-1-4200650. FAX 57-1-2624459. *4754*

TRIBUNAL DE JUSTICA DO ESTADO DO RIO GRANDE DO SUL. REVISTA DE JURISPRUDENCIA.
Tribuna de Justica, Praca Marechal Deodoro, 55, 5o andar, 90010-908 Porto Alegre RS, Brazil. TEL 55-51-2282444 ext. 1550. *4035*

TRIBUTARY (TRENTON).
New Jersey Wastewater Treatment Trust, CN 440, Trenton, NJ 08625. TEL 609-219-8600. FAX 609-219-8620. *2991*

TRINCOLL JOURNAL.
Trinity College, Trinity College 702596, Hartford, CT 06106. *4480*

TRINITY JOURNAL.
Trinity Evangelical Divinity School, 2065 Half Day Rd., Deerfield, IL 60015. TEL 847-945-8800. *6379*

TRISOMY 21.
Eterna International, Inc., Box 5731, Hauppauge, NY 11788-0154. *5041*

TROENDERBLADET.
Troenderbladet AS, Pottenvegen 11, N-7084 Melhus, Norway. TEL 47-72-87-00-55. FAX 47-72-87-00-55. *3345*

TROPHOBLAST RESEARCH.
Plenum Publishing Corp., 233 Spring St., New York, NY 10013-1578. TEL 212-620-8000. FAX 212-463-0742. *4968*

TROPICAL AGRICULTURE.
University of the West Indies, Imperial College of Tropical Agriculture, St. Augustine, Trinidad & Tobago, W.I. TEL 809-645-3640. FAX 809-662-1182. *159*

TROPICAL AGRICULTURIST.
Department of Agriculture, No. 1, Sarasavi Mawatha, P.O. Box 05, Peradeniya, Sri Lanka. TEL 94-8-88136. FAX 94-8-88030. *159*

TROPICAL ANIMAL HEALTH AND PRODUCTION.
Edinburgh University Press, 22 George Sq., Edinburgh EH8 9LF, Scotland. TEL 44-131-650-6207. FAX 44-131-662-0053. *7280*

TROPICAL BIODIVERSITY.
Indonesian Foundation for the Advancement of Biological Sciences, P.O. Box 103, Depok 16401, Indonesia. FAX 62-21-775-1837. *630*

TROPICAL DOCTOR.
Royal Society of Medicine Press Ltd., 1 Wimpole St., London W1M 8AE, England. TEL 44-171-290-2900. FAX 44-171-290-2929. *4844*

TROPICAL ECOLOGY.
International Society for Tropical Ecology, Dept. of Botany, Banaras Hindu University, Varanasi 221 005, India. TEL 91-542-317099. FAX 91-542-317074. *731*

TROPICAL FRUIT NEWS.
Rare Fruit Council International, Inc., Box 561914, Miami, FL 33156. TEL 813-474-6133. *3206*

TROPICAL LEPIDOPTERA.
Association for Tropical Lepidoptera, Box 141210, Gainesville, FL 32614-1210. TEL 352-372-3505. FAX 352-373-3249. *761*

TROPICAL MEDICINE.
Nagasaki Daigaku, Nettai Igaku Kenkyujo, 12-4 Sakamoto-machi, Nagasaki 852, Japan. *4844*

TROPICAL MEDICINE & INTERNATIONAL HEALTH.
Blackwell Science Ltd., Osney Mead, Oxford OX2 0EL, England. TEL 44-1865-206206. FAX 44-1865-721205. *6252*

TROPICAL SCIENCE.
Whurr Publishers Ltd., 19b Compton Terrace, London N1 2UN, England. TEL 44-171-359-5979. FAX 44-171-226-5290. *159*

TROPICAL VETERINARIAN.
University of Ibadan, Faculty of Veterinary Medicine, Ibadan, Oyo State, Nigeria. FAX 234-2-8103043. *7280*

TROPICULTURA.
A G C D - A B O S, Rue du Trone 4, Bte. 605, 1000 Brussels, Belgium. TEL 32-2-5190447. *247*

TRUCKERS - U S A.
Horizon Media, Box 3168, Tuscaloosa, AL 35403-3168. TEL 205-758-3070. *7180*

TRUCKWORLD ONLINE!
AutoWeb Worldwide Publishing, Inc., Box 590, Cottage Grove, OR 97424. *7180*

THE TS A G I JOURNAL.
Begell House Inc., 79 Madison Ave., Ste. 1205, New York, NY 10016-7892. TEL 212-725-1999. FAX 212-213-8368. *81*

TSAFON.
Centre de Recherches Hebraiques, 1 place du Temple, 59000 Lille, France. TEL 33-3-20575399. FAX 33-3-20919171. *6410*

TSITOLOGIYA.
Izdatel'stvo Nauka, S.-Peterburgskoe Otdelenie, Mendeleevskaya liniya, 1, 199034 St. Petersburg B-34, Russia. *745*

TSUDA REVIEW.
Tsuda College, 2-1-1 Tsuda-machi, Kodaira-shi, Tokyo 187, Japan. TEL 0423-42-5111. FAX 0423-41-2444. *4480*

TUBERCLE AND LUNG DISEASE.
Churchill Livingstone, Robert Stevenson House, 1-3 Baxter's Pl., Leith Walk, Edinburgh EH1 3AF, Scotland. TEL 44-131-556-2424. FAX 44-131-535-1704. *5123*

TUHINGA: RECORDS OF THE MUSEUM OF NEW ZEALAND TE PAPA TONGAREWA.
Museum of New Zealand, Board of Trustees, Buckle St., P.O. Box 467, Wellington, New Zealand. TEL 64-4-385-9609. FAX 64-4-385-6035. *5367*

TUIJIN JISHU.
Zhongguo Hangtian Gongye Zonggongsi, Di 3 Yanjiuyuan, 31 Yanjiusho, P.O. Box 7208-26, Beijing 100074, People's Republic of China. TEL 86-10-6837-6141. FAX 86-10-6837-4052. *81*

TULANE STUDIES IN GEOLOGY AND PALEONTOLOGY.
Tulane University, Department of Geology, New Orleans, LA 70118. TEL 504-865-5198. *2373*

TULANE STUDIES IN ZOOLOGY AND BOTANY.
Tulane University, Museum of Natural History, Belle Chasse, LA 70037. TEL 504-394-1711. FAX 504-394-5045. *851*

TULSA STUDIES IN WOMEN'S LITERATURE.
University of Tulsa, Tulsa Studies in Women's Literature, 600 S. College Ave., Tulsa, OK 74104-3189. TEL 918-631-2503. FAX 918-584-0623. *4480*

TUMOR BIOLOGY.
S. Karger AG, Allschwilerstr. 10, P.O. Box CH-4009 Basel, Switzerland. TEL 41-61-3061111. FAX 41-61-3061234. *4988*

TUMOR DIAGNOSIS.
Field & Wood, Medical Periodicals, Inc., Box 975, Blue Bell, PA 19422. TEL 610-828-4010. FAX 215-482-0226. *4988*

TUMOR RESEARCH: EXPERIMENTAL AND CLINICAL.
Sapporo Ika Daigaku, Fuzoku Gan Kenkyujo, Nishi-17-chome, Minami-1-jo, Chuo-ku, Sapporo-shi, Hokkaido 060, Japan. TEL 81-11-611-2111. FAX 81-11-615-3099. *4988*

TUMOR TARGETING.
Chapman & Hall, Journals Department 2-6 Boundary Row, London SE1 8HN, England. TEL 44-171-8650066. FAX 44-171-5229623. *4988*

LA TUNISIE MEDICALE.
Societe Tunisienne des Sciences Medicales, 16 Rue Touraine, 1002 Tunis - Belvedere, Tunisia. TEL 216-790-924. FAX 216-796-602. *4754*

TUNNELLING AND UNDERGROUND SPACE TECHNOLOGY.
Elsevier Science Ltd., Pergamon, P.O. Box 800, Kidlington, Oxford OX5 1DX, England. TEL 44-1865-843000. FAX 44-1865-843010. *2743*

TURANG XUEBAO.
Science Press, Marketing and Sales Department, 16 Donghuangchenggen North St., Beijing 100717, People's Republic of China. TEL 4010642. FAX 4019810. *2323*

TURBOMACHINERY INTERNATIONAL.
Turbomachinery International Publications, Box 5550, Norwalk, CT 06856. TEL 203-853-6015. FAX 203-852-8175. *2902*

TURBULENCE.
Wydawnictwo Politechniki Czestochowskiej, Ul. Dabrowskiego 69, 42-200 Czestochowa, Poland. TEL 48-34-250974. FAX 48-34-612385. *5255*

TURK VETERINERLIK VE HAYVANCILIK DERGISI.
Scientific and Technical Research Council of Turkey - TUBITAK, Ataturk Bulvari, No. 221, Kavaklidere, 06100 Ankara, Turkey. TEL 90-312-4685300. FAX 90-312-4271336. *7280*

TURKIC LANGUAGES.
Harrassowitz Verlag, 65174 Wiesbaden, Germany. TEL 49-611-530555. FAX 49-611-530559. *4309*

TURKISH CHAMBER OF CIVIL ENGINEERS. DIGEST (YEAR).
Turkish Chamber of Civil Engineers, Selanik Caddesi 19-1, Kizilay 06650 Ankara, Turkey. TEL 90-312-4337626. FAX 90-312-4170632. *2753*

TURKISH JOURNAL OF AGRICULTURE AND FORESTRY.
Scientific and Technical Research Council of Turkey - TUBITAK, Ataturk Bulvari, No. 221, Kavaklidere, 06100 Ankara, Turkey. TEL 90-312-4685300. FAX 90-312-4271336. *159*

TURKISH JOURNAL OF BIOLOGY.
Scientific and Technical Research Council of Turkey - TUBITAK, Ataturk Bulvari, No. 221, Kavaklidere, 06100 Ankara, Turkey. TEL 90-312-4685300. FAX 90-312-4271336. *630*

TURKISH JOURNAL OF BOTANY.
Scientific and Technical Research Council of Turkey - TUBITAK, Ataturk Bulvari, No. 221, Kavaklidere, 06100 Ankara, Turkey. TEL 90-312-4685300. FAX 90-312-4271336. *731*

TURKISH JOURNAL OF CANCER.
Turkish Association for Cancer Research and Control, Atac Sokak No. 21, 06420 Yenisehir, Ankara, Turkey. TEL 90-312-4312950. FAX 90-312-4313958. *4988*

TURKISH JOURNAL OF CHEMISTRY.
Scientific and Technical Research Council of Turkey - TUBITAK, Ataturk Bulvari, No. 221, Kavaklidere, 06100 Ankara, Turkey. TEL 90-312-4685300. FAX 90-312-4271336. *1770*

TURKISH JOURNAL OF DERMATOPATHOLOGY.
Turkish Society of Dermatopathology, Mithatpasa Cad. 16-11, Yenisehir, 06420 Ankara, Turkey. TEL 90-312-4300221. FAX 90-312-4300221. *4881*

TURKISH JOURNAL OF EARTH SCIENCES.
Scientific and Technical Research Council of Turkey - TUBITAK, Ataturk Bulvari, No. 221, Kavaklidere, 06100 Ankara, Turkey. TEL 90-312-4685300. FAX 90-312-4271336. *2323*

TURKISH JOURNAL OF ELECTRICAL ENGINEERING AND COMPUTER SCIENCES.
Scientific and Technical Research Council of Turkey - TUBITAK, Ataturk Bulvari, No. 221, Kavaklidere, 06100 Ankara, Turkey. TEL 90-312-4685300. FAX 90-312-4276677. *2091*

TURKISH JOURNAL OF ENGINEERING AND ENVIRONMENTAL SCIENCES.
Scientific and Technical Research Council of Turkey - TUBITAK, Ataturk Bulvari, No. 221, Kavaklidere, 06100 Ankara, Turkey. TEL 90-312-4685300. FAX 90-312-4271336. *2743*

TURKISH JOURNAL OF GASTROENTEROLOGY.
Turkish Society of Gastroenterology, Bayindir Sokak 17-7, 06420 Kizilay - Ankara, Turkey. TEL 90-312-4354373. *4915*

TURKISH JOURNAL OF MATHEMATICS.
Scientific and Technical Research Council of Turkey - TUBITAK, Ataturk Bulvari, No. 221, Kavaklidere, 06100 Ankara, Turkey. TEL 90-312-4685300. FAX 90-312-4271336. *4612*

TURKISH JOURNAL OF MEDICAL SCIENCES.
Scientific and Technical Research Council of Turkey - TUBITAK, Ataturk Bulvari, No. 221, Kavaklidere, 06100 Ankara, Turkey. TEL 90-312-4685300. FAX 90-312-4271336. *4754*

TURKISH JOURNAL OF NUCLEAR SCIENCES.
Turkiye Atom Enerjisi Kurumu - T A E K, 06530 Ankara, Turkey. TEL 90-312-2876013. FAX 90-312-2878761. *2704*

TURKISH JOURNAL OF PEDIATRICS.
Turkish and International Children's Center, P.O. Box 66, Samanpazari, 06240 Ankara, Turkey. TEL 90-312-3242326. FAX 90-312-3112253. *5041*

TURKISH JOURNAL OF PHYSICS.
Scientific and Technical Research Council of Turkey - TUBITAK, Ataturk Bulvari, No. 221, Kavaklidere, 06100 Ankara, Turkey. TEL 90-312-4685300. FAX 90-312-4271336. *5831*

TURKISH JOURNAL OF ZOOLOGY.
Scientific and Technical Research Council of Turkey - TUBITAK, Ataturk Bulvari, No. 221, Kavaklidere, 06100 Ankara, Turkey. TEL 90-312-4685300. FAX 90-312-4271336. *851*

TURKIYAT MECMUASI.
Istanbul University, Institute of Turkish Researches, Kavalah sokagi 5-4, Horhor, Fstih-Istanbul, Turkey. TEL 90-212-5323507. FAX 90-212-5349495. *3660*

TURNING WHEEL.
Buddhist Peace Fellowship, Box 4650, Berkeley, CA 94704. TEL 510-525-8596. FAX 510-525-7973. *6390*

DE TWEEDE RONDE.
Uitgeverij G.A. van Oorschot, Herengracht 613, 1017 CE Amsterdam, Netherlands. TEL 31-20-6231484. FAX 31-20-6254083. *4480*

TWELVE STEP RAG.
Families Anonymous, Inc., Box 3475, Culver City, CA 90231-3475. TEL 310-313-5800. FAX 310-313-6841. *2306*

TWENTIETH CENTURY JAPAN: THE EMERGENCE OF A WORLD POWER.
University of California Press, 2120 Berkeley Way, Berkeley, CA 94720. TEL 510-642-4247. FAX 510-643-7127. *3540*

TYDSKRIF VIR ISLAMKUNDE.
Rand Afrikaans University, Centre for Islamic Studies, P.O. Box 524, Auckland Park 2006, South Africa. *6401*

TYDSKRIF VIR LETTERKUNDE.
Foundation for Education, Science and Technology, P.O. Box 1758, Pretoria 0001, South Africa. TEL 27-12-322-6404. FAX 27-12-320-7803. *4481*

TYDSKRIF VIR SKOONLUG.
National Association for Clean Air, P.O. Box 5777, Johannesburg 2000, South Africa. TEL 27-11-6462210. FAX 27-11-6462210. *2972*

U C L A HISTORICAL JOURNAL.
University of California at Los Angeles, Graduate Students Association, Department of History, Los Angeles, CA 90095-1473. TEL 310-825-4601. FAX 310-206-9630. *3515*

U C L A JOURNAL OF DANCE ETHNOLOGY.
University of California at Los Angeles, Department of Dance, Dance Bldg. 124, Los Angeles, CA 90095-1608. TEL 310-825-3951. FAX 310-825-7507. *2296*

U C L A SYMPOSIUM SERIES ON MOLECULAR AND CELLULAR BIOLOGY.
John Wiley & Sons, Inc., Journals, 605 Third Ave., New York, NY 10158. TEL 212-475-7700. *630*

U K NATURE CONSERVATION.
Joint Nature Conservation Committee, Monkstone House, City Rd., Peterborough PE1 1JY, England. *2246*

U N R I S D DISCUSSION PAPER SERIES.
United Nations Research Institute for Social Development, Reference Centre, Palais des Nations, 1211 Geneva 10, Switzerland. TEL 41-22-798-8400. FAX 41-22-740-0791. *6643*

U R I S A JOURNAL.
University of Wisconsin Press, Journal Division, c/o Institute for Environmental Studies, WARF Bldg., Rm. 1048, 610 Walnut St., Madison, WI 53705. TEL 608-263-6843. *2246*

U S I JOURNAL.
United Service Institution of India, Rao Tula Ram Marg (Opposite Signal Enclave), New Delhi 110 057, India. TEL 91-11-6878682. FAX 91-11-6879773. *5288*

U S M C A RESEARCH JOURNAL.
University of Southern Mindanao, College of Agriculture, Kabacan, Cotabato 9407, Philippines. *159*

U S PHARMACIST.
Jobson Publishing, Inc., 100 Ave. of the Americas, New York, NY 10013-1678. TEL 212-274-7000. FAX 212-431-0500. *5697*

U T S REVIEW.
John Libbey & Company Pty. Ltd., 15-17 Young St., Sydney, N.S.W. 2000, Australia. TEL 61-2-92514099. FAX 61-2-92514428. *6643*

UBYSSEY.
University of British Columbia, Rm. 245 K, S.U.B., Vancouver, BC V6T 1Z1, Canada. TEL 604-822-6681. FAX 604-822-1658. *1975*

UDITVANI.
Jugsalai, Jamshedpur 831 006, Bihar, India. TEL 431042. *3321*

UIT.
Vlaamse Toeristenbond, Vlaamse Automobilistenbond, Sint-Jakobsmarkt 45, B-2000 Antwerp, Belgium. TEL 32-3-2203400. FAX 32-3-2340598. *7247*

UKRAINIAN MATHEMATICAL JOURNAL.
Plenum Publishing Corp., Consultants Bureau, 233 Spring St., New York, NY 10013-1578. TEL 212-620-8468. FAX 212-463-0742. *4612*

ULITARRA.
Ulitarra Literary Association Inc., P.O. Box 195, Armidale, N.S.W. 2350, Australia. TEL 61-67-729135. *4363*

ULSTER MEDICAL JOURNAL.
Ulster Medical Society, c/o Queens University Medical Library, Institute of Clinical Science, Grosvenor Rd., Belfast BT12 6BA, Northern Ireland. TEL 44-1232-322043. FAX 44-1232-247068. *4755*

ULTIMATE REALITY AND MEANING.
University of Toronto Press, Journals Department, 5201 Dufferin St., Downsview, ON M3H 5T8, Canada. TEL 416-667-7710. FAX 416-667-7881. *5756*

ULTIMO BUSCADERO.
Ultimo Buscadero S.r.l., Casella Postale 239, 21013 Gallarate (VA), Italy. TEL 39-331-771027. *5442*

ULTRA-FIT AUSTRALIA.
Australian Workout Publications, P.O. Box 266, Newport Beach, N.S.W. 2106, Australia. TEL 61-2-99993384. FAX 61-3-99993385. *5791*

ULTRA SCIENTIST OF PHYSICAL SCIENCES.
P.O. Box 93, G.P.O., Bhopal 462 001, India. TEL 91-755-540624. FAX 91-755-510334. *6580*

ULTRAMICROSCOPY.
North-Holland, P.O. Box 211, 1000 AE Amsterdam, Netherlands. TEL 31-20-4853911. FAX 31-20-4853598. *798*

ULTRASONICS.
Elsevier Science B.V., P.O. Box 211, 1000 AE Amsterdam, Netherlands. TEL 31-20-4853911. FAX 31-20-4853598. *5874*

ULTRASONICS SONOCHEMISTRY.
Elsevier Science B.V., P.O. Box 211, 1000 AE Amsterdam, Netherlands. TEL 31-20-4853911. FAX 31-20-4853598. *5874*

ULTRASOUND IN MEDICINE & BIOLOGY.
Elsevier Science Inc., Box 945, New York, NY 10159-0945. TEL 212-633-3730. FAX 212-633-3680. *630*

ULTRASOUND IN OBSTETRICS & GYNECOLOGY.
Parthenon Publishing Group, Casterton Hall, Carnforth, Lancs. LA6 2LA, England. TEL 44-152-427-2084. FAX 44-152-427-1587. *4968*

ULTRASOUND QUARTERLY.
Lippincott - Raven Publishers, 227 E. Washington Sq., Philadelphia, PA 19106. TEL 215-238-4200. FAX 215-238-7390. *5116*

ULTRASTRUCTURAL PATHOLOGY.
Taylor & Francis Inc., 1900 Frost Rd., Ste. 101, Bristol, PA 19007-1598. TEL 215-785-5800. FAX 215-785-5515. *745*

ULUSAL CERRAHI DERGISI.
Turkish Surgical Society, Guzelbahce Sok. 35-7, 80200 Nisantasi - Istanbul, Turkey. TEL 90-212-2475295. FAX 90-212-2470835. *5156*

HA'UMAH.
Misdar Jabotinsky, P.O. Box 1461, Efrata Z.C. 90435, Israel. TEL 972-2-9311890. *3324*

UNA'S LECTURES.
University of California Press, 2120 Berkeley Way, Berkeley, CA 94720. TEL 510-643-7127. FAX 510-643-7127. *3794*

UNDER FIVE CONTACT.
Pre-School Learning Alliance, 69 Kings Cross Rd., London WC1X 9LL, England. TEL 44-171-833-0991. FAX 44-171-837-4942. *2489*

THE UNDERGROUND WINE JOURNAL.
Wine Journal Enterprises, Inc., 1654 Amberwood Dr., Ste. A, South Pasadena, CA 91030. TEL 818-441-6617. FAX 818-441-6765. *528*

UNDERSEA & HYPERBARIC MEDICINE.
Undersea and Hyperbaric Medical Society, Inc., 10531 Metropolitan Ave., Kensington, MD 20895. TEL 301-942-2980. FAX 301-942-7804. *4755*

UNDERSTANDING CHEMICAL REACTIVITY.
Kluwer Academic Publishers, Postbus 17, 3300 AA Dordrecht, Netherlands. TEL 31-78-6392392. FAX 31-78-6392254. *1770*

UNDERSTANDING MAGAZINE.
Dionysia Press, 20A Montgomery St., Edinburgh EH7 5JS, Scotland. TEL 44-131-478-0089. *4481*

UNFORGETTABLE FIRE.
Jordan O'Neill, Ed. & Pub., 54 Logan Ave., No. 1, Staten Island, NY 10301. *7345*

UNI MAGAZIN HANNOVER.
Universitaet Hannover, Pressestelle, Postfach 6009, 30060 Hannover, Germany. TEL 49-511-7625355. FAX 49-511-7625391. *6979*

UNICIENCIA.
Universidad Nacional, Facultad de Ciencias Exactas y Naturales, Apdo. 86, 3000 Heredia, Costa Rica. TEL 506-2375230. FAX 506-2773485. *6580*

UNIFORM COMMERCIAL CODE LAW JOURNAL.
Warren, Gorham & Lamont, One Penn Plaza, New York, NY 10119. TEL 212-971-5000. FAX 212-971-5113. *4057*

UNIFORM LAW REVIEW.
Kluwer Law International, Postbus 85889, 2508 CN The Hague, Netherlands. TEL 31-70-3081500. FAX 31-70-3081515. *4127*

UNION MATEMATICA ARGENTINA. REVISTA.
Union Matematica Argentina, Ciudad Universitaria, 5000 Cordoba, Argentina. TEL 54-51-334051. FAX 54-51-334054. *4612*

UNIT TRUSTS HANDBOOK.
Profile Media, 26 11th Ave., Houghton Estate, Johannesburg 2198, South Africa. TEL 27-11-728-5510. FAX 27-11-728-5845. *1412*

U.S. FOREST SERVICE. GENERAL TECHNICAL REPORT N E.
U.S. Forest Service, Northeastern Forest Experiment Station, 359 Main Rd., Delaware, OH 43015. TEL 614-368-0124. FAX 614-368-0152. *3165*

U.S. FOREST SERVICE. RESOURCE BULLETIN N E.
U.S. Forest Service, Northeastern Forest Experiment Station, 359 Main Rd., Delaware, OH 43015. TEL 614-368-0124. FAX 614-368-0152. *3165*

U.S. NATIONAL CENTER FOR HEALTH STATISTICS. MONTHLY VITAL STATISTICS REPORT.
U.S. National Center for Health Statistics, Data Dissemination Branch, 6525 Belcrest Rd., Hyattsville, MD 20782. TEL 301-436-8500. *6073*

U.S. NATIONAL MARINE FISHERIES SERVICE. TECHNICAL REPORT.
U.S. National Marine Fisheries Service, Scientific Publications Office, 7600 Sandpoint Way, N.E., Bin C15700, Seattle, WA 98115. TEL 206-526-6107. FAX 206-526-6426. *3080*

UNITED STATES IN THE WORLD: FOREIGN PERSPECTIVES.
University of Chicago Press, 5801 S. Ellis Ave., Chicago, IL 60637. TEL 773-702-7899. *6042*

UNIVERSIDAD CENTRAL DE VENEZUELA. CENTRO DE ESTUDIOS DEL DESARROLLO. CUADERNOS DEL C E N D E S.
Universidad Central de Venezuela, Centro de Estudios del Desarrollo, Apdo. Postal 6622, Caracas 1010-A, Venezuela. TEL 7523266. FAX 582-7512691. *6737*

UNIVERSIDAD CENTRAL DE VENEZUELA. FACULTAD DE AGRONOMIA. REVISTA.
Universidad Central de Venezuela, Facultad de Agronomia, Apdo. 4579, Maracay, Edo. Aragua 2101, Venezuela. TEL 58-43-462212. *160*

UNIVERSIDAD CENTRAL DE VENEZUELA. INSTITUTO DE ESTUDIOS HISPANOAMERICANOS. ANUARIO.
Universidad Central de Venezuela, Instituto de Estudios Hispanoamericanos, Centro Comercial Los Chaguaramos, piso 3, Caracas 1041 A, Venezuela. TEL 58-2-6930502. FAX 58-2-6930508. *3650*

UNIVERSIDAD, CIENCIA Y TECNOLOGIA.
Universidad Nacional Experimental Politecnica "Antonio Jose de Sucre", Urbanizacion Villa Asia, Final Calle China - Puerto Ordaz, Apdo. Postal 78, Ciudad Guayana, Venezuela. TEL 58-86-625245. FAX 58-86-625245. *2744*

UNIVERSIDAD COMPLUTENSE DE MADRID. REVISTA MATEMATICA.
Universidad Complutense de Madrid, Servicio de Publicaciones, Isaac Peral s-n, Ciudad Universitaria, 28040 Madrid, Spain. TEL 34-1-3946934. FAX 34-1-3946954. *4613*

UNIVERSIDAD DE ANTIOQUIA. REVISTA.
Universidad de Antioquia, Departamento de Publicaciones, Bloque 22, Cuidad Universitaria, Apdo. Aereo 1226, Medellin, Colombia. TEL 57-4-2105010. FAX 57-4-2638282. *3795*

UNIVERSIDAD DE GUADALAJARA. INSTITUTO DE BOTANICA. BOLETIN.
Universidad de Guadalajara, Instituto de Botanica, Apdo. Postal 139, 45110 Zapopan, Jalisco, Mexico. TEL 52-3-6820003. FAX 52-3-6264635. *731*

UNIVERSIDAD DE MURCIA. ANALES DE PSICOLOGIA.
Universidad de Murcia, Servicio de Publicaciones, Santo Cristo 1, 30080 Murcia, Spain. TEL 34-68-363014. FAX 34-68-363414. *6157*

UNIVERSIDAD DE PUERTO RICO. REVISTA JURIDICA.
Universidad de Puerto Rico, Escuela de Derecho, P.O. Box 23349, San Juan, PR 00931-3349. TEL 787-764-0000 ext. 2443. FAX 787-764-2675. *4140*

UNIVERSIDAD DE ZULIA. FACULTAD DE CIENCIAS VETERINARIAS. REVISTA CIENTIFICA.
Universidad del Zulia, Facultad de Ciencias Veterinarias, Apdo. 15252, Delicias 4003-A, Maracaibo, Venezuela. TEL 58-61-596158. FAX 58-61-425176. *7280*

UNIVERSIDAD DE ZULIA. FACULTAD DE INGENIERIA. REVISTA TECNICA.
Universidad del Zulia, Facultad de Ingenieria, Apdo. 10-482, Correo Bella Vista, Maracaibo, Venezuela. TEL 58-61-525732. FAX 58-61-525732. *2744*

UNIVERSIDAD NACIONAL AUTONOMA DE MEXICO. INSTITUTO DE GEOGRAFIA. SERIE VARIA.
Universidad Nacional Autonoma de Mexico, Instituto de Geografia, Circuito de la Investigacion Cientifica, Ciudad Universitaria, 04510 Mexico, D.F., Mexico. TEL 52-5-6224338. FAX 52-5-5160539. *3424*

UNIVERSIDAD NACIONAL DE ASUNCION. FACULTAD DE CIENCIAS EXACTAS Y NATURALES. MEMORIA.
Universidad Nacional de Asuncion, Facultad de Ciencias Exactas y Naturales, Casilla de Correo 1039, Asuncion, Paraguay. TEL 595-21-585601. FAX 595-21-585600. *6581*

UNIVERSIDAD NACIONAL DE LA PLATA. FACULTAD DE AGRONOMIA. REVISTA.
Universidad Nacional de la Plata, Facultad de Agronomia, C.C. 31, Calle 60 y 119, 1900 La Plata, Argentina. TEL 54-21-38168. FAX 54-21-252346. *160*

UNIVERSIDADE DE SAO PAULO. DEPARTAMENTO DE BOTANICA. BOLETIM DE BOTANICA.
Universidade de Sao Paulo, Departamento de Botanica, Caixa Postal 11461, 05421-970 Sao Paulo, Brazil. TEL 55-11-8187595. FAX 55-11-8187547. *731*

UNIVERSIDADE DE SAO PAULO. FACULDADE DE EDUCACAO. REVISTA.
Universidade de Sao Paulo, Faculdade de Educacao, Av. da Universidade, 308, 05508-900 Sao Paulo SP, Brazil. TEL 55-11-8183525. FAX 55-11-8183148. *2490*

UNIVERSIDADE DE SAO PAULO. REVISTA DE FARMACIA E BIOQUIMICA.
Universidade de Sao Paulo, Faculdade de Ciencias Farmaceuticas, C.P. 66083, 05389-970 Sao Paulo, Brazil. TEL 55-11-8137251. FAX 55-11-2128194. *5697*

UNIVERSIDADE FEDERAL DO RIO DE JANEIRO. INSTITUTO DE MATEMATICA. ESTUDOS E COMUNICACOES.
Universidade Federal do Rio de Janeiro, Instituto de Matematica, C.P. 68530, 21945-970 Rio de Janeiro, RJ, Brazil. TEL 55-21-5900940. FAX 55-21-2901095. *4613*

UNIVERSIDADE FEDERAL DO RIO DE JANEIRO. INSTITUTO DE MATEMATICA. MEMORIAS DE MATEMATICA.
Universidade Federal do Rio de Janeiro, Instituto de Matematica, C.P. 68530, 21945-970 Rio de Janeiro, RJ, Brazil. TEL 55-21-5900940. FAX 55-21-2901095. *4618*

UNIVERSIDADE FEDERAL DO RIO DE JANEIRO. INSTITUTO DE MATEMATICA. TEXTOS DE METODOS MATEMATICOS.
Universidade Federal do Rio de Janeiro, Instituto de Matematica, C.P. 68.530, 21945-970 Rio de Janeiro, RJ, Brazil. TEL 55-21-5900940. FAX 55-21-2901095. *4613*

UNIVERSITA DEGLI STUDI DI GENOVA. ISTITUTO DI ARCHEOLOGIA E FILOLOGIA CLASSICA "F. DELLA CORTE". PUBBLICAZIONI.
Universita degli Studi di Genova, Istituto di Archeologia e Filologia Classica "F. Della Corte", Via Balbi 4, 3p, 16126 Genoa, Italy. TEL 209-97-22. *4310*

UNIVERSITA DEGLI STUDI DI MODENA. SEMINARIO MATEMATICO E FISICO. ATTI.
Universita degli Studi di Modena, Seminario Matematico e Fisico, Via Campi 213-b, 41100 Modena, Italy. TEL 39-59-364496. FAX 39-59-370513. *4613*

UNIVERSITA KARLOVA. LEKARSKA FAKULTA. LEKARSKE ZPRAVY.
Karolinum - Nakladatelstvi Univerzity Karlovy, Ovocny trh 5, 116 36 Prague 1, Czech Republic. TEL 42-2-24491265. FAX 42-2-24212041. *4756*

UNIVERSITAS COMENIANA. ACTA MATHEMATICA.
Univerzita Komenskeho, Matematicko-fizikalna Fakulta, Mlynska Dlina, 842 15 Bratislava, Slovakia. TEL 42-7-725741. FAX 42-7-725882. *4613*

UNIVERSITAS LITTERARUM ET ARTIUM MISKOLCIENSIS. ANNALES.
Universitas Litterarum et Artium Miskolciensis, Vasgyari ut 18, 3545 Miskolc, Hungary. TEL 36-46-401511. FAX 36-46-401511. *6643*

UNIVERSITE DE BORDEAUX II. CAHIERS ETHNOLOGIQUES.
Presses Universitaires de Bordeaux, 3 place de la Victoire, 33000 Bordeaux, France. TEL 54-31-33-14. FAX 56314694. *332*

UNIVERSITE DE BORDEAUX III. CENTRE DE RECHERCHES SUR L'AMERIQUE ANGLOPHONE. ANNALES.
Maison des Sciences de l'Homme d'Aquitaine, Esplanade des Antilles, Domaine Universitaire, 33405 Talence Cedex, France. TEL 56-84-68-00. FAX 56-84-68-10. *4482*

UNIVERSITE DE PARIS VI (PIERRE ET MARIE CURIE) INSTITUT DE STATISTIQUE. PUBLICATIONS.
Universite de Paris VI (Pierre et Marie Curie), Institut de Statistique, 4, Place Jussieu, 75230 Paris Cedex 05, France. *4618*

UNIVERSITE DE REIMS. INSTITUT DE GEOGRAPHIE. TRAVAUX.
Universite de Reims, Institut de Geographie, 57 rue Pierre Taittinger, 51096 Reims, France. TEL 26-05-36-81. FAX 26-05-36-82. *3424*

UNIVERSITE DES SCIENCES HUMAINES DE STRASBOURG. CENTRE DE RECHERCHE SUR LE PROCHE ORIENT ET LA GRECE ANTIQUES. TRAVAUX.
E.J. Brill, P.O. Box 9000, 2300 PA Leiden, Netherlands. TEL 31-71-5353500. FAX 31-71-5317532. *1908*

UNIVERSITE LIBRE DE BRUXELLES. INSTITUT DES LANGUES VIVANTES ET DE PHONETIQUE. ETUDES ET TRAVAUX.
Universite Libre de Bruxelles, Institut des Langues Vivantes et de Phonetique, C.P. 110, Av. F.D. Roosevelt 50, 1050 Brussels, Belgium. TEL 32-2-6502010. FAX 32-2-6502007. *4310*

UNIVERSITEIT VAN STELLENBOSCH. ANNALE.
Universiteit van Stellenbosch, Private Bag X1, Matieland 7602, Stellenbosch. TEL 27-21-80804587. FAX 27-21-8084499. *6581*

UNIVERSITY BOOKMAN.
Educational Reviewer, Inc., Box 367, Mecosta, MI 49332. FAX 302-652-1760. *6286*

THE UNIVERSITY NEWS.
University of Dallas, University News, 1845 E. Northgate Dr., Box 732, Irving, TX 75062. TEL 972-721-5089. FAX 972-721-5048. *1976*

UNIVERSITY OF ALASKA. ANTHROPOLOGICAL PAPERS.
University of Alaska Fairbanks, Department of Anthropology, Box 757720, 310 Eielson Bldg., Fairbanks, AK 99775-7720. TEL 907-474-7288. FAX 907-474-7453. *333*

UNIVERSITY OF ALASKA. BIOLOGICAL PAPERS.
University of Alaska at Fairbanks, Institute of Arctic Biology, Box 75700, 308 Irving I, Fairbanks, AK 99775-7000. TEL 907-474-7658. FAX 907-474-7666. *631*

UNIVERSITY OF ARIZONA. ANTHROPOLOGICAL PAPERS.
University of Arizona Press, 1230 N. Park Ave., Tucson, AZ 85719. TEL 602-621-1441. *333*

UNIVERSITY OF ARKANSAS. LECTURE NOTES IN THE MATHEMATICAL SCIENCES.
John Wiley & Sons, Inc., 605 Third Ave., New York, NY 10158. TEL 212-850-6000. FAX 212-850-6088. *4614*

UNIVERSITY OF BRADFORD. DEVELOPMENT AND PROJECT PLANNING CENTRE. BRADFORD DEVELOPMENT PAPERS.
University of Bradford, Development and Project Planning Centre, The Library, Bradford, W. Yorks BD1 1DP, England. *1369*

UNIVERSITY OF BRITISH COLUMBIA LAW REVIEW.
University of British Columbia Law Review Society, Faculty of Law, Vancouver, BC V6T 1Z2, Canada. TEL 604-822-3066. FAX 604-822-4633. *4038*

UNIVERSITY OF CAIRO. FACULTY OF MEDICINE. MEDICAL JOURNAL.
University of Cairo, Faculty of Medicine, Manyal University Hospital, Kasr El-Aini Post, Cairo, Egypt. TEL 726-0595. *4756*

UNIVERSITY OF CALIFORNIA AT BERKELEY. CENTER FOR CHINESE STUDIES. SERIES.
University of California Press, 2120 Berkeley Way, Berkeley, CA 94720. TEL 510-642-4247. FAX 510-643-7127. *3540*

UNIVERSITY OF CALIFORNIA AT BERKELEY. CENTER FOR JAPANESE STUDIES. SERIES.
University of California Press, 2120 Berkeley Way, Berkeley, CA 94720. TEL 510-642-4247. FAX 510-643-4247. *3330*

UNIVERSITY OF CALIFORNIA AT LOS ANGELES. CENTER FOR MEDIEVAL AND RENAISSANCE STUDIES. CONTRIBUTIONS.
University of California Press, 2120 Berkeley Way, Berkeley, CA 94720. TEL 510-642-4247. FAX 510-643-7127. *3516*

UNIVERSITY OF CALIFORNIA AT LOS ANGELES. CENTER FOR MEDIEVAL AND RENAISSANCE STUDIES. PUBLICATIONS.
University of California Press, 2120 Berkeley Way, Berkeley, CA 94720. TEL 510-642-4247. FAX 510-643-7127. *3516*

UNIVERSITY OF CALIFORNIA AT LOS ANGELES. CENTER FOR THE STUDY OF COMPARATIVE FOLKLORE AND MYTHOLOGY. PUBLICATIONS.
University of California Press, 2120 Berkeley Way, Berkeley, CA 94720. TEL 510-642-4247. FAX 510-643-7127. *3093*

UNIVERSITY OF CALIFORNIA AT LOS ANGELES. CLARK LIBRARY PROFESSORSHIP. MONOGRAPHIC SERIES.
University of California Press, 2120 Berkeley Way, Berkeley, CA 94720. TEL 510-642-4247. FAX 510-643-7127. *3796*

UNIVERSITY OF CALIFORNIA AT LOS ANGELES. LATIN AMERICAN CENTER. LATIN AMERICAN STUDIES SERIES.
Latin American Studies Center Publications, University of California, Los Angeles, Box 951447, 10342 Bunche Hall, Los Angeles, CA 90095-1447. *3650*

UNIVERSITY OF CALIFORNIA, DAVIS. CENTERS FOR WATER AND WILDLAND RESOURCES. CONTRIBUTIONS.
University of California, Davis, Centers for Water and Wildland Resources, Davis, CA 95616. TEL 916-752-8070. FAX 916-752-8086. *7301*

UNIVERSITY OF CALIFORNIA PUBLICATIONS. ANTHROPOLOGICAL RECORDS.
University of California Press, 2120 Berkeley Way, Berkeley, CA 94720. TEL 510-642-4247. FAX 510-643-7127. *333*

UNIVERSITY OF CALIFORNIA PUBLICATIONS. CLASSICAL STUDIES.
University of California Press, 2120 Berkeley Way, Berkeley, CA 94720. TEL 510-642-4247. FAX 510-643-7127. *1908*

UNIVERSITY OF CALIFORNIA PUBLICATIONS. FOLKLORE & MYTHOLOGY STUDIES.
University of California Press, 2120 Berkeley Way, Berkeley, CA 94720. TEL 510-642-4247. FAX 510-643-7127. *3093*

UNIVERSITY OF CALIFORNIA PUBLICATIONS. NEAR EASTERN STUDIES.
University of California Press, 2120 Berkeley Way, Berkeley, CA 94720. TEL 510-642-4247. FAX 510-643-7127. *3540*

UNIVERSITY OF CALIFORNIA PUBLICATIONS IN ANTHROPOLOGY.
University of California Press, 2120 Berkeley Way, Berkeley, CA 94720. TEL 510-642-4247. FAX 510-643-7127. *333*

UNIVERSITY OF CALIFORNIA PUBLICATIONS IN BOTANY.
University of California Press, 2120 Berkeley Way, Berkeley, CA 94720. TEL 510-642-4247. FAX 510-643-7127. *732*

UNIVERSITY OF CALIFORNIA PUBLICATIONS IN ENTOMOLOGY.
University of California Press, 2120 Berkeley Way, Berkeley, CA 94720. TEL 510-642-4247. FAX 510-643-7127. *762*

UNIVERSITY OF CALIFORNIA PUBLICATIONS IN GEOGRAPHY.
University of California Press, 2120 Berkeley Way, Berkeley, CA 94720. TEL 510-642-4247. FAX 510-643-7127. *3425*

UNIVERSITY OF CALIFORNIA PUBLICATIONS IN GEOLOGICAL SCIENCES.
University of California Press, 2120 Berkeley Way, Berkeley, CA 94720. TEL 510-642-4247. FAX 510-643-7127. *2323*

UNIVERSITY OF CALIFORNIA PUBLICATIONS IN LINGUISTICS.
University of California Press, 2120 Berkeley Way, Berkeley, CA 94720. TEL 510-642-4247. FAX 510-643-7127. *4310*

UNIVERSITY OF CALIFORNIA PUBLICATIONS IN MODERN PHILOLOGY.
University of California Press, 2120 Berkeley Way, Berkeley, CA 94720. TEL 510-642-4247. FAX 510-643-7127. *4311*

UNIVERSITY OF CALIFORNIA PUBLICATIONS IN ZOOLOGY.
University of California Press, 2120 Berkeley Way, Berkeley, CA 94720. TEL 510-642-4247. FAX 510-643-7127. *852*

UNIVERSITY OF CAPE TOWN. RESEARCH REPORT.
University of Cape Town, Research Support Services, Private Bag, Rondebosch 7700, South Africa. TEL 27-21-6502433. FAX 27-21-6897781. *2560*

UNIVERSITY OF CHICAGO. GEOGRAPHY RESEARCH PAPERS.
University of Chicago Press, 5801 S. Ellis Ave., Chicago, IL 60637. TEL 773-702-7899. FAX 773-660-2235. *3425*

UNIVERSITY OF CHICAGO STUDIES IN LIBRARY SCIENCE.
University of Chicago Press, 5801 S. Ellis Ave., Chicago, IL 60637. TEL 773-702-7899. *4220*

UNIVERSITY OF COLORADO. INSTITUTE OF ARCTIC AND ALPINE RESEARCH. OCCASIONAL PAPERS.
University of Colorado, Institute of Arctic and Alpine Research, Campus Box 450, Boulder, CO 80309-0450. TEL 303-492-3765. FAX 303-492-6388. *6581*

UNIVERSITY OF CONNECTICUT. INSTITUTE OF WATER RESOURCES. REPORT SERIES.
University of Connecticut, Institute of Water Resources, Storrs, CT 06269-4018. TEL 203-486-0335. *7301*

9960 REFEREED SERIALS

UNIVERSITY OF DAYTON REVIEW.
University of Dayton Press, 300 College Park Ave., Dayton, OH 45469-1539. TEL 513-229-2449. FAX 513-229-4330. *3796*

UNIVERSITY OF DELAWARE. DISASTER RESEARCH CENTER. REPORT SERIES.
University of Delaware, Disaster Research Center, Newark, DE 19716. TEL 302-831-6618. FAX 302-831-2091. *6253*

UNIVERSITY OF GHANA LAW JOURNAL.
University of Ghana, Faculty of Law, Legon, Ghana. TEL 233-21-775304. *4039*

UNIVERSITY OF HAWAII. WATER RESOURCES RESEARCH CENTER. TECHNICAL REPORT.
University of Hawaii, Water Resources Research Center, 2540 Dole St., Honolulu, HI 96822. TEL 808-956-7847. FAX 808-956-5044. *7301*

UNIVERSITY OF ILLINOIS AT URBANA-CHAMPAIGN. ENGINEERING EXPERIMENT STATION. SUMMARY OF ENGINEERING RESEARCH.
University of Illinois at Urbana-Champaign, College of Engineering, 112 Engineering Hall, 1308 W. Green St., Urbana, IL 61801. TEL 217-333-1510. *2744*

UNIVERSITY OF ILLINOIS AT URBANA-CHAMPAIGN. WATER RESOURCES CENTER. RESEARCH REPORT.
University of Illinois at Urbana-Champaign, Water Resources Center, 1101 W. Peabody Dr., Rm. 278, Urbana, IL 61801. TEL 217-333-0536. FAX 217-244-8583. *7301*

UNIVERSITY OF KANSAS. DEPARTMENT OF ANTHROPOLOGY. PUBLICATIONS IN ANTHROPOLOGY.
University of Kansas Libraries, Exchange & Gifts Department, Level 2W Watson Library, Lawrence, KS 66045. TEL 913-864-3746. *333*

UNIVERSITY OF KANSAS. MUSEUM OF NATURAL HISTORY. SPECIAL PUBLICATIONS.
University of Kansas, Natural History Museum, 602 Dyche Hall, Lawrence, KS 66045-2454. TEL 785-654-4450. FAX 785-864-5335. *632*

UNIVERSITY OF KANSAS. NATURAL HISTORY MUSEUM. SCIENTIFIC PAPERS.
University of Kansas, Natural History Museum, Lawrence, KS 66045. TEL 913-864-3347. FAX 913-864-5321. *6581*

UNIVERSITY OF KANSAS. PALEONTOLOGICAL CONTRIBUTIONS. NEW SERIES.
University of Kansas, Paleontological Institute, 121 Lindley Hall, Lawrence, KS 66045. TEL 913-864-3338. FAX 913-864-5276. *5564*

UNIVERSITY OF LONDON. INSTITUTE OF GERMANIC STUDIES. BITHELL SERIES OF DISSERTATIONS.
University of London, Institute of Germanic Studies, 29 Russell Sq., London WC1B 5DP, England. TEL 44-171-580-2711. FAX 44-171-436-3497. *4482*

UNIVERSITY OF LONDON. INSTITUTE OF GERMANIC STUDIES. PUBLICATIONS.
University of London, Institute of Germanic Studies, 29 Russell Sq., London WC1B 5DP, England. TEL 44-171-580-2711. FAX 44-171-436-3497. *4482*

UNIVERSITY OF LONDON. SCHOOL OF ORIENTAL AND AFRICAN STUDIES. BULLETIN.
Oxford University Press, Academic Division, Great Clarendon St., Oxford OX2 6DP, England. TEL 44-1865-267907. FAX 44-1865-267485. *3796*

UNIVERSITY OF MANCHESTER. DEPARTMENT OF COMPUTER SCIENCE. TECHNICAL REPORT SERIES.
University of Manchester, Department of Computer Science, Oxford Rd., Manchester M13 9PL, England. TEL 44-161-275-6130. FAX 44-161-275-6236. *2159*

UNIVERSITY OF MEMPHIS. ANTHROPOLOGICAL RESEARCH CENTER. OCCASIONAL PAPERS.
University of Memphis, Anthropological Research Center, Memphis, TN 38152. TEL 901-678-2618. FAX 901-678-2069. *333*

UNIVERSITY OF MICHIGAN. DIVISION OF RESEARCH DEVELOPMENT AND ADMINISTRATION. RESEARCH NEWS.
University of Michigan, Division of Research Development and Administration, 3003 S. State St., Ann Arbor, MI 48109-1274. TEL 313-763-5587. FAX 313-763-4053. *2561*

UNIVERSITY OF MICHIGAN. HERBARIUM. CONTRIBUTIONS.
University of Michigan, Herbarium, North University Building, Ann Arbor, MI 48109-1057. TEL 313-764-2407. FAX 313-763-0369. *732*

UNIVERSITY OF MICHIGAN. MUSEUM OF PALEONTOLOGY. CONTRIBUTIONS.
University of Michigan, Museum of Paleontology, 1529 Ruthven Museums Bldg., 1109 Geddes Rd., Ann Arbor, MI 48109-1079. TEL 313-764-0489. *5564*

UNIVERSITY OF MICHIGAN. MUSEUM OF PALEONTOLOGY. PAPERS ON PALEONTOLOGY.
University of Michigan, Museum of Paleontology, 1529 Ruthven Museums Bldg., 1109 Geddes Rd., Ann Arbor, MI 48109-1079. TEL 313-764-0489. *5564*

UNIVERSITY OF MICHIGAN. MUSEUM OF ZOOLOGY. MISCELLANEOUS PUBLICATIONS.
University of Michigan, Museum of Zoology, Ann Arbor, MI 48109-1079. TEL 313-764-0476. FAX 313-763-4080. *852*

UNIVERSITY OF MICHIGAN. MUSEUM OF ZOOLOGY. OCCASIONAL PAPERS.
University of Michigan, Museum of Zoology, Ann Arbor, MI 48109-1079. TEL 313-764-0476. FAX 313-763-4080. *852*

UNIVERSITY OF MICHIGAN. MUSEUMS OF ART AND ARCHAEOLOGY. BULLETIN.
Kelsey Museum of Archaeology, Department of the History of Art, 434 S. State St., Ann Arbor, MI 48109-1390. TEL 313-647-3307. FAX 313-763-8976. *5367*

UNIVERSITY OF MISSOURI AT COLUMBIA. MUSEUM OF ANTHROPOLOGY. MISCELLANEOUS PUBLICATIONS IN ANTHROPOLOGY.
University of Missouri at Columbia, Museum of Anthropology, 104 Swallow Hall, Columbia, MO 65211. TEL 314-882-3573. *333*

UNIVERSITY OF MISSOURI MONOGRAPHS IN ANTHROPOLOGY.
University of Missouri at Columbia, Museum of Anthropology, 104 Swallow Hall, Columbia, MO 65211. TEL 314-882-3573. *333*

UNIVERSITY OF NEW BRUNSWICK LAW JOURNAL.
University of New Brunswick, Faculty of Law, P.O. Box 4400, Fredericton, NB E3B 5A3, Canada. TEL 506-453-4657. FAX 506-453-5186. *4039*

UNIVERSITY OF NEW MEXICO. INSTITUTE OF METEORITICS. SPECIAL PUBLICATION.
University of New Mexico, Institute of Meteoritics, Albuquerque, NM 87131. TEL 505-277-2747. FAX 505-277-3577. *502*

UNIVERSITY OF NORTH DAKOTA. INSTITUTE FOR ECOLOGICAL STUDIES. RESEARCH REPORT.
Institute for Ecological Studies, University of North Dakota, Box 8278, University Sta., Grand Forks, ND 58202. TEL 701-777-2851. *2956*

UNIVERSITY OF OREGON ANTHROPOLOGICAL PAPERS.
University of Oregon, Department of Anthropology, Eugene, OR 97403-1218. TEL 541-346-5102. FAX 541-346-0668. *333*

UNIVERSITY OF OTAGO MEDICAL SCHOOL. PROCEEDINGS.
Otago Medical School Research Society, P.O. Box 913, Dunedin, New Zealand. TEL 64-3-4797570. FAX 64-3-4790401. *4756*

UNIVERSITY OF OXFORD. SCHOOL OF GEOGRAPHY. RESEARCH PAPERS.
University of Oxford, School of Geography, Mansfield Rd., Oxford OX1 3TB, England. TEL 44-1865-271919. FAX 44-1865-271929. *3425*

UNIVERSITY OF PRETORIA. INSTITUTE FOR STRATEGIC STUDIES. BULLETIN.
University of Pretoria, Institute for Strategic Studies, Pretoria 0002, South Africa. TEL 27-12-4202407. FAX 27-12-2402693. *6042*

UNIVERSITY OF SOUTH CAROLINA. BELLE W. BARUCH LIBRARY IN MARINE SCIENCE AND COASTAL RESEARCH. COLLECTED PAPERS.
University of South Carolina Press, c/o Dianne Smith, Rights & Permissions, Columbia, SC 29208. TEL 803-777-5243. *2416*

UNIVERSITY OF SOUTH FLORIDA. INTERNATIONAL BIOMEDICAL SYMPOSIA SERIES.
Plenum Publishing Corp., 233 Spring St., New York, NY 10013-1578. TEL 212-620-8000. FAX 212-463-0742. *632*

UNIVERSITY OF SUSSEX. CENTRE FOR CONTINUING EDUCATION. OCCASIONAL PAPER.
University of Sussex, Centre for Continuing Education, Falmer, Brighton, Sussex BN1 9RG, England. TEL 44-1273-678025. FAX 44-1273-678848. *3516*

UNIVERSITY OF SYDNEY. DEPARTMENT OF ECONOMICS. WORKING PAPERS IN ECONOMICS.
University of Sydney, Department of Economics, Room 324 Merewether Bldg., City Rd., Sydney, N.S.W. 2006, Australia. TEL 61-2-513074. FAX 61-2-5521118. *1009*

UNIVERSITY OF TASMANIA. CENTRE FOR ENVIRONMENTAL STUDIES. OCCASIONAL PAPER.
University of Tasmania, Centre for Environmental Studies, G.P.O. Box 252C, Hobart, Tas. 7001, Australia. FAX 61-2-202989. *2956*

UNIVERSITY OF TASMANIA. CENTRE FOR ENVIRONMENTAL STUDIES. PROJECT REPORT.
University of Tasmania, Centre for Environmental Studies, G.P.O. Box 252C, Hobart, Tas. 7001, Australia. FAX 61-02-202989. *2247*

UNIVERSITY OF TEXAS AT AUSTIN. BUREAU OF ECONOMIC GEOLOGY. ANNUAL REPORT.
University of Texas at Austin, Bureau of Economic Geology, Attn. A. Masterson, Pub. Sales, Box X, University Sta., Austin, TX 78713-8924. TEL 512-471-7144. FAX 512-471-0140. *2374*

UNIVERSITY OF TEXAS AT AUSTIN. BUREAU OF ECONOMIC GEOLOGY. GEOLOGICAL CIRCULAR.
University of Texas at Austin, Bureau of Economic Geology, Attn.: A. Masterson, Pub. Sales, Box X, University Sta., Austin, TX 78713-8924. TEL 512-471-7721. FAX 512-471-0140. *2374*

UNIVERSITY OF TEXAS AT AUSTIN. BUREAU OF ECONOMIC GEOLOGY. GUIDEBOOK.
University of Texas at Austin, Bureau of Economic Geology, Attn.: A. Masterson, Pub. Sales, Box X, University Sta., Austin, TX 78713-8924. TEL 512-471-7721. FAX 512-471-0140. *2374*

UNIVERSITY OF TEXAS AT AUSTIN. BUREAU OF ECONOMIC GEOLOGY. MINERAL RESOURCE CIRCULARS.
University of Texas at Austin, Bureau of Economic Geology, Attn.: A. Masterson, Pub. Sales, Box X, University Sta., Austin, TX 78713-8924. TEL 512-471-7721. FAX 512-471-0140. *2374*

UNIVERSITY OF TEXAS AT AUSTIN. BUREAU OF ECONOMIC GEOLOGY. OTHER PUBLICATIONS.
University of Texas at Austin, Bureau of Economic Geology, Attn.: A. Masterson, Pub. Sales, Box X, University Sta., Austin, TX 78713-8924. TEL 512-471-7721. FAX 512-471-0140. *2374*

UNIVERSITY OF TEXAS AT AUSTIN. BUREAU OF ECONOMIC GEOLOGY. REPORT OF INVESTIGATIONS.
University of Texas at Austin, Bureau of Economic Geology, Attn.: A. Masterson, Pub. Sales, Box X, University Sta., Austin, TX 78713-8924. TEL 512-471-7721. FAX 512-471-0140. *2374*

UNIVERSITY OF TEXAS AT AUSTIN. CENTER FOR RESEARCH IN WATER RESOURCES. TECHNICAL REPORT SERIES.
University of Texas at Austin, Center for Research in Water Resources, J.J. Pickle Research Campus, Austin, TX 78712. TEL 512-471-3131. FAX 512-471-0072. *7301*

THE UNIVERSITY OF TEXAS LIFETIME HEALTH LETTER.
University of Texas, Houston Health Science Center, 7000 Fannin St., Houston, TX 77030. TEL 713-792-4265. FAX 713-794-4738. *5791*

UNIVERSITY OF THE WITWATERSRAND. INSTITUTE FOR ADVANCED SOCIAL RESEARCH. SEMINAR PAPERS.
University of the Witwatersrand, Institute for Advanced Social Research, Private Bag 3, Wits 2050, South Africa. FAX 27-11-7168030. *6644*

UNIVERSITY OF TOKUSHIMA. FACULTY OF ENGINEERING. BULLETIN.
Tokushima Daigaku, Kogakubu, 2-1 Minamijosanjima-cho, Tokushima 770, Japan. TEL 81-886-56-7304. FAX 81-886-54-9632. *2744*

UNIVERSITY OF TOKYO. OCEAN RESEARCH INSTITUTE. BULLETIN.
University of Tokyo, Ocean Research Institute, 15-1 Minami-Dai 1-chome, Nakano-ku, Tokyo 164, Japan. TEL 81-3-5351-6342. FAX 81-3-3375-6716. *2417*

UNIVERSITY OF TORONTO MEDICAL JOURNAL.
University of Toronto, Medical Society, Medical Sciences Bldg., Toronto, ON M5S 1A1, Canada. TEL 416-978-8730. *4756*

UNIVERSITY OF UTAH ANTHROPOLOGICAL PAPERS.
University of Utah Press, 101 University Services Bldg., Salt Lake City, UT 84112. TEL 801-581-6771. *333*

UNIVERSITY OF WESTERN ONTARIO. SERIES IN PHILOSOPHY OF SCIENCE.
Kluwer Academic Publishers, Postbus 17, 3300 AA Dordrecht, Netherlands. TEL 31-78-6392392. FAX 31-78-6392254. *5757*

UNIVERSITY OF WESTERN ONTARIO MEDICAL JOURNAL.
Willow Press, Health Sciences Centre, London, ON N6A 3K7, Canada. *4756*

UNIVERSITY OF WYOMING. CONTRIBUTIONS TO GEOLOGY.
University of Wyoming, Department of Geology and Geophysics, Box 3006, University Sta., Laramie, WY 82071. TEL 307-766-3386. FAX 307-766-6679. *2374*

UNMANNED SYSTEMS.
Association for Unmanned Vehicle Systems International, 1200 19th St., N.W., Ste. 300, Washington, DC 20036-2412. TEL 703-524-6646. FAX 703-524-2303. *5289*

UPDATE (SOUTH AFRICAN EDITION).
George Warman Publications (Pty.) Ltd., P.O. Box 704, Cape Town 8000, South Africa. TEL 27-21-245320. FAX 27-21-261332. *4756*

UPPELDI OG MENNTUN.
Rannsoknarstofnun Kennarahaskola Islands, Stakkahlid, 105 Rekjavik, Iceland. TEL 354-568-3827. FAX 354-563-3833. *2491*

UPPER INDIA MOTORIST.
Automobile Association of Upper India, C-8, Institutional Area, South of IIT, New Delhi 110 016, India. TEL 6864521. FAX 6866302. *7120*

THE UPPERCRUST.
Upper Crust Publications, 361 Virginia St., Crystal Lake, IL 60014. TEL 815-459-1000. *3689*

URBAN ACADEMIC LIBRARIAN.
Library Association of the City University of New York, Hunter College Library, 695 Park Ave., New York, NY 10021. TEL 212-772-4168. *4221*

URBAN AFFAIRS (NEWARK).
Urban Affairs Association, University of Delaware, Newark, DE 19716. *3762*

URBAN AFFAIRS REVIEW.
Sage Publications, Inc., 2455 Teller Rd., Thousand Oaks, CA 91320. TEL 805-499-0721. FAX 805-499-0871. *3762*

URBAN ANTHROPOLOGY AND STUDIES OF CULTURAL SYSTEMS AND WORLD ECONOMIC DEVELOPMENT.
The Institute, Inc., 56 Centennial Ave., Brockport, NY 14420. TEL 716-637-6531. *333*

URBAN DESIGN AND PRESERVATION QUARTERLY.
American Planning Association, Urban Design and Preservation, 1776 Massachusetts Ave. N.W., Washington, DC 20036. *3762*

URBAN DESIGN INTERNATIONAL.
Thomson Professional, 2-6 Boundary Row, London SE1 8HN, England. TEL 44-171-8650066. FAX 44-171-5229623. *3762*

URBAN EDUCATION.
Corwin Press, Inc., 2455 Teller Rd., Thousand Oaks, CA 91320. TEL 805-499-0721. FAX 805-499-0871. *2491*

URBAN HISTORY REVIEW.
Becker Associates, Box 507, Sta. Q, Toronto, ON M4T 2M5, Canada. TEL 416-483-7282. FAX 416-489-1713. *3650*

URBAN POLICY & RESEARCH.
Urban Policy and Research, Landscape, Environment and Policy, RMIT, P.O. Box 2476V, Melbourne, Vic. 3001, Australia. TEL 61-3-4293316. FAX 61-3-6601855. *3763*

THE URBAN REVIEW.
Human Sciences Press, Inc., 233 Spring St., New York, NY 10013. TEL 212-620-8000. FAX 212-463-0742. *2491*

URBAN STUDIES.
Carfax Publishing Co., P.O. Box 25, Abingdon, Oxon OX14 3UE, England. TEL 44-1235-401000. FAX 44-1235-401550. *3763*

URETHANE ABSTRACTS.
Technomic Publishing Co., Inc., 851 New Holland Ave., Box 3535, Lancaster, PA 17604. TEL 717-291-5609. FAX 717-295-4538. *5886*

URO-GRAM.
Society of Urologic Nurses and Associates, Box 56, Pitman, NJ 08071-0056. TEL 609-256-2335. FAX 609-589-7463. *5166*

UROGYNAECOLOGIA INTERNATIONAL JOURNAL.
Associazione Italiana di Urologia Ginecologica, Via Salaria 290, 00199 Rome, Italy. TEL 39-6-8080114. *4968*

UROLOGIA INTERNATIONALIS.
S. Karger AG, Allschwilerstr. 10, P.O. Box, CH-4009 Basel, Switzerland. TEL 41-61-3061111. FAX 41-61-3061234. *5166*

UROLOGIC NURSING.
Mosby - Year Book, Inc., 11830 Westline Industrial Dr., St. Louis, MO 63146-3318. TEL 314-872-8370. FAX 314-432-1380. *5166*

UROLOGIC ONCOLOGY.
Elsevier Science Inc., Box 945, New York, NY 10159-0945. TEL 212-633-3730. FAX 212-633-3680. *4988*

UROLOGY.
Excerpta Medica, Inc., 105 Raider Blvd., Belle Meade, NJ 08502. TEL 908-874-8550. FAX 908-874-8419. *5166*

US WURK.
Fries Instituut, Postbus 716, 9700 AS Groningen, Netherlands. FAX 31-50-3634900. *4312*

USER MODELING AND USER-ADAPTED INTERACTION.
Kluwer Academic Publishers, Postbus 17, 3300 AA Dordrecht, Netherlands. TEL 31-78-6392392. FAX 31-78-6392254. *2520*

UTAH GENEALOGICAL ASSOCIATION. GENEALOGICAL JOURNAL.
Utah Genealogical Association, Box 1144, Salt Lake City, UT 84110. TEL 801-531-2091. *3244*

UTAH GEOLOGICAL ASSOCIATION. ANNUAL GUIDEBOOK.
Utah Geological Association, Box 520100, Salt Lake City, UT 84152-0100. TEL 801-537-3300. *2374*

UTAH GEOLOGICAL SURVEY. BULLETIN.
Utah Geological Survey, 1594 W. North Temple, Ste. 3110, Box 146100, Salt Lake City, UT 84114-6100. TEL 801-537-3300. FAX 801-537-3400. *2374*

UTAH GEOLOGICAL SURVEY. CIRCULAR.
Utah Geological Survey, 1594 W. North Temple, Ste. 3110, Box 146100, Salt Lake City, UT 84114-6100. TEL 801-537-3300. FAX 801-537-3400. *2375*

UTAH GEOLOGICAL SURVEY. SPECIAL STUDIES.
Utah Geological Survey, 1594 W. North Temple, Ste. 3110, Box 146100, Salt Lake City, UT 84114-6100. TEL 801-537-3300. FAX 801-537-3400. *2375*

UTAH GEOLOGICAL SURVEY. SURVEY NOTES.
Utah Geological Survey, 1594 W. North Temple, Ste. 3110, Box 146100, Salt Lake City, UT 84114-6100. TEL 801-537-3300. FAX 801-537-3400. *2375*

UTAH HISTORICAL QUARTERLY.
State Historical Society, 300 Rio Grande, Salt Lake City, UT 84101. TEL 801-533-3500. FAX 801-533-3504. *3650*

UTILITIES LAW REVIEW.
John Wiley & Sons Ltd., Journals, Baffins Ln., Chichester, W. Sussex PO19 1UD, England. TEL 44-1243-779777. FAX 44-1243-775878. *4041*

UTILITIES POLICY.
Elsevier Science Ltd., Pergamon, P.O. Box 800, Kidlington, Oxford OX5 1DX, England. TEL 44-1865-843000. FAX 44-1865-843010. *2849*

UTRECHT STUDIES IN AIR AND SPACE LAW.
Kluwer Academic Publishers, Postbus 17, 3300 AA Dordrecht, Netherlands. TEL 31-78-6392392. FAX 31-78-6392254. *4041*

UTTAR PRADESH JOURNAL OF ZOOLOGY.
Uttar Pradesh Zoological Society, c/o PG-Dept. of Zoology, Muzaffarnagar 251001, India. TEL 91-131-409053. FAX 91-131-402510. *852*

UTTERANTS...
Global Graphics, Box 822, Mountain View, CA 94042-0822. *4483*

V F A PROFIL.
Profil Verlag GmbH, Scheideweg 160B, 26127 Oldenburg, Germany. TEL 49-441-93023-0. FAX 49-441-9302320. *416*

V H L FAMILY FORUM.
V H L Family Alliance, 171 Clinton Rd., Brookline, MA 02146. TEL 617-232-5946. FAX 617-734-8233. *5101*

V I C MEDICAL UPDATE.
Vitamin Information Centre, P.O. Box 182, Isando 1600, South Africa. TEL 27-11-3934794. FAX 27-11-3934790. *5483*

V I E R BULLETIN.
Victorian Institute of Educational Research, c/o Kevin Hall, Ed., Faculty of Education, University of Melbourne, Parkville, Vic. 3052, Australia. TEL 61-3-93448418. FAX 61-3-93472468. *2492*

V O REALITES.
Parti Suisse du Travail, Case Postale 366, CH-1211 Geneva 4, Switzerland. TEL 022-3206335. FAX 022-3200587. *3900*

V O, VIE OUVRIERE.
Revue Vie Ouvriere Inc., 1215 Visitation, Ste. 101, Montreal, PQ H2L 3B5, Canada. TEL 514-523-5998. FAX 514-527-3403. *3267*

VAAR FOEDA.
Statens Livsmedelsverk, P.O. Box 622, SE-751 26 Uppsala, Sweden. FAX 46-18-17-55-00. *5483*

VAARD I NORDEN.
Sykepleiernes Samarbeid i Norden, P.O. Box 2681, St. Hanshaugen, N-131 Oslo 1, Norway. TEL 47-22-04-33-04. FAX 47-22-38-02-30. *4951*

VACATION INDUSTRY REVIEW.
Interval International, 6262 Sunset Dr., Penthouse 1, S. Miami, FL 33143. TEL 305-666-1861. FAX 305-668-3408. *7247*

REFEREED SERIALS

VACCINE.
Elsevier Science Ltd., Oxford Fulfilment Centre, P.O. Box 800, Kidlington, Oxford OX5 1DX, England. TEL 44-1865-843000. FAX 44-1865-843010. *4801*

VACUUM.
Elsevier Science Ltd., Pergamon, P.O. Box 800, Kidlington, Oxford OX5 1DX, England. TEL 44-1865-843000. FAX 44-1865-843010. *5832*

VAEKST.
Hedeselskabet, Klostermarken 12, P.O. Box 110, DK-8800 Viborg, Denmark. TEL 45-86-67-61-11. FAX 45-86-67-51-01. *3166*

VAERLD OCH VETANDE.
Vaerld och Vetande Ekonomisk Foerening, c/o Ejvegaard, Hagmarksgatan 8 C, S-582 17 Linkoeping, Sweden. FAX 46-13-12-88-11. *6582*

VALLEY WOMEN'S VOICE.
University of Massachusetts, 321 Student Union, Amherst, MA 01003. TEL 413-545-2436. *7335*

VALOER.
Foereningen Valoer, Konstvetenskapliga Institutionen, Slottet, Soedra tornet, inngaang HO, S-752 37 Uppsala, Sweden. TEL 46-18-18-28-88. FAX 46-18-18-28-92. *471*

VALUATION.
American Society of Appraisers, Box 17265, Washington, DC 20041-0265. TEL 703-478-2228. FAX 703-742-8471. *1171*

THE VALUER AND LAND ECONOMIST.
Australian Institute of Valuers and Land Economists, 6 Campion St., Deakin, A.C.T. 2600, Australia. TEL 61-6-2822411. FAX 61-6-28521944. *6315*

VALUERS' NEWS LINE.
New Zealand Institute of Valuers, P.O. Box 27-146, Willis St., Wellington, New Zealand. TEL 64-4-385-8436. FAX 64-4-382-9214. *6315*

VANDERBILT UNIVERSITY. DEPARTMENT OF ENVIRONMENTAL AND WATER RESOURCES ENGINEERING. TECHNICAL REPORTS.
Vanderbilt University, Department of Civil & Environmental Engineering, Box 6304, Sta. B, Nashville, TN 37235. TEL 615-322-2720. *2956*

VANDERBILT UNIVERSITY PUBLICATIONS IN ANTHROPOLOGY.
Vanderbilt University Publications in Anthropology, Box 1532, Sta. B, Nashville, TN 37235. TEL 615-322-7522. FAX 615-343-0230. *334*

VANGUARD.
Vanguard Publications, P.O. Box 2269, London E6 3RF, England. TEL 44-181-471-6872. FAX 44-181-592-3009. *5977*

VASCULAR SURGERY (GLEN HEAD).
Westminster Publications, Inc., 708 Glen Cove Ave., Glen Head, NY 11545. TEL 516-759-0025. FAX 516-759-5524. *5157*

VASCULUM.
Northern Naturalists Union, Sunderland Museum & Art Gallery, Borough Rd., Sunderland, Tyne and Wear SR1 1PP, England. TEL 44-191-565-0723. FAX 44-191-565-0713. *6582*

VECTEUR ENVIRONNEMENT.
Association Quebecoise des Techniques de l'Environnement, 911 rue Jean-Talon Est, Montreal, PQ H2R 1V5, Canada. TEL 514-270-7110. FAX 514-270-7154. *2956*

VEDANTA.
Ramakrishna Vedanta Centre, Bourne End, Bucks. SL8 5LG, England. TEL 44-1628-526464. *6395*

VELIGER.
California Malacozoological Society, Inc., Department of Invertebrate Zoology, Santa Barbara Museum of Natural History, 2559 Puesta del Sol Rd., Santa Barbara, CA 93105. TEL 802-682-4711. FAX 805-963-9679. *852*

VELON.
Vereniging voor Lerarenopleiders in Nederland, Postbus 30011, 6503 HN Nijmegen, Netherlands. TEL 31-24-3459802. *2562*

VENEZUELAN LITERATURE AND ARTS JOURNAL.
Hamline University Press, Hamline University, Mail Stop 50, 1536 Hewitt Ave., St. Paul, MN 55104-1284. TEL 612-523-2001. FAX 612-523-2956. *4484*

VERA LEX.
Pace University, Costello House, Pleasantville, NY 10570-2799. TEL 914-773-3945. FAX 914-773-3541. *5758*

VERBUM NOBILE.
Zwiazek Szlachty Polskiej, Ul. Parkowa 52-5, 81-727 Sopot, Poland. TEL 466617. *3244*

VERENIGING VOOR GESCHIED- TAAL- EN VOLKSKUNDIG ONDERZOEK IN HET KORTRIJKSE. VERHANDELINGEN.
Vereniging voor Geschied- Taal- en Volkskundig Onderzoek in het Kortrijkse, Keizer Karelstraat 83, 8000 Brugge, Belgium. TEL 32-50-317366. *3611*

VERGILIUS.
Vergilian Society of America, Box 817, Oxford, OH 45056. TEL 803-777-2765. FAX 803-777-0454. *1909*

VERHALTENSTHERAPIE.
S. Karger AG, Allschwilerstr. 10, P.O. Box, CH-4009 Basel, Switzerland. TEL 41-61-3061111. FAX 41-61-3061234. *5101*

VERSES.
Cader Publishing, Ltd., 36915 Ryan Rd., Sterling Heights, MI 48310. TEL 810-795-3635. FAX 810-795-9875. *4484*

VESTNIK.
Vestnik Information Agency, 6100 Park Heights Ave., Baltimore, MD 21215. TEL 410-358-0900. FAX 410-358-3867. *3611*

VET ON-LINE. *7280*

VETERANS FOR PEACE JOURNAL.
Veterans for Peace, Inc., Box 3881, Portland, ME 04104. TEL 207-773-1431. FAX 207-773-0804. *6042*

VETERINARIA E ZOOTECNIA.
Universidade Estadual Paulista, Av. Vicente Ferreira 1278, Caixa Postal 71, 17515-901 Marilla SP, Brazil. TEL 55-144-222504. FAX 55-144-222504. *7281*

VETERINARIA MEXICO.
Universidad Nacional Autonoma de Mexico, Facultad de Medicina Veterinaria y Zootecnia, Circuito Exterior, Ciudad Universitaria, 04510 Mexico, D.F., Mexico. TEL 52-5-6225875. FAX 52-5-5508697. *7281*

VETERINARY & COMPARATIVE OPHTHALMOLOGY.
Veterinary Practice Publishing Co., Box 6050, Mission Viejo, CA 92690. *7281*

VETERINARY AND COMPARATIVE ORTHOPAEDICS AND TRAUMATOLOGY.
F.K. Schattauer Verlagsgesellschaft mbH, Lenzhalde 3, 70192 Stuttgart, Germany. TEL 49-711-22987-0. FAX 49-711-22987-50. *7281*

VETERINARY AND HUMAN TOXICOLOGY.
Comparative Toxicology Laboratories, Publication Office, Kansas State University, Manhattan, KS 66506-5606. TEL 913-532-4334. FAX 913-532-4481. *2982*

VETERINARY CLINICAL NUTRITION.
Veterinary Practice Publishing Co., Box 6050, Mission Viejo, CA 92690. *7282*

VETERINARY CLINICAL PATHOLOGY.
Veterinary Practice Publishing Co., Box 6050, Mission Viejo, CA 92690. *7282*

VETERINARY DERMATOLOGY.
Blackwell Science Ltd., Osney Mead, Oxford OX2 OEL, England. TEL 44-1865-206206. FAX 44-1865-721205. *7282*

VETERINARY IMMUNOLOGY AND IMMUNOPATHOLOGY.
Elsevier Science B.V., P.O. Box 211, 1000 AE Amsterdam, Netherlands. TEL 31-20-4853911. FAX 31-20-4853598. *7282*

VETERINARY INSTITUTE, PULAWY. BULLETIN.
Instytut Weterynarii, c/o Krystyna Ciemiega-Wilczynska, Sec., Al. Partyzantow 57, 24-100 Pulawy, Poland. TEL 48-81-863051. FAX 48-81-862595. *7282*

VETERINARY MEDICAL JOURNAL GIZA.
Cairo University, Faculty of Veterinary Medicine, Giza, Cairo, Egypt. *7282*

VETERINARY MEDICINE.
Veterinary Medicine Publishing Co., 15333 W. 95th, Lenexa, KS 66219. TEL 913-492-4300. FAX 913-492-4157. *7283*

VETERINARY MICROBIOLOGY.
Elsevier Science B.V., P.O. Box 211, 1000 AE Amsterdam, Netherlands. TEL 31-20-4853911. FAX 31-20-4853598. *7283*

VETERINARY PARASITOLOGY.
Elsevier Science B.V., P.O. Box 211, 1000 AE Amsterdam, Netherlands. TEL 31-20-4853911. FAX 31-20-4853598. *7283*

VETERINARY PRACTICE STAFF.
Veterinary Practice Publishing Co., Box 6050, Mission Viejo, CA 92690. *7283*

VETERINARY QUARTERLY.
Koninklijke Nederlandse Maatschappij voor Diergeneeskunde, Julianalaan 10, Postbus 14301, 3508 SB Utrecht, Netherlands. TEL 31-50-2510111. FAX 31-30-2511787. *7283*

VETERINARY RADIOLOGY & ULTRASOUND.
American College of Veterinary Radiology, c/o Lucinda Ayres, 2520 Beechridge Rd., Raleigh, NC 27608. TEL 919-510-0560. FAX 919-510-0560. *7283*

VETERINARY RESEARCH.
Editions Scientifiques et Medicales Elsevier, 141 rue de Javel, 75747 Paris, France. TEL 33-1-45589022. FAX 33-1-45589421. *7284*

VETERINARY RESEARCH COMMUNICATIONS.
Kluwer Academic Publishers, Postbus 17, 3300 AA Dordrecht, Netherlands. TEL 31-78-6392392. FAX 31-78-6392254. *7284*

VETERINARY SURGERY.
W.B. Saunders Co., Curtis Center, 3rd Fl., Independence Sq. W., Philadelphia, PA 19106-3399. TEL 215-238-7800. FAX 215-238-6445. *7284*

VETERINER HEKIMLERI DERNEGI DERGISI.
Turk Veteriner Hekimleri Dernegi, Saglik Sok. 21-3, Yenisehir, Ankara, Turkey. *7284*

VETUS TESTAMENTUM.
E.J. Brill, P.O. Box 9000, 2300 PA Leiden, Netherlands. TEL 31-71-5353500. FAX 31-71-5317532. *6380*

VETUS TESTAMENTUM. SUPPLEMENTS.
E.J. Brill, P.O. Box 9000, 2300 PA Leiden, Netherlands. TEL 31-71-5353500. FAX 31-71-5317532. *6380*

VEXILLA HELVETICA.
Societe Suisse de Vexillologie, c/o Dr. Emil Dreyer, Flurweg 43, CH-3052 Zollikofen, Switzerland. TEL 41-31-9116018. FAX 41-31-9220225. *3244*

VEXILOLOGIE.
Vexilologicky Klub, Pod Lipami 58, 130 00 Prague, Czech Republic. *3244*

VIANDES ET PRODUITS CARNES.
Association pour le Developpement de l'Institut de la Viande, 2 rue Chappe, 63039 Clermont-Ferrand Cedex 2, France. TEL 33-4-73907297. FAX 33-4-73921777. *292*

VIATOR.
N.V. Brepols, Steenweg op Tielen 68, 2300 Turnhout, Belgium. TEL 32-14-402500. FAX 32-14-428919. *3516*

VIBRATIONAL SPECTRA AND STRUCTURE.
Elsevier Science B.V., Books Division, P.O. Box 211, 1000 AE Amsterdam, Netherlands. TEL 31-20-4853911. FAX 31-20-4853705. *1836*

VIBRATIONAL SPECTROSCOPY.
Elsevier Science B.V., P.O. Box 211, 1000 AE Amsterdam, Netherlands. TEL 31-20-4853911. FAX 31-20-4853598. *1770*

VICTORIA, AUSTRALIA. GEOLOGICAL SURVEY. REPORT.
Geological Survey of Victoria, Minerals and Petroleum, Victoria, P.O. Box 2145, MDC, Fitzroy, Vic. 3065, Australia. TEL 61-3-94127377. FAX 61-3-94127442. *2375*

VICTORIAN.
Victoria College, School and Old Victorians' Association, Jersey, Channel Islands. TEL 44-1534-37591. FAX 44-1534-27448. *1978*

VICTORIAN LITERATURE AND CULTURE.
Cambridge University Press, Edinburgh Bldg., Shaftesbury Rd., Cambridge CB2 2RU, England. TEL 44-1223-312393. FAX 44-1223-315052. *4484*

VICTORIAN REVIEW.
Victorian Studies Association of Western Canada, c/o Prof. Chris Hosgood, Ed., Dept. of History, University of Lethbridge, Lethbridge, AB T1K 3M4, Canada. TEL 403-329-2543. FAX 403-329-5109. *4484*

VICTORIANS INSTITUTE JOURNAL.
University of North Carolina Press, Box 2288, NC 27515-2288. TEL 919-966-3561. FAX 919-966-3829. *4364*

LE VIDE: SCIENCE, TECHNIQUE ET APPLICATIONS.
Societe Francaise du Vide, 19 rue du Renard, 75004 Paris, France. TEL 33-1-53-01-90-30. FAX 33-1-42-78-63-20. *5832*

VIDEO INDUSTRY STATISTICAL REPORT.
Corbell Publishing, 4676 Admiralty Way, Ste. 300, Marina Del Rey, CA 90292. TEL 310-574-5337. FAX 310-574-5383. *2014*

VIDEO JOURNAL OF COLOR FLOW IMAGING.
Dynamedia, Inc., 2 Fulham Court, Silver Spring, MD 20902-3016. TEL 301-649-6886. FAX 301-649-3447. *5116*

VIDEO JOURNAL OF ECHOCARDIOGRAPHY.
Dynamedia, Inc., 2 Fulham Court, Silver Spring, MD 20902-3016. TEL 301-649-6886. FAX 301-649-3447. *4825*

VIDEOMAKER.
Videomaker Inc., Box 4591, Chico, CA 95927. TEL 916-891-8410. FAX 916-891-8443. *2070*

VIDERE.
M I T Press, 5 Cambridge Center, Cambridge, MA 02142. TEL 617-253-2889. FAX 617-577-1545. *2125*

VIE ET MILIEU.
Universite de Paris VI (Pierre et Marie Curie), Laboratoire Arago, 66650 Banyuls sur Mer, France. TEL 33-4-68887327. FAX 33-4-68881699. *632*

VIENNA CIRCLE COLLECTION.
Kluwer Academic Publishers, Postbus 17, 3300 AA Dordrecht, Netherlands. TEL 31-78-6392392. FAX 31-78-6392254. *577*

VIET NAM GENERATION.
Viet Nam Generation, Inc., Box 208206, New Haven, CT 06520-8206. TEL 203-387-6882. FAX 203-389-3104. *3651*

VIGILIAE CHRISTIANAE.
E.J. Brill, P.O. Box 9000, 2300 PA Leiden, Netherlands. TEL 31-71-5353500. FAX 31-71-5317532. *6380*

VIGILIAE CHRISTIANAE. SUPPLEMENT.
E.J. Brill, P.O. Box 9000, 2300 PA Leiden, Netherlands. TEL 31-71-5353500. FAX 31-71-5317532. *6380*

VILLES EN PARALLELE.
Universite de Paris X - Nanterre, Laboratoire de Geographie Urbaine, 200 av. de la Republique, 92001 Nanterre Cedex, France. TEL 33-1-40977367. FAX 33-1-40977616. *3426*

VINYAR TENGWAR.
Elvish Linguistic Fellowship, 2509 Ambling Circle, Crofton, MD 21114. TEL 410-721-5690. *4484*

VIOLA D'AMORE SOCIETY OF AMERICA. NEWSLETTER.
Viola d'Amore Society of America, 39-23 47th St., Sunnyside, NY 11104. TEL 718-729-3138. *5443*

VIOLENCE AGAINST WOMEN.
Sage Publications, Inc., 2455 Teller Rd., Thousand Oaks, CA 91320. TEL 805-499-0721. FAX 805-499-0871. *6738*

VIOLENCE AND VICTIMS.
Springer Publishing Company, 536 Broadway, New York, NY 10012-3955. TEL 212-431-4370. FAX 212-941-7842. *6738*

VIRAL IMMUNOLOGY.
Mary Ann Liebert, Inc. Publishers, 2 Madison Ave., Larchmont, NY 10538. TEL 914-834-3100. FAX 914-834-3688. *4801*

VIRGINIA. WATER RESOURCES RESEARCH CENTER. BULLETIN.
Water Resources Research Center, Virginia Polytechnic Institute and State University, 10 Sandy Hall (0444), Blacksburg, VA 24061. TEL 703-231-8036. *7302*

VIRGINIA BUILDER.
Mid-Atlantic Trade Exposition Inc., 2117 Smith Ave., Chesapeake, VA 23320. TEL 757-420-2434. FAX 804-424-5954. *917*

VIRGINIA ENGLISH BULLETIN.
Virginia Association of Teachers of English, College of Education, Virginia Tech, Blacksburg, VA 24061-0313. FAX 540-231-9075. *4313*

VIRGINIA ENVIRONMENTAL LAW JOURNAL.
Virginia Environmental Law Journal, University of Virginia, School of Law, Charlottesville, VA 22903. TEL 804-924-3683. FAX 804-924-7536. *4043*

VIRGINIA EPISCOPALIAN.
Episcopal Diocese of Virginia, 110 W. Franklin, Richmond, VA 23220. TEL 804-643-8451. FAX 804-644-6928. *6446*

VIRGINIA GEOGRAPHER.
Virginia Geographical Society, c/o Donald Zeigler, Ed., Old Dominion Univ., Norfolk, VA 23529-0088. FAX 804-683-3241. *3426*

VIRGINIA JOURNAL OF INTERNATIONAL LAW.
Virginia Journal of International Law Association, University of Virginia, School of Law, 580 Massie Rd., Charlottesville, VA 22903. TEL 804-924-3415. FAX 804-924-3237. *4128*

VIRGINIA JOURNAL OF SCIENCE.
Virginia Academy of Science, c/o James H. Martin, J.S. Reynolds Community College, Box 85622, Richmond, VA 23285-5622. TEL 804-371-3064. *6583*

VIRGINIA SOCIAL SCIENCE JOURNAL.
Virginia Social Science Association, c/o Thomas Bertsch, Man. Ed., Marketing Department, James Madison University, Harrisonburg, VA 22807. FAX 703-568-2754. *6645*

VIRGINIA TAX REVIEW.
Virginia Tax Review Association, University of Virginia, School of Law, Charlottesville, VA 22901. TEL 804-924-4726. FAX 804-924-7536. *1637*

VIRITTAAJAA.
Kotikielen Seura, Castrenianum, P.O. Box 3, FIN-00014, University of Helsinki, Finland. FAX 358-0-19123329. *4313*

VIROLOGY.
Academic Press, Inc., Journal Division, 525 B St., Ste. 1900, San Diego, CA 92101-4495. TEL 619-230-1840. FAX 619-688-6800. *795*

VIRUS GENES.
Kluwer Academic Publishers Boston, Box 358, Accord Sta., Hingham, MA 02018-0358. TEL 617-871-6600. FAX 617-871-6528. *795*

VIRUS INFECTIONS OF VERTEBRATES.
Elsevier Science B.V., Books Division, P.O. Box 211, 1000 AE Amsterdam, Netherlands. TEL 31-20-4853911. FAX 31-20-4853705. *7284*

VIRUS RESEARCH.
Elsevier Science B.V., P.O. Box 211, 1000 AE Amsterdam, Netherlands. TEL 31-20-4853911. FAX 31-20-4853598. *795*

VISIBLE RELIGION.
E.J. Brill, P.O. Box 9000, 2300 PA Leiden, Netherlands. TEL 31-71-5353500. FAX 31-71-5317532. *6381*

VISION.
Management Development Institute, P.O. Box 60, Mehrauli Road, Gurgaon 122 001, Haryana, India. TEL 91-124-340173. FAX 91-124-341189. *1512*

VISION RESEARCH.
Elsevier Science Ltd., Pergamon, P.O. Box 800, Kidlington, Oxford OX5 1DX, England. TEL 44-1865-843000. FAX 44-1865-843010. *5002*

VISION TECNOLOGICA.
Intevep, S.A., Centro de Informacion Tecnica, Apdo. Postal 76343, Caracas 1070A, Venezuela. TEL 58-2-9087879. FAX 58-2-9086886. *5626*

VISTA (INDIANAPOLIS).
Wesleyan Publishing House, Box 50434, Indianapolis, IN 46250-0434. TEL 317-570-5191. FAX 317-570-5290. *6381*

VISTAS IN ASTRONOMY.
Elsevier Science Ltd., Pergamon, P.O. Box 800, Kidlington, Oxford OX5 1DX, England. TEL 44-1865-843000. FAX 44-1865-843010. *503*

VISUAL ANTHROPOLOGY.
Gordon and Breach - Harwood Academic, Amsteldisk 166, 1st Fl., 1079 LH Amsterdam, Netherlands. *334*

VISUAL LITERACY REVIEW.
International Visual Literacy Association (Spokane), c/o Barbara I. Clark, Gonzaga University, E. 502 Boone AD 25, Spokane, WA 99258-0001. *2623*

VISUAL MEDIA.
Association for the Advancement of Visual Media, 3-1750 The Queensway, Ste. 1341, Etobicoke, ON M9C 5HS, Canada. TEL 416-761-6056. FAX 905-820-7397. *5347*

VISUAL RESOURCES.
Gordon and Breach - Harwood Academic, Amsteldisk 166, 1st Fl., 1079 LH Amsterdam, Netherlands. *471*

VITAMINS AND HORMONES: ADVANCES IN RESEARCH AND APPLICATIONS.
Academic Press, Inc., 525 B St., Ste. 1900, San Diego, CA 92101-4495. TEL 619-231-0926. FAX 619-699-6715. *5698*

VIVARIUM.
E.J. Brill, P.O. Box 9000, 2300 PA Leiden, Netherlands. TEL 31-71-5353500. FAX 31-71-5317532. *3611*

VIVEK.
National Centre for Software Technology, Gulmohar Cross Rd. No. 9, Juhu, Bombay 400 049, India. TEL 91-22-620-1606. FAX 91-22-621-0139. *2105*

VNITRNI LEKARSTVI.
Nakladatelske Stredisko C L S J.E. Purkyne, Sokolska 31, 120 26 Prague 2, Czech Republic. TEL 420-2-24911420. FAX 420-2-24911420. *4757*

VOCE DELL'EMIGRANTE.
Comitato Regionale Emigranti Abruzzesi, Vico Sportello, 10, Casella Postale 7, 67035 Pratola Peligna (AQ), Italy. TEL 39-864-53147. FAX 39-864-52785. *3048*

VODOHOSPODARSKY CASOPIS.
Slovenska Akademia Vied, Ustav Hydrologie, Racianska 75, P.O. Box 94, 830 08 Bratislava, Slovakia. TEL 421-7-253000. FAX 421-7-259404. *2398*

REFEREED SERIALS

VOICES (BURNSVILLE).
Rural Southern Voice for Peace, 1898 Hannah Branch Rd., Burnsville, NC 28714. TEL 704-675-5933. FAX 704-675-9335. *6645*

VOICES (DECATUR).
American Academy of Psychotherapists, Box 607, Decatur, GA 30031. TEL 404-299-6336. FAX 404-299-0206. *6158*

VOICES IN ITALIAN AMERICANA.
Bordighera, Inc., Purdue University, Dept. of Foreign Languages and Literatures, 1359 Stanley Coulter Hall, Box 1374, Lafayette, IN 47902-1374. TEL 765-494-3839. FAX 765-496-1700. *4365*

VOICES - ISRAEL.
Voices Israel Group of Poets in English, c/o Mark Levinson, Ed., P.O. Box 5780, Herzliya 46157, Israel. TEL 972-9-9552411. *4526*

VOIX ET VISAGES.
Association Nationale des Anciennes Deportees et Internees de la Resistance, 241 bd. Saint-Germain, 75007 Paris, France. TEL 33-1-45513414. *3611*

VOLCANOLOGY & SEISMOLOGY.
Gordon and Breach - Harwood Academic, Amsteldisk 166, 1st Fl., 1079 LH Amsterdam, Netherlands. *2392*

VOLKSKUNDE IN NIEDERSACHSEN.
Volker Schmerse Text- und Bildgestaltung, Postfach 110335, 37048 Goettingen, Germany. TEL 49-551-46335. FAX 49-551-47550. *3093*

VOLKSKUNDIG BULLETIN.
Uitgeverij S U N, Postbus 1609, 6501 BP Nijmegen, Netherlands. TEL 31-24-3221700. FAX 31-24-3235493. *334*

VOLUME REVERSAL SURVEY.
Almarco L C C, Box 1451, Sedona, AZ 86339. TEL 602-282-1275. FAX 602-282-6364. *1414*

VOX (ALBUQUERQUE).
Cleave Press, 2118 Central S.E., Ste. 6, Albuquerque, NM 87106. TEL 505-243-3492. *4365*

VOX SANGUINIS.
S. Karger AG, Allschwilerstr. 10, P.O. Box, CH-4009 Basel, Switzerland. TEL 41-61-3061111. FAX 41-61-3061234. *4802*

VOXAIR.
Canadian Forces Base Winnipeg, Westwin, MB R3J 0T0, Canada. TEL 204-889-3963. FAX 204-885-4176. *5290*

VOYAGEUR.
Brown County Historical Society, Box 8085, Green Bay, WI 54308-8085. TEL 920-465-2446. FAX 920-465-2890. *3651*

VRIJETIJDSTUDIES.
Uitgeverij Boom, P.O. Box 400, 7940 AK Meppel, Netherlands. TEL 31-522-257012. FAX 31-522-253864. *4153*

VSTRECHI.
Encounters, 7738 Woodbine Ave., Philadelphia, PA 19151. TEL 215-477-6172. *4526*

VYSKUMNY USTAV ZIVOCISNEJ VYROBY V NITRE. VEDECKE PRACE.
Vyskumny Ustav Zivocisnej Vyroby v Nitre, Hlohovska 2, 949 92 Nitra, Slovak Republic. TEL 42-87-519030. FAX 42-87-519032. *164*

VYTAPENI, VETRANI, INSTALACE.
Spolecnost pro Techniku Prostredi, Novotneho Lavka 5, 116 68 Prague 1, Czech Republic. TEL 420-2-21082201. FAX 420-2-21082201. *3485*

VYZIVA A POTRAVINY.
Spolecnost pro Vyzivu, Sobeslavska 40, 130 00 Prague 3, Czech Republic. TEL 42-2-67311280. FAX 42-2-67310515. *5484*

VYZVOL'NYI SHLYAKH.
Ukrainian Information Service Ltd., 200 Liverpool Rd., London N1 1LF, England. TEL 44-171-607-6266. FAX 44-171-607-6737. *4365*

W C C I FORUM.
World Council for Curriculum and Instruction, c/o Estela Matriano, WCCI Exec. Dir., University of Cincinnati, Cincinnati, OH 45221-0002. TEL 513-556-3573. FAX 513-556-2483. *2567*

W E A LEGEND.
Wilderness Education Association, Colorado State University, Department of Natural Resource Recreation and Tourism, Colorado State University, Ft. Collins, CO 80523. TEL 970-223-6252. FAX 970-223-6252. *2248*

W H Y.
World Hunger Year, 505 Eighth Ave., 21st Fl., New York, NY 10018-6582. TEL 212-629-8850. FAX 212-465-9274. *6693*

W P S PROFESSIONAL HANDBOOK SERIES.
Western Psychological Services, 12031 Wilshire Blvd., Los Angeles, CA 90025. TEL 310-478-2061. FAX 310-478-7838. *6158*

W Z B PAPERS.
Wissenschaftszentrum Berlin fuer Sozialforschung, Reichpietschufer 50, 10785 Berlin, Germany. TEL 49-30-25491-0. FAX 49-30-25491684. *6645*

WAIKATO LAW REVIEW.
University of Waikato, School of Law, Private Bag 3105, Hamilton, New Zealand. TEL 64-7-8384167. FAX 64-7-8384417. *4043*

WALLACE STEVENS JOURNAL.
Wallace Stevens Society, Inc., Box 5750 Clarkson University, Potsdam, NY 13699-5750. TEL 315-268-3987. FAX 315-268-3983. *4526*

WAR AND SOCIETY.
University of New South Wales, Department of History, University College, Australian Defence Force Academy, Campbell, A.C.T. 2600, Australia. TEL 61-6-2688879. FAX 61-6-2688879. *3517*

WAR IN HISTORY.
Arnold, 338 Euston Rd., London NW1 3BH, England. TEL 44-171-873-6000. FAX 44-171-873-6325. *5290*

WAR, LITERATURE, AND THE ARTS.
U.S. Air Force Academy, Department of English, HQ USAFA-DFENG, 2354 Fairchild Dr., Ste. 6D35, USAF Academy, CO 80840-6242. TEL 719-333-3930. FAX 719-333-3132. *4485*

WARM EARTH.
Warm Earth Publishing, Kiah Cottage, Kenilworth, Qld. 4754, Australia. TEL 61-74-460457. *3207*

WARSHIP.
Conway Maritime Press, 33 John St., London WC1N 2AT, England. TEL 44-171-753-7777. FAX 44-171-753-7795. *5290*

WASCANA REVIEW.
University of Regina, Regina, SK S4S 0A2, Canada. TEL 306-584-4302. FAX 306-585-4827. *4485*

WASHINGTON ACADEMY OF SCIENCES. JOURNAL.
Washington Academy of Sciences, 1200 New York Ave., N.W., 8th Fl., Washington, DC 20005. TEL 202-326-8975. *6583*

WASHINGTON HISTORY.
Historical Society of Washington, D.C., 1307 New Hampshire N.W., Washington, DC 20036-1507. TEL 202-785-2068. FAX 202-887-5785. *3651*

WASHINGTON INTERNATIONAL.
c/o Delphi Intenational, 1828 L. St., N.W., Ste. 900, Washington, DC 20036-5104. TEL 202-223-3180. FAX 301-946-0779. *7249*

WASHINGTON REPORT (ST. PETERSBURG).
Editors Release Service, Box 10309, St. Petersburg, FL 33733-0309. TEL 813-866-1598. FAX 813-866-1598. *5979*

WASHINGTON STATE UNIVERSITY. MATHEMATICS NOTES.
Washington State University, Department of Pure and Applied Mathematics, Pullman, WA 99164-3113. TEL 509-335-8518. *4615*

WASMANN JOURNAL OF BIOLOGY.
University of San Francisco, Biology Department, San Francisco, CA 94117. TEL 415-666-6381. *633*

WASTE MANAGEMENT.
Elsevier Science Ltd., Pergamon, P.O. Box 800, Kidlington, Oxford OX5 1DX, England. TEL 44-1865-843000. FAX 44-1865-843010. *2991*

WASTE MANAGEMENT GUIDE.
The Bureau of National Affairs, Inc., 1231 25th St., N.W., Washington, DC 20037. TEL 202-452-4200. FAX 202-822-8092. *1770*

WATCH MAGAZINE.
Watch Magazines Inc., 245-401 Richmond St. W., Toronto, ON M5V 1X3, Canada. TEL 416-595-1313. FAX 416-595-1312. *1893*

WATER ENVIRONMENT RESEARCH.
Water Environment Federation, 601 Wythe St., Alexandria, VA 22314-1994. TEL 703-684-2400. FAX 703-684-2492. *2973*

WATER GARDEN JOURNAL.
International Water Lily Society, Suite 328 - G12, 1401 Johnson Ferry Rd., Marietta, GA 30062-8115. TEL 770-977-3564. FAX 770-977-9959. *3207*

WATER INTERNATIONAL.
International Water Resources Association, University of New Mexico, 1915 Roma N.E., Albuquerque, NM 87131-1436. TEL 505-277-9400. FAX 505-277-9405. *7303*

WATER LAW.
John Wiley & Sons Ltd., Journals, Baffins Ln., Chichester, W. Sussex PO19 1UD, England. TEL 44-1243-779777. FAX 44-1243-775878. *7304*

WATER POLLUTION: A SERIES OF MONOGRAPHS.
Academic Press, Inc., 525 B St., Ste. 1900, San Diego, CA 92101-4495. TEL 619-231-0926. FAX 619-699-6715. *7304*

WATER QUALITY INTERNATIONAL.
Elsevier Science Ltd., Pergamon, P.O. Box 800, Kidlington, Oxford OX5 1DX, England. TEL 44-1865-843000. FAX 44-1865-843010. *2973*

WATER QUALITY RESEARCH JOURNAL OF CANADA.
National Water Research Institute, 867 Lakeshore Rd., Box 5050, Burlington, ON L7R 4L7, Canada. TEL 905-336-4884. FAX 905-336-6444. *2973*

WATER RESEARCH.
Elsevier Science Ltd., Pergamon, P.O. Box 800, Kidlington, Oxford OX5 1DX, England. TEL 44-1865-843000. FAX 44-1865-843010. *7304*

WATER RESOURCES.
Maik Nauka - Interperiodica, Mezhdunarodnyi Otdel, Ul. Profsoyuznaya, 90, 117864 Moscow, Russia. TEL 7-095-3360066. FAX 7-095-3360066. *7305*

WATER RESOURCES MANAGEMENT.
Kluwer Academic Publishers, Postbus 17, 3300 AA Dordrecht, Netherlands. TEL 31-78-6392392. FAX 31-78-6392254. *7305*

WATER S.A.
Water Research Commission, P.O. Box 824, Pretoria 0001, South Africa. *7305*

WATER SCIENCE AND TECHNOLOGY.
Elsevier Science Ltd., Pergamon, P.O. Box 800, Kidlington, Oxford OX5 1DX, England. TEL 44-1865-843000. FAX 44-1865-843010. *7305*

WATER SCIENCE AND TECHNOLOGY LIBRARY.
Kluwer Academic Publishers, Postbus 17, 3300 AA Dordrecht, Netherlands. TEL 31-78-6392392. FAX 31-78-6392254. *7305*

WATER TREATMENT.
China Ocean Press, International Cooperation Department, Haimao Dalou, 1 Fuxingmenwai Dajie, Beijing 100860, People's Republic of China. TEL 8032211. FAX 8033515. *7306*

WATER WEST.
Naylor Communications Ltd., Ste. 203, 301 14 St. N.W., Calgary, AB T2N 2A1, Canada. TEL 403-259-4041. FAX 403-258-1631. *7306*

WATERLINES.
Intermediate Technology Publications Ltd., 103-105 Southampton Row, London WC1B 4HH, England. TEL 44-171-436-9761. FAX 44-171-436-2013. *7306*

WATERLOO HISTORICAL SOCIETY. ANNUAL VOLUME.
Waterloo Historical Society, 85 Queen St. N., Kitchener, ON N2H 2H1, Canada. FAX 519-570-1360. *3651*

WAVE MOTION.
North-Holland, P.O. Box 211, 1000 AE Amsterdam, Netherlands. TEL 31-20-4853911. FAX 31-20-4853598. *5832*

WAY STATION MAGAZINE.
1319 S. Logan St., Lansing, MI 48910. TEL 517-374-7735. *4486*

WEAR.
Elsevier Science S.A., P.O. Box 564, CH-1001 Lausanne 1, Switzerland. TEL 41-21-3207381. FAX 41-21-3235444. *2903*

WEATHERWISE.
Heldref Publications, 1319 Eighteenth St., N.W., Washington, DC 20036-1802. TEL 202-296-6267. FAX 202-296-5149. *5245*

WEBBIA; RACCOLTA DI SCRITTI BOTANICI.
Museo Botanico, Via Giorgio La Pira 4, 50121 Florence, Italy. TEL 39-55-2757460. *732*

WEBER STUDIES: AN INTERDISCIPLINARY HUMANITIES JOURNAL.
Weber State University, Ogden, UT 84408-1214. TEL 801-626-6473. FAX 801-626-7130. *3797*

WECHSELWIRKUNG.
Vijlen Institute for Physics, Rott 53, NL-6294 NL Vijlen, Netherlands. TEL 31-43455-9001. FAX 31-43455-2346. *6980*

WEED RESEARCH.
Blackwell Science Ltd., Osney Mead, Oxford OX2 0EL, England. TEL 44-1865-206206. FAX 44-1865-721205. *249*

WEED SCIENCE.
Weed Science Society of America, 1508 W. University, Champaign, IL 61821-3133. TEL 217-352-4212. FAX 217-352-4241. *249*

WEEKLY BULLETIN.
Magyar Tavirati Iroda, Pl. Naphegy ter. 8, 1016 Budapest, Hungary. TEL 36-1-1756722. FAX 36-1-1188297. *3305*

WEGE UND VISIONEN.
Sandila Import-Export Handels GmbH, Saegestr. 37, 79737 Herrischried, Germany. TEL 49-7764-1026. FAX 49-7764-6660. *6382*

WEIMAR AND NOW: GERMAN CULTURAL CRITICISM.
University of California Press, 2120 Berkeley Way, Berkeley, CA 94720. TEL 510-642-4247. FAX 510-643-7127. *4486*

WEISHENGWU XUEBAO.
Science Press, Marketing and Sales Department, 16 Donghuangchenggen North St., Beijing 100717, People's Republic of China. TEL 4010642. FAX 4019810. *795*

WEITI GUSHENGWU XUEBAO.
Science Press, Marketing and Sales Department, 16 Donghuangchenggen North St., Beijing 100717, People's Republic of China. TEL 4010642. FAX 4019810. *795*

WEIXING XIAOSHUO XUANKAN.
Weixing Xiaoshuo Xuankan Zazhishe, No.5, Xinwei Lu, Nanchang, Jiangxi 330002, People's Republic of China. TEL 0791-8332782. FAX 0791-8331282. *4486*

WELCOME HOME.
Mothers-at-Home, Inc., 8310A Old Courthouse Rd., Vienna, VA 22182. TEL 703-827-5903. FAX 703-790-8587. *7336*

WELDING AND SURFACING REVIEWS.
Gordon and Breach - Harwood Academic, Amsteldisk 166, 1st Fl., 1079 LH Amsterdam, Netherlands. *5224*

WELDING IN THE WORLD.
Elsevier Science Ltd., Pergamon, P.O. Box 800, Kidlington, Oxford OX5 1DX, England. TEL 44-1865-843000. FAX 44-1865-843010. *5225*

WELSH HISTORY REVIEW.
University of Wales Press, 6 Gwennyth St., Cathays, Cardiff CF2 4YD, Wales. TEL 44-1222-231919. FAX 44-1222-230908. *3517*

WELSH JOURNAL OF EDUCATION.
University of Wales Press, 6 Gwennyth St., Cathays, Cardiff CF2 4YD, Wales. TEL 44-1222-231919. FAX 44-1222-230908. *2493*

DIE WELT DES ISLAMS.
E.J. Brill, P.O. Box 9000, 2300 PA Leiden, Netherlands. TEL 31-71-5353500. FAX 31-71-5317532. *5540*

WELTTRENDS.
WeltTrend e.V., c/o Raimund Kraemer, Ed., Universitaet Potsdam, Postfach 900327, 14439 Potsdam, Germany. TEL 49-331-9774489. FAX 49-331-9774535. *6043*

DE WERELD VAN HET JONGE KIND.
Uitgeverij Dijkstra bv, Postbus 24018, 3502 MA Utrecht, Netherlands. TEL 31-30-82803321. FAX 31-30-803844. *2493*

WERTHEIM PUBLICATIONS IN INDUSTRIAL RELATIONS.
Harvard University, J.F.K. School of Government, Cambridge, MA 02138. TEL 617-495-4157. FAX 617-495-5898. *1458*

WEST AFRICAN JOURNAL OF EDUCATIONAL AND VOCATIONAL MEASUREMENT.
West African Examinations Council, Test Development and Research Division, P.M.B. 1076, Yaba, Lagos State, Nigeria. TEL 234-1-861711. *6158*

WEST EUROPEAN POLITICS.
Frank Cass, Newbury House, 890-900 Eastern Ave., Newbury Park, Ilford, Essex IG2 7HH. TEL 44-181-599-8866. FAX 44-181-599-0954. *6043*

WEST INDIAN MEDICAL JOURNAL.
University of the West Indies, Faculty of Medical Sciences, Mona Campus, Kingston 7, Jamaica, W.I. TEL 809-927-1214. FAX 809-927-2556. *4758*

WEST VIRGINIA ACADEMY OF SCIENCE. PROCEEDINGS.
West Virginia Academy of Science, Marshall University, 400 Hal Greer Blvd., Huntington, WV 25755. TEL 304-696-2338. FAX 304-696-3243. *6583*

WEST VIRGINIA MEDICAL JOURNAL.
West Virginia State Medical Association, 4307 MacCorkle Ave., Box 4106, Charleston, WV 25364. TEL 304-925-0342. FAX 304-925-0345. *4758*

WESTERN AMERICAN LITERATURE.
Western Literature Association, Utah State University, English Department, Logan, UT 84322-3200. TEL 801-797-1603. FAX 801-797-4099. *4487*

WESTERN AUSTRALIAN NATURALIST.
Western Australian Naturalists' Club Inc., P.O. Box 156, Nedlands, W.A. 6009, Australia. FAX 61-9-2728688. *6583*

WESTERN BIRDS.
Western Field Ornithologists, c/o Dorothy Myers, 6011 Saddletree Ln., Yorba Linda, CA 92686. TEL 714-779-2201. *810*

WESTERN JOURNAL OF COMMUNICATION.
Western States Communication Association, c/o Connie J. Conlee, WSCA Executive Director, Department of Speech Communication, California State University, Fresno, Fresno, CA 93740-0046. *4314*

WESTERN JOURNAL OF MEDICINE.
Carden Jennings Publishing Co., Ltd., 1224 W. Main St., Ste. 200, Charlottesville, VA 22903-2858. TEL 804-979-4913. FAX 804-979-4025. *4758*

WESTERN PHARMACOLOGY SOCIETY. PROCEEDINGS.
Western Pharmacology Society, Inc., University of Arizona, Department of Pharmacology, College of Medicine, Tucson, AZ 85724. TEL 602-626-7843. FAX 602-626-6883. *5698*

WESTFIELD CENTER. NEWSLETTER.
Westfield Center for Early Keyboard Studies, One Cottage St., Easthampton, MA 01027. TEL 413-527-7664. FAX 413-527-7689. *5444*

WESTMINSTER MAGAZINE.
Westminster College, Office of Communication Services, New Wilmington, PA 16172. TEL 412-946-7226. FAX 412-946-7187. *1979*

WESTMINSTER STUDIES IN EDUCATION.
Carfax Publishing Co., P.O. Box 25, Abingdon, Oxon. OX14 3UE, England. TEL 44-1235-401000. FAX 44-1235-401550. *2493*

WESTWIND (LOS ANGELES).
University of California at Los Angeles, A-265 Murphy Hall, 405 Hilgard Ave., Los Angeles, CA 90095. TEL 310-206-1225. *473*

WETLANDS.
Society of Wetlands Scientists, Box 1897, Lawrence, KS 66044. TEL 913-843-1235. FAX 913-843-1274. *7306*

WETLANDS ECOLOGY AND MANAGEMENT.
Kluwer Academic Publishers, Postbus 17, 3300 AA Dordrecht, Netherlands. TEL 31-78-6392392. FAX 31-78-6392254. *7307*

WHAT'S NEW IN FOREST RESEARCH.
Forest Research Institute, Private Bag 3020, Rotorua, New Zealand. TEL 64-7-3475899. FAX 64-7-3479380. *3166*

WHAT'S UP AT CHEEKWOOD.
Tennessee Botanical Gardens & Museum of Art, 1200 Forrest Park Dr., Nashville, TN 37205. TEL 615-353-2163. FAX 615-353-2168. *473*

WHERE VANCOUVER.
Where Canada, Inc., The Sixth Estate, 2208 Spruce St., Vancouver, BC V6H 2P3, Canada. TEL 604-736-5586. FAX 604-736-3465. *7262*

WHISPERING WIND.
Jack Heriard, Ed. & Pub., Box 1390, Folsom, LA 70437-1390. TEL 504-796-5433. FAX 504-796-9236. *3049*

WHITE RIBBON BULLETIN.
M & D Printing Co., R.I. Box 43, Lowpoint, IL 61545. TEL 309-443-5275. FAX 309-364-3355. *2306*

WHITE RIVER VALLEY HISTORICAL QUARTERLY.
White River Valley Historical Society, Box 555, Point Lookout, MO 65726-0555. *3652*

WHO'S WHO OF SOUTHERN AFRICA INCLUDING MAURITIUS, NAMIBIA, ZIMBABWE, BOTSWANA, SWAZILAND AND NEIGHBORING COUNTRIES.
Jonathan Ball Publishers, P.O. Box 411697, Craighall 2024, South Africa. TEL 27-11-8802406. FAX 27-11-8802366. *580*

WIADOMOSCI ARCHEOLOGICZNE.
Panstwowe Muzeum Archeologiczne, Ul. Dluga 52, 00-241 Warsaw, Poland. TEL 48-22-8313221. FAX 48-22-8315195. *388*

WIADOMOSCI BOTANICZNE.
Polska Akademia Nauk, Instytut Botaniki im. W. Szafera, Ul. Lubicz 46, 31-512 Krakow, Poland. TEL 48-12-215144. FAX 48-12-219790. *732*

WIENER - GOETHE - VEREIN. JAHRBUCH.
Verlag Fassbaender, Lichtgasse 10, A-1150 Vienna, Austria. TEL 43-1-8923546. FAX 43-1-8923717. *4487*

WIES I ROLNICTWO.
Polska Akademia Nauk, Instytut Rozwoju Wsi i Rolnictwa, Ul. Nowy Swiat 72, 00-330 Warsaw, Poland. TEL 48-22-8266371. FAX 48-22-8266371. *204*

WILD CAT.
Cat Survival Trust, The Centre, Codicote Rd., Welwun, Herts AL6 9TU, England. TEL 44-143-871-6873. FAX 44-143-871-7535. *2249*

WILD OUTDOOR WORLD (W.O.W.).
Rocky Mountain Elk Foundation, Box 1249, Helena, MT 59624. TEL 406-449-1335. FAX 406-449-9197. *1894*

WILDERNESS AND ENVIRONMENTAL MEDICINE.
Chapman & Hall, Journals Department 2-6 Boundary Row, London SE1 8HN, England. TEL 44-171-8650066. FAX 44-171-5229623. *5133*

WILDERNESS NEWS.
Wilderness Society, 130 Davey St., Hobart, Tas. 7000, Australia. TEL 61-2-349799. *2958*

WILDERNESS RECORD.
California Wilderness Coalition, 2655 Portage Bay E., Ste. 5, Davis, CA 95616. TEL 916-758-0380. FAX 916-758-0382. *2249*

WILDLIFE BEHAVIOR AND ECOLOGY.
University of Chicago Press, 5801 S. Ellis Ave., Chicago, IL 60637. TEL 773-702-7899. *633*

WILDLIFE BIOLOGY.
Nordic Council for Wildlife Research, c/o Jan Bertelsen, Techn. Ed., Grenaavej 14, Kaloe, DK-8410 Roende, Denmark. TEL 45-89-20-15-08. FAX 45-89-20-15-15. *853*

WILDLIFE CONSERVATION.
Wildlife Conservation Society, Wildlife Conservation Park, Bronx, NY 10460. TEL 718-220-5121. FAX 718-584-2625. *2249*

WILDLIFE GUARDIAN.
League Against Cruel Sports Ltd., Sparling House, 83-87 Union St., London SE1 1SG, England. FAX 44-171-357-6749. *305*

WILDLIFE MONOGRAPHS.
Wildlife Society, 5410 Grosvenor Ln., Bethesda, MD 20814-2197. TEL 301-897-9770. FAX 301-530-2471. *2249*

WILDLIFE RESCUE.
Wildlife Rescue Association of British Columbia, 5216 Glencarin Dr., Burnaby, BC V5B 3C1, Canada. TEL 604-526-7275. FAX 604-524-2890. *2249*

WILDLIFE SOCIETY BULLETIN.
Wildlife Society, 5410 Grosvenor Ln., Bethesda, MD 20814-2197. TEL 301-897-9770. FAX 301-530-2471. *2250*

WILEY SERIES IN GEOTECHNICAL ENGINEERING.
John Wiley & Sons, Inc., 605 Third Ave., New York, NY 10158. TEL 212-850-6000. FAX 212-850-6088. *250*

WILLDENOWIA.
Botanischer Garten und Botanisches Museum Berlin-Dahlem, Koenigin-Luise-Str. 6-8, 14191 Berlin, Germany. TEL 49-30-83006194. FAX 49-30-83006186. *733*

WILLIAM AND MARY QUARTERLY.
Omohundro Institute of Early American History and Culture, Box 8781, Williamsburg, VA 23187. TEL 757-221-1120. FAX 757-221-1047. *3652*

WILLIAM CARLOS WILLIAMS REVIEW.
William Carlos Williams Society, University of Texas at Austin, Department of English, PAR 108, Austin, TX 78712-1164. TEL 512-471-7842. FAX 512-471-4909. *4487*

WILLIAMS ALUMNI REVIEW.
Williams College, Society of Alumni, Mears House, 75 Park St., Box 38, Williamstown, MA 01267. TEL 413-597-4151. FAX 413-597-4158. *1980*

WIND ENGINEERING.
Multi-Science Publishing Co. Ltd., 107 High St., Brentwood, Essex CM14 4RX, England. TEL 44-1277-224632. FAX 44-1277-223453. *2707*

WINDOW FASHIONS.
G & W McNamara Publishing, Inc., 4225 White Bear Pky., Ste. 400, St. Paul, MN 55110-3349. TEL 612-293-1544. FAX 612-653-4308. *3861*

WINDSOR REVIEW.
University of Windsor, Faculty of Arts, Windsor, ON N9B 3P4, Canada. TEL 519-253-4232. FAX 519-973-7050. *4366*

WINE & DINE E-ZINE.
Jubilee Cottage, Upper Nyland, Gillingham, Dorset SP8 5SH, England. *3738*

WINTERTHUR PORTFOLIO.
University of Chicago Press, Journals Division, Box 37005, Chicago, IL 60637. TEL 773-753-3347. FAX 773-753-0811. *5369*

WIRELESS PERSONAL COMMUNICATIONS.
Kluwer Academic Publishers, Postbus 17, 3300 AA Dordrecht, Netherlands. TEL 31-78-6392392. FAX 31-78-6392254. *2030*

WIRELESS TELECOM.
275 Slater St., Ste. 2004, Ottawa, ON K1P 5H9, Canada. TEL 613-233-4888. FAX 613-233-2032. *2009*

THE WISCONSIN ARCHEOLOGIST.
Wisconsin Archeological Society, Box 1292, Milwaukee, WI 53201. TEL 414-229-4273. *389*

WISCONSIN ARCHITECT.
Wisconsin Architect, Inc., 321 S. Hamilton St., Madison, WI 53703-3606. TEL 608-257-8477. *417*

WISCONSIN BLUE BOOK.
Department of Administration, Document Sales, 202 S. Thornton Ave., Box 7840, Madison, WI 53707. TEL 608-266-3358. *6201*

WISCONSIN MEDICAL JOURNAL.
State Medical Society of Wisconsin, 330 E. Lakeside St., Box 1109, Madison, WI 53701. TEL 608-257-6781. FAX 608-283-5401. *4759*

WITNESS (FARMINGTON HILLS).
Oakland Community College, 27055 Orchard Lake Rd., Farmington Hills, MI 48334. TEL 810-471-7740. *4366*

WOMAN IN HISTORY.
Monument Press (Las Colinas), Box 160361, Las Colinas, TX 75016-9998. TEL 214-686-5332. FAX 214-685-5332. *7336*

WOMAN'S ART JOURNAL.
Woman's Art, Inc., 1711 Harris Rd., Laverock, PA 19038-7208. TEL 215-233-0639. FAX 215-233-0639. *473*

WOMEN & CRIMINAL JUSTICE.
Haworth Press, Inc., 10 Alice St., Binghamton, NY 13904. TEL 607-722-5857. FAX 607-722-6362. *4096*

WOMEN & HEALTH.
Haworth Press, Inc., 10 Alice St., Binghamton, NY 13904. TEL 607-722-5857. FAX 607-722-6362. *7311*

WOMEN AND LANGUAGE.
George Mason University, Communication Department, 4400 University Dr., Fairfax, VA 22030-4444. TEL 703-993-1099. FAX 703-993-1096. *4314*

WOMEN & PERFORMANCE.
Women & Performance Project, 721 Broadway, 6th Fl., New York, NY 10003. TEL 212-998-1625. *7018*

WOMEN & POLITICS (BINGHAMTON).
Haworth Press, Inc., 10 Alice St., Binghamton, NY 13904. TEL 607-722-5857. FAX 607-722-6362. *5980*

WOMEN & THERAPY.
Haworth Press, Inc., 10 Alice St., Binghamton, NY 13904. TEL 607-722-5857. FAX 607-722-6362. *6158*

WOMEN - CHURCH.
Women - Church Journal Collective Inc., G.P.O. Box 2134, Sydney, N.S.W. 2001, Australia. TEL 61-2-99692125. FAX 61-2-99692125. *6382*

WOMEN IN CONTEXT.
Plenum Publishing Corp., 233 Spring St., New York, NY 10013-1578. TEL 212-620-8000. FAX 212-463-0742. *7311*

WOMEN IN CULTURE AND SOCIETY.
University of Chicago Press, 5801 S. Ellis Ave., Chicago, IL 60637. TEL 773-702-7899. *7337*

WOMEN IN FRENCH STUDIES.
Women in French, c/o Adele King, Ed., Department of Modern Languages, Ball State University, Muncie, IN 47306. TEL 765-285-1365. FAX 765-285-8980. *4488*

WOMEN IN GERMAN YEARBOOK.
University of Nebraska Press, 312 N. 14th St., Box 880484, Lincoln, NE 68588-0484. TEL 402-472-3581. FAX 402-472-6214. *7348*

WOMEN OF NOTE QUARTERLY.
Vivace Press, N.W. 310 Wawawai Rd., Pullman, WA 99163-2959. TEL 509-334-4660. FAX 509-334-3551. *5444*

WOMEN WITH WHEELS.
Susan Frissell, Ed. & Pub., 1718 Northfield Sq., Ste. A, Northfield, IL 60093. TEL 847-501-3519. *7122*

WOMEN'S GLOBAL NETWORK FOR REPRODUCTIVE RIGHTS. NEWSLETTER.
Women's Global Network for Reproductive Rights, NZ Voorburgwal 32, 1012 RZ Amsterdam, Netherlands. TEL 31-20-6209672. FAX 31-20-6222450. *7311*

WOMEN'S HEALTH ISSUES.
Elsevier Science Inc., Box 945, New York, NY 10159-0945. TEL 212-633-3730. FAX 212-633-3680. *7311*

WOMEN'S HEALTH: RESEARCH ON GENDER, BEHAVIOR, AND POLICY.
Lawrence Erlbaum Associates, Inc., 10 Industrial Dr., Mahwah, NJ 07430-2262. TEL 201-236-9500. FAX 201-236-0072. *7311*

WOMEN'S HISTORY REVIEW.
Triangle Journals Ltd., P.O. Box 65, Wallingford, Oxon. OX10 0YG, England. TEL 44-1491-838013. FAX 44-1491-834968. *7349*

WOMEN'S IMAGING.
Durantech Publishing Co., 3870 La Sierra Ave., Ste. 392, Riverside, CA 92505. TEL 818-413-0826. *4968*

WOMEN'S STUDIES (NEW YORK).
Gordon and Breach - Harwood Academic, Amsteldisk 166, 1st Fl., 1079 LH Amsterdam, Netherlands. *7349*

WOMEN'S STUDIES IN COMMUNICATION.
Organization for Research on Women and Communication, c/o Sharon D. Downey, Ed., Department of Speech Comm., CSU, 1250 Bellflower Blvd., Long Beach, CA 90840-2407. TEL 310-985-4301 ext.7673. FAX 310-985-4259. *7349*

WOMEN'S STUDIES INTERNATIONAL FORUM.
Elsevier Science Ltd., Pergamon, P.O. Box 800, Kidlington, Oxford OX5 1DX, England. TEL 44-1865-843000. FAX 44-1865-843010. *7349*

WOMEN'S STUDIES QUARTERLY.
Feminist Press at the City University of New York, 311 E. 94th St., New York, NY 10128-5603. TEL 212-360-5790. FAX 212-348-1241. *7349*

WOMEN'S WORLD.
Isis - Women's International Cross-Cultural Exchange (Isis-WICCE), P.O. Box 4934, Kampala, Uganda. TEL 256-41-266007. FAX 256-41-268676. *7339*

WOMEN'S WRITING.
Triangle Journals Ltd., P.O. Box 65, Wallingford, Oxon. OX10 0YG, England. TEL 44-1491-838013. FAX 44-1491-834968. *7349*

WOMENWISE.
Concord Feminist Health Center, 38 S. Main St., Concord, NH 03301. TEL 603-225-2739. FAX 603-668-6255. *7311*

WOMYN'S WORDS.
Women's Energy Bank, Inc., Box 15548, St. Petersburg, FL 33733-5548. TEL 813-823-5333. *7350*

WOOL TECHNOLOGY AND SHEEP BREEDING.
Wool Research Organisation of New Zealand Inc., Private Bag 4749, Christchurch, New Zealand. TEL 64-3-3252421. FAX 64-3-3242717. *292*

WOOLF STUDIES ANNUAL.
Pace University Press, 1 Pace Plaza, New York, NY 10038. TEL 212-346-1405. FAX 212-346-1754. *4488*

WORD & IMAGE.
Taylor & Francis Ltd., 1 Gunpowder Sq., London EC4A 3DE, England. TEL 44-171-5830490. FAX 44-171-5830585. *4367*

WORD & SPIRIT.
St. Bede's Publications, Box 545, 271 N. Main St., Petersham, MA 01366. TEL 508-724-3407. FAX 508-724-3574. *6486*

WORD IN ACTION.
British and Foreign Bible Society, Stonehill Green, Westlea, Swindon, Wilts. SN5 7DG, England. TEL 44-1793-418100. FAX 44-1793-418118. *6382*

WORD IN LIFE.
Australian Catholic University, P.O. Box 256, Dickson, A.C.T. 2602, Australia. TEL 61-6-62091184. FAX 61-6-62091148. *6486*

WORD OF MOUTH (SAN FRANCISCO).
c/o Delta Dental Plan of CA, Box 7736, San Francisco, CA 94120. TEL 415-972-8300. *4873*

WORD WRAP.
Manitoba Writers' Guild, 206-100 Arthur St., Winnipeg, MB R3B 1H3, Canada. TEL 204-942-6134. FAX 204-942-5754. *4488*

WORK.
Elsevier Science Ireland Ltd., P.O. Box 85, Limerick, Ireland. TEL 353-61-471944. FAX 353-61-472144. *5501*

WORK AND STRESS.
Taylor & Francis Ltd., 1 Gunpowder Sq., London EC4A 3DE, England. TEL 44-171-583-0490. FAX 44-171-583-0585. *6159*

WORKERS' COMP. ADVISOR (NEW YORK).
New York State Insurance Fund, PIO 2nd fl., 199 Church St., New York, NY 10007. TEL 212-312-7285. FAX 212-312-9042. *3837*

WORKING MOMS AND DADS.
Corporate Marketing and Publishing Inc., Box 12217, Tucson, AZ 85732-2217. TEL 520-790-4044. *1859*

WORKING PAPERS ON LANGUAGE, GENDER & SEXISM.
Monash University, Department of Linguistics, Clayton, Vic. 3168, Australia. TEL 61-9-99052297. *4314*

WORKING PAPERS ON WOMEN IN INTERNATIONAL DEVELOPMENT.
Michigan State University, Women and International Development Program, 202 International Center for International Programs, East Lansing, MI 48824-1035. TEL 517-353-5040. FAX 517-353-7254. *1370*

WORKING PARTY REPORTS.
Centre for European Policy Studies, Place du Congres 1, 1000 Brussels, Belgium. TEL 32-2-2293911. FAX 32-2-2194151. *6044*

WORKS AND DAYS.
Indiana University of Pennsylvania, English Department, 110 Leonard Hall, Indiana, PA 15705. TEL 412-357-6486. FAX 412-357-6213. *4488*

WORLD AFFAIRS (WASHINGTON).
Heldref Publications, 1319 Eighteenth St., N.W., Washington, DC 20036-1802. TEL 202-296-6267. FAX 202-296-5149. *6044*

WORLD ANIMAL SCIENCE.
Elsevier Science B.V., Books Division, P.O. Box 211, 1000 AE Amsterdam, Netherlands. TEL 31-20-4853911. FAX 31-20-4853705. *853*

WORLD AQUACULTURE SOCIETY. JOURNAL.
World Aquaculture Society, 143 J M Parker Coliseum, Louisiana State University, Baton Rouge, LA 70803. TEL 504-388-3137. FAX 504-388-3493. *2417*

THE WORLD BANK ECONOMIC REVIEW.
World Bank, 1818 H St., N.W., Washington, DC 20433. TEL 202-477-1155. FAX 202-522-2627. *1295*

WORLD BANK RESEARCH OBSERVER.
World Bank, 1818 H St., N.W., Washington, DC 20433. TEL 202-473-1155. FAX 202-522-2627. *1173*

WORLD CERAMICS ABSTRACTS.
Ceram Research Ltd., Queens Rd., Penkhull, Stoke-on-Trent, Staffs. ST4 7LQ, England. *1736*

WORLD COMPETITION.
Kluwer Law International, Postbus 85889, 2508 CN The Hague, Netherlands. TEL 31-70-3081500. FAX 31-70-3081515. *4128*

WORLD CROP PESTS.
Elsevier Science B.V., Books Division, P.O. Box 211, 1000 AE Amsterdam, Netherlands. TEL 31-20-4853911. FAX 31-20-4853705. *250*

WORLD DEVELOPMENT.
Elsevier Science Ltd., Pergamon, P.O. Box 800, Kidlington, Oxford OX5 1DX, England. TEL 44-1865-843000. FAX 44-1865-843010. *1371*

THE WORLD ECONOMY.
Blackwell Publishers Ltd., 108 Cowley Rd., Oxford OX4 1JF, England. TEL 44-1865-791100. FAX 44-1865-791347. *1013*

WORLD ENGLISHES.
Blackwell Publishers Ltd., 108 Cowley Rd., Oxford OX4 1JF, England. TEL 44-1865-791100. FAX 44-1865-791347. *4314*

WORLD FUTURES.
Gordon and Breach - Harwood Academic, Amsteldisk 166, 1st Fl., 1079 LH Amsterdam, Netherlands. *5759*

WORLD HOSPITALS AND HEALTH SERVICES.
International Hospital Federation, 4 Abbots Pl., London NW6 4NP, England. TEL 0171-372-7181. FAX 0171-328-7433. *3720*

WORLD JOURNAL OF PSYCHOSYNTHESIS.
World Journal Press, Box 859, E. Lansing, MI 48823. TEL 517-372-4660. FAX 517-372-9959. *5101*

WORLD JOURNAL OF SURGERY.
Springer-Verlag, Medical Journals, 175 Fifth Ave., New York, NY 10010. TEL 212-460-1500. FAX 212-473-6272. *5157*

WORLD LIBRARIES.
Rosary College, Graduate School of Library and Information Science, 7900 W. Division, River Forest, IL 60305. TEL 708-524-6866. FAX 708-524-6657. *4223*

WORLD LITERATURE WRITTEN IN ENGLISH.
National Institute of Education, Division of Literature and Drama, Bukit Timah Rd., Singapore 1025, Singapore. TEL 65-4605622. FAX 65-4635840. *4488*

THE WORLD OF A S P.
American Self-Protection Association, 825 Greengate Oval, Sagamore Hills, OH 44067. TEL 216-467-7110. FAX 216-457-6834. *6794*

WORLD OF CO-OPERATIVE ENTERPRISE.
Plunkett Foundation, 23 Hanborough Business Park, Long Hanborough, Oxford OX8 8LH, England. TEL 44-1993-883636. FAX 44-1993-883576. *1208*

THE WORLD OF TRIBAL ARTS.
Tribarts Inc., 2261 Market St., Ste. 644, San Francisco, CA 94114. TEL 415-677-7917. FAX 415-413-8321. *5369*

WORLD OF WOOD.
International Wood Collectors Society, 11553 Marion St., Denver, CO 80233-2191. TEL 303-252-1479. *3166*

WORLD PATENT INFORMATION.
Elsevier Science Ltd., Pergamon, P.O. Box 800, Kidlington, Oxford OX5 1DX, England. TEL 44-1865-843000. FAX 44-1865-843010. *5592*

WORLD POLITICS (BALTIMORE).
Johns Hopkins University Press, Journals Publishing Division, 2715 N. Charles St., Baltimore, MD 21218-4319. TEL 410-516-6987. FAX 410-516-6968. *6044*

WORLD PSYCHOLOGY.
International Council of Psychologists, Inc., c/o John M. Davis, Sec'y-Gen., Dept. of Psychology, Southwest Texas State Univ., San Marcos, TX 78666-4616. FAX 512-245-3153. *6159*

WORLD RESOURCE REVIEW.
22 W. 381 75th St., Naperville, IL 60565-9245. TEL 630-910-1551. FAX 630-910-1561. *2958*

WORLD REVIEW OF NUTRITION AND DIETETICS.
S. Karger AG, Allschwilerstr. 10, P.O. Box, CH-4009 Basel, Switzerland. TEL 41-61-3061111. FAX 41-61-3061234. *5484*

WORLD SURFACE COATING ABSTRACTS.
Paint Research Association, 8 Waldgreave Rd., Teddington, Middlesex TW11 8LD, England. TEL 44-181-977-4427. FAX 44-181-943-4705. *5557*

WORLD SURVEY OF CLIMATOLOGY.
Elsevier Science B.V., Books Division, P.O. Box 211, 1000 AE Amsterdam, Netherlands. TEL 31-20-4853911. FAX 31-20-4853705. *5247*

WORLD WIDE WEB JOURNAL.
O'Reilly & Associates, 103 Morris St., Ste. A, Sebastopol, CA 95472. TEL 707-829-0515. FAX 707-829-0104. *2141*

WORLDPLAST.
Field & Wood, Medical Periodicals, Inc., Box 975, Blue Bell, PA 19422. TEL 610-828-4010. FAX 215-482-0226. *5157*

WORLD'S POULTRY SCIENCE JOURNAL.
Butterworth - Heinemann, Part of the Reed Elsevier group, Linacre House, Jordan Hill, Oxford OX2 8DP, England. TEL 44-1865-310366. FAX 44-1865-310898. *293*

WORLDVIEWS: ENVIRONMENT, CULTURE, RELIGION.
White Horse Press, 10 High St., Knapwell, Cambridge CB3 8NR, England. TEL 44-1954-267527. FAX 44-1954-267527. *2958*

WORLDWIDE LIVING COSTS.
P-E International plc, Park House, Wick Rd., Egham, Surrey TW20 0HW, England. TEL 44-1784-434411. FAX 44-1784-476369. *1638*

WOUND BALLISTICS REVIEW.
International Wound Ballistics Association, Box 701, El Segundo, CA 90245. TEL 310-640-6065. *4906*

WOUND REPAIR AND REGENERATION.
Mosby - Year Book, Inc., 11830 Westline Industrial Dr., St. Louis, MO 63146-3318. TEL 800-325-4177. FAX 314-432-1380. *5018*

WRITING LAB NEWSLETTER.
Purdue University, Department of English, 1356 Heavilon, West Lafayette, IN 47907-1356. TEL 765-494-7268. FAX 765-494-3780. *2623*

WRITING PROGRAM ADMINISTRATION.
Council of Writing Program Administrators, Department of English, Illinois State University, Normal, IL 61790-4240. TEL 309-438-7596. FAX 309-438-5414. *4489*

WUDANG.
Wudang Zazhishe, Tiyuchang, Danjiangkou, Hubei 441900, People's Republic of China. TEL 86-719-5223531. *6795*

WUJI CAILIAO XUEBAO.
Science Press, Marketing and Sales Department, 16 Donghuangchenggen North St., Beijing 100717, People's Republic of China. TEL 4010642. FAX 4019810. *1810*

WULI.
Science Press, Marketing and Sales Department, 16 Donghuangchenggen North St., Beijing 100717, People's Republic of China. TEL 4010642. FAX 4019810. *5833*

WULI XUEBAO.
Science Press, Marketing and Sales Department, Donghuangchenggen North St., Beijing 100717, People's Republic of China. TEL 4010642. FAX 4019810. *5833*

WUTAISHAN YANJIU.
Wutaishan Yanjiuhui, 38, Bingzhou Nanlu, Taiyuan, Shanxi 030006, People's Republic of China. TEL 0351-7075841. *3518*

WYOMING ARCHAEOLOGIST.
Wyoming Archaeological Society, Inc., 1617 Westridge Terr., Casper, WY 82604. TEL 307-268-2212. FAX 307-268-2224. *389*

X R S - X-RAY SPECTROMETRY.
John Wiley & Sons Ltd., Journals, Baffins Ln., Chichester, W. Sussex PO19 1UD, England. TEL 44-1243-779777. FAX 44-1243-775878. *5870*

XENOBIOTICA.
Taylor & Francis Ltd., 1 Gunpowder Sq., London EC4A 3DE, England. TEL 44-171-583-0490. FAX 44-171-583-0585. *672*

XENOTRANSPLANTATION.
Munksgaard International Publishers Ltd., 35 Noerre Soegade, P.O. Box 2148, DK-1016 Copenhagen K, Denmark. TEL 45-33-127030. FAX 45-33-129387. *5157*

XIANDAI BINGQI.
Xiandai Bingqi Zazhishe, P.O. Box 2413-8, Beijing 100081, People's Republic of China. TEL 86-10-6841-7625. FAX 86-10-6841-3642. *5291*

XIANDAI GUOJI GUANXI.
Xiandai Guoji Guanxi Yanjiusuo, No. A-2, Wanshousi, Haidian, Beijing 100081, People's Republic of China. TEL 86-10-6879-7796. FAX 86-10-6841-8641. *6045*

XIANDAI ZHENDUAN YU ZHILIAO.
Xiandai Zhenduan yu Zhiliao Bianjibu, No. 8, Bayi Ave., 9th Fl., Nanchang, Jiangxi 330003, People's Republic of China. TEL 86-791-6228412. *4759*

XIBEI SHI-DI.
Lanzhou Daxue, Sichou zhi Lu Wenhua Kaifa Jingying Zhongxin, Lanzhou, Gansu 730000, People's Republic of China. TEL 86-931-8913299. FAX 86-931-8885076. *3541*

XIBU TANKUANG GONGCHENG.
Xibu Tankuang Gongcheng Bianjibu, 16 Youhao Beilu, Urumqi, Xinjiang 830000, People's Republic of China. TEL 86-991-4818457. FAX 86-991-4841517. *5319*

XIN SHIXUE.
Xin Shixue Zazhishe, P.O. Box 1-44, Nan-kang, Taipei, Taiwan 11529, Republic of China. TEL 886-2-7829555. FAX 886-2-7868834. *3541*

XINAN JIAOTONG DAXUE XUEBAO.
Xinan Jiaotong Daxue, Xuebao Bianjibu, Chengdu, Sichuan 610031, People's Republic of China. TEL 86-28-7524160. *6585*

XINLI XUEBAO.
Science Press, Marketing and Sales Department, 16 Donghuangchenggen North St., Beijing 100717, People's Republic of China. TEL 4010642. FAX 4019810. *6159*

XINXUEGUANBINGXUE JINZHAN.
Chengdu Xingxueguanbing Yanjiusuo, 82 Qinglong Jie, Chengdu, Sichuan 610031, People's Republic of China. TEL 86-28-6649831. *4825*

XITONG GONGCHENG XUEBAO.
Tianjin Daxue, Qilitai, Nankai Qu, Tianjin 300072, People's Republic of China. FAX 022-7388657. *2746*

XITONG KEXUE YU SHUXUE.
Science Press, Marketing and Sales Department, 16 Donghuangchenggen North St., Beijing 100717, People's Republic of China. TEL 4010642. FAX 4019810. *2160*

XUXEM.
Fundacja Nowej Kultury, P.O. Box 1021, 50-951 Wroclaw 3, Poland. TEL 48-71-634072. FAX 48-71-634072. *3798*

YACHAY.
Universidad Catolica Boliviana, Casilla 2118, Cochabamba, Bolivia. TEL 591-42-57086. *3798*

YAD VASHEM STUDIES.
Yad Vashem Martyrs' and Heroes' Remembrance Authority, P.O. Box 3477, Jerusalem 91034, Israel. TEL 972-2-433511. FAX 972-2-751611. *6411*

YAKLASIM.
Yaklasin Yayincilik San. ve Tic. A.S., Bukulm Sk. No. 117-3, Kavaklidere - Ankara, Turkey. TEL 90-312-4687646. FAX 90-312-4281885. *4048*

THE YALE - CHINA REVIEW.
Yale China Association, Box 208223, Yale Sta., New Haven, CT 06520. TEL 203-432-0880. *2567*

YALE DAILY NEWS.
Yale Daily News Publishing, Co., Inc., 202 York St., New Haven, CT 06511-4804. TEL 203-432-2424. FAX 203-432-7425. *1980*

YALE JOURNAL OF BIOLOGY AND MEDICINE.
Yale Journal of Biology and Medicine, Inc., 333 Cedar St., New Haven, CT 06510. TEL 203-785-4251. FAX 203-785-6309. *4760*

YALE JOURNAL OF CRITICISM.
Johns Hopkins University Press, Journals Publishing Division, 2715 N. Charles St., Baltimore, MD 21218-4319. TEL 410-516-6987. FAX 410-516-6968. *4491*

YALE LITERARY MAGAZINE.
Box 209087, Yale Sta., New Haven, CT 06520. TEL 203-773-3488. *4491*

YALE UNIVERSITY. DEPARTMENT OF ANTHROPOLOGY. PUBLICATIONS IN ANTHROPOLOGY.
Yale University, Department of Anthropology, Box 208277, New Haven, CT 06520. TEL 203-432-3670. FAX 203-432-3669. *334*

YANSHI LIXUE YU GONGCHENG XUEBAO.
Chinese Academy of Sciences, Institute of Rock and Soil Mechanics, Wuhan, Hubei 430071, People's Republic of China. TEL 86-27-786-9250. FAX 86-27-786-2413. *5849*

YANSHI XUEBAO.
Science Press, Marketing and Sales Department, 16 Donghuangchenggen North St., Beijing 100717, People's Republic of China. TEL 4010642. FAX 4019810. *2377*

YANTU LIXUE.
Zhongguo Kexueyuan, Wuhan Yantu Lixue Yanjiusuo, Xiaohongshan, Wuhan, Hubei 430071, People's Republic of China. TEL 813712. *5849*

YAOWU FENXI ZAZHI.
Chinese Medical Association, P.O. Box 2258, 42 Dongsi Xidajie, Beijing 100710, People's Republic of China. TEL 1-550394. *5699*

YASO.
Yagai Shokubutsu Kenkyukai, c/o Mr. Nobushige Kato, 1-18 Wakaba, Shinjuku-ku, Tokyo 160, Japan. TEL 81-3-3357-9090. *733*

YEARBOOK OF COMPARATIVE AND GENERAL LITERATURE.
Indiana University, Comparative Literature Program, Ballantine Hall 923, Bloomington, IN 47405. TEL 812-855-2140. FAX 812-855-2688. *4491*

THE YEARBOOK OF LANGLAND STUDIES.
Pegasus Press, University of North Carolina at Asheville, Asheville, NC 28804. TEL 704-232-5143. FAX 704-232-5146. *4527*

YEARBOOK OF MORPHOLOGY.
Kluwer Academic Publishers, Postbus 17, 3300 AA Dordrecht, Netherlands. TEL 31-78-6392392. FAX 31-78-6392254. *4315*

YEAST.
John Wiley & Sons Ltd., Journals, Baffins Ln., Chichester, W. Sussex PO19 1UD, England. TEL 44-1243-779777. FAX 44-1243-775878. *688*

YEATS ELIOT REVIEW.
Murphy Newsletter Services, 8524 Asher Ave., Little Rock, AR 72204. TEL 501-562-6619. *4527*

YICHUAN XUEBAO.
Science Press, Marketing and Sales Department, 16 Donghuangchenggen North St., Beijing 100717, People's Republic of China. TEL 4010642. FAX 4019810. *777*

YINGXIANG JISHU.
Quanguo Qinggong Ganguang Cailiao Keji Qingbaozhan, 20 Dongting Lu, Hexi Qu, Tianjin 300220, People's Republic of China. TEL 86-22-2834-2934. FAX 86-22-2834-0654. *5776*

YINGYONG SHENGXUE.
Science Press, Marketing and Sales Department, 16 Donghuangchenggen North St., Beijing 100717, People's Republic of China. TEL 4010642. FAX 4019810. *5875*

YINGYONG SHUXUE HE LIXUE.
Chongqing Jiaotong Xueyuan, 107 Dahuang Lu, Chongqing, Sichuan 630042, People's Republic of China. TEL 86-811-881-3708. *4616*

YINGYONG SHUXUE XUEBAO.
Science Press, Marketing and Sales Department, 16 Donghuangchenggen North St., Beijing 100717, People's Republic of China. TEL 4010642. FAX 4019810. *4616*

YINGYU SHIJIE.
Commercial Press, P.O. Box 1504, Beijing 100005, People's Republic of China. TEL 86-10-6525-7190. FAX 86-10-6513-5899. *4315*

YISHU BAIJIA.
Jiangsu Sheng Wenhua Yishu Yanjiusuo, 1 Qingdao Lu, Nanjing, Jiangsu 210008, People's Republic of China. TEL 86-25-6632175. *474*

YOEKI KAGAKU SHINPOJUMU KOEN YOSHISHU.
Yoeki Kagaku Kenkyukai, c/o Prof. M. Nakahara, Institute for Chemical Research, Kyoto University, Uji, Kyoto 611, Japan. TEL 81-774-38-3076. FAX 81-774-38-3076. *1836*

YOGA AND TOTAL HEALTH.
Yoga Institute, Prabhat Colony, Santa Cruz East, Mumbai 400 055, India. TEL 91-22-6110506. FAX 91-22-6115237. *5759*

YOGA - MIMAMSA.
Kaivalyadhama Institution, Lonavla 410 403, District Puna, Maharashtra, India. TEL 91-2114-73039. FAX 91-2114-71983. *5759*

YOKOGAWA BURIJJI GIHO.
Yokogawa Bridge Corp., 4-44 Shibaura 4-chome, Minato-ku, Tokyo 108, Japan. TEL 81-3-3453-4111. FAX 81-3-3453-4616. *2801*

YONSEI MEDICAL JOURNAL.
Yonsei University, College of Medicine, C.P.O. Box 8044, Seoul, S. Korea. TEL 82-2-361-5061. FAX 82-2-393-4945. *4760*

YORK RESEARCH PAPERS IN LINGUISTICS.
University of York, Department of Language and Linguistic Science, Heslington, York YO1 5DD, England. TEL 44-1904-432650. FAX 44-1904-432652. *4315*

YOU!
Veritas Communications Inc., 31194 La Baya Dr., Ste. 200, Westlake Village, CA 91362-4022. TEL 818-991-1813. FAX 818-991-2024. *1895*

YOUJI HUAXUE.
Science Press, Marketing and Sales Department, 16 Donghuangchenggen North St., Beijing 100717, People's Republic of China. TEL 4010642. FAX 4019810. *1825*

REFEREED SERIALS   9969

YOUNG.
Tidskriftsfoereningen - Young, c/o Monica Rudberg, Ed., Institute of Educational Research, University of Oslo, Box 1092 Blindern, NO-0317 Oslo, Norway. TEL 47-22-85-53-69. FAX 47-22-85-42-50. *1859*

THE YOUNGSTER.
Society of St. Paul, Inc., MCPO Box 1722, 1299 Makati City, Metro Manila, Philippines. *1895*

YOUR HEALTH & FITNESS.
General Learning Communications, Health Communications Group, 900 kokie Blvd., Ste. 200, Northbrook, IL 60062-4028. TEL 847-205-3000. FAX 847-564-8197. *5793*

YOUTH THEATRE JOURNAL.
American Alliance for Theatre & Education, Theatre Department, Arizona State University, Box 852002, Tempe, AZ 85287-2002. TEL 602-965-6064. FAX 602-965-5361. *7018*

YUANZI HEWULI PINGLUN.
He Wuli Dongtai Bianjibu, P.O. Box 31, Lanzhou, Gansu 730000, People's Republic of China. TEL 86-931-8828960. FAX 86-931-8881100. *5858*

YUGOSLAV JOURNAL OF OPERATIONS RESEARCH.
University of Belgrade, Faculty of Organizational Sciences, Jove Ilica 154, 11000 Belgrade, Yugoslavia. TEL 38-11-465855. FAX 38-11-461221. *2092*

YUHANG CAILIAO GONGYI.
Hangtian Gongye Zong Gongsi, Hangtian Cailiao ji Gongyi Yanjiu-suo, P.O. Box 9200-73, Beijing 100076, People's Republic of China. TEL 86-10-68383269. FAX 86-10-64227606. *83*

YUNNAN MINZU XUEYUAN XUEBAO.
Yunnan Minzu Xueyuan, Lianhua Chi, Kunming, Yunnan 650031, People's Republic of China. TEL 86-871-5154458. *5540*

Z.
Norsk Filmklubbforbund, Dronningensgt. 16, N-0152 Oslo, Norway. TEL 47-22-47-46-80. FAX 47-22-47-46-92. *5348*

Z BADAN NAD POLSKIMI KSIEGOZBIORAMI HISTORYCZNYMI.
Uniwersytet Warszawski, Instytut Bibliotekoznawstwa i Informacji Naukowej, Nowy Swiat 69, 00-046 Warsaw, Poland. TEL 48-22-8268569. FAX 48-22-8268569. *4223*

ZAGADNIENIA EKONOMIKI ROLNEJ.
Instytut Ekonomiki Rolnictwa i Gospodarki Zywnosciowej, Ul. Swietokrzyska 20, 00-002 Warsaw, Poland. TEL 48-22-8266117. FAX 48-22-8271960. *204*

ZAMBEZIA: THE JOURNAL OF THE UNIVERSITY OF ZIMBABWE.
University of Zimbabwe Publications, P.O. Box MP 203, Mt. Pleasant, Harare, Zimbabwe. TEL 263-4-303211. FAX 263-4-333407. *6647*

ZAMBIA LAW JOURNAL.
University of Zambia, School of Law, P.O. Box 32379, Lusaka, Zambia. TEL 260-1-293580. FAX 260-1-253952. *4049*

ZANDERA.
Buecherei des Deutschen Gartenbaues e.V., Thaerstr. 7, 14469 Potsdam, Germany. *3208*

ZAOCHUAN JISHU.
Zhongguo Chuanbo Gongye Zonggongsi, Chuanbo Gongyi Yanjiusuo, P.O. Box 032-201, Shanghai 200032, People's Republic of China. TEL 86-21-6439-9626. FAX 86-21-6439-0908. *7170*

ZAOZHI HUAXUE PIN.
China Papermaking Chemicals Industry Association, 7 Shihuiba, Changbanxiang, Hangzhou, Zhejiang Province 310014, People's Republic of China. TEL 86-571-8315561. *5573*

ZEITLUPE.
Schweizerische Stiftung fuer das Alter, Schulhausstr. 55, Postfach 642, CH-8027 Zurich, Switzerland. TEL 41-1-2838900. FAX 41-1-2838910. *3447*

ZEITSCHRIFT FUER ANTIKES CHRISTENTUM.
Walter de Gruyter und Co., Genthiner Str. 13, 10785 Berlin, Germany. TEL 49-30-26005-0. *6384*

ZEITSCHRIFT FUER GANZHEITSFORSCHUNG.
Gesellschaft fuer Ganzheitsforschung, Augasse 2-6, A-1090 Vienna, Austria. TEL 43-1-313364531. FAX 43-1-31336727. *5759*

ZEITSCHRIFT FUER HAUTKRANKHEITEN H UND G.
Blackwell Wissenschaft, Kurfuerstendamm 57, 10707 Berlin, Germany. TEL 49-30-32790624. FAX 49-30-32790610. *4882*

ZEITSCHRIFT FUER NATURFORSCHUNG. SECTION A: A JOURNAL OF PHYSICAL SCIENCES.
Verlag der Zeitschrift fuer Naturforschung, Postfach 2645, 72016 Tuebingen, Germany. TEL 49-7071-31555. FAX 49-7071-360571. *5833*

ZEITSCHRIFT FUER NATURFORSCHUNG. SECTION B: A JOURNAL OF CHEMICAL SCIENCES.
Verlag der Zeitschrift fuer Naturforschung, Postfach 2645, 72016 Tuebingen, Germany. TEL 49-7071-31555. FAX 49-7071-360571. *1810*

ZEITSCHRIFT FUER NATURFORSCHUNG. SECTION C: A JOURNAL OF BIOSCIENCES.
Verlag der Zeitschrift fuer Naturforschung, Postfach 2645, 72016 Tuebingen, Germany. TEL 49-7071-31555. FAX 49-7071-360571. *634*

ZEITSCHRIFT FUER PARAPSYCHOLOGIE UND GRENZGEBIETE DER PSYCHOLOGIE.
Wissenschaftliche Gesellschaft zur Foederung der Parapsychologie e.V., Hildastr. 64, 79102 Freiburg, Germany. TEL 49-761-77202. *5579*

ZEITSCHRIFT FUER RELIGIONS- UND GEISTESGESCHICHTE.
E.J. Brill, P.O. Box 9000, 2300 PA Leiden, Netherlands. TEL 31-71-5353500. FAX 31-71-5317532. *6384*

ZEITSCHRIFT FUER RELIGIONS- UND GEISTESGESCHICHTE. BEIHEFTE.
E.J. Brill, P.O. Box 9000, 2300 PA Leiden, Netherlands. TEL 31-71-5353500. FAX 31-71-5317532. *6384*

ZEN VIEWS.
Ti-Jean Press, Box 273, Powell River, BC V8A 4Z6, Canada. *6391*

ZENTRALSTERILISATION - CENTRAL SERVICE.
M H P Verlag GmbH, Ostring 13, 65205 Wiesbaden, Germany. TEL 49-6122-7709131. FAX 49-6122-76331. *4761*

ZEOLITES.
Elsevier Science Inc., Box 945, New York, NY 10159-0945. TEL 212-633-3730. FAX 212-633-3680. *1798*

ZESZYTY KUROWSKIE.
Kurowskie Towarzystwo Regionalne, Gminny Osrodek Kultury, Ul. Kilinskiego 2, 24-170 Kurow, Poland. TEL 48-81-811099. *3614*

ZESZYTY LITERACKIE.
Zeszyty Literackie Foundation, Nowy Swiat 27, 00-732 Warsaw, Poland. TEL 48-22-8263822. FAX 48-22-8263822. *4492*

ZESZYTY PRASOZNAWCZE.
Uniwersytet Jagiellonski, Osrodek Badan Prasoznawczych, Ul. Wislna 2, 31-007 Krakow, Poland. TEL 48-12-220644. FAX 48-12-226306. *3883*

ZESZYTY TARNOGORSKIE.
Instytut w Tarnowskich Gorach, Ul. Ligonia 7, P.O. Box 112, 42-600 Tarnowskie Gory, Poland. TEL 48-32-1855030. *3614*

ZHENJUN XUEBAO.
Science Press, Marketing and Sales Department, 16 Donghuangchenggen North St., Beijing 100717, People's Republic of China. TEL 4010642. FAX 4109810. *733*

ZHENKONG.
Jixie Gongye Bu, Shenyang Zhenkong Jishu Yanjiusuo, 1 Lianhua Beili, Dadong-qu, Shenyang, Liaoning 110042, People's Republic of China. TEL 86-24-4809925. FAX 86-24-4805081. *2850*

ZHIWU BAOHU.
Zhongguo Zhiwu Baohu Xuehui, Zhongguo Nongke Yuan, Zhibao Suo, 2 Yuanmingyuan Xilu, Beijing 100094, People's Republic of China. TEL 86-10-6258-1177. FAX 86-10-6258-3080. *733*

ZHIWU BINGLI XUEBAO.
Zhongguo Zhiwu Bingli Xuehui, Department of Plant Protection, Beijing University of Agriculture, Beijing 100094, People's Republic of China. TEL 86-10-2582244. FAX 86-10-2582332. *734*

ZHIWU FENLEI XUEBAO.
Science Press, Marketing and Sales Department, 16 Donghuangchenggen North St., Beijing 100717, People's Republic of China. TEL 4010642. FAX 4019810. *734*

ZHIWU SHENGLI XUEBAO.
Science Press, Marketing and Sales Department, 16 Donghuangchenggen North St., Beijing 100717, People's Republic of China. TEL 4010642. FAX 4019810. *734*

ZHIWU SHENGTAI XUEBAO.
Science Press, Marketing and Sales Department, 16 Donghuangchenggen North St., Beijing 100717, People's Republic of China. TEL 86-10-6401-9815. FAX 86-10-6401-9810. *734*

ZHIWU XUEBAO.
Science Press, Marketing and Sales Department, 16 Donghuangchenggen North St., Beijing 100717, People's Republic of China. TEL 4010642. FAX 4019810. *734*

ZHIWU ZIYUAN YU HUANJING.
Zhiwu Ziyuan yu Huanjing Bianjibu, Zhongshan Mengwai, Nanjing, Jiangsu 210014, People's Republic of China. TEL 86-25-443-2128. FAX 86-25-443-2074. *734*

ZHIWUXUE TONGBAO.
Zhongguo Kexueyuan, Zhiwu Yanjiusuo, 141 Xizhimenwai Dajie, Beijing 100044, People's Republic of China. TEL 893831. *734*

ZHIYE YU JIANKANG.
Tianjin Institute of Industrial Hygiene and Occupational Diseases, 221 Ma Chang Rd., Hexi District, Tianjin 300204, People's Republic of China. TEL 3283432. *6255*

ZHONG CHENG YAO.
Guojia Yiyao Guanli-ju, Zhong Cheng Yao Xinxi Zhongxin, 324 Renmin Road, Shanghai 200002, People's Republic of China. TEL 86-21-6328-9639. FAX 86-21-6328-9639. *5699*

ZHONGGUO BINGLI SHENGLI ZAZHI.
Zhongguo Bingli Shengli Xuehui, Jinan University, Shipai, Guangzhou, Guangdong 510632, People's Republic of China. TEL 5516511. FAX 5516941. *4761*

ZHONGGUO CHAOSHENG YIXUE ZAZHI.
Zhongguo Chaosheng Yixue Gongcheng Xuehui, 2 Bei Yuan, P.O. Box 1609, Beijing 100012, People's Republic of China. TEL 86-10-6490-2643. FAX 86-10-6423-2519. *5117*

ZHONGGUO GANGCHANGBING ZAZHI.
Zhongguo Gangchangbing Zazhi Bianjibu, No. 42, Wenhua Xilu, Jinan, Shandong 250011, People's Republic of China. TEL 0531-2963276. *4915*

ZHONGGUO GONGCHENGSHI.
Zhongguo Gongchengshi Zazhishe, No.1, Wenhua Lu 1 Duan, Heping-qu, Shenyang, Liaoning 110006, People's Republic of China. TEL 86-24-3891121. *2746*

ZHONGGUO HAIYANG PINGTAI.
China State Shipbuilding Corporation, Shipbuilding Technology Research Institute, P.O. Box 032-201, No. 851 Zhongshan Nan 2 Lu, Shanghai 200032, People's Republic of China. TEL 86-21-6439-9626. FAX 86-21-6439-0908. *5628*

ZHONGGUO HANGTIAN.
Hangtian Gongye Zong Gongsi, Xinxi Yanjiu-suo, P.O. Box 1408, 1 Binhe Lu, Hepingli, Beijing 100013, People's Republic of China. TEL 86-10-6837-3440. FAX 81-10-6422-7606. *83*

ULRICH'S INTERNATIONAL PERIODICALS DIRECTORY 1998

REFEREED SERIALS

ZHONGGUO HUANJING KEXUE.
Chinese Society for Environmental Sciences, No.115, Xizhimennei Nanxiaojie, Beijing 100035, People's Republic of China. TEL 86-1-6066498. FAX 86-1-6020031. *2959*

ZHONGGUO KANGFU YIXUE ZAZHI.
Zhongguo Kangfu Yixuehui, Zhongri Youhao Yiyuan, Yinghuayuan East St., Beijing 100029, People's Republic of China. TEL 86-10-6420-6649. FAX 86-10-6421-7749. *4761*

ZHONGGUO KEXUE A.
Science Press, Marketing and Sales Department, 16 Donghuangchenggen North St., Beijing 100717, People's Republic of China. TEL 4010642. FAX 4109810. *6586*

ZHONGGUO KEXUE B.
Science Press, Marketing and Sales Department, 16 Donghuangchenggen North St., Beijing 100717, People's Republic of China. TEL 4010642. FAX 4019810. *6586*

ZHONGGUO KONGJIAN KEXUE JISHU.
Chinese Academy of Space Technology, P.O. Box 9622, Beijing 100086, People's Republic of China. TEL 86-10-6837-8744. FAX 86-10-6837-8745. *83*

ZHONGGUO MIANYIXUE ZAZHI.
Jilin Sheng Weisheng Ting, Fu 2, Dong Minzhu Dajie, Changchun, Jilin 130061, People's Republic of China. TEL 825027. *4802*

ZHONGGUO NONGYE QIXIANG.
Zhongguo Nongye Kexueyuan, 30 Baishiqiao Lu, Beijing 100081, People's Republic of China. TEL 8314433. *5248*

ZHONGGUO SHENGWU FANGZHI.
Zhongguo Nongye Kexueyuan, 30 Baishiqiao Lu, Beijing 100081, People's Republic of China. TEL 86-10-8314433. FAX 86-10-8323182. *634*

ZHONGGUO SHIYONG ERKE ZAZHI.
Zhongguo Shiyong Yixue Zazhishe, 44-1, Jixian St., Heping District, Shenyang, Liaoning 110005, People's Republic of China. TEL 86-24-3394597. FAX 86-24-3391212. *5041*

ZHONGGUO SHIYONG FUKE YU CHANKE ZAZHI.
Zhongguo Shiyong Yixue Zazhishe, 44-1, Jixian St., Heping District, Shenyang, Liaoning 110005, People's Republic of China. TEL 86-24-3394474. FAX 86-24-3391212. *4969*

ZHONGGUO SHIYONG NEIKE ZAZHI.
Zhongguo Shiyong Yixue Zazhishe, 44-1, Jixian St., Heping District, Shenyang, Liaoning 110005, People's Republic of China. TEL 86-24-3395218. FAX 86-24-3391212. *4927*

ZHONGGUO SHIYONG WAIKE ZAZHI.
Zhongguo Shiyong Yixue Zazhishe, 44-1, Jixian St., Heping District, Shenyang, Liaoning 110005, People's Republic of China. TEL 86-24-3395362. FAX 96-24-3391212. *5157*

ZHONGGUO XIAODUXUE ZAZHI.
Zhonghua Yufang Yixuehui (Fengtai), 20 Dongdajie, Fengtai, Beijing 100071, People's Republic of China. TEL 86-1-6688-8229. FAX 86-1-6688-8229. *4761*

ZHONGGUO XINLI WEISHENG ZAZHI.
Beijing Yike Daxue, Jingshen Weisheng Yanjiusuo, 38 Huayuan Beilu, Beijing 100083, People's Republic of China. TEL 861-2010890. FAX 861-2027314. *6160*

ZHONGGUO XIUFU CHONGJIAN WAIKE ZAZHI.
Zhongguo Xiufu Chongjian Waike Zazhi Bianjibu, Huaxi Yike Daxue Fushu Diyi Yiyuan Nei, 37 Guoxue Xiang, Chengdu, Sichuan 610041, People's Republic of China. TEL 86-28-5551255. FAX 86-28-5559438. *5158*

ZHONGGUO YAOLI XUEBAO.
Science Press, Marketing and Sales Department, 16 Donghuangchenggen Beijie, Beijing 100707, People's Republic of China. TEL 4010642. FAX 4012180. *5699*

ZHONGGUO YAOXUE WENZHAI.
Guojia Yiyao Guanli-ju, Keji Qingbao Yanjiusuo, A-38 Beilishilu, Beijing 100810, People's Republic of China. TEL 86-10-6831-3344. FAX 86-10-6831-1978. *299*

ZHONGGUO YINGYONG SHENGLIXUE ZAZHI.
Zhongguo Yingyong Shenglixue Zazhi Bianjibu, One Da Li Dao, Tianjin 300050, People's Republic of China. TEL 86-22-841-3063. FAX 86-22-331-4818. *822*

ZHONGGUO YIXUE KEXUEYUAN XUEBAO.
Chinese Academy of Medical Sciences (CAMS), 9 Dong Dan San Tiao, Beijing 100730, People's Republic of China. TEL 86-10-5133074. *4761*

ZHONGGUO ZIXINGCHE.
Bicycle Information Centre of China, China Bicycle Association, No.6, Alley 360, Anyuan Road, Shanghai 200060, People's Republic of China. TEL 021-2584696. FAX 021-2550918. *6834*

ZHONGHUA SHENJING WAIKE ZAZHI.
Beijing Neurosurgical Institute, No.6, Tiantan Xili, Beijing 100050, People's Republic of China. TEL 86-10-5113169. FAX 86-10-7018349. *5102*

ZHONGHUA YANDIBING ZAZHI.
West China University of Medical Sciences, First Teaching Hospital, No. 37, Guoxue Xiang, Chengdu, Sichuan 610041, People's Republic of China. TEL 86-28-5577707. FAX 86-28-5577707. *5003*

ZHONGHUA YINGCAI.
Zhonghua Yingcai Huabaoshe, 3 Fuyou St., Beijing 100032, People's Republic of China. TEL 81-10-309-5986. FAX 86-10-309-5608. *3272*

ZHONGNAN CAIJING DAXUE XUEBAO.
Zhongnan Caijing Daxue, 114 Wuluo Lu, Wuchang Qu, Wuhan, Hubei 430064, People's Republic of China. TEL 86-27-8044330. FAX 86-27-8044548. *1313*

ZHONGSHAN.
Zhongshan Bianjibu, 2 Yihe Lu, Nanjing, Jiangsu 210024, People's Republic of China. TEL 86-25-6638819. *4493*

ZHONGWEN XINXI.
Zhongguo Zhongwen Xinxi Xuehui, P.O. Box 263, Chendu Keji Daxue - Chengdu University of Science and Technology, Chengdu , Sichuan Province, People's Republic of China. TEL 028-581591. *4223*

ZHONGXUE YUWEN.
Hubei Daxue, Zhongwen Xi, Baoji'an, Wuchang-qu, Wuhan, Hubei 430062, People's Republic of China. TEL 86-27-6811903. FAX 86-27-6814263. *4317*

ZHONGYI ZHENGGUY.
Luoyang Zhenggu Yanjiusuo, No. 1, Qiming Nanlu, Luoyang, Henan 471002, People's Republic of China. TEL 86-379-3953520. FAX 86-379-3953520. *5018*

ZIDONGHUA XUEBAO.
Science Press, Marketing and Sales Department, 16 Donghuangchenggen North St., Beijing 100717, People's Republic of China. TEL 4010642. FAX 4019810. *2112*

ZIMBABWE JOURNAL OF EDUCATIONAL RESEARCH.
University of Zimbabwe, Faculty of Education, P.O. Box MP 167, Mount Pleasant, Harare, Zimbabwe. TEL 263-4-303271. FAX 263-4-333407. *2496*

ZIMBABWE VETERINARY JOURNAL.
Zimbabwe Veterinary Journal, P.O. Box CY168, Causeway, Harare, Zimbabwe. TEL 263-4-495859. FAX 263-4-495859. *7285*

ZION.
Historical Society of Israel, P.O. Box 4179, Jerusalem 91041, Israel. TEL 972-2-637171. FAX 972-2-662135. *3051*

ZIPZAP. *4493*

ZIRAN ZIYUAN XUEBAO.
Science Press, Marketing and Sales Department, 16 Donghuangchenggen North St., Beijing 100717, People's Republic of China. TEL 4010642. FAX 4019810. *2324*

ZOO ANVERS.
Societe Royale de Zoologie d'Anvers, Koningin Astridplein 26, 2018 Antwerp, Belgium. TEL 32-3-2024540. FAX 32-3-2310018. *854*

ZOO BIOLOGY.
John Wiley & Sons, Inc., Journals, 605 Third Ave., New York, NY 10158. TEL 212-850-6645. FAX 212-850-6021. *854*

ZOOCRIADEROS.
Centro de Investigacion y Reproduccion de Especies Silvestres, Apdo. Postal 397, Merida 5101, Venezuela. TEL 58-74-712939. *854*

ZOOLOGICA POLONIAE.
Polskie Towarzystwo Zoologiczne, Ul. Sienkiewicza 21, 50-335 Wroclaw, Poland. TEL 48-71-225041. FAX 48-71-222817. *854*

ZOOLOGICA SCRIPTA.
Elsevier Science Ltd., Pergamon, P.O. Box 800, Kidlington, Oxford OX5 1DX, England. *854*

ZOOLOGICAL SCIENCE.
Zoological Society of Japan, Toshin Bldg., 2-27-2 Hongo, Bunkyo-ku, Tokyo 113, Japan. TEL 81-3-3812-2111. FAX 81-3-3816-1965. *854*

ZOOLOGICAL SOCIETY OF LONDON. SYMPOSIA.
Oxford University Press, Walton St., Oxford OX2 6DP, England. TEL 44-1865-56767. FAX 44-1865-56646. *855*

ZOOLOGICAL STUDIES.
Academia Sinica, Institute of Zoology, Nankang, Taipei, Taiwan 11529, Republic of China. TEL 886-2-7899507. FAX 886-2-7858059. *855*

ZOOLOGY IN THE MIDDLE EAST.
Max Kasparek Verlag, Bleichstr. 1, 69120 Heidelberg, Germany. TEL 49-6221-475069. FAX 49-6221-471858. *855*

ZUID - AFRIKA.
Zuid - Afrikaansche Stichting Moederland, Keizersgracht 141, 1015 CK Amsterdam, Netherlands. TEL 31-20-6249318. FAX 31-20-6382596. *5982*

ZUOWU XUEBAO.
Science Press, Marketing and Sales Department, 16 Donghuangchenggen North St., Beijing 100717, People's Republic of China. FAX 86-1-4019810. *251*

ZUOWU ZAZHI.
Zhongguo Zuowu Xuehui, Zhongguo Nongye Kexueyuan, 30 Baishiqiao Lu, Beijing 100081, People's Republic of China. TEL 891731. *167*

ZYGON.
Blackwell Publishers, 238 Main St., Cambridge, MA 02142. FAX 617-547-0789. *6385*

ZYGOTE.
Cambridge University Press, Edinburgh Bldg., Shaftesbury Rd., Cambri'ge CB2 2RU, England. TEL 44-1223-312393. FAX 44-1223-315052. *777*

ZYMURGY.
American Homebrewers Association Inc., Box 1679, Boulder, CO 80306-1679. TEL 303-447-0816. FAX 303-447-2825. *530*

1ST STEPS: DAILY MARKETING AND DESIGN.
Internet Business Network, 346 Starling Rd., Mill Valley, CA 94941. FAX 415-383-8676. *1554*

9-1-1 MAGAZINE.
Official Publications, Inc., Box 11788, Santa Ana, CA 92711-1788. TEL 714-544-7776. FAX 714-838-9233. *2283*

16 DE ABRIL.
Ministerio de Salud Publica, Instituto Superior de Ciencias Medicas de la Habana, Calle G s-n, e. 25 y 27, Plaza de la Revolucion, 10400 Vedado, Havana, Cuba. TEL 537-308942. FAX 537-333063. *4762*

21ST CENTURY AFRO REVIEW.
I A A S Publishers, Inc., 7676 New Hampshire Ave., Langley Park, MD 20783. TEL 301-499-6308. FAX 301-499-4298. *3051*

50 PLUS NEWS MAGAZINE.
Box 230, Hartland, WI 53029-0230. TEL 414-367-5303. FAX 414-367-9517. *3447*

96 INC.
96 Inc., Box 15559, Boston, MA 02215. TEL 617-267-0543. FAX 617-262-3568. *4493*

Serials Available on CD-ROM

A A P G BULLETIN.
American Association of Petroleum Geologists, Box 979, Tulsa, OK 74101. TEL 918-584-2555. FAX 918-560-2665. *5593*

A A P G STUDIES IN GEOLOGY SERIES.
American Association of Petroleum Geologists, Box 979, Tulsa, OK 74101. TEL 918-584-2555. *5594*

A B C.
Prensa Espanola S.A., Juan I Luca de Tena, 7, 28027 Madrid, Spain. TEL 34-1-3399000. FAX 34-1-3208711. *3358*

A B C BELGE POUR LE COMMERCE ET L'INDUSTRIE.
A B C pour le Commerce et l'Industrie C.V., Doornveld 1B28, B-1731 Asse, Belgium. TEL 32-2-4630273. FAX 32-2-4630885. *1649*

A B C DER DEUTSCHEN WIRTSCHAFT - QUELLENWERK FUR EINKAUF-VERKAUF.
A B C Publishing Group, Postfach 100262, 64202 Darmstadt, Germany. TEL 49-6151-3892-0. FAX 49-6151-33164. *1649*

A B C EUROP PRODUCTION.
A B C Publishing Group, Postfach 100262, 64202 Darmstadt, Germany. TEL 49-6151-3892-0. FAX 49-6151-33164. *1313*

A B C LUXEMBOURGEOIS POUR LE COMMERCE ET L'INDUSTRIE.
A B C pour le Commerce et l'Industrie C.V., Doornveld 1B28, B-1731 Asse, Belgium. TEL 32-2-4630273. FAX 32-2-4630885. *1649*

A B C POL SCI.
A B C-Clio, 130 Cremona, Box 1911, Santa Barbara, CA 93116-1911. TEL 805-968-1911. FAX 805-685-9685. *5982*

A B I - INFORM.
U M I, 300 N. Zeeb Rd., Ann Arbor, MI 48106. TEL 313-761-4700. FAX 800-864-0019. Producer(s): UMI. *1014*

A B I X: AUSTRALASIAN BUSINESS INTELLIGENCE.
Business Intelligence Australia Pty. Ltd., McConnell Dowell House, 627 Chapel St., S. Yarra, Vic. 3141, Australia. TEL 61-3-98279088. FAX 61-3-98279099. *1014*

A B M S MEDICAL SPECIALIST PLUS.
Marquis Who's Who, A Division of Reed Elsevier Inc., 121 Chanlon Rd., New Providence, NJ 07974. TEL 908-464-6800. FAX 908-665-6688. Available only on CD-ROM. *4628*

A C P JOURNAL CLUB.
American College of Physicians, Independence Mall W., Sixth St. at Race, Philadelphia, PA 19106-1572. TEL 215-351-2400. *4762*

A D M.
Asociacion Dental Mexicana, A.C., Ezequiel Montes No. 92, Col. Revolucion, Delegacion Cuauhtemoc, Mexico, D.F. 06030, Mexico. TEL 52-5-29400095. FAX 52-5-2945143. *4848*

A E S I S QUARTERLY.
Australian Mineral Foundation, 63 Conyngham St., Glenside, S.A. 5065, Australia. TEL 61-8-83790444. FAX 61-8-83794634. *5319*

A F P - DOC SUR C D - R O M.
Chadwyck-Healey France S.A., 50 rue de Paradis, 75010 Paris, France. TEL 33-1-44838181. FAX 33-1-44838183. Available only on CD-ROM. Producer(s): Chadwyck-Healey Inc. *3868*

A F P SCIENCES.
Agence France Presse, 13 Place de la Bourse, B.P. 20, 75061 Paris Cedex 2, France. TEL 40-41-46-46. Producer(s): Chadwyck-Healey Inc. *4629*

A F P SCIENCES SUR C D - R O M.
Chadwyck-Healey France S.A., 50 rue de Paradis, 75010 Paris, France. TEL 33-1-44838181. FAX 33-1-44838183. Available only on CD-ROM. Producer(s): Chadwyck-Healey Inc. *6506*

A H F S DRUG INFORMATION.
American Society of Health-System Pharmacists, 7272 Wisconsin Ave., Bethesda, MD 20814. TEL 301-657-3000. FAX 301-657-1641. Producer(s): SilverPlatter Information, Inc. *5644*

A I A A JOURNAL.
American Institute of Aeronautics and Astronautics, Inc., 1801 Alexander Dr., Ste. 500, Reston, VA 20191. TEL 703-264-7500. *51*

A I D A.
Zeller Publications, Postfach 1949, 49009 Osnabrueck, Germany. TEL 49-541-4045914. FAX 49-541-41255. Available only on CD-ROM. *531*

A J N R.
American Society of Neuroradiology, 2210 Midwest Rd., Ste. 207, Oak Brook, IL 60521. TEL 630-574-0220. FAX 630-574-0661. *5102*

A L I S A.
Australian Clearing House for Library & Information Science, Library, St. Bernards Rd., Magill, S.A. 5072, Australia. TEL 61-8-3024766. FAX 61-8-3024695. *4223*

A N T E PLUS.
Bowker - Saur Ltd., A member of the Reed Elsevier plc group, Maypole House, Maypole Rd., E. Grinstead, W. Sussex RH19 1HU, England. TEL 44-1342-330100. FAX 44-1342-330191. Available only on CD-ROM. Producer(s): Bowker - Saur Ltd. *6980*

A O A C INTERNATIONAL. OFFICIAL METHODS OF ANALYSIS.
A O A C International, 481 N. Frederick Ave., Ste. 500, Gaithersburg, MD 20877-2417. TEL 301-924-7077. FAX 301-924-7089. *1786*

(YEAR) A R R L PERIODICALS C D - R O M.
American Radio Relay League, Inc., 225 Main St., Newington, CT 06111. TEL 860-594-0200. FAX 860-594-0303. Available only on CD-ROM. *2022*

A S A ANNUAL MEETING PAPERS.
African Studies Association, Credit Union Bldg., Emory University, Atlanta, GA 30322. TEL 404-329-6410. Available only on CD-ROM. *2993*

A S F A AQUACULTURE ABSTRACTS.
Cambridge Scientific Abstracts, 7200 Wisconsin Ave., 6th Fl., Bethesda, MD 20814. TEL 301-961-6750. FAX 301-961-6720. Producer(s): NISC, SilverPlatter Information, Inc. *3081*

A S F A MARINE BIOTECHNOLOGY ABSTRACTS.
Cambridge Scientific Abstracts, 7200 Wisconsin Ave., 6th Fl., Bethesda, MD 20814. TEL 301-961-6750. FAX 301-961-6720. Producer(s): Knight-Ridder, Inc., NISC, SilverPlatter Information, Inc. *634*

A S H R A E HANDBOOK.
American Society of Heating, Refrigerating and Air-Conditioning Engineers, Inc., 1791 Tullie Circle, N.E., Atlanta, GA 30329. TEL 404-636-8400. FAX 404-321-5478. *3476*

A S H R A E TRANSACTIONS.
American Society of Heating, Refrigerating and Air-Conditioning Engineers, Inc., 1791 Tullie Circle, N.E., Atlanta, GA 30329. TEL 404-636-8400. FAX 404-321-5478. *3476*

SERIALS AVAILABLE ON CD-ROM

A S S I A: APPLIED SOCIAL SCIENCES INDEX & ABSTRACTS.
Bowker - Saur Ltd., A member of the Reed Elsevier plc group, Maypole House, Maypole Rd., E. Grinstead, W. Sussex RH19 1HU, England. TEL 44-1342-330100. FAX 44-1342-330191.
Producer(s): Bowker - Saur Ltd. *6648*

A S S I A PLUS.
Bowker - Saur Ltd., A member of the Reed Elsevier plc group, Maypole House, Maypole Rd., E. Grinstead, W. Sussex RH19 1HU, England. TEL 44-1342-330100. FAX 44-1342-330191.
Available only on CD-ROM. Producer(s): Bowker - Saur Ltd. *6648*

A S T I S BIBLIOGRAPHY.
Arctic Science & Technology Information System, Arctic Institute of North America, University of Calgary, 2500 University Dr. N.W., Calgary, AB T2N 1N4, Canada. TEL 403-220-4036. FAX 403-282-4609. *634*

A S T I S CURRENT AWARENESS BULLETIN.
Arctic Science & Technology Information System, Arctic Institute of North America, University of Calgary, 2500 University Dr. N.W., Calgary, AB T2N 1N4, Canada. TEL 403-284-7515. FAX 403-282-4609. *2324*

A S T I S OCCASIONAL PUBLICATIONS.
Arctic Science & Technology Information System, University of Calgary, 2500 University Dr. N.W., Calgary, AB T2N 1N4, Canada. TEL 403-220-4036. FAX 403-282-4609. *2324*

A TO ZOO.
R.R. Bowker, A Division of Reed Elsevier plc group, 121 Chanlon Rd., New Providence, NJ 07974. TEL 908-464-6800. FAX 908-665-6688.
Producer(s): Bowker Electronic Publishing (Children's Reference PLUS). *531*

A U A PATIENT MANAGEMENT PROGRAM.
Decker Periodicals, P.O. Box 620, LCD 1, Hamilton, ON L8N 3K7, Canada. TEL 905-522-7017. FAX 905-522-7839. *5158*

ABERDEEN'S CONCRETE SOURCEBOOK.
Aberdeen Group, 426 S. Westgate St., Addison, IL 60101. TEL 630-543-0870. FAX 630-543-3112. *860*

ABSTRACTS IN BIOCOMMERCE.
BioCommerce Data Ltd., Prudential Bldgs., 95 High St., Slough, Berks. SL1 1DH, England. TEL 44-1753-511777. FAX 44-1753-512239. *634*

ABSTRACTS IN NEW TECHNOLOGIES AND ENGINEERING.
Bowker - Saur Ltd., A member of the Reed Elsevier plc group, Maypole House, Maypole Rd., E. Grinstead, W. Sussex RH19 1HU, England. TEL 44-1342-330100. FAX 44-1342-330191.
Producer(s): Bowker - Saur Ltd. *6980*

ABSTRACTS OF WORKING PAPERS IN ECONOMICS.
Cambridge University Press, Edinburgh Bldg., Shaftesbury Rd., Cambridge CB2 2RU, England. TEL 44-1223-312393. FAX 44-1223-315052. *1015*

ABYA YALA NEWS.
South and Meso American Indian Rights Center, Box 28703, Oakland, CA 94604-8703. TEL 510-834-4263. FAX 510-834-4264. *2993*

ACADEMIA SINICA. BOTANICAL BULLETIN.
Academia Sinica, Institute of Botany, Nankang, Taipei, Taiwan 11529, Republic of China. TEL 886-2-789-9590. FAX 886-2-7827954. *688*

ACADEMIC ABSTRACTS C D - R O M.
EBSCO Publishing, 10 Estes St., Box 682, Ipswich, MA 01938. TEL 508-356-6500. FAX 508-356-6565. *2*

ACADEMIC INDEX.
Information Access Company, 362 Lakeside Dr., Foster City, CA 94404. TEL 415-378-5200. FAX 415-378-5369. *3798*

ACCOUNTANCY.
Institute of Chartered Accountants in England and Wales, P.O. Box 433, Moorgate Pl., London EC2P 2BJ, England. TEL 44-171-833-3291. *1080*

ACCOUNTING & FINANCE ABSTRACTS.
M C B University Press Ltd., Anbar Electronic Intelligence, 60-62 Toller Ln., Bradford, W. Yorks BD8 9BY, England. TEL 44-1274-480916. FAX 44-1274-543576. *2093*

ACCOUNTING AND TAX INDEX.
U M I, 300 N. Zeeb Rd., Ann Arbor, MI 48106. TEL 313-761-4700. FAX 800-864-0019. *1015*

ACCOUNTING FOR GOVERNMENT CONTRACTS: FEDERAL ACQUISITION REGULATION.
Matthew Bender & Co., Inc., 2 Park Ave., New York, NY 10016. TEL 212-448-2000. *1081*

ACKNOWLEDGE THE WINDOW LETTER.
Mendham Technology Group, 144 Talmadge Rd., Box 11, Mendham, NJ 07945. TEL 201-543-2273. FAX 201-543-6033. *2186*

ACQUISITION OF GREATER DAYTON.
Hannover Publishing Co., Inc., 6356 Far Hills Ave., Dayton, OH 45459-2782. TEL 937-291-1100. FAX 937-436-3426.
Producer(s): UMI. *6294*

ACTA BALTICO - SLAVICA.
Slawistyczny Osrodek Wydawniczy, Al. Ujazdowskie 18 m.16, 00-478 Warsaw, Poland. TEL 48-22-6250054. FAX 48-22-6290075. *3546*

ACTA GASTROENTEROLOGICA LATINOAMERICANA.
Juncal 2134, Planta Baja B 1125, Buenos Aires, Argentina. TEL 541-8250050. FAX 541-8222139. *4907*

ACTION NATIONALE.
Ligue d'Action Nationale, 425 Blvd. de Maisonneuve Ouest, Montreal, PQ H3A 3G5, Canada. TEL 514-845-8533. FAX 514-845-8529. *5888*

ACTIVE AND PASSIVE ELECTRONIC COMPONENTS.
Gordon and Breach - Harwood Academic, Amsteldisk 166, 1st Fl., 1079 LH Amsterdam, Netherlands. *2807*

ACTORS C D - R O M.
Spotlight, 7 Leicester Pl., London WC2H 7BP, England. TEL 44-171-437-7631. FAX 44-171-437-5881.
Available only on CD-ROM. *7000*

ACTRESSES C D - R O M.
Spotlight, 7 Leicester Pl., London WC2H 7BP, England. TEL 44-171-437-7631. FAX 44-171-437-5881.
Available only on CD-ROM. *7001*

ACTUALIDAD ECONOMICA.
Recoletos 1, 7o, 28001 Madrid, Spain. TEL 34-1-3373220. FAX 34-1-5768150.
Producer(s): Chadwyck-Healey Inc. *1219*

ACTUALIDAD ECONOMICA EN C D - R O M.
Chadwyck-Healey Ltd., The Quorum, Barnwell Rd., Cambridge CB5 8SW, England. TEL 44-1223-215512. FAX 44-1223-215514.
Available only on CD-ROM. Producer(s): Chadwyck-Healey Inc. *930*

ADHESIVES ABSTRACTS.
Rapra Technology Ltd., Shawbury, Shrewsbury, Shrops. SY4 4NR, England. TEL 44-1939-250383. FAX 44-1939-251118. *1771*

ADOLESCENCE (SAN DIEGO).
Libra Publishers, Inc., 3089C Clairemont Dr., Ste. 383, San Diego, CA 92117. TEL 619-571-1414. *1837*

ADRESSBUCH FUER DEN DEUTSCHSPRACHIGEN BUCHHANDEL C D - R O M.
Buchhaendler-Vereinigung GmbH, Postfach 100442, 60004 Frankfurt a.M., Germany. TEL 49-69-1306-0. FAX 49-69-1306201.
Available only on CD-ROM. *6260*

ADVANCES (KALAMAZOO).
Fetzer Institute, 9292 West KL Ave., Kalamazoo, MI 49009-9398. TEL 616-375-2000. FAX 616-372-2163. *4632*

ADVERTISER & AGENCY RED BOOKS PLUS.
National Register Publishing, A Division of Reed Elsevier Inc., 121 Chanlon Rd., New Providence, NJ 07974. TEL 908-464-6800. FAX 908-665-6688.
Producer(s): Bowker Electronic Publishing. *30*

AFRICAN JOURNAL OF INTERNATIONAL AFFAIRS & DEVELOPMENT.
College Press Publisher Services, OGC Bldg., New Bodija, Secretariat, P.O. Box 30678, Ibadan, Oyo State, Nigeria. TEL 234-2-810-4165. FAX 234-2-810-1963.
Producer(s): UMI. *6003*

AFRIQUE MEDICALE.
B.P. 1826, Dakar, Senegal. TEL 23-48-80. FAX 22-56-30. *4633*

THE AGE.
David Syme & Co. Limited, 250 Spencer St., 5th Fl., Melbourne, Vic. 3000, Australia. TEL 61-3-96012903. FAX 61-3-96707514. *3250*

AGEINFO C D - R O M.
Centre for Policy on Ageing, 25-31 Ironmonger Row, London EC1V 3QP, England. TEL 44-171-253-1787. FAX 44-171-490-4206.
Available only on CD-ROM. *3447*

AGRICULTURA Y SOCIEDAD.
Ministerio de Agricultura, Pesca y Alimentacion, Centro de Publicaciones, Paseo de la Infanta Isabel 1, 28071 Madrid, Spain. TEL 34-1-3475551. FAX 34-1-3475722. *90*

AGRICULTURAL & ENVIRONMENTAL BIOTECHNOLOGY ABSTRACTS.
Cambridge Scientific Abstracts, 7200 Wisconsin Ave., 6th Fl., Bethesda, MD 20814. TEL 301-961-6700. FAX 301-961-6720.
Producer(s): Knight-Ridder, Inc., NISC, SilverPlatter Information, Inc. *167*

AGRICULTURE AND ENVIRONMENT FOR DEVELOPING COUNTRIES.
Koninklijk Instituut voor de Tropen, Mauritskade 63, 1092 AD Amsterdam, Netherlands. TEL 31-20-5688298. FAX 31-20-6654423.
Producer(s): SilverPlatter Information, Inc. *168*

AGRO-AGEN.
Akademia Rolnicza, Poznan, Biblioteka Glowna, Ul. Witosa 45, 60-667 Poznan, Poland. TEL 48-61-487809. FAX 48-61-487802. *168*

AGRO-LIBREX.
Akademia Rolnicza, Poznan, Biblioteka Glowna, Ul. Witosa 45, 60-667 Poznan, Poland. TEL 48-61-666066. FAX 48-61-659643.
Available only on CD-ROM. *168*

AGROFORESTRY ABSTRACTS.
CAB International, Wallingford, Oxon. OX10 8DE, England. TEL 44-1491-832111. FAX 44-1491-826090. *3167*

AHWAZ UNIVERSITY OF MEDICAL SCIENCES. SCIENTIFIC MEDICAL JOURNAL.
Ahwaz University of Medical Sciences, P.O. Box 189, Ahwaz, Iran. TEL 98-61-32036. FAX 98-61-61544. *4634*

AIDS - S T D HEALTH PROMOTION EXCHANGE.
Koninklijk Instituut voor de Tropen, Mauritskade 63, 1092 AD Amsterdam, Netherlands. TEL 31-20-5688711. FAX 31-20-5688286. *4832*

AIR CONDITIONING & HEATING SERVICE & REPAIR - DOMESTIC CARS, LIGHT TRUCKS & VANS.
Mitchell International, Inc., 9889 Willow Creek Rd., Box 26260, San Diego, CA 92196-0260. TEL 800-648-8010. FAX 619-578-4752. *7081*

AIR CONDITIONING & HEATING SERVICE & REPAIR - IMPORTED CARS & TRUCKS.
Mitchell International, Inc., 9889 Willow Creek Rd., Box 26260, San Diego, CA 92196-0260. TEL 800-878-6550. FAX 619-578-4752. *7081*

AIR UNIVERSITY LIBRARY INDEX TO MILITARY PERIODICALS.
U.S. Air Force, Air University Library, Maxwell AFB, AL 36112-6424. TEL 334-953-2504. FAX 334-953-1192. *5292*

AIXPERT.
I B M Corporation (Austin), Izip 1034, 11400 Burnet Rd., Austin, TX 78758. TEL 512-823-6840. FAX 512-823-6520. *2209*

ALABAMA BUSINESS DIRECTORY.
American Business Directories, 5711 S. 86th Cir., Box 27347, Omaha, NE 68127. TEL 402-593-4600. FAX 401-331-5481. *1650*

ALABAMA MANUFACTURERS REGISTER.
Manufacturers' News, Inc., 1633 Central St., Evanston, IL 60201. TEL 847-864-7000. FAX 847-332-1100. *1650*

ALAMEDA COUNTY COMMERCE AND INDUSTRY DIRECTORY.
Database Publishing Company, 1590 S. Lewis St., Anaheim, CA 92805-6423. TEL 714-778-6400. FAX 714-778-6811. *1650*

ALASKA BUSINESS DIRECTORY.
American Business Directories, 5711 S. 86th Cir., Box 27347, Omaha, NE 68127. TEL 402-593-4600. FAX 402-331-5481. *1651*

ALASKA COURT RULES, STATE AND FEDERAL.
West Group, 620 Opperman Dr., Eagan, MN 55123. TEL 612-687-8000. FAX 612-387-7302. *4129*

ALLOYS INDEX.
Cambridge Scientific Abstracts, 7200 Wisconsin Ave., 6th fl., Bethesda, MD 20814. TEL 301-961-6750. FAX 301-961-6720.
Producer(s): Knight-Ridder, Inc. *5216*

ALMANAQUE ABRIL.
Editora Abril, S.A., Rua do Curtume, 571, Bl. A, 6o andar, 05066-900 Sao Paulo, SP, Brazil. TEL 011-871-6020. FAX 011-871-6334. *2655*

ALTA HOTELERIA INTERNACIONAL.
Alta Hoteleria, S.A. de C.V., Cataluna No. 19, Insurgentes Sur, Mixcoac, 03920 Mexico, D.F., Mexico. TEL 52-5-6112109. FAX 52-5-6114584. *3722*

ALTERNATIVE PRESS INDEX.
Alternative Press Center, Inc., Box 33109, Baltimore, MD 21218. TEL 410-243-2471. FAX 410-235-5325.
Producer(s): NISC. *4368*

AMERICA.
America Press Inc., 106 W. 56th St., New York, NY 10019. TEL 212-581-4640. FAX 212-399-3596.
Producer(s): UMI. *6449*

AMERICA: HISTORY AND LIFE. ANNUAL INDEX.
A B C-Clio, 130 Cremona, Box 1911, Santa Barbara, CA 93116-1911. TEL 805-968-1911. FAX 805-685-9685. *3518*

AMERICA: HISTORY AND LIFE. ARTICLE ABSTRACTS AND CITATIONS OF REVIEWS AND DISSERTATIONS COVERING THE UNITED STATES AND CANADA.
A B C-Clio, 130 Cremona, Box 1911, Santa Barbara, CA 93116-1911. TEL 805-968-1911. FAX 805-685-9685. *3518*

AMERICAN ACADEMY OF PEDIATRICS. COMMITTEE ON INFECTIOUS DISEASES. REPORT (YEAR).
American Academy of Pediatrics, 141 Northwest Point Blvd., Box 927, Elk Grove Village, IL 60009-0927. TEL 847-228-5005. FAX 847-228-1281. *5027*

AMERICAN ASSOCIATION OF PETROLEUM GEOLOGISTS. MEMOIR.
American Association of Petroleum Geologists, Box 979, Tulsa, OK 74101. TEL 918-584-2555. *2330*

AMERICAN ASSOCIATION OF TEXTILE CHEMISTS AND COLORISTS. TECHNICAL MANUAL (YEAR).
American Association of Textile Chemists and Colorists, One Davis Dr., Box 12215, Research Triangle Park, NC 27709-2215. TEL 919-549-8141. FAX 919-549-8933. *6983*

AMERICAN BOOK TRADE DIRECTORY.
R.R. Bowker, A Division of Reed Elsevier Inc., 121 Chanlon Rd., New Providence, NJ 07974. TEL 908-464-6800. FAX 908-665-6688.
Producer(s): Bowker Electronic Publishing. *6260*

THE AMERICAN BUSINESS DISC.
American Business Directories, 5711 S. 86th Circle, Box 27347, Omaha, NE 68127. TEL 402-593-4523. FAX 402-331-6681.
Available only on CD-ROM. *1651*

AMERICAN COLLEGE OF CARDIOLOGY. JOURNAL.
Elsevier Science Inc., Box 945, New York, NY 10159-0945. TEL 212-633-3730. FAX 212-633-3680. *4808*

AMERICAN CRAFT.
American Craft Council, 72 Spring St., New York, NY 10012. TEL 212-274-0630. FAX 212-274-0650.
Producer(s): UMI. *477*

AMERICAN DENTAL ASSOCIATION. JOURNAL.
American Dental Association, 211 E. Chicago Ave., Chicago, IL 60611. TEL 312-440-2500. FAX 312-440-3538. *4850*

AMERICAN DOCTORAL DISSERTATIONS.
U M I, 300 N. Zeeb Rd., Ann Arbor, MI 48106. TEL 313-761-4700. FAX 800-864-0019.
Producer(s): UMI. *2531*

AMERICAN FAMILY PHYSICIAN.
American Academy of Family Physicians, 8880 Ward Pkwy., Kansas City, MO 64114. TEL 816-333-9700. FAX 816-333-0303. *4635*

AMERICAN JOURNAL OF CRITICAL CARE.
American Association of Critical Care Nurses, 101 Columbia, Aliso Viejo, CA 92656. TEL 714-362-2000. FAX 714-362-2020.
Producer(s): SilverPlatter Information, Inc. *4928*

AMERICAN JOURNAL OF OPHTHALMOLOGY.
Ophthalmic Publishing Co., 77 W. Wacker Dr., Ste. 660, Chicago, IL 60601-1632. TEL 312-629-1690. FAX 312-629-1744. *4989*

AMERICAN JOURNAL OF SPORTS MEDICINE.
American Orthopaedic Society for Sports Medicine, 230 Calvary St., Waltham, MA 02154. TEL 617-736-0707. FAX 617-736-0607. *5128*

AMERICAN LIBRARY DIRECTORY.
R.R. Bowker, A Division of Reed Elsevier Inc., 121 Chanlon Rd., New Providence, NJ 07974. TEL 908-464-6800. FAX 908-665-6688.
Producer(s): Bowker Electronic Publishing. *4158*

AMERICAN MANUFACTURERS DIRECTORY.
American Business Directories, 5711 S. 86th Circle, Box 27347, Omaha, NE 68127. TEL 402-593-4600. FAX 402-331-5481. *1651*

AMERICAN MARITIME CASES.
American Maritime Cases, Inc., 28 E. 21st St., Baltimore, MD 21218-5932. TEL 410-752-2939. FAX 410-625-1174. *4141*

AMERICAN MEN AND WOMEN OF SCIENCE.
R.R. Bowker, A Division of Reed Elsevier Inc., 121 Chanlon Rd., New Providence, NJ 07974. TEL 908-464-6800. FAX 908-665-6688.
Producer(s): Bowker Electronic Publishing. *571*

AMERICAN PUBLIC OPINION DATA.
Opinion Research Service, 7200 Wisconsin Ave., Ste. 704, Bethesda, MD 20814-4811. *3369*

AMERICAN PUBLIC OPINION INDEX.
Opinion Research Service, 7200 Wisconsin Ave., Ste. 704, Bethesda, MD 20814-4811. *6739*

AMERICAN SPECTATOR.
2020 N. 14th St., Ste. 750, Box 549, Arlington, VA 22201. TEL 703-243-3733. FAX 703-243-6814. *4322*

AMERICAN STATISTICS INDEX.
Congressional Information Service, Inc., A member of the LEXIS NEXIS family, 4520 East-West Hwy., Bethesda, MD 20814-3389. TEL 301-654-1550. FAX 301-654-4033. *6891*

AMERICAS.
Americas Magazine, 19th St. & Constitution Ave., N.W., Ste. 300, Washington, DC 20006. TEL 202-458-3278. FAX 202-458-6217. *3772*

AMERICA'S CORPORATE FINANCE DIRECTORY.
National Register Publishing, A Division of Reed Elsevier Inc., 121 Chanlon Rd., New Providence, NJ 07974. TEL 908-464-6800. FAX 908-665-2870.
Producer(s): Bowker Electronic Publishing. *1652*

AMIGA GAMES.
Computec Verlag, Isarstr. 32-34, 90451 Nuernberg, Germany. TEL 49-911-96832-0. FAX 49-911-6426333. *2116*

AMIGA PLUS C D - R O M.
I C P - Innovativ Presse GmbH, Wendelsteinstr. 3, 85591 Vaterstetten, Germany. TEL 49-8106-33954. FAX 49-8106-34238.
Available only on CD-ROM. *2117*

AMNESTY INTERNATIONAL AUSTRALIAN NEWSLETTER.
Amnesty International Australia, Private Bag 23, Broadway, N.S.W. 2007, Australia. TEL 61-2-92113560. FAX 61-2-92113608. *5987*

ANALYTICAL ABSTRACTS.
The Royal Society of Chemistry, Thomas Graham House, Science Park, Milton Rd., Cambridge CB4 4WF, England. TEL 44-1223-420066. FAX 44-1223-423429.
Producer(s): SilverPlatter Information, Inc. *1772*

ANDERSON'S OHIO LAW ON DISC.
Anderson Publishing Co., 2035 Reading Rd., Cincinnati, OH 45202. TEL 513-421-4142. FAX 513-562-8116.
Available only on CD-ROM. *3910*

ANESTHESIOLOGY.
Lippincott - Raven Publishers, 227 E. Washington Sq., Philadelphia, PA 19106. TEL 215-238-4200. FAX 215-238-4227. *4804*

ANIMAL BEHAVIOR ABSTRACTS.
Cambridge Scientific Abstracts, 7200 Wisconsin Ave., 6th Fl., Bethesda, MD 20814. TEL 301-961-6750. FAX 301-961-6720.
Producer(s): NISC, SilverPlatter Information, Inc. *635*

ANNALS OF HEALTH LAW.
Loyola University Chicago, School of Law, One E. Pearson St., Chicago, IL 60611. TEL 312-915-6304. FAX 312-915-7201. *3910*

ANNALS OF INTERNAL MEDICINE.
American College of Physicians, Independence Mall W., Sixth St. at Race, Philadelphia, PA 19106-1572. TEL 215-351-2400. FAX 215-351-2799. *4924*

ANNOTATED BIBLIOGRAPHY OF ENGLISH STUDIES.
Swets & Zeitlinger bv, P.O. Box 825, 2160 SZ Lisse, Netherlands. TEL 31-252-435111. FAX 31-252-415888.
Available only on CD-ROM. *4494*

ANNUAIRE TELEXPORT.
Chambre de Commerce et d'Industrie de Paris (CEDIP), 27 av. de Friedland, 75008 Paris, France. TEL 33-1-42897240. FAX 33-1-42897281. *1178*

THE ANNUAL REGISTER (YEAR).
Keesing's Worldwide, LLC, 7979 Old Georgetown Rd., Bethesda, MD 20814. TEL 301-718-8770. FAX 301-718-8494. *5892*

ANNUAL REGISTRARS SERVICE.
Financial Times Information Ltd., Extel, Fitzroy Hosue, 13-17 Epworth St., London EC2A 4DL, England. TEL 44-171-825-8000. FAX 44-171-608-2032. *1373*

ANNUARIO DEI DEPUTATI E SENATORI DEL PARLAMENTO REPUBBLICANO.
Editoriale Italiana, Via Vigliena 10, 00192 Rome, Italy. TEL 39-6-32301777. FAX 39-6-3211359. *6164*

ANNUARIO GENERALE ITALIANO.
Guida Monaci S.p.A., Via Vitorchiano 107, 00189 Rome, Italy. TEL 39-6-3288805. FAX 39-6-3275693. *1209*

ANTARCTIC BIBLIOGRAPHY.
U.S. Library of Congress, Washington, DC 20540. TEL 202-707-1181.
Producer(s): NISC (Arctic & Antarctic Regions). *6587*

ANTHROPOLOGICAL LITERATURE.
Harvard University, Tozzer Library, 21 Divinity Ave., Cambridge, MA 02138. TEL 617-495-2253. FAX 617-496-2741. *335*

SERIALS AVAILABLE ON CD-ROM

ANTHROPOLOGY TODAY.
Royal Anthropological Institute of Great Britain and Ireland, 50 Fitzroy St., London W1P 5HS, England. TEL 44-171-387-0455. FAX 44-171-383-4235. *309*

ANTI-CANCER DRUGS.
Rapid Science Publishers, The Old Malthouse, Paradise St., Oxford OX1 1LD, England. TEL 44-1865-790447. FAX 44-1865-244012. *4970*

ANTIMICROBIAL AGENTS AND CHEMOTHERAPY.
American Society for Microbiology, 1325 Massachusetts Ave., N.W., Washington, DC 20005. TEL 202-737-3600. *780*

ANTIOCH REVIEW.
Antioch Review, Inc., Box 148, Yellow Springs, OH 45387. TEL 513-767-6389. *4323*

ANUARIO DE ESTUDIOS AMERICANOS.
Consejo Superior de Investigaciones Cientificas (C.S.I.C.), Vitruvio 8, 28006 Madrid, Spain. TEL 34-1-5612833. FAX 34-1-5629634. *3617*

ANUARIO HISPANO.
T I Y M Publishing Company, Inc., 1489 Chain Bridge Rd., Ste. 200, McLean, VA 22101. TEL 703-734-1632. FAX 703-356-0787. *5504*

ANWALT- UND NOTARVERZEICHNIS.
Verlag Dr. Otto Schmidt KG, Unter den Ulmen 96-98, 50968 Cologne, Germany. TEL 49-221-9373801. FAX 49-221-93738943. *1652*

APPLICABLE ANALYSIS.
Gordon and Breach - Harwood Academic, Amsteldisk 166, 1st Fl., 1079 LH Amsterdam, Netherlands. *4561*

APPLIED AND ENVIRONMENTAL MICROBIOLOGY.
American Society for Microbiology, 1325 Massachusetts Ave., N.W., Washington, DC 20005. TEL 202-737-3600. *780*

APPLIED PHYSICS LETTERS.
American Institute of Physics, One Physics Ellipse, College Park, MD 20740-3843. TEL 301-209-3000. *5797*

APPLIED SCIENCE & TECHNOLOGY INDEX.
H.W. Wilson Co., 950 University Ave., Bronx, NY 10452. TEL 718-588-8400. FAX 718-590-1617. Producer(s): SilverPlatter Information, Inc., H.W. Wilson. *2747*

APPLIWARE.
Gruppo Editoriale J C E, Via Ferri 6, 20092 Cinisello Balsamo (MI), Italy. TEL 39-2-660251. FAX 39-2-6127620. *2209*

AQUALINE ABSTRACTS.
W R C plc, P.O. Box 85, Frankland Rd., Blagrove, Swindon, Wilts SN5 8YF, England. *7307*

AQUATIC BIOLOGY, AQUACULTURE & FISHERIES RESOURCES.
National Information Services Corporation (NISC), 3100 St. Paul St., Ste. 806, Baltimore, MD 21218. TEL 410-243-0797. FAX 410-243-0982. Available only on CD-ROM. Producer(s): NISC. *635*

AQUATIC SCIENCES & FISHERIES ABSTRACTS. PART 1: BIOLOGICAL SCIENCES AND LIVING RESOURCES.
Cambridge Scientific Abstracts, 7200 Wisconsin Ave., 6th Fl., Bethesda, MD 20814. TEL 301-961-6750. FAX 301-961-6720. Producer(s): NISC, SilverPlatter Information, Inc. *7307*

AQUATIC SCIENCES & FISHERIES ABSTRACTS. PART 2: OCEAN TECHNOLOGY, POLICY AND NON-LIVING RESOURCES.
Cambridge Scientific Abstracts, 7200 Wisconsin Ave., 6th Fl., Bethesda, MD 20814. TEL 301-961-6750. FAX 301-961-6720. Producer(s): NISC, SilverPlatter Information, Inc. *7307*

AQUATIC SCIENCES & FISHERIES ABSTRACTS. PART 3: AQUATIC POLLUTION AND ENVIRONMENTAL QUALITY.
Cambridge Scientific Abstracts, 7200 Wisconsin Ave., 6th Fl., Bethesda, MD 20814. TEL 301-961-6700. FAX 301-961-6720. Producer(s): Knight-Ridder, Inc. (Environmental Management), NISC, SilverPlatter Information, Inc. *3081*

ARAB STUDIES QUARTERLY.
Association of Arab-American University Graduates, Inc., 2121 Wisconsin Ave., N.W., Ste. 310, Washington, DC 20007-2258. TEL 202-337-7717. FAX 202-337-3302. *2997*

ARBEITSRECHTLICHE PRAXIS C D - R O M.
Verlag C.H. Beck, 80791 Munich, Germany. TEL 49-89-38189338. FAX 49-89-38189398. Available only on CD-ROM. *1418*

ARCHITECTURAL PUBLICATIONS INDEX.
R I B A Publications, Finsbury Mission, 39 Moreland St., London EC1V 8BB, England. TEL 44-171-251-0791. FAX 44-171-608-2375. *418*

ARCHIVES OF ENVIRONMENTAL HEALTH.
Heldref Publications, 1319 Eighteenth St., N.W., Washington, DC 20036-1802. TEL 202-296-6267. FAX 202-296-5149. Producer(s): UMI. *4640*

ARCHIVES OF FAMILY MEDICINE.
American Medical Association, 515 N. State St., Chicago, IL 60610. TEL 312-464-5000. FAX 312-464-5831. *4640*

ARCHIVES OF GENERAL PSYCHIATRY.
American Medical Association, 515 N. State St., Chicago, IL 60610. TEL 312-464-5000. FAX 312-464-5831. *5052*

ARCHIVES OF INTERNAL MEDICINE.
American Medical Association, 515 N. State St., Chicago, IL 60610. TEL 312-464-5000. FAX 312-464-5831. *4924*

ARCHIVES OF NEUROLOGY.
American Medical Association, 515 N. State St., Chicago, IL 60610. TEL 312-464-5000. FAX 312-464-5831. *5053*

ARCHIVES OF OPHTHALMOLOGY.
American Medical Association, 515 N. State St., Chicago, IL 60610. TEL 312-464-5000. FAX 312-464-5831. *4990*

ARCHIVES OF OTOLARYNGOLOGY - HEAD & NECK SURGERY.
American Medical Association, 515 N. State St., Chicago, IL 60610. TEL 312-464-5000. FAX 312-464-5831. *5020*

ARCHIVES OF PEDIATRICS & ADOLESCENT MEDICINE.
American Medical Association, 515 N. State St., Chicago, IL 60610. TEL 312-464-5000. FAX 312-464-4181. *5028*

ARCHIVES OF SURGERY.
American Medical Association, 515 N. State St., Chicago, IL 60610. TEL 312-464-5000. FAX 312-464-5831. *5136*

ARCTIC & ANTARCTIC REGIONS (COLD REGIONS).
National Information Services Corporation (NISC), 3100 St. Paul St., Ste. 806, Baltimore, MD 21218. TEL 410-243-0797. FAX 410-243-0982. Available only on CD-ROM. Producer(s): NISC. *2324*

HA'ARETZ.
21 Salman Shocken St., P.O. Box 233, Tel Aviv 61001, Israel. TEL 972-3-5121212. FAX 972-3-6810012. *3323*

ARGENTINA. INSTITUTO NACIONAL DE ESTADISTICA Y CENSOS. ANUARIO ESTADISTICO.
Instituto Nacional de Estadistica y Censos, Avda. Julio A. Roca, 609 P.B., 1067 Buenos Aires, Argentina. TEL 54-1-3499662. FAX 54-1-3499621. *6060*

ARIZONA BUSINESS DIRECTORY.
American Business Directories, 5711 S. 86th Circle, Box 27347, Omaha, NE 68127. TEL 402-593-4600. FAX 402-331-5481. *1652*

ARIZONA INDUSTRIAL DIRECTORY.
Phoenix Chamber of Commerce, 201 N. Central Ave., 27th Fl., Phoenix, AZ 85073. TEL 602-495-2195. FAX 602-495-8913. *1652*

ARKANSAS BUSINESS DIRECTORY.
American Business Directories, 5711 S. 86th Circle, Box 27347, Omaha, NE 68127. TEL 402-593-4600. FAX 402-331-5481. *1652*

ARKANSAS HISTORICAL QUARTERLY.
Arkansas Historical Association, University of Arkansas, Department of History, Old Main 416, Fayetteville, AR 72701. TEL 501-575-5884. FAX 501-575-2642. *3618*

ARKANSAS MANUFACTURERS REGISTER.
Manufacturers' News, Inc., 1633 Central St., Evanston, IL 60201-1569. TEL 847-864-7000. FAX 847-332-1100. *1652*

ARQUIVOS DE NEURO-PSIQUIATRIA.
Associacao Arquivos Neuro-Psiquiatria Dr. Oswaldo Lange, Caixa Postal 8877, 01065-970 Sao Paulo, SP, Brazil. TEL 55-11-2879726. FAX 55-11-2898879. *5053*

ART INDEX.
H.W. Wilson Co., 950 University Ave., Bronx, NY 10452. TEL 718-588-8400. FAX 718-590-1617. Producer(s): SilverPlatter Information, Inc., H.W. Wilson (WILSONDISC). *475*

ARTBIBLIOGRAPHIES MODERN.
A B C - Clio Ltd., 35A Great Clarendon St., Oxford OX2 6AT, England. TEL 44-1865-311350. FAX 44-1865-311358. *475*

ARTS & HUMANITIES CITATION INDEX.
Institute for Scientific Information, 3501 Market St., Philadelphia, PA 19104. TEL 215-386-0100. FAX 215-386-2911. Producer(s): Institute for Scientific Information (A&HCI/CDE). *475*

ARTS EDUCATION POLICY REVIEW.
Heldref Publications, 1319 Eighteenth St., N.W., Washington, DC 20036-1802. TEL 202-296-6267. FAX 202-296-5149. Producer(s): UMI. *429*

ASIAN AFFAIRS: AN AMERICAN REVIEW.
Heldref Publications, 1319 18th St., N.W., Washington, DC 20036-1802. TEL 202-296-6267. FAX 202-296-5149. Producer(s): UMI. *6005*

ASIAN CLASSICS INPUT PROGRAM.
Asian Classics Input Program, 1911 Marmary Rd., Gaithersburg, MD 20878-1839. TEL 301-948-5569. FAX 301-294-7870. *6388*

ASIANWEEK.
Pan Asia Venture Capital Corporation, 809 Sacramento St., San Francisco, CA 94108. TEL 415-397-0220. FAX 415-397-7258. *2998*

ASSOCIATIONS YELLOW BOOK.
Leadership Directories, Inc., 104 Fifth Ave., 2nd Fl., New York, NY 10011. TEL 212-627-4140. FAX 212-645-0931. Producer(s): Chadwyck-Healey Inc. *1653*

THE ATLANTA CONSTITUTION AND JOURNAL INDEX.
U M I, 300 N. Zeeb Rd., Ann Arbor, MI 48106-1346. TEL 313-761-4700. FAX 800-864-0019. *3883*

THE ATLANTIC MONTHLY.
Atlantic Monthly Co., 77 N. Washington St., Ste. 5, Boston, MA 02114-1908. TEL 617-536-9500. Producer(s): UMI. *4324*

ATOMS IN JAPAN.
Nihon Genshiryoku Sangyo Kaigi, Toshin Bldg., 1-1-13 Shinbashi, Minato-ku, Tokyo 105, Japan. FAX 81-3-3508-2411. *2694*

AUDITORY NEUROSCIENCE.
Gordon and Breach - Harwood Academic, Amsteldisk 166, 1st. Fl., 1079 LH Amsterdam, Netherlands. *5053*

SERIALS AVAILABLE ON CD-ROM

AUDUBON.
National Audubon Society, 700 Broadway, New York, NY 10003. TEL 212-979-3126. FAX 212-477-9069.
Producer(s): UMI. *2223*

AUSTRALIA. BUREAU OF STATISTICS. HISTORICAL PUBLICATIONS ON C D - R O M.
Australian Bureau of Statistics, P.O. Box 10, Belconnen, A.C.T. 2616, Australia.
Available only on CD-ROM. *6895*

AUSTRALIAN & NEW ZEALAND JOURNAL OF SOCIOLOGY.
Longman Australia, 95 Coventry St., S. Melbourne, Vic. 3205, Australia. TEL 61-3-96970657. FAX 61-3-96992041. *6702*

AUSTRALIAN ARCHITECTURAL PERIODICALS INDEX.
Stanton Library, Reader Services Department, P.O. Box 12, N. Sydney, N.S.W. 2059, Australia. TEL 61-2-99368400. FAX 61-2-99368440. *418*

AUSTRALIAN ART AUCTION RECORDS.
Australian Art Sales, P.O. Box 50, Sutherland, N.S.W. 2232, Australia. TEL 61-2-92677363. *431*

AUSTRALIAN CASE CITATOR.
L B C Information Services, 50 Waterloo Rd., N. Ryde, N.S.W. 2113, Australia. TEL 61-2-99366444. FAX 61-2-98889706. *4130*

AUSTRALIAN CATALOGUE OF NEW FILMS AND VIDEOS.
Australian Catalogue, P.O. Box 204, Albert Park, Vic. 3206, Australia. TEL 61-3-525-5302. FAX 61-3-537-2325. *5324*

AUSTRALIAN CORPORATIONS & SECURITIES LAW REPORTER.
C C H Australia Ltd., P.O. Box 230, North Ryde, N.S.W. 2113, Australia. TEL 61-1-300300224. FAX 61-1-300306224. *4073*

AUSTRALIAN DIGEST.
L B C Information Services, 50 Waterloo Rd., N. Ryde, N.S.W. 2113, Australia. TEL 61-2-99366444. FAX 61-2-98889706. *3915*

AUSTRALIAN FAMILY AND SOCIETY ABSTRACTS.
Australian Institute of Family Studies, 300 Queen St., Melbourne, Vic. 3000, Australia. TEL 61-3-92147888. FAX 61-3-92147839. *6739*

AUSTRALIAN FAMILY LAW & PRACTICE.
C C H Australia Ltd., P.O. Box 230, North Ryde, N.S.W. 2113, Australia. TEL 61-1-300300224. FAX 61-2-300306224. *4099*

AUSTRALIAN FEDERAL TAX REPORTER.
C C H Australia Ltd., P.O. Box 230, North Ryde, N.S.W. 2113, Australia. TEL 61-1-300300224. FAX 61-1-300306224. *1599*

AUSTRALIAN INCOME TAX LEGISLATION.
C C H Australia Ltd., P.O. Box 230, North Ryde, N.S.W. 2113, Australia. TEL 61-1-300300224. FAX 61-1-300306224. *1599*

AUSTRALIAN INCOME TAX RULINGS.
C C H Australia Ltd., P.O. Box 230, North Ryde, N.S.W. 2113, Australia. TEL 61-1-300300224. FAX 61-1-300306224. *3915*

AUSTRALIAN LEGAL MONTHLY DIGEST.
L B C Information Services, 50 Waterloo Rd., N. Ryde, N.S.W. 2113, Australia. TEL 61-2-99366444. FAX 61-2-98889706. *4130*

AUSTRALIAN TERTIARY HANDBOOKS COLLECTION ON MULTIMEDIA.
Hermes Precisa Australia, 570 City Rd., S. Melbourne, Vic. 3205, Australia. TEL 61-3-96935500. FAX 61-3-96904035. *2521*

AUTOIMMUNITY.
Gordon and Breach - Harwood Academic, Amsteldisk 166, 1st Fl., 1079 LH Amsterdam, Netherlands. *4792*

AUTORIDADES DE LA BIBLIOTECA NACIONAL DE ESPANA EN C D - R O M.
Biblioteca Nacional de Espana, Paeo de Recoletos 20, 28001 Madrid, Spain.
Available only on CD-ROM. Producer(s): Chadwyck-Healey Inc. *533*

AUTO4WORLD.COM.
Superior Products Corp., Box 11312, Fort Lauderdale, FL 33339. TEL 954-567-1144. FAX 954-564-5105. *7090*

AVIATION WEEK & SPACE TECHNOLOGY.
McGraw-Hill Companies, Aviation Week Group (New York), 1221 Ave. of the Americas, New York, NY 10020. TEL 212-512-3034. FAX 212-512-4225. *59*

AZ B - ARIZONA BUSINESS.
Arizona State University, Center for Business Research, College of Business, Box 874406, Tempe, AZ 85287-4406. TEL 602-965-3961. FAX 602-965-5458. *935*

B D I DEUTSCHLAND LIEFERT.
Verlag W. Sachon, Schloss Mindelburg, 87714 Mindelheim, Germany. TEL 49-8261-999-0. FAX 49-8261-999180. *1316*

B H I PLUS.
Bowker - Saur Ltd., A member of the Reed Elsevier plc group, Maypole House, Maypole Rd., E. Grinstead, W. Sussex RH19 1HU, England. TEL 44-1342-330100. FAX 44-1342-330191.
Available only on CD-ROM. Producer(s): Bowker - Saur Ltd. *3798*

B I R D.
Centre International de l'Enfance, Chateau de Longchamp, Bois de Boulogne, 75016 Paris, France. TEL 33-1-44302062. FAX 33-1-44302065. *1861*

B M J.
B M J Publishing Group, B.M.A. House, Tavistock Sq., London WC1H 9JR, England. TEL 44-171-387-4499. FAX 44-171-383-6661. *4644*

B N A'S EMPLOYEE BENEFITS LIBRARY ON C D.
The Bureau of National Affairs, Inc., 1231 25th St., N.W., Washington, DC 20037. TEL 202-452-4200. FAX 202-822-8092.
Available only on CD-ROM. *1420*

B N A'S ENVIRONMENT & SAFETY SMARTCITE.
The Bureau of National Affairs, Inc., 1231 25th St., N.W., Washington, DC 20037. TEL 202-452-4200. FAX 202-822-8092.
Available only on CD-ROM. *2907*

B N B ON C D - R O M.
British Library, National Bibliographic Service, Boston Spa, Wetherby, W. Yorks. LS23 7BQ, England. TEL 44-1937-546585. FAX 44-1937-546586.
Available only on CD-ROM. Producer(s): Chadwyck-Healey Inc. *533*

B N I.
Primary Source Media, P.O. Box 45, Reading RG1 8HF, England. TEL 44-1734-583247. FAX 44-1734-591325.
Available only on CD-ROM. *3883*

B S I STANDARDS CATALOGUE.
British Standards Institution, Linford Wood, Milton Keynes, Bucks. MK14 6LE, England. TEL 44-1908-220022. FAX 44-1908-320856. *5249*

BAHRAIN MEDICAL BULLETIN.
P.O. Box 32159, Manama, Bahrain. TEL 973-279472. *4645*

BAHRAIN MEDICAL SOCIETY. JOURNAL.
Bahrain Medical Society, P.O. Box 26136, Manama, Bahrain. TEL 973-742666. *4645*

BANGLADESH JOURNAL OF BOTANY.
Bangladesh Botanical Society, c/o Department of Botany, University of Dhaka, Dhaka 1000, Bangladesh. TEL 505848. *694*

BANGLADESH MEDICAL RESEARCH COUNCIL BULLETIN.
Bangladesh Medical Research Council, Mokakhali, Dhaka 1212, Bangladesh. TEL 871393. *4645*

BANK LETTER.
Institutional Investor Newsletters, 477 Madison Ave., New York, NY 10022. TEL 212-224-3233. FAX 212-224-3353. *1108*

BANK OF JAPAN. ECONOMIC AND FINANCIAL DATA ON C D - R O M.
Bank of Japan, c/o Public Relations Department, 1-1, 2-chome, Hongokucho, Nihonbashi, Chuo-ku, Tokyo 103, Japan.
Available only on CD-ROM. *1023*

BANKRUPTCY CODE, RULES AND FORMS.
West Group, 620 Opperman Dr., Eagan, MN 55123. TEL 612-687-7000. FAX 612-687-7302. *3918*

BANKRUPTCY EVIDENCE MANUAL.
West Group, 620 Opperman Dr., Eagan, MN 55123-1308. TEL 612-687-8000. FAX 612-687-7302. *3918*

BARRON'S PROFILES OF AMERICAN COLLEGES.
Barron's Educational Series, Inc., 250 Wireless Blvd., Hauppauge, NY 11788. TEL 516-434-3311. *2521*

BAYERISCHE STAATSBIBLIOTHEK. OSTEUROPA-KATALOG AUF C D - R O M.
Bayerische Staatsbibliothek, Ludwigstr. 16, 80539 Munich, Germany. TEL 49-89-286380. FAX 49-89-28638293.
Available only on CD-ROM. *533*

BEAUTIFUL BRITISH COLUMBIA MAGAZINE.
Beautiful British Columbia Magazine Ltd., 929 Ellery St., Victoria, BC V9A 7B4, Canada. TEL 250-384-5456. FAX 250-384-2812. *7186*

BEAUTIFUL BRITISH COLUMBIA TRAVELLER.
Beautiful British Columbia Magazine Ltd., 929 Ellery St., Victoria, BC V9A 7B4, Canada. TEL 250-384-5456. FAX 250-384-2812. *7186*

BEAUTY CARE SUPPLY GUIDE.
Made in Europe Marketing Organisation GmbH, Hahnstr. 70, 60528 Frankfurt a.M., Germany. TEL 49-69-6680380. FAX 49-69-66803838. *504*

BEGLEITPAPIERE FUER AUSFUHRSENDUNGEN.
Mendel Verlag, Robensstr. 39, 52070 Aachen, Germany. TEL 49-241-154355. FAX 49-241-154355. *1316*

BEHAVIORAL MEDICINE.
Heldref Publications, 1319 Eighteenth St., N.W., Washington, DC 20036-1802. TEL 202-396-6267. FAX 202-296-5149.
Producer(s): UMI. *6097*

BEHAVIOURAL NEUROLOGY.
Rapid Science Publishers, 2-6 Boundary Row, London SE1 8HN, England. TEL 44-171-865-0198. FAX 44-171-410-6600. *5054*

BEHAVIOURAL PHARMACOLOGY.
Rapid Science Publishers, The Old Malthouse, Paradise St., Oxford OX1 1LD, England. TEL 44-1865-790447. FAX 44-1865-244012. *5649*

DIE BEKLEIDUNGS- UND WAESCHE-INDUSTRIE UND IHRE HELFER.
Industrieschau-Verlagsgesellschaft mbH, Postfach 100262, 64202 Darmstadt, Germany. TEL 49-6151-38920. FAX 49-6151-33164. *1913*

BELGIAN BUSINESS & INDUSTRIE.
Business & Industrie, Research Park Zellik, De Haak, 1731 Zellik (Brussels). TEL 32-2-4675740. FAX 32-2-4675969. *1579*

BENELUX-MERKENBLAD.
Benelux Merkenbureau, Bordewijklaan 15, 2591 XR The Hague, Netherlands. TEL 31-70-3491111. FAX 31-70-3475708. *5581*

BESPRECHUNGEN ANNOTATIONEN.
Einkaufszentrale fuer Bibliotheken, Bismarckstr. 3, 72764 Reutlingen, Germany. TEL 49-7121-144-0. FAX 49-7121-144280. *4163*

BEST BOOKS FOR CHILDREN.
R.R. Bowker, A Division of Reed Elsevier Inc., 121 Chanlon Rd., New Providence, NJ 07974. TEL 908-464-6800. FAX 908-665-6688.
Producer(s): Bowker Electronic Publishing. *1838*

BEST'S INSURANCE REPORTS: LIFE - HEALTH.
A.M. Best Co., Ambest Rd., Oldwick, NJ 08858. TEL 908-439-2200. FAX 908-439-3296. *3809*

SERIALS AVAILABLE ON CD-ROM

BEST'S INSURANCE REPORTS: PROPERTY - CASUALTY.
A.M. Best Co., Ambest Rd., Oldwick, NJ 08858. TEL 908-439-2200. FAX 908-439-3296. *3809*

BEST'S UNDERWRITING GUIDE.
A.M. Best Co., Ambest Rd., Oldwick, NJ 08858. TEL 908-439-2200. FAX 908-439-3296. *3810*

BETRIEBS-BERATER.
Verlag Recht und Wirtschaft GmbH, Haeusserstr. 14, 69115 Heidelberg, Germany. TEL 49-6221-906-1. *3920*

BIBLIOGRAFIA BRASILEIRA DE ODONTOLOGIA.
Universidade de Sao Paulo, Faculdade de Odontologia, Av. Prof. Lineu Prestes, 2227, Caixa Postal 8216, 05508-900 Sao Paulo SP, Brazil. TEL 55-11-8187861. FAX 55-11-8187413. *4764*

BIBLIOGRAFIA ESPANOLA DESDE 1976 EN C D - R O M.
Biblioteca Nacional de Espana, Paseo de Recoletos 20, 28001 Madrid, Spain.
Available only on CD-ROM. Producer(s): Chadwyck-Healey Inc. *534*

BIBLIOGRAFIA GENERALE DELLA LINGUA E DELLA LETTERATURA ITALIANA.
Salerno Editrice, Via di Donna Olimpia 20, 00152 Rome, Italy. TEL 39-6-58205688. FAX 39-6-58238241. *534*

BIBLIOGRAFIA LATINOAMERICANA.
Universidad Nacional Autonoma de Mexico, Direccion General de Bibliotecas, Apdo. Postal 70-392, Circuito Exterior, Ciudad Universitaria, 04510 Mexico, D.F., Mexico. TEL 52-5-6223958. FAX 52-5-6162557. *534*

BIBLIOGRAFIA LATINOAMERICANA: PART II.
Universidad Nacional Autonoma de Mexico, Direccion eneral de Bibliotecas, Apdo. Postal 70-392, C.P. 04510 Mexico, D.F., Mexico. TEL 52-5-6223958. FAX 52-5-6162557. *534*

BIBLIOGRAFIA NACIONAL PORTUGUESA EM C D - R O M.
Chadwyck-Healey Ltd., The Quorum, Barnwell Rd., Cambridge CB5 8SW, England. TEL 44-1223-215512. FAX 44-1223-215514.
Available only on CD-ROM. Producer(s): Chadwyck-Healey Inc. *535*

BIBLIOGRAFIA NAZIONALE ITALIANA.
Istituto Centrale per il Catalogo Unico delle Biblioteche Italiane e per le Informazioni Bibliografiche, Viale del Castro Pretorio, 105, 00185 Rome, Italy. TEL 39-06-4959217. FAX 39-06-4959302.
Producer(s): Chadwyck-Healey Inc. *535*

BIBLIOGRAPHIA MEDICA CECHOSLOVACA.
Narodni Lekarska Knihovna, Sokolska 31, 121 32 Prague 2, Czech Republic. TEL 42-2-24915775. FAX 42-2-24924625. *4764*

BIBLIOGRAPHICAL SOCIETY OF CANADA. BULLETIN.
Bibliographical Society of Canada, P.O. Box 575, Sta. "P", Toronto, ON M5S 2T1, Canada. *536*

BIBLIOGRAPHICAL SOCIETY OF CANADA. FACSIMILE SERIES.
Bibliographical Society of Canada, P.O. Box 575, Sta. "P", Toronto, ON M5S 2T1, Canada. *536*

BIBLIOGRAPHICAL SOCIETY OF CANADA. MONOGRAPHS.
Bibliographical Society of Canada, P.O. Box 575, Sta. "P", Toronto, ON M5S 2T1, Canada. *536*

BIBLIOGRAPHICAL SOCIETY OF CANADA. PAPERS.
Bibliographical Society of Canada, P.O. Box 575, Sta. "P", Toronto, ON M5S 2T1, Canada. *537*

BIBLIOGRAPHIE DER DEUTSCHEN SPRACH- UND LITERATURWISSENSCHAFT.
Vittorio Klostermann, Frauenlobstr. 22, 60487 Frankfurt a.M., Germany. TEL 49-69-970816-0. FAX 49-69-708038. *4494*

BIBLIOGRAPHIE GEOGRAPHIQUE INTERNATIONALE. F R A N C I S. 531.
Centre National de la Recherche Scientifique, Pole de Recherche pour l'Organisation et la Diffusion de l'Information Geographique, 191 rue Saint-Jacques, 75005 Paris, France. TEL 33-1-42345620. FAX 33-1-43296529. *3428*

BIBLIOGRAPHIE NATIONALE FRANCAISE. LIVRES.
Bibliotheque Nationale de France, Quai Francois Mauriac, 75706 Paris Cedex 13, France. TEL 33-1-47038610. FAX 33-1-47038586.
Producer(s): Chadwyck-Healey Inc. *537*

BIBLIOGRAPHIE NATIONALE FRANCAISE. PUBLICATIONS EN SERIE.
Bibliotheque Nationale de France, Quai Francois Mauriac, 75706 Paris Cedex 13, France. TEL 33-1-47038610. FAX 33-1-47038586.
Producer(s): Chadwyck-Healey Inc. *537*

BIBLIOGRAPHIE NATIONALE FRANCAISE. PUBLICATIONS OFFICIELLES.
Bibliotheque Nationale de France, Quai Francois Mauriac, 75706 Paris Cedex 13, France. TEL 33-1-47038610. FAX 33-1-47038586.
Producer(s): Chadwyck-Healey Inc. *537*

BIBLIOGRAPHY AND INDEX OF GEOLOGY.
American Geological Institute, 4220 King St., Alexandria, VA 22302-1502. TEL 703-379-2480. FAX 703-379-7563.
Producer(s): SilverPlatter Information, Inc. (GeoRef). *2324*

BIBLIOGRAPHY OF AGRICULTURE.
Oryx Press, Box 33889, Phoenix, AZ 85067-3889. TEL 602-265-2651. FAX 602-265-6250.
Producer(s): SilverPlatter Information, Inc. *170*

BIBLIOGRAPHY OF BIOETHICS.
Kennedy Institute of Ethics, National Reference Center for Bioethics Literature, Georgetown University, Box 571212, Washington, DC 20057-1212. TEL 202-687-6738. FAX 202-687-6770.
Producer(s): SilverPlatter Information, Inc. *4764*

BIBLIOGRAPHY OF ECONOMIC GEOLOGY.
Geosystems, P.O. Box 40, Didcot, Oxon. OX11 9BX, England. TEL 44-1235-813913.
Producer(s): NISC (Geosearch). *2324*

BIBLIOGRAPHY OF EDUCATION THESES IN AUSTRALIA.
Australian Council for Educational Research, Private Bag 55, Camberwell, Vic. 3124, Australia. TEL 61-3-92775555. FAX 61-3-92775500. *2497*

BIBLIOGRAPHY OF SCOTLAND.
National Library of Scotland, George IV Bridge, Edinburgh EH1 1EW, Scotland. TEL 44-131-226-4531. FAX 44-131-220-6662. *4495*

BIBLIOGRAPHY OF SYSTEMATIC MYCOLOGY.
International Mycological Institute, Bakeham Lane, Egham, Surrey TW20 9TV, England. *635*

BIBLIOGRAPHY ON COLD REGIONS SCIENCE & TECHNOLOGY.
U.S. Army, Cold Regions Research and Engineering Laboratory, 72 Lyme Rd., Hanover, NH 03755-1290. TEL 603-646-4221. FAX 603-646-4712.
Producer(s): NISC (Arctic & Antarctic Regions). *2747*

BIBLIOTHECA SACRA.
Dallas Theological Seminary, 3909 Swiss Ave., Dallas, TX 75204. TEL 214-824-3094. FAX 214-841-3532. *6416*

BILLBOARD HISTORY OF ROCK 'N ROLL.
B P I Communications, Inc. (New York), 1515 Broadway, New York, NY 10036. TEL 212-764-7300. FAX 212-944-1719.
Available only on CD-ROM. *5377*

BIOCATALYSIS AND BIOTRANSFORMATION.
Gordon and Breach - Harwood Academic, Amsteldisk 166, 1st Fl., 1079 LH Amsterdam, Netherlands. *678*

BIOCHEMISTRY AND BIOPHYSICS CITATION INDEX.
Institute for Scientific Information, 3501 Market St., Philadelphia, PA 19104. TEL 215-386-0100. FAX 215-386-2911. *635*

BIOENGINEERING ABSTRACTS.
Cambridge Scientific Abstracts, 7200 Wisconsin Ave., 6th Fl., Bethesda, MD 20814-4823. TEL 301-961-6700. FAX 301-961-6720.
Producer(s): Knight-Ridder, Inc. (Biotechnology & Bioengineering). *635*

BIOFOULING.
Gordon and Breach - Harwood Academic, Amsteldisk 166, 1st Fl., 1079 LH Amsterdam, Netherlands. *2975*

BIOGRAPHY AND GENEALOGY MASTER INDEX.
Gale Research, 835 Penobscot Bldg., 645 Griswold St., Detroit, MI 48226-4094. TEL 313-961-2242. FAX 800-414-5043. *581*

BIOGRAPHY INDEX.
H.W. Wilson Co., 950 University Ave., Bronx, NY 10452. TEL 718-588-8400. FAX 718-590-1617.
Producer(s): SilverPlatter Information, Inc., H.W. Wilson (WILSONDISC). *581*

BIOLOGICAL ABSTRACTS.
BIOSIS, 2100 Arch St., Philadelphia, PA 19103-1399. TEL 215-587-4847. FAX 215-587-2016.
Producer(s): SilverPlatter Information, Inc. *635*

BIOLOGICAL ABSTRACTS - R R M.
BIOSIS, 2100 Arch St., Philadelphia, PA 19103-1399. TEL 215-587-4847. FAX 215-587-2016.
Producer(s): SilverPlatter Information, Inc. *635*

BIOLOGICAL & AGRICULTURAL INDEX.
H.W. Wilson Co., 950 University Ave., Bronx, NY 10452. TEL 718-588-8400. FAX 718-590-1617.
Producer(s): SilverPlatter Information, Inc., H.W. Wilson (WILSONDISC). *636*

BIOLOGY DIGEST.
Plexus Publishing, Inc., 143 Old Marlton Pike, Medford, NJ 08055. TEL 609-654-6500. FAX 609-654-4309. *636*

BIOMEDICAL AND ENVIRONMENTAL SCIENCES.
Zhongguo Yufang Yixue Kexueyuan, 27 Nanwei Rd., Beijing 100050, People's Republic of China. TEL 86-10-6317-3957. FAX 86-10-6317-0892.
Available only on CD-ROM. Producer(s): SilverPlatter Information, Inc. *4646*

BIOMEDICAL ENGINEERING CITATION INDEX.
Institute for Scientific Information, 3501 Market St., Philadelphia, PA 19104. TEL 215-386-0100. FAX 215-386-2991. *4764*

BIOMETALS.
Thomson Science, 2-6 Boundary Row, London SE1 8HN, England. TEL 44-171-865-0198. FAX 44-171-410-6600. *655*

BIOSIS SERIAL SOURCES.
BIOSIS, 2100 Arch St., Philadelphia, PA 19103-1399. TEL 215-587-4847. FAX 215-587-2016. *636*

BIOTECHNOLOGY ABSTRACTS.
Derwent Publications Ltd., Derwent House, 14 Great Queen St., London WC2B 5DF, England. TEL 44-171-3442800. *636*

BIOTECHNOLOGY CITATION INDEX.
Institute for Scientific Information, 3501 Market St., Philadelphia, PA 19104. TEL 215-386-0100. FAX 215-386-2911. *636*

BIRKNER (YEAR) - EUROPEAN AND INTERNATIONAL PAPERWORLD.
Birkner & Co. Verlag, Winsbergring 38, 22525 Hamburg, Germany. TEL 49-40-85308502. FAX 49-40-85308381. *5565*

BLENDER.
25 W. 39th St., Ste. 900, New York, NY 10018. TEL 212-302-2626. FAX 212-302-2635.
Available only on CD-ROM. *5377*

BLIND WELFARE.
National Association for the Blind, India, 11 Khan Abdul Gaffar Khan Rd., Worli Seaface, Mumbai 400 025, India. TEL 91-22-493-6930. FAX 91-22-493-2539. *3468*

BLOOD COAGULATION AND FIBRINOLYSIS.
Thomson Science, 2-6 Boundary Row, London SE1 8HN, England. TEL 44-171-865-0198. FAX 44-171-928-0748. *4916*

BLUE BOOK OF CANADIAN BUSINESS.
International Press Publications Inc., 90 Nolan Ct., Ste. 21, Markham, ON L3R 4L9, Canada. TEL 905-946-9588. FAX 905-946-9590. *1226*

BLUE SKY LAW REPORTS.
C C H Incorporated, 2700 Lake Cook Rd., Riverwoods, IL 60015. TEL 847-267-7000. FAX 800-224-8299. *3920*

BOERNEBIBLIOTEKSKATALOG. BOEGER & TIDSSKRIFTER. EMNEKATALOG.
Dansk BiblioteksCenter as, Tempovej 7-11, DK-2750 Ballerup, Denmark. TEL 45-44-867777. FAX 45-44-867892. *539*

BOERNEBIBLIOTEKSKATALOG. BOEGER & TIDSSKRIFTER. FORFATTERKATALOG.
Dansk BiblioteksCenter as, Tempovej 7-11, DK-2750 Ballerup, Denmark. TEL 45-44-867777. FAX 45-44-867892. *539*

BOERNEBIBLIOTEKSKATALOG. BOEGER & TIDSSKRIFTER. TITELKATALOG.
Dansk BiblioteksCenter as, Tempovej 7-11, DK-2750 Ballerup, Denmark. TEL 45-44-867777. FAX 45-44-867892. *539*

BOERNEBIBLIOTEKSKATALOG. GRAMMOFONPLADER, KASSETTEBAAND.
Dansk BiblioteksCenter as, Tempovej 7-11, DK-2750 Ballerup, Denmark. TEL 45-44-867777. FAX 45-44-867892. *5447*

BOERNEBIBLIOTEKSKATALOG. LYDBOEGER, BOG & BAAND.
Dansk BiblioteksCenter as, Tempovej 7-11, DK-2750 Ballerup, Denmark. TEL 45-44-867777. FAX 45-44-867892. *1861*

BOLETIN OFICIAL DEL ESTADO.
Boletin Oficial del Estado, Trafalgar, 27, 28071 Madrid, Spain. TEL 34-1-5382297. FAX 34-1-5382275. *6166*

BOND INFORMATION DATABASE SERVICE.
Moody's Investors Service, 99 Church St., New York, NY 10007. TEL 212-553-0300. FAX 212-553-4700. *2172*

BOOK OF THE STATES.
Council of State Governments, 3560 Iron Works Pike, Box 11910, Lexington, KY 40578-1910. TEL 606-244-8000. FAX 606-244-8001. *6166*

BOOK REVIEW DIGEST.
H.W. Wilson Co., 950 University Ave., Bronx, NY 10452. TEL 718-588-8400. FAX 718-590-1617. Producer(s): K.G. Saur Verlag, H.W. Wilson (WILSONDISC). *4325*

BOOKS IN PRINT.
R.R. Bowker, A Division of Reed Elsevier Inc., 121 Chanlon Rd., New Providence, NJ 07974. TEL 908-464-6800. FAX 908-665-3502. Producer(s): Bowker Electronic Publishing (Books in Print PLUS). *539*

BOOKS IN PRINT ON DISC.
R.R. Bowker, A Division of Reed Elsevier Inc., 121 Chanlon Rd., New Providence, NJ 07974. TEL 908-665-2866. FAX 908-665-3528. Available only on CD-ROM. Producer(s): Bowker Electronic Publishing (Books in Print PLUS). *540*

BOOKS IN PRINT SUPPLEMENT.
R.R. Bowker, A Division of Reed Elsevier Inc., 121 Chanlon Rd., New Providence, NJ 07974. TEL 908-464-6800. FAX 908-665-3502. Producer(s): Bowker Electronic Publishing (Books in Print PLUS). *540*

BOOKS IN PRINT WITH BOOK REVIEWS ON DISC.
R.R. Bowker, A Division of Reed Elsevier Inc., 121 Chanlon Rd., New Providence, NJ 07974. FAX 908-665-3528. Available only on CD-ROM. Producer(s): Bowker Electronic Publishing (Books in Print PLUS). *540*

BOOKS OUT-OF-PRINT.
R.R. Bowker, A Division of Reed Elsevier Inc., 121 Chanlon Rd., New Providence, NJ 07974. TEL 908-464-6800. FAX 908-665-3502. Producer(s): Bowker Electronic Publishing (Books Out-of-Print PLUS). *540*

BOOKS OUT-OF-PRINT PLUS.
R.R. Bowker, A Division of Reed Elsevier Inc., 121 Chanlon Rd., New Providence, NJ 07974. FAX 908-665-3528. Producer(s): Bowker Electronic Publishing (Books Out-of-Print PLUS). *540*

BOOKS OUT-OF-PRINT WITH BOOK REVIEWS PLUS.
R.R. Bowker, A Division of Reed Elsevier Inc., 121 Chanlon Rd., New Providence, NJ 07974. FAX 908-665-3528. Producer(s): Bowker Electronic Publishing (Books Out-of-Print with Book Reviews PLUS). *540*

BOSTON SPA CONFERENCES ON C D - R O M.
British Library, Document Supply Centre, Boston Spa, Wetherby, W. Yorks. LS23 7BQ, England. TEL 44-1937-546080. FAX 44-1937-546286. Available only on CD-ROM. *540*

BOSTON SPA SERIALS ON C D - R O M.
British Library, Document Supply Centre, Boston Spa, Wetherby, W. Yorks. LS23 7BQ, England. TEL 44-1937-546061. FAX 44-1937-546286. Available only on CD-ROM. *540*

THE BOWKER ANNUAL LIBRARY AND BOOK TRADE ALMANAC.
R.R. Bowker, A Division of Reed Elsevier Inc., 121 Chanlon Rd., New Providence, NJ 07974. TEL 908-464-6800. FAX 908-665-6688. Producer(s): Bowker Electronic Publishing. *4166*

BOWKER - WHITAKER GLOBAL BOOKS IN PRINT ON DISC.
R.R. Bowker, A Division of Reed Elsevier Inc., 121 Chanlon Rd., New Providence, NJ 07974. TEL 908-665-2866. FAX 908-665-3528. Producer(s): Bowker Electronic Publishing (Books In Print PLUS). *540*

BOWKER'S COMPLETE VIDEO DIRECTORY.
R.R. Bowker, A Division of Reed Elsevier Inc., 121 Chanlon Rd., New Providence, NJ 07974. TEL 908-464-6800. FAX 908-665-6688. Producer(s): Bowker Electronic Publishing. *2066*

BOWKER'S LAW BOOKS AND SERIALS IN PRINT.
R.R. Bowker, A Division of Reed Elsevier Inc., 121 Chanlon Rd., New Providence, NJ 07974. TEL 908-464-6800. FAX 908-665-3502. *4051*

BOYS' LIFE (INKPRINT EDITION).
Boy Scouts of America, Box 152079, Irving, TX 75015-2079. TEL 972-580-2366. FAX 972-580-2079. *1865*

BRABY'S DIRECTORY ON DISK.
Braby's, P.O. Box 1426, Pinetown 3600, South Africa. TEL 27-31-7017021. FAX 27-31-7017036. *1655*

BRASILIA MEDICA.
Associacao Medica de Brasilia, EQS 713-913, Modulo E, 70930 Brasilia, D.F., Brazil. TEL 061-245-1408. FAX 061-245-2501. *4648*

BRIEFING PAPERS.
Federal Publications Inc., 1120 20th St., N.W., Ste. 500 S., Washington, DC 20036-3488. TEL 202-337-7000. FAX 202-659-2233. *3921*

BRITANNICA BOOK OF THE YEAR.
Encyclopaedia Britannica, Inc., 310 S. Michigan Ave., Chicago, IL 60604. TEL 312-347-7000. FAX 312-347-7914. *2656*

BRITISH AND IRISH ARCHAEOLOGICAL BIBLIOGRAPHY.
British Archaeological Bibliography, University College London, Rm. 101, Institute of Archaeology, 31-34 Gordon Sq., London WC1H 0PY, England. TEL 44-171-380-7532. FAX 44-171-383-2572. *390*

BRITISH EDUCATION INDEX.
British Education Index, Brotherton Library, University of Leeds, Leeds LS2 9JT, England. TEL 44-113-233-5525. FAX 44-113-233-5524. *2497*

BRITISH HUMANITIES INDEX.
Bowker - Saur Ltd., A member of the Reed Elsevier plc group, Maypole House, Maypole Rd., E. Grinstead, W. Sussex RH19 1HU, England. TEL 44-1342-330100. FAX 44-1342-330191. Producer(s): Bowker - Saur Ltd. *3798*

BRITISH NATIONAL BIBLIOGRAPHY.
British Library, National Bibliographic Service, Boston Spa, Wetherby, W. Yorks. LS23 7BQ, England. TEL 44-1937-546613. FAX 44-1937-546586. *541*

BRITISH PHARMACOPOEIA: MAIN EDITION.
H.M.S.O., 51 Nine Elms Ln., London SW8 5DR, England. TEL 44-171-873-0011. FAX 44-171-873-8247. *5651*

BRITISH PHARMACOPOEIA: VETERINARY EDITION.
H.M.S.O., 51 Nine Elms Ln., London SW8 5DR, England. TEL 44-171-873-0011. FAX 44-171-873-8247. *7267*

BRITISH STANDARDS MICROFILE.
Technical Indexes Ltd., Willoughby Rd., Bracknell, Berkshire RG12 8DW, England. TEL 44-1344-426311. FAX 44-1344-424971. *2712*

BROADCASTING IN THE U K.
Key Note Ltd., Field House, 72 Oldfield Rd., Hampton, Middlesex TW12 2HQ, England. TEL 44-181-783-0755. FAX 44-181-783-0049. *2023*

BRYN MAWR CLASSICAL REVIEW.
Bryn Mawr Commentaries, Inc., Bryn Mawr College, Thomas Library, Bryn Mawr, PA 19010. TEL 610-526-5384. FAX 610-526-7475. *1901*

BULLETIN OF THE ATOMIC SCIENTISTS.
Educational Foundation for Nuclear Science, 6042 S. Kimbark Ave., Chicago, IL 60637. TEL 773-702-2555. FAX 773-702-0725. Producer(s): UMI. *6007*

DIE BURGER.
P.O. Box 692, Heerengarcht, 40, Cape Town 8000, South Africa. TEL 27-21-4062222. FAX 27-21-4063221. *3355*

BURRELLE'S MEDIA DIRECTORY.
Burrelle's Media Directories, 75 E. Northfield Rd., Livingston, NJ 07039. TEL 202-992-6600. Producer(s): SilverPlatter Information, Inc. *1983*

BURTON GROUP NEWS ANALYSIS.
Burton Group, Box 3448, Salt Lake City, UT 84110-3448. TEL 801-943-1966. FAX 801-943-2425. *2074*

BURTON GROUP REPORT.
Burton Group, Box 3448, Salt Lake City, UT 84110-3448. TEL 801-943-1966. FAX 801-943-2425. *2074*

BUSINESS DATELINE.
U M I Company (Louisville), 620 S. Third St., Louisville, KY 40202-2475. *939*

BUSINESS ECONOMICS.
National Association of Business Economists, 1233 20th St., N.W., Ste. 505, Washington, DC 20036-2304. TEL 202-463-6223. FAX 202-463-6239. *940*

BUSINESS EVENTS GUIDE.
International Press Publications Inc., 90 Nolan Ct., Ste. 21, Markham, ON L3R 4L9, Canada. TEL 905-946-9588. FAX 905-946-9590. *5167*

BUSINESS FINLAND.
Helsinki Media Special Magazines, P.O. Box 16, FIN-00381 Helsinki, Finland. TEL 358-0-120-5911. FAX 358-0-120-5959. *1657*

BUSINESS HISTORY.
Frank Cass, Newbury House, 890-900 Eastern Ave., Newbury Park, Ilford, Essex 1G2 7HH, England. TEL 44-181-599-8866. FAX 44-181-599-0984. *941*

BUSINESS INDIA.
Business India Group of Publications, Nirmal, Nariman Point, Mumbai 400 021, India. TEL 91-22-2009274. FAX 91-22-2875671. *1209*

BUSINESS INFORMATION REVIEW.
Headland Business Information, Customer Services Department, Maypole House, Maypole Rd., E. Grinstead, W. Sussex RH19 1HU, England. TEL 44-1342-330-100. FAX 44-1342-330-191. *1658*

SERIALS AVAILABLE ON CD-ROM

BUSINESS MEXICO.
American Chamber of Commerce of Mexico, A.C., Lucerna 78, Col. Juarez, Del. Cuauhtemoc, 06600 Mexico DF, Mexico. TEL 52-5-724-3800. FAX 52-5-703-2911.
Producer(s): UMI. *1180*

BUSINESS PERIODICALS INDEX.
H.W. Wilson Co., 950 University Ave., Bronx, NY 10452. TEL 718-588-8400. FAX 718-590-1617. Producer(s): SilverPlatter Information, Inc., H.W. Wilson (WILSONDISC). *1027*

BUSINESS PUBLICATION ADVERTISING SOURCE.
S R D S, 1700 Higgins Rd., Des Plaines, IL 60018. TEL 847-375-5000. FAX 847-375-5001. *48*

BUSINESS RATIO PLUS: BUS & COACH OPERATORS.
I C C Business Publications Ltd., Field House, 72 Oldfield Rd., Hampton, Middlesex TW12 2HQ, England. TEL 44-181-783-0922. FAX 44-181-783-1940. *7025*

THE BUSINESS WHO'S WHO AUSTRALIAN PRODUCTS AND TRADENAMES GUIDE.
Dun & Bradstreet Marketing Pty. Ltd., 19 Havilan St., Chatswood, N.S.W. 2065, Australia. TEL 61-2-9352700. FAX 61-2-9352777. *1519*

BYTE.
McGraw-Hill Companies, Byte Publications, One Phoenix Mill Ln., Peterborough, NH 03458. TEL 617-860-6336. FAX 617-860-6522. *2154*

C C H FEDERAL TAX WEEKLY.
C C H Incorporated, 2700 Lake Cook Rd., Riverwoods, IL 60015. TEL 847-267-7000. FAX 800-224-8299. *1601*

C C H FINANCIAL AND ESTATE PLANNING.
C C H Incorporated, 2700 Lake Cook Rd., Riverwoods, IL 60015. TEL 847-267-7000. FAX 800-224-8299. *1117*

C - C PLUS PLUS.
Miller Freeman, Inc. (Lawrence), 1601 W. 23rd St., Ste. 200, Lawrence, KS 66046. TEL 913-841-1631. FAX 913-841-2624. *2142*

C D - C I N.
Comissao Nacional de Energia Nuclear, Centro de Informacoes Nucleares, Rua General Severiano 90, Botafogo, 22294-900 Rio de Janeiro RJ, Brazil. TEL 55-21-5462440. FAX 55-21-5462447. *2682*

C D - CIBEPAT.
Ministerio de Industria y Energia, Oficina Espanola de Patentes y Marcas, Panama 1, 28071 Madrid, Spain. TEL 34-1-3495300. FAX 34-1-4572280. Available only on CD-ROM. *5582*

C D - I H L.
International Committee of the Red Cross, Public Information Division, 19 avenue de la Paix, CH-1202 Geneva, Switzerland. TEL 022-7302885. FAX 022-7332057.
Available only on CD-ROM. *4107*

C D M O T A.
Bureau of Tourism Research, Level 1, Burns Bldg., 28 National Crt., Forrest, A.C.T. 2603, Australia. TEL 61-6-2797264. FAX 61-6-2797298.
Available only on CD-ROM. *7252*

C D MONACI.
Guida Monaci S.p.A., Via Vitorchiano 107, 00189 Rome, Italy. TEL 39-6-3331333. FAX 39-6-3335555.
Available only on CD-ROM. *1658*

C D P FILE.
U.S. Centers for Disease Control, National Center for Chronic Disease Prevention and Health Promotion, 4770 Burford Hwy., N.E., MS K-50, Atlanta, GA 30341-3724. TEL 404-488-5705. FAX 404-488-5739.
Available only on CD-ROM. *6230*

C D - R O M DIRECTORY.
Macmillan Reference Ltd., 25 Eccleston Pl., London SW1W 9NF, England. TEL 44-171-881-8000. FAX 44-171-881-8001. *2107*

C D - R O M SOURCEBOOK.
Disc Company, 21 Red Maple Rd., Hilton Head Island, SC 29928. TEL 703-237-0682. FAX 703-532-5447. *4230*

C D - R O M SPORTWISSENSCHAFT.
Czwalina Verlag, Postfach 730240, 22122 Hamburg, Germany. TEL 49-40-6794300. FAX 49-40-67943030.
Available only on CD-ROM. *6795*

C D - R O MS IN PRINT.
Gale Research, 835 Penobscot Bldg., 645 Griswold St., Detroit, MI 48226-4094. TEL 313-961-2242. FAX 800-414-5043. *2093*

C I S INDEX TO PUBLICATIONS OF THE UNITED STATES CONGRESS.
Congressional Information Service, Inc., A member of the LEXIS-NEXIS family, 4520 East-West Hwy., Bethesda, MD 20814. TEL 301-654-1550. FAX 301-654-4033. *6203*

C L A S E.
Universidad Nacional Autonoma de Mexico, Direccion General de Bibliotecas, Apdo. Postal 70-392, C.P. 04510 Mexico, D.F., Mexico. TEL 52-5-6223958. FAX 52-5-6162557. *6649*

C M A J.
Canadian Medical Association, P.O. Box 8650, Ottawa, ON K1G 0G8, Canada. TEL 613-731-9331. FAX 613-523-0937. *4650*

C R I S P: BIOMEDICAL RESEARCH INFORMATION ON C D - R O M.
U.S. Government Printing Office, c/o Superintendent of Documents, Washington, DC 20242.
Available only on CD-ROM. *646*

C S A NEUROSCIENCES ABSTRACTS.
Cambridge Scientific Abstracts, 7200 Wisconsin Ave., 6th Fl., Bethesda, MD 20814. TEL 301-961-6750. FAX 301-961-6720.
Producer(s): SilverPlatter Information, Inc. *4766*

C THEORY.
Concordia University, 1455 de Maisonneuve West, Montreal, PQ H3G 1M8, Canada. TEL 514-282-9298. *5897*

C U S I P MASTER DIRECTORY.
Standard & Poor's, 25 Broadway, New York, NY 10004. TEL 212-208-8000. *1378*

CABO.
Historical Society of Cape Town, c/o Etaine Eberhard, Ed., P.O. Box 157, Newlands 7725, South Africa. TEL 27-12-6864939. FAX 27-12-6866404.
Producer(s): NISC. *3525*

CALCIUM AND CALCIFIED TISSUE ABSTRACTS.
Cambridge Scientific Abstracts, 7200 Wisconsin Ave., 6th Fl., Bethesda, MD 20814. TEL 301-961-6750. FAX 301-961-6720.
Producer(s): SilverPlatter Information, Inc. *638*

CALIFORNIA BUSINESS DIRECTORY.
American Business Directories, 5711 S. 86th Circle, Box 27347, Omaha, NE 68127. TEL 402-593-4600. FAX 402-331-5481. *1658*

CALIFORNIA MANUFACTURERS REGISTER.
Database Publishing Company, 1590 S. Lewis St., Anaheim, CA 92805-6423. TEL 714-778-6400. FAX 714-778-6811. *1658*

CALIFORNIA TAX ANALYSIS.
C C H Incorporated, 2700 Lake Cook Rd., Riverwoods, IL 60015. TEL 847-267-7000. FAX 800-224-8299. *1602*

CALIFORNIA WEEKLY EXPLORER.
California Weekly Explorer, Inc., 285 E. Main St., Ste. 3, Tustin, CA 92780. TEL 714-730-5991. FAX 714-730-3548.
Available only on CD-ROM. *1866*

CANADA STATUTE CITATOR.
Canada Law Book Inc., 240 Edward St., Aurora, ON L4G 3S9, Canada. TEL 905-841-6472. FAX 905-841-5085. *3927*

CANADA YEAR BOOK.
Statistics Canada, Operations and Integration Division, Circulation Management, Jean Talon Bldg., 2-C12, Tunney's Pasture, Ottawa, ON K1A 0T6, Canada. TEL 613-951-7277. FAX 613-951-1584. *6904*

CANADIAN CATHOLIC HISTORICAL STUDIES.
Canadian Catholic Historical Association, c/o Secretary General, 1155 Yonge St., Toronto, ON M4T 1W2, Canada. TEL 416-934-0606. FAX 416-934-3444. *6453*

CANADIAN EDUCATION INDEX.
Micromedia Ltd., 20 Victoria St., Toronto, ON M5C 2N8, Canada. TEL 416-362-5211. FAX 416-362-6161. *2497*

CANADIAN INDEX.
Micromedia Ltd., 20 Victoria St., Toronto, ON M5C 2N8, Canada. TEL 416-362-5211. FAX 416-362-6161.
Producer(s): Knight-Ridder, Inc. *1029*

CANADIAN JOURNAL OF ADMINISTRATIVE SCIENCES.
Administrative Sciences Association of Canada, Faculty of Commerce and Administration, Concordia University, 1455 de Maisonneuve Blvd. W., Montreal, QC H3G 1M8, Canada. TEL 514-848-2719. FAX 514-848-2839.
Producer(s): UMI. *946*

CANADIAN JOURNAL OF ANAESTHESIA.
Canadian Anaesthetists' Society, 1 Eglinton Ave., E., Ste. 208, Toronto, ON M4P 3A1, Canada. TEL 416-480-0602. FAX 416-480-0320. *4805*

CANADIAN JOURNAL OF HISTORY.
University of Saskatchewan, 707 Arts Bldg., 9 Campus Dr., Saskatoon, SK S7N 5A5, Canada. TEL 306-966-5794. FAX 306-966-5852.
Producer(s): H.W. Wilson. *3491*

CANADIAN LITERARY PERIODICALS INDEX.
Reference Press, P.O. Box, Teeswater, ON N0G 2S0, Canada. TEL 519-392-6634. *4368*

CANADIAN PERIODICAL INDEX.
Gale Research, 835 Penobscot Bldg., 645 Griswold St., Detroit, MI 48226-4094. TEL 313-961-2242. FAX 800-414-5043. *8*

CANADIAN RESEARCH INDEX, MICROLOG.
Micromedia Ltd., 20 Victoria St., Toronto, ON M5C 2N8, Canada. TEL 416-362-5211. FAX 416-362-6161. *8*

CANADIAN STANDARDS ASSOCIATION E - CODE, ELECTRICAL SAFETY STANDARDS.
Canadian Standards Association, 178 Rexdale Blvd., Toronto, ON M9W 1R3, Canada. TEL 416-747-4044. FAX 416-747-2475. *5249*

CANADIAN TRADE INDEX.
Canadian Manufacturers Association, 75 International Blvd., Toronto, ON M9W 6L9, Canada. TEL 416-798-8000. FAX 416-798-8050. *1659*

CANCER.
John Wiley & Sons, Inc., Journals, 605 Third Ave., New York, NY 10158. TEL 212-850-6645. FAX 212-850-6021. *4972*

CANCER CAUSES & CONTROL.
Rapid Science Publishers, The Old Malthouse, Paradise St., Oxford OX1 1LD, England. TEL 44-1865-790447. FAX 44-1865-244012. *4972*

CAP-AUX-DIAMANTS.
Editions Cap-aux-Diamants Inc., C.P. 26, Haute Ville, PQ G1R 4M8, Canada. TEL 418-656-5040. FAX 418-656-7282. *3621*

CAPITAL CHANGES REPORTS.
C C H Incorporated, 2700 Lake Cook Rd., Riverwoods, IL 60015. TEL 847-267-7000. FAX 800-224-8299. *1603*

CAR AND DRIVER BUYERS GUIDE.
Hachette Filipacchi Magazines, Inc., 1633 Broadway, New York, NY 10019. TEL 212-767-6000. FAX 212-267-5619. *7093*

CARBOHYDRATE LETTERS.
Gordon and Breach - Harwood Academic, Amsteldisk 166, 1st Fl., 1079 LH Amsterdam, Netherlands. *656*

CARNETEC.
Marketing and Technology Group, Inc., 1415 N. Dayton St., Chicago, IL 60622. TEL 312-266-3311. FAX 312-266-3363. *3098*

CASA DE LAS AMERICAS.
3ra y G, Vedado, Habana 10400, Cuba. TEL 537-323587. FAX 537-334554. *4387*

CATALOGO COLETIVO DE ANAIS DE EVENTOS.
Comissao Nacional de Energia Nuclear, Centro de Informacoes Nucleares, Rua General Severiano, 90 Botafogo, 22294-900 Rio de Janeiro RJ, Brazil. TEL 55-21-5462467. FAX 55-21-5462447. *6588*

CATALOGO COLETIVO NACIONAL DE PUBLICACOES PERIODICAS (IN MICROFICHES).
Instituto Brasileiro de Informacao em Ciencia e Tecnologia, SAS Quadra 5, Lote 6, Bloco H, 70070-000 Brasilia D.F., Brazil. TEL 55-61-2176161. FAX 55-61-2262677. *542*

CATALOGO DEI LIBRI IN COMMERCIO.
Editrice Bibliografica S.p.A., Viale Vittorio Veneto 24, 20124 Milan, Italy. TEL 02-29006965. FAX 02-654624. *542*

CATALOGO DEI LIBRI IN COMMERCIO - C D - R O M.
Informazioni Editoriale, Via Carlo Poma 1, 20129 Milan, Italy. TEL 49-2-70129293. FAX 49-2-70129424.
Available only on CD-ROM. Producer(s): K.G. Saur Verlag. *542*

CATALOGO EDILE.
BE-MA Editrice s.r.l., Via Teocrito 50, 20128 Milan, Italy. TEL 39-2-2552451. FAX 39-2-27000692. *875*

CATALOGUE AFNOR (NORMES FRANCAISES).
Association Francaise de Normalisation, Tour Europe, 92049 Paris La Defense, Cedex, France. TEL 42-91-55-55. FAX 42-91-56-56. *5249*

CATALOGUE OF BRITISH OFFICIAL PUBLICATIONS NOT PUBLISHED BY H.M.SO.
Chadwyck-Healey Ltd., The Quorum, Barnwell Rd., Cambridge CB5 8SW, England. TEL 01223-215512. FAX 01223-215513.
Producer(s): Chadwyck-Healey Inc. *542*

CATCHWORD AND TRADE NAME INDEX.
Bowker - Saur Ltd., A member of the Reed Elsevier plc group, Maypole House, Maypole Rd., E. Grinstead, W. Sussex RH19 1HU, England. TEL 44-1342-330100. FAX 44-1342-330191.
Producer(s): Bowker - Saur Ltd. (CTI Plus). *6981*

CATHOLIC INSIGHT.
Life Ethics Information Centre, P.O. Box 625, Adelaide Station, 36 Adelaide St., E., Toronto, ON M5C 2J8, Canada. TEL 416-368-4558. FAX 416-368-8575. *3259*

CD - MARC BIBLIOGRAPHIC.
U.S. Library of Congress, Cataloging Distribution Service, Washington, DC 20541-5017. TEL 202-707-6100. FAX 202-707-1334.
Available only on CD-ROM. *543*

CD - MARC BIBLIOGRAPHIC. ENGLISH ONLY.
U.S. Library of Congress, Cataloging Distribution Service, Washington, DC 20541-5017. TEL 202-707-6100. FAX 202-707-1334.
Available only on CD-ROM. *543*

CD - MARC BIBLIOGRAPHIC. ENGLISH ONLY. CURRENT YEARS.
U.S. Library of Congress, Cataloging Distribution Service, Washington, DC 20541-5017. TEL 202-707-6100. FAX 202-707-1334.
Available only on CD-ROM. *543*

CD - MARC NAMES.
U.S. Library of Congress, Cataloging Distribution Service, Washington, DC 20541-5017. TEL 202-707-6100. FAX 202-707-1334.
Available only on CD-ROM. *543*

CD - MARC SERIALS.
U.S. Library of Congress, Cataloging Distribution Service, Washington, DC 20541-5017. TEL 202-707-6100. FAX 202-707-1334.
Available only on CD-ROM. *543*

CD - MARC SUBJECTS.
U.S. Library of Congress, Cataloging Distribution Service, Washington, DC 20541-5017. TEL 202-707-6100. FAX 202-707-1334.
Available only on CD-ROM. *543*

CELL ADHESION AND COMMUNICATION.
Gordon and Breach - Harwood Academic, Amsteldisk 166, 1st Fl., 1079 LH Amsterdam, Netherlands. *595*

CENSUS OF AGRICULTURE: FINAL REPORTS.
U.S. Bureau of the Census, Customer Services, Washington, DC 20233. TEL 301-457-4100. FAX 301-457-4714. *172*

CENSUS OF CONSTRUCTION INDUSTRIES: FINAL REPORTS.
U.S. Bureau of the Census, Customer Services, Washington, DC 20233. TEL 301-457-4100. FAX 301-457-4714. *876*

CENSUS OF CONSTRUCTION INDUSTRIES: PRELIMINARY REPORTS.
U.S. Bureau of the Census, Customer Services, Washington, DC 20233. TEL 301-457-4100. FAX 301-457-4714. *920*

CENSUS OF MANUFACTURES: FINAL REPORTS.
U.S. Bureau of the Census, Customer Services, Washington, DC 20233. TEL 301-457-4100. FAX 301-457-4714. *1029*

CENSUS OF MANUFACTURES: PRELIMINARY REPORTS.
U.S. Bureau of the Census, Customer Services, Washington, DC 20233. TEL 301-457-4100. FAX 301-457-4714. *1029*

CENSUS OF MINERAL INDUSTRIES: FINAL REPORTS.
U.S. Bureau of the Census, Customer Services, Washington, DC 20233. TEL 301-457-4100. FAX 301-457-4714. *5297*

CENSUS OF MINERAL INDUSTRIES: PRELIMINARY REPORTS.
U.S. Bureau of the Census, Customer Services, Washington, DC 20233. TEL 301-457-4100. FAX 301-457-4714. *5297*

CENSUS OF RETAIL TRADE: FINAL REPORTS.
U.S. Bureau of the Census, Customer Services, Washington, DC 20233. TEL 301-457-4100. FAX 301-457-4714. *1029*

CENSUS OF SERVICE INDUSTRIES: FINAL REPORTS.
U.S. Bureau of the Census, Customer Services, Washington, DC 20233. TEL 301-457-4100. FAX 301-457-4714. *1030*

CENSUS OF TRANSPORTATION, COMMUNICATIONS, AND UTILITIES: FINAL REPORTS.
U.S. Bureau of the Census, Customer Services, Washington, DC 20233. TEL 301-457-4100. FAX 301-457-4714. *7050*

CENSUS OF WHOLESALE TRADE: FINAL REPORTS.
U.S. Bureau of the Census, Customer Services, Washington, DC 20233. TEL 301-457-4100. FAX 301-457-4714. *1030*

CENTRAL AFRICAN JOURNAL OF MEDICINE.
Central African Journal of Medicine Co., P.O. Box A195, Avondale, Harare, Zimbabwe. TEL 263-4-791631. *4652*

CERAMIC ABSTRACTS.
Cambridge Scientific Abstracts, Attn: Angela Hitti, 7200 Wisconsin Ave., 6th Fl., Bethesda, MD 20814. TEL 301-961-6750. FAX 301-961-6720.
Producer(s): NISC. *1735*

CERAMIC ABSTRACTS (C D - R O M).
National Information Services Corporation (NISC), 3100 St. Paul Dt., Ste. 806, Baltimore, MD 21218. TEL 410-243-0797. FAX 410-243-0982.
Available only on CD-ROM. Producer(s): NISC. *1735*

CESKA NARODNI BIBLIOGRAFIE. CLANKY V NOVINACH A CASOPISECH.
Narodni Knihovna Ceske Republiky, Klementinum 190, 110 01 Prague 1, Czech Republic. TEL 420-2-24229500. FAX 420-2-24227796. *543*

CESKA NARODNI BIBLIOGRAFIE. KNIHY.
Narodni Knihovna Ceske Republiky, Klementinum 190, 110 01 Prague 1, Czech Republic. TEL 42-2-24229500. FAX 42-2-24227796. *543*

CEYLON MEDICAL JOURNAL.
Sri Lanka Medical Association, Wijerama House, 6 Wijerama Mawatha, Colombo 7, Sri Lanka. TEL 941-693324. FAX 941-698802. *4652*

THE CHALLENGE.
Pakistan Anti-Tuberculosis Association, Block No. 55, Rm. 8, Pakistan Secretariat, Karachi, Pakistan. TEL 92-21-5688011. *5118*

CHANGE (WASHINGTON).
Heldref Publications, 1319 18th St., N.W., Washington, DC 20036-1802. TEL 202-296-6267. FAX 202-296-5149.
Producer(s): UMI. *2535*

CHEM MATTERS.
American Chemical Society, Office of High School Chemistry, 1155 16th St., N.W., Washington, DC 20036. TEL 202-872-4600. FAX 202-833-7732. *1741*

CHEM SOURCES INTERNATIONAL.
Chemical Sources International, Inc., Box 1824, Clemson, SC 29633. TEL 803-646-7840. FAX 803-646-9938. *1660*

CHEM SOURCES U S A.
Chemical Sources International, Inc., Box 1824, Clemson, SC 29633-1824. TEL 803-646-7840. FAX 803-646-9938. *1660*

CHEMICAL ABSTRACTS.
Chemical Abstracts Service, 2540 Olentangy River Rd., Box 3012, Columbus, OH 43210-0012. TEL 614-447-3600. FAX 614-447-3713. *1781*

CHEMICAL ENGINEERING COMMUNICATIONS.
Gordon and Breach - Harwood Academic, Amsteldisk 166, 1st Fl., 1079 LH Amsterdam, Netherlands. *2758*

CHEMICAL HAZARDS IN INDUSTRY.
The Royal Society of Chemistry, Thomas Graham House, Science Park, Milton Rd., Cambridge CB4 4WF, England. TEL 44-1223-420066. FAX 44-1223-423429.
Producer(s): Knight-Ridder, Inc. *5488*

CHEMINFORM.
Wiley - V C H, Postfach 101161, 69451 Weinheim, Germany. TEL 49-6201-606147. FAX 49-6201-606117. *1782*

DIE CHEMISCHE INDUSTRIE UND IHRE HELFER.
Industrieschau-Verlagsgesellschaft mbH, Postfach 100262, 64202 Darmstadt, Germany. TEL 49-6151-38920. FAX 49-6151-33164. *2761*

CHEMISTRY & BIOLOGY.
Current Biology Ltd., 400 Market St., Ste. 700, Philadelphia, PA 19106. FAX 215-574-2270. *681*

CHEMISTRY AND ECOLOGY.
Gordon and Breach - Harwood Academic, Amsteldisk 166, 1st Fl., 1079 LH Amsterdam, Netherlands. *1744*

CHEMISTRY CITATION INDEX.
Institute for Scientific Information, 3501 Market St., Philadelphia, PA 19104. TEL 215-386-0100. FAX 215-386-2911. *1782*

CHEMORECEPTION ABSTRACTS.
Cambridge Scientific Abstracts, 7200 Wisconsin Ave., 6th Fl., Bethesda, MD 20814. TEL 301-961-6750. FAX 301-961-6720.
Producer(s): SilverPlatter Information, Inc. *1782*

CHICAGO AREA BUSINESS DIRECTORY.
American Business Directories, 5711 S. 86th Circle, Box 27347, Omaha, NE 68127. TEL 402-593-4600. FAX 402-331-5481. *1660*

THE CHICAGO TRIBUNE INDEX.
U M I, 300 N. Zeeb Rd., Ann Arbor, MI 48106-1346. TEL 313-761-4700. FAX 800-864-0019. *3883*

CHICANO DATABASE ON C D - R O M.
University of California at Berkeley, Ethnic Studies Library Publications Unit, c/o Lillian Castillo-Speed, 30 Stephens Hall, No. 2360, Berkeley, CA 24720-2360. TEL 510-643-0552. FAX 510-642-6456.
Available only on CD-ROM. *3005*

SERIALS AVAILABLE ON CD-ROM

CHICANO INDEX.
University of California at Berkeley, Ethnic Studies Library Publication Unit, 30 Stephens Hall, No. 2360, Berkeley, CA 94702-2360. TEL 510-643-0552. FAX 510-642-6456. *3052*

CHILD ABUSE & NEGLECT C D - R O M.
National Information Services Corporation (NISC), 3100 St. Paul St., Ste. 806, Baltimore, MD 21218. TEL 410-243-0797. FAX 410-243-0982. Available only on CD-ROM. Producer(s): NISC. *1840*

CHILDREN'S BOOKS IN PRINT.
R.R. Bowker, A Division of Reed Elsevier Inc., 121 Chanlon Rd., New Providence, NJ 07974. TEL 908-464-6800. FAX 908-665-6688. Producer(s): Bowker Electronic Publishing (Books in Print PLUS). *544*

CHINA HAND.
Economist Intelligence Unit, 111 W. 57th St., New York, NY 10019. TEL 212-554-0600. FAX 212-586-1182. *948*

CHINESE JOURNAL OF MICROBIOLOGY AND IMMUNOLOGY.
Chinese Society of Microbiology, National Taiwan University, College of Medicine, Jen-Ai Rd., Taipei, Taiwan, Republic of China. *782*

CHINESE NATIONAL BIBLIOGRAPHY.
National Central Library, 20 Chung Shan S. Rd., Taipei, Taiwan 10040, Republic of China. TEL 886-2-3619132. FAX 886-2-311-0155. Available only on CD-ROM. *4225*

CHIP.
Vogel Publishing Sp. z o.o., Plac Czerwony 1-3-5, 53-661 Wroclaw, Poland. TEL 48-71-734475. FAX 48-71-557361. *2074*

CHIP.
Vogel Publishing Kft, Hajdu u.42-44 2nd Fl., 1139 Budapest, Hungary. TEL 36-1-2523731. FAX 36-1-2523731. *2074*

CHIP SPECIAL.
Vogel Publishing Sp. z o.o., Plac Czerwony 1-3-5, 53-661 Wroclaw, Poland. TEL 48-71-734475. FAX 48-71-557361. *2210*

CHOICE (MIDDLETOWN).
Choice, 100 Riverview Ctr., Middletown, CT 06457. TEL 203-347-6933. FAX 203-346-8586. Producer(s): SilverPlatter Information, Inc. *6289*

CHOICES FOR YOUNG READERS.
John Gordon Burke Publisher, Inc., Box 1492, Evanston, IL 60204-1492. TEL 847-866-8625. FAX 847-866-6639. *1843*

CHONGGI KANHAENGMUL KISA SAEGIN.
National Assembly Library, 1 Yoido-dong, Seoul, S. Korea. FAX 82-2-788-4298. *9*

CHRISTIAN BOOKS IN PRINT ON DISC.
R.R. Bowker, A Division of Reed Elsevier Inc., 121 Chanlon Rd., New Providence, NJ 07974. TEL 908-464-6800. FAX 908-665-3528. Available only on CD-ROM. *544*

CHRISTIAN CENTURY.
Christian Century Foundation, 407 S. Dearborn St., Chicago, IL 60605. TEL 312-427-5380. Producer(s): UMI. *6328*

CHRISTIAN SCIENCE MONITOR INDEX.
U M I, 300 N. Zeeb Rd., Ann Arbor, MI 48106-1346. TEL 313-761-4700. FAX 800-864-0019. *3883*

CHROMOSOME RESEARCH.
Rapid Science Publishers, The Old Malthouse, Paradise St., Oxford OX1 1LD, England. TEL 44-1865-790447. FAX 44-1865-244012. *765*

CHRONICLE FINANCIAL AID GUIDE.
Chronicle Guidance Publications, Inc., Box 1190, Moravia, NY 13118. TEL 315-497-0330. FAX 315-497-3359. *2535*

CHRONICLE FOUR-YEAR COLLEGE DATABOOK.
Chronicle Guidance Publications, Inc., Box 1190, Moravia, NY 13118. TEL 315-497-0330. FAX 315-497-3359. *2521*

CHRONICLE TWO-YEAR COLLEGE DATABOOK.
Chronicle Guidance Publications, Inc., Box 1190, Moravia, NY 13118. TEL 315-497-0330. FAX 315-497-3359. *2521*

CHRONICLE VOCATIONAL SCHOOL MANUAL.
Chronicle Guidance Publications, Inc., Box 1190, Moravia, NY 13118. TEL 315-497-0330. FAX 315-497-3359. *2521*

CHURCHART PRO ON DISK.
Communication Resources Inc., 4150 Belden Village St., Ste. 400, Canton, OH 44718-2502. FAX 330-493-7897. *6419*

CIVIL ENGINEERING SYSTEMS.
Gordon and Breach - Harwood Academic, Amsteldisk 166, 1st Fl., 1079 LH Amsterdam, Netherlands. *2780*

CLASSICA ET MEDIAEVALIA.
Museum Tusculanum Press, University of Copenhagen, Njalsgade 92, DK-2300 Copenhagen S, Denmark. TEL 45-35-32-91-09. FAX 45-35-32-91-13. *1901*

CLASSIFIED DIRECTORY OF WISCONSIN MANUFACTURERS.
W M C Service Corporation, 501 E. Washington Ave., Box 352, Madison, WI 53701-0352. TEL 608-258-3400. FAX 608-258-3413. *1661*

THE CLEARING HOUSE.
Heldref Publications, 1319 Eighteenth St., N.W., Washington, DC 20036-1802. TEL 202-296-6267. FAX 202-296-5149. Producer(s): UMI. *2429*

CLINICAL AND DIAGNOSTIC LABORATORY IMMUNOLOGY.
American Society for Microbiology, 1325 Massachusetts Ave., N.W., Washington, DC 20005. TEL 202-942-9319. FAX 202-942-9346. *4792*

CLINICAL AND EXPERIMENTAL IMMUNOLOGY.
Blackwell Science Ltd., Osney Mead, Oxford OX2 OEL, England. TEL 44-1865-206206. FAX 44-1865-721205. *4793*

CLINICAL AND EXPERIMENTAL METASTASIS.
Rapid Science Publishers, 2-6 Boundary Row, London SE1 8HN, England. TEL 44-171-865-0198. FAX 44-171-410-6600. *4976*

CLINICAL AUTONOMIC RESEARCH.
Rapid Science Publishers, The Old Malthouse, Paradise St., Oxford OX1 1LD, England. TEL 44-1865-790447. FAX 44-1865-244012. *4655*

CLINICAL CHEMISTRY AND ENZYMOLOGY COMMUNICATIONS.
Gordon and Breach - Harwood Academic, Amsteldisk 166, 1st Fl., 1079 LH Amsterdam, Netherlands. *657*

CLINICAL LABORATORY.
Clinical Laboratory Publications, Im Breitspiel 15, 69126 Heidelberg, Germany. TEL 49-6221-3432133. FAX 49-6221-300291. *4883*

CLINICAL LABORATORY PRODUCT COMPARISON SYSTEM.
E C R I, 5200 Butler Pike, Plymouth Meeting, PA 19462. TEL 610-825-6000. FAX 610-834-1275. Producer(s): Knight-Ridder, Inc. *4896*

CLINICAL MICROBIOLOGY REVIEWS.
American Society for Microbiology, 1325 Massachusetts Ave., N.W., Washington, DC 20005. TEL 202-737-3600. *782*

CLOTHING AND TEXTILE ARTS INDEX.
Box 1300, Monument, CO 80132. TEL 719-488-3716. *1919*

COAL HIGHLIGHTS.
I E A Coal Research, Gemini House, 10-18 Putney Hill, London SW15 6AA, England. TEL 44-181-780-0111. FAX 44-181-780-1746. *2661*

COAL WEEK.
McGraw-Hill Companies, Energy & Business Newsletters, 1221 Ave. of the Americas, 36th Fl., New York, NY 10020. TEL 212-512-6410. Producer(s): SilverPlatter Information, Inc. (McGraw-Hill Energy Library). *5298*

COAL WEEK INTERNATIONAL.
McGraw-Hill Companies, Energy & Business Newsletters, 1221 Ave. of the Americas, 36th Fl., New York, NY 10020. TEL 212-512-6410. Producer(s): SilverPlatter Information, Inc. (McGraw-Hill Energy Library). *5298*

CODE OF FEDERAL REGULATIONS.
U.S. Office of the Federal Register, National Archives and Records Administration, 8th St. and Pennsylvania Ave., N.W., Washington, DC 20408. TEL 202-523-5230. *3931*

COLLEGE BLUE BOOK.
Macmillan Library Reference, 1633 Broadway, New York, NY 10019-6785. TEL 212-654-8430. *2521*

COLLEGE CATALOG COLLECTION.
Career Guidance Foundation, 8090 Engineer Rd., San Diego, CA 92111. FAX 619-278-8960. *2536*

COLLEGE MEDIA DIRECTORY.
Oxbridge Communications, Inc., 150 Fifth Ave., New York, NY 10011. TEL 212-741-0231. FAX 212-633-2938. *544*

COLLEGE OF AGRICULTURAL, CONSUMER AND ENVIRONMENTAL SCIENCES. RESEARCH PROGRESS.
University of Illinois at Urbana-Champaign, College of Agricultural, Consumer and Environmental Sciences, 47 Mumford Hall, 1301 W. Gregory Dr., Urbana, IL 61801. TEL 217-244-2830. *109*

COLLEGE TEACHING.
Heldref Publications, 1319 Eighteenth St., N.W., Washington, DC 20036-1802. TEL 202-296-6267. FAX 202-296-5149. Producer(s): UMI. *2537*

COLORADO BUSINESS DIRECTORY.
American Business Directories, 5711 S. 86th Circle, Box 27347, Omaha, NE 68127. TEL 402-593-4600. FAX 402-331-5481. *1661*

COLOUR INDEX.
Society of Dyers and Colourists, Perkin House, P.O. Box 244, Bradford, W. Yorks BD1 2JB, England. TEL 44-1274-7215138. FAX 44-1274-392888. *6985*

COMBUSTION SCIENCE AND TECHNOLOGY.
Gordon and Breach - Harwood Academic, Amsteldisk 166, 1st Fl., 1079 LH Amsterdam, Netherlands. *1827*

COMERCIO EXTERIOR.
Banco Nacional de Comercio Exterior, S.A., Gerencia de la Revista Comercio Exterior, Camino a Santa Teresa 1679, Col. Jardines del Pedregal, 01900 Mexico D.F., Mexico. TEL 525-3276220. FAX 525-3276214. *1320*

COMMERCIO E SERVIZI.
Maggioli Editore, Viale Vespucci 12-n, 47037 Rimini, Italy. TEL 0541-626777. FAX 0541-622020. *4077*

COMMONWEAL.
Commonweal Foundation, 475 Riverside Dr., Rm. 405, New York, NY 10115. TEL 212-732-0800. Producer(s): UMI. *4329*

COMMONWEALTH STATUTES ANNOTATIONS.
L B C Information Services, 50 Waterloo Rd., N. Ryde, N.S.W. 2113, Australia. TEL 61-2-99366444. FAX 61-2-98889706. *4130*

COMMUNICATIONS COMPANIES ANALYSIS. MANUFACTURERS VOLUME.
M D I S Publications Ltd., MDIS House, City Fields Business Park, City Fields Way, Chichester, W. Sussex PO20 6FS, England. TEL 44-1243-533322. FAX 44-1243-533418. *1986*

COMMUNICATIONS COMPANIES ANALYSIS. OPERATORS VOLUME.
M D I S Publications Ltd., MDIS House, City Fields Business Park, City Fields Way, Chichester, W. Sussex PO20 6FS, England. TEL 44-1243-533322. FAX 44-1243-533418. *1986*

COMMUNICATIONS MARKETS ANALYSIS.
M D I S Publications Ltd., MDIS House, City Fields Business Park, City Fields Way, Chichester, W. Sussex PO20 6FS, England. TEL 44-1243-533322. FAX 44-1243-533418. *1986*

COMMUNICATIONS OF C O L I P S.
Chinese and Oriental Languages Information Processing Society, c/o Dept. of Information Systems & Computer Science, National University of Singapore, Kent Ridge, Singapore 0511, Singapore. TEL 65-772-2782. FAX 65-779-4580. *4319*

COMMUNITY CURRENTS.
Community Development Foundation, 60 Highbury Grove, London N5 2AG, England. TEL 0171-226-5375. FAX 0171-704-0313. *6696*

COMPACTMATH - COMPACT MATHEMATICS LIBRARY.
Springer-Verlag, Heidelberger Platz 3, 14197 Berlin, Germany. TEL 49-30-82787-0. FAX 49-30-82787448.
Available only on CD-ROM. *4617*

COMPANY DATABASE C D.
Herold Business Data AG, Guntramsdorferstr. 105, A-2340 Moedling, Austria. TEL 43-2236-401. FAX 43-2236-4018.
Available only on CD-ROM. *1662*

COMPENDIUM OF PHARMACEUTICALS AND SPECIALTIES.
Canadian Pharmaceutical Association, 1785 Alta Vista Dr., Ottawa, ON K1G 3Y6, Canada. TEL 613-523-7877. FAX 613-523-0445. *5654*

COMPENSATION AND WORKING CONDITIONS.
U.S. Bureau of Labor Statistics, 441 G St., N.W., Washington, DC 20212. TEL 202-655-4000. *1231*

THE COMPLETE DIRECTORY OF LARGE PRINT BOOKS AND SERIALS.
R.R. Bowker, A Division of Reed Elsevier Inc., 121 Chanlon Rd., New Providence, NJ 07974. TEL 908-464-6800. FAX 908-655-3502.
Producer(s): Bowker Electronic Publishing. *3459*

COMPLEX VARIABLES: THEORY AND APPLICATION.
Gordon and Breach - Harwood Academic, Amsteldisk 166, 1st Fl., 1079 LH Amsterdam, Netherlands. *4567*

COMPLIANCE OFFICER'S MANAGEMENT MANUAL.
Sheshunoff Information Services Inc., 505 Barton Springs Rd., Ste. 1100, Austin, TX 78704. TEL 512-472-2244. *1122*

COMPREHENSIVE MEDLINE.
EBSCO Publishing, 10 Estes St., Box 682, Ipswich, MA 01938. TEL 508-356-6565. FAX 508-356-6565.
Available only on CD-ROM. *4766*

COMPUTER ABSTRACTS.
M C B University Press Ltd., Anbar Electronic Intelligence, 60-62 Toller Ln., Bradford, W. Yorks BD8 9BY, England. TEL 44-1274-499821. FAX 44-1274-547143. *2093*

COMPUTER AND COMMUNICATIONS TECHNOLOGY DOCUMENTS MICROFILE.
Technical Indexes Ltd., Willoughby Rd., Bracknell, Berkshire RG12 8DW, England. TEL 44-1344-426311. FAX 44-1344-424971. *2015*

COMPUTER & CONTROL ABSTRACTS.
INSPEC, I.E.E., Michael Faraday House, Six Hills Way, Stevenage, Herts. SG1 2AY, England. TEL 44-1438-313311. FAX 44-1438-742840.
Producer(s): UMI. *2093*

COMPUTER SELECT.
Computer Library, One Park Ave., New York, NY 10016. TEL 212-503-4400. FAX 212-503-4414.
Available only on CD-ROM. *2094*

THE COMPUTER USERS YEAR BOOK.
V N U Business Publications BV, VNU House, 32-34 Broadwick St., London W1A 2HG, England. *2154*

CONFEDERATE VETERAN.
Sons of Confederate Veterans, P.O. Box 41828, Houston, TX 77241-1828. TEL 713-373-1199. *3623*

CONFIDENTIAL REPORT FOR ATTORNEYS.
Confidential Report for Attorneys, Box 1476, Oceanside, CA 92051. TEL 760-721-3622. FAX 760-721-3683. *3934*

CONGRESSIONAL MEMBER ORGANIZATIONS AND CAUCUSES: C I S GUIDE TO PUBLICATIONS & POLICY MATERIALS.
Congressional Information Service, Inc., A member of the LEXIS-NEXIS family, 4520 East-West Hwy., Bethesda, MD 20814. TEL 301-654-1550. FAX 301-654-4033. *5903*

CONGRESSIONAL STAFF DIRECTORY.
C Q Staff Directories Inc., 815 Slaters Lane, Alexandria, VA 22314. TEL 703-739-0900. FAX 703-739-0234. *5903*

CONGRESSIONAL YELLOW BOOK.
Leadership Directories, Inc., 104 Fifth Ave., 2nd Fl., New York, NY 10011. TEL 212-627-4140. FAX 212-645-0931.
Producer(s): Chadwyck-Healey Inc. *6170*

CONNECTICUT BUSINESS DIRECTORY.
American Business Directories, 5711 S. 86th Cir., Box 27347, Omaha, NE 68127. TEL 402-593-4600. FAX 402-331-5481. *1662*

CONNECTICUT RULES OF COURT, STATE AND FEDERAL.
West Group, 620 Opperman Dr., Eagan, MN 55123. TEL 612-687-8000. FAX 612-687-7302. *4130*

CONSIGLIO DI STATO.
Casa Editrice Italedi, Piazza Cavour 19, 00193 Rome, Italy. TEL 39-6-3210803. *3935*

CONSOLIDATED FEDERAL FUNDS REPORT.
U.S. Bureau of the Census, Customer Services, Washington, DC 20233. TEL 301-457-4100. FAX 301-457-4714. *6170*

CONSOLIDATED TREATIES & INTERNATIONAL AGREEMENTS: UNITED STATES CURRENT DOCUMENT SERVICE.
Oceana Publications, Inc., 75 Main St., Dobbs Ferry, NY 10522. TEL 914-693-8100. FAX 914-693-0402. *4110*

CONSUMER MAGAZINE AND ADVERTISING SOURCE.
S R D S, 1700 Higgins Rd., Des Plaines, IL 60018. TEL 847-375-5000. FAX 847-375-5001. *48*

CONSUMER REPORTS.
Consumers Union of the United States, Inc., 101 Truman Ave., Yonkers, NY 10703-1057. TEL 914-378-2000. FAX 914-378-2900. *2254*

CONSUMERS INDEX.
Pierian Press, Box 1808, Ann Arbor, MI 48106. TEL 313-434-5530. FAX 313-434-6409.
Producer(s): NISC (Consumers Reference Disc). *2260*

CONSUMERS REFERENCE DISC.
National Information Services Corporation (NISC), 3100 St. Paul St., Ste. 806, Baltimore, MD 21218. TEL 410-243-0797. FAX 410-243-0982.
Available only on CD-ROM. Producer(s): NISC. *2260*

CONSUMER'S RESEARCH MAGAZINE.
Consumers' Research, Inc., 800 Maryland Ave., N.E., Washington, DC 20002. TEL 202-546-1713. FAX 202-546-1638.
Producer(s): UMI. *2254*

CONTRA COSTA COUNTY COMMERCE AND INDUSTRY DIRECTORY.
Database Publishing Company, 1590 S. Lewis St., Anaheim, CA 92805-6423. TEL 714-778-6400. FAX 714-778-6811. *1662*

COREL MAGAZINE.
Omray Inc., 9801 Anderson Mill Rd., Ste. 207, Austin, TX 78750. TEL 512-250-1700. FAX 512-219-3156. *2122*

CORPORATE AFFILIATIONS PLUS.
National Register Publishing, A Division of Reed Elsevier Inc., 121 Chanlon Rd., New Providence, NJ 07974. TEL 908-464-6800. FAX 908-771-7704.
Available only on CD-ROM. Producer(s): Bowker Electronic Publishing. *1662*

CORPORATE DIRECTORY OF US PUBLIC COMPANIES.
Walker's Western Research, 1650 Borel Pl., Ste. 130, San Mateo, CA 94402. TEL 415-341-1110. FAX 415-341-2351. *1380*

CORPORATE FINANCING WEEK.
Institutional Investor Newsletters, 477 Madison Ave., New York, NY 10022. TEL 212-224-3233. FAX 212-224-3353. *1123*

CORPORATE REPORT MINNESOTA.
American City Business Journals, Inc. (Austin), 505 Powell St., Austin, TX 78703-5121.
Producer(s): UMI. *1471*

CORPORATE YELLOW BOOK.
Leadership Directories, Inc., 104 Fifth Ave., 2nd Fl., New York, NY 10011. TEL 212-627-4140. FAX 212-645-0931.
Producer(s): Chadwyck-Healey Inc. *1472*

CORPTECH DIRECTORY OF TECHNOLOGY COMPANIES.
Corporate Technology Information Services Inc., c/o Eileen Kenney, 12 Alfred Ave., Ste. 200, Woburn, MA 01801. TEL 617-932-3939. FAX 617-932-6335. *1663*

CORPUS CHRISTIANORUM. CONTINUATIO MEDIAEVALIS.
N.V. Brepols, Steenweg op Tielen 68, 2300 Turnhout, Belgium. TEL 32-14-402500. FAX 32-14-428919. *6460*

CORPUS CHRISTIANORUM. SERIES LATINA.
N.V. Brepols, Steenweg op Tielen 68, 2300 Turnhout, Belgium. TEL 32-14-402500. FAX 32-14-428919. *6460*

CORROSION ABSTRACTS.
N A C E International, Box 218340, Houston, TX 77218. TEL 713-492-0535. FAX 713-492-8254. *2748*

COTTON: REVIEW OF THE WORLD SITUATION.
International Cotton Advisory Committee, 1629 K St. N.W., Ste. 702, Washington, DC 20006. TEL 202-463-6660. FAX 202-463-6950. *6985*

COTTON: WORLD STATISTICS.
International Cotton Advisory Committee, 1629 K St. N.W., Ste. 702, Washington, DC 20006. TEL 202-463-6660. FAX 202-463-6950. *6999*

COUNTRY FORECASTS (NEW YORK).
Economist Intelligence Unit, 111 W. 57th St., New York, NY 10019. TEL 212-554-0600. FAX 212-586-1182. *5908*

COUNTRY REPORT. BOLIVIA.
Economist Intelligence Unit, 111 W. 57th St., New York, NY 10019. TEL 212-554-0600. FAX 212-586-1182.
Producer(s): Knight-Ridder, Inc., SilverPlatter Information, Inc. *1235*

COUNTRY REPORT. BULGARIA.
Economist Intelligence Unit, 111 W. 57th St., New York, NY 10019. TEL 212-554-0600. FAX 212-586-1182.
Producer(s): Knight-Ridder, Inc., SilverPlatter Information, Inc. *1236*

COUNTRY REPORT. CZECH REPUBLIC.
Economist Intelligence Unit, 111 W. 57th St., New York, NY 10019. TEL 212-554-0600. FAX 212-586-1182.
Producer(s): Knight-Ridder, Inc., SilverPlatter Information, Inc. *1237*

COUNTRY REPORT. PERU.
Economist Intelligence Unit, 111 W. 57th St., New York, NY 10019. TEL 212-554-0600. FAX 212-586-1182.
Producer(s): Knight-Ridder, Inc., SilverPlatter Information, Inc. *1241*

COUNTRY REPORTS.
Economist Intelligence Unit, 111 W. 57th St., New York, NY 10019. TEL 212-554-0600. FAX 212-586-1182. *1244*

COUNTY AND CITY DATA BOOK.
U.S. Bureau of the Census, Customer Services, Washington, DC 20233. TEL 301-457-4100. FAX 301-457-4714. *6907*

COUNTY AND CITY EXTRA.
Bernan Press, 4611-F Assembly Dr., Lanham, MD 20706-4391. TEL 301-459-7666. FAX 301-459-0056. *6908*

COUNTY BUSINESS PATTERNS.
U.S. Bureau of the Census, Customer Services, Washington, DC 20233. TEL 301-457-4100. FAX 301-457-4714. *1032*

CRAWFORD'S DIRECTORY OF CITY CONNECTIONS.
Miller Freeman Information Services, Riverbank House, Angel Ln., Tonbridge, Kent TN9 1SE, England. TEL 44-1732-362666. FAX 44-1732-367301. *1124*

CRIMINAL JUSTICE ABSTRACTS.
Willow Tree Press, Inc., 124 Willow Tree Rd., Monsey, NY 10952. TEL 914-354-9139. FAX 914-362-8376.
Producer(s): SilverPlatter Information, Inc. *2283*

CRITIQUE: STUDIES IN MODERN FICTION.
Heldref Publications, 1319 Eighteenth St., N.W., Washington, DC 20036-1802. TEL 202-296-6267. FAX 202-296-5149.
Producer(s): UMI. *4395*

CROATIAN MEDICAL JOURNAL.
Pabst Science Publishers, Am Eichengrund 28, 49525 Lengerich, Germany. TEL 49-5484-308. FAX 49-5484-550. *4658*

CROSS CURRENTS (NEW ROCHELLE).
Association for Religion and Intellectual Life, College of New Rochelle, New Rochelle, NY 10805-2339. TEL 914-235-1439. FAX 914-235-1584. *6333*

CRYPTOSYSTEMS JOURNAL.
485 Middle Holland Rd., Holland, PA 18966. TEL 215-579-9888. *2196*

CUADERNOS AMERICANOS.
Universidad Nacional Autonoma de Mexico, Centro Coordinador y Difusor de Estudios Latinoamericanos, Torre I de Humanidades, Piso 2, Ciudad Universitaria, 04510 Mexico, D.F. TEL 52-5-6271902. FAX 52-5-6162515. *4395*

CUADERNOS DE HISTORIA DEL ARTE.
Universidad Nacional de Cuyo, Facultad de Filosofia y Letras, Centro Universitario, Parque General San Martin, 5500 Mendoza, Argentina. TEL 54-61-230915. FAX 54-61-380457. *437*

CULTIVOS TROPICALES.
Instituto Nacional de Ciencias Agricolas, Gaveta Postal No. 1, San Jose de las Lajas, Havana 32700, Cuba. TEL 537-64-63290. FAX 537-64-63867. *221*

CUMULATIVE BOOK INDEX.
H.W. Wilson Co., 950 University Ave., Bronx, NY 10452. TEL 718-588-8400. FAX 718-590-1617.
Producer(s): SilverPlatter Information, Inc., H.W. Wilson. *545*

CUMULATIVE INDEX TO NURSING & ALLIED HEALTH LITERATURE.
C I N A H L Information Systems, 1509 Wilson Terrace, Box 871, Glendale, CA 91209-0871. TEL 818-409-8005. FAX 818-546-5679.
Producer(s): C I N A H L, SilverPlatter Information, Inc. *4768*

CURRENT (WASHINGTON, 1960).
Heldref Publications, 1319 18th St., N.W., Washington, DC 20036-1802. TEL 202-296-6267. FAX 202-296-5149.
Producer(s): UMI. *2431*

CURRENT BIBLIOGRAPHY ON SCIENCE AND TECHNOLOGY: CHEMISTRY AND CHEMICAL ENGINEERING (FOREIGN).
Japan Science and Technology Corporation, Information Center for Science and Technology, 5-3 Yonbancho, Chiyoda-ku, Tokyo 102, Japan. TEL 81-3-3214-8413. FAX 81-3-5214-8410. *1782*

CURRENT BIBLIOGRAPHY ON SCIENCE AND TECHNOLOGY: CHEMISTRY AND CHEMICAL ENGINEERING (JAPANESE).
Japan Science and Technology Corporation, Information Center for Science and Technology, 5-3 Yonbancho, Chiyoda-ku, Tokyo 102, Japan. TEL 81-3-5214-8413. FAX 81-3-5214-8410. *1782*

CURRENT BIBLIOGRAPHY ON SCIENCE AND TECHNOLOGY: CIVIL ENGINEERING AND ARCHITECTURE.
Japan Science and Technology Corporation, Information Center for Science and Technology, 5-3, Yonbancho, Chiyoda-ku, Tokyo 102, Japan. TEL 81-3-5214-8413. FAX 81-3-5214-8410. *2748*

CURRENT BIBLIOGRAPHY ON SCIENCE AND TECHNOLOGY: EARTH SCIENCE, MINING AND METALLURGY.
Japan Science and Technology Corporation, Information Center for Science and Technology, 5-3, Yonbacho, Chiyoda-ku, Tokyo 102, Japan. TEL 81-3-5214-8413. FAX 81-3-5214-8410. *2325*

CURRENT BIBLIOGRAPHY ON SCIENCE AND TECHNOLOGY: ELECTRONICS AND ELECTRICAL ENGINEERING.
Japan Science and Technology Corporation, Information Center for Science and Technology, 5-3, Yonbancho, Chiyoda-ku, Tokyo 102, Japan. TEL 81-3-5214-8413. FAX 81-3-5214-8410. *2748*

CURRENT BIBLIOGRAPHY ON SCIENCE AND TECHNOLOGY: ENERGY.
Japan Science and Technology Corporation, Information Center for Science and Technology, 5-3, Yonbancho, Chiyoda-ku, Tokyo 102, Japan. TEL 81-3-5214-8413. FAX 81-3-5214-8410. *2682*

CURRENT BIBLIOGRAPHY ON SCIENCE AND TECHNOLOGY: LIFE SCIENCES.
Japan Science and Technology Corporation, Information Center for Science and Technology, 5-3, Yonbancho, Chiyoda-ku, Tokyo 102, Japan. TEL 81-3-5214-8413. FAX 81-3-5214-8410. *639*

CURRENT BIBLIOGRAPHY ON SCIENCE AND TECHNOLOGY: MANAGEMENT SCIENCE AND SYSTEMS ENGINEERING.
Japan Science and Technology Corporation, Information Center for Science and Technology, 5-3, Yonbancho, Chiyoda-ku, Tokyo 102, Japan. TEL 81-3-5214-8413. FAX 81-3-5214-8410. *1033*

CURRENT BIBLIOGRAPHY ON SCIENCE AND TECHNOLOGY: MECHANICAL ENGINEERING.
Japan Science and Technology Corporation, Information Center for Science and Technology, 5-3, Yonbancho, Chiyoda-ku, Tokyo 102, Japan. TEL 81-3-5214-8413. FAX 81-3-5214-8410. *2748*

CURRENT BIBLIOGRAPHY ON SCIENCE AND TECHNOLOGY: NUCLEAR ENGINEERING.
Japan Science and Technology Corporation, Information Center for Science and Technology, 5-3, Yonbancho, Chiyoda-ku, Tokyo 102, Japan. TEL 81-3-5214-8413. FAX 81-3-5214-8410. *2748*

CURRENT BIBLIOGRAPHY ON SCIENCE AND TECHNOLOGY: PURE AND APPLIED PHYSICS.
Japan Science and Technology Corporation, Information Center for Science and Technology, 5-3, Yonbancho, Chiyoda-ku, Tokyo 102, Japan. TEL 81-3-5214-8413. FAX 81-3-5214-8410. *5834*

CURRENT BIOGRAPHY YEARBOOK.
H.W. Wilson Co., 950 University Ave., Bronx, NY 10452. TEL 718-588-8400. FAX 718-590-1716.
Producer(s): H.W. Wilson (WILSONDISC). *573*

CURRENT BIOTECHNOLOGY.
The Royal Society of Chemistry, Thomas Graham House, Science Park, Milton Rd., Cambridge CB4 4WF, England. TEL 44-1223-420066. FAX 44-1223-423429.
Producer(s): Knight-Ridder, Inc. *639*

CURRENT CONTENTS: AGRICULTURE, BIOLOGY & ENVIRONMENTAL SCIENCES.
Institute for Scientific Information, 3501 Market St., Philadelphia, PA 19104. TEL 215-386-0100. FAX 215-386-2911. *173*

CURRENT CONTENTS: CLINICAL MEDICINE.
Institute for Scientific Information, 3501 Market St., Philadelphia, PA 19104. TEL 215-386-0100. FAX 215-386-2911. *4768*

CURRENT CONTENTS: LIFE SCIENCES.
Institute for Scientific Information, 3501 Market St., Philadelphia, PA 19104. TEL 215-386-0100. FAX 215-386-2211. *639*

CURRENT CONTENTS: PHYSICAL, CHEMICAL & EARTH SCIENCES.
Institute for Scientific Information, 3501 Market St., Philadelphia, PA 19104. TEL 215-386-0100. FAX 215-386-2211. *1783*

CURRENT DIGEST OF THE POST-SOVIET PRESS.
Current Digest of the Soviet Press, 3857 N. High St., Columbus, OH 43214-3747. TEL 614-292-4234. FAX 614-267-6310. *5983*

CURRENT HEALTH 2.
Weekly Reader Corporation, Box 120023, Stamford, CT 06912-0023. FAX 609-786-3360.
Producer(s): UMI. *5780*

CURRENT ISSUES SOURCEFILE.
Congressional Information Service, Inc., A member of the LEXIS NEXIS family, 4520 East-West Hwy., Bethesda, MD 20814-3389. TEL 301-654-1550. FAX 301-657-3203.
Available only on CD-ROM. *6609*

CURRENT MATHEMATICAL PUBLICATIONS.
American Mathematical Society, Box 6248, Providence, RI 02940-6248. TEL 401-455-4000. FAX 401-331-3842.
Producer(s): SilverPlatter Information, Inc. (MathDisc). *4617*

CURRENT MEDICAL DIAGNOSIS AND TREATMENT.
Appleton & Lange, Box 120041, Stamford, CT 06912-0041. TEL 203-406-4500. *4659*

CURRENT OPINION IN ANAESTHESIOLOGY.
Rapid Science Publishers, 2-6 Boundary Row, London SE1 8HN, England. TEL 44-171-865-0198. FAX 44-171-410-6600. *4771*

CURRENT OPINION IN BIOTECHNOLOGY.
Current Biology Ltd., 400 Market St., Ste. 700, Philadelphia, PA 19106. TEL 800-552-5866. FAX 215-574-2270. *639*

CURRENT OPINION IN CARDIOLOGY.
Rapid Science Publishers, 2-6 Boundary Row, London SE1 8HN, England. TEL 44-171-865-0198. FAX 44-171-410-6600. *4771*

CURRENT OPINION IN CELL BIOLOGY.
Current Biology Ltd., 400 Market St., Ste. 700, Philadelphia, PA 19106. FAX 215-574-2270. *639*

CURRENT OPINION IN COSMETIC DENTISTRY.
Rapid Science Publishers, 2-6 Boundary Row, London SE1 8HN, England. TEL 44-171-865-0198. FAX 44-171-410-6600. *4771*

CURRENT OPINION IN CRITICAL CARE.
Rapid Science Publishers, 2-6 Boundary Row, London SE1 8HN, England. TEL 44-171-865-0198. FAX 44-171-865-0198. *5006*

CURRENT OPINION IN DERMATOLOGY.
Rapid Science Publishers, 2-6 Boundary Row, London SE1 8HN, England. TEL 44-171-865-0198. FAX 44-171-410-6600. *4876*

CURRENT OPINION IN ENDOCRINOLOGY & DIABETES.
Rapid Science Publishers, 2-6 Boundary Row, London SE1 8HN, England. TEL 44-171-865-0198. FAX 44-171-410-6600. *4883*

CURRENT OPINION IN GASTROENTEROLOGY.
Rapid Science Publishers, 2-6 Boundary Row, London SE1 8HN, England. TEL 44-171-865-0198. FAX 44-171-410-6600. *4771*

CURRENT OPINION IN GENETICS & DEVELOPMENT.
Current Biology Ltd., 400 Market St., Ste. 700, Philadelphia, PA 19106. TEL 800-552-5866. FAX 215-574-2270. *639*

CURRENT OPINION IN HEMATOLOGY.
Rapid Science Publishers, 2-6 Boundary Row, London SE1 8HN, England. TEL 44-171-865-0198. FAX 44-171-410-6600. *4918*

CURRENT OPINION IN IMMUNOLOGY.
Current Biology Ltd., 400 Market St., Ste. 700, Philadelphia, PA 19106. FAX 215-574-2270. *4772*

CURRENT OPINION IN INFECTIOUS DISEASES.
Rapid Science Publishers, 2-6 Boundary Row, London SE1 8HN, England. TEL 44-171-865-0198. FAX 44-171-410-6600. *4772*

CURRENT OPINION IN LIPIDOLOGY.
Rapid Science Publishers, 2-6 Boundary Row, London SE1 8HN, England. TEL 44-171-410-6600. FAX 44-171-410-6600. *4772*

CURRENT OPINION IN NEPHROLOGY & HYPERTENSION.
Rapid Science Publishers, 2-6 Boundary Row, London SE1 8HN, England. TEL 44-171-865-0198. FAX 44-171-865-0198. *4772*

CURRENT OPINION IN NEUROBIOLOGY.
Current Biology, Ltd., 400 Market St., Ste. 700, Philadelphia, PA 19106. TEL 800-552-5866. FAX 215-574-2270. *640*

CURRENT OPINION IN NEUROLOGY.
Rapid Science Publishers, 2-6 Boundary Row, London SE1 8HN, England. TEL 44-171-865-0198. FAX 44-171-410-6600. *4772*

CURRENT OPINION IN OBSTETRICS & GYNECOLOGY.
Rapid Science Publishers, 2-6 Boundary Row, London SE1 8HN, England. TEL 44-171-865-0198. FAX 44-171-410-6600. *4772*

CURRENT OPINION IN ONCOLOGY.
Rapid Science Publishers, 2-6 Boundary Row, London SE1 8HN, England. TEL 44-171-865-0198. FAX 44-171-410-6600. *4772*

CURRENT OPINION IN OPHTHALMOLOGY.
Rapid Science Publishers, 2-6 Boundary Row, London SE1 8HN, England. TEL 44-171-865-0198. FAX 44-171-410-6600. *4772*

CURRENT OPINION IN ORTHOPEDICS.
Rapid Science Publishers, 2-6 Boundary Row, London SE1 8HN, England. TEL 44-171-865-0198. FAX 44-171-410-6600. *4772*

CURRENT OPINION IN OTOLARYNGOLOGY & HEAD AND NECK SURGERY.
Rapid Science Publishers, 2-6 Boundary Row, London SE1 8HN, England. TEL 44-171-865-0198. FAX 44-171-410-6600. *5021*

CURRENT OPINION IN PEDIATRICS.
Rapid Science Publishers, 2-6 Boundary Row, London SE1 8HN, England. TEL 44-171-865-0198. FAX 44-171-410-6600. *4773*

CURRENT OPINION IN PERIODONTOLOGY.
Rapid Science Publishers, 2-6 Boundary Row, London SE1 8HN, England. TEL 44-171-865-0198. FAX 44-171-410-6600. *4773*

CURRENT OPINION IN PSYCHIATRY.
Rapid Science Publishers, 2-6 Boundary Row, London SE1 8HN, England. TEL 44-171-865-0198. FAX 44-171-410-6600. *4773*

CURRENT OPINION IN PULMONARY MEDICINE.
Rapid Science Publishers, 2-6 Boundary Row, London SE1 8HN, England. TEL 44-171-865-0198. FAX 44-171-410-6600. *5118*

CURRENT OPINION IN RHEUMATOLOGY.
Rapid Science Publishers, 2-6 Boundary Row, London SE1 8HN, England. TEL 44-171-865-0198. FAX 44-171-410-6600. *4773*

CURRENT OPINION IN STRUCTURAL BIOLOGY.
Current Biology Ltd., 400 Market St., Ste. 700, Philadelphia, PA 19106. TEL 800-552-5866. FAX 215-574-2270. *640*

CURRENT OPINION IN SURGICAL INFECTIONS.
Rapid Science Publishers, 2-6 Boundary Row, London SE1 8HN, England. TEL 44-171-865-0198. FAX 44-171-410-6600. *5139*

CURRENT OPINION IN UROLOGY.
Rapid Science Publishers, 2-6 Boundary Row, London SE1 8HN, England. TEL 44-171-865-0198. FAX 44-171-410-6600. *4773*

CURRENT PROTOCOLS IN HUMAN GENETICS.
John Wiley & Sons, Inc., Journals, 605 Third Ave., New York, NY 10158. TEL 212-850-6645. FAX 212-850-6021. *765*

CURRENT PROTOCOLS IN IMMUNOLOGY.
John Wiley & Sons, Inc., Journals, 605 Third Ave., New York, NY 10158. TEL 212-850-6645. FAX 212-850-6021. *4793*

CURRENT PROTOCOLS IN MOLECULAR BIOLOGY.
John Wiley & Sons, Inc., Journals, 605 Third Ave., New York, NY 10158. TEL 212-850-6645. FAX 212-850-6021. *597*

CURRENT PROTOCOLS IN PROTEIN SCIENCE.
John Wiley & Sons, Inc., Journals, 605 Third Ave., New York, NY 10158. TEL 212-850-6645. FAX 212-850-6021. *658*

CURRENT RESEARCH IN LIBRARY & INFORMATION SCIENCE.
Bowker - Saur Ltd., A member of the Reed Elsevier plc group, Maypole House, Maypole Rd., E. Grinstead, W. Sussex RH19 1HU, England. TEL 44-1342-330100. FAX 44-1342-330191. Producer(s): Bowker - Saur Ltd. *4173*

CURRENT SURGICAL DIAGNOSIS & TREATMENT.
Appleton & Lange, Box 120041t St., Stamford, CT 06912-0041. TEL 203-406-4500. *5140*

CURRENT THOUGHTS & TRENDS.
Box 35004, Colorado Springs, CO 80935-3504. TEL 719-531-3585. FAX 719-598-7128. *6386*

CYMBIOSIS.
Cymbiosis, Inc., 6201 W. Sunset Blvd., Ste. 80, Hollywood, CA 90028-8704. TEL 213-463-3808. FAX 213-463-5426. *5387*

C2C ABSTRACTS: JAPAN - ANALYTICAL CHEMISTRY.
Scan C2C, 1001 Pennsylvania Ave., N.W., No. 1300, Washington, DC 20024-2505. TEL 800-525-3865. FAX 202-863-3855. Producer(s): Knight-Ridder, Inc. *1783*

C2C ABSTRACTS: JAPAN - CERAMICS.
Scan C2C, 1001 Pennsylvania Ave., N.W., No.1300, Washington, DC 20024-2505. TEL 800-525-3865. FAX 202-863-3855. Producer(s): Knight-Ridder, Inc. *1735*

C2C ABSTRACTS: JAPAN - CHEMICAL ENGINEERING.
Scan C2C, 1001 Pennsylvania Ave., N.W., No. 1300, Washington, DC 20024-2505. TEL 800-525-3865. FAX 202-863-3855. Producer(s): Knight-Ridder, Inc. *2748*

C2C ABSTRACTS: JAPAN - CRYSTALLOGRAPHY.
Scan C2C, 1001 Pennsylvania Ave., N.W., No. 1300, Washington, DC 20024-2505. TEL 800-525-3865. FAX 202-863-3855. Producer(s): Knight-Ridder, Inc. *1783*

C2C ABSTRACTS: JAPAN - HYDROCARBONS.
Scan C2C, 1001 Pennsylvania Ave., N.W., No. 1300, Washington, DC 20024-2505. TEL 800-525-3865. FAX 202-863-3855. Producer(s): Knight-Ridder, Inc. *1783*

C2C ABSTRACTS: JAPAN - INORGANIC CHEMISTRY.
Scan C2C, 1001 Pennsylvania Ave., N.W., No. 1300, Washington, DC 20024-2505. TEL 800-525-3865. FAX 202-863-3855. Producer(s): Knight-Ridder, Inc. *1783*

C2C ABSTRACTS: JAPAN - MATERIALS SCIENCE.
Scan C2C, 1001 Pennsylvania Ave., N.W., No. 1300, Washington, DC 20024-2505. TEL 800-525-3865. FAX 202-863-3855. Producer(s): Knight-Ridder, Inc. *2748*

C2C ABSTRACTS: JAPAN - METALS.
Scan C2C, 1001 Pennsylvania Ave., N.W., No. 1300, Washington, DC 20024-2505. TEL 800-525-3865. FAX 202-863-3855. Producer(s): Knight-Ridder, Inc. *5217*

C2C ABSTRACTS: JAPAN - ORGANIC CHEMISTRY.
Scan C2C, 1001 Pennsylvania Ave., N.W., No. 1300, Washington, DC 20024-2505. TEL 800-525-3865. FAX 202-863-3855. Producer(s): Knight-Ridder, Inc. *1783*

C2C ABSTRACTS: JAPAN - PHYSICAL CHEMISTRY.
Scan C2C, 1001 Pennsylvania Ave., N.W., No. 1300, Washington, DC 20024-2505. TEL 800-525-3865. FAX 202-863-3855. Producer(s): Knight-Ridder, Inc. *1783*

C2C ABSTRACTS: JAPAN - PLASTICS.
Scan C2C, 1001 Pennsylvania Ave., N.W., No. 1300, Washington, DC 20024-2505. TEL 800-525-3865. FAX 202-863-3855. Producer(s): Knight-Ridder, Inc. *5886*

C2C ABSTRACTS: JAPAN - POLYMER CHEMISTRY.
Scan C2C, 1001 Pennsylvania Ave., N.W., No. 1300, Washington, DC 20024-2505. TEL 800-525-3865. FAX 202-863-3855. Producer(s): Knight-Ridder, Inc. *1783*

C2C ABSTRACTS: JAPAN - SURFACE CHEMISTRY.
Scan C2C, 1001 Pennsylvania Ave., N.W., No. 1300, Washington, DC 20024-2505. TEL 800-525-3865. FAX 202-863-3855. Producer(s): Knight-Ridder, Inc. *1783*

C2C ABSTRACTS: JAPAN - TEXTILES.
Scan C2C, 1001 Pennsylvania Ave., N.W., No. 1300, Washington, DC 20024-2025. TEL 800-525-3865. FAX 202-863-3855. Producer(s): Knight-Ridder, Inc. *6999*

C2C CURRENTS: JAPAN - CHEMISTRY.
Scan C2C, 1001 Pennsylvania Ave., N.W., No. 1300, Washington, DC 20024-2025. TEL 800-525-3865. FAX 202-863-3855. Producer(s): Knight-Ridder, Inc. *1783*

C2C CURRENTS: JAPAN - COMPUTERS.
Scan C2C, 1001 Pennsylvania Ave., N.W., No. 1300, Washington, DC 20024-2025. TEL 800-525-3865. FAX 202-863-3855. Producer(s): Knight-Ridder, Inc. *2094*

C2C CURRENTS: JAPAN - ELECTRONICS.
Scan C2C, 1001 Pennsylvania Ave., N.W., No. 1300, Washington, DC 20024-2505. TEL 800-525-3865. FAX 202-863-3855. Producer(s): Knight-Ridder, Inc. *2627*

C2C CURRENTS: JAPAN - MATERIALS.
Scan C2C, 1001 Pennsylvania Ave., N.W., No. 1300, Washington, DC 20024-2505. TEL 800-525-3865. FAX 202-863-3855. Producer(s): Knight-Ridder, Inc. *2748*

D K I LITERATUR-SCHNELLDIENST KUNSTSTOFFE KAUTSCHUK FASERN.
Deutsches Kunststoff-Institut, Schlossgartenstr. 6, 64289 Darmstadt, Germany. TEL 49-6151-162105. FAX 49-6151-292855. *5886*

D L A P S.
U.S. Defense Logistics Agency, 8725 John J. Kingman Rd., Ste. 2533, Fort Belvoir, VA 22060-6221.
Available only on CD-ROM. *6204*

D M S MARKET INTELLIGENCE REPORTS: AIRBORNE ELECTRONICS.
Forecast International Inc. - D M S, 22 Commerce Rd., Newtown, CT 06470. TEL 203-426-0800. FAX 203-426-0223. *2627*

D M S MARKET INTELLIGENCE REPORTS: AIRBORNE RETROFIT AND MODERNIZATION.
Forecast International Inc. - D M S, 22 Commerce Rd., Newtown, CT 06470. TEL 203-426-0800. FAX 203-426-1964. *63*

D M S MARKET INTELLIGENCE REPORTS: AIRCRAFT: CIVIL AND MILITARY.
Forecast International - D M S, 22 Commerce Rd., Newtown, CT 06470. TEL 203-426-0800. FAX 203-426-0223. *63*

D M S MARKET INTELLIGENCE REPORTS: "AN" EQUIPMENT.
Forecast International Inc. - D M S, 22 Commerce Rd., Newtown, CT 06470. TEL 203-426-0800. FAX 203-426-0223. *5264*

D M S MARKET INTELLIGENCE REPORTS: ANTI-SUBMARINE WARFARE.
Forecast International Inc. - D M S, 22 Commerce Rd., Newtown, CT 06470. TEL 203-426-0800. FAX 203-426-0233. *5264*

D M S MARKET INTELLIGENCE REPORTS: C 3 I.
Forecast International Inc. - D M S, 22 Commerce Rd., Newtown, CT 06470. TEL 203-426-0800. FAX 203-426-0223. *5264*

D M S MARKET INTELLIGENCE REPORTS: CIVIL AIRCRAFT.
Forecast International Inc. - D M S, 22 Commerce Rd., Newtown, CT 06470. TEL 203-426-0800. FAX 203-426-0223. *63*

D M S MARKET INTELLIGENCE REPORTS: DEFENSE AND AEROSPACE COMPANIES.
Forecast International Inc. - D M S, 22 Commerce Rd., Newtown, CT 06470. TEL 203-426-0800. FAX 203-426-2033. *5264*

D M S MARKET INTELLIGENCE REPORTS: ELECTRO-OPTICAL SYSTEMS.
Forecast International Inc. - D M S, 22 Commerce Rd., Newtown, CT 06470. TEL 203-426-0800. FAX 203-426-0223. *2628*

D M S MARKET INTELLIGENCE REPORTS: ELECTRONIC SYSTEMS.
Forecast International Inc. - D M S, 22 Commerce Rd., Newtown, CT 06470. TEL 203-426-0800. FAX 203-426-0223. *5264*

D M S MARKET INTELLIGENCE REPORTS: ELECTRONIC WARFARE.
Forecast International Inc. - D M S, 22 Commerce Rd., Newtown, CT 06470. TEL 203-426-0800. FAX 203-426-0223. *5264*

D M S MARKET INTELLIGENCE REPORTS: FOREIGN MILITARY MARKETS: ASIA, AUSTRALIA & PACIFIC RIM.
Forecast International Inc. - D M S, 22 Commerce Rd., Newtown, CT 06470. TEL 203-426-0800. FAX 203-426-0223. *5264*

D M S MARKET INTELLIGENCE REPORTS: FOREIGN MILITARY MARKETS: LATIN AMERICA & CARIBBEAN.
Forecast International Inc. - D M S, 22 Commerce Rd., Newtown, CT 06470. TEL 203-426-0800. FAX 203-426-0233. *5264*

D M S MARKET INTELLIGENCE REPORTS: FOREIGN MILITARY MARKETS: MIDDLE EAST & AFRICA.
Forecast International Inc. - D M S, 22 Commerce Rd., Newtown, CT 06470. TEL 203-426-0800. FAX 203-426-0233. *5264*

D M S MARKET INTELLIGENCE REPORTS: FOREIGN MILITARY MARKETS: N A T O & EUROPE.
Forecast International Inc. - D M S, 22 Commerce Rd., Newtown, CT 06470. TEL 203-426-0800. FAX 203-426-2033. *5264*

D M S MARKET INTELLIGENCE REPORTS: GAS TURBINE.
Forecast International Inc. - D M S, 22 Commerce Rd., Newtown, CT 06470. TEL 203-426-0800. FAX 203-426-0223. *5264*

D M S MARKET INTELLIGENCE REPORTS: INTERNATIONAL CONTRACTORS.
Forecast International Inc. - D M S, 22 Commerce Rd., Newtown, CT 06470. TEL 203-426-0800. FAX 203-426-0223. *5264*

D M S MARKET INTELLIGENCE REPORTS: LAND AND SEA-BASED ELECTRONICS.
Forecast International Inc. - D M S, 22 Commerce Rd., Newtown, PA 06470. TEL 203-426-0800. FAX 203-426-0223. *2628*

D M S MARKET INTELLIGENCE REPORTS: MILITARY AIRCRAFT.
Forecast International Inc. - D M S, 22 Commerce Rd., Newtown, CT 06470. TEL 203-426-0800. FAX 203-426-0223. *5264*

D M S MARKET INTELLIGENCE REPORTS: MILITARY FORCE STRUCTURES OF THE WORLD.
Forecast International Inc. - D M S, 22 Commerce Rd., Newtown, CT 06470. TEL 203-426-0800. FAX 203-426-0223. *5264*

D M S MARKET INTELLIGENCE REPORTS: MILITARY VEHICLES.
Forecast International Inc. - D M S, 22 Commerce Rd., Newtown, CT 06470. TEL 203-426-0800. FAX 203-426-0223. *5264*

D M S MARKET INTELLIGENCE REPORTS: MISSILES.
Forecast International Inc. - D M S, 22 Commerce Rd., Newtown, CT 06470. TEL 203-426-1964. *5264*

D M S MARKET INTELLIGENCE REPORTS: ORDNANCE & MUNITIONS.
Forecast International Inc. - D M S, 22 Commerce Rd., Newtown, CT 06470. TEL 203-426-0800. FAX 203-426-0233. *5265*

D M S MARKET INTELLIGENCE REPORTS: RADAR.
Forecast International Inc. - D M S, 22 Commerce Rd., Newtown, CT 06470. TEL 203-426-0800. FAX 203-426-0233. *5265*

D M S MARKET INTELLIGENCE REPORTS: SPACE SYSTEMS.
Forecast International Inc. - D M S, 22 Commerce Rd., Newtown, CT 06470. TEL 203-426-0800. FAX 203-426-0233. *5265*

D M S MARKET INTELLIGENCE REPORTS: U S DEFENSE BUDGET.
Forecast International Inc. - D M S, 22 Commerce Rd., Newtown, CT 06470. TEL 203-426-0800. FAX 203-426-0223. *5265*

D M S MARKET INTELLIGENCE REPORTS: UNMANNED VEHICLES.
Forecast International Inc. - D M S, 22 Commerce Rd., Newtown, CT 06470. TEL 203-426-0800. FAX 203-426-0233. *5265*

D M S MARKET INTELLIGENCE REPORTS: WARSHIPS.
Forecast International Inc. - D M S, 22 Commerce Rd., Newtown, CT 06470. TEL 203-426-0800. FAX 203-426-0223. *5265*

D N A SEQUENCE.
Gordon and Breach - Harwood Academic, Amsteldisk 166, 1st Fl., 1079 LH Amsterdam, Netherlands. *766*

D P A MEMBERSHIP BOOK.
A P Information Services, Roman House, 296 Golders Green Rd., London NW11 9PZ. TEL 44-181-455-4550. FAX 44-181-455-6381. *1663*

DAILY TELEGRAPH.
Telegraph plc., 1 Canada Sq., Canary Wharf, London E14 5DT, England. TEL 44-171-538-8288. FAX 44-171-538-6242.
Producer(s): Chadwyck-Healey Inc. *3295*

DAKAR MEDICAL.
Societe Medicale d'Afrique Noire de Langue Francaise, B.P. 450, Dakar, Senegal. *4660*

DANISH YEARBOOK OF PHILOSOPHY.
Museum Tusculanum Press, University of Copenhagen, Njalsgade 92, DK-2300 Copenhagen S, Denmark. TEL 45-35-32-91-09. FAX 45-35-32-91-13. *5723*

DANSK ARTIKELINDEKS: AVISER OG TIDSSKRIFTER.
Dansk BiblioteksCenter as, Tempovej 7-11, DK-2750 Ballerup, Denmark. TEL 45-44-867777. FAX 45-44-867892. *3884*

DANSK FAGPRESSEKATALOG.
Dansk Fagpresse Service ApS, Sommerstedgade 7, DK-1718 Copenhagen V, Denmark. TEL 45-33-86-31-00. FAX 45-31-23-43-10. *48*

DANSK LYDFORTEGNELSE.
Dansk BiblioteksCenter as, Tempovej 7-11, DK-2750 Ballerup, Denmark. TEL 45-44-867777. FAX 45-44-867892. *5447*

DANSK UDDANNELSES & ERHVERVS LEKSIKON.
Raadet for Uddannelses- og Erhvervsvejledning (R.U.E.), Aebeloegade 7, DK-2100 Copenhagen Oe, Denmark. TEL 45-39-17-76-00. FAX 45-39-17-76-29. *5507*

DANSKE KOMMUNER.
Kommunernes Landsforening, Gyldenloevesgade 11, 1600 Copenhagen V, Denmark. TEL 45-31-122788. FAX 45-31-122785. *6213*

DATA BASE OF DEFINED CONTRIBUTION AND DEFINED BENEFIT PLANS.
Judy Diamond Associates, Inc., 1730 M St., N.W., Ste. 1025, Washington, DC 20036. TEL 202-728-0840. FAX 202-728-0845. *3814*

DATA-INFO.
Marketons B.V., Postbus 1310, 6501 BH Nijmegen, Netherlands. TEL 31-24-3224200. FAX 31-24-3603176. *2127*

DATAPHILE.
AsiaTech Publications Ltd., 23rd Fl., Citicorp Centre, 18 Whitfield Rd., North Point, Hong Kong, People's Republic of China. TEL 852-2837-8800. FAX 852-2520-5463. *2015*

DATAPRO SOFTWARE FINDER.
Datapro Information Services Group, 600 Delran Pkwy., Delran, NJ 08075.
Available only on CD-ROM. *2211*

DATAWORLD.
Faulkner Information Services, Inc., 114 Cooper Center, 7905 Browning Rd., Pennsauken, NJ 08109-4319. TEL 609-662-2070. FAX 609-662-3380. *2173*

DAYTON BUSINESS REPORTER.
Hannover Publishing Co., Inc., 6356 Far Hills Ave., Dayton, OH 45459-2782. TEL 937-291-1100. FAX 937-436-3426.
Producer(s): UMI. *953*

LES DEBROUILLARDS.
Publications BLD, 3995 rue Sainte-Catherine Est, Montreal, PQ H1W 2G7, Canada. TEL 514-522-1304. FAX 514-522-1761. *1869*

DEFENCE DOCUMENTS MICROFILE.
Technical Indexes Ltd., Willoughby Rd., Bracknell, Berks. RG12 8DW, England. TEL 44-1344-426311. FAX 44-1344-424971. *5265*

DEFENSE COUNSEL JOURNAL.
International Association of Defense Counsel, 1 N. Franklin St., Ste. 2400, Chicago, IL 60606-3401. TEL 312-368-1494. FAX 312-368-1854.
Producer(s): UMI. *4060*

DELAWARE BUSINESS DIRECTORY.
American Business Directories, 5711 S. 86th Circle, Box 27347, Omaha, NE 68127. TEL 402-593-4600. FAX 402-331-5481. *1663*

DELAWARE REPORTER.
West Group, 620 Opperman Dr., Eagan, MN 55123. TEL 612-687-8000. FAX 612-687-7302. *3938*

DELPHI INFORMANT.
Informant Communications Group, Inc., 10519 E. Stockton Blvd., Ste. 142, Elk Grove, CA 95624-9704. TEL 916-686-6610. FAX 916-686-8497. *2143*

DESIGN AND APPLIED ARTS INDEX.
Design Documentation, Old Manor Lodge, Bodiam, Robertsbridge, E. Sussex TN32 5UJ, England. TEL 0580-830877. FAX 0435-863184. *476*

DESIGN NEWS O E M DIRECTORY.
Cahners Publishing Company (Newton), Division of Reed Elsevier Inc., 275 Washington St., Newton, MA 02158-1630. TEL 617-558-4762. FAX 617-558-4402.
Available only on CD-ROM. *4543*

DEUTSCH - DEUTSCHE RECHTS ZEITSCHRIFT.
Verlag C.H. Beck, 80791 Munich, Germany. TEL 49-89-38189338. FAX 49-89-38189398. *3939*

DEUTSCHE GELD- UND KREDITINSTITUTE. BANKEN-ORTSLEXIKON.
Verlag Hoppenstedt GmbH, Havelstr. 9, 64295 Darmstadt, Germany. TEL 49-6151-380-0. FAX 49-6151-380-360. *1128*

DEUTSCHE NATIONALBIBLIOGRAPHIE (C D - R O M AKTUELL).
Buchhaendler-Vereinigung GmbH, Postfach 100442, 60004 Frankfurt a.M., Germany. TEL 49-69-1306-243. FAX 49-69-1306201.
Available only on CD-ROM. Producer(s): Chadwyck-Healey Inc. *545*

DEUTSCHE NATIONALBIBLIOGRAPHIE MUSIK C D - R O M.
Buchhaendler-Vereinigung GmbH, Postfach 100442, 60004 Frankfurt a.M., Germany. TEL 49-69-1306-0. FAX 49-69-1306201.
Available only on CD-ROM. *5447*

DEUTSCHE ZEITSCHRIFT FUER PHILOSOPHIE.
Akademie Verlag GmbH, Muehlenstr. 33-34, 13187 Berlin, Germany. TEL 49-30-47889348. FAX 49-30-47889357. *5723*

DEUTSCHES STEUERRECHT.
Verlag C.H. Beck, 80791 Munich, Germany.
TEL 49-89-38189-338. FAX 49-89-38189-398.
1606

DEVELOPMENTAL IMMUNOLOGY.
Gordon and Breach - Harwood Academic,
Amsteldisk 166, 1st Fl., 1079 LH Amsterdam,
Netherlands. *4794*

LE DEVOIR.
2050 rue de Bleury, 9e etage, Montreal, PQ H3A
3M9, Canada. TEL 514-985-3333. *3260*

DEWEY DECIMAL CLASSIFICATION ADDITIONS, NOTES AND DECISIONS.
Forest Press, 85 Watervliet Ave., Albany, NY
12206-2082. TEL 518-489-8549. FAX 518-489-7804. *4174*

DHAKA UNIVERSITY STUDIES. PART B: SCIENCE.
University of Dhaka, Ramna, Dhaka 1000,
Bangladesh. *6522*

DIAGNOSTIC AND THERAPEUTIC ENDOSCOPY.
Gordon and Breach - Harwood Academic,
Amsteldisk 166, 1st Fl., 1079 LH Amsterdam,
Netherlands. *4896*

DIAGNOSTIC IMAGING & RADIOLOGY PRODUCT COMPARISON SYSTEM.
E C R I, 5200 Butler Pike, Plymouth Meeting, PA
19462. TEL 610-825-6000. FAX 610-834-1275.
Producer(s): Knight-Ridder, Inc. *5105*

DICTIONARY OF NATURAL PRODUCTS ON C D - R O M.
Chapman & Hall, Electronic Publishing Division 2-6
Boundary Row, London SE1 8HN, England. TEL 44-171-865-0066. FAX 44-171-522-0101.
Available only on CD-ROM. *5655*

DICTIONNAIRE JOLY SOCIETES.
Joly Editions, 1 av. Franklin D. Roosevelt, 75008
Paris, France. TEL 33-1-44951620. FAX 33-1-45638939. *1473*

DIETRICH'S INDEX PHILOSOPHICUS.
Zeller Publications, Postfach 1949, 49009
Osnabrueck, Germany. TEL 49-541-4045914.
FAX 49-541-41255.
Available only on CD-ROM. *5760*

DIODE D.A.T.A. DIGEST.
D.A.T.A. Business Publishing, 15 Inverness Way E.,
Box 6510, Englewood, CO 80155-6510. FAX 303-799-4082. *2629*

DIRECTORY OF AMERICAN RESEARCH AND TECHNOLOGY.
R.R. Bowker, A Division of Reed Elsevier Inc., 121
Chanlon Rd., New Providence, NJ 07974. TEL 908-464-6800. FAX 908-665-6688.
Producer(s): Bowker Electronic Publishing. *6958*

DIRECTORY OF CHAIN RESTAURANT OPERATORS (YEAR).
C S G Information Services, 3922 Coconut Palm
Dr., Tampa, FL 33619. TEL 813-664-6800.
FAX 813-664-6882. *1666*

DIRECTORY OF CHEMICAL PRODUCERS - CANADA.
S R I International, Process Industries Division,
Chemical Marketing Research Center, Menlo Park,
CA 94025. TEL 415-859-3627. FAX 415-859-4623. *1747*

DIRECTORY OF CHEMICAL PRODUCERS - CHINA.
S R I International, Process Industries Division,
Chemical Marketing Research Center, Menlo Park,
CA 94025. TEL 415-859-3627. FAX 415-859-4623. *1747*

DIRECTORY OF CHEMICAL PRODUCERS - EAST ASIA.
S R I International, Process Industries Division,
Chemical Marketing Research Center, Menlo Park,
CA 94025. TEL 415-859-3627. FAX 415-859-4623. *1747*

DIRECTORY OF CHEMICAL PRODUCERS - MEXICO.
S R I International, Process Industries Division,
Chemical Marketing Research Center, Menlo Park,
CA 94025. TEL 415-859-3627. FAX 415-859-4623. *1747*

DIRECTORY OF CHEMICAL PRODUCERS - MIDDLE EAST.
S R I International, Process Industries Division,
Chemical Marketing Research Center, Menlo Park,
CA 94025. TEL 415-859-3627. FAX 415-859-4623. *1747*

DIRECTORY OF CHEMICAL PRODUCERS - SOUTH AMERICA.
S R I International, Process Industries Division,
Chemical Marketing Research Center, Menlo Park,
CA 94025. TEL 415-859-3627. FAX 415-859-4623. *1747*

DIRECTORY OF CHEMICAL PRODUCERS - UNITED STATES.
S R I International, Process Industries Division,
Chemical Marketing Research Center, Menlo Park,
CA 94025. TEL 415-859-3627. FAX 415-859-4623. *1747*

DIRECTORY OF CHEMICAL PRODUCERS - WESTERN EUROPE.
S R I International, Process Industries Division,
Chemical Marketing Research Center, Menlo Park,
CA 94025. TEL 415-859-3627. FAX 415-859-4623. *1747*

DIRECTORY OF COMPUTER RETAILERS, DEALERS & DISTRIBUTORS (YEAR).
C S G Information Services, 3922 Coconut Palm
Dr., Tampa, FL 33619. TEL 813-664-6800.
FAX 813-664-6882. *2129*

DIRECTORY OF COMPUTER V A R'S & SYSTEM INTEGRATORS (YEAR).
C S G Information Services, 3922 Coconut Palm
Dr., Tampa, FL 33619. TEL 813-664-6800.
FAX 813-664-6882. *1666*

DIRECTORY OF CORPORATE AFFILIATIONS.
National Register Publishing, A Division of Reed
Elsevier Inc., 121 Chanlon Rd., New Providence, NJ
07974. TEL 908-464-6800. FAX 908-771-7704.
Producer(s): Bowker Electronic Publishing. *1667*

DIRECTORY OF DEPARTMENT STORES & MAIL ORDER FIRMS (YEAR).
C S G Information Services, 3922 Coconut Palm
Dr., Tampa, FL 33619. TEL 813-664-6800.
FAX 813-664-6882. *1667*

DIRECTORY OF DISCOUNT AND GENERAL MERCHANDISE STORES (YEAR).
C S G Information Services, 3922 Coconut Palm
Dr., Tampa, FL 33619. TEL 813-664-6800.
FAX 813-664-6810. *1667*

DIRECTORY OF DRUG STORE AND H B C CHAINS (YEAR).
C S G Information Services, 3922 Coconut Palm
Dr., Tampa, FL 33619. TEL 813-664-6800.
FAX 813-664-6882. *1667*

DIRECTORY OF E U INFORMATION SOURCES.
Euroconfidentiel s.a., Rue de Rixensart 18, 1332
Genval, Belgium. TEL 32-2-6520284. FAX 32-2-6530180. *4174*

DIRECTORY OF ENGINEERING GRADUATE STUDIES AND RESEARCH.
American Society for Engineering Education, 1818
N St., N.W., Ste. 600, Washington, DC 20036.
TEL 202-331-3500. FAX 202-265-8504. *2715*

DIRECTORY OF FLORIDA INDUSTRIES.
Harris InfoSource International, 2057-2 Aurora Rd.,
Twinsburg, OH 44087-1999. TEL 216-425-9000.
FAX 216-425-7150. *1668*

THE DIRECTORY OF GRANT-MAKING TRUSTS.
Charities Aid Foundation, Kings Hill, West Malling,
Kent ME19 4TA, England. TEL 44-1732-520000.
FAX 44-1732-520001. *6663*

DIRECTORY OF HISTORY DEPARTMENTS AND ORGANIZATIONS (YEAR).
American Historical Association, 400 A St., S.E.,
Washington, DC 20003-3889. TEL 202-544-2422.
FAX 202-544-8307. *2522*

DIRECTORY OF HOME CENTER OPERATORS & HARDWARE CHAINS (YEAR).
C S G Information Services, 3922 Coconut Palm
Dr., Tampa, FL 33619. TEL 813-664-6800.
FAX 813-664-6882. *1668*

DIRECTORY OF LEADING CHAIN STORES (YEAR).
C S G Information Services, 3922 Coconut Palm
Dr., Tampa, FL 33619. TEL 813-664-6800.
FAX 813-664-6882. *1669*

DIRECTORY OF LIBRARIES IN CANADA.
Micromedia Ltd., 20 Victoria St., Toronto, ON M5C
2N8, Canada. TEL 416-362-5211. FAX 416-362-6161. *4174*

DIRECTORY OF LOUISIANA MANUFACTURERS.
Harris InfoSource International, 2057-2 Aurora Rd.,
Twinsburg, OH 44087. TEL 216-425-9000.
FAX 216-425-7150. *1669*

DIRECTORY OF MAJOR MAILERS & WHAT THEY MAIL (YEAR).
North American Publishing Co., 401 N. Broad St.,
Philadelphia, PA 19108. TEL 215-238-5300.
FAX 215-238-5457. *1670*

DIRECTORY OF MAJOR MALLS.
Directory of Major Malls, Inc., Box 1708, 7 S.
Myrtle Ave., Spring Valley, NY 10977. TEL 914-426-0040. FAX 914-426-0802. *6299*

DIRECTORY OF RESEARCH GRANTS.
Oryx Press, Box 33889, Phoenix, AZ 85067-3889.
TEL 602-265-2651. FAX 602-265-6250.
Producer(s): Knight-Ridder, Inc. *2539*

DIRECTORY OF SUPERMARKET, GROCERY & CONVENIENCE STORE CHAINS (YEAR).
C S G Information Services, 3922 Coconut Palm
Dr., Tampa, FL 33619. TEL 813-664-6800.
FAX 813-664-6882. *1671*

DIRECTORY OF TEXAS MANUFACTURERS.
University of Texas at Austin, Bureau of Business
Research, Box 7459, Austin, TX 78713. TEL 512-471-1616. FAX 512-471-1063. *1671*

DIRECTORY OF U.S. SUBSIDIARIES OF BRITISH COMPANIES.
British - American Chamber of Commerce, 52
Vanderbilt Ave., Ste. 20, New York, NY 10017-3808. TEL 212-661-4060. *1185*

DIRECTORY OF UNITED STATES EXPORTERS.
Journal of Commerce, Inc., 2 World Trade Center,
27th fl., New York, NY 10048-0203. TEL 212-837-7000. FAX 212-837-7035. *1322*

DIRECTORY OF WHOLESALE GROCERS (YEAR).
C S G Information Services, 3922 Coconut Palm
Dr., Tampa, FL 33619. TEL 813-664-6800.
FAX 813-664-6882. *1672*

DISCONTINUED DISCRETE SEMICONDUCTORS D.A.T.A. DIGEST.
D.A.T.A. Business Publishing, 15 Inverness Way E.,
Box 6510, Englewood, CO 80155-6510. FAX 303-799-4082. *2629*

DISCONTINUED I CS D.A.T.A. DIGEST.
D.A.T.A. Business Publishing, 15 Inverness Way E.,
Box 6510, Englewood, CO 80155-6510. FAX 303-799-4082. *2629*

DISSERTATION ABSTRACTS INTERNATIONAL. SECTION A: HUMANITIES AND SOCIAL SCIENCES.
U M I, 300 N. Zeeb Rd., Ann Arbor, MI 48106.
TEL 313-761-4700. FAX 800-864-0019.
Producer(s): UMI. *3799*

DISSERTATION ABSTRACTS INTERNATIONAL. SECTION B: PHYSICAL SCIENCES AND ENGINEERING.
U M I, 300 N. Zeeb Rd., Ann Arbor, MI 48106.
TEL 313-761-4700. FAX 800-864-0019.
Producer(s): UMI. *6589*

DISSERTATION ABSTRACTS INTERNATIONAL. SECTION C: WORLDWIDE.
U M I, 300 N. Zeeb Rd., Ann Arbor, MI 48106.
TEL 313-761-4700. FAX 800-864-0019.
Producer(s): UMI. *3799*

DISSERTATION ABSTRACTS ON DISC.
U M I, 300 N. Zeeb Rd., Ann Arbor, MI 48016-1304. TEL 313-761-4700. FAX 800-864-0019.
Producer(s): UMI.

DISTRIBUTED COMPUTING MONITOR.
Patricia Seybold Group, 85 Devonshire St. Fl. 5,
Boston, MA 02109-3504. *2154*

DJERELO.
Ukrainian Academy of Sciences, Institute of Information Recording Problems, Vul. Shpaka 2, 252113 Kiev, Ukraine. TEL 38-44-4412197. FAX 38-44-4461491. *6589*

DOLLARSENSE.
E.F. Baumer & Company, 401 Shatto Pl., Ste. 105, Los Angeles, CA 90020. TEL 213-386-2111. FAX 213-386-6470. *1128*

DOMESTIC CARS SERVICE & REPAIR.
Mitchell International, Inc., 9889 Willow Creek Rd., Box 26260, San Diego, CA 92196-0260. FAX 619-578-4752. *7097*

DOMESTIC LIGHT TRUCKS & VANS SERVICE & REPAIR.
Mitchell International, Inc., 9889 Willow Creek Rd., Box 26260, San Diego, CA 92196-0260. TEL 800-648-8010. FAX 619-578-4752. *7097*

DOMINION TAX CASES.
C C H Canadian Ltd., 6 Garamond Ct., North York, ON M3C 1Z5, Canada. TEL 416-441-2992. FAX 416-444-9011. *1606*

DONGYUE LUNCONG.
Shandong Sheng Shehui Kexueyuan, No. 10, Yuhan Rd., Jinan, Shandong 250002, People's Republic of China. TEL 86-531-2015471. *6610*

DOWNSTATE ILLINOIS BUSINESS DIRECTORY.
American Business Directories, 5711 S. 86th Circle, Box 27347, Omaha, NE 68127. TEL 402-593-4600. FAX 402-331-5481. *1672*

DRUG ABUSE.
Swedish Council for Information on Alcohol and other Drugs (CAN), Documentation Center, P.O. Box 27302, S-102 54 Stockholm, Sweden. FAX 46-8-661-64-84. *2300*

DRUG DESIGN AND DISCOVERY.
Gordon and Breach - Harwood Academic, Amsteldisk 166, 1st Fl., 1079 LH Amsterdam, Netherlands. *5656*

DRUG NEWS & PERSPECTIVES.
J.R. Prous, S.A. International Publishers, Apdo. de Correos 540, 08080 Barcelona, Spain. TEL 343-459-2220. FAX 343-458-1535. *5657*

DRUGS OF THE FUTURE.
J.R. Prous, S.A. International Publishers, Apdo. de Correos 540, 08080 Barcelona, Spain. TEL 343-459-2220. FAX 343-458-1535. *5659*

DRYDEN OBSERVER.
Alex Wilson Coldstream Ltd., Colonization St., Dryden, ON P8N 2Y9, Canada. FAX 807-223-2907. *3260*

DUQUESNE LAW REVIEW.
Duquesne University, Duquesne School of Law, 900 Locust St., Pittsburgh, PA 15282. TEL 412-396-6297. FAX 412-396-6294. *3943*

E D I FORUM.
E D I Group, Ltd., Box 710, Oak Park, IL 60302. TEL 708-848-0135. FAX 708-848-0270. *2169*

E E M.
Hearst Business Publishing UTP Division, Attn. Georgeann Amsler, Mktg. Mgr., 645 Stewart Ave., Garden City, NY 11530. TEL 516-227-1300. FAX 516-227-1453. *2630*

E FOR ENVIRONMENT.
R.R. Bowker, A Division of Reed Elsevier Inc., 121 Chanlon Rd., New Providence, NJ 07974. TEL 908-464-6800. FAX 908-665-6688. *2913*

E I A PUBLICATIONS DIRECTORY.
U.S. Energy Information Administration, National Energy Information Center, EI-231, James Forrestal Bldg., Rm. 1F-048, 1000 Independence Ave., S.W., Washington, DC 20585. TEL 202-568-8800. FAX 202-586-0727. *2663*

E I S.
Cambridge Scientific Abstracts, 7200 Wisconsin Ave., 6th Fl., Bethesda, MD 20814. TEL 301-961-6750. FAX 301-961-6720. Producer(s): Knight-Ridder, Inc., NISC, SilverPlatter Information, Inc. *2960*

E I U NEWSLETTERS.
Economist Intelligence Unit, 111 W. 57th St., New York, NY 10019. TEL 212-554-0600. FAX 212-586-1182. *955*

E M F - E M I CONTROL.
E E C Press, 6193 Finchingfield Rd., Gainesville, VA 22065. TEL 540-347-0030. FAX 540-347-5813. *6958*

E N B NEWS.
English National Board for Nursing, Midwifery, and Health Visiting, Victory House, 170 Tottenham Ct. Rd., London W1P OHA, England. TEL 44-171-388-3131. FAX 44-171-383-4031. *4932*

E R I C ON C D - R O M.
National Information Services Corporation (NISC), 3100 St. Paul St., Ste. 806, Baltimore, MD 21218. TEL 410-243-0797. FAX 410-243-0982. Available only on CD-ROM. Producer(s): NISC. *2499*

E S O M A R DIRECTORY (YEAR).
European Society for Opinion and Marketing Research, J.J. Viottastraat 29, 1071 JP Amsterdam, Netherlands. TEL 31-20-664-2141. FAX 31-20-664-2922. *1525*

E Z A - ENTSCHEIDUNGSSAMMLUNG ZUM ARBEITSRECHT.
Luchterhand Verlag, Heddesdorferstr. 31, 56564 Neuwied, Germany. TEL 49-2631-801-0. FAX 49-2631-801204. *4079*

EARTH SYSTEM MONITOR.
U.S. National Oceanic Data Center, NOAA - NESDIS OC1, SSMC3, 4th Fl., 1315 East-West Hwy., Silver Spring, MD 20910-3282. TEL 301-713-3277. FAX 301-713-3301. *2402*

EARTHQUAKE ENGINEERING ABSTRACTS DATABASE.
University of California at Berkeley, Earthquake Engineering Research Center, 1301 S. 46th St., Richmond, CA 94804-4698. TEL 510-231-9401. FAX 510-231-9461.
Producer(s): NISC (Earthquakes and the Built Environment Index). *2749*

EARTHQUAKE HISTORY OF THE UNITED STATES.
U.S. National Geophysical Data Center, 325 Broadway, Boulder, CO 80303-3328. TEL 303-497-6826. FAX 303-497-6513. *2381*

THE EAST AFRICAN MEDICAL JOURNAL.
Kenya Medical Association House, Chyulu Rd., P.O. Box 41632, Nairobi, Kenya. TEL 254-2-712010. FAX 254-2-724617. *4663*

EBONY.
Johnson Publishing Co., Inc., 820 S. Michigan Ave., Chicago, IL 60605. TEL 312-322-9200. FAX 312-322-9375.
Producer(s): UMI. *3009*

ECO DEL MANTE.
Guerrero 701 Ote., 89800 Mante, Tamaulipas, Mexico. TEL 55-123-20040. FAX 55-123-22420. *3335*

ECO-LOG CANADIAN POLLUTION LEGISLATION.
Southam Information Products Ltd., 1450 Don Mills, Don Mills, ON M3B 2X7, Canada. TEL 416-445-6641. FAX 416-442-2200. *2961*

ECOCENTRAL.
University of New Mexico, Latin American Institute, 801 Yale N.E., Albuquerque, NM 87131-1016. TEL 505-277-6839. FAX 505-277-5989.
Producer(s): NISC. *1358*

ECOLOGY ABSTRACTS.
Cambridge Scientific Abstracts, 7200 Wisconsin Ave., 6th Fl., Bethesda, MD 20814. TEL 301-961-6750. FAX 301-961-6720.
Producer(s): NISC, SilverPlatter Information, Inc. *2961*

ECONOMIC JUSTICE REPORT.
Ecumenical Coalition for Economic Justice, 402-77 Charles St. W., Toronto, ON M5S 1K5, Canada. TEL 416-921-4615. FAX 416-922-1419. *6012*

ECONOMIC REPORT OF THE PRESIDENT.
U.S. Executive Office of the President, Council of Economic Advisers, Washington, DC 20500. TEL 202-395-7332. *1254*

THE ECONOMIST.
Economist Newspaper Ltd., 25 St. James's St., London SW1A 1HG, England. TEL 44-171-830-7000. FAX 44-171-839-2968.
Producer(s): Chadwyck-Healey Inc. *1256*

ECONOMIST. ANNUAL INDEX.
Economist Newspaper Ltd., 25 St. James's St., London SW1A 1HG, England. TEL 44-171-830-7000. FAX 44-171-839-2968.
Producer(s): Chadwyck-Healey Inc. *1256*

THE ECONOMIST ON C D - R O M.
Chadwyck-Healey Ltd., The Quorum, Barnwell Rd., Cambridge CB5 8SW, England. TEL 44-1223-215512. FAX 44-1223-215514.
Available only on CD-ROM. Producer(s): Chadwyck-Healey Inc. *1256*

EDITOR & PUBLISHER - FREE PAPER PUBLISHER COMMUNITY, SPECIALTY & FREE PUBLICATIONS YEAR BOOK.
Editor & Publisher Co., Inc., 11 W. 19th St., New York, NY 10011. TEL 212-675-4380. FAX 212-929-1259. *35*

EDITOR & PUBLISHER INTERNATIONAL YEAR BOOK.
Editor & Publisher Co., Inc., 11 W. 19th St., New York, NY 10011. TEL 212-675-4380. FAX 212-929-1259. *3872*

EDITOR & PUBLISHER MARKET GUIDE.
Editor & Publisher Co., Inc., 11 W. 19th St., New York, NY 10011. TEL 212-675-4380. FAX 212-929-1259. *1525*

THE EDMONTON JOURNAL.
P.O. Box 2421, Edmonton, AB T5J 2S6, Canada. TEL 403-429-5100. FAX 403-429-5500. *3261*

THE EDUCATION DIGEST.
Prakken Publications, Inc., Box 8623, Ann Arbor, MI 48107. TEL 313-769-1211. FAX 313-769-8383.
Producer(s): UMI. *2437*

EDUCATION INDEX.
H.W. Wilson Co., 950 University Ave., Bronx, NY 10452. TEL 718-590-8400. FAX 718-590-1617.
Producer(s): SilverPlatter Information, Inc., H.W. Wilson (WILSONDISC). *2499*

EFFETA.
Istituto Gualandi per Sordomuti e Sordomute, Via Nosadella 49, 40123 Bologna, Italy. TEL 39-51-330552. FAX 39-51-332878. *3462*

EGYPTIAN JOURNAL OF FOOD SCIENCE.
National Information and Documentation Centre (NIDOC), Tahrir St., Dokki, Awqaf P.O., Cairo, Egypt. TEL 20-2-3371696. *5472*

EGYPTIAN JOURNAL OF PHARMACEUTICAL SCIENCES.
National Information and Documentation Centre (NIDOC), Tahrir St., Dokki, Awqaf P.O., Cairo, Egypt. TEL 20-2-3371696. *5659*

EGYPTIAN JOURNAL OF VETERINARY SCIENCE.
National Information and Documentation Centre (NIDOC), Tahrir St., Dokki, Awqaf P.O., Cairo, Egypt. TEL 20-2-3371696. *7269*

EGYPTIAN ORTHOPAEDIC JOURNAL.
Egyptian Orthopaedic Association, P.O. Box 4, Alexandria 21111, Egypt. TEL 20-3-4225626. *5006*

EINKAUFS 1X1 DER DEUTSCHEN INDUSTRIE.
Deutscher Adressbuch Verlag, Arheilger Weg 17, 64380 Rossdorf, Germany. TEL 06154-699500. FAX 06154-6995490. *1675*

DIE EISEN, BLECH UND METALL VERARBEITENDE INDUSTRIE, STAHLVERFORMUNG UND IHRE HELFER.
Industrieschau-Verlagsgesellschaft mbH, Postfach 100262, 64202 Darmstadt, Germany. TEL 49-6151-38920. FAX 49-6151-33164. *5190*

SERIALS AVAILABLE ON CD-ROM

DIE EISEN-, STAHL- UND N E METALL-INDUSTRIE UND IHRE HELFER.
Industrieschau-Verlagsgesellschaft mbH, Postfach 100262, 64202 Darmstadt, Germany. TEL 49-6151-38920. FAX 49-6151-33164. *5190*

ELECTRE BIBLIO.
Electre, 35 rue Gregoire-de-Tours, 75006 Paris, France. TEL 33-1-44412861. FAX 33-1-44412865.
Available only on CD-ROM. *6289*

ELECTRIC POWER ANNUAL.
U.S. Energy Information Administration, National Energy Information Center, EI-231, James Forrestal Bldg., Rm. 1F-048, 1000 Independence Ave., S.W., Washington, DC 20585. TEL 202-586-8800. FAX 202-586-0727. *2688*

ELECTRIC POWER MONTHLY.
U.S. Energy Information Administration, National Energy Information Center, EI-231, James Forrestal Bldg., Rm. 1F-048, 1000 Independence Ave., S.W., Washington, DC 20585. TEL 202-586-8800. FAX 202-0586-0727. *2688*

ELECTRIC UTILITY WEEK.
McGraw-Hill, Inc., 1221 Ave. of the Americas, New York, NY 10020. TEL 212-512-6410.
Producer(s): SilverPlatter Information, Inc. (McGraw-Hill Energy Library). *2817*

ELECTRIC UTILITY WEEK'S DEMAND-SIDE REPORT.
McGraw-Hill, Inc., 1221 Ave. of the Americas, New York, NY 10020. TEL 212-512-6410.
Producer(s): SilverPlatter Information, Inc. (McGraw-Hill Energy Library). *2688*

ELECTRICAL & ELECTRONICS ABSTRACTS.
INSPEC, I.E.E., Michael Faraday House, Six Hill Way, Stevenage, Herts. SG1 2AY, England. TEL 44-1438-313311. FAX 44-1438-742840. *2749*

ELECTRICAL AND ELECTRONICS TRADES DIRECTORY.
INSPEC, I.E.E., Michael Faraday House, Six Hills Way, Stevenage, Herts SG1 2AY, England. TEL 44-1438-313311. FAX 44-1438-742840. *2817*

ELECTRICAL COMPONENT LOCATOR - DOMESTIC CARS, LIGHT TRUCKS & VANS.
Mitchell International, Inc., 9889 Willow Creek Rd., Box 26260, San Diego, CA 92196-0260. TEL 619-578-6550. FAX 619-578-4752. *7098*

ELECTRICAL COMPONENT LOCATOR - IMPORTED CARS, LIGHT TRUCKS & VANS.
Mitchell International, Inc., 9889 Willow Creek Rd., Box 26260, San Diego, CA 92196-0260. TEL 800-648-8010. FAX 619-578-4752. *7098*

ELECTRO.
Societe Nouvelle d'Editions Publicitaires, 16, Av. de Verdun, 75010 Paris, France. *2631*

ELECTRONIC ENGINEERING INDEX.
Technical Indexes Ltd., Willoughby Rd., Bracknell, Berks RG12 8DW, England. TEL 44-1344-426311. FAX 44-1344-424971. *2632*

ELECTRONIC JOURNAL OF THEORETICAL CHEMISTRY.
John Wiley & Sons Ltd., Journals, Baffins Ln., Chichester, W. Sussex PO19 1UD, England. TEL 44-1243-779777. FAX 44-1243-843232. *1790*

ELECTRONIC QUALITY ASSURANCE DOCUMENTS.
Technical Indexes Ltd., Willoughby Rd., Bracknell, Berkshire RG12 8DW, England. TEL 44-1344-426311. FAX 44-1344-424971. *2633*

ELECTRONICS BUYERS' GUIDE.
Miller Freeman Information Services, Riverbank House, Angel Ln., Tonbridge, Kent TN9 1SE, England. TEL 44-1732-362666. FAX 44-1732-367301. *2634*

DIE ELEKTRO-INDUSTRIE, ELEKTRONIK UND IHRE HELFER.
Industrieschau-Verlagsgesellschaft mbH, Postfach 100262, 64202 Darmstadt, Germany. TEL 49-6151-3892-0. FAX 49-6151-33164. *2635*

ELEMENTARY SCHOOL LIBRARY COLLECTION.
Brodart Co., 500 Arch St., Williamsport, PA 17705. FAX 717-326-6769. *4177*

EL-HI TEXTBOOKS AND SERIALS IN PRINT.
R.R. Bowker, A Division of Reed Elsevier Inc., 121 Chanlon Rd., New Providence, NJ 07974. TEL 908-464-6800. FAX 908-665-3502.
Producer(s): Bowker Electronic Publishing. *2499*

ELSEVIER SCIENCE. CATALOGUE - BOOKS.
Elsevier Science B.V., P.O. Box 211, 1000 AE Amsterdam, Netherlands. TEL 31-20-4853911. FAX 31-20-4853598. *6524*

ELSEVIER SCIENCE. CATALOGUE - JOURNALS.
Elsevier Science B.V., P.O. Box 211, 1000 AE Amsterdam, Netherlands. TEL 31-20-4853911. FAX 31-20-4853598. *6524*

ELSEVIER SCIENCE. CATALOGUE ON C D - R O M.
Elsevier Science B.V., P.O. Box 211, 1000 AE Amsterdam, Netherlands. TEL 31-20-4853911. FAX 31-20-4853598.
Available only on CD-ROM. *6524*

EMIRATES MEDICAL JOURNAL.
Emirates Medical Association, P.O. Box 6600, Dubai, United Arab Emirates. TEL 971-4-377377. FAX 971-4-344082. *4664*

EMPLOYEE BENEFITS MANAGEMENT.
C C H Incorporated, 2700 Lake Cook Rd., Riverwoods, IL 60015. TEL 847-267-7000. FAX 800-224-8299. *1475*

EMPLOYMENT AND EARNINGS: UNITED STATES.
U.S. Bureau of Labor Statistics, 2 Massachusetts Ave., N.E., Washington, DC 20212. TEL 202-655-4000. *1257*

EMPLOYMENT LAW CASES.
Incomes Data Services Ltd., 77 Bastwick St., London EC1V 3TT, England. TEL 0171-250-3434. FAX 0171-608-0949. *1428*

ENANTIOMER.
Gordon and Breach - Harwood Academic, Amsteldisk 166, 1st Fl., 1079 LH Amsterdam, Netherlands. *1748*

ENCYCLOPEDIA OF ASSOCIATIONS.
Gale Research, 835 Penobscot Bldg., 645 Griswold St., Detroit, MI 48226-4094. TEL 313-961-2242. FAX 800-414-5043. *2656*

ENCYCLOPEDIA OF SOCIAL WORK.
N A S W Press, 750 First St., N.E., Ste. 700, Washington, DC 20002-4241. TEL 202-408-8600. FAX 202-336-8312. *6664*

ENDOTHELIUM.
Gordon and Breach - Harwood Academic, Amsteldisk 166, 1st Fl., 1079 LH Amsterdam, Netherlands. *600*

ENERGY DATABASE UNESCO - ISEEK.
1 rue Miollis, 75732 Paris Cedex 15, France. TEL 33-1-45684300. FAX 33-1-45685741.
Available only on CD-ROM. *2686*

ENERGY INFORMATION DIRECTORY.
U.S. Energy Information Administration, National Energy Information Center, EI-231, James Forrestal Bldg., Rm. 1F-048, 1000 Independence Ave., S.W., Washington, DC 20585. TEL 202-586-8800. FAX 202-586-0727. *2667*

ENGINEERED MATERIALS ABSTRACTS.
Cambridge Scientific Abstracts, 7200 Wisconsin Ave., Bethesda, MD 20814. TEL 301-961-6750. FAX 301-961-6720.
Producer(s): Knight-Ridder, Inc. *2749*

ENGINEERING INDEX ANNUAL.
Engineering Information, Inc., Castle Point on the Hudson, Hoboken, NJ 07030. TEL 201-216-8500. FAX 201-216-8532.
Producer(s): Knight-Ridder, Inc. (COMPENDEX PLUS CD-ROM). *2749*

ENGINEERING INDEX MONTHLY.
Engineering Information, Inc., Castle Point on the Hudson, Hoboken, NJ 07030. TEL 201-216-8500. FAX 201-216-8532.
Producer(s): Knight-Ridder, Inc. (COMPENDEX PLUS CD-ROM). *2749*

ENGINEERING OPTIMIZATION.
Gordon and Breach - Harwood Academic, Amsteldisk 166, 1st Fl., 1079 LH Amsterdam, Netherlands. *2718*

ENHANCED HEAT TRANSFER.
Gordon and Breach - Harwood Academic, Amsteldisk 166, 1st Fl., 1079 LH Amsterdam, Netherlands. *2883*

ENSEMBLE.
Banque Internationale d'Information sur les Etats Francophones, 25 Eddy, Hull, ON K1A 0M5, Canada. TEL 819-997-3857. FAX 819-953-8439.
Available only on CD-ROM. *4177*

ENTERTAINMENT LAW REPORTER.
Entertainment Law Reporter Publishing Co., 2118 Wilshire Blvd., No. 311, Santa Monica, CA 90403. TEL 310-829-9335. FAX 310-829-9335. *3946*

ENTOMOLOGY ABSTRACTS.
Cambridge Scientific Abstracts, 7200 Wisconsin Ave., 6th Fl., Bethesda, MD 20814. TEL 301-961-6750. FAX 301-961-6720.
Producer(s): NISC, SilverPlatter Information, Inc. *640*

ENTREPRENEURSHIP: THEORY AND PRACTICE.
Baylor University, Hankamer School of Business, BU Box 98006, Waco, TX 76798-8006. TEL 817-755-1111 ext.156. FAX 817-755-2271. *1642*

ENVIRONMENT.
Heldref Publications, 1319 Eighteenth St., N.W., Washington, DC 20036-1802. TEL 202-296-6267. FAX 202-296-5149.
Producer(s): UMI. *2918*

ENVIRONMENT ABSTRACTS.
Congressional Information Service, Inc., A member of the LEXIS NEXIS family, 4520 East-West Hwy., Bethesda, MD 20814-3389. TEL 301-654-1550. FAX 301-654-4033. *2961*

ENVIRONMENT ABSTRACTS ANNUAL.
Congressional Information Service, Inc., A member of the LEXIS-NEXIS family, 4520 East-West Hwy., Ste. 800, Bethesda, MD 20814-3389. TEL 301-654-1550. FAX 301-654-4033. *2961*

ENVIRONMENT AND ECOLOGY.
M K K Publications, 91A Ananda Palit Rd., Calcutta, West Bengal 700 014, India. TEL 91-33-828220. *2918*

ENVIRONMENTAL ACTION.
Environmental Action Foundation, Box 61463, Durham, NC 27715-1463. TEL 301-891-1106. FAX 301-891-2218.
Producer(s): UMI. *2920*

ENVIRONMENTAL HEALTH BRIEFING.
Barbour Index, New Lodge Drift Rd., Windsor, Berks. SL4 4RQ, England. TEL 01344-884121. FAX 01344-884112. *6232*

ENVIRONMENTAL PERIODICALS BIBLIOGRAPHY.
International Academy at Santa Barbara, 800 Garden St., Ste. D, Santa Barbara, CA 93101-1552. TEL 805-965-5010. FAX 805-965-6071.
Producer(s): NISC. *2961*

ENVIRONMENTAL PERIODICALS BIBLIOGRAPHY (C D - R O M).
National Information Services Corporation (NISC), 3100 St. Paul St., Ste. 806, Baltimore, MD 21218. TEL 410-243-0797. FAX 410-243-0982.
Available only on CD-ROM. Producer(s): NISC. *2961*

EPIDEMIOLOGICAL NEWS BULLETIN.
Committee on Epidemic Diseases, Quarantine & Epidemiology Dept., 40 Scotts Rd., Environment Bldg., Singapore 228231, Singapore. TEL 65-732-9758. FAX 65-734-8287. *4835*

ERGA.
Instituto Nacional de Seguridad e Higiene en el Trabajo, Ministerio de Trabajo y Seguridad Social, Calle Dulcet 2-10, 08034 Barcelona, Spain. FAX 34-3-2803642. *5502*

ERGONOMICS ABSTRACTS.
Taylor & Francis Ltd., 1 Gunpowder Sq., London EC4A 3DE, England. TEL 44-171-583-0490. FAX 44-171-583-0585. *2749*

SERIALS AVAILABLE ON CD-ROM

ESSAY AND GENERAL LITERATURE INDEX.
H.W. Wilson Co., 950 University Ave., Bronx, NY 10452. TEL 718-588-8400. FAX 718-590-1617. Producer(s): SilverPlatter Information, Inc., H.W. Wilson (WILSONDISC). *4495*

ESSENTIAL ECOLOGY, ZOOLOGY & PLANT SCIENCE ABSTRACTS.
National Information Services Corporation (NISC), 3100 St. Paul St., Ste. 806, Baltimore, MD 21218. TEL 410-243-0797. FAX 410-243-0982. Available only on CD-ROM. Producer(s): NISC. *640*

ESSENTIAL FISHERIES ABSTRACTS.
National Information Services Corporation (NISC), 3100 St. Paul St., Ste. 806, Baltimore, MD 21218. TEL 410-243-0797. FAX 410-243-0982. Available only on CD-ROM. Producer(s): NISC. *3082*

ESSENTIAL FORESTRY & WILDFIRE ABSTRACTS.
National Information Services Corporation (NISC), 3100 St. Paul St., Ste. 806, Baltimore, MD 21218. TEL 410-243-0797. FAX 410-243-0982. Available only on CD-ROM. Producer(s): NISC. *3167*

ESSENTIAL ORNITHOLOGICAL ABSTRACTS.
National Information Services Corporation (NISC), 3100 St. Paul St., Ste. 806, Baltimore, MD 21218. TEL 410-243-0797. FAX 410-243-0982. Available only on CD-ROM. Producer(s): NISC. *640*

ESSENTIAL WILDLIFE & CONSERVATION BIOLOGY ABSTRACTS.
National Information Services Corporation (NISC), 3100 St. PAul St., Ste. 806, Baltimore, MD 21218. TEL 410-243-0797. FAX 410-243-0982. Available only on CD-ROM. Producer(s): NISC. *640*

ESTATE TAX FREEZE: TOOLS AND TECHNIQUES.
Matthew Bender & Co., Inc., 2 Park Ave., New York, NY 10016. TEL 212-448-2000. *6300*

ESTUARIES AND COASTAL WATERS OF THE BRITISH ISLES.
Plymouth Marine Laboratory, Citadel Hill, Plymouth PL1 2PB, England. TEL 44-1752-633266. FAX 44-1752-633102. Producer(s): NISC (Oceanographic & Marine Resources). *2961*

ETHIOPIAN MEDICAL JOURNAL.
Ethiopian Medical Association, P.O. Box 3472, Addis Ababa, Ethiopia. TEL 251-1-158174. *4665*

EURO O S H.
Chapman & Hall, 2-6 Boundary Row, London SE1 8HN, England. TEL 44-171-865-0066. FAX 44-171-5220101. Available only on CD-ROM. *5489*

EUROCAT.
Chadwyck-Healey Ltd., The Quorum, Barnwell Rd., Cambridge CB5 8SW, England. TEL 44-1223-215512. FAX 44-1223-215514. Available only on CD-ROM. Producer(s): Chadwyck-Healey Inc. *6173*

EUROMONEY.
Euromoney Publications plc., Nestor House, Playhouse Yard, London EC4V 5EX, England. TEL 44-171-779-8935. FAX 44-171-779-8541. *1130*

EUROPAEISCHES PATENTAMT. AMTSBLATT.
European Patent Office, Schottenfeldgasse 29, Postfach 82, A-1072 Vienna, Austria. TEL 43-1-521264051. FAX 43-1-521264192. *5583*

EUROPAGES.
Euredit s.a., 9 av. de Friedland, 75008 Paris, France. TEL 33-1-53775400. FAX 33-1-42893473. *1676*

EUROPEAN BOOK WORLD.
Anderson Rand Ltd., Scotts Bindery, Russell Ct., Cambridge CB2 1HL, England. TEL 44-1223-566640. FAX 44-1223-566643. *6270*

EUROPEAN CONVERTING INDUSTRY DIRECTORY.
Kingland House, 361 City Rd., London EC1V 1LR, England. TEL 44-171-417-7400. FAX 44-171-417-7500. *5566*

EUROPEAN JOURNAL OF BIOCHEMISTRY (C D - R O M).
Springer-Verlag, Heidelberger Platz 3, 14197 Berlin, Germany. TEL 49-30-82787-0. FAX 49-30-82787448. Available only on CD-ROM. *659*

EUROPEAN JOURNAL OF CANCER PREVENTION.
Rapid Science Publishers, The Old Malthouse, Paradise St., Oxford OX1 1LD, England. TEL 44-1865-790447. FAX 44-1865-244012. *4978*

EUROPEAN JOURNAL OF GASTROENTEROLOGY AND HEPATOLOGY.
Rapid Science Publishers, 2-6 Boundary Row, London SE1 8HN, England. TEL 44-171-865-0198. FAX 44-171-410-6600. *4909*

EUROPEAN JOURNAL OF NEUROLOGY.
Rapid Science Publishers, 2-6 Boundary Row, London SE1 8HN, England. TEL 44-171-865-0198. FAX 44-171-410-6600. *5063*

EUROPEAN MEDIA ART FESTIVAL.
International Experimental Film Workshop, Postfach 1861, 49008 Osnabrueck, Germany. TEL 49-541-21658. FAX 49-541-28327. *5330*

EUROPEAN RESEARCH AND DEVELOPMENT DATABASE (YEAR).
Bowker - Saur Ltd., A member of the Reed Elsevier plc group, Maypole House, Maypole Rd., E. Grinstead, W. Sussex RH19 1HU, England. TEL 44-1342-330100. FAX 44-1342-330191. *573*

EUROPEAN TAXATION.
I B F D Publications B.V., P.O. Box 20237, 1000 HE Amsterdam, Netherlands. TEL 31-20-6267726. FAX 31-20-6228658. *1607*

EUROPEAN TAXATION DATA BASE ON C D - R O M.
I B F D Publications B.V., P.O. Box 20237, 1000 HE Amsterdam, Netherlands. TEL 31-20-6267726. FAX 31-20-6228658. Available only on CD-ROM. *1607*

EXCEPTIONAL CHILD EDUCATION RESOURCES.
Council for Exceptional Children, 1920 Association Dr., Reston, VA 22091-1589. TEL 703-620-3660. FAX 703-264-9494. Producer(s): SilverPlatter Information, Inc. *2500*

EXCERPTA MEDICA ABSTRACT JOURNALS.
Elsevier Science B.V., P.O. Box 211, 1000 AE Amsterdam, Netherlands. TEL 31-20-4853757. FAX 31-20-4853432. Producer(s): SilverPlatter Information, Inc. (Excerpta Medica Library Service). *4774*

EXCERPTA MEDICA. SECTION 1: ANATOMY, ANTHROPOLOGY, EMBRYOLOGY & HISTOLOGY.
Elsevier Science B.V., P.O. Box 211, 1000 AE Amsterdam, Netherlands. TEL 31-20-4853757. FAX 31-20-4853432. Producer(s): SilverPlatter Information, Inc. *4774*

EXCERPTA MEDICA. SECTION 2: PHYSIOLOGY.
Elsevier Science B.V., P.O. Box 211, 1000 AE Amsterdam, Netherlands. TEL 31-20-4853757. FAX 31-20-4853432. Producer(s): SilverPlatter Information, Inc. *4774*

EXCERPTA MEDICA. SECTION 3: ENDOCRINOLOGY.
Elsevier Science B.V., P.O. Box 211, 1000 AE Amsterdam, Netherlands. TEL 31-20-4853757. FAX 31-20-4853432. Producer(s): SilverPlatter Information, Inc. *4775*

EXCERPTA MEDICA. SECTION 4: MICROBIOLOGY: BACTERIOLOGY, MYCOLOGY, PARASITOLOGY AND VIROLOGY.
Elsevier Science B.V., P.O. Box 211, 1000 AE Amsterdam, Netherlands. TEL 31-20-4853757. FAX 31-20-4853432. Producer(s): SilverPlatter Information, Inc. *4775*

EXCERPTA MEDICA. SECTION 5: GENERAL PATHOLOGY AND PATHOLOGICAL ANATOMY.
Elsevier Science B.V., P.O. Box 211, 1000 AE Amsterdam, Netherlands. TEL 31-20-4853757. FAX 31-20-4853432. Producer(s): SilverPlatter Information, Inc. *4775*

EXCERPTA MEDICA. SECTION 6: INTERNAL MEDICINE.
Elsevier Science B.V., P.O. Box 211, 1000 AE Amsterdam, Netherlands. TEL 31-20-4853757. FAX 31-20-4853432. Producer(s): SilverPlatter Information, Inc. *4775*

EXCERPTA MEDICA. SECTION 7: PEDIATRICS AND PEDIATRIC SURGERY.
Elsevier Science B.V., P.O. Box 211, 1000 AE Amsterdam, Netherlands. TEL 31-20-4853757. FAX 31-20-4853432. Producer(s): SilverPlatter Information, Inc. *4775*

EXCERPTA MEDICA. SECTION 8: NEUROLOGY AND NEUROSURGERY.
Elsevier Science B.V., P.O. Box 211, 1000 AE Amsterdam, Netherlands. TEL 31-20-4853757. FAX 31-20-4853432. Producer(s): SilverPlatter Information, Inc. *4775*

EXCERPTA MEDICA. SECTION 9: SURGERY.
Elsevier Science B.V., P.O. Box 211, 1000 AM Amsterdam, Netherlands. TEL 31-20-4853757. FAX 31-20-4853432. Producer(s): SilverPlatter Information, Inc. *4775*

EXCERPTA MEDICA. SECTION 10: OBSTETRICS AND GYNECOLOGY.
Elsevier Science B.V., P.O. Box 211, 1000 AE Amsterdam, Netherlands. TEL 31-20-4853757. FAX 31-20-4853432. Producer(s): SilverPlatter Information, Inc. *4775*

EXCERPTA MEDICA. SECTION 11: OTORHINOLARYNGOLOGY.
Elsevier Science B.V., P.O. Box 211, 1000 AE Amsterdam, Netherlands. TEL 31-20-4853757. FAX 31-20-4853432. Producer(s): SilverPlatter Information, Inc. *4775*

EXCERPTA MEDICA. SECTION 12: OPHTHALMOLOGY.
Elsevier Science B.V., P.O. Box 211, 1000 AE Amsterdam, Netherlands. TEL 31-20-4853757. FAX 31-20-4853432. Producer(s): SilverPlatter Information, Inc. *4776*

EXCERPTA MEDICA. SECTION 13: DERMATOLOGY AND VENEREOLOGY.
Elsevier Science B.V., P.O. Box 211, 1000 AE Amsterdam, Netherlands. TEL 31-20-4853757. FAX 31-20-4853432. Producer(s): SilverPlatter Information, Inc. *4776*

EXCERPTA MEDICA. SECTION 14: RADIOLOGY.
Elsevier Science B.V., P.O. Box 211, 1000 AE Amsterdam, Netherlands. TEL 31-20-4853757. FAX 31-20-4853432. Producer(s): SilverPlatter Information, Inc. *4776*

EXCERPTA MEDICA. SECTION 15: CHEST DISEASES, THORACIC SURGERY AND TUBERCULOSIS.
Elsevier Science B.V., P.O. Box 211, 1000 AE Amsterdam, Netherlands. TEL 31-20-4853757. FAX 31-20-4853432. Producer(s): SilverPlatter Information, Inc. *4776*

EXCERPTA MEDICA. SECTION 16: CANCER.
Elsevier Science B.V., P.O. Box 211, 1000 AE Amsterdam, Netherlands. TEL 31-20-4853757. FAX 31-20-4853432. Producer(s): SilverPlatter Information, Inc. *4776*

EXCERPTA MEDICA. SECTION 17: PUBLIC HEALTH, SOCIAL MEDICINE AND EPIDEMIOLOGY.
Elsevier Science B.V., P.O. Box 211, 1000 AE Amsterdam, Netherlands. TEL 31-20-4853757. FAX 31-20-4853432. Producer(s): SilverPlatter Information, Inc. *6256*

EXCERPTA MEDICA. SECTION 18: CARDIOVASCULAR DISEASES AND CARDIOVASCULAR SURGERY.
Elsevier Science B.V., P.O. Box 211, 1000 AE Amsterdam, Netherlands. TEL 31-20-4853757. FAX 31-20-4853432. Producer(s): SilverPlatter Information, Inc. *4776*

EXCERPTA MEDICA. SECTION 19: REHABILITATION AND PHYSICAL MEDICINE.
Elsevier Science B.V., P.O. Box 211, 1000 AE Amsterdam, Netherlands. TEL 31-20-4853757. FAX 31-20-4853432. Producer(s): SilverPlatter Information, Inc. *4776*

EXCERPTA MEDICA. SECTION 20: GERONTOLOGY AND GERIATRICS.
Elsevier Science B.V., P.O. Box 211, 1000 AE Amsterdam, Netherlands. TEL 31-20-4853757. FAX 31-20-4853432.
Producer(s): SilverPlatter Information, Inc. *3448*

EXCERPTA MEDICA. SECTION 21: DEVELOPMENTAL BIOLOGY AND TERATOLOGY.
Elsevier Science B.V., P.O. Box 211, 1000 AE Amsterdam, Netherlands. TEL 31-20-4853757. FAX 31-20-4853432.
Producer(s): SilverPlatter Information, Inc. *641*

EXCERPTA MEDICA. SECTION 22: HUMAN GENETICS.
Elsevier Science B.V., P.O. Box 211, 1000 AE Amsterdam, Netherlands. TEL 31-20-4853757. FAX 31-20-4853432.
Producer(s): SilverPlatter Information, Inc. *641*

EXCERPTA MEDICA. SECTION 23: NUCLEAR MEDICINE.
Elsevier Science B.V., P.O. Box 211, 1000 AE Amsterdam, Netherlands. TEL 31-20-4853757. FAX 31-20-4853432.
Producer(s): SilverPlatter Information, Inc. *4777*

EXCERPTA MEDICA. SECTION 24: ANESTHESIOLOGY.
Elsevier Science B.V., P.O. Box 211, 1000 AE Amsterdam, Netherlands. TEL 31-20-4853757. FAX 31-20-4853432.
Producer(s): SilverPlatter Information, Inc. *4777*

EXCERPTA MEDICA. SECTION 25: HEMATOLOGY.
Elsevier Science B.V., P.O. Box 211, 1000 AE Amsterdam, Netherlands. TEL 31-20-4853757. FAX 31-20-4853432.
Producer(s): SilverPlatter Information, Inc. *4777*

EXCERPTA MEDICA. SECTION 26: IMMUNOLOGY, SEROLOGY AND TRANSPLANTATION.
Elsevier Science B.V., P.O. Box 211, 1000 AE Amsterdam, Netherlands. TEL 31-20-4853757. FAX 31-20-4853432.
Producer(s): SilverPlatter Information, Inc. *4777*

EXCERPTA MEDICA. SECTION 27: BIOPHYSICS, BIO-ENGINEERING AND MEDICAL INSTRUMENTATION.
Elsevier Science B.V., P.O. Box 211, 1000 AE Amsterdam, Netherlands. TEL 31-20-4853757. FAX 31-20-4853432.
Producer(s): SilverPlatter Information, Inc. *4777*

EXCERPTA MEDICA. SECTION 28: UROLOGY AND NEPHROLOGY.
Elsevier Science B.V., P.O. Box 211, 1000 AE Amsterdam, Netherlands. TEL 31-20-4853757. FAX 31-20-4853432.
Producer(s): SilverPlatter Information, Inc. *4777*

EXCERPTA MEDICA. SECTION 29: CLINICAL AND EXPERIMENTAL BIOCHEMISTRY.
Elsevier Science B.V., P.O. Box 211, 1000 AE Amsterdam, Netherlands. TEL 31-20-4853757. FAX 31-20-4853432.
Producer(s): SilverPlatter Information, Inc. *641*

EXCERPTA MEDICA. SECTION 30: CLINICAL AND EXPERIMENTAL PHARMACOLOGY.
Elsevier Science B.V., P.O. Box 211, 1000 AE Amsterdam, Netherlands. TEL 31-20-4853757. FAX 31-20-4853432.
Producer(s): SilverPlatter Information, Inc. *5701*

EXCERPTA MEDICA. SECTION 31: ARTHRITIS AND RHEUMATISM.
Elsevier Science B.V., P.O. Box 211, 1000 AE Amsterdam, Netherlands. TEL 31-20-4853757. FAX 31-20-4853432.
Producer(s): SilverPlatter Information, Inc. *4777*

EXCERPTA MEDICA. SECTION 32: PSYCHIATRY.
Elsevier Science B.V., P.O. Box 211, 1000 AE Amsterdam, Netherlands. TEL 31-20-4853757. FAX 31-20-4853432.
Producer(s): SilverPlatter Information, Inc. *4777*

EXCERPTA MEDICA. SECTION 33: ORTHOPEDIC SURGERY.
Elsevier Science B.V., P.O. Box 211, 1000 AE Amsterdam, Netherlands. TEL 31-20-4853757. FAX 31-20-4853432.
Producer(s): SilverPlatter Information, Inc. *4778*

EXCERPTA MEDICA. SECTION 35: OCCUPATIONAL HEALTH AND INDUSTRIAL MEDICINE.
Elsevier Science B.V., P.O. Box 211, 1000 AE Amsterdam, Netherlands. TEL 31-20-4853757. FAX 31-20-4853432.
Producer(s): SilverPlatter Information, Inc. *4778*

EXCERPTA MEDICA. SECTION 36: HEALTH POLICY, ECONOMICS AND MANAGEMENT.
Elsevier Science B.V., P.O. Box 211, 1000 AE Amsterdam, Netherlands. TEL 31-20-4853757. FAX 31-20-4853432.
Producer(s): SilverPlatter Information, Inc. *3721*

EXCERPTA MEDICA. SECTION 38: ADVERSE REACTIONS TITLES.
Elsevier Science B.V., P.O. Box 211, 1000 AE Amsterdam, Netherlands. TEL 31-20-4853757. FAX 31-20-4853432.
Producer(s): SilverPlatter Information, Inc. *4778*

EXCERPTA MEDICA. SECTION 40: DRUG DEPENDENCE, ALCOHOL ABUSE AND ALCOHOLISM.
Elsevier Science B.V., P.O. Box 211, 1000 AE Amsterdam, Netherlands. TEL 31-20-4853757. FAX 31-20-4853432.
Producer(s): SilverPlatter Information, Inc. *2307*

EXCERPTA MEDICA. SECTION 46: ENVIRONMENTAL HEALTH AND POLLUTION CONTROL.
Elsevier Science B.V., P.O. Box 211, 1000 AE Amsterdam, Netherlands. TEL 31-20-4853757. FAX 31-20-4853432.
Producer(s): SilverPlatter Information, Inc. *2962*

EXCERPTA MEDICA. SECTION 48: GASTROENTEROLOGY.
Elsevier Science B.V., P.O. Box 211, 1000 AE Amsterdam, Netherlands. TEL 31-20-4853757. FAX 31-20-4853432.
Producer(s): SilverPlatter Information, Inc. *4778*

EXCERPTA MEDICA. SECTION 49: FORENSIC SCIENCE ABSTRACTS.
Elsevier Science B.V., P.O. Box 211, 1000 AE Amsterdam, Netherlands. TEL 31-20-4853757. FAX 31-20-4853432.
Producer(s): SilverPlatter Information, Inc. *4778*

EXCERPTA MEDICA. SECTION 50: EPILEPSY ABSTRACTS.
Elsevier Science B.V., P.O. Box 211, 1000 AE Amsterdam, Netherlands. TEL 31-20-4853757. FAX 31-20-4853432.
Producer(s): SilverPlatter Information, Inc. *4778*

EXCERPTA MEDICA. SECTION 52: TOXICOLOGY.
Elsevier Science B.V., P.O. Box 211, 1000 AE Amsterdam, Netherlands. TEL 31-20-4853757. FAX 31-20-4853432.
Producer(s): SilverPlatter Information, Inc. *2962*

EXECUTIVE SPEECHES.
Executive Speaker Co., Box 292437, Dayton, OH 45429. TEL 937-294-8493. FAX 937-294-6044. *963*

EXEGY.
A B C-Clio, 130 Cremona Dr., Box 1911, Santa Barbara, CA 93116-1911. TEL 805-968-1911. FAX 805-685-5685.
Available only on CD-ROM. *3373*

EXEMPT ORGANIZATION MASTER LIST ON C D - R O M.
Tax Analysts, 6830 N. Fairfax Dr., Arlington, VA 22213. FAX 703-533-4444.
Available only on CD-ROM. *1608*

EXPANSION.
Recoletos Compania Editorial, S.A, Recoletos 1, 5o, 28001 Madrid, Spain. TEL 34-1-3373220. FAX 34-1-3373266.
Producer(s): Chadwyck-Healey Inc. *963*

EXPANSION EN C D - R O M.
Chadwyck-Healey Ltd., The Quorum, Barnwell Rd., Cambridge CB5 8SW, England. TEL 44-1223-215512. FAX 44-1223-215514.
Available only on CD-ROM. Producer(s): Chadwyck-Healey Inc. *963*

L'EXPERT AUTOMOBILE.
Societe d'Edition de l'Expertise Automobile et Materiel Industriel, 19 rue des Filles du Calvaire, 75140 Paris Cedex 03, France. TEL 16-1-42-77-32-50. FAX 16-1-40-27-02-63. *7099*

EXPERTS CONTACT DIRECTORY.
Gale Research, 835 Penobscot Bldg., 645 Griswold St., Detroit, MI 48226-4094. TEL 313-961-2242. FAX 800-41-50433. *1951*

THE EXPLICATOR.
Heldref Publications, 1319 Eighteenth St., N.W., Washington, DC 20036-1802. TEL 202-296-6267. FAX 202-296-5149.
Producer(s): UMI. *4405*

EXPORT SALES AND MARKETING MANUAL (YEAR).
Export USA Publications, 6901 W. 84th St., Ste. 157, Minneapolis, MN 55438. FAX 612-943-1535. *1324*

EXTRAMED.
Informania Limited, P.O. Box 40, Petersfield, Hants. GU32 2YH, England. FAX 44-1730-265398.
Available only on CD-ROM. *4778*

F O G R A LITERATUR DATENBANK.
Forschungsgesellschaft Druck e.V., Postfach 800469, 81604 Munich, Germany. TEL 49-89-431820. FAX 49-89-4316896.
Available only on CD-ROM. *6087*

F R A N C I S. 519: PHILOSOPHIE.
Centre National de la Recherche Scientifique, Institut de l'Information Scientifique et Technique, 2 allee du Parc de Brabois, 54514 Vandoeuvre-les-Nancy Cedex, France. TEL 83-50-46-00. FAX 83-50-46-50. *5760*

F R A N C I S. 520: SCIENCES DE L'EDUCATION.
Centre National de la Recherche Scientifique, Institut de l'Information Scientifique et Technique, 2 allee du Parc de Brabois, 54514 Vandoeuvre-les-Nancy Cedex, France. TEL 83-50-46-00. FAX 83-50-46-50. *2500*

F R A N C I S. 521: SOCIOLOGIE.
Centre National de la Recherche Scientifique, Institut de l'Information Scientifique et Technique, 2 allee du Parc de Brabois, 54514 Vandoeuvre-les-Nancy Cedex, France. TEL 83-50-46-00. FAX 83-50-46-50. *6739*

F R A N C I S. 522: HISTOIRE DES SCIENCES ET DE TECHNIQUES.
Centre National de la Recherche Scientifique, Institut de l'Information Scientifique et Technique, 2 allee du Parc de Brabois, 54514 Vandoeuvre-les-Nancy Cedex, France. TEL 83-50-46-00. FAX 83-50-46-50. *3520*

F R A N C I S. 523: HISTOIRE ET SCIENCES DE LA LITTERATURE.
Centre National de la Recherche Scientifique, Institut de l'Information Scientifique et Technique, 2 allee du Parc de Brabois, 54514 Vandoeuvre-les-Nancy Cedex, France. TEL 83-50-46-00. FAX 83-50-46-50. *4495*

F R A N C I S. 524: SCIENCES DU LANGAGE.
Centre National de la Recherche Scientifique, Institut de l'Information Scientifique et Technique, 2 allee du Parc de Brabois, 54514 Vandoeuvre-les-Nancy Cedex, France. TEL 83-50-46-00. FAX 83-50-46-50. *4318*

F R A N C I S. 525: PREHISTOIRE ET PROTOHISTOIRE.
Centre National de la Recherche Scientifique, Institut de l'Information Scientifique et Technique, 2 allee du Parc de Brabois, 54514 Vandoeuvre-les-Nancy Cedex, France. TEL 83-50-46-00. FAX 83-50-46-50. *390*

F R A N C I S. 526: ART ET ARCHEOLOGIE.
Centre National de la Recherche Scientifique, Institut de l'Information Scientifique et Technique, 2 allee du Parc de Brabois, 54514 Vandoeuvre-les-Nancy Cedex, France. TEL 83-50-46-00. FAX 83-50-46-50. *476*

SERIALS AVAILABLE ON CD-ROM

F R A N C I S. 527: HISTOIRE ET SCIENCES DES RELIGIONS.
Centre National de la Recherche Scientifique, Institut de l'Information Scientifique et Technique, 2 allee du Parc de Brabois, 54514 Vandoeuvre-les-Nancy Cedex, France. TEL 83-50-46-00. FAX 83-50-46-50. *6386*

F R A N C I S. 528: BIBLIOGRAPHIE INTERNATIONALE DE SCIENCE ADMINISTRATIVE.
Centre National de la Recherche Scientifique, Institut de l'Information Scientifique et Technique, 2 allee du Parc de Brabois, 54514 Vandoeuvre-les-Nancy Cedex, France. TEL 83-50-46-00. FAX 83-50-46-50. *1038*

F R A N C I S. 529: ETHNOLOGIE.
Centre National de la Recherche Scientifique, Institut de l'Information Scientifique et Technique, 2 allee du Parc de Brabois, 54514 Vandoeuvre-les-Nancy Cedex, France. TEL 83-50-46-00. FAX 83-50-46-50. *335*

F R A N C I S. 603: INFORMATIQUE ET SCIENCES JURIDIQUES.
Centre National de la Recherche Scientifique, Institut de l'Information Scientifique et Technique, 2 allee du Parc de Brabois, 54514 Vandoeuvre-les-Nancy Cedex, France. TEL 83-50-46-00. FAX 83-50-46-50. *4068*

F R A N C I S. 617: E C O D O C.
Centre National de la Recherche Scientifique, Institut de l'Information Scientifique et Technique, 2 allee du Parc de Brabois, 54514 Vandoeuvre-les-Nancy Cedex, France. TEL 83-50-46-00. FAX 83-50-46-50. *1038*

FACTS ON FILE WORLD NEWS DIGEST WITH INDEX.
Facts on File, Inc., 11 Penn Plza, 15th Fl., New York, NY 10001. TEL 212-967-8800. *3494*

FAIRPLAY MARINE COMPUTING GUIDE.
Fairplay Publications Ltd., P.O. Box 96, Coulsdon, Surrey CR5 2TE, England. TEL 44-181-645-2800. FAX 44-181-660-2824. *7149*

FAM R VOLLTEXT C D - R O M.
Verlag C.H. Beck, 80791 Munich, Germany. TEL 49-89-38189338. FAX 49-89-38189398. Available only on CD-ROM. *4100*

FAMILY PRACTICE RECERTIFICATION.
M R A Publications, Inc., 2 Greenwich Office Park, Greenwich, CT 06831-5154. TEL 203-629-3550. FAX 203-629-2536. *4667*

FAMILY PROCESS.
Family Process, Inc., Box 460, Vernon, NJ 07462-0460. TEL 201-612-9868. FAX 201-764-7448. Producer(s): UMI. *6112*

FAMILY RELATIONS.
National Council on Family Relations, 3989 Central Ave., N.E., Ste. 550, Minneapolis, MN 55421-3921. TEL 612-781-9331. FAX 612-781-9348. Producer(s): NISC. *6710*

FAMILY STUDIES DATABASE.
National Information Services Corporation (NISC), Ste. 6, Wyman Towers, 3100 St. Paul St., Baltimore, MD 21218. TEL 410-243-0797. FAX 410-243-0982. Available only on CD-ROM. Producer(s): NISC. *4627*

FAMILY THERAPY.
Libra Publishers, Inc., 3089C Clairemont Dr., Ste. 383, San Diego, CA 92117. TEL 619-571-1414. *5065*

FARM CHEMICALS HANDBOOK.
Meister Publishing Co., 37733 Euclid Ave., Willoughby, OH 44094. TEL 216-942-2000. FAX 216-942-0662. *223*

FAULKNER'S ENTERPRISE NETWORKING.
Faulkner Information Services, Inc., 114 Cooper Center, 7905 Browning Rd., Pennsauken, NJ 08109-4319. TEL 609-662-2070. FAX 609-662-3380. *2170*

FAULKNER'S LOCAL AREA NETWORKING.
Faulkner Information Services, Inc., 114 Cooper Center, 7905 Browning Rd., Pennsauken, NJ 08109-4319. TEL 609-662-2070. FAX 609-662-3380. *2188*

FAULKNER'S MICROCOMPUTERS AND SOFTWARE.
Faulkner Information Services, Inc., 114 Cooper Center, 7905 Browning Rd., Pennsauken, NJ 08109-4319. TEL 609-662-2070. FAX 609-662-3380. *2188*

FAULKNER'S TELECOMMUNICATIONS WORLD.
Faulkner Information Services, Inc., 114 Cooper Center, 7905 Browning Rd., Pennsauken, NJ 08109-4319. TEL 609-662-2070. FAX 609-662-3380. *2034*

FEDERAL ACQUISITION REGULATION (WASHINGTON).
U.S. General Services Administration, G S A Bldg., 18th and F Sts., N.W., Washington, DC 20405. *6173*

FEDERAL BANKING LAW REPORTS.
C C H Incorporated, 2700 Lake Cook Rd., Riverwoods, IL 60015. TEL 847-267-7000. FAX 800-224-8299. *1132*

FEDERAL CRIMINAL CODE AND RULES.
West Group, 620 Opperman Dr., Eagan, MN 55123. TEL 612-687-7000. FAX 612-687-7302. *4090*

FEDERAL ESTATE AND GIFT TAX REPORTS.
C C H Incorporated, 2700 Lake Cook Rd., Riverwoods, IL 60015. TEL 847-267-7000. FAX 800-224-8299. *4097*

FEDERAL EXCISE TAX REPORTS.
C C H Incorporated, 2700 Lake Cook Rd., Riverwoods, IL 60015. TEL 847-267-7000. FAX 800-224-8299. *1608*

FEDERAL LABOR LAWS.
West Group, 620 Opperman Dr., Eagan, MN 55123. TEL 612-687-7000. FAX 612-687-7602. *3949*

FEDERAL REGIONAL YELLOW BOOK.
Leadership Directories, Inc., 104 Fifth Ave., 2nd Fl., New York, NY 10011. TEL 212-627-4140. FAX 212-645-0931. Producer(s): Chadwyck-Healey Inc. *6174*

FEDERAL REGISTER.
U.S. Office of the Federal Register, National Archives and Records Administration, Washington, DC 20408. TEL 202-523-5230. *6174*

FEDERAL SECURITIES LAW REPORTS.
C C H Incorporated, 2700 Lake Cook Rd., Riverwoods, IL 60015. TEL 312-583-8500. *3950*

FEDERAL SENTENCING GUIDELINES MANUAL.
West Group, 620 Opperman Dr., Eagan, MN 55123. TEL 612-687-8000. FAX 612-687-7302. *4090*

FEDERAL SOCIAL SECURITY LAWS.
West Group, 620 Opperman Dr., Eagan, MN 55123. TEL 612-687-7000. FAX 612-687-7302. *3815*

FEDERAL STAFF DIRECTORY.
CC Q Staff Directories Inc., 815 Slaters Lane, Alexandria, VA 22314. TEL 703-739-0900. FAX 703-739-0234. *6174*

FEDERAL TAX COORDINATOR 2D.
Research Institute of America, Inc., 90 Fifth Ave., New York, NY 10011. TEL 212-645-4800. FAX 212-337-4279. *1608*

FEDERAL TAX GUIDE REPORTS.
C C H Incorporated, 2700 Lake Cook Rd., Riverwoods, IL 60015. TEL 847-267-7000. FAX 800-224-8299. *1609*

FEDERAL TECHNOLOGY REPORT.
McGraw-Hill Companies, Energy & Business Newsletters, 1221 Ave. of the Americas, 36th Fl., New York, NY 10020. TEL 212-512-6410. Producer(s): SilverPlatter Information, Inc. (McGraw-Hill Energy Library). *2669*

FEDERAL YELLOW BOOK.
Leadership Directories, Inc., 104 Fifth Ave., 2nd Fl., Ste. 1000, New York, NY 10011. TEL 212-627-4140. FAX 212-645-0931. Producer(s): Chadwyck-Healey Inc. *6174*

FERROELECTRICS.
Gordon and Breach - Harwood Academic, Amsteldisk 166, 1st Fl., 1079 LH Amsterdam, Netherlands. *5802*

FERROELECTRICS LETTERS.
Gordon and Breach - Harwood Academic, Amsteldisk 166, 1st Fl., 1079 LH Amsterdam, Netherlands. *2824*

FERTILITY AND STERILITY.
American Society for Reproductive Medicine, 1209 Montgomery Hwy., Birmingham, AL 35216-2809. TEL 205-978-5000. FAX 205-978-5005. *4957*

FILM & VIDEO FINDER.
Plexus Publishing, Inc., 143 Old Marlton Pike, Medford, NJ 08055-8750. TEL 609-654-4888. FAX 609-654-4309. Producer(s): SilverPlatter Information, Inc. *2500*

FILM COMMENT.
Film Society of Lincoln Center, 70 Lincoln Center Plaza, New York, NY 10023-6595. TEL 212-875-5610. FAX 212-875-5636. Producer(s): UMI. *5332*

FILM INDEX INTERNATIONAL.
Chadwyck-Healey Ltd., The Quorum, Barnwell Rd., Cambridge CB5 8SW, England. TEL 44-1223-215512. FAX 44-1223-215514. Available only on CD-ROM. Producer(s): Chadwyck-Healey Inc. *5332*

FILMSTRIP AND SLIDE SET FINDER.
Plexus Publishing, Inc., 143 Old Marlton Pike, Medford, NJ 08055-8750. TEL 609-654-6500. FAX 609-654-4309. *2500*

FINANCIAL STATISTICS OF MAJOR INVESTOR-OWNED ELECTRIC UTILITIES (YEAR).
U.S. Energy Information Administration, National Energy Information Center, EI-231, James Forrestal Bldg., Rm. 1F-048, 1000 Independence Ave., S.W., Washington, DC 20585. TEL 202-586-8800. FAX 202-5586-0727. *2684*

FINANCIAL STATISTICS OF MAJOR PUBLICLY OWNED ELECTRIC UTILITIES (YEAR).
U.S. Energy Information Administration, National Energy Information Center, EI-231, James Forrestal Bldg., Rm. 1F-048, 1000 Independence Ave., S.W., Washington, DC 20585. TEL 202-586-8800. FAX 202-586-0727. *2684*

FINANCIAL TIMES (FRANKFURT EDITION).
Financial Times (Europe) GmbH, Nibelungenplatz 3, 60318 Frankfurt a.M., Germany. TEL 069-156850. FAX 069-5964481. Producer(s): Chadwyck-Healey Inc. *1136*

FINANCIAL TIMES (LONDON, 1888).
Financial Times, One Southwark Bridge, London SE1 9HL, England. TEL 44-171-873-3514. FAX 44-171-263-9764. Producer(s): Chadwyck-Healey Inc. *1136*

FINANCIAL TIMES (NORTH AMERICAN EDITION).
F T Publications Inc., 14 E. 60th St., New York, NY 10022. TEL 212-752-7400. FAX 212-319-0704. Producer(s): Chadwyck-Healey Inc. *1136*

FINANCIAL TIMES ON C D - R O M.
Chadwyck-Healey Ltd., The Quorum, Barnwell Rd., Cambridge CB5 8SW, England. TEL 44-1223-215512. FAX 44-1223-215514. Available only on CD-ROM. Producer(s): Chadwyck-Healey Inc. *1136*

FINANCIAL YELLOW BOOK.
Leadership Directories, Inc., 104 Fifth Ave., 2nd Fl., New York, NY 10011. TEL 212-627-4140. FAX 212-645-0931. Producer(s): Chadwyck-Healey Inc. *1478*

DE FINANCIEEL ECONOMISCHE TIJD.
Uitgeversbedrijf Tijd n.v., Franklin Building, Posthoflei 3, 2600 Berchem (Antwerp), Belgium. TEL 32-3-2860211. FAX 32-3-2860310. *964*

EL FINANCIERO INTERNATIONAL EDITION.
El Financiero International, Inc., Lago Bolsena 176, Col. Anahuac, 11320 Mexico DF, Mexico. TEL 525-227-7600. FAX 525-227-7634. *1137*

FINDEX (YEAR).
Euromonitor, 60-61 Britton St., London EC1M 5NA, England. TEL 44-171-251-8024. FAX 44-171-608-3149.
Producer(s): SilverPlatter Information, Inc. *1039*

FIRMEN DER NEUEN BUNDESLAENDER.
Verlag Hoppenstedt GmbH, Havelstr. 9, 64295 Darmstadt, Germany. TEL 49-6151-380-0. FAX 49-6151-380-360. *1584*

FIRMENBUCH OESTERREICH.
Jupiter Verlag GmbH, Robertgasse 2, A-1020 Vienna, Austria. *1680*

FIRMENHANDBUCH CHEMISCHE INDUSTRIE. BUNDESREPUBLIK DEUTSCHLAND.
E C O N Verlag GmbH, Postfach 300321, 40403 Duesseldorf, Germany. TEL 49-211-4359746. FAX 49-211-4359781. *1680*

FIRST MONDAY.
Munksgaard International Publishers Ltd., Noerre Soegade 35, P.O. Box 2148, DK-1016 Copenhagen, Denmark. TEL 45-33-127030. *2133*

FISH & FISHERIES WORLDWIDE.
National Information Services Corporation (NISC), 3100 St. Paul St. Ste. 806, Baltimore, MD 21218. TEL 410-243-0797. FAX 410-243-0982. Available only on CD-ROM. Producer(s): NISC. *3082*

FISHERIES REVIEW.
U.S. National Biological Service, Information Transfer Center, 1201 Oak Ridge Dr., Ste. 200, Ft. Collins, CO 80525-5589. TEL 303-226-9401.
Producer(s): NISC (Fish & Fisheries Worldwide). *3082*

FLASH MAGAZINE.
BlackLightning Publishing, Inc., Riddle Pond Rd., West Topsham, VT 05086. TEL 802-439-6462. FAX 802-439-6463. *6088*

FLORIDA BUSINESS DIRECTORY.
American Business Directories, 5711 S. 86th Circle, Box 27347, Omaha, NE 68127. TEL 402-593-4600. FAX 402-331-5481. *1680*

FLUID POWER STANDARDS.
National Fluid Power Association, 3333 N. Mayfair Rd., Milwaukee, WI 53222. TEL 414-778-3363. FAX 414-778-3361. *2884*

FOCUS ON EXCEPTIONAL CHILDREN.
Love Publishing Co., Box 22353, Denver, CO 80222. TEL 303-757-2579. FAX 303-782-5683. *2584*

FOOD CHEMICAL NEWS GUIDE.
Food Chemical News, Inc., 1101 Pennsylvania Ave., S.E., Washington, DC 20003. TEL 202-544-1980. FAX 202-546-3890. *3105*

FOOD SCIENCE AND TECHNOLOGY ABSTRACTS.
International Food Information Service (I F I S Publishing), Lane End House, Shinfield, Reading, Berks. RG2 9BB, England. TEL 01734-883895. FAX 01734-885065.
Producer(s): SilverPlatter Information, Inc. (COMPU-INFO). *3132*

FOREIGN AFFAIRS.
Council on Foreign Relations, Inc., 58 E. 68th St., New York, NY 10021. TEL 212-734-0400.
Producer(s): UMI. *6014*

FOREIGN POLICY (WASHINGTON).
Carnegie Endowment for International Peace, 2400 N St., N.W., Ste. 700, Washington, DC 20037. TEL 202-862-7940. FAX 202-463-7914. *6015*

FOREIGN REPORT (PRINT).
Economist Newspaper, 25 St. James' St., London SW1A 1HG, England. TEL 071-839-7000. FAX 071-839-2968. *5927*

FORLAGSSERIEKATALOG FOR BOERNE- OG SKOLEBIBLIOTEKER.
Dansk BiblioteksCenter as, Tempovej 7-11, DK-2750 Ballerup, Denmark. TEL 45-44-867777. FAX 45-44-867892. *2500*

FORO ITALIANO.
Zanichelli Editore S.p.A., Via Irnerio, 34, 40126 Bologna, Italy. TEL 39-51-293111. FAX 39-51-249782. *3953*

FORTHCOMING BOOKS.
R.R. Bowker, A Division of Reed Elsevier Inc., 121 Chanlon Rd., New Providence, NJ 07974. TEL 908-464-6800. FAX 908-665-3502.
Producer(s): Bowker Electronic Publishing (Books in Print PLUS). *547*

FORTUNE MAGAZINE.
Time Inc., Time & Life Bldg., Rockefeller Center, New York, NY 10020-1393. TEL 212-522-1212. *1479*

FOXTALK.
Pinnacle Publishing, Inc., Box 888, Kent, WA 98035-0888. TEL 206-251-1900. FAX 206-251-5057. *2143*

FRASER FORUM.
Fraser Institute, 626 Bute St., Vancouver, BC V6E 3M1, Canada. TEL 604-688-0221. FAX 604-388-8539. *1261*

FREE RADICAL RESEARCH.
Gordon and Breach - Harwood Academic, Amsteldisk 166, 1st Fl., 1079 LH Amsterdam, Netherlands. *660*

FRONTIERS IN NETWORKING.
Academic Press, Inc, Journal Division, 525 B St., Ste. 1900, San Diego, CA 92101-4495. TEL 619-230-1840.
Available only on CD-ROM. *2133*

FUJIAN LINXUEYUAN XUEBAO.
Fujian Linxueyuan, Xiqin, Nanping, Fujian 353001, People's Republic of China. TEL 86-599-8508080. FAX 86-599-8508194. *3154*

FUJIAN ZHONGYI YAO.
Fujian Zhongyi Xueyuan, 282 Wusi Lu, Fuzhou, Fujian 350003, People's Republic of China. TEL 0591-7841296. FAX 0591-7842524. *295*

G I CANCER.
Gordon and Breach - Harwood Academic, Amsteldisk 166, 1st Fl., 1079 LH Amsterdam, Netherlands. *4978*

G I S EUROPE.
GeoInformation International, 307 Cambridge Science Pk., Milton Rd., Cambridge CB4 4ZD, England. TEL 44-1223-423020. FAX 44-1223-425787. *3429*

G K E.
Josef Keller Verlag, Postfach 1455, 82317 Starnberg, Germany. TEL 49-8151-771144. FAX 49-8151-771152.
Available only on CD-ROM. *5394*

G S A TODAY.
Geological Society of America, 3300 Penrose Pl., Box 9140, Boulder, CO 80301. TEL 303-447-2020. FAX 303-447-1133. *2340*

GALE'S LITERARY INDEX C D - R O M.
Gale Research, 835 Penobscot Bldg., 645 Griswold St., Detroit, MI 48226-4094. TEL 313-961-2242. FAX 800-414-5043. *4408*

GAS & LIQUID CHROMATOGRAPHY LITERATURE - ABSTRACTS & INDEX.
Preston Publications, Inc., Box 48312, Niles, IL 60714. TEL 847-965-0566. FAX 847-965-7639. *1784*

GAZETTE.
250 rue St-Antoine O., Montreal, PQ H2Y 3R7, Canada. *3261*

GEEKGIRL.
P.O. Box 759, Newtown, N.S.W. 2042, Australia. *7321*

GEFAHRGUT - DANGEROUS GOODS C D - R O M.
Springer-Verlag, Heidelberger Platz 3, 14197 Berlin, Germany. TEL 49-30-82787-0. FAX 49-30-82787448.
Available only on CD-ROM. *7068*

GENBANK.
U.S. National Library of Medicine, U.S. National Center for Biotechnology Information, Bldg. 38A, Rm. 8N-803, Bldg. 38A, Rm. 8N-803, 8600 Rockville Pike, Bethesda, MD 20894. TEL 301-496-2475. FAX 301-480-2233. *735*

GENERAL LAWS OF MASSACHUSETTS. OFFICIAL EDITION (YEAR).
West Group, 620 Opperman Dr., Eagan, MN 55123. TEL 612-687-8000. FAX 612-687-7302. *4132*

GENERAL SCIENCE INDEX.
H.W. Wilson Co., 950 University Ave., Bronx, NY 10452. TEL 718-588-8400. FAX 718-590-1617.
Producer(s): SilverPlatter Information, Inc., H.W. Wilson (WILSONDISC). *6589*

GENETIC, SOCIAL, AND GENERAL PSYCHOLOGY MONOGRAPHS.
Heldref Publications, 1319 Eighteenth St., N.W., Washington, DC 20036-1802. TEL 202-296-6267. FAX 202-296-5149.
Producer(s): UMI. *6113*

GENETICS ABSTRACTS.
Cambridge Scientific Abstracts, 7200 Wisconsin Ave., 6th Fl., Bethesda, MD 20814. TEL 301-961-6750. FAX 301-961-6720.
Producer(s): SilverPlatter Information, Inc. *641*

GEO KATALÓG (YEAR). VOLUME 1. TOURISTISCHE VEROEFFENTLICHUNGEN.
GeoCenter Verlagsvertrieb GmbH, Neumarkterstr. 18, 81673 Munich, Germany. TEL 49-89-43189-0. FAX 49-89-43189555. *3403*

THE GEOGRAPHICAL JOURNAL.
Royal Geographical Society, 1 Kensington Gore, London SW7 2AR, England. TEL 44-171-589-5466. FAX 44-171-584-4447.
Producer(s): UMI. *3405*

GEOGRAPHICAL SYSTEMS.
Gordon and Breach - Harwood Academic, Amsteldisk 166, 1st Fl., 1079 LH Amsterdam, Netherlands. *3406*

GEOLOGICAL SOCIETY OF AMERICA. BULLETIN.
Geological Society of America, 3300 Penrose Pl., Box 9140, Boulder, CO 80301. TEL 303-447-2020. FAX 303-447-1133. *2343*

GEOLOGY (BOULDER).
Geological Society of America, 3300 Penrose Pl., Box 9140, Boulder, CO 80301. TEL 303-447-2020. FAX 303-447-1133. *2347*

GEOPHYSICAL AND ASTROPHYSICAL FLUID DYNAMICS.
Gordon and Breach - Harwood Academic, Amsteldisk 166, 1st Fl., 1079 LH Amsterdam, Netherlands. *2382*

GEOPHYSICS.
Society of Exploration Geophysicists, Box 702740, Tulsa, OK 74170-2740. TEL 918-493-3516. *2383*

GEORGIA ADVANCE SHEETS.
Darby Printing Co. (Atlanta), 6215 Purdue Dr., S.W., Atlanta, GA 30336-2827. TEL 404-344-2665. FAX 404-346-3332. *3955*

GEORGIA BUSINESS DIRECTORY.
American Business Directories, 5711 S. 86th Circle, Box 27347, Omaha, NE 68127. TEL 402-593-4600. FAX 402-331-5481. *1682*

GEORGIA COURT RULES AND PROCEDURE, STATE AND FEDERAL.
West Group, 620 Opperman Dr., Eagan, MN 55123. TEL 612-687-8000. FAX 612-687-7602. *4132*

GEOSCIENCE DOCUMENTATION.
Geosystems, P.O. Box 40, Didcot, Oxon. OX11 9BX, England. TEL 44-1235-813913.
Producer(s): NISC (Geosearch). *2325*

GEOSEARCH.
National Information Services Corporation (NISC), 3100 St. Paul St., Ste. 806, Baltimore, MD 21218. TEL 410-243-0797. FAX 410-243-0982.
Available only on CD-ROM. Producer(s): NISC. *2325*

SERIALS AVAILABLE ON CD-ROM

GEOSOURCES.
Geosystems, P.O. Box 40, Didcot, Oxon. OX11 9BS, England. TEL 44-1385-813913.
Producer(s): NISC (Geosearch). *2325*

GEOTECHNICAL ABSTRACTS.
Research Resources, Inc., Geotext Services, 8819 Sundale Dr., Silver Spring, MD 20910. TEL 301-589-2070. FAX 301-589-4129. *2750*

GEOTITLES.
Geosystems, P.O. Box 40, Didcot, Oxon. OX11 9BX, England. TEL 44-1235-813913.
Producer(s): NISC (Geosearch). *2326*

GERMAN AND EAST EUROPEAN BOOKS IN PRINT.
Buchhaendler-Vereinigung GmbH, Postfach 100442, 60004 Frankfurt a.M., Germany. TEL 49-69-1306-0. FAX 49-69-1306201.
Available only on CD-ROM. *548*

GERMAN BOOKS OUT OF PRINT ON C D - R O M.
K.G. Saur Verlag KG, A member of the Reed Elsevier plc group, Ortlerstr. 8, 81373 Munich, Germany. TEL 49-89-76902-0. FAX 49-89-76901250.
Available only on CD-ROM. *548*

GERMANIC REVIEW.
Heldref Publications, 1319 Eighteenth St., N.W., Washington, DC 20036-1802. TEL 202-296-6267. FAX 202-296-5149.
Producer(s): UMI. *4260*

GEWERBLICHER RECHTSSCHUTZ UND URHEBERRECHT.
Wiley - V C H, Postfach 101161, 69451 Weinheim, Germany. TEL 49-6201-606147. FAX 49-6201-606117. *5584*

GEWERBLICHER RECHTSSCHUTZ UND URHEBERRECHT. INTERNATIONALER TEIL.
Wiley - V C H, Postfach 101161, 69451 Weinheim, Germany. TEL 49-6201-606147. FAX 49-6201-606117. *5584*

DIE GIESSEREI-INDUSTRIE UND IHRE HELFER.
Industrieschau-Verlagsgesellschaft mbH, Postfach 100262, 64202 Darmstadt, Germany. TEL 49-6151-38920. FAX 49-6151-33164. *5192*

GIFTED EDUCATION REVIEW.
Peak Educational Resources, Inc., Box 2278, Evergreen, CO 80437-2278. TEL 303-670-8350. *2584*

GINECOLOGIA Y OBSTETRICIA DE MEXICO.
Asociacion Mexicana de Ginecologia y Obstetricia, Ave. Amsterdam 214-PH2, Col. Hipodromo, Deleg. Cuauhtemoc, 06100 Mexico D.F., Mexico. TEL 5645463. FAX 2641745. *4957*

GIORNALE DI BARGA.
Casella Postale No. 33, Lucca 55051, Italy.
TEL 39-583-73003. FAX 39-583-723003. *3326*

GIURISPRUDENZA ITALIANA.
Unione Tipografico Editrice Torinese, Corso Raffaello 28, 10125 Turin, Italy. TEL 39-11-65291. FAX 39-11-6529394. *3956*

GLOBAL COMPANY HANDBOOK.
C I F A R Publications, Inc., 3490 US Hwy 1, BL012, Princeton, NJ 08540-5920. TEL 609-520-9333. FAX 609-520-0905. *1328*

THE GLOBE AND MAIL.
Globe and Mail Publishing, 444 Front St., W., Toronto, ON M5V 2S9, Canada. TEL 416-585-5000. FAX 416-585-5085. *3262*

GNOMON.
Verlag C.H. Beck, 80791 Munich, Germany.
TEL 49-89-38189-338. FAX 49-89-38189-398. *1903*

GONGNENG GAOFENZI XUEBAO.
Gongneng Gaofenzi Xuebao Bianjibu, 130 Meilong Rd., Shanghai 200237, People's Republic of China. TEL 86-21-6413-2666. FAX 86-21-6477-7138. *2764*

GONGYE SHUI CHULI.
Tianjin Huagong Yanjiuyuan, Sanhao Lu, Dingzigu, Hongqiao-qu, Tianjin 300131, People's Republic of China. TEL 86-22-2651-2112. FAX 86-22-2651-2112. *2968*

GORDON'S (YEAR) INTERNATIONAL PHOTOGRAPHY PRICE ANNUAL.
Gordon's Art Reference, Inc., 306 W. Coronado Rd., Phoenix, AZ 85003-1147. TEL 941-434-6842. FAX 941-434-6969. *5766*

GORDON'S PRINT PRICE ANNUAL (YEAR).
Gordon's Art Reference, Inc., 306 W. Coronado Rd., Phoenix, AZ 85003-1147. TEL 941-434-6842. FAX 941-434-6969. *443*

GOVERNMENT AFFAIRS YELLOW BOOK.
Leadership Directories, Inc., 104 Fifth Ave., 2nd Fl., New York, NY 10011. TEL 212-627-4140. FAX 212-645-0931.
Producer(s): Chadwyck-Healey Inc. *6175*

GOVERNMENT COMPUTER NEWS.
Cahners Publishing Company (Silver Spring), Division of Reed Elsevier Inc., 8601 Georgia Ave., Ste. 300, Silver Spring, MD 20910. TEL 301-650-2176. FAX 301-650-2111. *6209*

GOVERNMENT CONTRACTOR.
Federal Publications Inc., 1120 20th St., N.W., Ste. 500 S., Washington, DC 20036-3483. TEL 202-337-7000. FAX 202-659-2233. *3956*

GOVERNMENT CONTRACTS REPORTS.
C C H Incorporated, 2700 Lake Cook Rd., Riverwoods, IL 60015. TEL 847-267-7000. FAX 800-224-8299. *3956*

GRADUATE MEDICAL EDUCATION DIRECTORY (YEARS).
American Medical Association, 515 N. State St., Chicago, IL 60610. TEL 312-464-5000. FAX 312-464-5600. *2542*

THE GRAMOPHONE CLASSICAL CATALOGUE.
Retail Establishment Data Publishing Ltd., Paulton House, 8 Shepherdess Walk, London N1 7LR, England. TEL 0171-490-0049. FAX 0171-253-1308. *5396*

THE GRAMOPHONE CLASSICAL GOOD C D GUIDE.
Gramophone Publications Ltd., 177-179 Kenton Rd., Harrow, Mddx. HA3 0HA, England. TEL 44-181-907-4476. FAX 44-181-907-0073. *5396*

GRAVITY (YEAR).
U.S. National Geophysical Data Center, 325 Broadway, Boulder, CO 80303-3328. TEL 303-497-6836. FAX 303-497-6513.
Available only on CD-ROM. *2383*

GREAT BRITAIN. HOUSE OF COMMONS. PARLIAMENTARY DEBATES.
H.M.S.O., 51 Nine Elms Ln., London SW8 5DR, England. TEL 44-171-873-0011. FAX 44-171-873-8247.
Producer(s): Chadwyck-Healey Inc. *5930*

GREAT BRITAIN. HOUSE OF COMMONS. PARLIAMENTARY DEBATES (C D - R O M EDITION).
Chadwyck-Healey Ltd., The Quorum, Barnwell Rd., Cambridge CB5 8SW, England. TEL 44-1223-215512. FAX 44-1223-215514.
Available only on CD-ROM. Producer(s): Chadwyck-Healey Inc. *5930*

GREAT BRITAIN. HOUSE OF LORDS. PARLIAMENTARY DEBATES.
H.M.S.O., P.O. Box 276, London SW8 5DT, England. TEL 44-171-873-0011. FAX 44-171-873-8463.
Producer(s): Chadwyck-Healey Inc. *5930*

GREAT BRITAIN. HOUSE OF LORDS. PARLIAMENTARY DEBATES (C D - R O M EDITION).
Chadwyck-Healey Ltd., The Quorum, Barnwell Rd., Cambridge CB5 8SW, England. TEL 44-1223-215512. FAX 44-1223-215514.
Available only on CD-ROM. Producer(s): Chadwyck-Healey Inc. *5930*

GREAT BRITAIN. NATURAL RESOURCES INSTITUTE. BULLETIN.
Natural Resources Institute, Central Ave., Chatham Maritime, Kent ME4 4TB, England. TEL 44-1634-880088. FAX 44-1634-880066. *121*

GREEK ORTHODOX THEOLOGICAL REVIEW.
Holy Cross Orthodox Press, 50 Goddard Ave., Brookline, MA 02146. TEL 617-731-3500. FAX 617-566-9075.
Producer(s): UMI. *6391*

GREEN PAGES.
Geraldine Flower Publications, 192 Acton Ln., London W4 5DL, England. TEL 0181-747-8028. FAX 0181-747-8054. *195*

DAS GROSSE EINKAUFS 1X1 DER DEUTSCHEN WIRTSCHAFT.
Deutscher Adressbuch Verlag, Arheilger Weg 17, 64380 Rossdorf, Germany. TEL 49-6154-69950-0. FAX 49-6154-6995490. *1683*

GROWTH FACTORS.
Gordon and Breach - Harwood Academic, Amsteldisk 166, 1st Fl., 1079 LH Amsterdam, Netherlands. *816*

THE GUARDIAN (MANCHESTER).
Guardian Newspapers Ltd., 164 Deansgate, Manchester M60 2RR, England. TEL 44-161-832-7200. FAX 44-161-876-5362.
Producer(s): Chadwyck-Healey Inc. *3297*

THE GUARDIAN ON C D - R O M.
Chadwyck-Healey Ltd., The Quorum, Barnwell Rd., Cambridge CB5 8SW, England. TEL 44-1223-215512. FAX 44-1223-215514.
Available only on CD-ROM. Producer(s): Chadwyck-Healey Inc. *3297*

GUIDA ALLE APPLICAZIONI MACINTOSH.
Gruppo Editoriale J C E, Via Ferri 6, 20092 Cinisello Balsmao (MI), Italy. TEL 39-2-660251. FAX 39-2-6127620. *2188*

GUIDA DELLE REGIONI D'ITALIA.
SEAT, Via Saffi 18, 10138 Turin, Italy. TEL 39-6-855691. FAX 39-6-85569817. *1683*

GUIDE DE L'EAU.
Pierre Johanet et ses Fils, 30 rue Rene Boulanger, 75010 Paris, France. TEL 33-1-42400008. FAX 33-1-42402646. *7294*

GUIDE TO NEW AUSTRALIAN BOOKS.
D.W. Thorpe, A member of the Reed Elsevier plc group, 18 Salmon St., Port Melbourne, Vic. 3207, Australia. TEL 61-3-92457370. FAX 61-3-92457395. *549*

GUIDELINES.
Bibliographic Services, P.O. Box 961, Mount Waverley, Vic. 3149, Australia. *4225*

H C F A'S LAWS, REGULATIONS, AND MANUALS (C D - R O M).
U.S. Health Care Financing Administration, Department of Health and Human Services, C-3-11-07, 7500 Security Blvd., Baltimore, MD 21244. TEL 410-786-6572. FAX 410-786-5768.
Available only on CD-ROM. *3708*

H I C.
Health Informatics Society of Australia, 413 Lygon St., Brunswick East, Vic. 3057, Australia. TEL 61-3-93880555. FAX 61-3-93882086. *4846*

H T F S DIGEST.
A.E.A. Technology, Harwell Bldg. 392.7, Didcot, Oxon OX11 0RA, England. TEL 44-1235-432908. FAX 44-1235-831981. *2764*

H V A C & R RESEARCH.
American Society of Heating, Refrigerating and Air-Conditioning Engineers, Inc., 1791 Tullie Circle, N.E., Atlanta, GA 30329. TEL 404-636-8400. FAX 404-321-5478. *3479*

HAMDARD ISLAMICUS.
Hamdard Foundation, Nazimabad No. 3, Karachi 74600, Pakistan. TEL 92-21-6616001. FAX 92-21-6611755. *6396*

HAMDARD MEDICUS.
Hamdard Foundation, Nazimabad No. 3, Karachi 74600, Pakistan. TEL 92-21-6616001. FAX 92-21-6611755. *4674*

HANDBOEK VAN DE NEDERLANDSE PERS EN PUBLICITEIT.
Nijgh Periodieken B.V., Postbus 122, 3100 AC Schiedam, Netherlands. TEL 31-10-4274100. FAX 31-10-4739911. *36*

HANDBOOK OF LABOR STATISTICS.
U.S. Bureau of Labor Statistics, 441 G St., N.W., Washington, DC 20212. TEL 202-655-4000. *1262*

HANDBOOK OF LATIN AMERICAN STUDIES: A SELECTED AND ANNOTATED GUIDE TO RECENT PUBLICATIONS.
University of Texas Press, Journals Division, Box 7819, Austin, TX 78713. TEL 512-471-4278. Producer(s): NISC (Latin American Studies - Vol.1). *3520*

HANDBOOK ON INJECTABLE DRUGS.
American Society of Health-System Pharmacists, 7272 Wisconsin Ave., Bethesda, MD 20814. TEL 301-657-3000. FAX 301-657-8817. *5664*

HANDBUCH DER AUSLANDSZOELLE.
Mendel Verlag, Robensstr. 39, 52070 Aachen, Germany. TEL 49-241-154355. FAX 49-241-154355.
Available only on CD-ROM. *1328*

HANDBUCH DER STEUERVERANLAGUNGEN: EINKOMMENSTEUER, KOERPERSCHAFTSTEUER, GEWERBESTEUER, UMSATZSTEUER.
C.H. Beck'sche Verlagsbuchhandlung, Wilhelmstr. 9, 80801 Munich, Germany. TEL 089-38189-338. FAX 089-38189-398. *1612*

HAN'GUK BAKSA MIT SOKSA HAGWI NONMUN CH'ONGMONGNOK.
National Assembly Library, 1 Yoido-dong, Seoul, S. Korea. FAX 82-2-788-4298. *2501*

HANYU XUEXI.
Yanbian Daxue, Hayu Xuexi Bianjibu, 105 Gongyuan St., Yanji, Jilin 133002, People's Republic of China. TEL 86-433-2732219. FAX 86-433-2719618. *4261*

HARPER'S MAGAZINE.
Harpers Magazine Foundation, 666 Broadway, New York, NY 10012-2317. TEL 212-614-6500. FAX 212-228-5889.
Producer(s): UMI. *4337*

HARRIS CONNECTICUT MANUFACTURERS DIRECTORY.
Harris InfoSource International, 2057-2 Aurora Rd., Twinsburg, OH 44087. TEL 216-425-9000. FAX 800-643-5997. *1684*

HARRIS DELAWARE MANUFACTURERS DIRECTORY.
Harris InfoSource International, 2057-2 Aurora Rd., Twinsburg, OH 44087. TEL 216-425-9000. FAX 216-425-7150. *1684*

HARRIS GEORGIA MANUFACTURERS DIRECTORY.
Harris InfoSource International, 2057-2 Aurora Rd., Twinsburg, OH 44087. TEL 216-425-9000. FAX 800-643-5997. *1684*

HARRIS ILLINOIS INDUSTRIAL DIRECTORY (YEAR).
Harris InfoSource International, 2057-2 Aurora Rd., Twinsburg, OH 44087. TEL 216-425-9000. FAX 216-425-7150. *1684*

HARRIS INDIANA INDUSTRIAL DIRECTORY (YEAR).
Harris InfoSource International, 2057-2 Aurora Rd., Twinsburg, OH 44087. TEL 216-425-9000. FAX 216-425-7150. *1684*

HARRIS KENTUCKY INDUSTRIAL DIRECTORY (YEAR).
Harris InfoSource International, 2057-2 Aurora Rd., Twinsburg, OH 44087. TEL 216-425-9000. FAX 216-425-7150. *1684*

HARRIS MASSACHUSETTS MANUFACTURERS DIRECTORY.
Harris InfoSource International, 2057-2 Aurora Rd., Twinsburg, OH 44087. TEL 216-425-9000. FAX 216-425-7150. *1684*

HARRIS MICHIGAN INDUSTRIAL DIRECTORY (YEAR).
InfoSource International, 2057-2 Aurora Rd., Twinsburg, OH 44087. TEL 216-425-9000. FAX 216-425-7150. *1684*

HARRIS MISSOURI DIRECTORY OF MANUFACTURERS.
Harris InfoSource International, 2057-2 Aurora Rd., Twinsburg, OH 44087. TEL 216-425-9000. FAX 216-425-7150. *1684*

HARRIS NATIONAL MANUFACTURERS DIRECTORY (YEAR).
Harris InfoSource International, 2057 Aurora Rd., Twinsburg, OH 44087. TEL 216-425-9000. FAX 216-425-7150. *1684*

HARRIS NATIONAL MANUFACTURERS DIRECTORY MIDWEST EDITION (YEAR).
Harris InfoSource International, 2057-2 Aurora Rd., Twinsburg, OH 44087. TEL 216-425-9000. FAX 216-425-7150. *1684*

HARRIS NATIONAL MANUFACTURERS DIRECTORY NORTHEAST EDITION (YEAR).
Harris InfoSource International, 2057-2 Aurora Rd., Twinsburg, OH 44087. TEL 216-425-9000. FAX 216-425-7150. *1684*

HARRIS NATIONAL MANUFACTURERS DIRECTORY SOUTHEAST EDITION (YEAR).
Harris InfoSource International, 2057-2 Aurora Rd., Twinsburg, OH 44087. TEL 216-425-9000. FAX 216-425-7150. *1685*

HARRIS NEW ENGLAND MANUFACTURERS DIRECTORY.
Harris InfoSource International, 2057-2 Aurora Rd., Twinsburg, OH 44087. TEL 216-425-9000. FAX 216-425-7150. *1685*

HARRIS OHIO INDUSTRIAL DIRECTORY (YEAR).
Harris InfoSource International, 2057-2 Aurora Rd., Twinsburg, OH 44087. TEL 216-425-9000. FAX 216-425-7150. *1685*

HARRIS RHODE ISLAND MANUFACTURERS DIRECTORY.
Harris Publishing Co. (Twinsburg), 2057-2 Aurora Rd., Twinsburg, OH 44087. TEL 216-425-9000. FAX 800-643-5997. *1685*

HARRIS SOUTH CAROLINA MANUFACTURERS DIRECTORY.
Harris InfoSource International, 2057-2 Aurora Rd., Twinsburg, OH 44087. TEL 216-425-9000. FAX 216-425-7150. *1685*

HARRIS TEXAS MANUFACTURERS DIRECTORY.
Harris InfoSource International, 2057-2 Aurora Rd., Twinsburg, OH 44087. TEL 216-425-9000. FAX 216-425-7150. *1685*

HARRIS WEST VIRGINIA MANUFACTURING DIRECTORY (YEAR).
Harris Publishing Co. (Twinsburg), 2057-2 Aurora Rd., Twinsburg, OH 44087. TEL 216-425-9000. FAX 216-425-7150. *1685*

HASTINGS COMMUNICATIONS AND ENTERTAINMENT LAW JOURNAL (COMM - ENT).
University of California at San Francisco, Hastings College of the Law, 200 McAllister St., San Francisco, CA 94102-4978. TEL 415-565-4731. FAX 415-565-4814. *3958*

HASTINGS CONSTITUTIONAL LAW QUARTERLY.
University of California at San Francisco, Hastings College of the Law, 200 McAllister St., San Francisco, CA 94102-4978. TEL 415-565-4726. FAX 415-565-4814. *4070*

HASTINGS INTERNATIONAL AND COMPARATIVE LAW REVIEW.
University of California at San Francisco, Hastings College of the Law, 200 McAllister St., San Francisco, CA 94102-4978. TEL 415-565-4730. FAX 415-565-4814. *4115*

HASTINGS LAW JOURNAL.
University of California at San Francisco, Hastings College of the Law, 200 McAllister St., San Francisco, CA 94102-4978. TEL 415-565-4727. FAX 415-565-4814. *3958*

HASTINGS WOMEN'S LAW JOURNAL.
University of California at San Francisco, Hastings College of the Law, 200 McAllister St., San Francisco, CA 94102. TEL 415-565-4870. FAX 415-464-4814. *3958*

HAWAII BUSINESS DIRECTORY.
American Business Directories, 5711 S. 86th Circle, Box 27347, Omaha, NE 68127. TEL 402-593-4600. FAX 402-331-5481. *1685*

HAWKEYE (LA PLATA).
Charles County Community College, Box 910, Mitchell Rd., La Plata, MD 20646-0910. TEL 301-934-2251. FAX 301-934-7698. *1955*

AL-HAYAT.
Al Hayat Publishing Company Ltd., Kensington Centre, 66 Hammersmith Rd., London W14 8YT, England. TEL 44-171-602-9988. FAX 44-171-371-4215. *3336*

HAZARDOUS WASTE BUSINESS.
McGraw-Hill Companies, Energy & Business Newsletters, 1221 Ave. of the Americas, 36th Fl., New York, NY 10020. TEL 212-521-6410.
Producer(s): SilverPlatter Information, Inc. (McGraw-Hill Energy Library). *2985*

HAZARDS IN THE OFFICE.
The Royal Society of Chemistry, Thomas Graham House, Science Park, Milton Rd., Cambridge CB4 4WF, England. TEL 44-1223-420066. FAX 44-1223-423429.
Producer(s): Knight-Ridder, Inc. *6235*

HEALTH AND POPULATION: PERSPECTIVES AND ISSUES.
National Institute of Health and Family Welfare, New Mehrauli Rd., Munirka, New Delhi 110 067, India. *857*

HEALTH AND SAFETY SCIENCE ABSTRACTS.
Cambridge Scientific Abstracts, 7200 Wisconsin Ave., 6th Fl., Bethesda, MD 20814. TEL 301-961-6750. FAX 301-961-6720.
Producer(s): Knight-Ridder, Inc. (Toxicology & Pharmacology), NISC (Health & Safety - Risk Abstracts), SilverPlatter Information, Inc. (PolTox1). *6256*

HEALTH DEVICES ALERTS.
E C R I, 5200 Butler Pike, Plymouth Meeting, PA 19462. TEL 610-825-6000. FAX 610-834-1275. *4779*

HEALTH INDEX.
Information Access Company, 362 Lakeside Dr., Foster City, CA 94404. TEL 415-378-5200. FAX 415-378-5369. *4779*

HEALTH INDUSTRY QUICKSOURCE.
Legal Communications, Ltd., 1617 JFK Blvd., Ste. 960, Philadelphia, PA 19103. TEL 215-577-2300. FAX 215-557-2301. *4780*

HEALTH MANPOWER MANAGEMENT.
M C B University Press Ltd., 60-62 Toller Ln., Bradford, W. Yorks BD8 9BY, England. TEL 44-1274-777700. FAX 44-1274-785200. *1480*

HEALTHCARE FINANCIAL MANAGEMENT.
Healthcare Financial Management Association, Two Westbrook Corporate Center, Ste. 700, Westchester, IL 60154. TEL 708-531-9600. FAX 708-531-0032. *3710*

HEBEI SHIFAN DAXUE XUEBAO (SHEHUI KEXUE BAN).
Hebei Shifan Daxue, Yuhua Lu, Shijiazhuang, Hebei 050016, People's Republic of China. TEL 86-311-6049941. FAX 86-311-6049413. *6616*

HEBEI SHIFAN DAXUE XUEBAO (ZIRAN KEXUE BAN).
Hebei Shifan Daxue, Yuhua Donglu, Shijiazhuang, Hebei 050016, People's Republic of China. TEL 86-311-6049941. FAX 86-311-6049413. *6530*

HEHAI DAXUE XUEBAO.
Hehai Daxue, 1 Xikang Rd., Nanjing, Jiangsu 210098, People's Republic of China. TEL 86-25-3713777. FAX 86-25-3315375. *2394*

HELLENIC JOURNAL OF GASTROENTEROLOGY.
Beta Medical Publishers Ltd., Adrianiou 3, 115 25 Athens, Greece. TEL 30-1-7232-302. FAX 30-1-7232-302. *4911*

HEMATOLOGY.
Gordon and Breach - Harwood Academic, Amsteldisk 166, 1st Fl., 1079 LH Amsterdam, Netherlands. *4919*

THE HEMINGWAY REVIEW.
University of Idaho Press, c/o Susan F. Beegel, Ed., 180 Polpis Rd., Nantucket, MA 02554. TEL 508-325-7157.
Producer(s): UMI. *4413*

HERALD EXPRESS.
Herald Express Publications Ltd., Barton Hill Rd., Torquay, Devon TQ2 8JN, England. TEL 44-1803-676000. FAX 44-1803-676299. *3297*

HEWLETT-PACKARD JOURNAL.
Hewlett Packard Co. (Palo Alto), 3000 Hanover St., Palo Alto, CA 94304. TEL 415-857-2387. FAX 415-857-2157. *2188*

HIGH PRESSURE RESEARCH.
Gordon and Breach - Harwood Academic, Amsteldisk 166, 1st Fl., 1079 LH Amsterdam, Netherlands. *5845*

HISPANIA.
American Association of Teachers of Spanish and Portuguese, Inc., University of Northern Colorado, 210 Butler-Hancock Hall, Greeley, CO 80639. TEL 920-351-1090. FAX 970-351-1095. *4262*

HISPANIC AMERICAN PERIODICALS INDEX.
Latin American Studies Center Publications, University of California, Los Angeles, Box 951447, 10347 Bunche Hall, Los Angeles, CA 90095-1447. TEL 310-825-0810. FAX 310-206-2634. Producer(s): NISC (Latin American Studies - Vol.1). *3520*

HISPANIC REVIEW.
University of Pennsylvania, Romance Languages Department, 512 Williams Hall, Philadelphia, PA 19104-6305. TEL 215-898-7420. FAX 215-898-0933. *4262*

HISTORICAL ABSTRACTS. PART A: MODERN HISTORY ABSTRACTS, 1450-1914.
A B C-Clio, 130 Cremona, Box 1911, Santa Barbara, CA 93116-1911. TEL 805-968-1911. FAX 805-685-9685. *3520*

HISTORICAL ABSTRACTS. PART B: TWENTIETH CENTURY ABSTRACTS, 1914 TO THE PRESENT.
A B C-Clio, 130 Cremona, Box 1911, Santa Barbara, CA 93116-1911. TEL 805-968-1911. FAX 805-685-9685. *3520*

HISTORICAL ABSTRACTS. PART B: TWENTIETH CENTURY ABSTRACTS, 1914 TO THE PRESENT. ANNUAL INDEX.
A B C-Clio, 130 Cremona, Box 1911, Santa Barbara, CA 93116-1911. TEL 805-968-1911. FAX 805-685-9685. *3521*

HISTORICAL BIOLOGY.
Gordon and Breach - Harwood Academic, Amsteldisk 166, 1st Fl., 1079 LH Amsterdam, Netherlands. *5559*

HISTORICAL METHODS.
Heldref Publications, 1319 Eighteenth St., N.W., Washington, DC 20036-1802. TEL 202-296-6267. FAX 202-296-5149. Producer(s): UMI. *3498*

HISTORY AND THEORY.
Blackwell Publishers, 238 Main St., Cambridge, MA 02142. TEL 617-547-7110. FAX 617-547-0789. Producer(s): UMI, H.W. Wilson. *3499*

HISTORY: REVIEWS OF NEW BOOKS.
Heldref Publications, 1319 Eighteenth St., N.W., Washington, DC 20036-1802. TEL 202-296-6267. FAX 202-296-5149. Producer(s): UMI. *3499*

HISTORY TODAY.
History Today Ltd., 20 Old Compton St., London W1V 5PE, England. TEL 44-171-439-8315. Producer(s): UMI. *3499*

HOLLAND EXPORTS.
A B C voor Handel en Industrie C.V., P.O. Box 190, 2000 AD Haarlem, Netherlands. TEL 31-23-5319031. FAX 31-23-5327033. *1329*

HOME POWER.
Home Power, Inc., Box 520, Ashland, OR 97520-0520. TEL 916-475-0830. FAX 916-475-3179. *2670*

HOOVER'S GUIDE TO THE BOOK BUSINESS.
Reference Press, Inc., Box 140375, Austin, TX 78714-0375. TEL 512-454-7778. FAX 512-454-9401. *1686*

HOOVER'S GUIDE TO THE TOP NEW YORK COMPANIES.
Reference Press, Inc., Box 140375, Austin, TX 78714-0375. TEL 512-454-7778. FAX 512-454-9401. *1686*

HOOVER'S GUIDE TO THE TOP SOUTHERN CALIFORNIA COMPANIES.
Reference Press, Inc., Box 140375, Austin, TX 78714-0375. TEL 512-454-7778. FAX 512-454-9401. *1686*

HOOVER'S HANDBOOK OF AMERICAN BUSINESS.
Reference Press Inc., Box 140375, Austin, TX 78714-0375. TEL 512-454-7778. FAX 512-454-9401. *1686*

HOOVER'S HANDBOOK OF EMERGING COMPANIES.
Reference Press, Inc., Box 140375, Austin, TX 78714-0375. TEL 512-454-7778. FAX 512-454-9401. *1686*

HOOVER'S HANDBOOK OF WORLD BUSINESS.
Reference Press Inc., Box 140375, Austin, TX 78714-0375. TEL 512-454-7778. FAX 512-454-9401. *1686*

HOPPENSTEDT VADEMECUM DER INVESTMENTFONDS.
Verlag Hoppenstedt GmbH, Havelstr. 9, 64295 Darmstadt, Germany. TEL 49-6151-380-0. FAX 49-6151-380-360. *1387*

HOPSCOTCH.
Bluffton News Printing and Publishing Co., Box 164, 103 N. Main St., Bluffton, OH 45817-0164. TEL 419-358-4610. FAX 419-358-5027. *1874*

HORIZONTES (SAN FRANCISCO).
Horizontes, Passaic County C.C., 1 College Blvd., Paterson, NJ 07505. TEL 415-641-6051. FAX 415-282-3320. *3016*

HORTICULTURAL ABSTRACTS.
CAB International, Wallingford, Oxon. OX10 8DE, England. TEL 44-1491-832111. FAX 44-1491-826090. *3208*

HOSPITAL ADMINISTRATION.
Indian Hospital Association, B-401, Sarita Vihar, New Delhi 110 044, India. TEL 91-11-6835648. *3711*

HOSPITAL PRODUCT COMPARISON SYSTEM.
E C R I, 5200 Butler Pike, Plymouth Meeting, PA 19462. TEL 610-825-6000. FAX 610-834-1275. Producer(s): Knight-Ridder, Inc. *3713*

HOSPITAL TOPICS.
Heldref Publications, 1319 Eighteenth St., N.W., Washington, DC 20036. TEL 202-296-6267. FAX 202-296-5149. Producer(s): UMI. *3714*

HOTELS DE LA FRANCE.
Ecran Publicite, 190 bd. Haussmann, 75008 Paris, France. TEL 33-1-44959950. FAX 33-1-49539016. *3729*

HUAXUE JINZHAN.
Zhongguo Kexueyuan, Wenxian Qingbao Zhongxin, 8 Kexueyuan Nanlu, Zhongguancun, Beijing 100080, People's Republic of China. TEL 86-10-6256-2547. FAX 81-10-6256-6846. *1751*

HUMAN RESOURCES MANAGEMENT.
C C H Incorporated, 2700 Lake Cook Rd., Riverwoods, IL 60015. TEL 847-267-7000. FAX 800-224-8299. *1432*

HUMAN RESOURCES MANAGEMENT - COMPENSATION.
C C H Incorporated, 2700 Lake Cook Rd., Riverwoods, IL 60015. TEL 847-267-7000. FAX 800-224-8299. *1568*

HUMAN RESOURCES MANAGEMENT - EMPLOYEE RELATIONS.
C C H Incorporated, 4025 W. Peterson Ave., Riverwoods, IL 60015. TEL 847-267-7000. FAX 800-224-8299. *1568*

HUMAN RESOURCES MANAGEMENT - EQUAL EMPLOYMENT OPPORTUNITY.
C C H Incorporated, 2700 Lake Cook Rd., Riverwoods, IL 60015. TEL 847-267-7000. FAX 847-224-8299. *1568*

HUMAN RESOURCES MANAGEMENT - O S H A COMPLIANCE.
C C H Incorporated, 2700 Lake Cook Rd., Riverwoods, IL 60015. TEL 847-267-7000. FAX 800-224-8299. *5491*

HUMAN RESOURCES MANAGEMENT - PERSONNEL PRACTICES - COMMUNICATIONS.
C C H Incorporated, 2700 Lake Cook Rd., Riverwoods, IL 60015. TEL 847-267-7000. FAX 800-224-8299. *1568*

HUMANITIES INDEX.
H.W. Wilson Co., 950 University Ave., Bronx, NY 10452. TEL 718-588-8400. FAX 718-590-1617. Producer(s): H.W. Wilson (WILSONDISC). *3799*

HYDROTITLES.
Geosystems, P.O. Box 40, Didcot, Oxon. OX11 9BX, England. TEL 44-1235-813913. Producer(s): NISC (HydroROM). *2326*

I A R C MONOGRAPHS ON THE EVALUATION OF CARCINOGENIC RISK OF CHEMICALS TO HUMANS.
I A R C Press, 150, cours Albert Thomas, 69372 Lyon Cedex 08, France. TEL 33-72-738485. FAX 33-72-738302. *4979*

I C A C RECORDER.
International Cotton Advisory Committee, 1629 K St. N.W., Ste. 702, Washington, DC 20006. TEL 202-463-6660. FAX 202-463-6950. *6987*

I C MASTER.
Hearst Business Publishing UTP Division, 645 Stewart Ave., Garden City, NY 11530. TEL 516-227-1300. FAX 516-227-1453. *2639*

I D F DIRECTORY.
International Diabetes Federation, 1 rue Defacqz, 1000 Brussels, Belgium. TEL 32-2-5385511. FAX 32-2-5385514. *4889*

I E E REVIEW.
I.E.E., Michael Faraday House, Six Hills Way, Stevenage, Herts. SG1 2AY, England. TEL 44-1438-313311. FAX 44-1438-742840. Producer(s): UMI. *2833*

I I C.
Wiley - V C H, Postfach 101161, 69451 Weinheim, Germany. TEL 49-6201-606-147. FAX 49-6201-606117. *5585*

I N I S ATOMINDEX.
International Atomic Energy Agency, Wagramerstrasse 5, Box 100, A-1400 Vienna, Austria. TEL 43-1-2060-22529. FAX 43-1-2060-29302. Producer(s): SilverPlatter Information, Inc. (INIS). *5835*

I R S LETTER RULINGS AND TECHNICAL ADVICE MEMORANDUMS (1980-YEAR).
Tax Analysts, 6830 N. Fairfax Dr., Arlington, VA 22213. FAX 703-533-4444. *1613*

I R S PUBLICATIONS.
C C H Incorporated, 2700 Lake Cook Rd., Riverwoods, IL 60015. TEL 847-267-7000. FAX 800-224-8299. *1613*

I S S N COMPACT.
International Centre for the Registration of Serials, I S S N International Centre, 20 rue Bachaumont, 75002 Paris, France. TEL 33-1-44-88-22-20. FAX 33-1-40-26-32-43. Available only on CD-ROM. *550*

I S S N REGISTER (MICROFICHE EDITION).
International Centre for the Registration of Serials, I S S N International Centre, 20 rue Bachaumont, 75002 Paris, France. TEL 33-1-44-88-22-20. FAX 33-1-40-26-32-43. *550*

I S S N REGISTER (TAPE EDITION).
International Centre for the Registration of Serials, I S S N International Center, 20 rue Bachaumont, 75002 Paris, France. TEL 33-1-44-88-22-20. FAX 33-1-40-26-32-43. *551*

I T S JOURNAL.
Gordon and Breach - Harwood Academic, Amsteldisk 166, 1st Fl., 1079 LH Amsterdam, Netherlands. *7053*

IBERLEX.
Boletin Oficial del Estado, Trafalgar, 27, 28071 Madrid, Spain. TEL 34-1-5382297. FAX 34-1-5382275. *4070*

ICHNOS.
Gordon and Breach - Harwood Academic, Amsteldisk 166, 1st Fl., 1079 LH Amsterdam, Netherlands. *5559*

IDAHO BUSINESS DIRECTORY.
American Business Directories, 5711 S. 86th Circle, Box 27347, Omaha, NE 68127. TEL 402-593-4600. FAX 402-331-5481. *1687*

IDAHO WOOL GROWERS BULLETIN.
Idaho Wool Growers Association, 802 W. Bannock, No. 205, Box 2596, Boise, ID 83701. TEL 208-344-2271. FAX 208-336-9447. *277*

IGAKU CHUO ZASSHI.
Igaku Chuo Zasshi Kankokai, 5-18, Takaido Higashi 2-chome, Suginami-ku, Tokyo 168, Japan. TEL 86-3-3334-7625. FAX 86-3-3332-1394. *4682*

ILLINOIS BUSINESS DIRECTORY.
American Business Directories, 5711 S. 86th Circle, Box 27347, Omaha, NE 68127. TEL 402-593-4600. FAX 402-331-5481. *1687*

ILLINOIS FAMILY LAWS AND COURT RULES.
West Group, 620 Opperman Dr., Eagan, MN 55123. TEL 612-687-8000. FAX 612-687-7302. *4101*

ILLINOIS MANUFACTURERS DIRECTORY.
Manufacturers' News, Inc., 1633 Central St., Evanston, IL 60201. TEL 847-864-7000. FAX 847-332-1100. *1687*

ILLINOIS RESEARCH.
University of Illinois at Urbana-Champaign, College of Agricultural, Consumer and Environmental Sciences, 47 Mumford Hall, 1301 W. Gregory Dr., IL 61801. TEL 217-244-2830. *124*

ILLINOIS SERVICES DIRECTORY.
Manufacturers' News, Inc., 1633 Central St., Evanston, IL 60201-1505. TEL 847-864-7000. FAX 847-332-1100. *1687*

ILLINOIS STATISTICAL ABSTRACT.
University of Illinois at Urbana-Champaign, Bureau of Economic and Business Research, 428 Commerce Bldg., W., 1206 S. Sixth St., Champaign, IL 61820. TEL 217-333-2331. FAX 217-233-7410. *6916*

ILOLEX C D - R O M.
Kluwer Law International, Postbus 85889, 2508 CN The Hague, Netherlands. TEL 31-70-3081500. FAX 31-70-3081515.
Available only on CD-ROM. *1434*

ILTALEHTI.
Kustannusosakeyhtio Italehti, P.O. Box 372, FIN-00101 Helsinki, Finland. TEL 358-9-50-77-21. FAX 358-9-17-73-13. *3278*

IMAGING.
Science Reviews Ltd., P.O. Box 81, Northwood, Middlesex HA6 3DN, England. TEL 44-1923-823586. FAX 44-1923-825066. *5107*

IMMIGRATION BRIEFINGS.
Federal Publications Inc., 1120 20th St., N.W., Ste. 500 S., Washington, DC 20036. TEL 202-337-7000. FAX 202-659-2233. *4070*

IMMUNOLOGY ABSTRACTS.
Cambridge Scientific Abstracts, 7200 Wisconsin Ave., 6th Fl., Bethesda, MD 20814. TEL 301-961-6750. FAX 301-961-6720.
Producer(s): SilverPlatter Information, Inc. *4780*

IMPORTED CARS, LIGHT TRUCKS & VANS SERVICE & REPAIR.
Mitchell International, Inc., 9889 Willow Creek Rd., Box 26260, San Diego, CA 92196-0260. TEL 800-648-8010. FAX 619-578-4752. *7102*

THE INDEPENDENT.
Newspaper Publishing plc., 1 Canada Sq., Canary Wharf, London E14 5DL, England. TEL 44-171-510-2000. FAX 44-171-293-2435.
Producer(s): Chadwyck-Healey Inc. *3298*

THE INDEPENDENT INDEX.
Primary Source Media, P.O. Box 45, Reading RG1 8HF, England. TEL 44-1734-583247. FAX 44-1734-591325. *3884*

THE INDEPENDENT ON C D - R O M.
Chadwyck-Healey Ltd., The Quorum, Barnwell Rd., Cambridge CB5 8SW, England. TEL 44-1223-215512. FAX 44-1223-215514.
Available only on CD-ROM. Producer(s): Chadwyck-Healey Inc. *3298*

THE INDEPENDENT ON SUNDAY.
Newspaper Publishing plc., 1 Canada Sq., Canary Wharf, London E14 5DL, England. TEL 44-171-293-2000. FAX 44-171-293-2435.
Producer(s): Chadwyck-Healey Inc. *3298*

INDEPENDENT POWER REPORT.
McGraw-Hill Companies, Energy & Business Newsletters, 1221 Ave. of the Americas, 36th Fl., New York, NY 10020. TEL 212-512-6410.
Producer(s): SilverPlatter Information, Inc. (McGraw-Hill Energy Library). *2671*

INDEX CHEMICUS.
Institute for Scientific Information, 3501 Market St., Philadelphia, PA 19104. TEL 215-386-0100. FAX 215-386-2911. *1784*

INDEX: FOREIGN BROADCAST INFORMATION SERVICE DAILY REPORTS: AFRICA SUB-SAHARA.
NewsBank, Inc., 58 Pine St., New Canaan, CT 06840-5426. TEL 203-966-1100. FAX 203-966-6254. *5984*

INDEX: FOREIGN BROADCAST INFORMATION SERVICE DAILY REPORTS: CHINA.
NewsBank, Inc., 58 Pine St., New Canaan, CT 06840-5426. TEL 203-966-1100. FAX 203-966-6254. *5984*

INDEX: FOREIGN BROADCAST INFORMATION SERVICE DAILY REPORTS: EAST ASIA.
NewsBank, Inc., 58 Pine St., New Canaan, CT 06840-5426. TEL 203-966-1100. FAX 203-966-6254. *5984*

INDEX: FOREIGN BROADCAST INFORMATION SERVICE DAILY REPORTS: EASTERN EUROPE.
NewsBank, Inc., 58 Pine St., New Canaan, CT 06840-5426. TEL 203-966-1100. FAX 203-966-6254. *5984*

INDEX: FOREIGN BROADCAST INFORMATION SERVICE DAILY REPORTS: LATIN AMERICA.
NewsBank, Inc., 58 Pine St., New Canaan, CT 06840-5426. TEL 203-966-1100. FAX 203-966-6254. *5984*

INDEX: FOREIGN BROADCAST INFORMATION SERVICE DAILY REPORTS: NEAR EAST AND SOUTH ASIA.
NewsBank, Inc., 58 Pine St., New Canaan, CT 06840-5426. TEL 203-966-1100. FAX 203-966-6254. *5984*

INDEX: FOREIGN BROADCAST INFORMATION SERVICE DAILY REPORTS: WESTERN EUROPE.
NewsBank, Inc., 58 Pine St., New Canaan, CT 06840-5426. TEL 203-966-1100. FAX 203-966-6254. *5984*

INDEX: FOREIGN BROADCAST INFORMATION SERVICE REPORTS: CENTRAL EURASIA.
NewsBank, Inc., 58 Pine St., New Canaan, CT 06840-5426. TEL 203-966-1100. FAX 203-966-6254.
Available only on CD-ROM. *5984*

INDEX ISLAMICUS.
Bowker - Saur Ltd., A member of the Reed Elsevier plc group, Maypole House, Maypole Rd., E. Grinstead, W. Sussex RH19 1HU, England. TEL 44-1342-330100. FAX 44-1342-330191. *551*

INDEX MEDICUS.
U.S. National Library of Medicine, 8600 Rockville Pike, Bethesda, MD 20894.
Producer(s): Cambridge Scientific Abstracts (Compact Cambridge MEDLINE), Knight-Ridder, Inc. (DIALOG OnDisc MEDLINE), SilverPlatter Information, Inc. (MEDLINE). *4780*

INDEX NEW ZEALAND.
National Library of New Zealand, P.O. Box 1467, Wellington, New Zealand. TEL 64-4-4743098. FAX 64-4-4753124. *15*

INDEX TO BOOK REVIEWS IN RELIGION.
American Theological Library Association, 820 Church St., Ste. 300, Evanston, IL 60201-5613. TEL 847-869-7788. FAX 847-869-8513. *6386*

INDEX TO CHINESE PERIODICALS.
National Central Library, 20 Chung Shan S. Rd., Taipei, Taiwan 10040, Republic of China. TEL 886-2-361-9132. FAX 886-2-311-0155.
Available only on CD-ROM. *15*

INDEX TO DENTAL LITERATURE.
American Dental Association, 211 E. Chicago Ave., Chicago, IL 60611. TEL 312-440-2500. FAX 312-440-2550.
Producer(s): Cambridge Scientific Abstracts (Compact Cambridge MEDLINE), Knight-Ridder, Inc. (DIALOG OnDisc MEDLINE), SilverPlatter Information, Inc. (MEDLINE). *4780*

INDEX TO FOREIGN LEGAL PERIODICALS.
University of California Press, Journals Division, 2120 Berkeley Way, No. 5812, Berkeley, CA 94720-5812. TEL 510-643-7154. FAX 510-642-9917.
Producer(s): SilverPlatter Information, Inc. *4053*

INDEX TO HEBREW PERIODICALS (C D - R O M EDITION).
University of Haifa Library, Haifa 31905, Israel. FAX 972-4-257753.
Available only on CD-ROM. *551*

INDEX TO HOUSE OF COMMONS PARLIAMENTARY PAPERS.
Chadwyck-Healey Ltd., The Quorum, Barnwell Rd., Cambridge CB5 8SW, England. TEL 44-1223-215512. FAX 44-1223-215514.
Producer(s): Chadwyck-Healey Inc. *5984*

INDEX TO INTERNATIONAL STATISTICS.
Congressional Information Service, Inc., A member of the LEXIS-NEXIS family, 4520 East-West Hwy., Bethesda, MD 20814-3389. TEL 301-654-1550. FAX 301-654-4033. *6917*

INDEX TO JEWISH PERIODICALS.
Box 18570, Cleveland Heights, OH 44118. TEL 216-381-4846. FAX 216-381-4321. *6386*

INDEX TO LEGAL PERIODICALS & BOOKS.
H.W. Wilson Co., 950 University Ave., Bronx, NY 10452. TEL 718-588-8400. FAX 718-590-1617.
Producer(s): SilverPlatter Information, Inc., H.W. Wilson (WILSONDISC). *4053*

INDEX TO SCIENTIFIC & TECHNICAL PROCEEDINGS.
Institute for Scientific Information, 3501 Market St., Philadelphia, PA 19104. TEL 215-386-0100. FAX 215-386-2911.
Producer(s): Institute for Scientific Information. *6590*

INDEX TO SOCIAL SCIENCES & HUMANITIES PROCEEDINGS.
Institute for Scientific Information, 3501 Market St., Philadelphia, PA 19104. TEL 215-386-0100. FAX 215-386-2911.
Producer(s): Institute for Scientific Information. *6650*

INDEX TO SOUTH AFRICAN PERIODICALS.
State Library, P.O. Box 397, Pretoria 0001, South Africa. TEL 27-12-21-8931. FAX 27-12-325-5984. *6290*

INDEX TO THE ST. PAUL PIONEER PRESS.
Newsbank, Inc., 58 Pine St., New Canaan, CT 06840-5426. TEL 203-966-1100. FAX 203-966-6254. *3884*

INDEX TRANSLATIONUM.
UNESCO Publishing, 1 rue Miollis, 75732 Paris Cedex 15, France. TEL 33-1-45684300. FAX 33-1-45685741.
Available only on CD-ROM. *4226*

INDIAN JOURNAL OF CANCER.
Indian Cancer Society, 74 Jerbai Wadia Rd., Parel, Mumbai 400 012, India. TEL 91-22-412-5238. *4979*

THE INDIAN JOURNAL OF CHEST DISEASES AND ALLIED SCIENCES.
University of Delhi, Vallabhbhai Patel Chest Institute, Delhi 110 007, India. TEL 91-11-7257102. *4925*

INDIAN JOURNAL OF DERMATOLOGY, VENEREOLOGY AND LEPROLOGY.
Indian Association of Dermatologists, Venereologists and Leprologists, c/o Dr. Gurmohan Singh, Ed., New D-7, Banaras Hindu University, Varanasi 221 005, India. TEL 91-542-310845. *4878*

INDIAN JOURNAL OF LEPROSY.
Indian Leprosy Association, 1, Red Cross Road, New Delhi 110 001, India. TEL 3714748. *4836*

INDIAN JOURNAL OF MALARIOLOGY.
Indian Council of Medical Research, Malaria Research Center, 22, Sham Nath Marg, Delhi 110 054, India. TEL 91-11-2528455. FAX 91-11-7234234. *4836*

INDIAN JOURNAL OF MEDICAL RESEARCH. SECTION A: INFECTIOUS DISEASES.
Indian Council of Medical Research, Division of Publication & Information, P.O. Box 4911, Ansari Nagar, New Delhi 110 029, India. TEL 91-11-6963980. FAX 91-11-6868662. *4683*

INDIAN JOURNAL OF NUTRITION AND DIETETICS.
Avinashilingam Institute for Home Science and Higher Education for Women, c/o Rajammal P. Devadas, Ed., Coimbatore 641 043, India. TEL 40241. *5474*

INDIAN JOURNAL OF OPHTHALMOLOGY.
All India Ophthalmological Society, c/o L.V. Prasad Eye Institute, Road No. 2, Banjara Hills 500 034, Hyderabad, India. *4994*

INDIAN JOURNAL OF PATHOLOGY & MICROBIOLOGY.
Indian Association of Pathologists and Microbiologists, Department of Laboratory Medicine, Safdarjung Hospital, New Delhi 110 029, India. TEL 91-11-668433. *4683*

INDIAN JOURNAL OF PHARMACEUTICAL SCIENCES.
Indian Pharmaceutical Association, Kalina Santacruz East, Mumbai 400 098, India. TEL 91-22-612-2401. FAX 91-22-614-0480. *5666*

INDIAN JOURNAL OF PHARMACOLOGY.
Indian Pharmacological Society, Department of Pharmacology, Jipmer, Pondicherry 605 006, India. TEL 91-413-36380. FAX 91-413-38132. *5666*

INDIAN JOURNAL OF PHYSIOLOGY AND PHARMACOLOGY.
Association of Physiologists and Pharmacologists of India, Department of Physiology, All India Institute of Medical Sciences, Ansari Nagar, New Delhi 110 029, India. *816*

INDIAN JOURNAL OF PSYCHIATRY.
Indian Psychiatric Society, K.G.'s Medical College, B-8, Sector A, Mahanagar, Lucknow 226 006, India. TEL 91-522-371481. FAX 91-522-0266025. *5068*

INDIAN JOURNAL OF RADIOLOGY & IMAGING.
Indian Radiological & Imaging Association, 13 Bheemanna Mudali Garden St., Madras 600018, India. TEL 91-22-412-1521. FAX 91-22-382-9595. *5107*

INDIANA BUSINESS DIRECTORY.
American Business Directories, 5711 S. 86th Circle, Box 27347, Omaha, NE 68127. TEL 402-593-4600. FAX 402-331-5481. *1687*

INDIANA MANUFACTURERS DIRECTORY.
Manufacturers' News, Inc., 1633 Central St., Evanston, IL 60201. TEL 847-864-7000. FAX 847-332-1100. *1687*

INDICE DE LA LITERATURA DENTAL EN CASTELLANO.
Asociacion Odontologica Argentina, Junin 959, Buenos Aires, Argentina. TEL 541-9611062. FAX 541-9611110. *4780*

INDICE ESPANOL DE CIENCIA Y TECNOLOGIA.
Centro de Informacion y Documentacion Cientifica (Cindoc), Joaquin Costa 22, 28002 Madrid, Spain. TEL 34-1-5635482. FAX 34-1-5642644. *6590*

INDICE ESPANOL DE CIENCIAS SOCIALES. SERIES A: PSYCHOLOGY AND EDUCATIONAL SCIENCES.
Centro de Informacion y Documentacion Cientifica (Cindoc), Joaquin Costa 22, 28002 Madrid, Spain. TEL 34-1-5635482. FAX 34-1-5642644. *6160*

INDICE ESPANOL DE CIENCIAS SOCIALES. SERIES B: ECONOMICS, SOCIOLOGY AND POLITICAL SCIENCE.
Centro de Informacion y Documentacion Cientifica (Cindoc), Joaquin Costa 22, 28002 Madrid, Spain. TEL 34-1-4111098. FAX 34-1-5645069. *1047*

INDICE ESPANOL DE CIENCIAS SOCIALES. SERIES C: LAW.
Centro de Informacion y Documentacion Cientifica (Cindoc), Joaquin Costa 22, 28002 Madrid, Spain. TEL 34-1-5635482. FAX 34-1-5642644. *4053*

INDICE ESPANOL DE CIENCIAS SOCIALES. SERIES D: SCIENCE AND SCIENTIFIC INFORMATION.
Centro de Informacion y Documentacion Cientifica (Cindoc), Joaquin Costa 22, 28002 Madrid, Spain. TEL 34-1-5635482. FAX 34-1-5642645. *6590*

INDICE ESPANOL DE CIENCIAS SOCIALES. SERIES E: URBAN PLANNING.
Centro de Informacion y Documentacion Cientifica (Cindoc), Joaquin Costa 22, 28002 Madrid, Spain. TEL 34-1-5635482. FAX 34-1-5642644. *3766*

INDICE ESPANOL DE HUMANIDADES. SERIES A: ART.
Centro de Informacion y Documentacion Cientifica (Cindoc), Joaquin Costa 22, 28002 Madrid, Spain. TEL 34-3-5635482. FAX 34-1-5642644. *476*

INDICE ESPANOL DE HUMANIDADES. SERIES B: HISTORICAL SCIENCES.
Centro de Informacion y Documentacion Cientifica (Cindoc), Joaquin Costa 22, 28002 Madrid, Spain. TEL 34-1-5635482. FAX 34-1-5642644. *3521*

INDICE ESPANOL DE HUMANIDADES. SERIES C: LINGUISTICS AND LITERATURE.
Centro de Informacion y Documentacion Cientifica (Cindoc), Joaquin Costa 22, 28002 Madrid, Spain. TEL 34-1-5635482. FAX 34-1-5642644. *4318*

INDICE ESPANOL DE HUMANIDADES. SERIES D: PHILOSOPHY.
Centro de Informacion y Documentacion Cientifica (Cindoc), Joaquin Costa 22, 28002 Madrid, Spain. TEL 34-1-5635482. FAX 34-1-5642644. *5760*

INDICE MEDICO ESPANOL.
Generalitat Valenciana, Conselleria de Sanitat i Consum, Avda. Blasco Ibanez - 17, 46010 Valencia, Spain. TEL 96-361-06-54. FAX 96-3613975. *4780*

INDIVIDUALS WITH DISABILITIES EDUCATION LAW REPORTER.
L R P Publications, 747 Dresher Rd., Box 980, Horsham, PA 19044-0980. TEL 215-784-0941. FAX 215-784-9639. *2585*

INDUSTRIAL AND COMMERCIAL TRAINING.
M C B University Press Ltd., 60-62 Toller Ln., Bradford, W. Yorks BD8 9BY, England. TEL 44-1274-777700. FAX 44-1274-785200. *1569*

INDUSTRIAL CASES REPORTS.
Incorporated Council of Law Reporting for England and Wales, 3 Stone Bldgs., Lincoln's Inn, London WC2A 3XN, England. TEL 44-171-242-6471. FAX 44-171-831-5247. *4081*

INDUSTRIAL ENERGY BULLETIN.
McGraw-Hill Companies, Energy & Business Newsletters, 1221 Ave. of the Americas, 36th Fl., New York, NY 10020. TEL 212-512-2000. Producer(s): SilverPlatter Information, Inc. (McGraw-Hill Energy Library). *2671*

INDUSTRIAL MANAGEMENT & DATA SYSTEMS.
M C B University Press Ltd., 60-62 Toller Ln., Bradford, W. Yorks BD8 9BY, England. TEL 44-1274-777700. FAX 44-1274-785200. *1201*

INDUSTRIAL NEWS (IAEGER).
Box 180, Iaeger, WV 24844. TEL 304-938-2142. *971*

INDUSTRY GROUP MARKET VALUES.
Standard & Poor's, 25 Broadway, New York, NY 10004. TEL 212-208-8000. *1388*

INFECTION AND IMMUNITY.
American Society for Microbiology, 1325 Massachusetts Ave., N.W., Washington, DC 20005. TEL 202-737-3600. *4797*

INFORMATICS IN HEATHCARE AUSTRALIA.
Health Informatics Society of Australia, 413 Lygon St., Brunswick East, Vic. 3057, Australia. TEL 61-3-93880555. FAX 61-3-93882086. *4847*

INFORMATIE.
Kluwer Bedrijfswetenschappen B.V., Postbus 23, 7400 GA Deventer, Netherlands. TEL 31-570-648932. FAX 31-570-611504. *2084*

INFORMATORE DI VETERINARIA E ZOOTECNIA.
Organizzazione Editoriale Medico Farmaceutica, Via Edolo 42, 20125 Milan, Italy. TEL 39-2-675051. FAX 39-2-67505223. *7271*

INFORME SOBRE CHILE.
Editorial Gestion, Ltda., Rafael Canas 114, Casilla 16485, Correo 9, Santiago, Chile. TEL 56-2-2361313. FAX 56-2-2361114. *6917*

INFOTAX.
InfoMedia Technologies (Pty) Ltd., P.O. Box 44597, Claremont 7735, South Africa. TEL 27-21-689 5075. FAX 27-21-689-5025. *1613*

INGRAM - BOOKS IN PRINT PLUS.
R.R. Bowker, A Division of Reed Elsevier Inc., 121 Chanlon Rd., New Providence, NJ 07974. TEL 800-521-8110. FAX 908-665-3528.
Available only on CD-ROM. Producer(s): Bowker Electronic Publishing (Books In Print PLUS). *551*

INGRAM - BOOKS IN PRINT PLUS WITH BOOK REVIEWS PLUS.
R.R. Bowker, A Division of Reed Elsevier Inc., 121 Chanlon Rd., New Providence, NJ 07974. TEL 800-521-8110. FAX 908-665-3528.
Available only on CD-ROM. Producer(s): Bowker Electronic Publishing (Books In Print PLUS). *551*

INPHARMA WEEKLY.
Adis International Limited, Private Bag 65901, Mairangi Bay, Auckland 10, New Zealand. TEL 64-9-479-8100. FAX 64-9-479-8145.
Producer(s): SilverPlatter Information, Inc. *5701*

INSIDE CONFERENCES ON C D - R O M.
British Library, Document Supply Centre, Boston Spa, Weatherby, W. Yorks. LS23 7BQ, England. TEL 44-1937-546080. FAX 44-1937-546286. Available only on CD-ROM. *551*

INSIDE ENERGY WITH FEDERAL LANDS.
McGraw-Hill Companies, Energy & Business Newsletters, 1221 Ave. of the Americas, 36th Fl., New York, NY 10020. TEL 212-512-6410. Producer(s): SilverPlatter Information, Inc. (McGraw-Hill Energy Library). *2671*

INSIDE F E R C.
McGraw-Hill Companies, 1221 Ave. of the Americas, New York, NY 10020. Producer(s): SilverPlatter Information, Inc. (McGraw-Hill Energy Library). *2671*

INSIDE F E R C'S GAS MARKET REPORT.
McGraw-Hill Companies, Energy & Business Newsletters, 1221 Ave. of the Americas, 36th Fl., New York, NY 10020. TEL 212-512-6410. Producer(s): SilverPlatter Information, Inc. (McGraw-Hill Energy Library). *5606*

INSIDE INFORMATION ON C D - R O M.
British Library, Document Supply Centre, Boston Spa, Wetherby, W. Yorks. LS23 7BQ, England. TEL 44-1937-546080. FAX 44-1937-546080. Available only on CD-ROM. *551*

INSIDE N R C.
McGraw-Hill Companies, Energy and Business Newsletters, 1221 Ave. of the Americas, 36th Fl., New York, NY 10020. Producer(s): SilverPlatter Information, Inc. (McGraw-Hill Energy Library). *2698*

INSIGHT ON THE NEWS.
Washington Times Corporation, 3600 New York Ave., N.E., Washington, DC 20002. TEL 202-636-8800. FAX 202-529-2484. *3376*

INSTITUT PASTEUR DE TUNIS. ARCHIVES.
Institut Pasteur de Tunis, 13 Place Pasteur, B.P. 74, 1002 Tunis Belvedere, Tunisia. TEL 216-1-283022. FAX 216-1-791833. *4684*

INSTITUTE OF MANAGEMENT INTERNATIONAL DATABASES PLUS.
Bowker - Saur Ltd., A member of the Reed Elsevier plc group, Maypole House, Maypole Rd., E. Grinstead, W. Sussex RH19 1HU, England. TEL 44-1342-330100. FAX 44-1342-330191. Available only on CD-ROM. Producer(s): Bowker - Saur Ltd. *1483*

INSTITUTE OF NUCLEAR MATERIALS MANAGEMENT. PROCEEDINGS OF ANNUAL MEETING.
Institute of Nuclear Materials Management, Inc., 60 Revere Dr., Ste. 500, Northbrook, IL 60062-1563. TEL 847-480-9573. *2698*

INSTITUTE OF PAPER SCIENCE AND TECHNOLOGY. ABSTRACT BULLETIN.
Institute of Paper Science and Technology, 500 10th St., N.W., Atlanta, GA 30318. TEL 404-894-5726. FAX 404-894-4778. *5574*

INSTITUTIONAL INVESTOR.
Institutional Investor, Inc., 488 Madison Ave., New York, NY 10022. TEL 212-224-3570. FAX 212-224-3592. *1389*

INSTITUTIONAL INVESTOR INTERNATIONAL EDITION.
Institutional Investor, Inc., 488 Madison Ave., New York, NY 10022. TEL 212-224-3570. FAX 212-224-3592. *1389*

INSTITUTO DE CARDIOLOGIA DE MEXICO. ARCHIVOS.
Instituto Nacional de Cardiologia "Ignacio Chavez", Oficina de Publicaciones, Juan Badiano No.1, Tlalpan, 14080 Mexico D.F., Mexico. TEL 52-5-5732911 ext. 310. FAX 52-5-5730994. *4818*

INSTITUTO DE INVESTIGACIONES LITERARIAS. ANUARIO.
Fondo Editorial Tropykos, Calle El Escorial, Edif. Luxor 7 Fl., Las Acacias, Caracas, Venezuela. TEL 58-02-6930565. FAX 58-02-624926. *4416*

INSTITUTO NACIONAL DE CANCEROLOGIA. REVISTA.
Instituto Nacional de Cancerologia, Ave. San Fernando 22, Col. Tlalpan, 14000 Mexico, D.F., Mexico. TEL 52-5-6551437. FAX 52-5-5733627. *4979*

INSTITUTO NACIONAL DE ENFERMEDADES RESPIRATORIAS. REVISTA.
Instituto Nacional de Enfermedades Respiratorias, Clz. Tlalpan 4502, Col. Seccion XVI, 14082 Mexico DF, Mexico. TEL 52-5-6663187. FAX 52-5-6663187. *5119*

INSURANCE CASE LAW DIGEST.
Butterworths Canada Ltd., Part of the Reed Elsevier group, 75 Clegg Rd., Markham, ON L6G 1A1, Canada. TEL 905-479-2665. FAX 905-479-2826. *3964*

INSURANCE PERIODICALS INDEX.
N I L S Publishing Company, 21625 Prairie St., Box 2507, Chatsworth, CA 91311. TEL 818-998-8830. FAX 818-718-8482. *3839*

INTEGRATED CIRCUITS. DIGITAL.
D.A.T.A. Business Publishing, 15 Inverness Way E., Box 6510, Englewood, CO 80155-6510. FAX 303-799-4082. *2642*

INTEGRATED FERROELECTRICS.
Gordon and Breach - Harwood Academic, Amsteldisk 166, 1st Fl., 1079 LH Amsterdam, Netherlands. *2835*

INTEGRATED WASTE MANAGEMENT.
McGraw-Hill Companies, Energy & Business Newsletters, 1221 Ave. of the Americas, 36th Fl., New York, NY 10020. TEL 212-512-6410. Producer(s): SilverPlatter Information, Inc. (McGraw-Hill Energy Library). *2986*

(YEAR) INTERACTIVE SOURCEBOOK.
North American Publishing Co., 401 N. Broad St., Philadelphia, PA 19108. TEL 215-238-5482. FAX 215-238-5412. *2051*

INTER-CORPORATE OWNERSHIP.
Statistics Canada, Operations and Integration Division, Circulation Management, Jean Talon Bldg., 2-C12, Tunney's Pasture, Ottawa, ON K1A 0T6, Canada. TEL 613-951-7277. FAX 613-951-1584. *1213*

INTERFACE I CS D.A.T.A. DIGEST.
D.A.T.A. Business Publishing, 15 Inverness Way E., Box 6510, Englewood, CO 80155-6510. FAX 303-799-4082. *2643*

INTERNAL REVENUE MANUAL - AUDIT AND ADMINISTRATION.
C C H Inc., 2700 Lake Cook Rd., Riverwoods, IL 60015. TEL 847-267-7000. *1614*

INTERNATIONAL ANNUAL BIBLIOGRAPHY OF FESTSCHRIFTEN.
Zeller Publications, Postfach 1949, 49009 Osnabrueck, Germany. TEL 49-541-4045914. FAX 49-541-41255. *552*

INTERNATIONAL ATOMIC ENERGY AGENCY. SAFETY SERIES.
International Atomic Energy Agency, Wagramerstr. 5, P.O. Box 100, A-1400 Vienna, Austria. TEL 43-1-2060-22529. FAX 43-1-2060-29302. *6239*

INTERNATIONAL BOOKS IN PRINT.
K.G. Saur Verlag KG, A member of the Reed Elsevier plc group, Ortlerstr. 8, 81373 Munich, Germany. TEL 49-89-76902-0. FAX 49-89-76902150. Producer(s): K.G. Saur Verlag. *552*

INTERNATIONAL BOOKS IN PRINT PLUS.
K.G. Saur Verlag KG, A member of the Reed Elsevier plc group, Ortlerstr. 8, 81373 Munich, Germany. TEL 49-89-76902-0. FAX 49-89-76902150. Available only on CD-ROM. Producer(s): K.G. Saur Verlag. *552*

INTERNATIONAL CIVIL ENGINEERING ABSTRACTS.
M C B University Press Ltd., 60-62 Toller Ln., Bradford, W. Yorks BD8 9BY, England. TEL 44-1274-777700. FAX 44-1274-785200. *2750*

INTERNATIONAL CLINICAL PSYCHOPHARMACOLOGY.
Rapid Science Publishers, The Old Malthouse, Paradise St., Oxford OX1 1LD, England. TEL 44-1865-790447. FAX 44-1865-244012. *6117*

INTERNATIONAL DEFENSE REVIEW.
Jane's Information Group, Sentinel House, 163 Brighton Rd., Coulsdon, Surrey CR5 2NH, England. TEL 44-181-700-3700. FAX 44-181-700-3846. *5271*

INTERNATIONAL DIRECTORY OF DESIGN.
Penrose Press, Box 470925, San Francisco, CA 94147. TEL 415-567-4157. FAX 415-567-4165. *448*

INTERNATIONAL ECONOMIC INSIGHTS.
Institute for International Economics, 11 Dupont Circle N.W., Ste. 620, Washington, DC 20036-1207. TEL 202-328-9000. FAX 202-328-5432. *1266*

INTERNATIONAL ENERGY ANNUAL.
U.S. Energy Information Administration, National Energy Information Center, EI-231, James Forrestal Bldg., Rm. 1F-048, 1000 Independence Ave., S.W., Washington, DC 20585. TEL 202-586-8800. FAX 202-586-0727. *2672*

INTERNATIONAL EXAMINER.
622 S. Washington, Seattle, WA 98104. *3018*

INTERNATIONAL FILM INDEX ON C D - R O M.
Bowker - Saur Ltd., A member of the Reed Elsevier plc group, Maypole House, Maypole Rd., E. Grinstead, W. Sussex RH19 1HU, England. TEL 44-1342-330100. FAX 44-1342-330191. Available only on CD-ROM. *5337*

INTERNATIONAL FILMARCHIVE C D - R O M.
International Federation of Film Archives (F I A F), 6 Nottingham St., London W1M 3RB, England. TEL 0171-224-1203. FAX 0171-224-0991. Available only on CD-ROM. *5349*

INTERNATIONAL FINANCIAL STATISTICS.
International Monetary Fund, Publications Unit, 700 19th St., N.W., Washington, DC 20431. TEL 202-623-7430. FAX 202-623-7201. *1048*

INTERNATIONAL FREQUENCY LIST.
International Telecommunication Union, Place des Nations, CH-1211 Geneva 20, Switzerland. TEL 41-22-7306141. FAX 41-22-7305464. *2052*

INTERNATIONAL GUIDE TO MICROFORM MASTERS.
K.G. Saur Verlag KG, A member of the Reed Elsevier plc group, Ortlerstr. 8, 81373 Munich, Germany. TEL 49-89-76902-0. FAX 49-89-76901250. Available only on CD-ROM. *552*

INTERNATIONAL HOSPITALITY AND TOURISM DATABASE C D - R O M.
John Wiley & Sons, Attn. Karen Bobbett, Sha Library, Statler Hall, Ithaca, NY 14853-6902. TEL 607-254-4656. FAX 607-255-0021. Available only on CD-ROM. *3739*

INTERNATIONAL INDEX TO FILM PERIODICALS.
International Federation of Film Archives (F I A F), 6 Nottingham St., London W1M 3RB, England. TEL 0171-224-1203. FAX 0171-224-0991. *5349*

INTERNATIONAL INDEX TO MUSIC PERIODICALS.
Chadwyck-Healey Ltd., The Quorum, Barnwell Rd., Cambridge CB5 8SW, England. TEL 44-1223-215512. FAX 44-1223-215514. Available only on CD-ROM. *5447*

INTERNATIONAL INDEX TO TELEVISION PERIODICALS.
International Federation of Film Archives (F I A F), 6 Nottingham St., London W1M 3RB, England. TEL 0171-224-1203. FAX 0171-224-0991. *2012*

INTERNATIONAL JOURNAL OF BANK MARKETING.
M C B University Press Ltd., 60-62 Toller Ln., Bradford, W. Yorks BD8 9BY, England. TEL 44-1274-777700. FAX 44-1274-785200. *1147*

INTERNATIONAL JOURNAL OF COMPUTATIONAL FLUID DYNAMICS.
Gordon and Breach - Harwood Academic, Amsteldisk 166, 1st Fl., 1079 LH Amsterdam, Netherlands. *5845*

INTERNATIONAL JOURNAL OF COMPUTER MATHEMATICS.
Gordon and Breach - Harwood Academic, Amsteldisk 166, 1st Fl., 1079 LH Amsterdam, Netherlands. *4621*

INTERNATIONAL JOURNAL OF ENVIRONMENTAL ANALYTICAL CHEMISTRY.
Gordon and Breach - Harwood Academic, Amsteldisk 166, 1st Fl., 1079 LH Amsterdam, Netherlands. *1791*

INTERNATIONAL JOURNAL OF ENVIRONMENTAL STUDIES. SECTIONS A & B.
Gordon and Breach - Harwood Academic, Amsteldisk 166, 1st Fl., 1079 LH Amsterdam, Netherlands. *2935*

INTERNATIONAL JOURNAL OF GENERAL SYSTEMS.
Gordon and Breach - Harwood Academic, Amsteldisk 166, 1st Fl., 1079 LH Amsterdam, Netherlands. *2156*

INTERNATIONAL JOURNAL OF NEUROSCIENCE.
Gordon and Breach - Harwood Academic, Amsteldisk 166, 1st Fl., 1079 LH Amsterdam, Netherlands. *5069*

INTERNATIONAL JOURNAL OF OPERATIONS AND PRODUCTION MANAGEMENT.
M C B University Press Ltd., 60-62 Toller Ln., Bradford, W. Yorks BD8 9BY, England. TEL 44-1274-777700. FAX 44-1274-785200. *1484*

INTERNATIONAL JOURNAL OF PEDIATRIC HEMATOLOGY - ONCOLOGY.
Gordon and Breach - Harwood Academic, Amsteldisk 166, 1st Fl., 1079 LH Amsterdam, Netherlands. *4980*

INTERNATIONAL JOURNAL OF PHYSICAL DISTRIBUTION & LOGISTICS MANAGEMENT.
M C B University Press Ltd., 60-62 Toller Ln., Bradford, W. Yorks BD8 9BY, England. TEL 44-1274-777700. FAX 44-1274-785200. *7175*

SERIALS AVAILABLE ON CD-ROM

INTERNATIONAL JOURNAL OF POLYMER ANALYSIS & CHARACTERIZATION.
Gordon and Breach - Harwood Academic, Amsteldisk 166, 1st Fl., 1079 LH Amsterdam, Netherlands. *2766*

INTERNATIONAL JOURNAL OF POLYMERIC MATERIALS.
Gordon and Breach - Harwood Academic, Amsteldisk 166, 1st Fl., 1079 LH Amsterdam, Netherlands. *2766*

INTERNATIONAL JOURNAL OF PUNJAB STUDIES.
Sage Publications India Pvt. Ltd., Box 4215, New Delhi 110 048, India. TEL 91-11-644-4958. FAX 91-11-647-2426.
Producer(s): SilverPlatter Information, Inc. *6620*

INTERNATIONAL JOURNAL OF RETAIL & DISTRIBUTION MANAGEMENT.
M C B University Press Ltd., 60-62 Toller Ln., Bradford, W. Yorks BD8 9BY, England. TEL 44-1274-777700. FAX 44-1274-785200. *1531*

INTERNATIONAL JOURNAL OF ROTATING MACHINERY.
Gordon and Breach - Harwood Academic, Amsteldisk 166, 1st Fl., 1079 LH Amsterdam, Netelands. *4545*

INTERNATIONAL JOURNAL OF SOCIAL ECONOMICS.
M C B University Press Ltd., 60-62 Toller Ln., Bradford, W. Yorks BD8 9BY, England. TEL 44-1274-777700. FAX 44-1274-785200. *973*

INTERNATIONAL JOURNAL OF SOLAR ENERGY.
Gordon and Breach - Harwood Academic, Amsteldisk 166, 1st Fl., 1079 LH Amsterdam, Netherlands. *2706*

INTERNATIONAL JOURNAL OF SYSTEMATIC BACTERIOLOGY.
American Society for Microbiology, 1325 Massachusetts Ave., N.W., Washington, DC 20005. TEL 202-737-3600. *787*

INTERNATIONAL LITERARY MARKET PLACE.
R.R. Bowker, A Division of Reed Elsevier Inc., New Providence, NJ 07974. TEL 908-464-6800. FAX 908-665-6688.
Producer(s): Bowker Electronic Publishing. *6274*

INTERNATIONAL MARKETING DATA AND STATISTICS (YEAR).
Euromonitor, 60-61 Britton St., London EC1M 5QU, England. TEL 44-171-251-8024. FAX 44-171-608-3149. *1048*

INTERNATIONAL MARKETING REVIEW.
M C B University Press Ltd., 60-62 Toller Ln., Bradford, W. Yorks BD8 9BY, England. TEL 44-1274-777700. FAX 44-1274-785200. *1531*

INTERNATIONAL MEDICAL JOURNAL.
Japan International Cultural Exchange Foundation, 2-15-5-207 Shoto, Shibuya-ku, Tokyo 150, Japan. TEL 81-3-3424-9090. FAX 81-3-3424-9119. *4687*

INTERNATIONAL MEDIEVAL BIBLIOGRAPHY.
International Medieval Bibliography, International Medieval Institute, Parkinson 103, University of Leeds, Leeds LS2 9JT, England. TEL 44-113-2333614. FAX 44-113-2333616. *3521*

INTERNATIONAL NEW PRODUCT REPORT.
Mintel International Group Ltd., 18-19 Long Ln., London EC1A 9HE, England. TEL 44-171-606-4533. FAX 44-171-606-5932. *3142*

INTERNATIONAL NURSING INDEX.
Lippincott - Raven Publishers, 227 E. Washington Sq., Philadelphia, PA 19106. TEL 215-238-4200. FAX 215-238-4227.
Producer(s): Cambridge Scientific Abstracts (Compact Cambridge MEDLINE), Knight-Ridder, Inc. (DIALOG OnDisc MEDLINE), SilverPlatter Information, Inc. (MEDLINE). *4781*

INTERNATIONAL PACKAGING ABSTRACTS.
Pira International, Randalls Rd., Leatherhead, Surrey KT22 7RU, England. TEL 44-1372-802050. FAX 44-1372-802239.
Producer(s): Knight-Ridder, Inc. *5550*

INTERNATIONAL PETROLEUM STATISTICS REPORT.
U.S. Energy Information Administration, National Energy Information Center, EI-231, James Forrestal Bldg., Rm. 1F-048, 1000 Independence Ave., S.W., Washington, DC 20585. TEL 202-586-8800. FAX 202-586-0727. *6918*

INTERNATIONAL PHARMACEUTICAL ABSTRACTS.
American Society of Health-System Pharmacists, 7272 Wisconsin Ave., Bethesda, MD 20814. TEL 301-657-3000. FAX 301-657-1641.
Producer(s): SilverPlatter Information, Inc. *5701*

INTERNATIONAL POLITICAL SCIENCE ABSTRACTS.
International Political Science Association, 27 rue Saint-Guillaume, 75337 Paris Cedex 07, France. TEL 33-1-45495187. FAX 33-1-45490149. *5985*

INTERNATIONAL REVIEWS OF IMMUNOLOGY.
Gordon and Breach - Harwood Academic, Amsteldisk 166, 1st Fl., 1079 LH Amsterdam, Netherlands. *4797*

INTERNATIONAL SATELLITE DIRECTORY.
Design Publishers, 800 Siesta Way, Sonoma, CA 95476-4413. *71*

INTERNATIONAL SEMICONDUCTOR DIRECTORY D.A.T.A. DIGEST: MASTER TYPE LOCATOR.
D.A.T.A. Business Publishing, 15 Inverness Way E., Box 6510, Englewood, CO 80155-6510. FAX 303-799-0381. *2643*

INTERNATIONAL SOCIETY OF EXPLOSIVES ENGINEERS. SYMPOSIUM ON EXPLOSIVES AND BLASTING RESEARCH. PROCEEDINGS.
International Society of Explosives Engineers, 29100 Aurora Rd., Cleveland, OH 44139-1800. TEL 216-349-4004. FAX 216-349-3788. *2766*

INTERNATIONAL TELECOMMUNICATIONS INTELLIGENCE.
M D I S Publications Ltd., MDIS House, City Fields Business Park, City Fields Way, Chichester, W. Sussex PO20 6FS, England. TEL 44-1243-533322. FAX 44-1243-533418. *1995*

INTERNATIONAL VISITOR SURVEY. QUARTERLY REPORTS.
Bureau of Tourism Research, Level 1, Burns Bldg., 28 National Crt., Forrest, A.C.T. 2603, Australia. TEL 61-6-2797264. FAX 61-6-2797298. *7254*

INTERNATIONALE BIBLIOGRAPHIE DER REZENSIONEN WISSENSCHAFTLICHER LITERATUR.
Zeller Publications, Postfach 1949, 49009 Osnabrueck, Germany. TEL 49-541-4045914. FAX 49-541-41255. *6590*

INTERNATIONALE BIBLIOGRAPHIE DER ZEITSCHRIFTENLITERATUR AUS ALLEN GEBIETEN DES WISSENS.
Zeller Publications, Postfach 1949, 49009 Osnabrueck, Germany. TEL 49-541-4045914. FAX 49-541-41255. *553*

INTERPRETER RELEASES.
Federal Publications Inc., 1120 20th St., N.W., Ste. 500 S., Washington, DC 20036. TEL 202-337-7000. FAX 202-659-2233. *4070*

INTLEC C D - R O M.
Chadwyck-Healey Inc., 1101 King St., Ste. 380, Alexandria, VA 22314-2944. TEL 703-683-4890. FAX 703-683-7589.
Available only on CD-ROM. Producer(s): Chadwyck-Healey Inc. *1266*

INTRANET AND NETWORKING STRATEGIES REPORT.
Computer Economics, Inc., 5841 Edison Pl., Carlsbad, CA 92008-6519. TEL 760-438-8100. FAX 760-431-1126. *1202*

INVERSE PROBLEMS IN ENGINEERING.
Gordon and Breach - Harwood Academic, Amsteldisk 166, 1st Fl., 1079 LH Amsterdam, Netherlands. *2727*

INVESTIGACION CLINICA.
Universidad del Zulia, Instituto de Investigaciones Clinicas, Apdo. Postal 1151, Maracaibo, Venezuela. TEL 5861-523844. FAX 58-61-916053. *4687*

IOWA BUSINESS DIRECTORY.
American Business Directories, 5711 S. 86th Circle, Box 27347, Omaha, NE 68127. TEL 402-593-4600. FAX 402-331-5481. *1689*

IOWA MANUFACTURERS REGISTER.
Manufacturers' News, Inc., 1633 Central St., Evanston, IL 60201. TEL 847-864-7000. FAX 847-332-1100. *1689*

IOWA RULES OF COURT, STATE AND FEDERAL.
West Group, 620 Opperman Dr., Eagan, MN 55123. TEL 612-687-8000. FAX 612-687-7302. *4133*

IRANIAN JOURNAL OF PUBLIC HEALTH.
Iranian Public Health Association, University of Teheran, Teheran, Iran. *6240*

ISOLATION AND PURIFICATION.
Gordon and Breach - Harwood Academic, Amsteldisk 166, 1st Fl., 1079 LH Amsterdam, Netherlands. *1791*

ITSUU LABORATORY, TOKYO. ANNUAL REPORT.
Itsuu Laboratory, 28-10 Tamagawa 2-chome, Setagaya-ku, Tokyo 173, Japan. *1816*

J A M A: THE JOURNAL OF THE AMERICAN MEDICAL ASSOCIATION.
American Medical Association, 515 N. State St., Chicago, IL 60610. TEL 312-464-5000. FAX 312-464-4184. *4689*

J A R AMENDMENT SERVICE TO REGULATORY DOCUMENTS.
Joint Aviation Authorities, J A A Headquarters, Saturnusstraat 8-10, P.O. Box 3000, 2130 KA Hoofddorp, Netherlands. TEL 31-23-5679700. FAX 31-23-5621714. *7073*

J & W BANKING INTERNATIONAL. INTERNATIONAL BANKING AND FINANCE COMMUNICATIONS DIRECTORY.
Telex - Verlag Jaeger & Waldmann GmbH, Birkenweg 8-10, 64295 Darmstadt, Germany. TEL 49-6151-3302-0. FAX 49-6151-3302-50. *2035*

J & W TELEFAX INTERNATIONAL. INTERNATIONAL FAX DIRECTORY.
Telex - Verlag Jaeger & Waldmann GmbH, Birkenweg 8-10, 64295 Darmstadt, Germany. TEL 49-6151-3302-0. FAX 49-6151-3302-50. *2035*

J & W TELEX INTERNATIONAL. INTERNATIONAL TELEX AND TELETEX DIRECTORY.
Telex - Verlag Jaeger & Waldmann GmbH, Birkenweg 8-10, 64295 Darmstadt, Germany. TEL 49-6151-3302-0. FAX 49-6151-3302-50. *2035*

J & W TRAVEL INTERNATIONAL.
Telex - Verlag Jaeger & Waldmann GmbH, Birkenweg 8-10, 64295 Darmstadt, Germany. TEL 49-6151-3302-0. FAX 49-6151-3302-50. *2035*

JAHRBUCH DER AUKTIONSPREISE FUER BUECHER, HANDSCHRIFTEN UND AUTOGRAPHEN.
Dr. Ernst Hauswedell und Co. Verlag, Haldenstr. 20, 70376 Stuttgart, Germany. TEL 49-711-638264. FAX 49-711-6369010. *6274*

JAHRBUCH DER WERBUNG.
E C O N Verlag GmbH, Postfach 300321, 40403 Duesseldorf, Germany. TEL 49-211-4359749. FAX 49-211-4359781. *38*

JAHRBUCH FUER BERGBAU, ERDOEL UND ERDGAS, PETROCHEMIE, ELEKTRIZITAET, UMWELTSCHUTZ.
Verlag Glueckauf GmbH, Postfach 185620, 45206 Essen, Germany. TEL 49-2054-92412023. FAX 49-2054-924129. *5304*

JANE'S AIRCRAFT UPGRADES.
Jane's Information Group, Sentinel House, 163 Brighton Rd., Coulsdon, Surrey CR5 2NH, England. TEL 44-181-700-3700. FAX 44-181-700-3788. *71*

JANE'S ALL THE WORLD'S AIRCRAFT.
Jane's Information Group, Sentinel House, 163 Brighton Rd., Coulsdon, Surrey CR5 2NH, England. TEL 44-181-700-3700. FAX 44-181-700-3788. *71*

JANE'S ARMOUR AND ARTILLERY.
Jane's Information Group, Sentinel House, 163 Brighton Rd., Coulsdon, Surrey CR5 2NH, England. TEL 44-181-700-3700. FAX 44-181-700-3788. *5272*

JANE'S ARMOUR AND ARTILLERY UPGRADES.
Jane's Information Group, Sentinel House, 163 Brighton Rd., Coulsdon, Surrey CR5 2NH, England. TEL 44-181-700-3700. FAX 44-181-700-3788. *5272*

JANE'S AVIONICS.
Jane's Information Group, Sentinel House, 163 Brighton Rd., Coulsdon, Surrey CR5 2NH, England. TEL 44-181-700-3700. FAX 44-181-700-3788. *71*

JANE'S C 4 I SYSTEMS.
Jane's Information Group, Sentinel House, 163 Brighton Rd., Coulsdon, Surrey CR5 2NH, England. TEL 44-181-700-3700. FAX 44-181-700-3788. *5272*

JANE'S FIGHTING SHIPS.
Jane's Information Group, Sentinel House, 163 Brighton Rd., Coulsdon, Surrey CR5 2NH, England. TEL 44-181-700-3700. FAX 44-181-700-3788. *5272*

JANE'S HIGH-SPEED MARINE TRANSPORTATION.
Jane's Information Group, Sentinel House, 163 Brighton Rd., Coulsdon, Surrey CR5 2NH, England. TEL 44-181-700-3700. FAX 44-181-700-3715. *7154*

JANE'S INFANTRY WEAPONS.
Jane's Information Group, Sentinel House, 163 Brighton Rd., Coulsdon, Surrey CR5 2NH, England. TEL 44-181-700-3700. FAX 44-181-700-3788. *5272*

JANE'S INTERNATIONAL A B C AEROSPACE DIRECTORY.
Jane's Information Group, Sentinel House, 163 Brighton Rd., Coulsdon, Surrey CR5 2NH, England. TEL 44-181-700-3700. FAX 44-181-700-3788. *71*

JANE'S INTERNATIONAL DEFENCE DIRECTORY.
Jane's Information Group, Sentinel House, 163 Brighton Rd., Coulsdon, Surrey CR5 2NH, England. TEL 44-181-700-3700. FAX 44-181-700-3816. *5272*

JANE'S LAND-BASED AIR DEFENCE.
Jane's Information Group, Sentinel House, 163 Brighton Rd., Coulsdon, Surrey CR5 2NH, England. TEL 44-181-700-3700. FAX 44-181-700-3788. *5272*

JANE'S MILITARY COMMUNICATIONS.
Jane's Information Group, Sentinel House, 163 Brighton Rd., Coulsdon, Surrey CR5 2NH, England. TEL 44-181-700-3700. FAX 44-181-700-3788. *5272*

JANE'S MILITARY VEHICLES AND LOGISTICS.
Jane's Information Group, Sentinel House, 163 Brighton Rd., Coulsdon, Surrey CR5 2NH, England. TEL 44-18700-3700. FAX 44-181-700-3788. *5273*

JANE'S N B C PROTECTION EQUIPMENT.
Jane's Information Group, Sentinel House, 163 Brighton Rd., Coulsdon, Surrey CR5 2NH, England. TEL 44-181-700-3700. FAX 44-181-700-3788. *5273*

JANE'S NAVAL WEAPON SYSTEM.
Jane's Information Group, Sentinel House, 163 Brighton Rd., Coulsdon, Surrey CR5 2NH, England. TEL 44-181-700-3700. FAX 44-181-700-3788. *5273*

JANE'S POLICE AND SECURITY EQUIPMENT.
Jane's Information Group, Sentinel House, 163 Brighton Rd., Coulsdon, Surrey CR5 2NH, England. TEL 44-181-700-3700. FAX 44-181-700-3788. *2287*

JANE'S RADAR AND ELECTRONIC WARFARE SYSTEMS.
Jane's Information Group, Sentinel House, 163 Brighton Rd., Coulsdon, Surrey CR5 2NH, England. TEL 44-181-700-3700. FAX 44-181-700-3788. *5273*

JANE'S SIMULATION AND TRAINING SYSTEMS.
Jane's Information Group, Sentinel House, 163 Brighton Rd., Coulsdon, Surrey CR5 2NH, England. TEL 44-181-700-3700. FAX 44-181-700-3788. *5273*

JANE'S SPACE DIRECTORY.
Jane's Information Group, Sentinel House, 163 Brighton Rd., Coulsdon, Surrey CR5 2NH, England. TEL 44-181-700-3700. FAX 44-181-700-3788. *71*

JANE'S UNDERWATER WARFARE SYSTEMS.
Jane's Information Group, Sentinel House, 163 Brighton Rd., Coulsdon, Surrey CR5 2NH, England. TEL 44-181-700-3700. FAX 44-181-700-3788. *5273*

JANE'S URBAN TRANSPORT SYSTEMS.
Jane's Information Group, Sentinel House, 163 Brighton Rd., Coulsdon, Surrey CR5 2NH, England. TEL 44-181-700-3700. FAX 44-181-700-3715. *7031*

JANE'S WORLD RAILWAYS.
Jane's Information Group, Sentinel House, 163 Brighton Rd., Coulsdon, Surrey CR5 2NH, England. TEL 44-181-700-3700. FAX 44-181-700-3715. *7127*

JAPAN ELECTRONICS BUYERS' GUIDE.
Dempa Publications, Inc., 1-11-15, Higashi Gotanda, Shinagawa-ku, Tokyo 141, Japan. TEL 81-3-3445-6111. FAX 81-3-3445-6101. Available only on CD-ROM. *1690*

JAPAN TIMES.
Japan Times Ltd., 5-4 Shibaura 4-chome, Minato-ku, Tokyo 108, Japan. TEL 03-3453-5242. FAX 03-3452-1298. *3330*

JAPANESE JOURNAL OF CLINICAL ONCOLOGY.
Foundation for Promotion of Cancer Research, c/o National Cancer Center Hospital, 1-1, Tsukiji 5-chome, Chuo-ku, Tokyo 104, Japan. TEL 81-3-3542-2511. FAX 81-3-3545-3567. *4980*

JAPANESE NATIONAL BIBLIOGRAPHY WEEKLY LIST.
National Diet Library, 1-10-1 Nagata-cho, Chiyoda-ku, Tokyo 100, Japan. TEL 81-3-3581-2331. FAX 81-3-3597-9104. *553*

THE JAPANESE PHARMACOPOEIA.
Yakuji Nippo, Ltd., 1, Kanda Izumicho, Chiyoda-ku, Tokyo 101, Japan. TEL 81-3-3862-2141. FAX 81-3-5821-8757. *5669*

THE JERUSALEM POST.
Jerusalem Post, P.O. Box 81, Jerusalem 91000, Israel. TEL 972-2-5315666. FAX 972-2-5389527. *3324*

THE JERUSALEM POST (EDITION FRANCAISE).
Jerusalem Post, P.O. Box 81, Jerusalem 91000, Israel. TEL 972-2-315666. FAX 972-2-389017. *3324*

THE JERUSALEM POST (INTERNATIONAL EDITION).
Jerusalem Post, P.O. Box 81, Jerusalem 91000, Israel. TEL 972-2-315666. FAX 972-2-389017. *3324*

JET.
Johnson Publishing Co., Inc., 820 S. Michigan Ave., Chicago, IL 60605-2190. TEL 312-322-9200. Producer(s): UMI. *3376*

JEWISH BIBLE QUARTERLY.
Jewish Bible Association, P.O. Box 29002, Jerusalem, Israel. TEL 972-2-6759144. FAX 972-2-6759144. *6347*

JIANGHAN KAOGU.
Archaeological Institute of Hubei Province, Tian'e Cun, Donghu Lu, Wuchang-qu, Wuhan, Hubei 430077, People's Republic of China. TEL 86-10-27-6813122. *368*

JIANGSU NONGYE XUEBAO.
Jiangsu Sheng Nongye Kexueyuan, Xiaolingwei, Nanjing, Jiangsu 210014, People's Republic of China. TEL 86-25-4390285. *129*

JOHANSENS RECOMMENDED HOTELS, COUNTRY HOUSES & INNS IN GREAT BRITAIN & IRELAND C D - R O M.
Hobsons Publishing plc., Bateman St., Cambridge CB2 1LZ, England. TEL 44-1223-354551. FAX 44-1223-321454. Available only on CD-ROM. *3730*

JOHANSENS RECOMMENDED HOTELS IN EUROPE.
Hobsons Publishing plc., Bateman St., Cambridge CB2 1LZ, England. TEL 44-1223-354551. FAX 44-1223-321454. *3730*

JOINT AVIATION AUTHORITIES. CERTIFICATION INFORMATION - PROCEDURES.
Joint Aviation Authorities, J A A Headquarters, Saturnusstraat 8-10, P.O. Box 3000, 2130 KA Hoofddorp, Netherlands. TEL 31-23-5679700. FAX 31-23-5621714. *7074*

JOINT AVIATION AUTHORITIES. GENERAL INFORMATION - PROCEDURES. INFORMATION LEAFLETS.
Joint Aviation Authorities, J A A Headquarters, Saturnusstraat 8-10, P.O. Box 3000, 2130 KA Hoofddorp, Netherlands. TEL 31-23-5679700. FAX 31-23-5621714. *7074*

JOINT AVIATION AUTHORITIES. MAINTENANCE INFORMATION - PROCEDURES.
Joint Aviation Authorities, J A A Headquarters, Saturnusstraat 8-10, P.O. Box 3000, 2130 KA Hoofddorp, Netherlands. TEL 31-23-5679700. FAX 31-23-5621714. *7074*

JOINT AVIATION AUTHORITIES. REGULATORY DOCUMENTS.
Joint Aviation Authorities, J A A Headquarters, Saturnusstraat 8-10, P.O. Box 3000, 2130 KA Hoofddorp, Netherlands. TEL 31-23-5679700. FAX 31-23-5621714. *7074*

JORDAN MEDICAL JOURNAL.
Jordan Medical Association, P.O. Box 915, Amman, Jordan. *4690*

JOURNAL OF ADHESION.
Gordon and Breach - Harwood Academic, Amsteldisk 166, 1st Fl., 1079 LH Amsterdam, Netherlands. *5809*

JOURNAL OF ADVERTISING.
American Academy of Advertising, Clemson University, College of Commerce & Industry, 245 Sirrine Hall, Clemson, SC 29634-1325. *38*

JOURNAL OF AMERICAN COLLEGE HEALTH.
Heldref Publications, 1319 Eighteenth St., N.W., Washington, DC 20036-1802. TEL 202-296-6267. FAX 202-296-5149. Producer(s): UMI. *5785*

JOURNAL OF APPLIED PHYSICS.
American Institute of Physics, One Physics Ellipse, College Park, MD 20740-3843. TEL 301-209-3000. *5809*

JOURNAL OF APPLIED THERAPEUTICS.
Gordon and Breach - Harwood Academic, Amsteldisk 166, 1st Fl., 1079 LH Amsterdam, Netherlands. *5670*

JOURNAL OF ARCHITECTURAL ENGINEERING.
American Society of Civil Engineers, Architectural Engineering Division, 345 E. 47th St., New York, NY 10007-0335. TEL 212-705-7000. *407*

JOURNAL OF ARTS MANAGEMENT, LAW, AND SOCIETY.
Heldref Publications, 1319 18th St., N.W., Washington, DC 20036-1802. TEL 202-296-6267. FAX 202-296-5149. Producer(s): UMI. *3968*

JOURNAL OF BACTERIOLOGY.
American Society for Microbiology, 1325 Massachusetts Ave., N.W., Washington, DC 20005. TEL 202-737-3600. *787*

JOURNAL OF BLACKS IN HIGHER EDUCATION.
CH II Publishers, Inc., 200 W. 57th St., New York, NY 10019. TEL 212-399-1084. FAX 212-245-1973. *3023*

SERIALS AVAILABLE ON CD-ROM

JOURNAL OF BONE AND JOINT SURGERY: BRITISH VOLUME.
British Editorial Society of Bone and Joint Surgery, 22 Buckingham St., London WC2N 6ET, England. TEL 0171-782-0010. FAX 0171-782-0995. *5009*

JOURNAL OF BUSINESS FORECASTING METHODS AND SYSTEMS.
Graceway Publishing Co., Box 670159, Flushing, NY 11367-0159. TEL 718-463-3914. FAX 718-544-9086. *976*

JOURNAL OF CANADIAN PETROLEUM TECHNOLOGY.
Canadian Institute of Mining, Metallurgy and Petroleum, Petroleum Society, 101 6 Ave., S.W., Ste. 320, Calgary, AB T2P 3P4, Canada. TEL 403-237-5112. FAX 403-262-4792. *5607*

JOURNAL OF CHEMICAL EDUCATION: SOFTWARE. SPECIAL ISSUE SERIES.
American Chemical Society, Division of Chemical Education, Inc., c/o Dept. of Chemistry, Univ. of Wisconsin at Madison, 1101 University Ave., Madison, WI 53706-1396. TEL 608-262-5153. FAX 608-265-8094. *2517*

JOURNAL OF CHEMICAL PHYSICS.
American Institute of Physics, One Physics Ellipse, College Park, MD 20740-3843. TEL 301-209-3000. FAX 516-349-9704. *5809*

JOURNAL OF CLINICAL MICROBIOLOGY.
American Society for Microbiology, 1325 Massachusetts Ave., N.W., Washington, DC 20005. TEL 202-737-3600. *788*

JOURNAL OF COMPARATIVE FAMILY STUDIES.
University of Calgary, Department of Sociology, 2500 University Dr. N.W., Calgary, AB T2N 1N4, Canada. TEL 403-220-7317. FAX 403-282-9298. *6716*

JOURNAL OF COMPARATIVE RELIGION.
Universal Publications (a division of S T C), P.O. Box 7305, Ottawa, ON K1L 8E4, Canada. TEL 613-831-1052. FAX 613-831-8452. *6348*

JOURNAL OF CONSUMER MARKETING.
M C B University Press Ltd., 60-62 Toller Ln., Bradford, W. Yorks BD8 9BY, England. TEL 44-1274-777700. FAX 44-1274-785200. *1532*

JOURNAL OF CONSUMER RESEARCH.
University of Chicago Press, Journals Division, Box 37005, Chicago, IL 60637. TEL 773-753-3347. FAX 773-753-0811. *1532*

JOURNAL OF COORDINATION CHEMISTRY.
Gordon and Breach - Harwood Academic, Amsteldisk 166, 1st Fl., 1079 LH Amsterdam, Netherlands. *1755*

JOURNAL OF CORPORATION LAW.
University of Iowa, College of Law, 190 Boyd Law Bldg., Iowa City, IA 52242-1113. TEL 319-335-9061. FAX 319-335-9019. *4082*

THE JOURNAL OF DEVELOPMENT STUDIES.
Frank Cass, Newbury House, 890-900 Eastern Ave., Newbury Park, Ilford, Essex 1G2 7HH, England. TEL 44-181-599-8866. FAX 44-181-599-0984. *1364*

JOURNAL OF DEVELOPMENTAL EDUCATION.
Appalachian State University, National Center for Developmental Education, Boone, NC 28608. TEL 704-262-2876. FAX 704-262-2128. *2546*

JOURNAL OF DIFFERENCE EQUATIONS AND APPLICATIONS.
Gordon and Breach - Harwood Academic, Amsteldisk 166, 1st Fl., 1079 LH Amsterdam, Netherlands. *4582*

JOURNAL OF DRUG TARGETING.
Gordon and Breach - Harwood Academic, Amsteldisk 166, 1st Fl., 1079 LH Amsterdam, Netherlands. *5671*

THE JOURNAL OF ECONOMIC EDUCATION.
Heldref Publications, 1319 18th St., N.W., Washington, DC 20036-1802. TEL 202-296-6267. FAX 202-296-5149.
Producer(s): UMI. *976*

JOURNAL OF ECONOMIC LITERATURE.
American Economic Association, 2014 Broadway, Ste. 305, Nashville, TN 37203. TEL 615-322-2595.
Producer(s): SilverPlatter Information, Inc. *1052*

JOURNAL OF ECONOMIC STUDIES.
M C B University Press Ltd., 60-62 Toller Ln., Bradford, W. Yorks BD8 9BY, England. TEL 44-1274-777700. FAX 44-1274-785200. *977*

JOURNAL OF EDUCATION FOR BUSINESS.
Heldref Publications, 1319 18th St., N.W., Washington, DC 20036-1802. TEL 202-296-6267. FAX 202-296-5149.
Producer(s): UMI. *977*

JOURNAL OF EDUCATIONAL ADMINISTRATION.
M C B University Press Ltd., 60-62 Toller Ln., Bradford, W. Yorks BD8 9BY, England. TEL 44-1274-777700. FAX 44-1274-785200. *2574*

THE JOURNAL OF EDUCATIONAL RESEARCH.
Heldref Publications, 1319 18th St., N.W., Washington, DC 20036-1802. TEL 202-296-6267. FAX 202-296-5149.
Producer(s): UMI. *2455*

JOURNAL OF ENGINEERING VALUATION AND COST ANALYSIS.
Gordon and Breach - Harwood Academic, Amsteldisk 166, 1st Fl., 1079 LH Amsterdam, Netherlands. *2728*

THE JOURNAL OF ENVIRONMENTAL EDUCATION.
Heldref Publications, 1319 Eighteenth St., N.W., Washington, DC 20036-1802. TEL 202-296-6267.
Producer(s): UMI. *2937*

JOURNAL OF ENZYME INHIBITION.
Gordon and Breach - Harwood Academic, Amsteldisk 166, 1st Fl., 1079 LH Amsterdam, Netherlands. *663*

JOURNAL OF EVOLUTIONARY PSYCHOLOGY.
Institute for Evolutionary Psychology, 4625 Fifth Ave., Apt. 605, Pittsburgh, PA 15213-3644. TEL 412-621-7057. *6125*

JOURNAL OF EXPERIMENTAL EDUCATION.
Heldref Publications, 1319 18th St., N.W., Washington, DC 20036-1802. TEL 202-296-6267. FAX 202-296-5149.
Producer(s): UMI. *2608*

JOURNAL OF FAMILY WELFARE.
Family Planning Association of India, Bajaj Bhavan, Nariman Point, Mumbai 400021, India. TEL 91-22-202-9080. FAX 91-22-202-9038. *857*

THE JOURNAL OF GENERAL PSYCHOLOGY.
Heldref Publications, 1319 Eighteenth St., N.W., Washington, DC 20036. TEL 202-296-6267. FAX 202-296-5149.
Producer(s): UMI. *6126*

THE JOURNAL OF GENETIC PSYCHOLOGY.
Heldref Publications, 1319 Eighteenth St., N.W., Washington, DC 20036-1802. TEL 202-296-6267. FAX 202-296-5149.
Producer(s): UMI. *6127*

JOURNAL OF GROUP PSYCHOTHERAPY, PSYCHODRAMA & SOCIOMETRY.
Heldref Publications, 1319 Eighteenth St., N.W., Washington, DC 20036-1802. TEL 202-296-6267. FAX 202-296-5149.
Producer(s): UMI. *6127*

JOURNAL OF HIGHER EDUCATION.
Ohio State University Press, 1070 Carmack Rd., Columbus, OH 43210. TEL 614-292-6930. FAX 614-292-2065.
Producer(s): UMI. *2547*

JOURNAL OF HYDROLOGIC ENGINEERING.
American Society of Civil Engineers, 345 East 47th St., New York, NY 10017-2398. *2791*

JOURNAL OF INFRASTRUCTURE SYSTEMS.
American Society of Civil Engineers, 345 E. 47th St., New York, NY 10017-2398. TEL 212-705-7000. *2791*

JOURNAL OF MANAGEMENT CONSULTING.
858 Longview Rd., Burlingame, CA 94010-6974. TEL 415-342-1954. FAX 415-344-5005. *1488*

JOURNAL OF MANAGEMENT HISTORY.
M C B University Press Ltd., 60-62 Toller Ln., Bradford, W. Yorks BD8 9BY, England. TEL 44-1274-777700. FAX 44-1274-785200. *1488*

JOURNAL OF MANAGEMENT IN MEDICINE.
M C B University Press Ltd., 60-62 Toller Ln., Bradford, W. Yorks BD8 9BY, England. TEL 44-1274-777700. FAX 44-1274-785200. *4696*

JOURNAL OF MARINE ENVIRONMENTAL ENGINEERING.
Gordon and Breach - Harwood Academic, Amsteldisk 166, 1st Fl., 1079 LH Amsterdam, Netherlands. *2939*

JOURNAL OF MARKETING PRACTICE: APPLIED MARKETING SCIENCE.
M C B University Press Ltd., 60-62 Toller Ln., Bradford, W. Yorks BD8 9BY, England. TEL 44-1274-777700. FAX 44-1274-785200. *1534*

JOURNAL OF MARRIAGE AND THE FAMILY.
National Council on Family Relations, 3989 Central Ave., N.E., Ste. 550, Minneapolis, MN 55421-3921. TEL 612-781-9331. FAX 612-781-9348.
Producer(s): NISC. *6717*

JOURNAL OF MATERIALS RESEARCH.
Materials Research Society, 9800 McKnight Rd., Pittsburgh, PA 15237. TEL 412-367-3003. FAX 412-367-4373. *2862*

JOURNAL OF MATERIALS SCIENCE.
Thomson Science, 2-6 Boundary Row, London SE1 8HN, England. TEL 44-171-8650066. FAX 44-171-5229623. *2862*

JOURNAL OF MATERIALS SCIENCE LETTERS.
Chapman & Hall, Journals Department 2-6 Boundary Row, London SE1 8HN, England. TEL 44-171-8650066. FAX 44-171-5229623. *2862*

JOURNAL OF MINERAL POLICY, BUSINESS AND ENVIRONMENT - RAW MATERIALS REPORT.
Raavarugruppen Ekonomisk Foerening, P.O. Box 44062, S-100 73 Stockholm, Sweden. TEL 46-8-744-00-65. FAX 46-8-7440066. *1364*

JOURNAL OF MONEY, CREDIT & BANKING.
Ohio State University Press, 1070 Carmack Rd., Columbus, OH 43210. TEL 614-292-6930. FAX 614-292-2065.
Producer(s): UMI. *1151*

JOURNAL OF MOTOR BEHAVIOR.
Heldref Publications, 1319 Eighteenth St., N.W., Washington, DC 20036-1802. TEL 202-296-6267. FAX 202-296-5149.
Producer(s): UMI. *6128*

JOURNAL OF NEUROGENETICS.
Gordon and Breach - Harwood Academic, Amsteldisk 166, 1st Fl., 1079 LH Amsterdam, Netherlands. *5075*

JOURNAL OF OBSTETRICS AND GYNAECOLOGY.
University of Tokyo Press, 3-1, Hongo 7-chome, Bunkyo-ku, Tokyo 113, Japan. *4962*

JOURNAL OF OBSTETRICS AND GYNAECOLOGY OF INDIA.
Federation of Obstetric & Gynaecological Societies of India, Purandare Griha, 31 C, Dr. N.A. Purandare Marg, Bombay 400 007, India. TEL 811-04-46. *4962*

JOURNAL OF ORGANIZATIONAL CHANGE MANAGEMENT.
M C B University Press Ltd., 60-62 Toller Ln., Bradford, W. Yorks BD8 9BY, England. TEL 44-1274-777700. FAX 44-1274-785200. *1489*

JOURNAL OF ORTHOPAEDIC RHEUMATOLOGY.
Rapid Science Publishers, The Old Malthouse, Paradise St., Oxford OX1 1LD, England. TEL -1865-790447. FAX -1865-244012. *5125*

JOURNAL OF POPULAR FILM AND TELEVISION.
Heldref Publications, 1319 Eighteenth St., N.W., Washington, DC 20036-1802. TEL 202-296-6267. FAX 202-296-5149.
Producer(s): UMI. *5337*

SERIALS AVAILABLE ON CD-ROM

JOURNAL OF POPULATION, HEALTH AND SOCIAL WELFARE.
Korea Institute for Health and Social Affairs, San 42-14, Bulgwang-Dong, Eunpyung-Ku, Seoul 122 040, S. Korea. TEL 02-355-8003. FAX 02-352-9129. *6673*

JOURNAL OF PORTFOLIO MANAGEMENT.
Institutional Investor Journals, 488 Madison Ave., New York, NY 10022. TEL 212-224-3185. FAX 212-224-3527. *1393*

JOURNAL OF POSTGRADUATE MEDICINE.
Seth G.S. Medical College and K.E.M. Hospital, Staff Society, Dept. of Nephrology, Bombay 400012, India. TEL 4132118. *4698*

JOURNAL OF PROPERTY FINANCE.
M C B University Press Ltd., 60-62 Toller Ln., Bradford, W. Yorks BD8 9BY, England. TEL 44-1274-777700. FAX 44-1274-785200. *6304*

JOURNAL OF PROTECTIVE COATINGS AND LININGS.
Technology Publishing Co., 2100 Wharton St., Ste. 31, Pittsburgh, PA 15203. TEL 412-431-8300. FAX 412-431-5428. *5553*

JOURNAL OF REGIONAL AND LOCAL STUDIES.
c/o Lincoln University, Department of Humanities, Brayford Pool, Lincoln LN6 7TS, England. *3578*

JOURNAL OF SERVICES MARKETING.
M C B University Press Ltd., 60-62 Toller Ln., Bradford, W. Yorks BD8 9BY, England. TEL 44-1274-777700. FAX 44-1274-785200. *1535*

JOURNAL OF SOIL BIOLOGY AND ECOLOGY.
Indian Society of Soil Biology and Ecology, University of Agricultural Sciences, Department of Entomology, Hebbal, Bangalore 560 024, India. TEL 91-80-3330153. FAX 91-80-3330277. *610*

JOURNAL OF SPORT BEHAVIOR.
University of South Alabama, Department of Health, Physical Education and Leisure Studies, Mobile, AL 36688. TEL 334-460-7131. FAX 334-460-7252. Producer(s): UMI. *6767*

JOURNAL OF STATISTICAL COMPUTATION AND SIMULATION.
Gordon and Breach - Harwood Academic, Amsteldisk 166, 1st Fl., 1079 LH Amsterdam, Netherlands. *2152*

JOURNAL OF STRUCTURAL LEARNING.
Gordon and Breach - Harwood Academic, Amsteldisk 166, 1st Fl., 1079 LH Amsterdam, Netherlands. *6132*

JOURNAL OF TECHNOLOGY TRANSFER.
Technology Transfer Society, 435 N. Michigan Ave., Chicago, IL 60611-4001. *6964*

JOURNAL OF TRAUMA - INJURY, INFECTION AND CRITICAL CARE.
Williams & Wilkins, 351 W. Camden St., Baltimore, MD 21201-2436. TEL 410-528-4068. FAX 410-528-4452. *5011*

JOURNAL OF VACUUM SCIENCE AND TECHNOLOGY. PART A. VACUUM, SURFACES AND FILMS.
American Institute of Physics, One Physics Ellipse, College Park, MD 20740-3843. TEL 301-209-3000. *5812*

JOURNAL OF VACUUM SCIENCE AND TECHNOLOGY. PART B. MICROELECTRONICS AND NANOMETER STRUCTURES.
American Institute of Physics, One Physics Ellipse, College Park, MD 20740-3843. TEL 301-209-3000. *5812*

JOURNAL OF VIROLOGY.
American Society for Microbiology, 1325 Massachusetts Ave., N.W., Washington, DC 20005. TEL 202-737-3600. *788*

JUDICIAL STAFF DIRECTORY.
C Q Staff Directories Inc., 815 Slaters Lane, Alexandria, VA 22314. TEL 703-739-0900. FAX 703-739-0234. *4133*

JUDICIAL YELLOW BOOK.
Leadership Directories, Inc., 104 Fifth Ave., 2nd Fl., New York, NY 10011. TEL 212-627-4140. FAX 212-645-0931.
Producer(s): Chadwyck-Healey Inc. *3971*

JUDIT.
Kluwer Rechtswetenschappen Belgie, Santvoortbeeklaan 21-25, 2100 Antwerp, Belgium. FAX 32-3-3600467.
Available only on CD-ROM. *3971*

JUNGE WELT.
Verlag 8. Mai GmbH, Am Treptower Park 28-30, 12435 Berlin, Germany. TEL 49-30-536355-0. FAX 49-30-68834343. *3286*

JURISTISCHE SCHULUNG.
Verlag C.H. Beck, 80791 Munich, Germany. TEL 49-89-38189-338. FAX 49-89-38189-398. *3972*

JUTA - STATE LIBRARY INDEX TO THE GOVERNMENT GAZETTE.
Juta & Co. Ltd., P.O. Box 14373, Kenwyn 7790, South Africa. TEL 27-21-7975101. FAX 27-21-7970121. *6205*

JUTA'S STATUTES OF SOUTH AFRICA.
Juta & Co. Ltd., P.O. Box 14373, Kenwyn 7790, South Africa. TEL 27-21-7975101. FAX 27-21-7970121. *3973*

K R ONDISC CHEMICAL BUSINESS NEWSBASE.
The Royal Society of Chemistry, Thomas Graham House, Science Park, Milton Rd., Cambridge CB4 4WF, England. TEL 44-1223-420066. FAX 44-1223-423623.
Available only on CD-ROM. *1757*

K R ONDISC ENVIRONMENTAL CHEMISTRY, HEALTH AND SAFETY.
The Royal Society of Chemistry, Thomas Graham House, Science Park, Milton Rd., Cambridge CB4 4WF, England. TEL 44-1223-420066. FAX 44-1223-423623.
Available only on CD-ROM. *2980*

KAIJO HOANCHO. SUIROBU KANSOKU HOKOKU. KAIYO HEN.
Kaijo Hoancho, Suirobu, 3-1, Tsukiji 5-chome, Chuo-ku, Tokyo 104, Japan. FAX 81-3-3545-2885. *2396*

KANSAS BUSINESS DIRECTORY.
American Business Directories, 5711 S. 86th Circle, Box 27347, Omaha, NE 68127. TEL 402-593-4600. FAX 402-331-5481. *1690*

KANSAS MANUFACTURERS REGISTER.
Manufacturers' News, Inc., 1633 Central St., Evanston, IL 60201-1569. TEL 847-864-7000. FAX 847-332-1100. *1690*

KATALOG FOR SKOLEBIBLIOTEKER. SKOLEBIBLIOTEKARENS.
Dansk BiblioteksCenter as, Tempovej 7-11, DK-2750 Ballerup, Denmark. TEL 45-44-867777. FAX 45-44-867892. *553*

KATALOG FOR SKOLEBIBLIOTEKER. TITELKATALOG.
Dansk BiblioteksCenter as, Tempovej 7-11, DK-2750 Ballerup, Denmark. TEL 45-44-867777. FAX 45-44-867892. *553*

KEESING'S RECORD OF WORLD EVENTS.
Keesing's Worldwide, LLC, 7979 Old Georgetown Rd., Bethesda, MD 20814. TEL 301-718-8770. FAX 301-718-8494. *5985*

KELLY'S DIRECTORY.
Kelly's Directories, Part of the Reed Elsevier group, Windsor Court, E. Grinstead House, E. Grinstead, W. Sussex RH19 1XB, England. TEL 01342-326972. FAX 01342-335747. *1690*

KENTUCKY ATTORNEY GENERAL OPINIONS.
Banks - Baldwin Law Publishing Co., Box 318063, Cleveland, OH 44131-8063. TEL 216-520-5600. FAX 216-520-5655. *4133*

KENTUCKY BUSINESS DIRECTORY.
American Business Directories, 5711 S. 86th Circle, Box 27347, Omaha, NE 68127. TEL 402-593-4600. FAX 402-331-5481. *1690*

KENTUCKY MANUFACTURERS REGISTER.
Manufacturers' News, Inc., 1633 Central St., Evanston, IL 60201. TEL 847-864-7000. FAX 847-332-1100. *1691*

KENTUCKY RULES OF COURT, STATE AND FEDERAL.
West Group, 620 Opperman Dr., Eagan, MN 55123. TEL 612-687-8000. FAX 612-687-7302. *4133*

KEY ABSTRACTS - BUSINESS AUTOMATION.
INSPEC, I.E.E., Michael Faraday House, Six Hill Way, Stevenage, Herts. SG1 2AY, England. TEL 44-1438-313311. FAX 44-1438-742840.
Producer(s): Knight-Ridder, Inc.. *2095*

KEY NOTE MARKET REPORT: ACCOUNTANCY.
Key Note Ltd., Field House, 72 Oldfield Rd., Hampton, Middlesex TW12 2HQ, England. TEL 44-181-783-0755. FAX 44-181-783-0049. *1093*

KEY NOTE MARKET REPORT: ADHESIVES.
Key Note Ltd., Field House, 72 Oldfield Rd., Hampton, Middlesex TW12 2HQ, England. TEL 44-181-783-0755. FAX 44-181-783-1940. *2768*

KEY NOTE MARKET REPORT: ADVERTISING AGENCIES.
Key Note Ltd., Field House, 72 Oldfield Rd., Hampton, Middlesex TW12 2HQ, England. TEL 44-181-783-0755. FAX 44-181-783-0049. *38*

KEY NOTE MARKET REPORT: AEROSPACE.
Key Note Ltd., Field House, 72 Oldfield Rd., Hampton, Middlesex TW12 2HQ, England. TEL 44-181-783-0755. FAX 44-181-783-0049. *73*

KEY NOTE MARKET REPORT: AFTER DINNER DRINKS.
Key Note Ltd., Field House, 72 Oldfield Rd., Hampton, Middlesex TW12 2HQ, England. TEL 44-181-783-0755. FAX 44-181-783-0049. *523*

KEY NOTE MARKET REPORT: AGRICULTURAL MACHINERY.
Key Note Ltd., Field House, 72 Oldfield Rd., Hampton, Middlesex TW12 2HQ, England. TEL 44-181-783-0755. FAX 44-181-783-0049. *207*

KEY NOTE MARKET REPORT: AGROCHEMICALS & FERTILIZERS.
Key Note Ltd., Field House, 72 Oldfield Rd., Hampton, Middlesex TW12 2HQ, England. TEL 44-181-783-0755. FAX 44-181-783-0049. *233*

KEY NOTE MARKET REPORT: AIRLINES.
Key Note Ltd., Field House, 72 Oldfield Rd., Hampton, Middlesex TW12 2HQ, England. TEL 44-181-783-0755. FAX 44-181-783-0049. *7074*

KEY NOTE MARKET REPORT: AIRPORTS.
Key Note Ltd., Field House, 72 Oldfield Rd., Hampton, Middlesex TW12 2HQ, England. TEL 44-181-783-0755. FAX 44-181-783-0049. *7074*

KEY NOTE MARKET REPORT: ANIMAL FEEDSTUFFS.
Key Note Ltd., Field House, 72 Oldfield Rd., Hampton, Middlesex TW12 2HQ, England. TEL 44-181-783-0755. FAX 44-181-783-0049. *264*

KEY NOTE MARKET REPORT: AUTOMATIC VENDING.
Key Note Ltd., Field House, 72 Oldfield Rd., Hampton, Middlesex TW12 2HQ, England. TEL 44-181-783-0755. FAX 44-181-783-0049. *1536*

KEY NOTE MARKET REPORT: AUTOPARTS.
Key Note Ltd., Field House, 72 Oldfield Rd., Hampton, Middlesex TW12 2HQ, England. TEL 44-181-783-0755. FAX 44-181-783-0049. *7104*

KEY NOTE MARKET REPORT: BABY PRODUCTS.
Key Note Ltd., Field House, 72 Oldfield Rd., Hampton, Middlesex TW12 2HQ, England. TEL 44-181-783-0755. FAX 44-181-783-0049. *1849*

KEY NOTE MARKET REPORT: BATHS & SANITARYWARE.
Key Note Ltd., Field House, 72 Oldfield Rd., Hampton, Middlesex TW12 2HQ, England. TEL 44-181-783-0755. FAX 44-181-783-0049. *507*

KEY NOTE MARKET REPORT: BETTING & GAMING.
Key Note Ltd., Field House, 72 Oldfield Rd., Hampton, Middlesex TW12 2HQ, England. TEL 44-181-783-0755. FAX 44-181-783-0049. *6768*

KEY NOTE MARKET REPORT: BICYCLES.
Key Note Ltd., Field House, 72 Oldfield Rd., Hampton, Middlesex TW12 2HQ, England. TEL 44-181-783-0755. FAX 44-181-783-0049. *6828*

10004 SERIALS AVAILABLE ON CD-ROM

KEY NOTE MARKET REPORT: BISCUITS & CAKES.
Key Note Ltd., Field House, 72 Oldfield Rd., Hampton, Middlesex TW12 2HQ, England. TEL 44-181-783-0755. FAX 44-181-783-0049. *3137*

KEY NOTE MARKET REPORT: BOOK PUBLISHING.
Key Note Ltd., Field House, 72 Oldfield Rd., Hampton, Middlesex TW12 2HQ, England. TEL 44-181-783-0755. FAX 44-181-783-0049. *6275*

KEY NOTE MARKET REPORT: BOOKSELLING.
Key Note Ltd., Field House, 72 Oldfield Rd., Hampton, Middlesex TW12 2HQ, England. TEL 44-181-783-0755. FAX 44-181-783-0049. *6275*

KEY NOTE MARKET REPORT: BOTTLED WATERS.
Key Note Ltd., Field House, 72 Oldfield Rd., Hampton, Middlesex TW12 2HQ, England. TEL 44-181-783-0755. FAX 44-181-783-0049. *523*

KEY NOTE MARKET REPORT: BREAD BAKERS.
Key Note Ltd., Field House, 72 Oldfield Rd., Hampton, Middlesex TW12 2HQ, England. TEL 44-181-783-0755. FAX 44-181-783-0049. *3137*

KEY NOTE MARKET REPORT: BREAKFAST CEREALS.
Key Note Ltd., Field House, 72 Oldfield Rd., Hampton, Middlesex TW12 2HQ, England. TEL 44-181-783-0755. FAX 44-181-783-0049. *3117*

KEY NOTE MARKET REPORT: BREWERIES & THE BEER MARKET.
Key Note Ltd., Field House, 72 Oldfield Rd., Hampton, Middlesex TW12 2HQ, England. TEL 44-181-783-0755. FAX 44-181-783-0049. *523*

KEY NOTE MARKET REPORT: BRICKS & TILES.
Key Note Ltd., Field House, 72 Oldfield Rd., Hampton, Middlesex TW12 2HQ, England. TEL 44-181-783-0755. FAX 44-181-783-0049. *900*

KEY NOTE MARKET REPORT: BROWN GOODS.
Key Note Ltd., Field House, 72 Oldfield Rd., Hampton, Middlesex TW12 2HQ, England. TEL 44-181-783-0755. FAX 44-181-783-0049. *2644*

KEY NOTE MARKET REPORT: BUILDING CONTRACTING.
Key Note Ltd., Field House, 72 Oldfield Rd., Hampton, Middlesex TW12 2HQ, England. TEL 44-181-783-0755. FAX 44-181-783-0049. *900*

KEY NOTE MARKET REPORT: BUILDING MATERIALS.
Key Note Ltd., Field House, 72 Oldfield Rd., Hampton, Middlesex TW12 2HQ, England. TEL 44-181-783-0755. FAX 44-181-783-1940. *900*

KEY NOTE MARKET REPORT: BUILDING SOCIETIES.
Key Note Ltd., Field House, 72 Oldfield Rd., Hampton, Middlesex TW12 2HQ, England. TEL 44-181-783-0755. FAX 44-181-783-0049. *900*

KEY NOTE MARKET REPORT: BUS & COACH OPERATORS.
Key Note Ltd., Field House, 72 Oldfield Rd., Hampton, Middlesex TW12 2HQ, England. TEL 44-171-783-0755. FAX 44-171-783-0049. *7032*

KEY NOTE MARKET REPORT: BUSINESS PRESS.
Key Note Ltd., Field House, 72 Oldfield Rd., Hampton, Middlesex TW12 2HQ, England. TEL 44-181-783-0755. FAX 44-181-783-0049. *979*

KEY NOTE MARKET REPORT: BUSINESS TRAVEL.
Key Note Ltd., Field House, 72 Oldfield Rd., Hampton, Middlesex TW12 2HQ, England. TEL 44-181-783-0755. FAX 44-181-783-0049. *7215*

KEY NOTE MARKET REPORT: C D - R O M.
Key Note Ltd., Field House, 72 Oldfield Rd., Hampton, Middlesex TW12 2HQ, England. TEL 44-181-783-0755. FAX 44-181-783-1940. *2016*

KEY NOTE MARKET REPORT: C T N'S.
Key Note Ltd., Field House, 72 Oldfield Rd., Hampton, Middlesex TW12 2HQ, England. TEL 44-181-783-0755. FAX 44-181-783-0049. *1151*

KEY NOTE MARKET REPORT: CABLE AND SATELLITE T V.
Key Note Ltd., Field House, 72 Oldfield Rd., Hampton, Middlesex TW12 2HQ, England. TEL 44-181-783-0755. FAX 44-181-783-0049. *2053*

KEY NOTE MARKET REPORT: CAMERAS & CAMCORDERS.
Key Note Ltd., Field House, 72 Oldfield Rd., Hampton, Middlesex TW12 2HQ, England. TEL 44-181-783-0755. FAX 44-181-783-0049. *5768*

KEY NOTE MARKET REPORT: CAMPING & CARAVANNING.
Key Note Ltd., Field House, 72 Oldfield Rd., Hampton, Middlesex TW12 2HQ, England. TEL 44-181-783-0755. FAX 44-181-783-0049. *4149*

KEY NOTE MARKET REPORT: CANNED FOODS.
Key Note Ltd., Field House, 72 Oldfield Rd., Hampton, Middlesex TW12 2HQ, England. TEL 44-181-783-0755. FAX 44-181-783-0049. *3117*

KEY NOTE MARKET REPORT: CAR DEALERS.
Key Note Ltd., Field House, 72 Oldfield Rd., Hampton, Middlesex TW12 2HQ, England. TEL 44-181-783-0755. FAX 44-181-783-0049. *7104*

KEY NOTE MARKET REPORT: CARPETS & FLOORCOVERINGS.
Key Note Ltd., Field House, 72 Oldfield Rd., Hampton, Middlesex TW12 2HQ, England. TEL 44-181-783-0755. FAX 44-181-783-0049. *3858*

KEY NOTE MARKET REPORT: CASH & CARRY OUTLETS.
Key Note Ltd., Field House, 72 Oldfield Rd., Hampton, Middlesex TW12 2HQ, England. TEL 44-181-783-0755. FAX 44-181-783-0049. *1536*

KEY NOTE MARKET REPORT: CHARITIES.
Key Note Ltd., Field House, 72 Oldfield Rd., Hampton, Middlesex TW12 2HQ, England. TEL 44-181-783-0755. FAX 44-181-783-1940. *6675*

KEY NOTE MARKET REPORT: CHEMICAL INDUSTRY.
Key Note Ltd., Field House, 72 Oldfield Rd., Hampton, Middlesex TW12 2HQ, England. TEL 44-181-783-0755. FAX 44-181-783-0049. *2768*

KEY NOTE MARKET REPORT: CHILDRENSWEAR.
Key Note Ltd., Field House, 72 Oldfield Rd., Hampton, Middlesex TW12 2HQ, England. TEL 44-181-783-0755. FAX 44-181-783-0049. *1916*

KEY NOTE MARKET REPORT: CHILLED FOODS.
Key Note Ltd., Field House, 72 Oldfield Rd., Hampton, Middlesex TW12 2HQ, England. TEL 44-181-783-0755. FAX 44-181-783-0049. *3117*

KEY NOTE MARKET REPORT: CHINA & EARTHENWARE.
Key Note Ltd., Field House, 72 Oldfield Rd., Hampton, Middlesex TW12 2HQ, England. TEL 44-181-783-0755. FAX 44-181-783-0049. *1732*

KEY NOTE MARKET REPORT: CIDER.
Key Note Ltd., Field House, 72 Oldfield Rd., Hampton, Middlesex TW12 2HQ, England. TEL 44-181-783-0755. FAX 44-181-783-0049. *523*

KEY NOTE MARKET REPORT: CIGARETTES & TOBACCO.
Key Note Ltd., Field House, 72 Oldfield Rd., Hampton, Middlesex TW12 2HQ, England. TEL 44-181-783-0755. FAX 44-181-783-0049. *7020*

KEY NOTE MARKET REPORT: CIVIL ENGINEERING.
Key Note Ltd., Field House, 72 Oldfield Rd., Hampton, Middlesex TW12 2HQ, England. TEL 44-181-783-0755. FAX 44-181-783-0049. *2792*

KEY NOTE MARKET REPORT: CLOTHING MANUFACTURING.
Key Note Ltd., Field House, 72 Oldfield Rd., Hampton, Middlesex TW12 2HQ, England. TEL 44-181-783-0755. FAX 44-181-783-0049. *1916*

KEY NOTE MARKET REPORT: CLOTHING RETAILING.
Key Note Ltd., Field House, 72 Oldfield Rd., Hampton, Middlesex TW12 2HQ, England. TEL 44-181-783-0755. FAX 44-181-783-0049. *1916*

KEY NOTE MARKET REPORT: COMMERCIAL RADIO.
Key Note Ltd., Field House, 72 Oldfield Rd., Hampton, Middlesex TW12 2HQ, England. TEL 44-181-783-0755. FAX 44-181-783-0049. *2025*

KEY NOTE MARKET REPORT: COMMERCIAL T V.
Key Note Ltd., Field House, 72 Oldfield Rd., Hampton, Middlesex TW12 2HQ, England. TEL 44-181-783-0755. FAX 44-181-783-0049. *2053*

KEY NOTE MARKET REPORT: COMMERCIAL VEHICLES.
Key Note Ltd., Field House, 72 Oldfield Rd., Hampton, Middlesex TW12 2HQ, England. TEL 44-181-783-0755. FAX 44-181-783-0049. *7104*

KEY NOTE MARKET REPORT: COMPUTER SERVICES.
Key Note Ltd., Field House, 72 Oldfield Rd., Hampton, Middlesex TW12 2HQ, England. TEL 44-181-783-0755. FAX 44-181-783-0049. *2127*

KEY NOTE MARKET REPORT: COMPUTER SOFTWARE.
Key Note Ltd., Field House, 72 Oldfield Rd., Hampton, Middlesex TW12 2HQ, England. TEL 44-181-783-0755. FAX 44-181-783-1940. *2214*

KEY NOTE MARKET REPORT: CONFECTIONERY.
Key Note Ltd., Field House, 72 Oldfield Rd., Hampton, Middlesex TW12 2HQ, England. TEL 44-181-783-0755. FAX 44-181-783-0049. *3137*

KEY NOTE MARKET REPORT: CONSUMER MAGAZINES.
Key Note Ltd., Field House, 72 Oldfield Rd., Hampton, Middlesex TW12 2HQ, England. TEL 44-181-783-0755. FAX 44-181-783-0049. *6275*

KEY NOTE MARKET REPORT: CONTRACEPTIVES.
Key Note Ltd., Field House, 72 Oldfield Rd., Hampton, Middlesex TW12 2HQ, England. TEL 44-181-783-0755. FAX 44-181-783-0049. *858*

KEY NOTE MARKET REPORT: CONTRACT CATERING.
Key Note Ltd., Field House, 72 Oldfield Rd., Hampton, Middlesex TW12 2HQ, England. TEL 44-171-783-0049. *3731*

KEY NOTE MARKET REPORT: CONTRACT CLEANING.
Key Note Ltd., Field House, 72 Oldfield Rd., Hampton, Middlesex TW12 2HQ, England. TEL 44-181-783-0755. FAX 44-181-783-0049. *1910*

KEY NOTE MARKET REPORT: CONVENIENCE RETAILING.
Key Note Ltd., Field House, 72 Oldfield Rd., Hampton, Middlesex TW12 2HQ, England. TEL 44-181-783-0755. FAX 44-181-783-0049. *1536*

KEY NOTE MARKET REPORT: COSMETICS & FRAGRANCES.
Key Note Ltd., Field House, 72 Oldfield Rd., Hampton, Middlesex TW12 2HQ, England. TEL 44-181-783-0755. FAX 44-181-783-0049. *511*

KEY NOTE MARKET REPORT: COURIER & EXPRESS SERVICES.
Key Note Ltd., Field House, 72 Oldfield Rd., Hampton, Middlesex TW12 2HQ, England. TEL 44-181-783-0755. FAX 44-181-783-0049. *2019*

KEY NOTE MARKET REPORT: CREDIT & OTHER FINANCE CARDS.
Key Note Ltd., Field House, 72 Oldfield Rd., Hampton, Middlesex TW12 2HQ, England. TEL 44-181-783-0755. FAX 44-181-783-0049. *1151*

KEY NOTE MARKET REPORT: DEBT MANAGEMENT & FACTORING.
Key Note Ltd., Field House, 72 Oldfield Rd., Hampton, Middlesex TW12 2HQ, England. TEL 44-181-783-0755. FAX 44-181-783-0049. *1151*

KEY NOTE MARKET REPORT: DEFENCE EQUIPMENT.
Key Note Ltd., Field House, 72 Oldfield Rd., Hampton, Middlesex TW12 2HQ, England. TEL 44-181-783-0755. FAX 44-181-783-0049. *5274*

KEY NOTE MARKET REPORT: DIRECT MARKETING.
Key Note Ltd., Field House, 72 Oldfield Rd., Hampton, Middlesex TW12 2HQ, England. TEL 44-181-783-0755. FAX 44-181-783-0049. *1536*

KEY NOTE MARKET REPORT: DISPOSABLE PAPER PRODUCTS.
Key Note Ltd., Field House, 72 Oldfield Rd., Hampton, Middlesex TW12 2HQ, England. TEL 44-181-783-0755. FAX 44-181-783-0049. *5567*

KEY NOTE MARKET REPORT: DISTILLERS (WHISKY).
Key Note Ltd., Field House, 72 Oldfield Rd., Hampton, Middlesex TW12 2HQ, England. TEL 44-181-783-0755. FAX 44-181-783-0049. *523*

KEY NOTE MARKET REPORT: DOMESTIC HEATING.
Key Note Ltd., Field House, 72 Oldfield Rd., Hampton, Middlesex TW12 2HQ, England. TEL 44-181-783-0755. FAX 44-181-783-0049. *3481*

KEY NOTE MARKET REPORT: DRY BATTERIES.
Key Note Ltd., Field House, 72 Oldfield Rd., Hampton, Middlesex TW12 2HQ, England. TEL 44-181-783-0755. FAX 44-181-783-0049. *5839*

KEY NOTE MARKET REPORT: ELECTRICAL CONTRACTING.
Key Note Ltd., Field House, 72 Oldfield Rd., Hampton, Middlesex TW12 2HQ, England. TEL 44-181-783-0755. FAX 44-181-783-0049. *2838*

KEY NOTE MARKET REPORT: ELECTRONIC COMPONENT DISTRIBUTION.
Key Note Ltd., Field House, 72 Oldfield Rd., Hampton, Middlesex TW12 2HQ, England. TEL 44-181-783-0755. FAX 44-181-783-0049. *2645*

KEY NOTE MARKET REPORT: ELECTRONIC COMPONENT MANUFACTURERS.
Key Note Ltd., Field House, 72 Oldfield Rd., Hampton, Middlesex TW12 2HQ, England. TEL 44-181-783-0755. FAX 44-181-783-0049. *2645*

KEY NOTE MARKET REPORT: ELECTRONIC GAMES.
Key Note Ltd., Field House, 72 Oldfield Rd., Hampton, Middlesex TW12 2HQ, England. TEL 44-181-783-0755. FAX 44-181-783-0049. *2118*

KEY NOTE MARKET REPORT: EMPLOYMENT AGENCIES.
Key Note Ltd., Field House, 72 Oldfield Rd., Hampton, Middlesex TW12 2HQ, England. TEL 44-181-783-0755. FAX 44-181-783-0049. *5512*

KEY NOTE MARKET REPORT: EQUIPMENT LEASING.
Key Note Ltd., Field House, 72 Oldfield Rd., Hampton, Middlesex TW12 2HQ, England. TEL 44-181-783-0755. FAX 44-181-783-0049. *1644*

KEY NOTE MARKET REPORT: ESTATE AGENTS.
Key Note Ltd., Field House, 72 Oldfield Rd., Hampton, Middlesex TW12 2HQ, England. TEL 44-181-783-0755. FAX 44-181-783-0049. *4097*

KEY NOTE MARKET REPORT: ETHNIC FOODS.
Key Note Ltd., Field House, 72 Oldfield Rd., Hampton, Middlesex TW12 2HQ, England. TEL 44-181-783-0755. FAX 44-181-783-0049. *3117*

KEY NOTE MARKET REPORT: EXHIBITIONS AND CONFERENCE ORGANISERS.
Key Note Ltd., Field House, 72 Oldfield Rd., Hampton, Middlesex TW12 2HQ, England. TEL 44-181-783-0755. FAX 44-181-783-0049. *5170*

KEY NOTE MARKET REPORT: FAST FOOD AND HOME DELIVERY OUTLETS.
Key Note Ltd., Field House, 72 Oldfield Rd., Hampton, Middlesex TW12 2HQ, England. TEL 44-181-783-0755. FAX 44-181-783-0049. *3117*

KEY NOTE MARKET REPORT: FIBRES.
Key Note Ltd., Field House, 72 Oldfield Rd., Hampton, Middlesex TW12 2HQ, England. TEL 44-181-783-0755. FAX 44-181-783-1940. *6990*

KEY NOTE MARKET REPORT: FINANCE HOUSES.
Key Note Ltd., Field House, 72 Oldfield Rd., Hampton, Middlesex TW12 2HQ, England. TEL 44-181-783-0755. FAX 44-181-783-0049. *1151*

KEY NOTE MARKET REPORT: FIRE PROTECTION EQUIPMENT.
Key Note Ltd., Field House, 72 Oldfield Rd., Hampton, Middlesex TW12 2HQ, England. TEL 44-181-783-0755. FAX 44-181-783-0049. *3056*

KEY NOTE MARKET REPORT: FOOD FLAVOURINGS & INGREDIENTS.
Key Note Ltd., Field House, 72 Oldfield Rd., Hampton, Middlesex TW12 2HQ, England. TEL 44-181-783-0755. FAX 44-181-783-0049. *3117*

KEY NOTE MARKET REPORT: FOOTWEAR.
Key Note Ltd., Field House, 72 Oldfield Rd., Hampton, Middlesex TW12 2HQ, England. TEL 44-181-783-0755. FAX 44-181-783-1940. *6596*

KEY NOTE MARKET REPORT: FREIGHT FORWARDING.
Key Note Ltd., Field House, 72 Oldfield Rd., Hampton, Middlesex TW12 2HQ, England. TEL 44-181-783-0755. FAX 44-181-783-0049. *7032*

KEY NOTE MARKET REPORT: FROZEN FOODS.
Key Note Ltd., Field House, 72 Oldfield Rd., Hampton, Middlesex TW12 2HQ, England. TEL 44-181-783-0755. FAX 44-181-783-0049. *3117*

KEY NOTE MARKET REPORT: FRUIT & VEGETABLES.
Key Note Ltd., Field House, 72 Oldfield Rd., Hampton, Middlesex TW12 2HQ, England. TEL 44-181-783-0755. FAX 44-181-783-0049. *3143*

KEY NOTE MARKET REPORT: FRUIT JUICES & HEALTH DRINKS.
Key Note Ltd., Field House, 72 Oldfield Rd., Hampton, Middlesex TW12 2HQ, England. TEL 44-181-783-0755. FAX 44-181-783-0049. *523*

KEY NOTE MARKET REPORT: GARDEN EQUIPMENT.
Key Note Ltd., Field House, 72 Oldfield Rd., Hampton, Middlesex TW12 2HQ, England. TEL 44-181-783-0755. FAX 44-181-783-0049. *3197*

KEY NOTE MARKET REPORT: GIFTWARE.
Key Note Ltd., Field House, 72 Oldfield Rd., Hampton, Middlesex TW12 2HQ, England. TEL 44-181-783-0755. FAX 44-181-783-0049. *3450*

KEY NOTE MARKET REPORT: GLASSWARE.
Key Note Ltd., Field House, 72 Oldfield Rd., Hampton, Middlesex TW12 2HQ, England. TEL 44-181-783-0755. FAX 44-181-783-1940. *1732*

KEY NOTE MARKET REPORT: GREETINGS CARDS.
Key Note Ltd., Field House, 72 Oldfield Rd., Hampton, Middlesex TW12 2HQ, England. TEL 44-181-783-0755. FAX 44-181-783-0049. *3450*

KEY NOTE MARKET REPORT: HAND LUGGAGE & LEATHER GOODS.
Key Note Ltd., Field House, 72 Oldfield Rd., Hampton, Middlesex TW12 2HQ, England. TEL 44-181-783-0755. FAX 44-181-783-0049. *4145*

KEY NOTE MARKET REPORT: HEALTH CLUBS AND LEISURE CENTRES.
Key Note Ltd., Field House, 72 Oldfield Rd., Hampton, Middlesex TW12 2HQ, England. TEL 44-181-783-0755. FAX 44-181-783-0049. *6768*

KEY NOTE MARKET REPORT: HEALTH FOODS.
Key Note Ltd., Field House, 72 Oldfield Rd., Hampton, Middlesex TW12 2HQ, England. TEL 44-181-783-0755. FAX 44-181-783-0049. *3117*

KEY NOTE MARKET REPORT: HEATING, VENTILATING & AIR CONDITIONING.
Key Note Ltd., Field House, 72 Oldfield Rd., Hampton, Middlesex TW12 2HQ, England. TEL 44-181-783-0755. FAX 44-181-783-0049. *3481*

KEY NOTE MARKET REPORT: HOME FURNISHINGS.
Key Note Ltd., Field House, 72 Oldfield Rd., Hampton, Middlesex TW12 2HQ, England. TEL 44-181-783-0755. FAX 44-181-783-0049. *3858*

KEY NOTE MARKET REPORT: HOME LEISURE.
Key Note Ltd., Field House, 72 Oldfield Rd., Hampton, Middlesex TW12 2HQ, England. TEL 44-181-783-0755. FAX 44-181-783-1940. *4150*

KEY NOTE MARKET REPORT: HOME SHOPPING.
Key Note Ltd., Field House, 72 Oldfield Rd., Hampton, Middlesex TW12 2HQ, England. TEL 44-181-783-0755. FAX 44-181-783-0049. *1536*

KEY NOTE MARKET REPORT: HORTICULTURAL RETAILING.
Key Note Ltd., Field House, 72 Oldfield Rd., Hampton, Middlesex TW12 2HQ, England. TEL 44-181-783-0755. FAX 44-181-783-0049. *3197*

KEY NOTE MARKET REPORT: HOT DRINKS.
Key Note Ltd., Field House, 72 Oldfield Rd., Hampton, Middlesex TW12 2HQ, England. TEL 44-181-783-0755. FAX 44-181-783-1940. *523*

KEY NOTE MARKET REPORT: HOTELS.
Key Note Ltd., Field House, 72 Oldfield Rd., Hampton, Middlesex TW12 2HQ, England. TEL 44-181-783-0755. FAX 44-181-783-0049. *3731*

KEY NOTE MARKET REPORT: HOUSEBUILDING.
Key Note Ltd., Field House, 72 Oldfield Rd., Hampton, Middlesex TW12 2HQ, England. TEL 44-181-783-0755. FAX 44-181-783-0049. *900*

KEY NOTE MARKET REPORT: HOUSEHOLD APPLIANCES (WHITE GOODS).
Key Note Ltd., Field House, 72 Oldfield Rd., Hampton, Middlesex TW12 2HQ, England. TEL 44-181-783-0755. FAX 44-181-783-0049. *3858*

KEY NOTE MARKET REPORT: HOUSEHOLD FURNITURE.
Key Note Ltd., Field House, 72 Oldfield Rd., Hampton, Middlesex TW12 2HQ, England. TEL 44-181-783-0755. FAX 44-181-783-0049. *3858*

KEY NOTE MARKET REPORT: ICE-CREAMS & FROZEN DESSERTS.
Key Note Ltd., Field House, 72 Oldfield Rd., Hampton, Middlesex TW12 2HQ, England. TEL 44-181-783-0755. FAX 44-181-783-0049. *3117*

KEY NOTE MARKET REPORT: INDUSTRIAL FASTENERS.
Key Note Ltd., Field House, 72 Oldfield Rd., Hampton, Middlesex TW12 2HQ, England. TEL 44-181-783-0755. FAX 44-181-783-1940. *2864*

KEY NOTE MARKET REPORT: INDUSTRIAL PUMPS.
Key Note Ltd., Field House, 72 Oldfield Rd., Hampton, Middlesex TW12 2HQ, England. TEL 44-181-783-0755. FAX 44-181-783-0049. *2873*

KEY NOTE MARKET REPORT: INDUSTRIAL VALVES.
Key Note Ltd., Field House, 72 Oldfield Rd., Hampton, Middlesex TW12 2HQ, England. TEL 44-181-783-0755. FAX 44-181-783-0049. *2878*

KEY NOTE MARKET REPORT: INSULATION PRODUCTS.
Key Note Ltd., Field House, 72 Oldfield Rd., Hampton, Middlesex TW12 2HQ, England. TEL 44-181-783-0755. FAX 44-181-783-0049. *901*

KEY NOTE MARKET REPORT: JEWELLERY, WATCHES & FASHION ACCESSORIES.
Key Note Ltd., Field House, 72 Oldfield Rd., Hampton, Middlesex TW12 2HQ, England. TEL 44-181-783-0755. FAX 44-181-783-0049. *3865*

KEY NOTE MARKET REPORT: KITCHENWARE.
Key Note Ltd., Field House, 72 Oldfield Rd., Hampton, Middlesex TW12 2HQ, England. TEL 44-181-783-0755. FAX 44-181-783-0049. *3858*

KEY NOTE MARKET REPORT: LIGHTING EQUIPMENT.
Key Note Ltd., Field House, 72 Oldfield Rd., Hampton, Middlesex TW12 2HQ, England. TEL 44-181-783-0755. FAX 44-181-783-0049. *3858*

KEY NOTE MARKET REPORT: LINGERIE.
Key Note Ltd., Field House, 72 Oldfield Rd., Hampton, Middlesex TW12 2HQ, England. TEL 44-181-783-0755. FAX 44-181-783-0049. *1916*

KEY NOTE MARKET REPORT: LOW ALCOHOL DRINKS.
Key Note Ltd., Field House, 72 Oldfield Rd., Hampton, Middlesex TW12 2HQ, England. TEL 44-181-783-0755. FAX 44-181-783-0049. *523*

KEY NOTE MARKET REPORT: MACHINE TOOLS.
Key Note Ltd., Field House, 72 Oldfield Rd., Hampton, Middlesex TW12 2HQ, England. TEL 44-181-783-0755. FAX 44-181-783-0049. *2878*

KEY NOTE MARKET REPORT: MANAGEMENT CONSULTANTS.
Key Note Ltd., Field House, 72 Oldfield Rd., Hampton, Middlesex TW12 2HQ, England. TEL 44-181-783-0755. FAX 44-181-783-0049. *1490*

KEY NOTE MARKET REPORT: MEAT & MEAT PRODUCTS.
Key Note Ltd., Field House, 72 Oldfield Rd., Hampton, Middlesex TW12 2HQ, England. TEL 44-181-783-0755. FAX 44-181-783-0049. *3117*

KEY NOTE MARKET REPORT: MECHANICAL HANDLING.
Key Note Ltd., Field House, 72 Oldfield Rd., Hampton, Middlesex TW12 2HQ, England. TEL 44-181-783-0755. FAX 44-181-783-0049. *2891*

KEY NOTE MARKET REPORT: MEDICAL EQUIPMENT.
Key Note Ltd., Field House, 72 Oldfield Rd., Hampton, Middlesex TW12 2HQ, England. TEL 44-181-783-0755. FAX 44-181-783-0049. *4700*

KEY NOTE MARKET REPORT: MILK & DAIRY PRODUCTS.
Key Note Ltd., Field House, 72 Oldfield Rd., Hampton, Middlesex TW12 2HQ, England. TEL 44-181-783-0755. FAX 44-181-783-0049. *256*

KEY NOTE MARKET REPORT: MORTGAGE FINANCE.
Key Note Ltd., Field House, 72 Oldfield Rd., Hampton, Middlesex TW12 2HQ, England. TEL 44-181-783-0755. FAX 44-181-783-0049. *1151*

KEY NOTE MARKET REPORT: NEWSPAPERS.
Key Note Ltd., Field House, 72 Oldfield Rd., Hampton, Middlesex TW12 2HQ, England. TEL 44-181-783-0755. FAX 44-181-783-0049. *3876*

KEY NOTE MARKET REPORT: O T C PHARMACEUTICALS.
Key Note Ltd., Field House, 72 Oldfield Rd., Hampton, Middlesex TW12 2HQ, England. TEL 44-181-783-1940. FAX 44-181-783-0049. *5675*

KEY NOTE MARKET REPORT: OFF-LICENSE TRADE.
Key Note Ltd., Field House, 72 Oldfield Rd., Hampton, Middlesex TW12 2HQ, England. TEL 44-181-783-0755. FAX 44-181-783-1940. *1589*

KEY NOTE MARKET REPORT: OFFICE FURNITURE.
Key Note Ltd., Field House, 72 Oldfield Rd., Hampton, Middlesex TW12 2HQ, England. TEL 44-181-783-0755. FAX 44-181-783-0049. *1557*

KEY NOTE MARKET REPORT: OPHTHALMIC GOODS & SERVICES.
Key Note Ltd., Field House, 72 Oldfield Rd., Hampton, Middlesex TW12 2HQ, England. TEL 44-181-783-0755. FAX 44-181-783-0049. *4996*

KEY NOTE MARKET REPORT: OWN BRANDS.
Key Note Ltd., Field House, 72 Oldfield Rd., Hampton, Middlesex TW12 2HQ, England. TEL 44-181-783-0755. FAX 44-181-783-0049. *1536*

KEY NOTE MARKET REPORT: PACKAGING (GLASS).
Key Note Ltd., Field House, 72 Oldfield Rd., Hampton, Middlesex TW12 2HQ, England. TEL 44-181-783-0755. FAX 44-181-783-0049. *5545*

KEY NOTE MARKET REPORT: PACKAGING (METALS & AEROSOLS).
Key Note Ltd., Field House, 72 Oldfield Rd., Hampton, Middlesex TW12 2HQ, England. TEL 44-181-783-0755. FAX 44-181-783-0049. *5545*

KEY NOTE MARKET REPORT: PACKAGING (PAPER & BOARD).
Key Note Ltd., Field House, 72 Oldfield Rd., Hampton, Middlesex TW12 2HQ, England. TEL 44-181-783-0755. FAX 44-181-783-0049. *5545*

KEY NOTE MARKET REPORT: PACKAGING (PLASTICS).
Key Note Ltd., Field House, 72 Oldfield Rd., Hampton, Middlesex TW12 2HQ, England. TEL 44-181-783-0755. FAX 44-181-783-0049. *5545*

KEY NOTE MARKET REPORT: PAINTS & VARNISHES.
Key Note Ltd., Field House, 72 Oldfield Rd., Hampton, Middlesex TW12 2HQ, England. TEL 44-181-783-0755. FAX 44-181-783-0049. *5553*

KEY NOTE MARKET REPORT: PASSENGER SHIPPING.
Key Note Ltd., Field House, 72 Oldfield Rd., Hampton, Middlesex TW12 2HQ, England. TEL 44-181-783-0755. FAX 44-181-783-0049. *7155*

KEY NOTE MARKET REPORT: PERISHABLE FAST-MOVING CONSUMER GOODS.
Key Note Ltd., Field House, 72 Oldfield Rd., Hampton, Middlesex TW12 2HQ, England. TEL 44-181-783-0755. FAX 44-181-783-0049. *3117*

KEY NOTE MARKET REPORT: PET FOODS.
Key Note Ltd., Field House, 72 Oldfield Rd., Hampton, Middlesex TW12 2HQ, England. TEL 44-181-783-0755. FAX 44-181-783-0049. *5639*

KEY NOTE MARKET REPORT: PHOTOCOPIERS & FAX MACHINES.
Key Note Ltd., Field House, 72 Oldfield Rd., Hampton, Middlesex TW12 2HQ, England. TEL 44-181-783-0755. FAX 44-181-783-0049. *1557*

KEY NOTE MARKET REPORT: PHOTOGRAPHIC SERVICES.
Key Note Ltd., Field House, 72 Oldfield Rd., Hampton, Middlesex TW12 2HQ, England. TEL 44-181-783-0755. FAX 44-181-783-0049. *5768*

KEY NOTE MARKET REPORT: PLANT HIRE.
Key Note Ltd., Field House, 72 Oldfield Rd., Hampton, Middlesex TW12 2HQ, England. TEL 44-181-783-0755. FAX 44-181-783-0049. *1268*

KEY NOTE MARKET REPORT: PLASTICS PROCESSING.
Key Note Ltd., Field House, 72 Oldfield Rd., Hampton, Middlesex TW12 2HQ, England. TEL 44-181-783-0755. FAX 44-181-783-0049. *5879*

KEY NOTE MARKET REPORT: PREMIUM LAGERS, BEERS AND CIDERS.
Key Note Ltd., Field House, 72 Oldfield Rd., Hampton, Middlesex TW12 2HQ, England. TEL 44-181-783-0755. FAX 44-181-783-0049. *523*

KEY NOTE MARKET REPORT: PRESCRIBED PHARMACEUTICALS.
Key Note Ltd., Field House, 72 Oldfield Rd., Hampton, Middlesex TW12 2HQ, England. TEL 44-181-783-0755. FAX 44-181-783-1940. *5675*

KEY NOTE MARKET REPORT: PRINTED CIRCUITS.
Key Note Ltd., Field House, 72 Oldfield Rd., Hampton, Middlesex TW12 2HQ, England. TEL 44-181-783-0755. FAX 44-181-783-0049. *2112*

KEY NOTE MARKET REPORT: PRINTING.
Key Note Ltd., Field House, 72 Oldfield Rd., Hampton, Middlesex TW12 2HQ, England. TEL 44-181-783-0755. FAX 44-181-783-0049. *6081*

KEY NOTE MARKET REPORT: PRISON SERVICES.
Key Note Ltd., Field House, 72 Oldfield Rd., Hampton, Middlesex TW12 2HQ, England. TEL 44-181-783-0755. FAX 44-181-783-0049. *2287*

KEY NOTE MARKET REPORT: PRIVATE HEALTHCARE.
Key Note Ltd., Field House, 72 Oldfield Rd., Hampton, Middlesex TW12 2HQ, England. TEL 44-181-783-0755. FAX 44-181-783-0049. *4700*

KEY NOTE MARKET REPORT: PROCESS PLANT.
Key Note Ltd., Field House, 72 Oldfield Rd., Hampton, Middlesex TW12 2HQ, England. TEL 44-181-783-0755. FAX 44-181-783-0049. *1589*

KEY NOTE MARKET REPORT: PUBLIC HOUSES.
Key Note Ltd., Field House, 72 Oldfield Rd., Hampton, Middlesex TW12 2HQ, England. TEL 44-181-783-0755. FAX 44-181-783-0049. *3731*

KEY NOTE MARKET REPORT: READY MEALS.
Key Note Ltd., Field House, 72 Oldfield Rd., Hampton, Middlesex TW12 2HQ, England. TEL 44-181-783-0755. FAX 44-181-783-0049. *3117*

KEY NOTE MARKET REPORT: RESTAURANTS.
Key Note Ltd., Field House, 72 Oldfield Rd., Hampton, Middlesex TW12 2HQ, England. TEL 44-181-783-0755. FAX 44-181-783-0049. *3731*

KEY NOTE MARKET REPORT: RETAIL BRANCH BANKING.
Key Note Ltd., Field House, 72 Oldfield Rd., Hampton, Middlesex TW12 2HQ, England. TEL 44-181-783-0755. FAX 44-181-783-0049. *1151*

KEY NOTE MARKET REPORT: RETAIL CHEMISTS & DRUG STORES.
Key Note Ltd., Field House, 72 Oldfield Rd., Hampton, Middlesex TW12 2HQ, England. TEL 44-181-783-0755. FAX 44-181-783-0049. *5675*

KEY NOTE MARKET REPORT: ROAD HAULAGE.
Key Note Ltd., Field House, 72 Oldfield Rd., Hampton, Middlesex TW12 2HQ, England. TEL 44-181-783-0755. FAX 44-181-783-0049. *7175*

KEY NOTE MARKET REPORT: RUBBER MANUFACTURING & PROCESSING.
Key Note Ltd., Field House, 72 Oldfield Rd., Hampton, Middlesex TW12 2HQ, England. TEL 44-181-783-0755. FAX 44-181-783-0049. *6502*

KEY NOTE MARKET REPORT: SAUCES AND SPREADS.
Key Note Ltd., Field House, 72 Oldfield Rd., Hampton, Middlesex TW12 2HQ, England. TEL 44-181-783-0755. FAX 44-181-783-0049. *3117*

KEY NOTE MARKET REPORT: SCIENTIFIC INSTRUMENTS.
Key Note Ltd., Field House, 72 Oldfield Rd., Hampton, Middlesex TW12 2HQ, England. TEL 44-181-783-0755. FAX 44-181-783-1940. *3803*

KEY NOTE MARKET REPORT: SCRAP METAL PROCESSING.
Key Note Ltd., Field House, 72 Oldfield Rd., Hampton, Middlesex TW12 2HQ, England. TEL 44-181-783-0755. FAX 44-181-783-0049. *5198*

KEY NOTE MARKET REPORT: SELF-ASSEMBLY FURNITURE.
Key Note Ltd., Field House, 72 Oldfield Rd., Hampton, Middlesex TW12 2HQ, England. TEL 44-181-783-0755. FAX 44-181-783-1940. *3858*

KEY NOTE MARKET REPORT: SHOP FITTING.
Key Note Ltd., Field House, 72 Oldfield Rd., Hampton, Middlesex TW12 2HQ, England. TEL 44-181-783-0755. FAX 44-181-783-0049. *1536*

KEY NOTE MARKET REPORT: SHOWERS & SHOWER ACCESSORIES.
Key Note Ltd., Field House, 72 Oldfield Rd., Hampton, Middlesex TW12 2HQ, England. TEL 44-181-783-0755. FAX 44-181-783-0049. *3858*

KEY NOTE MARKET REPORT: SLIMMING MARKET.
Key Note Ltd., Field House, 72 Oldfield Rd., Hampton, Middlesex TW12 2HQ, England. TEL 44-181-783-0755. FAX 44-181-783-0049. *1589*

KEY NOTE MARKET REPORT: SMALL DOMESTIC ELECTRICAL APPLIANCES.
Key Note Ltd., Field House, 72 Oldfield Rd., Hampton, Middlesex TW12 2HQ, England. TEL 44-181-783-0755. FAX 44-181-783-0049. *2645*

KEY NOTE MARKET REPORT: SNACK FOODS.
Key Note Ltd., Field House, 72 Oldfield Rd., Hampton, Middlesex TW12 2HQ, England. TEL 44-181-783-0755. FAX 44-181-783-0049. *3117*

KEY NOTE MARKET REPORT: SOAPS & DETERGENTS.
Key Note Ltd., Field House, 72 Oldfield Rd., Hampton, Middlesex TW12 2HQ, England. TEL 44-181-783-0755. FAX 44-181-783-0049. *1910*

KEY NOTE MARKET REPORT: SOFT DRINKS (CARBONATES & CONCENTRATES).
Key Note Ltd., Field House, 72 Oldfield Rd., Hampton, Middlesex TW12 2HQ, England. TEL 44-181-783-0755. FAX 44-181-783-0049. *523*

KEY NOTE MARKET REPORT: SPORTS CLOTHING AND FOOTWEAR.
Key Note Ltd., Field House, 72 Oldfield Rd., Hampton, Middlesex TW12 2HQ, England. TEL 44-181-783-0755. FAX 44-181-783-0049. *1916*

KEY NOTE MARKET REPORT: SPORTS EQUIPMENT.
Key Note Ltd., Field House, 72 Oldfield Rd., Hampton, Middlesex TW12 2HQ, England. TEL 44-181-783-0755. FAX 44-181-783-0049. *6768*

KEY NOTE MARKET REPORT: STATIONERY (PERSONAL & OFFICE).
Key Note Ltd., Field House, 72 Oldfield Rd., Hampton, Middlesex TW12 2HQ, England. TEL 44-181-783-0755. FAX 44-181-783-0049. *1557*

KEY NOTE MARKET REPORT: STEEL STOCKHOLDING.
Key Note Ltd., Field House, 72 Oldfield Rd., Hampton, Middlesex TW12 2HQ, England. TEL 44-181-783-0755. FAX 44-181-783-1940. *1393*

KEY NOTE MARKET REPORT: SUPERMARKETS & SUPERSTORES.
Key Note Ltd., Field House, 72 Oldfield Rd., Hampton, Middlesex TW12 2HQ, England. TEL 44-181-783-0755. FAX 44-181-783-0049. *3117*

KEY NOTE MARKET REPORT: T V & VIDEO RENTAL.
Key Note Ltd., Field House, 72 Oldfield Rd., Hampton, Middlesex TW12 2HQ, England. TEL 44-181-783-0755. FAX 44-181-783-0049. *2645*

KEY NOTE MARKET REPORT: TELECOMMUNICATIONS.
Key Note Ltd., Field House, 72 Oldfield Rd., Hampton, Middlesex TW12 2HQ, England. TEL 44-181-783-0755. FAX 44-181-783-1940. *1996*

KEY NOTE MARKET REPORT: TIMBER & JOINERY.
Key Note Ltd., Field House, 72 Oldfield Rd., Hampton, Middlesex TW12 2HQ, England. TEL 44-181-783-0755. FAX 44-181-783-0049. *3172*

KEY NOTE MARKET REPORT: TOILETRIES.
Key Note Ltd., Field House, 72 Oldfield Rd., Hampton, Middlesex TW12 2HQ, England. TEL 44-181-783-0755. FAX 44-181-783-0049. *507*

KEY NOTE MARKET REPORT: TOURIST ATTRACTIONS.
Key Note Ltd., Field House, 72 Oldfield Rd., Hampton, Middlesex TW12 2HQ, England. TEL 44-181-783-0755. FAX 44-181-783-0049. *7215*

KEY NOTE MARKET REPORT: TOYS & GAMES.
Key Note Ltd., Field House, 72 Oldfield Rd., Hampton, Middlesex TW12 2HQ, England. TEL 44-181-783-0755. FAX 44-181-783-0094. *3450*

KEY NOTE MARKET REPORT: TRAINING.
Key Note Ltd., Field House, 72 Oldfield Rd., Hampton, Middlesex TW12 2HQ, England. TEL 44-181-783-0755. FAX 44-181-783-0049. *2511*

KEY NOTE MARKET REPORT: TRAVEL AGENTS & OVERSEAS TOUR OPERATORS.
Key Note Ltd., Field House, 72 Oldfield Rd., Hampton, Middlesex TW12 2HQ, England. TEL 44-181-783-0755. FAX 44-181-783-0049. *7215*

KEY NOTE MARKET REPORT: VEHICLE LEASING & HIRE.
Key Note Ltd., Field House, 72 Oldfield Rd., Hampton, Middlesex TW12 2HQ, England. TEL 44-181-783-0755. FAX 44-181-783-0049. *7104*

KEY NOTE MARKET REPORT: VEHICLE SECURITY.
Key Note Ltd., Field House, 72 Oldfield Rd., Hampton, Middlesex TW12 2HQ, England. TEL 44-181-783-0755. FAX 44-181-783-0049. *7104*

KEY NOTE MARKET REPORT: VIDEO RETAIL & HIRE.
Key Note Ltd., Field House, 72 Oldfield Rd., Hampton, Middlesex TW12 2HQ, England. TEL 44-181-783-0755. FAX 44-181-783-0049. *2067*

KEY NOTE MARKET REPORT: WALLCOVERINGS.
Key Note Ltd., Field House, 72 Oldfield Rd., Hampton, Middlesex TW12 2HQ, England. TEL 44-181-783-0755. FAX 44-181-783-0049. *3847*

KEY NOTE MARKET REPORT: WASTE MANAGEMENT.
Key Note Ltd., Field House, 72 Oldfield Rd., Hampton, Middlesex TW12 2HQ, England. TEL 44-181-783-0755. FAX 44-181-783-0049. *2987*

KEY NOTE MARKET REPORT: WATER UTILITIES.
Key Note Ltd., Field House, 72 Oldfield Rd., Hampton, Middlesex TW12 2HQ, England. TEL 44-181-783-0755. FAX 44-181-783-0049. *7296*

KEY NOTE MARKET REPORT: WINDOWS & DOORS.
Key Note Ltd., Field House, 72 Oldfield Rd., Hampton, Middlesex TW12 2HQ, England. TEL 44-181-783-0755. FAX 44-181-783-0049. *3858*

KEY NOTE MARKET REPORT: WINE.
Key Note Ltd., Field House, 72 Oldfield Rd., Hampton, Middlesex TW12 2HQ, England. TEL 44-181-783-0755. FAX 44-181-783-0049. *523*

KEY NOTE MARKET REPORT: WOMEN'S MAGAZINES.
Key Note Ltd., Field House, 72 Oldfield Rd., Hampton, Middlesex TW12 2HQ, England. TEL 44-181-783-0755. FAX 44-181-783-0049. *7324*

KEY NOTE MARKET REVIEW: CORPORATE SERVICES IN THE U K.
Key Note Ltd., Field House, 72 Oldfield Rd., Hampton, Middlesex TW12 2HQ, England. TEL 44-181-783-0755. FAX 44-181-783-0049. *1691*

KEY NOTE MARKET REVIEW: D I Y & HOME IMPROVEMENTS.
Key Note Ltd., Field House, 72 Oldfield Rd., Hampton, Middlesex TW12 2HQ, England. TEL 44-181-783-0755. FAX 44-181-783-0049. *3847*

KEY NOTE MARKET REVIEW: ENERGY INDUSTRY IN THE U K.
Key Note Ltd., Field House, 72 Oldfield Rd., Hampton, Middlesex TW12 2HQ, England. TEL 44-181-783-0755. FAX 44-181-783-0049. *2673*

KEY NOTE MARKET REVIEW: GREY MARKET IN THE U K.
Key Note Ltd., Field House, 72 Oldfield Rd., Hampton, Middlesex TW12 2HQ, England. TEL 44-181-783-0755. FAX 44-181-783-0049. *1536*

KEY NOTE MARKET REVIEW: MULTIMEDIA IN U K.
Key Note Ltd., Field House, 72 Oldfield Rd., Hampton, Middlesex TW12 2HQ, England. TEL 44-181-783-0755. FAX 44-181-783-0049. *2016*

KEY NOTE MARKET REVIEW: PASSENGER TRAVEL IN U K.
Key Note Ltd., Field House, 72 Oldfield Rd., Hampton, Middlesex TW12 2HQ, England. TEL 44-181-783-0755. FAX 44-181-783-0049. *7215*

KEY NOTE MARKET REVIEW: PERSONAL FINANCE IN THE U K.
Key Note Ltd., Field House, 72 Oldfield Rd., Hampton, Middlesex TW12 2HQ, England. TEL 44-181-783-0755. FAX 44-181-783-0049. *1151*

KEY NOTE MARKET REVIEW: RETAILING IN THE U K.
Key Note Ltd., Field House, 72 Oldfield Rd., Hampton, Middlesex TW12 2HQ, England. TEL 44-181-783-0755. FAX 44-181-783-0049. *1536*

KEY NOTE MARKET REVIEW: U K CATERING MARKET.
Key Note Ltd., Field House, 72 Oldfield Rd., Hampton, Middlesex TW12 2HQ, England. TEL 44-181-783-0755. FAX 44-181-783-0049. *3731*

KEY NOTE MARKET REVIEW: U K CHEMICAL INDUSTRY.
Key Note Ltd., Field House, 72 Oldfield Rd., Hampton, Middlesex TW12 2HQ, England. TEL 44-181-783-0755. FAX 44-181-783-0049. *1757*

KEY NOTE MARKET REVIEW: U K CLOTHING & FOOTWEAR.
Key Note Ltd., Field House, 72 Oldfield Rd., Hampton, Middlesex TW12 2HQ, England. TEL 44-181-783-0755. FAX 44-181-783-0049. *1916*

KEY NOTE MARKET REVIEW: U K COMPUTER MARKET.
Key Note Ltd., Field House, 72 Oldfield Rd., Hampton, Middlesex TW12 2HQ, England. TEL 44-181-783-0755. FAX 44-181-783-0049. *2127*

KEY NOTE MARKET REVIEW: U K CONSTRUCTION INDUSTRY.
Key Note Ltd., Field House, 72 Oldfield Rd., Hampton, Middlesex TW12 2HQ, England. TEL 44-181-783-0755. FAX 44-181-783-0049. *901*

KEY NOTE MARKET REVIEW: U K DEFENCE INDUSTRY.
Key Note Ltd., Field House, 72 Oldfield Rd., Hampton, Middlesex TW12 2HQ, England. TEL 44-181-783-0755. FAX 44-181-783-0049. *5274*

KEY NOTE MARKET REVIEW: U K DISTRIBUTION.
Key Note Ltd., Field House, 72 Oldfield Rd., Hampton, Middlesex TW12 2HQ, England. TEL 44-181-783-0755. FAX 44-181-783-0049. *1589*

KEY NOTE MARKET REVIEW: U K DRINKS MARKET.
Key Note Ltd., Field House, 72 Oldfield Rd., Hampton, Middlesex TW12 2HQ, England. TEL 44-181-783-0755. FAX 44-181-783-0049. *523*

KEY NOTE MARKET REVIEW: U K EDUCATION INDUSTRY.
Key Note Ltd., Field House, 72 Oldfield Rd., Hampton, Middlesex TW12 2HQ, England. TEL 44-181-783-0755. FAX 44-181-783-0049. *2574*

KEY NOTE MARKET REVIEW: U K FOOD MARKET.
Key Note Ltd., Field House, 72 Oldfield Rd., Hampton, Middlesex TW12 2HQ, England. TEL 44-181-783-0755. FAX 44-181-783-0049. *3117*

KEY NOTE MARKET REVIEW: U K HEALTHCARE.
Key Note Ltd., Field House, 72 Oldfield Rd., Hampton, Middlesex TW12 2HQ, England. TEL 44-181-783-0755. FAX 44-181-783-0049. *4700*

KEY NOTE MARKET REVIEW: U K HOUSEHOLD MARKET - FURNITURE, FITTINGS & DECOR.
Key Note Ltd., Field House, 72 Oldfield Rd., Hampton, Middlesex TW12 2HQ, England. TEL 44-181-783-0755. FAX 44-181-783-1940. *3858*

KEY NOTE MARKET REVIEW: U K HOUSEHOLD MARKET - HOUSEHOLD APPLIANCES AND HOUSEWARES.
Key Note Ltd., Field House, 72 Oldfield Rd., Hampton, Middlesex TW12 2HQ, England. TEL 44-181-783-0755. FAX 44-181-783-1940. *3858*

KEY NOTE MARKET REVIEW: U K INSURANCE MARKET.
Key Note Ltd., Field House, 72 Oldfield Rd., Hampton, Middlesex TW12 2HQ, England. TEL 44-181-783-0755. FAX 44-181-783-0049. *3823*

KEY NOTE MARKET REVIEW: U K LEISURE AND RECREATION.
Key Note Ltd., Field House, 72 Oldfield Rd., Hampton, Middlesex TW12 2HQ, England. TEL 44-181-783-0755. FAX 44-181-783-0049. *4150*

KEY NOTE MARKET REVIEW: U K MOTOR INDUSTRY.
Key Note Ltd., Field House, 72 Oldfield Rd., Hampton, Middlesex TW12 2HQ, England. TEL 44-181-783-0755. FAX 44-181-783-0049. *7104*

KEY NOTE MARKET REVIEW: U K OFFICE EQUIPMENT.
Key Note Ltd., Field House, 72 Oldfield Rd., Hampton, Middlesex TW12 2HQ, England. TEL 44-181-783-0755. FAX 44-181-783-0049. *1557*

KEY NOTE MARKET REVIEW: U K PACKAGING INDUSTRY.
Key Note Ltd., Field House, 72 Oldfield Rd., Hampton, Middlesex TW12 2HQ, England. TEL 44-181-783-0755. FAX 44-181-783-0049. *5545*

KEY NOTE MARKET REVIEW: U K PET MARKET.
Key Note Ltd., Field House, 72 Oldfield Rd., Hampton, Middlesex TW12 2HQ, England. TEL 44-181-783-0755. FAX 44-181-783-0049. *1536*

KEY NOTE MARKET REVIEW: U K PHARMACEUTICAL INDUSTRY.
Key Note Ltd., Field House, 72 Oldfield Rd., Hampton, Middlesex TW12 2HQ, England. TEL 44-181-783-0755. FAX 44-181-783-0049. *5675*

KEY NOTE MARKET REVIEW: U K PUBLISHING.
Key Note Ltd., Field House, 72 Oldfield Rd., Hampton, Middlesex TW12 2HQ, England. TEL 44-181-783-0755. FAX 44-181-783-0049. *6275*

KEY NOTE MARKET REVIEW: U K SECURITY MARKET.
Key Note Ltd., Field House, 72 Oldfield Rd., Hampton, Middlesex TW12 2HQ, England. TEL 44-181-783-0755. FAX 44-181-783-0049. *2287*

KEY NOTE MARKET REVIEW: U K SOFT DRINKS.
Key Note Ltd., Field House, 72 Oldfield Rd., Hampton, Middlesex TW12 2HQ, England. TEL 44-181-783-0755. FAX 44-181-783-0049. *523*

KEY NOTE MARKET REVIEW: U K SPORTS MARKET.
Key Note Ltd., Field House, 72 Oldfield Rd., Hampton, Middlesex TW12 2HQ, England. TEL 44-181-783-0755. FAX 44-181-783-0049. *6768*

KEY NOTE MARKET REVIEW: U K TELECOMMUNICATIONS.
Key Note Ltd., Field House, 72 Oldfield Rd., Hampton, Middlesex TW12 2HQ, England. TEL 44-181-783-0755. FAX 44-181-783-0049. *1996*

KEY NOTE MARKET REVIEW: U K TOILETRIES & COSMETICS MARKET.
Key Note Ltd., Field House, 72 Oldfield Rd., Hampton, Middlesex TW12 2HQ, England. TEL 44-181-783-0755. FAX 44-181-783-1940. *511*

KEY NOTE MARKET REVIEW: U K TRAVEL & TOURISM.
Key Note Ltd., Field House, 72 Oldfield Rd., Hampton, Middlesex TW12 2HQ, England. TEL 44-181-783-0755. FAX 44-181-783-0049. *7215*

KEY NOTE MARKET REVIEW: U K WEDDING MARKET.
Key Note Ltd., Field House, 72 Oldfield Rd., Hampton, Middlesex TW12 2HQ, England. TEL 44-181-783-0755. FAX 44-181-783-0049. *4626*

KEY NOTE MARKET REVIEW: WHOLESALING IN THE U K.
Key Note Ltd., Field House, 72 Oldfield Rd., Hampton, Middlesex TW12 2HQ, England. TEL 44-181-783-0755. FAX 44-181-783-0049. *1536*

KEY NOTE MARKET REVIEW: YOUTH MARKET IN THE U.K.
Key Note Ltd., Field House, 72 Oldfield Rd., Hampton, Middlesex TW12 2HQ, England. TEL 44-181-783-0755. FAX 44-181-783-0049. *39*

KEY NOTE REPORT: FURNITURE.
Key Note Publications Ltd., Field House, 72 Oldfield Rd., Hampton, Middlesex TW12 2HQ, England. TEL 0181-783-0755. FAX 0181-783-1720. *3858*

KEY NOTE REPORT: PRINTING INKS.
Key Note Publications Ltd., Field House, 72 Oldfield Rd., Hampton, Middlesex TW12 2HQ, England. TEL 0181-783-0755. FAX 0181-783-1720. *6081*

KING ABDULAZIZ MEDICAL JOURNAL.
King Abdul Aziz University, College of Medicine and Allied Sciences, P.O. Box 1540, Jeddah 21441, Saudi Arabia. *4700*

KIPLINGER'S PERSONAL FINANCE MAGAZINE.
Kiplinger Washington Editors, Inc., 1729 H St., N.W., Washington, DC 20006. TEL 202-887-6400. FAX 202-331-1206. Producer(s): UMI. *1152*

KNACK.
N.V. R M G, Bd. Louis Schmidt 97, 1040 Brussels, Belgium. TEL 32-2-7361175. FAX 32-2-7344018. *3255*

KNJIZNICA.
Zveza Bibliotekarskih Drustev Slovenije, Turjaska 1, Ljubljana, Slovenia. TEL 061-150-131. *4190*

THE KNOWLEDGE.
Miller Freeman Information Services, Riverbank House, Angel Ln., Tonbridge, Kent TN9 1SE, England. TEL 44-1732-362666. FAX 44-1732-767301. *2053*

KOMPASS.
Forlaget Kompass Danmark, Oeveroedvej 5, DK-2840 Holte, Denmark. TEL 45-45-41-21-00. FAX 45-45-41-06-65. *1691*

KOMPASS AUSTRALIA.
Peter Isaacson Publications Pty. Ltd., 46-50 Porter St., Prahran, Vic. 3181, Australia. TEL 61-3-2457777. FAX 61-3-2457840. *1691*

KOMPASS BELGIUM.
Editus Belgium S.A., Av. Moliere 256, 1060 Brussels, Belgium. TEL 32-2-3459070. FAX 32-2-3473340. *1691*

KOMPASS ITALIA.
Kompass Italia S.p.A., Via Seruais, 125, 10146 Turin, Italy.
Producer(s): SilverPlatter Information, Inc. *1691*

KOMPASS SELECT EXPORT. BUILDING CONSTRUCTION, CONTRACTORS.
Forlaget Kompass-Danmark, Oeveroedvej 5, DK-Holte, Denmark. TEL 45-45-41-21-00. FAX 45-45-41-06-65. *901*

KOMPASS SELECT EXPORT. BUSINESS SERVICES.
Forlaget Kompass-Danmark, Oeveroedvej 5, DK-2840 Holte, Denmark. TEL 45-45-41-21-00. FAX 45-45-41-21-00. *1339*

KOMPASS SELECT EXPORT. CHEMICAL INDUSTRY.
Forlaget Kompass Danmark, Oeveroedvej 5, DK-2840 Holte, Denmark. TEL 45-45-41-21-00. FAX 45-45-41-21-00. *1758*

KOMPASS SELECT EXPORT. ELECTRICAL AND ELECTRONIC EQUIPMENT.
Kompas-Danmark, Oeveroedvej 5, DK-2840 Holte, Denmark. TEL 45-45-41-21-00. FAX 45-45-41-21-00. *2645*

KOMPASS SELECT EXPORT. FOOD INDUSTRY.
Forlaget Kompass Danmark, Oeveroedvej 5, DK-2840 Holte, Denmark. TEL 45-45-41-21-00. FAX 45-45-41-21-00. *3118*

KOMPASS SELECT EXPORT. MACHINE INDUSTRY.
Forlaget Kompass Danmark, Oeveroedvej 5, DK-2840 Holte, Denmark. TEL 45-45-41-21-00. FAX 45-45-41-06-65. *4546*

KOMPASS SELECT EXPORT. METAL PRODUCTS.
Oeveroedvej 5, DK-2840 Holte, Denmark. TEL 45-45-41-21-00. FAX 45-45-41-06-65. *5198*

KOMPASS SELECT EXPORT. PAPER INDUSTRY, GRAPHIC ARTS.
Forlaget Kompass Danmark, Oeveroedevej 5, DK-2840 Holte, Denmark. TEL 45-45-41-21-00. FAX 45-45-41-06-65. *5568*

KOMPASS SELECT EXPORT. RUBBER INDUSTRY, PLASTICS INDUSTRY.
Forlaget Kompass Danmark, Oeveroedvej 5, DK-2840 Holte, Denmark. TEL 45-45-41-21-00. FAX 45-45-41-06-65. *6502*

KOMPASS SELECT EXPORT. SCIENTIFIC AND INDUSTRIAL INSTRUMENTS, WATCH INDUSTRY.
Forlaget Kompass Danmark, Oeveroedvej 5, DK-2840 Holte, Denmark. TEL 45-45-41-21-00. FAX 45-45-41-06-65. *3803*

KOMPASS SELECT EXPORT. TEXTILES, CLOTHING, FOOTWEAR AND LEATHER GOODS.
Forlaget Kompass Danmark, Oeveroedvej 5, DK-2840 Holte, Denmark. TEL 45-45-41-21-00. FAX 45-45-41-06-65. *6991*

KOMPASS SELECT EXPORT. TRANSPORT EQUIPMENT.
Forlaget Kompass Danmark, Oeveroedvej 5, DK-2840 Holte, Denmark. TEL 45-45-41-21-00. FAX 45-45-41-06-65. *7032*

KOMPASS SELECT EXPORT. WOOD INDUSTRY.
Kompass-Danmark, Oeveroedvej 5, DK-2840 Holte, Denmark. TEL 45-45-41-21-00. FAX 45-45-41-06-65. *3859*

KOMPASS SOUTH AFRICA.
Reed Business Information South Africa (Pty.) Ltd., P.O. Box 653207, Benmore 2010, South Africa. TEL 27-11-774-1110. FAX 27-11-883-4729. *1692*

KOMPASS SVERIGE.
Kompass Sverige AB, Torsgatan 21, S-113 90 Stockholm, Sweden. FAX 46-8-7363022. *1693*

KOMPASS UNITED KINGDOM.
Kompass, Part of the Reed Elsevier group, Windsor Ct., E. Grinstead House, E. Grinstead, W. Sussex RH19 1XD, England. TEL 44-1342-326972. FAX 44-1342-335992. *1693*

KONZERNE IN SCHAUBILDERN.
Verlag Hoppenstedt GmbH, Havelstr. 9, 64295 Darmstadt, Germany. TEL 49-6151-380-0. FAX 49-6151-380360. *1693*

KOREA POLICY SERIES.
Korean Overseas Information Service, 82-1 Sejongnoo, Chongno-gu, Seoul 110-050, S. Korea. TEL 739-4481. FAX 736-2199. *5939*

KOREAN NURSE.
Korean Nurses' Association, 88-7 Sanglim-Dong, Choong Ku, Seoul, S. Korea. *4939*

KORRESPONDENZ ABWASSER.
Gesellschaft zur Foerderung der Abwassertechnik, Postfach 1165, 53758 Hennef, Germany. TEL 49-2242-872190. FAX 49-2242-872151. *2940*

KTO EST' KTO NA KOMP'YUTERNOM RYNKE.
Izdatel'stvo M G U, Bolshaya Nikitskaya ul., 5-7, 103009 Moscow, Russia. TEL 7-095-2030122. FAX 7-095-2030168. *2148*

DIE KUNSTSTOFF-INDUSTRIE UND IHRE HELFER.
Industrieschau-Verlagsgesellschaft mbH, Postfach 100262, 64202 Darmstadt, Germany. TEL 49-6151-3892-0. FAX 49-6151-33164. *5879*

KUWAIT JOURNAL OF SCIENCE & ENGINEERING.
University of Kuwait, Faculty of Science, P.O. Box 5969, Kuwait. *6542*

LILACS-CD-ROM.
Latin American and Caribbean Center on Health Sciences Information (BIREME), Rua Botucatu, 862, Vila Clementino, 04023-901 Sao Paulo SP, Brazil. TEL 55-11-5769800. FAX 55-11-5711919. Available only on CD-ROM. *4781*

L I S A: LIBRARY & INFORMATION SCIENCE ABSTRACTS.
Bowker - Saur Ltd., A member of the Reed Elsevier plc group, Maypole House, Maypole Rd., E. Grinstead, W. Sussex RH19 1HU, England. TEL 44-1342-330100. FAX 44-1342-330191.
Producer(s): Bowker - Saur Ltd. *4227*

L I S A PLUS.
Bowker - Saur Ltd., A member of the Reed Elsevier plc group, Maypole House, Maypole Rd., E. Grinstead, W. Sussex RH19 1HU, England. TEL 44-1342-330100. FAX 44-1342-330191.
Available only on CD-ROM. Producer(s): Bowker - Saur Ltd. *4227*

LABORATORY HAZARDS BULLETIN.
The Royal Society of Chemistry, Thomas Graham House, Science Park, Milton Rd., Cambridge CB4 4WF, England. TEL 44-1223-420066. FAX 44-1223-423429.
Producer(s): Knight-Ridder, Inc. *5493*

LAING'S REVIEW OF PRIVATE HEALTHCARE (YEAR).
Laing & Buisson, Lymehouse Studios, 38 Georgiana St., London NW1 0EB, England. TEL 44-171-284-1268. FAX 44-171-267-8269. *1693*

LAMY FISCAL.
Lamy S.A., 187-189 quai de Valmy, 75490 Paris Cedex 10, France. TEL 33-1-44721343. FAX 33-1-44721395. *3975*

LAMY SOCIAL.
Lamy S.A., 187-189 quai de Valmy, 75490 Paris Cedex 10, France. TEL 33-1-44721343. FAX 33-1-44721395. *3975*

THE LANCET.
The Lancet Ltd., 42 Bedford Sq., London WC1B 3SL, England. TEL 44-171-4364981. FAX 44-171-4367570. *4702*

THE LANCET (NORTH AMERICAN EDITION).
The Lancet Ltd., 655 Ave. of the Americas, New York, NY 10011. TEL 212-633-3800. FAX 212-633-3850. *4702*

LANDES- UND KOMMUNALVERWALTUNG.
Verlag C.H. Beck, 80791 Munich, Germany. TEL 49-89-38189338. FAX 49-89-38189398. *6182*

LARYNGOSCOPE.
Lippincott - Raven Publishers, 227 E. Washington Sq., Philadelphia, PA 19106-3780. TEL 215-238-4200. FAX 215-238-4227. *5023*

LASER CHEMISTRY.
Gordon and Breach - Harwood Academic, Amsteldisk 166, 1st Fl., 1079 LH Amsterdam, Netherlands. *5864*

LASERS IN ENGINEERING.
Gordon and Breach - Harwood Academic, Amsteldisk 166, 1st Fl., 1079 LH Amsterdam, Netherlands. *5865*

LATIN AMERICAN RESEARCH REVIEW.
Latin American Studies Association (Albuquerque), c/o University of New Mexico, 801 Yale N.E., Albuquerque, NM 87131-1016. TEL 505-277-5985. FAX 505-277-5989. *6624*

LATIN AMERICAN STUDIES. VOLUME 1.
National Information Services Corporation (NISC), 3100 St. Paul St., Ste. 806, Baltimore, MD 21218. TEL 410-243-0797. FAX 410-243-0982.
Available only on CD-ROM. Producer(s): NISC. *3521*

LATIN AMERICAN STUDIES. VOLUME 2.
National Information Services Corporation (NISC), 3100 St. Paul St., Ste. 806, Baltimore, MD 21218. TEL 410-243-0797. FAX 410-243-0982.
Available only on CD-ROM. Producer(s): NISC. *3521*

LATIN AMERICAN TAXATION DATA BASE ON C D - R O M.
I B F D Publications B.V., P.O. Box 20237, 1000 HE Amsterdam, Netherlands. TEL 31-20-6267726. FAX 31-20-6228658. *1618*

LAW FIRMS YELLOW BOOK.
Leadership Directories, Inc., 104 Fifth Ave., 2nd Fl., New York, NY 10011. TEL 212-627-4140. FAX 212-645-0931.
Producer(s): Chadwyck-Healey Inc. *3977*

LAW REPORTS: APPEAL CASES.
Incorporated Council of Law Reporting for England and Wales, 3 Stone Bldgs., Lincoln's Inn, London WC2A 3XN, England. TEL 44-171-242 6471. FAX 44-171-831-5247. *3978*

LAW REPORTS: CHANCERY AND FAMILY DIVISION.
Incorporated Council of Law Reporting for England and Wales, 3 Stone Bldgs., Lincoln's Inn, London WC2A 3XN, England. TEL 44-171-242 6471. FAX 44-171-831-5247. *4102*

LAW REPORTS: QUEEN'S BENCH DIVISION.
Incorporated Council of Law Reporting for England and Wales, 3 Stone Bldgs., Lincoln's Inn, London WC2A 3XN, England. TEL 44-171-242 6471. FAX 44-171-831-5247. *3978*

LAWS AFFECTING CHILDREN WITH SPECIAL NEEDS.
L R P Publications, 747 Dresher Rd., Box 980, Horsham, PA 19044-0980. FAX 215-784-9639. *3979*

LAWYERS' LIABILITY REVIEW.
Versus Law, Inc., Box 1435, Bellevue, WA 98009. TEL 425-250-0142. FAX 425-250-0157. *3980*

LEADERSHIP DIRECTORIES ON C D - R O M.
Chadwyck-Healey Inc., 1101 King St., Ste. 380, Alexandria, VA 22314-2944. TEL 703-683-4890. FAX 703-683-7589.
Available only on CD-ROM. Producer(s): Chadwyck-Healey Inc. *6182*

THE LEADING EDGE (TULSA).
Society of Exploration Geophysicists, Box 702740, Tulsa, OK 74170-2740. TEL 918-493-3516. *2386*

THE LEARNING ORGANIZATION.
M C B University Press Ltd., 60-62 Toller Ln., Bradford, W. Yorks BD8 9BY, England. TEL 44-1274-777700. FAX 44-1274-785200. *1570*

LEBENSMITTELRECHT C D - R O M.
Verlag C.H. Beck, 80791 Munich, Germany. TEL 49-89-38189340. FAX 49-89-38189398.
Available only on CD-ROM. *3980*

LEGALTRAC.
Information Access Company, 362 Lakeside Dr., Foster City, CA 94404. TEL 415-378-5200. FAX 415-378-5369. *4055*

LEISURE INTELLIGENCE.
Mintel International Group Ltd., 18-19 Long Ln., London EC1A 9HE, England. TEL 44-171-606-4533. FAX 44-171-606-5932. *4150*

LEITSATZKARTEI DES DEUTSCHEN RECHTS.
Verlag C.H. Beck, 80791 Munich, Germany. TEL 49-89-38189338. FAX 49-89-38189398.
Available only on CD-ROM. *3983*

LETTERATURA ITALIANA. AGGIORNAMENTO BIBLIOGRAFICO.
Alcione Edizioni s.r.l., Corso Italia 31, C.P. 554, Trieste, Italy. TEL 39-40-366069. *4496*

LEUKEMIA AND LYMPHOMA.
Gordon and Breach - Harwood Academic, Amsteldisk 166, 1st Fl., 1079 LH Amsterdam, Netherlands. *4921*

LI B E R.
Comune di Campi Bisenzio, c/o Biblioteca Gianni Rodari, Via Garcia Corca 1, 50013 Campi Bisenzio (FI), Italy. TEL 39-55-8960800. FAX 39-55-8951964. *6276*

LIBRARIAN CAREER DEVELOPMENT.
M C B University Press Ltd., 60-62 Toller Ln., Bradford, W. Yorks BD8 9BY, England. TEL 44-1274-777700. FAX 44-1274-785200. *4192*

LIBRARY LITERATURE.
H.W. Wilson Co., 950 University Ave., Bronx, NY 10452. TEL 718-588-8400. FAX 718-590-1617. Producer(s): SilverPlatter Information, Inc., H.W. Wilson (WILSONDISC). *4227*

LIBRARY MANAGEMENT.
M C B University Press Ltd., 60-62 Toller Ln., Bradford, W. Yorks BD8 9BY, England. TEL 44-1274-777700. FAX 44-1274-785200. *4194*

LIBRARY REVIEW.
M C B University Press Ltd., 60-62 Toller Ln., Bradford, W. Yorks BD8 9BY, England. TEL 44-1274-777700. FAX 44-1274-785200. *4195*

LIBROS EN VENTA EN HISPANOAMERICA Y ESPANA.
Melcher Ediciones, c/o Margaret Melcher, Box 6000, San Juan, PR 00906. TEL 787-724-1352. FAX 787-724-2886.
Producer(s): K.G. Saur Verlag. *555*

LIBROS EN VENTA EN HISPANOAMERICA Y ESPANA PLUS.
R.R. Bowker, A Division of Reed Elsevier plc group, 121 Chanlon Rd., New Providence, NJ 07974. TEL 908-665-2866. FAX 908-665-3528.
Available only on CD-ROM. Producer(s): Bowker Electronic Publishing. *555*

LIBROS ESPANOLES EN VENTA.
Ministerio de Cultura, Centro del Libro y de la Lectura, C. Santiago Rusinol, 8, 28040 Madrid, Spain. TEL 536-88-30. FAX 553-99-90. *555*

LIEFERN UND LEISTEN.
Deutscher Adressbuch Verlag, Arheilger Weg 17, 64380 Rossdorf, Germany. TEL 06154-699500. FAX 06154-6995490. *1694*

LIFE.
Time Inc., Time & Life Bldg., Rockefeller Center, 1271 Ave. of the Americas, New York, NY 10020. TEL 212-522-1212. FAX 212-522-1863.
Producer(s): UMI, H.W. Wilson. *3377*

LINCHUANG PIFUKE ZAZHI.
Jiangsu Sheng Renmin Yiyuan, 300 Guangzhou Lu, Nanjing, Jiangsu 210029, People's Republic of China. TEL 86-25-303836. FAX 86-25-6612555. *4879*

LINEAR AND MULTILINEAR ALGEBRA.
Gordon and Breach - Harwood Academic, Amsteldisk 166, 1st Fl., 1079 LH Amsterdam, Netherlands. *4586*

LINEAR I CS D.A.T.A. DIGEST.
D.A.T.A. Business Publishing, 15 Inverness Way E., Box 6510, Englewood, CO 80155-6510. FAX 303-799-4082. *2645*

LINGUISTICS AND LANGUAGE BEHAVIOR ABSTRACTS.
Sociological Abstracts, Inc., Box 22206, San Diego, CA 92192-0206. TEL 619-695-8803. FAX 619-695-0416.
Producer(s): NISC, SilverPlatter Information, Inc. *4319*

LITERARY MARKET PLACE.
R.R. Bowker, A Division of Reed Elsevier Inc., 121 Chanlon Rd., New Providence, NJ 07974. TEL 908-464-6800. FAX 908-665-6688.
Producer(s): Bowker Electronic Publishing. *6276*

LITERARY REVIEW.
Fairleigh Dickinson University, Literary Review, 285 Madison Ave., Madison, NJ 07940. TEL 201-443-8564. *4428*

LITERATURE - FILM QUARTERLY.
Salisbury State University, Salisbury, MD 21801. TEL 410-543-6446. FAX 410-543-6068. *5339*

LIVRES DISPONIBLES.
Electre, 35 rue Gregoire-de-Tours, 75006 Paris Cedex 06, France. *555*

LOCAL GOVERNMENT AND ENVIRONMENTAL REPORTS OF AUSTRALIA.
L B C Information Services, 50 Waterloo Rd., N. Ryde, N.S.W. 2113, Australia. TEL 61-2-99366444. FAX 61-2-98882229. *4134*

LOCAL GOVERNMENT LAW & PRACTICE (NEW SOUTH WALES).
L B C Information Services, 50 Waterloo Rd., N. Ryde, N.S.W. 2113, Australia. TEL 61-2-99366444. FAX 61-2-98882229. *4134*

LOCAL GOVERNMENT REGULATIONS SERVICES (NEW SOUTH WALES).
L B C Information Services, 50 Waterloo Rd., N. Ryde, N.S.W. 2113, Australia. TEL 61-2-99366444. FAX 61-2-98882229. *4134*

LODGING, RESTAURANT AND TOURISM INDEX.
Hotel and Institutional Management Institute, Purdue University, West Lafayette, IN 47907-1002. TEL 765-494-2914. FAX 765-496-2484. *3739*

(YEAR) LOGIS DE FRANCE GUIDE BOOK.
Federation Nationale des Logis de France, 83 av. d'Italie, 75013 Paris, France. TEL 33-1-45847000. FAX 33-1-45835966. *3732*

THE LOS ANGELES TIMES INDEX.
U M I, 300 N. Zeeb Rd., Ann Arbor, MI 48106-1346. TEL 313-761-4700. FAX 800-864-0019. *3884*

LOUISIANA BUSINESS DIRECTORY.
American Business Directories, 5711 S. 86th Circle, Box 27347, Omaha, NE 68127. TEL 402-593-4600. FAX 402-331-5481. *1694*

LOUISIANA MANUFACTURERS REGISTER.
Manufacturer's News, Inc., 1633 Central St., Evanston, IL 60201-1505. TEL 847-864-7000. FAX 847-332-1100. *1694*

LOUISIANA RULES OF COURT, FEDERAL.
West Group, 620 Opperman Dr., Eagan, MN 55123. TEL 612-687-8000. FAX 612-687-7302. *4134*

LUCKNOW LIBRARIAN.
Uttar Pradesh Library Association, Lucknow Branch, U.P. Library Association, P.O. Box 446, Lucknow 226 001, India. TEL 91-522-211547. FAX 91-522-228227. *4196*

M D R'S SCHOOL DIRECTORIES.
Market Data Retrieval, Inc., 16 Progress Dr., Box 2117, Shelton, CT 06484-1117. TEL 203-926-4800. FAX 203-929-5253. *2525*

M L A INTERNATIONAL BIBLIOGRAPHY OF BOOKS AND ARTICLES ON THE MODERN LANGUAGES AND LITERATURES.
Modern Language Association of America, 10 Astor Place, New York, NY 10003. TEL 212-475-9500. FAX 212-477-9863.
Producer(s): SilverPlatter Information, Inc. *4496*

MCGOLDRICK'S CANADIAN CUSTOMS GUIDE "HARMONIZED SYSTEM".
McMullin Publishers Ltd., 417 St. Pierre, Montreal, PQ H2Y 2M4, Canada. TEL 514-849-1424. FAX 514-849-9809. *1340*

MACINTOSH TIPS & TRICKS.
Giles Road Press, 520 Palm Dr., Apt. 3, Wickenburg, AZ 85390-2432. TEL 520-684-1011. FAX 520-684-3965. *2198*

MACLEAN'S.
Maclean Hunter Ltd., Maclean Hunter Bldg., 777 Bay St., Toronto, ON M5W 1A7, Canada. TEL 416-596-5021. FAX 416-596-5516.
Producer(s): UMI. *3263*

MADE IN EUROPE. GENERAL MERCHANDISE.
Made in Europe Marketing Organisation GmbH, Hahnstr. 70, 60528 Frankfurt a.M., Germany. TEL 49-69-668038. FAX 49-69-66803838. *1341*

MADE IN EUROPE - HOTEL AND CATERING SUPPLY GUIDE.
Made in Europe Marketing Organisation GmbH, Hahnstr. 70, 60528 Frankfurt a.M., Germany. TEL 49-69-668038. FAX 49-69-66803838. *1694*

MADE IN EUROPE - MEDICAL EQUIPMENT AND SUPPLY GUIDE.
Made in Europe Marketing Organisation GmbH, Hahnstr. 70, 60528 Frankfurt a.M., Germany. TEL 49-69-6680380. FAX 49-69-66803838. *4704*

10010 SERIALS AVAILABLE ON CD-ROM

MAGAZINE ARTICLE SUMMARIES.
EBSCO Publishing, 10 Estes St., Box 682, Ipswich, MA 01938. TEL 508-356-6500. FAX 508-356-6565. *18*

MAGAZINE INDEX.
Information Access Company, 362 Lakeside Dr., Foster City, CA 94404. TEL 415-378-5200. FAX 415-378-5369. *6290*

MAGNETIC AND ELECTRICAL SEPARATION.
Gordon and Breach - Harwood Academic, Amsteldisk 166, 1st Fl., 1079 LH Amsterdam, Netherlands. *5814*

MAGYAR KONYVESZET.
Orszagos Szechenyi Konyvtar, Budavari Palota F epulet, 1827 Budapest, Hungary. TEL 36-1-1556967. FAX 36-1-202-0804. *556*

MAGYAR NEMZETI BIBLIOGRAFIA. IDOSZAKI KIADVANYOK BIBLIOGRAFIAJA.
Orszagos Szechenyi Konyvtar, Budavari Palota F epulet, 1827 Budapest, Hungary. TEL 36-1-156-9378. FAX 36-1-202-0804. Available only on CD-ROM. *556*

MAGYAR NEMZETI BIBLIOGRAFIA. KONYVEK.
Orszagos Szechenyi Konyvtar, Budavari Palota F epulet, 1827 Budapest, Hungary. TEL 36-1-1556967. FAX 36-1-2020804. Available only on CD-ROM. *556*

MAGYAR NEMZETI BIBLIOGRAFIA. KONYVEK BIBLIOGRAFIAJA.
Orszagos Szechenyi Konyvtar, Budavari Palota F epulet, 1827 Budapest, Hungary. TEL 36-1-156-8497. FAX 36-1-202-0804. *556*

MAGYAR NEMZETI BIBLIOGRAFIA. PERIODIKUMOK.
Orszagos Szechenyi Konyvtar, Budavari Palota F epulet, 1827 Budapest, Hungary. TEL 36-1-1556967. FAX 36-1-2020804. Available only on CD-ROM. *556*

THE MAIL ON C D - R O M.
Chadwyck-Healey Ltd., The Quorum, Barnwell Rd., Cambridge CB5 8SW, England. TEL 44-1223-215512. FAX 44-1223-215514. Available only on CD-ROM. Producer(s): Chadwyck-Healey Inc. *3298*

MAINE BAR DIRECTORY.
Tower Publishing Co., 588 Saco Rd., Standish, ME 04084-6239. TEL 207-642-5400. FAX 207-642-5463. *3986*

MAINE BUSINESS DIRECTORY.
American Business Directories, 5711 S. 86th Circle, Box 27347, Omaha, NE 68127. TEL 402-593-4600. FAX 402-331-5481. *1695*

AL-MAJALLAH AL-TIBBIYYAH AL-MISRIYYAH AL-JADIDAH.
Egyptian Junior Medical Doctors Association, Medical Information and Publishing Center, c/o Egyptian Medical Association, 42 Sharia Kasr El-Aini, Cairo, Egypt. *4705*

MAJALLAH-I DANISHKADAH-I DAMPIZISHKI.
University of Teheran, Faculty of Veterinary Medicine, Azadi Ave., P.O. Box 14155-6453, Tehran, Iran. TEL 98-21-923510. FAX 98-21-933222. *7275*

MAKERERE MEDICAL JOURNAL.
Makerere University Medical Students' Association (MUMSA), P.O. Box 7072, Kampala, Uganda. *4705*

MANAGEMENT DEVELOPMENT REVIEW.
M C B University Press Ltd., 60-62 Toller Ln., Bradford, W. Yorks BD8 9BY, England. TEL 44-1274-777700. FAX 44-1274-785200. *1571*

MANAGERIAL AUDITING JOURNAL.
M C B University Press Ltd., 60-62 Toller Ln., Bradford, W. Yorks BD8 9BY, England. TEL 44-1274-777700. FAX 44-1274-785200. *1495*

MANAGING SERVICE QUALITY.
M C B University Press Ltd., 60-62 Toller Ln., Bradford, W. Yorks BD8 9BY, England. TEL 44-1274-777700. FAX 44-1274-785200. *1495*

MANITOBA CO-OPERATOR.
Manitoba Pool Elevators, 220 Portage Ave., P.O. Box 9800, Stn. Main, Winnipeg, MB R3C 3K7, Canada. TEL 204-934-0401. FAX 204-934-0480. *136*

MANSOURA JOURNAL OF PHARMACEUTICAL SCIENCES.
University of Mansoura, Faculty of Pharmacy, University P.O. 35516, Mansoura, Egypt. *5677*

MANUFACTURING SUPPLIES & FABRICS.
Asian Sources Media Group, G.P.O. Box 12367, Hong Kong, People's Republic of China. TEL 852-2555-4777. *1917*

MARINE AND FRESHWATER BEHAVIOUR AND PHYSIOLOGY.
Gordon and Breach - Harwood Academic, Amsteldisk 166, 1st Fl., 1079 LH Amsterdam, Netherlands. *613*

MARINE POLLUTION RESEARCH TITLES.
Plymouth Marine Laboratory, Citadel Hill, Plymouth PL1 2PB, England. TEL 44-1752-633266. FAX 44-1752-633102. Producer(s): NISC (Oceanographic & Marine Resources). *2962*

MARINE TECHNOLOGY ABSTRACTS ON C D - R O M.
Institute of Marine Engineers, The Memorial Bldg., 76 Mark Ln., London EC3R 7JN, England. TEL 44-171-481-8493. FAX 44-171-488-1854. Available only on CD-ROM. *7054*

MARKET INTELLIGENCE.
Mintel International Group Ltd., 18-19 Long Ln., London EC1A 9HE, England. TEL 44-171-606-4533. FAX 44-171-606-5932. *1538*

MARKETING ADDRESS DATA C D.
Herold Business Data AG, Guntramsdorferstr. 105, A-2340 Moedling, Austria. TEL 43-2236-401. FAX 43-2236-4018. Available only on CD-ROM. *1696*

MARKETING INTELLIGENCE & PLANNING.
M C B University Press Ltd., 60-62 Toller Ln., Bradford, W. Yorks BD8 9BY, England. TEL 44-1274-777700. FAX 44-1274-785200. *1539*

MARKETING SERIES.
Natural Resources Institute, Central Ave., Chatham Maritime, Kent ME4 4TB, England. TEL 44-1634-880088. FAX 44-1634-880066. *1540*

MARKETSEARCH.
Arlington Management Publications, 1 Hay Hill, Berkeley Sq., London W1X 7LF, England. TEL 44-171-495-1940. FAX 44-171-409-2557. *1057*

MARLY - RECHTSPRECHUNG ZUM COMPUTERRECHT.
Verlag C.H. Beck, 80791 Munich, Germany. TEL 49-89-38189338. FAX 49-89-38189398. Available only on CD-ROM. *2150*

MARTINDALE-HUBBELL LAW DIRECTORY.
Martindale-Hubbell, A Division of Reed Elsevier Inc., 121 Chanlon Rd., New Providence, NJ 07974. FAX 908-464-3553. Producer(s): Bowker Electronic Publishing. *3987*

MARTINDALE-HUBBELL LAW DIRECTORY ON C D - R O M.
Martindale-Hubbell, A Division of Reed Elsevier Inc., 121 Chanlon Rd., New Providence, NJ 07974. FAX 908-464-3553. Available only on CD-ROM. Producer(s): Bowker Electronic Publishing. *3987*

MARYLAND BUSINESS DIRECTORY.
American Business Directories, 5711 S. 86th Circle, Box 27347, Omaha, NE 68127. TEL 402-593-4600. FAX 402-331-5481. *1696*

MARYLAND - D.C. MANUFACTURERS REGISTER.
Manufacturers' News, Inc., 1633 Central St., Evanston, IL 60201-1569. TEL 847-864-7000. FAX 847-332-1100. *1696*

MASSACHUSETTS BUSINESS DIRECTORY.
American Business Directories, 5711 S. 86th Circle, Omaha, NE 68127. TEL 402-593-4600. FAX 402-331-5481. *1696*

MASTERS ABSTRACTS INTERNATIONAL.
U M I, 300 N. Zeeb Rd., Ann Arbor, MI 48106. TEL 313-761-4700. FAX 800-864-0019. Producer(s): UMI. *2502*

MATERIALS SCIENCE CITATION INDEX.
Institute for Scientific Information, 3501 Market St., Philadelphia, PA 19104. TEL 215-386-0100. FAX 215-386-2911. *2751*

MATHEMATICAL REVIEWS.
American Mathematical Society, Box 6248, Providence, RI 02940-6248. TEL 401-455-4000. FAX 401-331-3842. Producer(s): SilverPlatter Information, Inc. (MathDisc). *4617*

A MATTER OF FACT: STATEMENTS CONTAINING STATISTICS ON CURRENT SOCIAL, ECONOMIC AND POLITICAL ISSUES.
Pierian Press, Box 1808, Ann Arbor, MI 48106. TEL 313-434-5530. FAX 313-434-6409. Producer(s): NISC, SilverPlatter Information, Inc. *3505*

MAYO CLINIC PROCEEDINGS.
Dowden Publishing Company, 110 Summit Ave., Montvale, NJ 07645. TEL 201-782-5735. FAX 201-391-2778. *4706*

MEALEY'S LITIGATION REPORT: INSURANCE.
Mealey Publications, Inc., Box 446, Wayne, PA 19087. TEL 610-688-6566. FAX 610-688-7552. *4063*

MEALEY'S LITIGATION REPORT: INSURANCE INSOLVENCY.
Mealey Publications, Inc., Box 446, Wayne, PA 19087. TEL 610-688-6566. FAX 610-688-7552. *4063*

MECHANICAL ENGINEERING ABSTRACTS.
Cambridge Scientific Abstracts, 7200 Wisconsin Ave., 6th Fl., Bethesda, MD 20814. TEL 301-961-6700. FAX 301-961-6720. Producer(s): SilverPlatter Information, Inc. *2751*

MEDECINE ET ENFANCE, ADOLESCENCE.
Edition et Communication Medicales, 23 rue Saint-Ferdinand, 75017 Paris, France. TEL 45-74-44-65. FAX 40-55-94-13. *5034*

MEDIATORS OF INFLAMMATION.
Rapid Science Publishers, The Old Malthouse, Paradise St., Oxford OX1 1LD, England. TEL 44-1865-790447. FAX 44-1865-244012. *4706*

MEDICAL AND HEALTH CARE BOOKS AND SERIALS IN PRINT.
R.R. Bowker, A Division of Reed Elsevier Inc., 121 Chanlon Rd., New Providence, NJ 07974. TEL 908-464-6800. FAX 908-665-3502. *4782*

MEDICAL AND HEALTHCARE MARKETPLACE GUIDE.
Legal Communications, Ltd., 1617 JFK Blvd., Ste. 960, Philadelphia, PA 19103. TEL 215-557-2300. FAX 215-557-2301. *1697*

MEDICAL & PHARMACEUTICAL BIOTECHNOLOGY ABSTRACTS.
Cambridge Scientific Abstracts, 7200 Wisconsin Ave., 6th Fl., Bethesda, MD 20814. TEL 301-961-6700. FAX 301-961-6720. Producer(s): Knight-Ridder, Inc. (Biotechnology & Bioengineering), SilverPlatter Information, Inc. *4782*

MEDICAL DEVICE COMPANIES ANALYSIS NEWSLETTER.
M D I S Publications Ltd., MDIS House, City Fields Business Park, City Fields Way, Chichester, W. Sussex PO20 6FS, England. TEL 44-1243-533322. FAX 44-1243-533418. *3804*

MEDICAL DEVICE COMPANIES ANALYSIS PROFILES.
M D I S Publications Ltd., MDIS House, City Fields Business Park, City Fields Way, Chichester, W. Sussex PO20 6FS, England. TEL 44-1243-533322. FAX 44-1243-533418. *3804*

MEDICAL DIRECTORY.
Cartermill Publishing, Maple House, 149 Tottenham Court Rd., London W1P 9LL, England. TEL 44-171-896-2400. FAX 44-171-896-2449. *4708*

MEDICAL JOURNAL ARMED FORCES INDIA.
Armed Forces Medical College, Pune 411 040, Maharashtra, India. TEL 91-212-673290. FAX 91-212-679539. *4709*

MEDICAL JOURNAL OF THE ISLAMIC REPUBLIC OF IRAN.
National Center for Scientific Research, 1188 Enghelab Ave., P.O. Box 13145-554, Tehran 13158, Iran. TEL 98-21-6462778. FAX 98-21-6468180. *4709*

MEDICINAL AND AROMATIC PLANTS ABSTRACTS.
National Institute of Science Communication, Council of Scientific and Industrial Research, K.S. Krishnan Rd., New Delhi 110 012, India. TEL 91-11-5726014. FAX 91-11-5787062. *4782*

MEDISTAT.
M D I S Publications Ltd., MDIS House, City Fields Business Park, City Fields Way, Chichester, W. Sussex PO20 6FS, England. TEL 44-1243-533322. FAX 44-1243-532124. *4714*

MEDLINE PROFESSIONAL - C D.
SilverPlatter Information, Inc., 100 River Ridge Dr., Norwood, MA 02062-5026. TEL 617-769-2599. FAX 617-769-8763.
Available only on CD-ROM. *4782*

MEGAMOT.
Henrietta Szold Institute, 9 Columbia St., Kiryat Menachem, Jerusalem 96583, Israel. FAX 2-437698. *6720*

MEITAN JINGJI YANJIU.
Zhongguo Meitan Kexue Yanjiu Zongyuan, Jingji Yanjiusuo, Hepingli, Beijing 100013, People's Republic of China. TEL 86-10-6423-4338. FAX 86-10-6422-1627. *984*

MELANOMA RESEARCH.
Rapid Science Publishers, The Old Malthouse, Paradise St., Oxford OX1 1LD, England. TEL 44-1865-790447. FAX 44-1865-244012. *4983*

MEMORY I CS D.A.T.A. DIGEST.
D.A.T.A. Business Publishing, 15 Inverness Way E., Box 6510, Englewood, CO 80155-6510. FAX 303-799-4082. *2645*

MENDELEEV COMMUNICATIONS.
Turpion - Moscow Ltd., 47 Leninsky prospekt, 117913 Moscow, Russia. TEL 7-95-1356417. FAX 7-95-1358860. *1760*

MENNONITE REPORTER.
Mennonite Publishing Service, 3-312 Marsland Drive, Waterloo, ON N2J 3Z1, Canada. TEL 519-884-3810. FAX 519-884-3331. *6433*

MERCADO DE VALORES.
Nacional Financiera, S.N.C., Subdireccion de Informacion Tecnica y Publicaciones, Insurgentes Sur 1971, Nivel Fuente, Col. Guadalupe Inn, 01020 Mexico, D.F., Mexico. TEL 52-5-3256047. *1396*

METALS ABSTRACTS.
Cambridge Scientific Abstracts, 7200 Wisconsin Ave., Bethesda, MD 20814. TEL 301-961-6750. FAX 301-961-6720.
Producer(s): Knight-Ridder, Inc. *5220*

METALS ABSTRACTS INDEX.
Cambridge Scientific Abstracts, 7200 Wisconsin Ave., Bethesda, MD 20814. TEL 301-961-6750. FAX 301-961-6720.
Producer(s): Knight-Ridder, Inc. *5220*

METEOROLOGICAL AND GEOASTROPHYSICAL ABSTRACTS.
American Meteorological Society, c/o Inforonics, Inc., 550 Newtown Rd., Littleton, MA 01460. TEL 508-486-8976. FAX 508-486-0027. *5248*

MEYLER'S SIDE EFFECTS OF DRUGS.
Elsevier Science B.V., Books Division, P.O. Box 211, 1000 AE Amsterdam, Netherlands. TEL 31-20-4853911. FAX 31-20-4853705.
Producer(s): SilverPlatter Information, Inc. (SEDBASE). *5678*

MICHIGAN BUSINESS DIRECTORY.
American Business Directories, 5711 S. 86th Circle, Box 27347, Omaha, NE 68127. TEL 402-593-4600. FAX 402-331-5481. *1697*

MICHIGAN LAW REVIEW.
Michigan Law Review Association, 625 South State St., Hutchins Hall, Ann Arbor, MI 48109-1215. TEL 313-763-5870. FAX 313-647-5817. *3990*

MICHIGAN MANUFACTURERS DIRECTORY.
Pick Publications, Inc., 24293 Telegraph Rd., Ste. 140, Southfield, MI 48034-7924. TEL 810-827-7111. FAX 810-443-5191. *1698*

MICHIGAN TODAY.
University of Michigan, Office of University Relations, News and Information Services, 412 Maynard St., Ann Arbor, MI 48109. TEL 313-764-0105. FAX 313-764-7084. *1961*

MICROBIAL & COMPARATIVE GENOMICS.
Mary Ann Liebert, Inc. Publishers, 2 Madison Ave., Larchmont, NY 10538. TEL 914-834-3100. FAX 914-834-3688. *773*

MICROBIOLOGY ABSTRACTS: SECTION A. INDUSTRIAL & APPLIED MICROBIOLOGY.
Cambridge Scientific Abstracts, 7200 Wisconsin Ave., 6th Fl., Bethesda, MD 20814. TEL 301-961-6750. FAX 301-961-6720.
Producer(s): NISC, SilverPlatter Information, Inc. *642*

MICROBIOLOGY ABSTRACTS: SECTION B. BACTERIOLOGY.
Cambridge Scientific Abstracts, 7200 Wisconsin Ave., 6th Fl., Bethesda, MD 20814. TEL 301-961-6750. FAX 301-961-6720.
Producer(s): SilverPlatter Information, Inc. *642*

MICROBIOLOGY ABSTRACTS: SECTION C. ALGOLOGY, MYCOLOGY AND PROTOZOOLOGY.
Cambridge Scientific Abstracts, 7200 Wisconsin Ave., 6th Fl., Bethesda, MD 20814. TEL 301-961-6750. FAX 301-961-6720.
Producer(s): NISC, SilverPlatter Information, Inc. *642*

MICROBIOLOGY AND MOLECULAR BIOLOGY REVIEWS.
American Society for Microbiology, 1325 Massachusetts Ave., N.W., Washington, DC 20005. TEL 202-737-3600. *790*

MICROCOMPUTER ABSTRACTS.
Information Today, Inc., 143 Old Marlton Pike, Medford, NJ 08055. TEL 609-654-6266. FAX 609-654-4309.
Producer(s): SilverPlatter Information, Inc. *2095*

MICROPROCESSOR I C'S D.A.T.A. DIGEST.
D.A.T.A. Business Publishing, 15 Inverness Way E., Box 6510, Englewood, CO 80155-6510. FAX 303-799-4082. *2190*

MICROPROCESSOR REPORT.
874 Gravenstein Hwy. So., Ste.14, Sebastopol, CA 95472. TEL 707-824-4004. FAX 707-823-0504. *2191*

MIDDLE EASTERN STUDIES.
Frank Cass, Newbury House, 890-900 Eastern Ave., Newbury Park, Ilford, Essex IG2 7HH, England. TEL 44-181-599-8836. FAX 44-181-599-0984. *3658*

MIDLIFE WOMAN.
MidLife Women's Network, 5129 Logan Ave. S., Minneapolis, MN 55419-1019. TEL 612-915-0020. FAX 612-925-0020. *7327*

MIETRECHT VOLLTEXT C D - R O M.
Verlag C.H. Beck, 80791 Munich, Germany. TEL 49-89-38189338. FAX 49-89-38189398.
Available only on CD-ROM. *3990*

MILITARY SPECIFICATIONS AND STANDARDS SERVICES NUMERIC INDEX.
Information Handling Services, 15 Inverness Way East, Englewood, CO 80150. TEL 303-790-0600. FAX 303-799-4085. *5277*

MILLER G A A P GUIDE.
Harcourt Brace Professional Publishing, 525 B St., Ste. 1900, San Diego, CA 92101-4495. TEL 619-699-6716. FAX 619-699-6542. *1095*

MILLER G A A S GUIDE.
Harcourt Brace Professional Publishing, 525 B St., Ste. 1900, San Diego, CA 92101-4495. TEL 619-699-6716. FAX 619-699-6593. *1095*

MILLION DOLLAR DIRECTORY.
Dun and Bradstreet, 3 Sylvan Way, Parsippany, NJ 07054-3896. TEL 201-605-6000.
Producer(s): Dun & Bradstreet Information Services. *1698*

MINERALOGICAL ABSTRACTS.
Mineralogical Society, 41 Queen's Gate, London SW7 5HR, England. TEL 44-171-584-7516. FAX 44-171-823-8021. *5321*

MINNESOTA BUSINESS DIRECTORY.
American Business Directories, 5711 S. 86th Circle, Box 27347, Omaha, NE 68127. TEL 402-593-4600. FAX 402-331-5481. *1698*

MINNESOTA MANUFACTURERS REGISTER.
Manufacturers' News, Inc., 1633 Central St., Evanston, IL 60201. TEL 847-864-7000. FAX 847-332-1100. *1698*

MINNESOTA STATUTES.
Office of Revisor of Statutes, 700 State Office Bldg., St. Paul, MN 55155. TEL 612-296-2868. *4135*

MINNESOTA STATUTES ON C D - R O M.
Office of Revisor of Statutes, 700 State Office Bldg., St. Paul, MN 55155. TEL 612-296-2868. *4135*

MINT MUSEUM MEMBERNEWS.
Mint Museum of Art, 2730 Randolph Rd., Charlotte, NC 28207. TEL 704-337-2000. FAX 704-337-2101. *5359*

MISSISSIPPI BUSINESS DIRECTORY.
American Business Directories, 5711 S. 86th Circle, Box 27347, Omaha, NE 68127. TEL 402-593-4600. FAX 402-331-5481. *1699*

MISSISSIPPI MANUFACTURERS REGISTER.
Manufacturers' News, Inc., 1633 Central St., Evanston, IL 60201-1569. TEL 847-864-7000. FAX 847-332-1100. *1699*

THE MISSISSIPPI QUARTERLY.
Mississippi State University, College of Arts and Sciences, Box 5272, Mississippi State, MS 39762. TEL 601-325-3069. FAX 601-325-3299. *4346*

MISSOURI BUSINESS DIRECTORY.
American Business Directories, 5711 S. 86th Circle, Box 27347, Omaha, NE 68127. TEL 402-593-4600. FAX 402-331-5481. *1699*

MISSOURI GETAWAY TRAVEL GUIDE.
Division of Tourism, Truman State Office Building, Box 1055, Jefferson City, MO 65102. TEL 573-751-4133. FAX 573-751-5160. *7221*

MISSOURI MANUFACTURERS REGISTER.
Manufacturers' News, Inc., 1633 Central St., Evanston, IL 60201. TEL 847-864-7000. FAX 847-332-1100. *1699*

MITTELSTAENDISCHE UNTERNEHMEN.
Verlag Hoppenstedt GmbH, Havelstr. 9, 64295 Darmstadt, Germany. TEL 49-6151-380-0. FAX 49-6151-380-360. *1591*

MODERN DRAFTING PRACTICES AND STANDARDS MANUAL.
Genium Publishing Corp., 1 Genium Plaza, Schenectady, NY 12304-4690. TEL 518-377-8854. FAX 518-377-1891. *6967*

MODERN ESTATE PLANNING.
Matthew Bender & Co., Inc., 2 Park Ave., New York, NY 10016. TEL 212-448-2000. *1154*

DIE MOEBEL-INDUSTRIE UND IHRE HELFER.
Industrieschau-Verlagsgesellschaft mbH, Postfach 100262, 64202 Darmstadt, Germany. TEL 49-6151-3892-0. FAX 49-6151-33164. *3859*

MOLECULAR AND CELLULAR BIOLOGY.
American Society for Microbiology, 1325 Massachusetts Ave., N.W., Washington, DC 20005. TEL 202-737-3600. *791*

MOLECULAR CRYSTALS AND LIQUID CRYSTALS SCIENCE AND TECHNOLOGY. SECTION A: MOLECULAR CRYSTALS AND LIQUID CRYSTALS.
Gordon and Breach - Harwood Academic, Amsteldisk 166, 1st Fl., 1079 LH Amsterdam, Netherlands. *1803*

MOLECULAR CRYSTALS AND LIQUID CRYSTALS SCIENCE AND TECHNOLOGY. SECTION B: NONLINEAR OPTICS.
Gordon and Breach - Harwood Academic, Amsteldisk 166, 1st Fl., 1079 LH Amsterdam, Netherlands. *5866*

MOLECULAR CRYSTALS AND LIQUID CRYSTALS SCIENCE AND TECHNOLOGY. SECTION C: MOLECULAR MATERIALS.
Gordon and Breach - Harwood Academic, Amsteldisk 166, 1st Fl., 1079 LH Amsterdam, Netherlands. *1803*

MOLECULAR SIMULATION.
Gordon and Breach - Harwood Academic, Amsteldisk 166, 1st Fl., 1079 LH Amsterdam, Netherlands. *1760*

MOLECULES.
Springer-Verlag, Heidelberger Platz 3, 14197 Berlin, Germany. TEL 49-30-82787-0. FAX 49-30-82787448. *1819*

LE MONDE.
Le Monde S.A., 21 bis rue Claude-Bernard, 75242 Paris Cedex 5, France. TEL 33-1-42172000. FAX 33-1-42172121. *3280*

LE MONDE INDEX.
Primary Source Media, P.O. Box 45, Reading RG1 8HF, England. TEL 44-1734-583247. FAX 44-1734-591325. *3884*

MONEY (NEW YORK).
Time Inc., Time & Life Bldg., Rockefeller Center, 1271 Ave. of the Americas, New York, NY 10020. TEL 212-522-1212. Producer(s): UMI. *1155*

MONEY MANAGEMENT LETTER.
Institutional Investor Newsletters, 477 Madison Ave., New York, NY 10022. TEL 212-224-3233. FAX 212-224-3353. *1396*

MONTANA BUSINESS DIRECTORY.
American Business Directories, 5711 S. 86th Circle, Box 27347, Omaha, NE 68127. TEL 402-593-4600. FAX 402-331-5481. *1699*

MONTHLY CATALOG OF UNITED STATES GOVERNMENT PUBLICATIONS.
U.S. Government Printing Office, Superintendent of Documents, Washington, DC 20402-9341. Producer(s): SilverPlatter Information, Inc., H.W. Wilson. *6205*

MONTHLY LABOR REVIEW.
U.S. Bureau of Labor Statistics, 2 Massachusetts Ave., N.E., Washington, DC 20212. TEL 202-606-5902. *1058*

MOODY'S COMPANY DATA.
Moody's Investors Service, 99 Church St., New York, NY 10007-0300. TEL 212-553-0300. FAX 212-553-4700. Available only on CD-ROM. *1203*

MOODY'S INTERNATIONAL COMPANY DATA.
Moody's Investors Service, 99 Church St., New York, NY 10007. TEL 212-553-0300. FAX 212-553-4700. Available only on CD-ROM. *1397*

MORNINGSTAR MUTUAL FUNDS ONDISC.
Morningstar, Inc., 225 W. Wacker Dr., Chicago, IL 60606. TEL 312-696-6000. FAX 312-696-6001. Available only on CD-ROM. *1398*

MOSCOW NEWS.
Moscow News Information & Media Company, 16-2 Tverskaya ul., 103829 Moscow. TEL 7-095-2003666. FAX 7-095-2092661. *3352*

MOSKOVSKIE NOVOSTI.
Moscow News Information & Media Company, 16-2 Tverskaya ul., 103829 Moscow, Russia. TEL 7-095-2006390. FAX 7-095-2000650. *3352*

MOTHER AND CHILD.
Maternity & Child Welfare Association of Pakistan, MCH House, 30-F, Gulberg-II, Lahore 54666, Pakistan. TEL 92-42-874621. *7328*

MOTHER JONES.
Foundation for National Progress, 731 Market St., Ste. 600, San Francisco, CA 94103. TEL 415-665-6637. FAX 415-665-6696. Producer(s): UMI. *4347*

MOTO MAGAZYN.
Proszynski i S-ka, S.A., Ul. Rozana 34, 02-569 Warsaw, Poland. TEL 48-22-451256. FAX 48-22-452736. *7106*

MOTOR BUSINESS INTERNATIONAL.
Economist Intelligence Unit, 111 W. 57th St., New York, NY 10019. TEL 212-554-0600. FAX 212-586-1182. *7107*

MOTOR TREND.
Petersen Publishing Co., 6420 Wilshire Blvd., Los Angeles, CA 90048. TEL 213-782-2220. FAX 213-782-2866. Producer(s): UMI. *7108*

MULTI-STATE SALES TAX GUIDE.
C C H Incorporated, 2700 Lake Cook Rd., Riverwoods, IL 60015. TEL 847-267-7000. FAX 800-224-8299. *1620*

MULTIMEDIA COMPUTING & PRESENTATIONS.
Multimedia Computing Corporation, P.O. Box 60369, Sunnyvale, CA 94088-0369. TEL 408-737-7575. FAX 408-739-8019. *2216*

MULTIMEDIA MONITOR.
Phillips Business Information, Inc., 1201 Seven Locks Rd., Potomac, MD 20854. TEL 301-424-3338. FAX 301-309-3847. *2157*

MULTIMEDIA WORLD.
I D G Communications Inc. (San Francisco), 501 Second St., San Francisco, CA 94107. TEL 415-281-8650. FAX 415-281-3915. *2199*

MULTIMEDIA WORLD LIVE!
I D G Communications Inc. (San Francisco), 501 Second St., San Francisco, CA 94107. TEL 415-281-8650. FAX 415-281-3915. Available only on CD-ROM. *2199*

THE MULTIMEDIA YEARBOOK.
Macmillan Magazines Ltd., 4 Porters South, Crinan St., London N1 9XW. TEL 44-1256-29242. FAX 44-1256-842084. *2017*

MULTINATIONAL BUSINESS REVIEW.
University of Detroit Mercy, College of Business Administration, Box 19900, Detroit, MI 48219-0900. TEL 313-993-1264. FAX 313-993-1052. Producer(s): UMI. *1342*

MULTISTATE CORPORATE INCOME TAX GUIDE.
C C H Incorporated, 2700 Lake Cook Rd., Riverwoods, IL 60015. TEL 312-583-8500. FAX 800-224-8299. *1620*

MUNDO HISPANICO.
Mundo Hispanico, Inc., Box 13808, Sta. K, Atlanta, GA 30324-0808. TEL 404-881-0441. FAX 404-881-6085. *3030*

MUNICIPAL YELLOW BOOK.
Leadership Directories, Inc., 104 Fifth Ave., 2nd Fl., New York, NY 10011. TEL 212-627-4140. FAX 212-645-0931. Producer(s): Chadwyck-Healey Inc. *6220*

MUSE (MUSIC SEARCH).
National Information Services Corporation (NISC), 3100 St. Paul St., Ste. 806, Baltimore, MD 21218. TEL 410-243-0797. FAX 410-243-0982. Available only on CD-ROM. Producer(s): NISC. *5448*

MUSIC INDEX.
Harmonie Park Press, 23630 Pinewood, Warren, MI 48091-4759. TEL 810-755-3080. FAX 810-755-4213. *5448*

N A B E INDUSTRY SURVEY.
National Association of Business Economists, 1233 20th St., N.W., Ste. 505, Washington, DC 20036-2304. TEL 202-463-6223. FAX 202-462-6239. *1272*

N A B E OUTLOOK & POLICY SURVEY.
National Association of Business Economists, 1233 20th St., N.W., Ste. 505, Washington, DC 20036-2304. TEL 202-463-6223. FAX 202-463-6239. *1272*

N C J R S DOCUMENT RETRIEVAL INDEX.
U.S. National Institute of Justice, National Criminal Justice Reference Service, Box 6000, Department F, Rockville, MD 20849-6000. TEL 301-251-5500. FAX 301-251-5212. *2284*

N C J W JOURNAL.
National Council of Jewish Women, 53 W. 23rd St., New York, NY 10010. TEL 212-645-4048. FAX 212-645-7466. *7328*

N D L C D - R O M LINE JAPANESE PERIODICAL INDEX.
National Diet Library, 1-10-1 Nagata-cho, Chiyoda-ku, Tokyo 100, Japan. TEL 81-3-3581-2331. FAX 81-3-3597-9104. *3799*

N E L M INDEX SERIES.
National English Literary Museum, Private Bag 1019, Grahamstown 6140, South Africa. TEL 27-461-27042. FAX 27-461-22582. Producer(s): NISC. *1496*

N I O S H POCKET GUIDE TO CHEMICAL HAZARDS.
U.S. National Institute for Occupational Safety and Health, Attn: Publications, 4676 Columbia Pkwy., Cincinnati, OH 45226. FAX 513-533-8573. *5494*

NIOSHTIC.
U.S. National Institute for Occupational Safety and Health, Technical Information Center, Attn: Publications, 4676 Columbia Pky., Cincinnati, OH 45226. FAX 513-533-8573. Producer(s): SilverPlatter Information, Inc. *5494*

N J W - RECHTSPRECHUNGS-REPORT ZIVILRECHT.
Verlag C.H. Beck, 80791 Munich, Germany. TEL 49-89-38189-338. FAX 49-89-38189-398. *4064*

N O S P - MIKRO.
University of Oslo Library, N O S P - Centre, N-0242 Oslo, Norway. TEL 47-22-859110. FAX 47-22-859050. *557*

N T I S BIBLIOGRAPHIC DATA BASE.
U.S. National Technical Information Service, 5285 Port Royal Rd., Springfield, VA 22161. TEL 703-487-4630. Producer(s): Knight-Ridder, Inc., OCLC, SilverPlatter Information, Inc. *6292*

N VW Z RECHTSPRECHUNGS REPORT VERWALTUNGSRECHT.
Verlag C.H. Beck, 80791 Munich, Germany. TEL 49-89-38189-338. FAX 49-89-38189398. *3993*

DIE NAHRUNGS- UND GENUSSMITTEL-INDUSTRIE UND IHRE HELFER.
Industrieschau-Verlagsgesellschaft mbH, Postfach 100262, 64202 Darmstadt, Germany. TEL 49-6151-38920. FAX 49-6151-33164. *3121*

NANJING SHEHUI KEXUE.
Nanjing Shehui Kexuejie Lianhehui, 35 Jinxianghe Lu, Nanjing, Jiangsu 210008, People's Republic of China. TEL 86-25-3611547. *6627*

NASH & CIBINIC REPORT.
Federal Publications Inc., 1120 20th St., N.W., Ste. 500 S, Washington, DC 20036-3484. TEL 202-377-7000. FAX 202-659-2233. *6185*

THE NATION.
The Nation Company, L.P., 72 Fifth Ave., New York, NY 10011. TEL 212-242-8400. FAX 212-463-9712. Producer(s): UMI. *4347*

NATIONAL CIVIC REVIEW.
Jossey-Bass Inc., Publishers, 350 Sansone St., 5th Fl., San Francisco, CA 94104. FAX 800-605-2665. Producer(s): UMI. *6221*

NATIONAL CONTEST JOURNAL.
American Radio Relay League, Inc., 25 Main St., Newington, CT 06111. TEL 860-594-0200. FAX 860-594-0303. *2026*

NATIONAL DIRECTORY OF CATALOGS.
Oxbridge Communications, Inc., 150 Fifth Ave., Ste. 302, New York, NY 10011. TEL 212-741-0231. FAX 212-633-2938. *557*

NATIONAL DIRECTORY OF FIRE CHIEFS, RESCUE & EMERGENCY DEPARTMENTS.
Span Publishing, Box 365, 1308 Main St., Stevens Point, WI 54481-0365. TEL 715-345-2772. FAX 715-345-7288. *3057*

NATIONAL DIRECTORY OF MAGAZINES.
Oxbridge Communications, Inc., 150 Fifth Ave., New York, NY 10011. TEL 212-741-0231. FAX 212-633-2938. *557*

NATIONAL DIRECTORY OF MAILING LISTS.
Oxbridge Communications, Inc., 150 Fifth Ave., Ste. 302, New York, NY 10011. TEL 212-741-0231. FAX 212-633-2938. *1700*

NATIONAL ENGLISH LITERARY MUSEUM. BIBLIOGRAPHIC SERIES.
National English Literary Museum, Private Bag 1019, Grahamstown 6140, South Africa. TEL 27-461-27042. FAX 27-46122582. *4496*

NATIONAL MEDICAL JOURNAL OF INDIA.
All India Institute of Medical Sciences, New Delhi 110 029, India. TEL 91-11-6863002. FAX 91-11-6862663. *4720*

NATIONAL NEWSPAPER INDEX.
Information Access Company, 362 Lakeside Dr., Foster City, CA 94404. TEL 415-378-5200. FAX 415-378-5369. *3884*

NATIONAL REVIEW.
National Review, Inc., 215 Lexington Ave., New York, NY 10016. TEL 212-679-7330. FAX 212-849-2835.
Producer(s): UMI. *5946*

NATION'S BUSINESS.
U.S. Chamber of Commerce, 1615 H St., N.W., Washington, DC 20062-2000. TEL 202-463-5650. FAX 202-887-3437.
Producer(s): UMI. *1193*

NATURAL HISTORY.
American Museum of Natural History, Central Park W. at 79th St., New York, NY 10024-5192. TEL 212-769-5500. FAX 212-769-5511.
Producer(s): UMI. *6550*

NATURAL PRODUCT LETTERS.
Gordon and Breach - Harwood Academic, Amsteldisk 166, 1st Fl., 1079 LH Amsterdam, Netherlands. *1760*

NEBRASKA BUSINESS DIRECTORY.
American Business Directories, 5711 S. 86th Circle, Box 27347, Omaha, NE 68127. TEL 402-593-4600. FAX 402-331-5481. *1701*

NEBRASKA MANUFACTURERS REGISTER.
Manufacturers' News, Inc., 1633 Central St., Evanston, IL 60201-1569. TEL 847-864-7000. FAX 847-332-1100. *1701*

NETWORK WORLD.
Network World Inc., 161 Worcester Rd., 5th Fl., Framingham, MA 01701. TEL 508-875-6400. FAX 508-879-3167. *2138*

NEUE JURISTISCHE WOCHENSCHRIFT.
Verlag C.H. Beck, 80791 Munich, Germany. TEL 49-89-38189-338. FAX 49-89-38189-398. *3995*

NEUE WIRTSCHAFTS-BRIEFE.
Verlag Neue Wirtschafts-Briefe GmbH, Eschstr. 22, 44629 Herne, Germany. TEL 49-2323-141-0. FAX 49-2323-141123. *1621*

NEUE ZEITSCHRIFT FUER ARBEITSRECHT.
Verlag C.H. Beck, 80791 Munich, Germany. TEL 49-89-38189-338. FAX 49-89-38189-398. *3995*

NEUE ZEITSCHRIFT FUER STRAFRECHT.
Verlag C.H. Beck, 80791 Munich, Germany. TEL 49-89-38189-338. FAX 49-89-38189-398. *4093*

NEUE ZEITSCHRIFT FUER VERWALTUNGSRECHT.
Verlag C.H. Beck, 80791 Munich, Germany. TEL 49-89-38189-338. FAX 49-89-38189-398. *4136*

NEUE ZUERCHER ZEITUNG.
Neue Zuercher Zeitung, Falkenstr. 11, CH-8021 Zurich, Switzerland. TEL 41-1-2581111. FAX 41-1-2581675. *3364*

NEUROCASE.
Oxford University Press, Academic Division, Great Clarendon St., Oxford OX2 6DP, England. TEL 44-1865-267907. FAX 44-1865-267485. *5082*

NEUROLOGY INDIA.
Neurological Society of India, Dept. of Neurology, Post-graduate Institute of Medical Education & Research, Chandigarh 160 012, India. TEL 0172-541032. *5084*

NEUROREPORT.
Rapid Science Publishers, The Old Malthouse, Paradise St., Oxford OX1 1LD, England. TEL 44-1865-790447. FAX 44-1865-244012. *5086*

NEUROSCIENCE CITATION INDEX.
Institute for Scientific Information, 3501 Market St., Philadelphia, PA 19104. TEL 215-386-0100. FAX 215-386-2911. *4783*

NEVADA BUSINESS DIRECTORY.
American Business Directories, 5711 S. 86th Circle, Box 27347, Omaha, NE 68127. TEL 402-593-4600. FAX 402-331-5481. *1701*

NEW ENGLAND JOURNAL OF MEDICINE.
Massachusetts Medical Society, 10 Shattuck St., Boston, MA 02115. TEL 617-734-9800. FAX 617-893-8103. *4721*

NEW ENGLAND WATER WORKS ASSOCIATION. JOURNAL.
New England Water Works Association, 64 Dilla St., Milford, MA 01757-1104. TEL 508-478-6996. FAX 508-634-8643.
Producer(s): Knight-Ridder, Inc. *7298*

NEW HAMPSHIRE BUSINESS DIRECTORY.
American Business Directories, 5711 S. 86th Circle, Box 27347, Omaha, NE 68127. TEL 402-593-4600. FAX 402-331-5481. *1701*

NEW JERSEY BUSINESS DIRECTORY.
American Business Directories, 5711 S. 86th Circle, Box 27347, Omaha, NE 68127. TEL 402-593-4600. FAX 402-331-5481. *1702*

NEW JERSEY DIRECTORY OF MANUFACTURERS.
Commerce Register, Inc., 190 Godwin Ave., Midland Park, NJ 07432. TEL 201-445-3000. FAX 201-446-5806. *1702*

NEW JERSEY LAWYER (ISELIN).
New Jersey Lawyer, Inc., Metropolitan Corporate Plaza, 485B Route 1, Ste. 100, Iselin, NJ 08830-3013. TEL 908-750-4994. FAX 908-750-0010. *3997*

NEW JERSEY MANUFACTURERS DIRECTORY.
Harris InfoSource International, 2057-2 Aurora Rd., Twinsburg, OH 44087. TEL 216-425-9000. FAX 800-6423-5997. *1702*

NEW JERSEY RULES OF COURT, STATE AND FEDERAL.
West Group, 620 Opperman Dr., Eagan, MN 55123. TEL 612-687-8000. FAX 612-687-7302. *4136*

NEW LIBRARY WORLD.
M C B University Press Ltd., 60-62 Toller Ln., Bradford, W. Yorks BD8 9BY, England. TEL 44-1274-777700. FAX 44-1274-785200. *4202*

NEW MEXICO BUSINESS DIRECTORY.
American Business Directories, 5711 S. 86th Circle, Box 27347, Omaha, NE 68127. TEL 402-593-4600. FAX 402-331-5481. *1702*

NEW MEXICO REPORTS.
West Group, 620 Opperman Dr., Eagan, MN 55123. TEL 612-687-8000. FAX 612-687-7302. *3997*

NEW PERSPECTIVES QUARTERLY.
Blackwell Publishers, 238 Main St., Cambridge, MA 02142. TEL 617-547-7110. FAX 617-547-0789. *5948*

NEW PRODUCT LAUNCH LETTER.
IMSWORLD Publications Ltd., 7 Harewood Ave., London NW1 6JB, England. TEL 0171-393-5000. FAX 0171-393-5900. *5680*

THE NEW REPUBLIC.
1220 19th St., N.W., Washington, DC 20036. TEL 202-331-7494. FAX 202-331-0275.
Producer(s): UMI. *4349*

NEW SCIENTIST.
I P C Magazines, Specialist Magazine Group King's Reach Tower, Stamford St., London SE1 9LS, England. TEL 44-171-261-5000. FAX 44-1444-445599.
Producer(s): Bowker - Saur Ltd. *6553*

NEW SCIENTIST C D - R O M.
Bowker - Saur Ltd., A member of the Reed Elsevier plc group, Maypole House, Maypole Rd., E. Grinstead, W. Sussex RH19 1HU, England. TEL 44-1342-330100. FAX 44-1342-330191.
Available only on CD-ROM. *6553*

NEW TRADE NAMES IN THE RUBBER AND PLASTICS INDUSTRIES.
Rapra Technology Ltd., Shawbury, Shrewsbury, Shrops. SY4 4NR, England. TEL 44-1939-250383. FAX 44-1939-251118. *6503*

NEW YORK BUSINESS DIRECTORY.
American Business Directories, 5711 S. 86th Circle, Box 27347, Omaha, NE 68127. TEL 402-593-4600. FAX 402-331-5481. *1702*

NEW YORK LAW JOURNAL.
New York Law Publishing Co., 345 Park Ave. S., New York, NY 10010. TEL 212-779-9200. *3998*

NEW YORK MANUFACTURERS DIRECTORY.
Harris InfoSource International, 2057-2 Aurora Rd., Twinsburg, OH 44087. TEL 216-425-9000. FAX 216-425-7150. *1702*

NEW YORK METRO BUSINESS DIRECTORY.
American Business Directories, 5711 S. 86th Circle, Box 27347, Omaha, NE 68127. TEL 402-593-4600. FAX 402-331-5481. *1702*

THE NEW YORK TIMES.
New York Times Company, 229 W. 43rd St., New York, NY 10036. TEL 212-556-1234. FAX 212-556-4603.
Producer(s): UMI. *3380*

THE NEW YORK TIMES INDEX.
U M I, 300 N. Zeeb Rd., Ann Arbor, MI 48106. TEL 313-761-4700. FAX 800-864-0019. *3885*

NEW ZEALAND BUSINESS WHO'S WHO.
New Zealand Financial Press Ltd., P.O. Box 1881, Auckland 1, New Zealand. TEL 64-9-3071287. FAX 64-9-3732734. *1702*

NEWS FROM INDIAN COUNTRY.
Indian Country Communications, Rte. 2, Box 2900-A, Hayward, WI 54843. TEL 715-634-5226. FAX 715-634-3243. *3032*

NEWS MEDIA YELLOW BOOK.
Leadership Directories, Inc., 104 Fifth Ave., 2nd Fl., New York, NY 10011. TEL 212-627-4140. FAX 212-645-0931.
Producer(s): Chadwyck-Healey Inc. *1702*

NEWS - 400.
Duke Communications International, 221 E. 29th St., Ste. 242, Loveland, CO 80538. TEL 970-663-4700. FAX 970-663-3285. *2180*

NEWSBANK REVIEW OF THE ARTS: FILM AND TELEVISION.
NewsBank, Inc., 58 Pine St., New Canaan, CT 06840-5426. TEL 203-966-1100. FAX 203-966-6254. *5341*

NEWSLETTERS IN PRINT.
Gale Research, 835 Penobscot Bldg., 645 Griswold St., Detroit, MI 48226-4094. TEL 313-961-2242. FAX 800-414-5043. *558*

SERIALS AVAILABLE ON CD-ROM

NEWSMAKERS.
Gale Research, 835 Penobscot Bldg., 645 Griswold St., Detroit, MI 48226-4094. TEL 313-961-2242. FAX 800-414-5043. *576*

NEWSPAPER ABSTRACTS.
U M I Company (Louisville), 620 S. Third St., Louisville, KY 40202-2475. *3885*

NEWSWEEK.
Newsweek, Inc., 251 W. 57th St., New York, NY 10019. TEL 212-445-4000. *3381*

NEXOS; SOCIEDAD, CIENCIA, LITERATURA.
Nexos S.A. de C.V., Mazatlan 119, Col. Condesa, 06140 Mexico DF, Mexico. TEL 52-5-2867922. FAX 52-5-2860794. *6627*

NIEMAN REPORTS.
Nieman Foundation, Harvard University, 1 Francis Ave., Cambridge, MA 02138. TEL 617-495-2237. FAX 617-495-8976.
Producer(s): UMI. *3878*

NIGERIAN JOURNAL OF NUTRITIONAL SCIENCES.
Ibadan University Press, University of Ibadan, Ibadan, Oyo State, Nigeria. *5478*

NIGERIAN JOURNAL OF PAEDIATRICS.
Ibadan University Press, University of Ibadan, Ibadan, Oyo State, Nigeria. *5035*

NIGERIAN MEDICAL JOURNAL.
Nigerian Medical Association, P.O. Box 1108, Lagos, Nigeria. TEL 234-1-801500. FAX 231-1-837630. *4722*

NIHON SHIKA MASUI GAKKAI ZASSHI.
Nihon Shika Masui Gakkai, Osaka University, 1-8 Yamadoaka, Suita, 565 Osaka, Japan. TEL 81-3-3947-8891. FAX 81-3-3947-8341. *4806*

NIKKEI MULTIMEDIA.
Nikkei Business Publications, Inc., 2-7-6 Hirakawa-cho, Chiyoda-ku, Tokyo 102, Japan. TEL 81-3-5210-8073. FAX 81-3-5210-8119. *4233*

NINETEENTH CENTURY BIBLIOGRAPHIC RECORDS.
Chadwyck-Healey Ltd., The Quorum, Barnwell Rd., Cambridge CB5 8SW, England. TEL 44-1223-215512. FAX 44-1223-215514.
Available only on CD-ROM. Producer(s): Chadwyck-Healey Inc. *558*

NON-PRESCRIPTION DRUG REFERENCE FOR HEALTH CARE PROFESSIONAL.
Canadian Pharmaceutical Association, 1785 Alta Vista Dr., Ottawa, ON K1G 3Y6, Canada. TEL 613-523-7877. *5681*

NONFERROUS METALS ALERT.
Cambridge Scientific Abstracts, 7200 Wisconsin Ave., Bethesda, MD 20814. TEL 301-961-6750. FAX 301-961-6720.
Producer(s): Knight-Ridder, Inc. *5220*

NONGYE JIXIE XUEBAO.
Zhongguo Nongye Jixie Xuehui, 1 Bei Shatan, Dewai, Beijing 100083, People's Republic of China. TEL 86-10-6201-7131. FAX 86-10-6204-3686. *208*

NONPARAMETRIC STATISTICS.
Gordon and Breach - Harwood Academic, Amsteldisk 166, 1st Fl., 1079 LH Amsterdam, Netherlands. *6929*

NONWOVENS ABSTRACTS.
Pira International, Randalls Rd., Leatherhead, Surrey KT22 7RU, England. TEL 44-1372-802050. FAX 44-1372-802239.
Producer(s): Knight-Ridder, Inc. *5887*

NORSK BOKFORTEGNELSE. AARSKATALOG.
University of Oslo Library, Bibliographic Services Department, N-0242 Oslo, Norway. FAX 47-22-85-90-50. *558*

NORSK MUSIKKFORTEGNELSE. NOTETRYKK.
University of Oslo Library, Bibliographic Services Department, N-0242 Oslo, Norway. FAX 47-22-85-90-50. *5448*

NORSK PERIODIKAFORTEGNELSE.
University of Oslo Library, Bibliographic Services Department, N-242 Oslo, Norway. FAX 47-22-85-90-50. *559*

NORSK SKATTELOVSAMLING.
Jacob Jaroey, Vraasgt. 18, N-3701 Skien, Norway. TEL 47-35-59-92-26. *1622*

NORSKE TIDSSKRIFTARTIKLER.
University of Oslo Library, Bibliographic Services Department, N-0242 Oslo, Norway. FAX 47-22-85-90-50. *559*

NORTH CAROLINA BUSINESS DIRECTORY.
American Business Directories, 5711 S. 86th Circle, Box 27347, Omaha, NE 68127. TEL 402-593-4600. FAX 402-331-5481. *1703*

NORTH CAROLINA MANUFACTURERS DIRECTORY.
Harris InfoSource International, 2057-2 Aurora Rd., Twinsburg, OH 44087. TEL 216-425-9000. FAX 216-425-7150. *1703*

NORTH CAROLINA MANUFACTURERS REGISTER.
Manufacturers' News, Inc., 1633 Central St., Evanston, IL 60201-1569. TEL 847-864-7000. FAX 847-332-1100. *1703*

NORTH DAKOTA BUSINESS DIRECTORY.
American Business Directories, 5711 S. 86th Circle, Box 27347, Omaha, NE 68127. TEL 402-593-4600. FAX 402-331-5481. *1703*

NORTH DAKOTA MANUFACTURERS REGISTER.
Manufacturers' News, Inc., 1633 Central St., Evanston, IL 60201-1569. TEL 847-864-7000. FAX 847-332-1100. *1703*

NORTHEAST POWER REPORT.
McGraw-Hill Companies, Energy & Business Newsletters, 1221 Ave. of the Americas, 36th Fl., New York, NY 10020. TEL 212-512-6410. FAX 212-512-2723.
Producer(s): SilverPlatter Information, Inc. (McGraw-Hill Energy Library). *2690*

NORTHERN CALIFORNIA BUSINESS DIRECTORY.
American Business Directories, 5711 S. 86th Circle, Box 27347, Omaha, NE 68127. TEL 402-593-4600. FAX 402-331-5481. *1703*

NORTHERN IRELAND TRADE DIRECTORY.
Business to Business Publications, The King Bldg., Ste. 11, 152 Albertbridge Rd., Belfast BT5 4GS, N. Ireland. TEL 44-1232-455775. FAX 44-1232-461924. *1703*

NOTIMEX ON C D - R O M.
National Information Services Corporation (NISC), 3100 St. Paul St., Ste. 806, Baltimore, MD 21218. TEL 410-243-0797. FAX 410-243-0982.
Available only on CD-ROM. Producer(s): NISC. *3885*

NOTISUR.
University of New Mexico, Latin American Institute, 801 Yale N.E., Albuquerque, NM 87131-1016. TEL 505-277-6839. FAX 505-277-5989.
Producer(s): NISC (Latin American Studies - Vol.2). *5949*

NUCLEARFUEL.
McGraw-Hill Companies, 1221 Ave. of the Americas, New York, NY 10020.
Producer(s): SilverPlatter Information, Inc. (McGraw-Hill Energy Library). *2702*

NUCLEIC ACIDS ABSTRACTS.
Cambridge Scientific Abstracts, 7200 Wisconsin Ave., 6th Fl., Bethesda, MD 20814. TEL 301-961-6750. FAX 301-961-6720.
Producer(s): SilverPlatter Information, Inc. *643*

NUCLEIC ACIDS RESEARCH.
Oxford University Press, Academic Division, Great Clarendon St., Oxford OX2 6DP, England. TEL 44-1865-267907. FAX 44-1865-267485. *667*

NUCLEONICS WEEK.
McGraw-Hill Companies, Energy & Business Newsletters, 1221 Ave. of the Americas, 36th Fl., New York, NY 10020. TEL 212-512-6410.
Producer(s): SilverPlatter Information, Inc. (McGraw-Hill Energy Library). *2675*

NUEVA SOCIEDAD.
Editorial Nueva Sociedad Ltda., Apdo. 61712, Chacao, Caracas 1060-A, Venezuela. TEL 58-2-2651849. FAX 58-2-2673397. *5950*

NURSING BIBLIOGRAPHY.
Royal College of Nursing, Library and Information Services, 20 Cavendish Sq., London W1M 0AB, England. TEL 44-171-409-3333. FAX 44-171-491-3859. *4783*

NUTRITION HEALTH REVIEW.
Vegetus Publications, Box 406, Haverford, PA 19041. TEL 610-896-1853. FAX 610-896-1857. *5479*

NYERE DANSK FAGLITTERATUR.
Dansk BiblioteksCenter as, Tempovej 7-11, DK-2750 Ballerup, Denmark. TEL 45-44-867777. FAX 45-44-867892. *559*

O E C D ECONOMIC SURVEYS: THE CZECH REPUBLIC.
Organization for Economic Cooperation and Development, 2 rue Andre Pascal, 75775 Paris Cedex, France. TEL 33-1-45248200. FAX 33-1-45248500. *1275*

O G: ORIENTAL GUYS.
O G Magazine, 1164 Bishop St., Ste. 124-293, Honolulu, HI 96813. FAX 808-526-3742. *3699*

O J C D.
Chadwyck-Healey Ltd., The Quorum, Barnwell Rd., Cambridge CB5 8SW, England. TEL 44-1223-215512. FAX 44-1223-215514.
Available only on CD-ROM. Producer(s): Chadwyck-Healey Inc. *6030*

O S C BULLETIN.
Micromedia Ltd., 20 Victoria St., Toronto, ON M5C 2N8, Canada. TEL 416-362-5211. FAX 416-362-6161. *1400*

THE OBSERVER.
Guardian Newspapers Ltd., 164 Deansgate, Manchester M60 2RR, England. TEL 44-161-832-7200. FAX 44-161-831-5362.
Producer(s): Chadwyck-Healey Inc. *3299*

OCCUPATIONAL HYGIENE.
Gordon and Breach - Harwood Academic, Amsteldisk 166, 1st Fl., 1079 LH Amsterdam, Netherlands. *5496*

OCCUPATIONAL OUTLOOK HANDBOOK.
U.S. Bureau of Labor Statistics, 2 Massachusetts Ave., N.E., Washington, DC 20212. TEL 202-606-5701. *5518*

OCCUPATIONAL OUTLOOK QUARTERLY.
U.S. Bureau of Labor Statistics, 2 Massachusetts Ave., N.E., Washington, DC 20212. TEL 202-606-5701. *5518*

OCEANIC ABSTRACTS.
Cambridge Scientific Abstracts, 7200 Wisconsin Ave., 6th Fl., Bethesda, MD 20814. TEL 301-961-6750. FAX 301-961-6720.
Producer(s): NISC. *2326*

OCEANOGRAPHIC & MARINE RESOURCES.
National Information Services Corporation (NISC), 3100 St. Paul St., Ste. 806, Baltimore, MD 21218. TEL 410-243-0797. FAX 410-243-0982.
Available only on CD-ROM. Producer(s): NISC. *2326*

OCEANOGRAPHIC LITERATURE REVIEW.
Elsevier Science Ltd., Pergamon, P.O. Box 800, Kidlington, Oxford OX5 1DX, England. TEL 44-1865-843000. FAX 44-1865-843010.
Producer(s): NISC (Oceanographic & Marine Resources). *2326*

OEKO-TEST MAGAZIN.
Oeko-Test Verlag GmbH und Co. KG, Kasselerstr. 1a, 60486 Frankfurt a.M., Germany. TEL 49-69-97777-0. FAX 49-69-97777139. *2257*

OFFICIAL A B M S DIRECTORY OF BOARD CERTIFIED MEDICAL SPECIALISTS.
Marquis Who's Who, A Division of Reed Elsevier Inc., 121 Chanlon Rd., New Providence, NJ 07974. TEL 908-464-6800. FAX 908-665-6688.
Producer(s): Bowker Electronic Publishing. *4724*

OFFICIAL INDEX TO THE FINANCIAL TIMES.
Primary Source Media, P.O. Box 45, Reading RG1 8HF, England. TEL 44-1734-583247. FAX 44-1734-591325. *1062*

OFFICIAL IOWA MANUFACTURERS DIRECTORY.
Harris InfoSource International, 2057-2 Aurora Rd., Twinsburg, OH 44087. TEL 216-425-9000. FAX 216-425-7150. *1704*

OFFICIAL JOURNAL OF THE EUROPEAN COMMUNITIES. C SERIES: INFORMATION AND NOTICES (ENGLISH EDITION).
Office for Official Publications of the European Communities, L-2985 Luxembourg, Luxembourg. Producer(s): Chadwyck-Healey Inc. *6030*

OFFICIAL JOURNAL OF THE EUROPEAN COMMUNITIES. L & C: LEGISLATION AND COMPETITION.
Office for Official Publications of the European Communities, L-2985 Luxembourg, Luxembourg. Producer(s): Chadwyck-Healey Inc. *6030*

OHIO ATTORNEY GENERAL OPINIONS.
Banks - Baldwin Law Publishing Co., Box 318063, Cleveland, OH 44131-8063. TEL 216-520-5600. FAX 216-520-5655. *4137*

OHIO BUSINESS DIRECTORY.
American Business Directories, 5711 S. 86th Circle, Box 27347, Omaha, NE 68127. TEL 402-593-4600. FAX 402-331-5481. *1704*

OHIO MANUFACTURERS DIRECTORY.
Manufacturers' News, Inc., 1633 Central St., Evanston, IL 60201. TEL 847-864-7000. FAX 847-332-1100. *1704*

OHIO RULES OF COURT, STATE AND FEDERAL.
West Group, 620 Opperman Dr., Eagan, MN 55123. TEL 612-687-8000. FAX 612-687-7302. *4137*

OHIO STATE LAW JOURNAL.
Ohio State University, College of Law, 55 W. 12th Ave., Columbus, OH 43210-1391. TEL 614-292-6829. *4003*

OKLAHOMA BUSINESS DIRECTORY.
American Business Directories, 5711 S. 86th Circle, Box 27347, Omaha, NE 68127. TEL 402-593-4600. FAX 402-331-5481. *1704*

OKLAHOMA MANUFACTURERS REGISTER.
Manufacturers' News, Inc., 1633 Central St., Evanston, IL 60201-1505. TEL 847-864-7000. FAX 847-332-1100. *1704*

ON THE LEVEL.
Family Planning N.S.W., 328-336 Liverpool Rd., Ashfield, N.S.W. 2131, Australia. TEL 61-2-716-6099. *6721*

ONCOGENES AND GROWTH FACTORS ABSTRACTS.
Cambridge Scientific Abstracts, 7200 Wisconsin Ave., 6th Fl., Bethesda, MD 20814. TEL 301-961-6750. FAX 301-961-6720. Producer(s): SilverPlatter Information, Inc. *4784*

ONEDISC.
Tax Analysts, 6830 N. Fairfax Dr., Arlington, VA 22213. FAX 703-533-4444. Available only on CD-ROM. *1623*

ONLINE HOTLINE NEWS SERVICE.
Information Intelligence, Inc., Box 31098, Phoenix, AZ 85046. TEL 602-996-2283. Available only on CD-ROM. *2139*

THE ONLINE JOURNAL OF CURRENT CLINICAL TRIALS.
Chapman & Hall, Journals Department 2-6 Boundary Row, London SE1 8HN, England. TEL 44-171-8650066. FAX 44-171-5229623. *4724*

ONLINE LIBRARIES AND MICROCOMPUTERS.
Information Intelligence, Inc., Box 31098, Phoenix, AZ 85046. TEL 602-996-2283. *4234*

ONLINE NEWSLETTER.
Information Intelligence Inc., Box 31098, Phoenix, AZ 85046. TEL 602-996-2283. *2139*

ONLY THE BEST.
Association for Supervision and Curriculum Development, 1250 N. Pitt St., Alexandria, VA 22314-1453. TEL 703-549-9110. FAX 703-299-8631. *2216*

ONTARIO STATUTE CITATOR.
Canada Law Book Inc., 240 Edward St., Aurora, ON L4G 3S9, Canada. TEL 905-841-6472. FAX 905-841-5085. *4004*

OPEN INFORMATION SYSTEMS.
Patricia Seybold Group, 85 Devonshire St. 5th Fl., Boston, MA 02109-3504. *2157*

OPERATIONS & PRODUCTION MANAGEMENT ABSTRACTS.
M C B University Press Ltd., Anbar Electronic Intelligence, 60-62 Toller Ln., Bradford, W. Yorks BD8 9BY, England. TEL 44-1274-480916. FAX 44-1274-543576. *1062*

OPHTHALMOLOGY.
Lippincott - Raven Publishers, 227 E. Washington Sq., Philadelphia, PA 19106. TEL 215-238-4200. FAX 215-238-4227. *4999*

OPTICAL AND QUANTUM ELECTRONICS.
Thomson Science, 2-6 Boundary Row, London SE1 8HN, England. TEL 44-171-8650066. FAX 44-171-5229623. *2648*

OPTICAL ENGINEERING.
International Society for Optical Engineering (SPIE), Box 10, 1000 20th St., Bellingham, WA 98227-0010. TEL 360-676-3290. FAX 360-647-1445. *5866*

(YEAR) OPTICS JOURNALS - OPTICS INDEX.
Optical Society of America, Inc., 2010 Massachusetts Ave., N.W., Washington, DC 20036-1023. TEL 202-223-8130. FAX 202-223-1096. Available only on CD-ROM. *5868*

OPTIMIZATION.
Gordon and Breach - Harwood Academic, Amsteldisk 166, 1st Fl., 1079 LH Amsterdam, Netherlands. *4617*

OPTIMIZATION METHODS AND SOFTWARE.
Gordon and Breach - Harwood Academic, Amsteldisk 166, 1st Fl., 1079 LH Amsterdam, Netherlands. *4623*

OPTOELECTRONICS D.A.T.A. DIGEST.
D.A.T.A. Business Publishing, 15 Inverness Way E., Box 6510, Englewood, CO 80155-6510. FAX 303-799-4082. *2648*

ORACLE INFORMANT.
Informant Communications Group, Inc., 10519 E. Stockton Blvd., Ste. 100, Elk Grove, CA 95624-9703. TEL 916-686-6610. FAX 916-686-8497. *2216*

OREGON BUSINESS DIRECTORY.
American Business Directories, 5711 S. 86th Circle, Box 27347, Omaha, NE 68127. TEL 402-593-4600. FAX 402-331-5481. *1705*

ORGANISED SOUND.
Cambridge University Press, Edinburgh Bldg., Shaftesbury Rd., Cambridge CB2 2RU, England. TEL 44-1223-312393. FAX 44-1223-315052. *5423*

ORTHODISC.
Lippincott - Raven Press, 227 E. Washington Sq., Philadelphia, PA 19106. TEL 215-238-4200. Available only on CD-ROM. *5013*

OUTDOOR LIFE.
Times Mirror Magazines, Inc., 2 Park Ave., New York, NY 10016. TEL 212-779-5000. FAX 212-686-6877. Producer(s): UMI. *6878*

OXBRIDGE DIRECTORY OF NEWSLETTERS.
Oxbridge Communications, Inc., 150 Fifth Ave., New York, NY 10011. TEL 212-741-0231. FAX 212-633-2938. *559*

P A I S INTERNATIONAL IN PRINT.
Public Affairs Information Service, Inc., 521 W. 43rd St., 5th Fl., New York, NY 10036-4396. TEL 212-736-6629. FAX 212-643-2848. Producer(s): SilverPlatter Information, Inc. (PAIS INTERNATIONAL N SILVERPLATTER). *5985*

P A I S SELECT.
Public Affairs Information Service, Inc., 521 W. 43rd St., New York, NY 10036-4396. TEL 212-736-6629. Available only on CD-ROM. Producer(s): Public Affairs Information Service, Inc., SilverPlatter Information, Inc. (PAIS SELECT ON SILVERPLATTER). *5985*

P A S C A L E 11: PHYSIQUE ATOMIQUE ET MOLECULAIRE. PLASMAS.
Centre National de la Recherche Scientifique, Institut de l'Information Scientifique et Technique, 2 allee du Parc de Brabois, 54514 Vandoeuvre-Les-Nancy Cedex, France. TEL 83-50-46-00. FAX 83-50-46-50. *5835*

P A S C A L E 12: ETAT CONDENSE.
Centre National de la Recherche Scientifique, Institut de l'Information Scientifique et Technique, 2 allee du Parc de Brabois, 54514 Vandoeuvre-Les-Nancy Cedex, France. TEL 83-50-46-00. FAX 83-50-46-50. *5836*

P A S C A L E 13: STRUCTURE DES LIQUIDES ET DES SOLIDES - CRISTALLOGRAPHIE.
Centre National de la Recherche Scientifique, Institut de l'Information Scientifique et Technique, 2 allee du Parc de Brabois, 54514 Vandoeuvre-Les-Nancy Cedex, France. TEL 83-50-46-00. FAX 83-50-46-50. *1785*

P A S C A L E 18: CHROMATOGRAPHIE.
Centre National de la Recherche Scientifique, Institut de l'Information Scientifique et Technique, 2 allee du Parc de Brabois, 54514 Vandoeuvre-les-Nancy Cedex, France. TEL 83-50-46-00. FAX 83-50-46-50. *1785*

P A S C A L E 20: ELECTRONIQUE ET TELECOMMUNICATIONS.
Centre National de la Recherche Scientifique, Institut de l'Information Scientifique et Technique, 2 allee du Parc de Brabois, 54514 Vandoeuvre-les-Nancy Cedex, France. TEL 83-50-46-00. FAX 83-50-46-50. *2648*

P A S C A L E 27: METHODES DE FORMATION ET TRAITEMENT DES IMAGES.
Centre National de la Recherche Scientifique, Institut de l'Information Scientifique et Technique, 2 allee du Parc de Brabois, 54514 Vandoeuvre-Les-Nancy Cedex, France. TEL 83-50-46-00. FAX 83-50-46-50. *5836*

P A S C A L E 30: MICROSCOPIE ELECTRONIQUE ET DIFFRACTION ELECTRONIQUE.
Centre National de la Recherche Scientifique, Institut de l'Information Scientifique et Technique, 2 allee du Parc de Brabois, 54514 Vandoeuvre-Les-Nancy Cedex, France. TEL 83-50-46-00. FAX 83-50-46-50. *643*

P A S C A L E 32: METROLOGIE ET APPAREILLAGE EN PHYSIQUE ET PHYSICOCHIMIE.
Centre National de la Recherche Scientifique, Institut de l'Information Scientifique et Technique, 2 allee du Parc de Brabois, 54514 Vandoeuvre-Les-Nancy Cedex, France. TEL 83-50-46-00. FAX 83-50-46-50. *5256*

P A S C A L E 33. INFORMATIQUE.
Centre National de la Recherche Scientifique, Institut de l'Information Scientifique et Technique, 2 allee du Parc de Brabois, 54514 Vandoeuvre-Les-Nancy Cedex, France. TEL 33-3-83504600. FAX 33-3-83504650. *2095*

P A S C A L E 34. ROBOTIQUE, AUTOMATIQUE ET AUTOMATISATION DES PROCESSUS INDUSTRIELS.
Centre National de la Recherche Scientifique, Institut de l'Information Scientifique et Technique, 2 allee du Parc de Brabois, 54514 Vandoeuvre-Les-Nancy Cedex, France. TEL 33-3-83504600. FAX 33-3-83504650. *2096*

P A S C A L E 36: POLLUTION DE L'EAU, DE L'AIR ET DU SOL - DECHETS - BRUIT.
Centre National de la Recherche Scientifique, Institut de l'Information Scientifique et Technique, 2 allee du Parc de Brabois, 54514 Vandoeuvre-Les-Nancy, France. TEL 83-50-46-00. FAX 83-50-46-50. *2963*

P A S C A L. E 48: ENVIRONNEMENT COSMIQUE TERRESTRE, ASTRONOMIE ET GEOLOGIE EXTRATERRESTRE.
Centre National de la Recherche Scientifique, Institut de l'Information Scientifique et Technique, 2 allee du Parc de Brabois, 54514 Vandoeuvre-Les-Nancy, France. TEL 83-50-46-00. FAX 83-50-46-50. *2327*

P A S C A L. E 49: METEOROLOGIE, GLACIOLOGIE, PHYSIQUE DES OCEANS.
Centre National de la Recherche Scientifique, Institut de l'Information Scientifique et Technique, 2 allee du Parc de Brabois, 54514 Vandoeuvre-Les-Nancy Cedex, France. TEL 83-50-46-00. FAX 83-50-46-50. *5248*

P A S C A L. E 58: GENETIQUE.
Centre National de la Recherche Scientifique, Institut de l'Information Scientifique et Technique, 2 allee du Parc de Brabois, 54514 Vandoeuvre-Les-Nancy Cedex, France. TEL 83-50-46-00. FAX 83-50-46-50. *643*

P A S C A L. E 61: MICROBIOLOGIE: BACTERIOLOGIE, VIROLOGIE, MYCOLOGIE, PROTOZOAIRES PATHOGENES.
Centre National de la Recherche Scientifique, Institut de l'Information Scientifique et Technique, 2 allee du Parc de Brabois, 54514 Vandoeuvre-Les-Nancy Cedex, France. TEL 83-50-46-00. FAX 83-50-46-50. *643*

P A S C A L. E 62: IMMUNOLOGIE.
Centre National de la Recherche Scientifique, Institut de l'Information Scientifique et Technique, 2 allee du Parc de Brabois, 54514 Vandoeuvre-Les-Nancy Cedex, France. TEL 83-50-46-00. FAX 83-50-46-50. *643*

P A S C A L. E 63: TOXICOLOGIE.
Centre National de la Recherche Scientifique, Institut de l'Information Scientifique et Technique, 2 allee du Parc de Brabois, 54514 Vandoeuvre-Les-Nancy Cedex, France. TEL 83-50-46-00. FAX 83-50-46-50. *2963*

P A S C A L. E 64: ENDOCRINOLOGIE HUMAINE ET EXPERIMENTALE. ENDOCRINOPATHIES.
Centre National de la Recherche Scientifique, Institut de l'Information Scientifique et Technique, 2 allee du Parc de Brabois, 54514 Vandoeuvre-Les-Nancy Cedex, France. TEL 83-50-46-00. FAX 83-50-46-50. *4784*

P A S C A L. E 65: PSYCHOLOGIE, PSYCHOPATHOLOGIE, PSYCHIATRIE.
Centre National de la Recherche Scientifique, Institut de l'Information Scientifique et Technique, 2 allee du Parc de Brabois, 54514 Vandoeuvre-Les-Nancy Cedex, France. TEL 83-50-46-00. FAX 83-50-46-50. *4784*

P A S C A L. E 68: GENETIQUE HUMAINE.
Centre National de la Recherche Scientifique, Institut de l'Information Scientifique et Technique, 2 allee du Parc de Brabois, 54514 Vandoeuvre-Les-Nancy Cedex, France. TEL 83-50-46-00. FAX 83-50-46-50. *643*

P A S C A L. E 71: OPHTALMOLOGIE.
Centre National de la Recherche Scientifique, Institut de l'Information Scientifique et Technique, 2 allee du Parc de Brabois, 54514 Vandoeuvre-Les-Nancy Cedex, France. TEL 83-50-46-00. FAX 83-50-46-50. *4784*

P A S C A L. E 72: OTORHINOLARYNGOLOGIE. STOMATOLOGIE. PATHOLOGIE CERVICOFACIALE.
Centre National de la Recherche Scientifique, Institut de l'Information Scientifique et Technique, 2 allee du Parc de Brabois, 54514 Vandoeuvre-Les-Nancy, France. TEL 83-50-46-00. FAX 83-50-46-50. *4785*

P A S C A L. E 73: DERMATOLOGIE. MALADIES SEXUELLEMENT TRANSMISSIBLES.
Centre National de la Recherche Scientifique, Institut de l'Information Scientifique et Technique, 2 allee du Parc de Brabois, 54514 Vandoeuvre-Les-Nancy, France. TEL 83-50-46-00. FAX 83-50-46-50. *4785*

P A S C A L. E 74: PNEUMOLOGIE.
Centre National de la Recherche Scientifique, Institut de l'Information Scientifique et Technique, 2 allee du Parc de Brabois, 54514 Vandoeuvre-Les-Nancy Cedex, France. TEL 83-50-46-00. FAX 83-50-46-50. *4785*

P A S C A L. E 75: CARDIOLOGIE ET APPAREIL CIRCULATOIRE.
Centre National de la Recherche Scientifique, Institut de l'Information Scientifique et Technique, 2 allee du Parc de Brabois, 54514 Vandoeuvre-Les-Nancy Cedex, France. TEL 83-50-46-00. FAX 83-50-46-50. *4785*

P A S C A L. E 76: GASTROENTEROLOGIE, FOIE, PANCREAS, ABDOMEN.
Centre National de la Recherche Scientifique, Institut de l'Information Scientifique et Technique, 2 allee du Parc de Brabois, 54514 Vandoeuvre-Les-Nancy Cedex, France. TEL 83-50-46-00. FAX 83-50-46-50. *4785*

P A S C A L. E 77: NEPHROLOGIE. VOIES URINAIRES.
Centre National de la Recherche Scientifique, Institut de l'Information Scientifique et Technique, 2 allee du Parc de Brabois, 54514 Vandoeuvre-Les-Nancy Cedex, France. TEL 83-50-46-00. FAX 83-50-46-50. *4785*

P A S C A L. E 78: NEUROLOGIE.
Centre National de la Recherche Scientifique, Institut de l'Information Scientifique et Technique, 2 allee du Parc de Brabois, 54514 Vandoeuvre-Les-Nancy Cedex, France. TEL 83-50-46-00. FAX 83-50-46-50. *4785*

P A S C A L. E 79: PATHOLOGIE ET PHYSIOLOGIE OSTEOARTICULAIRES.
Centre National de la Recherche Scientifique, Institut de l'Information Scientifique et Technique, 2 allee du Parc de Brabois, 54514 Vandoeuvre-Les-Nancy Cedex, France. TEL 83-50-46-00. FAX 83-50-46-50. *4785*

P A S C A L. E 80: HEMATOLOGIE.
Centre National de la Recherche Scientifique, Institut de l'Information Scientifique et Technique, 2 allee du Parc de Brabois, 54514 Vandoeuvre-Les-Nancy Cedex, France. TEL 83-50-46-00. FAX 83-50-46-50. *4785*

P A S C A L. E 82: GYNECOLOGIE, OBSTETRIQUE, ANDROLOGIE.
Centre National de la Recherche Scientifique, Institut de l'Information Scientifique et Technique, 2 allee du Parc de Brabois, 54514 Vandoeuvre-Les-Nancy Cedex, France. TEL 83-50-46-00. FAX 83-50-46-50. *4785*

P A S C A L. E 83: ANESTHESIE ET REANIMATION.
Centre National de la Recherche Scientifique, Institut de l'Information Scientifique et Technique, 2 allee du Parc de Brabois, 54514 Vandoeuvre-Les-Nancy Cedex, France. TEL 83-50-46-00. FAX 83-50-46-50. *4785*

P A S C A L. E 84: GENIE BIOMEDICAL. INFORMATIQUE BIOMEDICALE.
Centre National de la Recherche Scientifique, Institut de l'Information Scientifique et Technique, 2 allee du Parc de Brabois, 54514 Vandoeuvre-Les-Nancy Cedex, France. TEL 83-50-46-00. FAX 83-50-46-50. *4786*

P A S C A L. E 89: CANCER.
Centre National de la Recherche Scientifique, Institut de l'Information Scientifique et Technique, 2 allee du Parc de Brabois, 54514 Vandoeuvre-Les-Nancy Cedex, France. TEL 83-50-46-00. FAX 83-50-46-50. *4786*

P A S C A L. F 10: MECANIQUE, ACOUSTIQUE ET TRANSFERT DE CHALEUR.
Centre National de la Recherche Scientifique, Institut de l'Information Scientifique et Technique, 2 allee du Parc de Brabois, 54514 Vandoeuvre-Les-Nancy Cedex, France. TEL 83-50-46-00. FAX 83-50-46-50. *5836*

P A S C A L. F 16: CHIMIE ANALYTIQUE, MINERALE ET ORGANIQUE.
Centre National de la Recherche Scientifique, Institut de l'Information Scientifique et Technique, 2 allee du Parc de Brabois, 54514 Vandoeuvre-Les-Nancy Cedex, France. TEL 83-50-46-00. FAX 83-50-46-50. *1785*

P A S C A L. F 17: CHIMIE GENERALE, MINERALE ET ORGANIQUE.
Centre National de la Recherche Scientifique, Institut de l'Information Scientifique et Technique, 2 allee du Parc de Brabois, 54514 Vandoeuvre-Les-Nancy Cedex, France. TEL 83-50-46-00. FAX 83-50-46-50. *1785*

P A S C A L. F 23: GENIE CHIMIQUE. INDUSTRIES CHIMIQUE ET PARACHIMIQUE.
Centre National de la Recherche Scientifique, Institut de l'Information Scientifique et Technique, 2 allee du Parc de Brabois, 54514 Vandoeuvre-Les-Nancy Cedex, France. TEL 83-50-46-00. FAX 83-50-46-50. *1785*

P A S C A L. F 24: POLYMERES - PEINTURES - BOIS.
Centre National de la Recherche Scientifique, Institut de l'Information Scientifique et Technique, 2 allee du Parc de Brabois, 54514 Vandoeuvre-Les-Nancy Cedex, France. TEL 83-50-46-00. FAX 83-50-46-50. *1785*

P A S C A L. F 40: MINERALOGIE. GEOCHIMIE. GEOLOGIE EXTRATERRESTRE.
Centre National de la Recherche Scientifique, Institut de l'Information Scientifique et Technique, 2 allee du Parc de Brabois, 54514 Vandoeuvre-Les-Nancy Cedex, France. TEL 83-50-46-00. FAX 83-50-46-50. *2327*

P A S C A L. F 41: GISEMENTS METALLIQUES ET NON METALLIQUES.
Centre National de la Recherche Scientifique, Institut de l'Information Scientifique et Technique, 2 allee du Parc de Brabois, 54514 Vandoeuvre-Les-Nancy Cedex, France. TEL 83-50-46-00. FAX 83-50-46-50. *5321*

P A S C A L. F 42: ROCHES CRISTALLINES.
Centre National de la Recherche Scientifique, Institut de l'Information Scientifique et Technique, 2 allee du Parc de Brabois, 54514 Vandoeuvre-Les-Nancy Cedex, France. TEL 83-50-46-00. FAX 83-50-46-50. *2327*

P A S C A L. F 43: ROCHES SEDIMENTAIRES. GEOLOGIE MARINE.
Centre National de la Recherche Scientifique, Institut de l'Information Scientifique et Technique, 2 allee du Parc de Brabois, 54514 Vandoeuvre-Les-Nancy Cedex, France. TEL 83-50-46-00. FAX 83-50-46-50. *2327*

P A S C A L. F 44: STRATIGRAPHIE, GEOLOGIE REGIONALE, GEOLOGIE GENERALE.
Centre National de la Recherche Scientifique, Institut de l'Information Scientifique et Technique, 2 allee du Parc de Brabois, 54514 Vandoeuvre-Les-Nancy Cedex, France. TEL 83-50-46-00. FAX 83-50-46-50. *2327*

P A S C A L. F 45: TECTONIQUE, GEOPHYSIQUE INTERNE.
Centre National de la Recherche Scientifique, Institut de l'Information Scientifique et Technique, 2 allee du Parc de Brabois, 54514 Vandoeuvre-Les-Nancy Cedex, France. TEL 83-50-46-00. FAX 83-50-46-50. *2327*

P A S C A L. F 46: HYDROLOGIE. GEOLOGIE DE L'INGENIEUR. FORMATIONS SUPERFICIELLES.
Centre National de la Recherche Scientifique, Institut de l'Information Scientifique et Technique, 2 allee du Parc de Brabois, 54514 Vandoeuvre-Les-Nancy Cedex, France. TEL 83-50-46-00. FAX 83-50-46-50. *2327*

P A S C A L. F 47: PALEONTOLOGIE.
Centre National de la Recherche Scientifique, Institut de l'Information Scientifique et Technique, 2 allee du Parc de Brabois, 54514 Vandoeuvre-Les-Nancy Cedex, France. TEL 83-50-46-00. FAX 83-50-46-50. *5564*

P A S C A L. F 52: BIOCHIMIE - BIOPHYSIQUE - MOLECULAIRE - BIOLOGIE MOLECULAIRE ET CELLULAIRE.
Centre National de la Recherche Scientifique, Institut de l'Information Scientifique et Technique, 2 allee du Parc de Brabois, 54514 Vandoeuvre-Les-Nancy Cedex, France. TEL 83-50-46-00. FAX 83-50-46-50. *643*

P A S C A L. F 53: ANATOMIE ET PHYSIOLOGIE DES VERTEBRES.
Centre National de la Recherche Scientifique, Institut de l'Information Scientifique et Technique, 2 allee du Parc de Brabois, 54514 Vandoeuvre-Les-Nancy Cedex, France. TEL 83-50-46-00. FAX 83-50-46-50. *643*

P A S C A L. F 54: REPRODUCTION DES VERTEBRES, EMBRYOLOGIE DES VERTEBRES ET DES INVERTEBRES.
Centre National de la Recherche Scientifique, Institut de l'Information Scientifique et Technique, 2 allee du Parc de Brabois, 54514 Vandoeuvre-Les-Nancy Cedex, France. TEL 83-50-46-00. FAX 83-50-46-50. *4786*

P A S C A L. F 55: BIOLOGIE VEGETALE.
Centre National de la Recherche Scientifique, Institut de l'Information Scientifique et Technique, 2 allee du Parc de Brabois, 54514 Vandoeuvre-Les-Nancy Cedex, France. TEL 83-50-46-00. FAX 83-50-46-50. *644*

P A S C A L. F 56: ECOLOGIE ANIMALE, VEGETALE ET MICROBIENNE. ETHOLOGIE ANIMALE.
Centre National de la Recherche Scientifique, Institut de l'Information Scientifique et Technique, 2 allee du Parc de Brabois, 54514 Vandoeuvre-Les-Nancy Cedex, France. TEL 83-50-46-00. FAX 83-50-46-50. *644*

P A S C A L. F 70: PHARMACOLOGIE. TRAITEMENTS MEDICAMENTEUX.
Centre National de la Recherche Scientifique, Institut de l'Information Scientifique et Technique, 2 allee du Parc de Brabois, 54514 Vandoeuvre-Les-Nancy Cedex, France. TEL 83-50-46-00. FAX 83-50-46-50. *5702*

P A S C A L. T 205: SCIENCES DE L'INFORMATION. DOCUMENTATION.
Centre National de la Recherche Scientifique, Institut de l'Information Scientifique et Technique, 2 allee du Parc de Brabois, 54514 Vandoeuvre-Les-Nancy Cedex, France. TEL 83-50-46-00. FAX 83-50-46-50. *4227*

P A S C A L. T 215: BIOTECHNOLOGIES.
Centre National de la Recherche Scientifique, Institut de l'Information Scientifique et Technique, 2 allee du Parc de Brabois, 54514 Vandoeuvre-Les-Nancy Cedex, France. TEL 83-50-46-00. FAX 83-50-46-50. *4786*

P A S C A L. T 230: ENERGIE.
Centre National de la Recherche Scientifique, Institut de l'Information Scientifique et Technique, 2 allee du Parc de Brabois, 54514 Vandoeuvre-Les-Nancy Cedex, France. TEL 83-50-46-00. FAX 83-50-46-50. *5836*

P A S C A L. T 235: MEDECINE TROPICALE.
Centre National de la Recherche Scientifique, Institut de l'Information Scientifique et Technique, 2 allee du Parc de Brabois, 54514 Vandoeuvre-Les-Nancy Cedex, France. TEL 83-50-46-00. FAX 83-50-46-50. *4786*

P A S C A L. T 240: METAUX - METALLURGIE.
Centre National de la Recherche Scientifique, Institut de l'Information Scientifique et Technique, 2 allee du Parc de Brabois, 54514 Vandoeuvre-Les-Nancy Cedex, France. TEL 83-50-46-00. FAX 83-50-46-50. *5220*

P A S C A L. T 260: ZOOLOGIE FONDAMENTALE ET APPLIQUEE DES INVERTEBRES.
Centre National de la Recherche Scientifique, Institut de l'Information Scientifique et Technique, 2 allee du Parc de Brabois, 54514 Vandoeuvre-Les-Nancy Cedex, France. TEL 83-50-46-00. FAX 83-50-46-50. *644*

P A S C A L. T 280: SCIENCES AGRONOMIQUES ET FORESTIERES: PRODUCTIONS VEGETALES.
Centre National de la Recherche Scientifique, Institut de l'Information Scientifique et Technique, 2 allee du Parc de Brabois, 54514 Vandoeuvre-Les-Nancy Cedex, France. TEL 83-50-46-00. FAX 83-50-46-50. *180*

P A S C A L. T 295: BATIMENT. TRAVAUX PUBLICS.
Centre National de la Recherche Scientifique, Institut de l'Information Scientifique et Technique, 2 allee du Parc de Brabois, 54514 Vandoeuvre-Les-Nancy Cedex, France. TEL 83-50-46-00. FAX 83-50-46-50. *2751*

P A S C A L V.4 SCIENCES DE LA TERRE.
Centre National de la Recherche Scientifique, Institut de l'Information Scientifique et Technique, 2 allee du Parc de Brabois, 54514 Vandoeuvre-Les-Nancy Cedex, France. TEL 83-50-46-00. FAX 83-50-46-50. *2327*

P C ACTION.
Computec Verlag, Isarstr. 32-34, 90451 Nuernberg, Germany. TEL 49-911-96832-0. FAX 49-911-6426333. *2119*

P C GAMES.
Computec Verlag, Isarstr. 32-34, 90451 Nuernberg, Germany. TEL 49-911-96832-0. FAX 49-911-6426333. *2119*

P C GAMES.
E M A P - Images, Priory Ct., 30-32 Farringdon Ln., London EC1R 3AU, England. TEL 44-171-972-6700. FAX 44-171-972-6710. *2119*

P C GAMES PLUS.
Computec Verlag, Osarstr. 32-34, 90451 Nuernberg, Germany. TEL 49-911-96832-0. FAX 49-911-6426333. *2119*

P C LETTER.
155 Bovet Rd., Ste. 800, San Mateo, CA 94402-3115. TEL 800-432-2478. FAX 415-312-0547. *2148*

P C REVIEW.
E M A P - Images, Priory Ct., 30-32 Ferringdon Ln., London EC1R 3AU, England. TEL 44-171-972-6710. FAX 44-171-972-6710. *2192*

P C WEEK.
Ziff-Davis Publishing Co., One Park Ave., New York, NY 10016-5146. TEL 212-503-5100. *2202*

P R PLANNER - EUROPE.
Media Information Ltd., Hale House, 290-296 Green Lanes, London N13 5TP, England. FAX 44-181-886-0703. *1705*

THE P R S GROUP. COUNTRY REPORTS: WORLD SERVICE.
The P R S Group, Box 248, East Syracuse, NY 13057-0248. TEL 315-431-0511. FAX 315-431-0200. *1276*

PACIFIC TELECOMMUNICATIONS COUNCIL. CONFERENCE PROCEEDINGS.
Pacific Telecommunications Council, 2454 S. Beretania St., Ste. 302, Honolulu, HI 96826-1596. TEL 808-941-3789. FAX 808-944-4874. *2037*

(YEAR) PACKAGING SOURCEBOOK (INTERNATIONAL EDITION).
North American Publishing Co., 401 N. Broad St., Philadelphia, PA 19108. TEL 215-238-5482. FAX 215-238-5412. *5547*

(YEAR) PACKAGING SOURCEBOOK (NORTH AMERICAN EDITION).
North American Publishing Co., 401 N. Broad St., Philadelphia, PA 19108. TEL 215-238-5482. FAX 215-238-5412. *5547*

PAEDIATRICA INDONESIANA.
Indonesian Society of Pediatrician, c/o Dept. of Child Health, Medical School, University of Indonesia, Jalan Salemba 6, Jakarta 10430, Indonesia. TEL 62-21-314-8610. FAX 61-21-390-7743. *5035*

PAKISTAN JOURNAL OF BIOCHEMISTRY.
Pakistan Society of Biochemists, Institute of Chemistry, University of Punjab, Lahore 54590, Pakistan. *668*

PAKISTAN JOURNAL OF CLINICAL PSYCHOLOGY.
University of Karachi, Institute of Clinical Psychology, 118, Block 20, Abul Asar Hafeez Jalindhri Rd., Gulistan-e-Jauhar, Karachi 75290, Pakistan. TEL 92-21-8113584. *6139*

PAKISTAN JOURNAL OF HEALTH.
College of Community Medicine, 6 Birdwood Rd., Lahore, Pakistan. TEL 92-42-7583945. FAX 92-42-7586395. *6246*

PAKISTAN JOURNAL OF OTOLARYNGOLOGY.
Pakistan Society of Otolaryngology, c/o Dr. M.H.A. Beg, F.R.C.S., Modern Ear Nose and Throat Hospital, B-10 Block 13-A, Opposite PIA Planetarium, University Rd., Karachi 74400, Pakistan. TEL 92-21-4971762. FAX 92-21-4971763. *5024*

PAKISTAN JOURNAL OF PHARMACEUTICAL SCIENCES.
University of Karachi, Faculty of Pharmacy, Karachi 75270, Pakistan. *5682*

PAKISTAN JOURNAL OF PSYCHOLOGY.
University of Karachi, Institute of Clinical Psychology, 118, Block 20, Abul Asar Hafeez Jalindhri Rd., Gulistan-e-Jauhar, Karachi 75290, Pakistan. TEL 92-21-8113584. *6139*

PAKISTAN MEDICAL ASSOCIATION. JOURNAL.
Pakistan Medical Association, P.M.A. House, Aga Khan III Rd., Karachi 74400, Pakistan. TEL 92-21-7214632. FAX 92-21-7226443. *4726*

PAPERBASE ABSTRACTS.
Pira International, Randalls Rd., Leatherhead, Surrey KT22 7RU, England. TEL 44-1372-802050. FAX 44-1372-802239.
Producer(s): Knight-Ridder, Inc. *5574*

PARALLEL ALGORITHMS AND APPLICATIONS.
Gordon and Breach - Harwood Academic, Amsteldisk 166, 1st Fl., 1079 LH Amsterdam, Netherlands. *2157*

PARENTS.
Gruner & Jahr U.S.A. Publishing, 110 Fifth Ave., New York, NY 10011. TEL 212-499-2000.
Producer(s): UMI. *1853*

PARKER DIRECTORY OF CALIFORNIA ATTORNEYS.
Parker Directory of California Attorneys, A Division of Reed Elsevier Inc., 121 Chanlon Rd., New Providence, NJ 07974-1541. *4006*

PARTICLE ACCELERATORS.
Gordon and Breach - Harwood Academic, Amsteldisk 166, 1st Fl., 1079 LH Amsterdam, Netherlands. *5855*

PATENT ABSTRACTS IN ENGLISH.
Vsesoyuznyi Nauchno-Issledovatel'skii Institut Patentnoi Informatsii (VNIIPI), Raushskaya nab. 4-5, 113035 Moscow, Russia. TEL 7-095-9593313. FAX 7-095-9593304.
Available only on CD-ROM. *5593*

PATHOGENESIS.
Gordon and Breach - Harwood Academic, Amsteldisk 166, 1st Fl., 1079 LH Amsterdam, Netherlands. *4727*

PATOLOGIA.
Obsidiana Editores, S.A., Czda. de Tlalpan 2365, Col. Ciudad Jardin, 04370 Mexico DF, Mexico. TEL 6899133. *619*

PAYROLL MANAGEMENT GUIDE.
C C H Incorporated, 2700 Lake Cook Rd., Riverwoods, IL 60015. TEL 847-267-7000. FAX 800-224-8299. *1160*

PEACE CORPS TIMES.
U.S. Peace Corps, 1990 K St., N.W., Washington, DC 20526. TEL 202-254-3371. FAX 202-606-3110. *1366*

PEDIATRIC REVIEWS AND COMMUNICATIONS.
Gordon and Breach - Harwood Academic, Amsteldisk 166, 1st Fl., 1079 LH Amsterdam, Netherlands. *5038*

PEDIATRICS (ENGLISH EDITION).
American Academy of Pediatrics, 141 Northwest Point Blvd., Box 927, Elk Grove Village, IL 60009-0927. TEL 847-228-5005. FAX 847-228-5097. *5038*

10018 SERIALS AVAILABLE ON CD-ROM

PENGUIN AUSTRALIAN ACCOMMODATION GUIDE.
Peter Isaacson Publications Pty. Ltd., 46-50 Porter St., Prahran, Vic. 3181, Australia. TEL 61-3-2457777. FAX 61-3-2457840. *7228*

PENNSYLVANIA BUSINESS DIRECTORY.
American Business Directories, 5711 S. 86th Circle, Box 27347, Omaha, NE 68127. TEL 402-593-4600. FAX 402-331-5481. *1705*

PENNSYLVANIA MANUFACTURERS REGISTER.
Manufacturers' News, Inc., 1633 Central St., Evanston, IL 60201. TEL 847-864-7000. FAX 847-332-1100. *1705*

PENNSYLVANIA RULES OF COURT, STATE AND FEDERAL.
West Group, 620 Opperman Dr., Eagan, MN 55123. TEL 612-687-8000. FAX 612-687-7302. *4137*

PENSION PLAN GUIDE.
C C H Incorporated, 2700 Lake Cook Rd., Riverwoods, IL 60015. TEL 847-267-7000. FAX 800-224-8299. *3829*

PERIODICA. INDICE DE REVISTAS LATINOAMERICANAS EN CIENCIAS.
Universidad Nacional Autonoma de Mexico, Direccion General de Bibliotecas, Apdo. Postal 70-392, C.P. 04510 Mexico, D.F., Mexico. TEL 52-5-6223958. FAX 52-5-6162557. *6591*

PERIODICAL ABSTRACTS.
U M I, 300 N. Zeeb Rd., Ann Arbor, MI 48106. TEL 313-761-4700. FAX 800-864-0019. *22*

PERIODICALS CONTENTS INDEX.
Chadwyck-Healey Ltd., The Quorum, Barnwell Rd., Cambridge CB5 8SW, England. TEL 44-1223-215512. FAX 44-1223-215514. *6650*

THE PERRYMAN TEXAS LETTER.
Texas Economic Publishers, Inc., 510 N. Valley Mills Dr., Ste. 300, Waco, TX 76710-6076. TEL 254-751-7411. FAX 254-751-7855. *1281*

PERSONAL FINANCE INTELLIGENCE.
Mintel International Group Ltd., 18-19 Long Ln., London EC1A 9HE, England. TEL 44-171-606-4533. FAX 44-171-606-5932. *1161*

PERSONNEL REVIEW.
M C B University Press Ltd., 60-62 Toller Ln., Bradford, W. Yorks BD8 9BY, England. TEL 44-1274-777700. FAX 44-1274-785200. *1573*

PERSPECTIVES OF NEW MUSIC.
Perspectives of New Music, Inc., University of Washington, Music, Box 353450, Seattle, WA 98195-3450. TEL 206-543-0196. FAX 206-543-9285. *5425*

PERSPECTIVES ON DEVELOPMENTAL NEUROBIOLOGY.
Gordon and Breach - Harwood Academic, Amsteldisk 166, 1st Fl., 1079 LH Amsterdam, Netherlands. *5090*

PERSPECTIVES ON POLITICAL SCIENCE.
Heldref Publications, 1319 18th St, N.W., Washington, DC 20036-1802. TEL 202-296-6267. FAX 202-296-5149.
Producer(s): UMI. *5955*

PETERSON'S GRADUATE AND PROFESSIONAL PROGRAMS: AN OVERVIEW (YEAR) (BOOK 1).
Peterson's, 202 Carnegie Center, Box 2123, Princeton, NJ 08543-2123. TEL 609-243-9111. FAX 609-243-9150.
Producer(s): SilverPlatter Information, Inc. (PETERSON'S GRADLINE). *2526*

PETERSON'S GRADUATE AND PROFESSIONAL PROGRAMS: BUSINESS, EDUCATION, HEALTH, INFORMATION STUDIES, LAW, AND SOCIAL WORK (YEAR) (BOOK 6).
Peterson's, 202 Carnegie Center, Box 2123, Princeton, NJ 08543-2123. TEL 609-243-9111. FAX 609-243-9150.
Producer(s): SilverPlatter Information, Inc. (PETERSON'S GRADLINE). *2526*

PETERSON'S GRADUATE AND PROFESSIONAL PROGRAMS: ENGINEERING AND APPLIED SCIENCES (YEAR) (BOOK 5).
Peterson's, 202 Carnegie Center, Box 2123, Princeton, NJ 08543-2123. TEL 609-243-9111. FAX 609-243-9150.
Producer(s): SilverPlatter Information, Inc. (PETERSON'S GRADLINE). *2526*

PETERSON'S GRADUATE AND PROFESSIONAL PROGRAMS: THE BIOLOGICAL SCIENCES (YEAR) (BOOK 3).
Peterson's, 202 Carnegie Center, Box 2123, Princeton, NJ 08543-2123. TEL 609-243-9111. FAX 609-243-9150.
Producer(s): SilverPlatter Information, Inc. (PETERSON'S GRADLINE). *2526*

PETERSON'S GRADUATE AND PROFESSIONAL PROGRAMS: THE HUMANITIES, ARTS, AND SOCIAL SCIENCES (YEAR) (BOOK 2).
Peterson's, 202 Carnegie Center, Box 2123, Princeton, NJ 08543-2123. TEL 609-243-9111. FAX 609-243-9150.
Producer(s): SilverPlatter Information, Inc. (PETERSON'S GRADLINE). *2526*

PETERSON'S GRADUATE AND PROFESSIONAL PROGRAMS: THE PHYSICAL SCIENCES, MATHEMATICS, AND AGRICULTURAL SCIENCES (YEAR) (BOOK 4).
Peterson's, 202 Carnegie Center, Box 2123, Princeton, NJ 08543-2123. TEL 609-243-9111. FAX 609-243-9150.
Producer(s): SilverPlatter Information, Inc. (PETERSON'S GRADLINE). *2526*

PETROLEUM ABSTRACTS.
University of Tulsa, Information Services Division, 600 S. College Ave., Tulsa, OK 74104-3189. TEL 918-631-2297. FAX 918-599-9361.
Producer(s): Knight-Ridder, Inc. *5631*

PETROLEUM MARKETING MONTHLY.
U.S. Energy Information Administration, National Energy Information Center, EI-231, James Forrestal Bldg., Rm. 1F-048, 1000 Independence Ave., S.W., Washington, DC 20585. TEL 202-586-8800. FAX 202-586-0727. *5618*

PHARMACEUTICAL COMPANIES ANALYSIS.
M D I S Publications Ltd., MDIS House, City Fields Business Park, City Fields Way, Chichester, W. Sussex PO20 6FS, England. TEL 44-1243-533322. FAX 44-1243-533418. *5684*

PHARMACEUTICAL COMPANY PROFILES.
IMSWORLD Publications Ltd., 7 Harewood Ave., London NW1 6JB, England. TEL 0171-393-5000. FAX 0171-393-5900. *5684*

PHARMACOLOGY REVIEWS AND COMMUNICATIONS.
Gordon and Breach - Harwood Academic, Amsteldisk 166, 1st Fl., 1079 LH Amsterdam, Netherlands. *5687*

PHARMASOURCE.
Chapman & Hall, Electronic Publishing Division 2-6 Boundary Row, London SEI 8HN, England. TEL 44-171-865-0066. FAX 44-171-522-0101.
Available only on CD-ROM. *5689*

PHASE TRANSITIONS.
Gordon and Breach - Harwood Academic, Amsteldisk 166, 1st Fl., 1079 LH Amsterdam, Netherlands. *5817*

PHILIPPINE DENTAL ASSOCIATION. JOURNAL.
Philippines Dental Association, Ayala Ave. corner Kamagong St., Makati, Metro Manila, Philippines. TEL 818-6144. FAX 816-3034. *4868*

PHILIPPINE JOURNAL OF INTERNAL MEDICINE.
Philippine College of Physicians, Facilities Central Bldg., 548 Shaw Blvd., Mandaluyong, Metro Manila, Philippines. TEL 2-780233. *4926*

PHILIPPINE JOURNAL OF NUTRITION.
Philippine Association of Nutrition, c/o Nutrition Foundation of the Philippines, 107 E. Rodriguez, Sr. Blvd., Quezon City, Philippines. *5481*

PHILIPPINE JOURNAL OF OPHTHALMOLOGY.
Philippine Academy of Ophthalmology, Philippine General Hospital, Taft Ave., Manila 1000, Philippines. *5000*

PHILIPPINE JOURNAL OF SURGICAL SPECIALTIES.
Philippine College of Surgeons, c/o Philippine Medical Association, PMA Bldg., North Ave., Quezon City, Philippine. *5151*

PHILOSOPHER'S INDEX.
Philosopher's Information Center, 1616 E. Wooster St., Box P, Bowling Green, OH 43402. TEL 419-353-8830. FAX 419-353-8920.
Producer(s): Knight-Ridder, Inc.. *5760*

PHONOLOG REPORTER.
Trade Service Corporation, 10996 Torreyana Rd., Box 85007, San Diego, CA 92186-9982. TEL 619-457-5920. FAX 619-457-1320. *5448*

PHOSPHORUS, SULPHUR AND SILICON AND THE RELATED ELEMENTS.
Gordon and Breach - Harwood Academic, Amsteldisk 166, 1st Fl., 1079 LH Amsterdam, Netherlands. *1809*

PHOTONICS DIRECTORY.
Laurin Publishing Co., Inc., Box 4949, Berkshire Common, Pittsfield, MA 01202-4949. TEL 413-499-0514. FAX 413-442-3180. *5869*

PHYSICIANS' DESK REFERENCE.
Medical Economics Publishing Co., Inc., 5 Paragon Dr., Montvale, NJ 07645. TEL 201-358-7200. FAX 201-573-1045. *4729*

PHYSICIANS' DESK REFERENCE FOR NONPRESCRIPTION DRUGS.
Medical Economics Publishing Co., Inc., 5 Paragon Dr., Montvale, NJ 07645. TEL 201-358-7200. FAX 201-573-1045. *4729*

PHYSICIANS' GENRX.
Mosby - Year Book, Inc., 11830 Westline Industrial Dr., St. Louis, MO 63146-3318. TEL 314-872-8370. FAX 314-432-1380. *4730*

PHYSICS ABSTRACTS.
INSPEC, I.E.E., Michael Faraday House, Six Hills Way, Stevenage, Herts. SG1 2AY, England. TEL 44-1438-313311. FAX 44-1438-742840.
Producer(s): UMI. *5836*

PHYSICS AND CHEMISTRY OF LIQUIDS.
Gordon and Breach - Harwood Academic, Amsteldisk 166, 1st Fl., 1079 LH Amsterdam, Netherlands. *5847*

PHYSICS - USPEKHI.
Turpion - Moscow Ltd., 47 Leninsky prospekt, 117913 Moscow, Russia. TEL 7-95-1356417. FAX 7-95-1358860. *5821*

PINKERTON EYE ON TRAVEL.
Pinkerton Risk Assessment Services, 200 N. Glebe Rd., No. 1011, Arlington, VA 22203-3728. TEL 703-525-6111. FAX 703-525-2454. *7228*

PIXEL - THE COMPUTER ANIMATION NEWSLETTER.
Pixel - The Computer Animation News People, Inc., 109 Vanderhoof Ave., Ste. 2, Toronto, ON M4G 2H7, Canada. TEL 416-424-4657. FAX 416-424-1812. *477*

PLANT TISSUE CULTURE.
Bangladesh Association for Plant Tissue Culture, University of Dhaka, Department of Botany, Dhaka-1000, Bangladesh. TEL 880-2-506378. FAX 880-2-865583.
Available only on CD-ROM. *723*

PLASMA DEVICES AND OPERATIONS.
Gordon and Breach - Harwood Academic, Amsteldisk 166, 1st Fl., 1079 LH Amsterdam, Netherlands. *5822*

PLASTICS D.A.T.A. DIGEST.
D.A.T.A. Business Publishing, 15 Inverness Way E., Box 6510, Englewood, CO 80155-6510. FAX 303-799-4082. *5882*

PLOUGHSHARES.
Ploughshares, Inc., Emerson College, 100 Beacon St., Boston, MA 02116. TEL 617-824-8753.
Producer(s): UMI, H.W. Wilson. *4450*

POEMFINDER.
Roth Publishing, Inc., 185 Great Neck Rd., Great Neck, NY 11021. TEL 516-466-3676. FAX 516-829-7746.
Available only on CD-ROM. *4497*

POINT DE REPERE.
Services Documentaires Multimedia Inc., 75 Port Royal E., bureau 300, Montreal, PQ H3L 3T1, Canada. TEL 514-382-0895. FAX 514-384-9139. *22*

POLAR AND GLACIOLOGICAL ABSTRACTS.
Cambridge University Press, Edinburgh Bldg., Shaftesbury Rd., Cambridge CB2 2RU, England. TEL 44-1223-312393. FAX 44-1223-315052. *2327*

POLITICAL RISK SERVICES ON C D - R O M.
The P R S Group, Box 248, East Syracuse, NY 13057-0248. TEL 315-431-0511. FAX 315-431-0200.
Available only on CD-ROM. *1282*

POLITICAL RISK YEARBOOK.
The P R S Group, Box 248, East Syracuse, NY 13057-0248. TEL 315-431-0511. FAX 315-431-0200. *1161*

POLLING THE NATIONS.
Opinion Research Service, 7200 Wisconsin Ave., Ste. 704, Bethesda, MD 20814-4811.
Available only on CD-ROM. *6740*

POLLUTION ABSTRACTS.
Cambridge Scientific Abstracts, 7200 Wisconsin Ave., 6th Fl., Bethesda, MD 20814. TEL 301-961-6750. FAX 301-961-6720.
Producer(s): Knight-Ridder, Inc. (Environmental Management), NISC, SilverPlatter Information, Inc. (POLTOX1). *2963*

POLYCYCLIC AROMATIC COMPOUNDS.
Gordon and Breach - Harwood Academic, Amsteldisk 166, 1st Fl., 1079 LH Amsterdam, Netherlands. *1821*

POLYMERS, CERAMICS, COMPOSITES ALERT.
Cambridge Scientific Abstracts, 7200 Wisconsin Ave., Bethesda, MD 20814. TEL 301-961-6750. FAX 301-961-6720.
Producer(s): Knight-Ridder, Inc. *5887*

POPULAR.
2413 Dundas St. W., Toronto, ON M6P 1X3, Canada. TEL 416-531-2495. FAX 416-531-7187. *3037*

POPULAR MECHANICS.
Hearst Corporation, Popular Mechanics, 224 W. 57th St., New York, NY 10019. TEL 212-649-3127.
Producer(s): UMI. *6970*

POPULAR SCIENCE.
Times Mirror Magazines, Inc., 2 Park Ave., New York, NY 10016. TEL 212-779-5000.
Producer(s): UMI. *6970*

POPULATION INDEX.
Princeton University, Office of Population Research, 21 Prospect Ave., Princeton, NJ 08544-2091. TEL 609-258-4949. FAX 609-258-1039.
Producer(s): SilverPlatter Information, Inc. *6069*

PORTFOLIO LETTER.
Institutional Investor Newsletters, 477 Madison Ave., New York, NY 10022. TEL 212-224-3233. FAX 212-224-3353. *1402*

POSTCARD SERIES - THE DIRECTORY.
Hobsons Publishing plc., Bateman St., Cambridge CB2 1LZ, England. TEL 44-1223-460366. FAX 44-1223-301506. *2553*

POWDER DIFFRACTION FILE SEARCH MANUAL. HANAWALT METHOD. INORGANIC.
Joint Committee on Powder Diffraction Standards, International Centre for Diffraction Data, Newton Sq. Corp. Camp, 12, Newton Square, PA 19073. TEL 215-328-9400. FAX 215-328-2503. *1795*

POWDER DIFFRACTION FILE SEARCH MANUAL. ORGANIC.
Joint Committee on Powder Diffraction Standards, International Centre for Diffraction Data, 12 Campus Blvd., Newtown Square, PA 19073. TEL 610-325-9814. FAX 610-325-9823. *1822*

POWER ENGINEERING JOURNAL.
I.E.E., Michael Faraday House, Six Hills Way, Stevenage, Herts. SG1 2AG, England. TEL 44-1438-313311. FAX 44-1438-742840.
Producer(s): UMI. *2843*

PRACTICAL FORMS AND PRECEDENTS.
L B C Information Services, 50 Waterloo Rd., N. Ryde, N.S.W. 2113, Australia. TEL 61-2-99366444. FAX 61-2-98889706. *4009*

PREDICASTS F & S INDEX INTERNATIONAL.
Information Access Company, 362 Lakeside Dr., Foster City, CA 94404. TEL 415-378-5200. FAX 415-378-5369. *1065*

PRENSA LIBRE.
Prensa Libre, S.A., 13 Calle 9-31, Zona 1, 01001 Guatemala, Guatemala. TEL 502-2-305096. FAX 502-2-301347. *3304*

PRESENCE MAGAZINE.
Presence Magazine Inc., 2715 chemin Cote Ste-Catherine, Montreal, PQ H3T 1B6, Canada. TEL 514-739-9797. FAX 514-739-1664. *6363*

PREVENTING SCHOOL FAILURE.
Heldref Publications, 1319 Eighteenth St., N.W., Washington, DC 20036-1802. TEL 202-296-6267. FAX 202-296-5149.
Producer(s): UMI. *2588*

PRIMARY CARE MEDICINE ON C D - R O M.
Lippincott - Raven Publishers, 227 E. Washington Sq., Philadelphia, PA 19106-3780. TEL 215-238-4200. FAX 215-238-4227.
Available only on CD-ROM. *4733*

PRINT MEDIA PRODUCTION SOURCE.
S R D S, 1700 Higgins Rd., Des Plaines, IL 60018. TEL 847-375-5000. FAX 847-375-5001. *50*

(YEAR) PRINTING INDUSTRY GOLD BOOK.
North American Publishing Co., 401 N. Broad St., Philadelphia, PA 19108. TEL 215-238-5482. FAX 215-238-5412. *6084*

PRIVATISATION INTERNATIONAL.
Privatisation International Ltd., Butlers Wharf Business Centre, Ste. 404, 45 Curlew St., London SE1 2ND, England. TEL 44-171-378-1620. FAX 44-171-403-7876. *993*

PROARBEIT.
Bundesanstalt fuer Arbeit, Institut fuer Arbeitsmarkt- und Berufsforschung, Regensburgerstr. 104, 90327 Nuernberg, Germany. TEL 49-911-1793011. FAX 49-911-1791147. *1065*

PROCESS AND CHEMICAL ENGINEERING.
The Royal Society of Chemistry, Thomas Graham House, Science Park, Milton Rd., Cambridge CB4 4WF, England. TEL 44-1223-420066. FAX 44-1223-423429.
Producer(s): Knight-Ridder, Inc. *2752*

PRODUCER PRICE INDEXES.
U.S. Bureau of Labor Statistics, 2 Massachusetts Ave., N.E., Washington, DC 20212. TEL 202-655-4000. *1284*

PRODUCTIVITY MEASURES FOR SELECTED INDUSTRIES.
U.S. Bureau of Labor Statistics, 441 G St., N.W., Washington, DC 20212. TEL 202-523-9244. *1284*

PROFESSIONAL BUILDER'S HOME PLAN DATABASE C D - R O M.
Cahners Publishing Company (Des Plaines), Division of Reed Elsevier Inc., 1350 E. Touhy Ave., Box 5080, Des Plaines, IL 60017-5080. TEL 847-390-2101. FAX 847-635-9950.
Available only on CD-ROM. *909*

PROJECT FINANCE INTERNATIONAL.
I F R Publishing, 11 New Fetter Ln., London EC4A 1JN, England. TEL 44-171-815-3900. FAX 44-171-815-3856. *1162*

PROSPECTS DIRECTORY.
C S U Ltd., Armstrong House, Oxford Rd., Manchester M1 7ED, England. TEL 44-161-236-9816. FAX 44-161-236-8541. *5514*

PSYCHIATRIC GENETICS.
Rapid Science Publishers, The Old Malthouse, Paradise St., Oxford OX1 1LD, England. TEL 44-1865-790447. FAX 44-1865-244012. *776*

PSYCHOLOGICAL ABSTRACTS.
American Psychological Association, 750 First St., N.E., Washington, DC 20002-4242. TEL 202-336-5600. FAX 202-336-5568.
Producer(s): American Psychological Assn., NISC (PsycLIT), SilverPlatter Information, Inc. (PsycLIT). *6161*

PSYCHOLOGY TODAY.
Sussex Publishers Inc., 49 E. 21st St., 11th Fl., New York, NY 10010. TEL 212-260-7210. FAX 212-260-7445.
Producer(s): UMI. *6147*

PSYCHOPATHOLOGIE AFRICAINE.
Societe de Psychopathologie et d'Hygiene Mentale de Dakar, B.P. 5097, Dakar-Fann, Senegal. *5094*

PUBLIC HEALTH.
Landesinstitut fuer den Oeffentlichen Gesundheitsdienst des Landes Nordrhein-Westfalen, Westerfeldstr. 35-37, 33611 Bielefeld, Germany. TEL 49-521-8007264. FAX 49-521-8007197. *4787*

PUBLIC UTILITIES REPORTS.
Public Utilities Reports, Inc., 8229 Boone Blvd., Ste. 401, Vienna, VA 22182. TEL 703-847-7720. FAX 703-917-6964. *2676*

PUBLICATIONS IN EDUCATION AND THE SOCIAL SCIENCES IN ISRAEL.
Henrietta Szold Institute, 9 Columbia St, Kiryat Menachem, Jerusalem 96583, Israel. TEL 972-2-6494444. FAX 972-2-6437698.
Available only on CD-ROM. *6740*

PUBLICUS.
Schwabe und Co. AG, Steinentorstr. 13, CH-4010 Basel, Switzerland. TEL 41-61-2789565. FAX 41-61-2789566. *6191*

PUBLISHERS, DISTRIBUTORS & WHOLESALERS OF THE UNITED STATES.
R.R. Bowker, A Division of Reed Elsevier Inc., 121 Chanlon Rd., New Providence, NJ 07974. TEL 908-464-6800. FAX 908-665-3502.
Producer(s): Bowker Electronic Publishing. *1707*

PUBLISHERS' INTERNATIONAL I S B N DIRECTORY (YEAR).
K.G. Saur Verlag KG, A member of the Reed Elsevier plc group, Ortlerstr. 8, 81373 Munich, Germany. TEL 49-89-76902-0. FAX 49-89-76902150.
Producer(s): K.G. Saur Verlag. *6291*

PUBLISHERS' INTERNATIONAL I S B N DIRECTORY PLUS.
K.G. Saur Verlag KG, A member of the Reed Elsevier plc group, Ortlerstr. 8, 81373 Munich, Germany. TEL 49-89-76902-0. FAX 49-89-76902150.
Available only on CD-ROM. *6291*

PUERTO RICO HEALTH SCIENCES JOURNAL.
University of Puerto Rico, Office of the Dean for Academic Affairs, Medical Sciences Campus, Box 365067, San Juan, PR 00936-5067. TEL 787-758-2525. FAX 787-764-2470. *4734*

PUNCH IN INTERNATIONAL TRAVEL AND ENTERTAINMENT MAGAZINE.
Enterprises Publishing, 400 E. 59th St., Ste. 9F, New York, NY 10022. TEL 212-755-4363. FAX 212-755-4365. *7229*

PUNGOLO.
Centro Internazionale di Studi per i Giovani, Via Col. Romej 7, 91100 Trapani, Italy. TEL 39-923-546700. *1884*

Q E X: A R R L EXPERIMENTERS' EXCHANGE.
American Radio Relay League, Inc., 225 Main St., Newington, CT 06111. TEL 860-594-0200. FAX 860-594-0303. *2027*

QST.
American Radio Relay League, Inc., 225 Main St., Newington, CT 06111. TEL 860-594-0200. FAX 860-584-0239. *2027*

QUALITY ASSURANCE IN EDUCATION.
M C B University Press Ltd., 60-62 Toller Ln., Bradford, W. Yorks BD8 9BY, England. TEL 44-1274-777700. FAX 44-1274-785200. *2475*

SERIALS AVAILABLE ON CD-ROM

QUALITY OF LIFE RESEARCH.
Rapid Science Publishers, 2-6 Boundary Row, London SE1 8HN, England. TEL 44-171-865-0198. FAX 44-171-410-6600. *4735*

QUANTUM ELECTRONICS.
Turpion - Moscow Ltd., 47 Leninsky prospekt, 11793 Moscow, Russia. TEL 7-95-1356417. FAX 7-95-1358860. *2844*

QUARTERLY FINANCIAL INSTITUTION RATINGS.
L A C E Financial Corp., 118 N. Court St., Frederick, MD 21701. TEL 301-662-1011. *1163*

QUEBEC (PROVINCE). SERVICES DOCUMENTAIRES MULTIMEDIA. CHOIX: DOCUMENTATION AUDIOVISUELLE.
Services Documentaires Multimedia Inc., 75 Port-Royal E., bureau 300, Montreal, PQ H3L 3T1, Canada. TEL 514-382-0895. FAX 514-384-9139. *561*

QUEBEC (PROVINCE). SERVICES DOCUMENTAIRES MULTIMEDIA. CHOIX: DOCUMENTATION IMPRIMEE.
Services Documentaires Multimedia Inc., 75 Port-Royal E., bureau 300, Montreal, PQ H3L 3T1, Canada. TEL 514-382-0895. FAX 514-384-9139. *561*

QUEBEC (PROVINCE). SERVICES DOCUMENTATION MULTIMEDIA. CHOIX JEUNESSE: DOCUMENTATION IMPRIMEE.
Services Documentaires Multimedia Inc., 75 Port-Royal E., bureau 300, Montreal, PQ H3L 3T1, Canada. TEL 514-382-0895. FAX 514-384-9139. *561*

QUFU SHIFAN DAXUE XUEBAO.
Qufu Shifan Daxue, Xuebao Bianjibu, Qufu, Shandong 273165, People's Republic of China. TEL 86-537-4424344. *6631*

QUILL (GREENCASTLE).
Society of Professional Journalists, Box 77, Greencastle, IN 46135-0077. TEL 317-653-3333. FAX 317-653-4631. *3879*

R A M.
Televak Uitgeverij N.V., Postbus 75985, 1070 AZ Amsterdam, Netherlands. TEL 31-20-6659220. FAX 31-20-6657316. *2027*

R A P R A ABSTRACTS.
Rapra Technology Ltd., Shawbury, Shrewsbury, Shrops. SY4 4NR, England. TEL 44-1939-250383. FAX 44-1939-251118. *6506*

R A P R A ABSTRACTS - C D - R O M.
Rapra Technology Ltd., Shawbury, Shrewsbury, Shrops. SY4 4NR, England. TEL 44-1939-250383. FAX 44-1939-251118.
Available only on CD-ROM. *6506*

R & D FOCUS.
IMSWORLD Publications Ltd., 7 Harewood Ave., London NW1 6JB, England. TEL 0171-393-5000. FAX 0171-393-5900. *5692*

R I A TAX GUIDE.
Research Institute of America, Inc., 90 Fifth Ave., New York, NY 10011. TEL 212-645-4800. FAX 212-337-4279. *1625*

R I B A PRODUCT SELECTOR.
R I B A Information Services, Finsbury Mission, 39 Moreland St., London EC1V 8BB, England. TEL 44-171-250-4050. FAX 44-171-490-4434. *413*

R I L M ABSTRACTS OF MUSIC LITERATURE.
R I L M Abstracts, City University of New York, 33 W. 42nd St., New York, NY 10036. TEL 212-642-2709. FAX 212-642-1973.
Producer(s): NISC (MUSE, Music Search). *5449*

R T E C S.
U.S. National Institute for Occupational Safety and Health, Attn: Publications, 4676 Columbia Pkwy., Cincinnati, OH 45226.
Producer(s): SilverPlatter Information, Inc. *5498*

RADIATION EFFECTS AND DEFECTS IN SOLIDS.
Gordon and Breach - Harwood Academic, Amsteldisk 166, 1st Fl., 1079 LH Amsterdam, Netherlands. *5857*

RADIOACTIVE WASTE MANAGEMENT AND ENVIRONMENTAL RESTORATION.
Gordon and Breach - Harwood Academic, Amsteldisk 166, 1st Fl., 1079 LH Amsterdam, Netherlands. *2988*

RAPPORTI SOCIALI.
Edizioni Rapporti Sociali, Via Bruschetti 11, 20125 Milan, Italy. TEL 39-2-6701806. *5963*

RAWAL MEDICAL JOURNAL.
Pakistan Medical Association, Rawalpindi-Islamabad Branch, Rawalpindi, Pakistan. *4736*

RAWLINSONS NEW ZEALAND CONSTRUCTION HANDBOOK.
Rawlinsons New Zealand Construction Handbook Ltd., Rawlinson House, 4th Fl., 25-27 Broadway, Newmarket, Auckland, New Zealand. TEL 64-9-5290061. FAX 64-9-5244977. *1708*

REACTIONS WEEKLY.
Adis International Limited, Private Bag 65901, Mairangi Bay, Auckland 10, New Zealand. TEL 64-9-479-8100. FAX 64-9-479-8145.
Producer(s): SilverPlatter Information, Inc. *5702*

READERS' GUIDE ABSTRACTS.
H.W. Wilson Co., 950 University Ave., Bronx, NY 10452-9978. TEL 718-588-8400. FAX 718-590-1617.
Producer(s): SilverPlatter Information, Inc., H.W. Wilson (WILSONDISC). *23*

READERS' GUIDE TO PERIODICAL LITERATURE.
H.W. Wilson Co., 950 University Ave., Bronx, NY 10452-9978. TEL 718-588-8400. FAX 718-590-1617.
Producer(s): SilverPlatter Information, Inc., H.W. Wilson (WILSONDISC). *23*

LA RECHERCHE.
Societe d'Editions Scientifiques, 57 rue de Seine, 75280 Paris Cedex 06, France. TEL 43-54-32-84. FAX 46-34-75-08.
Producer(s): Chadwyck-Healey Inc. *6562*

RECUEIL ANNUEL DE JURISPRUDENCE BELGE.
Larcier, Rue des Minimes 39, 1000 Brussels, Belgium. TEL 32-2-5480711. FAX 32-2-5139009. *4014*

REFERATEDIENST ZUR LITERATURWISSENSCHAFT.
Geisteswissenschaftliche Zentren Berlin e.V., Zentrum fuer Literaturforschung, Jaegerstr. 10-11, 10117 Berlin, Germany. TEL 49-30-20192169. FAX 49-30-20192154. *4456*

REFERENCE AND RESEARCH BOOK NEWS.
Book News, Inc. (Portland), 5739 N.E. Sumner St., Portland, OR 97218. TEL 503-281-9230. FAX 503-287-4485. *561*

REGISTER OF AUSTRALIAN MINING.
Resource Information Unit, 79 Hay St., Subiaco, W.A. 6008, Australia. TEL 61-8-93823955. FAX 61-8-93881025. *5314*

REGISTER OF AUSTRALIAN PETROLEUM.
Resource Information Unit, 79 Hay St., Subiaco, W.A. 6008, Australia. TEL 61-8-93823955. FAX 61-8-93881025. *5621*

RELIGION INDEX ONE: PERIODICALS.
American Theological Library Association, 820 Church St., Ste. 300, Evanston, IL 60201-5613. TEL 847-869-7788. FAX 847-869-8513. *6387*

RELIGION INDEX TWO: MULTI-AUTHOR WORKS.
American Theological Library Association, 820 Church St., Ste. 300, Evanston, IL 60201-5613. TEL 847-869-7788. FAX 847-869-8513. *6387*

RELIGION INDEXES: THESAURUS.
American Theological Library Association, 820 Church St., Ste. 300, Evanston, IL 60201-5613. TEL 847-869-7788. FAX 847-869-8513. *6366*

RELIGIOUS & THEOLOGICAL ABSTRACTS.
Religious & Theological Abstracts Inc., 100 W. Park, Box 215, Myerstown, PA 17067. TEL 717-866-6734. FAX 717-866-9280. *6387*

REMOTE SENSING REVIEWS.
Gordon and Breach - Harwood Academic, Amsteldisk 166, 1st Fl., 1079 LH Amsterdam, Netherlands. *2738*

RENT REVIEW AND LEASE RENEWAL.
M C B University Press Ltd., 60-62 Toller Ln., Bradford, W. Yorks BD8 9BY, England. TEL 44-1274-777700. FAX 44-1274-785200. *6312*

REPERTOIRE DES PRODUITS DISPONIBLES AU QUEBEC.
Centre de Recherche Industrielle du Quebec, 333 rue Franquet, Sainte-Foy, PQ G1P 4C7, Canada. TEL 418-652-2234. FAX 418-652-2212. *1710*

REPERTORIO CRONOLOGICO DE LEGISLACION.
Editorial Aranzadi, S.A., Avda. Carlos III, 34, Apdo. 111, 31080 Pamplona, Spain. TEL 34-48-331212. FAX 34-48-330919. *4015*

REPERTORIO DE JURISPRUDENCIA.
Editorial Aranzadi, S.A., Avda. Carlos III, 34, Apdo. 111, 31080 Pamplona, Spain. TEL 34-48-331212. FAX 34-48-330919. *4015*

REPERTORIO DEL FORO ITALIANO.
Zanichelli Editore, Via Irnerio 34, 40126 Bologna, Italy. TEL 39-51-293111. FAX 39-51-249782. *4015*

REPERTORIUM.
Dutch Association of the Innovative Pharmaceutical Industry (NEFARMA), Postbus 9193, 3506 GD Utrecht, Netherlands. FAX 31-30-2631830. *4737*

RESEARCH IN MINISTRY.
American Theological Library Association, 820 Church St., Ste. 300, Evanston, IL 60201-5613. TEL 847-869-7788. FAX 847-869-8513. *6387*

RESEARCH MANUAL OF INDUSTRIAL LAW.
C C H Australia Ltd., P.O. Box 230, North Ryde, N.S.W. 2113, Australia. TEL 61-1-300300224. FAX 61-1-330306224. *4056*

RESOURCES IN EDUCATION.
E R I C Facility, 1100 West St., 2nd Fl., Laurel, MD 20707-3587. TEL 301-497-4080. FAX 301-953-0263.
Producer(s): Knight-Ridder, Inc. (ERIC), NISC (ERIC on CD-ROM), OCLC (ERIC), SilverPlatter Information, Inc. (ERIC). *2503*

RESOURCES IN EDUCATION ANNUAL CUMULATION.
Oryx Press, Box 33889, Phoenix, AZ 85067-3889. TEL 602-265-2651. FAX 602-265-6250.
Producer(s): NISC (ERIC). *2503*

RETAIL INTELLIGENCE.
Mintel International Group Ltd., 18-19 Long Ln., London EC1A 9HE, England. TEL 44-171-606-4533. FAX 44-171-606-5932. *1547*

REVIEW (WASHINGTON).
Heldref Publications, 1319 Eighteenth St., N.W., Washington, DC 20036-1802. TEL 202-296-6267.
Producer(s): UMI. *3473*

REVISTA ANDINA.
Centro de Estudios Regionales Andinos "Bartolome de las Casas", Apdo. 140087, Lima 14, Peru. TEL 51-14-223703. FAX 51-14-427894. *6632*

REVISTA BRASILEIRA DE PATOLOGIA.
Sociedade Brasileira de Patologia Clinica, Rua Sampaio Viana, 92, 20261-040 Rio de Janeiro, RJ, Brazil. TEL 55-21-2933848. FAX 55-21-2932041. *4737*

REVISTA COSTARRICENSE DE CIENCIAS MEDICAS.
Caja Costarricense de Seguro Social, Apdo. 10105, San Jose, Costa Rica. FAX 506-2338359. *4738*

REVISTA DE GASTROENTEROLOGIA DE MEXICO.
Obsidiana Editores, S.A., Czda. de Tlalpan 2365, Col. Ciudad Jardin, 04370 Mexico DF, Mexico. TEL 6899133. *4914*

REVISTA DE INVESTIGACION CLINICA.
Instituto Nacional de la Nutricion "Salvador Zubiran", Av. San Fernando y Viaducto Tlalpan, Mexico 22, D.F., Mexico. TEL 915-573-1200. FAX 915-655-1076. *4738*

REVISTA DE INVESTIGACION CONTABLE (TEUKEN).
Universidad Nacional de la Patagonia San Juan Bosca, Facultad de Ciencias Economicas, Sarmiento 553 Casilla de Correo 172, 9000 C. Rivadavia, Argentina. TEL 0967-24463. FAX 54-96724463. *1097*

REVISTA DE MEDICINA LEGALA.
Societatea de Medicina Legala din Romania, Sos. Vitan-Birzesti 9, 75669 Bucharest, Rumania. TEL 40-1-6343890. FAX 40-1-3210260. *4906*

REVISTA DO SETOR DE CIENCIAS AGRARIAS.
Universidade Federal do Parana, Sector de Ciencias Agrarias, Caixa Postal 672, 80035-050 Curitiba PR, Brazil. TEL 55-41-2535552. FAX 55-41-2535552. *148*

REVISTA DOS TRIBUNAIS.
Editora Revista dos Tribunais, Rua Conde do Pinhal, 78, 01501 Sao Paulo SP, Brazil. *4017*

REVISTA ESPANOLA DE ECONOMIA AGRARIA.
Ministerio de Agricultura, Pesca y Alimentacion, Centro de Publicaciones, Paseo de la Infanta Isabel 1, 28071 Madrid, Spain. TEL 34-1-3475551. FAX 34-1-3475722. *201*

REVISTA MEDICA DE MOCAMBIQUE.
Ministerio da Saude, Instituto Nacional de Saude, Universidade Eduardo Mondlane, Faculdade de Medicina, C.P. 264, Maputo, Mozambique. TEL 427131. FAX 258-1-423-726. *6249*

RHODE ISLAND BUSINESS DIRECTORY.
American Business Directories, 5711 S. 86th Circle, Box 27347, Omaha, NE 68127. TEL 402-593-4600. FAX 402-331-5481. *1710*

RISK ABSTRACTS.
Cambridge Scientific Abstracts, 7200 Wisconsin Ave., 6th Fl., Bethesda, MD 20814. TEL 301-961-6700. FAX 301-961-6720.
Producer(s): Knight-Ridder, Inc. (Environmental Management); NISC (Health & Safety - Risk Abstracts). *2963*

RISK MAGAZINE.
I I A Publishing Pty. Ltd., P.O. Box 861, Double Bay, N.S.W. 2028, Australia. TEL 61-2-3287699. FAX 61-2-32887690. *3832*

RISK MANAGEMENT.
Risk Management Society Publishing, Inc., 655 Third Ave., 2nd Fl., New York, NY 10017-5637. TEL 212-286-9364. FAX 212-922-0716. *3832*

ROCKS AND MINERALS.
Heldref Publications, 1319 Eighteenth St., N.W., Washington, DC 20036-1802. TEL 202-296-6267. FAX 202-296-5149.
Producer(s): UMI. *5315*

ROCZNIKI NAUKOWE ZOOTECHNIKI.
Instytut Zootechniki, Ul. Sarego 2, 31-047 Krakow, Poland. TEL 48-12-227333. FAX 48-12-228065. *287*

ROLLING STONE.
Wenner Media, Inc., 1290 Ave. of Americas, New York, NY 10104. TEL 212-484-1616. FAX 212-759-2966.
Producer(s): UMI. *5432*

ROMULUS.
Canada Institute for Scientific and Technical Information, Information Resource Management, Ottawa, ON K1A 0S2, Canada. *6591*

ROTOR ROSTER.
Air Track, Box 610, Hilliard, FL 32046. TEL 912-496-3504. FAX 912-496-7513. *7078*

ROUGE ET NOIR.
V I P News Verlag GmbH, Taubstummengasse 13-4, A-1040 Vienna, Austria. TEL 01-5050801-0. FAX 01-505080121. *6779*

ROYAL ANTHROPOLOGICAL INSTITUTE. JOURNAL.
Royal Anthropological Institute of Great Britain and Ireland, 50 Fitzroy St., London W1P 5HS, England. TEL 44-171-3870455. FAX 44-171-3834235. *329*

RUBBER WORLD.
Lippincott & Peto, Inc., 1867 W. Market St., Akron, OH 44313. TEL 216-864-2122. *6504*

RUBBICANA-EUROPE (YEAR).
Rapra Technology Ltd., Shawbury, Shrewsbury, Shrops. SY4 4NR, England. TEL 44-1939-250383. FAX 44-1939-251118. *6505*

RURAL TECHNOLOGY GUIDE.
Natural Resources Institute, Central Ave., Chatham Maritime, Kent ME4 4TB, England. TEL 44-1634-880088. FAX 44-1634-880066. *150*

RUSSIAN ACADEMY OF SCIENCE. IZVESTIYA. MATHEMATICS.
Turpion - Moscow Ltd., 47 Leninsky prospekt, 117913 Moscow, Russia. TEL 7-95-1356417. FAX 7-95-1358860. *4602*

RUSSIAN BOOKS IN PRINT ON C D - R O M.
Bowker - Saur Ltd., A member of the Reed Elsevier plc group, Maypole House, Maypole Rd., E. Grinstead, W. Sussex RH19 1HU, England. TEL 44-1342-330100. FAX 44-1342-330191.
Available only on CD-ROM. Producer(s): Bowker - Saur Ltd. *562*

RUSSIAN CHEMICAL REVIEWS.
Turpion - Moscow Ltd., 47 Leninsky prospekt, 117913 Moscow, Russia. TEL 7-95-1356417. FAX 7-95-1358860. *1766*

S A R AND Q S A R IN ENVIRONMENTAL RESEARCH.
Gordon and Breach - Harwood Academic, Amsteldisk 166, 1st Fl., 1079 LH Amsterdam, Netherlands. *2950*

S A TAX REVIEW.
InfoMedia Technologies (Pty) Ltd., P.O. Box 44597, Claremont 7735, South Africa. TEL 27-21-689 5075. FAX 27-21-689-5025. *1626*

S I A - SURFACE AND INTERFACE ANALYSIS.
John Wiley & Sons Ltd., Journals, Baffins Ln., Chichester, W. Sussex PO19 1UD, England. TEL 44-1243-779777. FAX 44-1243-775878. *2773*

THE S I G C A T FOUNDATION COMPENDIUM OF C D - R O MS.
Special Interest Group on C D - R O M Applications & Technology, 11343 Sunset Hills Rd., Reston, VA 22090. TEL 202-512-1265. FAX 703-435-5553.
Available only on CD-ROM. *562*

S I R S GOVERNMENT REPORTER ON C D - R O M.
Social Issues Resources Series, Box 2348, Boca Raton, FL 33427-2348. TEL 561-994-0079. FAX 561-994-4704.
Available only on CD-ROM. *6651*

S I R S INDEX-ONLY C D - R O M.
Social Issues Resources Series, Box 2348, Boca Raton, FL 33427-2348. TEL 561-994-0079. FAX 561-994-4704.
Available only on CD-ROM. *6651*

S I R S RESEARCHER C D - R O M.
Social Issues Resources Series, Box 2348, Boca Raton, FL 33427-2348. TEL 561-994-0079. FAX 561-994-4704.
Available only on CD-ROM. *6651*

SACRAMENTO BUSINESS JOURNAL.
American City Business Journals, Inc. (Austin), 505 Powell St., Austin, TX 78703-5121.
Producer(s): UMI. *999*

SADO MARINE BIOLOGICAL STATION. REPORT.
Niigata Daigaku, Rigakubu Fuzoku Sado Rinkai Jikkenjo, 2-8050 Igarashi, Niigata 950-21, Japan. TEL 0259-75-2012. FAX 0259-75-2012. *624*

SAFETY AND HEALTH AT WORK.
International Labour Office, International Occupational Safety and Health Information Centre, 4 route des Morillons, CH-1211 Geneva 22, Switzerland. TEL 41-22-799-6111. FAX 41-22-799-8516.
Producer(s): SilverPlatter Information, Inc. *5503*

SALUD MENTAL.
Editorial Laser S.A. de C.V., Lago Alberto 442-7, Col. Anahuac, Deleg. Miguel Hidalgo, 11320 Mexico DF, Mexico. TEL 52-5-2600250. FAX 52-5-2600048. *5097*

SALUD PUBLICA DE MEXICO.
Instituto Nacional de Salud Publica, Secretaria de Salud, Av. Universidad, 665, Planta Baja, Col. Santa Maria Ahuacatitlad, 62508 Cuernavaca, Morelos, Mexico. TEL 52-73-110111. FAX 52-73-175745. *6250*

SAN MATEO COUNTY COMMERCE AND INDUSTRY DIRECTORY.
Database Publishing Company, 1590 S. Lewis St., Anaheim, CA 92805-6423. TEL 714-778-6400. FAX 714-778-6811. *1711*

SANTO TOMAS JOURNAL OF MEDICINE.
Santo Tomas University Press, Espana St., Manila 1008, Philippines. TEL 02-731-3101. FAX 632-731-3126. *4742*

SARDIUS.
Juta & Co. Ltd., P.O. Box 14373, Kenwyn 7790, South Africa. TEL 27-21-7975101. FAX 27-21-7615010.
Available only on CD-ROM. *5986*

SAUDI HEART JOURNAL.
King Abdul Aziz University Hospital, P.O. Box 6615, Jeddah 21452, Saudi Arabia. TEL 966-2-6697043. FAX 966-2-6697043. *4823*

SAUDI MEDICAL JOURNAL.
Saudi Arabian Armed Forces Ministry of Defence and Aviation, Medical Services Department, P.O. Box 7897, Riyadh 11159, Saudi Arabia. TEL 966-1-4777714. FAX 966-1-4777194. *4742*

SCANDINAVIAN JOURNAL OF DEVELOPMENT ALTERNATIVES AND AREA STUDIES.
Bethany Books, Sweden, P.O. Box 7444, S-103 91 Stockholm, Sweden. TEL 46-8-580-196-87. *6634*

SCANDINAVIAN STUDIES (PROVO).
Society for the Advancement of Scandinavian Study, c/o Steven P. Sondrup, Ed., Department of Comparative Literature, Brigham Young University, Provo, UT 84602-6118. TEL 801-378-2579. FAX 801-378-4649. *4463*

SCHOLARSHIPS, GRANTS, & PRIZES.
Peterson's, 202 Carnegie Center, Box 2123, Princeton, NJ 08543-2123. TEL 609-243-9111. FAX 609-243-9150. *2555*

SCHOLASTIC UPDATE.
Scholastic Inc., 555 Broadway, New York, NY 10012-3999. TEL 212-343-6100.
Producer(s): UMI. *1886*

DER SCHWEIZER TREUHAENDER.
Treuhand-Kammer, Postfach 892, CH-8025 Zurich, Switzerland. TEL 41-1-2677575. FAX 41-1-2677555. *1098*

SCHWEIZERISCHE ZEITSCHRIFT FUER VOLKSWIRTSCHAFT UND STATISTIK.
Helbing und Lichtenhahn Verlag AG, Freie Str. 84, CH-4051 Basel, Switzerland. TEL 41-61-2721116. FAX 41-61-2721150.
Producer(s): SilverPlatter Information, Inc. *1000*

SCIENCE ACTIVITIES.
Heldref Publications, 1319 Eighteenth St., N.W., Washington, DC 20036-1802. TEL 202-296-6267. FAX 202-296-5149.
Producer(s): UMI. *2481*

SCIENCE CITATION INDEX.
Institute for Scientific Information, 3501 Market St., Philadelphia, PA 19104. TEL 215-386-0100. FAX 215-386-2911.
Producer(s): Institute for Scientific Information (SCI CDE). *6592*

SCIENCE NEWS.
Science Service, 1719 N St., N.W., Washington, DC 20036. TEL 800-552-4412. FAX 202-659-0365.
Producer(s): UMI. *6569*

SCITECH BOOK NEWS.
Book News, Inc. (Portland), 5739 N.E. Sumner St., Portland, OR 97218. TEL 503-281-9230. FAX 503-287-4485. *562*

SCOTT'S DIRECTORIES - ATLANTIC INDUSTRIAL DIRECTORY.
Southam Information Products Ltd., Scott's Directories, 1450 Don Mills Rd., Don Mills, ON M3B 2X7, Canada. TEL 416-442-2122. FAX 416-510-6875. *1711*

SCOTT'S DIRECTORIES, GREATER TORONTO BUSINESS DIRECTORY.
Southam Information Products Ltd., Scott's Directories, 1450 Don Mills Rd., Don Mills, ON M3B 2X7, Canada. TEL 416-442-2122. FAX 416-510-6875. *1711*

SCOTT'S DIRECTORIES - ONTARIO MANUFACTURERS.
Southam Information Products Ltd., Scott's Directories, 1450 Don Mills Rd., Don Mills, ON M3B 2X7, Canada. TEL 416-442-2122. FAX 416-510-6875. *1711*

SCOTT'S DIRECTORIES - QUEBEC MANUFACTURERS.
Southam Information Products Ltd., Scott's Directories, 1450 Don Mills Rd., Don Mills, ON M3B 2X7, Canada. TEL 416-442-2122. FAX 416-510-6875. *1711*

SCOTT'S DIRECTORIES - WESTERN INDUSTRIAL DIRECTORY.
Southam Information Products Ltd., Scott's Directories, 1450 Don Mills Rd., Don Mills, ON M3B 2X7, Canada. TEL 416-442-2122. FAX 416-510-6875. *1711*

SCULPTURE REVIEW.
National Sculpture Society, 1177 Ave. of the Americas, New York, NY 10036. TEL 212-764-5645. FAX 212-764-5651. *465*

SEA GRANT ABSTRACTS.
Woods Hole Data Base, Inc., Box 712, Woods Hole, MA 02543. TEL 508-548-2743.
Producer(s): NISC (Oceanographic & Marine Resources). *2328*

SEARCHING DIALOG: THE COMPLETE GUIDE.
Dialog Information Services, Inc. (Palo Alto), 3460 Hillview Ave., Palo Alto, CA 94304. TEL 415-858-3785. FAX 415-858-7069. *4213*

SECURITE ET SANTE AU TRAVAIL.
International Labour Office, International Occupational Safety and Health Information Centre, 4 route des Morillons, CH-1211 Geneva, Switzerland. TEL 41-22-799-6111. FAX 41-22-799-8516.
Producer(s): SilverPlatter Information, Inc. *5503*

SEIBT INDUSTRIEKATALOG.
Seibt Verlag GmbH, Leopoldstr. 208, 80804 Munich, Germany. TEL 49-89-360903-0. FAX 49-89-364317. *1711*

SEIBT MEDIZINISCHE TECHNIK.
Seibt Verlag GmbH, Leopoldstr. 208, 80804 Munich, Germany. TEL 49-89-360903-0. FAX 49-89-364317. *4744*

SEIBT OBERFLAECHENTECHNIK.
Seibt Verlag GmbH, Leopoldstr. 208, 80804 Munich, Germany. TEL 49-89-360903-0. FAX 49-89-364317. *5848*

SEIBT UMWELT TECHNIK.
Seibt Verlag GmbH, Leopoldstr. 208, 80804 Munich, Germany. TEL 49-89-360903-0. FAX 49-89-364317. *2951*

SELL'S PRODUCTS & SERVICES DIRECTORY.
Miller Freeman Information Services, Riverbank House, Angel Ln., Tonbridge, Kent TN9 1SE, England. TEL 44-1732-362666. FAX 44-1732-767301. *1711*

SERIALS DIRECTORY.
EBSCO Industries, Inc., Title Information Department, 5724 Hwy. 280 East, Birmingham, AL 35242. TEL 205-991-6600. FAX 205-995-1582. *562*

SESAME BULLETIN.
Centre de Cooperation Internationale en Recherche Agronomique pour le Developpement (CIRAD), B.P. 5035, 34032 Montpellier Cedex 1, France. TEL 67-61-58-00. FAX 67-61-58-20. *152*

SEVENTEEN.
K-III Communications Corp., 745 Fifth Ave., New York, NY 10151. TEL 212-745-0100.
Producer(s): UMI. *7333*

SHENGLI KEXUE JINZHAN.
Zhongguo Shengli Xuehui, 38 Xueyuan Rd., Beijing Medical University, Beijing 100083, People's Republic of China. TEL 861-209-1150. FAX 861-202-9252. *822*

SHENGWU GONGCHENG JINZHAN.
Zhongguo Kexueyuan, Wenxian Qingbao Zhongxin, 8 Kexueyuan Nanlu, Zhongguancun, Beijing 100080, People's Republic of China. TEL 86-10-6256-2548. FAX 86-10-6256-7325. *687*

SHOPPING CENTER DIRECTORY.
National Research Bureau, Inc. (Chicago), 150 N. Wacker Dr., Ste. 2222, Chicago, IL 60606-1608. TEL 312-541-0100. FAX 312-541-1492. *1712*

SHUITU BAOCHI TONGBAO.
Zhongguo Kexueyuan, Xibei Shuitu Baochi Yanjiusuo, Yangling Qu, Xi'an, Shaanxi 712100, People's Republic of China. TEL 86-910-7012412. FAX 86-910-7012210. *244*

SICHUAN HUANJING.
Sichuan Huanjing Bianjibu, 18 Renmin Nanlu 4 Duan (Section 4), Chengdu, Sichuan 610041, People's Republic of China. TEL 86-28-5580473. *2951*

SIDE EFFECTS OF DRUGS ANNUAL.
Elsevier Science B.V., Books Division, P.O. Box 211, 1000 AE Amsterdam, Netherlands. TEL 31-20-4853911. FAX 31-20-4853705.
Producer(s): SilverPlatter Information, Inc. (SEDBASE). *5694*

SINGAPORE JOURNAL OF OBSTETRICS & GYNAECOLOGY.
Obstetrical and Gynaecological Society of Singapore, c/o National University Hospital, Dept. of O & G, Lower Kent Ridge Road, Singapore 0511, Singapore. TEL 7724267. FAX 779-4753. *4967*

SINGAPORE MONTHLY TRADE STATISTICS: IMPORTS & EXPORTS.
Trade Statistics, 303 Upper Serangoon Rd., P.O. Box 485, Singapore 1334, Singapore. *1068*

SINGAPORE NATIONAL BIBLIOGRAPHY.
National Library Board, 91 Stamford Rd., Singapore 178896, Singapore. TEL 65-332-3683. FAX 65-332-3684. *3522*

SINGAPORE PERIODICALS INDEX.
National Library Board, 91 Stamford Rd., Singapore 1778896, Singapore. TEL 65-332-3683. FAX 65-332-3684. *26*

SINGAPORE TRADE CONNECTION.
Singapore Trade Development Board, 1 Maritime Square No. 10-40, World Trade Centre, Telok Blangah Rd., Singapore 0409, Singapore. TEL 279-0426. FAX 278-7073.
Available only on CD-ROM. *1346*

THE SINGER REPORT ON MANAGED CARE SYSTEMS AND TECHNOLOGY.
Charles J. Singer & Co., 401 Edgewater Pl., Ste. 580, Wakefield, MA 01880. TEL 617-246-7585. FAX 617-246-5263. *4848*

SMALL PRESS RECORD OF BOOKS IN PRINT.
Dustbooks, Box 100, Paradise, CA 95967. TEL 916-877-6110. FAX 916-877-0222.
Available only on CD-ROM. *563*

SOCIAL POLICY.
Union Institute, 25 W. 43rd St., Rm. 620, New York, NY 10036. TEL 212-642-2929. FAX 212-642-1956.
Producer(s): H.W. Wilson. *6729*

SOCIAL SCIENCES CITATION INDEX.
Institute for Scientific Information, 3501 Market St., Philadelphia, PA 19104. TEL 215-386-0100. FAX 215-386-2911.
Producer(s): Institute for Scientific Information (SSCI). *6651*

SOCIAL SCIENCES INDEX.
H.W. Wilson Co., 950 University Ave., Bronx, NY 10452. TEL 718-588-8400. FAX 718-590-1617.
Producer(s): SilverPlatter Information, Inc., H.W. Wilson. *6651*

SOCIAL WORK ABSTRACTS.
N A S W Press, 750 First St., N.E., Ste. 700, Washington, DC 20002-4241. TEL 202-408-8600. FAX 202-336-8310.
Producer(s): SilverPlatter Information, Inc. (SWAB-PLUS). *6698*

SOCIETY.
Transaction Publishers, Transaction Periodicals Consortium, Department 3092, Rutgers University, New Brunswick, NJ 08903. TEL 908-445-2280. FAX 908-445-3138. *6639*

SOCIO-ECONOMIC SERIES.
Natural Resources Institute, Central Ave., Chatham Maritime, Kent ME4 4TB, England. TEL 44-1634-880088. FAX 44-1634-880066. *153*

SOCIOLOGICA.
Universidad Autonoma Metropolitana - Azcapotzalco, Departamento de Sociologia, Av. San Pablo 180, Edif., Piso 3, Azcapotzalco, 02200 Mexico, D.F., Mexico. TEL 52-5-7244339. FAX 52-5-3948093. *6730*

SOCIOLOGICAL ABSTRACTS.
Sociological Abstracts, Inc., Box 22206, San Diego, CA 92192-0206. TEL 619-695-8803. FAX 619-695-0416.
Producer(s): NISC (Sociofile), SilverPlatter Information, Inc. (Sociofile). *6740*

THE SOFTWARE USERS YEAR BOOK.
V N U Business Publications BV, 32-34 Broadwick St., London W1A 2HG, England. TEL 071-439-4242. FAX 071-437-7906. *2219*

SOJOURNER.
Sojourner Feminist Institute, 42 Seaverns Ave., Jamaica Plain, MA 02130-2865. TEL 617-524-0415. *7347*

SOLAR-GEOPHYSICAL DATA. PART 1 - PROMPT REPORTS.
U.S. National Geophysical Data Center, 325 Broadway, Boulder, CO 80303-3328. TEL 303-497-6836. FAX 303-497-6513. *501*

SOLAR-GEOPHYSICAL DATA: PART 2 - COMPREHENSIVE REPORTS.
U.S. National Geophysical Data Center, 325 Broadway, Boulder, CO 80303-3328. TEL 303-497-6836. FAX 303-497-6513. *501*

IL SOLE 24 ORE.
Editrice Il Sole - 24 Ore, S.p.A., Via Lomazzo 52, 20154 Milan, Italy. TEL 02-31031. FAX 02-312055.
Producer(s): Chadwyck-Healey Inc. *3328*

IL SOLE 24 ORE SU C D - R O M.
Chadwyck-Healey Ltd., The Quorum, Barnwell Rd., Cambridge CB5 8SW, England. TEL 44-1223-215512. FAX 44-1223-215514.
Available only on CD-ROM. Producer(s): Chadwyck-Healey Inc. *3328*

SOLEIL.
UniMedia Inc., 925 chemin St-Louis, C.P. 1547 Terminus, Quebec, PQ G1K 7J6, Canada. TEL 418-686-3233. FAX 418-686-3260. *3266*

SOPHIA.
Vaasa University Library, P.O. Box 331, FIN-65101 Vaasa, Finland. TEL 358-6-324-82-33. FAX 358-6-324-82-00.
Available only on CD-ROM. *3522*

SORKINS DIRECTORY OF BUSINESS & GOVERNMENT (CHICAGO EDITION).
Sorkins Directories, Inc., 1001 Craig Rd., Ste. 260, St. Louis, MO 63146. TEL 314-872-2101. FAX 314-872-2102. *1595*

SOURCEMEX.
University of New Mexico, Latin American Institute, 801 Yale N.E., Albuquerque, NM 87131-1016. TEL 505-277-6839. FAX 505-277-5989.
Producer(s): NISC (Latin American Studies - Vol.2). *1289*

SOURCES OF SUPPLY - BUYERS GUIDE.
William O. Dannhausen Corp., Drawer 795, Park Ridge, IL 60068. TEL 847-823-3145. FAX 847-696-3445. *5572*

SOUTH AFRICAN CRIMINAL LAW REPORTS.
Juta & Co. Ltd., P.O. Box 14373, Kenwyn 7790, South Africa. TEL 27-21-7975101. FAX 27-21-7970121. *4095*

SOUTH AFRICAN LABOUR LIBRARY.
Juta & Co. Ltd., P.O. Box 14373, Kenwyn 7790, South Africa. TEL 27-21-7975101. FAX 27-21-7970121.
Available only on CD-ROM. *1453*

SOUTH AFRICAN LAW REPORTS.
Juta & Co. Ltd., P.O. Box 14373, Kenwyn 7790, South Africa. TEL 27-21-7975101. FAX 27-21-7970121. *4026*

SOUTH AFRICAN STATUTES.
Juta & Co. Ltd., P.O. Box 14373, Kenwyn 7790, South Africa. TEL 27-21-7975101. FAX 27-21-7970121.
Available only on CD-ROM. *4026*

SOUTH ASIAN SURVEY.
Sage Publications India Pvt. Ltd., P.O. Box 4215, New Delhi 110 048, India. TEL 91-11-644-4958. FAX 91-11-647-2426.
Producer(s): SilverPlatter Information, Inc. *3539*

SOUTH CAROLINA BUSINESS DIRECTORY.
American Business Directories, 5711 S. 86th Circle, Box 27347, Omaha, NE 68127. TEL 402-593-4600. FAX 402-331-5481. *1712*

SOUTH CAROLINA MANUFACTURERS REGISTER.
Manufacturers' News, Inc., 1633 Central St., Evanston, IL 60201-1569. TEL 847-864-7000. FAX 847-332-1100. *1712*

SOUTH DAKOTA BUSINESS DIRECTORY.
American Business Directories, 5711 S. 86th Circle, Box 27347, Omaha, NE 68127. TEL 402-593-4600. FAX 402-331-5481. *1713*

SOUTHEAST ASIAN JOURNAL OF TROPICAL MEDICINE AND PUBLIC HEALTH.
Southeast Asian Ministers of Education Organisation (SEAMEO), Regional Tropical Medicine & Public Health Network (TROPMED), 420-6 Rajvithi Rd., Bangkok 10400, Thailand. TEL 66-2-2457193. FAX 66-2-2477721. *4844*

SOUTHEAST POWER REPORT.
McGraw-Hill Companies, 1221 Ave. of the Americas, New York, NY 10020. TEL 212-512-2000.
Producer(s): SilverPlatter Information, Inc. (McGraw-Hill Energy Library). *2679*

SOUTHERN AFRICAN BOOKS IN PRINT.
Books in Print Information Services, P.O. Box 15129, Vlaeberg 8018, South Africa. FAX 27-21-4615467. *564*

SOUTHERN CALIFORNIA BUSINESS DIRECTORY.
American Business Directories, 5711 S. 86th Circle, Box 27347, Omaha, NE 68127. TEL 402-593-4600. FAX 402-331-5481. *1713*

THE SOUTHERN REVIEW.
Louisiana State University, 43 Allen Hall, Baton Rouge, LA 70803-5005. TEL 504-388-5108. FAX 504-388-5098. *4469*

SPACE FORUM.
Gordon and Breach - Harwood Academic, Amsteldisk 166, 1st Fl., 1079 LH Amsterdam, Netherlands. *79*

SPECIAL EDUCATION LAW AND LITIGATION TREATISE.
L R P Publications, 747 Dresher Rd., Box 980, Horsham, PA 19044-0980. TEL 215-784-0941. FAX 215-784-9639. *2590*

SPECIALIST.
Doctor Publications (Pvt) Ltd., P.O. Box 8766, Raja Ghazanfar Ali Rd., Saddar, Karachi, Pakistan. TEL 92-21-5688791. FAX 92-21-5689860. *4747*

SPECIFICATION.
E M A P - Architecture, 33-39 Bowling Green Ln., London EC1R 0DA, England. TEL 44-171-837-1212. FAX 44-171-833-8072. *913*

SPEEDNEWS.
Speednews, Inc., 1801 Ave. of the Stars, Ste. 210, Los Angeles, CA 90067-5904. TEL 310-203-9603. FAX 310-203-9352. *7078*

SPINE (PHILADELPHIA, 1976).
Lippincott - Raven Publishers, 227 E. Washington Sq., Philadelphia, PA 19106. TEL 215-238-4200. FAX 215-238-4227. *5016*

SPORTS MEDICINE, TRAINING AND REHABILITATION.
Gordon and Breach - Harwood Academic, Amsteldisk 166, 1st Fl., 1079 LH Amsterdam, Netherlands. *5133*

SPORTSEARCH.
Sport Information Resource Centre (SIRC), 1600 James Naismith Drive, Gloucester, ON K1B 5N4, Canada. TEL 613-748-5658. FAX 613-748-5701.
Producer(s): SilverPlatter Information, Inc. *6797*

STAFFETTA QUOTIDIANA.
Rivista Italiana Petrolio s.r.l., Via Aventina 19, 00153 Rome, Italy. TEL 39-6-5741208. FAX 39-6-5754306. *5623*

STANDARD & POOR'S CORPORATE REGISTERED BOND INTEREST RECORD.
Standard & Poor's Corporation, 25 Broadway, New York, NY 10004. TEL 212-208-8000. *1408*

STANDARD & POOR'S CORPORATION RECORDS.
Standard & Poor's, 25 Broadway, New York, NY 10004. TEL 212-208-8000. FAX 212-412-0459. *1408*

STANDARD & POOR'S CORPORATION RECORDS. DAILY NEWS SECTION.
Standard & Poor's, 25 Broadway, New York, NY 10004. TEL 212-208-8000. *1003*

STANDARD & POOR'S REGISTER OF CORPORATIONS, DIRECTORS AND EXECUTIVES.
Standard & Poor's, 25 Broadway, New York, NY 10004. TEL 212-208-8000. *1507*

STANDARD & POOR'S STOCK REPORTS. AMERICAN STOCK EXCHANGE.
Standard & Poor's, 25 Broadway, New York, NY 10004. TEL 212-208-8000. *1409*

STANDARD & POOR'S STOCK REPORTS. N A S D A Q AND REGIONAL EXCHANGES.
Standard & Poor's, 25 Broadway, New York, NY 10004. TEL 212-208-8000. *1409*

STANDARD & POOR'S STOCK REPORTS. NEW YORK STOCK EXCHANGE.
Standard & Poor's, 25 Broadway, New York, NY 10004. TEL 212-208-8000. *1409*

STANDARD DIRECTORY OF ADVERTISERS (GEOGRAPHIC EDITION).
National Register Publishing, A Division of Reed Elsevier Inc., 121 Chanlon Rd., New Providence, NJ 07974. TEL 908-464-6800. FAX 908-464-3553.
Producer(s): Bowker Electronic Publishing. *1713*

STANDARD DIRECTORY OF ADVERTISING AGENCIES.
National Register Publishing, A Division of Reed Elsevier Inc., 121 Chanlon Rd., New Providence, NJ 07974. TEL 908-464-6800. FAX 908-464-3500.
Producer(s): Bowker Electronic Publishing. *1713*

STANDARD DIRECTORY OF INTERNATIONAL ADVERTISERS AND AGENCIES.
National Register Publishing, A Division of Reed Elsevier Inc., 121 Chanlon Rd., New Providence, NJ 07974. TEL 908-464-6800. FAX 908-665-6688.
Producer(s): Bowker Electronic Publishing. *1714*

STANDARD FEDERAL TAX REPORTS.
C C H Incorporated, 2700 Lake Cook Rd., Riverwoods, IL 60015. TEL 847-267-7000. FAX 800-224-8299. *1628*

STANDARD PERIODICAL DIRECTORY.
Oxbridge Communications, Inc., 150 Fifth Ave., New York, NY 10011. TEL 212-741-0231. FAX 212-633-2938. *564*

STAPLES' GUIDE TO NEW ZEALAND INCOME TAX PRACTICE.
Brooker's Limited, Level 1 - Telecom Networks House, 68-86 Jervois Quay, Wellington, New Zealand. TEL 64-4-4998178. FAX 64-4-4998173. *1628*

STATE ACADEMIES OF SCIENCE ABSTRACTS.
AcadSci, Inc., Box 4157, Huntington, WV 25729. TEL 304-696-6742. FAX 304-696-3243. *6592*

STATE ADMINISTRATIVE OFFICIALS.
Council of State Governments, 3560 Iron Works Pike, Box 11910, Lexington, KY 40578-1910. TEL 606-244-8000. FAX 606-244-8001. *6194*

STATE TAX GUIDE.
C C H Incorporated, 2700 Lake Cook Rd., Riverwoods, IL 60015. TEL 847-267-7000. FAX 800-224-8299. *1628*

STATE TAX NOTES.
Tax Analysts, 6830 N. Fairfax Dr., Arlington, VA 22213. TEL 703-533-4400. FAX 703-533-4444. *1628*

STATE TAX ONEDISC.
Tax Analysts, 6830 N. Fairfax Dr., Arlington, VA 22213. TEL 703-533-4600. FAX 703-533-4444.
Available only on CD-ROM. *1628*

STATE TAX REPORTS.
C C H Incorporated, 2700 Lake Cook Rd., Riverwoods, IL 60015. TEL 847-267-7000. FAX 800-224-8299. *1628*

STATE YELLOW BOOK.
Leadership Directories, Inc., 104 Fifth Ave., 2nd Fl., New York, NY 10011. TEL 212-627-4140. FAX 212-645-0931.
Producer(s): Chadwyck-Healey Inc. *6196*

STATISTICAL REFERENCE INDEX.
Congressional Information Service, Inc., A member of the LEXIS-NEXIS family, 4520 East-West Hwy., Bethesda, MD 20814-3389. TEL 301-654-1550. FAX 301-654-4033. *6943*

STATISTICS.
Gordon and Breach - Harwood Academic, Amsteldisk 166, 1st Fl., 1079 LH Amsterdam, Netherlands. *6944*

STATISTIK UDEN GRAENSER.
Danmarks Statistik, Sejroegade 11, DK-2100 Copenhagen Oe, Denmark. TEL 45-31-17-31-50. FAX 45-31-18-48-01.
Available only on CD-ROM. *6945*

STATISTISCHES JAHRBUCH FUER DIE BUNDESREPUBLIK DEUTSCHLAND.
Statistisches Bundesamt, 65180 Wiesbaden, Germany. TEL 49-611-75-1. FAX 49-611-724000. *6945*

STEELS ALERT.
Cambridge Scientific Abstracts, 7200 Wisconsin Ave., Bethesda, MD 20814. TEL 301-961-6750. FAX 301-961-6720.
Producer(s): Knight-Ridder, Inc. *5221*

STEPFAMILIES.
Stepfamily Association of America, 215 Centennial Mall S., Ste. 212, Lincoln, NE 68508. TEL 402-477-7837. FAX 402-477-8317. *6734*

STEUERGESETZE PLUS.
Verlag C.H. Beck, 80791 Munich, Germany. TEL 49-89-38189338. FAX 49-89-38189398.
Available only on CD-ROM. *1629*

STEUERVERANLAGUNGEN C D - R O M.
Verlag C.H. Beck, 80791 Munich, Germany. TEL 49-89-38189338. FAX 49-89-38189398.
Available only on CD-ROM. *1629*

STEVENS ENVIRONMENTAL SOURCEBOOK.
Stevens Publishing Corporation, 3700 J.H. Kultgen Frwy., Waco, TX 76706. TEL 817-776-9000. FAX 817-776-9018. *2952*

STOCHASTICS AND STOCHASTICS REPORTS.
Gordon and Breach - Harwood Academic, Amsteldisk 166, 1st Fl., 1079 LH Amsterdam, Netherlands. *4608*

10024   SERIALS AVAILABLE ON CD-ROM

STOCKS IN THE S & P 500. OFFICIAL SERIES.
Standard & Poor's, 25 Broadway, New York, NY 10004. TEL 212-208-8000. *1410*

STRESS.
Gordon and Breach - Harwood Academic, Amsteldisk 166, 1st Fl., 1079 LH Amsterdam, Netherlands. *4748*

STRUCTURAL SURVEY.
M C B University Press Ltd., 60-62 Toller Ln., Bradford, W. Yorks BD8 9BY, England. TEL 44-1274-777700. FAX 44-1274-785200. *914*

STRUCTURE.
Current Biology Ltd., 400 Market St., Ste. 700, Philadelphia, PA 19106. FAX 215-574-2270. *628*

STRUCTURIST.
Eli Bornstein, Ed. & Pub., Box 378, RPO University, University of Saskatchewan, Saskatoon, SK S7N 4J8, Canada. TEL 306-966-4198. FAX 306-966-8670.
Producer(s): H.W. Wilson. *467*

STUDIES IN INFORMATICS AND CONTROL.
Research Institute for Informatics, 8-10 Averescu Ave., 71316 Bucharest 1, Rumania. TEL 40-1-2223778. FAX 40-1-3128539. *4234*

STUDY ABROAD.
UNESCO Publishing, 7 Place de Fontenoy, 75352 Paris 07 SP, France. TEL 33-1-45684300. FAX 33-1-45685741. *2567*

STYLE (EDITION FRANCAISE).
N.V. Trends Magazines, Bd. Louis Schmidt 97, 1040 Brussels, Belgium. TEL 32-2-7321860. FAX 32-2-7344018. *3255*

STYLE (NEDERLANDSE EDITIE).
N.V. Trends Magazines, Bd. Louis Schmidt 97, 1040 Brussels, Belgium. TEL 32-2-7321860. FAX 32-2-7344018. *3255*

SUBJECT GUIDE TO BOOKS IN PRINT.
R.R. Bowker, A Division of Reed Elsevier Inc., 121 Chanlon Rd., New Providence, NJ 07974. TEL 908-464-6800. FAX 908-665-3502.
Producer(s): Bowker Electronic Publishing (Books In Print PLUS). *564*

SUBJECT GUIDE TO CHILDREN'S BOOKS IN PRINT.
R.R. Bowker, A Division of Reed Elsevier Inc., 121 Chanlon Rd., New Providence, NJ 07974. TEL 908-464-6800. FAX 908-665-3502.
Producer(s): Bowker Electronic Publishing. *564*

SUDAN MEDICAL JOURNAL.
Khartoum University Press, P.O. Box 321, Khartoum, Sudan. *4748*

SUEDDEUTSCHE ZEITUNG.
Sueddeutscher Verlag GmbH, Sendlingerstr. 8, 80331 Munich, Germany. TEL 49-89-2183-0. FAX 49-89-2183787. *3291*

SULFUR LETTERS.
Gordon and Breach - Harwood Academic, Amsteldisk 166, 1st Fl., 1079 LH Amsterdam, Netherlands. *1768*

SULFUR REPORTS.
Gordon and Breach - Harwood Academic, Amsteldisk 166, 1st Fl., 1079 LH Amsterdam, Netherlands. *1768*

SUNDAY TELEGRAPH.
Telegraph plc., 1 Canada Sq., Canary Wharf, London E14 5DT, England. TEL 44-171-513-2504. FAX 44-171-538-6242.
Producer(s): Chadwyck-Healey Inc. *3301*

THE SUNDAY TIMES.
Times Newspapers Ltd., 1 Virginia St., London E1 9XT, England. TEL 44-171-782-6000. FAX 44-171-782-6250.
Producer(s): Chadwyck-Healey Inc. *3301*

SUOMEN KIRJALLISUUS.
Helsingin Yliopiston Kirjasto, Unioninkatu 36, FIN-00014 Helsinki, University of Helsinki, Finland. FAX 358-0-70844341. *564*

SUPERCOMPUTING PROCEEDINGS.
I E E E Computer Society Press, 10662 Los Vaqueros Circle, Los Alamitos, CA 90720-1264. TEL 714-821-8380. FAX 714-821-4641. *2159*

SUPERCONDUCTIVITY REVIEW.
Gordon and Breach - Harwood Academic, Amsteldisk 166, 1st Fl., 1079 LH Amsterdam, Netherlands. *2653*

SUPRAMOLECULAR CHEMISTRY.
Gordon and Breach - Harwood Academic, Amsteldisk 166, 1st Fl., 1079 LH Amsterdam, Netherlands. *1768*

SURFACE-MOUNTED DISCRETES D.A.T.A. DIGEST.
D.A.T.A. Business Publishing, 15 Inverness Way E., Box 6510, Englewood, CO 80155-6510. FAX 303-799-4082. *2847*

SURFACE-MOUNTED INTEGRATED CIRCUITS D.A.T.A. DIGEST.
D.A.T.A. Business Publishing, 15 Inverness Way E., Box 6510, Englewood, CO 80155-6510. FAX 303-799-4082. *2847*

SURFACE TREATMENT TECHNOLOGY ABSTRACTS.
Finishing Publications Ltd., 105 Whitney Dr., Stevenage, Herts. SG1 4DF, England. TEL 01438-745115. FAX 01438-364536. *5221*

SURGICAL PRODUCT COMPARISON SYSTEM.
E C R I, 5200 Butler Pike, Plymouth Meeting, PA 19462. TEL 610-825-6000. FAX 610-834-1275.
Producer(s): Knight-Ridder, Inc. *5155*

SURGICAL RESEARCH COMMUNICATIONS.
Gordon and Breach - Harwood Academic, Amsteldisk 166, 1st Fl., 1079 LH Amsterdam, Netherlands. *5155*

SWEET'S CANADIAN CONSTRUCTION CATALOGUE.
McGraw-Hill Information Systems Company of Canada, 270 Yorkland Blvd., North York, ON M2J 1R8, Canada. TEL 416-496-3100. FAX 416-496-3123. *915*

SWISS FINANCIAL YEAR BOOK.
Elvetica Edizioni S.A., Via Vela 6, Casella Postale 134, CH-6834 Morbio, Switzerland. TEL 091-435056. FAX 091-437605. *1291*

SYNOPSIS OF BOILER & PRESSURE VESSEL LAWS, RULES AND REGULATIONS.
Uniform Boiler & Pressure Vessel Laws Society, Inc., 308 N. Evergreen Rd., Ste. 240, Louisville, KY 40243-1076. TEL 502-244-6029. *2901*

SYNTHESIS - REGENERATION: A MAGAZINE OF GREEN SOCIAL THOUGHT.
W D Press, Box 24115, St. Louis, MO 63130. TEL 314-727-5393. *2953*

SYS ADMIN.
Miller Freeman, Inc. (Lawrence), 1601 W. 23rd St., Ste. 200, Lawrence, KS 66046. TEL 913-841-1631. FAX 913-841-2624. *2146*

SYSTEM UBW.
Ahriman Verlag GmbH, Stuebeweg 60, 79108 Freiburg, Germany. TEL 49-761-502303. FAX 49-761-502247. *6156*

T E S S.
Educational Products Information Exchange (EPIE) Institute, 103-3 W. Montauk Hwy., Hampton Bays, NY 11946-4006. TEL 516-728-9100. FAX 516-728-9228.
Available only on CD-ROM. *2219*

T O M.
Information Access Company, 362 Lakeside Dr., Foster City, CA 94404. TEL 415-378-5200. FAX 415-378-5369. *2504*

T R I S ELECTRONIC BIBLIOGRAPHIC DATA BASE.
U.S. National Research Council, Transportation Research Board, 2101 Constitution Ave., N.W., Washington, DC 20418. TEL 202-334-3250. FAX 202-334-3495.
Producer(s): SilverPlatter Information, Inc. *7058*

DIE TAGESZEITUNG.
T A Z Verlagsgenossenschaft e.G., Kochstr. 18, 10969 Berlin, Germany. TEL 49-30-25902-0. FAX 49-30-2518095. *3291*

TAIWAN BICYCLES & PARTS GUIDE (YEAR).
Trade Winds, Inc., No. 7, Lane 75, Yungkang St., P.O. Box 7-179, Taipei, Taiwan 10602, Republic of China. TEL 02-393-2718. FAX 02-396-4022. *1714*

TAIWAN GOLF EQUIPMENT BUYERS' GUIDE.
Trade Winds, Inc., No. 7, Lane 75, Yungkang St., P.O. Box 7-179, Taipei, Taiwan 10602, People's Republic of China. TEL 886-2-3913251. FAX 886-2-3964022. *6819*

TAIWAN TOY BUYER'S GUIDE.
Trade Winds, Inc., No. 7, Lane 75, Yungkang St., P.O. Box 7-179, Taipei, Taiwan 10602, Republic of China. TEL 02-393-2718. FAX 02-396-4022. *3451*

TAIWAN YELLOW PAGES.
Taiwan Yellow Pages Corp., Chouwoo House 2F, P.O. Box 84-84, 57 Tunhwa S. Rd., Sec. 1, Taipei, Taiwan, Republic of China. TEL 886-2-570-9966. FAX 886-2-578-2739. *1715*

TAX ANALYST MICROFICHE DATABASE.
Tax Analysts, 6830 Fairfax Dr., Arlington, VA 22213. TEL 703-533-4400. FAX 703-533-4444. *1630*

TAX ANALYSTS LETTER RULING SERVICE.
Tax Analysts, 6830 N. Fairfax Dr., Arlington, VA 22213. TEL 703-553-4400. FAX 703-533-4444. *1630*

THE TAX DIRECTORY.
Tax Analysts, 6830 N. Fairfax Dr., Arlington, VA 22213. TEL 703-553-4400. FAX 703-533-4444. *1630*

TAX, ESTATE & FINANCIAL PLANNING FOR THE ELDERLY.
Matthew Bender & Co., Inc., 2 Park Ave., New York, NY 10016. TEL 212-448-2000. *3446*

THE TAX EXECUTIVE.
Tax Executives Institute, Inc., 1001 Pennsylvania Ave., N.W., No. 320, Washington, DC 20004-2505. TEL 202-638-5601. FAX 202-638-5607. *1630*

TAX LIBRARY.
Juta & Co. Ltd., P.O. Box 14373, Kenwyn 7790, South Africa. TEL 27-21-7975101. FAX 27-21-7970121.
Available only on CD-ROM. *1631*

TAX MANAGEMENT COUNTRY PORTFOLIOS.
Tax Management, Inc., Heron House, 10 Dean Farrar St., London SW1H 0DX, England. TEL 44-171-222-8831. FAX 44-171-222-5550. *1631*

TAX MANAGEMENT'S MULTISTATE TAX PORTFOLIO SERIES.
Tax Management, Inc., 1250 23rd St., N.W., Washington, DC 20037-1166. TEL 202-833-7240. FAX 202-833-7297. *1632*

TAX NOTES.
Tax Analysts, 6830 N. Fairfax Dr., Arlington, VA 22213. TEL 703-533-4400. FAX 703-533-4444. *1633*

TAX TREATIES (RIVERWOODS).
C C H Incorporated, 2700 Lake Cook Rd., Riverwoods, IL 60015. TEL 847-267-7000. FAX 800-224-8299. *1633*

TAX TREATIES DATA BASE ON C D - R O M.
I B F D Publications B.V., P.O. Box 20237, 1000 HE Amsterdam, Netherlands. TEL 31-20-6267726. FAX 31-20-6228658. *1633*

TAXATION IN LATIN AMERICA.
I B F D Publications B.V., P.O. Box 20237, 1000 HE Amsterdam, Netherlands. TEL 31-20-6267726. FAX 31-20-6228658. *1634*

TEACHING PRE K-8.
Early Years, Inc., 40 Richards Ave., Norwalk, CT 06854-2309. TEL 203-855-2650. FAX 203-855-2656. *2621*

TECHNICAL ANALYSIS OF STOCKS & COMMODITIES.
Technical Analysis, Inc., 4757 California Ave., S.W., Seattle, WA 98116-4499. TEL 206-938-0570. FAX 206-938-1307. *1411*

TECHNICAL GUIDE BOOK.
Screenprinting & Graphic Imaging Association International, 10015 Main St., Fairfax, VA 22031. TEL 703-385-1335. *6086*

TECHNIQUES.
American Vocational Association, 1410 King St., Alexandria, VA 22314. TEL 703-683-3111. FAX 703-683-7424.
Producer(s): UMI. *2621*

TECHNOMARK REGISTER. CONTRACT PACKAGERS & MANUFACTURERS - EUROPE.
Technomark Consulting Services Ltd., King House, London W2 4UA, England. TEL 44-171-229-9239. FAX 44-171-792-2587. *1715*

TECHNOMARK REGISTER. EUROPEAN CONTRACT RESEARCH ORGANISATIONS. CLINICAL RESEARCH.
Technomark Consulting Services Ltd., King House, London W2 4UA, England. TEL 44-171-229-9239. FAX 44-171-792-2587. *1715*

TECHNOMARK REGISTER. EUROPEAN CONTRACT RESEARCH ORGANISATIONS. TOXICOLOGY & ANALYSIS.
Technomark Consulting Services Ltd., King House, London W2 4UA, England. TEL 44-171-229-9239. FAX 44-171-792-2587. *1715*

TELECOM SOURCES.
Asian Sources Media Group, G.P.O. Box 12367, Hong Kong, People's Republic of China. TEL 852-2555-4777. *2004*

TELEFACTS.
Datapro Research Group, McGraw-Hill House, Shoppenhangers Rd., Maidenhead, Berks. SL6 2QL, England. TEL 01628-773277. *2041*

TELEFAXBUCH DER DEUTSCHEN TELEKOM AG.
Deutsche Telekom Medien GmbH, Wiesenhuettenstr. 18, 60329 Frankfurt a.M., Germany. TEL 069-2682-0. FAX 069-26821101. *2021*

THE TELEGRAPH ON C D - R O M.
Chadwyck-Healey Ltd., The Quorum, Barnwell Rd., Cambridge CB5 8SW, England. TEL 44-1223-215512. FAX 44-1223-215514.
Available only on CD-ROM. Producer(s): Chadwyck-Healey Inc. *3301*

(YEARS) TELEVISION PROGRAMMING SOURCE BOOKS.
North American Publishing Co., 401 N. Broad St., Philadelphia, PA 19108. TEL 215-238-5300. FAX 215-238-5457. *2063*

TENNESSEE BUSINESS DIRECTORY.
American Business Directories, 5711 S. 86th Circle, Box 27347, Omaha, NE 68127. TEL 402-593-4600. FAX 402-331-5481. *1715*

TENNESSEE RULES OF COURT, STATE AND FEDERAL.
West Group, 620 Opperman Dr., Eagan, MN 55123. TEL 612-687-8000. FAX 612-687-7302. *4139*

TESTZENTRALE TESTKATALOG.
Hogrefe Verlag GmbH und Co. KG, Rohnsweg 25, 37085 Goettingen, Germany. TEL 49-551-49609-0. FAX 49-551-4960988. *6162*

TEXAS ALMANAC AND STATE INDUSTRIAL GUIDE.
Dallas Morning News, Box 655237, Dallas, TX 75265. TEL 214-977-8261. FAX 214-977-8120. *6947*

TEXAS BUSINESS DIRECTORY.
American Business Directories, 5711 S. 86th Circle, Box 27347, Omaha, NE 68127. TEL 402-593-4600. FAX 402-331-5481. *1716*

TEXAS MANUFACTURERS REGISTER.
Manufacturers' News, Inc., 1633 Central St., Evanston, IL 60201. TEL 847-864-7000. FAX 847-332-1100. *1716*

DIE TEXTIL-INDUSTRIE UND IHRE HELFER.
Industrieschau-Verlagsgesellschaft mbH, Postfach 100262, 64202 Darmstadt, Germany. TEL 49-6151-3892-0. FAX 49-6151-33164. *6995*

TEXTILE TECHNOLOGY DIGEST.
Institute of Textile Technology, 2551 Ivy Rd., Charlottesville, VA 22903-4614. TEL 804-296-5511. FAX 804-977-5400. *7000*

TEXTURES AND MICROSTRUCTURES.
Gordon and Breach - Harwood Academic, Amsteldisk 166, 1st Fl., 1079 LH Amsterdam, Netherlands. *2372*

THEOLOGY.
Society for Promoting Christian Knowledge, Holy Trinity Church, Marylebone Rd., London NW1 4DU, England. TEL 44-171-387-5282. FAX 44-171-388-2352. *6378*

THEORETICAL CHEMICAL ENGINEERING.
The Royal Society of Chemistry, Thomas Graham House, Science Park, Milton Rd., Cambridge CB4 4WF, England. TEL 44-1223-420066. FAX 44-1223-423429.
Producer(s): Knight-Ridder, Inc. *2753*

THESAURUS OF E R I C DESCRIPTORS.
Oryx Press, Box 33889, Phoenix, AZ 85067-3889. TEL 602-265-2651. FAX 602-265-6250.
Producer(s): NISC (ERIC). *2504*

THOMAS FOOD INDUSTRY REGISTER.
Thomas Publishing Company, Five Penn Plaza, New York, NY 10001. TEL 212-290-7341. FAX 212-290-8749. *3129*

THOMAS REGISTER OF AMERICAN MANUFACTURERS AND THOMAS REGISTER CATALOG FILE.
Thomas Publishing Company, Five Penn Plaza, New York, NY 10001. TEL 212-290-7277. FAX 212-290-7365. *1552*

THOM'S COMMERCIAL DIRECTORY.
Thom's Directories Ltd., 38 Merrion Sq., Dublin 2, Ireland. TEL 353-1-6767481. FAX 353-1-6762620. *1716*

THOM'S DUBLIN & COUNTY STREET DIRECTORY.
Thom's Directories Ltd., 38 Merrion Sq., Dublin 2, Ireland. TEL 353-1-6767481. FAX 353-1-6762620. *3423*

THORPE - R O M.
D.W. Thorpe, A member of the Reed Elsevier plc group, 18 Salmon St., Port Melbourne, Vic. 3207, Australia. TEL 61-3-92457370. FAX 61-3-92457395.
Available only on CD-ROM. *565*

THYRISTOR D.A.T.A. DIGEST.
D.A.T.A. Business Publishing, 15 Inverness Way E., Box 6510, Englewood, CO 80155-6510. FAX 303-799-4082. *2848*

TIME.
Time Inc., Time & Life Bldg., Rockefeller Center, 1271 Ave. of the Americas, New York, NY 10020-1393. TEL 212-522-1212. FAX 212-522-0003.
Producer(s): UMI. *3387*

THE TIMES.
Times Newspapers Ltd., 1 Virginia St., London E1 9XT, England. TEL 44-171-782-5142. FAX 44-171-782-6132.
Producer(s): Chadwyck-Healey Inc. *3302*

THE TIMES AND THE SUNDAY TIMES COMPACT DISC EDITION.
Chadwyck-Healey Ltd., The Quorum, Barnwell Rd., Cambridge CB5 8SW, England. TEL 44-1223-215512. FAX 44-1223-215514.
Available only on CD-ROM. Producer(s): Chadwyck-Healey Inc. *3302*

TIMES EDUCATIONAL SUPPLEMENT.
Times Supplements Ltd., Admiral House, 66-68 E. Smithfield, London E1 9XY, England. TEL 44-171-782-3000. FAX 44-171-782-3200.
Producer(s): Chadwyck-Healey Inc. *2488*

TIMES HIGHER EDUCATION SUPPLEMENT.
Times Supplements Ltd., Admiral House, 66-68 E. Smithfield, London E1 9XY, England. TEL 44-171-782-3000. FAX 44-171-782-3300.
Producer(s): Chadwyck-Healey Inc. *2557*

TIMES INDEX.
Primary Source Media, P.O. Box 45, Reading RG1 8HF, England. TEL 44-1734-583247. FAX 44-1734-5912325. *3885*

THE TIMES LITERARY SUPPLEMENT INDEX.
Primary Source Media, P.O. Box 45, Reading RG1 8HF, England. TEL 44-1734-583247. FAX 44-1734-591325. *4497*

TOHKAI SEIKEI GEKA GAISHO KENKYU KAISHI.
Tohkai Seikei Geka Gaisho Kenkyukai, Gifu Kenritsu Tajimi Byoin Seikei Geka, 5-161, Maebatacho, Tajimi-shi, Gifu-ken 507, Japan. TEL 81-572-22-5311. FAX 81-572-25-1246. *5017*

TOHKAI SEKITSUI GEKA.
Tohkai Sekitsui Geka Kenkyukai, Gifu Kenritsu Tajimi Byoin, 5-161, Maebatacho, Tajimi-shi, Gifuken 507, Japan. TEL 81-572-22-5311. FAX 81-572-25-1246. *5017*

TOKAI JOURNAL OF EXPERIMENTAL AND CLINICAL MEDICINE.
Tokai Daigaku Shuppansha - Tokai University Press (Kanagawa), Boseidai, Isehara, Kanagawa 259-11, Japan. FAX 0463-91-3328. *4753*

TOMORROW PEOPLE NEWS.
European Network for Information and International Cooperation, Via Col. Romej 7, 91100 Trapani, Italy. TEL 39-923-546700. *1891*

TONGJI MEDICAL UNIVERSITY. JOURNAL.
Tongji Medical University, c/o Prof. Liu Xunfang, Wuhan, Hubei 430030, People's Republic of China. TEL 01-506-6688. FAX 01-506-3101. *4753*

TOP MANAGEMENT BELGIUM - LUXEMBURG.
Alain Renier & Co. S.P.R.L., Ave. des Casernes 41A, 1040 Brussels, Belgium. TEL 32-2-6462740. FAX 32-2-6462017. *1510*

TOXICOLOGICAL AND ENVIRONMENTAL CHEMISTRY.
Gordon and Breach - Harwood Academic, Amsteldisk 166, 1st Fl., 1079 LH Amsterdam, Netherlands. *2981*

TOXICOLOGY ABSTRACTS.
Cambridge Scientific Abstracts, 7200 Wisconsin Ave., 6th Fl., Bethesda, MD 20814. TEL 301-961-6750. FAX 301-961-6720.
Producer(s): Knight-Ridder, Inc. (Toxicology & Pharmacology), SilverPlatter Information, Inc. (POLTOX1). *5702*

TRAINING FOR QUALITY.
M C B University Press Ltd., 60-62 Toller Ln., Bradford, W. Yorks BD8 9BY, England. TEL 44-1274-777700. FAX 44-1274-785200. *1577*

TRANSGENICS.
Gordon and Breach - Harwood Academic, Amsteldisk 166, 1st Fl., 1079 LH Amsterdam, Netherlnads. *777*

TRANSISTOR D.A.T.A. DIGEST.
D.A.T.A. Business Publishing, 15 Inverness Way E., Box 6510, Englewood, CO 80155-6510. FAX 303-799-4082. *2848*

TRANSPORTATION PLANNING AND TECHNOLOGY.
Gordon and Breach - Harwood Academic, Amsteldisk 166, 1st Fl., 1079 LH Amsterdam, Netherlands. *7043*

TRANSPORTATION TELEPHONE TICKLER.
Journal of Commerce, Inc., 2 World Trade Center, 27th fl., New York, NY 10048-0203. TEL 212-837-7000. *1717*

TRENDS.
N.V. Trends Magazines, Bd. Louis Schmidt 97, 1040 Brussels, Belgium. TEL 32-2-7321860. FAX 32-2-7344018. *3255*

TRENDS - TENDANCES.
N.V. Trends Magazines, Bd. Louis Schmidt 97, 1040 Brussels, Belgium. TEL 32-2-7321860. FAX 32-2-7344018. *3255*

TRIBUNALI AMMINISTRATIVI REGIONALI.
Casa Editrice Italedi, Piazza Cavour 19, 00193 Rome, Italy. TEL 39-6-3210803. *4035*

TROENDERBLADET.
Troenderbladet AS, Pottenvegen 11, N-7084 Melhus, Norway. TEL 47-72-87-00-55. FAX 47-72-87-00-55. *3345*

LA TUNISIE MEDICALE.
Societe Tunisienne des Sciences Medicales, 16 Rue Touraine, 1002 Tunis - Belvedere, Tunisia. TEL 216-790-924. FAX 216-796-602. *4754*

TURANG QINSHI YU SHUITU BAOCHI XUEBAO.
Zhongguo Kexueyuan, Xibei Shuitu Baochi Yanjiusuo, Yangling Qu, Xi'an, Shaanxi 712100, People's Republic of China. TEL 86-910-7012412. FAX 86-910-7012210. *248*

TWEETALIGE LOSBLADIGE WETBOEKEN.
Kluwer Editions Juridiques Belgique, Santvoortbeeklaan 21-25, 2100 Deurne - Anvers, Belgium. *4036*

U C DAVIS LAW REVIEW.
University of California at Davis, School of Law, Martin Luther King, Jr. Hall, Davis, CA 95616. TEL 916-752-2551. FAX 916-752-4704. *4036*

U K O P.
Chadwyck-Healey Ltd., The Quorum, Barnwell Rd., Cambridge CB5 8SW, England. TEL 44-1223-215512. FAX 44-1223-215514.
Available only on CD-ROM. Producer(s): Chadwyck-Healey Inc. *6198*

U N B I S PLUS ON C D - R O M.
Chadwyck-Healey Inc., 1101 King St., Ste. 380, Alexandria, VA 22314-2944. TEL 703-683-4890. FAX 703-683-7589.
Available only on CD-ROM. Producer(s): Chadwyck-Healey Inc. *5986*

U S A TODAY INDEX.
U M I, 300 N. Zeeb Rd., Ann Arbor, MI 48106-1346. TEL 313-761-4700. FAX 800-864-0019. *3885*

U S CRUDE OIL, NATURAL GAS, AND NATURAL GAS LIQUIDS RESERVES (YEAR) ANNUAL REPORT.
U.S. Energy Information Administration, National Energy Information Center, EI-231, James Forrestal Bldg., Rm. 1F-048, 1000 Independence Ave., S.W., DC 20585. TEL 202-586-8800. FAX 202-586-0727. *5625*

U S GOVERNMENT PERIODICALS INDEX.
Congressional Information Service, Inc., A member of the LEXIS-NEXIS family, 4520 East-West Hwy., Bethesda, MD 20814-3389. TEL 301-654-1550. FAX 301-654-4033. *27*

U S MARKET FORECASTS.
Editor & Publisher Co., Inc., 11 W. 19th St., New York, NY 10011. TEL 212-675-4380. FAX 212-929-1259. *1552*

U S NEWS & WORLD REPORT.
U S News & World Report Inc., 1290 Ave. of the Americas, Ste. 600, New York, NY 10104. TEL 212-830-1500.
Producer(s): UMI. *3388*

UJ PERIODIKUMOK.
Orszagos Szechenyi Konyvtar, Konyvtartudomanyi es Modszertani Kozpont, Budavari Palota F epulet, 1827 Budapest, Hungary. TEL 36-1-1556967. FAX 36-1-2020804. *565*

ULRICH'S INTERNATIONAL PERIODICALS DIRECTORY.
R.R. Bowker, A Division of Reed Elsevier Inc., 121 Chanlon Rd., New Providence, NJ 07974. TEL 908-665-2847. FAX 908-771-7725.
Producer(s): Bowker Electronic Publishing (Ulrich's PLUS), SilverPlatter Information, Inc. (ERL). *566*

ULRICH'S ON DISC.
R.R. Bowker Electronic Publishing, 121 Chanlon Rd., New Providence, NJ 07974. FAX 908-665-3528.
Available only on CD-ROM. Producer(s): Bowker Electronic Publishing (Ulrich's PLUS). *566*

ULRICH'S UPDATE.
R.R. Bowker, A Division of Reed Elsevier Inc., 121 Chanlon Rd., New Providence, NJ 07974. TEL 908-665-2847. FAX 908-771-7725.
Producer(s): Bowker Electronic Publishing (Ulrich's PLUS). *566*

ULSTER MEDICAL JOURNAL.
Ulster Medical Society, c/o Queens University Medical Library, Institute of Clinical Science, Grosvenor Rd., Belfast BT12 6BA, Northern Ireland. TEL 44-1232-322043. FAX 44-1232-247068.
Producer(s): SilverPlatter Information, Inc. (MEDLINE). *4755*

UNESCO DATABASES.
UNESCO Publishing, 1 rue Miollis, 75732 Paris Cedex 15, France. TEL 33-1-45684300. FAX 33-1-45685741.
Available only on CD-ROM. *566*

UNESCO: RESOLUTIONS AND DECISIONS 1987-1996.
UNESCO Publishing, 7 Place de Fontenoy, 75352 Paris 07 SP, France. TEL 33-1-45684300. FAX 33-1-45685741.
Available only on CD-ROM. *6643*

UNIFORM COMMERCIAL CODE FILING GUIDE.
U C C Guide Inc., Rte. 9W, Southgate Plaza, Box 338, Ravena, NY 12143-1338. TEL 518-156-3366. FAX 800-822-0703. *4087*

UNITED NATIONS. STATISTICAL YEARBOOK.
United Nations Publications, Sales and Marketing Section, Room DC2-0853, New York, NY 10017. TEL 212-963-3802. FAX 212-963-3489. *6950*

UNITED NATIONS DOCUMENTS AND PUBLICATIONS.
NewsBank, Inc., 58 Pine St., New Canaan, CT 06840-5426. TEL 800-752-4650. FAX 203-966-6254. *566*

U.S. BUREAU OF LABOR STATISTICS. C P I DETAILED REPORT.
U.S. Bureau of Labor Statistics, 2 Massachusetts Ave., N.E., Washington, DC 20212. TEL 202-655-4000. *1293*

U.S. CONGRESS. CONGRESSIONAL RECORD.
U.S. Congress, Washington, DC 20515. TEL 202-275-2051. FAX 202-275-0019. *5976*

U.S. DEPARTMENT OF JUSTICE. BUREAU OF JUSTICE STATISTICS. CRIME AND JUSTICE DATA.
Inter-University Consortium for Political and Social Research, National Archive of Criminal Justice Data, Box 1248, Ann Arbor, MI 48106-1248. TEL 313-764-2570. FAX 313-764-8041.
Available only on CD-ROM. *2285*

U.S. ELECTRIC POWER BUSINESS DIRECTORY.
Utility Data Institute, 1200 G St., N.W., Ste. 250, Washington, DC 20005. TEL 202-942-8788. FAX 202-942-8789.
Available only on CD-ROM. *2692*

U.S. ENERGY INFORMATION ADMINISTRATION. ANNUAL ENERGY OUTLOOK.
U.S. Energy Information Administration, National Energy Information Center, EI-231, Forrestal Bldg., Rm. 1F-048, 1000 Independence Ave., S.W., Washington, DC 20585. TEL 202-586-8800. FAX 202-586-0727. *2686*

U.S. ENERGY INFORMATION ADMINISTRATION. ANNUAL ENERGY REVIEW.
U.S. Energy Information Administration, National Energy Information Center, EI-231, James Forrestal Bldg., Rm. 1F-048, 1000 Independence Ave., S.W., Washington, DC 20585. TEL 202-586-8800. FAX 202-586-0727. *2679*

U.S. ENERGY INFORMATION ADMINISTRATION. MONTHLY ENERGY REVIEW.
U.S. Energy Information Administration, National Energy Information Center, EI-231, James Forrestal Bldg., Rm. 1F-048, 1000 Independence Ave., S.W., Washington, DC 20585. TEL 202-586-8800. FAX 202-586-0727. *2686*

U.S. ENERGY INFORMATION ADMINISTRATION. NATURAL GAS ANNUAL.
U.S. Energy Information Administration, National Energy Information Center, EI-231, James Forrestal Bldg., Rm. 1F-048, 1000 Independence Ave., S.W., Washington, DC 20585. TEL 202-586-8800. FAX 202-586-0727. *5626*

U.S. ENERGY INFORMATION ADMINISTRATION. NATURAL GAS MONTHLY.
U.S. Energy Information Administration, National Energy Information Center, EI-231, James Forrestal Bldg., Rm. 1F-048, 1000 Independence Ave., S.W., Washington, DC 20585. TEL 202-586-8800. FAX 202-586-0727. *5626*

U.S. ENERGY INFORMATION ADMINISTRATION. PETROLEUM MARKETING ANNUAL.
U.S. Energy Information Administration, National Energy Information Center, EI-231, James Forrestal Bldg., Rm. 1F-048, Washington, DC 20585. TEL 202-586-8800. FAX 202-586-0727. *5626*

U.S. ENERGY INFORMATION ADMINISTRATION. PETROLEUM SUPPLY ANNUAL.
U.S. Energy Information Administration, National Energy Information Center, EI-231, National Energy Information Center, EI-231, James Forrestal Bldg., Rm. 1F-048, 1000 Independence Ave., S.W., Washington, DC 20585. TEL 202-586-8800. FAX 202-586-0727. *5626*

U.S. ENERGY INFORMATION ADMINISTRATION. PETROLEUM SUPPLY MONTHLY.
U.S. Energy Information Administration, National Energy Information Center, EI-231, James Forrestal Bldg., Rm. 1F-048, 1000 Independence Ave., S.W., Washington, DC 20585. TEL 202-586-8800. FAX 202-586-0727. *5626*

U.S. ENERGY INFORMATION ADMINISTRATION. QUARTERLY COAL REPORT.
U.S. Energy Information Administration, National Energy Information Center, EI-231, c/o Paulette Young, Coal Division, 1000 Independence Ave., S.W., EI-522, DC 20585. TEL 202-586-8800. FAX 202-586-0727. *2680*

U.S. ENERGY INFORMATION ADMINISTRATION. SHORT - TERM ENERGY OUTLOOK.
U.S. Energy Information Administration, National Energy Information Center, EI-231, James Forrestal Bldg., Rm. 1F-048, 1000 Independence Ave., S.W., Washington, DC 20585. TEL 202-586-8800. FAX 202-586-0727. *2680*

U.S. GENERAL SERVICES ADMINISTRATION. CATALOG OF FEDERAL DOMESTIC ASSISTANCE.
U.S. General Services Administration, Publications, 18th and F Sts., N.W., DC 20405. TEL 202-501-1794. FAX 202-501-4281. *6198*

U.S. LIBRARY OF CONGRESS. CATALOGER'S DESKTOP.
U.S. Library of Congress, Cataloging Distribution Service, Washington, DC 20541-5017. TEL 202-707-6100. FAX 202-707-1334.
Available only on CD-ROM. *567*

U.S. LIBRARY OF CONGRESS. CLASSIFICATION PLUS.
U.S. Library of Congress, Cataloguing Distribution Service, Washington, DC 20541-5017. TEL 202-707-6100. FAX 202-707-1334.
Available only on CD-ROM. *4219*

U.S. LIBRARY OF CONGRESS. MUSIC CATALOG ON C D - R O M.
U.S. Library of Congress, Cataloging Distribution Service, Washington, DC 20541-5017. TEL 202-707-6100. FAX 202-707-1334.
Available only on CD-ROM. *568*

U.S. LIBRARY OF CONGRESS. MUSIC CATALOG ON MICROFICHE.
Advanced Library Systems, Inc., 100 Brickstone Sq., Box 246, Andover, MA 01810-0005. TEL 508-470-0610. FAX 508-475-1072.
Producer(s): NISC (Muse). *5449*

U.S. LIBRARY OF CONGRESS. NEW SERIAL TITLES.
U.S. Library of Congress, Cataloging Distribution Service, Washington, DC 20541-5017. TEL 202-707-6100. FAX 202-707-1334. *568*

U.S. OCCUPATIONAL SAFETY AND HEALTH REVIEW COMMISSION. ADMINISTRATIVE LAW JUDGE AND COMMISSION DECISIONS.
U.S. Occupational Safety and Health Review Commission, 1 Lafayette Ctr., 1120 20th St., N.W., 9th Fl., Washington, DC 20036-3419. TEL 202-606-5100. *5501*

U.S. PATENT AND TRADEMARK OFFICE. OFFICIAL GAZETTE. PATENTS.
U.S. Patent and Trademark Office, General Information Services Division, Crystal City Plaza 3, Rm. 2C02, Washington, DC 20231. TEL 703-308-4357. FAX 703-305-7786. *5591*

U.S. PATENT AND TRADEMARK OFFICE. OFFICIAL GAZETTE. TRADEMARKS.
U.S. Patent and Trademark Office, General Information Services Division, Crystal Plaza 3, Rm. 2C02, Washington, DC 20231. TEL 703-308-4357. FAX 703-305-7786. *5591*

UNITED STATES CODE UNANNOTATED.
Gould Publications, 1333 N. U.S. Hwy. 17-92, Longwood, FL 32750-3724. TEL 407-695-9500. FAX 407-695-9500. *4037*

UNIVERSITY OF ALEXANDRIA. FACULTY OF MEDICINE. BULLETIN.
University of Alexandria, Faculty of Medicine, 22 Sharia al-Gaish, Al-Shatby, Alexandria, Egypt. *4756*

UNIVERSITY OF COLORADO LAW REVIEW.
University of Colorado Law Review, 290 Fleming Law Bldg., Campus Box 401, Boulder, CO 80309-0401. TEL 303-492-6145. FAX 303-492-1200. *4039*

UNIVERSITY OF MANCHESTER. DEPARTMENT OF COMPUTER SCIENCE. TECHNICAL REPORT SERIES.
University of Manchester, Department of Computer Science, Oxford Rd., Manchester M13 9PL, England. TEL 44-161-275-6130. FAX 44-161-275-6236. *2159*

UNIVERSITY OF PENNSYLVANIA LAW REVIEW.
University of Pennsylvania Law Review, 3400 Chestnut St., Philadelphia, PA 19104-6204. TEL 215-898-7060. FAX 215-573-2005. *4039*

UNSERE FAMILIE.
Verlag Friedrich Bischoff GmbH, Postfach 110242, 60037 Frankfurt a.M., Germany. TEL 49-69-2696-0. FAX 49-69-252915. *6499*

UPSTATE NEW YORK BUSINESS DIRECTORY.
American Business Directories, 5711 S. 86th Circle, Box 27347, Omaha, NE 68127. TEL 402-593-4600. FAX 402-331-5481. *1720*

URBADISC C D - R O M.
London Research Centre, Research Library, 81 Black Prince Rd., London SE1 7SZ, England. TEL 44-171-627-9661. FAX 44-171-627-8674. Available only on CD-ROM. *3768*

URBAN ABSTRACTS.
London Research Centre, Research Library, 81 Black Prince Rd., London SE1 7SZ, England. TEL 44-171-627-9666. FAX 44-171-627-9674. *6208*

UTAH BUSINESS DIRECTORY.
American Business Directories, 5711 S. 86th Circle, Box 27347, Omaha, NE 68127. TEL 402-593-4600. FAX 402-331-5481. *1720*

UTILITY ENVIRONMENT REPORT.
McGraw-Hill, Inc., Energy & Business Newsletters, 1221 Ave. of the Americas, 36th Fl., New York, NY 10020. TEL 212-512-6410.
Producer(s): SilverPlatter Information, Inc. (McGraw-Hill Energy Library). *2849*

V A R D S REPORT.
Financial Planning Resources, Inc., Box 1927, Roswell, GA 30077-1927. TEL 404-998-5186. FAX 404-998-5187. *3836*

V K E.
Josef Keller Verlag, Postfach 1455, 82317 Starnberg, Germany. TEL 49-8151-771144. FAX 49-8151-771152.
Available only on CD-ROM. *2069*

V L M - VERZEICHNIS LIEFERBARER MUSIKALIEN C D - R O M.
Buchhaendler-Vereinigung GmbH, Postfach 100442, 60004 Frankfurt a.M., Germany. TEL 49-69-13060. FAX 49-69-1306201.
Available only on CD-ROM. *5449*

V L S I DESIGN.
Gordon and Breach - Harwood Academic, Amsteldisk 166, 1st Fl., 1079 LH Amsterdam, Netherlands. *2116*

V M R STANDARD USED CAR PRICES.
V M R International, Inc., 41 N. Main St., N. Grafton, MA 01536. TEL 508-839-6707. FAX 508-839-6266. *7120*

V O, VIE OUVRIERE.
Revue Vie Ouvriere Inc., 1215 Visitation, Ste. 101, Montreal, PQ H2L 3B5, Canada. TEL 514-523-5998. FAX 514-527-3403. *3267*

V R S.
Erich Schmidt Verlag GmbH & Co. (Berlin), Genthiner Str. 30G, 10785 Berlin, Germany. TEL 49-30-2500850. FAX 49-30-25008521. *4057*

V V B - VERZEICHNIS VERGRIFFENER BUECHER C D - R O M.
Buchhaendler-Vereinigung GmbH, Postfach 100442, 60004 Frankfurt a.M., Germany. TEL 49-69-1306-0. FAX 49-69-1306201.
Available only on CD-ROM. *569*

VAARD I NORDEN.
Sykepleiernes Samarbeid i Norden, P.O. Box 2681, St. Hanshaugen, N-131 Oslo 1, Norway. TEL 47-22-04-33-04. FAX 47-22-38-02-30. *4951*

VADEMECUM DEUTSCHER LEHR- UND FORSCHUNGSSTAETTEN. STAETTEN DER FORSCHUNG.
Dr. Josef Raabe Verlags GmbH, Postfach 103922, 70034 Stuttgart, Germany. TEL 49-711-62900-0. FAX 49-711-6290010. *6582*

VADEMECUM VOOR HET VERZEKERINGSWEZEN.
Nijgh Periodieken B.V., Postbus 122, 3100 AC Schiedam, Netherlands. TEL 31-10-4274100. FAX 31-10-4739911. *3836*

VANDERBILT RUBBER HANDBOOK.
R.T. Vanderbilt Co., Inc., 30 Winfield St., Norwalk, CT 06855. TEL 203-853-1400. FAX 203-853-1452. *6505*

VARIETY'S VIDEO DIRECTORY ON DISC.
R.R. Bowker, A Division of Reed Elsevier Inc., 121 Chanlon Rd., New Providence, NJ 07974. TEL 908-665-2866. FAX 908-665-3528.
Available only on CD-ROM. Producer(s): Bowker Electronic Publishing. *5347*

VARLIK.
Varlik Yayinlari A.S., Cagaloglu Yokusu 40-2, Istanbul 34440, Turkey. TEL 90-212-5129528. FAX 90-212-5226924. *4483*

VARTA - FUEHRER.
VARTA - Fuehrer GmbH, Luetzerodestr. 10, 30161 Hannover, Germany. TEL 49-511-3401310. FAX 49-511-3401319. *3737*

VATRA.
Uniunea Scriitorilor din Romania, Inspectoratul pentru Cultura al Judetului Mures, Str. Primariei, Nr. 1, 4300 Tirgu-Mures, Rumania. TEL 40-65-165008. *4364*

VENDOR CATALOG SERVICES INDEX.
Information Handling Services, 15 Inverness Way E., Englewood, CO 80150. TEL 303-790-0600. FAX 303-799-4085. *1720*

VERBAENDE, BEHOERDEN, ORGANISATIONEN DER WIRTSCHAFT.
Verlag Hoppenstedt GmbH, Havelstr. 9, 64295 Darmstadt, Germany. TEL 49-6151-380-0. FAX 49-6151-380-360. *1294*

VERFAHRENSTECHNISCHE BERICHTE.
Bayer AG, Abteilung Publikationen, 51368 Leverkusen, Germany. *2753*

VERMONT BUSINESS DIRECTORY.
American Business Directories, 5711 S. 86th Circle, Box 27347, Omaha, NE 68127. TEL 402-593-4600. FAX 402-331-5481. *1720*

VERZEICHNIS AUSLAENDISCHER ZEITSCHRIFTEN IN SCHWEIZERISCHEN BIBLIOTHEKEN.
Schweizerische Landesbibliothek, Hallwylstr. 15, CH-3003 Bern, Switzerland. TEL 41-31-3228911. FAX 41-31-3228463. *569*

VERZEICHNIS LIEFERBARER BUECHER.
K.G. Saur Verlag KG, A member of the Reed Elsevier plc group, Ortlerstr. 8, 81373 Munich, Germany. TEL 49-89-76902-0. FAX 49-89-76902150.
Producer(s): K.G. Saur Verlag. *569*

VERZEICHNIS LIEFERBARER BUECHER - C D - R O M.
K.G. Saur Verlag KG, A member of the Reed Elsevier plc group, Ortlerstr. 8, 81373 Munich, Germany. TEL 49-89-76902-0. FAX 49-89-76901250.
Available only on CD-ROM. Producer(s): K.G. Saur Verlag. *569*

VICTORIAN STATUTES CUMULATIVE SUPPLEMENT.
L B C Information Services, 50 Waterloo Rd., N. Ryde, N.S.W. 2113, Australia. TEL 61-2-99366444. FAX 61-2-98889706. *4071*

VIDEOLOG.
Trade Service Information Ltd., Cherryholt Rd., Stamford, Lincs. PE9 2HT, England. TEL 44-1780-764331. FAX 44-1780-482067. *2070*

VIE ET SANTE.
Editions Vie et Sante, 60 av. Emile Zola, 77192 Dammarie les Lys Cedex, France. FAX 64-87-00-66. *5792*

VIGILE URBANO.
Maggioli Editore, Viale Vespucci 12-n, Casella Postale 290, 47037 Rimini, Italy. TEL 0541-626777. FAX 0541-622020. *2282*

VIRGINIA BUSINESS DIRECTORY.
American Business Directories, 5711 S. 86th Circle, Box 27347, Omaha, NE 68127. TEL 402-593-4600. FAX 402-331-5481. *1721*

VIRGINIA COURT RULES AND PROCEDURE, STATE AND FEDERAL.
West Group, 620 Opperman Dr., Eagan, MN 55123. TEL 612-687-7302. FAX 612-687-7302. *4140*

VIRGINIA INDUSTRIAL DIRECTORY.
Virginia Chamber of Commerce, 9 S. Fifth St., Richmond, VA 23219. TEL 800-477-7682. FAX 804-783-6112. *1721*

VIRGINIA MANUFACTURERS DIRECTORY.
Manufacturers' News, Inc., 1633 Central St., Evanston, IL 60201. TEL 847-864-7000. FAX 847-332-1100. *1721*

VIROLOGY.
Academic Press, Inc., Journal Division, 525 B St., Ste. 1900, San Diego, CA 92101-4495. TEL 619-230-1840. FAX 619-688-6800. *795*

VIROLOGY AND AIDS ABSTRACTS.
Cambridge Scientific Abstracts, 7200 Wisconsin Ave., 6th Fl., Bethesda, MD 20814. TEL 301-961-6750. FAX 301-961-6720.
Producer(s): SilverPlatter Information, Inc. *4789*

VISUALISATION OF ENGINEERING RESEARCH.
John Wiley & Sons Ltd., Journals, Baffins Ln., Chichester, W. Sussex PO19 1UD, England. TEL 44-1243-779777. FAX 44-1243-843232.
Available only on CD-ROM. *2806*

DE VOLKSKRANT.
P C M Publishers, Wybrantstraat 150, 1091 GR Amsterdam, Netherlands. TEL 31-20-5629111. FAX 31-20-5622122. *3339*

THE WALL STREET JOURNAL INDEX.
U M I, 300 N. Zeeb Rd., Ann Arbor, MI 48106. TEL 313-761-4700. FAX 800-864-0019. *1172*

WALL STREET LETTER.
Institutional Investor Newsletters, 477 Madison Ave., New York, NY 10022. TEL 212-224-3233. FAX 212-224-3353. *1414*

10028 SERIALS AVAILABLE ON CD-ROM

WANG IN THE NEWS.
Publications & Communications, Inc., 12416 Hymeadow, Austin, TX 78750-1849. TEL 512-250-9023. FAX 512-331-3900. *2128*

WARREN'S HEATON ON SURROGATES' COURTS.
Matthew Bender & Co., Inc., 2 Park Ave., New York, NY 10016. TEL 212-448-2000. *4140*

WARTA DEMOGRAFI.
University of Indonesia, Faculty of Economics, Demographic Institute, Jalan Salemba Raya 4, Jakarta 10430, Indonesia. TEL 06221-336434. FAX 06221-3102457. *6060*

WASHINGTON BUSINESS DIRECTORY.
American Business Directories, 5711 S. 86th Circle, Box 27347, Omaha, NE 68127. TEL 402-593-4600. FAX 402-331-5481. *1721*

WASHINGTON COURT RULES, STATE AND FEDERAL.
West Group, 620 Opperman Dr., Eagan, MN 55123. TEL 621-687-8000. FAX 612-687-7302. *4140*

WASHINGTON D.C. AREA BUSINESS DIRECTORY.
American Business Directories, 5711 S. 86th Circle, Box 27347, Omaha, NE 68127. TEL 402-593-4600. FAX 402-331-5481. *1721*

WASHINGTON MANUFACTURERS REGISTER.
Database Publishing Company, 1590 S. Lewis St., Anaheim, CA 92805-6423. TEL 714-778-6400. FAX 714-778-6811. *1721*

THE WASHINGTON POST INDEX.
U M I, 300 N. Zeeb Rd., Ann Arbor, MI 48106. TEL 313-761-4700. FAX 800-864-0019. *3885*

WATER RESOURCES ABSTRACTS (BETHESDA).
Cambridge Scientific Abstracts, 7200 Wisconsin Ave., 6th Fl., Bethesda, MD 20814. TEL 301-961-6750. FAX 301-961-6720.
Producer(s): NISC, SilverPlatter Information, Inc. *7308*

WATER RESOURCES ABSTRACTS (C D - R O M).
National Information Services Corporation (NISC), 3100 St. Paul St., Ste. 806, Baltimore, MD 21218. TEL 410-243-0797. FAX 410-243-0982.
Available only on CD-ROM. Producer(s): NISC. *7308*

WATER RESOURCES WORLDWIDE.
National Information Services Corporation (NISC), 3100 St. Paul St., Ste. 806, Baltimore, MD 21218. TEL 410-243-0797. FAX 410-243-0982.
Available only on CD-ROM. Producer(s): NISC. *7308*

WATERLOW'S SOLICITORS' AND BARRISTERS' DIRECTORY.
Waterlow Legal Publishing, Paulton House, 8 Shepherdess Walk, London N1 7LB, England. TEL 44-171-490-0049. FAX 44-171-253-1308. *4045*

WEATHERWISE.
Heldref Publications, 1319 Eighteenth St., N.W., Washington, DC 20036-1802. TEL 202-296-6267. FAX 202-296-5149.
Producer(s): UMI. *5245*

WEEKEND KNACK.
N.V. R M G, Bd. Louis Schmidt 97, 1040 Brussels, Belgium. TEL 32-2-7361175. FAX 32-2-73444018. *3255*

WEEKLY LAW REPORTS.
Incorporated Council of Law Reporting for England and Wales, 3 Stone Bldgs., Lincoln's Inn, London WC2A 3XN, England. TEL 44-171-242-6471. FAX 44-171-831-5247. *4045*

WER BAUT MASCHINEN IN DEUTSCHLAND.
Verlag Hoppenstedt GmbH, Havelstr. 9, 64295 Darmstadt, Germany. TEL 49-6151-380-0. FAX 49-6151-380-360. *2903*

WER LIEFERT WAS?
Wer Liefert Was? GmbH, Normannenweg 16-20, 20537 Hamburg, Germany. TEL 49-40-25440-0. FAX 49-40-25440100. *1721*

WER LIEFERT WAS? CENTRAL EUROPE.
Wer Liefert Was? GmbH, Normannenweg 16-20, 20537 Hamburg, Germany. TEL 49-40-25440-0. FAX 49-40-25440100. *1721*

WER LIEFERT WAS? LIGHT.
Wer Liefert Was? GmbH, Normannenweg 16-20, 20537 Hamburg, Germany. TEL 49-40-25440-0. FAX 49-40-25440100.
Available only on CD-ROM. *1721*

WEST EUROPEAN POLITICS.
Frank Cass, Newbury House, 890-900 Eastern Ave., Newbury Park, Ilford, Essex 1G2 7HH. TEL 44-181-599-8866. FAX 44-181-599-0954. *6043*

WEST VIRGINIA BUSINESS DIRECTORY.
American Business Directories, 5711 S. 86th Circle, Box 27347, Omaha, NE 68127. TEL 402-593-4600. FAX 402-331-5481. *1722*

WEST VIRGINIA MANUFACTURERS REGISTER.
Manufacturers' News, Inc., 1633 Central St., Evanston, IL 60201. TEL 847-864-7000. FAX 847-332-1100. *1722*

WEST'S ALASKA REPORTER.
West Group, 620 Opperman Dr., Eagan, MN 55123. TEL 312 387-8000. FAX 612-387-7302. *4045*

WEST'S CALIFORNIA REPORTER.
West Group, 620 Opperman Dr., Eagan, MN 55123. TEL 612-687-8000. FAX 612-687-7302. *4045*

WEST'S FEDERAL REPORTER.
West Group, 620 Opperman Dr., Eagan, MN 55123. TEL 612-687-8000. FAX 612-687-7302. *4067*

WEST'S FEDERAL RULES DECISIONS.
West Group, 620 Opperman Dr., Eagan, MN 55213. TEL 612-687-8000. FAX 612-687-7302. *4045*

WEST'S LOUISIANA RULES OF COURT, STATE.
West Group, 620 Opperman Dr., Eagan, MN 55123. TEL 612-687-8000. FAX 612-687-7302. *4140*

WETTBEWERBSRECHT VOLLTEXT C D - R O M.
Verlag C.H. Beck, 80791 Munich, Germany. TEL 49-89-38189338. FAX 49-89-38189398. Available only on CD-ROM. *5591*

WHAT'S ON SATELLITE.
Design Publishers, 800 Siesta Way, Sonoma, CA 95476-4413. TEL 707-939-9306. *2008*

WHICH DEGREE. WHICH UNIVERSITY - ON C D - R O M.
Hobsons Publishing plc., Bateman St., Cambridge CB2 1LZ, England. TEL 44-1223-460366. FAX 44-1223-301506.
Available only on CD-ROM. *2562*

WHITAKER'S BOOKS IN PRINT.
J. Whitaker & Sons Ltd., 12 Dyott St., London WC1A 1DF, England. TEL 44-171-420-6000. FAX 44-171-836-2909.
Producer(s): Bowker Electronic Publishing. *570*

WHO WAS WHO IN AMERICA.
Marquis Who's Who, A Division of Reed Elsevier Inc., 121 Chanlon Rd., New Providence, NJ 07974. TEL 908-464-6800. FAX 908-665-6688.
Producer(s): Bowker Electronic Publishing. *577*

WHO'S WHO IN AMERICA.
Marquis Who's Who, A Division of Reed Elsevier Inc., 121 Chanlon Rd., New Providence, NJ 07974. TEL 908-464-6800. FAX 908-665-6688.
Producer(s): Bowker Electronic Publishing. *578*

WHO'S WHO IN AMERICAN EDUCATION.
Marquis Who's Who, A Division of Reed Elsevier Inc., 121 Chanlon Rd., New Providence, NJ 07974. TEL 908-464-6800. FAX 908-665-6688.
Producer(s): Bowker Electronic Publishing. *578*

WHO'S WHO IN AMERICAN LAW.
Marquis Who's Who, A Division of Reed Elsevier Inc., 121 Chanlon Rd., New Providence, NJ 07974. TEL 908-464-6800. FAX 908-665-6688.
Producer(s): Bowker Electronic Publishing. *4046*

WHO'S WHO IN AMERICAN NURSING.
Marquis Who's Who, A Division of Reed Elsevier Inc., 121 Chanlon Rd., New Providence, NJ 07974. TEL 908-464-6800. FAX 908-665-6688.
Producer(s): Bowker Electronic Publishing. *4951*

WHO'S WHO IN ENTERTAINMENT.
Marquis Who's Who, A Reed Reference Publishing Company, Part of the Reed Elsevier group, 121 Chanlon Rd., New Providence, NJ 07974. TEL 908-464-6800. FAX 908-665-6688.
Producer(s): Bowker Electronic Publishing. *5348*

WHO'S WHO IN EUROPEAN RESEARCH AND DEVELOPMENT.
Bowker - Saur Ltd., A member of the Reed Elsevier plc group, Maypole House, Maypole Rd., E. Grinstead, W. Sussex RH19 1HU, England. TEL 44-1342-330100. FAX 44-1342-330191. *579*

WHO'S WHO IN FINANCE AND INDUSTRY.
Marquis Who's Who, A Division of Reed Elsevier Inc., 121 Chanlon Rd., New Providence, NJ 07974. TEL 908-464-6800. FAX 908-665-6688.
Producer(s): Bowker Electronic Publishing. *579*

WHO'S WHO IN SCIENCE AND ENGINEERING.
Marquis Who's Who, A Division of Reed Elsevier Inc., 121 Chanlon Rd., New Providence, NJ 07974. TEL 908-464-6800. FAX 908-665-6688.
Producer(s): Bowker Electronic Publishing. *579*

WHO'S WHO IN THE EAST.
Marquis Who's Who, A Division of Reed Elsevier Inc., 121 Chanlon Rd., New Providence, NJ 07974. TEL 908-464-6800. FAX 908-665-6688.
Producer(s): Bowker Electronic Publishing. *580*

WHO'S WHO IN THE MIDWEST.
Marquis Who's Who, A Division of Reed Elsevier Inc., 121 Chanlon Rd., New Providence, NJ 07974. TEL 908-464-6800. FAX 908-665-6688.
Producer(s): Bowker Electronic Publishing. *580*

WHO'S WHO IN THE SOUTH AND SOUTHWEST.
Marquis Who's Who, A Division of Reed Elsevier Inc., 121 Chanlon Rd., New Providence, NJ 07974. TEL 908-464-6800. FAX 908-665-6688.
Producer(s): Bowker Electronic Publishing. *580*

WHO'S WHO IN THE WEST.
Marquis Who's Who, A Division of Reed Elsevier Inc., 121 Chanlon Rd., New Providence, NJ 07974. TEL 908-464-6800. FAX 908-665-6688.
Producer(s): Bowker Electronic Publishing. *580*

WHO'S WHO IN THE WORLD.
Marquis Who's Who, A Division of Reed Elsevier Inc., 121 Chanlon Rd., New Providence, NJ 07974. FAX 908-665-6688.
Producer(s): Bowker Electronic Publishing. *580*

WHO'S WHO OF AMERICAN WOMEN.
Marquis Who's Who, A Division of Reed Elsevier Inc., 121 Chanlon Rd., New Providence, NJ 07974. TEL 908-464-6800. FAX 908-665-6688.
Producer(s): Bowker Electronic Publishing. *580*

WICKS SUBJECT INDEX OF COMMONWEALTH LEGISLATION.
L B C Information Services, 50 Waterloo Rd., N. Ryde, N.S.W. 2113, Australia. TEL 61-2-99366444. FAX 61-2-98887240. *4057*

WILDLIFE REVIEW (FORT COLLINS).
U.S. National Biological Service, Information Transfer Center, 1201 Oak Ridge Dr., No. 200, Ft. Collins, CO 80525-5562. TEL 970-226-9401. FAX 970-226-9455.
Producer(s): NISC (Wildlife Worldwide). *2251*

WILDLIFE WORLDWIDE.
National Information Services Corporation (NISC), 3100 St. Paul St., Ste. 806, Baltimore, MD 21218. TEL 410-243-0797. FAX 410-243-0982.
Available only on CD-ROM. Producer(s): NISC. *645*

WILEY EMPLOYMENT LAW UPDATE ON C D - R O M.
John Wiley & Sons, Inc., Law Publications, 605 Third Ave., New York, NY 10158. TEL 212-850-6645. FAX 212-850-6021.
Available only on CD-ROM. *4046*

WILSON ABSTRACTS.
H.W. Wilson Co., 950 University Ave., Bronx, NY 10452. TEL 718-588-8400. FAX 718-590-1617.
Producer(s): SilverPlatter Information, Inc., H.W. Wilson (WILSONDISC). *476*

WILSON APPLIED SCIENCE AND TECHNOLOGY ABSTRACTS.
H.W. Wilson Co., 950 University Ave., Bronx, NY 10452. TEL 718-588-8400. FAX 718-590-1617. Producer(s): SilverPlatter Information, Inc., H.W. Wilson. *2753*

WILSON BUSINESS ABSTRACTS.
H.W. Wilson Co., 950 University Ave., Bronx, NY 10452. TEL 718-588-8400. FAX 718-590-1617. Producer(s): SilverPlatter Information, Inc., H.W. Wilson (WILSONDISC). *1078*

WILSON EDUCATION ABSTRACTS.
H.W. Wilson Co., 950 University Ave., Bronx, NY 10452. TEL 718-588-8400. FAX 718-590-1617. Producer(s): SilverPlatter Information, Inc., H.W. Wilson (WILSONDISC). *2505*

WILSON GENERAL SCIENCE ABSTRACTS.
H.W. Wilson Co., 950 University Ave., Bronx, NY 10452. TEL 718-588-8400. FAX 718-590-1617. Producer(s): SilverPlatter Information, Inc., H.W. Wilson (WILSONDISC). *6592*

WILSON HUMANITIES ABSTRACTS.
H.W. Wilson Co., 950 University Ave., Bronx, NY 10452. TEL 718-588-8400. FAX 718-590-1617. Producer(s): SilverPlatter Information, Inc., H.W. Wilson (WILSONDISC). *3799*

WILSON SOCIAL SCIENCES ABSTRACTS.
H.W. Wilson Co., 950 University Ave., Bronx, NY 10452. TEL 718-588-8400. FAX 718-590-1617. Producer(s): SilverPlatter Information, Inc., UMI (PROQUEST), H.W. Wilson. *6651*

WINDOWS DEVELOPER'S JOURNAL.
Miller Freeman, Inc. (Lawrence), 1601 W. 23rd St., Ste. 200, Lawrence, KS 66046. TEL 913-841-1631. FAX 913-841-2624. *2147*

WINE ON LINE.
Enterprises Publishing, 400 E. 59th St., Ste. 9F, New York, NY 10022. TEL 212-755-4363. FAX 212-755-4365. *529*

WIRELESS COMMUNICATION C D - R O M.
Baltzer Science Publishers B.V., P.O. Box 221, 1400 AE Bussum, Netherlands. TEL 31-20-6370061. FAX 31-20-6323651. Available only on CD-ROM. *2008*

WIRTSCHAFTS UND STEUER HEFTE.
D I E Verlag H. Schaefer GmbH, Postfach 2243, 61292 Bad Homburg, Germany. TEL 49-6172-9583-0. FAX 49-6172-71288. *1012*

WISCONSIN BUSINESS DIRECTORY.
American Business Directories, 5711 S. 86th Circle, Box 27347, Omaha, NE 68127. TEL 402-593-4600. FAX 402-331-5481. *1723*

WISCONSIN COURT RULES AND PROCEDURE, STATE AND FEDERAL.
West Group, 620 Opperman Dr., Eagan, MN 55123. TEL 612-687-8000. FAX 612-687-7302. *4140*

WISCONSIN MANUFACTURERS REGISTER.
Manufacturers' News, Inc., 1633 Central St., Evanston, IL 60201. TEL 847-864-7000. FAX 847-332-1100. *1723*

WOMAN AND EARTH.
467 Central Park West, Ste. 7F, New York, NY 10025. TEL 212-866-8130. FAX 212-866-8130. *7336*

WOMEN IN MANAGEMENT REVIEW & ABSTRACTS.
M C B University Press Ltd., 60-62 Toller Ln., Bradford, W. Yorks BD8 9BY, England. TEL 44-1274-777700. FAX 44-1274-785200. *1512*

WOMEN STUDIES ABSTRACTS.
Transaction Publishers, Transaction Periodicals Consortium, Department 3092, Rutgers University, New Brunswick, NJ 08903. TEL 908-445-2280. FAX 908-445-3138. Producer(s): NISC (Women's Resources International). *7350*

THE WOMEN'S REVIEW OF BOOKS.
Wellesley College, Center for Research on Women, Wellesley, MA 02181. TEL 617-283-2087. FAX 617-283-3645. *4366*

WOMEN'S SPORTS AND FITNESS.
Sports & Fitness Publishing, 2025 Pearl St., Boulder, CO 80302. TEL 303-440-5111. FAX 303-440-3313. Producer(s): UMI. *6794*

WORDPERFECT FOR WINDOWS MAGAZINE.
Ivy International Communications, Inc., 270 W. Center St., Orem, UT 84057. TEL 801-228-9626. FAX 801-227-3478. *2220*

WORDPERFECT MAGAZINE.
Ivy International Communications, Inc., 270 W. Center St., Orem, UT 84057. TEL 801-228-9626. FAX 801-227-3478. *2220*

WORDS & MUSIC.
Society of Composers, Authors and Music Publishers of Canada, 41 Valleybrook Dr., Don Mills, ON M3B 2S6, Canada. TEL 416-445-8700. FAX 416-442-3829. *5445*

WORK STUDY.
M C B University Press Ltd., 60-62 Toller Ln., Bradford, W. Yorks BD8 9BY, England. TEL 44-1274-777700. FAX 44-1274-785200. *1512*

WORKERS COMPENSATION.
Standard Publishing Corp., 155 Federal St., Boston, MA 02110. TEL 617-457-0600. FAX 617-457-0608. *3837*

WORKGROUP COMPUTING REPORT.
Patricia Seybold Group, 85 Devonshire St., 5th Fl., Boston, MA 02109-3504. *2177*

WORLD AROMATICS AND DERIVATIVES.
S R I Consulting, World Petrochemicals Program, Chemical Business Research Center, Menlo Park, CA 94025. TEL 415-859-5211. FAX 415-859-2182. *1771*

WORLD AVIATION DIRECTORY.
McGraw-Hill Companies, Aviation Week Group (New York), 1221 Ave. of the Americas, New York, NY 10020. TEL 215-237-4112. FAX 215-586-3232. *83*

WORLD BIODIVERSITY DATABASE SERIES.
UNESCO Publishing, 7 Place de Fontenoy, 75352 Paris 07 SP, France. TEL 33-1-45684300. FAX 33-1-45685741. Available only on CD-ROM. *2323*

WORLD C4 HYDROCARBONS AND DERIVATIVES.
S R I Consulting, World Petrochemicals Program, Chemical Business Research Center, Menlo Park, CA 94025. TEL 415-859-5211. FAX 415-859-2182. *1771*

WORLD DATA (YEAR).
World Bank, 1818 H. St., N.W., Washington, DC 20433. Available only on CD-ROM. *1295*

WORLD DEBT TABLES.
World Bank, 1818 H St., N.W., Washington, DC 20433. TEL 202-473-1155. FAX 202-522-2627. *1371*

WORLD DIRECTORY OF HUMAN RIGHTS RESEARCH AND TRAINING INSTITUTIONS.
UNESCO Publishing, 7 Place de Fontenoy, 75352 Paris 07 SP, France. TEL 33-1-45684300. FAX 33-1-45685741. *1723*

WORLD DRUG MARKET MANUAL.
IMSWORLD Publications Ltd., 7 Harewood Ave., London NW1 6JB, England. TEL 0171-393-5000. FAX 0171-393-5900. *5698*

WORLD ENERGY AND NUCLEAR DIRECTORY (YEAR).
Longman Group UK Ltd., Westgate House, 6th Fl., The High, Harlow, Essex CM20 1YR, England. TEL 44-1279-442601. FAX 44-1279-444501. *2705*

WORLD ETHYLENE AND DERIVATIVES.
S R I Consulting, World Petrochemicals Program, Chemical Business Research Center, Menlo Park, CA 94025. TEL 415-859-5211. FAX 415-859-2182. *1771*

WORLD FACTBOOK.
U.S. National Technical Information Service, 5285 Port Royal Rd., Springfield, VA 22161. TEL 703-482-0623. *6044*

WORLD FEEDSTOCKS.
S R I Consulting, World Petrochemicals Program, Chemical Business Research Center, Menlo Park, CA 94025. TEL 415-859-5211. FAX 415-859-2182. *1771*

WORLD GUIDE TO LIBRARIES.
K.G. Saur Verlag KG, A member of the Reed Elsevier plc group, Ortlerstr. 8, 81373 Munich, Germany. TEL 49-89-76902-0. FAX 49-89-76902150. Producer(s): Bowker Electronic Publishing (Publishing Market Place Reference PLUS). *4222*

WORLD GUIDE TO LIBRARIES PLUS.
K.G. Saur Verlag KG, A member of the Reed Elsevier plc group, Ortlerstr. 8, 81373 Munich, Germany. TEL 49-89-76902-0. FAX 49-89-7690-2150. Available only on CD-ROM. *4222*

(YEAR) WORLD GUIDE TO TELEVISION.
North American Publishing Co., 401 N. Broad St., Philadelphia, PA 19108. TEL 215-238-5300. FAX 215-238-5474. *2065*

WORLD HEALTH.
World Health Organization, Distribution and Sales, CH-1211 Geneva 27, Switzerland. TEL 41-22-791-2476. FAX 41-22-791-4857. Producer(s): UMI. *6254*

WORLD JOURNAL OF MICROBIOLOGY AND BIOTECHNOLOGY.
Rapid Science Publishers, The Old Malthouse, Paradise St., Oxford OX1 1LD, England. TEL 44-1865-790447. FAX 44-1865-244012. *796*

WORLD JOURNAL OF SURGERY.
Springer-Verlag, Medical Journals, 175 Fifth Ave., New York, NY 10010. TEL 212-460-1500. FAX 212-473-6272. *5157*

WORLD LITERATURE TODAY.
110 Monnet Hall, University of Oklahoma, Norman, OK 73019-0375. TEL 405-325-4531. FAX 405-325-7495. *4488*

WORLD METHANOL AND DERIVATIVES.
S R I Consulting, World Petrochemicals Program, Chemical Business Research Center, Menlo Park, CA 94025. TEL 415-859-5211. FAX 415-859-2182. *1771*

WORLD PRESS REVIEW.
Stanley Foundation (New York), 200 Madison Ave., Ste. 2104, New York, NY 10016. TEL 212-889-5155. FAX 212-889-5634. Producer(s): UMI. *4367*

WORLD PROPYLENE AND DERIVATIVES.
S R I Consulting, World Petrochemicals Program, Chemical Business Research Center, Menlo Park, CA 94025. TEL 415-859-5211. FAX 415-859-2182. *1771*

WORLD PUBLISHING MONITOR.
Pira International, Randalls Rd., Leatherhead, Surrey KT22 7RU, England. TEL 44-1372-802050. FAX 44-1372-802239. Producer(s): Knight-Ridder, Inc. *2096*

WORLD'S ELECTRIC POWER PLANT DATABASE ON C D - R O M.
Utility Data Institute, 1200 G St., N.W., Ste. 250, Washington, DC 20005. TEL 202-942-8788. FAX 202-942-8789. Available only on CD-ROM. *2692*

WORLDWIDE DIRECTORY OF DEFENSE AUTHORITIES.
Keesing's Worldwide, LLC, 7979 Old Georgetown Rd., Ste. 900, Bethesda, MD 20814. TEL 301-718-8770. FAX 301-718-8494. *5291*

WORLDWIDE GOVERNMENT DIRECTORY.
Keesing's Worldwide, LLC, 7979 Old Georgetown Rd., Ste. 900, Bethesda, MD 20814. TEL 301-718-8770. FAX 301-718-8494. Producer(s): Knight-Ridder, Inc. *1723*

WORLDWIDE TAX TREATIES ON C D - R O M.
Tax Analysts, 6830 N. Fairfax Dr., Arlington, VA 22213. FAX 703-533-4444. Available only on CD-ROM. *1638*

10030 SERIALS AVAILABLE ON CD-ROM

THE WRITER.
Writer, Inc., 120 Boylston St., Boston, MA 02116. TEL 617-423-3157.
Producer(s): UMI. *4488*

WRITER'S MARKET.
F & W Publications, Inc., 1507 Dana Ave., Cincinnati, OH 45207. TEL 513-531-2222. FAX 513-531-4082. *6287*

WULIN.
Guangdong Kexue Puji Chubanshe, 3 Xingping Li, Dahua Jie, Yingyuan Lu, Guangzhou, Guangdong 510047, People's Republic of China. *6795*

WYOMING BUSINESS DIRECTORY.
American Business Directories, 5711 S. 86th Circle, Box 27347, Omaha, NE 68127. TEL 402-593-4600. FAX 402-331-5481. *1724*

XI'AN TIYU XUEYUAN XUEBAO.
Xi'an Tiyu Xueyuan, 38 Hanguang Rd., Xi'an, Shaanxi 710068, People's Republic of China. TEL 86-29-5214007. FAX 86-29-5250061. *5792*

XIANDAI GUOJI GUANXI.
Xiandai Guoji Guanxi Yanjiusuo, No. A-2, Wanshousi, Haidian, Beijing 100081, People's Republic of China. TEL 86-10-6879-7796. FAX 86-10-6841-8641. *6045*

XIBU TANKUANG GONGCHENG.
Xibu Tankuang Gongcheng Bianjibu, 16 Youhao Beilu, Urumqi, Xinjiang 830000, People's Republic of China. TEL 86-991-4818457. FAX 86-991-4841517. *5319*

XINXUEGUANBINGXUE JINZHAN.
Chengdu Xingxueguanbing Yanjiusuo, 82 Qinglong Jie, Chengdu, Sichuan 610031, People's Republic of China. TEL 86-28-6649831. *4825*

YAHOO! INTERNET LIFE.
Ziff-Davis Publishing Co., One Park Ave., New York, NY 10016. TEL 212-503-4804. FAX 212-503-5699. *2141*

YANTU GONGCHENG XUEBAO.
Zhongguo Tumu Gongcheng Xuehui, 34 Hujuguan, Nanjing, Jiangsu 210024, People's Republic of China. TEL 86-25-6633662. FAX 86-25-3310321. Available only on CD-ROM. *2801*

YEAR BOOK OF ANESTHESIOLOGY AND PAIN MANAGEMENT.
Mosby - Year Book, Inc., Continuity Division, 161 N. Clark St., Chicago, IL 60601. TEL 312-726-9733. FAX 312-726-6075. *4808*

YEAR BOOK OF CARDIOLOGY.
Mosby - Year Book, Inc., Continuity Division, 161 N. Clark St., Chicago, IL 60601. TEL 312-726-9733. FAX 312-726-6075.
Producer(s): SilverPlatter Information, Inc. (ClinMED-CD). *4825*

YEAR BOOK OF CRITICAL CARE MEDICINE.
Mosby - Year Book, Inc., Continuity Division, 161 N. Clark St., Chicago, IL 60601. TEL 312-726-9733. *4760*

YEAR BOOK OF DENTISTRY.
Mosby - Year Book, Inc., Continuity Division, 161 N. Clark St., Chicago, IL 60601. TEL 312-726-9733. FAX 312-726-6075. *4873*

YEAR BOOK OF ENDOCRINOLOGY.
Mosby - Year Book, Inc., Continuity Division, 161 N. Clark St., Chicago, IL 60601. TEL 312-726-9733. FAX 312-726-6075. *4893*

YEARBOOK OF INTERNATIONAL ORGANIZATIONS.
K.G. Saur Verlag KG, A member of the Reed Elsevier plc group, Ortlerstr. 8, 81373 Munich, Germany. TEL 49-89-76902-0. FAX 49-89-76902150.
Producer(s): K.G. Saur Verlag. *6045*

YEAR BOOK OF ONCOLOGY.
Mosby - Year Book, Inc., Continuity Division, 161 N. Clark St., Chicago, IL 60601. TEL 312-726-9733. FAX 312-726-6075. *4988*

YEAR BOOK OF PULMONARY DISEASE.
Mosby - Year Book, Inc., Continuity Division, 161 N. Clark St., Chicago, IL 60601. TEL 312-726-9746. FAX 312-726-6075. *5123*

YOD.
Institut National des Langues et Civilisations Orientales, 2 rue de Lille, 75343 Paris Cedex 07, France. TEL 49-26-42-74. FAX 49-26-42-99. *6411*

YUNNAN ZHONGYI ZAZHI.
Yunnan Sheng Zhongyi Zhongyao Yanjiusuo, Lianhua Chi, Kunming, Yunnan 650223, People's Republic of China. TEL 5154494. *299*

Z D.
Deutsches Bibliotheksinstitut, Abt. 1 - Publikationen, Alt-Moabit 101A, 10559 Berlin, Germany. TEL 49-30-39077-0. FAX 49-30-39077100. *570*

Z D F JAHRBUCH.
Z D F, Presse und Oeffentlichkeitsarbeit, Postfach 4040, 55100 Mainz, Germany. TEL 49-6131-702210. FAX 49-6131-705366. *2065*

Z V E I ELEKTRO UND ELEKTRONIK - EINKAUFSFUEHRER.
Verlag W. Sachon, Schloss Mindelburg, 87714 Mindelheim, Germany. TEL 49-8261-999-0. FAX 49-8261-999-180. *2806*

ZA RULEM.
Izdatel'stvo Za Rulem, Seliverstov ul., 10, 103045 Moscow, Russia. TEL 7-095-2071965. FAX 7-095-2071630. *7122*

ZEITSCHRIFT FUER VERMOEGENS- UND INVESTITIONSRECHT.
Verlag C.H. Beck, 80791 Munich, Germany. TEL 49-89-38189338. FAX 49-89-38189398. *1638*

ZEITSCHRIFTEN - DATENBANK (Z D B).
Deutsches Bibliotheksinstitut, Abt. 1 - Publikationen, Alt-Moabit 101A, 10559 Berlin, Germany. TEL 49-30-39077-0. FAX 49-30-39077100. *4223*

ZENTRALBLATT FUER MATHEMATIK UND IHRE GRENZGEBIETE.
Springer-Verlag, Heidelberger Platz 3, 14197 Berlin, Germany. TEL 49-30-82787-0. FAX 49-30-82787448. *4618*

ZHEJIANG ZHONGYI ZAZHI.
Zhejiang Sheng Zhongyiyao Yanjiusuo, 26 Tianmushan Lu, Hangzhou, Zhejiang 310007, People's Republic of China. *299*

ZHONGGUO DAODAN YU HANGTIAN WENZHAI.
Hangtian Gongye Zong Gongsi, Xinxi Yanjiu-suo, P.O. Box 1408, 1 Binhe Lu, Hepingli, Beijing 100013, People's Republic of China. TEL 86-10-6837-2847. FAX 86-10-6422-7606. *84*

ZHONGGUO GONGCHENGSHI.
Zhongguo Gongchengshi Zazhishe, No.1, Wenhua Lu 1 Duan, Heping-qu, Shenyang, Liaoning 110006, People's Republic of China. TEL 86-24-3891121. *2746*

ZHONGGUO YANRONG.
Guilin Karst Research Institute, 40 Qixing Lu, Guilin, Guangxi 541004, People's Republic of China. TEL 86-773-5812442. FAX 86-773-513708. *2377*

ZHONGGUO YAOXUE ZAZHI.
Zhongguo Yaoxuehui, 42 Dongsi Xidajie, Beijing 100710, People's Republic of China. TEL 01-5133311. FAX 01-8354609. *5699*

ZHONGGUO YIXUE KEXUEYUAN XUEBAO.
Chinese Academy of Medical Sciences (CAMS), 9 Dong Dan San Tiao, Beijing 100730, People's Republic of China. TEL 86-10-5133074. *4761*

ZHONGGUO ZHONGLIU LINCHUANG.
Tianjin Zhongliu Yanjiusuo, Zhongguo Kang-Ai Xiehui, Huan-hu-xi Lu, Tiyuanbei, Hexi Qu, Tianjin 300060, People's Republic of China. TEL 86-22-2374477. *4989*

ZHONGHUA CHUANRANBING ZAZHI.
Zhonghua Yixuehui, Shanghai Fenhui, 1623 Beijing Xilu, Shanghai 200040, People's Republic of China. TEL 86-21-62531885. FAX 86-21-62550842. *4762*

ZHONGHUA ERKE ZAZHI.
Guoji Shudian, Qikan Bu, Chegongzhuang Xilu 21, P.O. Box 399, Beijing, People's Republic of China. *5041*

ZHONGHUA FU-CHANKE ZAZHI.
Guoji Shudian, Qikan Bu, Chegongzhuang Xilu 21, P.O. Box 399, Beijing 100044, People's Republic of China. *4969*

ZHONGHUA GUKE ZAZHI.
Zhonghua Guke Zazhi Bianjibu, Tianjin Yiyuan, Jiefang Nanlu, Weiti Daokou, Tianjin 300211, People's Republic of China. TEL 86-22-2384734. *5018*

ZHONGHUA LAONIAN YIXUE ZAZHI.
Zhonghua Yixuehui, Beijing Yiyuan (Beijing Hospital), 1 Dahua Lu, Beijing 100730, People's Republic of China. TEL 5126611. *3447*

ZHONGHUA LILIAO ZAZHI.
Zhonghua Yixuehui, Tang Gang Zi, Anshan, Liaoning 114048, People's Republic of China. *5047*

ZHONGHUA LIUXINGBINGXUE ZAZHI.
Zhonghua Yufang Yixuehui, 16, Hepingli Zhongjie, Beijing 100013, People's Republic of China. TEL 4218457. *4762*

ZHONGHUA MAZUIXUE ZAZHI.
Guoji Shudian, Qikan Bu, Chegongzhuang Xilu 21, P.O. Box 399, Beijing 100044, People's Republic of China. *4808*

ZHONGHUA NEIFENMI DAIXIE ZAZHI.
Shanghai Institute of Endocrinology, 197 Ruijin Lu Sec. 2, Shanghai, People's Republic of China. TEL 8610-8232343. FAX 8610-8211656. *4893*

ZHONGHUA NEIKE ZAZHI.
Guoji Shudian, Qikan Bu, Chegongzhuang Xilu 21, P.O. Box 399, Beijing 100044, People's Republic of China. *4927*

ZHONGHUA SHENJING-JINGSHENKE ZAZHI.
Chinese Medical Association, P.O. Box 2258, 42 Dongsi Xidajie, Beijing 100710, People's Republic of China. TEL 1-550394. *5102*

ZHONGHUA SHENJING WAIKE ZAZHI.
Beijing Neurosurgical Institute, No.6, Tiantan Xili, Beijing 100050, People's Republic of China. TEL 86-10-5113169. FAX 86-10-7018349. *5102*

ZHONGHUA WAIKE ZAZHI.
Guoji Shudian, Qikan Bu, Chegongzhuang Xilu 21, P.O. Box 399, Beijing 100044, People's Republic of China. *5158*

ZHONGHUA WULI YIXUE ZAZHI.
Hebei Yixue Yuan, 5 Chang'an Xilu, Shijiazhuang, Hebei 050017, People's Republic of China. TEL 44121. *5047*

ZHONGHUA XIAOHUA ZAZHI.
Zhonghua Yixuehui, Shanghai Fenhui, 1623 Beijing Xilu, Shanghai 200040, People's Republic of China. TEL 86-21-62531885. FAX 86-21-62550842. *4915*

ZHONGHUA XIN-XUEGUANBING ZAZHI.
Chinese Medical Association, P.O. Box 2258, 42 Dongsi Xidajie, Beijing 100710, People's Republic of China. TEL 1-550394. *4825*

ZHONGHUA XUEYEXUE ZAZHI.
Zhongguo Yixue Kexueyuan, Xueye Yanjiusuo, 288 Nanjing Lu, Tianjin 300020, People's Republic of China. TEL 86-22-730-4167. FAX 86-22-730-4167. *4922*

ZHONGHUA YISHI ZAZHI.
Guoji Shudian, Qikan Bu, Chegongzhuang Xilu 21, P.O. Box 399, Beijing 100044, People's Republic of China. *4762*

ZHONGHUA YUFANG YIXUE ZAZHI.
Zhonghua Yufang Yixuehui, 16, Hepingli Zhongjie, Beijing 100013, People's Republic of China. *4762*

ZHONGHUA ZHENGXING SHAOSHANG WAIKE ZAZHI.
Chinese Academy of Medical Sciences (CAMS), Plastic Surgery Hospital, Badachu Rd., Beijing 100041, People's Republic of China. TEL 86-10-6886-4812. FAX 86-10-6886-4137. *5158*

ZHONGHUA ZHONGLIU ZAZHI.
Zhonghua Zhongliu Zazhi Bianjibu, No. 1 Panjiayuan, Zuo'anmen Wai, Beijing 100021, People's Republic of China. TEL 86-10-7781331. *4989*

ZHONGXIAOXUE GUANLI.
Zhongxiaoxue Guanli Zazhishe, A-24 Huangsi Dajie, Dewai, Beijing 100011, People's Republic of China. TEL 2018316. *2580*

ZHUZAO JISHU.
Xi'an Zhuzao Xuehui, P.O. Box 608, Xi'an Ligong Daxue, Jinhua Nanlu, Xi'an, Shaanxi 710048, People's Republic of China. TEL 86-29-3239700. FAX 86-29-3235545. *5216*

ZIMPEL. SOFTWARE: Z DATA.
Verlag Dieter Zimpel, Angererstr. 36, 80796 Munich, Germany. TEL 49-89-3073445. FAX 49-89-302409. *2220*

ZOOLOGICAL RECORD.
BIOSIS, 2100 Arch St., Philadelphia, PA 19103-1399. TEL 215-587-4847. FAX 215-587-2016. Producer(s): SilverPlatter Information, Inc.. *645*

Producer Listing/ Serials on CD-ROM

AMERICAN PSYCHOLOGICAL ASSN.
750 First St., NE, Washington, DC 20002-4242.
Tel: 202-336-5500
  Psychological Abstracts.

BOWKER ELECTRONIC PUBLISHING
(Division of Reed Elsevier Inc.)
121 Chanlon Rd., New Providence, NJ 07974. Tel: 908-464-6800 Telex: 138755
Fax: 908-665-3528.
  A to Zoo. *(Children's Reference PLUS)*
  Advertiser & Agency Red Books Plus.
  American Book Trade Directory.
  American Library Directory.
  American Men and Women of Science.
  America's Corporate Finance Directory.
  Best Books for Children.
  Books in Print. *(Books in Print PLUS)*
  Books in Print on Disc. *(Books in Print PLUS)*
  Books in Print Supplement. *(Books in Print PLUS)*
  Books in Print with Book Reviews on Disc. *(Books in Print PLUS)*
  Books Out-of-Print. *(Books Out-of-Print PLUS)*
  Books Out-of-Print Plus. *(Books Out-of-Print PLUS)*
  Books Out-of-Print with Book Reviews Plus. *(Books Out-of-Print with Book Reviews PLUS)*
  The Bowker Annual Library and Book Trade Almanac.
  Bowker - Whitaker Global Books in Print on Disc. *(Books In Print PLUS)*
  Bowker's Complete Video Directory.
  Children's Books in Print. *(Books in Print PLUS)*
  The Complete Directory of Large Print Books and Serials.
  Corporate Affiliations Plus.
  Directory of American Research and Technology.
  Directory of Corporate Affiliations.
  El-Hi Textbooks and Serials in Print.
  Forthcoming Books. *(Books in Print PLUS)*
  Ingram - Books in Print Plus. *(Books In Print PLUS)*
  Ingram - Books in Print Plus with Book Reviews Plus. *(Books In Print PLUS)*
  International Literary Market Place.
  Libros en Venta en Hispanoamerica y Espana Plus.
  Literary Market Place.
  Martindale-Hubbell Law Directory.
  Martindale-Hubbell Law Directory on C D - R O M.
  Official A B M S Directory of Board Certified Medical Specialists.
  Publishers, Distributors & Wholesalers of the United States.
  Standard Directory of Advertisers (Geographic Edition).
  Standard Directory of Advertising Agencies.
  Standard Directory of International Advertisers and Agencies.
  Subject Guide to Books in Print. *(Books In Print PLUS)*
  Subject Guide to Children's Books in Print.
  Ulrich's International Periodicals Directory. *(Ulrich's PLUS)*
  Ulrich's on Disc. *(Ulrich's PLUS)*
  Ulrich's Update. *(Ulrich's PLUS)*
  Variety's Video Directory on Disc.
  Whitaker's Books in Print.
  Who Was Who in America.
  Who's Who in America.
  Who's Who in American Education.
  Who's Who in American Law.
  Who's Who in American Nursing.
  Who's Who in Entertainment.
  Who's Who in Finance and Industry.
  Who's Who in Science and Engineering.
  Who's Who in the East.
  Who's Who in the Midwest.
  Who's Who in the South and Southwest.
  Who's Who in the West.
  Who's Who in the World.
  Who's Who of American Women.
  World Guide to Libraries. *(Publishing Market Place Reference PLUS)*

BOWKER - SAUR LTD. (A member of the Reed Elsevier plc group)
Maypole House, Maypole Rd., East Grinstead, W. Sussex RH19 1HH, United Kingdom Tel: 0342-330-100
Fax: 0342-330-191.
  A N T E Plus.
  A S S I A: Applied Social Sciences Index & Abstracts.
  A S S I A Plus.
  Abstracts in New Technologies and Engineering.
  B H I Plus.
  British Humanities Index.
  Catchword and Trade Name Index. *(CTI Plus)*
  Current Research in Library & Information Science.
  Institute of Management International Databases Plus.
  L I S A: Library & Information Science Abstracts.
  L I S A Plus.
  New Scientist.
  Russian Books in Print on C D - R O M.

CINAHL
P.O. Box 871, Glendale, CA 91209-0871.
1509 Wilson Terr., Glendale, CA 91209. Tel: 818-409-8005 Fax: 818-546-5679.
  Cumulative Index to Nursing & Allied Health Literature.

CAMBRIDGE SCIENTIFIC ABSTRACTS
(Div. of Cambridge Information Group)
7200 Wisconsin Ave., Suite 601, Bethesda, MD 20814. Tel: 301-961-6750 Telex: 89-8452
Fax: 301-961-6720.
  Index Medicus. *(Compact Cambridge MEDLINE)*
  Index to Dental Literature. *(Compact Cambridge MEDLINE)*
  International Nursing Index. *(Compact Cambridge MEDLINE)*

CHADWYCK-HEALEY INC.
1101 King St., Ste. 380, Alexandria, VA 22314.
Tel: 703-683-4890
Fax: 703-683-7589.
  A F P - Doc sur C D - R O M.
  A F P Sciences.
  A F P Sciences sur C D - R O M.
  Actualidad Economica.
  Actualidad Economica en C D - R O M.
  Associations Yellow Book.
  Autoridades de la Biblioteca Nacional de Espana en C D - R O M.
  B N B on C D - R O M.
  Bibliografia Espanola desde 1976 en C D - R O M.
  Bibliografia Nacional Portuguesa em C D - R O M.
  Bibliografia Nazionale Italiana.
  Bibliographie Nationale Francaise. Livres.
  Bibliographie Nationale Francaise. Publications en Serie.
  Bibliographie Nationale Francaise. Publications Officielles.
  Catalogue of British Official Publications Not Published by H.M.S.O.
  Congressional Yellow Book.
  Corporate Yellow Book.
  Daily Telegraph.
  Deutsche Nationalbibliographie (C D - R O M Aktuell).
  The Economist.
  Economist. Annual Index.
  The Economist on C D - R O M.
  Eurocat.
  Expansion.
  Expansion en C D - R O M.
  Federal Regional Yellow Book.
  Federal Yellow Book.
  Film Index International.
  Financial Times (Frankfurt Edition).
  Financial Times (London, 1888).
  Financial Times (North American Edition).
  Financial Times on C D - R O M.
  Financial Yellow Book.
  Government Affairs Yellow Book.
  Great Britain. House of Commons. Parliamentary Debates.

PRODUCER LISTING/SERIALS ON CD-ROM

Great Britain. House of Commons. Parliamentary Debates (C D - R O M Edition).
Great Britain. House of Lords. Parliamentary Debates.
Great Britain. House of Lords. Parliamentary Debates (C D - R O M Edition).
The Guardian (Manchester).
The Guardian on C D - R O M.
The Independent.
The Independent on C D - R O M.
The Independent on Sunday.
Index to House of Commons Parliamentary Papers.
Intlec C D - R O M.
Judicial Yellow Book.
Law Firms Yellow Book.
Leadership Directories on C D - R O M.
The Mail on C D - R O M.
Municipal Yellow Book.
News Media Yellow Book.
Nineteenth Century Bibliographic Records.
O J C D.
The Observer.
Official Journal of the European Communities. C Series: Information and Notices (English Edition).
Official Journal of the European Communities. L & C: Legislation and Competition.
La Recherche.
Il Sole 24 Ore.
Il Sole 24 Ore su C D - R O M.
State Yellow Book.
Sunday Telegraph.
The Sunday Times.
The Telegraph on C D - R O M.
The Times.
The Times and The Sunday Times Compact Disc Edition.
Times Educational Supplement.
Times Higher Education Supplement.
U K O P.
U N B I S Plus on C D - R O M.

DUN & BRADSTREET INFORMATION SERVICES
(Subsidiary of: Div. of Dun & Bradstreet Corp.)
899 Eaton Ave., Bethlehem, PA 18025. Tel: 610-882-7000
Fax: 610-882-7269.
Million Dollar Directory.

INSTITUTE FOR SCIENTIFIC INFORMATION
3501 Market St., Philadelphia, PA 19104. Tel: 215-386-0100 Telex: 845305
Fax: 215-386-6362.
Arts & Humanities Citation Index. (A&HCI/CDE)
Index to Scientific & Technical Proceedings.
Index to Social Sciences & Humanities Proceedings.
Science Citation Index. (SCI CDE)
Social Sciences Citation Index. (SSCI)

KNIGHT-RIDDER INFORMATION, INC.
2440 El Camino Real, Mountain View, CA 94040. Tel: 415-254-7000
Fax: 415-254-8000.
A S F A Marine Biotechnology Abstracts.
Agricultural & Environmental Biotechnology Abstracts.
Alloys Index.
Aquatic Sciences & Fisheries Abstracts. Part 3: Aquatic Pollution and Environmental Quality. (Environmental Management)
BioEngineering Abstracts. (Biotechnology & Bioengineering)
Canadian Index.
Chemical Hazards in Industry.
Clinical Laboratory Product Comparison System.
Country Report. Bolivia.
Country Report. Bulgaria.
Country Report. Czech Republic.
Country Report. Peru.
Current Biotechnology.
C2C Abstracts: Japan - Analytical Chemistry.
C2C Abstracts: Japan - Ceramics.
C2C Abstracts: Japan - Chemical Engineering.
C2C Abstracts: Japan - Crystallography.
C2C Abstracts: Japan - Hydrocarbons.
C2C Abstracts: Japan - Inorganic Chemistry.
C2C Abstracts: Japan - Materials Science.
C2C Abstracts: Japan - Metals.
C2C Abstracts: Japan - Organic Chemistry.
C2C Abstracts: Japan - Physical Chemistry.
C2C Abstracts: Japan - Plastics.
C2C Abstracts: Japan - Polymer Chemistry.
C2C Abstracts: Japan - Surface Chemistry.
C2C Abstracts: Japan - Textiles.
C2C Currents: Japan - Chemistry.
C2C Currents: Japan - Computers.
C2C Currents: Japan - Electronics.
C2C Currents: Japan - Materials.
Diagnostic Imaging & Radiology Product Comparison System.
Directory of Research Grants.
E I S.
Engineered Materials Abstracts.
Engineering Index Annual. (COMPENDEX PLUS CD-ROM)
Engineering Index Monthly. (COMPENDEX PLUS CD-ROM)
Hazards in the Office.
Health and Safety Science Abstracts. (Toxicology & Pharmacology)
Hospital Product Comparison System.
Index Medicus. (DIALOG OnDisc MEDLINE)
Index to Dental Literature. (DIALOG OnDisc MEDLINE)
International Nursing Index. (DIALOG OnDisc MEDLINE)
International Packaging Abstracts.
Key Abstracts - Business Automation.
Laboratory Hazards Bulletin.
Medical & Pharmaceutical Biotechnology Abstracts. (Biotechnology & Bioengineering)
Metals Abstracts.
Metals Abstracts Index.
N T I S Bibliographic Data Base.
New England Water Works Association. Journal.
Nonferrous Metals Alert.
Nonwovens Abstracts.
Paperbase Abstracts.
Petroleum Abstracts.
Philosopher's Index.
Pollution Abstracts. (Environmental Management)
Polymers, Ceramics, Composites Alert.
Process and Chemical Engineering.
Resources in Education. (ERIC)
Risk Abstracts. (Environmental Management)
Steels Alert.
Surgical Product Comparison System.
Theoretical Chemical Engineering.
Toxicology Abstracts. (Toxicology & Pharmacology)
World Publishing Monitor.
Worldwide Government Directory.

NISC
3100 St. Paul St. Wyaman Towers, Suite 806, Baltimore, MD 21218. Tel: 410-243-0797
Fax: 410-243-0982.
A S F A Aquaculture Abstracts.
A S F A Marine Biotechnology Abstracts.
Agricultural & Environmental Biotechnology Abstracts.
Alternative Press Index.
Animal Behavior Abstracts.
Antarctic Bibliography. (Arctic & Antarctic Regions)
Aquatic Biology, Aquaculture & Fisheries Resources.
Aquatic Sciences & Fisheries Abstracts. Part 1: Biological Sciences and Living Resources.
Aquatic Sciences & Fisheries Abstracts. Part 2: Ocean Technology, Policy and Non-living Resources.
Aquatic Sciences & Fisheries Abstracts. Part 3: Aquatic Pollution and Environmental Quality.
Arctic & Antarctic Regions (Cold Regions).
Bibliography of Economic Geology. (Geosearch)
Bibliography on Cold Regions Science & Technology. (Arctic & Antarctic Regions)
Cabo.
Ceramic Abstracts.
Ceramic Abstracts (C D - R O M).
Child Abuse & Neglect C D - R O M.
Consumers Index. (Consumers Reference Disc)
Consumers Reference Disc.
E I S.
E R I C on C D - R O M.
Earthquake Engineering Abstracts Database. (Earthquakes and the Built Environment Index)
EcoCentral.
Ecology Abstracts.
Entomology Abstracts.
Environmental Periodicals Bibliography.
Environmental Periodicals Bibliography (C D - R O M).
Essential Ecology, Zoology & Plant Science Abstracts.
Essential Fisheries Abstracts.
Essential Forestry & Wildfire Abstracts.
Essential Ornithological Abstracts.
Essential Wildlife & Conservation Biology Abstracts.
Estuaries and Coastal Waters of the British Isles. (Oceanographic & Marine Resources)
Family Relations.
Family Studies Database.
Fish & Fisheries Worldwide.
Fisheries Review. (Fish & Fisheries Worldwide)
Geoscience Documentation. (Geosearch)
GeoSEARCH.
Geosources. (Geosearch)
Geotitles. (Geosearch)
Handbook of Latin American Studies: A Selected and Annotated Guide to Recent Publications. (Latin American Studies - Vol.1)
Health and Safety Science Abstracts. (Health & Safety - Risk Abstracts)
Hispanic American Periodicals Index. (Latin American Studies - Vol.1)
Hydrotitles. (HydroROM)
Journal of Marriage and the Family.
Latin American Studies. Volume 1.
Latin American Studies. Volume 2.
Linguistics and Language Behavior Abstracts.
Marine Pollution Research Titles. (Oceanographic & Marine Resources)
A Matter of Fact: Statements Containing Statistics on Current Social, Economic and Political Issues.
Microbiology Abstracts: Section A. Industrial & Applied Microbiology.
Microbiology Abstracts: Section C. Algology, Mycology and Protozoology.
Muse (Music Search).
N E L M Index Series.
Notimex on C D - R O M.
NotiSur. (Latin American Studies - Vol.2)
Oceanic Abstracts.
Oceanographic & Marine Resources.
Oceanographic Literature Review. (Oceanographic & Marine Resources)
Pollution Abstracts.
Psychological Abstracts. (PsycLIT)
R I L M Abstracts of Music Literature. (MUSE, Music Search)
Resources in Education. (ERIC on CD-ROM)
Resources in Education Annual Cumulation. (ERIC)
Risk Abstracts. (Health & Safety - Risk Abstracts)
Sea Grant Abstracts. (Oceanographic & Marine Resources)
Sociological Abstracts. (Sociofile)
SourceMex. (Latin American Studies - Vol.2)
Thesaurus of E R I C Descriptors. (ERIC)
U.S. Library of Congress. Music Catalog on Microfiche. (Muse)
Water Resources Abstracts (Bethesda).
Water Resources Abstracts (C D - R O M).
Water Resources Worldwide.
Wildlife Review (Fort Collins). (Wildlife Worldwide)
Wildlife Worldwide.
Women Studies Abstracts. (Women's Resources International)

OCLC ONLINE COMPUTER LIBRARY CTR., INC.
6565 Frantz Rd., Dublin, OH 43017-0702. Tel: 614-764-6000 Telex: 810-339-2026
Fax: 614-764-6096.
N T I S Bibliographic Data Base.
Resources in Education. (ERIC)

PUBLIC AFFAIRS INFORMATION SERVICE, INC.
521 W. 43rd St., New York, NY 10036-4396. Tel: 212-736-6629 Telex: 4909991777
Fax: 212-643-2848.
P A I S Select.

SAUR@K. G.#VERLAG (Subsidiary of: member of the Reed Elsevier plc group)
Ortlerstr. 8, 81373 Munich, Germany Tel: 089-76902 Telex: 5212067-SAUR-D
Fax: 089-76902150.
Book Review Digest.
Catalogo dei Libri in Commercio - C D - R O M.
International Books in Print.
International Books in Print Plus.
Libros en Venta in Hispanoamerica y Espana.
Publishers' International I S B N Directory (Year).
Verzeichnis Lieferbarer Buecher.
Verzeichnis Lieferbarer Buecher - C D - R O M.
Yearbook of International Organizations.

SILVERPLATTER INFORMATION, INC.
100 River Ridge Dr., Norwood, MA 02062. Tel: 617-769-2599
Fax: 617-769-8763.
  A H F S Drug Information.
  A S F A Aquaculture Abstracts.
  A S F A Marine Biotechnology Abstracts.
  Agricultural & Environmental Biotechnology Abstracts.
  Agriculture and Environment for Developing Countries.
  American Journal of Critical Care.
  Analytical Abstracts.
  Animal Behavior Abstracts.
  Applied Science & Technology Index.
  Aquatic Sciences & Fisheries Abstracts. Part 1: Biological Sciences and Living Resources.
  Aquatic Sciences & Fisheries Abstracts. Part 2: Ocean Technology, Policy and Non-living Resources.
  Aquatic Sciences & Fisheries Abstracts. Part 3: Aquatic Pollution and Environmental Quality.
  Art Index.
  Bibliography and Index of Geology. (GeoRef)
  Bibliography of Agriculture.
  Bibliography of Bioethics.
  Biography Index.
  Biological Abstracts.
  Biological Abstracts - R R M.
  Biological & Agricultural Index.
  Biomedical and Environmental Sciences.
  Burrelle's Media Directory.
  Business Periodicals Index.
  C S A Neurosciences Abstracts.
  Calcium and Calcified Tissue Abstracts.
  Chemoreception Abstracts.
  Choice (Middletown).
  Coal Week. (McGraw-Hill Energy Library)
  Coal Week International. (McGraw-Hill Energy Library)
  Country Report. Bolivia.
  Country Report. Bulgaria.
  Country Report. Czech Republic.
  Country Report. Peru.
  Criminal Justice Abstracts.
  Cumulative Book Index.
  Cumulative Index to Nursing & Allied Health Literature.
  Current Mathematical Publications. (MathDisc)
  E I S.
  Ecology Abstracts.
  Education Index.
  Electric Utility Week. (McGraw-Hill Energy Library)
  Electric Utility Week's Demand-Side Report. (McGraw-Hill Energy Library)
  Entomology Abstracts.
  Essay and General Literature Index.
  Exceptional Child Education Resources.
  Excerpta Medica Abstract Journals. (Excerpta Medica Library Service)
  Excerpta Medica. Section 1: Anatomy, Anthropology, Embryology & Histology.
  Excerpta Medica. Section 2: Physiology.
  Excerpta Medica. Section 3: Endocrinology.
  Excerpta Medica. Section 4: Microbiology: Bacteriology, Mycology, Parasitology and Virology.
  Excerpta Medica. Section 5: General Pathology and Pathological Anatomy.
  Excerpta Medica. Section 6: Internal Medicine.
  Excerpta Medica. Section 7: Pediatrics and Pediatric Surgery.
  Excerpta Medica. Section 8: Neurology and Neurosurgery.
  Excerpta Medica. Section 9: Surgery.
  Excerpta Medica. Section 10: Obstetrics and Gynecology.
  Excerpta Medica. Section 11: Otorhinolaryngology.
  Excerpta Medica. Section 12: Ophthalmology.
  Excerpta Medica. Section 13: Dermatology and Venereology.
  Excerpta Medica. Section 14: Radiology.
  Excerpta Medica. Section 15: Chest Diseases, Thoracic Surgery and Tuberculosis.
  Excerpta Medica. Section 16: Cancer.
  Excerpta Medica. Section 17: Public Health, Social Medicine and Epidemiology.
  Excerpta Medica. Section 18: Cardiovascular Diseases and Cardiovascular Surgery.
  Excerpta Medica. Section 19: Rehabilitation and Physical Medicine.
  Excerpta Medica. Section 20: Gerontology and Geriatrics.
  Excerpta Medica. Section 21: Developmental Biology and Teratology.
  Excerpta Medica. Section 22: Human Genetics.
  Excerpta Medica. Section 23: Nuclear Medicine.
  Excerpta Medica. Section 24: Anesthesiology.
  Excerpta Medica. Section 25: Hematology.
  Excerpta Medica. Section 26: Immunology, Serology and Transplantation.
  Excerpta Medica. Section 27: Biophysics, Bio-Engineering and Medical Instrumentation.
  Excerpta Medica. Section 28: Urology and Nephrology.
  Excerpta Medica. Section 29: Clinical and Experimental Biochemistry.
  Excerpta Medica. Section 30: Clinical and Experimental Pharmacology.
  Excerpta Medica. Section 31: Arthritis and Rheumatism.
  Excerpta Medica. Section 32: Psychiatry.
  Excerpta Medica. Section 33: Orthopedic Surgery.
  Excerpta Medica. Section 35: Occupational Health and Industrial Medicine.
  Excerpta Medica. Section 36: Health Policy, Economics and Management.
  Excerpta Medica. Section 38: Adverse Reactions Titles.
  Excerpta Medica. Section 40: Drug Dependence, Alcohol Abuse and Alcoholism.
  Excerpta Medica. Section 46: Environmental Health and Pollution Control.
  Excerpta Medica. Section 48: Gastroenterology.
  Excerpta Medica. Section 49: Forensic Science Abstracts.
  Excerpta Medica. Section 50: Epilepsy Abstracts.
  Excerpta Medica. Section 52: Toxicology.
  Federal Technology Report. (McGraw-Hill Energy Library)
  Film & Video Finder.
  Findex (Year).
  Food Science and Technology Abstracts. (COMPU-INFO)
  General Science Index.
  Genetics Abstracts.
  Hazardous Waste Business. (McGraw-Hill Energy Library)
  Health and Safety Science Abstracts. (PolTox1)
  I N I S Atomindex. (INIS)
  Immunology Abstracts.
  Independent Power Report. (McGraw-Hill Energy Library)
  Index Medicus. (MEDLINE)
  Index to Dental Literature. (MEDLINE)
  Index to Foreign Legal Periodicals.
  Index to Legal Periodicals & Books.
  Industrial Energy Bulletin. (McGraw-Hill Energy Library)
  Inpharma Weekly.
  Inside Energy with Federal Lands. (McGraw-Hill Energy Library)
  Inside F E R C. (McGraw-Hill Energy Library)
  Inside F E R C's Gas Market Report. (McGraw-Hill Energy Library)
  Inside N R C. (McGraw-Hill Energy Library)
  Integrated Waste Management. (McGraw-Hill Energy Library)
  International Journal of Punjab Studies.
  International Nursing Index. (MEDLINE)
  International Pharmaceutical Abstracts.
  Journal of Economic Literature.
  Kompass Italia.
  Library Literature.
  Linguistics and Language Behavior Abstracts.
  M L A International Bibliography of Books and Articles on the Modern Languages and Literatures.
  Mathematical Reviews. (MathDisc)
  A Matter of Fact: Statements Containing Statistics on Current Social, Economic and Political Issues.
  Mechanical Engineering Abstracts.
  Medical & Pharmaceutical Biotechnology Abstracts.
  Meyler's Side Effects of Drugs. (SEDBASE)
  Microbiology Abstracts: Section A. Industrial & Applied Microbiology.
  Microbiology Abstracts: Section B. Bacteriology.
  Microbiology Abstracts: Section C. Algology, Mycology and Protozoology.
  Microcomputer Abstracts.
  Monthly Catalog of United States Government Publications.
  N I O S H T I C.
  N T I S Bibliographic Data Base.
  Northeast Power Report. (McGraw-Hill Energy Library)
  NuclearFuel. (McGraw-Hill Energy Library)
  Nucleic Acids Abstracts.
  Nucleonics Week. (McGraw-Hill Energy Library)
  Oncogenes and Growth Factors Abstracts.
  P A I S International in Print. (PAIS INTERNATIONAL N SILVERPLATTER)
  P A I S Select. (PAIS SELECT ON SILVERPLATTER)
  Peterson's Graduate and Professional Programs: An Overview (Year) (Book 1). (PETERSON'S GRADLINE)
  Peterson's Graduate And Professional Programs: Business, Education, Health, Information Studies, Law, and Social Work (Year) (Book 6). (PETERSON'S GRADLINE)
  Peterson's Graduate and Professional Programs: Engineering and Applied Sciences (Year) (Book 5). (PETERSON'S GRADLINE)
  Peterson's Graduate and Professional Programs: The Biological Sciences (Year) (Book 3). (PETERSON'S GRADLINE)
  Peterson's Graduate and Professional Programs: The Humanities, Arts, and Social Sciences (Year) (Book 2). (PETERSON'S GRADLINE)
  Peterson's Graduate and Professional Programs: The Physical Sciences, Mathematics, and Agricultural Sciences (Year) (Book 4). (PETERSON'S GRADLINE)
  Pollution Abstracts. (POLTOX1)
  Population Index.
  Psychological Abstracts. (PsycLIT)
  R T E C S.
  Reactions Weekly.
  Readers' Guide Abstracts.
  Readers' Guide to Periodical Literature.
  Resources in Education. (ERIC)
  Safety and Health at Work.
  Schweizerische Zeitschrift fuer Volkswirtschaft und Statistik.
  Securite et Sante au Travail.
  Side Effects of Drugs Annual. (SEDBASE)
  Social Sciences Index.
  Social Work Abstracts. (SWAB-PLUS)
  Sociological Abstracts. (Sociofile)
  South Asian Survey.
  Southeast Power Report. (McGraw-Hill Energy Library)
  SportSearch.
  T R I S Electronic Bibliographic Data Base.
  Toxicology Abstracts. (POLTOX1)
  Ulrich's International Periodicals Directory. (ERL)
  Ulster Medical Journal. (MEDLINE)
  Utility Environment Report. (McGraw-Hill Energy Library)
  Virology and AIDS Abstracts.
  Water Resources Abstracts (Bethesda).
  Wilson Abstracts.
  Wilson Applied Science and Technology Abstracts.
  Wilson Business Abstracts.
  Wilson Education Abstracts.
  Wilson General Science Abstracts.
  Wilson Humanities Abstracts.
  Wilson Social Sciences Abstracts.
  Year Book of Cardiology. (ClinMED-CD)
  Zoological Record.

UMI
300 N. Zeeb Rd., Ann Arbor, MI 48106. Tel: 313-761-4700
Fax: 313-761-1203.
  A B I - INFORM.
  Acquisition of Greater Dayton.
  African Journal of International Affairs & Development.
  America.
  American Craft.
  American Doctoral Dissertations.
  Archives of Environmental Health.
  Arts Education Policy Review.
  Asian Affairs: An American Review.
  The Atlantic Monthly.
  Audubon.
  Behavioral Medicine.
  Bulletin of the Atomic Scientists.
  Business Mexico.
  Canadian Journal of Administrative Sciences.
  Change (Washington).
  Christian Century.
  The Clearing House.
  College Teaching.
  Commonweal.
  Computer & Control Abstracts.
  Consumer's Research Magazine.
  Corporate Report Minnesota.
  Critique: Studies in Modern Fiction.
  Current (Washington, 1960).
  Current Health 2.
  Dayton Business Reporter.
  Defense Counsel Journal.
  Dissertation Abstracts International. Section A: Humanities and Social Sciences.
  Dissertation Abstracts International. Section B: Physical Sciences and Engineering.

10036 PRODUCER LISTING/SERIALS ON CD-ROM

Dissertation Abstracts International. Section C: Worldwide.
Dissertation Abstracts on Disc.
Ebony.
The Education Digest.
Environment.
Environmental Action.
The Explicator.
Family Process.
Film Comment.
Foreign Affairs.
Genetic, Social, and General Psychology Monographs.
The Geographical Journal.
Germanic Review.
Greek Orthodox Theological Review.
Harper's Magazine.
The Hemingway Review.
Historical Methods.
History and Theory.
History: Reviews of New Books.
History Today.
Hospital Topics.
I E E Review.
Jet.
Journal of American College Health.
Journal of Arts Management, Law, and Society.
The Journal of Economic Education.
Journal of Education for Business.
The Journal of Educational Research.
The Journal of Environmental Education.
Journal of Experimental Education.
The Journal of General Psychology.
The Journal of Genetic Psychology.
Journal of Group Psychotherapy, Psychodrama & Sociometry.
Journal of Higher Education.
Journal of Money, Credit & Banking.
Journal of Motor Behavior.
Journal of Popular Film and Television.
Journal of Sport Behavior.
Kiplinger's Personal Finance Magazine.
Life.
Maclean's.
Masters Abstracts International.
Money (New York).
Mother Jones.
Motor Trend.
Multinational Business Review.
The Nation.
National Civic Review.
National Review.
Nation's Business.
Natural History.
The New Republic.
The New York Times.
Nieman Reports.
Outdoor Life.
Parents.
Perspectives on Political Science.
Physics Abstracts.
Ploughshares.
Popular Mechanics.
Popular Science.
Power Engineering Journal.
Preventing School Failure.
Psychology Today.
Review (Washington).
Rocks and Minerals.
Rolling Stone.
Sacramento Business Journal.
Scholastic Update.
Science Activities.
Science News.
Seventeen.
Techniques.
Time.
U S News & World Report.
Weatherwise.
Wilson Social Sciences Abstracts. *(PROQUEST)*
Women's Sports and Fitness.
World Health.
World Press Review.
The Writer.

H. W. WILSON
950 University Ave., Bronx, NY 10452. Tel: 718-588-8400 Cable: WILSONDEX Fax: 718-590-1617.
Applied Science & Technology Index.
Art Index. *(WILSONDISC)*
Biography Index. *(WILSONDISC)*
Biological & Agricultural Index. *(WILSONDISC)*
Book Review Digest. *(WILSONDISC)*
Business Periodicals Index. *(WILSONDISC)*
Canadian Journal of History.
Cumulative Book Index.
Current Biography Yearbook. *(WILSONDISC)*
Education Index. *(WILSONDISC)*
Essay and General Literature Index. *(WILSONDISC)*
General Science Index. *(WILSONDISC)*
History and Theory.
Humanities Index. *(WILSONDISC)*
Index to Legal Periodicals & Books. *(WILSONDISC)*
Library Literature. *(WILSONDISC)*
Life.
Monthly Catalog of United States Government Publications.
Ploughshares.
Readers' Guide Abstracts. *(WILSONDISC)*
Readers' Guide to Periodical Literature. *(WILSONDISC)*
Social Policy.
Social Sciences Index.
Structurist.
Wilson Abstracts. *(WILSONDISC)*
Wilson Applied Science and Technology Abstracts.
Wilson Business Abstracts. *(WILSONDISC)*
Wilson Education Abstracts. *(WILSONDISC)*
Wilson General Science Abstracts. *(WILSONDISC)*
Wilson Humanities Abstracts. *(WILSONDISC)*
Wilson Social Sciences Abstracts.

Serials Available Online

This index contains abbreviated entries for all serials known to be available online. Vendor names are given if known, plus file names or numbers in parentheses. For full bibliographic information on these titles, please refer to the complete entry on the page indicated in italics.

A A B'S BIBLIOGRAPHY OF RARE & OUT-OF-PRINT TITLES FOR SALE.
A A B British Book Search Services (Oxford), Editorial Research Centre, P.O. Box 342, Oxford OX1 1NN, England. TEL 01865-792610. FAX 01865-792611. *6288*

A A B'S GUIDE TO PRIVATE ENGLISH LANGUAGE SCHOOLS IN THE U.K. FOR OVERSEAS STUDENTS.
A A B British Book Search Services (Oxford), Editorial Research Centre, P.O. Box 342, Oxford OX1 1NN, England. TEL 44-1865-792610. FAX 44-1865-792611. *2520*

A A B'S REGISTER OF WANTED PUBLICATIONS.
A A B British Book Search Services (Oxford), Editorial Research Centre, P.O. Box 342, Oxford OX1 1NN, England. TEL 44-1865-792610. FAX 44-1865-792611. *6288*

A A MAGAZINE.
V N U Business Publications BV, VNU House, 32-34 Broadwick St., London W1A 2HG, England. TEL 44-171-439-4242. FAX 44-171-437-7001. *1079*

THE A B A A NEWSLETTER.
Antiquarian Booksellers' Association of America, 400 Summit Ave., St. Paul, MN 55102-2662. URL: http://www.clark.net/pub/rmharris/newsltr/newsltr.html. *6259*

A B A BANK COMPLIANCE.
American Bankers Association, 1120 Connecticut Ave., N.W., Washington, DC 20036. TEL 202-663-5497. FAX 202-663-7543.
Vendor(s): UMI. *1100*

A B A BANKING JOURNAL.
Simmons - Boardman Publishing Corp., 345 Hudson St., New York, NY 10014-4502. TEL 212-620-7200. FAX 212-633-1165.
Vendor(s): Dow Jones News Retrieval, Information Access Co., Knight-Ridder Information, Inc. (File no.648), Lexis-Nexis, Ovid Technologies, Inc. (TSAP), UMI. *1100*

A B A JOURNAL.
American Bar Association, 750 N. Lake Shore Dr., Chicago, IL 60611. TEL 312-988-5000. FAX 312-988-6014. URL: http://www.abanet.org.
Vendor(s): Lexis-Nexis, UMI, West Group. *3902*

A B A WASHINGTON LETTER.
American Bar Association, Governmental Affairs Office, 740 15th St., Washington, DC 20005-1009. TEL 202-662-1017. URL: http://www.abanet.org/govaffairs. *3902*

A B B REVIEW.
A B B Corporate Management Services AG, Ruetistr. 6, CH-5401 Baden, Switzerland. TEL 41-56-2054836. FAX 41-56-2212274. URL: http://www.abbreview.com.
Vendor(s): Data-Star, Knight-Ridder Information, Inc. *2807*

A B C BELGE POUR LE COMMERCE ET L'INDUSTRIE.
A B C pour le Commerce et l'Industrie C.V., Doornveld 1B28, B-1731 Asse, Belgium. TEL 32-2-4630273. FAX 32-2-4630885. *1649*

A B C DER DEUTSCHEN WIRTSCHAFT - QUELLENWERK FUR EINKAUF-VERKAUF.
A B C Publishing Group, Postfach 100262, 64202 Darmstadt, Germany. TEL 49-6151-3892-0. FAX 49-6151-33164.
Vendor(s): Data-Star, FIZ Technik. *1649*

A B C EUROP PRODUCTION.
A B C Publishing Group, Postfach 100262, 64202 Darmstadt, Germany. TEL 49-6151-3892-0. FAX 49-6151-33164.
Vendor(s): Data-Star, FIZ Technik. *1313*

A B C LUXEMBOURGEOIS POUR LE COMMERCE ET L'INDUSTRIE.
A B C pour le Commerce et l'Industrie C.V., Doornveld 1B28, B-1731 Asse, Belgium. TEL 32-2-4630273. FAX 32-2-4630885. *1649*

A B E C O R COUNTRY REPORTS.
Barclays Bank plc., Economics Department, P.O. Box 12, Barclays House, 1 Wimborne Rd., Poole, Dorset BH15 2BB, England. TEL 01202-344023. FAX 01202-402303.
Vendor(s): Data-Star, Knight-Ridder Information, Inc. *1219*

A B I - INFORM.
U M I, 300 N. Zeeb Rd., Ann Arbor, MI 48106. TEL 313-761-4700. FAX 800-864-0019. URL: http://wwww.umi.com.
Vendor(s): Data-Star (INFO), European Space Agency (File no.30), Knight-Ridder Information, Inc. (File no.15), Lexis-Nexis (ABI), Ovid Technologies, Inc. (INFO), Questel Orbit Inc. (INFO), STN International (STN), UMI. *1014*

A B I X: AUSTRALASIAN BUSINESS INTELLIGENCE.
Business Intelligence Australia Pty. Ltd., McConnell Dowell House, 627 Chapel St., S. Yarra, Vic. 3141, Australia. TEL 61-3-98279088. FAX 61-3-98279099. URL: http://www.abix.com.au.
Vendor(s): AUSINET, Kiwinet. *1014*

A C A JOURNAL.
American Compensation Association, 14040 N. Northsight Blvd., Scottsdale, AZ 85260. TEL 605-951-9191. FAX 602-483-8352.
Vendor(s): UMI. *1561*

A C A NEWS.
American Compensation Association, 14040 N. Northsight Blvd., Scottsdale, AZ 85260. TEL 602-951-9191. FAX 602-483-8352.
Vendor(s): UMI. *1561*

A C FLYER.
McGraw-Hill Companies, 1221 Ave. of the Americas, New York, NY 10020. TEL 212-512-2000. URL: http://www.mcgraw-hill.com/acfonline/ *7061*

A C L S OCCASIONAL PAPERS.
American Council of Learned Societies, 228 E. 45th St., New York, NY 10017. TEL 212-697-1505. FAX 212-949-8058. URL: http://www.acls.org. *3769*

A C M GUIDE TO COMPUTING LITERATURE.
Association for Computing Machinery, 1515 Broadway, 17th Fl., New York, NY 10036-5701. TEL 212-869-7440. FAX 212-869-0481.
Vendor(s): Knight-Ridder Information, Inc.. *2093*

A C M TRANSACTIONS ON MATHEMATICAL SOFTWARE.
Association for Computing Machinery, 1515 Broadway, 17th Fl., New York, NY 10036-5701. TEL 212-869-7440. FAX 212-944-1318. URL: http://gams.nist.gov/toms/Overview.html. *2208*

A C P JOURNAL CLUB.
American College of Physicians, Independence Mall W., Sixth St. at Race, Philadelphia, PA 19106-1572. TEL 215-351-2400. URL: http://www.acponline.org/journals/acpjc/jcmenu.htm. *4762*

A C U T A NEWS.
Association of College and University Telecommunications Administrators, 152 W. Zandale Dr., Ste. 200, Lexington, KY 40503-2486. TEL 606-278-3338. FAX 606-278-3268. URL: http://www.acuta.org. *2014*

A D C NEWS.
Automatic Identification Manufacturers U.S.A., 634 Alpha Dr., Pittsburgh, PA 15238-2802. TEL 412-963-8588. FAX 412-963-8753. *2105*

SERIALS AVAILABLE ONLINE

A F C NEWS.
Australian Film Commission, G.P.O. Box 3984, Sydney, N.S.W. 2001, Australia. TEL 61-2-93216444. URL: http://www.afc.gov.au. *5322*

A F H R C FACTSHEETS.
Agriculture Canada, Kentville Research Station, Kentville, NS B4N 1J5, Canada. TEL 902-679-5333, 97237(VR). FAX 902-679-2311. URL: http: //res.agr.ca/kentville/pubs/agindex.htm. Available only online. *85*

A G A GAS ENERGY REVIEW.
American Gas Association, 1515 Wilson Blvd., Arlington, VA 22209. TEL 703-841-8400. FAX 703-841-8406.
Vendor(s): UMI. *5594*

A G A R D REPORTS.
U.S. National Aeronautics and Space Administration, Scientific and Technical Information Office, 800 Elkridge Landing Rd., Linthicum Heights, MD 21090-2934. URL: http://www.sti.nasa.gov. Available only online. *51*

A G B NEWSLETTER.
University of Grenoble, URL: http://gag.observ-gr.fr/liens/agbnews.html.
Available only online. *488*

A GATHERING OF THE TRIBES.
Steve Cannon, Ed. & Pub., Box 20693, Tompkins Sq. Sta., New York, NY 10009. TEL 212-674-3778. FAX 212-674-5576. URL: http://www.interport.net/~tribes. *419*

A H F S DRUG INFORMATION.
American Society of Health-System Pharmacists, 7272 Wisconsin Ave., Bethesda, MD 20814. TEL 301-657-3000. FAX 301-657-1641.
Vendor(s): Data-Star (DIFT), Knight-Ridder Information, Inc. (File no.229), Lexis-Nexis, Ovid Technologies, Inc. (DIFT). *5644*

A I M REPORTS.
Agencia de Informacao de Mocambique, High Holborn House, 52-54 High Holborn, London WC1V 6RL, England. TEL 44-171-404-3230. FAX 44-171-404-33231. *3337*

A I MAGAZINE.
American Association for Artificial Intelligence, 445 Burgess Dr., Menlo Park, CA 94025. TEL 415-328-3123. FAX 415-321-4457. URL: http://www.aaai.org. *2096*

A I T REVIEW.
Asian Institute of Technology, Media and Information Services Office, P.O. Box 2754, Bangkok 10501, Thailand. TEL 66-2-516-0110. FAX 66-2-516-2126. URL: http://www.ait.ac.th/ *2708*

A J R.
American Roentgen Ray Society, Attn.: Leigh Myzk, 1891 Preston White Dr., VA 22091. TEL 703-648-8992. FAX 703-264-8863. *5102*

A L A·W O N.
American Library Association, Washington Office, 1301 Pennsylvania Ave, N.W., Ste. 403, Washington, DC 20004. TEL 202-628-8410. FAX 202-628-8419.
Available only online. *4154*

A L A WASHINGTON NEWS.
American Library Association, Washington Office, 1301 Pennsylvania Ave., N.W., Ste. 403, Washington, DC 20004. TEL 202-628-8410. URL: http://www.ala.org/washoff/publics.html. *4154*

A L C T S NETWORK NEWS.
American Library Association, Association for Library Collections & Technical Services, 50 E. Huron St., Chicago, IL 60611-2759. TEL 312-280-5035. FAX 312-280-3257.
Available only online. *4229*

A L F NEWSLETTER.
Association of Libertarian Feminists, Box 20252, London Terrace Post Office, New York, NY 10011. TEL 212-924-4345. FAX 212-924-4345. URL: http:/ourworld.compuserve.com/homepages/assn__of__libertarian__feminists. *5887*

A L I.
Avon Literary Intelligencer, 20 Pyron Pl., Bristol BS8 1JT, England. TEL 44-1225-826105. FAX 44-1225-826492. URL: http://www.bath.ac.uk/~masdr/ali.html. *4321*

A L M D ADVANCE.
L B C Information Services, 50 Waterloo Rd., N. Ryde, N.S.W. 2113, Australia. TEL 61-2-99366444. FAX 61-2-98889706. *3903*

A M P S METER WEEKLY REPORTS.
S A Advertising Research Foundation, P.O. Box 98874, 2152 Sloane Park, South Africa. TEL 27-11-463-5340. FAX 27-11-463-5010. *48*

A M P S RADIO DIARY.
S A Advertising Research Foundation, P.O. Box 98874, 2152 Sloane Park, South Africa. TEL 27-11-463-5340. FAX 27-11-463-5010. *2010*

A M R E P DATABASE BULLETIN.
Australian Mineral Resource Politics Pty. Ltd., 10 Hampstead Hill Rd., Aldgate, S.A. 5154, Australia. TEL 8 339 2960. *5293*

A M S NEWSLETTER (BOSTON).
American Meteorological Society, 45 Beacon St., Boston, MA 02108-3693. TEL 617-227-2425. FAX 617-742-8718. URL: http://www.ametsoc.org/AMS/newsltr/newsltr.html.
Available only online. *5225*

A. MAGAZINE: THE ASIAN AMERICAN QUARTERLY.
270 Lafayette St., Ste. 400, New York, NY 10012. TEL 212-925-2123. FAX 212-925-2896. URL: http://www.amagazine.com/at-live/amagazine.amagmain.html. *2993*

A N Q: A QUARTERLY JOURNAL OF SHORT ARTICLES, NOTES AND REVIEWS.
Heldref Publications, 1319 Eighteenth St., N.W., Washington, DC 20036-1802. TEL 202-296-6267. FAX 202-296-5149.
Vendor(s): Information Access Co. *4369*

A O A C INTERNATIONAL. JOURNAL.
A O A C International, 481 N. Frederick Ave., Ste. 500, Gaithersburg, MD 20877-2417. TEL 301-924-7077. FAX 301-924-7089.
Vendor(s): STN International (CJAOAC). *1786*

A O R N JOURNAL.
Association of Operating Room Nurses, Inc., c/o Peggy S. Lehr, 2170 S. Parker Rd., Ste. 300, Denver, CO 80231. TEL 303-755-6300. FAX 303-750-3441. URL: http://www.aorn.org/journal/allinone.htm. *4927*

A P A I S: AUSTRALIAN PUBLIC AFFAIRS INFORMATION SERVICE.
National Library of Australia, Publications Section, Cultural and Educational Services Division, Canberra, A.C.T. 2600, Australia. TEL 61-6-262-1365. FAX 61-6-273-4493. *6202*

A P A MONITOR.
American Psychological Association, 750 First St., N.E., Washington, DC 20002-4242. TEL 202-336-5560. FAX 202-336-5568. URL: http://www.apa.org:80/monitor/ *6088*

A P F REPORTER.
Alicia Patterson Foundation, 1730 Pennsylvania Ave., N.W., Ste. 850, Washington, DC 20006. TEL 202-393-5995. FAX 301-951-8512. URL: http://www.charm.net/~apfengel/home.html. *3868*

A P I S.
University of Florida, Institute of Food and Agricultural Sciences, Dept. of Entomology and Nematology, Bldg. 970, Gainesville, FL 32611-0620. TEL 904-392-1801. FAX 904-392-0190. URL: http://www.ifas.ufl.edu/~mts/apishtm/apis.htm. *85*

A P P A NEWSLETTER.
A P P A: The Association of Higher Education Facilities Officers, 1643 Prince St., Alexandria, VA 22314-2818. TEL 703-684-1446. FAX 703-549-2772.
Available only online. *2568*

A P S BULLETIN.
American Pain Society, 4700 W. Lake Ave., Glenview, IL 60025-1485. TEL 847-375-4715. FAX 847-375-4777. URL: http://www.ampainsoc.org. *4802*

A P S NEWS SERVICE.
Arab Press Service, A P S House, P.O. Box 3896, Nicosia, Cyprus. TEL 357-2-351778. FAX 357-2-350265.
Vendor(s): Information Access Co. *2660*

A S D A NEWS.
American Sleep Disorders Association, 1610 14th St., N.W., Ste. 300, Rochester, MN 55901. TEL 507-287-6006. FAX 507-287-6008. *5047*

A S F A AQUACULTURE ABSTRACTS.
Cambridge Scientific Abstracts, 7200 Wisconsin Ave., 6th Fl., Bethesda, MD 20814. TEL 301-961-6750. FAX 301-961-6720. URL: http://www.csa.com.
Vendor(s): DIMDI, European Space Agency, Knight-Ridder Information, Inc. (File no.44), STN International (AQUASCI). *3081*

A S F A MARINE BIOTECHNOLOGY ABSTRACTS.
Cambridge Scientific Abstracts, 7200 Wisconsin Ave., 6th Fl., Bethesda, MD 20814. TEL 301-961-6750. FAX 301-961-6720. URL: http://www.csa.com.
Vendor(s): European Space Agency, Knight-Ridder Information, Inc. (File nos.44 and 76), STN International. *634*

A S M NEWS (WASHINGTON).
American Society for Microbiology, 1325 Massachusetts Ave., N.W., Washington, DC 20005. TEL 202-737-3600. URL: http://www.asmusa.org/jnlsrc/asmnew1.htm. *778*

A S S I A: APPLIED SOCIAL SCIENCES INDEX & ABSTRACTS.
Bowker - Saur Ltd., A member of the Reed Elsevier plc group, Maypole House, Maypole Rd., E. Grinstead, W. Sussex RH19 1HU, England. TEL 44-1342-330100. FAX 44-1342-330191. URL: http://www.reed-elsevier.com.
Vendor(s): Data-Star (ASSI). *6648*

A S T I S BIBLIOGRAPHY.
Arctic Science & Technology Information System, Arctic Institute of North America, University of Calgary, 2500 University Dr. N.W., Calgary, AB T2N 1N4, Canada. TEL 403-220-4036. FAX 403-282-4609.
Vendor(s): QL Systems Ltd. *634*

A S T I S CURRENT AWARENESS BULLETIN.
Arctic Science & Technology Information System, Arctic Institute of North America, University of Calgary, 2500 University Dr. N.W., Calgary, AB T2N 1N4, Canada. TEL 403-284-7515. FAX 403-282-4609.
Vendor(s): QL Systems Ltd. *2324*

A S T I S OCCASIONAL PUBLICATIONS.
Arctic Science & Technology Information System, University of Calgary, 2500 University Dr. N.W., Calgary, AB T2N 1N4, Canada. TEL 403-220-4036. FAX 403-282-4609.
Vendor(s): QL Systems Ltd. *2324*

A S U RESEARCH MAGAZINE.
Arizona State University, A S U Research Magazine, Box 878206, Tempe, AZ 85387-8206. TEL 602-965-1266. FAX 602-965-9684. URL: http://toad.asu.edu/rschmag/. *6507*

A S U TRAVEL GUIDE.
A S U Travel Guide, Inc., 1525 Francisco Blvd., E., San Rafael, CA 94901. TEL 415-459-0300. FAX 415-459-0494. URL: http://www.ASUGuide.com. *7182*

A SLICE OF STALE PIZZA.
17 Kneen St., Fitzroy, Vic. 3068, Australia. URL: http://www.ozemail.com.au/~crust.
Available only online. *5370*

A V E W D NEWSLETTER.
URL: http://www.cam.org/~novsoft/index.html. Available only online. *2130*

A V VIDEO & MULTIMEDIA PRODUCER.
Knowledge Industry Publications, Inc., 701 Westchester Ave., White Plains, NY 10604. TEL 914-328-9157. *2066*

A W E A WIND ENERGY WEEKLY.
American Wind Energy Association, 122 C St., N.W., Ste. 400, Washington, DC 20001. TEL 202-383-2500. FAX 202-383-2505. URL: http://www.igc.apc.org/awea/. *2707*

ABERDEEN'S CONCRETE SOURCEBOOK.
Aberdeen Group, 426 S. Westgate St., Addison, IL 60101. TEL 630-543-0870. FAX 630-543-3112. URL: http://www.supernetwork.com. *860*

ABERDEEN'S CONSTRUCTION MARKETING TODAY.
Aberdeen Group, 426 S. Westgate St., Addison, IL 60101. TEL 630-543-0870. FAX 630-543-3112. URL: http://www.supernetwork.com. *860*

ABERDEEN'S MAGAZINE OF MASONRY CONSTRUCTION.
Aberdeen Group, 426 S. Westgate St., Addison, IL 60101. TEL 630-543-0870. FAX 630-543-3112. URL: http://www.supernetwork.com; http://www.wocnet.com/mags/mc.htm. *860*

ABILITY NETWORK MAGAZINE.
Ability Network Publishing Inc., 19 Mount Pleasant Ave., Dartmouth, NS B3A 3T3, Canada. TEL 902-461-9009. FAX 902-461-9484. *3452*

ABOUT MARKETING TO WOMEN.
About Women, Inc., 33 Broad St., Boston, MA 02109. TEL 617-723-4337. FAX 617-723-7107. Vendor(s): Information Access Co. *1513*

ABSATZWIRTSCHAFT.
Verlagsgruppe Handelsblatt GmbH, Kasernenstr. 67, 40213 Duesseldorf, Germany. TEL 49-211-8870. FAX 49-211-329954. *1514*

ABSTRACTS AND REVIEWS FROM ZENTRALBLATT FUER MATHEMATIK.
Fachinformationszentrum Karlsruhe, Gesellschaft fuer wissenschaftlich-technische Information mbH, 76344 Eggenstein-Leopoldshafen, Germany. TEL 07247-808333. FAX 07247-808666. *4617*

ABSTRACTS IN BIOCOMMERCE.
BioCommerce Data Ltd., Prudential Bldgs., 95 High St., Slough, Berks. SL1 1DH, England. TEL 44-1753-511777. FAX 44-1753-512239. URL: www.biospace.com/biocommerce. Vendor(s): Data-Star (CELL), Knight-Ridder Information, Inc. (file no.286). *634*

ABSTRACTS IN NEW TECHNOLOGIES AND ENGINEERING.
Bowker - Saur Ltd., A member of the Reed Elsevier plc group, Maypole House, Maypole Rd., E. Grinstead, W. Sussex RH19 1HU, England. TEL 44-1342-330100. FAX 44-1342-330191. URL: http://www.reed-elsevier.com. Vendor(s): Knight-Ridder Information, Inc. (File no.142). *6980*

ABSTRACTS OF BULGARIAN SCIENTIFIC MEDICAL LITERATURE.
Tsentralna Meditsinska Biblioteka, 1, Sv. Georgi Sofiiski St., 1431 Sofia, Bulgaria. TEL 359-2-523171. URL: http://www.medun.acad.bg. *4762*

ABSTRACTS OF WORKING PAPERS IN ECONOMICS.
Cambridge University Press, Edinburgh Bldg., Shaftesbury Rd., Cambridge CB2 2RU, England. TEL 44-1223-312393. FAX 44-1223-315052. URL: http://www.cup.org/journals/CUPJNLS.html. *1015*

ABSTRACTS ON HYGIENE AND COMMUNICABLE DISEASES.
CAB International, Wallingford, Oxon. OX10 8DE, England. TEL 44-1491-832111. FAX 44-1491-826090. URL: http://www.cabi.org. Vendor(s): DIMDI, Data-Star. *4763*

ABYA YALA NEWS.
South and Meso American Indian Rights Center, Box 28703, Oakland, CA 94604-8703. TEL 510-834-4263. FAX 510-834-4264. URL: http://www.maxwell.syr.edu/nativeweb/abyayala/orfs/saiic. Vendor(s): Lexis-Nexis. *2993*

ACADEMIA.
Baker & Taylor, Inc., Box 734, Somerville, NJ 08876. TEL 908-218-0400. FAX 908-218-3980. URL: http://www.baker-taylor.com. Available only online. *6260*

ACADEMIC ABSTRACTS C D - R O M.
EBSCO Publishing, 10 Estes St., Box 682, Ipswich, MA 01938. TEL 508-356-6500. FAX 508-356-6565. URL: http://www.epnet.com. Vendor(s): Ovid Technologies, Inc. *2*

ACADEMIC FILE INTERNATIONAL NEWS & PHOTO SYNDICATION.
Eastern Art Publishing Group, 27 Wallorton Gardens, London SL14 8DX, England. TEL 44-81-392-1122. FAX 44-81-392-1422. Available only online. *419*

ACADEMIC INDEX.
Information Access Company, 362 Lakeside Dr., Foster City, CA 94404. TEL 415-378-5200. FAX 415-378-5369. Vendor(s): Information Access Co., Knight-Ridder Information, Inc. (File no.88), Ovid Technologies, Inc. (ACAD). *3798*

ACADEMY OF MANAGEMENT. JOURNAL.
Academy of Management, Box 3020, Briarcliff Manor, NY 10510-8020. TEL 914-923-2607. FAX 914-923-2615. Vendor(s): Information Access Co., UMI. *1463*

ACADEMY OF MANAGEMENT EXECUTIVE.
Academy of Management, Box 3020, Briarcliff Manor, NY 10510-8020. TEL 914-923-2607. FAX 914-923-2615. URL: http://aom.pace.edu/publications/. Vendor(s): Information Access Co., UMI. *1463*

ACADEMY OF MANAGEMENT REVIEW.
Academy of Management, Box 3020, Briarcliff Manor, NY 10510. TEL 914-923-2607. FAX 914-923-2615. Vendor(s): Information Access Co., UMI. *1463*

ACADEMY OF MARKETING SCIENCE. JOURNAL.
Sage Publications, Inc., 2455 Teller Rd., Thousand Oaks, CA 91320. TEL 805-499-0721. FAX 805-499-0871. URL: http://www.sagepub.com/journals/usdetails/j0140.html. Vendor(s): Knight-Ridder Information, Inc. *1514*

ACADEMY OF MEDICINE, SINGAPORE. ANNALS.
Academy of Medicine, Singapore, 16 College Road, 01-01 College of Medicine Bldg., Singapore 169854, Singapore. TEL 65-2245166. FAX 65-2255155. URL: http://biomed.nus.sg/annals. *4630*

ACCENT ON LIVING.
Cheever Publishing, Inc., Box 700, Bloomington, IL 61702. TEL 309-378-2961. FAX 309-378-4420. Vendor(s): Information Access Co., UMI. *3466*

ACCESS E P A.
U.S. Environmental Protection Agency, Enterprise Management Division, 401 M St., S.W., Rm. 2003, 3404, Washington, DC 20460. URL: http://www.epa.gov. *2904*

ACCESS REPORTS.
Access Reports, Inc., 1624 Dogwood Lane, Lynchburg, VA 24503. TEL 804-384-5334. FAX 804-384-8272. Vendor(s): NewsNet (GT10). *5987*

ACCESS: THE SUPPLEMENTARY INDEX TO PERIODICALS.
John Gordon Burke Publisher, Inc., Box 1492, Evanston, IL 60204-1492. TEL 847-866-8625. FAX 847-866-6639. URL: http://www.nlightn.com. *2*

ACCOUNT LIST FILE.
Data Management Services Group Ltd., Ramillies House, 1-2 Ramillies St., London W1V 1DF, England. TEL 44-171-287-0030. FAX 44-171-437-4505. *29*

ACCOUNTANCY.
Institute of Chartered Accountants in England and Wales, P.O. Box 433, Moorgate Pl., London EC2P 2BJ, England. TEL 44-171-833-3291. URL: http://www.accountancymag.demon.co.uk/. Vendor(s): UMI. *1080*

ACCOUNTING AND FINANCE.
Accounting Association of Australia and New Zealand, 4th Fl., CPA House, 170 Queen St., Melbourne, Vic. 3000, Australia. TEL 61-3-96420227. URL: http://www.ecom.unimelb.edu.au/accwww/aaanz/. Vendor(s): Information Access Co., UMI. *1081*

ACCOUNTING AND TAX INDEX.
U M I, 300 N. Zeeb Rd., Ann Arbor, MI 48106. TEL 313-761-4700. FAX 800-864-0019. URL: http://www.umi.com. Vendor(s): Knight-Ridder Information, Inc. (File no. 485), UMI. *1015*

ACCOUNTING, BUSINESS AND FINANCIAL HISTORY.
Thomson Professional, 2-6 Boundary Row, London SE1 8HN, England. TEL 44-171-865-0066. FAX 44-171-522-9621. URL: http://abfh.thomsonprofessional.com. *930*

ACCOUNTING EDUCATION.
Thomson Professional, 2-6 Boundary Row, London SE1 8HN, England. TEL 44-171-8650066. FAX 44-171-8659623. URL: http://ae.thomsonprofessional.com. *1081*

ACCOUNTING EDUCATION NEWS.
American Accounting Association, 5717 Bessie Dr., Sarasota, FL 34233-2399. TEL 941-921-7747. FAX 941-923-4093. Vendor(s): UMI. *1081*

ACCOUNTING HISTORIANS JOURNAL.
Academy of Accounting Historians, c/o William D. Samson, Culverhouse School of Accountancy, University of Alabama, Tuscaloosa, AL 35487. TEL 205-348-2903. URL: http://nexxus.som.cwru.edu/Accounting. Vendor(s): UMI. *1081*

ACCOUNTING HISTORY.
Garry Carnegie, Ed. & Pub., c/o School of Accounting and Finance, Faculty of Business and Law, Deakin University, Geelong, Vic. 3217, Australia. TEL 61-3-52272733. FAX 61-3-52272264. *1081*

ACCOUNTING TECHNOLOGY.
Faulkner & Gray, Inc. (New York), 11 Penn Plaza, 17th Fl., New York, NY 10001. TEL 212-967-7000. FAX 212-967-7155. Vendor(s): UMI. *1082*

ACCOUNTING TODAY.
Faulkner and Gray, Inc. (New York), 11 Penn Plaza, 17th Fl., New York, NY 10001. TEL 212-967-7000. FAX 212-967-7155. URL: http://www.faulknergray.com/account/today.htm. Vendor(s): Information Access Co., UMI. *1082*

ACCOUNTS OF CHEMICAL RESEARCH.
American Chemical Society, 1155 16th St., N.W., Washington, DC 20036. TEL 202-872-4363. FAX 614-447-3671. Vendor(s): STN International (CJACS). *1736*

ACCREDITATION AND QUALITY ASSURANCE.
Springer-Verlag, Heidelberger Platz 3, 14197 Berlin, Germany. TEL 49-30-82787-0. FAX 49-30-82787448. URL: http://link.springer.de. *1787*

ACKNOWLEDGE THE WINDOW LETTER.
Mendham Technology Group, 144 Talmadge Rd., Box 11, Mendham, NJ 07945. TEL 201-543-2273. FAX 201-543-6033. Vendor(s): Information Access Co. *2186*

ACQUISITION OF GREATER DAYTON.
Hannover Publishing Co., Inc., 6356 Far Hills Ave., Dayton, OH 45459-2782. TEL 937-291-1100. FAX 937-436-3426. URL: http://www.daytonbusiness.com. *6294*

ACROSS THE BOARD.
Conference Board, Inc., 845 Third Ave., New York, NY 10022. TEL 212-759-0900. FAX 212-980-7014. Vendor(s): Information Access Co., UMI. *1463*

ACTA DIABETOLOGICA.
Springer-Verlag, Heidelberger Platz 3, 14197 Berlin, Germany. TEL 49-30-82787-0. FAX 49-30-82787448. URL: http://link.springer.de. *4882*

SERIALS AVAILABLE ONLINE

ACTA INFORMATICA.
Springer-Verlag, Heidelberger Platz 3, 14197 Berlin, Germany. TEL 49-30-82787-0. FAX 49-30-82787448. URL: http://link.springer.de. *2180*

ACTA NEUROPATHOLOGICA.
Springer-Verlag, Heidelberger Platz 3, 14197 Berlin, Germany. TEL 49-30-82787-0. FAX 49-30-82787448. URL: http://link.springer.de. *5048*

ACTA PHARMACEUTICA.
Croatian Pharmaceutical Society, Masarykova 2-II, HR-41000 Zagreb, Croatia. TEL 041-427944. FAX 041-431301. *5644*

ACTA PHARMACEUTICA HUNGARICA.
Magyar Gyogyszereszeti Tarsasag, Gyomroi ut 19-21, P.O.B. 27, 1475 Budapest, Hungary. TEL 36-1-4314620. FAX 36-1-2605604. *5644*

ACTA POLYTECHNICA.
Ceske Vysoke Uceni Technicke, Zikova 4, 166 35 Prague 6, Czech Republic. TEL 420-2-24353490. FAX 420-2-24311042. URL: http://www.cvut.cz/images/ctu/publishing/ *2708*

ACTA VIROLOGICA.
Vydavatel'stvo S A P, s.r.a., P.O. Box 57, Nam. Slobody 6, 810 05 Bratislava, Slovakia. TEL 42-7-211728. URL: http://www.europe.idealibrary.com/ *779*

ACTIVE AND PASSIVE ELECTRONIC COMPONENTS.
Gordon and Breach - Harwood Academic, Amsteldisk 166, 1st Fl., 1079 LH Amsterdam, Netherlands. URL: http://www.gbhap.com/Active_Passive_Electronic_Components/. *2807*

ACTUALIDAD COLOMBIANA.
Instituto Latinoamericano de Servicios Legales Alternativos, Apdo. Aereo 077844, Bogota, Colombia. TEL 57-1-245-5955. FAX 57-1-2884854. *3904*

ACTUALIDAD ECONOMICA.
Recoletos 1, 7o, 28001 Madrid, Spain. TEL 34-1-3373220. FAX 34-1-5768150. *1219*

ACTUALIDAD INTERNET.
URL: http://www.infolanz.es/actualidad. Available only online. *2130*

ACTUALITES PHARMACEUTIQUES.
S.U.T.I.P., 175 rue du Faubourg Poissonniere, 75009 Paris, France. FAX 42-82-98-00. *5644*

AD INFINITUM.
Dark Dimension Sci-Fi Club, URL: http://www2.combase.com/~adinfin. Available only online. *4528*

AD NAUSEAM.
1176 Bird Ave., San Jose, CA 95125. URL: http://www.crl.com/~jnelson/nauseam/ Available only online. *2131*

ADCOM NET.
Publitech, Inc., Box 840, Sherborn, MA 01770. TEL 508-651-3932. URL: http://www.adcom.net. Available only online. *29*

ADDICTION.
Carfax Publishing Co., P.O. Box 25, Abingdon, Oxon. OX14 3UE, England. TEL 44-1235-401000. FAX 44-1325-401550. *2297*

ADDICTION RESEARCH FOUNDATION. JOURNAL.
Addiction Research Foundation of Ontario, Subscription - Marketing Department, 33 Russell St., Toronto, ON M5S 2S1, Canada. TEL 416-595-6059. FAX 416-593-4694. URL: http://www.intropage.html. *2297*

ADDRESS LIST, REGIONAL AND SUBREGIONAL LIBRARIES FOR THE BLIND AND PHYSICALLY HANDICAPPED.
U.S. Library of Congress, National Library Service for the Blind and Physically Handicapped, Washington, DC 20542. TEL 202-707-5100. FAX 202-707-0712. URL: http://www.lcweb.loc.gov/nls. *3467*

ADHESION COMMUNICATIONS.
Gordon and Breach - Harwood Academic, Amsteldisk 166, 1st Fl., 1079 LH Amsterdam, Netherlands. URL: http://www.gbhap.com/Adhesion_Communications/. *5886*

ADHESIVES ABSTRACTS.
Rapra Technology Ltd., Shawbury, Shrewsbury, Shrops. SY4 4NR, England. TEL 44-1939-250383. FAX 44-1939-251118. URL: http://www.rapra.net. Vendor(s): Data-Star, Knight-Ridder Information, Inc., Questel Orbit Inc., STN International. *1771*

ADHESIVES AGE.
Intertec Publishing (Atlanta), 6151 Powers Ferry Rd., N.W., Atlanta, GA 30339-2941. TEL 770-955-2500. FAX 770-955-0476. Vendor(s): Information Access Co., UMI. *2754*

ADHESIVES & SEALANTS INDUSTRY.
Business News Publishing Co., 755 W. Big Beaver, Ste. 1000, Troy, MI 48084. TEL 810-362-3700. FAX 810-362-0317. URL: http://www.bnp.com. *2754*

THE ADJUNCT ADVOCATE.
Adjunct Advocate, Inc., Box 130117, Ann Arbor, MI 48113-0117. TEL 313-930-6854. FAX 313-741-8195. *2530*

ADMAP.
N T C Publications Ltd., P.O. Box 89, Henley-on-Thames, Oxon RB9 1GB, England. TEL 44-1491-411000. FAX 44-1491-571188. *29*

ADMINISTRATION & SOCIETY.
Sage Publications, Inc., 2455 Teller Rd., Thousand Oaks, CA 91320. TEL 805-499-0721. FAX 805-499-0871. URL: http://www.sagepub.com. Vendor(s): Information Access Co. *6162*

ADMINISTRATIVE SCIENCE QUARTERLY.
Cornell University, Johnson Graduate School of Management, 20 Thornwood Dr., Ste. 100, Ithaca, NY 14850-1265. TEL 607-254-7143. FAX 607-254-7100. URL: http://www.gsm.cornell.edu/ASQ/asq/html.
Vendor(s): Dow Jones News Retrieval, Information Access Co., Knight-Ridder Information, Inc., Ovid Technologies, Inc., UMI. *6162*

ADOLESCENCE (SAN DIEGO).
Libra Publishers, Inc., 3089C Clairemont Dr., Ste. 383, San Diego, CA 92117. TEL 619-571-1414. Vendor(s): Information Access Co., UMI. *1837*

ADVANCED IMAGING.
P T N Publishing Corp., 445 Broad Hollow Rd., Ste. 21, Melville, NY 11747-4722. TEL 516-845-2700. FAX 516-845-2797. Vendor(s): Information Access Co. *2014*

ADVANCED INTELLIGENT NETWORK NEWS.
Phillips Business Information, Inc., 1201 Seven Locks Rd., Potomac, MD 20854. TEL 301-424-3338. FAX 301-309-3847. Vendor(s): Information Access Co., NewsNet (TE15). *2131*

ADVANCED MANAGEMENT JOURNAL.
Society for Advancement of Management, Texas A&M University - Corpus Christi, College of Business, 6300 Ocean Dr., FC 111, Corpus Christi, TX 78412. TEL 512-994-6045. FAX 512-994-2725. Vendor(s): Information Access Co., UMI. *1464*

ADVANCED MATERIALS & PROCESSES.
A S M International, Materials Information, Materials Park, OH 44073-0002. TEL 216-338-5151. FAX 216-338-4634. URL: http://www.asm-intl.org/www-asm/magazine/am&p.html. Vendor(s): Information Access Co. *2850*

ADVANCES (KALAMAZOO).
Fetzer Institute, 9292 West KL Ave., Kalamazoo, MI 49009-9398. TEL 616-375-2000. FAX 616-372-2163. *4632*

ADVANCES IN APPLIED MATHEMATICS.
Academic Press, Inc., Journal Division, 525 B St., Ste. 1900, San Diego, CA 92101-4495. TEL 619-230-1840. FAX 619-699-6800. URL: http://www.apnet.com; http://www.idealibrary.com/ *4557*

ADVANCES IN MATHEMATICS.
Academic Press, Inc., Journal Division, 525 B St., Ste. 1900, San Diego, CA 92101-4495. TEL 619-230-1840. FAX 619-699-6800. URL: http://www.apnet.com/www/journal/ai.htm; http://www.idealibrary.com/ *4557*

ADVANCES IN PHARMACEUTICAL SCIENCES.
Academic Press, Inc., 525 B St., Ste. 1900, San Diego, CA 92101-4495. TEL 619-231-0926. FAX 619-699-6715. *5645*

ADVERTISING AGE.
Crain Communications, Inc. (Chicago), 740 Rush St., Chicago, IL 60611. TEL 312-649-5417. FAX 312-280-3174. URL: http://www.adage.com. Vendor(s): Information Access Co., Lexis-Nexis (ADAGE). *30*

ADWEEK (LOS ANGELES).
BPI Communications, Inc., 5055 Wilshire Blvd., Ste. 600, Los Angeles, CA 90036. TEL 213-525-2270. FAX 213-525-2391. Vendor(s): Knight-Ridder Information, Inc. (File no.648), Ovid Technologies, Inc. (TSAP). *30*

ADWEEK (NEW YORK).
B P I Communications, Inc. (New York), 1515 Broadway, New York, NY 10036. TEL 212-536-5336. FAX 212-536-1416. URL: http://www.adweek.com/magazine/adweek.asp. Vendor(s): Information Access Co., Knight-Ridder Information, Inc. (File no.648), Lexis-Nexis, Ovid Technologies, Inc. (TSAP). *31*

ADWEEK: MIDWEST.
A S M Communications, Inc. (Chicago), 222 Merchandise Mart Plaza, Ste. 936, Chicago, IL 60654-1102. TEL 312-467-6500. FAX 312-321-0039. Vendor(s): Information Access Co. *31*

ADWEEK: SOUTHWEST.
B P I, 3102 Maple Ave., Ste. 120, Dallas, TX 75201-1233. TEL 214-871-9550. Vendor(s): Information Access Co. *31*

AERA.
Asahi Shimbun Publishing Co., 3-2 Tsukiji 5-chome, Chuo-ku, Tokyo 104-11, Japan. *3329*

THE AERIAL ARCHAEOLOGY NEWSLETTER.
URL: http://www.nmia.com/~jaybird/AAnewsletter/ Available only online. *346*

AERONAUTICAL ENGINEERING: A CONTINUING BIOGRAPHY WITH INDEXES.
U.S. National Aeronautics and Space Administration, Scientific and Technical Information Office, 800 Elkridge Landing Rd., Linthicum Heights, MD 21090-2934. URL: http:/www.sti.nasa.gov. Available only online. *83*

AEROSPACE AMERICA.
American Institute of Aeronautics and Astronautics, Inc., 1801 Alexander Dr., Ste. 500, Reston, VA 20191. TEL 703-264-7500. FAX 202-646-7508. URL: http://www.aiaa.org/publications/aa-magazine.html. Vendor(s): Lexis-Nexis (AEROAM). *53*

AEROSPACE DAILY.
McGraw-Hill Companies, Aviation Week Group (Washington), 1200 G St., N.W., Ste. 200, Washington, DC 20005. TEL 202-383-2350. Vendor(s): Dow Jones News Retrieval, European Space Agency (File no.72/AEROSPACE DAILY), Knight-Ridder Information, Inc. (File nos.624,648), Lexis-Nexis (AIRDLY), NewsNet (AE29), Ovid Technologies, Inc. (TSAP). *54*

AEROSPACE ENGINEERING MAGAZINE.
Society of Automotive Engineers, 400 Commonwealth Dr., Warrendale, PA 15096-0001. TEL 412-772-7114. FAX 412-776-4026. URL: http://www.sae.org/PRODSERV/MAGAZINE/Aerospac.htm. Vendor(s): Questel Orbit Inc. *54*

AEROSPACE MEDICINE AND BIOLOGY.
U.S. National Aeronautics and Space Administration, Scientific and Technical Information Office, 800 Elkridge Landing Rd., Linthicum Heights, MD 21090-2934. URL: http:/www.sti.nasa.gov. Available only online. *4763*

AEROSPACE PROPULSION.
McGraw-Hill Companies, Aviation Week Group (Washington), 1200 G St., N.W., Ste. 200, Washington, DC 20005. TEL 202-383-2350. Vendor(s): Dow Jones News Retrieval (ASR), Knight-Ridder Information, Inc. (ASP), Lexis-Nexis (AERPRO), NewsNet (AE34). *54*

SERIALS AVAILABLE ONLINE 10041

AEROTECH NEWS & REVIEW.
URL: http://www.avimall.com/aerotech/index.html.
Available only online. *54*

THE AETHER SANCTUM.
URL: http://aether.documenta.com.au.
Available only online. *5370*

LES AFFAIRES.
Publications Transcontinental Inc., 1100 boul. Rene Levesque W., 24th Fl., Montreal, PQ H3B 4X9, Canada. TEL 514-392-9000. FAX 514-392-4723.
Vendor(s): Southam Electronic Publishing. *1101*

AFFIRMATIVE ACTION - E E O PERSONNEL UPDATE.
Nyper Publications, Box 662, Latham, NY 12110. TEL 518-786-1654. FAX 518-456-8582. URL: http://www.nyper.com.
Vendor(s): Lexis-Nexis, NewsNet. *3906*

AFFORDABLE HOUSING INDUSTRY INFORMATION SERVICE.
Affordable Housing Finance Magazine, 657 Mission St., San Francisco, CA 94105-4118. TEL 415-546-7255. URL: http://www.housingfinance.com.
Available only online. *3740*

AFRICA ANALYSIS.
Africa Analysis Ltd., Ludgate House, 107-111 Fleet St., London EC4A 2AB, England. TEL 44-171-353-1117. FAX 44-171-353-1516. URL: http://www.textor.com/cms/dAAAA.html. *1219*

AFRICA ECONOMIC DIGEST.
Concord Press of Nigeria, 26-32 Whistler St., London N5 1NJ, England. TEL 071-359-5335. FAX 071-359-9173. *1220*

AFRICA NEWS ONLINE.
Africa News Service, Inc., Box 3851, Durham, NC 27702. TEL 919-286-0747. FAX 919-286-2614. URL: http://www.afnews.org/ans.
Available only online. Vendor(s): NewsNet. *5888*

AFRICA TODAY.
Lynne Rienner Publishers, 1800 30th St., Ste. 314, Boulder, CO 80301. TEL 303-444-6684. FAX 303-444-0824. URL: http://www.africa.co.uk.
Vendor(s): Information Access Co., UMI. *5889*

AFRICAN AFFAIRS.
Oxford University Press, Academic Division, Great Clarendon St., Oxford OX2 6DP, England. TEL 44-1865-267907. FAX 44-1865-267485. URL: http://www.oup.co.uk/jnts/list/afrafj/.
Vendor(s): Information Access Co. *5889*

AFRICAN AMERICAN REVIEW.
Indiana State University, Department of English, Terre Haute, IN 47809. TEL 812-237-2968. FAX 812-237-3156.
Vendor(s): Information Access Co., UMI. *2993*

AFRICAN ARTS.
University of California at Los Angeles, James S. Coleman African Studies Center, Los Angeles, CA 90024. TEL 310-825-1218. URL: http://www.isop.ucla.edu/jscass/afrart/afrart1.htm.
Vendor(s): UMI. *420*

AFRICAN BUSINESS.
I.C. Publications, 7 Coldbath Sq., London EC1R 4LQ, England. TEL 44-171-713-7711. FAX 44-171-713-7898. *1353*

AFRICAN STUDIES QUARTERLY.
University of Florida, Center for African Studies, 427 Grinter Hall, Box 115560, Gainesville, FL 32611-5560. TEL 352-392-2183. FAX 352-392-2435. URL: http://www.clas.ufl.edu/africa/asq.
Available only online. *6601*

AFTENPOSTEN.
Aftenposten A-S, P.O. Box 1178, Sentrum, N-0107 Oslo, Norway. TEL 47-22-86-30-00. FAX 47-22-42-63-25. URL: http://www.aftenposten.no. *3341*

AFTERIMAGE.
Visual Studies Workshop, 31 Prince St., Rochester, NY 14607. TEL 716-442-8676. FAX 716-442-1992.
Vendor(s): Information Access Co. *5761*

AFTERIMAGES.
2808 Peppertree Pl., Plano, TX 75074. URL: http://www.access.digex.net/~justgus/afterimages/.
Available only online. *4371*

AFTERMARKET BUSINESS.
Advanstar Communications, Inc., 7500 Old Oak Blvd., Cleveland, OH 44130. TEL 216-891-2604. FAX 216-891-2574.
Vendor(s): Information Access Co., Knight-Ridder Information, Inc. *7081*

AFTERNOON MAGAZINE.
Motley Focus Locus, 788 Columbus Ave., 7P, New York, NY 10025. URL: http://www.motley-focus.com/~timber/afternoon.html.
Available only online. *420*

THE AG BIOETHICS FORUM.
I S U Bioethics Program, URL: http://www.iastate.edu/~grad__cikkege/bioethics. *86*

THE AGE.
David Syme & Co. Limited, 250 Spencer St., 5th Fl., Melbourne, Vic. 3000, Australia. TEL 61-3-96012903. FAX 61-3-96707514. URL: http://www.theage.com.au.
Vendor(s): AUSINET. *3250*

AGE AND AGEING.
Oxford University Press, Academic Division, Great Clarendon St., Oxford OX2 6DP, England. TEL 44-1865-267907. FAX 44-1865-267485. URL: http://www.oup.co.uk/jnls/list/ageing.
Vendor(s): Information Access Co., Ovid Technologies, Inc. *3430*

AGENCY SALES.
Manufacturers' Agents National Association, 23016 Mill Creek Rd., Box 3467, Laguna Hills, CA 92654-3467. TEL 714-859-4040.
Vendor(s): Information Access Co., UMI. *1514*

AGENDA (MEMPHIS).
Towery Publishing, Inc., 1835 Union Ave., No. 142, Memphis, TN 38104. TEL 901-725-2400. FAX 901-725-2401. URL: http://www.towery.c. *1176*

AGEXPORTER.
U.S. Department of Agriculture, Foreign Agricultural Service, Information Division, Rm. 4638-S, Washington, DC 20250-1000. TEL 202-720-9437. FAX 202-720-3229.
Vendor(s): Information Access Co. *186*

AGGIE PANORAMA.
New Mexico State University, Box 3K, Las Cruces, NM 88003-8001. TEL 505-646-3221. FAX 505-646-2099. URL: http://www.nmsu.edu/~ncomm/Panorama/Panoramatoc.html. *1938*

AGGRESSIVE BEHAVIOR.
John Wiley & Sons, Inc., Journals, 605 Third Ave., New York, NY 10158. TEL 212-850-6645. FAX 212-850-6021. URL: http://www.wiley.co.uk. *6091*

AGING RESEARCH & TRAINING NEWS.
Business Publishers, Inc., 951 Pershing Dr., Silver Spring, MD 20910-4464. TEL 301-587-6300. FAX 301-585-9075. URL: http://www.bpinews.com/hr/pages/art.html.
Vendor(s): NewsNet. *3431*

AGNIESZKA'S DOWRY.
Small Garlic Press, URL: http://www.mcs.net/~marek/asgp/chapbook.html.
Available only online. *4502*

AGRA EUROPE.
Agra Europe (London) Ltd., 25 Frant Rd., Tunbridge Wells, Kent TN2 5JT, England. TEL 44-1892-533813. FAX 44-1892-544895.
Vendor(s): Information Access Co. *187*

AGRI FINANCE.
Doane Agricultural Service Co., 11701 Borman Dr., St. Louis, MO 63146-4199. TEL 314-569-2700. FAX 314-569-1083.
Vendor(s): UMI. *187*

AGRI MARKETING.
Doane Information Service, 11701 Borman Dr., St. Louis, MO 63146. TEL 314-569-2700. FAX 314-564-1083.
Vendor(s): UMI. *187*

AGRICULTURAL & ENVIRONMENTAL BIOTECHNOLOGY ABSTRACTS.
Cambridge Scientific Abstracts, 7200 Wisconsin Ave., 6th Fl., Bethesda, MD 20814. TEL 301-961-6700. FAX 301-961-6720. URL: http://www.csa.com.
Vendor(s): Knight-Ridder Information, Inc. (File no. 76/Life Sciences Collection), STN International (LIFESCI). *167*

AGRICULTURAL ENGINEERING ABSTRACTS.
CAB International, Walingford, Oxon. OX10 8DE, England. TEL 44-1491-832111. FAX 44-1491-826090. URL: http://www.cabi.org.
Vendor(s): DIMDI, European Space Agency (File nos.16 & 124/CAB), Knight-Ridder Information, Inc., STN International. *167*

AGRICULTURAL HISTORY.
University of California Press, Journals Division, 2120 Berkeley Way, No. 5812, Berkeley, CA 94720-5812. TEL 510-643-7154. FAX 510-642-9917. URL: http://library.berkeley.edu:8080/ucalpress/journals.
Vendor(s): Information Access Co. *91*

AGRICULTURAL RESEARCH.
U.S. Department of Agriculture, Agriculture Research Service, Rm. 408, 6303 Ivy Ln., Greenbelt, MD 20770. TEL 301-344-2514. FAX 301-344-2325. URL: http://www.ars.usda.gov/is/AR.
Vendor(s): Information Access Co., UMI. *212*

AGRICULTURAL RESEARCH DEPARTMENT. WINAND STARING CENTRE FOR INTEGRATED LAND, SOIL AND WATER RESEARCH. REPORTS.
Dienst Landbouwkundig Onderzoek, P.O. Box 125, 6700 AC Wageningen, Netherlands. TEL 31-8370-74200. FAX 31-8370-24812. *212*

AGRICULTURAL STATISTICS SERIES NO.2: ANIMAL PRODUCTION.
Statistical Office of the European Communities, Rue Alcide de Gasperi, 2920 Luxembourg, Luxembourg. TEL 43011. *168*

AGRICULTURAL SUPPLY INDUSTRY.
P J B Publications Ltd., 18-20 Hill Rise, Richmond, Surrey TW10 6UA, England. TEL 44-181-948-3262. FAX 44-181-332-8998. URL: http://www.pjbpubs.co.uk/agrow/aghome.html.
Vendor(s): Data-Star, Knight-Ridder Information, Inc. (File no.129), Ovid Technologies, Inc. (PHIN). *92*

AGRICULTURE AND ENVIRONMENT FOR DEVELOPING COUNTRIES.
Koninklijk Instituut voor de Tropen, Mauritskade 63, 1092 AD Amsterdam, Netherlands. TEL 31-20-5688298. FAX 31-20-6654423.
Vendor(s): Questel Orbit Inc. (TROPAG). *168*

AGRINDEX.
Food and Agriculture Organization of the United Nations (Rome), Via delle Terme de Caracalla, 00100 Rome, Italy. TEL 57974350. FAX 57975155.
Vendor(s): DIMDI, Knight-Ridder Information, Inc. (File no.203), European Space Agency (File no.29/AGRIS). *93*

AGROFORESTRY ABSTRACTS.
CAB International, Wallingford, Oxon. OX10 8DE, England. TEL 44-1491-832111. FAX 44-1491-826090.
Vendor(s): DIMDI, Data-Star, European Space Agency, Knight-Ridder Information, Inc., Ovid Technologies, Inc., STN International. *3167*

AGROW.
P J B Publications Ltd., 18-20 Hill Rise, Richmond, Surrey TW10 6UA, England. TEL 44-181-948-3262. FAX 44-181-332-8998. URL: http://www.pjbpubs.co.uk/agrow/aghome.html.
Vendor(s): Data-Star, Knight-Ridder Information, Inc. (File No.129), Ovid Technologies, Inc. (PHIN,PHIC, PHID). *96*

AGWAY COOPERATOR.
Agway Inc., Box 4741, Syracuse, NY 13221. TEL 315-479-6117. FAX 315-449-6041. URL: http://www.agway.com. *96*

SERIALS AVAILABLE ONLINE

AIDS.
Thomson Science, 2-6 Boundary Row, London SE1 8HN, England. TEL 44-171-865-0198. FAX 44-171-928-7876. URL: http://www.thomsonscience.com. *4830*

AIDS BOOK REVIEW JOURNAL.
University of Illinois at Chicago, Library, Box 8198, Chicago, IL 60680-8198. TEL 312-996-2730. FAX 312-413-0424. URL: http://www.uic.edu/depts/lib/aidsbkrv/.
Available only online. *4830*

AIDS CARE.
Carfax Publishing Co., P.O. Box 25, Abingdon, Oxon. OX14 3UE, England. TEL 44-1235-401000. FAX 44-1235-401550. *4830*

AIDS NEWSLETTER.
CAB International, Wallingford, Oxon. OX10 8DE, England. TEL 44-1491-832111. FAX 44-1491-826090. URL: http://www.cabi.org.
Vendor(s): DIMDI. *4831*

AIDS POLICY AND LAW.
L R P Publications, 747 Dresher Rd., Box 980, Horsham, PA 19044-0980. TEL 215-784-0941. FAX 215-784-9639. URL: http://www.lrp.com.
Vendor(s): Human Resources Information Network (CDD, HDD). *3907*

AIDS READER.
S C P Communications, Inc., 134 W. 29th St., New York, NY 10001-5304. URL: http://www.medscape.com. *4831*

AIDS THERAPIES.
Charles W. Henderson, Ed. & Pub., Box 5528, Atlanta, GA 31107-0528. TEL 404-377-8895. FAX 404-378-5411. URL: http://www.newsfile.com. *4832*

AIDS WEEKLY PLUS.
Charles W. Henderson, Ed. & Pub., Box 5528, Atlanta, GA 31107-0528. TEL 404-507-7777. FAX 404-507-7788.
Vendor(s): Data-Star (PTS NEWSLETTER DATABASE), Information Access Co., Knight-Ridder Information, Inc. (File no.636), NewsNet (HH14). *4832*

AIKIDO JOURNAL.
K.K. Aiki News, Matsugae-cho 14-17-103, Sagamihara-shi, Kanagawa-ken 228, Japan. TEL 81-427-48-2423. FAX 81-427-48-2421. *6747*

AIR CARGO REPORT.
Phillips Business Information, Inc., 1201 Seven Locks Rd., Potomac, MD 20854. TEL 301-424-3338. FAX 301-309-3847.
Vendor(s): Information Access Co., NewsNet. *7061*

AIR CARGO WORLD.
Intertec Publishing Corp. (Atlanta), 6151 Powers Ferry Rd., N.W., Atlanta, GA 30339-2941. TEL 770-955-2500. FAX 770-955-0400.
Vendor(s): Information Access Co. *7061*

AIR CONDITIONING, HEATING & REFRIGERATION NEWS.
Business News Publishing Company, 755 W. Big Beaver Rd., Ste. 1000, Troy, MI 48084. TEL 810-362-3700. FAX 810-362-0317. URL: http://www.bnp.com/thenews.
Vendor(s): Dow Jones News Retrieval, Information Access Co., Knight-Ridder Information, Inc. (File no.648), Ovid Technologies, Inc. (TSAP). *3476*

AIR FRESHENERS AND INSECTICIDES: THE INTERNATIONAL MARKET.
Euromonitor, 60-61 Britton St., London EC1M 5NA, England. TEL 44-171-251-8024. FAX 44-171-608-3149. URL: http://www.euromonitor.com.
Vendor(s): Data-Star, Knight-Ridder Information, Inc. *1909*

AIR IN THE PARAGRAPH LINE.
600 7th Ave., No. 520, Seattle, WA 98104-1933. URL: http://www.speakeasy.org/~jkonrath. *3368*

AIR SAFETY WEEK.
Phillips Business Information, Inc., 1201 Seven Locks Rd., Potomac, MD 20854. TEL 301-424-3338. FAX 301-309-3847.
Vendor(s): Data-Star, Information Access Co., Knight-Ridder Information, Inc., NewsNet (AE16). *56*

AIR TRANSPORT WORLD.
Penton Publishing Co. (Stamford), 600 Summer St., Box 1361, Stamford, CT 06904. TEL 203-348-7531. FAX 203-348-4023. URL: http://www.atwonline.com/
Vendor(s): Information Access Co., Knight-Ridder Information, Inc., UMI. *56*

AIR - WATER POLLUTION REPORT.
Business Publishers, Inc., 951 Pershing Dr., Silver Spring, MD 20910-4464. TEL 301-587-6300. FAX 301-585-9075.
Vendor(s): Data-Star, Information Access Co., Knight-Ridder Information, Inc., NewsNet (EV10). *2905*

AIRCRAFT SURVIVABILITY.
Joint Technical Coordinating Group - Aircraft Survivability. URL: http://surviac.flight.wpafb.af.mil/curr__awar/ac__surv__newsletter/newsletters.html.
Available only online. *56*

AIRCRAFT VALUE NEWSLETTER.
Phillips Business Information, Inc., 1201 Seven Locks Rd., Potomac, MD 20854. TEL 301-424-3338. FAX 301-309-3847.
Vendor(s): Information Access Co., NewsNet. *7063*

AIRFINANCE JOURNAL.
Euromoney Aviation Group, Playhouse Yard, Nestor House, London EC4V 5EX, England. TEL 44-171-779-8941. FAX 44-171-779-8525.
Vendor(s): UMI. *7063*

AIRLINE BUSINESS.
Reed Business Publishing Ltd., Quadrant House, The Quadrant, Sutton, Surrey SM2 5AS, England. TEL 0181-652-4996. FAX 0181-652-8914.
Vendor(s): Data-Star, Information Access Co., Reuters, Ltd. *7063*

AIRLINE FINANCIAL NEWS.
Phillips Business Information, Inc., 1201 Seven Locks Rd., Potomac, MD 20854. TEL 301-424-3338. FAX 301-309-3847.
Vendor(s): Data-Star, Information Access Co., Knight-Ridder Information, Inc., NewsNet (AE25). *7063*

AIRLINE INDUSTRY INFORMATION.
M2 Communications Ltd., P.O. Box 475, Coventry CV1 2ZW, England. TEL 44-1203-634700. FAX 44-1203-634144. URL: http://www.m2.com.
Available only online. *7063*

AIRMAN.
U.S. Air Force, Air Force News Agency, Kelly AFB, TX 78241-6105. TEL 210-925-7757. FAX 210-925-7219. URL: http://www.af.mil. *5257*

AIRPORTS.
McGraw-Hill Companies, Aviation Week Group (Washington), 1200 G St., N.W., Ste. 200, Washington, DC 20005. TEL 202-383-2350.
Vendor(s): Dow Jones News Retrieval, Knight-Ridder Information, Inc. (File no.624/McGRAW-HILL PUBLICATIONS ONLINE), Lexis-Nexis, NewsNet (AE21). *7064*

AISLE SAY.
41-07 42nd St., Ste. 4B, Long Island City, NY 11014. URL: http://www.escape.com/~theanet/aislesay.html.
Available only online. *7001*

AIXPERT.
I B M Corporation (Austin), Izip 1034, 11400 Burnet Rd., Austin, TX 78758. TEL 512-823-6840. FAX 512-823-6520. URL: http://www.developer.ibm.com/library/aixpert/. *2209*

AIXTRA.
I B M Corporation (Roanoke), 5 W. Kirwood Blvd., MS 01-04-60, Roanoke, VA 76299. TEL 817-962-6551. FAX 817-962-7218. URL: http://pscc.dfw.ibm.com/aixtra. *2072*

ALABAMA BUSINESS DIRECTORY.
American Business Directories, 5711 S. 86th Cir., Box 27347, Omaha, NE 68127. TEL 402-593-4600. FAX 401-331-5481. *1650*

ALABAMA LAW REVIEW.
University of Alabama, School of Law, Box 870382, University, AL 35487-0382. TEL 205-348-7191.
Vendor(s): West Group. *3907*

ALABAMA LAWYER.
State Bar of Alabama, Lock Box 4156, Montgomery, AL 36101. TEL 205-269-1515.
Vendor(s): West Group. *3907*

ALASKA. STATE COUNCIL ON THE ARTS. COMMUNIQUE.
State Council on the Arts, 411 W. Fourth Ave., Ste. 1E, Anchorage, AK 99501-2343. TEL 907-279-1558. FAX 907-279-4330. URL: http://www.educ.state.akus/asca/home/html. *420*

ALASKA BUSINESS DIRECTORY.
American Business Directories, 5711 S. 86th Cir., Box 27347, Omaha, NE 68127. TEL 402-593-4600. FAX 402-331-5481. *1651*

ALASKA BUSINESS MONTHLY.
Alaska Business Publishing Co., Box 241288, Anchorage, AK 99524-1288. TEL 907-276-4373. FAX 907-279-2900.
Vendor(s): Information Access Co., Knight-Ridder Information, Inc., Lexis-Nexis. *931*

ALASKA JOURNAL OF COMMERCE & PACIFIC RIM REPORTER.
Pacific Rim Publishing Co., Box 201894, Anchorage, AK 99520-1894. TEL 907 272-7500. FAX 907-279-1037.
Vendor(s): Knight-Ridder Information, Inc., UMI. *1208*

ALASKA SNOW SURVEY REPORT.
U.S. Natural Resources Conservation Service (Anchorage), 949 E. 36th Ave., Ste. 400, Anchorage, AK 99508-4362. TEL 907-271-2424. FAX 907-271-3951. *7287*

ALBANY LAW REVIEW.
Albany Law School, 80 New Scotland Ave., Albany, NY 12208. TEL 518-445-2372. FAX 518-472-5857.
Vendor(s): Lexis-Nexis, West Group, Wilsonline. *3908*

THE ALBANY REPORT.
Sawchuk, Brown Associates, 41 State St., Albany, NY 12207. TEL 518-462-0318. FAX 518-462-0688.
Available only online. *1220*

ALBERT HOFMANN'S STRANGE MISTAKE.
Box 1852, Brown University, Providence, RI 02912. URL: http://www.rabyd.com/lsd.
Available only online. *4894*

ALBERTA DECISIONS. CIVIL AND CRIMINAL CASES.
Western Legal Publications, 301-1 Alexander St., Vancouver, BC V6A 1B2, Canada. TEL 604-687-5671. FAX 604-687-2796. *3908*

ALBERTA REPORTS.
Maritime Law Book Ltd., Box 302, Fredericton, NB E3B 4Y9, Canada. TEL 506-453-9921. FAX 506-453-9525.
Vendor(s): QL Systems Ltd. *3908*

ALCOHOL HEALTH & RESEARCH WORLD.
U.S. National Institute on Alcohol Abuse and Alcoholism, 6000 Executive Blvd., Bethesda, MD 20892-7003. TEL 301-443-3860. FAX 301-480-1726. URL: http://www.niaace.nih.gov.
Vendor(s): Information Access Co., UMI. *2298*

ALCOHOL OUTLOOK.
Information Resources, Inc., 1925 N. Lynn St., Ste. 1000, Arlington, VA 22204-1717. TEL 703-528-2500. FAX 703-528-1483.
Vendor(s): Information Access Co. *5594*

ALCOHOLISM & DRUG ABUSE WEEKLY.
Manisses Communications Group, Inc., Box 9758, Providence, RI 02940-9758. TEL 401-831-6020. FAX 401-861-6370. URL: http://www.manisses.com.
Vendor(s): Data-Star, Information Access Co., Knight-Ridder Information, Inc., Ovid Technologies, Inc. *2298*

ALDRICHIMICA ACTA.
Aldrich Chemical Company, Inc., 1001 W. St. Paul Ave., Milwaukee, WI 53233. TEL 414-298-7907. FAX 414-273-4979. URL: http://www.sigma.sial.com/aldrich/acta29__2/content.htm. *1811*

ALGEBRA COLLOQUIUM.
Springer-Verlag Singapore, No. 04-01, Cencon I, One Tannery Rd., Singapore 347719, Singapore. TEL 65-84-20-112. FAX 65-84-20-107. *4558*

ALL CANADA WEEKLY SUMMARIES - NATIONAL.
Canada Law Book Inc., 240 Edward St., Aurora, ON L4G 3S9, Canada. TEL 905-841-6472. FAX 905-841-5085. *3908*

ALL ENGLAND LAW REPORTS.
Butterworth & Co. (Publishers) Ltd., Part of the Reed Elsevier group, Halsbury House, 35 Chancery Ln., London WC2A 1EL, England. TEL 071-400-2500. FAX 071-400-2842.
Vendor(s): Lexis-Nexis. *4129*

ALL MEDIA & PRODUCT SURVEY.
S A Advertising Research Foundation, P.O. Box 98874, 2152 Sloane Park, South Africa. TEL 27-11-463-5340. FAX 27-11-463-5010. *48*

ALLOYS INDEX.
Cambridge Scientific Abstracts, 7200 Wisconsin Ave., 6th fl., Bethesda, MD 20814. TEL 301-961-6750. FAX 301-961-6720. URL: http://www.csa.com.
Vendor(s): CEDOCAR, CISTI, Data-Star (META), European Space Agency (File no.3), FIZ Technik (META), Knight-Ridder Information, Inc. (File no.32/METADEX), Questel Orbit Inc. (MDEX), STN International. *5216*

ALMA.
Via Tevere 68, 87036 Roges Rende (CS), Italy. URL: http://www.diemme.it/"luigi/alma.html.
Available only online. *2097*

ALMANAC OF FAMOUS PEOPLE.
Gale Research, 835 Penobscot Bldg., 645 Griswold St., Detroit, MI 48226-4094. TEL 313-961-2242. FAX 800-414-5043.
Vendor(s): Lexis-Nexis. *571*

ALSIRAT.
Joel Gazis-Sax, Ed. & Pub., 2727 Midtown Court, No. 37, Palo Alto, CA 94303. URL: http://www.best.com/~gazissax/
Available only online. *4372*

ALTERNATIVE COUNTRY MONTHLY.
URL: http://www.ix.net.au/~reporter/index.html. *6602*

ALTERNATIVE PRESS INDEX.
Alternative Press Center, Inc., Box 33109, Baltimore, MD 21218. TEL 410-243-2471. FAX 410-235-5325. URL: http://www.igc.apc.org/altpress/ *4368*

ALTERNATIVES JOURNAL.
University of Waterloo, Faculty of Environmental Studies, Waterloo, ON N2L 3G1, Canada. TEL 519-888-4567. FAX 519-746-0292. URL: http://www.fes.uwaterloo.ca/research/alternatives/. *2905*

ALTERNATIVES TO THE HIGH COST OF LITIGATION.
C P R Institute for Dispute Resolution, 366 Madison Ave., New York, NY 10017-3122. TEL 212-949-6490. FAX 212-949-8859.
Vendor(s): Lexis-Nexis, West Group. *3909*

ALTERNATIVES TO THE USE OF LIVE VERTEBRATES IN BIOMEDICAL RESEARCH AND TESTING.
National Library of Medicine, Toxicology and Environmental Health Information Program, URL: gopher://gopher.nlm.nih.gov:70/00/teh/animals/.abtehalt.txt.
Available only online. *646*

ALUMINIUM INDUSTRY ABSTRACTS.
Aluminum Association, Inc., Materials Park, OH 44073. TEL 216-338-5151. FAX 216-338-4634.
Vendor(s): European Space Agency (File no.9/ALUMINUM), Knight-Ridder Information, Inc. (File no.33). *5216*

ALUMINIUM TODAY.
Argus Business Media Ltd., Queensway House, 2 Queensway, Redhill, Surrey RH1 1QS, England. TEL 44-1737-768611. FAX 44-1737-761685.
Vendor(s): Information Access Co. *5185*

ALZHEIMER'S DISEASE REVIEW.
University of Kentucky, Sanders - Brown Center on Aging, Lexington, KY 40536-0230. TEL 606-257-6461. FAX 606-323-2866. URL: http://www.coa.uky.edu/ADReview.
Available only online. *5050*

EL AMANTE CINE.
Vaccaro, Sanchez y Cia., SA, Moreno 794, 9o piso, Buenos Aires, Argentina. URL: http://www.apriweb.com/amante/. *5323*

AMBIT.
17 Priory Gardens, London N.6, England. TEL 44-181-340-3566. *4372*

AMERICA.
America Press Inc., 106 W. 56th St., New York, NY 10019. TEL 212-581-4640. FAX 212-399-3596.
Vendor(s): Information Access Co., UMI. *6449*

AMERICA AT WORK.
American Federation of Labor - Congress of Industrial Organizations, 815 16th St., N.W., Washington, DC 20006. TEL 202-637-5010. FAX 202-637-5058.
Vendor(s): Knight-Ridder Information, Inc. *3886*

AMERICA: HISTORY AND LIFE. ARTICLE ABSTRACTS AND CITATIONS OF REVIEWS AND DISSERTATIONS COVERING THE UNITED STATES AND CANADA.
A B C-Clio, 130 Cremona, Box 1911, Santa Barbara, CA 93116-1911. TEL 805-968-1911. FAX 805-685-9685.
Vendor(s): Knight-Ridder Information, Inc. (File no.38). *3518*

AMERICAN ACADEMY OF CHILD AND ADOLESCENT PSYCHIATRY. JOURNAL.
Williams & Wilkins, 351 W. Camden St., Baltimore, MD 21201-2436. TEL 410-528-4068. FAX 410-528-4452. URL: http://www.wwilkins.com.
Vendor(s): Ovid Technologies, Inc. *5050*

AMERICAN ADVERTISING.
American Advertising Federation, 1101 Vermont Ave., N.W., Ste. 500, Washington, DC 20005. TEL 202-898-0089. FAX 202-898-0159.
Vendor(s): UMI. *31*

AMERICAN AGENT AND BROKER.
Commerce Publishing Co., 330 N. Fourth St., St. Louis, MO 63102-2036. TEL 314-421-5445.
Vendor(s): UMI. *3807*

AMERICAN ALMANAC.
Reference Press Inc., Box 140375, Austin, TX 78714-0375. TEL 512-454-7778. FAX 512-454-9401. URL: http://www.hoovers.com. *2655*

AMERICAN ANTIQUITY.
Society for American Archaeology, 900 Second St., N.W., No. 12, Washington, DC 20002-3557. TEL 202-789-8200. FAX 202-789-0284. URL: http://www.saa.org/Publications/AmAntiq/amantiq.html.
Vendor(s): Information Access Co. *347*

AMERICAN ARTIST.
B P I Communications, Inc. (New York), 1515 Broadway, 11th Fl., New York, NY 10036. TEL 212-764-7300. FAX 212-536-5351.
Vendor(s): Information Access Co. *421*

AMERICAN ASSOCIATION OF STRATIGRAPHIC PALYNOLOGISTS. NEWSLETTER.
American Association of Stratigraphic Palynologists Foundation, c/o Vaughn M. Bryant, Jr., Palynology Laboratory, Texas A & M Univ., College Station, TX 77843-4352. TEL 409-845-5242. FAX 409-845-4070. URL: http://opal.geology.utoronto.ca:80/aasp/. *2330*

AMERICAN BANKER.
American Banker - Bond Buyer, Newsletter Division One State St. Plaza, New York, NY 10004-1549. FAX 212-843-9600.
Vendor(s): Data-Star (BANK), Information Access Co., Knight-Ridder Information, Inc. (File no.625), Lexis-Nexis, NewsNet (FI10), Ovid Technologies, Inc. *1102*

AMERICAN BANKER INDEX.
U M I, 300 N. Zeeb Rd., Ann Arbor, MI 48106. TEL 313-761-4700. FAX 800-864-0019. URL: http://www.umi.com.
Vendor(s): Knight-Ridder Information, Inc., UMI. *1015*

AMERICAN BANKER'S WASHINGTON WATCH.
American Banker - Bond Buyer, Newsletter Division One State St. Plaza, New York, NY 10004-1549. TEL 800-733-4371. FAX 212-943-2224.
Vendor(s): Information Access Co., Knight-Ridder Information, Inc., Lexis-Nexis, NewsNet (FI05). *1102*

AMERICAN BEHAVIORAL SCIENTIST.
Sage Publications, Inc., 2455 Teller Rd., Thousand Oaks, CA 91320. TEL 805-499-0721. FAX 805-499-0871. URL: http://www.sagepub.com.
Vendor(s): Information Access Co. *6602*

AMERICAN BIBLIOGRAPHY OF SLAVIC AND EAST EUROPEAN STUDIES.
M.E. Sharpe, Inc., 80 Business Park Dr., Armonk, NY 10504. TEL 415-723-9668. FAX 914-273-2106. *3518*

AMERICAN BUSINESS LAW JOURNAL.
Academy of Legal Studies in Business, c/o Daniel J. Herron, Dept. of Finance, 120 Upham Hall, Miami University, Oxford, OH 45056. TEL 513-529-2945. FAX 513-529-6992. URL: http://miavx1.muohio.edu/~herrondj/
Vendor(s): Information Access Co. *4072*

AMERICAN CHEMICAL SOCIETY. DIRECTORY OF GRADUATE RESEARCH.
American Chemical Society, 1155 16th St., N.W., Washington, DC 20036. TEL 800-227-5558. FAX 202-872-4615. *2520*

AMERICAN CHEMICAL SOCIETY. JOURNAL.
American Chemical Society, 1155 16th St., N.W., Washington, DC 20036.
Vendor(s): STN International (CJACS). *1738*

AMERICAN CITY & COUNTY.
Intertec Publishing Corp. (Atlanta), 6151 Powers Ferry Rd., N.W., Atlanta, GA 30339-2941. TEL 770-955-2500. FAX 770-955-0400.
Vendor(s): Information Access Co., LOGIN Information Services, UMI. *6210*

AMERICAN COLLEGE OF CARDIOLOGY. JOURNAL.
Elsevier Science Inc., Box 945, New York, NY 10159-0945. TEL 212-633-3730. FAX 212-633-3680. URL: http://www.elsevier.nl/.
Vendor(s): Ovid Technologies, Inc. *4808*

AMERICAN COLLEGE OF SURGEONS. JOURNAL.
American College of Surgeons, Publishing Department, 54 E. Erie St., Chicago, IL 60611-2798. TEL 312-787-9282. FAX 312-440-7026.
Vendor(s): Lexis-Nexis. *5134*

AMERICAN COUNCIL OF LEARNED SOCIETIES. NEWSLETTER.
American Council of Learned Societies, 228 E. 45th St., New York, NY 10017. TEL 212-697-1505. FAX 212-949-8058. URL: http://www.acls.org. *3771*

AMERICAN CRAFT.
American Craft Council, 72 Spring St., New York, NY 10012. TEL 212-274-0630. FAX 212-274-0650.
Vendor(s): UMI. *477*

AMERICAN CRIMINAL LAW REVIEW.
Georgetown University Law Center, 600 New Jersey Ave., N.W., Washington, DC 20009. TEL 202-662-9468.
Vendor(s): Information Access Co., West Group (ACRIMLREV). *2260*

AMERICAN DEMOGRAPHICS.
Cowles Business Media, 11 River Bend Dr., S., Box 4949, Stamford, CT 06907-0949. TEL 203-358-9900. FAX 203-358-5811.
Vendor(s): Dow Jones News Retrieval, Information Access Co., Lexis-Nexis, UMI. *6046*

AMERICAN DIETETIC ASSOCIATION. JOURNAL.
American Dietetic Association, 216 W. Jackson Blvd., Ste. 800, Chicago, IL 60606-6995. TEL 312-899-0040. FAX 312-899-1757.
Vendor(s): Information Access Co., UMI. *5469*

10044 SERIALS AVAILABLE ONLINE

AMERICAN DOCTORAL DISSERTATIONS.
U M I, 300 N. Zeeb Rd., Ann Arbor, MI 48106. TEL 313-761-4700. FAX 800-864-0019. Vendor(s): Data-Star, Knight-Ridder Information, Inc. (File no. 35), OCLC (EPIC), Ovid Technologies, Inc., STN International, UMI. *2531*

AMERICAN DRUGGIST.
Press Corps, American Druggist, 444 Park Ave. S., Rm 402, New York, NY 10016-7321. TEL 212-686-8584. FAX 212-686-9098. Vendor(s): Information Access Co. *5646*

AMERICAN ECONOMIC REVIEW.
American Economic Association, 2014 Broadway, Ste. 305, Nashville, TN 37203. TEL 615-322-2595. URL: http://www.vanderbilt.edu/AEA. *1220*

AMERICAN ECONOMIST.
Omicron Delta Epsilon Fraternity, c/o Michael Szenberg, Ed., Graduate School of Business, Dept. of Economics, Pace University, New York, NY 10038. TEL 212-346-1921. FAX 212-346-1573. Vendor(s): Information Access Co., UMI. *1220*

AMERICAN ENTERPRISE.
American Enterprise Institute for Public Policy Research, 1150 17th St., N.W., Washington, DC 20036. TEL 202-862-5800. FAX 202-862-7178. Vendor(s): UMI. *5890*

AMERICAN FAMILY PHYSICIAN.
American Academy of Family Physicians, 8880 Ward Pkwy., Kansas City, MO 64114. TEL 816-333-9700. FAX 816-333-0303. Vendor(s): Information Access Co., Lexis-Nexis, Ovid Technologies, Inc. *4635*

AMERICAN FITNESS.
Aerobics and Fitness Association of America, 15250 Ventura Blvd., Ste. 310, Sherman Oaks, CA 91403. TEL 818-905-0040. Vendor(s): Information Access Co., Knight Ridder Information, Inc. (File no.149), UMI. *5778*

AMERICAN FORESTS.
American Forests, Box 2000, Washington, DC 20013. TEL 202-667-3300. FAX 202-667-7751. Vendor(s): Information Access Co., UMI. *3146*

AMERICAN GAS.
American Gas Association, 1515 Wilson Blvd., Arlington, VA 22209. TEL 703-841-8400. FAX 703-841-8406. Vendor(s): UMI. *5595*

AMERICAN GERIATRICS SOCIETY. JOURNAL.
Williams & Wilkins, 351 W. Camden St., Baltimore, MD 21201-2436. TEL 410-528-4068. FAX 410-528-4452. URL: http://www.wwilkins.com. Vendor(s): Ovid Technologies, Inc. *3432*

AMERICAN HEALTH.
Reader's Digest Association, Inc. (New York), 28 West 23rd St., New York, NY 10010. TEL 212-366-8900. FAX 212-627-3833. Vendor(s): Information Access Co. *5778*

AMERICAN HEALTH CARE ASSOCIATION. PROVIDER.
American Health Care Association, 1201 L St., N.W., Washington, DC 20005. TEL 202-842-4444. FAX 202-842-3860. *6654*

AMERICAN HEALTH LINE.
American Political Network, Inc., 3129 Mount Vernon Ave., Alexandria, VA 22305. TEL 703-518-4600. FAX 703-518-8703. URL: http://www.apn.com. Available only online. *6227*

AMERICAN HEART JOURNAL.
Mosby - Year Book, Inc., 11830 Westline Industrial Dr., St. Louis, MO 63146-3318. TEL 314-872-8370. FAX 314-432-1380. Vendor(s): Ovid Technologies, Inc. *4809*

AMERICAN HERITAGE.
American Heritage, 60 Fifth Ave., New York, NY 10011. TEL 212-206-5500. FAX 212-620-2332. Vendor(s): Information Access Co., Knight-Ridder Information, Inc. *3615*

AMERICAN HISTORICAL REVIEW.
American Historical Association, 400 A St., S.E., Washington, DC 20003-3889. TEL 202-544-2422. FAX 202-544-8307. URL: http://www.jstor.org/fcgi-bin/jstor/listjournal.fcg/00028762?configjstor. Vendor(s): UMI. *3487*

AMERICAN IMAGO.
Johns Hopkins University Press, Journals Publishing Division, 2715 N. Charles St., Baltimore, MD 21218. TEL 410-516-6980. FAX 410-516-6968. URL: http://muse.jhu.edu. Vendor(s): Information Access Co. *5051*

AMERICAN INDIAN LAW REVIEW.
University of Oklahoma, College of Law, 300 Timberdell Rd., Norman, OK 73019. TEL 405-325-5191. Vendor(s): West Group. *3909*

AMERICAN INDIAN QUARTERLY.
University of Nebraska Press, 312 N. 14th St., Box 880484, Lincoln, NE 68588-0484. TEL 402-472-3581. FAX 402-472-6214. Vendor(s): Information Access Co. *307*

AMERICAN INSTITUTE OF PHYSICS. CENTER FOR HISTORY OF PHYSICS. NEWSLETTER.
American Institute of Physics, Center for History of Physics, One Physics Ellipse, College Park, MD 20740. TEL 301-209-3165. FAX 301-209-0882. URL: http://aip.org/aip/history/newsletters.html. *5796*

AMERICAN INSTITUTE OF PHYSICS NEWS.
American Institute of Physics, One Physics Ellipse, College Park, MD 20740-3843. TEL 516-576-2411. FAX 516-576-2374. URL: http://www.newton.ex.ac.uk/aip/ Available only online. *5796*

AMERICAN JEWISH HISTORY.
Johns Hopkins University Press, Journals Publishing Division, 2715 N. Charles St., Baltimore, MD 21218-4310. TEL 410-516-6987. FAX 410-516-6968. URL: http://muse.jhu.edu; http://www.press.jhu.edu/journals/american__jewish__history/ *2996*

AMERICAN JOURNAL OF AGRICULTURAL ECONOMICS.
American Agricultural Economics Association, 1110 Buckeye Ave., Ames, IA 50010-8063. TEL 515-233-3202. FAX 515-233-3101. Vendor(s): Information Access Co., UMI. *189*

AMERICAN JOURNAL OF ANTHROPOMORPHICS.
Med Systems Co., Box 580009, Flushing, NY 11358-0009. TEL 718-359-5741. FAX 718-359-2768. *421*

AMERICAN JOURNAL OF CARDIOLOGY.
Excerpta Medica, Inc., 105 Raider Blvd., Belle Mead, NJ 08502. TEL 908-874-8550. FAX 908-874-8419. Vendor(s): Lexis-Nexis, Ovid Technologies, Inc. *4809*

AMERICAN JOURNAL OF COMMUNITY PSYCHOLOGY.
Plenum Publishing Corp., 233 Spring St., New York, NY 10013-1578. TEL 212-620-8000. FAX 212-463-0742. Vendor(s): Information Access Co. *6700*

AMERICAN JOURNAL OF DRUG AND ALCOHOL ABUSE.
Marcel Dekker Journals, 270 Madison Ave., New York, NY 10016. TEL 212-696-9000. FAX 212-685-4540. Vendor(s): Information Access Co. *2299*

AMERICAN JOURNAL OF ECONOMICS AND SOCIOLOGY.
American Journal of Economics & Sociology, Inc., 41 E. 72nd St., New York, NY 10021-0310. TEL 212-988-1680. FAX 212-399-6465. Vendor(s): Information Access Co., UMI. *932*

AMERICAN JOURNAL OF INDUSTRIAL MEDICINE.
John Wiley & Sons, Inc., Journals, 605 Third Ave., New York, NY 10158. TEL 212-850-6645. FAX 212-850-6021. URL: http://www.wiley.co.uk. *5485*

AMERICAN JOURNAL OF INTERNATIONAL LAW.
American Society of International Law, 2223 Massachusetts Ave., N.W., Washington, DC 20008-2864. TEL 202-939-6000. FAX 202-797-7133. Vendor(s): Lexis-Nexis. *4104*

AMERICAN JOURNAL OF KIDNEY DISEASES.
W.B. Saunders Co., Curtis Center, 3rd Fl., Independence Sq. W., Philadelphia, PA 19106-3399. TEL 215-238-7800. FAX 215-238-6445. *5158*

AMERICAN JOURNAL OF LAW & MEDICINE.
American Society of Law, Medicine & Ethics, 765 Commonwealth Ave., Ste. 1634, Boston, MA 02215. TEL 617-262-4990. FAX 617-437-7596. Vendor(s): Information Access Co., Lexis-Nexis, West Group. *3909*

AMERICAN JOURNAL OF LEGAL HISTORY.
Temple University, School of Law, Philadelphia, PA 19122. TEL 215-787-1256. FAX 215-787-1785. Vendor(s): West Group. *3909*

AMERICAN JOURNAL OF MATHEMATICS.
Johns Hopkins University Press, Journals Publishing Division, 2715 N. Charles St., Baltimore, MD 21218. TEL 410-516-6987. FAX 410-516-6968. URL: http://muse.jhu.edu. Vendor(s): Information Access Co. *4559*

AMERICAN JOURNAL OF MEDICAL GENETICS.
John Wiley & Sons, Inc., Journals, 605 Third Ave., New York, NY 10158. TEL 212-850-6645. FAX 212-850-6021. URL: http://www.wiley.co.uk. *763*

THE AMERICAN JOURNAL OF MEDICINE.
Excerpta Medica, Inc., 105 Raider Blvd., Belle Mead, NJ 08502. TEL 908-874-8550. FAX 908-874-8419. Vendor(s): Lexis-Nexis, Ovid Technologies, Inc. *4636*

AMERICAN JOURNAL OF NURSING.
Lippincott - Raven Publishers, 227 E. Washington Sq., Philadelphia, PA 19106. TEL 215-238-4200. FAX 215-238-4227. URL: http://www.lrpub.com. Vendor(s): UMI. *4928*

AMERICAN JOURNAL OF OBSTETRICS AND GYNECOLOGY.
Mosby - Year Book, Inc., 11830 Westline Industrial Dr., St. Louis, MO 63146-3318. TEL 314-872-8370. FAX 314-432-1380. Vendor(s): Ovid Technologies, Inc. *4952*

AMERICAN JOURNAL OF OPHTHALMOLOGY.
Ophthalmic Publishing Co., 77 W. Wacker Dr., Ste. 660, Chicago, IL 60601-1632. TEL 312-629-1690. FAX 312-629-1744. URL: http://www.ajo.com. Vendor(s): Information Access Co. *4989*

AMERICAN JOURNAL OF OTOLOGY.
Lippincott - Raven Publishers, 227 E. Washington Sq., Philadelphia, PA 19106. TEL 215-238-4200. FAX 215-238-4227. URL: http://www.lrpub.com. *5019*

AMERICAN JOURNAL OF PHARMACEUTICAL EDUCATION.
American Association of Colleges of Pharmacy, 1426 Prince St., Alexandria, VA 22314-2815. TEL 703-739-2330. *5646*

AMERICAN JOURNAL OF PHILOLOGY.
Johns Hopkins University Press, Journals Publishing Division, 2715 N. Charles St., Baltimore, MD 21218. TEL 410-516-6987. FAX 410-516-6968. URL: http://muse.jhu.edu. Vendor(s): Information Access Co. *4239*

AMERICAN JOURNAL OF PHYSICAL MEDICINE AND REHABILITATION.
Williams & Wilkins, 351 W. Camden St., Baltimore, MD 21201-2436. TEL 410-528-4068. FAX 410-528-4452. URL: http://www.wilkins.com. Vendor(s): Ovid Technologies, Inc. *5041*

AMERICAN JOURNAL OF PRIMATOLOGY.
John Wiley & Sons, Inc., Journals, 605 Third Ave., New York, NY 10108. TEL 212-850-6645. FAX 212-850-6021. URL: http://wiley.co.uk. *825*

AMERICAN JOURNAL OF PSYCHIATRY.
American Psychiatric Press, Inc., Journal Division, 1400 K St., N.W., Ste. 1101, Washington, DC 20005. TEL 202-682-6020. FAX 202-682-6016. Vendor(s): Ovid Technologies, Inc., UMI. *5051*

AMERICAN JOURNAL OF PSYCHOLOGY.
University of Illinois Press, 1325 S. Oak St., Champaign, IL 61820. TEL 217-333-0950. FAX 217-244-8082.
Vendor(s): Information Access Co. *6092*

AMERICAN JOURNAL OF PSYCHOTHERAPY.
Association for the Advancement of Psychotherapy, Belfer Education Center, 1300 Morris Park Ave., Rm. 402, Bronx, NY 10461-1602. TEL 718-430-3503. FAX 718-430-8907. URL: http://www.ajp.org.
Vendor(s): UMI. *5051*

AMERICAN JOURNAL OF PUBLIC HEALTH.
American Public Health Association, 1015 15th St., N.W., Washington, DC 20005. TEL 202-789-5600.
Vendor(s): Ovid Technologies, Inc., UMI. *6228*

AMERICAN JOURNAL OF SPORTS MEDICINE.
American Orthopaedic Society for Sports Medicine, 230 Calvary St., Waltham, MA 02154. TEL 617-736-0707. FAX 617-736-0607.
Vendor(s): Information Access Co., UMI. *5128*

AMERICAN JOURNAL OF SURGERY.
Excerpta Medica, Inc., 105 Raider Blvd., Belle Mead, NJ 08502. TEL 908-874-8550. FAX 908-874-8419.
Vendor(s): Lexis-Nexis, Ovid Technologies, Inc. *5135*

AMERICAN JOURNAL OF TAX POLICY.
American College of Tax Counsel, Box 870382, Tuscaloosa, AL 35487-0382. TEL 205-348-7372. FAX 205-348-3917.
Vendor(s): Lexis-Nexis, West Group. *1599*

AMERICAN JOURNAL OF THERAPEUTICS.
Chapman & Hall, Journals Department 2-6 Boundary Row, London SE1 8HN, England. TEL 44-171-8560066. FAX 44-171-5229623. URL: http://www.chaphall.com/chaphall/journals.html. *4637*

AMERICAN JOURNALISM REVIEW.
American Journalism Review, 8701 Adelphi Rd., Adelphi, MD 20783. TEL 301-431-4771. FAX 301-431-0097. URL: http://www.inform.umd.edu/news/AJR/ajr.html.
Vendor(s): Information Access Co. *3869*

THE AMERICAN LAWYER.
American Lawyer Media, L.P. (New York), 600 Third Ave., 2nd Fl., New York, NY 10016. TEL 212-973-2800. FAX 212-972-6258.
Vendor(s): Lexis-Nexis. *3910*

AMERICAN LEGION MAGAZINE.
Box 1055, Indianapolis, IN 46206. TEL 317-630-1200. FAX 317-630-1280.
Vendor(s): UMI. *1929*

AMERICAN LIBRARIES.
American Library Association, 50 E. Huron St., Chicago, IL 60611-2795. TEL 312-944-6780. FAX 312-440-0901.
Vendor(s): Information Access Co., Knight-Ridder Information, Inc. *4158*

AMERICAN LIBRARY DIRECTORY.
R.R. Bowker, A Division of Reed Elsevier Inc., 121 Chanlon Rd., New Providence, NJ 07974. TEL 908-464-6800. FAX 908-665-6688. URL: http://www.bowker.com.
Vendor(s): Knight-Ridder Information, Inc. (File no.460). *4158*

AMERICAN MANUFACTURERS DIRECTORY.
American Business Directories, 5711 S. 86th Circle, Box 27347, Omaha, NE 68127. TEL 402-593-4600. FAX 402-331-5481. *1651*

AMERICAN MARITIME CASES.
American Maritime Cases, Inc., 28 E. 21st St., Baltimore, MD 21218-5932. TEL 410-752-2939. FAX 410-625-1174.
Vendor(s): Lexis-Nexis. *4141*

AMERICAN MARKETPLACE.
Business Publishers, Inc., 951 Pershing Dr., Silver Spring, MD 20910-4464. TEL 301-587-6300. FAX 301-585-9075.
Vendor(s): Information Access Co., NewsNet (AD13) *6046*

AMERICAN MATHEMATICAL SOCIETY. BULLETIN. NEW SERIES.
American Mathematical Society, Box 6248, Providence, RI 02940-6248. TEL 401-455-4000. FAX 401-331-3842. URL: http://www.ams.org/bull/. *4559*

AMERICAN MATHEMATICAL SOCIETY. ELECTRONIC RESEARCH ANNOUNCEMENTS.
American Mathematical Society, Box 6248, Providence, RI 02940-6248. TEL 401-455-4000. FAX 401-331-3842. URL: http://www.ams.org/era/. Available only online. *4559*

AMERICAN MATHEMATICAL SOCIETY. JOURNAL.
American Mathematical Society, Box 6248, Providence, RI 02940-6248. TEL 401-455-4000. FAX 401-331-3842. URL: http://www.ams.org/jams. *4559*

AMERICAN MATHEMATICAL SOCIETY. NOTICES.
American Mathematical Society, Box 6248, Providence, RI 02940-6248. TEL 401-455-4000. FAX 401-331-3842. URL: http://www.ams.org/notices. *4559*

AMERICAN MATHEMATICAL SOCIETY. PROCEEDINGS.
American Mathematical Society, Box 6248, Providence, RI 02940-6248. TEL 401-455-4000. FAX 401-331-3842. URL: http://www.ams.org/proc. *4559*

AMERICAN MATHEMATICAL SOCIETY. TRANSACTIONS.
American Mathematical Society, Box 6248, Providence, RI 02940-6248. TEL 401-455-4000. FAX 401-331-3842. URL: http://www.ams.org/tran/. *4559*

AMERICAN MEDICAL NEWS.
American Medical Association, 515 N. State St., Chicago, IL 60610. TEL 312-464-5000. FAX 312-464-5831. URL: http://www.ama-assn.org.
Vendor(s): Information Access Co. *4637*

AMERICAN MEN AND WOMEN OF SCIENCE.
R.R. Bowker, A Division of Reed Elsevier Inc., 121 Chanlon Rd., New Providence, NJ 07974. TEL 908-464-6800. FAX 908-665-6688. URL: http://www.reedref.com.
Vendor(s): Knight-Ridder Information, Inc. (File no.236). *571*

AMERICAN METAL MARKET.
Capital Cities - A B C, Inc., Diversified Publishing Group, 825 Seventh Ave., New York, NY 10019. TEL 212-887-8560. FAX 212-887-8493.
Vendor(s): Information Access Co., Knight-Ridder Information, Inc. *1515*

AMERICAN MIDLAND NATURALIST.
University of Notre Dame, Department of Biological Sciences, Box 369, Notre Dame, IN 46556. TEL 219-631-7481. FAX 219-631-7413.
Vendor(s): Information Access Co. *6511*

AMERICAN MUSIC.
University of Illinois Press, 1325 S. Oak St., Champaign, IL 61820. TEL 217-333-0950. FAX 217-244-8082.
Vendor(s): Information Access Co. *5371*

AMERICAN MUSIC TEACHER.
Music Teachers National Association, Inc., Carew Tower, 441 Vine St., Ste. 505, Cincinnati, OH 45202-2814. TEL 513-421-1420. FAX 513-421-2503.
Vendor(s): UMI. *5372*

AMERICAN NEWSPEAK.
2002 S. Dearborn, Seattle, WA 98144. URL: http://www.scn.org/news/newspeak/. Available only online. *3369*

AMERICAN ORIENTAL SOCIETY. JOURNAL.
American Oriental Society, Harlan Hatcher Graduate Library, University of Michigan, Ann Arbor, MI 48109-1205. TEL 313-747-4760. URL: http://www-personal.umich.edu/~jrodgers.frntmtr.htm.
Vendor(s): Information Access Co., UMI. *5520*

AMERICAN PAINT & COATINGS JOURNAL.
American Paint Journal Co., 8832 Norwood Dr., Leawood, KS 66206-1626. TEL 314-530-0301.
Vendor(s): Information Access Co. *5550*

AMERICAN PETROLEUM INSTITUTE. DIVISION OF STATISTICS. WEEKLY STATISTICAL BULLETIN.
American Petroleum Institute, Publications Section, 1220 L St., N.W., Washington, DC 20005. TEL 202-682-8375. FAX 202-962-4776. URL: http://www.api.org.
Vendor(s): PetroScan. *5628*

AMERICAN PETROLEUM INSTITUTE. MONTHLY COMPLETION REPORT.
American Petroleum Institute, Publications Section, 1220 L St., N.W., Washington, DC 20005. TEL 202-682-8375. FAX 202-962-4776. URL: http://www.api.org. *5628*

AMERICAN PETROLEUM INSTITUTE. QUARTERLY COMPLETION REPORT.
American Petroleum Institute, Publications Section, 1220 L St., N.W., Washington, DC 20005. TEL 202-682-8375. FAX 202-962-4776. URL: http://www.api.org. *5628*

AMERICAN PHARMACEUTICAL ASSOCIATION. JOURNAL.
American Pharmaceutical Association, 2215 Constitution Ave., N.W., Washington, DC 20037. TEL 202-628-4410. *5646*

AMERICAN PHILOSOPHICAL QUARTERLY.
North American Philosophical Publications, Inc., 153 Fairview Ave., Verdna, PA 15147. TEL 412-624-5450. FAX 412-383-7506. URL: http://www.bgsu.edu/offices/phildoc/
Vendor(s): Information Access Co. *5717*

AMERICAN PHOTO.
Hachette Filipacchi Magazines, Inc., 1633 Broadway, 45th Fl., New York, NY 10019. TEL 212-767-6000.
Vendor(s): Information Access Co. *5761*

AMERICAN PLANNING ASSOCIATION. JOURNAL.
American Planning Association, 122 S. Michigan Ave., Ste. 1600, Chicago, IL 60603-6107. TEL 312-431-9100. FAX 312-431-9985.
Vendor(s): Information Access Co., UMI. *3740*

AMERICAN POETRY REVIEW.
World Poetry, Inc., 1721 Walnut St., Philadelphia, PA 19103. TEL 215-496-0439.
Vendor(s): Information Access Co., UMI. *4502*

AMERICAN POLITICAL SCIENCE REVIEW.
American Political Science Association, 1527 New Hampshire Ave., N.W., Washington, DC 20036. TEL 202-483-2512. FAX 202-483-2657.
Vendor(s): Information Access Co. *5891*

AMERICAN PRINTER.
Intertec Publishing Corp. (Overland Park), 9800 Metcalf Ave., Overland Park, KS 66202. TEL 312-726-2802. FAX 312-726-3091. URL: http://www.americanprinter.com.
Vendor(s): Information Access Co., UMI. *6074*

AMERICAN QUARTERLY.
Johns Hopkins University Press, Journals Publishing Division, 2715 N. Charles St., Baltimore, MD 21218. TEL 410-516-6987. FAX 410-516-6968. URL: http://muse.jhu.edu. *3772*

AMERICAN RECORD GUIDE.
Record Guide Productions, 4412 Braddock St., Cincinnati, OH 45204. TEL 513-941-1116. FAX 513-941-1112.
Vendor(s): Information Access Co., UMI. *5372*

AMERICAN REHABILITATION.
U.S. Department of Education, Mary E. Switzer Bldg., Rm. 3127, 330 C St., S.W., Washington, DC 20202. TEL 202-732-1296.
Vendor(s): Information Access Co., UMI. *6654*

AMERICAN RENAISSANCE.
New Century Foundation, Box 1674, Louisville, KY 40201. TEL 502-637-3242. FAX 502-637-9324. URL: http://www.amren.com. *6700*

AMERICAN REVIEW OF PUBLIC ADMINISTRATION.
Georgia State University, School of Public Administration and Urban Studies, University Plaza, Atlanta, GA 30303-3083. TEL 404-651-4591. FAX 404-651-1378.
Vendor(s): Information Access Co., Knight-Ridder Information, Inc., UMI. *6163*

SERIALS AVAILABLE ONLINE

AMERICAN RIFLEMAN.
N R A Publications, 11250 Waples Mill Rd., Fairfax, VA 22030. TEL 703-267-1379. FAX 703-267-3971.
Vendor(s): UMI. *6749*

AMERICAN SCHOOL & UNIVERSITY.
Intertec Publishing Corp., 9800 Metcalf, Overland Park, KS 66212-2215. TEL 913-341-1300.
Vendor(s): Information Access Co. *2568*

AMERICAN SCIENTIST.
Sigma Xi, Scientific Research Society, Box 13975, 99 Alexander Dr., Research Triangle Park, NC 27709. TEL 919-549-0097. FAX 919-549-0090. URL: http://www.amsci.org/amsci/amsci.html.
Vendor(s): Information Access Co. *6511*

AMERICAN SHIPPER.
Howard Publications, Inc., 300 W. Adams St., Ste. 600, Jacksonville, FL 32202-4304. TEL 904-355-2601. FAX 904-791-8836.
Vendor(s): Information Access Co. *7145*

AMERICAN SHOOTING MAGAZINE.
45303 Margate, Macomb, MI 45304. URL: http://www.rust.net/~dapierce.
Available only online. *6860*

AMERICAN SOCIETY FOR INFORMATION SCIENCE. BULLETIN.
American Society for Information Science, 8720 Georgia Ave, Ste. 501, Silver Spring, MD 20910. TEL 301-495-0900. FAX 301-495-0810.
Vendor(s): UMI. *4158*

AMERICAN SOCIETY OF C L U & CH F C. JOURNAL.
American Society of C L U & Ch F C, 270 Bryn Mawr Ave., Bryn Mawr, PA 19010. TEL 215-526-2500. FAX 215-526-2538.
Vendor(s): UMI. *3807*

AMERICAN SOCIOLOGICAL REVIEW.
American Sociological Association, 1722 N St., N.W., Washington, DC 20036. TEL 202-833-3410. FAX 202-785-0146.
Vendor(s): UMI. *6701*

AMERICAN SPECTATOR.
2020 N. 14th St., Ste. 750, Box 549, Arlington, VA 22201. TEL 703-243-3733. FAX 703-243-6814. URL: http://www.spectator.org; http://www.amspec.org.
Vendor(s): Information Access Co. *4322*

AMERICAN STATISTICS INDEX.
Congressional Information Service, Inc., A member of the LEXIS NEXIS family, 4520 East-West Hwy., Bethesda, MD 20814-3389. TEL 301-654-1550. FAX 301-654-4033. URL: http://www.cispubs.com.
Vendor(s): Knight-Ridder Information, Inc. (File no.102). *6891*

AMERICAN THEATRE.
Theatre Communications Group, Inc., 355 Lexington Ave., New York, NY 10017. TEL 212-697-5230. FAX 212-983-4847.
Vendor(s): Information Access Co., UMI. *7001*

AMERICAN UNIVERSITY LAW REVIEW.
American University, Washington College of Law, 4801 Massachusetts Ave., N.W., Ste. 621, Washington, DC 20016. TEL 202-274-4433.
Vendor(s): Lexis-Nexis, West Group. *3910*

AMERICAN VISIONS.
African American Museums Association, Box 37049, Washington, DC 20078-4741. URL: http://www.americanvisions.com.
Vendor(s): Information Access Co., UMI. *2997*

AMERICAN WINE ON THE WEB.
Box 5068, Lake Gregory, CA 92325. TEL 909-338-9776. FAX 909-338-4956. URL: http://www.2way.com/food/wine.
Available only online. *514*

AMERICANS WITH DISABILITIES ACT UPDATE.
Nyper Publications, Box 370, Latham, NY 12112-0370. TEL 518-786-1654. FAX 518-456-8582. URL: http://www.nyper.com.
Vendor(s): Lexis-Nexis, NewsNet. *3452*

AMERICANS WITH DISABILITIES CASES.
The Bureau of National Affairs, Inc., 1231 25th St., N.W., Washington, DC 20037. TEL 202-452-4200. FAX 202-822-8092. URL: http://www.bna.com/.
Vendor(s): West Group (FLB-CS, MLRR-CS). *3910*

AMERICAS.
Americas Magazine, 19th St. & Constitution Ave., N.W., Ste. 300, Washington, DC 20006. TEL 202-458-3278. FAX 202-458-6217.
Vendor(s): Information Access Co., UMI. *3772*

AMERICA'S COMMUNITY BANKER.
America's Community Bankers, 900 19th St., N.W., Ste. 400, Washington, DC 20006. TEL 202-857-3100. FAX 202-857-5581. URL: http://www.acbankers.org.
Vendor(s): Information Access Co., UMI. *1102*

AMERICA'S FUTURE.
America's Future, Inc., 7800 Bonhomme Ave., St. Louis, MO 63105. TEL 314-725-6003. FAX 314-721-3373. URL: http://www.basenet.net/~eamiller/af/af.html. *5891*

AMERICA'S NETWORK.
Advanstar Communications, Inc., 7500 Old Oak Blvd., Cleveland, OH 44130. TEL 216-826-2839. FAX 216-891-2726.
Vendor(s): Information Access Co., Knight-Ridder Information, Inc. *2031*

AMERICA'S NETWORK DIRECTORY.
Advanstar Communications, Inc., 7500 Old Oak Blvd., Cleveland, OH 44130. TEL 216-826-2839. FAX 216-891-2726.
Vendor(s): Knight-Ridder Information, Inc. *2031*

THE AMICUS JOURNAL.
Natural Resources Defense Council Inc., 40 W. 20th St., 11th Fl., New York, NY 10011. TEL 212-727-2700. FAX 212-727-1773. URL: http://www.nrdc.org.
Vendor(s): Information Access Co., UMI. *2906*

AMIGA REPORT MAGAZINE.
1203 Alexander Ave., Streamwood, IL 60107. FAX 847-741-0689. URL: http://www.cucug.org/ar/
Available only online. *2194*

AMUSEMENT BUSINESS.
B P I Communications, Amusement Business Division, Box 24970, Nashville, TN 37202. TEL 615-321-4250. FAX 615-327-1575. URL: http://www.amusementbusiness.com.
Vendor(s): Information Access Co., Knight-Ridder Information, Inc. *7001*

ANAEROBE.
Academic Press Ltd., 24-28 Oval Rd., London NW1 7DX, England. TEL 44-171-482-2893. FAX 44-171-267-0362. URL: http://www.hbuk.co.uk/ap/anaerobe; http://www.europe.idealibrary.com/. *779*

DER ANAESTHESIST.
Springer-Verlag, Heidelberger Platz 3, 14197 Berlin, Germany. TEL 49-30-82787-0. FAX 49-30-82787448. URL: http://link.springer.de. *4803*

ANALES DE QUIMICA.
Springer-Verlag Iberica, S.A., Provenca, 388, 1a planta, 08025 Barcelona, Spain. TEL 39-3-4570227. FAX 39-3-4571502. *1739*

ANALGESICS: THE INTERNATIONAL MARKET.
Euromonitor, 60-61 Britton St., London EC1M 5NA, England. TEL 44-171-251-8024. FAX 44-171-608-3149. URL: http://www.euromonitor.com.
Vendor(s): Data-Star, Knight-Ridder Information, Inc. *5646*

ANALYSE.
Nederlandse Vereniging van BioMedische Laboratoriummedewerkers, Wilhelminapark 52, 3581 NM Utrecht, Netherlands. TEL 31-30-2522881. FAX 31-30-2541814. *4894*

THE ANALYST.
The Royal Society of Chemistry, Thomas Graham House, Science Park, Milton Rd., Cambridge CB4 4WF, England. TEL 44-1223-420066. FAX 44-1223-423429. URL: http://chemistry.rsc.org/rsc/.
Vendor(s): STN International (CJRSC). *1787*

ANALYTICA CHIMICA ACTA.
Elsevier Science B.V., P.O. Box 211, 1000 AE Amsterdam, Netherlands. TEL 31-20-4853911. FAX 31-20-4853598. URL: http://www.elsevier.nl/
Vendor(s): STN International. *1788*

ANALYTICAL ABSTRACTS.
The Royal Society of Chemistry, Thomas Graham House, Science Park, Milton Rd., Cambridge CB4 4WF, England. TEL 44-1223-420066. FAX 44-1223-423429. URL: http://chemistry.rsc.org/rsc/.
Vendor(s): Data-Star (ANAB), Knight-Ridder Information, Inc. (File no.305), Questel Orbit Inc. (ANAB), STN International (ANABSTR). *1772*

ANALYTICAL BIOCHEMISTRY.
Academic Press, Inc., Journal Division, 525 B. St., Ste. 1900, San Diego, CA 92101-4495. TEL 619-230-1840. FAX 619-699-6800. URL: http://www.apnet.com/www/journal/ab.htm; http://www.idealibrary.com/ *650*

ANALYTICAL CHEMISTRY.
American Chemical Society, 1155 16th St., N.W., Washington, DC 20036. TEL 800-333-9511. FAX 614-447-3671.
Vendor(s): STN International (CJACS). *1788*

ANALYTICAL COMMUNICATIONS.
The Royal Society of Chemistry, Thomas Graham House, Science Park, Milton Rd., Cambridge CB4 4WF, England. TEL 44-1223-420066. FAX 44-1223-423429. URL: http://chemistry.rsc.org/rsc/. *1788*

ANALYTICAL INSTRUMENT INDUSTRY REPORT.
A I I Report Ltd., P.O. Box 78, E. Grinstead, W. Sussex RH19 2YW, England. TEL 44-1342-835935. FAX 44-1342-833488. *3800*

ANARCH.
URL: http://home1.gte.net/anarch/index.html.
Available only online. *5891*

ANATOLIAN STUDIES.
British Institute of Archaeology at Ankara, 31-34 Gordon Sq., London WC1H 0PY, England. TEL 44-171-388-2361. FAX 44-171-388-2361. *347*

THE ANATOMICAL RECORD.
John Wiley & Sons, Inc., Journals, 605 Third Ave., New York, NY 10158. TEL 212-850-6645. FAX 212-850-6021. URL: http://www.wiley.uk.co. *585*

ANATOMY AND EMBRYOLOGY.
Springer-Verlag, Heidelberger Platz 3, 14197 Berlin, Germany. TEL 49-30-82787-0. FAX 49-30-82787448. URL: http://link.springer.de. *812*

ANCIENT HISTORY BULLETIN.
c/o Dept. of Greek, Latin and Ancient History, University of Calgary, 2500 University Dr., N.W., Calgary AB T2N 1N4, Canada. URL: http://136.122.12.15/docs/dorectories/ahb/ahb/html. *3488*

ANDEAN REPORT.
Andean Air Mail & Peruvian Times S.A., Pasaje Los Pinos, 156, Piso B, Of. 6, Miraflores, Lima, Peru. TEL 51-14-453761. FAX 51-14-467888. *1221*

ANDREW SEYBOLD'S OUTLOOK.
Pinecrest Press, Inc., Box 917, Brookdale, CA 95007. TEL 408-338-7701. FAX 408-338-7806. URL: http://www.outlook.com. *2126*

ANESTHESIA AND ANALGESIA.
Williams & Wilkins, 351 W. Camden St., Baltimore, MD 21201-2436. TEL 410-528-4068. FAX 410-528-4452. URL: http://www.wwilkins.com.
Vendor(s): Ovid Technologies, Inc. *4803*

ANESTHESIOLOGY.
Lippincott - Raven Publishers, 227 E. Washington Sq., Philadelphia, PA 19106. TEL 215-238-4200. FAX 215-238-4227. URL: http://www.lrpub.com.
Vendor(s): Ovid Technologies, Inc. *4804*

ANGER MANAGEMENT - CONTROLLING THE VOLCANO WITHIN.
URL: http://www.kumu.com/~grhoades/newsletters.html.
Available only online. *6093*

ANGEWANDTE CHEMIE.
Wiley - V C H, Postfach 101161, 69451 Weinheim, Germany. TEL 49-6201-606-0. FAX 49-6201-606328. URL: http://www.vchgroup.de.
Vendor(s): STN International (CJVCH). *1739*

ANGEWANDTE CHEMIE: INTERNATIONAL EDITION.
Wiley - V C H, Postfach 101161, 69451 Weinheim, Germany. TEL 49-6201-606-0. FAX 49-6201-606-328. URL: http://www.vchgroup.de. *1739*

ANIMAL BEHAVIOR ABSTRACTS.
Cambridge Scientific Abstracts, 7200 Wisconsin Ave., 6th Fl., Bethesda, MD 20814. TEL 301-961-6750. FAX 301-961-6720. URL: http://www.csa.com.
Vendor(s): Knight-Ridder Information, Inc. (File no.76/LIFE SCIENCES COLLECTION), STN International (LIFESCI). *635*

ANIMAL BEHAVIOUR.
Academic Press Ltd., 24-28 Oval Rd., London NW1 7DX, England. TEL 44-171-267-4466. FAX 44-171-482-2293. URL: http://www.hbuk.co.uk/ap/abehav; http://www.europe.idealibrary.com/. *826*

ANIMAL BREEDING ABSTRACTS.
CAB International, Wallingford, Oxon. OX10 8DE, England. TEL 44-1491-832111. FAX 44-1491-826090. URL: http://www.cabi.org.
Vendor(s): DIMDI, European Space Agency, Knight-Ridder Information, Inc. *635*

ANIMAL DISEASE OCCURRENCE.
CAB International, Wallingford, Oxon. OX10 8DE, England. TEL 44-1491-832111. FAX 44-1491-826090. URL: http://www.cabi.org.
Vendor(s): DIMDI, European Space Agency, Knight-Ridder Information, Inc. *7285*

ANIMAL PHARM.
P J B Publications Ltd., 18-20 Hill Rise, Richmond, Surrey TW10 6UA, England. TEL 44-181-948-3262. FAX 44-181-332-8998. URL: http://www.pjbpubs.co.uk/animal/aghome.html.
Vendor(s): Data-Star, Knight-Ridder Information, Inc. (File No.129), Ovid Technologies, Inc. (PHIN,PHIC, PHID). *7265*

ANIMAL WELFARE INFORMATION CENTER BULLETIN.
U.S. Animal Welfare Information Center, National Agricultural Library, 10301 Baltimore Blvd., 5th Fl., Beltsville, MD 20705-2351. TEL 301-504-6212. FAX 301-504-7125. URL: http://netvet.wustl.edu/awic.htm. *301*

ANIMALS.
Massachusetts Society for the Prevention of Cruelty to Animals, 350 S. Huntington Ave., Boston, MA 02130. TEL 617-541-5065. FAX 617-522-4885. URL: http://www.americast.com; http://www.mspca.org/. *301*

ANIMUS.
Memorial University of Newfoundland, St. John's, NF A1C 5S7, Canada. URL: http://www.mun.ca/animus.
Available only online. *5717*

ANNALES ACADEMIAE SCIENTIARUM FENNICAE. MATHEMATICA.
Suomalainen Tiedeakatemia, Mariankatu 5, FIN-00170 Helsinki, Finland. URL: http://geom.helsinki.fi/annales/anna.html. *4560*

ANNALES ACADEMIAE SCIENTIARUM FENNICAE. MATHEMATICA DISSERTATIONES.
Suomalainen Tiedeakatemia, Mariankatu 5, FIN-00170 Helsinki, Finland. FAX 358-9-660-1171. *4560*

ANNALES DE PHYSIQUE.
Editions de Physique, Z.I. de Courtaboeuf, B.P. 112, 91944 Les Ulis Cedex, France. TEL 33-1-69-07-36-88. FAX 33-1-69-28-84-91. URL: http://www.edphys.fr/docinfos/onlinean.html. *5796*

ANNALES GEOPHYSICAE.
Springer-Verlag, Heidelberger Platz 3, 14197 Berlin, Germany. TEL 49-30-82787-0. FAX 49-30-82787448. URL: http://link.springer.de. *2378*

ANNALS OF BOTANY.
Academic Press Ltd., 24-28 Oval Rd., London NW1 7DX, England. TEL 44-171-267-4466. FAX 44-171-482-2293. URL: http://www.hbuk.co.uk/ap/aob; http://www.europe.idealibrary.com/. *692*

ANNALS OF HEMATOLOGY.
Springer-Verlag, Heidelberger Platz 3, 14197 Berlin, Germany. TEL 49-30-82787-0. FAX 49-30-82787448. URL: http://link.springer.de. *4916*

ANNALS OF INTERNAL MEDICINE.
American College of Physicians, Independence Mall W., Sixth St. at Race, Philadelphia, PA 19106-1572. TEL 215-351-2400. FAX 215-351-2799. URL: http://www.acponline.org/journals/annals/annaltoc.htm.
Vendor(s): Ovid Technologies, Inc. *4924*

ANNALS OF NEUROLOGY.
Lippincott - Raven Publishers, 227 E. Washington Sq., Philadelphia, PA 19106. TEL 215-238-4200. FAX 215-238-4227.
Vendor(s): Lexis-Nexis, Ovid Technologies, Inc. *5052*

THE ANNALS OF PHARMACOTHERAPY.
Harvey Whitney Books Company, Box 42696, Cincinnati, OH 45242. TEL 513-793-3555. FAX 513-793-3600. *5647*

ANNALS OF PHYSICS.
Academic Press, Inc., Journal Division, 525 B St., Ste. 1900, San Diego, CA 92101-4495. TEL 619-230-1840. FAX 619-699-6800. URL: http://www.apnet.com/www/journal/ph.htm; http://ww.idealibrary.com/. *5796*

ANNALS OF PLASTIC SURGERY.
Lippincott - Raven Publishers, 227 E. Washington Sq., Philadelphia, PA 19106. TEL 215-238-4200. FAX 215-238-4227. URL: http://www.lrpub.com.
Vendor(s): Lexis-Nexis. *5135*

ANNALS OF THE RHEUMATIC DISEASES.
B M J Publishing Group, B.M.A. House, Tavistock Sq., London WC1H 9JR, England. TEL 44-171-383-6270. FAX 44-171-383-6402.
Vendor(s): Ovid Technologies, Inc. *5124*

ANNALS OF THORACIC SURGERY.
Elsevier Science Inc., Box 945, New York, NY 10159-0945. TEL 212-633-3730. FAX 212-633-3680. URL: http://www.elsevier.nl/
Vendor(s): Lexis-Nexis. *5136*

ANNALS OF TROPICAL MEDICINE AND PARASITOLOGY.
Carfax Publishing Co., P.O. Box 25, Abingdon, Oxon OX14 3UE, England. TEL 44-1235-401000. FAX 44-1235-401550. *4832*

ANNALS OF VASCULAR SURGERY.
Springer-Verlag, Medical Journals, 175 Fifth Ave., New York, NY 10010-7858. TEL 212-460-1500. FAX 212-473-6272. *5136*

ANNAPOLIS ONLINE FORUM.
Annapolis Virtual Mall, 1012 Forest Hill Ave., Annapolis, MD 21403. TEL 410-263-7264. URL: http://avmcyber.com/forum/
Available only online. *3369*

ANNOTATION.
National Historical Publications and Records Commission, National Archives Bldg., Washington, DC 20408. TEL 202-501-5600. FAX 202-501-5601. URL: http://www.nara.gov/nara/nhprc/annotation/. *3617*

ANNUAIRE TELEXPORT.
Chambre de Commerce et d'Industrie de Paris (CEDIP), 27 av. de Friedland, 75008 Paris, France. TEL 33-1-42897204. FAX 33-1-42897281.
Vendor(s): Data-Star. *1178*

ANNUAL BIBLIOGRAPHY OF ENGLISH LANGUAGE AND LITERATURE.
W.S. Maney & Son Ltd., Hudson St., Leeds LS9 7DL, England. TEL 01532-497481. FAX 01532-486983. *4494*

ANNUAL FORUM REPORTS.
Professional Education International, Inc., 549 W. Randolph St., Ste. 600, Chicago, IL 60661. TEL 312-559-4100. FAX 312-559-4111. *1981*

ANNUAL REVIEW OF COMMUNICATIONS.
Professional Education International, Inc., 549 W. Randolph St., Ste. 600, Chicago, IL 60661. TEL 312-559-4100. FAX 312-559-4111. *1981*

ANNUAL REVIEW OF GENETICS.
Annual Reviews Inc., 4139 El Camino Way, Box 10139, Palo Alto, CA 94303-0139. TEL 650-493-4400. FAX 650-424-0910. URL: http://www.annurev.org.
Vendor(s): Information Access Co. *763*

ANNUAL REVIEW OF MEDICINE: SELECTED TOPICS IN THE CLINICAL SCIENCES.
Annual Reviews Inc., 4139 El Camino Way, Box 10139, Palo Alto, CA 94303-0139. TEL 650-493-4400. FAX 650-424-0910. URL: http://www.annurev.org. *4639*

ANNUAL REVIEW OF MICROBIOLOGY.
Annual Reviews Inc., 4139 El Camino Way, Box 10139, Palo Alto, CA 94303-0139. TEL 650-493-4400. FAX 650-424-0910. URL: http://www.annurev.org.
Vendor(s): Information Access Co. *780*

ANNUAL REVIEW OF O C L C RESEARCH.
O C L C Online Computer Library Center, Inc., Office of Research and Special Projects, 6565 Frantz Rd., Dublin, OH 43017-3395. TEL 614-764-6000. URL: http://www.purlorg/net/publications. *4229*

ANNUAL REVIEW OF PSYCHOLOGY.
Annual Reviews Inc., 4139 El Camino Way, Box 10139, Palo Alto, CA 94303-0139. TEL 650-493-4400. FAX 650-424-0910. URL: http://www.annurev.org/series/psycolgy/psycolgy.htm.
Vendor(s): Information Access Co., UMI. *6093*

ANNUAL REVIEW OF SOCIOLOGY.
Annual Reviews Inc., 4139 El Camino Way, Box 10139, Palo Alto, CA 94303-0139. TEL 650-493-4400. FAX 650-424-0910. URL: http://www.annurev.org.
Vendor(s): Information Access Co., UMI. *6701*

ANNUAL SURVEY OF MANUFACTURES.
U.S. Bureau of the Census, Customer Services, Washington, DC 20233. TEL 301-457-4100. FAX 301-457-4714. URL: http://www.census.gov/.
Vendor(s): CompuServe, Inc., Knight-Ridder Information, Inc. *1016*

ANNUAL WORLD BANK CONFERENCE ON DEVELOPMENT ECONOMICS.
World Bank, International Bank for Reconstruction and Development, 1818 H St., N.W., Washington, DC 20433. TEL 202-473-1155. FAX 202-522-2627.
Vendor(s): Knight-Ridder Information, Inc. *932*

ANOTHER WINDOWS 95 LINKS AND RESOURCES NEWSLETTER.
TEL 39-81-5092318. URL: http://rhay.home.ml.org.
Available only online. *2131*

ANSIBLE.
94 London Rd., Reading, Berks. RG1 5AU, England. FAX 44-118-966-9914. URL: http://www.dcs.gla.ac.uk/sf-archives/ansible/. *4528*

ANTARCTIC BIBLIOGRAPHY.
U.S. Library of Congress, Washington, DC 20540. TEL 202-707-1181.
Vendor(s): Questel Orbit Inc. (COLD). *6587*

ANTHEM.
Henge Productions, c/o E. A. Fichtl, Ed., 6141 42nd Ave., N., St. Petersburg, FL 33709. TEL 813-347-3743. URL: http://www.tbi.net/~eafichtl/index.htm.
Available only online. *4376*

ANTHOLO-GEE!-ZINE.
Fine Art Inc., TEL 706-245-4900. FAX 706-245-4900.
Available only online. *4376*

ANTHROPOLOGICAL LITERATURE.
Harvard University, Tozzer Library, 21 Divinity Ave., Cambridge, MA 02138. TEL 617-495-2253. FAX 617-496-2741.
Vendor(s): Research Libraries Group Information Network. *335*

ANTI-CANCER DRUG DESIGN.
Oxford University Press, Academic Division, Great Clarendon St., Oxford OX2 6DP, England. TEL 44-1865-267907. FAX 44-1865-267485. URL: http://www.oup.co.uk/journals. *4970*

ANTI-CENSORSHIP NEWSLETTER.
The Parent S I G, 1640 Via Pacifica, Ste.F-105, Corona, CA 91720. *6702*

ANTIOCH REVIEW.
Antioch Review, Inc., Box 148, Yellow Springs, OH 45387. TEL 513-767-6389.
Vendor(s): Information Access Co., UMI. *4323*

ANTIQUES AND ART AROUND FLORIDA.
Antiques and Art Around Publishing, Inc., Box 2481, Fort Lauderdale, FL 33303-2481. TEL 954-768-9430. FAX 954-768-0621. *337*

ANTIQUITY.
Company of Biologists Ltd., Bidder Bldg., 140 Cowley Rd., Cambridge CB4 4DL. TEL 44-1223-426164. FAX 44-1223-423353. URL: http://www.cityscape.co.uk/users/ag64; http://intarch.ac.uk/antiquity.
Vendor(s): Information Access Co. *348*

ANTISEMITISM WORLD REPORT (YEAR).
Institute for Jewish Policy Research, 79 Wimpole St., London W1M 7DD, England. FAX 0171-935-3252. URL: http://www.ort.org/cummunit.jpr.
Available only online. *5988*

ANTITRUST.
American Bar Association, Antitrust Law Section, 750 N. Lake Shore Dr., Chicago, IL 60611. TEL 312-988-5606. URL: http://www.abanet.org/antitrust.
Vendor(s): Lexis-Nexis, West Group (ANTITR). *4072*

ANTITRUST & TRADE REGULATION REPORT.
The Bureau of National Affairs, Inc., 1231 25th St., N.W., Washington, DC 20037. TEL 202-452-4200. FAX 202-822-8092. URL: http://www.bna.com/
Vendor(s): Lexis-Nexis (TRADRG), West Group (BNA-ATRR). *1578*

ANTITRUST FREEDOM OF INFORMATION LOG.
Washington Regulatory Reporting Associates, Box 356, Basye, VA 22810. TEL 703-856-2216. FAX 703-856-8331.
Vendor(s): Lexis-Nexis. *1315*

ANTITRUST LAW JOURNAL.
American Bar Association, Antitrust Law Section, 750 N. Lake Shore Dr., Chicago, IL 60611. TEL 312-988-5606.
Vendor(s): Information Access Co., Lexis-Nexis, West Group (ANTITRLJ). *4073*

ANTITRUST LITIGATION REPORTER.
Andrews Publications, 175 Strafford Ave., Bldg. 4, Ste. 140, Wayne, PA 19087. TEL 610-225-0510. FAX 610-225-0501.
Vendor(s): Lexis-Nexis. *1103*

ANTIVIRAL AGENTS BULLETIN.
Biotechnology Information Institute, 1700 Rockville Pike, Ste. 400, Rockville, MD 20852. TEL 301-424-0255. FAX 301-424-0257. URL: http://www.bioinfo.com/biotech/antiviral.html.
Vendor(s): Information Access Co. *5647*

ANUARIO DE LITERATURA.
Universidade Federal de Santa Catarina, Curso de Pos-Graduacao em Literatura, Campus Universitario, Trindade, 88040-970 Florianopolis, SC, Brazil. TEL 55-48-2319582. FAX 55-48-2319988. URL: http://www.cce.ufsc.br/~pglb. *4376*

ANUARIO ESTATISTICO DOS TRANSPORTES.
Empresa Brasileira de Planejamento de Transportes, G E I P O T, SAN Quadra 3 Blocos N-O, 70040-920 Brasilia DF, Brazil. FAX 061-224-8642. *7023*

ANYTHING THAT MOVES.
Bay Area Bisexual Network, 2261 Market St., Ste. 496, San Francisco, CA 94114-1600. TEL 415-703-7977. URL: http://www.hooked.net/users/jonesey/atm.html. *3691*

APICULTURAL ABSTRACTS.
International Bee Research Association, 18 North Rd., Cardiff CF1 3DY, Wales. TEL 44-1222-372409. FAX 44-1222-665522.
Vendor(s): European Space Agency (File nos.16 & 124/CAB), Knight-Ridder Information, Inc. *168*

APOKALYPSO.
Box 782, Chester, NJ 07930. URL: http://www.planet.net/ptgermine. *6320*

APOTHECARY.
Health Care Marketing Services, H C M S Inc., Box AP, Los Altos, CA 94023-0179. TEL 415-941-3955. FAX 415-941-2303. *5647*

APPAREL INDUSTRY MAGAZINE.
Shore-Varrone, Inc., 6255 Barfield Rd. N.E., Ste. 200, Atlanta, GA 30328-4300. TEL 404-252-8831. FAX 404-252-4436. URL: http://www.svi-atl.com.
Vendor(s): Information Access Co., Knight-Ridder Information, Inc., UMI. *1912*

APPARENTDEPTH.
4320 Sarah St., Ste. 23, Burbank, CA 91505. URL: http://www.apparentdepth.com.
Available only online. *6702*

APPETITE.
Academic Press Ltd., 24-28 Oval Rd., London NW1 7DX, England. TEL 44-171-267-4466. FAX 44-171-482-2293. URL: http://www.hbuk.co.uk; http://www.europe.idealibrary.com/. *5469*

APPLESAUCE.
South Australian Apple Users Club, P.O. Box 322, Prospect, S.A. 5082, Australia. TEL 61-8-84434298. URL: http://www.webmedia.com.au/applesauce/ *2194*

APPLIANCE.
Dana Chase Publications, Inc., 1110 Jorie Blvd., CS-9019, Oak Brook, II 60522-9019. TEL 708 990 3484. FAX 708-990-0078.
Vendor(s): Information Access Co. *2808*

APPLIANCE MANUFACTURER.
Business News Publishing Company, 755 W. Big Beaver, Ste. 1000, Troy, MI 48084. TEL 810-362-3700. FAX 810-362-0317. URL: http://www.bnp.com.
Vendor(s): Information Access Co., Knight-Ridder Information, Inc., UMI. *2808*

APPLICABLE ALGEBRA IN ENGINEERING, COMMUNICATION AND COMPUTING.
Springer-Verlag, Heidelberger Platz 3, 14197 Berlin, Germany. TEL 49-30-82787-0. FAX 49-30-82787448. URL: http://link.springer.de. *4618*

APPLICABLE ANALYSIS.
Gordon and Breach - Harwood Academic, Amsteldisk 166, 1st Fl., 1079 LH Amsterdam, Netherlands. URL: http://www.gbhap.com/Applicable_Analysis. *4561*

APPLICATION DEVELOPMENT TRENDS.
Software Productivity Group, Inc., 1 Apple Hill No. 301, Natick, MA 01760-2072. *2164*

APPLIED AND COMPUTATIONAL HARMONIC ANALYSIS.
Academic Press, Inc., Journal Division, 525 B St., Ste. 1900, San Diego, CA 92101-4495. TEL 619-230-1840. FAX 619-699-6800. URL: http://www.apnet.com/www/journal/ha.htm; http://www.idealibrary.com/ *4561*

APPLIED ARTIFICIAL INTELLIGENCE.
Taylor & Francis Inc., 1900 Frost Rd., Ste. 101, Bristol, PA 19007-1598. TEL 215-785-5800. FAX 215-785-5515. URL: http://www.tandf.co.uk/. *2097*

APPLIED CATALYSIS A: GENERAL.
Elsevier Science B.V., P.O. Box 211, 1000 AE Amsterdam, Netherlands. TEL 31-20-4853911. FAX 31-20-4853598. URL: http://www.elsevier.nl/
Vendor(s): STN International. *2755*

APPLIED ECONOMICS.
Routledge, 11 New Fetter Ln., London EC4P 4EE, England. TEL 44-171-583-9855. FAX 44-171-842-2298. URL: http://www.routledge.com/routledge/journal/journals.html.
Vendor(s): Information Access Co. *933*

APPLIED ECONOMICS LETTERS.
Routledge, 11 New Fetter Ln., London EC4P 4EE, England. TEL 44-171-583-9855. FAX 44-171-842-2298. URL: http://www.routledge.com/routledge/journal/journals.html. *933*

APPLIED FINANCIAL ECONOMICS.
Routledge, 11 New Fetter Ln., London EC4P 4EE, England. TEL 44-171-583-9855. FAX 44-171-842-2298. URL: http://www.routledge.com/routledge/journal/journals.html. *1221*

APPLIED GENETICS NEWS.
Business Communications Co., Inc. (Norwalk), 25 Van Zant St., Ste. 13, Norwalk, CT 06855. TEL 203-853-4266. FAX 203-853-0348.
Vendor(s): Data-Star, Information Access Co., Knight-Ridder Information, Inc., NewsNet (BT03). *763*

APPLIED MATHEMATICAL FINANCE.
Thomson Professional, 2-6 Boundary Row, London SE1 8HN, England. TEL 44-171-8650066. FAX 44-171-5229623. URL: http://amf.thomsonprofessional.com. *4562*

APPLIED MICROBIOLOGY AND BIOTECHNOLOGY.
Springer-Verlag, Heidelberger Platz 3, 14197 Berlin, Germany. TEL 49-30-82787-0. FAX 49-30-82787448. URL: http://link.springer.de. *677*

APPLIED PHYSICS. A: MATERIALS SCIENCE & PROCESSING.
Springer-Verlag, Heidelberger Platz 3, 14197 Berlin, Germany. TEL 49-30-82787-0. FAX 49-30-82787448. URL: http://link.springer.de. *5797*

APPLIED PHYSICS. B: LASERS AND OPTICS.
Springer-Verlag, Heidelberger Platz 3, 14197 Berlin, Germany. TEL 49-30-82787-0. FAX 49-30-82787448. URL: http://link.springer.de. *5797*

APPLIED PHYSICS LETTERS.
American Institute of Physics, One Physics Ellipse, College Park, MD 20740-3843. TEL 301-209-3000. URL: http://www.aip.org.
Vendor(s): OCLC. *5797*

APPLIED SCIENCE & TECHNOLOGY INDEX.
H.W. Wilson Co., 950 University Ave., Bronx, NY 10452. TEL 718-588-8400. FAX 718-590-1617.
Vendor(s): Knight-Ridder Information, Inc., OCLC, Ovid Technologies, Inc., WIlsonline (AST). *2747*

APPLIED SEMIOTICS.
University of Toronto, Department of French, 50 St. Joseph St., Toronto, ON M4S 1J4, Canada. URL: http://www.chass.utoronto.ca/french/as-sa.
Available only online. *4241*

APPRAISAL JOURNAL.
Appraisal Institute, 875 N. Michigan Ave., Ste. 2400, Chicago, IL 60611-1980. TEL 312-335-4100. FAX 312-353-4400.
Vendor(s): Information Access Co., UMI. *6294*

AQUACULTURE INTERNATIONAL.
Thomson Science, 2-6 Boundary Row, London SE1 8HN, England. TEL 44-171-8650066. FAX 44-171-8659623. URL: http://www.thomsonscience.com. *3061*

AQUALINE ABSTRACTS.
W R C plc, P.O. Box 85, Frankland Rd., Blagrove, Swindon, Wilts SN5 8YF, England. URL: http://www.wrcplc.co.uk.
Vendor(s): European Space Agency, Questel Orbit Inc. (AQUA), Telesystemes - Questel. *7307*

AQUARIUM SCIENCES AND CONSERVATION.
Thomson Science, 2-6 Boundary Row, London SE1 8HN, England. TEL 44-171-865-0066. FAX 44-171-5229623. URL: http://www.thomsonscience.com. *3061*

AQUATIC SCIENCES & FISHERIES ABSTRACTS. PART 1: BIOLOGICAL SCIENCES AND LIVING RESOURCES.
Cambridge Scientific Abstracts, 7200 Wisconsin Ave., 6th Fl., Bethesda, MD 20814. TEL 301-961-6750. FAX 301-961-6720. URL: http://www.csa.com.
Vendor(s): DIMDI, European Space Agency, Knight-Ridder Information, Inc. (File no.44), STN International (AQUASCI). *7307*

AQUATIC SCIENCES & FISHERIES ABSTRACTS. PART 2: OCEAN TECHNOLOGY, POLICY AND NON-LIVING RESOURCES.
Cambridge Scientific Abstracts, 7200 Wisconsin Ave., 6th Fl., Bethesda, MD 20814. TEL 301-961-6750. FAX 301-961-6720. URL: http://www.csa.com.
Vendor(s): DIMDI, European Space Agency, Knight-Ridder Information, Inc. (File no.44), STN International (AQUASCI). *7307*

AQUATIC SCIENCES & FISHERIES ABSTRACTS. PART 3: AQUATIC POLLUTION AND ENVIRONMENTAL QUALITY.
Cambridge Scientific Abstracts, 7200 Wisconsin Ave., 6th Fl., Bethesda, MD 20814. TEL 301-961-6700. FAX 301-961-6720. URL: http://www.csa.com.
Vendor(s): DIMDI, European Space Agency, Knight-Ridder Information, Inc. (File no.44), STN International (AQUASCI). *3081*

ARAB STUDIES QUARTERLY.
Association of Arab-American University Graduates, Inc., 2121 Wisconsin Ave., N.W., Ste. 310, Washington, DC 20007-2258. TEL 202-337-7717. FAX 202-337-3302.
Vendor(s): Information Access Co., UMI. *2997*

ARCHAEOLOGICAL NEWSLETTER.
Royal Ontario Museum, Committee for Field Archaeology, 100 Queen's Park, Toronto, ON M5S 2C6, Canada. TEL 416-586-5698. FAX 416-586-5863. URL: http://www.rom.on.ca/ebuff/aboutarc.htm. *349*

ARCHAEOLOGY ON KAUA'I.
Anthropology Club of Kaua'i, 3-1901 Kaumualii Hwy., Lihue, HI 96766. TEL 808-245-8311. FAX 808-245-8220.
Available only online. *351*

ARCHIPELAGO.
URL: http://www.goarchi.com/archo/provines/i-jaya/i-jayahome.html.
Available only online. *3321*

ARCHITECTURAL PUBLICATIONS INDEX.
R I B A Publications, Finsbury Mission, 39 Moreland St., London EC1V 8BB, England. TEL 44-171-251-0791. FAX 44-171-608-2375.
Vendor(s): Knight-Ridder Information, Inc. (File no.179). *418*

ARCHITECTURAL RECORD.
McGraw-Hill Companies, 1221 Ave. of the Americas, New York, NY 10020. TEL 212-512-2000. FAX 212-512-4256. URL: http://mcgraw-hill.com/corporate/news__info/locator.html.
Vendor(s): Dow Jones News Retrieval (ARCH), Knight-Ridder Information, Inc. (AR), NewsNet (BC13). *394*

ARCHITECTURAL REVIEW.
E M A P - Architecture, 33-39 Bowling Green Ln., London EC1R ODA, England. TEL 0171-837-1212. FAX 0171-278-4003. URL: http://www.emap.com/construct/arhome.htm.
Vendor(s): UMI. *394*

ARCHITECTURE.
B P I Communications, Inc., 1130 Connecticut Ave., N.W., Ste. 625, Washington, DC 20036. TEL 202-828-0993. FAX 202-828-0825. URL: http://www.bpi.com/
Vendor(s): Information Access Co. *394*

ARCHITRONIC.
Kent State University, School of Architecture and Environmental Design, Kent, OH 44242-0001. TEL 330-672-2869. FAX 330-672-3809. URL: http://www.saed.kent.edu/Architronic/
Available only online. *396*

ARCHIV DER MATHEMATIK.
Birkhaeuser Verlag, P.O. Box 133, CH-4010 Basel, Switzerland. TEL 41-61-2050730. FAX 41-61-2050791. *4563*

ARCHIVE FOR MATHEMATICAL LOGIC.
Springer-Verlag, Heidelberger Platz 3, 14197 Berlin, Germany. TEL 49-30-82787-0. FAX 49-30-82787448. URL: http://link.springer.de. *4563*

ARCHIVE FOR RATIONAL MECHANICS AND ANALYSIS.
Springer-Verlag, Heidelberger Platz 3, 14197 Berlin, Germany. TEL 49-30-82787-0. FAX 49-30-82787448. URL: http://link.springer.de. *4563*

ARCHIVE OF APPLIED MECHANICS.
Springer-Verlag, Heidelberger Platz 3, 14197 Berlin, Germany. TEL 49-30-82787-0. FAX 49-30-82787448. URL: http://link.springer.de. *2710*

ARCHIVES OF BIOCHEMISTRY AND BIOPHYSICS.
Academic Press, Inc., Journal Division, 525 B St., Ste. 1900, San Diego, CA 92101-4495. TEL 619-230-1840. FAX 619-699-6800. URL: http://www.apnet.com/www/journal/bb.htm; http://www.idealibrary.com/ *651*

ARCHIVES OF DERMATOLOGICAL RESEARCH.
Springer-Verlag, Heidelberger Platz 3, 14197 Berlin, Germany. TEL 49-30-82787-0. FAX 49-30-82787448. URL: http://link.springer.de. *4875*

ARCHIVES OF DERMATOLOGY.
American Medical Association, 515 N. State St., Chicago, IL 60610. TEL 312-464-5000. FAX 617-667-4948. URL: http://www.ama-assn.org/public/journals/derm/dermhome.htm.
Vendor(s): Information Access Co., Knight-Ridder Information, Inc. *4875*

ARCHIVES OF DISEASE IN CHILDHOOD.
B M J Publishing Group, B.M.A. House, Tavistock Sq., London WC1H 9JR, England. TEL 44-171-383-6270. FAX 44-171-383-6402.
Vendor(s): Ovid Technologies, Inc. *5027*

ARCHIVES OF DISEASE IN CHILDHOOD. FETAL AND NEONATAL EDITION.
B M J Publishing Group, B.M.A. House, Tavistock Sq., London WC1H 9JR, England. TEL 44-171-387-4499. FAX 44-171-383-6661.
Vendor(s): Ovid Technologies, Inc.. *4953*

ARCHIVES OF ENVIRONMENTAL HEALTH.
Heldref Publications, 1319 Eighteenth St., N.W., Washington, DC 20036-1802. TEL 202-296-6267. FAX 202-296-5149.
Vendor(s): Information Access Co. *4640*

ARCHIVES OF FAMILY MEDICINE.
American Medical Association, 515 N. State St., Chicago, IL 60610. TEL 312-464-5000. FAX 312-464-5831. URL: http://www.ama-assn.org/ public/journals/fami/famihome.htm.
Vendor(s): Information Access Co., Knight-Ridder Information, Inc. *4640*

ARCHIVES OF GENERAL PSYCHIATRY.
American Medical Association, 515 N. State St., Chicago, IL 60610. TEL 312-464-5000. FAX 312-464-5831. URL: http://www.ama-assn.org/public/journals/psyc/psychome.htm.
Vendor(s): Information Access Co., Knight-Ridder Information, Inc. *5052*

ARCHIVES OF GYNECOLOGY AND OBSTETRICS.
Springer-Verlag, Heidelberger Platz 3, 14197 Berlin, Germany. TEL 49-30-82787-0. FAX 49-30-82787448. URL: http://link.springer.de. *4953*

ARCHIVES OF INTERNAL MEDICINE.
American Medical Association, 515 N. State St., Chicago, IL 60610. TEL 312-464-5000. FAX 312-464-5831. URL: http://www.ama-assn.org/public/journals/inte/intehome.htm.
Vendor(s): Information Access Co., Knight-Ridder Information, Inc. *4924*

ARCHIVES OF MICROBIOLOGY.
Springer-Verlag, Heidelberger Platz 3, 14197 Berlin, Germany. TEL 49-30-82787-0. FAX 49-30-82787448. URL: http://link.springer.de. *781*

ARCHIVES OF NEUROLOGY.
American Medical Association, 515 N. State St., Chicago, IL 60610. TEL 312-464-5000. FAX 312-464-5831. URL: http://www.ama-assn.org/public/journals/neur/neurhome.htm.
Vendor(s): Information Access Co., Knight-Ridder Information, Inc. *5053*

ARCHIVES OF OPHTHALMOLOGY.
American Medical Association, 515 N. State St., Chicago, IL 60610. TEL 312-464-5000. FAX 312-464-5831. URL: http://www.ama-assn.org/public/journals/opht/ophthome.htm.
Vendor(s): Information Access Co., Knight-Ridder Information, Inc. *4990*

ARCHIVES OF OTOLARYNGOLOGY - HEAD & NECK SURGERY.
American Medical Association, 515 N. State St., Chicago, IL 60610. TEL 312-464-5000. FAX 312-464-5831. URL: http://www.ama-assn.org/public/journals/otol/otolhome.htm.
Vendor(s): Information Access Co., Knight-Ridder Information, Inc. *5020*

ARCHIVES OF PATHOLOGY & LABORATORY MEDICINE.
College of American Pathologists, 325 Waukegan Rd., Northfield, IL 60093-2750. TEL 847-832-7000. FAX 847-832-8150.
Vendor(s): Lexis-Nexis. *4640*

ARCHIVES OF PEDIATRICS & ADOLESCENT MEDICINE.
American Medical Association, 515 N. State St., Chicago, IL 60610. TEL 312-464-5000. FAX 312-464-4181. URL: http://www.ama-assn.org/public/journals/ajdc/ajdchome.htm.
Vendor(s): Information Access Co., Knight-Ridder Information, Inc. *5028*

ARCHIVES OF PHYSIOLOGY AND BIOCHEMISTRY.
Swets & Zeitlinger bv, P.O. Box 825, 2160 SZ Lisse, Netherlands. TEL 31-252-435111. FAX 31-252-415888. URL: http://www.swets.nl. *813*

ARCHIVES OF SEXUAL BEHAVIOR.
Plenum Publishing Corp., 233 Spring St., New York, NY 10013-1578. TEL 212-620-8000. FAX 212-463-0742.
Vendor(s): Information Access Co. *4640*

ARCHIVES OF SURGERY.
American Medical Association, 515 N. State St., Chicago, IL 60610. TEL 312-464-5000. FAX 312-464-5831. URL: http://www.ama-assn.org/public/journals/surg/surghome.htm.
Vendor(s): Information Access Co., Knight-Ridder Information, Inc. *5136*

THE ARCHIVES OF UNUSUAL POETRY.
All - Electric Paperbacks, URL: http://www.paperbacks.com/poetry/
Available only online. *4503*

ARCHIVUM MATHEMATICUM.
Masarykova Universita, Janackovo Nam. 2a, 662 95 Brno, Czech Republic. TEL 42-5-41321251. FAX 42-5-41210337. URL: http://www.emis.de/journals/AM/. *4563*

THE ARCHWAY (SMITHFIELD).
Bryant College, Box 7, 1150 Douglas Pike, Smithfield, RI 02917-1284. TEL 401-232-6028. FAX 401-232-6319. *1940*

AREA MAGAZINE.
Area Arts, 615 Mt. Pleasant Rd., Ste. 205, Toronto, ON M4S 3C5, Canada. TEL 416-368-9401. FAX 416-359-0755. *423*

ARETHUSA.
Johns Hopkins University Press, Journals Publishing Division, 2715 N. Charles St., Baltimore, MD 21218-4319. TEL 410-516-6987. FAX 410-516-6968. URL: http://muse.jhu.edu. *1900*

ARGUMENTATION & ADVOCACY.
American Forensic Association, Box 256, River Falls, WI 54022-0256. FAX 715-425-9533.
Vendor(s): Information Access Co., UMI. *1982*

ARHIV ZA FARMACIJU.
Farmaceutsko Drustvo Srbije, Vojvode Stepe 450, Box 664, 11000 Belgrade, Yugoslavia. *5648*

ARI.
Springer-Verlag, Heidelberger Platz 3, 14197 Berlin, Germany. TEL 49-30-82787-0. FAX 49-30-82787448. *2331*

ARID LANDS NEWSLETTER.
University of Arizona, Office of Arid Lands Studies, 1955 E. Sixth St., Tucson, AZ 85719. TEL 520-621-8584. FAX 520-621-3816. URL: http://ag.arizona.edu/OALS/ALN/ALNHome.html. *2906*

ARIZONA BUSINESS DIRECTORY.
American Business Directories, 5711 S. 86th Circle, Box 27347, Omaha, NE 68127. TEL 402-593-4600. FAX 402-331-5481. *1652*

ARIZONA BUSINESS GAZETTE.
Phoenix Newspapers, Inc., Box 1950, Phoenix, AZ 85001. TEL 602-271-7373. FAX 602-271-7363.
Vendor(s): Dow Jones News Retrieval, Knight-Ridder Information, Inc., Lexis-Nexis, MediaStream. *933*

ARIZONA COMMISSION ON THE ARTS. REPORT TO THE GOVERNOR (YEAR).
Commission on the Arts, 417 W. Roosevelt St., Phoenix, AZ 85003. TEL 602-255-5882. FAX 602-256-0282. URL: http://www.state.az.us/azarts. *423*

ARIZONA LEGISLATIVE REPORT.
Arizona News Service, 14 N. 18th Ave., Phoenix, AZ 85007. TEL 602-258-7026. FAX 602-258-2504. *4069*

ARIZONA STATE LAW JOURNAL.
Arizona State University, College of Law, Tempe, AZ 85287. TEL 602-965-6287. FAX 602-965-2427. Vendor(s): West Group. *3912*

ARKANSAS. AGRICULTURAL EXPERIMENT STATION. RESEARCH BULLETIN.
Agricultural Experiment Station, Agricultural Publications, 110 Agriculture Bldg., 1 University of Arkansas, Division of Agriculture, Fayetteville, AR 72701-1201. TEL 501-575-5647. FAX 501-575-7531. URL: http://www.uark.edu/depts/agripub/publications/. *169*

ARKANSAS. AGRICULTURAL EXPERIMENT STATION. RESEARCH SERIES.
Agricultural Experiment Station, Agricultural Publications, 110 Agriculture Bldg., 1 University of Arkansas, Division of Agriculture, Fayetteville, AR 72701-1201. TEL 501-575-5647. FAX 501-575-7531. URL: http://www.uark.edu/depts/agripub/publications/. *169*

ARKANSAS. AGRICULTURAL EXPERIMENT STATION. SPECIAL REPORTS.
Agricultural Experiment Station, Agricultural Publications, 110 Agriculture Bldg., 1 University of Arkansas, Division of Agricultural, Fayetteville, AR 72701-1201. TEL 501-575-5647. FAX 501-575-7531. URL: http://www.uark.edu/depts/agripub/publications/. *169*

ARKANSAS BUSINESS AND ECONOMIC REVIEW.
University of Arkansas, College of Business Administration, Fayetteville, AR 72701. TEL 501-575-4151. FAX 501-575-7687. Vendor(s): Information Access Co., Knight-Ridder Information, Inc., UMI. *933*

ARKANSAS BUSINESS DIRECTORY.
American Business Directories, 5711 S. 86th Circle, Box 27347, Omaha, NE 68127. TEL 402-593-4600. FAX 402-331-5481. *1652*

ARKANSAS DAILY LEGISLATIVE DIGEST.
Arkansas Legislative Digest, Inc., 1401 W. Sixth St., Little Rock, AR 72201. TEL 501-376-2843. FAX 501-374-9256. *4069*

ARKANSAS HISTORICAL QUARTERLY.
Arkansas Historical Association, University of Arkansas, Department of History, Old Main 416, Fayetteville, AR 72701. TEL 501-575-5884. FAX 501-575-2642. *3618*

ARMED FORCES AND SOCIETY.
Transaction Publishers, Transaction Periodicals Consortium, Department 3092, Rutgers University, New Brunswick, NJ 08903. TEL 908-445-2280. FAX 908-445-3138. Vendor(s): Information Access Co., UMI. *5258*

ARMED FORCES COMPTROLLER.
American Society of Military Comptrollers, 225 Reinekers Ln., Ste. 250, Alexandria, VA 22314-2875. TEL 703-549-0360. FAX 703-549-3181. Vendor(s): UMI. *5259*

ARMS CONTROL TODAY.
Arms Control Association, 1726 M St., N.W., Ste. 201, Washington, DC 20036-4504. TEL 202-463-8270. FAX 202-463-8273. URL: http://www.armscontrol.org. Vendor(s): UMI. *5893*

ARMY LAWYER.
U.S. Army, Judge Advocate General's School, Charlottesville, VA 22903-1781. TEL 804-972-6393. Vendor(s): West Group. *4143*

ARS ORIENTALIS.
Department of History of Art, Tappan Hall, University of Michigan, Ann Arbor, MI 48109-1357. TEL 313-647-3307. FAX 313-763-8976. *5521*

ARS PHARMACEUTICA.
Universidad de Granada, Servicio de Publicaciones, Antiguo Colegio Maximo, Campus de Cartuja, 18071 Granada, Spain. TEL 34-58-243930. FAX 34-58-242827. *5648*

THE ART BIN.
Nisus Publishing, Observatoriegatan 22, S-113 29 Stockholm, Sweden. URL: http://www.nisus.se/artbin. Available only online. *424*

ART BULLETIN.
College Art Association, 275 Seventh Ave., New York, NY 10001. TEL 212-691-1051. FAX 212-627-2381. Vendor(s): Information Access Co., UMI. *424*

ART CELLAR EXCHANGE.
Token Art Corporation, 2171 India St., Ste. H, San Diego, CA 92101. TEL 619-338-0797. FAX 619-338-0826. URL: http://www.artcellarex.com/. Available only online. *424*

ART COM: CONTEMPORARY ART COMMUNICATIONS.
Contemporary Arts Press, Box 3123, Rincon Annex, San Francisco, CA 94119. TEL 415-431-7524. FAX 415-431-7841. Available only online. *424*

ART DAILY.
ArtDaily, Inc., URL: http://www.artdaily.com. Available only online. *424*

ART IN AMERICA.
Brant Publications, Inc., 575 Broadway, 5th Fl., New York, NY 10021. TEL 212-941-2800. FAX 212-941-2819. Vendor(s): Information Access Co., UMI. *425*

ART INDEX.
H.W. Wilson Co., 950 University Ave., Bronx, NY 10452. TEL 718-588-8400. FAX 718-590-1617. Vendor(s): Knight-Ridder Information, Inc., OCLC, Ovid Technologies, Inc., Wilsonline (File ART). *475*

ART JOURNAL (YEAR).
College Art Association, 275 Seventh Ave., New York, NY 10001. TEL 212-691-1051. FAX 212-627-2381. Vendor(s): Information Access Co., UMI. *425*

THE ART OF EATING.
Box 242, Peacham, VT 05862. TEL 802-479-3033. FAX 802-592-3400. URL: http://artofeating.com. *3096*

ART SALES INDEX: OIL PAINTINGS, DRAWINGS, WATER COLOURS AND SCULPTURE.
Art Sales Index Ltd., 1 Thames St., Weybridge, Surrey KT13 8JG, England. TEL 44-1932-856426. FAX 44-1932-842482. *426*

ARTBEAT.
Department of Communications and the Arts, G.P.O. Box 2154, Canberra, A.C.T. 2601, Australia. TEL 61-6-2791253. URL: http://www.dca.gov.au/artbeat.html. Available only online. *427*

ARTBIBLIOGRAPHIES MODERN.
A B C - Clio Ltd., 35A Great Clarendon St., Oxford OX2 6AT, England. TEL 44-1865-311350. FAX 44-1865-311358. Vendor(s): Knight-Ridder Information, Inc. (File no.56). *475*

ARTFORUM.
Artforum International Magazine, Inc., 65 Bleecker St., New York, NY 10012. TEL 212-475-4000. FAX 212-529-1257. Vendor(s): Information Access Co. *428*

ARTHRITIS AND RHEUMATISM.
Lippincott - Raven Publishers, 227 E. Washington Sq., Philadelphia, PA 19106. TEL 215-238-4200. FAX 215-238-4227. URL: http://www.lrpub.com. Vendor(s): Lexis-Nexis, Ovid Technologies, Inc. *5124*

ARTHRITIS TODAY.
Arthritis Foundation, 1314 Spring St., N.W., Atlanta, GA 30309. TEL 404-872-7100. FAX 404-872-9559. Vendor(s): Information Access Co. *5124*

ARTHURIANA.
International Arthurian Society, North American Branch, Southern Methodist University, Dallas, TX 75275-0432. TEL 214-768-2949. FAX 214-768-4129. URL: http://dc.smu.edu/Arthuriana/ *3550*

ARTIFICIAL LIFE AND ROBOTICS.
Springer-Verlag Tokyo, 3-13, Hongo 3-chome, Bunkyo-ku, Tokyo 113, Japan. TEL 81-3-38120331. FAX 81-3-38120719. *2098*

ARTNET MAGAZINE.
ArtNet, 145 E. 57th St., 9th Fl., New York, NY 10022. TEL 212-497-9700. FAX 212-497-9707. URL: http://www.artnet.com/magazine.html. Available only online. *429*

ARTNOIR SHOWCASE.
1323 S.E. 17th St., Ste. 138, Fort Lauderdale, FL 33316. TEL 954-523-9673. FAX 954-523-9673. URL: http://www.artnoir.com. Available only online. *429*

ARTS & HUMANITIES CITATION INDEX.
Institute for Scientific Information, 3501 Market St., Philadelphia, PA 19104. TEL 215-386-0100. FAX 215-386-2911. Vendor(s): Knight-Ridder Information, Inc. (File no.139), Ovid Technologies, Inc. (AHCI). *475*

ARTS EDUCATION POLICY REVIEW.
Heldref Publications, 1319 Eighteenth St., N.W., Washington, DC 20036-1802. TEL 202-296-6267. FAX 202-296-5149. Vendor(s): Information Access Co., UMI. *429*

ARTSPEAK.
420 Fifth Ave., 26th Fl., New York, NY 10018. TEL 212-924-6531. *430*

ARZNEIMITTEL-FORSCHUNG.
Editio Cantor, Postfach 1255, 88322 Aulendorf, Germany. TEL 49-7525-940135. FAX 49-7525-940180. URL: http://www.ecv.de. *5648*

AS WE ARE.
As We Are, Inc., Box 380048, Cambridge, MA 02238. TEL 617-492-2440. FAX 617-492-0486. URL: http://as-we-are.com/awal/. *5504*

ASAHI SHIMBUN SHUKUSATUBAN.
Asahi Shimbun Publishing Co., 3-2 Tsukiji 5-chome, Chuo-ku, Tokyo 104-11, Japan. *3329*

ASBESTOS & LEAD ABATEMENT REPORT.
Business Publishers, Inc., 951 Pershing Dr., Silver Spring, MD 20910-4464. TEL 301-587-6300. FAX 301-587-1081. Vendor(s): Data-Star, Human Resources Information Network, Information Access Co., Knight-Ridder Information, Inc., NewsNet (EV27). *2907*

ASIA INC.
Asia, Inc. Ltd., 8-F Kinwick Centre, 32 Hollywood Rd., Central, Hong Kong, People's Republic of China. TEL 852-2581-8088. FAX 852-2851-0302. URL: http://www.asia-inc.com/ *1639*

ASIA-PACIFIC BIOTECH NEWS.
World Scientific Publishing Co. Pte. Ltd., K H Biotech Services Pte. Ltd., Farrer Rd., P.O. Box 128, Singapore 912805, Singapore. TEL 65-382-5663. FAX 65-382-5919. URL: http://www.wspc.com.sg. *677*

ASIA PACIFIC ECONOMIC REVIEW.
Zencore, Inc., Box 14089, Seattle, WA 98119. TEL 202-860-4970. FAX 206-860-4895. URL: http://www.moshix2.net/aper/ *1315*

ASIA-PACIFIC EXCHANGE JOURNAL.
University of Hawaii, Kapiolani Community College, *2531*

ASIA - PACIFIC JOURNAL OF MANAGEMENT.
National University of Singapore, Faculty of Business Administration, 10 Kent Ridge Crescent, Singapore 119260, Singapore. TEL 65-7723161. FAX 65-7765641. Vendor(s): UMI. *1465*

ASIA-PACIFIC MAGAZINE.
Australian National University, Research School of Pacific & Asian Studies, G.O.P Box 192, Canberra A.C.T. 2601, Australia. TEL 61-6-2494160. URL: http://www.coombs.anu.edu.au/asia-pacific-magazine. *6603*

ASIA - PACIFIC POPULATION & POLICY.
East - West Center, 1601 East-West Rd., Honolulu, HI 96848. TEL 808-944-7482. FAX 808-944-7490. URL: http://www.ewc.hawaii.edu. *6046*

ASIA - PACIFIC POPULATION RESEARCH ABSTRACTS.
East - West Center, 1601 East-West Rd., Honolulu, HI 96848. TEL 808-944-7482. FAX 808-944-7490. URL: http://www.ewc.hawaii.edu. *6060*

ASIAMONEY.
Euromoney Publications plc., 20th Fl., Trust Tower, 68 Johnston Road, Wanchai, Hong Kong, People's Republic of China. TEL 852-529-5009. FAX 852-866-9046.
Vendor(s): UMI. *1103*

ASIAN BUSINESS.
Far East Trade Press Ltd., Kai Tak Commercial Bldg., 2nd Fl., 317 Des Voeux Rd., Central, Hong Kong, People's Republic of China. TEL 545-7200. FAX 544-6979. URL: http://web3.asia1.com.sg/timesnet/navigatn/text/ab.html.
Vendor(s): UMI. *1579*

ASIAN FOLKLORE STUDIES.
Nanzan University, 18, Yamazato-cho, Showa-ku, Nagoya 466, Japan. TEL 052-832-3111. FAX 052-833-6157. URL: http://www.ic.nanzan-u.ac/jp/
Vendor(s): Information Access Co. *3084*

ASIAN JOURNAL OF SURGERY.
Asian Surgical Association, Queen Mary Hospital, Hong Kong, People's Republic of China. TEL 852-2855-4621. FAX 852-2855-9950.
Vendor(s): Lexis-Nexis. *5136*

ASIAN MANUFACTURERS JOURNAL.
G.P.O. Box 6217, Hong Kong, People's Republic of China. TEL 852-2558-8131. FAX 852-2897-5087. URL: http://www.amj.com. *1579*

ASIAN STUDIES CENTER BACKGROUNDER.
Heritage Foundation, 214 Massachusetts Ave., N.E., Washington, DC 20002. TEL 202-546-4400. FAX 202-543-9647.
Vendor(s): Lexis-Nexis. *6005*

ASIAN SURVEY.
University of California Press, Journals Division, 2120 Berkeley Way, No. 5812, Berkeley, CA 94720-5812. TEL 510-643-7154. FAX 510-642-9917. URL: http://library.berkeley.edu:8080/ucalpress/journals.
Vendor(s): Information Access Co., UMI. *5893*

ASIANWEEK.
Pan Asia Venture Capital Corporation, 809 Sacramento St., San Francisco, CA 94108. TEL 415-397-0220. FAX 415-397-7258. URL: http://www.pavc.com; http://www.asianweek.com.
Vendor(s): Lexis-Nexis (Ethnic Newswatch). *2998*

ASOCIACION DE DEMOGRAFIA HISTORICA. BOLETIN.
Asociacion de Demografia Historica, Centre d'Estudis Demografics, Edifici E2, Universitat Autonoma de Barcelona, 08193 Bellaterra, Spain. TEL 34-3-5813060. FAX 34-3-5813061. *6046*

ASPHALT CONTRACTOR.
Group III Communications, 204 W. Kansas Ave., No. 103, Independence, MO 64050-3714. TEL 816-254-8735. FAX 816-254-2128. *862*

ASPHALT INSTITUTE CATALOG OF PUBLICATIONS, AUDIO VISUALS, AND COMPUTER PROGRAMS.
Asphalt Institute, Research Park Dr., Box 14052, Lexington, KY 40512-4052. TEL 606-288-4960. FAX 606-288-4999. URL: http://www.asphaltinstitute.org. *2777*

ASSEMBLAGE.
University of Sheffield, Research School of Archaeology, 2 Mappin St., Sheffield S1 4DT, England. TEL 44-114-222-5102. FAX 44-114-272-7347. URL: http://www.shef.ac.uk/uni/union/susoc/assem/
Available only online. *354*

ASSEMBLY (CAROL STREAM).
Hitchcock Publishing, 191 S. Gary Ave., Carol Stream, IL 60188. TEL 708-665-1000. FAX 708-462-2225.
Vendor(s): Information Access Co. *2711*

ASSET FINANCE AND LEASING DIGEST.
Euromoney Publications plc., Nestor House, Playhouse Yard, London EC4V 5EX, England. TEL 44-171-779-8935. FAX 44-171-779-8541.
Vendor(s): UMI. *1373*

ASSET SALES REPORT.
American Banker - Bond Buyer, Newsletter Division 1 State St. Plaza, New York, NY 10004-1549. TEL 800-733-4371. FAX 212-943-2224.
Vendor(s): Data-Star, Information Access Co., Knight-Ridder Information, Inc., Lexis-Nexis, NewsNet (FI33). *1373*

ASSOCIATION FOR COMPUTING MACHINERY. COMMUNICATIONS.
Association for Computing Machinery, 1515 Broadway, 17th Fl., New York, NY 10036-5701. TEL 212-869-7440. FAX 212-944-1318.
Vendor(s): Information Access Co., UMI. *2168*

ASSOCIATION MANAGEMENT.
American Society of Association Executives, 1575 Eye St., N.W., Washington, DC 20005-1168. TEL 202-626-2735. FAX 202-408-9635.
Vendor(s): Information Access Co., UMI. *1465*

THE ASTRONOMER.
16 Westminster Close, Basingstoke, Hants. RG22 4PP, England. TEL 44-1256-471074. FAX 44-1256-471074. URL: http://www.demon.co.uk/astronomer/. *489*

ASTRONOMICAL SOCIETY OF AUSTRALIA. PUBLICATIONS.
C.S.I.R.O. Publishing, 150 Oxford St., Collingwood, Vic. 3066, Australia. TEL 61-3-96627500. FAX 61-3-96627611. URL: http://www.publish.csiro.au/journals/pasa/index.html. *489*

ASTRONOMY.
Kalmbach Publishing Co., 210272 Crossroads Cir., Waukesha, WI 53187. TEL 414-796-8776. FAX 414-796-1142. URL: http://www.kalmbach.com/astro/astronomy.html.
Vendor(s): Information Access Co., UMI. *490*

ASTRONOMY AND ASTROPHYSICS.
Springer-Verlag, Heidelberger Platz 3, 14197 Berlin, Germany. TEL 49-30-82787-0. FAX 49-30-82787448. URL: http://link.springer.de. *490*

THE ASTRONOMY AND ASTROPHYSICS REVIEW.
Springer-Verlag, Heidelberger Platz 3, 14197 Berlin, Germany. TEL 49-30-82787-0. FAX 49-30-82787448. URL: http://link.springer.de; http://www.springer-ny.com/physics/journals.htm. *491*

ASTRONOMY AND ASTROPHYSICS SUPPLEMENT SERIES.
Editions de Physique, 7 av.du Hoggar, B.P. 112, Z.I. de Courtaboeuf, 91944 Les Ulis cedex A, France. TEL 33-1-69-07-36-68. FAX 33-1-69-28-84-91. URL: http:www.ed-phys.fr. *491*

ASTRONOMY & GEOPHYSICS.
I O P Publishing Ltd., Dirac House, Temple Back, Bristol BS1 6BE, England. TEL 44-117-929-7481. FAX 44-117-929-4318. URL: http://www.iop.org/mags/ag. *491*

THE ASTROPHYSICIST'S TANGO PARTNER SPEAKS.
URL: http://www.geocities.com/soho/6115/
Available only online. *4503*

AT ECO.NEWS.
P S Informatics, 49 New Rd., Wootton Bassett, Wiltshire SN4 7DG, England. TEL 44-1793-853371. FAX 44-1793-853371. URL: http://ourworld.compuserve.com/homepages/psplus_doyle.
Available only online. *2907*

AT THE PARK.
Yellow Dot Publishing, Box 597783, Chicago, IL 60659-7783. TEL 773-465-4880. FAX 773-465-0084. URL: http://www.mcs.net/~atthpark/home.html. *4147*

ATHENS FINANCIAL GAZETTE.
Enimeroseis - Dioscuri Ltd., 21 Sarandapichou St., 114 71 Athens, Greece. TEL 361-5497. FAX 363-8274. URL: http://www.enternet.gr/afg. *934*

ATLANTA BUSINESS CHRONICLE.
American City Business Journals, 1801 Peachtree St., No. 150, Atlanta, GA 30339-1859. TEL 404-249-1000. FAX 404-249-1058. URL: http://www.amcity.com/atlanta.
Vendor(s): Information Access Co., Knight-Ridder Information, Inc. *1222*

THE ATLANTA CONSTITUTION AND JOURNAL INDEX.
U M I, 300 N. Zeeb Rd., Ann Arbor, MI 48106-1346. TEL 313-761-4700. FAX 800-864-0019. URL: http://www.umi.com. *3883*

ATLANTIC.
American Chamber of Commerce (UK), 75 Brook St., London W1Y 2EB, England. TEL 071-493-0381. FAX 071-493-2394.
Vendor(s): Knight-Ridder Information, Inc. *1178*

ATLANTIC ECONOMIC JOURNAL.
Atlantic Economic Society, c/o John M. Virgo, Ed., Box 1101, Southern Illinois University, Edwardsville, IL 62026-1101. TEL 618-692-2291. FAX 618-692-3400. URL: http://www.iaes.org.
Vendor(s): Information Access Co., Knight-Ridder Information, Inc. *934*

ATLANTIC EXPLORER TRAVELMAG.
3889 Kencrest Ave., Halifax, NS B3K 3L4, Canada. URL: http://www.whatasite.com/explorer.
Available only online. *7185*

ATLANTIC FLYER.
Box 668, Litchfield, CT 06759-0668. TEL 203-238-9009. FAX 203-238-4121. URL: http://www.aflyer.com/ *7064*

THE ATLANTIC MONTHLY.
Atlantic Monthly Co., 77 N. Washington St., Ste. 5, Boston, MA 02114-1908. TEL 617-536-9500. URL: http://www.theatlantic.com.
Vendor(s): Information Access Co. *4324*

ATLANTIC TRADE REPORT & GLOBAL DEFENSE INDUSTRY.
Bergerac International Ltd., Rt. One, Box 309, Gainesville, VA 20065. TEL 703-349-2922. FAX 703-349-2922.
Vendor(s): Information Access Co. *1315*

ATOMIC DATA AND NUCLEAR DATA TABLES.
Academic Press, Inc., Journal Division, 525 B. St., Ste. 1900, San Diego, CA 92101-4495. TEL 619-230-1840. FAX 619-699-6800. URL: http://www/apnet.com/www/journal/dt.htm; http://www.idealibrary.com/ *5850*

ATTAINMENT BUSINESS STARTUPS JOURNAL.
Abiogenesis Publications, Box 9, Bellingham, WA 98227-0009. URL: http://www.abiogenesis.com/attainment.
Available only online. *934*

ATTENDERINGSBULLETIN BIBLIOTHEEK STARING-GEBOUW: LAND, BODEM, WATER.
International Institute for Land Reclamation and Improvement, Library - Staring Building, P.O. Box 45, 6700 AA Wageningen, Netherlands. TEL 31-317-474733. FAX 31-317-424812. *2959*

ATTORNEY - C P A.
American Association of Attorney-Certified Public Accountants, Inc., 24196 Alicia Pkwy., Ste. K, Mission Viejo, CA 92691. TEL 714-768-0336.
Vendor(s): UMI. *4073*

AUDIO (NEW YORK).
Hachette Filipacchi Magazines, Inc., 1633 Broadway, New York, NY 10019. TEL 212-767-6000. FAX 212-767-5619.
Vendor(s): Information Access Co. *5374*

AUDIO: THE INTERNATIONAL MARKET.
Euromonitor, 60-61 Britton St., London EC1M 5NA, England. TEL 44-171-251-8024. FAX 44-171-608-3149. URL: http://www.euromonitor.com.
Vendor(s): Data-Star, Knight-Ridder Information, Inc. *2625*

AUDIO WEEK.
Warren Publishing, Inc., 2115 Ward Ct., N.W., Washington, DC 20037. TEL 212-686-5410. FAX 212-889-5097.
Vendor(s): Data-Star, Information Access Co., Knight-Ridder Information, Inc., NewsNet (EC93). *6742*

AUDIOCASSETTE & C D FINDER.
Plexus Publishing, Inc., 143 Old Marlton Pike, Medford, NJ 08055-8750. TEL 609-654-4888. FAX 609-654-4309.
Vendor(s): Knight-Ridder Information, Inc. (File no.46). *2496*

AUDIOTEX UPDATE.
Worldwide Videotex, Box 3273, Boynton Beach, FL 33424-3273. TEL 407-738-2276.
Vendor(s): Data-Star, Information Access Co., Knight-Ridder Information, Inc., NewsNet (TE16). *2014*

AUDIOVISUAL LIBRARIAN.
Aslib, Association for Information Management, Multimedia Group, c/o Anthony Hugh Thompson, Ed., Coach House Frongog, Llanbadarn Fawr, Aberystwyth SY23 3HN, Wales. TEL 44-1970-617322. FAX 44-1970-617322. URL: www.dmu.ac.uk:70/00/special/i_space/avl. *4229*

AUDITORY NEUROSCIENCE.
Gordon and Breach - Harwood Academic, Amsteldisk 166, 1st. Fl., 1079 LH Amsterdam, Netherlands. URL: http://www.gbhap.com/Auditory_Neuroscience/. *5053*

AUDUBON.
National Audubon Society, 700 Broadway, New York, NY 10003. TEL 212-979-3126. FAX 212-477-9069.
Vendor(s): Information Access Co., UMI. *2223*

AUGUSTA MARGARET RIVER MAIL ONLINE.
URL: http://www.margaret-river.com.au/mail.html.
Available only online. *3250*

AUSTIN BUSINESS JOURNAL.
American City Business Journals, Inc. (Austin), 505 Powel St., Austin, TX 78703-5121. TEL 512-328-0180. FAX 512-328-7304.
Vendor(s): UMI. *935*

AUSTRALASIAN TRANSPORT NEWS.
Publishing Services (Australia) Pty. Ltd., 244 St. Paul's Terrace, Spring Hill, Brisbane, Qld. 4000, Australia. TEL 617-38541286. FAX 61-7-32524829. URL: http://www.pubser.com.au. *7172*

AUSTRALASIAN TREE CROPS SOURCEBOOK.
Tree Crops Centre, P.O. Box 27, Subiaco, W.A. 6008, Australia. TEL 61-8-03991065. FAX 61-8-92881852. URL: http://www.AOI.com.au/atcros/
Available only online. *214*

AUSTRALIAN ACCOUNTANT.
Australian Society of Certified Practising Accountants, 170 Queen St., Melbourne, Vic. 3000, Australia. TEL 61-3-96069606. FAX 61-3-96708901.
Vendor(s): UMI. *1084*

AUSTRALIAN ADVERSE DRUG REACTIONS BULLETIN.
Australian Drug Reactions Advisory Committee, URL: http://www.health.gov.au/hsh/tga/tgapubs/tgapubs.htm.
Available only online. *5649*

AUSTRALIAN AND NEW ZEALAND JOURNAL OF MEDICINE.
Adis International Pty. Ltd., 9 Rodborough Rd., Frenchs Forest, N.S.W. 2089, Australia. TEL 61-2-9759100. FAX 61-2-9759199. *4643*

AUSTRALIAN ARCHITECTURAL PERIODICALS INDEX.
Stanton Library, Reader Services Department, P.O. Box 12, N. Sydney, N.S.W. 2059, Australia. TEL 61-2-99368400. FAX 61-2-99368440. *418*

AUSTRALIAN CORPORATE NEWS.
C C H Australia Ltd., P.O. Box 230, North Ryde, N.S.W. 2113, Australia. TEL 61-1-300300224. FAX 61-1-300306224. *4073*

AUSTRALIAN DIRECTORY OF ACADEMICS.
Universal Consultancy Services, P.O. Box 683, Kenmore, Qld. 4069, Australia. TEL 61-7-32028404. FAX 61-7-32028393. *2532*

AUSTRALIAN DIRECTORY OF FACULTIES.
Universal Consultancy Services, P.O. Box 683, Kenmore, Qld. 4069, Australia. TEL 61-7-32028404. FAX 61-7-32028393. *2532*

AUSTRALIAN ECONOMIC REVIEW.
Blackwell Publishers Ltd., 108 Cowley Rd., Oxford OX4 1JF, England. TEL 44-1865-791100. FAX 44-1865-791347. URL: http://www.blackwellpublishers.co.uk.
Vendor(s): UMI. *935*

AUSTRALIAN EDUCATION INDEX.
Australian Council for Educational Research, Private Bag 55, Camberwell, Vic. 3124, Australia. TEL 61-3-92775555. FAX 61-3-92775500.
Vendor(s): AUSINET. *2496*

AUSTRALIAN FAMILY AND SOCIETY ABSTRACTS.
Australian Institute of Family Studies, 300 Queen St., Melbourne, Vic. 3000, Australia. TEL 61-3-92147888. FAX 61-3-92147839. *6739*

AUSTRALIAN GEOLOGICAL SURVEY ORGANISATION. YEARBOOK.
Australian Geological Survey Organisation, G.P.O. Box 378, Canberra, A.C.T. 2601, Australia. TEL 61-6-2499519. FAX 61-6-2499982. URL: http://www.agso.gov.au.
Available only online. *2310*

AUSTRALIAN GOVERNMENT PUBLICATIONS.
National Library of Australia, Publications Section, Cultural and Educational Services Division, Canberra, A.C.T. 2600, Australia. TEL 61-6-262-1365. FAX 61-6-273-4493. *533*

AUSTRALIAN JOURNAL OF AGRICULTURAL RESEARCH.
C.S.I.R.O. Publishing, 150 Oxford St., Collingwood, Vic. 3066, Australia. TEL 61-3-96627628. FAX 61-3-96627611. URL: http://www.publish.csiro.au/journals/ajar/electronic.html. *100*

AUSTRALIAN JOURNAL OF BOTANY.
C.S.I.R.O. Publishing, 150 Oxford St., Collingwood, Vic. 3066, Australia. TEL 61-3-96627624. FAX 61-3-96627611. URL: http://www.publish.csiro.au/journals/ajb/electronic.html. *693*

AUSTRALIAN JOURNAL OF CHEMISTRY.
C.S.I.R.O. Publishing, 150 Oxford St., Collingwood, Vic. 3066, Australia. TEL 61-3-96627500. FAX 61-3-96627611. URL: http://www.publish.csiro.au/journals/ajc/index.html. *1740*

AUSTRALIAN JOURNAL OF DAIRY TECHNOLOGY.
Dairy Industry Association of Australia, P.O. Box 8000, Glen Iris, Vic. 3146, Australia, Australia. FAX 61-3-92526555.
Vendor(s): Knight-Ridder Information, Inc. *252*

AUSTRALIAN JOURNAL OF EXPERIMENTAL AGRICULTURE.
C.S.I.R.O. Publishing, 150 Oxford St., Collingwood, Vic. 3066, Australia. TEL 61-3-96627614. FAX 61-3-96627611. URL: http://www.publish.csiro.au/journals/ajea/online_journal.html. *214*

AUSTRALIAN JOURNAL OF MANAGEMENT.
Australian Graduate School of Management, University of New South Wales, Sydney, N.S.W. 2052, Australia. TEL 61-2-99319259. FAX 61-2-96627621. URL: http://www.agsm.unsw.edu.au/~eajm/. *1466*

AUSTRALIAN JOURNAL OF PHYSICS.
C.S.I.R.O. Publishing, 150 Oxford St., Collingwood, Vic. 3066, Australia. TEL 61-3-96627500. FAX 61-3-96627611. URL: http://www.publish.csiro.au/journals/ajp/index.html. *5797*

AUSTRALIAN JOURNAL OF PLANT PHYSIOLOGY.
C.S.I.R.O. Publishing, 150 Oxford St., Collingwood, Vic. 3066, Australia. TEL 61-3-96627620. FAX 61-3-96627611. URL: http://www.publish.csiro.au/journals/ajpp. *813*

AUSTRALIAN JOURNAL OF SOIL RESEARCH.
C.S.I.R.O. Publishing, 150 Oxford St., Collingwood, Vic. 3066, Australia. TEL 61-3-96627628. FAX 61-3-96627611. URL: http://www.publish.csiro.au/journals/ajsr/electronic.html. *215*

AUSTRALIAN JOURNAL OF ZOOLOGY.
C.S.I.R.O. Publishing, 150 Oxford St., Collingwood, Vic. 3066, Australia. TEL 61-3-96627622. FAX 61-3-96627611. URL: http://www.publish.csiro.au/journals/ajz. *828*

AUSTRALIAN JOURNALISM REVIEW.
Journalism Education Association, c/o School of Communication, Charles Sturt University - Mitchell, Bathurts, N.S.W. 2795, Australia. TEL 61-2-63384524. FAX 61-2-63384409. URL: http://www.csu.au/faculty/arts/commun/jea/ajr. *3869*

AUSTRALIAN NETWORK FOR ART AND TECHNOLOGY NEWSLETTER.
Australian Network for Art and Technology, P.O. Box 8029, Hindley St., Adelaide, S.A. 5000, Australia. TEL 61-8-82319037. FAX 61-8-82117323. URL: http://www.va.com/anat/ *431*

AUSTRALIAN PLANTS.
Society for Growing Australian Plants, 860 Henry Lawson Dr., Picnic Point, N.S.W. 2213, Australia. TEL 61-2-773-9866. URL: http://www.ozemail.com.au/~sgap/apoline.html. *693*

AUSTRALIAN ROAD RESEARCH.
A R R B Transport Research Ltd., 500 Burwood Hwy., Vermont S., Vic. 3133, Australia. TEL 61-3-98811555. FAX 61-3-98878104. URL: http://www.arrb.org.au.
Available only online. *2747*

AUSTRALIAN SECURITIES COMMISSION RELEASES.
C C H Australia Ltd., P.O. Box 230, North Ryde, N.S.W. 2113, Australia. TEL 61-1-300300224. FAX 61-1-300306224. *4074*

AUSTRALIAN SOCIETY OF INDEXERS NEWSLETTER.
Australian Society of Indexers, P.O. Box R598, Royal Exchange, N.S.W. 1225, Australia. TEL 61-2-91304206. FAX 61-2-94383729. URL: http://www.zeta.org.au/~aussi. *4224*

AUSTRALIAN TAX FORUM.
Taxation Institute of Australia, 7th Fl., 64 Castlereagh St., Sydney, N.S.W. 2000, Australia. TEL 61-2-92323422. FAX 61-2-92216953. URL: http://www.taxia/asn.au/
Vendor(s): UMI. *1600*

AUSTRALIAN WOMEN'S MONTHLY.
16-1 Bishop St., Box Hill, Vic. 3155, Australia. URL: http://www.tbsa.com.au/~ferrett/monthly.html.
Available only online. *7313*

AUSTRIA KULTUR.
Austrian Cultural Institute, 950 Third Ave., Fl. 20th, New York, NY 10022-2705. TEL 212-759-5165. URL: http://www.austriaculture.net/. *3252*

AUSTRIAN INFORMATION.
Austrian Press and Information Service, 3524 International Ct., N.W., Washington, DC 20008-3035. TEL 202-895-6775. FAX 202-895-6772. URL: http://www.austria.org/ *6006*

AUSZUEGE AUS DEN EUROPAEISCHEN PATENTANMELDUNGEN. TEIL 1A. CHEMIE UND HUETTENWESEN.
Wila Verlag Wilhelm Lampl GmbH, Landsberger Str. 191A, 80687 Munich, Germany. TEL 49-89-54756-0. FAX 49-89-54756309. *5580*

AUSZUEGE AUS DEN EUROPAEISCHEN PATENTANMELDUNGEN. TEIL 2A. PHYSIK, OPTIK, AKUSTIK, FEINMECHANIK.
Wila Verlag Wilhelm Lampl GmbH, Landsberger Str. 191A, 80687 Munich, Germany. TEL 49-89-54756-0. FAX 49-89-54756309. *5580*

AUSZUEGE AUS DEN EUROPAEISCHEN PATENTANMELDUNGEN. TEIL 3A. UEBRIGE VERARBEITUNGSINDUSTRIE UND ARBEITSVERFAHREN, FAHRZEUGBAU, ERNAEHRUNG, LANDWIRTSCHAFT.
Wila Verlag Wilhelm Lampl GmbH, Landsberger Str. 191A, 80687 Munich, Germany. TEL 49-89-54756-0. FAX 49-89-54756309. *5580*

AUSZUEGE AUS DEN EUROPAEISCHEN PATENTSCHRIFTEN. TEIL 1. GRUND- UND ROHSTOFFINDUSTRIE, CHEMIE UND HUETTEN- WESEN, BAUWESEN UND BERGBAU.
Wila Verlag Wilhelm Lampl GmbH, Landsberger Str. 191A, 80687 Munich, Germany. TEL 49-89-54756-0. FAX 49-89-54756309. *5580*

AUSZUEGE AUS DEN GEBRAUCHSMUSTERN.
Wila Verlag Wilhelm Lampl GmbH, Landsberger Str. 191A, 80687 Munich, Germany. TEL 49-89-54756-0. FAX 49-89-54756309. *5580*

AUSZUEGE AUS DEN OFFENLEGUNGSSCHRIFTEN. TEIL 1. GRUND- UND ROHSTOFFINDUSTRIE, CHEMIE UND HUETTEN-WESEN, BAUWESEN UND BERGBAU.
Wila Verlag Wilhelm Lampl GmbH, Landsberger Str. 191A, 80687 Munich, Germany. TEL 49-89-54756-0. FAX 49-89-54756309. *5580*

AUSZUEGE AUS DEN OFFENLEGUNGSSCHRIFTEN. TEIL 2. ELEKTROTECHNIK, PHYSIK, FEINMECHANIK UND OPTIK, AKUSTIK.
Wila Verlag Wilhelm Lampl GmbH, Landsberger Str. 191A, 80687 Munich, Germany. TEL 49-89-54756-0. FAX 49-89-54756309. *5580*

AUSZUEGE AUS DEN OFFENLEGUNGSSCHRIFTEN. TEIL 3. UEBRIGE VERARBEITUNGSINDUSTRIE UND ARBEITSVERFAHREN, MASCHINEN- UND FAHRZEUGBAU, ERNAEHRUNG, LANDWIRTSCHAFT.
Wila Verlag Wilhelm Lampl GmbH, Landsberger Str. 191A, 80687 Munich, Germany. TEL 49-89-54756-0. FAX 49-89-54756309. *5580*

AUSZUEGE AUS DEN PATENTSCHRIFTEN.
Wila Verlag Wilhelm Lampl GmbH, Landsberger Str. 191A, 80687 Munich, Germany. TEL 49-89-54756-0. FAX 49-89-54756309. *5580*

AUTO PARTS REPORT.
International Trade Services, Box 5950, Bethesda, MD 20824-5950. TEL 301-229-2077. FAX 301-229-3995. *7084*

DE AUTOGIDS.
Uitgeverij Auto - Magazine N.V., Gen Dumonceaulaan 56-1, B-1190 Brussels, Belgium. TEL 32-2-3333260. FAX 32-2-3333210. URL: http://www.automagazine.be. *7086*

AUTOIMMUNITY.
Gordon and Breach - Harwood Academic, Amsteldisk 166, 1st Fl., 1079 LH Amsterdam, Netherlands. URL: http://www.gbhap.com/Autoimmunity/. *4792*

AUTOMATIC I D NEWS.
Advanstar Communications, Inc., 7500 Old Oak Blvd., Cleveland, OH 44130. TEL 216-826-2839. FAX 216-891-2726. URL: http://Advanstar.com/AutoIDNews.
Vendor(s): Information Access Co. *2105*

AUTOMATIC MERCHANDISER.
Johnson Hill Press, Inc., 1233 Janesville Ave., Ft. Atkinson, WI 53538. TEL 920-563-6388. FAX 920-563-1702. *1516*

AUTOMOBILE.
K-III Communications Corp., 745 Fifth Ave., New York, NY 10151. TEL 212-745-0100. URL: http://www.automobilemag.com.
Vendor(s): Information Access Co. *7086*

AUTOMOTIVE ENGINEERING MAGAZINE.
Society of Automotive Engineers, 400 Commonwealth Dr., Warrendale, PA 15096-0001. TEL 412-772-7114. FAX 412-776-4026. URL: http://www.sae.org/PRODSERV/MAGAZINE/automo.html.
Vendor(s): Information Access Co., Questel Orbit Inc. *7088*

AUTOMOTIVE INDUSTRIES.
Chilton Co., 2600 Fisher Bldg., 3011 W. Grand Blvd., Detroit, MI 48202. TEL 313-875-2090. FAX 313-875-8148. URL: http://www.ai.chilton.net/
Vendor(s): Information Access Co., Knight-Ridder Information, Inc., Lexis-Nexis. *7088*

AUTOMOTIVE MANUFACTURING AND PRODUCTION.
Gardner Publications, Inc., 6915 Valley Ave., Cincinnati, OH 45244-3029. TEL 513-527-8800. FAX 513-527-8801. URL: http://www/gardnerweb.com.
Vendor(s): UMI. *7088*

AUTOMOTIVE NEWS.
Crain Communications Inc., (Detroit), Automotive News, 1400 Woodbridge Ave., Detroit, MI 48207-3187. TEL 313-446-6000. FAX 313-446-0383. URL: http://www.erain.co.uk/crain/autonews.html.
Vendor(s): Information Access Co. *7089*

AUTOMOTIVES: THE INTERNATIONAL MARKET.
Euromonitor, 60-61 Britton St., London EC1M 5NA, England. TEL 44-171-251-8024. FAX 44-171-608-3149. URL: http://www.euromonitor.com.
Vendor(s): Data-Star, Knight-Ridder Information, Inc. *7089*

AUTOPARTS REPORT.
International Trade Services, Box 5950, Bethesda, MD 20824-5950. TEL 301-229-2077. FAX 301-229-3995.
Vendor(s): Data-Star, Information Access Co., Knight-Ridder Information, Inc., NewsNet (AU09). *7089*

AUTOWEEK.
Crain Communications, Inc. (Detroit), 1400 Woodridge Ave., Detroit, MI 48207-3187. TEL 313-446-6000. FAX 313-446-1650. URL: http://www.crain.co.uk/crain/autoweek.html.
Vendor(s): Information Access Co., Lexis-Nexis. *7090*

AUTO4WORLD.COM.
Superior Products Corp., Box 11312, Fort Lauderdale, FL 33339. TEL 954-567-1144. FAX 954-564-5105. URL: http://www.auto4world.com. *7090*

AVERY INDEX TO ARCHITECTURAL PERIODICALS.
G.K. Hall & Co., MacMillan Library Reference USA, Box 159, Thorndike, ME 04986. TEL 212-654-8452. FAX 207-948-2863. URL: http://www.mir.com/thorndike.
Vendor(s): Knight-Ridder Information, Inc., Research Libraries Group Information Network. *418*

AVIATION DAILY.
McGraw-Hill Companies, Aviation Week Group (Washington), 1200 G St., N.W., Ste. 200, Washington, DC 20005. TEL 202-383-2350.
Vendor(s): Dow Jones News Retrieval, Knight-Ridder Information, Inc. (File no.624/McGRAW-HILL PUBLICATIONS ONLINE), Lexis-Nexis (AVDLY), NewsNet (AE28). *58*

AVIATION EUROPE.
McGraw-Hill Companies, Aviation Week Group (Washington), 1200 G St., N.W., Ste. 200, Washington, DC 20005. TEL 202-383-2350.
Vendor(s): Dow Jones News Retrieval (AE), Knight-Ridder Information, Inc. (AE), Lexis-Nexis (AVEUR), NewsNet (AE35). *7065*

AVIATION WEEK & SPACE TECHNOLOGY.
McGraw-Hill Companies, Aviation Week Group (New York), 1221 Ave. of the Americas, New York, NY 10020. TEL 212-512-3034. FAX 212-512-4225. URL: http://www.awgnet.com/aviation/
Vendor(s): Dow Jones News Retrieval, Knight-Ridder Information, Inc. (File no.624/McGRAW-HILL PUBLICATIONS ONLINE), Lexis-Nexis, NewsNet (AE30). *59*

AZ B - ARIZONA BUSINESS.
Arizona State University, Center for Business Research, College of Business, Box 874406, Tempe, AZ 85287-4406. TEL 602-965-3961. FAX 602-965-5458.
Vendor(s): Information Access Co., UMI. *935*

AZERBAIJAN INTERNATIONAL.
Azerbaijan International, Box 5217, Sherman Oaks, CA 91413. TEL 818-785-0077. FAX 818-997-7337. URL: http://www.azer.com. *6006*

B B A - REVIEWS ON CANCER.
Elsevier Science B.V., P.O. Box 211, 1000 AE Amsterdam, Netherlands. TEL 31-20-4853911. FAX 31-20-4853598. URL: http://www1.elsevier.nl/journals/roco/ *4971*

THE B B I NEWSLETTER.
Biomedical Business International, 16269 Laguna Canyon Rd., Ste. 100, Irvine, CA 92618-3603. TEL 714-755-5757. FAX 714-755-5724.
Vendor(s): Information Access Co., Knight-Ridder Information, Inc. *4644*

B C BUSINESS.
Canada Wide Magazines & Communications Ltd., 4180 Lougheed Hwy., 4th Fl., Burnaby, BC V5C 6A7, Canada. TEL 604-299-7311.
Vendor(s): Information Access Co., Knight-Ridder Information, Inc. *935*

B D I DEUTSCHLAND LIEFERT.
Verlag W. Sachon, Schloss Mindelburg, 87714 Mindelheim, Germany. TEL 49-8261-999-0. FAX 49-8261-999180. URL: http://www.sachon.de.
Vendor(s): Data-Star, FIZ Technik. *1316*

B H A.
Centre National de la Recherche Scientifique, Institut de l'Information Scientifique et Technique, 2 allee du Parc de Brabois, 54514 Vandoeuvre-Les-Nancy Cedex, France. TEL 83-50-46-00. FAX 83-50-46-50.
Vendor(s): Knight-Ridder Information, Inc. (File no.191, Art Literature International), Telesystemes - Questel. *475*

B I R D.
Centre International de l'Enfance, Chateau de Longchamp, Bois de Boulogne, 75016 Paris, France. TEL 33-1-44302062. FAX 33-1-44302065. *1861*

B L A S T.
American Bar Association, Science and Technology Section, 750 N. Lake Shore Dr., Chicago, IL 60611. TEL 312-988-6067. FAX 312-988-6281.
Vendor(s): Ovid Technologies, Inc., Knight-Ridder Information, Inc., Lexis-Nexis, West Group. *3916*

B M D MONITOR.
Pasha Publications Inc., 1616 N. Ft. Myer Dr., Ste. 1000, Arlington, VA 22209-3107. TEL 703-528-1244. FAX 703-528-1253. *5261*

B M E S BULLETIN.
Biomedical Engineering Society, Box 2399, Culver City, CA 90231. TEL 310-618-9322. URL: http://www.mecca.org/BME/BMES/bmeshome.html. *4644*

B M J.
B M J Publishing Group, B.M.A. House, Tavistock Sq., London WC1H 9JR, England. TEL 44-171-387-4499. FAX 44-171-383-6661. URL: http://www.bmjpg.com.
Vendor(s): Information Access Co., Ovid Technologies, Inc., UMI. *4644*

B M T ABSTRACTS.
B M T Ltd., Northumbria House, Davy Bank, Wallsend. Tyne and Wear NE28 6UY, England. TEL 44-181-614-4277. FAX 44-181-943-5347. URL: http://www.bmt.org/abstr.htm.
Vendor(s): Knight-Ridder Information, Inc. (TRIS, File No. 63). *7048*

B N A PENSION & BENEFITS REPORTER.
The Bureau of National Affairs, Inc., 1231 25th St., N.W., Washington, DC 20037. TEL 202-452-4200. FAX 202-822-8092. URL: http://www.bna.com/
Vendor(s): Human Resources Information Network (CDD, HDD), Lexis-Nexis (PENSN), West Group (BNA-PEN). *1420*

B N A POLICY AND PRACTICE SERIES.
The Bureau of National Affairs, Inc., 1231 25th St., N.W., Washington, DC 20037. TEL 202-452-4200. FAX 202-822-8092. URL: http://www.bna.com/
Vendor(s): Human Resources Information Network (BPP). *1562*

B N A POLICY AND PRACTICE SERIES. COMPENSATION.
The Bureau of National Affairs, Inc., 1231 25th St., N.W., Washington, DC 20037. TEL 202-452-4200. FAX 202-822-8092. URL: http://www.bna.com/
Vendor(s): Human Resources Information Network. *1420*

B N A POLICY AND PRACTICE SERIES. FAIR EMPLOYMENT PRACTICES.
The Bureau of National Affairs, Inc., 1231 25th St., N.W., Washington, DC 20037. TEL 202-452-4200. FAX 202-822-8092. URL: http://www.bna.com/
Vendor(s): Human Resources Information Network, Knight-Ridder Information, Inc. *1420*

B N A POLICY AND PRACTICE SERIES. LABOR RELATIONS.
The Bureau of National Affairs, Inc., 1231 25th St., N.W., Washington, DC 20037. TEL 202-452-4200. FAX 202-822-8092. URL: http://www.bna.com/
Vendor(s): Human Resources Information Network. *1420*

B N A POLICY AND PRACTICE SERIES. PERSONNEL MANAGEMENT.
The Bureau of National Affairs, Inc., 1231 25th St., N.W., Washington, DC 20037. TEL 202-452-4200. FAX 202-822-8092. URL: http://www.bna.com/ Vendor(s): Human Resources Information Network. *1562*

B N A'S AMERICANS WITH DISABILITIES ACT MANUAL AND CASES.
The Bureau of National Affairs, Inc., 1231 25th St., N.W., Washington, DC 20037. TEL 202-452-4200. FAX 202-822-8092. URL: http://www.bna.com/ Vendor(s): Human Resources Information Network (ADAM), West Group (FLB-CS, MLRR-CS). *4140*

B N A'S BANKING REPORT.
The Bureau of National Affairs, Inc., 1231 25th St., N.W., Washington, DC 20037. TEL 202-452-4200. FAX 202-822-8092. URL: http://www.bna.com/ Vendor(s): Bureau of National Affairs, Human Resources Information Network (CDD,HDD), Lexis-Nexis (BNABNK), West Group (BNA-BNK). *3916*

B N A'S BANKRUPTCY LAW REPORTER.
The Bureau of National Affairs, Inc., 1231 25th St., N.W., Washington, DC 20037. TEL 202-452-4200. FAX 202-822-8092. URL: http://www.bna.com/ *3917*

B N A'S COLLECTIVE BARGAINING BULLETIN.
The Bureau of National Affairs, Inc., 1231 25th St., N.W., Washington, DC 20037. TEL 202-452-4200. FAX 202-822-8092. URL: http://www.bna.com/ Vendor(s): Human Resources Information Network (File DD). *1420*

B N A'S CORPORATE COUNSEL WEEKLY.
The Bureau of National Affairs, Inc., 1231 25th St., N.W., Washington, DC 20037. TEL 202-452-4200. FAX 202-822-8092. URL: http://www.bna.com/ *1466*

B N A'S EASTERN EUROPE REPORTER.
The Bureau of National Affairs, Inc., 1231 25th St., N.W., Washington, DC 20037. TEL 202-452-4200. FAX 202-822-8092. URL: http://www.bna.com/ *1223*

B N A'S ELECTRONIC INFORMATION POLICY & LAW REPORT.
The Bureau of National Affairs, Inc., 1231 25th St., N.W., Washington, DC 20037. TEL 202-452-4200. FAX 202-822-8092. URL: http://www.bna.com/. *4058*

B N A'S EMPLOYEE RELATIONS WEEKLY.
The Bureau of National Affairs, Inc., 1231 25th St., N.W., Washington, DC 20037. TEL 202-452-4200. FAX 202-822-8092. URL: http://www.bna.com/ Vendor(s): Human Resources Information Network (Files CDD, HDD). *1420*

B N A'S EMPLOYMENT DISCRIMINATION REPORT.
The Bureau of National Affairs, Inc., 1231 25th St., N.W., Washington, DC 20037. TEL 202-452-4200. FAX 202-822-8092. URL: http://www.bna.com/ *1562*

B N A'S FEDERAL ENVIRONMENT & SAFETY REGULATORY MONITORING REPORT.
The Bureau of National Affairs, Inc., 1231 25th St., N.W., Washington, DC 20037. TEL 202-452-4200. FAX 202-822-8092. URL: http://www.bna.com/ *2908*

B N A'S HEALTH CARE DAILY REPORT.
The Bureau of National Affairs, Inc., 1231 25th St., N.W., Washington, DC 20037. TEL 202-452-4200. FAX 202-822-8092. URL: http://www.bna.com/. *3703*

B N A'S HEALTH CARE FRAUD REPORT.
The Bureau of National Affairs, Inc., 1231 25th St., N.W., Washington, DC 20037. TEL 202-452-4200. FAX 202-822-8092. URL: http://www.bna.com/. *3704*

B N A'S HEALTH CARE POLICY REPORT.
The Bureau of National Affairs, Inc., 1231 25th St., N.W., Washington, DC 20037. TEL 202-452-4200. FAX 202-822-8092. URL: http://www.bna.com/ Vendor(s): Lexis-Nexis (file BNAHCP). *6229*

B N A'S HEALTH LAW REPORTER.
The Bureau of National Affairs, Inc., 1231 25th St., N.W., Washington, DC 20037. TEL 202-452-4200. FAX 202-822-8092. URL: http://www.bna.com/ Vendor(s): Lexis-Nexis (file BNAHLR). *3917*

B N A'S MEDICARE REPORT.
The Bureau of National Affairs, Inc., 1231 25th St., N.W., Washington, DC 20037. TEL 202-452-4200. FAX 202-822-8092. URL: http://www.bna.com/ Vendor(s): Human Resources Information Network (File DD), Lexis-Nexis (File BNAHMED). *4645*

B N A'S PATENT, TRADEMARK & COPYRIGHT JOURNAL.
Bureau of National Affairs, 1231 25th St., N.W., Washington, DC 20037. TEL 202-452-4200. FAX 202-833-8092. URL: http://www.bna.com/ Vendor(s): Lexis-Nexis, West Group (BNA-PTCJ). *5581*

B N A'S SAFETYNET.
The Bureau of National Affairs, Inc., 1231 25th St., N.W., Washington, DC 20037. TEL 202-452-4200. FAX 202-822-8092. URL: http://www.bna.com/ Vendor(s): Human Resources Information Network (CDD, HDD). *5487*

B N A'S WORKERS' COMPENSATION REPORT.
The Bureau of National Affairs, Inc., 1231 25th St., N.W., Washington, DC 20037. TEL 202-452-4200. FAX 202-822-8092. URL: http://www.bna.com/ Vendor(s): Human Resources Information Network (File DD). *1420*

B S P DATA INTERCHANGE SPECIFICATIONS HANDBOOK.
International Air Transport Association, 2000 Peel St., Montreal, PQ H3A 2R4, Canada. TEL 514-844-6311. FAX 514-844-5286. URL: http://www.iata.org. *1105*

B T TECHNOLOGY JOURNAL.
Thomson Science, 2-6 Boundary Row, London SE1 8HN, England. TEL 44-171-8650066. FAX 44-171-5229623. URL: http://www.thomsonscience.com. *1982*

B T TODAY.
British Telecommunications plc., 81 Newgate St., Rm. A236, London EC14 7AJ, England. TEL 44-171-356-5307.
Vendor(s): Data-Star, Knight-Ridder Information, Inc., NewsNet (TE60). *2032*

B T W.
Curtin University of Technology, Computing Centre, Kent St., Bentley, W.A. 6102, Australia. TEL 61-9-351-7915. FAX 61-9-3512495. URL: http://www.curtin.edu.au/curtin/dept/cc/BTW/
Available only online. *2073*

BABY CARE PRODUCTS: THE INTERNATIONAL MARKET.
Euromonitor, 60-61 Britton St., London EC1M 5NA, England. TEL 44-171-251-8024. FAX 44-171-608-3149. URL: http://www.euromonitor.com. Vendor(s): Data-Star, Knight-Ridder Information, Inc. *504*

BABY DOE'S OBSESSED.
2215 R Market St., San Francisco, CA 94114. URL: http://www.creative.net/~babydoe.
Available only online. *3369*

BABY FOODS: THE INTERNATIONAL MARKET.
Euromonitor, 60-61 Britton St., London EC1M 5NA, England. TEL 44-171-251-8024. FAX 44-171-608-3149. URL: http://www.euromonitor.com. Vendor(s): Data-Star, Knight-Ridder Information, Inc. *3097*

BABYSUE.
Box 8989, Atlanta, GA 30306-8989. TEL 404-875-8951. URL: http://www.babysue.com. *4503*

THE BACK LETTER.
Lippincott - Raven Publishers, 227 E. Washington Sq., Philadelphia, PA 19106-3780. TEL 215-238-4200. FAX 215-238-4227. URL: http://www.lrpub.com.
Vendor(s): Information Access Co. *5005*

BACK STAGE.
B P I Communications, Inc. (New York), 1515 Broadway, 14th Fl., New York, NY 10036. TEL 212-764-7300. FAX 212-536-5318.
Vendor(s): Information Access Co. *7002*

BACKGROUND NOTES ON THE COUNTRIES OF THE WORLD.
U.S. Department of State, Bureau of Public Affairs, 2201 C St., N.W., Washington, DC 20520. TEL 202-647-6575. URL: http://www.state.gov/www/background_notes/index.html. *3396*

BACKGROUNDER.
Heritage Foundation, 214 Massachusetts Ave., N.E., Washington, DC 20002. TEL 202-546-4400. FAX 202-543-9647.
Vendor(s): Lexis-Nexis. *6006*

BACKGROUNDER UPDATE.
Heritage Foundation, 214 Massachusetts Ave., N.E., Washington, DC 20002. TEL 202-546-4400. FAX 202-543-9647.
Vendor(s): Lexis-Nexis. *6164*

BACKPACKER.
Rodale Press, Inc., 33 E. Minor St., Emmaus, PA 18049. TEL 610-967-5171. FAX 610-967-7725. URL: http://www.bpbasecamp.com.
Vendor(s): Information Access Co., UMI. *6862*

BAD FAITH LAW REPORT.
Stratton Press, Box 22391, San Francisco, CA 94122. TEL 415-759-5270. *3808*

BAD SUBJECTS.
Bad Subjects Production Team, 322 Wheeler Hall, University of California, Berkeley, CA 94720. URL: http://eng.hss.cmu.edu./bs. *5894*

BAKERY-NET.
208 E. Bailey Rd., Naperville, IL 60565. URL: http://www.bakery-net.com.
Available only online. *3134*

BAKERY PRODUCTION AND MARKETING.
Cahners Publishing Company (Des Plaines), Division of Reed Elsevier Inc., 1350 E. Touhy Ave., Box 5080, Des Plaines, IL 60017-5080. TEL 847-390-2908. FAX 847-390-2445. URL: http://www.cahners.com/mainmag/bpm.htm.
Vendor(s): Information Access Co., Knight-Ridder Information, Inc., Lexis-Nexis. *3134*

BAKERY PRODUCTS: THE INTERNATIONAL MARKET.
Euromonitor, 60-61 Britton St., London EC1M 5NA, England. TEL 44-171-251-8024. FAX 44-171-608-3149. URL: http://www.euromonitor.com.
Vendor(s): Data-Star, Knight-Ridder Information, Inc. *3134*

BAKKEN LIBRARY AND MUSEUM.
Bakken, 3537 Zenith Ave. S., Minneapolis, MN 55416. TEL 612-927-6508. FAX 612-927-7265. URL: http://www.bakkenmueum.org. *4162*

BALTIMORE BUSINESS JOURNAL.
American City Business Journals, Inc. (Baltimore), 117 Water St., 9th Fl., Baltimore, MD 21202. TEL 410-576-1161. FAX 410-752-3112.
Vendor(s): Information Access Co., Knight-Ridder Information, Inc. *936*

BALTIMORE GAY PAPER.
Gay and Lesbian Community Center of Baltimore, Ltd., Box 22575, Baltimore, MD 21203. TEL 301-837-7748. FAX 301-837-8512. *3691*

BALTIMORE'S CHILD.
11 Dutton Ct., Baltimore, MD 21228. TEL 410-367-5883. FAX 410-719-9342. URL: http://family.com. *1838*

BANGKOK POST.
Post Publishing Co., Ltd., Bangkok Post Bldg., 136 Nanong Rd., Off Sunthorn Kosa Rd., Klong Toey, Bangkok 10110, Thailand. TEL 662-240-3700. FAX 662-240-3790. URL: http://www.bangkokpost.net/ *3365*

BANGLADESH JOURNAL OF PUBLIC ADMINISTRATION.
Bangladesh Public Administration Training Centre, Attn: Asst. Publication Officer, Molla Mosharraf Hossain, Savar, Dhaka 1343, Bangladesh. TEL 831711-20-251. *6165*

BANGLADESH PHARMACEUTICAL JOURNAL.
Bangladesh Pharmaceutical Society, University of Dhaka, Ramna, Dhaka 2, Bangladesh. *5649*

BANGOR THEOLOGICAL SEMINARY. GENERAL THEOLOGICAL LIBRARY. BULLETIN.
Bangor Theological Seminary, 159 State St., Portland, ME 04101. TEL 207-874-2214. *6385*

BANK AUTOMATION NEWS.
Phillips Business Information, Inc., 1201 Seven Locks Rd., Potomac, MD 20854. TEL 301-424-3338. FAX 301-309-3847.
Vendor(s): Data-Star, Information Access Co., Knight-Ridder Information, Inc., NewsNet. *1174*

BANK LOAN REPORT.
Investment Dealers' Digest, 2 World Trade Center, 18th Fl., New York, NY 10048-0638. TEL 212-227-1200. FAX 212-321-2336.
Vendor(s): Information Access Co., UMI. *1108*

BANK MERGERS & ACQUISITIONS.
S N L Securities, LP, 410 E. Main St., Box 2124, Charlottesville, VA 22902. TEL 804-977-1600. FAX 804-977-4466.
Vendor(s): NewsNet (FI59). *1109*

BANK MUTUAL FUND REPORT.
American Banker Newsletters, One State Street Plaza, 26th Fl., New York, NY 10004-1505. TEL 212-803-8300. FAX 212-843-9620.
Vendor(s): Data-Star, Knight-Ridder Information, Inc., Lexis-Nexis, NewsNet. *1109*

BANK NETWORK NEWS.
Faulkner & Gray, Inc., 300 S. Wacker Dr., 18th Fl., Chicago, IL 60606. TEL 312-913-1334.
Vendor(s): Information Access Co., NewsNet (FI71). *1175*

BANK NEWS.
Bank News, Inc., 912 Baltimore Ave., Ste. 900, Kansas City, MO 64105. TEL 816-421-7941.
Vendor(s): UMI. *1109*

BANK OF CANADA. REVIEW.
Bank of Canada, Publications Distribution, Communications Services, 234 Wellington St., Ottawa, On K1A 0G9, Canada. TEL 613-782-8248. FAX 613-782-8874. URL: http://www.bank-banque-canada.ca.
Vendor(s): UMI. *1109*

BANK OF HAWAII BUSINESS TRENDS.
Bank of Hawaii, Economics Department, Box 2900, Honolulu, HI 96846. TEL 808-537-8307. FAX 808-536-9433. URL: http://www.boh.com/econ/ *1224*

BANK OPERATIONS BULLETIN.
American Bankers Association, 1120 Connecticut Ave. N.W., Washington, DC 20036. TEL 202-663-5430. FAX 302-834-8405.
Vendor(s): UMI. *1175*

BANK PERSONNEL NEWS.
American Bankers Association, 1120 Connecticut Ave., N.W., Washington, DC 20036. TEL 202-663-5090. FAX 301-828-4540.
Vendor(s): UMI. *1110*

BANK SYSTEMS & TECHNOLOGY.
Miller Freeman Inc. (New York), One Penn Plaza, New York, NY 10119. TEL 212-714-1300. FAX 212-302-6273.
Vendor(s): UMI. *1111*

BANK TECHNOLOGY NEWS.
Faulkner & Gray, Inc. (New York), 11 Penn Plaza, 17th Fl., New York, NY 10001. TEL 212-967-7000.
Vendor(s): Information Access Co., NewsNet (FI70). UMI. *1111*

THE BANKER.
Financial Times Business Information, Magazines 2 Greystoke Pl., Fetter Ln., London EC4A 1ND, England. TEL 0171-405-6969. FAX 0171-405-5276.
Vendor(s): UMI. *1111*

BANKERS RESEARCH.
Bankers Research, Inc., Box 431, Westport, CT 06881-0431. TEL 203-227-1237.
Vendor(s): UMI. *1112*

BANKING POLICY REPORT.
Law and Business, Inc., 1185 Avenue of the Americas, New York, NY 10036-2601. TEL 201-894-8484. FAX 201-894-8666.
Vendor(s): Lexis-Nexis. *1112*

BANKING STRATEGIES.
Bank Administration Institute, One N. Franklin St., Chicago, IL 60606. TEL 312-683-2248. FAX 312-683-2373.
Vendor(s): Information Access Co., Lexis-Nexis, UMI. *1113*

BANKING WORLD.
Headway House & Law, Premier Mags c/o Katharine Buckley, Haymarket House, 1 Oxendon St., London SW1Y 4EE, England. TEL 44-171-388-3171.
Vendor(s): UMI. *1113*

BAPTIST BIBLE TRIBUNE.
Baptist Bible Tribune, Inc., 720 E. Kearney St., Box 309, Springfield, MO 65801. TEL 417-831-3996. FAX 417-831-1470. *6414*

BARCLAYS COUNTRY REPORTS.
Barclays Bank plc., Economics Department, P.O. Box 12, Barclays House, 1 Wimborne Rd., Poole, Dorset BH15 2BB, England. TEL 01202-344023. FAX 01202-402303.
Vendor(s): Data-Star, Knight-Ridder Information, Inc. *1225*

BARCLAYS ECONOMIC REVIEW.
Barclays Bank plc., Economics Department, P.O. Box 12, Barclays House, 1 Wimborne Rd., Poole, Dorset BH15 2BB, England. TEL 01202-344023. FAX 01202-402303.
Vendor(s): Data-Star, Knight-Ridder Information, Inc., UMI. *1115*

BARRON'S.
Dow Jones & Co., Inc., 200 Liberty St., New York, NY 10281. TEL 212-416-2700. FAX 212-416-2829. URL: http://www.barrons.com.
Vendor(s): Dow Jones News Retrieval. *1374*

BASES.
Bases Publications, 27 rue de la Vistule, 75013 Paris, France. TEL 33-1-45827575. FAX 33-1-45824604. URL: http://www.fla-consultants.fr.
Vendor(s): Telesystemes - Questel. *4230*

BASIC AND APPLIED SOCIAL PSYCHOLOGY.
Lawrence Erlbaum Associates, Inc., 10 Industrial Dr., Mahwah, NJ 07430-2262. TEL 201-236-9500. FAX 201-236-0072. URL: http://www.erlbaum.com. *6096*

BASIC PETROLEUM DATA BOOK.
American Petroleum Institute, Publications Section, 1220 L St., N.W., Washington, DC 20005. TEL 202-682-8375. FAX 202-962-4776. URL: http://www.api.org. *5628*

BATH AND SHOWER PRODUCTS: THE INTERNATIONAL MARKET.
Euromonitor, 60-61 Britton St., London EC1M 5NA, England. TEL 44-171-251-8024. FAX 44-171-608-3149. URL: http://www.euromonitor.com.
Vendor(s): Data-Star, Knight-Ridder Information, Inc. *504*

BATTERY & E V TECHNOLOGY NEWS.
Business Communications Co., Inc. (Norwalk), 25 Van Zant St., Ste. 13, Norwalk, CT 06855. TEL 203-853-4266. FAX 203-853-0348.
Vendor(s): Data-Star, Information Access Co., Knight-Ridder Information, Inc., NewsNet (RD30). *2810*

BEAM LINE.
Stanford Linear Accelerator Center, URL: http://www.slac.stanford.edu/pubs/beamline/beamline.html.
Available only online. *5850*

BEANIE.
URL: http://www.sentex.net/~bracken/beanie.hmtl.
Available only online. *4325*

BEATTHIEF.
1708 Mcallister St., San Francisco, CA 94115. URL: http://www.beatthief.com.
Available only online. *5376*

BEAUTIFUL BRITISH COLUMBIA MAGAZINE.
Beautiful British Columbia Magazine Ltd., 929 Ellery St., Victoria, BC V9A 7B4, Canada. TEL 250-384-5456. FAX 250-384-2812. URL: http://www.beautifulbc.com. *7186*

BEAUTIFUL BRITISH COLUMBIA TRAVELLER.
Beautiful British Columbia Magazine Ltd., 929 Ellery St., Victoria, BC V9A 7B4, Canada. TEL 250-384-5456. FAX 250-384-2812. URL: http://www.beautifulbc.com. *7186*

BEAUTY COUNTER.
Miller Freeman plc, Sovereign Way, Tonbridge, Kent TN9 1RW, England. TEL 44-1732-364422. FAX 44-1732-361534.
Vendor(s): Information Access Co. *509*

BEER: THE INTERNATIONAL MARKET.
Euromonitor, 60-61 Britton St., London EC1M 5NA, England. TEL 44-171-251-8024. FAX 44-171-908-3149. URL: http://www.euromonitor.com.
Vendor(s): Data-Star, Knight-Ridder Information, Inc. *515*

BEHAVIORAL ECOLOGY AND SOCIOBIOLOGY.
Springer-Verlag, Heidelberger Platz 3, 14197 Berlin, Germany. TEL 49-30-82787-0. FAX 49-30-82787448. URL: http://link.springer.de. *2908*

BEHAVIORAL HEALTH MANAGEMENT.
Medquest Communications Inc., 629 Euclid Ave., Ste. 500, Cleveland, OH 44114-3003. TEL 216-522-9700. FAX 216-522-9707.
Vendor(s): Information Access Co., UMI. *2299*

BEHAVIORAL HEALTH TREATMENT.
Manisses Communications Group, Inc., Box 9758, Providence, RI 02940-9758. TEL 401-831-6020. FAX 401-861-6370. URL: http://www.manisses.com.
Vendor(s): Information Access Co. *2299*

BEHAVIOUR AND INFORMATION TECHNOLOGY.
Taylor & Francis Ltd., 1 Gunpowder Sq., London EC4A 3DE, England. TEL 44-171-583-0490. FAX 44-171-583-0585. URL: http://www.tandf.co.uk/. *6097*

BEILSTEINS HANDBUCH DER ORGANISCHEN CHEMIE. SUPPLEMENT.
Springer-Verlag, 175 Fifth Ave., New York, NY 10010. TEL 212-460-1500. FAX 212-473-6272.
Vendor(s): Knight-Ridder Information, Inc. (File no.390). *1812*

BEITRAEGE ZUR ALGEBRA UND GEOMETRIE.
Heldermann Verlag, Langer Graben 13d, 32657 Lemgo, Germany. TEL 49-5261-10226. FAX 49-5261-15264. URL: http://www.zblmath.fiz-karlsruhe.de/e-journals/BAG/index.html. *4564*

DIE BEKLEIDUNGS- UND WAESCHE-INDUSTRIE UND IHRE HELFER.
Industrieschau-Verlagsgesellschaft mbH, Postfach 100262, 64202 Darmstadt, Germany. TEL 49-6151-38920. FAX 49-6151-33164. *1913*

BELIZE FIRST MAGAZINE.
280 Beaverdam Rd., Candler, NC 28715. URL: http://www.turq.com/belizefirst/ *7186*

BELLES LETTRES (NORTH POTOMAC).
2208 Spinnaker Ct., Reston, VA 22091-4704. TEL 301-294-0278. FAX 301-294-0023.
Vendor(s): Information Access Co. *4380*

BENCHMARKS.
University of North Texas, Computing Center, Box 13495, Denton, TX 76203-6495. TEL 817-565-2324. FAX 817-565-4060. *2073*

BENEFITS QUARTERLY.
International Society of Certified Employee Benefit Specialists, Inc., Box 209, Brookfield, WI 53008-0209. TEL 414-786-8771. FAX 414-786-8650.
Vendor(s): UMI. *1562*

BERKELEY JOURNAL OF EMPLOYMENT AND LABOR LAW.
University of California Press, Journals Division, 2120 Berkeley Way, No. 5812, Berkeley, CA 94720-5812. TEL 510-643-7154. FAX 510-642-9917. URL: http://library.berkeley.edu:8080/ucalpress/journals.
Vendor(s): Information Access Co. *1421*

THE BERMUDA SUN.
Bermuda Sun Ltd., P.O. Box HM 1241, Hamilton HMDX, Bermuda. TEL 441-295-3902. FAX 441-292-5597. URL: http://www.bermudasun.org. *3256*

BERNOULLI.
Thomson Science, 2-6 Boundary Row, London SE1 8HN, England. TEL 44-171-8650066. FAX 44-171-5229623. URL: http://www.thomsonscience.com. *4564*

BEST'S REVIEW. LIFE - HEALTH INSURANCE EDITION.
A.M. Best Co., Ambest Rd., Oldwick, NJ 08858. TEL 908-439-2200. FAX 908-439-3296. URL: http://www.ambest.com/; http://204.48.26.77/review/issue-lh/cover.html. Vendor(s): Information Access Co., Knight-Ridder Information, Inc., UMI. *3809*

BEST'S REVIEW. PROPERTY - CASUALTY INSURANCE EDITION.
A.M. Best Co., Ambest Rd., Oldwick, NJ 08858. TEL 908-439-2200. FAX 908-439-3296. URL: http://204.48.26.77/review/issue-pc/cover.html. Vendor(s): Information Access Co., Knight-Ridder Information, Inc., UMI. *3810*

BEST'S UNDERWRITING GUIDE.
A.M. Best Co., Ambest Rd., Oldwick, NJ 08858. TEL 908-439-2200. FAX 908-439-3296. *3810*

BEST'S UNDERWRITING NEWSLETTER.
A.M. Best Co., Ambest Rd., Oldwick, NJ 08858. TEL 908-439-2200. FAX 908-439-3296. *3810*

BETTER HOMES AND GARDENS.
Meredith Corporation, 1716 Locust St., Des Moines, IA 50309-3023. TEL 515-284-3048. FAX 515-284-3023. URL: http://www.bhglive.com. Vendor(s): Information Access Co., UMI. *3841*

BETTER NUTRITION.
Intertec Publishing Corp. (Atlanta), 6151 Powers Ferry Rd., N.W., Atlanta, GA 30339-2941. TEL 770-955-2500. FAX 770-955-0400. Vendor(s): Information Access Co., UMI. *5470*

BETWEEN THE LINES.
2137 Qualicum Dr., Vancouver, B.C. V5P 2M3, Canada. TEL 604-322-1588. URL: http://nrgup.com/nrgup/archives. *5376*

BEVERAGE INDUSTRY.
Stagnito Publishing Company, 1935 Shermer Rd., Ste. 100, Northbrook, IL 60062. TEL 847-205-5660. FAX 847-205-5680. Vendor(s): Information Access Co. *516*

BEVERAGE WORLD (ENGLISH EDITION).
Strategic Business Communications, 226 W. 26th St., New York, NY 10011. TEL 212-822-5930. FAX 212-822-5931. Vendor(s): Information Access Co., Knight-Ridder Information, Inc., Lexis-Nexis, UMI. *516*

BEVERLY HILLS BAR ASSOCIATION JOURNAL.
Beverly Hills Bar Association, 300 S. Beverly Dr., Ste. 201, Beverly Hills, CA 90212. TEL 213-553-6644. FAX 213-284-8290. Vendor(s): West Group. *3920*

BEYOND DOMINIA.
301 Coleman Dr., Monroeville, PA 15146. URL: http://www.bdominia.com/magic/beyond.html. Available only online. *3663*

BEYOND ETERNITY.
URL: http://www.interlog.com/~vash/eternity.html. Available only online. *4325*

BIBLIO.
Aster Publishing Corp., 845 Willamette St., Eugene, OR 97401. TEL 541-345-3800. FAX 541-302-9872. URL: http://www.bibliomag.com/bibmag.htm. *6263*

BIBLIOGRAFIA BRASILEIRA.
Biblioteca Nacional de Brasil, Av. Rio Branco, 219, 20042 Rio de Janeiro, Brazil. TEL 021-262-8255. FAX 021-220-4173. *4224*

BIBLIOGRAFIA BRASILEIRA DE ODONTOLOGIA.
Universidade de Sao Paulo, Faculdade de Odontologia, Av. Prof. Lineu Prestes, 2227, Caixa Postal 8216, 05508-900 Sao Paulo SP, Brazil. TEL 55-11-8187861. FAX 55-11-8187413. *4764*

BIBLIOGRAFIA LATINOAMERICANA.
Universidad Nacional Autonoma de Mexico, Direccion General de Bibliotecas, Apdo. Postal 70-392, Circuito Exterior, Ciudad Universitaria, 04510 Mexico, D.F., Mexico. TEL 52-5-6223958. FAX 52-5-6162557. URL: http://www.cichcu.unam.mx. *534*

BIBLIOGRAFIA LATINOAMERICANA: PART II.
Universidad Nacional Autonoma de Mexico, Direccion eneral de Bibliotecas, Apdo. Postal 70-392, C.P. 04510 Mexico, D.F., Mexico. TEL 52-5-6223958. FAX 52-5-6162557. URL: http://www.cichu.unam.mx. *534*

BIBLIOGRAFIA NAZIONALE ITALIANA.
Istituto Centrale per il Catalogo Unico delle Biblioteche Italiane e per le Informazioni Bibliografiche, Viale del Castro Pretorio, 105, 00185 Rome, Italy. TEL 39-06-4959217. FAX 39-06-4959302. *535*

BIBLIOGRAFIA VENEZOLANA.
Instituto Autonomo Biblioteca Nacional, Oficina de Information, Apdo. 80593, Prados del Este, Caracas 1080-A, Venezuela. TEL 943-1361. FAX 941-5219. *4163*

BIBLIOGRAFIE NEDERLANDSE SOCIALE WETENSCHAPPEN.
Universiteit Utrecht, Bureau Bibliografie Nederlandse Sociale Wetenschappen, Plompetorengracht 11, 3512 CA Utrecht, Netherlands. TEL 31-30-2537272. FAX 31-30-2536560. *6649*

BIBLIOGRAFIE VAN DE NEDERLANDSE TAAL- EN LITERATUUR WETENSCHAP.
Stichting Bibliographica Neerlandica, Postbus 90751, 2509 LT The Hague, Netherlands. *4318*

BIBLIOGRAFIJA JUGOSLAVIJE. CLANCI I PRILOZI U SERIJSKIM PUBLIKACIJAMA. SERIJA A: DRUSTVENE NAUKE.
Jugoslovenski Bibliografsko-Informacijski Institut (YUBIN), Terazije 26, Belgrade, Yugoslavia. FAX 11-687-760. *6649*

BIBLIOGRAFIJA JUGOSLAVIJE. CLANCI I PRILOZI U SERIJSKIM PUBLIKACIJAMA. SERIJA B: PRIRODNE, PRIMENJENE, MEDICINSKE I TEHNICKE NAUKE.
Jugoslovenski Bibliografsko-Informacijski Institut (YUBIN), Terazije 26, Belgrade, Yugoslavia. FAX 11-687-760. *6588*

BIBLIOGRAFIJA JUGOSLAVIJE. CLANCI I PRILOZI U SERIJSKIM PUBLIKACIJAMA. SERIJA C: UMETNOST, SPORT, FILOLOGIJA, KNJIZEVNOST.
Jugoslovenski Bibliografsko-Informacijski Institut (YUBIN), Terazije 26, Belgrade, Yugoslavia. FAX 11-687-760. *535*

BIBLIOGRAFIJA JUGOSLAVIJE. KNJIGE, BROSURE I MUZIKALIJE.
Jugoslovenski Bibliografsko-Informacijski Institut (YUBIN), Terazije 26, Belgrade, Yugoslavia. FAX 11-687-760. *536*

BIBLIOGRAFIJA PREVODA U S R J.
Jugoslovenski Bibliografsko-Informacijski Institut (YUBIN), Terazije 26, Belgrade, Yugoslavia. FAX 11-687-760. *536*

BIBLIOGRAPHIA MEDICA CECHOSLOVACA.
Narodni Lekarska Knihovna, Sokolska 31, 121 32 Prague 2, Czech Republic. TEL 42-2-24915775. FAX 42-2-24924625. URL: http://www.nlk.anet.cz. *4764*

BIBLIOGRAPHIC INDEX.
H.W. Wilson Co., 950 University Ave., Bronx, NY 10452. TEL 718-588-8400. FAX 718-590-1617. Vendor(s): Wilsonline (BIB). *536*

BIBLIOGRAPHIE GEOGRAPHIQUE INTERNATIONALE. FRANCIS. 531.
Centre National de la Recherche Scientifique, Pole de Recherche pour l'Organisation et la Diffusion de l'Information Geographique, 191 rue Saint-Jacques, 75005 Paris, France. TEL 33-1-42345620. FAX 33-1-43296529. Vendor(s): Telesystemes - Questel. *3428*

BIBLIOGRAPHY AND INDEX OF GEOLOGY.
American Geological Institute, 4220 King St., Alexandria, VA 22302-1502. TEL 703-379-2480. FAX 703-379-7563. Vendor(s): Knight-Ridder Information, Inc., OCLC (EPIC and First Search), Questel Orbit Inc. (GEOR), STN International (GeoRef). *2324*

BIBLIOGRAPHY OF AGRICULTURE.
Oryx Press, Box 33889, Phoenix, AZ 85067-3889. TEL 602-265-2651. FAX 602-265-6250. URL: http://www.oryxpress.com/. Vendor(s): CISTI. *170*

BIBLIOGRAPHY OF BIOETHICS.
Kennedy Institute of Ethics, National Reference Center for Bioethics Literature, Georgetown University, Box 571212, Washington, DC 20057-1212. TEL 202-687-6738. FAX 202-687-6770. Vendor(s): Knight-Ridder Information, Inc., National Library of Medicine, Telesystemes - Questel (BIOETHICS). *4764*

BIBLIOGRAPHY OF ECONOMIC GEOLOGY.
Geosystems, P.O. Box 40, Didcot, Oxon. OX11 9BX, England. TEL 44-1235-813913. Vendor(s): Knight-Ridder Information, Inc. (File no 58). *2324*

BIBLIOGRAPHY OF EDUCATION THESES IN AUSTRALIA.
Australian Council for Educational Research, Private Bag 55, Camberwell, Vic. 3124, Australia. TEL 61-3-92775555. FAX 61-3-92775500. URL: http://www.informit.com.au. *2497*

BIBLIOGRAPHY OF SCOTLAND.
National Library of Scotland, George IV Bridge, Edinburgh EH1 1EW, Scotland. TEL 44-131-226-4531. FAX 44-131-220-6662. URL: http://www.nls.uk. *4495*

BIBLIOGRAPHY OF THE HISTORY OF MEDICINE.
U.S. National Library of Medicine, 8600 Rockville Pike, Bethesda, MD 20894. Vendor(s): National Library of Medicine. *4764*

BIBLIOGRAPHY ON COLD REGIONS SCIENCE & TECHNOLOGY.
U.S. Army, Cold Regions Research and Engineering Laboratory, 72 Lyme Rd., Hanover, NH 03755-1290. TEL 603-646-4221. FAX 603-646-4712. Vendor(s): Questel Orbit Inc. (COLD). *2747*

BIBLIOTHEEK VOOR HEDENDAAGSE DOKUMENTATIE. BULLETIN.
Biblioteek voor Hedendaagse Dokumentatie, Parklaan 2, B-9100 St. Niklaas Waas, Belgium. TEL 32-3-776-5063. FAX 32-3-778-0785. *4230*

BIBLIOTHEQUE AFRICAINE. LISTE DES ACQUISITIONS.
Bibliotheque Africaine, 19 rue des petits Carmes, 1000 Brussels, Belgium. TEL 32-2-5013544. FAX 32-2-5013669. Vendor(s): BELINDIS (AFLI). *539*

BICYCLING.
Rodale Press, Inc., 33 E. Minor St., Emmaus, PA 18046. TEL 610-967-5171. FAX 610-967-8960. Vendor(s): Information Access Co., UMI. *6825*

BIG DREAMS.
2202 Haversley Ave., Coquitlam, BC V3J 1W4, Canada. TEL 604-760-1631. FAX 604-931-2135. URL: http://www.wimsey.com/~duncans/BigDreams. *1639*

BIG SHOUT MAGAZINE.
Red Ink, Inc., 1120 West St., Wilmington, DE 19801. TEL 302-888-2929. FAX 302-888-2926. *3370*

BIG SKY MAC E - ZINE.
B - Smug, Big - Sky Mac User Group, Box 80553, Billings, MT 59108. URL: http://www.imt.net/~bgskymac/BigSky__MacEzine.html. Available only online. *2195*

THE BIG TAKEOVER.
249 Eldridge St., No. 14, New York, NY 10002. TEL 212-533-6057. URL: http://members.aol.com/bigtake. *5376*

BIKER BOERSE.
Zweite Hand Verlag, Am Treptower Park 75, 12435 Berlin, Germany. TEL 49-30-53433146. FAX 49-30-53433132. URL: http://www.zweitehand.de/bikerboerse. *6825*

BILDUNGSFORSCHUNG UND BILDUNGSPRAXIS.
Universitaetsverlag Freiburg, Perolles 42, CH-1700 Freiburg, Switzerland. TEL 41-37-864311. FAX 41-37-864300. *2425*

BILL STRONG'S MISSISSIPPI PHOTOGRAPHY TRAVEL CULTURE.
209 Wildwood Trace, Hattiesburg, MS 39402-2355. URL: http://www.phototour.com/. Available only online. *5762*

BILLBOARD (NEW YORK).
B P I Communications, Inc. (New York), 1515 Broadway, New York, NY 10036. TEL 212-764-7300. FAX 212-536-5358. Vendor(s): Information Access Co., Knight-Ridder Information, Inc. *5376*

BILLBOARD BULLETIN.
B P I Communications, Inc. (New York), 1515 Broadway, New York, NY 10036. TEL 212-536-5021. FAX 212-536-5310. URL: http://www.billboard.com. *5377*

BINGO BUGLE.
Bingo Bugle, Inc., Box 527, Vashon, WA 98070. FAX 206-463-5630. URL: http://www.halcyon.com/bluesnow/bingo.html. *6752*

BIOCATALYSIS AND BIOTRANSFORMATION.
Gordon and Breach - Harwood Academic, Amsteldisk 166, 1st Fl., 1079 LH Amsterdam, Netherlands. URL: http://www.gbhap.com/Biocatalysis_Biotransformation/. *678*

BIOCHEMICAL AND BIOPHYSICAL RESEARCH COMMUNICATIONS.
Academic Press, Inc., Journal Division, 525 B St., Ste. 1900, San Diego, CA 92101-4495. TEL 619-230-1840. FAX 619-699-6800. URL: http://www.apnet.com/www/journal/rc.htm; http://www.idealibrary.com. *652*

BIOCHEMICAL AND MOLECULAR MEDICINE.
Academic Press, Inc., Journal Division, 525 B. St., Ste. 1900, San Diego, CA 92101-4495. TEL 619-230-1840. FAX 619-699-6800. URL: http://www.apnet.com/www/journal/mm.htm; http://www.idealibrary.com/ *652*

BIOCHEMICAL GENETICS.
Plenum Publishing Corp., 233 Spring St., New York, NY 10013-1578. TEL 212-620-8000. FAX 212-463-0742. *652*

BIOCHEMICAL JOURNAL.
Portland Press Ltd., 59 Portland Pl., London W1N 3AJ, England. TEL 44-171-580-5530. FAX 44-171-323-1136. URL: http://bj.portlandpress.co.uk *652*

BIOCHEMISTRY.
American Chemical Society, 1155 16th St., N.W., Washington, DC 20036. TEL 800-335-9511. FAX 614-447-3671. Vendor(s): STN International (CJACS). *653*

BIOCHEMISTRY AND MOLECULAR BIOLOGY INTERNATIONAL.
Australian Academic Press Pty. Ltd., 31 Jeays St., Bowen Hills, Qld. 4006, Australia. TEL 61-7-3257176. FAX 61-7-32525908. URL: http://www.apnet.com/www/journal/bm.htm; http://www.idealibrary.com/ *653*

BIOCOMMERCE FINANCIAL ABSTRACTS.
BioCommerce Data Ltd., Prudential Bldgs., 95 High St., Slough, Berks. SL1 1DH, England. TEL 44-1753-511777. FAX 44-1753-512239. URL: http://www.biospace.com/biocommerce. Vendor(s): Data-Star (CELL), Knight-Ridder Information, Inc. (File no.286). *635*

BIOCONTROL NEWS AND INFORMATION.
CAB International, Wallingford, Oxon. OX10 8DE, England. TEL 44-1491-832111. FAX 44-1491-826090. URL: http://www.cabi.org. Vendor(s): DIMDI, European Space Agency, Knight-Ridder Information, Inc., STN International. *589*

BIOCONTROL SCIENCE AND TECHNOLOGY.
Carfax Publishing Co., P.O. Box 25, Abingdon, Oxon. OX14 3UE, England. TEL 44-1235-401000. FAX 44-1235-401550. *216*

BIOCYCLE.
J G Press, Inc., 419 State Ave., Emmaus, PA 18049. TEL 610-967-4135. Vendor(s): UMI. *2983*

BIODIVERSITY AND CONSERVATION.
Chapman & Hall, Journals Department 2-6 Boundary Row, London SE1 8HN, England. TEL 44-171-8650066. FAX 44-171-5229623. URL: http://www.chaphall.com/chaphall/journals.html. *2224*

BIOELECTROMAGNETICS.
John Wiley & Sons, Inc., Journals, 605 Third Ave., New York, NY 10158. TEL 212-850-6645. FAX 212-850-6021. URL: http://www.wiley.co.uk. *673*

BIOENGINEERING ABSTRACTS.
Cambridge Scientific Abstracts, 7200 Wisconsin Ave., 6th Fl., Bethesda, MD 20814-4823. TEL 301-961-6700. FAX 301-961-6720. URL: http://www.csa.com. *635*

BIOFOULING.
Gordon and Breach - Harwood Academic, Amsteldisk 166, 1st Fl., 1079 LH Amsterdam, Netherlands. URL: http://www.gbhap.com/Biofouling/. *2975*

BIOGRAPHICAL BIOPSIES.
4064 W. Second St., Los Angeles, CA 90004. URL: http://users.aol.com/mmbriefs/bb-index.htm. Available only online. *4325*

BIOGRAPHY AND GENEALOGY MASTER INDEX.
Gale Research, 835 Penobscot Bldg., 645 Griswold St., Detroit, MI 48226-4094. TEL 313-961-2242. FAX 800-414-5043. Vendor(s): Knight-Ridder Information, Inc. (File nos.287,288). *581*

BIOGRAPHY INDEX.
H.W. Wilson Co., 950 University Ave., Bronx, NY 10452. TEL 718-588-8400. FAX 718-590-1617. Vendor(s): Knight-Ridder Information, Inc., OCLC, Wilsonline (File BIO). *581*

BIOIMAGING.
I O P Publishing Ltd., Dirac House, Temple Back, Bristol BS1 6BE, England. TEL 44-117-929-7481. FAX 44-117-929-4318. URL: http://www.iop.org. *5798*

BIOLOGICAL ABSTRACTS.
BIOSIS, 2100 Arch St., Philadelphia, PA 19103-1399. TEL 215-587-4847. FAX 215-587-2016. URL: http://www.biosis.org. Vendor(s): DIMDI, Data-Star, Knight-Ridder Information, Inc. (File nos.5 & 55), Ovid Technologies, Inc. (BIOL), STN International (BIOSIS). *635*

BIOLOGICAL ABSTRACTS - R R M.
BIOSIS, 2100 Arch St., Philadelphia, PA 19103-1399. TEL 215-587-4847. FAX 215-587-2016. URL: http://www.biosis.org. Vendor(s): DIMDI, Data-Star, Knight-Ridder Information, Inc. (File nos.5 & 55), Ovid Technologies, Inc. (BIOL), STN International (BIOSIS). *635*

BIOLOGICAL & AGRICULTURAL INDEX.
H.W. Wilson Co., 950 University Ave., Bronx, NY 10452. TEL 718-588-8400. FAX 718-590-1617. Vendor(s): Knight-Ridder Information, Inc., OCLC, Ovid Technologies, Inc., Wilsonline. *636*

BIOLOGICAL BULLETIN.
Marine Biological Laboratory, Woods Hole, MA 02543. TEL 508-289-7428. FAX 508-457-1924. URL: http://www.mbl.edu:80/html/bb/bb.home.html. Vendor(s): Information Access Co., UMI. *590*

BIOLOGICAL CONTROL.
Academic Press, Inc., Journal Division, 525 B Ste., Ste. 1900, San Diego, CA 92101-4495. TEL 619-230-1840. FAX 619-699-6800. URL: http://www.apnet.com/journal/bc.htm; http://www.idealibrary.com/ *590*

BIOLOGICAL CYBERNETICS.
Springer-Verlag, Heidelberger Platz 3, 14197 Berlin, Germany. TEL 49-30-82787-0. FAX 49-30-82787448. URL: http://link.springer.de. *2160*

BIOLOGICAL RHYTHM RESEARCH.
Swets & Zeitlinger bv, P.O. Box 825, 2160 SZ Lisse, Netherlands. TEL 31-252-435111. FAX 31-252-415888. URL: http://www.swets.nl. *590*

BIOLOGICAL SCIENCE REPORT.
U.S. National Biological Service, Information Transfer Center, 1201 Oak Ridge Dr., Ste. 200, Ft. Collins, CO 80525-5589. TEL 970-226-9401. FAX 970-226-9455. *591*

BIOLOGICALS.
Academic Press Ltd., 24-28 Oval Rd., London NW1 7DX, England. TEL 44-171-267-4466. FAX 44-171-482-2293. URL: http://www.hbuk.co.uk/ap/biologicals; http://www.europe.idealibrary.com/. *591*

BIOLOGY AND FERTILITY OF SOILS.
Springer-Verlag, Heidelberger Platz 3, 14197 Berlin, Germany. TEL 49-30-82787-0. FAX 49-30-82787448. URL: http://link.springer.de. *216*

BIOLOGY DIGEST.
Plexus Publishing, Inc., 143 Old Marlton Pike, Medford, NJ 08055. TEL 609-654-6500. FAX 609-654-4309. Vendor(s): OCLC. *636*

BIOMARKERS.
Taylor & Francis Ltd., 1 Gunpowder Sq., London EC4A 3DE, England. TEL 44-171-5830490. FAX 44-171-5830585. URL: http://www.tandf.co.uk/. *4646*

BIOMEDICAL MARKET NEWSLETTER.
David G. Anast, Ed.& Pub., 3237 Idaho Pl., Costa Mesa, CA 92626-2207. TEL 714-434-9500. FAX 714-434-9755. Vendor(s): CompuServe, Inc., Data-Star, Dow Jones News Retrieval, Information Access Co., Knight-Ridder Information, Inc., Lexis-Nexis. *1517*

BIOMETALS.
Thomson Science, 2-6 Boundary Row, London SE1 8HN, England. TEL 44-171-865-0198. FAX 44-171-410-6600. URL: http://www.thomsonscience.com. *655*

BIOORGANIC & MEDICINAL CHEMISTRY.
Elsevier Science Ltd., Pergamon, P.O. Box 800, Kidlington, Oxford OX5 1DX, England. TEL 44-1865-843000. FAX 44-1865-843010. URL: http://www.elsevier.nl/ *1812*

BIOORGANIC & MEDICINAL CHEMISTRY LETTERS.
Elsevier Science Ltd., Pergamon, P.O. Box 800, Kidlington, Oxford OX5 1DX, England. TEL 44-1865-843000. FAX 44-1865-843010. URL: http://www.elsevier.nl/ *1812*

BIOORGANIC CHEMISTRY.
Academic Press, Inc., Journal Division, 525 B St., Ste. 1900, San Diego, CA 92101-4495. TEL 619-230-1840. FAX 619-699-6800. URL: http://www.apnet.com/www/journal/bh.htm; http://www.idealibrary.com/ *1812*

BIOPHARM.
Advanstar Communications, Inc., 859 Willamette St., Eugene, OR 97401. TEL 503-343-5020. FAX 503-344-3514. Vendor(s): Information Access Co. *5650*

BIOPOLYMERS.
John Wiley & Sons, Inc., Journals, 605 Third Ave., New York, NY 10158. TEL 212-692-6645. FAX 212-850-6021. URL: http://www.wiley.co.uk. Vendor(s): STN International (CJWILEY). *1812*

BIOPROCESS ENGINEERING.
Springer-Verlag, Heidelberger Platz 3, 14197 Berlin, Germany. TEL 49-30-82787-0. FAX 49-30-82787448. URL: http://link.springer.de. *678*

BIOS.
Beta Beta Beta, Box 670, Madison, NJ 07940-0670. TEL 201-377-8407. *592*

BIOSAFETY.
Science Reviews Ltd., P.O. Box 81, Northwood, Middlesex HA6 3DY, England. TEL 44-1923-823586. FAX 44-1923-825006. URL: http://www.scilet.com/scilet.htm.
Available only online. *592*

BIOSCAN.
American Health Consultants Inc., 3525 Piedmont Rd., N.E. Bldg. 6, Ste. 400, Atlanta, GA 30305. *679*

BIOSCIENCE.
American Institute of Biological Sciences, 1444 Eye St., N.W., Ste. 200, Washington, DC 20005. TEL 202-628-1500. FAX 202-628-1509. URL: http://www.aibs.rog/bioscience.html.
Vendor(s): Information Access Co., UMI. *593*

BIOTECH BUSINESS.
Worldwide Videotex, Box 3273, Boynton Beach, FL 33424-3273. TEL 407-738-2276.
Vendor(s): Data-Star, Information Access Co., Knight-Ridder Information, Inc., NewsNet (BT06). *764*

BIOTECHNOLOGY ABSTRACTS.
Derwent Publications Ltd., Derwent House, 14 Great Queen St., London WC2B 5DF, England. TEL 44-171-3442800.
Vendor(s): Knight-Ridder Information, Inc. (File no.357), Questel Orbit Inc. (BIOT). *636*

BIOTECHNOLOGY TODAY.
Society of Chemical Industry, 14 Belgrave Sq., London SW1X 8PS, England. TEL 44-171-235-3681. FAX 44-171-235-9410. URL: http://biotech.mond.org.
Available only online. *681*

BIOVENTURE VIEW.
BioVenture Publishing, Inc., 2555 Flores St., Ste. 555, San Mateo, CA 94403-2342. TEL 415-574-7128. FAX 415-574-8319.
Vendor(s): CompuServe, Inc., Data-Star, Dow Jones News Retrieval, European Space Agency, Information Access Co., Knight-Ridder Information, Inc. (File no.636). *681*

THE BIRD HUNTING REPORT.
Pasha Publications Inc., 1616 N. Ft. Myer Dr., Ste. 1000, Arlington, VA 22209-3107. TEL 703-528-1244. FAX 703-528-1253. *6862*

BIRD WATCHER'S DIGEST.
Pardson, Inc., Box 110, Marietta, OH 45750. TEL 614-373-5285. FAX 614-373-8443. URL: http://www.petersononline.com/birds/bird/about/bird.html. *800*

BIRMINGHAM BUSINESS.
Birmingham Area Chamber of Commerce, 2027 First Ave. N., Birmingham, AL 35203. TEL 205-323-5461. FAX 205-250-7669.
Vendor(s): UMI. *1179*

THE BISCUITS & GRAVY QUARTERLY.
Biscuits and Gravy Press, 22812 9th St., Newhall, CA 91321-2810. URL: http://muse.calarts.edu:80/~jlamb. *3085*

BITEY.
URL: http://www.bitey.com.
Available only online. *2014*

THE BITSIFTER DIGEST.
Pandora Productions, 24985 Soquel Rd., Los Gatos, CA 95030. URL: http://www.bitsifter.com.
Available only online. *3370*

BIZ TIPS NEWSLETTER.
URL: http://www.bizresource.com.
Available only online. *1639*

BKOLASKY.
1500 K St., Ste. 625, Washington, DC 20005. URL: http://www.intellectualcapital.com.
Available only online. *6165*

THE BLACK COLLEGIAN.
140 Carondelet St., New Orleans, LA 70130-2526. TEL 504-523-0154. FAX 504-523-0271. URL: http://www.black-collegian.com/.
Vendor(s): Information Access Co., UMI. *1942*

BLACK CROSS MAGAZINE.
3121 Corto Place, Ste. 2, Long Beach, CA 90803. URL: http://www.csulb.edu/'wstien/ *4381*

BLACK ENTERPRISE.
Earl G. Graves Publishing Co., Inc., 130 Fifth Ave., New York, NY 10011. TEL 212-242-8000. FAX 212-886-9610.
Vendor(s): Information Access Co., UMI. *937*

BLACK NEWSPAPER INDEX.
U M I, 300 N. Zeeb Rd., Ann Arbor, MI 48106. TEL 313-761-4700. FAX 800-864-0019.
Vendor(s): Knight-Ridder Information, Inc. *3052*

BLACK POWDER JOURNAL.
C R Labs, Inc., 12440 New London Eastern Rd., Homerville, OH 44235. TEL 330-648-2707. FAX 330-648-2707. URL: http://ezines.firelands.net/blackpowderjournal.
Available only online. *6862*

BLACK RAVEN.
Motley Focus Locus, 788 Columbus Ave., 7P, New York, NY 10025. URL: http://www.motley-focus.com/~timber/raven.html.
Available only online. *4529*

BLACK SCHOLAR.
Black World Foundation, Box 2869, Oakland, CA 94609. TEL 510-547-6633.
Vendor(s): UMI. *3001*

BLAETTERTEIG.
Media Austria, Postfach 95, A-1013 Vienna, Austria. TEL 43-1-3665512. URL: http://www.fgidec1.tuwien.ac.at/media/. *3870*

BLIND WELFARE.
National Association for the Blind, India, 11 Khan Abdul Gaffar Khan Rd., Worli Seaface, Mumbai 400 025, India. TEL 91-22-493-6930. FAX 91-22-493-2539. *3468*

BLOCKHEAD JOURNAL.
2512 W. Club Blvd., Durham, NC 27705-3127. URL: http://www.blockhead.com/.
Available only online. *3370*

BLOOD.
W.B. Saunders Co., Curtis Center, 3rd Fl., Independence Sq. W., Philadelphia, PA 19106-3399. TEL 215-238-7800. FAX 215-238-6445.
Vendor(s): Lexis-Nexis, Ovid Technologies, Inc. *4916*

BLOOD ALLEY.
Highland Echo Publishing, 3355 Grandview Hwy., Vancouver, BC V5M 1Z5, Canada. URL: http://www.vannet.com/vanecho/magzine.htm.
Available only online. *4382*

BLOOD & APHORISMS.
P.O. Box 702, Stn. P, Toronto, ON M5S 2Y4, Canada. TEL 416-535-1233. URL: http://www.interlog.com/~fiction. *4382*

BLOOD CELLS, MOLECULES, AND DISEASES.
Academic Press, Inc., Journal Division, 525 B St., Ste. 1900, San Diego, CA 92101. TEL 619-230-1840. FAX 619-699-6800. URL: http://www.apnet.com/www/journal/md.htm; http://www.idealibrary.com/ *4916*

BLOOD COAGULATION AND FIBRINOLYSIS.
Thomson Science, 2-6 Boundary Row, London SE1 8HN, England. TEL 44-171-865-0198. FAX 44-171-928-0748. URL: http://www.thomsonscience.com. *4916*

BLOOD PRESSURE MONITORING.
Thomson Science, 2-6 Boundary Row, London SE1 8HN, England. TEL 44-171-865-0198. FAX 44-171-410-6600. URL: http://www.thomsonscience.com. *4811*

BLOOD WEEKLY.
Charles W. Henderson, Ed. & Pub., Box 5528, Atlanta, GA 31107-0528. TEL 404-377-8895. FAX 404-378-5411.
Vendor(s): CompuServe, Inc., Data-Star, Dow Jones News Retrieval, Information Access Co., Knight-Ridder Information, Inc., NewsNet, Ovid Technologies, Inc. *4917*

BLOODLINES.
United Kennel Club, Inc., 100 E. Kilgore Rd., Kalamazoo, MI 49002-5584. TEL 616-343-9020. FAX 616-343-7037. *5635*

BLOOMBERG ASPHALT REPORT.
Bloomberg Financial Markets, 100 Business Park Dr., Box 888, Princeton, NJ 09542-0888. TEL 609-279-3000. FAX 609-683-7523. URL: http://www.bloomberg.com/energy.
Available only online. *2778*

BLOOMBERG ENERGY.
Bloomberg Financial Markets, 100 Business Park Dr., Box 888, Princeton, NJ 08542-0888. TEL 609-279-3000. FAX 609-683-7523. URL: http://www.bloomberg.com/energy.
Available only online. *5597*

BLOOMBERG NATURAL GAS REPORT.
Bloomberg Financial Markets, 100 Business Park Dr., Box 888, Princeton, NJ 08542-0888. TEL 609-279-3000. FAX 609-683-7523. URL: http://www.bloomberg.com/energy.
Available only online. *5597*

BLOOMBERG OIL BUYERS' GUIDE.
Bloomberg Financial Markets, 100 Business Park Dr., Box 888, Princeton, NJ 08542-0888. TEL 609-279-3000. FAX 609-683-7523. URL: http://www.bloomberg.com/energy.
Available only online. *5597*

BLUE LIST OF CURRENT MUNICIPAL AND CORPORATE OFFERINGS.
Standard & Poors Corporation, 25 Broadway, New York, NY 10004. TEL 212-208-8000. *1375*

BLUES ACCESS.
Cary Wolfson, Ed. & Pub., 1455 Chestnut Pl., Boulder, CO 80304-3153. TEL 303-443-7245. FAX 303-939-9729. URL: http://www.bluesaccess.com. *5377*

BOARDWATCH MAGAZINE.
8500 W. Bowles Ave., Ste. 210, Littleton, CO 80123. TEL 303-973-6038. FAX 303-973-3731. URL: http://www.boardwatch.com. *2165*

BOATING.
Hachette Filipacchi Magazines, Inc., 1633 Broadway, 43rd Fl., New York, NY 10009. TEL 212-767-5574. FAX 212-767-5618.
Vendor(s): Information Access Co., Knight-Ridder Information, Inc., UMI. *6836*

BOATING INDUSTRY.
National Trade Publications, Inc., 13 Century Hill, Latham, NY 23220-2197. TEL 518-783-1281. FAX 518-783-1386.
Vendor(s): Information Access Co. *6837*

BOBBIN.
Bobbin Publishing, Inc., 1110 Shop Rd., Box 1986, Columbia, SC 29202. TEL 803-771-7500. FAX 803-799-1461. URL: http://www.bobbin.com.
Vendor(s): Information Access Co., UMI. *1913*

BOCOEX INDEX.
Boston Computer Exchange Index, 210 South St., 6th Fl., Boston, MA 02111. TEL 617-542-4414. FAX 617-542-8849. *2126*

BOERNEBIBLIOTEKSKATALOG. BOEGER & TIDSSKRIFTER. EMNEKATALOG.
Dansk BiblioteksCenter as, Tempovej 7-11, DK-2750 Ballerup, Denmark. TEL 45-44-867892. FAX 45-44-867892. *539*

BOERNEBIBLIOTEKSKATALOG. BOEGER & TIDSSKRIFTER. FORFATTERKATALOG.
Dansk BiblioteksCenter as, Tempovej 7-11, DK-2750 Ballerup, Denmark. TEL 45-44-867892. FAX 45-44-867892. *539*

BOERNEBIBLIOTEKSKATALOG. BOEGER & TIDSSKRIFTER. TITELKATALOG.
Dansk BiblioteksCenter as, Tempovej 7-11, DK-2750 Ballerup, Denmark. TEL 45-44-867892. FAX 45-44-867892. *539*

BOERNEBIBLIOTEKSKATALOG. GRAMMOFONPLADER, KASSETTEBAAND.
Dansk BiblioteksCenter as, Tempovej 7-11, DK-2750 Ballerup, Denmark. TEL 45-44-867892. FAX 45-44-867892. *5447*

BOERNEBIBLIOTEKSKATALOG. LYDBOEGER, BOG & BAAND.
Dansk BiblioteksCenter as, Tempovej 7-11, DK-2750 Ballerup, Denmark. TEL 45-44-867777. FAX 45-44-867892. *1861*

BOLETIN OFICIAL DE LA PROPIEDAD INDUSTRIAL. 1: MARCAS Y OTROS SIGNOS DISTINTIVOS.
Ministerio de Industria y Energia, Oficina Espanola de Patentes y Marcas, Panama, 1, 28071 Madrid, Spain. TEL 34-1-3495300. FAX 34-1-4572280.
Vendor(s): Oficina Espanola de Patentes y Marcas. *5581*

BOLETIN OFICIAL DE LA PROPIEDAD INDUSTRIAL. 2: PATENTES Y MODELOS DE UTILIDAD.
Ministerio de Industria y Energia, Oficina Espanola de Patentes y Marcas, Panama, 1, 28071 Madrid, Spain. TEL 34-1-3495300. FAX 34-1-4572280.
Vendor(s): Oficina Espanola de Patentes y Marcas. *5581*

BOLETIN OFICIAL DE LA PROPIEDAD INDUSTRIAL. 3: MODELOS Y DIBUJOS INDUSTRIALES Y ARTISTICOS.
Ministerio de Industria y Energia, Oficina Espanola de Patentes y Marcas, Panama, 1, 28071 Madrid, Spain. TEL 34-1-3495300. FAX 34-1-4572280.
Vendor(s): Oficina Espanola de Patentes y Marcas. *5581*

BOLETIN OFICIAL DE LA PROPIEDAD INDUSTRIAL. 4: RESUMENES DE PATENTES.
Ministerio de Industria y Energia, Oficina Espanola de Patentes y Marcas, Panama, 1, 28071 Madrid, Spain. TEL 34-1-3495300. FAX 34-1-4572280.
Vendor(s): Oficina Espanola de Patentes y Marcas. *5581*

BOLETIN OFICIAL DEL ESTADO.
Boletin Oficial del Estado, Trafalgar, 27, 28071 Madrid, Spain. TEL 34-1-5382297. FAX 34-1-5382275. URL: http://www.boe.es. *6166*

THE BOND BUYER.
American Banker - Bond Buyer, Newsletter Division One State St. Plaza, New York, NY 10004-1549. FAX 212-943-2224.
Vendor(s): Information Access Co., Knight-Ridder Information, Inc. (File no.626), Lexis-Nexis, NewsNet (FI08). *1376*

BOOK PUBLISHING REPORT.
Cowles - SIMBA Information, 11 Riverbend Dr. S., Box 4949, Stamford, CT 06907-0949. TEL 203-358-9900. FAX 203-358-5811. URL: http://www.simbanet.com.
Vendor(s): Knight-Ridder Information, Inc., NewsNet (PB19). *6264*

BOOK REVIEW DIGEST.
H.W. Wilson Co., 950 University Ave., Bronx, NY 10452. TEL 718-588-8400. FAX 718-590-1617.
Vendor(s): OCLC, Wilsonline (File BRD). *4325*

BOOK REVIEW INDEX.
Gale Research, 835 Penobscot Bldg., 645 Griswold St., Detroit, MI 48226-4094. TEL 313-961-2242. FAX 800-414-5043.
Vendor(s): Knight-Ridder Information, Inc. (File no.137). *6288*

BOOK WORLD.
Washington Post Co., 1150 15th St., N.W., Washington, DC 20071. TEL 202-334-6000. FAX 202-334-5059.
Vendor(s): Knight-Ridder Information, Inc. *6264*

BOOKLIST.
American Library Association, 50 E. Huron St., Chicago, IL 60611-2795. TEL 312-944-6780. FAX 312-440-9374. URL: http://www.ala.org/booklist/index.html. *6289*

BOOKS IN PRINT.
R.R. Bowker, A Division of Reed Elsevier Inc., 121 Chanlon Rd., New Providence, NJ 07974. TEL 908-464-6800. FAX 908-665-3502. URL: http://www.bowker.com.
Vendor(s): Knight-Ridder Information, Inc. (File no.470), Lexis-Nexis (BIP), Ovid Technologies, Inc. (BBIP). *539*

BOOKS IN PRINT SUPPLEMENT.
R.R. Bowker, A Division of Reed Elsevier Inc., 121 Chanlon Rd., New Providence, NJ 07974. TEL 908-464-6800. FAX 908-665-3502. URL: http://www.reedref.com.
Vendor(s): Knight-Ridder Information, Inc. (File no.470), Ovid Technologies, Inc. (BBIP). *540*

BOOKS ON CANADA.
Association for the Export of Canadian Books, 504-1 Nicholas St., Ottawa, ON K1N 7B7, Canada. TEL 613-562-2324. FAX 613-562-2329. URL: http://aecb.org. *6265*

BOOKS OUT-OF-PRINT.
R.R. Bowker, A Division of Reed Elsevier Inc., 121 Chanlon Rd., New Providence, NJ 07974. TEL 908-464-6800. FAX 908-665-3502. URL: http://www.reedref.com.
Vendor(s): Knight-Ridder Information, Inc. (File no.470), Ovid Technologies, Inc. (BBIP). *540*

BOOKS OUT-OF-PRINT PLUS.
R.R. Bowker, A Division of Reed Elsevier Inc., 121 Chanlon Rd., New Providence, NJ 07974. FAX 908-665-3528. URL: http://www.reedref.com. *540*

BOOKS OUT-OF-PRINT WITH BOOK REVIEWS PLUS.
R.R. Bowker, A Division of Reed Elsevier Inc., 121 Chanlon Rd., New Providence, NJ 07974. FAX 908-665-3528. URL: http://www.reedref.com. *540*

BOOKS: THE INTERNATIONAL MARKET.
Euromonitor, 60-61 Britton St., London EC1M 5NA, England. TEL 44-171-251-8024. FAX 44-171-608-3149. URL: http://www.euromonitor.com.
Vendor(s): Data-Star, Knight-Ridder Information, Inc. *6265*

BOOT.
Imagine Publishing, Inc., 150 N. Hill Dr., Brisbane, CA 94005. TEL 415-468-4684. FAX 415-468-4686. URL: http://www.bootnet.com. *2209*

BOOT COVE ECONOMIC FORECAST.
Voight Industries, Inc., Box 200, Lubec, ME 04652. TEL 207-733-5593.
Vendor(s): NewsNet (IV29). *1226*

BORDER CROSSINGS.
Arts Manitoba Publications Inc., 500 - 70 Arthur St., Winnipeg, MB R3B 1G7, Canada. TEL 204-942-5778. FAX 204-949-0793. *432*

BOSTON BUSINESS JOURNAL.
American City Business Journals, Inc., 505 Powell St., Austin, TX 78703-5121.
Vendor(s): CompuServe, Inc., Data-Star, Dow Jones News Retrieval, Knight-Ridder Information, Inc., National Data Corp., UMI. *937*

BOSTON COLLEGE ENVIRONMENTAL AFFAIRS LAW REVIEW.
Boston College, School of Law, 885 Centre St., Newton, MA 02159. TEL 617-552-4354. *2909*

BOSTON COLLEGE LAW REVIEW.
Boston College, School of Law, 885 Centre St., Newton, MA 02159. TEL 617-552-8575.
Vendor(s): West Group. *3921*

THE BOSTON GLOBE INDEX.
U M I, 300 N. Zeeb Rd., Ann Arbor, MI 48106. TEL 313-761-4700. FAX 800-864-0019.
Vendor(s): Knight-Ridder Information, Inc. (File no. 484). *3883*

THE BOSTON REVIEW.
Boston Critic, Inc., c/o MIT, E53-407, Cambridge, MA 02139-4307. TEL 617-253-3642. FAX 617-252-1549. URL: http://www.polisci.mit.edu/BostonReview. *4325*

BOSTON UNIVERSITY INTERNATIONAL LAW JOURNAL.
Boston University, School of Law, International Law Journal, 765 Commonwealth Ave., Boston, MA 02215. TEL 617-353-3157. FAX 617-353-7400.
Vendor(s): West Group. *4107*

BOSTON UNIVERSITY LAW REVIEW.
Boston University, School of Law, Law Review, 765 Commonwealth Ave., Boston, MA 02215. TEL 617-353-3118. FAX 617-353-6767.
Vendor(s): Lexis-Nexis, West Group. *3921*

THE BOTANICAL REVIEW.
New York Botanical Garden, Scientific Publications Department, Bronx, NY 10458-5126. TEL 718-817-8721. FAX 718-817-8842.
Vendor(s): Information Access Co. *696*

BOTTIN ENTREPRISES.
Bottin S A, 4 rue Andre Boulle, 94961 Cretil Cedex 9, France. TEL 49-81-56-56. FAX 49-81-56-76. *1655*

THE BOWKER ANNUAL LIBRARY AND BOOK TRADE ALMANAC.
R.R. Bowker, A Division of Reed Elsevier Inc., 121 Chanlon Rd., New Providence, NJ 07974. TEL 908-464-6800. FAX 908-665-6688. URL: http://www.bowker.com.
Vendor(s): European Space Agency, Knight-Ridder Information, Inc., Ovid Technologies, Inc. (BBIP), Questel Orbit Inc. *4166*

BOWKER - WHITAKER GLOBAL BOOKS IN PRINT ON DISC.
R.R. Bowker, A Division of Reed Elsevier Inc., 121 Chanlon Rd., New Providence, NJ 07974. TEL 908-665-2866. FAX 908-665-3528. URL: http://www.reedref.com. *540*

BOWNE DIGEST FOR CORPORATE & SECURITIES LAWYERS.
Brumberg Publications, Inc., 124 Harvard St., Brookline, MA 02146. TEL 617-734-1979. FAX 617-734-1989.
Vendor(s): NewsNet (LA11). *4051*

BOXOFFICE.
R L D Communications, 6640 Sunset Blvd., Ste. 100, Hollywood, CA 90028. TEL 213-465-1186. FAX 213-465-5049. URL: http://www.boxoff.com. *5324*

BOYS' LIFE (INKPRINT EDITION).
Boy Scouts of America, Box 152079, Irving, TX 75015-2079. TEL 972-580-2366. FAX 972-580-2079.
Vendor(s): Information Access Co. *1865*

BRAILLE BOOK REVIEW (LARGE PRINT EDITION).
U.S. Library of Congress, National Library Service for the Blind and Physically Handicapped, Washington, DC 20542. TEL 202-707-5100. FAX 202-707-0712. URL: http://www.lcweb.loc.gov/nls. *3468*

BRAILLE BOOKS (LARGE PRINT EDITION).
U.S. Library of Congress, National Library Service for the Blind and Physically Handicapped, Washington, DC 20542. TEL 202-707-5100. FAX 202-707-0712. URL: http://www.lcweb.loc.gov/nls. *3458*

BRAILLE FORUM.
American Council of the Blind, 1155 15th St. N.W., Ste. 720, Washington, DC 20005. TEL 202-467-5081. FAX 202-467-5085. URL: http://www.acb.org. *3468*

BRAILLE MONITOR (INKPRINT EDITION).
National Federation of the Blind, 1800 Johnson St., Baltimore, MD 21230. TEL 410-659-9314. FAX 410-685-5653. *3468*

BRAIN.
Oxford University Press, Academic Division, Great Clarendon St., Oxford OX2 6DP, England. TEL 44-1865-267907. FAX 44-1865-267485. URL: http://www.oup.co.uk/journals. *5055*

BRAIN AND COGNITION.
Academic Press, Inc., Journal Division, 525 B St., Ste. 1900, San Diego, CA 92101-4495. TEL 619-230-1840. FAX 619-699-6800. URL: http://www/apnet.com/www/journal/br.htm; http://www.idealibrary.com/ *6098*

BRAIN AND LANGUAGE.
Academic Press, Inc., Journal Division, 525 B St., Ste. 1900, San Diego, CA 92101-4495. TEL 619-230-1840. FAX 619-699-6800. URL: http://www.apnet.com/www/journal/bl.htm; http://www.idealibrary.com/ *6098*

BRAIN AND NERVE.
Igaku-Shoin Ltd., 5-24-3 Hongo, Bunkyo-ku, Tokyo 113-91, Japan. TEL 81-3-3817-5701.
Vendor(s): JICST. *5055*

BRAIN, BEHAVIOR, AND IMMUNITY.
Academic Press, Inc., Journal Division, 525 B St., Ste. 1900, San Diego, CA 92101-4495. TEL 619-230-1840. FAX 619-699-6800. URL: http://www.apnet.com/www/journal/bi.htm; http://www.idealibrary.com/ 4792

BRAIN INJURY.
Taylor & Francis Ltd., 1 Gunpowder Sq., London EC4A 3DE, England. TEL 44-171-583-0490. FAX 44-171-583-0585. URL: http://www.tandf.co.uk/. 5055

BRANDS AND THEIR COMPANIES.
Gale Research, 835 Penobscot Bldg., 645 Griswold St., Detroit, MI 48226-4094. TEL 313-961-2242. FAX 800-414-5043.
Vendor(s): Knight-Ridder Information, Inc. 5581

BRANDWEEK.
B P I Communications, Inc. (New York), 1515 Broadway, New York, NY 10036. TEL 212-764-7300. FAX 212-536-5084. URL: http://www.brandweek.com.
Vendor(s): Information Access Co., Knight-Ridder Information, Inc. (File no.648), Ovid Technologies, Inc. (TSAP). 32

BRANDYWINE.NET BUSINESS REPORT.
Ad Pro, Inc., Box 520, Oxford, PA 19363. TEL 610-932-2444. FAX 610-932-2246. URL: http://www.chestercounty.com/busrpt.htm. 937

BRAZIL REPORT.
Lettres (U.K.) Ltd., 61 Old St., London EC1V 9HX, England. TEL 44-171-251-0012. FAX 44-171-253-8193.
Vendor(s): Lexis-Nexis. 1226

BREAKFAST CEREALS: THE INTERNATIONAL MARKET.
Euromonitor, 60-61 Britton St., London EC1M 5NA, England. TEL 44-171-251-8024. FAX 44-171-608-3149. URL: http://www.euromonitor.com.
Vendor(s): Data-Star, Knight-Ridder Information, Inc. 3097

BREAST NEWS.
N H M R C National Breast Cancer Centre, P.O. Box 572, Kings Cross, N.S.W. 2011, Australia. TEL 02-9334-1716. FAX 02-9326-9329. URL: http://www.nbcc.org.au/pages/brnews/contents.htm. 4971

BRETTNEWS.
245 Eighth Ave., Ste. 305, New York, NY 10011. URL: http://www.brettnews.com. 4326

BREW-INFO.
European Brewery Convention, P.O. Box 510, 2380 BB Zoeterwoude, Netherlands. TEL 31-71-456047. FAX 31-71-410013. 517

BREW: TRAVELING AMERICA'S BREWPUBS AND MICROBREWERIES.
1120 Mulberry, Des Moines, IA 50309. TEL 515-243-4929. FAX 515-243-4517. URL: http://www.brewmag.com. 517

BRIEF (CHICAGO).
American Bar Association, Tort and Insurance Practice Section, 750 N. Lake Shore Dr., Chicago, IL 60611. TEL 312-988-6046. URL: http://www.abanet.org.
Vendor(s): Lexis-Nexis, West Group (BRIEF). 3921

BRIGHAM YOUNG UNIVERSITY LAW REVIEW.
Brigham Young University, J. Reuben Clark Law School, 471F JRCB, Provo, UT 84602. TEL 801-378-5678. FAX 801-378-3595.
Vendor(s): West Group. 3921

BRIGHT LIGHTS.
Box 420987, San Francisco, CA 94142-0987. TEL 510-601-5530. FAX 510-601-5530. URL: http://www.slip.net/~gmm/bright.html. Available only online. 5325

BRITANNICA BOOK OF THE YEAR.
Encyclopaedia Britannica, Inc., 310 S. Michigan Ave., Chicago, IL 60604. TEL 312-347-7000. FAX 312-347-7914. 2656

BRITISH ACCOUNTING REVIEW.
Academic Press Ltd., 24-28 Oval Rd., London NW1 7DX, England. TEL 44-171-267-4466. FAX 44-171-482-2293. URL: http://www.hbuk.co.uk/ap/bar; http://www.europe.idealibrary.com/. 1085

BRITISH CATALOGUE OF MUSIC.
Bowker - Saur Ltd., A member of the Reed Elsevier plc group, Maypole House, Maypole Rd., E. Grinstead, W. Sussex Rh19 1HU, England. TEL 44-01342-330100. FAX 44-1342-330191. URL: http://www.reed-elsevier.com. 5378

BRITISH COLUMBIA DECISIONS - CIVIL CASES.
Western Legal Publications, 301-1 Alexander St., Vancouver, BC V6A 1B2, Canada. TEL 604-681-5671. FAX 604-687-2796. 4058

BRITISH COLUMBIA DECISIONS - CRIMINAL CONVICTION AND SENTENCE CASES.
Western Legal Publications, 301-1 Alexander St., Vancouver, BC V6A 1B2, Canada. TEL 604-687-5671. FAX 604-687-2796. 4088

BRITISH COLUMBIA DECISIONS - FAMILY LAW CASES.
Western Legal Publications, 301-1 Alexander St., Vancouver, BC V6A 1B2, Canada. TEL 604-687-5671. FAX 604-687-2796. 4099

BRITISH COLUMBIA DECISIONS - INSURANCE LAW CASES.
Western Legal Publications, 301-1 Alexander St., Vancouver, BC V6A 1B2, Canada. TEL 604-687-5671. FAX 604-687-2796. 3922

BRITISH COLUMBIA DECISIONS - LABOUR ARBITRATION.
Western Legal Publications, 301 One Alexander St., Vancouver, BC V6A 1B2, Canada. TEL 604-687-5671. FAX 604-687-2796. 1421

BRITISH COLUMBIA DECISIONS - LABOUR RELATIONS BOARD DIGESTS.
Western Legal Publications, 301-1 Alexander St., Vancouver, BC V6A 1B2, Canada. TEL 604-687-5671. FAX 604-687-2796. 1421

BRITISH COLUMBIA DECISIONS - MUNICIPAL LAW CASES.
Western Legal Publications, 301-1 Alexander St., Vancouver, BC V6A 1B2, Canada. TEL 604-687-5671. FAX 604-687-2796. 3922

BRITISH COLUMBIA SNOW SURVEY BULLETIN.
Ministry of the Environment, Lands and Parks, Department of Lands and Water Management, 765 Broughton St., Victoria, BC V8V 1X4, Canada. FAX 250-356-5496. URL: http://wtrwww.env.gov.bc.ca/wat/snow__bulletin/. Available only online. 5228

BRITISH EDUCATION INDEX.
British Education Index, Brotherton Library, University of Leeds, Leeds LS2 9JT, England. TEL 44-113-233-5525. FAX 44-113-233-5524. URL: http://www.leeds.ac.uk/library/library.html.
Vendor(s): Knight-Ridder Information, Inc. (File no.121). 2497

BRITISH EXPORTS.
Kompass, Part of the Reed Elsevier group, Windsor Ct., E. Grinstead House, E. Grinstead, W. Sussex RH19 1XD, England. TEL 44-1342-326972. FAX 44-1342-335747.
Vendor(s): Reed Information Services Ltd. 1657

THE BRITISH JOURNAL FOR THE PHILOSOPHY OF SCIENCE.
Oxford University Press, Academic Division, Great Clarendon St., Oxford OX2 6DP, England. TEL 44-1865-267907. FAX 44-1865-267485. URL: http://www.oup.co.uk/journals.
Vendor(s): Information Access Co. 6516

THE BRITISH JOURNAL OF AESTHETICS.
Oxford University Press, Academic Division, Great Clarendon St., Oxford OX2 6DP, England. TEL 44-1865-267907. FAX 44-1865-267485. URL: http://www.oup.co.uk/journals.
Vendor(s): Information Access Co. 5720

BRITISH JOURNAL OF CLINICAL PHARMACOLOGY.
Blackwell Science Ltd., Osney Mead, Oxford OX2 OEL, England. TEL 44-1865-206206. FAX 44-1865-721205. URL: http://www.black.co.uk. 5650

THE BRITISH JOURNAL OF CRIMINOLOGY.
Oxford University Press, Academic Division, Great Clarendon St., Oxford OX2 6DP, England. TEL 44-1865-267907. FAX 44-1865-267485. URL: http://www.oup.co.uk/journals.
Vendor(s): Information Access Co. 2262

BRITISH JOURNAL OF DERMATOLOGY.
Blackwell Science Ltd., Osney Mead, Oxford OX2 OEL, England. TEL 44-1865-206206. FAX 44-1865-721205. URL: http://www.black.co.uk. 4875

BRITISH JOURNAL OF NEUROSURGERY.
Carfax Publishing Co., P.O. Box 25, Abingdon, Oxon. OX14 3UE, England. TEL 44-1235-401000. FAX 44-1235-401550. 5137

BRITISH JOURNAL OF OBSTETRICS & GYNAECOLOGY.
Blackwell Science Ltd., Osney Mead, Oxford OX2 OEL, England. TEL 44-1865-206206. FAX 44-1865-721205. URL: http://www.black.co.uk.
Vendor(s): Ovid Technologies, Inc. 4954

BRITISH JOURNAL OF ORTHODONTICS.
Oxford University Press, Academic Division, Great Clarendon St., Oxford OX2 6DP, England. TEL 44-1865-267907. FAX 44-1865-267485. 4852

BRITISH JOURNAL OF PHARMACOLOGY.
Stockton Press, Houndmills, Basingstoke, Hants. RG21 6XS, England. TEL 44-1256-351898. FAX 44-1256-328339. 5651

BRITISH JOURNAL OF POLITICAL SCIENCE.
Cambridge University Press, Edinburgh Bldg., Shaftesbury Rd., Cambridge CB2 2RU, England. TEL 44-1223-312393. FAX 44-1223-315052. URL: http://www.cup.org/journals/CUPJNLS.html.
Vendor(s): Information Access Co. 5895

BRITISH JOURNAL OF PSYCHOLOGY.
British Psychological Society, St. Andrew's House, 48 Princess Rd. E., Leicester LE1 7DR, England. TEL 44-166-254-9568. FAX 44-166-247-0787. URL: http://www.journals.eecs.qub.ac.uk.
Vendor(s): Information Access Co., UMI. 6100

BRITISH JOURNAL OF RHEUMATOLOGY.
Oxford University Press, Academic Division, Great Clarendon St., Oxford OX2 6DP, England. TEL 44-1865-267907. FAX 44-1865-267485. URL: http://www.oup.co.uk/journals.
Vendor(s): Ovid Technologies, Inc. 5125

BRITISH JOURNAL OF SURGERY.
Blackwell Science Ltd., Osney Mead, Oxford OX2 OEL, England. TEL 44-1865-206206. FAX 44-1865-721205. URL: http://www.black.co.uk.
Vendor(s): Lexis-Nexis, Ovid Technologies, Inc. 5137

BRITISH JOURNAL OF UROLOGY.
Blackwell Science Ltd., Osney Mead, Oxford OX2 OEL, England. TEL 44-1865-206206. FAX 44-1865-721205. URL: http://www.black.co.uk.
Vendor(s): Ovid Technologies, Inc. 5159

BRITISH LIBRARY. DOCUMENT SUPPLY CENTRE. INDEX OF CONFERENCE PROCEEDINGS.
British Library, Document Supply Centre, Boston Spa, Wetherby, W. Yorks. LS23 7BQ, England. TEL 44-1937-546080. FAX 44-1937-546286. 5173

BRITISH NATIONAL BIBLIOGRAPHY.
British Library, National Bibliographic Service, Boston Spa, Wetherby, W. Yorks. LS23 7BQ, England. TEL 44-1937-546613. FAX 44-1937-546586. URL: http://portico.bl.uk. 541

BRITISH PLASTICS AND RUBBER MAGAZINE.
M C M Publishing Ltd., 37 Nelson Rd., Caterham, Surrey CR3 5PP, England. TEL 44-1883-347059.
Vendor(s): Information Access Co.. 5876

BRITISH RATE AND DATA.
E M A P Media, 33-39 Bowling Green Ln., London EC1R 0DA, England. TEL 44-171-505-8265. FAX 44-171-505-8264. 541

BRITISH VIRGIN ISLANDS WELCOME TOURIST GUIDE.
Island Publishing Co., P.O. Box 133, Road Town - Tortola, British Virgin Islands, W.I. TEL 809-494-2413. FAX 809-494-4413. URL: http://www.bviwelcome.com. *7189*

BROADBAND NETWORKING NEWS.
Phillips Business Information, Inc., 1201 Seven Locks Rd., Potomac, MD 20854. TEL 301-424-3338. FAX 301-309-3847.
Vendor(s): Information Access Co., NewsNet (TE51). *2168*

BROADCAST WEEK.
Globe and Mail Publishing, 444 Front St. W., Toronto, ON M5V 2S9, Canada. TEL 416-585-5045. *1983*

BROADCASTAWAY.
Techtonic Webzine, URL: http://www.merlin.com.au/tech/index.html.
Available only online. *2044*

BROADCASTING & CABLE.
Cahners Publishing Company (Washington), Entertainment Division, Division of Reed Elsevier Inc., 1705 DeSales St., N.W., Washington, DC 20036. TEL 202-659-2340. FAX 202-429-0651. URL: http://www.broadcastingcable.com/
Vendor(s): Information Access Co., Knight-Ridder Information, Inc., Lexis-Nexis. *2044*

BROADCASTING IN THE U K.
Key Note Ltd., Field House, 72 Oldfield Rd., Hampton, Middlesex TW12 2HQ, England. TEL 44-181-783-0755. FAX 44-181-783-0049. *2023*

BROOKINGS REVIEW.
Brookings Institution, 1775 Massachusetts Ave., N.W., Washington, DC 20036-2188. TEL 202-797-6258. FAX 202-797-6195.
Vendor(s): Information Access Co., UMI. *938*

BROOKLYN JOURNAL OF INTERNATIONAL LAW.
Brooklyn Law School, 250 Joralemon, Brooklyn, NY 11201. TEL 718-780-7971. FAX 718-780-0353.
Vendor(s): National Data Corp., West Group. *4107*

BROOKLYN LAW REVIEW.
Brooklyn Law School, 250 Joralemon St., Brooklyn, NY 11201. TEL 718-780-7968.
Vendor(s): Lexis-Nexis. *3922*

BROWN UNIVERSITY CHILD AND ADOLESCENT BEHAVIOR LETTER.
Manisses Communications Group, Inc., Box 9758, Providence, RI 02940-9758. TEL 401-831-6020. FAX 401-861-6370. URL: http://www.manisses.com.
Vendor(s): Information Access Co. *1839*

BROWN UNIVERSITY DIGEST OF ADDICTION THEORY & APPLICATION.
Manisses Communications Group, Inc., Box 9758, Providence, RI 02940-9758. TEL 401-831-6020. FAX 401-861-6370. URL: http://www.manisses.com.
Vendor(s): Information Access Co. *2299*

BROWN UNIVERSITY LONG-TERM CARE QUALITY ADVISOR.
Manisses Communications Group, Inc., Box 9758, Providence, RI 02940-9758. TEL 401-861-6370. FAX 401-861-6370. URL: http://www.manisses.com.
Vendor(s): Information Access Co. *3704*

BRUNSWICK BUSINESS JOURNAL.
A B J Publishing Inc., 599 Main St., Ste. 203, Moncton, NB E1C 1C8, Canada. TEL 506-857-9696. FAX 506-859-7395.
Vendor(s): UMI. *938*

BRYN MAWR CLASSICAL REVIEW.
Bryn Mawr Commentaries, Inc., Bryn Mawr College, Thomas Library, Bryn Mawr, PA 19010. TEL 610-526-5384. FAX 610-526-7475. URL: gopher://gopher.lib.Virginia.EDU:70/11/alpha/bmcr/. *1901*

BRYN MAWR MEDIEVAL REVIEW.
Bryn Mawr Commentaries, Inc., Bryn Mawr College, Thomas Library, Bryn Mawr, PA 19010. TEL 215-526-5384. FAX 610-526-7475. URL: gopher://gopher.lib.virginia.edu/70/11/alpha/bmmr.
Available only online. *3555*

BRYN MAWR REVIEWS.
Bryn Mawr Commentaries, Inc., Bryn Mawr College, Thomas Library, Bryn Mawr, PA 19010. TEL 610-526-5384. FAX 610-526-7475.
Available only online. *3555*

BUBBLEHEAD INTERNET MUSIC MAGAZINE.
P.O. Box 1171, Fremantle, Perth, W.A. 6160, Australia. URL: http://cleo.murdoch.edu.au/~achamber.
Available only online. *5379*

BUDAPEST WEEK.
Duax Ltd., Vaci ut 168 F ep., 1138 Budapest, Hungary. TEL 36-1-2702255 ext. 7300. FAX 36-1-2705148. URL: http://www.enet.hu.bpweek1. *3002*

BUDDHA ZINE.
BuddhaNet, P.O. Box J1020, Haymarket, Sydney 2000, Australia. TEL 61-2-9212-3061. FAX 61-2-9212-3071. URL: http://www2.hawkesbury.uws.edu.au/BuddhaNet/budzine.htm.
Available only online. *6388*

BUFFALO LAW REVIEW.
State University of New York at Buffalo, Buffalo Law Review, 605 John Lord O'Brian Hall, Amherst Campus, Amherst, NY 14260. TEL 716-645-2059. FAX 716-645-2064. URL: http://wings.buffalo.edu/law/blr/.
Vendor(s): West Group. *3922*

BUGNET.
Box 393, Sumas, WA 98295. URL: http://www.bugnet.com/free1.html.
Available only online. *2195*

BUILDER (WASHINGTON).
Hanley-Wood Inc., One Thomas Circle, N.W., Ste. 600, Washington, DC 20005. TEL 202-452-0800. FAX 202-785-1974. URL: http://www.builderonline.com. *868*

BUILDING RESEARCH AND INFORMATION.
Thomson Professional, 2-6 Boundary Row, London SE1 8HN, England. TEL 44-171-8650066. FAX 44-171-5229623. URL: http://jpr.thomsonprofessional.com. *871*

BUILDING SUPPLY BUSINESS.
Cahners Publishing Company (Des Plaines), Division of Reed Elsevier Inc., 1350 E. Touhy Ave., Box 5080, Des Plaines, IL 60018-5080. TEL 847-635-8800. FAX 847-635-9950.
Vendor(s): Dow Jones News Retrieval, Information Access Co., Knight-Ridder Information, Inc. *872*

BUILDINGS.
Stamats Communications, Inc., Box 1888, Cedar Rapids, IA 52406-1888. TEL 319-364-6167. FAX 319-364-4278. URL: http://www.buildings.com.
Vendor(s): Information Access Co., Knight-Ridder Information, Inc., UMI. *872*

BUKKYO DAIGAKU SHINRIGAKU KENKYUJO KIYO.
Bukkyo Daigaku, Shinrigaku Kenkyujo, Kitahananobocho, Murasakino, Kita-ku, Kyoto 603, Japan.
Vendor(s): UMI. *6100*

BULLETIN OF ECONOMIC RESEARCH.
Blackwell Publishers Ltd., 108 Cowley Rd., Oxford OX4 1JF, England. TEL 44-1865-791100. FAX 44-1865-791347. URL: http://www.blackwellpublishers.co.uk.
Vendor(s): Information Access Co. *938*

BULLETIN OF ENTOMOLOGICAL RESEARCH.
CAB International, Wallingford, Oxon. OX10 8DE, England. TEL 44-1491-832111. FAX 44-1491-826090. URL: http://www.cabi.org.
Vendor(s): DIMDI, European Space Agency, Knight-Ridder Information, Inc. *748*

BULLETIN OF NORTHERN IRELAND LAW.
S L S Legal Publications, School of Law, Queens University of Belfast, Belfast BT7 1NN, N. Ireland. TEL 44-1232-335224. FAX 44-1232-325590.
Vendor(s): Context Ltd. *3923*

THE BULLETIN OF SYMBOLIC LOGIC.
Association for Symbolic Logic, Department of Mathematics, University of Illinois at Urbana-Champaign, 1409 W. Green St., Urbana, IL 61801. TEL 217-244-7902. FAX 217-333-9576. URL: http://www.math.ucla.edu/~asl/bslcontests.html. *4565*

BULLETIN OF THE ATOMIC SCIENTISTS.
Educational Foundation for Nuclear Science, 6042 S. Kimbark Ave., Chicago, IL 60637. TEL 773-702-2555. FAX 773-702-0725. URL: http://www.neoglyphics.com/atomics/; http://neog.com/atomic/index.html.
Vendor(s): Information Access Co., UMI. *6007*

BULLETIN OF THE HISTORY OF MEDICINE.
Johns Hopkins University Press, Journals Publishing Division, 2715 N. Charles St., Baltimore, MD 21218. TEL 410-516-6987. FAX 410-516-6968. URL: http://muse.jhu.edu. *4649*

BULLETIN OF VOLCANOLOGY.
Springer-Verlag, Heidelberger Platz 3, 14197 Berlin, Germany. TEL 49-30-82787-0. FAX 49-30-82787448. URL: http://linl.springer.de. *2379*

BULLETIN ON NARCOTICS.
United Nations Publications, Sales and Marketing Section, Room DC2-0853, New York, NY 10017. TEL 212-963-8302. FAX 212-963-3489. URL: http://www.un.org/publications. *2300*

BULLETIN ON THE RHEUMATIC DISEASES.
Arthritis Foundation, 1314 Spring St., N.W., Atlanta, GA 30309. TEL 404-872-7100. FAX 404-872-9559.
Vendor(s): Lexis-Nexis. *5125*

BULLETIN SIGNALETIQUE DES TELECOMMUNICATIONS.
Centre National d'Etudes des Telecommunications, Service des Abonnements, 38-40 rue du General Leclerc, 92131 Issy-les-Moulineaux Cedex, France. TEL 45-29-51-08.
Vendor(s): Telesystemes - Questel. *1983*

BULLETIN TO MANAGEMENT.
The Bureau of National Affairs, Inc., 1231 25th St., N.W., Washington, DC 20037. TEL 202-452-4200. FAX 202-822-8092. URL: http://www.bna.com/
Vendor(s): Human Resources Information Network (CDD, HDD). *1563*

THE BULLETIN WITH NEWSWEEK.
A C P Publishing Pty. Ltd., 54-58 Park St., Sydney, N.S.W. 2000, Australia. TEL 61-2-2828302. FAX 61-2-2674359. *3250*

DIE BURGER.
P.O. Box 692, Heerengracht, 40, Cape Town 8000, South Africa. TEL 27-21-4062222. FAX 27-21-4063221. URL: http://www.maspers.com/dieburger/ *3355*

BURRELLE'S MEDIA DIRECTORY.
Burrelle's Media Directories, 75 E. Northfield Rd., Livingston, NJ 07039. TEL 202-992-6600. *1983*

BURTON GROUP NEWS ANALYSIS.
Burton Group, Box 3448, Salt Lake City, UT 84110-3448. TEL 801-943-1966. FAX 801-943-2425. *2074*

BURTON GROUP REPORT.
Burton Group, Box 3448, Salt Lake City, UT 84110-3448. TEL 801-943-1966. FAX 801-943-2425. *2074*

BURTZ BIRTUAL ATELIER.
Keltenstr. 23, CH-8044 Zurich, Switzerland. URL: http://www.burtz.ch.
Available only online. *476*

BUSINESS AMERICA.
U.S. Department of Commerce, 14th St. between Constitution Ave. and Pennsylvania Ave., N.W., Washington, DC 20230. TEL 202-482-3251. FAX 202-482-5819. URL: http://www.ita.doc.gov/bizam/bizam.html.
Vendor(s): Dow Jones News Retrieval, Information Access Co., Knight-Ridder Information, Inc., UMI. *1317*

BUSINESS AND COMMERCIAL AVIATION.
McGraw-Hill Companies (Port Chester), Four International Dr., Port Chester, NY 10573. TEL 914-939-0300. FAX 914-939-1184. URL: http://www.awgnet.com/bca.
Vendor(s): Information Access Co., Knight-Ridder Information, Inc. *60*

BUSINESS AND HEALTH.
Medical Economics Publishing Co., Inc., 5 Paragon Dr., Montvale, NJ 07645. TEL 201-358-7208. FAX 201-573-1045.
Vendor(s): Information Access Co. *3811*

BUSINESS AND SOCIETY.
Sage Publications, Inc., 2455 Teller Rd., Thousand Oaks, CA 91320. TEL 805-499-0721. FAX 805-499-0871. URL: http://www.sagepub.co.uk/journals/usdetalis/j0037.html.
Vendor(s): Information Access Co. *939*

BUSINESS AND SOCIETY REVIEW.
Business and Society Review, c/o Hanover Publishers, 200 W. 57th St., New York, NY 10019. TEL 212-399-1088. FAX 212-245-1973.
Vendor(s): Information Access Co. *939*

BUSINESS AND THE ENVIRONMENT.
Cutter Information Corp., 37 Broadway, Arlington, MA 02174-5552. TEL 617-648-8700. FAX 617-648-1950. URL: http://www.cutter.com.
Vendor(s): Information Access Co. *2909*

BUSINESS ASIA.
Economist Intelligence Unit, 111 W. 57th St., New York, NY 10019. TEL 212-554-0600. FAX 212-586-1182. URL: http://www.eiu.com.
Vendor(s): Knight-Ridder Information, Inc. *939*

BUSINESS CHINA.
Economist Intelligence Unit, 111 W. 57th St., New York, NY 10019. TEL 212-554-0600. FAX 212-586-1182. URL: http://www.eiu.com.
Vendor(s): Knight-Ridder Information, Inc., Lexis-Nexis. *1227*

BUSINESS COMMUNICATION QUARTERLY.
Association for Business Communication, c/o Dr. Robert J. Myers, Dept. of Speech Communication, Baruch College, 17 Lexington Ave., New York, NY 10010. TEL 817-565-4423. URL: http://www.cohums.ohio-state.edu/english/facstf/kol/abc/bcq.htm.
Vendor(s): Information Access Co. *1468*

BUSINESS COMMUNICATIONS REVIEW.
B C R Enterprises, Inc., 950 York Rd., Hinsdale, IL 60521-2939. TEL 312-986-1432.
Vendor(s): Information Access Co. *2032*

BUSINESS COMPUTING BRIEF.
Financial Times Telecoms & Media Publishing, Maple House, 149 Tottenham Court Rd., London W1P 9LL, England. TEL 44-171-896-2234. FAX 44-171-896-2256.
Vendor(s): Data-Star, Information Access Co., Lexis-Nexis. *1199*

BUSINESS CREDIT.
National Association of Credit Management, 8815 Centre Park Dr., Ste. 200, Columbia, MD 21045. TEL 410-740-5560. FAX 410-740-5574.
Vendor(s): Information Access Co., UMI. *1116*

BUSINESS DATELINE.
U M I Company (Louisville), 620 S. Third St., Louisville, KY 40202-2475.
Vendor(s): Dow Jones News Retrieval, Human Resources Information Network, Knight-Ridder Information, Inc., Lexis-Nexis. *939*

BUSINESS DAY.
B D F M Ltd., 4 Biermann Ave., Johannesburg 2000, South Africa. TEL 27-11-2803000. FAX 27-11-2805600. URL: http://www.bday.co.za. *939*

BUSINESS DIGEST OF DELAWARE VALLEY.
Business Digest of Philadelphia Inc., 2449 Golf Rd., Philadelphia, PA 19131. TEL 215-477-8620.
Vendor(s): Knight-Ridder Information, Inc. *1640*

BUSINESS DIRECTIONS.
Victory Press Pty. Ltd., P.O. Box 565, Victoria Park, W.A. 6100, Australia. TEL 61-9-4702353. FAX 61-9-4702363. URL: http://www.business.com.au/business. *1640*

BUSINESS EAST MIDLANDS.
Business Magazine Group, Briarwood House, St. John St., Mansfield, Notts NG18 1QH, England. TEL 0623-422522. FAX 0623-27479. *940*

BUSINESS EASTERN EUROPE.
Economist Intelligence Unit, 111 W. 57th St., New York, NY 10019. TEL 212-554-0600. FAX 212-586-1182. URL: http://www.eiu.com.
Vendor(s): Knight-Ridder Information, Inc., Lexis-Nexis. *1227*

BUSINESS ECONOMICS.
National Association of Business Economists, 1233 20th St., N.W., Ste. 505, Washington, DC 20036-2304. TEL 202-463-6223. FAX 202-463-6239. URL: http://www.nabe.com.
Vendor(s): Information Access Co., UMI. *940*

BUSINESS - EDUCATION INSIDER.
Heritage Foundation, 214 Massachusetts Ave., N.E., Washington, DC 20002. TEL 202-546-4400. FAX 202-543-9647.
Vendor(s): Lexis-Nexis. *1227*

BUSINESS EUROPA.
Central European Business Ltd., 2 Market St., Saffron Walden, Essex CB10 1H2, England. TEL 44-1799-521150. FAX 44-1799-524805.
Vendor(s): Information Access Co. *940*

BUSINESS EUROPE.
Economist Intelligence Unit, 111 W. 57th St., New York, NY 10019. TEL 212-554-0600. FAX 212-586-1182. URL: http://www.eiu.com.
Vendor(s): Knight-Ridder Information, Inc., Lexis-Nexis. *1317*

BUSINESS FIRST (BUFFALO).
Business First of New York, Inc., 472 Delaware Ave., Buffalo, NY 14202. TEL 716-882-6200. FAX 716-882-3020.
Vendor(s): Information Access Co., Knight-Ridder Information, Inc., Lexis-Nexis. *941*

BUSINESS FORUM (LOS ANGELES).
California State University, Los Angeles, School of Business & Economics, 5151 State University Dr., Los Angeles, CA 90032-8120. TEL 213-343-2806. FAX 213-343-5263.
Vendor(s): Information Access Co., UMI. *941*

BUSINESS FOUNDATION BOOK. GENERAL TRADE INDEX & BUSINESS GUIDE.
Business Foundation Co. Ltd., Ul. Krucza 38-42, 00-512 Warsaw, Poland. TEL 48-22-219993. FAX 48-22-219761. *1657*

BUSINESS HISTORY.
Frank Cass, Newbury House, 890-900 Eastern Ave., Newbury Park, Ilford, Essex 1G2 7HH, England. TEL 44-181-599-8866. FAX 44-181-599-0984. URL: http://www.frankcass.com/jnls/bh.htm.
Vendor(s): Information Access Co. *941*

BUSINESS HISTORY REVIEW.
Harvard Business School Publishing, 60 Harvard Way, Boston, MA 02163. TEL 617-495-6154. FAX 617-496-5985.
Vendor(s): Information Access Co., Knight-Ridder Information, Inc., UMI. *941*

BUSINESS HOTLINE ONLINE.
URL: http://www.bizhotline.com.
Available only online. *1640*

BUSINESS IN BROWARD.
Lauderdale Publishing, 1301 Andrews Ave., P.O. Box 7375, Ft. Lauderdale, FL 33316. TEL 954-763-3338. FAX 954-763-4481.
Vendor(s): Lexis-Nexis, UMI. *1640*

BUSINESS INDEX.
Information Access Company, 362 Lakeside Dr., Foster City, CA 94404. TEL 415-378-5200. FAX 415-378-5369.
Vendor(s): Knight-Ridder Information, Inc. (File no.148), Lexis-Nexis, Ovid Technologies, Inc. *1026*

BUSINESS INSURANCE.
Crain Communications, Inc. (Chicago), 740 Rush St., Chicago, IL 60611. TEL 312-649-5398. FAX 312-280-3174.
Vendor(s): Information Access Co., Lexis-Nexis. *3811*

THE BUSINESS JOURNAL (LIMA).
Box 388, Lima, OH 45802-0388. TEL 419-999-4762. FAX 419-991-6839.
Vendor(s): Information Access Co. *1209*

BUSINESS JOURNAL (PHOENIX).
Phoenix Business Journal, Inc., 2910 N. Central Ave., Phoenix, AZ 85012. TEL 602-230-8400. FAX 602-230-0955.
Vendor(s): Information Access Co., Knight-Ridder Information, Inc. *942*

BUSINESS JOURNAL (PORTLAND).
American City Business Journals, Inc. (Portland), Box 14490, Portland, OR 97214. TEL 503-274-8733. FAX 503-227-2650.
Vendor(s): Information Access Co. *1227*

BUSINESS JOURNAL OF UPPER EAST TENNESSEE AND SOUTHWEST VIRGINIA.
Business Publishers Company, Box 643, Tri-Port Complex, 2333-D Hwy. 75, Blountville, TN 37617. TEL 615-323-7111. FAX 615-323-1479.
Vendor(s): UMI. *942*

BUSINESS JOURNAL SERVING GREATER MILWAUKEE.
Business Journal of Milwaukee Inc., 600 W. Virginia St., Ste. 500, Milwaukee, WI 53204-1551. TEL 414-278-7788. FAX 414-278-7028. URL: http://www.amcity.com/milwaukee.
Vendor(s): Information Access Co., UMI. *942*

BUSINESS KOREA.
Korea Trade Promotion Corp., Won Chang Bldg., 3rd. Fl., 26-3 Yoido-dong, Yongdung po-ku, Seoul 150-602, S. Korea. TEL 02-234-4010. FAX 02-253-4040.
Vendor(s): UMI. *942*

BUSINESS LATIN AMERICA.
Economist Intelligence Unit, 111 W. 57th St., New York, NY 10019. TEL 212-554-0600. FAX 212-586-1182. URL: http://www.eiu.com/2x605brid/catalog/country/samer.html.
Vendor(s): Knight-Ridder Information, Inc., Lexis-Nexis. *1227*

BUSINESS LAW EUROPE.
Financial Times Professional Publishing, Maple House, 149 Tottenham Court Rd., London W1P 9LL, England. TEL 44-171-896-2222. FAX 44-171-896-2276.
Vendor(s): Data-Star, Information Access Co., Lexis-Nexis. *4075*

BUSINESS LAWYER.
American Bar Association, Business Law Section, 750 N. Lake Shore Dr., Chicago, IL 60611. TEL 312-988-5588. URL: http://www.abanet.org.
Vendor(s): Information Access Co., Lexis-Nexis (BUSLAW), West Group (BUSLAW). *4076*

BUSINESS LIFE MAGAZINE.
4101-A Piedmont Pkwy., Greensboro, NC 27410. TEL 910-812-8801. FAX 910-812-8832. URL: http://www.spyder.net/bizlife. *32*

BUSINESS MAILERS REVIEW.
Pasha Publications Inc., 1616 N. Ft. Myer Dr., Ste. 1000, Arlington, VA 22209-3107. TEL 703-816-8640. FAX 703-528-4926.
Vendor(s): Information Access Co. *2019*

BUSINESS MARKETING.
Crain Communications, Inc. (Chicago), 740 Rush St., Chicago, IL 60611-2590. TEL 312-649-5260. FAX 312-649-5228. URL: http://www.crain.co.uk/crain/busmar.html.
Vendor(s): Information Access Co. *1517*

BUSINESS MEXICO.
American Chamber of Commerce of Mexico, A.C., Lucerna 78, Col. Juarez, Del. Cuauhtemoc, 0600 Mexico DF, Mexico. TEL 52-5-724-3800. FAX 52-5-703-2911.
Vendor(s): Lexis-Nexis, UMI. *1180*

BUSINESS NORTH CAROLINA.
News and Observer Publishing Co., 5435 77 Center Dr., Ste. 50, Charlotte, NC 28217-0711. TEL 704-523-6987. FAX 704-523-4211.
Vendor(s): Information Access Co., Knight-Ridder Information, Inc., Lexis-Nexis, UMI. *1640*

BUSINESS NORTH EAST.
Business Magazine Group, Briarwood House, St. John St., Mansfield, Notts NG18 1QH, England. TEL 0642-232882. FAX 0623-232899. *942*

BUSINESS OPPORTUNITIES HANDBOOK.
Enterprise Magazines, Inc., 1020 N. Broadway, Ste. 111, Milwaukee, WI 53202. TEL 414-272-9977. FAX 414-272-9973. URL: http://www.ezines.com. *1640*

BUSINESS ORGANIZATIONS, AGENCIES, AND PUBLICATIONS DIRECTORY.
Gale Research, 835 Penobscot Bldg., 645 Griswold St., Detroit, MI 48226-4094. TEL 313-961-2242. FAX 800-414-5043. *1658*

BUSINESS PEOPLE MAGAZINE.
McCaine Davies Communications Ltd., 232 Henderson Hwy., Winnipeg, MB R2L 1L9, Canada. TEL 204-982-4000. FAX 204-982-4001. Vendor(s): UMI. *1209*

BUSINESS PERIODICALS INDEX.
H.W. Wilson Co., 950 University Ave., Bronx, NY 10452. TEL 718-588-8400. FAX 718-590-1617. Vendor(s): Knight-Ridder Information, Inc., OCLC, Ovid Technologies, Inc., Wilsonline (File BPI). *1027*

BUSINESS PERSPECTIVES.
University of Memphis, Bureau of Business & Economic Research, Memphis, TN 38152. TEL 901-678-2281. URL: http://www.peopl.memphis.edu/~bberlib? Vendor(s): Information Access Co. *943*

BUSINESS POWER MAGAZINE.
Decision Media Group & Publishing Co., Transcend Visual Communications, Inc., Box 512, Appleton, WI 54912. URL: http://www.athenet.net/~dmgedit/bpm.html. Available only online. *943*

BUSINESS QUARTERLY.
Monash University, URL: http://www.monash.edu.au/pubs/busquart/index.html. Available only online. *943*

BUSINESS QUARTERLY.
University of Western Ontario, Western Business School, c/o Angela Smith, London, ON N6A 3K7, Canada. TEL 519-661-3309. FAX 519-661-3838. Vendor(s): Information Access Co., Knight-Ridder Information, Inc., UMI. *1468*

BUSINESS RATIO PLUS: BUS & COACH OPERATORS.
I C C Business Publications Ltd., Field House, 72 Oldfield Rd., Hampton, Middlesex TW12 2HQ, England. TEL 44-181-783-0922. FAX 44-181-783-1940. *7025*

BUSINESS TECH.
URL: http://businesstech.com. Available only online. *2131*

BUSINESS TIMES.
Choice Media, 315 Peck St., Box 580, New Haven, CT 06513-0580. TEL 203-782-1420. FAX 203-782-3793. Vendor(s): UMI. *1228*

BUSINESS TRAVEL NEWS.
Miller Freeman Inc. (New York), One Penn Plaza, New York, NY 10119. FAX 847-647-5972. Vendor(s): Data-Star, Information Access Co., Knight-Ridder Information, Inc., NewsNet (TR08). *7189*

BUSINESS WEEK.
McGraw-Hill Companies, 1221 Ave. of the Americas, 39th Fl., New York, NY 10020. TEL 212-512-2000. URL: http://www.businessweek.com/ Vendor(s): Dow Jones News Retrieval, Knight-Ridder Information, Inc. (File no.624/McGRAW-HILL PUBLICATIONS ONLINE), Lexis-Nexis, NewsNet (GB55). *944*

BUSINESS WEST MIDLANDS.
Business Magazine Group, Briarwood House, St. John St., Mansfield, Notts NG18 1QH, England. TEL 021-308-0077. FAX 021-308-0385. *944*

THE BUSINESS WHO'S WHO OF AUSTRALIA.
Dun & Bradstreet Marketing Pty. Ltd., 19 Havilah St., Chatswood, N.S.W. 2067, Australia. TEL 61-2-9352700. FAX 61-2-9352777. URL: http://www.dbmarketing.com.au. Vendor(s): AUSINET. *1658*

BUSINESS WORLD.
BusinessWorld Publishing Corp., No. 95 Balete Drive Extension, New Manila, Quezon City 1112, Philippines. TEL 632-7270091. FAX 632-7276014. *1580*

BUYOUTS NEWSLETTER.
Securities Data Publishing, 40 W. 57th St., 11th Fl., New York, NY 10019. TEL 212-765-5311. FAX 212-765-6123. Vendor(s): Data-Star, Information Access Co., Knight-Ridder Information, Inc. *944*

BUZZ (LOS ANGELES).
Buzz, Inc., 11835 W. Olympic Blvd., Ste. 450, Los Angeles, CA 90064. TEL 310-473-2721. FAX 310-473-2876. *4326*

BYTE.
McGraw-Hill Companies, Byte Publications, One Phoenix Mill Ln., Peterborough, NH 03458. TEL 617-860-6336. FAX 617-860-6522. URL: http://www.byte.com. Vendor(s): Dow Jones News Retrieval, Knight-Ridder Information, Inc. (File no.624/McGRAW-HILL PUBLICATIONS ONLINE), Lexis-Nexis, NewsNet (EC34). *2154*

B2B E-NEWSLETTER.
URL: http://www.DoyleMarketing.com. Available only online. *944*

C A - A CANCER JOURNAL FOR CLINICIANS.
Lippincott - Raven Publishers, 227 E. Washington Sq., Philadelphia, PA 19106. TEL 215-238-4200. URL: http://www.ca-journal.org. Vendor(s): Information Access Co. *4972*

C A D - C A M UPDATE.
Worldwide Videotex, Box 3273, Boynton Beach, FL 33424-3273. TEL 407-738-2276. Vendor(s): Information Access Co., NewsNet (MG15). *2120*

C A U S E. PROCEEDINGS OF NATIONAL CONFERENCE.
C A U S E, 4840 Pearl E. Circle, Ste. 302E, Boulder, CO 80301. TEL 303-449-4430. FAX 303-440-0461. URL: http://www.cause.org/conference/cause96/c96.html. *2515*

C B A RECORD.
Chicago Bar Association, 321 S. Plymouth Ct., Chicago, IL 60604-3997. TEL 312-554-2000. FAX 312-554-2054. Vendor(s): West Group. *3924*

C - C PLUS PLUS.
Miller Freeman, Inc. (Lawrence), 1601 W. 23rd St., Ste. 200, Lawrence, KS 66046. TEL 913-841-1631. FAX 913-841-2624. URL: http://www.cuj.com. Vendor(s): Information Access Co. *2142*

C D A INVESTNET INSIDERS' CHRONICLE.
C D A Investment Technologies, Inc., 1355 Piccard Dr., Rockville, MD 20850. FAX 301-590-1329. Vendor(s): Information Access Co. *1378*

C D - C I N.
Comissao Nacional de Energia Nuclear, Centro de Informacoes Nucleares, Rua General Severiano 90, Botafogo, 22294-900 Rio de Janeiro RJ, Brazil. TEL 55-21-5462440. FAX 55-21-5462447. *2682*

C D - CIBEPAT.
Ministerio de Industria y Energia, Oficina Espanola de Patentes y Marcas, Panama 1, 28071 Madrid, Spain. TEL 34-1-3495300. FAX 34-1-4572280. *5582*

C D COMPUTING NEWS.
Worldwide Videotex, Box 3273, Boynton Beach, FL 33424-3273. TEL 407-738-2276. Vendor(s): Information Access Co., Knight-Ridder Information, Inc., NewsNet (EC67). *2126*

C D - R O M DATABASES.
Worldwide Videotex, Box 3273, Boynton Beach, FL 33424-3273. TEL 407-738-2276. Vendor(s): Information Access Co., Knight-Ridder Information, Inc., NewsNet (EC71). *4230*

C D - R O M PROFESSIONAL.
Online, Inc., 462 Danbury Rd., Wilton, CT 06897. TEL 203-761-1466. FAX 203-761-1444. Vendor(s): Information Access Co., UMI. *4230*

C D - R O M WORLD.
P C World Communications, Inc., 501 Second St., Ste. 600, San Francisco, CA 94107. TEL 415-243-0500. FAX 415-442-1891. Vendor(s): Knight-Ridder Information, Inc., NewsNet. *4168*

C D R REPORTS.
Council for Disability Rights, 176 W. Adams St., No. 1830, Chicago, IL 60603. TEL 312-444-9484. FAX 312-444-1977. URL: http://disabilityrights.org. *5988*

C E C COMMUNICATIONS.
Gordon and Breach - Harwood Academic, Amsteldisk 166, 1st Fl., 1079 LH Amsterdam, Netherlands. URL: http://www.gbhap.com/CEC__Communications/. *2747*

C E R F NET NEWS.
California Education and Research Federation Network, Box 85608, San Diego, CA 92186-9784. TEL 619-534-5087. *2131*

C F O.
C F O Publishing Corporation, 253 Summer St., Boston, MA 02210. TEL 617-345-9700. FAX 617-951-4090. URL: http://www.cfonet.com. Vendor(s): UMI. *945*

C F O ALERT (WEEKLY).
American Banker Newsletters, One State Street Plaza, 26th Fl., New York, NY 10004-1505. TEL 212-803-8300. FAX 212-843-9620. Vendor(s): Data-Star, Knight-Ridder Information, Inc., Lexis-Nexis, NewsNet. *1117*

C I N D A.
International Atomic Energy Agency, Wagramerstr. 5, P.O. Box 100, A-1400 Vienna, Austria. TEL 43-1-2060-22529. FAX 43-1-2060-29302. *5834*

C I S INDEX TO PUBLICATIONS OF THE UNITED STATES CONGRESS.
Congressional Information Service, Inc., A member of the LEXIS-NEXIS family, 4520 East-West Hwy., Bethesda, MD 20814. TEL 301-654-1550. FAX 301-654-4033. URL: http://www.cispubs.com. Vendor(s): Lexis-Nexis. *6203*

C I S LEGISLATIVE HISTORIES ANNUAL.
Congressional Information Service, Inc., A member of the LEXIS-NEXIS family, 4520 East-West Hwy., Bethesda, MD 20814-3389. TEL 301-654-1550. FAX 301-654-4033. URL: http://www.cispubs.com. Vendor(s): Lexis-Nexis. *3924*

C L A S E.
Universidad Nacional Autonoma de Mexico, Direccion General de Bibliotecas, Apdo. Postal 70-392, C.P. 04510 Mexico, D.F., Mexico. TEL 52-5-6223958. FAX 52-5-6162557. *6649*

C M.
Sara Fiedelholtz, Ed. & Pub., 23 E. 10th St., No. 706, New York, NY 10003. TEL 212-529-1519. FAX 212-979-8772. *1943*

C M A J.
Canadian Medical Association, P.O. Box 8650, Ottawa, ON K1G 0G8, Canada. TEL 613-731-9331. FAX 613-523-0937. URL: http://www.cma.ca/journals/cmaj. Vendor(s): Ovid Technologies, Inc. *4650*

C M A MAGAZINE.
Society of Management Accountants of Canada, 120 King St. W., Box 176 M.P.O., Hamilton, ON L8N 3C3, Canada. TEL 905-525-4100. FAX 905-525-4533. Vendor(s): Information Access Co. *1085*

C M MAGAZINE.
Manitoba Library Association, 208-100 Arthur St., Winnipeg, MB R3B 1H3, Canada. TEL 204-943-4567. URL: http://www.mbnet.mb.ca/cm. Available only online. *6267*

C N S: THE JOURNAL FOR ADVANCED NURSING PRACTICE.
Williams & Wilkins, 351 W. Camden St., Baltimore, MD 21201-2436. TEL 410-528-4000. FAX 410-528-4312. URL: http://www.wwilkins.com. Vendor(s): Ovid Technologies, Inc. *4930*

C O M S A T TECHNICAL REVIEW.
COMSAT Corporation, 22300 COMSAT Dr., Clarksburg, MD 20871-9471. TEL 301-428-4512. FAX 301-428-7747. URL: http:www.comsat.com. *1983*

C O N S E R MICROFICHE.
National Library of Canada, Canadiana Editorial Division, 395 Wellington St., Ottawa, ON K1A 0N4, Canada. TEL 819-994-6912. FAX 819-953-0291. *541*

C O O L DOCTOR - COMPUTING ONLINE DOCTOR.
Kissware Works!, URL: http://kww.com/cool/ Available only online. *2074*

C P A CLIENT BULLETIN.
American Institute of Certified Public Accountants, Harborside Financial Ctr., 201 Plaza Three, Jersey City, NJ 07311-3881. TEL 201-938-3201. FAX 201-938-3329. URL: http://www.aicpa.org. Vendor(s): UMI. *1086*

C P A LETTER.
American Institute of Certified Public Accountants, Public Relations - Communications, Harborside Financial Center, 201 Plaza Three, Jersey City, NJ 07311-9801. TEL 201-938-3796. FAX 800-329-1112. URL: http://www.aicpa.org/pubs/cpaltr/index.htm.
Vendor(s): UMI. *1086*

C PLUS PLUS PROGRAMMING LANGUAGE NEWSLETTER.
URL: http://www.rmii.com/~glenm. Available only online. *2142*

C Q RESEARCHER.
Congressional Quarterly Inc., 1414 22nd St., N.W., Washington, DC 20037. FAX 202-728-1863. Vendor(s): Information Access Co. *5896*

C Q'S WASHINGTON ALERT.
Congressional Quarterly Inc., 1414 22nd St., N.W., Washington, DC 20037. FAX 202-728-1863. *6211*

C R B FUTURES MARKET SERVICE.
Bridge Publishing, 30 S. Wacker Dr., Ste. 1810, Chicago, IL 60606. TEL 312-454-1801. FAX 312-454-0239. *1378*

C S A NEUROSCIENCES ABSTRACTS.
Cambridge Scientific Abstracts, 7200 Wisconsin Ave., 6th Fl., Bethesda, MD 20814. TEL 301-961-6750. FAX 301-961-6720. URL: http://www.csa.com.
Vendor(s): Knight-Ridder Information, Inc. (File no.76/LIFE SCIENCES COLLECTION), STN International (LIFESCI). *4766*

C S E L T INFOTEL.
C S E L T - Centro Studi e Laboratori Telecomunicazioni S.p.A., Via Reiss Romoli, 274, 10148 Turin, Italy. TEL 39-11-2285111. FAX 39-11-2285095. URL: http://www.cselt.stet.it. *2010*

C S S P NEWS.
Council of Scientific Society Presidents, 1155 16th St., N.W., Washington, DC 20036. TEL 202-872-4452. FAX 202-872-4079. *6517*

C S T COMMUNICATIONS.
Gordon and Breach - Harwood Academic, Amsteldisk 166, 1st Fl., 1079 LH Amsterdam, Netherlands. URL: http://www.gbhap.com/CST_Communications/. *1781*

C T D NEWS.
Center for Workplace Health, Box 980, Horsham, PA 19044-0980. TEL 610-896-2770. FAX 610-896-2762.
Vendor(s): Information Access Co. *5487*

C THEORY.
Concordia University, 1455 de Maisonneuve West, Montreal, PQ H3G 1M8, Canada. TEL 514-282-9298. URL: http://www.ctheory.com. *5897*

C W R L E-JOURNAL: THE ELECTRONIC JOURNAL FOR COMPUTER WRITING, RHETORIC AND LITERATURE.
University of Texas at Austin, Computer Writing and Research Laboratories, TEL 512-471-6109. URL: http://www.cwrl.utexas.edu/~cwrl/index.html. Available only online. *4247*

C 4 I NEWS.
Phillips Business Information, Inc., 1201 Seven Locks Rd., Potomac, MD 20854. TEL 301-424-3338. FAX 301-309-3847.
Vendor(s): Information Access Co. *5262*

CAB INTERNATIONAL. BUREAU OF NUTRITION. ANNOTATED BIBLIOGRAPHIES.
CAB International, Bureau of Nutrition, Wallingford, Oxon. OX10 8DE, England. TEL 44-1491-832111. FAX 44-1491-833508.
Vendor(s): CISTI, DIMDI, European Space Agency, Knight-Ridder Information, Inc., Ovid Technologies, Inc. *5484*

CABLE - TELCO REPORT.
Telecommunications Reports, 1333 H St., N.W., Ste. 100-E, Washington, DC 20005. FAX 202-842-3023. URL: http://www.tr.com.
Vendor(s): Information Access Co., NewsNet (TE106). *2046*

CABLEFAX.
Phillips Business Information, Inc., 1201 Seven Locks Rd., Potomac, MD 20854-1053. TEL 301-424-3338. FAX 301-309-3847.
Vendor(s): Information Access Co. *2046*

CADALYST.
Advanstar Communications, Inc., CADalyst, 859 Willamette St., Eugene, OR 97401. TEL 503-343-1200. FAX 503-686-5732. URL: http://www.cadonline.com.
Vendor(s): Information Access Co. *2120*

CADENCE UNIVERSE PERFORMANCE REPORT.
C D A - Cadence, 1355 Piccard Dr., Rockville, MD 20850. TEL 301-975-9600. FAX 301-590-1350. *1378*

CAERT-THRESOOR.
c/o Drs. E.O. van Keulen, Rijkmuseum 'Nederlands Scheepvaart Museum', Kattenburgerplein 1, 1018 KK Amsterdam, Netherlands. URL: http://kartoserver.frw.ruu.nl/html/staff/krogt/ct_eng.htm. *3397*

CAFE COMPENDIUM.
Box 542327, Houston, TX 77254-2327. URL: http://www.neosoft.com/~fortuna/intro.htm. *4326*

CAFE MAGAZINE.
Box 173, Cambridge CB5 8YB, England. URL: http://www.gold.net/users/fy15. *3294*

CAHIERS D'ONCOLOGIE.
Springer-Verlag France, 26 rue des Carmes, 75005 Paris, France. TEL 33-1-44-41-15-80. FAX 33-1-43-54-49-08. URL: http://science.springer.de. *4972*

CAL LAW.
URL: http://www.callaw.com/ Available only online. *3925*

CALCIFIED TISSUE INTERNATIONAL.
Springer-Verlag, Medical Journals, 175 Fifth Ave., New York, NY 10010. TEL 212-460-1500. FAX 212-473-6272. URL: http://www.springer-ny.com. *4883*

CALCIUM AND CALCIFIED TISSUE ABSTRACTS.
Cambridge Scientific Abstracts, 7200 Wisconsin Ave., 6th Fl., Bethesda, MD 20814. TEL 301-961-6750. FAX 301-961-6720. URL: http://www.csa.com.
Vendor(s): Knight-Ridder Information, Inc. (File no.76/LIFE SCIENCES COLLECTION), STN International (LIFESCI). *638*

CALCULUS OF VARIATIONS AND PARTIAL DIFFERENTIAL EQUATIONS.
Springer-Verlag, Heidelberger Platz 3, 14197 Berlin, Germany. TEL 49-30-82787-0. FAX 49-30-82787448. URL: http://link.springer.de. *4565*

CALGARY CITYSCOPE MAGAZINE.
I E Publication, Inc., 1324 11th Ave., S.W., No. 300, Calgary, Alta. T3C 0M6, Canada. TEL 403-228-7020. FAX 403-228-7193. *5325*

CALGARY HERALD.
215 16th St. S.E., Calgary, AB T2P 0W8, Canada. TEL 403-235-7400. FAX 403-235-7379. URL: http://www.calgaryherlad.com.
Vendor(s): Lexis-Nexis, Southam Electronic Publishing. *3259*

CALIFORNIA AGRICULTURE.
University of California, Division of Agriculture and Natural Resources, 300 Lakeside Dr., 6th Fl., Oakland, CA 94612-3560. TEL 510-987-0044. URL: http://www.ucop.edu/anrhome/cal-ag/about_ca.html. *106*

CALIFORNIA BUSINESS.
1777 Rollins Rd., Burlingame, CA 95010. TEL 415-776-1472. FAX 415-776-9933.
Vendor(s): Information Access Co., Knight-Ridder Information, Inc. *1229*

CALIFORNIA BUSINESS DIRECTORY.
American Business Directories, 5711 S. 86th Circle, Box 27347, Omaha, NE 68127. TEL 402-593-4600. FAX 402-331-5481. *1658*

CALIFORNIA CELEBRATIONS.
Division of Tourism, Box 1499, Sacramento, CA 95812-1499. TEL 800-862-2543. FAX 916-322-3402. *7190*

CALIFORNIA CONSTRUCTION NEWS COVERING EAST BAY.
McGraw-Hill Companies, Princeton Rd. S-2, Box 689, Hightstown, NJ 08520-0689. *874*

CALIFORNIA CONSTRUCTION NEWS COVERING GOLD COAST.
McGraw-Hill Companies, Princeton Rd. S-2, Box 689, Hightstown, NJ 08520-0689. *874*

CALIFORNIA CONSTRUCTION NEWS COVERING INLAND EMPIRE.
McGraw-Hill Companies, Princeton Rd. S-2, Box 689, Hightstown, NJ 08520-0689. *874*

CALIFORNIA CONSTRUCTION NEWS COVERING LOS ANGELES.
McGraw-Hill Companies, Princeton Rd. S-2, Box 689, Hightstown, NJ 08520-0689. *874*

CALIFORNIA CONSTRUCTION NEWS COVERING NORTH COAST.
McGraw-Hill Companies, Princeton Rd. S-2, Box 689, Hightstown, NJ 08520-0689. *874*

CALIFORNIA CONSTRUCTION NEWS COVERING ORANGE COUNTY.
McGraw-Hill Companies, Princeton Rd. S-2, Box 689, Hightstown, NJ 08520-0689. *874*

CALIFORNIA CONSTRUCTION NEWS COVERING SAN DIEGO.
McGraw-Hill Companies, Princeton Rd. S-2, Box 689, Hightstown, NJ 08520-0689. *874*

CALIFORNIA CONSTRUCTION NEWS COVERING SAN FRANCISCO.
McGraw-Hill Companies, Princeton Rd. S-2, Box 689, Hightstown, NJ 08520-0689. *874*

CALIFORNIA CONSTRUCTION NEWS COVERING SOUTH BAY.
McGraw-Hill Companies, Princeton Rd. S-2, Box 689, Hightstown, NJ 08520-0689. *874*

CALIFORNIA LABOR MARKET BULLETIN.
Employment Development Department, Labor Market Information Division, 7000 Franklin Blvd., No. 1100, Sacramento, CA 95823. TEL 916-262-2162. FAX 916-262-2443. URL: http://www.calmis.cahwnet.gov. *1229*

CALIFORNIA LAW REVIEW.
University of California Press, Journals Division, 2120 Berkeley Way, No. 5812, Berkeley, CA 94720-5812. TEL 510-643-7154. FAX 510-642-9917. URL: http://law164.berkeley.edu/'clr/
Vendor(s): Information Access Co. *3926*

CALIFORNIA MANAGEMENT REVIEW.
University of California at Berkeley, S549 Haas School of Business, Ste. 1900, Berkeley, CA 94720-1900. TEL 510-642-7159. FAX 510-642-1318. URL: http://haas.berkeley.edu/news/cmr.html.
Vendor(s): Information Access Co., UMI. *1469*

CALIFORNIA PLANNING AND DEVELOPMENT REPORT.
Torf Fulton Associates, 1275 Sunnycrest Ave., Ventura, CA 93003-1212. TEL 805-642-7838.
Vendor(s): Information Access Co., NewsNet (EV23). *6167*

CALIFORNIA PUBLIC FINANCE.
American Banker - Bond Buyer, Newsletter Division One State St. Plaza, New York, NY 10004-1549. TEL 800-733-4371. FAX 212-943-2224.
Vendor(s): Information Access Co., NewsNet (Fl65). *1602*

CALIFORNIA STATE CONTRACTS REGISTER.
Department of General Services, Office of Small and Minority Business, 1531 I St., 2nd Fl., Sacramento, CA 95814-2016. TEL 916-323-5478. FAX 916-442-7855. URL: http://www.dgs.ca.gov/osmb. *945*

CALLALOO.
Johns Hopkins University Press, Journals Publishing Division, 2715 N. Charles St., Baltimore, MD 21218. TEL 410-515-6987. FAX 410-516-6968. URL: http://muse.jhu.edu; http://www.press.jhu.edu/journals/callaloo/
Vendor(s): Information Access Co. *4385*

CAMPAIGN.
Haymarket Publishing Ltd., 174 Hammersmith Rd., London W6 7JP, England. TEL 44-171-413-4328. FAX 44-171-413-4013.
Vendor(s): Information Access Co., MediaStream. *33*

CAMPAIGNS AND ELECTIONS.
Campaigns and Elections, 1511 K St., N.W., Ste. 1020, Washington, DC 20005. TEL 202-638-7788.
Vendor(s): Information Access Co., UMI. *5898*

CAMPBELL LAW REVIEW.
Campbell University, Box 1165, Buies Creek, NC 27506. TEL 910-893-1799. FAX 910-893-1729.
Vendor(s): West Group. *3927*

CAMPING MAGAZINE.
American Camping Association, Inc., 5000 State Rd. 67 N., Martinsville, IN 46151-7902. TEL 317-342-8456.
Vendor(s): Information Access Co. *1840*

CAMPUS CRIME.
Business Publishers, Inc., 951 Pershing Dr., Silver Spring, MD 20910-4464. TEL 301-587-6300. FAX 301-585-9075.
Vendor(s): NewsNet. *2285*

CAMPUS LIFE.
Christianity Today, Inc., 465 Gundersen Dr., Carol Stream, IL 60188. TEL 630-260-6200. FAX 630-260-0114. URL: http://www.christianity.net/campuslife. *1944*

CAMPUS REPORT.
Accuracy in Academia, Inc., 4455 Connecticut Ave., N.W., Ste. 330, Washington, DC 20008. TEL 202-364-4401. FAX 202-364-4098. URL: http://take.aim.org/. *2534*

CANADA. STATISTICS CANADA. CONSUMER PRICES AND PRICE INDEXES.
Statistics Canada, Operations and Integration Division, Circulation Management, Jean Talon Bldg., 2-C12, Tunney's Pasture, Ottawa, ON K1A 0T6, Canada. TEL 613-951-7277. FAX 613-951-1584. URL: http://statcan.ca:80/cgi-bin/downpub/downpub.cgi. *1027*

CANADA. STATISTICS CANADA. INFOMAT.
Statistics Canada, Operations and Integration Division, Circulation Management, Jean Talon Bldg., 2-C12, Tunney's Pasture, Ottawa, ON K1A 0T6, Canada. TEL 613-951-7277. FAX 613-951-1584. URL: http://statcan.ca:80/cgi-bin/downpub/downpub.cgi. *6903*

CANADA. STATISTICS CANADA. PASSENGER BUS AND URBAN TRANSIT STATISTICS.
Statistics Canada, Operations and Integration Division, Circulation Management, Jean Talon Bldg., 2-C12, Tunney's Pasture, Ottawa, ON K1A 0T6, Canada. TEL 613-951-7277. FAX 613-951-1584. URL: http://statcan.ca:80/cgi-bin/downpub/downpub.cgi. *7049*

CANADA STOCKWATCH. EASTERN EDITION.
Canjex Publishing, 700 W. Georgia St., Box 10371, Vancouver, BC V7Y 1J6, Canada. TEL 604-687-1500. FAX 604-687-2304. *1378*

CANADA STOCKWATCH. WESTERN EDITION.
Canjex Publishing, 700 W. Georgia St., Box 10371, Vancouver, BC V7Y 1J6, Canada. TEL 604-687-1500. FAX 604-687-2304. *1378*

CANADA - UNITED STATES LAW JOURNAL.
Case Western Reserve University, School of Law, 11075 East Blvd., Cleveland, OH 44106-7148. TEL 216-368-3304. FAX 216-368-3310.
Vendor(s): Lexis-Nexis. *4108*

CANADIAN ACTORS' ANECDOTES.
URL: http://web.idirect.com/~canuck/canact.html.
Available only online. *7003*

CANADIAN BANKER.
Canadian Bankers Association, P.O. Box 348, Commerce Ct. W., Ste. 3000, 199 Bay St., Toronto, ON M5L 1G2, Canada. TEL 416-362-6092. FAX 416-362-5658.
Vendor(s): Information Access Co., UMI. *1118*

CANADIAN BUSINESS.
Canadian Business Media, 777 Bay St., 5th Fl., Toronto, ON M5W 1A7, Canada. TEL 416-596-5100. FAX 416-596-5152.
Vendor(s): Information Access Co. *946*

CANADIAN CHEMICAL NEWS.
Chemcan Publishers Limited, 130 Slater St., Ste. 550, Ottawa, ON K1P 6E2, Canada. TEL 613-232-6252. FAX 613-232-5862.
Vendor(s): Information Access Co. *1741*

CANADIAN CRIMINAL CASES.
Canada Law Book Inc., 240 Edward St., Aurora, ON L4G 3S9, Canada. TEL 905-841-6472. FAX 905-841-6472. *4088*

CANADIAN CYCLIST.
7 Barker St., Paris, ON N3L 2H4, Canada.
TEL 519-442-7905. FAX 514-442-5259. URL: http://www.canadiancyclist.com. *6825*

CANADIAN DIMENSION.
Dimension Publishing Inc., 91 Albert St., Rm. 2-B, Winnipeg, MB R3B 1G5, Canada. TEL 204-957-1519. FAX 204-943-4617. URL: http://www.canadiandimension.mb.ca/cd/index.htm.
Vendor(s): Information Access Co. *5898*

CANADIAN DIRECTORY OF HEALTH CARE CONFERENCES.
Canadian Nurses Association, 50 Driveway, Ottawa, ON K2P 1E2, Canada. TEL 613-237-2133. FAX 613-237-3520. URL: http://www.cna-nurses.ca.
Available only online. *5168*

CANADIAN EDUCATION INDEX.
Micromedia Ltd., 20 Victoria St., Toronto, ON M5C 2N8, Canada. TEL 416-362-5211. FAX 416-362-6161. *2497*

CANADIAN FEDERAL GOVERNMENT HANDBOOK.
Globe Information Services, 444 Front St. W., Toronto, ON M5V 2S9, Canada. TEL 416-585-5250. FAX 416-585-5249. *572*

CANADIAN FEDERATION OF BIOLOGICAL SOCIETIES. NEWSLETTER.
Canadian Federation of Biological Societies, 104 - 1750 Courtwood Cres., Ottawa, ON K2C 2B5, Canada. TEL 613-225-8889. FAX 613-225-9621. URL: http://www.fermentas.com/cfbs. *595*

CANADIAN FOREIGN POLICY.
Professional Association of Foreign Service Officers, 45 Rideau St., Ste. 600, Ottawa, ON K1N 5B6, Canada. TEL 613-241-4396. FAX 613-241-5911. URL: http://www.carleton.ca/npsia/cfpj. *6007*

CANADIAN FOREIGN RELATIONS.
Department of External Affairs, Domestic Information Division, 125 Sussex Dr., Ottawa, ON K1A 0G2, Canada. TEL 613-996-9134.
Vendor(s): QL Systems Ltd. *6007*

CANADIAN FOREST INDUSTRIES.
J C F T Forest Communications, 1 rue Pacifique, Ste-Anne-de-Bellevue, PQ H9X 1C5, Canada. TEL 514-457-2211.
Vendor(s): Southam Electronic Publishing. *3170*

CANADIAN GEOGRAPHIC.
Canadian Geographical Enterprises, 39 McArthur Ave., Vanier, ON K1L 8L7, Canada. TEL 613-745-4629. FAX 613-744-0947. URL: http://www.cangeo.ca.
Vendor(s): Information Access Co., UMI. *3259*

CANADIAN HISTORICAL REVIEW.
University of Toronto Press, Journals Department, 5201 Dufferin St., Downsview, ON M3H 5T8, Canada. TEL 416-667-7710. FAX 416-667-7881.
Vendor(s): Information Access Co. *3491*

CANADIAN HIV - AIDS POLICY & LAW NEWSLETTER.
Canadian HIV - AIDS Legal Network, 4007 de Mentana, Montreal, PQ H2L 3R9, Canada. TEL 514-526-1796. FAX 514-526-5543. *4833*

CANADIAN INDEX.
Micromedia Ltd., 20 Victoria St., Toronto, ON M5C 2N8, Canada. TEL 416-362-5211. FAX 416-362-6161.
Vendor(s): Data-Star, IST-INFORMATHEQUE, Inc., Knight-Ridder Information, Inc. (File no.262), QL Systems Ltd. *1029*

CANADIAN INTERNATIONAL MERCHANDISE TRADE.
Statistics Canada, Operations and Integration Division, Circulation Management, Jean Talon Bldg., 2-C12, Tunney's Pasture, Ottawa, ON K1A 0T6, Canada. TEL 613-951-7277. FAX 613-951-1584. URL: http://statcan.ca:80/cgi-bin/downpub/downpub.cgi. *1029*

CANADIAN JOURNAL OF ADMINISTRATIVE SCIENCES.
Administrative Sciences Association of Canada, Faculty of Commerce and Administration, Concordia University, 1455 de Maisonneuve Blvd. W., Montreal, QC H3G 1M8, Canada. TEL 514-848-2719. FAX 514-848-2839.
Vendor(s): UMI. *946*

CANADIAN JOURNAL OF CRIMINOLOGY.
Canadian Criminal Justice Association, 383 Parkdale Ave., Ste. 304, Ottawa, ON K1Y 4R4, Canada. TEL 613-725-3715. FAX 613-725-3720.
Vendor(s): Information Access Co., UMI. *2263*

CANADIAN JOURNAL OF HISTORY.
University of Saskatchewan, 707 Arts Bldg., 9 Campus Dr., Saskatoon, SK S7N 5A5, Canada. TEL 306-966-5794. FAX 306-966-5852. URL: http://www.usak.ca/history/cjh.
Vendor(s): Information Access Co., UMI. *3491*

CANADIAN JOURNAL OF HOSPITAL PHARMACY.
Canadian Society of Hospital Pharmacists, 1145 Hunt Club Rd., Ste. 350, Ottawa, ON K1V 0Y3, Canada. TEL 613-736-9733. FAX 613-736-5660. *5651*

CANADIAN JOURNAL OF MATHEMATICS.
Canadian Mathematical Society, 577 King Edward, Ottawa, ON K1N 6N5, Canada. TEL 613-564-2223. *4565*

CANADIAN JOURNAL OF PEDIATRICS.
Rodar Publishing Inc., 8102 Trans Canada Hwy., St. Laurent, PQ H4S 1Z4, Canada. TEL 514-333-5350. FAX 514-457-2679. *5029*

CANADIAN JOURNAL OF PHYSIOLOGY AND PHARMACOLOGY.
National Research Council of Canada, Research Journals, Ottawa, ON K1A 0R6, Canada. TEL 613-993-9084. FAX 613-952-7656. URL: http://www.cisti.nrc.ca/cisti/journals/cjpp.html. *814*

THE CANADIAN JOURNAL OF RURAL MEDICINE.
Canadian Medical Association, P.O. Box 8650, Ottawa, ON K1G 0G8, Canada. TEL 613-731-9331. FAX 613-523-0937. URL: http://www.cma.ca/journals/cjrm/ *4651*

CANADIAN JOURNAL OF SURGERY.
Canadian Medical Association, P.O. Box 8650, Ottawa, ON K1G 0G8, Canada. TEL 613-731-9331. FAX 613-523-0937. URL: http://www.cma.ca/journals/cjs/ *5137*

CANADIAN LITERATURE.
University of British Columbia, No. 167, 1855 West Mall, Vancouver, BC V6T 1Z2, Canada. TEL 604-822-2780. FAX 604-822-5504. URL: http://www.swifty.com/cdn_lit.
Vendor(s): UMI. *4386*

SERIALS AVAILABLE ONLINE

CANADIAN MACHINERY & METALWORKING.
Maclean Hunter Ltd., Business Publication Division, Maclean-Hunter Bldg., 777 Bay St., Toronto, ON M5W 1A7, Canada. TEL 416-596-5720.
Vendor(s): Information Access Co. *4542*

CANADIAN MANAGER.
Taylor Enterprises Ltd., 2175 Sheppard Ave. E., Ste. 310, Willowdale, ON M2J 1W8, Canada. TEL 416-493-0155. FAX 416-491-1670.
Vendor(s): Information Access Co., UMI. *1469*

CANADIAN MATHEMATICAL BULLETIN.
Canadian Mathematical Society, 577 King Edward, Ottawa, ON K1N 6N5, Canada. TEL 613-564-2223. *4566*

CANADIAN MINING JOURNAL.
Southam Magazine Group, 1450 Don Mills Rd., Don Mills, ON M3B 2X7, Canada. TEL 416-445-6641. FAX 416-442-2272.
Vendor(s): Information Access Co., Southam Electronic Publishing. *5297*

CANADIAN OUTLOOK.
Conference Board of Canada, 255 Smyth Rd., Ste. 100, Ottawa, ON K1H 8M7, Canada. TEL 613-526-3280. FAX 613-526-4857. *1229*

CANADIAN PACKAGING.
Maclean-Hunter Ltd., Business Publication Division, Maclean-Hunter Bldg., 777 Bay St., Toronto, ON M5W 1A7, Canada. TEL 416-596-6016.
Vendor(s): Information Access Co. *5542*

CANADIAN PATENT REPORTER.
Canada Law Book Inc., 240 Edward St., Aurora, ON L4G 3S9, Canada. TEL 905-841-6472. FAX 905-841-5085. *3928*

CANADIAN PERIODICAL INDEX.
Gale Research, 835 Penobscot Bldg., 645 Griswold St., Detroit, MI 48226-4094. TEL 313-961-2242. FAX 800-414-5043. *8*

CANADIAN PHARMACEUTICAL JOURNAL.
Keith Healthcare Communications, 21 Concourse Gate, No. 13, Nepean, ON K2E 7S4, Canada. TEL 613-727-1364. FAX 613-727-3757. *5651*

CANADIAN PSYCHIATRIC ASSOCIATION BULLETIN.
Canadian Psychiatric Association, 237 Argyle Ave., Ste. 200, Ottawa, ON K2P 1B8, Canada. TEL 613-234-2815. FAX 613-234-2815. URL: http://cpa.medical.org/cpa/public2/publications/bulletin_new.htm. *5057*

CANADIAN PUBLIC ADMINISTRATION.
Institute of Public Administration of Canada, 1075 Bay St., Ste. 401, Toronto, ON M5S 2B1, Canada. TEL 416-924-8787. FAX 416-924-4992.
Vendor(s): Information Access Co. *6168*

CANADIAN RESEARCH INDEX, MICROLOG.
Micromedia Ltd., 20 Victoria St., Toronto, ON M5C 2N8, Canada. TEL 416-362-5211. FAX 416-362-6161. URL: http://www.micromedia.on.ca. *8*

THE CANADIAN REVIEW OF SOCIOLOGY AND ANTHROPOLOGY.
Canadian Sociology and Anthropology Association, Concordia University, 1455 bd. de Maisonneuve Ouest, Montreal, PQ H3G 1M8, Canada. TEL 514-848-8780. FAX 514-848-4539.
Vendor(s): Information Access Co. *6704*

CANADIAN SHAREOWNER.
1090 University Ave. W., Ste. 204, P.O. Box 7337, Windsor, ON N9C 5S4, Canada. TEL 519-252-1555. FAX 519-252-9570.
Vendor(s): UMI. *1379*

CANADIAN SPEECHES: ISSUES OF THE DAY.
Canadian Speeches, Box 250, Woodville, ON K0M 2T0, Canada. TEL 705-439-2580. FAX 705-439-1208.
Vendor(s): Knight-Ridder Information, Inc. *946*

CANADIAN THESES.
National Library of Canada, 395 Wellington St., Ottawa, ON K1A 0N4, Canada. TEL 819-994-6912. FAX 819-953-0291.
Vendor(s): CISTI. *542*

CANADIAN TRADE INDEX.
Canadian Manufacturers Association, 75 International Blvd., Toronto, ON M9W 6L9, Canada. TEL 416-798-8000. FAX 416-798-8050.
Vendor(s): Southam Electronic Publishing. *1659*

CANADIAN TREASURY MANAGEMENT REVIEW.
Royal Bank of Canada, S. Tower, 9th Fl., Royal Bank Plaza, Toronto, ON M5J 2J5, Canada. TEL 416-974-2274. FAX 416-974-0365.
Vendor(s): UMI. *1118*

CANADIAN UNDERWRITER.
Southam Magazine Group, 1450 Don Mills Rd., Don Mills, ON M3B 2X7, Canada. TEL 416-445-6641. FAX 416-442-2213.
Vendor(s): Southam Electronic Publishing, UMI. *3812*

CANADIAN WHO'S WHO.
University of Toronto Press, Directories Departement, 10 St. Mary St., Ste. 700, Toronto, ON M3H 5T8, Canada. TEL 416-978-2239. FAX 416-978-4738. *572*

CANADIANA.
National Library of Canada, 395 Wellington St., Ottawa, ON K1A 0N4, Canada. TEL 819-956-4800. FAX 819-994-1498. *542*

CANADIANA ON MICROFICHE.
National Library of Canada, 395 Wellington St., Ottawa, ON K1A 0N4, Canada. TEL 819-994-6912, 819-994-6912. FAX 819-953-0291.
Vendor(s): CISTI. *542*

CANADIANA PRE-1901.
National Library of Canada, 395 Wellington St., Ottawa, ON K1A 0N4, Canada. TEL 819-994-6912. FAX 819-996-0291.
Vendor(s): CISTI. *542*

CANCER.
John Wiley & Sons, Inc., Journals, 605 Third Ave., New York, NY 10158. TEL 212-850-6645. FAX 212-850-6021. URL: http://www.wiley.co.uk. *4972*

CANCER CHEMOTHERAPY AND PHARMACOLOGY.
Springer-Verlag, Heidelberger Platz 3, 14197 Berlin, Germany. TEL 49-30-82787-0. FAX 49-30-82787448. URL: http://link.springer.de. *4973*

CANCER CONTROL.
Moffitt Cancer Center, 12902 Magnolia Dr., Tampa, FL 33612. TEL 813-632-1349. FAX 813-632-1380. URL: http://daisy.moffitt.usf.edu/cancjrnl/ccj.html. *4973*

CANCER GENE THERAPY.
Appleton & Lange, Journal Division Box 120041, Stamford, CT 06912-0041. TEL 203-406-4500. *4973*

CANCER IMMUNOLOGY, IMMUNOTHERAPY.
Springer-Verlag, Heidelberger Platz 3, 14197 Berlin, Germany. TEL 49-30-82787-0. FAX 49-30-82787448. URL: http://link.springer.de. *4973*

THE CANCER JOURNAL FROM SCIENTIFIC AMERICAN.
Scientific American, Inc., 415 Madison Ave., New York, NY 10017-1111. TEL 212-754-0550. FAX 212-980-3062. *4974*

CANCER WEEKLY PLUS.
Charles W. Henderson, Ed. & Pub., Box 5528, Atlanta, GA 31107-0528. TEL 404-377-8895. FAX 404-378-5411. URL: http://www.newsfile.com.
Vendor(s): CompuServe, Inc., Data-Star, Dow Jones News Retrieval, Information Access Co., Knight-Ridder Information, Inc., NewsNet (HH15), Ovid Technologies, Inc. *4975*

CANDY INDUSTRY.
Advanstar Communications, Inc., 7500 Old Oak Blvd., Cleveland, OH 44130. TEL 216-826-2839. FAX 216-819-2651.
Vendor(s): Information Access Co., Knight-Ridder Information, Inc. *3135*

CANNED FOODS: THE INTERNATIONAL MARKET.
Euromonitor, 60-61 Britton St., London EC1M 5NA, England. TEL 44-171-251-8024. FAX 44-171-608-3149. URL: http://www.euromonitor.com.
Vendor(s): Data-Star, Knight-Ridder Information, Inc. *3098*

CAPACITY MANAGEMENT REVIEW.
Institute for Computer Capacity Management, 1020 8th Ave. S., Ste. 6, Naples, FL 34102. TEL 941-261-8945. FAX 941-261-5456.
Vendor(s): UMI. *2172*

CAPITAL CURRENT.
Astroff Corkum Ross Associates, Inc., 202-141 Pretoria Ave., Ottawa, ON K1S 1X1, Canada. URL: http://www.acr.com/capital.
Available only online. *3259*

CAPITAL DISTRICT BUSINESS REVIEW.
Albany Business Journal, Inc., Box 15081, Albany, NY 12212-5081. TEL 518-432-1091.
Vendor(s): Knight-Ridder Information, Inc. *1229*

CAPITAL UNIVERSITY LAW REVIEW.
Capital University, Law School, 665 S. High St., Columbus, OH 43215. TEL 614-445-8836. FAX 614-445-7125.
Vendor(s): National Data Corp., West Group. *2263*

CAPITAL XTRA.
Pink Triangle Press (Ottawa), 177 Nepean St., Ste. 506, Ottawa, ON K2P 0B4, Canada. TEL 613-237-7133. FAX 613-237-6651. *3692*

CAPTION CENTER NEWS.
Caption Center, 125 Western Ave., Boston, MA 02134. TEL 617-492-9225. FAX 617-562-0590. URL: http://www.wgbh.org/caption. *2047*

CAR AFTERMARKET: THE INTERNATIONAL MARKET.
Euromonitor, 60-61 Britton St., London EC1M 5NA, England. TEL 44-171-251-8024. FAX 44-171-608-3149. URL: http://www.euromonitor.com.
Vendor(s): Data-Star, Knight-Ridder Information, Inc. *7093*

CAR AND DRIVER.
Hachette Filipacchi Magazines, Inc. (Ann Arbor), 2002 Hogback Rd., Ann Arbor, MI 48105. TEL 313-971-3600. FAX 313-971-9188.
Vendor(s): Information Access Co., Knight-Ridder Information, Inc., UMI. *7093*

CAR RENTAL: THE INTERNATIONAL MARKET.
Euromonitor, 60-61 Britton St., London EC1M 5NA, England. TEL 44-171-251-8024. FAX 44-171-608-3149. URL: http://www.euromonitor.com.
Vendor(s): Data-Star, Knight-Ridder Information, Inc. *7094*

CARBOHYDRATE LETTERS.
Gordon and Breach - Harwood Academic, Amsteldisk 166, 1st Fl., 1079 LH Amsterdam, Netherlands. URL: http://www.gbhap.com/Carbohydrate_Letters/. *656*

CARBOHYDRATE RESEARCH.
Elsevier Science Ltd., P.O. Box 800, Kidlington, Oxford OX5 1DX, England. TEL 44-1865-843000. FAX 44-1865-843010. URL: http://www.elsevier.nl/
Vendor(s): STN International. *1813*

CARCINOGENESIS.
Oxford University Press, Academic Division, Great Clarendon St., Oxford OX2 6DP, England. TEL 44-1865-267907. FAX 44-1865-267485. URL: http://www.oup.co.uk/journals. *4975*

CARD FAX.
Faulkner & Gray, Inc. (New York), 11 Penn Plaza, 17th Fl., New York, NY 10001. TEL 212-967-7000. FAX 212-967-7155.
Vendor(s): Information Access Co., NewsNet (Fl67). *1118*

CARD NEWS.
Phillips Business Information, Inc., 1201 Seven Locks Rd., Potomac, MD 20854. TEL 301-424-3338. FAX 301-309-3847.
Vendor(s): Data-Star, Information Access Co., Knight-Ridder Information, Inc., NewsNet (Fl24). *1118*

CARDIOLOGY CLINICS.
W.B. Saunders Co., Curtis Center, 3rd Fl., Independence Sq. W., Philadelphia, PA 19106-3399. TEL 215-238-7800. FAX 215-238-6445.
Vendor(s): Ovid Technologies, Inc. *4812*

CARDIOVASCULAR AND INTERVENTIONAL RADIOLOGY.
Springer-Verlag, Medical Journals, 175 Fifth Ave., New York, NY 10010. TEL 212-460-1500. FAX 212-473-6272. URL: http://www.springer-ny.com.
Vendor(s): FIZ Technik. *5104*

CAREER DEVELOPMENT QUARTERLY.
American Counseling Association, 5999 Stevenson Ave., Alexandria, VA 22304-3300. TEL 703-823-9800. FAX 703-823-0252.
Vendor(s): UMI. *5505*

CAREER MAGAZINE.
TEL 303-440-5110. URL: http://www.careermag.com.
Available only online. *5505*

CAREERS & MAJORS.
Oxendine Publishing, Inc., Box 14081, Gainesville, FL 32604-2081. TEL 352-373-6907. FAX 352-373-8120. *5506*

CARIBBEAN & CENTRAL AMERICA REPORT.
Lettres (U.K.) Ltd., 61 Old St., London EC1V 9HX, England. TEL 44-171-251-0012. FAX 44-171-253-8193.
Vendor(s): Lexis-Nexis. *1229*

CARIBBEAN UPDATE.
Kal Wagenheim, Ed. & Pub., 52 Maple Ave., Maplewood, NJ 07040. TEL 201-762-1565. FAX 201-762-9585.
Vendor(s): Information Access Co. *1318*

CAROLINA TIPS.
Carolina Biological Supply Co., 2700 York Rd., Burlington, NC 27215. TEL 910-584-0381. FAX 910-584-3399. *595*

CARPET & FLOORCOVERINGS REVIEW.
Miller Freeman Publishers Ltd., Sovereign Way, Tonbridge, Kent TN9 1RW, England. TEL 44-1732-364422. FAX 44-1732-361534.
Vendor(s): Information Access Co. *3853*

CARRIER AVIATION NEWS.
G.P.O. Box 2204, Adelaide, S.A. 5001, Australia. TEL 61-8-8276-8661. URL: http://www.geocities.com/~davemc/canset.htm.
Available only online. *61*

CASE WESTERN RESERVE JOURNAL OF INTERNATIONAL LAW.
Case Western Reserve University, School of Law, 11075 East Blvd., Cleveland, OH 44106-7148. TEL 216-368-3304. FAX 216-368-3310.
Vendor(s): Lexis-Nexis. *4108*

CASE WESTERN RESERVE LAW REVIEW.
Case Western Reserve University, School of Law, 11075 East Blvd., Cleveland, OH 44106-7148. TEL 216-368-3304. FAX 216-369-3310.
Vendor(s): Lexis-Nexis. *3929*

CATAHOULA EZINE.
Box 6042, Moore, OK 73153. URL: http://pages.prodigy.com/Okcatahoula.
Available only online. *5635*

CATALOG AGE.
Cowles Business Media, 11 River Bend Dr., S., Box 4949, Stamford, CT 06907-0949. TEL 203-358-9900. FAX 203-358-5811.
Vendor(s): Information Access Co., UMI. *33*

CATALOGO COLETIVO DE ANAIS DE EVENTOS.
Comissao Nacional de Energia Nuclear, Centro de Informacoes Nucleares, Rua General Severiano, 90 Botafogo, 22294-900 Rio de Janeiro RJ, Brazil. TEL 55-21-5462467. FAX 55-21-5462447. *6588*

CATALOGUE AFNOR (NORMES FRANCAISES).
Association Francaise de Normalisation, Tour Europe, 92049 Paris La Defense, Cedex, France. TEL 42-91-55-55. FAX 42-91-56-56.
Vendor(s): Telesystemes - Questel. *5249*

CATALOGUE OF I T U PUBLICATIONS.
International Telecommunication Union, Place des Nations, CH-1211 Geneva 20, Switzerland. TEL 41-22-7306141. FAX 41-22-7305194. URL: http://www.itu.ch. *2011*

CATALYST (MELBOURNE).
Royal Melbourne Institute of Technology, Student Union, P.O. Box 12387, A'Beckett St., Melbourne, Vic. 8006, Australia. TEL 61-3-96602884. FAX 61-3-96603705. *1944*

CATALYST (WASHINGTON).
National Crime Prevention Council, 1700 K St., N.W., 2nd Fl., Washington, DC 20006-3817. TEL 202-466-6272. FAX 202-296-1356. URL: http://www.weprevent.org. *2263*

THE CATALYST (WESTMINSTER).
National Council on Community Services & Continuing Education, c/o Sue Hartman, Professional Development Program, Front Range Community College, 3645 W. 112th Ave., Westminster, CO 80030. *2508*

CATHOLIC ACCENT.
Greensburg Catholic Accent and Communications, Inc., 723 E. Pittsburgh St., Greensburg, PA 15601. TEL 412-834-4010. FAX 412-836-5650. *6454*

CATHOLIC FAMILY PERSPECTIVES WEEKLY.
195 Lark St., Rochester, NY 14613. URL: http://www.vivanet.com/~jwagner/cfpw.htm.
Available only online. *6704*

CATHOLIC UNIVERSITY LAW REVIEW.
Catholic University of America, Columbus School of Law, 3600 John McCormack Rd., NE, Washington, DC 20064. TEL 202-319-5159. FAX 202-319-4459.
Vendor(s): Lexis-Nexis. *3929*

CATO JOURNAL.
Cato Institute, 1000 Massachusetts Ave., N.W., Washington, DC 20001-5403. TEL 202-842-0200. FAX 202-842-3490.
Vendor(s): UMI. *5899*

CATT'S CLAWS.
Box 6185, Hot Springs, AR 71902. URL: http://www.imageworld.com/istuber.html.
Available only online. *5989*

CAUSE - EFFECT MAGAZINE.
C A U S E, 4830 Pearl E. Cir., Ste. 302E, Boulder, CO 80301. TEL 303-449-4430. FAX 303-440-0461. URL: http://www.cause.org/cause-effect/cause-effect.html. *2515*

THE CAVALIER DAILY.
Cavalier Daily, Inc., Newcomb Hall, Charlottesville, VA 22903. TEL 804-924-1086. FAX 804-924-7290. URL: http://www.virginia.edu/~cavdaily. *1944*

CELL ADHESION AND COMMUNICATION.
Gordon and Breach - Harwood Academic, Amsteldisk 166, 1st Fl., 1079 LH Amsterdam, Netherlands. URL: http://www.gbhap.com/Cell__Adhesion__Communication/. *595*

CELL AND TISSUE RESEARCH.
Springer-Verlag, Heidelberger Platz 3, 14197 Berlin, Germany. TEL 49-30-82787-0. FAX 49-30-82787448. URL: http://link.springer.de. *737*

CELL BIOLOGY INTERNATIONAL.
Academic Press Ltd., 24-28 Oval Rd., London NW1 7DX, England. TEL 44-171-267-4466. FAX 44-171-482-2293. URL: http://www.hbuk.co.uk/ap/cellbio; http://www.europe.idealibrary.com/. *738*

CELL MOTILITY AND THE CYTOSKELETON.
John Wiley & Sons, Inc., Journals, 605 Third Ave., New York, NY 10158. TEL 212-850-6645. FAX 212-850-6021. URL: http://www.wiley.co.uk. *738*

CELLULAR AND MOLECULAR LIFE SCIENCES.
Birkhaeuser Verlag, P.O. Box 133, CH-4010 Basel, Switzerland. TEL 41-61-2050730. FAX 41-61-2050791. URL: http://www.birkhauser.ch. *596*

CELLULAR BUSINESS.
Intertec Publishing Corp., 9800 Metcalf, Overland Park, KS 66212-2215. TEL 913-341-1300. FAX 913-967-1898.
Vendor(s): UMI. *2033*

CELLULAR IMMUNOLOGY.
Academic Press, Inc., Journal Division, 525 B St., Ste. 1900, San Diego, CA 92101-4495. TEL 619-230-1840. FAX 619-699-6800. URL: http://www.apnet.com/www/journal/ci.htm; http://www.idealibrary.com. *4792*

CELLULAR SALES & MARKETING.
Creative Communications Inc. (Herndon), Box 1519-ULR, Herndon, VA 20172-1519. TEL 703-742-9696.
Vendor(s): NewsNet (TE72). *2033*

CELLULOSE.
Thomson Science, 2-6 Boundary Row, London SE1 8HN, England. TEL 44-171-8650066. FAX 44-171-5229623. URL: http://www.thomsonscience.com. *699*

CENSUS AND YOU.
U.S. Bureau of the Census, Public Information Office, Washington, DC 20233. TEL 301-457-2822. FAX 301-457-4714. URL: http://www.census.gov/. *6905*

CENSUS OF AGRICULTURE: FINAL REPORTS.
U.S. Bureau of the Census, Customer Services, Washington, DC 20233. TEL 301-457-4100. FAX 301-457-4714. URL: http://www.census.gov/. *172*

CENSUS OF CONSTRUCTION INDUSTRIES: FINAL REPORTS.
U.S. Bureau of the Census, Customer Services, Washington, DC 20233. TEL 301-457-4100. FAX 301-457-4714. URL: http://www.census.gov/. *876*

CENSUS OF GOVERNMENTS (FINAL REPORTS).
U.S. Bureau of the Census, Customer Services, Washington, DC 20233. TEL 301-457-4100. FAX 301-457-4714. URL: http://www.census.gov/. *6203*

CENSUS OF MANUFACTURES: FINAL REPORTS.
U.S. Bureau of the Census, Customer Services, Washington, DC 20233. TEL 301-457-4100. FAX 301-457-4714. URL: http://www.census.gov/. *1029*

CENTER OF THE CIRCLE.
512 N. Douglas Blvd., Midwest City, OK 73130-2410. URL: http://www.keytech.com/~lbullock.
Available only online. *6488*

CENTERS FOR PLURALISM NEWSLETTER.
Institute for Democracy in Eastern Europe, Bagno 3, pok. 205, P.O. Box 311, 00-950 Warsaw, Poland. TEL 48-22-6208358. FAX 48-22-6208358. *5899*

CENTRAL ATLANTIC ENVIRONMENTAL DIRECTORY.
Harbinger Communications, Box 8175, Missoula, MT 59807. TEL 406-721-0440. FAX 406-721-0440. *2226*

CENTRAL CALIFORNIA POETRY JOURNAL.
214 Wilkes Circle, Santa Cruz, CA 95060. URL: http://www.solopublications.com.
Available only online. *4505*

CENTRAL EUROPEAN.
Euromoney Publications plc., Nestor House, Playhouse Yard, London EC4V 5EX, England. TEL 44-171-779-8935. FAX 44-171-779-8541.
Vendor(s): UMI. *1120*

CENTRAL NEW YORK BUSINESS JOURNAL.
C N Y Business Journal, 231 Walton St., Syracuse, NY 13202-1226. TEL 315-472-3104. FAX 315-472-3644.
Vendor(s): Knight-Ridder Information, Inc., UMI. *1230*

CENTRAL PENN BUSINESS JOURNAL.
Journal Publications, Inc., 409 S. Second St., Ste. 3D, Harrisburg, PA 17104-1612. TEL 717-236-4300. FAX 717-236-6803.
Vendor(s): UMI. *947*

CENTRAL PERKULATIONS.
Y G H F, Box 17113, Memphis, TN 38187. URL: http://www.yghf.com/
Available only online. *2047*

CENTRE FOR ASIA-PACIFIC STUDIES NEWS.
Centre for Asia-Pacific Studies, URL: http://human.ntu.ac.uk/foh/caps.html.
Available only online. *5524*

SERIALS AVAILABLE ONLINE

CENTRE FOR PLANT BREEDING AND REPRODUCTION RESEARCH. ANNUAL REPORT.
C P R O - D L O, Postbus 16, 6700 AA Wageningen, Netherlands. TEL 31-317-477017. FAX 31-317-418094. URL: http://www.bib.wau.nl/cpro/. *218*

CERAMIC ABSTRACTS.
Cambridge Scientific Abstracts, Attn: Angela Hitti, 7200 Wisconsin Ave., 6th Fl., Bethesda, MD 20814. TEL 301-961-6750. FAX 301-961-6720. URL: http://www.csa.com. Vendor(s): Knight-Ridder Information, Inc. (File no.335), Questel Orbit Inc. (CERM), STN International (CERAB). *1735*

CERAMIC INDUSTRY.
Business News Publishing Company, 755 W. Big Beaver Rd., Ste. 1000, Troy, MI 48084. TEL 810-362-3700. FAX 810-362-0317. URL: http://www.bnp.com. Vendor(s): Information Access Co. *1726*

CERAMICS MONTHLY.
American Ceramic Society, 735 Ceramic Pl., Box 6102, Westerville, OH 43086-6102. TEL 614-794-5890. FAX 614-794-5854. Vendor(s): Information Access Co., UMI. *1727*

CEREAL SOURCE (YEAR).
American Association of Cereal Chemists, Inc, 3340 Pilot Knob Rd., St. Paul, MN 55121. TEL 612-454-7250. FAX 612-454-0766. URL: http://www.scisoc.org/aacc/searchcs. *3132*

CESKA A SLOVENSKA FARMACIE.
Nakladatelske Stredisko C L S J.E. Purkyne, Sokolska 31, 120 26 Prague 2, Czech Republic. TEL 420-2-24911420. FAX 420-2-24911420. *5652*

CESKA NARODNI BIBLIOGRAFIE. KNIHY.
Narodni Knihovna Ceske Republiky, Klementinum 190, 110 01 Prague 1, Czech Republic. TEL 42-2-24229500. FAX 42-2-24227796. *543*

CHAIN STORE AGE.
Lebhar-Friedman, Inc., 425 Park Ave., New York, NY 10022. TEL 212-756-5000. URL: http://www.chainstoreage.com. Vendor(s): Information Access Co., UMI. *1520*

CHAMBER JOBWATCH.
American Chamber of Commerce Executives, 4232 King St., Alexandria, VA 22302-9950. TEL 703-998-0072. FAX 703-931-5624. *1182*

CHANGE (WASHINGTON).
Heldref Publications, 1319 18th St., N.W., Washington, DC 20036-1802. TEL 202-296-6267. FAX 202-296-5149. Vendor(s): Information Access Co. *2535*

CHAOS.
American Institute of Physics, One Physics Ellipse, College Park, MD 20740-3843. TEL 301-209-3000. URL: http://www.aip.org. *5799*

CHAOS CONTROL DIGIZINE.
Box 1065, Hoboken, NJ 07030. URL: http://www.chaoscontrol.com. Available only online. *5382*

CHAOTIC FRINGE.
URL: http://home.earthlink.net/~jsinclair. Available only online. *3371*

CHARISMA.
Strang Communications Co., 600 Rinehart Rd., Lake Mary, FL 32746. TEL 407-333-0600. URL: http://www.charismamag.com. *6327*

CHARTERED PROPERTY AND CASUALTY UNDERWRITERS SOCIETY. JOURNAL.
Chartered Property & Casualty Underwriters Society, Box 3009, 720 Providence Rd., Malvern, PA 19355. TEL 610-251-2743. URL: http://www.cpcusociety.org/. Vendor(s): UMI. *3812*

CHATELAINE (ENGLISH EDITION).
Maclean Hunter Ltd., Maclean Hunter Bldg., 777 Bay St., Toronto, ON M5W 1A7, Canada. TEL 416-596-5425. FAX 416-596-5516. URL: http://www.canoe.ca/chatelaine. Vendor(s): Information Access Co. *7314*

THE CHATTAHOOCHEE REVIEW.
DeKalb College, 2101 Womack Rd., Dunwoody, GA 30338. TEL 770-551-3166. FAX 770-551-7471. *4389*

CHAYE KEXUE.
Chinese Academy of Agricultural Sciences, Tea Research Institute, 1 Yunqi Lu, Hangzhou, Zhejiang 310008, People's Republic of China. TEL 86-571-709-1258. FAX 86-571-709-1263. *3099*

CHEM-FACTS: ETHYLENE & PROPYLENE.
Chem-Intell, Reed Information Services Windsor Ct, East Grinstead House, E. Grinstead, W. Sussex RH19 1XA, England. TEL 44-1342-335831. FAX 44-1342-335612. Vendor(s): Data-Star, Knight-Ridder Information, Inc. *1813*

CHEM-FACTS: EUROPEAN REVIEW.
Chem-Intell, Reed Information Services Windsor Ct., East Grinstead House, E. Grinstead, W. Sussex RH19 1XA, England. TEL 44-1342-335831. FAX 44-1342-335612. Vendor(s): Data-Star, Knight-Ridder Information, Inc. *1741*

CHEM-FACTS: FRANCE.
Chem-Intell, Reed Information Services Windsor Ct, East Grinstead House, E. Grinstead, W. Sussex RH19 1XA, England. TEL 44-1342-335831. FAX 44-1342-335612. Vendor(s): Data-Star, Knight-Ridder Information, Inc. *1741*

CHEM-FACTS: GERMANY.
Chem-Intell, Reed Information Services Windsor Ct., East Grinstead House, E. Grinstead, W. Sussex RH19 1XA, England. TEL 44-1342-335831. FAX 44-1342-335612. Vendor(s): Data-Star, Knight-Ridder Information, Inc. *1741*

CHEM-FACTS: P V C.
Chem-Intell, Reed Information Services Windsor Ct., East Grinstead House, E. Grinstead, W. Sussex RH19 1XA, England. TEL 44-1342-335831. FAX 44-1342-335612. Vendor(s): Data-Star, Knight-Ridder Information, Inc. *1813*

CHEM-FACTS: POLYETHYLENE.
Chem-Intell, Reed Information Services Windsor Ct., East Grinstead House, E. Grinstead, W. Sussex RH19 1XA, England. TEL 44-1342-335831. FAX 44-1342-335612. Vendor(s): Data-Star, Questel Orbit Inc. *1813*

CHEM-FACTS: POLYPROPYLENE.
Chem-Intell, Reed Information Services Windsor Ct., East Grinstead House, E. Grinstead, W. Sussex RH19 1XA, England. TEL 44-1342-335831. FAX 44-1342-335612. Vendor(s): Data-Star, Knight-Ridder Information, Inc., Questel Orbit Inc. *1813*

CHEM-FACTS: STYRENICS.
Chem-Intell, Reed Information Services Windsor Ct., East Grinstead House, E. Grinstead, W. Sussex RH19 1XA, England. TEL 44-1342-335831. FAX 44-1342-335612. Vendor(s): Data-Star, Knight-Ridder Information, Inc. *1814*

CHEM-FACTS: UNITED KINGDOM.
Chem-Intell, Reed Information Services Windsor Ct., East Grinstead House, E. Grinstead, W. Sussex RH19 1XA, England. TEL 44-1342-335831. FAX 44-1342-335612. Vendor(s): Data-Star, Knight-Ridder Information, Inc. *1741*

CHEM SOURCES INTERNATIONAL.
Chemical Sources International, Inc., Box 1824, Clemson, SC 29633. TEL 803-646-7840. FAX 803-646-9938. Vendor(s): STN International. *1660*

CHEM SOURCES U S A.
Chemical Sources International, Inc., Box 1824, Clemson, SC 29633-1824. TEL 803-646-7840. FAX 803-646-9938. Vendor(s): STN International. *1660*

CHEMICAL ABSTRACTS.
Chemical Abstracts Service, 2540 Olentangy River Rd., Box 3012, Columbus, OH 43210-0012. TEL 614-447-3600. FAX 614-447-3713. Vendor(s): STN International. *1781*

CHEMICAL ABSTRACTS - APPLIED CHEMISTRY AND CHEMICAL ENGINEERING SECTIONS.
Chemical Abstracts Service, 2540 Olentangy River Rd., Box 3012, Columbus, OH 43210-0012. TEL 614-447-3663. FAX 614-447-3713. Vendor(s): STN International (CA). *1781*

CHEMICAL ABSTRACTS - BIOCHEMISTRY SECTIONS.
Chemical Abstracts Service, 2540 Olentangy River Rd., Box 3012, Columbus, OH 43210-0012. TEL 614-447-3600. FAX 614-447-3713. Vendor(s): STN International (CA). *1781*

CHEMICAL ABSTRACTS - MACROMOLECULAR SECTIONS.
Chemical Abstracts Service, 2540 Olentangy River Rd., Box 3012, Columbus, OH 43210-0012. TEL 614-447-3600. FAX 614-447-3713. Vendor(s): STN International (CA). *1781*

CHEMICAL ABSTRACTS - ORGANIC CHEMISTRY SECTIONS.
Chemical Abstracts Service, 2540 Olentangy River Rd., Box 3012, Columbus, OH 43210-0012. TEL 614-447-3600. FAX 614-447-3713. Vendor(s): STN International (CA). *1781*

CHEMICAL ABSTRACTS - PHYSICAL, INORGANIC AND ANALYTICAL CHEMISTRY SECTIONS.
Chemical Abstracts Service, 2540 Olentangy River Rd., Box 3012, Columbus, OH 43210-0012. TEL 614-447-3600. FAX 614-447-3713. Vendor(s): STN International (CA). *1781*

CHEMICAL ABSTRACTS SERVICE SOURCE INDEX.
Chemical Abstracts Service, 2540 Olentangy River Rd., Columbus, OH 43210-0012. TEL 614-447-3600. FAX 614-447-3713. *1781*

CHEMICAL AND BIOLOGICAL DEFENSE INFORMATION ANALYSIS CENTER. NEWSLETTER.
Department of Defense, Information Analysis Center, Attn.: SCBRD-RTA (Joseph Williams), APG-EA, MD 21010-5423. TEL 410-671-4878. FAX 410-671-2649. URL: http://www.cbiac.apgea.army.mil/newsletr.html. Available only online. *2757*

CHEMICAL & PHARMACEUTICAL BULLETIN.
Pharmaceutical Society of Japan, 12-15, Shibuya 2-chome, Shibuya-ku, Tokyo 150, Japan. *1742*

CHEMICAL COMMUNICATIONS.
The Royal Society of Chemistry, Thomas Graham House, Science Park, Milton Rd., Cambridge CB4 4WF, England. TEL 44-1223-420066. FAX 44-1223-423429. URL: http://chemistry.rsc.org/rsc/. Vendor(s): STN International (CJRSC). *1742*

CHEMICAL EDUCATOR.
Springer-Verlag, 175 Fifth Ave., New York, NY 10010. TEL 212-460-1500. FAX 212-473-6272. URL: http://journals-springer-ny.com/chedr/. Available only online. *1742*

CHEMICAL ENGINEERING.
McGraw-Hill Companies, 1221 Ave. of the Americas, New York, NY 10020. TEL 212-512-2197. URL: http://www.che.com/ Vendor(s): Dow Jones News Retrieval (CE), Knight-Ridder Information, Inc. (File no.624/McGRAW-HILL PUBLICATIONS ONLINE), Lexis-Nexis (CHEMEN), NewsNet (CH19). *2757*

CHEMICAL ENGINEERING COMMUNICATIONS.
Gordon and Breach - Harwood Academic, Amsteldisk 166, 1st Fl., 1079 LH Amsterdam, Netherlands. URL: http://www.gbhap.com/Chemical_Engineering_Communications/; http://www.gbhap.us.com/journals/108/108-top.html. *2758*

CHEMICAL ENGINEERING RESEARCH & DESIGN.
Institution of Chemical Engineers, George E. Davis Bldg., 165-189 Railway Terr., Rugby, Warks. CV21 3HQ, England. TEL 44-1788-578214. FAX 44-1788-560833. URL: http://www.icheme.org/prod.htm. *2759*

CHEMICAL HAZARDS IN INDUSTRY.
The Royal Society of Chemistry, Thomas Graham House, Science Park, Milton Rd., Cambridge CB4 4WF, England. TEL 44-1223-420066. FAX 44-1223-423429. URL: http://chemistry.rsc.org/rsc/. Vendor(s): Data-Star (CSNB), Knight-Ridder Information, Inc. (File no.317), Questel Orbit Inc. (CSNS), STN International (CSNB). *5488*

CHEMICAL INDUSTRIES NEWSLETTER.
S R I International, Process Industries Division, Chemical Marketing Research Center, Menlo Park, CA 94025. TEL 415-859-3346. URL: http://www-cmrc.sri.com/CIN/ *1742*

CHEMICAL INDUSTRY NOTES.
Chemical Abstracts Service, 2540 Olentangy River Rd., Box 3012, Columbus, OH 43210-0012. TEL 614-447-3600. FAX 614-447-3713. *1781*

CHEMICAL MARKETING REPORTER.
Schnell Publishing Co., Inc., 80 Broad St., New York, NY 10004-2203. TEL 212-248-4177. FAX 212-248-4903. URL: http://www.chemexpo.com; http://elsevier.nl:80/inca/publications/store. Vendor(s): Information Access Co., Knight-Ridder Information, Inc., UMI. *1742*

CHEMICAL MONITOR.
Desktop Publishing, Box 314, Lindenhurst, NY 11757-0314. TEL 516-669-8147. Vendor(s): Data-Star, Information Access Co., Knight-Ridder Information, Inc., NewsNet (CH15). *1789*

CHEMICAL PLANT FILE.
Chem-Intell, Reed Information Services Windsor Ct., East Grinstead House, E. Grinstead, W. Sussex RH19 1XA, England. TEL 44-1342-335831. FAX 44-1342-335612. Vendor(s): Data-Star, Knight-Ridder Information, Inc., Reed Information Services Ltd. *1742*

CHEMICAL REGULATION REPORTER.
The Bureau of National Affairs, Inc., 1231 25th St., N.W., Washington, DC 20037. TEL 202-452-4200. FAX 202-822-8092. URL: http://www.bna.com/ Vendor(s): Human Resources Information Network (File DD), Lexis-Nexis (BNA-CHEM), West Group. *2910*

CHEMICAL RESEARCH IN TOXICOLOGY.
American Chemical Society, 1155 16th St., N.W., Washington, DC 20036. TEL 800-333-9511. FAX 614-447-3671. Vendor(s): STN International. *2975*

CHEMICAL REVIEWS.
American Chemical Society, 1155 16th St., N.W., Washington, DC 20036. TEL 800-333-9511. FAX 614-447-3671. Vendor(s): STN International (CJACS). *1743*

CHEMICAL TITLES.
Chemical Abstracts Service, 2540 Olentangy River Rd., Columbus, OH 43210-0012. TEL 614-447-3600. FAX 614-447-3713. *1782*

CHEMICAL WEEK.
Chemical Week Associates, 888 Seventh Ave., New York, NY 10106. TEL 212-621-4900. FAX 212-621-4949. URL: http://www.chemweek.com/ Vendor(s): Information Access Co., Lexis-Nexis. *2760*

CHEMISCHE BERICHTE.
Wiley - V C H, Postfach 101161, 69451 Weinheim, Germany. TEL 49-6201-606147. FAX 49-6201-606117. URL: http://www.vchgroup.de. *1744*

CHEMISCHE INDUSTRIE.
Verlagsgruppe Handelsblatt GmbH, Kasernenstr. 67, 40213 Duesseldorf, Germany. TEL 49-211-8870. FAX 49-211-65531. *2761*

DIE CHEMISCHE INDUSTRIE UND IHRE HELFER.
Industrieschau-Verlagsgessellschaft mbH, Postfach 100262, 64202 Darmstadt, Germany. TEL 49-6151-38920. FAX 49-6151-33164. *2761*

CHEMIST & DRUGGIST.
Miller Freeman plc, Sovereign Way, Tonbridge, Kent TN9 1RW, England. TEL 44-1732-364422. FAX 44-1732-361534. Vendor(s): Information Access Co. *5652*

CHEMISTRY & BIOLOGY.
Current Biology Ltd., 400 Market St., Ste. 700, Philadelphia, PA 19106. FAX 215-574-2270. URL: http://BioMedNet.com/cgi-bin/members/titles.pl. *681*

CHEMISTRY AND ECOLOGY.
Gordon and Breach - Harwood Academic, Amsteldisk 166, 1st Fl., 1079 LH Amsterdam, Netherlands. URL: http://www.gbhap.com/Chemistry_Ecology/. *1744*

CHEMISTRY AND INDUSTRY.
Society of Chemical Industry, 14 Belgrave Sq., London SW1X 8PS, England. TEL 44-171-235-3681. FAX 44-171-235-9410. URL: http://ci.mond.org. *1744*

CHEMISTRY TODAY.
Society of Chemical Industry, 14 Belgrave Sq., London SW1X 8PS, England. TEL 44-171-235-3681. FAX 44-171-235-9410. URL: http://chemistry.mond.org. Available only online. *1745*

CHEMORECEPTION ABSTRACTS.
Cambridge Scientific Abstracts, 7200 Wisconsin Ave., 6th Fl., Bethesda, MD 20814. TEL 301-961-6750. FAX 301-961-6720. URL: http://www.csa.com. Vendor(s): Knight-Ridder Information, Inc. (File no.76/LIFE SCIENCES COLLECTION), STN International (LIFESCI). *1782*

CHEMSCOPE.
Chemscope, Inc., URL: http://chemscope.com. Available only online. *4652*

CHEST.
American College of Chest Physicians, 3300 Dundee Rd., Northbrook, IL 60062. TEL 847-498-1400. FAX 847-498-5460. URL: http://www.chestnet.org. Vendor(s): Information Access Co. *5118*

CHIAROSCURO.
Reporter Publishing, Via Manzoni 31, 50018 Scandicci, Italy. TEL 39-55-2578346. FAX 39-55-250868. URL: http://www.mclink.it/com/reporter. *4249*

CHICAGO (YEAR).
Harper Collins Publishers, Birnbaum Travel Guides, 10 E. 53rd St., New York, NY 10022-5299. TEL 212-207-7542. Vendor(s): Information Access Co. *7192*

CHICAGO AREA BUSINESS DIRECTORY.
American Business Directories, 5711 S. 86th Circle, Box 27347, Omaha, NE 68127. TEL 402-593-4600. FAX 402-331-5481. *1660*

CHICAGO ARTISTS' NEWS.
Chicago Artists' Coalition, 11 E. Hubbard St., 7th Fl., Chicago, IL 60611. TEL 312-670-2060. FAX 312-670-2521. URL: http://www.caconline.or/home.html. *435*

CHICAGO ENTERPRISE.
Commercial Club of Chicago, One First National Plaza, No. 2700, Chicago, IL 60603. TEL 312-853-1203. FAX 312-853-1209. Vendor(s): Lexis-Nexis. *947*

CHICAGO JOURNAL OF THEORETICAL COMPUTER SCIENCE.
M I T Press, 5 Cambridge Center, Cambridge, MA 02142-1493. TEL 617-253-2889. FAX 617-577-1545. URL: http://www-mitpress.mit.edu/jnls-catalog/chicago.html. Available only online. *2074*

CHICAGO - KENT LAW REVIEW.
Chicago - Kent College of Law, 565 W. Adams St., Chicago, IL 60661-3691. TEL 312-906-5190. FAX 312-906-5280. Vendor(s): West Group. *3930*

CHICAGO REVIEW.
Chicago Review, 5801 S. Kenwood, Chicago, IL 60637. TEL 773-702-0887. FAX 773-702-0887. URL: http://humanities.uchicago.edu/humanities/reviews. Vendor(s): Information Access Co. *4389*

THE CHICAGO TRIBUNE INDEX.
U M I, 300 N. Zeeb Rd., Ann Arbor, MI 48106-1346. TEL 313-761-4700. FAX 800-864-0019. *3883*

CHICANO - LATINO LAW REVIEW.
University of California at Los Angeles, School of Law, 405 Hilgard Ave., Los Angeles, CA 90024-1476. TEL 310-825-2894. FAX 310-206-6489. URL: http://www.law.ucla.edu/student/organizations/cllr. Vendor(s): West Group. *3930*

CHIEF EXECUTIVE MAGAZINE.
Chief Executive Group, Inc., 733 Third Ave., 21st Fl., New York, NY 10017. TEL 212-687-8288. FAX 212-687-8456. Vendor(s): Information Access Co. *1469*

CHIEF EXECUTIVE OFFICERS NEWSLETTER.
Center for Entrepreneurial Management, Inc., 180 Varick St., Penthouse, New York, NY 10014. TEL 212-633-0060. FAX 212-633-0063. Vendor(s): NewsNet. *1469*

CHILD ABUSE & NEGLECT.
Elsevier Science Ltd., Pergamon, P.O. Box 800, Kidlington, Oxford OX5 1DX, England. TEL 44-1865-843000. FAX 44-1865-843010. URL: http://www/elsevier.nl/. *1840*

CHILD DEVELOPMENT ABSTRACTS AND BIBLIOGRAPHY.
University of Chicago Press, Journals Division, 5720 S. Woodlawn Ave., Chicago, IL 60637. TEL 773-753-3347. FAX 773-753-0811. URL: http://www.journals.uchicago.eud/CDAB/journal/ *1861*

CHILD HEALTH ALERT.
Box 610228, Newton Highlands, MA 02161. Vendor(s): Information Access Co. *5029*

CHILD PROTECTION REPORT.
Business Publishers, Inc., 951 Pershing Dr., Silver Spring, MD 20910-4432. TEL 301-587-6300. FAX 301-585-9075. Vendor(s): NewsNet. *1841*

CHILDHOOD EDUCATION.
Association for Childhood Education International, 11501 Georgia Ave., Ste. 315, Wheaton, MD 20902. TEL 301-942-2443. Vendor(s): Information Access Co., UMI. *2428*

CHILDREN TODAY.
U.S. Department of Health and Human Services, Administration for Children and Families, Office of Public Affairs, 370 L'Enfant Promende, S.W., 7th Fl., Washington, DC 20447. TEL 202-401-9215. Vendor(s): Information Access Co., Knight-Ridder Information, Inc., UMI. *1842*

CHILDREN'S BOOKS IN PRINT.
R.R. Bowker, A Division of Reed Elsevier Inc., 121 Chanlon Rd., New Providence, NJ 07974. TEL 908-464-6800. FAX 908-665-6688. URL: http://www.reedref.com. Vendor(s): Knight-Ridder Information, Inc. (File no.470), Ovid Technologies, Inc. (BBIP). *544*

CHILDREN'S BUSINESS.
Fairchild Fashion & Merchandising Group, 7 W. 34th St., New York, NY 10001. TEL 212-630-4199. FAX 212-630-4201. Vendor(s): Information Access Co. *1921*

CHILD'S NERVOUS SYSTEM.
Springer-Verlag, Heidelberger Platz 3, 14197 Berlin, Germany. TEL 49-30-82787-0. FAX 49-30-82787448. URL: http://link.springer.de. *5058*

CHILLED AND DELICATESSEN FOODS: THE INTERNATIONAL MARKET.
Euromonitor, 60-61 Britton St., London EC1M 5NA, England. TEL 44-171-251-8024. FAX 44-171-608-3149. URL: http://www.euromonitor.com. Vendor(s): Data-Star, Knight-Ridder Information, Inc. *3099*

CHILTON'S AUTOMOTIVE MARKETING.
Chilton Co., 201 King of Prussia Rd., Radnor, PA 19089. TEL 610-964-4000. FAX 610-964-4981. Vendor(s): Information Access Co., Knight-Ridder Information, Inc., Lexis-Nexis. *7095*

SERIALS AVAILABLE ONLINE

CHILTON'S DISTRIBUTION.
Chilton Co., Chilton Way, Radnor, PA 19089. TEL 215-964-4379.
Vendor(s): Information Access Co., Knight-Ridder Information, Inc., Lexis-Nexis. *7026*

CHILTON'S FOOD ENGINEERING.
Chilton Co., One Chilton Way, Radnor, PA 19089. TEL 610-964-4447.
Vendor(s): Information Access Co., Knight-Ridder Information, Inc., Lexis-Nexis. *3099*

CHILTON'S FOOD ENGINEERING INTERNATIONAL.
Chilton Co., Chilton Way, Radnor, PA 19089. TEL 610-964-4440.
Vendor(s): Information Access Co., Knight-Ridder Information, Inc. *3099*

CHILTON'S HARDWARE AGE.
Chilton Co., Chilton Way, Radnor, PA 19089. TEL 610-964-4282. URL: http://www.homemkt.com.
Vendor(s): Knight-Ridder Information, Inc. *927*

CHILTON'S JEWELERS' CIRCULAR-KEYSTONE.
Chilton Co., Chilton Way, Radnor, PA 19089. TEL 215-964-4474. FAX 215-964-4481.
Vendor(s): Knight-Ridder Information, Inc. *3863*

CHILTON'S MOTOR AGE.
Chilton Co., 201 King of Prussia Rd., Radnor, PA 19089. TEL 610-964-4390. FAX 610-964-4251.
Vendor(s): Information Access Co., Knight-Ridder Information, Inc., Lexis-Nexis. *7095*

CHINA AERO INFORMATION.
Hangkong Hangtian Gongye-bu, Keji Qingbao Yanjiusuo, 14 Xiaoguan Dongli, P.O. Box 9816, Beijing 100029, People's Republic of China. TEL 86-10-6492-2211. FAX 86-10-6491-8417. URL: http://www.iag.com. *61*

CHINA AEROSPACE ABSTRACTS.
Hangkong Gongye Chubanshe, 14 Xiaoguan Dongli, Anwai, Beijing 100029, People's Republic of China. TEL 8610-4918404. FAX 8610-4221696. *83*

CHINA BUSINESS REVIEW.
United States - China Business Council, 1818 N St., N.W., Ste. 200, Washington, DC 20036-2406. TEL 202-429-0340. FAX 202-833-9027. URL: http://www.uschina.org/cbr.
Vendor(s): Information Access Co., Knight-Ridder Information, Inc., UMI, Wilsonline. *1319*

CHINA HAND.
Economist Intelligence Unit, 111 W. 57th St., New York, NY 10019. TEL 212-554-0600. FAX 212-586-1182. URL: http://www.eiu.com. *948*

THE CHINA QUARTERLY.
Oxford University Press, Academic Division, Great Clarendon St., Oxford OX2 6DP, England. TEL 44-1865-267907. FAX 44-1865-267485. URL: http://www.oup.co.uk/journals.
Vendor(s): UMI. *5524*

CHINA TODAY (BRITISH EDITION).
Jinri Zhongguo Zazhishe, 24 Baiwanzhuang Lu, Beijing 100037, People's Republic of China. TEL 86-1-8326037. FAX 86-1-8328338.
Vendor(s): Knight-Ridder Information, Inc. *3269*

CHINESE MEDICAL JOURNAL.
Chinese Medical Association, P.O. Box 2258, 42 Dongsi Xidajie, Beijing 100710, People's Republic of China. TEL 5133311. *4653*

CHING FENG.
Christian Study Centre on Chinese Religion & Culture, 6-F Kiu Kin Mansion, 566 Nathan Rd., Kowloon, Hong Kong, People's Republic of China. TEL 852-2770-3310. FAX 852-2782-6869.
Vendor(s): Knight-Ridder Information, Inc., Ovid Technologies, Inc. *6328*

CHIP.
Vogel Publishing Kft, Hajdu u.42-44 2nd Fl., 1139 Budapest, Hungary. TEL 36-1-2523731. FAX 36-1-2523731. *2074*

CHIPNET ELECTRONIC MAGAZINE.
650 Stadler Rd., Helena, MT 59602. URL: http://www.tybee.com/chipnet.
Available only online. *2131*

CHIROPRACTIC ONLINE TODAY.
Box 1980, New York, NY 10013-0873. URL: http://www.panix.com/'tonto1/dc.html.
Available only online. *4826*

DER CHIRURG.
Springer-Verlag, Heidelberger Platz 3, 14197 Berlin, Germany. TEL 49-30-82787-0. FAX 49-30-82787448. URL: http://link.springer.de. *4766*

CHIRURGIA MAXILLOFACIALIS ET PLASTICA.
Hrvatski Lijecnicki Zbor, Drustvo za Maksilofacijalnu i Plasticnu Kirurgiju, Subiceva 9, Zagreb. TEL 385-41-420-470. FAX 385-41-425-629. *5138*

CHOICE (MIDDLETOWN).
Choice, 100 Riverview Ctr., Middletown, CT 06457. TEL 203-347-6933. FAX 203-346-8586. *6289*

CHOICES (NEW YORK).
Choice in Dying, Inc., 200 Varick St., New York, NY 10014. TEL 212-366-5540. FAX 212-366-5337. URL: http://www.choices.org. *2253*

CHOICES: A CORE COLLECTION FOR YOUNG RELUCTANT READERS.
John Gordon Burke Publisher, Inc., Box 1492, Evanston, IL 60204-1492. TEL 847-866-8625. FAX 847-866-6639. URL: http://www.nlightn.com. *1867*

CHREODS.
c/o Manchester Metropolitan University, School of Education, 799 Wilmslow Rd., Didsbury, Manchester M20 2RR, England. URL: http://s13a.math.aca.mmu.ac.uk/Chreods/Chreods_intro.html. *2428*

CHRISTIAN CENTURY.
Christian Century Foundation, 407 S. Dearborn St., Chicago, IL 60605. TEL 312-427-5380.
Vendor(s): Information Access Co., UMI. *6328*

CHRISTIAN HISTORY.
Christianity Today, Inc., 465 Gundersen Dr., Carol Stream, IL 60188. TEL 630-260-6200. FAX 630-260-0114. URL: http://www.christianity.net/christianhistory. *6328*

CHRISTIAN READER.
Christianity Today, Inc., 465 Gundersen Dr., Carol Stream, IL 60188-2498. TEL 630-260-6200. FAX 630-260-0114. URL: http://www.christianity.net/cr. *6329*

CHRISTIAN SCIENCE MONITOR.
Christian Science Publishing Society, One Norway St., Boston, MA 02115-3195. TEL 617-450-2000. URL: http://www.csmonitor.com.
Vendor(s): Knight-Ridder Information, Inc. *3371*

CHRISTIAN SCIENCE MONITOR INDEX.
U M I, 300 N. Zeeb Rd., Ann Arbor, MI 48106-1346. TEL 313-761-4700. FAX 800-864-0019.
Vendor(s): Knight-Ridder Information, Inc. *3883*

CHRISTIAN WEB REVIEW.
Faith Reality Publications, URL: http://dbj.com/www/wtknight/cwreview.html.
Available only online. *6418*

CHRISTIANITY TODAY.
Christianity Today, Inc., 465 Gundersen Dr., Carol Stream, IL 60188. TEL 630-260-6200. FAX 630-261-0114. URL: http://www.christianity.net/ct.
Vendor(s): Information Access Co., UMI. *6330*

CHROMOSOMA.
Springer-Verlag, Heidelberger Platz 3, 14197 Berlin, Germany. TEL 49-30-82787-0. FAX 49-30-82787448. URL: http://link.springer.de. *764*

THE CHRONICLE OF HIGHER EDUCATION.
Chronicle of Higher Education, Inc., 1255 23rd St., N.W., Ste. 700, Washington, DC 20037. TEL 202-466-1000. FAX 202-296-2691.
Vendor(s): UMI. *2535*

CHRONICLES OF CHAOS.
57 Lexfield Ave., Downsview, ON M3M 1M6, Canada. URL: http://www.interlog.com/~ginof/coc.html.
Available only online. *5383*

CHRONICLES OF FICTION.
2406 Belmont Blvd., Nashville, TN 37212. URL: http://edge.edge.net/~renshawc/chronicles.html.
Available only online. *4390*

CHRYSALIS (OMAHA).
Transformations Forum, SIS, Inc., 4524 Shirley St., Omaha, NE 68106. URL: http://www.transformations.com/Chrys.
Available only online. *5456*

CHURCH HISTORY.
American Society of Church History, Box 8517, Red Bank, NJ 07701-8517.
Vendor(s): UMI. *6330*

THE CHURCH MUSIC REPORT.
T C M R Communications Inc., 109 Seventh Ave. N., Franklin, TN 37064. TEL 615-591-2363. FAX 615-790-0879. URL: http://www.tcmr.com. *5383*

CHURCHART PRO ON DISK.
Communication Resources Inc., 4150 Belden Village St., Ste. 400, Canton, OH 44718-2502. FAX 330-493-7897. *6419*

CINCINNATI BUSINESS COURIER.
A C B J Business Publications Inc., 35 E. 7th St., Ste. 700, Cincinnati, OH 45202-2411. TEL 513-621-6665. FAX 513-621-2462.
Vendor(s): Information Access Co. *948*

CINCINNATI LAW REVIEW.
University of Cincinnati, College of Law, Rm. 300, Cincinnati, OH 45221-0040. TEL 513-556-5101. FAX 513-556-6265.
Vendor(s): West Group. *3930*

CINEASTE.
Cineaste Publishers, Inc., 200 Park Ave. S., Ste. 1601, New York, NY 10003. TEL 212-982-1241. FAX 212-982-1241.
Vendor(s): Information Access Co., UMI. *5326*

CINEMA REVUE.
Independent Publisher's Group, Box 40611, Memphis, TN 38174. TEL 901-272-7462. *5327*

CINEMEDIA ACCESS COLLECTION. VIDEO CATALOG.
State Film Centre of Victoria, Film and Video Library, 17 St. Andrews Pl., E. Melbourne, Vic. 3002, Australia. TEL 61-3-96511303. FAX 61-3-96511502. URL: http://www.cinemedia.net. *5328*

CINOPSIS.
Rue M. Poedts, 10, 1160 Brussels, Belgium. TEL 32-32206620321. URL: http://www.cinopsis.com; http://www.cinopsis.be.
Available only online. *5328*

CIRCUIT TRACES.
Circuit Traces Communications, URL: http://www.ctraces.com.
Available only online. *4529*

THE CIRCULAR FILE.
URL: http://www.interbridge.com/circfile/circfile.html.
Available only online. *4327*

CIRCULATION (DALLAS).
American Heart Association, 7272 Greenville Ave., Dallas, TX 75231-4596. TEL 214-706-1310. FAX 214-691-6342.
Vendor(s): Ovid Technologies, Inc. (JWAT) *4814*

CIRCULATION RESEARCH.
American Heart Association, 7272 Greenville Ave., Dallas, TX 75231-4596. TEL 214-706-1310. FAX 214-691-6342.
Vendor(s): Ovid Technologies, Inc. *4814*

CITATIONS FOR SERIAL LITERATURE.
MIT Libraries, Rm. 14E-210A, Massachusetts Institute of Technology, Cambridge, MA 02139-4307. URL: http://www.readmore.com/info/csl.html.
Available only online. *4225*

THE CITIZEN.
25 Church St., Inverkeithing, Fife Ky11 1LH, Scotland. URL: http://ourworld.compuserve.com/homepages/The_Citizen/ *5900*

CITIZEN POKE MAGAZINE.
Box 234, Amherst College, Amherst, MA 01002-5000. URL: http://www.cpoke.com.
Available only online. *4327*

SERIALS AVAILABLE ONLINE

CITY LAW.
Center for New York City Law, 57 Worth St., 10th Fl., Rm. 1001A, New York, NY 10013-2960. TEL 212-431-2115. FAX 212-431-3295. *3930*

CIVICA SCUOLA DI MUSICA. QUADERNI.
Civica Scuola di Musica, Via Stilicone 36, 20154 Milan, Italy. TEL 02-313334. FAX 02-3315697. *5384*

CIVIL ENGINEERING SYSTEMS.
Gordon and Breach - Harwood Academic, Amsteldisk 166, 1st Fl., 1079 LH Amsterdam, Netherlands. URL: http://www.gbhap.com/Civil_Engineering_Systems/. *2780*

CLADISTICS: THE INTERNATIONAL JOURNAL OF THE WILLI HENNIG SOCIETY.
Academic Press Ltd., 24-28 Oval Rd., London NW1 7DX, England. TEL 44-171-267-4466. FAX 44-171-482-2293. URL: http://www.hbuk.co.uk/ap/cladistics; http://www.europe.idealibrary.com/. *699*

CLASSICAL AND QUANTUM GRAVITY.
I O P Publishing Ltd., Dirac House, Temple Back, Bristol BS1 6BE, England. TEL 44-117-929-7481. FAX 44-117-929-4318. URL: http://www.iop.org. *5799*

CLASSICAL ANTIQUITY.
University of California Press, Journals Division, 2120 Berkeley Way, No. 5812, Berkeley, CA 94720-5812. TEL 510-643-7154. FAX 510-642-9917. URL: http://sunsite.berkeley.edu:8080/scan. Vendor(s): Information Access Co. *1901*

THE CLASSICAL QUARTERLY.
Oxford University Press, Academic Division, Great Clarendon St., Oxford OX2 6DP, England. TEL 44-1865-267907. FAX 44-1865-267485. URL: http://www.oup.co.uk/journals. Vendor(s): Information Access Co. *1902*

CLEANING APPLIANCES: THE INTERNATIONAL MARKET.
Euromonitor, 60-61 Britton St., London EC1M 5NA, England. TEL 44-171-251-8024. FAX 44-171-608-3149. URL: http://www.euromonitor.com. Vendor(s): Data-Star, Knight-Ridder Information, Inc. *2627*

CLEANING BUSINESS.
Wm. R. Griffin, Pub., Box 1273, Seattle, WA 98111-1273. TEL 206-622-4241. FAX 206-622-6876. URL: http://www.cleaningconsultants.com. *1641*

THE CLEARING HOUSE.
Heldref Publications, 1319 Eighteenth St., N.W., Washington, DC 20036-1802. TEL 202-296-6267. FAX 202-296-5149. Vendor(s): Information Access Co. *2429*

CLEVELAND STATE LAW REVIEW.
Cleveland State University, Cleveland - Marshall College of Law, 1983 E. 24th St., Cleveland, OH 44115. TEL 216-687-2336. Vendor(s): West Group. *3931*

CLIMATE DYNAMICS.
Springer-Verlag, Heidelberger Platz 3, 14197 Berlin, Germany. TEL 49-30-82787-0. FAX 49-30-82787448. URL: http://link.springer.de. *5228*

CLINICA.
P J B Publications Ltd., 18-20 Hill Rise, Richmond, Surrey TW10 6UA, England. TEL 44-181-948-3262. FAX 44-181-332-8998. URL: http://www.pjbpubs.co.uk/clinica/clinic.html. Vendor(s): Data-Star, Knight-Ridder Information, Inc. (File No. 129), Ovid Technologies, Inc. (PHIN,PHIC, PHID). *4654*

CLINICAL AND INVESTIGATIVE MEDICINE.
Canadian Medical Association, 1867 Alta Vista Dr., Ottawa, ON K1G 3Y6, Canada. TEL 613-731-9331. FAX 613-523-0937. URL: http://www.cma.ca/journals/cim. *4654*

CLINICAL CHEMISTRY AND ENZYMOLOGY COMMUNICATIONS.
Gordon and Breach - Harwood Academic, Amsteldisk 166, 1st Fl., 1079 LH Amsterdam, Netherlands. URL: http://www.gbhap.com/Clinical_Chemistry_Enzymology_Communications/ *657*

CLINICAL DIABETES.
American Diabetes Association, 1660 Duke St., Alexandria, VA 22314. TEL 703-549-1500. FAX 703-836-7439. Vendor(s): Information Access Co., Ovid Technologies, Inc. *4883*

CLINICAL DYSMORPHOLOGY.
Chapman & Hall, Journals Department 2-6 Boundary Row, London SE1 8HN, England. TEL 44-171-8650066. FAX 44-171-5229623. URL: http://www.chaphall.com/chaphall/journals.html. *814*

CLINICAL IMMUNOLOGY AND IMMUNOPATHOLOGY.
Academic Press, Inc., Journal Division, 525 B St., Ste. 1900, San Diego, CA 92101-4495. TEL 619-230-1840. FAX 619-699-6800. URL: http://www.apnet.com/www.journal/ii.htm. *4793*

CLINICAL LABORATORY.
Clinical Laboratory Publications, Im Breitspiel 15, 69126 Heidelberg, Germany. TEL 49-6221-3432133. FAX 49-6221-300291. URL: http://www.hway.net/clinlab. *4883*

CLINICAL LASER MONTHLY.
American Health Consultants, Inc., 3525 Piedmont Rd., N.E., Bldg. 6, Ste. 400, Atlanta, GA 30305. TEL 800-688-2421. FAX 800-284-3291. Vendor(s): Lexis-Nexis. *5139*

CLINICAL ONCOLOGY.
Springer-Verlag London Ltd., Sweetapple House, Catteshall Rd., Godalming, Surrey GU7 3DJ, England. TEL 44-1483-418800. FAX 44-1483-415144. *4976*

CLINICAL ORAL INVESTIGATIONS.
Springer-Verlag, Heidelberger Platz 3, 14197 Berlin, Germany. TEL 49-30-82787-0. FAX 49-30-82787448. *4853*

CLINICAL ORTHOPAEDICS AND RELATED RESEARCH.
Lippincott - Raven Publishers, 227 E. Washington Sq., Philadelphia, PA 19106. TEL 215-238-4200. FAX 215-238-4227. URL: http://www.lrpub.com. Vendor(s): Lexis-Nexis, Ovid Technologies, Inc. *5006*

CLINICAL PEDIATRICS.
Westminster Publications, Inc., 708 Glen Cove Ave., Glen Head, NY 11545. TEL 516-759-0025. FAX 516-759-5524. Vendor(s): Lexis-Nexis, Ovid Technologies, Inc. *5029*

CLINICAL PHARMACOLOGY & THERAPEUTICS.
Mosby - Year Book, Inc., 11830 Westline Industrial Dr., St. Louis, MO 63146-3318. TEL 314-872-8370. FAX 314-432-1380. Vendor(s): Ovid Technologies, Inc. *5653*

CLIONET.
James Cook University of North Queensland, Department of History and Politics, Townsville, Qld. 4811, Australia. TEL 61-77-814170. FAX 61-77-814487. Available only online. *3492*

CLONE.
Alpha du Centaure, Available only online. *2151*

CLUB MANAGEMENT.
Finan Publishing, 8730 Big Bend Blvd., St. Louis, MO 63119. TEL 314-961-6644. FAX 314-961-4809. URL: http://www.club-mgmt.com. Vendor(s): UMI. *1930*

THE CLUB TREAD REPORT.
Braun's Bicycle & Fitness, 27 Scott St., Kitchener, ON N2H 2P8, Canada. TEL 519-579-BIKE. FAX 519-579-8723. URL: http://www.bltg.com/ctreport/ *6826*

COACH AND ATHLETIC DIRECTOR.
Scholastic Inc., 555 Broadway, New York, NY 10012-3999. TEL 212-343-6100. Vendor(s): Information Access Co. *5779*

COAL AGE.
Intertec Publishing Corp., 9800 Metcalf Ave., Overland Park, KS 66212-2215. TEL 913-341-1300. FAX 913-967-1898. Vendor(s): Lexis-Nexis. *5298*

COAL HIGHLIGHTS.
I E A Coal Research, Gemini House, 10-18 Putney Hill, London SW15 6AA, England. TEL 44-181-780-0111. FAX 44-181-780-1746. Vendor(s): QL Systems Ltd. *2661*

COAL OUTLOOK.
Pasha Publications Inc., 1616 N. Ft. Myer Dr., Ste. 1000, Arlington, VA 22209-3107. TEL 703-528-1244. FAX 703-528-1253. *5298*

COAL TECH INTERNATIONAL.
McGraw-Hill Companies, Energy & Business Newsletters, 1221 Ave. of the Americas, 36th Fl., New York, NY 10020. Vendor(s): Dow Jones News Retrieval (CSL), Knight-Ridder Information, Inc. (File no.624/McGRAW-HILL PUBLICATIONS ONLINE), Lexis-Nexis (SYNFLS), NewsNet (EY76). *2662*

COAL U.K.
Financial Times Energy Publishing, Maple House, 149 Tottenham Court Rd., London W1P 9LL, England. TEL 0171-896-2241. FAX 0171-896-2275. Vendor(s): Data-Star, Knight-Ridder Information, Inc., Lexis-Nexis. *2662*

COAL WEEK.
McGraw-Hill Companies, Energy & Business Newsletters, 1221 Ave. of the Americas, 36th Fl., New York, NY 10020. TEL 212-512-6410. Vendor(s): Dow Jones News Retrieval (COW), Knight-Ridder Information, Inc. (File no.624/McGRAW-HILL PUBLICATIONS ONLINE), Lexis-Nexis (COALWK), NewsNet (EY77). *5298*

COAL WEEK INTERNATIONAL.
McGraw-Hill Companies, Energy & Business Newsletters, 1221 Ave. of the Americas, 36th Fl., New York, NY 10020. TEL 212-512-6410. Vendor(s): Dow Jones News Retrieval (CWI), Knight-Ridder Information, Inc. (File no.624/McGRAW-HILL PUBLICATIONS ONLINE), Lexis-Nexis (COALIN), NewsNet (EY78). *5298*

COALDAT MONTHLY (PRODUCING DISTRICT FORMAT).
Pasha Publications Inc., 1616 N. Ft. Myer Dr., Ste. 1000, Arlington, VA 22209-3107. TEL 703-528-1244. FAX 703-528-1253. *1520*

COALDAT MONTHLY (SUPPLIERS FORMAT).
Pasha Publications Inc., 1616 N. Ft. Myer Dr., Ste. 1000, Arlington, VA 22209-3107. TEL 703-528-1244. FAX 703-528-1253. *1520*

COALDAT MONTHLY (UTILITY FORMAT).
Pasha Publications Inc., 1616 N. Ft. Myer Dr., Ste. 1000, Arlington, VA 22209-3107. TEL 703-528-1244. FAX 703-528-1253. *1521*

COALDAT PRODUCTIVITY REPORT.
Pasha Publications Inc., 1616 N. Ft. Myer Dr., Ste. 1000, Arlington, VA 22209-3107. TEL 703-528-1244. FAX 703-528-1253. *5320*

COALDAT QUARTERLY.
Pasha Publications Inc., 1616 N. Ft. Myer Dr., Ste. 1000, Arlington, VA 22209-3107. TEL 703-528-1244. FAX 703-528-1253. *1521*

COAST BUSINESS.
Ship Island Holding Co., Box 1209, Gulfport, MS 39502-1209. TEL 601-868-1182. FAX 601-867-2986. Vendor(s): UMI. *948*

COATINGS.
Kay Publishing Company Ltd., 406 N. Service Rd., E., Ste. 1, Oakville, ON L6H 5R2, Canada. TEL 905-844-9773. FAX 905-844-5672. Vendor(s): Information Access Co. *5551*

COCTAIL OF THE WEEK NEWSLETTER.
Box 2577, Taren Point Business Ctr., N.S.W. 2229, Australia. URL: http://www.ozemail.com.au/~berghous/drink.html. Available only online. *519*

CODE ONE.
Lockheed Martin TAS, Mail Zone 1224, Box 748, Ft. Worth, TX 76101-0748. TEL 817-777-5542. FAX 817-777-5557. URL: http://www.lmtas.com/codeone/codeone.html. *62*

COFFEE TALK MAGAZINE.
Coffee Talk, Inc., 1306 Western Ave., Ste. 406, Seattle, WA 98101. TEL 206-382-2112. FAX 206-623-0446. URL: http://www.coffeetalk.com. *3100*

COGNITIVE PSYCHOLOGY.
Academic Press, Inc., Journal Division, 525 B St., Ste. 1900, San Diego, CA 92101-4495. TEL 619-230-1840. FAX 619-699-6800. URL: http://www.apnet.com/www/journal/cg.htm; http://www.idealibrary.com/ *6103*

COGNITIVE THERAPY AND RESEARCH.
Plenum Publishing Corp., 233 Spring St., New York, NY 10013-1578. TEL 212-620-8000. FAX 212-463-0742. *6103*

COLD FUSION TIMES.
URL: http://world.std.com/'mica/cft.html.
Available only online. *2695*

COLE PAPERS.
2590 Greenwich St., Ste. 9, San Francisco, CA 94123-3333. TEL 415-673-2424. FAX 415-673-2449. URL: http://colegroup.com. *6956*

COLEGIO OFICIAL DE FARMACEUTICO. CIRCULAR FARMACEUTICA.
Colegio Oficial de Farmaceuticos de la Provincia de Barcelona, Pau Claris, 94, 08010 Barcelona, Spain. *5654*

COLLABORATIVE COMPUTING.
Chapman & Hall, Journals Department 2-6 Boundary Row, London SE1 8HN, England. TEL 44-171-8650066. FAX 44-171-5229623. URL: http://www.chaphall.com/chaphall/journals.html. *2131*

COLLECTIVE BARGAINING NEGOTIATIONS & CONTRACTS.
The Bureau of National Affairs, Inc., 1231 25th St., N.W., Washington, DC 20037. TEL 202-452-4200. FAX 202-822-8092. URL: http://www.bna.com/
Vendor(s): Human Resources Information Network, West Group. *1423*

THE COLLECTOR NEWSMAGAZINE.
D R S Internet Publishing Group, Box 488, Matthews, NC 28106. URL: http://www.ceo-online.com/thecollector.
Available only online. *339*

COLLEGAMENTO.
Utet Periodici Scientifici s.r.l., Via P. Giuria 20, 10125 Turin, Italy. TEL 39-2-29003555. FAX 39-2-6599049. *5654*

COLLEGE HEIGHTS HERALD.
Western Kentucky University, 109 Garrett Center, Bowling Green, KY 42101. TEL 502-745-2653. FAX 502-745-2697. URL: http://www.msc.edu/info/herald. *1946*

COLLEGE LITERATURE.
West Chester University, 554 New Main, West Chester, PA 19383. TEL 610-436-2901. FAX 610-436-3150.
Vendor(s): Information Access Co. *4391*

COLLEGE MEDIA DIRECTORY.
Oxbridge Communications, Inc., 150 Fifth Ave., New York, NY 10011. TEL 212-741-0231. FAX 212-633-2938. *544*

COLLEGE PRESS SERVICE.
Tribune Media Services, 435 N. Michigan Ave., Ste. 1417, Chicago, IL 60611-4008. *2536*

COLLEGE QUARTERLY.
A C A A T O, P.O. Box 362, Thornhill, ON L3T 4A2, Canada. TEL 905-764-1246. URL: http://www.collegequarterly.org.
Available only online. *2536*

COLONIAL HOMES.
Hearst Corporation, Colonial Homes, 1790 Broadway, 14th Fl., New York, NY 10019. TEL 212-830-2951. FAX 212-586-3455. URL: http://www.hearstcorp.com.
Vendor(s): Information Access Co. *400*

COLONNADE.
Georgia College & State University, Box 2442, Milledgeville, GA 31061. TEL 912-453-4511. FAX 912-454-1472. URL: http://acs5.gac.peachnet.edu/~colonnade. *1946*

COLORADO BUSINESS.
Wiesner Publishing, Inc., 7009 S. Potomac St., Englewood, CO 80112. TEL 303-397-7600. FAX 303-397-7619.
Vendor(s): Information Access Co., Knight-Ridder Information, Inc., Lexis-Nexis. *1231*

COLORADO BUSINESS DIRECTORY.
American Business Directories, 5711 S. 86th Circle, Box 27347, Omaha, NE 68127. TEL 402-593-4600. FAX 402-331-5481. *1661*

COLORADO CONSTRUCTION WEEKLY.
McGraw-Hill Companies, Princeton Rd. S-2, Box 689, Hightstown, NJ 08520-0689. *877*

COLORADO GUIDE TO SMOKE-FREE DINING.
Group to Alleviate Smoking Pollution (GASP), 2885 Aurora Ave., No. 37, Boulder, CO 80303-2252. TEL 303-444-9799. URL: http://www.smokescreen.org. *3724*

COLORADO SPRINGS BUSINESS JOURNAL.
31 E. Platte Ave., Ste. 300, Box 1541, Colorado Springs, CO 80901. TEL 719-634-5905. FAX 719-634-5157.
Vendor(s): UMI. *948*

COLUMBIA COLLEGE TODAY.
Columbia University, Columbia College, Office of Alumni Affairs, 475 Riverside Dr., Rm. 917, New York, NY 10115. TEL 212-870-2752. FAX 212-870-2747. URL: http://www.columbia.edu/cu/college/alumni/CCT/. *1947*

COLUMBIA JOURNAL OF LAW AND SOCIAL PROBLEMS.
Darby Publishing, 435 W. 116th St., New York, NY 10027. TEL 212-663-8708. FAX 212-866-9714.
Vendor(s): West Group. *3932*

COLUMBIA JOURNAL OF TRANSNATIONAL LAW.
Columbia Journal of Transnational Law Association, Columbia University, 435 W. 116th St., Box D25, New York, NY 10027. TEL 212-663-8709.
Vendor(s): West Group. *4109*

COLUMBIA JOURNAL OF WORLD BUSINESS.
J A I Press Inc., 55 Old Post Rd., No. 2, Box 1678, Greenwich, CT 06830-1678. TEL 203-661-7602. FAX 203-661-0792. URL: http://www.jaipress.com/jmspub.hmt.
Vendor(s): Information Access Co. *1320*

COLUMBIA JOURNALISM REVIEW.
Columbia University, Graduate School of Journalism, 700 Journalism Bldg., New York, NY 10027. TEL 212-854-1881. FAX 212-854-8580. URL: http://www.cjr.org/.
Vendor(s): Information Access Co., UMI. *3870*

COLUMBIA LAW REVIEW.
Columbia Law Review Association, 435 W. 116th St., New York, NY 10027. TEL 212-854-4398.
Vendor(s): Lexis-Nexis, West Group. *3932*

COLUMBUS BUSINESS JOURNAL.
110 N. High St., Gahanna, OH 43230-9069.
Vendor(s): Knight-Ridder Information, Inc. *949*

COLUMBUS FREE PRESS.
Columbus Institute for Contemporary Journalism, 1240 Bryden Rd., Columbus, OH 43205. TEL 614-253-2571. FAX 614-253-2571. URL: http://www.freepress.org.
Available only online. *4328*

COMBUSTION SCIENCE AND TECHNOLOGY.
Gordon and Breach - Harwood Academic, Amsteldisk 166, 1st Fl., 1079 LH Amsterdam, Netherlands. URL: http://www.gbhap.com/Combustion__Science__Technology/. *1827*

COMBUSTION THEORY AND MODELLING.
I O P Publishing Ltd., Dirac House, Temple Back, Bristol BS1 6BE, England. TEL 44-117-9297481. FAX 44-117-9294318. URL: http://www.iop.org/EJ/3/313bin/journal/ct. *5840*

COMEDYZINE.
Box 27-3621, Boca Raton, FL 33429. URL: http://www.comedyzine.com.
Available only online. *4328*

COMERCIO EXTERIOR.
Banco Nacional de Comercio Exterior, S.A., Gerencia de la Revista Comercio Exterior, Camino a Santa Teresa 1679, Col. Jardines del Pedregal, 01900 Mexico D.F., Mexico. TEL 525-3276220. FAX 525-3276214. URL: http://mexico.businessline.gob.mx/infotec/revista.html. *1320*

COMING SOON MAGAZINE.
130 Prim Rd., Ste. 211, Colchester, VT 05446. URL: http://www.csoon.com.
Available only online. *2117*

COMMENTARII MATHEMATICI HELVETICI.
Birkhaeuser Verlag, P.O. Box 133, CH-4010 Basel, Switzerland. TEL 41-61-2050730. FAX 41-61-2050791. *4567*

COMMENTARY.
American Jewish Committee, 165 E. 56th St., New York, NY 10022. TEL 212-751-4000. FAX 212-751-1174.
Vendor(s): Information Access Co. *4328*

COMMERCE BUSINESS DAILY.
U.S. International Trade Administration, U.S. Department of Commerce, Herbert C. Hoover Bldg., Rm. 3850, 14th St. & Constitution Ave., Washington, DC 20230. TEL 202-482-2867.
Vendor(s): Knight-Ridder Information, Inc. (File nos.194 & 195), NewsNet, United Communications Group (CBD OnLine). *1521*

COMMERCE EXTRA.
URL: http://www.outreach/commercelink/issue1.html.
Available only online. *949*

COMMERCIAL NEWS U S A.
U.S. Department of Commerce, International Trade Administration, Rm. 1310, Washington, DC 20230. TEL 202-482-4918. FAX 202-482-5362. *1320*

COMMODORE HACKIN.
Brain Innovations, Inc., 10710 Bruhn Ave., Bennington, NE 68007. URL: http://www.jbrain.com/chacking/
Available only online. *2075*

COMMONWEAL.
Commonweal Foundation, 475 Riverside Dr., Rm. 405, New York, NY 10115. TEL 212-732-0800.
Vendor(s): Information Access Co., UMI. *4329*

COMMONWEALTH CURRENTS.
Commonwealth Secretariat, Information and Public Affairs Division, Marlborough House, Pall Mall, London SW1Y 5HX, England. TEL 44-171-747-6386. FAX 44-171-839-9081. URL: http://www.thecommonwealth.org. *6009*

COMMONWEALTH GOVERNMENT DIRECTORY.
Australian Government Publishing Service, G.P.O. Box 84, Canberra, A.C.T. 2601, Australia. TEL 61-6-295-4411. FAX 61-6-295-4455. *6169*

COMMONWEALTH LAW REPORTS.
L B C Information Services, 50 Waterloo Rd., N. Ryde, N.S.W. 2113, Australia. TEL 61-2-99366444. FAX 61-2-98889706. *4130*

COMMUNICABLE DISEASES INTELLIGENCE.
Department of Health and Family Services, G.P.O. Box 9848, Canberra, A.C.T. 2601, Australia. TEL 61-6-2896895. FAX 61-6-2897791. *4834*

COMMUNICATION EDUCATION.
Speech Communication Association, 5105 Backlick Rd., Bldg. E., Annandale, VA 22003. TEL 703-750-0533. FAX 703-914-9471.
Vendor(s): UMI. *2598*

COMMUNICATION MONOGRAPHS.
Speech Communication Association, 5105 Backlick Rd., Bldg. E., Annandale, VA 22003. TEL 703-750-0533. FAX 703-914-9471.
Vendor(s): UMI. *2429*

COMMUNICATION QUARTERLY.
Eastern Communication Association, c/o Kathleen M. Long, Exec. Sec., Department of Communication & Marketing, West Virginia Wesleyan College, 59 College Ave., Buckhannon, WV 26201-2997. TEL 304-473-8234.
Vendor(s): UMI. *2429*

COMMUNICATION STUDIES.
Boylor Universitg, Waco, TX 76798. TEL 405-332-8000. FAX 405-332-1623.
Vendor(s): UMI. *1985*

COMMUNICATION WORLD.
International Association of Business Communicators, One Hallidie Plaza, Ste. 600, San Francisco, CA 94102. TEL 415-433-3400. FAX 415-362-8762.
Vendor(s): Information Access Co., Knight-Ridder Information, Inc., Lexis-Nexis, UMI. *1470*

COMMUNICATIONS AND THE LAW.
Fred B. Rothman & Co., 10368 W. Centennial Rd., Littleton, CO 80127. TEL 303-979-5657. FAX 303-978-1457.
Vendor(s): UMI. *1985*

COMMUNICATIONS BUSINESS & FINANCE.
Telecommunications Reports, 1333 H St., N.W., Ste. 100-E, Washington, DC 20005. FAX 202-842-3023. URL: http://www.tr.com.
Vendor(s): Information Access Co. *1986*

COMMUNICATIONS COMPANIES ANALYSIS. OPERATORS VOLUME.
M D I S Publications Ltd., MDIS House, City Fields Business Park, City Fields Way, Chichester, W. Sussex PO20 6FS, England. TEL 44-1243-533322. FAX 44-1243-533418. *1986*

COMMUNICATIONS DAILY.
Warren Publishing, Inc., 2115 Ward Ct., N.W., Washington, DC 20037. TEL 202-872-9200. FAX 202-293-3435.
Vendor(s): Data-Star, Information Access Co., Knight-Ridder Information, Inc., Lexis-Nexis, NewsNet (TE01). *2047*

COMMUNICATIONS IN MATHEMATICAL PHYSICS.
Springer-Verlag, Heidelberger Platz 3, 14197 Berlin, Germany. TEL 49-30-82787-0. FAX 49-30-82787448. URL: http://link.springer.de. *5800*

COMMUNICATIONS INTERNATIONAL.
E M A P Business & Computer Publications Ltd., 33-39 Bowling Green Ln., London EC1R 0DA, England. TEL 44-171-837-1212. FAX 44-171-278-4003.
Vendor(s): Information Access Co., Lexis-Nexis, UMI. *1986*

COMMUNICATIONS MARKETS ANALYSIS.
M D I S Publications Ltd., MDIS House, City Fields Business Park, City Fields Way, Chichester, W. Sussex PO20 6FS, England. TEL 44-1243-533322. FAX 44-1243-533418. *1986*

COMMUNICATIONS NEWS.
Nelson Publishing Co., 2504 N. Tamiami Trail, Nokomis, FL 34275. TEL 813-966-9521. FAX 813-966-2590. URL: http://www.comnews.com.
Vendor(s): Information Access Co., Knight-Ridder Information, Inc. *1986*

COMMUNICATIONS STANDARDS NEWS.
Omnicom P B I, Rosemount House, Rosemount Ave., W. Byfleet, Surrey KT14 6NP, England. TEL 44-1932-355515. FAX 44-1932-355962.
Vendor(s): Information Access Co. *2168*

COMMUNICATIONSWEEK.
C M P Publications, Inc., 600 Community Dr., Manhasset, NY 11030. TEL 516-562-5000. FAX 516-562-5718.
Vendor(s): Information Access Co., NewsNet (TE23). *1986*

COMMUNICATIONSWEEK INTERNATIONAL.
C M P Publications, Inc., 600 Community Dr., Manhasset, NY 11030. TEL 516-562-5000. FAX 516-562-5474.
Vendor(s): Data-Star, Information Access Co., Knight-Ridder Information, Inc., Lexis-Nexis, NewsNet (TE28). *1986*

COMMUNITIES MAGAZINE.
Fellowship for International Community, Box 155, Rutladge, MO 63563. TEL 816-883-5545. FAX 816-883-5545. URL: http://www.ic.org/. *6661*

COMMUNITY AND WORKER RIGHT-TO-KNOW NEWS.
Thompson Publishing Company, 1725 K St., N.W., Ste. 700, Washington, DC 20006. TEL 202-872-4000.
Vendor(s): Information Access Co. *5488*

COMMUNITY MENTAL HEALTH JOURNAL.
Human Sciences Press, Inc., 233 Spring St., New York, NY 10013-1578. TEL 212-620-8000. FAX 212-463-0742. *6661*

COMMUNITY PHARMACY.
Miller Freeman plc, Sovereign Way, Tonbridge, Kent TN9 1RW, England. TEL 44-1732-364422. FAX 44-1732-361534.
Vendor(s): Information Access Co. *5654*

COMMUTER - REGIONAL AIRLINE NEWS.
Phillips Business Information, Inc., 1201 Seven Locks Rd., Potomac, MD 20854. TEL 301-424-3338. FAX 301-309-3487.
Vendor(s): Data-Star, Information Access Co., Knight-Ridder Information, Inc., NewsNet (AE25). *7066*

COMMUTER REGIONAL AIRLINE NEWS INTERNATIONAL.
Phillips Business Information, Inc., 120 Seven Locks Rd., Potomac, MD 20854. TEL 301-424-3338. FAX 301-309-3487.
Vendor(s): Information Access Co., NewsNet (AE26). *7066*

COMP MEDIA.
URL: http://www.village2000.com/comp.media/
Available only online. *6956*

COMPANIES AND THEIR BRANDS.
Gale Research, 835 Penobscot Bldg., 645 Griswold St., Detroit, MI 48226-4094. TEL 313-961-2242. FAX 800-414-5043.
Vendor(s): Knight-Ridder Information, Inc. *1661*

COMPARATIVE DRAMA.
Western Michigan University, Department of English, Kalamazoo, MI 49008-3851. TEL 616-387-2576. FAX 616-387-8750.
Vendor(s): UMI. *4392*

COMPARATIVE ECONOMIC STUDIES.
Association for Comparative Economic Studies, c/o Robert Stuart, Ed., Department of Economics, Rutgers University, New Brunswick, NJ 08903-5055. TEL 908-932-7368. FAX 908-932-7416.
Vendor(s): UMI. *1298*

COMPARATIVE EDUCATION.
Carfax Publishing Co., P.O. Box 25, Abingdon, Oxon. OX14 3UE, England. TEL 44-1235-401000. FAX 44-1235-401550. *2430*

COMPARATIVE HAEMATOLOGY INTERNATIONAL.
Springer-Verlag London Ltd., Sweetapple House, Catteshall Rd., Godalming, Surrey GU7 3DJ, England. TEL 44-1483-418800. FAX 44-1483-415144. *4917*

COMPARATIVE LITERATURE.
University of Oregon, Comparative Literature, 1223 Friendly Hall, Eugene, OR 97403-1233. TEL 503-346-4022. FAX 503-346-4030.
Vendor(s): UMI. *4392*

COMPENSATION AND BENEFITS REVIEW.
American Management Association, 1601 Broadway, New York, NY 10019. TEL 212-903-8069. FAX 212-903-8168.
Vendor(s): Information Access Co., Knight-Ridder Information, Inc., UMI. *1424*

COMPENSATION & BENEFITS SOFTWARE CENSUS.
Advanced Personnel Systems, 1873-Hidden View Ln., Roseville, CA 95661-5819. TEL 916-781-2900. FAX 916-781-2901. URL: http://www.hrcensus.com.
Vendor(s): Human Resources Information Network. *1199*

COMPLEMENTARY MEDICINE INDEX.
British Library, Medical Information Centre, Boston Spa, Wetherby, W. Yorks. LS23 7BQ, England. TEL 44-1937-546039. FAX 44-1937-546458. *299*

THE COMPLETE DIRECTORY OF LARGE PRINT BOOKS AND SERIALS.
R.R. Bowker, A Division of Reed Elsevier Inc., 121 Chanlon Rd., New Providence, NJ 07974. TEL 908-464-6800. FAX 908-655-3502. URL: http://www.reedref.com. *3459*

COMPLEX VARIABLES: THEORY AND APPLICATION.
Gordon and Breach - Harwood Academic, Amsteldisk 166, 1st Fl., 1079 LH Amsterdam, Netherlands. URL: http://www.gbhap.com/Complex_Variables_Theory_Applications/. *4567*

COMPLEXITY INTERNATIONAL.
c/o School of Information Techonology, Charles Sturt University, Panorama Ave., Bathurst, N.S.W. 2795, Australia. TEL 61-63-384272. FAX 61-63-384649. URL: http://www.csu.edu.au/ci/ci.html. Available only online. *2154*

COMPLICATIONS IN SURGERY.
S C P Communications, Inc., 134 W. 29th St., New York, NY 10001-5304. TEL 212-714-1740. URL: http://www.medscape.com.
Available only online. *5139*

THE COMPOSITES AND ADHESIVES NEWSLETTER.
T - C Press, Box 36006, Los Angeles, CA 90036-0006. TEL 213-938-6923. FAX 213-938-6923.
Vendor(s): Data-Star, Information Access Co., Knight-Ridder Information, Inc. *5877*

COMPOSITES INDUSTRY MONTHLY.
Composite Market Reports, 1345 E. Mian St., Ste. 100, Mesa, AZ 85203-8950. TEL 602-461-9445. FAX 602-461-8177.
Vendor(s): Dow Jones News Retrieval, Information Access Co., Knight-Ridder Information, Inc., NewsNet. *2856*

COMPOSITES NEWS: INFRASTRUCTURE.
Composites News International, 991 Lomas Santa Fe Dr., C469, Solana Beach, CA 92075-2125. TEL 619-755-1372. FAX 619-755-5271.
Vendor(s): Information Access Co. *6956*

COMPREHENSIVE PSYCHIATRY.
W.B. Saunders Co., Curtis Center, 3rd Fl., Independence Sq. W., Philadelphia, PA 19106-3399. TEL 215-238-7800. FAX 215-238-6445. *5059*

COMPUMATH CITATION INDEX.
Institute for Scientific Information, 3501 Market St., Philadelphia, PA 19104. TEL 215-386-0100. FAX 215-386-2911.
Vendor(s): Ovid Technologies, Inc. *4617*

COMPUNOTES.
1315 Woodgate Dr., St. Louis, MO 63122. URL: http://users.aol.com/compnote.
Available only online. *2131*

COMPUTATIONAL MECHANICS.
Springer-Verlag, Heidelberger Platz 3, 14197 Berlin, Germany. TEL 49-30-82787-0. FAX 49-30-82787448. URL: http://link.springer.de. *4620*

COMPUTE - ED.
URL: http://www.j.eklund@uts.edu.au; j.harvey@edfac.usyd.edu.au
Available only online. *2430*

COMPUTER (LOS ALAMITOS).
I E E E Computer Society Press, 10662 Los Vaqueros Circle, Box 3014, Los Alamitos, CA 90720-1264. TEL 714-821-8380. FAX 714-821-4641. URL: http://www.computer.org/pubs/computer/computer.htm. *2075*

COMPUTER AIDED DESIGN REPORT.
C A D - C A M Publishing, Inc., 1010 Turquoise St., Ste. 320, San Diego, CA 92109-1268. TEL 619-488-0533. FAX 619-488-6052.
Vendor(s): Information Access Co. *2121*

COMPUTER-AIDED ENGINEERING (CLEVELAND).
Penton Publishing Co., 1100 Superior Ave., Cleveland, OH 44114-2543. TEL 216-696-7000. FAX 216-696-8765.
Vendor(s): Information Access Co., Knight-Ridder Information, Inc. *2802*

COMPUTER & CO.
Hackenstr. 7, 80331 Muenchen, Germany. URL: http://www.computer-co.de.
Available only online. *2131*

SERIALS AVAILABLE ONLINE

COMPUTER & CONTROL ABSTRACTS.
INSPEC, I.E.E., Michael Faraday House, Six Hills Way, Stevenage, Herts. SG1 2AY, England. TEL 44-1438-313311. FAX 44-1438-742840. URL: http://www.iee.org.uk.
Vendor(s): CEDOCAR, Data-Star, European Space Agency (File no.8/INSPEC), FIZ Technik, Knight-Ridder Information, Inc., Questel Orbit Inc., STN International. *2093*

COMPUTER AND INFORMATION SYSTEMS ABSTRACTS JOURNAL.
Cambridge Scientific Abstracts, 7200 Wisconsin Ave., 6th Fl., Bethesda, MD 20814. TEL 301-961-6750. FAX 301-961-6720. URL: http://www.csa.com.
Vendor(s): STN International. *2093*

COMPUTER AUDIT UPDATE.
Elsevier Science Ltd., P.O. Box 800, Kidlington, Oxford OX5 1DX, England. TEL 44-1865-843000. FAX 44-1865-843010. URL: http://www.elsevier.nl/.
Vendor(s): Information Access Co. *2148*

COMPUTER BOOK REVIEW.
Computer Book Review, Box 61067, Honolulu, HI 96839. URL: http://www.bookwire.com/cbr.
Vendor(s): Knight-Ridder Information, Inc. *2075*

COMPUTER BUSINESS REVIEW.
ComputerWire Plc., 12 Sutton Row, London W1V 5FH, England. TEL 44-171-208-4200. FAX 44-171-439-1105. URL: http://www.computerwire.com.
Vendor(s): Information Access Co. *2126*

COMPUTER CHESS REPORTS.
Computer Chess Digest Inc., c/o I C D Corp., 21 Walt Whitman Rd., Huntington Station, NY 11746. TEL 516-424-3300. FAX 516-424-3405. URL: http://www.ICDchess.com.
Available only online. *6757*

COMPUTER CORNER.
URL: http://www.wfaa.com/ccindex.html.
Available only online. *2075*

COMPUTER COUNSEL.
Computer Counsel, Inc., Box 819, Avon, CT 06001-0819. TEL 312-207-6900. FAX 312-207-1045.
Vendor(s): West Group. *2075*

COMPUTER CURRENTS.
Computer Currents Publishing, Inc., 5720 Hollis St., Emeryville, CA 94608. TEL 510-547-6800. FAX 510-547-4613. URL: http://www.currents.net. *2126*

COMPUTER CURRENTS (BAY AREA EDITION).
Computer Currents Publishing, Inc., 5720 Hollis St., Emeryville, CA 94608. TEL 510-547-6800. FAX 510-547-4613. URL: http://www.currents.net. *2126*

COMPUTER CURRENTS (BOSTON EDITION).
Computer Currents Publishing, Inc., 5720 Hollis St., Emeryville, CA 94608. TEL 510-547-6800. FAX 510-547-4613. URL: http://www.currents.net. *2126*

COMPUTER CURRENTS (DALLAS - FT. WORTH EDITION).
Computer Currents Publishing, Inc., 5720 Hollis St., Emeryville, CA 94608. TEL 510-547-6800. FAX 510-547-4613. URL: http://www.currents.net. *2126*

COMPUTER CURRENTS (NEW YORK METRO EDITION).
Computer Currents Publishing, Inc., 5720 Hollis St., Emeryville, CA 94608. TEL 510-547-6800. FAX 510-547-4613. URL: http://www.currents.net. *2126*

COMPUTER DATABASE.
Information Access Company, 362 Lakeside Dr., Foster City, CA 94404. TEL 415-378-5200. FAX 415-378-5369.
Available only online. Vendor(s): Data-Star (CMPT), Knight-Ridder Information, Inc. (File no.275), Ovid Technologies, Inc. (CMPT). *2093*

COMPUTER DEALER NEWS.
Plesman Publications Ltd., 2005 Sheppard Ave. E., 4th Fl., Willowdale, ON M2J 5B1, Canada. TEL 416-497-9562. FAX 416-497-9427.
Vendor(s): Information Access Co. *2147*

COMPUTER DEALER NEWS SOURCE GUIDE.
Plesman Publications Ltd., 2005 Sheppard Ave. E., 4th Fl., Willowdale, ON M2J 5B1, Canada. TEL 416-497-9562. FAX 416-497-9427. URL: http://www.plesman.com. *2128*

COMPUTER DESIGN.
PennWell Publishing Co. (Nashua), Advanced Technology Group, 10 Tara Blvd., 5th Fl., Nashua, NH 03062-2801. TEL 603-891-9111. FAX 603-891-0514.
Vendor(s): Knight-Ridder Information, Inc. *2121*

COMPUTER FRAUD & SECURITY.
Elsevier Science Ltd., P.O. Box 800, Kidlington, Oxford OX5 1DX, England. TEL 44-1865-843000. FAX 44-1865-843010. URL: http://www.elsevier.nl/.
Vendor(s): Data-Star, Information Access Co., Knight-Ridder Information, Inc. *2149*

COMPUTER GAMING WORLD.
Ziff-Davis Publishing Co. (San Francisco), 135 Main St., San Francisco, CA 94105. TEL 415-357-4900. FAX 415-357-4977. URL: http://www.zdnet.com/gaming.
Vendor(s): Information Access Co. *2117*

COMPUTER GRAPHICS WORLD.
PennWell Publishing Co. (Nashua), Advanced Technology Group, 10 Tara Blvd., 5th Fl., Nashua, NH 03062-2801. TEL 603-891-0123. FAX 603-891-0539.
Vendor(s): Information Access Co., Knight-Ridder Information, Inc. *2121*

COMPUTER INDUSTRY DAILY.
Computer Economics, Inc., 5841 Edison Pl., Carlsbad, CA 92008. TEL 760-438-8100. FAX 760-431-1126. URL: http://www.computereconomics.com. *2127*

COMPUTER INDUSTRY FORECASTS.
Data Analysis Group, 5100 Cherry Creek Rd., Box 128, Cloverdale, CA 95425. TEL 707-539-3009. FAX 707-486-5618. URL: http://www.cif1.com.
Vendor(s): Lexis-Nexis. *2094*

COMPUTER INDUSTRY REPORT.
International Data Corporation, 5 Speen St., Framingham, MA 01701. TEL 508-935-4530. URL: http://www.idcresearch.com.
Vendor(s): Information Access Co. *2172*

THE COMPUTER JOURNAL.
Oxford University Press, Academic Division, Great Clarendon St., Oxford OX2 6DP, England. TEL 44-1865-267907. FAX 44-1865-267485. URL: http://www.oup.co.uk/journals. *2076*

COMPUTER LAWYER.
Aspen Law & Business, 270 Sylvan Ave., Englewood Cliffs, NJ 07632-2513. FAX 201-894-8666.
Vendor(s): Lexis-Nexis, West Group. *2076*

COMPUTER MANAGER.
National Association of Purchasing Management Organization, URL: http://www.compumgr.com/index2.htm. *2147*

COMPUTER MUSIC JOURNAL.
M I T Press, 5 Cambridge Center, Cambridge, MA 02142. TEL 617-253-2889. FAX 617-577-1545. URL: http://www-mitpress.mit.edu. *5449*

COMPUTER PROTOCOLS.
Worldwide Videotex, Box 3273, Boynton Beach, FL 33424-3273. TEL 407-738-2276.
Vendor(s): Data-Star, Information Access Co., Knight-Ridder Information, Inc., NewsNet (EC74). *2077*

COMPUTER PUBLISHING & ADVERTISING REPORT.
Cowles - SIMBA Information, 11 Riverbend Dr. S., Box 4949, Stamford, CT 06907-0949. TEL 203-358-9900. FAX 203-358-5811. URL: http://www.simbanet.com.
Vendor(s): Information Access Co. *6291*

COMPUTER RESELLER NEWS.
C M P Publications, Inc., 600 Community Dr., Manhasset, NY 11030. TEL 516-562-5000. FAX 516-733-6916. URL: http://www.crn.com.
Vendor(s): Information Access Co., NewsNet (EC07). *2147*

COMPUTER RETAIL WEEK.
C M P Publications, Inc., 600 Community Dr., Manhasset, NY 11030. TEL 516-562-5000. FAX 516-562-5464.
Vendor(s): Information Access Co. *2147*

COMPUTER SECURITY JOURNAL.
Miller Freeman, Inc., 600 Harrison St., San Francisco, CA 94107. TEL 415-905-2370. FAX 415-905-2234.
Vendor(s): UMI. *2149*

COMPUTER SHOPPER.
Coastal Associates Publishing, L.P., Computer Publications Division One Park Ave., New York, NY 10016. FAX 212-503-3999.
Vendor(s): Information Access Co. *2147*

COMPUTER SPEECH & LANGUAGE.
Academic Press Ltd., 24-28 Oval Rd., London NW1 7DX, England. TEL 44-171-267-4466. FAX 44-171-482-2293. URL: http://www.hbuk.co.uk/ap/csl; http://www.idealibrary.com/. *2142*

COMPUTER TECHNOLOGY REVIEW.
West World Productions, Inc., 420 N. Camden Dr., Beverly Hills, CA 90210-4507. TEL 310-777-6670.
Vendor(s): UMI. *2077*

COMPUTER USER'S SURVIVAL MAGAZINE.
Enterprises Publishing, 400 E. 59th St., Ste. 9F, New York, NY 10022. TEL 212-755-4363. FAX 212-755-4365. *2196*

COMPUTER VISION AND IMAGE UNDERSTANDING.
Academic Press, Inc., Journal Division, 525 B St., Ste. 1900, San Diego, CA 92101-4495. TEL 619-230-1840. FAX 619-699-6800. URL: http://www.apnet.com/www/journal/iv.htm; http://www.idealibrary.com/ *2121*

COMPUTER WEEKLY.
Reed Business Information, Quadrant House, The Quadrant, Sutton, Surrey SM2 5AS, England. TEL 44-181-661-8642. FAX 44-181-661-8979.
Vendor(s): Information Access Co. *2077*

COMPUTER WORKSTATIONS.
Worldwide Videotex, Box 3273, Boynton Beach, FL 33424-3273. TEL 407-738-2276.
Vendor(s): Information Access Co. *2178*

COMPUTERGRAM INTERNATIONAL.
A P T Data Group plc., 12 Sutton Row, 4th Fl., London W1V 5FH, England. TEL 44-171-208-4200. FAX 44-171-439-1105.
Vendor(s): Information Access Co., NewsNet (EC72). *2078*

COMPUTERS AND BIOMEDICAL RESEARCH.
Academic Press, Inc., Journal Division, 525 B. St., Ste. 1900, San Diego, CA 92101-4495. TEL 619-230-1840. FAX 619-699-6800. URL: http://www.apnet.com/www/journal/co.htm; http://www.idealibrary.com/ *4846*

COMPUTERS IN LIBRARIES.
Information Today, Inc., 143 Old Marlton Pike, Medford, NJ 08055-8750. TEL 609-654-6266. FAX 609-654-4309.
Vendor(s): Information Access Co., NewsNet, UMI. *2187*

COMPUTERS IN PHYSICS.
American Institute of Physics, One Physics Ellipse, College Park, MD 20740-3843. TEL 301-209-3000. URL: http://www.aip.org/cip. *5838*

COMPUTERWORLD.
Computerworld, Inc., 551 Old Connecticut Path, Box 9171, Framingham, MA 01701-9171. TEL 508-879-0700. FAX 508-875-8931.
Vendor(s): Knight-Ridder Information, Inc. (File no.674), Lexis-Nexis. *2078*

COMPUTERWORLD HONG KONG.
I D G Communications (HK) Ltd., Mount Parker House, Ste. 1011-15, 1111 King's Rd., Quarry Bay, Hong Kong, People's Republic of China. TEL 852-2861-3238. FAX 852-2861-0953. *2127*

COMPUTING CANADA.
Plesman Publications Ltd., 2005 Sheppard Ave. E., 4th Fl., Willowdale, ON M2J 5B1, Canada. TEL 416-497-9562. FAX 416-497-9427.
Vendor(s): Information Access Co. *2210*

COMPUTING RESEARCH NEWS.
Computing Research Association, 1875 Connecticut Ave., N.W., Ste. 718, Washington, DC 20009. TEL 202-234-2111. FAX 202-667-1066. URL: http://www.cra.org/crn. *4230*

COMPUTING REVIEWS.
Association for Computing Machinery, 1515 Broadway, 17th Fl., New York, NY 10036-5701. TEL 212-869-7440. FAX 212-944-1318. Vendor(s): Knight-Ridder Information, Inc. *2094*

COMPUTING TIMES.
Triad Publications, Box 14018, Tulsa, OK 74159-1018. TEL 918-585-8564. *2187*

COMPUTING TODAY.
Christianity Today, Inc., 465 Gundersen Dr., Carol Stream, IL 60188. TEL 630-260-6200. FAX 630-260-0114. URL: http://www.christianity.net/compt. *2132*

CONCERNING CARS AND TRUCKS.
Concerning Cars Inc., Box 450, Pound Ridge, NY 10576. TEL 914-764-8260. FAX 914-764-8308. *2911*

THE CONCRETE PRODUCER.
Aberdeen Group, 426 S. Westgate St., Addison, IL 60101. TEL 630-543-0870. FAX 630-543-3112. URL: http://www.supernetwork.com. *877*

CONCRETE PRODUCTS.
Intertec Publishing Corp., 29 N. Wacker Dr., Chicago, IL 60606. TEL 312-726-2802. FAX 312-726-2574.
Vendor(s): Information Access Co. *877*

CONFECTIONERY: THE INTERNATIONAL MARKET.
Euromonitor, 60-61 Britton St., London EC1M 5NA, England. TEL 44-171-251-8024. FAX 44-171-608-3149. URL: http://www.euromonitor.com.
Vendor(s): Data-Star, Knight-Ridder Information, Inc. *3136*

CONFERENCE PAPERS ANNUAL INDEX.
Cambridge Scientific Abstracts, 7200 Wisconsin Ave., 6th Fl., Bethesda, MD 20814. TEL 301-961-6750. FAX 301-961-6720. URL: http://www.csa.com.
Vendor(s): Knight-Ridder Information, Inc. (File no. 77), STN International (CONFSCI). *5173*

CONFERENCE PAPERS INDEX.
Cambridge Scientific Abstracts, 7200 Wisconsin Ave., 6th Fl., Bethesda, MD 20814. TEL 301-961-6750. FAX 301-961-6720. URL: http://www.csa.com.
Vendor(s): Knight-Ridder Information, Inc. (File no.77), STN International (CONFSCI). *5173*

CONFESS.
8214 S.W. Hawthorne Ln., Vashon, WA 98070. URL: http://www.fess-up.com.
Available only online. *6104*

CONFIGURATIONS.
Johns Hopkins University Press, Journals Publishing Division, 2715 N. Charles St., Baltimore, MD 21218-4319. TEL 410-516-6987. FAX 410-516-6968. URL: http://muse.jhu.ed. *4392*

CONFLICT RESOLUTION NOTES.
Conflict Resolution Center International, Inc., 2205 E. Carson St., Pittsburgh, PA 15203-2107. TEL 412-481-5559. FAX 412-481-5559. *3934*

CONFORMAL GEOMETRY AND DYNAMICS.
American Mathematical Society, Box 6248, Providence, RI 02940-6248. TEL 401-455-4000. FAX 401-331-3842. URL: http://www.ams.org/ecgd/
Available only online. *4568*

CONGRESS DAILY.
National Journal, Inc., 1501 M St., N.W., Ste. 300, Washington, DC 20005. TEL 202-739-8480. FAX 202-739-8539. *5902*

CONGRESS IN PRINT.
Congressional Quarterly Inc., 1414 22 St., N.W., Washington, DC 20037. FAX 202-728-1863. *5902*

CONGRESSIONAL ACTIVITIES.
Oliphant Washington Service, Box 9808, Friendship Sta., Washington, DC 20016. TEL 202-298-7226. FAX 202-333-5006.
Vendor(s): NewsNet (GT20). *6170*

CONGRESSIONAL MONITOR.
Congressional Quarterly Inc., 1414 22nd St., N.W., Washington, DC 20037. FAX 202-728-1863. *5903*

CONGRESSIONAL QUARTERLY SERVICE. WEEKLY REPORT.
Congressional Quarterly Inc., 1414 22nd St., N.W., Washington, DC 20037. FAX 202-728-1863.
Vendor(s): Information Access Co. *5903*

CONGRESSIONAL RECORD SCANNER.
Congressional Quarterly Inc., 1414 22nd St., N.W., Washington, DC 20037. FAX 202-728-1863. *5983*

CONGRESSIONAL RESEARCH REPORT.
Penny Hill Press, 6440 Wiscasset Rd., Bethesda, MD 20816. TEL 301-229-8229. FAX 301-229-6988.
Vendor(s): Information Access Co. *544*

CONNECT (ANN ARBOR).
Pegasus Press, Inc., 3487 Braeburn Circle, Ann Arbor, MI 48108. TEL 313-973-8825. FAX 313-973-0411. *2178*

CONNECTICUT BUSINESS DIRECTORY.
American Business Directories, 5711 S. 86th Cir., Box 27347, Omaha, NE 68127. TEL 402-593-4600. FAX 402-331-5481. *1662*

CONNECTICUT LAW REVIEW.
Connecticut Law Review Association, 65 Elizabeth St., Hartford, CT 06105-2290. TEL 860-570-5331. FAX 860-570-5332.
Vendor(s): West Group. *3934*

CONNECTION SCIENCE.
Carfax Publishing Co., P.O. Box 25, Abingdon, Oxon. OX14 3UE, England. TEL 44-1235-401000. FAX 44-1235-401550. *2099*

CONNECTIONS (LOS GATOS).
Mactivity, Inc., 20 N. Santa Cruz Ave., Los Gatos, CA 95030. TEL 408-354-2500. FAX 408-354-2571. *2132*

CONNECTIONS NEWSLETTER (MEMPHIS).
Southern States Communication Association, c/o Dr. Richard R. Ranta, Exec. Dir., College of Communication & Fine Arts, University of Memphis, Memphis, TN 38152. TEL 901-678-2350. FAX 901-678-5118. *1987*

CONNOTATIONS (PHOENIX).
Central Arizona Speculative Fiction Society, Box 62613, Phoenix, AZ 85082-2613. TEL 602-220-9785. URL: http://www.casfs.org. *4529*

CONSCIOUS CHOICE.
920 N. Franklin, Ste. 202, Chicago, IL 60610-3121. URL: http://www.consciouschoice.com. *2911*

CONSCIOUS CONSUMER.
New Consumer Institute, Inc., Box 51, Wauconda, IL 60084. TEL 847-526-0522. FAX 847-487-0010. URL: http://www.envirolink.com/sbn.
Available only online. *2253*

CONSCIOUSNESS AND COGNITION.
Academic Press, Inc., Journal Division, 525 B St., Ste. 1900, San Diego, CA 92101-4495. TEL 619-230-1840. FAX 619-699-6800. URL: http://www.apnet.com/www/jounal/cc.htm; htp://www.idealibrary.com/ *6104*

CONSERLINE.
U.S. Library of Congress, Serial Record Division, 101 Independence Ave., S.E., Washington, DC 20540-4160. TEL 202-707-5947. FAX 202-707-6333. URL: http://lcweb.loc.gov/acq/conser/consrlin.html.
Available only online. *4172*

CONSERVATION ECOLOGY.
URL: http://journal.biology.carleton.ca/journal/overview.html.
Available only online. *2227*

CONSOLIDATED FEDERAL FUNDS REPORT.
U.S. Bureau of the Census, Customer Services, Washington, DC 20233. TEL 301-457-4100. FAX 301-457-4714. URL: http://www.census.gov/. *6170*

CONSTITUTIONAL COMMENTARY.
Constitutional Commentary Inc., 229 19th Ave. S., Minneapolis, MN 55455. TEL 612-625-4819. FAX 612-625-2011.
Vendor(s): West Group. *5989*

CONSTRUCTION BULLETIN (ATLANTA).
Construction Market Data, Inc., 4126 Pleasantdale Rd., Ste. A8, Atlanta, GA 30340. FAX 770-613-5978. *879*

CONSTRUCTION CLAIMS CITATOR.
Select Press, Construction Industry Press, Box 9838, San Rafael, CA 94912. TEL 415-924-1612. Vendor(s): NewsNet (BC12). *879*

CONSTRUCTION CLAIMS MONTHLY.
Business Publishers, Inc., 951 Pershing Dr., Silver Spring, MD 20910-4464. TEL 301-587-6300. FAX 301-585-9075.
Vendor(s): NewsNet. *879*

CONSTRUCTION CLAIMS TRAINING GUIDE.
Business Publishers, Inc., 951 Pershing Dr., Silver Spring, MD 20910-4464. TEL 301-587-6300. FAX 301-585-9075.
Vendor(s): NewsNet. *879*

CONSTRUCTION DATA & NEWS COVERING OREGON.
McGraw-Hill Companies, Princeton Rd. S-2, Box 689, Hightstown, NJ 08520-0689. *879*

CONSTRUCTION DATA & NEWS COVERING SACRAMENTO.
McGraw-Hill Companies, Princeton Rd. S-2, Box 689, Hightstown, NJ 08520-0689. *879*

CONSTRUCTION DATA & NEWS COVERING WASHINGTON & ALASKA.
McGraw-Hill Companies, Princeton Rd. S-2, Box 689, Hightstown, NJ 08520-0689. *879*

CONSTRUCTION EQUIPMENT.
Cahners Publishing Company (Des Plaines), Division of Reed Elsevier Inc., 1350 E. Touhy Ave., Box 5080, Des Plaines, IL 60018-5080. TEL 847-390-2176. FAX 847-390-2690. URL: http://www.coneq.com; http://www.packdigest.com/mainmag/ce.htm. *880*

CONSTRUCTION INJURY LIABILITY MONTHLY.
Business Publishers, Inc., 951 Pershing Dr., Silver Spring, MD 20910-4464. TEL 301-587-6300. FAX 301-587-1081.
Vendor(s): NewsNet. *3935*

CONSTRUCTION LABOR REPORT.
The Bureau of National Affairs, Inc., 1231 25th St., N.W., Washington, DC 20037. TEL 202-452-4200. FAX 202-822-8092. URL: http://www.bna.com/
Vendor(s): Human Resources Information Network (File DD). *1424*

CONSTRUCTION MANAGEMENT AND ECONOMICS.
Thomson Professional, 2-6 Boundary Row, London SE1 8HN, England. TEL 44-171-8650066. FAX 44-171-5229623. URL: http://jpr.thomsonprofessional.com. *881*

CONSTRUCTION NEWS WEEKLY COVERING LONG ISLAND.
McGraw-Hill Companies, Princeton Rd. S-2, Box 689, Hightstown, NJ 08520-0689. *881*

CONSTRUCTION NEWS WEST.
McGraw-Hill Companies, Princeton Rd. S-2, Box 689, Hightstown, NJ 08520-0689. *881*

CONSTRUCTION REVIEW.
U.S. International Trade Administration, Basic Industries Division, Department of Commerce, Herbert C. Hoover Bldg., ITA Rm. H4039, 14th St. and Constitution Ave., Washington, DC 20230. TEL 202-482-0132. FAX 202-482-0382.
Vendor(s): Information Access Co., Knight-Ridder Information, Inc., UMI. *921*

CONSTRUCTIVE APPROXIMATION.
Springer-Verlag, Science Journals, 175 Fifth Ave., New York, NY 10010. TEL 212-460-1500. FAX 212-473-6272. URL: http://www.springer-ny.com; http://www.math.usf.edu/CA/ *4568*

CONSULTANTS AND CONSULTING ORGANIZATIONS DIRECTORY.
Gale Research, 835 Penobscot Bldg., 645 Griswold St., Detroit, MI 48226-4094. TEL 313-961-2242. FAX 800-414-5043.
Vendor(s): Human Resources Information Network (CCOD). *1471*

CONSULTANTS NEWS.
Kennedy Publications, Templeton Rd., Fitzwilliam, NH 03447. TEL 603-585-6544. FAX 603-585-9555.
Vendor(s): UMI. *1471*

CONSULTING - TOOLS.
National Consultant Referrals, Inc., 4918 N. Harbor Dr., Ste. 103, San Diego, CA 92106. TEL 619-523-2188. URL: http://referrals.com.
Available only online. *1471*

CONSUMER CATERING: THE INTERNATIONAL MARKET.
Euromonitor, 60-61 Britton St., London EC1M 5NA, England. TEL 44-171-251-8024. FAX 44-171-608-3149. URL: http://www.euromonitor.com.
Vendor(s): Data-Star, Knight-Ridder Information, Inc. *3100*

CONSUMER INFORMATION CATALOG.
U.S. General Services Administration, Consumer Information Center, 18th and F Sts., N.W., Rm. G-142, Washington, DC 20405. TEL 202-501-1794. FAX 202-501-4281. URL: http://www.pueblo.gsa.gov. *544*

CONSUMER POLICY REVIEW.
Which? Ltd., 2 Marylebone Rd., London NW1 4DF, England. TEL 44-171-830-6000. FAX 44-171-830-6220.
Vendor(s): UMI. *2254*

CONSUMER PRODUCT SAFETY REVIEW.
National Injury Information Clearinghouse, 4330 East-West Hwy., Bethesda, MD 20814. TEL 301-504-0990. URL: http://www.cpsc.gov. *2254*

CONSUMER REPORTS.
Consumers Union of the United States, Inc., 101 Truman Ave., Yonkers, NY 10703-1057. TEL 914-378-2000. FAX 914-378-2900.
Vendor(s): Information Access Co., Knight-Ridder Information, Inc. (File no.646), Lexis-Nexis. *2254*

CONSUMER REPORTS ON HEALTH.
Consumers Union of the United States, Inc., 101 Truman Ave., Yonkers, NY 10703-1057. TEL 914-378-2000. FAX 914-378-2906.
Vendor(s): Information Access Co., Knight-Ridder Information, Inc. (File no.646). *5780*

CONSUMER REPORTS TRAVEL LETTER.
Consumers Union of the United States, Inc., 101 Truman Ave., Yonkers, NY 10703-1057. TEL 914-378-2000. FAX 914-378-2906.
Vendor(s): Information Access Co., Knight-Ridder Information, Inc. (File no.646). *7194*

CONSUMERS DIGEST.
Consumers Digest, Inc., 8001 N. Lincoln Ave., 6th Fl., Skokie, IL 60077-3657. TEL 847-763-9200.
Vendor(s): Information Access Co. *2254*

CONSUMERS INDEX.
Pierian Press, Box 1808, Ann Arbor, MI 48106. TEL 313-434-5530. FAX 313-434-6409.
Vendor(s): OCLC. *2260*

CONSUMER'S RESEARCH MAGAZINE.
Consumers' Research, Inc., 800 Maryland Ave., N.E., Washington, DC 20002. TEL 202-546-1713. FAX 202-546-1638.
Vendor(s): Information Access Co., UMI. *2254*

CONTEMPORARY ECONOMIC POLICY.
Western Economic Association International, 7400 Center Ave., Ste. 109, Huntington Beach, CA 92647-3039. TEL 714-898-3222.
Vendor(s): Information Access Co. *950*

CONTEMPORARY EDUCATIONAL PSYCHOLOGY.
Academic Press, Inc., Journal Division, 525 B St., Ste. 1900, San Diego, CA 92101-4495. TEL 619-230-1840. FAX 619-699-6800. URL: http://www.apnet.com/www/journal/ep.htm; http://www.idealibrary.com/ *2430*

CONTEMPORARY LITERATURE.
University of Wisconsin Press, Journal Division, 114 N. Murray St., Madison, WI 53715. TEL 608-262-4952. FAX 608-262-7560.
Vendor(s): Information Access Co., UMI. *4393*

CONTEMPORARY MUSICIANS.
Gale Research, 835 Penobscot Bldg., 645 Griswold St., Detroit, MI 48226-4094. TEL 313-961-2242. FAX 800-414-5043.
Vendor(s): Lexis-Nexis. *5385*

CONTEMPORARY PHYSICS.
Taylor & Francis Ltd., 1 Gunpowder Sq., London EC4A 3DE, England. TEL 44-171-583-0490. FAX 44-171-583-0585. URL: http://www.tandf.co.uk/. *5800*

THE CONTEMPORARY REVIEW.
Contemporary Review Co. Ltd., Cheam Business Centre, 14 Upper Mulgrave Rd., Cheam, Surrey SM2 7AZ, England. TEL 44-181-643-4846. FAX 44-181-241-7507.
Vendor(s): Information Access Co. *4329*

CONTEMPORARY SOCIOLOGY.
American Sociological Association, 1722 N St., N.W., Washington, DC 20036. TEL 202-833-3410. FAX 202-785-0146.
Vendor(s): UMI. *6739*

CONTENTSDIRECT.
Elsevier Science Ltd., P.O. Box 800, Kidlington, Oxford OX2 5DK, England. TEL 44-1865-843000. FAX 44-1865-843010. URL: http://www.elsevier.com/homepage/about/caware/condir/.
Available only online. *6588*

CONTINUUM MECHANICS AND THERMODYNAMICS.
Springer-Verlag, Heidelberger Platz 3, 14197 Berlin, Germany. TEL 49-30-82787-0. FAX 49-30-82787448. URL: http://link.springer.de. *5840*

CONTRACEPTIVE TECHNOLOGY UPDATE.
American Health Consultants, Inc., 3525 Piedmont Rd., N.E., Bldg. 6, Ste. 400, Atlanta, GA 30305. TEL 404-262-7436. FAX 800-284-3291.
Vendor(s): Lexis-Nexis. *856*

CONTRACTING BUSINESS.
Penton Publishing Co., 1100 Superior Ave., Cleveland, OH 44114-2543. TEL 216-696-7000. FAX 216-696-7932.
Vendor(s): Information Access Co. *3477*

THE CONTRARIAN'S VIEW.
132 Moreland St., Worcester, MA 01609. TEL 508-757-2881. URL: http://www.assumption.edu. *1380*

CONTRIBUTIONS TO MINERALOGY AND PETROLOGY.
Springer-Verlag, Heidelberger Platz 3, 14197 Berlin, Germany. TEL 49-30-82787-0. FAX 49-30-82787448. URL: http://link.springer.de. *2336*

CONTROL AND INSTRUMENTATION.
Miller Freeman Technical Ltd., Miller Freeman House, 30 Calderwood St., London SE18 6QH, England. TEL 44-181-855-7777. FAX 44-181-316-3422.
Vendor(s): Information Access Co. *2108*

CONTROLLER'S COST REPORT.
Warren, Gorham & Lamont, One Penn Plaza, New York, NY 10119. TEL 212-971-5000. FAX 212-971-5113.
Vendor(s): Information Access Co. *950*

CONTROLLERS UPDATE.
Institute of Management Accountants, 10 Paragon Dr., Montvale, NJ 07645-1760. TEL 201-573-9000. FAX 201-573-8185.
Vendor(s): UMI. *1088*

CONVENIENCE STORE NEWS.
Macfadden Publishing, Macfadden Trade Publications, 233 Park Ave. S., 6th Fl., New York, NY 10003. TEL 212-780-2300. FAX 212-228-3142.
Vendor(s): Information Access Co. *3140*

CONVERGENCE: INTERNATIONAL CONGRESS ON TRANSPORTATION ELECTRONICS. PROCEEDINGS.
Society of Automotive Engineers, 400 Commonwealth Dr., Warrendale, PA 15096-0001. TEL 412-776-4841. FAX 412-776-3036.
Vendor(s): European Space Agency, FIZ Technik, Questel Orbit Inc. *7096*

COOK POLITICAL REPORT.
Cook and Company, 900 Second St., N.E., Ste. 107, Washington, DC 20002. TEL 202-289-1625. FAX 202-289-0454. *5904*

COOK'S INDEX.
John Gordon Burke Publisher, Inc., Box 1492, Evanston, IL 60204-1492. TEL 847-866-8625. FAX 847-866-6639. URL: http://www.nlightn.com. *3690*

CO-OPSERVATIONS.
Co-operative Housing Federation of Canada, 225 Metcalfe St., Ste. 311, Ottawa, ON K2P 1P9, Canada. TEL 613-230-2201. FAX 613-230-2231. *3744*

COR EUROPAEUM.
Springer-Verlag, Sachsenplatz 4-6, A-1201 Vienna, Austria. TEL 43-1-3302415. FAX 43-1-3302426. *4814*

CORAL REEFS.
Springer-Verlag, Heidelberger Platz 3, 14197 Berlin, Germany. TEL 49-30-82787-0. FAX 49-30-82787448. URL: http://link.springer.de. *2401*

CORDELL CONSTRUCTION REPORTS.
Cordell Building Information Services, P.O. Box 124, St. Leonards, N.S.W. 2065, Australia. TEL 61-2-934-5555. *882*

THE CORNELL HOTEL & RESTAURANT ADMINISTRATION QUARTERLY.
Elsevier Science Inc., Box 945, New York, NY 10159-0945. TEL 212-633-3730. FAX 212-633-3680. URL: http://www.elsevier.nl/
Vendor(s): Information Access Co., UMI. *3724*

CORNELL INTERNATIONAL LAW JOURNAL.
Cornell University, Cornell Law School, Myron Taylor Hall, Ithaca, NY 14853. TEL 607-255-9666. FAX 607-255-7193.
Vendor(s): Lexis-Nexis, West Group. *4110*

CORNELL JOURNAL OF LAW AND PUBLIC POLICY.
Cornell University, Cornell Law School, Myron Taylor Hall, Ithaca, NY 14853. TEL 607-255-0526. FAX 607-255-7193. URL: http://www.cls.cornell.edu/cjlpp
Vendor(s): Lexis-Nexis, West Group. *3936*

CORNELL LAW REVIEW.
Cornell University, Cornell Law School, Myron Taylor Hall, Ithaca, NY 14853-4901. TEL 607-255-3387. FAX 607-255-7193.
Vendor(s): Lexis-Nexis, West Group. *3936*

CORNELL MAGAZINE.
Cornell Alumni Federation, 55 Brown Rd., Ithaca, NY 14850. FAX 607-257-1782. *1947*

CORNELL SCIENCE & TECHNOLOGY MAGAZINE.
C U M E, Inc, Cornell University, B 46 Olin Hall, Ithaca, NY 14853. TEL 607-255-3312. FAX 607-255-9606. URL: http://www.englib.cornell.edu/scitech/. *2714*

CORONARY ARTERY DISEASE.
Thomson Science, 2-6 Boundary Row, London SE1 8HN, England. TEL 44-171-410-6600. FAX 44-171-865-0198. URL: http://www.thomsonscience.com. *4767*

CORPORATE BOARD.
Vanguard Publications, Inc., 4440 Hagadorn Rd., Okemos, MI 48864-2414. URL: http://www.corporateboard.com.
Vendor(s): Information Access Co. *1471*

CORPORATE CASHFLOW.
Intertec Publishing Corp. (Atlanta), 6151 Powers Ferry Rd., N.W., Atlanta, GA 30339-2941. TEL 770-955-2500. FAX 770-955-0400.
Vendor(s): Information Access Co., UMI. *1123*

CORPORATE DETROIT MAGAZINE.
Corporate Detroit, Inc., 19512 Livernois Ave., Detroit, MI 48221-1766. TEL 313-872-6000. FAX 313-872-6009.
Vendor(s): Knight-Ridder Information, Inc., UMI. *950*

CORPORATE E F T REPORT.
Phillips Business Information, Inc., 1201 Seven Locks Rd., Potomac, MD 20854. TEL 301-424-3338. FAX 301-424-4297.
Vendor(s): Information Access Co., Knight-Ridder Information, Inc., Lexis-Nexis, NewsNet (Fl12). *1123*

CORPORATE GOVERNANCE.
James McRichtie, Ed. & Pub., 2461 Second Ave., Sacramento, CA 95818. URL: http://www.corpgov.net/
Available only online. *1471*

CORPORATE GROWTH REPORT.
Quality Services Company, 5290 Overpass Rd., Ste. 126, Santa Barbara, CA 93111-9950. TEL 805-964-7841. FAX 805-964-1073.
Vendor(s): UMI. *1381*

CORPORATE I T UPDATE.
M2 Communications Ltd., P.O. Box 475, Coventry CV1 2ZW, England. TEL 44-1203-634700. FAX 44-1203-634144. URL: http://www.m2.com.
Available only online. *951*

CORPORATE JOBS OUTLOOK!
Plunkett Research, Ltd., P.O. Drawer 8270, Galveston, TX 77553-8270. TEL 409-765-8530. FAX 409-765-8571.
Vendor(s): Human Resources Information Network. *5507*

CORPORATE LEGAL TIMES.
Giant Steps Publishing Corp., 3 E. Huron, Chicago, IL 60611. TEL 312-654-3500.
Vendor(s): Lexis-Nexis (CORPLT), West Group (CORPLT). *4078*

CORPORATE LOCATION.
Euromoney Publications plc., Nestor House, Playhouse Yard, London EC4 5EX, England. TEL 44-171-779-8368. FAX 44-171-779-8369.
Vendor(s): UMI. *1356*

CORPORATE MONEY.
Centaur Communications Ltd., St. Giles House, 50 Poland St., London W1V 4AX, England. TEL 44-171-287-9800. FAX 44-171-439-1480.
Vendor(s): Information Access Co. *1123*

CORPORATE REPORT MINNESOTA.
American City Business Journals, Inc. (Austin), 505 Powell St., Austin, TX 78703-5121.
Vendor(s): CompuServe, Inc., Data-Star, Dow Jones News Retrieval, Information Access Co., Knight-Ridder Information, Inc., Lexis-Nexis, UMI. *1471*

CORPORATE REPORT VENTURES.
American City Business Journals, Inc. (Austin), 505 Powell St., Austin, TX 78703-5121.
Vendor(s): UMI. *1641*

CORPORATE REPORT WISCONSIN.
The Brady Co., Inc., N80 W12878 Fond du Lac Ave., Box 878, Menomonee Falls, WI 53052-0878. TEL 414-255-9077. FAX 414-255-3388.
Vendor(s): UMI. *951*

THE CORPS REPORT.
Pasha Publications Inc., 1616 N. Ft. Myer Dr., Ste. 1000, Arlington, VA 22209-3107. TEL 703-528-1244. FAX 703-528-1253. *5263*

CORPTECH DIRECTORY OF TECHNOLOGY COMPANIES.
Corporate Technology Information Services Inc., c/o Eileen Kenney, 12 Alfred Ave., Ste. 200, Woburn, MA 01801. TEL 617-932-3939. FAX 617-932-6335. URL: http://www.corptech.com.
Vendor(s): Questel Orbit Inc. (CORP). *1663*

CORPTECH - TECHNOLOGY SPOTLIGHT.
Corporate Technology Information Services Inc., 12 Alfred St., Ste. 200, Woburn, MA 01801. TEL 617-932-3939. FAX 617-932-6335. URL: http://www.corptech.com:3600/spotmenu.htm.
Available only online. *1663*

CORRECTIONS TODAY.
American Correctional Association, 4380 Forbes Blvd., Lanham, MD 20706-4322. TEL 301-918-1800.
Vendor(s): Information Access Co., UMI. *2264*

CORROSIONEERING NEWSLETTER.
C L I International, Inc., URL: http://www.clihouston.com/newslet.html.
Available only online. *2857*

COSMETIC INSIDER'S REPORT.
Advanstar Communications, Inc., 7500 Old Oak Blvd., Cleveland, OH 44130. TEL 216-826-2839. FAX 216-891-2726.
Vendor(s): Data-Star, Information Access Co., Knight-Ridder Information, Inc. *510*

COSMETIC WORLD NEWS.
World News Publications, 130 Wigmore St., London W1H OAT, England. FAX 44-171-487-5436.
Vendor(s): Information Access Co. *510*

COSMETICS AND TOILETRIES.
Allured Publishing, 362 S. Schmale Rd., Carol Stream, IL 60188-2787. TEL 708-653-2155. FAX 708-653-2192.
Vendor(s): Information Access Co. *510*

COSMETICS INTERNATIONAL.
Cosmetics Communications Ltd., 335 Linen Hall, 162-168 Regent St., London W1R 5TB, England. TEL 44-171-434-1530. FAX 44-171-437-0915.
Vendor(s): Information Access Co., Lexis-Nexis. *510*

COSMIC VISIONS.
Pegasus Press, URL: http://www.cosmicvisions.com/
Available only online. *4529*

COSMOPOLITAN.
Hearst Corporation, Cosmopolitan, 224 W. 57th St., New York, NY 10019. TEL 212-649-3570. FAX 212-956-3268. URL: http://www.cosmomag.com; http://www.hearstcorp.com.
Vendor(s): Information Access Co. *7315*

COSMOS.
Cosmos Club, 2121 Massachusetts Ave., N.W., Washington, DC 20008. TEL 202-387-7783. FAX 202-234-6817. URL: http://www.his.com/'cosmos. *6609*

COST ENGINEERING (MORGANTOWN).
A A C E International, 209 Prairie Ave., Ste. 100, Morgantown, WV 26505. TEL 304-296-8444. FAX 304-291-5728. URL: http://www.eng.hawaii.edu/'aace/Aace.html.
Vendor(s): UMI. *2714*

COST MANAGEMENT UPDATE.
Institute of Management Accountants, 10 Paragon Dr., Montvale, NJ 07645-1760. TEL 201-573-9000.
Vendor(s): UMI. *1605*

COTTON AND TROPICAL FIBRES.
CAB International, Wallingford, Oxon. OX10 8DE, England. TEL 44-1491-832111. FAX 44-1491-826090. URL: http://www.cabi.org.
Vendor(s): DIMDI, European Space Agency (File nos.16 & 124/CAB), Knight-Ridder Information, Inc. *172*

COTTON: REVIEW OF THE WORLD SITUATION.
International Cotton Advisory Committee, 1629 K St. N.W., Ste. 702, Washington, DC 20006. TEL 202-463-6660. FAX 202-463-6950. URL: http://www.icac.org.
Vendor(s): Information Access Co. *6985*

COTTON: WORLD STATISTICS.
International Cotton Advisory Committee, 1629 K St. N.W., Ste. 702, Washington, DC 20006. TEL 202-463-6660. FAX 202-463-6950. URL: http://www.icac.org. *6999*

COUGH AND COLD REMEDIES: THE INTERNATIONAL MARKET.
Euromonitor, 60-61 Britton St., London EC1M 5NA, England. TEL 44-171-251-8024. FAX 44-171-608-3149. URL: http://www.euromonitor.com.
Vendor(s): Data-Star, Knight-Ridder Information, Inc. *5654*

THE COUNTRY DOCTOR.
Available only online. *295*

COUNTRY FORECAST. ALGERIA.
Economist Intelligence Unit, 111 W. 57th St., New York, NY 10019. TEL 212-554-0600. FAX 212-586-1182. URL: http://www.eiu.com.
Vendor(s): Knight-Ridder Information, Inc., Lexis-Nexis. *5904*

COUNTRY FORECAST. ARGENTINA.
Economist Intelligence Unit, 111 W. 57th St., New York, NY 10019. TEL 212-554-0600. FAX 212-586-1182. URL: http://www.eiu.com.
Vendor(s): Knight-Ridder Information, Inc., Lexis-Nexis. *5904*

COUNTRY FORECAST. ASIA - PACIFIC.
Economist Intelligence Unit, 111 W. 57th St., New York, NY 10019. TEL 212-554-0600. FAX 212-586-1182. URL: http://www.eiu.com.
Vendor(s): Knight-Ridder Information, Inc., Lexis-Nexis. *5904*

COUNTRY FORECAST. AUSTRALIA.
Economist Intelligence Unit, 111 W. 57th St., New York, NY 10019. TEL 212-554-0600. FAX 212-586-1182. URL: http://www.eiu.com.
Vendor(s): Knight-Ridder Information, Inc., Lexis-Nexis. *5904*

COUNTRY FORECAST. AUSTRIA.
Economist Intelligence Unit, 111 W. 57th St., New York, NY 10019. TEL 212-554-0600. FAX 212-586-1182. URL: http://www.eiu.com.
Vendor(s): Knight-Ridder Information, Inc., Lexis-Nexis. *5904*

COUNTRY FORECAST. BELGIUM.
Economist Intelligence Unit, 111 W. 57th St., New York, NY 10019. TEL 212-554-0600. FAX 212-586-1182. URL: http://www.eiu.com.
Vendor(s): Knight-Ridder Information, Inc., Lexis-Nexis. *5904*

COUNTRY FORECAST. BRAZIL.
Economist Intelligence Unit, 111 W. 57th St., New York, NY 10019. TEL 212-554-0600. FAX 212-586-1182. URL: http://www.eiu.com.
Vendor(s): Knight-Ridder Information, Inc., Lexis-Nexis. *5904*

COUNTRY FORECAST. BULGARIA.
Economist Intelligence Unit, 111 W. 57th St., New York, NY 10019. TEL 212-554-0600. FAX 212-586-1182. URL: http://www.eiu.com.
Vendor(s): Knight-Ridder Information, Inc., Lexis-Nexis. *5905*

COUNTRY FORECAST. CANADA.
Economist Intelligence Unit, 111 W. 57th St., New York, NY 10019. TEL 212-554-0600. FAX 212-586-1182. URL: http://www.eiu.com.
Vendor(s): Knight-Ridder Information, Inc., Lexis-Nexis. *5905*

COUNTRY FORECAST. CHILE.
Economist Intelligence Unit, 111 W. 57th St., New York, NY 10019. TEL 212-554-0600. FAX 212-586-1182. URL: http://www.eiu.com.
Vendor(s): Knight-Ridder Information, Inc., Lexis-Nexis. *5905*

COUNTRY FORECAST. CHINA.
Economist Intelligence Unit, 111 W. 57th St., New York, NY 10019. TEL 212-554-0600. FAX 212-586-1182. URL: http://www.eiu.com.
Vendor(s): Knight-Ridder Information, Inc., Lexis-Nexis. *5905*

COUNTRY FORECAST. COLOMBIA.
Economist Intelligence Unit, 111 W. 57th St., New York, NY 10019. TEL 212-554-0600. FAX 212-586-1182. URL: http://www.eiu.com.
Vendor(s): Knight-Ridder Information, Inc., Lexis-Nexis. *5905*

COUNTRY FORECAST. CZECH REPUBLIC.
Economist Intelligence Unit, 111 W. 57th St., New York, NY 10019. TEL 212-554-0600. FAX 212-586-1182. URL: http://www.eiu.com.
Vendor(s): Knight-Ridder Information, Inc., Lexis-Nexis. *5905*

COUNTRY FORECAST. DENMARK.
Economist Intelligence Unit, 111 W. 57th St., New York, NY 10019. TEL 212-554-0600. FAX 212-586-1182. URL: http://www.eiu.com.
Vendor(s): Knight-Ridder Information, Inc., Lexis-Nexis. *5905*

COUNTRY FORECAST. EASTERN EUROPE AND THE FORMER SOVIET UNION.
Economist Intelligence Unit, 111 W. 57th St., New York, NY 10019. TEL 212-554-0600. FAX 212-486-1182. URL: http://www.eiu.com.
Vendor(s): Knight-Ridder Information, Inc., Lexis-Nexis. *5905*

COUNTRY FORECAST. ECUADOR.
Economist Intelligence Unit, 111 W. 57th St., New York, NY 10019. TEL 212-554-0600. FAX 212-586-1182. URL: http://www.eiu.com.
Vendor(s): Knight-Ridder Information, Inc., Lexis-Nexis. *5905*

COUNTRY FORECAST. EGYPT.
Economist Intelligence Unit, 111 W. 57th St., New York, NY 10019. TEL 212-554-0600. FAX 212-586-1182. URL: http://www.eiu.com.
Vendor(s): Knight-Ridder Information, Inc., Lexis-Nexis. *5905*

COUNTRY FORECAST. EUROPE.
Economist Intelligence Unit, 111 W. 57th St., New York, NY 10019. TEL 212-554-0600. FAX 212-586-1182. URL: http://www.eiu.com.
Vendor(s): Knight-Ridder Information, Inc., Lexis-Nexis. *5905*

COUNTRY FORECAST. FINLAND.
Economist Intelligence Unit, 111 W. 57th St., New York, NY 10019. TEL 212-554-0600. FAX 212-586-1182. URL: http://www.eiu.com.
Vendor(s): Knight-Ridder Information, Inc., Lexis-Nexis. *5905*

COUNTRY FORECAST. FRANCE.
Economist Intelligence Unit, 111 W. 57th St., New York, NY 10019. TEL 212-554-0600. FAX 212-586-1182. URL: http://www.eiu.com.
Vendor(s): Knight-Ridder Information, Inc., Lexis-Nexis. *5905*

COUNTRY FORECAST. GERMANY.
Economist Intelligence Unit, 111 W. 57th St., New York, NY 10019. TEL 212-554-0600. FAX 212-586-1182. URL: http://www.eiu.com.
Vendor(s): Knight-Ridder Information, Inc., Lexis-Nexis. *5905*

COUNTRY FORECAST. GLOBAL OUTLOOK.
Economist Intelligence Unit, 111 W. 57th St., New York, NY 10019. TEL 212-554-0600. FAX 212-586-1182. URL: http://www.eiu.com.
Vendor(s): Knight-Ridder Information, Inc., Lexis-Nexis. *5905*

COUNTRY FORECAST. GREECE.
Economist Intelligence Unit, 111 W. 57th St., New York, NY 10019. TEL 212-554-0600. FAX 212-586-1182. URL: http://www.eiu.com.
Vendor(s): Knight-Ridder Information, Inc., Lexis-Nexis. *5906*

COUNTRY FORECAST. HONG KONG.
Economist Intelligence Unit, 111 W. 57th St., New York, NY 10019. TEL 212-554-0600. FAX 212-586-1182. URL: http://www.eiu.com.
Vendor(s): Knight-Ridder Information, Inc., Lexis-Nexis. *5906*

COUNTRY FORECAST. HUNGARY.
Economist Intelligence Unit, 111 W. 57th St., New York, NY 10019. TEL 212-554-0600. FAX 212-586-1182. URL: http://www.eiu.com.
Vendor(s): Knight-Ridder Information, Inc., Lexis-Nexis. *5906*

COUNTRY FORECAST. INDIA.
Economist Intelligence Unit, 111 W. 57th St., New York, NY 10019. TEL 212-554-0600. FAX 212-586-1182. URL: http://www.eiu.com.
Vendor(s): Knight-Ridder Information, Inc., Lexis-Nexis. *5906*

COUNTRY FORECAST. INDONESIA.
Economist Intelligence Unit, 111 W. 57th St., New York, NY 10019. TEL 212-554-0600. FAX 212-586-1182. URL: http://www.eiu.com.
Vendor(s): Knight-Ridder Information, Inc., Lexis-Nexis. *5906*

COUNTRY FORECAST. IRAN.
Economist Intelligence Unit, 111 W. 57th St., New York, NY 10019. TEL 212-554-0600. FAX 212-486-1182. URL: http://www.eiu.com.
Vendor(s): Knight-Ridder Information, Inc., Lexis-Nexis. *5906*

COUNTRY FORECAST. IRAQ.
Economist Intelligence Unit, 111 W. 57th St., New York, NY 10019. TEL 212-554-0600. FAX 212-586-1182. URL: http://www.eiu.com.
Vendor(s): Knight-Ridder Information, Inc., Lexis-Nexis. *5906*

COUNTRY FORECAST. IRELAND.
Economist Intelligence Unit, 111 W. 57th St., New York, NY 10019. TEL 212-554-0600. FAX 212-586-1182. URL: http://www.eiu.com.
Vendor(s): Knight-Ridder Information, Inc., Lexis-Nexis. *5906*

COUNTRY FORECAST. ISRAEL.
Economist Intelligence Unit, 111 W. 57th St., New York, NY 10019. TEL 212-554-0600. FAX 212-586-1182. URL: http://www.eiu.com.
Vendor(s): Knight-Ridder Information, Inc., Lexis-Nexis. *5906*

COUNTRY FORECAST. ITALY.
Economist Intelligence Unit, 111 W. 57th St., New York, NY 10019. TEL 212-554-0600. FAX 212-586-1182. URL: http://www.eiu.com.
Vendor(s): Knight-Ridder Information, Inc., Lexis-Nexis. *5906*

COUNTRY FORECAST. JAPAN.
Economist Intelligence Unit, 111 W. 57th St., New York, NY 10019. TEL 212-554-0600. FAX 212-586-1182. URL: http://www.eiu.com.
Vendor(s): Knight-Ridder Information, Inc., Lexis-Nexis. *5906*

COUNTRY FORECAST. LATIN AMERICA.
Economist Intelligence Unit, 111 W. 57th St., New York, NY 10019. TEL 212-554-0600. FAX 212-586-1182. URL: http://www.eiu.com.
Vendor(s): Knight-Ridder Information, Inc., Lexis-Nexis. *5906*

COUNTRY FORECAST. MALAYSIA.
Economist Intelligence Unit, 111 W. 57th St., New York, NY 10019. TEL 212-554-0600. FAX 212-586-1182. URL: http://www.eiu.com.
Vendor(s): Knight-Ridder Information, Inc., Lexis-Nexis. *5906*

COUNTRY FORECAST. MEXICO.
Economist Intelligence Unit, 111 W. 57th St., New York, NY 10019. TEL 212-554-0600. FAX 212-586-1182. URL: http://www.eiu.com.
Vendor(s): Knight-Ridder Information, Inc., Lexis-Nexis. *5906*

COUNTRY FORECAST. MIDDLE EAST AND NORTH AFRICA.
Economist Intelligence Unit, 111 W. 57th St., New York, NY 10019. TEL 212-554-0600. FAX 212-586-1182. URL: http://www.eiu.com.
Vendor(s): Knight-Ridder Information, Inc., Lexis-Nexis. *5906*

COUNTRY FORECAST. NETHERLANDS.
Economist Intelligence Unit, 111 W. 57th St., New York, NY 10019. TEL 212-544-0600. FAX 212-586-1182. URL: http://www.eiu.com.
Vendor(s): Knight-Ridder Information, Inc., Lexis-Nexis. *5907*

COUNTRY FORECAST. NEW ZEALAND.
Economist Intelligence Unit, 111 W. 57th St., New York, NY 10019. TEL 212-554-0600. FAX 212-586-1182. URL: http://www.eiu.com.
Vendor(s): Knight-Ridder Information, Inc., Lexis-Nexis. *5907*

COUNTRY FORECAST. NIGERIA.
Economist Intelligence Unit, 111 W. 57th St., New York, NY 10019. TEL 212-554-0600. FAX 212-586-1182. URL: http://www.eiu.com.
Vendor(s): Knight-Ridder Information, Inc., Lexis-Nexis. *5907*

COUNTRY FORECAST. NORWAY.
Economist Intelligence Unit, 111 W. 57th St., New York, NY 10019. TEL 212-544-0600. FAX 212-586-1182. URL: http://www.eiu.com.
Vendor(s): Knight-Ridder Information, Inc., Lexis-Nexis. *5907*

COUNTRY FORECAST. PAKISTAN.
Economist Intelligence Unit, 111 W. 57th St., New York, NY 10019. TEL 212-554-0600. FAX 212-586-1182. URL: http://www.eiu.com.
Vendor(s): Knight-Ridder Information, Inc., Lexis-Nexis. *5907*

COUNTRY FORECAST. PERU.
Economist Intelligence Unit, 111 W. 57th St., New York, NY 10019. TEL 212-554-0600. FAX 212-586-1182. URL: http://www.eiu.com.
Vendor(s): Knight-Ridder Information, Inc., Lexis-Nexis. *5907*

COUNTRY FORECAST. PHILIPPINES.
Economist Intelligence Unit, 111 W. 57th St., New York, NY 10019. TEL 212-554-0600. FAX 212-586-1182. URL: http://www.eiu.com.
Vendor(s): Knight-Ridder Information, Inc., Lexis-Nexis. *5907*

COUNTRY FORECAST. POLAND.
Economist Intelligence Unit, 111 W. 57th St., New York, NY 10019. TEL 212-554-0600. FAX 212-586-1182. URL: http://www.eiu.com.
Vendor(s): Knight-Ridder Information, Inc., Lexis-Nexis. *5907*

COUNTRY FORECAST. PORTUGAL.
Economist Intelligence Unit, 111 W. 57th St., New York, NY 10019. TEL 212-554-0600. FAX 212-586-1182. URL: http://www.eiu.com.
Vendor(s): Knight-Ridder Information, Inc., Lexis-Nexis. *5907*

COUNTRY FORECAST. ROMANIA.
Economist Intelligence Unit, 111 W. 57th St., New York, NY 10019. TEL 212-554-0600. FAX 212-586-1182. URL: http://www.eiu.com.
Vendor(s): Knight-Ridder Information, Inc., Lexis-Nexis. *5907*

COUNTRY FORECAST. RUSSIA.
Economist Intelligence Unit, 111 W. 57th St., New York, NY 10019. TEL 212-554-0600. FAX 212-586-1182. URL: http://www.eiu.com.
Vendor(s): Knight-Ridder Information, Inc., Lexis-Nexis. *5907*

COUNTRY FORECAST. SAUDI ARABIA.
Economist Intelligence Unit, 111 W. 57th St., New York, NY 10019. TEL 212-554-0600. FAX 212-586-1182. URL: http://www.eiu.com.
Vendor(s): Knight-Ridder Information, Inc., Lexis-Nexis. *5907*

COUNTRY FORECAST. SINGAPORE.
Economist Intelligence Unit, 111 W. 57th St., New York, NY 10019. TEL 212-554-0600. FAX 212-586-1182. URL: http://www.eiu.com.
Vendor(s): Knight-Ridder Information, Inc., Lexis-Nexis. *5907*

COUNTRY FORECAST. SLOVAKIA.
Economist Intelligence Unit, 111 W. 57th St., New York, NY 10019. TEL 212-554-0600. FAX 212-586-1182. URL: http://www.eiu.com.
Vendor(s): Knight-Ridder Information, Inc., Lexis-Nexis. *5907*

COUNTRY FORECAST. SOUTH AFRICA.
Economist Intelligence Unit, 111 W. 57th St., New York, NY 10019. TEL 212-554-0600. FAX 212-586-1182. URL: http://www.eiu.com.
Vendor(s): Knight-Ridder Information, Inc., Lexis-Nexis. *5907*

COUNTRY FORECAST. SOUTH KOREA.
Economist Intelligence Unit, 111 W. 57th St., New York, NY 10019. TEL 212-554-0600. FAX 212-586-1182. URL: http://www.eiu.com.
Vendor(s): Knight-Ridder Information, Inc., Lexis-Nexis. *5908*

COUNTRY FORECAST. SPAIN.
Economist Intelligence Unit, 111 W. 57th St., New York, NY 10019. TEL 212-554-0600. FAX 212-586-1182. URL: http://www.eiu.com.
Vendor(s): Knight-Ridder Information, Inc., Lexis-Nexis. *5908*

COUNTRY FORECAST. SRI LANKA.
Economist Intelligence Unit, 111 W. 57th St., New York, NY 10019. TEL 212-554-0600. FAX 212-586-1182. URL: http://www.eiu.com.
Vendor(s): Knight-Ridder Information, Inc., Lexis-Nexis. *5908*

COUNTRY FORECAST. SUB-SAHARAN AFRICA.
Economist Intelligence Unit, 111 W. 57th St., New York, NY 10019. TEL 212-554-0600. FAX 212-486-1182. URL: http://www.eiu.com.
Vendor(s): Knight-Ridder Information, Inc., Lexis-Nexis. *5908*

COUNTRY FORECAST. SWEDEN.
Economist Intelligence Unit, 111 W. 57th St., New York, NY 10019. TEL 212-554-0600. FAX 212-586-1182. URL: http://www.eiu.com.
Vendor(s): Knight-Ridder Information, Inc., Lexis-Nexis. *5908*

COUNTRY FORECAST. SWITZERLAND.
Economist Intelligence Unit, 111 W. 57th St., New York, NY 10019. TEL 212-554-0600. FAX 212-586-1182. URL: http://www.eiu.com.
Vendor(s): Knight-Ridder Information, Inc., Lexis-Nexis. *5908*

COUNTRY FORECAST. TAIWAN.
Economist Intelligence Unit, 111 W. 57th St., New York, NY 10019. TEL 212-554-0600. FAX 212-586-1182. URL: http://www.eiu.com.
Vendor(s): Knight-Ridder Information, Inc., Lexis-Nexis. *5908*

COUNTRY FORECAST. THAILAND.
Economist Intelligence Unit, 111 W. 57th St., New York, NY 10019. TEL 212-554-0600. FAX 212-586-1182. URL: http://www.eiu.com.
Vendor(s): Knight-Ridder Information, Inc., Lexis-Nexis. *5908*

COUNTRY FORECAST. TURKEY.
Economist Intelligence Unit, 111 W. 57th St., New York, NY 10019. TEL 212-554-0600. FAX 212-586-1182. URL: http://www.eiu.com.
Vendor(s): Knight-Ridder Information, Inc., Lexis-Nexis. *5908*

COUNTRY FORECAST. UNITED KINGDOM.
Economist Intelligence Unit, 111 W. 57th St., New York, NY 10019. TEL 212-554-0600. FAX 212-586-1182. URL: http://www.eiu.com.
Vendor(s): Information Access Co., Knight-Ridder Information, Inc., Lexis-Nexis. *5908*

COUNTRY FORECAST. UNITED STATES OF AMERICA.
Economist Intelligence Unit, 111 W. 57th St., New York, NY 10019. TEL 212-554-0600. FAX 212-586-1182. URL: http://www.eiu.com.
Vendor(s): Knight-Ridder Information, Inc., Lexis-Nexis. *5908*

COUNTRY FORECAST. VENEZUELA.
Economist Intelligence Unit, 111 W. 57th St., New York, NY 10019. TEL 212-554-0600. FAX 212-586-1182. URL: http://www.eiu.com.
Vendor(s): Knight-Ridder Information, Inc., Lexis-Nexis. *5908*

COUNTRY FORECAST. VIETNAM.
Economist Intelligence Unit, 111 W. 57th St., New York, NY 10019. TEL 212-554-0600. FAX 212-586-1182. URL: http://www.eiu.com.
Vendor(s): Knight-Ridder Information, Inc., Lexis-Nexis. *5908*

COUNTRY FORECASTS (NEW YORK).
Economist Intelligence Unit, 111 W. 57th St., New York, NY 10019. TEL 212-554-0600. FAX 212-586-1182. URL: http://www.eiu.com.
Vendor(s): Knight-Ridder Information, Inc., Lexis-Nexis. *5908*

COUNTRY FORECASTS (SYRACUSE).
The P R S Group, Box 248, East Syracuse, NY 13057-0248. TEL 315-431-0511. FAX 315-431-0200. URL: http://www.countrydata.com.
Vendor(s): Data-Star (FSRI), Information Access Co., Knight-Ridder Information, Inc., NewsNet (IT933). *951*

COUNTRY JOURNAL.
Cowles Business Media, 11 River Bend Dr., S., Box 4949, Stamford, CT 06907-0949. TEL 203-321-1778. FAX 203-358-5811.
Vendor(s): Information Access Co. *3372*

COUNTRY MUSIC.
Silver Eagle Publishers, 329 Riverside Ave., Westport, CT 06880. TEL 203-221-4950. FAX 203-221-4948.
Vendor(s): Information Access Co. *5386*

COUNTRY PROFILE. ALBANIA.
Economist Intelligence Unit, 111 W. 57th St., New York, NY 10019. TEL 212-554-0600. FAX 212-586-1182. URL: http://www.eiu.com.
Vendor(s): Knight-Ridder Information, Inc., Lexis-Nexis. *5908*

COUNTRY PROFILE. ALGERIA.
Economist Intelligence Unit, 111 W. 57th St., New York, NY 10019. TEL 212-554-0600. FAX 212-586-1182. URL: http://www.eiu.com.
Vendor(s): Knight-Ridder Information, Inc., Lexis-Nexis. *5909*

COUNTRY PROFILE. ANGOLA.
Economist Intelligence Unit, 111 W. 57th St., New York, NY 10019. TEL 212-554-0600. FAX 212-586-1182. URL: http://www.eiu.com.
Vendor(s): Knight-Ridder Information, Inc., Lexis-Nexis. *5909*

COUNTRY PROFILE. ARGENTINA.
Economist Intelligence Unit, 111 W. 57th St., New York, NY 10019. TEL 212-554-0600. FAX 212-586-1182.
Vendor(s): Knight-Ridder Information, Inc., Lexis-Nexis. *5909*

COUNTRY PROFILE. AUSTRALIA.
Economist Intelligence Unit, 111 W. 57th St., New York, NY 10019. TEL 212-554-0600. FAX 212-586-1182. URL: http://www.eiu.com.
Vendor(s): Knight-Ridder Information, Inc., Lexis-Nexis. *5909*

COUNTRY PROFILE. AUSTRIA.
Economist Intelligence Unit, 111 W. 57th St., New York, NY 10019. TEL 212-554-0600. FAX 212-586-1182. URL: http://www.eiu.com.
Vendor(s): Knight-Ridder Information, Inc., Lexis-Nexis. *5909*

COUNTRY PROFILE. AZERBAIJAN.
Economist Intelligence Unit, 111 W. 57th St., New York, NY 10019. TEL 212-554-0600. FAX 212-586-1182. URL: http://www.eiu.com.
Vendor(s): Knight-Ridder Information, Inc., Lexis-Nexis. *5909*

COUNTRY PROFILE. BAHRAIN, QATAR.
Economist Intelligence Unit, 111 W. 57th St., New York, NY 10019. TEL 212-554-0600. FAX 212-586-1182. URL: http://www.eiu.com.
Vendor(s): Knight-Ridder Information, Inc., Lexis-Nexis. *5909*

COUNTRY PROFILE. BALTIC REPUBLICS: LITHUANIA, LATVIA, ESTONIA.
Economist Intelligence Unit, 111 W. 57th St., New York, NY 10019. TEL 212-554-0600. FAX 212-586-1182. URL: http://www.eiu.com.
Vendor(s): Knight-Ridder Information, Inc., Lexis-Nexis. *5909*

COUNTRY PROFILE. BANGLADESH.
Economist Intelligence Unit, 111 W. 57th St., New York, NY 10019. TEL 212-554-0600. FAX 212-586-1182. URL: http://www.eiu.com.
Vendor(s): Knight-Ridder Information, Inc., Lexis-Nexis. *5909*

COUNTRY PROFILE. BELGIUM, LUXEMBOURG.
Economist Intelligence Unit, 111 W. 57th St., New York, NY 10019. TEL 212-554-0600. FAX 212-586-1182. URL: http://www.eiu.com.
Vendor(s): Knight-Ridder Information, Inc., Lexis-Nexis. *5909*

COUNTRY PROFILE. BELIZE, BAHAMAS, BERMUDA.
Economist Intelligence Unit, 111 W. 57th St., New York, NY 10019. TEL 212-554-0600. FAX 212-586-1182. URL: http://www.eiu.com.
Vendor(s): Knight-Ridder Information, Inc., Lexis-Nexis. *5909*

COUNTRY PROFILE. BOLIVIA.
Economist Intelligence Unit, 111 W. 57th St., New York, NY 10019. TEL 212-554-0600. FAX 212-586-1181. URL: http://www.eiu.com.
Vendor(s): Knight-Ridder Information, Inc., Lexis-Nexis. *5909*

COUNTRY PROFILE. BOSNIA-HERCEGOVINA, CROATIA.
Economist Intelligence Unit, 111 W. 57th St., New York, NY 10019. TEL 212-554-0600. FAX 212-586-1182. URL: http://www.eiu.com.
Vendor(s): Knight-Ridder Information, Inc., Lexis-Nexis. *5909*

COUNTRY PROFILE. BOTSWANA, LESOTHO.
Economist Intelligence Unit, 111 W. 57th St., New York, NY 10019. TEL 212-554-0600. FAX 212-586-1182. URL: http://www.eiu.com.
Vendor(s): Knight-Ridder Information, Inc., Lexis-Nexis. *5909*

COUNTRY PROFILE. BRAZIL.
Economist Intelligence Unit, 111 W. 57th St., New York, NY 10019. TEL 212-554-0600. FAX 212-586-1182. URL: http://www.eiu.com.
Vendor(s): Knight-Ridder Information, Inc., Lexis-Nexis. *5910*

COUNTRY PROFILE. BULGARIA.
Economist Intelligence Unit, 111 W. 57th St., New York, NY 10019. TEL 212-554-0600. FAX 212-586-1182. URL: http://www.eiu.com.
Vendor(s): Knight-Ridder Information, Inc., Lexis-Nexis. *5910*

COUNTRY PROFILE. CAMBODIA, LAOS.
Economist Intelligence Unit, 111 W. 57th St., New York, NY 10019. TEL 212-554-0600. FAX 212-586-1182. URL: http://www.eiu.com.
Vendor(s): Knight-Ridder Information, Inc., Lexis-Nexis. *5910*

COUNTRY PROFILE. CAMEROON, CENTRAL AFRICAN REPUBLIC, CHAD.
Economist Intelligence Unit, 111 W. 57th St., New York, NY 10019. TEL 212-554-0600. FAX 212-586-1182. URL: http://www.eiu.com.
Vendor(s): Knight-Ridder Information, Inc., Lexis-Nexis. *5910*

COUNTRY PROFILE. CANADA.
Economist Intelligence Unit, 111 W. 57th St., New York, NY 10019. TEL 212-554-0600. FAX 212-586-1182.
Vendor(s): Knight-Ridder Information, Inc., Lexis-Nexis. *5910*

COUNTRY PROFILE. CHILE.
Economist Intelligence Unit, 111 W. 57th St., New York, NY 10019. TEL 212-554-0600. FAX 212-586-1182. URL: http://www.eiu.com.
Vendor(s): Knight-Ridder Information, Inc., Lexis-Nexis. *5910*

COUNTRY PROFILE. CHINA, MONGOLIA.
Economist Intelligence Unit, 111 W. 57th St., New York, NY 10019. TEL 212-554-0600. FAX 212-586-1182. URL: http://www.eiu.com.
Vendor(s): Knight-Ridder Information, Inc., Lexis-Nexis. *5910*

COUNTRY PROFILE. COLOMBIA.
Economist Intelligence Unit, 111 W. 57th St., New York, NY 10019. TEL 212-554-0600. FAX 212-586-1182. URL: http://www.eiu.com.
Vendor(s): Knight-Ridder Information, Inc., Lexis-Nexis. *5910*

COUNTRY PROFILE. CONGO.
Economist Intelligence Unit, 111 W. 57th St., New York, NY 10019. TEL 212-554-0600. FAX 212-586-1182. URL: http://www.eiu.com.
Vendor(s): Knight-Ridder Information, Inc., Lexis-Nexis. *5910*

COUNTRY PROFILE. COSTA RICA.
Economist Intelligence Unit, 111 W. 57th St., New York, NY 11019. TEL 212-554-0600. FAX 212-586-1182. URL: http://www.eiu.com.
Vendor(s): Knight-Ridder Information, Inc., Lexis-Nexis. *5910*

COUNTRY PROFILE. COTE D'IVOIRE, MALI.
Economist Intelligence Unit, 111 W. 57th St., New York, NY 10019. TEL 212-554-0600. FAX 212-586-1182. URL: http://www.eiu.com.
Vendor(s): Knight-Ridder Information, Inc., Lexis-Nexis. *5910*

10080 SERIALS AVAILABLE ONLINE

COUNTRY PROFILE. CUBA.
Economist Intelligence Unit, 111 W. 57th St., New York, NY 10019. TEL 212-554-0600. FAX 212-586-1182. URL: http://www.eiu.com.
Vendor(s): Knight-Ridder Information, Inc., Lexis-Nexis. *5910*

COUNTRY PROFILE. CYPRUS, MALTA.
Economist Intelligence Unit, 111 W. 57th St., New York, NY 10019. TEL 212-554-0600. FAX 212-9586-1182. URL: http://www.eiu.com.
Vendor(s): Knight-Ridder Information, Inc., Lexis-Nexis. *5910*

COUNTRY PROFILE. CZECH REPUBLIC.
Economist Intelligence Unit, 111 W. 57th St., New York, NY 10019. TEL 212-554-0600. FAX 212-586-1182. URL: http://www.eiu.com.
Vendor(s): Knight-Ridder Information, Inc., Lexis-Nexis. *5910*

COUNTRY PROFILE. DENMARK, ICELAND.
Economist Intelligence Unit, 111 W. 57th St., New York, NY 10019. TEL 212-554-0600. FAX 212-586-1182. URL: http://www.eiu.com.
Vendor(s): Knight-Ridder Information, Inc., Lexis-Nexis. *5911*

COUNTRY PROFILE. DOMINICAN REPUBLIC, HAITI, PUERTO RICO.
Economist Intelligence Unit, 111 W. 57th St., New York, NY 10019. TEL 212-554-0600. FAX 212-586-1182. URL: http://www.eiu.com.
Vendor(s): Knight-Ridder Information, Inc., Lexis-Nexis. *5911*

COUNTRY PROFILE. ECUADOR.
Economist Intelligence Unit, 111 W. 57th St., New York, NY 10019. TEL 212-554-0600. FAX 212-586-1182. URL: http://www.eiu.com.
Vendor(s): Knight-Ridder Information, Inc., Lexis-Nexis. *5911*

COUNTRY PROFILE. EGYPT.
Economist Intelligence Unit, 111 W. 57th St., New York, NY 10019. TEL 212-554-0600. FAX 212-586-1182. URL: http://www.eiu.com.
Vendor(s): Knight-Ridder Information, Inc., Lexis-Nexis. *5911*

COUNTRY PROFILE. ETHIOPIA, ERITREA, SOMALIA, DJIBOUTI.
Economist Intelligence Unit, 111 W. 57th St., New York, NY 10019. TEL 212-554-0600. FAX 212-586-1182. URL: http://www.eiu.com.
Vendor(s): Knight-Ridder Information, Inc., Lexis-Nexis. *5911*

COUNTRY PROFILE. FINLAND.
Economist Intelligence Unit, 111 W. 57th St., New York, NY 10019. TEL 212-554-0600. FAX 212-586-1182. URL: http://www.eiu.com.
Vendor(s): Knight-Ridder Information, Inc., Lexis-Nexis. *5911*

COUNTRY PROFILE. FRANCE.
Economist Intelligence Unit, 111 W. 57th St., New York, NY 10019. TEL 212-554-0600. FAX 212-586-1182. URL: http://www.eiu.com.
Vendor(s): Knight-Ridder Information, Inc., Lexis-Nexis. *5911*

COUNTRY PROFILE. GABON, EQUATORIAL GUINEA.
Economist Intelligence Unit, 111 W. 57th St., New York, NY 10019. TEL 212-554-0600. FAX 212-586-1182. URL: http://www.eiu.com.
Vendor(s): Knight-Ridder Information, Inc., Lexis-Nexis. *5911*

COUNTRY PROFILE. GEORGIA, ARMENIA.
Economist Intelligence Unit, 111 W. 57th St., New York, NY 10019. TEL 212-554-0600. FAX 212-586-1182. URL: http://www.eiu.com.
Vendor(s): Knight-Ridder Information, Inc., Lexis-Nexis. *5911*

COUNTRY PROFILE. GERMANY.
Economist Intelligence Unit, 111 W. 57th St., New York, NY 10019. TEL 212-554-0600. FAX 212-586-1182. URL: http://www.eiu.com.
Vendor(s): Knight-Ridder Information, Inc., Lexis-Nexis. *5911*

COUNTRY PROFILE. GHANA.
Economist Intelligence Unit, 111 W. 57th St., New York, NY 10019. TEL 212-554-0600. FAX 212-586-1182. URL: http://www.eiu.com.
Vendor(s): Knight-Ridder Information, Inc., Lexis-Nexis. *5911*

COUNTRY PROFILE. GREECE.
Economist Intelligence Unit, 111 W. 57th St., New York, NY 10019. TEL 212-554-0600. FAX 212-586-1182. URL: http://www.eiu.com.
Vendor(s): Knight-Ridder Information, Inc., Lexis-Nexis. *5911*

COUNTRY PROFILE. GUATEMALA, EL SALVADOR.
Economist Intelligence Unit, 111 W. 57th St., New York, NY 10019. TEL 212-554-0600. FAX 212-586-1182. URL: http://www.eiu.com.
Vendor(s): Knight-Ridder Information, Inc., Lexis-Nexis. *5911*

COUNTRY PROFILE. GUINEA, SIERRA LEONE, LIBERIA.
Economist Intelligence Unit, 111 W. 57th St., New York, NY 10019. TEL 212-554-0600. FAX 212-586-1182. URL: http://www.eiu.com.
Vendor(s): Knight-Ridder Information, Inc., Lexis-Nexis. *5911*

COUNTRY PROFILE. GUYANA, WINDWARD AND LEEWARD ISLANDS.
Economist Intelligence Unit, 111 W. 57th St., New York, NY 10019. TEL 212-554-0600. FAX 212-586-1182. URL: http://www.eiu.com.
Vendor(s): Knight-Ridder Information, Inc., Lexis-Nexis. *5911*

COUNTRY PROFILE. HONG KONG, MACAU.
Economist Intelligence Unit, 111 W. 57th St., New York, NY 10019. TEL 212-554-0600. FAX 212-586-1182. URL: http://www.eiu.com.
Vendor(s): Knight-Ridder Information, Inc., Lexis-Nexis. *5912*

COUNTRY PROFILE. HUNGARY.
Economist Intelligence Unit, 111 W. 57th St., New York, NY 10019. TEL 212-554-0600. FAX 212-586-1182. URL: http://www.eiu.com.
Vendor(s): Knight-Ridder Information, Inc., Lexis-Nexis. *5912*

COUNTRY PROFILE. INDIA, NEPAL.
Economist Intelligence Unit, 111 W. 57th St., New York, NY 10019. TEL 212-554-0600. FAX 212-586-1182. URL: http://www.eiu.com.
Vendor(s): Knight-Ridder Information, Inc., Lexis-Nexis. *5912*

COUNTRY PROFILE. INDONESIA.
Economist Intelligence Unit, 111 W. 57th St., New York, NY 10019. TEL 212-554-0600. FAX 212-586-1182. URL: http://www.eiu.com.
Vendor(s): Knight-Ridder Information, Inc., Lexis-Nexis. *5912*

COUNTRY PROFILE. IRAN.
Economist Intelligence Unit, 111 W. 57th St., New York, NY 10019. TEL 212-554-0600. FAX 212-586-1182. URL: http://www.eiu.com.
Vendor(s): Knight-Ridder Information, Inc., Lexis-Nexis. *5912*

COUNTRY PROFILE. IRAQ.
Economist Intelligence Unit, 111 W. 57th St., New York, NY 10019. TEL 212-554-0600. FAX 212-586-1182. URL: http://www.eiu.com.
Vendor(s): Knight-Ridder Information, Inc., Lexis-Nexis. *5912*

COUNTRY PROFILE. IRELAND.
Economist Intelligence Unit, 111 W. 57th St., New York, NY 10019. TEL 212-554-0600. FAX 212-586-1182. URL: http://www.eiu.com.
Vendor(s): Knight-Ridder Information, Inc., Lexis-Nexis. *5912*

COUNTRY PROFILE. ISRAEL, THE OCCUPIED TERRITORIES.
Economist Intelligence Unit, 111 W. 57th St., New York, NY 10019. TEL 212-554-0600. FAX 212-586-1182. URL: http://www.eiu.com.
Vendor(s): Knight-Ridder Information, Inc., Lexis-Nexis. *5912*

COUNTRY PROFILE. ITALY.
Economist Intelligence Unit, 111 W. 57th St., New York, NY 10019. TEL 212-554-0600. FAX 212-586-1182. URL: http://www.eiu.com.
Vendor(s): Knight-Ridder Information, Inc., Lexis-Nexis. *5912*

COUNTRY PROFILE. JAMAICA, BARBADOS.
Economist Intelligence Unit, 111 W. 57th St., New York, NY 10019. TEL 212-554-0600. FAX 212-586-1182. URL: http://www.eiu.com.
Vendor(s): Knight-Ridder Information, Inc., Lexis-Nexis. *5912*

COUNTRY PROFILE. JAPAN.
Economist Intelligence Unit, 111 W. 57th St., New York, NY 10019. TEL 212-554-0600. FAX 212-586-1182. URL: http://www.eiu.com.
Vendor(s): Knight-Ridder Information, Inc., Lexis-Nexis. *5912*

COUNTRY PROFILE. JORDAN.
Economist Intelligence Unit, 111 W. 57th St., New York, NY 10019. TEL 212-554-0600. FAX 212-586-1182. URL: http://www.eiu.com.
Vendor(s): Knight-Ridder Information, Inc., Lexis-Nexis. *5912*

COUNTRY PROFILE. KAZAKHSTAN.
Economist Intelligence Unit, 111 W. 57th St., New York, NY 10019. TEL 212-554-0600. FAX 212-586-1182. URL: http://www.eiu.com.
Vendor(s): Knight-Ridder Information, Inc., Lexis-Nexis. *5912*

COUNTRY PROFILE. KENYA.
Economist Intelligence Unit, 111 W. 57th St., New York, NY 10019. TEL 212-554-0600. FAX 212-586-1192. URL: http://www.eiu.com.
Vendor(s): Knight-Ridder Information, Inc., Lexis-Nexis. *5912*

COUNTRY PROFILE. KUWAIT.
Economist Intelligence Unit, 111 W. 57th St., New York, NY 10019. TEL 212-554-0600. FAX 212-586-1182. URL: http://www.eiu.com.
Vendor(s): Knight-Ridder Information, Inc., Lexis-Nexis. *5912*

COUNTRY PROFILE. LEBANON.
Economist Intelligence Unit, 111 W. 57th St., New York, NY 10019. TEL 212-554-0600. FAX 212-586-1182. URL: http://www.eiu.com.
Vendor(s): Knight-Ridder Information, Inc., Lexis-Nexis. *5913*

COUNTRY PROFILE. LIBYA.
Economist Intelligence Unit, 111 W. 57th St., New York, NY 10019. TEL 212-554-0600. FAX 212-586-1182. URL: http://www.eiu.com.
Vendor(s): Knight-Ridder Information, Inc., Lexis-Nexis. *5913*

COUNTRY PROFILE. MACEDONIA, SERBIA-MONTENEGRO.
Economist Intelligence Unit, 111 W. 57th St., New York, NY 10019. TEL 212-554-0600. FAX 212-586-1182. URL: http://www.eiu.com.
Vendor(s): Knight-Ridder Information, Inc., Lexis-Nexis. *5913*

COUNTRY PROFILE. MADAGASCAR.
Economist Intelligence Unit, 111 W. 57th St., New York, NY 10019. TEL 212-554-0600. FAX 212-586-1182. URL: http://www.eiu.com.
Vendor(s): Knight-Ridder Information, Inc., Lexis-Nexis. *5913*

COUNTRY PROFILE. MALAWI.
Economist Intelligence Unit, 111 W. 57th St., New York, NY 10019. TEL 212-554-0600. FAX 212-586-1182. URL: http://www.eiu.com.
Vendor(s): Knight-Ridder Information, Inc., Lexis-Nexis. *5913*

COUNTRY PROFILE. MALAYSIA, BRUNEI.
Economist Intelligence Unit, 111 W. 57th St., New York, NY 10019. TEL 212-554-0600. FAX 212-586-1182. URL: http://www.eiu.com.
Vendor(s): Knight-Ridder Information, Inc., Lexis-Nexis. *5913*

COUNTRY PROFILE. MAURITIUS, SEYCHELLES.
Economist Intelligence Unit, 111 W. 57th St., New York, NY 10019. TEL 212-544-0600. FAX 212-586-1182. URL: http://www.eiu.com.
Vendor(s): Knight-Ridder Information, Inc., Lexis-Nexis. *5913*

COUNTRY PROFILE. MEXICO.
Economist Intelligence Unit, 111 W. 57th St., New York, NY 10019. TEL 212-554-0600. FAX 212-586-1182. URL: http://www.eiu.com.
Vendor(s): Knight-Ridder Information, Inc., Lexis-Nexis. *5913*

COUNTRY PROFILE. MOROCCO.
Economist Intelligence Unit, 111 W. 57th St., New York, NY 10019. TEL 212-554-0600. FAX 212-586-1182. URL: http://www.eiu.com.
Vendor(s): Knight-Ridder Information, Inc., Lexis-Nexis. *5913*

COUNTRY PROFILE. MOZAMBIQUE.
Economist Intelligence Unit, 111 W. 57th St., New York, NY 10019. TEL 212-554-0600. FAX 212-586-1182. URL: http://www.eiu.com.
Vendor(s): Knight-Ridder Information, Inc., Lexis-Nexis. *5913*

COUNTRY PROFILE. MYANMAR.
Economist Intelligence Unit Ltd., 111 W. 57th St., New York, NY 10019. TEL 212-554-0600. FAX 212-586-1182. URL: http://www.eiu.com.
Vendor(s): Knight-Ridder Information, Inc., Lexis-Nexis. *5913*

COUNTRY PROFILE. NAMIBIA, SWAZILAND.
Economist Intelligence Unit, 111 W. 57th St., New York, NY 10019. TEL 212-554-0600. FAX 212-586-1182. URL: http://www.eiu.com.
Vendor(s): Knight-Ridder Information, Inc., Lexis-Nexis. *5913*

COUNTRY PROFILE. NETHERLANDS.
Economist Intelligence Unit, 111 W. 57th St., New York, NY 10019. TEL 212-554-0600. FAX 212-586-1182. URL: http://www.eiu.com.
Vendor(s): Knight-Ridder Information, Inc., Lexis-Nexis. *5913*

COUNTRY PROFILE. NEW ZEALAND.
Economist Intelligence Unit, 111 W. 57th St., New York, NY 10019. TEL 212-554-0600. FAX 212-586-1182. URL: http://www.eiu.com.
Vendor(s): Knight-Ridder Information, Inc., Lexis-Nexis. *5913*

COUNTRY PROFILE. NICARAGUA, HONDURAS.
Economist Intelligence Unit, 111 W. 57th St., New York, NY 10019. TEL 212-554-0600. FAX 212-586-1182. URL: http://www.eiu.com.
Vendor(s): Knight-Ridder Information, Inc., Lexis-Nexis. *5913*

COUNTRY PROFILE. NIGER, BURKINA FASO.
Economist Intelligence Unit, 111 W. 57th St., New York, NY 10019. TEL 212-554-0600. FAX 212-586-1182. URL: http://www.eiu.com.
Vendor(s): Knight-Ridder Information, Inc., Lexis-Nexis. *5914*

COUNTRY PROFILE. NIGERIA.
Economist Intelligence Unit, 111 W. 57th St., New York, NY 10019. TEL 212-554-0600. FAX 212-586-1182. URL: http://www.eiu.com.
Vendor(s): Knight-Ridder Information, Inc., Lexis-Nexis. *5914*

COUNTRY PROFILE. NORWAY.
Economist Intelligence Unit, 111 W. 57th St., New York, NY 10019. TEL 212-554-0600. FAX 212-586-1182. URL: http://www.eiu.com.
Vendor(s): Knight-Ridder Information, Inc., Lexis-Nexis. *5914*

COUNTRY PROFILE. OMAN.
Economist Intelligence Unit, 111 W. 57th St., New York, NY 10019. TEL 212-554-0600. FAX 212-586-1182. URL: http://www.eiu.com.
Vendor(s): Knight-Ridder Information, Inc., Lexis-Nexis. *5914*

COUNTRY PROFILE. PACIFIC ISLANDS: FIJI, SOLOMON ISLANDS, WESTERN SAMOA, VANUATU, TONGA AND NEW CALEDONIA.
Economist Intelligence Unit, 111 W. 57th St., New York, NY 10019. TEL 212-554-0600. FAX 212-586-1182. URL: http://www.eiu.com.
Vendor(s): Knight-Ridder Information, Inc., Lexis-Nexis. *5914*

COUNTRY PROFILE. PAKISTAN, AFGHANISTAN.
Economist Intelligence Unit, 111 W. 57th St., New York, NY 10019. TEL 212-554-0600. FAX 212-586-1182. URL: http://www.eiu.com.
Vendor(s): Knight-Ridder Information, Inc., Lexis-Nexis. *5914*

COUNTRY PROFILE. PANAMA.
Economist Intelligence Unit, 111 W. 57th St., New York, NY 10019. TEL 212-554-0600. FAX 212-586-1182. URL: http://www.eiu.com.
Vendor(s): Knight-Ridder Information, Inc., Lexis-Nexis. *5914*

COUNTRY PROFILE. PAPUA NEW GUINEA.
Economist Intelligence Unit, 111 W. 57th St., New York, NY 10019. TEL 212-554-0600. FAX 212-586-1182. URL: http://www.eiu.com.
Vendor(s): Knight-Ridder Information, Inc., Lexis-Nexis. *5914*

COUNTRY PROFILE. PERU.
Economist Intelligence Unit, 111 W. 57th St., New York, NY 10019. TEL 212-554-0600. FAX 212-586-1182. URL: http://www/eiu.com.
Vendor(s): Knight-Ridder Information, Inc., Lexis-Nexis. *5914*

COUNTRY PROFILE. PHILIPPINES.
Economist Intelligence Unit, 111 W. 57th St., New York, NY 10019. TEL 212-554-0600. FAX 212-586-1182. URL: http://www.eiu.com.
Vendor(s): Knight-Ridder Information, Inc., Lexis-Nexis. *5914*

COUNTRY PROFILE. POLAND.
Economist Intelligence Unit, 111 W. 57th St., New York, NY 10019. TEL 212-554-0600. FAX 212-586-1182. URL: http://www.eiu.com.
Vendor(s): Knight-Ridder Information, Inc., Lexis-Nexis. *5914*

COUNTRY PROFILE. PORTUGAL.
Economist Intelligence Unit, 111 W. 57th St., New York, NY 10019. TEL 212-554-0600. FAX 212-586-1182. URL: http://www.eiu.com.
Vendor(s): Knight-Ridder Information, Inc., Lexis-Nexis. *5914*

COUNTRY PROFILE. ROMANIA.
Economist Intelligence Unit, 111 W. 57th St., New York, NY 10003-1658. TEL 212-554-0600. FAX 212-596-1182. URL: http://www.eiu.com.
Vendor(s): Knight-Ridder Information, Inc., Lexis-Nexis. *5914*

COUNTRY PROFILE. RUSSIA.
Economist Intelligence Unit, 111 W. 57th St., New York, NY 10019. TEL 212-554-0600. FAX 212-586-1182. URL: http://www.eiu.com.
Vendor(s): Knight-Ridder Information, Inc., Lexis-Nexis. *5914*

COUNTRY PROFILE. RWANDA, BURUNDI.
Economist Intelligence Unit, 111 W. 57th St., New York, NY 10019. TEL 212-554-0600. FAX 212-586-1182. URL: http://www.eiu.com.
Vendor(s): Knight-Ridder Information, Inc., Lexis-Nexis. *5914*

COUNTRY PROFILE. SAO TOME AND PRINCIPE, GUINEA-BISSAU, CAPE VERDE.
Economist Intelligence Unit, 111 W. 57th St., New York, NY 10019. TEL 212-554-0600. FAX 212-586-1182. URL: http://www.eiu.com.
Vendor(s): Knight-Ridder Information, Inc., Lexis-Nexis. *5915*

COUNTRY PROFILE. SAUDI ARABIA.
Economist Intelligence Unit, 111 W. 57th St., New York, NY 10019. TEL 212-544-0600. FAX 212-586-1182. URL: http://www.eiu.com.
Vendor(s): Knight-Ridder Information, Inc., Lexis-Nexis. *5915*

COUNTRY PROFILE. SENEGAL.
Economist Intelligence Unit, 111 W. 57th St., New York, NY 10019. TEL 212-554-0600. FAX 212-586-1182. URL: http://www.eiu.com.
Vendor(s): Knight-Ridder Information, Inc., Lexis-Nexis. *5915*

COUNTRY PROFILE. SINGAPORE.
Economist Intelligence Unit, 111 W. 57th St., New York, NY 10019. TEL 212-544-0600. FAX 212-586-1182. URL: http://www.eiu.com.
Vendor(s): Knight-Ridder Information, Inc., Lexis-Nexis. *5915*

COUNTRY PROFILE. SLOVAKIA.
Economist Intelligence Unit, 111 W. 57th St., New York, NY 10019. TEL 212-554-0600. FAX 212-586-1182. URL: http://www.eiu.com.
Vendor(s): Knight-Ridder Information, Inc., Lexis-Nexis. *5915*

COUNTRY PROFILE. SLOVENIA.
Economist Intelligence Unit, 111 W. 57th St., New York, NY 10019. TEL 212-554-0600. FAX 212-586-1182. URL: http://www.eiu.com.
Vendor(s): Knight-Ridder Information, Inc., Lexis-Nexis. *5915*

COUNTRY PROFILE. SOUTH AFRICA.
Economist Intelligence Unit, 111 W. 57th St., New York, NY 10019. TEL 212-554-0600. FAX 212-586-1182. URL: http://www.eiu.com.
Vendor(s): Knight-Ridder Information, Inc., Lexis-Nexis. *5915*

COUNTRY PROFILE. SOUTH KOREA, NORTH KOREA.
Economist Intelligence Unit, 111 W. 57th St., New York, NY 10019. TEL 212-554-0600. FAX 212-586-1182. URL: http://www.eiu.com.
Vendor(s): Knight-Ridder Information, Inc., Lexis-Nexis. *5915*

COUNTRY PROFILE. SPAIN.
Economist Intelligence Unit, 111 W. 57th St., New York, NY 10019. TEL 212-554-0600. FAX 212-586-1182. URL: http://www.eiu.com.
Vendor(s): Knight-Ridder Information, Inc., Lexis-Nexis. *5915*

COUNTRY PROFILE. SRI LANKA.
Economist Intelligence Unit, 111 W. 57th St., New York, NY 10019. TEL 212-554-0600. FAX 212-586-1182. URL: http://www.eiu.com.
Vendor(s): Knight-Ridder Information, Inc., Lexis-Nexis. *5915*

COUNTRY PROFILE. SUDAN.
Economist Intelligence Unit, 111 W. 57th St., New York, NY 10019. TEL 212-554-0600. FAX 212-586-1182. URL: http://www.eiu.com.
Vendor(s): Knight-Ridder Information, Inc., Lexis-Nexis. *5915*

COUNTRY PROFILE. SWEDEN.
Economist Intelligence Unit, 111 W. 57th St., New York, NY 10019. TEL 212-554-0600. FAX 212-586-1182. URL: http://www.eiu.com.
Vendor(s): Knight-Ridder Information, Inc., Lexis-Nexis. *5915*

COUNTRY PROFILE. SWITZERLAND.
Economist Intelligence Unit, 111 W. 57th St., New York, NY 10019. TEL 212-554-0600. FAX 212-9586-1182. URL: http://www.eiu.com.
Vendor(s): Knight-Ridder Information, Inc., Lexis-Nexis. *5915*

COUNTRY PROFILE. SYRIA.
Economist Intelligence Unit, 111 W. 57th St., New York, NY 10019. TEL 212-554-0600. FAX 212-586-1182. URL: http://www.eiu.com.
Vendor(s): Knight-Ridder Information, Inc., Lexis-Nexis. *5915*

COUNTRY PROFILE. TAIWAN.
Economist Intelligence Unit, 111 W. 57th St., New York, NY 10019. TEL 212-554-0600. FAX 212-586-1182. URL: http://www.eiu.com.
Vendor(s): Knight-Ridder Information, Inc., Lexis-Nexis. *5915*

COUNTRY PROFILE. TANZANIA, COMOROS.
Economist Intelligence Unit, 111 W. 57th St., New York, NY 10019. TEL 212-554-0600. FAX 212-586-1182. URL: http://www.eiu.com.
Vendor(s): Knight-Ridder Information, Inc., Lexis-Nexis. *5916*

COUNTRY PROFILE. THAILAND.
Economist Intelligence Unit, 111 W. 57th St., New York, NY 10019. TEL 212-554-0600. FAX 212-586-1192. URL: http://www.eiu.com.
Vendor(s): Knight-Ridder Information, Inc., Lexis-Nexis. *5916*

COUNTRY PROFILE. THE GAMBIA, MAURITANIA.
Economist Intelligence Unit, 111 W. 57th St., New York, NY 10019. TEL 212-554-0600. FAX 212-586-1182. URL: http://www.eiu.com.
Vendor(s): Knight-Ridder Information, Inc., Lexis-Nexis. *5916*

SERIALS AVAILABLE ONLINE

COUNTRY PROFILE. TOGO, BENIN.
Economist Intelligence Unit, 111 W. 57th St., New York, NY 10019. TEL 212-554-0600. FAX 212-586-1182. URL: http://www.eiu.com.
Vendor(s): Knight-Ridder Information, Inc., Lexis-Nexis. *5916*

COUNTRY PROFILE. TRINIDAD AND TOBAGO, SURINAME, NETHERLANDS ANTILLES, ARUBA.
Economist Intelligence Unit, 111 W. 57th St., New York, NY 10019. TEL 212-554-0600. FAX 212-586-1182. URL: http://www.eiu.com.
Vendor(s): Knight-Ridder Information, Inc., Lexis-Nexis. *5916*

COUNTRY PROFILE. TUNISIA.
Economist Intelligence Unit, 111 W. 57th St., New York, NY 10019. TEL 212-554-0600. FAX 212-586-1182. URL: http://www.eiu.com.
Vendor(s): Knight-Ridder Information, Inc., Lexis-Nexis. *5916*

COUNTRY PROFILE. TURKEY.
Economist Intelligence Unit, 111 W. 57th St., New York, NY 10019. TEL 212-554-0600. FAX 212-586-1182. URL: http://www.eiu.com.
Vendor(s): Knight-Ridder Information, Inc., Lexis-Nexis. *5916*

COUNTRY PROFILE. UGANDA.
Economist Intelligence Unit, 111 W. 57th St., New York, NY 10019. TEL 212-554-0600. FAX 212-586-1182. URL: http://www.eiu.com.
Vendor(s): Knight-Ridder Information, Inc., Lexis-Nexis. *5916*

COUNTRY PROFILE. UKRAINE.
Economist Intelligence Unit, 111 W. 57th St., New York, NY 10019. TEL 212-554-0600. FAX 212-586-1182. URL: http://www.eiu.com.
Vendor(s): Knight-Ridder Information, Inc., Lexis-Nexis. *5916*

COUNTRY PROFILE. UNITED ARAB EMIRATES.
Economist Intelligence Unit, 111 W. 57th St., New York, NY 10019. TEL 212-554-0600. FAX 212-586-1182. URL: http://www.eiu.com.
Vendor(s): Knight-Ridder Information, Inc., Lexis-Nexis. *5916*

COUNTRY PROFILE. UNITED KINGDOM.
Economist Intelligence Unit, 111 W. 57th St., New York, NY 10019. TEL 212-554-0600. FAX 212-586-1182. URL: http://www.eiu.com.
Vendor(s): Knight-Ridder Information, Inc., Lexis-Nexis. *5916*

COUNTRY PROFILE. UNITED STATES OF AMERICA.
Economist Intelligence Unit, 111 W. 57th St., New York, NY 10019. TEL 212-554-0600. FAX 212-586-1182. URL: http://www.eiu.com.
Vendor(s): Knight-Ridder Information, Inc., Lexis-Nexis. *5916*

COUNTRY PROFILE. URUGUAY, PARAGUAY.
Economist Intelligence Unit, 111 W. 57th St., New York, NY 10019. TEL 212-554-0600. FAX 212-586-1182. URL: http://www.eiu.com.
Vendor(s): Knight-Ridder Information, Inc., Lexis-Nexis. *5916*

COUNTRY PROFILE. VENEZUELA.
Economist Intelligence Unit, 111 W. 57th St., New York, NY 10003-1658. TEL 212-554-0600. FAX 212-586-1182. URL: http://www.eiu.com.
Vendor(s): Knight-Ridder Information, Inc., Lexis-Nexis. *5916*

COUNTRY PROFILE. YEMEN.
Economist Intelligence Unit, 111 W. 57th St., New York, NY 10019. TEL 212-554-0600. FAX 212-586-1182. URL: http://www.eiu.com.
Vendor(s): Knight-Ridder Information, Inc., Lexis-Nexis. *5917*

COUNTRY PROFILE. ZAIRE.
Economist Intelligence Unit, 111 W. 57th St., New York, NY 10019. TEL 212-554-0600. FAX 212-586-1182. URL: http://www.eiu.com.
Vendor(s): Knight-Ridder Information, Inc., Lexis-Nexis. *5917*

COUNTRY PROFILE. ZAMBIA.
Economist Intelligence Unit, 111 W. 57th St., New York, NY 10019. TEL 212-554-0600. FAX 212-586-1182. URL: http://www.eiu.com.
Vendor(s): Knight-Ridder Information, Inc., Lexis-Nexis. *5917*

COUNTRY PROFILE. ZIMBABWE.
Economist Intelligence Unit, 111 W. 57th St., New York, NY 10019. TEL 212-554-0600. FAX 212-586-1182. URL: http://www.eiu.com.
Vendor(s): Knight-Ridder Information, Inc., Lexis-Nexis. *5917*

COUNTRY PROFILES.
Economist Intelligence Unit, 111 W. 57th St., New York, NY 10019. TEL 212-554-0600. FAX 212-586-1182. URL: http://www.eiu.com.
Vendor(s): Knight-Ridder Information, Inc., Lexis-Nexis. *5917*

COUNTRY REPORT. ALBANIA.
Economist Intelligence Unit, 111 W. 57th St., New York, NY 10019. TEL 212-554-0600. FAX 212-586-1182. URL: http://www.eiu.com.
Vendor(s): Central Institute for Scientific & Technical Information, Knight-Ridder Information, Inc.. *1234*

COUNTRY REPORT. ALGERIA.
Economist Intelligence Unit, 111 W. 57th St., New York, NY 10019. TEL 212-554-0600. FAX 212-586-1182. URL: http://www.eiu.com.
Vendor(s): Knight-Ridder Information, Inc., Lexis-Nexis. *1234*

COUNTRY REPORT. ANGOLA.
Economist Intelligence Unit, 111 W. 57th St., New York, NY 10019. TEL 212-554-0600. FAX 212-938-1182. URL: http://www.eiu.com.
Vendor(s): Knight-Ridder Information, Inc., Lexis-Nexis. *1234*

COUNTRY REPORT. ARGENTINA.
Economist Intelligence Unit, 111 W. 57th St., New York, NY 10019. TEL 212-554-0600. FAX 212-586-1182. URL: http://www.eiu.com.
Vendor(s): Knight-Ridder Information, Inc., Lexis-Nexis. *1235*

COUNTRY REPORT. AUSTRALIA.
Economist Intelligence Unit, 111 W. 57th St., New York, NY 10019. TEL 212-554-0600. FAX 212-586-1182.
Vendor(s): Knight-Ridder Information, Inc., Lexis-Nexis. *1235*

COUNTRY REPORT. AUSTRIA.
Economist Intelligence Unit, 111 W. 57th St., New York, NY 10019. TEL 212-554-0600. FAX 212-586-1182. URL: http://www.eiu.com.
Vendor(s): Knight-Ridder Information, Inc., Lexis-Nexis. *1235*

COUNTRY REPORT. BAHRAIN, QATAR.
Economist Intelligence Unit, 111 W. 57th St., New York, NY 10019. TEL 212-554-0600. FAX 212-586-1182. URL: http://www.eiu.com.
Vendor(s): Knight-Ridder Information, Inc., Lexis-Nexis. *1235*

COUNTRY REPORT. BALTIC REPUBLICS: LITHUANIA, LATVIA, ESTONIA.
Economist Intelligence Unit, 111 W. 57th St., New York, NY 10019. TEL 212-554-0600. FAX 212-586-1182. URL: http://www.eiu.com.
Vendor(s): Knight-Ridder Information, Inc., Lexis-Nexis. *1235*

COUNTRY REPORT. BANGLADESH.
Economist Intelligence Unit, 111 W. 57th St., New York, NY 10019. TEL 212-554-0600. FAX 212-586-1182. URL: http://www.eiu.com.
Vendor(s): Knight-Ridder Information, Inc., Lexis-Nexis. *1235*

COUNTRY REPORT. BELGIUM, LUXEMBOURG.
Economist Intelligence Unit, 111 W. 57th St., New York, NY 10019. TEL 212-554-0600. FAX 212-586-1182. URL: http://www.eiu.com.
Vendor(s): Knight-Ridder Information, Inc., Lexis-Nexis. *1235*

COUNTRY REPORT. BOLIVIA.
Economist Intelligence Unit, 111 W. 57th St., New York, NY 10019. TEL 212-554-0600. FAX 212-586-1182. URL: http://www.eiu.com.
Vendor(s): Knight-Ridder Information, Inc., Lexis-Nexis. *1235*

COUNTRY REPORT. BOSNIA-HERCEGOVINA, CROATIA AND SLOVENIA.
Economist Intelligence Unit, 111 W. 57th St., New York, NY 10019. TEL 212-554-0600. FAX 212-586-1182. URL: http://www.eiu.com.
Vendor(s): Knight-Ridder Information, Inc., Lexis-Nexis. *1235*

COUNTRY REPORT. BRAZIL.
Economist Intelligence Unit, 111 W. 57th St., New York, NY 10019. TEL 212-554-0600. FAX 212-586-1182. URL: http://www.eiu.com.
Vendor(s): Knight-Ridder Information, Inc., Lexis-Nexis. *1236*

COUNTRY REPORT. BULGARIA.
Economist Intelligence Unit, 111 W. 57th St., New York, NY 10019. TEL 212-554-0600. FAX 212-586-1182. URL: http://www.eiu.com.
Vendor(s): Knight-Ridder Information, Inc., Lexis-Nexis. *1236*

COUNTRY REPORT. CAMBODIA, LAOS.
Economist Intelligence Unit, 111 W. 57th St., New York, NY 10019. TEL 212-554-0600. FAX 212-586-1182. URL: http://www.eiu.com.
Vendor(s): Knight-Ridder Information, Inc., Lexis-Nexis. *1236*

COUNTRY REPORT. CAMEROON, C.A.R., CHAD.
Economist Intelligence Unit, 111 W. 57th St., New York, NY 10019. TEL 212-554-0600. FAX 212-586-1182. URL: http://www.eiu.com.
Vendor(s): Knight-Ridder Information, Inc., Lexis-Nexis. *1236*

COUNTRY REPORT. CANADA.
Economist Intelligence Unit, 111 W. 57th St., New York, NY 10019. TEL 212-554-0600. FAX 212-586-1182. URL: http://www.eiu.com.
Vendor(s): Knight-Ridder Information, Inc., Lexis-Nexis. *1236*

COUNTRY REPORT. CHILE.
Economist Intelligence Unit, 111 W. 57th St., New York, NY 10019. TEL 212-554-0600. FAX 212-586-1182. URL: http://www.eiu.com.
Vendor(s): Knight-Ridder Information, Inc., Lexis-Nexis. *1236*

COUNTRY REPORT. CHINA, MONGOLIA.
Economist Intelligence Unit, 111 W. 57th St., New York, NY 10019. TEL 212-554-0600. FAX 212-586-1182. URL: http://www.eiu.com.
Vendor(s): Knight-Ridder Information, Inc., Lexis-Nexis. *1236*

COUNTRY REPORT. COLOMBIA.
Economist Intelligence Unit, 111 W. 57th St., New York, NY 10019. TEL 212-554-0600. FAX 212-586-1182. URL: http://www.eiu.com.
Vendor(s): Knight-Ridder Information, Inc., Lexis-Nexis. *1236*

COUNTRY REPORT. CONGO, SAO TOME AND PRINCIPE, GUINEA-BISSAU, CAPE VERDE.
Economist Intelligence Unit, 111 W. 57th St., New York, NY 10019. TEL 212-554-0600. FAX 212-586-1182. URL: http://www.eiu.com.
Vendor(s): Knight-Ridder Information, Inc., Lexis-Nexis. *1236*

COUNTRY REPORT. COSTA RICA.
Economist Intelligence Unit, 111 W. 57th St., New York, NY 10019. TEL 212-554-0600. FAX 212-586-1182. URL: http://www.eiu.com.
Vendor(s): Knight-Ridder Information, Inc., Lexis-Nexis. *1237*

COUNTRY REPORT. COTE D'IVOIRE, MALI.
Economist Intelligence Unit, 111 W. 57th St., New York, NY 10019. TEL 212-554-0600. FAX 212-586-1182. URL: http://eiu.com.
Vendor(s): Knight-Ridder Information, Inc., Lexis-Nexis. *1237*

COUNTRY REPORT. CUBA, DOMINICAN REPUBLIC, HAITI, PUERTO RICO.
Economist Intelligence Unit, 111 W. 57th St., New York, NY 10019. TEL 212-554-0600. FAX 212-586-1182. URL: http://www.eiu.com.
Vendor(s): Knight-Ridder Information, Inc., Lexis-Nexis. *1237*

COUNTRY REPORT. CYPRUS, MALTA.
Economist Intelligence Unit, 111 W. 57th St., New York, NY 10019. TEL 212-554-0600. FAX 212-586-1182. URL: http://www.eiu.com.
Vendor(s): Knight-Ridder Information, Inc., Lexis-Nexis. *1237*

COUNTRY REPORT. CZECH REPUBLIC.
Economist Intelligence Unit, 111 W. 57th St., New York, NY 10019. TEL 212-554-0600. FAX 212-586-1182.
Vendor(s): Knight-Ridder Information, Inc., Lexis-Nexis. *1237*

COUNTRY REPORT. DENMARK, ICELAND.
Economist Intelligence Unit, 111 W. 57th St., New York, NY 10019. TEL 212-554-0600. FAX 212-586-1182. URL: http://www.eiu.com.
Vendor(s): Knight-Ridder Information, Inc., Lexis-Nexis. *1237*

COUNTRY REPORT. ECUADOR.
Economist Intelligence Unit, 111 W. 57th St., New York, NY 10019. TEL 212-554-0600. FAX 212-586-1182. URL: http://www.eiu.com.
Vendor(s): Knight-Ridder Information, Inc., Lexis-Nexis. *1237*

COUNTRY REPORT. EGYPT.
Economist Intelligence Unit, 111 W. 57th St., New York, NY 10019. TEL 212-554-0600. FAX 212-586-1182. URL: http://www.eiu.com.
Vendor(s): Knight-Ridder Information, Inc., Lexis-Nexis. *1237*

COUNTRY REPORT. ETHIOPIA, ERITREA, SOMALIA, DJIBOUTI.
Economist Intelligence Unit, 111 W. 57th St., New York, NY 10019. TEL 212-554-0600. FAX 212-586-1182. URL: http://www.eiu.com.
Vendor(s): Knight-Ridder Information, Inc., Lexis-Nexis. *1237*

COUNTRY REPORT. FINLAND.
Economist Intelligence Unit, 111 W. 57th St., New York, NY 10019. TEL 212-554-0600. FAX 212-586-1182. URL: http://www.eiu.com.
Vendor(s): Knight-Ridder Information, Inc., Lexis-Nexis. *1237*

COUNTRY REPORT. FRANCE.
Economist Intelligence Unit, 111 W. 57th St., New York, NY 10019. TEL 212-554-0600. FAX 212-586-1182. URL: http://www.eiu.com.
Vendor(s): Knight-Ridder Information, Inc., Lexis-Nexis. *1237*

COUNTRY REPORT. GABON, EQUATORIAL GUINEA.
Economist Intelligence Unit, 111 W. 57th St., New York, NY 10019. TEL 212-554-0600. FAX 212-586-1182. URL: http://www.eiu.com.
Vendor(s): Knight-Ridder Information, Inc., Lexis-Nexis. *1237*

COUNTRY REPORT. GERMANY.
Economist Intelligence Unit, 111 W. 57th St., New York, NY 10019. TEL 212-554-0600. FAX 212-586-1182. URL: http://www.eiu.com.
Vendor(s): Knight-Ridder Information, Inc., Lexis-Nexis. *1238*

COUNTRY REPORT. GHANA.
Economist Intelligence Unit, 111 W. 57th St., New York, NY 10019. TEL 212-554-0600. FAX 212-586-1182. URL: http://www.eiu.com.
Vendor(s): Knight-Ridder Information, Inc., Lexis-Nexis. *1238*

COUNTRY REPORT. GREECE.
Economist Intelligence Unit, 111 W. 57th St., New York, NY 10019. TEL 212-554-0600. FAX 212-586-1182. URL: http://www.eiu.com.
Vendor(s): Knight-Ridder Information, Inc., Lexis-Nexis. *1238*

COUNTRY REPORT. GUATEMALA, EL SALVADOR.
Economist Intelligence Unit, 111 W. 57th St., New York, NY 10019. TEL 212-554-0600. FAX 212-586-1182.
Vendor(s): Knight-Ridder Information, Inc., Lexis-Nexis. *1238*

COUNTRY REPORT. GUINEA, SIERRA LEONE, LIBERIA.
Economist Intelligence Unit, 111 W. 57th St., New York, NY 10019. TEL 212-554-0600. FAX 212-586-1182. URL: http://www.eiu.com.
Vendor(s): Knight-Ridder Information, Inc., Lexis-Nexis. *1238*

COUNTRY REPORT. HONG KONG, MACAU.
Economist Intelligence Unit, 111 W. 57th St., New York, NY 10019. TEL 212-554-0600. FAX 212-586-1182. URL: http://www.eiu.com.
Vendor(s): Knight-Ridder Information, Inc., Lexis-Nexis. *1238*

COUNTRY REPORT. HUNGARY.
Economist Intelligence Unit, 111 W. 57th St., New York, NY 10019. TEL 212-554-0600. FAX 212-586-1182. URL: http://www.eiu.com.
Vendor(s): Knight-Ridder Information, Inc., Lexis-Nexis. *1238*

COUNTRY REPORT. INDIA, NEPAL.
Economist Intelligence Unit, 111 W. 57th St., New York, NY 10019. TEL 212-554-0600. FAX 212-586-1182. URL: http://www.eiu.com.
Vendor(s): Knight-Ridder Information, Inc., Lexis-Nexis. *1238*

COUNTRY REPORT. INDONESIA.
Economist Intelligence Unit, 111 W. 57th St., New York, NY 10019. TEL 212-554-0600. FAX 212-586-4685. URL: http://www.eiu.com.
Vendor(s): Knight-Ridder Information, Inc., Lexis-Nexis. *1238*

COUNTRY REPORT. IRAN.
Economist Intelligence Unit, 111 W. 57th St., New York, NY 10019. TEL 212-554-0600. FAX 212-586-1182. URL: http://www.eiu.com.
Vendor(s): Knight-Ridder Information, Inc., Lexis-Nexis. *1238*

COUNTRY REPORT. IRAQ.
Economist Intelligence Unit, 111 W. 57th St., New York, NY 10019. TEL 212-554-0600. FAX 212-586-1182. URL: http://www.eiu.com.
Vendor(s): Knight-Ridder Information, Inc., Lexis-Nexis. *1238*

COUNTRY REPORT. IRELAND.
Economist Intelligence Unit, 111 W. 57th St., New York, NY 10019. TEL 212-554-0600. FAX 212-586-1182. URL: http://www.eiu.com.
Vendor(s): Knight-Ridder Information, Inc., Lexis-Nexis. *1239*

COUNTRY REPORT. ISRAEL, THE OCCUPIED TERRITORIES.
Economist Intelligence Unit, 111 W. 57th St., New York, NY 10019. TEL 212-554-0600. FAX 212-586-1182. URL: http://www.eiu.com.
Vendor(s): Knight-Ridder Information, Inc., Lexis-Nexis. *1239*

COUNTRY REPORT. ITALY.
Economist Intelligence Unit, 111 W. 57th St., New York, NY 10019. TEL 212-554-0600. FAX 212-586-1182. URL: http://www.eiu.com.
Vendor(s): Knight-Ridder Information, Inc., Lexis-Nexis. *1239*

COUNTRY REPORT. JAMAICA, BELIZE, BAHAMAS, BERMUDA, BARBADOS.
Economist Intelligence Unit, 111 W. 57th St., New York, NY 10019. TEL 212-554-0600. FAX 212-586-1182. URL: http://www.eiu.com.
Vendor(s): Knight-Ridder Information, Inc., Lexis-Nexis. *1239*

COUNTRY REPORT. JAPAN.
Economist Intelligence Unit, 111 W. 57th St., New York, NY 10019. TEL 212-554-0600. FAX 212-586-1182. URL: http://www.eiu.com.
Vendor(s): Knight-Ridder Information, Inc., Lexis-Nexis. *1239*

COUNTRY REPORT. JORDAN.
Economist Intelligence Unit, 111 W. 57th St., New York, NY 10019. TEL 212-554-0600. FAX 212-586-1182. URL: http://www.eiu.com.
Vendor(s): Knight-Ridder Information, Inc., Lexis-Nexis. *1239*

COUNTRY REPORT. KAZAKHSTAN.
Economist Intelligence Unit, 111 W. 57th St., New York, NY 10019. TEL 212-554-0600. FAX 212-586-1182. URL: http://www.eiu.com.
Vendor(s): Knight-Ridder Information, Inc., Lexis-Nexis. *1239*

COUNTRY REPORT. KENYA.
Economist Intelligence Unit, 111 W. 57th St., New York, NY 10019. TEL 212-554-0600. FAX 212-586-1182. URL: http://www.eiu.com.
Vendor(s): Knight-Ridder Information, Inc., Lexis-Nexis. *1239*

COUNTRY REPORT. KUWAIT.
Economist Intelligence Unit, 111 W. 57th St., New York, NY 10019. TEL 212-554-0600. FAX 212-586-1182. URL: http://www.eiu.com.
Vendor(s): Knight-Ridder Information, Inc., Lexis-Nexis. *1239*

COUNTRY REPORT. LEBANON.
Economist Intelligence Unit, 111 W. 57th St., New York, NY 10019. TEL 212-554-0600. FAX 212-586-1182. URL: http://www.eiu.com.
Vendor(s): Knight-Ridder Information, Inc., Lexis-Nexis. *1239*

COUNTRY REPORT. LIBYA.
Economist Intelligence Unit, 111 W. 57th St., New York, NY 10019. TEL 212-554-0600. FAX 212-586-1182. URL: http://www.eiu.com.
Vendor(s): Knight-Ridder Information, Inc., Lexis-Nexis. *1239*

COUNTRY REPORT. MALAYSIA, BRUNEI.
Economist Intelligence Unit, 111 W. 57th St., New York, NY 10019. TEL 212-554-0600. FAX 212-586-1182. URL: http://www.eiu.com.
Vendor(s): Knight-Ridder Information, Inc., Lexis-Nexis. *1240*

COUNTRY REPORT. MAURITIUS, MADAGASCAR, SEYCHELLES.
Economist Intelligence Unit, 111 W. 57th St., New York, NY 10019. TEL 212-554-0600. FAX 212-586-1182. URL: http://www.eiu.com.
Vendor(s): Knight-Ridder Information, Inc., Lexis-Nexis. *1240*

COUNTRY REPORT. MEXICO.
Economist Intelligence Unit, 111 W. 57th St., New York, NY 10019. TEL 212-554-0600. FAX 212-586-1182. URL: http://www.eiu.com.
Vendor(s): Knight-Ridder Information, Inc., Lexis-Nexis. *1240*

COUNTRY REPORT. MOROCCO.
Economist Intelligence Unit, 111 W. 57th St., New York, NY 10019. TEL 212-554-0600. FAX 212-586-1182. URL: http://www.eiu.com.
Vendor(s): Knight-Ridder Information, Inc., Lexis-Nexis. *1240*

COUNTRY REPORT. MOZAMBIQUE, MALAWI.
Economist Intelligence Unit, 111 W. 57th St., New York, NY 10019. TEL 212-554-0600. FAX 212-586-1182. URL: http://www.eiu.com.
Vendor(s): Knight-Ridder Information, Inc., Lexis-Nexis. *1240*

COUNTRY REPORT. NETHERLANDS.
Economist Intelligence Unit, 111 W. 57th St., New York, NY 10019. TEL 212-554-0600. FAX 212-586-1182. URL: http://www.eiu.com.
Vendor(s): Knight-Ridder Information, Inc., Lexis-Nexis. *1240*

COUNTRY REPORT. NEW ZEALAND.
Economist Intelligence Unit, 111 W. 57th St., New York, NY 10019. TEL 212-554-0600. FAX 212-586-1182. URL: http://www.eiu.com.
Vendor(s): Knight-Ridder Information, Inc., Lexis-Nexis. *1240*

COUNTRY REPORT. NICARAGUA, HONDURAS.
Economist Intelligence Unit, 111 W. 57th St., New York, NY 10019. TEL 212-554-0600. FAX 212-586-1182. URL: http://www.eiu.com.
Vendor(s): Knight-Ridder Information, Inc., Lexis-Nexis. *1240*

COUNTRY REPORT. NIGERIA.
Economist Intelligence Unit, 111 W. 57th St., New York, NY 10019. TEL 212-554-0600. FAX 212-586-1182. URL: http://www.eiu.com.
Vendor(s): Knight-Ridder Information, Inc., Lexis-Nexis. *1241*

10084   SERIALS AVAILABLE ONLINE

COUNTRY REPORT. NORWAY.
Economist Intelligence Unit, 111 W. 57th St., New York, NY 10019. TEL 212-554-0600. FAX 212-586-1182. URL: http://www.eiu.com.
Vendor(s): Knight-Ridder Information, Inc., Lexis-Nexis. *1241*

COUNTRY REPORT. OMAN, YEMEN.
Economist Intelligence Unit, 111 W. 57th St., New York, NY 10019. TEL 212-554-0600. FAX 212-586-1182. URL: http://www.eiu.com.
Vendor(s): Knight-Ridder Information, Inc., Lexis-Nexis. *1241*

COUNTRY REPORT. PACIFIC ISLANDS: PAPUA NEW GUINEA, FIJI, SOLOMON ISLANDS, WESTERN SAMOA, VANUATU, TONGA.
Economist Intelligence Unit, 111 W. 57th St., New York, NY 10019. TEL 212-554-0600. FAX 212-586-1827. URL: http://www.eiu.com.
Vendor(s): Knight-Ridder Information, Inc., Lexis-Nexis. *1241*

COUNTRY REPORT. PAKISTAN, AFGHANISTAN.
Economist Intelligence Unit, 111 W. 57th St., New York, NY 10019. TEL 212-554-0600. FAX 212-586-1182. URL: http://www.eiu.com.
Vendor(s): Knight-Ridder Information, Inc., Lexis-Nexis. *1241*

COUNTRY REPORT. PANAMA.
Economist Intelligence Unit, 111 W. 57th St., New York, NY 10019. TEL 212-554-0600. FAX 212-586-1182. URL: http://www.eiu.com.
Vendor(s): Knight-Ridder Information, Inc., Lexis-Nexis. *1241*

COUNTRY REPORT. PERU.
Economist Intelligence Unit, 111 W. 57th St., New York, NY 10019. TEL 212-554-0600. FAX 212-586-1182. URL: http://www.eiu.com.
Vendor(s): Knight-Ridder Information, Inc., Lexis-Nexis. *1241*

COUNTRY REPORT. PHILIPPINES.
Economist Intelligence Unit, 111 W. 57th St., New York, NY 10019. TEL 212-554-0600. FAX 212-586-1182. URL: http://www.eiu.com.
Vendor(s): Knight-Ridder Information, Inc., Lexis-Nexis. *1241*

COUNTRY REPORT. POLAND.
Economist Intelligence Unit, 111 W. 57th St., New York, NY 10019. TEL 212-554-0600. FAX 212-938-4685. URL: http://www.eiu.com.
Vendor(s): Knight-Ridder Information, Inc., Lexis-Nexis. *1241*

COUNTRY REPORT. PORTUGAL.
Economist Intelligence Unit, 111 W. 57th St., New York, NY 10019. TEL 212-554-0600. FAX 212-586-1182. URL: http://www.eiu.com.
Vendor(s): Knight-Ridder Information, Inc., Lexis-Nexis. *1241*

COUNTRY REPORT. ROMANIA.
Economist Intelligence Unit, 111 W. 57th St., New York, NY 10019. TEL 212-554-0600. FAX 212-586-1182. URL: http://www.eiu.com.
Vendor(s): Knight-Ridder Information, Inc., Lexis-Nexis. *1241*

COUNTRY REPORT. RUSSIA.
Economist Intelligence Unit, 111 W. 57th St., New York, NY 10019. TEL 212 554 0600. FAX 212-586-1182. URL: http://www.eiu.com.
Vendor(s): Knight-Ridder Information, Inc., Lexis-Nexis. *1242*

COUNTRY REPORT. SAUDI ARABIA.
Economist Intelligence Unit, 111 W. 57th St., New York, NY 10019. TEL 212-554-0600. FAX 212-586-1182. URL: http://www.eiu.com.
Vendor(s): Knight-Ridder Information, Inc., Lexis-Nexis. *1242*

COUNTRY REPORT. SENEGAL, THE GAMBIA, MAURITANIA.
Economist Intelligence Unit, 111 W. 57th St., New York, NY 10019. TEL 212-554-0600. FAX 212-586-1182. URL: http://www.eiu.com.
Vendor(s): Knight-Ridder Information, Inc., Lexis-Nexis. *1242*

COUNTRY REPORT. SINGAPORE.
Economist Intelligence Unit, 111 W. 57th St., New York, NY 10019. TEL 212-554-0600. FAX 212-586-1182. URL: http://www.eiu.com.
Vendor(s): Knight-Ridder Information, Inc., Lexis-Nexis. *1242*

COUNTRY REPORT. SLOVAKIA.
Economist Intelligence Unit, 111 W. 57th St., New York, NY 10019. TEL 212-554-0600. FAX 212-586-1182. URL: http://www.eiu.com.
Vendor(s): Knight-Ridder Information, Inc., Lexis-Nexis. *1242*

COUNTRY REPORT. SOUTH AFRICA.
Economist Intelligence Unit, 111 W. 57th St., New York, NY 10019. TEL 212-554-0600. FAX 212-586-1182. URL: http://www.eiu.com.
Vendor(s): Knight-Ridder Information, Inc., Lexis-Nexis. *1242*

COUNTRY REPORT. SOUTH KOREA, NORTH KOREA.
Economist Intelligence Unit, 111 W. 57th St., New York, NY 10019. TEL 212-554-0600. FAX 212-586-1182. URL: http://www.eiu.com.
Vendor(s): Knight-Ridder Information, Inc., Lexis-Nexis. *1242*

COUNTRY REPORT. SPAIN.
Economist Intelligence Unit, 111 W. 57th St., New York, NY 10019. TEL 212-554-0600. FAX 212-586-1182. URL: http://www.eiu.com.
Vendor(s): Knight-Ridder Information, Inc., Lexis-Nexis. *1242*

COUNTRY REPORT. SRI LANKA.
Economist Intelligence Unit, 111 W. 57th St., New York, NY 10019. TEL 212-554-0600. FAX 212-586-1182. URL: http://www.eiu.com.
Vendor(s): Knight-Ridder Information, Inc., Lexis-Nexis. *1242*

COUNTRY REPORT. SUDAN.
Economist Intelligence Unit, 111 W. 57th St., New York, NY 10019. TEL 212-554-0600. FAX 212-586-1182. URL: http://www.eiu.com.
Vendor(s): Knight-Ridder Information, Inc., Lexis-Nexis. *1242*

COUNTRY REPORT. SWEDEN.
Economist Intelligence Unit, 111 W. 57th St., New York, NY 10019. TEL 212-554-0600. FAX 212-586-1182. URL: http://www.eiu.com.
Vendor(s): Knight-Ridder Information, Inc., Lexis-Nexis. *1242*

COUNTRY REPORT. SWITZERLAND.
Economist Intelligence Unit, 111 W. 57th St., New York, NY 10019. TEL 212-554-0600. FAX 212-586-1182. URL: http://www.eiu.com.
Vendor(s): Knight-Ridder Information, Inc., Lexis-Nexis. *1242*

COUNTRY REPORT. SYRIA.
Economist Intelligence Unit, 111 W. 57th St., New York, NY 10019. TEL 212-554-0600. FAX 212-586-1182. URL: http://www.eiu.com.
Vendor(s): Knight-Ridder Information, Inc., Lexis-Nexis. *1243*

COUNTRY REPORT. TAIWAN.
Economist Intelligence Unit, 111 W. 57th St., New York, NY 10019. TEL 212-554-0600. FAX 212-586-1182. URL: http://www.eiu.com.
Vendor(s): Knight-Ridder Information, Inc., Lexis-Nexis. *1243*

COUNTRY REPORT. TANZANIA, COMOROS.
Economist Intelligence Unit, 111 W. 57th St., New York, NY 10019. TEL 212-554-0600. FAX 212-586-1182. URL: http://www.eiu.com.
Vendor(s): Knight-Ridder Information, Inc., Lexis-Nexis. *1243*

COUNTRY REPORT. THAILAND.
Economist Intelligence Unit, 111 W. 57th St., New York, NY 10019. TEL 212-554-0600. FAX 212-586-1182. URL: http://www.eiu.com.
Vendor(s): Knight-Ridder Information, Inc., Lexis-Nexis. *1243*

COUNTRY REPORT. TOGO, BENIN.
Economist Intelligence Unit, 111 W. 57th St., New York, NY 10019. TEL 212-554-0600. FAX 212-586-1182. URL: http://www.eiu.com.
Vendor(s): Knight-Ridder Information, Inc., Lexis-Nexis. *1243*

COUNTRY REPORT. TRINIDAD & TOBAGO, GUYANA, WINDWARD & LEEWARD ISLANDS, SURINAME, NETHERLANDS ANTILLES, ARUBA.
Economist Intelligence Unit, 111 W. 57th St., New York, NY 10019. TEL 212-554-0600. FAX 212-586-1182. URL: http://www.eiu.com.
Vendor(s): Knight-Ridder Information, Inc., Lexis-Nexis. *1243*

COUNTRY REPORT. TUNISIA.
Economist Intelligence Unit, 111 W. 57th St., New York, NY 10019. TEL 212-554-0600. FAX 212-586-1182. URL: http://www.eiu.com.
Vendor(s): Knight-Ridder Information, Inc., Lexis-Nexis. *1243*

COUNTRY REPORT. TURKEY.
Economist Intelligence Unit, 111 W. 57th St., New York, NY 10019. TEL 212-554-0600. FAX 212-586-1182. URL: http://www.eiu.com.
Vendor(s): Knight-Ridder Information, Inc., Lexis-Nexis. *1243*

COUNTRY REPORT. UGANDA, RWANDA, BURUNDI.
Economist Intelligence Unit, 111 W. 57th St., New York, NY 10019. TEL 212-554-0600. FAX 212-586-1182. URL: http://www.eiu.com.
Vendor(s): Knight-Ridder Information, Inc., Lexis-Nexis. *1243*

COUNTRY REPORT. UKRAINE.
Economist Intelligence Unit, 111 W. 57th St., New York, NY 10019. TEL 212-554-0600. FAX 212-586-1182. URL: http://www.eiu.com.
Vendor(s): Knight-Ridder Information, Inc., Lexis-Nexis. *1243*

COUNTRY REPORT. UNITED ARAB EMIRATES.
Economist Intelligence Unit, 111 W. 57th St., New York, NY 10019. TEL 212-554-0600. FAX 212-586-1182. URL: http://www.eiu.com.
Vendor(s): Knight-Ridder Information, Inc., Lexis-Nexis. *1243*

COUNTRY REPORT. UNITED KINGDOM.
Economist Intelligence Unit, 111 W. 57th St., New York, NY 10019. TEL 212-554-0600. FAX 212-586-1182.
Vendor(s): Knight-Ridder Information, Inc., Lexis-Nexis. *1243*

COUNTRY REPORT. UNITED STATES OF AMERICA.
Economist Intelligence Unit, 111 W. 57th St., New York, NY 10019. TEL 212-554-0600. FAX 212-586-1182. URL: http://www.eiu.com.
Vendor(s): Knight-Ridder Information, Inc., Lexis-Nexis. *1244*

COUNTRY REPORT. URUGUAY, PARAGUAY.
Economist Intelligence Unit, 111 W. 57th St., New York, NY 10019. TEL 212-554-0600. FAX 212-586-1182. URL: http://www.eiu.com.
Vendor(s): Knight-Ridder Information, Inc., Lexis-Nexis. *1244*

COUNTRY REPORT. VENEZUELA.
Economist Intelligence Unit, 111 W. 57th St., New York, NY 10019. TEL 212-554-0600. FAX 212-586-1182. URL: http://www.eiu.com.
Vendor(s): Knight-Ridder Information, Inc., Lexis-Nexis. *1244*

COUNTRY REPORT. ZAMBIA, ZAIRE.
Economist Intelligence Unit, 111 W. 57th St., New York, NY 10019. TEL 212-554-0600. FAX 212-586-1182. URL: http://www.eiu.com.
Vendor(s): Knight-Ridder Information, Inc., Lexis-Nexis. *1244*

COUNTRY REPORT. ZIMBABWE.
Economist Intelligence Unit, 111 W. 57th St., New York, NY 10019. TEL 212-554-0600. FAX 212-586-1182. URL: http://www.eiu.com.
Vendor(s): Knight-Ridder Information, Inc., Lexis-Nexis. *1244*

COUNTRY REPORTS.
Economist Intelligence Unit, 111 W. 57th St., New York, NY 10019. TEL 212-554-0600. FAX 212-586-1182. URL: http://www.eiu.com.
Vendor(s): Knight-Ridder Information, Inc., Lexis-Nexis. *1244*

COUNTRY RISK SERVICE.
Economist Intelligence Unit, 111 W. 57th St., New York, NY 10019. TEL 212-554-0600. FAX 212-586-1182. URL: http://www.eiu.com.
Vendor(s): Lexis-Nexis. *1244*

SERIALS AVAILABLE ONLINE 10085

COUNTRY RISK SERVICE. ALGERIA.
Economist Intelligence Unit, 111 w. 57th St., New York, NY 10019. TEL 212-554-0600. FAX 212-586-1182. URL: http://www.eiu.com. Vendor(s): Lexis-Nexis. *1244*

COUNTRY RISK SERVICE. ANGOLA.
Economist Intelligence Unit, 111 W. 57th St., New York, NY 10019. TEL 212-554-0600. FAX 212-586-1182. URL: http://www.eiu.com. Vendor(s): Lexis-Nexis. *1244*

COUNTRY RISK SERVICE. ARGENTINA.
Economist Intelligence Unit, 111 W. 57th St., New York, NY 10019. TEL 212-554-0600. FAX 212-586-1182. URL: http://www.eiu.com. Vendor(s): Lexis-Nexis. *1244*

COUNTRY RISK SERVICE. AUSTRALIA.
Economist Intelligence Unit, 111 W. 57th St., New York, NY 10019. TEL 212-554-0600. FAX 212-586-1182. URL: http://www.eiu.com. Vendor(s): Lexis-Nexis. *1244*

COUNTRY RISK SERVICE. BANGLADESH.
Economist Intelligence Unit, 111 W. 57th St., New York, NY 10019. TEL 212-554-0600. FAX 212-586-1182. URL: http://www.eiu.com. Vendor(s): Lexis-Nexis. *1245*

COUNTRY RISK SERVICE. BOLIVIA.
Economist Intelligence Unit, 111 W. 57th St., New York, NY 10019. TEL 212-554-0600. FAX 212-586-1182. URL: http://www.eiu.com. Vendor(s): Lexis-Nexis. *1245*

COUNTRY RISK SERVICE. BRAZIL.
Economist Intelligence Unit, 111 W. 57th St., New York, NY 10019. TEL 212-554-0600. FAX 212-586-1182. URL: http://www.eiu.com. Vendor(s): Lexis-Nexis. *1245*

COUNTRY RISK SERVICE. BULGARIA.
Economist Intelligence Unit, 111 W. 57th St., New York, NY 10019. TEL 212-554-0600. FAX 212-586-1182. URL: http://www.eiu.com. Vendor(s): Lexis-Nexis. *1245*

COUNTRY RISK SERVICE. CAMEROON.
Economist Intelligence Unit, 111 W. 57th St., New York, NY 10019. TEL 212-554-0600. FAX 212-586-1182. URL: http://www.eiu.com. Vendor(s): Lexis-Nexis. *1245*

COUNTRY RISK SERVICE. CHILE.
Economist Intelligence Unit, 111 W. 57th St., New York, NY 10019. TEL 212-554-0600. FAX 212-586-1182. URL: http://www.eiu.com. Vendor(s): Lexis-Nexis. *1245*

COUNTRY RISK SERVICE. CHINA.
Economist Intelligence Unit, 111 W. 57th St., New York, NY 10019. TEL 212-554-0600. FAX 212-586-1182. URL: http://www.eiu.com. Vendor(s): Lexis-Nexis. *1245*

COUNTRY RISK SERVICE. COLOMBIA.
Economist Intelligence Unit, 111 W. 57th St., New York, NY 10019. TEL 212-554-0600. FAX 212-586-1182. URL: http://www.eiu.com. Vendor(s): Lexis-Nexis. *1245*

COUNTRY RISK SERVICE. CONGO.
Economist Intelligence Unit, 111 W. 57th St., New York, NY 10019. TEL 212-554-0600. FAX 212-586-1182. URL: http://www.eiu.com. Vendor(s): Lexis-Nexis. *1245*

COUNTRY RISK SERVICE. COSTA RICA.
Economist Intelligence Unit, 111 W. 57th St., New York, NY 10019. TEL 212-554-0600. FAX 212-586-1182. URL: http://www.eiu.com. Vendor(s): Lexis-Nexis. *1245*

COUNTRY RISK SERVICE. COTE D'IVOIRE.
Economist Intelligence Unit, 111 W. 57th St., New York, NY 10019. TEL 212-554-0600. FAX 212-586-1182. URL: http://www.eiu.com. Vendor(s): Lexis-Nexis. *1245*

COUNTRY RISK SERVICE. CYPRUS.
Economist Intelligence Unit, 111 W. 57th St., New York, NY 10019. TEL 212-554-0600. FAX 212-586-1182. URL: http://www.eiu.com. Vendor(s): Lexis-Nexis. *1245*

COUNTRY RISK SERVICE. CZECH REPUBLIC.
Economist Intelligence Unit, 111 W. 57th St., New York, NY 10019. TEL 212-554-0600. FAX 212-586-1182. URL: http://www.eiu.com. Vendor(s): Lexis-Nexis. *1245*

COUNTRY RISK SERVICE. DOMINICAN REPUBLIC.
Economist Intelligence Unit, 111 W. 57th St., New York, NY 10019. TEL 212-554-0600. FAX 212-586-1182. URL: http://www.eiu.com. Vendor(s): Lexis-Nexis. *1245*

COUNTRY RISK SERVICE. ECUADOR.
Economist Intelligence Unit, 111 W. 57th St., New York, NY 10019. TEL 212-554-0600. FAX 212-586-1182. URL: http://www.eiu.com. Vendor(s): Lexis-Nexis. *1246*

COUNTRY RISK SERVICE. EGYPT.
Economist Intelligence Unit, 111 W. 57th St., New York, NY 10019. TEL 212-554-0600. FAX 212-586-1182. URL: http://www.eiu.com. Vendor(s): Lexis-Nexis. *1246*

COUNTRY RISK SERVICE. EL SALVADOR.
Economist Intelligence Unit, 111 W. 57th St., New York, NY 10019. TEL 212-554-0600. FAX 212-586-1182. URL: http://www.eiu.com. Vendor(s): Lexis-Nexis. *1246*

COUNTRY RISK SERVICE. FORMER YUGOSLAV REPUBLICS: SERBIA, MONTENEGRO, MACEDONIA.
Economist Intelligence Unit, 111 W. 57th St., New York, NY 10019. TEL 212-554-0600. FAX 212-586-1182. URL: http://www.eiu.com. Vendor(s): Lexis-Nexis. *1246*

COUNTRY RISK SERVICE. GABON.
Economist Intelligence Unit, 111 W. 57th St., New York, NY 10019. TEL 212-554-0600. FAX 212-538-1182. URL: http://www.eiu.com. Vendor(s): Lexis-Nexis. *1246*

COUNTRY RISK SERVICE. GHANA.
Economist Intelligence Unit, 111 W. 57th St., New York, NY 10019. TEL 212-554-0600. FAX 212-586-1182. URL: http://www.eiu.com. Vendor(s): Lexis-Nexis. *1246*

COUNTRY RISK SERVICE. GREECE.
Economist Intelligence Unit, 111 W. 57th St., New York, NY 10019. TEL 212-554-0600. FAX 212-586-1182. URL: http://www.eiu.com. Vendor(s): Lexis-Nexis. *1246*

COUNTRY RISK SERVICE. GUATEMALA.
Economist Intelligence Unit, 111 W. 57th St., New York, NY 10019. TEL 212-554-0600. FAX 212-586-1182. URL: http://www.eiu.com. Vendor(s): Lexis-Nexis. *1246*

COUNTRY RISK SERVICE. HONDURAS.
Economist Intelligence Unit, 111 W. 57th St., New York, NY 10019. TEL 212-554-0600. FAX 212-586-1182. URL: http://www.eiu.com. Vendor(s): Lexis-Nexis. *1246*

COUNTRY RISK SERVICE. HONG KONG.
Economist Intelligence Unit, 111 W. 57th St., New York, NY 10019. TEL 212-554-0600. FAX 212-586-1182. URL: http://www.eiu.com. Vendor(s): Lexis-Nexis. *1246*

COUNTRY RISK SERVICE. HUNGARY.
Economist Intelligence Unit, 111 W. 57th St., New York, NY 10019. TEL 212-554-0600. FAX 212-586-1182. URL: http://www.eiu.com. Vendor(s): Lexis-Nexis. *1246*

COUNTRY RISK SERVICE. INDIA.
Economist Intelligence Unit, 111 W. 57th St., New York, NY 10019. TEL 212-554-0600. FAX 212-586-1182. URL: http://www.eiu.com. Vendor(s): Lexis-Nexis. *1246*

COUNTRY RISK SERVICE. INDONESIA.
Economist Intelligence Unit, 111 W. 57th St., New York, NY 10019. TEL 212-554-0600. FAX 212-586-1182. URL: http://www.eiu.com. Vendor(s): Lexis-Nexis. *1246*

COUNTRY RISK SERVICE. IRAN.
Economist Intelligence Unit, 111 W. 57th St., New York, NY 10019. TEL 212-554-0600. FAX 212-586-1182. URL: http://www.eiu.com. Vendor(s): Lexis-Nexis. *1246*

COUNTRY RISK SERVICE. IRAQ.
Economist Intelligence Unit, 111 W. 57th St., New York, NY 10019. TEL 212-554-0600. FAX 212-586-1182. URL: http://www.eiu.com. Vendor(s): Lexis-Nexis. *1246*

COUNTRY RISK SERVICE. ISRAEL.
Economist Intelligence Unit, 111 W. 57th St., New York, NY 10019. TEL 212-554-0600. FAX 212-586-1182. URL: http://www.eiu.com. Vendor(s): Lexis-Nexis. *1247*

COUNTRY RISK SERVICE. JAMAICA.
Economist Intelligence Unit, 111 W. 57th St., New York, NY 10019. TEL 212-554-0600. FAX 212-586-1182. URL: http://www.eiu.com. Vendor(s): Lexis-Nexis. *1247*

COUNTRY RISK SERVICE. JORDAN.
Economist Intelligence Unit, 111 W. 57th St., New York, NY 10019. TEL 212-554-0600. FAX 212-586-1182. URL: http://www.eiu.com. Vendor(s): Lexis-Nexis. *1247*

COUNTRY RISK SERVICE. KAZAKHSTAN.
Economist Intelligence Unit, 111 W. 57th St., New York, NY 10019. TEL 212-554-0600. FAX 212-586-1182. URL: http://www.eiu.com. Vendor(s): Lexis-Nexis. *1247*

COUNTRY RISK SERVICE. KENYA.
Economist Intelligence Unit, 111 W. 57th St., New York, NY 10019. TEL 212-554-0600. FAX 212-586-1182. URL: http://www.eiu.com. Vendor(s): Lexis-Nexis. *1247*

COUNTRY RISK SERVICE. KUWAIT.
Economist Intelligence Unit, 111 W. 57th St., New York, NY 10019. TEL 212-554-0600. FAX 212-586-1182. URL: http://www.eiu.com. Vendor(s): Lexis-Nexis. *1247*

COUNTRY RISK SERVICE. LIBYA.
Economist Intelligence Unit, 111 W. 57th St., New York, NY 10019. TEL 212-554-0600. FAX 212-586-1182. URL: http://www.eiu.com. Vendor(s): Lexis-Nexis. *1247*

COUNTRY RISK SERVICE. MALAWI.
Economist Intelligence Unit, 111 W. 57th St., New York, NY 10019. TEL 212-554-0600. FAX 212-586-1182. URL: http://www.eiu.com. Vendor(s): Lexis-Nexis. *1247*

COUNTRY RISK SERVICE. MALAYSIA.
Economist Intelligence Unit, 111 W. 57th St., New York, NY 10019. TEL 212-554-0600. FAX 212-586-1182. URL: http://www.eiu.com. Vendor(s): Lexis-Nexis. *1247*

COUNTRY RISK SERVICE. MEXICO.
Economist Intelligence Unit, 111 W. 57th St., New York, NY 10019. TEL 212-554-0600. FAX 212-586-1182. URL: http://www.eiu.com. Vendor(s): Lexis-Nexis. *1247*

COUNTRY RISK SERVICE. MOROCCO.
Economist Intelligence Unit, 111 W. 57th St., New York, NY 10019. TEL 212-554-0600. FAX 212-586-1182. URL: http://www.eiu.com. Vendor(s): Lexis-Nexis. *1247*

COUNTRY RISK SERVICE. NAMIBIA.
Economist Intelligence Unit, 111 W. 57th St., New York, NY 10019. TEL 212-586-0600. FAX 212-586-1182. URL: http://www.eiu.com. Vendor(s): Lexis-Nexis. *1247*

COUNTRY RISK SERVICE. NEW ZEALAND.
Economist Intelligence Unit, 111 W. 57th St., New York, NY 10019. TEL 212-554-0600. FAX 212-586-1182. URL: http://www.eiu.com. Vendor(s): Lexis-Nexis. *1247*

COUNTRY RISK SERVICE. NICARAGUA.
Economist Intelligence Unit, 111 W. 57th St., New York, NY 10019. TEL 212-554-0600. FAX 212-586-1182. URL: http://www.eiu.com. Vendor(s): Lexis-Nexis. *1247*

COUNTRY RISK SERVICE. NIGERIA.
Economist Intelligence Unit, 111 W. 57th St., New York, NY 10019. TEL 212-554-0600. FAX 212-586-1182. URL: http://www.eiu.com. Vendor(s): Lexis-Nexis. *1247*

COUNTRY RISK SERVICE. PAKISTAN.
Economist Intelligence Unit, 111 W. 57th St., New York, NY 10019. TEL 212-554-0600. FAX 212-586-1182. URL: http://www.eiu.com. Vendor(s): Lexis-Nexis. *1248*

COUNTRY RISK SERVICE. PANAMA.
Economist Intelligence Unit, 111 W. 57th St., New York, NY 10019. TEL 212-554-0600. FAX 212-586-1182. URL: http://www.eiu.com. Vendor(s): Lexis-Nexis. *1248*

COUNTRY RISK SERVICE. PAPUA NEW GUINEA.
Economist Intelligence Unit, 111 W. 57th St., New York, NY 10019. TEL 212-554-0600. FAX 212-586-1182. URL: http://www.eiu.com. Vendor(s): Lexis-Nexis. *1248*

COUNTRY RISK SERVICE. PARAGUAY.
Economist Intelligence Unit, 111 W. 57th St., New York, NY 10019. TEL 212-554-0600. FAX 212-586-1182. URL: http://www.eiu.com. Vendor(s): Lexis-Nexis. *1248*

COUNTRY RISK SERVICE. PERU.
Economist Intelligence Unit, 111 W. 57th St., New York, NY 10019. TEL 212-554-0600. FAX 212-586-1182. URL: http://www.eiu.com. Vendor(s): Lexis-Nexis. *1248*

COUNTRY RISK SERVICE. PHILIPPINES.
Economist Intelligence Unit, 111 W. 57th St., New York, NY 10019. TEL 212-554-0600. FAX 212-8586-1182. URL: http://www.eiu.com. Vendor(s): Lexis-Nexis. *1248*

COUNTRY RISK SERVICE. POLAND.
Economist Intelligence Unit, 111 W. 57th St., New York, NY 10019. TEL 212-554-0600. FAX 212-586-1182. URL: http://www.eiu.com. Vendor(s): Lexis-Nexis. *1248*

COUNTRY RISK SERVICE. PORTUGAL.
Economist Intelligence Unit, 111 W. 57th St., New York, NY 10019. TEL 212-554-0600. FAX 212-586-1182. URL: http://www.eiu.com. Vendor(s): Lexis-Nexis. *1248*

COUNTRY RISK SERVICE. ROMANIA.
Economist Intelligence Unit, 111 W. 57th St., New York, NY 10019. TEL 212-554-0600. FAX 212-586-1182. URL: http://www.eiu.com. Vendor(s): Lexis-Nexis. *1248*

COUNTRY RISK SERVICE. RUSSIA.
Economist Intelligence Unit, 111 W. 57th St., New York, NY 10019. TEL 212-554-0600. FAX 212-586-1182. URL: http://www.eiu.com. Vendor(s): Lexis-Nexis. *1248*

COUNTRY RISK SERVICE. SAUDI ARABIA.
Economist Intelligence Unit, 111 W. 57th St., New York, NY 10019. TEL 212-554-0600. FAX 212-586-1182. URL: http://www.eiu.com. Vendor(s): Lexis-Nexis. *1248*

COUNTRY RISK SERVICE. SENEGAL.
Economist Intelligence Unit, 111 W. 57th St., New York, NY 10019. TEL 212-554-0600. FAX 212-586-1182. URL: http://www.eiu.com. Vendor(s): Lexis-Nexis. *1248*

COUNTRY RISK SERVICE. SINGAPORE.
Economist Intelligence Unit, 111 W. 57th St., New York, NY 10019. TEL 212-554-0600. FAX 212-586-1182. URL: http://www.eiu.com. Vendor(s): Lexis-Nexis. *1248*

COUNTRY RISK SERVICE. SLOVENIA.
Economist Intelligence Unit, 111 W. 57th St., New York, NY 10019. TEL 212-554-0600. FAX 212-586-1182. URL: http://www.eiu.com. Vendor(s): Lexis-Nexis. *1248*

COUNTRY RISK SERVICE. SOUTH AFRICA.
Economist Intelligence Unit, 111 W. 57th St., New York, NY 10019. TEL 212-554-0600. FAX 212-586-1182. URL: http://www.eiu.com. Vendor(s): Lexis-Nexis. *1248*

COUNTRY RISK SERVICE. SOUTH KOREA.
Economist Intelligence Unit, 111 W. 57th St., New York, NY 10019. TEL 212-554-0600. FAX 212-586-1182. URL: http://www.eiu.com. Vendor(s): Lexis-Nexis. *1249*

COUNTRY RISK SERVICE. SPAIN.
Economist Intelligence Unit, 111 W. 57th St., New York, NY 10019. TEL 212-554-0600. FAX 212-938-4685. URL: http://www.eiu.com. Vendor(s): Lexis-Nexis. *1249*

COUNTRY RISK SERVICE. SRI LANKA.
Economist Intelligence Unit, 111 W. 57th St., New York, NY 10019. TEL 212-554-0600. FAX 212-586-1182. URL: http://www.eiu.com. Vendor(s): Lexis-Nexis. *1249*

COUNTRY RISK SERVICE. SUDAN.
Economist Intelligence Unit, 111 W. 57th St., New York, NY 10019. TEL 212-554-0600. FAX 212-586-1182. URL: http://www.eiu.com. Vendor(s): Lexis-Nexis. *1249*

COUNTRY RISK SERVICE. SYRIA.
Economist Intelligence Unit, 111 W. 57th St., New York, NY 10019. TEL 212-554-0600. FAX 212-586-1182. URL: http://www.eiu.com. Vendor(s): Lexis-Nexis. *1249*

COUNTRY RISK SERVICE. TAIWAN.
Economist Intelligence Unit, 111 W. 57th St., New York, NY 10019. TEL 212-554-0600. FAX 212-586-1182. URL: http://www.eiu.com. Vendor(s): Lexis-Nexis. *1249*

COUNTRY RISK SERVICE. THAILAND.
Economist Intelligence Unit, 111 W. 57th St., New York, NY 10019. TEL 212-554-0600. FAX 212-586-1182. URL: http://www.eiu.com. Vendor(s): Lexis-Nexis. *1249*

COUNTRY RISK SERVICE. THE BALTIC REPUBLICS: LATVIA, ESTONIA, LITHUANIA.
Economist Intelligence Unit, 111 W. 57th St., New York, NY 10019. TEL 212-554-0600. FAX 212-586-1182. URL: http://www.eiu.com. Vendor(s): Lexis-Nexis. *1249*

COUNTRY RISK SERVICE. TRINIDAD AND TOBAGO.
Economist Intelligence Unit, 111 W. 57th St., New York, NY 10019. TEL 212-554-0600. FAX 212-586-1182. URL: http://www.eiu.com. Vendor(s): Lexis-Nexis. *1249*

COUNTRY RISK SERVICE. TUNISIA.
Economist Intelligence Unit, 111 W. 57th St., New York, NY 10019. TEL 212-554-0600. FAX 212-586-1182. URL: http://www.eiu.com. Vendor(s): Lexis-Nexis. *1249*

COUNTRY RISK SERVICE. TURKEY.
Economist Intelligence Unit, 111 W. 57th St., New York, NY 10019. TEL 212-554-0600. FAX 212-586-1182. URL: http://www.eiu.com. Vendor(s): Lexis-Nexis. *1249*

COUNTRY RISK SERVICE. UKRAINE.
Economist Intelligence Unit, 111 W. 57th St., New York, NY 10019. TEL 212-554-0600. FAX 212-586-1182. URL: http://www.eiu.com. Vendor(s): Lexis-Nexis. *1249*

COUNTRY RISK SERVICE. UNITED ARAB EMIRATES.
Economist Intelligence Unit, 111 W. 57th St., New York, NY 10019. TEL 212-554-0600. FAX 212-586-1182. URL: http://www.eiu.com. Vendor(s): Lexis-Nexis. *1249*

COUNTRY RISK SERVICE. URUGUAY.
Economist Intelligence Unit, 111 W. 57th St., New York, NY 10019. TEL 212-554-0600. FAX 212-586 1182. URL: http://www.eiu.com. Vendor(s): Lexis-Nexis. *1249*

COUNTRY RISK SERVICE. VENEZUELA.
Economist Intelligence Unit, 111 W. 57th St., New York, NY 10019. TEL 212-554-0600. FAX 212-586-1182. URL: http://www.eiu.com. Vendor(s): Lexis-Nexis. *1249*

COUNTRY RISK SERVICE. YEMEN.
Economist Intelligence Unit, 111 W. 57th St., New York, NY 10019. TEL 212-554-0600. FAX 212-586-1182. URL: http://www.eiu.com. Vendor(s): Lexis-Nexis. *1250*

COUNTRY RISK SERVICE. ZAIRE.
Economist Intelligence Unit, 111 W. 57th St., New York, NY 10019. TEL 212-554-0600. FAX 212-586-1182. URL: http://www.eiu.com. Vendor(s): Lexis-Nexis. *1250*

COUNTRY RISK SERVICE. ZAMBIA.
Economist Intelligence Unit, 111 W. 57th St., New York, NY 10019. TEL 212-554-0600. FAX 212-586-1182. URL: http://www.eiu.com. Vendor(s): Lexis-Nexis. *1250*

COUNTRY RISK SERVICE. ZIMBABWE.
Economist Intelligence Unit, 111 W. 57th St., New York, NY 10019. TEL 212-554-0600. FAX 212-586-1182. URL: http://www.eiu.com. Vendor(s): Lexis-Nexis. *1250*

COUNTRY WAVE.
Country Wave Publications Ltd., 20461 Douglas Crescent, No. 4, Langley, BC V3A 4B6, Canada. TEL 604-514-1700. FAX 604-514-1776. *5387*

COUNTRYSIDE AND SMALL STOCK JOURNAL.
Countryside Publications, Ltd., N2601 Winter Sports Rd., Withee, WI 54498-9317. TEL 715-785-7979. FAX 715-785-7414. Vendor(s): Information Access Co.. *3372*

COUNTY BUSINESS PATTERNS.
U.S. Bureau of the Census, Customer Services, Washington, DC 20233. TEL 301-457-4100. FAX 301-457-4714. URL: http://www.census.gov/. *1032*

COUNTY ECONOMIC INDICATORS.
Oregon Economic Development Department, 775 Summer St., N.E., Salem, OR 97310. TEL 503-373-1290. FAX 503-581-5115. URL: http://www.econ.state.or.us/stats.htm. *1250*

THE COURIER.
Union Society, King's Walk, Newcastle-upon-Tyne NE1 8QB, England. TEL 44-191-232-4050. FAX 44-191-222-1876. URL: http://www.ncl.ac.uk/'ncourier/. *1947*

COURIER (PARIS).
UNESCO Publishing, 7 place de Fontenoy, 75352 Paris 07 SP, France. TEL 33-1-45684300. FAX 33-1-45685741. URL: http://www.unesco.org/publications. Vendor(s): Information Access Co., Knight-Ridder Information, Inc.. *6010*

COUSIN AVOCADO'S HIDEAWAY.
412 Oak St., Ridgefield, NJ 07657. URL: http://www.avocadoshideaway.com. Available only online. *4329*

COVEN OF ANGELS.
Jitterbug Press, 1315 Dwight Way, no. L, Berkeley, CA 94702. URL: http://www.jitterbug.com. *4530*

COVEN PRIDE.
Box 1852, Brown University, Providence, RI 02912. URL: http://www.rabyd.com/covenpride. Available only online. *4530*

COVER.
Arts New York, Box 1215, Cooper Sta., New York, NY 10276. TEL 212-673-1152. FAX 212-253-7614. URL: http://plaza.interport.net/byocafe. *3776*

COWLES - SIMBA MEDIA DAILY.
Cowles - SIMBA Information, 11 Riverbend Dr. S., Box 4949, Stamford, CT 06907-0949. TEL 203-358-9900. FAX 203-358-5811. URL: http://www.simbanet.com; http://www.mediacentral.com. Vendor(s): CompuServe, Inc., Information Access Co., NewsNet. *1987*

THE COWLES - SIMBA REPORT ON DIRECTORY PUBLISHING.
Cowles - SIMBA Information, 11 Riverbend Dr. S., Box 4949, Stamford, CT 06907-0949. TEL 203-358-9900. FAX 203-358-5811. URL: http://www.simbanet.com. Vendor(s): Information Access Co., Knight-Ridder Information, Inc. (File no.636), NewsNet (PB30). *6269*

CRAFTS 'N THINGS.
Clapper Communications Companies, 2400 E. Devon Ave., Ste. 375, Des Plaines, IL 60018-4618. TEL 847-635-5800. FAX 847-635-6311. URL: http://www.craftnet.org/crafts-n-things. *479*

CRAIN'S CHICAGO BUSINESS.
Crain Communications, Inc. (Chicago), 740 N. Rush St., Chicago, IL 60611-2525. TEL 312-649-5270. FAX 312-649-5228.
Vendor(s): Information Access Co., Knight-Ridder Information, Inc., Lexis-Nexis (CHIBUS). *952*

CRAIN'S CLEVELAND BUSINESS.
Crain Communications, Inc. (Detroit), 1400 Woodbridge Ave., Detroit, MI 48207-3187. TEL 800-678-9595. FAX 216-694-4264.
Vendor(s): Information Access Co., Knight-Ridder Information, Inc., Lexis-Nexis. *1250*

CRAIN'S DETROIT BUSINESS.
Crain Communications, Inc. (Detroit), 1400 Woodbridge Ave., Detroit, MI 48207-3187. TEL 313-446-0426. FAX 313-446-1650.
Vendor(s): Information Access Co., Knight-Ridder Information, Inc., Lexis-Nexis. *952*

CRAIN'S NEW YORK BUSINESS.
Crain Communications, Inc. (New York), 220 E. 42nd St., Ste. 1306, New York, NY 10017. TEL 212-210-0277. FAX 212-210-0799.
Vendor(s): Information Access Co., Knight-Ridder Information, Inc., Lexis-Nexis (NYBUS). *952*

CRANBERRY WINTERS.
1859 Jefferson St., Eugene, OR 97402. URL: http://www.efn.org/~brideh/Deb/cwinters.html.
Available only online. *4394*

THE CREATIVE CHILD - INTERACTIVE PARENTING NEWSLETTER.
URL: http://www.the-creative-child.com/newsletter.
Available only online. *1843*

CREATIVE NONFICTION.
5501 Walnut St., Ste. 202, Pittsburgh, PA 15232. TEL 412-688-0304. FAX 412-683-9173. URL: http://www.goucher.edu/~cnf. *4394*

CREATIVITY.
Art Direction Book Co. Inc., 456 Glenbrook Rd., Glenbrook, CT 06906. TEL 203-353-1441. FAX 203-353-1371.
Vendor(s): Information Access Co. *34*

CRECER FELIZ.
Hachette Filipacchi Revistas, Cardenal Herrera Oria 3, 28034 Madrid, Spain. TEL 34-1-358-1122. FAX 34-1-358-2059. *1843*

CREDIT AND CHARGE CARDS: THE INTERNATIONAL MARKET.
Euromonitor, 60-61 Britton St., London EC1M 5NA, England. TEL 44-171-251-8024. FAX 44-171-608-3149. URL: http://www.euromonitor.com.
Vendor(s): Data-Star, Knight-Ridder Information, Inc. *1125*

CREDIT CARD MANAGEMENT.
Faulkner & Gray, Inc., 300 S. Wacker Dr., 18th Fl., Chicago, IL 60606. TEL 312-913-1334.
Vendor(s): Information Access Co., Lexis-Nexis, NewsNet, UMI. *1125*

CREDIT CARD NEWS.
Faulkner & Gray, Inc. (New York), 11 Penn Plaza, 17th Fl., New York, NY 10001. TEL 212-967-7000. FAX 212-967-7155.
Vendor(s): Information Access Co., UMI. *1125*

CREDIT CONTROL.
House of Words Ltd., 7 Greding Walk, Hutton, Brentwood, Essex CM13 2UF, England. TEL 44-1277-225402. FAX 44-1277-201554.
Vendor(s): UMI. *1125*

CREDIT RISK MANAGEMENT.
Phillips Business Information, Inc., 1201 Seven Locks Rd., Potomac, MD 20854. TEL 301-424-3338. FAX 301-309-3847.
Vendor(s): NewsNet (FI57). *1125*

CREDIT UNION ACCOUNTANT.
American Banker - Bond Buyer, Newsletter Division One State St. Plaza, New York, NY 10004-1549. TEL 800-733-4371. FAX 212-943-2224.
Vendor(s): Information Access Co. *1125*

CREDIT UNION EXECUTIVE.
C U N A Publications, Box 431, Madison, WI 53701. TEL 608-231-4000. FAX 608-231-4370.
Vendor(s): Information Access Co. *1125*

CREDIT UNION MANAGEMENT.
Credit Union Executives Society, Box 14167, Madison, WI 53714-0167. TEL 608-271-2664. FAX 608-271-2303. URL: http://www.cues.org.
Vendor(s): UMI. *1126*

CREDIT WORLD.
International Credit Association, 243 N. Lindbergh Blvd., Box 419057, St. Louis, MO 63141-1757. TEL 314-991-3030. FAX 314-991-3029.
Vendor(s): UMI. *1126*

CREIGHTON LAW REVIEW.
Creighton University, Creighton Law School, 2133 California St., Omaha, NE 68178. TEL 402-280-2980.
Vendor(s): West Group. *3936*

CRETACEOUS RESEARCH.
Academic Press Ltd., 24-28 Oval Rd., London NW1 7DX, England. TEL 44-171-267-4466. FAX 44-171-482-2293. URL: http://www.hbuk.co.uk/ap/cretres; http://www.europe.idealibrary.co/. *2312*

CRIME & DELINQUENCY.
Sage Publications, Inc., 2455 Teller Rd., Thousand Oaks, CA 91320. TEL 805-499-0721. FAX 805-499-0871. URL: http://www.sagepub.com.
Vendor(s): UMI. *2264*

CRIMINAL APPEAL REPORTS.
Sweet & Maxwell, South Quay Plaza, 7th Fl., 183 Marsh Wall, London E14 9FT, England. TEL 071-538-8686. FAX 071-538-9508.
Vendor(s): Lexis-Nexis. *2265*

CRIMINAL JUSTICE ABSTRACTS.
Willow Tree Press, Inc., 124 Willow Tree Rd., Monsey, NY 10952. TEL 914-354-9139. FAX 914-362-8376.
Vendor(s): West Group. *2283*

CRIMINAL JUSTICE ETHICS.
Institute for Criminal Justice Ethics, John Jay College of Criminal Justice, City University of New-York, 899 Tenth Ave., New-York, NY 10019. TEL 212-237-8033. FAX 212-237-8901.
Vendor(s): Information Access Co. *5722*

CRIMINAL JUSTICE PERIODICAL INDEX.
U M I, 300 N. Zeeb Rd., Ann Arbor, MI 48106. TEL 313-761-4700. FAX 800-864-0019.
Vendor(s): Knight-Ridder Information, Inc. (File no. 171). *2283*

CRIMINAL LAW REPORTER.
The Bureau of National Affairs, Inc., 1231 25th St., N.W., Washington, DC 20037. TEL 202-452-4200. FAX 202-822-8092. URL: http://www.bna.com/ *4089*

CRIMINOLOGY.
American Society of Criminology, 1314 Kinnear Rd., Columbus, OH 43212. TEL 614-292-9207.
Vendor(s): UMI. *2266*

CRITICAL CARE MEDICINE.
Williams & Wilkins, 351 W. Camden St., Baltimore, MD 21201-2436. TEL 410-528-4068. FAX 410-528-4452. URL: http://www.wwilkins.com.
Vendor(s): Ovid Technologies, Inc. *4658*

CRITICAL ISSUES.
Heritage Foundation, 214 Massachusetts Ave., N.E., Washington, DC 20002. TEL 202-546-4400. FAX 202-543-9647.
Vendor(s): Lexis-Nexis. *5919*

CRITICAL PERSPECTIVES ON ACCOUNTING.
Academic Press Ltd., 24-28 Oval Rd., London NW1 7DX, England. TEL 44-171-267-4466. FAX 44-171-482-2293. URL: http://www.hbuk.co.uk/ap/cpa; http://www.europe.idealibrary.com/. *1089*

CRITICAL REVIEWS IN ANALYTICAL CHEMISTRY.
C R C Press, Inc., 2000 Corporate Blvd., N.W., Boca Raton, FL 33431. TEL 561-994-0555. FAX 561-998-9784. URL: http://www.crcpress.com/jour/crac/crac.htm. *1790*

CRITICAL REVIEWS IN NEUROSURGERY.
Springer-Verlag, Heidelberger Platz 3, 14197 Berlin, Germany. TEL 49-30-82787-0. FAX 49-30-82787448. URL: http://link.springer.de. *5139*

CRITICAL STUDIES IN MASS COMMUNICATION.
Speech Communication Association, 5105 Backlick Rd., Bldg. E., Annandale, VA 22003. TEL 703-750-0533. FAX 703-914-9471.
Vendor(s): UMI. *1987*

CRITICISM.
Wayne State University Press, 4809 Woodward Ave., Detroit, MI 48201-1309. TEL 313-577-6120. FAX 313-577-6131.
Vendor(s): Information Access Co., UMI. *4395*

CRITIQUE: STUDIES IN MODERN FICTION.
Heldref Publications, 1319 Eighteenth St., N.W., Washington, DC 20036-1802. TEL 202-296-6267. FAX 202-296-5149.
Vendor(s): Information Access Co., UMI. *4395*

CROP PHYSIOLOGY ABSTRACTS.
CAB International, Wallingford, Oxon. OX10 8DE, England. TEL 44-1491-832111. FAX 44-1491-826090. URL: http://www.cabi.org.
Vendor(s): DIMDI, European Space Agency, Knight-Ridder Information, Inc., STN International. *172*

CROSS CURRENTS (NEW ROCHELLE).
Association for Religion and Intellectual Life, College of New Rochelle, New Rochelle, NY 10805-2339. TEL 914-235-1439. FAX 914-235-1584. URL: http://www.aril.org. *6333*

CROSS FIRE YOUTH MINISTRY MAGAZINE.
55 Redlands St., Springfield, MA 01104. URL: http://www.crossfire.org.
Available only online. *6333*

CROSS-STITCHER.
Clapper Communications Companies, 2400 E. Devon Ave., Ste. 375, Des Plaines, IL 60018-4618. TEL 847-635-5800. FAX 847-635-6311. URL: http://www.craftnet.org/cross-stitcher. *5451*

CROSSTALK.
California Higher Education Policy Center, URL: http://professionals.com/~chepc/ct__1095/ctmain__1095.html.
Available only online. *2538*

THE CROUSER REPORT.
Crouser & Associates, 235 Dutch Rd., Charleston, WV 25302. TEL 304-342-5100. FAX 304-342-5187. URL: http://www.crouser.com. *1641*

CRUISING WORLD.
Sailing Company, Box 3400, Newport, RI 02840-0992. TEL 401-847-1588. FAX 401-848-5048. URL: http://www.cruisingworld.com/cwdeckpg.html.
Vendor(s): Information Access Co. *6838*

CRUX MATHEMATICORUM WITH MATHEMATICAL MAYHEM.
Canadian Mathematical Society, 577 King Edward, P.O. Box 450, Stn. A, Ottawa, ON K1N 6N5, Canada. TEL 613-562-5702. FAX 613-565-1539. URL: http://camel.math.ca/CMS/CRUX/editorial.html. *4569*

CRYOBIOLOGY.
Academic Press, Inc., Journal Division, 525 B St., Ste. 1900, San Diego, CA 92101-4495. TEL 619-230-1840. FAX 619-699-6800. URL: http://www.apnet.com/www/journal/cy.htm; http://www.idealibrary.com/. *674*

CULTIVOS TROPICALES.
Instituto Nacional de Ciencias Agricolas, Gaveta Postal No. 1, San Jose de las Lajas, Havana 32700, Cuba. TEL 537-64-63290. FAX 537-64-63867. *221*

CULTUREKIOSQUE.
Culturekiosque Publications Ltd., 164 Madison Ave., Ste. 500, New York, NY 10016-5411. URL: http://www.culturekiosque.com.
Available only online. *4330*

CUMBERLAND LAW REVIEW.
Samford University, Cumberland School of Law, 800 Lakeshore Dr., ROBBH 315, Birmingham, AL 35229. TEL 205-870-2757. FAX 205-870-2673.
Vendor(s): West Group. *3937*

CUMULATIVE BOOK INDEX.
H.W. Wilson Co., 950 University Ave., Bronx, NY 10452. TEL 718-588-8400. FAX 718-590-1617.
Vendor(s): Ovid Technologies, Inc., Wilsonline (File CBI). *545*

CUMULATIVE INDEX TO NURSING & ALLIED HEALTH LITERATURE.
C I N A H L Information Systems, 1509 Wilson Terrace, Box 871, Glendale, CA 91209-0871. TEL 818-409-8005. FAX 818-546-5679. URL: http://www.cinahl.com/.
Vendor(s): Data-Star (NAHL), Ovid Technologies, Inc. (NAHL). *4768*

CUPCAKE CANASTA.
35 Pine Walk, Surbiton, Surrey KT5 8NW, England. URL: http://www.anastrophe.demon.co.uk/
Available only online. *4395*

CURRENT ADVANCES IN APPLIED MICROBIOLOGY & BIOTECHNOLOGY.
Elsevier Science B.V., P.O. Box 211, 1000 AE Amsterdam, Netherlands. TEL 31-20-4853911. FAX 31-20-4853598. URL: http://www.elsevier.nl/.
Vendor(s): Ovid Technologies, Inc. (CABS). *638*

CURRENT ADVANCES IN CANCER RESEARCH.
Elsevier Science B.V., P.O. Box 211, 1000 AE Amsterdam, Netherlands. TEL 31-20-4853911. FAX 31-20-4853598. URL: http://www.elsevier.nl/.
Vendor(s): Ovid Technologies, Inc. (CABS). *4768*

CURRENT ADVANCES IN CELL & DEVELOPMENTAL BIOLOGY.
Elsevier Science B.V., P.O. Box 211, 1000 AE Amsterdam, Netherlands. TEL 31-20-4853911. FAX 31-20-4853598. URL: http://www.elsevier.nl/
Vendor(s): Ovid Technologies, Inc. (CABS). *638*

CURRENT ADVANCES IN CLINICAL CHEMISTRY.
Elsevier Science B.V., P.O. Box 211, 1000 AE Amsterdam, Netherlands. TEL 31-20-4853911. FAX 31-20-48535988. URL: http://www.elsevier.nl/
Vendor(s): Ovid Technologies, Inc. (CABS). *1782*

CURRENT ADVANCES IN ECOLOGICAL AND ENVIRONMENTAL SCIENCES.
Elsevier Science B.V., P.O. Box 211, 1000 AE Amsterdam, Netherlands. TEL 31-20-4853911. FAX 31-20-4853598. URL: http://www.elsevier.nl/
Vendor(s): Ovid Technologies, Inc. (CABS). *2960*

CURRENT ADVANCES IN ENDOCRINOLOGY & METABOLISM.
Elsevier Science B.V., P.O. Box 211, 1000 AE Amsterdam, Netherlands. TEL 31-20-4853911. FAX 31-20-4853598. URL: http://www.elsevier.nl/
Vendor(s): Ovid Technologies, Inc. (CABS). *4768*

CURRENT ADVANCES IN GENETICS AND MOLECULAR BIOLOGY.
Elsevier Science B.V., P.O. Box 211, 1000 AE Amsterdam, Netherlands. TEL 31-20-485-3911. FAX 31-20-4853598. URL: http://www.elsevier.nl/
Vendor(s): Ovid Technologies, Inc. (CABS). *638*

CURRENT ADVANCES IN IMMUNOLOGY & INFECTIOUS DISEASES.
Elsevier Science B.V., P.O. Box 211, 1000 AE Amsterdam, Netherlands. TEL 31-20-4853911. FAX 31-20-4853598. URL: http://www.elsevier.nl/
Vendor(s): Ovid Technologies, Inc. (CABS). *4768*

CURRENT ADVANCES IN NEUROSCIENCE.
Elsevier Science B.V., P.O. Box 211, 1000 AE Amsterdam, Netherlands. TEL 31-20-4853911. FAX 31-20-4853598. URL: http://www.elsevier.nl/
Vendor(s): Ovid Technologies, Inc. (CABS). *4768*

CURRENT ADVANCES IN PLANT SCIENCE.
Elsevier Science B.V., P.O. Box 211, 1000 AE Amsterdam, Netherlands. TEL 31-20-4853911. FAX 31-20-48535988. URL: http://www.elsevier.nl/
Vendor(s): Ovid Technologies, Inc. (CABS). *638*

CURRENT ADVANCES IN PROTEIN BIOCHEMISTRY.
Elsevier Science B.V., P.O. Box 211, 1000 AE Amsterdam, Netherlands. TEL 31-20-4853911. FAX 31-20-4853598. URL: http://www.elsevier.nl/
Vendor(s): Ovid Technologies, Inc. (CABS). *639*

CURRENT ADVANCES IN TOXICOLOGY.
Elsevier Science B.V., P.O. Box 211, 1000 AE Amsterdam, Netherlands. TEL 31-20-4853911. FAX 31-20-4853598. URL: http://www.elsevier.nl/
Vendor(s): Ovid Technologies, Inc. (CABS). *2960*

CURRENT AWARENESS ABSTRACTS.
Aslib, Association for Information Management, Publications Department, Information House, 20-24 Old St., London EC1V 9AP, England. TEL 44-171-253-4488. FAX 44-171-430-0514. URL: http://www.aslib.co.uk/. *4172*

CURRENT AWARENESS IN BIOLOGICAL SCIENCES.
Elsevier Science B.V., P.O. Box 211, 1000 AE Amsterdam, Netherlands. TEL 31-20-4853757. FAX 31-20-4853432. URL: http://www.elsevier.nl/.
Vendor(s): Ovid Technologies, Inc. (CABS) *639*

CURRENT AWARENESS IN HEALTH EDUCATION.
U.S. Bureau of Health Education, Department of Health and Human Services, Washington, DC 20201. TEL 202-655-4000.
Vendor(s): Ovid Technologies, Inc. *5780*

CURRENT BIBLIOGRAPHY ON SCIENCE AND TECHNOLOGY: CHEMISTRY AND CHEMICAL ENGINEERING (FOREIGN).
Japan Science and Technology Corporation, Information Center for Science and Technology, 5-3 Yonbancho, Chiyoda-ku, Tokyo 102, Japan. TEL 81-3-3214-8413. FAX 81-3-5214-8410.
Vendor(s): JICST. *1782*

CURRENT BIBLIOGRAPHY ON SCIENCE AND TECHNOLOGY: CHEMISTRY AND CHEMICAL ENGINEERING (JAPANESE).
Japan Science and Technology Corporation, Information Center for Science and Technology, 5-3 Yonbancho, Chiyoda-ku, Tokyo 102, Japan. TEL 81-3-5214-8413. FAX 81-3-5214-8410.
Vendor(s): JICST. *1782*

CURRENT BIBLIOGRAPHY ON SCIENCE AND TECHNOLOGY: CIVIL ENGINEERING AND ARCHITECTURE.
Japan Science and Technology Corporation, Information Center for Science and Technology, 5-3, Yonbancho, Chiyoda-ku, Tokyo 102, Japan. TEL 81-3-5214-8413. FAX 81-3-5214-8410.
Vendor(s): JICST. *2748*

CURRENT BIBLIOGRAPHY ON SCIENCE AND TECHNOLOGY: EARTH SCIENCE, MINING AND METALLURGY.
Japan Science and Technology Corporation, Information Center for Science and Technology, 5-3, Yonbacho, Chiyoda-ku, Tokyo 102, Japan. TEL 81-3-5214-8413. FAX 81-3-5214-8410.
Vendor(s): JICST. *2325*

CURRENT BIBLIOGRAPHY ON SCIENCE AND TECHNOLOGY: ELECTRONICS AND ELECTRICAL ENGINEERING.
Japan Science and Technology Corporation, Information Center for Science and Technology, 5-3, Yonbancho, Chiyoda-ku, Tokyo 102, Japan. TEL 81-3-5214-8413. FAX 81-3-5214-8410.
Vendor(s): JICST. *2748*

CURRENT BIBLIOGRAPHY ON SCIENCE AND TECHNOLOGY: ENERGY.
Japan Science and Technology Corporation, Information Center for Science and Technology, 5-3, Yonbancho, Chiyoda-ku, Tokyo 102, Japan. TEL 81-3-5214-8413. FAX 81-3-5214-8410.
Vendor(s): JICST. *2682*

CURRENT BIBLIOGRAPHY ON SCIENCE AND TECHNOLOGY: ENVIRONMENTAL POLLUTION.
Japan Science and Technology Corporation, Information Center for Science and Technology, 5-3, Yonbacho, Chiyoda-ku, Tokyo 102, Japan. TEL 81-3-5214-8413. FAX 81-3-3581-6446.
Vendor(s): JICST. *2960*

CURRENT BIBLIOGRAPHY ON SCIENCE AND TECHNOLOGY: LIFE SCIENCES.
Japan Science and Technology Corporation, Information Center for Science and Technology, 5-3, Yonbancho, Chiyoda-ku, Tokyo 102, Japan. TEL 81-3-5214-8413. FAX 81-3-5214-8410.
Vendor(s): JICST. *639*

CURRENT BIBLIOGRAPHY ON SCIENCE AND TECHNOLOGY: MANAGEMENT SCIENCE AND SYSTEMS ENGINEERING.
Japan Science and Technology Corporation, Information Center for Science and Technology, 5-3, Yonbancho, Chiyoda-ku, Tokyo 102, Japan. TEL 81-3-5214-8413. FAX 81-3-5214-8410.
Vendor(s): JICST. *1033*

CURRENT BIBLIOGRAPHY ON SCIENCE AND TECHNOLOGY: MECHANICAL ENGINEERING.
Japan Science and Technology Corporation, Information Center for Science and Technology, 5-3, Yonbancho, Chiyoda-ku, Tokyo 102, Japan. TEL 81-3-5214-8413. FAX 81-3-5214-8410.
Vendor(s): JICST. *2748*

CURRENT BIBLIOGRAPHY ON SCIENCE AND TECHNOLOGY: NUCLEAR ENGINEERING.
Japan Science and Technology Corporation, Information Center for Science and Technology, 5-3, Yonbancho, Chiyoda-ku, Tokyo 102, Japan. TEL 81-3-5214-8413. FAX 81-3-5214-8410.
Vendor(s): JICST. *2748*

CURRENT BIBLIOGRAPHY ON SCIENCE AND TECHNOLOGY: PURE AND APPLIED PHYSICS.
Japan Science and Technology Corporation, Information Center for Science and Technology, 5-3, Yonbancho, Chiyoda-ku, Tokyo 102, Japan. TEL 81-3-5214-8413. FAX 81-3-5214-8410.
Vendor(s): JICST. *5834*

CURRENT BIOLOGY.
Current Biology Ltd., 800 Market St., Ste. 700, Philadelphia, PA 19106. TEL 800-552-5866. FAX 215-574-2270. URL: http://BioMedNet.com/cbiology/ *639*

CURRENT BIOTECHNOLOGY.
The Royal Society of Chemistry, Thomas Graham House, Science Park, Milton Rd., Cambridge CB4 4WF, England. TEL 44-1223-420066. FAX 44-1223-423429. URL: http://chemistry.rsc.org/rsc/.
Vendor(s): Data-Star (CUBI), Knight-Ridder Information, Inc. (File no.358). *639*

CURRENT BUSINESS REPORTS: MONTHLY RETAIL TRADE: SALES AND INVENTORIES.
U.S. Bureau of the Census, Customer Services, Washington, DC 20233. TEL 301-457-4100. FAX 301-457-4714. URL: http://www.census.gov/.
Vendor(s): CompuServe, Inc., Knight-Ridder Information, Inc.. *1033*

CURRENT BUSINESS REPORTS: MONTHLY WHOLESALE TRADE, SALES AND INVENTORIES.
U.S. Bureau of the Census, Customer Services, Washington, DC 20233. TEL 301-457-4100. FAX 301-457-4714. URL: http://www.census.gov/. *1211*

CURRENT COMPETITION.
Pasha Publications Inc., 1616 N. Ft. Myer Dr., Ste. 1000, Arlington, VA 22209-3107. TEL 703-528-1244. FAX 703-528-1253. *2687*

CURRENT CONSTRUCTION REPORTS: EXPENDITURES FOR RESIDENTIAL IMPROVEMENTS AND REPAIRS.
U.S. Bureau of the Census, Customer Services, Washington, DC 20233. TEL 301-457-4100. FAX 301-457-4714. URL: http://www.census.gov/. *3744*

CURRENT CONSTRUCTION REPORTS: HOUSING COMPLETIONS.
U.S. Bureau of the Census, Customer Services, Washington, DC 20233. TEL 301-457-4100. FAX 301-457-4714. URL: http://www.census.gov/. *3744*

CURRENT CONSTRUCTION REPORTS: HOUSING STARTS.
U.S. Bureau of the Census, Customer Services, Washington, DC 20233. TEL 310-457-4100. FAX 301-457-4714. URL: http://www.census.gov/. *3744*

CURRENT CONSTRUCTION REPORTS: HOUSING UNITS AUTHORIZED BY BUILDING PERMITS.
U.S. Bureau of the Census, Customer Services, Washington, DC 20233. TEL 301-457-4100. FAX 301-457-4714. URL: http://www.census.gov/.
Available only online. *3744*

CURRENT CONSTRUCTION REPORTS: NEW ONE-FAMILY HOUSES SOLD.
U.S. Bureau of the Census, Customer Services, Washington, DC 20233. TEL 301-457-4100. FAX 301-457-4714. URL: http://www.census.gov/. *3744*

CURRENT CONSTRUCTION REPORTS: NEW RESIDENTIAL CONSTRUCTION IN SELECTED METROPOLITAN AREAS.
U.S. Bureau of the Census, Customer Services, Washington, DC 20233. TEL 301-457-4100. FAX 301-457-4714. URL: http://www.census.gov/. *3745*

CURRENT CONSTRUCTION REPORTS: VALUE OF NEW CONSTRUCTION PUT IN PLACE.
U.S. Bureau of the Census, Customer Services, Washington, DC 20233. TEL 301-457-4100. FAX 301-457-4714. URL: http://www.census.gov/. *3745*

CURRENT CONTENTS: AGRICULTURE, BIOLOGY & ENVIRONMENTAL SCIENCES.
Institute for Scientific Information, 3501 Market St., Philadelphia, PA 19104. TEL 215-386-0100. FAX 215-386-2911.
Vendor(s): Knight-Ridder Information, Inc. (File no.440), Ovid Technologies, Inc. (CTOC,CBIB,AGRI). *173*

CURRENT CONTENTS: ARTS & HUMANITIES.
Institute for Scientific Information, 3501 Market St., Philadelphia, PA 19104. TEL 215-386-0100. FAX 215-386-2991.
Vendor(s): Knight-Ridder Information, Inc. (File no.440), Ovid Technologies, Inc. (CTOC,CBIB,ARTS). *3799*

CURRENT CONTENTS: CLINICAL MEDICINE.
Institute for Scientific Information, 3501 Market St., Philadelphia, PA 19104. TEL 215-386-0100. FAX 215-386-2911.
Vendor(s): Knight-Ridder Information, Inc. (File no.440), Ovid Technologies, Inc. (CTOC,CBIB,CLIN). *4768*

CURRENT CONTENTS: ENGINEERING, COMPUTING & TECHNOLOGY.
Institute for Scientific Information, 3501 Market St., Philadelphia, PA 19104. TEL 215-386-0100. FAX 215-386-2911.
Vendor(s): Knight-Ridder Information, Inc. (File no.440), Ovid Technologies, Inc. (CTOC,CBIB,ENGI). *2748*

CURRENT CONTENTS: LIFE SCIENCES.
Institute for Scientific Information, 3501 Market St., Philadelphia, PA 19104. TEL 215-386-0100. FAX 215-386-2211.
Vendor(s): Knight-Ridder Information, Inc. (File no.440), Ovid Technologies, Inc. (CTOC,CBIB,LIFE). *639*

CURRENT CONTENTS: PHYSICAL, CHEMICAL & EARTH SCIENCES.
Institute for Scientific Information, 3501 Market St., Philadelphia, PA 19104. TEL 215-386-0100. FAX 215-386-2211.
Vendor(s): Knight-Ridder Information, Inc. (File no.440), Ovid Technologies, Inc. (CTOC,CBIB,PHYS). *1783*

CURRENT CONTENTS: SOCIAL & BEHAVIORAL SCIENCES.
Institute for Scientific Information, 3501 Market St., Philadelphia, PA 19104. TEL 215-386-0100. FAX 215-386-2911.
Vendor(s): Knight-Ridder Information, Inc. (File no.440), Ovid Technologies, Inc. (CTOC,CBIB,BEHA). *6739*

CURRENT DIGEST OF THE POST-SOVIET PRESS.
Current Digest of the Soviet Press, 3857 N. High St., Columbus, OH 43214-3747. TEL 614-292-4234. FAX 614-267-6310.
Vendor(s): Lexis-Nexis. *5983*

CURRENT GENETICS.
Springer-Verlag, Heidelberger Platz 3, 14197 Berlin, Germany. TEL 49-30-82787-0. FAX 49-30-82787448. URL: http://link.springer.de. *765*

CURRENT GOVERNMENTS REPORTS.
U.S. Bureau of the Census, Governments Division, Washington, DC 20233. TEL 301-457-1523. Available only online. *6170*

CURRENT GOVERNMENTS REPORTS: CITY EMPLOYMENT.
U.S. Bureau of the Census, Governments Division, Washington, DC 20233. TEL 301-457-1523. Available only online. Vendor(s): CompuServe, Inc., Knight-Ridder Information, Inc. *1033*

CURRENT GOVERNMENTS REPORTS: CITY GOVERNMENT FINANCES.
U.S. Bureau of the Census, Governments Division, Washington, DC 20233. TEL 301-457-1523. Available only online. *1605*

CURRENT GOVERNMENTS REPORTS: COUNTY GOVERNMENT EMPLOYMENT.
U.S. Bureau of the Census, Governments Division, Washington, DC 20233. TEL 301-457-1523. Available only online. Vendor(s): CompuServe, Inc., Knight-Ridder Information, Inc. *6170*

CURRENT GOVERNMENTS REPORTS: COUNTY GOVERNMENT FINANCES.
U.S. Bureau of the Census, Governments Division, Washington, DC 20233. TEL 202-457-1523. Available only online. *1605*

CURRENT GOVERNMENTS REPORTS: FINANCES OF EMPLOYEE RETIREMENT SYSTEMS OF STATE AND LOCAL GOVERNMENTS.
U.S. Bureau of the Census, Governments Division, Washington, DC 20233. TEL 202-457-1523. Available only online. *1605*

CURRENT GOVERNMENTS REPORTS: GOVERNMENT FINANCES.
U.S. Bureau of the Census, Governments Division, Washington, DC 20233. TEL 301-457-1523. FAX 301-457-4714. Available only online. Vendor(s): CompuServe, Inc., Knight-Ridder Information, Inc. *1605*

CURRENT GOVERNMENTS REPORTS: PUBLIC EMPLOYMENT.
U.S. Bureau of the Census, Governments Division, Washington, DC 20233. TEL 301-457-1523. FAX 301-457-4714.
Vendor(s): CompuServe, Inc., Knight-Ridder Information, Inc. *1425*

CURRENT GOVERNMENTS REPORTS: STATE GOVERNMENT FINANCES.
U.S. Bureau of the Census, Governments Division, Washington, DC 20233. TEL 202-457-1586. Available only online. *1033*

CURRENT GOVERNMENTS REPORTS: STATE GOVERNMENT TAX COLLECTIONS.
U.S. Bureau of the Census, Customer Services, Washington, DC 20233. TEL 202-457-4100. URL: http://www.census.gov/. Available only online. *1605*

CURRENT HEALTH 2.
Weekly Reader Corporation, Box 120023, Stamford, CT 06912-0023. FAX 609-786-3360.
Vendor(s): Information Access Co., UMI. *5780*

CURRENT HOUSING REPORTS: AMERICAN HOUSING SURVEY FOR METROPOLITAN AREAS.
U.S. Bureau of the Census, Customer Services, Washington, DC 20233. TEL 301-457-4100. FAX 301-457-4714. URL: http://www.census.gov/. *3745*

CURRENT HOUSING REPORTS: AMERICAN HOUSING SURVEY FOR THE UNITED STATES.
U.S. Bureau of the Census, Customer Services, Washington, DC 20233. TEL 301-457-4100. FAX 301-457-4714. URL: http://www.census.gov/. *3745*

CURRENT HOUSING REPORTS: HOUSING CHARACTERISTICS.
U.S. Bureau of the Census, Customer Services, Washington, DC 20233. TEL 301-457-4100. FAX 301-457-4714. URL: http://www.census.gov/. *3745*

CURRENT HOUSING REPORTS: HOUSING VACANCIES AND HOME OWNERSHIP.
U.S. Bureau of the Census, Customer Services, Washington, DC 20233. TEL 301-457-4100. FAX 301-457-4714. URL: http://www.census.gov/. *3745*

CURRENT HOUSING REPORTS: MARKET ABSORPTION OF APARTMENTS.
U.S. Bureau of the Census, Customer Services, Washington, DC 20233. TEL 301-457-4100. FAX 301-457-4714. URL: http://www.census.gov/. *3745*

CURRENT INDEX TO JOURNALS IN EDUCATION.
Oryx Press, 4041 N. Central Ave., No. 700, Phoenix, AZ 85012-3397. TEL 602-265-2651. FAX 602-265-6250. URL: http://www.oryxpress.com/.
Vendor(s): CISTI, Knight-Ridder Information, Inc. (File no.1/ERIC), Ovid Technologies, Inc., Questel Orbit Inc. (ERIC). *2498*

CURRENT INDEX TO STATISTICS.
American Statistical Association, 1429 Duke St., Alexandria, VA 22314-3415. TEL 703-684-1221. FAX 703-684-2037.
Vendor(s): European Space Agency, Knight-Ridder Information, Inc., Ovid Technologies, Inc. (MATH). *4617*

CURRENT INDUSTRIAL REPORTS.
U.S. Bureau of the Census, Customer Services, Washington, DC 20233. TEL 301-457-4100. FAX 301-457-4714. URL: http://www.census.gov/. *1582*

CURRENT INDUSTRIAL REPORTS: BROADWOVEN FABRICS (GRAY).
U.S. Bureau of the Census, Customer Services, Washington, DC 20233. TEL 301-457-4100. FAX 301-457-4714. URL: http://www.census.gov/. *6999*

CURRENT INDUSTRIAL REPORTS: FATS AND OILS. OILSEED CRUSHINGS.
U.S. Bureau of the Census, Customer Services, Washington, DC 20233. TEL 301-457-4100. FAX 301-457-4714. URL: http://www.census.gov/. *3132*

CURRENT INDUSTRIAL REPORTS: FATS AND OILS. PRODUCTION, CONSUMPTION, AND STOCKS.
U.S. Bureau of the Census, Customer Services, Washington, DC 20233. TEL 301-457-4100. FAX 301-457-4714. URL: http://www.census.gov/. *3132*

CURRENT INDUSTRIAL REPORTS: MANUFACTURERS' SHIPMENTS, INVENTORIES, AND ORDERS AND UNITED STATES DEPARTMENT OF COMMERCE NEWS: ADVANCE REPORT ON DURABLE GOODS MANUFACTURERS' SHIPMENTS AND ORDERS.
U.S. Bureau of the Census, Customer Services, Washington, DC 20233. TEL 301-457-4100. FAX 301-457-4714. URL: http://www.census.gov/. *1582*

CURRENT INDUSTRIAL REPORTS: MANUFACTURING TECHNOLOGY - FACTORS AFFECTING ADOPTION (YEAR).
U.S. Bureau of the Census, Customer Services, Washington, DC 20233. TEL 301-457-4100. FAX 301-457-4714. URL: http://www.census.gov/. *1582*

CURRENT INDUSTRIAL REPORTS: NONFERROUS CASTINGS.
U.S. Bureau of the Census, Customer Services, Washington, DC 20233. TEL 301-457-4100. URL: http://www.census.gov/. *5217*

CURRENT LAW INDEX.
Information Access Company, 362 Lakeside Dr., Foster City, CA 94404. TEL 415-378-5200. FAX 415-378-5369.
Vendor(s): Knight-Ridder Information, Inc., Lexis-Nexis, Ovid Technologies, Inc., West Group. *4052*

CURRENT MATHEMATICAL PUBLICATIONS.
American Mathematical Society, Box 6248, Providence, RI 02940-6248. TEL 401-455-4000. FAX 401-331-3842. URL: http://www.ams.org/.
Vendor(s): European Space Agency, Knight-Ridder Information, Inc., Ovid Technologies, Inc. *4617*

CURRENT MICROBIOLOGY.
Springer-Verlag, Life Science Journals, 175 Fifth Ave., New York, NY 10010. TEL 212-460-1500. FAX 212-473-6272. URL: http://www.springer-ny.com. *782*

CURRENT OPINION IN ANAESTHESIOLOGY.
Rapid Science Publishers, 2-6 Boundary Row, London SE1 8HN, England. TEL 44-171-865-0198. FAX 44-171-410-6600. URL: http://BioMednet.com/cgi-bin/members1/titles.pl.
Vendor(s): OCLC. *4771*

CURRENT OPINION IN BIOTECHNOLOGY.
Current Biology Ltd., 400 Market St., Ste. 700, Philadelphia, PA 19106. TEL 800-552-5866. FAX 215-574-2270.
Vendor(s): OCLC. *639*

CURRENT OPINION IN CARDIOLOGY.
Rapid Science Publishers, 2-6 Boundary Row, London SE1 8HN, England. TEL 44-171-865-0198. FAX 44-171-410-6600. URL: http://BioMedNet.com/cgi-bin/members1/titles.pl.
Vendor(s): OCLC. *4771*

CURRENT OPINION IN CELL BIOLOGY.
Current Biology Ltd., 400 Market St., Ste. 700, Philadelphia, PA 19106. FAX 215-574-2270. URL: http://BioMedNet.com/cig-bin/members1/titles.pl.
Vendor(s): OCLC. *639*

CURRENT OPINION IN CRITICAL CARE.
Rapid Science Publishers, 2-6 Boundary Row, London SE1 8HN, England. TEL 44-171-865-0198. FAX 44-171-410-6600. URL: http://BioMedNet.com/cgi-bin/members1/titles.pl.
Vendor(s): OCLC. *5006*

CURRENT OPINION IN DERMATOLOGY.
Rapid Science Publishers, 2-6 Boundary Row, London SE1 8HN, England. TEL 44-171-865-0198. FAX 44-171-410-6600. URL: http://BioMedNet.com/cgi-bin/members1/titles.pl.
Vendor(s): OCLC. *4876*

CURRENT OPINION IN ENDOCRINOLOGY & DIABETES.
Rapid Science Publishers, 2-6 Boundary Row, London SE1 8HN, England. TEL 44-171-865-0198. FAX 44-171-410-6600. URL: http://BioMedNet.com/cgi-bin/members1/titles.pl.
Vendor(s): OCLC. *4883*

CURRENT OPINION IN GASTROENTEROLOGY.
Rapid Science Publishers, 2-6 Boundary Row, London SE1 8HN, England. TEL 44-171-865-0198. FAX 44-171-410-6600. URL: http://BioMedNet.com/cgi-bin/members1/titles.pl.
Vendor(s): OCLC. *4771*

CURRENT OPINION IN GENETICS & DEVELOPMENT.
Current Biology Ltd., 400 Market St., Ste. 700, Philadelphia, PA 19106. TEL 800-552-5866. FAX 215-574-2270. URL: http://BioMedNet.com/cgi-bin/members1/titles.pl.
Vendor(s): OCLC. *639*

CURRENT OPINION IN HEMATOLOGY.
Rapid Science Publishers, 2-6 Boundary Row, London SE1 8HN, England. TEL 44-171-865-0198. FAX 44-171-410-6600. URL: http://BioMedNet.com/cgi-bin/members1/titles.pl.
Vendor(s): OCLC. *4918*

CURRENT OPINION IN IMMUNOLOGY.
Current Biology Ltd., 400 Market St., Ste. 700, Philadelphia, PA 19106. FAX 215-574-2270. URL: http://BioMedNet.com/cgi-bin/members1/titles.pl.
Vendor(s): OCLC. *4772*

CURRENT OPINION IN INFECTIOUS DISEASES.
Rapid Science Publishers, 2-6 Boundary Row, London SE1 8HN, England. TEL 44-171-865-0198. FAX 44-171-410-6600. URL: http://BioMedNet.com/cgi-bin/members1/titles.pl.
Vendor(s): OCLC. *4772*

CURRENT OPINION IN LIPIDOLOGY.
Rapid Science Publishers, 2-6 Boundary Row, London SE1 8HN, England. TEL 44-171-410-6600. FAX 44-171-410-6600. URL: http://BioMedNet.com/cgi-bin/members1/titles.pl.
Vendor(s): OCLC. *4772*

CURRENT OPINION IN NEPHROLOGY & HYPERTENSION.
Rapid Science Publishers, 2-6 Boundary Row, London SE1 8HN, England. TEL 44-171-865-0198. FAX 44-171-865-0198. URL: http://BioMedNet.com/cgi-bin/members1/titles.pl.
Vendor(s): OCLC. *4772*

CURRENT OPINION IN NEUROBIOLOGY.
Current Biology Ltd., 400 Market St., Ste. 700, Philadelphia, PA 19106. TEL 800-552-5866. FAX 215-574-2270. URL: http://BioMedNet.com/cgi-bin/members1/titles.pl.
Vendor(s): OCLC. *640*

CURRENT OPINION IN NEUROLOGY.
Rapid Science Publishers, 2-6 Boundary Row, London SE1 8HN, England. TEL 44-171-865-0198. FAX 44-171-410-6600. URL: http://BioMedNet.com/cig-bin/members1/titles.pl.
Vendor(s): OCLC. *4772*

CURRENT OPINION IN OBSTETRICS & GYNECOLOGY.
Rapid Science Publishers, 2-6 Boundary Row, London SE1 8HN, England. TEL 44-171-865-0198. FAX 44-171-410-6600. URL: http://BioMedNet.com/cgi-bin/members1/titles.pl.
Vendor(s): OCLC. *4772*

CURRENT OPINION IN ONCOLOGY.
Rapid Science Publishers, 2-6 Boundary Row, London SE1 8HN, England. TEL 44-171-865-0198. FAX 44-171-410-6600. URL: http://BioMedNet.com/cgi-bin/members1/titles.pl.
Vendor(s): OCLC. *4772*

CURRENT OPINION IN OPHTHALMOLOGY.
Rapid Science Publishers, 2-6 Boundary Row, London SE1 8HN, England. TEL 44-171-865-0198. FAX 44-171-410-6600. URL: http://BioMedNet.com/cgi-bin/members/titles.pl.
Vendor(s): OCLC. *4772*

CURRENT OPINION IN ORTHOPEDICS.
Rapid Science Publishers, 2-6 Boundary Row, London SE1 8HN, England. TEL 44-171-865-0198. FAX 44-171-410-6600. URL: http://BioMedNet.com/cgi-bin/members1/titles.pl.
Vendor(s): OCLC. *4772*

CURRENT OPINION IN OTOLARYNGOLOGY & HEAD AND NECK SURGERY.
Rapid Science Publishers, 2-6 Boundary Row, London SE1 8HN, England. TEL 44-171-865-0198. FAX 44-171-410-6600. URL: http://BioMedNet.com/cgi-bin/members1/titles.pl.
Vendor(s): OCLC. *5021*

CURRENT OPINION IN PEDIATRICS.
Rapid Science Publishers, 2-6 Boundary Row, London SE1 8HN, England. TEL 44-171-865-0198. FAX 44-171-410-6600. URL: http://BioMedNet.com/cgi-bin/members1/titles.pl.
Vendor(s): OCLC. *4773*

CURRENT OPINION IN PERIODONTOLOGY.
Rapid Science Publishers, 2-6 Boundary Row, London SE1 8HN, England. TEL 44-171-865-0198. FAX 44-171-410-6600. URL: http://BioMedNet.com/cgi-bin/members1/titles.pl.
Vendor(s): OCLC. *4773*

CURRENT OPINION IN PSYCHIATRY.
Rapid Science Publishers, 2-6 Boundary Row, London SE1 8HN, England. TEL 44-171-865-0198. FAX 44-171-410-6600. URL: http://BioMedNet.com/cgi-bin/members1/titles.pl.
Vendor(s): OCLC. *4773*

CURRENT OPINION IN PULMONARY MEDICINE.
Rapid Science Publishers, 2-6 Boundary Row, London SE1 8HN, England. TEL 44-171-865-0198. FAX 44-171-410-6600. URL: http://BioMedNet.com/cgi-bin/members1/titles.pl.
Vendor(s): OCLC. *5118*

CURRENT OPINION IN RHEUMATOLOGY.
Rapid Science Publishers, 2-6 Boundary Row, London SE1 8HN, England. TEL 44-171-865-0198. FAX 44-171-410-6600. URL: http://BioMedNet.com/cgi-bin/members1/titles.pl.
Vendor(s): OCLC. *4773*

CURRENT OPINION IN STRUCTURAL BIOLOGY.
Current Biology Ltd., 400 Market St., Ste. 700, Philadelphia, PA 19106. TEL 800-552-5866. FAX 215-574-2270. URL: http://BioMedNet.com/cgi-bin/members1/titles.pl.
Vendor(s): OCLC. *640*

CURRENT OPINION IN SURGICAL INFECTIONS.
Rapid Science Publishers, 2-6 Boundary Row, London SE1 8HN, England. TEL 44-171-410-6600.
Vendor(s): OCLC. *5139*

CURRENT OPINION IN UROLOGY.
Rapid Science Publishers, 2-6 Boundary Row, London SE1 8HN, England. TEL 44-171-865-0198. FAX 44-171-410-6600. URL: http://BioMedNet.com/cgi-bin/members1/titles.pl.
Vendor(s): OCLC. *4773*

CURRENT PHYSICS INDEX.
American Institute of Physics, One Physics Ellipse, College Park, MD 20740-3843. TEL 301-209-3000. *5834*

CURRENT POPULATION REPORTS: CONSUMER INCOME. MONEY INCOME OF HOUSEHOLDS, FAMILIES AND PERSONS IN THE UNITED STATES (YEAR).
U.S. Bureau of the Census, Customer Services, Washington, DC 20233. TEL 301-457-4100. FAX 301-457-4714. URL: http://www.census.gov/. *6063*

CURRENT POPULATION REPORTS: POPULATION CHARACTERISTICS. GEOGRAPHICAL MOBILITY.
U.S. Bureau of the Census, Customer Services, Washington, DC 20233. TEL 301-457-4100. FAX 301-457-4714. URL: http://www.census.gov/. *6063*

CURRENT POPULATION REPORTS: POPULATION CHARACTERISTICS. HOUSEHOLD AND FAMILY CHARACTERISTICS.
U.S. Bureau of the Census, Customer Services, Washington, DC 20233. TEL 301-457-4100. FAX 301-457-4714. URL: http://www.census.gov/. *6063*

CURRENT POPULATION REPORTS: POPULATION CHARACTERISTICS. MARITAL STATUS AND LIVING ARRANGEMENTS.
U.S. Bureau of the Census, Customer Services, Washington, DC 20233. TEL 301-457-4100. FAX 301-457-4714. URL: http://www.census.gov/. *6063*

CURRENT POPULATION REPORTS: POPULATION CHARACTERISTICS. RESIDENTS OF FARMS AND RURAL AREAS.
U.S. Bureau of the Census, Customer Services, Washington, DC 20233. TEL 301-457-4100. FAX 301-457-4714. URL: http://www.census.gov/. *6063*

CURRENT POPULATION REPORTS: POPULATION CHARACTERISTICS. SCHOOL ENROLLMENT: SOCIAL AND ECONOMIC CHARACTERISTICS OF STUDENTS.
U.S. Bureau of the Census, Customer Services, Washington, DC 20233. TEL 301-457-4100. FAX 301-457-4714. URL: http://www.census.gov/. *6063*

CURRENT POPULATION REPORTS: POPULATION ESTIMATES AND PROJECTIONS. UNITED STATES POPULATION ESTIMATES BY AGE, SEX, RACE AND HISPANIC ORIGIN.
U.S. Bureau of the Census, Customer Services, Washington, DC 20233. TEL 301-457-4100. FAX 301-457-4714. URL: http://www.census.gov/. *6063*

CURRENT POPULATION REPORTS: SERIES P-23. SPECIAL STUDIES.
U.S. Bureau of the Census, Customer Services, Washington, DC 20233. TEL 301-457-4100. FAX 301-457-4714. URL: http://www.census.gov/. *6064*

CURRENT POPULATION REPORTS: SERIES P-25. POPULATION ESTIMATES AND PROJECTIONS.
U.S. Bureau of the Census, Customer Services, Washington, DC 20233. TEL 301-457-4100. FAX 301-457-4714. URL: http://www.census.gov/. *6064*

CURRENT POPULATION REPORTS: SERIES P-60. CONSUMER INCOME.
U.S. Bureau of the Census, Customer Services, Washington, DC 20233. TEL 301-457-4100. FAX 301-457-4714. URL: http://www.census.gov/. *6064*

CURRENT POPULATION REPORTS: SERIES P-70. HOUSEHOLD ECONOMIC STUDIES.
U.S. Bureau of the Census, Customer Services, Washington, DC 20402. TEL 301-457-4100. FAX 301-457-4714. URL: http://www.census.gov/.
Vendor(s): CompuServe, Inc., Knight-Ridder Information, Inc. *6064*

CURRENT RESEARCH IN BRITAIN. BIOLOGICAL SCIENCES.
Longman Cartermill Ltd., Technology Centre, St. Andrews, Fife KY16 9EA, Scotland. TEL 44-1937-843434. FAX 44-1937-546333.
Vendor(s): Questel Orbit Inc. (CRIB). *640*

CURRENT RESEARCH IN BRITAIN. HUMANITIES.
Longman Cartermill Ltd., Technology Centre, St. Andrews, Fife KY16 9EA, Scotland. TEL 0937-843434. FAX 0937-546333.
Vendor(s): Questel Orbit Inc. (CRIB). *3799*

CURRENT RESEARCH IN BRITAIN. PHYSICAL SCIENCES.
Longman Cartermill Ltd., Technology Centre, St. Andrews, Fife KY16 9EA, Scotland. TEL 44-1937-843434. FAX 44-1937-546333.
Vendor(s): Questel Orbit Inc. (CRIB). *6589*

CURRENT RESEARCH IN LIBRARY & INFORMATION SCIENCE.
Bowker - Saur Ltd., A member of the Reed Elsevier plc group, Maypole House, Maypole Rd., E. Grinstead, W. Sussex RH19 1HU, England. TEL 44-1342-330100. FAX 44-1342-330191. URL: http://www.reed-elsevier.com.
Vendor(s): Knight-Ridder Information, Inc. (File no.61), Ovid Technologies, Inc. (LISA). *4173*

CURRENT SCIENCE AND TECHNOLOGY RESEARCH IN JAPAN.
Japan Science and Technology Corporation, Information Center for Science and Technology, 5-3, Yonbancho, Chiyoda-ku, Tokyo 102, Japan. TEL 81-3-5214-8413. FAX 81-3-5214-8410.
Vendor(s): JICST. *6589*

CURSUS.
Universite de Montreal, Ecole de Bibliotheconomie et des Sciences de l'Information, C.P. 6128, succ. Centre Ville, Montreal PQ H3C 3J7, Canada. URL: http://mistral.ere.umontreal.ca/~beaudryg/cursus/protocole.html.
Available only online. *4173*

CURTAINUP.
URL: http://www.geocities.com/broadway/1068.
Available only online. *7004*

CUSTOM BUILDER.
Gruner & Jahr U.S.A. Publishing, 110 Fifth Ave., New York, NY 10011-5601. TEL 207-828-4470. FAX 207-828-4478.
Vendor(s): Information Access Co. *883*

CYANOSIS.
Darin DeStefano, Ed. & Pub., 1032 Irving, Ste. 904, San Francisco, CA 94122. TEL 415-566-3661. URL: http://www.system-zero.com. *4331*

CYBER-SCREAM.
Trona Press, Inc., Box 544, Frostburg, MD 21532. URL: http://netbiz.net/~esss/scream.html. *4331*

CYBER TIMES.
Modified Ltd., Queen Anne House, 11 Charlotte St., Bath BA1 2NE, England. URL: http://www.modified.com.
Available only online. *6957*

CYBERARIAN'S GUIDE TO CYBER - MARKETING.
I O Communications, 182 B Ch. de Charleroi, 1060 Brussels, Belgium. TEL 32-2-534-07-37. FAX 32-2-534-07-57. URL: http://www.iocom.be/pilot/cybermarketing/ *952*

CYBERNETICS AND SYSTEMS (BRISTOL).
Taylor & Francis Inc., 1900 Frost Rd., Ste. 101, Bristol, PA 19007-1598. TEL 215-785-5800. FAX 215-785-5515. URL: http://www.tandf.co.uk/jnls/cbs.htm. *2161*

CYBERSEA SCUBA JOURNAL.
14530 Erwin St., Van Nuys, CA 91411. URL: http://www.scubajournal.com.
Available only online. *6757*

CYBERWEST MAGAZINE.
Box 40239, Denver, CO 80204-0239. URL: http://www.cyberwest.com.
Available only online. *7194*

CYCLE WORLD.
Hachette Filipacchi Magazines, Inc. (Newport Beach), 1499 Monrovia Ave., Newport Beach, CA 92663. TEL 714-720-5300. FAX 714-631-0651.
Vendor(s): Information Access Co., UMI. *6826*

CYPRUS. OFFICIAL GAZETTE.
Government Printing Office, Nicosia, Cyprus. TEL 357-2-302202. FAX 357-2-303175. *3273*

THE CYPRUS REVIEW.
Intercollege - Research and Development Center, P.O. Box 4005, 1700 Nicosia, Cyprus. TEL 357-2-357962. FAX 357-2-357964.
Vendor(s): Data-Star, Knight-Ridder Information, Inc., Ovid Technologies, Inc. *6609*

CYTOKINE.
Academic Press Ltd., 24-28 Oval Rd., London NW1 7DX, England. TEL 44-171-267-4466. FAX 44-71-482-2293. URL: http://www.hbuk.co.uk/ap/cytokine; http://www.europe.idealibrary.com/. *765*

C2C ABSTRACTS: JAPAN - ANALYTICAL CHEMISTRY.
Scan C2C, 1001 Pennsylvania Ave., N.W., No. 1300, Washington, DC 20024-2505. TEL 800-525-3865. FAX 202-863-3855.
Vendor(s): Data-Star (JPTC), European Space Agency (File no.241), Knight-Ridder Information, Inc. (File no.582), Questel Orbit Inc. (JTEC). *1783*

C2C ABSTRACTS: JAPAN - CERAMICS.
Scan C2C, 1001 Pennsylvania Ave., N.W., No.1300, Washington, DC 20024-2505. TEL 800-525-3865. FAX 202-863-3855.
Vendor(s): Data-Star (JPTC), European Space Agency (File no.241), Knight-Ridder Information, Inc. (File no.582), Questel Orbit Inc. (JTEC). *1735*

C2C ABSTRACTS: JAPAN - CHEMICAL ENGINEERING.
Scan C2C, 1001 Pennsylvania Ave., N.W., No. 1300, Washington, DC 20024-2505. TEL 800-525-3865. FAX 202-863-3855.
Vendor(s): Data-Star (JPTC), European Space Agency (File no.241), Knight-Ridder Information, Inc. (File no.582), Questel Orbit Inc. (JTEC). *2748*

C2C ABSTRACTS: JAPAN - CRYSTALLOGRAPHY.
Scan C2C, 1001 Pennsylvania Ave., N.W., No. 1300, Washington, DC 20024-2505. TEL 800-525-3865. FAX 202-863-3855.
Vendor(s): Data-Star (JPTC), European Space Agency (File no.241), Knight-Ridder Information, Inc. (File no.582), Questel Orbit Inc. (JTEC). *1783*

C2C ABSTRACTS: JAPAN - HYDROCARBONS.
Scan C2C, 1001 Pennsylvania Ave., N.W., No. 1300, Washington, DC 20024-2505. TEL 800-525-3865. FAX 202-863-3855.
Vendor(s): Data-Star (JPTC), European Space Agency (File no.241), Knight-Ridder Information, Inc. (File no.582), Questel Orbit Inc. (JTEC). *1783*

C2C ABSTRACTS: JAPAN - INORGANIC CHEMISTRY.
Scan C2C, 1001 Pennsylvania Ave., N.W., No. 1300, Washington, DC 20024-2505. TEL 800-525-3865. FAX 202-863-3855.
Vendor(s): Data-Star (JPTC), European Space Agency (File no.241), Knight-Ridder Information, Inc. (File no.582), Questel Orbit Inc. (JTEC). *1783*

C2C ABSTRACTS: JAPAN - MATERIALS SCIENCE.
Scan C2C, 1001 Pennsylvania Ave., N.W., No. 1300, Washington, DC 20024-2505. TEL 800-525-3865. FAX 202-863-3855.
Vendor(s): Data-Star (JPTC), European Space Agency (File no.241), Knight-Ridder Information, Inc. (File no.582), Questel Orbit Inc. (JTEC). *2748*

C2C ABSTRACTS: JAPAN - METALS.
Scan C2C, 1001 Pennsylvania Ave., N.W., No. 1300, Washington, DC 20024-2505. TEL 800-525-3865. FAX 202-863-3855.
Vendor(s): Data-Star (JPTC), European Space Agency (File no.241), Knight-Ridder Information, Inc. (File no.582), Questel Orbit Inc. (JTEC). *5217*

C2C ABSTRACTS: JAPAN - ORGANIC CHEMISTRY.
Scan C2C, 1001 Pennsylvania Ave., N.W., No. 1300, Washington, DC 20024-2505. TEL 800-525-3865. FAX 202-863-3855.
Vendor(s): Data-Star (JPTC), European Space Agency (File no.241), Knight-Ridder Information, Inc. (File no.582), Questel Orbit Inc. (JTEC). *1783*

C2C ABSTRACTS: JAPAN - PHYSICAL CHEMISTRY.
Scan C2C, 1001 Pennsylvania Ave., N.W., No. 1300, Washington, DC 20024-2505. TEL 800-525-3865. FAX 202-863-3855.
Vendor(s): Data-Star (JPTC), European Space Agency (File no.241), Knight-Ridder Information, Inc. (File no.582), Questel Orbit Inc. (JTEC). *1783*

C2C ABSTRACTS: JAPAN - PLASTICS.
Scan C2C, 1001 Pennsylvania Ave., N.W., No. 1300, Washington, DC 20024-2505. TEL 800-525-3865. FAX 202-863-3855.
Vendor(s): Data-Star (JPTC), European Space Agency (File no.241), Knight-Ridder Information, Inc. (File no.582), Questel Orbit Inc. (JTEC). *5886*

C2C ABSTRACTS: JAPAN - POLYMER CHEMISTRY.
Scan C2C, 1001 Pennsylvania Ave., N.W., No. 1300, Washington, DC 20024-2505. TEL 800-525-3865. FAX 202-863-3855.
Vendor(s): Data-Star (JPTC), European Space Agency (File no.241), Knight-Ridder Information, Inc. (File no.582), Questel Orbit Inc. (JTEC). *1783*

C2C ABSTRACTS: JAPAN - SURFACE CHEMISTRY.
Scan C2C, 1001 Pennsylvania Ave., N.W., No. 1300, Washington, DC 20024-2505. TEL 800-525-3865. FAX 202-863-3855.
Vendor(s): Data-Star (JPTC), European Space Agency (File no.241), Knight-Ridder Information, Inc. (File no.582), Questel Orbit Inc. (JTEC). *1783*

C2C ABSTRACTS: JAPAN - TEXTILES.
Scan C2C, 1001 Pennsylvania Ave., N.W., No. 1300, Washington, DC 20024-2025. TEL 800-525-3865. FAX 202-863-3855.
Vendor(s): Data-Star (JPTC), European Space Agency (File no.241), Knight-Ridder Information, Inc. (File no.582), Questel Orbit Inc. (JTEC). *6999*

C2C CURRENTS: JAPAN - CHEMISTRY.
Scan C2C, 1001 Pennsylvania Ave., N.W., No. 1300, Washington, DC 20024-2025. TEL 800-525-3865. FAX 202-863-3855.
Vendor(s): Data-Star (JPTC), European Space Agency (File no.241), Knight-Ridder Information, Inc. (File no.582), Questel Orbit Inc. (JTEC). *1783*

C2C CURRENTS: JAPAN - COMPUTERS.
Scan C2C, 1001 Pennsylvania Ave., N.W., No. 1300, Washington, DC 20024-2025. TEL 800-525-3865. FAX 202-863-3855.
Vendor(s): Data-Star (JPTC), European Space Agency (File no.241), Knight-Ridder Information, Inc. (File no.582), Questel Orbit Inc. (JTEC). *2094*

C2C CURRENTS: JAPAN - ELECTRONICS.
Scan C2C, 1001 Pennsylvania Ave., N.W., No. 1300, Washington, DC 20024-2505. TEL 800-525-3865. FAX 202-863-3855.
Vendor(s): Data-Star (JPTC), European Space Agency (File no.241), Knight-Ridder Information, Inc. (File no.582), Questel Orbit Inc. (JTEC). *2627*

C2C CURRENTS: JAPAN - MATERIALS.
Scan C2C, 1001 Pennsylvania Ave., N.W., No. 1300, Washington, DC 20024-2505. TEL 800-525-3865. FAX 202-863-3855.
Vendor(s): Data-Star (JPTC), European Space Agency (File no.241), Knight-Ridder Information, Inc. (File no.582), Questel Orbit Inc. (JTEC). *2748*

D A N B I B.
Dansk BiblioteksCenter as, Tempovej 7-11, DK-2750 Ballerup, Denmark. TEL 45-44-86-77-77. FAX 45-44-97-14-85.
Available only online. *545*

D B.
Diablo Publications, 2520 Camino Diablo, Walnut Creek, CA 94596. TEL 510-943-1111. FAX 510-943-1045.
Vendor(s): Lexis-Nexis, UMI. *1211*

D B M S.
Miller Freeman Inc. (San Mateo), 411 Borel Ave. Ste. 100, San Mateo, CA 74402. TEL 415-358-9500. FAX 415-358-9855.
Vendor(s): Information Access Co.. *2210*

D E C U S MAGAZINE.
Digital Equipment Computer Users Society, Communications Organization, 334 South St., SHR3-1 - T25, Shrewsbury, MA 01545. TEL 508-841-3584. FAX 508-841-3357. URL: http://www.decus.org. *2079*

D I Y: THE INTERNATIONAL MARKET.
Euromonitor, 60-61 Britton St., London EC1M 5NA, England. TEL 44-171-251-8024. FAX 44-171-608-3149. URL: http://www.euromonitor.com.
Vendor(s): Data-Star, Knight-Ridder Information, Inc. *3854*

SERIALS AVAILABLE ONLINE

D I Y WEEK.
Miller Freeman Publishers Ltd., Sovereign Way, Tonbridge, Kent TN9 1RW, England. TEL 44-1732-364422. FAX 44-1732-361534.
Vendor(s): Information Access Co. *3768*

D K I LITERATUR-SCHNELLDIENST KUNSTSTOFFE KAUTSCHUK FASERN.
Deutsches Kunststoff-Institut, Schlossgartenstr. 6, 64289 Darmstadt, Germany. TEL 49-6151-162105. FAX 49-6151-292855.
Vendor(s): FIZ Technik, STN International. *5886*

D L A BULLETIN.
University of California, Division of Library Automation, 300 Lakeside Dr., 8th Fl., Oakland, CA 94612-3550. TEL 510-987-0564. URL: http://ftp.dla.ucop.edu/pub/dlabulletin. *4230*

D M NEWS.
D M News Corp., 100 Sixth Ave., 6th Fl., New York, NY 10013-1689. TEL 212-741-2095. FAX 212-633-9367.
Vendor(s): Lexis-Nexis. *1523*

D N A SEQUENCE.
Gordon and Breach - Harwood Academic, Amsteldisk 166, 1st Fl., 1079 LH Amsterdam, Netherlands. URL: http://www.gbhap.com/DNA__Sequence/. *766*

D N R.
Fairchild Fashion Publication, Seven W. 34th St., New York, NY 10001. TEL 212-630-3600. FAX 212-630-2602.
Vendor(s): Information Access Co., Knight-Ridder Information, Inc.. *6985*

D P R K - DEMOCRATIC PEOPLE'S REPUBLIC OF KOREA.
URL: http://www.kimsoft.com/dprk.htm.
Available only online. *5525*

D R I - MCGRAW-HILL U S FORECAST SUMMARY.
D R I - McGraw-Hill, 24 Hartwell Ave., Lexington, MA 02173. TEL 617-863-5100. FAX 617-860-6332. *1251*

D T & G JOURNAL OF DESIGN, TYPOGRAPHY & GRAPHICS.
Design & Publishing Center, 15 Southgate, Harrisonburg, VA 22801. URL: http://www.graphic-design.com/DTG/
Available only online. *2132*

D U P I D O K.
Dansk Udenrigspolitisk Institut (DUPI), Nytorv 5, DK-1450 Copenhagen K, Denmark. TEL 45-33-36-65-65. FAX 45-33-36-65-66. URL: http://www.dupi.dk/documentation/dupidok. *6010*

D V D AND FUTURE C D.
TechMedia, 52 Foundling Ct., London WC1N 1AN, England. TEL 44-171-837-0815. FAX 44-171-278-9917. *2066*

DAEDALUS.
American Academy of Arts and Sciences, Norton's Woods, 136 Irving St., Cambridge, MA 02138. TEL 617-491-2600. FAX 617-576-5088.
Vendor(s): Information Access Co. *3777*

DAGBLADET.
P.O. Box 1184 Sentrum, N-0107 Oslo, Norway. TEL 47-22-31-06-00. FAX 47-22-42-95-48. URL: http://www.dagbladet.no. *3342*

DAILY BRIEF.
Intelligent Network Concepts, URL: http://www.tiac.net/users/incinc/.
Available only online. *3247*

DAILY BULLETIN - M T I.
Magyar Tavirati Iroda, Pl. Naphegy ter. 8, 1016 Budapest, Hungary. TEL 36-1-175-6722. FAX 36-1-118-8297. URL: http://www.mti.hu. *3305*

DAILY CAMPUS (DALLAS).
Student Media Company, Inc., 3140 Dyer St., Dallas, TX 75275. TEL 214-768-4555. FAX 214-768-4573. URL: http://www.sde.htrigg.smv.edu. *1948*

DAILY ENVIRONMENT REPORT.
The Bureau of National Affairs, Inc., 1231 25th St., N.W., Washington, DC 20037. TEL 202-452-4200. FAX 202-822-8092. URL: http://www.bna.com/
Vendor(s): West Group (file BNA-DEN). *2912*

DAILY LABOR REPORT.
The Bureau of National Affairs, Inc., 1231 25th St., N.W., Washington, DC 20037. TEL 202-452-4200. FAX 202-822-8092. URL: http://www.bna.com/
Vendor(s): Bureau of National Affairs, Human Resources Information Network (CDD, HDD), Lexis-Nexis (DLABRT), West Group (BNA-DLR). *1425*

DAILY OIL BULLETIN.
Southam Magazine Group (Calgary), 999 Eighth St. S.W., Ste. 300, Calgary, AB T2R 1N7, Canada. TEL 403-244-6111. FAX 403-245-8666. URL: http://www.nickles.com.
Vendor(s): Information Access Co., Southam Electronic Publishing. *5599*

DAILY REPORT FOR EXECUTIVES.
The Bureau of National Affairs, Inc., 1231 25th St., N.W., Washington, DC 20037. TEL 202-452-4200. FAX 202-822-8092. URL: http://www.bna.com/
Vendor(s): Human Resources Information Network (CDD, HDD), Lexis-Nexis (DREXEC), NewsNet, West Group (BNA-DER). *1472*

DAILY TAX REPORT.
The Bureau of National Affairs, Inc., 1231 25th St., N.W., Washington, DC 20037. TEL 202-452-4200. FAX 202-822-8092. URL: http://www.bna.com/
Vendor(s): Bureau of National Affairs, Lexis-Nexis (BNADTR), NewsNet, West Group (BNA-DTR). *1606*

DAILY TEXAN.
Texas Student Publications, Box D, Austin, TX 78713-9804. TEL 512-471-4591. FAX 512-471-1576. *1949*

DAIRY FOODS.
Cahners Publishing Company (Des Plaines), Division of Reed Elsevier Inc., 1350 E. Touhy Ave., Box 5080, Des Plaines, IL 60018-5080. TEL 847-390-2424. FAX 847-390-2445. URL: http://www.cahners.com/mainmag/df.htm.
Vendor(s): Information Access Co., Knight-Ridder Information, Inc., Lexis-Nexis. *3101*

DAIRY MARKETS WEEKLY.
Agra Europe (London) Ltd., 25 Frant Rd., Tunbridge Wells, Kent TN2 5JT, England. TEL 44-1892-533813. FAX 44-1892-544895.
Vendor(s): Information Access Co.. *253*

DAIRY PRODUCTS: THE INTERNATIONAL MARKET.
Euromonitor, 60-61 Britton St., London EC1M 5NA, England. TEL 44-171-251-8024. FAX 44-171-608-3149. URL: http://www.euromonitor.com.
Vendor(s): Data-Star, Knight-Ridder Information, Inc. *254*

DAIRY SCIENCE ABSTRACTS.
CAB International, Wallingford, Oxon. OX10 8DE, England. TEL 44-1491-832111. FAX 44-1491-826090. URL: http://www.cabi.org.
Vendor(s): DIMDI, European Space Agency, Knight-Ridder Information, Inc. *173*

DALAL STREET JOURNAL.
Dalal Street Communications Pvt. Ltd., 31-A, Noble Chambers, 4th Fl., Janmabhoomi Marg, Bombay 400 001, India. TEL 2870287. FAX 2872779. URL: http://www.cyberindia.net/DSJ/home.htm. *1126*

DALLAS BUSINESS JOURNAL.
Dallas Business Journal, Inc., 10670 N. Central Expwy., Ste. 710, Dallas, TX 75231-2111. TEL 214-520-1010. FAX 214-522-5606. *953*

DALTON TRANSACTIONS.
The Royal Society of Chemistry, Thomas Graham House, Science Park, Milton Rd., Cambridge CB4 4WF, England. TEL 44-1223-420066. FAX 44-1223-423623. URL: http://chemistry.rsc.org/rsc/.
Vendor(s): STN International (CJRSC). *1807*

DANCE MAGAZINE.
Dance Magazine, Inc., 33 W. 60th St., New York, NY 10023. TEL 212-245-9050. FAX 212-956-6487.
Vendor(s): Information Access Co., UMI. *2292*

DANIEL'S INFOZENE.
URL: http://www.iofcom.com/forms/maillist.html.
Available only online. *3372*

DANSK ARTIKELINDEKS: AVISER OG TIDSSKRIFTER.
Dansk BiblioteksCenter as, Tempovej 7-11, DK-2750 Ballerup, Denmark. TEL 45-44-867777. FAX 45-44-867892. *3884*

DANSK LYDFORTEGNELSE.
Dansk BiblioteksCenter as, Tempovej 7-11, DK-2750 Ballerup, Denmark. TEL 45-44-867777. FAX 45-44-867892. *5447*

DARGONZINE.
Dargon Project, URL: http://www.shore.net/'dargon.
Available only online. *4530*

DARK PLANET WEBZINE.
Indiana University, Chemistry A620, Bloomington, IN 47405. URL: http://www.sfsite.com/darkplanet/.
Available only online. *4530*

DATA COMMUNICATIONS.
McGraw-Hill Companies, 1221 Ave. of the Americas, New York, NY 10020. TEL 212-512-2000.
Vendor(s): Dow Jones News Retrieval, Knight-Ridder Information, Inc. (File no.624/McGRAW-HILL PUBLICATIONS ONLINE), Lexis-Nexis, NewsNet (TE37). *2169*

DATA STORAGE REPORT.
Jonas Press Publishing Company, 53 Park Belmont Pl., San Jose, CA 95136-2506. TEL 408-629-8249. FAX 408-629-8249.
Vendor(s): Information Access Co., Knight-Ridder Information, Inc. *2178*

DATABASE (WILTON).
Online, Inc., 462 Danbury Rd., Wilton, CT 06897. TEL 203-761-1466. URL: http://www.onlineinc.com/database.
Vendor(s): Information Access Co., UMI. *2165*

DATABASED WEB ADVISOR.
Advisor Publications Inc., 5675 Ruffin Rd., Ste. 200, San Diego, CA 92123. TEL 619-278-5600. FAX 619-278-0300. URL: http://www.advisor.com/ *2210*

DATAMATION.
Cahners Publishing Company (Newton), Division of Reed Elsevier Inc., 275 Washington St., Newton, MA 02158-1630. TEL 617-558-4424. FAX 617-558-4506. URL: http://www.datamation.com.
Vendor(s): Information Access Co., Knight-Ridder Information, Inc.. *2173*

DATAPHILE.
AsiaTech Publications Ltd., 23rd Fl., Citicorp Centre, 18 Whitfield Rd., North Point, Hong Kong, People's Republic of China. TEL 852-2837-8800. FAX 852-2520-5463. URL: http://www.dataphile.com.hk. *2015*

DATAPRO DIRECTORY OF MICROCOMPUTER SOFTWARE.
Datapro Information Services Group, 600 Delran Pkwy., Delran, NJ 08075. TEL 609-764-0100. FAX 609-764-2814.
Vendor(s): Knight-Ridder Information, Inc. *2129*

DATAPRO DIRECTORY OF SOFTWARE.
Datapro Information Services Group, 600 Delran Pkwy., Delran, NJ 08075. TEL 609-764-0100. FAX 609-764-2814.
Vendor(s): Knight-Ridder Information, Inc. *2210*

DATENSCHUTZ UND INFORMATIONSRECHT.
Oesterreichische Gesellschaft fuer Datenschutz, Sautergasse 20, A-1170 Vienna, Austria. TEL 43-1-4897893. FAX 43-1-4897891310. URL: http://www.adis.at/. *2149*

DAVISON'S SALESMAN'S BOOK.
Davison Publishing Co., Inc., Box 1289, Concord, NC 28026-1289. TEL 704-785-8700. FAX 704-785-8701. URL: http://www.davisonbluebook.com. *1663*

DAVISON'S TEXTILE BLUE BOOK.
Davison Publishing Co., Inc., Box 1289, Concord, NC 28026-1289. TEL 704-785-8700. FAX 704-785-8701. URL: http://www.davisonbluebook.com. *1663*

DAVISON'S TEXTILE BLUE BOOK EUROPE.
Davison Publishing Co., Inc., Box 1289, Concord, NC 28026-1289. TEL 704-785-8700. FAX 704-785-8701. URL: http://www.davisonbluebook.com. *6999*

DAVISON'S TEXTILE BUYER'S GUIDE.
Davison Publishing Co., Inc., Box 1289, Concord, NC 28026-1289. TEL 704-785-8700. FAX 704-785-8701. URL: http://www.davisonbluebook.com. *6999*

DAYTON BUSINESS REPORTER.
Hannover Publishing Co., Inc., 6356 Far Hills Ave., Dayton, OH 45459-2782. TEL 937-291-1100. FAX 937-436-3426. URL: http://www.daytonbusiness.com.
Vendor(s): UMI. *953*

DE PAUL BUSINESS LAW JOURNAL.
DePaul University, College of Law, 25 E. Jackson Blvd., Chicago, IL 60604. TEL 312-362-8553. FAX 312-362-5931.
Vendor(s): West Group. *3938*

DEAD ANGEL.
815-A Brazos St., No. 515, Austin, TX 78701. URL: http://www.eden.com/zines/deadangel/deadangel.html.
Available only online. *5388*

DEAD PIG DIGEST.
3 Northcote Rd., Glebe 2037, NSW Sydney, Australia. URL: http://gco.apana.org.au/'snrub/.
Available only online. *4331*

DEAFDIGEST.
Silent News, 2726 Gingerview Lane, Annapolis, MD 21401. URL: http://www.yellowstar.com/DeafDigest/deafdisg.htm.
Available only online. *3462*

DEAFSPORTZINE.
Silent News, 2726 Gingerview Lane, Annapolis, MD 21401. URL: http://www.yellowstar.com/DeafSportZine/sportzine.htm.
Available only online. *6758*

DEALER BUSINESS.
Ward's Communications, 3000 Town Center, Ste. 2750, Southfield, MI 48075-1212. TEL 810-357-0800. FAX 810-357-0810.
Vendor(s): Information Access Co. *7096*

DEALERNEWS.
Advanstar Communications, Inc., 7500 Old Oak Blvd., Cleveland, OH 44130. TEL 216-826-2839. FAX 216-891-2726.
Vendor(s): Information Access Co. *6827*

DEALERSCOPE CONSUMER ELECTRONICS MARKETPLACE.
North American Publishing Co., 401 N. Broad St., Philadelphia, PA 19108. TEL 215-238-5300. FAX 215-238-5457. URL: http://www.napco.com/dcem/dcem1.html.
Vendor(s): Knight-Ridder Information, Inc. *2628*

DEATH STUDIES.
Taylor & Francis Inc., 1900 Frost Rd., Ste. 101, Bristol, PA 19007-1598. TEL 215-785-5800. FAX 215-785-5515. URL: http://www.tandf.co.uk/. *6107*

DEBIT CARD NEWS.
Faulkner & Gray, Inc., 300 S. Wacker Dr., 18th Fl., Chicago, IL 60606. TEL 312-913-1334.
Vendor(s): Information Access Co., UMI. *1127*

DEBTZAPPER.
URL: http://www.gen.com/debtzapper/tour/2044.
Available only online. *1127*

DEFAULTED BONDS NEWSLETTER.
Bond Investors Association, Inc., 6175 N.W. 153rd St., Ste. 221, Miami Lakes, FL 33014-2435. TEL 305-557-1832. *1381*

DEFENSE & FOREIGN AFFAIRS STRATEGIC POLICY.
International Media Corporation Ltd., 175 Piccadilly, Ste. 1A, London W1V 9DB, England. TEL 071-491-2044. FAX 071-409-1923.
Vendor(s): Lexis-Nexis. *5920*

DEFENSE CLEANUP.
Pasha Publications Inc., 1616 N. Ft. Myer Dr., Ste. 1000, Arlington, VA 22209-3107. TEL 703-528-1244. FAX 703-528-1253. *2984*

DEFENSE COUNSEL JOURNAL.
International Association of Defense Counsel, 1 N. Franklin St., Ste. 2400, Chicago, IL 60606-3401. TEL 312-368-1494. FAX 312-368-1854.
Vendor(s): Information Access Co., West Group. *4060*

DEFENSE DAILY.
Phillips Business Information, Inc., 120 Seven Locks Rd., Potomac, MD 20854. TEL 301-424-3338. FAX 301-309-3847.
Vendor(s): Information Access Co., Knight-Ridder Information, Inc., NewsNet (DE01). *63*

DEFENSE ELECTRONICS.
Intertec Publishing Corp. (Atlanta), 6151 Powers Ferry Rd., N.W., Atlanta, GA 30339-2491. TEL 770-955-2500. FAX 770-955-0400.
Vendor(s): Information Access Co., Knight-Ridder Information, Inc., Lexis-Nexis. *2628*

DEFENSE WEEK.
King Publishing Group, Inc., 627 National Press Bldg., Washington, DC 20045. TEL 202-638-4260. FAX 202-662-9744.
Vendor(s): Information Access Co., Lexis-Nexis, NewsNet (DE16). *5267*

DELAWARE BUSINESS DIRECTORY.
American Business Directories, 5711 S. 86th Circle, Box 27347, Omaha, NE 68127. TEL 402-593-4600. FAX 402-331-5481. *1663*

DELAWARE BUSINESS REVIEW.
Independent Newspapers, Inc., Box 737, Dover, DE 19903. TEL 302-998-9580. FAX 302-998-1276.
Vendor(s): UMI. *953*

DELAWARE JOURNAL OF CORPORATE LAW.
Widener University, School of Law, Box 7286, Wilmington, DE 19803. TEL 302-477-2145. FAX 302-477-2042.
Vendor(s): Lexis-Nexis, West Group. *4079*

DELAWARE VALLEY RAIL PASSENGER.
Delaware Valley Association of Railroad Passengers, Box 7505, Philadelphia, PA 19010-7505. TEL 215-673-6445. FAX 215-885-7448. URL: http://www.libertynet.org/'dvarp/currsnt.html. *7125*

DELOS SCIENCE FICTION.
Silvio Sosio, Ed. & Pub., URL: http://www.fantascienza.com/delos.
Available only online. *4530*

DEMITASSE.
Box 542327, Houston, TX 77254-2327. URL: http://www.neosoft.com/'fortuna/intro.htm.
Available only online. *4331*

DENDRON NEWS.
454 Willamette St., Ste. 216, Box 11284, Eugene, OR 97440-3484. TEL 541-345-9106. URL: http://www.efn.org/'dendron. *5061*

DENTAL ECONOMICS.
PennWell Publishing Co., Dental Economics Division, Box 3408, Tulsa, OK 74101. TEL 918-835-3161. FAX 918-831-9804. URL: http://www.pennwell.com.
Vendor(s): UMI. *4854*

THE DENVER BUSINESS JOURNAL.
American City Business Journals (Denver), 1700 Broadway, No. 515, Denver, CO 80290. TEL 303-837-3500. FAX 303-837-3535.
Vendor(s): Information Access Co. *953*

DENVER JOURNAL OF INTERNATIONAL LAW AND POLICY.
University of Denver, College of Law, 7039 E. 18th Ave., Ste. 235, Denver, CO 80220. TEL 303-871-6170.
Vendor(s): West Group. *4111*

DENVER POST INDEX.
U M I, 300 N. Zeeb Rd., Ann Arbor, MI 48106-1346. TEL 313-761-4700. FAX 800-864-0019.
Vendor(s): Knight-Ridder Information, Inc. *3884*

DENVER UNIVERSITY LAW REVIEW.
University of Denver, College of Law, Porter Adm. Bldg., 7039 E. 18th Ave., Denver, CO 80220-1826. TEL 303-871-6172.
Vendor(s): Lexis-Nexis, West Group. *3939*

DEODORANTS: THE INTERNATIONAL MARKET.
Euromonitor, 60-61 Britton St., London EC1M 5NA, England. TEL 44-171-251-8024. FAX 44-171-608-3149. URL: http://www.euromonitor.com.
Vendor(s): Data-Star, Knight-Ridder Information, Inc. *505*

DERMATOLOGY TIMES.
Advanstar Communications, Inc., 7500 Old Oak Blvd., Cleveland, OH 44130. TEL 216-826-2839. FAX 216-891-2726.
Vendor(s): Information Access Co., Knight-Ridder Information, Inc. *4877*

DESIGN EXCHANGE.
Global Village Institute, Box 90, Summertown, TN 38483. TEL 615-964-3992. URL: http://www.gaia.org/dx. *2912*

DESIGN TIMES.
Regis Publishing, Inc., 1 Design Center Pl., Ste. 615, Boston, MA 02210-2313. TEL 617-443-0636. FAX 617-443-0637. URL: http://www.designtimes.com/ *3844*

DESIRE STREET.
New Orleans Poetry Forum, c/o Andrea Gereighty, Pres., 257 Bonabel Blvd., Metairie, LA 70005-3738. *4507*

DETROIT NEWS INDEX.
U M I, 300 N. Zeeb Rd., Ann Arbor, MI 48106-1346. TEL 313-731-4700. FAX 800-864-0019.
Vendor(s): Knight-Ridder Information, Inc. *3884*

DETROITER.
Greater Detroit Chamber Communications Inc., 600 W. Lafayette, Box 33840, Detroit, MI 48232-0840. TEL 313-596-0373. URL: http://www.detroitchamber.com.
Vendor(s): UMI. *1185*

DER DEUTSCHE APOTHEKER.
Verlag "Der Deutsche Apotheker", Hans-Thoma-Str. 1, 61440 Oberursel, Germany. TEL 49-6171-55012. FAX 49-6171-55142. *5655*

DEUTSCHE APOTHEKER ZEITUNG.
Deutscher Apotheker Verlag, Postfach 101061, 70009 Stuttgart, Germany. TEL 49-711-2582-0. FAX 49-711-2582290. *5655*

DEVELOPMENT BUSINESS.
United Nations, Division of Public Information, United Nations Plaza, DC1-574, New York, NY 10017. TEL 212-963-1517. FAX 212-963-1381.
Vendor(s): Data-Star, Knight-Ridder Information, Inc. *1357*

DEVELOPMENT, GENES AND EVOLUTION.
Springer-Verlag, Heidelberger Platz 3, 14197 Berlin, Germany. TEL 49-30-82787-0. FAX 49-30-82787448. URL: http://link.springer.de. *598*

DEVELOPMENTAL BIOLOGY.
Academic Press, Inc., Journal Division, 525 B St., Ste. 1900, San Diego, CA 92101-4495. TEL 619-230-1840. FAX 619-699-6800. URL: http://www.apnet.com/www/journal/db.htm; http://www.idealibrary.com/ *598*

DEVELOPMENTAL DYNAMICS.
John Wiley & Sons, Inc., Journals, 605 Third Ave., New York, NY 10158. TEL 212-850-6645. FAX 212-850-6021. URL: http://www.wiley.co.uk. *598*

DEVELOPMENTAL IMMUNOLOGY.
Gordon and Breach - Harwood Academic, Amsteldisk 166, 1st Fl., 1079 LH Amsterdam, Netherlands. URL: http://www.gbhap.com/Developmental__Immunology/. *4794*

DEVELOPMENTAL REVIEW.
Academic Press, Inc., Journal Division, 525 B St., Ste. 1900, San Diego, CA 92101-4495. TEL 619-230-1840. FAX 619-699-6800. URL: http://www.apnet.com/www/journal/dr.htm; http://www.idealibrary.com/ *6107*

10094 SERIALS AVAILABLE ONLINE

DEVELOPNET NEWS.
Volunteers in Technical Assistance, Inc., 1600 Wilson Blvd., Ste. 500, Arlington, VA 22209. TEL 703-276-1800. FAX 703-243-1865. Available only online. *6958*

DEVICES & DIAGNOSTICS LETTER.
Washington Business Information, Inc., c/o Karen Harrington, 1117 N. 19th St., Ste. 200, Arlington, VA 22209. TEL 703-247-3434. FAX 703-247-3421.
Vendor(s): Ovid Technologies, Inc. (DIOG), Data-Star, Knight-Ridder Information, Inc. *4661*

LE DEVOIR.
2050 rue de Bleury, 9e etage, Montreal, PQ H3A 3M9, Canada. TEL 514-985-3333.
Vendor(s): Southam Electronic Publishing. *3260*

DIABETES.
American Diabetes Association, 1660 Duke St., Alexandria, VA 22314. TEL 703-549-1500. FAX 703-836-7439.
Vendor(s): Information Access Co., Ovid Technologies, Inc. *4884*

DIABETES CARE.
American Diabetes Association, 1660 Duke St., Alexandria, VA 22314. TEL 703-549-1500. FAX 703-836-7439.
Vendor(s): Ovid Technologies, Inc. *4884*

DIABETES FORECAST.
American Diabetes Association, 1660 Duke St., Alexandria, VA 22314. TEL 703-549-1500. FAX 703-836-7439.
Vendor(s): Information Access Co. *4884*

DIABETOLOGIA.
Springer-Verlag, Heidelberger Platz 3, 14197 Berlin, Germany. TEL 49-30-82787-0. FAX 49-30-82787448. URL: http://link.springer.de. *4886*

DIACRITICS.
Johns Hopkins University Press, Journals Publishing Division, 2715 N. Charles St., Baltimore, MD 21218. TEL 410-516-6987. FAX 410-516-6968. URL: http://muse.jhu.edu. *4397*

DIAGNOSTIC AND THERAPEUTIC ENDOSCOPY.
Gordon and Breach - Harwood Academic, Amsteldisk 166, 1st Fl., 1079 LH Amsterdam, Netherlands. URL: http://www.gbhap.com/Diagnostic__Therapeutic_Endoscopy/. *4896*

DIAL ELECTRICAL - ELECTRONICS.
Dial Industry Publications, Windsor Ct., Grinstead House, E. Grinstead, W. Sussex RH19 1XA, England. TEL 44-1342-326972. FAX 44-1342-335247. URL: www.readingo.co.uk.
Vendor(s): Reed Information Services Ltd.. *2628*

DIAL ENGINEERING.
Dial Industry Publications, Windsor Ct., East Grinstead House, E. Grinstead, W. Sussex RH19 1XA, England. TEL 44-1342-326972. FAX 44-1342-335747. URL: www.readingo.co.uk.
Vendor(s): Reed Information Services Ltd. *2857*

DIAN HUAXUE.
Chinese Chemical Society, P.O. Box 2709, Beijing 100080, People's Republic of China. TEL 86-10-62568157. FAX 86-10-62568157. URL: http://www.xmu.edu.cn/library.html. *1804*

DIARIO CATARINESE.
R. Desembargador Pedro Silva 2958, 80080-900 Florianopolis, Santa Catarina, Brazil. TEL 55-482-494546. *3257*

DICK.
8214 S.W. Hawthorne Ln., Vashon, WA 98070. TEL 206-567-4364. URL: http://www.fess-up.com/dick.html. Available only online. *6610*

DICKINSON JOURNAL OF INTERNATIONAL LAW.
Dickinson School of Law, 150 S. College St., Carlisle, PA 17013. TEL 717-243-4611. FAX 717-243-4443.
Vendor(s): West Group. *4111*

DICKINSON LAW REVIEW.
Dickinson School of Law, 150 S. College St., Carlisle, PA 17013. TEL 717-240-5203. FAX 717-243-4443.
Vendor(s): Lexis-Nexis, West Group. *3939*

DICTIONARY OF CONTEMPORARY QUOTATIONS.
John Gordon Burke Publisher, Inc., Box 1492, Evanston, IL 60204-1492. TEL 847-866-8625. URL: http://www.nlightn.com. *4398*

DIDASKALIA.
University of Tasmania, Department of Classics, Hobart, Tasmania 7001, Australia. TEL 61-02-202-294. FAX 61-02-202-288.
Available only online. *1902*

DIENST LANDBOUWKUNDIG ONDERZOEK. STARING CENTRUM, INSTITUUT VOOR ONDERZOEK VAN HET LANDELIJK GEBIED. JAARBOEK.
Dienst Landbouwkundig Onderzoek, Staring Centrum, Instituut voor Onderzoek van het Landelijk Gebied, P.O. Box 125, 6700 AC Wageningen, Netherlands. TEL 31-317-474200. FAX 31-317-424812. *2912*

DIENST LANDBOUWKUNDIG ONDERZOEK. STARING CENTRUM, INSTITUUT VOOR ONDERZOEK VAN HET LANDELIJK GEBIED. RAPPORT.
Dienst Landbouwkundig Onderzoek, Staring Centrum, Instituut voor Onderzoek van het Landelijk Gebied, P.O. Box 125, 6700 AC Wageningen, Netherlands. TEL 31-317-474200. FAX 31-317-424812. *2913*

DIESEL PROGRESS ENGINES & DRIVES.
Diesel & Gas Turbine Publications, 13555 Bishop's Ct., Brookfield, WI 53005-6286. TEL 414-784-9177. FAX 414-784-8133.
Vendor(s): Information Access Co. *2882*

DIFFERENCES.
Indiana University Press, 601 N. Morton St., Bloomington, IN 47404. TEL 812-855-9449. FAX 812-855-8507.
Vendor(s): Information Access Co. *7342*

DIFFERENTIATION.
Springer-Verlag, Heidelberger Platz 3, 14197 Berlin, Germany. TEL 49-30-82787-0. FAX 49-30-82787448. URL: http://link.springer.de. *599*

DIFFUSION EXPRESS.
Electricite de France, Direction des Etudes et Recherches, Departement Systemes d'Information et de Documentation, 1, av. du General de Gaulle, 92141 Clamart, France. TEL 47-65-41-58. FAX 47-65-31-24.
Vendor(s): European Space Agency (File no.27), Telesystemes - Questel (Base EDF.DOC). *2748*

DIGEST OF ACTIVITIES OF CONGRESS.
Oliphant Washington Service, Box 9808, Friendship Sta., Washington, DC 20016. TEL 202-298-7226. FAX 202-333-5006.
Vendor(s): NewsNet. *6171*

DIGESTIVE DISEASES AND SCIENCES.
Plenum Publishing Corp., 233 Spring St., New York, NY 10013-1578. TEL 212-620-8000. FAX 212-463-0742. URL: http://www.catchword.co.uk/. *4909*

DIGESTIVE REMEDIES: THE INTERNATIONAL MARKET.
Euromonitor, 60-61 Britton St., London EC1M 5NA, England. TEL 44-171-251-8024. FAX 44-171-608-3149. URL: http://www.euromonitor.com.
Vendor(s): Data-Star, Knight-Ridder Information, Inc. *5656*

DIGITAL AGE.
Cardinal Business Media, Inc., 1300 Virginia Dr., Ste. 400, Ft. Washington, PA 19034-3225. TEL 215-643-8000. FAX 215-643-3901. URL: http://www.cardinal.com/digital__age; http://basix.com/decpro/.
Vendor(s): Information Access Co. *2080*

DIGITAL LIFE.
Marketsource Corporation, URL: http://www.taponline.com/tap/tech/net-tools/digital/digital.html.
Available only online. *2132*

DIGITAL MEDIA: A SEYBOLD REPORT.
Seybold Publications, 528 E. Baltimore Ave., Box 644, Media, PA 19063. TEL 610-565-2480. FAX 610-565-1858.
Vendor(s): Information Access Co.. *2188*

DIGITAL MOVIE NEWS.
Homeport Hollywood, Box 507, El Dorado, CA 95623-0507. URL: http://www.el-dorado.ca.us/~dmnews. *5330*

DIGITAL SIGNAL PROCESSING.
Academic Press, Inc., Journal Division, 525 B St., Ste. 1900, San Diego, CA 92101-4495. TEL 619-230-1840. FAX 619-699-6800. URL: http://www.apnet.com/www/journal/sp.htm; http://www.idealibrary.com. *2629*

DIGITAL SYSTEMS REPORT.
Computer Economics, Inc., 5841 Edison Pl., Carlsbad, CA 92008. TEL 760-438-8100. FAX 760-431-1126. URL: http://www.computereconomics.com.
Vendor(s): Information Access Co. *2080*

DIOGENES (ENGLISH EDITION).
Berghahn Books Inc., 165 Taber Ave., Providence, RI 02906. TEL 401-861-9330. FAX 401-521-0046.
Vendor(s): UMI. *6708*

THE DIPLOMATIC POUCH.
Box 1078, Parker, CO 80134. URL: http://devel.igo.org/dippouch.
Available only online. *3666*

DIRECT MARKETING.
Hoke Communications, 224 Seventh St., Garden City, Long Island, NY 11530. TEL 516-746-6700. FAX 516-294-8141. URL: http://netplaza.com/cgi-bin/document/plaza/business/1025/storepg2html?&uid429513.
Vendor(s): Information Access Co., Lexis-Nexis, UMI. *1523*

DIRECTION OF TRADE STATISTICS.
International Monetary Fund, Publication Services, 700 19th St., N.W., Ste. C-100, Washington, DC 20431. TEL 202-623-7430. FAX 202-623-7201. *1035*

DIRECTORIES IN PRINT.
Gale Research, 835 Penobscot Bldg., 645 Griswold St., Detroit, MI 48226-4094. TEL 313-961-2242. FAX 800-414-5043.
Vendor(s): Knight-Ridder Information, Inc. *546*

DIRECTORS & BOARDS.
229 S. 18th St., 3rd Fl., Philadelphia, PA 19103. TEL 215-790-7000. FAX 215-790-7005.
Vendor(s): Information Access Co., UMI. *1474*

DIRECTORY OF ARCHIVAL COLLECTIONS IN NEWFOUNDLAND AND LABRADOR.
Association of Newfoundland and Labrador Archives, Colonial Building, Military Rd., St. John's, NF A1C 2C9, Canada. TEL 709-726-2867. FAX 709-729-0578. URL: http://www.infonet.st-johns.nf.ca/providers/anla/anlahome.html. *4174*

DIRECTORY OF ASSOCIATIONS IN CANADA.
Micromedia Ltd., 20 Victoria St., Toronto, ON M5C 2N8, Canada. TEL 416-362-5211. FAX 416-362-6161. URL: http://www.mmltd.com. *1665*

DIRECTORY OF BIOMEDICAL AND HEALTH CARE GRANTS.
Oryx Press, Box 33889, Phoenix, AZ 85067-3889. TEL 602-265-2651. FAX 602-265-6250.
Vendor(s): Knight-Ridder Information, Inc. *2498*

DIRECTORY OF COMMUNITY LEGISLATION IN FORCE.
Office for Official Publications of the European Communities, L-2985 Luxembourg, Luxembourg.
Vendor(s): Commission of the European Communities. *3940*

DIRECTORY OF CORPORATE AFFILIATIONS.
National Register Publishing, A Division of Reed Elsevier Inc., 121 Chanlon Rd., New Providence, NJ 07974. TEL 908-464-6800. FAX 908-771-7704. URL: http://www.reedref.com.
Vendor(s): Knight-Ridder Information, Inc. (File no.513, Corporate Affiliations), Lexis-Nexis. *1667*

DIRECTORY OF DIRECTORS.
Reed Information Services, Windsor Court, E. Grinstead House, E. Grinstead, W. Sussex RH19 1XA, England. TEL 01342-335832. FAX 01342-335948.
Vendor(s): Reed Information Services Ltd. *1474*

DIRECTORY OF ELECTRONIC JOURNALS, NEWSLETTERS AND ACADEMIC DISCUSSION LISTS.
Association of Research Libraries, 21 Dupont Circle, Ste. 800, Washington, DC 20036. TEL 202-296-2296. FAX 202-872-0884. URL: http://arl.cni.org/scomm/edir/index.html. *546*

DIRECTORY OF GRANTS IN THE HUMANITIES.
Oryx Press, Box 33889, Phoenix, AZ 85067-3889. TEL 602-265-2651. FAX 602-265-6250. Vendor(s): Knight-Ridder Information, Inc. *2498*

DIRECTORY OF HEALTHCARE GROUP PURCHASING ORGANIZATIONS.
Medical Economics Co., 5 Paragon Dr., Montvale, NJ 07645-1742. TEL 201-358-7657. FAX 201-722-2662.
Vendor(s): Lexis-Nexis. *1668*

DIRECTORY OF HOSPITAL PERSONNEL.
Medical Economics Co., 5 Paragon Dr., Montvale, NJ 07645-1742. TEL 201-358-7657. FAX 201-722-2662.
Vendor(s): Lexis-Nexis. *1669*

DIRECTORY OF LIBRARIES AND LIBRARY SYSTEMS IN THE SOUTH CENTRAL RESEARCH LIBRARY COUNCIL REGION.
South Central Research Library Council, DeWitt Bldg., 215 N. Cayuga St., Ithaca, NY 14850. TEL 607-273-9106. FAX 607-272-0740. URL: http://www.lakenet.org/.
Available only online. *4174*

DIRECTORY OF LIBRARIES IN CANADA.
Micromedia Ltd., 20 Victoria St., Toronto, ON M5C 2N8, Canada. TEL 416-362-5211. FAX 416-362-6161. URL: http://www.mmltd.com. *4174*

DIRECTORY OF OBSOLETE SECURITIES.
Financial Information Incorporated, 30 Montgomery St., Jersey City, NJ 07302. FAX 800-344-3292. *1382*

DIRECTORY OF RESEARCH GRANTS.
Oryx Press, Box 33889, Phoenix, AZ 85067-3889. TEL 602-265-2651. FAX 602-265-6250. Vendor(s): Knight-Ridder Information, Inc. *2539*

DISABILITY & SOCIETY.
Carfax Publishing Co., P.O. Box 25, Abingdon, Oxon. OX14 3UE, England. TEL 44-1235-401000. FAX 44-1235-401550. *3466*

DISABILITY ISSUES.
Information Center for Individuals with Disabilities, Box 750119, Arlington Heights, MA 02175-0119. TEL 617-462-5015. FAX 617-345-5318. *3453*

DISCLOSURE (CHICAGO).
National Training and Information Center, 810 N. Milwaukee, Chicago, IL 60622. TEL 312-243-3035. FAX 312-243-7044.
Vendor(s): UMI. *2255*

DISCOUNT STORE NEWS.
Lebhar-Friedman, Inc., 425 Park Ave., New York, NY 10022. TEL 212-756-5000. URL: http://www.discountstorenews.com.
Vendor(s): Information Access Co., Knight-Ridder Information, Inc., Lexis-Nexis. *1524*

DISCOVER (BURBANK).
Walt Disney Magazine Publishing Group, 114 5th Ave., New York, NY 10011. TEL 818-973-4320. Vendor(s): Knight-Ridder Information, Inc., Lexis-Nexis, MediaStream. *6523*

DISCRETE & COMPUTATIONAL GEOMETRY.
Springer-Verlag, Science Journals, 175 Fifth Ave., New York, NY 10010. TEL 212-460-1500. FAX 212-473-6272. URL: http://www.springer-ny.com. *4570*

DISCRETE AND CONTINUOUS DYNAMICAL SYSTEMS.
Department of Mathematics, Southwest Missouri State University, Springfield, MO 65804. TEL 417-836-5377. FAX 417-886-0559. URL: http://science.smsu.edu/˜hu. *4570*

DISEASES OF THE COLON AND RECTUM.
Williams & Wilkins, 351 W. Camden St., Baltimore, MD 21201-2436. TEL 410-528-4000. FAX 410-528-4312. URL: http://www.wwilkins.com.
Vendor(s): Ovid Technologies, Inc. *5141*

DISGRUNTLED.
Counterpoint Press, Inc., 61 Arlington Court, Kensington, CA 94707. URL: http://www.disgruntled.com.
Available only online. *1425*

DISPLAY.
I N F O S C A N, Nordre Fasanvej 108-B, DK-2000 Frederiksberg, Denmark. TEL 45-38-16-06-06. FAX 45-38-16-06-07. URL: http://www.infoscan.dk. *2132*

DISPOSABLE PAPER PRODUCTS: THE INTERNATIONAL MARKET.
Euromonitor, 60-61 Britton St., London EC1M 5NA, England. TEL 44-171-251-8024. FAX 44-171-608-3149. URL: http://www.euromonitor.com.
Vendor(s): Data-Star, Knight-Ridder Information, Inc. *5566*

DISSERTATION ABSTRACTS INTERNATIONAL. SECTION A: HUMANITIES AND SOCIAL SCIENCES.
U M I, 300 N. Zeeb Rd., Ann Arbor, MI 48106. TEL 313-761-4700. FAX 800-864-0019.
Vendor(s): Data-Star, Knight-Ridder Information, Inc. (File no.35), OCLC (EPIC), Ovid Technologies, Inc. (DISS), STN International. *3799*

DISSERTATION ABSTRACTS INTERNATIONAL. SECTION B: PHYSICAL SCIENCES AND ENGINEERING.
U M I, 300 N. Zeeb Rd., Ann Arbor, MI 48106. TEL 313-761-4700. FAX 800-864-0019.
Vendor(s): Data-Star, Knight-Ridder Information, Inc. (File no.35), OCLC (EPIC), Ovid Technologies, Inc. (DISS), STN International. *6589*

DISSERTATION ABSTRACTS INTERNATIONAL. SECTION C: WORLDWIDE.
U M I, 300 N. Zeeb Rd., Ann Arbor, MI 48106. TEL 313-761-4700. FAX 800-864-0019.
Vendor(s): Data-Star, Knight-Ridder Information, Inc. (File no.35), OCLC (EPIC), Ovid Technologies, Inc. (DISS), STN International. *3799*

DISSERTATION ABSTRACTS ON DISC.
U M I, 300 N. Zeeb Rd., Ann Arbor, MI 48016-1304. TEL 313-761-4700. FAX 800-864-0019.
Vendor(s): Data-Star, Knight-Ridder Information, Inc., OCLC (ERIC), Ovid Technologies, Inc. (DISS), STN International. *3799*

DISTRIBUTED COMPUTING.
Springer-Verlag, Heidelberger Platz 3, 14197 Berlin, Germany. TEL 49-30-82787-0. FAX 49-30-82787448. URL: http://link.springer.de. *2080*

DISTRIBUTED COMPUTING MONITOR.
Patricia Seybold Group, 85 Devonshire St. Fl. 5, Boston, MA 02109-3504. *2154*

DISTRIBUTED SYSTEMS ENGINEERING.
I O P Publishing Ltd., Dirac House, Temple Back, Bristol BS1 6BE, England. TEL 44-117-929-7481. FAX 44-117-929-4318. URL: http://www.iop.org. *5801*

DIVA, DIBA?
48-C Maningning St., Teacher's Village, Quezon City, Philippines. URL: http://www.geocities.com/westhollywood/3142.
Available only online. *3347*

DO-IT-YOURSELF RETAILING.
National Retail Hardware Association, 5822 W. 74th St., Indianapolis, IN 46278. TEL 317-297-1190. FAX 317-328-4354. URL: http://www.nrha.org.
Vendor(s): Information Access Co. *3768*

DOCUMENT IMAGING REPORT.
Phillips Business Information, Inc., 1201 Seven Locks Rd., Potomac, MD 20854. TEL 301-424-3338. FAX 301-309-3847.
Vendor(s): Information Access Co., NewsNet (EC02). *2169*

DOCUMENTA MATHEMATICA.
Deutsche Mathematiker Vereinigung, Postfach 100131, 33501 Bielefeld, Germany. URL: http://www.math.uiuc.edu/documenta/. *4570*

DODGE BUILDING REVIEW COVERING CENTRAL INDIANA.
McGraw-Hill Companies, Princeton Rd. S-2, Box 689, Hightstown, NJ 08520-0689. *885*

DODGE BUILDING REVIEW COVERING NORTHERN INDIANA.
McGraw-Hill Companies, Princeton Rd. S-2, Box 689, Hightstown, NJ 08520-0689. *885*

DODGE BUILDING REVIEW COVERING SOUTHERN INDIANA.
McGraw-Hill Companies, Princeton Rd. S-2, Box 689, Hightstown, NJ 08520-0689. *885*

DODGE CONSTRUCTION NEWS WEEKLY COVERING ALABAMA.
McGraw-Hill Companies, Princeton Rd. S-2, Box 689, Hightstown, NJ 08520-0689. *885*

DODGE CONSTRUCTION NEWS WEEKLY COVERING ALBANY.
McGraw-Hill Companies, Princeton Rd. S-2, Box 689, Hightstown, NJ 08520-0689. *885*

DODGE CONSTRUCTION NEWS WEEKLY COVERING ARKANSAS.
McGraw-Hill Companies, Princeton Rd. S-2, Box 689, Hightstown, NJ 08520-0689. *885*

DODGE CONSTRUCTION NEWS WEEKLY COVERING ASHEVILLE - CHARLOTTE.
McGraw-Hill Companies, Princeton Rd. S-2, Box 689, Hightstown, NJ 08520-0689. *885*

DODGE CONSTRUCTION NEWS WEEKLY COVERING AUSTIN.
McGraw-Hill Companies, Princeton Rd. S-2, Box 689, Hightstown, NJ 08520-0689. *885*

DODGE CONSTRUCTION NEWS WEEKLY COVERING BALTIMORE.
McGraw-Hill Companies, Princeton Rd. S-2, Box 689, Hightstown, NJ 08520-0689. *885*

DODGE CONSTRUCTION NEWS WEEKLY COVERING BATON ROUGE.
McGraw-Hill Companies, Princeton Rd. S-2, Box 689, Hightstown, NJ 08520-0689. *885*

DODGE CONSTRUCTION NEWS WEEKLY COVERING BEAUMONT - LAKE CHARLES.
McGraw-Hill Companies, Princeton Rd. S-2, Box 689, Hightstown, NJ 08520-0689. *885*

DODGE CONSTRUCTION NEWS WEEKLY COVERING BROOKLYN - QUEENS.
McGraw-Hill Companies, Princeton Rd. S-2, Box 689, Hightstown, NJ 08520-0689. *885*

DODGE CONSTRUCTION NEWS WEEKLY COVERING BUFFALO.
McGraw-Hill Companies, Princeton Rd. S-2, Box 689, Hightstown, NJ 08520-0689. *885*

DODGE CONSTRUCTION NEWS WEEKLY COVERING CENTRAL AND SOUTHERN ILLINOIS.
McGraw-Hill Companies, Princeton Rd. S-2, Box 689, Hightstown, NJ 08520-0689. *885*

DODGE CONSTRUCTION NEWS WEEKLY COVERING CENTRAL NEW JERSEY.
McGraw-Hill Companies, Princeton Rd. S-2, Box 689, Hightstown, NJ 08520-0689. *885*

DODGE CONSTRUCTION NEWS WEEKLY COVERING CENTRAL PENNSYLVANIA.
McGraw-Hill Companies, Princeton Rd. S-2, Box 689, Hightstown, NJ 08520-0689. *885*

DODGE CONSTRUCTION NEWS WEEKLY COVERING CHICAGO ENGINEERING.
McGraw-Hill Companies, Princeton Rd. S-2, Box 689, Hightstown, NJ 08520-0689. *886*

DODGE CONSTRUCTION NEWS WEEKLY COVERING CHICAGO GENERAL BUILDING.
McGraw-Hill Companies, Princeton Rd. S-2, Box 689, Hightstown, NJ 08520-0689. *886*

DODGE CONSTRUCTION NEWS WEEKLY COVERING CINCINNATI AND VICINITY.
McGraw-Hill Companies, Princeton Rd. S-2, Box 689, Hightstown, NJ 08520-0689. *886*

DODGE CONSTRUCTION NEWS WEEKLY COVERING CLEVELAND - AKRON - CANTON.
McGraw-Hill Companies, Princeton Rd. S-2, Box 689, Hightstown, NJ 08520-0689. *886*

DODGE CONSTRUCTION NEWS WEEKLY COVERING COLUMBIA - CHARLESTON.
McGraw-Hill Companies, Princeton Rd. S-2, Box 689, Hightstown, NJ 08520-0689. *886*

DODGE CONSTRUCTION NEWS WEEKLY COVERING COLUMBUS AND VICINITY.
McGraw-Hill Companies, Princeton Rd. S-2, Box 689, Hightstown, NJ 08520-0689. *886*

DODGE CONSTRUCTION NEWS WEEKLY COVERING CONNECTICUT.
McGraw-Hill Companies, Princeton Rd. S-2, Box 689, Hightstown, NJ 08520-0689. *886*

DODGE CONSTRUCTION NEWS WEEKLY COVERING DALLAS.
McGraw-Hill Companies, Princeton Rd. S-2, Box 689, Hightstown, NJ 08520-0689. *886*

DODGE CONSTRUCTION NEWS WEEKLY COVERING DAYTON AND VICINITY.
McGraw-Hill Companies, Princeton Rd. S-2, Box 689, Hightstown, NJ 08520-0689. *886*

DODGE CONSTRUCTION NEWS WEEKLY COVERING DETROIT METRO.
McGraw-Hill Companies, Princeton Rd. S-2, Box 689, Hightstown, NJ 08520-0689. *886*

DODGE CONSTRUCTION NEWS WEEKLY COVERING EASTERN KENTUCKY.
McGraw-Hill Companies, Princeton Rd. S-2, Box 689, Hightstown, NJ 08520-0689. *886*

DODGE CONSTRUCTION NEWS WEEKLY COVERING EASTERN MASSACHUSETTS.
McGraw-Hill Companies, Princeton Rd. S-2, Box 689, Hightstown, NJ 08520-0689. *886*

DODGE CONSTRUCTION NEWS WEEKLY COVERING EASTERN MISSOURI.
McGraw-Hill Companies, Princeton Rd. S-2, Box 689, Hightstown, NJ 08520-0689. *886*

DODGE CONSTRUCTION NEWS WEEKLY COVERING EASTERN NORTH CAROLINA.
McGraw-Hill Companies, Princeton Rd. S-2, Box 689, Hightstown, NJ 08520-0689. *886*

DODGE CONSTRUCTION NEWS WEEKLY COVERING EASTERN OKLAHOMA.
McGraw-Hill Companies, Princeton Rd. S-2, Box 689, Hightstown, NJ 08520-0689. *886*

DODGE CONSTRUCTION NEWS WEEKLY COVERING FORT WORTH.
McGraw-Hill Companies, Princeton Rd. S-2, Box 689, Hightstown, NJ 08520-0689. *886*

DODGE CONSTRUCTION NEWS WEEKLY COVERING GEORGIA.
McGraw-Hill Companies, Princeton Rd. S-2, Box 689, Hightstown, NJ 08520-0689. *886*

DODGE CONSTRUCTION NEWS WEEKLY COVERING HOUSTON.
McGraw-Hill Companies, Princeton Rd. S-2, Box 689, Hightstown, NJ 08520-0689. *886*

DODGE CONSTRUCTION NEWS WEEKLY COVERING IOWA.
McGraw-Hill Companies, Princeton Rd. S-2, Box 689, Hightstown, NJ 08520-0689. *886*

DODGE CONSTRUCTION NEWS WEEKLY COVERING JACKSONVILLE AND VICINITY.
McGraw-Hill Companies, Princeton Rd. S-2, Box 689, Hightstown, NJ 08520-0689. *886*

DODGE CONSTRUCTION NEWS WEEKLY COVERING KANSAS.
McGraw-Hill Companies, Princeton Rd. S-2, Box 689, Hightstown, NJ 08520-0689. *886*

DODGE CONSTRUCTION NEWS WEEKLY COVERING KANSAS CITY.
McGraw-Hill Companies, Princeton Rd. S-2, Box 689, Hightstown, NJ 08520-0689. *886*

DODGE CONSTRUCTION NEWS WEEKLY COVERING KNOXVILLE AND VICINITY.
McGraw-Hill Companies, Princeton Rd. S-2, Box 689, Hightstown, NJ 08520-0689. *886*

DODGE CONSTRUCTION NEWS WEEKLY COVERING LEXINGTON AND VICINITY.
McGraw-Hill Companies, Princeton Rd. S-2, Box 689, Hightstown, NJ 08520-0689. *886*

DODGE CONSTRUCTION NEWS WEEKLY COVERING MAINE.
McGraw-Hill Companies, Princeton Rd. S-2, Box 689, Hightstown, NJ 08520-0689. *886*

DODGE CONSTRUCTION NEWS WEEKLY COVERING MEMPHIS AND VICINITY.
McGraw-Hill Companies, Princeton Rd. S-2, Box 689, Hightstown, NJ 08520-0689. *886*

DODGE CONSTRUCTION NEWS WEEKLY COVERING METRO PHILADELPHIA.
McGraw-Hill Companies, Princeton Rd. S-2, Box 689, Hightstown, NJ 08520-0689. *886*

DODGE CONSTRUCTION NEWS WEEKLY COVERING MIAMI AND VICINITY.
McGraw-Hill Companies, Princeton Rd. S-2, Box 689, Hightstown, NJ 08520-0689. *887*

DODGE CONSTRUCTION NEWS WEEKLY COVERING MINNESOTA - NORTHWEST WISCONSIN.
McGraw-Hill Companies, Princeton Rd. S-2, Box 689, Hightstown, NJ 08520-0689. *887*

DODGE CONSTRUCTION NEWS WEEKLY COVERING NASHVILLE AND VICINITY.
McGraw-Hill Companies, Princeton Rd. S-2, Box 689, Hightstown, NJ 08520-0689. *887*

DODGE CONSTRUCTION NEWS WEEKLY COVERING NEBRASKA.
McGraw-Hill Companies, Princeton Rd. S-2, Box 689, Hightstown, NJ 08520-0689. *887*

DODGE CONSTRUCTION NEWS WEEKLY COVERING NEW HAMPSHIRE.
McGraw-Hill Companies, Princeton Rd. S-2, Box 689, Hightstown, NJ 08520-0689. *887*

DODGE CONSTRUCTION NEWS WEEKLY COVERING NEW ORLEANS.
McGraw-Hill Companies, Princeton Rd. S-2, Box 689, Hightstown, NJ 08520-0689. *887*

DODGE CONSTRUCTION NEWS WEEKLY COVERING NORFOLK.
McGraw-Hill Companies, Princeton Rd. S-2, Box 689, Hightstown, NJ 08520-0689. *887*

DODGE CONSTRUCTION NEWS WEEKLY COVERING NORTH AND SOUTH DAKOTA.
McGraw-Hill Companies, Princeton Rd. S-2, Box 689, Hightstown, NJ 08520-0689. *887*

DODGE CONSTRUCTION NEWS WEEKLY COVERING NORTHEAST WISCONSIN - UPPER PENINSULA.
McGraw-Hill Companies, Princeton Rd. S-2, Box 689, Hightstown, NJ 08520-0689. *887*

DODGE CONSTRUCTION NEWS WEEKLY COVERING NORTHERN MISSISSIPPI.
McGraw-Hill Companies, Princeton Rd. S-2, Box 689, Hightstown, NJ 08520-0689. *887*

DODGE CONSTRUCTION NEWS WEEKLY COVERING NORTHERN NEW JERSEY.
McGraw-Hill Companies, Princeton Rd. S-2, Box 689, Hightstown, NJ 08520-0689. *887*

DODGE CONSTRUCTION NEWS WEEKLY COVERING NORTHWEST FLORIDA.
McGraw-Hill Companies, Princeton Rd. S-2, Box 689, Hightstown, NJ 08520-0689. *887*

DODGE CONSTRUCTION NEWS WEEKLY COVERING NORTHWEST ILLINOIS.
McGraw-Hill Companies, Princeton Rd. S-2, Box 689, Hightstown, NJ 08520-0689. *887*

DODGE CONSTRUCTION NEWS WEEKLY COVERING ORLANDO AND VICINITY.
McGraw-Hill Companies, Princeton Rd. S-2, Box 689, Hightstown, NJ 08520-0689. *887*

DODGE CONSTRUCTION NEWS WEEKLY COVERING PITTSBURGH AND VICINITY.
McGraw-Hill Companies, Princeton Rd. S-2, Box 689, Hightstown, NJ 08520-0689. *887*

DODGE CONSTRUCTION NEWS WEEKLY COVERING RALEIGH - DURHAM.
McGraw-Hill Companies, Princeton Rd. S-2, Box 689, Hightstown, NJ 08520-0689. *887*

DODGE CONSTRUCTION NEWS WEEKLY COVERING REGIONAL ALLIANCE.
McGraw-Hill Companies, Princeton Rd. S-2, Box 689, Hightstown, NJ 08520-0689. *887*

DODGE CONSTRUCTION NEWS WEEKLY COVERING RHODE ISLAND.
McGraw-Hill Companies, Princeton Rd. S-2, Box 689, Hightstown, NJ 08520-0689. *887*

DODGE CONSTRUCTION NEWS WEEKLY COVERING RICHMOND.
McGraw-Hill Companies, Princeton Rd. S-2, Box 689, Hightstown, NJ 08520-0689. *887*

DODGE CONSTRUCTION NEWS WEEKLY COVERING RIO GRANDE.
McGraw-Hill Companies, Princeton Rd. S-2, Box 689, Hightstown, NJ 08520-0689. *887*

DODGE CONSTRUCTION NEWS WEEKLY COVERING ROANOKE.
McGraw-Hill Companies, Princeton Rd. S-2, Box 689, Hightstown, NJ 08520-0689. *887*

DODGE CONSTRUCTION NEWS WEEKLY COVERING ROCHESTER.
McGraw-Hill Companies, Princeton Rd. S-2, Box 689, Hightstown, NJ 08520-0689. *887*

DODGE CONSTRUCTION NEWS WEEKLY COVERING ST. LOUIS.
McGraw-Hill Companies, Princeton Rd. S-2, Box 689, Hightstown, NJ 08520-0689. *887*

DODGE CONSTRUCTION NEWS WEEKLY COVERING SHREVEPORT.
McGraw-Hill Companies, Princeton Rd. S-2, Box 689, Hightstown, NJ 08520-0689. *887*

DODGE CONSTRUCTION NEWS WEEKLY COVERING SOUTH CAROLINA.
McGraw-Hill Companies, Princeton Rd. S-2, Box 689, Hightstown, NJ 08520-0689. *887*

DODGE CONSTRUCTION NEWS WEEKLY COVERING SOUTHERN CALIFORNIA INCLUDING NEVADA.
McGraw-Hill Companies, Princeton Rd. S-2, Box 689, Hightstown, NJ 08520-0689. *887*

DODGE CONSTRUCTION NEWS WEEKLY COVERING SOUTHERN MISSISSIPPI.
McGraw-Hill Companies, Princeton Rd. S-2, Box 689, Hightstown, NJ 08520-0689. *887*

DODGE CONSTRUCTION NEWS WEEKLY COVERING SOUTHERN NEW JERSEY.
McGraw-Hill Companies, Princeton Rd. S-2, Box 689, Hightstown, NJ 08520-0689. *888*

DODGE CONSTRUCTION NEWS WEEKLY COVERING SOUTHERN PENINSULA.
McGraw-Hill Companies, Princeton Rd. S-2, Box 689, Hightstown, NJ 08520-0689. *888*

DODGE CONSTRUCTION NEWS WEEKLY COVERING SOUTHERN WISCONSIN.
McGraw-Hill Companies, Princeton Rd. S-2, Box 689, Hightstown, NJ 08520-0689. *888*

DODGE CONSTRUCTION NEWS WEEKLY COVERING STATE OF MISSISSIPPI.
McGraw-Hill Companies, Princeton Rd. S-2, Box 689, Hightstown, NJ 08520-0689. *888*

DODGE CONSTRUCTION NEWS WEEKLY COVERING SYRACUSE.
McGraw-Hill Companies, Princeton Rd. S-2, Box 689, Hightstown, NJ 08520-0689. *888*

DODGE CONSTRUCTION NEWS WEEKLY COVERING THE BRONX - MANHATTAN - STATEN ISLAND.
McGraw-Hill Companies, Princeton Rd. S-2, Box 689, Hightstown, NJ 08520-0689. *888*

DODGE CONSTRUCTION NEWS WEEKLY COVERING THE HUDSON VALLEY.
McGraw-Hill Companies, Princeton Rd. S-2, Box 689, Hightstown, NJ 08520-0689. *888*

DODGE CONSTRUCTION NEWS WEEKLY COVERING THE LEHIGH VALLEY.
McGraw-Hill Companies, Princeton Rd. S-2, Box 689, Hightstown, NJ 08520-0689. *888*

DODGE CONSTRUCTION NEWS WEEKLY COVERING THE NORTH SHORE.
McGraw-Hill Companies, Princeton Rd. S-2, Box 689, Hightstown, NJ 08520-0689. *888*

DODGE CONSTRUCTION NEWS WEEKLY COVERING THE SOUTH SHORE.
McGraw-Hill Companies, Princeton Rd. S-2, Box 689, Hightstown, NJ 08520-0689. *888*

DODGE CONSTRUCTION NEWS WEEKLY COVERING TOLEDO AND VICINITY.
McGraw-Hill Companies, Princeton Rd. S-2, Box 689, Hightstown, NJ 08520-0689. *888*

DODGE CONSTRUCTION NEWS WEEKLY COVERING VERMONT.
McGraw-Hill Companies, Princeton Rd. S-2, Box 689, Hightstown, NJ 08520-0689. *888*

DODGE CONSTRUCTION NEWS WEEKLY COVERING WAL-MART.
McGraw-Hill Companies, Princeton Rd. S-2, Box 689, Hightstown, NJ 08520-0689. *888*

DODGE CONSTRUCTION NEWS WEEKLY COVERING WASHINGTON GENERAL BUILDING.
McGraw-Hill Companies, Princeton Rd. S-2, Box 689, Hightstown, NJ 08520-0689. *888*

DODGE CONSTRUCTION NEWS WEEKLY COVERING WEST CENTRAL FLORIDA.
McGraw-Hill Companies, Princeton Rd. S-2, Box 689, Hightstown, NJ 08520-0689. *888*

DODGE CONSTRUCTION NEWS WEEKLY COVERING WEST PALM BEACH AND VICINITY.
McGraw-Hill Companies, Princeton Rd. S-2, Box 689, Hightstown, NJ 08520-0689. *888*

DODGE CONSTRUCTION NEWS WEEKLY COVERING WEST VIRGINIA.
McGraw-Hill Companies, Princeton Rd. S-2, Box 689, Hightstown, NJ 08520-0689. *888*

DODGE CONSTRUCTION NEWS WEEKLY COVERING WESTERN KENTUCKY.
McGraw-Hill Companies, Princeton Rd. S-2, Box 689, Hightstown, NJ 08520-0689. *888*

DODGE CONSTRUCTION NEWS WEEKLY COVERING WESTERN MASSACHUSETTS.
McGraw-Hill Companies, Princeton Rd. S-2, Box 689, Hightstown, NJ 08520-0689. *888*

DODGE CONSTRUCTION NEWS WEEKLY COVERING WESTERN MISSOURI.
McGraw-Hill Companies, Princeton Rd. S-2, Box 689, Hightstown, NJ 08520-0689. *888*

DODGE CONSTRUCTION NEWS WEEKLY COVERING WESTERN NORTH CAROLINA.
McGraw-Hill Companies, Princeton Rd. S-2, Box 689, Hightstown, NJ 08520-0689. *888*

DODGE CONSTRUCTION NEWS WEEKLY COVERING WESTERN OKLAHOMA.
McGraw-Hill Companies, Princeton Rd. S-2, Box 689, Hightstown, NJ 08520-0689. *888*

DODGE CONSTRUCTION NEWS WEEKLY COVERING WESTERN PENNSYLVANIA.
McGraw-Hill Companies, Princeton Rd. S-2, Box 689, Hightstown, NJ 08520-0689. *888*

DODGE CONSTRUCTION NEWS WEEKLY COVERING WINSTON - SALEM.
McGraw-Hill Companies, Princeton Rd. S-2, Box 689, Hightstown, NJ 08520-0689. *888*

DODGE CONSTRUCTION NEWS WEEKLY COVERING YOUNGSTOWN AND VICINITY.
McGraw-Hill Companies, Princeton Rd. S-2, Box 689, Hightstown, NJ 08520-0689. *888*

DODGE DAILY BULLETIN. AKRON - YOUNGSTOWN.
McGraw-Hill Companies, Princeton Rd. S-2, Box 689, Hightstown, NJ 08520-0689. *888*

DODGE DAILY BULLETIN. ALABAMA.
McGraw-Hill Companies, Princeton Rd. S-2, Box 689, Hightstown, NJ 08520-0689. *888*

DODGE DAILY BULLETIN. ARIZONA.
McGraw-Hill Companies, Princeton Rd. S-2, Box 689, Hightstown, NJ 08520-0689. *889*

DODGE DAILY BULLETIN. ATLANTA AND VICINITY ENGINEERING.
McGraw-Hill Companies, Princeton Rd. S-2, Box 689, Hightstown, NJ 08520-0689. *889*

DODGE DAILY BULLETIN. AUSTIN - SAN ANTONIO.
McGraw-Hill Companies, Princeton Rd. S-2, Box 689, Hightstown, NJ 08520-0689. *889*

DODGE DAILY BULLETIN. BALTIMORE.
McGraw-Hill Companies, Princeton Rd. S-2, Box 689, Hightstown, NJ 08520-0689. *889*

DODGE DAILY BULLETIN. BALTIMORE - DELAWARE.
McGraw-Hill Companies, Princeton Rd. S-2, Box 689, Hightstown, NJ 08520-0689. *889*

DODGE DAILY BULLETIN. BIRMINGHAM ENGINEERING.
McGraw-Hill Companies, Princeton Rd. S-2, Box 689, Hightstown, NJ 08520-0689. *889*

DODGE DAILY BULLETIN. BROWARD COUNTY.
McGraw-Hill Companies, Princeton Rd. S-2, Box 689, Hightstown, NJ 08520-0689. *889*

DODGE DAILY BULLETIN. BUFFALO AND VICINITY.
McGraw-Hill Companies, Princeton Rd. S-2, Box 689, Hightstown, NJ 08520-0689. *889*

DODGE DAILY BULLETIN. BUFFALO METRO.
McGraw-Hill Companies, Princeton Rd. S-2, Box 689, Hightstown, NJ 08520-0689. *889*

DODGE DAILY BULLETIN. CENTRAL PENNSYLVANIA.
McGraw-Hill Companies, Princeton Rd. S-2, Box 689, Hightstown, NJ 08520-0689. *889*

DODGE DAILY BULLETIN. CINCINNATI.
McGraw-Hill Companies, Princeton Rd. S-2, Box 689, Hightstown, NJ 08520-0689. *889*

DODGE DAILY BULLETIN. CLEVELAND AND VICINITY.
McGraw-Hill Companies, Princeton Rd. S-2, Box 689, Hightstown, NJ 08520-0689. *889*

DODGE DAILY BULLETIN. COLUMBUS.
McGraw-Hill Companies, Princeton Rd. S-2, Box 689, Hightstown, NJ 08520-0689. *889*

DODGE DAILY BULLETIN. CONNECTICUT.
McGraw-Hill Companies, Princeton Rd. S-2, Box 689, Hightstown, NJ 08520-0689. *889*

DODGE DAILY BULLETIN. DALLAS.
McGraw-Hill Companies, Princeton Rd. S-2, Box 689, Hightstown, NJ 08520-0689. *889*

DODGE DAILY BULLETIN. DETROIT.
McGraw-Hill Companies, Princeton Rd. S-2, Box 689, Hightstown, NJ 08520-0689. *889*

DODGE DAILY BULLETIN. DETROIT CENTRAL.
McGraw-Hill Companies, Princeton Rd. S-2, Box 689, Hightstown, NJ 08520-0689. *889*

DODGE DAILY BULLETIN. EASTERN & CENTRAL TENNESSEE.
McGraw-Hill Companies, Princeton Rd. S-2, Box 689, Hightstown, NJ 08520-0689. *889*

DODGE DAILY BULLETIN. EASTERN AND CENTRAL TENNESSEE ENGINEERING.
McGraw-Hill Companies, Princeton Rd. S-2, Box 689, Hightstown, NJ 08520-0689. *889*

DODGE DAILY BULLETIN. EASTERN MASSACHUSETTS.
McGraw-Hill Companies, Princeton Rd. S-2, Box 689, Hightstown, NJ 08520-0689. *889*

DODGE DAILY BULLETIN. EASTERN OKLAHOMA.
McGraw-Hill Companies, Princeton Rd. S-2, Box 689, Hightstown, NJ 08520-0689. *889*

DODGE DAILY BULLETIN. FIVE BOROS.
McGraw-Hill Companies, Princeton Rd. S-2, Box 689, Hightstown, NJ 08520-0689. *889*

DODGE DAILY BULLETIN. FORT WORTH.
McGraw-Hill Companies, Princeton Rd. S-2, Box 689, Hightstown, NJ 08520-0689. *889*

DODGE DAILY BULLETIN. FOUR BOROS.
McGraw-Hill Companies, Princeton Rd. S-2, Box 689, Hightstown, NJ 08520-0689. *889*

DODGE DAILY BULLETIN. GEORGIA.
McGraw-Hill Companies, Princeton Rd. S-2, Box 689, Hightstown, NJ 08520-0689. *889*

DODGE DAILY BULLETIN. GEORGIA ENGINEERING.
McGraw-Hill Companies, Princeton Rd. S-2, Box 689, Hightstown, NJ 08520-0689. *889*

DODGE DAILY BULLETIN. GREATER LEXINGTON AND VICINITY.
McGraw-Hill Companies, Princeton Rd. S-2, Box 689, Hightstown, NJ 08520-0689. *889*

DODGE DAILY BULLETIN. GREATER LOUISVILLE.
McGraw-Hill Companies, Princeton Rd. S-2, Box 689, Hightstown, NJ 08520-0689. *889*

DODGE DAILY BULLETIN. HOUSTON.
McGraw-Hill Companies, Princeton Rd. S-2, Box 689, Hightstown, NJ 08520-0689. *889*

DODGE DAILY BULLETIN. INDIANA.
McGraw-Hill Companies, Princeton Rd. S-2, Box 689, Hightstown, NJ 08520-0689. *889*

DODGE DAILY BULLETIN. JACKSONVILLE AND VICINITY.
McGraw-Hill Companies, Princeton Rd. S-2, Box 689, Hightstown, NJ 08520-0689. *890*

DODGE DAILY BULLETIN. KANSAS.
McGraw-Hill Companies, Princeton Rd. S-2, Box 689, Hightstown, NJ 08520-0689. *890*

DODGE DAILY BULLETIN. KANSAS CITY.
McGraw-Hill Companies, Princeton Rd. S-2, Box 689, Hightstown, NJ 08520-0689. *890*

DODGE DAILY BULLETIN. LONG ISLAND.
McGraw-Hill Companies, Princeton Rd. S-2, Box 689, Hightstown, NJ 08520-0689. *890*

DODGE DAILY BULLETIN. LOUISIANA.
McGraw-Hill Companies, Princeton Rd. S-2, Box 689, Hightstown, NJ 08520-0689. *890*

DODGE DAILY BULLETIN. MAINE - NEW HAMPSHIRE - VERMONT.
McGraw-Hill Companies, Princeton Rd. S-2, Box 689, Hightstown, NJ 08520-0689. *890*

DODGE DAILY BULLETIN. MANHATTAN.
McGraw-Hill Companies, Princeton Rd. S-2, Box 689, Hightstown, NJ 08520-0689. *890*

DODGE DAILY BULLETIN. MIAMI.
McGraw-Hill Companies, Princeton Rd. S-2, Box 689, Hightstown, NJ 08520-0689. *890*

DODGE DAILY BULLETIN. MIAMI ENGINEERING.
McGraw-Hill Companies, Princeton Rd. S-2, Box 689, Hightstown, NJ 08520-0689. *890*

DODGE DAILY BULLETIN. MINNEAPOLIS - ST. PAUL.
McGraw-Hill Companies, Princeton Rd. S-2, Box 689, Hightstown, NJ 08520-0689. *890*

DODGE DAILY BULLETIN. MINNESOTA - NORTHWEST WISCONSIN.
McGraw-Hill Companies, Princeton Rd. S-2, Box 689, Hightstown, NJ 08520-0689. *890*

DODGE DAILY BULLETIN. MISSISSIPPI.
McGraw-Hill Companies, Princeton Rd. S-2, Box 689, Hightstown, NJ 08520-0689. *890*

DODGE DAILY BULLETIN. NASSAU - SUFFOLK.
McGraw-Hill Companies, Princeton Rd. S-2, Box 689, Hightstown, NJ 08520-0689. *890*

DODGE DAILY BULLETIN. NEBRASKA & SOUTHWEST IOWA.
McGraw-Hill Companies, Princeton Rd. S-2, Box 689, Hightstown, NJ 08520-0689. *890*

DODGE DAILY BULLETIN. NEW MEXICO.
McGraw-Hill Companies, Princeton Rd. S-2, Box 689, Hightstown, NJ 08520-0689. *890*

DODGE DAILY BULLETIN. NEW MEXICO - WEST TEXAS.
McGraw-Hill Companies, Princeton Rd. S-2, Box 689, Hightstown, NJ 08520-0689. *890*

10098 SERIALS AVAILABLE ONLINE

DODGE DAILY BULLETIN. NEW ORLEANS.
McGraw-Hill Companies, Princeton Rd. S-2, Box 689, Hightstown, NJ 08520-0689. *890*

DODGE DAILY BULLETIN. NEW ORLEANS ENGINEERING.
McGraw-Hill Companies, Princeton Rd. S-2, Box 689, Hightstown, NJ 08520-0689. *890*

DODGE DAILY BULLETIN. NORTH & SOUTH DAKOTA.
McGraw-Hill Companies, Princeton Rd. S-2, Box 689, Hightstown, NJ 08520-0689. *890*

DODGE DAILY BULLETIN. NORTH CAROLINA.
McGraw-Hill Companies, Princeton Rd. S-2, Box 689, Hightstown, NJ 08520-0689. *890*

DODGE DAILY BULLETIN. NORTH CAROLINA ENGINEERING.
McGraw-Hill Companies, Princeton Rd. S-2, Box 689, Hightstown, NJ 08520-0689. *890*

DODGE DAILY BULLETIN. NORTHERN FLORIDA ENGINEERING.
McGraw-Hill Companies, Princeton Rd. S-2, Box 689, Hightstown, NJ 08520-0689. *890*

DODGE DAILY BULLETIN. NORTHERN NEW JERSEY.
McGraw-Hill Companies, Princeton Rd. S-2, Box 689, Hightstown, NJ 08520-0689. *890*

DODGE DAILY BULLETIN. NORTHWEST AND WEST TEXAS.
McGraw-Hill Companies, Princeton Rd. S-2, Box 689, Hightstown, NJ 08520-0689. *890*

DODGE DAILY BULLETIN. NORTHWEST FLORIDA.
McGraw-Hill Companies, Princeton Rd. S-2, Box 689, Hightstown, NJ 08520-0689. *890*

DODGE DAILY BULLETIN. ORLANDO AND VICINITY.
McGraw-Hill Companies, Princeton Rd. S-2, Box 689, Hightstown, NJ 08520-0689. *890*

DODGE DAILY BULLETIN. PALM BEACH.
McGraw-Hill Companies, Princeton Rd. S-2, Box 689, Hightstown, NJ 08520-0689. *890*

DODGE DAILY BULLETIN. PHILADELPHIA HOUSING.
McGraw-Hill Companies, Princeton Rd. S-2, Box 689, Hightstown, NJ 08520-0689. *890*

DODGE DAILY BULLETIN. PITTSBURGH.
McGraw-Hill Companies, Princeton Rd. S-2, Box 689, Hightstown, NJ 08520-0689. *890*

DODGE DAILY BULLETIN. RHODE ISLAND.
McGraw-Hill Companies, Princeton Rd. S-2, Box 689, Hightstown, NJ 08520-0689. *890*

DODGE DAILY BULLETIN. SOUTH CAROLINA.
McGraw-Hill Companies, Princeton Rd. S-2, Box 689, Hightstown, NJ 08520-0689. *891*

DODGE DAILY BULLETIN. SOUTH CAROLINA ENGINEERING.
McGraw-Hill Companies, Princeton Rd. S-2, Box 689, Hightstown, NJ 08520-0689. *891*

DODGE DAILY BULLETIN. SOUTHERN MICHIGAN PENINSULA.
McGraw-Hill Companies, Princeton Rd. S-2, Box 689, Hightstown, NJ 08520-0689. *891*

DODGE DAILY BULLETIN. SOUTHERN NEW JERSEY AND PHILADELPHIA HOUSING.
McGraw-Hill Companies, Princeton Rd. S-2, Box 689, Hightstown, NJ 08520-0689. *891*

DODGE DAILY BULLETIN. TEXAS ENGINEERING.
McGraw-Hill Companies, Princeton Rd. S-2, Box 689, Hightstown, NJ 08520-0689. *891*

DODGE DAILY BULLETIN. TOLEDO.
McGraw-Hill Companies, Princeton Rd. S-2, Box 689, Hightstown, NJ 08520-0689. *891*

DODGE DAILY BULLETIN. UTAH.
McGraw-Hill Companies, Princeton Rd. S-2, Box 689, Hightstown, NJ 08520-0689. *891*

DODGE DAILY BULLETIN. WASHINGTON AND VICINITY.
McGraw-Hill Companies, Princeton Rd. S-2, Box 689, Hightstown, NJ 08520-0689. *891*

DODGE DAILY BULLETIN. WEST CENTRAL FLORIDA.
McGraw-Hill Companies, Princeton Rd. S-2, Box 689, Hightstown, NJ 08520-0689. *891*

DODGE DAILY BULLETIN. WESTCHESTER.
McGraw-Hill Companies, Princeton Rd. S-2, Box 689, Hightstown, NJ 08520-0689. *891*

DODGE DAILY BULLETIN. WESTERN MASSACHUSETTS.
McGraw-Hill Companies, Princeton Rd. S-2, Box 689, Hightstown, NJ 08520-0689. *891*

DODGE DAILY BULLETIN. WESTERN MISSOURI.
McGraw-Hill Companies, Princeton Rd. S-2, Box 689, Hightstown, NJ 08520-0689. *891*

DODGE DAILY BULLETIN. WESTERN OKLAHOMA.
McGraw-Hill Companies, Princeton Rd. S-2, Box 689, Hightstown, NJ 08520-0689. *891*

DODGE DAILY BULLETIN. WICHITA.
McGraw-Hill Companies, Princeton Rd. S-2, Box 689, Hightstown, NJ 08520-0689. *891*

DOLLARS & SENSE.
Economic Affairs Bureau, Inc., One Summer St., Somerville, MA 02143. TEL 617-628-8411. FAX 617-628-2025. URL: http://www.igc.apc.org/dollars.
Vendor(s): Information Access Co. *1252*

DOLLARSENSE.
E.F. Baumer & Company, 401 Shatto Pl., Ste. 105, Los Angeles, CA 90020. TEL 213-386-2111. FAX 213-386-6470. *1128*

DOMINION LAW REPORTS.
Canada Law Book Inc., 240 Edward St., Aurora, ON L4G 3S9, Canada. TEL 905-841-6472. FAX 905-841-5085. *3942*

DONOSY.
Bajonska 3, 03-963 Warsaw, Poland. TEL 48-22-6177985.
Available only online. *3348*

DOOMED TO OBSCURITY.
Box 2257, Philadelphia, PA 19103. URL: http://www.dto.net.
Available only online. *4398*

DOOMSDAY HOUSTON.
Paradise Online Service, 11306 Briar Rose, Houston, TX 77077-6432. TEL 713-597-4049. URL: http://paradise.pplnet.com/doomsday/.
Available only online. *5389*

DOORS AND HARDWARE.
Door and Hardware Institute, 14170 Newbrook Dr., Chantilly, VA 20151. TEL 703-222-2010. FAX 703-222-2410. URL: http://www.dhi.org.
Vendor(s): Information Access Co. *927*

DOWN BEAT.
Maher Publications, Inc., 102 N. Haven Rd., Elmhurst, IL 60126. TEL 708-941-2030. FAX 708-941-3210.
Vendor(s): Information Access Co., UMI. *5389*

DOWN UNDER TRAVELLERS WEBZINE.
URL: http://www.south-pacific.com.travel-zine.
Available only online. *7196*

DOWNSTATE ILLINOIS BUSINESS DIRECTORY.
American Business Directories, 5711 S. 86th Circle, Box 27347, Omaha, NE 68127. TEL 402-593-4600. FAX 402-331-5481. *1672*

DOWNSTREAM TRENDS.
Arab Press Service, A P S House, P.O. Box 3896, Nicosia, Cyprus. TEL 357-2-351778. FAX 357-2-350265.
Vendor(s): Information Access Co. *2662*

DR. DOBB'S JOURNAL.
Miller Freeman, Inc., 600 Harrison St., San Francisco, CA 94107. TEL 415-905-2200. FAX 415-905-2232.
Vendor(s): Information Access Co. *2188*

DRAGOCO REPORT.
Dragoco Gerberding & Co. AG, Dragocostr., 37601 Holzminden, Germany. TEL 49-5531-97-0. FAX 49-5531-971391. *510*

DRAKE LAW REVIEW.
Drake University, Law School, Cartwright Hall, Des Moines, IA 50311. TEL 515-271-2930. FAX 515-271-4926.
Vendor(s): West Group. *3942*

DREAMPOP.
22 Terra Vista Ave., No. G12, San Francisco, CA 94115. URL: http://www.rock.com/dreampop.
Available only online. *5389*

DREAMS AND DRAGONS.
URL: http://www.vic.com/'jclark/.
Available only online. *4399*

DREAMSCAPE.
520 Washington Blvd., Ste. 339, Marina del Rey, CA 90292. TEL 310-822-1583. FAX 310-822-0163. URL: http://www.dreams.com/dreamscape.pl. *2516*

DRUG ABUSE.
Swedish Council for Information on Alcohol and other Drugs (CAN), Documentation Center, P.O. Box 27302, S-102 54 Stockholm, Sweden. FAX 46-8-661-64-84. *2300*

DRUG AND CHEMICAL TOXICOLOGY.
Marcel Dekker Journals, 270 Madison Ave., New York, NY 10016. TEL 212-696-9000. FAX 212-685-4540. *5656*

DRUG AND COSMETIC INDUSTRY.
Advanstar Communications, Inc., 7500 Old Oak Blvd., Cleveland, OH 44130. TEL 216-826-2839. FAX 216-891-2726.
Vendor(s): Information Access Co., Knight-Ridder Information, Inc., UMI. *510*

DRUG DATA REPORT.
J.R. Prous, S.A. International Publishers, Apdo. de Correos 540, 08080 Barcelona, Spain. TEL 343-459-2220. FAX 343-458-1535.
Vendor(s): Knight-Ridder Information, Inc. *5656*

DRUG DESIGN AND DISCOVERY.
Gordon and Breach - Harwood Academic, Amsteldisk 166, 1st Fl., 1079 LH Amsterdam, Netherlands. URL: http://www.gbhap.com/Drug_Design_Discovery/. *5656*

DRUG DETECTION REPORT.
Pace Publications, 443 Park Ave. S., New York, NY 10016. TEL 212-685-5450. FAX 212-679-4701.
Vendor(s): Information Access Co. *1564*

DRUG DEVELOPMENT AND INDUSTRIAL PHARMACY.
Marcel Dekker Journals, 270 Madison Ave., New York, NY 10016. TEL 212-696-9000. FAX 212-685-4540. *5657*

DRUG FACTS AND COMPARISONS.
Facts and Comparisons, 111 W. Port Plaza, Ste. 300, St. Louis, MO 63146-3098. FAX 314-878-5563. *5657*

DRUG INFORMATION JOURNAL.
Drug Information Association, Box 3113, Maple Glen, PA 19002. TEL 215-628-2288. FAX 215-641-1229. *5657*

DRUG NEWS & PERSPECTIVES.
J.R. Prous, S.A. International Publishers, Apdo. de Correos 540, 08080 Barcelona, Spain. TEL 343-459-2220. FAX 343-458-1535.
Vendor(s): Knight-Ridder Information, Inc. *5657*

DRUG RESISTANCE WEEKLY.
Charles W. Henderson, Ed. & Pub., Box 5528, Atlanta, GA 31107-0528. TEL 404-377-8895. FAX 404-378-5411.
Vendor(s): Information Access Co. *5658*

DRUG STORE NEWS.
Lebhar-Friedman, Inc., 425 Park Ave., New York, NY 10022. TEL 212-756-5000.
Vendor(s): Information Access Co., Lexis-Nexis. *1525*

DRUG TOPICS.
Medical Economics Publishing Co., Inc., 5 Paragon Dr., Montvale, NJ 07645. TEL 201-358-7200. FAX 201-573-1045.
Vendor(s): Information Access Co., UMI. *5658*

DRUGS MADE IN GERMANY.
Editio Cantor, Postfach 1255, 88322 Aulendorf, Germany. TEL 49-7525-940135. FAX 49-7525-940180. URL: http://www.ecv.de. *5659*

THE DUELIST.
Wizards of the Coast, Box 707, Renton, WA 98057. TEL 206-204-8000. FAX 206-204-5928. URL: http://www.wizards.com/Duelist_Online> *6759*

DUKE LAW JOURNAL.
Duke University, School of Law, Box 90364, Durham, NC 27708-0364. TEL 919-613-7101. FAX 919-613-7231.
Vendor(s): Lexis-Nexis, West Group. *3943*

DULUTHIAN.
Duluth Area Chamber of Commerce, 118 E. Superior St., Duluth, MN 55802. TEL 218-722-5501.
Vendor(s): UMI. *1186*

DUQUESNE LAW REVIEW.
Duquesne University, Duquesne School of Law, 900 Locust St., Pittsburgh, PA 15282. TEL 412-396-6297. FAX 412-396-6294.
Vendor(s): West Group. *3943*

DUTCHESS COUNTY HISTORICAL SOCIETY. YEARBOOK.
Dutchess County Historical Society, Box 88, Poughkeepsie, NY 12602.
Vendor(s): Knight-Ridder Information, Inc. *3625*

DYNAMIC BUSINESS.
S M C Business Councils, 1400 S. Braddock Ave., Pittsburgh, PA 15218-1264. TEL 412-371-1500. FAX 412-371-0460. URL: http://www.smc.org. *1641*

DYSPHAGIA.
Springer-Verlag, Medical Journals, 175 Fifth Ave., New York, NY 10010. TEL 212-460-1500. FAX 212-473-6272. URL: http://www.springer-ny.com. *5021*

E A JOURNAL.
National Association of Enrolled Agents, 200 Orchard Ridge Dr., Ste. 302, Gaithersburg, MD 20878-1978. TEL 301-212-9608. FAX 301-990-1611. URL: http://www.naea.org. *1607*

E & P ENVIRONMENT.
J & E Communications, Inc., 6804 Hwy. 6 S., Ste. 394, Houston, TX 77083. TEL 713-879-7828.
Vendor(s): Information Access Co., NewsNet. *5599*

E B QUARTERLY.
American Bankers Association, 1120 Connecticut Ave., N.W., Washington, DC 20036. TEL 202-663-5087. FAX 202-663-7543.
Vendor(s): UMI. *1128*

E C ENERGY MONTHLY.
Financial Times Energy Publishing, Maple House, 149 Tottenham Court Rd., London W1P 9LL, England. TEL 44-171-896-2241. FAX 44-171-896-2275.
Vendor(s): Data-Star, Information Access Co., Knight-Ridder Information, Inc., Lexis-Nexis. *2663*

E C H O FACTS FOR USERS.
European Commission Host Organization, P.O. Box 2373, L-1023 Luxembourg, Luxembourg. TEL 352-401162-200. FAX 352-401162-234. URL: http://www.echo.lu/ *2132*

E D F LETTER.
Environmental Defense Fund, 257 Park Ave. S., New York, NY 10010. TEL 212-505-2100. FAX 212-505-2375. URL: http://www.edf.org/pubs/EDF-Letter/ *2913*

E D I NEWS.
Phillips Business Information, Inc., 1201 Seven Locks Rd., Potomac, MD 20854. TEL 301-424-3338. FAX 301-309-3847.
Vendor(s): Information Access Co., NewsNet (TE80). *2169*

E D N MAGAZINE.
Cahners Publishing Company (Newton), Division of Reed Elsevier Inc., 275 Washington St., Newton, MA 02158-1630. TEL 617-558-4454. FAX 617-558-4470. URL: http://www.ednmag.com.
Vendor(s): Information Access Co., Knight-Ridder Information, Inc. *2629*

E D P WEEKLY.
Computer Age & E D P News Services, 714 Church St., Alexandria, VA 22314-4202. TEL 703-739-8500. FAX 703-739-8505.
Vendor(s): Information Access Co. *2173*

E D U Q.
Services Documentaires Multimedia Inc., 75 Port-Royal E., bureau 300, Montreal, PQ H3L 3T1, Canada. TEL 514-382-0895. FAX 514-384-9139. URL: http://www.sdm.qc.ca. *2498*

E E I ENVIRONMENTAL DIRECTORY OF U.S. POWER PLANTS.
Utility Data Institute, 1200 G St., N.W., Ste. 250, Washington, DC 20005. TEL 202-942-8788. FAX 202-942-8789. URL: http://udidata.inter.net/udidata. *2815*

E F T REPORT.
Phillips Business Information, Inc., 1201 Seven Locks Rd., Potomac, MD 20854. TEL 301-424-3338. FAX 301-309-3847.
Vendor(s): Information Access Co., Knight-Ridder Information, Inc., Lexis-Nexis, NewsNet (FI11). *1175*

E FOR ENVIRONMENT.
R.R. Bowker, A Division of Reed Elsevier Inc., 121 Chanlon Rd., New Providence, NJ 07974. TEL 908-464-6800. FAX 908-665-6688. URL: http://www.reedref.com. *2913*

E I A PUBLICATIONS DIRECTORY.
U.S. Energy Information Administration, National Energy Information Center, EI-231, James Forrestal Bldg., Rm. 1F-048, 1000 Independence Ave., S.W., Washington, DC 20585. TEL 202-568-8800. FAX 202-586-0727. URL: http://www.eia.doe.gov. *2663*

E L H.
Johns Hopkins University Press, Journals Publishing Division, 2715 N. Charles St., Baltimore, MD 21218. TEL 410-516-6987. FAX 410-516-6968. URL: http://muse.jhu.edu/journals/elh/v60/
Vendor(s): Information Access Co. *4399*

E L T JOURNAL.
Oxford University Press, Academic Division, Great Clarendon St., Oxford OX2 6DP, England. TEL 44-1865-267907. FAX 44-1865-267485. URL: http://www.oup.co.uk/journals. *4253*

E LAW.
Murdoch University, School of Law, Perth, W.A. 6150, Australia. FAX 61-9-3106671. URL: http://www.murdoch.edu.au/elaw.
Available only online. *3943*

E-LETTER ON SYSTEMS, CONTROL, & SIGNAL PROCESSING.
Eindhoven University of Technology, Department of Mathematics & Computing Science, P.O. Box 513, 5600 MB Eindhoven, Netherlands. TEL 31-10-472378. FAX 31-40-465995.
Available only online. *2154*

THE E M B O JOURNAL.
Oxford University Press, Academic Division, Great Clarendon St., Oxford OX2 6DP, England. TEL 44-1865-267907. FAX 44-1865-267485. URL: http://www.oup.co.uk/journals. *659*

E M F KEEPTRACK.
Center for Energy Information, One Grandview Place, Winthrop, ME 04364.
Vendor(s): NewsNet. *2663*

E M M S.
Telecommunications Reports, 1333 H St., N.W., No.100-E., Washington, DC 20005. TEL 202-842-3022. FAX 202-842-1875.
Vendor(s): Information Access Co., NewsNet (EC32). *1988*

E N A.
Austrian Press and Information Service, 3524 International Ct., N.W., Washington, DC 20008-3035. TEL 202-895-6775. FAX 202-895-6772. URL: http://www.austria.org/ *1252*

E N B NEWS.
English National Board for Nursing, Midwifery, and Health Visiting, Victory House, 170 Tottenham Ct. Rd., London W1P OHA, England. TEL 44-171-388-3131. FAX 44-171-383-4031. URL: http://www.eng.org.uk. *4932*

E N D S ENVIRONMENT DAILY.
40 Bowling Green Ln., London EC1R 0NR, England. TEL 44-171-278-4745. URL: http://www.ends.co.uk/envdaily.
Available only online. *2914*

E - N F A I S NOTES.
National Federation of Abstracting and Information Services, 1518 Walnut St., Ste. 307, Philadelphia, PA 19102. TEL 215-893-1561. FAX 215-893-1564.
Available only online. *11*

E N I BULLETIN.
Ecumenical News International, P.O. Box 2100, CH-1211 Geneva 2, Switzerland. TEL 41-22-76087. FAX 41-22-7981346. *6335*

E N R.
McGraw-Hill Companies, 1221 Ave. of the Americas, New York, NY 10020. TEL 212-512-2000. FAX 212-512-2565. URL: http://www.enr.com/meet/meet.html.
Vendor(s): Dow Jones News Retrieval (ENR), Information Access Co., Knight-Ridder Information, Inc. (File no.624/McGRAW-HILL PUBLICATIONS ONLINE), Lexis-Nexis (ENR), NewsNet (BC06). *2783*

E.P. MAGAZINE.
Vigilante Publications, Huntingdon House, 35 Field Rd., Reading, Berks RG1 6AP, England. TEL 44-1734-581878. FAX 44-1734-581878. URL: http://www.vigilante.co.uk. *5389*

E P S L ONLINE.
Elsevier Science B.V., P.O. Box 211, 1000 AE Amsterdam, Netherlands. TEL 31-20-4853911. FAX 31-20-4853705. URL: http://www.elsevier.nl/locate/epsl.
Available only online. *2313*

E R I C CLEARINGHOUSE ON URBAN EDUCATION. DIGEST.
E R I C Clearinghouse on Urban Education, Box 40, Teachers College, Columbia University, New York, NY 10027. TEL 212-678-3433. FAX 212-678-4012. URL: http://eric-web.tc.columbia.edu/.
Vendor(s): The Source. *2434*

E S E NOTES.
University of North Carolina at Chapel Hill, School of Public Health, CB 7400, Chapel Hill, NC 27599-7400. TEL 919-966-1024. FAX 919-966-2583. URL: http://www.sph.unc.edu/envr/esenotes.htm. *2914*

E U D I S E D - EUROPEAN EDUCATIONAL RESEARCH YEARBOOK.
K.G. Saur Verlag KG, A member of the Reed Elsevier plc group, Ortlerstr. 8, 81373 Munich, Germany. TEL 49-89-76902-0. FAX 49-89-76902150. URL: http://www.reed-elsevier.com.
Vendor(s): European Space Agency (File no.24/EUDISED R&D). *2499*

E V A: THE ELECTRONIC VISUAL ARTS JOURNAL.
University of Western Ontario, 1341 Birmingham St., Halifax N.S., B3J 2J3, Canada. URL: http://www.uwo.ca/visarts/eva.html.
Available only online. *439*

EAR AND HEARING.
Williams & Wilkins, 351 W. Camden St., Baltimore, MD 21201-2436. TEL 410-528-4068. FAX 410-528-4452. URL: http://www.wwilkins.com.
Vendor(s): Ovid Technologies, Inc. *5021*

THE EARLY AMERICA REVIEW.
Box 11410, Bainbridge Island, WA 98110. URL: http://earlyamerica.com/review/.
Available only online. *3625*

EARLY AMERICAN HOMES.
Cowles Enthusiast Media, History Group, 6405 Flank Dr., Box 8200, Harrisburg, PA 17105-8200. TEL 717-657-9555. FAX 717-657-9526.
Vendor(s): Information Access Co. *3854*

SERIALS AVAILABLE ONLINE

EARLY AMERICAN LITERATURE.
University of North Carolina Press, Box 2288, Chapel Hill, NC 27515-2288. TEL 919-966-3561. FAX 800-272-6817.
Vendor(s): UMI. *4400*

EARLY MUSIC.
Oxford University Press, Academic Division, Great Clarendon St., Oxford OX2 6DP, England. TEL 44-1865-267773. FAX 44-1865-267485. URL: http://www.oup.co.uk/journals.
Vendor(s): Information Access Co. *5390*

EARNINGS GUIDE ON P C.
Box 1, Horsham, W. Sussex RH12 3YY, England. TEL 0403-791155. FAX 0403-701152. *1129*

EARTH AND PLANETARY SCIENCE LETTERS.
Elsevier Science B.V., P.O. Box 211, 1000 AE Amsterdam, Netherlands. TEL 31-20-4853911. FAX 31-20-4853598. URL: http://www.elsevier.nl/locate/epsl. *2313*

EARTH ISLAND JOURNAL.
Earth Island Institute, 300 Broadway, Ste. 28, San Francisco, CA 94133-3312. TEL 415-788-3666. FAX 415-788-7324. URL: http://www.earthisland.org/
Vendor(s): UMI. *2914*

EARTH OBSERVER.
U.S. National Aeronautics and Space Administration, Earth Observing System Project, Goddard Space Flight Center, Greenbelt, MD 20771. TEL 301-286-3411. FAX 301-286-1738. URL: http://eospso.gsfc.nasa.gov/earth_observ.html. *64*

EARTHQUAKE ENGINEERING ABSTRACTS DATABASE.
University of California at Berkeley, Earthquake Engineering Research Center, 1301 S. 46th St., Richmond, CA 94804-4698. TEL 510-231-9401. FAX 510-231-9461. *2749*

EAST ASIAN BUSINESS INTELLIGENCE.
International Executive Reports, Ltd., 717 D St., N.W., Ste. 300, Washington, DC 20004-2807. TEL 202-628-6900. FAX 202-628-6618.
Vendor(s): Lexis-Nexis. *1322*

EAST ASIAN EXECUTIVE REPORTS.
International Executive Reports, Ltd., 717 D St., N.W., Ste. 300, Washington, DC 20004-2807. TEL 202-628-6900. FAX 202-628-6618.
Vendor(s): Lexis-Nexis, UMI, West Group. *1252*

EAST EUROPE AGRICULTURE & FOOD.
Agra Europe (London) Ltd., 25 Frant Rd., Tunbridge Wells, Kent TN2 5JT, England. TEL 44-1892-533813. FAX 44-1892-544895.
Vendor(s): Information Access Co. *1675*

EAST EUROPE & THE REPUBLICS: A POLITICAL RISK ANNUAL.
The P R S Group, Box 248, East Syracuse, NY 13057-0248. TEL 315-431-0511. FAX 315-431-0200.
Vendor(s): Data-Star (FSRI), Lexis-Nexis (IBCRPT). *1252*

EAST EUROPEAN ENERGY REPORT.
Financial Times Energy Publishing, Maple House, 149 Tottenham Court Rd., London W1P 9LL, England. TEL 0171-896-2241. FAX 0171-896-2275.
Vendor(s): Data-Star, Knight-Ridder Information, Inc., Lexis-Nexis. *2663*

EAST EUROPEAN INSURANCE REPORT.
Financial Times Financial Publishing, Maple House, 149 Tottenham Court Rd., London W1P 9LL, England. TEL 44-171-896-2314. FAX 44-171-896-2319.
Vendor(s): Information Access Co. *3815*

EAST EUROPEAN MARKETS.
Pearson Professional Ltd., Financial Times Newsletters and Management Reports Maple House, 149 Tottenham Court Rd., London W1P 9LL, England. TEL 44-171-896-2325. FAX 44-171-896-2333.
Vendor(s): Data-Star, Information Access Co., Lexis-Nexis. *1525*

EAST EUROPEAN POLITICS & SOCIETIES.
University of California Press, Journals Division, 2120 Berkeley Way, No. 5812, Berkeley, CA 94720-5812. TEL 510-643-7154. FAX 510-642-9917. URL: http://library.berkeley.edu:8080/ucalpress/journals.
Vendor(s): Information Access Co. *5922*

EAST EUROPEAN QUARTERLY.
East European Quarterly, University of Colorado, Box 29, Regent Hall, Boulder, CO 80309. TEL 941-753-4782.
Vendor(s): Information Access Co., UMI. *6611*

THE EAST YORK OBSERVER.
Centennial College, P.O. Box 631, Stn. A, Scarborough, ON M1K 5E9, Canada. TEL 416-289-5107. FAX 416-289-5111. URL: http://www.bccc.com. *3260*

EASTERN ECONOMIC JOURNAL.
Eastern Economic Association, Iona College, New Rochelle, NY 10801. TEL 610-559-8050. FAX 610-250-8961. URL: http://www.iona.edu/eea.thm.
Vendor(s): UMI. *955*

EBONY.
Johnson Publishing Co., Inc., 820 S. Michigan Ave., Chicago, IL 60605. TEL 312-322-9200. FAX 312-322-9375.
Vendor(s): Information Access Co., UMI. *3009*

ECCENTRICITY.
9822 St. Cloud Ct., Fairfax, VA 22031. URL: http://mason.gmu.edu/~bcheatha. *4508*

ECHO MAGAZINE.
Ace Publishing, Inc., Box 16630, Phoenix, AZ 85011-6639. TEL 602-266-0550. FAX 602-266-0773. *3693*

ECHOCARDIOGRAPHY JOURNAL OF CARDIAC ULTRASOUND.
Available only online. *4816*

ECO-LOG WEEK.
Southam Information Products Ltd., 1450 Don Mills Rd., Don Mills, ON M3B 2X7, Canada. TEL 416-445-6641. FAX 416-442-2200.
Vendor(s): Information Access Co., Southam Electronic Publishing. *2961*

ECOCENTRAL.
University of New Mexico, Latin American Institute, 801 Yale N.E., Albuquerque, NM 87131-1016. TEL 505-277-6839. FAX 505-277-5989. URL: http://www.ladb.unm.edu/.
Vendor(s): Knight-Ridder Information, Inc., Lexis-Nexis, NewsNet. *1358*

ECOLOGIA E DESENVOLVIMENTO.
Editora Terceiro Mundo, Rua da Gloria, 122, 105-106, 20241-180 Rio de Janeiro, Brasil. TEL 55-21-2217511. FAX 55-21-2528455. URL: http://www.etm.netune.com.br. *2915*

ECOLOGICAL ABSTRACTS.
Elsevier - Geo Abstracts, Regency House, 34 Duke St., Norwich NR3 3AP, England. TEL 44-1603-626327. FAX 44-1603-667934.
Vendor(s): Knight-Ridder Information, Inc. (File no.292), Questel Orbit Inc. (GEOB). *640*

ECOLOGICAL APPLICATIONS.
Ecological Society of America, 2010 Massachusetts Ave., N.W., Ste. 400, Washington, DC 20036. TEL 202-833-8773. FAX 202-833-8775. URL: http://www.sdsc.eta/~esa/ *2915*

ECOLOGICAL MONOGRAPHS.
Ecological Society of America, 2010 Massachusetts Ave., N.W., Ste. 400, Washington, DC 20036. TEL 202-833-8773. FAX 202-833-8775. URL: http://www.sdsc.eta/~esa/
Vendor(s): Information Access Co., UMI. *2915*

THE ECOLOGIST.
Ecosystems Ltd., Agriculture House, Bath Rd., Sturminster Newton, Dorset DT10 1DU, England. TEL 44-1258-473476. FAX 44-1258-473748. URL: http://www.gold.net/ecosystem/eclog.htm.
Vendor(s): Information Access Co. *2915*

ECOLOGY.
Ecological Society of America, 2010 Massachusetts Ave., N.W., Ste. 400, Washington, DC 20036. TEL 202-833-8773. FAX 202-833-8775. URL: http://www.sdsc.eta/~esa/
Vendor(s): Information Access Co., UMI. *2916*

ECOLOGY ABSTRACTS.
Cambridge Scientific Abstracts, 7200 Wisconsin Ave., 6th Fl., Bethesda, MD 20814. TEL 301-961-6750. FAX 301-961-6720. URL: http://www.csa.com.
Vendor(s): Knight-Ridder Information, Inc. (File no.76/LIFE SCIENCES COLLECTION), STN International. *2961*

ECONEWS.
Northcoast Environmental Center, Inc., 879 Ninth St., Arcata, CA 95521. TEL 707-822-6918. FAX 707-822-0827.
Vendor(s): CompuServe, Inc. *2916*

ECONOMETRICA.
Blackwell Publishers Ltd., 108 Cowley Rd., Oxford OX4 1JF, England. TEL 44-1865-791100. FAX 44-1865-791347. URL: http://www.blackwellpublishers.co.uk. *956*

ECONOMIC COMMENTARY.
Federal Reserve Bank of Cleveland, Box 6387, Cleveland, OH 44101. TEL 216-579-3079. FAX 216-579-2477.
Vendor(s): Information Access Co., UMI. *957*

ECONOMIC DEVELOPMENT REVIEW.
American Economic Development Council, 9801 W. Higgins Rd., Ste. 540, Rosemont, IL 60018-4726. TEL 847-692-9944. FAX 847-696-2990. URL: http://www.aedc.org/hqtrs.
Vendor(s): UMI. *1583*

ECONOMIC GEOGRAPHY.
Clark University, 950 Main St., Worcester, MA 01610-1477. TEL 508-793-7311. FAX 508-793-8881.
Vendor(s): Information Access Co., UMI. *3401*

ECONOMIC INDICATORS (WASHINGTON).
U.S. Executive Office of the President, Council of Economic Advisers, Executive Office Bldg., Washington, DC 20500. TEL 202-395-5062.
Vendor(s): Information Access Co., Knight-Ridder Information, Inc. *1254*

ECONOMIC INQUIRY.
Western Economic Association International, 7400 Center Ave., Ste. 109, Huntington Beach, CA 92647. TEL 714-898-3222.
Vendor(s): Information Access Co., Knight-Ridder Information, Inc. *958*

ECONOMIC JOURNAL.
Blackwell Publishers Ltd., 108 Cowley Rd., Oxford OX4 1JF, England. TEL 44-1865-791100. FAX 44-1865-791347. URL: http://www.blackwellpublishers.co.uk.
Vendor(s): Information Access Co. *958*

ECONOMIC OPPORTUNITY REPORT.
Business Publishers, Inc., 951 Pershing Dr., Silver Spring, MD 20910-4464. TEL 301-587-6300. FAX 301-585-9075.
Vendor(s): NewsNet. *6664*

ECONOMIC OUTLOOK.
Blackwell Publishers Ltd., 108 Cowley Rd., Oxford OX4 1JF, England. TEL 44-1865-791100. FAX 44-1865-791347. URL: http://www.blackwellpublishers.co.uk. *1254*

ECONOMIC PERSPECTIVES (CHICAGO).
Federal Reserve Bank of Chicago, Public Information Center, Box 834, Chicago, IL 60690. TEL 312-322-5112.
Vendor(s): Information Access Co., UMI. *1254*

ECONOMIC RECORD.
Economic Society of Australia, c/o R.A. Williams, Ed., Dept. of Economics, Melbourne University, Melbourne, Vic. 3052, Australia. TEL 61-3-93447426. FAX 61-3-93446899.
Vendor(s): Information Access Co., UMI. *958*

ECONOMIC REPORT OF THE PRESIDENT.
U.S. Executive Office of the President, Council of Economic Advisers, Washington, DC 20500. TEL 202-395-7332. *1254*

ECONOMIC REVIEW.
Economic and Industrial Publications, Al-Masiha, 47 Abdullah Haroon Rd., P.O. Box 7843, Karachi 74400, Pakistan.
Vendor(s): Information Access Co. *958*

ECONOMIC REVIEW.
Federal Reserve Bank of Cleveland, Box 6387, Cleveland, OH 44101. TEL 216-579-3079. FAX 216-579-2477.
Vendor(s): UMI. *1129*

ECONOMIC THEORY.
Springer-Verlag, Heidelberger Platz 3, 14197 Berlin, Germany. TEL 49-30-82787-0. FAX 49-30-82787448. URL: http://link.springer.de. *1302*

ECONOMIC TRENDS (CLEVELAND).
Federal Reserve Bank of Cleveland, Box 6387, Cleveland, OH 44101. TEL 216-579-3079. FAX 216-579-2477. *1255*

ECONOMISCH-STATISTISCHE BERICHTEN.
Nederlands Economisch Instituut, P.O. Box 4224, 3006 AE Rotterdam, Netherlands. TEL 31-10-4538743. FAX 31-10-4525840. *1255*

ECONOMIST.
Mainichi Shinbun Sha, 1-1-1 Hitotsubashi, Chiyoda-ku, Tokyo 100-51, Japan. TEL 81-3-3213-3711. FAX 81-3-3213-3724.
Vendor(s): UMI. *1255*

THE ECONOMIST.
Economist Newspaper Ltd., 25 St. James's St., London SW1A 1HG, England. TEL 44-171-830-7000. FAX 44-171-839-2968. URL: http://www.economist.com.
Vendor(s): Information Access Co., Lexis-Nexis, MediaStream. *1256*

ECOTOXICOLOGY.
Chapman & Hall, Journals Department 2-6 Boundary Row, London SE1 8HN, England. TEL 44-171-8650066. FAX 44-171-5229623. URL: http://www.chaphall.com/chaphall/journals.html. *2976*

ECOTOXICOLOGY AND ENVIRONMENTAL SAFETY.
Academic Press, Inc., Journal Division, 525 B St., Ste. 1900, San Diego, CA 92101-4495. TEL 619-250-1840. FAX 619-699-6800. URL: http://www.apnet.com/www/journal/es.htm; http://www.idealibrary.com/ *2977*

ECQUID NOVI.
Institute for Communication Research, Potchefstroom University, Potchefstroom 2520, South Africa. TEL 27-148-2991648. FAX 27-148-2991651. *3872*

ECUMENICAL NEWS INTERNATIONAL.
Ecumenical News International, 150 route de Ferney, P.O. Box 2100, CH-1211 Geneva 2, Switzerland. TEL 41-22-76087. FAX 41-22-7981346. *6336*

ECUMENICAL REVIEW.
World Council of Churches, 150 route de Ferney, P.O. Box 2100, CH-1211 Geneva 2, Switzerland. TEL 41-22-791-6111. FAX 41-22-791-0361.
Vendor(s): Information Access Co., UMI. *6336*

ED NET BRIEFS.
Class I V Publications, Inc., URL: http://www.classIV.com.
Available only online. *2435*

EDITOR & PUBLISHER MARKET GUIDE.
Editor & Publisher Co., Inc., 11 W. 19th St., New York, NY 10011. TEL 212-675-4380. FAX 212-929-1259. URL: http://www.mediainfo.com. *1525*

EDITOR & PUBLISHER - THE FOURTH ESTATE.
Editor & Publisher Co., Inc., 11 W. 19th St., New York, NY 10011. TEL 212-675-4380. FAX 212-929-1259. URL: http://www.mediainfo.com.
Vendor(s): Information Access Co. *3872*

EDITORS ONLY.
Editors Only Publications, Box 17108, Fountain Hills, AZ 85269. TEL 602-837-6492. FAX 602-837-6872.
Vendor(s): NewsNet (PB13). *3872*

EDMONTON CHAMBER OF COMMERCE. COMMERCE NEWS.
Edmonton Chamber of Commerce, Suite 600, 10123-99 St., Edmonton, AB T5J 3G9, Canada. TEL 403-426-4620. FAX 403-424-7946.
Vendor(s): UMI. *1186*

THE EDMONTON JOURNAL.
P.O. Box 2421, Edmonton, AB T5J 2S6, Canada. TEL 403-429-5100. FAX 403-429-5500. *3261*

EDUCATION AUTHORITIES' DIRECTORY AND ANNUAL.
School Government Publishing Co. Ltd., Darby House, Bletchingley Rd., Merstham, Redhill, Surrey RH1 3DN, England. TEL 44-1737-642223. FAX 44-1737-644283. *2436*

EDUCATION DAILY.
Capitol Publications Inc., 1101 King St., Ste. 444, Alexandria, VA 22314. TEL 703-683-4100. FAX 703-739-6501.
Vendor(s): NewsNet (ED08). *2436*

EDUCATION ET FRANCOPHONIE.
Association Canadienne d'Education de Langue Francaise, 268 rue Marie-de-l'Incarnation, Quebec, PQ G1N 3G4, Canada. TEL 418-681-4661. FAX 418-681-3389. URL: http://www.acelf.ca/revue. *2437*

EDUCATION IN CANADA.
Statistics Canada, Operations and Integration Division, Circulation Management, Jean Talon Bldg., 2-C12, Tunney's Pasture, Ottawa, ON K1A 0T6, Canada. TEL 613-951-7277. FAX 613-951-1584. URL: http://statcan.ca:80/cgi-bin/downpub/downpub.cgi. *2499*

EDUCATION INDEX.
H.W. Wilson Co., 950 University Ave., Bronx, NY 10452. TEL 718-590-8400. FAX 718-590-1617.
Vendor(s): OCLC, Wilsonline (File EDI). *2499*

EDUCATION POLICY ANALYSIS ARCHIVES.
Arizona State University, College of Education, Box 872411, Tempe, AZ 85287-2411. TEL 602-965-2692. URL: http://seamonkey.edu.asu.edu/epaa. Available only online. *2438*

EDUCATION TECHNOLOGY NEWS.
Business Publishers, Inc., 951 Pershing Dr., Silver Spring, MD 20910-4464. TEL 301-587-6300. FAX 301-585-9075.
Vendor(s): Information Access Co., NewsNet. *2113*

EDUCATION WEEK.
Editorial Projects in Education, Inc., 4301 Connecticut Ave., N.W., Ste. 432, Washington, DC 20008. TEL 202-364-4114. URL: http://www.edweek.org. *2438*

EDUCATIONAL INNOVATION AND INFORMATION.
UNESCO, International Bureau of Education, Case Postale 199, 1211 Geneva 20, Switzerland. TEL 41-22-7981455. FAX 41-22-7981486. URL: http://www.unicc.org/ibe. *2564*

EDUCATIONAL LEADERSHIP.
Association for Supervision and Curriculum Development, 1250 N. Pitt St., Alexandria, VA 22314-1453. TEL 703-549-9110. FAX 703-549-3891. URL: http://www.ascd.org.
Vendor(s): Information Access Co., UMI. *2601*

EDUCATIONAL MARKETER.
Cowles - SIMBA Information, 11 Riverbend Dr. S., Box 4949, Stamford, CT 06907-0949. TEL 203-358-9900. FAX 203-358-5811. URL: http://www.simbanet.com.
Vendor(s): Information Access Co., Knight-Ridder Information, Inc., NewsNet (PB20). *2601*

EDUCATIONAL RECORD.
American Council on Education, One Dupont Circle, N.W., Washington, DC 20036-1193. TEL 202-939-9380. FAX 202-833-4760.
Vendor(s): UMI. *2440*

EDUCATIONAL STUDIES.
American Educational Studies Association, c/o Bryan Deever, Ed., LB 8144, Georgia Southern University, Statesboro, GA 30460. TEL 912-681-5091. FAX 912-681-5093.
Vendor(s): UMI. *2440*

EDUCOM REVIEW.
Turnkey Publishing, Box 200549, Austin, TX 78720. TEL 512-335-2286. FAX 512-335-3083. URL: http://educom.edu/web/pubs/eduLib.html. *2540*

EDUCOM UPDATE.
Educom, 1112 16th St., N.W., Ste. 600, Washington, DC 20036. TEL 202-872-4200. FAX 512-335-3083. URL: http://educom.edu/web/pubs/eduLib.html.
Available only online. *2516*

EDUPAGE.
Educom, 1290 Oxford Rd., Atlanta, GA 30306. TEL 512-335-2286. FAX 512-335-3083. URL: http://www.educom.edu.
Available only online. *2441*

EFFECTOR.
Electronic Frontier Foundation, URL: http://www.eff.org/pub/eff/newsletters/effector/. Available only online. *5990*

EFFETA.
Istituto Gualandi per Sordomuti e Sordomute, Via Nosadella 49, 40123 Bologna, Italy. TEL 39-51-330552. FAX 39-51-332878. *3462*

EGYPTIAN JOURNAL OF PHARMACEUTICAL SCIENCES.
National Information and Documentation Centre (NIDOC), Tahrir St., Dokki, Awqaf P.O., Cairo, Egypt. TEL 20-2-3371696. *5659*

EIGHTEENTH CENTURY LIFE.
Johns Hopkins University Press, Journals Publishing Division, 2715 N. Charles St., Baltimore, MD 21218. TEL 410-516-6987. FAX 410-516-6968. URL: http://muse.jhu.edu. *3563*

EIGHTEENTH-CENTURY STUDIES.
Johns Hopkins University Press, Journals Publishing Division, 2715 N. Charles St., Baltimore, MD 21218-4319. TEL 410-516-6987. FAX 410-516-6968. URL: http://muse.jhu.edu. *3494*

EINKAUFS 1X1 DER DEUTSCHEN INDUSTRIE.
Deutscher Adressbuch Verlag, Arheilger Weg 17, 64380 Rossdorf, Germany. TEL 06154-699500. FAX 06154-6995490.
Vendor(s): Data-Star, FIZ Technik. *1675*

DIE EISEN, BLECH UND METALL VERARBEITENDE INDUSTRIE, STAHLVERFORMUNG UND IHRE HELFER.
Industrieschau-Verlagsgesellschaft mbH, Postfach 100262, 64202 Darmstadt, Germany. TEL 49-6151-38920. FAX 49-6151-33164. *5190*

DIE EISEN-, STAHL- UND N E METALL-INDUSTRIE UND IHRE HELFER.
Industrieschau-Verlagsgesellschaft mbH, Postfach 100262, 64202 Darmstadt, Germany. TEL 49-6151-38920. FAX 49-6151-33164. *5190*

EKISTICS.
Athens Technological Organization, Athens Center of Ekistics, 24 Strat. Syndemou, 106-73 Athens, Greece. TEL 30-1-3639-379. FAX 30-1-3633-395.
Vendor(s): UMI. *3746*

ELDERCARE FORUM.
ElderCare Financial Management, Inc., 170 Elaine Dr., Roswell, GA 30075. TEL 770-518-2767. URL: http://www.mindspung.com/~eldercare/elderweb.htm. *1129*

ELECTRIC DREAMS.
4644 Geary Blvd, Ste. 171, San Francisco, CA 94118. URL: http://www.phys.unsw.edu.au/~mettw/edreams/home.html; http://www.dreamgate.com. *6109*

ELECTRIC LIGHT AND POWER.
PennWell Publishing Co., Box 1260, Tulsa, OK 74101. TEL 918-835-3161. FAX 918-831-9497.
Vendor(s): Information Access Co.. *2817*

ELECTRIC PERSPECTIVES.
Edison Electric Institute, 701 Pennsylvania Ave., N.W., Washington, DC 20004-2696. TEL 202-508-5000. FAX 202-508-5030.
Vendor(s): UMI. *2817*

ELECTRIC POWER ANNUAL.
U.S. Energy Information Administration, National Energy Information Center, EI-231, James Forrestal Bldg., Rm. 1F-048, 1000 Independence Ave., S.W., Washington, DC 20585. TEL 202-586-8800. FAX 202-586-0727. URL: http://www.eia.doe.gov. *2688*

ELECTRIC POWER MONTHLY.
U.S. Energy Information Administration, National Energy Information Center, EI-231, James Forrestal Bldg., Rm. 1F-048, 1000 Independence Ave., S.W., Washington, DC 20585. TEL 202-586-8800. FAX 202-0586-0727. URL: http://www.eia.doe.gov. *2688*

ELECTRIC UTILITY WEEK.
McGraw-Hill, Inc., 1221 Ave. of the Americas, New York, NY 10020. TEL 212-512-6410. Vendor(s): Knight-Ridder Information, Inc. (File no.624/McGRAW-HILL PUBLICATIONS ONLINE), Dow Jones News Retrieval (EUW), Lexis-Nexis (ELUTL), NewsNet (EY65). *2817*

ELECTRIC UTILITY WEEK'S DEMAND-SIDE REPORT.
McGraw-Hill, Inc., 1221 Ave. of the Americas, New York, NY 10020. TEL 212-512-6410. Vendor(s): Knight-Ridder Information, Inc. (DSR), Dow Jones News Retrieval (DSR), NewsNet (EY87). *2688*

ELECTRICAL & ELECTRONICS ABSTRACTS.
INSPEC, I.E.E., Michael Faraday House, Six Hill Way, Stevenage, Herts. SG1 2AY, England. TEL 44-1438-313311. FAX 44-1438-742840. URL: http://www.iee.org.uk. Vendor(s): CEDOCAR, Data-Star, European Space Agency, FIZ Technik, Knight-Ridder Information, Inc., Questel Orbit Inc., STN International. *2749*

ELECTRICAL CONSTRUCTION & MAINTENANCE.
Intertec Publishing Corp., 9800 Metcalf Ave., Overland Park, KS 66212-2215. TEL 913-341-1300. FAX 913-967-1898. URL: http://www.intertec.com/pubs/ecm.htm. Vendor(s): Information Access Co. *2817*

ELECTRICAL WORLD.
McGraw-Hill Companies, 1221 Ave. of the Americas, New York, NY 10020. TEL 212-512-2000. Vendor(s): Dow Jones News Retrieval (EWL), Knight-Ridder Information, Inc. (EW), Lexis-Nexis (ELECWD), NewsNet (EY03). *2819*

THE ELECTRICITY JOURNAL.
1501 Western Ave., Ste. 100, Seattle, WA 98101-1570. TEL 206-382-0195. URL: http://www.speakeasy.org/electricity/. Vendor(s): UMI. *2688*

ELECTRO MANUFACTURING.
Worldwide Videotex, Box 3273, Boynton Beach, FL 33424-3273. TEL 407-738-2276. Vendor(s): Information Access Co., NewsNet. *2804*

ELECTRONIC ADVERTISING & MARKETPLACE REPORT.
Cowles - SIMBA Information, 11 Riverbend Dr. S., Box 4949, Stamford, CT 06907-0949. TEL 203-358-9900. FAX 203-358-5811. URL: http://www.simbanet.com. Vendor(s): Information Access Co. *1989*

ELECTRONIC ANTIQUITY.
University of Tasmania, Department of Classics, Hobart, Tasmania 7001, Australia. TEL 61-02-202-294. FAX 61-02-202-288. Available only online. *1903*

ELECTRONIC BUSINESS TODAY.
Cahners Publishing Company (Newton), Division of Reed Elsevier Inc., 275 Washington St., Newton, MA 02158-1630. TEL 617-964-3030. FAX 617-558-4470. URL: http://www.ebtmag.com. Vendor(s): Information Access Co., Knight-Ridder Information, Inc. *2631*

ELECTRONIC BUYERS' NEWS.
C M P Publications, Inc., 600 Community Dr., Manhasset, NY 11030. TEL 516-562-5000. FAX 516-562-5123. Vendor(s): Information Access Co., NewsNet (EC12). *2631*

ELECTRONIC CHEMICALS NEWS.
Chemical Week Associates, 888 Seventh Ave., New York, NY 10106. TEL 212-621-4900. FAX 212-621-4949. Vendor(s): Information Access Co. *2631*

ELECTRONIC COMMUNICATIONS IN PROBABILITY.
Institute of Mathematical Statistics, URL: http://www.math.washington.edu/~ejpecp. Available only online. *4571*

ELECTRONIC DESIGN.
Penton Publishing (Hasbrouck Heights), 611 Rte. 46 W., Hasbrouck Heights, NJ 07604. TEL 201-393-6057. Vendor(s): Information Access Co., Knight-Ridder Information, Inc., Lexis-Nexis. *2631*

ELECTRONIC ENGINEERING TIMES.
C M P Publications, Inc., 600 Community Dr., Manhasset, NY 11030. TEL 516-562-5000. FAX 516-562-5325. Vendor(s): Information Access Co., NewsNet (EC14). *2632*

ELECTRONIC GOURMET GUIDE.
Box 3407, Crestline, CA 92325-3407. URL: http://www.foodwine.com. Available only online. *7197*

ELECTRONIC GREEN JOURNAL.
University of Idaho Library, University of Idaho Library, Moscow, ID 83844. TEL 208-885-6631. FAX 208-885-6817. URL: http://www.lib.uidaho.edu:70/docs/egj.html. Available only online. *2917*

ELECTRONIC INFORMATION REPORT.
Cowles - SIMBA Information, 11 Riverbend Dr. S., Box 4949, Stamford, CT 06907-0949. TEL 203-358-9900. FAX 203-358-5811. URL: http://www.simbanet.com. Vendor(s): Information Access Co., Knight-Ridder Information, Inc., NewsNet (PB22). *2166*

THE ELECTRONIC JOURNAL OF COMBINATORICS.
American Mathematical Society, Box 6248, Providence, RI 02940-6248. TEL 401-455-4000. FAX 401-331-3842. URL: http://www.combinatorics org/. Available only online. *4571*

ELECTRONIC JOURNAL OF DIFFERENTIAL EQUATIONS.
Southwest Texas State University, Department of Mathematics, San Marcos, TX 78666-4616. TEL 512-245-2551. URL: http://www.ejde.math.swt.edu/. Available only online. *4571*

ELECTRONIC JOURNAL OF GEOTECHNICAL ENGINEERING.
URL: http://www. geotech.civen.okstate.edu/ejge. Available only online. *2783*

ELECTRONIC JOURNAL OF PROBABILITY.
Institute of Mathematical Statistics, URL: http://www.math.washington.edu/~ejpecp/. Available only online. *4571*

THE ELECTRONIC JOURNAL OF RADICAL ORGANISATION THEORY.
URL: http://www.mngt.waikato.ac.nz/depts/sm&l/journal/ejrot.htm. Available only online. *6611*

ELECTRONIC JOURNAL OF SOCIOLOGY.
University of Alberta, Department of Sociology, Edmonton, AB T6G 2H4, Canada. URL: http://gpu.srv.ualberta.ca. Available only online. *6708*

ELECTRONIC JOURNAL OF STRATEGIC INFORMATION SYSTEMS.
University of Sheffield, Information Studies Department, 211 Portobello St., Regents Court, Rm. 315, Sheffield S10 2UH, England. TEL 44-742-768555. FAX 44-742-780300. Available only online. *2181*

ELECTRONIC JOURNAL OF THEORETICAL CHEMISTRY.
John Wiley & Sons Ltd., Journals, Baffins Ln., Chichester, W. Sussex PO19 1UD, England. TEL 44-1243-779777. FAX 44-1243-843232. URL: http://www.wiley.co.uk. *1790*

THE ELECTRONIC JOURNAL ON VIRTUAL CULTURE.
TEL 330-273-5932. URL: http://rdz.stjohns.edu/ejvc/ejvc.html. Available only online. *2132*

ELECTRONIC LEARNING.
Scholastic Inc., 555 Broadway, New York, NY 10012-3999. TEL 212-343-6100. Vendor(s): Information Access Co., Knight-Ridder Information, Inc., UMI. *2516*

ELECTRONIC MATERIALS AND PACKAGING.
Research Information Ltd., 222 Maylands Ave., Hemel Hempstead, Herts. HP2 7TD, England. TEL 44-1442-213222. FAX 44-1442-259395. Vendor(s): Information Access Co. *2632*

ELECTRONIC MATERIALS TECHNOLOGY NEWS.
Business Communications Co., Inc. (Norwalk), 25 Van Zant St., Ste. 13, Norwalk, CT 06855. TEL 203-853-4266. FAX 203-853-0348. Vendor(s): Information Access Co., NewsNet (ML04). *2632*

ELECTRONIC MEDIA.
Crain Communications, Inc. (Chicago), 740 N. Rush St., Chicago, IL 60611-2590. TEL 312-649-5200. FAX 312-649-5465. Vendor(s): Information Access Co., Lexis-Nexis. *2019*

ELECTRONIC MESSAGING NEWS.
Phillips Business Information, Inc., 1201 Seven Locks Rd., Potomac, MD 20854. TEL 301-424-3338. FAX 301-309-3847. Vendor(s): NewsNet (TE05). *2015*

ELECTRONIC MONEY TREE.
URL: http://www.soos.com/$tree. Available only online. *1641*

ELECTRONIC NEWS.
Cahners Publishing Co., 475 Park Ave. S., 2nd fl., New York, NY 10006. TEL 212-736-3900. FAX 212-736-5125. URL: http://www.sumnet.com/enews. Vendor(s): Information Access Co., Knight-Ridder Information, Inc. *2632*

ELECTRONIC PHOTOGRAPHY NEWS.
Photofinishing News, Inc., 10915 Bonita Beach Rd., Ste. 1091, Bonita Springs, FL 34135. TEL 941-992-4421. FAX 941-992-6328. URL: http://www.photo-news.com. *5764*

ELECTRONIC RECRUITING NEWS.
Internet Business Network, 346 Starling Rd., Mill Valley, CA 94941. TEL 415-380-8244. FAX 415-383-8676. URL: http://www.interbiznet.com/hrstart.html. Available only online. *1564*

ELECTRONIC RESOURCES REVIEW.
M C B University Press Ltd., 60-62 Toller Lane, Bradford, West Yorkshire BD8 9BY, England. URL: http://www.anbar.co.uk/liblink/err/jourhome.htm. Available only online. *4231*

ELECTRONIC RETAILING.
G P G Publishing, Inc., 9200 Sunset Blvd., Ste. 612, Los Angeles, CA 90069. TEL 818-782-7328. FAX 818-782-7450. URL: http://www.eretail.com. *1525*

ELECTRONIC T V HOST.
T V Host, Inc., Box 1665, 3935 Jonestown Rd., Harrisburg, PA 17109. TEL 717-657-1700. FAX 717-657-2921. URL: http://www.tvhost.com; http://www.nytimes.com/maglive.html. Available only online. *2049*

ELECTRONIC URBAN REPORT.
3151 Cahuenga Blvd. W., Ste. 200, Los Angeles, CA 90068. URL: http://www.Eurweb.com. Available only online. *3009*

ELECTRONIC WORLD NEWS.
C M P Publications, Inc., 600 Community Dr., Manhasset, NY 11030. TEL 516-562-5000. Vendor(s): NewsNet (EC13). *2633*

ELECTRONICS AND COMMUNICATIONS ABSTRACTS JOURNAL.
Cambridge Scientific Abstracts, 7200 Wisconsin Ave., 6th Fl., Bethesda, MD 20814. TEL 301-961-6750. FAX 301-961-6720. URL: http://www.csa.com. Vendor(s): STN International (ELCOM). *2012*

ELECTRONICS BUYERS' GUIDE.
Miller Freeman Information Services, Riverbank House, Angel Ln., Tonbridge, Kent TN9 1SE, England. TEL 44-1732-362666. FAX 44-1732-367301. URL: http://www.mfplc.com. *2634*

ELECTRONICS LETTERS.
I.E.E., Michael Faraday House, Six Hills Way, Stevenage, Herts. SG1 2AY, England. TEL 44-1438-313311. FAX 44-1438-742840. URL: http://www.iee.org.uk.
Vendor(s): OCLC. *2634*

ELECTRONICS LETTERS ONLINE.
I.E.E., Michael Faraday House, Six Hills Way, Stevenage, Herts. SG1 2AY, England. TEL 44-1438-313311. FAX 44-1438-742840. URL: http://www.iee.org.uk.
Available only online. Vendor(s): OCLC. *2634*

ELECTRONICS NOW.
Gernsback Publications, Inc., 500 Bi-County Blvd., Farmingdale, NY 11735. TEL 516-293-3000. FAX 516-293-3115. URL: http://www.gernsback.com.
Vendor(s): Information Access Co. *2634*

ELECTRONICS TIMES.
Morgan-Grampian Technical Press Ltd., Morgan-Grampian House, 30 Calderwood St., London SE18 6QH, England. TEL 44-181-855-7777. FAX 44-181-854-1793.
Vendor(s): Information Access Co. *2635*

ELECTRONICS WEEKLY.
Reed Business Information, Quadrant House, The Quadrant, Sutton, Surrey SM2 5AS, England. TEL 44-181-652-3649. FAX 44-181-652-8956.
Vendor(s): Information Access Co. *2635*

DIE ELEKTRO-INDUSTRIE, ELEKTRONIK UND IHRE HELFER.
Industrieschau-Verlagsgesellschaft mbH, Postfach 100262, 64202 Darmstadt, Germany. TEL 49-6151-3892-0. FAX 49-6151-33164. *2635*

ELEKTRON.
Smena Publishing House, Prazska 11, 812 84 Bratislava, Slovakia. TEL 406-06. *6523*

ELEMENTARY SCIENCE THIS MONTH.
Mankato State University, College of Education, Box 8400, Mankato, MN 56002-8400. URL: http://www.lme.mankato.msus.edu/ci/elem.sci.html.
Available only online. *1870*

ELEVEN.
General Learning Corporation, 900 Skokie Blvd., Ste. 200, Northbrook, IL 60062. TEL 847-205-3000. URL: http://www.wttw.com. *2049*

ELSEVIER SCIENCE. CATALOGUE - BOOKS.
Elsevier Science B.V., P.O. Box 211, 1000 AE Amsterdam, Netherlands. TEL 31-20-4853911. FAX 31-20-4853598. URL: http://www.elsevier.nl/. *6524*

ELSEVIER SCIENCE. CATALOGUE - JOURNALS.
Elsevier Science B.V., P.O. Box 211, 1000 AE Amsterdam, Netherlands. TEL 31-20-4853911. FAX 31-20-4853598. URL: http://www.elsevier.nl/. *6524*

EM ABERTO.
Instituto Nacional de Estudos e Pesquisas Educacionais, Sgas Q.607 Bl.50 - L2 Sul, 70200-670 Brasilia, DF, Brazil. TEL 55-61-2442612. FAX 55-61-2444712. *2441*

EMERGENCY MEDICINE REPORTS.
American Health Consultants, Inc., 3525 Piedmont Rd., N.E., Bldg. 6, Ste. 400, Atlanta, GA 30305. TEL 404-262-7436. FAX 404-262-7837.
Vendor(s): Ovid Technologies, Inc. *4664*

EMERGENCY PREPAREDNESS NEWS.
Business Publishers, Inc., 951 Pershing Dr., Silver Spring, MD 20910-4464. TEL 301-587-6300. FAX 301-585-9075.
Vendor(s): NewsNet (GT34). *1897*

EMERGING & SPECIAL SITUATIONS.
Standard & Poor's Corporation, 25 Broadway, New York, NY 10004. TEL 212-208-8000.
Vendor(s): Knight-Ridder Information, Inc. (ESS), Dow Jones News Retrieval (ESS), NewsNet (FI16). *1383*

EMERGING INFECTIOUS DISEASES.
U.S. National Center for Infectious Diseases, 1600 Clifton Rd., Mailstop C-12, Atlanta, GA 30333. TEL 404-639-3967. FAX 404-639-3039. URL: http://www.cdc.gov/nccidod/EID/eid.htm. *6232*

EMORY INTERNATIONAL LAW REVIEW.
Emory University, School of Law, Gambrell Hall, Atlanta, GA 30322. TEL 404-727-6830. FAX 404-727-6820.
Vendor(s): West Group. *4112*

EMORY LAW JOURNAL.
Emory University, School of Law, Gambrell Hall, Atlanta, GA 30322. TEL 404-727-6830. FAX 404-727-6820.
Vendor(s): West Group. *3944*

EMPLOYEE BENEFIT CASES.
The Bureau of National Affairs, Inc., 1231 25th St., N.W., Washington, DC 20037. TEL 202-452-4200. FAX 202-822-8092. URL: http://www.bna.com/ *1426*

EMPLOYEE BENEFIT PLAN REVIEW.
Charles D. Spencer & Associates, Inc., 250 S. Wacker Dr., Ste. 600, Chicago, IL 60606-5834. TEL 312-993-7900.
Vendor(s): UMI. *1426*

EMPLOYEE HEALTH AND FITNESS.
American Health Consultants, Inc., 3525 Piedmont Rd., N.E., Bldg. 6, Ste. 400, Atlanta, GA 30305. TEL 404-262-7436. FAX 800-284-3291.
Vendor(s): Lexis-Nexis. *5780*

EMPLOYEE RELATIONS.
M C B University Press Ltd., 60-62 Toller Ln., Bradford, W. Yorks BD8 9BY, England. TEL 44-1274-777700. FAX 44-1274-785200. URL: http://www.mcb.co.uk.
Vendor(s): Information Access Co. *1427*

EMPLOYEE RELATIONS LAW JOURNAL.
John Wiley & Sons, Inc., Journals, 605 Third Ave., New York, NY 10158. TEL 212-850-6645. FAX 212-850-6021. URL: http://www.wiley.co.uk.
Vendor(s): Information Access Co., Knight-Ridder Information, Inc. *3944*

EMPLOYMENT GUIDE.
The Bureau of National Affairs, Inc., 1231 25th St., N.W., Washington, DC 20037. TEL 202-452-4200. FAX 202-822-8092. URL: http://www.bna.com/
Vendor(s): Human Resources Information Network (EMPG, CDD, HDD). *1565*

EMPLOYMENT INFORMATION IN THE MATHEMATICAL SCIENCES.
American Mathematical Society, Box 6248, Providence, RI 02940-6248. TEL 401-455-4000. FAX 401-331-3842. URL: http://www.ams.org/committee/profession/employ.html.
Vendor(s): Human Resources Information Network. *4571*

EMPLOYMENT JOURNAL.
MicroLine Systems Canada, 125 Stewart Blvd., Ste. 211B, Brockville, ON K6V 4W4, Canada. FAX 613-345-3880. URL: http://www.brocknet.com/employment-journal/
Available only online. *5508*

EMPLOYMENT OPPORTUNITIES (ENGLEWOOD).
National Guild of Community Schools of the Arts, Box 8018, Englewood, NJ 07631. TEL 201-871-3337.
Vendor(s): NewsNet. *5508*

ENANTIOMER.
Gordon and Breach - Harwood Academic, Amsteldisk 166, 1st Fl., 1079 LH Amsterdam, Netherlands. URL: http://www.gbhap.com/Enantiomer/. *1748*

ENBI TO PORIMA.
Institute of Polymer Industry, Inc., C.P.O. Box 1176, Tokyo 100-91, Japan. URL: http://www.rapra.net. *1815*

ENCYCLOPEDIA OF ASSOCIATIONS.
Gale Research, 835 Penobscot Bldg., 645 Griswold St., Detroit, MI 48226-4094. TEL 313-961-2242. FAX 800-414-5043.
Vendor(s): Knight-Ridder Information, Inc. (File no.114). *2656*

ENDOTHELIUM.
Gordon and Breach - Harwood Academic, Amsteldisk 166, 1st Fl., 1079 LH Amsterdam, Netherlands. URL: http://www.gbhap.com/Endothelium/. *600*

ENERGIA: BIBLIOGRAFIA SELETIVA.
Comissao Nacional de Energia Nuclear, Centro de Informacoes Nucleares, Rua General Severiano, 90, Botafogo, 22294-900 Rio de Janeiro RJ, Brazil. TEL 55-21-5462440. FAX 55-21-5462447. URL: http://www.cnen.gov.br/cin.
Available only online. *2683*

ENERGY & ENVIRONMENT.
Multi-Science Publishing Co. Ltd., 107 High St., Brentwood, Essex CM14 4RX, England. TEL 44-1277-224632. FAX 44-1277-223453.
Vendor(s): Information Access Co. *2665*

ENERGY & FUELS.
American Chemical Society, 1155 16th St., N.W., Washington, DC 20036. TEL 800-333-9511. FAX 614-447-3671.
Vendor(s): STN International (CJACS). *2665*

ENERGY BUSINESS REVIEW.
Arab Press Service, P.O. Box 3896, Nicosia, Cyprus. FAX 357-2-350265.
Vendor(s): Information Access Co. *2665*

ENERGY CONSERVATION NEWS.
Business Communications Co., Inc. (Norwalk), 25 Van Zant St., Ste. 13, Norwalk, CT 06855. TEL 203-853-4266. FAX 203-853-0348.
Vendor(s): Data-Star, Information Access Co., Knight-Ridder Information, Inc., NewsNet (EY59). *2665*

ENERGY DAILY.
King Publishing Group, Inc., 627 National Press Bldg., Washington, DC 20045. TEL 202-638-4260. FAX 202-662-9744.
Vendor(s): Data-Star, Information Access Co., Knight-Ridder Information, Inc., Lexis-Nexis, NewsNet (EY57). *2666*

ENERGY DATA BASE.
U.S. National Technical Information Service, 5285 Port Royal Rd., Springfield, VA 22161. TEL 703-487-4630.
Available only online. Vendor(s): Knight-Ridder Information, Inc., STN International. *2666*

ENERGY DESIGN UPDATE.
Cutter Information Corp., 37 Broadway, Arlington, MA 02174. TEL 617-648-8700. FAX 617-648-1950. URL: http://www.cutter.com.
Vendor(s): NewsNet (BC08). *892*

ENERGY ECONOMIST.
Financial Times Energy Publishing, Maple House, 149 Tottenham Court Rd. London W1P 9LL, England. TEL 0171-896-2241. FAX 0171-896-2275.
Vendor(s): Data-Star, Knight-Ridder Information, Inc., Lexis-Nexis. *2666*

ENERGY INFORMATION DIRECTORY.
U.S. Energy Information Administration, National Energy Information Center, EI-231, James Forrestal Bldg., Rm. 1F-048, 1000 Independence Ave., S.W., Washington, DC 20585. TEL 202-586-8800. FAX 202-586-0727. URL: http://www.eia.doe.gov. *2667*

ENERGY JOURNAL.
International Association for Energy Economics, 28790 Chagrin Blvd., Ste. 210, Cleveland, OH 44122. TEL 216-464-5365. FAX 216-464-2737. URL: http://www.IAEE.org.
Vendor(s): Information Access Co. *2667*

ENERGY LAW JOURNAL.
Federal Energy Bar Association, 1350 Connecticut Ave., N.W., Ste. 300, Washington, DC 20036. TEL 202-223-5625. FAX 202-833-5566.
Vendor(s): West Group. *3945*

ENERGY REPORT.
Pasha Publications Inc., 1616 N. Fort Myer Dr., Ste. 1000, Arlington, VA 22209-3107. TEL 703-528-1244. FAX 703-528-1253. *2667*

SERIALS AVAILABLE ONLINE

ENERGY REPORT.
Springfield Information Services, P.O. Box 31, Peterborough, Cambs. PE1 1SD, England. TEL 44-1733-267272.
Vendor(s): Information Access Co. *2667*

ENERGY RESEARCH ABSTRACTS.
U.S. Department of Energy, Office of Scientific and Technical Information, Box 62, Oak Ridge, TN 37831. TEL 615-576-9362.
Vendor(s): Knight-Ridder Information, Inc., STN International (ENERGY). *2683*

ENERGY USER NEWS.
Chilton Co., Chilton Way, Radnor, PA 19089. TEL 215-964-4028.
Vendor(s): Information Access Co., Knight-Ridder Information, Inc., Lexis-Nexis. *2668*

THE ENGINEER.
Miller Freeman Technical Ltd., Miller Freeman House, 30 Calderwood St., London SE18 6QH, England. TEL 44-181-855-7777. FAX 44-181-854-7476.
Vendor(s): Information Access Co. *2716*

ENGINEERED MATERIALS ABSTRACTS.
Cambridge Scientific Abstracts, 7200 Wisconsin Ave., Bethesda, MD 20814. TEL 301-961-6750. FAX 301-961-6720. URL: http://www.csa.com.
Vendor(s): European Space Agency (File no.134), Knight-Ridder Information, Inc. (File no.293), Questel Orbit Inc. (EMAB), STN International (EMA). *2749*

ENGINEERING & MINING JOURNAL.
Intertec Publishing Corp., 29 N. Wacker Dr., Chicago, IL 60606. TEL 312-726-2802. FAX 312-726-4103.
Vendor(s): Information Access Co., Lexis-Nexis. *5299*

ENGINEERING DIMENSIONS.
Association of Professional Engineers of Ontario, 25 Sheppard Ave. W., Ste. 1000, North York, ON M2N 6S9, Canada. TEL 416-224-1100. FAX 416-224-8168. URL: http://www.peo.on.ca. *2717*

ENGINEERING ECONOMIST.
Institute of Industrial Engineers, 25 Technology Park-Atlanta, Norcross, GA 30092. TEL 770-449-0460. FAX 770-263-8532.
Vendor(s): Information Access Co., UMI. *2717*

ENGINEERING INDEX ANNUAL.
Engineering Information, Inc., Castle Point on the Hudson, Hoboken, NJ 07030. TEL 201-216-8500. FAX 201-216-8532.
Vendor(s): Ovid Technologies, Inc. (COMP), CEDOCAR, Data-Star, Knight-Ridder Information, Inc. (File no.8), European Space Agency, Questel Orbit Inc., STN International. *2749*

ENGINEERING INDEX MONTHLY.
Engineering Information, Inc., Castle Point on the Hudson, Hoboken, NJ 07030. TEL 201-216-8500. FAX 201-216-8532.
Vendor(s): CEDOCAR, CISTI, Data-Star, European Space Agency, Knight-Ridder Information, Inc. (File no.8), Questel Orbit Inc., Ovid Technologies, Inc. (COMP), STN International (COMPENDEX). *2749*

ENGINEERING OPTIMIZATION.
Gordon and Breach - Harwood Academic, Amsteldisk 166, 1st Fl., 1079 LH Amsterdam, Netherlands. URL: http://www.gbhap.com/Engineering_Optimization. *2718*

ENGLISH HISTORICAL REVIEW.
Addison Wesley Longman, Edinburgh Gate, Edinburgh Way, Harlow, Essex CM20 2JE, England. TEL 44-1279-426721. FAX 44-1279-431059.
Vendor(s): Information Access Co. *3564*

ENGLISH LANGUAGE NOTES.
University of Colorado, English Language Notes, CB 226, Boulder, CO 80309. TEL 303-492-7176. FAX 303-492-3521.
Vendor(s): Information Access Co. *4401*

ENHANCED ENERGY RECOVERY NEWS.
Business Communications Co., Inc. (Norwalk), 25 Van Zant St., Ste. 13, Norwalk, CT 06855. TEL 203-853-4266. FAX 203-853-0348.
Vendor(s): Information Access Co., NewsNet (EY60). *2669*

ENHANCED HEAT TRANSFER.
Gordon and Breach - Harwood Academic, Amsteldisk 166, 1st Fl., 1079 LH Amsterdam, Netherlands. URL: http://www.gbhap.com/Enhanced_Heat_Transfer/. *2883*

ENTELECHY.
Flat Earth Media, 1791 Ninth Ave., San Francisco, CA 94122. TEL 415-731-4146. URL: http://www.entelechy.org. *4402*

ENTERPRISE (NEW YORK).
Equitable Life Assurance Society of the U.S., 787 Seventh Ave., Area 37K, New York, NY 10019. TEL 212-554-4738.
Vendor(s): UMI. *3815*

ENTERPRISE SOLUTIONS FOR MANAGERS OF WINDOWS NT.
Cardinal Business Media, Inc., 1300 Virginia Dr., Ste. 400, Fort Washington, PA 19034. TEL 215-643-8000. FAX 215-643-8099. URL: http://www.cardinal.com/ent. *2133*

ENTERPRISE SYSTEMS JOURNAL.
Cardinal Business Media, Inc., 12225 Greenville Ave., Ste. 700, Dallas, TX 75243-9338. TEL 972-669-9000. FAX 972-669-9909.
Vendor(s): Information Access Co. *2174*

ENTERTAINMENT & SPORTS LAW REVIEW.
University of Miami, School of Law, Box 248087, Coral Gables, FL 33124-8087. TEL 305-284-6886.
Vendor(s): West Group. *3945*

ENTERTAINMENT LAW REPORTER.
Entertainment Law Reporter Publishing Co., 2118 Wilshire Blvd., No. 311, Santa Monica, CA 90403. TEL 310-829-9335. FAX 310-829-9335.
Vendor(s): Lexis-Nexis, West Group. *3946*

THE ENTERTAINMENT MAGAZINE ON-LINE.
Southwest Alternatives Institute, Inc., Box 3355, Tucson, AZ 85722. TEL 520-623-3733. URL: http://emol.org/org.
Available only online. *5391*

ENTERTAINMENT MARKETING LETTER.
E P M Communications, 160 Mercer St., 3rd Fl., New York, NY 10012-3212. TEL 212-941-0099. FAX 212-941-1622.
Vendor(s): Information Access Co. *1526*

ENTERTAINMENT SOFTWARE: THE INTERNATIONAL MARKET.
Euromonitor, 60-61 Britton St., London EC1M 5NA, England. TEL 44-171-251-8024. FAX 44-171-608-3149. URL: http://www.euromonitor.com.
Vendor(s): Data-Star, Knight-Ridder Information, Inc. *4148*

ENTERTAINMENT WEEKLY.
Entertainment Weekly Inc., 1675 Broadway, New York, NY 10019. TEL 212-522-5600. FAX 212-522-0074.
Vendor(s): Information Access Co., MediaStream. *3373*

ENTERZONE.
1017 Bayview Ave., Oakland, CA 94610-4032. URL: http://ezone.org/ez.
Available only online. *440*

ENTOMOLOGY ABSTRACTS.
Cambridge Scientific Abstracts, 7200 Wisconsin Ave., 6th Fl., Bethesda, MD 20814. TEL 301-961-6750. FAX 301-961-6720. URL: http://www.csa.com.
Vendor(s): Knight-Ridder Information, Inc. (File no.76/LIFE SCIENCES COLLECTION), STN International (LIFESCI). *640*

ENTREPRENEURSHIP: THEORY AND PRACTICE.
Baylor University, Hankamer School of Business, BU Box 98006, Waco, TX 76798-8006. TEL 817-755-1111 ext.156. FAX 817-755-2271. URL: http://hsb.baylor.edu/html/dept/bcpr/HSB/genmf.htm.
Vendor(s): Information Access Co., UMI. *1642*

ENTREZ DOCUMENT RETRIEVAL SYSTEM.
U.S. National Center for Biotechnology Information, National Library of Medicine, Bldg. 38A, Rm. 8N-803, 8600 Rockville Pike, Bethesda, MD 20894. TEL 301-496-2475. FAX 301-480-9241. URL: http://www.ncbi.nlm.nih.gov.
Available only online. *4774*

ENVIRO UPDATE.
Association of Tasmania's Environment Team, URL: http://ingomar.lgat.tas.gov.au/newslets/envup/envup.htm.
Available only online. *2917*

ENVIRONMENT.
Heldref Publications, 1319 Eighteenth St., N.W., Washington, DC 20036-1802. TEL 202-296-6267. FAX 202-296-5149.
Vendor(s): Information Access Co., UMI. *2918*

ENVIRONMENT ABSTRACTS.
Congressional Information Service, Inc., A member of the LEXIS NEXIS family, 4520 East-West Hwy., Bethesda, MD 20814-3389. TEL 301-654-1550. FAX 301-654-4033. URL: http://www.cispubs.com.
Vendor(s): DIMDI, Data-Star (ENVN/Enviroline), Knight-Ridder Information, Inc., Lexis-Nexis. *2961*

ENVIRONMENT ABSTRACTS ANNUAL.
Congressional Information Service, Inc., A member of the LEXIS-NEXIS family, 4520 East-West Hwy., Ste. 800, Bethesda, MD 20814-3389. TEL 301-654-1550. FAX 301-654-4033. URL: http://www.cispubs.com.
Vendor(s): Data-Star (ENVN/Enviroline), European Space Agency (File no.11/ENVIROLINE and File no.109/Acid Rain Abstracts), Knight-Ridder Information, Inc. (File no.40), Questel Orbit Inc. (Enviroline). *2961*

ENVIRONMENT AND SAFETY BRIEFING.
Barbour Index, New Lodge Drift Rd., Windsor, Berks. SL4 4RQ, England. TEL 01344-884121. FAX 01483-884112. *2918*

ENVIRONMENT BUSINESS.
Information for Industry Ltd., 18-20 Ridgway, London SW19 4QN, England. TEL 44-181-944-2930. FAX 44-181-944-1982.
Vendor(s): Information Access Co. *2918*

ENVIRONMENT INDEX.
Asian Institute of Technology, Environmental Systems Information Center (ENSIC), P.O. Box 2754, Bangkok 10501, Thailand. FAX 66-2-5245870.
Available only online. *2918*

ENVIRONMENT REPORTER.
The Bureau of National Affairs, Inc., 1231 25th St., N.W., Washington, DC 20037. TEL 202-452-4200. FAX 202-822-8092. URL: http://www.bna.com/
Vendor(s): Human Resources Information Network, Lexis-Nexis (ENVREP), West Group (BNA-ER). *2919*

ENVIRONMENT TODAY.
Society of Chemical Industry, 14 Belgrave Sq., London SW1X 8PS, England. TEL 44-171-235-3681. FAX 44-171-235-9410. URL: http://enviro.mond.org.
Available only online. *2919*

ENVIRONMENT WATCH: LATIN AMERICA.
Cutter Information Corp., 37 Broadway, Arlington, MA 02174-5552. FAX 617-648-1950. URL: http://www.cutter.com.
Vendor(s): Information Access Co., NewsNet (EV44). *2919*

ENVIRONMENT WATCH: WEST EUROPE.
Cutter Information Corp., 37 Broadway, Arlington, MA 02174-5552. TEL 617-648-8700. FAX 617-648-1950. URL: http://world.std.com/˜cic/ewwe/ewwe.htm.
Vendor(s): Information Access Co. *2919*

ENVIRONMENT WEEK.
Business Publishers, Inc., 951 Pershing Dr., Silver Spring, MD 20910-4464. TEL 301-587-6300. FAX 301-585-9075.
Vendor(s): Data-Star, Information Access Co., Knight-Ridder Information, Inc., Lexis-Nexis, NewsNet (EV25). *2919*

ENVIRONMENTAL ACTION.
Environmental Action Foundation, Box 61463, Durham, NC 27715-1463. TEL 301-891-1106. FAX 301-891-2218. URL: http://www.econet.apc.org/eaf/
Vendor(s): Information Access Co., UMI. *2920*

ENVIRONMENTAL AND ECOLOGICAL STATISTICS.
Thomson Science, 2-6 Boundary Row, London SE1 8HN, England. TEL 44-171-8650066. FAX 44-171-5229623. URL: http://www.thomsonscience.com. *2961*

ENVIRONMENTAL AND MOLECULAR MUTAGENESIS.
John Wiley & Sons, Inc., Journals, 605 Third Ave., New York, NY 10158. TEL 212-850-6645. FAX 212-850-6021. URL: http://www.wiley.co.uk *766*

ENVIRONMENTAL BUSINESS JOURNAL.
Environmental Business International Inc., 4452 Park Blvd., Ste. 306, San Diego, CA 92116-4039. TEL 619-295-7685. FAX 619-295-5743. Vendor(s): Information Access Co.. *2920*

ENVIRONMENTAL DEFENSE FUND. ANNUAL REPORT.
Environmental Defense Fund, 257 Park Ave. S., New York, NY 10010. TEL 212-505-2100. FAX 212-505-2375. URL: http://www.edf.org/pubs/AnnualReport/ *2921*

ENVIRONMENTAL GEOCHEMISTRY AND HEALTH.
Chapman & Hall, Journals Department 2-6 Boundary Row, London SE1 8HN, England. TEL 44-171-8560066. FAX 44-171-5229623. URL: http://www.chaphall.com/chaphall/journals.html. *2922*

ENVIRONMENTAL GEOLOGY.
Springer-Verlag, Heidelberger Platz 3, 14197 Berlin, Germany. TEL 49-30-82787-0. FAX 49-30-82787448. URL: http://link.springer.de. *2339*

ENVIRONMENTAL HEALTH LETTER.
Business Publishers, Inc., 951 Pershing Dr., Silver Spring, MD 20910-4464. TEL 301-587-6300. FAX 301-585-9075. Vendor(s): NewsNet. *4664*

ENVIRONMENTAL HEALTH PERSPECTIVES.
U.S. Department of Health and Human Services, National Institute of Environmental Health Sciences, Box 12233, Research Triangle Park, NC 27709. TEL 919-541-3406. FAX 919-541-0273. URL: http://ehis.niehs.nih.gov/. *2922*

ENVIRONMENTAL HYDROLOGY REPORT.
International Association for Environmental Hydrology, Box 35324, San Antonio, TX 78235-5324. TEL 210-344-5418. FAX 210-344-9941. URL: http://www.hydroweb.com. Available only online. *2393*

ENVIRONMENTAL LAW (PORTLAND).
Northwestern School of Law, Lewis and Clark College, 10015 S.W. Terwilliger Blvd., Portland, OR 97219. TEL 503-768-6700. FAX 503-768-6671. URL: http://www.lclark.edu/~envtl/ Vendor(s): Information Access Co., Lexis-Nexis, West Group. *2922*

ENVIRONMENTAL LAW REPORTER.
Environmental Law Institute, 1616 P St., S.W., Ste. 200, Washington, DC 20036. TEL 202-328-5150. Vendor(s): Lexis-Nexis, West Group. *2923*

ENVIRONMENTAL MANAGEMENT (NEW YORK).
Springer-Verlag, Life Science Journals, 175 Fifth Ave., New York, NY 10010. TEL 212-460-1500. FAX 212-473-6272. URL: http://www.springer-ny.com. *2923*

ENVIRONMENTAL MANAGEMENT BRIEFING.
Barbour Index, New Lodge Drift Rd., Windsor, Berks. SL4 4RQ, England. TEL 01344-884121. FAX 01344-884112. *2984*

ENVIRONMENTAL NUTRITION.
Environmental Nutrition, Inc., 52 Riverside Dr., Ste. 15A, New York, NY 10024-6599. TEL 212-362-0424. FAX 212-362-2066. Vendor(s): Information Access Co. *5472*

ENVIRONMENTAL PERIODICALS BIBLIOGRAPHY.
International Academy at Santa Barbara, 800 Garden St., Ste. D, Santa Barbara, CA 93101-1552. TEL 805-965-5010. FAX 805-965-6071. Vendor(s): Knight-Ridder Information, Inc. (File no.68). *2961*

ENVIRONMENTAL PROBLEMS & REMEDIATION.
Merton Allen Associates, InfoTeam Inc., Box 15640, Plantation, FL 33318-5640. TEL 954-473-9560. FAX 954-473-0544. Vendor(s): Data-Star, Information Access Co., NewsNet, UMI. *2924*

ENVIRONMENTAL REMEDIATION TECHNOLOGY.
Business Publishers, Inc., 951 Pershing Dr., Silver Spring, MD 20910-4464. TEL 301-587-6300. FAX 301-589-5103. Vendor(s): Information Access Co.. *2924*

ENVIRONMENTAL RESEARCH.
Academic Press, Inc., Journal Division, 525 B St., Ste. 1900, San Diego, CA 92101-4495. TEL 619-230-1840. FAX 619-699-6800. URL: http://www.apnet.com/www/journal/er.htm; http://www.idealibrary.com. *2925*

ENVIRONMENTAL SCIENCE & TECHNOLOGY (WASHINGTON).
American Chemical Society, 1155 16th St., N.W., Washington, DC 20036. FAX 614-447-3671. Vendor(s): STN International (CJACS). *2925*

ENVIRONMENTAL SOLUTIONS.
Advanstar Communications, Inc., 7500 Old Oak Blvd., Cleveland, OH 44130. TEL 216-826-2839. FAX 216-891-2726. Vendor(s): Information Access Co. *2984*

THE ENVIRONMENTALIST.
Chapman & Hall, Journals Department 2-6 Boundary Row, London SE1 8HN, England. TEL 44-171-8560066. FAX 44-171-5229623. URL: http://www.chaphall.com/chaphall/journals.html. *2926*

EQUAL OPPORTUNITIES REVIEW.
Eclipse Group Ltd., Industrial Relations Services, 18-20 Highbury Pl., London N5 1QP, England. TEL 44-171-354-5858. FAX 44-171-226-8618. Vendor(s): UMI. *1429*

EQUINE OZ.
Laurel Enterprises, URL: http://www.equineoz.com.au/ Available only online. *35*

EQUIPMENT AND MATERIALS UPDATE.
Merton Allen Associates, InfoTeam Inc., Box 15640, Plantation, FL 33318-5640. TEL 954-473-9560. FAX 954-473-0544. Vendor(s): Information Access Co., NewsNet, UMI. *6525*

EQUIPMENT LEASING TODAY.
Equipment Leasing Association, 1300 N. 17th St., Ste. 1010, Arlington, VA 22209. TEL 703-527-8655. FAX 703-527-2649. URL: http://elaonline.com/ Vendor(s): UMI. *4543*

ERGONOMICS.
Taylor & Francis Ltd., 1 Gunpowder Sq., London EC4A 3DE, England. TEL 44-171-583-0490. FAX 44-171-583-0585. URL: http://www.tandf.co.uk/. *2719*

ESCENE (YEAR).
1619 Eighth Ave., N., Seattle, WA 98109. URL: http://www.etext.org/zines/escene/ Available only online. *4530*

ESQUIRE.
Hearst Corporation, Esquire, 250 W. 55th St., New York, NY 10019. TEL 212-649-2040. FAX 212-977-3158. URL: http://www.heastcorp.com. Vendor(s): Information Access Co. *5176*

ESSAY AND GENERAL LITERATURE INDEX.
H.W. Wilson Co., 950 University Ave., Bronx, NY 10452. TEL 718-588-8400. FAX 718-590-1617. Vendor(s): Wilsonline (File EGL). *4495*

ESSAYS IN HISTORY.
University of Virginia, Corcoran Department of History, Charlottesville, VA 22903. TEL 804-924-7146. URL: http://www.lib.virginia.edu/journals/EH/EH.html. Available only online. *3494*

ESSAYS IN LITERATURE.
Western Illinois University, Department of English, 114 Simpkins Hall, Macomb, IL 61455-1396. TEL 309-298-2212. FAX 309-298-2212. Vendor(s): Information Access Co., UMI. *4402*

ESSENCE (NEW YORK).
Essence Communications Inc., 1500 Broadway, New York, NY 10036-4015. TEL 212-642-0600. FAX 212-921-5173. Vendor(s): Information Access Co. *7318*

ESSOR.
Union Francaise d'Annuaires Professionnels, 130 av des Boulaux, B.P.36, 78192 Trappes Cedex, France. TEL 01-30-13-82-00. FAX 01-30-13-82-11. *1323*

ESTATE PLANNER'S ALERT.
Research Institute of America, Inc., 90 Fifth Ave., New York, NY 10011. TEL 212-645-4800. FAX 212-337-4279. Vendor(s): Lexis-Nexis. *4096*

ESTATE PLANNING (NEW YORK).
Warren, Gorham & Lamont, One Penn Plaza, New York, NY 10119. TEL 212-971-5000. FAX 212-971-5113. Vendor(s): Lexis-Nexis (TAXRIA-Library), West Group (WGL-ESTPLN). *4096*

ESTATES GAZETTE.
Estates Gazette Ltd., 151 Wardour St., London W1V 4BN, England. TEL 44-171-437-0141. FAX 44-171-437-2432. *6300*

ESTUARINE, COASTAL AND SHELF SCIENCE.
Academic Press Ltd., 24-28 Oval Rd., London NW1 7DX, England. TEL 44-171-267-4466. FAX 44-171-482-2293. URL: http://www.hbuk.co.uk/ap/ecss; http://www.europe.idealibrary.com/ *2402*

ESTUDIOS PUBLICOS.
Centro de Estudios Publicos, Monsenor Sotero Sanz No. 175, Providencia, Santiago 9, Chile. TEL 56-2-2315324. FAX 56-2-2335253. *6612*

ESTUDIOS RURALES LATINOAMERICANOS.
Fundacion Estudios Rurales Latinoamericanos, Apdo. Aereo 11386, Bogota, Colombia. TEL 2837771. *1257*

ETC.
International Society for General Semantics, Box 728, Concord, CA 94522. TEL 510-798-0311. FAX 510-798-0312. URL: http://www.crl.com/~isgs/isgshome.html. Vendor(s): Information Access Co., UMI. *4256*

ETHNOLOGY.
University of Pittsburgh, Department of Anthropology, Pittsburgh, PA 15260. TEL 412-648-7503. FAX 412-648-7535. URL: http://www.pitt.edu/~caswww/cdesc/index.html. Vendor(s): Information Access Co., UMI. *315*

ETHNOMUSICOLOGY ONLINE.
URL: http://umbc.edu/eol. Available only online. *5391*

ETOY TANKSYSTEM.
P.O. Box 3365, 8049 Zurich, Switzerland. URL: http://www.etoy.com. Available only online. *2133*

EUROBIOLOGISTE.
Centre National des Biologistes, 80 av. du Maine, 75014 Paris, France. TEL 33-1-43229770. FAX 33-1-43217312. *600*

EUROFOOD.
Agra Europe (London) Ltd., 25 Frant Rd., Tunbridge Wells, Kent TN2 5JT, England. TEL 44-1892-533813. FAX 44-1892-544895. Vendor(s): Information Access Co. *3102*

EUROFOOD MONITOR.
Agra Europe (London) Ltd., 25 Frant Rd., Tunbridge Wells, Kent TN2 5JT, England. TEL 44-1892-533813. FAX 44-1892-544895. *3102*

EUROMARKETING.
Crain Communications Inc., New Garden House, 78 Hatton Garden, London EC1N 8JQ, England. TEL 44-171-457-1400. FAX 44-171-457-1440. Vendor(s): Information Access Co. *35*

EUROMONEY.
Euromoney Publications plc., Nestor House, Playhouse Yard, London EC4V 5EX, England. TEL 44-171-779-8935. FAX 44-171-779-8541. URL: http://www.emwl.com/contents/publications/euromoney/
Vendor(s): Information Access Co., Knight-Ridder Information, Inc., UMI. *1130*

THE EUROMONITOR BOOK REPORT (YEAR).
Euromonitor, 60-61 Britton St., London EC1M 5NA, England. TEL 44-171-251-8024. FAX 44-171-608-3149. URL: http://www.euromonitor.com. *6270*

EURONOMICS.
International Business Consortium Alphen, P.O. Box 1154, 2400 BD Alphen aan den Rijn, Netherlands. TEL 31-1720-25529. FAX 31-1720-26099. *961*

EUROPA CHEMIE.
Verlagsgruppe Handelsblatt GmbH, Kasernenstr. 67, 40213 Duesseldorf, Germany. TEL 49-211-8870. FAX 49-211-329954. *2763*

EUROPA VAN MORGEN.
European Commission Office in the Netherlands, Postbus 30465, 2500 GL The Hague, Netherlands. TEL 31-70-3469326. FAX 31-70-3646619. *6013*

EUROPAGES.
EureDit s.a., 9 av. de Friedland, 75008 Paris, France. TEL 33-1-53775400. FAX 33-1-42893473. URL: http://www.europages.com. *1676*

EUROPE.
Office for Official Publications of the European Communities, L-2985 Luxembourg, Luxembourg. Vendor(s): Information Access Co. *1258*

EUROPE - ASIA STUDIES.
Carfax Publishing Co., P.O. Box 25, Abingdon, Oxon. OX14 3UE, England. TEL 44-1235-401000. FAX 44-1235-401550.
Vendor(s): Information Access Co. *962*

EUROPE TODAY.
Greater Europe Mission, 18950 Base Camp Rd., Monument, CO 80132-8009. TEL 719-488-8008. FAX 719-488-8018. URL: http://www.gospelcom.net/gem. *6337*

THE EUROPEAN.
The European Ltd., 200 Gray's Inn Rd., London WC1X 8NE, England. TEL 44-171-418-7777. FAX 44-171-713-1840. *3277*

THE EUROPEAN ACCOUNTING REVIEW.
Thomson Professional, 2-6 Boundary Row, London SE1 8HN, England. TEL 44-171-865-0066. FAX 44-171-522-9621. URL: http://ear.thomsonprofessional.com. *1089*

EUROPEAN ADHESIVES & SEALANTS.
Argus Business Media Ltd., Queensway House, 2 Queensway, Redhill, Surrey RH1 1QS, England. TEL 44-1737-768611. FAX 44-1737-761685.
Vendor(s): Information Access Co. *5190*

EUROPEAN BIOPHYSICS JOURNAL.
Springer-Verlag, Heidelberger Platz 3, 14197 Berlin, Germany. TEL 49-30-82787-0. FAX 49-30-82787448. URL: http://link.springer.de. *675*

THE EUROPEAN BUSINESS JOURNAL.
Whurr Publishers Ltd., 19b Compton Terrace, London N1 2UN, England. TEL 44-171-359-5979. FAX 44-171-226-5290.
Vendor(s): UMI. *962*

EUROPEAN CHEMICAL NEWS.
Reed Business Information, Quadrant House, The Quadrant, Sutton, Surrey SM2 5AS, England. TEL 44-181-652-3187. FAX 44-181-652-3357. *2763*

EUROPEAN COMMUNITIES. COURT OF JUSTICE AND COURT OF FIRST INSTANCE. PROCEEDINGS.
European Communities, Court of Justice, L-2925 Luxembourg, Luxembourg. TEL 352-43031. FAX 352-4303-2600. URL: http://europa.eu.int/cj/index.htm. *4131*

EUROPEAN COSMETIC MARKETS.
Wilmington Publishing, Wilmington House, Church Rd., Dartford, Kent UA2 7EF, England. TEL 44-1322-277788. FAX 44-1322-276476.
Vendor(s): Information Access Co. *510*

EUROPEAN ENERGY REPORT.
Financial Times Energy Publishing, Maple House, 149 Tottenham Court Rd., London W1P 9LL, England. TEL 44-171-896-2241. FAX 44-171-896-2275.
Vendor(s): Data-Star, Information Access Co., Knight-Ridder Information, Inc., Lexis-Nexis. *2669*

EUROPEAN INDUSTRIAL RELATIONS REVIEW.
Eclipse Group Ltd., Industrial Relations Services, 18-20 Highbury Pl., London N5 1QP, England. TEL 44-171-354-5858. FAX 44-171-226-8618.
Vendor(s): UMI. *1429*

EUROPEAN JOURNAL OF APPLIED PHYSIOLOGY AND OCCUPATIONAL PHYSIOLOGY.
Springer-Verlag, Heidelberger Platz 3, 14197 Berlin, Germany. TEL 49-30-82787-0. FAX 49-30-82787448. URL: http://link.springer.de. *815*

EUROPEAN JOURNAL OF BIOCHEMISTRY.
Springer-Verlag, Heidelberger Platz 3, 14197 Berlin, Germany. TEL 49-30-82787-0. FAX 49-30-82787448. URL: http://link.springer.de. *659*

EUROPEAN JOURNAL OF CLINICAL PHARMACOLOGY.
Springer-Verlag, Heidelberger Platz 3, 14197 Berlin, Germany. TEL 49-30-82787-0. FAX 49-30-82787448. URL: http://link.springer.de. *5660*

EUROPEAN JOURNAL OF COMBINATORICS.
Academic Press Ltd., 24-28 Oval Rd., London NW1 7DX, England. TEL 44-171-267-4466. FAX 44-171-482-2293. URL: http://www.hbuk.co.uk/ap/ejc; http://www.europe.idealibrary.com/ *4572*

EUROPEAN JOURNAL OF DRUG METABOLISM AND PHARMACOKINETICS.
Editions Medecine et Hygiene, Case Postale 456, CH-1211 Geneva 4, Switzerland. TEL 41-22-7029311. FAX 41-22-7029355. *5660*

EUROPEAN JOURNAL OF EMERGENCY MEDICINE.
Chapman & Hall, Journals Department 2-6 Boundary Row, London SE1 8HN, England. TEL 44-171-8650066. FAX 44-171-5229623. URL: http://www.chaphall.com/chaphall/journals.html. *5007*

THE EUROPEAN JOURNAL OF FINANCE.
Thomson Professional, 2-6 Boundary Row, London SE1 8HN, England. TEL 44-171-8650066. FAX 44-171-5229623. URL: http://www.thomsonprofessional.com. *1131*

EUROPEAN JOURNAL OF MARKETING.
M C B University Press Ltd., 60-62 Toller Ln., Bradford, W. Yorks BD8 9BY, England. TEL 44-1274-777700. FAX 44-1274-785200. URL: http://www.mcb.co.uk/liblink/ejm/jourhome.htm. *1526*

EUROPEAN JOURNAL OF MORPHOLOGY.
Swets & Zeitlinger bv, P.O. Box 825, 2160 SZ Lisse, Netherlands. TEL 31-252-435111. FAX 31-252-415888. URL: http://www.swets.nl. *815*

EUROPEAN JOURNAL OF NUCLEAR MEDICINE.
Springer-Verlag, Heidelberger Platz 3, 14197 Berlin, Germany. TEL 49-30-82787-0. FAX 49-30-82787448. URL: http://link.springer.de. *5106*

EUROPEAN JOURNAL OF ORTHODONTICS.
Oxford University Press, Academic Division, Great Clarendon St., Oxford OX2 6DP, England. TEL 44-1865-267907. FAX 44-1865-267485. URL: http://www.oup.co.uk/journals. *4857*

EUROPEAN JOURNAL OF ORTHOPAEDIC SURGERY & TRAUMATOLOGY.
Springer-Verlag France, 26, rue des Carmes, 75005 Paris, France. TEL 33-1-44-41-15-80. FAX 33-1-43-54-49-08. URL: http://science.springer.de. *5007*

EUROPEAN JOURNAL OF PEDIATRICS.
Springer-Verlag, Heidelberger Platz 3, 14197 Berlin, Germany. TEL 49-30-82787-0. FAX 49-30-82787448. URL: http://link.springer.de. *5031*

EUROPEAN JOURNAL OF PHARMACEUTICS AND BIOPHARMACEUTICS.
Elsevier Science B.V., P.O. Box 211, 1000 AE Amsterdma, Netherlands. TEL 31-20-4853757. FAX 31-20-4853432. URL: http://www.elsevier.nl/. *5660*

EUROPEAN JOURNAL OF PHYSICS.
I O P Publishing Ltd., Dirac House, Temple Back, Bristol BS1 6BE, England. TEL 44-117-929-7481. FAX 44-117-929-4318. URL: http://www.iop.org. *5802*

EUROPEAN MEDIA ART FESTIVAL.
International Experimental Film Workshop, Postfach 1861, 49008 Osnabrueck, Germany. TEL 49-541-21658. FAX 49-541-28327. URL: http://www.emaf.de. *5330*

EUROPEAN MEDIA BUSINESS & FINANCE.
Omnicom P B I, Rosemount House, Rosemount Ave., W. Byfleet, Surrey KT14 6NP, England. TEL 44-1932-355515. FAX 44-1932-355962.
Vendor(s): Information Access Co. *1131*

EUROPEAN PHYSICS REVIEW A. HADRONS AND NUCLEI.
Springer-Verlag, Heidelberger Platz 3, 14197 Berlin, Germany. TEL 49-30-82787-0. FAX 49-30-82787448. URL: http://link.springer.de; http://science.springer.de/zphys-e/zphys-e.htm. *5851*

EUROPEAN PHYSICS REVIEW B. CONDENSED MATTER.
Springer-Verlag, Heidelberger Platz 3, 14197 Berlin, Germany. TEL 49 30-82787-0. FAX 49-30-82787448. URL: http://link.springer.de; http://science.springer.de/zphys-e/zphys-e.htm. *5802*

EUROPEAN PHYSICS REVIEW C. PARTICLES AND FIELDS.
Springer-Verlag, Heidelberger Platz 3, 14197 Berlin, Germany. TEL 49-30-82787-0. FAX 49-30-82787448. URL: http://link.springer.de. *5802*

EUROPEAN PHYSICS REVIEW D. ATOMS, MOLECULES, CLUSTERS AND OPTICAL PHYSICS.
Springer-Verlag, Heidelberger Platz 3, 14197 Berlin, Germany. TEL 49-30-82787-0. FAX 49-30-82787448. URL: http://link.springer.de; http://science.springer.de/zphys-e/zphys-e.htm. *5802*

EUROPEAN POLYMERS PAINT COLOUR JOURNAL.
Argus Business Media Ltd., Queensway House, 2 Queensway, Redhill, Surrey RH1 1QS, England. TEL 44-1737-768611. FAX 44-1737-761685.
Vendor(s): Information Access Co. *5552*

EUROPEAN POWER NEWS.
Argus Business Media Ltd., Queensway House, 2 Queensway, Redhill, Surrey RH1 1QS, England. TEL 44-1737-768611. FAX 44-1737-761685.
Vendor(s): Information Access Co. *2823*

EUROPEAN RADIOLOGY.
Springer-Verlag, Heidelberger Platz 3, 14197 Berlin, Germany. TEL 49-30-82787-0. FAX 49-30-82787448. URL: http://link.springer.de. *5106*

EUROPEAN RUBBER JOURNAL.
Crain Communications, Inc., New Garden House, 78 Hatton Garden, London EC1N 8JQ, England. TEL 44-171-457-1400. FAX 44-171-457-1440.
Vendor(s): Information Access Co. *6501*

EUROPEAN SEMICONDUCTOR BULLETIN.
Angel Business Communications Ltd., Kingsland House, 361-373 City Rd., London EC1V 1LR, England. TEL 44-171-417-7400. FAX 44-171-417-7500. *2637*

EUROPEAN SERIES IN APPLIED AND INDUSTRIAL MATHEMATICS. PROCEEDINGS.
Societe de Mathematiques Appliquees et Industrielles, 11 rue Pierre et Marie Curie, 75231 Paris Cedex 05, France. TEL 33-1-44276661. URL: http://www.emath.fr/proc/ *4572*

EUROPHYSICS LETTERS.
Editions de Physique, Zone Industrielle de Courtaboeuf, B.P. 112, 91944 Les Ulis Cedex, France. TEL 33-1-69-07-36-88. FAX 33-1-69-28-84-91. URL: http://www.ed-phys.fr/infodocs/onlineeuro.html. *5802*

EUROSTATISTICS DATA FOR SHORT TERM ECONOMIC ANALYSIS.
Office for Official Publications of the European Communities, Rue Alcide de Gasperi, 2920 Luxembourg, Luxembourg.
Vendor(s): Commission of the European Communities. *1038*

EUROWEEK.
Euromoney Publications plc., Nestor House, Playhouse Yard, London EC4V 5EX, England. TEL 44-171-779-8935. FAX 44-171-779-8541. Vendor(s): UMI. *1131*

EVA, YOUR GUIDE TO TONGA.
Vava'u Press Ltd., P.O. Box 427, Nuku'alofa, Tonga. TEL 676-23101. FAX 676-24749. URL: http://www.netstorage.com/lcami/tonaga/matangi. *7198*

EVALUATION COMMENT.
University of California at Los Angeles, Center for the Study of Evaluation, 405 Hilgard Ave., 1320 Moore Hall, Los Angeles, CA 90095-1522. TEL 310-206-1532. *2602*

EVALUATION OF DRUG INTERACTIONS.
Professional Drug Systems, Inc., 530 Maryville Centre Dr., St. Louis, MO 63141. TEL 314-275-8848. FAX 314-275-8819. *5661*

EVANS-NOVAK POLITICAL REPORT.
Eagle Publishing, A Phillips Publishing International Company, 422 First St., S.E., Washington, DC 20003. TEL 202-546-5005. FAX 202-546-8759. Vendor(s): Information Access Co. *5925*

EVENTLINE.
Elsevier Science B.V., P.O. Box 521, 1000 AM Amsterdam, Netherlands. TEL 31-20-4853911. FAX 31-20-4853598. URL: http://www.elsevier.nl/. Vendor(s): Data-Star, European Space Agency, Knight-Ridder Information, Inc. *1677*

EVERYBODY'S NEWS ONLINE.
Goodwin Communications, Inc., 1310 Pendleton St., Ste. 700, Cincinnati, OH 45210. URL: http://www.everybodys.org. Available only online. *3373*

EVO.
P Publishing, Box 566, Nebraska City, NE 68410-0566. URL: http://www.p-pub.com. Available only online. *2133*

EVOLUTION.
Allen Press, Inc., 1041 New Hampshire Ave., Box 1897, Lawrence, KS 66044-8897. FAX 913-843-1274. Vendor(s): Information Access Co. *767*

EVOLUTIONARY ECOLOGY.
Chapman & Hall, Journals Department 2-6 Boundary Row, London SE1 8HN, England. TEL 44-171-8650066. FAX 44-171-5229623. URL: http://www.chaphall.com/chaphall/jounals.html. *2927*

EXCEPTIONAL CHILDREN.
Council for Exceptional Children, 1920 Association Dr., Reston, VA 22091. TEL 703-620-3660. FAX 703-264-9494. Vendor(s): Information Access Co., UMI. *1845*

EXCEPTIONAL PARENT.
Psy-Ed. Corp., 555 Kinderkamack Rd., Oradell, NJ 07649-1517. TEL 201-489-0871. FAX 201-489-1240. URL: http://families.com. Vendor(s): Information Access Co., UMI. *1845*

EXCERPTA MEDICA ABSTRACT JOURNALS.
Elsevier Science B.V., P.O. Box 211, 1000 AE Amsterdam, Netherlands. TEL 31-20-4853757. FAX 31-20-4853432. URL: http://www.elsevier.nl/ Vendor(s): DIMDI, Data-Star, JICST, Knight-Ridder Information, Inc., Ovid Technologies, Inc. *4774*

EXCERPTA MEDICA. SECTION 1: ANATOMY, ANTHROPOLOGY, EMBRYOLOGY & HISTOLOGY.
Elsevier Science B.V., P.O. Box 211, 1000 AE Amsterdam, Netherlands. TEL 31-20-4853757. FAX 31-20-4853432. URL: http://www.elsevier.nl/ Vendor(s): DIMDI, Data-Star, JICST, Knight-Ridder Information, Inc., Ovid Technologies, Inc. *4774*

EXCERPTA MEDICA. SECTION 2: PHYSIOLOGY.
Elsevier Science B.V., P.O. Box 211, 1000 AE Amsterdam, Netherlands. TEL 31-20-4853757. FAX 31-20-4853432. URL: http://www.elsevier.nl/ Vendor(s): DIMDI, Data-Star, JICST, Knight-Ridder Information, Inc., Ovid Technologies, Inc. *4774*

EXCERPTA MEDICA. SECTION 3: ENDOCRINOLOGY.
Elsevier Science B.V., P.O. Box 211, 1000 AE Amsterdam, Netherlands. TEL 31-20-4853757. FAX 31-20-4853432. URL: http://www.elsevier.nl/ Vendor(s): DIMDI, Data-Star, JICST, Knight-Ridder Information, Inc., Ovid Technologies, Inc. *4775*

EXCERPTA MEDICA. SECTION 4: MICROBIOLOGY: BACTERIOLOGY, MYCOLOGY, PARASITOLOGY AND VIROLOGY.
Elsevier Science B.V., P.O. Box 211, 1000 AE Amsterdam, Netherlands. TEL 31-20-4853757. FAX 31-20-4853432. URL: http://www.elsevier.nl/ Vendor(s): DIMDI, Data-Star, JICST, Knight-Ridder Information, Inc., Ovid Technologies, Inc. *4775*

EXCERPTA MEDICA. SECTION 5: GENERAL PATHOLOGY AND PATHOLOGICAL ANATOMY.
Elsevier Science B.V., P.O. Box 211, 1000 AE Amsterdam, Netherlands. TEL 31-20-4853757. FAX 31-20-4853432. URL: http://www.elsevier.nl/ Vendor(s): DIMDI, Data-Star, JICST, Knight-Ridder Information, Inc., Ovid Technologies, Inc. *4775*

EXCERPTA MEDICA. SECTION 6: INTERNAL MEDICINE.
Elsevier Science B.V., P.O. Box 211, 1000 AE Amsterdam, Netherlands. TEL 31-20-4853757. FAX 31-20-4853432. URL: http://www.elsevier.nl/ Vendor(s): DIMDI, Data-Star, JICST, Knight-Ridder Information, Inc., Ovid Technologies, Inc. *4775*

EXCERPTA MEDICA. SECTION 7: PEDIATRICS AND PEDIATRIC SURGERY.
Elsevier Science B.V., P.O. Box 211, 1000 AE Amsterdam, Netherlands. TEL 31-20-4853757. FAX 31-20-4853432. URL: http://www.elsevier.nl/ Vendor(s): DIMDI, Data-Star, JICST, Knight-Ridder Information, Inc., Ovid Technologies, Inc. *4775*

EXCERPTA MEDICA. SECTION 8: NEUROLOGY AND NEUROSURGERY.
Elsevier Science B.V., P.O. Box 211, 1000 AE Amsterdam, Netherlands. TEL 31-20-4853757. FAX 31-20-4853432. URL: http://www.elsevier.nl/ Vendor(s): DIMDI, Data-Star, JICST, Knight-Ridder Information, Inc., Ovid Technologies, Inc. *4775*

EXCERPTA MEDICA. SECTION 9: SURGERY.
Elsevier Science B.V., P.O. Box 211, 1000 AM Amsterdam, Netherlands. TEL 31-20-4853757. FAX 31-20-4853432. URL: http://www.elsevier.nl/ Vendor(s): DIMDI, Data-Star, JICST, Knight-Ridder Information, Inc., Ovid Technologies, Inc. *4775*

EXCERPTA MEDICA. SECTION 10: OBSTETRICS AND GYNECOLOGY.
Elsevier Science B.V., P.O. Box 211, 1000 AE Amsterdam, Netherlands. TEL 31-20-4853757. FAX 31-20-4853432. URL: http://www.elsevier.nl/ Vendor(s): DIMDI, Data-Star, JICST, Knight-Ridder Information, Inc., Ovid Technologies, Inc. *4775*

EXCERPTA MEDICA. SECTION 11: OTORHINOLARYNGOLOGY.
Elsevier Science B.V., P.O. Box 211, 1000 AE Amsterdam, Netherlands. TEL 31-20-4853757. FAX 31-20-4853432. URL: http://www.elsevier.nl/ Vendor(s): DIMDI, Data-Star, JICST, Knight-Ridder Information, Inc., Ovid Technologies, Inc. *4775*

EXCERPTA MEDICA. SECTION 12: OPHTHALMOLOGY.
Elsevier Science B.V., P.O. Box 211, 1000 AE Amsterdam, Netherlands. TEL 31-20-4853757. FAX 31-20-4853432. URL: http://www.elsevier.nl/ Vendor(s): DIMDI, Data-Star, JICST, Knight-Ridder Information, Inc., Ovid Technologies, Inc. *4775*

EXCERPTA MEDICA. SECTION 13: DERMATOLOGY AND VENEREOLOGY.
Elsevier Science B.V., P.O. Box 211, 1000 AE Amsterdam, Netherlands. TEL 31-20-4853757. FAX 31-20-4853432. URL: http://www.elsevier.nl/ Vendor(s): DIMDI, Data-Star, JICST, Knight-Ridder Information, Inc., Ovid Technologies, Inc. *4776*

EXCERPTA MEDICA. SECTION 14: RADIOLOGY.
Elsevier Science B.V., P.O. Box 211, 1000 AE Amsterdam, Netherlands. TEL 31-20-4853757. FAX 31-20-4853432. URL: http://www.elsevier.nl/ Vendor(s): DIMDI, Data-Star, JICST, Knight-Ridder Information, Inc., Ovid Technologies, Inc. *4776*

EXCERPTA MEDICA. SECTION 15: CHEST DISEASES, THORACIC SURGERY AND TUBERCULOSIS.
Elsevier Science B.V., P.O. Box 211, 1000 AE Amsterdam, Netherlands. TEL 31-20-4853757. FAX 31-20-4853432. URL: http://www.elsevier.nl/ Vendor(s): DIMDI, Data-Star, JICST, Knight-Ridder Information, Inc., Ovid Technologies, Inc. *4776*

EXCERPTA MEDICA. SECTION 16: CANCER.
Elsevier Science B.V., P.O. Box 211, 1000 AE Amsterdam, Netherlands. TEL 31-20-4853757. FAX 31-20-4853432. URL: http://www.elsevier.nl/ Vendor(s): DIMDI, Data-Star, JICST, Knight-Ridder Information, Inc., Ovid Technologies, Inc. *4776*

EXCERPTA MEDICA. SECTION 17: PUBLIC HEALTH, SOCIAL MEDICINE AND EPIDEMIOLOGY.
Elsevier Science B.V., P.O. Box 211, 1000 AE Amsterdam, Netherlands. TEL 31-20-4853757. FAX 31-20-4853432. URL: http://www.elsevier.nl/ Vendor(s): DIMDI, Data-Star, JICST, Knight-Ridder Information, Inc., Ovid Technologies, Inc. *6256*

EXCERPTA MEDICA. SECTION 18: CARDIOVASCULAR DISEASES AND CARDIOVASCULAR SURGERY.
Elsevier Science B.V., P.O. Box 211, 1000 AE Amsterdam, Netherlands. TEL 31-20-4853757. FAX 31-20-4853432. URL: http://www.elsevier.nl/ Vendor(s): DIMDI, Data-Star, JICST, Knight-Ridder Information, Inc., Ovid Technologies, Inc. *4776*

EXCERPTA MEDICA. SECTION 19: REHABILITATION AND PHYSICAL MEDICINE.
Elsevier Science B.V., P.O. Box 211, 1000 AE Amsterdam, Netherlands. TEL 31-20-4853757. FAX 31-20-4853432. URL: http://www.elsevier.nl/ Vendor(s): DIMDI, Data-Star, JICST, Knight-Ridder Information, Inc., Ovid Technologies, Inc. *4776*

EXCERPTA MEDICA. SECTION 20: GERONTOLOGY AND GERIATRICS.
Elsevier Science B.V., P.O. Box 211, 1000 AE Amsterdam, Netherlands. TEL 31-20-4853757. FAX 31-20-4853432. URL: http://www.elsevier.nl/ Vendor(s): DIMDI, Data-Star, JICST, Knight-Ridder Information, Inc., Ovid Technologies, Inc. *3448*

EXCERPTA MEDICA. SECTION 21: DEVELOPMENTAL BIOLOGY AND TERATOLOGY.
Elsevier Science B.V., P.O. Box 211, 1000 AE Amsterdam, Netherlands. TEL 31-20-4853757. FAX 31-20-4853432. URL: http://www.elsevier.nl/ Vendor(s): DIMDI, Data-Star, JICST, Knight-Ridder Information, Inc., Ovid Technologies, Inc. *641*

EXCERPTA MEDICA. SECTION 22: HUMAN GENETICS.
Elsevier Science B.V., P.O. Box 211, 1000 AE Amsterdam, Netherlands. TEL 31-20-4853757. FAX 31-20-4853432. URL: http://www.elsevier.nl. Vendor(s): DIMDI, Data-Star, JICST, Knight-Ridder Information, Inc., Ovid Technologies, Inc. *641*

EXCERPTA MEDICA. SECTION 23: NUCLEAR MEDICINE.
Elsevier Science B.V., P.O. Box 211, 1000 AE Amsterdam, Netherlands. TEL 31-20-4853757. FAX 31-20-4853432. URL: http://www.elsevier.nl/ Vendor(s): DIMDI, Data-Star, JICST, Knight-Ridder Information, Inc., Ovid Technologies, Inc. *4777*

EXCERPTA MEDICA. SECTION 24: ANESTHESIOLOGY.
Elsevier Science B.V., P.O. Box 211, 1000 AE Amsterdam, Netherlands. TEL 31-20-4853757. FAX 31-20-4853432. URL: http://www.elsevier.nl/ Vendor(s): DIMDI, Data-Star, JICST, Knight-Ridder Information, Inc., Ovid Technologies, Inc. *4777*

EXCERPTA MEDICA. SECTION 25: HEMATOLOGY.
Elsevier Science B.V., P.O. Box 211, 1000 AE Amsterdam, Netherlands. TEL 31-20-4853757. FAX 31-20-4853432. URL: http://www.elsevier.nl/ Vendor(s): DIMDI, Data-Star, JICST, Knight-Ridder Information, Inc., Ovid Technologies, Inc. *4777*

EXCERPTA MEDICA. SECTION 26: IMMUNOLOGY, SEROLOGY AND TRANSPLANTATION.
Elsevier Science B.V., P.O. Box 211, 1000 AE Amsterdam, Netherlands. TEL 31-20-4853757. FAX 31-20-4853432. URL: http://www.elsevier.nl/ Vendor(s): DIMDI, Data-Star, JICST, Knight-Ridder Information, Inc., Ovid Technologies, Inc. *4777*

EXCERPTA MEDICA. SECTION 27: BIOPHYSICS, BIO-ENGINEERING AND MEDICAL INSTRUMENTATION.
Elsevier Science B.V., P.O. Box 211, 1000 AE Amsterdam, Netherlands. TEL 31-20-4853757. FAX 31-20-4853432. URL: http://www.elsevier.nl/ Vendor(s): DIMDI, Data-Star, JICST, Knight-Ridder Information, Inc., Ovid Technologies, Inc. *4777*

EXCERPTA MEDICA. SECTION 28: UROLOGY AND NEPHROLOGY.
Elsevier Science B.V., P.O. Box 211, 1000 AE Amsterdam, Netherlands. TEL 31-20-4853757. FAX 31-20-4853432. URL: http://www.elsevier.nl/ Vendor(s): DIMDI, Data-Star, JICST, Knight-Ridder Information, Inc., Ovid Technologies, Inc. *4777*

EXCERPTA MEDICA. SECTION 29: CLINICAL AND EXPERIMENTAL BIOCHEMISTRY.
Elsevier Science B.V., P.O. Box 211, 1000 AE Amsterdam, Netherlands. TEL 31-20-4853757. FAX 31-20-4853432. URL: http://www.elsevier.nl/ Vendor(s): DIMDI, Data-Star, JICST, Knight-Ridder Information, Inc., Ovid Technologies, Inc. *641*

EXCERPTA MEDICA. SECTION 30: CLINICAL AND EXPERIMENTAL PHARMACOLOGY.
Elsevier Science B.V., P.O. Box 211, 1000 AE Amsterdam, Netherlands. TEL 31-20-4853757. FAX 31-20-4853432. URL: http://www.elsevier.nl/ Vendor(s): DIMDI, Data-Star, JICST, Knight-Ridder Information, Inc., Ovid Technologies, Inc. *5701*

EXCERPTA MEDICA. SECTION 31: ARTHRITIS AND RHEUMATISM.
Elsevier Science B.V., P.O. Box 211, 1000 AE Amsterdam, Netherlands. TEL 31-20-4853757. FAX 31-20-4853432. URL: http://www.elsevier.nl/ Vendor(s): DIMDI, Data-Star, JICST, Knight-Ridder Information, Inc., Ovid Technologies, Inc. *4777*

EXCERPTA MEDICA. SECTION 32: PSYCHIATRY.
Elsevier Science B.V., P.O. Box 211, 1000 AE Amsterdam, Netherlands. TEL 31-20-4853757. FAX 31-20-4853432. URL: http://www.elsevier.nl/ Vendor(s): DIMDI, Data-Star, JICST, Knight-Ridder Information, Inc., Ovid Technologies, Inc. *4777*

EXCERPTA MEDICA. SECTION 33: ORTHOPEDIC SURGERY.
Elsevier Science B.V., P.O. Box 211, 1000 AE Amsterdam, Netherlands. TEL 31-20-4853757. FAX 31-20-4853432. URL: http://www.elsevier.nl/ Vendor(s): DIMDI, Data-Star, JICST, Knight-Ridder Information, Inc., Ovid Technologies, Inc. *4778*

EXCERPTA MEDICA. SECTION 35: OCCUPATIONAL HEALTH AND INDUSTRIAL MEDICINE.
Elsevier Science B.V., P.O. Box 211, 1000 AE Amsterdam, Netherlands. TEL 31-20-4853757. FAX 31-20-4853432. Vendor(s): DIMDI, Data-Star, JICST, Knight-Ridder Information, Inc., Ovid Technologies, Inc. *4778*

EXCERPTA MEDICA. SECTION 36: HEALTH POLICY, ECONOMICS AND MANAGEMENT.
Elsevier Science B.V., P.O. Box 211, 1000 AE Amsterdam, Netherlands. TEL 31-20-4853757. FAX 31-20-4853432. URL: http://www.elsevier.nl/ Vendor(s): DIMDI, Data-Star, JICST, Knight-Ridder Information, Inc., Ovid Technologies, Inc. *3721*

EXCERPTA MEDICA. SECTION 38: ADVERSE REACTIONS TITLES.
Elsevier Science B.V., P.O. Box 211, 1000 AE Amsterdam, Netherlands. TEL 31-20-4853757. FAX 31-20-4853432. URL: http://www.elsevier.nl/ Vendor(s): DIMDI, Data-Star, JICST, Knight-Ridder Information, Inc., Ovid Technologies, Inc. *4778*

EXCERPTA MEDICA. SECTION 40: DRUG DEPENDENCE, ALCOHOL ABUSE AND ALCOHOLISM.
Elsevier Science B.V., P.O. Box 211, 1000 AE Amsterdam, Netherlands. TEL 31-20-4853757. FAX 31-20-4853432. URL: http://www.elsevier.nl/ Vendor(s): DIMDI, Data-Star, JICST, Knight-Ridder Information, Inc., Ovid Technologies, Inc. *2307*

EXCERPTA MEDICA. SECTION 46: ENVIRONMENTAL HEALTH AND POLLUTION CONTROL.
Elsevier Science B.V., P.O. Box 211, 1000 AE Amsterdam, Netherlands. TEL 31-20-4853757. FAX 31-20-4853432. URL: http://www.elsevier.nl/ Vendor(s): DIMDI, Data-Star, JICST, Knight-Ridder Information, Inc., Ovid Technologies, Inc. *2962*

EXCERPTA MEDICA. SECTION 48: GASTROENTEROLOGY.
Elsevier Science B.V., P.O. Box 211, 1000 AE Amsterdam, Netherlands. TEL 31-20-4853757. FAX 31-20-4853432. URL: http://www.elsevier.nl/ Vendor(s): DIMDI, Data-Star, JICST, Knight-Ridder Information, Inc., Ovid Technologies, Inc. *4778*

EXCERPTA MEDICA. SECTION 49: FORENSIC SCIENCE ABSTRACTS.
Elsevier Science B.V., P.O. Box 211, 1000 AE Amsterdam, Netherlands. TEL 31-20-4853757. FAX 31-20-4853432. URL: http://www.elsevier.nl/ Vendor(s): DIMDI, Data-Star, JICST, Knight-Ridder Information, Inc., Ovid Technologies, Inc. *4778*

EXCERPTA MEDICA. SECTION 50: EPILEPSY ABSTRACTS.
Elsevier Science B.V., P.O. Box 211, 1000 AE Amsterdam, Netherlands. TEL 31-20-4853757. FAX 31-20-4853432. URL: http://www.elsevier.nl/ Vendor(s): DIMDI, Data-Star, JICST, Knight-Ridder Information, Inc., Ovid Technologies, Inc. *4778*

EXCERPTA MEDICA. SECTION 52: TOXICOLOGY.
Elsevier Science B.V., P.O. Box 211, 1000 AE Amsterdam, Netherlands. TEL 31-20-4853757. FAX 31-20-4853432. URL: http://www.elsevier.nl/ Vendor(s): DIMDI, Data-Star, JICST, Knight-Ridder Information, Inc., Ovid Technologies, Inc. *2962*

EXECUTIVE ACCOUNTANT.
Institute of Cost and Executive Accountants Educational Trust, 141-149 Fonthill Rd., London N4 3HF, England. TEL 44-171-272-3925. FAX 44-171-281-5723. Vendor(s): UMI. *1089*

EXECUTIVE BRIEF.
Society for Information Management, 401 N. Michigan Ave., Chicago, IL 60611-4267. TEL 312-644-6610. FAX 312-245-1083. URL: http://www.simnet.org. *2181*

EXECUTIVE EXCELLENCE.
Executive Excellence Publishing, 1344 E. 1120 S., Provo, UT 84606. TEL 801-375-4014. FAX 801-377-5960. URL: http://www.eep.com. Vendor(s): UMI. *1565*

EXECUTIVE FEMALE.
National Association for Female Executives, 30 Irving Pl., 5th Fl., New York, NY 10003. TEL 212-477-2200. Vendor(s): Information Access Co. *7319*

EXECUTIVE HEALTH'S GOOD HEALTH REPORT.
Executive Health, 383 Route 46 W., Fairfield, NJ 07004-2402. TEL 201-227-5599. Vendor(s): Information Access Co. *5781*

EXECUTIVE MEMORANDUM.
Heritage Foundation, 214 Massachusetts Ave., N.E., Washington, DC 20002. TEL 202-546-4400. FAX 202-543-9647. Vendor(s): Lexis-Nexis. *6014*

EXECUTIVE REPORT.
Riverview Publications, Inc., 3 Gateway Center, 5th Fl., Pittsburgh, PA 15222-1004. TEL 412-471-4585. FAX 412-644-3006. Vendor(s): Knight-Ridder Information, Inc., Lexis-Nexis, UMI. *1642*

EXECUTIVE SPEAKER.
Executive Speaker Co., Box 292437, Dayton, OH 45429. TEL 937-294-8493. FAX 937-294-6044. Vendor(s): Lexis-Nexis. *36*

EXECUTIVE SPEECHES.
Executive Speaker Co., Box 292437, Dayton, OH 45429. TEL 937-294-8493. FAX 937-294-6044. Vendor(s): UMI. *963*

EXPANSION.
Recoletos Compania Editorial, S.A, Recoletos 1, 5o, 28001 Madrid, Spain. TEL 34-1-3373220. FAX 34-1-3373266. URL: http://www.recoletos.es. *963*

EXPERIMENTAL & APPLIED ACAROLOGY.
Thomson Science, 2-6 Boundary Row, London SE1 8HN, England. TEL 44-171-8560066. FAX 44-171-5229623. URL: http://www.thomsonscience.com. *601*

EXPERIMENTAL AND MOLECULAR PATHOLOGY.
Academic Press, Inc., Journal Division, 525 B St., Ste. 1900, San Diego, CA 92101-4495. TEL 619-230-1840. FAX 619-699-6800. URL: http://www.apnet.com/www/journal/mo.htm; http://www.idealibrary.com. *4666*

EXPERIMENTAL BIOLOGY ONLINE.
Springer-Verlag, Heidelberger Platz 3, 14197 Berlin, Germany. TEL 49-30-82787-0. FAX 49-30-82787448. URL: http://link.springer.de. Available only online. *601*

EXPERIMENTAL BRAIN RESEARCH.
Springer-Verlag, Heidelberger Platz 3, 14197 Berlin, Germany. TEL 49-30-82787-0. FAX 49-30-82787448. URL: http://link.springer.de. *5064*

EXPERIMENTAL CELL RESEARCH.
Academic Press, Inc., Journal Division, 525 B St., Ste. 1900, San Diego, CA 92101-4495. TEL 619-230-1840. FAX 619-699-6800. URL: http://www.apnet.com/www/journals/ex.htm; http://www.idealibrary.com/ *740*

EXPERIMENTAL EYE RESEARCH.
Academic Press Ltd., 24-28 Oval Rd., London NW1 7DX, England. TEL 44-171-267-4466. FAX 44-171-482-2293. URL: http://www.hbuk.co.uk/ap/eer; http://www.europe.idealibrary.com/ *4993*

EXPERIMENTAL MATHEMATICS.
A K Peters, Ltd., 289 Linden St., Wellesley, MA 02181-5910. TEL 617-235-2210. FAX 617-235-2404. URL: http://www.akpeters.com; http://www.expmath.com. *4572*

EXPERIMENTAL NEUROLOGY.
Academic Press, Inc., Journal Division, 525 B St., Ste. 1900, San Diego, CA 92101-4495. TEL 619-230-1840. FAX 619-699-6800. URL: http://www.apnet.com/www/journal/en.htm; http://www.idealibrary.com/ *5065*

EXPERIMENTAL PARASITOLOGY.
Academic Press, Inc., Journal Division, 525 B St., Ste. 1900, San Diego, CA 92101-4495. TEL 619-230-1840. FAX 619-699-6800. URL: http://www.apnet.com/www/journal/pr.htm; http://www.idealibrary.com/ *4835*

EXPERIMENTAL ROCKET FLYER.
California Rocketry, Box 1242, Claremont, CA 91711. FAX 909-398-1877. *64*

EXPERT.
Kriyanovski ul., 24-35, b.2, 124036 Moscow, Russia. TEL 7-095-1246390. URL: http://www.expert.ru. *963*

THE EXPERT AND THE LAW.
National Forensic Center, 17 Temple Terr., Lawrenceville, NJ 08648. TEL 609-883-0550. Vendor(s): Lexis-Nexis. *3948*

EXPERTS CONTACT DIRECTORY.
Gale Research, 835 Penobscot Bldg., 645 Griswold St., Detroit, MI 48226-4094. TEL 313-961-2242. FAX 800-41-50433. *1951*

THE EXPLICATOR.
Heldref Publications, 1319 Eighteenth St., N.W., Washington, DC 20036-1802. TEL 202-296-6267. FAX 202-296-5149. Vendor(s): Information Access Co., UMI. *4405*

EXPLORATIONS IN ECONOMIC HISTORY.
Academic Press, Inc., Journal Division, 525 B St., Ste. 1900, San Diego, CA 92101-4495. TEL 619-230-1840. FAX 619-699-6800. URL: http://www.apnet.com/www/journal/eh/htm; http://www.idealibrary.com/ *1304*

EXPO (KANSAS CITY).
Atwood Convention Publishing, 11600 College Blvd., Overland Park, KS 66210. TEL 913-469-1185. FAX 913-469-0806. URL: http://www.expoweb.com. *1477*

THE EXPORTER.
Trade Data Reports, Inc., 90 John St., 5th Fl., New York, NY 10038-3202. Vendor(s): NewsNet (IT04). *1325*

EXPOSURE! (YAKIMA).
129 Foothills Rd., Lake Oswego, OR 97034-3105. URL: http://www.exposure-usa.com/ *2133*

L'EXPRESS.
Case Postale 561, CH-2001 Neuchatel, Switzerland. TEL 038-256501. FAX 038-247736. *3363*

EXQUISITE CORPSE.
Illinois State University, Campus Box 4241, Normal, IL 61790-4241. URL: http://corpse.books.com/EChome.html. *4333*

EXTRA!
Fairness & Accuracy In Reporting (F.A.I.R.), 130 W. 25th St., New York, NY 10001. TEL 212-633-6700. FAX 212-727-7668. URL: http://www.fair.org/fair/ *3872*

EXTRAPOLATION.
Kent State University Press, Box 5190, 307 Lowry Hall, Kent, OH 44242-0001. TEL 330-672-7913. FAX 330-672-3104.
Vendor(s): Information Access Co. *4531*

EXTREMOPHILES.
Springer-Verlag Tokyo, 3-13, Hongo 3-chome, Bunkyo-ku, Tokyo 113, Japan. TEL 81-3-38120331. FAX 81-3-38120719. *682*

EYE.
301-S. Elm St., Ste. 405, Greensboro, NC 27401-2636. TEL 910-370-1702. FAX 910-370-1603. URL: http://www.infi.net/~eye. *3374*

EYEWEAR: THE INTERNATIONAL MARKET.
Euromonitor, 60-61 Britton Rd., London EC1 5NA, England. TEL 44-171-251-8024. FAX 44-171-608-3149. URL: http://www.euromonitor.com.
Vendor(s): Data-Star, Knight-Ridder Information, Inc.. *5007*

F B I LAW ENFORCEMENT BULLETIN.
U.S. Federal Bureau of Investigation, F B I Academy, Madison Bldg., Rm. 209, Quantico, VA 22135. TEL 703-640-8666. FAX 703-640-1474.
Vendor(s): Information Access Co., UMI. *2267*

F B I S REPORT: CENTRAL EURASIA.
U.S. National Technical Information Service, 5285 Port Royal Rd., Springfield, VA 22161. TEL 703-487-4600. FAX 703-321-8547. *5925*

F C C REPORT.
Capitol Publications Inc., Telecom Publishing Group, 1101 King St., Ste. 444, Box 1455, Alexandria, VA 22313-2055. FAX 703-739-6484. URL: http://www.telecommunications.com.
Vendor(s): Information Access Co., Knight-Ridder Information, Inc., NewsNet (TE52). *1990*

F D A CONSUMER.
U.S. Food and Drug Administration, Office of Public Affairs, 5600 Fishers Ln., Rockville, MD 20857. TEL 301-443-3220.
Vendor(s): Information Access Co., Knight-Ridder Information, Inc., UMI. *2255*

F D A ENFORCEMENT REPORT.
U.S. Food and Drug Administration, Office of Public Affairs, Rm. 15A-11, Parklawn Bldg., 5600 Fishers Ln., Rockville, MD 20857. TEL 301-443-3285.
Vendor(s): Information Access Co., Ovid Technologies, Inc. (DIOG). *2267*

F D A MEDICAL BULLETIN.
U.S. Food and Drug Administration, Office of Public Affairs, 5600 Fisher's Ln., Rockville, MD 20857. TEL 301-443-3220.
Vendor(s): Data-Star, Information Access Co., Knight-Ridder Information, Inc., Ovid Technologies, Inc. (DIOG) *5661*

F I I ANNUAL GUIDE TO BONDS.
Financial Information Incorporated, 30 Montgomery St., Jersey City, NJ 07302. FAX 800-344-3292. *1383*

F I I ANNUAL GUIDE TO STOCKS.
Financial Information Incorporated, 30 Montgomery St., Jersey City, NJ 07302. FAX 800-344-3292. *1383*

F O I A UPDATE.
U.S. Department of Justice, Office of Information and Privacy, Constitution Ave. & Tenth Sts., N.W., Washington, DC 20530-0001. TEL 202-514-5105. FAX 202-514-1009. URL: http://www.usdoj.gov. *3872*

F R A N C I S. 519: PHILOSOPHIE.
Centre National de la Recherche Scientifique, Institut de l'Information Scientifique et Technique, 2 allee du Parc de Brabois, 54514 Vandoeuvre-les-Nancy Cedex, France. TEL 83-50-46-00. FAX 83-50-46-50.
Vendor(s): Telesystemes - Questel. *5760*

F R A N C I S. 520: SCIENCES DE L'EDUCATION.
Centre National de la Recherche Scientifique, Institut de l'Information Scientifique et Technique, 2 allee du Parc de Brabois, 54514 Vandoeuvre-les-Nancy Cedex, France. TEL 83-50-46-00. FAX 83-50-46-50.
Vendor(s): Telesystemes - Questel. *2500*

F R A N C I S. 521: SOCIOLOGIE.
Centre National de la Recherche Scientifique, Institut de l'Information Scientifique et Technique, 2 allee du Parc de Brabois, 54514 Vandoeuvre-les-Nancy Cedex, France. TEL 83-50-46-00. FAX 83-50-46-50.
Vendor(s): Telesystemes - Questel. *6739*

F R A N C I S. 522: HISTOIRE DES SCIENCES ET DE TECHNIQUES.
Centre National de la Recherche Scientifique, Institut de l'Information Scientifique et Technique, 2 allee du Parc de Brabois, 54514 Vandoeuvre-les-Nancy Cedex, France. TEL 83-50-46-00. FAX 83-50-46-50.
Vendor(s): European Space Agency, Telesystemes - Questel. *3520*

F R A N C I S. 523: HISTOIRE ET SCIENCES DE LA LITTERATURE.
Centre National de la Recherche Scientifique, Institut de l'Information Scientifique et Technique, 2 allee du Parc de Brabois, 54514 Vandoeuvre-les-Nancy Cedex, France. TEL 83-50-46-00. FAX 83-50-46-50.
Vendor(s): Telesystemes - Questel. *4495*

F R A N C I S. 524: SCIENCES DU LANGAGE.
Centre National de la Recherche Scientifique, Institut de l'Information Scientifique et Technique, 2 allee du Parc de Brabois, 54514 Vandoeuvre-les-Nancy Cedex, France. TEL 83-50-46-00. FAX 83-50-46-50.
Vendor(s): Telesystemes - Questel. *4318*

F R A N C I S. 525: PREHISTOIRE ET PROTOHISTOIRE.
Centre National de la Recherche Scientifique, Institut de l'Information Scientifique et Technique, 2 allee du Parc de Brabois, 54514 Vandoeuvre-les-Nancy Cedex, France. TEL 83-50-46-00. FAX 83-50-46-50.
Vendor(s): Telesystemes - Questel. *390*

F R A N C I S. 526: ART ET ARCHEOLOGIE.
Centre National de la Recherche Scientifique, Institut de l'Information Scientifique et Technique, 2 allee du Parc de Brabois, 54514 Vandoeuvre-les-Nancy Cedex, France. TEL 83-50-46-00. FAX 83-50-46-50.
Vendor(s): Telesystemes - Questel. *476*

F R A N C I S. 527: HISTOIRE ET SCIENCES DES RELIGIONS.
Centre National de la Recherche Scientifique, Institut de l'Information Scientifique et Technique, 2 allee du Parc de Brabois, 54514 Vandoeuvre-les-Nancy Cedex, France. TEL 83-50-46-00. FAX 83-50-46-50.
Vendor(s): Telesystemes - Questel. *6386*

F R A N C I S. 528: BIBLIOGRAPHIE INTERNATIONALE DE SCIENCE ADMINISTRATIVE.
Centre National de la Recherche Scientifique, Institut de l'Information Scientifique et Technique, 2 allee du Parc de Brabois, 54514 Vandoeuvre-les-Nancy Cedex, France. TEL 83-50-46-00. FAX 83-50-46-50.
Vendor(s): Telesystemes - Questel. *1038*

F R A N C I S. 529: ETHNOLOGIE.
Centre National de la Recherche Scientifique, Institut de l'Information Scientifique et Technique, 2 allee du Parc de Brabois, 54514 Vandoeuvre-les-Nancy Cedex, France. TEL 83-50-46-00. FAX 83-50-46-50.
Vendor(s): Telesystemes - Questel. *335*

F R A N C I S. 603: INFORMATIQUE ET SCIENCES JURIDIQUES.
Centre National de la Recherche Scientifique, Institut de l'Information Scientifique et Technique, 2 allee du Parc de Brabois, 54514 Vandoeuvre-les-Nancy Cedex, France. TEL 83-50-46-00. FAX 83-50-46-50.
Vendor(s): Telesystemes - Questel. *4068*

F R A N C I S. 617: E C O D O C.
Centre National de la Recherche Scientifique, Institut de l'Information Scientifique et Technique, 2 allee du Parc de Brabois, 54514 Vandoeuvre-les-Nancy Cedex, France. TEL 83-50-46-00. FAX 83-50-46-50.
Vendor(s): Telesystemes - Questel. *1038*

F R A N C I S. 731: ECONOMIE DE L'ENERGIE.
Centre National de la Recherche Scientifique, Institut de l'Information Scientifique et Technique, 2 allee du Parc de Brabois, 54514 Vandoeuvre-les-Nancy Cedex, France. TEL 33-83-50-46-00. FAX 33-83-50-46-50.
Vendor(s): Telesystemes - Questel. *2683*

F T C FREEDOM OF INFORMATION LOG.
Washington Regulatory Reporting Associates, Box 356, Basye, VA 22810. TEL 703-856-2216. FAX 703-856-8331.
Vendor(s): Lexis-Nexis. *1325*

F T C WATCH.
Washington Regulatory Reporting Associates, Box 356, Basye, VA 22810. TEL 703-856-2216.
Vendor(s): Lexis-Nexis, NewsNet (GT17). *1325*

F Y I FRANCE.
Box 460668, San Francisco, CA 94146. TEL 415-282-4850. FAX 415-824-1072. URL: http://www.fyifrance.com.
Available only online. *4231*

FACILITIES DESIGN AND MANAGEMENT.
Miller Freeman Inc. (New York), One Penn Plaza, New York, NY 10119. TEL 212-714-1300. FAX 212-714-1313.
Vendor(s): UMI. *1477*

FACTS ON FILE WORLD NEWS DIGEST WITH INDEX.
Facts on File, Inc., 11 Penn Plza, 15th Fl., New York, NY 10001. TEL 212-967-8800.
Vendor(s): Information Access Co., Knight-Ridder Information, Inc. (File no.264), Lexis-Nexis. *3494*

FADE TO BLACK COMEDY MAGAZINE.
URL: http://www.fadetoblack.com.
Available only online. *7006*

FAIR EMPLOYMENT PRACTICES SUMMARY OF LATEST DEVELOPMENTS.
The Bureau of National Affairs, Inc., 1231 25th St., N.W., Washington, DC 20037. TEL 202-452-4200. FAX 202-822-8092. URL: http://www.bna.com/
Vendor(s): Human Resources Information Network (CDD, HDD). *1430*

FAIR EMPLOYMENT REPORT.
Business Publishers, Inc., 951 Pershing Dr., Silver Spring, MD 20910-4464. TEL 301-587-6300. FAX 301-585-9075.
Vendor(s): NewsNet. *1430*

FAIR TRADER.
Culture Clash Communications, URL: http://www.izad.com/cultureclash.
Available only online. *1527*

FAIRFIELD COUNTY BUSINESS JOURNAL.
Westfair Communications, Inc., 108 Corporate Park Dr., Ste. 105, White Plains, NY 10604-3805. TEL 914-694-3600. FAX 914-694-3699.
Vendor(s): UMI. *1259*

FAIRY DUST.
URL: http://sahsimi.wwa.com/'sapphire/fairy.html.
Available only online. *6598*

FAMILIES IN SOCIETY.
Families International, Inc., 11700 W. Lake Park Dr., Milwaukee, WI 53224. TEL 414-359-1040. FAX 414-359-1074. URL: http://www.fsanet.org.
Vendor(s): UMI. *6665*

FAMILY ADVOCATE.
American Bar Association, Family Law Section, 750 N. Lake Shore Dr., Chicago, IL 60611. TEL 708-675-2864. URL: http://www.abanet.org.
Vendor(s): West Group (FAMADVO). *4100*

SERIALS AVAILABLE ONLINE

FAMILY CIRCLE.
Family Circle, Inc., 110 Fifth Ave., New York, NY 10011. TEL 212-499-2000. FAX 212-463-1808. Vendor(s): Information Access Co. *3684*

THE FAMILY HANDYMAN.
Home Service Publications, Inc., 7900 International Dr., Ste. 950, Minneapolis, MN 55425. TEL 612-854-3000. FAX 612-854-8009. Vendor(s): Information Access Co., UMI. *3768*

FAMILY LAW QUARTERLY.
American Bar Association, Family Law Section, 750 N. Lake Shore Dr., Chicago, IL 60611. TEL 312-988-6068. URL: http://www.abanet.org. Vendor(s): West Group (FAMLQ). *4101*

FAMILY LAW REPORTER.
The Bureau of National Affairs, Inc., 1231 25th St., N.W., Washington, DC 20037. TEL 202-452-4200. FAX 202-822-8092. URL: http://www.bna.com/ *4101*

FAMILY LAW REPORTS.
Jordan Publishing Ltd., 21 St. Thomas St., Bristol BS1 6JS, England. TEL 0117-923-0600. FAX 0117-923-0063. Vendor(s): Lexis-Nexis. *4101*

FAMILY MEDICAL PRACTICE ON-LINE.
Priory Lodge Education Ltd., URL: http://www.priory.com/journals/fam.htm. Available only online. *4667*

FAMILY PLANNING PERSPECTIVES.
Alan Guttmacher Institute, 120 Wall St., New York, NY 10005. TEL 212-248-1111. FAX 212-248-1951. URL: http://www.AGI-USA.org. Vendor(s): UMI. *4956*

FAMILY PRACTICE.
Oxford University Press, Academic Division, Great Clarendon St., Oxford OX2 6DP, England. TEL 44-1865-267907. FAX 44-1865-267485. URL: http://www.oup.co.uk/journals. *4667*

FAMILY RELATIONS.
National Council on Family Relations, 3989 Central Ave., N.E., Ste. 550, Minneapolis, MN 55421-3921. TEL 612-781-9331. FAX 612-781-9348. Vendor(s): Knight-Ridder Information, Inc., Ovid Technologies, Inc., UMI. *6710*

FANLIGHT NEWS.
Fanlight Productions, 47 Halifax St., Boston, MA 02130. TEL 617-524-0980. FAX 617-524-8838. URL: htp://www.fanlight.com. *4667*

FAR EASTERN ECONOMIC REVIEW.
Review Publishing Co. Ltd., G.P.O. Box 160, Hong Kong, People's Republic of China. TEL 852-2508-4300. FAX 852-2503-1549. URL: http://www.feer.com. Vendor(s): Dow Jones News Retrieval. *1259*

FARADAY DISCUSSIONS.
The Royal Society of Chemistry, Thomas Graham House, Science Park, Milton Rd., Cambridge CB4 4WF, England. TEL 44-1223-420066. FAX 44-1223-423429. URL: http://chemistry.rsc.org/rsc/. Vendor(s): STN International (CJRSC). *1828*

FARADAY TRANSACTIONS.
The Royal Society of Chemistry, Thomas Graham House, Science Park, Milton Rd., Cambridge CB4 4WF, England. TEL 44-1223-420066. FAX 44-1223-423623. URL: http://chemistry.rsc.org/rsc/. Vendor(s): STN International (CJRSC). *1828*

FARM AND FOOD.
Teagasc, 19 Sandymount Ave., Dublin 4, Ireland. TEL 353-1-6688188. FAX 353-1-6688023. *115*

FARM BUREAU NEWS.
American Farm Bureau Federation, 600 Maryland Ave., S.W., Ste. 800, Washington, DC 20024. TEL 202-484-3600. URL: http://www.fb.com/ *116*

FARMACEUTEN.
Dansk Farmaceutforening, Toldbbodgade 36, 1253 Copenhagen K, Denmark. *5661*

FARMACEUTICKY OBZOR.
Ministerstvo Zdravotnictva, Institut pre Dalsie Vzdelavanie Pracovnikov, Limbova 12, 833 39 Bratislava, Slovakia. *5661*

FARMACEUTSKI GLASNIK.
Hrvatsko Farmaceutsko Drustvo, Masarykova 2, 41000 Zagreb, Croatia. TEL 41-427944. FAX 41-431301. *5661*

FARMACEVTISK REVY.
Sveriges Farmacevtfoerbund, Vasagatan 48, Box 3215, S-103 64 Stockholm, Sweden. *5661*

FARMACEVTSKI VESTNIK.
Slovensko Farmacevtsko Drustvo, P.O. Box 311, Masera Spasica 10, 61001 Ljubljana, Slovenia. TEL 061-221-078. *5662*

FARMACI.
Danmarks Apotekerforening, Bredgade 54, 1260 Copenhagen K, Denmark. TEL 45-33-76-76-00. FAX 45-33-76-76-99. URL: http://www.dpa.dk. *5662*

FARMACIA.
Uniunea Societatilor de Stiinte Medicale din Romania, Str. Progresului 8, 70754 Bucharest, Rumania. *5662*

FARMACJA POLSKA.
Polskie Towarzystwo Farmaceutyczne, Dluga 16, 00-238 Warsaw, Poland. TEL 48-22-8310241. FAX 48-22-8310243. *5662*

FASHION U K.
Portland House, 164 New Cavendish St., London W1M 7FJ, England. URL: http://www.widemedia.com/fashionuk/ Available only online. *1922*

FASHIONSTANCE.
URL: http://www.fashionstance.com; http://www.users.wineasy.se/bjornt/fshead.html. Available only online. *1922*

FAST FOOD: THE INTERNATIONAL MARKET.
Euromonitor, 60-61 Britton St., London EC1M 5NA, England. TEL 44-171-251-8024. FAX 44-171-608-3149. URL: http://www.euromonitor.com. Vendor(s): Data-Star, Knight-Ridder Information, Inc. *3103*

FASTLINK SOFTWARE UPDATE.
URL: http://www.symgroup.com/ng/html/newsletter.html. Available only online. *2211*

FAT CITY NEWS.
URL: http://www.fatcitynews.com. Available only online. *3872*

FAT! SO?
Box 423464, San Francisco, CA 94142. URL: http://www.fatso.com/. *4334*

FATE.
Llewellyn Worldwide, 84 S. Wabasha St., Box 64383, St. Paul, MN 55164-0383. TEL 612-291-1970. FAX 612-291-1908. URL: http://www.lewellyn.com. *5575*

THE FATE OF THE ARABIAN PENINSULA.
Arab Press Service, A P S House, P.O. Box 3896, Ncosia, Cyprus. TEL 357-2-351778. FAX 357-2-350265. Vendor(s): Information Access Co. *2669*

FATHERING MAGAZINE.
Box 3284, Galveston, TX 77552. URL: http://www.fathermag.com/ Available only online. *1845*

FAULKNER & GRAY'S MEDICINE AND HEALTH.
Faulkner & Gray, Healthcare Information Center 1133 15th St., N.W., Ste. 450, Washington, DC 20005. TEL 202-828-4148. Vendor(s): Information Access Co., NewsNet (HH21) *4667*

FEATHERS & FUR.
Victorian Field & Game Association, P.O. Box 444, Frankston, Vic. 3199, Australia. TEL 61-59-95-6277. FAX 61-59-95-6278. URL: http://www.netcore.com.au/~dkspub/Feathers.htm. *6868*

FEDERAL & STATE INSURANCE WEEK.
J R Publishing, Box 6654, McLean, VA 22106. TEL 703-532-2235. Vendor(s): Information Access Co., NewsNet (IN04). *3815*

FEDERAL APPLIED TECHNOLOGY DATABASE.
U.S. National Technical Information Service, 5285 Port Royal Rd., Springfield, VA 22161. TEL 703-487-4630. Available only online. Vendor(s): Ovid Technologies, Inc. *6960*

FEDERAL BENEFITS FOR VETERANS AND DEPENDENTS.
U.S. Department of Veterans Affairs, 810 Vermont Ave., N.W., Washington, DC 20420. TEL 202-273-5737. *5268*

FEDERAL CAREER OPPORTUNITIES.
Federal Research Service, Inc., 243 Church St., N.W., Box 1059, Vienna, VA 22183-1059. TEL 703-281-0200. FAX 703-281-7639. URL: http://www.fedjobs.com. *5509*

FEDERAL COMPUTER MARKET REPORT.
Computer Age & E D P News Services, 714 Church St., Alexandria, VA 22314-4202. TEL 703-739-8500. FAX 703-739-8505. Vendor(s): Information Access Co. *2155*

FEDERAL CONTRACT DISPUTES.
Business Publishers, Inc., 951 Pershing Dr., Silver Spring, MD 20910-4464. TEL 301-587-6300. FAX 301-585-9075. Vendor(s): NewsNet. *4080*

FEDERAL CONTRACTS REPORT.
The Bureau of National Affairs, Inc., 1231 25th St., N.W., Washington, DC 20037. TEL 202-452-4200. FAX 202-822-8092. URL: http://www.bna.com/ Vendor(s): Lexis-Nexis (FDCONT), West Group. *1584*

FEDERAL COURT OF APPEAL DECISIONS.
Western Legal Publications, 301-1 Alexander St., Vancouver, BC V6A 1B2, Canada. TEL 604-687-5671. FAX 604-687-2796. *4131*

FEDERAL ELECTION COMMISSION RECORD.
U.S. Federal Election Commission, Washington, DC 20463. TEL 202-219-3420. URL: http://www.fec.gov/pages/infosub1.htm. *5926*

FEDERAL GRANTS & CONTRACTS WEEKLY.
Capitol Publications Inc., 1101 King St., Ste. 444, Alexandria, VA 22314. TEL 703-683-4100. FAX 703-739-6501. Vendor(s): NewsNet (GT37). *6174*

FEDERAL LAW-RELATED CAREERS DIRECTORY.
Federal Reports, Inc., 1010 Vermont Ave., N.W., Ste. 408, Washington, DC 20005. TEL 202-393-3311. FAX 202-393-1553. URL: http://www.attorneyjobs.com. Vendor(s): Lexis-Nexis. *3950*

FEDERAL LAWYER.
Federal Bar Association, 1815 H St., N.W., Ste. 408, Washington, DC 20006-3697. TEL 202-638-0252. FAX 202-775-0295. Vendor(s): West Group. *3950*

FEDERAL MOTOR VEHICLE FLEET REPORT.
U.S. General Services Administration, Office of Policy, Planning and Evaluation, G S A Bldg., 18th and F Sts., N.W., Washington, DC 20405. URL: http://www.PolicyWorks.gov/org/maint/mt/homepage/mtv/mtvhp. *7099*

FEDERAL PROBATION.
U.S. Administrative Office of the United States Courts, Federal Corrections and Supervision Division, Washington, DC 20402-9371. TEL 202-273-1627. FAX 202-273-1603. Vendor(s): Information Access Co. *2267*

FEDERAL REGISTER.
U.S. Office of the Federal Register, National Archives and Records Administration, Washington, DC 20408. TEL 202-523-5230. Vendor(s): Knight-Ridder Information, Inc. (File no.669), Lexis-Nexis, Ovid Technologies, Inc. (DIOG), West Group. *6174*

FEDERAL RESEARCH IN PROGRESS DATABASE.
U.S. National Technical Information Service, 5285 Port Royal Rd., Springfield, VA 22161. TEL 703-487-4630. Available only online. Vendor(s): Knight-Ridder Information, Inc. (File nos.265,266). *2720*

SERIALS AVAILABLE ONLINE 10111

FEDERAL RESEARCH REPORT.
Business Publishers, Inc., 951 Pershing Dr., Silver Spring, MD 20910-4464. TEL 301-587-6300. FAX 301-585-9075.
Vendor(s): NewsNet (RD10). *2443*

FEDERAL RESERVE BANK OF ATLANTA. FINANCIAL UPDATE.
Federal Reserve Bank of Atlanta, 104 Marietta St., N.W., Atlanta, GA 30303-2713. TEL 404-521-8020. FAX 404-521-8050. URL: http://www.frbatlanta.org. *1132*

FEDERAL RESERVE BANK OF CLEVELAND. WORKING PAPER.
Federal Reserve Bank of Cleveland, Box 6387, Cleveland, OH 44101. TEL 216-579-2380. FAX 216-579-3050.
Available only online. *1132*

FEDERAL RESERVE BANK OF MINNEAPOLIS. QUARTERLY REVIEW.
Federal Reserve Bank of Minneapolis, Minneapolis, MN 55480-0291. TEL 612-240-6455. FAX 612-204-5515. URL: http://woodrow.mpls.frb.fed.us.
Vendor(s): UMI. *1133*

FEDERAL RESERVE BANK OF NEW YORK. ECONOMIC POLICY REVIEW.
Federal Reserve Bank of New York, Public Information, 33 Liberty St., New York, NY 10045-0001. TEL 212-720-6150.
Vendor(s): Knight-Ridder Information, Inc., UMI. *1259*

FEDERAL RESERVE BANK OF PHILADELPHIA. BUSINESS REVIEW.
Federal Reserve Bank of Philadelphia, Box 66, Philadelphia, PA 19105. TEL 215-574-6428. FAX 215-574-4364. URL: http://www.phil.frb.org.
Vendor(s): UMI. *1259*

FEDERAL RESERVE BANK OF RICHMOND. ECONOMIC QUARTERLY.
Federal Reserve Bank of Richmond, Research Department, 701 E. Byrd St., Richmond, VA 23219. TEL 804-697-8000. FAX 804-697-8287. URL: http://www.rich.frb.org.
Vendor(s): Information Access Co. *1260*

FEDERAL RESERVE BANK OF ST. LOUIS. REVIEW.
Federal Reserve Bank of St. Louis, Box 442, St. Louis, MO 63166. TEL 314-444-8320.
Vendor(s): Information Access Co., UMI. *1260*

FEDERAL RESERVE BANK OF SAN FRANCISCO. ECONOMIC LETTER.
Federal Reserve Bank of San Francisco, Box 7702, San Francisco, CA 94120. TEL 415-974-3230. FAX 415-974-3341. URL: http://www.frbsf.org. *1260*

FEDERAL RESERVE BANK OF SAN FRANCISCO. ECONOMIC REVIEW.
Federal Reserve Bank of San Francisco, Box 7702, San Francisco, CA 94120. TEL 415-974-3230. FAX 415-974-3341. URL: http://www.frbsf.org.
Vendor(s): UMI. *1260*

FEDERAL RESERVE BULLETIN.
U.S. Federal Reserve System, Board of Governors, Publications Services, Rm. MS-138, Washington, DC 20551. TEL 202-452-3244. FAX 202-728-5886.
Vendor(s): Information Access Co., Knight-Ridder Information, Inc., Lexis-Nexis, UMI. *1133*

FEDERAL SENTENCING REPORTER.
University of California Press, Journals Division, 2120 Berkeley Way, No. 5812, Berkeley, CA 94720-5812. TEL 510-643-7154. FAX 510-642-9917. URL: http://library.berkeley.edu:8080/ucalpress/journals.
Vendor(s): Lexis-Nexis, West Group. *2267*

FEDERAL TAX COORDINATOR 2D.
Research Institute of America, Inc., 90 Fifth Ave., New York, NY 10011. TEL 212-645-4800. FAX 212-337-4279.
Vendor(s): Lexis-Nexis. *1608*

FEDERAL TAX REGULATIONS.
Research Institute of America, Inc., 90 Fifth Ave., New York, NY 10011. TEL 212-645-4800.
Vendor(s): Research Institute of America. *1609*

FEDERAL TECHNOLOGY REPORT.
McGraw-Hill Companies, Energy & Business Newsletters, 1221 Ave. of the Americas, 36th Fl., New York, NY 10020. TEL 212-512-6410.
Vendor(s): Dow Jones News Retrieval (TTR), Knight-Ridder Information, Inc. (TTR), Lexis-Nexis (FEDTEC), NewsNet (RD46). *2669*

FEDGAZETTE: FEDERAL RESERVE BANK OF MINNEAPOLIS REGIONAL BUSINESS & ECONOMICS NEWSPAPER.
Federal Reserve Bank of Minneapolis, Box 291, Minneapolis, MN 55480-0291. TEL 612-340-2446. FAX 612-335-2855. URL: http://woodrow.mpls.frb.fed.us.
Vendor(s): UMI. *1260*

FEEDSTUFFS.
A B C, Inc., 12400 Whitewater Dr., Ste. 160, Box 2400, Minnetonka, MN 55343. TEL 612-931-0211. FAX 612-938-1832. URL: http://www.feedstuffs.com. *263*

FEMINA.
Edipresse Publications SA, Av. de la Gare 33, CH-1001 Lausanne, Switzerland. TEL 41-21-3494848. FAX 41-21-3494859. URL: http://www.edicom.ch/femina. *7319*

FEMINIST STUDIES.
Feminist Studies, Inc., c/o Department of Women's Studies, University of Maryland, College Park, MD 20742. TEL 301-405-7415. FAX 301-314-9190. URL: http://www.inform.umd.edu/FemStud.
Vendor(s): Information Access Co., UMI. *7343*

FERROELECTRICS.
Gordon and Breach - Harwood Academic, Amsteldisk 166, 1st Fl., 1079 LH Amsterdam, Netherlands. URL: http://www.gbhap.com/Ferroelectrics/. *5802*

FERROELECTRICS COMMUNICATIONS.
Gordon and Breach - Harwood Academic, Amsteldisk 166, 1st Fl., 1079 LH Amsterdam, Netherlands. URL: http://www.gbhap.com/Ferroelectrics__Communications/. *5834*

FERROELECTRICS LETTERS.
Gordon and Breach - Harwood Academic, Amsteldisk 166, 1st Fl., 1079 LH Amsterdam, Netherlands. URL: http://www.gbhap.com/Ferroelectrics__Letters_Section/. *2824*

FERTILITY AND STERILITY.
American Society for Reproductive Medicine, 1209 Montgomery Hwy., Birmingham, AL 35216-2809. TEL 205-978-5000. FAX 205-978-5005. *4957*

FERTILITY WEEKLY (ATLANTA).
Charles W. Henderson, Ed. & Pub., Box 5528, Atlanta, GA 31107-0528. TEL 404-377-8895. FAX 404-378-5411. URL: http://www.newsfile.com. *4957*

FERTILIZER INTERNATIONAL.
British Sulphur Publishing, 31 Mount Pleasant, London WC1X 0AD, England. TEL 44-171-837-5600. FAX 44-171-837-0292.
Vendor(s): Information Access Co. *224*

FEW-BODY SYSTEMS. ACTA PHYSICA AUSTRIACA. NEW SERIES.
Springer-Verlag, Sachsenplatz 4-6, P.O. Box 89, A-1201 Vienna, Austria. TEL 43-1-3302415. FAX 43-1-3302426. *5803*

FIBER OPTICS NEWS.
Phillips Business Information, Inc., 1201 Seven Locks Rd., Potomac, MD 20854. TEL 301-424-3338. FAX 301-424-4297.
Vendor(s): Information Access Co., Knight-Ridder Information, Inc., NewsNet (TE29). *1990*

THE FIBONACCI QUARTERLY.
Fibonacci Association, c/o South Dakota State University, Computer Science Dept., Box 2201, Brookings, SD 57007-1596. TEL 605-688-5719. FAX 605-688-5878. URL: http://www.sdstate.edu/~wcsc/http/fibhome.html. *4572*

FICTION DIGEST.
Amcam Inc., 187 Vanderbilt Ave., Apt. 3, Brooklyn, NY 11205-3305. TEL 718-643-2988. FAX 718-797-9403. URL: http://www.std.com/amcan/cafe/fd.htm. *4178*

FIDDLER MAGAZINE.
Fiddler Magazine, Box 125, Los Altos, CA 94022. TEL 415-948-4383. URL: http://www.fiddle.com. *5393*

FIDO NEWS.
Fido Software, 55 Rodel Pl., San Francisco, CA 94103-3406.
Available only online. *2133*

FIELD & STREAM.
Times Mirror Magazines, Inc., 2 Park Ave., New York, NY 10016. TEL 212-779-5000. FAX 212-725-3836.
Vendor(s): Information Access Co., UMI. *6868*

FIELD & STREAM ONLINE.
Times Mirror Magazines, Inc., 2 Park Ave., New York, NY 10016. TEL 212-779-5000. FAX 212-725-3836. URL: http://www.fieldandstream.com/.
Available only online. *6868*

FIELD CROP ABSTRACTS.
CAB International, Wallingford, Oxon. OX10 8DE, England. TEL 44-1491-832111. FAX 44-1491-826090. URL: http://www.cabi.org.
Vendor(s): DIMDI, European Space Agency, Knight-Ridder Information, Inc., STN International. *174*

FIESTA.
Galaxy Publications Ltd., P.O. Box 312, Witham, Essex CM8 3SZ, England. FAX 44-1376-510680. URL: http://www.gs.fiesta.org. *5176*

FILM & VIDEO FINDER.
Plexus Publishing, Inc., 143 Old Marlton Pike, Medford, NJ 08055-8750. TEL 609-654-4888. FAX 609-654-4309.
Vendor(s): Knight-Ridder Information, Inc. (File no.46). *2500*

FILM COMMENT.
Film Society of Lincoln Center, 70 Lincoln Center Plaza, New York, NY 10023-6595. TEL 212-875-5610. FAX 212-875-5636.
Vendor(s): Information Access Co., UMI. *5332*

FILM QUARTERLY.
University of California Press, Journals Division, 2120 Berkeley Way, No. 5812, Berkeley, CA 94720-5812. TEL 510-643-7154. FAX 510-642-9917. URL: http://library.berkeley.edu:8080/ucalpress/journals.
Vendor(s): Information Access Co. *5333*

FILMMAKER.
110 W. 57th St., 3rd. Fl., New York, NY 10019-3319. TEL 212-581-8080. FAX 212-581-1857. URL: http://www.filmmag.com/ *5334*

FILMSTRIP AND SLIDE SET FINDER.
Plexus Publishing, Inc., 143 Old Marlton Pike, Medford, NJ 08055-8750. TEL 609-654-6500. FAX 609-654-4309. *2500*

THE FINAL CALL.
Final Call Newspaper, 734 W. 79th St., Chicago, IL 60620. TEL 312-602-1230. URL: http://www.noi.org/finalcall.com. *6396*

FINANCE AND DEVELOPMENT.
International Monetary Fund, Publication Services, 700 19th St., N.W., Washington, DC 20431. TEL 202-623-7430. FAX 202-623-7201.
Vendor(s): Information Access Co., UMI. *1133*

FINANCE AND STOCHASTICS.
Springer-Verlag, Heidelberger Platz 3, 14197 Berlin, Germany. TEL 49-30-82787-0. FAX 49-30-82787448. URL: http://link.springer.de. *1133*

FINANCE EAST EUROPE.
Financial Times Business Information, Newsletters 126 Jermyn St., London SW1Y 4UJ, England. TEL 44-171-411-4414. FAX 44-171-411-4415.
Vendor(s): Information Access Co. *1134*

FINANCIAL ADVERTISING REVIEW.
Business Word Inc., 5350 S. Roslyn St., Ste. 400, Englewood, CO 80111-2125. TEL 303-290-8500. FAX 303-290-9025.
Vendor(s): NewsNet. *36*

FINANCIAL ANALYSTS JOURNAL.
Association for Investment Management and Research, Box 3668, Charlottesville, VA 22903. TEL 804-980-3668. FAX 804-980-9755.
Vendor(s): UMI. *1384*

10112 SERIALS AVAILABLE ONLINE

FINANCIAL EXECUTIVE.
Financial Executives Institute, 10 Madison Ave., Box 1938, Morristown, NJ 07962-1938. TEL 201-898-4621. FAX 201-267-4031.
Vendor(s): Information Access Co., Knight-Ridder Information, Inc., UMI. *1478*

FINANCIAL FAX.
D R I - McGraw-Hill, 24 Hartwell Ave., Lexington, MA 02173. TEL 617-863-5100. FAX 617-860-6332. *1134*

FINANCIAL MANAGEMENT.
Financial Management Association, University of South Florida, College of Business, Tampa, FL 33620. TEL 813-974-2084. FAX 813-974-3318. URL: http://www.webspace.com/~fma/.
Vendor(s): Information Access Co., UMI. *1478*

FINANCIAL MARKET TRENDS.
Organization for Economic Cooperation and Development, 2 rue Andre-Pascal, 75775 Paris Cedex 16, France.
Vendor(s): Information Access Co., UMI. *1135*

FINANCIAL MARKETS, INSTITUTIONS AND INSTRUMENTS.
Blackwell Publishers, 238 Main St., Cambridge, MA 02142. TEL 617 547 7110. FAX 617-547-0789.
Vendor(s): UMI. *1135*

FINANCIAL PLANNING (NEW YORK).
Securities Data Publishing, 40 W. 57th St., 11th Fl., New York, NY 10019. TEL 212-765-5311. FAX 212-765-6123.
Vendor(s): Information Access Co. *1478*

FINANCIAL POST.
Financial Post Co., Ltd., 333 King St. E., Toronto, ON M5A 4N2, Canada. TEL 416-350-6300. FAX 416-350-6601.
Vendor(s): Information Access Co., Southam Electronic Publishing. *1135*

FINANCIAL POST DIRECTORY OF DIRECTORS.
Financial Post Co., Ltd., 333 King St. E., Toronto, ON M5A 4N2, Canada. TEL 416-350-6116. FAX 416-350-6501.
Vendor(s): Southam Electronic Publishing. *1478*

FINANCIAL POST MAGAZINE.
Financial Post Co., Ltd., 333 King St. E., Toronto, ON M5A 4N2, Canada. TEL 416-350-6516. FAX 416-350-6501. *1135*

FINANCIAL REGULATION REPORT.
Financial Times Business Information, Newsletters 126 Jermyn St., London SW1Y 4UJ, England. TEL 0171-441-4414. FAX 0171-441-4415.
Vendor(s): Data-Star, Lexis-Nexis. *1135*

FINANCIAL REVIEW (STATESBORO).
Eastern Finance Association, c/o Univ. of Tennessee, 426 Stokley Management Ctr., Knoxville, TN 37996-0540. TEL 423-974-1713. FAX 423-974-1716.
Vendor(s): Information Access Co. *1135*

FINANCIAL STATISTICS OF MAJOR INVESTOR-OWNED ELECTRIC UTILITIES (YEAR).
U.S. Energy Information Administration, National Energy Information Center, EI-231, James Forrestal Bldg., Rm. 1F-048, 1000 Independence Ave., S.W., Washington, DC 20585. TEL 202-586-8800. FAX 202-5586-0727. URL: http://www.eia.doe.gov. *2684*

FINANCIAL STATISTICS OF MAJOR PUBLICLY OWNED ELECTRIC UTILITIES (YEAR).
U.S. Energy Information Administration, National Energy Information Center, EI-231, James Forrestal Bldg., Rm. 1F-048, 1000 Independence Ave., S.W., Washington, DC 20585. TEL 202-586-8800. FAX 202-586-0727. URL: http://www.eia.doe.gov. *2684*

FINANCIAL TECHNOLOGY INSIGHT.
Elsevier Science Ltd., P.O. Box 800, Kidlington, Oxford OX5 1DX, England. TEL 44-1865-843000. FAX 44-1865-843010. URL: http://www.elsevier.nl/.
Vendor(s): Data-Star, Information Access Co., Knight-Ridder Information, Inc. *1201*

FINANCIAL TIMES WORLD TAX REPORT.
Financial Times Professional Publishing, Maple House, 149 Tottenham Court Rd., London W1P 9LL, England. TEL 44-171-896-2222. FAX 44-171-896-2276.
Vendor(s): Information Access Co., Knight-Ridder Information, Inc., Lexis-Nexis. *1609*

FINANCIAL TREND FORECASTER.
URL: http://www.fintrend.com/.
Available only online. *1260*

FINANCIAL WORLD.
Financial World Partners, 1328 Broadway, New York, NY 10001. TEL 212-594-5030. FAX 212-629-0021.
Vendor(s): Data-Star, Information Access Co., Knight-Ridder Information, Inc., Lexis-Nexis, UMI. *1136*

DE FINANCIEEL ECONOMISCHE TIJD.
Uitgeversbedrijf Tijd n.v., Franklin Building, Posthoflei 3, 2600 Berchem (Antwerp), Belgium. TEL 32-3-2860211. FAX 32-3-2860310. *964*

HET FINANCIEELE DAGBLAD.
Het Financieele Dagblad B.V., P.O. Box 216, 1000 AE Amsterdam, Netherlands. TEL 31-20-5928888. FAX 31-20-592800. URL: http://www.Nederlander.com.nl. *964*

FINANCIER: ANALYSES OF CAPITAL AND MONEY MARKET TRANSACTIONS.
Financier, Inc., 220 Locust St., Apt. 3-E, Philadelphia, PA 19106-3928. TEL 215-829-1354. FAX 215-829-1376. URL: http://www.the-financier.com. *1136*

EL FINANCIERO INTERNATIONAL EDITION.
El Financiero International, Inc., Lago Bolsena 176, Col. Anahuac, 11320 Mexico DF, Mexico. TEL 525-227-7600. FAX 525-227-7634. URL: http://basic.attis.com.mx/wwwFinanNews.html. *1137*

FINANCING OPERATIONS. AFRICA.
Economist Intelligence Unit, 111 W. 57th St., New York, NY 10019. TEL 212-554-0600. FAX 212-586-1181. URL: http://www.eiu.com.
Vendor(s): Knight-Ridder Information, Inc., Lexis-Nexis. *1137*

FINANCING OPERATIONS. ARGENTINA.
Economist Intelligence Unit, 111 W. 57th St., New York, NY 10019. TEL 212-554-0600. FAX 212-586-1181. URL: http://www.eiu.com.
Vendor(s): Knight-Ridder Information, Inc., Lexis-Nexis. *1137*

FINANCING OPERATIONS. AUSTRALIA.
Economist Intelligence Unit, 111 W. 57th St., New York, NY 10019. TEL 212-554-0600. FAX 212-586-1181. URL: http://www.eiu.com.
Vendor(s): Knight-Ridder Information, Inc., Lexis-Nexis. *1137*

FINANCING OPERATIONS. BELGIUM.
Economist Intelligence Unit, 111 W. 57th St., New York, NY 10019. TEL 212-554-0600. FAX 212-586-1181. URL: http://www.eiu.com.
Vendor(s): Knight-Ridder Information, Inc., Lexis-Nexis. *1137*

FINANCING OPERATIONS. BRAZIL.
Economist Intelligence Unit, 111 W. 57th St., New York, NY 10019. TEL 212-554-0600. FAX 212-586-1181. URL: http://www.eiu.com.
Vendor(s): Knight-Ridder Information, Inc., Lexis-Nexis. *1137*

FINANCING OPERATIONS. CANADA.
Economist Intelligence Unit, 111 W. 57th St., New York, NY 10019. TEL 212-554-0600. FAX 212-586-1181. URL: http://www.eiu.com.
Vendor(s): Knight-Ridder Information, Inc., Lexis-Nexis. *1137*

FINANCING OPERATIONS. CHILE.
Economist Intelligence Unit, 111 W. 57th St., New York, NY 10019. TEL 212-554-0600. FAX 212-586-1181.
Vendor(s): Knight-Ridder Information, Inc., Lexis-Nexis. *1137*

FINANCING OPERATIONS. COLOMBIA.
Economist Intelligence Unit, 111 W. 57th St., New York, NY 10019. TEL 212-554-0600. FAX 212-586-1181. URL: http://www.eiu.com.
Vendor(s): Knight-Ridder Information, Inc., Lexis-Nexis. *1137*

FINANCING OPERATIONS. COSTA RICA.
Economist Intelligence Unit, 111 W. 57th St., New York, NY 10019. TEL 212-554-0600. FAX 212-586-1181. URL: http://www.eiu.com.
Vendor(s): Knight-Ridder Information, Inc., Lexis-Nexis. *1137*

FINANCING OPERATIONS. CZECH REPUBLIC.
Economist Intelligence Unit, 111 W. 57th St., New York, NY 10019. TEL 212-554-0600. FAX 212-586-1181. URL: http://www.eiu.com.
Vendor(s): Knight-Ridder Information, Inc., Lexis-Nexis. *1137*

FINANCING OPERATIONS. EL SALVADOR.
Economist Intelligence Unit, 111 W. 57th St., New York, NY 10019. TEL 212-554-0600. FAX 212-586-1182. URL: http://www.eiu.com.
Vendor(s): Knight-Ridder Information, Inc., Lexis-Nexis. *1137*

FINANCING OPERATIONS. FRANCE.
Economist Intelligence Unit, 111 W. 57th St., New York, NY 10019. TEL 212-554-0600. FAX 212-586-1181. URL: http://www.eiu.com.
Vendor(s): Knight-Ridder Information, Inc., Lexis-Nexis. *1138*

FINANCING OPERATIONS. GERMANY.
Economist Intelligence Unit, 111 W. 57th St., New York, NY 10019. TEL 212-554-0600. FAX 212-586-1181. URL: http://www.eiu.com.
Vendor(s): Knight-Ridder Information, Inc., Lexis-Nexis. *1138*

FINANCING OPERATIONS. GREECE.
Economist Intelligence Unit, 111 W. 57th St., New York, NY 10019. TEL 212-554-0600. FAX 212-586-1181. URL: http://www.eiu.com.
Vendor(s): Knight-Ridder Information, Inc., Lexis-Nexis. *1138*

FINANCING OPERATIONS. GUATEMALA.
Economist Intelligence Unit, 111 W. 57th St., New York, NY 10019. TEL 212-554-0600. FAX 212-586-1182. URL: http://www.eiu.com.
Vendor(s): Knight-Ridder Information, Inc., Lexis-Nexis. *1138*

FINANCING OPERATIONS. HONDURAS.
Economist Intelligence Unit, 111 W. 57th St., New York, NY 10019. TEL 212-554-0600. FAX 212-586-1182. URL: http://www.eiu.com.
Vendor(s): Knight-Ridder Information, Inc., Lexis-Nexis. *1138*

FINANCING OPERATIONS. HONG KONG.
Economist Intelligence Unit, 111 W. 57th St., New York, NY 10019. TEL 212-554-0600. FAX 212-586-1181. URL: http://www.eiu.com.
Vendor(s): Knight-Ridder Information, Inc., Lexis-Nexis. *1138*

FINANCING OPERATIONS. HUNGARY.
Economist Intelligence Unit, 111 W. 57th St., New York, NY 10019. TEL 212-554-0600. FAX 212-586-1181. URL: http://www.eiu.com.
Vendor(s): Knight-Ridder Information, Inc., Lexis-Nexis. *1138*

FINANCING OPERATIONS. INDIA.
Economist Intelligence Unit, 111 W. 57th St., New York, NY 10019. TEL 212-554-0600. FAX 212-586-1181. URL: http://www.eiu.com.
Vendor(s): Knight-Ridder Information, Inc., Lexis-Nexis. *1138*

FINANCING OPERATIONS. ITALY.
Economist Intelligence Unit, 111 W. 57th St., New York, NY 10019. TEL 212-554-0600. FAX 212-586-1181. URL: http://www.eiu.com.
Vendor(s): Knight-Ridder Information, Inc., Lexis-Nexis. *1138*

FINANCING OPERATIONS. JAPAN.
Economist Intelligence Unit, 111 W. 57th St., New York, NY 10019. TEL 212-554-0600. FAX 212-586-1182. URL: http://www.eiu.com.
Vendor(s): Knight-Ridder Information, Inc., Lexis-Nexis. *1138*

FINANCING OPERATIONS. MALAYSIA.
Economist Intelligence Unit, 111 W. 57th St., New York, NY 10019. TEL 212-554-0600. FAX 212-586-1181. URL: http://www.eiu.com. Vendor(s): Knight-Ridder Information, Inc., Lexis-Nexis. *1138*

FINANCING OPERATIONS. MEXICO.
Economist Intelligence Unit, 111 W. 57th St., New York, NY 10019. TEL 212-554-0600. FAX 212-586-1181. URL: http://www.eiu.com. Vendor(s): Knight-Ridder Information, Inc., Lexis-Nexis. *1138*

FINANCING OPERATIONS. NETHERLANDS.
Economist Intelligence Unit, 111 W. 57th St., New York, NY 10019. TEL 212-554-0600. FAX 212-586-1181. URL: http://www.eiu.com. Vendor(s): Knight-Ridder Information, Inc., Lexis-Nexis. *1139*

FINANCING OPERATIONS. NICARAGUA.
Economist Intelligence Unit, 111 W. 57th St., New York, NY 10019. TEL 212-554-0600. FAX 212-586-1182. URL: http://www.eiu.com. Vendor(s): Knight-Ridder Information, Inc., Lexis-Nexis. *1139*

FINANCING OPERATIONS. NIGERIA.
Economist Intelligence Unit, 111 W. 57th St., New York, NY 10019. TEL 212-554-0600. FAX 212-586-1181. URL: http://www.eiu.com. Vendor(s): Knight-Ridder Information, Inc., Lexis-Nexis. *1139*

FINANCING OPERATIONS. NORWAY.
Economist Intelligence Unit, 111 W. 57th St., New York, NY 10019. TEL 212-554-0600. FAX 212-586-1181. URL: http://www.eiu.com. Vendor(s): Knight-Ridder Information, Inc., Lexis-Nexis. *1139*

FINANCING OPERATIONS. PANAMA.
Economist Intelligence Unit, 111 W. 57th St., New York, NY 10019. TEL 212-554-0600. FAX 212-586-1181. URL: http://www.eiu.com. Vendor(s): Knight-Ridder Information, Inc., Lexis-Nexis. *1139*

FINANCING OPERATIONS. PHILIPPINES.
Economist Intelligence Unit, 111 W. 57th St., New York, NY 10019. TEL 212-554-0600. FAX 212-586-1181. URL: http://www.eiu.com. Vendor(s): Knight-Ridder Information, Inc., Lexis-Nexis. *1139*

FINANCING OPERATIONS. POLAND.
Economist Intelligence Unit, 111 W. 57th St., New York, NY 10019. TEL 212-554-0600. FAX 212-586-1181. URL: http://www.eiu.com. Vendor(s): Knight-Ridder Information, Inc., Lexis-Nexis. *1139*

FINANCING OPERATIONS. RUSSIA.
Economist Intelligence Unit, 111 W. 57th St., New York, NY 10019. TEL 212-554-0600. FAX 212-586-1181. URL: http://www.eiu.com. Vendor(s): Knight-Ridder Information, Inc., Lexis-Nexis. *1139*

FINANCING OPERATIONS. SAUDI ARABIA.
Economist Intelligence Unit, 111 W. 57th St., New York, NY 10019. TEL 212-554-0600. FAX 212-586-1181. URL: http://www.eiu.com. Vendor(s): Knight-Ridder Information, Inc., Lexis-Nexis. *1139*

FINANCING OPERATIONS. SINGAPORE.
Economist Intelligence Unit, 111 W. 57th St., New York, NY 10019. TEL 212-554-0600. FAX 212-586-1181. URL: http://www.eiu.com. Vendor(s): Knight-Ridder Information, Inc., Lexis-Nexis. *1139*

FINANCING OPERATIONS. SOUTH AFRICA.
Economist Intelligence Unit, 111 W. 57th St., New York, NY 10019. TEL 212-554-0600. FAX 212-586-1181. URL: http://www.eiu.com. Vendor(s): Knight-Ridder Information, Inc., Lexis-Nexis. *1139*

FINANCING OPERATIONS. SOUTH KOREA.
Economist Intelligence Unit, 111 W. 57th St., New York, NY 10019. TEL 212-554-0600. FAX 212-586-1181. URL: http://www.eiu.com. Vendor(s): Knight-Ridder Information, Inc., Lexis-Nexis. *1140*

FINANCING OPERATIONS. SPAIN.
Economist Intelligence Unit, 111 W. 57th St., New York, NY 10019. TEL 212-554-0600. FAX 212-586-1181. URL: http://www.eiu.com. Vendor(s): Knight-Ridder Information, Inc., Lexis-Nexis. *1140*

FINANCING OPERATIONS. SWEDEN.
Economist Intelligence Unit, 111 W. 57th St., New York, NY 10019. TEL 212-554-0600. FAX 212-586-1181. URL: http://www.eiu.com. Vendor(s): Knight-Ridder Information, Inc., Lexis-Nexis. *1140*

FINANCING OPERATIONS. SWITZERLAND.
Economist Intelligence Unit, 111 W. 57th St., New York, NY 10019. TEL 212-554-0600. FAX 212-586-1181. URL: http://www.eiu.com. Vendor(s): Knight-Ridder Information, Inc., Lexis-Nexis. *1140*

FINANCING OPERATIONS. TAIWAN.
Economist Intelligence Unit, 111 W. 57th St., New York, NY 10019. TEL 212-554-0600. FAX 212-586-1181. URL: http://www.eiu.com. Vendor(s): Knight-Ridder Information, Inc., Lexis-Nexis. *1140*

FINANCING OPERATIONS. THAILAND.
Economist Intelligence Unit, 111 W. 57th St., New York, NY 10019. TEL 212-554-0600. FAX 212-586-1181. URL: http://www.eiu.com. Vendor(s): Knight-Ridder Information, Inc., Lexis-Nexis. *1140*

FINANCING OPERATIONS. UNITED KINGDOM.
Economist Intelligence Unit, 111 W. 57th St., New York, NY 10019. TEL 212-554-0600. FAX 212-586-1181. URL: http://www.eiu.com. Vendor(s): Knight-Ridder Information, Inc., Lexis-Nexis. *1140*

FINANCING OPERATIONS. UNITED STATES OF AMERICA.
Economist Intelligence Unit, 111 W. 57th St., New York, NY 10019. TEL 212-554-0600. FAX 212-586-1181. URL: http://www.eiu.com. Vendor(s): Knight-Ridder Information, Inc., Lexis-Nexis. *1140*

FINANCING OPERATIONS. VENEZUELA.
Economist Intelligence Unit, 111 W. 57th St., New York, NY 10019. TEL 212-554-0600. FAX 212-586-1181. URL: http://www.eiu.com. Vendor(s): Knight-Ridder Information, Inc., Lexis-Nexis. *1140*

FINDEX (YEAR).
Euromonitor, 60-61 Britton St., London EC1M 5NA, England. TEL 44-171-251-8024. FAX 44-171-608-3149. URL: http://www.euromonitor.com. Vendor(s): Knight-Ridder Information, Inc. (File no.196). *1039*

FINE FISHING.
1914 Conestoga St., Moscow, ID 83843. URL: http://www.finefishing.com. Available only online. *6868*

FINE FOOD & TRAVEL MAGAZINE.
1914 Conestoga St., Moscow, ID 83843. URL: http://www.finetravel.com. Available only online. *7200*

FINESSE MARKETPLACE JOURNAL.
URL: http://www.fingraphics.com. Available only online. *2211*

FINITE FIELDS AND THEIR APPLICATIONS.
Academic Press, Inc., Journal Division, 525 B St., Ste. 1900, San Diego, CA 92101-4495. TEL 619-230-1840. FAX 619-688-6800. URL: http://www.apnet.com/www/journal/ff.htm; http://www.idealibrary.com. *4572*

FIRMEN DER NEUEN BUNDESLAENDER.
Verlag Hoppenstedt GmbH, Havelstr. 9, 64295 Darmstadt, Germany. TEL 49-6151-380-0. FAX 49-6151-380-360. Vendor(s): Data-Star, Knight-Ridder Information, Inc. *1584*

FIRST MONDAY.
Munksgaard International Publishers Ltd., Noerre Soegade 35, P.O. Box 2148, DK-1016 Copenhagen, Denmark. TEL 45-33-127030. URL: http://www.firstmonday.dk. *2133*

FIRST PERSON MAGAZINE.
84 Townshend Terrace, Richmond, Surrey TW9 1XN, England. URL: http://www.vulliamt.demon.co.uk. *5065*

FIRST THINGS.
Institute on Religion and Public Life, 156 Fifth Ave., Ste. 400, New York, NY 10010. TEL 212-627-2288. FAX 212-627-2184. *6339*

FISCAL STUDIES.
Institute of Fiscal Studies, 7 Ridgmount St., London WC1E 7AE, England. TEL 44-171-636-3784. FAX 44-171-323-4780. URL: http://www1.ifs.org.uk/ifsinfo/fiscalStudies.htm. Vendor(s): UMI. *1610*

FISCO & SOCIETA.
Via G. Bettolo, 6, Rome, Italy. TEL 6-3751-7714. URL: http://www.mclink.it/com/forlai. Available only online. *5926*

FISH AND GAME FINDER.
Fish and Game Finder Magazines, 41 W. Michigan, Orlando, FL 32806. TEL 407-425-0045. FAX 407-425-1529. *6868*

FISH AND SHELLFISH IMMUNOLOGY.
Academic Press Ltd., 24-28 Oval Rd., London NW1 7DX, England. TEL 44-171-267-4466. FAX 44-171-482-2293. URL: http://www.hbuk.co.uk/ap/fsi; http://www.europe.idealibrary.com/ *601*

FISHERIES MARKET NEWS REPORT.
Urner Barry Publications, Inc., Box 389, Toms River, NJ 08754. TEL 908-240-5330. FAX 908-341-0891. URL: http://www.urnerbarry.com. *3082*

THE FISHERNET.
Box 701096, San Antonio, TX 78270-1096. URL: http://www.thefishernet.com. Available only online. *6868*

THE FISHING NETWORK WEB-ZINE.
75 Talara Dr., Ste. 404, North York, ON M2K 2X4, Canada. URL: http://www.the-fishing-network.com. Available only online. *6868*

FITOTERAPIA.
IdB Holding, Viale Ortles 12, 20139 Milan, Italy. TEL 39-2-57496442. FAX 39-2-57496443. *703*

FIVE PERCENT OWNERSHIP PORTFOLIOS.
C D A Investment Technologies, Inc., 1355 Piccard Dr., Rockville, MD 20850. FAX 301-590-1350. *1384*

FIVE-YEAR INFORMATION RESOURCES MANAGEMENT PROGRAM.
U.S. Department of Veterans Affairs, 810 Vermont Ave., N.W. (008B3), Washington, DC 20420. TEL 202-233-3557. *4178*

FIZBIN MAGIC MAGAZINE.
John Fleischer, Ed. & Pub., 119 Nashua Rd., Gronton, MA 01450. URL: http://www.tiac.net/users/rjf/fizbin.html. *3667*

FLAME RETARDANCY NEWS.
Business Communications Co., Inc. (Norwalk), 25 Van Zant St., Ste. 13, Norwalk, CT 06855-1781. TEL 203-853-4266. FAX 203-853-0348. Vendor(s): Information Access Co., NewsNet (RD40) *6960*

FLAMES.
Steinkrug Publications, Ltd., 20 Leaden Hill, Orwell, Royston, Yorkshire SG8 5QH, England. URL: http://www.gold.net/flames/. Available only online. *6960*

FLASH MAGAZINE.
BlackLightning Publishing, Inc., Riddle Pond Rd., West Topsham, VT 05086. TEL 802-439-6462. FAX 802-439-6463. URL: http://www.flashweb.com. *6088*

FLEA NEWS.
Iowa State University, Department of Entomology, Ames, IA 50011-3222. TEL 515-232-7714. FAX 515-233-1851. URL: http://www.public.iastate.edu/~entomology/FleaNews/AboutFleaNews.html. *752*

SERIALS AVAILABLE ONLINE

FLEET EQUIPMENT.
Maple Publishing, 134 W. Slade St., Palatine, IL 60067. TEL 847-359-6100. FAX 847-359-6420. URL: http://www.truklink.com.
Vendor(s): UMI. *7174*

FLETCHER FORUM OF WORLD AFFAIRS.
Fletcher School of Law and Diplomacy, Tufts University, Medford, MA 02155. TEL 617-623-3610. FAX 617-627-3979. URL: http://www.tufts.edu/fletcher/forum.html.
Vendor(s): West Group. *6014*

FLEXNEWS.
Flex Learning Systems, URL: http://www.flexlearn.com6.
Available only online. *2516*

FLIGHT INTERNATIONAL.
Reed Business Publishing Group, Quadrant House, The Quadrant, Sutton, Surrey SM2 5AS, England. TEL 44-181-652-3882. FAX 44-181-652-3840. URL: http://www.reedbusiness.com/aerospace.htm.
Vendor(s): Data-Star, Information Access Co., Lexis-Nexis. *64*

FLOORING.
Douglas Publications, Inc., 2807 N. Parham Rd., Ste., Richmond, VA 23294-4410. TEL 804-741-6704. FAX 804-750-2399.
Vendor(s): Information Access Co. *3856*

FLORIDA BAR JOURNAL.
Florida Bar, 650 Apalachee Pkwy., Tallahassee, FL 32399-2300. TEL 904-561-5680. FAX 904-681-3859.
Vendor(s): West Group. *3951*

FLORIDA BUSINESS DIRECTORY.
American Business Directories, 5711 S. 86th Circle, Box 27347, Omaha, NE 68127. TEL 402-593-4600. FAX 402-331-5481. *1680*

FLORIDA LAW REVIEW.
University of Florida, College of Law, Gainesville, FL 32611. TEL 904-392-2148.
Vendor(s): West Group. *3951*

FLORIDA LEADER.
Oxendine Publishing, Inc., Box 14081, Gainesville, FL 32604-2081. TEL 352-373-6907. FAX 352-373-8120. *1952*

FLORIDA STATE UNIVERSITY LAW REVIEW.
Florida State University, College of Law, Tallahassee, FL 32306. TEL 904-644-2045. URL: http://law.fsu.edu/lawreview/index.html.
Vendor(s): West Group. *3952*

FLORIDA TREND.
Florida Trend Inc., Box 611, St. Petersburg, FL 33731. TEL 813-821-5800. FAX 813-822-5083.
Vendor(s): Information Access Co., Knight-Ridder Information, Inc., Lexis-Nexis, UMI. *1261*

FLOWER AND GARDEN.
K C Publishing Inc., 700 47th St., Ste. 310, Kansas City, MO 64112. TEL 816-531-5730. FAX 816-531-3873.
Vendor(s): Information Access Co., Knight-Ridder Information, Inc., UMI. *3187*

FLOWER & GARDEN CRAFTS EDITION.
K C Publishing Inc., 700 W. 47th St., Ste. 310, Kansas City, MO 64112. TEL 816-531-5730. FAX 816-531-3873.
Vendor(s): Knight-Ridder Information, Inc. *5451*

FLUID ABSTRACTS: CIVIL ENGINEERING.
Elsevier Science Ltd., P.O. Box 800, Kidlington, Oxford OX5 1DX, England. TEL 44-1865-843000. FAX 44-1865-843010. URL: http://www.elsevier.nl/.
Vendor(s): European Space Agency (File no.48/FLUIDEX), Knight-Ridder Information, Inc. (File no.96/FLUIDEX). *2749*

FLUID ABSTRACTS: PROCESS ENGINEERING.
Elsevier Science Ltd., P.O. Box 800, Kidlington, Oxford OX5 1DX, England. TEL 44-1865-843000. FAX 44-1865-843010. URL: http://www.elsevier.nl/.
Vendor(s): European Space Agency (File no.48/FLUIDEX), Knight-Ridder Information, Inc. (File no.96/FLUIDEX). *2750*

FLUX.
P.O. Box 4392, London WC1N 3XX, England. URL: http://easyweb.easynet.co.uk/'flux/
Available only online. *4334*

FLY MAGAZINE.
University of Plymouth, Student Union, Drake Circus, Plymouth, Devon OL4 8AA, England. TEL 44-1752-663337. FAX 44-1752-251669. *1952*

FLY MUSIC MAGAZINE.
176 Purves Rd., London NW10 5TG, England. TEL 44-181-9685655. FAX 44-181-9685655. URL: http://www.fly.co.uk/
Available only online. *5393*

FLYING.
Hachette Filipacchi Magazines, Inc., 1633 Broadway, New York, NY 10019. TEL 212-767-6953.
Vendor(s): Information Access Co., Knight-Ridder Information, Inc., UMI. *65*

FOCUS (MADISON).
University of Wisconsin at Madison, Institute for Research on Poverty, 3412 Social Science Bldg., 1180 Observatory Dr., Madison, WI 53706. TEL 608-262-6358. FAX 608-265-3119. URL: http://www.ssc.wics.edu.irp/. *6666*

FOCUS (NEW YORK, 1950).
American Geographical Society, 120 Wall St., No. 100, New York, NY 10005-3904. TEL 212-422-3456.
Vendor(s): UMI. *3402*

FOCUS JAPAN.
Japan External Trade Organization, 2-5 Toranomon 2-chome, Minato-ku, Tokyo 105, Japan. TEL 03-3582-5521. FAX 03-3582-0504. *1326*

FOCUS ON EXCEPTIONAL CHILDREN.
Love Publishing Co., Box 22353, Denver, CO 80222. TEL 303-757-2579. FAX 303-782-5683. *2584*

FOCUS ON IRAN.
Azadegan Foundation, URL: http://www.mehrdad.org/focus-on-iran.html.
Available only online. *6014*

FOLDING AND DESIGN.
Current Biology Ltd., 400 Market St., Ste. 700, Philadelphia, PA 19106-2514. TEL 800-427-1796, 215-574-2225. URL: http://www.cursci.co.uk/biomed.html. *660*

FOLIA PHARMACOLOGICA JAPONICA.
Japanese Pharmacological Society, Editorial Office, Kantohya Bldg., Gokomachi-Ebisugawa, Nakagyo-ku, Kyoto 604, Japan. TEL 81-75-252-4641. FAX 81-75-252-4618. *5663*

FOLIO (STAMFORD).
Cowles Business Media, 11 River Bend Dr., S., Box 4949, Stamford, CT 06907-0949. TEL 203-358-9900. FAX 203-349-3848. URL: http://www.mediacentral.com.
Vendor(s): Information Access Co., Knight-Ridder Information, Inc., UMI. *6271*

FOLKLIFE CENTER NEWS.
U.S. Library of Congress, American Folklife Center, Washington, DC 20540-4610. TEL 202-707-6590. FAX 202-707-2076. URL: http://lcweb.loc.gov/folklife. *3086*

FOLKLORE.
Institute of the Estonian Language, URL: http://www.haldjas.folklore.ee/folklore.
Available only online. *3087*

FOOD & BEVERAGE MARKETING.
Charleson Publishing Co., 445 Broadhollow Rd., Melville, NY 11747-3601.
Vendor(s): Information Access Co., Lexis-Nexis. *3104*

FOOD AND BIOPRODUCTS PROCESSING.
Institution of Chemical Engineers, George E. Davis Bldg., 165-189 Railway Terr., Rugby, Warks. CV21 3HQ, England. TEL 44-1788-78214. FAX 44-1788-578214. URL: http://www.icheme.org/ *683*

FOOD & DRINK WEEKLY.
Sparks Companies, Inc., 6708 Whittier Ave., McLean, VA 22101. TEL 703-734-8787. FAX 703-556-7865.
Vendor(s): Information Access Co., Lexis-Nexis, NewsNet (FB03). *3105*

FOOD AND DRUG LETTER.
Washington Business Information, Inc., c/o Karen Harrington, 1117 N. 19th St., Ste. 200, Arlington, VA 22209. TEL 703-247-3434. FAX 703-247-3421.
Vendor(s): Ovid Technologies, Inc. (DIOG), Data-Star, Knight-Ridder Information, Inc. *1584*

FOOD & DRUG PACKAGING.
Independent Publishing Company, 210 S. Fifth St., Ste. 202, St. Charles, IL 60174. TEL 630-377-0100. FAX 630-377-1678. URL: http://www.fdp.com.
Vendor(s): Information Access Co. *5544*

FOOD CHEMICAL NEWS.
Food Chemical News, Inc., 1101 Pennsylvania Ave., S.E., Washington, DC 20003. TEL 202-544-1980. FAX 202-546-3890.
Vendor(s): Data-Star, Information Access Co., Knight-Ridder Information, Inc., NewsNet (FB07). *3105*

FOOD, COSMETICS AND DRUGS PACKAGING.
Elsevier Science Ltd., P.O. Box 800, Kidlington, Oxford OX5 1DX, England. TEL 44-1865-843000. FAX 44-1865-843010. URL: http://www.elsevier.nl/.
Vendor(s): Information Access Co., Knight-Ridder Information, Inc. *5544*

FOOD IN CANADA.
Maclean Hunter Ltd., Business Publication Division, Maclean Hunter Bldg., 777 Bay St., Toronto, ON M5W 1A7, Canada. TEL 416-596-5884. FAX 416-596-5526.
Vendor(s): Information Access Co., Lexis-Nexis. *3106*

FOOD INGREDIENT NEWS.
Business Communications Co., Inc. (Norwalk), 25 Van Zant St., Ste. 13, Norwalk, CT 06855. TEL 203-853-4266. FAX 203-853-0348.
Vendor(s): Information Access Co. *3106*

THE FOOD INSTITUTE REPORT.
Food Institute, 28-12 Broadway, Fair Lawn, NJ 07410. TEL 201-791-5570. FAX 201-791-5222. URL: http://www.foodinstitute.com.
Vendor(s): Information Access Co. *3106*

FOOD LABELING AND NUTRITION NEWS.
Food Chemical News, Inc., 1101 Pennsylvania Ave., S.E., Washington, DC 20003. TEL 202-544-1980. FAX 202-546-3890.
Vendor(s): Information Access Co. *3106*

FOOD MANUFACTURE INTERNATIONAL.
Miller Freeman Technical Ltd., Miller Freeman House, 30 Calderwood St., London SE18 6QH, England. TEL 44-181-855-7777. FAX 44-181-316-3206.
Vendor(s): Information Access Co., Lexis-Nexis. *3107*

FOOD MICROBIOLOGY.
Academic Press Ltd., 24-28 Oval Rd., London NW1 7DX, England. TEL 44-171-267-4466. FAX 44-171-482-2293. URL: http://www.hbuk.co.uk/ap/foodmicro; http://www.europe.idealibrary.com/ *785*

FOOD NUTRITION AND AGRICULTURE.
Food and Agriculture Organization of the United Nations, Sales & Distribution Section, Via delle Terme di Caracalla, 00100 Rome, Italy. TEL 57971. FAX 6799563.
Vendor(s): Information Access Co. *5473*

THE FOOD PAPER.
Gault Millau Inc., 5900 Wilshire Blvd., Ste. 1820, Los Angeles, CA 90036. TEL 213-965-3529. FAX 213-936-2883.
Available only online. *3725*

FOOD PROCESSING.
I M L Group plc, Blair House, High St., Tonbridge, Kent TN9 1BQ, England. TEL 44-1732-359990. FAX 44-1732-770049.
Vendor(s): Information Access Co. *3107*

FOOD RETAILERS: THE INTERNATIONAL MARKET.
Euromonitor, 60-61 Turnmill St., London EC1M 5QU, England. TEL 44-171-251-8024. FAX 44-171-608-3149. URL: http://www.euromonitor.com. Vendor(s): Data-Star, Knight-Ridder Information, Inc.. *3141*

FOOD SAFETY BRIEFING.
Barbour Index, New Lodge Drift Rd., Windsor, Berks. SL4 4RQ, England. TEL 01344-884121. FAX 01344-884112. *5490*

FOOD SCIENCE AND TECHNOLOGY.
Academic Press Ltd., 24-28 Oval Rd., London NW1 7DX, England. TEL 44-171-267-4466. FAX 44-171-482-2293. URL: http://www.hbuk.co.uk.ap/lwt; http://www.europe.idealibrary.com/ *3108*

FOOD SCIENCE AND TECHNOLOGY ABSTRACTS.
International Food Information Service (I F I S Publishing), Lane End House, Shinfield, Reading, Berks. RG2 9BB, England. TEL 01734-883895. FAX 01734-885065.
Vendor(s): CISTI, DIMDI, Data-Star (FSTA), Knight-Ridder Information, Inc. (File no.51), Questel Orbit Inc. (FSTA), STN International. *3132*

FOOD SCIENCE CATALOG.
American Association of Cereal Chemists, Inc., 3340 Pilot Knob Rd., St. Paul, MN 55121-2097. FAX 612-454-0766. URL: http://www.scisoc.rog/aacc/pubs/books/aaccbks.htm. *3109*

FOOD TRADE REVIEW.
Food Trade Press Ltd., Station House, Hortons Way, Westerham, Kent TN16 1BZ, England. TEL 44-1959-563944. FAX 44-1959-561285.
Vendor(s): Information Access Co., Lexis-Nexis. *3109*

FOODS ADLIBRA.
Foods Adlibra Publications, 9000 Plymouth Ave. N., Minneapolis, MN 55427. TEL 612-540-4759. FAX 612-540-3166.
Vendor(s): Knight-Ridder Information, Inc. (File no.79). *3132*

FOODS ADLIBRA BEVERAGE EDITION.
Foods Adlibra Publications, 9000 Plymouth Ave., N., Minneapolis, MN 55427. TEL 612-540-4759. FAX 612-540-3166.
Vendor(s): Knight-Ridder Information, Inc. (File no.79). *530*

FOODS ADLIBRA FOODSERVICE EDITION.
Foods Adlibra Publications, 9000 Plymouth Ave. N., Minneapolis, MN 55427. TEL 612-540-4759. FAX 612-540-3166.
Vendor(s): Knight-Ridder Information, Inc. (File no.79). *3132*

FOODS ADLIBRA SEAFOOD EDITION.
Foods Adlibra Publications, 9000 Plymouth Ave. N., Minneapolis, MN 55427. TEL 612-540-4759. FAX 612-540-3166.
Vendor(s): Knight-Ridder Information, Inc. (File no.79). *3132*

FOODS ADLIBRA SNACK & CONFECTIONS EDITION.
Foods Adlibra Publications, 9000 Plymouth Ave. N., Minneapolis, MN 55427. TEL 612-540-4759. FAX 612-540-3166.
Vendor(s): Knight-Ridder Information, Inc. (File no.79). *3132*

THE FOODSERVICE DISTRIBUTOR.
Penton Publishing Co., 1100 Superior Ave., Cleveland, OH 44114-2543. TEL 216-696-7000. FAX 216-696-8765.
Vendor(s): Information Access Co. *3110*

FOOT & ANKLE INTERNATIONAL.
Williams & Wilkins, 351 W. Camden St., Baltimore, MD 21201-2436. TEL 410-528-4068. FAX 410-528-4452. URL: http://www.wwilkins.com.
Vendor(s): Ovid Technologies, Inc. *5007*

FOOTWEAR NEWS.
Fairchild Fashion & Merchandising Group, 7 W. 34th St., New York, NY 10001. TEL 212-630-4199. FAX 212-630-4201.
Vendor(s): Information Access Co., Knight-Ridder Information, Inc., Lexis-Nexis. *6595*

FOR YOUR EYES ONLY.
Tiger Publications, Box 8759, Amarillo, TX 79114-8759. TEL 806-655-2009.
Vendor(s): NewsNet (DE15). *5268*

FORBES.
Forbes, Inc., 60 Fifth Ave., New York, NY 10011. TEL 212-620-2200. URL: http://www.forbes.com/forbes.
Vendor(s): Dow Jones News Retrieval, Information Access Co., Knight-Ridder Information, Inc., Lexis-Nexis. *1478*

FORD INVESTMENT MANAGEMENT REPORT.
Ford Investor Services, 11722 Sorrento Valley Rd., Ste. 1, San Diego, CA 92121. TEL 619-755-1327. *1384*

FORD VALUE REPORT.
Ford Investor Services, 11722 Sorrento Valley Rd., Ste. 1, San Diego, CA 92121. TEL 619-755-1327. *1384*

FORDHAM INTELLECTUAL PROPERTY, MEDIA & ENTERTAINMENT LAW JOURNAL.
Lincoln Center, 140 W. 62nd St., New York, NY 10023. TEL 212-636-6948. FAX 212-636-6582. URL: http://www.fordhamiplj.com.
Vendor(s): West Group. *3953*

FORDHAM INTERNATIONAL LAW JOURNAL.
Fordham University, School of Law, 140 W. 62nd St., Rm. 015, New York, NY 10023-7477. TEL 212-636-6931. FAX 212-636-6932.
Vendor(s): West Group. *4113*

FORDHAM LAW REVIEW.
Fordham University, School of Law, Lincoln Center, 140 W. 62nd St., Rm. 04, New York, NY 10023. TEL 212-636-6876. FAX 212-636-6965.
Vendor(s): Lexis-Nexis, West Group. *3953*

FORDHAM URBAN LAW JOURNAL.
Fordham University, School of Law, Lincoln Center, 140 W. 62nd St., New York, NY 10023. TEL 212-636-6881.
Vendor(s): West Group. *3953*

FOREIGN AFFAIRS.
Council on Foreign Relations, Inc., 58 E. 68th St., New York, NY 10021. TEL 212-734-0400. URL: http://foreignaffairs.org/
Vendor(s): Information Access Co., Lexis-Nexis, UMI. *6014*

FOREIGN POLICY (WASHINGTON).
Carnegie Endowment for International Peace, 2400 N St., N.W., Ste. 700, Washington, DC 20037. TEL 202-862-7940. FAX 202-463-7914.
Vendor(s): Information Access Co., UMI. *6015*

FOREIGN POLICY BULLETIN.
Kluwer Law International, Postbus 85889, 2508 CN The Hague, NE. TEL 31-70-3081500. FAX 31-70-3081515. URL: http://www.wkap.nl.
Vendor(s): Data-Star, Knight-Ridder Information, Inc., Ovid Technologies, Inc.. *6015*

FOREIGN SERVICE JOURNAL.
American Foreign Service Association, 2101 E St., N.W., Washington, DC 20037. TEL 202-338-4045. FAX 202-338-8244. *6015*

FOREIGN TRADE REPORTS. U.S. EXPORT AND IMPORT MERCHANDISE TRADE AND SUPPLEMENT.
U.S. Bureau of the Census, Foreign Trade Division, Washington, DC 20233. TEL 301-763-5140.
Vendor(s): CompuServe, Inc., Knight-Ridder Information, Inc. *1326*

FORENSIC SERVICES DIRECTORY.
National Forensic Center, 17 Temple Terr., Lawrenceville, NJ 08648. TEL 609-883-0550.
Vendor(s): Lexis-Nexis, West Group. *3953*

FOREST HEALTH BULLETIN.
Canadian Forest Service, Great Lakes Forestry Centre, Box 490, Sault Ste. Marie, ON P6A 5M7, Canada. TEL 705-949-9461. FAX 705-759-7500. Available only online. *3151*

FOREST PRODUCTS ABSTRACTS.
CAB International, Wallingford, Oxon. OX10 8DE, England. TEL 44-1491-832111. FAX 44-1491-826090.
Vendor(s): CISTI, DIMDI, European Space Agency (File nos.16 & 124/CAB), Knight-Ridder Information, Inc., Ovid Technologies, Inc. (CABA). *3168*

FOREST PRODUCTS EQUIPMENT.
L & W Publishing Co., Box 789, Hwy. 1 S., Swainsboro, GA 30401. TEL 912-237-6778. FAX 912-237-6878. URL: http://www.forestnet.com/fpe/index.html. *3171*

FOREST PRODUCTS JOURNAL.
Forest Products Society, 2801 Marshall Ct., Madison, WI 53705. TEL 608-231-1361. FAX 608-231-2152.
Vendor(s): UMI. *3171*

FOREST SANGHA NEWSLETTER.
Forest Sangha, Amaravati Buddhist Monastery, Great Gaddesden, Hemel Hempstead, Hertfordshire, England. TEL 44-1442-842455. FAX 44-1442-813721. URL: http://www-ipg.umds.ac.uk/~crr/newsletter/ *6389*

FORESTRY.
Oxford University Press, Academic Division, Great Clarendon St., Oxford OX2 6DP, England. TEL 44-1865-267907. FAX 44-1865-267485.
Vendor(s): European Space Agency (File nos.16 & 124/CAB). *3152*

FORESTRY ABSTRACTS.
CAB International, Wallingford, Oxon. OX10 8DE, England. TEL 44-1491-832111. FAX 44-1491-826090.
Vendor(s): CISTI, DIMDI, European Space Agency, Knight-Ridder Information, Inc., Ovid Technologies, Inc. (CABA). *3168*

FORLAGSSERIEKATALOG FOR BOERNE- OG SKOLEBIBLIOTEKER.
Dansk BiblioteksCenter as, Tempovej 7-11, DK-2750 Ballerup, Denmark. TEL 45-44-867777. FAX 45-44-867892. *2500*

FORMULARY.
Advanstar Communications, Inc., 7500 Old Oak Blvd., Cleveland, OH 44130. TEL 216-826-2839. FAX 216-891-2726. *5663*

FORTHCOMING BOOKS.
R.R. Bowker, A Division of Reed Elsevier Inc., 121 Chanlon Rd., New Providence, NJ 07974. TEL 908-464-6800. FAX 908-665-3502. URL: http://www.reedref.com.
Vendor(s): Knight-Ridder Information, Inc. (File no.470), Ovid Technologies, Inc. (BBIP). *547*

FORTSCHRITTE DER ARZNEIMITTELFORSCHUNG.
Birkhaeuser Verlag, P.O. Box 133, CH-4010 Basel, Switzerland. TEL 41-7217784. FAX 41-61-7217950. *5663*

FORTSCHRITTE IN DER GEOLOGIE VON RHEINLAND UND WESTFALEN.
Geologisches Landesamt Nordrhein-Westfalen, Postfach 1080, 47710 Krefeld, Germany. TEL 49-2151-8971. FAX 49-2151-897505. URL: http://www.gla.nrw.de. *2340*

FORTUNE INTERNATIONAL.
Time Warner Publishing BV, Ottho Heldring Straat 5, 1066 AZ Amsterdam, Netherlands. TEL 31-20-5104911. FAX 31-20-6175077. URL: http://fortune.com. *965*

FORTUNE MAGAZINE.
Time Inc., Time & Life Bldg., Rockefeller Center, New York, NY 10020-1393. TEL 212-522-1212. URL: http://www.fortune.com. *1479*

FORWARD (NEW YORK).
Forward Association, 45 E. 33rd St., New York, NY 10016. TEL 212-889-8200. FAX 212-447-6406. *3012*

FORWARD MOTION.
Forward Motion, Box 150311, Brooklyn, NY 11215-0311. TEL 718-789-2551. *5927*

FOSTER NATURAL GAS REPORT.
Foster Associates, 4550 Montgomery Ave., Ste. 350N, Bethesda, MD 20814-3341. TEL 202-408-7710. FAX 202-408-7723.
Vendor(s): Dow Jones News Retrieval, Lexis-Nexis. *5601*

FOUNDATION DIRECTORY.
Foundation Center, 79 Fifth Ave., New York, NY 10003. TEL 212-807-3690. FAX 212-807-3677. URL: http://www.fdncenter.org.
Vendor(s): Knight-Ridder Information, Inc. *6696*

10116 SERIALS AVAILABLE ONLINE

FOUNDATION GRANTS INDEX.
Foundation Center, 79 Fifth Ave., New York, NY 10003. TEL 212-807-3690. FAX 212-807-3677. URL: http://fdncenter.org.
Vendor(s): Knight-Ridder Information, Inc. *6696*

FOUNDATION GRANTS INDEX QUARTERLY.
Foundation Center, 79 Fifth Ave., New York, NY 10003. TEL 212-807-3690. FAX 212-807-3677. URL: http://www.fdncenter.org.
Vendor(s): Knight-Ridder Information, Inc. *6696*

FOUNDATION NEWS & COMMENTARY.
Council on Foundations, Inc., 1828 L St., N.W., Ste. 300, Washington, DC 20036. TEL 202-466-6512. FAX 202-785-3926. *6666*

FOUNDATIONS OF PHYSICS.
Plenum Publishing Corp., 233 Spring St., New York, NY 10013-1578. TEL 212-620-8000. FAX 212-463-0742. *5804*

FOUNDRY MANAGEMENT & TECHNOLOGY.
Penton Publishing Co., 1100 Superior Ave., Cleveland, OH 44114-2543. TEL 216-696-7000. FAX 216-696-8765.
Vendor(s): Information Access Co., Knight-Ridder Information, Inc. *5191*

FRANCE. CONSEIL NATIONAL DU CREDIT. STATISTIQUES MENSUELLES.
Banque de France, Service de l'Information, 48, rue Croix des Petits Champs, 75001 Paris, France. TEL 1-42-92-39-08. FAX 1-42-92-39-40.
Vendor(s): GSI-ECO. *1040*

FRANCE. CONSEIL NATIONAL DU CREDIT. STATISTIQUES TRIMESTRIELLES.
Banque de France, Service de l'Information, 48, Croix des Petits Champs, 75001 Paris, France. TEL 1-42-92-39-08. FAX 1-42-92-39-40.
Vendor(s): GSI-ECO. *1040*

THE FRANCHISE HANDBOOK.
Enterprise Magazines, Inc., 1020 N. Broadway, Ste. 111, Milwaukee, WI 53202. TEL 414-272-9977. FAX 414-272-9973. URL: http://www.franchise1.com. *1642*

FRANCHISING.
Hassel Hunt & Moore Pty. Ltd., Level 1, 5 Vuko Pl., Warriewood, N.S.W. 2102, Australia. TEL 61-2-99706688. FAX 61-2-99796979. URL: http://www.franchise.net.au. *1642*

FRANCHISING WORLD.
International Franchise Association, 1350 New York Ave., N.W., Ste. 900, Washington, DC 20005. TEL 202-628-8000. FAX 202-628-0812.
Vendor(s): UMI. *1528*

FRATRICIDE.
URL: http://www.redmon.deltos.com/frat.html.
Available only online. *4335*

FREE ASSOCIATIONS.
Process Press, 26 Freegrove Rd., London N7 9RQ, England. TEL 44-181-609-1597. FAX 44-171-609-4837. URL: http://www.shef.ac.uk/'psysc/process_press. *6112*

FREE CHOICE.
Freedom Organisation for the Right to Enjoy Smoking Tobacco (F O R E S T), 2 Grosvenor Gardens, London SW1W 0DH, England. TEL 44-171-823-6550. FAX 44-171-823-4534. *5991*

FREE INQUIRY.
Council for Secular Humanism, Box 664, Buffalo, NY 14226. TEL 716-636-1425. FAX 716-636-1733. URL: http://www.secularhumanism.org.
Vendor(s): Information Access Co., UMI. *5728*

FREE OR FAIR TRADE?
Instituto Latinoamericano de Servicios Legales Alternativos, Apdo. Aereo 077844, Bogota, Colombia. TEL 57-1-245-5955. FAX 57-1-2884854. *4080*

FREE PENNY POEMS.
80 House Rock Rd., Sedona, AZ 86351. URL: http://www.geocities.com/SoHo/1601.
Available only online. *4509*

FREE RADICAL RESEARCH.
Gordon and Breach - Harwood Academic, Amsteldisk 166, 1st Fl., 1079 LH Amsterdam, Netherlands. URL: http://www.gbhap.com/Free_Radical_Research/. *660*

FREEDOM REVIEW.
Transaction Publishers, Transaction Periodicals Consortium, Department 3092, Rutgers University, New Brunswick, NJ 08903. TEL 908-445-2280. FAX 908-445-3138. *5991*

FREEDOM WRITER.
Institute for First Amendment Studies, Inc., Box 589, Great Barrington, MA 01230. TEL 413-528-3800. FAX 413-528-4466. URL: http://www.berkshire.net/~ifas/ *5991*

FREEMAN.
Foundation for Economic Education, Inc., 30 S. Broadway, Irvington-on-Hudson, NY 10533. TEL 914-591-7230. FAX 914-591-8910. *5928*

FRENCH HISTORICAL STUDIES.
Duke University Press, Box 90660, Durham, NC 27708-0660. TEL 919-687-3600. FAX 919-688-4574. URL: http://www.duke.edu/web/dupress/dup.htm.
Vendor(s): UMI. *3567*

FREQUENT FLYER.
Reed Travel Group (Oak Brook), Part of the Reed Elsevier group 2000 Clearwater Dr., Oak Brook, IL 60521. TEL 708-574-6000. FAX 708-574-6222. *7068*

FRESENIUS' JOURNAL OF ANALYTICAL CHEMISTRY.
Springer-Verlag, Heidelberger Platz 3, 14197 Berlin, Germany. TEL 49-30-82787-0. FAX 49-30-82787448. URL: http://link.springer.de. *1791*

FRESHWATER FISHERIES LABORATORY PITLOCHRY. ANNUAL REVIEW.
Scottish Office, Agriculture and Fisheries Department, Faskally, Pitlochry, Perthshire PH16 5LB, Scotland. TEL 0796-472060. FAX 0796-473523.
Vendor(s): Knight-Ridder Information, Inc. *3068*

FROHLINGER'S MARKETING REPORT.
Marketing Strategist Communications, Ltd., 7 Coppel Dr., Tenafly, NJ 07670-2903. TEL 201-567-4447. FAX 201-568-8538.
Vendor(s): Information Access Co. *1528*

FROM NOW ON - THE EDUCATIONAL TECHNOLOGY JOURNAL.
562 W. Lake Samish Dr., Bellingham, WA 98226. TEL 360-637-8759. URL: http://fromnowon.org.
Available only online. *6960*

FRONT STRIKER BULLETIN.
American Matchcover Collecting Club, Box 18481, Asheville, NC 28814-0481. TEL 704-254-4487. FAX 704-254-1066. *3667*

FRONTIERS (ARLINGTON).
National Science Foundation, 4201 Wilson Blvd., Arlington, VA 22230. TEL 703-306-1070. FAX 703-306-0159. URL: http://www.nsf.gov:80/od/lpa/news/publicat/frontier/start.htm. *6527*

FRONTIERS (W. HOLLYWOOD).
Mercury Capital, Inc., 7985 Santa Monica Blvd., Ste. 109, W. Hollywood, CA 90046. TEL 213-848-2222. FAX 213-656-8784.
Vendor(s): Information Access Co. *3694*

FRONTIERS: A JOURNAL OF WOMEN STUDIES.
Washington State University Press, Box 645910, Pullman, WA 99164-5910. TEL 509-335-3518. FAX 509-335-8568.
Vendor(s): UMI. *7343*

FRONTIERS IN NEUROENDOCRINOLOGY.
Academic Press, Inc., Journal Division, 528 B. St., Ste. 1900, San Diego, CA 92101-4495. TEL 619-230-1840. FAX 619-699-6800. URL: http://www.apnet.com/www/journal/fn.htm; http://www.idealibrary.com/ *4888*

FRONTIERS OF HEALTH SERVICES MANAGEMENT.
Health Administration Press, 1 N. Franklin St., Ste. 1700, Chicago, IL 60606-3491. TEL 312-424-2800. FAX 312-424-0014. URL: http://www.ache.org.
Vendor(s): UMI. *3707*

FROZEN AND CHILLED FOODS.
Argus Business Media Ltd., Queensway House, 2 Queensway, Redhill, Surrey RH1 1QS, England. TEL 44-1737-768611. FAX 44-1737-761685.
Vendor(s): Information Access Co. *3110*

FROZEN FOOD AGE.
Progressive Grocer Associates, 263 Tresser Blvd., Stamford, CT 06901-3202. TEL 203-325-3500. FAX 203-325-4377.
Vendor(s): Information Access Co., UMI. *3110*

FROZEN FOOD DIGEST.
Frozen Food Digest, Inc., 271 Madison Ave., New York, NY 10016. TEL 212-557-8600. FAX 212-986-9868.
Vendor(s): Information Access Co. *3110*

FROZEN FOOD: THE INTERNATIONAL MARKET.
Euromonitor, 60-61 Britton St., London EC1M 5NA, England. TEL 44-171-251-8024. FAX 44-171-608-3149. URL: http://www.euromonitor.com.
Vendor(s): Data-Star, Knight-Ridder Information, Inc. *3110*

FRUIT AND VEGETABLES: THE INTERNATIONAL MARKET.
Euromonitor, 60-61 Britton St., London EC1M 5NA, England. TEL 44-171-251-8024. FAX 44-171-608-3149. URL: http://www.euromonitor.com.
Vendor(s): Data-Star, Knight-Ridder Information, Inc. *3110*

FRUIT JUICES: THE INTERNATIONAL MARKET.
Euromonitor, 60-61 Britton St., London EC1M 5NA, England. TEL 44-171-251-8024. FAX 44-171-608-3149. URL: http://www.euromonitor.com.
Vendor(s): Data-Star, Knight-Ridder Information, Inc. *520*

FUGUE.
University of Idaho, English Department, Brink Hall, Rm. 200, Moscow, ID 83844-1102. URL: http://www.uidaho.edu/LS/Eng/Fugue/. *4408*

FUND EXCHANGE.
Paul A. Merriman & Associates, Inc., 1200 Westlake Ave., N., Ste. 700, Seattle, WA 98109. TEL 206-285-8877. URL: http://www.paulmerriman.com. *1385*

FUND RAISING MANAGEMENT.
Hoke Communications, Inc., 224 Seventh St., Garden City, NY 11530. TEL 516-746-6700. FAX 516-294-8141.
Vendor(s): Information Access Co., Knight-Ridder Information, Inc., UMI. *1142*

FUNGAL GENETICS AND BIOLOGY.
Academic Press, Inc., Journal Division, 525 B St., Ste. 1900, San Diego, CA 92101-4495. TEL 619-230-1840. FAX 619-699-6800. URL: http://www.apnet.com/www.journal/fg.htm; http://www.idealibrary.com/ *705*

FUNGAL GENETICS NEWSLETTER.
Fungal Genetics Stock Center, University of Kansas Medical School, Department of Microbiology, Kansas City, KS 66160-7420. TEL 913-588-7044. FAX 913-588-7295. URL: http://www.kumc.edu/*fgsc. *602*

FUNKY LLAMA CLUB.
5527 Ponderosa Dr., Rockford, IL 61107-1783. URL: http://flc.home.ml.org.
Available only online. *4498*

FURIOUS GREEN THOUGHTS.
URL: http://www.furious.com.
Available only online. *4335*

FURMAN UNIVERSITY ELECTRONIC JOURNAL OF UNDERGRADUATE MATHEMATICS.
Furman University, Department of Mathematics, 3300 Ponsett Hwy., Greenville, SC 29613-0666. TEL 864-294-3632. URL: http://math.furman.edu/~mwoodard/fuejum/
Available only online. *4573*

FUSION POWER REPORT.
Business Publishers, Inc., 951 Pershing Dr., Silver Spring, MD 20910-4464. TEL 301-587-6300. FAX 301-585-9075.
Vendor(s): Information Access Co., Knight-Ridder Information, Inc., NewsNet (EY46). *2696*

THE FUTURE OF CHILDREN.
David and Lucile Packard Foundation, Center for the Future of Children, 300 Second St., Ste. 102, Los Altos, CA 94022. TEL 415-948-3696. FAX 415-948-6498. URL: http://www.futureofchildren.org. *1846*

FUTURES (CEDAR FALLS).
Oster Communications, Inc., 219 Parkade, Cedar Falls, IA 50613. TEL 319-277-1271. FAX 319-277-5803.
Vendor(s): Information Access Co. *1385*

FUTURES WORLD NEWS.
Oster Communications, Inc., 219 Parkade, Cedar Falls, IA 50613. TEL 319-277-1271. FAX 319-277-5803.
Available only online. *1385*

FUTURESCOPE.
Decision Resources, Inc., 1100 Winter St., Waltham, MA 02154-1238. TEL 617-487-3737. FAX 617-487-5750.
Vendor(s): Knight-Ridder Information, Inc. (File no. 192). *1385*

THE FUTURIST.
World Future Society, 7910 Woodmont Ave., Ste. 450, Bethesda, MD 20814. TEL 301-656-8274.
Vendor(s): Information Access Co., Knight-Ridder Information, Inc., UMI. *6527*

G A C I A C BULLETIN.
U.S. Department of Defense, Guidance and Control Information Analysis Center, c/o Chalmer George, AMC Smart Weapons Management Office, Attn.: AMSMI-SW, Redstone Arsenal, AL 35898-5222. TEL 205-876-3788. URL: http://gaciac.iitri.com/bulletins.html.
Available only online. *66*

G A O DAYBOOK.
U.S. General Accounting Office, Office of Public Affairs, Box 6015, Gaithersburg, MD 20884-6015. TEL 202-512-6000. FAX 301-258-4066.
Available only online. *6175*

G I CANCER.
Gordon and Breach - Harwood Academic, Amsteldisk 166, 1st Fl., 1079 LH Amsterdam, Netherlands. URL: http://www.gbhap.com/GI_Cancer/. *4978*

THE G M P LETTER.
Washington Business Information, Inc., c/o Karen Harrington, 1117 N. 19th St., Ste. 200, Arlington, VA 22209. TEL 703-247-3434. FAX 703-247-3421.
Vendor(s): Ovid Technologies, Inc. (DIOG), Data-Star, Knight-Ridder Information, Inc. *3801*

G N N MAGAZINE.
Global Network Navigator, 22000 Aol Way, Dulles, VA 20166. TEL 510-883-7220. URL: http://gnn.com/.
Available only online. *2133*

G N N NEWS.
Global Network Navigator, 22000 Aol Way, Dulles, VA 20166. TEL 510-883-7220. URL: http://gnn.com/.
Available only online. *2133*

G P.
Haymarket Publishing Ltd., 174 Hammersmith Rd., London W6 7JP, England. TEL 44-171-413-4328. FAX 44-171-413-4013.
Vendor(s): Data-Star (GPGP). *4670*

G R I D.
Gas Research Institute, Member Relations and Communications, 8600 W. Bryn Mawr Ave., Chicago, IL 60631. TEL 773-399-8100. FAX 773-399-8170.
Vendor(s): Information Access Co. *5601*

G S A TODAY.
Geological Society of America, 3300 Penrose Pl., Box 9140, Boulder, CO 80301. TEL 303-447-2020. FAX 303-447-1133. URL: http://www.aescon.com/geosociety/pubs.index.html. *2340*

G U I PROGRAM NEWS.
Worldwide Videotex, Box 3273, Boynton Beach, FL 33424-3273. TEL 407-738-2276.
Vendor(s): Information Access Co. *2212*

G W D.
GREENY World Domination Task Force, Inc., Box 16038, Lubbock, TX 79490-6038. URL: http://www.geocities/Athens/2334/index.html.
Available only online. *4335*

GAJOOB.
Box 3201, Salt Lake City, UT 84110. TEL 801-364-5110. *5394*

GALATEA.
Vrije Universiteit Amsterdam, Word & Image Studies, URL: http://www.let.vu.nl/e-zine/galatea.
Available only online. *442*

GALE DIRECTORY OF DATABASES.
Gale Research, 835 Penobscot Bldg., 645 Griswold St., Detroit, MI 48226-4094. TEL 313-961-2242. FAX 800-414-5043.
Vendor(s): Data-Star, Questel Orbit Inc., Telesystemes - Questel. *2166*

GALE DIRECTORY OF PUBLICATIONS AND BROADCAST MEDIA.
Gale Research, 835 Penobscot Bldg., 645 Griswold St., Detroit, MI 48226-4094. TEL 313-961-2242. FAX 800-414-5043.
Vendor(s): Knight-Ridder Information, Inc. *548*

GALLUP POLL MONTHLY.
Gallup Poll News Service, 47 Hulfish St., Box 628, Princeton, NJ 08542. TEL 609-924-9600. FAX 609-683-9256. URL: http://www.gallup.com. *5928*

GAME DEVELOPER.
Miller Freeman, Inc., 600 Harrison St., San Francisco, CA 94107. TEL 415-905-2588. FAX 415-905-2165. URL: http://www.mfi.com/gdnag. *2118*

THE GAME REVIEW.
URL: http://tgr.clever.net; http://ns2.clever.net/~ionizer.
Available only online. *2118*

GAMES AND ECONOMIC BEHAVIOR.
Academic Press, Inc., Journal Division, 525 B St., Ste. 1900, San Diego, CA 92101-4495. TEL 619-230-1840. FAX 619-699-6800. URL: http://www.apnet.com/www/journal/ga.htm; http://www.idealibrary.com/ *6112*

GANGWAY.
Gangan Publishing, P.O. Box 522, Strawberry Hills, N.S.W. 2012, Australia. TEL 61-2-93192443. FAX 61-2-93192445. URL: http://www.matra.com.au/'gangan/gangway.html.
Available only online. *4408*

GAP-TOOTHED.
837 W. Cornelia, Chicago, IL 60657. URL: http://gap-toothed.com.
Available only online. *4335*

GARDENING: THE INTERNATIONAL MARKET.
Euromonitor, 60-61 Britton St., London EC1M 5NA, England. TEL 44-171-251-8024. FAX 44-171-608-3149. URL: http://www.euromonitor.com.
Vendor(s): Data-Star, Knight-Ridder Information, Inc.. *3189*

GARDENWEB.
138 Montgomery St., Ste. 1M, Highland Park, NJ 08904. URL: http://www.gardenweb.com.
Available only online. *3189*

THE GARRETT COUNTY JOURNAL.
260 Langdon St., Ste. 3, Madison, WI 53703. URL: http://www.cyborganic.com/people/garrett.
Available only online. *4408*

GAS ABSTRACTS.
Institute of Gas Technology, 1700 S. Mount Prospect Rd., Des Plaines, IL 60018-1804. TEL 847-768-0673. FAX 847-768-0669. *5629*

GAS DAILY.
Pasha Publications Inc., 1616 N. Ft. Myer Dr., Ste. 1000, Arlington, VA 22209-3107. TEL 703-528-1244. FAX 703-528-1253. *5602*

GAS MARKET TRENDS.
Arab Press Service, A P S House, P.O. Box 3896, Nicosia, Cyprus. TEL 357-2-351778. FAX 357-2-350265.
Vendor(s): Information Access Co. *2670*

GAS MARKETS WEEK.
Pasha Publications Inc., 1616 N. Ft. Myer Dr., Ste. 1000, Arlington, VA 22209-3107. TEL 703-528-1244. FAX 703-528-1253. *5602*

GAS STORAGE REPORT.
Pasha Publications Inc., 1616 N. Ft. Myer Dr., Ste. 1000, Arlington, VA 22209-3107. TEL 703-528-1244. FAX 703-528-1253. *5603*

GAS TRANSPORTATION REPORT.
Pasha Publications Inc., 1616 N. Ft. Myer Dr., Ste. 1000, Arlington, VA 22209-3107. TEL 703-528-1244. FAX 703-528-1253. *5603*

GASSHO.
Dharmanet International, Box 4951, Berkeley, CA 94704-4951. TEL 510-620-0936. *6389*

GASTROENTEROLOGY.
W.B. Saunders Co., Curtis Center, 3rd Fl., Independence Sq. W., Philadelphia, PA 19106-3399. TEL 215-238-7800. FAX 215-238-6445.
Vendor(s): Ovid Technologies, Inc. *4910*

GASTROENTEROLOGY NURSING.
Williams & Wilkins, 351 W. Camden St., Baltimore, MD 21201-2436. TEL 410-528-4068. FAX 410-528-4452. URL: http://www.wwilkins.com.
Vendor(s): Ovid Technologies, Inc. *4910*

GAY SCOTLAND.
Calosa Publishing Ltd., 11 Dixon St, Glasgow G1 4AL, Scotland. TEL 44-141-204-0742. FAX 44-141-204-0741. *3695*

GAZETA LEKARSKA.
Naczelna Izba Lekarska w Warszawie, Ul. Grojecka 65A, 02-094 Warsaw, Poland. TEL 48-22-6250121. FAX 48-22-6296333. URL: http://www.ternet.pl/zdrowie/nil/bb.htm. *4670*

GAZETTE.
250 rue St-Antoine O., Montreal, PQ H2Y 3R7, Canada.
Vendor(s): Southam Electronic Publishing. *3261*

GEBORENER DEUTSCHER.
William L. Gage, Ed. & Pub., 805 Alvarado Dr. N.E., Albuquerque, NM 87108-1648. TEL 505-268-1310. *3223*

GEEKGIRL.
P.O. Box 759, Newtown, N.S.W. 2042, Australia. URL: http://www.geekgirl.com.au. *7321*

GENBANK.
U.S. National Library of Medicine, U.S. National Center for Biotechnology Information, Bldg. 38A, Rm. 8N-803, Bldg. 38A, Rm. 8N-803, 8600 Rockville Pike, Bethesda, MD 20894. TEL 301-496-2475. FAX 301-480-2233. URL: http://www.ncbi.nlm.nih.gov. *735*

GENDER AND DEVELOPMENT.
Carfax Publishing Co., P.O. Box 25, Abingdon, Oxon OX14 3UE, England. TEL 44-1235-401000. FAX 44-1235-401550. *7343*

GENDER AND EDUCATION.
Carfax Publishing Co., P.O. Box 25, Abingdon, Oxon. OX14 3UE, England. TEL 44-1235-401000. FAX 44-1235-401550. *2445*

GENDER, PLACE AND CULTURE.
Carfax Publishing Co., P.O. Box 25, Abingdon, Oxon. OX14 3UE, England. TEL 44-1235-401000. FAX 44-1235-401550. URL: http://www.carfax.co.uk. *7344*

GENE.
Elsevier Science B.V., P.O. Box 211, 1000 AE Amsterdam, Netherlands. TEL 31-20-4853911. FAX 31-20-4853598. URL: http://www.elsevier.nl/. *767*

THE GENE EXCHANGE.
Union of Concerned Scientists (Washington), 1616 P St., N.W., Ste. 310, Washington, DC 20036. TEL 202-332-0900. FAX 202-332-0905. *767*

THE GENE LETTER.
URL: http://www.geneletter.org.
Available only online. *767*

SERIALS AVAILABLE ONLINE

GENE THERAPY WEEKLY.
Charles W. Henderson, Ed. & Pub., Box 5528, Atlanta, GA 31107-0528. TEL 404-377-8895. FAX 404-378-5411. URL: http://www.newsfile.com. *4671*

GENERAL AND COMPARATIVE ENDOCRINOLOGY.
Academic Press, Inc., Journal Division, 525 B St., Ste. 1900, San Diego, CA 92101-4495. TEL 619-230-1840. FAX 619-699-6800. URL: http://www.apnet.com/www/journal/gc.htm; http://www.idealibrary.com/ *4888*

GENERAL RELATIVITY AND GRAVITATION.
Plenum Publishing Corp., 233 Spring St., New York, NY 10013-1578. TEL 212-620-8000. FAX 212-463-0742. URL: http://www.catchword.co.uk/. *5804*

GENERAL SCIENCE INDEX.
H.W. Wilson Co., 950 University Ave., Bronx, NY 10452. TEL 718-588-8400. FAX 718-590-1617. Vendor(s): OCLC, Wilsonline (File GSI). *6589*

GENERATING AVAILABILITY REPORT (YEAR).
North American Electric Reliability Council, Princeton Forrestal Village, 116-390 Village Blvd., Princeton, NJ 08540-5731. TEL 609-452-8060. URL: http://www.nerc.com. *2689*

GENERATING UNIT STATISTICS (YEAR).
North American Electric Reliability Council, Princeton Forrestal Village, 116-390 Village Blvd., Princeton, NJ 08540-5731. TEL 609-452-8060. URL: http://www.nerc.com. *2689*

GENERATOR 21 WORLD WIDE.
255 14th Ave., San Francisco, CA 94118. URL: http://www.well.com/~buttrfly. Available only online. *4336*

GENESIS REPORT - DX.
Genesis Group Associates, Inc., 29 Park St., Montclair, NJ 07042. TEL 201-509-7735. FAX 201-509-7745. Vendor(s): Data-Star, Dow Jones News Retrieval, Information Access Co., Knight-Ridder Information, Inc., Lexis-Nexis. *4672*

GENESIS REPORT - RX.
Genesis Group Associates, Inc., 29 Park St., Montclair, NJ 07042. TEL 201-509-7735. FAX 201-509-7745. Vendor(s): Data-Star, Dow Jones News Retrieval, Information Access Co., Knight-Ridder Information, Inc., Lexis-Nexis. *5664*

GENETIC EPIDEMIOLOGY.
John Wiley & Sons, Inc., Journals, 605 Third Ave., New York, NY 10158. TEL 212-850-6645. FAX 212-850-6021. URL: http://wwww.wiley.co.uk. *768*

GENETICS ABSTRACTS.
Cambridge Scientific Abstracts, 7200 Wisconsin Ave., 6th Fl., Bethesda, MD 20814. TEL 301-961-6750. FAX 301-961-6720. URL: http://www.csa.com. Vendor(s): Knight-Ridder Information, Inc. (File no.76/LIFE SCIENCES COLLECTION), STN International (LIFESCI). *641*

GENGO TO KYOIKU NO KENKYU.
Saitama Daigaku Kyoiku Gakubu, Kyoiku Gakubu, Takenaga Laboratory, 255, Shimo Okubo, Urawa-shi 338, Japan. TEL 048-858-3175. FAX 048-858-3690. *2603*

GENOME RESEARCH.
Cold Spring Harbor Laboratory Press, Publications Department, Box 100, Cold Spring Harbor, NY 11724. TEL 516-367-8492. FAX 516-367-8334. URL: http://www.cshl.org. *785*

GENOMICS.
Academic Press, Inc., Journal Division, 525 B St., Ste. 1900, San Diego, CA 92101-4495. TEL 619-230-1840. FAX 619-699-6800. URL: http://www.apnet.com/www/journal/ge.htm; http://www.idealibrary.com/ *770*

GENRE MAGAZINE.
7080 Hollywood Blvd., Ste. 1104, Hollywood, CA 90028. TEL 213-467-8300. FAX 213-467-8365. *5176*

GEO INFO SYSTEMS.
Advanstar Communications, Inc., 7500 Old Oak Blvd., Cleveland, OH 44130. TEL 216-826-2839. FAX 216-891-2726. Vendor(s): Information Access Co. *3429*

GEO-MARINE LETTERS.
Springer-Verlag, Heidelberger Platz 3, 14197 Berlin, Germany. TEL 49-30-82787-0. FAX 49-30-82787448. URL: http://link.springer.de. *2341*

GEOGRAPHIC INFORMATION AND DECISION ANALYSIS RESEARCH GROUP. NEWSLETTER.
Geographic Information and Decision Analysis Research Group, c/o Jacek Malczewski, Dept. of Geography, University of Western Ontario, London, ON N6A 5C2, Canada. URL: http://sparky.sscl.uwo.ca/gimda/journal.htm. Available only online. *3404*

GEOGRAPHICAL ABSTRACTS: HUMAN GEOGRAPHY.
Elsevier - Geo Abstracts, Regency House, 34 Duke St., Norwich NR3 3AP, England. TEL 44-1603-626327. FAX 44-1603-667934. URL: http://www.elsevier.nl. Vendor(s): Knight-Ridder Information, Inc. (File no.292), Questel Orbit Inc. (GEOB). *3428*

GEOGRAPHICAL ABSTRACTS: PHYSICAL GEOGRAPHY.
Elsevier - Geo Abstracts, Regency House, 34 Duke St., Norwich NR3 3AP, England. TEL 44-1603-626327. FAX 44-1603-667934. URL: http://www.elsevier.nl/. Vendor(s): Knight-Ridder Information, Inc. (File no.292), Questel Orbit Inc. (GEOB). *3428*

THE GEOGRAPHICAL JOURNAL.
Royal Geographical Society, 1 Kensington Gore, London SW7 2AR, England. TEL 44-171-589-5466. FAX 44-171-584-4447. Vendor(s): Information Access Co., UMI. *3405*

GEOGRAPHICAL MAGAZINE.
Royal Geographical Society, 1 Kensington Gore, London SW7 2AR, England. TEL 44-171-589-5466. FAX 44-171-584-4447. Vendor(s): Information Access Co. *3405*

GEOGRAPHICAL REVIEW.
American Geographical Society, 120 Wall St., No. 100, New York, NY 10005-3904. TEL 212-422-5456. Vendor(s): Information Access Co., UMI. *3405*

GEOGRAPHICAL SYSTEMS.
Gordon and Breach - Harwood Academic, Amsteldisk 166, 1st Fl., 1079 LH Amsterdam, Netherlands. URL: http://www.gbhap.com/Geographical__Systems/. *3406*

GEOLOGICAL ABSTRACTS.
Elsevier - Geo Abstracts, Regency House, 34 Duke St., Norwich NR3 3AP, England. TEL 44-1603-626327. FAX 44-1603-667934. URL: http://www.elsevier.nl/. Vendor(s): Knight-Ridder Information, Inc. (File no.292), Questel Orbit Inc. (GEOB). *2325*

GEOLOGICAL SOCIETY OF INDIA. JOURNAL.
Geological Society of India, Post Box 1922, Gavipuran, Bangalore 560 019, India. TEL 91-80-6613352. Vendor(s): Knight-Ridder Information, Inc. (File no.89). *2344*

GEOLOGISCHE RUNDSCHAU.
Springer-Verlag, Heidelberger Platz 3, 14197 Berlin, Germany. TEL 49-30-82787-0. FAX 49-30-82787448. URL: http://link.springer.de. *2346*

GEOMETRIC AND FUNCTIONAL ANALYSIS.
Birkhaeuser Verlag, P.O. Box 133, CH-4010 Basel, Switzerland. TEL 41-61-2050730. FAX 41-61-2050791. *4574*

GEOMETRY & TOPOLOGY.
URL: http://www.maths.warwick.ac.uk/gt/. Available only online. *4574*

GEOPHYSICAL AND ASTROPHYSICAL FLUID DYNAMICS.
Gordon and Breach - Harwood Academic, Amsteldisk 166, 1st Fl., 1079 LH Amsterdam, Netherlands. URL: http://www.gbhap.com/Geophysical__Astrophysical__Fluid__Dynamics/. *2382*

GEORGE JR.
Box 2962, Columbus, OH 43216. URL: http://www.georgejr.com. Available only online. *4336*

GEORGE MASON LAW REVIEW.
Darby, 3401 N. Fairfax Dr., Arlington, VA 22201. TEL 703-993-8161. FAX 703-993-8088. Vendor(s): Lexis-Nexis, West Group. *3954*

GEORGE WASHINGTON JOURNAL OF INTERNATIONAL LAW AND ECONOMICS.
George Washington University, National Law Center, 2008 G St., N.W., Washington, DC 20052. TEL 202-676-3847. FAX 202-676-3876. Vendor(s): Lexis-Nexis, West Group. *4114*

GEORGE WASHINGTON LAW REVIEW.
2008 G St., N.W., Washington, DC 20052. TEL 202-676-3868. FAX 202-676-3876. Vendor(s): Lexis-Nexis, West Group. *3954*

GEORGE WELLS' WASHINGTON BEVERAGE INSIGHT.
George Wells & Associates, 2942 S. Columbus St., Ste. A-2, Arlington, VA 22206. TEL 703-671-8140. Vendor(s): Information Access Co., NewsNet. *520*

GEORGETOWN IMMIGRATION LAW JOURNAL.
Georgetown University Law Center, 600 New Jersey Ave., N.W., Washington, DC 20009. TEL 202-662-9468. Vendor(s): West Group. *3955*

GEORGETOWN INTERNATIONAL ENVIRONMENTAL LAW REVIEW.
Georgetown University Law Center, 600 New Jersey Ave., N.W., Washington, DC 20009. TEL 202-662-9468. Vendor(s): West Group. *2929*

GEORGETOWN LAW JOURNAL.
Georgetown University Law Center, 600 New Jersey Ave., N.W., Washington, DC 20009. TEL 202-662-9468. Vendor(s): Lexis-Nexis, West Group. *3955*

GEORGETOWN REVIEW.
Milkbone Publishing, Box 6309, Southern Sta., Hattiesburg, MS 39406-6309. TEL 601-583-6940. FAX 601-583-6940. *4409*

GEORGIA BUSINESS DIRECTORY.
American Business Directories, 5711 S. 86th Circle, Box 27347, Omaha, NE 68127. TEL 402-593-4600. FAX 402-331-5481. *1682*

GEORGIA JOURNAL OF INTERNATIONAL AND COMPARATIVE LAW.
Georgia Journal of International and Comparative Law, Inc., University of Georgia, School of Law, Athens, GA 30602. TEL 706-542-5205. Vendor(s): Lexis-Nexis, West Group. *4114*

GEORGIA LAW REVIEW.
University of Georgia, School of Law, Athens, GA 30602. TEL 706-542-7286. FAX 706-542-5556. URL: http://www.lawsch.edu/~galarev. Vendor(s): West Group. *3955*

GEORGIA TREND.
Grimes Publications, Inc., Box 1266, Athens, GA 30603. TEL 404-354-0463. FAX 404-354-6824. Vendor(s): Information Access Co., Knight-Ridder Information, Inc., Lexis-Nexis, UMI. *1142*

GEOSCIENCE DOCUMENTATION.
Geosystems, P.O. Box 40, Didcot, Oxon. OX11 9BX, England. TEL 44-1235-813913. Vendor(s): Knight-Ridder Information, Inc. (File no.58). *2325*

GEOTECHNICAL AND GEOLOGICAL ENGINEERING.
Thomson Science, 2-6 Boundary Row, London SE1 8HN, England. TEL 44-171-8650066. FAX 44-171-522-9623. URL: http://www.thomsonscience.com. *5301*

GEOTHERMAL RESOURCES COUNCIL. BULLETIN.
Geothermal Resources Council, Box 1350, Davis, CA 95617-1350. TEL 916-758-2360. FAX 916-758-2839. URL: http://www.geothermal.org. *2692*

GEOTITLES.
Geosystems, P.O. Box 40, Didcot, Oxon. OX11 9BX, England. TEL 44-1235-813913. Vendor(s): Knight-Ridder Information, Inc. (File no.58). *2326*

GERIATRIC NURSING.
Mosby Year - Book, Inc., 11830 Westline Industrial Dr., St. Louis, MO 63146-3318. TEL 314-872-8370. FAX 314-432-1380. *3436*

GERIATRICS.
Advanstar Communications, Inc., 7500 Old Oak Blvd., Cleveland, OH 44130. TEL 216-826-2839. FAX 216-891-2726. URL: http://www.modernmedicine.com/geri/gerindex.html. Vendor(s): Information Access Co., UMI. *3436*

GERMAN BRIEF.
Frankfurter Allgemeine Zeitung GmbH, Information Services, Hellerhofstr. 2-4, 60327 Frankfurt a.M., Germany. TEL 49-69-75912219. FAX 49-69-75912188. *966*

GERMAN LIFE.
Zeitgeist Publishing, 1 Corporate Dr., Grantsville, MD 21536. TEL 301-895-3859. FAX 301-895-5029. URL: http://langlab.uta.edu/GERM/German__Life/ *3285*

GERMANIC REVIEW.
Heldref Publications, 1319 Eighteenth St., N.W., Washington, DC 20036-1802. TEL 202-296-6267. FAX 202-296-5149. Vendor(s): UMI. *4260*

GERMANY'S TOP 500.
Frankfurter Allgemeine Zeitung GmbH, Information Services, Hellerhofstr. 2-4, 60327 Frankfurt a.M., Germany. TEL 49-69-75912219. FAX 49-69-75912188. *1682*

THE GERONTOLOGIST.
Gerontological Society of America, 1275 K St., N.W., Ste. 350, Washington, DC 20005-4006. TEL 202-842-1275. FAX 202-842-1150. URL: http://gsa.iog.wayne.edu/Journals/gerontologist.html. Vendor(s): UMI. *3436*

GETTING RESULTS...FOR THE HANDS-ON MANAGER.
American Management Association, 1601 Broadway, New York, NY 10019. TEL 212-586-8100. FAX 212-903-8083. Vendor(s): Information Access Co., UMI. *1479*

GIANT ROBOT.
Box 2053, Los Angeles, CA 90064. *3013*

DIE GIESSEREI-INDUSTRIE UND IHRE HELFER.
Industrieschau-Verlagsgesellschaft mbH, Postfach 100262, 64202 Darmstadt, Germany. TEL 49-6151-38920. FAX 49-6151-33164. *5192*

GIFTS & DECORATIVE ACCESSORIES.
Geyer-McAllister Publications, Inc., 51 Madison Ave., New York, NY 10010. TEL 212-689-4411. Vendor(s): Information Access Co., Knight-Ridder Information, Inc. *3449*

GIORNALE DI MEDICINA MILITARE.
Direzione Generale della Sanita Militare, Via S. Stefano Rotondo, n.4, 00184 Rome, Italy. TEL 39-4735-7939. *4672*

GIRLJOCK.
Rox-A-Tronic Publishing, Box 882723, San Francisco, CA 94188. TEL 415-282-6833. FAX 415-282-6833. *3695*

GLACIAL GEOLOGY AND GEOMORPHOLOGY.
John Wiley & Sons Ltd., Journals, Baffins Ln., Chichester, W. Sussex PO19 1UD, England. TEL 44-1243-779777. FAX 44-1243-843232. URL: http://ggg.qub.ac.uk/ggg. Available only online. *2315*

GLASS (REDHILL).
Argus Business Media Ltd., Queensway House, 2 Queensway, Redhill, Surrey RH1 1QS, England. TEL 44-1737-768611. FAX 44-1737-761685. Vendor(s): Information Access Co. *1729*

GLASS INTERNATIONAL.
Argus Business Media Ltd., Queensway House, 2 Queensway, Redhill, Surrey RH1 1QS, England. TEL 44-1737-768611. FAX 44-1737-761685. Vendor(s): Information Access Co. *1730*

GLEN COVE COMPUTING NEWS.
Glen Cove Computing, 26 Castle Hill Ct., Vallejo, CA 94591. URL: http://www.glencove.com/gcctimes.htm. Available only online. *2133*

GLOBAL COMPANY HANDBOOK.
C I F A R Publications, Inc., 3490 US Hwy 1, BL012, Princeton, NJ 08540-5920. TEL 609-520-9333. FAX 609-520-0905. Vendor(s): Lexis-Nexis. *1328*

GLOBAL ENVIRONMENTAL CHANGE.
Elsevier Science Ltd., Pergamon, P.O. Box 800, Kidlington, Oxford OX5 1DX, England. TEL 44-1865-843000. FAX 44-1865-843010. URL: http://www.elsevier.nl/. Vendor(s): Data-Star, Knight-Ridder Information, Inc., NewsNet. *2930*

GLOBAL ENVIRONMENTAL CHANGE REPORT.
Cutter Information Corp., 37 Broadway, Arlington, MA 02174. TEL 617-648-8700. FAX 617-648-1950. URL: http://www.cutter.com. Vendor(s): Information Access Co. *2930*

GLOBAL INVESTOR.
Euromoney Publications plc., Nestor House, Playhouse Yard, London EC4V 5EX, England. TEL 44-171-779-8935. FAX 44-171-779-8541. Vendor(s): UMI. *1143*

GLOBAL MAIL.
Soapbox June, Box 410837, San Francisco, CA 94141-0837. *443*

GLOBAL MARKETPLACE.
7111 W. Indian School Rd., Ste. 101, Phoenix, AZ 85033. TEL 602-872-7900. FAX 603-530-4940. URL: http://www.globalmarketnt. *967*

GLOBAL PESTICIDE CAMPAIGNER.
Pesticide Action Network, North America Regional Center, 116 New Montgomery St., No. 810, San Francisco, CA 94105-3607. TEL 415-541-9140. FAX 415-541-9253. URL: http://www.panna.org. *2978*

GLOBAL POSITIONING & NAVIGATION NEWS.
Phillips Business Information, Inc., 1201 Seven Locks Rd., Potomac, MD 20854. TEL 301-424-3338. FAX 301-309-3847. Vendor(s): Information Access Co., NewsNet (DE24). *2034*

GLOBAL PRIVATE POWER.
Financial Times Energy Publishing, Maple House, 149 Tottenham Court Rd., London W1P 9LL, England. TEL 44-171-896-2241. FAX 44-171-896-2275. Vendor(s): Data-Star, Knight-Ridder Information, Inc., Lexis-Nexis. *2689*

GLOBE AND MAIL REPORT ON BUSINESS.
Globe and Mail Publishing, 444 Front St. W., Toronto, ON M5V 2S9, Canada. TEL 416-585-5000. *1262*

GLOBE E JOURNAL OF CONTEMPORARY ART.
Monash University, Visual Arts Department, Wellington Rd., Clayton, Vic. 3168, Australia. TEL 61-3-99054222. FAX 61-3-99054209. URL: http://www.arts.monash.edu.au/visarts/globe/ghome.html. Available only online. *443*

GLOSSOLALIA.
Stenbocksv. 24, FIN-02860 Esbo, Finland. URL: http://www.thing.net/'grist/homecyan.htm. Available only online. *4410*

GLYCOCONJUGATE JOURNAL.
Chapman & Hall, Journals Department 2-6 Boundary Row, London SE1 8HN, England. TEL 44-171-8650066. FAX 44-171-5229623. URL: http://www.chaphall.com/chaphall/journals.html. *660*

GO, GIRL! MAGAZINE.
Kappas Marina, West Pier 1A, Sausalito, CA 94965. TEL 415-332-4234. FAX 415-332-8852. URL: http://www.gogirlmag.com. Available only online. *7321*

GOLDEN GATE UNIVERSITY LAW REVIEW.
Golden Gate University, School of Law, 536 Mission St., San Francisco, CA 94105. TEL 415-442-6691. Vendor(s): West Group. *3956*

GOLF MAGAZINE (NEW YORK).
Times Mirror Magazines, Inc., 2 Park Ave., New York, NY 10016. TEL 212-779-5000. URL: http://www.golfonline.com. Vendor(s): Information Access Co. *6806*

GOLOB'S OIL POLLUTION BULLETIN.
World Information Systems, Box 535, Harvard Sq. Sta., Cambridge, MA 02238. FAX 617-491-5100. Vendor(s): NewsNet (EV05). *2985*

GONZOLIGA.
Available only online. *6808*

GOOD HOUSEKEEPING.
Hearst Corporation, Good Housekeeping, 959 Eighth Ave., New York, NY 10019. TEL 212-649-2200. FAX 212-265-3307. URL: http://homearts.com/gh/; http://www.hearstcorp.com. Vendor(s): Information Access Co.. *3684*

GOURMET FARE MAGAZINE.
D R S Internet Publishing Group, Box 488, Matthews, NC 28106. URL: http://www.drspublishing.com/gourmet. Available only online. *3111*

GOVERNING.
2300 N St., N.W., Ste. 760, Washington, DC 20037. TEL 202-862-8802. FAX 202-862-0032. URL: http://www.governing.com. Vendor(s): Lexis-Nexis, LOGIN Information Services. *6215*

GOVERNMENT COMPUTER NEWS.
Cahners Publishing Company (Silver Spring), Division of Reed Elsevier Inc., 8601 Georgia Ave., Ste. 300, Silver Spring, MD 20910. TEL 301-650-2176. FAX 301-650-2111. URL: http://www.gcn.com. Vendor(s): Information Access Co., Knight-Ridder Information, Inc. *6209*

GOVERNMENT EMPLOYEE RELATIONS REPORT.
The Bureau of National Affairs, Inc., 1231 25th St., N.W., Washington, DC 20037. TEL 202-452-4200. FAX 202-822-8092. URL: http://www.bna.com/ Vendor(s): Human Resources Information Network (CDD, HDD), Lexis-Nexis (GOVEMP), West Group. *1431*

GOVERNMENT EXECUTIVE.
National Journal, Inc., 1501 M St., N.W., Ste. 300, Washington, DC 20005. TEL 202-739-8400. FAX 202-833-8069. Vendor(s): UMI. *6176*

GOVERNMENT FINANCE REVIEW.
Government Finance Officers Association, 180 N. Michigan Ave., Ste. 800, Chicago, IL 60601. TEL 312-977-9700. FAX 312-977-4806. Vendor(s): Information Access Co. *1611*

GOVERNMENT PRODUCT NEWS.
Penton Publishing Co., 1100 Superior Ave., Cleveland, OH 44114-2543. TEL 216-696-7000. FAX 216-696-7658. Vendor(s): Knight-Ridder Information, Inc. *6176*

GOVERNMENT REPORTS ANNOUNCEMENTS & INDEX.
U.S. National Technical Information Service, 5285 Port Royal Rd., Springfield, VA 22161. TEL 703-487-4630. FAX 703-321-8547. Vendor(s): CEDOCAR, CISTI, Data-Star, European Space Agency, JICST, Knight-Ridder Information, Inc. (File no.6), Ovid Technologies, Inc., Questel Orbit Inc. (NTIS), STN International (NTIS). *6204*

GOVERNMENT RESEARCH DIRECTORY.
Gale Research, 835 Penobscot Bldg., 645 Griswold St., Detroit, MI 48226-4094. TEL 313-961-2242. FAX 800-414-5043. Vendor(s): Knight-Ridder Information, Inc. *6960*

GOVERNMENT TECHNOLOGY.
9719 Lincoln Village Dr., No. 500, Sacramento, CA 95827-3303. TEL 916-363-5000. FAX 916-363-5197. URL: http://www.govtech.net/. *6209*

THE GRAMOPHONE CLASSICAL CATALOGUE.
Retail Establishment Data Publishing Ltd., Paulton House, 8 Shepherdess Walk, London N1 7LR, England. TEL 0171-490-0049. FAX 0171-253-1308. *5396*

GRAND RAPIDS BUSINESS JOURNAL.
Gemini Publications, 549 Ottawa Ave. N.W., Grand Rapids, MI 49503-1444. TEL 616-459-4545. FAX 616-459-4800. Vendor(s): Knight-Ridder Information, Inc., UMI. *1212*

SERIALS AVAILABLE ONLINE

GRAND TIMES.
Grand Times Publishing, Inc., 403 Village Dr., El Cerrito, CA 94530-3355. TEL 510-527-4337. URL: http://www.grandtimes.com. *3437*

GRANT ADVISOR.
Box 520, Linden, VA 22642. TEL 540-636-1529. FAX 540-636-7313. URL: httpf://www.grantadvisor.com. *2542*

GRAPEVINE (NORMAL).
c/o Dr. Edward R. Hines, Ed., Educational Administration and Foundations Dept., Illinois State University, Campus Box 5900, Normal, IL 61761. TEL 309-438-5405. FAX 309-438-8683. URL: http://www.ilstu.edu/depts/coe/grpvine.htm. Available only online. *2542*

GRAPEVINE (RED BANK).
Reunions U S A, Box 124, Red Bank, NJ 07701. TEL 908-530-2065. *3225*

GRAPHIC ARTS MONTHLY.
Cahners Publishing Company (New York), Division of Reed Elsevier Inc., 245 W. 17th St., New York, NY 10011. TEL 212-463-6836. FAX 212-463-6530. URL: http://www.gammag.com. Vendor(s): Information Access Co., Knight-Ridder Information, Inc., Lexis-Nexis. *6079*

GRAPHICAL MODELS AND IMAGE PROCESSING.
Academic Press, Inc., Journal Division, 525 B St., Ste. 1900, San Diego, CA 92101-4495. TEL 619-230-1840. FAX 619-699-6800. URL: http://www.apnet.com/www/journal/ip.htm; http://www.idealibrary.com/ *2122*

GRASSLANDS AND FORAGE ABSTRACTS.
CAB International, Wallingford, Oxon. OX10 8DE, England. TEL 44-1491-832111. FAX 44-1491-826090. URL: http://www.cabi.org. Vendor(s): DIMDI, European Space Agency, Knight-Ridder Information, Inc., Ovid Technologies, Inc., STN International. *175*

GRAVITY.
URL: http://www.minspring.com/'ulysses/gravity/ Available only online. *4510*

GREAT BRITAIN. H.M.S.O. BOOKS IN PRINT.
H.M.S.O. Books, 51 Nine Elms Ln., London SW8 5DR, England. TEL 44-171-873-0011. FAX 44-171-873-8247. Vendor(s): Knight-Ridder Information, Inc. *548*

GREAT BRITAIN. H.M.S.O. DAILY LIST.
H.M.S.O. Books, 51 Nine Elms Ln., London SW8 5DR, England. TEL 44-171-873-0011. Vendor(s): Knight-Ridder Information, Inc. *548*

GREAT BRITAIN. H.M.S.O. MONTHLY CATALOGUE.
H.M.S.O. Books, 51 Nine Elms Ln., London SW8 5DR, England. TEL 44-171-873-0011. FAX 44-171-873-8247. Vendor(s): Knight-Ridder Information, Inc. *549*

GREAT BRITAIN. H.M.S.O. PUBLICATIONS CATALOGUE.
H.M.S.O. Books, 51 Nine Elms Ln., London SW8 5DR, England. TEL 44-171-873-0011. FAX 44-171-873-8247. Vendor(s): Knight-Ridder Information, Inc. *549*

GREAT BRITAIN. H.M.S.O. STATUTORY INSTRUMENTS LIST.
H.M.S.O. Books, 51 Nine Elms Ln., London SW8 5DR, England. TEL 44-171-873-0011. FAX 44-171-873-8247. Vendor(s): Knight-Ridder Information, Inc. *549*

GREAT BRITAIN. NATURAL RESOURCES INSTITUTE. BULLETIN.
Natural Resources Institute, Central Ave., Chatham Maritime, Kent ME4 4TB, England. TEL 44-1634-880088. FAX 44-1634-880066. URL: http://www.nri.org. *121*

GREAT BRITAIN. STATIONERY OFFICE. ANNUAL CATALOGUE.
Stationery Office, 51 Nine Elms Ln., London SW8 5DR, England. TEL 44-171-873-0011. Vendor(s): Knight-Ridder Information, Inc. *549*

GREAT BRITIAN. H.M.S.O. COMMITTEE REPORTS INDEX.
H.M.S.O. Books, Subscriptions, 51 Nine Elms Ln., London SW8 5DR, England. TEL 071-873-8499. Vendor(s): Knight-Ridder Information, Inc. *549*

GREAT LAKES ENVIRONMENTAL DIRECTORY.
Harbinger Communications, Box 8175, Missoula, MT 59807. TEL 406-721-0440. FAX 406-721-0440. *2231*

GREAT LAKES UNITED.
Great Lakes United, Buffalo State College, Cassety Hall, 1300 Elmwood Ave., Buffalo, NY 14222. TEL 716-886-0142. FAX 716-886-0303. URL: http://www.great-lakes.net/glu. *2231*

GREECE AND ROME.
Oxford University Press, Academic Division, Great Clarendon St., Oxford OX2 6DP, England. TEL 44-1865-267907. FAX 44-1865-267485. URL: http://www.oup.co.uk/journals. Vendor(s): Information Access Co. *1903*

GREEK, ROMAN AND BYZANTINE STUDIES.
Duke University, Department of Classical Studies, Box 90199, Durham, NC 27708-0199. TEL 919-684-6456. Vendor(s): UMI. *1903*

GREEN BUSINESS LETTER.
Tilden Press Inc., 1519 Connecticut Ave., N.W., Washington, DC 20036. TEL 202-332-1700. FAX 202-332-3028. URL: http://www.enn.com/gbl. *967*

GREEN MARKETS.
Pike & Fischer, Inc., 4600 East-West Hwy., Ste. 200, Bethesda, MD 20814. TEL 301-654-6262. FAX 301-654-6297. *121*

GREEN WEEK.
Tasmanian Greens, URL: http://www.vision.net.au:80/'tasgreens/mediaindex.html. Available only online. *2930*

GREENBOOK.
American Marketing Association, New York Chapter, 60 E. 42nd St., Ste. 1765, New York, NY 10165-0006. TEL 212-687-3280. FAX 212-557-9242. URL: http://www.greenbook.org. *1528*

GREENOTES.
American Library Association, Social Responsibilities Round Table, 50 E. Huron St., Chicago, IL 60611-2795. TEL 312-944-6780. FAX 312-440-9374. URL: http://www.ala.org/alaorg/rtables/srrt/greenotes/greenotes.html. Available only online. *2931*

GREENWICH VILLAGE GAZETTE.
Netgazettes Publications, Box 1023, Island Heights, NJ 08732-1023. URL: http://www.greenwichvillageny.com. Available only online. *3375*

GRIFFIN.
Canisius College, 2001 Main St., Buffalo, NY 14028-1098. TEL 716-888-2195. FAX 716-888-2525. URL: http://www.canisius.edu. *1954*

GRIFFITHIANA.
Cineteca del Friuli, Via Osoppo 26, 33014 Gemona, Italy. TEL 39-432-980458. FAX 39-432-970542. URL: http://muse.jhu.edu. *5335*

GRILLES PTERODACTYL.
180 Bank St., S. Melbourne, Vic. 3205, Australia. URL: http://www.ozemail.com.au/~drgrigg/ptero.html. Available only online. *3375*

GRIST ON-LINE.
17 W. 64th St. Apt. 2-E, New York, NY 10023-6710. TEL 212-787-2861. URL: http://www.thing.net/~grist. *4510*

GROCER.
William Reed Publishing Ltd., Broadfield Park, Crawley, W. Sussex RH11 9RT, England. TEL 44-1293-613400. FAX 44-1293-610340. *3141*

GROCERY HEADQUARTERS.
Trend Publishing Inc., 625 N. Michigan Ave., Ste. 1500, Chicago, IL 60611. TEL 312-654-2300. FAX 312-654-2323. Vendor(s): Information Access Co., Lexis-Nexis. *3142*

GROOVES.
URL: http://pathfinder.com/grooves/index8.html. Available only online. *5396*

GROUND WATER.
Ground Water Publishing Co., 601 Dempsey Rd., Westerville, OH 43081-8978. TEL 614-337-8229. Vendor(s): Information Access Co., UMI. *2393*

GROUND WATER MONITOR.
Business Publishers, Inc., 951 Pershing Dr., Silver Spring, MD 20910-4464. TEL 301-587-6300. FAX 301-585-9075. Vendor(s): Data-Star (PTBN), Information Access Co., Knight-Ridder Information, Inc., NewsNet (EV18). *7294*

GROUP & ORGANIZATION MANAGEMENT.
Sage Publications, Inc., 2455 Teller Rd., Thousand Oaks, CA 91320. TEL 805-499-0721. FAX 805-499-0871. URL: http://www.sagepub.com. Vendor(s): Information Access Co. *1566*

GROUP DECISION AND NEGOTIATION.
Kluwer Academic Publishers, Postbus 17, 3300 AA Dordrecht, Netherlands. TEL 31-78-6392392. FAX 31-78-6392254. URL: http://www.wkap.nl. *1479*

GROWING EDGE MAGAZINE.
New Moon Publishing, Inc., Box 1027, Corvallis, OR 97339-1027. TEL 541-757-0027. FAX 541-757-0028. URL: http://www.growingedge.com. *3192*

GROWTH AND CHANGE.
Blackwell Publishers, 238 Main St., Cambridge, MA 02141. TEL 617-547-7110. FAX 617-547-0789. Vendor(s): Information Access Co., UMI. *1585*

GROWTH FACTORS.
Gordon and Breach - Harwood Academic, Amsterdisk 166, 1st Fl., 1079 LH Amsterdam, Netherlands. URL: http://www.gbhap.com/Growth_Factors/. *816*

GROWTH REGULATION.
Churchill Livingstone, Robert Stevenson House, 1-3 Baxter's Pl., Leith Walk, Edinburgh EH1 3AF, Scotland. TEL 44-131-556-2424. FAX 44-131-535-1704. URL: http://www.churchill.com. Available only online. *4888*

GRROWL!
415 W. 46th St., Ste. 5-A, New York, NY 10036. URL: http://www.nrrdgrrl.com/grrowl. Available only online. *7322*

GUARANTOR (NEW YORK).
American Banker - Bond Buyer, Newsletter Division One State St. Plaza, New York, NY 10004-1549. FAX 212-943-2224. Vendor(s): Information Access Co. *1143*

THE GUARDIAN (MANCHESTER).
Guardian Newspapers Ltd., 164 Deansgate, Manchester M60 2RR, England. TEL 44-161-832-7200. FAX 44-161-876-5362. *3297*

GUARDIAN WEEKLY.
Guardian Newspapers Ltd., 164 Deansgate, Manchester M60 2RR, England. TEL 44-161-832-7200. FAX 44-161-876-5362. Vendor(s): Lexis-Nexis. *3297*

GUIA DE LA INDUSTRIA ALIMENTARIA.
Informatica Cosmos, S.A. de C.V., Calz. del Hueso 334-A1, Col. Ex-Hacienda Coapa, 14300 Mexico D.F., Mexico. TEL 52-5-677-6043. FAX 52-5-679-3575. URL: http://www.cosmos.com.mx. *3111*

GUIDE TO THE CANADIAN FINANCIAL SERVICES INDUSTRY.
Globe Information Services, 444 Front St. W., Toronto, ON M5V 2S9, Canada. TEL 416-585-5250. FAX 416-585-5249. *1684*

GUITAR PLAYER.
Miller Freeman Inc. (San Mateo), 411 Borel Ave., Ste. 100, San Mateo, CA 94402. TEL 415-358-9500. FAX 415-358-9216. Vendor(s): Information Access Co. *5396*

GUNS & AMMO.
Petersen Publishing Co., 6420 Wilshire Blvd., Los Angeles, CA 90048. TEL 213-782-2000. Vendor(s): Knight-Ridder Information, Inc. *6871*

GURL.
233 E. 12th St., Ste. 3D, New York, NY 10003. URL: http://www.gurl.com. Available only online. *7322*

GUT.
B M J Publishing Group, B.M.A. House, Tavistock Sq., London WC1H 9JR, England. TEL 44-171-387-4499. FAX 44-171-383-6661.
Vendor(s): Ovid Technologies, Inc. *4911*

DER GYNAEKOLOGE.
Springer-Verlag, Heidelberger Platz 3, 14197 Berlin, Germany. TEL 49-30-82787-0. FAX 49-30-82787448. URL: http://link.springer.de. *4958*

GYNECOLOGIC ONCOLOGY.
Academic Press, Inc., Journal Division, 525 B St., Ste. 1900, San Diego, CA 92101-4495. TEL 619-230-1840. FAX 619-699-6800. URL: http://www.apnet.com/www/journal/go.htm; http://www.idealibrary.com. *4958*

H C I LETTERS.
Springer-Verlag London Ltd., Sweetapple House, Cattashall Rd., Godalming, Surrey GU7 3DJ, England. TEL 44-1483-418822. FAX 44-1483-415151. *2082*

H F N.
Fairchild Publications, Fairchild Fashion & Merchandising Group 7 W. 34th St., New York, NY 10001. TEL 212-630-4000. FAX 212-630-3675.
Vendor(s): Information Access Co., Knight-Ridder Information, Inc., Lexis-Nexis. *3856*

H I V JOURNAL CLUB.
Australian Society for H I V Medicine, URL: http://www.unsw.edu.au/clients/ashm/HIV__JC.html.
Available only online. *4836*

H N O (BERLIN).
Springer-Verlag, Heidelberger Platz 3, 14197 Berlin, Germany. TEL 49-30-82787-0. FAX 49-30-82787448. URL: http://link.springer.de. *5021*

H P PROFESSIONAL.
Cardinal Business Media, Inc., 1300 Virginia Dr., Ste. 400, Fort Washington, PA 19034-3225. TEL 215-643-8000. FAX 215-643-4827.
Vendor(s): Information Access Co. *2188*

H R FOCUS.
American Management Association, 1601 Broadway, New York, NY 10019. TEL 212-586-8100.
Vendor(s): Information Access Co., UMI. *1566*

H R MAGAZINE.
Society for Human Resource Management, 606 N. Washington St., Alexandria, VA 22314-1914. TEL 703-548-3440. FAX 703-836-0367.
Vendor(s): Human Resources Information Network, Information Access Co., UMI. *1567*

H T F S DIGEST.
A.E.A. Technology, Harwell Bldg. 392.7, Didcot, Oxon OX11 0RA, England. TEL 44-1235-432908. FAX 44-1235-831981. *2764*

H U E S - A WOMAN'S GUIDE TO POWER & ATTITUDE.
H U E S, Inc., Box 7778, Ann Arbor, MI 48107. TEL 313-971-0023. FAX 313-971-0450. *7322*

H V G.
Heti Vilaggazdasag Rt., Szepvolgyi ut 35, 1037 Budapest, Hungary. TEL 361-1884329. FAX 361-1887101. URL: http://www.hvg.hu/ *967*

HAIR CARE PRODUCTS: THE INTERNATIONAL MARKET.
Euromonitor, 60-61 Britton St., London EC1M 5NA, England. TEL 44-171-251-8024. FAX 44-171-608-3149. URL: http://www.euromonitor.com.
Vendor(s): Data-Star, Knight-Ridder Information, Inc.. *506*

HAMBURGER WIRTSCHAFT.
Continentale Werbung GmbH, Rabiosen 16, 20095 Hamburg, Germany.
Vendor(s): GBI. *1188*

HAMLINE LAW REVIEW.
Western Newspaper Publishing Co., 1536 Hewitt Ave., St. Paul, MN 55104-1284. TEL 612-641-2350. FAX 612-641-2808.
Vendor(s): West Group. *3957*

HANDBOOK ON INJECTABLE DRUGS.
American Society of Health-System Pharmacists, 7272 Wisconsin Ave., Bethesda, MD 20814. TEL 301-657-3000. FAX 301-657-8817.
Vendor(s): Knight-Ridder Information, Inc. (File no.229), Ovid Technologies, Inc. (DIFT). *5664*

HANDBUCH DER GROSSUNTERNEHMEN.
Verlag Hoppenstedt GmbH, Havelstr. 9, 64295 Darmstadt, Germany. TEL 49-6151-380-0. FAX 49-6151-380-360.
Vendor(s): Data-Star, GBI, Knight-Ridder Information, Inc. *1585*

HANDELSBLATT.
Verlagsgruppe Handelsblatt GmbH, Kasernenstr. 67, 40213 Duesseldorf, Germany. TEL 49-211-8870. FAX 49-211-329954. *1212*

HANDS ON! (CAMBRIDGE).
T E R C, 2067 Massachusetts Ave., Cambridge, MA 02140. TEL 617-547-0430. FAX 617-349-3535. URL: http://www.terc.edu. *2447*

HANGZHOU DAXUE XUEBAO (ZIRAN KEXUE BAN).
Hangzhou Daxue, 34 Tianmushan Lu, Hangzhou, Zhejiang 310028, People's Republic of China.
Vendor(s): Knight-Ridder Information, Inc. *6529*

HAPPYFAG.
323 Broadway Ave. E., Ste. 902, Seattle, WA 98102. URL: http://psweb.com/scooter/happyfag.html.
Available only online. *3695*

HARBINGER FILE.
Harbinger Communications, Box 8175, Missoula, MT 59807. TEL 406-721-0440. FAX 406-721-0440. URL: ned@ism.net. *2931*

HARFORD BUSINESS LEDGER.
Harford Business Ledger, Inc., Box 40, Aberdeen, MD 21001-0075. TEL 410-893-9191. FAX 410-272-4208.
Vendor(s): UMI. *968*

HARPER'S BAZAAR.
Hearst Corporation, Harper's Bazaar, 1700 Broadway, New York, NY 10019. TEL 212-903-5464. URL: http://www.hearstcorp.com.
Vendor(s): Information Access Co. *1923*

HARPER'S MAGAZINE.
Harpers Magazine Foundation, 666 Broadway, New York, NY 10012-2317. TEL 212-614-6500. FAX 212-228-5889.
Vendor(s): Information Access Co., UMI. *4337*

HARVARD BUSINESS REVIEW.
Harvard Business School Publishing Corporation, 60 Harvard Way, Boston, MA 02163. TEL 617-495-6800. FAX 617-495-9933. URL: http://www.hbsp.harvard.edu/groups/hbr/index.html.
Vendor(s): Data-Star (HBRO), Human Resources Information Network, Knight-Ridder Information, Inc. (File no.122), Lexis-Nexis, Ovid Technologies, Inc. (HBRO). *968*

HARVARD CIVIL RIGHTS - CIVIL LIBERTIES LAW REVIEW.
Harvard University, Law School, Publications Center, Hastings Hall, Cambridge, MA 02138. TEL 617-495-3694.
Vendor(s): West Group. *4061*

HARVARD EDUCATIONAL REVIEW.
Harvard University, Graduate School of Education, Gutman Library, Ste. 349, 6 Appian Way, Cambridge, MA 02138. TEL 617-495-3432.
Vendor(s): UMI. *2447*

HARVARD ENVIRONMENTAL LAW REVIEW.
Harvard University, Law School, Publications Center, Hastings Hall, Cambridge, MA 02138. TEL 617-495-3694.
Vendor(s): West Group. *3957*

HARVARD HEALTH LETTER.
Harvard Health Publications Group, 164 Longwood Ave., Boston, MA 02115. TEL 617-432-1485. FAX 617-432-1506.
Vendor(s): Information Access Co. *5782*

HARVARD HEART LETTER.
Harvard Health Publications Group, 164 Longwood Ave., Boston, MA 02115. TEL 617-432-1485. FAX 617-432-1506.
Vendor(s): Information Access Co. *4816*

HARVARD INTERNATIONAL LAW JOURNAL.
Harvard University, Law School, Publications Center, Hastings Hall, Cambridge, MA 02138. TEL 617-495-3694.
Vendor(s): West Group. *4114*

HARVARD JOURNAL OF LAW AND PUBLIC POLICY.
Harvard Society for Law and Public Policy, Inc., Harvard Law School, Cambridge, MA 02138. TEL 617-495-3105. FAX 617-495-1110.
Vendor(s): UMI, West Group. *3957*

HARVARD JOURNAL OF LAW AND TECHNOLOGY.
Harvard University, Law School, Communications Department, Holmes Hall, Cambridge, MA 02138. TEL 617-495-3118. URL: http://studorg.law.harvard.edu/jolt/. *3957*

HARVARD JOURNAL ON LEGISLATION.
Harvard University, Law School, Publications Center, Hastings Hall, Cambridge, MA 02138. TEL 617-495-3694.
Vendor(s): West Group. *3958*

HARVARD LAW REVIEW.
Harvard Law Review Association, Gannett House, Cambridge, MA 02138. TEL 617-495-4650. FAX 617-495-2748.
Vendor(s): Lexis-Nexis (Lexis), West Group. *3958*

HARVARD MENTAL HEALTH LETTER.
Harvard Health Publications Group, 164 Longwood Ave., Boston, MA 02115. TEL 617-432-1485. FAX 617-432-1506.
Vendor(s): Information Access Co. *5067*

HARVARD THEOLOGICAL REVIEW.
Harvard Divinity School, 45 Francis Ave., Cambridge, MA 02138. TEL 617-495-5786. FAX 617-495-9489.
Vendor(s): Information Access Co. *6342*

HARVARD WOMEN'S HEALTH WATCH.
Harvard Health Publications Group, 164 Longwood Ave., Boston, MA 02115. TEL 617-432-1485. FAX 617-432-1506.
Vendor(s): Information Access Co. *7309*

HARVARD WOMEN'S LAW JOURNAL.
Harvard University, Law School (Women's Law Journal), Publications Center, Hastings Hall, Cambridge, MA 02138. TEL 617-495-3726. FAX 617-495-1110. URL: http://www.harvard.edu/
Vendor(s): Lexis-Nexis, West Group. *3958*

HASTINGS CENTER REPORT.
Hastings Center, 255 Elm Rd., Briarcliff Manor, NY 10510. TEL 914-762-8500. FAX 914-762-2124.
Vendor(s): Information Access Co., UMI. *4674*

HASTINGS COMMUNICATIONS AND ENTERTAINMENT LAW JOURNAL (COMM - ENT).
University of California at San Francisco, Hastings College of the Law, 200 McAllister St., San Francisco, CA 94102-4978. TEL 415-565-4731. FAX 415-565-4814.
Vendor(s): West Group. *3958*

HASTINGS CONSTITUTIONAL LAW QUARTERLY.
University of California at San Francisco, Hastings College of the Law, 200 McAllister St., San Francisco, CA 94102-4978. TEL 415-565-4726. FAX 415-565-4814.
Vendor(s): West Group. *4070*

HASTINGS INTERNATIONAL AND COMPARATIVE LAW REVIEW.
University of California at San Francisco, Hastings College of the Law, 200 McAllister St., San Francisco, CA 94102-4978. TEL 415-565-4730. FAX 415-565-4814.
Vendor(s): West Group. *4115*

HASTINGS LAW JOURNAL.
University of California at San Francisco, Hastings College of the Law, 200 McAllister St., San Francisco, CA 94102-4978. TEL 415-565-4727. FAX 415-565-4814.
Vendor(s): Lexis-Nexis, West Group. *3958*

HASTINGS WOMEN'S LAW JOURNAL.
University of California at San Francisco, Hastings College of the Law, 200 McAllister St., San Francisco, CA 94102. TEL 415-565-4870. FAX 415-464-4814.
Vendor(s): West Group. *3958*

SERIALS AVAILABLE ONLINE

DER HAUTARZT.
Springer-Verlag, Heidelberger Platz 3, 14197 Berlin, Germany. TEL 49-30-82787-0. FAX 49-30-82787448. URL: http://link.springer.de. *4878*

HAWAII BUSINESS.
Hawaii Business Publishing Corp., Box 913, Honolulu, HI 96808. TEL 808-946-3978. Vendor(s): Information Access Co., Knight-Ridder Information, Inc., Lexis-Nexis, UMI. *1263*

HAWAII BUSINESS DIRECTORY.
American Business Directories, 5711 S. 86th Circle, Box 27347, Omaha, NE 68127. TEL 402-593-4600. FAX 402-331-5481. *1685*

HAWAIIAN SHELL NEWS.
Hawaiian Malacological Society, Box 22130, Honolulu, HI 96823-2130. URL: http://www.hits.net/~hsn.
Available only online. *835*

HAZARD TECHNOLOGY.
Emergency Information System, International, 1401 Rockville Pike, Ste. 500, Rockville, MD 20852. TEL 301-738-6900. FAX 301-738-1026. URL: http://www.eisintl.com. *1898*

HAZARDOUS MATERIALS INTELLIGENCE REPORT.
World Information Systems, Box 535, Harvard Sq. Sta., Cambridge, MA 02238. TEL 617-491-5100. FAX 617-492-3312.
Vendor(s): NewsNet. *2985*

HAZARDOUS MATERIALS TRANSPORTATION.
The Bureau of National Affairs, Inc., 1231 25th St., N.W., Washington, DC 20037. TEL 202-452-4200. FAX 202-822-8092. URL: http://www.bna.com/.
Vendor(s): NewsNet (EV35). *7029*

HAZARDOUS WASTE BUSINESS.
McGraw-Hill Companies, Energy & Business Newsletters, 1221 Ave. of the Americas, 36th Fl., New York, NY 10020. TEL 212-521-6410.
Vendor(s): Dow Jones News Retrieval (HWB), Knight-Ridder Information, Inc. (HWB), Lexis-Nexis (HWB), NewsNet (EV41). *2985*

HAZARDOUS WASTE NEWS.
Business Publishers, Inc., 951 Pershing Dr., Silver Spring, MD 20910-4464. TEL 301-587-6300. FAX 301-585-9075.
Vendor(s): Information Access Co., Knight-Ridder Information, Inc., NewsNet (CH10). *2985*

HAZARDS IN THE OFFICE.
The Royal Society of Chemistry, Thomas Graham House, Science Park, Milton Rd., Cambridge CB4 4WF, England. TEL 44-1223-420066. FAX 44-1223-423429. URL: http://chemistry.rsc.org/rsc/.
Vendor(s): Data-Star (CSNB), Knight-Ridder Information, Inc. (File no. 317), STN International (CSNB). *6235*

HAZMAT TRANSPORT NEWS.
Business Publishers, Inc., 951 Pershing Dr., Silver Spring, MD 20910-4464. TEL 301-587-6300. FAX 301-585-9075.
Vendor(s): Information Access Co., NewsNet (CH14) *2986*

HAZNEWS.
Profitastral Ltd., Park House, 140 Battersea Park Rd., London SW11 4NB, England. TEL 44-171-498-2511. FAX 44-171-498-2343.
Vendor(s): Data-Star (PTBN,PTSP), Information Access Co., Knight-Ridder Information, Inc. (File nos.636 & 16). *2986*

HEADWAY.
Richberg Communications, Inc., 13555 Bammel N. Houston, Ste. 227, Houston, TX 77066. TEL 281-444-4265. FAX 281-583-9534. URL: http://www.townhall.com/headwaymag.
Vendor(s): NewsNet (PO05). *5931*

HEADZ UP!
URL: http://pobox.com/~hip-hop/headzup.
Available only online. *5398*

HEALTH (SAN FRANCISCO).
Time Inc. Health, 2 Embarcadero Center, Ste. 600, San Francisco, CA 94111. TEL 415-248-2700.
Vendor(s): Information Access Co., UMI. *5782*

HEALTH A TO Z NEWS.
Medical Network, URL: http://www.HealthAtoZ.com.
Available only online. *4675*

HEALTH AFFAIRS.
Project Hope, 7500 Old Georgetown Rd., No. 600, Bethesda, MD 20814-6133. TEL 301-656-7401. FAX 301-654-2845. URL: http://www.projhope.org/HA/.
Vendor(s): UMI. *6235*

HEALTH ALLIANCE ALERT.
Faulkner & Gray, Healthcare Information Center 1133 15th St., N.W., Ste. 450, Washington, DC 20005. TEL 202-828-4148.
Vendor(s): Information Access Co., Knight-Ridder Information, Inc., NewsNet (HH23). *4675*

HEALTH AND ENVIRONMENT REVIEW.
Ecol Data, URL: http://www.imagic.com.au/~magi/ecol/ecol.html.
Available only online. *2962*

HEALTH AND SAFETY SCIENCE ABSTRACTS.
Cambridge Scientific Abstracts, 7200 Wisconsin Ave., 6th Fl., Bethesda, MD 20814. TEL 301-961-6750. FAX 301-961-6720. URL: http://www.csa.com.
Vendor(s): Questel Orbit Inc. (ORBIT). *6256*

HEALTH & SOCIAL WORK.
N A S W Press, 750 First St., N.E., Ste. 700, Washington, DC 20002-4241. TEL 202-408-8600. FAX 202-336-8312. URL: http://www.naswpress.org.
Vendor(s): Information Access Co., UMI. *6668*

HEALTH CARE FINANCING REVIEW.
U.S. Health Care Financing Administration, Department of Health and Human Services, C-3-11-07, 7500 Security Blvd., Baltimore, MD 21244-1850. TEL 410-786-6577. FAX 410-786-5768. URL: http://www.hcfa.gov/pubfroms/ordpub.html.
Vendor(s): Information Access Co., UMI. *4675*

HEALTH CARE MANAGEMENT REVIEW.
Aspen Publishers, Inc., 200 Orchard Ridge Dr., Gaithersburg, MD 20878. FAX 301-417-7550.
Vendor(s): Information Access Co., UMI. *3708*

HEALTH CARE STRATEGIC MANAGEMENT.
Business Word Inc., 5350 S. Roslyn St., Ste. 400, Englewood, CO 80111-2125. TEL 303-290-8500. FAX 303-290-9025.
Vendor(s): NewsNet, UMI. *3709*

HEALTH CARE SUPERVISOR.
Aspen Publishers, Inc., 200 Orchard Ridge Dr., Gaithersburg, MD 20878. FAX 301-417-7550.
Vendor(s): UMI. *4933*

HEALTH DEVICES ALERTS.
E C R I, 5200 Butler Pike, Plymouth Meeting, PA 19462. TEL 610-825-6000. FAX 610-834-1275.
Vendor(s): Knight-Ridder Information, Inc. (File no.198). *4779*

HEALTH DEVICES SOURCEBOOK.
E C R I, 5200 Butler Pike, Plymouth Meeting, PA 19462. TEL 610-825-6000. FAX 610-834-1275.
Vendor(s): Knight-Ridder Information, Inc. (File no.188). *4676*

HEALTH DIRECT.
Box 1118, Piedmont, CA 94611. URL: http://www.healthdirect.com.
Available only online. *4676*

HEALTH GRANTS & CONTRACTS WEEKLY.
Capitol Publications Inc., 1101 King St., Ste. 444, Alexandria, VA 22314. TEL 703-683-4100. FAX 703-739-6501.
Vendor(s): NewsNet (HH10). *6177*

HEALTH INDEX.
Information Access Company, 362 Lakeside Dr., Foster City, CA 94404. TEL 415-378-5200. FAX 415-378-5369.
Vendor(s): Data-Star (HLTH), Knight-Ridder Information, Inc. (File no.149), Ovid Technologies, Inc. (HEAL). *4779*

HEALTH INDUSTRY TODAY.
Business Word Inc., 5350 S. Roslyn St., Ste. 400, Englewood, CO 80111-2125. TEL 303-290-8500. FAX 303-290-9025.
Vendor(s): Information Access Co., NewsNet, UMI. *4676*

HEALTH INFORMATION SERVICES FOCUS.
Aspen Systems Corp., Health Information Services, 1600 Research Blvd., Rockville, MD 20850. URL: http://www.aspensys.com/hisfocus/.
Available only online. *6236*

HEALTH LEGISLATION.
Faulkner & Gray, Healthcare Information Center 1133 15th St., N.W., Ste. 450, Washington, DC 20005. TEL 202-828-4148.
Vendor(s): Information Access Co., NewsNet (HH22) *4677*

HEALTH LETTER ON THE C D C.
Charles W. Henderson, Ed. & Pub., Box 5528, Atlanta, GA 31107-0528. TEL 404-377-8895. FAX 404-378-5411. URL: http://www.newsfile.com. *4677*

HEALTH MANAGEMENT TECHNOLOGY.
Intertec Publishing Corp. (Atlanta), 6151 Powers Ferry Rd., N.W., Atlanta, GA 30339-2491. TEL 770-955-2500. FAX 770-955-0400.
Vendor(s): Information Access Co., Knight-Ridder Information, Inc., UMI. *4846*

HEALTH MATRIX: JOURNAL OF LAW-MEDICINE.
Case Western Reserve University, School of Law, 11075 East Blvd., Cleveland, OH 44106-7148. TEL 216-368-3304. FAX 216-368-3310.
Vendor(s): Lexis-Nexis. *3959*

HEALTH NETWORK LETTER.
Capitol Publications Inc., 1101 King St., Ste. 444, Box 1455, Alexandria, VA 22314. TEL 703-683-4100. FAX 703-739-6517.
Vendor(s): NewsNet. *4677*

HEALTH NEWS DAILY.
F-D-C Reports, Inc., 5550 Friendship Blvd., Ste. One, Chevy Chase, MD 20815. FAX 301-664-7238.
Vendor(s): Data-Star (HNDO), Knight-Ridder Information, Inc. (File no.43), NewsNet (HH01). *4677*

HEALTH PLAN BUSINESS ADVISOR.
Capitol Publications Inc., 1101 King St., Ste. 444, Alexandria, VA 22314. TEL 703-683-4100. FAX 703-739-6501.
Vendor(s): Information Access Co., NewsNet (HH16) *3709*

HEALTH POLICY & BIOMEDICAL RESEARCH: THE BLUE SHEET.
F-D-C Reports, Inc., 5550 Friendship Blvd., Ste. One, Chevy Chase, MD 20815. FAX 301-664-7238.
Vendor(s): Data-Star (FDCR), Knight-Ridder Information, Inc. (File no.187), Lexis-Nexis, Ovid Technologies, Inc. (FDCR). *4677*

HEALTH POLICY AND PLANNING.
Oxford University Press, Academic Division, Great Clarendon St., Oxford OX2 6DP, England. TEL 44-18650267907. FAX 44-1865-267485. URL: http://www.oup.co/journals. *6237*

HEALTH PROGRESS.
Catholic Health Association of the United States, 4455 Woodson Rd., St. Louis, MO 63134-3797. TEL 314-427-2500. FAX 314-427-0029. *3709*

HEALTH PROMOTION INTERNATIONAL.
Oxford University Press, Academic Division, Great Clarendon St., Oxford OX2 6DP, England. TEL 44-1865-267907. FAX 44-1865-267485. URL: http://www.oup.co/journals. *6237*

HEALTH SERVICE ABSTRACTS.
Department of Health, Library and Information Services, Rm. 5C07, Quarry House, Quarry Hill, Leeds LS2 7UE, England. TEL 0113-254-5072. FAX 0113-254-5084.
Vendor(s): Data-Star. *4780*

HEALTH SERVICES RESEARCH.
Health Administration Press, 1 North Franklin St., Ste. 1700, Chicago, IL 60606-3491. TEL 312-424-2800. FAX 312-424-0014. URL: http://www.xnet.com/'hret/aboutsr.htm; http://www.ache.org.
Vendor(s): Information Access Co., UMI. *3709*

HEALTH SYSTEMS REVIEW.
F A H S Review, Inc., 1405 N. Pierce St., Ste. 308, Little Rock, AR 72207. TEL 501-661-9555. FAX 501-663-4903.
Vendor(s): UMI. *3709*

HEALTH WHICH?
Which? Ltd., 2 Marylebone Rd., London NW1 4DF, England. TEL 44-171-830-6000. FAX 44-171-830-7664. *5783*

HEALTHCARE ADVERTISING REVIEW.
Business Word Inc., 5350 S. Rosly St., Ste. 400, Englewood, CO 80111-2125. TEL 303-290-8500. FAX 303-290-9025.
Vendor(s): NewsNet. *36*

HEALTHCARE EXECUTIVE.
American College of Healthcare Executives, One N. Franklin St., Ste. 1700, Chicago, IL 60606-3491. TEL 312-424-3800. FAX 312-424-0023.
Vendor(s): UMI. *3710*

HEALTHCARE FINANCIAL MANAGEMENT.
Healthcare Financial Management Association, Two Westbrook Corporate Center, Ste. 700, Westchester, IL 60154. TEL 708-531-9600. FAX 708-531-0032.
Vendor(s): Information Access Co., Knight-Ridder Information, Inc., UMI. *3710*

HEALTHCARE FORUM JOURNAL.
Healthcare Forum, 425 Market St., 16th Fl., San Francisco, CA 94105. TEL 415-356-4300. FAX 415-356-9300. URL: http://www.healthonline.com/THF.HTM.
Vendor(s): UMI. *3710*

HEALTHCARE P R & MARKETING NEWS.
Phillips Business Information, Inc., 1201 Seven Locks Rd., Potomac, MD 20854. TEL 301-424-3338. FAX 301-309-3847.
Vendor(s): Information Access Co. *4678*

HEALTHCARE TECHNOLOGY & BUSINESS OPPORTUNITIES.
Biomedical Business International, 16269 Laguna Canyon Rd., Ste. 100, Irvine, CA 92618-3603. TEL 714-755-5757. FAX 714-755-5724.
Vendor(s): Information Access Co., Knight-Ridder Information, Inc. *4678*

HEALTHFACTS.
Center for Medical Consumers, 237 Thompson St., New York, NY 10012. TEL 212-674-7105. FAX 212-674-7100.
Vendor(s): Information Access Co. *4678*

HEARD MAGAZINE.
Terry Allen, Ed. & Pub., 128 The Entrance Rd., The Entrance, N.S.W. 2261, Australia. URL: http://www.ozemail.com.au/~hmag.
Available only online. *5398*

HEART.
B M J Publishing Group, B.M.A. House, Tavistock Sq., London WC1H 9JR, England. TEL 0171-383-6270. FAX 0171-383-6402.
Vendor(s): Ovid Technologies, Inc. *4817*

HEART & LUNG.
Mosby - Year Book, Inc., 11830 Westline Industrial Dr., St. Louis, MO 63146-3318. TEL 314-872-8370. FAX 314-432-1380.
Vendor(s): Ovid Technologies, Inc. *4933*

HEARTS AT HOME NEWSLETTER.
Hearts at Home, URL: http://www.popi.net/~mlaustin. *7322*

HEAT AND MASS TRANSFER.
Springer-Verlag, Heidelberger Platz 3, 14197 Berlin, Germany. TEL 49-30-28787-0. FAX 49-30-82787448. URL: http://link.springer.de. *5841*

HEAT ENGINEERING.
Foster Wheeler Corp., Perryville Corporate Park, Clinton, NJ 08809-4000. TEL 908-730-4000. FAX 908-730-5315. URL: http://www.fwc.com. *2721*

HEAT TRANSFER - RECENT CONTENTS.
American Society of Mechanical Engineers, 22 Law Dr., Fairfield, NJ 07007-2900. TEL 973-882-1167. FAX 973-882-1717. URL: http://www.asme.org. *5835*

HEATING - PIPING - AIR CONDITIONING.
Penton Publishing Co., 1100 Superior Ave., Cleveland, OH 44114-2543. TEL 216-969-7000. FAX 216-696-8765. URL: http://www.penton.com/hpac/.
Vendor(s): Information Access Co. *3479*

HEAVEN TEK MAGAZINE.
Revelation Ministries and Commonwealth Technical Services, 806 B1 Boulder Springs Dr., Richmond, VA 23225. URL: http://www.cts.richmond.va.us/heaventek.
Available only online. *6427*

L'HEBDO.
Pont Bessieres 3, CH-1005 Lausanne, Switzerland. TEL 41-21-3203611. FAX 41-21-3203617. URL: http://www.hebdo.ch/hebdo/hebdo.html. *3364*

HECATE.
Hecate Press, c/o English Dept., Univ. of Queensland, St. Lucia, Qld. 4067, Australia. TEL 61-7-33653146. FAX 61-7-33652799.
Vendor(s): Information Access Co., UMI. *7344*

HELEN K. MUSSALLEM LIBRARY SELECTED ACQUISITIONS.
Canadian Nurses Association, 50 Driveway, Ottawa, ON K2P 1E2, Canada. TEL 613-237-2133. FAX 613-237-3520. URL: http://www.cna-nurses.ca.
Available only online. *4780*

HELICOPTER NEWS.
Phillips Business Information, Inc., 1201 Seven Locks Rd., Potomac, MD 20854. TEL 301-424-3338. FAX 301-309-3847.
Vendor(s): Data-Star, Information Access Co., Knight-Ridder Information, Inc., NewsNet (AE12). *67*

HELLER REPORT ON EDUCATION TECHNOLOGY AND TELECOMMUNICATIONS MARKETS.
Nelson B. Heller & Associates, 1910 1st St. Ste 303, Highland Park, IL 60035-3146. TEL 847-441-2920. FAX 847-926-0202.
Vendor(s): NewsNet (ED11). *1529*

HELMINTHOLOGICAL ABSTRACTS.
CAB International, Wallingford, Oxon. OX10 8DE, England. TEL 44-1491-832111. FAX 44-1491-826090.
Vendor(s): CISTI, DIMDI, European Space Agency (File nos.16 & 124/CAB), Knight-Ridder Information, Inc., Ovid Technologies, Inc. (VETR). *176*

HEMATOLOGY.
Gordon and Breach - Harwood Academic, Amsteldisk 166, 1st Fl., 1079 LH Amsterdam, Netherlands. URL: http://www.gbhap.com/Hematology/. *4919*

HEMATOLOGY AND CELL THERAPY.
Springer-Verlag France, 26, rue des Carmes, 75005 Paris. TEL 33-1-44-41-15-80. FAX 33-1-43-54-49-08. URL: http://www.science.springer.de. *4919*

THE HEMINGWAY REVIEW.
University of Idaho Press, c/o Susan F. Beegel, Ed., 180 Polpis Rd., Nantucket, MA 02554. TEL 508-325-7157.
Vendor(s): Information Access Co. *4413*

THE HENRY JAMES REVIEW.
Johns Hopkins University Press, Journals Publishing Division, 2715 N. Charles St., Baltimore, MD 21218. TEL 410-516-6987. FAX 410-516-6968. URL: http://muse.jhu.edu. *4413*

HEPATITIS WEEKLY.
Charles W. Henderson, Ed. & Pub., Box 5528, Atlanta, GA 31107-0528. TEL 404-377-8895. FAX 404-378-5411. URL: http://www.newsfile.com. *4836*

THE HERALD.
Montgomery County Genealogical & Historical Society, Inc., Box 867, Conroe, TX 77305-0867. TEL 409-756-8625.
Vendor(s): UMI. *3226*

HERALD EXPRESS.
Herald Express Publications Ltd., Barton Hill Rd., Torquay, Devon TQ2 8JN, England. TEL 44-1803-676000. FAX 44-1803-676299. *3297*

HERALDO DE SAN LUIS POTOSI.
Villerias 305, 78000 San Luis Potosi, Mexico. TEL 48-12-33-12. FAX 48-12-20-81. *3335*

HERBA POLONICA.
Instytut Roslin i Przetworow Zielarskich, Libelta 27, 61-707 Poznan, Poland. TEL 48-61-525616. FAX 48-61-527463. *707*

HERITAGE (AUSTIN).
Texas Historical Foundation, Box 50314, Austin, TX 78763. TEL 512-453-2154. FAX 512-451-1323. URL: http://www.texashf.org. *3629*

HERITAGE (CARSON).
Heritage Publishers, 20218 Tajauta Ave., Carson, CA 90746-2566. FAX 310-763-8296. URL: http://home.earthlink.net/~vgendrano/heritage.html. *3015*

HERITAGE FOUNDATION. ISSUE BULLETINS.
Heritage Foundation, 214 Massachusetts Ave., N.E., Washington, DC 20002. TEL 202-546-4400. FAX 202-543-9647.
Vendor(s): Lexis-Nexis. *5931*

HERITAGE LECTURES.
Heritage Foundation, 214 Massachusetts Ave., N.E., Washington, DC 20002. TEL 202-546-4400. FAX 202-543-9647.
Vendor(s): Lexis-Nexis. *6177*

HERNIA.
Springer-Verlag, Heidelberger Platz 3, 14197 Berlin, Germany. TEL 49-30-82787-0. FAX 49-30-82787448. URL: http://link.springer.de. *5143*

HERPESVIRUSES WEEKLY.
Charles W. Henderson, Ed. & Pub., Box 5528, Atlanta, GA 31107-0528. TEL 404-377-8895. FAX 404-378-5411. URL: http://www.newsfile.com. *4836*

HESSISCHE BIBLIOGRAPHIE.
K.G. Saur Verlag KG, A member of the Reed Elsevier plc group, Ortlerstr. 8, 81373 Munich, Germany. TEL 49-89-76902-0. FAX 49-89-76902150. URL: http://www.reed-elsevier.com. *550*

HETEROCLITE MAGAZINE.
Heteroclite Association, URL: http://www.worldnet.fr/'villemon/english.shtml. *4413*

HEWLETT-PACKARD JOURNAL.
Hewlett Packard Co. (Palo Alto), 3000 Hanover St., Palo Alto, CA 94304. TEL 415-857-2387. FAX 415-857-2157. URL: http://www.hp.com/hpj/journal.html.
Vendor(s): Information Access Co., Knight-Ridder Information, Inc. *2188*

HIGH PERFORMANCE POLYMERS.
I O P Publishing Ltd., Dirac House, Temple Back, Bristol BS1 6BE, England. TEL 44-117-929-7481. FAX 44-117-929-4318. URL: http://www.iop.org. *1816*

HIGH PRESSURE RESEARCH.
Gordon and Breach - Harwood Academic, Amsteldisk 166, 1st Fl., 1079 LH Amsterdam, Netherlands. URL: http://www.gbhap.com/High_Pressure_Research/. *5845*

HIGH - TC UPDATE.
Iowa State University, Ames Laboratory, A219 Physics, Ames, IA 50011-3020. TEL 515-294-3877. FAX 515-294-1134. URL: http://www.physics.iastate.edu/htcu/htcu.html. *5805*

HIGH TECH CERAMICS NEWS.
Business Communications Co., Inc. (Norwalk), 25 Van Zant St., Ste. 13, Norwalk, CT 06855. TEL 203-853-4266. FAX 203-853-0348.
Vendor(s): Data-Star, Information Access Co., Knight-Ridder Information, Inc., NewsNet (ML05). *1731*

HIGH TECH SEPARATIONS NEWS.
Business Communications Co., Inc. (Norwalk), 25 Van Zant St., Ste. 13, Norwalk, CT 06855. TEL 203-853-4266. FAX 203-853-0348.
Vendor(s): Data-Star, Information Access Co., Knight-Ridder Information, Inc., NewsNet (BT04). *1791*

HIGH TECHNOLOGY CAREERS.
High Technology Careers, 4701 Patrick Henry Dr., Ste. 1901, Santa Clara, CA 95054. TEL 408-970-8800. FAX 408-980-5103. URL: http://www.vjf.com. *5510*

SERIALS AVAILABLE ONLINE

HIGH YIELD REPORT.
American Banker - Bond Buyer, Newsletter Division One State St. Plaza, New York, NY 10004-1549. TEL 800-733-4371. FAX 212-943-2224. Vendor(s): Information Access Co., Knight-Ridder Information, Inc., Lexis-Nexis, NewsNet. *1144*

HIGHBEAMS.
Beloit College, 700 College St., Beloit, WI 53511. TEL 608-363-2828. URL: http://beloit.edu/~highbe. Available only online. *4413*

HIGHLANDER WEB MAGAZINE.
URL: http://www.catalyst-highlands.co.uk. Available only online. *3297*

HIGHWAY SAFETY - ANNUAL REPORT.
U.S. Federal Highway Administration, Office of Highway Information Management, Department of Transportation, 400 Seventh St., S.W., Washington, DC 20590. TEL 202-366-0180. FAX 202-366-7742. *7052*

HIGHWAY SAFETY PERFORMANCE. FATAL AND INJURY ACCIDENT RATES ON PUBLIC ROADS IN THE UNITED STATES.
U.S. Federal Highway Administration, Office of Highway Information Management, Department of Transportation, 400 Seventh St., S.W., Washington, DC 20590. TEL 202-366-0180. FAX 202-366-7742. *7052*

HILVERSUMMARY.
Nederlandse Omroep Stichting, Postbus 26444, 1202 JJ Hilversum, Netherlands. TEL 31-35-6773197. FAX 31-35-6773586. URL: http://www.omroep.nl/nos/rtv/voorlichting/hsumm. *2024*

HIP MAGAZINE.
1563 Solano Ave., No. 137, Berkeley, CA 94707. TEL 510-527-8993. FAX 510-527-9088. *3463*

HIPPOCRATES.
Health Publishing Group, 2 Embarcadero Center, Ste. 600, San Francisco, CA 94111. TEL 415-248-2700. FAX 415-248-2779. *4679*

HISPANIC.
Hispanic Publishing Corp., 98 San Jacinto Blvd., Ste. 1150, Austin, TX 78701-4039. Vendor(s): Information Access Co. *3015*

HISPANIC AMERICAN PERIODICALS INDEX.
Latin American Studies Center Publications, University of California, Los Angeles, Box 951447, 10347 Bunche Hall, Los Angeles, CA 90095-1447. TEL 310-825-0810. FAX 310-206-2634. *3520*

HISPANIC REVIEW.
University of Pennsylvania, Romance Languages Department, 512 Williams Hall, Philadelphia, PA 19104-6305. TEL 215-898-7420. FAX 215-898-0933.
Vendor(s): UMI. *4262*

THE HISTOCHEMICAL JOURNAL.
Chapman & Hall, Journals Department 2-6 Boundary Row, London SE1 8HN, England. TEL 44-171-8650066. FAX 44-171-5229623. URL: http://www.chaphall.com/chaphall/journals.html. *740*

HISTOCHEMISTRY AND CELL BIOLOGY.
Springer-Verlag, Heidelberger Platz 3, 14197 Berlin, Germany. TEL 49-30-82787-08. FAX 49-30-82787448. URL: http://link.springer.de. *741*

HISTORIA MATHEMATICA.
Academic Press, Inc., Journal Division, 525 B St., Ste. 1900, San Diego, CA 92101-4495. TEL 619-230-1840. FAX 619-699-6800. URL: http://www.apnet.com/www/journal/hm.htm. *4575*

THE HISTORIAN (EAST LANSING).
Michigan State University Press, Manly Miles Bldg., Ste. 25, 1405 S. Harrison Rd., East Lansing, MI 48823-5202. TEL 517-432-9543. FAX 517-336-2611.
Vendor(s): Information Access Co., UMI. *3497*

HISTORIC HOUSE NEWS.
Historic House Trust of New York City, The Arsenal, Rm. 203, Central Park, New York, NY 10021. TEL 212-360-8282. FAX 212-360-8201. URL: http://www.preserve.org/hht. *405*

HISTORICAL ABSTRACTS. PART A: MODERN HISTORY ABSTRACTS, 1450-1914.
A B C-Clio, 130 Cremona, Box 1911, Santa Barbara, CA 93116-1911. TEL 805-968-1911. FAX 805-685-9685.
Vendor(s): Knight-Ridder Information, Inc. (File no.39). *3520*

HISTORICAL ABSTRACTS. PART B: TWENTIETH CENTURY ABSTRACTS, 1914 TO THE PRESENT.
A B C-Clio, 130 Cremona, Box 1911, Santa Barbara, CA 93116-1911. TEL 805-968-1911. FAX 805-685-9685.
Vendor(s): Knight-Ridder Information, Inc. (File no.39). *3520*

HISTORICAL ABSTRACTS. PART B: TWENTIETH CENTURY ABSTRACTS, 1914 TO THE PRESENT. ANNUAL INDEX.
A B C-Clio, 130 Cremona, Box 1911, Santa Barbara, CA 93116-1911. TEL 805-968-1911. FAX 805-685-9685.
Vendor(s): Knight-Ridder Information, Inc. (File no.39). *3521*

HISTORICAL BIOLOGY.
Gordon and Breach - Harwood Academic, Amsteldisk 166, 1st Fl., 1079 LH Amsterdam, Netherlands. URL: http://www.gbhap.com/Historical_Biology/. *5559*

HISTORICAL JOURNAL OF FILM, RADIO AND TELEVISION.
Carfax Publishing Co., P.O. Box 25, Abingdon, Oxon. OX14 3UE, England. TEL 44-1235-401000. FAX 44-1235-401550.
Vendor(s): Information Access Co. *3498*

HISTORY AND THEORY.
Blackwell Publishers, 238 Main St., Cambridge, MA 02142. TEL 617-547-7110. FAX 617-547-0789. Vendor(s): Information Access Co., UMI. *3499*

HISTORY TODAY.
History Today Ltd., 20 Old Compton St., London W1V 5PE, England. TEL 44-171-439-8315.
Vendor(s): Information Access Co., UMI. *3499*

HITMAKERS - WEEKLY TOP 40 RADIO & MUSIC INDUSTRY MAGAZINE.
URL: http://www.hitmakers.com. Available only online. *5398*

HOCKEY PLAYER MAGAZINE.
Hockey Player Magazine L.P., Box 1007, Okemos, MI 48805-1007. URL: http://www.hockeyplayer.com. *6764*

HOFSTRA LABOR LAW JOURNAL.
Hofstra School of Law, Hempstead, NY 11550. TEL 516-463-5006. FAX 516-565-0074.
Vendor(s): West Group. *3960*

HOFSTRA LAW REVIEW.
Hofstra University, Hofstra Law Review, Hempstead, NY 11550. TEL 516-463-5910. FAX 516-463-5092.
Vendor(s): Lexis-Nexis, West Group. *3960*

HOGAN'S ALLEY.
Bull Moose Publishing Corp., Box 47684, Atlanta, GA 30368. TEL 770-458-2624. FAX 770-458-3657.
Vendor(s): CompuServe, Inc. (FUNFOR). *444*

HOLLAND EXPORTS.
A B C voor Handel en Industrie C.V., P.O. Box 190, 2000 AD Haarlem, Netherlands. TEL 31-23-5319031. FAX 31-23-5327033. URL: http://www.hollandexports.com.
Vendor(s): Data-Star. *1329*

HOLLIS PRESS & PUBLIC RELATIONS ANNUAL.
Hollis Directories Ltd., Harlequin House, 7 High St., Teddington, Middlesex TW11 8EH, England. TEL 44-181-977-7711. FAX 44-181-977-1133. URL: http://www.holis-pr.co.uk. *36*

HOLLOW EAR.
Box 1285, New Haven, CT 06505. TEL 203-624-6423. URL: http://www.hear.com/hollow/ Available only online. *4510*

HOLLYWOOD REPORTER.
B P I Communications, 1515 Broadway, New York, NY 10036. TEL 212-536-5199. URL: http://www.hollywoodreporter.com.
Vendor(s): Information Access Co., Lexis-Nexis. *5335*

HOLY TEMPLE OF MASS CONSUMPTION.
Church of the SunGenius, Box 30904, Raleigh, NC 27622. URL: http://www4.ncsu.edu/unity/users/a/aiken/ *6616*

HOME BUSINESS MAGAZINE.
United Marketing & Research Company, Inc., Box 2712, 9582 Hamilton Ave., No. 368, CA 92646. TEL 714-968-0331. FAX 714-968-7722. URL: http://www.homebusinessmag.com. *1643*

HOME FASHIONS MAGAZINE.
Fairchild Fashion & Merchandising Group, 7 W. 34th St., New York, NY 10001. TEL 212-630-4199. FAX 212-630-4201.
Vendor(s): Information Access Co. *3857*

HOME OFFICE COMPUTING.
Scholastic Inc., 555 Broadway, New York, NY 10012-3999. TEL 212-505-3000. URL: http://www.samlloffice.com/
Vendor(s): Information Access Co., UMI. *2197*

HONGKONGIANA.
Hong Kong Polytechnic Library, Hung Hom, Kowloon, Hong Kong, People's Republic of China. TEL 852-2766-6863. FAX 852-2765-8274. Available only online. *14*

HOOK.
Market Vision Studios, Trent Bldg., 50 S. Buckhout St., Irvington, NY 10533. URL: http://www.thehook.com. Available only online. *445*

HOOSIER BANKER.
Indiana Bankers Association, 3135 N. Meridian St., Indianapolis, IN 46208-4717. TEL 317-921-3135. FAX 317-921-3131.
Vendor(s): UMI. *1144*

HOOVER'S DIRECTORY OF HUMAN RESOURCES EXECUTIVES.
Reference Press, Inc., Box 140375, Austin, TX 78714-0375. TEL 512-454-7778. FAX 512-454-9401. URL: http://www.hoovers.com. *1686*

HOOVER'S GUIDE TO COMPUTER COMPANIES.
Reference Press, Inc., Box 140375, Austin, TX 78714-0375. TEL 512-454-7778. FAX 512-454-9401. URL: http://www.hoovers.com. *2129*

HOOVER'S GUIDE TO PRIVATE COMPANIES.
Reference Press, Inc., Box 140375, Austin, TX 78714-0375. TEL 512-454-7778. FAX 512-454-9401. URL: http://www.hoovers.com. *1686*

HOOVER'S GUIDE TO THE BOOK BUSINESS.
Reference Press, Inc., Box 140375, Austin, TX 78714-0375. TEL 512-454-7778. FAX 512-454-9401. URL: http://www.hoovers.com. *1686*

HOOVER'S GUIDE TO THE TOP CHICAGO COMPANIES.
Reference Press, Inc., Box 140375, Austin, TX 78714-0375. TEL 512-454-7778. FAX 512-454-9401. URL: http://www.hoovers.com. *1686*

HOOVER'S GUIDE TO THE TOP NEW YORK COMPANIES.
Reference Press, Inc., Box 140375, Austin, TX 78714-0375. TEL 512-454-7778. FAX 512-454-9401. URL: http://www.hoover.com. *1686*

HOOVER'S GUIDE TO THE TOP SOUTHERN CALIFORNIA COMPANIES.
Reference Press, Inc., Box 140375, Austin, TX 78714-0375. TEL 512-454-7778. FAX 512-454-9401. URL: http://www.hoovers.com. *1686*

HOOVER'S GUIDE TO THE TOP TEXAS COMPANIES.
Reference Press, Inc., Box 140375, Austin, TX 78714-0375. TEL 512-454-7778. FAX 512-454-9401. URL: http://www.hoovers.com. *1686*

HOOVER'S HANDBOOK OF AMERICAN BUSINESS.
Reference Press, Inc., Box 140375, Austin, TX 78714-0375. TEL 512-454-7778. FAX 512-454-9401. URL: http://www.hoovers.com. *1686*

HOOVER'S HANDBOOK OF EMERGING COMPANIES.
Reference Press, Inc., Box 140375, Austin, TX 78714-0375. TEL 512-454-7778. FAX 512-454-9401. URL: http://www.hoovers.com. *1686*

HOOVER'S HANDBOOK OF WORLD BUSINESS.
Reference Press Inc., Box 140375, Austin, TX 78714-0375. TEL 512-454-7778. FAX 512-454-9401. URL: http://www.hoovers.com. *1686*

HOOVER'S MASTERLIST OF MAJOR LATIN AMERICAN COMPANIES.
Reference Press, Inc., Box 140375, Austin, TX 78714-0375. TEL 512-454-7778. URL: http://www.hoovers.com. *1686*

HOOVER'S MASTERLIST OF MAJOR U S COMPANIES (YEAR).
Reference Press, Inc., Box 140375, Austin, TX 78714-0375. TEL 512-454-7778. FAX 512-454-9401. URL: http://www.hoovers.com. *1686*

HORMONES AND BEHAVIOR.
Academic Press, Inc., Journal Division, 525 B St., Ste. 1900, San Diego, CA 92101-4495. TEL 619-230-1840. FAX 619-699-6800. URL: http://www.apnet.com/www/journal/hb.htm; http://www.idealibrary.com/ *4889*

HORN BOOK MAGAZINE.
Horn Book, Inc., 11 Beacon St., Ste. 1000, Boston, MA 02108-3017. TEL 617-227-1555. FAX 617-523-0299.
Vendor(s): Information Access Co. *6272*

HORTICULTURAL ABSTRACTS.
CAB International, Wallingford, Oxon. OX10 8DE, England. TEL 44-1491-832111. FAX 44-1491-826090. URL: http://www.cabi.org.
Vendor(s): DIMDI, European Space Agency, Knight-Ridder Information, Inc., STN International. *3208*

HORTICULTURE.
P J S Publications, Inc., 2 News Plaza, Box 1790, Peoria, IL 61656. TEL 309-682-6626. FAX 309-682-7394.
Vendor(s): Information Access Co., UMI. *3194*

HORTIDEAS.
HortIdeas Publishing, 460 Black Lick Rd., Gravel Switch, KY 40328. TEL 606-332-7606. *3194*

HOSPITAL ADMITTING MONTHLY.
American Health Consultants, Inc., 3525 Piedmont Rd., N.E., Bldg. 6, Ste. 400, Atlanta, GA 30305. TEL 404-262-7436. FAX 800-284-3291.
Vendor(s): Lexis-Nexis. *3711*

HOSPITAL AND HEALTH ADMINISTRATION INDEX.
American Hospital Association, One North Franklin, Chicago, IL 60606. TEL 312-422-3000. FAX 312-422-4700. URL: http://www.aha.org.
Vendor(s): DIMDI, National Library of Medicine. *3721*

HOSPITAL & HEALTH SERVICES ADMINISTRATION.
Health Administration Press, 1 North Franklin St., Ste. 1700, Chicago, IL 60606. TEL 312-424-2800. FAX 312-424-0014. URL: http://www.ache.org.
Vendor(s): Information Access Co., UMI. *3711*

HOSPITAL EMPLOYEE HEALTH.
American Health Consultants, Inc., 3525 Piedmont Rd., N.E., Bldg. 6, Ste. 400, Atlanta, GA 30305. TEL 404-262-7436. FAX 800-284-3291.
Vendor(s): Lexis-Nexis. *3712*

HOSPITAL INFECTION CONTROL.
American Health Consultants, Inc., 3525 Piedmont Rd., N.E., Bldg. 6, Ste. 400, Atlanta, GA 30305. TEL 404-262-7436. FAX 800-284-3291.
Vendor(s): Lexis-Nexis. *3712*

HOSPITAL MATERIALS MANAGEMENT.
Business Word Inc., 5350 S. Roslyn St., Ste. 400, Englewood, CO 80111-2125. TEL 303-290-8500. FAX 303-290-9025.
Vendor(s): Information Access Co., NewsNet, UMI. *3713*

HOSPITAL MATERIEL MANAGEMENT QUARTERLY.
Aspen Publishers, Inc., 200 Orchard Ridge Dr., Gaithersburg, MD 20878. FAX 301-417-7550.
Vendor(s): UMI. *3713*

HOSPITAL PAYMENT AND INFORMATION MANAGEMENT.
American Health Consultants, Inc., 3525 Piedmont Rd., N.E., Bldg. 6, Ste. 400, Atlanta, GA 30305. TEL 404-262-7436. FAX 800-284-3291.
Vendor(s): Lexis-Nexis, NewsNet. *3713*

HOSPITAL PEER REVIEW.
American Health Consultants, Inc., 3525 Piedmont Rd., N.E., Bldg. 6, Ste. 400, Atlanta, GA 30305. TEL 404-262-7436. FAX 800-284-3291.
Vendor(s): Lexis-Nexis. *3713*

HOSPITAL PRACTICE.
McGraw-Hill Companies (Minneapolis), 4530 W. 77th St., Minneapolis, MN 55435. TEL 612-835-3222. FAX 612-835-3460. *4680*

HOSPITAL RISK CONTROL.
E C R I, 5200 Butler Pike, Plymouth Meeting, PA 19462. TEL 610-825-6000. FAX 610-834-1275. *3713*

HOSPITAL RISK MANAGEMENT.
American Health Consultants, Inc., 3525 Piedmont Rd., N.E., Bldg. 6, Ste. 400, Atlanta, GA 30305. TEL 404-262-7436. FAX 800-284-3291.
Vendor(s): Lexis-Nexis. *3713*

HOSPITAL TOPICS.
Heldref Publications, 1319 Eighteenth St., N.W., Washington, DC 20036. TEL 202-296-6267. FAX 202-296-5149. *3714*

HOSPITALIS.
Hospitalis Verlag AG, Hermetschloostr. 73, Postfach 1632, CH-8048 Zurich, Switzerland. TEL 41-1-4330080. FAX 41-1-4330242.
Vendor(s): Knight-Ridder Information, Inc. *3714*

HOSPITALITY DESIGN.
Bill Communications, Inc., 355 Park Ave. S., 3rd Fl., New York, NY 10010-1706. TEL 212-592-6200.
Vendor(s): Information Access Co. *3846*

HOSPITALS AND HEALTH NETWORKS.
American Hospital Publishing, Inc., 737 N. Michigan Ave., Ste. 700, Chicago, IL 60611. TEL 312-440-6800. FAX 312-951-8491.
Vendor(s): Information Access Co., Knight-Ridder Information, Inc., Lexis-Nexis, UMI. *3714*

HOT HOLLYWOOD GOSSIP.
URL: http://members.aol.com/editorman/gossip.html.
Available only online. *5336*

HOT ROD.
Petersen Publishing Co., 6420 Wilshire Blvd., Los Angeles, CA 90048. TEL 213-782-2000. FAX 213-782-2865.
Vendor(s): Information Access Co., Knight-Ridder Information, Inc. *7102*

HOTEL AND MOTEL MANAGEMENT.
Advanstar Communications, Inc., 7500 Old Oak Blvd., Cleveland, OH 44130. TEL 216-826-2839. FAX 216-891-2675.
Vendor(s): Information Access Co., Knight-Ridder Information, Inc. *3728*

HOTLINE (FALLS CHURCH).
American Political Network, Inc., 3129 Mount Vernon Ave., Alexandria, VA 22305-2640. TEL 703-237-5130.
Vendor(s): NewsNet (PO01). *5932*

HOTWIRED.
Wired Ventures Ltd., 520 Third St., 4th Fl., San Francisco, CA 94107. TEL 415-222-6200. FAX 415-222-6369. URL: http://www.hotwired.com/.
Available only online. *2082*

HOUSE BEAUTIFUL.
Hearst Corporation, House Beautiful, 1700 Broadway, New York, NY 10019-5970. TEL 212-903-5000. FAX 212-765-8292. URL: http://www.hearstcorp.com.
Vendor(s): Information Access Co. *3846*

HOUSEHOLD CLEANING AGENTS: THE INTERNATIONAL MARKET.
Euromonitor, 60-61 Britton St., London EC1M 5QU, England. TEL 44-171-251-8024. FAX 44-171-608-3149. URL: http://www.euromonitor.com.
Vendor(s): Data-Star, Knight-Ridder Information, Inc. *1910*

HOUSEWARES.
Miller Freeman Publishers Ltd., Sovereign Way, Tonbridge, Kent TN9 1RW, England. TEL 44-1732-364422. FAX 44-1732-361534.
Vendor(s): Information Access Co. *3857*

HOUSEWARES: THE INTERNATIONAL MARKET.
Euromonitor, 60-61 Britton St., London EC1M 5NA, England. TEL 44-171-251-8024. FAX 44-171-608-3146. URL: http://www.euromonitor.com.
Vendor(s): Data-Star, Knight-Ridder Information, Inc. *3857*

HOUSTON BUSINESS JOURNAL.
American City Business Journals, Inc. (Houston), One West Loop S., Ste. 650, Houston, TX 77027. TEL 713-688-8811. FAX 713-963-0482. URL: http://www.amcity.com.
Vendor(s): Knight-Ridder Information, Inc., Lexis-Nexis. *1263*

HOUSTON JOURNAL OF INTERNATIONAL LAW.
University of Houston, Law Center, 4800 Calhoun Rd., BLB, Ste. 29, Houston, TX 77004-6370. TEL 713-749-3774.
Vendor(s): West Group. *3960*

HOUSTON LAW REVIEW.
Houston Law Review Inc., University of Houston Law Center-University Park, Houston, TX 77004. TEL 713-749-3195. FAX 713-749-4661.
Vendor(s): West Group. *3960*

HOUSTON POST INDEX.
U M I, 300 N. Zeeb Rd., Ann Arbor, MI 48106-1346. TEL 313-761-4700. FAX 800-864-0019.
Vendor(s): Knight-Ridder Information, Inc. *3884*

HOWARD LAW JOURNAL.
Howard University, School of Law, 2900 Van Ness St., N.W., Washington, DC 20008. TEL 202-806-8084. FAX 202-806-8424.
Vendor(s): Lexis-Nexis, West Group. *3960*

HUADONG LIGONG DAXUE XUEBAO.
Huadong Ligong Daxue, Xuebao Bianjibu, 130 Meilong Rd., Shanghai 200237, People's Republic of China. TEL 86-21-6413-2666. FAX 86-21-6477-5678.
Vendor(s): Knight-Ridder Information, Inc. *2765*

HUMAN BIOLOGY (DETROIT).
Wayne State University Press, 4809 Woodward Ave., Detroit, MI 48201-1309. TEL 313-577-6120. FAX 313-577-6131.
Vendor(s): Information Access Co., UMI. *604*

HUMAN ECOLOGY (NEW YORK).
Plenum Publishing Corp., 233 Spring St., New York, NY 10013-1578. TEL 212-620-8000. FAX 212-463-0742.
Vendor(s): Information Access Co. *318*

HUMAN ECOLOGY FORUM.
New York State College of Human Ecology, 1150 Comstock Hall, Cornell University, Ithaca, NY 14850-0901. *6616*

HUMAN FACTORS.
Human Factors and Ergonomics Society, Box 1369, Santa Monica, CA 90406-1369. TEL 310-394-1811. FAX 310-394-2410. URL: http://www.hfes.vt.edu/hfes/; http://hfes.org/Publications/HFJournal.html.
Vendor(s): Information Access Co. *2722*

HUMAN GENETICS.
Springer-Verlag, Heidelberger Platz 3, 14197 Berlin, Germany. TEL 49-30-82787-0. FAX 49-30-82787448. URL: http://link.springer.de. *770*

HUMAN GENOME NEWS.
Human Genome Management Information System, Oak Ridge National Laboratory, 1060 Commerce Park, Oak Ridge, TN 37830. TEL 423-576-6669. FAX 423-574-9888. URL: http://www.ornl.gov/hqmis. *770*

HUMAN GENOME PROGRAM REPORT.
U.S. Department of Energy, Human Genome Program, Office of Health and Environmental Research, ER-72 GTN, Washington, DC 20585. TEL 301-903-6488. FAX 301-903-5051. URL: http://www.ornl.gov/hgmis. *770*

HUMAN LIFE REVIEW.
Human Life Foundation, Inc., 215 Lexington Ave., 4th Fl., New York, NY 10016. TEL 212-685-5210. FAX 212-725-9793.
Vendor(s): Information Access Co. *6712*

HUMAN MOLECULAR GENETICS.
Oxford University Press, Academic Division, Great Clarendon St., Oxford OX2 6DP, England. TEL 44-1865-267907. FAX 44-1865-267485. URL: http://www.oup.co.uk/journals. *771*

HUMAN RELATIONS.
Plenum Publishing Corp., 233 Spring St., New York, NY 10013-1578. TEL 212-260-8000. FAX 212-463-0742. URL: http://www.catchword.co.uk/.
Vendor(s): Information Access Co., UMI. *6617*

HUMAN RELATIONS, AUTHORITY AND JUSTICE.
URL: http://www.human-nature.com/HRAJ/home.html.
Available only online. *6115*

HUMAN REPRODUCTION.
Oxford University Press, Academic Division, Great Clarendon St., Oxford OX2 6DP, England. TEL 44-1865-267907. FAX 44-1865-267485. URL: http://www.oup.co.uk/journals. *4959*

HUMAN REPRODUCTION UPDATE.
Oxford University Press, Academic Division, Great Clarendon St., Oxford OX2 6DP, England. TEL 44-1865-267907. FAX 44-1865-267485. URL: http://www.oup.co.uk/journals. *641*

HUMAN RESOURCE EXECUTIVE.
L R P Publications, Inc., 747 Dresher Rd., Ste. 500, Box 980, Horsham, PA 19044. TEL 215-784-0860. FAX 215-784-0870.
Vendor(s): Human Resources Information Network. *1567*

HUMAN RESOURCE PLANNING.
Human Resource Planning Society, 317 Madison Ave., Ste. 1509, New York, NY 10017. TEL 212-490-6387. FAX 212-682-6851. URL: http://www.hrps.org.
Vendor(s): Information Access Co., UMI. *1568*

HUMAN RIGHTS.
American Bar Association, Individual Rights and Responsibilities Section, 750 N. Lake Shore Dr., Chicago, IL 60611. TEL 312-988-5990. FAX 312-988-6281. URL: http://www.abanet.org.
Vendor(s): West Group (HUMRT). *5992*

HUMAN RIGHTS QUARTERLY.
Johns Hopkins University Press, Journals Publishing Division, 2715 N. Charles St., Baltimore, MD 21218. TEL 410-516-6987. FAX 410-516-6968. URL: http://muse.jhu.edu.
Vendor(s): Information Access Co. *6712*

HUMAN SYSTEMS MANAGEMENT.
I O S Press, Van Diemenstraat 94, 1013 CN Amsterdam, Netherlands. TEL 31-20-6382189. FAX 31-20-6203419. URL: http://www.iospress.nl/iospress.
Vendor(s): UMI. *1481*

THE HUMANIST.
American Humanist Association, 7 Harwood Dr., Box 1188, Amherst, NY 14226-7188. TEL 716-839-5080. FAX 716-839-5079.
Vendor(s): Information Access Co., UMI. *5729*

HUMANITAS.
Editrice Morcelliana S.p.A., Via Gabriele Rosa 71, 25100 Brescia, Italy. TEL 39-30-46451. FAX 39-30-2400605. URL: http://hella.stm.it/market/morcelliana/home.htm. *4338*

HUMANITIES INDEX.
H.W. Wilson Co., 950 University Ave., Bronx, NY 10452. TEL 718-588-8400. FAX 718-590-1617.
Vendor(s): OCLC, Ovid Technologies, Inc. (WHUM), Wilsonline (File HUM). *3799*

HUMOURNET.
HumourNet Communications, Ltd, 6830M No. 323, Guilford Rd., Columbia, MD 21046. URL: http://www.humournet.com/HumourNet/
Available only online. *4338*

HUNGARIAN OBSERVER.
Pallas Lap-es Konyvkiado Vallalat, Garay v.5, 1076 Budapest, Hungary. TEL 36-1-2210285.
Vendor(s): Lexis-Nexis. *3305*

HYDRAULICS & PNEUMATICS.
Penton Publishing Co., 1100 Superior Ave., Cleveland, OH 44114-2543. TEL 216-696-7000. FAX 216-696-8765.
Vendor(s): Information Access Co., Knight-Ridder Information, Inc.. *2872*

HYDROCARBON PROCESSING.
Gulf Publishing Co., Box 2608, Houston, TX 77252-2608. TEL 713-529-4301. FAX 713-520-4433. URL: http://www.gulfpub.com.
Vendor(s): Information Access Co.. *5605*

HYDROGEN TODAY.
American Hydrogen Association, 216 S. Clark Dr., Ste. 103, Tempe, AZ 85281. TEL 602-921-0433. FAX 602-967-6601. URL: http://www.getnet.com/charity/aha. *2693*

HYDROTITLES.
Geosystems, P.O. Box 40, Didcot, Oxon. OX11 9BX, England. TEL 44-1235-813913.
Vendor(s): Knight-Ridder Information, Inc. (File no.58). *2326*

HYGEIA.
Box 3943, Amity Sta., New Haven, CT 06525. URL: http://www.connix.com/hygeia.
Available only online. *6115*

HYPATIA.
Indiana University Press, 601 N. Morton St., Bloomington, IN 47404. TEL 812-855-9449. FAX 812-855-8507.
Vendor(s): Information Access Co., Knight-Ridder Information, Inc. (File no.57), UMI. *7344*

HYPE.
305 E. Pine St., Seattle, WA 98122. TEL 206-233-9814. FAX 206-343-5173. URL: http://www.webcom.com/nattyreb/hype/ *5399*

HYPER (SUB) TEXT.
Global Graphics, URL: http://www.globalgraphics.com/Zines/hst/hypersubtext.html.
Available only online. *4415*

HYPERMARKETS AND SUPERSTORES: THE INTERNATIONAL MARKET.
Euromonitor, 60-61 Britton St., London EC1M 5NA, England. TEL 44-171-251-8024. FAX 44-171-608-3149. URL: http://www.euromonitor.com.
Vendor(s): Data-Star, Knight-Ridder Information, Inc.. *3142*

HYPERMEDIA JOYCE STUDIES.
URL: http://astro.temple.edu/'callahan/hjs/hjs.html.
Available only online. *4415*

HYPERSKI.
URL: http://www.hyperski.com/index.htm.
Available only online. *6871*

I A F C ON SCENE.
International Association of Fire Chiefs, 4025 Fair Ridge Dr., Fairfax, VA 22033-2868. TEL 703-273-0911. FAX 703-273-9363. URL: http://www.ichiffs.org. *3056*

I A H S NEWSLETTER.
Wilfrid Laurier University Press, c/o Dr. G.J. Young, Secretary General IAHS, Department of Geography, Wilfred Laurier University, Waterloo, Ontario N2L 3CS, Canada. TEL 519-884-1970. FAX 519-725-0968. URL: http://www.wlu.ca/~wwwiahs/index.html. *2394*

I A T U L QUARTERLY.
International Association of Technological University Libraries, Walton St. URL: http://educate.lib.chalmers.se/iatul/n1.html. *4181*

I & T MAGAZINE.
European Commission, Directorate-General for Telecommunications, Information Industries and Innovation (DG XIII), Rue de la Loi, 200, B-1049 Brussels, Belgium. *1992*

I B C'S MONEY FUND REPORT.
I B C Financial Data, Inc., 290 Eliot St., Ashland, MA 01721. TEL 508-881-2800. FAX 508-881-0982. URL: http://www.ibcdata.com. *1387*

I B J MONTHLY REPORT.
Industrial Bank of Japan, 1-3-3 Marunouchi, Chiyoda-ku, Tokyo, Japan. *1263*

I B T.
International Business Communications (IBC) Ltd., P.O. Box 145, Tel Aviv 61001, Israel. TEL 972-3-6397194. FAX 972-3-6397195.
Vendor(s): Information Access Co., NewsNet (IT92). *1213*

I C A C RECORDER.
International Cotton Advisory Committee, 1629 K St. N.W., Ste. 702, Washington, DC 20006. TEL 202-463-6660. FAX 202-463-6950. URL: http://www.icac.org. *6987*

I C E S JOURNAL OF MARINE SCIENCE.
Academic Press Ltd., 24-28 Oval Rd., London NW1 7DX, England. TEL 44-171-267-4466. FAX 44-171-482-2293. URL: http://www.hbuk.co.uk/ap/icesjms; http://www.europe.idealibrary.com/ *2404*

I D C JAPAN REPORT.
International Data Corporation, 5 Speen St., Framingham, MA 01701. TEL 508-875-5000.
Vendor(s): Information Access Co. *2127*

I D R C REPORTS.
International Development Research Centre, Box 8500, Ottawa, ON K1G 3H9, Canada. TEL 613-236-6163. FAX 613-563-2476. URL: http://www.idrc.ca.
Available only online. *1361*

I D - THE VOICE OF FOODSERVICE DISTRIBUTION.
Bill Communications, Inc., 355 Park Ave. S., 5th Fl., New York, NY 10010-1789. TEL 212-592-6200. FAX 212-592-6339.
Vendor(s): Information Access Co., Knight-Ridder Information, Inc., Lexis-Nexis. *3112*

I E A OIL MARKET REPORT.
Financial Times Energy Publishing, Maple House, 149 Tottenham Court Rd., London W1P 9LL, England. TEL 0171-896-2241. FAX 0171-896-2275.
Vendor(s): Data-Star, Knight-Ridder Information, Inc., Lexis-Nexis. *2670*

I E E E ANNALS OF THE HISTORY OF COMPUTING.
Institute of Electrical and Electronics Engineers, Inc., 345 E. 47th St., New York, NY 10017-2394. TEL 732-981-0060. FAX 732-981-9667. URL: http://computer.org/pubs/annals/annals.htm. *2083*

I E E E COMPUTATIONAL SCIENCE & ENGINEERING.
Institute of Electrical and Electronics Engineers, Inc., 345 E. 47th St., New York, NY 10017-2394. TEL 732-981-0060. FAX 732-981-9667. URL: http://www.ieee.org. *2083*

I E E E COMPUTER GRAPHICS AND APPLICATIONS.
I E E E Computer Society Press, 10662 Los Vaqueros Circle, Box 3014, Los Alamitos, CA 90720-1264. TEL 714-821-8380. FAX 714-821-4641. URL: http://www.ieee.org; http://www.computer.org/pubs/cg&a.htm. *2122*

I E E E CONCURRENCY.
I E E E Computer Society Press, 10662 Los Vaqueros Circle, Box 3014, Los Alamitos, CA 90720-1314. TEL 714-821-8380. FAX 714-821-4010. URL: http://computer.org/pubs/p&dt/p&dt.htm. *2133*

I E E E DESIGN & TEST OF COMPUTERS.
I E E E Computer Society, 10662 Los Vaqueros Circle, Box 3014, Los Alamitos, CA 90720-1264. TEL 714-821-8380. URL: http://computer.org/pubs/d&t/d&t.htm. *2115*

I E E E INTELLIGENT SYSTEMS MAGAZINE.
I E E E Computer Society Press, 10662 Los Vaqueros Circle, Box 3014, Los Alamitos, CA 90720-1264. TEL 714-821-8380. FAX 714-821-4641. URL: http://computer.org/pubs/expert/expert.htm. *2115*

I E E E INTERNET COMPUTING.
I E E E Computer Society Press, 10662 Los Vaqueros Circle, Box 3014, Los Alamitos, CA 90720-1314. TEL 714-821-8380. FAX 714-821-4010. URL: http://www.computer.org/internet/. *2133*

I E E E JOURNAL OF TECHNOLOGY COMPUTER AIDED DESIGN.
Institute of Electrical and Electronics Engineers, Inc., 345 E. 47th St., New York, NY 10017-2394. URL: http://www.ieee.org/journal/tcal. Available only online. *2123*

I E E E MICRO.
I E E E Computer Society Press, 10662 Los Vaqueros Circle, Box 3014, Los Alamitos, CA 90720-1264. TEL 714-821-8380. FAX 714-821-4641. URL: http://computer.org/pubs/micro/micro.htm. *2189*

I E E E SOFTWARE.
I E E E Computer Society Press, 10662 Los Vaqueros Circle, Box 3014, Los Alamitos, CA 90720-1264. TEL 714-821-8380. FAX 714-821-4641. URL: http://computer.org/pubs/software/software.htm. *2212*

I E E E TRANSACTIONS ON PARALLEL AND DISTRIBUTED SYSTEMS.
Institute of Electrical and Electronics Engineers, Inc., 345 E. 47th St., New York, NY 10017-2394. TEL 732-981-0060. FAX 732-981-9667. URL: http://www.ieee.org; http://www.computer.org/pubs/tpds.htm. *2134*

I E E PROCEEDINGS - CIRCUITS, DEVICES AND SYSTEMS.
I.E.E, Michael Faraday House, Six Hills Way, Stevenage, Herts. SG1 2AY, England. TEL 44-1438-313311. FAX 44-1438-742840. URL: http://www.iee.org.uk. *2832*

I E E PROCEEDINGS - COMMUNICATIONS.
I.E.E, Michael Faraday House, Six Hills Way, Stevenage, Herts. SG1 2AY, England. TEL 44-1438-313311. FAX 44-1438-742840. URL: http://www.iee.org.uk. *2832*

I E E PROCEEDINGS - COMPUTERS AND DIGITAL TECHNIQUES.
I.E.E, Michael Faraday House, Six Hills Way, Stevenage, Herts. SG1 2AY, England. TEL 44-1438-313311. FAX 44-1438-742840. URL: http://www.iee.org.uk. *2179*

I E E PROCEEDINGS - CONTROL THEORY AND APPLICATIONS.
I.E.E, Michael Faraday House, Six Hills Way, Stevenage, Herts. SG1 2AY, England. TEL 44-1438-313311. FAX 44-1438-742840. URL: http://www.iee.org.uk. *2832*

I E E PROCEEDINGS - ELECTRIC POWER APPLICATIONS.
I.E.E, Michael Faraday House, Six Hills Way, Stevenage, Herts. SG1 2AY, England. TEL 44-1438-313311. FAX 44-1438-742840. URL: http://www.iee.org.uk. *2832*

I E E PROCEEDINGS - GENERATION, TRANSMISSION AND DISTRIBUTION.
I.E.E, Michael Faraday House, Six Hills Way, Stevenage, Herts. SG1 2AY, England. TEL 44-1438-313311. FAX 44-1438-742840. URL: http://www.iee.org.uk. *2832*

I E E PROCEEDINGS - MICROWAVES, ANTENNAS & PROPAGATION.
I.E.E, Michael Faraday House, Six Hills Way, Stevenage, Herts. SG1 2AY, England. TEL 44-1438-313311. FAX 44-1438-742840. URL: http://www.iee.org.uk. *2832*

I E E PROCEEDINGS - OPTOELECTRONICS.
I.E.E, Michael Faraday House, Six Hills Way, Stevenage, Herts. SG1 2AY, England. TEL 44-1438-313311. FAX 44-1438-742840. URL: http://www.iee.org.uk. *5861*

I E E PROCEEDINGS - RADAR, SONAR AND NAVIGATION.
I.E.E, Michael Faraday House, Six Hills Way, Stevenage, Herts. SG1 2AY, England. TEL 44-1438-313311. FAX 44-1438-742840. URL: http://www.iee.org.uk. *2832*

I E E PROCEEDINGS - SCIENCE, MEASUREMENT AND TECHNOLOGY.
I.E.E, Michael Faraday House, Six Hills Way, Stevenage, Herts. SG1 2AY, England. TEL 44-1438-313311. FAX 44-1438-742840. URL: http://www.iee.org.uk. *2833*

I E E PROCEEDINGS - VISION, IMAGE & SIGNAL PROCESSING.
I.E.E, Michael Faraday House, Six Hills Way, Stevenage, Herts. SG1 2AY, England. TEL 44-1438-313311. FAX 44-1438-742840. URL: http://www.iee.org.uk. *2833*

I G C C NEWSLETTER.
Institute on Global Conflict and Cooperation, University of California, 9500 Gilman Dr., La Jolla, CA 92093-0518. TEL 619-534-1979. FAX 619-534-7655. URL: http://www.igcc.ucsd.edu/igcc/igccmenu.html. *6017*

I G C C POLICY BRIEFS.
Institute on Global Conflict and Cooperation, University of California, 9500 Gilman Dr., La Jolla, CA 92093-0518. TEL 619-534-1979. FAX 619-534-7655. URL: http://www.igcc.ucsd.edu/igcc/igccmenu.html. *6018*

I G C C POLICY PAPERS.
Institute on Global Conflict and Cooperation, University of California, 9500 Gilman Dr., La Jolla, CA 92093-0518. TEL 619-534-1979. FAX 619-534-7655. URL: http://www.igcc.ucsd.edu/igcc/igccmenu.html. *6018*

I G P L LOGIC JOURNAL.
Oxford University Press, Academic Division, Great Clarendon St., Oxford OX2 6DP, England. TEL 44-1865-267907. FAX 44-1865-267485. URL: http://www.oup.co.uk/jnls/igpl. *5730*

I I E SOLUTIONS.
Institute of Industrial Engineers, Norcross, GA 30092. TEL 404-449-0460. URL: http://www.iienet.org/pubs/htm. Vendor(s): Knight-Ridder Information, Inc., UMI. *2876*

I I E TRANSACTIONS.
Thomson Science, 2-6 Boundary Row, London SE1 8HN, England. TEL 44-171-8560066. FAX 44-171-5229623. URL: http://www.thomsonscience.com. *2876*

I J O NEWSLETTER.
International Juridical Organization for Environment and Development, Via Barberini 3, 00187 Rome, Italy. TEL 39-6-4742117. FAX 39-6-4745779. *2932*

I LOVE MY NANNY NEWS.
I Love My Nanny, Inc., URL: http://www.ilovemynanny.com/. Available only online. *1847*

I M M ABSTRACTS AND INDEX.
Institution of Mining and Metallurgy, 44 Portland Pl., London W1N 4BR, England. TEL 0171-580-3802. FAX 0171-436-5388. Vendor(s): European Space Agency (IMMAGE). *5321*

I N F O R JOURNAL.
University of Toronto Press, Journals Department, 5201 Dufferin St., Downsview, ON M3H 5T8, Canada. TEL 416-667-7710. FAX 416-667-7881. Vendor(s): UMI. *2174*

I N I S ATOMINDEX.
International Atomic Energy Agency, Wagramerstrasse 5, Box 100, A-1400 Vienna, Austria. TEL 43-1-2060-22529. FAX 43-1-2060-29302. Vendor(s): BELINDIS, CISTI, European Space Agency (File no.28/INIS), STN International (ENERGY). *5835*

I P A REVIEW.
Institute of Public Affairs, 128-36 Jolimont Rd., Jolimont, Vic. 3002, Australia. TEL 61-3-96547499. FAX 61-3-96507627. Vendor(s): UMI. *970*

I P NEWS (PRINT EDITION).
NetPubs International, LLC, 430 Canyon Ave., Ste. B, Ft. Collins, CO 80521-2625. TEL 970-416-7703. FAX 970-416-7754. URL: http://www.netpubsintl.com/ipnews.html. *2134*

I R S PUBLICATIONS.
C C H Incorporated, 2700 Lake Cook Rd., Riverwoods, IL 60015. TEL 847-267-7000. FAX 800-224-8299. Vendor(s): Wilsonline. *1613*

I S D N NEWS.
Phillips Business Information, Inc., 1201 Seven Locks Rd., Potomac, MD 20854. TEL 301-424-3338. FAX 301-309-3847. Vendor(s): Data-Star, Information Access Co., Knight-Ridder Information, Inc., NewsNet (TE90). *2016*

I T S JOURNAL.
Gordon and Breach - Harwood Academic, Amsteldisk 166, 1st Fl., 1079 LH Amsterdam, Netherlands. URL: http://www.gbhap.com/Intelligent__Transportation__Systems/. *7053*

I TO CHO.
Igaku-Shoin Ltd., 5-24-3 Hongo, Bunkyo-ku, Tokyo 113-91, Japan. TEL 81-3-3817-5714. FAX 81-3-3815-7802. Vendor(s): JICST. *4911*

I - WATCH NEWSLETTER.
Exton Enterprises, P.O. Box 394, Mt. Ommaney, Qld. 4074, Australia. URL: http://www.gil.com.au/comm/eemall/iwatch/. Available only online. *2134*

IBERLEX.
Boletin Oficial del Estado, Trafalgar, 27, 28071 Madrid, Spain. TEL 34-1-5382297. FAX 34-1-5382275. URL: http://www.boe.es. *4070*

IBN QIRTAIBA.
2 Jenkins Place, Wembley Downs, W.A. 6019, Australia. URL: http://www.sf.sig.au.mensa.org. Available only online. *4532*

ICARUS (SAN DIEGO).
Academic Press, Inc., Journal Division, 525 B St., Ste. 1900, San Diego, CA 92101-4495. TEL 619-230-1840. FAX 619-699-6800. URL: http://www.apnet.com/www/journal/is.htm; http://www.idealibrary.com/ *495*

ICE CREAM REPORTER.
F I N D - S V P, Inc., 625 Avenue of the Americas, New York, NY 10011-2002. TEL 212-645-4500. FAX 212-645-7681. Vendor(s): NewsNet (FB04). *3136*

ICE CREAM, YOGHURTS AND CHILLED DESSERTS: THE INTERNATIONAL MARKET.
Euromonitor, 60-61 Britton St., London EC1M 5NA, England. TEL 44-171-251-8024. FAX 44-171-608-3149. URL: http://www.euromonitor.com. Vendor(s): Data-Star, Knight-Ridder Information, Inc. *3112*

ICHNOS.
Gordon and Breach - Harwood Academic, Amsteldisk 166, 1st Fl., 1079 LH Amsterdam, Netherlands. URL: http://www.gbhap.com/Ichnos/. *5559*

IDAHO BUSINESS DIRECTORY.
American Business Directories, 5711 S. 86th Circle, Box 27347, Omaha, NE 68127. TEL 402-593-4600. FAX 402-331-5481. *1687*

IDAHO LAW REVIEW.
University of Idaho, College of Law, Moscow, ID 83843. TEL 208-885-7241. Vendor(s): West Group. *3961*

IDAHO PUBLIC AFFAIRS DIGEST.
Ridenbaugh Press, Box 2276, Boise, ID 83701. TEL 208-344-0844. FAX 208-344-0844. URL: http://www.ridenbaugh.com. *4132*

IDEAS MAGAZINE.
Upstarts Internet Services, 1-29 Beachfront Pde., Angels Beach, N.S.W. 2478, Australia. URL: http://www.upstarts.net.au/site/ideas.html. Available only online. *2933*

IGAKU CHUO ZASSHI.
Igaku Chuo Zasshi Kankokai, 5-18, Takaido Higashi 2-chome, Suginami-ku, Tokyo 168, Japan. TEL 86-3-3334-7625. FAX 86-3-3332-1394. *4682*

ILLINOIS BUSINESS DIRECTORY.
American Business Directories, 5711 S. 86th Circle, Box 27347, Omaha, NE 68127. TEL 402-593-4600. FAX 402-331-5481. *1687*

ILLINOIS LEGAL TIMES.
Giant Steps Publishing Corp., 3 E. Huron St., Chicago, IL 60611. TEL 312-654-3510. Vendor(s): Lexis-Nexis, West Group. *3961*

10128   SERIALS AVAILABLE ONLINE

ILLUSTRATED CASE REPORTS IN GASTROENTEROLOGY.
Chapman & Hall, Journals Department 2-6 Boundary Row, London SE1 8HN, England. TEL 44-171-8650066. FAX 44-171-5229323. URL: http://www.chaphall.com/chaphall/journals.html. *4911*

IMAGEN VASCA ONLINE.
Codeco, Comercial de Comunicaciones, S.L., Trasera de Burgos 8, 48014 Bilbao, Spain. TEL 34-4-4478414. FAX 34-4-4761187. URL: http://www.codeconet.com/imagenvasca. Available only online. *1213*

IMAGING ABSTRACTS.
Pira International, Randalls Rd., Leatherhead, Surrey KT22 7RU, England. TEL 44-1372-802050. FAX 44-1372-802239. URL: http://www.pira.co.uk/. Vendor(s): Data-Star (PIRA), FIZ Technik, Knight-Ridder Information, Inc. (F248), Questel Orbit Inc. (PIRA/IMAB), STN International (PIRA). *5777*

IMAGING UPDATE.
Worldwide Videotex, Box 3273, Boynton Beach, FL 33424-3273. TEL 407-738-2276. Vendor(s): Data-Star, Information Access Co., Knight-Ridder Information, Inc., NewsNet (EC05). *2123*

IMAGING WORLD.
Cardinal Business Media, Inc., 1300 Virginia Dr., Ste. 400, Fort Washington, PA 19034. TEL 215-643-8000. FAX 215-643-8099. URL: http://www.cardinal.com/iw. *2123*

IMMUNOGENETICS.
Springer-Verlag, Heidelberger Platz 3, 14197 Berlin, Germany. TEL 49-30-82787-0. FAX 49-30-82787448. URL: http://link.springer.de. *4795*

IMMUNOLOGY ABSTRACTS.
Cambridge Scientific Abstracts, 7200 Wisconsin Ave., 6th Fl., Bethesda, MD 20814. TEL 301-961-6750. FAX 301-961-6720. URL: http://www.csa.com. Vendor(s): Knight-Ridder Information, Inc. (File no.76/LIFE SCIENCES COLLECTION), STN International (LIFESCI). *4780*

IMMUNOLOGY TODAY.
Elsevier Science Ltd., P.O. Box 800, Kidlington, Oxford OX5 1DX, England. TEL 44-1865-843000. FAX 44-1865-843010. URL: http://www.elsevier.nl/. Vendor(s): OCLC. *4796*

IMMUNOTHERAPY WEEKLY.
Charles W. Henderson, Ed. & Pub., Box 5528, Atlanta, GA 31107-0528. TEL 404-377-8895. FAX 404-378-4511. URL: http://www.newsfile.com. *4797*

IMPACT PRESS.
Loudmouth Productions, Inc., 10151 University Blvd., Ste. 151, Orlando, FL 32817. URL: http://www.mindspring.com/~impact-press. *6618*

IMPLEMENT & TRACTOR.
Freiberg Publishing Company, Inc., 2302 W. First St., Box 7, Cedar Falls, IA 50613. TEL 319-277-3599. FAX 319-277-3783. URL: http//www.agimplement.com. Vendor(s): Information Access Co. *207*

IMPORTS & EXPORTS OF CRUDE OIL AND PETROLEUM PRODUCTS.
American Petroleum Institute, Publications Section, 1220 L St., N.W., Washington, DC 20005. TEL 202-682-8375. FAX 202-962-4776. URL: http://www.api.org. *5605*

IMPRESA & STATO.
Camera di Commercio, Industria, Artiganato e Agricoltura di Milano, Via Meravigli 9-B, 20123 Milan, Italy. TEL 39-2-85154206. URL: http://www.mi.camcom.it/impresa.htm. *1189*

IMPROVED RECOVERY WEEK.
F. Jay Schempf, Ed. & Pub., Box 2607, Bellaire, TX 77402-2607. TEL 713-680-0914. FAX 713-680-9343. Vendor(s): Data-Star, Information Access Co., Knight-Ridder Information, Inc., Lexis-Nexis. *2671*

IN-CAR ENTERTAINMENT: THE INTERNATIONAL MARKET.
Euromonitor, 60-61 Britton St., London EC1M 5NA, England. TEL 44-171-251-8024. FAX 44-171-608-3149. URL: http://www.euromonitor.com. Vendor(s): Data-Star, Knight-Ridder Information, Inc. *2642*

IN FLIGHT U S A.
URL: http://www.inflightusa.com. Available only online. *7071*

IN FOCUS (MOUNTAIN VIEW).
TeleSensory, 455 N. Bernardo Ave., Box 7455, Mountain View, CA 94043. TEL 415-335-1800. FAX 415-335-1816. URL: http://www.telesensory.com. *3470*

IN HAND.
31 Randolph Dr., Southwood, Farnborough, Hants. GU14 0QQ, England. TEL 01252-518960. FAX 01252-518960. *2179*

IN MOTION MAGAZINE.
N P C Productions, Box 927482, San Diegao, CA 92192. URL: http://www.inmotionmagazine.com. Available only online. *6713*

IN SIGHT OF THE BIG EYE.
E-Mail Club, Inc., Box 2776, Sarasota, FL 34230. URL: http://www.bigeye.com. Available only online. *2134*

IN TOUCH (CALGARY).
7620 Elbow Dr. S.W., Calgary, AB T2V 1K2, Canada. URL: http://www.intouchmag.com. *296*

IN VIVO.
Windhover Information, Inc., 50 Washington St., 5th Fl., South Norwalk, CT 06864. TEL 203-838-4401. FAX 203-838-3214. Vendor(s): Information Access Co. *4682*

INC.
Goldhirsh Group, Inc., 38 Commercial Wharf, Boston, MA 02110. TEL 617-248-8000. FAX 617-248-8090. URL: http://www.incmag.com. Vendor(s): Information Access Co., Knight-Ridder Information, Inc., Lexis-Nexis. *1643*

INCENTIVE.
Bill Communications, Inc., 355 Park Ave. S., 5th Fl., New York, NY 10010-1789. TEL 212-592-6200. FAX 212-592-6339. Vendor(s): UMI. *1530*

INCOME OPPORTUNITIES.
Essence Communications Inc., 1500 Broadway, Ste. 600, New York, NY 10036-4015. TEL 212-642-0600. FAX 212-302-8269. URL: http://www.incomeops.com/ *1643*

INCOME SECURITIES ADVISOR.
Bond Investors Association, Inc., 617 N.W. 153rd St., Ste. 221, Miami Lakes, FL 33014-2435. TEL 305-557-1832. *1388*

INCREASE & DIFFUSION.
Smithsonian Institution. URL: http://www.si.edu/i. Available only online. *6532*

INDEPENDENT BANKER.
Independent Bankers Association of America, Box 267, Sauk Centre, MN 56378. TEL 612-352-6546. Vendor(s): UMI. *1145*

INDEPENDENT ENERGY.
PennWell Publishing Company (Tulsa), 1421 S. Sheridan Rd., Tulsa, OK 74112-6619. TEL 918-832-9377. FAX 918-831-9776. Vendor(s): UMI. *2671*

INDEPENDENT FILM AND VIDEO MONTHLY.
Foundation for Independent Video & Film, 304 Hudson St., 6th Fl., New York, NY 10013. TEL 212-807-1400. FAX 212-463-8519. URL: http://www.aivf.org; http://www.virtualfilm.com/AIVF/ *5336*

INDEPENDENT POWER REPORT.
McGraw-Hill Companies, Energy & Business Newsletters, 1221 Ave. of the Americas, 36th Fl., New York, NY 10020. TEL 212-512-6410. Vendor(s): Dow Jones News Retrieval (COG), Knight-Ridder Information, Inc. (File no.624/McGRAW-HILL PUBLICATIONS ONLINE), Lexis-Nexis (IPR), NewsNet (EY67). *2671*

INDEPENDENT SMALL PRESS REVIEW.
Independent Small Press Review (I.S.P.R.), Box 336, Santa Barbara, CA 93190-1336. TEL 805-687-4087. FAX 805-964-3337. *6273*

INDEX ANALYTIQUE SIGNALETIQUE BIBLIOGRAPHIQUE.
Ministere de la Population, Centre National de Documentation, Charii Ahmed Cherkaoui - Haut Agdal, B.P. 826 - 10004, Rabat, Morocco. TEL 212-7-774944. FAX 212-7-773134. URL: http://wizarat-sukkan.sukkan.gov.ma. *1047*

INDEX MEDICUS.
U.S. National Library of Medicine, 8600 Rockville Pike, Bethesda, MD 20894. Vendor(s): Knight-Ridder Information, Inc. (File nos.154 & 155/MEDLINE), National Library of Medicine, Ovid Technologies, Inc. (MESH, MESZ), STN International (MEDLINE). *4780*

INDEX NEW ZEALAND.
National Library of New Zealand, P.O. Box 1467, Wellington, New Zealand. TEL 64-4-4743098. FAX 64-4-4753124. URL: http://www.natlib.ogvt.nz/. Vendor(s): Kiwinet. *15*

INDEX OF ARTICLES ON JEWISH STUDIES.
Jewish National and University Library, P.O. Box 34165, Jerusalem 91341, Israel. TEL 972-2-585039. FAX 972-2-511771. *3052*

INDEX OF CURRENT RESEARCH ON PIGS.
CAB International, Wallingford, Oxon., England. TEL 44-1491-832111. FAX 44-1491-826090. URL: http://www.cabi.org. Vendor(s): DIMDI, European Space Agency, Knight-Ridder Information, Inc., STN International. *176*

INDEX OF ECONOMIC ARTICLES IN JOURNALS AND COLLECTIVE VOLUMES.
American Economic Association, 2014 Broadway, Ste. 305, Nashville, TN 37203. TEL 615-322-2595. Vendor(s): Knight-Ridder Information, Inc. (File no.139). *1047*

INDEX OF FUNGI.
CAB International, Wallingford, Oxon. OX10 8DE, England. TEL 44-1491-432111. FAX 44-1491-826090. URL: http:/www.cabi.org. Vendor(s): DIMDI, European Space Agency, Knight-Ridder Information, Inc., STN International. *641*

INDEX ON CENSORSHIP.
Writers & Scholars International Ltd., Lancaster House, 33 Islington High St., London N1 9LH, England. TEL 44-171-278-2313. FAX 44-171-278-1878. URL: http://www.oneworld.org/index_oc/ *4339*

INDEX TO CURRENT URBAN DOCUMENTS.
Greenwood Press, Inc., Subscription Publications 88 Post Rd. W., Box 5007, Westport, CT 06881-5007. TEL 203-226-3571. FAX 203-226-6009. *3766*

INDEX TO DENTAL LITERATURE.
American Dental Association, 211 E. Chicago Ave., Chicago, IL 60611. TEL 312-440-2500. FAX 312-440-2550. Vendor(s): Knight-Ridder Information, Inc. (File nos.154 & 155/MEDLINE), National Library of Medicine, Ovid Technologies, Inc. (MESH, MESZ), STN International (MEDLINE). *4780*

INDEX TO LEGAL PERIODICALS & BOOKS.
H.W. Wilson Co., 950 University Ave., Bronx, NY 10452. TEL 718-588-8400. FAX 718-590-1617. Vendor(s): Lexis-Nexis, OCLC, Ovid Technologies, Inc., West Group, Wilsonline (File ILP). *4053*

INDEX TO SCIENTIFIC & TECHNICAL PROCEEDINGS.
Institute for Scientific Information, 3501 Market St., Philadelphia, PA 19104. TEL 215-386-0100. FAX 215-386-2911. Vendor(s): Questel Orbit Inc. *6590*

INDEX TO SCIENTIFIC BOOK CONTENTS.
Institute for Scientific Information, 3501 Market St., Philadelphia, PA 19104. TEL 215-386-0100. FAX 215-386-2911. Vendor(s): DIMDI (ISTP&B Search). *6590*

INDEX TO SOUTH AFRICAN PERIODICALS.
State Library, P.O. Box 397, Pretoria 0001, South Africa. TEL 27-12-21-8931. FAX 27-12-325-5984. *6290*

INDEX TO THE ST. PAUL PIONEER PRESS.
Newsbank, Inc., 58 Pine St., New Canaan, CT 06840-5426. TEL 203-966-1100. FAX 203-966-6254. *3884*

INDEX TO THE SPORTING NEWS.
John Gordon Burke Publisher, Inc., Box 1492, Evanston, IL 60204-1492. TEL 847-866-8625. URL: http://www.nlightn.com. *6796*

INDEX VETERINARIUS.
CAB International, Wallingford, Oxon. OX10 8DE, England. TEL 44-1491-832111. FAX 44-1491-826090. URL: http://www.cabi.org. Vendor(s): DIMDI, European Space Agency, Knight-Ridder Information, Inc., STN International. *7285*

INDIAN CONCRETE JOURNAL.
Associated Cement Companies, Ltd., C R S Complex, L.B. Shastri Marg., Thane 400 604, India. TEL 91-22-5323631. FAX 91-22-5320962. *2786*

INDIAN JOURNAL OF HOSPITAL PHARMACY.
Indian Hospital Pharmacists' Association, R-566 New Rajinder Nagar, New Delhi 110 060, India. TEL 91-11-5754344. *5666*

INDIAN JOURNAL OF PHARMACEUTICAL SCIENCES.
Indian Pharmaceutical Association, Kalina Santacruz East, Mumbai 400 098, India. TEL 91-22-612-2401. FAX 91-22-614-0480. *5666*

INDIANA BUSINESS DIRECTORY.
American Business Directories, 5711 S. 86th Circle, Box 27347, Omaha, NE 68127. TEL 402-593-4600. FAX 402-331-5481. *1687*

INDIANA BUSINESS MAGAZINE.
Curtis Magazine Group, 1200 Waterway Blvd., Indianapolis, IN 46202-2157. TEL 317-692-1200. FAX 317-692-4250. Vendor(s): Information Access Co., Knight-Ridder Information, Inc., Lexis-Nexis, UMI. *1264*

INDIANA BUSINESS REVIEW.
Indiana University, School of Business, Bloomington, IN 47405. TEL 812-855-5507. Vendor(s): UMI. *971*

INDIANA JOURNAL OF COMMERCE AND INDUSTRY.
R & W Publishing, Inc., Box 3275, Evansville, IN 47731-3275. TEL 812-425-2210. FAX 812-422-4984. Vendor(s): UMI. *971*

INDIANA LAW JOURNAL.
Indiana University, School of Law, Law Building, Bloomington, IN 47405. TEL 812-855-5175. FAX 812-855-0555. Vendor(s): Lexis-Nexis, West Group. *3962*

INDIANA LAW REVIEW.
Indiana University, Indianapolis School of Law, 735 W. New York St., Indianapolis, IN 46202. TEL 317-274-4039. FAX 317-274-8825. Vendor(s): West Group. *3962*

INDIANA LEGISLATIVE INSIGHT.
Edward D. Feigenbaum, Ed. & Pub., Box 383, Noblesville, IN 46061-0383. TEL 317-773-8715. FAX 317-773-9998. *6179*

INDIANAPOLIS BUSINESS JOURNAL.
I B J Corp., 431 N. Pennsylvania, Indianapolis, IN 46204-1806. TEL 317-634-6200. FAX 317-263-5060. Vendor(s): Information Access Co., UMI. *1213*

INDIANAPOLIS C.E.O.
Metropolitan C.E.O., 911 E. 86th St., Ste. 100, Indianapolis, IN 46240-1840. TEL 317-257-8000. FAX 317-257-1482. *1482*

INDIAWORLD.
Ravi Database Consultants Pvt. Ltd., 304 Tulsiani Chambers, 212 Nariman Point, Bombay 400 021, India. TEL 91-22-2842959. FAX 91-22-2023904. URL: http://www.indiaworld.com. Available only online. *3312*

INDICE ESPANOL DE CIENCIA Y TECNOLOGIA.
Centro de Informacion y Documentacion Cientifica (Cindoc), Joaquin Costa 22, 28002 Madrid, Spain. TEL 34-1-5635482. FAX 34-1-5642644. *6590*

INDICE ESPANOL DE CIENCIAS SOCIALES. SERIES A: PSYCHOLOGY AND EDUCATIONAL SCIENCES.
Centro de Informacion y Documentacion Cientifica (Cindoc), Joaquin Costa 22, 28002 Madrid, Spain. TEL 34-1-5635482. FAX 34-1-5642644. *6160*

INDICE ESPANOL DE CIENCIAS SOCIALES. SERIES B: ECONOMICS, SOCIOLOGY AND POLITICAL SCIENCE.
Centro de Informacion y Documentacion Cientifica (Cindoc), Joaquin Costa 22, 28002 Madrid, Spain. TEL 34-1-4111098. FAX 34-1-5645069. *1047*

INDICE ESPANOL DE CIENCIAS SOCIALES. SERIES C: LAW.
Centro de Informacion y Documentacion Cientifica (Cindoc), Joaquin Costa 22, 28002 Madrid, Spain. TEL 34-1-5635482. FAX 34-1-5642644. *4053*

INDICE ESPANOL DE CIENCIAS SOCIALES. SERIES D: SCIENCE AND SCIENTIFIC INFORMATION.
Centro de Informacion y Documentacion Cientifica (Cindoc), Joaquin Costa 22, 28002 Madrid, Spain. TEL 34-1-5635482. FAX 34-1-5642645. *6590*

INDICE ESPANOL DE CIENCIAS SOCIALES. SERIES E: URBAN PLANNING.
Centro de Informacion y Documentacion Cientifica (Cindoc), Joaquin Costa 22, 28002 Madrid, Spain. TEL 34-1-5635482. FAX 34-1-5642644. *3766*

INDICE ESPANOL DE HUMANIDADES. SERIES A: ART.
Centro de Informacion y Documentacion Cientifica (Cindoc), Joaquin Costa 22, 28002 Madrid, Spain. TEL 34-3-5635482. FAX 34-1-5642644. *476*

INDICE ESPANOL DE HUMANIDADES. SERIES B: HISTORICAL SCIENCES.
Centro de Informacion y Documentacion Cientifica (Cindoc), Joaquin Costa 22, 28002 Madrid, Spain. TEL 34-1-5635482. FAX 34-1-5642644. *3521*

INDICE ESPANOL DE HUMANIDADES. SERIES C: LINGUISTICS AND LITERATURE.
Centro de Informacion y Documentacion Cientifica (Cindoc), Joaquin Costa 22, 28002 Madrid, Spain. TEL 34-1-5635482. FAX 34-1-5642644. *4318*

INDICE ESPANOL DE HUMANIDADES. SERIES D: PHILOSOPHY.
Centro de Informacion y Documentacion Cientifica (Cindoc), Joaquin Costa 22, 28002 Madrid, Spain. TEL 34-1-5635482. FAX 34-1-5642644. *5760*

INDICE MEDICO ESPANOL.
Generalitat Valenciana, Conselleria de Sanitat i Consum, Avda. Blasco Ibanez - 17, 46010 Valencia, Spain. TEL 96-361-06-54. FAX 96-3613975. *4780*

INDIVIDUAL EMPLOYMENT RIGHTS.
The Bureau of National Affairs, Inc., 1231 25th St., N.W., Washington, DC 20037. TEL 202-452-4200. FAX 202-822-8092. URL: http://www.bna.com/ Vendor(s): Human Resources Information Network (CDD, HDD), Lexis-Nexis (File LRRIER, IERNEW), West Group (File FLB-CS, LRR-IERN). *1435*

INDIVIDUALS WITH DISABILITIES EDUCATION LAW REPORTER.
L R P Publications, 747 Dresher Rd., Box 980, Horsham, PA 19044-0980. TEL 215-784-0941. FAX 215-784-9639. URL: http://www.lrp.com. *2585*

INDOOR AIR QUALITY UPDATE.
Cutter Information Corp., 37 Broadway, Arlington, MA 02174. TEL 617-648-8700. FAX 617-648-1950. URL: http://www.cutter.com. *406*

INDUSTRIAL & ENGINEERING CHEMISTRY RESEARCH.
American Chemical Society, 1155 16th St. N.W., Washington, DC 20036. TEL 800-333-9511. FAX 614-447-3671. Vendor(s): STN International (CJACS). *2765*

INDUSTRIAL AND LABOR RELATIONS REVIEW.
Cornell University, New York State School of Industrial and Labor Relations, Ithaca, NY 14853-3901. TEL 607-255-2732. FAX 607-255-8016. URL: http://www.ILR.cornell.edu/depts/ILRrev/. Vendor(s): Information Access Co., Knight-Ridder Information, Inc., Lexis-Nexis, West Group, Wilsonline. *1435*

INDUSTRIAL CASES REPORTS.
Incorporated Council of Law Reporting for England and Wales, 3 Stone Bldgs., Lincoln's Inn, London WC2A 3XN, England. TEL 44-171-242-6471. FAX 44-171-831-5247. Vendor(s): Lexis-Nexis. *4081*

INDUSTRIAL DISTRIBUTION.
Cahners Publishing Company (Newton), Division of Reed Elsevier Inc., 275 Washington St., Newton, MA 02158-1630. TEL 617-558-4564. FAX 617-558-4677. URL: http://www.manufacturing.net/magazine.id/ Vendor(s): Information Access Co., Knight-Ridder Information, Inc. *1530*

INDUSTRIAL ENERGY BULLETIN.
McGraw-Hill Companies, Energy & Business Newsletters, 1221 Ave. of the Americas, 36th Fl., New York, NY 10020. TEL 212-512-2000. Vendor(s): Dow Jones News Retrieval, Knight-Ridder Information, Inc. (File no.624/McGRAW-HILL PUBLICATIONS ONLINE), Lexis-Nexis, NewsNet (EY68). *2671*

INDUSTRIAL ENVIRONMENT.
Worldwide Videotex, Box 3273, Boynton Beach, FL 33424-3273. TEL 407-738-2276. Vendor(s): Information Access Co.. *2933*

INDUSTRIAL HEALTH.
National Institute of Industrial Health, 21-1 Nagao 6-chome, Tama-ku, Kawasaki-shi, Kanagawa-ken 214, Japan. TEL 81-044-865-6111. FAX 81-044-865-6116. URL: http://www.niih.go.jp. Vendor(s): JICST, Knight-Ridder Information, Inc.. *5491*

INDUSTRIAL HEALTH & HAZARDS UPDATE.
Merton Allen Associates, InfoTeam Inc., Box 15640, Plantation, FL 33318-5640. TEL 954-473-9560. FAX 954-473-0544. Vendor(s): Data-Star, Human Resources Information Network, Information Access Co., NewsNet (LA04), UMI. *5491*

INDUSTRIAL MANAGEMENT.
Institute of Industrial Engineers, 25 Technology Park-Atlanta, Norcross, GA 30092. TEL 770-449-0460. FAX 770-263-8532. Vendor(s): Information Access Co., UMI. *1482*

INDUSTRIAL PAINT & POWDER.
Hitchcock Publishing, 191 S. Gary Ave., Carol Stream, IL 60188. TEL 708-665-1000. FAX 708-462-2225. Vendor(s): Information Access Co., Knight-Ridder Information, Inc. *5553*

INDUSTRIAL PHYSICIST.
American Institute of Physics, One Physics Ellipse, College Park, MD 20740-3843. TEL 301-209-3040. FAX 301-209-0842. URL: http://www.aip.org/tip. *5806*

INDUSTRIAL RELATIONS JOURNAL.
Blackwell Publishers Ltd., 108 Cowley Rd., Oxford OX4 1JF, England. TEL 44-1865-791100. FAX 44-1865-791347. URL: http://www.blackwellpublishers.co.uk. Vendor(s): Information Access Co. *1435*

INDUSTRIAL RELATIONS LAW REPORTS.
Eclipse Group Ltd., Industrial Relations Services, 18-20 Highbury Pl., London N5 1QP, England. TEL 44-171-354-5858. FAX 44-171-226-8618. Vendor(s): Lexis-Nexis. *1435*

INDUSTRIAL REPORTS.
L B C Information Services, 50 Waterloo Rd., N. Ryde, N.S.W. 2113, Australia. TEL 61-2-99366444. FAX 61-2-98889706. Vendor(s): Info-One International Pty Ltd. *4082*

INDUSTRIAL RESEARCHER.
Pranava Industrial Services Pvt. Ltd., 18, Sagar Tarang, Bhulabhai Desai Rd., Bombay 400 036, India. TEL 3633236. Vendor(s): Knight-Ridder Information, Inc. *971*

SERIALS AVAILABLE ONLINE

INDUSTRIAL SPECIALTIES NEWS.
Blendon Information Services, 68 Longmore St., Willowdale, ON M2N 6T8, Canada. TEL 416-223-5397. FAX 416-223-8532.
Vendor(s): Data-Star, Dow Jones News Retrieval, Information Access Co., Knight-Ridder Information, Inc. *5302*

INDUSTRIES IN TRANSITION.
Business Communications Co., Inc. (Norwalk), 25 Van Zant St., Norwalk, CT 06855. TEL 203-853-4266. FAX 203-853-0348.
Vendor(s): Data-Star, Information Access Co., Knight-Ridder Information, Inc., NewsNet (GB46). *1587*

INDUSTRY GROUP MARKET VALUES.
Standard & Poor's, 25 Broadway, New York, NY 10004. TEL 212-208-8000. *1388*

INDUSTRY WEEK.
Penton Publishing Co., 1100 Superior Ave., Cleveland, OH 44114-2543. TEL 216-696-7000. FAX 216-969-7670. URL: http://www.industryweek.com.
Vendor(s): Information Access Co., Knight-Ridder Information, Inc., Lexis-Nexis, UMI. *1482*

INFECTION CONTROL WEEKLY.
Charles W. Henderson, Ed. & Pub., Box 5528, Atlanta, GA 31107-0528. TEL 404-377-8895. FAX 404-378-5411.
Vendor(s): Information Access Co. *4837*

INFERTILITY.
c/o Dr. Louis A. Mucelli, Ed., 614 2nd Ave., Ste. H, New York, NY 10016. TEL 212-684-4242. FAX 212-684-4290. *4959*

INFLAMMATION RESEARCH.
Birkhaeuser Verlag, P.O. Box 133, CH-4010 Basel, Switzerland. TEL 41-61-2050730. FAX 41-61-2050791. *5667*

INFO.
University of Tasmania, Information Services Division, URL: http://info.utas.edu.au/docs/info/index.html.
Available only online. *2134*

INFO-WORLD E-GAZETTE.
Available only online. *3376*

INFOCIS.
123 Breadfast Creek Rd., Ste. 4, Newstead Brisbane, Qld. 4006, Australia. URL: http://www.infocis.com.
Available only online. *3251*

INFONATION MAGAZINE.
InfoNation Magazine, Inc., 2616 Harriet Ave., Ste. 119, Maples, MN 55408. TEL 612-871-4090.
URL: http://www.info-nation.com. *2134*

INFORMATIK - FORSCHUNG UND ENTWICKLUNG.
Springer-Verlag, Heidelberger Platz 3, 14197 Berlin, Germany. TEL 49-30-82787-0. FAX 49-30-82787448. URL: http://science.springer.de/ife/ife-main.htm. *2182*

THE INFORMATION ADVISOR.
Find SVP, 625 Avenue of Americas, New York, NY 10010.
Vendor(s): Information Access Co. (Trade & Industry Index). *4231*

INFORMATION AND COMPUTATION.
Academic Press, Inc., Journal Division, 525 B St., Ste. 1900, San Diego, CA 92101-4495. TEL 619-230-1840. FAX 619-699-6800. URL: http://www.apnet.com/www/journal/ic.htm; http://www.idealibrary.com/ *2109*

INFORMATION & INTERACTIVE SERVICES REPORT.
Telecommunications Reports, 1333 H St., N.W., No. 100-E, Washington, DC 20005. TEL 202-842-3022. FAX 202-842-3047.
Vendor(s): Information Access Co., NewsNet (TE41). *6292*

INFORMATION EAUX.
Office International de l'Eau, Direction de la Documentation et des Donnees, Rue Edouard Chamberland, 87065 Limoges Cedex, France. TEL 55-11-47-80. FAX 55-77-71-15.
Vendor(s): European Space Agency (File no.73/AFEE). *7295*

THE INFORMATION FREEWAY REPORT.
Washington Researchers, Ltd., Box 19005, 20th St. Sta., Washington, DC 20036-9005. TEL 202-333-3499. FAX 202-625-0656. URL: http://www.researchers.com/pub/busintel/researchers.html.
Vendor(s): NewsNet. *2134*

INFORMATION LAW ALERT.
Voorhees Reports, 411 First St., Brooklyn, NY 11215-2507. URL: http://infolawalert.com/.
Vendor(s): Information Access Co. *5585*

INFORMATION MANAGEMENT REPORT.
Elsevier Science Ltd., P.O. Box 800, Kidlington, Oxford OX5 1DX, England. TEL 44-1865-843000. FAX 44-1865-843010. URL: http://www.elsevier.nl/.
Vendor(s): Data-Star (PTBN), Knight-Ridder Information, Inc. (File no.636). *4232*

INFORMATION OUTLOOK.
Special Libraries Association, 1700 18th St., N.W., Washington, DC 20009-2514. TEL 202-234-4700. FAX 202-265-9317.
Vendor(s): Information Access Co. *4184*

THE INFORMATION REPORT.
Washington Researchers, Ltd., Box 19005, 20th St. Sta., Washington, DC 20036-9005. TEL 202-333-3499. FAX 202-625-0656. URL: http://www.researchers.com/pub/busintel/researchers.html.
Vendor(s): NewsNet (IT08). *551*

INFORMATION RESEARCH NEWS.
University of Sheffield, Department of Information Studies, Western Bank, Sheffield S10 2TN, England. TEL 44-114-2768555. FAX 44-114-2780300. URL: http://www.shef.ac.uk/uni/academic/i-m/is/lecturer/ircont.html.
Available only online. *4184*

INFORMATION SCIENCE ABSTRACTS.
I F I - Plenum, 233 Spring St., New York, NY 10013. TEL 212-620-8000. FAX 212-463-0742.
Vendor(s): Knight-Ridder Information, Inc. (File no.202). *4226*

THE INFORMATION SOCIETY.
Taylor & Francis Inc., 1900 Frost Rd., Ste. 101, Bristol, PA 19007-1598. TEL 215-785-5800. FAX 215-785-5515. URL: http://www.ics.uci.edi/~kling/tis.html. *2183*

INFORMATION STRATEGY.
Economist Group, URL: http://www.info-strategy.com/. *972*

INFORMATION TECHNOLOGY AND LIBRARIES.
American Library Association, 50 E. Huron St, Chicago, IL 60611-2795. TEL 312-944-6780. FAX 312-440-9374.
Vendor(s): Information Access Co., UMI. *4185*

INFORMATION TECHNOLOGY DIGEST.
University of Michigan, Information Technology Division, 535 W. William Argus Bldg., Ann Arbor, MI 48103. TEL 313-763-8980. FAX 313-763-8937. URL: http://www.itd.umich.edu/ITDigest/. *2084*

INFORMATION TODAY.
Information Today, Inc., 143 Old Marlton Pike, Medford, NJ 08055. TEL 609-654-6266. FAX 609-654-4309.
Vendor(s): Information Access Co., Lexis-Nexis, UMI. *4232*

INFORMATION WEEK.
C M P Publications, Inc., 600 Community Dr., Manhasset, NY 11030. TEL 516-562-5000. FAX 516-562-7013.
Vendor(s): Information Access Co., NewsNet (TE34). *2167*

INFORMATIONS RECENTES SUR LES COMPTES NATIONAUX DES PAYS EN DEVELOPPEMENT.
Organization for Economic Cooperation and Development, 2 rue Andre-Pascal, 75775 Paris Cedex 16, France. *1362*

INFORMATIONSDIENST KRANKENHAUSWESEN.
Technische Universitaet Berlin, Institut fuer Gesundheitswesen, Str. des 17. Juni 135, 10623 Berlin, Germany. TEL 49-30-31423980. FAX 49-30-31424743. URL: http://www.tu-berlin.de/~heclinet.
Vendor(s): DIMDI. *3715*

INFORMATIONSDIENST PRAXISBEZOGENER LITERATUR IM WEINBAU.
Bundesanstalt fuer Zuechtungsforschung an Kulturpflanzen, Institut fuer Rebenzuechtung Geilweilerhof, 76833 Siebeldingen, Germany. TEL 49-6345-41-0. FAX 49-6345-41177.
Vendor(s): DIMDI, Knight-Ridder Information, Inc., STN International. *176*

INFORMAZIONE FILOSOFICA.
Ediform - Informazione e Cultura, Viale Monte Nero 68, 20135 Milan, Italy. TEL 39-2-55190714. FAX 39-2-55015245. URL: http://www.handson.it/infophil/. *5731*

INFORME LATINOAMERICANO.
Latin American Newsletters, 61 Old St., London EC1V 9HX, England. TEL 44-171-251-0012. FAX 44-171-253-8193.
Vendor(s): Lexis-Nexis. *1265*

INFOSYS.
Massey University, Information Systems Department, Albany, New Zealand. TEL 64-9-4418150. FAX 64-9-4418181.
Available only online. *2183*

INFOWORLD.
InfoWorld Publishing, 155 Bovet Rd., Ste. 800, San Mateo, CA 94402. TEL 415-572-7341. FAX 415-358-1269. URL: http://192.216.48.63/.
Vendor(s): Information Access Co., Lexis-Nexis, UMI. *2189*

INFOZINE: KANSAS CITY'S DIGITAL MAGAZINE.
Box 22661, Kansas City, MO 64113-2661. URL: http://www.infozine.com.
Available only online. *3376*

INHALATION TOXICOLOGY.
Taylor & Francis Inc., 1900 Frost Rd., Ste. 101, Bristol, PA 19007-1598. TEL 215-785-5800. FAX 215-785-5515. URL: http://www.tandf.co.uk/. *2978*

THE INHALER.
URL: http://darkshadow.com.au/inhaler/.
Available only online. *5400*

INJURY PREVENTION.
B M J Publishing Group, B.M.A. House, Tavistock Sq., London WC1H 9JR, England. TEL 44-171-383-9270. FAX 44-171-383-6402.
Vendor(s): Ovid Technologies, Inc. *5032*

INK & PRINT INTERNATIONAL.
Batiste Publications Ltd., Pembroke House, Campsbourne Rd., Hornsey, London N8 7PE, England. TEL 44-181-340-3291. FAX 44-181-341-4840.
Vendor(s): Information Access Co. *6080*

INKLINGS.
Inkspot, Toronto, ON, Canada. URL: http://www.inkspot.com/~ohi/ink/inklings.html.
Available only online. *2134*

INLINE.
Sports & Fitness Publishing, 2025 Pearl St., Boulder, CO 80302-4429. TEL 303-440-5111. FAX 303-440-3313. *6872*

INNOMINATE.
Sydney University Medical Society, Blackburn Bldg. D06, University of Sydney, Sydney, N.S.W. 2006, Australia. TEL 61-2-9351-2635. FAX 61-2-9351-6198. URL: http://www.blackburn.med.su.ua/medsoc/innom/ *1956*

INNOVATION.
NewsScan Inc., 1290 Oxford Rd., Box 15010, Atlanta, GA 30306. URL: http://www.newsscan.com.
Available only online. *972*

INNOVATION (ST. ANDREWS).
Longman Cartermill Ltd., Technology Centre, St. Andrews, Fife KY16 9EA, Scotland. TEL 44-1334-77660. *6533*

INNOVATIONS.
Stephen Kimber Associates, 2533 Beech St., Halifax, NS B3L 2X9, Canada. URL: http://www.innovations.org/ *6533*

INNOVATOR'S DIGEST.
Merton Allen Associates, InfoTeam Inc., Box 15640, Plantation, FL 33318-5640. TEL 954-473-9560. FAX 954-473-0544.
Vendor(s): Data-Star, Information Access Co., NewsNet (RD09), UMI. *6534*

INORGANIC CHEMISTRY.
American Chemical Society, 1155 16th St., N.W., Washington, DC 20036. TEL 800-333-9511. FAX 614-447-3671.
Vendor(s): STN International (CJACS). *1807*

INPHARMA WEEKLY.
Adis International Limited, Private Bag 65901, Mairangi Bay, Auckland 10, New Zealand. TEL 64-9-479-8100. FAX 64-9-479-8145. URL: http://www.adis.com.
Vendor(s): Data-Star (PHD,IPHC,IPHA,IPZZ), Knight-Ridder Information, Inc. (File no.428,429). *5701*

INQUISITOR.
Luna Grafika Design, Box 132, New York, NY 10024. TEL 212-595-8370. FAX 212-595-8370. URL: http://www.inquisitor.com. *3376*

INSIDE D O T & TRANSPORTATION WEEK.
Business Publishers, Inc., 951 Pershing Dr., Silver Spring, MD 20910-4464. TEL 301-587-6300. FAX 301-587-9075.
Vendor(s): Information Access Co., Lexis-Nexis, NewsNet (GT41). *7030*

INSIDE ENERGY WITH FEDERAL LANDS.
McGraw-Hill Companies, Energy & Business Newsletters, 1221 Ave. of the Americas, 36th Fl., New York, NY 10020. TEL 212-512-6410.
Vendor(s): Dow Jones News Retrieval (IE), Knight-Ridder Information, Inc. (File no.624/McGRAW-HILL PUBLICATIONS ONLINE), Lexis-Nexis (INERGY), NewsNet (EY69). *2671*

INSIDE EQUINE.
Equine Research Centre, University of Guelph, Guelph, ON N1G 2W1, Canada. TEL 519-837-0061. FAX 519-767-1081. *7271*

INSIDE F E R C.
McGraw-Hill Companies, 1221 Ave. of the Americas, New York, NY 10020.
Vendor(s): Dow Jones News Retrieval (FERC), Knight-Ridder Information, Inc. (File no.624/McGRAW-HILL PUBLICATIONS ONLINE), Lexis-Nexis (INFERC), NewsNet (EY70). *2671*

INSIDE F E R C'S GAS MARKET REPORT.
McGraw-Hill Companies, Energy & Business Newsletters, 1221 Ave. of the Americas, 36th Fl., New York, NY 10020. TEL 212-512-6410.
Vendor(s): Dow Jones News Retrieval (GSMR), Knight-Ridder Information, Inc. (File no.624/McGRAW-HILL PUBLICATIONS ONLINE), Lexis-Nexis (GASMKT), NewsNet (EY66). *5606*

INSIDE INDIANA.
Hoosier Publications Inc., P.O. Box 1231, 4615 E. Morningside Dr., Bloomington, IN 47408. TEL 812-334-9722. FAX 812-334-9756. *6809*

INSIDE M S.
National Multiple Sclerosis Society, 733 Third Ave., New York, NY 10017-3288. TEL 212-986-3240. FAX 212-986-7981. URL: http://www.nmss.org.
Vendor(s): Information Access Co. *5069*

INSIDE N R C.
McGraw-Hill Companies, Energy and Business Newsletters, 1221 Ave. of the Americas, 36th Fl., New York, NY 10020.
Vendor(s): Dow Jones News Retrieval (NRC), Knight-Ridder Information, Inc. (File no.624/McGRAW-HILL PUBLICATIONS ONLINE), Lexis-Nexis (INNRC), NewsNet (EY71). *2698*

INSIDE THE NEW COMPUTER INDUSTRY.
25420 Via Cicindela, Carmel, CA 93923-8412. TEL 408-626-4361. FAX 408-626-4362. URL: http://www.aallison.com. *2084*

INSIDE U S TRADE.
Inside Washington Publishers, Box 7167, Ben Franklin Sta., Washington, DC 20044-7167. TEL 703-416-8500. FAX 703-416-8543. URL: http://www.insidetrade.com. *1330*

INSIDER HOLDINGS.
C D A Investment Technologies, Inc., 1355 Piccard Dr., Rockville, MD 20850. FAX 301-590-1329. *1388*

INSIDER VIEWPOINT MAGAZINE.
URL: http://www.insidervlv.com. *6765*

INSIDERS SKI LETTER.
Skiletter, Inc., 115 Lilly Pond Ln., Katonah, NY 10536. TEL 914-232-5094. *6872*

INSIGHT ON THE NEWS.
Washington Times Corporation, 3600 New York Ave., N.E., Washington, DC 20002. TEL 202-636-8800. FAX 202-529-2484. URL: http://www.capital.washtimes.weekly.com.
Vendor(s): Information Access Co. *3376*

INSTANT MAGAZINE.
Instant Entertainment, Box 2224, Woburn, MA 01888-0324. TEL 617-246-0334. FAX 617-246-0587. URL: http://www.instantmag.com. *5400*

INSTITUT FOURIER. ANNALES.
Association des Annales de l'Institut Fourier, B.P. 74, 38402 Saint-Martin-d'Heres Cedex, France. FAX 33-4-76514478. URL: http://www.fourier.ujf-grenoble.fr/afif.html. *4577*

INSTITUT NATIONAL DE RECHERCHE EN INFORMATIQUE ET EN AUTOMATIQUE. RAPPORTS DE RECHERCHE.
Institut National de Recherche en Informatique et en Automatique, Sedis Diffusion, B.P. 105, 78153 Le Chesnay Cedex, France. TEL 33-1-39635511. FAX 33-1-39635228. URL: http://www.inria.fr/RRRT/publications-fra.html; http://www.inria.fr/RRRT/publications-eng.html. *2084*

INSTITUTE FOR PHILOSOPHY AND PUBLIC POLICY. REPORT.
Institute for Philosophy and Public Policy, 3rd Fl., Van Munching Hall, University of Maryland, College Park, MD 20742. TEL 301-405-4753. FAX 301-314-9346. URL: http://www.puaf.umd.edu/ippp. *5731*

INSTITUTE OF ASIAN STUDIES. JOURNAL.
Institute of Asian Studies, Chemmancherry, Sholinganallur Post, Madras 600 119, India. TEL 91-44-416728. FAX 91-44-419866. *6713*

INSTITUTE OF BRITISH GEOGRAPHERS. TRANSACTIONS.
Royal Geographical Society, 1 Kensington Gore, London SW7 2AR, England. TEL 44-171-591-3000. FAX 44-171-591-3001. URL: http://ppt.geog.qmw.ac.uk. *3410*

INSTITUTE OF ELECTRICAL AND ELECTRONICS ENGINEERS. PROCEEDINGS.
Institute of Electrical and Electronics Engineers, Inc., 345 E. 47th St., New York, NY 10017-2394. TEL 732-981-0060. FAX 732-981-9667. URL: http://www.ieee.org.
Vendor(s): OCLC. *2834*

INSTITUTE OF PAPER SCIENCE AND TECHNOLOGY. ABSTRACT BULLETIN.
Institute of Paper Science and Technology, 500 10th St., N.W., Atlanta, GA 30318. TEL 404-894-5726. FAX 404-894-4778.
Vendor(s): Knight-Ridder Information, Inc. (File nos.240 & 840/PAPERCHEM), STN International (PAPERCHEM2). *5574*

INSTITUTE OF PHYSICS CONFERENCE SERIES.
I O P Publishing Ltd., Dirac House, Temple Back, Bristol BS1 6BE, England. TEL 44-117-929-7481. FAX 44-117-929-4318. URL: http://www.iop.org. *5806*

INSTITUTIONAL INVESTOR.
Institutional Investor, Inc., 488 Madison Ave., New York, NY 10022. TEL 212-224-3570. FAX 212-224-3592.
Vendor(s): Information Access Co. *1389*

THE INSTITUTIONAL REAL ESTATE LETTER.
Institutional Real Estate, Inc., 1475 N. Broadway, Ste. 300, Walnut Creek, CA 94596. TEL 510-933-4040. FAX 510-934-4099. *6303*

INSTRUCTOR.
Scholastic Inc., 555 Broadway, New York, NY 10012-3999. TEL 212-643-6100.
Vendor(s): Information Access Co. *2451*

INSTRUMENTATION AND CONTROL SYSTEMS.
Chilton Co., One Chilton Way, Radnor, PA 19089. TEL 610-964-4417. FAX 610-964-2919. URL: http://www.chilton.net/ics/index.htm.
Vendor(s): Knight-Ridder Information, Inc. *3802*

INSURANCE ACCOUNTANT.
American Banker - Bond Buyer, Newsletter Division One State St. Plaza, New York, NY 10004-1549. TEL 800-733-4371. FAX 212-943-2224.
Vendor(s): Information Access Co. *3819*

INSURANCE AND TECHNOLOGY.
Miller Freeman Inc. (New York), One Penn Plaza, New York, NY 10119. TEL 212-714-1300. FAX 212-302-6273.
Vendor(s): UMI. *3840*

INSURANCE BROKERS' MONTHLY AND INSURANCE ADVISER.
Insurance Publishing & Printing Co., 7 Stourbridge Rd., Lye, Stourbridge, W. Midlands DY9 7DG, England.
Vendor(s): UMI. *3819*

INSURANCE PERIODICALS INDEX.
N I L S Publishing Company, 21625 Prairie St., Box 2507, Chatsworth, CA 91311. TEL 818-998-8830. FAX 818-718-8482.
Vendor(s): Knight-Ridder Information, Inc. (File no.169), Lexis-Nexis, West Group. *3839*

INSURANCE REGULATOR.
American Banker - Bond Buyer, Newsletter Division One State St. Plaza, New York, NY 10004-1549. TEL 800-733-4371. FAX 212-943-2224.
Vendor(s): Information Access Co. *3820*

INTANGIBLE.
Intangible Publications, Inc., 1430 Williamette, Ste. 200, Eugene, OR 97401. URL: http://www.intangible.org.
Available only online. *4416*

INTEGRATED CIRCUITS INTERNATIONAL.
Elsevier Science Ltd., P.O. Box 800, Kidlington, Oxford OX5 1DX, England. TEL 44-1865-843000. FAX 44-1865-843010. URL: http://www.elsevier.nl/.
Vendor(s): Data-Star, Information Access Co., Knight-Ridder Information, Inc. *2112*

INTEGRATED FERROELECTRICS.
Gordon and Breach - Harwood Academic, Amsteldisk 166, 1st Fl., 1079 LH Amsterdam, Netherlands. URL: http://www.gbhap.com/Integrated__Ferroelectrics/. *2835*

INTEGRATED PEST MANAGEMENT REVIEWS.
Thomson Science, 2-6 Boundary Row, London SE1 8HN, England. TEL 44-171-8650066. FAX 44-171-5229623. URL: http://www.thomsonscience.com. *229*

INTEGRATED WASTE MANAGEMENT.
McGraw-Hill Companies, Energy & Business Newsletters, 1221 Ave. of the Americas, 36th Fl., New York, NY 10020. TEL 212-512-6410.
Vendor(s): Dow Jones News Retrieval, Knight-Ridder Information, Inc. (File no. 624/McGRAW-HILL PUBLICATIONS ONLINE), Lexis-Nexis, NewsNet (EV40). *2986*

INTELLIGENT DATA ANALYSIS.
Elsevier Science Inc., Box 945, New York, NY 10159-0945. TEL 212-633-3730. FAX 212-633-3990. URL: http://www-east.elsevier.com/ida/Menu.html.
Available only online. *2100*

INTELLIGENT MANUFACTURING.
Lionheart Publishing, Inc., P.O. Box 159, Kent, OH 44240-0003. TEL 330-677-4210. FAX 330-678-9011. URL: http://lionhrtpub.com/IM/IM-welcome.html. *1587*

INTELLIGENT SOFTWARE STRATEGIES.
Cutter Information Corp., 37 Broadway, Arlington, MA 02174. TEL 617-648-8700. FAX 617-648-1950. *2100*

INTELLIGENT SYSTEMS REPORT.
Lionheart Publishing, Inc., 2555 Cumberland Pkwy., Ste. 299, Atlanta, GA 30339. TEL 770-431-0967. FAX 770-432-6969. URL: http://lionhrtpub.com/ISR/ISR-welcome.html. *2100*

INTENSIVE CARE MEDICINE.
Springer-Verlag, Heidelberger Platz 3, 14197 Berlin, Germany. TEL 49-30-82787-0. FAX 49-30-82787448. URL: http://link.springer.de. *4685*

INTERACTIVE CONTENT.
Jupiter Communications, 627 Broadway, New York, NY 10012. TEL 212-780-6060. FAX 212-780-6075. URL: http://www.jup.com.
Vendor(s): Information Access Co. *2134*

INTERACTIVE HOME.
Jupiter Communications, 627 Broadway, New York, NY 10012. TEL 212-780-6060. FAX 212-780-6075.
Vendor(s): Information Access Co., NewsNet. *6963*

INTERACTIVE VIDEO NEWS.
Phillips Business Information, Inc., 1201 Seven Locks Rd., Potomac, MD 20854. TEL 301-424-3338. FAX 301-309-3847.
Vendor(s): Information Access Co., NewsNet (AD07). *1531*

INTERACTIVITY.
Miller Freeman, Inc. (San Mateo), 411 Borel Ave., Ste. 100, San Mateo, CA 94402. TEL 415-358-9500. FAX 415-655-4360. URL: http://www.eyemedia.com. *2123*

INTER-AMERICAN LAW REVIEW.
University of Miami, School of Law, Box 248087, Coral Gables, FL 33124. TEL 305-284-5562.
Vendor(s): West Group. *4116*

INTER-AMERICAN TRADE AND INVESTMENT LAW.
National Law Center for Inter-American Free Trade, 111 S. Church Ave., Ste. 200, Tucson, AZ 85701-1629. TEL 620-622-1200. FAX 602-622-0957. URL: http://www.natlaw.com. *4116*

INTER-CORPORATE OWNERSHIP.
Statistics Canada, Operations and Integration Division, Circulation Management, Jean Talon Bldg., 2-C12, Tunney's Pasture, Ottawa, ON K1A 0T6, Canada. TEL 613-951-7277. FAX 613-951-1584. URL: http://www.statcan.ca.
Vendor(s): Southam Electronic Publishing. *1213*

INTER-FACE.
URL: http://www.albany.edu/'interface.
Available only online. *4511*

INTERFACE (BOSTON SPA).
British Library, National Bibliographic Service, Boston Spa, Wetherby, W. Yorks. LS23 7BQ, England. TEL 44-9137-546585. FAX 44-1935-546586. URL: http://portico.bl.uk/nbs/interf/ *4232*

INTERIOR DESIGN.
Cahners Publishing Company (New York), Design Division, Division of Reed Elsevier Inc., 245 W. 17th St., New York, NY 10011. TEL 212-463-6706. FAX 212-242-6667. URL: http://www.cahners.com/mainmag/id.htm.
Vendor(s): Information Access Co. *3847*

INTERIORS: FOR THE CONTRACT DESIGN PROFESSIONAL.
B P I Communications, Inc. (New York), 1515 Broadway, 11th Fl., New York, NY 10036. TEL 212-536-5141. FAX 212-536-5357.
Vendor(s): Information Access Co.. *3847*

INTERLINK HEADLINE NEWS.
URL: http://www.webcom.com/~poetas/interlink/ilhn.html.
Available only online. *3249*

INTERNAL AUDITOR.
Institute of Internal Auditors, Inc., 249 Maitland Ave., Altamonte Springs, FL 32701-4201. TEL 407-830-7600. FAX 407-831-5171. URL: http://www.rutgers.edu/Accounting/raw/iia.
Vendor(s): Information Access Co., UMI. *1091*

INTERNAL REVENUE MANUAL - AUDIT AND ADMINISTRATION.
C C H Inc., 2700 Lake Cook Rd., Riverwoods, IL 60015. TEL 847-267-7000. *1614*

INTERNATIONAL AFFAIRS.
East View Publications, 3020 Harbor Lane N., Plymouth, MN 55447. TEL 612-550-0961. FAX 612-559-2931. *6019*

INTERNATIONAL ARCHIVES OF OCCUPATIONAL AND ENVIRONMENTAL HEALTH.
Springer-Verlag, Heidelberger Platz 3, 14197 Berlin, Germany. TEL 49-30-82787-0. FAX 49-30-82787448. URL: http://link.springer.de. *5492*

INTERNATIONAL ASTRONOMICAL UNION. CENTRAL BUREAU FOR ASTRONOMICAL TELEGRAMS. CIRCULAR.
Smithsonian Institution Astrophysical Observatory, 60 Garden St., Cambridge, MA 02138. TEL 617-495-7280. FAX 617-495-7231. *495*

INTERNATIONAL ASTRONOMICAL UNION. MINOR PLANET CENTER. MINOR PLANET CIRCULARS - MINOR PLANETS AND COMETS.
Smithsonian Institution Astrophysical Observatory, 60 Garden St., Cambridge, MA 02138. TEL 617-495-7280. FAX 617-495-7231. URL: http://cfa-www.harvard.edu/cfa/ps/services/MPC.html. *495*

INTERNATIONAL BANKING REGULATOR.
American Banker - Bond Buyer, Newsletter Division One State St. Plaza, New York, NY 10004-1549. TEL 800-733-4371. FAX 212-943-2224.
Vendor(s): Information Access Co., NewsNet (IT36). *1146*

INTERNATIONAL BIBLIOGRAPHY OF THE SOCIAL SCIENCES. ECONOMICS.
Routledge, 11 New Fetter Ln., London EC4P 4EE, England. TEL 44-171-583-9855. FAX 44-171-583-0701. URL: http://www.routledge.com/routledge/journal/journals.html.
Vendor(s): QL Systems Ltd. *1048*

INTERNATIONAL BIBLIOGRAPHY OF THE SOCIAL SCIENCES. SOCIAL AND CULTURAL ANTHROPOLOGY.
Routledge, 11 New Fetter Lane, London EC4P 4EE, England. TEL 44-171-583-9855. FAX 44-171-583-0701. URL: http://www.routledge.com/routledge/journal/journals.html.
Vendor(s): QL Systems Ltd. *335*

INTERNATIONAL BIODETERIORATION & BIODEGRADATION.
Elsevier Science Ltd., P.O. Box 800, Kidlington, Oxford OX5 1DX, England. TEL 44-1865-843000. FAX 44-1865-843010. URL: http://www.elsevier.nl/.
Vendor(s): CISTI, DIMDI, European Space Agency (File nos.16 & 124/CAB), Knight-Ridder Information, Inc., Ovid Technologies, Inc. *683*

INTERNATIONAL BRANDS AND THEIR COMPANIES.
Gale Research, 835 Penobscot Bldg., 645 Griswold St., Detroit, MI 48226-4094. TEL 313-961-2242. FAX 800-414-5043.
Vendor(s): Knight-Ridder Information, Inc. *5586*

INTERNATIONAL BUILDING SERVICES ABSTRACTS.
Building Services Research and Information Association, Old Bracknell Ln. W., Bracknell, Berks. RG12 7AH, England. TEL 44-1344-426511. FAX 44-1344-487575. *3486*

INTERNATIONAL BULLETIN OF MISSIONARY RESEARCH.
Overseas Ministries Study Center, 490 Prospect St., New Haven, CT 06511-2196. TEL 203-624-6672.
Vendor(s): Information Access Co., UMI. *6429*

INTERNATIONAL BULLETIN ON ATOMIC AND MOLECULAR DATA FOR FUSION.
International Atomic Energy Agency, Wagramerstr. 5, P.O. Box 100, A-1400 Vienna, Austria. TEL 43-1-20600. FAX 43-1-20607. *2698*

INTERNATIONAL BUSINESS.
New Media Productions, 9 E. 40th St., 10 Fl., New York, NY 10016. TEL 212-683-2426.
Vendor(s): UMI. *1331*

INTERNATIONAL CALIFORNIA MINING JOURNAL.
California Mining Journal, Inc., Box 2260, Aptos, CA 95001. TEL 408-662-2899. FAX 408-662-3014. URL: http://www.icmj.com. *5303*

INTERNATIONAL COAL REPORT.
Financial Times Energy Publishing, Maple House, 149 Tottenham Court Rd., London W1P 9LL, England. TEL 44-171-896-2241. FAX 44-171-896-2275.
Vendor(s): Data-Star, Information Access Co., Knight-Ridder Information, Inc., Lexis-Nexis. *5303*

INTERNATIONAL COMMERCIAL LITIGATION (LONDON, 1990).
Euromoney Publications plc., Nestor House, Playhouse Yard, London EC4V 5EX, England. TEL 44-171-779-8935. FAX 44-171-779-8541.
Vendor(s): UMI. *4082*

INTERNATIONAL COUNTERTERRORISM & SECURITY.
Counterterrorism & Security, Inc., Box 10265, Arlington, VA 22210. TEL 703-243-0993. FAX 703-243-1197. URL: http://www.securitynet.net.
Vendor(s): NewsNet. *2286*

INTERNATIONAL COUNTRY RISK GUIDE.
The P R S Group, Box 248, East Syracuse, NY 13057-0248. TEL 315-431-0511. FAX 315-431-0200.
Vendor(s): Data-Star, Knight-Ridder Information, Inc., Lexis-Nexis. *1265*

INTERNATIONAL DEFENSE REVIEW.
Jane's Information Group, Sentinel House, 163 Brighton Rd., Coulsdon, Surrey CR5 2NH, England. TEL 44-181-700-3700. FAX 44-181-700-3846.
Vendor(s): Knight-Ridder Information, Inc., Lexis-Nexis. *5271*

INTERNATIONAL DEVELOPMENT ABSTRACTS.
Elsevier - Geo Abstracts, Regency House, 34 Duke St., Norwich NR3 3AP, England. TEL 44-1603-626327. FAX 44-1603-667934. URL: http://www.elsevier.nl/.
Vendor(s): Knight-Ridder Information, Inc. (File no.292), Questel Orbit Inc. *3428*

INTERNATIONAL DEVELOPMENT RESEARCH CENTRE. ANNUAL REPORT.
International Development Research Centre, Box 8500, Ottawa, ON K1G 3H9, Canada. TEL 613-236-6163. FAX 613-563-2476. URL: http://www.idrc.ca.
Available only online. *973*

INTERNATIONAL DIRECTORY OF DESIGN.
Penrose Press, Box 470925, San Francisco, CA 94147. TEL 415-567-4157. FAX 415-567-4165. URL: http://www.penrose-press.com/idd/. *448*

INTERNATIONAL ENERGY ANNUAL.
U.S. Energy Information Administration, National Energy Information Center, EI-231, James Forrestal Bldg., Rm. 1F-048, 1000 Independence Ave., S.W., Washington, DC 20585. TEL 202-586-8800. FAX 202-586-0727. *2672*

INTERNATIONAL ENVIRONMENT REPORTER.
The Bureau of National Affairs, Inc., 1231 25th St., N.W., Washington, DC 20037. TEL 202-452-4200. FAX 202-822-8092. URL: http://www.bna.com/
Vendor(s): Lexis-Nexis (File INTENV). *2934*

INTERNATIONAL EXAMINER.
622 S. Washington, Seattle, WA 98104. *3018*

INTERNATIONAL FINANCIAL LAW REVIEW.
Euromoney Publications plc., Nestor House, Playhouse Yard, London EC4V 5EX, England. TEL 44-171-779-8935. FAX 44-171-779-8541.
Vendor(s): UMI. *4118*

INTERNATIONAL FINANCIAL STATISTICS.
International Monetary Fund, Publications Unit, 700 19th St., N.W., Washington, DC 20431. TEL 202-623-7430. FAX 202-623-7201.
Vendor(s): National Data Corp. *1048*

INTERNATIONAL FOOD MANUFACTURE.
Miller Freeman Technical Ltd., Miller Freeman House, 30 Calderwood St., London SE18 6QH, England. TEL 44-181-855-7777. FAX 44-181-316-3206.
Vendor(s): Information Access Co. *3114*

INTERNATIONAL GAS REPORT.
Financial Times Energy Publishing, Maple House, 149 Tottenham Court Rd., London W1P 9LL, England. TEL 44-171-896-2241. FAX 44-171-896-2275.
Vendor(s): Data-Star, Information Access Co., Knight-Ridder Information, Inc., Lexis-Nexis. *5606*

INTERNATIONAL GAS TECHNOLOGY HIGHLIGHTS.
Institute of Gas Technology, 1700 S. Mt. Prospect Rd., Des Plaines, IL 60018. TEL 708-768-0512. FAX 708-768-0516.
Available only online. *5606*

INTERNATIONAL IMMUNOLOGY.
Oxford University Press, Academic Division, Great Clarendon St., Oxford OX2 6DP, England. TEL 44-1865-267907. FAX 44-1865-267485. URL: http://www.oup.co.uk/journals. *4797*

THE INTERNATIONAL INFORMATION AND LIBRARY REVIEW.
Academic Press Ltd., 24-28 Oval Rd., London NW1 7DX, England. TEL 44-171-482-2293. FAX 44-171-482-2293. URL: http://www.hbuk.co.uk/ap/iilr; http://www.europe.idealibrary.com. *4186*

THE INTERNATIONAL INFORMATION REPORT.
Washington Researchers, Ltd., Box 19005, 20th St. Sta., Washington, DC 20036-9005. TEL 202-333-3499. FAX 202-625-0656. URL: http://www.researchers.com/pub/busintel/researchers.html.
Vendor(s): NewsNet (IT75). *552*

INTERNATIONAL INSURANCE MONITOR.
International Insurance Monitor, Box 9001, Mt. Vernon, NY 10552. TEL 914-699-2020.
Vendor(s): UMI. *3821*

INTERNATIONAL JOINT COMMISSION. BIENNIAL REPORT ON GREAT LAKES WATER QUALITY.
International Joint Commission, Great Lakes Regional Office, 100 Ouellette Ave., 8th Fl., Windsor, ON N9A 6T3, Canada. TEL 519-257-6700. FAX 519-257-6740. URL: http://www.ijc.org. *2877*

INTERNATIONAL JOURNAL OF ADVANCED MANUFACTURING TECHNOLOGY.
Springer-Verlag London Ltd., Sweetapple House, Catteshall Rd., Godalming, Surrey GU7 3DJ, England. TEL 44-1483-418800. FAX 44-1483-415144. *2887*

INTERNATIONAL JOURNAL OF ADVERTISING.
Blackwell Publishers Ltd., 108 Cowley Rd., Oxford OX4 1JF, England. TEL 44-1865-791100. FAX 44-1865-791347. URL: http://www.blackwellpublishers.co.uk/scripts/webjrnl.idc?issn02650487.
Vendor(s): Information Access Co. *37*

INTERNATIONAL JOURNAL OF BIOMETEOROLOGY.
Springer-Verlag, Heidelberger Platz 3, 14197 Berlin, Germany. TEL 49-30-82787-0. FAX 49-30-82787448. URL: http://link.springer.de; http://www.springer.ny.com/ *5235*

INTERNATIONAL JOURNAL OF CLINICAL PRACTICE.
Medicom International Ltd., Churston House, Portsmouth Rd., Esher, Surrey KT10 9AD, England. TEL 44-1372-471671. FAX 44-1372-471672. *4686*

INTERNATIONAL JOURNAL OF COLORECTAL DISEASE.
Springer-Verlag, Heidelberger Platz 3, 14197 Berlin, Germany. TEL 49-30-82787-0. FAX 49-30-82787448. URL: http://link.springer.de. *5143*

INTERNATIONAL JOURNAL OF COMPARATIVE SOCIOLOGY.
E.J. Brill, P.O. Box 9000, 2300 PA Leiden, Netherlands. TEL 31-71-5353500. FAX 31-71-5317532.
Vendor(s): Information Access Co. *6714*

INTERNATIONAL JOURNAL OF COMPUTATIONAL FLUID DYNAMICS.
Gordon and Breach - Harwood Academic, Amsteldisk 166, 1st Fl., 1079 LH Amsterdam, Netherlands. URL: http://www.gbhap.com/Computational_Fluid_Dynamics/. *5845*

INTERNATIONAL JOURNAL OF COMPUTATIONAL INTELLIGENCE AND ORGANIZATIONS.
Lawrence Erlbaum Associates, Inc., 10 Industrial Ave., Mahwah, NJ 07430-2262. TEL 201-236-9500. URL: http://www.ecst.csuchico.edu/~ijcio/aims.html. *2101*

INTERNATIONAL JOURNAL OF COMPUTER INTEGRATED MANUFACTURING.
Taylor & Francis Ltd., 1 Gunpowder Sq., London EC4A 3DE, England. TEL 44-171-583-0490. FAX 44-171-583-0585. URL: http://www.tandfco.uk/jnls/cim.htm. *1202*

INTERNATIONAL JOURNAL OF COMPUTER MATHEMATICS.
Gordon and Breach - Harwood Academic, Amsteldisk 166, 1st Fl., 1079 LH Amsterdam, Netherlands. URL: http://www.gbhap.com/Computer_Mathematics/. *4621*

INTERNATIONAL JOURNAL OF CONTROL.
Taylor & Francis Ltd., 1 Gunpowder Sq., London EC4A 3DE, England. TEL 44-171-583-0490. FAX 44-171-583-0585. URL: http://www.tandf.co.uk/jnls/cona.htm. *2726*

INTERNATIONAL JOURNAL OF COSMETIC SCIENCE.
Thomson Science, 2-6 Boundary Row, London SE1 8HN, England. TEL 44-171-8650066. FAX 44-171-5229623. URL: http://www.thomsonscience.com. *511*

INTERNATIONAL JOURNAL OF ELECTRONICS.
Taylor & Francis Ltd., 1 Gunpowder Sq., London EC4A 3DE, England. TEL 44-171-583-0490. FAX 44-171-583-0585. URL: http://www.tandf.co.uk/. *2643*

INTERNATIONAL JOURNAL OF ENVIRONMENTAL ANALYTICAL CHEMISTRY.
Gordon and Breach - Harwood Academic, Amsteldisk 166, 1st Fl., 1079 LH Amsterdam, Netherlands. URL: http://www.gbhap.com/Environmental_Analytical_Chemistry/. *1791*

INTERNATIONAL JOURNAL OF ENVIRONMENTAL STUDIES. SECTIONS A & B.
Gordon and Breach - Harwood Academic, Amsteldisk 166, 1st Fl., 1079 LH Amsterdam, Netherlands. URL: http://www.gbhap.com/Environmental_Studies_A_B/. *2935*

INTERNATIONAL JOURNAL OF FLUID DYNAMICS.
Monash University, Department of Mechanical Engineering, Clayton 3168, Australia. TEL 61-3-99059624. FAX 61-3-99059639. URL: http://www.monash.edu.au/cc/staff/men/mecheng/ijfd/announce.html.
Available only online. *5845*

INTERNATIONAL JOURNAL OF FORENSIC DOCUMENT EXAMINERS.
Shunderson Communications, P.O. Box 42057, Ottawa, ON K1K 4L8, Canada. TEL 613-830-4750. FAX 613-830-9654.
Vendor(s): West Group. *2269*

INTERNATIONAL JOURNAL OF GENERAL SYSTEMS.
Gordon and Breach - Harwood Academic, Amsteldisk 166, 1st Fl., 1079 LH Amsterdam, Netherlands. URL: http://www.gbhap.com/General_Systems/. *2156*

INTERNATIONAL JOURNAL OF GEOGRAPHICAL INFORMATION SCIENCE.
Taylor & Francis Ltd., 1 Gunpowder Sq., London EC4A 3DE, England. TEL 44-171-583-0490. FAX 44-171-583-0585. URL: http://www.tandf.co.uk/. *3429*

INTERNATIONAL JOURNAL OF GOVERNMENT AUDITING.
International Organization of Supreme Audit Institutions, c/o U.S. General Accounting Office, 441 G St., N.W., Rm.7806, Washington, DC 20548. TEL 202-512-4707. FAX 1-202-512-4021.
Vendor(s): UMI. *6179*

INTERNATIONAL JOURNAL OF HEALTH SERVICES.
Baywood Publishing Co., Inc., 26 Austin Ave., Box 337, Amityville, NY 11701. TEL 516-691-1270. FAX 516-691-1770. URL: http://baywood.com. *6240*

INTERNATIONAL JOURNAL OF HUMAN-COMPUTER STUDIES.
Academic Press Ltd., 24-28 Oval Rd., London NW1 7DX, England. TEL 44-171-2674466. FAX 44-171-4822293. URL: http://www.hbuk.co.uk/ap/iijhcs; http://www.europe.idealibrary.com/ *2162*

INTERNATIONAL JOURNAL OF HUMAN RESOURCES MANAGEMENT.
Thomson Professional, 2-6 Boundary Row, London SE1 8HN, England. TEL 44-171-865-0066. FAX 44-171-522-9621. URL: http://hrm.thomsonprofessional.com. *1569*

INTERNATIONAL JOURNAL OF MANPOWER.
M C B University Press Ltd., 60-62 Toller Ln., Bradford, W. Yorks BD8 9BY, England. TEL 44-1274-777700. FAX 44-1274-785200. URL: http://www.mcb.co.uk.
Vendor(s): Information Access Co. *1437*

INTERNATIONAL JOURNAL OF NAUTICAL ARCHAEOLOGY.
Academic Press Ltd., 24-28 Oval Rd., London NW1 7DX, England. TEL 44-171-267-4466. FAX 44-171-482-2293. URL: http://www.hbuk.co.uk/ap/ijna; http://europe.idealibrary.com/ *367*

INTERNATIONAL JOURNAL OF NEUROSCIENCE.
Gordon and Breach - Harwood Academic, Amsteldisk 166, 1st Fl., 1079 LH Amsterdam, Netherlands. URL: http://www.gbhap.com/Neuroscience/. *5069*

INTERNATIONAL JOURNAL OF OPERATIONS AND PRODUCTION MANAGEMENT.
M C B University Press Ltd., 60-62 Toller Ln., Bradford, W. Yorks BD8 9BY, England. TEL 44-1274-777700. FAX 44-1274-785200. URL: http://www.mcb.co.uk/cgi-bin/mcb_serve/table1.txt&ijopm&journal1.htm.
Vendor(s): Information Access Co. *1484*

INTERNATIONAL JOURNAL OF PARALLEL PROGRAMMING.
Plenum Publishing Corp., 233 Spring St., New York, NY 10013-1578. TEL 212-620-8000. FAX 212-463-0742. URL: http://ns1.infor.com:6800/cgi/getrarec/ple200000087. *2144*

INTERNATIONAL JOURNAL OF PEDIATRIC HEMATOLOGY - ONCOLOGY.
Gordon and Breach - Harwood Academic, Amsteldisk 166, 1st Fl., 1079 LH Amsterdam, Netherlands. URL: http://www.gbhap.com/Pediatric_Hematology_Oncology/. *4980*

INTERNATIONAL JOURNAL OF PEST MANAGEMENT.
Taylor & Francis Ltd., 1 Gunpowder Sq., London EC4A 3DE, England. TEL 44-171-583-0490. FAX 44-171-583-0585. URL: http://www.tandf.co.uk/. *230*

INTERNATIONAL JOURNAL OF PHARMACEUTICS.
Elsevier Science B.V., P.O. Box 211, 1000 AE Amsterdam, Netherlands. TEL 31-20-4853911. FAX 31-20-4853598. URL: http://www.elsevier.nl/. *5668*

INTERNATIONAL JOURNAL OF PHARMACOGNOSY.
Swets & Zeitlinger bv, P.O. Box 825, 2160 SZ Lisse, Netherlands. TEL 31-252-435111. FAX 31-252-415888. URL: http://www.swets.nl. *5668*

INTERNATIONAL JOURNAL OF PHYSICAL DISTRIBUTION & LOGISTICS MANAGEMENT.
M C B University Press Ltd., 60-62 Toller Ln., Bradford, W. Yorks BD8 9BY, England. TEL 44-1274-777700. FAX 44-1274-785200. URL: http://www.mcb.co.uk/cgi-bin/mcb_serve/table1&jjpdlm&journal1.htm.
Vendor(s): Information Access Co. *7175*

INTERNATIONAL JOURNAL OF POLYMER ANALYSIS & CHARACTERIZATION.
Gordon and Breach - Harwood Academic, Amsteldisk 166, 1st Fl., 1079 LH Amsterdam, Netherlands. URL: http://www.gbhap.com/Polymer_Analysis_Characterization/. *2766*

INTERNATIONAL JOURNAL OF POLYMERIC MATERIALS.
Gordon and Breach - Harwood Academic, Amsteldisk 166, 1st Fl., 1079 LH Amsterdam, Netherlands. URL: http://www.gbhap.com/Polymeric_Materials/. *2766*

INTERNATIONAL JOURNAL OF PRODUCTION RESEARCH.
Taylor & Francis Ltd., 1 Gunpowder Sq., London EC4A 3DE, England. TEL 44-171-583-0490. FAX 44-171-583-0585. URL: http://www.tandf.co.uk/e-pub.cwonline.htm prs. *1588*

INTERNATIONAL JOURNAL OF PUBLIC ADMINISTRATION.
Marcel Dekker Journals, 270 Madison Ave., New York, NY 10016. TEL 212-696-9000. FAX 212-685-4540.
Vendor(s): Information Access Co. *6179*

SERIALS AVAILABLE ONLINE

INTERNATIONAL JOURNAL OF PUNJAB STUDIES.
Sage Publications India Pvt. Ltd., Box 4215, New Delhi 110 048, India. TEL 91-11-644-4958. FAX 91-11-647-2426. *6620*

INTERNATIONAL JOURNAL OF PURCHASING & MATERIALS MANAGEMENT.
National Association of Purchasing Management, 2055 E. Centennial Circle, Box 22160, Tempe, AZ 85285-2160. TEL 602-752-6276. FAX 602-752-7890. URL: http://www.napm.org/pub/ijpmm.html. Vendor(s): Information Access Co., Knight-Ridder Information, Inc., UMI. *1531*

INTERNATIONAL JOURNAL OF QUALITATIVE STUDIES IN EDUCATION.
Taylor & Francis Ltd., Rankine Rd., Basingstoke, Hants RG24 8PR, England. TEL 44-1256-840366. FAX 44-1256-479438. URL: http://www.tandf.co.uk/. *2452*

INTERNATIONAL JOURNAL OF QUALITY & RELIABILITY MANAGEMENT.
M C B University Press Ltd., 60-62 Toller Ln., Bradford, W. Yorks BD8 9BY, England. TEL 44-1274-777700. FAX 44-1274-785200. URL: http://www.mcb.co.uk. Vendor(s): Information Access Co. *1484*

INTERNATIONAL JOURNAL OF QUALITY SCIENCE.
M C B University Press Ltd., 60-62 Toller Ln., Bradford, W. Yorks BD8 9BY, England. TEL 44-1274-777700. FAX 44-1274-785200. URL: http://www.mcb.co.uk. *1485*

INTERNATIONAL JOURNAL OF RADIATION BIOLOGY.
Taylor & Francis Ltd., 1 Gunpowder Sq., London EC4A 3DE, England. TEL 44-171-583-0490. FAX 44-171-583-0585. URL: http://www.tandf.co.uk/. *4980*

INTERNATIONAL JOURNAL OF REHABILITATION RESEARCH.
Thomson Science, 2-6 Boundary Row, London SE1 8HN, England. TEL 44-171-865-0198. FAX 44-171-410-6600. URL: http://www.chaphall.com/chaphall/journals.html. *3455*

INTERNATIONAL JOURNAL OF REMOTE SENSING.
Taylor & Francis Ltd., 1 Gunpowder Sq., London EC4A 3DE, England. TEL 44-171-583-0490. FAX 44-171-583-0585. URL: http://www.tandf.co.uk/. *2317*

INTERNATIONAL JOURNAL OF RETAIL & DISTRIBUTION MANAGEMENT.
M C B University Press Ltd., 60-62 Toller Ln., Bradford, W. Yorks BD8 9BY, England. TEL 44-1274-777700. FAX 44-1274-785200. URL: http://www.mcb.co.uk. Vendor(s): Information Access Co. *1531*

INTERNATIONAL JOURNAL OF ROCK MECHANICS & MINING SCIENCES.
Elsevier Science Ltd., Pergamon, P.O. Box 800, Kidlington, Oxford OX5 1DX, England. TEL 44-1865-843000. FAX 44-1865-843010. URL: http://www.elsevier.nl/. Vendor(s): Questel Orbit Inc. (GEOM). *5303*

INTERNATIONAL JOURNAL OF ROTATING MACHINERY.
Gordon and Breach - Harwood Academic, Amsteldisk 166, 1st Fl., 1079 LH Amsterdam, Nethelands. URL: http://www.gbhap.com/Rotating__Machinery/. *4545*

INTERNATIONAL JOURNAL OF SOCIAL PSYCHIATRY.
Avenue Publishing Co., 55 Woodstock Ave., London NW11 9RG, England. TEL 44-181-455-2940. FAX 44-181-455-2940. Vendor(s): UMI. *5070*

INTERNATIONAL JOURNAL OF SOLAR ENERGY.
Gordon and Breach - Harwood Academic, Amsteldisk 166, 1st Fl., 1079 LH Amsterdam, Netherlands. URL: http://www.gbhap.com/Solar__Energy/. *2706*

INTERNATIONAL JOURNAL OF SUPERCOMPUTER APPLICATIONS AND HIGH-PERFORMANCE COMPUTING.
Sage Publications, Inc., Sage Science Press, 2455 Teller Rd., Thousand Oaks, CA 91320. TEL 805-499-0721. FAX 805-499-0871. URL: http://www.sagepub.com. Vendor(s): Knight-Ridder Information, Inc. *2214*

INTERNATIONAL JOURNAL OF THE SOCIOLOGY OF LAW.
Academic Press Ltd., 24-28 Oval Rd., London NW1 7DX, England. TEL 44-171-267-4466. FAX 44-171-482-2293. URL: http://www.hbuk.co.uk/ap//ijsl; http://www.europe.idealibrary.com/ *3965*

INTERNATIONAL JOURNAL OF THEORETICAL PHYSICS.
Plenum Publishing Corp., 233 Spring St., New York, NY 10013-1578. TEL 212-620-8000. FAX 212-463-0742. *5807*

INTERNATIONAL JOURNAL OF TOXICOLOGY.
Taylor & Francis Ltd., 1 Gunpowder Sq., London EC4A 3DE, England. TEL 44-171-583-0490. FAX 44-171-583-0585. URL: http://www.tandf.co.uk/. *2978*

INTERNATIONAL JOURNAL OF WATER RESOURCES DEVELOPMENT.
Carfax Publishing Co., P.O. Box 25, Abingdon, Oxon. OX14 3UE, England. TEL 44-1235-401000. FAX 44-1235-401550. *7295*

INTERNATIONAL JOURNAL OF WIRELESS INFORMATION NETWORKS.
Plenum Publishing Corp., 233 Spring St., New York, NY 10013-1578. TEL 212-620-8000. FAX 212-463-0742. URL: http://www.catchword.co.uk/. *1994*

INTERNATIONAL JOURNAL ON DIGITAL LIBRARIES.
Springer-Verlag, Heidelberger Platz 3, 14197 Berlin, Germany. TEL 49-30-82787-0. FAX 49-30-82787448. URL: http://link.springer.de. *4233*

INTERNATIONAL JOURNAL ON SOFTWARE TOOLS FOR TECHNOLOGY TRANSFER.
Springer-Verlag, Heidelberger Platz 3, 14197 Berlin, Germany. TEL 49-30-82787-0. FAX 49-30-82787448. URL: http://link.springer.de. *2156*

INTERNATIONAL LABORATORY BUYERS' GUIDE.
International Scientific Communications, Inc., 30 Controls Dr., Shelton, CT 06484. TEL 203-926-9300. FAX 203-926-9310. *684*

INTERNATIONAL LABOUR DOCUMENTATION.
I L O Publications, CH-1211 Geneva 22, Switzerland. TEL 41-22-799-6111. FAX 41-22-798-6358. Vendor(s): European Space Agency (File no.53/LABORDOC), Human Resources Information Network, Questel Orbit Inc. (LDOC). *1048*

INTERNATIONAL LABOUR REVIEW.
I L O Publications, CH-1211 Geneva 22, Switzerland. TEL 41-22-799-6111. FAX 41-22-798-6358. Vendor(s): Information Access Co., UMI. *1437*

INTERNATIONAL LAWYER.
American Bar Association, International Law and Practice Section, 740 15th St., N.W., Washington, DC 20005. TEL 202-662-1673. FAX 202-662-1669. URL: http://www.abanet.org. Vendor(s): Lexis-Nexis, West Group. *4119*

INTERNATIONAL LEGAL MATERIALS.
American Society of International Law, 2223 Massachusetts Ave., N.W., Washington, DC 20008-2864. TEL 202-939-6000. FAX 202-797-7133. Vendor(s): Lexis-Nexis. *4119*

INTERNATIONAL MARKET ALERT.
International Reports, Inc., 11300 Rockville Pike, Ste. 1100, Rockville, MD 20852-3035. Vendor(s): Lexis-Nexis, NewsNet (FI58). *1389*

INTERNATIONAL MATHEMATICS RESEARCH NOTICES.
Duke University Press, Box 90660, Durham, NC 27708-0660. TEL 919-687-3600. FAX 919-688-4578. URL: http://www.duke.edu/web/dupress/ *4578*

INTERNATIONAL MEDICAL JOURNAL.
Japan International Cultural Exchange Foundation, 2-15-5-207 Shoto, Shibuya-ku, Tokyo 150, Japan. TEL 81-3-3424-9090. FAX 81-3-3424-9119. *4687*

INTERNATIONAL MIGRATION REVIEW.
Center for Migration Studies, 209 Flagg Pl., Staten Island, NY 10304-1199. TEL 718-351-8800. FAX 718-667-4598. URL: http://www.cmsny.org/imr3.htm. Vendor(s): Information Access Co., UMI. *6052*

INTERNATIONAL MONETARY FUND. BALANCE OF PAYMENTS STATISTICS YEARBOOK.
International Monetary Fund, Publication Services, 700 19th St., N.W., Washington, DC 20431. TEL 202-623-7430. FAX 202-623-7201. *1048*

INTERNATIONAL MONETARY FUND. STAFF PAPERS.
International Monetary Fund, Publication Services, 700 19th St., N.W., Ste. C-100, Washington, DC 20431. TEL 202-623-7430. FAX 202-623-7201. Vendor(s): Information Access Co., UMI. *1147*

INTERNATIONAL NARCOTICS CONTROL STRATEGY REPORT.
U.S. Department of State, Bureau for International Narcotics and Law Enforcement Affairs, 2201 C St., N.W., Washington, DC 20520. TEL 202-647-6575. URL: http://www.state.gov. *2269*

INTERNATIONAL NURSING INDEX.
Lippincott - Raven Publishers, 227 E. Washington Sq., Philadelphia, PA 19106. TEL 215-238-4200. FAX 215-238-4227. URL: http://www.lrpub.com. Vendor(s): Knight-Ridder Information, Inc. (File nos.154 & 155/MEDLINE), National Library of Medicine, Ovid Technologies, Inc., STN International (MEDLINE). *4781*

INTERNATIONAL ORGANIZATION.
M I T Press, 5 Cambridge Center, Cambridge, MA 02142. TEL 617-253-2889. FAX 617-577-1545. URL: http://www-mitpress.mit.edu. Vendor(s): Information Access Co. *6020*

INTERNATIONAL ORTHOPAEDICS.
Springer-Verlag, Heidelberger Platz 3, 14197 Berlin, Germany. TEL 49-30-82787-0. FAX 49-30-82787448. URL: http://link.springer.de. *5008*

INTERNATIONAL PACKAGING ABSTRACTS.
Pira International, Randalls Rd., Leatherhead, Surrey KT22 7RU, England. TEL 44-1372-802050. FAX 44-1372-802239. URL: http://www.pira.co.uk/. Vendor(s): Data-Star, FIZ Technik, Knight-Ridder Information, Inc., Questel Orbit Inc. (PIRA), STN International. *5550*

INTERNATIONAL PETROLEUM ABSTRACTS.
John Wiley & Sons Ltd., Journals, Baffins Ln., Chichester, W. Sussex PO19 1UD, England. TEL 44-1243-779777. FAX 44-1243-775878. URL: http://www.wiley.co.uk. Vendor(s): Questel Orbit Inc. (IPAB). *5630*

INTERNATIONAL PETROLEUM STATISTICS REPORT.
U.S. Energy Information Administration, National Energy Information Center, EI-231, James Forrestal Bldg., Rm. 1F-048, 1000 Independence Ave., S.W., Washington, DC 20585. TEL 202-586-8800. FAX 202-586-0727. URL: http://www.eia..doe.gov. *6918*

INTERNATIONAL PHARMACEUTICAL ABSTRACTS.
American Society of Health-System Pharmacists, 7272 Wisconsin Ave., Bethesda, MD 20814. TEL 301-657-3000. FAX 301-657-1641. Vendor(s): DIMDI, Data-Star (IPAB), Knight-Ridder Information, Inc. (File no.74), National Library of Medicine, Ovid Technologies, Inc. (IPAB). *5701*

INTERNATIONAL PHOTO PROCESSING INDUSTRY REPORT.
Photofinishing News, Inc., 10915 Bonita Beach Rd., Ste. 1091, Bonita Springs, FL 34135. TEL 941-992-4421. FAX 941-992-6328. URL: dfranz@photo-news.com. *5777*

INTERNATIONAL PLAY JOURNAL.
Chapman & Hall, Journals Department 2-6 Boundary Row, London SE1 8HN, England. TEL 44-171-8650066. FAX 44-171-5229623. URL: http://www.chaphall.com/chaphall/journals.html. *6119*

INTERNATIONAL POPULATION DATA.
U.S. Bureau of the Census, Customer Services, Washington, DC 20233. TEL 301-457-4100. FAX 301-457-4714. URL: http://www.census.gov/. *6066*

INTERNATIONAL PRODUCT ALERT.
Marketing Intelligence Service Ltd., 6473D State Rt. 64, Naples, NY 14512-9726. TEL 716-374-6326. FAX 716-374-5217. URL: http://ourworld.compuserve.com/homepages/mktgintelsvc. Vendor(s): CompuServe, Inc., Data-Star, Dow Jones News Retrieval, Information Access Co., Knight-Ridder Information, Inc. (File no. 9), NewsNet (AD25). *1531*

INTERNATIONAL RESEARCH CENTERS DIRECTORY.
Gale Research, 835 Penobscot Bldg., 645 Griswold St., Detroit, MI 48226-4094. TEL 313-961-2242. FAX 800-414-5043.
Vendor(s): Knight-Ridder Information, Inc. *2452*

INTERNATIONAL REVIEW OF MISSION.
World Council of Churches, 150 route de Ferney, P.O. Box 2100, CH-1211 Geneva 2, Switzerland. TEL 41-22-791-6111. FAX 41-22-791-0361.
Vendor(s): Information Access Co., UMI. *6345*

INTERNATIONAL REVIEW OF RETAIL, DISTRIBUTION AND CONSUMER RESEARCH.
Thomson Professional, 2-6 Boundary Row, London SE1 8HN, England. TEL 44-171-865-0066. FAX 44-171-522-9621. URL: http://rdcr.thomsonprofessional.com. *1531*

INTERNATIONAL REVIEWS IN PHYSICAL CHEMISTRY.
Taylor & Francis Ltd., 1 Gunpowder Sq., London EC4A 3DE, England. TEL 44-171-583-0490. FAX 44-171-583-0585. URL: http://www.tandf.co.uk/. *1829*

INTERNATIONAL REVIEWS OF IMMUNOLOGY.
Gordon and Breach - Harwood Academic, Amsteldisk 166, 1st Fl., 1079 LH Amsterdam, Netherlands. URL: http://www.gbhap.com/IR__Immunology/. *4797*

INTERNATIONAL ROAD HAULAGE BY UNITED KINGDOM REGISTERED VEHICLES.
H.M.S.O., 51 Nine Elms Ln., London SW8 5DR, England. TEL 44-171-973-0011. FAX 44-171-873-8247. *7175*

INTERNATIONAL SATELLITE DIRECTORY.
Design Publishers, 800 Siesta Way, Sonoma, CA 95476-4413. URL: http://www.satnews.com. *71*

INTERNATIONAL SECURITIES REGULATION REPORT.
L R P Publications, 747 Dresher Rd., Box 980, Horsham, PA 19044-0980. TEL 215-784-0941. FAX 215-784-9639. URL: http://www.lrp.com.
Vendor(s): Lexis-Nexis. *1389*

INTERNATIONAL SECURITY.
M I T Press, 5 Cambridge Center, Cambridge, MA 02142. TEL 617-253-2889. FAX 617-577-1545. URL: http://www-mitpress.mit.edu.
Vendor(s): Information Access Co. *6021*

INTERNATIONAL SMALL BUSINESS JOURNAL.
Woodcock Publications Ltd., P.O. Box 1, Macclesfield, Cheshire SK10 4YQ, England. TEL 44-1625-528516. FAX 44-1625-532644.
Vendor(s): Information Access Co., UMI. *1644*

INTERNATIONAL SOLAR ENERGY INTELLIGENCE REPORT.
Business Publishers, Inc., 951 Pershing Dr., Silver Spring, MD 20910-4464. TEL 301-587-6300. FAX 301-585-9075.
Vendor(s): Data-Star, Information Access Co., Knight-Ridder Information, Inc., NewsNet. *2706*

INTERNATIONAL STUDIES OF MANAGEMENT AND ORGANIZATION.
M.E. Sharpe, Inc., 80 Business Park Dr., Armonk, NY 10504. TEL 914-273-1800. FAX 914-273-2106.
Vendor(s): Information Access Co., UMI. *1485*

INTERNATIONAL TAX REPORT.
Monitor Press Ltd., Suffolk House, Church Field Rd., Sudbury, Suffolk CO10 6YA, England. TEL 44-1787-378607. FAX 44-1787-881147.
Vendor(s): Data-Star, Lexis-Nexis, UMI. *1615*

INTERNATIONAL TAX REVIEW.
Euromoney Publications plc., Nestor House, Playhouse Yard, London EC4V 5EX, England. TEL 44-171-779-8935. FAX 44-171-779-8541.
Vendor(s): UMI. *1331*

INTERNATIONAL TELECOMMUNICATION UNION. OPERATIONAL BULLETIN.
International Telecommunication Union, Place des Nations, CH-1211 Geneva 20, Switzerland. TEL 41-22-7306141. FAX 41-22-7305194. URL: http://www.itu.ch. *2035*

INTERNATIONAL TRADE FINANCE.
Financial Times Business Information, Newsletters 126 Jermyn St., London SW1Y 4UJ, England. TEL 44-171-411-4414. FAX 44-171-441-4415.
Vendor(s): Information Access Co. *1148*

INTERNATIONAL TRADE FORUM.
International Trade Centre, Palais des Nations, CH-1211 Geneva 10, Switzerland. FAX 41-22-733-4439.
Vendor(s): Information Access Co., UMI. *1332*

INTERNATIONAL TRADE REPORTER.
The Bureau of National Affairs, Inc., 1231 25th St., N.W., Washington, DC 20037. TEL 202-452-4200. FAX 202-822-8092. URL: http://www.bna.com/
Vendor(s): Lexis-Nexis (INTRAD), West Group (BNA-ITR). *1332*

INTERNATIONAL TRADESHOW DIRECTORY.
M und A Verlag fuer Messen, Ausstellungen und Kongresse GmbH, Postfach 101528, 60015 Frankfurt a.M., Germany. TEL 49-69-759502. FAX 49-69-75951280.
Vendor(s): Data-Star, Knight-Ridder Information, Inc., Lexis-Nexis. *1689*

INTERNATIONAL UROGYNECOLOGY JOURNAL.
Springer-Verlag London Ltd., Sweetapple House, Catteshall Rd., Godalming, Surrey GU7 3DJ, England. TEL 44-1483-418800. FAX 44-1483-415144. *4960*

INTERNATIONAL WILDLIFE.
National Wildlife Federation, 8925 Leesburg Pike, Vienna, VA 22184-0001. TEL 703-790-4000. FAX 703-790-4075. URL: http://www.nwf.org.
Vendor(s): Information Access Co. *2234*

INTERNATIONALE BIBLIOGRAPHIE DER REZENSIONEN WISSENSCHAFTLICHER LITERATUR.
Zeller Publications, Postfach 1949, 49009 Osnabrueck, Germany. TEL 49-541-4045914. FAX 49-541-41255. *6590*

INTERNATIONALE BIBLIOGRAPHIE DER ZEITSCHRIFTENLITERATUR AUS ALLEN GEBIETEN DES WISSENS.
Zeller Publications, Postfach 1949, 49009 Osnabrueck, Germany. TEL 49-541-4045914. FAX 49-541-41255. URL: http://www.brzn.de. *553*

INTERNET.
Systems Comunicazioni, V. Olanda, 6, 20080 Gaggiana (MI), Italy. TEL 39-2-90841814. FAX 39-2-90841682. *2170*

INTERNET ARCHAEOLOGY.
Council for British Archaeology, Internet Archaeology Office, Dept. of Archaeology, University of York, The King's Manor, York YO1 2EP, England. TEL 44-1904-433955. FAX 44-1904-433939. URL: http://intarch.ac.uk.
Available only online. *367*

INTERNET BUSINESS NEWS.
M2 Communications Ltd., P.O. Box 475, Coventry CV1 2ZW, England. TEL 44-1203-634700. FAX 44-1203-634144. URL: http://www.m2.com.
Available only online. *2135*

INTERNET INFOSCAVENGER.
InfoScavenger Communications, Inc., 1153 Bergen Pkwy., Ste. 473, Evergreen, CO 80439. TEL 303-674-2794. FAX 303-674-4184. URL: http://www.infoscavenger.com. *2135*

INTERNET, JAVA AND ACTIVE X ADVISOR.
Advisor Publications Inc., 5675 Ruffin Rd., Ste. 200, San Diego, CA 92123. TEL 619-278-5600. FAX 619-278-0300. URL: http://www.advisor.com/ia.html. *2135*

INTERNET JOURNAL OF LANGUAGE, CULTURE AND SOCIETY.
URL: http://www.educ.utas.edu.au/'Thao.Le/journal/journal.html.
Available only online. *4265*

INTERNET JOURNAL OF VIBRATIONAL SPECTROSCOPY.
URL: http://www.teamworks.co.uk/ijvs/
Available only online. *1753*

THE INTERNET LAW HANDBOOK NEWSLETTER.
URL: http://www.lexonline.com/newslet.htm.
Available only online. *3965*

INTERNET LAWYER.
URL: http://www.internetlawyer.com/tillive.htm.
Available only online. *3965*

INTERNET MARKETING DIGEST.
TEL 31-20-5128634. URL: http://www.informatiebank.nl/digest/indexgb.htm.
Available only online. *2135*

INTERNET OPERATOR EUROPE.
TechMedia, 52 Foundling Ct., London WC1N 1AN, England. TEL 44-171-837-0815. FAX 44-171-278-9917. *2035*

INTERNET RESEARCH.
M C B University Press Ltd., 60-62 Toller Ln., Bradford, W. Yorks BD8 9BY, England. TEL 44-1274-777700. FAX 44-1274-785200. URL: http://www.mcb.co.uk/liblink/intr/jourhome.htm. *2135*

INTERNET ROADSTOP: MAC ZINE AND INFORMATION.
URL: http://digiserve.com/roadstop.
Available only online. *2197*

INTERNET SURVEYS.
URL: http://www.nua.ie/choice/surveys.
Available only online. *2135*

INTERNET TEACHER.
Regulus Communications,
Available only online. *2517*

THE INTERNET TIMES.
Euro-Marketing Associates, 1850 Union St., Ste. 1229, San Francisco, CA 94123. TEL 415-680-2423. URL: http://www.euromktg.com/eng/ed/it.html.
Available only online. *2135*

INTERNET TREND WATCH FOR LIBRARIES.
Librarians and Educators Online, URL: http://www.leonline.com.
Available only online. *4187*

INTERNET TRUCKING MAGAZINE.
URL: http://www.qcontinuum.com/~keard/trucking.html.
Available only online. *7175*

INTERNET VOYAGER.
Blue Dolphin Communications, Inc., 526 Boston Post Rd., Wayland, MA 01778-1833. TEL 508-443-6363. FAX 508-443-7286. URL: http://www.internetvoyager.com. *2170*

INTERNET WEEK.
Phillips Business Information, Inc., 1201 Seven Locks Rd., Potomac, MD 20854. TEL 301-424-3338. FAX 301-309-3847. URL: http://www.phillips.com/pbi/iw. *2136*

INTERNETWORK.
Cardinal Business Media, Inc., 1300 Virginia Dr., Ste. 400, Fort Washington, PA 19034. TEL 215-643-8000. FAX 215-643-3901.
Vendor(s): Information Access Co. *2136*

DER INTERNIST.
Springer-Verlag, Heidelberger Platz 3, 14197 Berlin, Germany. TEL 49-30-82787-0. FAX 49-30-82787448. URL: http://link.springer.de. *4925*

INTERPRETER (NASHVILLE).
United Methodist Communications, 810 12th Ave. S., Nashville, TN 37203-4744. TEL 615-742-5400. FAX 615-742-5460.
Vendor(s): UMI. *6429*

INTERTEXT.
URL: http://www.etext.org/zines/InterText/
Available only online. *4532*

SERIALS AVAILABLE ONLINE

INTER-UNIVERSITY CONSORTIUM FOR POLITICAL AND SOCIAL RESEARCH. GUIDE TO RESOURCES AND SERVICES.
Inter-University Consortium for Political and Social Research, Box 1248, Ann Arbor, MI 48106-1248. TEL 313-764-2570. FAX 313-764-8041. *6620*

INTERVIEW (NEW YORK).
Brant Publications, Inc., 575 Broadway, 5th Fl., New York, NY 10012. TEL 212-941-2800.
Vendor(s): Information Access Co. *3376*

INTO THE LIGHT.
American Waldensian Society, Box 744, Whitehall, PA 18052-0744. TEL 610-432-9569. FAX 610-432-9518. URL: http://www.waldensian.org. *6346*

INTROSPECTION.
32419 Seventh Ave. S.W., Federal Way, WA 98023. URL: http://web.wa.net/~akkbar/.
Available only online. *2118*

INVENTIONES MATHEMATICAE.
Springer-Verlag, Heidelberger Platz 3, 14197 Berlin, Germany. TEL 49-30-82787-0. FAX 49-30-82787448. URL: http://link.springer.de. *4579*

INVENTORIES OF NATURAL GAS LIQUIDS & LIQUIFIED REFINERY GASES.
American Petroleum Institute, Publications Section, 1220 L St., N.W., Washington, DC 20005. TEL 202-682-8375. FAX 202-962-4776. URL: http://www.api.org. *5630*

INVERSE PROBLEMS.
I O P Publishing Ltd., Dirac House, Temple Back, Bristol BS1 6BE, England. TEL 44-117-929-7481. FAX 44-117-929-4318. URL: http://www.iop.org. *4621*

INVERSE PROBLEMS IN ENGINEERING.
Gordon and Breach - Harwood Academic, Amsteldisk 166, 1st Fl., 1079 LH Amsterdam, Netherlands. URL: http://www.gbhap.com/Inverse__Problems__Engineering/. *2727*

INVERTEBRATE TAXONOMY.
C.S.I.R.O. Publishing, 150 Oxford St., Collingwood, Vic. 3066, Australia. TEL 61-3-96627622. FAX 61-3-96627611. URL: http://www.publish.csiro.au/journals/it. *606*

INVESTIGACION BIBLIOTECOLOGICA.
Universidad Nacional Autonoma de Mexico, Centro Universitario de Investigaciones Bibliotecologicas, Torre II de Humanidades, pisos 12 y 13, Ciudad Universitaria, 04510 Mexico, D.F., Mexico. TEL 52-5-6230352. FAX 52-5-5507461. URL: http://cuib.laborales.unam.mx/publicaciones/revista. *4187*

INVESTING, LICENSING AND TRADING. AMERICAS.
Economist Intelligence Unit, 111 W. 57th St., New York, NY 10019. TEL 212-554-0600. FAX 212-586-1181. URL: http://www.eiu.com.
Vendor(s): Knight-Ridder Information, Inc., Lexis-Nexis. *1332*

INVESTING, LICENSING AND TRADING. ARGENTINA.
Economist Intelligence Unit, 111 W. 57th St., New York, NY 10019. TEL 212-554-0600. FAX 212-586-1181. URL: http://www.eiu.com.
Vendor(s): Knight-Ridder Information, Inc., Lexis-Nexis. *1332*

INVESTING, LICENSING AND TRADING. ASIA.
Economist Intelligence Unit, 111 W. 57th St., New York, NY 10019. TEL 212-554-0600. FAX 212-586-1181. URL: http://www.eiu.com.
Vendor(s): Knight-Ridder Information, Inc., Lexis-Nexis. *1333*

INVESTING, LICENSING AND TRADING. AUSTRALIA.
Economist Intelligence Unit, 111 W. 57th St., New York, NY 10019. TEL 212-554-0600. FAX 212-596-1181. URL: http://www.eiu.com.
Vendor(s): Knight-Ridder Information, Inc., Lexis-Nexis. *1333*

INVESTING, LICENSING AND TRADING. AUSTRIA.
Economist Intelligence Unit, 111 W. 57th St., New York, NY 10019. TEL 212-554-0600. FAX 212-586-1181. URL: http://www.eiu.com.
Vendor(s): Knight-Ridder Information, Inc., Lexis-Nexis. *1333*

INVESTING, LICENSING AND TRADING. BELGIUM.
Economist Intelligence Unit, 111 W. 57th St., New York, NY 10019. TEL 212-554-0600. FAX 212-586-1181. URL: http://www.eiu.com.
Vendor(s): Knight-Ridder Information, Inc., Lexis-Nexis. *1333*

INVESTING, LICENSING AND TRADING. BRAZIL.
Economist Intelligence Unit, 111 W. 57th St., New York, NY 10019. TEL 212-554-0600. FAX 212-586-1181. URL: http://www.eiu.com.
Vendor(s): Knight-Ridder Information, Inc., Lexis-Nexis. *1333*

INVESTING, LICENSING AND TRADING. BRITAIN.
Economist Intelligence Unit, 111 W. 57th St., New York, NY 10019. TEL 212-554-0600. FAX 212-586-1181. URL: http://www.eiu.com.
Vendor(s): Knight-Ridder Information, Inc., Lexis-Nexis. *1333*

INVESTING, LICENSING AND TRADING. CANADA.
Economist Intelligence Unit, 111 W. 57th St., New York, NY 10019. TEL 212-554-0600. FAX 212-586-1181. URL: http://www.eiu.com.
Vendor(s): Knight-Ridder Information, Inc., Lexis-Nexis. *1333*

INVESTING, LICENSING AND TRADING. CENTRAL AMERICA.
Economist Intelligence Unit, 111 W. 57th St., New York, NY 10019. TEL 212-554-0600. FAX 212-586-1181. URL: http://www.eiu.com.
Vendor(s): Knight-Ridder Information, Inc., Lexis-Nexis. *1333*

INVESTING, LICENSING AND TRADING. CHILE.
Economist Intelligence Unit, 111 W. 57th St., New York, NY 10019. TEL 212-554-0600. FAX 212-586-1181. URL: http://www.eiu.com.
Vendor(s): Knight-Ridder Information, Inc., Lexis-Nexis. *1333*

INVESTING, LICENSING AND TRADING. CHINA.
Economist Intelligence Unit, 111 W. 57th St., New York, NY 10019. TEL 212-554-0600. FAX 212-586-1181. URL: http://www.eiu.com.
Vendor(s): Knight-Ridder Information, Inc., Lexis-Nexis. *1333*

INVESTING, LICENSING AND TRADING. COLOMBIA.
Economist Intelligence Unit, 111 W. 57th St., New York, NY 10019. TEL 212-554-0600. FAX 212-586-1181. URL: http://www.eiu.com.
Vendor(s): Knight-Ridder Information, Inc., Lexis-Nexis. *1333*

INVESTING, LICENSING AND TRADING. CZECH REPUBLIC.
Economist Intelligence Unit, 111 W. 57th St., New York, NY 10019. TEL 212-554-0600. FAX 212-586-1181. URL: http://www.eiu.com.
Vendor(s): Knight-Ridder Information, Inc., Lexis-Nexis. *1333*

INVESTING, LICENSING AND TRADING. DENMARK.
Economist Intelligence Unit, 111 W. 57th St., New York, NY 10019. TEL 212-554-0600. FAX 212-586-1181. URL: http://www.eiu.com.
Vendor(s): Knight-Ridder Information, Inc., Lexis-Nexis. *1334*

INVESTING, LICENSING AND TRADING. ECUADOR.
Economist Intelligence Unit, 111 W. 57th St., New York, NY 10019. TEL 212-554-0600. FAX 212-586-1181. URL: http://www.eiu.com.
Vendor(s): Knight-Ridder Information, Inc., Lexis-Nexis. *1334*

INVESTING, LICENSING AND TRADING. EGYPT.
Economist Intelligence Unit, 111 W. 57th St., New York, NY 10019. TEL 212-554-0600. FAX 212-586-1181. URL: http://www.eiu.com.
Vendor(s): Knight-Ridder Information, Inc., Lexis-Nexis. *1334*

INVESTING, LICENSING AND TRADING. FINLAND.
Economist Intelligence Unit, 111 W. 57th St., New York, NY 10019. TEL 212-554-0600. FAX 212-586-1181. URL: http://www.eiu.com.
Vendor(s): Knight-Ridder Information, Inc., Lexis-Nexis. *1334*

INVESTING, LICENSING AND TRADING. FRANCE.
Economist Intelligence Unit, 111 W. 57th St., New York, NY 10019. TEL 212-554-0600. FAX 212-586-1181. URL: http://www.eiu.com.
Vendor(s): Knight-Ridder Information, Inc., Lexis-Nexis. *1334*

INVESTING, LICENSING AND TRADING. GERMANY.
Economist Intelligence Unit, 111 W. 57th St., New York, NY 10019. TEL 212-554-0600. FAX 212-586-1181. URL: http://www.eiu.com.
Vendor(s): Knight-Ridder Information, Inc., Lexis-Nexis. *1334*

INVESTING, LICENSING AND TRADING. GLOBAL EDITION.
Economist Intelligence Unit, 111 W. 57th St., New York, NY 10019. TEL 212-554-0600. FAX 212-586-1181. URL: http://www.eiu.com.
Vendor(s): Knight-Ridder Information, Inc., Lexis-Nexis. *1334*

INVESTING, LICENSING AND TRADING. GREECE.
Economist Intelligence Unit, 111 W. 57th St., New York, NY 10019. TEL 212-554-0600. FAX 212-586-1181. URL: http://www.eiu.com.
Vendor(s): Knight-Ridder Information, Inc., Lexis-Nexis. *1334*

INVESTING, LICENSING AND TRADING. HONG KONG.
Economist Intelligence Unit, 111 W. 57th St., New York, NY 10019. TEL 212-554-0600. FAX 212-586-1181. URL: http://www.eiu.com.
Vendor(s): Knight-Ridder Information, Inc., Lexis-Nexis. *1334*

INVESTING, LICENSING AND TRADING. HUNGARY.
Economist Intelligence Unit, 215 Park Ave. S., New York, NY 10003-1658. TEL 212-554-0600. FAX 212-586-1182. URL: http://www.eiu.com.
Vendor(s): Knight-Ridder Information, Inc., Lexis-Nexis. *1334*

INVESTING, LICENSING AND TRADING. INDIA.
Economist Intelligence Unit, 111 W. 57th St., New York, NY 10019. TEL 212-554-0600. FAX 212-586-1181. URL: http://www.eiu.com.
Vendor(s): Knight-Ridder Information, Inc., Lexis-Nexis. *1334*

INVESTING, LICENSING AND TRADING. INDONESIA.
Economist Intelligence Unit, 111 W. 57th St., New York, NY 10019. TEL 212-554-0600. FAX 212-586-1181. URL: http://www.eiu.com.
Vendor(s): Knight-Ridder Information, Inc., Lexis-Nexis. *1335*

INVESTING, LICENSING AND TRADING. IRELAND.
Economist Intelligence Unit, 111 W. 57th St., New York, NY 10019. TEL 212-554-0600. FAX 212-586-1181. URL: http://www.eiu.com.
Vendor(s): Knight-Ridder Information, Inc., Lexis-Nexis. *1335*

INVESTING, LICENSING AND TRADING. ISRAEL.
Economist Intelligence Unit, 111 W. 57th St., New York, NY 10019. TEL 212-554-0600. FAX 212-586-1181. URL: http://www.eiu.com.
Vendor(s): Knight-Ridder Information, Inc., Lexis-Nexis. *1335*

INVESTING, LICENSING AND TRADING. ITALY.
Economist Intelligence Unit, 111 W. 57th St., New York, NY 10019. TEL 212-554-0600. FAX 212-586-1181. URL: http://www.eiu.com.
Vendor(s): Knight-Ridder Information, Inc., Lexis-Nexis. *1335*

INVESTING, LICENSING AND TRADING. JAPAN.
Economist Intelligence Unit, 111 W. 57th St., New York, NY 10019. TEL 212-554-0600. FAX 212-586-1181. URL: http://www.eiu.com.
Vendor(s): Knight-Ridder Information, Inc., Lexis-Nexis. *1335*

INVESTING, LICENSING AND TRADING. KENYA.
Economist Intelligence Unit, 111 W. 57th St., New York, NY 10019. TEL 212-554-0600. FAX 212-586-1181. URL: http://www.eiu.com.
Vendor(s): Knight-Ridder Information, Inc., Lexis-Nexis. *1335*

INVESTING, LICENSING AND TRADING. LUXEMBOURG.
Economist Intelligence Unit, 111 W. 57th St., New York, NY 10019. TEL 212-554-0600. FAX 212-586-1181. URL: http://www.eiu.com.
Vendor(s): Knight-Ridder Information, Inc., Lexis-Nexis. *1335*

INVESTING, LICENSING AND TRADING. MALAYSIA.
Economist Intelligence Unit, 111 W. 57th St., New York, NY 10019. TEL 212-554-0600. FAX 212-586-1181. URL: http://www.eiu.com.
Vendor(s): Knight-Ridder Information, Inc., Lexis-Nexis. *1335*

INVESTING, LICENSING AND TRADING. MEXICO.
Economist Intelligence Unit, 111 W. 57th St., New York, NY 10019. TEL 212-554-0600. FAX 212-586-1181. URL: http://www.eiu.com.
Vendor(s): Knight-Ridder Information, Inc., Lexis-Nexis. *1335*

INVESTING, LICENSING AND TRADING. MIDDLE EAST - AFRICA.
Economist Intelligence Unit, 111 W. 57th St., New York, NY 10019. TEL 212-554-0600. FAX 212-586-1181. URL: http://www.eiu.com.
Vendor(s): Knight-Ridder Information, Inc., Lexis-Nexis. *1335*

INVESTING, LICENSING AND TRADING. NETHERLANDS.
Economist Intelligence Unit, 111 W. 57th St., New York, NY 10019. TEL 212-554-0600. FAX 212-586-1181. URL: http://www.eiu.com.
Vendor(s): Knight-Ridder Information, Inc., Lexis-Nexis. *1335*

INVESTING, LICENSING AND TRADING. NEW ZEALAND.
Economist Intelligence Unit, 111 W. 57th St., New York, NY 10019. TEL 212-554-0600. FAX 212-586-1181. URL: http://www.eiu.com.
Vendor(s): Knight-Ridder Information, Inc., Lexis-Nexis. *1335*

INVESTING, LICENSING AND TRADING. NIGERIA.
Economist Intelligence Unit, 111 W. 57th St., New York, NY 10019. TEL 212-554-0600. FAX 212-586-1181. URL: http://www.eiu.com.
Vendor(s): Knight-Ridder Information, Inc., Lexis-Nexis. *1336*

INVESTING, LICENSING AND TRADING. NORWAY.
Economist Intelligence Unit, 111 W. 57th St., New York, NY 10019. TEL 212-554-0600. FAX 212-586-1181. URL: http://www.eiu.com.
Vendor(s): Knight-Ridder Information, Inc., Lexis-Nexis. *1336*

INVESTING, LICENSING AND TRADING. PAKISTAN.
Economist Intelligence Unit, 111 W. 57th St., New York, NY 10019. TEL 212-554-0600. FAX 212-586-1181. URL: http://www.eiu.com.
Vendor(s): Knight-Ridder Information, Inc., Lexis-Nexis. *1336*

INVESTING, LICENSING AND TRADING. PANAMA.
Economist Intelligence Unit, 111 W. 57th St., New York, NY 10019. TEL 212-554-0600. FAX 212-586-1181. URL: http://www.eiu.com.
Vendor(s): Knight-Ridder Information, Inc., Lexis-Nexis. *1336*

INVESTING, LICENSING AND TRADING. PERU.
Economist Intelligence Unit, 111 W. 57th St., New York, NY 10019. TEL 212-554-0600. FAX 212-586-1181. URL: http://www.eiu.com.
Vendor(s): Knight-Ridder Information, Inc., Lexis-Nexis. *1336*

INVESTING, LICENSING AND TRADING. PHILIPPINES.
Economist Intelligence Unit, 111 W. 57th St., New York, NY 10019. TEL 212-554-0600. FAX 212-586-1181. URL: http://www.eiu.com.
Vendor(s): Knight-Ridder Information, Inc., Lexis-Nexis. *1336*

INVESTING, LICENSING AND TRADING. POLAND.
Economist Intelligence Unit, 111 W. 57th St., New York, NY 10019. TEL 212-554-0600. FAX 212-586-1181. URL: http://www.eiu.com.
Vendor(s): Knight-Ridder Information, Inc., Lexis-Nexis. *1336*

INVESTING, LICENSING AND TRADING. PORTUGAL.
Economist Intelligence Unit, 111 W. 57th St., New York, NY 10019. TEL 212-554-0600. FAX 212-586-1181. URL: http://www.eiu.com.
Vendor(s): Knight-Ridder Information, Inc., Lexis-Nexis. *1336*

INVESTING, LICENSING AND TRADING. PUERTO RICO.
Economist Intelligence Unit, 111 W. 57th St., New York, NY 10019. TEL 212-554-0600. FAX 212-586-1181. URL: http://www.eiu.com.
Vendor(s): Knight-Ridder Information, Inc., Lexis-Nexis. *1336*

INVESTING, LICENSING AND TRADING. RUSSIA.
Economist Intelligence Unit, 111 W. 57th St., New York, NY 10019. TEL 212-554-0600. FAX 212-586-1181. URL: http://www.eiu.com.
Vendor(s): Knight-Ridder Information, Inc., Lexis-Nexis. *1336*

INVESTING, LICENSING AND TRADING. SAUDI ARABIA.
Economist Intelligence Unit, 111 W. 57th St., New York, NY 10019. TEL 212-554-0600. FAX 212-586-1181. URL: http://www.eiu.com.
Vendor(s): Knight-Ridder Information, Inc., Lexis-Nexis. *1336*

INVESTING, LICENSING AND TRADING. SINGAPORE.
Economist Intelligence Unit, 111 W. 57th St., New York, NY 10019. TEL 212-554-0600. FAX 212-586-1181. URL: http://www.eiu.com.
Vendor(s): Knight-Ridder Information, Inc., Lexis-Nexis. *1336*

INVESTING, LICENSING AND TRADING. SLOVAKIA.
Economist Intelligence Unit, 111 W. 57th St., New York, NY 10019. TEL 212-554-0600. FAX 212-586-1181. URL: http://www.eiu.com.
Vendor(s): Knight-Ridder Information, Inc., Lexis-Nexis. *1337*

INVESTING, LICENSING AND TRADING. SOUTH AFRICA.
Economist Intelligence Unit, 111 W. 57th St., New York, NY 10019. TEL 212-554-0600. FAX 212-586-1181. URL: http://www.eiu.com.
Vendor(s): Knight-Ridder Information, Inc., Lexis-Nexis. *1337*

INVESTING, LICENSING AND TRADING. SOUTH KOREA.
Economist Intelligence Unit, 111 W. 57th St., New York, NY 10019. TEL 212-554-0600. FAX 212-586-1181. URL: http://www.eiu.com.
Vendor(s): Knight-Ridder Information, Inc., Lexis-Nexis. *1337*

INVESTING, LICENSING AND TRADING. SPAIN.
Economist Intelligence Unit, 111 W. 57th St., New York, NY 10019. TEL 212-554-0600. FAX 212-586-1181. URL: http://www.eiu.com.
Vendor(s): Knight-Ridder Information, Inc., Lexis-Nexis. *1337*

INVESTING, LICENSING AND TRADING. SWEDEN.
Economist Intelligence Unit, 111 W. 57th St., New York, NY 10019. TEL 212-544-0600. FAX 212-586-1181. URL: http://www.eiu.com.
Vendor(s): Knight-Ridder Information, Inc., Lexis-Nexis. *1337*

INVESTING, LICENSING AND TRADING. SWITZERLAND.
Economist Intelligence Unit, 111 W. 57th St., New York, NY 10019. TEL 212-554-0600. FAX 212-586-1181. URL: http://www.eiu.com.
Vendor(s): Knight-Ridder Information, Inc., Lexis-Nexis. *1337*

INVESTING, LICENSING AND TRADING. TAIWAN.
Economist Intelligence Unit, 111 W. 57th St., New York, NY 10019. TEL 212-554-0600. FAX 212-586-1181. URL: http://www.eiu.com.
Vendor(s): Knight-Ridder Information, Inc., Lexis-Nexis. *1337*

INVESTING, LICENSING AND TRADING. THAILAND.
Economist Intelligence Unit, 111 W. 57th St., New York, NY 10019. TEL 212-554-0600. FAX 212-586-1181. URL: http://www.eiu.com.
Vendor(s): Knight-Ridder Information, Inc., Lexis-Nexis. *1337*

INVESTING, LICENSING AND TRADING. TURKEY.
Economist Intelligence Unit, 111 W. 57th St., New York, NY 10019. TEL 212-554-0600. FAX 212-586-1181. URL: http://www.eiu.com.
Vendor(s): Knight-Ridder Information, Inc., Lexis-Nexis. *1337*

INVESTING, LICENSING AND TRADING. UNITED STATES OF AMERICA.
Economist Intelligence Unit, 111 W. 57th St., New York, NY 10019. TEL 212-554-0600. FAX 212-586-1181. URL: http://www.eiu.com.
Vendor(s): Knight-Ridder Information, Inc., Lexis-Nexis. *1337*

INVESTING, LICENSING AND TRADING. URUGUAY.
Economist Intelligence Unit, 111 W. 57th St., New York, NY 10019. TEL 212-554-0600. FAX 212-586-1181. URL: http://www.eiu.com.
Vendor(s): Knight-Ridder Information, Inc., Lexis-Nexis. *1337*

INVESTING, LICENSING AND TRADING. VENEZUELA.
Economist Intelligence Unit, 111 W. 57th St., New York, NY 10019. TEL 212-554-0600. FAX 212-586-1181. URL: http://www.eiu.com.
Vendor(s): Knight-Ridder Information, Inc., Lexis-Nexis. *1337*

INVESTING, LICENSING AND TRADING. VIETNAM.
Economist Intelligence Unit, 111 W. 57th St., New York, NY 10019. TEL 212-554-0600. FAX 212-586-1181. URL: http://www.eiu.com.
Vendor(s): Knight-Ridder Information, Inc., Lexis-Nexis. *1338*

INVESTMENT ADVISORS EQUITY CHARACTERISTICS.
C D A - Cadence, 1355 Piccard Dr., Rockville, MD 20850. TEL 301-975-9600. FAX 301-590-1350. *1390*

INVESTMENT COMPANY PORTFOLIOS.
C D A Investment Technologies, Inc., 1355 Piccard Dr., Rockville, MD 20850. FAX 301-590-1329. *1390*

INVESTMENT COMPANY STOCK HOLDINGS.
C D A Investment Technologies, Inc., 1355 Piccard Dr., Rockville, MD 20850. FAX 301-590-1329. *1390*

INVESTMENT DEALERS' DIGEST.
Investment Dealers' Digest, 2 World Trade Ctr., 18th Fl., New York, NY 10048. TEL 212-432-0045.
Vendor(s): Information Access Co., UMI. *1390*

INVESTMENT QUALITY TRENDS.
Value Trend Analysis, 7440 Girard Ave., Ste. 4, La Jolla, CA 92037. TEL 619-459-3818. FAX 619-459-3819. URL: http://www.IQTrends.com. *1390*

INVESTMENT STRATEGY QUARTERLY.
Green Mountain Asset Management Corp., URL: http://www.stockresearch.com/
Available only online. *1391*

INVESTOR'S DAILY.
Box 66370, Los Angeles, CA 90066-0370.
Vendor(s): Lexis-Nexis. *1391*

IOWA BUSINESS DIRECTORY.
American Business Directories, 5711 S. 86th Circle, Box 27347, Omaha, NE 68127. TEL 402-593-4600. FAX 402-331-5481. *1689*

IOWA LAW REVIEW.
University of Iowa, College of Law, 190 Boyd Law Bldg., Iowa City, IA 52242-1113. TEL 319-335-9132. FAX 319-335-9019.
Vendor(s): Lexis-Nexis, West Group. *3966*

IOWA LEGISLATIVE NEWS SERVICE BULLETIN.
Iowa Legislative News Service, Box 8370, Des Moines, IA 50301-8370. TEL 515-266-6066. FAX 515-266-6626. *6180*

IRAN BUSINESS DIGEST.
Sayar Communications Co., URL: http://gpg.com/ibd/news.html.
Available only online. *974*

THE IRANIAN.
Box 7637, Berkeley, CA 94707-0637. URL: http://www.iranian.com.
Available only online. *5529*

IRISH AMERICA MAGAZINE.
Irish America Inc., 432 Park Ave. S., Ste. 1503, New York, NY 10016-8013. TEL 212-684-3366. FAX 212-779-1198. URL: http://www.irishvoice.com/. *3018*

IRISH AMERICAN POST.
Irish American Post Ltd., 301 N. Water St., 3rd Floor, Milwaukee, WI 53202-5713. TEL 414-273-8132. FAX 414-273-8196. *3019*

IRISH GEOGRAPHY.
Geographical Society of Ireland, Department of Geography, University College Dublin, Befield, Dublin 4, Ireland. TEL 353-1-7068484. FAX 353-1-2695597. *3411*

IRISH JOURNAL OF AGRICULTURAL AND FOOD RESEARCH.
Teagasc, 19 Sandymount Ave., Dublin 4, Ireland. TEL 353-1-6688188. FAX 353-1-6688023. *128*

IRON FEATHER JOURNAL.
Phun Inc., Box 1905, Boulder, CO 80306. TEL 303-575-5652. URL: http://phidias.colorado.edu/ifj/ *4340*

IRRIGATION AND DRAINAGE ABSTRACTS.
CAB International, Wallingford, Oxon. OX10 8DE, England. TEL 44-1491-832111. FAX 44-1491-826090. URL: http://www.cabi.org. Vendor(s): DIMDI, European Space Agency, Knight-Ridder Information, Inc., STN International. *177*

IRRIGATION SCIENCE.
Springer-Verlag, Heidelberger Platz 3, 14197 Berlin, Germany. TEL 49-30-82787-0. FAX 49-30-82787448. URL: http://link.springer.de. *128*

ISLAND REPORT.
7353 Dunver Crescent, Verdun, PQ H4H 2H6, Canada. TEL 514-766-2125. URL: http://home.earthlink.net/~tarial/
Available only online. *7213*

ISLAND TRAVEL TRADER.
Island Publications Ltd, 26 St. Ursula St., Valletta VLT 06, Malta. TEL 356-431864. FAX 356-431864. URL: http://engine2.maltanet.omnes.net/ittravel. *7213*

ISOLATION AND PURIFICATION.
Gordon and Breach - Harwood Academic, Amsteldisk 166, 1st Fl., 1079 LH Amsterdam, Netherlands. URL: http://www.gbhap.com/Isolation_Purification/. *1791*

ISRAEL PHARMACEUTICAL JOURNAL.
Pharmaceutical Association of Israel, P.O. Box 566, Tel Aviv 65 112, Israel. *5669*

ISSUES IN LAW AND MEDICINE.
National Legal Center for the Medically Dependent and Disabled, Inc., Box 1586, Terre Haute, IN 47808-1586. TEL 812-232-0103.
Vendor(s): Information Access Co., National Library of Medicine, West Group. *4688*

ISSUES IN SCIENCE AND TECHNOLOGY.
John Wiley & Sons, Inc., Journals, 605 Third Ave., New York, NY 10158. TEL 212-850-6645. FAX 212-850-6021.
Vendor(s): Information Access Co., UMI. *6536*

ISSUES IN SCIENCE AND TECHNOLOGY LIBRARIANSHIP.
Association of College and Research Libraries, Science and Techology Section, 50 E. Huron St., Chicago, IL 60611-2795. TEL 312-280-3248. FAX 312-440-9374. URL: http://www.library.ucsb.edu/istl/ *4187*

ITEM PROCESSING REPORT.
Phillips Business Information, Inc., 1201 Seven Locks Rd., Potomac, MD 20854. TEL 301-424-3338. FAX 301-309-3847.
Vendor(s): Data-Star, Information Access Co., Knight-Ridder Information, Inc., NewsNet (EC19). *2176*

ITHACA COLLEGE QUARTERLY.
Ithaca College, Alumni Hall, Ithaca, NY 14850. TEL 607-274-3830. FAX 607-274-1490. URL: http://www.ithaca.edu. *1957*

IT'S A BUNNY.
3634 St. Laurent, Montreal, PQ H2X 2V4, Canada. TEL 514-982-9644. URL: http://www.iti.qc.ca/iti/bunny/
Available only online. *4419*

IT'S ON-LINE.
TEL 33-3-711-36-21. URL: http://its-online.com.
Available only online. *2453*

IWATE MEDICAL UNIVERSITY SCHOOL OF LIBERAL ARTS & SCIENCES. ANNUAL REPORT.
Iwate Ika Daigaku Kyoyobu, 16-1, 3-chome, Honcho-dori, Morioka-shi, Iwate-ken 020, Japan. TEL 0196-51-5111. FAX 0196-25-5816.
Vendor(s): JICST (JOIS-III). *6536*

J A M A: THE JOURNAL OF THE AMERICAN MEDICAL ASSOCIATION.
American Medical Association, 515 N. State St., Chicago, IL 60610. TEL 312-464-5000. FAX 312-464-4184.
Vendor(s): Information Access Co., Knight-Ridder Information, Inc., Ovid Technologies, Inc. (JWAR). *4689*

J A S T.
American Studies Association of Turkey, c/o Dr. Irem Balkir, Dept. of English, Bilkent Universitesi, 06553 Ankara, Turkey. FAX 90-312-2664934. URL: http://www.bups.bilkent.edu.tr/jast/. *3632*

J C T: JOURNAL OF COATINGS TECHNOLOGY.
Federation of Societies for Coatings Technology, 492 Norristown Rd., Blue Bell, PA 19422-2350. TEL 215-940-0777. FAX 215-940-0292.
Vendor(s): Information Access Co. *5553*

J E I.
Association for Evolutionary Economics, 1101 McClung Tower, University of Tennessee, Knoxville, TN 37996-0411. TEL 615-974-1689. FAX 615-974-3915.
Vendor(s): Information Access Co., UMI. *1305*

J E I REPORT.
Japan Economic Institute, 1000 Connecticut Ave., N.W., Washington, DC 20036. TEL 202-296-5633. FAX 202-296-8333.
Vendor(s): NewsNet. *1338*

J E T P LETTERS.
American Institute of Physics, One Physics Ellipse, College Park, MD 20740-3843. TEL 301-209-3000. URL: http://www.aip.org. *5808*

J. GRUBER'S HAGERS-TOWN TOWN AND COUNTRY ALMANACK.
Gruber Almanack Company, 1120 Professional Court, Box 609, Hagerstown, MD 21741-0609. TEL 301-733-2530. FAX 301-791-1478. URL: http://www.almanack.com. *2657*

J I C S T ONLINE INFORMATION SYSTEM.
U.S. National Technical Information Service, 5285 Port Royal Rd., Springfield, VA 22161. TEL 703-487-4630.
Available only online. Vendor(s): JICST. *6593*

JACK O'DWYER'S NEWSLETTER.
J.R. O'Dwyer Co., Inc., 271 Madison Ave., New York, NY 10016. TEL 212-679-2471. FAX 212-683-2750.
Vendor(s): Lexis-Nexis. *38*

JANE'S DEFENCE WEEKLY.
Jane's Information Group, Sentinel House, 163 Brighton Rd., Coulsdon, Surrey CR5 2NH, England. TEL 44-181-700-3700. FAX 44-181-700-3788.
Vendor(s): Knight-Ridder Information, Inc.. *5272*

JANE'S INTELLIGENCE REVIEW.
Jane's Information Group, Sentinel House, 163 Brighton Rd., Coulsdon, Surrey CR5 2NH, England. TEL 44-181-700-3700. FAX 44-181-700-3788. URL: http://www.janes.com/janes.html.
Vendor(s): Knight-Ridder Information, Inc.. *5272*

JANE'S XINE.
72 N. Merkle, Columbus, OH 43209. URL: http://www.solgate.com/~axatta/zine.html.
Available only online. *5402*

JAPAN ECONOMIC ALMANAC.
Nihon Keizai Shimbun, Inc., 1-9-5 Otemachi, Chiyoda-ku, Tokyo 100-66, Japan. TEL 81-3-3270-0251. FAX 81-3-5255-2661. *1588*

JAPAN QUARTERLY.
Asahi Shimbun Publishing Co., 3-2, Tsukiji 5-chome, Chuo-ku, Tokyo 104-11, Japan. TEL 81-3-3545-0428. FAX 81-3-3546-2404. URL: http://www.c3.crc.co.jp/HomePage/research/JQ/index.html.
Vendor(s): UMI. *4340*

JAPAN SOCIETY FOR SIMULATION TECHNOLOGY. JOURNAL.
Japan Technical Information Service, Sogo Kojimachi No. 3 Bldg., 6th Fl., 1-6 Koji-machi, Chiyoda-ku, Tokyo 102, Japan. TEL 81-3-3239-4711. FAX 81-3-3239-4714.
Vendor(s): JICST (JOIS). *2152*

JAPAN - U S BUSINESS REPORT.
Japan Economic Institute, 1000 Connecticut Ave., N.W., Washington, DC 20036. TEL 202-296-5633. FAX 202-296-8333.
Vendor(s): NewsNet. *1338*

JAPANESE JOURNAL OF CLINICAL ONCOLOGY.
Foundation for Promotion of Cancer Research, c/o National Cancer Center Hospital, 1-1, Tsukiji 5-chome, Chuo-ku, Tokyo 104, Japan. TEL 81-3-3542-2511. FAX 81-3-3545-3567. URL: http://www.info.ncc.go.jp.
Vendor(s): JICST. *4980*

JAPANESE JOURNAL OF OPHTHALMOLOGY.
University of Tokyo, School of Medicine, Department of Ophthalmology, 7-3-1 Hongo, Bunkyo-ku, Tokyo 113, Japan. TEL 81-3-3815-5411. FAX 81-3-3817-0798.
Vendor(s): CompuServe, Inc., DataArkiv A.B., JICST. *4995*

JAPANESE JOURNAL OF PHARMACOLOGY.
Japanese Pharmacological Society, Editorial Office, Kantohya Bld., Gokomachi-Ebisugawa, Nakagyo-ku, Kyoto 604, Japan. TEL 81-75-252-4641. FAX 81-75-252-4618. URL: http://dbs.pharm.kyoto-u.ac.jp/. *5669*

JAVA DEVELOPER'S JOURNAL.
Sys-Con Publications, Inc., 39 E. Central Ave., Pearl River, NY 10965. TEL 914-735-1900. FAX 914-735-3922. URL: http://www.sys-con.com/java/. *2144*

JAVA REPORT.
Sigs Publications, Inc., 71 W. 23rd St., 3rd Fl., New York, NY 10010-4102. TEL 212-274-0640. FAX 212-274-0646. URL: http://www.sigs.com/ *2144*

JAZZ FRIENDS REVIEW.
111 Hudson Ave., Chatham, NY 12037. URL: http://tri-millenia.net/jfr/
Available only online. *5402*

JAZZ NOW.
Jazz Now Magazine, Box 19266, Oakland, CA 94619-0266. TEL 510-531-2839. FAX 510-531-8875. *5403*

JAZZCHORD.
Jazz Co-Ordination Association of New South Wales, URL: http://www.magna.com.au/'georgeh/ozjazzjc.html jazzchord.
Available only online. *5403*

THE JERUSALEM POST.
Jerusalem Post, P.O. Box 81, Jerusalem 91000, Israel. TEL 972-2-5315666. FAX 972-2-5389527.
Vendor(s): Lexis-Nexis. *3324*

THE JERUSALEM POST (EDITION FRANCAISE).
Jerusalem Post, P.O. Box 81, Jerusalem 91000, Israel. TEL 972-2-315666. FAX 972-2-389017.
Vendor(s): Lexis-Nexis. *3324*

THE JERUSALEM POST (INTERNATIONAL EDITION).
Jerusalem Post, P.O. Box 81, Jerusalem 91000, Israel. TEL 972-2-315666. FAX 972-2-389017.
Vendor(s): Lexis-Nexis. *3324*

JET.
Johnson Publishing Co., Inc., 820 S. Michigan Ave., Chicago, IL 60605-2190. TEL 312-322-9200.
Vendor(s): Information Access Co., UMI. *3376*

JEWELERS' CIRCULAR KEYSTONE.
Chilton Co., One Chilton Way, Radnor, PA 19089. TEL 610-964-4000. FAX 610-964-4481.
Vendor(s): Information Access Co. *3865*

JEWISH STUDIES.
Jerusalem Academy of Jewish Studies, P.O. Box 5454, Jerusalem, Israel. TEL 972-2-6522817. FAX 972-2-6522827. URL: http://www.dvar.org. *6405*

JIBI INKOKA, TOKEIBU GEKA.
Igaku-Shoin Ltd., 5-24-3 Hongo, Bunkyo-ku, Tokyo 113-91, Japan. TEL 81-3-3817-5710.
Vendor(s): JICST. *5022*

JIMMY'S RIDDLE.
13 Kingsway, Carlton Way, Cambridge CB4 2EW, England. URL: http://www.cl.cam.ac.uk/users/jrt1003/radio/riddle/ *5404*

JITTER.
Columbia House, 600 108th Ave. N.E., Ste. 120, Bellevue, WA 98004. URL: http://www.jitter.com. Available only online. *1875*

JOB PRATIQUE MAGAZINE.
23 rue des Appenins, 75017 Paris, France. TEL 33-1-42285900. FAX 33-1-42282458. URL: http://www.alma-inter.fr/jobpratique/ *5511*

THE JOCULAR JOURNAL.
135-39 78th Ave., Flushing, NY 11367. URL: http://www.perfekt.net.
Available only online. *4340*

JOHN MARSHALL LAW REVIEW.
Christensen Inc. (Chicago), 315 S. Plymouth Ct., Chicago, IL 60604. TEL 312-987-1415. FAX 312-360-2669.
Vendor(s): Lexis-Nexis, West Group. *3967*

JOINT ASSOCIATION SURVEY ON DRILLING COSTS.
American Petroleum Institute, Publications Section, 1220 L St., N.W., Washington, DC 20005. TEL 202-682-8375. FAX 202-962-4776. URL: http://www.api.org. *5630*

JOINT COMMISSION PERSPECTIVES.
Mosby-Yearbook, Inc., 11830 Westline Dr., St. Louis, MO 63146-3318. TEL 800-453-4351. FAX 314-432-1380.
Vendor(s): Lexis-Nexis. *6241*

JOURNAL DE MEDECINE LEGALE DROIT MEDICAL.
Editions E S K A, 27 rue Dunois, 75013 Paris, France. TEL 44-06-80-42. FAX 44-24-06-94. *4905*

JOURNAL DE PHYSIQUE I.
Editions de Physique, 7 av. du Hoggar, Z.I. de Courtaboeuf, B.P. 112, 91944 Les Ulis Cedex A, France. TEL 33-1-69-07-36-88. FAX 33-1-69-28-84-91. URL: http://www.ed-phys.fr. *5808*

JOURNAL DE PHYSIQUE II.
Editions de Physique, 7 av. du Hoggar, Z.I. de Courtaboeuf, B.P. 112, 91944 Les Ulis Cedex A, France. TEL 33-1-69-07-36-88. FAX 33-1-69-28-84-91. URL: http://www.ed-phys.fr/docinfos/onlinejp2.html. *5808*

JOURNAL DE PHYSIQUE III.
Editions de Physique, 7 av. du Hoggar, Z.I. de Courtaboeuf, B.P 112, 91944 Les Ulis Cedex A, France. TEL 33-1-69-07-36-88. FAX 33-1-69-28-84-91. URL: http://www.ed-phys.fr/docinfos/onlinejp3.html. *5809*

JOURNAL FOR QUALITY AND PARTICIPATION.
Association for Quality and Participation, 801-B W. 8th St., Ste. 501, Cincinnati, OH 45203. TEL 513-381-1959. FAX 513-381-0070.
Vendor(s): UMI. *1570*

JOURNAL FOR THE SCIENTIFIC STUDY OF RELIGION.
Society for the Scientific Study of Religion, c/o Ralph Hood, Department of Psychology, University of Tennessee, Chattanooga, TN 37403. TEL 423-755-4262.
Vendor(s): Information Access Co., UMI. *6347*

JOURNAL FOR UNIVERSAL COMPUTER SCIENCE.
Springer-Verlag, Heidelberger Platz 3, 14197 Berlin, Germany. TEL 49-30-82787-0. FAX 49-30-82787448. URL: http://link.springer.de. *2085*

JOURNAL OF ABNORMAL CHILD PSYCHOLOGY.
Plenum Publishing Corp., 233 Spring St., New York, NY 10013-1578. TEL 212-620-8000. FAX 212-463-0742.
Vendor(s): Information Access Co. *6120*

JOURNAL OF ACCOUNTANCY.
American Institute of Certified Public Accountants, Harborside Financial Ctr., 201 Plaza Three, Jersey City, NJ 07311-9801. TEL 201-938-3796. FAX 201-329-1112. URL: http://www.aicpa.org/pubs/jofa/index.htm.
Vendor(s): Information Access Co., UMI. *1092*

JOURNAL OF ACCOUNTING LITERATURE.
University of Florida, Accounting Research Center, Fisher School of Accounting-267 BUS, College of Business Administration, Gainesville, FL 32611. TEL 904-392-0155.
Vendor(s): UMI. *1093*

JOURNAL OF ADHESION.
Gordon and Breach - Harwood Academic, Amsteldisk 166, 1st Fl., 1079 LH Amsterdam, Netherlands. URL: http://www.gbhap.com/Adhesion/. *5809*

JOURNAL OF ADOLESCENCE.
Academic Press Ltd., 24-28 Oval Rd., London NW1 7DX, England. TEL 44-171-267-4466. FAX 44-171-482-2293. URL: http://www.hbuk.co.uk/ap/adolescence; http://www.europe.idealibrary.com/ *1848*

JOURNAL OF ADVANCED MATERIALS.
Intercontact Science, Leninskii Prospekt 49, 117911 Moscow, Russia. TEL 095-135-62-97. FAX 095-135-86-80. URL: http://www.demon.co.uk/cambsci/advmat.htm. *2861*

JOURNAL OF ADVERTISING.
American Academy of Advertising, Clemson University, College of Commerce & Industry, 245 Sirrine Hall, Clemson, SC 29634-1325. URL: http://business.clemson.edu/market/jao/
Vendor(s): Information Access Co., Lexis-Nexis, UMI. *38*

JOURNAL OF ADVERTISING RESEARCH.
Advertising Research Foundation, 641 Lexington Ave., 11th Fl., New York, NY 10022. TEL 212-751-5656. FAX 212-319-5265. URL: http://www.arfsite.org/publish.html.
Vendor(s): Information Access Co., UMI. *38*

JOURNAL OF AFRICAN HISTORY.
Cambridge University Press, Edinburgh Bldg., Shaftesbury Rd., Cambridge CB2 2RU, England. TEL 44-1223-312393. FAX 44-1223-315052. URL: http://www.cup.org/journals/jnlscat/afh/afh.html.
Vendor(s): Information Access Co. *3527*

JOURNAL OF AFRICAN TRAVEL WRITING.
University of North Carolina, Institute of African American Research, Box 346, Chapel Hill, NC 27514. URL: http://www.unc.edu/~ottotwo. *7214*

JOURNAL OF AGRICULTURAL AND FOOD CHEMISTRY.
American Chemical Society, 1155 16th St., N.W., Washington, DC 20036. TEL 800-333-9511. FAX 614-447-3671. URL: http://pubs.acs.org/journals/jafcau/index.html.
Vendor(s): STN International (CJACS). *231*

JOURNAL OF AGRICULTURAL ENGINEERING RESEARCH.
Academic Press Ltd., 24-28 Oval Rd., London NW1 7DX, England. TEL 44-171-267-4466. FAX 44-171-482-2293. URL: http://www.hbuk.co.uk/ap/jaer; http://www.europe.idealibrary.com/ *231*

JOURNAL OF AGRICULTURAL LENDING.
American Bankers Association, 1120 Connecticut Ave., N.W., Washington, DC 20036. TEL 202-663-5378. FAX 202-828-4540.
Vendor(s): UMI. *1148*

JOURNAL OF AIR LAW AND COMMERCE.
S M U Law Review Association, Southern Methodist University, School of Law, Dallas, TX 75275. TEL 214-768-8250. FAX 214-768-3946.
Vendor(s): West Group. *3968*

JOURNAL OF AIR TRANSPORTATION WORLD WIDE.
University of Nebraska at Omaha, Aviation Institute, Allwie Hall, Rm. 422, 60th & Dodge Sts., Omaha, NE 68182-0508. TEL 402-554-3424. FAX 402-554-3781.
Available only online. *7031*

JOURNAL OF ALGEBRA.
Academic Press, Inc., Journal Division, 525 B St., Ste. 1900, San Diego, CA 92101-4495. TEL 619-230-1840. FAX 619-699-6800. URL: http://www.apnet.com/www/journal/ja.htm; http://www.idealibrary.com/ *4580*

JOURNAL OF ALGORITHMS.
Academic Press, Inc., Journal Division, 525 B St., Ste. 1900, San Diego, CA 92101-4495. TEL 619-230-1840. FAX 619-699-6800. URL: http://www.apnet.com/www/journal/al.htm; http://www.idealibrary.com/ *4621*

THE JOURNAL OF ALLERGY AND CLINICAL IMMUNOLOGY.
Mosby - Year Book, Inc., 11830 Westline Industrial Dr., St. Louis, MO 63146-3318. TEL 314-872-8370. FAX 314-872-9164.
Vendor(s): Ovid Technologies, Inc. *4798*

JOURNAL OF AMERICAN CULTURE.
Popular Press, Bowling Green State University, Bowling Green, OH 43403. TEL 419-372-2981.
Vendor(s): UMI. *3782*

JOURNAL OF AMERICAN ETHNIC HISTORY.
Transaction Publishers, Transaction Periodicals Consortium, Department 3092, Rutgers University, New Brunswick, NJ 08903. TEL 908-445-2280. FAX 908-445-3138.
Vendor(s): Information Access Co. *3023*

JOURNAL OF AMERICAN HISTORY.
Organization of American Historians, 112 N Bryan St., Bloomington, IN 47408. TEL 812-855-7311. URL: http://www.jstor.org/fcgi-bin/jstor/listjournal.fcg/00218723?configjstor.
Vendor(s): UMI. *3632*

JOURNAL OF ANALYTICAL ATOMIC SPECTROMETRY.
The Royal Society of Chemistry, Thomas Graham House, Science Park, Milton Rd., Cambridge CB4 4WF, England. TEL 44-1223-420066. FAX 44-1223-423429. URL: http://chemistry.rsc.org/rsc/.
Vendor(s): STN International (CJRSC). *1792*

JOURNAL OF ANIMAL SCIENCE.
American Society of Animal Science, 1111 N. Dunlap Ave., Savoy, IL 61874. TEL 217-356-3182. FAX 217-398-4119. URL: http://www.asas.org/jas.html. *280*

JOURNAL OF ANTHROPOLOGICAL ARCHAEOLOGY.
Academic Press, Inc., Journal Division, 525 B St., Ste. 1900, San Diego, CA 92101-4495. TEL 619-230-1840. FAX 619-699-6859. URL: http://www.apnet.com/www/journal/aa.html. *321*

JOURNAL OF APPLIED ELECTROCHEMISTRY.
Thomson Science, 2-6 Boundary Row, London SE1 8HN, England. TEL 44-171-8650066. FAX 44-171-5229623. URL: http://www.thomsonscience.com. *1805*

JOURNAL OF APPLIED PHYSICS.
American Institute of Physics, One Physics Ellipse, College Park, MD 20740-3843. TEL 301-209-3000. URL: http://www.aip.org. *5809*

JOURNAL OF APPLIED PHYSIOLOGY.
American Physiological Society, 9650 Rockville Pike, Bethesda, MD 20814. TEL 301-530-7164. FAX 301-571-8313. URL: http://www.faseb.org/aps.
Vendor(s): OCLC. *817*

JOURNAL OF APPLIED POLYMER SCIENCE.
John Wiley & Sons, Inc., Journals, 605 Third Ave., New York, NY 10158. TEL 212-850-6645. FAX 212-850-6021.
Vendor(s): STN International (CJWILEY). *2767*

JOURNAL OF APPLIED STATISTICS.
Carfax Publishing Co., P.O. Box 25, Abingdon, Oxon. OX14 3UE, England. TEL 44-1235-401000. FAX 44-1235-401550. *6921*

JOURNAL OF APPLIED THERAPEUTICS.
Gordon and Breach - Harwood Academic, Amsteldisk 166, 1st Fl., 1079 LH Amsterdam, Netherlands. URL: http://www.gbhap/Applied_Therapeutics/. *5670*

SERIALS AVAILABLE ONLINE

JOURNAL OF APPROXIMATION THEORY.
Academic Press, Inc., Journal Division, 525 B St., Ste. 1900, San Diego, CA 92101-4495. TEL 619-230-1840. FAX 619-699-6800. URL: http://www.apnet.com/www/journal/at.htm; http://www.idealibrary.com/ *4580*

JOURNAL OF AQUARICULTURE AND AQUATIC SCIENCES.
The Written Word, 7601 E. Forest Lake Dr., N.W., Parkville, MO 64152. TEL 816-842-5936. FAX 816-474-5597.
Vendor(s): CompuServe, Inc. *608*

JOURNAL OF ARCHAEOLOGICAL SCIENCE.
Academic Press Ltd., 24-28 Oval Rd., London NW1 7DX, England. TEL 44-171-267-4466. FAX 44-171-482-2293. URL: http://www.hbuk.co.uk/ap/jas/; http://www.europe.idealibrary.com. *368*

THE JOURNAL OF ARCHITECTURE.
Thomson Professional, 2-6 Boundary Row, London SE1 8HN, England. TEL 44-171-8650066. FAX 44-171-5229623. URL: http://architecture.efnspon.com. *407*

JOURNAL OF ARID ENVIRONMENTS.
Academic Press Ltd., 24-28 Oval Rd., London NW1 7DX, England. TEL 44-171-267-4466. FAX 44-171-482-2293. URL: http://www.hbuk.co.uk/ap/jae; http://www.europe.idealibrary.com/ *3411*

JOURNAL OF ART & ENTERTAINMENT LAW.
Depaul University, College of Law, 25 E. Jackson Blvd., Chicago, IL 60604. TEL 312-362-5635. URL: http://shrike.depaul.edu/~snolley *3968*

JOURNAL OF ARTIFICIAL INTELLIGENCE RESEARCH.
Morgan Kaufmann Publishers, Inc., 340 Pine Street, 6th Fl., San Francisco, CA 94104. TEL 415-392-2665. FAX 415-982-2665. URL: http://www.jair.org/masthead.html; http://www.cs.washington.edu/research/jair/home.html. *2101*

JOURNAL OF ASIAN AND AFRICAN STUDIES.
E.J. Brill, P.O. Box 9000, 2300 PA Leiden, Netherlands. TEL 31-71-5353500. FAX 31-71-5317532.
Vendor(s): Information Access Co. *6716*

JOURNAL OF ASIAN STUDIES.
Association for Asian Studies, Inc., 1 Lane Hall, University of Michigan, Ann Arbor, MI 48109. TEL 313-665-2490.
Vendor(s): UMI. *5530*

JOURNAL OF AUSTRALASIAN GRAPHICS IMAGERY.
Curtin University of Technology, School of Computing, Hayman Rd., Bentley, W.A. 6102, Australia. TEL 619-351-7680. URL: http://www.cs.curtin.edu.au/jagi/
Available only online. *2124*

JOURNAL OF AUTOIMMUNITY.
Academic Press Ltd., 24-28 Oval Rd., London NW1 7DX, England. TEL 44-171-267-4466. FAX 44-171-482-2293. URL: http://www.hbuk.co.uk/ap/jautoimmunity; http://www.europe.idealibrary.com/ *4798*

JOURNAL OF BANK COST & MANAGEMENT ACCOUNTING.
National Association of Bank Cost and Management Accounting, 2385 Castilian Cir., Box 458, Northbrook, IL 60062-7614. TEL 847-272-4233. FAX 847-272-6445.
Vendor(s): UMI. *1149*

JOURNAL OF BIOLOGICAL CHEMISTRY.
American Society for Biochemistry and Molecular Biology, Inc., Box 630591, Baltimore, MD 21263. URL: http://www.highwire.stanford.edu/jbc/. *662*

JOURNAL OF BIOLOGICAL INORGANIC CHEMISTRY.
Springer-Verlag, Heidelberger Platz 3, 14197 Berlin, Germany. TEL 49-30-82787-0. FAX 49-30-82787488. URL: http://link.springer.de. *662*

JOURNAL OF BLACKS IN HIGHER EDUCATION.
CH II Publishers, Inc., 200 W. 57th St., New York, NY 10019. TEL 212-399-1084. FAX 212-245-1973.
Vendor(s): Lexis-Nexis. *3023*

JOURNAL OF BONE AND JOINT SURGERY: AMERICAN VOLUME.
Journal of Bone and Joint Surgery, Inc., 20 Pickering St., Needham, MA 02192-3157. TEL 617-449-9738.
Vendor(s): Ovid Technologies, Inc. *5009*

JOURNAL OF BROADCASTING AND ELECTRONIC MEDIA.
Broadcast Education Association, 1771 N St., N.W., Washington, DC 20036. TEL 202-429-5354.
Vendor(s): UMI. *2052*

JOURNAL OF BUDDHIST ETHICS.
University of London, Goldsmiths, London SE14, England. TEL 44-171-919-7497. FAX 44-171-919-7398. URL: http://www.gold.ac.uk/jbe/jbe.html.
Available only online. *6389*

THE JOURNAL OF BUSINESS (CHICAGO).
University of Chicago Press, Journals Division, Box 37005, Chicago, IL 60637. TEL 773-753-3347. FAX 773-753-0811. URL: http://www.nchicago.edu/JB/home.html.
Vendor(s): Information Access Co. *975*

JOURNAL OF BUSINESS (SPOKANE).
Northwest Business Press, Inc., 112 E. First Ave., Spokane, WA 99202. TEL 509-456-5257.
Vendor(s): UMI. *1149*

JOURNAL OF BUSINESS ADMINISTRATION.
University of British Columbia, Faculty of Commerce and Business Administration, Vancouver, BC V6T 1Z2, Canada. TEL 604-822-9434. FAX 604-822-8489.
Vendor(s): Information Access Co. *1486*

JOURNAL OF BUSINESS COMMUNICATION.
Association for Business Communication, c/o Dr. Rovert J. Myers, Dept. of Speech Communication, Baruch College, 17 Lexington Ave., New York, NY 10010. TEL 817-565-4423. URL: http://www.cohums.ohio-state.edu/english/facstf/kol/abc/jbc.html.
Vendor(s): Information Access Co., UMI. *1486*

JOURNAL OF BUSINESS ETHICS.
Kluwer Academic Publishers, Postbus 17, 3300 AA Dordrecht, Netherlands. TEL 31-78-6392392. FAX 31-78-6392254. URL: http://www.wkap.nl/kapis/CGI-BIN/WORLD/jounalhome.htm?O1674544.
Vendor(s): Information Access Co., UMI. *976*

JOURNAL OF BUSINESS FORECASTING METHODS AND SYSTEMS.
Graceway Publishing Co., Box 670159, Flushing, NY 11367-0159. TEL 718-463-3914. FAX 718-544-9086. URL: http://www.ibforecast.com/jbf.htm.
Vendor(s): UMI. *976*

JOURNAL OF BUSINESS IN DEVELOPING NATIONS.
North Carolina Central University, School of Business, JBND, Durham, NC 27707. URL: http://www.nccu.edu/business/journal.htm.
Available only online. *1363*

JOURNAL OF BUSINESS LOGISTICS.
Council of Logistics Management, 2803 Butterfield, Oak Brook, IL 60521. TEL 630-574-0985. FAX 630-574-0989.
Vendor(s): UMI. *1532*

JOURNAL OF BUSINESS STRATEGY.
Faulkner & Gray, Inc. (New York), 11 Penn Plaza, 17th Fl., New York, NY 10001. TEL 212-967-7000. FAX 212-967-7155. URL: http://www.faulknergray.com/business/business.html.
Vendor(s): Information Access Co., UMI. *1487*

JOURNAL OF CANCER RESEARCH AND CLINICAL ONCOLOGY.
Springer-Verlag, Heidelberger Platz 3, 14197 Berlin, Germany. TEL 49-30-82787-0. FAX 49-30-82787448. URL: http://link.springer.de. *4981*

JOURNAL OF CARDIOVASCULAR RISK.
Thomson Science, 2-6 Boundary Row, London SE1 8HN, England. TEL 44-171-865-0198. FAX 44-171-410-6600. URL: http://www.thomsonscience.com. *4820*

JOURNAL OF CAREER PLANNING & EMPLOYMENT.
National Association of Colleges and Employers, 62 Highland Ave., Bethlehem, PA 18017. TEL 610-868-1421. FAX 610-868-0208.
Vendor(s): UMI. *5512*

JOURNAL OF CATALYSIS.
Academic Press, Inc., Journal Division, 525 B St., Ste. 1900, San Diego, CA 92101-4495. TEL 619-230-1840. FAX 619-699-6800. URL: http://www.apnet.com/www/journal/ca.htm; http://wwww.idealibrary.com/ *1830*

JOURNAL OF CELL SCIENCE.
Company of Biologists Ltd., Bidder Bldg., 140 Cowley Rd., Cambridge CB4 4DL, England. TEL 44-1223-426164. FAX 44-1223-423353. URL: http://www.cityscape.co.uk/users/ag64. *741*

JOURNAL OF CELLULAR BIOCHEMISTRY.
John Wiley & Sons, Inc., Journals, 605 Third Ave., New York, NY 10158. TEL 212-850-6645. FAX 212-850-6021. URL: http://www.wiley.co.uk. *663*

JOURNAL OF CELLULAR PHYSIOLOGY.
John Wiley & Sons, Inc., Journals, 605 Third Ave., New York, NY 10158. TEL 212-850-6645. FAX 212-850-6021. URL: http://www.wiley.co.uk. *817*

JOURNAL OF CEREAL SCIENCE.
Academic Press Ltd., 24-28 Oval Rd., London NW1 7DX, England. TEL 44-171-267-4466. FAX 44-171-482-2293. URL: http://www.hbuk.co.uk/ap/jcs; http://www.europe.idealibrary.com/ *264*

JOURNAL OF CHEMICAL AND ENGINEERING DATA.
American Chemical Society, 1155 16th St. N.W., Washington, DC 20036. TEL 800-333-9511. FAX 614-447-3671. URL: http://pubs.acs.org/journals/jceaax/index.html.
Vendor(s): STN International (CJACS). *1754*

JOURNAL OF CHEMICAL EDUCATION.
American Chemical Society, c/o Dept. of Chemistry, Montana State University, Bozeman, MT 59717-0340. TEL 406-994-5393. FAX 406-994-5407. URL: http://jchemed.chem.wisc.edu/
Vendor(s): UMI. *1754*

JOURNAL OF CHEMICAL INFORMATION AND COMPUTER SCIENCES.
American Chemical Society, 1155 16th St. N.W., Washington, DC 20036. TEL 800-333-9511. FAX 614-447-3671.
Vendor(s): STN International (CJACS). *1800*

JOURNAL OF CHEMICAL PHYSICS.
American Institute of Physics, One Physics Ellipse, College park, MD 20740-3843. TEL 301-209-3000. FAX 516-349-9704. URL: http://www.aip.org; http://jcp.uchicago.edu/. *5809*

JOURNAL OF CHEMICAL RESEARCH.
The Royal Society of Chemistry, Thomas Graham House, Science Park, Milton Rd., Cambridge CB4 4WF, England. TEL 44-1223-420066. FAX 44-1223-423429. URL: http://chemistry.rsc.org/rsc/.
Vendor(s): STN International (CJRSC). *1755*

JOURNAL OF CHEMICAL THERMODYNAMICS.
Academic Press Ltd., 24-28 Oval Rd., London NW1 7DX, England. TEL 44-171-267-4466. FAX 44-171-482-2293. URL: http://www.hbuk.co.uk/ap/jct; http://www.europe.idealibrary.com/ *1830*

JOURNAL OF CLASSIFICATION.
Springer-Verlag, Science Journals, 175 Fifth Ave., New York, NY 10010. TEL 212-460-1500. FAX 212-473-6272. URL: http://www.springer-ny.com. *4581*

JOURNAL OF CLINICAL ENGINEERING.
Lippincott - Raven Publishers, 227 E. Washington Sq., Philadelphia, PA 19106-3780. TEL 215-238-4200. URL: http://www.lrpub.com/jce. *648*

JOURNAL OF CLINICAL EPIDEMIOLOGY.
Elsevier Science Inc., Box 945, New York, NY 10159-0945. TEL 212-633-3730. FAX 212-633-3680. URL: http://www.elsevier.nl/. *4693*

JOURNAL OF CLINICAL ONCOLOGY.
W.B. Saunders Co., Curtis Center, 3rd Fl., Independence Sq. W., Philadelphia, PA 19106-3399. TEL 215-238-7800. FAX 215-238-6445. *4981*

JOURNAL OF CLINICAL PATHOLOGY.
B M J Publishing Group, B.M.A. House, Tavistock Sq., London WC1H 9JR, England. TEL 44-171-383-6270. FAX 44-171-383-6402. Vendor(s): Ovid Technologies, Inc. *4693*

JOURNAL OF CLINICAL PHARMACOLOGY.
Lippincott - Raven Publishers, 227 E. Washington Sq., Philadelphia, PA 19106. TEL 215-238-4200. URL: http://www.lrpub.com. *5670*

JOURNAL OF CLINICAL PSYCHOLOGY.
John Wiley & Sons, Inc., Journals, 605 Third Ave., New York, NY 10158-0012. TEL 212-850-6645. FAX 212-850-6021. URL: http://www.wiley.co.uk. Vendor(s): UMI. *6122*

JOURNAL OF CLINICAL PSYCHOPHARMACOLOGY.
Williams & Wilkins, 351 W. Camden St., Baltimore, MD 21201-2436. TEL 410-528-4068. FAX 410-528-4452. URL: http://www.wwilkins.com. Vendor(s): Ovid Technologies, Inc.. *5670*

JOURNAL OF COGNITIVE NEUROSCIENCE.
M I T Press, 5 Cabridge Center, Cambridge, MA 02142. TEL 617-253-2889. FAX 617-577-1545. URL: http://www-mitpress.mit.edu. Vendor(s): Information Access Co.. *5073*

JOURNAL OF COLLOID AND INTERFACE SCIENCE.
Academic Press, Inc., Journal Division, 525 B St., Ste. 1900, San Diego, CA 92101-4495. TEL 619-230-1840. FAX 619-699-6800. URL: http://www.apnet.com/www/journal/cs.htm; http://www.idealibrary.com/ *1830*

JOURNAL OF COMBINATORIAL THEORY. SERIES A.
Academic Press, Inc., Journal Division, 525 B St., Ste. 1900, San Diego, CA 92101-4495. TEL 619-230-1840. FAX 619-699-6800. URL: http://www.apnet.com/www/journal/ta.htm. *4581*

JOURNAL OF COMBINATORIAL THEORY. SERIES B.
Academic Press, Inc., Journal Division, 525 B St., Ste. 1900, San Diego, CA 92101-4490. TEL 619-230-1840. FAX 619-699-6800. URL: http://www.apnet.com/www/journal/tb.htm; http://www.idealibrary.com/ *4581*

JOURNAL OF COMMERCE AND COMMERCIAL.
Journal of Commerce, Inc., 2 World Trade Center, 27th Fl., New York, NY 10048-0203. TEL 212-837-7000. FAX 212-837-7130. Vendor(s): Knight-Ridder Information, Inc., Lexis-Nexis, MediaStream. *1213*

JOURNAL OF COMMON MARKET STUDIES.
Blackwell Publishers Ltd., 108 Cowley Rd., Oxford OX4 1JF, England. TEL 44-1865-791100. FAX 44-1865-791347. URL: http://www.blackwellpublishers.ac.uk. Vendor(s): Information Access Co. *5936*

JOURNAL OF COMMUNICATION.
Oxford University Press, Journals, 2001 Evans Rd., Cary, NC 27513. TEL 919-677-0977. FAX 919-677-1714. URL: http://www.oup-usa.org/ Vendor(s): UMI. *1996*

JOURNAL OF COMMUNITY HEALTH.
Human Sciences Press, Inc., 233 Spring St., New York, NY 10013-1578. TEL 212-620-8000. FAX 212-463-0742. Vendor(s): Information Access Co. *4693*

JOURNAL OF COMPARATIVE ECONOMICS.
Academic Press, Inc., Journal Division, 525 B St., Ste. 1900, San Diego, CA 92101-4495. TEL 619-230-1840. FAX 619-699-6800. URL: http://www.apnet.com/www/journal/je.htm; http://www.idealibrary.com/ *976*

JOURNAL OF COMPARATIVE FAMILY STUDIES.
University of Calgary, Department of Sociology, 2500 University Dr. N.W., Calgary, AB T2N 1N4, Canada. TEL 403-220-7317. FAX 403-282-9298. Vendor(s): Information Access Co., UMI. *6716*

JOURNAL OF COMPARATIVE PHYSIOLOGY. A: SENSORY, NEURAL, AND BEHAVIORAL PHYSIOLOGY.
Springer-Verlag, Heidelberger Platz 3, 14197 Berlin, Germany. TEL 49-30-82787-0. FAX 49-30-82787448. URL: http://link.springer.de. *817*

JOURNAL OF COMPARATIVE PHYSIOLOGY. B: BIOCHEMICAL, SYSTEMATIC, AND ENVIRONMENTAL PHYSIOLOGY.
Springer-Verlag, Heidelberger Platz 3, 14197 Berlin, Germany. TEL 49-30-82787-0. FAX 49-30-82787448. URL: http://link.springer.de. *817*

JOURNAL OF COMPARATIVE RELIGION.
Universal Publications (a division of S T C), P.O. Box 7305, Ottawa, ON K1L 8E4, Canada. TEL 613-831-1052. FAX 613-831-8452. URL: htpp://www.upinfo.com/~up. *6348*

JOURNAL OF COMPLEXITY.
Academic Press, Inc., Journal Division, 525 B St., Ste. 1900, San Diego, CA 92101-4495. TEL 619-230-1840. FAX 619-699-6800. URL: http://www.apnet.com/www/journal/cm.htm; http://www.idealibrary.com/ *4621*

JOURNAL OF COMPOSITION THEORY.
Association of Teachers of Advanced Composition, c/o Thomas Kent, English Department. Iowa University, Ames, IA 50011. URL: http://nosferatu.cas.usf.edu/JAC/index.html. *4421*

JOURNAL OF COMPUTATIONAL INTELLIGENCE IN FINANCE.
Finance & Technology Publishing, Box 764, Haymarket, VA 20168. TEL 703-754-0696. FAX 703-753-2634. URL: http://ourworld.compuserve.com/homepages/ftpub. *1176*

JOURNAL OF COMPUTATIONAL PHYSICS.
Academic Press, Inc., Journal Division, 525 B St., Ste. 1900, San Diego, CA 92101-4495. TEL 619-230-1840. FAX 619-699-6800. URL: http://www.apnet.com/www/journal/cp.htm; http://www.idealibrary.com/ *5838*

JOURNAL OF COMPUTER - AIDED MOLECULAR DESIGN.
E S C O M Science Publishers BV, P.O. Box 214, 2300 AE Leiden, Netherlands. TEL 31-71-127052. FAX 31-71-121772. URL: http://wucmd.wustl.edu/jcamd/jcamd.html. *1800*

JOURNAL OF COMPUTER AND SYSTEM SCIENCES.
Academic Press, Inc., Journal Division, 525 B St., Ste. 1900, San Diego, CA 92101-4495. TEL 619-230-1840. FAX 619-699-6800. URL: http://www.apnet.com/www/journal/ss.htm; http://www.idealibrary.com/ *2085*

JOURNAL OF COMPUTER ASSISTED TOMOGRAPHY.
Lippincott - Raven Publishers, 227 E. Washington Sq., Philadelphia, PA 19106. TEL 215-238-4200. FAX 215-238-4227. URL: http://www.lrpub.com. *5108*

JOURNAL OF CONSUMER POLICY.
Kluwer Academic Publishers, Postbus 17, 3300 AA Dordrecht, Netherlands. TEL 31-78-6392392. FAX 31-78-6392254. URL: http://www.wkap.nl. Vendor(s): Information Access Co. *2256*

JOURNAL OF CONSUMER RESEARCH.
University of Chicago Press, Journals Division, Box 37005, Chicago, IL 60637. TEL 773-753-3347. FAX 773-753-0811. URL: http://www.journals.uchicago.edu/JCR/home.html. Vendor(s): Information Access Co., Knight-Ridder Information, Inc., Lexis-Nexis. *1532*

JOURNAL OF CONTEMPORARY NEUROLOGY.
M I T Press, 5 Cambridge Center, Cambridge, MA 02142. TEL 617-253-2889. FAX 617-577-1545. URL: http://www-mitpress.mit.edu/jrnls-cata;pg/cont-neuro.html. Available only online. *5073*

JOURNAL OF CONVEX ANALYSIS.
Heldermann Verlag, Langer Graben 13d, 32657 Lemgo, Germany. TEL 49-5261-10226. FAX 49-5261-15264. URL: http://www.emis.de/journals/jca/index.html. *4581*

SERIALS AVAILABLE ONLINE

JOURNAL OF COORDINATION CHEMISTRY.
Gordon and Breach - Harwood Academic, Amsteldisk 166, 1st Fl., 1079 LH Amsterdam, Netherlands. URL: http://www.gbhap.com/Coordination_Chemistry/. *1755*

JOURNAL OF CORPORATION LAW.
University of Iowa, College of Law, 190 Boyd Law Bldg., Iowa City, IA 52242-1113. TEL 319-335-9061. FAX 319-335-9019. Vendor(s): West Group. *4082*

JOURNAL OF COUNSELING & DEVELOPMENT.
American Counseling Association, 5999 Stevenson Ave., Alexandria, VA 22304-3300. TEL 703-823-9800. FAX 703-823-0252. Vendor(s): UMI. *6124*

JOURNAL OF CREDIBILITY ASSESSMENT AND WITNESS PSYCHOLOGY.
URL: http://truth.idbsu.edu/jcaawp/ Available only online. *6124*

THE JOURNAL OF CREDIT & RISK MANAGEMENT.
Robert Morris Associates, One Liberty Place, Ste. 2300, 1650 Market St., Philadelphia, PA 19107. TEL 215-851-9100. Vendor(s): Information Access Co., UMI. *1149*

JOURNAL OF CRIMINAL JUSTICE AND POPULAR CULTURE.
State University of New York at Albany, School of Criminal Justice, 135 Western Ave., Albany, NY 12222. TEL 518-442-5210. URL: http://www.albany.edu/scj/jcjpc/. Available only online. *4092*

JOURNAL OF CRIMINAL LAW & CRIMINOLOGY.
Northwestern University, School of Law - Office of Legal Publications, 357 E. Chicago Ave., Chicago, IL 60611. TEL 312-503-8463. Vendor(s): Information Access Co., UMI, West Group. *2270*

JOURNAL OF CRYPTOLOGY.
Springer-Verlag, Science Journals, 175 Fifth Ave., New York, NY 10010. TEL 212-460-1500. FAX 212-474-6272. URL: http://www.springer-ny.com. *4582*

JOURNAL OF DAIRY SCIENCE.
American Dairy Science Association, 1111 N. Dunlap Ave., Savoy, IL 61874. TEL 217-356-3182. FAX 217-398-4119. URL: http://orion.adsa.uiuc.edu/ *256*

JOURNAL OF DEMOCRACY.
Johns Hopkins University Press, Journals Publishing Division, 2715 N. Charles St., Baltimore, MD 21218. TEL 410-516-6987. FAX 410-516-6968. URL: http://muse.jhu.edu; http://www.press.jhu.journals/journal_of_democracy/ *5937*

THE JOURNAL OF DEVELOPMENT STUDIES.
Frank Cass, Newbury House, 890-900 Eastern Ave., Newbury Park, Ilford, Essex 1G2 7HH, England. TEL 44-181-599-8866. FAX 44-181-599-0984. URL: http://www.frankcass.com. Vendor(s): Information Access Co., UMI. *1364*

JOURNAL OF DIFFERENCE EQUATIONS AND APPLICATIONS.
Gordon and Breach - Harwood Academic, Amsteldisk 166, 1st Fl., 1079 LH Amsterdam, Netherlands. URL: http://www.gbhap.com/Difference_Equations_Applications/. *4582*

JOURNAL OF DIFFERENTIAL EQUATIONS.
Academic Press, Inc., Journal Division, 525 B St., Ste. 1900, San Diego, CA 92101-4495. TEL 619-230-1840. FAX 619-699-6800. URL: http://www.apnet.com/www/journal/de.htm; http://www.idealibrary.com/ *4582*

JOURNAL OF DRUG EDUCATION.
Baywood Publishing Co., Inc., 26 Austin Ave., Box 337, Amityville, NY 11701. TEL 516-691-1270. FAX 516-691-1770. URL: http://baywood.com. *2302*

JOURNAL OF DRUG ISSUES.
Journal of Drug Issues Inc., Box 4021, Leon Sta., Tallahassee, FL 32315. TEL 904-668-6669. *2303*

JOURNAL OF DRUG RESEARCH OF EGYPT.
National Organisation for Drug Control and Research, Drug Research and Control Center, 6, Abou-Hazem St., Pyramids Ave., Box 29, Cairo, Egypt. *5671*

JOURNAL OF DRUG TARGETING.
Gordon and Breach - Harwood Academic, Amsteldisk 166, 1st Fl., 1079 LH Amsterdam, Netherlands. URL: http://www.gbhap.com/Drug_Targeting/. *5671*

JOURNAL OF EARLY CHRISTIAN STUDIES.
Johns Hopkins University Press, Journals Publishing Division, 2715 N. Charles St., Ste. 750, Baltimore, MD 21218-4319. TEL 410-516-6987. FAX 410-516-6968. URL: http://muse.jhu.edu. *6348*

JOURNAL OF ECONOMIC LITERATURE.
American Economic Association, 2014 Broadway, Ste. 305, Nashville, TN 37203. TEL 615-322-2595.
Vendor(s): Knight-Ridder Information, Inc. (Economic Literature Index File no. 139). *1052*

JOURNAL OF ECONOMIC THEORY.
Academic Press, Inc., Journal Division, 525 B St., Ste. 1900, San Diego, CA 92101-4495. TEL 619-230-1840. FAX 619-699-6800. URL: http://www.apnet.com/www/journal/et.htm; http://www.idelibrary.com/ *1307*

JOURNAL OF EDUCATION FOR BUSINESS.
Heldref Publications, 1319 18th St., N.W., Washington, DC 20036-1802. TEL 202-296-6267. FAX 202-296-5149.
Vendor(s): UMI. *977*

JOURNAL OF EDUCATION FOR TEACHING.
Carfax Publishing Co., P.O. Box 25, Abingdon, Oxon. OX14 3UE, England. TEL 44-1235-401000. FAX 44-1235-401550. *2546*

JOURNAL OF ELECTRONIC DEFENSE.
Horizon - House - Publications, Inc., 685 Canton St., Norwood, MA 02062. TEL 617-769-9750. FAX 617-762-9230. URL: http://www.jedefense.com/jed.html/
Vendor(s): Information Access Co. *5273*

JOURNAL OF EMPIRICAL GENERALISATIONS IN MARKETING SCIENCE.
University of South Australia, North Terrace, Marketing Science Centre, Adelaide, S.A. 5001, Australia. TEL 61-8-3020715. FAX 61-8-3020442. URL: http://msc.citywest.unisa.edu.au/msc/Jems_Intro.html.
Available only online. *1533*

JOURNAL OF ENERGY, NATURAL RESOURCES AND ENVIRONMENTAL LAW.
University of Utah, College of Law, Salt Lake City, UT 84112. TEL 801-581-6833.
Vendor(s): West Group. *2673*

JOURNAL OF ENGINEERING VALUATION AND COST ANALYSIS.
Gordon and Breach - Harwood Academic, Amsteldisk 166, 1st Fl., 1079 LH Amsterdam, Netherlands. URL: http://www.gbhap.com/Engineering_Valuation_Cost_Analysis/. *2728*

JOURNAL OF ENGLISH AND GERMANIC PHILOLOGY.
University of Illinois Press, 1325 S. Oak St., Champaign, IL 61820. TEL 217-333-0950. FAX 217-244-8082.
Vendor(s): Information Access Co. *4267*

JOURNAL OF ENVIRONMENTAL ECONOMICS AND MANAGEMENT.
Academic Press, Inc., Journal Division, 525 B St., Ste. 1900, San Diego, CA 92101-4495. TEL 619-230-1840. FAX 619-699-6800. URL: http://www.apnet.com/journal/ee.htm; http://www.idealibrary.com/ *2937*

JOURNAL OF ENVIRONMENTAL HEALTH.
National Environmental Health Association, 720 S. Colorado Blvd., S. Tower, Ste. 970, Denver, CO 80246. TEL 303-756-9090. FAX 303-691-9490. URL: http://www.neha.org/~beckyr.
Vendor(s): Information Access Co., UMI. *2937*

JOURNAL OF ENVIRONMENTAL HYDROLOGY.
International Association for Environmental Hydrology, Box 35324, San Antonio, TX 78235-5324. TEL 210-344-5418. FAX 210-344-9941. URL: http://www.hydroweb.com.
Available only online. *2395*

JOURNAL OF ENVIRONMENTAL MANAGEMENT.
Academic Press Ltd., 24-28 Oval Rd., London NW1 7DX, England. TEL 44-171-267-4466. FAX 44-171-482-2293. URL: http://www.hbuk.co.uk/ap/jem; http://www.europe.idealibrary.com/ *2937*

JOURNAL OF ENVIRONMENTAL PLANNING AND MANAGEMENT.
Carfax Publishing Co., P.O. Box 25, Abingdon, Oxon. OX14 3UE, England. TEL 44-1235-401000. FAX 44-1235-401550. *3751*

JOURNAL OF ENVIRONMENTAL PSYCHOLOGY.
Academic Press Ltd., 24-28 Oval Rd., London NW1 7DX, England. TEL 44-171-267-4466. FAX 44-171-482-2293. URL: http://www.hbuk.co.uk/ap/jep; http://www.europe.idealibrary.com/ *6125*

JOURNAL OF ENZYME INHIBITION.
Gordon and Breach - Harwood Academic, Amsteldisk 166, 1st Fl., 1079 LH Amsterdam, Netherlands. URL: http://www.gbhap.com/Enzyme_Inhibition/. *663*

JOURNAL OF EUROPEAN INDUSTRIAL TRAINING.
M C B University Press Ltd., 60-62 Toller Ln., Bradford, W. Yorks BD8 9BY, England. TEL 44-1274-777700. FAX 44-1274-785200. URL: http://www.mcb/co.uk.
Vendor(s): Information Access Co.. *1487*

JOURNAL OF EUROPEAN STUDIES.
Alpha Academic, Halfpenny Furze, Mill Ln., Chalfont St. Giles, Bucks. HP8 4NR, England. TEL 44-1494-872509.
Vendor(s): Information Access Co., UMI. *3578*

JOURNAL OF EVOLUTIONARY BIOLOGY.
Birkhaeuser Verlag, P.O. Box 133, CH-4010 Basel, Switzerland. TEL 41-61-2050730. FAX 41-61-2050791. *772*

JOURNAL OF EVOLUTIONARY ECONOMICS.
Springer-Verlag, Heidelberger Platz 3, 14197 Berlin, Germany. TEL 49-30-82787-0. FAX 49-30-82787448. URL: http://link.springer.de. *1307*

JOURNAL OF EXCELLENCE IN HIGHER EDUCATION.
University of Phoenix, Southern California Campus, 949 South Coast Dr., Costa Mesa, CA 92626. FAX 714-437-1818. *2546*

JOURNAL OF EXPERIMENTAL & THEORETICAL ARTIFICIAL INTELLIGENCE.
Taylor & Francis Ltd., 1 Gunpowder Sq., London EC4A 3DE, England. TEL 44-171-583-0490. FAX 44-171-583-0585. URL: http://turing.paccs.binghamton.edu/jetai/. *2102*

JOURNAL OF EXPERIMENTAL AND THEORETICAL PHYSICS.
American Institute of Physics, One Physics Ellipse, College Park, MD 20740-3843. TEL 301-209-3000. URL: http://www.aip.org. *5809*

JOURNAL OF EXPERIMENTAL BOTANY.
Oxford University Press, Academic Division, Great Clarendon St., Oxford OX2 6DP, England. TEL 44-1865-267907. FAX 44-1865-267485. URL: http://www.oup.co.uk/journals. *711*

JOURNAL OF EXPERIMENTAL CHILD PSYCHOLOGY.
Academic Press, Inc., Journal Division, 525 B St., Ste. 1900, San Diego, CA 92101-4495. TEL 619-230-1840. FAX 619-699-6800. URL: http://www.apnet.com/www/journal/ch.htm; http://www.idealibrary.com/ *6125*

JOURNAL OF EXPERIMENTAL PSYCHOLOGY: GENERAL.
American Psychological Association, 750 First St., N.E., Washington, DC 20002-4242. TEL 202-336-5600. FAX 202-336-5568. URL: http://www.apa.org/journals/xge.html.
Vendor(s): Information Access Co. *6125*

JOURNAL OF EXPERIMENTAL SOCIAL PSYCHOLOGY.
Academic Press, Inc., Journal Division, 525 B St., Ste. 1900, San Diego, CA 92101-4495. TEL 619-230-1840. FAX 619-699-6800. URL: http://www.apnet.com/www/journa/js.htm; http://www.idealibrary.com/ *6126*

JOURNAL OF EXPERIMENTAL ZOOLOGY.
John Wiley & Sons, Inc., Journals, 605 Third Ave., New York, NY 10158. TEL 212-850-6645. FAX 212-850-6021. URL: http://www.wiley.co.uk. *839*

JOURNAL OF EXTENSION (ASCII EDITION).
Journal of Extension, Inc., c/o Virginia Tech, Blacksburg, VA 24061-0452. TEL 541-686-2697. URL: http://joe.org/joe/; http://joe.ext.vt.edu/joe.
Available only online. *2456*

JOURNAL OF FAMILY HISTORY.
Sage Publications, Inc., 2455 Teller Rd., Thousand Oaks, CA 91320. TEL 805-499-0721. FAX 805-499-0871. URL: http://www.sagepub.com.
Vendor(s): Information Access Co., Ovid Technologies, Inc. *6716*

JOURNAL OF FAMILY ISSUES.
Sage Publications, Inc., 2455 Teller Rd., Thousand Oaks, CA 91320. TEL 805-499-0721. FAX 805-499-0871. URL: http://www.sagepub.com.
Vendor(s): Ovid Technologies, Inc. *6716*

JOURNAL OF FAMILY PRACTICE.
Appleton & Lange, Journal Division Box 120041, Stamford, CT 06912-0041. TEL 203-406-4500.
Vendor(s): Information Access Co. *4694*

JOURNAL OF FINANCE.
American Finance Association, c/o W. Michael Keenan, Stern School of Business, New York University, 44 W. 4th St., Ste. 9-190, New York, NY 10012. TEL 212-998-0355.
Vendor(s): Information Access Co. *1149*

JOURNAL OF FINANCIAL INTERMEDIATION.
Academic Press, Inc., Journal Division, 525 B St., Ste. 1900, San Diego, CA 92101-4495. TEL 619-230-1840. FAX 619-699-6800. URL: http://www.apnet.com/www/journal/jf.htm; http://www.idealibrary.com. *1307*

JOURNAL OF FINANCIAL MANAGEMENT AND ANALYSIS.
Om Sai Ram Centre for Financial Management Research, 15 Prakash Co-operative Housing Society, Relief Rd., Santacruz (W.), Mumbai 400 054, India. TEL 91-22-6121715. *1150*

JOURNAL OF FINANCIAL PLANNING TODAY.
New Directions Publications, Inc., Box 6097, W. Palm Beach, FL 33405. TEL 407-434-0100. FAX 407-641-4801.
Vendor(s): UMI. *1150*

JOURNAL OF FINANCIAL RESEARCH.
Virginia Polytechnic Institute and State University, College of Business, Department of Finance, 1016 Pamplin Hall, Blacksburg, VA 24061-0221. TEL 540-231-7699. FAX 540-231-4706. URL: http://www.vt.edu:10021/business/finance/jfr.
Vendor(s): Information Access Co. *978*

JOURNAL OF FISH BIOLOGY.
Academic Press Ltd., 24-28 Oval Rd., London NW1 7DX, England. TEL 44-171-267-4466. FAX 44-171-482-2293. URL: http://hbukco.uk/ap/jfb; http://www.europe.idealibrary.com/ *840*

JOURNAL OF FLUIDS AND STRUCTURES.
Academic Press Ltd., 24-28 Oval Rd., London NW1 7DX, England. TEL 44-171-267-4466. FAX 44-171-482-2293. URL: http://www.hbuk.co.uk/ap/jfs; http://www.europe.idealibrary.com/ *2728*

JOURNAL OF FOOD COMPOSITION AND ANALYSIS.
Academic Press, Inc., Journal Division, 525 B St., Ste. 1900, San Diego, CA 92101-4495. TEL 619-230-1840. FAX 619-699-6800. URL: http://www.apnet.com/journal/fc.htm; http://www.idealibrary.con. *3115*

JOURNAL OF FUNCTIONAL ANALYSIS.
Academic Press, Inc., Journal Division, 525 B St., Ste. 1900, San Diego, CA 92101-4495. TEL 619-230-1840. FAX 619-699-6800. URL: http://www.apnet.com/www/journal/fu.htm; http://www.idealibrary.com/ *4582*

JOURNAL OF FUNCTIONAL AND LOGIC PROGRAMMING.
M I T Press, 5 Cambridge Center, Cambridge, MA 02142. TEL 617-253-2889. FAX 617-577-1545. URL: http://www-mitpress.mit.edu/jrnls-catalog/functional.html.
Available only online. *2144*

THE JOURNAL OF GENERAL PSYCHOLOGY.
Heldref Publications, 1319 Eighteenth St., N.W., Washington, DC 20036. TEL 202-296-6267. FAX 202-296-5149.
Vendor(s): Information Access Co., UMI. *6126*

THE JOURNAL OF GENETIC PSYCHOLOGY.
Heldref Publications, 1319 Eighteenth St., N.W., Washington, DC 20036-1802. TEL 202-296-6267. FAX 202-296-5149.
Vendor(s): Information Access Co., UMI. *6127*

JOURNAL OF GEODESY.
Springer-Verlag, Heidelberger Platz 3, 14197 Berlin, Germany. TEL 49-30-82787-0. FAX 49-30-82787448. URL: http://link.springer.de. *2385*

JOURNAL OF GEOGRAPHIC INFORMATION AND DECISION ANALYSIS.
Geographic Information and Decision Analysis Research Group, Dept. of Geography, University of Western Ontario, London, ON N6A 5C2, Canada. URL: http://sparky.sscl.uwo.ca/gimda/journal.htm.
Available only online. *3411*

JOURNAL OF GERONTOLOGICAL NURSING.
Slack, Inc., 6900 Grove Rd., Thorofare, NJ 08086-9447. TEL 609-848-1000. FAX 609-853-5991. URL: http://www.slackinc.com/allied/jgn/jgnhome.htm. *3439*

JOURNAL OF GRAPH ALGORITHMS AND APPLICATIONS.
URL: http://www.emis.de/journals/JGAA/index.html.
Available only online. *4582*

JOURNAL OF HEALTH AND SOCIAL BEHAVIOR.
American Sociological Association, 1722 N St., N.W., Washington, DC 20036. TEL 202-833-3410. FAX 202-785-0146.
Vendor(s): UMI. *6717*

JOURNAL OF HEALTH CARE FINANCE.
Aspen Publishers, Inc., 200 Orchard Ridge Dr., Gaithersburg, MD 20878. FAX 301-417-7550.
Vendor(s): Information Access Co., UMI. *3715*

JOURNAL OF HEALTH CARE MARKETING.
American Marketing Association, 250 S. Wacker Dr., Ste. 200, Chicago, IL 60606. TEL 312-648-0536. FAX 312-993-7542. URL: http://www.ama.org.
Vendor(s): Information Access Co., UMI. *1533*

JOURNAL OF HEALTH COMMUNICATION.
Taylor & Francis Inc., 1900 Frost Rd., Ste. 101, Bristol, PA 19007-1598. TEL 215-785-5800. FAX 215-785-5515. URL: http://www.tandf.co.uk/jnls/hcm.htm. *4695*

JOURNAL OF HIGHER EDUCATION.
Ohio State University Press, 1070 Carmack Rd., Columbus, OH 43210. TEL 614-292-6930. FAX 614-292-2065. URL: gopher://gopher.acs.ohio-state.edu:70/11/.
Vendor(s): Information Access Co., UMI. *2547*

JOURNAL OF HISTORICAL GEOGRAPHY.
Academic Press Ltd., 24-28 Oval Rd., London NW1 7DX, England. TEL 44-171-267-4466. FAX 44-171-482-2293. URL: http://www.hbuk.co.uk/ap/jhg; http://www.europe.idealibrary.com/ *3412*

JOURNAL OF HOUSING ECONOMICS.
Academic Press, Inc., Journal Division, 525 B St., Ste. 1900, San Diego, CA 92101-4495. TEL 619-230-1840. FAX 619-699-6800. URL: http://www.apnet.com/www/journal/he.htm; http://www.idealibrary.com/ *3751*

JOURNAL OF HUMAN EVOLUTION.
Academic Press Ltd., 24-28 Oval Rd., London NW1 7DX, England. TEL 44-171-267-4466. FAX 44-171-482-2293. URL: http://www.hbuk.co.uk/ap/journals/hu. *772*

JOURNAL OF HUMAN RESOURCES.
University of Wisconsin Press, Social Science Bldg., 1180 Observatory Dr., Madison, WI 53706. TEL 608-262-4952. FAX 608-262-7560.
Vendor(s): Information Access Co., UMI. *1570*

JOURNAL OF HYPERTENSION.
Thomson Science, 2-6 Boundary Row, London SE1 8HN, England. TEL 44-171-865-0198. FAX 44-171-410-6600. URL: http://www.thomsonscience.com. *4820*

JOURNAL OF IMAGE GUIDED SURGERY.
John Wiley & Sons, Inc., Journals, 605 Third Ave., New York, NY 10158-0012. TEL 212-850-6645. FAX 212-850-6021. URL: http://www.wiley.co.uk *5145*

JOURNAL OF IMMUNOLOGY.
American Association of Immunologists, 9650 Rockville Pike, Bethesda, MD 20814. TEL 301-530-7197. FAX 301-571-1813. URL: http://journals.at-home.com/ji. *4798*

JOURNAL OF INDIGENOUS STUDIES.
Gabriel Dumont Institute of Native Studies and Applied Research, 505 - 23rd St., E., Saskatoon, SK S7K 4K7, Canada. TEL 306-934-4941. FAX 306-934-4941. *321*

JOURNAL OF INDUSTRIAL ECONOMICS.
Blackwell Publishers Ltd., 108 Cowley Rd., Oxford OX4 1JF, England. TEL 44-1865-791100. FAX 44-1865-791347. URL: http://www.blackwellpublishers.co.uk.
Vendor(s): Information Access Co.. *978*

JOURNAL OF INFECTION.
W.B. Saunders Co. Ltd., 24-28 Oval Rd., London, NW1 7DX, England. TEL 44-171-267-4466. FAX 44-171-482-2293. URL: http://www.hbuk.co.uk/wbs/jiu/. *4839*

JOURNAL OF INFECTIOUS DISEASES.
University of Chicago Press, Journals Division, Box 37005, Chicago, IL 60637. TEL 773-753-3347. FAX 773-753-0811. URL: http://www.journals.uchicago.edu/JID/
Vendor(s): Ovid Technologies, Inc. (JWAT). *4839*

JOURNAL OF INFLAMMATION.
John Wiley & Sons, Inc., Journals, 605 Third Ave., New York, NY 10158. TEL 212-850-6645. FAX 212-850-6021. URL: http://www.wiley.co.uk *4821*

JOURNAL OF INFORMATION, LAW AND TECHNOLOGY.
University of Strathclyde, Centre for Law, Computers and Technology, 173 Cathedral St., Glasgow G4 0RQ, Scotland. TEL 44-141-552-4400. FAX 44-141-553-1546. URL: http://jilt.law.strath.ac.uk/.
Available only online. *3969*

JOURNAL OF INFORMATION TECHNOLOGY.
Thomson Professional, 2-6 Boundary Row, London SE1 8HN, England. TEL 44-171-8650066. FAX 44-171-5229521. URL: http://jpr.thomsonprofessional.com. *4188*

JOURNAL OF INSURANCE REGULATION.
National Association of Insurance Commissioners, 120 W. 12th St., Kansas City, MO 64105. TEL 816-374-7259. URL: http://www.naic.org.
Vendor(s): UMI. *3822*

JOURNAL OF INTELLIGENT MANUFACTURING.
Thomson Science, 2-6 Boundary Row, London SE1 8HN, England. TEL 44-171-8650066. FAX 44-171-5229624. URL: http://www.thomsonscience.com. *2110*

JOURNAL OF INTERACTIVE MARKETING.
John Wiley & Sons, Inc., Journals, 605 Third Ave., New York, NY 10158. TEL 212-850-6645. FAX 212-850-6021. URL: http://www.wiley.co.uk.
Vendor(s): Knight-Ridder Information, Inc. *1533*

JOURNAL OF INTERAMERICAN STUDIES AND WORLD AFFAIRS.
University of Miami, North - South Center Press, Box 248205, Coral Gables, FL 33124-3027. TEL 305-284-8914. FAX 305-284-5083.
Vendor(s): Information Access Co., UMI. *6023*

JOURNAL OF INTERDISCIPLINARY HISTORY.
M I T Press, 5 Cambridge Center, Cambridge, MA 02142. TEL 617-253-2889. FAX 617-577-1545. URL: http://www-mitpress.mit.edu.
Vendor(s): Information Access Co.. *3502*

JOURNAL OF INTERDISCIPLINARY STUDIES.
Institute for Interdisciplinary Research, 2828 Third St., Ste. 11, Santa Monica, CA 90405-4150. TEL 310-396-0517. *3783*

JOURNAL OF INTERNATIONAL AFFAIRS.
Columbia University, Journal of International Affairs, 420 W. 118th St., Box 4, International Affairs Bldg., New York, NY 10027. TEL 212-854-4775. FAX 212-662-0398.
Vendor(s): Information Access Co., UMI. *6024*

JOURNAL OF INTERNATIONAL BUSINESS STUDIES.
University of Western Ontario, Western Business School, London, ON N6A 3K7, Canada. TEL 519-661-4031. FAX 519-661-3700.
Vendor(s): Information Access Co., UMI. *978*

JOURNAL OF INTERNATIONAL TAXATION.
Warren, Gorham & Lamont, One Penn Plaza, New York, NY 10119. TEL 212-971-5000. FAX 212-971-5113. URL: http://www.wgl.com/tax/joit.html.
Vendor(s): Lexis-Nexis. *1617*

JOURNAL OF INTERNET PURCHASING.
Box 5145, Station F, Ottawa, ON K2C 3H3, Canada. URL: http://www.arraydev.com/commerce/jip/
Available only online. *1534*

JOURNAL OF INVERTEBRATE PATHOLOGY.
Academic Press, Inc., Journal Division, 525 B St., Ste. 1900, San Diego, CA 92101-4495. TEL 619-230-1840. FAX 619-699-6800. URL: http://www.apnet.com/www/journal/in.htm; http://www.idealibrary.com/ *756*

JOURNAL OF INVESTIGATIVE DERMATOLOGY.
Blackwell Science Inc., 350 Main St., Malden, MA 02148. TEL 617-876-7000. FAX 617-388-8255. *4879*

THE JOURNAL OF LABORATORY AND CLINICAL MEDICINE.
Mosby - Year Book, Inc., 11830 Westline Industrial Dr., St. Louis, MO 63146. TEL 314-872-8370. FAX 314-432-1380.
Vendor(s): Ovid Technologies, Inc.. *4898*

JOURNAL OF LASER APPLICATIONS.
Chapman & Hall, Journals Department 2-6 Boundary Row, London SE1 8HN, England. TEL 44-171-8650066. FAX 44-171-5229623. URL: http://www.chaphall.com/chaphall/journals.html. *5863*

JOURNAL OF LATIN AMERICAN STUDIES.
Cambridge University Press, Edinburgh Bldg., Shaftesbury Rd., Cambridge CB2 2RU, England. TEL 44-1223-312393. FAX 44-1223-315052. URL: http://www.cup.cam.ac.uk.
Vendor(s): Information Access Co.. *3633*

JOURNAL OF LAW & COMMERCE.
University of Pittsburgh, School of Law, 3900 Forbes Ave., Pittsburgh, PA 15260. TEL 412-648-1361. FAX 412-648-2648. URL: http://www.law.pitt.edu/journal/welcome.html.
Vendor(s): Lexis-Nexis, West Group. *4083*

JOURNAL OF LEGAL ECONOMICS.
American Academy of Economic and Financial Experts, University of North Alabama, Box 5077, Florence, AL 35632. TEL 205-760-4144. FAX 205-760-4170. *1308*

JOURNAL OF LEISURE RESEARCH.
National Recreation and Park Association, 2775 S. Quincy St., No. 300, Arlington, VA 22206. TEL 703-820-4940. FAX 703-671-6772.
Vendor(s): Information Access Co., UMI. *4149*

JOURNAL OF LEUKOCYTE BIOLOGY.
Federation of American Societies for Experimental Biology, 9650 Rockville Pike, Bethesda, MD 20814. TEL 301-530-7000. FAX 301-571-1855. *4696*

JOURNAL OF M U D RESEARCH.
URL: http://journal.tinymush.org/jomr.
Available only online. *6622*

JOURNAL OF MACROMARKETING.
University of Colorado, Business Research Division, Campus Box 420, Boulder, CO 80309-0420. TEL 303-492-8227. FAX 303-492-3620.
Vendor(s): UMI. *1534*

SERIALS AVAILABLE ONLINE

JOURNAL OF MAGNETIC RESONANCE.
Academic Press, Inc., Journal Division, 525 B St., Ste. 1900, San Diego, CA 92101-4495. TEL 619-230-1840. FAX 619-699-6800. URL: http://www.apnet.com/www/journal/mn.htm; http://www.idealibrary.com/ *5810*

JOURNAL OF MAGNETIC RESONANCE IMAGING.
Williams & Wilkins, 351 W. Camden St., Baltimore, MD 21201-2436. TEL 410-528-4068. FAX 410-528-4452. URL: http://www.wwilkins.com. Vendor(s): National Library of Medicine. *5109*

JOURNAL OF MANAGEMENT.
J A I Press Inc., 55 Old Post Rd., No. 2, Box 1678, Greenwich, CT 06830-1678. TEL 203-661-7602. FAX 203-661-0792.
Vendor(s): Information Access Co. *1488*

JOURNAL OF MANAGEMENT ACCOUNTING RESEARCH.
American Accounting Association, 5717 Bessie Dr., Sarasota, FL 34233. TEL 941-921-7747. FAX 941-923-4093. URL: http://www.nan.shh.fi/raw/aaa/aaa.htm.
Vendor(s): UMI. *1093*

JOURNAL OF MANAGEMENT CONSULTING.
858 Longview Rd., Burlingame, CA 94010-6974. TEL 415-342-1954. FAX 415-344-5005. URL: http://www.jmcforum.com/jmc/
Vendor(s): UMI. *1488*

JOURNAL OF MANAGEMENT INFORMATION SYSTEMS.
M.E. Sharpe, Inc., 80 Business Park Dr., Armonk, NY 10504. TEL 914-273-1800. FAX 914-273-2106. URL: http://www.stern.nyu.edu/jmis.
Vendor(s): UMI. *2184*

JOURNAL OF MANAGEMENT STUDIES.
Blackwell Publishers Ltd., 108 Cowley Rd., Oxford OX4 1JF, England. TEL 44-1865-791100. FAX 44-1865-791347. URL: http://www.blackwellpublishers.co.uk.
Vendor(s): Information Access Co. *1488*

JOURNAL OF MANAGERIAL ISSUES.
Pittsburg State University, Department of Economics, Finance & Banking, 1701 S. Broadway, Pittsburg, KS 66762-7533. TEL 316-235-4547. FAX 316-235-4578. URL: http://www.pittstate.edu/econ/jmi.html.
Vendor(s): Information Access Co. *1489*

JOURNAL OF MANAGERIAL PSYCHOLOGY.
M C B University Press Ltd., 60-62 Toller Ln., Bradford, W. Yorks BD8 9BY, England. TEL 44-1274-777700. FAX 44-1274-785200. URL: http://www.mcb.co.uk.
Vendor(s): Information Access Co. *1489*

JOURNAL OF MANUFACTURING SYSTEMS.
Elsevier Science Ltd., P.O. Box 800, Kidlington, Oxford OX5 1DX, England. TEL 44-1865-843000. FAX 44-1865-843010. URL: http://www.elsevier.nl/; http://www.sme.org/
Vendor(s): UMI. *2156*

JOURNAL OF MARINE BIOTECHNOLOGY.
Springer-Verlag, Life Science Journals, 175 Fifth Ave., New York, NY 10010. TEL 212-460-1500. FAX 212-473-6272. URL: http://www.springer-ny.com. *685*

JOURNAL OF MARINE ENVIRONMENTAL ENGINEERING.
Gordon and Breach - Harwood Academic, Amsteldisk 166, 1st Fl., 1079 LH Amsterdam, Netherlands. URL: http://www.gbhap.com/Marine__Environmental__Engineering/. *2939*

JOURNAL OF MARITAL AND FAMILY THERAPY.
American Association for Marriage and Family Therapy, 1133 15th St., N.W., Ste. 300, Washington, DC 20005.
Vendor(s): UMI. *6127*

JOURNAL OF MARKETING.
American Marketing Association, 250 S. Wacker Dr., Ste. 200, Chicago, IL 60606. TEL 312-648-0536. FAX 312-993-7542. URL: http://www.ama.org/pubs/jminfo/index.html.
Vendor(s): Information Access Co., Lexis-Nexis, UMI. *1534*

JOURNAL OF MARKETING COMMUNICATIONS.
Thomson Professional, 2-6 Boundary Row, London SE1 8HN, England. TEL 44-171-8650066. FAX 44-171-5229623. URL: http://jmc.thomsonprofessional.com. *1534*

JOURNAL OF MARKETING PRACTICE: APPLIED MARKETING SCIENCE.
M C B University Press Ltd., 60-62 Toller Ln., Bradford, W. Yorks BD8 9BY, England. TEL 44-1274-777700. FAX 44-1274-785200. URL: http://www.mcb.co.uk/liblink/jmpams/jourhome.htm. *1534*

JOURNAL OF MARKETING RESEARCH.
American Marketing Association, 250 S. Wacker Dr., Ste. 200, Chicago, IL 60606. TEL 312-648-0536. FAX 312-993-7542. URL: http://www.ama.org/pubs/jmr/index.html.
Vendor(s): Information Access Co., Lexis-Nexis. *1534*

JOURNAL OF MARRIAGE AND THE FAMILY.
National Council on Family Relations, 3989 Central Ave., N.E., Ste. 550, Minneapolis, MN 55421-3921. TEL 612-781-9331. FAX 612-781-9348.
Vendor(s): Knight-Ridder Information, Inc., UMI. *6717*

JOURNAL OF MATERIALS SCIENCE.
Thomson Science, 2-6 Boundary Row, London SE1 8HN, England. TEL 44-171-8650066. FAX 44-171-5229623. URL: http://www.thomsonscience.com. *2862*

JOURNAL OF MATERIALS SCIENCE LETTERS.
Chapman & Hall, Journals Department 2-6 Boundary Row, London SE1 8HN, England. TEL 44-171-8650066. FAX 44-171-5229623. URL: http://www.chaphall.com/chaphall/journals.html. *2862*

JOURNAL OF MATERIALS SCIENCE: MATERIALS IN ELECTRONICS.
Thomson Science, 2-6 Boundary Row, London SE1 8HN, England. TEL 44-171-8650066. FAX 44-171-5229623. URL: http://www.thomsonscience.com. *2863*

JOURNAL OF MATERIALS SCIENCE: MATERIALS IN MEDICINE.
Thomson Science, 2-6 Boundary Row, London SE1 8HN, England. TEL 44-171-8650066. FAX 44-171-5229623. URL: http://www.thomsonscience.com. *2863*

JOURNAL OF MATERNAL - FETAL INVESTIGATION.
Springer-Verlag, Medical Journals, 175 Fifth Ave., New York, NY 10010. TEL 212-460-1500. FAX 212-473-6272. URL: http://www.springer-ny.com. *4961*

JOURNAL OF MATHEMATICAL ANALYSIS AND APPLICATIONS.
Academic Press, Inc., Journal Division, 525 B St., Ste. 1900, San Diego, CA 92101-4495. TEL 619-230-1840. FAX 619-699-6800. URL: http://www.apnet.com/www/journal/ay.htm; http://www.idealibrary.com. *4583*

JOURNAL OF MATHEMATICAL BIOLOGY.
Springer-Verlag, Heidelberger Platz 3, 14197 Berlin, Germany. TEL 49-30-82787-0. FAX 49-30-82787448. URL: http://link.springer.de. *609*

JOURNAL OF MATHEMATICAL PHYSICS.
American Institute of Physics, One Physics Ellipse, College Park, MD 20740-3843. TEL 301-209-3000. URL: http://www.aip.org. *5810*

JOURNAL OF MATHEMATICAL PSYCHOLOGY.
Academic Press, Inc., Journal Division, 525 B St., Ste. 1900, San Diego, CA 92101-4495. TEL 619-230-1840. FAX 619-699-6800. URL: http://www.apnet.com/www/journal/mp.htm; http://www/idealibrary.com/ *6128*

JOURNAL OF MATHEMATICAL SYSTEMS, ESTIMATION AND CONTROL.
Birkhaeuser, 675 Massachusetts Ave., Cambridge, MA 02139-3309. TEL 617-876-2333. FAX 201-348-4505. URL: http://scholar.lib.vt.edu/ejournals/JMSEC.html. *4621*

JOURNAL OF MEDICAL AND PHARMACEUTICAL MARKETING.
Fred Atoki Publishing Co. Ltd., Plot 25 Kekere-Ekun St., Orile-Iganmu, Box 7313, Lagos, Nigeria. *1535*

JOURNAL OF MEDICAL ETHICS.
B M J Publishing Group, B.M.A. House, Tavistock Sq., London WC1H 9JR, England. TEL 44-171-383-6270. FAX 44-171-383-6402.
Vendor(s): UMI. *4696*

JOURNAL OF MEDICAL MICROBIOLOGY.
Thomson Science, 2-6 Boundary Row, London SE1 8HN, England. TEL 44-171-8650066. FAX 44-171-5229623. URL: http://www.thomsonscience.com. *4696*

JOURNAL OF MEDICAL VIROLOGY.
John Wiley & Sons, Inc., Journals, 605 Third Ave., New York, NY 10158. TEL 212-850-6645. FAX 212-850-6021. *4697*

JOURNAL OF MEDICINAL CHEMISTRY.
American Chemical Society, 1155 16th St., N.W., Washington, DC 20036. TEL 800-333-9511. FAX 614-447-3671.
Vendor(s): STN International (CJACS). *5672*

JOURNAL OF MEMBRANE BIOLOGY.
Springer-Verlag, Life Science Journals, 175 Fifth Ave., New York, NY 10010. TEL 212-460-1500. FAX 212-473-6272. URL: http://www.springer-ny.com. *742*

JOURNAL OF MEMORY AND LANGUAGE.
Academic Press, Inc., Journal Division, 525 B St., Ste. 1900, San Diego, CA 92101-4495. TEL 619-230-1840. FAX 619-699-6800. URL: http://www.apnet.com/www/journal/ml.htm; http://www.idealibrary.com/ *4268*

JOURNAL OF MENTAL HEALTH.
Carfax Publishing Co., P.O. Box 25, Abingdon, Oxon. OX14 3UE, England. TEL 44-1235-401000. FAX 44-1235-401550. *5074*

JOURNAL OF MICROMECHANICS AND MICROENGINEERING.
I O P Publishing Ltd., Dirac House, Temple Back, Bristol BS1 6BE, England. TEL 44-117-929-7481. FAX 44-117-929-4318. URL: http://www.iop.org. *2890*

JOURNAL OF MODERN HISTORY.
University of Chicago Press, Journals Division, Box 37005, Chicago, IL 60637. TEL 773-753-3347. FAX 773-753-0811. URL: http://www.jstor.org/fcgi-bin/jstor/; http://www.journals.uchicago.edu/JMH/ *3502*

JOURNAL OF MODERN OPTICS.
Taylor & Francis Ltd., 1 Gunpowder Sq., London EC4A 3DE, England. TEL 44-171-583-0490. FAX 44-171-583-0585. URL: http://www.tandf.co.uk/. *5863*

JOURNAL OF MOLECULAR AND CELLULAR CARDIOLOGY.
Academic Press Ltd., 24-28 Oval Rd., London NW1 7DX, England. TEL 44-171-267-4466. FAX 44-171-482-2293. URL: http://www.hbuk.co.uk/ap/jmcc; http://www.europe.idealibrary.com/ *4821*

JOURNAL OF MOLECULAR BIOLOGY.
Academic Press Ltd., 24-28 Oval Rd., London NW1 7DX, England. TEL 44-171-2674466. FAX 44-171-4822293. URL: http://www.hbuk.co.uk/ap/jmb; http://www.europe.idealibrary.com/ *664*

JOURNAL OF MOLECULAR EVOLUTION.
Springer-Verlag, Life Science Journals, 175 Fifth Ave., New York, NY 10010. TEL 212-460-1500. FAX 212-473-6272. URL: http://www.springer-ny.com. *772*

JOURNAL OF MOLECULAR MEDICINE.
Springer-Verlag, Heidelberger Platz 3, 14197 Berlin, Germany. TEL 49-30-82787-0. FAX 49-30-82787448. URL: http://link.springer.de. *4697*

JOURNAL OF MOLECULAR MODELING.
Springer-Verlag, Heidelberger Platz 3, 14197 Berlin, Germany. TEL 49-30-82787-0. FAX 49-30-82787448. URL: http://link.springer.de.
Available only online. *1831*

JOURNAL OF MOLECULAR SPECTROSCOPY.
Academic Press, Inc., Journal Division, 525 B St., Ste. 1900, San Diego, CA 92101-4495. TEL 619-230-1840. FAX 619-699-6800. URL: http://www.apnet.com/www/journal/ms.htm; http://www.idealibrary.com/ *5863*

JOURNAL OF MONEY, CREDIT & BANKING.
Ohio State University Press, 1070 Carmack Rd., Columbus, OH 43210. TEL 614-292-6930. FAX 614-292-2065. URL: http://www.jstor.org/journals/00222879.html.
Vendor(s): Information Access Co. *1151*

JOURNAL OF MORMON HISTORY.
Mormon History Association, 2470 N. 1000 W., Layton, UT 84041-1236. FAX 801-379-1348.
Vendor(s): Knight-Ridder Information, Inc. (File nos.38,39). *6492*

JOURNAL OF MULTIVARIATE ANALYSIS.
Academic Press, Inc., Journal Division, 525 B St., Ste. 1900, San Diego, CA 92101-4495. TEL 619-230-1840. FAX 619-699-6800. URL: http://www.apnet.com/www/journal/mv.htm; http://www.idealibrary.com/ *4584*

JOURNAL OF MUSCLE RESEARCH AND CELL MOTILITY.
Chapman & Hall, Journals Department 2-6 Boundary Row, London SE1 8HN, England. TEL 44-171-8650066. FAX 44-171-5229623. URL: http://www.chaphall.com/chaphall/journals.html. *4697*

JOURNAL OF MUSICOLOGY.
University of California Press, Journals Division, 2120 Berkeley Way, No. 5812, Berkeley, CA 94720-5812. TEL 510-643-7154. FAX 510-642-9917. URL: http://library.berkeley.edu:8080/ucalpress/journals.
Vendor(s): Information Access Co. *5405*

JOURNAL OF NATURAL PRODUCTS.
American Society of Pharmacognosy, Dept. L-0011, Columbus, OH 43268-0011. TEL 614-447-3776. FAX 614-447-3671. *5672*

JOURNAL OF NEAR EASTERN STUDIES.
University of Chicago Press, Journals Division, Box 37005, Chicago, IL 60637. TEL 773-753-3347. FAX 773-753-0811. URL: http://www.journals.uchicago.edu/JNES/
Vendor(s): Knight-Ridder Information, Inc. *369*

JOURNAL OF NEGRO EDUCATION.
Howard University Press, Marketing Department, 2600 Sixth St., N.W., Washington, DC 20059. TEL 202-806-8120. FAX 202-806-8434.
Vendor(s): Information Access Co., UMI. *2456*

JOURNAL OF NEGRO HISTORY.
Association for the Study of Afro-American Life and History, Inc., c/o Alton Hornsby, Jr., Ed., Dept. of History, Morehouse College, Atlanta, GA 30314. TEL 404-215-2620. FAX 404-215-2715.
Vendor(s): Information Access Co. *3024*

JOURNAL OF NERVOUS AND MENTAL DISEASE.
Williams & Wilkins, 351 W. Camden St., Baltimore, MD 21201-2436. TEL 410-528-4068. FAX 410-528-4452. URL: http://www.wwilkins.com.
Vendor(s): Ovid Technologies, Inc. *5074*

JOURNAL OF NETWORK AND SYSTEMS MANAGEMENT.
Plenum Publishing Corp., 233 Spring St., New York, NY 10013-1578. TEL 212-620-8000. FAX 212-463-0742. URL: http://www.catchword.co.uk/. *2156*

JOURNAL OF NEUROCHEMISTRY.
Lippincott - Raven Publishers, 227 E. Washington Sq., Philadelphia, PA 19106. TEL 215-238-4200. FAX 215-238-4227. URL: http://www.lrpub.com. *664*

JOURNAL OF NEUROCYTOLOGY.
Chapman & Hall, Journals Department 2-6 Boundary Row, London SE1 8HN, England. TEL 44-171-8650066. FAX 44-171-5229623. URL: http://www.chaphall.com/chaphall/journals.html. *742*

JOURNAL OF NEUROGENETICS.
Gordon and Breach - Harwood Academic, Amsteldisk 166, 1st Fl., 1079 LH Amsterdam, Netherlands. URL: http://www.gbhap.com/Neurogenetics/. *5075*

JOURNAL OF NEUROLOGY.
Springer-Verlag, Heidelberger Platz 3, 14197 Berlin, Germany. TEL 49-30-82787-0. FAX 49-30-82787448. URL: http://link.springer.de. *5075*

JOURNAL OF NEUROLOGY, NEUROSURGERY AND PSYCHIATRY.
B M J Publishing Group, B.M.A. House, Tavistock Sq., London WC1H 9JR, England. TEL 44-171-383-6270. FAX 44-171-383-6402.
Vendor(s): Ovid Technologies, Inc.. *5075*

JOURNAL OF NEUROSCIENCE.
Society for Neuroscience, 11 Dupont Cir., N.W., Ste. 500, Washington, DC 20036. TEL 202-462-6688. FAX 202-462-1547. URL: http://www.jneurosci.org/ *5076*

JOURNAL OF NONLINEAR SCIENCE.
Springer-Verlag, Science Journals, 175 Fifth Ave., New York, NY 10010. TEL 212-460-1500. FAX 212-473-6272. URL: http://www.springer-ny.com. *5810*

JOURNAL OF NUMBER THEORY.
Academic Press, Inc., Journal Division, 525 B St., Ste. 1900, San Diego, CA 92101-4495. TEL 619-230-1840. FAX 619-699-6800. URL: http://www.apnet.com/www/journal/nt.htm; http://idealibrary.com/ *4584*

JOURNAL OF OCCUPATIONAL AND ENVIRONMENTAL MEDICINE.
Williams & Wilkins, 351 W. Camden St., Baltimore, MD 21201-2436. TEL 410-528-4068. FAX 410-528-4452. URL: http://www.wwilkins.com.
Vendor(s): Ovid Technologies, Inc. *4697*

JOURNAL OF OCCUPATIONAL AND ORGANIZATIONAL PSYCHOLOGY.
British Psychological Society, St. Andrew's House, 48 Princess Rd. E., Leicester LE1 7DR, England. TEL 44-116-254-9568. FAX 44-116-247-0787. URL: http://www.journals.eecs.qub.ac.uk.
Vendor(s): Information Access Co. *6128*

JOURNAL OF OPTICS.
I O P Publishing Ltd., Dirac House, Temple Back, Bristol BS1 6BE, England. TEL 44-117-929-7481. FAX 44-117-929-4318. URL: http://www.iop.org. *5863*

JOURNAL OF ORGANIC CHEMISTRY (WASHINGTON).
American Chemical Society, 1155 16th St., N.W., Washington, DC 20036. TEL 800-333-9511. FAX 614-447-3671.
Vendor(s): STN International (CJACS). *1817*

JOURNAL OF ORGANOMETALLIC CHEMISTRY.
Elsevier Science S.A., P.O. Box 564, CH-1001 Lausanne 1, Switzerland. TEL 41-21-3207381. FAX 41-21-3235444.
Vendor(s): STN International. *1817*

JOURNAL OF ORTHOPAEDIC AND SPORTS PHYSICAL THERAPY.
Williams & Wilkins, 351 W. Camden St., Baltimore, MD 21201-2436. TEL 410-528-4068. FAX 410-528-4452. URL: http://www.wwilkins.com.
Vendor(s): Ovid Technologies, Inc. *5130*

JOURNAL OF PALESTINE STUDIES.
University of California Press, Journals Division, 2120 Berkeley Way, No. 5812, Berkeley, CA 94720-5812. TEL 510-643-7154. FAX 510-642-9917. URL: http://library.berkeley.edu:8080/ucalpress/journals.
Vendor(s): Information Access Co. *3657*

JOURNAL OF PARALLEL AND DISTRIBUTED COMPUTING.
Academic Press, Inc., Journal Division, 525 B St., Ste. 1900, San Diego, CA 92101-4495. TEL 619-230-1840. FAX 619-699-6800. URL: http://www.apnet.com/www/journal/pc.htm; http://www.idealibrary.com. *2086*

JOURNAL OF PARAPSYCHOLOGY.
Parapsychology Press, 402 N. Buchanan Blvd., Durham, NC 27701-1728. TEL 919-688-8241. FAX 919-683-4338. URL: http://world.std.com/~rhinerc/
Vendor(s): Information Access Co., UMI. *5576*

JOURNAL OF PARTNERSHIP TAXATION.
Warren, Gorham & Lamont, One Penn Plaza, New York, NY 10119. TEL 212-971-5000. FAX 212-971-5113.
Vendor(s): Lexis-Nexis (TAXRIA-Library), West Group (WGL-JPTAX). *1617*

JOURNAL OF PEDIATRIC SURGERY.
W.B. Saunders Co., Curtis Center, Independence Sq. W., Philadelphia, PA 19106-3399. TEL 215-238-7800. FAX 215-238-6445.
Vendor(s): Lexis-Nexis. *5146*

THE JOURNAL OF PEDIATRICS.
Mosby - Year Book, Inc., 11830 Westline Industrial Dr., St. Louis, MO 63146-3318. TEL 314-872-8370. FAX 314-432-1380.
Vendor(s): Ovid Technologies, Inc.. *5033*

JOURNAL OF PETROLOGY.
Oxford University Press, Academic Division, Great Clarendon St., Oxford OX2 6DP, England. TEL 44-1865-267907. FAX 44-1865-267485. *2354*

JOURNAL OF PHARMACEUTICAL SCIENCES.
American Pharmaceutical Association, 2215 Constitution Ave., N.W., Washington, DC 20037. TEL 202-628-4410. FAX 202-638-3783. *5673*

JOURNAL OF PHARMACOLOGY AND EXPERIMENTAL THERAPEUTICS.
Williams & Wilkins, 351 W. Camden St., Baltimore, MD 21201-2436. TEL 410-528-4068. FAX 410-528-4452. URL: http://www.wwilkins.com. *5673*

JOURNAL OF PHYSICAL CHEMISTRY.
American Chemical Society, 1155 16th St., N.W., Washington, DC 20036. TEL 800-333-9511. FAX 614-447-3671. URL: http://acsinfo.acs.org/plweb/jrpublic/jpchax/
Vendor(s): STN International (CJACS). *1831*

JOURNAL OF PHYSICAL EDUCATION, RECREATION AND DANCE.
American Alliance for Health, Physical Education, Recreation, and Dance, 1900 Association Dr., Reston, VA 22091. TEL 703-476-3400. FAX 703-476-9527.
Vendor(s): Information Access Co., UMI. *2608*

JOURNAL OF PHYSICS A: MATHEMATICAL AND GENERAL.
I O P Publishing Ltd., Dirac House, Temple Back, Bristol BS1 6BE, England. TEL 44-117-929-7481. FAX 44-117-929-4318. URL: http://www.iop.org. *5810*

JOURNAL OF PHYSICS B: ATOMIC, MOLECULAR AND OPTICAL PHYSICS.
I O P Publishing Ltd., Dirac House, Temple Back, Bristol, BS1 6BE, England. TEL 44-117-929-7481. FAX 44-117-929-4318. URL: http://www.iop.org. *5811*

JOURNAL OF PHYSICS: CONDENSED MATTER.
I O P Publishing Ltd., Dirac House, Temple BAck, Bristol BS1 6BE, England. TEL 44-117-929-7481. FAX 44-117-929-4318. URL: http://www.iop.org. *5811*

JOURNAL OF PHYSICS D: APPLIED PHYSICS.
I O P Publishing Ltd., Dirac House, Temple Back, Bristol BS1 6BE, England. TEL 44-117-929-7481. FAX 44-117-929-4318. URL: http://www.iop.org. *5811*

JOURNAL OF PHYSICS G: NUCLEAR AND PARTICLE PHYSICS.
I O P Publishing Ltd., Dirac House, Temple Back, Bristol BS1 6BE, England. TEL 44-117-929-7481. FAX 44-117-929-4318. URL: http://www.iop.org/EJ/3/313/bin/journal/jg. *5853*

JOURNAL OF PLANNING AND ENVIRONMENT LAW.
Sweet & Maxwell, South Quay Plaza, 7th Fl., 183 Marsh Wall, London E14 9FT, England. TEL 0171-538-8686. FAX 0171-538-9508. *3970*

JOURNAL OF POLITICAL ECONOMY.
University of Chicago Press, Journals Division, Box 37005, Chicago, IL 60637. TEL 773-753-3347. FAX 773-753-0811. URL: http://www.jstor.org/fcgi-bin/jstor/; http://www.journals.uchicago.edu/JPE/ *978*

JOURNAL OF POLYMER SCIENCE. PART A: POLYMER CHEMISTRY.
John Wiley & Sons, Inc., Journals, 605 Third Ave., New York, NY 10158. TEL 212-850-6645. FAX 212-850-6021. URL: http://www.wiley.co.uk.
Vendor(s): STN International (CJWILEY). *1817*

JOURNAL OF POLYMER SCIENCE. PART B: POLYMER PHYSICS.
John Wiley & Sons, Inc., Journals, 605 Third Ave., New York, NY 10158. TEL 212-850-6645. FAX 212-850-6021. URL: http://www.wiley.co.uk. Vendor(s): STN International (CJWILEY). *1817*

JOURNAL OF POLYMER SCIENCE. SYMPOSIA PROCEEDINGS.
John Wiley & Sons, Inc., Journals, 605 Third Ave., New York, NY 10158-0012. TEL 212-850-6000. FAX 212-850-6088.
Vendor(s): STN International. *1817*

JOURNAL OF POPULAR CULTURE.
Popular Press, Bowling Green State University, Bowling Green, OH 43403. TEL 419-372-7866. Vendor(s): UMI. *4421*

JOURNAL OF POPULAR FILM AND TELEVISION.
Heldref Publications, 1319 Eighteenth St., N.W., Washington, DC 20036-1802. TEL 202-296-6267. FAX 202-296-5149.
Vendor(s): Information Access Co., UMI. *5337*

JOURNAL OF POPULATION ECONOMICS.
Springer-Verlag, Heidelberger Platz 3, 14197 Berlin, Germany. TEL 49-30-82787-0. FAX 49-30-82787448. URL: http://link.springer.de. *6053*

JOURNAL OF PORTFOLIO MANAGEMENT.
Institutional Investor Journals, 488 Madison Ave., New York, NY 10022. TEL 212-224-3185. FAX 212-224-3527.
Vendor(s): Information Access Co., Lexis-Nexis. *1393*

JOURNAL OF POST KEYNESIAN ECONOMICS.
M.E. Sharpe, Inc., 80 Business Park Dr., Armonk, NY 10504. TEL 914-273-1800. FAX 914-273-2106.
Vendor(s): Information Access Co., UMI. *1308*

JOURNAL OF PRISONERS ON PRISONS.
University of Manitoba, University Centre, Box 54, Winnipeg, MB R3T 2N2, Canada. URL: http://www.synapse.net/~arrakis/jpp/jpp.html. *2271*

JOURNAL OF PROGRAMMING LANGUAGES.
Chapman & Hall, Journals Department 2-6 Boundary Row, London SE1 8HN, England. TEL 44-171-8650066. FAX 44-171-5229613. URL: http://www.chaphall.com/chaphall/journals.html. *2144*

JOURNAL OF PROPERTY MANAGEMENT.
Institute of Real Estate Management, 430 N. Michigan Ave., Chicago, IL 60611. TEL 312-329-6073. FAX 312-661-0217.
Vendor(s): Information Access Co., UMI. *6304*

JOURNAL OF PROPERTY RESEARCH.
Thomson Professional, 2-6 Boundary Row, London SE1 8HN, England. TEL 44-171-865-0066. FAX 44-171-522-9621. URL: http://jpr.thomsonprofessional.com. *3751*

JOURNAL OF PSYCHIATRY AND NEUROSCIENCE.
Canadian Psychiatric Association, 237 Argyle Ave., Ste. 200, Ottawa, ON K2P 1B8, Canada. TEL 613-234-2815. FAX 613-234-9857. URL: http://cpa.medical.org/cpa/public2/publications/jpnintro.htm. *5077*

JOURNAL OF PSYCHOLOGY AND THEOLOGY.
Biola University, Rosemead School of Psychology, 13800 Biola Ave., La Mirada, CA 90639-0001. TEL 310-903-4727. FAX 310-903-4786.
Vendor(s): Knight-Ridder Information, Inc., Ovid Technologies, Inc. *6130*

JOURNAL OF PSYCHOLOGY: INTERDISCIPLINARY & APPLIED.
Heldref Publications, 1319 Eighteenth St., N.W., Washington, DC 20036-1802. TEL 202-296-6267. FAX 202-296-5149.
Vendor(s): Information Access Co. *6130*

JOURNAL OF PUBLIC POLICY & MARKETING.
American Marketing Association, 250 S. Wacker Dr., Chicago, IL 60606-5819. TEL 312-648-0536. URL: http://www.ama.org.
Vendor(s): Information Access Co., UMI. *1535*

JOURNAL OF RADIOLOGICAL PROTECTION.
I O P Publishing Ltd., Dirac House, Temple Back, Bristol BS1 6BE, England. TEL 44-117-929-7481. FAX 44-117-929-4318. URL: http://www.iop.org. *2699*

JOURNAL OF REGIONAL AND LOCAL STUDIES.
c/o Lincoln University, Department of Humanities, Brayford Pool, Lincoln LN6 7TS, England. *3578*

JOURNAL OF REHABILITATION.
National Rehabilitation Association, 633 S. Washington St., Alexandria, VA 22314-4109. TEL 703-836-0850. FAX 703-836-0848.
Vendor(s): Information Access Co., UMI. *5044*

JOURNAL OF REHABILITATION RESEARCH AND DEVELOPMENT.
Department of Veterans Affairs, Office of Technology Transfer, 103 S. Gay St., Baltimore, MD 21202. TEL 410-962-1800. FAX 410-962-9670.
Vendor(s): UMI. *5011*

JOURNAL OF RELIGIOUS THOUGHT.
Howard University Press, 1240 Randolph St., N.E., Washington, DC 20017. TEL 202-806-0785. FAX 202-806-0502.
Vendor(s): UMI. *6350*

JOURNAL OF RESEARCH IN PERSONALITY.
Academic Press, Inc., Journal Division, 525 B St., Ste. 1900, San Diego, CA 92101-4495. TEL 619-230-1840. FAX 619-699-6800. URL: http://www.apnet.com/www/journal/rp.htm; http://www.idealibrary.com/ *6131*

JOURNAL OF RETAIL BANKING.
American Banker - Bond Buyer, Newsletter Division One State St. Plaza, New York, NY 10004-1549. TEL 212-943-5908.
Vendor(s): Information Access Co. *1151*

JOURNAL OF RETAILING.
J A I Press Inc., 55 Old Post Rd., No. 2, Box 1678, Greenwich, CT 06830-1678. TEL 203-661-7602. FAX 203-661-0792. URL: http://www.haas.berkeley.edu/~jrl.
Vendor(s): Information Access Co., Knight-Ridder Information, Inc.. *1535*

JOURNAL OF RISK AND INSURANCE.
American Risk and Insurance Association, c/o Chase Communications, Stephen H. Acunto, Exec. Dir., Box 9001, Mt. Vernon, NY 10552. TEL 914-699-2020. FAX 914-699-2025.
Vendor(s): Information Access Co., Knight-Ridder Information, Inc. *3822*

JOURNAL OF SCANDINAVIAN POETRY ON THE WEB.
Splints & Co., URL: http://www.geocities.com/Athens/2334/readme.htm.
Available only online. *4512*

JOURNAL OF SCHOOL HEALTH.
American School Health Association, Box 708, Kent, OH 44240. TEL 216-678-1601. FAX 216-678-4526.
Vendor(s): Information Access Co., UMI. *6242*

JOURNAL OF SEX RESEARCH.
Society for the Scientific Study of Sexuality, Box 208, Mt. Vernon, IA 52314. TEL 319-895-8407. FAX 319-895-6203. URL: http://www.ssc.wisc.edu/ssss.
Vendor(s): UMI. *6131*

JOURNAL OF SMALL BUSINESS MANAGEMENT.
West Virginia University, Bureau of Business and Economic Research, Box 6025, Morgantown, WV 26506-6025. TEL 304-293-7534. URL: http://www.wvu.edu/~colbe/research/bureau/jsbm.htm.
Vendor(s): Information Access Co., UMI. *1644*

JOURNAL OF SOCIAL HISTORY.
Carnegie - Mellon University Press, Schenley Park, 242 Baker Hall, Pittsburgh, PA 15213. TEL 412-268-2884. FAX 412-268-5288. URL: http://hss.cmu.edu/html/JSH/index.html.
Vendor(s): Information Access Co., UMI. *6718*

JOURNAL OF SOCIAL ISSUES.
Blackwell Publishers, 238 Main St., Cambridge, MA 02142. TEL 617-547-7110. FAX 617-547-0789.
Vendor(s): Information Access Co., UMI. *6132*

THE JOURNAL OF SOCIAL PSYCHOLOGY.
Heldref Publications, 1319 Eighteenth St., N.W., Washington, DC 20036-1802. TEL 202-296-6267. FAX 202-296-5149.
Vendor(s): Information Access Co., UMI. *6132*

THE JOURNAL OF SOCIO-ECONOMICS.
J A I Press Inc., 55 Old Post Rd., No. 2, Greenwich, CT 06830-1678. TEL 203-661-7602. FAX 203-661-0792.
Vendor(s): Information Access Co. *1308*

JOURNAL OF SOCIOLOGY AND SOCIAL WELFARE.
Western Michigan University, School of Social Work, c/o Fritz MacDonald, Managing Ed., Kalamazoo, MI 49008-5034. TEL 616-387-3198. FAX 616-387-3217. *6718*

JOURNAL OF SOIL AND WATER CONSERVATION.
Soil and Water Conservation Society, 7515 N.E. Ankeny Rd., Ankeny, IA 50021. TEL 515-289-2331. FAX 515-289-1227. URL: http://www.swcs.org/JSWCwelcom.htm.
Vendor(s): Information Access Co., UMI. *232*

JOURNAL OF SOLID STATE CHEMISTRY.
Academic Press, Inc., Journal Division, 525 B St., Ste. 1900, San Diego, CA 92101-4495. TEL 619-230-1840. FAX 619-699-6800. URL: http://www.apnet.com/journal/sc.htm; http://www.idealibrary.com/ *1832*

JOURNAL OF SOLID STATE ELECTROCHEMISTRY.
Springer-Verlag, Heidelberger Platz 3, 14197 Berlin, Germany. TEL 49-30-82787-0. FAX 49-30-82787448. URL: http://link.springer.de. *1805*

JOURNAL OF SOUND AND VIBRATION.
Academic Press Ltd., 24-28 Oval Rd., London NW1 7DX, England. TEL 44-171-267-4466. FAX 44-171-482-2293. URL: http://www.hbuk.co.uk/ap/jvs; http://www.europe.idealibrary.com/ *5873*

JOURNAL OF SOUTHEAST ASIAN STUDIES.
Singapore University Press, 10 Kent Ridge Crescent, Singapore 119260, Singapore. TEL 65-7761148. FAX 65-7740652. URL: http://www.nus.sg/SUP/97/supcat.htm jseas.
Vendor(s): Information Access Co.. *3536*

JOURNAL OF SPORT BEHAVIOR.
University of South Alabama, Department of Health, Physical Education and Leisure Studies, Mobile, AL 36688. TEL 334-460-7131. FAX 334-460-7252.
Vendor(s): Information Access Co., UMI. *6767*

JOURNAL OF SPORTS SCIENCES.
Thomson Professional, 2-6 Boundary Row, London SE1 8HN, England. TEL 44-171-865-0066. FAX 44-171-522-9623. URL: http://jpr.thomsonprofessional.com. *6767*

JOURNAL OF STATISTICAL COMPUTATION AND SIMULATION.
Gordon and Breach - Harwood Academic, Amsteldisk 166, 1st Fl., 1079 LH Amsterdam, Netherlands. URL: http://www.gbhap.com/Statistical__Computation__Simulation/. *2152*

JOURNAL OF STRATEGIC MARKETING.
Thomson Professional, 2-6 Boundary Row, London SE1 8HN, England. TEL 44-171-8650066. FAX 44-171-5229623. URL: http://jsm.thomsonprofessional.com. *1535*

JOURNAL OF STRUCTURAL BIOLOGY.
Academic Press, Inc., Journal Division, 525 B St., Ste. 1900, San Diego, CA 92101-4495. TEL 619-230-1840. FAX 619-699-6859. URL: http://www.apnet.com/www/journal/sb.htm; http://www.idealibrary.com/ *610*

JOURNAL OF STRUCTURAL LEARNING.
Gordon and Breach - Harwood Academic, Amsteldisk 166, 1st Fl., 1079 LH Amsterdam, Netherlands. URL: http://www.gbhap.com/Structural__Learning__Intelligent__Systems/. *6132*

JOURNAL OF SURGICAL ONCOLOGY.
John Wiley & Sons, Inc., Journals, 605 Third Ave., New York, NY 10158. TEL 212-850-6645. FAX 212-850-6021. URL: http://www.wiley.co.uk. *5146*

JOURNAL OF SURGICAL PATHOLOGY.
Chapman & Hall, Journals Department 2-6 Boundary Row, London SE1 8HN, England. TEL 44-171-8650066. FAX 44-171-5229623. URL: http://www.chaphall.com/chaphall/journals.html. *4698*

JOURNAL OF SURGICAL RESEARCH.
Academic Press, Inc., Journal Division, 525 B St., Ste. 1900, San Diego, CA 92101-4495. TEL 619-230-1840. FAX 619-699-6800. URL: http://www.apnet.com/www/journal/jr.htm; http://www.idealibrary.com/ *5147*

JOURNAL OF SYMBOLIC COMPUTATION.
Academic Press Ltd., 24-28 Oval Rd., London NW1 7DX, England. TEL 44-171-267-4466. FAX 44-171-482-2293. URL: http://www.hbuk.co.uk/ap/jsc; http://www.europe.idealibrary.com/ *4622*

JOURNAL OF SYSTEMS MANAGEMENT.
Association for Systems Management, Box 38370, Cleveland, OH 44138. TEL 216-243-6900. Vendor(s): Information Access Co., Knight-Ridder Information, Inc., UMI. *1490*

THE JOURNAL OF TAXATION.
Warren, Gorham & Lamont, One Penn Plaza, New York, NY 10119. TEL 212-971-5185. FAX 212-971-5113. URL: http://www.wgl.com/tax/jtax.html. Vendor(s): Lexis-Nexis (TAXRIA-Library), West Group (WGL-JTAX). *1618*

JOURNAL OF TECHNOLOGY EDUCATION.
Virginia Polytechnic Institute, Technology Education Program, c/o Mark Sanders, Ed., 144 Smyth Hall, Blacksburg, VA 24061-0432. FAX 703-231-4188. URL: http://borg.lib.vt.edu/ejournals/JTE/jte.html. *6976*

JOURNAL OF TECHNOLOGY LAW AND POLICY.
URL: http://www.journal.law.yfl.edu/~techlaw. Available only online. *5586*

JOURNAL OF TECHNOLOGY TRANSFER.
Technology Transfer Society, 435 N. Michigan Ave., Chicago, IL 60611-4001. Vendor(s): Knight-Ridder Information, Inc., Ovid Technologies, Inc. *6964*

JOURNAL OF THE AUSTRALIAN WAR MEMORIAL.
Australian War Memorial, G.P.O. Box 345, Canberra, A.C.T. 2601, Australia. TEL 61-6-2434345. FAX 61-6-2434325. URL: http://www.adfa.oz.au/~awm/journal/htm. Available only online. *5274*

JOURNAL OF THE EXPERIMENTAL ANALYSIS OF BEHAVIOR.
Society for the Experimental Analysis of Behavior, Inc., c/o Psychology Department, Indiana University, Bloomington, IN 47405. TEL 812-339-4718. URL: http://www.envmed.rochester.edu/wwwrap/behavior/jeabjaba.htm. *6133*

JOURNAL OF THE HISTORY OF IDEAS.
Johns Hopkins University Press, Journals Publishing Division, 2715 N. Charles St., Baltimore, MD 21218-4319. TEL 410-516-6987. FAX 410-516-6968. URL: http://muse.jhu.edu. *3783*

JOURNAL OF THE JAPANESE AND INTERNATIONAL ECONOMIES.
Academic Press, Inc., Journal Division, 525 B St., Ste. 1900, San Diego, CA 92101-4495. TEL 619-230-1840. FAX 619-699-6800. URL: http://www.apnet.com/www/journal/jj.htm; http://www.idealibrary.com/ *1339*

JOURNAL OF THEOLOGICAL STUDIES.
Oxford University Press, Academic Division, Great Clarendon St., Oxford OX2 6DP, England. TEL 44-1865-267907. FAX 44-1865-267485. URL: http://www.oup.co.uk/journals. Vendor(s): Information Access Co. *6350*

JOURNAL OF THEORETICAL BIOLOGY.
Academic Press Ltd., 24-28 Oval Rd., London NW1 7DX, England. TEL 44-171-267-4466. FAX 44-171-482-2293. URL: http://www.hbuk.co.uk/ap/jtb; http://www.europe.idealibrary.com/ *610*

JOURNAL OF TOXICOLOGY. CLINICAL TOXICOLOGY.
Marcel Dekker Journals, 270 Madison Ave., New York, NY 10016. TEL 212-696-9000. FAX 212-685-4540. URL: http://www.dekker.com. *2303*

JOURNAL OF TOXICOLOGY AND ENVIRONMENTAL HEALTH. PART A.
Taylor & Francis Inc., 1900 Frost Rd., Ste. 101, Bristol, PA 19007-1598. FAX 215-785-5515. URL: http://www.tandf.co.uk/. *2979*

JOURNAL OF TRAUMA - INJURY, INFECTION AND CRITICAL CARE.
Williams & Wilkins, 351 W. Camden St., Baltimore, MD 21201-2436. TEL 410-528-4068. FAX 410-528-4452. URL: http://www.wwilkins.com. Vendor(s): Ovid Technologies, Inc. *5011*

JOURNAL OF TRAVEL RESEARCH.
University of Colorado, Business Research Division, Campus Box 420, Boulder, CO 80309-0420. TEL 303-492-8227. FAX 303-492-3620. Vendor(s): UMI. *7214*

JOURNAL OF URBAN ECONOMICS.
Academic Press, Inc., Journal Division, 525 B St., Ste. 1900, San Diego, CA 92101-4495. TEL 619-230-1840. FAX 619-699-6800. URL: http://www.apnet.com/www/journal/ue.htm; http://www.idealibrary.com/ *978*

JOURNAL OF UROLOGY.
Williams & Wilkins, 351 W. Camden St., Baltimore, MD 21201-2436. TEL 410-528-4068. FAX 410-528-4452. URL: http://www.wwilkins.com. Vendor(s): Ovid Technologies, Inc. *5163*

JOURNAL OF VISUAL LANGUAGES AND COMPUTING.
Academic Press Ltd., 24-28 Oval Rd., London NW1 7DX, England. TEL 44-171-267-4466. FAX 44-171-482-2293. URL: http://www.hbuk.co.uk/ap/jvlc; http://www.europe.idealibrary.com/ *4320*

JOURNAL OF VOCATIONAL BEHAVIOR.
Academic Press, Inc., Journal Division, 525 B St., Ste. 1900, San Diego, CA 92101-4495. TEL 619-230-1840. FAX 619-699-6800. URL: http://www.apnet.com/www/journal/vb.htm; http://www.idealibrary.com/ *6133*

JOURNAL OF WOMEN'S HISTORY.
Indiana University Press, 601 N. Morton St., Bloomington, IN 47404. TEL 812-855-9449. FAX 812-855-8507. Vendor(s): UMI. *7345*

JOURNAL OF X-RAY SCIENCE AND TECHNOLOGY.
Academic Press, Inc., Journal Division, 525 B St., Ste. 1900, San Diego, CA 92101-4495. TEL 619-230-1840. FAX 619-699-6800. URL: http://www.apnet.com/www/journal/xr.htm; http://www.idealibrary.com/ *5812*

JOURNAL OF YOUTH AND ADOLESCENCE.
Plenum Publishing Corp., 233 Spring St., New York, NY 10013-1578. TEL 212-620-8000. FAX 212-463-0742. Vendor(s): Information Access Co., UMI. *1849*

JOURNAL RECORD.
Dolan Media, Box 26370, Oklahoma City, OK 73126-0370. TEL 405-235-3100. FAX 405-278-6918. *978*

JOURNALISM AND MASS COMMUNICATION EDUCATOR.
Association for Education in Journalism and Mass Communications, LeConte College, Rm. 121, University of South Carolina, Columbia, SC 29208-0251. TEL 830-777-2005. FAX 803-777-4728. Vendor(s): UMI. *3875*

JOURNALISM HISTORY.
Greenspun School of Communication, University of Nevada, Las Vegas, NV 89154-5007. TEL 702-895-3964. FAX 702-895-4805. Vendor(s): UMI. *3875*

JOURNALS OF GERONTOLOGY. SERIES A: BIOLOGICAL SCIENCES & MEDICAL SCIENCES.
Gerontological Society of America, 1275 K St., N.W., Ste. 250, Washington, DC 20005-4006. TEL 202-842-1275. FAX 202-842-1150. URL: http://gsa.iog.wayne.edu/Journals/ Vendor(s): UMI. *3440*

JOURNALS OF GERONTOLOGY. SERIES B: PSYCHOLOGICAL SCIENCES & SOCIAL SCIENCES.
Gerontological Society of America, 1275 K St., N.W., Ste. 250, Washington, DC 20005-4006. TEL 202-842-1275. FAX 202-842-1150. URL: http://gsa.iog.wayne.edu/Journals/ Vendor(s): UMI. *3440*

JOURNEY TO HEALTH.
URL: http://home.earthlink.net/cherylstkf/webdocs/index.html. Available only online. *5786*

JUDAISM.
American Jewish Congress, 15 E. 84th St., New York, NY 10028. TEL 212-879-4500. Vendor(s): Information Access Co., UMI. *6406*

JUDICATURE.
American Judicature Society, 180 N. Michigan Ave., Ste. 600, Chicago, IL 60601-7401. Vendor(s): West Group. *4133*

JUDICIAL CONDUCT REPORTER.
American Judicature Society, Center for Judicial Conduct Organizations, 180 N. Michigan, Ste. 600, Chicago, IL 60601. TEL 312-558-6900. FAX 312-558-9175. URL: http://homepage.interaccess.com/~ajs/. Vendor(s): West Group. *4133*

JUXTA.
977 Seminole Trail, No. 331, Charlottesville, VA 22901. *4422*

K G B.
K G B Media Inc., 133 Bowery, New York, NY 10002. TEL 212-343-1512. URL: http://www.kgbmedia.com/kgbmedia/. *3377*

K I T NEWSLETTER.
Peregrine Foundation, Box 460141, San Francisco, CA 94146-0141. TEL 415-821-2090. FAX 415-282-2369. URL: http://www.matisse.net/~peregrin/knsltrs.html. *6718*

K.L. SMITH'S CRUISELETTER.
Jackson Publishing, 20801 Severndale Terrace, Germantown, MD 20876. TEL 301-428-9877. FAX 301-515-7798. URL: http://www.lane.on.ca/pubs/c-letter/index.html. Available only online. *7214*

K N K.
c/o Karalius, P.O. Box 114, 3005 Kaunas, Lithuania. URL: http://www.soften.ktu.lt/~kaleck/koksnorskelias. *5405*

KAIJO HOANCHO. SUIROBU KANSOKU HOKOKU. KAIYO HEN.
Kaijo Hoancho, Suirobu, 3-1, Tsukiji 5-chome, Chuoku, Tokyo 104, Japan. FAX 81-3-3545-2885. URL: http://www.jodc.jhd.go.jp/ *2396*

KALAMAZOO COLLEGE QUARTERLY.
Kalamazoo College, 1200 Academy St., Kalamazoo, MI 49006-3295. TEL 616-377-7304. FAX 616-337-7305. *1958*

KALDRON.
Box 7164, Halcyon, CA 93420-7164. Available only online. *4512*

KANE'S BEVERAGE WEEK.
Whitaker Newsletters Inc., 313 South Ave., Box 192, Fanwood, NJ 07023. TEL 908-889-6336. FAX 908-889-6339. Vendor(s): NewsNet (FB06). *523*

KANSAS BUSINESS DIRECTORY.
American Business Directories, 5711 S. 86th Circle, Box 27347, Omaha, NE 68127. TEL 402-593-4600. FAX 402-331-5481. *1690*

KANSAS CITY BOARD OF TRADE REVIEW.
Kansas City Board of Trade, 4800 Main St., No.303, Kansas City, MO 64112. TEL 816-753-7500. FAX 816-753-3944. URL: http://www.kcbt.com. *264*

THE KANSAS CITY BUSINESS JOURNAL.
American City Business Journals, Inc. (Kansas City), 1101 Walnut St., Ste. 800, Kansas City, MO 64106-2122. TEL 816-421-5900. FAX 816-472-4010. Vendor(s): Information Access Co. *1268*

SERIALS AVAILABLE ONLINE

KANSAS CITY SMALL BUSINESS MONTHLY.
URL: http://www.kcsmallbiz.com.
Available only online. *1644*

THE KARATE CYBERDOJO JOURNAL.
Japan Karate-do Ryobu-kai Kansas, URL: http://www.jkr.com/cyberdojo/journal.
Available only online. *6768*

KASPAH RASTER.
Box 8831, Portland, OR 97207. URL: http://www.teleport.com/~jaheriot/kr.htm.
Available only online. *4341*

KATALOG FOR SKOLEBIBLIOTEKER. SKOLEBIBLIOTEKARENS.
Dansk BiblioteksCenter as, Tempovej 7-11, DK-2750 Ballerup, Denmark. TEL 45-44-867777. FAX 45-44-867892. *553*

KATALOG FOR SKOLEBIBLIOTEKER. TITELKATALOG.
Dansk BiblioteksCenter as, Tempovej 7-11, DK-2750 Ballerup, Denmark. TEL 45-44-867777. FAX 45-44-867892. *553*

KATHIE'S HERB PAGE.
URL: http://www.muscanet.com/~kschmitt.
Available only online. *3197*

KAUPPALEHTI.
Kustannus oy Kauppalehti, P.O. Box 189, SF-00101, Vetotie no.3, 01610 Vantaa, Finland. TEL 90 50781.
Vendor(s): Helsinki School of Economics. *979*

KEESING'S RECORD OF WORLD EVENTS.
Keesing's Worldwide, LLC, 7979 Old Georgetown Rd., Bethesda, MD 20814. TEL 301-718-8770. FAX 301-718-8494. URL: http://www.keesings.com. *5985*

KEJI GUANLI YANJIU.
Science & Technology Management Research Periodicals House, No. 100, Xianlie Zhonglu, Guangzhou, Guangdong 510070, People's Republic of China. TEL 86-20-8766-8145. FAX 86-20-8777-5791. *6539*

KELLY'S DIRECTORY.
Kelly's Directories, Part of the Reed Elsevier group, Windsor Court, E. Grinstead House, E. Grinstead, W. Sussex RH19 1XB, England. TEL 01342-326972. FAX 01342-335747. URL: http://www.reedinfo.co.uk.
Vendor(s): Reed Information Services Ltd. *1690*

KELLY'S LINK.
Kelly's Directories, Part of the Reed Elsevier group, Windsor Court, E. Grinstead House, E. Grinstead, W. Sussex RH19 1XB, England. TEL 01342-326972. FAX 01342-335747. URL: http://www.reedinfo.co.uk.
Vendor(s): Reed Information Services Ltd. *1690*

KELLY'S OIL & GAS DIRECTORY.
Kelly's Directories, Part of the Reed Elsevier group, Windsor Court, E. Grinstead House, E. Grinstead, W. Sussex RH19 1XB, England. TEL 01342-326972. FAX 01342-335747. URL: http://www.reedinfo.co.uk.
Vendor(s): Reed Information Services Ltd. *1690*

KENNEDY INSTITUTE OF ETHICS JOURNAL.
Johns Hopkins University Press, Journals Publishing Division, 2715 N. Charles St., Baltimore, MD 21218. TEL 410-516-6987. FAX 410-516-6968. URL: http://muse.jhu.edu; http://www.press.jhu.edu/journals/kennedy_institute_of_ethics_journal/ *4700*

KENTUCKY BANKER.
Kentucky Bankers Association, Ste. 1000, Waterfront Plaza, 325 W. Main St., Louisville, KY 40202. TEL 502-582-2453. FAX 502-584-6390.
Vendor(s): UMI. *1151*

KENTUCKY BANKING AND RELATED LAWS AND RULES ANNOTATED.
Michie, A Division of Reed Elsevier Inc., Box 7587, Charlottesville, VA 22906-7587. TEL 804-972-7566. FAX 800-643-1280. URL: http://www.michie.com. *1151*

KENTUCKY BUSINESS DIRECTORY.
American Business Directories, 5711 S. 86th Circle, Box 27347, Omaha, NE 68127. TEL 402-593-4600. FAX 402-331-5481. *1690*

KENTUCKY BUSINESS LEDGER.
Kentucky Communications, Inc., Box 470867, Charlotte, NC 28247.
Vendor(s): Knight-Ridder Information, Inc. *979*

KENTUCKY LAW JOURNAL.
University of Kentucky, College of Law, Lexington, KY 40506. TEL 606-257-4747. FAX 606-323-1061.
Vendor(s): West Group. *3973*

THE KENTUCKY MANUFACTURER.
Industrial Marketing, Inc., PO Box 4310, Lexington, KY 40544-4310. TEL 606-266-3303. FAX 606-266-3230.
Vendor(s): UMI. *979*

KERMIT NEWS.
Columbia University Academic Information Systems, Kermit Development and Distribution, 612 W. 115th St., New York, NY 10025. TEL 212-854-3703. FAX 212-663-8202. URL: http://www.columbia.edu/kermit/knews.html. *2144*

KEVINDEX.
MSOB x-215, Stanford, CA 94305-5479. URL: http://smi.stanford.edu/people/kxl/webazine.html. *4532*

KEXUE (SHANGHAI).
Shanghai Keji Chubanshe, 450 Ruijin 2 Lu, Shanghai 200020, People's Republic of China. TEL 86-21-473465. FAX 86-21-4730679.
Vendor(s): UMI. *6540*

KEY ABSTRACTS - BUSINESS AUTOMATION.
INSPEC, I.E.E., Michael Faraday House, Six Hill Way, Stevenage, Herts. SG1 2AY, England. TEL 44-1438-313311. FAX 44-1438-742840. URL: http://www.iee.org.uk.
Vendor(s): CEDOCAR, Data-Star, European Space Agency, FIZ Technik, Knight-Ridder Information, Inc., Questel Orbit Inc., STN International. *2095*

KEY BRITISH ENTERPRISES.
Dun & Bradstreet Ltd., Holmers Farm Way, High Wycombe, Bucks. HP12 4UL, England. TEL 44-1494-422000. FAX 44-1494-422260. *979*

KEY NOTE MARKET REPORT: ACCOUNTANCY.
Key Note Ltd., Field House, 72 Oldfield Rd., Hampton, Middlesex TW12 2HQ, England. TEL 44-181-783-0755. FAX 44-181-783-0049. *1093*

KEY NOTE MARKET REPORT: ADHESIVES.
Key Note Ltd., Field House, 72 Oldfield Rd., Hampton, Middlesex TW12 2HQ, England. TEL 44-181-783-0755. FAX 44-181-783-1940. *2768*

KEY NOTE MARKET REPORT: ADVERTISING AGENCIES.
Key Note Ltd., Field House, 72 Oldfield Rd., Hampton, Middlesex TW12 2HQ, England. TEL 44-181-783-0755. FAX 44-181-783-0049. *38*

KEY NOTE MARKET REPORT: AEROSPACE.
Key Note Ltd., Field House, 72 Oldfield Rd., Hampton, Middlesex TW12 2HQ, England. TEL 44-181-783-0755. FAX 44-181-783-0049. *73*

KEY NOTE MARKET REPORT: AFTER DINNER DRINKS.
Key Note Ltd., Field House, 72 Oldfield Rd., Hampton, Middlesex TW12 2HQ, England. TEL 44-181-783-0755. FAX 44-181-783-0049. *523*

KEY NOTE MARKET REPORT: AGRICULTURAL MACHINERY.
Key Note Ltd., Field House, 72 Oldfield Rd., Hampton, Middlesex TW12 2HQ, England. TEL 44-181-783-0755. FAX 44-181-783-0049. *207*

KEY NOTE MARKET REPORT: AGROCHEMICALS & FERTILIZERS.
Key Note Ltd., Field House, 72 Oldfield Rd., Hampton, Middlesex TW12 2HQ, England. TEL 44-181-783-0755. FAX 44-181-783-0049. *233*

KEY NOTE MARKET REPORT: AIRLINES.
Key Note Ltd., Field House, 72 Oldfield Rd., Hampton, Middlesex TW12 2HQ, England. TEL 44-181-783-0755. FAX 44-181-783-0049. *7074*

KEY NOTE MARKET REPORT: AIRPORTS.
Key Note Ltd., Field House, 72 Oldfield Rd., Hampton, Middlesex TW12 2HQ, England. TEL 44-181-783-0755. FAX 44-181-783-0049. *7074*

KEY NOTE MARKET REPORT: ANIMAL FEEDSTUFFS.
Key Note Ltd., Field House, 72 Oldfield Rd., Hampton, Middlesex TW12 2HQ, England. TEL 44-181-783-0755. FAX 44-181-783-0049. *264*

KEY NOTE MARKET REPORT: AUTOMATIC VENDING.
Key Note Ltd., Field House, 72 Oldfield Rd., Hampton, Middlesex TW12 2HQ, England. TEL 44-181-783-0755. FAX 44-181-783-0049. *1536*

KEY NOTE MARKET REPORT: AUTOPARTS.
Key Note Ltd., Field House, 72 Oldfield Rd., Hampton, Middlesex TW12 2HQ, England. TEL 44-181-783-0755. FAX 44-181-783-0049. *7104*

KEY NOTE MARKET REPORT: BABY PRODUCTS.
Key Note Ltd., Field House, 72 Oldfield Rd., Hampton, Middlesex TW12 2HQ, England. TEL 44-181-783-0755. FAX 44-181-783-0049. *1849*

KEY NOTE MARKET REPORT: BATHS & SANITARYWARE.
Key Note Ltd., Field House, 72 Oldfield Rd., Hampton, Middlesex TW12 2HQ, England. TEL 44-181-783-0755. FAX 44-181-783-0049. *507*

KEY NOTE MARKET REPORT: BETTING & GAMING.
Key Note Ltd., Field House, 72 Oldfield Rd., Hampton, Middlesex TW12 2HQ, England. TEL 44-181-783-0755. FAX 44-181-783-0049. *6768*

KEY NOTE MARKET REPORT: BICYCLES.
Key Note Ltd., Field House, 72 Oldfield Rd., Hampton, Middlesex TW12 2HQ, England. TEL 44-181-783-0755. FAX 44-181-783-0049. *6828*

KEY NOTE MARKET REPORT: BISCUITS & CAKES.
Key Note Ltd., Field House, 72 Oldfield Rd., Hampton, Middlesex TW12 2HQ, England. TEL 44-181-783-0755. FAX 44-181-783-0049. *3137*

KEY NOTE MARKET REPORT: BOOK PUBLISHING.
Key Note Ltd., Field House, 72 Oldfield Rd., Hampton, Middlesex TW12 2HQ, England. TEL 44-181-783-0755. FAX 44-181-783-0049. *6275*

KEY NOTE MARKET REPORT: BOOKSELLING.
Key Note Ltd., Field House, 72 Oldfield Rd., Hampton, Middlesex TW12 2HQ, England. TEL 44-181-783-0755. FAX 44-181-783-0049. *6275*

KEY NOTE MARKET REPORT: BOTTLED WATERS.
Key Note Ltd., Field House, 72 Oldfield Rd., Hampton, Middlesex TW12 2HQ, England. TEL 44-181-783-0755. FAX 44-181-783-0049. *523*

KEY NOTE MARKET REPORT: BREAD BAKERS.
Key Note Ltd., Field House, 72 Oldfield Rd., Hampton, Middlesex TW12 2HQ, England. TEL 44-181-783-0755. FAX 44-181-783-0049. *3137*

KEY NOTE MARKET REPORT: BREAKFAST CEREALS.
Key Note Ltd., Field House, 72 Oldfield Rd., Hampton, Middlesex TW12 2HQ, England. TEL 44-181-783-0755. FAX 44-181-783-0049. *3117*

KEY NOTE MARKET REPORT: BREWERIES & THE BEER MARKET.
Key Note Ltd., Field House, 72 Oldfield Rd., Hampton, Middlesex TW12 2HQ, England. TEL 44-181-783-0755. FAX 44-181-783-0049. *523*

KEY NOTE MARKET REPORT: BRICKS & TILES.
Key Note Ltd., Field House, 72 Oldfield Rd., Hampton, Middlesex TW12 2HQ, England. TEL 44-181-783-0755. FAX 44-181-783-0049. *900*

KEY NOTE MARKET REPORT: BROWN GOODS.
Key Note Ltd., Field House, 72 Oldfield Rd., Hampton, Middlesex TW12 2HQ, England. TEL 44-181-783-0755. FAX 44-181-783-0049. *2644*

KEY NOTE MARKET REPORT: BUILDING CONTRACTING.
Key Note Ltd., Field House, 72 Oldfield Rd., Hampton, Middlesex TW12 2HQ, England. TEL 44-181-783-0755. FAX 44-181-783-0049. *900*

KEY NOTE MARKET REPORT: BUILDING MATERIALS.
Key Note Ltd., Field House, 72 Oldfield Rd., Hampton, Middlesex TW12 2HQ, England. TEL 44-181-783-1940. *900*

KEY NOTE MARKET REPORT: BUILDING SOCIETIES.
Key Note Ltd., Field House, 72 Oldfield Rd., Hampton, Middlesex TW12 2HQ, England. TEL 44-181-783-0755. FAX 44-181-783-0049. *900*

KEY NOTE MARKET REPORT: BUS & COACH OPERATORS.
Key Note Ltd., Field House, 72 Oldfield Rd., Hampton, Middlesex TW12 2HQ, England. TEL 44-171-783-0755. FAX 44-171-783-0049. *7032*

KEY NOTE MARKET REPORT: BUSINESS PRESS.
Key Note Ltd., Field House, 72 Oldfield Rd., Hampton, Middlesex TW12 2HQ, England. TEL 44-181-783-0755. FAX 44-181-783-0049. *979*

KEY NOTE MARKET REPORT: BUSINESS TRAVEL.
Key Note Ltd., Field House, 72 Oldfield Rd., Hampton, Middlesex TW12 2HQ, England. TEL 44-181-783-0755. FAX 44-181-783-0049. *7215*

KEY NOTE MARKET REPORT: C D - R O M.
Key Note Ltd., Field House, 72 Oldfield Rd., Hampton, Middlesex TW12 2HQ, England. TEL 44-181-783-0755. FAX 44-181-783-1940. *2016*

KEY NOTE MARKET REPORT: C T N'S.
Key Note Ltd., Field House, 72 Oldfield Rd., Hampton, Middlesex TW12 2HQ, England. TEL 44-181-783-0755. FAX 44-181-783-0049. *1151*

KEY NOTE MARKET REPORT: CABLE AND SATELLITE T V.
Key Note Ltd., Field House, 72 Oldfield Rd., Hampton, Middlesex TW12 2HQ, England. TEL 44-181-783-0755. FAX 44-181-783-0049. *2053*

KEY NOTE MARKET REPORT: CAMERAS & CAMCORDERS.
Key Note Ltd., Field House, 72 Oldfield Rd., Hampton, Middlesex TW12 2HQ, England. TEL 44-181-783-0755. FAX 44-181-783-0049. *5768*

KEY NOTE MARKET REPORT: CAMPING & CARAVANNING.
Key Note Ltd., Field House, 72 Oldfield Rd., Hampton, Middlesex TW12 2HQ, England. TEL 44-181-783-0755. FAX 44-181-783-0049. *4149*

KEY NOTE MARKET REPORT: CANNED FOODS.
Key Note Ltd., Field House, 72 Oldfield Rd., Hampton, Middlesex TW12 2HQ, England. TEL 44-181-783-0755. FAX 44-181-783-0049. *3117*

KEY NOTE MARKET REPORT: CAR DEALERS.
Key Note Ltd., Field House, 72 Oldfield Rd., Hampton, Middlesex TW12 2HQ, England. TEL 44-181-783-0755. FAX 44-181-783-0049. *7104*

KEY NOTE MARKET REPORT: CARPETS & FLOORCOVERINGS.
Key Note Ltd., Field House, 72 Oldfield Rd., Hampton, Middlesex TW12 2HQ, England. TEL 44-181-783-0755. FAX 44-181-783-0049. *3858*

KEY NOTE MARKET REPORT: CASH & CARRY OUTLETS.
Key Note Ltd., Field House, 72 Oldfield Rd., Hampton, Middlesex TW12 2HQ, England. TEL 44-181-783-0755. FAX 44-181-783-0049. *1536*

KEY NOTE MARKET REPORT: CHARITIES.
Key Note Ltd., Field House, 72 Oldfield Rd., Hampton, Middlesex TW12 2HQ, England. TEL 44-181-783-0755. FAX 44-181-783-1940. *6675*

KEY NOTE MARKET REPORT: CHEMICAL INDUSTRY.
Key Note Ltd., Field House, 72 Oldfield Rd., Hampton, Middlesex TW12 2HQ, England. TEL 44-181-783-0755. FAX 44-181-783-0049. *2768*

KEY NOTE MARKET REPORT: CHILDRENSWEAR.
Key Note Ltd., Field House, 72 Oldfield Rd., Hampton, Middlesex TW12 2HQ, England. TEL 44-181-783-0755. FAX 44-181-783-0049. *1916*

KEY NOTE MARKET REPORT: CHILLED FOODS.
Key Note Ltd., Field House, 72 Oldfield Rd., Hampton, Middlesex TW12 2HQ, England. TEL 44-181-783-0755. FAX 44-181-783-0049. *3117*

KEY NOTE MARKET REPORT: CHINA & EARTHENWARE.
Key Note Ltd., Field House, 72 Oldfield Rd., Hampton, Middlesex TW12 2HQ, England. TEL 44-181-783-0755. FAX 44-181-783-0049. *1732*

KEY NOTE MARKET REPORT: CIDER.
Key Note Ltd., Field House, 72 Oldfield Rd., Hampton, Middlesex TW12 2HQ, England. TEL 44-181-783-0755. FAX 44-181-783-0049. *523*

KEY NOTE MARKET REPORT: CIGARETTES & TOBACCO.
Key Note Ltd., Field House, 72 Oldfield Rd., Hampton, Middlesex TW12 2HQ, England. TEL 44-181-783-0755. FAX 44-181-783-0049. *7020*

KEY NOTE MARKET REPORT: CIVIL ENGINEERING.
Key Note Ltd., Field House, 72 Oldfield Rd., Hampton, Middlesex TW12 2HQ, England. TEL 44-181-783-0755. FAX 44-181-783-0049. *2792*

KEY NOTE MARKET REPORT: CLOTHING MANUFACTURING.
Key Note Ltd., Field House, 72 Oldfield Rd., Hampton, Middlesex TW12 2HQ, England. TEL 44-181-783-0755. FAX 44-181-783-0049. *1916*

KEY NOTE MARKET REPORT: CLOTHING RETAILING.
Key Note Ltd., Field House, 72 Oldfield Rd., Hampton, Middlesex TW12 2HQ, England. TEL 44-181-783-0755. FAX 44-181-783-0049. *1916*

KEY NOTE MARKET REPORT: COMMERCIAL RADIO.
Key Note Ltd., Field House, 72 Oldfield Rd., Hampton, Middlesex TW12 2HQ, England. TEL 44-181-783-0755. FAX 44-181-783-0049. *2025*

KEY NOTE MARKET REPORT: COMMERCIAL T V.
Key Note Ltd., Field House, 72 Oldfield Rd., Hampton, Middlesex TW12 2HQ, England. TEL 44-181-783-0755. FAX 44-181-783-0049. *2053*

KEY NOTE MARKET REPORT: COMMERCIAL VEHICLES.
Key Note Ltd., Field House, 72 Oldfield Rd., Hampton, Middlesex TW12 2HQ, England. TEL 44-181-783-0755. FAX 44-181-783-0049. *7104*

KEY NOTE MARKET REPORT: COMPUTER SERVICES.
Key Note Ltd., Field House, 72 Oldfield Rd., Hampton, Middlesex TW12 2HQ, England. TEL 44-181-783-0755. FAX 44-181-783-0049. *2127*

KEY NOTE MARKET REPORT: COMPUTER SOFTWARE.
Key Note Ltd., Field House, 72 Oldfield Rd., Hampton, Middlesex TW12 2HQ, England. TEL 44-181-783-0755. FAX 44-181-783-1940. *2214*

KEY NOTE MARKET REPORT: CONFECTIONERY.
Key Note Ltd., Field House, 72 Oldfield Rd., Hampton, Middlesex TW12 2HQ, England. TEL 44-181-783-0755. FAX 44-181-783-0049. *3137*

KEY NOTE MARKET REPORT: CONSUMER MAGAZINES.
Key Note Ltd., Field House, 72 Oldfield Rd., Hampton, Middlesex TW12 2HQ, England. TEL 44-181-783-0755. FAX 44-181-783-0049. *6275*

KEY NOTE MARKET REPORT: CONTRACEPTIVES.
Key Note Ltd., Field House, 72 Oldfield Rd., Hampton, Middlesex TW12 2HQ, England. TEL 44-181-783-0755. FAX 44-181-783-0049. *858*

KEY NOTE MARKET REPORT: CONTRACT CATERING.
Key Note Ltd., Field House, 72 Oldfield Rd., Hampton, Middlesex TW12 2HQ, England. TEL 44-171-783-0755. FAX 44-171-783-0049. *3731*

KEY NOTE MARKET REPORT: CONTRACT CLEANING.
Key Note Ltd., Field House, 72 Oldfield Rd., Hampton, Middlesex TW12 2HQ, England. TEL 44-181-783-0755. FAX 44-181-783-0049. *1910*

KEY NOTE MARKET REPORT: CONVENIENCE RETAILING.
Key Note Ltd., Field House, 72 Oldfield Rd., Hampton, Middlesex TW12 2HQ, England. TEL 44-181-783-0755. FAX 44-181-783-0049. *1536*

KEY NOTE MARKET REPORT: COSMETICS & FRAGRANCES.
Key Note Ltd., Field House, 72 Oldfield Rd., Hampton, Middlesex TW12 2HQ, England. TEL 44-181-783-0755. FAX 44-181-783-0049. *511*

KEY NOTE MARKET REPORT: COURIER & EXPRESS SERVICES.
Key Note Ltd., Field House, 72 Oldfield Rd., Hampton, Middlesex TW12 2HQ, England. TEL 44-181-783-0755. FAX 44-181-783-0049. *2019*

KEY NOTE MARKET REPORT: CREDIT & OTHER FINANCE CARDS.
Key Note Ltd., Field House, 72 Oldfield Rd., Hampton, Middlesex TW12 2HQ, England. TEL 44-181-783-0755. FAX 44-181-783-0049. *1151*

KEY NOTE MARKET REPORT: DEBT MANAGEMENT & FACTORING.
Key Note Ltd., Field House, 72 Oldfield Rd., Hampton, Middlesex TW12 2HQ, England. TEL 44-181-783-0755. FAX 44-181-783-0049. *1151*

KEY NOTE MARKET REPORT: DEFENCE EQUIPMENT.
Key Note Ltd., Field House, 72 Oldfield Rd., Hampton, Middlesex TW12 2HQ, England. TEL 44-181-783-0755. FAX 44-181-783-0049. *5274*

KEY NOTE MARKET REPORT: DIRECT MARKETING.
Key Note Ltd., Field House, 72 Oldfield Rd., Hampton, Middlesex TW12 2HQ, England. TEL 44-181-783-0755. FAX 44-181-783-0049. *1536*

KEY NOTE MARKET REPORT: DISPOSABLE PAPER PRODUCTS.
Key Note Ltd., Field House, 72 Oldfield Rd., Hampton, Middlesex TW12 2HQ, England. TEL 44-181-783-0755. FAX 44-181-783-0049. *5567*

KEY NOTE MARKET REPORT: DISTILLERS (WHISKY).
Key Note Ltd., Field House, 72 Oldfield Rd., Hampton, Middlesex TW12 2HQ, England. TEL 44-181-783-0755. FAX 44-181-783-0049. *523*

KEY NOTE MARKET REPORT: DOMESTIC HEATING.
Key Note Ltd., Field House, 72 Oldfield Rd., Hampton, Middlesex TW12 2HQ, England. TEL 44-181-783-0755. FAX 44-181-783-0049. *3481*

KEY NOTE MARKET REPORT: DRY BATTERIES.
Key Note Ltd., Field House, 72 Oldfield Rd., Hampton, Middlesex TW12 2HQ, England. TEL 44-181-783-0755. FAX 44-181-783-0049. *5839*

KEY NOTE MARKET REPORT: ELECTRICAL CONTRACTING.
Key Note Ltd., Field House, 72 Oldfield Rd., Hampton, Middlesex TW12 2HQ, England. TEL 44-181-783-0755. FAX 44-181-783-0049. *2838*

KEY NOTE MARKET REPORT: ELECTRONIC COMPONENT DISTRIBUTION.
Key Note Ltd., Field House, 72 Oldfield Rd., Hampton, Middlesex TW12 2HQ, England. TEL 44-181-783-0755. FAX 44-181-783-0049. *2645*

KEY NOTE MARKET REPORT: ELECTRONIC COMPONENT MANUFACTURERS.
Key Note Ltd., Field House, 72 Oldfield Rd., Hampton, Middlesex TW12 2HQ, England. TEL 44-181-783-0755. FAX 44-181-783-0049. *2645*

KEY NOTE MARKET REPORT: ELECTRONIC GAMES.
Key Note Ltd., Field House, 72 Oldfield Rd., Hampton, Middlesex TW12 2HQ, England. TEL 44-181-783-0755. FAX 44-181-783-0049. *2118*

KEY NOTE MARKET REPORT: EMPLOYMENT AGENCIES.
Key Note Ltd., Field House, 72 Oldfield Rd., Hampton, Middlesex TW12 2HQ, England. TEL 44-181-783-0755. FAX 44-181-783-0049. *5512*

KEY NOTE MARKET REPORT: EQUIPMENT LEASING.
Key Note Ltd., Field House, 72 Oldfield Rd., Hampton, Middlesex TW12 2HQ, England. TEL 44-181-783-0755. FAX 44-181-783-0049. *1644*

KEY NOTE MARKET REPORT: ESTATE AGENTS.
Key Note Ltd., Field House, 72 Oldfield Rd., Hampton, Middlesex TW12 2HQ, England. TEL 44-181-783-0755. FAX 44-181-783-0049. *4097*

KEY NOTE MARKET REPORT: ETHNIC FOODS.
Key Note Ltd., Field House, 72 Oldfield Rd., Hampton, Middlesex TW12 2HQ, England. TEL 44-181-783-0755. FAX 44-181-783-0049. *3117*

KEY NOTE MARKET REPORT: EXHIBITIONS AND CONFERENCE ORGANISERS.
Key Note Ltd., Field House, 72 Oldfield Rd., Hampton, Middlesex TW12 2HQ, England. TEL 44-181-783-0755. FAX 44-181-783-0049. *5170*

SERIALS AVAILABLE ONLINE

KEY NOTE MARKET REPORT: FAST FOOD AND HOME DELIVERY OUTLETS.
Key Note Ltd., Field House, 72 Oldfield Rd., Hampton, Middlesex TW12 2HQ, England. TEL 44-181-783-0755. FAX 44-181-783-0049. *3117*

KEY NOTE MARKET REPORT: FIBRES.
Key Note Ltd., Field House, 72 Oldfield Rd., Hampton, Middlesex TW12 2HQ, England. TEL 44-181-783-0755. FAX 44-181-783-1940. *6990*

KEY NOTE MARKET REPORT: FINANCE HOUSES.
Key Note Ltd., Field House, 72 Oldfield Rd., Hampton, Middlesex TW12 2HQ, England. TEL 44-181-783-0755. FAX 44-181-783-0049. *1151*

KEY NOTE MARKET REPORT: FIRE PROTECTION EQUIPMENT.
Key Note Ltd., Field House, 72 Oldfield Rd., Hampton, Middlesex TW12 2HQ, England. TEL 44-181-783-0755. FAX 44-181-783-0049. *3056*

KEY NOTE MARKET REPORT: FOOD FLAVOURINGS & INGREDIENTS.
Key Note Ltd., Field House, 72 Oldfield Rd., Hampton, Middlesex TW12 2HQ, England. TEL 44-181-783-0755. FAX 44-181-783-0049. *3117*

KEY NOTE MARKET REPORT: FOOTWEAR.
Key Note Ltd., Field House, 72 Oldfield Rd., Hampton, Middlesex TW12 2HQ, England. TEL 44-181-783-0755. FAX 44-181-783-1940. *6596*

KEY NOTE MARKET REPORT: FREIGHT FORWARDING.
Key Note Ltd., Field House, 72 Oldfield Rd., Hampton, Middlesex TW12 2HQ, England. TEL 44-181-783-0755. FAX 44-181-783-0049. *7032*

KEY NOTE MARKET REPORT: FROZEN FOODS.
Key Note Ltd., Field House, 72 Oldfield Rd., Hampton, Middlesex TW12 2HQ, England. TEL 44-181-783-0755. FAX 44-181-783-0049. *3117*

KEY NOTE MARKET REPORT: FRUIT & VEGETABLES.
Key Note Ltd., Field House, 72 Oldfield Rd., Hampton, Middlesex TW12 2HQ, England. TEL 44-181-783-0755. FAX 44-181-783-0049. *3143*

KEY NOTE MARKET REPORT: FRUIT JUICES & HEALTH DRINKS.
Key Note Ltd., Field House, 72 Oldfield Rd., Hampton, Middlesex TW12 2HQ, England. TEL 44-181-783-0755. FAX 44-181-783-0049. *523*

KEY NOTE MARKET REPORT: GARDEN EQUIPMENT.
Key Note Ltd., Field House, 72 Oldfield Rd., Hampton, Middlesex TW12 2HQ, England. TEL 44-181-783-0755. FAX 44-181-783-0049. *3197*

KEY NOTE MARKET REPORT: GIFTWARE.
Key Note Ltd., Field House, 72 Oldfield Rd., Hampton, Middlesex TW12 2HQ, England. TEL 44-181-783-0755. FAX 44-181-783-0049. *3450*

KEY NOTE MARKET REPORT: GLASSWARE.
Key Note Ltd., Field House, 72 Oldfield Rd., Hampton, Middlesex TW12 2HQ, England. TEL 44-181-783-0755. FAX 44-181-783-1940. *1732*

KEY NOTE MARKET REPORT: GREETINGS CARDS.
Key Note Ltd., Field House, 72 Oldfield Rd., Hampton, Middlesex TW12 2HQ, England. TEL 44-181-783-0755. FAX 44-181-783-0049. *3450*

KEY NOTE MARKET REPORT: HAND LUGGAGE & LEATHER GOODS.
Key Note Ltd., Field House, 72 Oldfield Rd., Hampton, Middlesex TW12 2HQ, England. TEL 44-181-783-0755. FAX 44-181-783-0049. *4145*

KEY NOTE MARKET REPORT: HEALTH CLUBS AND LEISURE CENTRES.
Key Note Ltd., Field House, 72 Oldfield Rd., Hampton, Middlesex TW12 2HQ, England. TEL 44-181-783-0755. FAX 44-181-783-0049. *6768*

KEY NOTE MARKET REPORT: HEALTH FOODS.
Key Note Ltd., Field House, 72 Oldfield Rd., Hampton, Middlesex TW12 2HQ, England. TEL 44-181-783-0755. FAX 44-181-783-0049. *3117*

KEY NOTE MARKET REPORT: HEATING, VENTILATING & AIR CONDITIONING.
Key Note Ltd., Field House, 72 Oldfield Rd., Hampton, Middlesex TW12 2HQ, England. TEL 44-181-783-0755. FAX 44-181-783-0049. *3481*

KEY NOTE MARKET REPORT: HOME FURNISHINGS.
Key Note Ltd., Field House, 72 Oldfield Rd., Hampton, Middlesex TW12 2HQ, England. TEL 44-181-783-0755. FAX 44-181-783-0049. *3858*

KEY NOTE MARKET REPORT: HOME LEISURE.
Key Note Ltd., Field House, 72 Oldfield Rd., Hampton, Middlesex TW12 2HQ, England. TEL 44-181-783-0755. FAX 44-181-783-1940. *4150*

KEY NOTE MARKET REPORT: HOME SHOPPING.
Key Note Ltd., Field House, 72 Oldfield Rd., Hampton, Middlesex TW12 2HQ, England. TEL 44-181-783-0755. FAX 44-181-783-0049. *1536*

KEY NOTE MARKET REPORT: HORTICULTURAL RETAILING.
Key Note Ltd., Field House, 72 Oldfield Rd., Hampton, Middlesex TW12 2HQ, England. TEL 44-181-783-0755. FAX 44-181-783-0049. *3197*

KEY NOTE MARKET REPORT: HOT DRINKS.
Key Note Ltd., Field House, 72 Oldfield Rd., Hampton, Middlesex TW12 2HQ, England. TEL 44-181-783-0755. FAX 44-181-783-1940. *523*

KEY NOTE MARKET REPORT: HOTELS.
Key Note Ltd., Field House, 72 Oldfield Rd., Hampton, Middlesex TW12 2HQ, England. TEL 44-181-783-0755. FAX 44-181-783-0049. *3731*

KEY NOTE MARKET REPORT: HOUSEBUILDING.
Key Note Ltd., Field House, 72 Oldfield Rd., Hampton, Middlesex TW12 2HQ, England. TEL 44-181-783-0755. FAX 44-181-783-0049. *900*

KEY NOTE MARKET REPORT: HOUSEHOLD APPLIANCES (WHITE GOODS).
Key Note Ltd., Field House, 72 Oldfield Rd., Hampton, Middlesex TW12 2HQ, England. TEL 44-181-783-0755. FAX 44-181-783-0049. *3858*

KEY NOTE MARKET REPORT: HOUSEHOLD FURNITURE.
Key Note Ltd., Field House, 72 Oldfield Rd., Hampton, Middlesex TW12 2HQ, England. TEL 44-181-783-0755. FAX 44-181-783-0049. *3858*

KEY NOTE MARKET REPORT: ICE-CREAMS & FROZEN DESSERTS.
Key Note Ltd., Field House, 72 Oldfield Rd., Hampton, Middlesex TW12 2HQ, England. TEL 44-181-783-0755. FAX 44-181-783-0049. *3117*

KEY NOTE MARKET REPORT: INDUSTRIAL FASTENERS.
Key Note Ltd., Field House, 72 Oldfield Rd., Hampton, Middlesex TW12 2HQ, England. TEL 44-181-783-0755. FAX 44-181-783-1940. *2864*

KEY NOTE MARKET REPORT: INDUSTRIAL PUMPS.
Key Note Ltd., Field House, 72 Oldfield Rd., Hampton, Middlesex TW12 2HQ, England. TEL 44-181-783-0755. FAX 44-181-783-0049. *2873*

KEY NOTE MARKET REPORT: INDUSTRIAL VALVES.
Key Note Ltd., Field House, 72 Oldfield Rd., Hampton, Middlesex TW12 2HQ, England. TEL 44-181-783-0755. FAX 44-181-783-0049. *2878*

KEY NOTE MARKET REPORT: INSULATION PRODUCTS.
Key Note Ltd., Field House, 72 Oldfield Rd., Hampton, Middlesex TW12 2HQ, England. TEL 44-181-783-0755. FAX 44-181-783-0049. *901*

KEY NOTE MARKET REPORT: JEWELLERY, WATCHES & FASHION ACCESSORIES.
Key Note Ltd., Field House, 72 Oldfield Rd., Hampton, Middlesex TW12 2HQ, England. TEL 44-181-783-0755. FAX 44-181-783-0049. *3865*

KEY NOTE MARKET REPORT: KITCHENWARE.
Key Note Ltd., Field House, 72 Oldfield Rd., Hampton, Middlesex TW12 2HQ, England. TEL 44-181-783-0755. FAX 44-181-783-0049. *3858*

KEY NOTE MARKET REPORT: LIGHTING EQUIPMENT.
Key Note Ltd., Field House, 72 Oldfield Rd., Hampton, Middlesex TW12 2HQ, England. TEL 44-181-783-0755. FAX 44-181-783-0049. *3858*

KEY NOTE MARKET REPORT: LINGERIE.
Key Note Ltd., Field House, 72 Oldfield Rd., Hampton, Middlesex TW12 2HQ, England. TEL 44-181-783-0755. FAX 44-181-783-0049. *1916*

KEY NOTE MARKET REPORT: LOW ALCOHOL DRINKS.
Key Note Ltd., Field House, 72 Oldfield Rd., Hampton, Middlesex TW12 2HQ, England. TEL 44-181-783-0755. FAX 44-181-783-0049. *523*

KEY NOTE MARKET REPORT: MACHINE TOOLS.
Key Note Ltd., Field House, 72 Oldfield Rd., Hampton, Middlesex TW12 2HQ, England. TEL 44-181-783-0755. FAX 44-181-783-0049. *2878*

KEY NOTE MARKET REPORT: MANAGEMENT CONSULTANTS.
Key Note Ltd., Field House, 72 Oldfield Rd., Hampton, Middlesex TW12 2HQ, England. TEL 44-181-783-0755. FAX 44-181-783-0049. *1490*

KEY NOTE MARKET REPORT: MEAT & MEAT PRODUCTS.
Key Note Ltd., Field House, 72 Oldfield Rd., Hampton, Middlesex TW12 2HQ, England. TEL 44-181-783-0755. FAX 44-181-783-0049. *3117*

KEY NOTE MARKET REPORT: MECHANICAL HANDLING.
Key Note Ltd., Field House, 72 Oldfield Rd., Hampton, Middlesex TW12 2HQ, England. TEL 44-181-783-0755. FAX 44-181-783-0049. *2891*

KEY NOTE MARKET REPORT: MEDICAL EQUIPMENT.
Key Note Ltd., Field House, 72 Oldfield Rd., Hampton, Middlesex TW12 2HQ, England. TEL 44-181-783-0755. FAX 44-181-783-0049. *4700*

KEY NOTE MARKET REPORT: MILK & DAIRY PRODUCTS.
Key Note Ltd., Field House, 72 Oldfield Rd., Hampton, Middlesex TW12 2HQ, England. TEL 44-181-783-0755. FAX 44-181-783-0049. *256*

KEY NOTE MARKET REPORT: MORTGAGE FINANCE.
Key Note Ltd., Field House, 72 Oldfield Rd., Hampton, Middlesex TW12 2HQ, England. TEL 44-181-783-0755. FAX 44-181-783-0049. *1151*

KEY NOTE MARKET REPORT: NEWSPAPERS.
Key Note Ltd., Field House, 72 Oldfield Rd., Hampton, Middlesex TW12 2HQ, England. TEL 44-181-783-0755. FAX 44-181-783-0049. *3876*

KEY NOTE MARKET REPORT: O T C PHARMACEUTICALS.
Key Note Ltd., Field House, 72 Oldfield Rd., Hampton, Middlesex TW12 2HQ, England. TEL 44-181-783-1940. FAX 44-181-783-0049. *5675*

KEY NOTE MARKET REPORT: OFF-LICENSE TRADE.
Key Note Ltd., Field House, 72 Oldfield Rd., Hampton, Middlesex TW12 2HQ, England. TEL 44-181-783-0755. FAX 44-181-783-1940. *1589*

KEY NOTE MARKET REPORT: OFFICE FURNITURE.
Key Note Ltd., Field House, 72 Oldfield Rd., Hampton, Middlesex TW12 2HQ, England. TEL 44-181-783-0755. FAX 44-181-783-0049. *1557*

KEY NOTE MARKET REPORT: OPHTHALMIC GOODS & SERVICES.
Key Note Ltd., Field House, 72 Oldfield Rd., Hampton, Middlesex TW12 2HQ, England. TEL 44-181-783-0755. FAX 44-181-783-0049. *4996*

KEY NOTE MARKET REPORT: OWN BRANDS.
Key Note Ltd., Field House, 72 Oldfield Rd., Hampton, Middlesex TW12 2HQ, England. TEL 44-181-783-0755. FAX 44-181-783-0049. *1536*

KEY NOTE MARKET REPORT: PACKAGING (GLASS).
Key Note Ltd., Field House, 72 Oldfield Rd., Hampton, Middlesex TW12 2HQ, England. TEL 44-181-783-0755. FAX 44-181-783-0049. *5545*

KEY NOTE MARKET REPORT: PACKAGING (METALS & AEROSOLS).
Key Note Ltd., Field House, 72 Oldfield Rd., Hampton, Middlesex TW12 2HQ, England. TEL 44-181-783-0755. FAX 44-181-783-0049. *5545*

KEY NOTE MARKET REPORT: PACKAGING (PAPER & BOARD).
Key Note Ltd., Field House, 72 Oldfield Rd., Hampton, Middlesex TW12 2HQ, England. TEL 44-181-783-0755. FAX 44-181-783-0049. *5545*

KEY NOTE MARKET REPORT: PACKAGING (PLASTICS).
Key Note Ltd., Field House, 72 Oldfield Rd., Hampton, Middlesex TW12 2HQ, England. TEL 44-181-783-0755. FAX 44-181-783-0049. *5545*

KEY NOTE MARKET REPORT: PAINTS & VARNISHES.
Key Note Ltd., Field House, 72 Oldfield Rd., Hampton, Middlesex TW12 2HQ, England. TEL 44-181-783-0755. FAX 44-181-783-0049. *5553*

KEY NOTE MARKET REPORT: PASSENGER SHIPPING.
Key Note Ltd., Field House, 72 Oldfield Rd., Hampton, Middlesex TW12 2HQ, England. TEL 44-181-783-0755. FAX 44-181-783-0049. *7155*

KEY NOTE MARKET REPORT: PERISHABLE FAST-MOVING CONSUMER GOODS.
Key Note Ltd., Field House, 72 Oldfield Rd., Hampton, Middlesex TW12 2HQ, England. TEL 44-181-783-0755. FAX 44-181-783-0049. *3117*

KEY NOTE MARKET REPORT: PET FOODS.
Key Note Ltd., Field House, 72 Oldfield Rd., Hampton, Middlesex TW12 2HQ, England. TEL 44-181-783-0755. FAX 44-181-783-0049. *5639*

KEY NOTE MARKET REPORT: PHOTOCOPIERS & FAX MACHINES.
Key Note Ltd., Field House, 72 Oldfield Rd., Hampton, Middlesex TW12 2HQ, England. TEL 44-181-783-0755. FAX 44-181-783-0049. *1557*

KEY NOTE MARKET REPORT: PHOTOGRAPHIC SERVICES.
Key Note Ltd., Field House, 72 Oldfield Rd., Hampton, Middlesex TW12 2HQ, England. TEL 44-181-783-0755. FAX 44-181-783-0049. *5768*

KEY NOTE MARKET REPORT: PLANT HIRE.
Key Note Ltd., Field House, 72 Oldfield Rd., Hampton, Middlesex TW12 2HQ, England. TEL 44-181-783-0755. FAX 44-181-783-0049. *1268*

KEY NOTE MARKET REPORT: PLASTICS PROCESSING.
Key Note Ltd., Field House, 72 Oldfield Rd., Hampton, Middlesex TW12 2HQ, England. TEL 44-181-783-0755. FAX 44-181-783-0049. *5879*

KEY NOTE MARKET REPORT: PREMIUM LAGERS, BEERS AND CIDERS.
Key Note Ltd., Field House, 72 Oldfield Rd., Hampton, Middlesex TW12 2HQ, England. TEL 44-181-783-0755. FAX 44-181-783-0049. *523*

KEY NOTE MARKET REPORT: PRESCRIBED PHARMACEUTICALS.
Key Note Ltd., Field House, 72 Oldfield Rd., Hampton, Middlesex TW12 2HQ, England. TEL 44-181-783-0755. FAX 44-181-783-1940. *5675*

KEY NOTE MARKET REPORT: PRINTED CIRCUITS.
Key Note Ltd., Field House, 72 Oldfield Rd., Hampton, Middlesex TW12 2HQ, England. TEL 44-181-783-0755. FAX 44-181-783-0049. *2112*

KEY NOTE MARKET REPORT: PRINTING.
Key Note Ltd., Field House, 72 Oldfield Rd., Hampton, Middlesex TW12 2HQ, England. TEL 44-181-783-0755. FAX 44-181-783-0049. *6081*

KEY NOTE MARKET REPORT: PRISON SERVICES.
Key Note Ltd., Field House, 72 Oldfield Rd., Hampton, Middlesex TW12 2HQ, England. TEL 44-181-783-0755. FAX 44-181-783-0049. *2287*

KEY NOTE MARKET REPORT: PRIVATE HEALTHCARE.
Key Note Ltd., Field House, 72 Oldfield Rd., Hampton, Middlesex TW12 2HQ, England. TEL 44-181-783-0755. FAX 44-181-783-0049. *4700*

KEY NOTE MARKET REPORT: PROCESS PLANT.
Key Note Ltd., Field House, 72 Oldfield Rd., Hampton, Middlesex TW12 2HQ, England. TEL 44-181-783-0755. FAX 44-181-783-0049. *1589*

KEY NOTE MARKET REPORT: PUBLIC HOUSES.
Key Note Ltd., Field House, 72 Oldfield Rd., Hampton, Middlesex TW12 2HQ, England. TEL 44-181-783-0755. FAX 44-181-783-0049. *3731*

KEY NOTE MARKET REPORT: READY MEALS.
Key Note Ltd., Field House, 72 Oldfield Rd., Hampton, Middlesex TW12 2HQ, England. TEL 44-181-783-0755. FAX 44-181-783-0049. *3117*

KEY NOTE MARKET REPORT: RESTAURANTS.
Key Note Ltd., Field House, 72 Oldfield Rd., Hampton, Middlesex TW12 2HQ, England. TEL 44-181-783-0755. FAX 44-181-783-0049. *3731*

KEY NOTE MARKET REPORT: RETAIL BRANCH BANKING.
Key Note Ltd., Field House, 72 Oldfield Rd., Hampton, Middlesex TW12 2HQ, England. TEL 44-181-783-0755. FAX 44-181-783-0049. *1151*

KEY NOTE MARKET REPORT: RETAIL CHEMISTS & DRUG STORES.
Key Note Ltd., Field House, 72 Oldfield Rd., Hampton, Middlesex TW12 2HQ, England. TEL 44-181-783-0755. FAX 44-181-783-0049. *5675*

KEY NOTE MARKET REPORT: ROAD HAULAGE.
Key Note Ltd., Field House, 72 Oldfield Rd., Hampton, Middlesex TW12 2HQ, England. TEL 44-181-783-0755. FAX 44-181-783-0049. *7175*

KEY NOTE MARKET REPORT: RUBBER MANUFACTURING & PROCESSING.
Key Note Ltd., Field House, 72 Oldfield Rd., Hampton, Middlesex TW12 2HQ, England. TEL 44-181-783-0755. FAX 44-181-783-0049. *6502*

KEY NOTE MARKET REPORT: SAUCES AND SPREADS.
Key Note Ltd., Field House, 72 Oldfield Rd., Hampton, Middlesex TW12 2HQ, England. TEL 44-181-783-0755. FAX 44-181-783-0049. *3117*

KEY NOTE MARKET REPORT: SCIENTIFIC INSTRUMENTS.
Key Note Ltd., Field House, 72 Oldfield Rd., Hampton, Middlesex TW12 2HQ, England. TEL 44-181-783-0755. FAX 44-181-783-1940. *3803*

KEY NOTE MARKET REPORT: SCRAP METAL PROCESSING.
Key Note Ltd., Field House, 72 Oldfield Rd., Hampton, Middlesex TW12 2HQ, England. TEL 44-181-783-0755. FAX 44-181-783-0049. *5198*

KEY NOTE MARKET REPORT: SELF-ASSEMBLY FURNITURE.
Key Note Ltd., Field House, 72 Oldfield Rd., Hampton, Middlesex TW12 2HQ, England. TEL 44-181-783-0755. FAX 44-181-783-1940. *3858*

KEY NOTE MARKET REPORT: SHOP FITTING.
Key Note Ltd., Field House, 72 Oldfield Rd., Hampton, Middlesex TW12 2HQ, England. TEL 44-181-783-0755. FAX 44-181-783-0049. *1536*

KEY NOTE MARKET REPORT: SHOWERS & SHOWER ACCESSORIES.
Key Note Ltd., Field House, 72 Oldfield Rd., Hampton, Middlesex TW12 2HQ, England. TEL 44-181-783-0755. FAX 44-181-783-0049. *3858*

KEY NOTE MARKET REPORT: SLIMMING MARKET.
Key Note Ltd., Field House, 72 Oldfield Rd., Hampton, Middlesex TW12 2HQ, England. TEL 44-181-783-0755. FAX 44-181-783-0049. *1589*

KEY NOTE MARKET REPORT: SMALL DOMESTIC ELECTRICAL APPLIANCES.
Key Note Ltd., Field House, 72 Oldfield Rd., Hampton, Middlesex TW12 2HQ, England. TEL 44-181-783-0755. FAX 44-181-783-0049. *2645*

KEY NOTE MARKET REPORT: SNACK FOODS.
Key Note Ltd., Field House, 72 Oldfield Rd., Hampton, Middlesex TW12 2HQ, England. TEL 44-181-783-0755. FAX 44-181-783-0049. *3117*

KEY NOTE MARKET REPORT: SOAPS & DETERGENTS.
Key Note Ltd., Field House, 72 Oldfield Rd., Hampton, Middlesex TW12 2HQ, England. TEL 44-181-783-0755. FAX 44-181-783-0049. *1910*

KEY NOTE MARKET REPORT: SOFT DRINKS (CARBONATES & CONCENTRATES).
Key Note Ltd., Field House, 72 Oldfield Rd., Hampton, Middlesex TW12 2HQ, England. TEL 44-181-783-0755. FAX 44-181-783-0049. *523*

KEY NOTE MARKET REPORT: SPORTS CLOTHING AND FOOTWEAR.
Key Note Ltd., Field House, 72 Oldfield Rd., Hampton, Middlesex TW12 2HQ, England. TEL 44-181-783-0755. FAX 44-181-783-0049. *1916*

KEY NOTE MARKET REPORT: SPORTS EQUIPMENT.
Key Note Ltd., Field House, 72 Oldfield Rd., Hampton, Middlesex TW12 2HQ, England. TEL 44-181-783-0755. FAX 44-181-783-0049. *6768*

KEY NOTE MARKET REPORT: STATIONERY (PERSONAL & OFFICE).
Key Note Ltd., Field House, 72 Oldfield Rd., Hampton, Middlesex TW12 2HQ, England. TEL 44-181-783-0755. FAX 44-181-783-0049. *1557*

KEY NOTE MARKET REPORT: STEEL STOCKHOLDING.
Key Note Ltd., Field House, 72 Oldfield Rd., Hampton, Middlesex TW12 2HQ, England. TEL 44-181-783-0755. FAX 44-181-783-1940. *1393*

KEY NOTE MARKET REPORT: SUPERMARKETS & SUPERSTORES.
Key Note Ltd., Field House, 72 Oldfield Rd., Hampton, Middlesex TW12 2HQ, England. TEL 44-181-783-0755. FAX 44-181-783-0049. *3117*

KEY NOTE MARKET REPORT: T V & VIDEO RENTAL.
Key Note Ltd., Field House, 72 Oldfield Rd., Hampton, Middlesex TW12 2HQ, England. TEL 44-181-783-0755. FAX 44-181-783-0049. *2645*

KEY NOTE MARKET REPORT: TELECOMMUNICATIONS.
Key Note Ltd., Field House, 72 Oldfield Rd., Hampton, Middlesex TW12 2HQ, England. TEL 44-181-783-0755. FAX 44-181-783-1940. *1996*

KEY NOTE MARKET REPORT: TIMBER & JOINERY.
Key Note Ltd., Field House, 72 Oldfield Rd., Hampton, Middlesex TW12 2HQ, England. TEL 44-181-783-0755. FAX 44-181-783-0049. *3172*

KEY NOTE MARKET REPORT: TOILETRIES.
Key Note Ltd., Field House, 72 Oldfield Rd., Hampton, Middlesex TW12 2HQ, England. TEL 44-181-783-0755. FAX 44-181-783-0049. *507*

KEY NOTE MARKET REPORT: TOURIST ATTRACTIONS.
Key Note Ltd., Field House, 72 Oldfield Rd., Hampton, Middlesex TW12 2HQ, England. TEL 44-181-783-0755. FAX 44-181-783-0049. *7215*

KEY NOTE MARKET REPORT: TOYS & GAMES.
Key Note Ltd., Field House, 72 Oldfield Rd., Hampton, Middlesex TW12 2HQ, England. TEL 44-181-783-0755. FAX 44-181-783-0094. *3450*

KEY NOTE MARKET REPORT: TRAINING.
Key Note Ltd., Field House, 72 Oldfield Rd., Hampton, Middlesex TW12 2HQ, England. TEL 44-181-783-0755. FAX 44-181-783-0049. *2511*

KEY NOTE MARKET REPORT: TRAVEL AGENTS & OVERSEAS TOUR OPERATORS.
Key Note Ltd., Field House, 72 Oldfield Rd., Hampton, Middlesex TW12 2HQ, England. TEL 44-181-783-0755. FAX 44-181-783-0049. *7215*

KEY NOTE MARKET REPORT: VEHICLE LEASING & HIRE.
Key Note Ltd., Field House, 72 Oldfield Rd., Hampton, Middlesex TW12 2HQ, England. TEL 44-181-783-0755. FAX 44-181-783-0049. *7104*

KEY NOTE MARKET REPORT: VEHICLE SECURITY.
Key Note Ltd., Field House, 72 Oldfield Rd., Hampton, Middlesex TW12 2HQ, England. TEL 44-181-783-0755. FAX 44-181-783-0049. *7104*

KEY NOTE MARKET REPORT: VIDEO RETAIL & HIRE.
Key Note Ltd., Field House, 72 Oldfield Rd., Hampton, Middlesex TW12 2HQ, England. TEL 44-181-783-0755. FAX 44-181-783-0049. *2067*

KEY NOTE MARKET REPORT: WALLCOVERINGS.
Key Note Ltd., Field House, 72 Oldfield Rd., Hampton, Middlesex TW12 2HQ, England. TEL 44-181-783-0755. FAX 44-181-783-0049. *3847*

KEY NOTE MARKET REPORT: WASTE MANAGEMENT.
Key Note Ltd., Field House, 72 Oldfield Rd., Hampton, Middlesex TW12 2HQ, England. TEL 44-181-783-0755. FAX 44-181-783-0049. *2987*

KEY NOTE MARKET REPORT: WATER UTILITIES.
Key Note Ltd., Field House, 72 Oldfield Rd., Hampton, Middlesex TW12 2HQ, England. TEL 44-181-783-0755. FAX 44-181-783-0049. *7296*

KEY NOTE MARKET REPORT: WINDOWS & DOORS.
Key Note Ltd., Field House, 72 Oldfield Rd., Hampton, Middlesex TW12 2HQ, England. TEL 44-181-783-0755. FAX 44-181-783-0049. *3858*

KEY NOTE MARKET REPORT: WINE.
Key Note Ltd., Field House, 72 Oldfield Rd., Hampton, Middlesex TW12 2HQ, England. TEL 44-181-783-0755. FAX 44-181-783-0049. *523*

KEY NOTE MARKET REPORT: WOMEN'S MAGAZINES.
Key Note Ltd., Field House, 72 Oldfield Rd., Hampton, Middlesex TW12 2HQ, England. TEL 44-181-783-0755. FAX 44-181-783-0049. *7324*

KEY NOTE MARKET REVIEW: CORPORATE SERVICES IN THE U K.
Key Note Ltd., Field House, 72 Oldfield Rd., Hampton, Middlesex TW12 2HQ, England. TEL 44-181-783-0755. FAX 44-181-783-0049. *1691*

KEY NOTE MARKET REVIEW: D I Y & HOME IMPROVEMENTS.
Key Note Ltd., Field House, 72 Oldfield Rd., Hampton, Middlesex TW12 2HQ, England. TEL 44-181-783-0755. FAX 44-181-783-0049. *3847*

KEY NOTE MARKET REVIEW: ENERGY INDUSTRY IN THE U K.
Key Note Ltd., Field House, 72 Oldfield Rd., Hampton, Middlesex TW12 2HQ, England. TEL 44-181-783-0755. FAX 44-181-783-0049. *2673*

KEY NOTE MARKET REVIEW: GREY MARKET IN THE U K.
Key Note Ltd., Field House, 72 Oldfield Rd., Hampton, Middlesex TW12 2HQ, England. TEL 44-181-783-0755. FAX 44-181-783-0049. *1536*

KEY NOTE MARKET REVIEW: MULTIMEDIA IN U K.
Key Note Ltd., Field House, 72 Oldfield Rd., Hampton, Middlesex TW12 2HQ, England. TEL 44-181-783-0755. FAX 44-181-783-0049. *2016*

KEY NOTE MARKET REVIEW: PASSENGER TRAVEL IN U K.
Key Note Ltd., Field House, 72 Oldfield Rd., Hampton, Middlesex TW12 2HQ, England. TEL 44-181-783-0755. FAX 44-181-783-0049. *7215*

KEY NOTE MARKET REVIEW: PERSONAL FINANCE IN THE U K.
Key Note Ltd., Field House, 72 Oldfield Rd., Hampton, Middlesex TW12 2HQ, England. TEL 44-181-783-0755. FAX 44-181-783-0049. *1151*

KEY NOTE MARKET REVIEW: RETAILING IN THE U K.
Key Note Ltd., Field House, 72 Oldfield Rd., Hampton, Middlesex TW12 2HQ, England. TEL 44-181-783-0755. FAX 44-181-783-0049. *1536*

KEY NOTE MARKET REVIEW: U K CATERING MARKET.
Key Note Ltd., Field House, 72 Oldfield Rd., Hampton, Middlesex TW12 2HQ, England. TEL 44-181-783-0755. FAX 44-181-783-0049. *3731*

KEY NOTE MARKET REVIEW: U K CHEMICAL INDUSTRY.
Key Note Ltd., Field House, 72 Oldfield Rd., Hampton, Middlesex TW12 2HQ, England. TEL 44-181-783-0755. FAX 44-181-783-0049. *1757*

KEY NOTE MARKET REVIEW: U K CLOTHING & FOOTWEAR.
Key Note Ltd., Field House, 72 Oldfield Rd., Hampton, Middlesex TW12 2HQ, England. TEL 44-181-783-0755. FAX 44-181-783-0049. *1916*

KEY NOTE MARKET REVIEW: U K COMPUTER MARKET.
Key Note Ltd., Field House, 72 Oldfield Rd., Hampton, Middlesex TW12 2HQ, England. TEL 44-181-783-0755. FAX 44-181-783-0049. *2127*

KEY NOTE MARKET REVIEW: U K CONSTRUCTION INDUSTRY.
Key Note Ltd., Field House, 72 Oldfield Rd., Hampton, Middlesex TW12 2HQ, England. TEL 44-181-783-0755. FAX 44-181-783-0049. *901*

KEY NOTE MARKET REVIEW: U K DEFENCE INDUSTRY.
Key Note Ltd., Field House, 72 Oldfield Rd., Hampton, Middlesex TW12 2HQ, England. TEL 44-181-783-0755. FAX 44-181-783-0049. *5274*

KEY NOTE MARKET REVIEW: U K DISTRIBUTION.
Key Note Ltd., Field House, 72 Oldfield Rd., Hampton, Middlesex TW12 2HQ, England. TEL 44-181-783-0755. FAX 44-181-783-0049. *1589*

KEY NOTE MARKET REVIEW: U K DRINKS MARKET.
Key Note Ltd., Field House, 72 Oldfield Rd., Hampton, Middlesex TW12 2HQ, England. TEL 44-181-783-0755. FAX 44-181-783-0049. *523*

KEY NOTE MARKET REVIEW: U K EDUCATION INDUSTRY.
Key Note Ltd., Field House, 72 Oldfield Rd., Hampton, Middlesex TW12 2HQ, England. TEL 44-181-783-0755. FAX 44-181-783-0049. *2574*

KEY NOTE MARKET REVIEW: U K FOOD MARKET.
Key Note Ltd., Field House, 72 Oldfield Rd., Hampton, Middlesex TW12 2HQ, England. TEL 44-181-783-0755. FAX 44-181-783-0049. *3117*

KEY NOTE MARKET REVIEW: U K HEALTHCARE.
Key Note Ltd., Field House, 72 Oldfield Rd., Hampton, Middlesex TW12 2HQ, England. TEL 44-181-783-0755. FAX 44-181-783-0049. *4700*

KEY NOTE MARKET REVIEW: U K HOUSEHOLD MARKET - FURNITURE, FITTINGS & DECOR.
Key Note Ltd., Field House, 72 Oldfield Rd., Hampton, Middlesex TW12 2HQ, England. TEL 44-181-783-0755. FAX 44-181-783-1940. *3858*

KEY NOTE MARKET REVIEW: U K HOUSEHOLD MARKET - HOUSEHOLD APPLIANCES AND HOUSEWARES.
Key Note Ltd., Field House, 72 Oldfield Rd., Hampton, Middlesex TW12 2HQ, England. TEL 44-181-783-0755. FAX 44-181-783-1940. *3858*

KEY NOTE MARKET REVIEW: U K INSURANCE MARKET.
Key Note Ltd., Field House, 72 Oldfield Rd., Hampton, Middlesex TW12 2HQ, England. TEL 44-181-783-0755. FAX 44-181-783-0049. *3823*

KEY NOTE MARKET REVIEW: U K LEISURE AND RECREATION.
Key Note Ltd., Field House, 72 Oldfield Rd., Hampton, Middlesex TW12 2HQ, England. TEL 44-181-783-0755. FAX 44-181-783-0049. *4150*

KEY NOTE MARKET REVIEW: U K MOTOR INDUSTRY.
Key Note Ltd., Field House, 72 Oldfield Rd., Hampton, Middlesex TW12 2HQ, England. TEL 44-181-783-0755. FAX 44-181-783-0049. *7104*

KEY NOTE MARKET REVIEW: U K OFFICE EQUIPMENT.
Key Note Ltd., Field House, 72 Oldfield Rd., Hampton, Middlesex TW12 2HQ, England. TEL 44-181-783-0755. FAX 44-181-783-0049. *1557*

KEY NOTE MARKET REVIEW: U K PACKAGING INDUSTRY.
Key Note Ltd., Field House, 72 Oldfield Rd., Hampton, Middlesex TW12 2HQ, England. TEL 44-181-783-0755. FAX 44-181-783-0049. *5545*

KEY NOTE MARKET REVIEW: U K PET MARKET.
Key Note Ltd., Field House, 72 Oldfield Rd., Hampton, Middlesex TW12 2HQ, England. TEL 44-181-783-0755. FAX 44-181-783-0049. *1536*

KEY NOTE MARKET REVIEW: U K PHARMACEUTICAL INDUSTRY.
Key Note Ltd., Field House, 72 Oldfield Rd., Hampton, Middlesex TW12 2HQ, England. TEL 44-181-783-0755. FAX 44-181-783-0049. *5675*

KEY NOTE MARKET REVIEW: U K PUBLISHING.
Key Note Ltd., Field House, 72 Oldfield Rd., Hampton, Middlesex TW12 2HQ, England. TEL 44-181-783-0755. FAX 44-181-783-0049. *6275*

KEY NOTE MARKET REVIEW: U K SECURITY MARKET.
Key Note Ltd., Field House, 72 Oldfield Rd., Hampton, Middlesex TW12 2HQ, England. TEL 44-181-783-0755. FAX 44-181-783-0049. *2287*

KEY NOTE MARKET REVIEW: U K SOFT DRINKS.
Key Note Ltd., Field House, 72 Oldfield Rd., Hampton, Middlesex TW12 2HQ, England. TEL 44-181-783-0755. FAX 44-181-783-0049. *523*

KEY NOTE MARKET REVIEW: U K SPORTS MARKET.
Key Note Ltd., Field House, 72 Oldfield Rd., Hampton, Middlesex TW12 2HQ, England. TEL 44-181-783-0755. FAX 44-181-783-0049. *6768*

KEY NOTE MARKET REVIEW: U K TELECOMMUNICATIONS.
Key Note Ltd., Field House, 72 Oldfield Rd., Hampton, Middlesex TW12 2HQ, England. TEL 44-181-783-0755. FAX 44-181-783-0049. *1996*

KEY NOTE MARKET REVIEW: U K TOILETRIES & COSMETICS MARKET.
Key Note Ltd., Field House, 72 Oldfield Rd., Hampton, Middlesex TW12 2HQ, England. TEL 44-181-783-0755. FAX 44-181-783-1940. *511*

KEY NOTE MARKET REVIEW: U K TRAVEL & TOURISM.
Key Note Ltd., Field House, 72 Oldfield Rd., Hampton, Middlesex TW12 2HQ, England. TEL 44-181-783-0755. FAX 44-181-783-0049. *7215*

KEY NOTE MARKET REVIEW: U K WEDDING MARKET.
Key Note Ltd., Field House, 72 Oldfield Rd., Hampton, Middlesex TW12 2HQ, England. TEL 44-181-783-0755. FAX 44-181-783-0049. *4626*

KEY NOTE MARKET REVIEW: WHOLESALING IN THE U K.
Key Note Ltd., Field House, 72 Oldfield Rd., Hampton, Middlesex TW12 2HQ, England. TEL 44-181-783-0755. FAX 44-181-783-0049. *1536*

KEY NOTE MARKET REVIEW: YOUTH MARKET IN THE U.K.
Key Note Ltd., Field House, 72 Oldfield Rd., Hampton, Middlesex TW12 2HQ, England. TEL 44-181-783-0755. FAX 44-181-783-0049. *39*

KEY NOTE REPORT: FURNITURE.
Key Note Publications Ltd., Field House, 72 Oldfield Rd., Hampton, Middlesex TW12 2HQ, England. TEL 0181-783-0755. FAX 0181-783-1720. *3858*

KEY NOTE REPORT: PRINTING INKS.
Key Note Publications Ltd., Field House, 72 Oldfield Rd., Hampton, Middlesex TW12 2HQ, England. TEL 0181-783-0755. FAX 0181-783-1720. *6081*

KICK IT OVER.
Kick it Over Collective, P.O. Box 5811, Sta. A, Toronto, ON M5W 1P2, Canada. *5938*

KID CROSSWORDS AND OTHER PUZZLES.
URL: http://members.aol.com/kidcross. Available only online. *1876*

KID'N AROUND.
17205 Vashon Hwy. S.W., Vashon, WA 98070. URL: http://www.kidnaround.com. *1876*

KIDTECH NEWS.
KidTECH-BG Associates, P.O. Box 39079, Washington, DC 20016-9079. TEL 202-244-4767. FAX 202-244-4767. *2458*

KINGSWOOD KRANIUM.
Kingswood Advertising, Inc., Cricket Terrace Center, Ardmore, PA 19003. URL: http://www.kingswood.com. Available only online. *39*

KINO - GLAZ.
Izdatel'stvo Kino - Glaz Ltd., Eistnstein ul., 8, 223A, 129226 Moscow, Russia. TEL 7-095-1812236. FAX 7-095-2050658. *5338*

KIPLINGER AGRICULTURE LETTER.
Kiplinger Washington Editors, Inc., 1729 H St., N.W., Washington, DC 20006. TEL 202-887-6400. FAX 202-778-8976. URL: http://www.kiplinger.com/ *132*

KIPLINGER CALIFORNIA LETTER.
Kiplinger Washington Editors, Inc., 1729 H St., N.W., Washington, DC 20006. TEL 202-887-6400. FAX 202-778-8976. URL: http://www.kiplinger.com/ *1393*

KIPLINGER TAX LETTER.
Kiplinger Washington Editors, Inc., 1729 H St. N.W., Washington, DC 20006. TEL 202-887-6400. FAX 202-778-8976. URL: http://www.kiplinger.com/newsletter/tax.html. *1618*

KIPLINGER WASHINGTON LETTER.
Kiplinger Washington Editors, Inc., 1729 H St., N.W., Washington, DC 20006. TEL 202-887-6400. FAX 202-778-8976. URL: http://www.kplinger.com/newsletter/wash.html. *1393*

KIPLINGER'S PERSONAL FINANCE MAGAZINE.
Kiplinger Washington Editors, Inc., 1729 H St., N.W., Washington, DC 20006. TEL 202-887-6400. FAX 202-331-1206. Vendor(s): Information Access Co., Knight-Ridder Information, Inc., UMI. *1152*

THE KLEINMAN REPORT.
URL: http://www.kleinman.com. Available only online. *2136*

KNAVE.
Galaxy Publications Ltd., P.O. Box 312, Witham, Essex CM8 3SZ, England. FAX 44-1376-510680. URL: http://www.knave.com/. *5178*

KNEE SURGERY, SPORTS TRAUMATOLOGY, ARTHROSCOPY.
Springer-Verlag, Heidelberger Platz 3, 14197 Berlin, Germany. TEL 49-30-82787-0. FAX 49-30-82787448. URL: http://www.springer.de. *5130*

KNIGHT EXAMINER.
Jersey City State College, 2039 Kennedy Blvd., Jersey City, NJ 07305-1597. TEL 201-200-3575. FAX 201-200-3238. *1958*

KNIGHTMARES.
URL: http://members.aol.com/mdgpubs/index.htm. Available only online. *4532*

KOGNITIONSWISSENSCHAFT.
Springer-Verlag, Heidelberger Platz 3, 14197 Berlin, Germany. TEL 49-30-82787-0. FAX 49-30-82787448. URL: http://link.springer.de. *6133*

KOKYU TO JUNKAN.
Igaku Shoin Ltd., 5-24-3 Hongo, Bunkyo-ku, Tokyo 113-91, Japan. TEL 81-3-3817-5703. Vendor(s): JICST. *5120*

KOMPASS AGRIBUSINESSS AND FOOD AND BEVERAGE.
Peter Isaacson Publications Pty. Ltd., 46-50 Porter St., Prahran, Vic. 3181, Australia. TEL 61-3-2457777. FAX 61-3-2457840. *1691*

KOMPASS AUSTRALIA.
Peter Isaacson Publications Pty. Ltd., 46-50 Porter St., Prahran, Vic. 3181, Australia. TEL 61-3-2457777. FAX 61-3-2457840. *1691*

KOMPASS BELGIUM.
Editus Belgium S.A., Av. Moliere 256, 1060 Brussels, Belgium. TEL 32-2-3459070. FAX 32-2-3473340. *1691*

KOMPASS CHEMICAL, PLASTIC AND RUBBER PRODUCTS.
Peter Isaacson Publications Pty. Ltd., 46-50 Porter St., Prahran, Vic. 3181, Australia. TEL 61-3-2457777. FAX 61-3-2457840. *1691*

KOMPASS ELECTRONIC AND ELECTRICAL PRODUCTS.
Peter Isaacson Publications Pty. Ltd., 46-50 Porter St., Prahran, Vic. 3181, Australia. TEL 61-3-2457777. FAX 61-3-2457840. *1691*

KOMPASS SOUTH AFRICA.
Reed Business Information South Africa (Pty.) Ltd., P.O. Box 653207, Benmore 2010, South Africa. TEL 27-11-774-1110. FAX 27-11-883-4729. URL: http://africa.cis.co.za. *1692*

KOMPASS SVERIGE.
Kompass Sverige AB, Torsgatan 21, S-113 90 Stockholm, Sweden. FAX 46-8-7363022. Vendor(s): Knight-Ridder Information, Inc. *1693*

KOMPASS UNITED KINGDOM.
Kompass, Part of the Reed Elsevier group, Windsor Ct., E. Grinstead House, E. Grinstead, W. Sussex RH19 1XD, England. TEL 44-1342-326972. FAX 44-1342-335992. Vendor(s): Reed Information Services Ltd. *1693*

KONSTKALENDERN.
Foerlag ARB - Anders Blume, Box 17176, S-104 62 Stockholm, Sweden. TEL 46-8-669-64-09. FAX 46-8-669-64-89. URL: http://piazza.comedia.se/konstkalendern. *5357*

KONSTRUKTO.
URL: http://dove.mtx.net.au/~andypc. Available only online. *5938*

KONZERNE IN SCHAUBILDERN.
Verlag Hoppenstedt GmbH, Havelstr. 9, 64295 Darmstadt, Germany. TEL 49-6151-380-0. FAX 49-6151-380360. Vendor(s): Lexis-Nexis. *1693*

KOREA ECONOMIC WEEKLY.
URL: http://eco.ked.co.kr/h-kew.html. Available only online. *1268*

KOREAN JOURNAL OF PARASITOLOGY.
Korean Society for Parasitology, c/o Dept. of Parasitology, College of Medicine, Seoul National University, Seoul 110 799, S. Korea. TEL 82-2-740-8348. FAX 82-2-765-6142. URL: http://www.sun.hallym.ac.kr/~shuh/kjp.html. *4840*

THE KOUCH.
Jim Tae Stereo, 323 Goodwood Rd., Kings Park, S.A. 5034, Australia. URL: http://www.eastend.au.com/knekt/ Available only online. *6744*

KUDOS.
Box 45, 00511 Helsinki, Finland. URL: http://www.clinet.fi/~lyhty/kudos.html. Available only online. *3784*

KUKA KUKIN ON.
Kustannusosakeyhtio Otava, Uudenmaankatu 7R 8-12, SF-00120 Helsinki, Finland. TEL 358-9-19961. FAX 358-9-1996477. *575*

DIE KUNSTSTOFF-INDUSTRIE UND IHRE HELFER.
Industrieschau-Verlagsgesellschaft mbH, Postfach 100262, 64202 Darmstadt, Germany. TEL 49-6151-3892-0. FAX 49-6151-33164. *5879*

KYKLOS.
Blackwell Publishers Ltd., 108 Cowley Rd., Oxford OX4 1JF, England. TEL 44-1865-791100. FAX 44-1865-791347. Vendor(s): UMI. *1268*

L A N PRODUCT NEWS.
Worldwide Videotex, Box 3273, Boynton Beach, FL 33424-3273. TEL 407-738-2276. Vendor(s): Data-Star, Information Access Co., Knight-Ridder Information, Inc., NewsNet (EC99). *2136*

L A N TIMES.
McGraw-Hill Companies, 1221 Ave. of the Americas, New York, NY 10020. TEL 212-512-2000. Vendor(s): Dow Jones News Retrieval (LNTM), Knight-Ridder Information, Inc. (LAN), Lexis-Nexis (LANTME), NewsNet (EC42). *2197*

L C FOLK ARCHIVE FINDING AID.
U.S. Library of Congress, Archive of Folk Culture, American Folklife Center, Washington, DC 20540-4610. TEL 202-707-5510. URL: http://www.lcweb.loc.gov/folklife/. *4190*

L C FOLK ARCHIVE REFERENCE AID.
U.S. Library of Congress, Archive of Folk Culture, American Folklife Center, Washington, DC 20540-4610. TEL 202-707-5510. URL: http://lccweb.loc.gov/folklife/. *4190*

L C S: GUIDE TO HOCKEY.
Canadas Net, 632 Hempfield St., Greensburg, PA 15601. URL: http://www.lcshockey.com. Available only online. *6809*

L D C DEBT REPORT.
American Banker - Bond Buyer, Newsletter Division One State Pl. Plaza, New York, NY 10004-1549. TEL 800-733-4371. FAX 212-943-2224. Vendor(s): Information Access Co., Knight-Ridder Information, Inc., Lexis-Nexis, NewsNet (FI42). *1152*

L I M R A'S MARKETFACTS.
LIMRA International, Inc., Box 208, Hartford, CT 06141-0208. TEL 203-287-7725. Vendor(s): UMI. *3823*

L I S A: LIBRARY & INFORMATION SCIENCE ABSTRACTS.
Bowker - Saur Ltd., A member of the Reed Elsevier plc group, Maypole House, Maypole Rd., E. Grinstead, W. Sussex RH19 1HU, England. TEL 44-1342-330100. FAX 44-1342-330191. URL: http://www.reed-elsevier.com. Vendor(s): Knight-Ridder Information, Inc. (File no.61/LISA), Questel Orbit Inc. (LISA), Ovid Technologies, Inc. (LISA). *4227*

L I T A LINE.
American Library Association, 50 E. Huron St., Chicago, IL 60611-2795. TEL 312-944-6780. FAX 312-440-9374. URL: http://www.lita.org. Available only online. *4233*

L N G OBSERVER.
Institute of Gas Technology, 1700 S. Mount Prospect Rd., Des Plaines, IL 60018-1804. TEL 847-768-0512. FAX 847-768-0516. *5608*

L P I TECHNICAL REPORT.
Lunar and Planetary Institute, 3600 Bay Area Blvd., Houston, TX 77058-1113. TEL 713-486-2172. FAX 713-486-2186. *497*

LABOR - MANAGEMENT RELATIONS ANALYSIS - NEWS AND BACKGROUND INFORMATION.
The Bureau of National Affairs, Inc., 1231 25th St., N.W., Washington, DC 20037. TEL 202-452-4200. FAX 202-822-8092. URL: http://www.bna.com/ Vendor(s): Human Resources Information Network (File DD), West Group (File LLR-NEWS). *1440*

LABOR RELATIONS REFERENCE MANUAL.
The Bureau of National Affairs, Inc., 1231 25th St., N.W., Washington, DC 20037. TEL 202-452-4200. FAX 202-822-8092. URL: http://www.bna.com/ Vendor(s): Human Resources Information Network (Files BOARDS, COURTS), Lexis-Nexis (File LRRM), West Group (File FLB-CS, MLR-CS). *1441*

LABOR RELATIONS REPORTER.
The Bureau of National Affairs, Inc., 1231 25th St., N.W., Washington, DC 20037. TEL 202-452-4200. FAX 202-822-8092. URL: http://www.bna.com/. Vendor(s): Knight-Ridder Information, Inc. (File no. 244, Laborlaw), Lexis-Nexis, West Group. *1441*

LABOR RELATIONS REPORTER. FAIR EMPLOYMENT PRACTICES.
The Bureau of National Affairs, Inc., 1231 25th St., N.W., Washington, DC 20037. TEL 202-452-4200. FAX 202-822-8092. URL: http://www.bna.com/. Vendor(s): Knight-Ridder Information, Inc., West Group. *1441*

LABOR RELATIONS REPORTER. LABOR ARBITRATION AND DISPUTE SETTLEMENTS.
The Bureau of National Affairs, Inc., 1231 25th St., N.W., Washington, DC 20037. TEL 202-452-4200. FAX 202-822-8092. URL: http://www.bna.com/. Vendor(s): Human Resources Information Network (File LAR), Knight-Ridder Information, Inc. (Files 243, 244), Lexis-Nexis, West Group (File LRR-LA). *1441*

LABOR RELATIONS REPORTER. WAGES AND HOURS.
The Bureau of National Affairs, Inc., 1231 25th St., N.W., Washington, DC 20037. TEL 202-452-4200. FAX 202-822-8092. URL: http://www.bna.com/ Vendor(s): Knight-Ridder Information, Inc., West Group. *1441*

LABOR RELATIONS WEEK.
The Bureau of National Affairs, Inc., 1231 25th St., N.W., Washington, DC 20037. TEL 202-452-4200. FAX 202-822-8092. URL: http://www.bna.com/ Vendor(s): Human Resources Information Network (CDD, HDD). *1441*

LABOR STUDIES JOURNAL.
Transaction Publishers, Transaction Periodicals Consortium, Department 3092, Rutgers University, New Brunswick, NJ 08903. TEL 908-445-2280. FAX 908-445-3138.
Vendor(s): Information Access Co.. *1441*

LABORATORY HAZARDS BULLETIN.
The Royal Society of Chemistry, Thomas Graham House, Science Park, Milton Rd., Cambridge CB4 4WF, England. TEL 44-1223-420066. FAX 44-1223-423429. URL: http://chemistry.rsc.org/rsc/. Vendor(s): Data-Star (CSNB), Knight-Ridder Information, Inc. (File no.317), Questel Orbit Inc. (CSNB), STN International (CSNB). *5493*

LABORATORY INVESTIGATION.
Williams & Wilkins, 351 W. Camden St., Baltimore, MD 21201-2436. TEL 410-528-4068. FAX 410-528-4452. URL: http://www.wwilkins.com. Vendor(s): Ovid Technologies, Inc.. *4900*

LABOUR ARBITRATION CASES.
Canada Law Book Inc., 240 Edward St., Aurora, ON L4G 3S9, Canada. TEL 905-841-6472. FAX 905-841-5085. *1442*

LABTRADER MAGAZINE.
URL: http://www.labx.com/
Available only online. *6543*

LACROSSETALK.
All England Women's Lacrosse Association, 4 Western Ct., Bromley St., Digbeth, Birmingham 9, England. TEL 44-121-773-4422. *6809*

LADIES HOME JOURNAL (INKPRINT EDITION).
Meredith Corporation, 1716 Locust St., Des Moines, IA 50336. TEL 515-284-3000.
Vendor(s): Information Access Co., Knight-Ridder Information, Inc.. *7325*

LAEKEMEDELSVAERLDEN.
Swedish Pharmaceutical Press, P.O. Box 1136, S-111 81 Stockholm, Sweden. TEL 46-8-723-50-00. FAX 46-8-14-95-80. URL: http://www.swepharm.pharmasoft.se/Forlag/Lakemedelsvarlden/aktuellt.html. *5676*

LAFAYETTE BUSINESS DIGEST.
Laurendeau Communications, Box 587, Lafayette, IN 47902. TEL 317-742-6918. FAX 317-423-8133.
Vendor(s): UMI. *1268*

LAGNIAPPE LETTER.
Latin American Information Services, Inc., 159 W. 53rd St., 28th fl., New York, NY 10019. TEL 212-765-5520. FAX 212-765-2927. URL: http://www.lais.com.
Vendor(s): Information Access Co., Knight-Ridder Information, Inc., Lexis-Nexis. *1339*

LAGNIAPPE QUARTERLY MONITOR.
Latin American Information Services, Inc., 159 W. 53rd St., 28th fl., New York, NY 10019. TEL 212-765-5520. FAX 212-765-2927. URL: http://www.lais.com.
Vendor(s): Information Access Co.. *1364*

LAGUNA LIFE INTERNATIONAL.
20401 Sun Valley Dr., Laguna Beach, CA 92651-1166. URL: http://www.lagunabeachca.com.
Available only online. *3377*

LAKEWOOD REPORT ON POSITIVE EMPLOYEE PRACTICES.
Lakewood Publications, Inc., 50 S. Ninth St., Minneapolis, MN 55402. TEL 612-333-0471. FAX 612-333-6526.
Vendor(s): UMI. *1490*

LAKEWOOD REPORT ON TECHNOLOGY FOR LEARNING NEWSLETTER.
Lakewood Publications, Inc., 50 S. Ninth St., Minneapolis, MN 55402. TEL 612-333-0471. FAX 612-333-6526. *2459*

LAMBDA BOOK REPORT.
Lambda Literary Foundation, P.O. Box 73910, Washington, DC 20056-3910. TEL 202-462-7924. FAX 202-462-5264.
Vendor(s): Information Access Co., UMI. *3697*

LANCASTER COUNTY HISTORICAL SOCIETY. JOURNAL.
Lancaster County Historical Society, 230 N. President Ave., Lancaster, PA 17603-3125. TEL 717-392-4633. *3634*

THE LANCET.
The Lancet Ltd., 42 Bedford Sq., London WC1B 3SL, England. TEL 44-171-4364981. FAX 44-171-4367570. URL: http://www.thelancet.com.uk. Vendor(s): Information Access Co., Ovid Technologies, Inc., UMI. *4702*

LAND ECONOMICS.
University of Wisconsin Press, Journal Division, 114 N. Murray St., Madison, WI 53715. TEL 608-262-4952. FAX 608-262-7560.
Vendor(s): Information Access Co.. *197*

LAND MOBILE RADIO NEWS.
Phillips Business Information, Inc., 1201 Seven Locks Rd., Potomac, MD 20854. TEL 301-424-3338. FAX 301-424-4297.
Vendor(s): Information Access Co., Knight-Ridder Information, Inc., NewsNet (TE13). *2035*

LAND USE DIGEST.
Urban Land Institute, 1025 Thomas Jefferson St., N.W., Ste. 500 West, Washington, DC 20007. TEL 202-624-7000. FAX 202-624-7140. URL: http://www.uli.org/pubs/LUD/ *3752*

LAND USE LAW REPORT.
Business Publishers, Inc., 951 Pershing Dr., Silver Spring, MD 20910-4464. TEL 301-587-6300. FAX 301-585-9075.
Vendor(s): NewsNet (EV02). *3752*

LANE REPORT.
Lane Communications Group, 269 W. Main St., Lexington, KY 40507. TEL 606-244-3522. FAX 606-244-3544.
Vendor(s): UMI. *981*

LANGENBECKS ARCHIVE OF SURGERY.
Springer-Verlag, Heidelberger Platz 3, 14197 Berlin, Germany. TEL 49-30-82787-0. FAX 49-30-82787448. URL: http://link.springer.de. *5147*

LANGMUIR.
American Chemical Society, 1155 16th St., N.W., Washington, DC 20036. TEL 800-333-9511. FAX 614-447-3671.
Vendor(s): STN International (CJACS). *1832*

LANGUAGE LEARNING AND TECHNOLOGY.
University of Hawaii, National Foreign Language Resource Center, East-West Rd., Bldg. 1, Rm. 6-A, Honolulu, HI 96822. TEL 808-956-9424. URL: http://polyglot.cal.msu.edu/llt.
Available only online. *4320*

LARGE KITCHEN APPLIANCES: THE INTERNATIONAL MARKET.
Euromonitor, 60-61 Britton St., London EC1M 5NA, England. TEL 44-171-251-8024. FAX 44-171-608-3149. URL: http://www.euromonitor.com.
Vendor(s): Data-Star, Knight-Ridder Information, Inc.. *2645*

LARGE MIXED RETAILERS: THE INTERNATIONAL MARKET.
Euromonitor, 60-61 Britton St., London EC1M 5NA, England. TEL 44-171-251-8024. FAX 44-171-608-3149. URL: http://www.euromonitor.com.
Vendor(s): Data-Star, Knight-Ridder Information, Inc.. *1537*

LARYNGOSCOPE.
Lippincott - Raven Publishers, 227 E. Washington Sq., Philadelphia, PA 19106-3780. TEL 215-238-4200. FAX 215-238-4227. URL: http://www.irpub.com. *5023*

LAS VEGAS BUSINESS PRESS.
Wick Communications, 3535 Wynn Rd., Las Vegas, NV 89102. TEL 702-871-6780. FAX 702-871-3470.
Vendor(s): Lexis-Nexis, UMI. *981*

LAS VEGAS COMPUTER JOURNAL.
4430-1 E Charleston, Ste. 101, Las Vegas, NV 89104. URL: http://www.computerjournal.com. *2086*

LASER CHEMISTRY.
Gordon and Breach - Harwood Academic, Amsteldisk 166, 1st Fl., 1079 LH Amsterdam, Netherlands. URL: http://www.gbhap.com/Laser_Chemistry/. *5864*

LASERS IN ENGINEERING.
Gordon and Breach - Harwood Academic, Amsteldisk 166, 1st Fl., 1079 LH Amsterdam, Netherlands. URL: http://www.gbhap.com/Lasers_in_Engineering/. *5865*

LATE IMPERIAL CHINA.
Johns Hopkins University Press, Journals Publishing Division, 2715 N. Charles St., Baltimore, MD 21218-4319. TEL 410-516-6987. FAX 410-516-6968. URL: http://muse.jhu.edu. *3536*

LATEST MANAGEMENT RESEARCH AND PRACTICE.
M C B University Press Ltd., 60-62 Toller Ln., Bradford, W. Yorks BD8 9BY, England. TEL 44-1274-777700. FAX 44-1274-785200. URL: http://www.mcb.co.uk/lmrp.htm.
Available only online. *1054*

LATIN AMERICAN ECONOMY AND BUSINESS.
Latin American Newsletters, 61 Old St., London EC1V 9HX, England. TEL 44-171-251-0012. FAX 44-171-253-8193.
Vendor(s): Lexis-Nexis. *1340*

LATIN AMERICAN INFORMES ESPECIALES.
Lettres (U.K.) Ltd., 61 Old St., London EC1V 9HX, England. TEL 44-171-251-0012. FAX 44-171-253-8193.
Vendor(s): Lexis-Nexis. *1394*

LATIN AMERICAN REGIONAL REPORTS - ANDEAN GROUP.
Latin American Newsletters, 61 Old St., London EC1V 9HX, England. TEL 44-171-251-0012. FAX 44-171-253-8193.
Vendor(s): Lexis-Nexis. *1269*

LATIN AMERICAN RESEARCH REVIEW.
Latin American Studies Association (Albuquerque), c/o University of New Mexico, 801 Yale N.E., Albuquerque, NM 87131-1016. TEL 505-277-5985. FAX 505-277-5989.
Vendor(s): Information Access Co., UMI. *6624*

LATIN AMERICAN SPECIAL REPORTS.
Latin American Newsletters, 61 Old St., London EC1V 9HX, England. TEL 44-171-251-0012. FAX 44-171-253-8193.
Vendor(s): Lexis-Nexis. *1394*

LATIN AMERICAN TRAVEL ADVISOR.
Latin American Travel Consultants, Box 17-17-908, Quito, Ecuador. FAX 593-2-562-566. URL: http://www.amerispan.com/LATC. *7216*

LATIN AMERICAN WEEKLY REPORT.
Latin American Newsletters, 61 Old St., London EC1V 9HX, England. TEL 44-171-251-0012. FAX 44-171-253-8193.
Vendor(s): Lexis-Nexis. *1269*

LATIN TRADE.
Freedom Publications, Inc. (Miami), 200 S. Biscayne Blvd., Ste. 1150, Miami, FL 33131. TEL 305-358-8373. FAX 305-358-9166. URL: http://www.latintrade.com. *1340*

LATINFINANCE.
Latin American Financial Publications, Inc., 2121 Ponce de Leon Blvd., Ste. 1020, Coral Gables, FL 33134. TEL 305-448-6593. FAX 305-448-0718.
Vendor(s): Information Access Co.. *1152*

LAW & BUSINESS DIRECTORY OF CORPORATE COUNSEL.
Law & Business, Inc., 1185 Avenue of the Americas, New York, NY 10036-2601. TEL 201-894-8484.
Vendor(s): West Group. *4083*

LAW AND ORDER.
Hendon, Inc., 1000 Skokie Blvd., Wilmette, IL 60091. TEL 708-256-8555. FAX 708-256-8574.
Vendor(s): CompuServe, Inc.. *2272*

LAW AND POLICY IN INTERNATIONAL BUSINESS.
Georgetown University Law Center, 600 New Jersey Ave., N.W., Washington, DC 20009. TEL 202-662-9468.
Vendor(s): Information Access Co., West Group. *4121*

LAW & POLITICS OUTTA' LINE.
B R J G Publishing, 527 Marquette Ave., Ste. 2301, Minneapolis, MN 55402-1323. TEL 612-335-8808. FAX 612-335-8809. URL: http://www.lawandpolitics.com. Available only online. *3976*

LAW ENFORCEMENT PRODUCT NEWS.
General Communications, Inc., 100 Garfield St., 3rd. Fl., Denver, CO 80206. *2272*

LAW OFFICE TECHNOLOGY REVIEW.
c/o Barry D. Bayer, 2711 183rd St., Ste. 219, Homewood, IL 60430-2950. TEL 708-957-3322. FAX 708-957-3337. Vendor(s): Information Access Co., Knight-Ridder Information, Inc., NewsNet (LA15), West Group. *4068*

LAW PRACTICE MANAGEMENT.
American Bar Association, Law Practice Management Section, 750 N. Lake Shore Dr., Chicago, IL 60611. TEL 312-988-5000. URL: http://www.abanet.org. Vendor(s): Lexis-Nexis, West Group. *3978*

LAW TECHNOLOGY PRODUCT NEWS.
URL: http://www.ljx.com/ltpn. Available only online. *3979*

LAWYERS' MICRO USERS GROUP NEWSLETTER.
Paul Bernstein, Ed. & Pub. (Chicago), 333 E. Ontario St., Ste. 2102-B, Chicago, IL 60611. TEL 312-951-8451. Available only online. Vendor(s): NewsNet (LA05). *4068*

LEAD AND ZINC STATISTICS.
International Lead and Zinc Study Group, 2 King St., London SW1Y 6QP, England. TEL 44-171-839-8550. FAX 44-171-930-4635. *5219*

LEADERSHIP (CAROL STREAM).
Christianity Today, Inc., 465 Gundersen Dr., Carol Stream, IL 60188. TEL 630-260-6200. FAX 630-260-0114. URL: http://www.christianity.net/leadership. *6352*

LEADS FROM L A M A.
American Library Association, Library Administration and Management Association, 50 E. Huron St., Chicago, IL 60611-2795. TEL 312-944-6780. FAX 312-440-9374. URL: http://www.ala.org. Available only online. *4191*

LEAGUE OF WOMEN VOTERS OF GEORGIA. LEGISLATIVE NEWSLETTER.
League of Women Voters of Georgia, 1776 Peachtree St., N.W., 533N, Atlanta, GA 30309-2307. TEL 404-874-7352. FAX 404-874-7353. URL: http://www.ga.lwv.org. *3980*

LEARNING AND MOTIVATION.
Academic Press, Inc., Journal Division, 525 B St., Ste. 1900, San Diego, CA 92101-4495. TEL 619-230-1840. FAX 619-699-6800. URL: http://www.apnet.com/www/journal/lm.htm; http://www.idealibrary.com/ *2460*

LEARNING - FOUNTAIN REVIEWS.
URL: http://www.tricky.com/lfm/newsletr.htm. Available only online. *2136*

LEATHER.
Miller Freeman plc, Sovereign Way, Tonbridge, Kent TN9 1RW, England. TEL 44-1732-364422. FAX 44-1732-361534. Vendor(s): Information Access Co.. *4145*

LEBLANC BELL.
G. Leblanc Corporation, P.O. Box 1415, Kenosha, WI 53141-1415. TEL 414-658-1644. FAX 414-658-2824. URL: http://www.gleblanc.com. *5407*

LEGAL ASSISTANT TODAY.
James Publishing Group, Inc., 3505 Cadillac Ave., Ste. H, Costa Mesa, CA 92626-1419. TEL 714-755-5450. Vendor(s): UMI. *3981*

LEGAL COLUMN ARCHIVES.
URL: http://www.fmew.com/archive/index.html. Available only online. *3981*

LEGAL DEPOSIT PUBLICATIONS IN WESTERN AUSTRALIA.
Library and Information Service of Western Australia, Alexander Library Bldg., Perth Cultural Centre, Perth, W.A. 6000, Australia. TEL 61-9-4273111. FAX 61-9-4273256. URL: http://www.liswa.wa.gov.au. Available only online. *554*

LEGAL ONLINE.
Legal Communications, Ltd., 1617 JFK Blvd., Ste. 960, Philadelphia, PA 19103. TEL 215-557-2300. FAX 215-557-2301. URL: http://www.legalonline.com. *3981*

LEGAL PUBLISHER.
J K Publishing, Box 71020, Milwaukee, WI 53211. TEL 414-332-1625. FAX 414-964-0843. Vendor(s): Information Access Co., NewsNet. *3982*

LEGAL SURVIVAL NEWSLETTER.
74 Main St., Box 31, Akron, NY 14001. URL: http://www.friran.com. Available only online. *3982*

LEGAL TIMES.
American Lawyer Media, L.P., 1730 M St., N.W., Ste. 802, Washington, DC 20036. TEL 202-457-0686. FAX 202-457-0718. Vendor(s): Lexis-Nexis. *3982*

LEGALTRAC.
Information Access Company, 362 Lakeside Dr., Foster City, CA 94404. TEL 415-378-5200. FAX 415-378-5369. Vendor(s): Knight-Ridder Information, Inc. (File no.150), Lexis-Nexis (LGLIND), Ovid Technologies, Inc. (LAWS), West Group (LRI). *4055*

LEGISLATIVE NETWORK FOR NURSES.
Business Publishers, Inc., 951 Pershing Dr., Silver Spring, MD 20910-4464. TEL 301-587-6300. FAX 301-585-9075. Vendor(s): NewsNet. *4940*

LEISURE FUTURES.
Henley Centre for Forecasting Ltd., 9 Bridewell Pl., Blackfriars, London EC4V 6AY, England. TEL 0171-3535-9961. FAX 0171-353-2899. *4150*

LEISURE INTELLIGENCE.
Mintel International Group Ltd., 18-19 Long Ln., London EC1A 9HE, England. TEL 44-171-606-4533. FAX 44-171-606-5932. *4150*

LEISURE, RECREATION AND TOURISM ABSTRACTS.
CAB International, Wallingford, Oxon. OX10 8DE, England. TEL 44-1491-832111. FAX 44-1491-833508. URL: http://www.cabi.org. Vendor(s): DIMDI, European Space Agency, Knight-Ridder Information, Inc., STN International. *7254*

LEISURE STUDIES.
Thomson Professional, 2-6 Boundary Row, London SE1 8HN, England. TEL 171-8650066. FAX 171-5229623. URL: http://www.thomsonprofessional.com. *4150*

LEMON TREE BULLETIN.
Commonwealth Department of Human Services and Health, Lemon Tree Learning Project, URL: http://www.vicnet.net.au/~vmiac/lemon-00.htm. Available only online. *5079*

LEONARDO ELECTRONIC ALMANAC.
M I T Press, 5 Cambridge Center, Cambridge, MA 02142. TEL 617-253-2889. FAX 617-577-1545. URL: http://www-mitpress.mit.edu/jrnls-catalog/leonardo-almanac.html. Available only online. *477*

LETTER TO LIBRARIES ONLINE.
Oregon State Library, Salem, OR 97310-0640. TEL 503-378-2112. FAX 503-588-7119. URL: http://www.osl.state.or.us/oslhome.html. Available only online. *4233*

LETTERA MATEMATICA PRISTEM.
Springer-Verlag Italia Srl, Via Podgora 4, 20122 Milan, Italy. TEL 39-2-55194656. FAX 39-2-55193360. *4586*

LETTRE MENSUEL DE FRANCE PHARMACIE LABORATOIRES.
41 rue Gambetta, 92100 Boulogne Billancourt, France. TEL 46-04-52-46. FAX 46-05-65-47. *5676*

LEUKEMIA AND LYMPHOMA.
Gordon and Breach - Harwood Academic, Amsteldisk 166, 1st Fl., 1079 LH Amsterdam, Netherlands. URL: http://www.gbhap.com/Leukemia__Lymphoma/. *4921*

LEXXICON.COM.
Box 387, Newnan, GA 30364. URL: http://www.lexxicon.com. Available only online. *452*

LIABILITY WEEK.
J R Publishing Inc., Box 6654, McLean, VA 22106. TEL 703-532-2235. FAX 703-532-2236. Vendor(s): Information Access Co., NewsNet. *3824*

LIBRARIAN CAREER DEVELOPMENT.
M C B University Press Ltd., 60-62 Toller Ln., Bradford, W. Yorks BD8 9BY, England. TEL 44-1274-777700. FAX 44-1274-785200. URL: http://www.mcb.co.uk/liblink/lcd/jourhome.htm. *4192*

LIBRARY ADMINISTRATOR'S DIGEST.
B C P L Foundation, 320 York Rd., Towson, MD 21204. TEL 410-887-4622. FAX 410-887-6103. Vendor(s): UMI. *4193*

LIBRARY ISSUES.
Mountainside Publishing, Inc., 321 S. Main St., Ste. 300, Ann Arbor, MI 48107. TEL 313-662-3925. FAX 313-662-4450. URL: http://www.netpubsintl.com/li.html. *4194*

LIBRARY LITERATURE.
H.W. Wilson Co., 950 University Ave., Bronx, NY 10452. TEL 718-588-8400. FAX 718-590-1617. Vendor(s): OCLC, Wilsonline (File LIB). *4227*

LIBRARY RESOURCES FOR THE BLIND AND PHYSICALLY HANDICAPPED.
U.S. Library of Congress, National Library Service for the Blind and Physically Handicapped, Washington, DC 20542. TEL 202-707-5100. FAX 202-707-0712. URL: http://www.lcweb.loc.gov/nls. *4195*

LIBRARY SOFTWARE REVIEW.
Sage Publications, Inc., 2455 Teller Rd., Thousand Oaks, CA 91320. TEL 805-499-0721. FAX 805-499-0871. URL: http://www.sagepub.com. Vendor(s): Information Access Co.. *2215*

LIBRARY TECHNOLOGY REPORTS.
American Library Association, 50 E. Huron St., Chicago, IL 60611-2795. TEL 312-944-6780. FAX 312-440-9374. Vendor(s): Information Access Co. *4196*

LIBRARY TRENDS.
University of Illinois Press, 1325 S. Oak St., Champaign, IL 61820. TEL 217-333-1359. FAX 217-244-8082. URL: http://edfu.lis.uiuc.edu/puboff. Vendor(s): Information Access Co. *4196*

LIBRES: LIBRARY AND INFORMATION SCIENCE RESEARCH ELECTRONIC JOURNAL.
Dept. of Information Studies, Curtin University of Technology, G.P.O. Box U1987, Perth, WA 6845, Australia. TEL 61-9-3517217. FAX 61-9-3513152. URL: http:www.lib.lsu.edu/epubs/libres/. Available only online. *4196*

LIBROS ESPANOLES EN VENTA.
Ministerio de Cultura, Centro del Libro y de la Lectura, C. Santiago Rusinol, 8, 28040 Madrid, Spain. TEL 536-88-30. FAX 553-99-90. *555*

LICENSED PRACTICAL NURSE.
McClain Publishing Co., Box 10619, Charlotte, NC 28212-5677. *4940*

LICENSING LETTER.
E P M Communications, 160 Mercer St., 3rd Fl., New York, NY 10012-3212. TEL 212-941-0099. FAX 212-941-1622. Vendor(s): Information Access Co. *5587*

THE LICHENOLOGIST.
Academic Press Ltd., 24-28 Oval Rd., London NW1 7DX, England. TEL 44-171-267-4466. FAX 44-171-482-2293. URL: http://www.hbuk.co.uk/ap/lichenol; http://www.europe.idealibrary.com/ *713*

SERIALS AVAILABLE ONLINE

LIDOVE NOVINY.
Zerotinova 38, 130 00 Prague 3, Czech Republic. TEL 420-2-67098444. FAX 420-2-67098608. *3273*

LIEBIGS ANNALEN.
Wiley - V C H, Postfach 101161, 69451 Weinheim, Germany. TEL 49-6201-606147. FAX 49-6201-606117. URL: http://www.vchgroup.de. *1759*

LIES.
L C N Syndicate, 6001-0 Lomas Blvd. NE 4, Albuquerque, NM 87110-6640. URL: http://www.cent.com/abetting/ *4343*

LIFE.
Time Inc., Time & Life Bldg., Rockefeller Center, 1271 Ave. of the Americas, New York, NY 10020. TEL 212-522-1212. FAX 212-522-1863. URL: http://www.lifemag.com.
Vendor(s): Information Access Co., Knight-Ridder Information, Inc., Lexis-Nexis, UMI. *3377*

LIFE-LONG BUSINESS SUCCESS.
Available only online. *982*

LIFE SCIENCES & BIOTECHNOLOGY UPDATE.
Infoteam Inc., Box 15640, Plantation, FL 33318-5640. TEL 954-473-9560. FAX 954-473-0544. URL: http://home.aol.com/infoteamma.
Vendor(s): Data-Star, Dow Jones News Retrieval, Information Access Co., Knight-Ridder Information, Inc., Lexis-Nexis, NewsNet, UMI. *685*

LIFELINES.
Livingston County Library, Livingston County Genealogical Society, 450 Locust St., Chillicothe, MO 64601. TEL 816-646-2168. FAX 816-646-0547. URL: http://VAX2.RAINIS.NET/~fwoods/ *3230*

THE LIGHTHOUSE ELECTRONIC MAGAZINE.
Polarized Publications, 720 W. Water St., No. 1, Bellefonte, PA 16823-2733. TEL 814-353-4353. FAX 814-353-1953. URL: http://tlem.netcentral.net.
Available only online. *5448*

LILLY.
URL: http://members.aol.com/lillymag2.
Available only online. *1925*

LIMEN.
Kaos Theatre, URL: http://kali.murdoch.edu.au/limen.
Available only online. *7008*

LIMITED PARTNERSHIP INVESTMENT REVIEW.
Limited Partnership Investment Review, Inc., 55 Morris Ave., Springfield, NJ 07081. TEL 201-467-8700. FAX 201-467-0368.
Vendor(s): NewsNet. *1618*

LINEAR AND MULTILINEAR ALGEBRA.
Gordon and Breach - Harwood Academic, Amsteldisk 166, 1st Fl., 1079 LH Amsterdam, Netherlands. URL: http://www.gbhap.com/Linear_Multilinear_Algebra/. *4586*

LINGUISTICS AND LANGUAGE BEHAVIOR ABSTRACTS.
Sociological Abstracts, Inc., Box 22206, San Diego, CA 92192-0206. TEL 619-695-8803. FAX 619-695-0416.
Vendor(s): Knight-Ridder Information, Inc. (File no.36). *4319*

LINK-UP.
Information Today, Inc., 143 Old Marlton Pike, Medford, NJ 08055. TEL 609-654-6266. FAX 609-654-4309. URL: http://www.infotoday.com/lu/lunew.htm.
Vendor(s): Lexis-Nexis, UMI. *2170*

LINK-UP.
National Library of Australia, Publications Section, Cultural and Educational Services Division, Canberra, A.C.T. 2600, Australia. TEL 61-6-2621207. FAX 61-6-2734493. URL: http://www.nla.gov.au. *3455*

LINKS.
Southern Links Magazine Publishing Associates, 1040 William Hilton Pkwy., Ste. 200, Hilton Head Island, SC 29938. TEL 803-842-6200. FAX 803-842-6233. URL: http://www.golf.com/pub/links. *6810*

LINNEAN SOCIETY. BIOLOGICAL JOURNAL.
Academic Press Ltd., 24-28 Oval Rd., London NW1 7DX, England. TEL 44-171-267-4466. FAX 44-171-482-2293. URL: http://www.hbuk.co.uk/ap/biojls; http://www.europe.idealibrary.com/. *612*

LINNEAN SOCIETY. BOTANICAL JOURNAL.
Academic Press Ltd., 24-28 Oval Rd., London NW1 7DX, England. TEL 44-171-267-4466. FAX 44-171-482-2293. URL: http://www.hbuk.co.uk/ap/botjls; http://www.europe.idealibrary.com/. *713*

LINNEAN SOCIETY. ZOOLOGICAL JOURNAL.
Academic Press Ltd., 24-28 Oval Rd., London NW1 7DX, England. TEL 44-171-267-4466. FAX 44-171-482-2293. URL: http://www.hbuk.co.uk/ap/zjls; http://www.europe.idealibrary.com/. *841*

LINUX JOURNAL.
Specialized Systems Consultants, Box 85867, Seattle, WA 98145. TEL 206-782-7733. FAX 206-782-7191. URL: http://www.ssc.com. *2136*

LINX DATABASE.
Auckland District Law Society, P.O. Box 58, Auckland, New Zealand. TEL 64-9-3031040. FAX 64-9-3033359.
Available only online. Vendor(s): Kiwinet. *4055*

THE LION AND THE UNICORN.
Johns Hopkins University Press, Journals Publishing Division, 2715 N. Charles St., Baltimore, MD 21218. TEL 410-516-6987. FAX 410-516-6968. URL: http://muse.jhu.edu; http://www.press.jhu.edu/journals/lion_and_the_unicorn/ *4427*

LIQUID CRYSTALS.
Taylor & Francis Ltd., 1 Gunpowder Sq., London EC4A 3DE, England. TEL 44-171-583-0490. FAX 44-171-583-0585. URL: http://www.tandf.co.uk/. *1802*

LIST OF I T U - R RECOMMENDATIONS.
International Telecommunication Union, Place des Nations, CH-1211 Geneva 20, Switzerland. TEL 41-22-7306141. FAX 41-22-7305194. URL: http://www.itu.ch. *1997*

LIST OF SCIENTIFIC AND TECHNICAL LITERATURE RELATING TO THAILAND.
Thailand Institute of Scientific and Technological Research, 196 Phahonyothin Rd., Chatuchak, Bangkok 10900, Thailand. TEL 579-8594. FAX 662-579-8594. *6591*

LIST OF SERIALS INDEXED FOR ONLINE USERS.
U.S. National Library of Medicine, 8600 Rockville Pike, Bethesda, MD 20894.
Vendor(s): National Library of Medicine. *4781*

LITERACY NOW.
URL: http://www.deet.gov.au/pubs/lit_now/
Available only online. *2512*

LITERARY REVIEW.
Fairleigh Dickinson University, Literary Review, 285 Madison Ave., Madison, NJ 07940. TEL 201-443-8564. URL: http://www.cais.net/aesir/fiction/tlr.
Vendor(s): Information Access Co., UMI. *4428*

LITERATURE & MEDICINE.
Johns Hopkins University Press, Journals Publishing Division, 2715 N. Charles St., Baltimore, MD 21218. TEL 410-516-6987. FAX 410-516-6968. URL: http://muse.jhu.edu. *4429*

LITERATURINFORMATIONEN AUS DER BILDUNGSFORSCHUNG.
Max-Planck-Institut fuer Bildungsforschung, Lentzeallee 94, 14195 Berlin, Germany. TEL 49-30-82995-1. URL: http://www.mpib-berlin.mpg.de/dok/einfo.htm.
Available only online. *2502*

LITERATURINFORMATIONEN ZUR BERUFLICHEN BILDUNG.
W. Bertelsmann Verlag, Postfach 100633, 33506 Bielefeld, Germany. TEL 49-521-91101-0. FAX 49-521-9110179. URL: http://www.berufsbildung.de. *5512*

LITERATURSCHAU: MESSEN MECHANISCHER GROESSEN.
Bundesanstalt fuer Materialforschung und -pruefung, Unter den Eichen 87, 12205 Berlin, Germany. TEL 49-30-81043615. FAX 49-30-81041917. *2751*

LITERATURSCHAU: SCHWEISSEN UND VERWANDTE VERFAHREN.
Wirtschaftsverlag N W GmbH, Buergermeister-Smidt-Str. 74-76, 27568 Bremerhaven, Germany. TEL 49-471-945440. FAX 49-471-9454488. *5219*

LITERATURSCHAU ZERSTOERUNGSFREIE PRUEFUNG.
Wirtschaftsverlag N W GmbH, Buergermeister-Smidt-Str. 74-76, 27568 Bremerhaven, Germany. TEL 49-471-945440. FAX 49-471-9454488. *2751*

LITIGATION.
American Bar Association, Litigation Section, 750 N. Lake Shore Dr., Chicago, IL 60611. TEL 312-988-5555.
Vendor(s): West Group. *3984*

LITTERATUR PAA INDVANDRERSPROG I DANSKE FOLKEBIBLIOTEKER.
Dansk BiblioteksCenter as, Tempovej 7-11, 2750 Ballerup, Denmark. TEL 45-44-867777. FAX 45-44-867892. *4496*

LIVESTOCK, DAIRY AND POULTRY SITUATION & OUTLOOK.
U.S. Department of Agriculture, Economic Research Service, c/o Debbie Haugan, Rm. 110, 1301 New York Ave., N.W., Washington, DC 20005-4788. TEL 202-219-4060.
Vendor(s): Information Access Co., Knight-Ridder Information, Inc. *281*

LLOYDS BANK ANNUAL REVIEW.
Lloyds Bank plc., Economics Department, P.O. Box 19, Hays Lane House, 1 Hays Ln., London SE1 2HA, England. TEL 44-171-407-1000. FAX 44-171-357-4378.
Vendor(s): Information Access Co. *1153*

LOCAL COMPETITION REPORT.
Capitol Publications Inc., Telecom Publishing Group, 1101 King St., Ste. 444, Box 1455, Alexandria, VA 22313-2055. FAX 703-739-6484. URL: http://www.telecommunications.com.
Vendor(s): Information Access Co., NewsNet. *2035*

LOCAL GOVERNMENT AND ENVIRONMENTAL REPORTS OF AUSTRALIA.
L B C Information Services, 50 Waterloo Rd., N. Ryde, N.S.W. 2113, Australia. TEL 61-2-99366444. FAX 61-2-98882229.
Vendor(s): Info-One International Pty Ltd.. *4134*

LOCAL GOVERNMENT CHRONICLE.
E M A P - Business Publishing Ltd., 33-39 Bowling Green Ln., London EC1R 0DA, England. TEL 44-171-505-8400. FAX 44-171-278-9509. *6218*

LOCAL GOVERNMENT FOCUS (GOLD EDITION).
Eryl Morgan Publications Pty. Ltd., 1 Timmins St., Northcote 3070, Australia. TEL 61-3-9486-1211. URL: http://www.loc-gov-focus.aus.net. *6218*

LOCAL GOVERNMENT FOCUS (GREEN EDITION).
Eryl Morgan Publications Pty. Ltd., 1 Timmins St., Northcote 3070, Australia. TEL 61-3-9486-1211. URL: http://www.loc-gov-focus.aus.net. *6218*

LOCKERGNOME'S FREE WINDOWS 95 - N T E-ZINE.
Box 63, Hudson, IA 50643. URL: http://www.lockergnome.com/.
Available only online. *2215*

LODGING HOSPITALITY.
Penton Publishing Co., 1100 Superior Ave., Cleveland, OH 44114-2543. TEL 216-696-7000. FAX 216-696-8765.
Vendor(s): Information Access Co., Knight-Ridder Information, Inc., UMI. *3732*

LOG CABIN CHRONICLES.
Box 706, Derby Line, VT 05830. TEL 819-876-2538. URL: http://www.tomifobia.com.
Available only online. *7216*

SERIALS AVAILABLE ONLINE 10157

LOGGING & SAWMILLING JOURNAL.
P.O. Box 86670 Stn. Main North Van, North Vancouver, BC V7M 2A7, Canada. URL: http://www.forestnet.com/log&saw/index.html?24,18. *3172*

LOGIBASE.
Services Documentaires Multimedia Inc., 75 Port-Royal E., bureau 300, Montreal, PQ H3L 3T1, Canada. TEL 514-382-0895. FAX 514-384-9139. URL: http://www.sdm.qc.ca. *2215*

LOGISTICS AND TRANSPORTATION REVIEW.
University of British Columbia, Centre for Transportation Studies, Vancouver, BC V6T 1Z2, Canada. TEL 604-822-4510. FAX 604-822-8521. Vendor(s): Information Access Co., UMI. *7033*

LOGISTICS MANAGEMENT.
Cahners Publishing Company (Newton), Division of Reed Elsevier Inc., 275 Washington St., Newton, MA 02158-1630. TEL 617-558-4477. FAX 617-558-4327. URL: http://www.logisticsmgmt.com. Vendor(s): Information Access Co.. *7033*

LONDON MAGAZINE.
Blackburn Magazine Group, 231 Dundas St., Ste. 203, London, ON N6A 1H1, Canada. TEL 519-679-4901. FAX 519-434-7842. *3263*

LONG ISLAND BUSINESS NEWS.
Long Island Commercial Review, Inc., 2150 Smithtown Ave., Ronkonkoma, NY 11779-7327. TEL 516-737-1700. FAX 516-737-1890. URL: http://www.libiznews.com. Vendor(s): Information Access Co.. *982*

LONGEVITY.
Longevity International, Ltd., 277 Park Ave., 4th Fl., New York, NY 10172. TEL 212-702-6000. FAX 212-702-6282. Available only online. *3441*

LOOKOUT - FOODS.
Marketing Intelligence Service Ltd., 6473D Route 64, Naples, NY 14512-9726. TEL 716-374-6326. FAX 716-374-5217. URL: http://ourworld.compuserve.com/homepages/mktgintelsvc. *3119*

LOOKOUT - NONFOODS.
Marketing Intelligence Service Ltd., 6473D Route 64, Naples, NY 14512-9726. TEL 716-374-6326. FAX 716-374-5217. URL: http://ourworld.compuserve.com/homepages/mktgintelsvc. *512*

LOS ANGELES.
11100 Santa Monica Blvd., 7th Fl., Los Angeles, CA 90025. TEL 310-477-1181. Vendor(s): Information Access Co., Lexis-Nexis, UMI. *3377*

LOS ANGELES BUSINESS JOURNAL.
California Business Journals, 5700 Wilshire Blvd., Ste. 170, Los Angeles, CA 90010. Vendor(s): Information Access Co.. *1269*

THE LOS ANGELES TIMES INDEX.
U M I, 300 N. Zeeb Rd., Ann Arbor, MI 48106-1346. TEL 313-761-4700. FAX 800-864-0019. Vendor(s): Knight-Ridder Information, Inc.. *3884*

LOUGHBOROUGH UNIVERSITY GAZETTE.
Loughborough University, Loughborough, Leicestershire LE11 3TU, England. TEL 44-1509-222224. FAX 44-1509-223902. URL: http://www.lboro.ac.uk/service/publicity/gazette.html. Available only online. *1959*

LOUISIANA BUSINESS DIRECTORY.
American Business Directories, 5711 S. 86th Circle, Box 27347, Omaha, NE 68127. TEL 402-593-4600. FAX 402-331-5481. *1694*

LOUISIANA LAW REVIEW.
Louisiana State University, Law Center, Baton Rouge, LA 70803. TEL 504-388-1683. FAX 504-388-1685. Vendor(s): Lexis-Nexis, West Group. *3985*

LOUISIANA MUSIC DIRECTORY.
Offbeat, Inc., 333 St. Charles Ave., Ste. 614, New Orleans, LA 70130. TEL 504-522-5533. FAX 504-522-1159. URL: http://www.offbeat.com. *5408*

LOUISVILLE MAGAZINE.
Louisville Magazine, Inc., 137 W. Muhammed Ali, Louisville, KY 40202. TEL 502-625-0100. FAX 502-625-0109. Vendor(s): Knight-Ridder Information, Inc., Lexis-Nexis, UMI. *3378*

LOUNGE LOS ANGELES.
Box 39532, Los Angeles, CA 90039. TEL 213-243-9671. URL: http://www.val.net/lounge. *3732*

LOVTIDENDE A FOR KONGERIGET DANMARK.
Justisministeriet, Sekretariatet for Retsinformation, Axeltorv 6, 5. sal, D-1609 Copenhagen V, Denmark. TEL 45-33-32-52-22. FAX 45-33-91-28-01. *3985*

LOVTIDENDE C FOR KONGERIGET DANMARK.
Justitsministeriet, Sekretariatet for Retsinformation, Axeltorv 6, 5. sal, DK-1609 Copenhagen V, Denmark. TEL 45-33-32-52-22. FAX 45-33-91-28-01. *4122*

LOW TEMPERATURE PHYSICS.
American Institute of Physics, One Physics Ellipse, College Park, MD 20740-3843. TEL 301-209-3000. URL: http://www.aip.org. *5842*

LOYOLA LAW REVIEW.
Loyola University, School of Law, 7214 St. Charles, New Orleans, LA 70118. TEL 504-861-5558. Vendor(s): West Group. *3985*

LOYOLA OF LOS ANGELES INTERNATIONAL AND COMPARATIVE LAW JOURNAL.
Loyola of Los Angeles Law School, 919 South Albany St., Box 15019, Los Angeles, CA 90015-0019. TEL 213-736-1405. FAX 213-385-6247. Vendor(s): West Group. *3985*

LOYOLA UNIVERSITY CHICAGO LAW JOURNAL.
Loyola University Chicago, Law School, One E. Pearson St., Chicago, IL 60611. TEL 312-915-7183. FAX 312-915-7201. *3985*

LUMIERE.
URL: http://www.lumiere.com/. Available only online. *1925*

LUMPEN MAGAZINE.
Lumpen Media Group, 2558 W. Armitage Ave., Chicago, IL 60647. TEL 773-227-2072. FAX 773-227-2072. URL: http://www.lumpen.com. *5942*

LUNAR AND PLANETARY INFORMATION BULLETIN.
Lunar and Planetary Institute, 3600 Bay Area Blvd., Houston, TX 77058-1113. TEL 713-486-2172. FAX 713-486-2186. URL: http://cass.jsc.nasa.gov/pub/publications/publications.html. *497*

LUNG.
Springer-Verlag, Medical Journals, 175 Fifth Ave., New York, NY 10010. TEL 212-460-1500. FAX 212-473-6272. URL: http://www.springer-ny.com. *5120*

LYON CHIRURGICAL.
Hotel Dieu, 69288 Lyon Cedex 02, France. TEL 33-4-72413188. FAX 33-4-72413136. URL: http://www.filnet.fr/ardiap. *5148*

M.
M2 Communications Ltd., P.O. Box 475, Coventry CV1 2ZW, England. TEL 44-1203-634700. FAX 44-1203-634144. URL: http://www.m2.com. *2035*

M C L C COMMUNICATIONS.
Gordon and Breach - Harwood Academic, Amsteldisk 166, 1st Fl., 1079 LH Amsterdam, Netherlands. URL: http://www.gbhap.com/MCLC_Communications/. *1784*

M C N: AMERICAN JOURNAL OF MATERNAL CHILD NURSING.
Lippincott - Raven Publishers, 227 E. Washington Sq., Philadelphia, PA 19106. TEL 215-238-4200. FAX 215-238-4227. URL: http://www.lrpub.com. *4940*

MELUS.
Society for the Study of the Multi-Ethnic Literature of the United States, 272 Bartlett Hall, Department of English, University of Massachusetts, Amherst, MA 01003. TEL 413-545-3166. FAX 413-545-3880. Vendor(s): Information Access Co., UMI. *4431*

M.E.N. MAGAZINE.
Seattle M.E.N., 7552 31st Ave., N.E., Seattle, WA 98115. TEL 206-522-9701. URL: http://www.vix.com/mensmag/. *5183*

M I R A AUTOMOBILE ABSTRACTS.
Motor Industry Research Association, Watling St., Nuneaton, Warwickshire CV10 0TU, England. FAX 44-1203-343772. Vendor(s): Data-Star, European Space Agency. *7054*

M I R A AUTOMOTIVE BUSINESS NEWS.
Motor Industry Research Association, Watling St., Nuneaton, Warwickshire CV10 0TU, England. FAX 44-1203-343772. Vendor(s): European Space Agency. *1055*

M I S QUARTERLY.
M I S Research Center, University of Minnesota, Carlson School of Management, 271 19th Ave. S, Minneapolis, MN 55455. TEL 612-624-2035. FAX 612-624-2056. URL: http://www.misq.org/. Vendor(s): Information Access Co., UMI. *1492*

M L A INTERNATIONAL BIBLIOGRAPHY OF BOOKS AND ARTICLES ON THE MODERN LANGUAGES AND LITERATURES.
Modern Language Association of America, 10 Astor Place, New York, NY 10003. TEL 212-475-9500. FAX 212-477-9863. *4496*

M L N.
Johns Hopkins University Press, Journals Publishing Division, 2715 N. Charles St., Baltimore, MD 21218. TEL 410-516-6987. FAX 410-516-6968. URL: http://muse.jhu.edu. Vendor(s): Information Access Co.. *4279*

M L O.
Medical Economics Publishing Co., Inc., 5 Paragon Dr., Montvale, NJ 07645. TEL 201-358-7200. FAX 201-573-0344. Vendor(s): Information Access Co.. *4901*

M P T REVIEW.
Navellier and Associates, Inc., 1 E. Liberty St., Reno, NV 89501-2110. FAX 702-785-2323. Vendor(s): NewsNet (IV48). *1394*

M R S INTERNET JOURNAL OF NITRIDE SEMICONDUCTOR RESEARCH.
Materials Research Society, 9800 McKnight Rd., Pittsburg, PA 15237. TEL 412-307-3003. FAX 412-307-3000. URL: http://nsr.mij.mrs.org/. Available only online. *2864*

M T I A C CURRENT AWARENESS BULLETIN.
U.S. Department of Defense, Manufacturing Technology Information Analysis Center, URL: http://mtiac.hq.iitri.com/mtiac/cab/index.html. Available only online. *2892*

M T I ECONEWS.
Magyar Tavirati Iroda, Pl. Naphegy ter. 8, 1016 Budapest, Hungary. TEL 36-1-1188204. FAX 36-1-2613690. *1214*

M UND A - MESSEPLANER INTERNATIONAL.
M und A Verlag fuer Messen, Ausstellungen und Kongresse GmbH, Postfach 101528, 60015 Frankfurt a.M., Germany. TEL 49-69-759502. FAX 49-69-75951280. *1694*

M WEB MAGAZINE.
70 Triq il-Kosbor, Zonqor, Marsascala ZBR 09, Malta. FAX 356-639740. URL: http://www.geocities.com/siliconValley/7041/mwm.html. Available only online. *2145*

MAANEDSBLADET PRESS.
Maanedsbladet Press, Studiestraede 24, 1, DK-1455 Copenhagen K, Denmark. TEL 45-33-11-58-11. FAX 45-33-11-68-66. *3275*

MAC NET JOURNAL.
White Rabbit Publishing, 3711 N. Mullen St., Tacoma, WA 98407. TEL 206-752-6402. URL: http://www.blol.com/web_mnj. Available only online. *2198*

THE MACCABEAN.
Freeman Center for Strategic Studies, Box 35661, Houston, TX 77235-5661. TEL 713-723-6016. URL: http://www.freeman.io.com. *5942*

SERIALS AVAILABLE ONLINE

MCCALL'S.
McCall's Magazine, 110 Fifth Ave., New York, NY 10011. TEL 212-499-2000.
Vendor(s): Information Access Co. *7326*

MACCENTRAL.
6526 Roslyn Rd., Halifax, NS B3L 2M9, Canada. TEL 902-455-9169. URL: http://www.maccentral.com.
Available only online. *2198*

MACCOM.
URL: http://www.maccom.net.
Available only online. *2198*

MCGRAW-HILL'S BIOTECHNOLOGY NEWSWATCH.
McGraw-Hill Companies, Energy & Business Newsletters, 1221 Ave. of the Americas, 36th Fl., New York, NY 10020. TEL 212-512-6410.
Vendor(s): Dow Jones News Retrieval (BIO), Knight-Ridder Information, Inc. (File no.624/McGRAW-HILL PUBLICATIONS ONLINE), Lexis-Nexis (BIOTEC), NewsNet (BT08). *685*

MACHINE DESIGN.
Penton Publishing Co., 1100 Superior Ave., Cleveland, OH 44114-2543. TEL 216-696-7000. FAX 216-696-8765.
Vendor(s): Information Access Co., Knight-Ridder Information, Inc., UMI. *2892*

MACHINE LEARNING.
Kluwer Academic Publishers Boston, Box 358, Accord Sta., Hingham, MA 02018-0358. TEL 617-871-6300. FAX 617-871-6528. URL: http://mlis.www.wkap.nl. *2086*

MACHINE LEARNING ONLINE.
Kluwer Academic Publishers Boston, Box 358, Accord Sta., Hingham, MA 02018-0358. TEL 617-871-6600. FAX 617-871-6528. URL: http://mlis.www.wkap.nl.
Available only online. *2087*

MACHINE VISION & APPLICATIONS.
Springer-Verlag, Heidelberger Platz 3, 14197 Berlin, Germany. TEL 49-30-82787-0. FAX 49-30-82787448. URL: http://link.springer.de. *2162*

MACINTOSH TIPS & TRICKS.
Giles Road Press, 520 Palm Dr., Apt. 3, Wickenburg, AZ 85390-2432. TEL 520-684-1011. FAX 520-684-3965. URL: http://www.intac.com/~gilesrd/. *2198*

MACINTOUCH.
Macintouch Verlag, Birkenweg 2, CH-8304 Wallisellen, Switzerland. TEL 01-8305600. FAX 01-8305458. URL: http://www.macintouch.com. *2198*

THE MCKINSEY QUARTERLY.
McKinsey & Co. Inc., 55 E. 52nd St., New York, NY 10022. TEL 212-446-7000.
Vendor(s): Information Access Co., UMI. *1492*

MACLEAN'S.
Maclean Hunter Ltd., Maclean Hunter Bldg., 777 Bay St., Toronto, ON M5W 1A7, Canada. TEL 416-596-5021. FAX 416-596-5516. URL: http://www.canoe.ca/macleans.
Vendor(s): Information Access Co., Lexis-Nexis, Southam Electronic Publishing, UMI. *3263*

MACROMOLECULES.
American Chemical Society, 1155 16th St., N.W., Washington, DC 20036. TEL 800-333-9511. FAX 614-447-3671.
Vendor(s): STN International (CJACS). *1818*

MCTRANS: CENTER FOR MICROCOMPUTERS IN TRANSPORTATION. NEWSLETTER.
University of Florida, Transportation Research Center, 512 Weil Hall, Gainesville, FL 32611-2083. TEL 904-392-0378. FAX 904-392-3224. *7033*

MACUSER.
Ziff-Davis Publishing (San Francisco), 50 Beale St., 14th Fl., San Francisco, CA 94105-1813. TEL 415-378-5600.
Vendor(s): Information Access Co. *2198*

MACWEEK.
Coastal Associates Publishing, L.P., One Park Ave., New York, NY 10016. TEL 212-503-3500.
Vendor(s): Information Access Co., Lexis-Nexis. *2198*

MACWORLD.
Macworld Communications, 501 Second St., Ste. 500, San Francisco, CA 94107. TEL 415-243-0505. URL: http://www.macworld.com.
Vendor(s): Information Access Co., UMI. *2199*

THE MAGAZINE ANTIQUES.
Brant Publications, Inc., 575 Broadway, 5th Fl., New York, NY 10012. TEL 212-941-2800.
Vendor(s): Information Access Co. *341*

MAGAZINE ARTICLE SUMMARIES.
EBSCO Publishing, 10 Estes St., Box 682, Ipswich, MA 01938. TEL 508-356-6500. FAX 508-356-6565. URL: http://www.epnet.com.
Vendor(s): Ovid Technologies, Inc. (PMRO). *18*

MAGAZINE INDEX.
Information Access Company, 362 Lakeside Dr., Foster City, CA 94404. TEL 415-378-5200. FAX 415-378-5369.
Vendor(s): Knight-Ridder Information, Inc. (File no.47), Lexis-Nexis, Ovid Technologies, Inc. (MAGS). *6290*

MAGAZINE WORLD.
International Federation of the Periodical Press, Queen's House, 55-56 Lincolns Inn Fields, London WC2A 3LJ, England. TEL 44-171-404-4169. FAX 44-171-404-4170. *6277*

MAGAZINES IN SPECIAL MEDIA.
U.S. Library of Congress, National Library Service for the Blind and Physically Handicapped, Washington, DC 20542. TEL 202-707-5100. FAX 202-707-0712. *3459*

MAGICAL BLEND.
Magical Blend Publishers, 133 1/2 Broadway, Chico, CA 95928. TEL 916-893-9037. FAX 916-894-9076. URL: http://www.eden.com; http://www.magicalblend.com. *5458*

MAGILL'S CINEMA ANNUAL.
Gale Research, 835 Penobscot Bldg., 645 Griswold St., Detroit, MI 48226-4094. FAX 800-414-5043.
Vendor(s): Knight-Ridder Information, Inc. *5339*

MAGNETIC AND ELECTRICAL SEPARATION.
Gordon and Breach - Harwood Academic, Amsteldisk 166, 1st Fl., 1079 LH Amsterdam, Netherlands. URL: http://www.gbhap.com/Magnetic_Electrical_Separation/. *5814*

MAGNETIC RESONANCE MATERIALS IN PHYSICS, BIOLOGY AND MEDICINE.
Chapman & Hall, Journals Department 2-6 Boundary Row, London SE1 8HN, England. TEL 44-171-8560066. FAX 44-171-5229623. URL: http://www.chaphall.com/chaphall/journals.html. *5853*

MAGNNET.
Colonnaden 25, 20354 Hamburg, Germany. TEL 49-40-357197-44. FAX 49-40-357197-46. URL: http://www.magnnet.com.
Available only online. *3287*

MAGYAR ELEKTRONIKUS TOZSDE.
Pf. 311, Budapest 1536, Hungary. TEL 361-252-6697. URL: http://www.metpress.hu.
Available only online. *1395*

MAIL & GUARDIAN.
M & G Media Ltd., P.O. Box 32362, Braamfontein 2017, South Africa. TEL 27-11-4037111. FAX 27-11-4031025. URL: http://www.mg.co.za/mg/ *3356*

MAIL ORDER AND HOME SHOPPING: THE INTERNATIONAL MARKET.
Euromonitor, 60-61 Britton St., London EC1M 5NA, England. TEL 44-171-251-8024. FAX 44-171-608-3149. URL: http://www.euromonitor.com.
Vendor(s): Data-Star, Knight-Ridder Information, Inc. *1537*

MAIN GROUP CHEMISTRY NEWS COMMUNICATIONS.
Gordon and Breach - Harwood Academic, Amsteldisk 166, 1st Fl., 1079 LH Amsterdam, Netherlands. URL: http://www.gbhap.com/Main_Gro Chemistry_News_Communications/. *1785*

MAINE BUSINESS DIRECTORY.
American Business Directories, 5711 S. 86th Circle, Box 27347, Omaha, NE 68127. TEL 402-593-4600. FAX 402-331-5481. *1695*

MAINE LAW REVIEW.
University of Maine, School of Law, 246 Deering Ave., Portland, ME 04102. TEL 207-780-4357.
Vendor(s): Lexis-Nexis, West Group. *3986*

MAINE TIMES.
Maine Times, Inc., Box 350, 9 Union St., Hallowell, ME 04347. FAX 207-623-8970.
Vendor(s): UMI. *2941*

MAINFRAME COMPUTING.
Worldwide Videotex, Box 3273, Boynton Beach, FL 33424-3273. TEL 407-738-2276.
Vendor(s): Data-Star, Information Access Co., Knight-Ridder Information, Inc., NewsNet (EC87). *2179*

MAIZE ABSTRACTS.
CAB International, Wallingford, Oxon. OX10 8DE, England. TEL 44-1491-832111. FAX 44-1491-826090. URL: http://www.cabi.org.
Vendor(s): DIMDI, European Space Agency, Knight-Ridder Information, Inc., STN International. *178*

MAJOR 20TH-CENTURY WRITERS.
Gale Research, 835 Penobscot Bldg., 645 Griswold St., Detroit, MI 48226-4094. TEL 313-961-2242. FAX 800-414-5043.
Vendor(s): Lexis-Nexis (GALBIO). *4432*

MAKE-UP AND COLOUR COSMETICS: THE INTERNATIONAL MARKET.
Euromonitor, 60-61 Britton St., London EC1M 5NA, England. TEL 44-171-251-8024. FAX 44-171-608-3149. URL: http://www.euromonitor.com.
Vendor(s): Data-Star, Knight-Ridder Information, Inc. *507*

MAKING EYES AT THE MOON.
Available only online. *4345*

MAKING THE ROUNDS IN HEALTH, FAITH AND ETHICS.
Park Ridge Center, 211 E. Ontario St., Ste. 800, Chicago, IL 60611-3219. TEL 312-266-2222. FAX 312-266-6086.
Vendor(s): Information Access Co.. *4705*

MALARIA & TROPICAL DISEASE WEEKLY.
Charles W. Henderson, Ed. & Pub., Box 5528, Atlanta, GA 31107-0528. TEL 404-377-8895. FAX 404-378-5411. URL: http://www.newsfile.com. *4840*

MALT ADVOCATE.
Malt Society, 3416 Oak Hill Rd., Emmaus, PA 18049. TEL 610-967-1083. *524*

MAMMALIAN GENOME.
Springer-Verlag, Life Science Journals, 175 Fifth Ave., New York, NY 10010. TEL 212-460-1500. FAX 212-473-6272. URL: http://www.springer-ny.com. *773*

MANAGE.
National Management Association, 2210 Arbor Blvd., Dayton, OH 45439. TEL 513-294-0421.
Vendor(s): Information Access Co., UMI. *1492*

MANAGED CARE OUTLOOK.
Capitol Publications Inc., 1101 King St., Ste. 444, Alexandria, VA 22314. TEL 703-683-4100. FAX 703-739-6501.
Vendor(s): Information Access Co., NewsNet (HH12) *3716*

MANAGED CARE WEEK.
Atlantic Information Services, Inc., 1100 17th St., N.W., Ste. 300, Washington, DC 20036. TEL 202-775-9008. FAX 202-331-9542. URL: http://www.aispub.com.
Vendor(s): Information Access Co.. *3825*

MANAGED HEALTHCARE NEWS.
Quadrant HealthCom, 105 Raider Blvd., Belle Mead, NJ 08502-1510. TEL 908-874-0707. FAX 908-874-5611.
Vendor(s): Information Access Co. *4705*

MANAGED NETWORK SERVICES NEWS.
Phillips Business Information, Inc., 1201 Seven Locks Rd., Potomac, MD 20854. TEL 301-424-3338. FAX 301-309-3847. *2136*

MANAGEMENT ACCOUNTING.
Chartered Institute of Management Accountants, c/o Management Accounting, 63 Portland Pl., London W1N 4AB. TEL 44-171-637-2311. FAX 44-171-495-6098. URL: http://www.cima.org.uk/inst.htm. Vendor(s): UMI. *1094*

MANAGEMENT ACCOUNTING.
Institute of Management Accountants, 10 Paragon Dr., Montvale, NJ 07645-1760. TEL 201-573-9000. FAX 201-573-0639. URL: http://www.imanet.org; http://www.rutgers.edu/Accounting/raw/ima/maraw.htm. Vendor(s): Information Access Co., UMI. *1094*

MANAGEMENT ACCOUNTING RESEARCH.
Academic Press Ltd., 24-28 Oval Rd., London NW1 7DX, England. TEL 44-171-267-4466. FAX 44-171-482-2293. URL: http://www.hbuk.co.uk/ap/mar; http://www.europe.idealibrary.com/ *1094*

MANAGEMENT AND MARKETING ABSTRACTS.
Pira International, Randalls Rd., Leatherhead, Surrey KT22 7RU, England. TEL 44-1372-802050. FAX 44-1372-802239. URL: http://www.pira.co.uk/. Vendor(s): Data-Star, GBI. *1057*

MANAGEMENT CONTENTS.
Information Access Company, 362 Lakeside Dr., Foster City, CA 94409. TEL 415-378-5200. FAX 415-378-5369. Available only online. Vendor(s): Data-Star (MGMT), Knight-Ridder Information, Inc. (File no.75), Ovid Technologies, Inc. (MGMT). *1057*

MANAGEMENT DECISION.
M C B University Press Ltd., 60-62 Toller Ln., Bradford, W. Yorks BD8 9BY, England. TEL 44-1274-777700. FAX 44-1274-785200. URL: http://www.mcb.co.uk. Vendor(s): Information Access Co.. *1493*

MANAGEMENT EXPRESS.
Anbar Electronic Intelligence, 60-62 Toller Lane, Bradford, West Yorkshire, England. TEL 44-1274-777700. FAX 44-1274-785200. URL: http://www.anbar.co.uk/anbar.htm. Available only online. *1493*

MANAGEMENT INTERNATIONAL REVIEW.
Betriebswirtschaftlicher Verlag Dr. Th. Gabler GmbH, Abraham-Lincoln-Str. 46, 65189 Wiesbaden, Germany. TEL 49-611-7878129. FAX 49-611-7878423. Vendor(s): Information Access Co., UMI. *1493*

MANAGEMENT MATTERS.
Marton Allen Associates, InfoTeam Inc., Box 15640, Plantation, FL 33318-5640. TEL 954-473-9560. FAX 954-473-0544. Vendor(s): Data-Star, Human Resources Information Network, Information Access Co., NewsNet (MT11). *1494*

MANAGEMENT QUARTERLY.
National Rural Electric Cooperative Association, 4301 Wilson Blvd., Arlington, VA 22203-1860. TEL 703-907-5500. Vendor(s): Information Access Co., UMI. *1494*

MANAGEMENT REVIEW.
American Management Association, 1601 Broadway, New York, NY 10019. TEL 212-586-8100. FAX 212-903-8168. Vendor(s): Information Access Co., UMI. *1494*

MANAGEMENT SERVICES.
Institute of Management Services, 1 Cecil Ct., London Rd., Enfield, Mddx., England. TEL 44-181-366-1260. FAX 44-181-367-8149. Vendor(s): UMI. *1494*

MANAGEMENT TODAY.
Institute of Management Foundation, 2 Savoy Ct., 3rd. Fl., Strand, London, England. TEL 44-171-497-0580. FAX 44-171-497-0463. Vendor(s): UMI. *1494*

MANAGERIAL LAW.
Barmarick Publications, Enholmes Hall, Patrington, E. Yorks HU12 0PR, England. TEL 44-1964-630033. Vendor(s): Lexis-Nexis. *1444*

MANAGING INTELLECTUAL PROPERTY.
Euromoney Publications plc., Nestor House, Playhouse Yard, London EC4V 5EX, England. TEL 44-171-779-8686. FAX 44-171-779-8500. Vendor(s): UMI. *5587*

MANAGING OFFICE TECHNOLOGY.
Penton Publishing Co., 1100 Superior Ave., Cleveland, OH 44114-2543. TEL 216-696-7000. FAX 216-696-7648. Vendor(s): Information Access Co., Knight-Ridder Information, Inc., UMI. *1558*

MANITOBA BUSINESS MAGAZINE.
470 River Ave., 3rd Fl., Winnipeg, MB R3L 0C8, Canada. TEL 204-477-4620. Vendor(s): Information Access Co., Lexis-Nexis. *1496*

MANITOBA DECISIONS - CIVIL AND CRIMINAL CASES.
Western Legal Publications, 301-1 Alexander St., Vancouver, BC V6A 1B2, Canada. TEL 604-687-5671. FAX 604-687-2796. *4134*

MANITOBA REPORTS.
Maritime Law Book Ltd., Box 302, Fredericton, NB E3B 4Y9, Canada. TEL 506-453-9921. FAX 506-453-9525. Vendor(s): QL Systems Ltd.. *3987*

MANUELLE MEDIZIN.
Springer-Verlag, Heidelberger Platz 3, 14197 Berlin, Germany. TEL 49-30-82787-0. FAX 49-30-82787448. *5044*

MANUFACTURING AUTOMATION.
Vital Information Publications, 754 Caravel Ln., Foster City, CA 94404. TEL 415-345-7018. FAX 415-345-7018. Vendor(s): Data-Star, Information Access Co., Knight-Ridder Information, Inc., NewsNet (MG17). *1537*

MANUFACTURING CHEMIST.
Miller Freeman Technical Ltd., Miller Freeman House, 30 Calderwood St., London SE18 6QH, England. TEL 44-181-855-7777. FAX 44-181-316-3206. Vendor(s): Information Access Co.. *2768*

MANUFACTURING ENGINEERING.
Society of Manufacturing Engineers, One SME Dr., Box 930, Dearborn, MI 48121-0930. TEL 313-271-1500. FAX 313-271-2861. URL: http://www.sme.org/ Vendor(s): UMI. *2731*

MANUFACTURING NEWS.
Publishers & Producers, Box 36, Annandale, VA 22003. TEL 703-750-2664. FAX 703-750-0064. Vendor(s): Information Access Co.. *1590*

MAPLE ORCHARD.
Loyal Ontario Group Interested in Computers Inc. (LOGIC), P.O. Box 958, Thornhill, ON L3T 4A5, Canada. TEL 416-323-0828. *2199*

MARANATHA CHRISTIAN JOURNAL.
Matrix Development, 12240 Perris Blvd., Ste. 112, Moreno Valley, CA 92557. TEL 909-247-0958. FAX 909-242-5538. URL: http://www.pe.net/mcj. Available only online. *6433*

MARINE AND FRESHWATER BEHAVIOUR AND PHYSIOLOGY.
Gordon and Breach - Harwood Academic, Amstelđisk 166, 1st Fl., 1079 LH Amsterdam, Netherlands. URL: http://www.gbhap.com/Marine_Freshwater_Behaviour_Physiology_A_B/. *613*

MARINE BIOLOGY.
Springer-Verlag, Heidelberger Platz 3, 14197 Berlin, Germany. TEL 49-30-82787-0. FAX 49-30-82787448. URL: http://link.springer.de. *613*

MARINE FISHERIES REVIEW.
U.S. National Marine Fisheries Service, Scientific Publications Office, 7600 Sandpoint Way, N.E., Bin C15700, Seattle, WA 98115. TEL 206-526-6107. FAX 206-526-6426. Vendor(s): Information Access Co.. *3073*

MARINE LOG.
Simmons - Boardman Publishing Corp., 345 Hudson St., New York, NY 10014-4502. TEL 212-620-7200. Vendor(s): Lexis-Nexis. *7157*

MARINEFACTS.
Running End Ltd., Box 257, Crownsville, MD 21032-0257. TEL 410-923-1325. URL: http://www.rngend.com. *6840*

MARITIME INFORMATION REVIEW.
Maritime Information Centre, Bibliotheek T U Delft, Mekelweg 2, 2628 CD Delft, Netherlands. TEL 31-15-2786663. FAX 31-15-2786855. URL: http://www.library.tudelft/oudbouw/mic.htp. Vendor(s): European Space Agency. *7054*

MARKET: AFRICA - MID-EAST.
The P R S Group, Market: newsletters Box 248, East Syracuse, NY 13057-0248. TEL 315-431-0511. FAX 315-431-0200. URL: http://www.prsgroup.com. Vendor(s): CompuServe, Inc., Data-Star, Information Access Co., Knight-Ridder Information, Inc.. *1341*

MARKET: ASIA PACIFIC.
The P R S Group, Market: newsletters Box 248, East Syracuse, NY 13057-0248. TEL 315-431-0511. FAX 315-431-0200. URL: http://www.prsgroup.com. Vendor(s): Data-Star, Information Access Co., Knight-Ridder Information, Inc., NewsNet. *1341*

MARKET CHARTS.
Market Charts, Inc., 350 Hudson St., New York, NY 10014. TEL 212-243-0829. *1395*

MARKET DIRECTION REPORTS.
Euromonitor, 60-61 Britton St., London EC1M 5NA, England. TEL 44-171-251-8024. FAX 44-171-608-3149. URL: http://www.euromonitor.com. Vendor(s): Data-Star, Knight-Ridder Information, Inc.. *1538*

MARKET: EUROPE.
Market: Newsletters, Box 248, East Syracuse, NY 13057-0248. TEL 607-277-0934. FAX 607-277-0935. Vendor(s): CompuServe, Inc., Data-Star, Information Access Co., Knight-Ridder Information, Inc., NewsNet. *1341*

MARKET INTELLIGENCE.
Mintel International Group Ltd., 18-19 Long Ln., London EC1A 9HE, England. TEL 44-171-606-4533. FAX 44-171-606-5932. URL: http://www.cityscape.co.uk/users/ca93/. *1538*

MARKET: LATIN AMERICA.
The P R S Group, Market: newsletters Box 248, East Syracuse, NY 13057-0248. TEL 315-431-0511. FAX 315-431-0200. URL: http://www.prsgroup.com. Vendor(s): CompuServe, Inc., Data-Star, Information Access Co., Knight-Ridder Information, Inc., NewsNet. *1341*

MARKET LETTER.
URL: http://www.qadas.com/~jwalker/newslett.html. Available only online. *1395*

MARKET RESEARCH ABSTRACTS.
Market Research Society, 15 Northburgh St., London EC1V 0AH, England. TEL 44-171-490-4911. FAX 44-171-490-0608. Vendor(s): Data-Star, Knight-Ridder Information, Inc.. *1057*

MARKET RESEARCH EUROPE.
Euromonitor, 60-61 Britton St., London EC1M 5NA, England. TEL 44-171-251-8024. FAX 44-171-608-3149. URL: http://www.euromonitor.com. Vendor(s): Lexis-Nexis. *1538*

MARKET RESEARCH SOCIETY. JOURNAL.
Market Research Society, 15 Northburgh St., London EC1V 0AH, England. TEL 44-171-4904911. FAX 44-171-490-0608. Vendor(s): Information Access Co.. *1538*

SERIALS AVAILABLE ONLINE

MARKET SCREEN.
Market Guide Inc., 49 Glen Head Rd., Glen Head, NY 11545. TEL 516-759-1253. FAX 516-676-9240. *1395*

MARKETING.
Haymarket Publishing Ltd., 174 Hammersmith Rd., London W6 7JP, England. TEL 44-171-413-4307. FAX 44-171-413-4509.
Vendor(s): Information Access Co., MediaStream. *1538*

MARKETING COMPUTERS.
B P I Communications, Inc. (New York), 1515 Broadway, New York, NY 10036. TEL 212-764-7300.
Vendor(s): Information Access Co.. *2127*

MARKETING MANAGEMENT.
American Marketing Association, 250 S. Wacker Dr., Chicago, IL 60606-5819. TEL 312-648-0536. FAX 312-993-7542. URL: http://www.ama.org.
Vendor(s): UMI. *1540*

MARKETING NEWS.
American Marketing Association, 250 S. Wacker Dr., Ste. 200, Chicago, IL 60606. TEL 312-648-0536. FAX 312-993-7542. URL: http://www.ama.org/pubs/mn/pub2.html.
Vendor(s): Information Access Co., Lexis-Nexis, UMI. *1540*

MARKETING RESEARCH.
American Marketing Association, 250 S. Wacker Dr., Ste. 200, Chicago, IL 60606. TEL 312-648-0536. FAX 312-993-7542. URL: http://www.ama.org/pubs/mr/index.html.
Vendor(s): UMI. *1540*

MARKETING SERIES.
Natural Resources Institute, Central Ave., Chatham Maritime, Kent ME4 4TB, England. TEL 44-1634-880088. FAX 44-1634-880066. URL: http://www.nri.org. *1540*

MARKETING UPDATE NEWSLETTER.
Exton Enterprises, P.O. Box 394, Mt. Ommaney, Qld. 4074, Australia. URL: http://www.gil.com.au/comm/eemall.
Available only online. *1540*

MARKETING WEEK.
Centaur Communications Ltd., 50 Poland St., London W1V 4AX, England. TEL 44-171-287-9800. FAX 44-171-439-1480. URL: http://www.marketing-week.co.uk/mw0001/
Vendor(s): UMI. *1541*

MARKETPLACE MAGAZINE.
A D D Inc., 211 N. Lynndale Dr., Ste. 8, Appleton, WI 54913-1897. TEL 414-735-5969. FAX 414-735-5970.
Vendor(s): UMI. *984*

MARKETSEARCH.
Arlington Management Publications, 1 Hay Hill, Berkeley Sq., London W1X 7LF, England. TEL 44-171-495-1940. FAX 44-171-409-2557. *1057*

MARKT & WIRTSCHAFT.
Industrie- und Handelskammer Koeln, Unter Sachsenhausen 10-26, 50667 Cologne, Germany. TEL 0221-1640-0. FAX 0221-1640123. *1192*

MARQUETTE LAW REVIEW.
Marquette University, Law School, 1103 W. Wisconsin Ave., Milwaukee, WI 53233. TEL 414-288-5143. FAX 414-288-5914. URL: http://www.mu.edu/dept/law/
Vendor(s): West Group. *3987*

MARRIAGE PARTNERSHIP.
Christianity Today, Inc., 465 Gundersen Dr., Carol Stream, IL 60188. TEL 630-260-6200. FAX 630-260-0114. URL: http://www.christianity.net/mp. *4626*

MARTINDALE-HUBBELL LAW DIRECTORY.
Martindale-Hubbell, A Division of Reed Elsevier Inc., 121 Chanlon Rd., New Providence, NJ 07974. FAX 908-464-3553. URL: http://www.martindale.com.
Vendor(s): Lexis-Nexis. *3987*

MARTINDALE: THE EXTRA PHARMACOPOEIA.
Royal Pharmaceutical Society of Great Britain, 1 Lambeth High St., London SE1 7JN, England. TEL 071-735-9141. FAX 071-735-7629.
Vendor(s): Data-Star, Knight-Ridder Information, Inc. (File no.141). *5677*

MARYLAND BUSINESS & LIVING.
Philos Publications Inc., c/o D.N. Kuryk, 5 Light St., Ste. 950, Baltimore, MD 21202.
Vendor(s): Knight-Ridder Information, Inc.. *984*

MARYLAND BUSINESS DIRECTORY.
American Business Directories, 5711 S. 86th Circle, Box 27347, Omaha, NE 68127. TEL 402-593-4600. FAX 402-331-5481. *1696*

MARYLAND LAW REVIEW.
University of Maryland, School of Law, 500 W. Baltimore St., Baltimore, MD 21201. TEL 410-706-7414.
Vendor(s): West Group. *3988*

MASS HIGH TECH.
Mass Tech Communications, 200 High St., 4th Fl., Boston, MA 02110-3036. TEL 617-478-0430. FAX 617-478-0438. URL: http://www.boston.com/mht. *6966*

MASSACHUSETTS BUSINESS DIRECTORY.
American Business Directories, 5711 S. 86th Circle, Omaha, NE 68127. TEL 402-593-4600. FAX 402-331-5481. *1696*

MASSACHUSETTS C P A REVIEW.
Massachusetts Society of Certified Public Accountants, Inc., 105 Chauncy St., 10th Fl., Boston, MA 02111-1742. TEL 617-556-4000. FAX 617-556-4126.
Vendor(s): UMI. *1094*

MASSACHUSETTS LAWYER WEEKLY.
Lawyers Weekly Publications, 41 West St., Boston, MA 02111. TEL 617-451-7300. FAX 617-451-7324.
Vendor(s): Lexis-Nexis. *3988*

MASSACHUSETTS REVIEW.
Massachusetts Review, Inc., Memorial Hall, University of Massachusetts, Amherst, MA 01003. TEL 413-545-2689.
Vendor(s): UMI. *4345*

MASTERS ABSTRACTS INTERNATIONAL.
U M I, 300 N. Zeeb Rd., Ann Arbor, MI 48106. TEL 313-761-4700. FAX 800-864-0019.
Vendor(s): Knight-Ridder Information, Inc. (File no.35), OCLC (EPIC), Ovid Technologies, Inc., STN International. *2502*

THE MASTHEAD.
National Conference of Editorial Writers, 6223 Executive Blvd., Rockville, MD 20852. TEL 301-984-3015. FAX 301-231-0026.
Vendor(s): Information Access Co.. *3876*

MATANGI TONGA.
Vava'u Press Ltd., P.O. Box 427, Nuku'alofa, Tonga. TEL 676-23101. FAX 676-24749. URL: http://www.netstorage.com/lcami/tonga/matangi. *3366*

MATCH.
Universitaet Bayreuth, Lehrstuhl II fuer Mathematik, 95540 Bayreuth, Germany. TEL 49-921-553387. FAX 49-921-553385. URL: http://www.mathe2.uni-bayreuth.de/match. *1759*

MATERIAL HANDLING ENGINEERING.
Penton Publishing Co., 1100 Superior Ave., Cleveland, OH 44114-2543. TEL 216-696-7000. FAX 216-696-8765.
Vendor(s): Information Access Co., UMI. *4548*

MATERIALS BUSINESS INFORMATION.
Institute of Materials, 1 Carlton House Terrace, London SW1Y 5DB, England. TEL 44-171-839-4071. FAX 44-171-839-2078.
Vendor(s): Knight-Ridder Information, Inc. (File no.269). *5219*

MATERIALS INFORMATION TRANSLATIONS SERVICE.
Institute of Materials, 1 Carlton House Terr., London SW1Y 5DB, England. TEL 44-171-839-4071. FAX 44-171-839-2289.
Vendor(s): Knight-Ridder Information, Inc.. *5200*

MATERIALS RESEARCH INNOVATIONS.
Springer-Verlag, Heidelberger Platz 3, 14197 Berlin, Germany. TEL 49-30-82787-0. FAX 49-30-82787448. URL: http://link.springer.de. *6544*

MATERIALS SCIENCE AND TECHNOLOGY.
Centro de Investigacion y Produccion de Materiales, Apdo. Postal 397, Merida 5101, Venezuela. TEL 58-74-712939. URL: http://www.ciens.ula.ve/~cires.html. *2866*

MATHEMATICA IN EDUCATION AND RESEARCH.
Springer-Verlag, 175 Fifth Ave., New York, NY 10010. TEL 212-460-1500. FAX 212-473-6272. URL: http://www.springer-ny.com. *4588*

MATHEMATICA PANNONICA.
Mathematical Institute of the Hungarian Academy of Sciences, P.O. Box 127, H-1364 Budapest, Hungary. URL: http://www.emis.de/journals/MP/. *4588*

MATHEMATICAL PHYSICS ELECTRONIC JOURNAL.
University of Texas - Austin, URL: http://www.ma.utexas.edu.mpej.
Available only online. *4590*

MATHEMATICAL REVIEWS.
American Mathematical Society, Box 6248, Providence, RI 02940-6248. TEL 401-455-4000. FAX 401-331-3842. URL: http://www.ams.org/.
Vendor(s): European Space Agency (File no.80/MATHSCI), Knight-Ridder Information, Inc., Ovid Technologies, Inc. (MATH). *4617*

MATHEMATICS OF COMPUTATION.
American Mathematical Society, Box 6248, Providence, RI 02940-6248. TEL 401-455-4000. URL: http://www.ams.org/mcom/. *4591*

MATHEMATISCHE ANNALEN.
Springer-Verlag, Heidelberger Platz 3, 14197 Berlin, Germany. TEL 49-30-82787-0. FAX 49-30-82787448. URL: http://link.springer.de. *4592*

MATHEMATISCHE ZEITSCHRIFT.
Springer-Verlag, Heidelberger Platz 3, 14197 Berlin, Germany. TEL 49-30-82787-0. FAX 49-30-82787448. URL: http://link.springer.de. *4592*

A MATTER OF FACT: STATEMENTS CONTAINING STATISTICS ON CURRENT SOCIAL, ECONOMIC AND POLITICAL ISSUES.
Pierian Press, Box 1808, Ann Arbor, MI 48106. TEL 313-434-5530. FAX 313-434-6409.
Vendor(s): OCLC. *3505*

THE MAUI WINDSURFING REPORT.
Box 1202, Kula, HI 96790. URL: http://maui.net/~mauiwind/MWR/mwr.html.
Available only online. *6874*

MAYAQUEST NEWS.
URL: http://www.mecc.com/mq97/mqemailmgr.html.
Available only online. *2518*

MEALEY'S DAUBERT REPORT.
Mealey Publications, Inc., 512 Lancaster Ave., Box 446, Wayne, PA 19087-0446. TEL 610-688-6566. FAX 610-688-7552. URL: http://www.mealeys.com.
Vendor(s): Lexis-Nexis (MEALEY), West Group. *3988*

MEALEY'S EMERGING INSURANCE DISPUTES.
Mealey's Publications, Inc., Box 446, Wayne, PA 19087-0446. TEL 610-688-6566. FAX 610-688-7552. URL: http://www.mealeys.com.
Vendor(s): Lexis-Nexis (MEALEY), West Group. *3825*

MEALEY'S EMERGING TOXIC TORTS.
Mealey Publications, Inc., Box 446, Wayne, PA 19087. TEL 610-688-6566. FAX 610-688-7552. URL: http://www.mealeys.com.
Vendor(s): Lexis-Nexis (MEALEY), West Group. *4062*

MEALEY'S INSURANCE LAW WEEKLY.
Mealey Publications, Inc., 512 W. Lancaster Ave., Box 446, Wayne, PA 19087-0446. TEL 610-688-6566. FAX 610-688-7552. URL: http://www.mealeys.com.
Vendor(s): Lexis-Nexis (MEALEY), West Group. *3825*

MEALEY'S INSURANCE SUPPLEMENT.
Mealey Publications, Inc., Box 446, Wayne, PA 19087. TEL 610-688-6566. URL: http://www.mealeys.com.
Vendor(s): Lexis-Nexis (MEALEY), West Group. *3825*

MEALEY'S INTERNATIONAL ARBITRATION REPORT.
Mealey Publications, Inc., Box 446, Wayne, PA 19087. TEL 610-688-6566. FAX 610-688-7552. URL: http://www.mealeys.com.
Vendor(s): Lexis-Nexis (MEALEY), West Group. *4122*

MEALEY'S LITIGATION REPORT: ASBESTOS.
Mealey Publications, Inc., Box 446, Wayne, PA 19087. TEL 610-688-6566. FAX 610-688-7552. URL: http://www.mealeys.com.
Vendor(s): Lexis-Nexis (MEALEY), West Group. *4062*

MEALEY'S LITIGATION REPORT: BAD FAITH.
Mealey Publications, Inc., Box 446, Wayne, PA 19087. TEL 610-688-6566. FAX 610-688-7552. URL: http://www.mealeys.com.
Vendor(s): Lexis-Nexis (MEALEY), West Group. *4063*

MEALEY'S LITIGATION REPORT: BIOTECHNOLOGY.
Mealey Publications, Inc., 512 W. Lancaster Ave., Box 446, Wayne, PA 19087-0446. TEL 610-688-6566. FAX 610-68807552. URL: http://www.mealeys.com.
Vendor(s): Lexis-Nexis (MEALEY), West Group. *3989*

MEALEY'S LITIGATION REPORT: BREAST IMPLANTS.
Mealey Publications, Inc., Box 446, Wayne, PA 19807. TEL 610-688-6566. FAX 610-688-7552. URL: http://www.mealeys.com.
Vendor(s): Lexis-Nexis (MEALEY), West Group. *4063*

MEALEY'S LITIGATION REPORT: DRUGS AND MEDICAL DEVICES.
Mealey Publications, Inc., Box 446, Wayne, PA 19087. TEL 215-688-6566. FAX 215-688-7552. URL: http://www.mealeys.com.
Vendor(s): Lexis-Nexis (MEALEY), West Group. *4084*

MEALEY'S LITIGATION REPORT: INSURANCE.
Mealey Publications, Inc., Box 446, Wayne, PA 19087. TEL 610-688-6566. FAX 610-688-7552. URL: http://www.mealeys.com.
Vendor(s): Lexis-Nexis (MEALEY), West Group. *4063*

MEALEY'S LITIGATION REPORT: INSURANCE FRAUD.
Mealey Publications, Inc., Box 446, Wayne, PA 19087. TEL 610-688-6566. FAX 610-688-7552. URL: http://www.mealeys.com.
Vendor(s): Lexis-Nexis (MEALEY), West Group. *4063*

MEALEY'S LITIGATION REPORT: INSURANCE INSOLVENCY.
Mealey Publications, Inc., Box 446, Wayne, PA 19087. TEL 610-688-6566. FAX 610-688-7552. URL: http://www.mealeys.com.
Vendor(s): Lexis-Nexis (MEALEY), West Group. *4063*

MEALEY'S LITIGATION REPORT: INTELLECTUAL PROPERTY.
Mealey Publications, Inc., Box 446, Wayne, PA 19087-0446. TEL 610-688-6566. FAX 610-688-7552. URL: http://www.mealeys.com.
Vendor(s): Lexis-Nexis (MEALEY), West Group. *5587*

MEALEY'S LITIGATION REPORT: LATEX.
Mealey Publications, Inc., 512 W. Lancaster Ave., Box 446, Wayne, PA 19087-0446. TEL 610-688-6566. FAX 610-688-7552. URL: http://www.mealeys.com.
Vendor(s): Lexis-Nexis (MEALEY), West Group. *3989*

MEALEY'S LITIGATION REPORT: LEAD.
Mealey Publications, Inc., Box 446, Wayne, PA 19087. TEL 610-688-6566. FAX 610-688-7552. URL: http://www.mealeys.com.
Vendor(s): Lexis-Nexis (MEALEY), West Group. *4063*

MEALEY'S LITIGATION REPORT: PATENTS.
Mealey Publications, Inc., P.O. Box 446, Wayne, PA 19087-0446. TEL 610-688-6566. FAX 610-688-7552. URL: http://www.mealeys.com.
Vendor(s): Lexis-Nexis (MEALEY), West Group. *5587*

MEALEY'S LITIGATION REPORT: PEDICLE SCREWS.
Mealey Publications, Inc., Box 446, Wayne, PA 19087. TEL 215-688-6566. FAX 215-688-7552. URL: http://www.mealeys.com.
Vendor(s): Lexis-Nexis (MEALEY), West Group. *4084*

MEALEY'S LITIGATION REPORT: REINSURANCE.
Mealey Publications, Inc., Box 446, Wayne, PA 19087. TEL 610-688-6566. FAX 610-688-7552. URL: http://www.mealeys.com.
Vendor(s): Lexis-Nexis (MEALEY), West Group. *4063*

MEALEY'S LITIGATION REPORT: SUPERFUND.
Mealey Publications, Inc., Box 446, Wayne, PA 19087. TEL 610-688-6566. FAX 610-688-7552. URL: http://www.mealeys.com.
Vendor(s): Lexis-Nexis (MEALEY), West Group. *4063*

MEALEY'S LITIGATION REPORT: TOBACCO.
Mealey Publications, Inc., Box 446, Wayne, PA 19087. TEL 215-688-6566. FAX 215-688-7552. URL: http://www.mealeys.com.
Vendor(s): Lexis-Nexis (MEALEY), West Group. *4063*

MEASUREMENT SCIENCE AND TECHNOLOGY.
I O P Publishing Ltd., Dirac House, Temple Back, Bristol BS1 6BE, England. TEL 44-117-929-7481. FAX 44-117-929-4318. URL: http://www.iop.org/ *3804*

MEAT AND POULTRY: THE INTERNATIONAL MARKET.
Euromonitor, 60-61 Britton St., London EC1M 5QU, England. TEL 44-171-251-8024. FAX 44-171-608-3149. URL: http://www.euromonitor.com.
Vendor(s): Data-Star, Knight-Ridder Information, Inc.. *3119*

MECHANICAL ENGINEERING.
American Society of Mechanical Engineers, 22 Law Dr., Fairfield, NJ 07007-2900. TEL 973-882-1167. FAX 973-882-1717. URL: http://www.asme.org.
Vendor(s): Information Access Co., Lexis-Nexis, UMI. *2893*

MECHANICAL ENGINEERING ABSTRACTS.
Cambridge Scientific Abstracts, 7200 Wisconsin Ave., 6th Fl., Bethesda, MD 20814. TEL 301-961-6700. FAX 301-961-6720. URL: http://www.csa.com.
Vendor(s): European Space Agency (File no.10/ISMEC), Knight-Ridder Information, Inc. (File no.14), STN International (ISMEC). *2751*

MECHANICAL SYSTEMS & SIGNAL PROCESSING.
Academic Press Ltd., 24-28 Oval Rd., London NW1 7DX, England. TEL 44-171-267-4466. FAX 44-171-482-2293. URL: http://www.hbuk.co.uk/ap/mssp; http://www.europe.idealibrary.com/. *2893*

MED AD NEWS.
Engel Publishing Partners, 820 Bear Tavern Rd., W. Trenton, NJ 08628. TEL 609-530-0044. FAX 609-530-0207.
Vendor(s): Information Access Co.. *1541*

MEDECONOMICS.
Haymarket Publishing Ltd., 174 Hammersmith Rd., London W6 7JP, England. TEL 44-171-413-4328. FAX 44-171-413-4013.
Vendor(s): Data-Star. *4706*

MEDIA CENTRAL.
Cowles Business Media, URL: http://www.mediacentral.com.
Available only online. *3378*

MEDIA COMPUTING.
Dreamscape Net, 510 Woodhaven, Aptos, CA 95003. TEL 408-685-8818.
Available only online. *2171*

MEDIA INDUSTRY NEWSLETTER.
Phillips Business Information, Inc., 1201 Seven Locks Rd., Potomac, MD 20854. TEL 301-424-3338. FAX 301-309-3847. URL: http://www.phillips.com/pbi.htm.
Vendor(s): Information Access Co., NewsNet (PB14) *40*

MEDIA MONITOR.
Financial Times Telecoms & Media Publishing, Maple House, 149 Tottenham Court Rd., London W1P 9LL, England. TEL 0171-896-2234. FAX 0171-896-2256.
Vendor(s): Data-Star. *1998*

MEDIA PROFESSIONAL.
Audit Bureau of Circulations, 405 Lexington Ave., 48th Fl., New York, NY 10174-4805. URL: http://www.accessabc.com/ympmedia.html.
Available only online. *3876*

MEDIA WEEK.
E M A P Media, 33-39 Bowling Green Ln., London EC1R 0DA, England. TEL 44-171-505-8341. FAX 44-171-505-8363. *41*

MEDIAWEEK.
B P I Communications, Inc. (New York), 1515 Broadway, New York, NY 10036. TEL 212-536-5336. FAX 212-536-6594. URL: http://www.adweek.com/magazine/mediaweek.asp.
Vendor(s): Information Access Co., Knight-Ridder Information, Inc., Lexis-Nexis, UMI. *41*

MEDICAL AND HEALTH CARE BOOKS AND SERIALS IN PRINT.
R.R. Bowker, A Division of Reed Elsevier Inc., 121 Chanlon Rd., New Providence, NJ 07974. TEL 908-464-6800. FAX 908-665-3502. URL: http://www.reedref.com.
Vendor(s): Knight-Ridder Information, Inc., Ovid Technologies, Inc. (BBIP,ULRI). *4782*

MEDICAL AND PEDIATRIC ONCOLOGY.
John Wiley & Sons, Inc., Journals, 605 Third Ave., New York, NY 10158. TEL 212-850-6645. FAX 212-850-6021. *4982*

MEDICAL & PHARMACEUTICAL BIOTECHNOLOGY ABSTRACTS.
Cambridge Scientific Abstracts, 7200 Wisconsin Ave., 6th Fl., Bethesda, MD 20814. TEL 301-961-6700. FAX 301-961-6720. URL: http://www.csa.com.
Vendor(s): Knight-Ridder Information, Inc. (File no.76/LIFE SCIENCES COLLECTION), STN International (LIFESCI). *4782*

MEDICAL DEVICE APPROVAL LETTER.
Washington Information Source, 6506 Old Stage Rd., Ste. 100, Rockville, MD 20852-4326. TEL 301-770-5553.
Vendor(s): Information Access Co.. *4901*

MEDICAL DEVICE COMPANIES ANALYSIS NEWSLETTER.
M D I S Publications Ltd., MDIS House, City Fields Business Park, City Fields Way, Chichester, W. Sussex PO20 6FS, England. TEL 44-1243-533322. FAX 44-1243-533418. *3804*

MEDICAL DEVICE COMPANIES ANALYSIS PROFILES.
M D I S Publications Ltd., MDIS House, City Fields Business Park, City Fields Way, Chichester, W. Sussex PO20 6FS, England. TEL 44-1243-533322. FAX 44-1243-533418. *3804*

MEDICAL DEVICES, DIAGNOSTICS & INSTRUMENTATION REPORTS: THE GRAY SHEET.
F-D-C Reports, Inc., 5550 Friendship Blvd., Ste. One, Chevy Chase, MD 20815. FAX 301-664-7238.
Vendor(s): Data-Star (FDCR), Knight-Ridder Information, Inc. (File no.187), Lexis-Nexis, Ovid Technologies, Inc. (FDCR). *4707*

MEDICAL ECONOMICS.
Medical Economics Publishing Co., Inc., 5 Paragon Dr., Montvale, NJ 07645. TEL 201-358-7200. FAX 201-573-1045.
Vendor(s): Information Access Co., Knight-Ridder Information, Inc.. *4708*

MEDICAL EDUCATION ONLINE.
URL: http://www.utmb.edu/meo/
Available only online. *4708*

MEDICAL IMAGE ANALYSIS.
Oxford University Press, Academic Division, Great Clarendon St., Oxford OX2 6DP, England. TEL 44-1865-267907. FAX 44-1865-267485. URL: http://www.oup.co.uk/journals. *5111*

MEDICAL JOURNAL OF AUSTRALIA.
Australasian Medical Publishing Co., Private Bag 901, N. Sydney, N.S.W. 2059, Australia. TEL 61-2-99548666. FAX 61-2-99567644. URL: http://www.library.usyd.edu.au/mja/. *4709*

MEDICAL LETTER ON DRUGS AND THERAPEUTICS (ENGLISH EDITION).
Medical Letter, Inc., 1000 Main St., New Rochelle, NY 10801. TEL 914-235-0500. FAX 914-632-1733.
Vendor(s): UMI. *5677*

MEDICAL MARKETING & MEDIA.
C P S Communications, Inc., 7200 W. Camino Real, Ste. 215, Boca Raton, FL 33433. TEL 407-368-9301. FAX 407-368-7870.
Vendor(s): Information Access Co., Lexis-Nexis, UMI. *5677*

MEDICAL MICROBIOLOGY AND IMMUNOLOGY.
Springer-Verlag, Heidelberger Platz 3, 14197 Berlin, Germany. TEL 49-30-82787-0. FAX 49-30-82787448. URL: http://link.springer.de/link/service/journals/00430/index.htm. *4799*

MEDICAL ONCOLOGY.
Chapman & Hall, Journals Department 2-6 Boundary Row, London SE1 8HN, England. TEL 44-171-8560066. FAX 44-171-5229623. URL: http://www.chaphall.com/chaphall/journals.html. *4983*

MEDICAL OUTCOMES AND GUIDELINES ALERT.
Faulkner & Gray, Healthcare Information Center 11 Penn Plaza, 17th Fl., New York, NY 10001. TEL 212-967-7000.
Vendor(s): Information Access Co., Knight-Ridder Information, Inc., NewsNet. *4709*

MEDICAL REPORTER.
Box 370314, Denver, CO 80237. URL: http://www.dash.com/tmr.
Available only online. *4710*

MEDICAL SCIENCE RESEARCH.
Chapman & Hall, Journals Department 2-6 Boundary Row, London SE1 8HN, England. TEL 44-171-8560066. FAX 44-171-5229623. URL: http://www.chaphall.com/chaphall/journals.html.
Vendor(s): DIMDI, Data-Star, Ovid Technologies, Inc.. *4711*

MEDICAL TEXTILES.
International Newsletters, P.O. Box 133, Witney OX8 6ZH, England. TEL 44-1993-824130. FAX 44-1993-824150.
Vendor(s): Data-Star, Information Access Co., Knight-Ridder Information, Inc.. *4711*

MEDICAL TRIBUNE.
Medical Tribune, Inc., 100 Ave. of the Americas, 9th Fl., New York, NY 10013-1606. TEL 212-674-8500. FAX 212-529-8490. URL: http://www.medtrib.com/ *4711*

MEDICAL UPDATE.
Benjamin Franklin Literary and Medical Society, Inc., Medical Education and Research Foundation, Box 567, 1100 Waterway Blvd., Indianapolis, IN 46202. FAX 317-637-0126.
Vendor(s): Information Access Co.. *5787*

MEDICAL UTILIZATION MANAGEMENT.
Faulkner & Gray, Healthcare Information Center 11 Penn Plaza, 17th Fl., New York, NY 10001. TEL 212-967-7000.
Vendor(s): Information Access Co., Knight-Ridder Information, Inc., NewsNet. *4712*

MEDICAL WASTE NEWS.
Business Publishers, Inc., 951 Pershing Dr., Silver Spring, MD 20910-4432. TEL 301-587-6300. FAX 301-585-9075.
Vendor(s): Data-Star, Information Access Co., Knight-Ridder Information, Inc., NewsNet (EV30). *2987*

MEDICATED SKINCARE: THE INTERNATIONAL MARKET.
Euromonitor, 60-61 Britton St., London EC1M 5NA, England. TEL 44-171-251-8024. FAX 44-171-608-3149. URL: http://www.euromonitor.com.
Vendor(s): Data-Star, Knight-Ridder Information, Inc. *5677*

MEDICINAL AND AROMATIC PLANTS ABSTRACTS.
National Institute of Science Communication, Council of Scientific and Industrial Research, K.S. Krishnan Rd., New Delhi 110 012, India. TEL 91-11-5726014. FAX 91-11-5787062. *4782*

MEDICINE (BALTIMORE).
Williams & Wilkins, 351 W. Camden St., Baltimore, MD 21201-2436. TEL 410-528-4068. FAX 410-528-4452. URL: http://www.wwilkins.com.
Vendor(s): Ovid Technologies, Inc.. *4713*

MEDICINE AND SCIENCE IN SPORTS AND EXERCISE.
American College of Sports Medicine, Box 1440, Indianapolis, IN 46206-1440. TEL 317-637-9200. FAX 317-634-7817.
Vendor(s): Ovid Technologies, Inc.. *5131*

MEDICINE AUSTRALIA.
N R D G P, 186 Molesworth St., Lismore, N.S.W. 2480, Australia. URL: http://www.om.com.au/MedicineAu.
Available only online. *4713*

MEDICINE ON THE NET.
C O R Healthcare Resources, Box 40959, Santa Babara, CA 93140-0959. TEL 805-564-2177. URL: http://www.mednet-i.com. *4848*

MEDIO AMBIENTE.
Universidad Austral de Chile, Instituto de Ecologia y Evolucion, Facultad de Ciencias, Casilla 567, Valdivia, Chile. FAX 56-63-221344. *2941*

MEDISTAT.
M D I S Publications Ltd., MDIS House, City Fields Business Park, City Fields Way, Chichester, W. Sussex PO20 6FS, England. TEL 44-1243-533322. FAX 44-1243-532124. *4714*

MEDIUM AEVUM.
Society for the Study of Mediaeval Languages and Literature, c/o Dr. D.G. Pattison, Hon. Treas., Magdalen College, Oxford OX1 4AU, England. TEL 44-1865-276087.
Vendor(s): Information Access Co., UMI. *4434*

MEDSUPPORT F S F NEWSLETTER.
URL: http://people.delphi.com/suemark/news.htm.
Available only online. *4715*

MEETINGS AND CONVENTIONS.
Reed Travel Group, Part of the Reed Elsevier group 500 Plaza Dr., Secaucus, NJ 07096. TEL 201-902-1700. FAX 201-319-1796. URL: http://www.traveler.net/mtc/index.html.
Vendor(s): Information Access Co.. *5171*

MEGAMOT.
Henrietta Szold Institute, 9 Columbia St., Kiryat Menachem, Jerusalem 96583, Israel. FAX 2-437698. URL: http://www.szold.org.il. *6720*

MEGAWATT DAILY.
Pasha Publications Inc., 1616 N. Ft. Myer Dr., Ste. 1000, Arlington, VA 22209-3107. TEL 703-528-1244. FAX 703-528-1253. *2690*

MEGAWATT WEEK.
Pasha Publications Inc., 1616 N. Ft. Myer Dr., Ste. 1000, Arlington, VA 22209-3107. TEL 703-528-1244. FAX 703-528-1253. *2690*

MELBOURNE UNIVERSITY LAW REVIEW.
University of Melbourne, Law School, Parkville 3052, Vic., Australia. TEL 61-3-93446593. FAX 61-3-93478087. URL: http://www.law.unimelb.edu.au/mulr.
Vendor(s): Lexis-Nexis, West Group. *3989*

MELTING POT MAG-E-ZINE.
Box 95, Gloucester, MA 01930. URL: http://www.manateepro.com.
Available only online. *5409*

MEMBRANE & SEPARATION TECHNOLOGY NEWS.
Business Communications Co., Inc. (Norwalk), 25 Van Zant St., Norwalk, CT 06855. TEL 203-853-4266. FAX 203-853-0348.
Vendor(s): Data-Star, Information Access Co., Knight-Ridder Information, Inc., NewsNet (BT05). *685*

MEMPHIS BUSINESS JOURNAL.
Mid-South Communications, Inc., 88 Union, Ste. 102, Memphis, TN 38103-5195. TEL 901-523-1000. FAX 901-526-5240.
Vendor(s): Information Access Co., Knight-Ridder Information, Inc., Lexis-Nexis, UMI. *984*

MENDELEEV COMMUNICATIONS.
Turpion - Moscow Ltd., 47 Leninsky prospekt, 117913 Moscow, Russia. TEL 7-95-1356417. FAX 7-95-1358860. URL: http://turpion.ioc.ac.ru. *1760*

MENOPAUSE NEWS.
Menopause News, 2074 Union St., San Francisco, CA 94123. FAX 415-567-2368.
Vendor(s): Information Access Co.. *7309*

MEN'S HEALTH.
Rodale Press, Inc., 33 E. Minor St., Emmaus, PA 18049. TEL 610-967-5171. FAX 610-967-7725.
Vendor(s): Information Access Co., UMI. *5174*

MEN'S TOILETRIES: THE INTERNATIONAL MARKET.
Euromonitor, 60-61 Britton St., London EC1M 5NA, England. TEL 44-171-251-8024. FAX 44-171-608-3149. URL: http://www.euromonitor.com.
Vendor(s): Data-Star, Knight-Ridder Information, Inc. *507*

MENTAL HEALTH LAW REPORTER.
Business Publishers, Inc., 951 Pershing Dr., Silver Spring, MD 20910-4464. TEL 301-587-6300. FAX 301-585-9075.
Vendor(s): NewsNet. *4064*

MENTAL HEALTH REPORT.
Business Publishers, Inc., 951 Pershing Dr., Silver Spring, MD 20910-4464. TEL 301-587-6300. FAX 301-585-9075.
Vendor(s): NewsNet. *6677*

MENTAL HEALTH WEEKLY.
Manisses Communications Group, Inc., Box 9758, Providence, RI 02906-9758. TEL 401-861-6020. FAX 401-861-6370. URL: http://www.manisses.com. *6136*

MENZ MAGAZINE.
3113124 Canada Inc., 4150 St. Catherine W., Ste. 610, Westmount, PQ H3Z 2Y5, Canada. TEL 514-937-3131. FAX 514-449-3515. URL: http://www.menz.com. *5179*

MERCER BUSINESS MAGAZINE.
Mercer County Chamber of Commerce, 2550 Kuser Rd., Box 8307, Trenton, NJ 08650. TEL 609-586-2056. FAX 609-586-8052.
Vendor(s): Knight-Ridder Information, Inc., UMI. *1192*

MERCER LAW REVIEW.
Mercer University, Walter F. George School of Law, Macon, GA 31207. TEL 912-752-2622. URL: http://www.mercer.edu/~law/review.html.
Vendor(s): West Group. *3989*

MERCK INDEX: AN ENCYCLOPEDIA OF CHEMICALS AND DRUGS.
Merck Publishing Co., Box 2000, Rg 7-220, Rahway, NJ 07065. TEL 908-594-4600.
Vendor(s): CISTI, Knight-Ridder Information, Inc., Ovid Technologies, Inc. (MRCK), STN International, Telesystemes - Questel. *5702*

MERGERS & ACQUISITIONS.
Investment Dealers' Digest, 2 World Trade Center, 18th Fl., New York, NY 10048. TEL 212-432-0845. FAX 212-321-2336.
Vendor(s): Information Access Co., UMI. *984*

MERGERS & ACQUISITIONS REPORT.
Investment Dealers' Digest, 2 World Trade Center, 18th Fl., New York, NY 10048-0638. TEL 212-432-0045. FAX 212-321-2336.
Vendor(s): Information Access Co., UMI. *984*

MERGERS AND RESTRUCTURINGS.
Securities Data Publishing, 40 W. 57th St., 11th Fl., New York, NY 10019. TEL 212-765-5311. FAX 212-765-6123.
Vendor(s): Information Access Co., NewsNet. *984*

MERRILL'S EDGAR ADVISOR.
Merrill Corporation, One Merrill Circle, St. Paul, MN 55108. FAX 612-644-1633. URL: http://www.merrillcorp.com. *2157*

THE MESH.
URL: http://www.albany.globalone.net/themesh/. Available only online. *2137*

MESH.
Experimenta Media Arts, P.O. Box 1102, St. Kilda South, Vic. 3182, Australia. TEL 61-3-95255025. FAX 61-3-95255105. URL: http://www.peg.apc.org/~experimenta. *5339*

MESSAGES FROM THE FUTURE.
URL: http://www.islandnet.com/rhb/future_page.html. Available only online. *2137*

THE MESSENGER.
URL: http://members.tripod.com/'dowjones/home.htm. Available only online. *1396*

METABOLISM: CLINICAL AND EXPERIMENTAL.
W.B. Saunders Co., Curtis Center, 3rd Fl., Independence Sq. W., Philadelphia, PA 19106-3399. TEL 215-238-7800. FAX 215-238-6445. *4890*

METAL CENTER NEWS.
Hitchcock Publishing, 191 S. Gary Ave., Carol Stream, IL 60188. TEL 708-665-1000. FAX 708-462-2225.
Vendor(s): Information Access Co.. *5201*

METAL HEAT TREATING.
Penton Publishing Co., 1100 Superior Ave., Cleveland, OH 44114-2543. TEL 216-696-7000.
Vendor(s): Information Access Co.. *5202*

METALLURGIA: THE JOURNAL OF METALS TECHNOLOGY, METAL FORMING AND THERMAL PROCESSING.
Argus Business Publications Ltd., Queensway House, 2 Queensway, Redhill, Surrey RH1 1QS, England. TEL 44-1737-768611. FAX 44-1737-761685.
Vendor(s): Information Access Co.. *5203*

METALS ABSTRACTS.
Cambridge Scientific Abstracts, 7200 Wisconsin Ave., Bethesda, MD 20814. TEL 301-961-6750. FAX 301-961-6720. URL: http://www.csa.com.
Vendor(s): CEDOCAR, CISTI, Data-Star (META), European Space Agency (File no.3/METADEX), FIZ Technik (META), Knight-Ridder Information, Inc. (File no.32/METADEX), Questel Orbit Inc. (MDEX), STN International (METADEX). *5220*

METALS ABSTRACTS INDEX.
Cambridge Scientific Abstracts, 7200 Wisconsin Ave., Bethesda, MD 20814. TEL 301-961-6750. FAX 301-961-6720. URL: http://www.csa.com.
Vendor(s): CEDOCAR, CISTI, Data-Star (META), European Space Agency (File no.3/METADEX), FIZ Technik (META), Knight-Ridder Information, Inc. (File no.32/METADEX), Questel Orbit Inc. (MDEX), STN International (METADEX). *5220*

METALS INDUSTRY NEWS.
Argus Business Media Ltd., Queensway House, 2 Queensway, Redhill, Surrey RH1 1QS, England. TEL 44-1737-768611. FAX 44-1737-761685.
Vendor(s): Information Access Co.. *5204*

METALS WEEK.
McGraw-Hill Companies, Commodity Services Group, 1221 Avenue of the Americas, 42nd Fl., New York, NY 10020. TEL 212-512-2000.
Vendor(s): Dow Jones News Retrieval (MW), Knight-Ridder Information, Inc. (File no.624/McGRAW-HILL PUBLICATIONS ONLINE), Lexis-Nexis (METLWK), NewsNet (ML01). *5307*

METAPHORIA.
RR1 Box 1010, Wells, VT 05774. URL: http://www.sover.net/~jozef. Available only online. *5737*

METEOR.
Box 822, Mountain View, CA 94042-0822. URL: http://www.globalgraphics.com/Zines/Meteor/ Available only online. *3378*

METEOROLOGICAL AND GEOASTROPHYSICAL ABSTRACTS.
American Meteorological Society, c/o Inforonics, Inc., 550 Newtown Rd., Littleton, MA 01460. TEL 508-486-8976. FAX 508-486-0027. URL: http://www.mganet.org.
Vendor(s): Knight-Ridder Information, Inc. (File no.29). *5248*

METHODS: A COMPANION TO METHODS IN ENZYMOLOGY.
Academic Press, Inc., Journal Division, 525 B St., Ste. 1900, San Diego, CA 92101-4495. TEL 619-230-1840. FAX 619-699-6800. URL: http://www.apnet.com/www/journal/me.htm; http://www.idealibrary.com/ *666*

METROPOLITAN HOME.
Hachette Filipacchi Magazines, Inc., 1633 Broadway, 41st Fl., New York, NY 10019. TEL 212-767-6000. FAX 212-767-5636.
Vendor(s): Information Access Co., UMI. *3848*

METROPOLITAN LIFE INSURANCE COMPANY. STATISTICAL BULLETIN S B.
Metropolitan Life Insurance Company, 1 Madison Ave., New York, NY 10010. TEL 212-578-5014. FAX 212-685-7987. URL: http://www.statbull.com.
Vendor(s): Information Access Co. *3839*

METROPOLITAN NEWS - ENTERPRISE.
Metropolitan News Co., 210 S. Spring St., Los Angeles, CA 90012-3710. TEL 213-628-4384.
Vendor(s): Lexis-Nexis (METNWS). *4084*

MEXICAN STUDIES.
University of California Press, Journals Division, 2120 Berkeley Way, No. 5812, Berkeley, CA 94720-5812. TEL 510-643-7154. FAX 510-642-9917. URL: http://library.berkeley.edu:8080/ucalpress/journals.
Vendor(s): Information Access Co. *3785*

MEXICO & N A F T A REPORT.
Lettres (U.K.) Ltd., 61 Old St., London EC1V 9HX, England. TEL 44-171-251-0012. FAX 44-171-253-8193.
Vendor(s): Lexis-Nexis. *1270*

MEXICO BUSINESS MONTHLY.
Kal Wagenheim, Ed. & Pub., 52 Maple Ave., Maplewood, NJ 07040. TEL 201-762-1565. FAX 201-762-9585.
Vendor(s): Information Access Co.. *1342*

MEXICO CONSENSUS ECONOMIC FORECAST.
Arizona State University, Economic Outlook Center, Box 874406, Tempe, AZ 85287-4406. TEL 602-965-5543. FAX 602-964-5458. URL: http://www.cob.asa.edu/seid/eoc/eocmex.html. *1271*

MEXICO SERVICE.
International Reports, Inc., 11300 Rockville Pike, Ste. 1100, Rockville, MD 20852-3035. TEL 301-816-8950. FAX 301-816-8945. *1396*

MEYLER'S SIDE EFFECTS OF DRUGS.
Elsevier Science B.V., Books Division, P.O. Box 211, 1000 AE Amsterdam, Netherlands. TEL 31-20-4853911. FAX 31-20-4853705. URL: http://www.elsevier.nl/.
Vendor(s): Data-Star (SEDB), Knight-Ridder Information, Inc. (File no.70/SEDBASE), Ovid Technologies, Inc. *5678*

MICHIGAN BAR JOURNAL.
State Bar of Michigan, 306 Townsend, Lansing, MI 48933. TEL 517-372-9030.
Vendor(s): West Group. *3989*

MICHIGAN BUSINESS DIRECTORY.
American Business Directories, 5711 S. 86th Circle, Box 27347, Omaha, NE 68127. TEL 402-593-4600. FAX 402-331-5481. *1697*

MICHIGAN C P A.
Michigan Association of C P A, Box 9054, 28116 Orchard Lake Rd., Farmington Hills, MI 48333. TEL 248-855-2288. FAX 248-855-9122.
Vendor(s): Information Access Co., UMI. *1094*

MICHIGAN CITIZEN.
Newday Publishing, 12541 Second, Box 03560, Highland Park, MI 48203. TEL 313-869-0033. FAX 313-869-0430.
Vendor(s): Lexis-Nexis (ETHNIC NEWSWATCH). *3028*

MICHIGAN COMPUTERUSER MAGAZINE.
Primetime Press, 500 Hickory, Box 597, Linden, MI 48451. TEL 810-735-9720. FAX 810-735-9720. URL: http://www.michcu.com. *2087*

MICHIGAN JOURNAL OF POLITICAL SCIENCE.
University of Michigan, Michigan Journal of Political Science, 5620 Haven Hall, Ann Arbor, MI 48109-1045. TEL 313-764-6386. URL: gopher://gopher.itd.umich.edu. *5944*

MICHIGAN LAW REVIEW.
Michigan Law Review Association, 625 South State St., Hutchins Hall, Ann Arbor, MI 48109-1215. TEL 313-763-5870. FAX 313-647-5817. URL: http://www.law.umich.edu/pubs/
Vendor(s): Information Access Co., Lexis-Nexis, West Group. *3990*

MICHIGAN LAWYERS WEEKLY.
Michigan Lawyers Weekly, 333 S. Washington Sq., No.300, Lansing, MI 48933. TEL 517-374-6200. FAX 517-374-6222.
Vendor(s): Lexis-Nexis. *3990*

MICHIGAN MEDICINE.
Michigan State Medical Society, P.O. Box 950, East Lansing, MI 48826-0950. TEL 517-337-1351. FAX 517-337-2490. URL: http://www.msms.org/ *4716*

MICHIGAN TODAY.
University of Michigan, Office of University Relations, News and Information Services, 412 Maynard St., Ann Arbor, MI 48109. TEL 313-764-0105. FAX 313-764-7084. URL: http://www.umich.edu/~newsinfo/MT/mtfpg.html. *1961*

MICHNET NEWS.
Merit Network, Inc., c/o Mariella Wells, Ed., 4251 Plymouth Rd., Ann Arbor, MI 48105-2785. TEL 313-764-9430. FAX 313-647-3185. URL: http://www.merit.edu/michnet/michnet.news/ *2137*

MICRO M D NEWSLETTER.
Micro M D Publishing, 170 University Ave. W, Waterloo, Ontario, Canada N2L 3E9.
Vendor(s): CompuServe, Inc., NewsNet. *4848*

MICROBIAL ECOLOGY.
Springer-Verlag, Life Science Journals, 175 Fifth Ave., New York, NY 10010. TEL 212-460-1500. FAX 212-473-6272. URL: http://link.springer.de/link/service/journals/00248/index.htm. *789*

MICROBIAL PATHOGENESIS.
Academic Press Ltd., 24-28 Oval Rd., London NW1 7DX, England. TEL 44-171-267-4466. FAX 44-171-482-2293. URL: http://www.hbuk.co.uk/ap/micpath; http://www.europe.idealibrary.com/. *789*

MICROBIOLOGY ABSTRACTS: SECTION A. INDUSTRIAL & APPLIED MICROBIOLOGY.
Cambridge Scientific Abstracts, 7200 Wisconsin Ave., 6th Fl., Bethesda, MD 20814. TEL 301-961-6750. FAX 301-961-6720. URL: http://www.csa.com.
Vendor(s): Knight-Ridder Information, Inc. (File no.76/LIFE SCIENCES COLLECTION), STN International (LIFESCI). *642*

MICROBIOLOGY ABSTRACTS: SECTION B. BACTERIOLOGY.
Cambridge Scientific Abstracts, 7200 Wisconsin Ave., 6th Fl., Bethesda, MD 20814. TEL 301-961-6750. FAX 301-961-6720. URL: http://www.csa.com.
Vendor(s): Knight-Ridder Information, Inc. (File no.76/LIFE SCIENCES COLLECTION), STN International (LIFESCI). *642*

MICROBIOLOGY ABSTRACTS: SECTION C. ALGOLOGY, MYCOLOGY AND PROTOZOOLOGY.
Cambridge Scientific Abstracts, 7200 Wisconsin Ave., 6th Fl., Bethesda, MD 20814. TEL 301-961-6750. FAX 301-961-6720. URL: http://www.csa.com.
Vendor(s): Knight-Ridder Information, Inc. (File no.76/LIFE SCIENCES COLLECTION), STN International (LIFESCI). *642*

SERIALS AVAILABLE ONLINE

MICROCHEMICAL JOURNAL.
Academic Press, Inc., Journal Division, 525 B St., Ste. 1900, San Diego, CA 92101-4495. TEL 619-230-1840. FAX 619-699-6800. URL: http://www.apnet.com/www/journal/mj.htm; http://www.idealibrary.com/ *797*

MICROCIRCULATION.
Chapman & Hall, 2-6 Boundary Row, London SE1 8HN, England. TEL 44-171-8650066. FAX 44-171-5229623. URL: http://www.chaphall.com/chaphall/journals.html. *4716*

MICROCOMPUTER ABSTRACTS.
Information Today, Inc., 143 Old Marlton Pike, Medford, NJ 08055. TEL 609-654-6266. FAX 609-654-4309.
Vendor(s): Knight-Ridder Information, Inc. (File no.233). *2095*

MICROPROCESSOR REPORT.
874 Gravenstein Hwy. So., Ste.14, Sebastopol, CA 95472. TEL 707-824-4004. FAX 707-823-0504. URL: http://www.MDRonline.com.
Vendor(s): Information Access Co.. *2191*

MICROSCALE THERMOPHYSICAL ENGINEERING.
Taylor & Francis Ltd., 1 Gunpowder Sq., London EC4A 3DE, England. TEL 44-171-5830490. FAX 44-171-5830858. URL: http://www.tandf.co.uk. *5842*

MICROSCOPY AND MICROANALYSIS.
Springer-Verlag, 175 Fifth Ave., New York, NY 10060. TEL 212-460-1500. FAX 212-533-5977. URL: http://link.springer.de/link/service/journals/10005/tocs/current.html. *3804*

MICROSCOPY MICROANALYSIS MICROSTRUCTURES.
Societe Francaise de Microscopie Electronique, Case 243, Universite Paris VI, 4 place Jussieu, 75252 Paris Cedex 05, France. TEL 30-1-46-70-28-44. FAX 30-1-46-70-88-46. URL: http://www.ed-phys.fr. *5865*

MICROSOFT SYSTEMS JOURNAL.
Miller Freeman, 411 Bord Ave., San Mateo, CA 94402. TEL 415-358-9500. FAX 415-358-9865.
Vendor(s): Information Access Co.. *2145*

MICROSTATION MANAGER.
MicroManagement, Inc., Box 1536, Santa Fe, NM 87501. TEL 505-982-5181. FAX 505-986-3816. URL: http://www.copyright.com. *418*

MICROSYSTEM TECHNOLOGIES.
Springer-Verlag, Heidelberger Platz 3, 14197 Berlin, Germany. TEL 49-30-82787-0. FAX 49-30-82787448. URL: http://link.springer.de/link/service/journals/00542/index.htm. *2116*

MICROVASCULAR RESEARCH.
Academic Press, Inc., Journal Division, 525 B St., Ste. 1900, San Diego, CA 92101-4495. TEL 619-230-1840. FAX 619-699-6800. URL: http://www.apnet.com/www/journal/mr.htm; http://www.idealibrary.com/ *4822*

MICROWAVE JOURNAL (INTERNATIONAL EDITION).
Horizon - House - Publications, Inc., 685 Canton St., Norwood, MA 02062. TEL 617-769-9750. FAX 617-762-9230.
Vendor(s): Information Access Co. *2840*

MID-AMERICA COMMERCE & INDUSTRY.
M A C I Inc., 1824 Cheyenne Rd., Topeka, KS 66604. TEL 913-272-5280.
Vendor(s): UMI. *1271*

MID-AMERICAN JOURNAL OF BUSINESS.
Ball State University, Bureau of Business Research, Muncie, IN 47306. TEL 317-285-5926. FAX 317-285-8024. URL: http://www.bbr.bsu.edu/majb.
Vendor(s): UMI. *985*

THE MIDDLE EAST.
I.C. Publications Ltd., 7 Coldbath Sq., London EC1R 4LQ, England. TEL 44-171-713-7711. FAX 44-171-713-7898.
Vendor(s): Information Access Co. *4346*

MIDDLE EAST: ABSTRACTS AND INDEX.
Aristarchus Publications, Box 1020, Aberdeen, WA 98520. TEL 800-435-8221.
Vendor(s): Knight-Ridder Information, Inc. (File no.248). *18*

MIDDLE EAST BUSINESS INTELLIGENCE.
International Executive Reports Ltd., 717 D. St., N.W., Ste. 300, Washington, DC 20004-2807. TEL 202-628-6900. FAX 202-628-6618.
Vendor(s): Lexis-Nexis. *1342*

MIDDLE EAST ECONOMIC DIGEST.
M E E D Publications, 21 John St., London WC1N 2BP, England. TEL 44-171-470-6406. FAX 44-171-430-0337.
Vendor(s): Information Access Co. *1271*

MIDDLE EAST EXECUTIVE REPORTS.
International Executive Reports, Ltd., 717 D St., N.W., Ste. 300, Washington, DC 20004-2807. TEL 202-628-6900. FAX 202-628-6618.
Vendor(s): Lexis-Nexis, UMI, West Group. *1342*

MIDDLE EAST JOURNAL.
Middle East Institute, 1761 N St., N.W., Washington, DC 20036. TEL 202-785-0191.
Vendor(s): UMI. *6026*

MIDDLE EAST NEWS SERVICE.
Ramat Mamre, P.O. Box 18095, Kiryat Arba 10100, Israel. *5944*

MIDDLE EASTERN STUDIES.
Frank Cass, Newbury House, 890-900 Eastern Ave., Newbury Park, Ilford, Essex IG2 7HH, England. TEL 44-181-599-8836. FAX 44-181-599-0984. URL: http://www.frankcass.com.
Vendor(s): Information Access Co., UMI. *3658*

MIDDLESEX MAGAZINE.
Chronicle Communications, 615 Main St., Cromwell, CT 06416. TEL 209-635-1819. FAX 203-632-7203.
Vendor(s): UMI. *985*

MIDRANGE SYSTEMS.
Cardinal Business Media, Inc., 1300 Virginia Dr., Ste. 400, Fort Washington, PA 19034-3225. TEL 215-643-8000. FAX 215-643-3901.
Vendor(s): Information Access Co.. *2193*

MIDWEST QUARTERLY.
Pittsburg State University, Midwest Quarterly, Pittsburg, KS 66762. TEL 316-235-4317. FAX 316-232-7515.
Vendor(s): Information Access Co., UMI. *3786*

MIGRANTS AGAINST AIDS - HIV.
URL: http://users.aol.com/rsadki/index.html.
Available only online. *4840*

MIGRATION WORLD.
Center for Migration Studies, 209 Flagg Pl., Staten Island, NY 10304-1199. TEL 718-351-8800. FAX 718-667-4598. URL: http://www.cmsny.org/mw4.html.
Vendor(s): Information Access Co., UMI. *6054*

THE MILBANK QUARTERLY.
Blackwell Publishers, 238 Main St., Cambridge, MA 02142. TEL 617-547-7110. FAX 617-547-0789. URL: http://www.med.harvard.edu/publications/milbank.
Vendor(s): Information Access Co.. *5944*

MILITARY & COMMERCIAL FIBER BUSINESS.
Phillips Publishing, Inc., Defense - Aviation Group, 1111 19th St., N., Ste. 503, Arlington, VA 22209-1704. TEL 703-522-8333. FAX 703-522-6448.
Vendor(s): Data-Star, Knight-Ridder Information, Inc., NewsNet (DE06). *5276*

MILITARY LAW REVIEW.
U.S. Army, Judge Advocate General's School, Charlottesville, VA 22903-1781. TEL 804-972-6395.
Vendor(s): Lexis-Nexis, West Group. *4143*

MILITARY ROBOTICS NEWSLETTER.
L & B Limited, 19 Rock Creek Church Rd., N.W., Washington, DC 20011-6005. TEL 202-723-1600. FAX 202-726-2979.
Vendor(s): Information Access Co., Knight-Ridder Information, Inc. (NL0650), NewsNet (DE14). *2207*

MILITARY SPACE.
Pasha Publications Inc., 1616 N. Ft. Myer Dr., Ste. 1000, Arlington, VA 22209-3107. TEL 703-528-1244. FAX 703-528-1253. *5277*

MILITARY SPECIFICATIONS AND STANDARDS SERVICES NUMERIC INDEX.
Information Handling Services, 15 Inverness Way East, Englewood, CO 80150. TEL 303-790-0600. FAX 303-799-4085.
Vendor(s): Knight-Ridder Information, Inc. *5277*

MILITARY THOUGHT.
East View Publications, 3020 Harbor Lane N., Minneapolis, MN 55447. TEL 612-550-0961. FAX 612-559-2931. *5277*

MILJOERAPPORTEN.
Tomorrow Media, Kungsg. 27, S-111 56 Stockholm, Sweden. TEL 46-8-243480. FAX 46-8-24-08-09. URL: http://www.tomorrow.se. *2942*

MILLENNIAL PROPHECY REPORT.
Millennium Watch Institute, Box 34021, Philadelphia, PA 19101-4021. URL: http://www.channel1.com/mpr. *6355*

MILLING & BAKING NEWS.
Sosland Publishing Company, 4800 Main St., Ste. 100, Kansas City, MO 64112-2513. TEL 816-756-1000. FAX 816-756-0494.
Vendor(s): Information Access Co.. *3137*

MILLION DOLLAR DIRECTORY.
Dun and Bradstreet, 3 Sylvan Way, Parsippany, NJ 07054-3896. TEL 201-605-6000.
Vendor(s): Knight-Ridder Information, Inc. (File no.517), Questel Orbit Inc. *1698*

MIND.
Oxford University Press, Academic Division, Great Clarendon St., Oxford OX2 6DP, England. TEL 44-1865-267907. FAX 44-1865-267485. URL: http://www.oup.co.uk/journals.
Vendor(s): Information Access Co.. *5738*

MINDFIELD MAGAZINE.
Box 14114, Berkeley, CA 94712-5114. URL: http://www.dnai.com/'mindfld.
Available only online. *4346*

THE MINDFULNESS BELL.
Community of Mindful Living, Box 7355, Berkeley, CA 94707. TEL 510-527-3751. FAX 510-525-7129. URL: http://www.parallax.org. *6389*

MINDGATE.
29 Alma Rd., St. Kilda, Melbourne, Vic. 3182, Australia. URL: http://www.melbourne.net/mindgate/
Available only online. *4533*

MINE REGULATION REPORTER.
Pasha Publications Inc., 1616 N. Ft. Myer Dr., Ste. 1000, Arlington, VA 22209-3107. TEL 703-528-1244. FAX 703-528-1253. *5307*

MINERAL WATER: THE INTERNATIONAL MARKET.
Euromonitor, 60-61 Britton St., London EC1M 5NA, England. TEL 44-171-251-8024. FAX 44-171-608-3149. URL: http://www.euromonitor.com.
Vendor(s): Data-Star, Knight-Ridder Information, Inc. *524*

MINERALIUM DEPOSITA.
Springer-Verlag, Heidelberger Platz 3, 14197 Berlin, Germany. TEL 49-30-82787-0. FAX 49-30-82787448. URL: http://link.springer.de/link/service/journals/00126/index.htm. *2357*

THE MINERALOGICAL RECORD.
Mineralogical Record, Inc., 4631 Paseo Tubutama, Tucson, AZ 85740. FAX 520-544-0815.
Vendor(s): Information Access Co., UMI. *3671*

THE MINI-ANNALS OF IMPROBABLE RESEARCH.
Annals of Improbable Research, Box 380853, Cambridge, MA 02238. TEL 617-491-4437. FAX 617-661-0927. URL: http://www.improb.com/.
Available only online. *6545*

MINING ANNUAL REVIEW.
Mining Journal Ltd., 60 Worship St., London EC2A 2HD, England. TEL 44-171-216-6060. FAX 44-171-216-6050.
Vendor(s): Lexis-Nexis. *5309*

MINING MAGAZINE.
Mining Journal Ltd., 60 Worship St., London EC2A 2HD, England. TEL 44-171-216-6060. FAX 44-171-216-6050.
Vendor(s): Information Access Co., Lexis-Nexis. *5310*

MINISTERIALTIDENDE FOR KONGERIGET DANMARK.
Justisministeriet, Sekretariatet for Retsinformation, Axeltorv 6, 5. sal, DK-1609 Copenhagen V, Denmark. TEL 45-33-32-52-22. FAX 45-33-91-28-01. *6184*

MINNEAPOLIS - ST. PAUL CITYBUSINESS.
American City Business Journals, Inc. (Austin), 505 Powell St., Austin, TX 78703-5121. Vendor(s): CompuServe, Inc., Data-Star, Dow Jones News Retrieval, Knight-Ridder Information, Inc., Lexis-Nexis. *985*

MINNESOTA BUSINESS DIRECTORY.
American Business Directories, 5711 S. 86th Circle, Box 27347, Omaha, NE 68127. TEL 402-593-4600. FAX 402-331-5481. *1698*

MINNESOTA LAW REVIEW.
University of Minnesota, Law School, 229 19th Ave. S., Minneapolis, MN 55455. TEL 612-625-8034. Vendor(s): Lexis-Nexis, West Group. *3990*

MINNESOTA MEDICINE.
Minnesota Medical Association, 3433 Broadway St., N.E., Ste. 300, Minneapolis, MN 55413-1761. TEL 612-378-1875. FAX 612-378-3875. URL: http://www.mnmed.org. *4717*

MINORITY MARKETS ALERT.
E P M Communications, 160 Mercer St., 3rd. Fl., New York, NY 10012-3212. TEL 212-941-0099. FAX 212-941-1622. Vendor(s): Information Access Co., Knight-Ridder Information, Inc., Lexis-Nexis. *1542*

MIRROR MAGAZINE.
Box 182, Bolinas, CA 94118. URL: http://www.mirrormagazine.com. Available only online. *455*

MISSISSIPPI BUSINESS DIRECTORY.
American Business Directories, 5711 S. 86th Circle, Box 27347, Omaha, NE 68127. TEL 402-593-4600. FAX 402-331-5481. *1699*

MISSISSIPPI COLLEGE LAW REVIEW.
Mississippi College Law Review, 151 E. Griffith St., Jackson, MS 39201. TEL 601-925-7167. FAX 601-925-7113. Vendor(s): West Group. *3990*

MISSISSIPPI LAW JOURNAL.
Mississippi Law Journal, Box 849, University, MS 38677. TEL 601-232-6870. FAX 601-232-7948. URL: http://www.olemiss.edu/depts/law-school/LWjn.html. Vendor(s): West Group. *3991*

THE MISSISSIPPI QUARTERLY.
Mississippi State University, College of Arts and Sciences, Box 5272, Mississippi State, MS 39762. TEL 601-325-3069. FAX 601-325-3299. Vendor(s): Information Access Co., UMI. *4346*

MISSISSIPPI REVIEW.
University of Southern Mississippi, Center for Writers, Box 5144, Southern Sta., Hattiesburg, MS 39406. TEL 601-266-4321. FAX 601-266-5757. URL: http://sushi.st.usm.edu/mrw. *4436*

MISSOURI BUSINESS DIRECTORY.
American Business Directories, 5711 S. 86th Circle, Box 27347, Omaha, NE 68127. TEL 402-593-4600. FAX 402-331-5481. *1699*

MISSOURI LAW REVIEW.
University of Missouri at Columbia, School of Law, Box 203, Hulston Hall, Columbia, MO 65211. TEL 573-882-7055. FAX 573-882-9676. Vendor(s): West Group. *3991*

MITTEILUNGEN ZUR ASTRONOMIEGESCHICHTE.
Astronomische Gesellschaft, Arbeitskreis Astronomiegeschichte, Otterkiez 14, 14478 Potsdam, Germany. TEL 49-331-863199. URL: http://www.astro.uni-bonn.de/~pbrosche/aa/aa-ejourn.html. *497*

MITTELSTAENDISCHE UNTERNEHMEN.
Verlag Hoppenstedt GmbH, Havelstr. 9, 64295 Darmstadt, Germany. TEL 49-6151-380-0. FAX 49-6151-380-360. Vendor(s): Data-Star, GBI, Knight-Ridder Information, Inc. *1591*

MOBILE COMMUNICATIONS.
Financial Times Telecoms & Media Publishing, Maple House, 149 Tottenham Court Rd., London W1P 9LL, England. TEL 44-171-896-2234. FAX 44-171-896-2256. Vendor(s): Information Access Co. *1999*

MOBILE COMMUNICATIONS REPORT.
Warren Publishing, Inc., 2115 Ward Court, N.W., Washington, DC 20037. TEL 202-872-9200. FAX 202-293-3435. Vendor(s): Data-Star, Information Access Co., Knight-Ridder Information, Inc., NewsNet (TE32). *1999*

MOBILE MATTERS.
M2 Communications Ltd., P.O. Box 475, Coventry CV1 2ZW, England. TEL 44-1203-634700. FAX 44-1203-634144. URL: http://www.m2.com. *1999*

MOBILE PHONE NEWS.
Phillips Business Information, Inc., 1201 Seven Locks Rd., Potomac, MD 20854. TEL 301-424-3338. FAX 301-309-3847. Vendor(s): Information Access Co., NewsNet (TE25). *2036*

MOBILE SATELLITE NEWS (POTOMAC).
Phillips Business Information, Inc., 1201 Seven Locks Rd., Potomac, MD 20854. TEL 301-424-3338. FAX 301-309-3847. Vendor(s): Information Access Co., NewsNet (TE27). *2036*

MOBILE'S IN CHINA NEWSLETTER.
URL: http://homepages.tig.com/au/~moh1/index.html. Available only online. *1999*

MODEL RAILROADER.
Kalmbach Publishing Co., 21027 Crossroads Cir., Waukesha, WI 53187. TEL 414-796-8776. FAX 414-796-0126. Vendor(s): Information Access Co. *3672*

MODELLING & SIMULATION IN MATERIALS SCIENCE AND ENGINEERING.
I O P Publishing Ltd., Dirac House, Temple Back, Bristol BS1 6BE, England. TEL 44-117-929-7481. FAX 44-117-929-4318. URL: http://www.iop.org. *5815*

MODEM USER NEWS.
Worldwide Videotex, Box 3273, Boynton Beach, FL 33424-3273. TEL 407-738-2276. Vendor(s): Data-Star, Information Access Co., Knight-Ridder Information, Inc., NewsNet (EC97). *2179*

MODERN AGING RESEARCH.
John Wiley & Sons, Inc., Journals, 605 Third Ave., New York, NY 10158. TEL 212-475-7700. *3442*

MODERN BREWERY AGE.
Business Journals, 50 Day St., Box 5550, Norwalk, CT 06856. TEL 203-853-6015. Vendor(s): Information Access Co., Lexis-Nexis. *524*

MODERN BRIDE.
K-III Communications Corp., 745 Fifth Ave., New York, NY 10151. TEL 212-745-0100. Vendor(s): Knight-Ridder Information, Inc.. *4626*

MODERN CASTING.
American Foundrymen's Society, Inc., 505 State St., Des Plaines, IL 60016. TEL 708-824-0181. Vendor(s): Information Access Co.. *5205*

MODERN DRAMA.
University of Toronto Press, Journals Department, 5201 Dufferin St., North York ON M3H 5T8, Canada. TEL 416-667-7810. FAX 416-667-7881. Vendor(s): UMI. *4436*

MODERN FICTION STUDIES.
Johns Hopkins University Press, Journals Publishing Division, 2715 N. Charles St., Baltimore, MD 21218-4319. TEL 410-516-6987. FAX 410-516-6968. URL: http://muse.jhu.edu. *4436*

MODERN HEALTHCARE (YEAR).
Crain Communications, Inc. (Chicago), 740 N. Rush St., Chicago, IL 60611-2590. TEL 312-649-5341. FAX 312-280-3189. Vendor(s): Information Access Co.. *3717*

MODERN JUDAISM.
Johns Hopkins University Press, Journals Publishing Division, 2715 N. Charles St., Baltimore, MD 21218. TEL 410-516-6987. FAX 410-516-6968. URL: http://muse.jhu.edu. *3029*

MODERN LANGUAGE QUARTERLY.
Duke University Press, Box 90660, Durham, NC 27708-0660. TEL 919-687-3600. FAX 919-688-4574. URL: http://www.duke.edu/web/dupress/ Vendor(s): Information Access Co. *4436*

MODERN MACHINE SHOP.
Gardner Publications, Inc., 6915 Valley Ave., Cincinnati, OH 45244-3029. TEL 513-527-8800. FAX 513-527-8801. Vendor(s): Information Access Co.. *4549*

MODERN MATERIALS HANDLING.
Cahners Publishing Company (Newton), Division of Reed Elsevier Inc., 275 Washington St., Newton, MA 02158-1630. TEL 617-558-4734. FAX 617-558-4327. URL: http://www.mmh.com. Vendor(s): Information Access Co.. *4549*

MODERN MATURITY.
American Association of Retired Persons, 601 E St., N.W., Washington, DC 20049. TEL 202-728-4700. URL: http://www.aarp.org/mmaturity. Vendor(s): Information Access Co., UMI. *3442*

MODERN PAINT AND COATINGS.
Intertec Publishing Corp. (Atlanta), 6151 Powers Ferry Rd., N.W., Atlanta, GA 30339-2941. TEL 770-955-2500. FAX 770-955-0400. Vendor(s): Information Access Co., UMI. *5554*

MODERN PLASTICS.
McGraw-Hill Companies, 1221 Ave. of the Americas, New York, NY 10020. TEL 212-512-6245. FAX 212-512-6111. URL: http://www.modplas.com. Vendor(s): Dow Jones News Retrieval (MP), Knight-Ridder Information, Inc. (MP), Lexis-Nexis (MODPLA), NewsNet (CH23). *5880*

MODERN POWER SYSTEMS.
Wilmington Business Publishing, Apex House, London Rd., Northfleet, Kent DA11 9JA, England. TEL 44-1322-277788. FAX 44-1474-569418. Vendor(s): Information Access Co.. *2674*

MODERN TIRE DEALER.
Bill Communications, Inc. (Akron), 341 White Pond Dr., Box 3599, Akron, OH 44309-3599. TEL 330-867-4401. FAX 330-867-0019. URL: http://www.billcom.com/mtdmag. Vendor(s): Information Access Co., Knight-Ridder Information, Inc.. *6503*

MODERNISM - MODERNITY.
Johns Hopkins University Press, Journals Publishing Division, 2715 N. Charles St., Baltimore, MD 21218. TEL 410-516-6987. FAX 410-516-6968. URL: http://muse.jhu.edu. *3506*

MODEST PROPOSALS.
Modest Proposals, Nua Ltd., Westland Court, S. Cumberland St., Dublin 2, Ireland. TEL 353-1-676-8996. FAX 353-1-661-3932. URL: http://www.nua.ie/modestproposals/ Available only online. *2054*

DIE MOEBEL-INDUSTRIE UND IHRE HELFER.
Industrieschau-Verlagsgesellschaft mbH, Postfach 100262, 64202 Darmstadt, Germany. TEL 49-6151-3892-0. FAX 49-6151-33164. *3859*

MOKSHA JOURNAL.
Vajra Printing & Publishing of Yoga Anand Ashram, 49 Forrest Pl., Amityville, NY 11701. TEL 516-691-8475. FAX 516-691-8475. URL: http://www.santosha.com/moksha. *5738*

MOLECULAR AND CELLULAR NEUROSCIENCES.
Academic Press, Inc., Journal Division, 525 B St., Ste. 1900, San Diego, CA 92101-4495. TEL 619-230-1840. FAX 619-699-6800. URL: http://www.apnet.com/www/journal/cn.htm; http://www.idealibrary.com/ *5080*

MOLECULAR AND CELLULAR PROBES.
Academic Press Ltd., 24-28 Oval Rd., London NW1 7DX, England. TEL 44-171-267-4466. FAX 44-171-482-2293. URL: http://www.hbuk.co.uk/ap/mcp; http://www.europe.idealibrary.com/. *4901*

MOLECULAR AND GENERAL GENETICS.
Springer-Verlag, Heidelberger Platz 3, 14197 Berlin, Germany. TEL 49-30-82787-0. FAX 49-30-82787448. URL: http://link.springer.de/link/service/journals/00438/index.htm. *773*

MOLECULAR CRYSTALS AND LIQUID CRYSTALS SCIENCE AND TECHNOLOGY. SECTION A: MOLECULAR CRYSTALS AND LIQUID CRYSTALS.
Gordon and Breach - Harwood Academic, Amsteldisk 166, 1st Fl., 1079 LH Amsterdam, Netherlands. URL: http://www.gbhap.com/Molecular__Crystals__Liquid__Crystals/. *1803*

MOLECULAR CRYSTALS AND LIQUID CRYSTALS SCIENCE AND TECHNOLOGY. SECTION B: NONLINEAR OPTICS.
Gordon and Breach - Harwood Academic, Amsteldisk 166, 1st Fl., 1079 LH Amsterdam, Netherlands. URL: http://www.gbhap.com/Nonlinear__Optics/. *5866*

MOLECULAR CRYSTALS AND LIQUID CRYSTALS SCIENCE AND TECHNOLOGY. SECTION C: MOLECULAR MATERIALS.
Gordon and Breach - Harwood Academic, Amsteldisk 166, 1st Fl., 1079 LH Amsterdam, Netherlands. URL: http://www.gbhap.com/Molecular__Materials/. *1803*

MOLECULAR HUMAN REPRODUCTION.
Oxford University Press, Academic Division, Great Clarendon St., Oxford OX2 6DP, England. TEL 44-1865-267907. FAX 44-1865-267485. URL: http://www.oup.co.uk. *4963*

MOLECULAR MEDICINE.
Springer-Verlag, Medical Journals, 175 Fifth Ave., New York, NY 10010. TEL 212-460-1500. FAX 212-473-6272. URL: http://link.springer.de/link/service/journals/10020/index.htm. *4717*

MOLECULAR PATHOLOGY.
B M J Publishing Group, B.M.A. House, Tavistock Sq., London WC1H 9JR, England. TEL 44-171-387-4499. FAX 44-171-383-6661.
Vendor(s): Ovid Technologies, Inc.. *4901*

MOLECULAR PHYLOGENETICS AND EVOLUTION.
Academic Press, Inc., Journal Division, 525 B St., Ste. 1900, San Diego, CA 92101-4495. TEL 619-230-1840. FAX 619-699-6800. URL: http://www.apnet.com/www/journal/fy.htm; http://www.idealibrary.com/ *773*

MOLECULAR PHYSICS.
Taylor & Francis Ltd., 1 Gunpowder Sq., London EC4A 3DE, England. TEL 44-171-583-0490. FAX 44-171-583-0585. URL: http://www.tandf.co.uk/. *1833*

MOLECULAR SIMULATION.
Gordon and Breach - Harwood Academic, Amsteldisk 166, 1st Fl., 1079 LH Amsterdam, Netherlands. URL: http://www.gbhap.com/Molecular__Simulation/. *1760*

MOLECULES.
Springer-Verlag, Heidelberger Platz 3, 14197 Berlin, Germany. TEL 49-30-82787-0. FAX 49-30-82787448. URL: http://science.springer.de/molec/molecule.htm. *1819*

MONATSSCHRIFT KINDERHEILKUNDE.
Springer-Verlag, Heidelberger Platz 3, 14197 Berlin, Germany. TEL 49-30-82787-0. FAX 49-30-82787448. URL: http://link.springer.de. *5034*

MONDAY MORNING BRIEFS.
4064 W. Second St., Los Angeles, CA 90004. URL: http://users.aol.com/mmbriefs.
Available only online. *4347*

LE MONDE.
Le Monde S.A., 21 bis rue Claude-Bernard, 75242 Paris Cedex 5, France. TEL 33-1-42172000. FAX 33-1-42172121. URL: http://www.lemonde.fr.
Vendor(s): Telesystemes - Questel. *3280*

MONEY (NEW YORK).
Time Inc., Time & Life Bldg., Rockefeller Center, 1271 Ave. of the Americas, New York, NY 10020. TEL 212-522-1212. URL: http://pathfinder.com/.
Vendor(s): Information Access Co., Knight-Ridder Information, Inc., Lexis-Nexis, MediaStream, UMI. *1155*

MONEY LAUNDERING ALERT.
Alert Global Media, Inc., Box 11390, Miami, FL 33101. TEL 305-530-0500. FAX 305-530-9434. URL: http://www.moneylaundering.com.
Vendor(s): Data-Star, Dow Jones News Retrieval, Information Access Co., Knight-Ridder Information, Inc., Lexis-Nexis. *2273*

MONEY MARKET INSIGHT.
IBC - Donoghue, Inc., 290 Eliot St., Ashland, MA 01721. TEL 508-881-2800. FAX 508-881-0982. *1396*

MONEYLETTER (ASHLAND).
IBC - Donoghue, Inc., Box 9104, Ashland, MA 01721-9104. TEL 508-881-2800. FAX 508-881-0982. *1396*

MONIST.
Hegeler Institute, Box 600, La Salle, IL 61301. TEL 815-223-2520. FAX 815-223-4486. URL: htt://www.bgsu.edu/pdc/ *5738*

MONITOR DE LA FARMACIA Y DE LA TERAPEUTICA.
Centros Farmaceuticos Nacional S.A., Julian Camarillo, 37, 28037 Madrid, Spain. TEL 17754-43-84. FAX 1-754-56-59. *5679*

MONTANA BUSINESS DIRECTORY.
American Business Directories, 5711 S. 86th Circle, Box 27347, Omaha, NE 68127. TEL 402-593-4600. FAX 402-331-5481. *1699*

MONTANA BUSINESS QUARTERLY.
University of Montana, Bureau of Business and Economic Research, Missoula, MT 59812. TEL 406-243-5113. FAX 406-243-2086.
Vendor(s): Information Access Co., UMI. *986*

MONTANA CYBERZINE.
URL: http://www.montanacyberzine.com.
Available only online. *7222*

MONTHLY CATALOG OF UNITED STATES GOVERNMENT PUBLICATIONS.
U.S. Government Printing Office, Superintendent of Documents, Washington, DC 20402-9341.
Vendor(s): Knight-Ridder Information, Inc. (File no.66), Ovid Technologies, Inc.. *6205*

MONTHLY LABOR REVIEW.
U.S. Bureau of Labor Statistics, 2 Massachusetts Ave., N.E., Washington, DC 20212. TEL 202-606-5902.
Vendor(s): Information Access Co., Knight-Ridder Information, Inc., UMI. *1058*

MONTHLY PLANET.
Nuclear Weapons Freeze of Santa Cruz County, 320 Cedar St., Ste. G., Santa Cruz, CA 95060-4362. TEL 408-429-8755. *6027*

MONTHLY PRODUCT ANNOUNCEMENT.
U.S. Bureau of the Census, Customer Services, Washington, DC 20233. TEL 301-457-4100. FAX 301-457-4714. URL: http://www.census.gov/. *6054*

MONTHLY REPORT ON INTERNET MATTERS IN BELGIUM AND EUROPE.
URL: http://www.best.be.
Available only online. *2137*

MONTHLY REVIEW.
Monthly Review, 122 W. 27th St., 10th fl., New York, NY 10001. TEL 212-691-2555. FAX 212-727-3676. URL: http://www.igc.apc.org/MonthlyReview/
Vendor(s): Information Access Co., UMI. *5945*

MOONDANCE.
URL: http://www.studnets.dsu.edu/ilchuka/moondance/
Available only online. *7328*

MORE LIGHT UPDATE.
Presbyterians for Lesbian & Gay Concerns, Inc., Box 38, New Brunswick, NJ 08903-0038. TEL 908-249-1016. URL: http://www.epp.cmu.edu/~riley/PLGC.html. *3698*

MORTGAGE-BACKED SECURITIES LETTER.
Investment Dealers' Digest, 2 World Trade Center, 18th Fl., New York, NY 10048-0638. TEL 212-432-0045. FAX 212-321-2336.
Vendor(s): Information Access Co., UMI. *1398*

MORTGAGE BANKING.
Mortgage Bankers Association of America, 1125 15th St., N.W., Washington, DC 20005-2766. TEL 202-861-1930. FAX 202-861-1930.
Vendor(s): Information Access Co.. *1156*

THE MORTGAGE MARKETPLACE.
American Banker - Bond Buyer, Newsletter Division One State St. Plaza, New York, NY 10004-1549. TEL 800-733-4371. FAX 212-943-2224.
Vendor(s): Information Access Co.. *1398*

MOSAIC (WINNIPEG, 1967).
University of Manitoba, 208 Tier Bldg., Winnipeg, MB R3T 2N2, Canada. TEL 204-474-9763. FAX 204-261-9086. URL: http://www.umanitoba.ca/publications/mosaic.
Vendor(s): Information Access Co.. *4437*

MOSCOW NEWS.
Moscow News Information & Media Company, 16-2 Tverskaya ul., 103829 Moscow. TEL 7-095-2003666. FAX 7-095-2092661. *3352*

MOSKOVSKIE NOVOSTI.
Moscow News Information & Media Company, 16-2 Tverskaya ul., 103829 Moscow, Russia. TEL 7-095-2006390. FAX 7-095-2000650. URL: http://www.moscownews.ru.
Vendor(s): GBI, Knight-Ridder Information, Inc.. *3352*

MOTEL MAGAZINE.
URL: http://www.motelmag.com.
Available only online. *7222*

MOTHER EARTH NEWS.
Sussex Publishers Inc., 49 E. 21st St., 11th Fl., New York, NY 10010. TEL 212-260-7210. FAX 212-260-7445.
Vendor(s): Information Access Co., UMI. *3379*

MOTHER JONES.
Foundation for National Progress, 731 Market St., Ste. 600, San Francisco, CA 94103. TEL 415-665-6637. FAX 415-665-6696. URL: http://www.motherjones.com.
Vendor(s): CompuServe, Inc., Information Access Co., Knight-Ridder Information, Inc.. *4347*

MOTHERING.
Mothering Magazine, Box 1690, Santa Fe, NM 87504. FAX 505-986-8335.
Vendor(s): Information Access Co.. *7310*

MOTOR BOATING & SAILING.
Hearst Corporation, Motor Boating & Sailing, 250 W. 55th St., New York, NY 10019. TEL 212-649-4112. FAX 212-489-9258. URL: http://www.hearstcorp.com; http://www.iwol.com/iww/customers/mbs.
Vendor(s): Information Access Co.. *6841*

MOTOR BUSINESS ASIA PACIFIC.
Economist Intelligence Unit, 111 W. 57th St., New York, NY 10019. TEL 212-554-0600. FAX 212-586-1182. URL: http://www.eiu.com. *7107*

MOTOR BUSINESS EUROPE.
Economist Intelligence Unit, 111 W. 57th St., New York, NY 10019. TEL 212-554-0600. FAX 212-586-1182. URL: http://www.eiu.com. *7107*

MOTOR BUSINESS INTERNATIONAL.
Economist Intelligence Unit, 111 W. 57th St., New York, NY 10019. TEL 212-554-0600. FAX 212-586-1182. URL: http://www.eiu.com. *7107*

MOTOR BUSINESS JAPAN.
Economist Intelligence Unit, 111 W. 57th St., New York, NY 10019. TEL 212-554-0600. FAX 212-586-1182. URL: http://www.eiu.com. *7107*

MOTOR TREND.
Petersen Publishing Co., 6420 Wilshire Blvd., Los Angeles, CA 90048. TEL 213-782-2220. FAX 213-782-2866. URL: http://www.motortrend.com.
Vendor(s): Information Access Co., Knight-Ridder Information, Inc.. *7108*

MOTORCYCLE ONLINE.
URL: http://www.motorcycle.com/
Available only online. *6830*

MOTORCYCLE SHOPPER.
Payne Corp., 1353 Herndon Ave., Deltona, FL 32725-9046. TEL 407-860-1989. FAX 407-574-1014. URL: http://www.shopper.eurografix.com. *6830*

MOUNT SINAI JOURNAL OF MEDICINE.
Mount Sinai Hospital, Committee on Medical Education and Publications, 50 E. 98th St., Box 1094, New York, NY 10029. TEL 212-241-6108. FAX 212-722-6386.
Vendor(s): Knight-Ridder Information, Inc.. *4718*

MOUNTAIN LIVING.
Mountain Living Publishing, 7009 S. Potomac St., Englewood, CO 80112. TEL 303-397-7600. FAX 303-397-7619. URL: http://www.mountainliving.com/ml/ *4151*

MOUNTAIN XPRESS.
Mountain Xpress, Inc., Box 144, Asheville, NC 28802. TEL 704-251-1333. FAX 704-251-1311. URL: http://www.circle.net/'xpress. *3379*

MOVEMENT DISORDERS.
Lippincott - Raven Publishers, 227 Washington Sq., Philadelphia, PA 19106. TEL 215-238-4200. FAX 215-238-4227. *5081*

MOVING TOGETHER.
URL: http://www.mum.edu/exss__dept/daley.html.
Available only online. *4718*

MPLS. - ST. PAUL MAGAZINE.
M S P Communications, Pillsbury Ctr., S. Tower, 220 S. Sixth St., Ste. 500, Minneapolis, MN 55402. TEL 612-339-7571.
Vendor(s): Information Access Co., UMI. *3379*

MR. SHOWBIZ.
Starwave Corporation, 13810 S.E. Eastgate Way, Ste. 400, Bellevue, WA 98005. URL: http://www.MrShowbiz.com.
Available only online. *5340*

MULTICHANNEL NEWS.
Capital Cities - A B C, Inc., Diversified Publishing Group, 825 Seventh Ave., New York, NY 10019. TEL 212-887-8400.
Vendor(s): Information Access Co.. *2054*

MULTIMEDIA.
HighText Verlag, Ridlerstr. 55, 80339 Munich, Germany. TEL 49-89-500353-0. FAX 49-89-50035399. *2016*

MULTIMEDIA COMPUTING & PRESENTATIONS.
Multimedia Computing Corporation, P.O. Box 60369, Sunnyvale, CA 94088-0369. TEL 408-737-7575. FAX 408-739-8019. *2216*

MULTIMEDIA ENTERTAINMENT & TECHNOLOGY REPORT.
Cowles - SIMBA Information, 11 Riverbend Dr. S., Box 4949, Stamford, CT 06907-0949. TEL 203-358-9900. FAX 203-358-5811. URL: http://www.simbanet.com.
Vendor(s): Information Access Co.. *2128*

MULTIMEDIA MONITOR.
Phillips Business Information, Inc., 1201 Seven Locks Rd., Potomac, MD 20854. TEL 301-424-3338. FAX 301-309-3847.
Vendor(s): Information Access Co., Knight-Ridder Information, Inc., NewsNet (EC27). *2157*

MULTIMEDIA PUBLISHER.
Worldwide Videotex, Box 3273, Boynton Beach, FL 33424-3273. TEL 407-738-2276.
Vendor(s): Information Access Co.. *2017*

MULTIMEDIA SCHOOLS.
Online Inc., 462 Danbury Rd., Wilton, CT 06897-2126. TEL 203-761-1466. FAX 203-761-1444. URL: http://www.infotoday.com/MMSchools/ *2519*

MULTIMEDIA SYSTEMS.
Springer-Verlag, Heidelberger Platz 3, 14197 Berlin, Germany. TEL 49-30-82787-0. FAX 49-30-82787448. URL: http://link.springer.de/link/service/journals/00530/index.htm. *2087*

MULTIMEDIA WEEK.
Phillips Business Information, Inc., 1201 Seven Locks Rd., Potomac, MD 20854. TEL 301-424-3338. FAX 301-309-3847.
Vendor(s): Information Access Co.. *2124*

MULTINATIONAL BUSINESS REVIEW.
University of Detroit Mercy, College of Business Administration, Box 19900, Detroit, MI 48219-0900. TEL 313-993-1264. FAX 313-993-1052.
Vendor(s): UMI. *1342*

MULTINATIONAL MONITOR.
Essential Information, Box 19405, Washington, DC 20036. TEL 202-387-8034. FAX 202-234-5176. URL: http://www.essential.org/monitor/monitor.html.
Vendor(s): Information Access Co.. *1342*

MULTIWORLD.
URL: http://www.jnw.com/mw/about.html.
Available only online. *3379*

MUNICIPAL AND INDUSTRIAL WATER AND POLLUTION CONTROL.
Zanny Publications Ltd., 11966 Woodbine Ave., Gormley, ON L0H 1G0, Canada. TEL 905-887-5048. FAX 905-887-0764.
Vendor(s): Information Access Co.. *2970*

MUSIC AND LETTERS.
Oxford University Press, Academic Division, Great Clarendon St., Oxford OX2 6DP, England. TEL 44-1865-267907. FAX 44-1865-267485. URL: http://www.oup.co.uk/journals.
Vendor(s): Information Access Co.. *5411*

MUSIC & MEDIA.
B P I Communications, Rijnsburgstraat 11, 1059 AT Amsterdam, Netherlands. TEL 31-20-6691961. FAX 31-20-6691941.
Vendor(s): Information Access Co.. *5412*

MUSIC TRADES.
Music Trades Corporation, c/o Paul A. Majeski, Ed., Box 432, 80 West St., Englewood, NJ 07631. TEL 201-871-1965.
Vendor(s): Information Access Co.. *5414*

MUSIC WEEK.
Spotlight Publications Ltd., Ludgate House, 245 Blackfriars Rd., London SE1 9UR, England. TEL 44-171-620-3636. FAX 44-171-401-8036.
Vendor(s): Information Access Co.. *5414*

MUSICOPYRIGHT INTELLIGENCE.
E.S. Proteus, 1657 The Fairway, Ste. 123, Jenkintown, PA 19046. TEL 215-885-3154.
Vendor(s): CompuServe, Inc. (71553,3665). *5587*

MUSIKALER I DANSKE BIBLIOTEKER.
Dansk BiblioteksCenter as, Tempovej 7-11, DK-2750 Ballerup, Denmark. TEL 45-44-97-40-00. FAX 45-44-68-24-42.
Available only online. *5448*

MUZZLE BLASTS.
National Muzzle Loading Rifle Association, Box 67, Friendship, IN 47021. TEL 812-667-5131. FAX 812-667-5137. URL: ezines.firelands.net/MuzzleBlastsOnline/ *6875*

MYCORRHIZA.
Springer-Verlag, Heidelberger Platz 3, 14197 Berlin, Germany. TEL 49-30-82787-0. FAX 49-30-82787448. URL: http://link.springer.de/link/service/journals/00572/index.htm. *715*

N A B E OUTLOOK & POLICY SURVEY.
National Association of Business Economists, 1233 20th St., N.W., Ste. 505, Washington, DC 20036-2304. TEL 202-463-6223. FAX 202-463-6239.
Vendor(s): Information Access Co.. *1272*

N A B P NEWSLETTER.
National Association of Boards of Pharmacy, 700 Busse Hwy., Park Ridge, IL 60068-2402. TEL 708-698-6227. *5679*

N A C L A REPORT ON THE AMERICAS.
North American Congress on Latin America, Inc., 475 Riverside Dr., Rm. 454, New York, NY 10115. TEL 212-870-3146. FAX 212-870-3305.
Vendor(s): Information Access Co.. *6027*

N A S A PATENT ABSTRACTS BIBLIOGRAPHY: A CONTINUING BIBLIOGRAPHY. SECTION 2. INDEXES.
U.S. National Aeronautics and Space Administration, Scientific Technical Information Office, 800 Elkridge Landing Rd., Linthicum Heights, MD 21090-2934. URL: http://www.sti.nasa.gov.
Available only online. *5593*

N A S A THESAURUS SUPPLEMENT. PART 1. HIERARCHICAL LISTING.
U.S. National Aeronautics and Space Administration, Scientific and Technical Information Office, 800 Elkridge Landing Rd., Linthcum Heights, MD 21090-2934. URL: http://www.sti.nasa.gov. *84*

N A S A THESAURUS SUPPLEMENT. PART 2. ACCESS VOCABULARY.
U.S. National Aeronautics and Space Administration, Scientific and Technical Information Office, 800 Elkridge Landing Rd., Linthicum Heights, MD 21090-2934. URL: http://www.sti.nasa.gov. *84*

N A S A THESAURUS SUPPLEMENT. PART 3. DEFINITIONS.
U.S. National Aeronautics and Space Administration, Scientific and Technical Information Office, 800 Elkridge Landing Rd., Linthcum Heights, MD 21090-2934. URL: http://www.sti.nasa.gov. *84*

N A S F A A NEWSLETTER.
National Association of Student Financial Aid Administrators, 1920 L St., N.W., Ste. 200, Washington, DC 20036-5020. TEL 202-785-0453. FAX 202-785-1487. URL: http://www.nfsa.org. *2549*

N A S I G NEWSLETTER.
North American Serials Interest Group, Northern Arizona Univ., Cline Library, Bibliographic Services, Flagstaff, AZ 86011. TEL 520-523-6779. FAX 520-523-3770. URL: http://nasig.ils.unc.edu. *4200*

N A T O ADVANCED SCIENCE INSTITUTES SERIES A: LIFE SCIENCES.
Plenum Publishing Corp., 233 Spring St., New York, NY 10013-1578. TEL 212-620-8000. FAX 212-463-0742.
Vendor(s): European Space Agency (File no.128). *615*

N A T O ADVANCED SCIENCE INSTITUTES SERIES B: PHYSICS.
Plenum Publishing Corp., 233 Spring St., New York, NY 10013-1578. TEL 212-620-8000. FAX 212-463-0742.
Vendor(s): European Space Agency (File no.128). *5815*

N A T O ADVANCED SCIENCE INSTITUTES SERIES C: MATHEMATICAL AND PHYSICAL SCIENCES.
Kluwer Academic Publishers, Postbus 17, 3300 AA Dordrecht, Netherlands. TEL 31-78-6392392. FAX 31-78-6392254. URL: http://www.wkap.nl.
Vendor(s): European Space Agency (File no.128). *4594*

N A T O ADVANCED SCIENCE INSTITUTES SERIES D: BEHAVIOURAL AND SOCIAL SCIENCES.
Kluwer Academic Publishers, Postbus 17, 3300 AA Dordrecht, Netherlands. TEL 31-78-6392392. FAX 31-78-6392254. URL: http://www.wkap.nl.
Vendor(s): European Space Agency (File no.128). *6137*

N A T O ADVANCED SCIENCE INSTITUTES SERIES E: APPLIED SCIENCES.
Kluwer Academic Publishers, Postbus 17, 3300 AA Dordrecht, Netherlands. TEL 31-78-6392392. FAX 31-78-6392254. URL: http://www.wkap.nl.
Vendor(s): European Space Agency (File no.128). *6967*

N A T O ADVANCED SCIENCE INSTITUTES SERIES F: COMPUTER AND SYSTEMS SCIENCES.
Springer-Verlag, Heidelberger Platz 3, 14197 Berlin, Germany. TEL 49-30-8207-0. FAX 49-30-8214091.
Vendor(s): European Space Agency (File no.128). *2157*

N A T O ADVANCED SCIENCE INSTITUTES SERIES G: ECOLOGICAL SCIENCES.
Kluwer Academic Publishers, Postbus 17, 3300 AA Dordrecht, Netherlands. TEL 31-78-6392392. FAX 31-78-6392254. URL: http://www.wkap.nl.
Vendor(s): European Space Agency (File no.128). *2943*

N A T O ADVANCED SCIENCE INSTITUTES SERIES H: CELL BIOLOGY.
Kluwer Academic Publishers, Postbus 17, 3300 AA Dordrecht, Netherlands. TEL 31-78-6392392. FAX 31-78-6392254. URL: http://www.wkap.nl.
Vendor(s): European Space Agency (File no.128). *743*

SERIALS AVAILABLE ONLINE

N A T O DATA.
North Atlantic Treaty Organization, Integrated Data Service, Leopold III Laan, Brussels 1110, Belgium. TEL 32-2-7284599. FAX 32-2-7285229. Available only online. *5278*

N A T O SCIENTIFIC PUBLICATIONS. NEWSLETTER.
N A T O Publication Coordination Office, Elcerlyclaan 2, B-3090 Overijse, Belgium. TEL 32-2-6876636. URL: http://www.wkap.nl/natopco/nato_pco.htm. *6547*

N C A A NEWS.
National Collegiate Athletic Association, Circulation Department, Box 7347, Overland Park, KS 66207-0347. TEL 913-339-1906. FAX 913-339-1950. URL: http://www.ncaa.org. *6771*

N C A H F NEWSLETTER.
National Council Against Health Fraud, Inc., Box 1276, Loma Linda, CA 92354. TEL 909-824-4690. FAX 909-824-4838. URL: http://www.primenet.com/~ncahf/
Vendor(s): Information Access Co., UMI. *6244*

N C F.
Societa Editoriale Farmaceutica s.r.l., Via Ausonio, 12, 20123 Milan, Italy. TEL 02-89404545. FAX 02-89401168. *5679*

N C J R S DOCUMENT RETRIEVAL INDEX.
U.S. National Institute of Justice, National Criminal Justice Reference Service, Box 6000, Department F, Rockville, MD 20849-6000. TEL 301-251-5500. FAX 301-251-5212.
Vendor(s): Knight-Ridder Information, Inc.. *2284*

N D A PIPELINE.
F-D-C Reports, Inc., 5550 Friendship Blvd., Ste. 1, Chevy Chase, MD 20815. FAX 301-664-7238.
Vendor(s): Data-Star (NDAP). *5679*

N E A TODAY.
National Education Association of the United States, 1201 16th St., N.W., Washington, DC 20036. TEL 202-822-7207. FAX 202-822-7206.
Vendor(s): Information Access Co., UMI. *2464*

N G V NEWS.
Pasha Publications Inc., 1616 N. Ft. Myer Dr., Ste. 1000, Arlington, VA 22209-3107. TEL 703-528-1244. FAX 703-528-1253. *5610*

N H N E NEWS BRIEF.
New Heaven New Earth, Box 10627, Sedona, AZ 10627. URL: http://nen.sedona.net/nhne/ *5458*

N I O S H T I C.
U.S. National Institute for Occupational Safety and Health, Technical Information Center, Attn: Publications, 4676 Columbia Pky., Cincinnati, OH 45226. FAX 513-533-8573.
Vendor(s): Canadian Centre for Occupational Health & Safety, European Space Agency, Knight-Ridder Information, Inc., National Library of Medicine, Telesystemes - Questel. *5494*

N P NEWS.
Springhouse Corporation, 1111 Bethlehem Pike, Box 908, Springhouse, PA 19477. TEL 215-646-8700.
Vendor(s): UMI. *4941*

N S F BULLETIN.
U.S. National Science Foundation, 4201 Wilson Blvd., Ste. 245, Arlington, VA 22230. *6547*

N T I A C NEWSLETTER.
Nondestructive Testing Information Analysis Center, URL: http://www.dtic.mil/iac/ntiac/newslist.html.
Available only online. *2868*

N T I S ALERTS: FOREIGN TECHNOLOGY.
U.S. National Technical Information Service, 5285 Port Royal Rd., Springfield, VA 22161. TEL 703-487-4630. FAX 703-321-8547.
Vendor(s): Information Access Co.. *6982*

N T I S BIBLIOGRAPHIC DATA BASE.
U.S. National Technical Information Service, 5285 Port Royal Rd., Springfield, VA 22161. TEL 703-487-4630.
Vendor(s): Data-Star, Knight-Ridder Information, Inc., Questel Orbit Inc., Ovid Technologies, Inc., STN International. *6292*

N T T TOPICS.
Ruder, Finn & Rotman, N T T Information Desk, 301 E. 57th St., New York, NY 10022.
Vendor(s): Information Access Co.. *2037*

N U C O M 6.
National Library of Australia, Publications Section, Cultural and Educational Services Division, Canberra, A.C.T. 2600, Australia. TEL 61-6-262-1365. FAX 61-6-273-4493. *557*

N Y ROCK.
Scott Communications Inc., Box 563, New York, NY 10028-0005. URL: http://www.nyrock.com/
Available only online. *5419*

AN NAHAR.
An Nahar S.C.P.A., Banque du Liban St., P.O. Box 11-0226, Beirut, Lebanon. TEL 961-1-340960. FAX 961-1-340960. URL: http://www.annahar.com.lb. *3332*

DIE NAHRUNGS- UND GENUSSMITTEL-INDUSTRIE UND IHRE HELFER.
Industrieschau-Verlagsgesellschaft mbH, Postfach 100262, 64202 Darmstadt, Germany. TEL 49-6151-38920. FAX 49-6151-33164. *3121*

NAMIBIA TRADE DIRECTORY.
Namibia Trade Directory CC, P.O. Box 21593, Windhoek, Namibia. TEL 264-61-225665. FAX 264-61-220410. *1700*

NANJING HUAGONG DAXUE XUEBAO.
Nanjing Huagong Daxue, 5 Xinmofan Malu, Nanjing, Jiangsu 210009, People's Republic of China. TEL 86-25-3316755. FAX 86-25-3211316.
Vendor(s): Knight-Ridder Information, Inc.. *2769*

NANONEWS UPDATE.
Nanothinc, URL: http://www.nanothinc.com/News/current.html.
Available only online. *5816*

NANOTECHNOLOGY.
I O P Publishing Ltd., Dirac House, Temple Back, Bristol BS1 6BE, England. TEL 44-117-929-7481. FAX 44-117-929-4318. URL: http://www.iop.org. *5816*

NASH.
URL: http://155.247.25.10/nash.
Available only online. *5419*

NASHVILLE BUSINESS JOURNAL.
Mid-South Communications, Box 23229, Nashville, TN 37202. TEL 615-248-2222. FAX 615-248-6246.
Vendor(s): Lexis-Nexis, UMI. *986*

THE NATION.
The Nation Company, L.P., 72 Fifth Ave., New York, NY 10011. TEL 212-242-8400. FAX 212-463-9712. URL: http://www.TheNation.com.
Vendor(s): Information Access Co.. *4347*

NATIONAL AGRICULTURAL STATISTICS SERVICE. CATTLE ON FEED.
U.S. Department of Agriculture, National Agricultural Statistics Service, Independence Ave., between 12th & 14th Sts., S.W., South Bldg., Rm. 4117, Washington, DC 20250. TEL 202-655-4000.
Vendor(s): Knight-Ridder Information, Inc.. *178*

NATIONAL ASSOCIATION OF BOARDS OF PHARMACY. PROCEEDINGS.
National Association of Boards of Pharmacy, 700 Busse Hwy., Park Ridge, IL 60068-2402. TEL 708-698-6227. *5679*

NATIONAL ASSOCIATION OF INSURANCE COMMISSIONERS. PROCEEDINGS.
National Association of Insurance Commissioners, 120 W. 12th St., Kansas City, MO 64105. TEL 816-374-7259. URL: http://www.naic.org.
Vendor(s): Lexis-Nexis. *3827*

NATIONAL BASEBALL HALL OF FAME & MUSEUM YEARBOOK.
National Baseball Hall of Fame, Main St., Box 590, Cooperstown, NY 13326. TEL 607-547-7200. URL: http://www.baseballhalloffame.org. *6811*

NATIONAL BIBLIOGRAPHY OF BARBADOS.
National Library Service, Culloden Farm, Culloden Rd., St. Michael, Barbados, W.I. TEL 246-429-5716. FAX 246-436-1501. *557*

THE NATIONAL BOOK OF BUSINESS LISTS.
Reference Press, Inc., Box 140375, Austin, TX 78714-0375. TEL 512-454-7778. FAX 512-454-9401. URL: http://www.hoovers.com. *1700*

NATIONAL BUSINESS REVIEW.
Fourth Estate Holdings Ltd., P.O. Box 1734, Auckland, New Zealand. TEL 64-9-307-1629. FAX 64-9-373-3997. URL: http://www.nbr.co.nz.
Vendor(s): Kiwinet. *1272*

NATIONAL CANCER INSTITUTE. JOURNAL.
Oxford University Press, Academic Division, Great Clarendon St., Oxford OX2 6DP, England. TEL 44-1865-267907. FAX 44-1865-267485. URL: http://www.oup.co.uk/journals.
Vendor(s): Lexis-Nexis, Ovid Technologies, Inc.. *4983*

NATIONAL CATHOLIC REPORTER.
National Catholic Reporter Publishing Company, Inc., 115 E. Armour Blvd., Box 419281, Kansas City, MO 64141. TEL 816-531-0538. FAX 816-968-2280.
Vendor(s): Information Access Co.. *6472*

NATIONAL CIVIC REVIEW.
Jossey-Bass Inc., Publishers, 350 Sansone St., 5th Fl., San Francisco, CA 94104. FAX 800-605-2665. URL: http://www.joseybass.com.
Vendor(s): Information Access Co., UMI. *6221*

NATIONAL CONTRACT MANAGEMENT JOURNAL.
National Contract Management Association, 1912 Woodford Rd., Vienna, VA 22182-3728.
Vendor(s): UMI. *1497*

NATIONAL DIRECTORY OF CATALOGS.
Oxbridge Communications, Inc., 150 Fifth Ave., Ste. 302, New York, NY 10011. TEL 212-741-0231. FAX 212-633-2938. *557*

NATIONAL DIRECTORY OF LAW ENFORCEMENT ADMINISTRATORS AND CORRECTIONAL INSTITUTIONS.
National Police Chiefs & Sheriffs Information Bureau, Box 365, Stevens Point, WI 54481. TEL 800-647-7579. FAX 715-345-7288.
Vendor(s): Lexis-Nexis. *2274*

NATIONAL DIRECTORY OF MAGAZINES.
Oxbridge Communications, Inc., 150 Fifth Ave., New York, NY 10011. TEL 212-741-0231. FAX 212-633-2938. *557*

NATIONAL DIRECTORY OF MAILING LISTS.
Oxbridge Communications, Inc., 150 Fifth Ave., Ste. 302, New York, NY 10011. TEL 212-741-0231. FAX 212-633-2938. *1700*

NATIONAL FISHERMAN.
Journal Publications (Rockland), Box 7238, Portland, ME 04112-7438. TEL 207-842-5608. FAX 207-842-5609.
Vendor(s): Information Access Co.. *3074*

NATIONAL FORUM (AUBURN).
Honor Society of Phi Kappa Phi (Auburn), c/o Dr. James P. Kaetz, Ed., 129 Quad Center, Mell St., Auburn, AL 36849-5306. TEL 334-844-5200. FAX 334-844-5994. URL: http://www.auburn.edu/~kaetzjp/natforum.html.
Vendor(s): Information Access Co., UMI. *1963*

NATIONAL FORUM OF SPECIAL EDUCATION JOURNAL.
National Forum Journals, 4000 Locke Ln., Ste. 9, Lake Charles, LA 70605-2244. TEL 318-477-0008.
Available only online. *2588*

NATIONAL HOME CENTER NEWS.
Lebhar-Friedman, Inc., 425 Park Ave., New York, NY 10022. TEL 212-756-5000.
Vendor(s): Information Access Co.. *905*

NATIONAL INSTITUTE ECONOMIC REVIEW.
National Institute of Economic and Social Research, 2 Dean Trench St., Smith Sq., London SW1P 3HE, England. TEL 44-171-222-7665. FAX 44-171-222-1435.
Vendor(s): Information Access Co., UMI. *987*

NATIONAL INSTITUTE OF STANDARDS AND TECHNOLOGY. JOURNAL OF RESEARCH.
U.S. National Institute of Standards and Technology, U.S. Department of Commerce, Gaithersburg, MD 20899. TEL 301-975-3058. URL: http://nvl.nist.gov/pub/nistpubs/jres/jres.htm. *5253*

THE NATIONAL INTEREST.
National Affairs, Inc., 1112 16th St., N.W., Ste. 540., Washington, DC 20036. TEL 202-467-4884. FAX 202-467-0006.
Vendor(s): Information Access Co. *6028*

NATIONAL JEWELER.
Miller Freeman Inc. (New York), One Penn Plaza, New York, NY 10119. TEL 212-714-1300. FAX 212-279-3960. *3866*

NATIONAL JOURNAL.
National Journal, Inc., 1501 M St., N.W., Ste. 300, Washington, DC 20005. TEL 202-739-8400. FAX 202-833-8069.
Vendor(s): UMI. *5946*

NATIONAL LAW JOURNAL.
New York Law Publishing Co., 345 Park Ave. S., New York, NY 10010. TEL 212-779-9200. URL: http://www.ljx.com.
Vendor(s): Lexis-Nexis. *3994*

NATIONAL LIBRARY OF AUSTRALIA GATEWAYS.
National Library of Australia, Services to Libraries, Canberra, A.C.T. 2600, Australia. TEL 61-6-262-1580. FAX 61-6-273-1180. URL: http://www.nla.gov.au/2/pubs/gatehome.html. *4201*

NATIONAL MEDICAL ASSOCIATION. JOURNAL.
Slack, Inc., 6900 Grove Rd., Thorofare, NJ 08086-9447. TEL 609-848-1000. FAX 609-853-5991. URL: http://www.slackinc.com. *4720*

NATIONAL MORTGAGE NEWS.
Faulkner & Gray, 22nd Fl., 11 Penn Plaza, New York, NY 10001. TEL 212-967-7000. FAX 212-564-8879.
Vendor(s): UMI. *1157*

NATIONAL NEWSPAPER INDEX.
Information Access Company, 362 Lakeside Dr., Foster City, CA 94404. TEL 415-378-5200. FAX 415-378-5369.
Vendor(s): Knight-Ridder Information, Inc. (File no.111), Lexis-Nexis, Ovid Technologies, Inc. (NOOZ) *3884*

NATIONAL OUTLOOK.
Outlook Media Ltd., G.P.O. Box 2134, Sydney, N.S.W. 2001, Australia. TEL 61-2-3180918. FAX 61-2-6999182. URL: http://www.ozemail.com.au/~wfnev. *6357*

NATIONAL PARKS.
National Parks and Conservation Association, 1776 Massachusetts Ave., N.W., Washington, DC 20036. TEL 202-223-6722. FAX 202-659-0650. URL: http://www.npca.org/.
Vendor(s): Information Access Co., UMI. *4151*

NATIONAL PETROLEUM NEWS.
Adams Trade Press, 2101 S. Arlington Heights Rd., Ste. 150, Arlington Heights, IL 60005. TEL 847-427-9512. FAX 847-427-2041.
Vendor(s): Information Access Co., Knight-Ridder Information, Inc. *5611*

NATIONAL PHARMACEUTICAL ASSOCIATION. JOURNAL.
National Pharmaceutical Association, Inc., c/o Texas Southern University, College of Pharmacy, 3100 Cleburne, Houston, TX 77004. TEL 713-527-7164. FAX 713-639-1091. *5679*

NATIONAL PRODUCTIVITY REVIEW.
John Wiley & Sons, Inc., Journals, 605 Third Ave., New York, NY 10158. TEL 212-850-6645. FAX 212-850-6021. URL: http://www.wiley.co.uk.
Vendor(s): Information Access Co. *1497*

NATIONAL PUBLIC ACCOUNTANT.
National Society of Public Accountants, 1010 N. Fairfax St., Alexandria, VA 22314. TEL 703-549-6400. URL: http://www.nspa.org/.
Vendor(s): UMI. *1095*

NATIONAL REAL ESTATE INVESTOR.
Intertec Publishing Corp. (Atlanta), 6151 Powers Ferry Rd., N.W., Atlanta, GA 30339-2941. TEL 770-955-2500. FAX 770-955-0400.
Vendor(s): Information Access Co., UMI. *6307*

NATIONAL REPORT ON COMPUTERS AND HEALTH.
United Communications Group, 11300 Rockville Pike, Ste. 1100, Rockville, MD 20852-3030. TEL 301-816-8950. FAX 301-816-8945.
Vendor(s): Data-Star, Information Access Co., Knight-Ridder Information, Inc. *4848*

NATIONAL REPORT ON WORK & FAMILY.
Business Publishers, Inc., 951 Pershing Dr., Silver Spring, MD 20910-4464. TEL 301-587-6300. FAX 301-585-9075.
Vendor(s): Human Resources Information Network. *5513*

NATIONAL REPORTER.
Maritime Law Book Ltd., Box 302, Fredericton, NB E3B 4Y9, Canada. TEL 506-453-9921. FAX 506-453-9525.
Vendor(s): QL Systems Ltd. *3994*

NATIONAL REVIEW.
National Review, Inc., 215 Lexington Ave., New York, NY 10016. TEL 212-679-7330. FAX 212-849-2835. URL: http://www.nationalreview.com/
Vendor(s): Information Access Co., Knight-Ridder Information, Inc. *5946*

NATIONAL SCIENCE FOUNDATION. DIRECTORATE FOR ENGINEERING. ENGINEERING NEWS.
National Science Foundation, Directorate for Engineering, 4201 Wilson Blvd., Rm 505, Arlington, VA 22230. TEL 703-306-1300. URL: http://www.nsf.gov. *2733*

NATIONAL TAX JOURNAL.
National Tax Association - Tax Institute of America, 725 15th St., N.W., Ste. 600, Washington, DC 20005-2109. TEL 202-737-3325. URL: http://www.cob.asu.edu/nta/NTJ.html.
Vendor(s): Information Access Co. *1621*

NATIONAL UNDERWRITER. LIFE AND HEALTH - HEALTH & FINANCIAL SERVICES EDITION.
National Underwriter Co., 505 Gest St., Cincinnati, OH 45203-1716. TEL 513-721-2140. FAX 513-721-0126.
Vendor(s): Information Access Co., UMI. *3827*

NATIONAL UNDERWRITER. PROPERTY & CASUALTY - RISK & BENEFITS MANAGEMENT EDITION.
National Underwriter Co., 505 Gest St., Cincinnati, OH 45203. TEL 513-721-2140. FAX 513-721-0126. URL: http://www.naco.com/products/products/10021_nf.html.
Vendor(s): Information Access Co., UMI. *3827*

NATIONAL WATER RIGHTS DIGEST.
Ridenbaugh Press, Box 2276, Boise, ID 83701. TEL 208-344-0844. FAX 208-344-0844. URL: http://www.ridenbaugh.com. *7297*

NATIONAL WILDLIFE.
National Wildlife Federation, 8925 Leesburg Pike, Vienna, VA 22184-0111. TEL 703-790-4000. FAX 703-790-4075. URL: http://www.nwf.org.
Vendor(s): Information Access Co. *2238*

NATIONAL WRITING PROJECT. CENTER FOR THE STUDY OF WRITING. QUARTERLY.
National Writing Project, Center for the Study of Writing, Tolman Hall, University of California, Berkeley, CA 94720. TEL 510-642-0976. *2612*

NATION'S BUSINESS.
U.S. Chamber of Commerce, 1615 H St., N.W., Washington, DC 20062-2000. TEL 202-463-5650. FAX 202-887-3437. URL: http://www.uschamber.org/publications/index.html.
Vendor(s): Information Access Co., UMI. *1193*

NATION'S CITIES WEEKLY.
National League of Cities, 1301 Pennsylvania Ave., N.W., Washington, DC 20004. TEL 202-626-3040.
Vendor(s): Information Access Co. *6221*

NATION'S RESTAURANT NEWS.
Lebhar-Friedman, Inc., 425 Park Ave., New York, NY 10022. TEL 212-756-5000. FAX 212-838-9487.
Vendor(s): Information Access Co., UMI. *3732*

NATURAL HAZARD RESEARCH WORKING PAPERS.
University of Colorado, Institute of Behavioral Science, Campus Box 482, Boulder, CO 80309. TEL 303-492-6818. FAX 303-492-2151. URL: http://www.adder.colorado.edu/~hazctr/Home.htm. Available only online. *6627*

NATURAL HAZARDS OBSERVER.
University of Colorado, Institute of Behavioral Science, Campus Box 482, Boulder, CO 80309. TEL 303-492-6818. FAX 303-492-2151. URL: http://www.adder.colorado.edu/~hazctr/Home.html. *6550*

NATURAL HEALTH.
Natural Health L.P., 17 Station St., Box 1200, Brookline, MA 02147. TEL 617-232-1000. FAX 617-232-1572.
Vendor(s): Information Access Co.. *298*

NATURAL HISTORY.
American Museum of Natural History, Central Park W. at 79th St., New York, NY 10024-5192. TEL 212-769-5500. FAX 212-769-5511.
Vendor(s): Information Access Co., Knight-Ridder Information, Inc., UMI. *6550*

NATURAL PRODUCT LETTERS.
Gordon and Breach - Harwood Academic, Amsteldisk 166, 1st Fl., 1079 LH Amsterdam, Netherlands. URL: http://www.gbhap.com/Natural_Product_Letters/. *1760*

NATURAL RESOURCES & ENVIRONMENT.
American Bar Association, Natural Resources, Energy, and Environmental Law Section, 750 N. Lake Shore Dr., Chicago, IL 60611. TEL 312-988-5000. URL: http://www.abanet.org.
Vendor(s): West Group. *2238*

NATURAL SCIENCES AND ENGINEERING RESEARCH COUNCIL OF CANADA. LIST OF SCHOLARSHIPS AND GRANTS IN AID OF RESEARCH.
Natural Sciences & Engineering Research Council of Canada, 350 Albert St., Ottawa, ON K1A 1H5, Canada. TEL 613-995-5992. FAX 613-943-0742. Available only online. *2550*

NATURE CONSERVANCY MAGAZINE.
Nature Conservancy, 1815 N. Lynn St., Arlington, VA 22209. TEL 703-841-5300. *2239*

NATURWISSENSCHAFTEN.
Springer-Verlag, Heidelberger Platz 3, 14197 Berlin, Germany. TEL 49-30-82787-0. FAX 49-30-82787448. URL: http://link.springer.de/link/service/journals/00114/index.htm. *6551*

NAUNYN-SCHMIEDEBERG'S ARCHIVES OF PHARMACOLOGY.
Springer-Verlag, Heidelberger Platz 3, 14197 Berlin, Germany. TEL 49-30-82787-0. FAX 49-30-82787448. URL: http://link.springer.de/link/service/journals/00210/index.htm. *5680*

NAUTILUS.
URL: http://netics.it/nautilus. Available only online. *3327*

NAVAL WAR COLLEGE REVIEW.
U.S. Naval War College, 686 Cushing Rd., Code 32, Newport, RI 02841-1207. TEL 401-841-2236. FAX 401-841-3579. URL: http://www.usnwc.edu/nwc/press.htm. *5279*

NAVY NEWS & UNDERSEA TECHNOLOGY.
Pasha Publications Inc., 1616 N. Ft. Myer Dr., Ste. 1000, Arlington, VA 22209-3107. TEL 703-528-1244. FAX 703-528-1253. *5279*

NEBRASKA BUSINESS DIRECTORY.
American Business Directories, 5711 S. 86th Circle, Box 27347, Omaha, NE 68127. TEL 402-593-4600. FAX 402-331-5481. *1701*

NEBRASKA LAW REVIEW.
University of Nebraska at Lincoln, College of Law, Lincoln, NE 68583-0903. TEL 402-472-1267.
Vendor(s): Lexis-Nexis, West Group. *3995*

NEBRASKA LIBRARIES: A DIRECTORY.
Nebraska Library Commission, 1200 N St., No. 120, Lincoln, NE 68508-2023. TEL 402-471-2045. URL: http://neon.nlc.state.ne.us/nlc.html. Available only online. *4202*

NEDERLANDS A B C DIENSTVERLENERS.
A B C voor Handel en Industrie C.V., P.O. Box 190, 2000 AD Haarlem, Netherlands. TEL 31-23-5319031. FAX 31-23-5327033. URL: http://www.abc-d.nl.
Vendor(s): Data-Star. *1701*

NEDERLANDS A B C VOOR HANDEL EN INDUSTRIE.
A B C voor Handel en Industrie C.V., P.O. Box 190, 2000 AD Haarlem, Netherlands. TEL 31-23-5319031. FAX 31-23-5327033. URL: http://www.abc-d.nl.
Vendor(s): Data-Star. *1701*

NEEDLE TIPS AND THE HEPATITIS B COALITION NEWS.
Immunization Action Coalition, 1573 Selby Ave., Ste. 229, St. Paul, MN 55104. TEL 612-647-9009. FAX 612-647-9131. URL: http://www.winternet.com/~immunize/. *4800*

NEMATOLOGICAL ABSTRACTS.
CAB International, Wallingford, Oxon. OX10 8DE, England. TEL 44-1491-832111. FAX 44-1491-826090.
Vendor(s): CISTI, DIMDI, European Space Agency (File nos.16 & 124/CAB), Knight-Ridder Information, Inc., Ovid Technologies, Inc. (CABA). *179*

NEPHROLOGY, DIALYSIS AND TRANSPLANTATION.
Oxford University Press, Academic Division, Great Clarendon St., Oxford OX2 6DP, England. TEL 44-1865-267907. FAX 44-1865-267485. URL: http://www.oup.co.uk/journals. *5164*

NET BUSINESS DAILY.
I O Communications, 182 Ch. de Charleroi, 1060 Brussels, Belgium. TEL 32-2-534-07-37. FAX 32-5-534-07-57. URL: http://www.iocom.be/nbd/
Available only online. *987*

NETCETERA.
15400 S.E. 30th Pl., Ste. 202, Bellevue, WA 98007. URL: http://www.nwnet.net/netcetera/
Available only online. *2137*

THE NETHERLANDER.
Het Financieele Dagblad B.V., P.O. Box 216, 1000 AE Amsterdam, Netherlands. TEL 31-20-5928888. FAX 31-20-5928600. URL: http://www.netherlander.com. *987*

NETSCI.
Network Science Corporation, 412 Carolina Blvd., Isle of Palms, SC 29451. TEL 803-886-8775. FAX 803-886-5924. URL: http://www.awod.com/netsci/.
Available only online. *5680*

NETSURFER DIGEST.
333 Cobalt Way, Ste. 107, Sunnyvale, CA 94086. URL: http://www.netsurf.com/nsd/
Available only online. *2137*

NETWORK (DURHAM).
Family Health International, Research Triangle Park Branch, Box 13950, Durham, NC 27709. FAX 919-544-7040. URL: http://www.fhi.org. *858*

NETWORK AUDIO BITS.
Box 328, Orono, ME 04473-0328. URL: http://maine.maine.edu/~n-audio.
Available only online. *5419*

NETWORK BRIEFING.
A P T Data Group plc., 12 Sutton Row, 4th Fl., London W1V 5FH, England. TEL 44-171-208-4200. FAX 44-171-439-1105.
Vendor(s): Information Access Co. *2037*

NETWORK: COMPUTATION IN NEURAL SYSTEMS.
I O P Publishing Ltd., Dirac House, Temple Back, Bristol BS1 6BE, England. TEL 44-117-929-7481. FAX 44-117-929-4318. URL: http://www.iop.org. *6594*

NETWORK COMPUTING (MANHASSET).
C M P Publications, Inc., 600 Community Dr., Manhasset, NY 11030. TEL 516-562-5000. FAX 516-365-4601.
Vendor(s): Information Access Co. *2138*

NETWORK V A R.
Miller Freeman, Inc., 600 Harrison St., San Francisco, CA 94107. TEL 415-905-2200. FAX 415-905-2232.
Vendor(s): Information Access Co. *2138*

NETWORK WORLD.
Network World Inc., 161 Worcester Rd., 5th Fl., Framingham, MA 01701. TEL 508-875-6400. FAX 508-879-3167. URL: http://www.nwfusion.com.
Vendor(s): Knight-Ridder Information, Inc. (File no.674), Lexis-Nexis, UMI. *2138*

NETWORKS UPDATE.
Worldwide Videotex, Box 3273, Boynton Beach, FL 33424-3273. TEL 407-738-2276.
Vendor(s): Data-Star, Information Access Co., Knight-Ridder Information, Inc., NewsNet (EC95). *2138*

NEURAL COMPUTING AND APPLICATIONS.
Springer-Verlag London Ltd., Sweetapple House, Catteshall Rd., Godalming, Surrey GU7 3DJ, England. TEL 44-1483-418800. FAX 44-1483-415144. *2103*

NEUROBIOLOGY OF DISEASE.
Academic Press, Inc., Journal Division, 525 B St., Ste. 1900, San Diego, CA 92101-4495. TEL 619-230-1840. FAX 619-699-6800. URL: http://www.apnet.com/www/journal/nb.htm; http://www.idealibrary.com/ *5082*

NEUROBIOLOGY OF LEARNING AND MEMORY.
Academic Press, Inc., Journal Division, 525 B St., Ste. 1900, San Diego, CA 92101-4495. TEL 619-230-1840. FAX 619-699-6800. URL: http://www.apnet.com/www/journal/nl.htm; http://www.idealibrary.com/ *5082*

NEUROCASE.
Oxford University Press, Academic Division, Great Clarendon St., Oxford OX2 6DP, England. TEL 44-1865-267907. FAX 44-1865-267485. URL: http://www.oup.co.uk/journals. *5082*

NEUROIMAGE.
Academic Press, Inc., Journal Division, 525 B St., Ste. 1900, San Diego, CA 92101-4495. TEL 619-230-1840. FAX 619-699-6800. URL: http://www.apnet.com; http://www.idealibrary.com/ *5083*

NEUROLOGICAL SURGERY.
Igaku Shoin Ltd., 24-3 Hongo 5-chome, Bunkyo-ku, Tokyo 113-91, Japan. TEL 81-3-3817-5702.
Vendor(s): JICST. *5149*

NEUROLOGY.
Lippincott - Raven Publishers, 227 E. Washington Sq., Philadelphia, PA 19106. TEL 215-238-4200. FAX 215-238-4227. URL: http://www.lrpub.com.
Vendor(s): Ovid Technologies, Inc. *5084*

NEURORADIOLOGY.
Springer-Verlag, Heidelberger Platz 3, 14197 Berlin, Germany. TEL 49-30-82787-0. FAX 49-30-82787448. URL: http://link.springer.de/link/service/journals/00234/index.htm. *5112*

NEUROSCIENCE COMMUNICATIONS.
Gordon and Breach - Harwood Academic, Amsteldisk 166, 1st Fl., 1079 LH Amsterdam, Netherlands. URL: http://www.gbhap.com/Neuroscience_Communications/. *4783*

THE NEUROSCIENTIST.
Williams & Wilkins, 351 W. Camden St., Baltimore, MD 21201-2436. TEL 410-528-4068. FAX 410-528-4452. URL: http://www.wwilkins.com/the_neuroscientist. *5087*

NEUROSURGERY (BALTIMORE).
Williams & Wilkins, 351 W. Camden St., Baltimore, MD 21201-2436. TEL 410-528-4068. FAX 410-528-4452. URL: http://www.wwilkins.com/neurosurgery/
Vendor(s): Ovid Technologies, Inc. *5087*

NEVADA BUSINESS DIRECTORY.
American Business Directories, 5711 S. 86th Circle, Box 27347, Omaha, NE 68127. TEL 402-593-4600. FAX 402-331-5481. *1701*

NEVADA LAWYER.
State Bar of Nevada, 1325 Airmotive Way, Ste. 140, Reno, NV 89502-3239. TEL 702-329-4100. FAX 702-329-0522.
Vendor(s): Lexis-Nexis, West Group. *3996*

NEVADA WAGE SURVEY.
Employment, Training and Rehabilitation Department, Employment Security Division, 500 E. Third St., Carson City, NV 89713. TEL 702-687-4550. *1446*

NEW ACCOUNTANT.
Real Estate News Corp., 3525 W. Petersen Ave., Chicago, IL 60659.
Vendor(s): UMI. *1095*

NEW AFRICAN.
I.C. Publications Ltd., 7 Coldbath Sq., London EC1R 4LQ, England. TEL 44-171-713-7711. FAX 44-171-713-7898. *1365*

NEW ASTRONOMY.
Elsevier Science B.V., P.O. Box 211, 1000 AE Amsterdam, Netherlands. TEL 31-20-4853911. FAX 31-20-4853705. URL: http://www.elsevier.nl:80/inca/publications/5/2/5/6/5/4/525654.html. *498*

NEW BRUNSWICK REPORTS.
Maritime Law Book Ltd., Box 302, Fredericton, NB E3B 4Y9, Canada. TEL 506-453-9921. FAX 506-453-9525.
Vendor(s): QL Systems Ltd. *3996*

NEW ENGLAND ECONOMIC INDICATORS.
Federal Reserve Bank of Boston, Research Department, 600 Atlantic Ave., Boston, MA 02106. TEL 617-973-3397. FAX 617-973-4292. URL: http://www.bos.frb.org. *1273*

NEW ENGLAND ECONOMIC REVIEW.
Federal Reserve Bank of Boston, Research Department, Research Library D, Box 2076, Boston, MA 02106-2076. TEL 617-973-3397. FAX 617-973-4292. URL: http://www.bos.frb.org.
Vendor(s): Information Access Co. *1273*

NEW ENGLAND ENVIRONMENTAL DIRECTORY.
Harbinger Communications, Box 8175, Missoula, MT 59807. TEL 406-721-0440. FAX 406-721-0440. *2239*

NEW ENGLAND JOURNAL OF MEDICINE.
Massachusetts Medical Society, 10 Shattuck St., Boston, MA 02115. TEL 617-734-9800. FAX 617-893-8103. URL: http://www.nejm.org.
Vendor(s): Ovid Technologies, Inc. (NEJM). *4721*

NEW ENGLAND LAW REVIEW.
New England School of Law, New England Law Review, 154 Stuart St., Boston, MA 02116. TEL 617-422-7294. FAX 617-422-7451.
Vendor(s): Lexis-Nexis, West Group. *3996*

NEW FRONTIER.
New Frontier Education Society, 41 White Oak Rd., Arden, NC 28704-9557. TEL 704-251-0109. FAX 704-251-0727. URL: http://www.consciousnet.com. *5459*

NEW HAMPSHIRE BUSINESS DIRECTORY.
American Business Directories, 5711 S. 86th Circle, Box 27347, Omaha, NE 68127. TEL 402-593-4600. FAX 402-331-5481. *1701*

NEW HAMPSHIRE BUSINESS REVIEW.
Business Publications, Inc. (Manchester), 150 Dow St., Manchester, NH 03101-1227. TEL 603-624-1442. FAX 603-624-1310.
Vendor(s): Knight-Ridder Information, Inc., UMI. *1215*

NEW JERSEY BUSINESS.
New Jersey Business Magazine, 310 Passaic Ave., Fairfield, NJ 07004. TEL 201-882-5004.
Vendor(s): Lexis-Nexis, UMI. *1592*

NEW JERSEY BUSINESS DIRECTORY.
American Business Directories, 5711 S. 86th Circle, Box 27347, Omaha, NE 68127. TEL 402-593-4600. FAX 402-331-5481. *1702*

NEW JERSEY INDUSTRY ENVIRONMENTAL ALERT.
Business & Legal Reports, Inc., Attn: Carin Roaldset, 39 Academy St., Madison, CT 06443. TEL 203-245-7448. FAX 203-245-2559.
Vendor(s): Information Access Co. *2944*

NEW JERSEY LAW JOURNAL.
American Lawyer Media, L.P. (Newark), 238 Mulberry St., Box 20081, Newark, NJ 07101-6081. TEL 201-642-0075. FAX 201-642-0920.
Vendor(s): Lexis-Nexis. *3996*

NEW JERSEY LAWYER (ISELIN).
New Jersey Lawyer, Inc., Metropolitan Corporate Plaza, 485B Route 1, Ste. 100, Iselin, NJ 08830-3013. TEL 908-750-4994. FAX 908-750-0010. URL: http://www.njlnews.com. *3997*

NEW JERSEY LAWYER (NEW BRUNSWICK).
New Jersey State Bar Association, 1 Constitution Sq., New Brunswick, NJ 08901. TEL 908-249-5000.
Vendor(s): West Group. *3997*

NEW LAW JOURNAL.
Butterworth & Co. (Publishers) Ltd., Part of the Reed Elsevier group, Halsbury House, 35 Chancery Ln., London WC2A 1EL, England. TEL 071-400-2500. FAX 071-400-2842.
Vendor(s): Lexis-Nexis. *3997*

THE NEW LEADER.
American Labor Conference on International Affairs, Inc., 275 Seventh Ave., New York, NY 10001. TEL 212-807-8240. FAX 212-727-2229.
Vendor(s): Information Access Co., Knight-Ridder Information, Inc.. *3380*

NEW LITERARY HISTORY.
Johns Hopkins University Press, Journals Publishing Division, 2715 N. Charles St., Baltimore, MD 21218. TEL 410-516-6987. FAX 410-516-6968. URL: http://muse.jhu.edu.
Vendor(s): Information Access Co. *4440*

NEW MANUFACTURING PROCESSES AND MATERIALS SERIES.
Chapman & Hall, 2-6 Boundary Row, London SE1 8HN, England. TEL 44-171-8560066. FAX 44-171-5229623. URL: http://www.iop.org. *2868*

NEW MARITIMES.
New Maritimes Editorial Council Society, P.O. Box 31269, Halifax, NS B3K 5Y5, Canada. TEL 902-425-6622. *4348*

NEW MATERIALS - JAPAN.
International Newsletters, P.O. Box 133, Witney, Oxon. OX8 6ZH, England. TEL 44-1993-824130. FAX 44-1993-824150. URL: http://www.intnews.u-net.com.
Vendor(s): Information Access Co.. *6968*

NEW MEDIA MARKETS.
Financial Times Telecoms & Media Publishing, Maple House, 149 Tottenham Court Rd., London W1P 9LL, England. TEL 0171-896-2234. FAX 0171-896-2256.
Vendor(s): Information Access Co.. *2055*

NEW MEXICO BUSINESS DIRECTORY.
American Business Directories, 5711 S. 86th Circle, Box 27347, Omaha, NE 68127. TEL 402-593-4600. FAX 402-331-5481. *1702*

NEW MEXICO BUSINESS JOURNAL.
Sierra Publishing Group, Inc., 420 Central SW, Ste.104, Albuquerque, NM 87102. TEL 505-243-3444. FAX 505-243-4118.
Vendor(s): Information Access Co., Knight-Ridder Information, Inc., UMI. *987*

NEW MEXICO LAW REVIEW.
University of New Mexico, School of Law, 1117 Stanford, N.E., Albuquerque, NM 87131. TEL 505-277-8659.
Vendor(s): Lexis-Nexis, West Group. *3997*

NEW MOBILITY.
Miramar Communications Inc., 23815 Stuart Ranch Rd., Box 8987, CA 90265-8987. TEL 310-317-4522. FAX 310-317-9644. URL: http://www.newmobility.com/index.html. *3456*

NEW ORLEANS CITYBUSINESS.
New Orleans City Business, 111 Veterans Blvd., Ste. 1810, Metairie, LA 70005. TEL 504-834-9292. FAX 504-837-2258.
Vendor(s): Knight-Ridder Information, Inc., Lexis-Nexis, UMI. *1645*

NEW ORLEANS MAGAZINE.
New Orleans Publishing Group, 111 Veterans Blvd., Ste. 1810, Metairie, LA 70005. TEL 504-831-3731. FAX 504-837-2258.
Vendor(s): Information Access Co., UMI. *3380*

NEW PERSPECTIVES QUARTERLY.
Blackwell Publishers, 238 Main St., Cambridge, MA 02142. TEL 617-547-7110. FAX 617-547-0789.
Vendor(s): Information Access Co., UMI. *5948*

NEW POLITICAL SCIENCE.
Caucus for a New Political Science, c/o John C. Berg, Treas., Department of Government, Suffolk University, Boston, MA 02108-2770. TEL 617-573-8126. FAX 617-367-4623. URL: http://gramercy.ios.com/~urbsoc/NPS/home.html. *5948*

NEW PRODUCT LAUNCH LETTER.
IMSWORLD Publications Ltd., 7 Harewood Ave., London NW1 6JB, England. TEL 0171-393-5000. FAX 0171-393-5900.
Vendor(s): Data-Star. *5680*

NEW PRODUCT NEWS.
B P I Communications, 1130 Connecticut Ave., N.W., Ste. 625, Washington, DC 20036. TEL 202-828-0993. FAX 202-828-0825.
Vendor(s): Information Access Co., Lexis-Nexis. *3121*

THE NEW REPUBLIC.
1220 19th St., N.W., Washington, DC 20036. TEL 202-331-7494. FAX 202-331-0275. URL: http://www.enews.com/magazines/tnr/txindex.html.
Vendor(s): Information Access Co., Knight-Ridder Information, Inc., UMI. *4349*

NEW SCIENTIST.
I P C Magazines, Specialist Magazine Group King's Reach Tower, Stamford St., London SE1 9LS, England. TEL 44-171-261-5000. FAX 44-1444-445599. URL: http://www.newscientist.com/.
Vendor(s): Information Access Co., MediaStream. *6553*

NEW SOUTH WALES LAW REPORTS.
L B C Information Services, 50 Waterloo Rd., N. Ryde, N.S.W. 2113, Australia. TEL 61-2-99366444. FAX 61-2-98889706.
Vendor(s): Info-One International Pty Ltd.. *4136*

NEW STATESMAN.
New Statesman Ltd., 7th Fl., Victoria Station House, 191 Victoria St., London SW1E 5NE, England. TEL 44-171-828-1232. FAX 44-171-828-1881.
Vendor(s): Information Access Co., UMI. *4349*

NEW STEEL.
Chilton Publishing Company, 191 S. Gary Ave., Carol Stream, IL 60188. TEL 630-462-2285.
Vendor(s): Information Access Co., Knight-Ridder Information, Inc.. *5205*

NEW TECHNOLOGY WEEK.
King Communications Group, Inc., 627 National Press Bldg., Washington, DC 20045. TEL 202-638-4260. FAX 202-662-9744.
Vendor(s): Information Access Co., Lexis-Nexis, NewsNet (RD23). *6968*

NEW TRADE NAMES IN THE RUBBER AND PLASTICS INDUSTRIES.
Rapra Technology Ltd., Shawbury, Shrewsbury, Shrops. SY4 4NR, England. TEL 44-1939-250383. FAX 44-1939-251118. URL: http://www.rapra.net.
Vendor(s): Data-Star, European Space Agency, Knight-Ridder Information, Inc., Questel Orbit Inc. (RAPRA), STN International. *6503*

THE NEW VISION.
P.O. Box 9815, Kampala, Uganda. TEL 256-41-235846. FAX 256-41-235221. *3367*

NEW WAVES (COLLEGE STATION).
Texas Water Resources Institute, c/o Texas A & M Univ., Texas Agricultural Experiment Sta., College Station, TX 77843-2118. TEL 409-845-8571. FAX 409-845-8554. URL: http://twri.tamu.edu/twripubs/NewWaves/. *7298*

NEW WOMAN.
Hachette - E M A P, Endeavour House, 189 Shaftesbury Ave., London WC2H 8JE, England. TEL 44-171-437-9011. URL: http://www.erack.com/nwoman. *7329*

NEW WRITING MAGAZINE.
Box 1812, Amherst, NY 14226-7812. TEL 716-834-1067. URL: http://members.aol.com/newwriting. *4441*

NEW YORK BUSINESS DIRECTORY.
American Business Directories, 5711 S. 86th Circle, Box 27347, Omaha, NE 68127. TEL 402-593-4600. FAX 402-331-5481. *1702*

NEW YORK GENEALOGY NEWS.
476 Morris St., Ste. 1, Albany, NY 12208-3328.
Available only online. *3234*

THE NEW YORK JOURNAL OF MATHEMATICS.
State University of New York at Albany, URL: http://nyjm.albany.edu.
Available only online. *4594*

NEW YORK LAW JOURNAL.
New York Law Publishing Co., 345 Park Ave. S., New York, NY 10010. TEL 212-779-9200. URL: http://www.ljx.com.
Vendor(s): Lexis-Nexis, Wilsonline. *3998*

NEW YORK MAGAZINE.
K-III Communications Corp., 745 Fifth Ave., New York, NY 10151. TEL 212-745-0100.
Vendor(s): Information Access Co.. *3380*

NEW YORK METRO BUSINESS DIRECTORY.
American Business Directories, 5711 S. 86th Circle, Box 27347, Omaha, NE 68127. TEL 402-593-4600. FAX 402-331-5481. *1702*

NEW YORK REVIEW OF BOOKS.
N Y R E V, Inc., 250 W. 57th St., New York, NY 10107. TEL 212-757-8070. FAX 212-333-5374. URL: http://www.nybooks.com/nyrev.
Vendor(s): UMI. *4349*

NEW YORK REVIEW OF SCIENCE FICTION.
Dragon Press, Box 78, Pleasantville, NY 10570. TEL 914-769-5545. URL: http://www.nyrsf.com. *4534*

NEW YORK STATE BAR JOURNAL.
New York State Bar Association, One Marine Midland Plaza, Binghamton, NY 13902. FAX 607-772-6093.
Vendor(s): West Group (NYSTBJ). *3998*

NEW YORK STATE CONSERVATIONIST.
Department of Environmental Conservation, 50 Wolf Rd., Albany, NY 12233. TEL 518-457-5547. FAX 518-457-0858.
Vendor(s): UMI. *2239*

THE NEW YORK TIMES.
New York Times Company, 229 W. 43rd St., New York, NY 10036, TEL 212-556-1234. FAX 212-556-4603. URL: http://www.nytimes.com.
Vendor(s): Lexis-Nexis, UMI. *3380*

NEW YORK TIMES BOOK REVIEW.
New York Times Company, 229 W. 43rd St., New York, NY 10036. TEL 212-556-1234. URL: http://www.nytimes.com/books/home/. *6278*

THE NEW YORK TIMES INDEX.
U M I, 300 N. Zeeb Rd., Ann Arbor, MI 48106. TEL 313-761-4700. FAX 800-864-0019. *3885*

NEW YORK UNIVERSITY LAW REVIEW.
New York University Law Review, 110 W. Third St., New York, NY 10012. TEL 212-998-6350. FAX 212-995-4032.
Vendor(s): Lexis-Nexis, West Group. *3999*

NEW ZEALAND MANUFACTURER (WELLINGTON, 1992).
New Zealand Manufacturers Federation, 3 Church St., P.O. Box 11-543, Wellington 1, New Zealand. TEL 64-4-4733000. FAX 64-4-4733004.
Vendor(s): UMI. *988*

NEW ZEALAND NATIONAL BIBLIOGRAPHY.
National Library of New Zealand, P.O. Box 1467, Wellington, New Zealand. TEL 64-4-4743067. FAX 64-4-4743124. *558*

NEW ZEALAND SERIALS.
National Library of New Zealand, P.O. Box 1467, Wellington, New Zealand. TEL 64-4-7473067. FAX 64-4-4743124. *558*

NEWFOUNDLAND & PRINCE EDWARD ISLAND REPORTS.
Maritime Law Book Ltd., Box 302, Fredericton, NB E3B 4Y9, Canada. TEL 506-453-9921. FAX 506-453-9525.
Vendor(s): QL Systems Ltd.. *3999*

SERIALS AVAILABLE ONLINE

NEWMEDIA.
HyperMedia Communications, Inc., 901 Mariners Island, Ste. 365, San Mateo, CA 94404. TEL 415-573-5170. FAX 415-573-5131. URL: www.hyperstand.com. *2055*

NEWS I S.
Xephon, 1301 W. Hwy. 407, Ste. 201-450, Lewisville, TX 75067. TEL 817-455-7050. FAX 817-455-2492. URL: http://www.xephon.co.uk. Available only online. *2191*

THE NEWS INTERNATIONAL.
Independent Newspapers Corp. Pvt. Ltd., Printing House, I.I. Chundrigar Rd., P.O. Box 52, Karachi (Sindh) 74200, Pakistan. TEL 92-21-2637111. FAX 92-21-2636066. URL: http://www.jang-group.com/the news. *3346*

NEWS LIBRARY NEWS.
Special Libraries Association, News Division, c/o Catherine Kitchell, Ed., Bureau of National Affairs, 1231 25th St., N.W., Washington, DC 20037. URL: http://www4.nando.net/prof/poynter/nd/ndmenu.html. Vendor(s): MediaStream. *4203*

NEWS OF NORWAY.
Royal Norwegian Embassy, 2720-34th St., N.W., Washington, DC 20008. TEL 202-333-6000. FAX 202-337-0870. URL: http://www.norway.org/web/norway/ *3033*

NEWS PHOTOGRAPHER.
National Press Photographers Association, Inc., 1446 Conneaut Ave., Bowling Green, OH 43402-2145. TEL 419-352-8175. FAX 419-354-5435. URL: http://sunsite.unc.edu/nppa. Vendor(s): Information Access Co., UMI. *5769*

NEWS - 400.
Duke Communications International, 221 E. 29th St., Ste. 242, Loveland, CO 80538. TEL 970-663-4700. FAX 970-663-3285. URL: http://www.news400.com. *2180*

NEWSBRIEFNEWS.
TransAtlantic, Koniginneweg 201, 1075 CR Amsterdam, Netherlands. TEL 31-20-6711818. FAX 31-20-6711818. URL: gopher://gopher.konbib.nl/11/greynet/; http://www.konbib.nl/infolev/greynet/home.html. *4203*

NEWSCOPE.
United Methodist Publishing House, 201 Eighth Ave. S., Box 801, Nashville, TN 37202. TEL 615-749-6732. FAX 615-749-6079. *6435*

NEWSINC.
Cowles - SIMBA Information, 11 Riverbend Dr. S., Box 4949, Stamford, CT 06907-0949. TEL 203-358-9900. FAX 203-358-5811. URL: http://www.simbanet.com. Vendor(s): Information Access Co.. *6278*

THE NEWSLETTER NEWSLETTER.
Communication Resources Inc., 4150 Belden Village St., Ste. 400, Canton, OH 44718-2502. FAX 330-493-7897. *6435*

THE NEWSLETTER ON CIVIL LIBERTIES.
P.O. Box 888, Sta. F, Toronto, ON M4Y 2N9, Canada. URL: http://www.sympatico.ca/toshiya.k.ncl/. *5996*

NEWSLETTER ON SERIALS PRICING ISSUES.
Marcia Tuttle, Ed. & Pub., Serials Department, C.B. 3938, Davis Library, University of North Carolina at Chapel Hill, Chapel Hill, NC 27514-8890. TEL 919-962-8047. FAX 919-962-4450. URL: http://sunsite.unc.edu/reference/prices/prices.html. Available only online. *4203*

NEWSLETTER - THE INTERNATIONAL COMMUNICATION PROJECT.
AStA Universitaet Hannover, Foundation for International Communication, Welfengarten 1, 30167 Hannover, Germany. TEL 49-511-7625063. FAX 49-511-717441. URL: http://www.comlink.apc.org/fic/newslett/. *1365*

NEWSLETTERS IN PRINT.
Gale Research, 835 Penobscot Bldg., 645 Griswold St., Detroit, MI 48226-4094. TEL 313-961-2242. FAX 800-414-5043. Vendor(s): Knight-Ridder Information, Inc. (File no.469). *558*

NEWSMAKERS.
Gale Research, 835 Penobscot Bldg., 645 Griswold St., Detroit, MI 48226-4094. TEL 313-961-2242. FAX 800-414-5043. Vendor(s): Lexis-Nexis. *576*

NEWSNET ACTION LETTER.
NewsNet, Inc., 945 Haverford Rd., Bryn Mawr, PA 19010. TEL 610-527-8030. FAX 610-527-0338. Vendor(s): NewsNet (PB99). *2017*

NEWSPAPER ABSTRACTS.
U M I Company (Louisville), 620 S. Third St., Louisville, KY 40202-2475. *3885*

NEWSPAPER RESEARCH JOURNAL.
Association for Education in Journalism and Mass Communication, Le Conte College, Rm. 121, University of South Carolina, Columbia, SC 29208-0251. TEL 803-777-2005. Vendor(s): UMI. *3878*

NEWSPAPERS & TECHNOLOGY.
Media Business Corp., 607 10th St., Ste. 103, Golden, CO 80401-1053. TEL 303-355-2101. FAX 303-355-2144. URL: http://newsandtech.com/ *3878*

NEWSWEEK.
Newsweek, Inc., 251 W. 57th St., New York, NY 10019. TEL 212-445-4000. URL: http://www.newsweek-int.com. Vendor(s): Lexis-Nexis. *3381*

NEWTNEWS.
5375 Hewlett Dr., San Diego, CA 92115. URL: http://www.ridgecrest.ca.us/NewtNews/ Available only online. *2199*

NEXOS; SOCIEDAD, CIENCIA, LITERATURA.
Nexos S.A. de C.V., Mazatlan 119, Col. Condesa, 06140 Mexico DF, Mexico. TEL 52-5-2867922. FAX 52-5-2860794. URL: http://www.nexos.com.mx. *6627*

NEXUS (HAMILTON).
c/o Department of Anthropology, McMaster University, Hamilton, ON L8S 4L9, Canada. TEL 416-525-9140. Available only online. *325*

NEXUS NEW TIMES.
Nexus Magazine Pty Ltd., P.O. Box 30, Mapleton, Qld. 4650, Australia. TEL 61-7-5442-9280. FAX 61-7-5442-9381. URL: http://www.peg.apc.org/'nexus/. *5577*

NIEMAN REPORTS.
Nieman Foundation, Harvard University, 1 Francis Ave., Cambridge, MA 02138. TEL 617-495-2237. FAX 617-495-8976. Vendor(s): Information Access Co., UMI. *3878*

NIGHT PEOPLE.
URL: http://www.az.com/'katrinat. Available only online. *4441*

NIGHTLIFE (CARBONDALE).
Carbondale Nightlife, 705 W. Main St., Carbondale, IL 62901. TEL 618-549-2799. URL: http://www.midwest.net/nightlife/nightlife. *3381*

NIGRIZIA.
Missionari Comboniani, Vicolo Pozzo 1, 37129 Verona, Italy. URL: http://www.freeworld.it/peaclink/nigrizia.html. *6358*

NIHON KONCHU GAKKAI TAIKAI KOEN YOSHI.
Entomological Society of Japan, Kokuritsu Kagaku Hakubutsukan Dobutsu Kenkyubu, 23-1 Hyakunincho 3-chome, Shinjuku-ku, Tokyo 160, Japan. TEL 03-3364-7129. FAX 03-3364-7104. *642*

THE NIKKEI WEEKLY.
Nihon Keizai Shimbun, Inc., 1-9-5 Otemachi, Chiyoda-ku, Tokyo 100, Japan. TEL 81-3-3270-0251. FAX 81-3-5255-2661. Vendor(s): Lexis-Nexis. *988*

NINETEENTH-CENTURY LITERATURE (BERKELEY).
University of California Press, Journals Division, 2120 Berkeley Way, No. 5812, Berkeley, CA 94720-5812. TEL 510-643-7154. FAX 510-642-9917. URL: http://sunsite.berkeley.edu:8080/scan. Vendor(s): Information Access Co.. *4442*

19TH-CENTURY MUSIC.
University of California Press, Journals Division, 2120 Berkeley Way, No. 5812, Berkeley, CA 94720-5812. TEL 510-643-7154. FAX 510-642-9917. URL: http://library.berkeley.edu:808Q/ucalpress/journals. Vendor(s): Information Access Co.. *5420*

NIPPON JUI CHIKUSAN DAIGAKU KENKYU HOKOKU.
Nippon Jui Chikusan Daigaku, 1-7-1 Kyonan-cho, Musashino-shi, Tokyo 180, Japan. TEL 422-31-4151. FAX 422-33-2035. *7275*

NIPPON MEDICAL SCHOOL. JOURNAL.
Nippon Medical School, Medical Association, 1-1-5 Sendagi, Bunkyo-ku, Tokyo 113, Japan. TEL 81-3-3822-2131. FAX 81-3-3822-3759. Vendor(s): JICST. *4722*

NITRIC OXIDE.
S U B I S, Mansion House, 19 Kingfield Rd., Sheffield S11 9AS, England. TEL 44-114-255-4433. FAX 44-114-255-4626. URL: http://www.apnet.com/www/journal/no.htm. *667*

NITROGEN.
British Sulphur Publishing, 31 Mount Pleasant, London WC1X 0AD, England. TEL 44-171-837-5600. FAX 44-171-837-0292. Vendor(s): Information Access Co.. *236*

NO D E A - NONLINEAR DIFFERENTIAL EQUATIONS AND APPLICATIONS.
Birkhaeuser Verlag, P.O. Box 133, CH-4010 Basel, Switzerland. TEL 41-61-2050730. FAX 41-61-2050791. URL: http://link.springer.de/link/service/journals/00030/index.htm. *4594*

NO-SPACE.
URL: http://www.geocities.com/soho/lofts/7621. Available only online. *410*

NOEDUS.
URL: http://www.eig.unige.ch/'kaeser/noedus. Available only online. *4594*

NOISE AND VIBRATION WORLDWIDE.
Multi-Science Publishing Co. Ltd., 107 High St., Brentwood, Essex CM14 4RX, England. TEL 44-1277-224632. FAX 44-1277-223453. *5873*

NOISE REGULATION REPORT.
Business Publishers, Inc., 951 Pershing Dr., Silver Spring, MD 20910-4464. TEL 301-587-6300. FAX 301-585-9075. Vendor(s): NewsNet (EV19). *2971*

NON-FOODS MERCHANDISING.
Cardinal Business Media, Inc., 200 Connecticut Ave., Ste. 5-D, Norwalk, CT 06854. TEL 203-838-9100. FAX 203-838-2550. Vendor(s): Information Access Co.. *1543*

NONFERROUS METALS ALERT.
Cambridge Scientific Abstracts, 7200 Wisconsin Ave., Bethesda, MD 20814. TEL 301-961-6750. FAX 301-961-6720. URL: http://www.csa.com. Vendor(s): CEDOCAR, CISTI, Data-Star (MBUS), European Space Agency (File no.111), Knight-Ridder Information, Inc. (File no.269), Questel Orbit Inc. (MABU), STN International (MATBUS). *5220*

NONLINEAR SCIENCE TODAY.
Springer-Verlag, Science Journals, 175 Fifth Ave., New York, NY 10010. TEL 212-460-1500. FAX 212-473-6272. URL: http://www.springer-ny.com/nst. Available only online. *4595*

NONLINEARITY.
I O P Publishing Ltd., Dirac House, Temple Back, Bristol BS1 6BE, England. TEL 44-117-929-7481. FAX 44-117-929-4318. URL: http://www.iop.org/EJ/3/313/bin/journal/no. *4595*

NONPARAMETRIC STATISTICS.
Gordon and Breach - Harwood Academic, Amsteldisk 166, 1st Fl., 1079 LH Amsterdam, Netherlands. URL: http://www.gbhap.com/Nonparametric_Statistics/. *6929*

NONPRESCRIPTION PHARMACEUTICALS AND NUTRITIONALS: THE TAN SHEET.
F-D-C Reports, Inc., 5550 Friendship Blvd., Ste. 1, Chevy Chase, MD 20815. FAX 301-664-7238. Vendor(s): Data-Star (FDCR), Knight-Ridder Information, Inc. (File no.187), Lexis-Nexis. *5681*

NONPROFIT WORLD.
Society for Nonprofit Organizations, 6314 Odana Rd., Ste. 1, Madison, WI 53719. TEL 608-274-9777. FAX 608-274-9978. URL: http://www.uwex.edu/danenet/snpo.
Vendor(s): UMI. *6679*

NONWOVENS ABSTRACTS.
Pira International, Randalls Rd., Leatherhead, Surrey KT22 7RU, England. TEL 44-1372-802050. FAX 44-1372-802239. URL: http://www.pira.co.uk/.
Vendor(s): Data-Star, FIZ Technik, Knight-Ridder Information, Inc., Questel Orbit Inc., STN International. *5887*

NONWOVENS INDUSTRY.
Rodman Publications, Inc., 17 S. Franklin Tpk., Box 555, Ramsey, NJ 07446. TEL 201-825-2552. FAX 201-825-0553.
Vendor(s): Information Access Co.. *6992*

NORDIC JOURNAL OF PHILOSOPHICAL LOGIC.
Scandinavian University Press, P.O. Box 2959 Toeyen, N-0608 Oslo, Norway. TEL 47-22-575400. FAX 47-22-575353. URL: http:/ww.hf.uio.no/filosofi/njpl/. *5739*

NORDIC LINGUISTIC BULLETIN.
Nordic Linguistic Bulletin, Harald Haarfagersgt. 31, N-5007 Bergen, Norway. TEL 47-55-58-29-54. FAX 47-55-58-94-70.
Available only online. *4285*

NORDICOM.
Nordic Documentation Center for Mass Communication Research, Statsbiblioteket, Universitetsparken, DK-8000 Aarhus C, Denmark. TEL 45-86-12-20-22. FAX 45-86-13-27-04. *2013*

NORMALISATIE-NIEUWS.
Nederlands Normalisatie-instituut, P.O. Box 5059, 2600 GB Delft, Netherlands. TEL 31-15-2690390. FAX 31-15-2690190. URL: http://www.nni.nl. *5253*

NORTH AMERICAN FAUNA.
U.S. National Biological Service, Information Transfer Center, c/o Managing Editor, 1201 Oak Ridge Dr., Ste. 200, CO 80525-5589. TEL 970-226-9401. FAX 970-226-9455. *846*

THE NORTH AMERICAN REVIEW.
c/o Robley Wilson, Ed., University of Northern Iowa, Cedar Falls, IA 50614-0516. TEL 319-273-6455. FAX 319-273-6455.
Vendor(s): Information Access Co., UMI. *4350*

NORTH CAROLINA BUSINESS DIRECTORY.
American Business Directories, 5711 S. 86th Circle, Box 27347, Omaha, NE 68127. TEL 402-593-4600. FAX 402-331-5481. *1703*

NORTH CAROLINA JOURNAL OF INTERNATIONAL LAW AND COMMERCIAL REGULATION.
University of North Carolina at Chapel Hill, School of Law, No. 3380, Chapel Hill, NC 27599-3380. TEL 910-962-4402. FAX 910-962-4713.
Vendor(s): Lexis-Nexis, West Group. *4123*

NORTH CAROLINA LAW REVIEW.
North Carolina Law Review Association, Univ. of N. Carolina at Chapel Hill, School of Law, Van Hecke-Wettach Hall, Chapel Hill, NC 27599-3380. TEL 919-962-3926.
Vendor(s): Lexis-Nexis, West Group. *4000*

NORTH DAKOTA BUSINESS DIRECTORY.
American Business Directories, 5711 S. 86th Circle, Box 27347, Omaha, NE 68127. TEL 402-593-4600. FAX 402-331-5481. *1703*

NORTH SEA LETTER.
Financial Times Energy Publishing, Maple House, 149 Tottenham Court Rd., London W1P 9LL, England. TEL 44-171-896-2241. FAX 44-171-896-2275.
Vendor(s): Data-Star, Information Access Co., Knight-Ridder Information, Inc., Lexis-Nexis. *5612*

NORTH SEA RIG FORECAST.
Financial Times Energy Publications, Maple House, 149 Tottenham Court Rd., London W1P 9LL, England. TEL 44-171-896-2241. FAX 44-171-896-2275.
Vendor(s): Data-Star, Information Access Co., Knight-Ridder Information, Inc., Lexis-Nexis. *2674*

NORTH WIND.
George MacDonald Society, The Library, King's College, Strand, London WC2R 2LS, England. TEL 44-1342-823859. URL: http://www.primenet.com/biz/jjf/gmsociety.html. *4350*

NORTHEAST POWER REPORT.
McGraw-Hill Companies, Energy & Business Newsletters, 1221 Ave. of the Americas, 36th Fl., New York, NY 10020. TEL 212-512-6410. FAX 212-512-2723.
Vendor(s): Dow Jones News Retrieval (NEPR), Knight-Ridder Information, Inc. (NPR), NewsNet (EY88). *2690*

NORTHERN CALIFORNIA BUSINESS DIRECTORY.
American Business Directories, 5711 S. 86th Circle, Box 27347, Omaha, NE 68127. TEL 402-593-4600. FAX 402-331-5481. *1703*

NORTHERN HOUSE PAMPHLET POETS.
Northern House, 12 Queens Terrace, Newcastle-upon-Tyne NE2 2PJ, England. TEL 44-191-281-2614. *4515*

NORTHERN IRELAND NEWS SERVICE.
Box 57, Albany, NY 12211-0057. TEL 518-329-3003.
Vendor(s): NewsNet (IT74). *5949*

NORTHERN KENTUCKY LAW REVIEW.
Northern Kentucky University, Salmon P. Chase College of Law, Highland Heights, KY 41076. TEL 606-572-5444.
Vendor(s): West Group. *4001*

NORTHERN KENTUCKY ZINE.
Northern Kentucky Zine Inc., Box 815, Covington, KY 41012-0815. TEL 606-291-0430. FAX 606-291-0431. URL: http://pullmangroup.com.
Available only online. *7224*

THE NORTHERN MINER.
Southam Magazine Group, 1450 Don Mills Rd., Don Mills, ON M3B 2X7, Canada. TEL 416-445-6641. FAX 416-442-2175.
Vendor(s): Information Access Co., Southam Electronic Publishing. *5312*

NORTHERN ONTARIO BUSINESS.
Laurentian Publishing Co., 158 Elgin St., Sudbury, ON P3E 3N5, Canada. TEL 705-673-5705. FAX 705-673-9542.
Vendor(s): Lexis-Nexis, UMI. *989*

NORTHWEST PHOENIX.
Indiana University Northwest, 3400 Broadway, Moraine 110, Gary, IN 46408. TEL 219-980-6795. FAX 219-981-4233. *1964*

NORTHWESTERN JOURNAL OF INTERNATIONAL LAW & BUSINESS.
Northwestern University, School of Law - Office of Legal Publications, 357 E. Chicago Ave., Chicago, IL 60611. TEL 312-503-8467.
Vendor(s): West Group. *4123*

NORTHWESTERN UNIVERSITY LAW REVIEW.
Northwestern University, School of Law - Office of Legal Publications, 357 E. Chicago Ave., Chicago, IL 60611. TEL 312-503-8463.
Vendor(s): Lexis-Nexis, West Group. *4001*

NORWAVES.
NorWaves - N K I, P.O. Box 111, 1341 Bekkestua, Norway.
Available only online. *3344*

NORWAY. R B T - RIKSBIBLIOTEKTJENESTEN. SKRIFTER.
R B T - Riksbibliotektjenesten, P.O. Box 2439, Solli, N-0201 Oslo, Norway. TEL 47-22-43-08-80. FAX 47-22-56-09-81. URL: http://info.rbt.no/ *4204*

NOTES FROM THE WINDOWSILL.
Box 401, Santa Cruz, CA 95061-0401. URL: http://www.armory.com/~web/notes.html.
Available only online. *6279*

NOTES WAR.
110 Carr St., Chapel Hill, NC 27516. URL: http://www.gse.upenn.edu/billb/NotesWar.
Available only online. *4534*

SERIALS AVAILABLE ONLINE 10173

NOTISUR.
University of New Mexico, Latin American Institute, 801 Yale N.E., Albuquerque, NM 87131-1016. TEL 505-277-6839. FAX 505-277-5989. URL: http://www.ladb.unm.edu/.
Vendor(s): Information Access Co., Knight-Ridder Information, Inc., Lexis-Nexis, NewsNet. *5949*

NOTIZIE EVANGELICHE.
Federation of Protestant Churches in Italy, Via Firenze 38, 00184 Rome, Italy. TEL 39-6-4825120. FAX 39-6-4828728. URL: http://hella.stm.it/market/evan/home.htm. *6436*

NOTRE DAME LAW REVIEW.
University of Notre Dame, School of Law, Box 988, Notre Dame, IN 46556. TEL 219-631-7097. FAX 219-631-6371.
Vendor(s): West Group. *4001*

NOVA ASTRONAUTICA.
Associazione Sviluppo Propulsione Spaziale, Via N. Martoglio 22, 00137 Rome, Italy. TEL 39-6-87131068. *75*

NOVA LAW REVIEW.
Nova Law Review, 3305 College Ave., Fort Lauderdale, FL 33314. TEL 954-452-6195. URL: http://www.nsulaw.nova.edu/pubs/review/.
Vendor(s): West Group. *4001*

NOVA NEWS NET.
University of King's College, School of Journalism, 6350 Coburg Rd., Halifax, NS B3L 2X9, Canada. URL: http://www.ukings.ns.ca/nnn/html.
Available only online. *3878*

NOVA SCOTIA REPORTS.
Maritime Law Book Ltd., P.O. Box 302, Fredericton, NB E3B 4Y9, Canada. TEL 506-453-9921. FAX 506-453-9525.
Vendor(s): QL Systems Ltd.. *4001*

NOVEL: A FORUM ON FICTION.
Brown University, Department of Literature, Box 1984, Providence, RI 02912. TEL 414-863-3756.
Vendor(s): UMI. *4443*

NOW AND THEN.
East Tennessee State University, Center for Appalachian Studies and Services, Box 70556, Johnson City, TN 37614-0556. TEL 423-929-5348. FAX 423-929-6340. *4443*

NUA INTERNET SURVEYS.
Westland Court, S. Cumberland St., Dublin 2, Ireland. TEL 353-1-676-8996. FAX 353-1-661-3932. URL: http://www.nua.ie/surveys/
Available only online. *2138*

NUA NEW THINKING.
Westland Court, S. Cumberland St., Dublin 2, Ireland. TEL 353-1-676-8996. FAX 353-1-661-3932. URL: http://www.nua.ie/NewThinking/
Available only online. *5740*

NUCLEAR AWARENESS NEWS.
Nuclear Awareness Project, P.O. Box 104, Uxbridge ON L9P 1M6, Canada. TEL 905-852-0571. *2700*

NUCLEAR DATA NEWSLETTER.
International Atomic Energy Agency, Wagramerstr. 5, P.O. Box 100, A-1400 Vienna, Austria. TEL 43-1-20600. FAX 43-1-20607. *2700*

NUCLEAR DATA SHEETS.
Academic Press, Inc., Journal Division, 525 B St., Ste. 1900, San Diego, CA 92101-4495. TEL 619-230-1840. FAX 619-699-6800. URL: http://www.apnet.com/www/journal/ds.htm; http://www.idealibrary.com/ *2700*

NUCLEAR MEDICINE COMMUNICATIONS.
Chapman & Hall, Journals Department 2-6 Boundary Row, London SE1 8HN, England. TEL 44-171-8650066. FAX 44-171-522-9623. URL: http://www.chaphall.com/chaphall/journals.html. *5112*

NUCLEAR NEWS.
American Nuclear Society, 555 N. Kensington Ave., La Grange Park, IL 60525. TEL 708-352-6611. URL: http://www.ans.org/pubs/magazines/NN/
Vendor(s): Lexis-Nexis. *2701*

NUCLEAR WASTE NEWS.
Business Publishers, Inc., 951 Pershing Dr., Silver Spring, MD 20910-4464. TEL 301-587-6300. FAX 301-585-9075.
Vendor(s): Information Access Co., NewsNet (EV03). *2987*

NUCLEARFUEL.
McGraw-Hill Companies, 1221 Ave. of the Americas, New York, NY 10020.
Vendor(s): Dow Jones News Retrieval (NUF), Knight-Ridder Information, Inc. (File no.624/McGRAW-HILL PUBLICATIONS ONLINE), Lexis-Nexis (NUFUEL), NewsNet (EY72). *2702*

NUCLEIC ACIDS ABSTRACTS.
Cambridge Scientific Abstracts, 7200 Wisconsin Ave., 6th Fl., Bethesda, MD 20814. TEL 301-961-6750. FAX 301-961-6720. URL: http://www.csa.com.
Vendor(s): Knight-Ridder Information, Inc. (File no.76/LIFE SCIENCES COLLECTION), STN International (LIFESCI). *643*

NUCLEIC ACIDS RESEARCH.
Oxford University Press, Academic Division, Great Clarendon St., Oxford OX2 6DP, England. TEL 44-1865-267907. FAX 44-1865-267485. URL: http://www.oup.co.uk/journals. *667*

NUCLEONICS WEEK.
McGraw-Hill Companies, Energy & Business Newsletters, 1221 Ave. of the Americas, 36th Fl., New York, NY 10020. TEL 212-512-6410.
Vendor(s): Dow Jones News Retrieval (NUC), Knight-Ridder Information, Inc. (File no.624/McGRAW-HILL PUBLICATIONS ONLINE), Lexis-Nexis (NUWEEK), NewsNet (EY73). *2675*

NUCLEOTECNICA.
Comision Chilena de Energia Nuclear, Amunategui 95, Casilla 188-D, Santiago, Chile. TEL 56-2-6990070. FAX 56-2-6994548. *2702*

NUMERISCHE MATHEMATIK.
Springer-Verlag, Heidelberger Platz 3, 14197 Berlin, Germany. TEL 49-30-82787-0. FAX 49-30-82787448. URL: http://science.springer.de/nmee/nm-main.htm. *4623*

THE NURSE PRACTITIONER.
Springhouse Corporation, 1111 Bethlehem Pike, Box 908, Springhouse, PA 19477. TEL 215-646-8700. *4942*

NURSING HOMES.
Medquest Communications, Inc., 629 Euclid Ave., Ste. 500, Cleveland, OH 44114-3003. TEL 216-522-9700. FAX 216-522-9707.
Vendor(s): Information Access Co., Knight-Ridder Information, Inc., UMI. *4943*

NURSING OUTLOOK.
Mosby Year - Book, Inc., 11830 Westline Industrial Dr., St. Louis, MO 63146-3318. TEL 314-872-8370. FAX 314-432-1380. *4944*

NURSING RESEARCH.
Lippincott -Raven Publishers, 227 E. Washington Sq., Philadelphia, PA 19106. TEL 215-238-4200. FAX 215-238-4227. URL: http://www.lrpub.co. *4944*

THE NUTMEG POINT DISTRICT MAIL.
Box 43072, Upper Montclair, NJ 07043-0072. URL: http://www.kosmic.org/members/dongle/henry/
Available only online. *4534*

NUTRITION ABSTRACTS AND REVIEWS. SERIES A: HUMAN AND EXPERIMENTAL.
CAB International, Wallingford, Oxon. OX10 8DE, England. TEL 44-1491-832111. FAX 44-1491-826190. URL: http://www.cabi.org.
Vendor(s): DIMDI, European Space Agency, Knight-Ridder Information, Inc., STN International. *5485*

NUTRITION ABSTRACTS AND REVIEWS. SERIES B: LIVESTOCK FEEDS AND FEEDING.
CAB International, Wallingford, Oxon. OX10 8DE, England. TEL 44-1491-832111. FAX 44-1491-826090.
Vendor(s): CISTI, DIMDI, European Space Agency (File nos.16 & 124/CAB), Knight-Ridder Information, Inc., Ovid Technologies, Inc. (VETR). *179*

NUTRITION ACTION HEALTHLETTER.
Center for Science in the Public Interest, 1875 Connecticut Ave., N.W., Ste. 300, Washington, DC 20009-5728. TEL 202-332-9110. FAX 202-265-4954. URL: http://www.cspinet.org.
Vendor(s): Information Access Co., UMI. *5479*

NUTRITION FORUM.
Prometheus Books Incorporated, 59 John Glenn Dr., Amherst, NY 14228. TEL 716-691-0133. FAX 716-691-0133.
Vendor(s): Information Access Co. *5479*

NUTRITION HEALTH REVIEW.
Vegetus Publications, Box 406, Haverford, PA 19041. TEL 610-896-1853. FAX 610-896-1857.
Vendor(s): Information Access Co.. *5479*

NUTRITION RESEARCH NEWSLETTER.
Lyda Associates, Inc., Box 700, Palisades, NY 10964. TEL 914-359-8282. FAX 914-359-1229.
Vendor(s): Information Access Co. *5480*

NUTRITION REVIEWS.
Allen Press, Inc., Box 1897, Lawrence, KS 66044. TEL 913-843-1234. FAX 913-843-1274.
Vendor(s): UMI. *5480*

NUTRITION TODAY.
Williams and Wilkins, 351 W. Camden St., Baltimore, MD 21201-2436. TEL 410-528-4068. FAX 410-528-4452. URL: http://www.wwilkins.com.
Vendor(s): Information Access Co. *5481*

NY LITTERATUR OM KVINNOR.
Goeteborgs Universitet, Universitetsbibliotek, Centralbiblioteket, P.O. Box 5096, S-402 22 Goeteborg, Sweden. *7350*

NYERE DANSK FAGLITTERATUR.
Dansk BiblioteksCenter as, Tempovej 7-11, DK-2750 Ballerup, Denmark. TEL 45-44-867777. FAX 45-44-867892. *559*

NYTT JURIDISKT ARKIV. AVD. 1 - RAETTSFALL FRAAN HOEGSTA DOMSTOLEN.
Fritzes Foerlag AB, Norstedts Juridik, P.O. Box 6472, S-113 82 Stockholm, Sweden. TEL 46-8-690-91-90. FAX 46-8-690-90-70.
Vendor(s): DAFA Data AB. *4002*

O C L C ANNUAL REPORT.
Online Computer Library Center, Inc., 6565 Frantz Rd., Dublin, OH 43017. TEL 614-764-6000. FAX 614-764-6096. *4204*

O C L C NEWSLETTER.
Online Computer Library Center, Inc., 6565 Frantz Rd., Dublin, OH 43017. TEL 614-764-6000. *4204*

O E C D ECONOMIC OUTLOOK.
Organization for Economic Cooperation and Development, 2 rue Andre-Pascal, 75775 Paris Cedex 16, France. TEL 33-1-45-24-82-00. FAX 33-1-45-24-85-00.
Vendor(s): Information Access Co., UMI. *1274*

O E C D ECONOMIC STUDIES.
Organization for Economic Cooperation and Development, 2 rue Andre-Pascal, 75775 Paris Cedex 16, France. TEL 33-1-45-24-82-00. FAX 33-1-45-24-85-00.
Vendor(s): Information Access Co.. *1274*

O E C D ECONOMIC SURVEYS: AUSTRIA.
Organization for Economic Cooperation and Development, 2 rue Andre Pascal, 75775 Paris 16, France. TEL 33-1-45248200. FAX 33-1-45248500.
Vendor(s): Information Access Co. *1274*

O E C D ECONOMIC SURVEYS: CANADA.
Organization for Economic Cooperation and Development, 2 rue Andre-Pascal, 75775 Paris Cedex 16, France. TEL 33-1-45248200. FAX 33-1-45248500.
Vendor(s): Information Access Co.. *1274*

O E C D ECONOMIC SURVEYS: DENMARK.
Organization for Economic Cooperation and Development, 2 rue Andre-Pascal, 75775 Paris Cedex 16, France. TEL 33-1-45248200. FAX 33-1-45248500.
Vendor(s): Information Access Co.. *1274*

O E C D ECONOMIC SURVEYS: ICELAND.
Organization for Economic Cooperation and Development, 2 rue Andre-Pascal, 75775 Paris Cedex 16, France. TEL 33-1-45248200. FAX 33-1-45245800.
Vendor(s): Information Access Co.. *1274*

O E C D ECONOMIC SURVEYS: SPAIN.
Organization for Economic Cooperation and Development, 2 rue Andre-Pascal, 75775 Paris Cedex 16, France. TEL 33-1-45248200. FAX 33-1-45248500.
Vendor(s): Information Access Co.. *1275*

O E C D ECONOMIC SURVEYS: UNITED STATES.
Organization for Economic Cooperation and Development, 2 rue Andre-Pascal, 75775 Paris Cedex 16, France. TEL 33-1-45248200. FAX 33-1-45248500.
Vendor(s): Information Access Co.. *1275*

O E C D OBSERVER.
Organization for Economic Cooperation and Development, 2 rue Andre-Pascal, 75775 Paris Cedex 16, France. TEL 33-1-45-24-82-00. FAX 33-1-45-24-85-00.
Vendor(s): Information Access Co., UMI. *1275*

O E C D OIL, GAS, COAL & ELECTRICITY. QUARTERLY STATISTICS.
Organization for Economic Cooperation and Development, 2 rue Andre-Pascal, 75775 Paris Cedex 16, France. *5631*

O E REPORTS.
International Society for Optical Engineering (SPIE), 1000 20th St., Box 10, Bellingham, WA 98227-0010. TEL 360-676-3290. FAX 360-647-1445. *5866*

O-HAYO SENSEI.
O-Hayo Sensei, 1032 Irving St., Ste. 508, San Francisco, CA 94122. TEL 415-731-1113. FAX 415-731-1113. URL: http://www.ohayosensei.com. *2566*

O M R I DAILY DIGEST.
Open Media Research Institute, Motokov Bldg., Na Strzi 63, 14062 Prague 4, Czech Republic. TEL 42-2-61142114. FAX 42-2-61143184. URL: http://www.omri.cz/
Available only online. *6030*

O R - M S TODAY.
Institute for Operations Research and the Management Sciences, 901 Elkridge Landing Rd., Ste. 400, Linthicum, MD 21090-2909. TEL 410-850-0300. FAX 410-684-2963. URL: http://lionhrtpub.com/orms.html. *6555*

O S H BRIEFING.
Babour Index plc., New Lodge Drift Rd., Windsor, Berks. SL4 4RQ, England. TEL 44-1344-884121. FAX 44-1344-884112. URL: dd@ehas.demon.co.uk. *5495*

O S S C BULLETIN.
University of Oregon College of Education, Oregon School Study Council, 1787 Agate St., Eugene, OR 97403-5207. TEL 541-346-5043. FAX 541-346-2334. *2469*

O S - 2 COMPUTING! MAGAZINE.
URL: http://www.os2computing.com/magazine.
Available only online. *2145*

O S - 2 E -ZINE!
Haligonian Media, 26 Victoria Rd., Dartmouth, NS B2Y 2V9, Canada. URL: http://www.haligonian.com/os2/
Available only online. *2216*

OBJECT CURRENTS.
Sigs Publications, Inc., 71 W. 23rd St., New York, NY 10010. TEL 212-242-7447. FAX 212-242-7574. URL: http://www.sigs.com/
Available only online. *2145*

OBJECT MAGAZINE.
Sigs Publications, Inc., 71 W. 23rd St., New York, NY 10010-4102. TEL 212-242-7447. FAX 212-242-7574. URL: http://www.sigs.com. *2088*

OBJECT-ORIENTED STRATEGIES.
Cutter Information Corp., 37 Broadway, Arlington, MA 02174. TEL 617-648-8700. FAX 617-648-1950. URL: http://www.cutter.com. *2177*

SERIALS AVAILABLE ONLINE

OBJECT-ORIENTED SYSTEMS.
Chapman & Hall, Journals Department 2-6 Boundary Row, London SE1 8HN, England. TEL 44-171-8650066. FAX 44-171-5229623. URL: http://www.chaphall.com/chaphall/journals.html. *2145*

OBLIVION.
120 State Ave., N.E., Ste. 76, Olympia, WA 98501-8212. URL: http://www.oblivion.net. *1852*

OBSCURE.
Box 594, Lafayette, CA 94549-0594. URL: http://www.whamcat.com/obscure/ *4444*

OBSERVATOIRE DE STRASBOURG. CENTRE DE DONNEES ASTRONOMIQUES DE STRASBOURG. INFORMATION BULLETIN.
Observatoire de Strasbourg, 11 rue de l'Universite, 67000 Strasbourg, France. TEL 33-3-88150720. FAX 33-3-88150760. URL: http://cdsweb.u-strasbg.fr/cds.html. *498*

OBSERWATORIUM KRAKOWSKIE. ROCZNIK ASTRONOMICZNY. DODATEK MIEDZYNARODOWY.
Uniwersytet Jagiellonski, Oberwatorium Krakowskie, Ul. Orla 171, 30-244 Krakow, Poland. TEL 48-12-251294. FAX 48-12-251318. URL: http://www.oa.uj.eud.pl/ktt.rcznk.html. *499*

OBSTETRICAL & GYNECOLOGICAL SURVEY.
Williams & Wilkins, 351 W. Camden St., Baltimore, MD 21201-2436. TEL 410-528-4068. FAX 410-528-4452. URL: http://www.wilkins.com. Vendor(s): Ovid Technologies, Inc.. *4965*

OBSTETRICS AND GYNECOLOGY.
Elsevier Science Inc., Box 945, New York, NY 10159-0945. TEL 212-633-3730. FAX 212-633-3680. URL: http://www.elsevier.nl/. Vendor(s): Ovid Technologies, Inc.. *4965*

OCCUPATIONAL ERGONOMICS.
Chapman & Hall, Journals Department 2-6 Boundary Row, London SE1 8HN, England. TEL 44-171-8650066. FAX 44-171-5229623. URL: http://www.chaphall.com/chaphall/journals.html. *5495*

OCCUPATIONAL HAZARDS.
Penton Publishing Co., 1100 Superior Ave., Cleveland, OH 44114-2543. TEL 216-696-7000. FAX 216-696-8765.
Vendor(s): Information Access Co., UMI. *5496*

OCCUPATIONAL HEALTH & SAFETY.
Stevens Publishing Corporation, 3700 J.H. Kultgen Frwy., Waco, TX 76706. TEL 817-776-9000. FAX 817-776-9018.
Vendor(s): UMI. *5496*

OCCUPATIONAL HEALTH & SAFETY LETTER.
Business Publishers, Inc., 951 Pershing Dr., Silver Spring, MD 20910-4464. TEL 301-587-6300. FAX 301-585-9075.
Vendor(s): Information Access Co., NewsNet. *5496*

OCCUPATIONAL HYGIENE.
Gordon and Breach - Harwood Academic, Amsteldisk 166, 1st Fl., 1079 LH Amsterdam, Netherlands. URL: http://www.gbhap.com/Occupational__Hygiene/. *5496*

OCCUPATIONAL OUTLOOK QUARTERLY.
U.S. Bureau of Labor Statistics, 2 Massachusetts Ave., N.E., Washington, DC 20212. TEL 202-606-5701.
Vendor(s): Information Access Co., UMI. *5518*

OCCUPATIONAL SAFETY & HEALTH REPORTER.
The Bureau of National Affairs, Inc., 1231 25th St., N.W., Washington, DC 20037. TEL 202-452-4200. FAX 202-822-8092. URL: http://www.bna.com/. Vendor(s): Human Resources Information Network (CDD, HDD), Knight-Ridder Information, Inc. (Laborlaw, File no.244). *5497*

OCCUPATIONAL THERAPY INDEX.
British Library, Medical Information Centre, Boston Spa, Wetherby, W. Yorks. LS23 7BQ, England. TEL 01937-546039. FAX 01937-546458. *4784*

OCEAN OIL WEEKLY REPORT.
PennWell Publishing Co. (Houston), Box 1941, Houston, TX 77251. TEL 713-621-9720. FAX 713-963-6285. *5613*

OCEANIA.
University of Sydney, Sydney, N.S.W. 2006, Australia. TEL 61-2-93512666. FAX 61-2-93517488.
Vendor(s): Information Access Co., UMI. *326*

OCEANIC ABSTRACTS.
Cambridge Scientific Abstracts, 7200 Wisconsin Ave., 6th Fl., Bethesda, MD 20814. TEL 301-961-6750. FAX 301-961-6720. URL: http://www.csa.com.
Vendor(s): European Space Agency (File no.17/OCEANIC), Knight-Ridder Information, Inc. (File no.28), STN International (OCEAN). *2326*

OCEANUS.
Woods Hole Oceanographic Institution, Research Library, 86 Water St., Woods Hole, MA 02543. TEL 508-289-2719. FAX 508-289-2182. URL: http://www.mbl.edu/html/library/libweb.html.
Vendor(s): Information Access Co.. *2413*

OCTANE WEEK.
Information Resources, Inc., 1925 N. Lynn St., Ste. 1000, Arlington, VA 22204-1707. TEL 703-528-2500. FAX 703-528-1483.
Vendor(s): Data-Star, Dow Jones News Retrieval, Information Access Co., Knight-Ridder Information, Inc.. *5613*

O'DWYER'S P R SERVICES REPORT.
J.R. O'Dwyer Co., Inc., 271 Madison Ave., New York, NY 10016. TEL 212-679-2471. FAX 212-683-2750.
Vendor(s): Lexis-Nexis. *42*

OECOLOGIA.
Springer-Verlag, Heidelberger Platz 3, 14197 Berlin, Germany. TEL 49-30-82787-0. FAX 49-30-82787448. URL: http://link.springer.de. *618*

OFF-HIGHWAY ENGINEERING.
Society of Automotive Engineers, 400 Commonwealth Dr., Warrendale, PA 15096-0001. TEL 412-772-7114. FAX 412-776-4026.
Vendor(s): Questel Orbit Inc.. *7111*

OFF ROAD.
McMullen Argus Publishing Inc., 774 S. Placentia Ave., Placentia, CA 92870-6846. TEL 714-572-2255. FAX 714-572-1864.
Vendor(s): Information Access Co.. *7111*

OFFBEAT.
Offbeat, Inc., 333 St. Charles Ave., Ste. 614, New Orleans, LA 70130. TEL 504-522-5533. FAX 504-522-1159. URL: http://www.offbeat.com. *5421*

OFFSHORE.
Global Group Ltd., P.O. Box CB13039, Nassau, Bahamas. URL: http://www.dnai.com/offshore/offshore.html.
Available only online. *1159*

OFFSHORE (TULSA).
PennWell Publishing Co., Box 1260, Tulsa, OK 74101. TEL 918-835-3161. FAX 918-832-9295.
Vendor(s): Information Access Co., Lexis-Nexis. *5613*

OFFSHORE FIELD DEVELOPMENT INTERNATIONAL.
Offshore Data Services, Inc., Box 19909, Houston, TX 77224-1909. TEL 713-781-2713. FAX 713-781-9594. *5614*

OFFSHORE RIG LOCATOR.
Offshore Data Services, Inc., Box 19909, Houston, TX 77224-1909. TEL 713-781-2713. FAX 713-781-9594. *5614*

OHIO BUSINESS DIRECTORY.
American Business Directories, 5711 S. 86th Circle, Box 27347, Omaha, NE 68127. TEL 402-593-4600. FAX 402-331-5481. *1704*

THE OHIO C P A JOURNAL.
Ohio Society of Certified Public Accountants, 535 Metro Place S., Box 1810, Dublin, OH 43017-7810. TEL 614-764-2727. FAX 614-764-5880.
Vendor(s): Information Access Co., UMI. *1096*

OHIO NORTHERN UNIVERSITY LAW REVIEW.
Ohio Northern University, Pettit College of Law, Box 153, Ada, OH 45810. TEL 419-772-2248. FAX 419-772-2714. URL: http://www.law.onu.edu/.
Vendor(s): Lexis-Nexis, West Group. *4003*

OHIO OUTDOORS.
Firelands.Net, 12440 New London Eastern Rd., Homerville, OH 44235. URL: http://ezines.firelands.net/Ohio/Outdoors/
Available only online. *6877*

OHIO STATE JOURNAL ON DISPUTE RESOLUTION.
Ohio State University, College of Law, 55 W. 12th Ave., Columbus, OH 43210-1391. TEL 614-292-7170.
Vendor(s): West Group, Wilsonline. *4003*

OHIO STATE LANTERN.
Ohio State University, School of Journalism, 242 W. 18th Ave., Columbus, OH 43210. TEL 614-292-2031. FAX 614-292-3722. URL: http://www.thelantern.com. *1964*

OHIO STATE LAW JOURNAL.
Ohio State University, College of Law, 55 W. 12th Ave., Columbus, OH 43210-1391. TEL 614-292-6829.
Vendor(s): Lexis-Nexis, West Group, Wilsonline. *4003*

OHLASENE KNIHY.
Narodni Knihovna Ceske Republiky, Klementinum 190, 110 01 Prague 1, Czech Republic. TEL 420-2-21663306. FAX 420-2-21663306. *559*

OIL & GAS INTERESTS NEWSLETTER.
Hart Publications, Inc. (Denver), 4545 Post Oak Pl., Ste. 210, Houston, TX 77027. TEL 713-993-9320.
Vendor(s): Information Access Co.. *5615*

OIL AND GAS INVESTOR.
Hart Publications, Inc. (Houston), 4545 Post Oak Place, Ste. 210, Houston, TX 77027. TEL 713-993-9320.
Vendor(s): UMI. *5615*

OIL & GAS JOURNAL.
PennWell Publishing Co., Box 1260, Tulsa, OK 74101. TEL 918-835-3161. FAX 918-832-9295. URL: http://www.pennwell.com/ogj.html.
Vendor(s): Information Access Co., Lexis-Nexis, UMI. *5615*

OIL DAILY.
Energy Intelligence Group, 575 Broadway, 4th Fl., New York, NY 10012. TEL 212-941-5500. FAX 212-941-5509. URL: http://www.energyintel.com. *5615*

OIL MARKET TRENDS.
Arab Press Service, A P S House, P.O. Box 3896, Nicosia, Cyprus. TEL 357-2-351778. FAX 357-2-350265.
Vendor(s): Information Access Co.. *2675*

OIL PRICE INFORMATION SERVICE.
United Communications Group, 11300 Rockville Pike, Ste. 1100, Rockville, MD 20852-3030. TEL 301-816-8950.
Vendor(s): NewsNet (EY02), United Communications Group (PETROSCAN). *5616*

OIL SPILL INTELLIGENCE REPORT.
Cutter Information Corp., 37 Broadway, Arlington, MA 02174. TEL 617-648-8700. FAX 617-648-1950. URL: http://www.cutter.com.
Vendor(s): Information Access Co.. *5616*

OIL SPILL U S LAW REPORT.
Cutter Information Corp., 37 Broadway, Arlington, MA 02174. TEL 617-648-8700. FAX 617-648-8707.
Vendor(s): NewsNet (EV06). *4003*

OILS AND FATS: THE INTERNATIONAL MARKET.
Euromonitor, 60-61 Britton St., London EC1M 5NA, England. TEL 44-171-251-8024. FAX 44-171-608-3149. URL: http://www.euromonitor.com.
Vendor(s): Data-Star, Knight-Ridder Information, Inc.. *3122*

OKLAHOMA BUSINESS DIRECTORY.
American Business Directories, 5711 S. 86th Circle, Box 27347, Omaha, NE 68127. TEL 402-593-4600. FAX 402-331-5481. *1704*

OKLAHOMA CITY UNIVERSITY LAW REVIEW.
Oklahoma City University, School of Law, 2501 N. Blackwelder, Oklahoma City, OK 73106. TEL 405-521-5280. FAX 405-521-5172.
Vendor(s): West Group. *4004*

SERIALS AVAILABLE ONLINE

OKLAHOMA LAW REVIEW.
University of Oklahoma, College of Law, 300 Timberdell Rd., Norman, OK 73019. TEL 405-325-5191.
Vendor(s): West Group. *4004*

OKLAHOMA LIVING.
Oklahoma Association of Electric Cooperatives, Box 54309, Oklahoma City, OK 73154-1309. TEL 405-478-1455. FAX 405-478-0246. URL: http://www.ok-living.com. *3381*

OLDER AMERICANS REPORT.
Business Publishers, Inc., 951 Pershing Dr., Silver Spring, MD 20910-4464. TEL 301-587-6300. FAX 301-585-9075. URL: http://www.bpinews.com/hr/pages/oar.htm.
Vendor(s): NewsNet. *6680*

OLYMPUS.
TEL 813-835-1830. URL: http://users.southeast.net/'markw/index-c.htm.
Available only online. *4445*

OMNI.
Omni International, Ltd., 277 Park Ave., 4th Fl., New York, NY 10172. TEL 212-702-6000. FAX 212-702-6282. URL: http://www.omnimag.com.
Available only online. Vendor(s): Information Access Co. *6556*

ON THE HORIZON.
Jossey-Bass Inc., Publishers, 350 Sansome Street, 5th Fl., San Francisco, CA 94104. FAX 800-605-2665. URL: http://www.josseybass.com; http://sunsite.unc.edu/horizon. *2552*

ONCOGENES AND GROWTH FACTORS ABSTRACTS.
Cambridge Scientific Abstracts, 7200 Wisconsin Ave., 6th Fl., Bethesda, MD 20814. TEL 301-961-6750. FAX 301-961-6720. URL: http://www.csa.com.
Vendor(s): Knight-Ridder Information, Inc. (File no.76), STN International (LIFESCI). *4784*

ONDER STOOM.
StoomGroep Holland, Schutterspad 107, 6866 EV Heelsum, Netherlands. TEL 31-317-318163. *2735*

ONE IF BY CONGRESS, TWO IF BY WHITE HOUSE.
118 W. MacArthur Blvd., Santa Ana, CA 92707. URL: http://www.geocities.com/CapitolHill/1783.
Available only online. *5950*

ONE TO ONE (FRESNO).
CreeYadio Services, Box 9787, Fresno, CA 93794. TEL 209-448-0700. FAX 209-448-0761.
Vendor(s): CompuServe, Inc.. *2026*

ONGOING CURRENT BIBLIOGRAPHY OF PLASTIC & RECONSTRUCTIVE SURGERY.
Creative Products, Inc., 23 Pinewood Farm Ct., Owings Mills, MD 21117. TEL 410-252-4022. FAX 410-252-3142.
Vendor(s): National Library of Medicine. *4784*

DER ONKOLOGE.
Springer-Verlag, Heidelberger Platz 3, 14197 Berlin, Germany. TEL 49-30-82787-0. FAX 49-30-82787448. URL: http://link.springer.de. *4985*

ONKRUID.
Stichting Onkruid, West 32, 1633 JC Avenhorn, Netherlands. TEL 31-2295-42800. FAX 31-2295-42315. *5459*

ONLINE (WILTON).
Online, Inc., 462 Danbury Rd., Wilton, CT 06897. TEL 203-761-1466. FAX 203-761-1444. URL: http://www.onlineinc.com/onlinemag.
Vendor(s): Information Access Co. *2139*

ONLINE BIRTH CENTER NEWS.
Midwifery Today Association, Box 2672-350, Eugene, OR 97402. TEL 541-344-7438. FAX 541-344-1422. URL: http://www.efn.org/'djz/birth/obcnews.html.
Available only online. *4965*

THE ONLINE JOURNAL OF CURRENT CLINICAL TRIALS.
Chapman & Hall, Journals Department 2-6 Boundary Row, London SE1 8HN, England. TEL 44-171-8650066. FAX 44-171-5229623. URL: http://www.chaphall.com/chaphall/journals.html.
Vendor(s): OCLC. *4724*

ONLINE JOURNAL OF KNOWLEDGE SYNTHESIS FOR NURSING.
Sigma Theta Tau International Honor Society of Nursing, 550 W. North St., Indianapolis, IN 46202. TEL 317-634-8171. FAX 317-634-8188.
Available only online. Vendor(s): OCLC. *4945*

ONLINE JOURNAL OF VETERINARY RESEARCH.
URL: http://www.powerup.com.au/~jvet/jvet196a.htm.
Available only online. *7276*

ONLINE LIBRARIES AND MICROCOMPUTERS.
Information Intelligence, Inc., Box 31098, Phoenix, AZ 85046. TEL 602-996-2283. URL: http://www.infointelligence.com/www/iii-info.
Vendor(s): Data-Star, Dow Jones News Retrieval, European Space Agency, Information Access Co., Knight-Ridder Information, Inc., NewsNet (PB42). *4234*

ONLINE NEWSLETTER.
Information Intelligence Inc., Box 31098, Phoenix, AZ 85046. TEL 602-996-2283. URL: http://www.infointellignece.com/www/iii-info.
Vendor(s): Data-Star, Dow Jones News Retrieval, European Space Agency, Information Access Co., Knight-Ridder Information, Inc., NewsNet (PB41). *2139*

ONLINE NOETIC NETWORK.
LightSpeed Publishing, 74 S. Hamilton, Doylestown, PA 18901. URL: http://www.libertynet.org/noetic/
Available only online. *5459*

ONLINE PRODUCT NEWS.
Worldwide Videotex, Box 3273, Boynton Beach, FL 33424-3273. TEL 407-738-2276.
Vendor(s): Information Access Co., NewsNet (TE27). *2167*

ONLINE WORLD.
TEL 61-2-9281-6188. FAX 61-2-9281-6204. URL: http://www.onlineworld.net.au.
Available only online. *2167*

ONLINE WORLD MONITOR NEWSLETTER.
4815 Saltrod, Norway. URL: http://login.eunet.no/~presno/monitor.html.
Available only online. *2139*

ONLY THE BEST.
Association for Supervision and Curriculum Development, 1250 N. Pitt St., Alexandria, VA 22314-1453. TEL 703-549-9110. FAX 703-299-8631. URL: http://www.ascd.org. *2216*

ONSITE IRELAND.
Archeire, 54 SCR Portobello, Dublin 8, Ireland. TEL 353-1-676-8996. FAX 353-1-661-3932. URL: http://www.archeire.com/onsite/
Available only online. *411*

ONTARIO. LABOUR RELATIONS BOARD. REPORTS. A MONTHLY SERIES OF DECISIONS.
Labour Relations Board, 400 University Ave., Toronto, ON M7A 1V4, Canada. TEL 416-326-7500. FAX 416-326-7531.
Vendor(s): QL Systems Ltd. *1449*

ONTARIO APPEAL CASES.
Maritime Law Book Ltd., Box 302, Fredericton, NB E3B 4Y9, Canada. TEL 506-453-9921. FAX 506-453-9525.
Vendor(s): QL Systems Ltd. *4004*

ONTARIO REPORTS.
Butterworths Canada Ltd., Part of the Reed Elsevier group, 75 Clegg Rd., Markham, ON L6G 1A1, Canada. TEL 905-479-2665. FAX 905-479-2826.
Vendor(s): QL Systems Ltd. *4004*

ONVIDEO.
Box 17377, Beverly Hills, CA 90209. URL: http://www.cyberpod.com/cyberpod/onvideo.
Available only online. *2068*

OOZE MAGAZINE.
URL: http://www.io.com/'ooze.
Available only online. *4351*

OPEN INFORMATION SYSTEMS.
Patricia Seybold Group, 85 Devonshire St. 5th Fl., Boston, MA 02109-3504. *2157*

OPENINGS ONLINE.
Scholars Press, Box 15399, Atlanta, GA 30333-0399. TEL 404-727-2345. FAX 404-727-2348.
Available only online. *2552*

OPERA NEWS.
Metropolitan Opera Guild, Inc., 70 Lincoln Center Plaza, New York, NY 10023. TEL 212-769-7080. FAX 212-769-7007. URL: http://www.operanews.com.
Vendor(s): Information Access Co., UMI. *5422*

OPERATIONS IN OIL DIPLOMACY.
Arab Press Service, A P S House, P.O. Box 3896, Nicosia, Cyprus. TEL 357-2-351778. FAX 357-2-350265.
Vendor(s): Information Access Co. *6030*

DER OPHTHALMOLOGE.
Springer-Verlag, Heidelberger Platz 3, 14197 Berlin, Germany. TEL 49-30-82787-0. FAX 49-30-82787448. URL: http://link.springer.de. *4998*

OPHTHALMOLOGY.
Lippincott - Raven Publishers, 227 E. Washington Sq., Philadelphia, PA 19106. TEL 215-238-4200. FAX 215-238-4227. URL: http://www.lrpub.com. *4999*

OPHTHALMOLOGY TIMES.
Advanstar Communications, Inc., 7500 Old Oak Blvd., Cleveland, OH 44130. TEL 216-826-2839. FAX 216-891-2726.
Vendor(s): Information Access Co., Knight-Ridder Information, Inc. *4999*

OPPORTUNIST.
Grant Douglas Publishing, 455 Douglas Ave., Ste. 2155-10, Altamonte Springs, FL 32714-3315. TEL 407-786-3701. FAX 407-786-3712. *1400*

OPTICAL AND QUANTUM ELECTRONICS.
Thomson Science, 2-6 Boundary Row, London SE1 8HN, England. TEL 44-171-8650066. FAX 44-171-5229623. URL: http://www.thomsonscience.com. *2648*

OPTICAL DIAGNOSTICS IN ENGINEERING.
TEL 44-131-451-3156. FAX 44-131-447-8660. URL: http://www.civ.hw.ac.uk/research/flic/ode/odemain.htm.
Available only online. *5866*

OPTICAL FIBER TECHNOLOGY.
Academic Press, Inc., Journal Division, 525 B St., Ste. 1900, San Diego, CA 92101-4495. TEL 619-699-6715. FAX 619-231-6616. URL: http://www.apnet.com/www.journal/of.htm; http://www.idealibrary.com/ *5867*

OPTICAL MATERIALS AND ENGINEERING NEWS.
Business Communications Co., Inc. (Norwalk), 25 Van Zant St., Norwalk, CT 06855. TEL 203-853-4266. FAX 203-853-0348.
Vendor(s): Data-Star, Information Access Co., Knight-Ridder Information, Inc., NewsNet (RD37). *5867*

OPTICAL MEMORY NEWS.
Phillips Business Information, Inc., 1201 Seven Locks Rd., Potomac, MD 20854. TEL 301-424-3338. FAX 301-309-3847.
Vendor(s): Information Access Co., NewsNet (EC50). *2180*

OPTIMIZATION.
Gordon and Breach - Harwood Academic, Amsteldisk 166, 1st Fl., 1079 LH Amsterdam, Netherlands. URL: http://www.gbhap.com/Optimization/. *4617*

OPTIMIZATION METHODS AND SOFTWARE.
Gordon and Breach - Harwood Academic, Amsteldisk 166, 1st Fl., 1079 LH Amsterdam, Netherlands. URL: http://www.gbhap.com/Optimization__Methods__Software/. *4623*

OPTIMUM.
Canada Communication Group, Publishing Division, Ottawa, ON K1A 0S9, Canada. TEL 819-956-4802.
Vendor(s): Information Access Co. *1499*

OPTIONS.
International Institute for Applied Systems Analysis, A-2361 Laxenburg, Austria. TEL 43-2236-807-0. FAX 43-2236-73149. URL: http://www.iiasa.ac.at. *2185*

SERIALS AVAILABLE ONLINE 10177

OPTO & LASER EUROPE.
I O P Publishing Ltd., Dirac House, Temple Back, Bristol BS1 6BE, England. TEL 44-117-929-7481. FAX 44-117-929-4318. URL: http://www.iop.org. *5868*

ORAL HYGIENE PRODUCTS: THE INTERNATIONAL MARKET.
Euromonitor, 60-61 Britton St., London EC1M 5NA, England. TEL 44-171-251-8024. FAX 44-171-608-3149. URL: http://www.euromonitor.com. Vendor(s): Data-Star, Knight-Ridder Information, Inc.. *507*

THE ORAL MAJORITY.
8391 Beverly Blvd., Ste. 310, Los Angeles, CA 90048. URL: http://www.oralmajority.com. Available only online. *4351*

ORANGE COUNTY BUSINESS JOURNAL.
Orange County Business Journal, 4590 MacArthur Blvd., Ste. 100, Newport Beach, CA 92660. TEL 714-833-8373. FAX 714-833-8751. Vendor(s): Knight-Ridder Information, Inc., UMI. *1276*

ORBIS.
J A I Press Inc., 55 Old Post Rd., No. 2, Box 1678, Greenwich, CT 06830-1678. TEL 203-661-7602. FAX 203-661-0792. Vendor(s): Information Access Co.. *6031*

OREGON BUSINESS DIRECTORY.
American Business Directories, 5711 S. 86th Circle, Box 27347, Omaha, NE 68127. TEL 402-593-4600. FAX 402-331-5481. *1705*

OREGON BUSINESS MAGAZINE.
Oregon Business Media, 610 S.W. Broadway, No. 200, Portland, OR 97205-3431. TEL 503-223-0304. FAX 503-221-6544. URL: http://www.oregonbusiness.com. Vendor(s): Information Access Co.. *990*

OREGON LAW REVIEW.
University of Oregon, School of Law, 1101 Kincaid St., 1221 University of Oregon, Eugene, OR 97403-1221. TEL 541-346-3844. FAX 541-346-1564. URL: http://www.law.uoregon.edu/ Vendor(s): Lexis-Nexis, West Group. *4005*

OREGON STATE BAR BULLETIN.
Oregon State Bar, Box 1689, Lake Oswego, OR 97035-0889. TEL 503-620-0222. FAX 503-684-1366. Vendor(s): Lexis-Nexis, West Group. *4005*

ORGANIC GARDENING.
Rodale Press, Inc., 33 E. Minor St., Emmaus, PA 18049. TEL 610-967-5171. FAX 610-967-7725. Vendor(s): Information Access Co., UMI. *3201*

ORGANIZATION STUDIES.
Walter de Gruyter und Co., Genthiner Str. 13, 10785 Berlin, Germany. TEL 49-30-26005-0. FAX 49-30-26005251. URL: http://www.degruyter.de. Vendor(s): Information Access Co., UMI. *6628*

ORGANIZATIONAL BEHAVIOR AND HUMAN DECISION PROCESSES.
Academic Press, Inc., Journal Division, 525 B St., Ste. 900, San Diego, CA 92101-4495. TEL 619-230-1840. FAX 619-699-6800. URL: http://www.apnet.com/www/journal/ob.htm; http://www.idealibrary.com/ *1500*

ORGANIZATIONAL DYNAMICS.
American Management Association, 1601 Broadway, New York, NY 10019. TEL 212-586-8100. Vendor(s): Information Access Co., UMI. *1500*

ORGANOMETALLICS.
American Chemical Society, 1155 16th St., N.W., Washington, DC 20036. TEL 800-333-9511. FAX 614-447-3671. Vendor(s): STN International (CJACS). *1820*

ORIGINATION NEWS MONTHLY.
Faulkner & Gray, 22nd Fl., 11 Penn Plaza, New York, NY 10001. TEL 212-967-7000. Vendor(s): UMI. *1160*

ORIGINS, C N S DOCUMENTARY SERVICE.
Catholic News Service, 3211 4th St., N.E., Washington, DC 20017. TEL 202-541-3290. FAX 202-541-3255. Vendor(s): NewsNet (CN03). *6474*

ORION (CHICO).
California State University, Chico, College of Communication, Department of Journalism, Chico, CA 95929-0600. TEL 916-898-5625. FAX 916-898-4839. URL: http://www.orion.csuchico.edu. *1965*

ORLANDO BUSINESS JOURNAL.
American City Business Journals (Orlando), 315 E. Robinson St., Ste. 250, Orlando, FL 32801-1949. TEL 407-649-8470. FAX 407-649-8469. Vendor(s): Information Access Co. *990*

ORNAMENTAL HORTICULTURE.
CAB International, Wallingford, Oxon. OX10 8DE, England. TEL 44-1491-832111. FAX 44-1491-826090. URL: http://www.cabi.org. Vendor(s): DIMDI, European Space Agency, Knight-Ridder Information, Inc., STN International. *3208*

ORPHAN DISEASE UPDATE.
National Organization for Rare Disorders, Inc. (NORD), Box 8923, New Fairfield, CT 06812-8923. TEL 203-746-6518. FAX 203-746-6481. URL: http://www.nord-rdb.com/~orphan. *4725*

ORPHIC CHRONICLE.
URL: http://web2.airmail.net/zill/orphic/or_ndex.htm. Available only online. *4516*

DER ORTHOPAEDE.
Springer-Verlag, Heidelberger Platz 3, 14197 Berlin, Germany. TEL 49-30-82787-0. FAX 49-30-82787448. URL: http://link.springer.de. *5013*

ORTHOPEDICS TODAY.
Slack, Inc., 6900 Grove Rd., Thorofare, NJ 08086-9447. TEL 609-848-1000. FAX 609-853-5991. URL: http://www.slackinc.com. *5014*

THE OSLER MEDICAL JOURNAL.
Johns Hopkins Osler Medical Housestaff, URL: http://omj.med.jhu.edu/ Available only online. *4725*

OSTEOPOROSIS INTERNATIONAL.
Springer-Verlag London Ltd., Sweetapple House, Catteshall Rd., Godalming, Surrey GU7 3DJ, England. TEL 44-1483-418800. FAX 44-1483-415144. *4725*

OSTOMY QUARTERLY.
United Ostomy Association, Inc., 19772 MacArthur Blvd., Ste. 200, Irvine, CA 92612-2405. TEL 714-660-8624. FAX 714-660-9262. Vendor(s): Information Access Co. *4725*

THE OTHER SIDE (PHILADELPHIA).
The Other Side, Inc., 300 W. Apsley St., Philadelphia, PA 19144. TEL 215-849-2178. URL: htrtp://www.theotherside.org. Vendor(s): Information Access Co. *6360*

OTTAWA UPDATE.
Publinet, P.O. Box 828, Sta. B, Ottawa, Ont. K1P 5P9, Canada. TEL 613-238-4831. FAX 613-238-7698. URL: http://www.informetrica.com/publinet/ *6187*

OTTAWA X PRESS.
Ottawa X Press Publishing Inc., 69 Sparks St., Ottawa, ON K1P 5A5, Canada. TEL 613-237-8226. FAX 613-232-9055. URL: http://www.theottawaxpress.com. *5424*

OUR CHANGING PLANET.
U.S. Global Change Research Program, 300 E. St., S.W., Washington, DC 20546. URL: http://www.usgcrp.gov; http://www.gcrio.org. *2946*

OUR COUNTRY MAGAZINE.
Lemoine Publishing, 1060 B George Washington Way, Richland, WA 99352. URL: http://www.revolution.3-cities.com/~jrl. Available only online. *3382*

OUR PLANET.
United Nations Environment Programme, Information Service, P.O. Box 30552, Nairobi, Kenya. TEL 254-2-230800. FAX 254-2-226831. URL: http://www.ourplanet.com/imgversn/planethme.html. *2946*

OUTDOOR GUIDES NEWS.
Outdoor Guides Association, 401 E. Gulf Beach Dr., St. George Island, FL 32328. TEL 904-927-3536. FAX 904-927-3532. URL: http://wwwdi.com/oga. *6877*

OUTDOOR LIFE.
Times Mirror Magazines, Inc., 2 Park Ave., New York, NY 10016. TEL 212-779-5000. FAX 212-686-6877. Vendor(s): Information Access Co., Knight-Ridder Information, Inc., UMI. *6878*

OUTLOOK.
Canadian Jewish Outlook Society, 6184 Ash St., Ste. 3, Vancouver, BC V5Z 3G9, Canada. TEL 604-324-5101. FAX 604-325-2470. Vendor(s): UMI. *3035*

OUTLOOK (REDWOOD CITY).
California Society of Certified Public Accountants, 275 Shoreline Dr., Redwood City, CA 94065. TEL 415-802-2427. FAX 415-802-2300. Vendor(s): Information Access Co. *1096*

OUTLOOK (YEAR) PROCEEDINGS.
U.S. Department of Agriculture, World Agricultural Outlook Board, 14th St. and Independence Ave., S.W., Rm. 5143-S, Washington, DC 20250-3900. TEL 202-447-5447. Vendor(s): Ovid Technologies, Inc., Knight-Ridder Information, Inc. *200*

OUTSTATE BUSINESS.
Harbor House Publishers, Inc., 221 Water St., Boyne City, MI 49712. TEL 616-582-2814. FAX 616-582-3392. Vendor(s): UMI. *1276*

OVERDRIVE MAGAZINE.
Randall Publishing, 3200 Rice Mine Rd., Tuscaloosa, AL 35406. TEL 205-349-2990. FAX 205-349-3765. URL: http://www.overdriveonline.com. *7177*

OVERSEAS DEVELOPMENT INSTITUTE. BRIEFING PAPER.
Overseas Development Institute, Regent's College, Inner Circle, Regent's Park, London NW1 4NS, England. TEL 0171-487-7413. FAX 0171-487-7590. *1366*

OVI'S WORLD OF THE BIZARRE.
Spotlight Publishing, 4067 Hartwick St., Ste. 356, Lakewood, CA 90712. URL: http://www.ovis.com. Available only online. *3382*

OXBRIDGE DIRECTORY OF NEWSLETTERS.
Oxbridge Communications, Inc., 150 Fifth Ave., New York, NY 10011. TEL 212-741-0231. FAX 212-633-2938. *559*

OXFORD BULLETIN OF ECONOMICS AND STATISTICS.
Blackwell Publishers Ltd., 108 Cowley Rd., Oxford OX4 1JF, England. TEL 44-1865-791100. FAX 44-1865-791347. URL: http://www.blackwellpublishers.co.uk. Vendor(s): Information Access Co. *990*

OXFORD ECONOMIC PAPERS.
Oxford University Press, Academic Division, Great Clarendon St., Oxford OX2 6DP, England. TEL 44-1865-267907. FAX 44-1865-267485. URL: http://www.oup.co.uk/journals. Vendor(s): Information Access Co. *990*

OXFORD REVIEW OF ECONOMIC POLICY.
Oxford University Press, Academic Division, Great Clarendon St., Oxford OX2 6DP, England. TEL 44-1865-267907. FAX 44-1865-267485. URL: http://www.oup.co.uk/journals. *990*

OXIDATION OF METALS.
Plenum Publishing Corp., 233 Spring St., New York, NY 10013-1578. TEL 212-620-8000. FAX 212-463-0742. *1833*

Online

OXY-FUEL NEWS.
Information Resources, Inc., 1925 N. Lynn St., Ste. 1000, Arlington, VA 22204-1707. TEL 703-528-2500. FAX 703-528-1483.
Vendor(s): Information Access Co., NewsNet. *2675*

OYSTER BOY REVIEW.
103B Hanna St., Carrboro, NC 27510. URL: http://www.sunsite.unc.edu/ob. *4446*

P A COMMUNICATIONS.
Gordon and Breach - Harwood Academic, Amsteldisk 166, 1st Fl., 1079 LH Amsterdam, Netherlands. URL: http://www.gbhap.com/Particle__Accelerators__Communications/. *5835*

P A I S INTERNATIONAL IN PRINT.
Public Affairs Information Service, Inc., 521 W. 43rd St., 5th Fl., New York, NY 10036-4396. TEL 212-736-6629. FAX 212-643-2848. URL: http://www.pais.org.
Vendor(s): Data-Star (PAIS), Knight-Ridder Information, Inc. (File no.49/PAIS), OCLC, Ovid Technologies, Inc.. *5985*

P A S C A L. E 11: PHYSIQUE ATOMIQUE ET MOLECULAIRE. PLASMAS.
Centre National de la Recherche Scientifique, Institut de l'Information Scientifique et Technique, 2 allee du Parc de Brabois, 54514 Vandoeuvre-Les-Nancy Cedex, France. TEL 83-50-46-00. FAX 83-50-46-50.
Vendor(s): European Space Agency (File no.14), Knight-Ridder Information, Inc. (File no.144), Telesystemes - Questel. *5835*

P A S C A L. E 12: ETAT CONDENSE.
Centre National de la Recherche Scientifique, Institut de l'Information Scientifique et Technique, 2 allee du Parc de Brabois, 54514 Vandoeuvre-Les-Nancy Cedex, France. TEL 83-50-46-00. FAX 83-50-46-50.
Vendor(s): European Space Agency (File no.14), Knight-Ridder Information, Inc. (File no.144), Telesystemes - Questel. *5836*

P A S C A L. E 13: STRUCTURE DES LIQUIDES ET DES SOLIDES - CRISTALLOGRAPHIE.
Centre National de la Recherche Scientifique, Institut de l'Information Scientifique et Technique, 2 allee du Parc de Brabois, 54514 Vandoeuvre-Les-Nancy Cedex, France. TEL 83-50-46-00. FAX 83-50-46-50.
Vendor(s): European Space Agency (File no.14), Knight-Ridder Information, Inc. (File no.144), Telesystemes - Questel. *1785*

P A S C A L. E 18: CHROMATOGRAPHIE.
Centre National de la Recherche Scientifique, Institut de l'Information Scientifique et Technique, 2 allee du Parc de Brabois, 54514 Vandoeuvre-les-Nancy Cedex, France. TEL 83-50-46-00. FAX 83-50-46-50.
Vendor(s): European Space Agency (File no.14), Knight-Ridder Information, Inc. (File no.144), Telesystemes - Questel. *1785*

P A S C A L. E 20: ELECTRONIQUE ET TELECOMMUNICATIONS.
Centre National de la Recherche Scientifique, Institut de l'Information Scientifique et Technique, 2 allee du Parc de Brabois, 54514 Vandoeuvre-Les-Nancy Cedex, France. TEL 83-50-46-00. FAX 83-50-46-50.
Vendor(s): European Space Agency (File no.14), Knight-Ridder Information, Inc. (File no.144), Telesystemes - Questel. *2648*

P A S C A L. E 27: METHODES DE FORMATION ET TRAITEMENT DES IMAGES.
Centre National de la Recherche Scientifique, Institut de l'Information Scientifique et Technique, 2 allee du Parc de Brabois, 54514 Vandoeuvre-les-Nancy Cedex, France. TEL 83-50-46-00. FAX 83-50-46-50.
Vendor(s): European Space Agency (File no.14), Knight-Ridder Information, Inc. (File no.144), Telesystemes - Questel. *5836*

P A S C A L. E 30: MICROSCOPIE ELECTRONIQUE ET DIFFRACTION ELECTRONIQUE.
Centre National de la Recherche Scientifique, Institut de l'Information Scientifique et Technique, 2 allee du Parc de Brabois, 54514 Vandoeuvre-Les-Nancy Cedex, France. TEL 83-50-46-00. FAX 83-50-46-50.
Vendor(s): European Space Agency (File no.14), Knight-Ridder Information, Inc. (File no.144), Telesystemes - Questel. *643*

P A S C A L. E 32: METROLOGIE ET APPAREILLAGE EN PHYSIQUE ET PHYSICOCHIMIE.
Centre National de la Recherche Scientifique, Institut de l'Information Scientifique et Technique, 2 allee du Parc de Brabois, 54514 Vandoeuvre-Les-Nancy Cedex, France. TEL 83-50-46-00. FAX 83-50-46-50.
Vendor(s): European Space Agency (File no.14), Knight-Ridder Information, Inc. (File no.144), Telesystemes - Questel. *5256*

P A S C A L. E 33: INFORMATIQUE.
Centre National de la Recherche Scientifique, Institut de l'Information Scientifique et Technique, 2 allee du Parc de Brabois, 54514 Vandoeuvre-Les-Nancy Cedex, France. TEL 33-3-83504600. FAX 33-3-83504650.
Vendor(s): European Space Agency, Knight-Ridder Information, Inc., Telesystemes - Questel. *2095*

P A S C A L. E 34: ROBOTIQUE, AUTOMATIQUE ET AUTOMATISATION DES PROCESSUS INDUSTRIELS.
Centre National de la Recherche Scientifique, Institut de l'Information Scientifique et Technique, 2 allee du Parc de Brabois, 54514 Vandoeuvre-Les-Nancy Cedex, France. TEL 33-3-83504600. FAX 33-3-83504650.
Vendor(s): European Space Agency (File no.14), Knight-Ridder Information, Inc. (File no.144), Telesystemes - Questel. *2096*

P A S C A L. E 36: POLLUTION DE L'EAU, DE L'AIR ET DU SOL - DECHETS - BRUIT.
Centre National de la Recherche Scientifique, Institut de l'Information Scientifique et Technique, 2 allee du Parc de Brabois, 54514 Vandoeuvre-les-Nancy, France. TEL 83-50-46-00. FAX 83-50-46-50.
Vendor(s): European Space Agency (File no.14), Knight-Ridder Information, Inc. (File no.144), Telesystemes - Questel. *2963*

P A S C A L. E 48: ENVIRONNEMENT COSMIQUE TERRESTRE, ASTRONOMIE ET GEOLOGIE EXTRATERRESTRE.
Centre National de la Recherche Scientifique, Institut de l'Information Scientifique et Technique, 2 allee du Parc de Brabois, 54514 Vandoeuvre-les-Nancy, France. TEL 83-50-46-00. FAX 83-50-46-50.
Vendor(s): European Space Agency (File no.14), Knight-Ridder Information, Inc. (File no.144), Telesystemes - Questel. *2327*

P A S C A L. E 49: METEOROLOGIE, GLACIOLOGIE, PHYSIQUE DES OCEANS.
Centre National de la Recherche Scientifique, Institut de l'Information Scientifique et Technique, 2 allee du Parc de Brabois, 54514 Vandoeuvre-Les-Nancy Cedex, France. TEL 83-50-46-00. FAX 83-50-46-50.
Vendor(s): European Space Agency (File no.14), Knight-Ridder Information, Inc. (File no.144), Telesystemes - Questel. *5248*

P A S C A L. E 58: GENETIQUE.
Centre National de la Recherche Scientifique, Institut de l'Information Scientifique et Technique, 2 allee du Parc de Brabois, 54514 Vandoeuvre-Les-Nancy Cedex, France. TEL 83-50-46-00. FAX 83-50-46-50.
Vendor(s): European Space Agency (File no.14), Knight-Ridder Information, Inc. (File no.144), Telesystemes - Questel. *643*

P A S C A L. E 61: MICROBIOLOGIE: BACTERIOLOGIE, VIROLOGIE, MYCOLOGIE, PROTOZOAIRES PATHOGENES.
Centre National de la Recherche Scientifique, Institut de l'Information Scientifique et Technique, 2 allee du Parc de Brabois, 54514 Vandoeuvre-Les-Nancy Cedex, France. TEL 83-50-46-00. FAX 83-50-46-50.
Vendor(s): European Space Agency (File no.14), Knight-Ridder Information, Inc. (File no. 144), Telesystemes - Questel. *643*

P A S C A L. E 62: IMMUNOLOGIE.
Centre National de la Recherche Scientifique, Institut de l'Information Scientifique et Technique, 2 allee du Parc de Brabois, 54514 Vandoeuvre-Les-Nancy Cedex, France. TEL 83-50-46-00. FAX 83-50-46-50.
Vendor(s): European Space Agency (File no.14), Knight-Ridder Information, Inc. (File no.144), Telesystemes - Questel. *643*

P A S C A L. E 63: TOXICOLOGIE.
Centre National de la Recherche Scientifique, Institut de l'Information Scientifique et Technique, 2 allee du Parc de Brabois, 54514 Vandoeuvre-Les-Nancy Cedex, France. TEL 83-50-46-00. FAX 83-50-46-50.
Vendor(s): European Space Agency (File no.14), Knight-Ridder Information, Inc. (File no.144), Telesystemes - Questel. *2963*

P A S C A L. E 64: ENDOCRINOLOGIE HUMAINE ET EXPERIMENTALE. ENDOCRINOPATHIES.
Centre National de la Recherche Scientifique, Institut de l'Information Scientifique et Technique, 2 allee du Parc de Brabois, 54514 Vandoeuvre-Les-Nancy Cedex, France. TEL 83-50-46-00. FAX 83-50-46-50.
Vendor(s): European Space Agency (File no.14), Knight-Ridder Information, Inc. (File no.144), Telesystemes - Questel. *4784*

P A S C A L. E 65: PSYCHOLOGIE, PSYCHOPATHOLOGIE, PSYCHIATRIE.
Centre National de la Recherche Scientifique, Institut de l'Information Scientifique et Technique, 2 allee du Parc de Brabois, 54514 Vandoeuvre-Les-Nancy Cedex, France. TEL 83-50-46-00. FAX 83-50-46-50.
Vendor(s): European Space Agency (File no.14), Knight-Ridder Information, Inc. (File no.144), Telesystemes - Questel. *4784*

P A S C A L. E 68: GENETIQUE HUMAINE.
Centre National de la Recherche Scientifique, Institut de l'Information Scientifique et Technique, 2 allee du Parc de Brabois, 54514 Vandoeuvre-les-Nancy Cedex, France. TEL 83-50-46-00. FAX 83-50-46-50.
Vendor(s): European Space Agency, Knight-Ridder Information, Inc., Telesystemes - Questel. *643*

P A S C A L. E 71: OPHTALMOLOGIE.
Centre National de la Recherche Scientifique, Institut de l'Information Scientifique et Technique, 2 allee du Parc de Brabois, 54514 Vandoeuvre-Les-Nancy Cedex, France. TEL 83-50-46-00. FAX 83-50-46-50.
Vendor(s): European Space Agency (File no.14), Knight-Ridder Information, Inc. (File no. 144), Telesystemes - Questel. *4784*

P A S C A L. E 72: OTORHINOLARYNGOLOGIE. STOMATOLOGIE. PATHOLOGIE CERVICOFACIALE.
Centre National de la Recherche Scientifique, Institut de l'Information Scientifique et Technique, 2 allee du Parc de Brabois, 54514 Vandoeuvre-les-Nancy, France. TEL 83-50-46-00. FAX 83-50-46-50.
Vendor(s): European Space Agency (File no.14), Knight-Ridder Information, Inc. (File no.144), Telesystemes - Questel. *4785*

P A S C A L. E 73: DERMATOLOGIE. MALADIES SEXUELLEMENT TRANSMISSIBLES.
Centre National de la Recherche Scientifique, Institut de l'Information Scientifique et Technique, 2 allee du Parc de Brabois, 54514 Vandoeuvre-les-Nancy, France. TEL 83-50-46-00. FAX 83-50-46-50.
Vendor(s): European Space Agency (File no.14), Knight-Ridder Information, Inc. (File no.144), Telesystemes - Questel. *4785*

P A S C A L. E 74: PNEUMOLOGIE.
Centre National de la Recherche Scientifique, Institut de l'Information Scientifique et Technique, 2 allee du Parc de Brabois, 54514 Vandoeuvre-les-Nancy Cedex, France. TEL 83-50-46-00. FAX 83-50-46-50.
Vendor(s): European Space Agency (File no.14), Knight-Ridder Information, Inc. (File no.144), Telesystemes - Questel. *4785*

P A S C A L. E 75: CARDIOLOGIE ET APPAREIL CIRCULATOIRE.
Centre National de la Recherche Scientifique, Institut de l'Information Scientifique et Technique, 2 allee du Parc de Brabois, 54514 Vandoeuvre-Les-Nancy Cedex, France. TEL 83-50-46-00. FAX 83-50-46-50.
Vendor(s): European Space Agency (File no.14), Knight-Ridder Information, Inc. (File no.144), Telesystemes - Questel. *4785*

P A S C A L. E 76: GASTROENTEROLOGIE, FOIE, PANCREAS, ABDOMEN.
Centre National de la Recherche Scientifique, Institut de l'Information Scientifique et Technique, 2 allee du Parc de Brabois, 54514 Vandoeuvre-Les-Nancy Cedex, France. TEL 83-50-46-00. FAX 83-50-46-50.
Vendor(s): European Space Agency (File no.14), Knight-Ridder Information, Inc. (File no.144), Telesystemes - Questel. *4785*

P A S C A L. E 77: NEPHROLOGIE. VOIES URINAIRES.
Centre National de la Recherche Scientifique, Institut de l'Information Scientifique et Technique, 2 allee du Parc de Brabois, 54514 Vandoeuvre-Les-Nancy Cedex, France. TEL 83-50-46-00. FAX 83-50-46-50.
Vendor(s): European Space Agency (File no.14), Knight-Ridder Information, Inc. (File no.144), Telesystemes - Questel. *4785*

P A S C A L. E 78: NEUROLOGIE.
Centre National de la Recherche Scientifique, Institut de l'Information Scientifique et Technique, 2 allee du Parc de Brabois, 54514 Vandoeuvre-Les-Nancy Cedex, France. TEL 83-50-46-00. FAX 83-50-46-50.
Vendor(s): European Space Agency (File no.14), Knight-Ridder Information, Inc. (File no.144), Telesystemes - Questel. *4785*

P A S C A L. E 79: PATHOLOGIE ET PHYSIOLOGIE OSTEOARTICULAIRES.
Centre National de la Recherche Scientifique, Institut de l'Information Scientifique et Technique, 2 allee du Parc de Brabois, 54514 Vandoeuvre-Les-Nancy Cedex, France. TEL 83-50-46-00. FAX 83-50-46-50.
Vendor(s): European Space Agency (File no.14), Knight-Ridder Information, Inc. (File no.144), Telesystemes - Questel. *4785*

P A S C A L. E 80: HEMATOLOGIE.
Centre National de la Recherche Scientifique, Institut de l'Information Scientifique et Technique, 2 allee du Parc de Brabois, 54514 Vandoeuvre-Les-Nancy Cedex, France. TEL 83-50-46-00. FAX 83-50-46-50.
Vendor(s): European Space Agency (File no.14), Knight-Ridder Information, Inc. (File no.144), Telesystemes - Questel. *4785*

P A S C A L. E 82: GYNECOLOGIE, OBSTETRIQUE, ANDROLOGIE.
Centre National de la Recherche Scientifique, Institut de l'Information Scientifique et Technique, 2 allee du Parc de Brabois, 54514 Vandoeuvre-Les-Nancy Cedex, France. TEL 83-50-46-00. FAX 83-50-46-50.
Vendor(s): European Space Agency (File no.14), Knight-Ridder Information, Inc. (File no.144), Telesystemes - Questel. *4785*

P A S C A L. E 83: ANESTHESIE ET REANIMATION.
Centre National de la Recherche Scientifique, Institut de l'Information Scientifique et Technique, 2 allee du Parc de Brabois, 54514 Vandoeuvre-Les-Nancy Cedex, France. TEL 83-50-46-00. FAX 83-50-46-50.
Vendor(s): European Space Agency (File no.14), Knight-Ridder Information, Inc. (File no.144), Telesystemes - Questel. *4785*

P A S C A L. E 84: GENIE BIOMEDICAL. INFORMATIQUE BIOMEDICALE.
Centre National de la Recherche Scientifique, Institut de l'Information Scientifique et Technique, 2 allee du Parc de Brabois, 54514 Vandoeuvre-Les-Nancy Cedex, France. TEL 83-50-46-00. FAX 83-50-46-50.
Vendor(s): European Space Agency (File no.14), Knight-Ridder Information, Inc. (File no.144), Telesystemes - Questel. *4786*

P A S C A L. E 89: CANCER.
Centre National de la Recherche Scientifique, Institut de l'Information Scientifique et Technique, 2 allee du Parc de Brabois, 54514 Vandoeuvre-Les-Nancy Cedex, France. TEL 83-50-46-00. FAX 83-50-46-50.
Vendor(s): European Space Agency (File no.14), Knight-Ridder Information, Inc. (File no.144), Telesystemes - Questel. *4786*

P A S C A L. F 10: MECANIQUE, ACOUSTIQUE ET TRANSFERT DE CHALEUR.
Centre National de la Recherche Scientifique, Institut de l'Information Scientifique et Technique, 2 allee du Parc de Brabois, 54514 Vandoeuvre-Les-Nancy Cedex, France. TEL 83-50-46-00. FAX 83-50-46-50.
Vendor(s): European Space Agency (File no.14), Knight-Ridder Information, Inc. (File no.144), Telesystemes - Questel. *5836*

P A S C A L. F 16: CHIMIE ANALYTIQUE, MINERALE ET ORGANIQUE.
Centre National de la Recherche Scientifique, Institut de l'Information Scientifique et Technique, 2 allee du Parc de Brabois, 54514 Vandoeuvre-Les-Nancy Cedex, France. TEL 83-50-46-00. FAX 83-50-46-50.
Vendor(s): European Space Agency (File no.14), Knight-Ridder Information, Inc. (File no.144), Telesystemes - Questel. *1785*

P A S C A L. F 17: CHIMIE GENERALE, MINERALE ET ORGANIQUE.
Centre National de la Recherche Scientifique, Institut de l'Information Scientifique et Technique, 2 allee du Parc de Brabois, 54514 Vandoeuvre-Les-Nancy Cedex, France. TEL 83-50-46-00. FAX 83-50-46-50.
Vendor(s): European Space Agency (File no.14), Knight-Ridder Information, Inc. (File no.144), Telesystemes - Questel. *1785*

P A S C A L. F 23: GENIE CHIMIQUE. INDUSTRIES CHIMIQUE ET PARACHIMIQUE.
Centre National de la Recherche Scientifique, Institut de l'Information Scientifique et Technique, 2 allee du Parc de Brabois, 54514 Vandoeuvre-Les-Nancy Cedex, France. TEL 83-50-46-00. FAX 83-50-46-50.
Vendor(s): European Space Agency (File no.14), Knight-Ridder Information, Inc. (File no.144), Telesystemes - Questel. *1785*

P A S C A L. F 24: POLYMERES - PEINTURES - BOIS.
Centre National de la Recherche Scientifique, Institut de l'Information Scientifique et Technique, 2 allee du Parc de Brabois, 54514 Vandoeuvre-Les-Nancy Cedex, France. TEL 83-50-46-00. FAX 83-50-46-50.
Vendor(s): European Space Agency (File no.14), Knight-Ridder Information, Inc. (File no.144), Telesystemes - Questel. *1785*

P A S C A L. F 40: MINERALOGIE. GEOCHIMIE. GEOLOGIE EXTRATERRESTRE.
Centre National de la Recherche Scientifique, Institut de l'Information Scientifique et Technique, 2 allee du Parc de Brabois, 54514 Vandoeuvre-Les-Nancy Cedex, France. TEL 83-50-46-00. FAX 83-50-46-50.
Vendor(s): European Space Agency (File no.14), Knight-Ridder Information, Inc. (File no.144), Telesystemes - Questel. *2327*

P A S C A L. F 41: GISEMENTS METALLIQUES ET NON METALLIQUES.
Centre National de la Recherche Scientifique, Institut de l'Information Scientifique et Technique, 2 allee du Parc de Brabois, 54514 Vandoeuvre-Les-Nancy Cedex, France. TEL 83-50-46-00. FAX 83-50-46-50.
Vendor(s): European Space Agency (File no.14), Knight-Ridder Information, Inc. (File no.144), Telesystemes - Questel. *5321*

P A S C A L. F 42: ROCHES CRISTALLINES.
Centre National de la Recherche Scientifique, Institut de l'Information Scientifique et Technique, 2 allee du Parc de Brabois, 54514 Vandoeuvre-Les-Nancy Cedex, France. TEL 83-50-46-00. FAX 83-50-46-50.
Vendor(s): European Space Agency (File no.14), Knight-Ridder Information, Inc. (File no.144), Telesystemes - Questel. *2327*

P A S C A L. F 43: ROCHES SEDIMENTAIRES. GEOLOGIE MARINE.
Centre National de la Recherche Scientifique, Institut de l'Information Scientifique et Technique, 2 allee du Parc de Brabois, 54514 Vandoeuvre-Les-Nancy Cedex, France. TEL 83-50-46-00. FAX 83-50-46-50.
Vendor(s): European Space Agency (File no.14), Knight-Ridder Information, Inc. (File no.144), Telesystemes - Questel. *2327*

P A S C A L. F 44: STRATIGRAPHIE, GEOLOGIE REGIONALE, GEOLOGIE GENERALE.
Centre National de la Recherche Scientifique, Institut de l'Information Scientifique et Technique, 2 allee du Parc de Brabois, 54514 Vandoeuvre-Les-Nancy Cedex, France. TEL 83-50-46-00. FAX 83-50-46-50.
Vendor(s): European Space Agency (File no.14), Knight-Ridder Information, Inc. (File no.144), Telesystemes - Questel. *2327*

P A S C A L. F 45: TECTONIQUE, GEOPHYSIQUE INTERNE.
Centre National de la Recherche Scientifique, Institut de l'Information Scientifique et Technique, 2 allee du Parc de Brabois, 54514 Vandoeuvre-Les-Nancy Cedex, France. TEL 83-50-46-00. FAX 83-50-46-50.
Vendor(s): European Space Agency (File no.14), Knight-Ridder Information, Inc. (File no.144), Telesystemes - Questel. *2327*

P A S C A L. F 46: HYDROLOGIE. GEOLOGIE DE L'INGENIEUR. FORMATIONS SUPERFICIELLES.
Centre National de la Recherche Scientifique, Institut de l'Information Scientifique et Technique, 2 allee du Parc de Brabois, 54514 Vandoeuvre-Les-Nancy Cedex, France. TEL 83-50-46-00. FAX 83-50-46-50.
Vendor(s): European Space Agency (File no.14), Knight-Ridder Information, Inc. (File no.144), Telesystemes - Questel. *2327*

P A S C A L. F 47: PALEONTOLOGIE.
Centre National de la Recherche Scientifique, Institut de l'Information Scientifique et Technique, 2 allee du Parc de Brabois, 54514 Vandoeuvre-Les-Nancy Cedex, France. TEL 83-50-46-00. FAX 83-50-46-50.
Vendor(s): European Space Agency (File no.14), Knight-Ridder Information, Inc. (File no.144), Telesystemes - Questel. *5564*

P A S C A L. F 52: BIOCHIMIE - BIOPHYSIQUE - MOLECULAIRE - BIOLOGIE MOLECULAIRE ET CELLULAIRE.
Centre National de la Recherche Scientifique, Institut de l'Information Scientifique et Technique, 2 allee du Parc de Brabois, 54514 Vandoeuvre-Les-Nancy Cedex, France. TEL 83-50-46-00. FAX 83-50-46-50.
Vendor(s): European Space Agency (File no.14), Knight-Ridder Information, Inc. (File no.144), Telesystemes - Questel. *643*

P A S C A L. F 53: ANATOMIE ET PHYSIOLOGIE DES VERTEBRES.
Centre National de la Recherche Scientifique, Institut de l'Information Scientifique et Technique, 2 allee du Parc de Brabois, 54514 Vandoeuvre-Les-Nancy Cedex, France. TEL 83-50-46-00. FAX 83-50-46-50.
Vendor(s): European Space Agency (File no.14), Knight-Ridder Information, Inc. (File no.144), Telesystemes - Questel. *643*

P A S C A L. F 54: REPRODUCTION DES VERTEBRES, EMBRYOLOGIE DES VERTEBRES ET DES INVERTEBRES.
Centre National de la Recherche Scientifique, Institut de l'Information Scientifique et Technique, 2 allee du Parc de Brabois, 54514 Vandoeuvre-Les-Nancy Cedex, France. TEL 83-50-46-00. FAX 83-50-46-50.
Vendor(s): European Space Agency (File no.14), Knight-Ridder Information, Inc. (File no.144), Telesystemes - Questel. *4786*

P A S C A L. F 55: BIOLOGIE VEGETALE.
Centre National de la Recherche Scientifique, Institut de l'Information Scientifique et Technique, 2 allee du Parc de Brabois, 54514 Vandoeuvre-Les-Nancy Cedex, France. TEL 83-50-46-00. FAX 83-50-46-50.
Vendor(s): European Space Agency (File no.14), Knight-Ridder Information, Inc. (File no.144), Telesystemes - Questel. *644*

SERIALS AVAILABLE ONLINE

P A S C A L. F 56: ECOLOGIE ANIMALE, VEGETALE ET MICROBIENNE. ETHOLOGIE ANIMALE.
Centre National de la Recherche Scientifique, Institut de l'Information Scientifique et Technique, 2 allee du Parc de Brabois, 54514 Vandoeuvre-Les-Nancy Cedex, France. TEL 83-50-46-00. FAX 83-50-46-50.
Vendor(s): European Space Agency (File no.14), Knight-Ridder Information, Inc. (File no.144), Telesystemes - Questel. *644*

P A S C A L. F 70: PHARMACOLOGIE. TRAITEMENTS MEDICAMENTEUX.
Centre National de la Recherche Scientifique, Institut de l'Information Scientifique et Technique, 2 allee du Parc de Brabois, 54514 Vandoeuvre-Les-Nancy Cedex, France. TEL 83-50-46-00. FAX 83-50-46-50.
Vendor(s): European Space Agency (File no.14), Knight-Ridder Information, Inc. (File no.144), Telesystemes - Questel. *5702*

P A S C A L. T 205: SCIENCES DE L'INFORMATION. DOCUMENTATION.
Centre National de la Recherche Scientifique, Institut de l'Information Scientifique et Technique, 2 allee du Parc de Brabois, 54514 Vandoeuvre-Les-Nancy Cedex, France. TEL 83-50-46-00. FAX 83-50-46-50.
Vendor(s): European Space Agency (File no.14), Knight-Ridder Information, Inc. (File no.144), Telesystemes - Questel. *4227*

P A S C A L. T 215: BIOTECHNOLOGIES.
Centre National de la Recherche Scientifique, Institut de l'Information Scientifique et Technique, 2 allee du Parc de Brabois, 54514 Vandoeuvre-Les-Nancy Cedex, France. TEL 83-50-46-00. FAX 83-50-46-50.
Vendor(s): European Space Agency (File no.14), Knight-Ridder Information, Inc. (File no.144), Telesystemes - Questel. *4786*

P A S C A L. T 230: ENERGIE.
Centre National de la Recherche Scientifique, Institut de l'Information Scientifique et Technique, 2 allee du Parc de Brabois, 54514 Vandoeuvre-Les-Nancy Cedex, France. TEL 83-50-46-00. FAX 83-50-46-50.
Vendor(s): European Space Agency (File no.14), Knight-Ridder Information, Inc. (File no.144), Telesystemes - Questel. *5836*

P A S C A L. T 235: MEDECINE TROPICALE.
Centre National de la Recherche Scientifique, Institut de l'Information Scientifique et Technique, 2 allee du Parc de Brabois, 54514 Vandoeuvre-Les-Nancy Cedex, France. TEL 83-50-46-00. FAX 83-50-46-50.
Vendor(s): European Space Agency (File no.14), Knight-Ridder Information, Inc. (File no.144), Telesystemes - Questel. *4786*

P A S C A L. T 240: METAUX - METALLURGIE.
Centre National de la Recherche Scientifique, Institut de l'Information Scientifique et Technique, 2 allee du Parc de Brabois, 54514 Vandoeuvre-Les-Nancy Cedex, France. TEL 83-50-46-00. FAX 83-50-46-50.
Vendor(s): European Space Agency (File no.14), Knight-Ridder Information, Inc. (File no.144), Telesystemes - Questel. *5220*

P A S C A L. T 260: ZOOLOGIE FONDAMENTALE ET APPLIQUEE DES INVERTEBRES.
Centre National de la Recherche Scientifique, Institut de l'Information Scientifique et Technique, 2 allee du Parc de Brabois, 54514 Vandoeuvre-Les-Nancy Cedex, France. TEL 83-50-46-00. FAX 83-50-46-50.
Vendor(s): European Space Agency (File no.14), Knight-Ridder Information, Inc. (File no.144), Telesystemes - Questel. *644*

P A S C A L. T 280: SCIENCES AGRONOMIQUES ET FORESTIERES: PRODUCTIONS VEGETALES.
Centre National de la Recherche Scientifique, Institut de l'Information Scientifique et Technique, 2 allee du Parc de Brabois, 54514 Vandoeuvre-Les-Nancy Cedex, France. TEL 83-50-46-00. FAX 83-50-46-50.
Vendor(s): European Space Agency (File no.14), Knight-Ridder Information, Inc. (File no.144), Telesystemes - Questel. *180*

P A S C A L. T 295: BATIMENT. TRAVAUX PUBLICS.
Centre National de la Recherche Scientifique, Institut de l'Information Scientifique et Technique, 2 allee du Parc de Brabois, 54514 Vandoeuvre-les-Nancy Cedex, France. TEL 83-50-46-00. FAX 83-50-46-50.
Vendor(s): European Space Agency (File no.14), Knight-Ridder Information, Inc. (File no.144), Telesystemes - Questel. *2751*

P A S C A L V.4 SCIENCES DE LA TERRE.
Centre National de la Recherche Scientifique, Institut de l'Information Scientifique et Technique, 2 allee du Parc de Brabois, 54514 Vandoeuvre-les-Nancy Cedex, France. TEL 83-50-46-00. FAX 83-50-46-50.
Vendor(s): European Space Agency (File no.14), Knight-Ridder Information, Inc. (File no.144), Telesystemes - Questel. *2327*

P & S JOURNAL.
Columbia University, College of Physicians and Surgeons, 630 W. 168th St., New York, NY 10032. TEL 212-305-3877. FAX 212-928-5799. URL: http://cpmcnet.columbia.edu/news/journal. *4726*

P & T.
Quadrant HealthCom, 105 Raider Blvd., Belle Mead, NJ 08052-1510. TEL 908-874-0707. FAX 908-874-5611. *5682*

P C BUSINESS PRODUCTS.
Worldwide Videotex, Box 3273, Bounton Beach, FL 33424-3273. TEL 508-477-8979.
Vendor(s): Data-Star, Information Access Co., Knight-Ridder Information, Inc., NewsNet (EC94). *1176*

P C - COMPUTING.
Ziff-Davis Publishing (San Francisco), Computer Publications Division, 50 Beale St., 14th Fl., San Francisco, CA 94105-1813. TEL 415-578-7000. FAX 415-578-7059.
Vendor(s): Information Access Co.. *2200*

P C GAMES.
Computec Verlag, Isarstr. 32-34, 90451 Nuernberg, Germany. TEL 49-911-96832-0. FAX 49-911-6426333. URL: http://www.pcgames.de. *2119*

P C INTERN.
Data Becker GmbH, Merowingerstr. 30, 40223 Duesseldorf, Germany. TEL 49-211-933470. FAX 49-211-9334710. URL: http://www.pcintern.de. *2201*

P C MAGAZIN.
Franzis Verlag GmbH, Dornacherstr. 3, 85622 Feldkirchen, Germany. TEL 49-89-99115-0. FAX 49-89-99115-199.
Vendor(s): Knight-Ridder Information, Inc.. *2201*

P C MAGAZINE (U.K.).
Ziff-Davis UK Ltd., Cottons Centre, Hay's Ln., London SE1 2QT, England. TEL 44-171-378-6800. FAX 44-171-403-0668.
Vendor(s): Information Access Co.. *2201*

P C PRAXIS.
Data Becker GmbH, Merowingerstr. 30, 40223 Duesseldorf, Germany. TEL 49-211-933470. FAX 49-211-9334710. URL: http://www.pcpraxis.de. *2202*

P C PRESENTATIONS PRODUCTIONS.
Pisces Publishing Group, Inc., 417 Bridgeport Ave., Devon, CT 06460-4105. TEL 203-877-1927. FAX 203-877-1927. URL: http://www.cadvision.com/nolimits/pcpp.html. Available only online. *2202*

P C QUEST.
Cyber Media India Ltd., D-74 Panchsheel Enclave, New Delhi 110017, India. TEL 91-11-6433999. FAX 91-11-6475765. URL: http://www.pcquest.com. *2202*

P C S WEEK.
Phillips Business Information, Inc., 1201 Seven Locks Rd., Potomac, MD 20854. TEL 301-424-3338. FAX 301-309-3847.
Vendor(s): Information Access Co., NewsNet (TE12). *2001*

P C T GAZETTE.
World Intellectual Property Organization (WIPO), Publications Sales and Distribution Unit, 34 chemin des Colombettes, CH-1211 Geneva 20, Switzerland. TEL 41-22-730-9618. FAX 41-22-740-1812. *5593*

P C USER.
E M A P Business & Computer Publications Ltd., 33-39 Bowling Green Ln., London EC1R 0DA, England. TEL 44-171-837-1212. FAX 44-171-278-4008.
Vendor(s): Information Access Co.. *2192*

P C WEEK.
Ziff-Davis Publishing Co., One Park Ave., New York, NY 10016-5146. TEL 212-503-5100. URL: http://www.pcweek.com/
Vendor(s): CompuServe, Inc., Information Access Co.. *2202*

P C WORLD.
D J Communications, Inc., One Exeter Plaza, Boston, MA 02116. TEL 617-534-1200. URL: http://www.pcworld.com/.
Vendor(s): CompuServe, Inc. (GO PWOFORUM), Information Access Co.. *2203*

P C WORLD MALAYSIA.
Communication Resources Pte. Ltd., Blk. 1008, Toa Payoh North, No. 07-01, Singapore 318996, Singapore. TEL 65-256-6201. FAX 65-251-0348. URL: http://www.jaring.my/pcworld. *2203*

P C WORLD SINGAPORE.
Communication Resources Pte. Ltd., Blk. 1008, Toa Payoh North, No. 07-01, Singapore 318996, Singapore. TEL 65-2566201. FAX 65-251-0348. URL: http://www.comres.com.sg/pcworld. *2203*

P D A JOURNAL OF PHARMACEUTICAL SCIENCE AND TECHNOLOGY.
Parenteral Drug Association, Inc., 7500 Old Georgetown Rd., Ste. 620, Bethesda, MD 20814-6133. TEL 301-986-0293. FAX 301-986-0296. *5682*

P L E R U S.
Universidad de Puerto Rico, Escuela Graduada de Planificacion, P.O. Box 23354, UPR Sta., San Juan, PR 00931-3354. TEL 787-763-7590. FAX 787-763-5375. *3755*

P L I M REPORT.
URL: http://www.plim.org/plim5.html. Available only online. *5577*

P M L A.
Modern Language Association of America, 10 Astor Pl., New York, NY 10003. TEL 212-475-9500. FAX 212-477-9863.
Vendor(s): UMI. *4446*

P N I.
U M I, 300 N. Zeeb Rd., Ann Arbor, MI 48106-1346. TEL 313-761-4700. FAX 800-864-0019. URL: http://www.umi.com.
Vendor(s): Knight-Ridder Information, Inc. (File no.42), Ovid Technologies, Inc. (PNII), Questel Orbit Inc., STN International. *5702*

THE P R S GROUP. COUNTRY REPORTS: WORLD SERVICE.
The P R S Group, Box 248, East Syracuse, NY 13057-0248. TEL 315-431-0511. FAX 315-431-0200.
Vendor(s): Data-Star (FSRI), Lexis-Nexis (IBCRPT). *1276*

THE P R S GROUP. COUNTRY REPORTS: ALGERIA.
The P R S Group, Box 248, East Syracuse, NY 13057-0248. TEL 315-431-0511. FAX 315-431-0200.
Vendor(s): Data-Star, Lexis-Nexis. *1276*

THE P R S GROUP. COUNTRY REPORTS: ARGENTINA.
The P R S Group, Box 248, East Syracuse, NY 13057-0248. TEL 315-431-0511. FAX 315-431-0200.
Vendor(s): Data-Star, Lexis-Nexis. *1276*

THE P R S GROUP. COUNTRY REPORTS: BOLIVIA.
The P R S Group, Box 248, East Syracuse, NY 13057-0248. TEL 315-431-0511. FAX 315-431-0200.
Vendor(s): Data-Star, Lexis-Nexis. *1276*

THE P R S GROUP. COUNTRY REPORTS: BRAZIL.
The P R S Group, Box 248, East Syracuse, NY 13057-0248. TEL 315-431-0511. FAX 315-431-0200.
Vendor(s): Data-Star, Lexis-Nexis. *1276*

THE P R S GROUP. COUNTRY REPORTS: BULGARIA.
The P R S Group, Box 248, East Syracuse, NY 13057-0248. TEL 315-431-0511. FAX 315-431-0200.
Vendor(s): Data-Star, Lexis-Nexis. *1276*

THE P R S GROUP. COUNTRY REPORTS: CAMEROON.
The P R S Group, Box 248, East Syracuse, NY 13057-0248. TEL 315-431-0511. FAX 315-431-0200.
Vendor(s): Data-Star, Lexis-Nexis. *1277*

THE P R S GROUP. COUNTRY REPORTS: CHILE.
The P R S Group, Box 248, East Syracuse, NY 13057-0248. TEL 315-431-0511. FAX 315-431-0200.
Vendor(s): Data-Star, Lexis-Nexis. *1277*

THE P R S GROUP. COUNTRY REPORTS: CHINA.
The P R S Group, Box 248, East Syracuse, NY 13057-0248. TEL 315-431-0511. FAX 315-431-0200.
Vendor(s): Data-Star, Lexis-Nexis. *1277*

THE P R S GROUP. COUNTRY REPORTS: COLOMBIA.
The P R S Group, Box 248, East Syracuse, NY 13057-0248. TEL 315-431-0511. FAX 315-431-0200.
Vendor(s): Data-Star, Lexis-Nexis. *1277*

THE P R S GROUP. COUNTRY REPORTS: CONGO (KINSHASA).
The P R S Group, Box 248, East Syracuse, NY 13057-0248. TEL 315-431-0511. FAX 315-431-0200.
Vendor(s): Data-Star, Lexis-Nexis. *1277*

THE P R S GROUP. COUNTRY REPORTS: COSTA RICA.
The P R S Group, Box 248, East Syracuse, NY 13057-0248. TEL 315-431-0511. FAX 315-431-0200.
Vendor(s): Data-Star, Lexis-Nexis. *1277*

THE P R S GROUP. COUNTRY REPORTS: COTE D'IVOIRE.
The P R S Group, Box 248, East Syracuse, NY 13057-0248. TEL 315-431-0511. FAX 315-431-0200.
Vendor(s): Data-Star, Lexis-Nexis. *1277*

THE P R S GROUP. COUNTRY REPORTS: CZECH REPUBLIC.
The P R S Group, Box 248, East Syracuse, NY 13057-0248. TEL 315-431-0511. FAX 315-431-0200.
Vendor(s): Data-Star, Lexis-Nexis. *1277*

THE P R S GROUP. COUNTRY REPORTS: DOMINICAN REPUBLIC.
The P R S Group, Box 248, East Syracuse, NY 13057-0248. TEL 315-431-0511. FAX 315-431-0200.
Vendor(s): Data-Star, Lexis-Nexis. *1277*

THE P R S GROUP. COUNTRY REPORTS. ECUADOR.
The P R S Group, Box 248, East Syracuse, NY 13057-0248. TEL 315-431-0511. FAX 315-431-0200.
Vendor(s): Data-Star, Lexis-Nexis. *1277*

THE P R S GROUP. COUNTRY REPORTS: EGYPT.
The P R S Group, Box 248, East Syracuse, NY 13057-0248. TEL 315-431-0511. FAX 315-431-0200.
Vendor(s): Data-Star, Lexis-Nexis. *1277*

THE P R S GROUP. COUNTRY REPORTS: EL SALVADOR.
The P R S Group, Box 248, East Syracuse, NY 13057-0248. TEL 315-431-0511. FAX 315-431-0200.
Vendor(s): Data-Star, Lexis-Nexis. *1277*

THE P R S GROUP. COUNTRY REPORTS: GABON.
The P R S Group, Box 248, East Syracuse, NY 13057-0248. TEL 315-431-0511. FAX 315-431-0200.
Vendor(s): Data-Star, Lexis-Nexis. *1277*

THE P R S GROUP. COUNTRY REPORTS: GUATEMALA.
The P R S Group, Box 248, East Syracuse, NY 13057-0248. TEL 315-431-0511. FAX 315-431-0200.
Vendor(s): Data-Star, Lexis-Nexis. *1277*

THE P R S GROUP. COUNTRY REPORTS: GUINEA.
The P R S Group, Box 248, East Syracuse, NY 13057-0248. TEL 315-431-0511. FAX 315-431-0200.
Vendor(s): Data-Star, Lexis-Nexis. *1277*

THE P R S GROUP. COUNTRY REPORTS: HAITI.
The P R S Group, Box 248, East Syracuse, NY 13057-0248. TEL 315-431-0511. FAX 315-431-0200.
Vendor(s): Data-Star, Lexis-Nexis. *1277*

THE P R S GROUP. COUNTRY REPORTS: HONDURAS.
The P R S Group, Box 248, East Syracuse, NY 13057-0248. TEL 315-431-0511. FAX 315-431-0200.
Vendor(s): Data-Star, Lexis-Nexis. *1277*

THE P R S GROUP. COUNTRY REPORTS: HONG KONG.
The P R S Group, Box 248, East Syracuse, NY 13057-0248. TEL 315-431-0511. FAX 315-431-0200.
Vendor(s): Data-Star, Lexis-Nexis. *1277*

THE P R S GROUP. COUNTRY REPORTS: HUNGARY.
The P R S Group, Box 248, East Syracuse, NY 13057-0248. TEL 315-431-0511. FAX 315-431-0200.
Vendor(s): Data-Star, Lexis-Nexis. *1277*

THE P R S GROUP. COUNTRY REPORTS: INDIA.
The P R S Group, Box 248, East Syracuse, NY 13057-0248. TEL 315-431-0511. FAX 315-431-0200.
Vendor(s): Data-Star, Lexis-Nexis. *1277*

THE P R S GROUP. COUNTRY REPORTS: INDONESIA.
The P R S Group, Box 248, East Syracuse, NY 13057-0248. TEL 315-431-0511. FAX 315-431-0200.
Vendor(s): Data-Star, Lexis-Nexis. *1277*

THE P R S GROUP. COUNTRY REPORTS: IRAN.
The P R S Group, Box 248, East Syracuse, NY 13057-0248. TEL 315-431-0511. FAX 315-431-0200.
Vendor(s): Data-Star, Lexis-Nexis. *1277*

THE P R S GROUP. COUNTRY REPORTS: IRAQ.
The P R S Group, Box 248, East Syracuse, NY 13057-0248. TEL 315-431-0511. FAX 315-431-0200.
Vendor(s): Data-Star, Lexis-Nexis. *1277*

THE P R S GROUP. COUNTRY REPORTS: ISRAEL.
The P R S Group, Box 248, East Syracuse, NY 13057-0248. TEL 315-431-0511. FAX 315-431-0200.
Vendor(s): Data-Star, Lexis-Nexis. *1277*

THE P R S GROUP. COUNTRY REPORTS: JAMAICA.
The P R S Group, Box 248, East Syracuse, NY 13057-0248. TEL 315-431-0511. FAX 315-431-0200.
Vendor(s): Data-Star, Lexis-Nexis. *1277*

THE P R S GROUP. COUNTRY REPORTS: KENYA.
The P R S Group, Box 248, East Syracuse, NY 13057-0248. TEL 315-431-0511. FAX 315-431-0200.
Vendor(s): Data-Star, Lexis-Nexis. *1278*

THE P R S GROUP. COUNTRY REPORTS: KUWAIT.
The P R S Group, Box 248, East Syracuse, NY 13057-0248. TEL 315-431-0511. FAX 315-431-0200.
Vendor(s): Data-Star, Lexis-Nexis. *1278*

THE P R S GROUP. COUNTRY REPORTS: LIBYA.
The P R S Group, Box 248, East Syracuse, NY 13057-0248. TEL 315-431-0511. FAX 315-431-0200.
Vendor(s): Data-Star, Lexis-Nexis. *1278*

THE P R S GROUP. COUNTRY REPORTS: MALAYSIA.
The P R S Group, Box 248, East Syracuse, NY 13057-0248. TEL 315-431-0511. FAX 315-431-0200.
Vendor(s): Data-Star, Lexis-Nexis. *1278*

THE P R S GROUP. COUNTRY REPORTS: MEXICO.
The P R S Group, Box 248, East Syracuse, NY 13057-0248. TEL 315-431-0511. FAX 315-431-0200.
Vendor(s): Data-Star, Lexis-Nexis. *1278*

THE P R S GROUP. COUNTRY REPORTS: MOROCCO.
The P R S Group, Box 248, East Syracuse, NY 13057-0248. TEL 315-431-0511. FAX 315-431-0200.
Vendor(s): Data-Star, Lexis-Nexis. *1278*

THE P R S GROUP. COUNTRY REPORTS: NICARAGUA.
The P R S Group, Box 248, East Syracuse, NY 13057-0248. TEL 315-431-0511. FAX 315-431-0200.
Vendor(s): Data-Star, Lexis-Nexis. *1278*

THE P R S GROUP. COUNTRY REPORTS: NIGERIA.
The P R S Group, Box 248, East Syracuse, NY 13057-0248. TEL 315-431-0511. FAX 315-431-0200.
Vendor(s): Data-Star, Lexis-Nexis. *1278*

THE P R S GROUP. COUNTRY REPORTS: OMAN.
The P R S Group, Box 248, East Syracuse, NY 13057-0248. TEL 315-431-0511. FAX 315-431-0200.
Vendor(s): Data-Star, Lexis-Nexis. *1278*

THE P R S GROUP. COUNTRY REPORTS: PAKISTAN.
The P R S Group, Box 248, East Syracuse, NY 13057-0248. TEL 315-431-0511. FAX 315-431-0200.
Vendor(s): Data-Star, Lexis-Nexis. *1278*

THE P R S GROUP. COUNTRY REPORTS: PANAMA.
The P R S Group, Box 248, East Syracuse, NY 13057-0248. TEL 315-431-0511. FAX 315-431-0200.
Vendor(s): Data-Star, Lexis-Nexis. *1278*

THE P R S GROUP. COUNTRY REPORTS: PERU.
The P R S Group, Box 248, East Syracuse, NY 13057-0248. TEL 315-431-0511. FAX 315-431-0200.
Vendor(s): Data-Star, Lexis-Nexis. *1278*

THE P R S GROUP. COUNTRY REPORTS: PHILIPPINES.
The P R S Group, Box 248, East Syracuse, NY 13057-0248. TEL 315-431-0511. FAX 315-431-0200.
Vendor(s): Data-Star, Lexis-Nexis. *1278*

THE P R S GROUP. COUNTRY REPORTS: POLAND.
The P R S Group, Box 248, East Syracuse, NY 13057-0248. TEL 315-431-0511. FAX 315-431-0200.
Vendor(s): Data-Star, Lexis-Nexis. *1278*

THE P R S GROUP. COUNTRY REPORTS: ROMANIA.
The P R S Group, Box 248, East Syracuse, NY 13057-0248. TEL 315-431-0511. FAX 315-431-0200.
Vendor(s): Data-Star, Lexis-Nexis. *1278*

THE P R S GROUP. COUNTRY REPORTS: RUSSIA.
The P R S Group, Box 248, East Syracuse, NY 13057-0248. TEL 315-431-0511. FAX 315-431-0200.
Vendor(s): Data-Star, Lexis-Nexis. *1278*

THE P R S GROUP. COUNTRY REPORTS: SAUDI ARABIA.
The P R S Group, Box 248, East Syracuse, NY 13057-0248. TEL 315-431-0511. FAX 315-431-0200.
Vendor(s): Data-Star, Lexis-Nexis. *1278*

THE P R S GROUP. COUNTRY REPORTS: SINGAPORE.
The P R S Group, Box 248, East Syracuse, NY 13057-0248. TEL 315-431-0511. FAX 315-431-0200.
Vendor(s): Data-Star, Lexis-Nexis. *1278*

THE P R S GROUP. COUNTRY REPORTS: SOUTH AFRICA.
The P R S Group, Box 248, East Syracuse, NY 13057-0248. TEL 315-431-0511. FAX 315-431-0200.
Vendor(s): Data-Star, Lexis-Nexis. *1278*

THE P R S GROUP. COUNTRY REPORTS: SOUTH KOREA.
The P R S Group, Box 248, East Syracuse, NY 13057-0248. TEL 315-431-0511. FAX 315-431-0200.
Vendor(s): Data-Star, Lexis-Nexis. *1278*

THE P R S GROUP. COUNTRY REPORTS: SRI LANKA.
The P R S Group, Box 248, East Syracuse, NY 13057-0248. TEL 315-431-0511. FAX 315-431-0200.
Vendor(s): Data-Star, Lexis-Nexis. *1278*

THE P R S GROUP. COUNTRY REPORTS: SUDAN.
The P R S Group, Box 248, East Syracuse, NY 13057-0248. TEL 315-431-0511. FAX 315-431-0200.
Vendor(s): Data-Star, Lexis-Nexis. *1278*

THE P R S GROUP. COUNTRY REPORTS: SYRIA.
The P R S Group, Box 248, East Syracuse, NY 13057-0248. TEL 315-431-0511. FAX 315-431-0200.
Vendor(s): Data-Star, Lexis-Nexis. *1278*

THE P R S GROUP. COUNTRY REPORTS: TAIWAN.
The P R S Group, Box 248, East Syracuse, NY 13057-0248. TEL 315-431-0511. FAX 315-431-0200.
Vendor(s): Data-Star, Lexis-Nexis. *1278*

THE P R S GROUP. COUNTRY REPORTS: THAILAND.
The P R S Group, Box 248, East Syracuse, NY 13057-0248. TEL 315-431-0511. FAX 315-431-0200.
Vendor(s): Data-Star, Lexis-Nexis. *1279*

THE P R S GROUP. COUNTRY REPORTS: TUNISIA.
The P R S Group, Box 248, East Syracuse, NY 13057-0248. TEL 315-431-0511. FAX 315-431-0200.
Vendor(s): Data-Star, Lexis-Nexis. *1279*

THE P R S GROUP. COUNTRY REPORTS: TURKEY.
The P R S Group, Box 248, East Syracuse, NY 13057-0248. TEL 315-431-0511. FAX 315-431-0200.
Vendor(s): Data-Star, Lexis-Nexis. *1279*

THE P R S GROUP. COUNTRY REPORTS: UKRAINE.
The P R S Group, Box 248, East Syracuse, NY 13057-0248. TEL 315-431-0511. FAX 315-431-0200.
Vendor(s): Data-Star, Lexis-Nexis. *1279*

THE P R S GROUP. COUNTRY REPORTS: UNITED ARAB EMIRATES.
The P R S Group, Box 248, East Syracuse, NY 13057-0248. TEL 315-431-0511. FAX 315-431-0200.
Vendor(s): Data-Star, Lexis-Nexis. *1279*

THE P R S GROUP. COUNTRY REPORTS: URUGUAY.
The P R S Group, Box 248, East Syracuse, NY 13057-0248. TEL 315-431-0511. FAX 315-431-0200.
Vendor(s): Data-Star, Lexis-Nexis. *1279*

THE P R S GROUP. COUNTRY REPORTS: VENEZUELA.
The P R S Group, Box 248, East Syracuse, NY 13057-0248. TEL 315-431-0511. FAX 315-431-0200.
Vendor(s): Data-Star, Lexis-Nexis. *1279*

THE P R S GROUP. COUNTRY REPORTS: VIETNAM.
The P R S Group, Box 248, East Syracuse, NY 13057-0248. TEL 315-431-0511. FAX 315-431-0200.
Vendor(s): Data-Star, Lexis-Nexis. *1279*

THE P R S GROUP. COUNTRY REPORTS: ZAMBIA.
The P R S Group, Box 248, East Syracuse, NY 13057-0248. TEL 315-431-0511. FAX 315-431-0200.
Vendor(s): Data-Star, Lexis-Nexis. *1279*

THE P R S GROUP. COUNTRY REPORTS: ZIMBABWE.
The P R S Group, Box 248, East Syracuse, NY 13057-0248. TEL 315-431-0511. FAX 315-431-0200.
Vendor(s): Data-Star, Lexis-Nexis. *1279*

THE P R S GROUP. EXECUTIVE REPORTS: AUSTRALIA.
The P R S Group, Box 248, East Syracuse, NY 13057-0248. TEL 315-431-0511. FAX 315-431-0200.
Vendor(s): Data-Star, Lexis-Nexis. *1279*

THE P R S GROUP. EXECUTIVE REPORTS: AUSTRIA.
The P R S Group, Box 248, East Syracuse, NY 13057-0248. TEL 315-431-0511. FAX 315-431-0200.
Vendor(s): Data-Star, Lexis-Nexis. *1279*

THE P R S GROUP. EXECUTIVE REPORTS: BELGIUM.
The P R S Group, Box 248, East Syracuse, NY 13057-0248. TEL 315-431-0511. FAX 315-431-0200.
Vendor(s): Data-Star, Lexis-Nexis. *1279*

THE P R S GROUP. EXECUTIVE REPORTS: CANADA.
The P R S Group, Box 248, East Syracuse, NY 13057-0248. TEL 315-431-0511. FAX 315-431-0200.
Vendor(s): Data-Star, Lexis-Nexis. *1279*

THE P R S GROUP. EXECUTIVE REPORTS: DENMARK.
The P R S Group, Box 248, East Syracuse, NY 13057-0248. TEL 315-431-0511. FAX 315-431-0200.
Vendor(s): Data-Star, Lexis-Nexis. *1279*

THE P R S GROUP. EXECUTIVE REPORTS: FINLAND.
The P R S Group, Box 248, East Syracuse, NY 13057-0248. TEL 315-431-0511. FAX 315-431-0200.
Vendor(s): Data-Star, Lexis-Nexis. *1279*

THE P R S GROUP. EXECUTIVE REPORTS: FRANCE.
The P R S Group, Box 248, East Syracuse, NY 13057-0248. TEL 315-431-0511. FAX 315-431-0200.
Vendor(s): Data-Star, Lexis-Nexis. *1279*

THE P R S GROUP. EXECUTIVE REPORTS: GERMANY.
The P R S Group, Box 248, East Syracuse, NY 13057-0248. TEL 315-431-0511. FAX 315-431-0200.
Vendor(s): Data-Star, Lexis-Nexis. *1279*

THE P R S GROUP. EXECUTIVE REPORTS: GREECE.
The P R S Group, Box 248, East Syracuse, NY 13057-0248. TEL 315-431-0511. FAX 315-431-0200.
Vendor(s): Data-Star, Lexis-Nexis. *1280*

THE P R S GROUP. EXECUTIVE REPORTS: IRELAND.
The P R S Group, Box 248, East Syracuse, NY 13057-0248. TEL 315-431-0511. FAX 315-431-0200.
Vendor(s): Data-Star, Lexis-Nexis. *1280*

THE P R S GROUP. EXECUTIVE REPORTS: ITALY.
The P R S Group, Box 248, East Syracuse, NY 13057-0248. TEL 315-431-0511. FAX 315-431-0200.
Vendor(s): Data-Star, Lexis-Nexis. *1280*

THE P R S GROUP. EXECUTIVE REPORTS: JAPAN.
The P R S Group, Box 248, East Syracuse, NY 13057-0248. TEL 315-431-0511. FAX 315-431-0200.
Vendor(s): Data-Star, Lexis-Nexis. *1280*

THE P R S GROUP. EXECUTIVE REPORTS: NETHERLANDS.
The P R S Group, Box 248, East Syracuse, NY 13057-0248. TEL 315-431-0511. FAX 315-431-0200.
Vendor(s): Data-Star, Lexis-Nexis. *1280*

THE P R S GROUP. EXECUTIVE REPORTS: NEW ZEALAND.
The P R S Group, Box 248, East Syracuse, NY 13057-0248. TEL 315-431-0511. FAX 315-431-0200.
Vendor(s): Data-Star, Lexis-Nexis. *1280*

THE P R S GROUP. EXECUTIVE REPORTS: NORWAY.
The P R S Group, Box 248, East Syracuse, NY 13057-0248. TEL 315-431-0511. FAX 315-431-0200.
Vendor(s): Data-Star, Lexis-Nexis. *1280*

THE P R S GROUP. EXECUTIVE REPORTS: PORTUGAL.
The P R S Group, Box 248, East Syracuse, NY 13057-0248. TEL 315-431-0511. FAX 315-431-0200.
Vendor(s): Data-Star, Lexis-Nexis. *1280*

THE P R S GROUP. EXECUTIVE REPORTS: PUERTO RICO.
The P R S Group, Box 248, East Syracuse, NY 13057-0248. TEL 315-431-0511. FAX 315-431-0200.
Vendor(s): Data-Star, Lexis-Nexis. *1280*

THE P R S GROUP. EXECUTIVE REPORTS: SPAIN.
The P R S Group, Box 248, East Syracuse, NY 13057-0248. TEL 315-431-0511. FAX 315-431-0200.
Vendor(s): Data-Star, Lexis-Nexis. *1280*

THE P R S GROUP. EXECUTIVE REPORTS: SWEDEN.
The P R S Group, Box 248, East Syracuse, NY 13057-0248. TEL 315-431-0511. FAX 315-431-0200.
Vendor(s): Data-Star, Lexis-Nexis. *1280*

THE P R S GROUP. EXECUTIVE REPORTS: UNITED KINGDOM.
The P R S Group, Box 248, East Syracuse, NY 13057-0248. TEL 315-431-0511. FAX 315-431-0200.
Vendor(s): Data-Star, Lexis-Nexis. *1280*

THE P R S GROUP. EXECUTIVE REPORTS: UNITED STATES.
The P R S Group, Box 248, East Syracuse, NY 13057-0248. TEL 315-431-0511. FAX 315-431-0200.
Vendor(s): Data-Star, Lexis-Nexis. *1280*

P S P BULLETIN.
Association of American Publishers, Inc., Professional & Scholarly Publishing Division, 71 Fifth Ave., New York, NY 10003-3004. TEL 212-255-0200. FAX 212-255-7007. URL: http://www.publishers.org. *6280*

P S: POLITICAL SCIENCE & POLITICS.
American Political Science Association, 1527 New Hampshire Ave., N.W., Washington, DC 20036. TEL 202-483-2512. FAX 202-483-2657.
Vendor(s): Information Access Co.. *5953*

P T I JOURNAL.
1666 Newport Blvd., Ste. 141, Costa Mesa, CA 92627. TEL 714-752-1292. FAX 714-752-9533. URL: http://www.pti-journal.com. *7036*

P T N.
P T N Publishing Corp., 445 Broad Hollow Rd., Ste. 21, Melville, NY 11747-4722. TEL 516-845-2700. FAX 516-845-7109.
Vendor(s): Information Access Co.. *5769*

P W.
URL: http://users.aol.com/prodwekly/pw/pw.htm. Available only online. *2056*

PACIFIC AFFAIRS.
Pacific Affairs, University of British Columbia, 1855 West Mall, Ste. 164, Vancouver, BC V6T 1Z2, Canada. TEL 604-822-4534. FAX 604-822-9452. URL: http://www.cmpa.ca/s125.html.
Vendor(s): Information Access Co., UMI. *5953*

PACIFIC BUSINESS NEWS.
American City Business Journals, Inc. (Austin), 505 Powell Ste., Austin, TX 78703-5121. TEL 704-375-7404.
Vendor(s): Knight-Ridder Information, Inc., Lexis-Nexis. *990*

PACIFIC DISCOVERY.
California Academy of Sciences, Golden Gate Park, San Francisco, CA 94118. TEL 415-750-7116. URL: http://www.calacademy.org/pacdis/ *6557*

PACIFIC HISTORICAL REVIEW.
University of California Press, Journals Division, 2120 Berkeley Way, No. 5812, Berkeley, CA 94720-5812. TEL 510-643-7154. FAX 510-642-9917. URL: http://library.berkeley.edu:8080/ucalpress/journals.
Vendor(s): Information Access Co.. *3642*

PACIFIC LAW JOURNAL.
Western Newspaper Publishing Co., 3200 Fifth Ave., Sacramento, CA 95817. TEL 916-739-7171. FAX 916-739-7111.
Vendor(s): Lexis-Nexis, West Group. *4005*

PACIFIC NORTHWEST ENVIRONMENTAL DIRECTORY.
Harbinger Communications, Box 8175, Missoula, MT 59807. TEL 406-721-0440. FAX 406-721-0440. *2241*

PACK-O-FUN.
Clapper Communications Companies, 2400 E. Devon Ave., Ste. 375, Des Plaines, IL 60018-4618. TEL 847-635-5800. FAX 847-635-6311. URL: http://www.craftnet.org/pack-o-fun. *482*

PACKAGING DIGEST.
Cahners Publishing Company (Des Plaines), Division of Reed Elsevier Inc., 1350 E. Touhy Ave., Box 5080, Des Plaines, IL 60018-5080. TEL 847-635-2363. FAX 847-635-6856. URL: http://www.packagingdigest.com.
Vendor(s): Information Access Co. *5547*

PACKAGING SCIENCE AND TECHNOLOGY ABSTRACTS.
Fraunhofer Institut fuer Lebensmitteltechnologie und Verpackung, Giggenhauserstr. 35, 85354 Freising, Germany. TEL 49-8161-491-0. FAX 49-8161-491491. URL: http://www.ilv.fhg.de.
Vendor(s): DIMDI, Data-Star, FIZ Technik, Knight-Ridder Information, Inc. (File no.252), Questel Orbit Inc., STN International. *5550*

PACKAGING TECHNOLOGY AND ENGINEERING.
North American Publishing Co., 401 N. Broad St., Philadelphia, PA 19108. TEL 215-238-5300. FAX 215-238-5457.
Vendor(s): Information Access Co. *5548*

PACKAGING WEEK.
Miller Freeman Publishers Ltd., Sovereign Way, Tonbridge, Kent TN9 1RW, England. TEL 44-1732-364422. FAX 44-1732-353328.
Vendor(s): Information Access Co. *5548*

THE PAGE OF THE IMMORTALS.
12720 Granger Court, Apple Valley, MN 55124. URL: http://www.tc.umn.edu/nlhome/m650/lebe0007/immortals.html.
Available only online. *4446*

PAINT AND INK INTERNATIONAL.
Argus Business Media Ltd., Queensway House, 2 Queensway, Redhill, Surrey RH1 1QS, England. TEL 44-1737-768611. FAX 44-1737-761685.
Vendor(s): Information Access Co. *5554*

PAINTING.
Clapper Communications Companies, 2400 E. Devon Ave., Ste. 375, Des Plaines, IL 60018-4618. TEL 847-635-5800. FAX 847-635-6311. URL: http://www.craftnet.org/painting. *482*

PALAESTRA.
Challenge Publications, Ltd., Circulation Department, Box 508, 1948 Riverview Dr., Macomb, IL 61455-0508. TEL 309-833-1902. FAX 309-833-1902.
Vendor(s): Information Access Co. *3457*

PALINET NEWS.
PALINET, 3401 Market St., Ste. 262, Philadelphia, PA 19104. TEL 215-382-7031. FAX 215-382-0022. URL: http://www.palinet.org. *4234*

PAPER & PULP EUROPE.
Miller Freeman, Inc., 123 A chaussee de Charleroi, Bte. 5, 1060 Brussels, Belgium. TEL 32-2-5386040. FAX 32-2-5375626.
Vendor(s): Information Access Co. *5569*

PAPER, FILM AND FOIL CONVERTER.
Intertec Publishing Corp., 29 N. Wacker Dr., Chicago, IL 60606. TEL 312-726-2802. FAX 312-726-2574.
Vendor(s): Information Access Co. *5548*

PAPERBASE ABSTRACTS.
Pira International, Randalls Rd., Leatherhead, Surrey KT22 7RU, England. TEL 44-1372-802050. FAX 44-1372-802239. URL: http://www.pira.co.uk/.
Vendor(s): Data-Star, FIZ Technik, Knight-Ridder Information, Inc., Questel Orbit Inc. (PIRA), STN International. *5574*

PAPERBOARD PACKAGING.
Advanstar Communications, Inc., 7500 Old Oak Blvd., Cleveland, OH 44130. TEL 216-826-2839. FAX 216-821-2726.
Vendor(s): Information Access Co., Knight-Ridder Information, Inc. *5548*

PAPERPLATES.
19 Kenwood Ave., Toronto, ON M6C 2R8, Canada. TEL 416-651-2551. URL: http://www.hookup.net/'beekelly/. *4447*

PAPERS ON LANGUAGE AND LITERATURE.
Southern Illinois University at Edwardsville, Edwardsville, IL 62026. TEL 618-692-2119. FAX 618-692-3509. URL: http://www.siue.edu/~pll.
Vendor(s): Information Access Co., UMI. *4447*

PAPUA NEW GUINEA OIL AND GAS.
C A M Group, URL: http://www.camgroup.com.au/pog/pog_intr.html. *5617*

PARABOLA.
Society for the Study of Myth and Tradition, 656 Broadway, New York, NY 10012-2317. TEL 212-505-6200. FAX 212-979-7325. URL: http://www.parabola.org.
Vendor(s): Information Access Co. *3090*

PARALLEL ALGORITHMS AND APPLICATIONS.
Gordon and Breach - Harwood Academic, Amsteldisk 166, 1st Fl., 1079 LH Amsterdam, Netherlands. URL: http://www.gbhap.com/Parallel_Algorithms_Applications/. *2157*

PARAPLEGIA NEWS.
P V A Publications, 2111 E. Highland Ave., Ste. 180, Phoenix, AZ 85016-4702. TEL 602-224-0500. FAX 602-224-0507.
Vendor(s): Information Access Co. *3467*

PARASITOLOGY RESEARCH.
Springer-Verlag, Heidelberger Platz 3, 14197 Berlin, Germany. TEL 49-30-82787-0. FAX 49-30-82787448. URL: http://link.springer.de. *4842*

PARENTS.
Gruner & Jahr U.S.A. Publishing, 110 Fifth Ave., New York, NY 10011. TEL 212-499-2000.
Vendor(s): Information Access Co. *1853*

PARENTS AND CHILDREN TOGETHER ONLINE.
Edinfo Press, 2805 E. 10th St., Ste. 150, Bloomington, IN 47408. TEL 812-855-5847. URL: http://www.indiana.edu/~eric_rec/fl/pcto/menu.html.
Available only online. *1882*

PARIS-ANGLOPHONE.
Anglophone S.A., 32 rue Edouard Vaillant, 93100 Montreuil, France. TEL 33-1-48596658. FAX 33-1-48596668. *1705*

PARIS REVIEW.
Paris Review, Inc., 541 E. 72nd St., New York, NY 10021. TEL 212-861-0016. FAX 212-861-0282. URL: http://www.voyagerco.com/pr/prtoc.html.
Vendor(s): UMI. *4448*

PARKS AND RECREATION.
National Recreation and Park Association, 2775 S. Quincy St., No. 300, Arlington, VA 22206. TEL 703-820-4940. FAX 703-671-6772.
Vendor(s): Information Access Co., UMI. *4152*

PARLIAMENTARY AFFAIRS.
Oxford University Press, Academic Division, Great Clarendon St., Oxford OX2 6DP, England. TEL 44-1865-267907. FAX 44-1865-267485. URL: http://www.oup.co.uk/journals.
Vendor(s): Information Access Co. *5953*

PARTHENOGENESIS.
Box 1424, Fort Collins, CO 80522-1424. URL: http://www.nyx.net/'dherrick/parth.html.
Available only online. *4352*

PARTICLE ACCELERATORS.
Gordon and Breach - Harwood Academic, Amsteldisk 166, 1st Fl., 1079 LH Amsterdam, Netherlands. URL: http://www.gbhap.com/Particle_Accelerators/. *5855*

PARTY & PAPER RETAILER.
4Ward Corporation, 70 New Canaan Ave., Norwalk, CT 06850-2600. TEL 203-845-8020. FAX 203-845-8022.
Vendor(s): Information Access Co. *4152*

PASSI SULLA RETE.
Universita Ca Foscari di Venezia, Dipartimento di Studi Indologici ed Estremo Orientali, URL: http://www.unive.it/'dsie/passi/home.html.
Available only online. *5536*

PASTA LOVERS NEWSLETTER.
URL: http://home.sprynet.com/sprynet/jonaspas/
Available only online. *3687*

PASTA PRODUCTS: THE INTERNATIONAL MARKET.
Euromonitor, 60-61 Britton St., London EC1M 5NA, England. TEL 44-171-251-8024. FAX 44-171-608-3149. URL: http://www.euromonitor.com.
Vendor(s): Data-Star, Knight-Ridder Information, Inc. *3123*

PATENTS ABSTRACTS.
American Petroleum Institute, EnCompass, 275 Seventh Ave., New York, NY 10001-6708. TEL 212-366-4040. FAX 212-366-4298.
Vendor(s): Knight-Ridder Information, Inc., Questel Orbit Inc., STN International, Telesystemes - Questel. *5631*

PATHOGENESIS.
Gordon and Breach - Harwood Academic, Amsteldisk 166, 1st Fl., 1079 LH Amsterdam, Netherlands. URL: http://www.gbhap.com/Pathogenesis/. *4727*

DER PATHOLOGE.
Springer-Verlag, Heidelberger Platz 3, 14197 Berlin, Germany. TEL 49-30-82787-0. FAX 49-30-82787448. URL: http://link.springer.de. *4727*

PATIENT CARE.
Medical Economics Publishing Co., Inc., 5 Paragon Dr., Montvale, NJ 07645. TEL 201-358-7200. FAX 201-573-4625.
Vendor(s): Information Access Co., UMI. *4728*

PATIENT EDUCATION AND COUNSELING.
Elsevier Science Ireland Ltd., P.O. Box 85, Limerick, Ireland. TEL 353-61-471944. FAX 353-61-472144. *6246*

PATIENTS' RIGHTS REPORTER.
Cox Publications, Box 20316, Billings, MT 59104-0316. TEL 406-256-2248. FAX 406-256-7550.
Available only online. *3718*

PATTERN ANALYSIS AND APPLICATIONS.
Springer-Verlag London Ltd., Sweetapple House, Catteshall Rd., Godalming, Surrey GU7 3DJ, England. TEL 44-1483-418800. FAX 44-1483-415144. *2124*

PATTERNS OF GLOBAL TERRORISM.
U.S. Department of State, Office of the Coordinator for Counterterrorism, 2201 C St., N.W., Washington, DC 20520. TEL 202-647-6575. *6031*

PAX.
Svenska Freds- och Skiljedomsfoereningen, Svartensgatan 6, P.O. Box 4134, S-102 63 Stockholm, Sweden. TEL 46-8-702-97-60. FAX 46-8-702-18-46. *5954*

PAYMENT SYSTEMS WORLDWIDE.
F.I.A. Financial Publishing Co., 582 Oakwood Ave., Ste. 203, Lake Forest, IL 60045. TEL 708-615-0405. FAX 708-615-0416.
Vendor(s): UMI. *1160*

PAYMENTS SYSTEM REPORT.
National Automated Clearing House Association, 607 Herndon Pkwy., Ste. 200, Herndon, VA 20170. TEL 703-742-9190. FAX 703-787-0996.
Vendor(s): UMI. *1176*

PAYROLL ADMINISTRATION GUIDE.
The Bureau of National Affairs, Inc., 1231 25th St., N.W., Washington, DC 20037. TEL 202-452-4200. FAX 202-822-8092. URL: http://www.bna.com/
Vendor(s): Human Resources Information Network (File DD). *1449*

PAYROLL ADMINISTRATION GUIDE NEWSLETTER.
The Bureau of National Affairs, Inc., 1231 25th St., N.W., Washington, DC 20037. TEL 202-452-4200. FAX 202-822-8092. URL: http://www.bna.com/
Vendor(s): Human Resources Information Network (File DD). *1449*

SERIALS AVAILABLE ONLINE

PEACE NEWS FOR NONVIOLENT REVOLUTION.
Peace News Ltd., 5 Caledonian Rd., London N1 9DY, England. TEL 44-171-278-3344. FAX 44-171-278-0444. URL: http://www.gn.apc.org/peacenews. *5954*

PEACE NEWSLETTER.
Syracuse Peace Council, 924 Burnet Ave., Syracuse, NY 13203. TEL 315-472-5478. *5954*

PEACE WATCH.
U.S. Institute of Peace, 1550 M St., N.W., Ste. 700, Washington, DC 20005-1708. TEL 202-457-1700. FAX 202-429-6063. URL: http://www.usip.org. *6032*

PEACEKEEPING & INTERNATIONAL RELATIONS.
Canadian PeaceKeeping Press, Pearson Peacekeeping Centre Cornwallis Park, P.O. Box 100, Clementsport, NS B0S 1E0, Canada. TEL 902-638-8611. FAX 902-638-8576. URL: http://www.cdnpeacekeeping.ns.ca.
Vendor(s): UMI. *6032*

PEDIATRIC BULLETIN.
URL: http://ourworld.compuserve.com/homepages/myrna_nieves/.
Available only online. *5037*

PEDIATRIC CARDIOLOGY.
Springer-Verlag, Medical Journals, 175 Fifth Ave., New York, NY 10010. TEL 212-460-1500. FAX 212-473-6272. URL: http://www.springer-ny.com. *4822*

THE PEDIATRIC INFECTIOUS DISEASE JOURNAL.
Williams & Wilkins, 351 W. Camden St., Baltimore, MD 21201-2436. TEL 410-528-4068. FAX 410-528-4452. URL: http://www.wwilkins.com.
Vendor(s): Ovid Technologies, Inc.. *5037*

PEDIATRIC NEPHROLOGY.
Springer-Verlag, Heidelberger Platz 3, 14197 Berlin, Germany. TEL 49-30-82787-0. FAX 49-30-82787448. URL: http://link.springer.de. *5164*

PEDIATRIC PATHOLOGY & LABORATORY MEDICINE.
Taylor & Francis Inc., 1900 Frost Rd., Ste. 101, Bristol, PA 19007-1598. TEL 215-785-5800. FAX 215-785-5515. URL: http://www.tandf.co.uk/. *5037*

PEDIATRIC RADIOLOGY.
Springer-Verlag, Heidelberger Platz 3, 14197 Berlin, Germany. TEL 49-30-82787-0. FAX 49-30-82787448. URL: http://link.springer.de. *5038*

PEDIATRIC RESEARCH.
Williams & Wilkins, 351 W. Camden St., Baltimore, MD 21201-2436. TEL 410-528-4068. FAX 410-528-4452. URL: http://www.wwilkins.com.
Vendor(s): Ovid Technologies, Inc.. *5038*

PEDIATRIC REVIEWS AND COMMUNICATIONS.
Gordon and Breach - Harwood Academic, Amsteldisk 166, 1st Fl., 1079 LH Amsterdam, Netherlands. URL: http://www.gbhap.com/Pediatric_Reviews_Communications/. *5038*

PEDIATRIC SURGERY UPDATE.
Box 10426, Caparra Heights Sta., San Juan, PR 00922-0426. URL: http://home.coqui.net/titolugo/. *5150*

PEDIATRICS (ENGLISH EDITION).
American Academy of Pediatrics, 141 Northwest Point Blvd., Box 927, Elk Grove Village, IL 60009-0927. TEL 847-228-5005. FAX 847-228-5097. URL: http://www.pediatrics.org/
Vendor(s): Lexis-Nexis, Ovid Technologies, Inc.. *5038*

PEDIATRICS FOR PARENTS.
Pediatrics for Parents, Inc., Box 1069, Bangor, ME 04402-1069. TEL 207-942-6212.
Vendor(s): Information Access Co.. *5038*

THE PEKING DUCK.
Box 331661, Corpus Christi, TX 78463-1661. TEL 512-882-1446. URL: http://www.evolute.org. *4449*

PENNSYLVANIA ACADEMY OF SCIENCE. JOURNAL.
Pennsylvania Academy of Science, c/o Dr. S.K. Majumdar, Ed., Dept. of Biology, Lafayette College, Easton, PA 18042. TEL 610-250-5464. FAX 610-250-6557. *6559*

PENNSYLVANIA BUSINESS AND TECHNOLOGY.
Pittsburgh High Technology Council, 2000 Technology Dr., Pittsburgh, PA 15219. TEL 412-687-2700. FAX 412-687-2791.
Vendor(s): UMI. *6969*

PENNSYLVANIA BUSINESS DIRECTORY.
American Business Directories, 5711 S. 86th Circle, Box 27347, Omaha, NE 68127. TEL 402-593-4600. FAX 402-331-5481. *1705*

PENNSYLVANIA C P A JOURNAL.
Pennsylvania Institute of Certified Public Accountants, 1608 Walnut St., 3rd Fl., Philadelphia, PA 19103. TEL 215-735-2635. FAX 215-735-3694. URL: http://www.picpa.com.
Vendor(s): UMI. *1096*

PENNSYLVANIA STATE UNIVERSITY. ENVIRONMENTAL RESOURCES RESEARCH INSTITUTE. NEWSLETTER.
Pennsylvania State University, Environmental Resources Research Institute, 125 Land and Water Research Bldg., University Park, PA 16802-4900. TEL 814-863-0291. FAX 814-865-3378. URL: http://www.erri.psu.edu. *2242*

PENSIONS & INVESTMENTS.
Crain Communications, Inc. (New York), 220 E. 42nd St., New York, NY 10017-5806. TEL 212-210-0100. FAX 212-210-0799.
Vendor(s): Information Access Co., Lexis-Nexis (PENINV). *1401*

PENTHOUSE.
Penthouse International, Ltd., 277 Park Ave., 4th Fl., New York, NY 10172. TEL 212-702-6000. FAX 212-702-6282. URL: http://www.penthousemag.com. *5179*

PEOPLE WEEKLY.
Time Inc., Time & Life Bldg., Rockefeller Center, 1271 Ave. of the Americas, New York, NY 10020-1393. TEL 212-522-1212. URL: http://pathfinder.com.
Vendor(s): Information Access Co., Lexis-Nexis, MediaStream, UMI. *3382*

PEOPLE'S MEDICAL SOCIETY NEWSLETTER.
People's Medical Society, 462 Walnut St., Allentown, PA 18102-5488. TEL 610-770-1670. FAX 610-770-0607.
Vendor(s): Information Access Co.. *2258*

PEPPERDINE LAW REVIEW.
Pepperdine University, School of Law, 24255 Pacific Coast Hwy., Malibu, CA 90263-4694. TEL 310-456-4694. FAX 310-317-7283.
Vendor(s): West Group. *4007*

PEPSY. PEDAGOGISK LITTERATUR I NORDEN.
Nordisk Arbetsgrupp foer Pedagogi och Psykologi, Jyvaskylae University Library, Seminaarink. 15, SF-40100 Jyvaeskylae, Finland.
Available only online. *2472*

PERFECT SOUND FOREVER.
URL: http://www.furious.com/perfect.
Available only online. *5425*

PERFORMING ARTS AND ENTERTAINMENT IN CANADA.
Canadian Stage and Art Publications, 104 Glenrose Ave., Toronto, ON M4T 1K8, Canada. TEL 416-484-4534. FAX 416-484-6214.
Vendor(s): Information Access Co., UMI. *7011*

PERFORMING ARTS JOURNAL.
Johns Hopkins University Press, Journals Publishing Division, 2715 N. Charles St., Baltimore, MD 21218. TEL 410-516-6987. FAX 410-516-6968. URL: http://muse.jhu.edu.
Vendor(s): Information Access Co.. *7011*

PERFUMER & FLAVORIST.
Allured Publishing, 362 S. Schmale Rd., Carol Stream, IL 60188-2787. TEL 708-653-2155. FAX 708-653-2192. *512*

PERFUMES AND FRAGRANCES: THE INTERNATIONAL MARKET.
Euromonitor, 60-61 Britton St., London EC1M 5NA, England. TEL 44-171-251-8024. FAX 44-171-608-3149. URL: http://www.euromonitor.com.
Vendor(s): Data-Star, Knight-Ridder Information, Inc.. *508*

PERINATAL-MEDIZIN.
Springer-Verlag, Heidelberger Platz 3, 14197 Berlin, Germany. TEL 49-30-82787-0. FAX 49-30-82787448. URL: http://link.springer.de. *4965*

PERIODICA. INDICE DE REVISTAS LATINOAMERICANAS EN CIENCIAS.
Universidad Nacional Autonoma de Mexico, Direccion General de Bibliotecas, Apdo. Postal 70-392, C.P. 04510 Mexico, D.F., Mexico. TEL 52-5-6223958. FAX 52-5-6162557. URL: http://www.cichcu.unam.mx. *6591*

PERIODICAL ABSTRACTS.
U M I, 300 N. Zeeb Rd., Ann Arbor, MI 48106. TEL 313-761-4700. FAX 800-864-0019. URL: http://www.umi.com.
Vendor(s): Knight-Ridder Information, Inc., UMI. *22*

PERIODICALS CONTENTS INDEX.
Chadwyck-Healey Ltd., The Quorum, Barnwell Rd., Cambridge CB5 8SW, England. TEL 44-1223-215512. FAX 44-1223-215514. URL: http://www.chadwyck.com. *6650*

PERIODICALS IN SOUTHERN AFRICAN LIBRARIES.
State Library, P.O. Box 397, Pretoria 0001, South Africa. TEL 27-12-21-8931. FAX 27-12-325-5984. *560*

PERISCOPE (GREAT NECK).
Stragegic Business Co., 226 W. 26th St., 10th Fl., New York, NY 10001. TEL 212-822-5930.
Vendor(s): Information Access Co.. *526*

PERSONAL CARE APPLIANCES: THE INTERNATIONAL MARKET.
Euromonitor, 60-61 Britton St., London EC1M 5NA, England. TEL 44-171-251-8024. FAX 44-171-608-3149. URL: http://www.euromonitor.com.
Vendor(s): Data-Star, Knight-Ridder Information, Inc.. *2648*

PERSONAL COMPUTER MARKETS.
Blackwell Publishers Ltd., 108 Cowley Rd., Oxford OX4 1JF, England. TEL 44-1865-791100. FAX 44-1865-791347. URL: http://www.blackwellpublishers.co.uk.
Vendor(s): Data-Star, Information Access Co.. *1544*

PERSONAL FINANCE INTELLIGENCE.
Mintel International Group Ltd., 18-19 Long Ln., London EC1A 9HE, England. TEL 44-171-606-4533. FAX 44-171-606-5932. *1161*

PERSONAL TECHNOLOGIES.
Springer-Verlag London Ltd., Sweetapple House, Catteshall Rd., Godalming, Surrey GU7 3DJ, England. TEL 44-1483-418822. FAX 44-1483-415151. *2089*

PERSONALIST FORUM.
Mercer University Press, 6316 Peake Rd., Macon, GA 31210. TEL 912-752-2880. FAX 912-752-2264. URL: http://www.mercer.edu/~mupress/
Vendor(s): Knight-Ridder Information, Inc.. *5741*

PERSONNEL PSYCHOLOGY.
Personnel Psychology, Inc., 745 Haskins Rd., Ste. A, Bowling Green, OH 43402-1600. TEL 419-352-1562. FAX 419-352-2645.
Vendor(s): Information Access Co., UMI. *6140*

PERSONNEL REVIEW.
M C B University Press Ltd., 60-62 Toller Ln., Bradford, W. Yorks BD8 9BY, England. TEL 44-1274-777700. FAX 44-1274-785200. URL: http://www.mcb.co.uk.
Vendor(s): Information Access Co.. *1573*

PERSONNEL SOFTWARE CENSUS.
Advanced Personnel Systems, 1873 Hidden View Ln., Roseville, CA 95661-5819. TEL 916-781-2900. FAX 916-781-2901. URL: http://www.hrcensus.com.
Vendor(s): Human Resources Information Network. *1573*

THE PERSPECTIVE OBJECTIVE.
O M C E, URL: http://omce.org.
Available only online. *5577*

PERSPECTIVES (TORONTO).
Gerontological Nursing Association, P.O. Box 368, Station "K", Toronto, ON M4P 2G7, Canada. TEL 416-767-4454. FAX 416-591-6812. *3443*

SERIALS AVAILABLE ONLINE 10185

PERSPECTIVES OF NEW MUSIC.
Perspectives of New Music, Inc., University of Washington, Music, Box 353450, Seattle, WA 98195-3450. TEL 206-543-0196. FAX 206-543-9285. URL: http://weber.u.washington.edu/~pnm/pnm.html.
Vendor(s): Information Access Co.. 5425

PERSPECTIVES ON DEVELOPMENTAL NEUROBIOLOGY.
Gordon and Breach - Harwood Academic, Amsteldisk 166, 1st Fl., 1079 LH Amsterdam, Netherlands. URL: http://www.gbhap.com/Perspectives_Developmental_Neurobiology/. 5090

PEST CONTROL.
Advanstar Communications, Inc., 7500 Old Oak Blvd., Cleveland, OH 44130. TEL 216-243-8100. FAX 216-891-2675.
Vendor(s): Information Access Co. 238

PESTICIDE & TOXIC CHEMICAL NEWS.
Food Chemical News, Inc., 1101 Pennsylvania Ave., S.E., Washington, DC 20003. TEL 202-544-1980. FAX 202-546-3890.
Vendor(s): Data-Star, Information Access Co., Knight-Ridder Information, Inc., NewsNet (CH18). 3123

PESTICIDE BIOCHEMISTRY AND PHYSIOLOGY.
Academic Press, Inc., Journal Division, 525 B St., Ste. 1900, San Diego, CA 92101-4495. TEL 619-230-1840. FAX 619-699-6800. URL: http://www.apnet.com/www/journal/pb/htm; http://www.idealibrary.com/ 238

THE PESTICIDE MANUAL.
British Crop Protection Council, Bear Farm, Binfield, Bracknell, Berkshire RG12 5QE, England. TEL 44-1734-341998. FAX 44-1734-341998.
Vendor(s): Data-Star, Knight-Ridder Information, Inc. (File no.306). 145

PET FOODS AND PRODUCTS: THE INTERNATIONAL MARKET.
Euromonitor, 60-61 Britton St., London EC1M 5NA, England. TEL 44-171-251-8024. FAX 44-171-608-3149. URL: http://www.euromonitor.com.
Vendor(s): Data-Star, Knight-Ridder Information, Inc. 3123

PET PRODUCT NEWS.
Fancy Publications, 3 Burroughs, Irvine, CA 92618-2804. TEL 714-855-8822. FAX 714-855-3045. URL: http://www.petchannel.com.
Vendor(s): Information Access Co. 5641

PETERSEN'S PHOTOGRAPHIC.
Petersen Publishing Co., 6420 Wilshire Blvd., Los Angeles, CA 90048. TEL 213-782-2000. FAX 213-782-2465.
Vendor(s): Information Access Co., Knight-Ridder Information, Inc. 5770

PETERSON'S GRADUATE AND PROFESSIONAL PROGRAMS: AN OVERVIEW (YEAR) (BOOK 1).
Peterson's, 202 Carnegie Center, Box 2123, Princeton, NJ 08543-2123. TEL 609-243-9111. FAX 609-243-9150. URL: http://www.petersons.com.
Vendor(s): Knight-Ridder Information, Inc. (File no.273). 2526

PETERSON'S GRADUATE AND PROFESSIONAL PROGRAMS: BUSINESS, EDUCATION, HEALTH, INFORMATION STUDIES, LAW, AND SOCIAL WORK (YEAR) (BOOK 6).
Peterson's, 202 Carnegie Center, Box 2123, Princeton, NJ 08543-2123. TEL 609-243-9111. FAX 609-243-9150. URL: http://www.petersons.com.
Vendor(s): Knight-Ridder Information, Inc. (File no.273). 2526

PETERSON'S GRADUATE AND PROFESSIONAL PROGRAMS: ENGINEERING AND APPLIED SCIENCES (YEAR) (BOOK 5).
Peterson's, 202 Carnegie Center, Box 2123, Princeton, NJ 08543-2123. TEL 609-243-9111. FAX 609-243-9150. URL: http://www.petersons.com.
Vendor(s): Knight-Ridder Information, Inc. (File no.273). 2526

PETERSON'S GRADUATE AND PROFESSIONAL PROGRAMS: THE BIOLOGICAL SCIENCES (YEAR) (BOOK 3).
Peterson's, 202 Carnegie Center, Box 2123, Princeton, NJ 08543-2123. TEL 609-243-9111. FAX 609-243-9150. URL: http://www.petersons.com.
Vendor(s): Knight-Ridder Information, Inc. (File no.273). 2526

PETERSON'S GRADUATE AND PROFESSIONAL PROGRAMS: THE HUMANITIES, ARTS, AND SOCIAL SCIENCES (YEAR) (BOOK 2).
Peterson's, 202 Carnegie Center, Box 2123, Princeton, NJ 08543-2123. TEL 609-243-9111. FAX 609-243-9150. URL: http://www.petersons.com.
Vendor(s): Knight-Ridder Information, Inc. (File no.273). 2526

PETERSON'S GRADUATE AND PROFESSIONAL PROGRAMS: THE PHYSICAL SCIENCES, MATHEMATICS, AND AGRICULTURAL SCIENCES (YEAR) (BOOK 4).
Peterson's, 202 Carnegie Center, Box 2123, NJ 08543-2123. TEL 609-243-9111. FAX 609-243-9150. URL: http://www.petersons.com.
Vendor(s): Knight-Ridder Information, Inc. (File no.273). 2526

PETERSON'S GUIDE TO FOUR-YEAR COLLEGES (YEAR).
Peterson's, 202 Carnegie Center, Box 2123, Princeton, NJ 08543-2123. TEL 609-243-9111. FAX 609-243-9150. URL: http://www.petersons.com.
Vendor(s): CompuServe, Inc. (PCG), Dow Jones News Retrieval (SCHOOL), Knight-Ridder Information, Inc. (File no.214). 2527

PETERSON'S GUIDE TO TWO-YEAR COLLEGES (YEAR).
Peterson's, 202 Carnegie Center, Box 2123, Princeton, NJ 08543-2123. TEL 609-243-9111. FAX 609-243-9150. URL: http://www.petersons.com.
Vendor(s): CompuServe, Inc. (PCG), Dow Jones News Retrieval (SCHOOL), Knight-Ridder Information, Inc. (File no.214), Ovid Technologies, Inc. (PETE). 2527

PETITE.
Firestone Publishing, 1441 Commerce Way, Ste. 420, Miami Lakes, FL 33016-1598. TEL 305-557-0071. FAX 305-577-6005. URL: http://www.sexmags.com; http://www.dugent.com. 5180

PETROLEUM ABSTRACTS.
University of Tulsa, Information Services Division, 600 S. College Ave., Tulsa, OK 74104-3189. TEL 918-631-2297. FAX 918-599-9361. URL: http://www.pa.utulsa.edu/.
Vendor(s): Knight-Ridder Information, Inc. (File no. 87,987), Questel Orbit Inc. (TULSA). 5631

PETROLEUM ECONOMIST.
Euromoney Publications plc., Nestor House, Playhouse Yard, London EC4V 5EX, England. TEL 44-171-779-8935. FAX 44-171-779-8541.
Vendor(s): Information Access Co. 5618

PETROLEUM - ENERGY BUSINESS NEWS INDEX.
American Petroleum Institute, EnCompass, 275 Seventh Ave., New York, NY 10001-6708. TEL 212-366-4040. FAX 212-366-4298.
Vendor(s): Knight-Ridder Information, Inc., Questel Orbit Inc. (ABIZ), Telesystemes - Questel. 5631

PETROLEUM INDEPENDENT.
Petroleum Independent Publishers, Inc., 1101 16th St., N.W., Washington, DC 20036. TEL 202-857-4774. FAX 202-857-4799.
Vendor(s): Information Access Co. 5618

PETROLEUM INTELLIGENCE WEEKLY.
Energy Intelligence Group, 575 Broadway, 4th Fl., New York, NY 10012-3230. TEL 212-941-5500. FAX 212-941-5508. URL: http://www.energyintel.com. 5618

PETROLEUM MARKETING MONTHLY.
U.S. Energy Information Administration, National Energy Information Center, EI-231, James Forrestal Bldg., Rm. 1F-048, 1000 Independence Ave., S.W., Washington, DC 20585. TEL 202-586-8800. FAX 202-586-0727. URL: http://www.eia.doe.gov. 5618

PETS MAGAZINE.
Moorshead Magazines Ltd., 10 Gateway Blvd., Ste. 490, North York, ON M3C 3T4, Canada. TEL 416-696-5488. FAX 416-696-7395. 5641

DER PFLEGEBRIEF.
URL: http://www.uke.uni-hamburg.de/Schools/KrPflSchule/Pflegebrief/. 4946

PHARMA MARKETLETTER.
Marketletter (Publications) Ltd., 54-55 Wilton Rd., London SW1V 1DE, England. TEL 44-171-828-7272. FAX 44-171-828-0415. URL: http://www.rednet.co.uk.homepages/pharmale/pharmale.html.
Vendor(s): Data-Star, Information Access Co. 5683

PHARMA TIMES.
Indian Pharmaceutical Association, Kalina Santacruz East, Mumbai 400 098, India. TEL 91-22-612-2401. FAX 91-22-614-0480. 5683

PHARMACEUTICA ACTA HELVETIAE.
Elsevier Science B.V., P.O. Box 211, 1000 AE Amsterdam, Netherlands. TEL 31-20-4853911. FAX 31-20-4853598. URL: http://www.elsevier.nl/. 5684

PHARMACEUTICAL APPROVALS MONTHLY.
F-D-C Reports, Inc., 5550 Friendship Blvd., Ste. One, Chevy Chase, MD 20815. FAX 301-664-7238.
Vendor(s): Data-Star (FDCR), Knight-Ridder Information, Inc. (File no.187), Lexis-Nexis, Ovid Technologies, Inc. (FDCR). 5684

PHARMACEUTICAL BUSINESS NEWS.
Financial Times Pharmaceuticals and Healthcare Publishing, Maple House, 149 Tottenham Court Rd., London W1P 9LL, England. TEL 44-171-896-2209. FAX 44-171-896-2213. 5684

PHARMACEUTICAL COMPANIES ANALYSIS.
M D I S Publications Ltd., MDIS House, City Fields Business Park, City Fields Way, Chichester, W. Sussex PO20 6FS, England. TEL 44-1243-533322. FAX 44-1243-533418. 5684

PHARMACEUTICAL COMPANY PROFILES.
IMSWORLD Publications Ltd., 7 Harewood Ave., London NW1 6JB, England. TEL 0171-393-5000. FAX 0171-393-5900. 5684

PHARMACEUTICAL EXECUTIVE.
Advanstar Communications, Inc. (Eugene), 859 Willamette St., Eugene, OR 97401-6806. TEL 541-343-1200. FAX 541-344-3514.
Vendor(s): Information Access Co., UMI. 5684

PHARMACEUTICAL MANUFACTURING REVIEW.
Argus Business Media Ltd., Queensway House, 2 Queensway, Redhill, Surrey RH1 1QS, England. TEL 44-1737-768611. FAX 44-1737-761685.
Vendor(s): Information Access Co. 5685

PHARMACEUTICAL PROCESSING.
Gordon Publications, Part of Cahners Publishing Company, Division of Reed Elsevier Inc., 301 Gibraltar Dr., Box 650, Morris Plains, NJ 07950-0650. TEL 973-292-5100 ext.381. FAX 973-605-1220. URL: http://www.pharmpro.com. 5685

PHARMACEUTICAL SOCIETY OF JAPAN. JOURNAL.
Pharmaceutical Society of Japan, 12-15, Shibuya 2-chome, Shibuya-ku, Tokyo 150, Japan. 5685

PHARMACEUTICALS MONTHLY.
Yakugyo Jiho Co. Ltd., 2-36 Kanda Jimbo-cho, Chiyoda-ku, Tokyo 101, Japan. 5686

PHARMACEUTICALS TODAY.
Society of Chemical Industry, 14 Belgrave Sq., London SW1X 8PS, England. TEL 44-171-235-3681. FAX 44-171-235-9410. URL: http://pharma.mond.org.
Available only online. 5686

PHARMACIEN DE FRANCE.
Federation des Syndicats Pharmaceutiques de France, 13 rue Ballu, 75009 Paris, France. TEL 42-81-15-96. 5686

PHARMACIEN RURAL.
Association de Pharmacie Rural, 24 rue Vintimille, 75009 Paris, France. TEL 48-74-64-26. FAX 45-26-13-37. 5686

PHARMACIES AND DRUGSTORES: THE INTERNATIONAL MARKET.
Euromonitor, 60-61 Britton St., London EC1M 5NA, England. TEL 44-171-251-8024. FAX 44-171-608-3149. URL: http://www.euromonitor.com.
Vendor(s): Data-Star, Knight-Ridder Information, Inc.. *5686*

PHARMACIST NEWS.
Maclean-Hunter Ltd., Business Publication Division, Maclean-Hunter Bldg., 777 Bay St., Toronto, ON M5W 1A7, Canada. TEL 416-596-5950. *5686*

PHARMACOECONOMICS AND OUTCOMES NEWS.
Adis International Limited, Private Bag 65901, Mairangi Bay, Auckland 10, New Zealand. TEL 64-9-479-8100. FAX 64-9-479-8145. URL: http://www.adis.com.
Vendor(s): Knight-Ridder Information, Inc.. *5686*

PHARMACOGENETICS.
Chapman & Hall, Journals Department 2-6 Boundary Row, London SE1 8HN, England. TEL 44-171-8650066. FAX 44-171-5229613. URL: http://www.chaphall.com/chaphall/journals.html. *775*

PHARMACOLOGICAL RESEARCH.
Academic Press Ltd., 24-28 Oval Rd., London NW1 7DX, England. TEL 44-171 267-4466. FAX 44-171-482-2293. URL: http://www.hbuk.co.uk/ap/pharmres; http://www.europe.idealibrary.com/. *5687*

PHARMACOLOGY REVIEWS AND COMMUNICATIONS.
Gordon and Breach - Harwood Academic, Amsteldisk 166, 1st Fl., 1079 LH Amsterdam, Netherlands. URL: http://www.gbhap.com/Pharmacology_Reviews_Communications/. *5687*

PHARMACY IN HISTORY.
American Institute of the History of Pharmacy, Pharmacy Bldg., Madison, WI 53706. TEL 608-262-5378. *5688*

PHARMACY PRACTICE NEWS.
McMahon Group, 148 W. 24th St., 8th Fl., New York, NY 10011-1916. TEL 212-620-4600. FAX 212-620-5928. *5688*

PHARMACY TIMES.
Romaine Pierson Publishing Co., 80 Shore Rd., Port Washington, NY 11050. TEL 516-883-6350. FAX 516-883-6609. *5689*

PHARMAPROJECTS MAGAZINE.
P J B Publications Ltd., 18-20 Hill Rise, Richmond, Surrey TW10 6UA, England. TEL 44-181-948-3262. FAX 44-181-332-8990. URL: http://www.pjbpubs.co.uk/pharma/top.html.
Vendor(s): Data-Star, Knight-Ridder Information, Inc., Ovid Technologies, Inc., STN International. *5689*

DIE PHARMAZEUTISCHE INDUSTRIE.
Editio Cantor, Postfach 1255, 88322 Aulendorf, Germany. TEL 49-7525-940135. FAX 49-7525-940180. URL: http://www.ecv.de. *5689*

DIE PHARMAZIE.
Govi Pharmazeutischer Verlag GmbH, Ginnheimerstr. 26, 65760 Eschborn, Germany. TEL 49-6196-928262. FAX 49-6196-928203. *5689*

PHASE TRANSITIONS.
Gordon and Breach - Harwood Academic, Amsteldisk 166, 1st Fl., 1079 LH Amsterdam, Netherlands. URL: http://www.gbhap.com/Phase_Transitions/. *5817*

PHI DELTA KAPPAN.
Phi Delta Kappa, Inc., Box 789, Bloomington, IN 47402-0789. TEL 812-339-1156. FAX 812-339-0018.
Vendor(s): Information Access Co., UMI. *2472*

PHILADELPHIA BUSINESS JOURNAL.
American City Business Joournals, Inc., 505 Powell St., Austin, TX 78703-5121.
Vendor(s): CompuServe, Inc., Data-Star, Dow Jones News Retrieval, Information Access Co., Knight-Ridder Information, Inc., Lexis-Nexis, UMI. *1281*

PHILOLOGICAL QUARTERLY.
University of Iowa, Iowa City, IA 52242. TEL 319-335-0435.
Vendor(s): Information Access Co.. *4288*

PHILOSOPHER'S INDEX.
Philosopher's Information Center, 1616 E. Wooster St., Box P, Bowling Green, OH 43402. TEL 419-353-8830. FAX 419-353-8920.
Vendor(s): Knight-Ridder Information, Inc. (File no.57). *5760*

PHILOSOPHICAL FORUM.
Philosophical Forum, Inc., c/o Baruch College, 111 E. 18th St., G-1437, New York, NY 10010. TEL 212-387-1682.
Vendor(s): Ovid Technologies, Inc.. *5742*

PHILOSOPHICAL MAGAZINE LETTERS.
Taylor & Francis Ltd., 1 Gunpowder Sq., London EC4A 3DE, England. TEL 44-171-583-0490. FAX 44-171-583-0585. URL: http://www.tandf.co.uk/. *5818*

PHILOSOPHY AND LITERATURE.
Johns Hopkins University Press, Journals Publishing Division, 2715 N. Charles St., Baltimore, MD 21218. TEL 410-516-6987. FAX 410-516-6968. URL: http://muse.jhu.edu. *5744*

PHILOSOPHY AND PUBLIC AFFAIRS.
Princeton University Press, 41 William St., Princeton, NJ 08540. TEL 609-258-4900. FAX 609-258-6305. URL: http://pup.princeton.edu.
Vendor(s): UMI. *5955*

PHILOSOPHY EAST AND WEST.
University of Hawaii Press, Journals Department, 2840 Kolowalu St., Honolulu, HI 96822. TEL 808-956-8833. FAX 808-988-6052. URL: http://www2.hawaii.edu/uhpress/Journals/PW/PWHome.html.
Vendor(s): Information Access Co.. *5745*

PHILOSOPHY, PSYCHIATRY & PSYCHOLOGY.
Johns Hopkins University Press, Journals Publishing Division, 2715 N. Charles St., Baltimore, MD 21218. TEL 410-516-6987. FAX 410-516-6968. URL: http://muse.jhu.edu; http://www.press.jhu/journals/philosophy_psychiatry_and_psychology. *5745*

PHILOTELIA.
Hellenic Philotelic Society, 57 Akademias St., 106 79 Athens, Greece. TEL 30-1-3621-971. FAX 30-1-9422-157. *5711*

PHLEBOLOGY.
Springer-Verlag London Ltd., Sweetapple House, Catteshall Rd., Godalming, Surrey GU7 3DJ, England. TEL 44-1483-418800. FAX 44-1483-415144. *4823*

THE PHOENIX (ST. PAUL).
Phoenix, 447 Marshall Ave., Ste. 4, St. Paul, MN 55102. TEL 612-291-2691. FAX 612-291-0553. URL: http://www.gartland.com/phoenix. *5460*

PHONE LOSERS OF AMERICA.
1013 Kingswood Court, Celina, OH 45822. URL: http://www.cocksoldier.com.
Available only online. *2037*

PHOSPHORUS, SULPHUR AND SILICON AND THE RELATED ELEMENTS.
Gordon and Breach - Harwood Academic, Amsteldisk 166, 1st Fl., 1079 LH Amsterdam, Netherlands. URL: http://www.gbhap.com/Phosporus_Sulfur_Silicon/. *1809*

PHOTOBULLETIN.
PhotoSource International, 1910 35th Rd., Pine Lake Farm, Osceola, WI 54020. TEL 715-248-3800. FAX 715-248-7394.
Vendor(s): NewsNet (PB26). *5771*

PHOTOBULLETIN DAILY.
PhotoSource International, 1910 35th Rd., Pine Lake Farm, Osceola, WI 54020. TEL 715-248-3800. FAX 715-248-7394.
Vendor(s): NewsNet. *5771*

PHOTOFINISHING NEWS LETTER.
Photofinishing News, Inc., 10915 Bonita Beach Rd., Ste. 1091, Bonita Springs, FL 34135. TEL 941-992-4421. FAX 941-992-6328. URL: http://www.photo-news.com. *5771*

PHOTOGRAPHY: THE INTERNATIONAL MARKET.
Euromonitor, 60-61 Britton St., London EC1M 5NA, England. TEL 44-171-251-8024. FAX 44-171-608-3149. URL: http://www.euromonitor.com.
Vendor(s): Data-Star, Knight-Ridder Information, Inc.. *5772*

PHOTOMARKET.
PhotoSource International, 1910 35th Rd., Pine Lake Farm, Osceola, WI 54020. TEL 715-248-3800. FAX 715-248-7394.
Vendor(s): NewsNet (PB17). *5772*

PHOTON.
Icon Publications Ltd., Maxwell Ln., Kelso, Roxburghshire TD5 7BB, England. TEL 01573-226032. FAX 01573-226000. *5772*

PHOTONICS SPECTRA.
Laurin Publishing Co., Inc., Box 4949, Berkshire Common, Pittsfield, MA 01202-4949. TEL 413-499-0514. FAX 413-442-3180. URL: http://www.laurin.com.
Vendor(s): Information Access Co.. *5869*

PHOTOSHOP TIPS & TRICKS.
Design & Publishing Center, 15 Southgate, Harrisonburg, VA 22801. URL: http://www.graphic-design.com/Photoshop.
Available only online. *2139*

PHOTOSTOCKNOTES.
PhotoSource International, 1910 35th Rd., Pine Lake Farm, Osceola, WI 54020. TEL 715-248-3800. FAX 715-248-7394.
Vendor(s): NewsNet (PB12). *5773*

PHYSICAL EDUCATION INDEX.
Benoak Publishing Company, Box 474, Cape Girardeau, MO 63702-0474. TEL 573-334-8789. FAX 573-334-7996. *5793*

PHYSICAL REVIEW A.
American Physical Society, One Physics Ellipse, College Park, MD 20740-3844. TEL 301-209-3202. URL: http://ojps.aip.org/prao. *5819*

PHYSICAL REVIEW B (CONDENSED MATTER).
American Physical Society, One Physics Ellipse, College Park, MD 20740-3844. TEL 301-209-3202. URL: http://publish.aps.org/PRBO. *5819*

PHYSICAL REVIEW C (NUCLEAR PHYSICS).
American Physical Society, One Physics Ellipse, College Park, MD 20740-3843. TEL 301-209-3000. URL: http://ojps.aip.org/prco. *5856*

PHYSICAL REVIEW D (PARTICLES AND FIELDS).
American Physical Society, One Physics Ellipse, College Park, MD 20740-3843. TEL 301-209-3000. URL: http://publish.aps.org/PRDO. *5856*

PHYSICAL REVIEW E (STATISTICAL PHYSICS, PLASMAS, FLUIDS, AND RELATED INTERDISCIPLINARY TOPICS).
American Physical Society, One Physics Ellipse, College Park, MD 20740-3844. TEL 301-209-3000. URL: http://publish.aps.org/PREO. *5819*

PHYSICAL REVIEW LETTERS.
American Physical Society, One Physics Ellipse, College Park, MD 20740-3844. TEL 301-209-3202. URL: http://ojps.aip.org/prlo.
Vendor(s): OCLC. *5819*

PHYSICAL THERAPY.
American Physical Therapy Association, 1111 N. Fairfax St., Alexandria, VA 22314-1488. TEL 703-684-2782. FAX 703-706-3169. URL: http://www.apta.org/pt_journal.
Vendor(s): Central Institute for Scientific & Technical Information, Ovid Technologies, Inc.. *5045*

THE PHYSICIAN AND SPORTSMEDICINE.
McGraw-Hill Companies (Minneapolis), 4530 W. 77th St., Minneapolis, MN 55435. TEL 612-835-3222. URL: http://www.physsportsmed.com.
Vendor(s): Dow Jones News Retrieval, Information Access Co., Knight-Ridder Information, Inc., NewsNet (ME05). *5131*

PHYSICIAN EXECUTIVE.
American College of Physician Executives, Two Urban Centre, Ste. 200, 4890 W. Kennedy Blvd., Tampa, FL 33609. TEL 813-287-2000. FAX 813-287-8993.
Vendor(s): Information Access Co.. *3718*

PHYSICIAN MANAGER.
Atlantic Information Services, Inc., 1100 17th St., N.W., Ste. 300, Washington, DC 20036. TEL 202-775-9008. FAX 202-331-9542. URL: http://www.aispub.com.
Vendor(s): Information Access Co.. *3830*

PHYSICIANS' DESK REFERENCE.
Medical Economics Publishing Co., Inc., 5 Paragon Dr., Montvale, NJ 07645. TEL 201-358-7200. FAX 201-573-1045. *4729*

PHYSICIANS' DESK REFERENCE FOR NONPRESCRIPTION DRUGS.
Medical Economics Publishing Co., Inc., 5 Paragon Dr., Montvale, NJ 07645. TEL 201-358-7200. FAX 201-573-1045. *4729*

PHYSICIANS' DESK REFERENCE FOR OPHTHALMOLOGY.
Medical Economics Publishing Co., Inc., 5 Paragon Dr., Montvale, NJ 07645. TEL 201-358-7246. FAX 201-573-0344. *5000*

PHYSICS ABSTRACTS.
INSPEC, I.E.E., Michael Faraday House, Six Hills Way, Stevenage, Herts. SG1 2AY, England. TEL 44-1438-313311. FAX 44-1438-742840. URL: http://www.iee.org.uk.
Vendor(s): CEDOCAR, Data-Star, European Space Agency, FIZ Technik, Knight-Ridder Information, Inc., Questel Orbit Inc., STN International. *5836*

PHYSICS AND CHEMISTRY OF LIQUIDS.
Gordon and Breach - Harwood Academic, Amsteldisk 166, 1st Fl., 1079 LH Amsterdam, Netherlands. URL: http://www.gbhap.com/Physics__Chemistry__of__Liquids/. *5847*

PHYSICS AND CHEMISTRY OF MINERALS.
Springer-Verlag, Heidelberger Platz 3, 14197 Berlin, Germany. TEL 49-30-82787-0. FAX 49-30-82787448. URL: http://link.springer.de. *5313*

PHYSICS EDUCATION.
I O P Publishing Ltd., Dirac House, Temple Back, Bristol BS1 6BE, England. TEL 44-117-929-7481. FAX 44-117-929-4318. URL: http://www.iop.org/Journals/pe. *5820*

PHYSICS IN MEDICINE AND BIOLOGY.
I O P Publishing Ltd., Dirac House, Temple Back, Bristol BS1 6BE, England. TEL 44-117-929-7481. FAX 44-117-929-4318. URL: http://www.iop.org. *676*

PHYSICS OF FLUIDS.
American Institute of Physics, One Physics Ellipse, College Park, MD 20740-3843. TEL 301-209-3000. URL: http://www.aip.org. *5820*

PHYSICS OF PARTICLES AND NUCLEI.
American Institute of Physics, One Physics Ellipse, College Park, MD 20740-3843. TEL 301-209-3000. URL: http://www.aip.org. *5856*

PHYSICS OF PLASMAS.
American Institute of Physics, One Physics Ellipse, College Park, MD 20740-3843. TEL 301-209-3000. URL: http://www.aip.org. *5820*

PHYSICS OF THE SOLID STATE.
American Institute of Physics, One Physics Ellipse, College Park, MD 20740-3843. TEL 301-209-3000. URL: http://www.aip.org. *5820*

PHYSICS - USPEKHI.
Turpion - Moscow Ltd., 47 Leninsky prospekt, 117913 Moscow, Russia. TEL 7-95-1356417. FAX 7-95-1358860. URL: http://ufn.ioc.ac.ru/ufn.html. *5821*

PHYSICS WORLD.
I O P Publishing Ltd., Dirac House, Temple Back, Bristol BS1 6BE, England. TEL 44-117-929-7481. FAX 44-117-929-4318. URL: http://www/iop.org/Mags/PW. *5821*

PHYSIOLOGICAL AND MOLECULAR PLANT PATHOLOGY.
Academic Press Ltd., 24-28 Oval Rd., London NW1 7DX, England. TEL 44-171-267-4466. FAX 44-171-482-2293. URL: http://www.hbuk.co.uk/ap/pmpp; http://www.europe.idealibrary.com/. *720*

PHYSIOLOGICAL MEASUREMENT.
I O P Publishing Ltd., Dirac House, Temple Back, Bristol BS1 6BE, England. TEL 44-117-929-7481. FAX 44-117-929-4318. URL: http://www.iop.org. *4730*

PHYSIOLOGICAL REVIEWS.
American Physiological Society, 9650 Rockville Pike, Bethesda, MD 20814. TEL 301-530-7164. FAX 301-571-8313.
Vendor(s): Information Access Co.. *820*

PHYSIOLOGIST.
American Physiological Society, 9650 Rockville Pike, Bethesda, MD 20814. TEL 301-530-7164. FAX 301-571-8313. URL: http://www.faseb.org/aps. *820*

PHYSIOTHERAPY INDEX.
British Library, Medical Information Centre, Boston Spa, Wetherby, W. Yorks. LS23 7BQ, England. TEL 01937-546039. FAX 01937-546458. *4787*

PICTURES QUARTERLY.
Art League School of Alexandria, URL: http://www.worldweb.net/~talmage/PicturesQuarterly/
Available only online. *5773*

PIF.
DiMax Tech, Box 893162, Mililani, HI 96789-0162. URL: http://www.dimax.com/pif.
Available only online. *4449*

PIG NEWS & INFORMATION.
CAB International, Wallingford, Oxon. OX10 8DE, England. TEL 44-1491-832111. FAX 44-1491-826090. URL: http://www.cabi.org.
Vendor(s): DIMDI, European Space Agency, Knight-Ridder Information, Inc., STN International. *285*

PIPELINE & GAS JOURNAL.
Oildom Publishing Co. of Texas, Inc., Box 219368, Houston, TX 77218-9368. TEL 281-558-6930. FAX 281-558-7029.
Vendor(s): Information Access Co.. *5619*

PIPELINE INDUSTRY (TULSA).
Midwest Publishing Company, Box 50350, Tulsa, OK 74150-0350. TEL 918-582-2000. FAX 918-587-9349.
Vendor(s): Information Access Co.. *5619*

PIRRADAZISH: BULLETIN OF ACHAEMENIAN STUDIES.
University of Chicago, Oriental Institute, 1155 E. 58th St., Chicago, IL 60637-1569. TEL 312-702-9508. FAX 312-702-9853. *3659*

PIT & QUARRY.
Advanstar Communications, Inc., 7500 Old Oak Blvd., Cleveland, OH 44130. TEL 216-826-2839. FAX 216-891-2726.
Vendor(s): Information Access Co.. *5313*

PITTSBURGH BUSINESS TIMES - JOURNAL.
Pittsburgh Business Times, 2313 E. Carson St., Ste. 200, Pittsburgh, PA 15203-2109. TEL 412-481-6397. FAX 412-481-9956.
Vendor(s): Information Access Co., UMI. *992*

PIXEL - THE COMPUTER ANIMATION DIRECTORY.
Pixel - The Computer Animation News People, 109 Venderhoof St., Ste. 2, Toronto, ON M4G 2H7, Canada. TEL 416-424-4657. FAX 416-424-1812. *477*

PIXEL - THE COMPUTER ANIMATION NEWSLETTER.
Pixel - The Computer Animation News People, Inc., 109 Vanderhoof Ave., Ste. 2, Toronto, ON M4G 2H7, Canada. TEL 416-424-4657. FAX 416-424-1812. *477*

PLADEANMELDELSER, RYTMISK MUSIK.
Dansk BiblioteksCenter as, Tempovej 7-11, 2750 Ballerup, Denmark. TEL 5-44-867777. FAX 45-44-867892.
Available only online. *5426*

PLAGUE WATCH.
DeMigalt Media Group, Box 6, Bucyrus, MO 65444-0006. TEL 713-863-0244. FAX 713-864-2607. *4353*

PLAINTEXT.
URL: http://www.plaintext.com.
Available only online. *4450*

SERIALS AVAILABLE ONLINE 10187

PLANET MAGAZINE.
URL: http://www.etext.org/Zines/planet/
Available only online. *4534*

EL PLANETA PLATICA.
Talking Planet, 1511 Twin Springs Ct., Henderson, NV 89014-0320. URL: http://www.planeta.com/ *7228*

PLANETARY REPORT.
Planetary Society, 65 N. Catalina Ave., Pasadena, CA 91106-2301. TEL 818-793-5100. FAX 818-793-5568. URL: http://planetary.org/tps/. *499*

PLANNING COMMISSIONERS JOURNAL.
Champlain Planning Press, Box 4295, Burlington, VT 05406-4295. TEL 802-864-9083. FAX 802-862-1882. URL: http://www.plannersweb.com. *3756*

PLANNING CONSUMER MARKETS.
Henley Centre for Forecasting Ltd., 9 Bridewell Pl., Blackfriars, London EC4V 6AY, England. TEL 0171-353-9961. FAX 0171-353-2899. *1281*

PLANNING PERSPECTIVES.
Thomson Professional, 2-6 Boundary Row, London SE1 8HN, England. TEL 44-171-8650066. FAX 44-171-5229623. URL: http://pp.thomsonprofessional.com. *3508*

PLANNING PRACTICE AND RESEARCH.
Carfax Publishing Co., P.O. Box 25, Abingdon, Oxon. OX14 3UE, England. TEL 44-1235-401000. FAX 44-1235-401550. *3756*

PLANT BREEDING ABSTRACTS.
CAB International, Wallingford, Oxon. OX10 8DE, England. TEL 44-1491-832111. FAX 44-1491-826090. URL: http://www.cabi.org.
Vendor(s): DIMDI, European Space Agency, Knight-Ridder Information, Inc., STN International. *3208*

PLANT CELL REPORTS.
Springer-Verlag, Heidelberger Platz 3, 14197 Berlin, Germany. TEL 49-30-82787-0. FAX 49-30-82787448. URL: http://link.springer.de. *722*

THE PLANT ENGINEER E-ZINE.
Roy Anderson Company, Inc., URL: http://www.iac.net:80/~isis/index.html.
Available only online. *2736*

PLANT ENGINEERING.
Cahners Publishing Company (Newton), Division of Reed Elsevier Inc., 275 Washington St., Newton, MA 02158-1630. TEL 617-964-3030. URL: http://www.planteng.com; http://cahners.com/
Vendor(s): Information Access Co., Knight-Ridder Information, Inc.. *2736*

PLANT GENETIC RESOURCES ABSTRACTS.
CAB International, Wallingford, Oxon OX10 8DE, England. TEL 44-1491-832111. FAX 44-1491-826090. URL: http://www.cabi.org. *644*

PLANT GROWTH REGULATOR ABSTRACTS.
CAB International, Wallingford, Oxon. OX10 8DE, England. TEL 44-1491-832111. FAX 44-1491-833508. URL: http://www.cabi.org.
Vendor(s): DIMDI, European Space Agency, Knight-Ridder Information, Inc., STN International. *181*

PLANT PHYSIOLOGY.
American Society of Plant Physiologists, 15501 Monona Dr., Rockville, MD 20855. TEL 301-251-0560. FAX 301-279-2996. *723*

PLANTA.
Springer-Verlag, Heidelberger Platz 3, 14197 Berlin, Germany. TEL 49-30-82787-0. FAX 49-30-82787448. URL: http://link.springer.de. *724*

PLANTA MEDICA.
Georg Thieme Verlag, Ruedigerstr. 14, 70469 Stuttgart, Germany. TEL 0711-8931-0. FAX 0711-8931298. *5690*

PLANTS, SITES & PARKS.
B P I Communications, 49 Music Sq., W., Nashville, TN 37203. TEL 615-329-4940. FAX 615-329-4733. URL: http://www.bizsites.com.
Vendor(s): Information Access Co.. *1593*

SERIALS AVAILABLE ONLINE

PLASMA DEVICES AND OPERATIONS.
Gordon and Breach - Harwood Academic, Amsteldisk 166, 1st Fl., 1079 LH Amsterdam, Netherlands. URL: http://www.gbhap.com/Plasma_Devices_Operations/. *5822*

PLASMA PHYSICS AND CONTROLLED FUSION.
I O P Publishing Ltd., Dirac House, Temple Back, Bristol BS1 6BE, England. TEL 44-117-929-7481. FAX 44-117-929-4318. URL: http://www.iop.org. *5822*

PLASMA SOURCES SCIENCE AND TECHNOLOGY.
I O P Publishing Ltd., Dirac House, Temple Back, Bristol BS1 6BE, England. TEL 44-117-929-7481. FAX 44-117-929-4318. URL: http://www.iop.org. *5822*

PLASMID.
Academic Press, Inc., Journal Division, 525 B St., Ste. 1900, San Diego, CA 92101-4495. TEL 619-230-1840. FAX 619-699-6800. URL: http://www.apnet.com/www/journal/pl.htm. *620*

PLASTIC AND RECONSTRUCTIVE SURGERY.
Williams & Wilkins, 351 W. Camden St., Baltimore, MD 21201-2436. TEL 410-528-4068. FAX 410-528-4452. URL: http://www.wilkins.com.
Vendor(s): Ovid Technologies, Inc. *5151*

PLASTICS AND RUBBER ASIA.
S K C Communications Ltd., Southfields, South View Rd., Wadhurst, E. Sussex TN5 6TP, England. TEL 44-1892-784099. FAX 44-1892-784089.
Vendor(s): Information Access Co. *5882*

PLASTICS BUSINESS NEWS.
Market Search, Inc., 2727 Holland Sylvania Rd., Ste. A, Toledo, OH 43615. TEL 419-535-7899. FAX 419-535-1243.
Vendor(s): NewsNet (CH17). *5882*

PLASTICS ENGINEERING.
Society of Plastics Engineers, Inc., 14 Fairfield Dr., Box 403, Brookfield, CT 06804-0403. TEL 203-775-0471. FAX 203-775-8490.
Vendor(s): Information Access Co. *5882*

PLASTICS INDUSTRY NEWS JAPAN.
Rapra Technology Ltd., Shawbury, Shrewsbury, Shropshire SY4 4NR, England. TEL 44-1939-250383. FAX 44-1939-251118. URL: http://www.rapra.net. *5882*

PLASTICS NEWS.
Crain Communications Inc. (Akron), c/o Linda Whelan, 1725 Merriman Rd., Akron, OH 44313-3185. TEL 216-836-9180. FAX 216-836-2365.
Vendor(s): Information Access Co. *5883*

PLASTICS TECHNOLOGY.
Bill Communications, Inc., 355 Park Ave. S., 5th Fl., New York, NY 10010-1789. TEL 212-592-6200. FAX 212-592-6339.
Vendor(s): Information Access Co. *5883*

PLASTICS WORLD.
P T N Publishing Corp., 445 Broad Hollow Rd., Ste. 21, Melville, NY 11747-4722. TEL 516-845-2700.
Vendor(s): Information Access Co. *5883*

PLATT'S INTERNATIONAL PETROCHEMICAL REPORT.
McGraw-Hill Companies, 1221 Ave. of the Americas, New York, NY 10020.
Vendor(s): Dow Jones News Retrieval, Knight-Ridder Information, Inc. (File no.624/McGRAW-HILL PUBLICATIONS ONLINE), Lexis-Nexis, NewsNet (CH20). *5620*

PLATT'S OILGRAM NEWS.
McGraw-Hill Companies, Commodity Services Group, 1221 Ave. of the Americas, 42nd Fl., New York, NY 10020. TEL 212-512-2000.
Vendor(s): Dow Jones News Retrieval (PON), Knight-Ridder Information, Inc. (File no.624/McGRAW-HILL PUBLICATIONS ONLINE), Lexis-Nexis (PONEWS), NewsNet (EY74). *5620*

PLATT'S OILGRAM PRICE REPORT.
McGraw-Hill Companies, Commodity Services Group, 1221 Ave. of the Americas, 42nd Fl., New York, NY 10020.
Vendor(s): Dow Jones News Retrieval (POP), Knight-Ridder Information, Inc. (File no.624/McGRAW-HILL PUBLICATIONS ONLINE), Lexis-Nexis (PPRICE), NewsNet (EY75). *5620*

PLAYBOY.
Playboy Enterprises, Inc., 680 N. Lake Shore Dr., Chicago, IL 60611. TEL 312-751-8000. FAX 312-751-2818.
Vendor(s): Information Access Co. *5180*

PLAYER'S CHOICE MAGAZINE.
9406 US Hwy. 92 E., Ste. 110, Tampa, FL 33610. URL: http://members.aol.com/playersmag. *6775*

PLAYTHINGS.
Geyer-McAllister Publications, Inc., 51 Madison Ave., New York, NY 10010. TEL 212-689-4411.
Vendor(s): Information Access Co., Knight-Ridder Information, Inc. *3450*

PLOUGHSHARES.
Ploughshares, Inc., Emerson College, 100 Beacon St., Boston, MA 02116. TEL 617-824-8753. URL: www.emerson.edu/ploughshares/
Vendor(s): Information Access Co., UMI. *4450*

PLOWSHARE NEWS.
Plowshare Peace & Justice Center, 1402 Grandin Rd., S.W., Rm. 203, Box 1623, Roanoke, VA 24008-1623. TEL 540-985-0808. FAX 540-902-1034. URL: http://www.public.usit.net/pshare. *5955*

PLUMBING AND MECHANICAL DIRECTORY.
Business News Publishing Company, 55 W. Big Beaver Rd., Ste. 1000, Troy, MI 48084. TEL 810-362-3700. FAX 810-362-0317. URL: http://www.bnp.com. *1706*

PLUMBING & MECHANICAL ENGINEER.
Business News Publishing Co., 755 W. Big Beaver, Ste. 1000, Troy, MI 48084. TEL 810-362-3700. FAX 810-362-0317. URL: http://www.bnp.com. *3483*

PLYMOUTH COUNTY BUSINESS REVIEW.
Plymouth County Development Council, Box 1620, Pembroke, MA 02359. TEL 617-826-3136. FAX 617-826-0444. URL: http://www.plymouth-1620.com/.
Vendor(s): UMI. *1215*

THE POCKET INTERNET.
266 Main St., Medfield, MA 02052. URL: http://www.tiac.net/users/gadillon/pocket.htm.
Available only online. *2139*

POETRY (CHICAGO).
Modern Poetry Association, 60 W. Walton St., Chicago, IL 60610. TEL 312-255-3703.
Vendor(s): Information Access Co.. *4519*

POETRY IN MOTION MAGAZINE.
National Poet's Association, Box 173, Bayport, MN 55003. URL: http://www.winternet.com/~poem. *4519*

POETRY MACHINE - LYRIKMASCHINE.
URL: http://ourworld.compuserve.com/homepages/poetry_machine/
Available only online. *4451*

POET'S PARK.
URL: http://www.soos.com/poetpark.
Available only online. *4451*

POGONIP.
W. 111 Knox, Spokane, WA 99205. URL: http://www.ior.com/~mww/pogonip.htm.
Available only online. *4451*

POINT DE REPERE.
Services Documentaires Multimedia Inc., 75 Port Royal E., bureau 300, Montreal, PQ H3L 3T1, Canada. TEL 514-382-0895. FAX 514-384-9139. URL: http://www.sdm.qc.ca.
Vendor(s): IST-INFORMATHEQUE, Inc. *22*

POLAR AND GLACIOLOGICAL ABSTRACTS.
Cambridge University Press, Edinburgh Bldg., Shaftesbury Rd., Cambridge CB2 2RU, England. TEL 44-1223-312393. FAX 44-1223-315052. URL: http://www.cup.cam.ac.uk.
Vendor(s): QL Systems Ltd. *2327*

POLAR BIOLOGY.
Springer-Verlag, Heidelberger Platz 3, 14197 Berlin, Germany. TEL 49-30-82787-0. FAX 49-30-82787448. URL: http://link.springer.de. *620*

POLAR RESEARCH.
Norwegian Polar Institute, Middelthuns gate 29, P.O. Box 5072 Majorstua, N-0301 Oslo, Norway. TEL 47-22-95-95-00. FAX 47-22-95-95-01. *6559*

POLICY REVIEW.
Heritage Foundation, 214 Massachusetts Ave., N.E., Washington, DC 20002. TEL 202-546-4400. FAX 202-546-8328.
Vendor(s): Information Access Co., Lexis-Nexis. *5956*

POLICY STUDIES JOURNAL.
Policy Studies Organization, University of Illinois at Urbana-Champaign, 361 Lincoln Hall, Urbana, IL 61801. TEL 217-359-8541.
Vendor(s): Information Access Co., UMI. *5956*

POLISH JOURNAL OF PHARMACOLOGY.
Polska Akademia Nauk, Instytut Farmakologii, Ul. Smetna 12, 31-343 Krakow, Poland. TEL 48-12-374022. FAX 48-12-374500. *5690*

POLISH MUSIC.
Agencja Autorska, Ul. Hipoteczna 2, P.O. Box 133, 00-950 Warsaw, Poland. TEL 22-27-83-96. FAX 22-27-58-82.
Available only online. *5426*

POLITICAL COMMUNICATION.
Taylor & Francis Inc., 1900 Frost Rd., Ste. 101, Bristol, PA 19007. TEL 215-785-5800. FAX 215-785-5515. URL: http://www.tandf.co.uk/. *5957*

POLITICAL FINANCE & LOBBY REPORTER.
Amward Publications, Inc., 2030 Clarendon Blvd., Ste. 401, Arlington, VA 22201. TEL 703-525-7227. FAX 703-525-3536. URL: http://www.pflr.com.
Vendor(s): Lexis-Nexis, NewsNet (PO02). *5957*

POLITICAL RISK LETTER.
The P R S Group, Box 248, East Syracuse, NY 13057-0248. TEL 315-431-0511. FAX 315-431-0200.
Vendor(s): Information Access Co., NewsNet (IT29). *1345*

POLITICAL RISK YEARBOOK.
The P R S Group, Box 248, East Syracuse, NY 13057-0248. TEL 315-431-0511. FAX 315-431-0200.
Vendor(s): Data-Star (FSRI), Lexis-Nexis. *1161*

POLITICAL RISK YEARBOOK. VOLUME 1: NORTH & CENTRAL AMERICA.
The P R S Group, Box 248, East Syracuse, NY 13057-0248. TEL 315-431-0511. FAX 315-431-0200.
Vendor(s): Data-Star (FSRI), Lexis-Nexis. *1161*

POLITICAL RISK YEARBOOK. VOLUME 2: MIDDLE EAST & NORTH AFRICA.
The P R S Group, Box 248, East Syracuse, NY 13057-0248. TEL 315-431-0511. FAX 315-431-0200.
Vendor(s): Data-Star (FSRI), Lexis-Nexis. *1161*

POLITICAL RISK YEARBOOK. VOLUME 3: SOUTH AMERICA.
The P R S Group, Box 248, East Syracuse, NY 13057-0248. TEL 315-431-0511. FAX 315-431-0200.
Vendor(s): Data-Star (FSRI), Lexis-Nexis. *1161*

POLITICAL RISK YEARBOOK. VOLUME 4: SUB-SAHARAN AFRICA.
The P R S Group, Box 248, East Syracuse, NY 13057-0248. TEL 315-431-0511. FAX 315-431-0200.
Vendor(s): Data-Star (FSRI), Lexis-Nexis. *1161*

POLITICAL RISK YEARBOOK. VOLUME 5: ASIA & THE PACIFIC.
The P R S Group, Box 248, East Syracuse, NY 13057-0248. TEL 315-431-0511. FAX 315-431-0200.
Vendor(s): Data-Star (FSRI), Lexis-Nexis. *1161*

POLITICAL RISK YEARBOOK. VOLUME 6: EUROPE.
The P R S Group, Box 248, East Syracuse, NY 13057-0248. TEL 315-431-0511. FAX 315-431-0200.
Vendor(s): Data-Star (FSRI), Lexis-Nexis. *1161*

POLITICAL SCIENCE QUARTERLY.
Academy of Political Science, 475 Riverside Dr., Ste. 1274, New York, NY 10115-1274. TEL 212-870-2500. FAX 212-870-2202. URL: http://epn.org/psq.html.
Vendor(s): UMI. *5958*

POLITICS IN AMERICA.
Congressional Quarterly Inc., 1414 22nd St., N.W., Washington, DC 20037. TEL 202-887-8500. FAX 202-887-6706. *5959*

POLITYKA.
Spoldzielnia Pracy "Polityka", Miedziana 11, 00-835 Warsaw, Poland. TEL 48-22-635-3491. FAX 48-22-635-1797. URL: http://www.politka.pl. *3349*

POLIZIA MODERNA.
Fondo Assistenza del Personale della Pubblica Sicurezza, Piazza del Viminale, 00184 Rome, Italy. TEL 39-6-46671. FAX 39-6-4456903. URL: http://www.polizia.telpress.it. *2277*

POLLUTION ABSTRACTS.
Cambridge Scientific Abstracts, 7200 Wisconsin Ave., 6th Fl., Bethesda, MD 20814. TEL 301-961-6750. FAX 301-961-6720. URL: http://www.csa.com.
Vendor(s): Data-Star (POLL), European Space Agency (File no.18/POLLUTION), Knight-Ridder Information, Inc. (File no.41), STN International (POLLUAB). *2963*

POLYCYCLIC AROMATIC COMPOUNDS.
Gordon and Breach - Harwood Academic, Amsteldisk 166, 1st Fl., 1079 LH Amsterdam, Netherlands. URL: http://www.gbhap.com/Polycyclic__Aromatic__Compounds/. *1821*

POLYMER ENGINEERING AND SCIENCE.
Society of Plastics Engineers, Inc., 14 Fairfield Dr., Box 403, Brookfield, CT 06804-0403. TEL 203-775-0471. FAX 203-775-8490.
Vendor(s): Information Access Co. *2771*

POLYMERS, CERAMICS, COMPOSITES ALERT.
Cambridge Scientific Abstracts, 7200 Wisconsin Ave., Bethesda, MD 20814. TEL 301-961-6750. FAX 301-961-6720. URL: http://www.csa.com.
Vendor(s): CEDOCAR, CISTI, Data-Star (MBUS), European Space Agency (File no.111), Knight-Ridder Information, Inc. (File no.269), Questel Orbit Inc. (MABU), STN International (MATBUS). *5887*

POOP GOD.
Doo Dooists, Box 822, Mountain View, CA 94042-0822. URL: http://www.globalgraphics.com/poopgod.html. *4354*

POPULAR HOME AUTOMATION.
E H Publishing, Inc., Box 340, Wayland, MA 01778. TEL 508-358-3400. FAX 508-358-5195. *2649*

POPULAR MECHANICS.
Hearst Corporation, Popular Mechanics, 224 W. 57th St., New York, NY 10019. TEL 212-649-3127. URL: http://popularmechanics.com; http:www.hearstcorp.com.
Vendor(s): Information Access Co. *6970*

POPULAR PHOTOGRAPHY.
Hachette Filipacchi Magazines, Inc., 1633 Broadway, New York, NY 10019. TEL 212-767-6000.
Vendor(s): Information Access Co., Knight-Ridder Information, Inc., UMI. *5773*

POPULAR SCIENCE.
Times Mirror Magazines, Inc., 2 Park Ave., New York, NY 10016. TEL 212-779-5000.
Vendor(s): Information Access Co., Knight-Ridder Information, Inc., UMI. *6970*

POPULATION AND DEVELOPMENT REVIEW.
Population Council, 1 Dag Hammarskjold Plaza, New York, NY 10017. TEL 212-339-0500. FAX 212-755-6052.
Vendor(s): Information Access Co. *6055*

POPULATION INDEX.
Princeton University, Office of Population Research, 21 Prospect Ave., Princeton, NJ 08544-2091. TEL 609-258-4949. FAX 609-258-1039. URL: http://popindex.princeton.edu.
Vendor(s): National Library of Medicine. *6069*

PORTABLE WALL.
Basement Press Publishing Co., 215 Burlington, Billings, MT 59101. *4498*

PORTAVOZ.
Instituto Latinoamericano de Servicios Legales Alternativos, Apdo. Aereo 077844, Bogota, Colombia. TEL 57-1-2455955. FAX 57-1-2884854. *4009*

PORTUGALIAE MATHEMATICA.
Sociedade Portuguesa de Matematica, Avenida da Republica 37-4o, 1050 Lisbon, Portugal. TEL 351-1-7939785. FAX 351-1-7952349. URL: http://www.lmc.fc.ul.pt/~portmath. *4598*

POST-ADOPTION HELPER.
Helper Publishing, 36 Norwood Rd., Toronto, ON M4E 2S2, Canada. TEL 416-690-9593. FAX 416-690-9593. URL: http://www.helping.com/family/pa/pa.html. *1854*

POSTGRADUATE MEDICAL JOURNAL.
B M J Publishing Group, B.M.A. House, Tavistock Sq., London WC1H 9JR, England. TEL 44-171-383-6270. FAX 44-171-383-6402. *4731*

POSTGRADUATE MEDICINE.
McGraw-Hill Companies (Minneapolis), 4530 W. 77th St., Minneapolis, 609-426-7070, MN 55435. TEL 609-426-7070. FAX 612-835-3460. URL: http://www.postgradmed.com.
Vendor(s): Dow Jones News Retrieval (PGM), Information Access Co., Knight-Ridder Information, Inc. (PGM), NewsNet (ME06). *4732*

POTATO ABSTRACTS.
CAB International, Wallingford, Oxon. OX10 8DE, England. TEL 44-1491-832111. FAX 44-1491-826090. URL: http://www.cabi.org.
Vendor(s): DIMDI, European Space Agency, Knight-Ridder Information, Inc., STN International. *181*

POTATO NEWSLETTER.
Department of Agriculture, Plant Industry Branch, Box 6000, Fredericton, NB E3B 5H1, Canada. TEL 506-457-7244. FAX 506-457-7267. *241*

POTENTIALS IN MARKETING.
Lakewood Publications, Inc., 50 S. Ninth St., Minneapolis, MN 55402. TEL 612-333-0471. FAX 612-333-6526. URL: http://www.lakewoodpub.com/pim/index.htm.
Vendor(s): Information Access Co. *1545*

POULTRY ABSTRACTS.
CAB International, Wallingford, Oxon. OX10 8DE, England. TEL 44-1491-832111. FAX 44-1491-826090. URL: http://www.cabi.org.
Vendor(s): DIMDI, European Space Agency, Knight-Ridder Information, Inc., STN International. *181*

POWER (NEW YORK).
McGraw-Hill Companies, 1221 Ave. of the Americas, New York, NY 10020. TEL 212-512-2000.
Vendor(s): Dow Jones News Retrieval (PWR), Knight-Ridder Information, Inc. (POW), Lexis-Nexis (POWER), NewsNet (EY84). *2898*

POWER ENGINEERING.
PennWell Publishing Co., Box 1260, Tulsa, OK 74101. TEL 918-835-3161. FAX 918-832-9295.
Vendor(s): Information Access Co. *2843*

POWER GENERATION.
Pasha Publications Inc., 1616 N. Ft. Myer Dr., Ste. 1000, Arlington, VA 22209-3107. TEL 703-528-1244. FAX 703-528-1253. *2676*

POWER IN ASIA.
Financial Times Energy Publishing, Maple House, 149 Tottenham Court Rd., London W1P 9LL, England. TEL 44-171-896-2241. FAX 44-171-896-2275.
Vendor(s): Data-Star, Information Access Co., Knight-Ridder Information, Inc., Lexis-Nexis. *2843*

POWER IN EUROPE.
Financial Times Energy Publishing, Maple House, 149 Tottenham Court Rd., London W1P 9LL, England. TEL 44-171-896-2241. FAX 44-171-896-2275.
Vendor(s): Data-Star, Information Access Co., Knight-Ridder Information, Inc., Lexis-Nexis. *2690*

POWER IN LATIN AMERICA.
Financial Times Energy Publishing, Maple House, 149 Tottenham Court Rd., London W1P 9LL, England. TEL 44-171-896-2241. FAX 44-171-896-2275.
Vendor(s): Data-Star, Knight-Ridder Information, Inc., Lexis-Nexis. *2690*

POWER TRIPS.
Cedar Cottage Media Inc., 6282 Kathleen Ave., Ste. 502, Burnaby, BC V5H 4J4, Canada. URL: http://www.cedarcottage.com/power/index.htm. *5460*

POWER U K.
Financial Times Energy Publishing, Maple House, 149 Tottenham Court Rd., London W1P 9LL, England. TEL 0171-896-2241. FAX 0171-896-2275.
Vendor(s): Data-Star, Knight-Ridder Information, Inc., Lexis-Nexis. *2690*

THE PRACTICAL ACCOUNTANT.
Faulkner and Gray, Inc. (New York), 11 Penn Plaza, 17th Fl., New York, NY 10001. TEL 212-967-7000. FAX 212-967-7155. URL: http://www.faulknergray.com/account/prac.htm.
Vendor(s): Information Access Co., UMI. *1096*

PRACTICAL ANARCHY.
Spunk Press, P.O. Box 721, Madison, WI 53701-0721. TEL 608-251-4307. *5985*

THE PRACTICAL LAWYER.
American Law Institute - American Bar Association, Committee on Continuing Professional Education, 4025 Chestnut St., Philadelphia, PA 19104. TEL 215-243-1604. FAX 215-243-1664.
Vendor(s): UMI. *4009*

THE PRACTICAL LITIGATOR.
American Law Institute - American Bar Association, Committee on Continuing Professional Education, 4025 Chestnut St., Philadelphia, PA 19104. TEL 215-243-1604. FAX 215-243-1664.
Vendor(s): UMI. *4009*

THE PRACTICAL REAL ESTATE LAWYER.
American Law Institute - American Bar Association, Committee on Continuing Professional Education, 4025 Chestnut St., Philadelphia, PA 19104. TEL 215-243-1604. FAX 215-243-1664.
Vendor(s): UMI. *4009*

THE PRACTICAL TAX LAWYER.
American Law Institute - American Bar Association, Committee on Continuing Professional Education, 4025 Chestnut St., Philadelphia, PA 19104. TEL 215-243-1604. FAX 215-243-1664.
Vendor(s): UMI. *4009*

PRACTICING C P A.
American Institute of Certified Public Accountants, Private Companies Practice Section, Harborside Financial Ctr., 201 Plaza Three, Jersey City, NJ 07311-3881. TEL 201-938-3796. FAX 800-329-1112. URL: http://www.aicpa.org.
Vendor(s): UMI. *1096*

PRECISION TOOLMAKER.
Argus Business Media Ltd., Queensway House, 2 Queensway, Redhill, Surrey RH1 1QS, England. TEL 44-1737-768611. FAX 44-1737-773993.
Vendor(s): Information Access Co. *5207*

PREDICASTS BASEBOOK.
Information Access Company, 362 Lakeside Dr., Foster City, CA 94404. TEL 415-378-5200. FAX 415-358-4759.
Vendor(s): Data-Star, Knight-Ridder Information, Inc. *1064*

PREDICASTS F & S INDEX EUROPE.
Information Access Company, 362 Lakeside Dr., Foster City, CA 94404. TEL 415-378-5200. FAX 415-358-4759.
Vendor(s): Data-Star, Knight-Ridder Information, Inc., Ovid Technologies, Inc. (PTSI). *1065*

PREDICASTS F & S INDEX INTERNATIONAL.
Information Access Company, 362 Lakeside Dr., Foster City, CA 94404. TEL 415-378-5200. FAX 415-378-5369.
Vendor(s): Data-Star, Knight-Ridder Information, Inc., Ovid Technologies, Inc. (PTSI). *1065*

PREDICASTS F & S INDEX OF CORPORATE CHANGE.
Information Access Company, 362 Lakeside Dr., Foster City, CA 94404. TEL 415-378-5200. FAX 415-358-4759.
Vendor(s): Knight-Ridder Information, Inc., Ovid Technologies, Inc. (PTSI). *1065*

PREDICASTS F & S INDEX UNITED STATES.
Information Access Company, 362 Lakeside Dr., Foster City, CA 94404. TEL 415-378-5200. FAX 415-378-5369.
Vendor(s): Data-Star, Knight-Ridder Information, Inc., Ovid Technologies, Inc. (PTSI). *1065*

PREDICASTS FORECASTS.
Information Access Company, 362 Lakeside Dr., Foster City, CA 94404. TEL 415-378-5200. FAX 415-358-4759.
Vendor(s): Data-Star (PTFC), Knight-Ridder Information, Inc. *1065*

PREDICASTS OVERVIEW OF MARKETS AND TECHNOLOGY.
Information Access Company, 362 Lakeside Dr., Foster City, CA 94404. TEL 415-978-5200. FAX 415-358-4759.
Vendor(s): Data-Star, Knight-Ridder Information, Inc., Ovid Technologies, Inc. (PTSP). *2752*

PREDIKANT EN SAMENLEVING.
Bond van Nederlandse Predikanten, Cornelis Houtmanstraat 2, 3572 LV Utrecht, Netherlands. TEL 31-30-2716133. FAX 31-30-2733429. *6437*

PREMIERE (NEW YORK).
Hachette Filipacchi Magazines, Inc., 1633 Broadway, 45th Fl., New York, NY 10019. TEL 212-767-6000. FAX 212-767-5450. URL: http://www.premieremag.com/hfm/index.html.
Vendor(s): Information Access Co. *5342*

PREPARED FOODS.
Cahners Publishing Company (Des Plaines), Division of Reed Elsevier Inc., 1350 E. Touhy Ave., Box 5080, Des Plaines, IL 60018-5080. TEL 847-390-2435. FAX 847-390-2445. URL: http://www.preparedfoods.com.
Vendor(s): Information Access Co., Lexis-Nexis. *3124*

PREPARED SOUPS: THE INTERNATIONAL MARKET.
Euromonitor, 60-61 Britton St., London EC1M 5NA, England. TEL 44-171-251-8024. FAX 44-171-608-3149. URL: http://www.euromonitor.com.
Vendor(s): Data-Star, Knight-Ridder Information, Inc. *3124*

PREPRESS COMMENTARY.
Pira International, Randalls Rd., Leatherhead, Surrey KT22 7RU, England. TEL 44-1372-802080. FAX 44-1372-802239. URL: http://www.pira.co.uk.
Vendor(s): Information Access Co.. *6293*

PRESCRIBERS' JOURNAL.
H.M.S.O., 51 Nine Elms Ln., London SW8 5DR, England. TEL 44-171-873-0011. FAX 44-171-873-8463. *5690*

PRESCRIPTION PHARMACEUTICALS AND BIOTECHNOLOGY: THE PINK SHEET.
F-D-C Reports, Inc., 5550 Friendship Blvd., Ste. 1, Chevy Chase, MD 20815. FAX 301-664-7238.
Vendor(s): Data-Star (FDCR), Knight-Ridder Information, Inc. (File no.187), Lexis-Nexis, Ovid Technologies, Inc. (FDCR). *5691*

PRESENTATIONS.
Lakewood Publications Inc., 50 S. Ninth St., Minneapolis, MN 55402. TEL 612-333-0471. FAX 612-333-6526. URL: http://www.presentations.com. *43*

PRESIDENTIAL STUDIES QUARTERLY.
Center for the Study of the Presidency, 208 E. 75th St., New York, NY 10021. TEL 212-249-1200. FAX 212-628-9503.
Vendor(s): UMI. *5961*

PREVENTION.
Rodale Press, Inc., 33 E. Minor St., Emmaus, PA 18049. TEL 610-967-5171. FAX 610-967-7725.
Vendor(s): Information Access Co., UMI. *5788*

PREVENTION AT WORK.
Workers' Compensation Board, Communications Department, P.O. Box 5350, Stn. Terminal, Vancouver, BC V6B 5L5, Canada. TEL 604-279-7572. FAX 604-279-7406. URL: http://www.wcb.bc.ca. *1450*

PREVENTIVE MEDICINE.
Academic Press, Inc., Journal Division, 525 B St., Ste. 1900, San Diego, CA 92101-4495. TEL 619-230-1840. FAX 619-699-6800. URL: http://www.apnet.com/www/journal/pm.htm. *4733*

PREVIEW (HARRISBURG).
T V Host, Inc., Box 1665, 3935 Jonestown Rd., Harrisburg, PA 17109. TEL 717-657-1700. FAX 717-657-2921. URL: http://www.tvhost.com. *2056*

PREVIEW OF UNITED STATES SUPREME COURT CASES.
American Bar Association, Public Education Division, 541 N. Fairbanks Ct., Chicago, IL 60611-3314. TEL 312-988-5728. FAX 312-988-5494.
Vendor(s): West Group. *4137*

PRIMARY EDUCATION DIRECTORY.
School Government Publishing Co. Ltd., Darby House, Bletchingley Rd., Merstham, Redhill, Surrey RH1 3DN, England. TEL 44-1737-642223. FAX 44-1737-644283. *2527*

PRIMUS.
U.S. Military Academy, Department of Mathematics, West Point, NY 10996-9902. TEL 914-938-3200. FAX 914-938-2409. URL: http://www.dean.usma.edu/math/resource/pubs/primus/index.htm. *4598*

PRINCIPIA CYBERNETICA NEWSLETTER.
Principia Cybernetica Project, c/o Free University of Brussels, Pleinlaan 2, 1050 Brussels, Belgium. TEL 32-2-6412525. FAX 32-2-6412489. URL: http://pespmc1.vub.ac.be/.
Available only online. *2163*

PRINT.
R C Publications, Inc., 104 Fifth Ave., 19th Fl., New York, NY 10011. TEL 212-463-0600. FAX 212-989-9891.
Vendor(s): Information Access Co. *2125*

PRINT BUSINESS REGISTER.
P T N Publishing (Chicago), 20 E. Jackson Blvd., Ste. 700, Chicago, IL 60604-2203. TEL 312-922-5402. FAX 312-922-0856. *6083*

PRINTED CIRCUIT DESIGN.
Miller Freeman, Inc., 600 Harrison St., San Francisco, CA 94107. TEL 415-905-2200. FAX 415-905-2232.
Vendor(s): UMI. *2649*

PRINTING ABSTRACTS.
Pira International, Randalls Rd., Leatherhead, Surrey KT22 7RU, England. TEL 44-1372-802050. FAX 44-1372-802239. URL: http://www.pira.co.uk/.
Vendor(s): Data-Star, FIZ Technik, Knight-Ridder Information, Inc., Questel Orbit Inc. (PIRA), STN International. *6087*

PRINTING IMPRESSIONS.
North American Publishing Co., 401 N. Broad St., Philadelphia, PA 19108. TEL 215-238-5300. FAX 215-238-5457.
Vendor(s): Information Access Co. *6084*

PRINTING NEWS - EAST.
P T N Publishing Corp., 445 Broad Hollow Rd., Melville, NY 11474-4722. TEL 516-845-2700. FAX 516-845-7109.
Vendor(s): Information Access Co. *6084*

THE PRISON JOURNAL.
Sage Publications, Inc., 2455 Teller Rd., Thousand Oaks, CA 91320. TEL 805-499-0721. FAX 805-499-0871. URL: http://www.sagepub.com.
Vendor(s): Information Access Co. *2277*

PRIVACY JOURNAL.
Robert Ellis Smith, Ed. & Pub., Box 28577, Providence, RI 02908. TEL 401-274-7861.
Vendor(s): NewsNet. *5997*

PRIVATE EQUITY ANALYST.
Asset Alternatives, Inc., 180 Linden St., Ste. 3, Wellesley, MA 02181-7922. TEL 617-431-7353. FAX 617-431-7451. URL: http://www.assetalt.com. *1402*

PRIVATE LABEL.
E.W. Williams Publications Co., 2125 Center Ave., Ste. 305, Fort Lee, NJ 07024-5859. TEL 201-592-7007. FAX 201-592-7171. *1593*

PRIVATE LINE (CARMICHAEL).
Tom Farley, Ed. & Pub., Box 1059, Isleton, CA 95641. TEL 916-777-4420. URL: etext.archive.umich.edu/pub/zines/PrivateLine. *2038*

PRIVATE PLACEMENT REPORTER.
American Banker - Bond Buyer, Newsletter Division One State St. Plaza, New York, NY 10004-1549. TEL 800-733-4371. FAX 212-943-2224.
Vendor(s): Information Access Co., Knight-Ridder Information, Inc., Lexis-Nexis, NewsNet (FI61). *1162*

PRIVATISATION INTERNATIONAL.
Privatisation International Ltd., Butlers Wharf Business Centre, Ste. 404, 45 Curlew St., London SE1 2ND, England. TEL 44-171-378-1620. FAX 44-171-403-7876.
Vendor(s): Information Access Co. *993*

PRIVREDNA IZGRADNJA.
Savez Ekonomista Vojvodine, Zmaj Jovine 26, 21000 Novi Sad, Yugoslavia. TEL 021 24-971. *993*

PRIVY.
ArtHaven International, 1685 Parkline Dr., Ste. 12, Pittsburgh, PA 15227. TEL 412-881-0399. FAX 412-653-6812.
Available only online. *4452*

THE PRIZE.
Watchers of C I S, Box 66403, Roseville, MI 48066-6403. URL: http://users.aol.com/jeremiasD/Rooms/ThePrize/aboutTP.html. *3091*

PRO SOUND NEWS EUROPE.
Spotlight Publications Ltd., Ludgate House, 245 Blackfriars Rd., London SE1 9UR, England. TEL 44-171-620-3636. FAX 44-171-401-8036.
Vendor(s): Information Access Co. *6745*

PROARBEIT.
Bundesanstalt fuer Arbeit, Institut fuer Arbeitsmarkt- und Berufsforschung, Regensburgerstr. 104, 90327 Nuernberg, Germany. TEL 49-911-1793011. FAX 49-911-1791147. *1065*

PROBABILITY THEORY AND RELATED FIELDS.
Springer-Verlag, Heidelberger Platz 3, 14197 Berlin, Germany. TEL 49-30-82787-0. FAX 49-30-82787448. URL: http://link.springer.de. *4599*

PROBATE & PROPERTY.
American Bar Association, Real Property, Probate and Trust Law Section, 750 N. Lake Shore Dr., Chicago, IL 60611. TEL 312-988-5591. URL: http://www.abanet.org.
Vendor(s): West Group. *4098*

PROBE (BELTSVILLE).
U.S. National Agricultural Library, 10301 Baltimore Ave., 4th Fl., Beltsville, MD 20705-2351. TEL 301-504-6613. FAX 301-504-7098. URL: http://www.nalusda.gov:80/answers/info_center/pgdic/probe/v4n3_4.html. *776*

PROCESS AND CHEMICAL ENGINEERING.
The Royal Society of Chemistry, Thomas Graham House, Science Park, Milton Rd., Cambridge CB4 4WF, England. TEL 44-1223-420066. FAX 44-1223-423429. URL: http://chemistry.rsc.org/rsc/.
Vendor(s): Data-Star (CEAB), FIZ Technik (DECHEMA), Knight-Ridder Information, Inc. (File no.315), Questel Orbit Inc. (CEAB), STN International (CEABA). *2752*

PROCESS ENGINEERING.
Miller Freeman Technical Ltd., Miller Freeman House, 30 Calderwood St., London SE18 6QH, England. TEL 44-181-855-7777. FAX 44-181-316-3206.
Vendor(s): Information Access Co. *2772*

PROCESS HEATING.
Business News Publishing Co., 3150 River Rd., Ste. 101, Des Plaines, IL 60018. TEL 847-297-3450. FAX 847-297-8371. URL: http://www.bnp.com. *2878*

PROCESS SAFETY AND ENVIRONMENTAL PROTECTION.
Institution of Chemical Engineers, George E. Davis Bldg., 165-189 Railway Terr., Rugby, Warks. CV21 3HQ, England. TEL 44-1788-578214. FAX 44-1788-578214. URL: http://www.icheme.org/ *2772*

PRODUCER PRICE INDEXES.
U.S. Bureau of Labor Statistics, 2 Massachusetts Ave., N.E., Washington, DC 20212. TEL 202-655-4000. *1284*

PRODUCT ALERT.
Marketing Intelligence Service Ltd., 6473D Route 64, Naples, NY 14512-9726. TEL 716-374-6326. FAX 716-374-5217. URL: http://ourworld.compuserve.com/homepages/mktgintelsvc. Vendor(s): CompuServe, Inc., Data-Star, Dow Jones News Retrieval, Information Access Co., Knight-Ridder Information, Inc. (File no. 636), NewsNet (AD24). *3124*

PRODUCT SAFETY & LIABILITY REPORTER.
The Bureau of National Affairs, Inc., 1231 25th St., N.W., Washington, DC 20037. TEL 202-452-4200. FAX 202-822-8092. URL: http://www.bna.com/ *6247*

PRODUCT SAFETY LETTER.
Washington Business Information, Inc., c/o Karen Harrington, 1117 N. 19th St., Ste. 200, Arlington, VA 22209. TEL 703-247-3434. FAX 703-247-3421.
Vendor(s): NewsNet (GB52). *6247*

PRODUCTION AND INVENTORY MANAGEMENT JOURNAL.
A P I C S - The Educational Society for Resource Management, 500 W. Annandale Rd., Falls Church, VA 22046-4274. TEL 703-237-8344. FAX 703-237-1087. URL: http://www.apics.org.
Vendor(s): UMI. *1502*

PRODUCTION PLANNING & CONTROL.
Taylor & Francis Ltd., Rankine Rd., Basingstoke, Hants. RG24 8PR, England. TEL 44-1256-840366. FAX 44-1256-479438. URL: http://www.tandf.co.uk/. *2806*

PRODUCTIVITY SOFTWARE.
Worldwide Videotex, Box 3273, Boynton Beach, FL 33424-3273. TEL 407-738-2276.
Vendor(s): Data-Star, Information Access Co., Knight-Ridder Information, Inc., NewsNet (EC80). *2217*

PRODUCTS LIABILITY REPORTS.
C C H Incorporated, 2700 Lake Cook Rd., Riverwoods, IL 60015. TEL 847-267-7000. FAX 800-224-8299. *4010*

PROFESSIONAL BUILDER.
Cahners Publishing Company (Des Plaines), Division of Reed Elsevier Inc., 1350 E. Touhy Ave., Box 5080, Des Plaines, IL 60018-5080. TEL 847-390-2155. FAX 847-635-9950. URL: http://www.probuilder.com.
Vendor(s): Information Access Co. *909*

PROFESSIONAL ETHICS REPORT.
American Association for the Advancement of Science, 1200 New York Ave., N.W., Washington, DC 20005. TEL 202-326-6600. FAX 202-289-4950. URL: http://www.aaas.org/spp/dspp/sfrl/per4.htm. *5746*

PROFESSIONAL SAFETY.
American Society of Safety Engineers, 1800 E. Oakton St., Des Plaines, IL 60018-2187. TEL 708-692-4121. FAX 708-296-3769.
Vendor(s): UMI. *5497*

PROFESSIONAL SURVEYOR.
American Surveyors Publishing Co., 1713 Rosemont Ave., Ste. J, Frederick, MD 21702-4199. *3418*

PROFESSIONAL UPDATE.
Association of Professional Engineers, Scientists and Managers, Australia, 163 Eastern Rd., S. Melbourne, Vic. 3205, Australia. TEL 61-3-96958800. FAX 61-3-96969312. URL: http://ww.apesma.asn.au.
Vendor(s): Knight-Ridder Information, Inc., Questel Orbit Inc. *2738*

PROFILES IN HEALTHCARE MARKETING.
Business Word Inc., 5350 S. Roslyn St., Ste. 400, Englewood, CO 80111-2125. TEL 303-290-8500. FAX 303-290-9025.
Vendor(s): NewsNet. *43*

PROGRES TECHNIQUE.
Association Nationale de la Recherche Technique, 101 av. Raymond Poincare, 75016 Paris, France. TEL 33-1-44-05-04-40. FAX 33-1-47-04-25-20. *6970*

PROGRESS IN CARDIOVASCULAR DISEASES.
W.B. Saunders Co., Curtis Center, 3rd Fl., Independence Sq. W., Philadelphia, PA 19106-3399. TEL 215-238-7800. FAX 215-238-6445.
Vendor(s): Lexis-Nexis. *4823*

PROGRESSIVE (MADISON).
Progressive, Inc., 409 E. Main St., Madison, WI 53703. TEL 608-257-4626. FAX 608-257-3373. URL: http://www.progressive.org.
Vendor(s): Information Access Co., UMI. *5961*

PROGRESSIVE FARMER.
Southern Progressive Co., 2100 Lakeshore Dr., Birmingham, AL 35209. TEL 205-877-6000. FAX 205-877-6700. URL: http://www.pathfinder.com/PF. *147*

PROGRESSIVE GROCER.
Progressive Grocer Associates, LLC, 263 Tresser Blvd., 6th Fl., Stamford, CT 06901. TEL 203-325-3500. FAX 203-325-4377.
Vendor(s): Information Access Co., Knight-Ridder Information, Inc., Lexis-Nexis, UMI. *3144*

PROMAX INTERNATIONAL.
Promotion & Marketing Executives in the Electronic Media, 2029 Century Pk. E., Ste. 555, Los Angeles, CA 90067-2906. TEL 310-788-7600. FAX 310-788-7616. URL: http://www.promax.org. *2057*

PROMO.
Cowles - SIMBA Information, 11 Riverbend Dr. S., Box 4949, Stamford, CT 06907-0949. TEL 203-358-9900. FAX 203-358-5811. URL: http://www.simbanet.com.
Vendor(s): Information Access Co. *1545*

PROMPT.
Pasadena I B M User Group, 2303 Glen Canyon Rd., Altadena, CA 91001-3539. TEL 818-791-1600. FAX 818-791-1600. *2089*

PROOFTEXTS.
Johns Hopkins University Press, Journals Publishing Division, 2715 N. Charles St., Baltimore, MD 21218. TEL 410-516-6987. FAX 410-516-6968. URL: http://muse.jhu.edu. *6408*

PROPERTY, PLANNING AND COMPENSATION REPORTS.
Sweet & Maxwell, South Quay Plaza, 7th Fl., 183 Marsh Wall, London E14 9FT, England. TEL 071-538-8686. FAX 071-538-9508.
Vendor(s): Lexis-Nexis. *4011*

PROSOPOPEIA.
University of Bergen, Institute of Comparative Literature, c/o Seksjon for Litteraturvitenskap, Sydnesplass 9, 5007 Bergen, Norway. URL: http://www.hf.uib.no/i/litte/prosopopeia/index.htm. *4453*

THE PROSTATE.
John Wiley & Sons, Inc., Journals, 605 Third Ave., New York, NY 10158. TEL 212-850-6645. FAX 212-850-6021. URL: http://www.wiley.co.uk. *4734*

PROSUS.
Scandinavian University Press, P.O. Box 2959 Toeyen, N-0608 Oslo, Norway. TEL 47-22-57-53-00. FAX 47-22-57-53-53. URL: http://www.scup.no. *6630*

PROTEIN ENGINEERING.
Oxford University Press, Academic Division, Great Clarendon St., Oxford OX2 6DP, England. TEL 44-1865-267907. FAX 44-1865-267485. URL: http://www.oup.co.uk/journals. *669*

PROTEIN EXPRESSION AND PURIFICATION.
Academic Press, Inc., Journal Division, 525 B St., Ste. 1900, San Diego, CA 92101-4495. TEL 619-230-1840. FAX 619-699-6800. URL: http://www.apnet.com/www/journal/pt.htm. *670*

PROTEIN PROFILE ONLINE.
Oxford University Press, Academic Division, Great Clarendon St., Oxford OX2 6DP, England. TEL 44-1865-267907. FAX 44-1865-267485. URL: http://www.oup.co.uk.
Available only online. *670*

PROTEIN SCIENCE.
Cambridge University Press, Edinburgh Bldg., Shaftesbury Rd., Cambridge CB2 2RU, England. TEL 44-1223-312393. FAX 44-1223-315052. URL: http://www.cup.cam.ac.uk. *670*

PROTEUS.
Shippensburg University, Shippensburg, PA 17257. TEL 717-532-1206. FAX 717-532-1253. *3383*

PROTOZOOLOGICAL ABSTRACTS.
CAB International, Wallingford, Oxon. OX10 8DE, England. TEL 44-1491-832111. FAX 44-1491-826090. URL: http://www.cabi.org.
Vendor(s): DIMDI, European Space Agency, Knight-Ridder Information, Inc., STN International. *4787*

PROVINCIAL OUTLOOK.
Conference Board of Canada, 255 Smyth Rd., Ste. 100, Ottawa, ON K1H 8M7, Canada. TEL 613-526-3280. FAX 613-526-4857. *1285*

PSYCHE.
M I T Press, 55 Hayward St., Cambridge, MA 02142. TEL 617-253-2889. FAX 617-258-67796. URL: http://www-mitpress.mit.edu. *6143*

PSYCHIATRY ON-LINE.
URL: http://www.priory.com/journals/psych.htm.
Available only online. *5093*

PSYCHOLOGICAL ABSTRACTS.
American Psychological Association, 750 First St., N.E., Washington, DC 20002-4242. TEL 202-336-5600. FAX 202-336-5568. URL: http://www.apa.org/journals/abs.html.
Vendor(s): DIMDI, Data-Star (PSYC), Knight-Ridder Information, Inc. (File no.11/PsycINFO), Questel Orbit Inc., Ovid Technologies, Inc. *6161*

PSYCHOLOGICAL METHODS.
American Psychological Association, 750 First St., N.W., Washington, DC 20002-4242. TEL 202-336-5600. FAX 202-336-5568. URL: http://www.apa.org/journals/met.html. *6144*

THE PSYCHOLOGICAL RECORD.
Kenyon College, Gambier, OH 43022-9623. TEL 614-427-5377. FAX 614-427-4950.
Vendor(s): Information Access Co., UMI. *6145*

PSYCHOLOOGICAL REVIEW.
American Psychological Association, 750 First St., N.E., Washington, DC 20002-4242. TEL 202-336-5600. FAX 202-336-5568. URL: http://www.apa.org/journals/rev.html. *6145*

PSYCHOLOGY GRADUATE STUDENT JOURNAL.
c/o School of Psychology, University of Ottawa, 145 Jean Jacques Lussier, Ottawa ON K1N 6N5, Canada.
Available only online. *6147*

PSYCHOLOGY TODAY.
Sussex Publishers Inc., 49 E. 21st St., 11th Fl., New York, NY 10010. TEL 212-260-7210. FAX 212-260-7445.
Vendor(s): Information Access Co., Knight-Ridder Information, Inc., UMI. *6147*

PSYCHOPHARMACOLOGY.
Springer-Verlag, Heidelberger Platz 3, 14197 Berlin, Germany. TEL 49-30-82787-0. FAX 49-30-82787488. URL: http://link.springer.de. *5691*

PSYCHOPHARMACOLOGY BULLETIN.
U.S. Public Health Service, 5600 Fishers Ln., Rockville, MD 20857. TEL 301-496-4000.
Vendor(s): National Library of Medicine. *5691*

PSYCHOSOMATIC MEDICINE.
Williams & Wilkins, 351 W. Camden St., Baltimore, MD 21201-2436. TEL 410-528-4068. FAX 410-528-4452. URL: http://www.wwilkins.com.
Vendor(s): Ovid Technologies, Inc.. *5094*

PSYCHOTHERAPEUT.
Springer-Verlag, Heidelberger Platz 3, 14197 Berlin, Germany. TEL 49-30-82787-0. FAX 49-30-82787448. URL: http://link.springer.de. *5094*

PSYCINFO NEWS.
American Psychological Association, PsycINFO User Services, 750 First St., N.E., Washington, DC 20002-4242. TEL 202-336-5650. FAX 202-336-5633. URL: http://www.apa.org/psycinfo/issues.html. *6161*

PSYCOLOQUY.
c/o Cognitive Sciences Centre, Dept. of Psychology, Univ. of Southampton, Highfield, Southampton SO17 1BJ, England. URL: http://www.princeton.edu/~harnad/psyc.html.
Available only online. *6148*

PUB.
URL: http://www.ru.ac.za/journprojects/pub/
Available only online. *2139*

PUBLIC ACCESS COMPUTER SYSTEMS NEWS.
University of Houston Libraries, Houston, TX 77204-2091. TEL 713-743-9808. FAX 713-743-9811. URL: http://info.lib.uh.edu/pacsnews.html. *4234*

THE PUBLIC - ACCESS COMPUTER SYSTEMS REVIEW.
University Libraries, University of Houston, Houston, TX 77204-2091. TEL 713-743-9762. FAX 713-743-9673. URL: http://info.lib.uh.edu/pacsrev.html. *2185*

PUBLIC ADMINISTRATION.
Blackwell Publishers Ltd., 108 Cowley Rd., Oxford OX4 1JF, England. TEL 44-1865-791100. FAX 44-1865-791347. URL: http://www.blackwellpublishers.co.uk.
Vendor(s): Information Access Co.. *6189*

PUBLIC ADMINISTRATION QUARTERLY.
Southern Public Administration Education Foundation, c/o Dr. Jack Rabin, Pennsylvania State University at Harrisburg, Division of Public Affairs, Middletown, PA 17057. TEL 717-948-6363. FAX 717-540-1383.
Vendor(s): UMI. *6189*

PUBLIC ADMINISTRATION REVIEW.
American Society for Public Administration, 1120 G St., N.W., Ste. 700, Washington, DC 20005. TEL 202-393-7878. FAX 202-638-4952.
Vendor(s): Information Access Co., UMI. *6189*

PUBLIC BROADCASTING REPORT.
Warren Publishing, Inc., 2115 Ward Ct., N.W., Washington, DC 20037. TEL 202-872-9200. FAX 202-293-3435.
Vendor(s): Information Access Co., NewsNet (PB04) *2057*

PUBLIC BUDGETING AND FINANCE.
Transaction Publishers, Transaction Periodicals Consortium, Department 3092, Rutgers University, New Brunswick, NJ 08903. TEL 908-445-2280. FAX 908-445-3138.
Vendor(s): UMI. *1625*

PUBLIC CONTRACT LAW JOURNAL.
American Bar Association, Public Contract Law Section, 750 N. Lake Shore Dr., Chicago, IL 60611. TEL 312-988-5000. URL: http://www.abanet.org.
Vendor(s): West Group. *4011*

PUBLIC FINANCE QUARTERLY.
Sage Publications, Inc., 2455 Teller Rd., Thousand Oaks, CA 91320. TEL 805-499-0721. FAX 805-499-0871. URL: http://www.sagepub.com.
Vendor(s): Information Access Co. *1625*

PUBLIC HEALTH REPORTS.
U.S. Public Health Service, Department of Health and Human Services, J.F.K. Federal Bldg., Rm. 1855, Boston, MA 02203. TEL 617-565-1442. FAX 617-565-4260.
Vendor(s): Information Access Co., Lexis-Nexis, UMI. *6248*

PUBLIC INTEREST.
National Affairs, Inc., 1112 16th St., N.W., Ste. 530, Washington, DC 20036. TEL 202-785-8555. FAX 202-467-0006.
Vendor(s): Information Access Co., UMI. *6630*

PUBLIC LIBRARY NEWS.
State Library of New South Wales, Public Libraries Branch, Macquarie St., Sydney, N.S.W. 2000, Australia. TEL 61-2-92301526. FAX 61-2-92239702. URL: http://www.slnsw.gov.au/plb/pupbranch/pubnews/pubnews.htm. *4207*

PUBLIC MANAGEMENT.
International City - County Management Association, 777 North Capitol, N.E., Ste. 500, Washington, DC 20002-4201. TEL 202-962-3619. FAX 202-962-3500.
Vendor(s): Information Access Co., UMI. *6223*

THE PUBLIC MANAGER.
Bureaucrat, Inc., 12007 Titian Way, Potomac, MD 20854. TEL 301-279-9445. FAX 301-251-5872.
Vendor(s): Information Access Co. *6190*

PUBLIC PERSONNEL MANAGEMENT.
International Personnel Management Association, 1617 Duke St., Alexandria, VA 22314. TEL 703-549-7100. FAX 703-684-0948. URL: http://www.ipma-hr.org.
Vendor(s): Information Access Co. *1574*

PUBLIC PERSPECTIVE.
Roper Center for Public Opinion Research, Box 440, Storrs, CT 06269. TEL 860-486-4440. FAX 860-486-6308.
Vendor(s): Lexis-Nexis (PUBPER). *5962*

PUBLIC PRODUCTIVITY AND MANAGEMENT REVIEW.
Sage Publications, Inc., 2455 Teller Rd., Thousand Oaks, CA 91320. TEL 805-499-0721. FAX 805-499-0871. URL: http://www.sagepub.com.
Vendor(s): UMI. *6190*

PUBLIC PULSE.
Roper Starch Worldwide, 205 E. 42nd St., New York, NY 10017. TEL 212-599-0700. FAX 212-867-7008.
Vendor(s): Lexis-Nexis. *1546*

PUBLIC RELATIONS NEWS.
Phillips Business Information, Inc., 1201 Seven Locks Rd., Potomac, MD 20854. TEL 301-424-3338. FAX 301-309-3847.
Vendor(s): Information Access Co. *43*

PUBLIC RELATIONS QUARTERLY.
44 W. Market St., Box 311, Rhinebeck, NY 12572. TEL 914-876-2081. FAX 914-876-2561. URL: http://www.wwmedia.com/PRQ/prq.html.
Vendor(s): Information Access Co., UMI. *44*

PUBLIC RELATIONS REVIEW.
J A I Press Inc., 55 Old Post Rd., No.2, Box 1678, Greenwich, CT 06830-1678. TEL 203-661-7602. FAX 203-661-0792. URL: http://www.jaipress.com/jmpub.htm.
Vendor(s): Information Access Co. *44*

PUBLIC ROADS.
U.S. Federal Highway Administration, Office of Highway Information Management, Department of Transportation, 400 Seventh St., S.W., Washington, DC 20590. TEL 703-285-2443. FAX 703-285-2379.
Vendor(s): Information Access Co., UMI. *2796*

PUBLIC TREASURER.
L G C Communications, 33-39 Bowling Green Ln., London EC1R 0DA, England. TEL 44-171-505-8400. FAX 44-171-837-2725. URL: http://www.emap.com/lgc. *1625*

PUBLIC UNDERSTANDING OF SCIENCE.
I O P Publishing Ltd., Dirac House, Temple Back, Bristol BS1 6BE, England. TEL 44-117-929-7481. FAX 44-117-929-4318. URL: http://www.iop.org. *6560*

PUBLIC UTILITIES FORTNIGHTLY.
Public Utilities Reports, Inc., 8229 Boone Blvd., Ste. 401, Vienna, VA 22182. TEL 703-847-7720. FAX 703-917-6964. URL: http://www.pur.com.
Vendor(s): Information Access Co., Lexis-Nexis, UMI, West Group. *1502*

PUBLIC UTILITIES REPORTS.
Public Utilities Reports, Inc., 8229 Boone Blvd., Ste. 401, Vienna, VA 22182. TEL 703-847-7720. FAX 703-917-6964. URL: http://www.pur.com.
Vendor(s): Lexis-Nexis, West Group. *2676*

PUBLIC WELFARE.
American Public Welfare Association, c/o Publication Services, 810 First St., N.E., Ste. 500, Washington, DC 20002-4267. TEL 202-682-0100. FAX 202-289-6555.
Vendor(s): Information Access Co., UMI. *6682*

PUBLIC WORKS.
Public Works Journal Corporation, 200 S. Broad St., Ridgewood, NJ 07451. TEL 201-445-5800. FAX 201-445-5170.
Vendor(s): Information Access Co. *6223*

PUBLISHERS DIRECTORY.
Gale Research, 835 Penobscot Bldg., 645 Griswold St., Detroit, MI 48226-4094. TEL 313-961-2242. FAX 800-414-5043.
Vendor(s): Knight-Ridder Information, Inc. *6281*

PUBLISHERS, DISTRIBUTORS & WHOLESALERS OF THE UNITED STATES.
R.R. Bowker, A Division of Reed Elsevier Inc., 121 Chanlon Rd., New Providence, NJ 07974. TEL 908-464-6800. FAX 908-665-3502. URL: http://www.reedref.com.
Vendor(s): Knight-Ridder Information, Inc. (File no.450), Lexis-Nexis (PDW). *1707*

PUBLISHERS WEEKLY.
Cahners Publishing Company (New York), Printing and Publishing Division, Division of Reed Elsevier Inc., 249 W. 17th St., New York, NY 10011. TEL 212-463-6824. FAX 212-463-6631. URL: http://www.bookwire.com/pw/pw.html.
Vendor(s): Information Access Co. *6281*

PUBLISHING TECHNOLOGY REVIEW.
Pira International, Randalls Rd., Leatherhead, Surrey KT22 7RU, England. TEL 44-1372-802050. FAX 44-1372-802239. URL: http://www.pira.co.uk.
Vendor(s): Information Access Co. *6282*

PUBLIUS.
Meyner Center for the Study of State and Local Government, 16 Kirby Hall of Civil Rights, Lafayette College, Easton, PA 18042-1785. TEL 610-250-5598. FAX 610-559-4048. URL: http://www.lafayette.edu/publius/
Vendor(s): Information Access Co. *5962*

PUEBLO BUSINESS JOURNAL.
201 W. 8th St., Ste. 408, Box 1544, Pueblo, CO 81002. TEL 719-542-3616. FAX 719-542-4506.
Vendor(s): *1285*

PUGET SOUND BUSINESS JOURNAL.
Scripps Howard Business Publications (Seattle), 720 Third Ave., Ste. 800, Seattle, WA 98104. TEL 206-583-0701.
Vendor(s): Information Access Co., Knight-Ridder Information, Inc. *994*

PULMONARY PHARMACOLOGY (LONDON).
Academic Press Ltd., 24-28 Oval Rd., London NW1 7DX, England. TEL 44-171-267-4466. FAX 44-171-482-2293. URL: http://www.hbuk.co.uk/ap/pulpharm; http://www.europe.idealibrary.com/. *5121*

PULP AND PAPER.
Miller Freeman, Inc., 600 Harrison St., San Francisco, CA 94107. TEL 415-905-2200. FAX 415-905-2232.
Vendor(s): Information Access Co., Lexis-Nexis, UMI. *5571*

PULP & PAPER CANADA.
Southam Magazine Group (St. Laurent), 3300 Cote Vertu, Ste. 410, St. Laurent, PQ H4R 2B7, Canada. TEL 514-339-1399. FAX 514-339-1396.
Vendor(s): Information Access Co., Southam Electronic Publishing. *5571*

PULP & PAPER CANADA'S ANNUAL & DIRECTORY.
Southam Magazine Group (St. Laurent), 3300 Cote Vertu, Ste. 410, St. Laurent, PQ H4R 2B7, Canada. TEL 514-339-1399. FAX 514-339-1396. *5571*

PULP & PAPER INTERNATIONAL.
Miller Freeman, Inc., 600 Harrison St., San Francisco, CA 94107. TEL 415-905-2200. FAX 415-905-2232.
Vendor(s): Information Access Co., Lexis-Nexis. *5571*

PUNCH IN INTERNATIONAL TRAVEL AND ENTERTAINMENT MAGAZINE.
Enterprises Publishing, 400 E. 59th St., Ste. 9F, New York, NY 10022. TEL 212-755-4363. FAX 212-755-4365. *7229*

PURCHASING (NEWTON).
Cahners Publishing Company (Newton), Division of Reed Elsevier Inc., 275 Washington St., Newton, MA 02158-1630. TEL 617-558-4291. FAX 617-558-4327. URL: http://www..manufacturing.net/magazine/purchasing/
Vendor(s): Information Access Co. *1546*

PURDUE UNIVERSITY. INDIANA WATER RESOURCES RESEARCH CENTER. ANNUAL REPORT.
Purdue University, Indiana Water Resources Research Center, 1284 School of Civil Engineering, W. Lafayette, IN 47907-1284. TEL 317-494-8041. FAX 317-494-2720. URL: http://ingis.acn.purdue.edu:9999/wetnet/serach/wrrc.html.
Available only online. *7299*

PURE AND APPLIED OPTICS.
I O P Publishing Ltd., Dirac House, Temple Back, Bristol BS1 6BE, England. TEL 44-117-929-7481. FAX 44-117-929-4318. URL: http://www.iop.org. *5869*

PYROWORDS.
6310 Duquesne, Montreal, PQ H1M 3K5, Canada. URL: http://www.microtec.net/~lamiel/
Available only online. *4521*

QUALITATIVE REPORT.
Nova Southeastern University, School of Social and Systemic Studies, 3301 College Ave., Fort Lauderdale, FL 33314. URL: http://alpha.acast.nova.edu/nova/cwis/centers/ssss/index.html. *6631*

QUALITY PROGRESS.
American Society for Quality Control, 611 E. Wisconsin Ave., Box 3005, Milwaukee, WI 53201-3005. TEL 414-272-8575. FAX 414-272-1734. URL: http://qualityprogress.asqc.org/
Vendor(s): UMI. *2738*

QUANTUM AND SEMICLASSICAL OPTICS.
I O P Publishing Ltd., Dirac House, Temple Back, Bristol BS1 6BE, England. TEL 44-117-928-7481. FAX 44-117-929-4318. *5869*

QUARTERLY JOURNAL OF BUSINESS AND ECONOMICS.
University of Nebraska at Lincoln, College of Business Administration, CBA Bldg., Lincoln, NE 68588-0407. TEL 402-472-3309. FAX 402-472-9777. URL: http://www.cba.unl.edu/mani2/pubs/qjbe/QJBE.html.
Vendor(s): Information Access Co. *994*

QUARTERLY JOURNAL OF ECONOMICS.
M I T Press, 5 Cambridge Center, Cambridge, MA 02142. TEL 617-253-2889. FAX 617-577-1545. URL: http://www-mitpress.mit.edu.
Vendor(s): Information Access Co. *1310*

QUARTERLY JOURNAL OF MEDICINE.
Oxford University Press, Academic Division, Great Clarendon St., Oxford OX2 6DP, England. TEL 44-1865-267907. FAX 44-1865-267485. URL: http://www.oup.co.uk/journals.
Vendor(s): Ovid Technologies, Inc. *4735*

THE QUARTERLY REVIEW OF ECONOMICS AND FINANCE.
J A I Press Inc., 55 Old Post Rd., No. 2, Box 1678, Greenwich, CT 06830-1678. TEL 203-661-7602. FAX 203-661-0792.
Vendor(s): Information Access Co. *994*

QUARTZ HILL JOURNAL OF THEOLOGY.
Quartz Hill School of Theology, 43543 51st St. W., Quartz Hill, CA 93536. TEL 805-943-3484. FAX 805-948-3438. URL: http://www.theology.edu. *6438*

QUATERNARY RESEARCH.
Academic Press, Inc., Journal Division, 525 B St., Ste. 1900, San Diego, CA 92101-4495. TEL 619-230-1840. FAX 619-699-6800. URL: http://www.apnet.com/www/journal/qr.htm; http://www.idealibrary.com/ *2365*

QUE TAL? IN THE CURRENT SKIES.
Kansas City Missouri School District Planetarium, URL: http://oz.sunflower.org/'starwalk/current__sky.html.
Available only online. *500*

QUEBEC (PROVINCE). SERVICES DOCUMENTAIRES MULTIMEDIA. CHOIX: DOCUMENTATION AUDIOVISUELLE.
Services Documentaires Multimedia Inc., 75 Port-Royal E., bureau 300, Montreal, PQ H3L 3T1, Canada. TEL 514-382-0895. FAX 514-384-9139. URL: http://www.sdm.qc.ca. *561*

QUEBEC (PROVINCE). SERVICES DOCUMENTAIRES MULTIMEDIA. CHOIX: DOCUMENTATION IMPRIMEE.
Services Documentaires Multimedia Inc., 75 Port-Royal E., bureau 300, Montreal, PQ H3L 3T1, Canada. TEL 514-382-0895. FAX 514-384-9139. URL: http://www.sdm.qc.ca. *561*

QUEBEC (PROVINCE). SERVICES DOCUMENTATION MULTIMEDIA. CHOIX JEUNESSE: DOCUMENTATION IMPRIMEE.
Services Documentaires Multimedia Inc., 75 Port-Royal E., bureau 300, Montreal, PQ H3L 3T1, Canada. TEL 514-382-0895. FAX 514-384-9139. URL: http://www.sdm.qc.ca. *561*

QUEER IN YOUR EAR.
358 Danforth Ave., Box 65265, Toronto, ON M4K 3Z2, Canada. URL: http://www.interlog.com/~joeclark.
Available only online. *5428*

QUERCUS.
Camino de Hormigueras 122 bis., Planta 5, 28031 Madrid, Spain. TEL 34-1-3803090. FAX 34-1-3803250. URL: http://www.quercus.es. *2948*

QUERY (SUNNYVALE).
Syllabus Press, 345 Northlake Dr., San Jose, CA 95117-1261. TEL 408-746-2000. FAX 408-746-2711. URL: http://www.syllabus.com. *2519*

QUICK FROZEN FOODS INTERNATIONAL.
E.W. Williams Publications Co., 2125 Center Ave., Ste. 305, Fort Lee, NJ 07024-5859. TEL 201-592-7007. FAX 201-592-7171.
Vendor(s): Information Access Co.. *3125*

QUICK SOLUTIONS.
URL: http://www.idsonline.com/quick/.
Available only online. *1646*

QUIET INSANITY NEWSLETTER.
Quiet Insanity Productions, Box 2108, Vassar College, Poughkeepsie, NY 12604-2108. URL: http://www.iberia.vassar.edu/q-i/ *4355*

QUILL (GREENCASTLE).
Society of Professional Journalists, Box 77, Greencastle, IN 46135-0077. TEL 317-653-3333. FAX 317-653-4631.
Vendor(s): Information Access Co., Knight-Ridder Information, Inc.. *3879*

QUINNIPIAC LAW REVIEW.
Quinnipiac Law School, 275 Mt. Carmel Ave., Hamden, CT 06518-1950.
Vendor(s): West Group. *4012*

QUO.
Hachette Filipacchi Revistas, Cardenal Herrera Oria 3, 28034 Madrid, Spain. TEL 34-1-3581122. FAX 34-1-7290150. URL: http://www.hachette.es/quo. *3360*

R A C JOURNAL.
I I T Research Institute, Reliability Analysis Center, 201 Mill St., Rome, NY 13440. TEL 315-337-0900. FAX 315-337-9932. URL: http://rome.iitri.com/RAC/. *2738*

R A D!
Conspiracy M.E.D.I.A., 826 Old Charlotte Pike E., Franklin, TN 37064. TEL 615-791-1624. *5428*

R A P R A ABSTRACTS.
Rapra Technology Ltd., Shawbury, Shrewsbury, Shrops. SY4 4NR, England. TEL 44-1939-250383. FAX 44-1939-251118. URL: http://www.rapra.net.
Vendor(s): Data-Star, European Space Agency, Knight-Ridder Information, Inc., Questel Orbit Inc. (RAPRA), Telesystemes - Questel. *6506*

R & D FOCUS.
IMSWORLD Publications Ltd., 7 Harewood Ave., London NW1 6JB, England. TEL 0171-393-5000. FAX 0171-393-5900.
Vendor(s): Data-Star, Knight-Ridder Information, Inc. *5692*

R & D MANAGEMENT.
Blackwell Publishers Ltd., 108 Cowley Rd., Oxford OX4 1JF, England. TEL 44-1865-791100. FAX 44-1865-791347. URL: http://www.blackwellpub.com/scripts/webjrn1.idc?issn00336807.
Vendor(s): Information Access Co. *1503*

R B O C UPDATE.
Worldwide Videotex, Box 3273, Boynton Beach, FL 33424-3273. TEL 407-738-2276.
Vendor(s): Information Access Co. *2038*

R G.
Editions H.M.X. Inc., C.P. 915, Succ. C, Montreal, PQ H2L 4V2, Canada. TEL 514-523-9463. FAX 514-523-2214. URL: http://www.gaibec.com/rg. *3700*

R I C NEWS.
Rare-earth Information Center, Institute for Physical Research and Technology, Iowa State University, 112 Wilhelm Hall, Ames, IA 50011-3020. TEL 515-294-2272. FAX 515-294-3709. URL: http://www.ameslab.gov/mat__ref/ric.html. *5208*

R I L M ABSTRACTS OF MUSIC LITERATURE.
R I L M Abstracts, City University of New York, 33 W. 42nd St., New York, NY 10036. TEL 212-642-2709. FAX 212-642-1973. URL: http://rilm.cic.net.
Vendor(s): OCLC. *5449*

R N.
Medical Economics Publishing Co., Inc., 5 Paragon Dr., Montvale, NJ 07645. TEL 201-358-7200. FAX 201-573-8979.
Vendor(s): Information Access Co., UMI. *4947*

R Q.
American Library Association, 50 E. Huron St., Chicago, IL 60611-2795. TEL 312-944-6780. FAX 312-440-9374.
Vendor(s): Information Access Co. *4208*

R R.
Domstolsverket, Organistionsenheten, S-551 81 Joenkoeping, Sweden. *4012*

R T C WATCH.
Thomson Financial Services, One State St. Plaza, New York, NY 10004. TEL 800-733-4371. FAX 301-654-1678.
Vendor(s): NewsNet (Fl03). *1163*

R T E C S.
U.S. National Institute for Occupational Safety and Health, Attn: Publications, 4676 Columbia Pkwy., Cincinnati, OH 45226.
Vendor(s): Canadian Centre for Occupational Health & Safety, Chemical Information Systems, Data-Star, Knight-Ridder Information, Inc. (File no.336), National Library of Medicine, STN International. *5498*

R T SOLUTIONS E - ZINE.
URL: http://www.win.net/'beachweb/rtsolut1.html.
Available only online. *5122*

R V BUSINESS.
Affinity Group, Inc., T L Enterprises, 2575 Vista Del Mar Dr., Ventura, CA 93001-3920. TEL 805-667-4100.
Vendor(s): Information Access Co. *6797*

R V NEWS.
D & S Media Enterprises, Inc., 408 E. Southern Ave., Tempe, AZ 85283-5200. TEL 602-784-4060. FAX 602-784-4420. URL: http://www.rvamerica.com/rvnews/index.htm. *7037*

10194   SERIALS AVAILABLE ONLINE

RACHEL'S ENVIRONMENT & HEALTH WEEKLY.
Environmental Research Foundation, Box 5036, Annapolis, MD 21403-7036. TEL 410-263-1584. FAX 410-263-8944. *2948*

RADIATION AND ENVIRONMENTAL BIOPHYSICS.
Springer-Verlag, Heidelberger Platz 3, 14197 Berlin, Germany. TEL 49-30-82787-0. FAX 49-30-82787448. URL: http://link.springer.de. *676*

RADIATION EFFECTS AND DEFECTS IN SOLIDS.
Gordon and Breach - Harwood Academic, Amsteldisk 166, 1st Fl., 1079 LH Amsterdam, Netherlands. URL: http://www.gbhap.com/Radiation__Effects__Defects__in__Solids/. *5857*

RADICAL PHILOSOPHY.
Radical Philosophy Ltd., c/o Jean Grimshaw, North View, Dundry Ln., Dundry, Bristol BS18 8JG, England. TEL 44-117-064-2986. URL: http://crane.ukc.ac.uk/cprs/phil/rp/ *5746*

RADIO - MEDIA.
Box 2501, Los Angeles, CA 90078. URL: http://via.net/~bryanf/radio-media-info. *44*

RADIO TIMES.
B B C Worldwide Publishing, Woodlands, 80 Wood Lane, London W12 0TT. TEL 44-181-576-3999. FAX 44-181-576-3160. URL: http://www.radiotimes.beeb.com. *2028*

RADIO WEEK.
National Association of Broadcasters, 1771 N St., N.W., Washington, DC 20036. TEL 202-429-5350. FAX 202-429-5406. URL: http://www.nab.org. *2028*

RADIOACTIVE WASTE MANAGEMENT AND ENVIRONMENTAL RESTORATION.
Gordon and Breach - Harwood Academic, Amsteldisk 166, 1st Fl., 1079 LH Amsterdam, Netherlands. URL: http://www.gbhap.com/Radioactive__Waste__Management__Environmental__Restoration/. *2988*

RADIOGRAPHICS.
Radiological Society of North America, Inc., 2021 Spring Rd., Ste. 600, Oak Brook, IL 60521-1860. TEL 630-571-2670. FAX 630-571-7837. URL: http://ej.rsna.org. *5113*

DER RADIOLOGE.
Springer-Verlag, Heidelberger Platz 3, 14197 Berlin, Germany. TEL 49-30-82787-0. FAX 49-30-82787448. URL: http://link.springer.de. Vendor(s): FIZ Technik. *5113*

RADIOLOGIC CLINICS OF NORTH AMERICA.
W.B. Saunders Co., Curtis Center, 3rd Fl., Independence Sq. W., Philadelphia, PA 19106-3399. TEL 215-238-7800. FAX 215-238-6445. Vendor(s): Ovid Technologies, Inc. *5114*

RADIOLOGICAL HEALTH BULLETIN.
U.S. Food and Drug Administration, Center for Devices and Radiological Health, 5600 Fishers Ln., Rockville, MD 20857. TEL 301-443-5860. FAX 301-227-6834. *5114*

RADIOLOGY.
Radiological Society of North America, Inc., 2021 Spring Rd., Ste. 600, Oak Brook, IL 60521-1860. TEL 630-571-2670. FAX 630-571-7837. URL: http://www.rsna.org. *5114*

RAFT.
c/o John A.C. Greppin, Cleveland State University, Cleveland, OH 44115. TEL 216-687-3967. FAX 216-687-9214. *4521*

RAGGED EDGE.
Advocado Press, Box 145, Louisville, KY 40201. TEL 502-459-5343. FAX 502-899-9562. URL: http://www.iglou.com/why/edge. *3457*

RAGING SMOLDER MUSIC REVIEW.
1012 Forest Hills Ave., Annapolis, MD 21403. TEL 410-263-7264. URL: http://www.avmcyber.com/rsmr/
Available only online. *5428*

RAHAVARD PERSIAN JOURNAL.
Hassan Shahbaz, Ed. & Pub., Box 24640, Los Angeles, CA 90024. URL: http://www.rahavard.com. *3322*

THE RAIL SPLITTER.
Box 275, New York, NY 10044. TEL 212-980-7031. FAX 212-741-8756. *3644*

RAILWAY AGE.
Simmons - Boardman Publishing Corp., 345 Hudson St., New York, NY 10014-4502. TEL 212-620-7200.
Vendor(s): Information Access Co., UMI. *7131*

RAINBOWFISH ON-LINE.
5 Atlanta St., Manly, Qld. 4179, Australia. TEL 61-7-3396-7566. URL: http://www.ecn.net.au/~atappin/articles.htm.
Available only online. *3076*

RANDOM LENGTHS.
Random Lengths Publications, Inc., Box 867, Eugene, OR 97440-0867. TEL 541-686-9925. FAX 800-874-7979. URL: http://www.randomlengths.com. *3174*

RANDOM LENGTHS MIDWEEK MARKET REPORT.
Random Lengths Publications, Inc., Box 867, Eugene, OR 97440. TEL 541-686-9629. FAX 541-686-9629. URL: http://www.randomlengths.com. *3174*

RANT MAGAZINE.
Box 7012, Columbia, MD 21045. URL: http://www.erols.com/rant/rant/
Available only online. *4355*

RAPAPORT DIAMOND REPORT.
Rapaport Corp., 15 W. 47th St., Ste. 700, New York, NY 10036. TEL 212-354-0575. FAX 212-840-0243. *3866*

RAPID PROTOTYPING REPORT.
C A D - C A M Publishing, Inc., 1010 Turquoise St., Ste. 320, San Diego, CA 92109-1268. TEL 619-488-0533. FAX 619-488-6052.
Vendor(s): Information Access Co.. *2125*

RARE BREED.
514 Main St., Ste. 7, Bradley Beach, NJ 07720. TEL 908-502-0714. FAX 908-502-9272. URL: http://nj5.injersey.com/'rb007/. *3383*

RATEGRAM.
Bradshaw Group, Limited, Box 3517, San Rafael, CA 94912-3517. TEL 415-479-3815.
Vendor(s): NewsNet (IV61). *1163*

RATIONAL ALTERNATIVE DIGITAL CYBERZINE.
Box 171144, Salt Lake City, UT 84117-1144. URL: http://www.radcyberzine.com.
Available only online. *5428*

RE-DRAWING THE ISLAMIC MAP.
Arab Press Service, A P S House, P.O. Box 3896, Nicosia, Cyprus. TEL 357-2-351778. FAX 357-2-350265.
Vendor(s): Information Access Co. *6033*

REACH OUT MAGAZINE.
Reach Out Publishing, 3090 Sheridan St., Ste. 207, Hollywood, FL 33021. TEL 954-985-0319. URL: http://www.reachoutmag.com. *3457*

REACTIONS WEEKLY.
Adis International Limited, Private Bag 65901, Mairangi Bay, Auckland 10, New Zealand. TEL 64-9-479-8100. FAX 64-9-479-8145. URL: http://www.adis.com.
Vendor(s): Data-Star (READ,REAC,REAA,REZZ), Knight-Ridder Information, Inc. (File no.428,429). *5702*

READ ME FIRST.
URL: http://www. spiritone.com/~dbudin/
Available only online. *2204*

READERS' GUIDE ABSTRACTS.
H.W. Wilson Co., 950 University Ave., Bronx, NY 10452-9978. TEL 718-588-8400. FAX 718-590-1617.
Vendor(s): OCLC, Wilsonline (File RDG). *23*

READERS' GUIDE TO PERIODICAL LITERATURE.
H.W. Wilson Co., 950 University Ave., Bronx, NY 10452-9978. TEL 718-588-8400. FAX 718-590-1617.
Vendor(s): OCLC, Wilsonline (File RDG). *23*

REAL ESTATE ECONOMICS.
American Real Estate and Urban Economics Association, Indiana University, School of Business, Ste. 461, 1309 East Tenth St., Bloomington, IN 47405. URL: http://www.areuea.org.
Vendor(s): Information Access Co. *6310*

REAL ESTATE FINANCE.
Institutional Investor Journals, 488 Madison Ave., New York, NY 10022. TEL 212-224-3185. FAX 212-224-3527.
Vendor(s): UMI. *6310*

REAL ESTATE FINANCE TODAY.
Mortgage Bankers Association of America, 1125 15th St., N.W., Washington, DC 20005-2766. TEL 202-861-6555. FAX 202-861-1930.
Vendor(s): UMI. *6310*

REAL ESTATE INVESTORS CLASSIFIED.
T K O Real Estate Advisory Group, Box 2630, Mercerville, NJ 08690. TEL 609-587-6200. FAX 609-587-3511. URL: http://www.property.com. *6310*

REAL ESTATE ISSUES.
Counselors of Real Estate, 430 N. Michigan Ave., Chicago, IL 60611. TEL 312-329-8427. FAX 312-329-8881.
Vendor(s): UMI. *6310*

REAL ESTATE TODAY.
National Association of Realtors (Chicago), 430 N. Michigan Ave., Chicago, IL 60611. TEL 312-329-8458. FAX 312-329-5978.
Vendor(s): Information Access Co. *6311*

REAL ESTATE WEEKLY.
Hagedorn Communications Corp., One Madison Ave., 25th Fl., New York, NY 10010. TEL 212-679-1234.
Vendor(s): Information Access Co. *6311*

REAL PROPERTY, PROBATE AND TRUST JOURNAL.
American Bar Association, Real Property, Probate and Trust Law Section, 750 N. Lake Shore Dr., Chicago, IL 60611. TEL 312-988-6083. URL: http://www.abanet.org.
Vendor(s): UMI, West Group. *4098*

REAL-TIME IMAGING.
Academic Press Ltd., 24-28 Oval Rd., London NW1 7DX, England. TEL 44-171-482-2893. FAX 44-171-267-0362. URL: http://www.hbuk.co.uk/ap/rti; http://europe.idealibrary.com/. *2125*

REAL TIMES.
Michael Redman, Ed. & Pub., Box 1686, Bloomington, IN 47402. TEL 812-332-3498. *3383*

REALITIES.
Realities Library, 2745 Monterey Hwy. No. 76, San Jose, CA 95111. URL: http://www.soos.com/poetpark.
Available only online. *4521*

REALITY CHECK NETWORK.
URL: http://www.rcn.org.
Available only online. *2139*

REALPOETIK.
840 W. Nickerson St., Ste. 11, Seattle, WA 98119. TEL 206-282-3776. URL: http://www.wln.com/~salasin/rp.html.
Available only online. *4521*

REALTIME.
Australian Council for the Arts, P.O. Box A2246, Sydney S. Post Office, Sydney, N.S.W. 1235, Australia. URL: http://rtimearts.com/'opencity/. *7012*

REASON.
Reason Foundation, 3415 S. Sepulveda Blvd., Ste. 400, Los Angeles, CA 90034-6060. TEL 310-391-2245. FAX 310-391-4395. URL: http://www.reasonmag.com/reason.
Vendor(s): Information Access Co.. *4356*

RECALL NEWSLETTER.
C T I Modern Languages, University of Hull, School of European Languages & Cultures, Cottingham Rd., Hull HU6 7RX, England. TEL 44-1482-466373. FAX 44-1482-473816. *4321*

RECHERCHE EN MATIERE D'ECONOMIE DES TRANSPORTS.
Organization for Economic Cooperation and Development, European Conference of Ministers of Transport, 2 rue Andre Pascal, 75775 Paris Cedex 16, France. TEL 33-1-45248200. FAX 33-1-49104276. URL: http://www.oecd.org/; http://www.oecd.org/cem/
Vendor(s): European Space Agency (File no.74/ TRANSDOC Subfile: RESEARCH). *7037*

RECHERCHES UNIVERSITAIRES SUR L'INTEGRATION EUROPEENNE.
Commission of the European Communities, Rue de la Loi 200, B-1049 Brussels, Belgium. *5986*

RECORDS MANAGEMENT QUARTERLY.
Association of Records Managers and Administrators, 4200 Somerset Dr., Ste. 215, Prairie Village, KS 66208. TEL 913-341-3808. URL: http://www.arma.org/ha/rmq.html.
Vendor(s): Information Access Co., UMI. *4209*

RECUEIL DES BREVETS D'INVENTION.
Ministry of Economic Affairs, Office de la Propriete Industrielle, 154 Bd. E. Jacqmain, 1000 Brussels, Belgium. TEL 32-2-2064111. FAX 32-2-2065750.
Vendor(s): BELINDIS. *5589*

RECYCLING WORLD.
Environmental Defense Fund, 257 Park Ave. S., New York, NY 10010. TEL 212-505-2100. FAX 212-505-2375. URL: http://www.edf.org/pubs/Brochures/RecyclingWorld/ *2989*

RECYCLING WORLD.
Scrap Market Ltd., Hilltop, Offchurch Rd., Webheath, Redditch, Worcs. B77 5PQ, England. TEL 44-1527-404550. FAX 44-1527-404644. URL: http://tecweb.com/recycle/eurorec.htm. *2989*

RED POLITICS.
R P Publishing, 2-77 Holden St. N., Fitzroy, Vic. 3068, Australia.
Available only online. *5963*

REDBOOK.
Hearst Corporation, Redbook, 224 W. 57th St., New York, NY 10019. TEL 212-649-3450. URL: http://www.hearstcorp.com.
Vendor(s): Information Access Co.. *7332*

REEVES JOURNAL.
Business News Publishing Company, 755 W. Big Beaver Rd., Ste. 1000, Troy, MI 48084. TEL 810-362-3700. FAX 810-362-0317. URL: http://www.bnp.com. *3483*

REFERENCE AND RESEARCH BOOK NEWS.
Book News, Inc. (Portland), 5739 N.E. Sumner St., Portland, OR 97218. TEL 503-281-9230. FAX 503-287-4485. URL: http://www.books.com.booknews. *561*

REFERENCE BOOK OF CORPORATE MANAGEMENTS.
Dun's Marketing Services, 3 Sylvan Way, Parsippany, NJ 07054-3896. TEL 201-455-0900.
Vendor(s): Questel Orbit Inc. (RBCM). *1503*

REFLECTOR NEWSLETTER.
Astronomical League, 5027 W. Stanford, Dallas, TX 75209-3319. TEL 214-357-2744.
Vendor(s): CompuServe, Inc. *500*

REFRIGERATION SERVICE AND CONTRACTING.
Business News Publishing Company, 755 W. Big Beaver Rd., Ste. 1000, Troy, MI 48084. TEL 810-362-3700. FAX 810-362-0317. URL: http://www.bnp.com. *3484*

REGENT ONLINE JOURNAL OF COMMUNICATION.
Regent University, College of Communication and the Arts, School of Communication Studies, Virginia Beach, VA 23464-9800. TEL 804-523-7943. FAX 804-424-7051. URL: http://www.regent.edu/acad/schcom/rojc/rojc.html.
Available only online. *5343*

REGIONAL STUDIES.
Carfax Publishing Co., P.O. Box 25, Abingdon, Oxon. OX14 3UE, England. TEL 44-1235-401000. FAX 44-1235-401550.
Vendor(s): Information Access Co. *3758*

REGULATORY COMPLIANCE WATCH.
American Banker - Bond Buyer, Newsletter Division One State St. Plaza, New York, NY 10004-1549. TEL 800-733-4371. FAX 212-943-2224.
Vendor(s): Information Access Co., NewsNet (FI04). *1163*

REGULATORY TOXICOLOGY AND PHARMACOLOGY.
Academic Press, Inc., Journal Division, 525 B St., Ste. 1900, San Diego, CA 92101-4495. TEL 619-230-1840. FAX 619-699-6800. URL: http://www.apnet.com/www/journal/rt.htm; http://www.idealibrary.com/ *2980*

REGULATORY UPDATE.
Lewis B. Weisfeld, Ed. & Pub., 1 Franklin Town Blvd., Ste. 1204, Philadelphia, PA 19103. TEL 215-567-7235. FAX 215-567-7235. URL: http://www.regup.plastics.com/. *5885*

REHABILITATION INDEX.
British Library, Medical Information Centre, Boston Spa, Wetherby, W. Yorks. LS23 7BQ, England. TEL 01937-546520. FAX 01937-546458. *4788*

RELEASE 1.0.
EDventure Holdings, 104 Fifth Ave., New York, NY 10011-6987. TEL 212-924-8800. FAX 212-924-0240.
Vendor(s): Information Access Co. *2130*

RELIGION.
Academic Press Ltd., 24-28 Oval Rd., London NW1 7DX, England. TEL 44-171-267-4466. FAX 44-171-482-2293. URL: http://www.hbuk.co.uk/ap/religion; http://www.europe.idealibrary.com/. *6365*

RELIGION IN EASTERN EUROPE.
Christian Association for Relationships with Eastern Europe, c/o Rosemont College, Rosemont, PA 19010. TEL 215-527-0200. FAX 215-696-8970.
Vendor(s): Knight-Ridder Information, Inc., Ovid Technologies, Inc. *6366*

RELIGIOUS LEADERS OF AMERICA.
Gale Research, 835 Penobscot Bldg., 645 Griswold St., Detroit, MI 48226-4094. TEL 313-961-2242. FAX 800-414-5043.
Vendor(s): Lexis-Nexis. *6366*

RELIGIOUS STUDIES.
Cambridge University Press, Edinburgh Bldg., Shaftesbury Rd., Cambridge CB2 2RU, England. TEL 44-1223-312393. FAX 44-1223-315052. URL: http://www.cup.cam.ac.uk.
Vendor(s): Information Access Co. *6366*

REMOTE SENSING REVIEWS.
Gordon and Breach - Harwood Academic, Amsteldisk 166, 1st Fl., 1079 LH Amsterdam, Netherlands. URL: http://www.gbhap.com/Remote___Sensing___Reviews/. *2738*

RENAISSANCE QUARTERLY.
Renaissance Society of America, 24 W. 12th St., New York, NY 10011-8604. TEL 212-998-3797. FAX 212-995-4205.
Vendor(s): Information Access Co., UMI. *4456*

RENEW NEWSLETTER.
Network for Alternative Technology and Technology Assessment, c/o Energy and Environment Research Unit, Faculty of Technology, Open University, Walton Hall, Milton Keynes, Bucks. MK7 6AA, England. TEL 44-1908-654638. FAX 44-1908-653744. URL: http://eeru.open.ac.uk. *2677*

RENEWABLE ENERGY REPORT.
Financial Times Energy Publishing, Maple House, 149 Tottenham Court Rd., London W1P 9LL, England. TEL 0171-896-2241. FAX 0171-896-2275.
Vendor(s): Data-Star, Knight-Ridder Information, Inc., Lexis-Nexis. *2678*

RENTAL MANAGEMENT.
American Rental Association, 1900 19th St., Moline, IL 61265. TEL 309-764-2475. FAX 309-764-1533. URL: http://ararental.org. *1546*

REPERTOIRE DES BANQUES DE DONNEES PROFESSIONNELLES.
Association des Professionnels de l'Information et de la Documentation (ADBS), 25 rue Claude Tillier, 75012 Paris, France. TEL 33-1-43722525. FAX 33-1-43723041. URL: http://www.adbs.fr. *1709*

REPERTOIRE DES BANQUES DE DONNEES TELETEL POUR L'ENTREPRISE.
Editions F L A Consultants, 27 rue de la Vistule, 75013 Paris, France. TEL 33-1-45827575. FAX 33-1-45824604. URL: http://www.fla-consultants.fr. *2017*

REPINDEX.
Organizacion Panamericana de la Salud, Centro Panamericano de Ingenieria Sanitaria y Ciencias del Ambiente, Los Pinos 259, Urb. Camacho, Casilla Postal 4337, Lima 100, Peru. TEL 51-14-371077. FAX 51-14-378289. URL: http://www.cepis.org.pe. *2963*

REPORT ON A T & T.
Capitol Publications Inc., Telecom Publishing Group, 1101 King St., Ste. 444, Box 1455, Alexandria, VA 22313-2055. FAX 703-739-6490. URL: http://www.telecommunications.com.
Vendor(s): Information Access Co., NewsNet (TE50). *2017*

REPORT ON CORPORATE EDUCATIONAL SUPPORT.
Business Publishers, Inc., 951 Pershing Dr., Silver Spring, MD 20910-4464. TEL 301-587-6300. FAX 301-585-9075.
Vendor(s): NewsNet. *2577*

REPORT ON DEFENSE PLANT WASTE.
Business Publishers, Inc., 951 Pershing Dr., Silver Spring, MD 20910-4464. TEL 301-587-6300. FAX 301-585-9075.
Vendor(s): Information Access Co., NewsNet (EV28). *2989*

REPORT ON DISABILITY PROGRAMS.
Business Publishers, Inc., 951 Pershing Dr., Silver Spring, MD 20910-4464. TEL 301-587-6300. FAX 301-585-9075.
Vendor(s): NewsNet. *6683*

REPORT ON EDUCATION OF THE DISADVANTAGED.
Business Publishers, Inc., 951 Pershing Dr., Silver Spring, MD 20910-4464. TEL 301-587-6300. FAX 301-585-9075.
Vendor(s): NewsNet. *2589*

REPORT ON HEALTHCARE MANAGEMENT SOLUTIONS.
Garner-Aldrich Publishing, Box 3247, Silver Spring, MD 20918-3247. TEL 301-593-7025.
Vendor(s): NewsNet. *3719*

REPORT ON I B M.
DataTrends Publications, Inc., Box 4460, Leesburg, VA 20175. TEL 703-779-0574. FAX 703-779-2267.
Vendor(s): Information Access Co. *2180*

REPORT ON LITERACY PROGRAM.
Business Publishers, Inc., 951 Pershing Dr., Silver Spring, MD 20910-4464. TEL 301-587-6300. FAX 301-585-9075.
Vendor(s): NewsNet (ED10). *2477*

REPORT ON MICROSOFT.
DataTrends Publications, Inc., Box 4460, Leesburg, VA 20175. TEL 703-779-0574. FAX 703-779-2267.
Vendor(s): Information Access Co. *2128*

REPORT ON PRESCHOOL PROGRAMS.
Business Publishers, Inc., 951 Pershing Dr., Silver Spring, MD 20910-4464. TEL 301-587-6300. FAX 301-585-9075.
Vendor(s): NewsNet. *2477*

REPORT ON SCHOOL-AGE CHILD CARE.
Business Publishers, Inc., 951 Pershing Dr., Silver Spring, MD 20910-4464. TEL 301-587-6300. FAX 301-585-9075.
Vendor(s): NewsNet. *1855*

REPORTAGE.
115 Hester St., New York, NY 10002. TEL 212-941-8163. URL: http://www.users.interport.net/~akreye.
Available only online. *3880*

REPORTS ON PROGRESS IN PHYSICS.
I O P Publishing Ltd., Dirac House, Temple Back, Bristol BS1 6BE, England. TEL 44-117-929-7481. FAX 44-117-929-4318. URL: http://www.iop.org/Journals/rp. *5824*

REPRESENTATION THEORY.
American Mathematical Society, Box 6248, Providence, RI 02940-6248. TEL 401-455-4000. FAX 401-331-3842. URL: http://www.ams.org/ert/. Available only online. *4601*

REPRODUCTIVE RIGHTS UPDATE.
American Civil Liberties Union, Reproductive Freedom Project, 132 W. 43rd St., New York, NY 10036. TEL 212-944-9800. FAX 212-869-4314. URL: http://www.aclu.org. *5998*

RESEARCH ALERT (NEW YORK).
E P M Communications, 160 Mercer St., 3rd Fl., New York, NY 10012-3212. TEL 212-941-0099. FAX 212-941-1622.
Vendor(s): Information Access Co., Knight-Ridder Information, Inc., Lexis-Nexis. *1547*

RESEARCH & DEVELOPMENT.
Cahners Publishing Company (Des Plaines), Division of Reed Elsevier Inc., 1350 E. Touhy Ave., Box 5080, Des Plaines, IL 60018-5080. TEL 847-390-2343. FAX 847-390-2618. URL: http://www.rdmag.com.
Vendor(s): Information Access Co., Knight-Ridder Information, Inc. *6971*

RESEARCH CENTERS DIRECTORY.
Gale Research, 835 Penobscot Bldg., 645 Griswold St., Detroit, MI 48226-4094. TEL 313-961-2242. FAX 800-414-5043.
Vendor(s): Knight-Ridder Information, Inc. *6562*

RESEARCH HORIZONS.
Georgia Institute of Technology, Research Communications Office, 223 Centennial Research Bldg., Atlanta, GA 30332-0828. TEL 404-894-4259. FAX 404-894-6983. URL: http://www.gtri.gatech.edu/res-hor/rh-welcome.html. *2738*

RESEARCH IN AFRICAN LITERATURES.
Indiana University Press, 601 N. Morton St., Bloomington, IN 47404. TEL 812-855-9449. FAX 812-855-8507. URL: http://www.indiana.edu/~inpress/journals/ral.html.
Vendor(s): Information Access Co., UMI. *4457*

RESEARCH IN ECONOMICS.
Academic Press Ltd., 24-28 Oval Rd., London NW1 7DX, England. TEL 44-171-267-4466. FAX 44-171-482-2293. URL: http://www.hbuk.co.uk/ap/re; http://www.europe.idealibrary.com/. *996*

RESEARCH IN HIGHER EDUCATION.
Human Sciences Press, Inc., 233 Spring St., New York, NY 10013. TEL 212-620-8000. FAX 212-463-0742. *2577*

RESEARCH IN NONDESTRUCTIVE EVALUATION.
Springer-Verlag, Science Journals, 175 Fifth Ave., New York, NY 10010. TEL 212-460-1500. FAX 212-473-6272. URL: http://www.springer-ny.com. *2739*

RESEARCH QUARTERLY FOR EXERCISE AND SPORT.
American Alliance for Health, Physical Education, Recreation, and Dance, 1900 Association Dr., Reston, VA 22091. TEL 703-476-3400. FAX 703-476-9527.
Vendor(s): Information Access Co., UMI. *5789*

RESEARCH SERVICES DIRECTORY.
Gale Research, 835 Penobscot Bldg., 645 Griswold St., Detroit, MI 48226-4094. TEL 313-961-2242. FAX 800-414-5043.
Vendor(s): Knight-Ridder Information, Inc. *1710*

RESILOG.
Environment Canada, Transboundary Movement Division, Ottawa, ON K1A 0H3, Canada. TEL 819-997-3377. FAX 819-997-3068. URL: http://www.doe.ca/resilog/resinews.htm. *2989*

RESOURCE (ST. JOSEPH).
American Society of Agricultural Engineers, 2950 Niles Rd., St. Joseph, MI 49085-9659. TEL 616-429-0300. FAX 616-429-3852. URL: http://asae.org/resource.
Vendor(s): Information Access Co. *242*

RESOURCES IN EDUCATION.
E R I C Facility, 1100 West St., 2nd Fl., Laurel, MD 20707-3587. TEL 301-497-4080. FAX 301-953-0263. URL: http://ericfac.piccard.csc.com.
Vendor(s): Knight-Ridder Information, Inc., Ovid Technologies, Inc. *2503*

RESPIRATORY MEDICINE.
W.B. Saunders Co. Ltd., 24-28 Oval Rd., London NW1 7DX, England. TEL 44-171-267-4466. FAX 44-171-482-2293. URL: http://www.hbuk.co.uk/wbs/rem.
Vendor(s): Ovid Technologies, Inc. *5122*

RESPONSE T V.
Advanstar Communications, Inc., 7500 Old Oak Blvd., Cleveland, OH 44130. TEL 216-826-2839. FAX 216-891-2726.
Vendor(s): Information Access Co. *2057*

RESTAURANT BUSINESS.
Bill Communications, Inc., 355 Park Ave. S., 5th Fl., New York, NY 10010-1789. TEL 212-592-6200. FAX 212-592-6339. URL: http://www.restaurantbiz.com.
Vendor(s): Information Access Co., UMI. *3734*

RESTAURANT HOSPITALITY.
Penton Publishing Co., 1100 Superior Ave., Cleveland, OH 44114-2543. TEL 216-696-7000. FAX 216-696-8765.
Vendor(s): Information Access Co., UMI. *3734*

RESTAURANTS AND INSTITUTIONS.
Cahners Publishing Company (Des Plaines), Division of Reed Elsevier Inc., 1350 E. Touhy Ave., Box 5080, Des Plaines, IL 60018-5080. TEL 847-390-2035. FAX 847-390-2080. URL: http://www.rimag.com.
Vendor(s): Information Access Co. *3735*

RETAIL BUSINESS: MARKET REPORTS.
Corporate Intelligence on Retailing, 51 Doughty St., London WC1 N2LS, England. TEL 44-171-696-9006. *1547*

RETAIL INTELLIGENCE.
Mintel International Group Ltd., 18-19 Long Ln., London EC1A 9HE, England. TEL 44-171-606-4533. FAX 44-171-606-5932. *1547*

RETAIL STATIONERY: THE INTERNATIONAL MARKET.
Euromonitor, 60-61 Britton St., London EC1M 5NA, England. TEL 44-171-251-8024. FAX 44-171-608-3149. URL: http://www.euromonitor.com.
Vendor(s): Data-Star, Knight-Ridder Information, Inc. *1560*

RETAIL STORE IMAGE.
Intertec Publishing Corp. (Atlanta), 6151 Powers Ferry Rd., N.W., Atlanta, GA 30339-2941. TEL 770-955-2500. FAX 770-9550-0400.
Vendor(s): Information Access Co. *3849*

RETAIL TRADE INTERNATIONAL.
Euromonitor, 60-61 Britton St., London EC1M 5NA, England. TEL 44-171-251-8024. FAX 44-171-608-3149. URL: http://www.euromonitor.com. *1547*

RETINA.
Lippincott - Raven Publishers, 227 E. Washington Sq., Philadelphia, PA 19106. TEL 215-238-4200. FAX 215-238-4227. URL: http://www.lrpub.com. *5000*

REVIEW OF AGRICULTURAL ENTOMOLOGY.
CAB International, Wallingford, Oxon. OX10 8DE, England. TEL 44-1491-832111. FAX 44-1491-826090. URL: http://www.cabi.org.
Vendor(s): DIMDI, European Space Agency, Knight-Ridder Information, Inc., STN International. *182*

REVIEW OF AROMATIC AND MEDICINAL PLANTS.
CAB International, Wallingford, Oxon. OX10 8DE, England. TEL 44-1491-832111. FAX 44-1491-826090. URL: http://www.cabi.org. *4788*

THE REVIEW OF BANKING AND FINANCIAL SERVICES.
Standard & Poor's Corporation, 25 Broadway, New York, NY 10004. TEL 212-208-8000.
Vendor(s): Dow Jones News Retrieval (RBFS), Knight-Ridder Information, Inc. (BFS), Lexis-Nexis (RBFS), NewsNet (FI17). *1164*

REVIEW OF BLACK POLITICAL ECONOMY.
Transaction Publishers, Transaction Periodicals Consortium, Department 3092, Rutgers University, New Brunswick, NJ 08903. TEL 908-445-2280. FAX 908-445-3138.
Vendor(s): Information Access Co., UMI. *996*

REVIEW OF BUSINESS.
St. John's University, College of Business Administration, Bent Hall, 8000 Utopia Pkwy., Jamaica, NY 11439. TEL 718-990-6768. FAX 718-990-1868.
Vendor(s): Information Access Co., UMI. *996*

THE REVIEW OF CONTEMPORARY FICTION.
Review of Contemporary Fiction, Inc., 4241 Illinois State University, Normal, IL 61790-4241. TEL 309-438-7555. FAX 309-437-7422. URL: http://www.cas.ilstu.edu/english/dalkeycatalog/catreview.html.
Vendor(s): Information Access Co., UMI. *4457*

THE REVIEW OF ECONOMICS AND STATISTICS.
M I T Press, 5 Cambridge Center, Cambridge, MA 02142-1399. TEL 617-577-1545. FAX 617-577-1545. URL: http://www-mitpress.mit.edu/ *996*

REVIEW OF EDUCATIONAL RESEARCH.
American Educational Research Association, 1230 17th St., N.W., Washington, DC 20036-3078. TEL 202-223-9485. FAX 202-775-1824.
Vendor(s): UMI. *2478*

REVIEW OF ENGLISH STUDIES.
Oxford University Press, Academic Division, Great Clarendon St., Oxford OX2 6DP, England. TEL 44-1865-267907. FAX 44-1865-267485. URL: http://www.oup.co.uk/journals.
Vendor(s): Information Access Co. *4457*

REVIEW OF FINANCIAL ECONOMICS.
J A I Press Inc., 55 Old Post Rd., No. 2, Box 1678, Greenwich, CT 06830-1678. TEL 203-661-7602. FAX 203-661-0792.
Vendor(s): Information Access Co. *996*

REVIEW OF INFORMATION SCIENCE.
University Association for Information Science, URL: http://www.inf.wiss.uni-konstanz.de/ris. Available only online. *4210*

REVIEW OF MEDICAL AND VETERINARY ENTOMOLOGY.
CAB International, Wallingford, Oxon. OX10 8DE, England. TEL 44-1491-832111. FAX 44-1491-833508. URL: http://www.cabi.org.
Vendor(s): DIMDI, European Space Agency, Knight-Ridder Information, Inc., STN International. *7286*

REVIEW OF MEDICAL AND VETERINARY MYCOLOGY.
CAB International, Wallingford, Oxon. OX10 8DE, England. TEL 44-1491-832111. FAX 44-1491-826090. URL: http://www.cabi.org.
Vendor(s): DIMDI, European Space Agency, Knight-Ridder Information, Inc., STN International. *644*

THE REVIEW OF METAPHYSICS.
Philosophy Education Society, Inc., Catholic University of America, Washington, DC 20064. TEL 202-635-8778. FAX 202-319-4484.
Vendor(s): Information Access Co. *5748*

REVIEW OF OPHTHALMOLOGY.
Chilton Co., 201 King of Prussia Rd., Radnor, PA 19089. TEL 610-964-4370. FAX 610-964-2959. *5000*

REVIEW OF PLANT PATHOLOGY.
CAB International, Wallingford, Oxon. OX10 8DE, England. TEL 44-1491-832111. FAX 44-1491-826090. URL: http://www.cabi.org.
Vendor(s): DIMDI, European Space Agency, Knight-Ridder Information, Inc., STN International. *645*

REVIEW OF PUBLIC PERSONNEL ADMINISTRATION.
University of South Carolina, Institute of Public Affairs, Columbia, SC 29208. TEL 803-777-8157.
Vendor(s): UMI. *6192*

REVIEW OF SCIENTIFIC INSTRUMENTS.
American Institute of Physics, One Physics Ellipse, College Park, MD 20740-3843. TEL 301-209-3000. URL: http://www.aip.org. *3805*

THE REVIEW OF SECURITIES & COMMODITIES REGULATION.
Standard & Poor's, 25 Broadway, New York, NY 10004. TEL 212-208-8650. FAX 212-412-0240. Vendor(s): Dow Jones News Retrieval (RSCR), Knight-Ridder Information, Inc. (SCR), Lexis-Nexis (RSCR), NewsNet (FI20). *1404*

REVIEW OF SOCIAL ECONOMY.
Routledge, 11 New Fetter Ln., London EC4P 4EE, England. TEL 44-171-583-9855. FAX 44-171-842-2298. URL: http://www.routledge.com/routledge/journal/journals.html.
Vendor(s): Information Access Co. *997*

REVIEWS IN AMERICAN HISTORY.
Johns Hopkins University Press, Journals Publishing Division, 2715 N. Charles St., Baltimore, MD 21218. TEL 410-516-6987. FAX 410-516-6968. URL: http://muse.jhu.edu.
Vendor(s): Information Access Co. *3645*

REVIEWS IN FISH BIOLOGY AND FISHERIES.
Thomson Science, 2-6 Boundary Row, London SE1 8HN, England. TEL 44-171-8650066. FAX 44-171-5229623. URL: http://www.thomsonscience.com. *848*

REVIEWS IN MEDICAL MICROBIOLOGY.
Thomson Science, 2-6 Boundary Row, London SE1 8HN, England. TEL 44-171-865-0198. FAX 44-171-928-7876. URL: http://www.thomsonscience.com. *793*

REVISTA BRASILEIRA DE PESQUISAS MEDICAS E BIOLOGICAS.
Associacao Brasileira de Divulgacao Cientifica, c/o Eduardo Moacyr Krieger, Faculdade de Medicina de Ribeirao Preto, Campus de Ribeirao Preto, 14049-900 Ribeirao Preto SP, Brazil. TEL 55-16-633-3825. URL: http://brasil.emb.nw.dc.us/NIB/bjmbr/ *4737*

REVISTA CANARIA DE ESTUDIOS INGLESES.
Universidad de La Laguna, Secretariado de Publicaciones, San Agustin, 30, 38201 La Laguna-Tenerife, Islas Canarias, Spain. TEL 922-25-81-27. *4293*

REVISTA COLOMBIANA DE CIENCIAS QUIMICO FARMACEUTICAS.
Universidad Nacional de Colombia, Departamento de Farmacia, Apdo. Aereo 14490, Bogota, Colombia. *5693*

REVISTA COLOMBIANA DE MATEMATICAS.
Sociedad Colombiana de Matematicas, Apdo. Aereo No. 2521, Bogota, Colombia. FAX 2686465. URL: http://www.emis.de/journals/RCM/info.html. *4601*

REVISTA CUBANA DE FARMACIA.
Ministerio de Salud Publica, Centro Nacional de Informacion de Ciencias Medicas, Calle E No. 452, e-19 y 21, Plaza de la Revolucion, Apdo. 6520, Havana, Cuba. TEL 809-32-5338. *5693*

REVISTA CUBANA DE MEDICINA GENERAL INTEGRAL.
Ministerio de Salud Publica, Centro Nacional de Informacion de Ciencias Medicas, Calle E No. 452, e-19 y 21, Plaza de la Revolucion, Apdo. 6520, Havana, Cuba. TEL 809-32-5338. *4738*

REVISTA DE ESTUDIOS EXTREMENOS.
Centro de Estudios Extremenos, Servicio de Publicaciones, Felipe Checa 15, 06071 Badajoz, Spain. *3360*

REVISTA DE MICROBIOLOGIA.
Sociedade Brasileira de Microbiologia, c/o Luiz Rachid Trabulsi, Ed., Depto. de Microbiologia, Instituto de Ciencias Biomedicas USP, Av. Prof. Lineu Prestes, 1374, 05508-900 Sao Paulo, SP, Brazil. TEL 55-11-8139647. FAX 55-11-81396747. *793*

REVISTA ECONOMIA.
Universidad de Los Andes, Facultad de Economia, IIES, La Hechicera, Edf. B, 1r, Merida 5101, Venezuela. TEL 074-401081. FAX 074-401120. *997*

REVISTA FARMACEUTICA.
Academia Argentina de Farmacia y Bioquimica, Junin 956, Buenos Aires 1113, Argentina. *5693*

REVISTA PORTUGUESA DE FARMACIA.
Ordem dos Farmaceuticos, Rua da Sociedade Farmaceutica, No. 18, 1150 Lisbon, Portugal. TEL 351-1-3151104. FAX 351-1-3524480. *5693*

RHODE ISLAND BUSINESS DIRECTORY.
American Business Directories, 5711 S. 86th Circle, Box 27347, Omaha, NE 68127. TEL 402-593-4600. FAX 402-331-5481. *1710*

RICE ABSTRACTS.
CAB International, Wallingford, Oxon. OX10 8DE, England. TEL 44-1491-832111. FAX 44-1491-826090. URL: http://www.cabi.org.
Vendor(s): DIMDI, European Space Agency, Knight-Ridder Information, Inc., STN International. *182*

RICE THRESHER.
Rice University, Student Publications, 6100 Main St., Houston, TX 77005. TEL 713-527-4801. FAX 713-285-5238. URL: http://www.rice.edu/thresher. *1969*

RIDE ON!
Washington Bicycling Association, 818 Connecticut Ave., N.W., Washington, DC 20006. TEL 202-872-9830. FAX 202-862-9762. *2243*

RIDE THE WEB.
Tackett Management Solutions, URL: http://www.calegal.com/ridetheweb/
Available only online. *6833*

RIGAKU RYOHO JANARU.
Igaku-Shoin Ltd., 5-24-3 Hongo, Bunkyo-ku, Tokyo 113-91, Japan. TEL 81-3-3817-5703.
Vendor(s): JICST. *5046*

RIGHT-TO-KNOW PLANNING GUIDE (SERIES).
The Bureau of National Affairs, Inc., 1231 25th St., N.W., Washington, DC 20037. TEL 202-452-4200. FAX 202-822-8092. URL: http://www.bna.com/
Vendor(s): Human Resources Information Network (File DD). *6684*

RIGHT-TO-KNOW PLANNING GUIDE NEWSLETTER.
The Bureau of National Affairs, Inc., 1231 25th St., N.W., Washington, DC 20037. TEL 202-452-4200. FAX 202-822-8092.
Vendor(s): Human Resources Information Network (File DD). *6684*

RIHABIRITESHON IGAKU.
Japanese Association of Rehabilitation Medicine, 1-1-17 Komone, Itabashi-ku, Tokyo, Japan. TEL 81-3-5966-2031. FAX 81-3-5966-2033.
Vendor(s): JICST. *5047*

RIMSHOT! SKA E-ZINE.
Carnegie Mellon University, SMC 4037, Box 3015, Pittsburgh, PA 15213. URL: http://www.andrew.cmu.edu/~yw26/rimshot.
Available only online. *5431*

RIO OBSERVER.
Estrada das Canoas, 3406 Sao Conrado, Rio de Janeiro, RJ, Brazil. URL: http://www.rio-observer.com.
Available only online. *7232*

RISK, DECISION AND POLICY.
Thomson Professional, 2-6 Boundary Row, London SE1 8HN, England. TEL 44-171-8650066. FAX 44-171-5229623. URL: http://rdp.thomsonprofessional.com. *1505*

RISK: HEALTH, SAFETY & ENVIRONMENT.
Franklin Pierce Law Center, 2 White St., Concord, NH 03301. TEL 603-228-1541. FAX 603-224-3342. URL: http://www.flpc.edu/tfield/PRORISK.htm.
Vendor(s): West Group. *6249*

RISK MANAGEMENT.
Risk Management Society Publishing, Inc., 655 Third Ave., 2nd Fl., New York, NY 10017-5637. TEL 212-286-9364. FAX 212-922-0716. URL: http://www.rims.org/rmmag.html.
Vendor(s): Information Access Co., UMI. *3832*

ROAD & TRACK.
Hachette Filipacchi Magazines, Inc. (Newport Beach), Road & Track, 1499 Monrovia Ave., Newport Beach, CA 92663. TEL 714-720-5300. FAX 714-631-2757.
Vendor(s): Information Access Co., UMI. *7115*

ROAD TRAFFIC REPORTS.
Kenneth Mason Publications Ltd., 12 North St., Emsworth, Hants. PO10 7DQ, England. TEL 44-1243-377977. FAX 44-1243-379136.
Vendor(s): Lexis-Nexis. *7140*

ROBOTRONICS AGE NEWSLETTER.
Twenty-First Century Media Communications, Inc., 548 Cardero St., Vancouver, B.C. V6N 2K3, Canada. TEL 604-261-5712.
Vendor(s): NewsNet (EC16). *2104*

ROCHESTER BUSINESS JOURNAL.
55 St. Paul St., Rochester, NY 14604-1309. TEL 716-546-8303. FAX 716-546-3398. URL: http://www.rbj.net. *1287*

ROCKEFELLER ARCHIVE CENTER NEWSLETTER.
Rockefeller University, Rockefeller Archive Center, Pocantico Hills, 15 Dayton Ave., N. Tarrytown, NY 10591-1598. TEL 914-631-4505. FAX 914-631-6017. URL: http://www.rockefeller.edu/arc_cent/ *3511*

ROCKET LITERARY QUARTERLY.
Rocket Press, Box 730, Greenport, NY 11944-0730. *4460*

ROCKRGRL.
Rockrgrl, 7683 S.E. 27th St., Ste. 317, Mercer Island, WA 98040-2826. TEL 206-230-4280. FAX 206-230-4288. URL: http://www.indieweb.com/rockrgrl. *5431*

ROCKY MOUNTAIN ENVIRONMENTAL DIRECTORY.
Harbinger Communications, Box 8175, Missoula, MT 59807. TEL 406-721-0440. FAX 406-721-0440. *2243*

ROCKY MOUNTAIN HIGH: THE JOHN DENVER FAN CLUB.
3820 Baltimore, Kansas City, MO 64111. URL: http://www.sky.net/'emily. *5432*

ROCZNIKI NAUKOWE ZOOTECHNIKI.
Instytut Zootechniki, Ul. Sarego 2, 31-047 Krakow, Poland. TEL 48-12-227333. FAX 48-12-228065. *287*

ROLL CALL.
Roll Call, Inc., 900 Second St., N.E., Ste. 107, Washington, DC 20002. TEL 202-289-4900. FAX 202-289-2205. URL: http://www.rollcall.com.
Vendor(s): Lexis-Nexis. *5966*

ROLLING GOOD TIMES ONLINE.
R G T Online Inc., 901 Boonslick Rd., St. Charles, MO 63301. URL: http://www.rgtonline.com.
Available only online. *6778*

ROMANCE PHILOLOGY.
University of California Press, Journals Division, 2120 Berkeley Way, No. 5812, Berkeley, CA 94720-5812. TEL 510-643-7154. FAX 510-642-9117. URL: http://library.berkeley.edu:8080/ucalpress/journals.
Vendor(s): Information Access Co.. *4295*

ROMANIC REVIEW.
Columbia University, c/o Prof. Michael Riffaterre, Ed., 518 Philosophy Hall, Columbia University, New York, NY 10027. TEL 212-854-2500.
Vendor(s): Information Access Co.. *4460*

ROMANTICISM ON THE NET.
URL: http://users.ox.ac.uk/'scat0385.
Available only online. *4460*

ROMULUS.
Canada Institute for Scientific and Technical Information, Information Resource Management, Ottawa, ON K1A 0S2, Canada.
Vendor(s): CISTI. *6591*

ROOTSWORLD.
Box 1285, New Haven, CT 06505. TEL 203-624-6423. URL: http://www.rootsworld.com/rw/
Available only online. *5432*

ROUGH NOTES.
Rough Notes Co., Inc., Box 1990, Carmel, IN 46032-4990. TEL 317-582-1600. FAX 317-816-1003. URL: http://www.roughnotes.com/rnmag/
Vendor(s): UMI. *3832*

THE ROUND TOP REGISTER.
Round Top Publishing Company, Box 225, Round Top, TX 78954. TEL 409-249-5550. FAX 409-249-5021. URL: http://www.roundtop.com; http://www.rtis.com/reg/roundtop. *3384*

ROWENA'S PAGE.
URL: http://red-agnes.la.ca.us/sdy/rowena/. Available only online. *4461*

ROYAL ANTHROPOLOGICAL INSTITUTE. JOURNAL.
Royal Anthropological Institute of Great Britain and Ireland, 50 Fitzroy St., London W1P 5HS, England. TEL 44-171-3870455. FAX 44-171-3834235. Vendor(s): UMI. *329*

ROYAL COLLEGE OF PATHOLOGISTS OF AUSTRALASIA. BULLETIN.
Royal College of Pathologists of Australasia, Durham Hall, 207 Albion St., Surry Hills, N.S.W. 2010, Australia. TEL 61-2-93324266. FAX 61-2-93311431. URL: http://www.vifp.monash.edu.au/other_webs/rcpweb/bindex.html. Available only online. *4741*

ROYAL GAZETTE LIMITED.
Bermuda Press (Holdings) Ltd., P.O. Box HM1025, Hamilton HMDX, Bermuda. TEL 441-295-5881. FAX 441-295-1513. *3256*

ROYAL SOCIETY OF CHEMISTRY. JOURNAL: PERKIN TRANSACTIONS 1.
The Royal Society of Chemistry, Thomas Graham House, Science Park, Milton Rd., Cambridge CB4 4WF, England. TEL 44-1223-420066. FAX 44-1223-423429. URL: http://chemistry.rsc.org/rsc/. Vendor(s): STN International (CJRSC). *1823*

ROYAL SOCIETY OF CHEMISTRY. JOURNAL: PERKIN TRANSACTIONS 2.
The Royal Society of Chemistry, Thomas Graham House, Science Park, Milton Rd., Cambridge CB4 4WF, England. TEL 44-1223-420066. FAX 44-1223-423429. URL: http://chemistry.rsc.org/rsc/. Vendor(s): STN International (CJRSC). *1834*

ROYAL SOCIETY OF LONDON. PROCEEDINGS. SERIES A. MATHEMATICAL, PHYSICAL AND ENGINEERING SCIENCES.
Royal Society of London, 6 Carlton House Terrace, London SW1Y 5AG, England. TEL 44-171-839-5561. FAX 44-171-976-1837. URL: http://www.pubs.royalsoc.ac.uk. *4602*

ROYAL SOCIETY OF LONDON. PROCEEDINGS. SERIES B. BIOLOGICAL SCIENCES.
Royal Society of London, 6 Carlton House Terrace, London SW1Y 5AG, England. TEL 44-171-839-5561. FAX 44-171-976-1837. URL: http://www.pubs.royalsoc.ac.uk. *624*

ROYAL SOCIETY OF MEDICINE. JOURNAL.
Royal Society of Medicine Press Ltd., 1 Wimpole St., London W1M 8AE, England. TEL 44-171-290-2900. FAX 44-171-290-2929. *4741*

ROYAL SWISS NAVY GAZETTE.
Royal Swiss Navy, Box 15335, Vancouver, BC V6B 5B1, Canada. TEL 604-321-7962. Available only online. *4535*

RUBBER & PLASTICS NEWS.
Crain Communications Inc. (Akron), 1725 Merriman Rd., Ste. 300, Akron, OH 44313-5251. TEL 330-836-9180. FAX 330-836-1005. URL: http://www.rubbernews.com. Vendor(s): Information Access Co.. *6504*

RUBBER & PLASTICS NEWS II.
Crain Communications Inc. (Akron), 1725 Merriman Rd., Ste. 300, Akron, OH 44313-5251. TEL 330-836-9180. FAX 330-836-1005. URL: http://www.rubbernews.com. Vendor(s): Information Access Co. *6504*

RUBBER TRENDS.
Economist Intelligence Unit, 111 W. 57th St., New York, NY 10019. TEL 212-554-0600. FAX 212-586-1182. URL: http://www.eiu.com. Vendor(s): Information Access Co.. *6504*

RUBBER WORLD.
Lippincott & Peto, Inc., 1867 W. Market St., Akron, OH 44313. TEL 216-864-2122. Vendor(s): Information Access Co. *6504*

RUBBICANA: RUBBER DIRECTORY AND BUYERS GUIDE (YEAR).
Crain Communications Inc. (Akron), 1725 Merriman Rd., Ste. 300, Akron, OH 44313-5251. TEL 330-836-9180. FAX 330-836-1005. URL: http://www.rubbernews.com. *6505*

RUBY'S PEARLS.
9832-1 Sandler Rd., Jacksonville, FL 32222. Available only online. *4535*

RUNNER'S WORLD.
Rodale Press, Inc., 33 E. Minor St., Emmaus, PA 18049. TEL 610-967-5171. FAX 610-967-7725. Vendor(s): Information Access Co., UMI. *6779*

RURAL DEVELOPMENT ABSTRACTS.
CAB International, Wallingford, Oxon. OX10 8DE, England. TEL 44-1491-832111. FAX 44-1491-833508. URL: http://www.cabi.org. Vendor(s): DIMDI, European Space Agency, Knight-Ridder Information, Inc., STN International. *6206*

RURAL DEVELOPMENT PERSPECTIVES.
U.S. Economic Research Service, Department of Agriculture, 1303 New York Ave., N.W., Rm. 208, Washington, DC 20005-4788. TEL 202-219-4060. URL: http://www.econ.ag.gov/epubs/pdf/rdp/rdp.htm. *150*

RURAL LIBRARIES.
Center for the Study of Rural Librarianship, Clarion University of Pennsylvania, Clarion, PA 16214. TEL 814-226-2383. Vendor(s): Knight-Ridder Information, Inc., Wilsonline. *4211*

RURAL TECHNOLOGY GUIDE.
Natural Resources Institute, Central Ave., Chatham Maritime, Kent ME4 4TB, England. TEL 44-1634-880088. FAX 44-1634-880066. URL: http://www.nri.org. *150*

RURAL TELECOMMUNICATIONS.
National Telephone Cooperative Association, 2626 Pennsylvania Ave., N.W., Washington, DC 20037. TEL 202-298-2300. FAX 202-298-2320. Vendor(s): UMI. *2038*

RUSE MAGAZINE.
40 Lucky Dr., Greenbrae, CA 94904. URL: http://www.ruse.com. Available only online. *464*

RUSSIA.
Russian Information Novosti, 4 Zubovsky Blvd., Moscow 116021, Russia. FAX 7-95-2017299. Vendor(s): Information Access Co. *3352*

RUSSIA AND COMMONWEALTH BUSINESS LAW REPORT.
L R P Publications, 747 Dresher Rd., Box 980, Horsham, PA 19044-0980. TEL 215-784-0941. FAX 215-784-9639. URL: http://www.lrp.com. Vendor(s): Lexis-Nexis. *4020*

RUSSIA BRIEFING.
Eastern Europe Newsletter Ltd., 70 Bassein Park Rd., London W12 9RZ, England. TEL 0181-743-2829. FAX 0181-743-8637. *5967*

THE RUSSIA DESK.
Commerce Publishing International, 4001 N. 9th St., Ste. 904, Arlington, VA 22203-1962. TEL 703-524-7750. FAX 703-524-1630. *7078*

RUSSIAN AND EAST EUROPEAN FINANCE AND TRADE.
M.E. Sharpe, Inc., 80 Business Park Dr., Armonk, NY 10504. TEL 914-273-1800. FAX 914-273-2106. Vendor(s): UMI. *1346*

RUSSIAN CHEMICAL REVIEWS.
Turpion - Moscow Ltd., 47 Leninsky prospekt, 117913 Moscow, Russia. TEL 7-95-1356417. FAX 7-95-1358860. URL: http://turpion.ioc.ac.ru *1766*

RUSSIAN DEFENSE BUSINESS DIRECTORY (YEAR).
U.S. Department of Commerce, U.S.-Russia Defense Conversion Subcommittee, 14th St. between Constitution & E Sts., N.W., Washington, DC 20230. TEL 202-482-4695. *1367*

RUSSIAN SOCIAL SCIENCE REVIEW.
M.E. Sharpe, Inc., 80 Business Park Dr., Armonk, NY 10504. TEL 914-273-1800. FAX 914-273-2106. Vendor(s): UMI. *5967*

S A A O NEWSLETTER.
South Africa Astronomical Observatory, P.O. Box 9, Observatory 7935, South Africa. TEL 27-21-470025. FAX 27-21-473639. URL: http://www.saao.ac.za. *500*

S A C NEWSMONTHLY.
S A C, Inc., Box 159, Bogalusa, LA 70429-0159. TEL 504-732-2322. FAX 504-732-3744. *483*

S A E HANDBOOK.
Society of Automotive Engineers, 400 Commonwealth Dr., Warrendale, PA 15096-0001. TEL 412-776-4841. FAX 412-776-3036. Vendor(s): Questel Orbit Inc.. *7115*

S A E TECHNICAL LITERATURE ABSTRACTS.
Society of Automotive Engineers, 400 Commonwealth Dr., Warrendale, PA 15096-0001. TEL 412-776-4841. FAX 412-776-3036. Vendor(s): Questel Orbit Inc. *7056*

S A E TECHNICAL PAPERS.
Society of Automotive Engineers, 400 Commonwealth Dr., Warrendale, PA 15096-0001. TEL 412-776-4841. FAX 412-776-3036. Vendor(s): European Space Agency, FIZ Technik, Questel Orbit Inc. *7115*

S A I S REVIEW.
Johns Hopkins University Press, Journals Publishing Division, 2715 N. Charles St., Baltimore, Washington, MD 21218. TEL 410-516-6980. FAX 410-516-6968. URL: http://muse.jhu.edu. *6035*

S A R AND Q S A R IN ENVIRONMENTAL RESEARCH.
Gordon and Breach - Harwood Academic, Amsteldisk 166, 1st Fl., 1079 LH Amsterdam, Netherlands. URL: http://www.gbhap.com/SAR_QSAR_in_Environmental_Research/. *2950*

S C A D BULLETIN.
Commission of the European Communities, 200 rue de la Loi, B-1049 Brussels, Belgium. Vendor(s): Commission of the European Communities. *4056*

S C A N.
U.S. National Aeronautics and Space Administration, Scientific and Technical Information Office, 800 Elkridge Landing Rd., Linthicum Heights, MD 21090-2934. URL: http://www.sti.nasa.gov. *84*

S E C DOCKET.
U.S. Securities and Exchange Commission, 450 Fifth St., N.W., MISC-11, Washington, DC 20549. TEL 202-272-7460. FAX 202-272-7050. Vendor(s): West Group. *1405*

S E C NEWS DIGEST.
U.S. Securities and Exchange Commission, 450 Fifth St., N.W., MISC-11, Washington, DC 20549. TEL 202-272-7460. FAX 202-272-7050. Vendor(s): Bureau of National Affairs, NewsNet (EV96), West Group. *1405*

S E R EN EL 2000.
Hipolito Yrigoyen 1994, 2do. 4, 1089 Buenos Aires, Argentina. TEL 54-1-9510712. *5284*

S I A M JOURNAL ON APPLIED MATHEMATICS.
Society for Industrial and Applied Mathematics, 3600 University City Science Center, Philadelphia, PA 19104-2688. TEL 215-382-9800. FAX 215-386-7999. URL: http://www.siam.org. *4603*

S I A M JOURNAL ON COMPUTING.
Society for Industrial and Applied Mathematics, 3600 University City Science Center, Philadelphia, PA 19104-2688. TEL 215-382-9800. FAX 215-386-7999. URL: http://www.siam.org. *4624*

S I A M JOURNAL ON CONTROL AND OPTIMIZATION.
Society for Industrial and Applied Mathematics, 3600 University City Science Center, Philadelphia, PA 19104-2688. TEL 215-382-9800. FAX 215-386-7999. URL: http://www.siam.org. *4603*

S I A M JOURNAL ON DISCRETE MATHEMATICS.
Society for Industrial and Applied Mathematics, 3600 University City Science Center, Philadelphia, PA 19104-2688. TEL 215-382-9800. FAX 215-386-7998. URL: http://www.siam.org. *4603*

S I A M JOURNAL ON MATHEMATICAL ANALYSIS.
Society for Industrial and Applied Mathematics, 3600 University City Science Center, Philadelphia, PA 19104-2688. TEL 215-382-9800. FAX 215-386-7999. URL: http://www.siam.org. *4603*

S I A M JOURNAL ON MATRIX ANALYSIS AND APPLICATIONS.
Society for Industrial and Applied Mathematics, 3600 University City Science Center, Philadelphia, PA 19104-2688. TEL 215-382-9800. FAX 215-386-7999. URL: http://www.siam.org. *4603*

S I A M JOURNAL ON NUMERICAL ANALYSIS.
Society for Industrial and Applied Mathematics, 3600 University City Science Center, Philadelphia, PA 19104-2688. TEL 215-382-9800. FAX 215-386-7999. URL: http://www.siam.org. *4603*

S I A M JOURNAL ON OPTIMIZATION.
Society for Industrial and Applied Mathematics, 3600 University City Science Center, Philadelphia, PA 19104-2688. TEL 215-382-9800. FAX 215-386-7999. URL: http://www.siam.org. *4603*

S I A M JOURNAL ON SCIENTIFIC COMPUTING.
Society for Industrial and Applied Mathematics, 3600 University City Science Center, Philadelphia, PA 19104-2688. TEL 215-382-9800. FAX 215-386-7999. URL: http://www.siam.org. *4604*

S I A M REVIEW.
Society for Industrial and Applied Mathematics, 3600 University City Science Center, Philadelphia, PA 19104-2688. TEL 215-382-9800. FAX 215-386-7999. URL: http://www.siam.org. *4604*

S I M NETWORK.
Society for Information Management, 401 N. Michigan Ave., Chicago, IL 60611-4267. TEL 312-644-6610. FAX 312-245-1083. URL: http://www.simnet.org. *2185*

S I R O W NEWSLETTER.
Southwest Institute for Research on Women, c/o Women's Studies, 102 Douglass Bldg., University of Arizona, Tucson, AZ 85721. TEL 521-621-7338. FAX 521-621-1533. URL: http://www./arizona.edu/~sirow. *7347*

S M R COMMODITY CHARTS.
Security Market Research, Box 7476, Boulder, CO 80306-7476. TEL 303-494-8035. FAX 303-494-5474. URL: http://www.smr.com. *1405*

S M R STOCK CHARTS.
Security Market Research, Box 7476, Boulder, CO 80306-7476. TEL 303-494-8035. FAX 303-494-5474. URL: http://www.smr.com. *1405*

S M T TRENDS.
New Insights, 3033 Vallejo St., Crockett, CA 94525. TEL 510-787-2273. Vendor(s): Data-Star, Information Access Co., Knight-Ridder Information, Inc., NewsNet (MG18). *2651*

S O C M A NEWSLETTER.
Synthetic Organic Chemical Manufacturers Association, 1100 New York Ave., Ste. 1090, Washington, DC 20007. TEL 202-414-4100. FAX 202-289-8584. *1766*

S S D A YEDION - NEWSLETTER.
Hebrew University, Faculty of Social Sciences, Mount Scopus, Jerusalem 91905, Israel. TEL 972-2-883007. FAX 972-2-883004. *6634*

S T A R.
U.S. National Aeronautics and Space Administration, Scientific and Technical Information Office, 800 Elkridge Landing Rd., Linthicum Heights, MD 21090-2934. URL: http://www.sti.nasa.gov. Available only online. Vendor(s): European Space Agency, Knight-Ridder Information, Inc. (File no.108). *84*

S T N.
Times Mirror Magazines, Inc., 2 Park Ave., New York, NY 10016. TEL 212-779-5465. Vendor(s): Information Access Co., Knight-Ridder Information, Inc. *6881*

S U R V I A C BULLETIN.
U.S. Department of Defense, Survivability - Vulnerability Information Analysis Center, URL: http://surviac.flight.wpafb.af.mil/curr__awar/surviac__bulletin/bulletins.html. Available only online. *78*

SACRAMENTO BUSINESS JOURNAL.
American City Business Journals, Inc. (Austin), 505 Powell St., Austin, TX 78703-5121. Vendor(s): CompuServe, Inc., Data-Star, Dow Jones News Retrieval, Information Access Co., Knight-Ridder Information, Inc., Lexis-Nexis. *999*

SADO MARINE BIOLOGICAL STATION. REPORT.
Niigata Daigaku, Rigakubu Fuzoku Sado Rinkai Jikkenjo, 2-8050 Igarashi, Niigata 950-21, Japan. TEL 0259-75-2012. FAX 0259-75-2012. *624*

SAFETY AND HEALTH AT WORK.
International Labour Office, International Occupational Safety and Health Information Centre, 4 route des Morillions, CH-1211 Geneva 22, Switzerland. TEL 41-22-799-6111. FAX 41-22-799-8516. URL: http://turva.me.tut.fi/cis/home.html. Vendor(s): European Space Agency (File no.40/CISDOC), IST-INFORMATHEQUE, Inc., Questel Orbit Inc., Telesystemes - Questel. *5503*

SAFETY NET NEWSLETTER.
URL: http://www.eagle.ca/~matink/. Available only online. *1885*

SAILING WORLD.
Sailing Company, Box 3400, Newport, RI 02840-0992. TEL 401-847-1588. FAX 401-848-5048. URL: http://www.sailingworld.com/swdeckpg.htm. *6844*

ST. LOUIS BUSINESS JOURNAL.
St. Louis Business Journal Corp., 1 Metropolitan Sq., Ste. 2170, St. Louis, MO 63102-2733. TEL 314-421-6200. Vendor(s): Knight-Ridder Information, Inc. *999*

ST. LOUIS COMMERCE.
Commerce Magazine, Inc., 1 Metropolitan Sq., Ste. 1300, St. Louis, MO 63102-2733. TEL 314-231-5555. FAX 314-206-3222. Vendor(s): Lexis-Nexis, UMI. *1195*

ST. LOUIS JOURNALISM REVIEW.
Charles L. Klotzer, Ed. & Pub. Emeritus, 470 E. Lockwood, Ste. 414, St. Louis, MO 63119-3914. TEL 314-968-5905. FAX 314-963-6104. Vendor(s): Information Access Co.. *3880*

SAINT LOUIS UNIVERSITY LAW JOURNAL.
Saint Louis University, School of Law, 3700 Lindell Blvd., St. Louis, MO 63108. TEL 314-977-3933. Vendor(s): West Group. *4021*

ST. THOMAS LAW REVIEW.
St. Thomas University, School of Law, 16400 N.W. 32nd Ave., Miami, FL 33054. TEL 305-623-2373. FAX 305-623-2390. Vendor(s): Lexis-Nexis, West Group. *4021*

SALES & MARKETING MANAGEMENT.
Bill Communications, Inc., 355 Park Ave. S., 5th Fl., New York, NY 10010-1789. TEL 212-592-6200. FAX 212-592-6339. URL: http://www.edit.smmmag.com. Vendor(s): Information Access Co., UMI. *1548*

SALES AND MARKETING MANAGEMENT.
I S M Publishing Ltd., Nat West House, 31 Upper George St., Luton, Beds. LU1 2RD, England. TEL 44-1582-483232. FAX 44-1582-483232. Vendor(s): Knight-Ridder Information, Inc., UMI. *1548*

SALES AUTOMATION SUCCESS.
Denali Group, Inc., 2815 N.W. Pine Cone Dr., Ste. 100, Issaquah, WA 98027-8698. TEL 206-392-3514. FAX 206-391-7982. *1548*

SALESDOCTORS MAGAZINE.
SeaBird Associates, Inc., 5455 N. Federal Hwy., Ste. Q, Boca Raton, FL 33487. TEL 561-997-9345. FAX 561-997-9375. URL: http://www.salesdoctors.com. Available only online. *1548*

SALMAGUNDI.
Skidmore College, Saratoga Springs, NY 12866. TEL 518-581-5186. FAX 518-580-5188. Vendor(s): Information Access Co., UMI. *3791*

SALON (SAN FRANCISCO).
Salon Internet Inc., 185 Berry St., Ste. 4811, San Francisco, CA 94107. TEL 415-977-1999. URL: http://www.salonmagazine.com. Available only online. *4358*

SALT E-ZINE.
3204 Cypress Court, Alpharetta, GA 30202. URL: http://www.mindspring.com/'salt. Available only online. *5433*

SALUD PUBLICA DE MEXICO.
Instituto Nacional de Salud Publica, Secretaria de Salud, Av. Universidad, 665, Planta Baja, Col. Santa Maria Ahuacatitlan, 62508 Cuernavaca, Morelos, Mexico. TEL 52-73-110111. FAX 52-73-175745. Vendor(s): DIMDI, Data-Star, Knight-Ridder Information, Inc., Ovid Technologies, Inc. *6250*

SAME-DAY SURGERY.
American Health Consultants, Inc., 3525 Piedmont Rd., N.E., Bldg. 6, Ste. 400, Atlanta, GA 30305. TEL 404-262-7436. FAX 800-284-3291. Vendor(s): Lexis-Nexis. *5152*

SAMIR HUSNI'S GUIDE TO NEW CONSUMER MAGAZINES.
Oxbridge Communications, Inc., 150 5th Ave., Ste. 302, New York, NY 10011. TEL 212-741-0231. FAX 212-633-2938. URL: http://www.mediafinder.com. *6283*

SAN ANTONIO BUSINESS JOURNAL.
American City Business Journals, Inc. (San Antonio), 8200 W. Interstate Hwy. 10, Ste. 300, San Antonio, TX 78230-3877. TEL 512-341-3202. FAX 512-341-3031. Vendor(s): Information Access Co. *999*

SAN DIEGO BUSINESS JOURNAL.
San Diego Business Journal, Inc., 4909 Murphy Canyon Rd., No. 200, San Diego, CA 92123. TEL 619-277-6359. FAX 619-571-3628. Vendor(s): Information Access Co., Knight-Ridder Information, Inc., UMI. *999*

SAN DIEGO DAILY TRANSCRIPT.
Transcript Publishing Co., 2131 Third Ave., San Diego, CA 92101-2095. TEL 619-232-4381. FAX 619-236-8126. Vendor(s): Lexis-Nexis. *4021*

SAN FRANCISCO BUSINESS TIMES.
San Francisco Business Times, 275 Battery St., Ste. 940, San Francisco, CA 94111. TEL 415-989-2522. FAX 415-398-2494. Vendor(s): Information Access Co.. *1216*

SAN FRANCISCO DOWNTOWN.
Gordon Media, 215 Leidesdorff, No. 400, San Francisco, CA 94111. TEL 415-362-6641. FAX 415-362-2254. URL: http://www.sfdowntown.com. *3384*

SANDBOX WEB-ZINE.
Sandbox Open Arts Inc., Box 150098, Brooklyn, NY 11215-0098. URL: http://www.echonyc.com/~sandbox. Available only online. *464*

SANTA CLARA COMPUTER AND HIGH-TECHNOLOGY LAW JOURNAL.
Santa Clara University, School of Law, Santa Clara, CA 95053. TEL 408-554-4197. FAX 408-554-4191. *4021*

SANTA CLARA LAW REVIEW.
Santa Clara University, School of Law, Santa Clara, CA 95053. TEL 408-554-4074. Vendor(s): West Group. *4022*

SARASOTA MAGAZINE.
Clubhouse Publishing, Inc., 601 S. Osprey Ave., Sarasota, FL 34236. TEL 813-366-8225. FAX 813-365-7272. Vendor(s): Information Access Co., Lexis-Nexis. *3385*

10200 SERIALS AVAILABLE ONLINE

SARKO.
D.I.H. Press, P.O. Box 1010, Shatin, N.T., Hong Kong, People's Republic of China. TEL 852-605-7212. FAX 852-605-7238. URL: http://www.sarko.com.hk. *4462*

SARMATIAN REVIEW.
Polish Institute of Arts and Science in Houston, Houston Circle, Box 79119, Houston, TX 77279. TEL 713-467-5836. FAX 713-467-6348. URL: http://www.ruf.rice.edu/'sarmatia. *3040*

SASKATCHEWAN BUSINESS.
Sunrise Publishing Ltd., 2213-C Hanselman Ct., Saskatoon, SK S7L 6A8, Canada. TEL 306-244-5668. FAX 306-244-5679.
Vendor(s): Information Access Co.. *999*

SASKATCHEWAN DECISIONS, CIVIL AND CRIMINAL CASES.
Western Legal Publications, 301-1 Alexander St., Vancouver, BC V6A 1B2, Canada. TEL 604-687-5671. FAX 604-687-2796. *4022*

SASKATCHEWAN REPORTS.
Maritime Law Book Ltd., Box 302, Fredericton, NB E3B 4Y9, Canada. TEL 506-453-9921. FAX 506-453-9525.
Vendor(s): QL Systems Ltd. *4022*

SATELLITE COMMUNICATIONS.
Intertec Publishing Corp. (Atlanta), 6151 Powers Ferry Rd., N.W., Atlanta, GA 30339-2491. TEL 770-955-2500. FAX 770-955-0400.
Vendor(s): Information Access Co., UMI. *2002*

SATELLITE INDUSTRY DIRECTORY.
Phillips Business Information, Inc., 1201 Seven Locks Rd., Potomac, MD 20854. TEL 301-424-3338. FAX 301-309-3847.
Vendor(s): NewsNet (TE83E). *1711*

SATELLITE NEWS.
Phillips Business Information, Inc., 1201 Seven Locks Rd., Potomac, MD 20854. TEL 301-424-3338. FAX 301-309-3847.
Vendor(s): Information Access Co., NewsNet (TE03). *2003*

SATELLITE WEEK.
Warren Publishing, Inc., 2115 Ward Ct., N.W., Washington, DC 20037. TEL 202-872-9200. FAX 202-293-3435.
Vendor(s): Information Access Co., NewsNet (AE01). *2058*

SATURDAY EVENING POST.
Benjamin Franklin Literary & Medical Society, Box 1144, 1100 Waterway Blvd., Indianapolis, IN 46202. TEL 317-636-8881.
Vendor(s): Information Access Co., Knight-Ridder Information, Inc., UMI. *3385*

SATURDAY NIGHT.
Saturday Night, 184 Front St., E., Ste. 400, Toronto, ON M5A 4N3, Canada. TEL 416-368-7237. FAX 416-368-5112. URL: http://www.enews.com.
Vendor(s): Information Access Co., UMI. *3265*

SATYA.
Stealth Technologies, Inc., Prince St. Sta., Box 138, New York, NY 10012. TEL 212-674-0952. FAX 212-598-1856. URL: http://www.montelis.com/satya/ *5482*

SAVANNAH BUSINESS JOURNAL.
Blum Publishing Co., 6203 Abercorn, Ste. 103E, Savannah, GA 31405. TEL 912-354-5553. FAX 912-233-0140.
Vendor(s): UMI. *999*

SAVOURY SNACKS: THE INTERNATIONAL MARKET.
Euromonitor, 60-61 Britton St., London EC1M 5NA, England. TEL 44-171-251-8024. FAX 44-171-608-3149. URL: http://www.euromonitor.com.
Vendor(s): Data-Star, Knight-Ridder Information, Inc. *3126*

SCANDINAVIA NOW ONLINE.
Elfwendahl & Co., Runebergsgatan 6, SE-114 29 Stockholm, Sweden. TEL 46-8-678-32-30. FAX 46-8-611-23-58. URL: http://www.elfco.se/scandnow. Available only online. *1000*

SCANDINAVIAN JOURNAL OF NUTRITION.
Swedish Nutrition Foundation, Ideon, S-223 70 Lund, Sweden. TEL 46-(0)-46-18-22-80. FAX 46-0-46-18-22-81. *5482*

SCANDINAVIAN STUDIES (PROVO).
Society for the Advancement of Scandinavian Study, c/o Steven P. Sondrup, Ed., Department of Comparative Literature, Brigham Young University, Provo, UT 84602-6118. TEL 801-378-2579. FAX 801-378-4649.
Vendor(s): Information Access Co.. *4463*

SCANP.
Helsinki School of Economics, Runeberginkatu 22-24, FIN-00100 Helsinki, Finland.
Vendor(s): Helsinki School of Economics. *1067*

SCHIZOPHRENIA BULLETIN.
U.S. Public Health Service, National Institute of Mental Health, 5600 Fishers Ln., Rockville, MD 20857. TEL 301-443-9772. FAX 301-443-7895. *5097*

DER SCHMERZ (BERLIN).
Springer-Verlag, Heidelberger Platz 3, 14197 Berlin, Germany. TEL 49-30-82787-0. FAX 49-30-82787448. URL: http://link.springer.de. *4743*

SCHOLASTIC CHOICES.
Scholastic Inc., 555 Broadway, New York, NY 10012-3999. TEL 212-343-6100.
Vendor(s): Knight-Ridder Information, Inc.. *1885*

SCHOLASTIC UPDATE.
Scholastic Inc., 555 Broadway, New York, NY 10012-3999. TEL 212-343-6100. URL: http://www.scholastic.com.
Vendor(s): Information Access Co., Knight-Ridder Information, Inc., UMI. *1886*

SCHOOL ARTS.
Davis Publications, Inc. (Worcester), 50 Portland St., Printers Bldg., Worcester, MA 01608. TEL 508-754-7201. FAX 508-753-3834.
Vendor(s): Information Access Co. *2618*

SCHOOL LEADERSHIP & MANAGEMENT.
Carfax Publishing Co., P.O. Box 25, Abingdon, Oxon OX14 3UE, England. TEL 44-1235-401000. FAX 44-1235-401550. *2578*

SCHOOL NEWS.
1809 Greer Court, Regina, SK S4N 1T7, Canada. URL: http://www.dlcwest.com/~wmp/ Available only online. *2480*

SCHOOL PLANNING AND MANAGEMENT.
Peter Li, Inc., 330 Progress Rd., Dayton OH 45449. TEL 573-847-5900. FAX 513-847-5910.
Vendor(s): Information Access Co., Knight-Ridder Information, Inc. *2480*

SCHRIFTTUMS FUER DEN BEREICH HAUSHALT UND VERBAUCH. BIBLIOGRAPHIE.
Bundesforschungsanstalt fuer Ernaehrung, Institut fuer Ernaehrungsoekonomie und -soziologie, Garbenstr. 13, 70599 Stuttgart, Germany. TEL 0711-455063. FAX 0711-4569355.
Vendor(s): DIMDI. *3688*

SCHWEIZERISCHE ZEITSCHRIFT FUER VOLKSWIRTSCHAFT UND STATISTIK.
Helbing und Lichtenhahn Verlag AG, Freie Str. 84, CH-4051 Basel, Switzerland. TEL 41-61-2721116. FAX 41-61-2721150.
Vendor(s): Knight-Ridder Information, Inc. *1000*

SCI.OPINION.
URL: http://humanism.org/opinions/welcom.html. Available only online. *6566*

SCI FI WEB ZINE.
Dragon Ware Internet Solutions, 21 Third St., N., Great Fall, MT 59401. URL: http://www.sci-fi-mag.com.
Available only online. *4536*

SCIENCE.
American Association for the Advancement of Science, 1200 New York Ave., N.W., Washington, DC 20005. TEL 202-326-6417. URL: http://www.sciencemag.org.
Vendor(s): Information Access Co., Ovid Technologies, Inc. (SCIE), UMI. *6566*

SCIENCE AND JUSTICE.
Forensic Science Society, 18A Mount Parade, Harrogate, N. Yorks. HG1 1BX, England. TEL 44-1423-506068. FAX 44-1423-566391. URL: http://www.demon.co.uk/forensic/jnltop.html. *4906*

SCIENCE & SOCIETY.
Guilford Publications, Inc., 72 Spring St., 4th Fl., New York, NY 10012. TEL 212-431-9800. FAX 212-966-6708.
Vendor(s): UMI. *5968*

SCIENCE & TECHNOLOGY REVIEW.
Lawrence Livermore National Laboratory, c/o National Technical Information Service, 5285 Port Royal Rd., Springfield, VA 22161. URL: http://www.llnl.gov/str.html. *6567*

SCIENCE CITATION INDEX.
Institute for Scientific Information, 3501 Market St., Philadelphia, PA 19104. TEL 215-386-0100. FAX 215-386-2911.
Vendor(s): DIMDI, Data-Star, Knight-Ridder Information, Inc. (Files nos.34,432,433,434/SCISEARCH), Questel Orbit Inc.. *6592*

SCIENCE FOR DEMOCRATIC ACTION.
Institute for Energy and Environmental Research, 6935 Laurel Ave., Takoma Park, MD 20912. TEL 301-270-5500. FAX 301-270-3029. URL: http://www.ieer.org. *2951*

SCIENCE FRONTIERS.
Sourcebook Project, Box 107, Glen Arm, MD 21057. TEL 410-668-6047. URL: http://www.knowledge.co.uk/xxx/cat/sourcebook. *6568*

SCIENCE NEWS.
Science Service, 1719 N St., N.W., Washington, DC 20036. TEL 800-552-4412. FAX 202-659-0365. URL: http://www.sciencenews.org/
Vendor(s): Information Access Co., UMI. *6569*

SCIENCE WORLD.
Scholastic Inc., 555 Broadway, New York, NY 10012-3999. TEL 212-343-6100.
Vendor(s): Information Access Co. *6570*

THE SCIENCES.
New York Academy of Sciences, 2 E. 63rd St., New York, NY 10021.
Vendor(s): Information Access Co., UMI. *6570*

SCIENCES OF SOIL.
Kurfurstenstr. 13, 54295 Trier, Germany. TEL 49-651-47163. FAX 49-651-47163. URL: http://hintze-online.com/sos/.
Available only online. *243*

SCIENTIA PHARMACEUTICA.
Oesterreichische Apotheker-Verlagsgesellschaft mbH, Spitalgasse 31, A-1094 Vienna, Austria. TEL 43-1-4023588. FAX 43-1-4085355. *5693*

SCIENTIFIC AMERICAN.
Scientific American, Inc., 415 Madison Ave., New York, NY 10017-1111. TEL 212-754-0550. FAX 212-754-1138.
Vendor(s): Information Access Co., Ovid Technologies, Inc. (SAMM). *6570*

SCIENTIFIC AMERICAN MEDICINE.
Scientific American, Inc., 415 Madison Ave., New York, NY 10017-1111. TEL 212-754-0550. FAX 212-754-1138.
Vendor(s): Ovid Technologies, Inc. (SAMM). *4743*

SCIENTIFIC COMPUTING WORLD.
I O P Publishing Ltd., Dirac House, Temple Back, Bristol BS1 6BE, England. TEL 44-117-929-7481. FAX 44-117-927-4318. URL: http://www.iop.org. *2090*

SCIENTIFIC DIVING NEWS.
Australian Scientific Divers Association, P.O. Box 361, Castletown, Townsville, Qld. 4810, Australia. TEL 61-77-724452. FAX 61-77-213538. URL: http://www.ozemail.com.au/'edrew/news.htm. *2414*

SCIENTIFIC SERIALS IN THAI LIBRARIES.
Thailand Institute of Scientific and Technological Research, 196 Phahonyothin Rd., Chatuchak, Bangkok 10900, Thailand. TEL 579-8594. FAX 662-579-8594. *6592*

THE SCIENTIST.
The Scientist, Inc., 3600 Market St., Philadelphia, PA 19104-2645. TEL 215-386-9601. FAX 215-387-7542. URL: http://www.the-scientist.library.upen.edu.
Vendor(s): CompuServe, Inc. (71764.2561). *6571*

SCITECH BOOK NEWS.
Book News, Inc. (Portland), 5739 N.E. Sumner St., Portland, OR 97218. TEL 503-281-9230. FAX 503-287-4485. URL: http://www.books.com/booknews. *562*

SCOUTING.
Scout Association, Baden-Powell House, Queen's Gate, London SW7 5JS, England. TEL 44-171-584-7030613scoutingmag@enterprise.net. FAX 44-171-590-5124. URL: http://www.enterprise.net/scoutingmagazine/.
Vendor(s): Knight-Ridder Information, Inc. *1886*

SCRAWL.
URL: http://www.thescrawl.com.
Available only online. *3385*

SCREAMING IN DIGITAL.
1692, Burlington, NJ 08016-7292. URL: http://www.scream.org/.
Available only online. *5434*

SCREEN DIGEST.
Screen Digest Ltd., 37 Gower St., London WC1E 6HH, England. TEL 44-171-580-2842. FAX 44-171-580-0060.
Vendor(s): CompuServe, Inc., Data-Star, Information Access Co.. *2058*

SCREEN FINANCE.
Financial Times Telecoms & Media Publishing, Maple House, 149 Tottenham Court Rd., London W1P 9LL, England. TEL 44-171-896-2234. FAX 44-171-896-2256.
Vendor(s): Information Access Co., Lexis-Nexis. *5344*

THE SCRIBE.
University of Bridgeport, Student Center, 244 University Ave., Bridgeport, CT 06601. TEL 203-576-4382. FAX 203-576-4485. *1970*

SCRIBES JOURNAL OF LEGAL WRITING.
American Society of Writers on Legal Subjects, Wake Forest University, School of Law, Box 7206, Winston-Salem, NC 27109. TEL 910-759-5440. FAX 910-759-4301. *4023*

SCRIP - WORLD PHARMACEUTICAL NEWS.
P J B Publications Ltd., 18-20 Hill Rise, Richmond, Surrey TW10 6UA, England. TEL 44-181-948-3262. FAX 44-181-332-8998. URL: http://pjbpubs.co.uk/scrip/scrhome.html.
Vendor(s): Data-Star (PHIN), Knight-Ridder Information, Inc. (File No. 129), Ovid Technologies, Inc. (PHIN,PHIC,PHID). *5694*

SCRIPTA INSTITUTI DONNERIANI ABOENSIS.
Donner Institute for Research in Religious and Cultural History, Steiner Memorial Library, P.O. Box 70, FIN-20501 Aabo-Turku, Finland. TEL 358-2-2654315. FAX 358-2-2311290. URL: http://www.abo.fi/instut/di/donner.htm. *6370*

SCRIPTURE STUDIES.
Scripture Studies Inc., 20 Pastora, Foothill Ranch, CA 92610. URL: http://www.kaiwan.com/~sstys.html. *6371*

SCROLL OF PHI DELTA THETA.
Phi Delta Theta Fraternity, 2 So. Campus, Oxford, OH 45056. TEL 513-523-6345. FAX 513-523-9200. URL: http://www.phidelt-ghq.com. *1970*

SCROLLS OF SERENIA.
6 Glen Court, Monmouth Jct., NJ 08852. URL: http://www.superlink.net/~cbowers; http://www.alfheim.net/@scrolls.
Available only online. *4536*

SEAFOOD PRICE-CURRENT.
Urner Barry Publications, Inc., Box 389, Toms River, NJ 08754. TEL 908-240-5330. FAX 908-341-0891. URL: http://www.urnerbarry.com. *3078*

SEARCHABLE PHYSICS INFORMATION NOTICES.
American Institute of Physics, One Physics Ellipse, College Park, MD 20740-3843. TEL 301-209-3000.
Vendor(s): Knight-Ridder Information, Inc. (File no.62/SPIN). *5837*

SEARCHING DIALOG: THE COMPLETE GUIDE.
Dialog Information Services, Inc. (Palo Alto), 3460 Hillview Ave., Palo Alto, CA 94304. TEL 415-858-3785. FAX 415-858-7069. *4213*

SEATTLE UNIVERSITY LAW REVIEW.
Seattle University, School of Law, 950 Broadway Plaza, Tacoma, WA 98402. TEL 206-591-2995. FAX 206-591-6313.
Vendor(s): Lexis-Nexis, West Group. *4023*

SECURED LENDER.
Commercial Finance Association, 225 W. 34th St., Rm. 1815, New York, NY 10122-0008. TEL 212-594-3480.
Vendor(s): UMI. *1166*

SECURITE ET SANTE AU TRAVAIL.
International Labour Office, International Occupational Safety and Health Information Centre, 4 route des Morillons, CH-1211 Geneva, Switzerland. TEL 41-22-799-6111. FAX 41-22-799-8516. URL: http://turva.me.tut.fi/cis/home.html.
Vendor(s): European Space Agency, IST-INFORMATHEQUE, Inc., Questel Orbit Inc., Telesystemes - Questel. *5503*

SECURITIES EXCHANGE OF THAILAND. HANDBOOK.
Securities Exchange of Thailand, Sinthom Bldg., 2nd Fl., 132 Wireless Rd., Bangkok 10500, Thailand. *1406*

SECURITIES REGULATION & LAW REPORT.
The Bureau of National Affairs, Inc., 1231 25th St., N.W., Washington, DC 20037. TEL 202-452-4200. FAX 202-822-8092. URL: http://www.bna.com/
Vendor(s): Bureau of National Affairs, Lexis-Nexis (SECREG), West Group (BNA-SRLR). *4023*

SECURITIES WEEK.
McGraw-Hill Companies, 1221 Ave. of the Americas, New York, NY 10020. TEL 212-512-4214.
Vendor(s): Dow Jones News Retrieval (SW), Knight-Ridder Information, Inc. (File no.624/McGRAW-HILL PUBLICATIONS ONLINE), Lexis-Nexis (SECWK), NewsNet (FI27). *1406*

SECURITY INTELLIGENCE.
Interests, Ltd., 8512 Cedar St., Silver Spring, MD 20910-4322. TEL 301-588-7916. FAX 301-588-2085.
Vendor(s): NewsNet (IT64). *5968*

SECURITY MANAGEMENT.
American Society for Industrial Security, 1655 N. Fort Myer Dr., Ste. 1200, Arlington, VA 22209-3198. TEL 703-522-5800. FAX 703-522-5226.
Vendor(s): Information Access Co., UMI. *1506*

SEE FLORIDA MAGAZINES.
Miles Media Group, Inc., 3675 Clark Rd., Sarasota, FL 34233-2358. TEL 941-922-3575. FAX 941-923-6309. *7233*

SEED ABSTRACTS.
CAB International, Wallingford, Oxon. OX10 8DE, England. TEL 44-1491-832111. FAX 44-1491-826090. URL: http://www.cabi.org.
Vendor(s): DIMDI, European Space Agency, Knight-Ridder Information, Inc., STN International. *182*

SEED PATHOLOGY AND MICROBIOLOGY.
CAB International, Wallingford, Oxon. OX10 8DE, England. TEL 44-1491-832111. FAX 44-1491-826090. URL: http://www.cabi.org. *182*

SEIBT INDUSTRIEKATALOG.
Seibt Verlag GmbH, Leopoldstr. 208, 80804 Munich, Germany. TEL 49-89-360903-0. FAX 49-89-364317. URL: http://www.seibt.com.
Vendor(s): GBI. *1711*

SEIBT MEDIZINISCHE TECHNIK.
Seibt Verlag GmbH, Leopoldstr. 208, 80804 Munich, Germany. TEL 49-89-360903-0. FAX 49-89-364317. URL: http://www.seibt.com.
Vendor(s): GBI. *4744*

SEIBT OBERFLAECHENTECHNIK.
Seibt Verlag GmbH, Leopoldstr. 208, 80804 Munich, Germany. TEL 49-89-360903-0. FAX 49-89-364317. URL: http://www.seibt.com.
Vendor(s): GBI. *5848*

SEIBT UMWELT TECHNIK.
Seibt Verlag GmbH, Leopoldstr. 208, 80804 Munich, Germany. TEL 49-89-360903-0. FAX 49-89-364317. URL: http://www.seibt.com. *2951*

SEICHO.
Aichi-Gakuin University, Department of Anatomy, 1-100 Kusumoto-cho, Chikusaku-ku, Nagoya 464, Japan. TEL 052-751-2561. FAX 052-752-5988.
Vendor(s): JICST. *625*

SEIDMAN'S ONLINE INSIDER.
C M P Media Inc., 1 Landmark Sq., Ste. 220, Port Chester, NY 10573. URL: http://www.clark.net/pub/robert.
Available only online. *2140*

SEISHIN IGAKU.
Igaku-Shoin Ltd., 5-24-3 Hongo, Bunkyo-ku, Tokyo 113-91, Japan. TEL 81-3-3817-5711. FAX 81-3-3815-7802.
Vendor(s): JICST. *5097*

SELECTA MATHEMATICA.
Birkhaeuser Verlag, P.O. Box 133, CH-4010 Basel, Switzerland. TEL 41-61-2050730. FAX 41-61-2050791. *4605*

SELF-HELP AND PSYCHOLOGY MAGAZINE.
106 Thorn St., San Diego, CA 92103. URL: http://cybertowers.com/selfhelp.
Available only online. *6686*

SEMICONDUCTOR INDUSTRY & BUSINESS SURVEY NEWSLETTER.
H T E Research, Inc., 400 Oyster Point Blvd., Ste. 220, S. San Francisco, CA 94080. TEL 415-871-4377. FAX 415-871-0513.
Vendor(s): Information Access Co., NewsNet (EC35). *2651*

SEMICONDUCTOR SCIENCE AND TECHNOLOGY.
I O P Publishing Ltd., Dirac House, Temple Back, Bristol BS1 6BE, England. TEL 44-117-929-7481. FAX 44-117-929-4318. URL: http://www.iop.org. *2651*

SEMICONDUCTORS.
American Institute of Physics, One Physics Ellipse, College Park, MD 20740-3843. TEL 301-209-3000. URL: http://www.aip.org. *5826*

SEMIGROUP FORUM.
Springer-Verlag, Science Journals, 175 Fifth Ave., New York, NY 10010. TEL 212-460-1500. FAX 212-473-6272. URL: http://www.springer-ny.com. *4605*

SEMINARS IN ANESTHESIA.
W.B. Saunders Co., Curtis Center, 3rd Fl., Independence Sq. W., Philadelphia, PA 19106-3399. TEL 215-238-7800. FAX 215-238-6445. *4807*

SEMINARS IN CANCER BIOLOGY.
Academic Press Ltd., 24-28 Oval Rd., London NW1 7DX, England. TEL 44-171-267-4466. FAX 44-171-482-2293. URL: http://www.hbuk.co.uk/ap/cancerbio; http://www.europe.idealibrary.com/. *4987*

SEMINARS IN CELL AND DEVELOPMENTAL BIOLOGY.
Academic Press Ltd., 24-28 Oval Rd., London NW1 7DX, England. TEL 44-171-267-4466. FAX 44-171-482-2293. URL: http://www.hbuk.co.uk/ap/semcell/; http://www.europe.idealibrary.com/. *744*

SEMINARS IN CUTANEOUS MEDICINE & SURGERY.
W.B. Saunders Co., Curtis Center, 3rd Fl., Independence Sq. W., Philadelphia, PA 19106-3399. TEL 215-238-7800. FAX 215-238-6445. *4881*

SEMINARS IN DIAGNOSTIC PATHOLOGY.
W.B. Saunders Co., Curtis Center, 3rd Fl., Independence Sq. W., Philadelphia, PA 19106-3399. TEL 215-238-7800. FAX 215-238-6445. *4744*

SEMINARS IN HEMATOLOGY.
W.B. Saunders Co., Curtis Center, 3rd Fl., Independence Sq. W., Philadelphia, PA 19106-3399. TEL 215-238-7800. FAX 215-238-6445. Vendor(s): Lexis-Nexis. *4921*

SEMINARS IN IMMUNOLOGY.
Academic Press Ltd., 24-28 Oval Rd., London NW1 7DX, England. TEL 44-171-267-4466. FAX 44-171-482-2293. URL: http://www.hbuk.co.uk/ap/semimm; http://www.europe.idealibrary.com/. *4801*

SEMINARS IN NEPHROLOGY.
W.B. Saunders Co., Curtis Center, 3rd Fl., Independence Sq. W., Philadelphia, PA 19106-3399. TEL 215-238-7800. FAX 215-238-6445. *5165*

SEMINARS IN NEUROLOGY.
Thieme, 381 Park Ave. S., Ste. 1501, New York, NY 10016. TEL 212-683-5088. FAX 212-779-9020.
Vendor(s): Ovid Technologies, Inc. *5098*

SEMINARS IN RESPIRATORY AND CRITICAL CARE MEDICINE.
Thieme, 381 Park Ave. S., Ste. 1501, New York, NY 10016. TEL 212-683-5088. FAX 212-779-9020.
Vendor(s): Ovid Technologies, Inc. *5123*

SEMINARS IN ROENTGENOLOGY.
W.B. Saunders Co., Curtis Center, 3rd Fl., Independence Sq. W., Philadelphia, PA 19106-3399. TEL 215-238-7800. FAX 215-238-6445. *5115*

SEMINARS IN THE NEUROSCIENCES.
Academic Press, Inc., Journal Division, 525 B St., Ste. 1900, San Diego, CA 92101-4495. TEL 619-699-6800. FAX 619-230-1840. URL: http://www.hbuk.co.uk/ap/journals/sn.htm; http://www.idealibrary.com/ *5098*

SEMINARS IN ULTRASOUND, C T AND M R.
W.B. Saunders Co., Curtis Center, 3rd Fl., Independence Sq. W., Philadelphia, PA 19106-3399. TEL 215-238-7800. FAX 215-238-6445. *5115*

SEMINARS IN VIROLOGY.
Academic Press, Inc., Journal Division, 525 B ST., Ste. 1900, San Diego, CA 92101-4495. TEL 619-230-1840. FAX 619-699-6800. URL: http://www.hbuk.co.uk/ap/journals/vi.htm; http://www.idealibrary.com/ *794*

SENSOR BUSINESS DIGEST.
Vital Information Publications, 754 Caravel Ln., Foster City, CA 94404. TEL 415-345-7018. FAX 415-345-7018.
Vendor(s): Data-Star, Information Access Co., Knight-Ridder Information, Inc., NewsNet (MG16). *1549*

SENSOR REVIEW.
M C B University Press Ltd., 60-62 Toller Ln., Bradford, W. Yorks BD8 9BY, England. TEL 44-1274-777700. FAX 44-1274-785200. URL: http://www.mcb.co.uk.
Vendor(s): Data-Star, Knight-Ridder Information, Inc. *4552*

A SERIOUS BUSINESS.
Gabriel Publishing Company, 1469 Rosena Ave., Madison, OH 44057. TEL 216-428-6163. FAX 216-428-5509. URL: http://earthone.com.
Available only online. *1646*

SERVICE COMMUNICATIONS.
M2 Communications Ltd., P.O. Box 475, Coventry CV1 2ZW, England. TEL 44-1203-634700. FAX 44-1203-634144. URL: http://www.m2.com. *2003*

THE SERVICE INDUSTRIES JOURNAL.
Frank Cass, Newbury House, 890-900 Eastern Ave., Newbury Park, Ilford, Essex IG2 7HH, England. TEL 44-181-599-8866. FAX 44-181-599-0984. URL: http://www.frankcass.com.
Vendor(s): UMI. *1000*

SERVICE STATIONS: THE INTERNATIONAL MARKET.
Euromonitor, 60-61 Britton St., London EC1M 5NA, England. TEL 44-171-251-8024. FAX 44-171-608-3149. URL: http://www.euromonitor.com.
Vendor(s): Data-Star, Knight-Ridder Information, Inc. *7116*

SERVICE TECHNICIAN.
G.I.E., Inc Publishers, 4012 Bridge Ave., Cleveland, OH 44113. TEL 216-961-4130. FAX 216-961-0364. *2774*

SET-ASIDE ALERT.
Pasha Publications Inc., 1616 N. Ft. Myer Dr., Ste. 1000, Arlington, VA 22209-3107. TEL 703-528-1244. FAX 703-528-1253. *6193*

SETON HALL LEGISLATIVE JOURNAL.
Seton Hall University, Seton Hall Legislative Bureau, Newark, NJ 07102. TEL 201-642-8261. FAX 201-642-8734.
Vendor(s): West Group. *4024*

SETTOP & SERVER BULLETIN.
TechMedia, 52 Foundling Ct., London WC1N 1AN, England. TEL 44-171-837-0815. FAX 44-171-278-9917. *2058*

SEVENTEEN.
K-III Communications Corp., 745 Fifth Ave., New York, NY 10151. TEL 212-745-0100.
Vendor(s): Information Access Co. *7333*

SEWANEE REVIEW.
University of the South, Sewanee Review, Sewanee, TN 37383-1000. TEL 615-598-1246. FAX 615-598-1145. URL: http://www.sewanee.edu/sreview/home.html. *4464*

SEX ROLES.
Plenum Publishing Corp., 233 Spring St., New York, NY 10013-1578. TEL 212-620-8000. FAX 212-463-0742.
Vendor(s): Information Access Co. *6153*

SEX WEEKLY PLUS.
Charles W. Henderson, Ed. & Pub., Box 5528, Atlanta, GA 31107-0528. TEL 404-377-8895. FAX 404-378-4511. URL: http://www.newsfile.com. *4744*

SEXUAL PLANT REPRODUCTION.
Springer-Verlag, Heidelberger Platz 3, 14197 Berlin, Germany. TEL 49-30-82787-0. FAX 49-30-82787448. URL: http://link.springer.de. *727*

SEXUALLY TRANSMITTED DISEASES.
Lippincott - Raven Publishers, 227 E. Washington Sq., Philadelphia, PA 19106. TEL 215-238-4200. FAX 215-238-4227. URL: http://www.lrpub.com.
Vendor(s): Lexis-Nexis, Ovid Technologies, Inc.. *4881*

SEXUALLY TRANSMITTED INFECTIONS.
B M J Publishing Group, B.M.A. House, Tavistock Sq., London WC1H 9JR, England. TEL 44-171-383-6270. FAX 44-171-383-6402.
Vendor(s): Ovid Technologies, Inc., UMI. *4881*

SEYBOLD REPORT ON DESKTOP PUBLISHING.
Seybold Publications, 428 E. Baltimore Ave., Box 644, Media, PA 19063. TEL 610-565-2480. FAX 610-565-1858.
Vendor(s): Information Access Co. *2192*

SEYBOLD REPORT ON PUBLISHING SYSTEMS.
Seybold Publications, 428 E. Baltimore Ave., Box 644, Media, PA 19063. TEL 610-565-2480. FAX 610-656-1858.
Vendor(s): Information Access Co.. *6293*

SHAKESPEARE QUARTERLY.
Folger Shakespeare Library, 201 E. Capitol St., S.E., Washington, DC 20003-1094. TEL 202-675-0351. FAX 202-544-4623.
Vendor(s): UMI. *4465*

SHALOM.
Society for Transfer of Technology, P.O. Box 13006, Jerusalem 91130, Israel. TEL 972-2-6524383. FAX 972-2-6512636. URL: http://www.israel-mfa.gov.il. *1368*

SHARE GUIDE.
11540 Los Amigos Rd., Healdsburg, CA 95448. TEL 707-433-4044. FAX 707-433-1073. URL: http://www.shareguide.com. *298*

SHARE INTERNATIONAL.
Share International Foundation, U.S. Office, Box 971, North Hollywood, CA 91603. TEL 818-785-6300. FAX 818-994-0383. URL: http://www.shareintl.org. *5460*

SHAREPAPER.
URL: http://www.sharepaper.com.
Available only online. *2217*

SHARK NEWS.
Nature Conservation Bureau Ltd., 36 Kingfisher Ct., Hambridge Rd., Newbury, Berks. RG14 5SJ, England. TEL 44-1635-550380. FAX 44-1635-550230. *849*

SHEFFIELD ELECTRONIC PRESS.
URL: http://www.shef.ac.uk/~shep/.
Available only online. *5434*

SHIYOU HUAGONG.
Ministry of Chemical Industry, Beijing Research Institute of Chemical Industry, P.O. Box 1442, Hepingli, Beijing, People's Republic of China. TEL 86-10-6429-5032. FAX 86-10-6429-5032. *5622*

THE SHOCK AND VIBRATION DIGEST.
Vibration Institute, 6262 S. Kingery Hwy., Ste. 212, Willowbrook, IL 60514. TEL 708-654-2254. FAX 708-654-2271. *2869*

SHOCK WAVES.
Springer-Verlag, Heidelberger Platz 3, 14197 Berlin, Germany. TEL 49-30-82787-0. FAX 49-30-82787448. URL: http://link.springer.de. *5848*

SHOESTRING TRAVEL E-ZINE.
Strategic Publications, 2784 Heatherwood Court, Clearwater, FL 34621. URL: http://www.statpub.com.
Available only online. *7234*

SHONIKA.
Kanehara & Co., Ltd., 31-14 Yushima 2-chome, Bunkyo-ku, Tokyo 113, Japan.
Vendor(s): Ovid Technologies, Inc. *5040*

SHOOT.
B P I Communications, Inc. (New York), 1515 Broadway, New York, NY 10036. TEL 212-764-7300. FAX 212-536-5321.
Vendor(s): Information Access Co. *45*

SHOOTING INDUSTRY.
Publishers' Development Corp., 591 Camino de la Reina, Ste. 200, San Diego, CA 92108. TEL 619-297-5350. FAX 619-297-5353.
Vendor(s): Information Access Co. *6781*

SHOPPER REPORT.
Consumer Network, Inc, 3624 Market St., Philadelphia, PA 19104. TEL 215-561-2921. FAX 215-557-7692.
Vendor(s): Data-Star, Information Access Co., Knight-Ridder Information, Inc. *1549*

SHOPPING CENTER WORLD.
Intertec Publishing Corp. (Atlanta), 6151 Powers Ferry Rd., N.W., Atlanta, GA 30339-2941. TEL 770-955-2500. FAX 770-955-0400.
Vendor(s): Information Access Co. *1550*

SHORE JOURNAL.
1520 S. Salisbury Blvd., Salisbury, MD 21801. URL: http://www.shorejournal.com.
Available only online. *7234*

SICKNESS AND WELLNESS PUBLICATIONS.
John Gordon Burke Publisher, Inc., Box 1492, Evanston, IL 60204-1492. TEL 847-866-8625. URL: http://www.nlightn.com. *4788*

SIDE EFFECTS OF DRUGS ANNUAL.
Elsevier Science B.V., Books Division, P.O. Box 211, 1000 AE Amsterdam, Netherlands. TEL 31-20-4853911. FAX 31-20-4853705. URL: http://www.elsevier.nl/.
Vendor(s): Data-Star (SEDB), Knight-Ridder Information, Inc. (File no.70/SEDBASE), Ovid Technologies, Inc. *5694*

SIERRA.
Sierra Club, 85 Second St., San Francisco, CA 94105-3441. TEL 415-977-5500. FAX 415-977-5794. URL: http://www.sierraclub.org.
Vendor(s): Information Access Co., UMI. *2244*

SIGLO XXI CIENCIA AND TECNOLOGIA.
El Mercurio S.A.P., Av. Santa Maria 5542, Apdo. Postal 13 D, Las Condes, Chile. TEL 562-3301461. FAX 562-2421128. URL: http://www.mercurio.cl/revistas/index.html. *6573*

SILENCER.
21 Malcolm Court, Malcolm Crescent, London NW4 4PJ, England. URL: http://www.sonnet.co.uk/silencer/.
Available only online. *5435*

SIMMONS STUDY OF MEDIA & MARKETS (YEAR).
Simmons Market Research Bureau, Inc., 309 W. 49th St., New York, NY 10019. TEL 212-373-8900. FAX 212-373-8918. *2013*

SIMPLE COOKING.
Box 8, Steuben, ME 04680-0008. *3127*

SINCERE SINGLES.
Adriennne Schiff, Ed. & Pub., 512 Glendale Circle, Ann Arbor, MI 48103-4177. *6598*

SINGLE SCENE - ARIZONA.
Box 10159, Scottsdale, AZ 85271. TEL 602-945-6746. FAX 602-945-3766. *6599*

SINGLE SCOOP CELEBRITY NEWS.
GlobalComm 2000 Corp., 760 Skipper Dr. N.W., Atlanta, GA 30318-5922. TEL 404-222-9881. FAX 404-586-9444. URL: http://www.singlestv.com/singscop.htm. *6599*

THE SINGMON PAGES.
URL: http://www.crl.com/˜wbjw/index.htm.
Available only online. *4523*

SITUATION & OUTLOOK REPORT. AGRICULTURAL EXPORTS.
U.S. Department of Agriculture, Economic Research Service, c/o Debbie Haugan, Rm. 110, 1301 New York Ave., N.W., Washington, DC 20005. TEL 202-219-0515. URL: http://www.mannlib.cornell.edu/reports/erssrod/trade/aes-bb/
Vendor(s): Information Access Co. *201*

SITUATION & OUTLOOK REPORT. AGRICULTURAL INCOME & FINANCE.
U.S. Department of Agriculture, Economic Research Service, c/o Debbie Haugan, Rm. 110, 1301 New York Ave., N.W., Washington, DC 20005-4788. TEL 202-219-0515.
Vendor(s): Knight-Ridder Information, Inc. *201*

SITUATION & OUTLOOK REPORT. FRUIT & TREE NUTS.
U.S. Department of Agriculture, Economic Research Service, c/o Debbie Haugan, Rm. 110, 1301 New York Ave., N.W., DC 20005-4788. TEL 202-219-0515.
Vendor(s): Information Access Co., Knight-Ridder Information, Inc. *244*

SITUATION & OUTLOOK REPORT. SUGAR & SWEETENER.
U.S. Department of Agriculture, Economic Research Service, c/o Debbie Haugan, Rm. 110, 1301 New York Ave., N.W., Washington, DC 20005-4788. TEL 202-219-0515. URL: http://usda.mannlib.cornell.edu/reports/erssor/specialty/sss-bb/
Vendor(s): Information Access Co., Knight-Ridder Information, Inc. *202*

SITUATION & OUTLOOK REPORT. TOBACCO.
U.S. Department of Agriculture, Economic Research Service, c/o Debbie Haugan, Rm. 110, 1301 New York Ave., N.W., DC 20005-4789. TEL 202-219-4060.
Vendor(s): Information Access Co., Knight-Ridder Information, Inc. *202*

SITUATION & OUTLOOK REPORT. VEGETABLES & SPECIALTIES.
U.S. Department of Agriculture, Economic Research Service, c/o Debbie Haugan, Rm. 110, 1301 New York Ave., N.W., Washington, DC 20005-4788. TEL 202-219-0515.
Vendor(s): Information Access Co., Knight-Ridder Information, Inc. *202*

SKELETAL RADIOLOGY.
Springer-Verlag, Heidelberger Platz 3, 14197 Berlin, Germany. TEL 49-30-82787-0. FAX 49-30-82787448. URL: http://link.springer.de. *5115*

SKEPTICAL INQUIRER.
Committee for the Scientific Investigation of Claims of the Paranormal, Box 703, Buffalo, NY 14226-0703. TEL 716-636-1425. FAX 716-636-1733.
Vendor(s): Information Access Co. *5578*

SKIING.
Times Mirror Magazines, Inc., 2 Park Ave., New York, NY 10016. TEL 212-779-5000.
Vendor(s): Information Access Co., UMI. *6882*

SKIN CARE: THE INTERNATIONAL MARKET.
Euromonitor, 60-61 Britton St., London EC1M 5NA, England. TEL 44-171-251-8024. FAX 44-171-608-3149. URL: http://www.euromonitor.com.
Vendor(s): Data-Star, Knight-Ridder Information, Inc.. *508*

SKIN DIVER MAGAZINE.
Petersen Publishing Co., 6420 Wilshire Blvd., Los Angeles, CA 90048. TEL 213-782-2000.
Vendor(s): Information Access Co., Knight-Ridder Information, Inc. *6782*

SKY & TELESCOPE.
Sky Publishing Corp., 49 Bay State Rd., Cambridge, MA 02138. TEL 617-864-7360. FAX 617-864-6117. URL: http://www.skypub.com/s_t/s_t.shtlm.
Vendor(s): Information Access Co., UMI. *501*

SKYWINGS.
British Hang Gliding and Paragliding Association Ltd., Old Schoolroom, Loughborough Rd., Leicester LE4 5PJ, England. TEL 44-114-267-9227. URL: http://www.bhpa.co.uk/bhpa. *6883*

SLATE.
Microsoft Corp., 1 Microsoft Way, Redmond, WA 98052. TEL 206-882-8080. URL: http://www.slate.com/. *4359*

THE SLAVE RIVER JOURNAL.
P.O. Box 990, Fort Smith, NT X0E 0P0, Canada. TEL 403-872-2784. FAX 403-872-2754. URL: http://www.auroranet.nt.ca/srj. *3266*

SLOAN MANAGEMENT REVIEW.
Massachusetts Institute of Technology, Sloan School of Management, 77 Massachussetts Ave., E53-416, Cambridge, MA 02139. TEL 617-253-7170. FAX 617-258-9739. URL: http://web.mit.edu/smr-online/
Vendor(s): UMI. *1507*

SLUDGE NEWSLETTER.
Business Publishers, Inc., 951 Pershing Dr., Silver Spring, MD 20910-4464. TEL 301-587-6300. FAX 301-585-9075.
Vendor(s): Information Access Co., NewsNet (CH13) *2990*

SLUMGULLION.
412 N. Alfred St., Ste. 6, Alexandria, VA 22314. URL: http://www.from-and-substance.com/slumgullion.
Available only online. *4468*

SMALL ANIMALS.
CAB International, Wallingford, Oxon. OX10 8DE, England. TEL 44-1491-832111. FAX 44-1491-826090. URL: http://www.cabi.org.
Vendor(s): DIMDI, European Space Agency, Knight-Ridder Information, Inc., STN International. *7286*

SMALL BUSINESS JOURNAL.
Small Business Association of Michigan, 222 N. Washington Sq., Box 16158, Lansing, MI 48901-6158. TEL 517-482-8788. FAX 517-482-4205. *1647*

SMALL BUSINESS NEWS - AKRON.
Small Business News, Inc. (Akron), 86 W. Bowery St., Akron, OH 44308-1101. TEL 330-535-6397. FAX 330-535-6491. URL: http://www.sbnpub.com.
Vendor(s): UMI. *1647*

SMALL BUSINESS NEWS - CLEVELAND.
Small Business News, Inc. (Cleveland), 14725 Detroit Ave., Ste. 300, Cleveland, OH 44107-4103. TEL 216-228-6397. FAX 216-529-8924. URL: http://www.sbnpub.com.
Vendor(s): UMI. *1647*

SMALL BUSINESS TAX REVIEW.
A-N Group, Inc., Box 895, Melville, NY 11747-0895. TEL 516-549-4090. URL: http://www.smbiz.com.
Vendor(s): NewsNet (TX15). *1627*

SMALL KITCHEN APPLIANCES: THE INTERNATIONAL MARKET.
Euromonitor, 60-61 Britton St., London EC1M 5NA, England. TEL 44-171-251-8024. FAX 44-171-608-3149. URL: http://www.euromonitor.com.
Vendor(s): Data-Star, Knight-Ridder Information, Inc. *2652*

SMALL PRESS BOOK REVIEW.
Greenfield Press, Box 176, Southport, CT 06490. TEL 203-332-7629.
Available only online. *6284*

SMART MATERIALS AND STRUCTURES.
I O P Publishing Ltd., Dirac House, Temple Back, Bristol, BS1 6BE, England. TEL 44-117-929-7481. FAX 44-117-929-4318. *5874*

SMART WINE.
SmartWired Inc., 867 W. Napa St., Sonoma, CA 95476. TEL 707-939-0822. FAX 707-939-0833. URL: http://smartwine.com. *526*

SMITHSONIAN.
Smithsonian Institution, Arts & Industries Bldg., 900 Jefferson Dr., S.W., Washington, DC 20560. TEL 202-786-2900. FAX 202-786-2564. URL: http://www.smithsonianmag.si.edu.
Vendor(s): Information Access Co., Knight-Ridder Information, Inc. *6636*

THE SMOKIES MAGAZINE.
3605 Grove Circle, Knoxville, TN 37918. URL: http://thesmokies.com/.
Available only online. *7234*

SNAKE RIVER BASIN ADJUDICATION DIGEST.
Ridenbaugh Press, Box 2276, Boise, ID 83701. TEL 208-344-0844. FAX 208-344-0844. URL: http://www.ridenbaugh.com. *4025*

SNOW LION NEWSLETTER & CATALOG.
Snow Lion Publications, Box 6483, Ithaca, NY 14851. TEL 607-273-8519. FAX 607-273-8508. URL: http://www.well.com/user/snowlion/. *6390*

SNUFF IT.
Chruch of Euthanasia, Box 261, Somerville, MA 02143. URL: http://www.paranoia.com/coe/ *6497*

SOAP, COSMETICS, CHEMICAL SPECIALTIES.
P T N Publishing Corp., 445 Broadhollow Rd., Melville, NY 11747-3601.
Vendor(s): Information Access Co., Lexis-Nexis. *513*

SOAP, PERFUMERY & COSMETICS.
Wilmington Business Publishing, Apex House, London Rd., Northfleet, Kent DA11 9JA, England. TEL 44-1322-277788. FAX 44-1474-569418.
Vendor(s): Information Access Co. *513*

SOCIAL FORCES.
University of North Carolina Press, Box 2288, Chapel Hill, NC 27515-2288. TEL 919-966-3561. FAX 919-966-3829.
Vendor(s): Information Access Co., UMI. *6728*

SOCIAL INVENTIONS.
Institute for Social Inventions, 20 Heber Rd., London NW2 6AA, England. TEL 44-181-208-2853. FAX 44-181-452-6434. URL: http://newciv.org/GIB/ *6728*

SOCIAL JUSTICE.
Global Options, Box 40601, San Francisco, CA 94140. TEL 415-550-1703.
Vendor(s): Information Access Co. *6036*

SOCIAL POLICY.
Union Institute, 25 W. 43rd St., Rm. 620, New York, NY 10036. TEL 212-642-2929. FAX 212-642-1956. URL: http://www.socialpolicy.org.
Vendor(s): Information Access Co., UMI. *6729*

SOCIAL PROBLEMS.
University of California Press, Journals Division, 2120 Berkeley Way, Berkeley, CA 94720. TEL 510-643-7154. FAX 510-642-9917. URL: http://library.berkeley.edu:8080/ucalpress/journals.
Vendor(s): Information Access Co., UMI. *6729*

SOCIAL RESEARCH.
New School for Social Research, 65 Fifth Ave., New York, NY 10003. TEL 212-229-5776. FAX 212-229-5476.
Vendor(s): Information Access Co., UMI. *6637*

SERIALS AVAILABLE ONLINE

SOCIAL SCIENCE & MEDICINE.
Elsevier Science Ltd., Pergamon, P.O. Box 800, Kidlington, Oxford OX5 1DX, England. TEL 44-1865-843000. FAX 44-1865-843010. *4746*

THE SOCIAL SCIENCE JOURNAL.
J A I Press Inc., 55 Old Post Rd., No. 2, Box 1678, Greenwich, CT 06830-1678. TEL 203-661-7602. FAX 203-661-0792.
Vendor(s): Information Access Co. *6638*

SOCIAL SCIENCE RESEARCH.
Academic Press, Inc., Journal Division, 525 B St., Ste. 1900, San Diego, CA 92101-4495. TEL 619-230-1840. FAX 619-699-6800. URL: http://www.apnet.com/www/journal/so.htm; http://www.idealibrary.com/ *6638*

SOCIAL SCIENCES CITATION INDEX.
Institute for Scientific Information, 3501 Market St., Philadelphia, PA 19104. TEL 215-386-0100. FAX 215-386-2911.
Vendor(s): DIMDI, Data-Star, Knight-Ridder Information, Inc. (File no.7/SOCIAL SCISEARCH), Ovid Technologies, Inc. (SSCI). *6651*

SOCIAL SCIENCES INDEX.
H.W. Wilson Co., 950 University Ave., Bronx, NY 10452. TEL 718-588-8400. FAX 718-590-1617.
Vendor(s): OCLC, UMI (PROQUEST), Wilsonline. *6651*

SOCIAL SECURITY BULLETIN.
U.S. Social Security Administration, Office of Research, Evaluation, and Statistics, Publications Staff, Van Ness Center, Rm. 209, 4301 Connecticut Ave., N.W., Washington, DC 20008. TEL 202-282-7138. FAX 202-282-7219.
Vendor(s): Information Access Co., UMI. *3833*

THE SOCIAL STUDIES.
Heldref Publications, 1319 Eighteenth St., N.W., Washington, DC 20036-1802. TEL 202-296-6267. FAX 202-296-5149.
Vendor(s): Information Access Co., UMI. *2483*

SOCIAL WORK.
N A S W Press, 750 First St., N.E., Ste. 700, Washington, DC 20002-4241. TEL 202-408-8600. FAX 202-336-8312. URL: http://www.naswpress.org.
Vendor(s): Information Access Co., UMI. *6688*

SOCIAL WORK ABSTRACTS.
N A S W Press, 750 First St., N.E., Ste. 700, Washington, DC 20002-4241. TEL 202-408-8600. FAX 202-336-8310. URL: http://www.naswpress.org.
Vendor(s): Ovid Technologies, Inc. (SWAB). *6698*

SOCIETE FRANCAISE DE CARDIOLOGIE. BULLETIN D'INFORMATIONS.
Grou-Radenez-Joly, 19 rue des Saints Peres, 75006 Paris, France. *4824*

SOCIETY.
Transaction Publishers, Transaction Periodicals Consortium, Department 3092, Rutgers University, New Brunswick, NJ 08903. TEL 908-445-2280. FAX 908-445-3138.
Vendor(s): Information Access Co. *6639*

SOCIETY FOR ROMANIAN STUDIES NEWSLETTER.
Huntington College Society, Dept. of History, Huntington College, 2303 College Ave., Huntington, IN 46750. TEL 219-359-4242. FAX 219-356-9448. URL: http://www.huntcol.edu/~pmichels/srs.html. *3601*

SOCIETY OF RESEARCH ADMINISTRATORS. JOURNAL.
Society of Research Administrators, Inc., 1200 19th St., N.W., Ste. 300, Washington, DC 20036-2401. TEL 202-857-1141. FAX 202-223-4579.
Vendor(s): Information Access Co., UMI. *1507*

SOCIO-ECONOMIC SERIES.
Natural Resources Institute, Central Ave., Chatham Maritime, Kent ME4 4TB, England. TEL 44-1634-880088. FAX 44-1634-880066. URL: http://www.nri.org. *153*

SOCIOLOGICAL ABSTRACTS.
Sociological Abstracts, Inc., Box 22206, San Diego, CA 92192-0206. TEL 619-695-8803. FAX 619-695-0416.
Vendor(s): DIMDI (SA63), Data-Star (SOCA), Knight-Ridder Information, Inc. (File no.37), OCLC, Ovid Technologies, Inc. (SOCA). *6740*

SOCIOLOGICAL PERSPECTIVES.
J A I Press Inc., 55 Old Post Rd., No. 2, Box 1678, Greenwich, CT 06830-1678. TEL 203-661-7602. FAX 203-661-0792.
Vendor(s): Information Access Co.. *6731*

SOCIOLOGICAL RESEARCH ONLINE.
Sage Publications Ltd., 6 Bonhill St., London EC2A 4PU, England. TEL 44-171-374-0645. FAX 44-171-374-8741. URL: http://www.socresonline.org.uk/socresonline/.
Available only online. *6731*

SOCIOLOGY.
Cambridge University Press, Edinburgh Bldg., Shaftesbury Rd., Cambridge CB2 2RU, England. TEL 44-1223-312393. FAX 44-1223-315052. URL: http://www.cup.cam.ac.uk.
Vendor(s): Information Access Co., UMI. *6732*

SOCIOLOGY OF EDUCATION.
American Sociological Association, 1722 N St., N.W., Washington, DC 20036. TEL 202-833-3410. FAX 202-785-0146.
Vendor(s): UMI. *6733*

SOCIOLOGY OF HEALTH AND ILLNESS.
Blackwell Publishers Ltd., 108 Cowley Rd., Oxford OX4 1JF, England. TEL 44-1865-791100. FAX 44-1865-791347. URL: http://www.blackwellpublishers.co.uk. *6733*

SOCIOLOGY OF RELIGION.
Association for the Sociology of Religion, 3520 Wiltshire Dr., Holiday, FL 34691-1239. TEL 813-844-5990. FAX 813-844-7332.
Vendor(s): Information Access Co., UMI. *6733*

SOFT COMPUTING.
Springer-Verlag, Heidelberger Platz 3, 14197 Berlin, Germany. TEL 49-30-82787-0. FAX 49-30-82787448. URL: http://link.springer.de. *4624*

SOFT DRINKS: THE INTERNATIONAL MARKET.
Euromonitor, 60-61 Britton St., London EC1M 5NA, England. TEL 44-171-251-8024. FAX 44-171-608-3149. URL: http://www.euromonitor.com.
Vendor(s): Data-Star, Knight-Ridder Information, Inc. *527*

SOFT.LETTER.
Mercury Group, Inc., 17 Main St., Watertown, MA 02172-4491. TEL 617-924-3944. FAX 617-924-7288.
Vendor(s): Information Access Co. *2217*

SOFTLINK TIMES.
Softlink International, URL: http://softlink.client.uq.edu.au/slktime.htm.
Available only online. *4234*

SOFTWARE CATALOG: MICROCOMPUTERS.
Elsevier Science Inc., Box 945, New York, NY 10159-0945. TEL 212-633-3730. FAX 212-633-3680. URL: http://www.elsevier.nl/.
Vendor(s): CompuServe, Inc., Knight-Ridder Information, Inc. *2192*

SOFTWARE DEVELOPMENT.
Miller Freeman, Inc., 600 Harrison St., San Francisco, CA 94107. TEL 415-905-2200. FAX 415-905-2232. URL: http://www.http://www.sdmagazine.com/ *2217*

SOFTWARE ENCYCLOPEDIA.
R.R. Bowker, A Division of Reed Elsevier Inc., 121 Chanlon Rd., New Providence, NJ 07974. TEL 908-464-6800. FAX 908-665-3502. URL: http://www.reedref.com.
Vendor(s): Knight-Ridder Information, Inc. (File no.278). *2218*

SOFTWARE FUTURES.
A P T Data Group plc., 12 Sutton Row, 4th Fl., London W1V 5FH, England. TEL 44-171-528-7083. FAX 44-171-439-1105.
Vendor(s): Information Access Co. *2218*

SOFTWARE INDUSTRY REPORT.
Computer Age & E D P News Services, 714 Church St., Alexandria, VA 22314-4202. TEL 703-739-8500. FAX 703-739-8505.
Vendor(s): Information Access Co. *2218*

SOFTWARE MAGAZINE.
Sentry Publishing Company, Inc., 1 Research Dr., Ste. 400B, Westborough, MA 01581-3907. TEL 508-366-2031. FAX 508-836-4732.
Vendor(s): Information Access Co., UMI. *2218*

SOFTWARE QUALITY JOURNAL.
Thomson Science, 2-6 Boundary Row, London SE1 8HN, England. TEL 44-171-8650066. FAX 44-171-5229623. URL: http://www.thomsonscience.com. *2219*

SOIL SCIENCE.
Williams & Wilkins, 351 W. Camden St., Baltimore, MD 21201-2436. TEL 410-528-4068. FAX 410-528-4452. URL: http://www.wwilkins.com.
Vendor(s): Ovid Technologies, Inc. *244*

SOILS AND FERTILIZERS.
CAB International, Wallingford, Oxon. OX10 8DE, England. TEL 44-491-832111. FAX 44-491-833508.
Vendor(s): CISTI, DIMDI, European Space Agency, Knight-Ridder Information, Inc., Ovid Technologies, Inc.. *183*

SOILS AND FERTILIZERS - ABSTRACTS OF WORLD LITERATURE.
CAB International, Wallingford, Oxon. OX10 8DE, England. TEL 44-1491-832111. FAX 44-1491-826090. URL: http://www.cabi.org.
Vendor(s): DIMDI. *183*

SOLARIS.
Recherches en Sciences de l'Information et de la Documentation, Groupe Interuniversitaire, URL: http://www.info.unicaen.fr/bnum/jelec/Solaris/
Available only online. *4234*

SOLAS.
No. 151 - 32500 S. Fraser Way, Ste. 130, Abbotsford, BC V2T 4W1, Canada. URL: http://users.uniserve.com/~wonko/solas/
Available only online. *4468*

SOLEIL.
UniMedia Inc., 925 chemin St-Louis, C.P. 1547 Terminus, Quebec, PQ G1K 7J6, Canada. TEL 418-686-3233. FAX 418-686-3260. *3266*

SOLID STATE AND SUPERCONDUCTIVITY ABSTRACTS.
Cambridge Scientific Abstracts, 7200 Wisconsin Ave., 6th Fl., Bethesda, MD 20814. TEL 301-961-6750. FAX 301-961-6720. URL: http://www.csa.com.
Vendor(s): STN International (SOLIDSTATE). *5837*

SOLID STATE TECHNOLOGY.
PennWell Publishing Co. (Nashua), 10 Tara Blvd., 5th Fl., Nashua, NH 03062-2801. TEL 603-891-0123. FAX 609-891-0597.
Vendor(s): Information Access Co. *2652*

SOLID WASTE REPORT.
Business Publishers, Inc., 951 Pershing Dr., Silver Spring, MD 20910-4464. TEL 301-587-6300. FAX 301-585-9075.
Vendor(s): Information Access Co., NewsNet (EV20). *2952*

SOLSTICE: AN ELECTRONIC JOURNAL OF GEOGRAPHY AND MATHEMATICS.
Institute of Mathematical Geography, 2790 Briarcliff, Ann Arbor, MI 48105-1429. TEL 313-761-1231. *4607*

SOLUCIONES AVANZADAS.
Xview, S.A. de C.V., Tuxpan 2, Desp. 603, Col. Roma Sur, 06760 Mexico DF, Mexico. TEL 574-5316. FAX 574-5318. *1203*

SOMALIA NEWS UPDATE.
Somalia News Update, c/o Dept. of Cultural Anthropology, University of Uppsala, Traedgaardsgatan 18, S-753 09 Uppsala, Sweden. FAX 46-18-151160.
Available only online. *3355*

THE SOMETHING BETTER NEWS.
Something Better Publications, Inc., 2900 Wilson, S.W., Ste. 107, Grandville, MI 49418-1240. TEL 616-530-3957. FAX 616-530-0728. URL: http://www.somebetnews.com. *5970*

SOMNIAL TIMES.
American Mensa, Dreamers Special Interest Group, c/o Gloria Reiser, Box 561, Quincy, IL 62306-0561. TEL 217-222-9082. *5461*

SON OF SPAMM! MAGAZINE.
Mass Media, Inc., Box 230699, Portland, OR 97281-0699. URL: http://www.aracnet.com/~sospamm. *5436*

SORGHUM AND MILLETS.
CAB International, Wallingford, Oxon. OX10 8DE, England. TEL 44-1419-832111. FAX 44-1491-826090. URL: http://www.cabi.org.
Vendor(s): DIMDI, European Space Agency, Knight-Ridder Information, Inc., STN International. *183*

SORKINS DIRECTORY OF BUSINESS & GOVERNMENT (CHICAGO EDITION).
Sorkins Directories, Inc., 1001 Craig Rd., Ste. 260, St. Louis, MO 63146. TEL 314-872-2101. FAX 314-872-2102. URL: http://www.sorkins.com. *1595*

SOUND & HI FI.
Technical Press S.A., 31 Praxitelous St., 167 77 Athens, Greece. TEL 30-1-9961-861. FAX 30-1-9961-864. URL: http://www.techlink.gr. *5436*

SOUND & VISION.
Sound & Vision, 99 Atlantic Ave., Ste. 302, Toronto, ON M6K 3J8, Canada. TEL 416-535-7611. FAX 416-535-6325. *2652*

SOURCEMEX.
University of New Mexico, Latin American Institute, 801 Yale N.E., Albuquerque, NM 87131-1016. TEL 505-277-6839. FAX 505-277-5989. URL: http://www.ladb.unm.edu/.
Vendor(s): Information Access Co., Knight-Ridder Information, Inc., Lexis-Nexis, NewsNet (IT99). *1289*

SOURCES.
4 Phipps St., Ste. 109, Toronto, ON M4Y 1J5, Canada. TEL 416-964-7799. FAX 416-964-8763. URL: http://www.sources.com. *1712*

SOUTH AFRICAN FOOD & BEVERAGE MANUFACTURING REVIEW.
National Publishing (Pty) Ltd., P.O. Box 2271, Clareinch 7740, South Africa. TEL 27-21-611140. FAX 27-21-611389.
Vendor(s): Information Access Co., UMI. *3127*

SOUTH AFRICAN JOURNAL OF ECONOMIC HISTORY.
Economic History Society of Southern Africa, University of South Africa, Economics Department, P.O. Box 392, Pretoria 0001. TEL 27-12-4294502. FAX 27-12-4293433. *1311*

SOUTH AFRICAN JOURNAL OF MUSICOLOGY.
Musicological Society of Southern Africa, University of Natal, Department of Music, Private Bag X10, Dalbridge 4014, South Africa. TEL 27-31-2603053. FAX 27-31-2601048. URL: http://www.und.ac.za/und/samus. *5437*

SOUTH AFRICAN PHARMACEUTICAL JOURNAL.
Pharmaceutical Society of South Africa, P.O. Box 31360, Braamfontein, Johannesburg 2017, South Africa. TEL 27-11-339-1752. FAX 27-11-403-1309. *5695*

SOUTH ASIAN SURVEY.
Sage Publications India Pvt. Ltd., P.O. Box 4215, New Delhi 110 048, India. TEL 91-11-644-4958. FAX 91-11-647-2426. *3539*

SOUTH CAROLINA BUSINESS DIRECTORY.
American Business Directories, 5711 S. 86th Circle, Box 27347, Omaha, NE 68127. TEL 402-593-4600. FAX 402-331-5481. *1712*

SOUTH CAROLINA LAW REVIEW.
University of South Carolina, School of Law, Columbia, SC 29208. TEL 803-777-5874. FAX 803-777-2368.
Vendor(s): Lexis-Nexis, West Group. *4026*

SOUTH CAROLINA LAWYER.
South Carolina Bar, Box 608, Columbia, SC 29202-0608. TEL 803-799-6653. FAX 803-799-4118. URL: http://www.schar.org. *4026*

SOUTH DAKOTA BUSINESS DIRECTORY.
American Business Directories, 5711 S. 86th Circle, Box 27347, Omaha, NE 68127. TEL 402-593-4600. FAX 402-331-5481. *1713*

SOUTH DAKOTA BUSINESS REVIEW.
University of South Dakota, School of Business, 414 E. Clark St., Vermillion, SD 57069-2390. TEL 605-677-5287. FAX 605-677-5427. URL: http://www.brb.usd.edu.
Vendor(s): Information Access Co., UMI. *1002*

SOUTH DAKOTA LAW REVIEW.
University of South Dakota, School of Law, 414 E. Clark St., Vermilion, SD 57069-2390. TEL 605-677-5646. FAX 605-677-5417.
Vendor(s): West Group. *4026*

SOUTH FLORIDA BUSINESS JOURNAL.
American City Business Journals, Inc. (Miami), 1050 Lee Wagener Blvd., Ste. 302, Ft. Lauderdale, FL 33315-3500. FAX 305-594-1892.
Vendor(s): Information Access Co.. *1002*

SOUTH TEXAS LAW REVIEW.
South Texas Law Review, Inc., 1303 San Jacinto St., Houston, TX 77002.
Vendor(s): West Group. *4026*

SOUTHEAST ENVIRONMENTAL DIRECTORY.
Harbinger Communications, Box 8175, Missoula, MT 59807. TEL 406-721-0440. FAX 406-721-0440. *2245*

SOUTHEAST POWER REPORT.
McGraw-Hill Companies, 1221 Ave. of the Americas, New York, NY 10020. TEL 212-512-2000.
Vendor(s): Dow Jones News Retrieval (SEPR), Knight-Ridder Information, Inc. (SPR), NewsNet (EY89). *2679*

SOUTHEAST REAL ESTATE NEWS.
Intertec Publishing Corp. (Atlanta), 6151 Powers Ferry Rd., N.W., Atlanta, GA 30339-2941. TEL 770-955-2500. FAX 770-955-0400. *6313*

SOUTHERN CALIFORNIA BUSINESS.
Los Angeles Area Chamber of Commerce, 350 S. Bixel St., Los Angeles, CA 90017. TEL 213-580-7571. FAX 213-580-7586.
Vendor(s): Information Access Co., UMI. *1196*

SOUTHERN CALIFORNIA BUSINESS DIRECTORY.
American Business Directories, 5711 S. 86th Circle, Box 27347, Omaha, NE 68127. TEL 402-593-4600. FAX 402-331-5481. *1713*

SOUTHERN CONE REPORT.
Lettres (U.K.) Ltd., 61 Old St., London EC1V 9HX, England. TEL 44-171-251-0012. FAX 44-171-253-8193.
Vendor(s): Lexis-Nexis. *1289*

SOUTHERN ECONOMIC JOURNAL.
University of North Carolina at Chapel Hill, Southern Economic Association, 300 Hanes Hall, CB 3540, Chapel Hill, NC 27514. TEL 919-966-5261. FAX 919-932-5469.
Vendor(s): Information Access Co.. *1002*

SOUTHERN ILLINOIS UNIVERSITY LAW JOURNAL.
Southern Illinois University at Carbondale, School of Law, Lesar Law Bldg., Carbondale, IL 62901. TEL 618-453-8721. FAX 618-453-8769. URL: http://www.siu.edu.
Vendor(s): Lexis-Nexis, West Group. *4026*

SOUTHERN LIVING.
Southern Living, Inc., c/o H. Johnson, V.P. Circulation, 2100 Lakeshore Dr., Birmingham, AL 35209. TEL 205-877-6000. FAX 205-877-6422. *3385*

SOUTHERN MEDICAL JOURNAL.
Southern Medical Association, 35 Lakeshore Dr., Box 190088, Birmingham, AL 35219-0088. TEL 205-945-1840. FAX 205-945-1548. URL: http://www.sma.org/smj/index.htm. *4747*

SOUTHERN ORTHOPAEDIC ASSOCIATION. JOURNAL.
Southern Orthopaedic Association, 35 Lake Shore Dr., Box 190088, Birmingham, AL 35219-0088. FAX 205-945-1548. URL: http://www.sma.org/soa/jsoa.htm. *5016*

THE SOUTHERN REVIEW.
Louisiana State University, 43 Allen Hall, Baton Rouge, LA 70803-5005. TEL 504-388-5108. FAX 504-388-5098.
Vendor(s): Information Access Co., UMI. *4469*

SOUTHERN SOCIAL STUDIES JOURNAL.
Kentucky Council for the Social Studies, Morehead State University, U.P.O 738, Morehead, KY 40351. TEL 606-783-2765. FAX 606-783-2678.
Vendor(s): Knight-Ridder Information, Inc., Ovid Technologies, Inc. *6639*

SOUTHSCAN.
SouthScan Ltd., P.O. Box 724, London N16 5RZ, England. TEL 44-171-923-1467. FAX 44-171-923-2545. URL: http://www.gn.apc.org/southscan. *5971*

SOUTHWEST JOURNAL OF BUSINESS AND ECONOMICS.
University of Texas at El Paso, Texas Centers, El Paso, TX 79968.
Vendor(s): Information Access Co. *1003*

SOUTHWEST JOURNAL OF PURE AND APPLIED MATHEMATICS.
Cameron University, URL: http://rattler.cameron.edu/swjpam.
Available only online. *4607*

SOUTHWEST REAL ESTATE NEWS.
Intertec Publishing Corp. (Atlanta), 6151 Powers Ferry Rd., N.W., Atlanta, GA 30339-2941. TEL 770-955-2500. FAX 770-955-0400. *6313*

SOUTHWEST REVIEW.
Southern Methodist University, 307 Fondren Library W., Box 374, Dallas, TX 75275. TEL 214-768-1037. FAX 214-768-1408.
Vendor(s): Information Access Co., Information Intelligence Inc., UMI. *4360*

SOUTHWESTERN LAW JOURNAL.
S M U Law Review Association, Southern Methodist University, School of Law, Dallas, TX 75275. TEL 214-768-2594. FAX 214-768-3946.
Vendor(s): West Group. *4027*

SOWITIMES.
Studenteninformationsverein Public Media, Stifterstr. 20, A-4100 Ottensheim, Austria. TEL 04234-4547. *2556*

SOYABEAN ABSTRACTS.
CAB International, Wallingford, Oxon. OX10 8DE, England. TEL 44-1491-832111. FAX 44-1491-826090. URL: http://www.cabi.org.
Vendor(s): DIMDI, European Space Agency, Knight-Ridder Information, Inc., STN International. *183*

SPACE BUSINESS NEWS.
Phillips Business Information, Inc., 1201 Seven Locks Rd., Potomac, MD 20854. TEL 301-424-3338. FAX 301-309-3847.
Vendor(s): Data-Star, Information Access Co., Knight-Ridder Information, Inc., NewsNet (AE11). *79*

SPACE CALENDAR.
Space Age Publishing Company, 75-5751 Kuakini Hwy., Ste. 201, Kaulua-Kona, HI 96740. TEL 808-326-2014. FAX 808-326-1825.
Vendor(s): NewsNet (AE04). *79*

SPACE FAX DAILY.
Space Age Publishing Company, 75-5751 Kuakini Hwy., Ste. 201, Kaulua-Kona, HI 96740. TEL 808-326-2014. FAX 808-326-1825.
Vendor(s): NewsNet (AE07). *79*

SPACE FORUM.
Gordon and Breach - Harwood Academic, Amsteldisk 166, 1st Fl., 1079 LH Amsterdam, Netherlands. URL: http://www.gbhap.com/Space_Forum/. *79*

SPACE INDUSTRY NEWS.
C.S.I.R.O., Office of Space Science and Applications, URL: http://www.cossa.csiro.au/pubs/spins.htm. *79*

SERIALS AVAILABLE ONLINE

SPACE R & D ALERT.
Aerospace Communications, c/o Jeffrey K. Manber, Ed., 519 N. Alfred St., Alexandria, VA 22314-2226. Vendor(s): NewsNet. *79*

SPAIN. REGISTRO MERCANTIL. BOLETIN OFICIAL.
Boletin Oficial del Estado, Trafalgar, 27, 28071 Madrid, Spain. TEL 34-1-5382297. FAX 34-1-5382275. URL: http://www.boe.es. *1003*

SPANK! YOUTH CULTURE ONLINE.
2206 4 St., S.W., Calgary, AB T2S 1W9, Canada. TEL 403-571-0170. URL: http://www.spankmag.com. Available only online. *5438*

SPECIAL DELIVERY.
Association of Labor Assistants & Childbirth Educators, Box 382724, Cambridge, MA 02238. TEL 617-441-2500. FAX 617-441-3167. URL: http://www.alace.org. Vendor(s): Information Access Co.. *4968*

THE SPECIAL EDUCATOR.
L R P Publications, 747 Dresher Rd., Horsham, PA 19044. TEL 215-784-0941. FAX 215-784-9639. URL: http://www.lrp.com. *2591*

SPECIAL REFLECTIONS.
U.S. Department of Defense, Infrared Information Analysis Center, URL: http://www.erim.org/iria/iria.html. Available only online. *5870*

SPECIAL WARFARE.
John F. Kennedy Special Warfare Center and School, Attn.: AOJK-DT-MDM, USAJFKSWCS, Ft. Bragg, NC 28307-5000. TEL 910-512-1800. FAX 910-432-3147. URL: http://www.usasoc.soc.mil. *5286*

SPECIALITY CHEMICALS.
Argus Business Media Ltd., Queensway House, 2 Queensway, Redhill, Surrey RH1 1QS, England. TEL 44-1737-768611. FAX 44-1737-761685. Vendor(s): Information Access Co.. *2774*

SPECIALTY TRAVEL INDEX.
Alpine Hansen Publishers, 305 San Anselmo Ave., Ste. 313, San Anselmo, CA 94960. TEL 415-459-4900. FAX 415-459-4974. URL: http://www.specialtytravel.com. *7235*

SPECTRUM (LEXINGTON).
Council of State Governments, 3560 Iron Works Pike, Box 11910, Lexington, KY 40578-1910. TEL 606-244-8000. FAX 606-244-8001. Vendor(s): Information Access Co., UMI. *6194*

SPECTRUM CONVERTIBLES.
C D A Investment Technologies, Inc., 1355 Piccard Dr., Rockville, MD 20850. FAX 301-590-1329. *1408*

SPECTRUM INTERNATIONAL.
C D A Investment Technologies, Inc., 1355 Piccard Dr., Rockville, MD 20850. FAX 301-590-1329. *1408*

SPECTRUM TIDBITS.
URL: http://emporium.turnpike.net/d/dcservice/wg/alrokon.htm. *3446*

SPEEDMETER.
4532 Bryant, Maples, MN 55409-1755. URL: http://www.pressenter.com/'emo123/speedmeter/. Available only online. *1887*

SPEEDNEWS.
Speednews, Inc., 1801 Ave. of the Stars, Ste. 210, Los Angeles, CA 90067-5904. TEL 310-203-9603. FAX 310-203-9352. Vendor(s): NewsNet (AE15). *7078*

SPINE (PHILADELPHIA, 1976).
Lippincott - Raven Publishers, 227 E. Washington Sq., Philadelphia, PA 19106. TEL 215-238-4200. FAX 215-238-4227. URL: http://www.lrpub.com. *5016*

SPIRIT TO SPIRIT.
Box 4065, Frisco, CO 80443. URL: http://www.oneimage.com/'sandi/s-index.html. Available only online. *6373*

SPIRITS: THE INTERNATIONAL MARKET.
Euromonitor, 60-61 Britton St., London EC1M 5NA, England. TEL 44-171-251-8024. FAX 44-171-608-3146. URL: http://www.euromonitor.com. Vendor(s): Data-Star, Knight-Ridder Information, Inc. *527*

THE SPITTING IMAGE.
Box 20400, Tompkins Sq. Sta., New York, NY 10009. URL: http://www.bway.net/'seatopia. *4470*

SPLENDID E-ZINE.
11 Woodhaven Manor, Apt. G, White River Junction, VT 05001-2876. URL: http://www.luckgarage.com/splendid/. Available only online. *5438*

SPORT.
Petersen Publishing Co., 6420 Wilshire Blvd., Los Angeles, CA 90048. TEL 213-782-2000. Vendor(s): Information Access Co.. *6783*

SPORT KLUB.
Moscow News Information & Media Company, 16-2 Tverskaya ul., 103829 Moscow, Russia. TEL 7-095-2295605. FAX 7-095-2092661. *6784*

SPORT THESAURUS.
Sport Information Resource Centre (SIRC), 1600 James Naismith Dr., Gloucester, ON K1B 5N4, Canada. TEL 613-748-5658. FAX 613-748-5701. Vendor(s): Data-Star, Knight-Ridder Information, Inc., Ovid Technologies, Inc. *6797*

SPORTING GOODS BUSINESS.
Miller Freeman Inc. (New York), One Penn Plaza, New York, NY 10119. TEL 212-714-1300. FAX 212-714-1313. Vendor(s): Information Access Co., UMI. *6785*

THE SPORTING LIFE.
The Sporting Life, 1 Canada Sq., Canary Wharf, London E14 5AP, England. TEL 44-171-293-3291. FAX 44-171-293-3758. URL: http://www.sportinglife.co.uk/. *6857*

THE SPORTING NEWS.
Sporting News Publishing Co., 10176 Corporate Square Dr., Ste. 200, St. Louis, MO 63132-2924. TEL 314-993-7750. FAX 314-993-7726. Vendor(s): Information Access Co., Lexis-Nexis, UMI. *6785*

SPORTS AFIELD.
Hearst Corporation, Sports Afield, 250 W. 55th St., New York, NY 10019. TEL 212-649-4000. FAX 212-581-3923. URL: http://sportsafield.com; http://www.hearstcorp.com. Vendor(s): Information Access Co. *6884*

SPORTS ILLUSTRATED.
Time Inc., Time & Life Bldg., Rockefeller Center, 1271 Ave. of the Americas, New York, NY 10020-1393. TEL 212-522-1212. Vendor(s): CompuServe, Inc., Information Access Co., Knight-Ridder Information, Inc., Lexis-Nexis, UMI, MediaStream. *6787*

SPORTS MEDICINE, TRAINING AND REHABILITATION.
Gordon and Breach - Harwood Academic, Amsteldisk 166, 1st Fl., 1079 LH Amsterdam, Netherlands. URL: http://www.gbhap.com/Sports_Medicine/. *5133*

SPORTSEARCH.
Sport Information Resource Centre (SIRC), 1600 James Naismith Drive, Gloucester, ON K1B 5N4, Canada. TEL 613-748-5658. FAX 613-748-5701. Vendor(s): Data-Star, Knight-Ridder Information, Inc., Ovid Technologies, Inc. (SFDB). *6797*

SPORTSTYLE.
Fairchild Fashion & Merchandising Group, 7 W. 34th St., New York, NY 10001. TEL 212-630-4870. FAX 212-630-4879. Vendor(s): Information Access Co., Knight-Ridder Information, Inc. *6788*

SPORTSZINE U K.
URL: http://www.sportszineuk.co.uk. Available only online. *6788*

SPRAY TECHNOLOGY & MARKETING.
Industry Publications, Inc. (Fairfield), 389 Passaic Ave., Fairfield, NJ 07006. TEL 201-227-5151. FAX 201-227-9219. URL: http://members.aol.com/spraytec/index.htm. *5549*

SPRINGFIELD BUSINESS JOURNAL.
313 Park Central, W., Springfield, MO 65806-1244. TEL 417-831-3230. FAX 417-831-5478. URL: http://www.sbj.net. Vendor(s): UMI. *1003*

STAMPS.
American Publishing Company of New York, 85 Canisteo St., Hornell, NY 14843. TEL 607-324-2212. FAX 607-324-1753. Vendor(s): Information Access Co., UMI. *5713*

STANDARD & POOR'S CORPORATION RECORDS.
Standard & Poor's, 25 Broadway, New York, NY 10004. TEL 212-208-8000. FAX 212-412-0459. Vendor(s): Knight-Ridder Information, Inc. (File no.133/Corporate Descriptions), Lexis-Nexis, NewsNet. *1408*

STANDARD & POOR'S CORPORATION RECORDS. DAILY NEWS SECTION.
Standard & Poor's, 25 Broadway, New York, NY 10004. TEL 212-208-8000. Vendor(s): Knight-Ridder Information, Inc. (File no.133). *1003*

STANDARD & POOR'S DIVIDEND RECORD (DAILY).
Standard & Poor's Corporation, 25 Broadway, New York, NY 10004. TEL 212-208-8000. *1408*

STANDARD & POOR'S REGISTER OF CORPORATIONS, DIRECTORS AND EXECUTIVES.
Standard & Poor's, 25 Broadway, New York, NY 10004. TEL 212-208-8000. *1507*

STANDARD DIRECTORY OF ADVERTISERS (BUSINESS CLASSIFICATIONS EDITION).
National Register Publishing, A Division of Reed Elsevier Inc., 121 Chanlon Rd., New Providence, NJ 07974. TEL 908-464-6800. FAX 908-464-3553. URL: http://www.reedref.com. Vendor(s): Lexis-Nexis. *1713*

STANDARD FEDERAL TAX REPORTS.
C C H Incorporated, 2700 Lake Cook Rd., Riverwoods, IL 60015. TEL 847-267-7000. FAX 800-224-8299. Vendor(s): UMI. *1628*

STANDARD PERIODICAL DIRECTORY.
Oxbridge Communications, Inc., 150 Fifth Ave., New York, NY 10011. TEL 212-741-0231. FAX 212-633-2938. *564*

STANFORD JOURNAL OF INTERNATIONAL LAW.
Stanford University, Stanford Law School, Crown Quadrangle, Stanford, CA 94305-8610. TEL 415-723-1375. Vendor(s): West Group. *4126*

STANFORD LAW & POLICY REVIEW.
Stanford Law School, Crown Quadrangle, Stanford, CA 94305-8610. TEL 415-725-7297. FAX 415-725-9458. URL: http://www-leland.stanford.edu/group/slpr. Vendor(s): West Group. *4028*

STANFORD LAW REVIEW.
Stanford University, Stanford Law School, Crown Quadrangle, Stanford, CA 94305-8610. Vendor(s): Lexis-Nexis, West Group. *4028*

STANFORD UNIVERSITY LIBRARIES. NEWS NOTES.
Stanford University Libraries, Green Library, Stanford, CA 94305. TEL 415-723-2018. Available only online. *4216*

STAPP CAR CRASH CONFERENCE. PROCEEDINGS.
Society of Automotive Engineers, 400 Commonwealth Dr., Warrendale, PA 15096-0001. TEL 412-776-4841. FAX 412-776-3036. Vendor(s): European Space Agency, FIZ Technik, Questel Orbit Inc. *7117*

STARK RAVING SANITY.
1835 Cedar River Dr., Jacksonville, FL 32210-1301. URL: http://www.unf.edu/'mdubos/srs.htm. Available only online. *4471*

STATE ACADEMIES OF SCIENCE ABSTRACTS.
AcadSci, Inc., Box 4157, Huntington, WV 25729.
TEL 304-696-6742. FAX 304-696-3243. URL:
http://www.acadsci.com. *6592*

STATE & LOCAL COMMUNICATIONS REPORT.
Telecommunications Reports, 1333 H St., N.W.,
Ste. 100-E, Washington, DC 20005. FAX 212-842-3023. URL: http://www.tr.com.
Vendor(s): NewsNet (TE59). *2003*

STATE CAPITALS. CIVIL RIGHTS.
Wakeman-Walworth, Inc., 300 N. Washington St.,
Alexandria, VA 22314. TEL 703-549-8606.
FAX 703-549-1372. URL: http://legistate.com.
Vendor(s): West Group. *6195*

STATE CAPITALS. ENVIRONMENTAL REGULATION.
Wakeman-Walworth, Inc., 300 N. Washington St.,
Alexandria, VA 22314. TEL 703-549-8606.
FAX 703-549-1372. URL: http://legistate.com.
Vendor(s): West Group. *6195*

STATE CAPITALS. INSURANCE REGULATION.
Wakeman-Walworth, Inc., 300 N. Washington St.,
Alexandria, VA 22314. TEL 703-549-8606.
FAX 703-549-1372. URL: http://legistate.com.
Vendor(s): West Group. *6195*

STATE CAPITALS. PUBLIC UTILITIES.
Wakeman-Walworth, Inc., 300 N. Washington St.,
Alexandria, VA 22314. TEL 703-549-8606.
FAX 703-549-1372. URL: http://legistate.com.
Vendor(s): West Group. *6196*

STATE CAPITALS. TAXATION AND REVENUE POLICIES.
Wakeman-Walworth, Inc., 300 N. Washington St.,
Alexandria, VA 22314. TEL 703-549-8606.
FAX 703-549-1372. URL: http://legistate.com.
Vendor(s): West Group. *6196*

STATE CAPITALS. TAXES - PROPERTY.
Wakeman-Walworth, Inc., 300 N. Washington St.,
Alexandria, VA 22314. TEL 703-549-8606.
FAX 703-549-1372.
Vendor(s): West Group. *6196*

STATE CAPITOLS REPORT.
State Net, 2101 K St., Sacramento, CA 95816.
TEL 916-444-0840. FAX 916-446-5369. *6196*

THE STATE JOURNAL.
State Journal Corp., 904 Virginia St. E., Charleston,
WV 25301-2815. TEL 304-344-1630. FAX 304-345-2721.
Vendor(s): UMI. *1003*

STATE LEGISLATURES.
National Conference of State Legislatures, 1560
Broadway, Ste. 700, Denver, CO 80202-5140.
TEL 303-830-2200. FAX 303-863-8003.
Vendor(s): Information Access Co. *5972*

STATE OF UNBEING.
URL: http://www.io.com/~hagbard/sob.html.
Available only online. *4471*

STATE TAX NOTES.
Tax Analysts, 6830 N. Fairfax Dr., Arlington, VA
22213. TEL 703-533-4400. FAX 703-533-4444.
Vendor(s): Knight-Ridder Information, Inc., Lexis-Nexis. *1628*

STATE TAX REVIEW.
C C H Incorporated, 2700 Lake Cook Rd.,
Riverwoods, IL 60015. TEL 847-267-7000.
FAX 800-224-8299.
Vendor(s): NewsNet, UMI. *1628*

STATE TELEPHONE REGULATION REPORT.
Capitol Publications Inc., Telecom Publishing Group,
1101 King St., Ste. 444, Box 1455, Alexandria, VA
22313-2055. FAX 703-739-6490. URL: http://www.telecommunications.com.
Vendor(s): Information Access Co., NewsNet (TE47). *2039*

STATEMENTS.
Australian National State of the Environment, URL:
http://www.erin.gov.au:80/soe/soe.html.
Available only online. *2952*

STATION REPORTER.
Alfers Advertising & Publishing Inc., 5121 Sackville
St., Ste. 601, Halifax, NS B3J 1K1, Canada.
TEL 902-423-6788. FAX 902-423-3354. *7117*

STATISTICAL ABSTRACT OF THE UNITED STATES (YEAR).
U.S. Bureau of the Census, Customer Services,
Washington, DC 20233. TEL 301-457-4100.
FAX 301-457-4714. URL: http://www.census.gov/. *6942*

STATISTICAL OFFICE OF THE EUROPEAN COMMUNITIES. ENERGY STATISTICS MONTHLY BULLETIN.
Statistical Office of the European Communities, Rue
de Gasperi, 2920 Luxembourg, Luxembourg.
Vendor(s): GSI-ECO. *2685*

STATISTICS.
Gordon and Breach - Harwood Academic,
Amsteldisk 166, 1st Fl., 1079 LH Amsterdam,
Netherlands. URL: http://www.gbhap.com/Statistics/. *6944*

STATISTICS AND COMPUTING.
Thomson Science, 2-6 Boundary Row, London SE1
8HN, England. TEL 44-171-8650066. FAX 44-171-5229623. URL: http://thomsonscience.com. *6944*

STAY FREE!
341 Lafayette, Ste. 558, New York, NY 10012.
URL: http://sunsite.unc.edu/stayfree. *6640*

STEELS ALERT.
Cambridge Scientific Abstracts, 7200 Wisconsin
Ave., Bethesda, MD 20814. TEL 301-961-6750.
FAX 301-961-6720. URL: http://www.csa.com.
Vendor(s): CISTI, CREDOC, Data-Star (MBUS),
European Space Agency (File no.111), Knight-Ridder Information, Inc. (File no.269), Questel Orbit
Inc. (MABU), STN International (MATBUS). *5221*

STEPFAMILIES.
Stepfamily Association of America, 215 Centennial
Mall S., Ste. 212, Lincoln, NE 68508. TEL 402-477-7837. FAX 402-477-8317. *6734*

STEREO REVIEW.
Hachette Filipacchi Magazines, Inc., 1633 Broadway,
New York, NY 10019. TEL 212-767-6000.
Vendor(s): Information Access Co., Knight-Ridder
Information, Inc., UMI. *6746*

STETSON LAW REVIEW.
Stetson University, College of Law, 1401 61 St. S.,
St. Petersburg, FL 33707. TEL 813-345-1300.
FAX 813-345-8973.
Vendor(s): West Group. *4029*

STOCHASTICS AND STOCHASTICS REPORTS.
Gordon and Breach - Harwood Academic,
Amsteldisk 166, 1st Fl., 1079 LH Amsterdam,
Netherlands. URL: http://www.gbhap.com/Stochastics_Stochastics_Reports/. *4608*

STOCKS, BONDS, BILLS AND INFLATION (YEAR) YEARBOOK.
Ibbotson Associates, 225 N. Michigan Ave., Ste.
700, Chicago, IL 60601. TEL 312-616-1620.
FAX 312-616-0404. *1410*

STOCKS IN THE S & P 500. OFFICIAL SERIES.
Standard & Poor's, 25 Broadway, New York, NY
10004. TEL 212-208-8000. *1410*

STONE WORLD.
Business News Publishing Company, 755 W. Big
Beaver, Ste. 1000, Troy, MI 48084. TEL 810-362-3700. FAX 810-362-0317. URL: http://www.stoneworld.com. *1734*

STORES.
N R F Enterprises, Inc., 325 7th St., N.W., Ste.
1000, Washington, DC 20004-2802. TEL 202-626-8101. FAX 202-626-8191. URL: http://www.stores.com/.
Vendor(s): Information Access Co., Lexis-Nexis. *1507*

STORY BYTES.
Box 1227, Del Mar, CA 92014. URL: http://thor.he.net/~stories/
Available only online. *4537*

STRAND THREE.
c/o Speakeasy Cafe, 2304 Second Ave., Seattle,
WA 98121. TEL 206-441-2504. URL: http://www.speakeasy.org/~netropic/strand/
Available only online. *6734*

SERIALS AVAILABLE ONLINE 10207

STRATEGIC AND DEFENCE STUDIES CENTRE NEWSLETTER.
Strategic and Defence Studies Centre, Australian
National University, Canberra, A.C.T. 0200,
Australia. TEL 61-6-2438562. FAX 61-6-2480816.
URL: http://coombs.anu.edu.au/Depts/RSPAS/SDSC/news.htm. *5286*

STRATEGIC BALANCE IN THE MIDDLE EAST.
Arab Press Service, A P S House, P.O. Box 3896,
Nicosia, Cyprus. FAX 357-2-350265.
Vendor(s): Information Access Co.. *6037*

STRATEGIC NEWS SERVICE.
Technology Alliance Partners, Box 1969, Friday
Harbor, WA 98250.
Available only online. *2004*

STRATEGY & LEADERSHIP.
Strategic Leadership Forum, 435 N. Michigan Ave.,
Ste. 1700, Chicago, OH 60611-4008. TEL 312-644-0829. FAX 312-644-8557.
Vendor(s): Information Access Co.. *1508*

STRESS.
Gordon and Breach - Harwood Academic,
Amsteldisk 166, 1st Fl., 1079 LH Amsterdam,
Netherlands. URL: http://www.gbhap.com/Stress/. *4748*

STRESSFORSKNINGSRAPPORTER.
Karolinska Institutet, Institutionen foer Klinisk
Neurovetenskap, P.O. Box 230, S-171 77
Stockholm, Sweden. TEL 46-08-7286400. FAX 46-08-344143. *6155*

STROKE.
American Heart Association, 7272 Greenville Ave.,
Dallas, TX 75231-4596. TEL 214-706-1310.
FAX 214-691-6342.
Vendor(s): Ovid Technologies, Inc. *4824*

STRUCTURE.
Current Biology Ltd., 400 Market St., Ste. 700,
Philadelphia, PA 19106. FAX 215-574-2270. URL:
http://BioMednet.com/cgi-bin/members1/titles.pl.
628

STRUCTURIST.
Eli Bornstein, Ed. & Pub., Box 378, RPO University,
University of Saskatchewan, Saskatoon, SK S7N
4J8, Canada. TEL 306-966-4198. FAX 306-966-8670. *467*

STUDENT AFFAIRS JOURNAL ONLINE.
371-G North Barranca Ave., Azusa, CA 91702.
URL: http://www.digiserve.com/connect/sajo/
Available only online. *1972*

STUDENT NET.
254 College St., Ste. 400, New Haven, CT 06510.
TEL 203-624-7650. FAX 203-624-8715. URL:
http://www.student.net.
Available only online. *1973*

STUDIES IN AMERICAN FICTION.
Northeastern University, Department of English,
Boston, MA 02115. TEL 617-437-3687.
Vendor(s): Information Access Co.. *4472*

STUDIES IN BIBLIOGRAPHY.
University Press of Virginia, Box 3608, University
Sta., Charlottesville, VA 22903. TEL 804-924-3468. FAX 804-982-2655. URL: http://etext.lib.virginai.edu/bsuva.html; http://www.upress.virginia.edu. *564*

STUDIES IN ENGLISH LITERATURE 1500-1900.
Rice University, SEL-MS 46, 6100 Main St.,
Houston, TX 77005-1892. TEL 713-527-4697.
FAX 713-285-5207.
Vendor(s): Information Access Co., UMI. *4473*

STUDIES IN FAMILY PLANNING.
Population Council, 1 Dag Hammarskjold Plaza,
New York, NY 10017. TEL 212-339-0500.
FAX 212-755-6052. URL: http://www.jstor.org/fcgi-bin/jstor/listjournal.fcg.
Vendor(s): Information Access Co. *6058*

STUDIES IN INFORMATICS AND CONTROL.
Research Institute for Informatics, 8-10 Averescu
Ave., 71316 Bucharest 1, Rumania. TEL 40-1-2223778. FAX 40-1-3128539. URL: http://www.ici.ro/revista/sic.html. *4234*

STUDIES IN NONLINEAR DYNAMICS AND ECONOMETRICS.
M I T Press, 5 Cambridge Center, Cambridge, MA 02142-1399. TEL 617-253-2889. FAX 617-258-6779. URL: http://www-mitpress.mit.edu/jrnls-catalog/snde.htm.
Available only online. *4609*

STUDIES IN PHILOLOGY.
University of North Carolina Press, Box 2288, Chapel Hill, NC 27515-2288. TEL 919-966-3561. FAX 800-272-6817.
Vendor(s): UMI. *4305*

STUDIES IN SHORT FICTION.
Newberry College, 2100 College St., Newberry, SC 29108. TEL 803-321-5195. FAX 803-321-5629. URL: http://www.newberry.edu.
Vendor(s): Information Access Co., UMI. *4474*

STUDIES IN THE NOVEL.
University of North Texas, English Department, Denton, TX 76203. TEL 817-565-2025. FAX 807-565-4355.
Vendor(s): Information Access Co., UMI. *4474*

STUDIES ON NEOTROPICAL FAUNA AND ENVIRONMENT.
Swets & Zeitlinger bv, P.O. Box 825, 2160 SZ Lisse, Netherlands. TEL 31-252-435111. FAX 31-252-415888. URL: http://www.swets.nl. *850*

STUDIO OZ.
InterCity Oz, URL: http://interoz.com/studiooz.
Available only online. *468*

THE STUTE.
Stevens Institute of Technology, CastlePoint on the Hudson, Hoboken, NJ 07030. TEL 201-659-3404. *1973*

STYLE (DEKALB).
Northern Illinois University, Department of English, DeKalb, IL 60115. TEL 815-753-6653. FAX 815-753-0606.
Vendor(s): Information Access Co., UMI. *4474*

SUBJECT GUIDE TO BOOKS IN PRINT.
R.R. Bowker, A Division of Reed Elsevier Inc., 121 Chanlon Rd., New Providence, NJ 07974. TEL 908-464-6800. FAX 908-665-3502. URL: http://www.reedref.com.
Vendor(s): Knight-Ridder Information, Inc. (File no.470), Ovid Technologies, Inc. (BBIP). *564*

SUBJECT GUIDE TO CHILDREN'S BOOKS IN PRINT.
R.R. Bowker, A Division of Reed Elsevier Inc., 121 Chanlon Rd., New Providence, NJ 07974. TEL 908-464-6800. FAX 908-665-3502. URL: http://www.reedref.com. *564*

SUBSTANCE ABUSE REPORT.
Business Research Publications, Inc., 65 Bleecker St., 5th FL., New York, NY 10012-2450. TEL 212-673-4700. FAX 212-475-1790.
Vendor(s): Information Access Co. *2306*

THE SUCCESS EXPRESS JOURNAL.
Life - Press Communications, Box 1062, Grand Cayman, Ireland. URL: http://www.success.ie.
Available only online. *6155*

SUCCESS MAGAZINE.
Scott DeGarno - Success Magazine, 733 Third Ave., 10th Fl., New York, NY 10017. TEL 212-883-7100. FAX 212-949-7002.
Vendor(s): Information Access Co. *5516*

SUCCESSFUL FARMING.
Meredith Corporation, 1716 Locust St., Des Moines, IA 50309-3023. TEL 515-284-3000. FAX 515-284-3563. URL: http://www.agriculture.com.
Vendor(s): Information Access Co., UMI. *155*

SUCCESSFUL FRANCHISING.
H I S Publishing, 1224 Westwind Trail, Berne, IN 46711. TEL 219-589-3997, 219-589-2507. URL: http://www.entremkt.com/sf. *1347*

SUCCESSFUL MEETINGS.
Bill Communications, Inc., 355 Park Ave. S., 5th Fl., New York, NY 10010-1789. TEL 212-592-6200. FAX 212-592-6339.
Vendor(s): UMI. *1550*

SUD OUEST.
8 rue de Cheverus, 33094 Bordeaux Cedex, France. TEL 33-5-56003333. FAX 33-5-56003622. URL: http://www.atlantel.fr. *3281*

SUEDDEUTSCHE ZEITUNG.
Sueddeutscher Verlag GmbH, Sendlingerstr. 8, 80331 Munich, Germany. TEL 49-89-2183-0. FAX 49-89-2183787. URL: http://www.sueddeutsche.de. *3291*

SUFFOLK TRANSNATIONAL LAW REVIEW.
Suffolk University Law School, Suffolk Transnational Law Review, 41 Temple St., Boston, MA 02114-4280. TEL 617-573-8610.
Vendor(s): Lexis-Nexis, West Group. *4031*

SUFFOLK UNIVERSITY LAW REVIEW.
Darby Printing Co. (Boston), Beacon Hill, 41 Temple St., Boston, MA 02114-4280. TEL 617-573-8180. FAX 617-723-5847.
Vendor(s): West Group. *4031*

SUICIDE AND LIFE-THREATENING BEHAVIOR.
Guilford Publications, Inc., 72 Spring St., 4th Fl., New York, NY 10012. TEL 212-431-9800. FAX 212-966-6708.
Vendor(s): UMI. *6156*

SULFUR LETTERS.
Gordon and Breach - Harwood Academic, Amsteldisk 166, 1st Fl., 1079 LH Amsterdam, Netherlands. URL: http://www.gbhap.com/Sulfur__Letters/. *1768*

SULFUR REPORTS.
Gordon and Breach - Harwood Academic, Amsteldisk 166, 1st Fl., 1079 LH Amsterdam, Netherlands. URL: http://www.gbhap.com/Sulfur__Reports. *1768*

SULPHUR.
British Sulphur Publishing, 31 Mount Pleasant, London WC1X 0AD, England. TEL 44-171-837-5600. FAX 44-171-837-0292.
Vendor(s): Information Access Co. *183*

SUMMARY OF WORLD BROADCASTS. PART 1: FORMER U S S R (DAILY).
B B C Worldwide Monitoring, Caversham Park, Reading, Berks. RG4 8TZ, England. TEL 44-118-946-9289. FAX 44-118-946-3823. URL: http://www.monitor.bbc.co.uk.
Vendor(s): Data-Star, Lexis-Nexis, Reuters, Ltd. *1290*

SUMMARY OF WORLD BROADCASTS. PART 1: FORMER U S S R (WEEKLY ECONOMIC REPORT).
B B C Worldwide Monitoring, Caversham Park, Reading, Berks. RG4 8TZ, England. TEL 44-118-946-9289. FAX 44-118-946-3823. URL: http://www.monitor.bbc.co.uk.
Vendor(s): Data-Star, Lexis-Nexis, Reuters, Ltd. *1290*

SUMMARY OF WORLD BROADCASTS. PART 2: CENTRAL EUROPE, THE BALKANS (DAILY).
B B C Worldwide Monitoring, Caversham Park, Reading, Berks. RG4 8TZ, England. TEL 44-118-946-9289. FAX 44-118-946-3823. URL: http://www.monitor.bbc.co.uk.
Vendor(s): Data-Star, Lexis-Nexis, Reuters, Ltd. *1290*

SUMMARY OF WORLD BROADCASTS. PART 2: CENTRAL EUROPE, THE BALKANS (WEEKLY ECONOMIC REPORT).
B B C Worldwide Monitoring, Caversham Park, Reading, Berks. RG4 8TZ, England. TEL 44-118-946-9289. FAX 44-118-946-3823. URL: http://www.monitor.bbc.co.uk.
Vendor(s): Data-Star, Lexis-Nexis, Reuters, Ltd. *1290*

SUMMARY OF WORLD BROADCASTS. PART 3: ASIA - PACIFIC (DAILY).
B B C Worldwide Monitoring, Caversham Park, Reading, Berks. RG4 8TZ, England. TEL 44-118-946-9289. FAX 44-118-946-3823. URL: http://www.monitor.bbc.co.uk.
Vendor(s): Data-Star, Lexis-Nexis, Reuters, Ltd. *1291*

SUMMARY OF WORLD BROADCASTS. PART 3: ASIA - PACIFIC (WEEKLY ECONOMIC REPORT).
B B C Worldwide Monitoring, Caversham Park, Reading, Berks. RG4 8TZ, England. TEL 44-118-946-9289. FAX 44-118-946-3823. URL: http://www.monitor.bbc.co.uk.
Vendor(s): Data-Star, Lexis-Nexis, Reuters, Ltd. *1291*

SUMMARY OF WORLD BROADCASTS. PART 4: MIDDLE EAST (DAILY).
B B C Worldwide Monitoring, Caversham Park, Reading, Berks. RG4 8TZ, England. TEL 44-118-946-9289. FAX 44-118-946-3823. URL: http://www.monitor.bbc.co.uk.
Vendor(s): Data-Star, Lexis-Nexis, Reuters, Ltd. *1291*

SUMMARY OF WORLD BROADCASTS. PART 4: MIDDLE EAST (WEEKLY ECONOMIC REPORT).
B B C Worldwide Monitoring, Caversham Park, Reading, Berks. RG4 8TZ, England. TEL 44-118-946-9289. FAX 44-118-946-3823. URL: http://www.monitor.bbc.co.uk.
Vendor(s): Data-Star, Lexis-Nexis, Reuters, Ltd. *1291*

SUMMARY OF WORLD BROADCASTS. PART 5: AFRICA, LATIN AMERICA AND THE CARIBBEAN (DAILY).
B B C Monitoring, Caversham Park, Reading, Berks. RG4 8TZ, England. TEL 44-118-946-9289. FAX 44-118-946-3823. URL: http://www.monitor.bbc.co.uk.
Vendor(s): Data-Star, Lexis-Nexis, Reuters, Ltd. *1291*

SUMMARY OF WORLD BROADCASTS. PART 5: AFRICA, LATIN AMERICA AND THE CARIBBEAN (WEEKLY ECONOMIC REPORT).
B B C Worldwide Monitoring, Caversham Park, Reading, Berks. RG4 8TZ, England. TEL 44-118-946-9289. FAX 44-118-946-3823. URL: http://www.monitor.bbc.co.uk.
Vendor(s): Data-Star, Lexis-Nexis, Reuters, Ltd. *1291*

SUMMER ASSESSMENT - WINTER ASSESSMENT (YEAR).
North American Electric Reliability Council, Princeton Forrestal Village, 116-390 Village Blvd., Princeton, NJ 08540-5731. TEL 609-452-8060. URL: http://www.nerc.com. *2691*

SUN CARE: THE INTERNATIONAL MARKET.
Euromonitor, 60-61 Britton St., London EC1M 5NA, England. TEL 44-171-251-8024. FAX 44-171-608-3149. URL: http://www.euromonitor.com.
Vendor(s): Data-Star, Knight-Ridder Information, Inc. *508*

SUNDAY MAIL.
Queensland Newspapers Pty. Ltd., Campbell St., Bowen Hills, Brisbane, Qld., Australia. TEL 61-7-32526011. FAX 61-7-32526692. *3252*

SUNSET.
Sunset Publishing Corp., 80 Willow Rd., Menlo Park, CA 94025-3691. TEL 415-321-3600. FAX 415-328-6215.
Vendor(s): Information Access Co., Knight-Ridder Information, Inc. *3386*

THE SUNSHINE POST.
Box 5806, Jacksonville, AR 72078. URL: http://home.sprynet.com/sprynet/mkuba/
Available only online. *2140*

SUNWORLD.
Web Publishing Inc., 501 Second St., Ste. 310, San Francisco, CA 94107. TEL 603-924-0100. FAX 603-924-8779. URL: http://www.sunworld.com.
Available only online. *2090*

SUNZINE - ABOUT QUEENSLAND AUSTRALIA.
P.O. Box 159, Peregian Beach, Qld. 4573, Australia. TEL 61-7-5448-1888. FAX 61-7-5448-1686. URL: http://www.sunzine.net/
Available only online. *1004*

SUPER MARKETING.
Reed Business Publishing Group, Quadrant House, The Quadrant, Sutton, Surrey SM2 5AS, England. TEL 44-181-652-8275. FAX 44-181-652-3958. *3144*

SUPERCONDUCTIVITY REVIEW.
Gordon and Breach - Harwood Academic, Amsteldisk 166, 1st Fl., 1079 LH Amsterdam, Netherlands. URL: http://www.gbhap.com/ Superconductivity_Review/. *2653*

SUPERCONDUCTOR SCIENCE & TECHNOLOGY.
I O P Publishing Ltd., Dirac House, Temple Back, Bristol BS1 6BE, England. TEL 44-117-929-7481. FAX 44-117-929-4318. URL: http://www.iop.org. *5828*

SUPERCONDUCTOR WEEK.
WestTech, Box 411433, San Francisco, CA 94141. FAX 415-837-0372.
Vendor(s): Data-Star, Information Access Co., Knight-Ridder Information, Inc., NewsNet. *5828*

SUPERFUND WEEK.
Pasha Publications Inc., 1616 N. Ft. Myer Dr., Ste. 1000, Arlington, VA 22209-3107. TEL 703-528-1244. FAX 703-528-1253. *2953*

SUPERMARKET BUSINESS.
Howfrey Communications, 1086 Teaneck Rd., Teaneck, NJ 07666-4838. TEL 201-833-1900. FAX 201-833-1273.
Vendor(s): Information Access Co., Lexis-Nexis. *3145*

SUPERMARKET NEWS.
Fairchild Publications, 7 W. 34th St., New York, NY 10001. TEL 212-630-4199. FAX 212-630-4201.
Vendor(s): Information Access Co., Knight-Ridder Information, Inc., Lexis-Nexis. *3145*

SUPERMARKET STRATEGIC ALERT.
Pollack Associates, 140 E. 81st St., Ste. 5E, New York, NY 10028. TEL 212-734-0753. FAX 212-988-9394. *3145*

SUPPORTIVE CARE IN CANCER.
Springer-Verlag, Heidelberger Platz 3, 14197 Berlin, Germany. TEL 49-30-82787-0. FAX 49-30-82787448. URL: http://www.springer.de. *4987*

SUPRAMOLECULAR CHEMISTRY.
Gordon and Breach - Harwood Academic, Amsteldisk 166, 1st Fl., 1079 LH Amsterdam, Netherlands. URL: http://www.gbhap.com/ Supramolecular_Chemistry/. *1768*

SUPREME COURT OF CANADA DECISIONS.
Western Legal Publications, 301-1 Alexander St., Vancouver, BC V6A 1B2, Canada. TEL 604-687-5671. FAX 604-687-2796. *4138*

SUR IN ENGLISH.
Prensa Malaguena, S.A., Ave. Dr. Maranon 48, 29009 Malaga, Spain. TEL 34-52-649600. FAX 34-52-611256. *3360*

SURFACE.
Surface Publishing, 1388 Haight St., Ste. 168, San Francisco, CA 94117. TEL 415-771-0851. FAX 415-621-5404. *3386*

SURFACES.
University of Montreal, Department of Comparative Literature, URL: http://tornade.ere.umontreal.ca/ ~guedon/Surfaces/
Available only online. *4475*

SURGICAL AND RADIOLOGIC ANATOMY.
Springer-Verlag France, 26 rue des Carmes, 75005 Paris, France. TEL 33-1-44-41-15-80. FAX 33-1-43-54-49-08. URL: http://science.springer.de. *4749*

SURGICAL ENDOSCOPY.
Springer-Verlag, Medical Journals, 175 Fifth Ave., New York, NY 10010. TEL 212-460-1500. FAX 212-473-6272. URL: http://www.springer-ny.com. *5155*

SURGICAL RESEARCH COMMUNICATIONS.
Gordon and Breach - Harwood Academic, Amsteldisk 166, 1st Fl., 1079 LH Amsterdam, Netherlands. URL: http://www.gbhap.com/ Surgical_Research_Communications/. *5155*

SURPLUS RECORD.
Surplus Record, Inc., 20 N. Wacker Dr., Chicago, IL 60606. TEL 312-372-9077. FAX 312-372-6537. URL: http://www.surplusrecord.com. *4552*

SURVEY OF CURRENT BUSINESS.
U.S. Bureau of Economic Analysis, U.S. Department of Commerce, Washington, DC 20230. TEL 202-606-9900. URL: http://www.bea.doc.gov/ scbinf.html.
Vendor(s): Information Access Co., Knight-Ridder Information, Inc., UMI. *1291*

SUSSEX PAST AND PRESENT.
Sussex Archaeological Society, Bull House, 92 High St., Lewes, Sussex BN7 1XH, England. TEL 44-1273-486260. FAX 44-1273-486990.
Vendor(s): Information Access Co. *385*

SVENSKA MACPRESSEN.
Fakta - Press AB, P.O. Box 2048, S-550 02 Jonkoeping, Sweden. TEL 46-36-16-50-08. FAX 46-36-71-93-33. URL: http://www.macpressen.se. *2193*

SVERIGE - NYTT.
Aktiebolaget Sverige-Nytt, Box 22045, S-104 22 Stockholm, Sweden. TEL 46-8-650-05-25. FAX 46-8-650-04-07. URL: http://www.sverigenytt.se. *3363*

SWEDEN. FOERSAEKRINGSVAERKET. SOCIALFOERSAEKRINGSFAKTA.
Foersaekringsvaerket, Adolf Fredriks Kyrkogata 8, S-103 51 Stockholm, Sweden. TEL 46-8-786-90-00. FAX 46-8-786-95-80. URL: http://rpmg.se/ rfv.statistik/. *3835*

SWEDEN. SOCIALSTYRELSEN. FOERFATTNINGSSAMLING: MEDICAL.
Socialstyrelsen, S-106 30 Stockholm, Sweden. FAX 48-8-783-30-06. *4749*

SWEDEN. SOCIALSTYRELSEN. FOERFATTNINGSSAMLING: SOCIAL.
Socialstyrelsen, 106 30 Stockholm, Sweden. *6691*

THE SWEDISH ECONOMY.
Fritzes AB, S-106 47 Stockholm, Sweden. TEL 46-468-690-9090. FAX 46-468-205021.
Vendor(s): Information Access Co. *1005*

SWEDISH EXAMPLE.
Nordic News Network, P.O. Box 1181, S-181 23 Lidingoe, Sweden. TEL 46-8-731-92-00. FAX 46-8-731-92-00.
Available only online. *5973*

SWEET & SAVOURY BISCUITS: THE INTERNATIONAL MARKET.
Euromonitor, 60-61 Britton St., London EC1M 5NA, England. TEL 44-171-251-8024. FAX 44-171-608-3149. URL: http://www.euromonitor.com.
Vendor(s): Data-Star, Knight-Ridder Information, Inc. *3138*

SWISS BUSINESS.
S H Z Fachverlag AG, Seestr. 37, CH-8027 Zurich, Switzerland. TEL 41-1-2022046. FAX 41-1-2811970.
Vendor(s): Information Access Co. *1410*

SYLLABUS (SUNNYVALE).
Syllabus Press, 345 Northlake Dr., San Jose, CA 95117-1261. TEL 408-746-2000. FAX 408-746-2711. URL: http://www.syllabus.com. *2519*

SYMPOSIUM.
Heldref Publications, 1319 Eighteenth St., N.W., Washington, DC 20036-1802. TEL 202-296-6267. FAX 202-296-5149.
Vendor(s): Information Access Co. *4476*

SYNAGOGEN RUNDSCHAU.
Arthur-Custos-Gedaechtnis-Archiv, Tinnagel 5, 47608 Geldern, Germany. TEL 49-2831-2759. FAX 49-2831-98537. *6410*

SYNTHESIS C E.
Pasha Publications Inc., 1616 N. Ft. Myer Dr., Ste. 1000, Arlington, VA 22209-3107. TEL 703-528-1244. FAX 703-528-1253. *6443*

SYNTHESIS R C L.
Pasha Publications Inc., 1616 N. Ft. Myer Dr., Ste. 1000, Arlington, VA 22209-3107. TEL 703-528-1244. FAX 703-528-1253. *6443*

SYNTHETIC METHODS OF ORGANIC CHEMISTRY.
S. Karger AG, Allschwilerstr. 10, P.O. Box, CH-4009 Basel, Switzerland. TEL 41-61-3061111. FAX 41-61-3061234. URL: http://www.karger.ch.
Vendor(s): Questel Orbit Inc. *1824*

SYRACUSE JOURNAL OF INTERNATIONAL LAW & COMMERCE.
Joe Christensen, Inc. (Syracuse), E I White Hall, Ste. 0041, Syracuse, NY 13244-1030. TEL 315-443-2056.
Vendor(s): West Group. *4126*

SYSTEMS & NETWORK MANAGEMENT REPORT.
DataTrends Publications, Inc., Box 4460, Leesburg, VA 20177. TEL 703-779-0574. FAX 703-779-2267.
Vendor(s): Information Access Co. *2159*

T A J A.
Australian Anthropological Society, c/o Dept. of Anthropology, Univ. of Sydney, Sydney, N.S.W. 2006, Australia. TEL 61-2-93515489. FAX 61-2-93515489.
Vendor(s): Information Access Co. *331*

T A M BULLETIN.
Travelling Art Mail, c/o T A M, Postbus 10388, 5000 JJ Tilburg, Netherlands. TEL 31-13-5366103. *468*

T & E UPDATE.
Rochester Institute of Technology, Technical and Education Center for the Graphic Arts, 67 Lomb Memorial Dr., CIMS 2000, Rochester, NY 14623. TEL 716-475-2549. FAX 716-475-5571. URL: http://www.rit.edu/cims/te. *6086*

T C.
Box 15399, Atlanta, GA 30333-0399. TEL 404-727-2344. URL: http://scholar.cc.emory.edu/ scripts/tc/tc.html.
Available only online. *6376*

T C I.
Theatre Crafts International, 32 W. 18th St., New York, NY 10011-4612. TEL 212-229-2965. FAX 212-229-2084.
Vendor(s): Information Access Co., UMI. *7014*

T D R.
M I T Press, 5 Cambridge Center, Cambridge, MA 02142. TEL 617-253-2889. FAX 617-577-1545. URL: http://www-mitpress.mit.edu.
Vendor(s): Information Access Co. *7014*

T G A NEWS.
Department of Human Services and Health, Therapeutic Goods Administration, URL: http:// www.health.gov.au/hsh/tga/tga.htm.
Available only online. *5695*

T H E JOURNAL.
Ed Warnshius Ltd., 150 El Camino Real, Ste. 112, Tustin, CA 92780. TEL 714-730-4011. FAX 714-730-3739. URL: http://www.thejournal.c.
Vendor(s): Information Access Co. *2519*

T M A EXECUTIVE SUMMARY.
Tobacco Merchants Association of the United States, Inc., 231 Clarksville Rd., Ste. 6, Box 8019, Princeton, NJ 08543-8019. TEL 609-275-4900. FAX 609-275-8379. *7020*

T M A LEGISLATIVE BULLETIN.
Tobacco Merchants Association of the United States, Inc., 231 Clarksville Rd., Ste. 6, Box 8019, Princeton, NJ 08543-8019. TEL 609-275-4900. FAX 609-275-8379. *7020*

T M A TOBACCO BAROMETER: SMOKING, CHEWING, SNUFF.
Tobacco Merchants Association of the United States, Inc., 231 Clarksville Rd., Ste. 6, Box 8019, Princeton, NJ 08543-8019. TEL 609-275-4900. FAX 609-275-8379. *7021*

T M A TRADEMARK REPORT.
Tobacco Merchants Association of the United States, Inc., 231 Clarksville Rd., Ste. 6, Box 8019, Princeton, NJ 08543-8019. TEL 609-275-4900. FAX 609-275-8379. *7021*

T M A WORLD ALERT.
Tobacco Merchants Association of the United States, Inc., 231 Clarksville Rd., Ste. 6, Box 8019, Princeton, NJ 08543-8019. TEL 609-275-4900. FAX 609-275-8379. *7021*

T O W S.
URL: http://www.santacruz.k12.ca.us/~jpost/ projects/tows/tows.html.
Available only online. *1889*

SERIALS AVAILABLE ONLINE

T R I P SOUTH.
Browning Publications, 3103 Medlock Bridge Rd., Norcross, GA 30071. TEL 770-825-0220. FAX 770-825-0880. URL: http://www.tripsouth.com. *7236*

T R I S ELECTRONIC BIBLIOGRAPHIC DATA BASE.
U.S. National Research Council, Transportation Research Board, 2101 Constitution Ave., N.W., Washington, DC 20418. TEL 202-334-3250. FAX 202-334-3495. URL: http://www.nas.edu/trb/index.html.
Vendor(s): Knight-Ridder Information, Inc. (File no. 63). *7058*

T R WIRELESS NEWS.
Telecommunications Reports, 1333 H St., N.W., Ste. 100-E, Washington, DC 20005. FAX 202-842-3023. URL: http://www.tr.com.
Vendor(s): Information Access Co., NewsNet (TE45). *2004*

T V HOST MONTHLY.
T V Host, Inc., Box 1665, 3935 Jonestown Rd., Harrisburg, PA 17109. TEL 717-657-1700. FAX 717-657-2921. URL: http://www.tvhost.com; http://www.nytimes.cm/maglive.html. *2060*

T V HOST WEEKLY.
T V Host, Inc., Box 1665, 3935 Jonestown Rd., Harrisburg, PA 17109. TEL 717-657-1700. FAX 717-657-2921. URL: http://www.tvhost.com; http://www.nytimes.com/maglive.html. *2060*

T V SPORTSFILE.
Gould Media Services, Box 446, York, ME 03909. TEL 207-363-6037. FAX 207-363-7824. *6790*

DIE TAGESZEITUNG.
T A Z Verlagsgenossenschaft e.G., Kochstr. 18, 10969 Berlin, Germany. TEL 49-30-25902-0. FAX 49-30-2518095. URL: http://www.taz.de. *3291*

TAHITI BEACH PRESS.
Tahiti Publications Touristiques, P.O. Box 887, Papeete 98713, Tahiti. TEL 689-426850. FAX 689-423356. URL: http://www.fix.net/%7e.davis/tahiti-beach-press.html. *7237*

TAKE CARE.
Culture Clash Communications, URL: http://www.izad.com/cultureclash.
Available only online. *5791*

TALEBONES.
Fairwood Press, 10531 S.E. 250th Pl., Apt. 104, Kent, WA 98031-2892. URL: http://www.nventure.com/talebones. *4537*

TALK OF THE TYNE.
P.O. Box 25, Spennymoor, Co. Durham DL16 6GI, England. TEL 44-1388-815878. FAX 44-1388-815878. URL: http://www.swan.co.uk/tott/ *6819*

TALK STORY.
Smithsonian Institution, Center for Folklife Programs & Cultural Studies, 955 L'Enfant Plaza, S.W., Ste. 2600, MRC 914, Washington, DC 20560. TEL 202-287-3424. FAX 202-287-3699. URL: http://www.si.edu/folklife.
Available only online. *3092*

TALKING BOOK TOPICS (LARGE PRINT EDITION).
U.S. Library of Congress, National Library Service for the Blind and Physically Handicapped, Washington, DC 20542. TEL 202-707-5100. FAX 202-707-0712. URL: http://www.lcweb.loc.gov/nls. *3474*

TALKING POINTS.
Heritage Foundation, 214 Massachusetts Ave., N.E., Washington, DC 20002. TEL 202-546-4400. FAX 202-543-9647.
Vendor(s): Lexis-Nexis. *6039*

TAMPA BAY BUSINESS JOURNAL.
American City Business Journals, Inc. (Tampa), Box 24185, Tampa, FL 33623. TEL 813-877-6627.
Vendor(s): Information Access Co.. *1292*

TANDANYA.
Adelaide Bushwalkers Inc., Box 178, Unley, S.A. 5061, Australia. TEL 61-8-3811813. FAX 61-8-3810373. URL: http://www.fastlink.com.au:80/subscrib/bushwalking/sabw.html. *6885*

TAPE - DISC BUSINESS.
Knowledge Industry Publications, Inc., 701 Westchester Ave., White Plains, NY 10604-3002. TEL 914-328-9157. FAX 914-328-9093.
Vendor(s): Information Access Co. *1596*

TARGET MARKETING.
North American Publishing Co., 401 N. Broad St., Philadelphia, PA 19108. TEL 215-238-5300. FAX 215-238-5457.
Vendor(s): Information Access Co. *1551*

TAROT NEWS.
Tarot Special Interest Group of American Mensa, Tarot Special-Interest Group, Box 561, Quincy, IL 62306-0561. TEL 217-222-9082. *5578*

TASMANIAN REPORTS.
L B C Information Services, 50 Waterloo Rd., N. Ryde, N.S.W. 2113, Australia. TEL 61-2-99366444. FAX 61-2-98889706.
Vendor(s): Info-One International Pty Ltd.. *4139*

TASTY BITS FROM THE TECHNOLOGY FRONT.
URL: http://www.tbtf.com/.
Available only online. *2140*

TATTOOS.COM EZINE.
2234 Kingston Rd., Toronto, ON M1N 1T9, Canada. URL: http://tattoos.com.
Available only online. *468*

THE TAX ADVISER.
American Institute of Certified Public Accountants, Harborside Financial Ctr., 201 Plaza Three, Jersey City, NJ 07311-9801. TEL 201-938-3796. FAX 201-329-1112. URL: http://www.aicpa.org.
Vendor(s): Information Access Co., UMI. *1630*

THE TAX DIRECTORY.
Tax Analysts, 6830 N. Fairfax Dr., Arlington, VA 22213. TEL 703-553-4400. FAX 703-533-4444.
Vendor(s): Knight-Ridder Information, Inc., Lexis-Nexis. *1630*

THE TAX EXECUTIVE.
Tax Executives Institute, Inc., 1001 Pennsylvania Ave., N.W., No. 320, Washington, DC 20004-2505. TEL 202-638-5601. FAX 202-638-5607.
Vendor(s): Information Access Co., UMI. *1630*

TAX LAWYER.
American Bar Association, Taxation Section, 470 15th St., N.W., Washington, DC 20005-1009. URL: http://www.abanet.org.
Vendor(s): Lexis-Nexis, West Group. *4031*

TAX MANAGEMENT COMPENSATION PLANNING.
Tax Management, Inc., 1250 23rd St., N.W., Washington, DC 20037-1166. TEL 202-833-7240. FAX 202-833-7297. URL: http://www.bna.com/
Vendor(s): West Group (File TM-CP, TM-CP-OLD, TM-CPJ). *1631*

TAX MANAGEMENT COMPENSATION PLANNING JOURNAL.
Tax Management, Inc., 1250 23rd St., N.W., Washington, DC 20037-1166. TEL 202-833-7240. FAX 202-833-7297.
Vendor(s): UMI, West Group (File TM-CPJ). *1509*

TAX MANAGEMENT ESTATES, GIFTS AND TRUSTS.
Tax Management, Inc., 1250 23rd St., N.W., Washington, DC 20037-1166. TEL 202-833-7240. FAX 202-833-7297.
Vendor(s): West Group (Files TM-EGT, TM-EGT-OLD, TM-EGTJ). *1631*

TAX MANAGEMENT ESTATES, GIFTS AND TRUSTS JOURNAL.
Tax Management, Inc., 1250 23rd St., N.W., Washington, DC 20037-1166. TEL 202-452-4200. FAX 202-822-8092.
Vendor(s): Knight-Ridder Information, Inc. (Files 15, 485), UMI, West Group (File TM-EGTJ). *1410*

TAX MANAGEMENT FINANCIAL PLANNING JOURNAL.
Tax Management, Inc., 1250 23rd St., N.W., Washington, DC 20037. TEL 202-833-7240.
Vendor(s): UMI. *1169*

TAX MANAGEMENT FINANCIAL PRODUCTS REPORT.
Tax Management, Inc., 1231 25th St., N.W., Washington, DC 20037. TEL 202-833-7240. FAX 202-833-7297. URL: http://www.bna.com/. *1631*

TAX MANAGEMENT FOREIGN INCOME PORTFOLIOS.
Tax Management, Inc., 1250 23rd St., N.W., Washington, DC 20037-1166. TEL 202-833-7240. FAX 202-833-7297.
Vendor(s): West Group (File TM-FOR). *1631*

TAX MANAGEMENT INTERNATIONAL FORUM.
B N A International, Inc., Heron House, 10 Dean Farrar St., London SW1H 0DX, England. TEL 44-171-222-8831. FAX 44-171-222-0294. URL: http://www.bna.com. *1631*

TAX MANAGEMENT INTERNATIONAL JOURNAL.
Tax Management, Inc., 1250 23rd St., N.W., Washington, DC 20037-1166. TEL 202-833-7240. FAX 202-833-7297.
Vendor(s): Knight-Ridder Information, Inc. (Files 15, 485), UMI. *1632*

TAX MANAGEMENT MEMORANDUM.
Tax Management, Inc., 1231 23rd St., N.W., Washington, DC 20037-1166. TEL 202-833-7240. FAX 202-833-7297.
Vendor(s): UMI, West Group (File TM-TMM). *1632*

TAX MANAGEMENT REAL ESTATE.
Tax Management, Inc., 1250 23rd St., N.W., Washington, DC 20037-1166. TEL 202-833-7240. FAX 202-833-7297.
Vendor(s): West Group (Files TM-RE, TM-RE-OLD, TM-REJ). *6313*

TAX MANAGEMENT REAL ESTATE JOURNAL.
Tax Management, Inc., 1250 23rd St., N.W., Washington, DC 20037-1166. TEL 202-833-7240. FAX 202-833-7297.
Vendor(s): UMI, West Group (File TM-REJ). *6313*

TAX MANAGEMENT U S INCOME.
Tax Management, Inc., 1250 23rd St., N.W., Washington, DC 20037-1166. TEL 202-833-7240. FAX 202-833-7297.
Vendor(s): West Group (Files TM-US, TM-US-OLD, TM-TMWR). *1632*

TAX MANAGEMENT WEEKLY REPORT.
Tax Management, Inc., 1250 23rd St., N.W., Washington, DC 20037-1166. TEL 202-833-7240. FAX 202-833-7297.
Vendor(s): Human Resources Information Network (File DD), NewsNet (File TMWEEK), West Group (File TM-TMWR). *1632*

TAX NEWS SERVICE.
I B F D Publications B.V., P.O. Box 20237, 1000 HE Amsterdam, Netherlands. TEL 31-20-6267726. FAX 31-20-6228658.
Vendor(s): I B F D Pubns. BV, Lexis-Nexis. *1632*

TAX NOTES.
Tax Analysts, 6830 N. Fairfax Dr., Arlington, VA 22213. TEL 703-533-4400. FAX 703-533-4444.
Vendor(s): Knight-Ridder Information, Inc., Lexis-Nexis. *1633*

TAX NOTES INTERNATIONAL.
Tax Analysts, 6830 N. Fairfax Dr., Arlington, VA 22213. TEL 703-533-4646. FAX 703-533-4444.
Vendor(s): Knight-Ridder Information, Inc., Lexis-Nexis. *1633*

TAX PLANNING INTERNATIONAL REVIEW.
B N A International, Inc., Heron House, 10 Dean Farrar St., London SW1H 0DX, England. TEL 44-171-222-8831. FAX 44-171-222-0294. URL: http://www.bna.com. *1633*

TAX PROFILE.
C C H Canadian Ltd., 6 Garamond Ct., North York, ON M3C 1Z5, Canada. TEL 416-441-2992. FAX 416-449-9011.
Vendor(s): QL Systems Ltd. *1633*

TAX TREATIES DATA BASE ON C D - R O M.
I B F D Publications B.V., P.O. Box 20237, 1000 HE Amsterdam, Netherlands. TEL 31-20-6267726. FAX 31-20-6228658.
Vendor(s): I B F D Pubns. BV, Lexis-Nexis. *1633*

TAX WEEK.
C C H Australia Ltd., P.O. Box 230, North Ryde, N.S.W. 2113, Australia. TEL 61-1-300300224. FAX 61-1-300306224. *1634*

TAXATION FOR ACCOUNTANTS.
Warren, Gorham & Lamont, One Penn Plaza, New York, NY 10119. TEL 212-971-5000. FAX 212-971-5113. URL: http://www.wgl.com/tax/txac.html.
Vendor(s): Lexis-Nexis. *1634*

TAXATION FOR LAWYERS.
Warren, Gorham & Lamont, One Penn Plaza, New York, NY 10119. TEL 212-971-5000. FAX 212-971-5240.
Vendor(s): Lexis-Nexis. *1634*

TAXES (RIVERWOODS).
C C H Incorporated, 2700 Lake Cook Rd., Riverwoods, IL 60015. TEL 847-267-7000. FAX 800-224-8299.
Vendor(s): UMI. *1635*

TAYLOROLOGY.
URL: http://www.angelfire.com/az/taylorology. Available only online. *5346*

TEA AND COFFEE TRADE JOURNAL.
Lockwood Trade Journal Co., Inc., 130 W. 42nd St., New York, NY 10036-7802. TEL 212-391-2060. FAX 212-827-0945.
Vendor(s): Information Access Co., Lexis-Nexis. *3129*

TEA TIME.
URL: http://www.cei.net/'mlong. Available only online. *4537*

TEACHER.
Editorial Projects in Education, Inc., 4301 Connecticut Ave., N.W., Ste. 432, Washington, DC 20008. TEL 202-364-4114. URL: http://www.edweek.org/tm/tm.htm. *2620*

TEACHERS COLLEGE RECORD.
Columbia University, Teachers College Record Office, 525 W. 120th St., New York, NY 10027. TEL 212-678-3774. FAX 212-678-3790.
Vendor(s): UMI. *2487*

TEACHING AND LEARNING IN MEDICINE.
Lawrence Erlbaum Associates, Inc., 10 Industrial Dr., Mahwah, NJ 07430-2262. TEL 201-236-9500. FAX 201-236-0072. URL: http://www.erlbaum.com. *4750*

TEACHING CHILDREN MATHEMATICS.
National Council of Teachers of Mathematics, 1906 Association Dr., Reston, VA 22091-1593. TEL 703-620-9840. FAX 703-476-2970. URL: http://www.nctm.org.
Vendor(s): Information Access Co.. *4610*

TEACHING EDUCATION.
University of South Carolina, College of Education, Columbia, SC 29208. TEL 803-777-6301. FAX 803-777-3090. *2487*

TEACHING IN THE COMMUNITY COLLEGES JOURNAL.
URL: http://naio.kcc.hawaii.edu. Available only online. *2557*

TECBAHIA.
Centro de Pesquisas e Desenvolvimento, Rodovia BA-512, Km 0, Caixa Postal 09, 42800-000 Camacari BA, Brazil. TEL 55-71-8347500. FAX 55-71-8322243. URL: http://www.bahianet.com.br/ceped. *6975*

TECHKNOW TIMES.
URL: http://www.techknowtimes.com. Available only online. *2140*

TECHNICAL ANALYSIS OF STOCKS & COMMODITIES.
Technical Analysis, Inc., 4757 California Ave., S.W., Seattle, WA 98116-4499. TEL 206-938-0570. FAX 206-938-1307. URL: http://www.Traders.com. *1411*

TECHNICAL COMMUNICATION.
Society for Technical Communication, 901 N. Stuart St., Ste. 904, Arlington, VA 22203-1822. TEL 703-522-4114.
Vendor(s): Information Access Co., UMI. *2004*

TECHNICAL LITERATURE ABSTRACTS.
American Petroleum Institute, EnCompass, 275 Seventh Ave., New York, NY 10001-6708. TEL 212-366-4040. FAX 212-366-4298.
Vendor(s): Knight-Ridder Information, Inc., Questel Orbit Inc. (APILIT), STN International (APILIT), Telesystemes - Questel. *5632*

TECHNICAL LITERATURE ABSTRACTS: CATALYSTS - ZEOLITES.
American Petroleum Institute, EnCompass, 275 Seventh Ave., New York, NY 10001-6708. TEL 212-366-4040. FAX 212-366-4298. URL: http://www.api.org.
Vendor(s): Knight-Ridder Information, Inc., Questel Orbit Inc. (APILIT), STN International, Telesystemes - Questel. *1786*

TECHNICAL LITERATURE ABSTRACTS: FUEL REFORMULATION.
American Petroleum Institute, EnCompass, 275 Seventh Ave., New York, NY 10001-6708. TEL 212-366-4040. FAX 212-366-4298. URL: http://www.api.org.
Vendor(s): Knight-Ridder Information, Inc., Questel Orbit Inc. (APILIT), STN International (APILIT), Telesystemes - Questel. *1786*

TECHNICAL LITERATURE ABSTRACTS: OILFIELD CHEMICALS.
American Petroleum Institute, EnCompass, 275 Seventh Ave., New York, NY 10001-6708. TEL 212-366-4040. FAX 212-366-4298. URL: http://www.api.org.
Vendor(s): Knight-Ridder Information, Inc., Questel Orbit Inc. (APILIT), STN International (APILIT), Telesystemes - Questel. *5632*

TECHNICAL LITERATURE ABSTRACTS: TRIBOLOGY.
American Petroleum Institute, EnCompass, 275 Seventh Ave., New York, NY 10001-6708. TEL 212-366-4040. FAX 212-366-4298. URL: http://www.api.org.
Vendor(s): Knight-Ridder Information, Inc., Questel Orbit Inc. (APILIT), STN International (APILIT), Telesystemes - Questel. *1786*

TECHNICAL PHYSICS.
American Institute of Physics, One Physics Ellipse, College Park, MD 20740-3843. TEL 301-209-3000. *5829*

TECHNICAL PHYSICS LETTERS.
American Institute of Physics, One Physics Ellipse, College Park, MD 20740-3843. TEL 301-209-3000. URL: http://www.aip.org. *5829*

TECHNO ONLINE.
R A N X, Oderbruchstrasse 10, 10369 Berlin, Germany. TEL 040-441-98-341. FAX 030-25-55-55-99. URL: http://www.techno.de. Available only online. *5440*

TECHNOLOGIES FOR WORSHIP MAGAZINE.
A M I Publishing, P.O. Box 35, 20 Wellington St., E., Aurora, ON L4G 3H1, Canada. TEL 905-830-4300. FAX 905-853-5096. *6976*

TECHNOLOGY ACCESS REPORT.
University R & D Opportunities, Inc., 8 Digital Dr., Ste. 250, Novato, CA 94949-5759. TEL 415-883-7600. FAX 415-883-6421.
Vendor(s): DataArkiv A.B., Knight-Ridder Information, Inc., NewsNet (RD38). *6976*

TECHNOLOGY ALERT.
Merton Allen Associates, InfoTeam Inc., Box 15640, Plantation, FL 33318-5640. TEL 954-473-9560. FAX 954-473-0544.
Vendor(s): Data-Star, Information Access Co., NewsNet (RD09), UMI. *6976*

TECHNOLOGY AND LEARNING.
Miller Freeman, Inc., 600 Harrison St., San Francisco, CA 94107. TEL 415-905-2200. FAX 415-908-6604. URL: http://www.techlearning.com.
Vendor(s): Information Access Co., Knight-Ridder Information, Inc., UMI. *2519*

TECHNOLOGY MANAGEMENT ACTION.
Technology News Center, 6810 Butler Valley Rd., Korbel, CA 95550. TEL 707-668-4027. FAX 707-668-4055. *1348*

TECHNOLOGY REVIEW.
Massachusetts Institute of Technology, W59-200, Cambridge, MA 02139. TEL 617-253-8250. URL: http://www.mit.edu/org/t/techreview/www/tr.html.
Vendor(s): Knight-Ridder Information, Inc., UMI. *6578*

TECHNOLOGY TRANSFER HIGHLIGHTS.
Argonne National Laboratory, Industrial Technology Development Center, 9700 S. Cass Ave., Bldg. 900, Argonne, IL 60439. TEL 708-252-6393. FAX 708-252-5230. URL: http://www.anl.gov/ITD/hilead.html. *6977*

TECHNOLOGY TRANSFER WEEK.
Technical Insights, Inc., 32 N. Dean St., Englewood, NJ 07631-9967. TEL 201-568-4774. FAX 201-568-8247.
Vendor(s): Data-Star, Information Access Co., Knight-Ridder Information, Inc., NewsNet (DE17). *5287*

TECHNOLOGY WATCH.
Technology Watch, Inc., Box 2206, Springfield, VA 22152. *2125*

TEEN.
Petersen Publishing Co., 6420 Wilshire Blvd., Los Angeles, CA 90048. TEL 213-782-2000.
Vendor(s): Information Access Co., Knight-Ridder Information, Inc. *1889*

TEIRESIAS.
McGill University, Department of History, 855 Sherbrooke St. W., Montreal, PQ H3A 2T7, Canada. TEL 514-398-1797. *1908*

TEKSTILEC.
Urednistvo Tekstilec, Snezniska 5, p.p. 311, 61000 Ljubljana, Slovenia. TEL 61 224-417.
Vendor(s): Knight-Ridder Information, Inc. *6994*

TELCO BUSINESS REPORT.
Capitol Publications Inc., Telecom Publishing Group, 1101 King St., Ste. 444, Box 1455, Alexandria, VA 22313-2055. FAX 703-739-6490. URL: http://www.telecommunications.com.
Vendor(s): Information Access Co., Knight-Ridder Information, Inc., NewsNet (TE49). *2039*

TELCO COMPETITION REPORT.
Telecommunications Reports, 1333 H St., N.W., Ste. 100-E, Washington, DC 20005. FAX 202-842-3023. URL: http://www.tr.com.
Vendor(s): Information Access Co., NewsNet (TE62). *2004*

TELE-SERVICE NEWS.
Worldwide Videotex, Box 3273, Boynton Beach, FL 33424-3273. TEL 407-738-2276.
Vendor(s): Data-Star, Information Access Co., Knight-Ridder Information, Inc., NewsNet (TE21). *2039*

TELECOM & NETWORK SECURITY REVIEW.
Pasha Publications Inc., 1616 N. Ft. Myer Dr., Ste. 1000, Arlington, VA 22209-3107. TEL 703-528-1244. FAX 703-528-1253. *2004*

TELECOM MARKETS.
Financial Times Telecoms & Media Publishing, Maple House, 149 Tottenham Court Rd., London W1P 9LL, England. TEL 44-171-896-2234. FAX 44-171-896-2256.
Vendor(s): Data-Star, Information Access Co., Lexis-Nexis. *1596*

TELECOMEUROPA'S DEVELOPING WORLD TELECOMMUNICATIONS.
Telecomeuropa News Bureau Publications, 3 Princes Bldgs., George St., Bath, Avon BA1 2ED, England. TEL 44-1225-445282. FAX 44-1225-445283. *2004*

TELECOMEUROPA'S INTERACTIVE VIDEO NEWSLETTER.
Telecomeuropa News Bureau Publications, 3 Princes Bldgs., George St., Bath, Avon BA1 2ED, England. TEL 44-1225-445282. FAX 44-1225-445283. *2068*

TELECOMEUROPA'S INTERNATIONAL REGULATORY UPDATE.
Telecomeuropa News Bureau Publications, 3 Princes Bldgs., George St., Bath, Avon BA1 2ED, England. TEL 44-1225-445282. FAX 44-1225-445283. *2004*

TELECOMEUROPA'S MESSAGING NEWSLETTER.
Telecomeuropa News Bureau Publications, 3 Princes Bldgs., George St., Bath, Avon BA1 2ED, England. TEL 44-1225-445282. FAX 44-1225-445283. *2018*

TELECOMEUROPA'S MOBILE PHONE MONITOR.
Telecomeuropa News Bureau Publications, 3 Princes Bldgs., George St., Bath, Avon BA1 2ED, England. TEL 44-1225-445282. FAX 44-1225-445283. *2040*

TELECOMEUROPA'S SATELLITE COMMUNICATIONS NEWSLETTER.
Telecomeuropa News Bureau Publications, 3 Princes Bldgs., George St., Bath, Avon BA1 2ED, England. TEL 44-1225-445282. FAX 44-1225-445283. *2005*

TELECOMEUROPA'S TELECOMS STANDARDS MONITOR.
Telecomeuropa News Bureau Publications, 3 Princes Bldgs., George St., Bath, Avon BA1 2ED, England. TEL 44-1225-445282. FAX 44-1225-445283. *2005*

TELECOMEUROPA'S TELECOMS TARIFFS INNOVATION.
Telecomeuropa News Bureau Publications, 3 Princes Bldgs., George St., Bath, Avon BA1 2ED, England. TEL 44-1225-445282. FAX 44-1225-445283. *2005*

TELECOMMUNICATIONS (NORTH AMERICAN EDITION).
Horizon House Publications, Inc., 685 Canton St., Norwood, MA 02062. TEL 617-769-9750. FAX 617-762-9230.
Vendor(s): Information Access Co., UMI. *2005*

TELECOMMUNICATIONS AMERICAS.
Portland House, Stag Pl., London SW1E 5XT, England. TEL 44-171-957-0030. FAX 44-171-957-0031.
Vendor(s): UMI. *2040*

TELECOMMUNICATIONS INTERNATIONAL.
Portland House, Stag Pl., London SW1E 5XT, England. TEL 071-957-0030. FAX 071-957-0031.
Vendor(s): UMI. *2040*

TELECOMMUNICATIONS REPORTS.
Telecommunications Reports, 1333 H St., N.W., Ste. 100-E, Washington, DC 20005. FAX 202-842-3023. URL: http://www.tr.com.
Vendor(s): Information Access Co., NewsNet (TE11). *2005*

TELECOMMUNICATIONS REPORTS INTERNATIONAL.
Telecommunications Reports, 1333 H St., N.W., Ste.100-E, Washington, DC 20005. FAX 202-842-3023. URL: http://www.tr.com.
Vendor(s): Information Access Co., NewsNet (TE14). *2005*

TELECOMMUTING REVIEW.
Gil Gordon Associates, 10 Donner Ct., Monmouth Junction, NJ 08852. TEL 908-329-2266. URL: http://www.gilgordon.com.
Vendor(s): Information Access Co. *1576*

TELECOMWORLDWIRE.
M2 Communications Ltd., P.O. Box 475, Coventry CV1 2ZW, England. TEL 44-1203-634700. FAX 44-1203-634144. URL: http://www.m2.com.
Available only online. *2006*

TELECONNECT.
Gerald A. Friesen, Inc., 12 W. 21st St., New York, NY 10010. TEL 212-691-8215.
Vendor(s): Information Access Co. *2040*

TELEFAXBUCH DER DEUTSCHEN TELEKOM AG.
Deutsche Telekom Medien GmbH, Wiesenhuettenstr. 18, 60329 Frankfurt a.M., Germany. TEL 069-2682-0. FAX 069-26821101. *2021*

TELEMARKETING.
Technology Marketing Corporation, One Technology Plaza, Norwalk, CT 06854. TEL 203-852-6800. FAX 203-853-2845. URL: http://www.tmcnet.com/telemark/telemktg.htm.
Vendor(s): Information Access Co. *2006*

TELEPHONE I P NEWS.
Worldwide Videotex, Box 3273, Boynton Beach, FL 33424-3273. TEL 407-738-2276.
Vendor(s): Information Access Co. *2006*

TELEPHONE INDUSTRY DIRECTORY.
Phillips Business Information, Inc., 1201 Seven Locks Rd., Potomac, MD 20854. TEL 301-424-3338. FAX 301-309-3847.
Vendor(s): NewsNet (TE83E). *1715*

TELEPHONE NURSING TELEZINE.
4012 W Fig St., Tampa, FL 33609. URL: http://ally.ios.com/~webster/telezine.html.
Available only online. *4950*

TELEPHONY.
Telephony Publishing, One I B M Plaza, Chicago, IL 60611. TEL 312-595-1080. URL: http://www.internettelephony.com.
Vendor(s): Information Access Co., UMI. *2041*

TELESIS (OTTAWA).
Bell-Northern Research Ltd., 3500 Carling Ave., Ottawa, ON K1Y 4H7, Canada. TEL 613-765-2520. FAX 613-763-2008.
Vendor(s): UMI. *2041*

TELEVISION AND VIDEO: THE INTERNATIONAL MARKET.
Euromonitor, 60-61 Britton St., London EC1M 5NA, England. TEL 44-171-251-8024. FAX 44-171-608-3149. URL: http://www.euromonitor.com.
Vendor(s): Data-Star, Knight-Ridder Information, Inc. *2653*

TELEVISION DIGEST WITH CONSUMER ELECTRONICS.
Warren Publishing, Inc., 2115 Ward Ct., N.W., Washington, DC 20037. TEL 202-872-9200. FAX 202-293-3435.
Vendor(s): Information Access Co., NewsNet (PB01) *2063*

TELEVISION NEWS INDEX AND ABSTRACTS.
Vanderbilt University, Vanderbilt Television News Archive, 110 21st Ave. S., Ste. 704, Nashville, TN 37240-0007. TEL 615-322-2927. FAX 615-343-8250. URL: http://tvnews.vanderbilt.edu. *2014*

TELEWERKEN.
Kommunicatie Service Nederland, P.O. Box 146, 5430 AC Cuijk, Netherlands. TEL 31-485-318008. FAX 31-485-313234. *2006*

TEMENOS.
Finnish Society for the Study of Comparative Religion, c/o Donner Institute for Research in Religious and Cultural History, Steiner Memorial Library, P.O. Box 70, FIN-20501 Aabo-Turku, Finland. TEL 358-2-2654315. FAX 358-2-2311290. URL: http://www.abo.fi/comprel/temenos. *6376*

TEMPLE LAW REVIEW.
Temple University School of Law, Philadelphia, PA 19122. TEL 215-204-4528.
Vendor(s): West Group. *4032*

THE TEMPTATION OF SAINT ANTHONY.
Martin Bormann's Cranial Splints, Box 8166, Philadelphia, PA 19101-8166. TEL 215-627-9846. *4477*

TENNESSEE BAR JOURNAL.
Tennessee Bar Association, c/o Mary M. Tucker, 3622 West End Ave., Nashville, TN 37205-2403.
Vendor(s): West Group. *4032*

TENNESSEE BUSINESS DIRECTORY.
American Business Directories, 5711 S. 86th Circle, Box 27347, Omaha, NE 68127. TEL 402-593-4600. FAX 402-331-5481. *1715*

TENNESSEE LAW REVIEW.
Tennessee Law Review Association, Inc., College Law - Dunford Hall, 915 Volunteer Blvd., Knoxville, TN 37996-4070. TEL 423-974-4464. URL: http://www.law.utk.edu/lreview/lreview.htm.
Vendor(s): West Group. *4032*

TENNIS SERVER INTERACTIVE.
Tenagra Corporation, 1100 Hercules, Ste. 120, Houston, TX 77058. URL: http://www.tennisserver.com/.
Available only online. *6820*

TENNIS WEEK.
Eugene L. Scott, Ed. & Pub., 341 Madison Ave., New York, NY 10017. TEL 212-808-4750. FAX 212-983-6302. URL: http://www.tennisweek.com. *6820*

TERATOGENESIS, CARCINOGENESIS, AND MUTAGENESIS.
John Wiley & Sons, Inc., Journals, 605 Third Ave., New York, NY 10158. TEL 212-850-6645. FAX 212-850-6021. URL: http://www.wiley.co.uk *4751*

TERATOLOGY.
John Wiley & Sons, Inc., Journals, 605 Third Ave., New York, NY 10158. TEL 212-850-6645. FAX 212-850-6021. URL: http://www.wiley.co.uk *629*

TERRY FAMILY HISTORIAN.
c/o Robert M. Terry, Ed., 1518 Skyline Cir., Sapulpa, OK 74066. *3243*

THE TESTERS' NETWORK.
S T Labs, Inc., Sterling Plaza, 3rd Fl., 3535 128th Ave., S.E., Bellevue, WA 98006. URL: http://www.stlabs.com/testnet.htm.
Available only online. *2220*

TETRAHEDRON ALERT.
Elsevier Science Ltd., Pergamon, P.O. Box 800, Kidlington, Oxford OX5 1DX, England. TEL 44-1865-843000. FAX 44-1865-843100. URL: http://www.elsevier.nl/.
Available only online. *1769*

TETRAHEDRON LETTERS.
Elsevier Science Ltd., Pergamon, P.O. Box 800, Kidlington, Oxford OX5 1DX, England. TEL 44-1865-843000. FAX 44-1865-843010. URL: http://www.elsevier.nl/. *1824*

TEXAS BANKING.
912 Baltimore, Ste. 900, Kansas City, MO 64105. TEL 512-472-8388. FAX 512-473-2560.
Vendor(s): UMI. *1169*

TEXAS BUSINESS DIRECTORY.
American Business Directories, 5711 S. 86th Circle, Box 27347, Omaha, NE 68127. TEL 402-593-4600. FAX 402-331-5481. *1716*

TEXAS BUSINESS REVIEW.
University of Texas at Austin, Bureau of Business Research, Box 7459, Austin, TX 78713. TEL 512-471-1616. FAX 512-471-1063.
Vendor(s): Information Access Co. *1006*

TEXAS HEART INSTITUTE JOURNAL.
Texas Heart Institute, Publications & Communications, MC 1-194, Box 20345, Houston, TX 77225-0345. TEL 713-794-6630. FAX 713-791-3714. *4824*

TEXAS JOURNAL OF WOMEN AND THE LAW.
727 E. 26th St., Austin, TX 78705. TEL 512-471-3227. FAX 512-475-6741. URL: http://www.law.utexas.edu/journals/tjwl/tjwl.html.
Vendor(s): West Group. *4033*

TEXAS LABOR MARKET REVIEW.
Texas Workforce Commission, Labor Market Information Department, 101 E. 15th St., Rm. 252T, Austin, TX 78778. TEL 512-463-2843. FAX 512-475-1701. URL: http://www.twc.state.tx.us. *1455*

TEXAS LAW REVIEW.
University of Texas at Austin, School of Law Publications, Box 149084, Austin, TX 78714-9084. TEL 512-471-3164. FAX 512-471-6988.
Vendor(s): Lexis-Nexis. *4033*

TEXAS LAWYER.
American Lawyer Media, L.P. (New York), 600 Third Ave., 3rd Fl., New York, NY 10016. TEL 212-973-2800. FAX 214-741-2325.
Vendor(s): Lexis-Nexis. *4033*

TEXAS MONTHLY.
Texas Monthly, Inc., Box 1569, Austin, TX 78767. TEL 512-320-6900. FAX 512-476-9007.
Vendor(s): UMI. *3387*

TEXAS ON-SITE INSIGHTS.
Texas Water Resources Institute, c/o Texas A & M Univ., College Station, TX 77843-2118. TEL 409-845-8571. FAX 409-845-8554. URL: http://twri.towtrc.edu. *7300*

TEXAS REGISTER.
Secretary of State, Texas Register Division, Box 13824, TX 78711-3824. TEL 512-463-5561. FAX 512-463-5569. URL: http://www.sos.state.tx.us. *6197*

TEXAS TECH LAW REVIEW.
Texas Tech University, School of Law, Lubbock, TX 79409-0004. TEL 806-742-3789. FAX 806-742-1629.
Vendor(s): West Group. *4033*

TEXAS WATER RESOURCES.
Texas Water Resources Institute, c/o Texas A & M University, College Station, TX 77843-2118. TEL 409-845-8571. FAX 409-845-8554. URL: http://twri.tamu.edu/twripubs/WtrResrc/. *7300*

TEXAS WATER RESOURCES INSTITUTE. TECHNICAL REPORT.
Texas Water Resources Institute, c/o Texas A & M University, College Station, TX 77843-2118. TEL 409-845-8571. FAX 409-845-8554. URL: http://twri.tamu.edu. *7300*

TEXAS WATER SAVERS.
Texas Water Resources Institute, c/o Texas A & M Univ., Texas Agricultural Experiment Sta., College Station, TX 77843-2118. TEL 409-845-8571. FAX 409-845-8554. URL: http://www.twri.tamu.edu/twripubs/WtrSavrs/. *7300*

DIE TEXTIL-INDUSTRIE UND IHRE HELFER.
Industrieschau-Verlagsgesellschaft mbH, Postfach 100262, 64202 Darmstadt, Germany. TEL 49-6151-3892-0. FAX 49-6151-33164. *6995*

TEXTILE AND FABRIC WASHING PRODUCTS: THE INTERNATIONAL MARKET.
Euromonitor, 60-61 Britton St., London EC1M 5NA, England. TEL 44-171-251-8024. FAX 44-171-608-3149. URL: http://www.euromonitor.com.
Vendor(s): Data-Star, Knight-Ridder Information, Inc. *1911*

TEXTILE RENTAL.
Textile Rental Services Association of America, Box 1283, Hallandale, FL 33008. TEL 954-457-7555. FAX 954-457-3890. *1919*

TEXTILE TECHNOLOGY DIGEST.
Institute of Textile Technology, 2551 Ivy Rd., Charlottesville, VA 22903-4614. TEL 804-296-5511. FAX 804-977-5400.
Vendor(s): Knight-Ridder Information, Inc. (File no.119). *7000*

TEXTILE WORLD.
Intertec Publishing Corp., Textile Publications, P.O. Box 12901, Overland Park, KS 66282-2901.
Vendor(s): Information Access Co., UMI. *6997*

TEXTUAL REASONING.
Postmodern Jewish Philosophy Network, c/o Michael Zank, Dept. of Religion, Boston University, 745 Commonwealth Ave., Boston, MA 02215. TEL 617-353-4434. FAX 617-353-5441. URL: http://www.drew.edu/~pmjp. *5755*

TEXTURES AND MICROSTRUCTURES.
Gordon and Breach - Harwood Academic, Amsteldisk 166, 1st Fl., 1079 LH Amsterdam, Netherlands. URL: http://www.gbhap.com/Textures__Microstructures/. *2372*

THAI ABSTRACTS, SERIES A. SCIENCE AND TECHNOLOGY.
Thailand Institute of Scientific and Technological Research, 196 Phahonyothin Rd., Chatuchak, Bangkok 10900, Thailand. TEL 579-8594. FAX 662-579-8594. *6592*

THAT'S MY BABY.
That's My Baby, Inc., Box 1156, Lake Oswego, OR 97035. TEL 503-620-9132. FAX 503-620-3800. *1858*

THEATRE JOURNAL (BALTIMORE).
Johns Hopkins University Press, Journals Publishing Division, 2715 N. Charles St., Baltimore, MD 21218. TEL 410-516-6987. FAX 410-516-6968. URL: http://muse.jhu.edu.
Vendor(s): Information Access Co. *7016*

THEATRE RESEARCH INTERNATIONAL.
Oxford University Press, Academic Division, Great Clarendon St., Oxford OX2 6DP, England. TEL 44-1865-267907. FAX 44-1865-267485. URL: http://www.oup.co.uk/journals.
Vendor(s): Information Access Co. *7016*

THEATRE TOPICS.
Johns Hopkins University Press, Journals Publishing Division, 2715 N. Charles St., Baltimore, MD 21218. TEL 410-516-6987. FAX 410-516-6968. URL: http://muse.jhu.edu. *7017*

THEOLOGICAL STUDIES.
Theological Studies, Inc., Georgetown University, 37th and O Sts., N.W., Washington, DC 20057. TEL 202-338-0754. FAX 202-687-7679.
Vendor(s): Information Access Co., UMI. *6377*

THEOLOGY.
Society for Promoting Christian Knowledge, Holy Trinity Church, Marylebone Rd., London NW1 4DU, England. TEL 44-171-387-5282. FAX 44-171-388-2352.
Vendor(s): Knight-Ridder Information, Inc. *6378*

THEORETICAL AND APPLIED GENETICS.
Springer-Verlag, Heidelberger Platz 3, 14197 Berlin, Germany. TEL 49-30-82787-0. FAX 49-30-82787448. URL: http://link.springer.de. *777*

THEORETICAL AND COMPUTATIONAL FLUID DYNAMICS.
Springer-Verlag, Heidelberger Platz 3, 14197 Berlin, Germany. TEL 49-30-82787-0. FAX 49-30-82787448. URL: http://link.springer.de. *5849*

THEORETICAL CHEMICAL ENGINEERING.
The Royal Society of Chemistry, Thomas Graham House, Science Park, Milton Rd., Cambridge CB4 4WF, England. TEL 44-1223-420066. FAX 44-1223-423429. URL: http://chemistry.rsc.org/rsc/.
Vendor(s): Data-Star, FIZ Technik (DECHEMA), Knight-Ridder Information, Inc. (File no. 315), Questel Orbit Inc. (CEAB), STN International (CEABA) *2753*

THEORETICAL CHEMISTRY ACCOUNTS.
Springer-Verlag, Heidelberger Platz 3, 14197 Berlin, Germany. TEL 49-30-82787-0. FAX 49-30-82787448. URL: http://link.springer.de. *1769*

THEORY AND APPLICATONS OF CATEGORIES.
Mount Allison University, Department of Mathematics and Science, URL: http://www.tac.mta.ca/tac/geninfo.html; ftp://ftp.tac.mta.ca/pub/tac.
Available only online. *4611*

THEORY & EVENT.
URL: http://www.press.jhu.edu/journals/theory_&_event.
Available only online. *4362*

THEORY OF COMPUTING SYSTEMS.
Springer-Verlag, Science Journals, 175 Fifth Ave., New York, NY 10010. TEL 212-460-1500. FAX 212-473-6272. URL: http://www.springer-ny.com. *2221*

THEORY OF PROBABILITY AND ITS APPLICATIONS.
Society for Industrial and Applied Mathematics, 3600 University City Science Center, Philadelphia, PA 19104-2688. TEL 215-382-9800. FAX 215-386-7999. URL: http://www.siam.org. *4611*

THINK TANK TRANSCRIPTS.
URL: http://www.thinktank.com/transcripts.html.
Available only online. *4362*

THIRD WORLD QUARTERLY.
Carfax Publishing Co., P.O. Box 25, Abingdon, Oxon. OX14 3UE, England. TEL 44-1235-401000. FAX 44-1235-401550. *1368*

THIS JUST IN.
Center for the Advancement of Journalism, URL: http://internet-plaza.net/zone/thisjustin/about.html.
Available only online.

THOMAS REGISTER OF AMERICAN MANUFACTURERS AND THOMAS REGISTER CATALOG FILE.
Thomas Publishing Company, Five Penn Plaza, New York, NY 10001. TEL 212-290-7277. FAX 212-290-7365. URL: http://www.thomasregister.com. *1552*

THOMIST.
Thomist Press, 487 Michigan Ave., N.E., Washington, DC 20017. TEL 202-529-5300. FAX 202-636-4460. URL: http://www.thomist.org. *6483*

THORAX.
B M J Publishing Group, B.M.A. House, Tavistock Sq., London WC1H 9JR, England. TEL 44-171-383-6270. FAX 44-171-383-6402.
Vendor(s): Ovid Technologies, Inc. *4752*

THURGOOD MARSHALL LAW REVIEW.
Texas Southern University, Thurgood Marshall School of Law, 3100 Cleburne, Houston, TX 77004. TEL 713-527-7246. FAX 713-639-1049.
Vendor(s): West Group. *4034*

THURINGEN-BIBLIOGRAPHIE.
Thueringer Universitaets- und Landesbibliothek Jena, Ernst-Abbe-Platz 2, 07743 Jena, Germany. TEL 49-3641-632235. FAX 49-3641-638775. *3522*

TIDBITS.
URL: http://www.tidbits.com/
Available only online. *2205*

TIDINGS (CAMDEN).
National Marine Representatives Association, Box 969, 2742 Old Natchez Trace Trail, Camden, TN 38320-0660. TEL 901-584-0203. FAX 901-584-0420. URL: http://www.nmra.com. *1217*

TIDSSKRIFTINDEKS FOR SKOLEBIBLIOTEKER.
Dansk BiblioteksCenter as, Tempovej 7-11, DK-2750 Ballerup, Denmark. TEL 45-44-867777. FAX 45-44-867892. *565*

TIME.
Time Inc., Time & Life Bldg., Rockefeller Center, 1271 Ave. of the Americas, New York, NY 10020-1393. TEL 212-522-1212. FAX 212-522-0003. URL: http://www.time.com; http://pathfinder.com.
Vendor(s): Dow Jones News Retrieval, Information Access Co., Lexis-Nexis, MediaStream, UMI. *3387*

TIMELY INVESTMENT INFORMATION.
Green Mountain Asset Management Corp., 139 Bank St., Burlington, VT 05401. TEL 802-658-7806. URL: http://www.stockresearch.com.
Available only online. *1411*

TIMEOFF.
URL: http://www.peg.apc.org/~timeoff/.
Available only online. *3252*

TIMES (BETHLEHEM).
Council on Tall Buildings and Urban Habitat, Lehigh University, 11 E. Packer Ave., Bethlehem, PA 18015. TEL 610-758-3515. FAX 610-758-4522.
Vendor(s): UMI. *3760*

TIMES: IN HARNESS.
TIMES: standard inc., 8125 Jonestown Rd., Harrisburg, PA 17112. TEL 717-469-2000. FAX 717-469-2005. URL: http://www.timesite.com. *6857*

TIMES LAW REPORTS.
T & T Clark Ltd., 59 George St., Edinburgh EH2 2LQ, Scotland. TEL 44-131-225-4703. FAX 44-131-220-4260.
Vendor(s): Context Ltd. *4034*

TIN INTERNATIONAL.
M I I D A Ltd., P.O. Box 2137, London NW10 6TN, England. TEL 0181-961-7407. FAX 0181-961-7487.
Vendor(s): Knight-Ridder Information, Inc. *5213*

TIRE BUSINESS.
Crain Communications Inc. (Akron), 1725 Merriman Rd., Ste. 300, Akron, OH 44313-5251. TEL 330-836-9180. FAX 330-836-1005.
Vendor(s): Information Access Co. *6505*

TISK NEWS SERVICE.
D R S Internet Publishing Group, Box 488, Matthews, NC 28106. URL: http://www.ceo-online.com/tisk.
Available only online. *3387*

TIVI TUAN SAN.
URL: http://www.vicnet.net.au/~tvts/
Available only online. *3046*

10214 SERIALS AVAILABLE ONLINE

TO MATSAKONI.
c/o John Giannopoulos, 3, Samara Str., Patissia, 11144 Athens, Greece. URL: http://www.compulink.gr/users/matsakon/mwintyro.html. *6736*

TOBACCO INDUSTRY LITIGATION REPORTER.
Andrews Publications, 175 Strafford Ave., Bldg. 4, Ste. 140, Wayne, PA 19087. TEL 610-225-0501. FAX 610-225-0501. Vendor(s): NewsNet. *4034*

TODAY'S CHRISTIAN WOMAN.
Christianity Today, Inc., 465 Gundersen Dr., Carol Stream, IL 60188. TEL 630-260-6200. FAX 630-260-0114. URL: http://www.christianity.net.tcw. *7334*

TODAY'S HOMEOWNER.
Times Mirror Magazines, Inc., 2 Park Ave., New York, NY 10016-5601. TEL 212-779-5000. FAX 212-725-3281. URL: http://www.todayshomeowner.com/. Vendor(s): Information Access Co., UMI. *3769*

TODAY'S PARENT.
Professional Publishing Associates, 269 Richmond St. W., Toronto, ON M5V 1X1, Canada. TEL 416-596-8680. FAX 416-596-1991. URL: http://www.todaysparent.com. *1858*

TODAY'S TRAVELER.
Bluestone Group, Inc., 18 S. Michigan Ave., Ste. 1006, Chicago, IL 60603-3209. TEL 312-853-4775. FAX 312-782-7367. URL: http://www.todaystraveler.com. *7239*

TOHKAI SEIKEI GEKA GAISHO KENKYU KAISHI.
Tohkai Seikei Geka Gaisho Kenkyukai, Gifu Kenritsu Tajimi Byoin Seikei Geka, 5-161, Maebatacho, Tajimi-shi, Gifu-ken 507, Japan. TEL 81-572-22-5311. FAX 81-572-25-1246. *5017*

TOHKAI SEKITSUI GEKA.
Tohkai Sekitsui Geka Kenkyukai, Gifu Kenritsu Tajimi Byoin, 5-161, Maebatacho, Tajimi-shi, Gifuken 507, Japan. TEL 81-572-22-5311. FAX 81-572-25-1246. *5017*

TOHO UNIVERSITY MEDICAL SOCIETY. JOURNAL.
Toho University Medical Society, c/o Library, School of Medicine, 5-21-16 Omori Nishi, Ota-ku, Tokyo 143, Japan. TEL 81-3762-4151. FAX 81-3764-1642. *4753*

TOILETRIES, FRAGRANCES AND SKIN CARE: THE ROSE SHEET.
F-D-C Reports, Inc., 5550 Friendship Blvd., Ste. 1, Chevy Chase, MD 20815. FAX 301-664-7238. Vendor(s): Data-Star (FDCR), Knight-Ridder Information, Inc. (File no.187), Lexis-Nexis, Ovid Technologies, Inc. (FDCR). *513*

TOKELAU NATIONAL BIBLIOGRAPHY.
National Library of New Zealand, P.O. Box 1467, Wellington, New Zealand. TEL 64-4-4743067. FAX 64-4-4743124. *565*

TOKYO FINANCIAL REVIEW.
Bank of Tokyo, Ltd., 3-26 Kanda Nishikicho, Chiyoda-ku, Toyko 101, Japan. *1170*

TOLEDO BUSINESS JOURNAL.
Telex Communications, Inc., 27 Broadway St., Toledo, OH 43602-1701. TEL 419-244-8200. FAX 419-244-5773. Vendor(s): UMI. *1006*

TOMORROW'S MORNING.
Tomorrow's Morning, Inc., 160 N. Thurston Ave., Los Angeles, CA 90049. TEL 310-440-2778. FAX 310-476-6406. URL: http://morning.com. Vendor(s): CompuServe, Inc. *1891*

TOMORROW'S MORNING CLASSROOM EDITION.
Tomorrow's Morning, Inc., 160 N. Thurston Ave., Los Angeles, CA 90049. TEL 310-440-2778. FAX 610-476-6406. URL: http://morning.com. Vendor(s): CompuServe, Inc. *1891*

TOMORROWSF.
Unifont Co. Inc., Box 6038, Evanston, IL 60204. TEL 847-864-3668. URL: http://www.tomorrowsF.com. Available only online. *4538*

TONGUE.
URL: http://www.tongue-zine.com. Available only online. *4479*

TOOLING & PRODUCTION.
Huebcore Communications, Inc., 29100 Aurora Rd., Ste. 200, Solon, OH 44139. TEL 216-248-1125. FAX 216-686-0214. Vendor(s): Information Access Co., Knight-Ridder Information, Inc. *4553*

TOPSOIL.
143 Eastern Main Rd., Laventille, Trinidad & Tobago, W.I. URL: http://www.wow.net/anarchy/topsoil. *4479*

TORONTO COMPUTES.
ConText Publishing Inc., 99 Atlantic Ave., No. 408, Toronto, Ont. M4G 3J8, Canada. TEL 416-588-6818. *2091*

TORT & INSURANCE LAW JOURNAL.
American Bar Association, Tort and Insurance Practice Section, 750 N. Lake Shore Dr., Chicago, IL 60611. URL: http://www.abanet.org. Vendor(s): Lexis-Nexis, West Group. *4067*

TOSS-UP.
URL: http://www.uq.edu.au/%7ezzdpedwe/tossup/toss-old.html. Available only online. *2520*

TOTAL HEALTH.
Total Health Communications, Inc., 165 N. 100 St. E., Ste. 2, Saint George, UT 84770-2505. TEL 801-673-1789. FAX 801-634-9336. Vendor(s): Information Access Co., UMI. *5483*

TOTAL QUALITY MANAGEMENT.
Carfax Publishing Co., P.O. Box 25, Abingdon, Oxon. OX14 3UE, England. TEL 44-1235-401000. FAX 44-1235-401550. *1510*

TOUR & TRAVEL NEWS - T T G NORTH AMERICA.
Miller Freeman, Inc. (New York), One Penn Plaza, New York, NY 10119. TEL 212-714-1300. FAX 212-714-1313. Vendor(s): Data-Star, Information Access Co., Knight-Ridder Information, Inc., NewsNet (TR09). *7239*

TOWN AND COUNTRY.
Hearst Corporation, Town and Country, 1700 Broadway, New York, NY 10019. TEL 212-903-5000. FAX 212-765-8308. URL: http:www.hearst.corp.cm. Vendor(s): Information Access Co. *3387*

TOXIC CUSTARD WORKSHOP FILES.
URL: http://www.forthnet.gr/humour/tcwf/ToxicCustard.html. Available only online. *4363*

TOXIC SUBSTANCE MECHANISMS.
Taylor & Francis Inc., 1900 Frost Rd., Ste. 101, Bristol, PA 19007-1598. TEL 215-785-5800. FAX 215-785-5515. URL: http://www.tandf.co.uk/. *2981*

TOXICOLOGICAL AND ENVIRONMENTAL CHEMISTRY.
Gordon and Breach - Harwood Academic, Amsteldisk 166, 1st Fl., 1079 LH Amsterdam, Netherlands. URL: http://www.gbhap.com/Toxicological__Environmental__Chemistry/. *2981*

TOXICOLOGY ABSTRACTS.
Cambridge Scientific Abstracts, 7200 Wisconsin Ave., 6th Fl., Bethesda, MD 20814. TEL 301-961-6750. FAX 301-961-6720. URL: http://www.csa.com. Vendor(s): Knight-Ridder Information, Inc. (File no.76/LIFE SCIENCES COLLECTION), STN International (LIFESCI). *5702*

TOXICOLOGY AND APPLIED PHARMACOLOGY.
Academic Press, Inc., Journal Division, 525 B St., Ste. 1900, San Diego, CA 92101-4495. TEL 619-230-1840. FAX 619-699-6800. URL: http://www.apnet.com/www/journal/to.htm; http://www.idealibrary.com/ *2981*

TOXICOLOGY LETTERS.
Elsevier Science Ireland Ltd., P.O. Box 85, Limerick, Ireland. TEL 353-61-471944. FAX 353-61-472144. *2982*

TOXICOLOGY METHODS.
Taylor & Francis Inc., 1900 Frost Rd., Ste. 101, Bristol, PA 19007-1598. TEL 215-785-5800. FAX 215-785-5515. URL: http://www.tandf.co.uk/. *2982*

TOXICS LAW REPORTER.
The Bureau of National Affairs, Inc., 1231 25th St. N.W., Washington, DC 20037. TEL 202-452-4200. FAX 202-822-8092. URL: http://www.bna.com/ Vendor(s): Human Resources Information Network (CDD, HDD), Lexis-Nexis (File TOXICS). *2991*

TOY MARKET.
URL: http://www.toymarket.com/ Available only online. *3451*

TOYS AND GAMES: THE INTERNATIONAL MARKET.
Euromonitor, 60-61 Britton St., London EC1M 5NA, England. TEL 0171-251-8024. FAX 0171-608-3149. Vendor(s): Data-Star, Knight-Ridder Information, Inc. *3451*

TRADE & INDUSTRY INDEX.
Information Access Company, 362 Lakeside Dr., Foster City, CA 94404. TEL 415-378-5200. FAX 415-358-4759. Available only online. Vendor(s): Knight-Ridder Information, Inc. (File no.148), Ovid Technologies, Inc. (TSAP). *1074*

TRADEMARK REGISTER OF THE UNITED STATES.
Trademark Register, National Press Bldg., 1297, Washington, DC 20045. TEL 202-662-1233. FAX 202-347-4408. *5590*

TRADESCOPE.
Japan External Trade Organization, 2-5 Toranomon 2-chome, Minato-ku, Tokyo 104, Japan. TEL 03-3582-5521. FAX 03-3582-0504. *1717*

TRAFFIC REPORT.
Department of Economic Development and Tourism, P.O. Box 6000, Fredericton, NB E3B 5H1, Canada. TEL 506-457-7340. *6209*

TRAFFIC WORLD.
Journal of Commerce, Inc. (Washington), 741 National Press Bldg., Washington, DC 20045. TEL 202-383-6140. FAX 202-737-3349. Vendor(s): Information Access Co. *7040*

TRAILER BOATS.
Poole Publications, Inc., 20700 Belshaw Ave., Carson, CA 90746. TEL 310-537-6322. FAX 310-537-8735. URL: http://www.iwol.com/iww/customers/onlinemagazines/trailerboats/TB__images. Vendor(s): Information Access Co., UMI. *6845*

TRAILER LIFE.
A G I, 2575 Vista Del Mar, Ventura, CA 93001. TEL 805-667-4300. FAX 805-667-4213. Vendor(s): Information Access Co. *6886*

TRAILS.
Texas State Library and Archives Commission, Box 12927, Austin, TX 78711. TEL 512-463-5514. FAX 512-463-5436. URL: http://www.tsl.state.tx.us. *4217*

TRAINING.
Lakewood Publications, Inc., 50 S. Ninth St., Minneapolis, MN 55402. TEL 612-333-0471. FAX 612-333-6526. Vendor(s): Human Resources Information Network, Information Access Co., UMI. *1510*

TRAINING & DEVELOPMENT.
American Society for Training and Development, 1640 King St., Box 1443, Alexandria, VA 22313. TEL 703-683-8100. FAX 703-683-8103. Vendor(s): Information Access Co. *1577*

TRAINING AND DEVELOPMENT ORGANIZATIONS DIRECTORY.
Gale Research, 835 Penobscot Bldg., 645 Griswold St., Detroit, MI 48226-4094. TEL 313-961-2242. FAX 800-414-5043. Vendor(s): Human Resources Information Network (TDOD). *1510*

TRAINS.
Kalmbach Publishing Co., 21027 Crossroads Cir., Waukesha, WI 53187. TEL 414-796-8776. FAX 414-796-0126. Vendor(s): Information Access Co. *7134*

TRANS.
Passim Inc., 109 W. 17th St., New York, NY 10011. TEL 212-929-0226. FAX 212-924-6779. URL: http://www.echonyc.com/~trans. *469*

THE TRANSFORMATION STORY ARCHIVE.
URL: http://www.t0.or.at/~thomash/tsa/. Available only online. *4538*

TRANSGENIC RESEARCH.
Chapman & Hall, Journals Department 2-6 Boundary Row, London SE1 8HN, England. TEL 44-171-8650066. FAX 44-171-5229623. URL: http://www.chaphall.com/chaphall/journals.html. *777*

TRANSGENICS.
Gordon and Breach - Harwood Academic, Amsteldisk 166, 1st Fl., 1079 LH Amsterdam, Netherlnads. URL: http://www.gbhap.com/Transgenics/. *777*

TRANSIT RESEARCH ABSTRACTS.
U.S. National Research Council, Transportation Research Board, 2101 Constitution Ave., N.W., Washington, DC 20418. TEL 202-334-3213. FAX 202-334-2519.
Vendor(s): Knight-Ridder Information, Inc. (File no.63). *7058*

TRANSITION METAL CHEMISTRY.
Thomson Science, 2-6 Boundary Row, London SE1 8HN, England. TEL 44-171-8650066. FAX 44-171-5229623. URL: http://www.thomsonscience.com. *5214*

TRANSITION NEWSLETTER.
c/o Jennifer Prochnow, Rm. N11-039X, 1818 H St., N.W., Washington, DC 20433. URL: http://www.worldbank.org. Available only online. *1292*

TRANSMISSION AND DISTRIBUTION.
Intertec Publishing Corp., 9800 Metcalf, Overland Park, KS 66212-2215. TEL 913-341-1300. FAX 913-967-1904.
Vendor(s): UMI. *2848*

TRANSPACIFIC.
Transpacific Media Inc., 23852 P.C.H. No.390, Malibu, CA 90265-5000. TEL 310-582-2600. FAX 310-457-0535. URL: http://www.tmiweb.com. Vendor(s): Information Access Co. *3046*

TRANSPLANT INTERNATIONAL.
Springer-Verlag, Heidelberger Platz 3, 14197 Berlin, Germany. TEL 49-30-82787-0. FAX 49-30-82787448. URL: http://link.springer.de. *4754*

TRANSPLANTATION.
Williams & Wilkins, 351 W. Camden St., Baltimore, MD 21201-2436. TEL 410-528-4068. FAX 410-528-4452. URL: http://www.wwilkins.com.
Vendor(s): Ovid Technologies, Inc. *5156*

TRANSPLANTATION PROCEEDINGS.
Elsevier Science Inc., Box 945, New York, NY 10159-0945. TEL 212-633-3730. FAX 212-633-3680. *5156*

TRANSPORTATION & DISTRIBUTION.
Penton Publishing Co., 1100 Superior Ave., Cleveland, OH 44114-2543. TEL 216-696-7000. FAX 216-696-8765.
Vendor(s): Information Access Co., Knight-Ridder Information, Inc., UMI. *7043*

TRANSPORTATION JOURNAL.
American Society of Transportation and Logistics, Inc., 320 E. Water St., Lock Haven, PA 17745-2010. TEL 717-748-8515.
Vendor(s): Information Access Co., UMI. *7043*

TRANSPORTATION LAW JOURNAL.
University of Denver, College of Law, 7039 E. 18th Ave., Denver, CO 80220. TEL 303-871-6162. FAX 303-871-6165.
Vendor(s): West Group. *4035*

TRANSPORTATION PLANNING AND TECHNOLOGY.
Gordon and Breach - Harwood Academic, Amsteldisk 166, 1st Fl., 1079 LH Amsterdam, Netherlands. URL: http://www.gbhap.com/Transportation__Planning__Technology/. *7043*

TRAVAIL ET EMPLOI.
Documentation Francaise, 29-31 quai Voltaire, 75344 Paris Cedex 07, France. TEL 33-1-40157000. FAX 33-1-40157230.
Vendor(s): Telesystemes - Questel. *1455*

TRAVEL AGENT.
Universal Media, Inc., 801 Second Ave., New York, NY 10017. TEL 212-370-5050. FAX 212-370-4491.
Vendor(s): Information Access Co. *7242*

TRAVEL ALERT BULLETIN.
Nationwide Intelligence, Box 1922, Saginaw, MI 48605. TEL 517-752-6123. FAX 517-752-1605. URL: http://www.nationwidenetwork.com. *7242*

TRAVEL & LEISURE.
American Express Publishing Corp. (New York), 1120 Ave. of the Americas, New York, NY 10036. TEL 212-382-5600. FAX 212-768-1568. *7242*

TRAVEL AND TOURISM: THE INTERNATIONAL MARKET.
Euromonitor, 60-61 Britton St., London EC1M 5NA, England. TEL 44-171-251-8024. FAX 44-171-608-3149. URL: http://www.euromonitor.com.
Vendor(s): Data-Star, Knight-Ridder Information, Inc. *7242*

TRAVEL HOLIDAY.
Hachette Filipacchi Magazines, Inc., 1633 Broadway, New York, NY 10019. TEL 212-767-6000.
Vendor(s): Information Access Co. *7243*

TRAVEL MANAGEMENT DAILY.
Reed Travel Group, Part of the Reed Elsevier group 500 Plaza Dr., Secaucus, NJ 07096. TEL 201-902-1700. FAX 201-902-1967. *7243*

TRAVEL TRADE GAZETTE EUROPA.
Miller Freeman Technical Ltd., Miller Freeman House, 30 Calderwood St., London SE18 6QH, England. TEL 44-181-855-7777. FAX 44-181-316-3354.
Vendor(s): Information Access Co. *7244*

TRAVEL TRADE GAZETTE U K & IRELAND.
Miller Freeman Technical Ltd., Miller Freeman House, 30 Calderwood St., London SE18 6QH, England. TEL 44-181-855-7777. FAX 44-181-316-3354.
Vendor(s): Information Access Co. *7244*

TRAVEL WEEKLY.
Reed Travel Group, Part of the Reed Elsevier group 500 Plaza Dr., Secaucus, NJ 07096. TEL 201-902-2000. FAX 201-317-1755. URL: http://www.traveler.net/two/.
Vendor(s): Information Access Co. *7244*

TRAVELER SAVINGS SITE.
Travelocity, 1403 E. Reno Ave., Ste. C, Las Vegas, NV 89119. URL: http://www.home.sprynet.com/sprynet/inetmktg/. Available only online. *7245*

TRAVELERS GUIDE TO MEXICO.
Promociones de Mercados Turisticos, S.A. de C.V., Gral. Juan Cano 68, Col. San Miguel Chapultepec, 11850, D.F., Mexico. TEL 52-5-5160162. FAX 52-5-2725942. URL: http://www.travel-mex.com. *7261*

TRAVELFLASH.
URL: http://www.travelbase.com/auto/ajl__signup.cgi.
Available only online. *7245*

TRAVELMAG.
40 Brecknock Rd., Bristol, BS4 2DD, England. FAX 44-117-9719-689. URL: http://www.travelmag.co.uk.
Available only online. *7245*

TRAX D J MUSIC GUIDE.
American Trax D Js, 111 N. La Cienega Blvd., Beverly Hills, CA 90211-2206. TEL 310-659-7852. FAX 310-659-7856. URL: http://www.traxusa.com/dance/music/guide.html. *5441*

TREASURY & RISK MANAGEMENT.
C F O Publishing Corporation, 253 Summer St., Boston, MA 02210. TEL 617-345-9700. FAX 617-951-4090. URL: http://www.cfonet.com. *1411*

TREASURY MANAGER'S REPORT.
Phillips Business Information, Inc., 1201 Seven Locks Rd., Potomac, MD 20854. TEL 301-424-3338. FAX 301-309-3847.
Vendor(s): Information Access Co. *1170*

TREASURYLOG.
Go Public Relations, Badnerstr. 3-21, A-2500 Baden, Austria. URL: http://www.go-public.com/treasurylog. *1170*

TREE PHYSIOLOGY.
Heron Publishing, 202-3994 Shelbourne St., Victoria, BC V8N 3E2, Canada. TEL 250-721-9921. FAX 250-721-9924. URL: http://heronpublishing.com/tphome.html.
Vendor(s): Knight-Ridder Information, Inc. *730*

TREES.
Springer-Verlag, Heidelberger Platz 3, 14197 Berlin, Germany. TEL 49-30-82787-0. FAX 49-30-82787448. URL: http://link.springer.de. *731*

TRENDS: A COMPENDIUM OF DATA ON GLOBAL CHANGE.
Carbon Dioxide Information Analysis Center, Oak Ridge National Laboratory, Box 2008 (MS-6335), Oak Ridge, TN 37831-6335. TEL 423-574-0390. FAX 423-574-2232. URL: http://cdiac.esd.ornl.gov. Available only online. *5244*

TRI-CITY COMPUTING MAGAZINE.
A J A Consulting, 5208 W. Calavar Rd., Glendale, AZ 85306-4818. TEL 518-446-1944. URL: http://www.albany.net/~tricity/mast.html. *2091*

TRIAL.
Association of Trial Lawyers of America, 1050 31st St., N.W., Washington, DC 20007-4499. TEL 202-965-3500. FAX 202-965-0030. URL: http://www.atlanet.org/.
Vendor(s): Information Access Co. *4139*

TRIANGLE BUSINESS JOURNAL.
American City Business Journals, Inc. (Austin), 505 Powell St., Austin, TX 78703-5121. TEL 919-878-0010. FAX 919-790-6885.
Vendor(s): Lexis-Nexis. *1007*

TRIBUNA FARMACEUTICA.
Universidade Federal do Parana, Faculdade de Farmacia, Rua Coronel Dulcidio 638, Caixa Postal 888, 80000 Curitiba, Parana, Brazil. FAX 041-2642243. *5696*

TRIBUNE DESFOSSES.
42 rue Notre Dame des Victoires, 75002 Paris, France. TEL 1-42-33-21-30. FAX 1-42-33-12-36. URL: http://www.edelweb.fr/Guests/LaTribune. *1007*

TRINCOLL JOURNAL.
Trinity College, Trinity College 702596, Hartford, CT 06106. URL: http://www.trincoll.edu/tj/. Available only online. *4480*

TRIPOD (NEW YORK).
c/o Michael Agger, Asst. Ed., 191 Water St., Williamstown, MA 01267. TEL 413-458-2265. FAX 413-458-2465. URL: http://www.tripod.com. Available only online. *3387*

TRIQUARTERLY.
Northwestern University, 2020 Ridge Ave., Evanston, IL 60208-4302. TEL 847-491-3490. FAX 847-467-2096.
Vendor(s): Information Access Co., UMI. *4363*

TROPI-TIES E-ZINE & CATALOG.
4270 W. Oak Trail Rd., Santa Ynez, CA 93460. URL: http://www.tropi-ties.com. Available only online. *7246*

TROPICAL DISEASES BULLETIN.
CAB International, Wallingford, Oxon. OX10 8DE, England. TEL 44-1491-832111. FAX 44-1491-826090. URL: http://www.cabi.org.
Vendor(s): DIMDI. *4789*

TROPICAL GEOMORPHOLOGY NEWSLETTER.
National University of Singapore, Department of Geography, Singapore 119260, Singapore. FAX 65-777-3091. URL: http://zikzak.zikzak.net/tgn/. *2373*

TROPICAL OIL SEEDS.
CAB International, Wallingford, Oxon. OX10 8DE, England. TEL 44-1491-832111. FAX 44-1491-826090. URL: http://www.cabi.org. Vendor(s): DIMDI, European Space Agency, Knight-Ridder Information, Inc., STN International. *184*

TRUCKING TIMES.
Herrmeyer Publishing, 2413 Center St., Box 707, Cedar Falls, IA 50613. TEL 319-277-8332. FAX 319-277-8950. URL: http://www.ttol.com. *7180*

TRUCKWORLD ONLINE!
AutoWeb Worldwide Publishing, Inc., Box 590, Cottage Grove, OR 97424. URL: http://www.truckworld.com. Available only online. *7180*

TRUST LETTER.
American Bankers Association, Trust and Private Banking Center, 1120 Connecticut Ave., N.W., Washington, DC 20036. TEL 202-663-5087. FAX 202-663-7543. Vendor(s): UMI. *1170*

TRUSTEE.
American Hospital Publishing, Inc., 737 N. Michigan Ave., Ste. 700, Chicago, IL 60611. TFI 312-440-6800. FAX 312-951-8491. Vendor(s): UMI. *3720*

TRUSTS AND ESTATES (ATLANTA).
Intertec Publishing Corp. (Atlanta), 6151 Powers Ferry Rd., N.W., Atlanta, GA 30339-2941. TEL 770-955-2500. FAX 770-955-0400. Vendor(s): Information Access Co., UMI. *1412*

TRUTH SEEKER.
Truth Seeker Co., Inc., 16935 W. Bernardo Dr., Ste. 103, San Diego, CA 92117. TEL 619-676-0430. FAX 619-676-0433. *5756*

TUBERCULOSIS & AIRBORNE DISEASE WEEKLY.
Charles W. Henderson, Ed. & Pub., Box 5528, Atlanta, GA 31107-0528. TEL 404-377-8895. FAX 404-378-5411. URL: http://www.newsfile.com. Vendor(s): CompuServe, Inc., Data-Star, Dow Jones News Retrieval, Information Access Co., Knight-Ridder Information, Inc., NewsNet, Ovid Technologies, Inc. *4844*

TUCSON TEEN.
Southwest Alternatives Institute, Inc., Box 3355, Tucson, AZ 85722-3355. TEL 520-623-3733. FAX 520-623-3733. URL: http://emol.org/emol/tucsonteen/. Available only online. *1891*

TUESDAY BULLETIN.
Michigan State University, African Studies Center, 100 International Center, East Lansing, MI 48824-1035. *3530*

TUFTS UNIVERSITY HEALTH AND NUTRITION LETTER.
W H Y Publications, 53 Park Pl., 8th Fl., New York, NY 10007. TEL 212-608-6515. FAX 212-608-5317. Vendor(s): Information Access Co., UMI. *5483*

TUIJIN JISHU.
Zhongguo Hangtian Gongye Zonggongsi, Di 3 Yanjiuyuan, 31 Yanjiusho, P.O. Box 7208-26, Beijing 100074, People's Republic of China. TEL 86-10-6837-6141. FAX 86-10-6837-4052. *81*

TULANE ENVIRONMENTAL LAW JOURNAL.
Tulane University, School of Law, 6329 Freret St., Joseph Merrick Jones Hall, New Orleans, LA 70118. TEL 504-865-5939. FAX 504-865-6748. Vendor(s): Lexis-Nexis, West Group. *2954*

TULANE EUROPEAN AND CIVIL LAW FORUM.
Tulane University, School of Law, 6329 Freret St., New Orleans, LA 70118. TEL 504-865-5939. FAX 504-865-6748. Vendor(s): Lexis-Nexis, West Group. *4067*

TULANE LAW REVIEW.
Tulane University, School of Law, 6329 Freret St., New Orleans, LA 70118. TEL 504-865-5939. FAX 504-865-6748. Vendor(s): Lexis-Nexis, West Group. *4036*

TULANE MARITIME LAW JOURNAL.
Tulane University, School of Law, 6329 Freret St., New Orleans, LA 70118. TEL 504-865-5939. FAX 504-865-6748. Vendor(s): Lexis-Nexis, West Group. *4143*

TULSA LAW JOURNAL.
University of Tulsa, College of Law, 3120 E. Fourth Pl., Tulsa, OK 74104. TEL 918-631-3532. FAX 918-631-3556. Vendor(s): West Group. *4036*

TUMOR TARGETING.
Chapman & Hall, Journals Department 2-6 Boundary Row, London SE1 8HN, England. TEL 44-171-8650066. FAX 44-171-5229623. URL: http://www.chaphall.com/chaphall/journals.html. *4988*

TURING INSTITUTE ABSTRACTS IN ARTIFICIAL INTELLIGENCE.
Springer-Verlag London Ltd., Sweetapple House, Catteshall Rd., Godalming, Surrey GU7 3DJ, England. TEL 44-1483-418800. FAX 44-1483-415144. Vendor(s): Data-Star. *2096*

TURKISH JOURNAL OF MATHEMATICS.
Scientific and Technical Research Council of Turkey - TUBITAK, Ataturk Bulvari, No. 221, Kavaklidere, 06100 Ankara, Turkey. TEL 90-312-4685300. FAX 90-312-4271336. URL: http://www.math.metu.edu.tr/TJOM. *4612*

TWENTIETH CENTURY LITERATURE.
Hofstra University, 203 Student Center, Hempstead, NY 11550. TEL 516-463-5460. Vendor(s): Information Access Co., UMI. *4481*

TWILIGHT WORLD.
P.O. Box 67, 3500 AB Utrecht, Netherlands. TEL 31-30-2891429. URL: http://arrogant.itc.icl.ie/twilightworld/; http://www.scriba.org/twilight/ Available only online. *4538*

TWIN CITIES READER.
American City Business Journals, Inc. (Austin), 505 Powell St., Austin, TX 78703-5121. Vendor(s): CompuServe, Inc., Data-Star, Dow Jones News Retrieval, Knight-Ridder Information, Inc., Lexis-Nexis. *3388*

TWIN PEAKS GOURMET TRADING POST.
URL: http://www.tpeaks.com/archives.html. Available only online. *3689*

U A P NEWSLETTER.
International Federation of Library Association and Institutions, International Programme for UAP, c/o British Library, Boston Spa, Wetherby, W. Yorks. LS23 7BQ, England. TEL 44-1937-546254. FAX 44-1937-546478. URL: http://www.nlc-bnc.ca/ifla/vl/2/ndl/index/html. *4218*

U C A R QUARTERLY.
University Corporation for Atmospheric Research, Box 3000, Boulder, CO 80307. TEL 303-497-8611. FAX 303-497-8610. *5244*

U C DAVIS LAW REVIEW.
University of California at Davis, School of Law, Martin Luther King, Jr. Hall, Davis, CA 95616. TEL 916-752-2551. FAX 916-752-4704. Vendor(s): Lexis-Nexis, West Group. *4036*

U C L A LAW REVIEW.
University of California at Los Angeles, School of Law, Attn: Sherry Taylor, Box 951476, CA 90095-1476. TEL 213-825-4929. FAX 310-206-6489. URL: http://www.law.ucla.edu/student/organizations. Vendor(s): Lexis-Nexis. *4036*

U C L WORKING PAPERS IN LINGUISTICS.
University College London, Department of Phonetics and Linguistics, URL: http://www.phon.ucl.ac.uk/home/pub/wpl/uclwpl.html. *4309*

U C M P QUARTERLY.
Medical Library Center of New York, 5 E. 102nd St., 7th Fl., New York, NY 10029-5288. FAX 212-876-6697. *4789*

U H R A THUNDER LETTER.
Unlimited Hydroplane Racing Association, 19530 Pacific Hwy. S., Ste. 200, Seattle, WA 98188. URL: http://www.uhra.com. Available only online. *6845*

U K GAS REPORT.
Financial Times Energy Publishing, Maple House, 149 Tottenham Court Rd., London W1P 9LL, England. TEL 0171-896-2241. FAX 0171-896-2275. Vendor(s): Data-Star, Knight-Ridder Information, Inc., Lexis-Nexis. *2679*

U K INDUSTRIAL TRADE NAMES.
Kompass, Part of the Reed Elsevier group, Windsor Ct., E. Grinstead House, E. Grinstead, W. Sussex RH19 1XD, England. TEL 44-1342-326972. FAX 44-1342-335992. Vendor(s): Reed Information Services Ltd.. *1718*

U K NONLINEAR NEWS.
University College London, Centre for Nonlinear Dynamics and its Applications, Gower St., London WC1E 6BT, England. FAX 44-171-380-09865. URL: http://www.amsta.leeds.ac.uk/applied/news.dir/index.html. *4612*

U K VENTURE CAPITAL JOURNAL.
Venture Capital, The Quadrangle, 180 Wardour, London W1A 4YG, England. TEL 44-171-434-0411. FAX 44-171-434-3918. Vendor(s): Information Access Co. *1412*

U LAFF SEATTLE COMEDY.
URL: http://www.uspan.com/u-laff. Available only online. *7017*

U N CHRONICLE.
United Nations Publications, Sales and Marketing Section, Room DC2-0853, New York, NY 10017. TEL 212-963-8302. FAX 212-963-3489. URL: http://www.un.org/publications. Vendor(s): Information Access Co., UMI. *6040*

U N I D O LINKS.
United Nations Industrial Development Organization, Box 300, A-1400 Vienna, Austria. TEL 43-1-211-31-5538. FAX 43-1-209-2669. URL: http://www.unido.org. Available only online. *1369*

U P NEWSLETTER.
University of the Philippines, Information Office, 1st Fl. Mezzanine, Quezon Hall, U.P. Diliman, Quezon City, Philippines. FAX 96-15-72. *1975*

U S A GYMNASTICS.
U S A Gymnastics, 201 S. Capitol Ave., Ste. 300, Pan American Plaza, Indianapolis, IN 46225. TEL 317-237-5050. FAX 317-237-5069. URL: http://www.usa-gymnastics.org. *6792*

U S A TODAY.
Society for the Advancement of Education, 99 W. Hawthorne Ave., Ste. 518, Valley Stream, NY 11580-6101. TEL 516-568-9191. Vendor(s): Information Access Co., Knight-Ridder Information, Inc., Lexis-Nexis, UMI, MediaStream. *2489*

U S A TODAY INDEX.
U M I, 300 N. Zeeb Rd., Ann Arbor, MI 48106-1346. TEL 313-761-4700. FAX 800-864-0019. URL: http://www.umi.com. *3885*

U S BANKER.
Faulkner & Gray, Inc. (New York), 11 Penn Plaza, 17th Fl., New York, NY 10001. TEL 212-967-7000. FAX 212-967-7155. Vendor(s): Information Access Co., Lexis-Nexis, UMI. *1412*

U S CATHOLIC.
Claretian Publications, 205 W. Monroe St., Chicago, IL 60606. TEL 312-236-7782. FAX 312-236-8207. Vendor(s): Information Access Co. *6483*

U S CRUDE OIL, NATURAL GAS, AND NATURAL GAS LIQUIDS RESERVES (YEAR) ANNUAL REPORT.
U.S. Energy Information Administration, National Energy Information Center, EI-231, James Forrestal Bldg., Rm. 1F-048, 1000 Independence Ave., S.W., DC 20585. TEL 202-586-8800. FAX 202-586-0727. URL: http://www.eia.doe.gov. *5625*

U S NEWS & WORLD REPORT.
U S News & World Report Inc., 1290 Ave. of the Americas, Ste. 600, New York, NY 10104. TEL 212-830-1500. URL: http://usnews.com. Vendor(s): Information Access Co., Knight-Ridder Information, Inc., Lexis-Nexis, UMI. *3388*

U S OIL WEEK.
Capitol Publications Inc., 1101 King St., Ste. 444, Alexandria, VA 22314. TEL 703-683-4100. FAX 703-739-6436.
Vendor(s): Information Access Co., Knight-Ridder Information, Inc., NewsNet (EY55). *5625*

U S P QUALITY REVIEW.
U.S. Pharmacopeial Practitioners' Reporting Network, 12601 Twinbrook Pky., Rockville, MD 20852. URL: http://www.usp.org/prn. *5697*

U S PHARMACIST.
Jobson Publishing, Inc., 100 Ave. of the Americas, New York, NY 10013-1678. TEL 212-274-7000. FAX 212-431-0500. URL: http://www.uspharmacist.com/ *5697*

U S RAIL NEWS.
Business Publishers, Inc., 951 Pershing Dr., Silver Spring, MD 20910-4464. TEL 301-587-6300. FAX 301-585-9075.
Vendor(s): Information Access Co., NewsNet (TS11). *7135*

U: THE NATIONAL COLLEGE MAGAZINE.
American Collegiate Network, 1800 Century Park E., Ste, 820, Los Angeles, CA 90067-1511. TEL 310-551-1381. FAX 310-551-1659. URL: http://www.umagazine.com. *2558*

ULRICH'S INTERNATIONAL PERIODICALS DIRECTORY.
R.R. Bowker, A Division of Reed Elsevier Inc., 121 Chanlon Rd., New Providence, NJ 07974. TEL 908-665-2847. FAX 908-771-7725. URL: http://www.bowker.com.
Vendor(s): Knight-Ridder Information, Inc. (File no.480), Lexis-Nexis (ULRICHS), Ovid Technologies, Inc. (ULRI). *566*

ULRICH'S UPDATE.
R.R. Bowker, A Division of Reed Elsevier Inc., 121 Chanlon Rd., New Providence, NJ 07974. TEL 908-665-2847. FAX 908-771-7725. URL: http://www.reedref.com.
Vendor(s): Knight-Ridder Information, Inc. (File no.480), Lexis-Nexis (ULRICHS), Ovid Technologies, Inc. (ULRI). *566*

ULTRA W W W MAGAZINE.
P.O. Box 49, 2550 Kontich, Belgium. URL: http://www.dma.be/p/ultra.
Available only online. *5442*

UNCLE BOB'S WHIZ-BANG.
12358 Ventura Blvd., No. 170, Los Angeles, CA 91604. URL: http://media.home.ml.org.
Available only online. *5346*

UNDERGROUND.
Scarborough College Student Press, 1265 Military Trail, West Hill, Ont. M1C 1A4, Canada. TEL 416-978-2011. *4363*

UNDERGROUND CONSTRUCTION.
Oildom Publishing Co. of Texas, Inc., Box 219368, Houston, TX 77218-9368. TEL 713-558-6930. FAX 713-558-7029.
Vendor(s): Information Access Co. *5625*

UNDERGROUND EXPERTS UNITED.
. URL: http://www.lysator.liu.se/'chief.
Available only online. *4538*

THE UNDERGROUND INFORMER.
4161 Tujunga Ave., No. 103, Studio City, CA 91604. URL: http://www.primenet.com/~lonnie/ui/.
Available only online. *2140*

UNDERGROUND ONLINE.
Zuff - David Publishing Co., URL: http://www.undergournd-online.com.
Available only online. *4364*

UNDERSTANDING AND INVOLVEMENT BULLETIN.
URL: http://www.vicnet.net.au/~vmiac/u&i.htm.
Available only online. *5100*

UNHAPPY.
Fringeware Inc., 2002-A Guadalupe St., Ste. 227, Austin, TX 78705. URL: http://www.fringeware.com/anathema/unhappy.
Available only online. *4481*

UNIGRAM.X.
G-2 Computer Intelligence Inc., 3 Maple Place, P.O. Box 7, Glen Head, NY 11545-0007. TEL 516-759-7025. FAX 516-759-7028. *2220*

UNION LABOR REPORT.
The Bureau of National Affairs, Inc., 1231 25th St., N.W., Washington, DC 20037. TEL 202-452-4200. FAX 202-822-8092. URL: http://www.bna.com/
Vendor(s): Human Resources Information Network. *1456*

UNION LABOR REPORT WEEKLY NEWSLETTER.
The Bureau of National Affairs, Inc., 1231 25th St., N.W., Washington, DC 20037. TEL 202-452-4200. FAX 202-822-8092. URL: http://www.bna.com/
Vendor(s): Human Resources Information Network (CDD, HDD). *1456*

UNION LIST OF SERIALS IN ISRAEL LIBRARIES.
Jewish National and University Library, P.O.Box 34165, Jerusalem 91341, Israel. TEL 972-2-585028. FAX 972-511771.
Available only online. *566*

UNIONE MATEMATICA ITALIANA. NOTIZIARIO.
Unione Matematica Italiana, Piazza Porta San Donato 5, 40126 Bologna, Italy. TEL 39-51-243190. FAX 39-51-243190. URL: http://www.dm.unibo.it/'umi/. *4613*

UNISCI.
3907 S.E. Second Ave., Cape Coral, FL 33904. TEL 941-549-7048. FAX 941-945-3002. URL: http://unisci.com.
Available only online. *6580*

UNITAS.
Union Bank of Finland, FIN-00020 UBF, Finland. FAX 358-0-6572898.
Vendor(s): UMI. *1293*

UNITED NATIONS. NATIONAL ACCOUNTS STATISTICS. MAIN AGGREGATES AND DETAILED TABLES.
United Nations Publications, Sales and Marketing Section, Room DC2-0853, New York, NY 10017. TEL 212-963-8302. FAX 212-963-3489. URL: http://www.un.org/publications. *1076*

U.S. BUREAU OF LABOR STATISTICS. C P I DETAILED REPORT.
U.S. Bureau of Labor Statistics, 2 Massachusetts Ave., N.E., Washington, DC 20212. TEL 202-655-4000. *1293*

U.S. BUREAU OF LABOR STATISTICS. NATIONAL OFFICE NEWS RELEASES.
U.S. Bureau of Labor Statistics, 2 Massachusetts Ave., N.E., Washington, DC 20212. TEL 202-655-4000. *1293*

U.S. CENTERS FOR DISEASE CONTROL. MORBIDITY AND MORTALITY WEEKLY REPORT.
U.S. Department of Health and Human Services, Centers for Disease Control (MS: A28), Epidemiology Program Office, 1600 Clifton Rd. N.E., Atlanta, GA 30333. TEL 800-843-6356.
Vendor(s): Information Access Co., NewsNet, Ovid Technologies, Inc. *6252*

U.S. CONGRESS. CONGRESSIONAL RECORD.
U.S. Congress, Washington, DC 20515. TEL 202-275-2051. FAX 202-275-0019. *5976*

U.S. DEPARTMENT OF AGRICULTURE. AGRICULTURAL OUTLOOK.
U.S. Department of Agriculture, Economic Research Service, c/o Debbie Haugan, Rm. 110, 1301 New York Ave., N.W., Washington, DC 20005-4788. TEL 202-219-0515.
Vendor(s): Knight-Ridder Information, Inc. *202*

U.S. DEPARTMENT OF AGRICULTURE. AGRICULTURAL STATISTICS BOARD REPORT: AGRICULTURAL PRICES.
U.S. Department of Agriculture, Agricultural Statistics Board, Publications, South Bldg., Rm. 5829, Washington, DC 20250. TEL 202-655-4000.
Vendor(s): Knight-Ridder Information, Inc. *184*

U.S. DEPARTMENT OF AGRICULTURE. AGRICULTURAL STATISTICS BOARD REPORT: CROP PRODUCTION.
U.S. Department of Agriculture, Agricultural Statistics Board, Publications, Rm. 5829, South Bldg., Washington, DC 20250. TEL 202-655-4000.
Vendor(s): Knight-Ridder Information, Inc. *184*

U.S. DEPARTMENT OF AGRICULTURE. AGRICULTURAL STATISTICS BOARD REPORT: HOGS AND PIGS.
U.S. Department of Agriculture, Agricultural Statistics Board, Publications, Rm. 5829, South Bldg., Washington, DC 20250. URL: http://www.mannlib.cornell.edu/reports/nassr/livestock/php-bb/ *184*

U.S. DEPARTMENT OF AGRICULTURE. AGRICULTURAL STATISTICS BOARD REPORT: MILK PRODUCTION.
U.S. Department of Agriculture, Agricultural Statistics Board, Publications, Rm. 5829, South Bldg., Washington, DC 20250. URL: http://www.mannlib.cornell.edu/reports/nassr/livestock/php-bb/ *185*

U.S. DEPARTMENT OF AGRICULTURE. ECONOMIC RESEARCH SERVICE. FOOD REVIEW.
U.S. Department of Agriculture, Economic Research Service, c/o Debbie Haugan, Rm. 110, 1301 New York Ave., N.W., Washington, DC 20005-4788. TEL 202-219-0515.
Vendor(s): Lexis-Nexis. *202*

U.S. DEPARTMENT OF AGRICULTURE. SITUATION & OUTLOOK REPORT. AGRICULTURE AND TRADE: FORMER U S S R.
U.S. Department of Agriculture, Economic Research Service, c/o Debbie Haugan, Rm. 110, 1301 New York Ave., N.W., Washington, DC 20005-4788. TEL 202-219-0515.
Vendor(s): Information Access Co., Knight-Ridder Information, Inc. *203*

U.S. DEPARTMENT OF STATE. KEY OFFICERS OF FOREIGN SERVICE POSTS.
U.S. Department of State, Office of Information Services, Washington, DC 20520. TEL 202-655-4000.
Vendor(s): Knight-Ridder Information, Inc. *6041*

U.S. DEPARTMENT OF STATE DISPATCH.
U.S. Department of State, Bureau of Public Affairs, 2201 C St., N.W., Washington, DC 20502. TEL 202-647-6265.
Vendor(s): Information Access Co., Knight-Ridder Information, Inc. *6042*

U.S. ENERGY INFORMATION ADMINISTRATION. ANNUAL ENERGY OUTLOOK. SUPPLEMENT.
U.S. Energy Information Administration, National Energy Information Center, EI-231, James Forrestal Bldg., Rm. 1F-048, 1000 Independence Ave., S.W., Washington, DC 20585. TEL 202-586-8800. URL: http://www.eia.doe.gov.
Available only online. *2686*

U.S. ENERGY INFORMATION ADMINISTRATION. ANNUAL ENERGY OUTLOOK.
U.S. Energy Information Administration, National Energy Information Center, EI-231, Forrestal Bldg., Rm. 1F-048, 1000 Independence Ave., S.W., Washington, DC 20585. TEL 202-586-8800. FAX 202-586-0727. URL: http://www.eia.doe.gov. *2686*

U.S. ENERGY INFORMATION ADMINISTRATION. ANNUAL ENERGY REVIEW.
U.S. Energy Information Administration, National Energy Information Center, EI-231, James Forrestal Bldg., Rm. 1F-048, 1000 Independence Ave., S.W., Washington, DC 20585. TEL 202-586-8800. FAX 202-586-0727. URL: http://www.eia.doe.gov. *2679*

U.S. ENERGY INFORMATION ADMINISTRATION. MONTHLY ENERGY REVIEW.
U.S. Energy Information Administration, National Energy Information Center, EI-231, James Forrestal Bldg., Rm. 1F-048, 1000 Independence Ave., S.W., Washington, DC 20585. TEL 202-586-8800. FAX 202-586-0727. URL: http://www.eia.doe.gov/emeu/mer/contents.html. *2686*

U.S. ENERGY INFORMATION ADMINISTRATION. NATURAL GAS ANNUAL.
U.S. Energy Information Administration, National Energy Information Center, EI-231, James Forrestal Bldg., Rm. 1F-048, 1000 Independence Ave., S.W., Washington, DC 20585. TEL 202-586-8800. FAX 202-586-0727. URL: http://www.eia.doe.gov. *5626*

U.S. ENERGY INFORMATION ADMINISTRATION. NATURAL GAS MONTHLY.
U.S. Energy Information Administration, National Energy Information Center, EI-231, James Forrestal Bldg., Rm. 1F-048, 1000 Independence Ave., S.W., Washington, DC 20585. TEL 202-586-8800. FAX 202-586-0727. URL: http://www.eia.doe.gov. *5626*

U.S. ENERGY INFORMATION ADMINISTRATION. PETROLEUM MARKETING ANNUAL.
U.S. Energy Information Administration, National Energy Information Center, EI-231, James Forrestal Bldg., Rm. 1F-048, Washington, DC 20585. TEL 202-586-8800. FAX 202-586-0727. URL: http://www.eia.doe.gov. *5626*

U.S. ENERGY INFORMATION ADMINISTRATION. PETROLEUM SUPPLY ANNUAL.
U.S. Energy Information Administration, National Energy Information Center, EI-231, National Energy Information Center, EI-231, James Forrestal Bldg., Rm. 1F-048, 1000 Independence Ave., S.W., Washington, DC 20585. TEL 202-586-8800. FAX 202-586-0727. URL: http://www.eia.doe.gov. *5626*

U.S. ENERGY INFORMATION ADMINISTRATION. PETROLEUM SUPPLY MONTHLY.
U.S. Energy Information Administration, National Energy Information Center, EI-231, James Forrestal Bldg., Rm. 1F-048, 1000 Independence Ave., S.W., Washington, DC 20585. TEL 202-586-8800. FAX 202-586-0727. URL: http://www.eia.doe.gov. *5626*

U.S. ENERGY INFORMATION ADMINISTRATION. QUARTERLY COAL REPORT.
U.S. Energy Information Administration, National Energy Information Center, EI-231, c/o Paulette Young, Coal Division, 1000 Independence Ave., S.W., EI-522, DC 20585. TEL 202-586-8800. FAX 202-586-0727. URL: http://www.eia.doe.gov. Vendor(s): Knight-Ridder Information, Inc. *2680*

U.S. ENERGY INFORMATION ADMINISTRATION. SHORT - TERM ENERGY OUTLOOK.
U.S. Energy Information Administration, National Energy Information Center, EI-231, James Forrestal Bldg., Rm. 1F-048, 1000 Independence Ave., S.W., Washington, DC 20585. TEL 202-586-8800. FAX 202-586-0727. URL: http://www.eia.doe.gov. *2680*

U.S. ENERGY INFORMATION ADMINISTRATION. WEEKLY PETROLEUM STATUS REPORT.
U.S. Energy Information Administration, National Energy Information Center, EI-231, James Forrestal Bldg., Rm. 1F-048, 1000 Independence Ave., S.W., Washington, DC 20585. TEL 202-586-8800. FAX 202-586-0727. URL: http://www.eia.doe.gov. Vendor(s): PetroScan. *5626*

U.S. FEDERAL ELECTION COMMISSION. ANNUAL REPORT.
U.S. Federal Election Commission, Washington, DC 20463. TEL 202-219-3420. URL: http://www.fec.gov/info.arfrm.htm. *5976*

U.S. FEDERAL HIGHWAY ADMINISTRATION. HIGHWAY STATISTICS.
U.S. Federal Highway Administration, Office of Highway Information Management, Department of Transportation, 400 Seventh St., S.W., Washington, DC 20590. TEL 202-366-0180. FAX 202-366-7742. *7059*

U.S. FOREIGN BROADCAST INFORMATION SERVICE. DAILY REPORTS: LATIN AMERICA.
U.S. National Technical Information Service, 5285 Port Royal Rd., Springfield, VA 22161. TEL 703-487-4600. FAX 703-321-8547. *5976*

U.S. FOREIGN BROADCAST INFORMATION SERVICE. DAILY REPORTS: NEAR EAST & SOUTH ASIA.
U.S. National Technical Information Service, 5285 Port Royal Rd., Springfield, VA 22161. TEL 703-487-4600. *5976*

U.S. FOREIGN BROADCAST INFORMATION SERVICE. DAILY REPORTS: SUB-SAHARAN AFRICA.
U.S. National Technical Information Service, 5285 Port Royal Rd., Springfield, VA 22161. TEL 703-487-4600. FAX 702-321-8547. *5976*

U.S. FOREIGN BROADCAST INFORMATION SERVICE. DAILY REPORTS: CHINA.
U.S. National Technical Information Service, 5285 Port Royal Rd., Springfield, VA 22161. TEL 703-487-4600. FAX 703-321-8547. *5977*

U.S. FOREIGN BROADCAST INFORMATION SERVICE. DAILY REPORTS: (F B I S).
U.S. National Technical Information Service, 5285 Port Royal Rd., Springfield, VA 22161. TEL 703-487-4600. FAX 703-321-8547. *5977*

U.S. FOREIGN BROADCAST INFORMATION SERVICE. DAILY REPORTS: WESTERN EUROPE.
U.S. National Technical Information Service, 5285 Port Royal Rd., Springfield, VA 22161. TEL 703-487-4600. FAX 703-321-8547. *5977*

U.S. FOREIGN BROADCAST INFORMATION SERVICE. TRENDS.
U.S. National Technical Information Service, 5285 Port Royal Rd., Springfield, VA 22161. TEL 703-487-4600. FAX 703-321-8547. *6042*

U.S. GENERAL SERVICES ADMINISTRATION. CATALOG OF FEDERAL DOMESTIC ASSISTANCE.
U.S. General Services Administration, Publications, 18th and F Sts., N.W., DC 20405. TEL 202-501-1794. FAX 202-501-4281. *6198*

U.S. NATIONAL AERONAUTICS AND SPACE ADMINISTRATION. VIDEO CATALOG.
U.S. National Aeronautics and Space Administration, Scientific and Technical Information Office, 800 Elkridge Landing Rd., Linthicum Heights, MD 21090-2934. URL: http:/www.sti.nasa.gov. *84*

U.S. NATIONAL COMMITTEE FOR MAN AND THE BIOSPHERE PROGRAM. BULLETIN.
U.S. National Committee for the Man and the Biosphere Program, Man and the Biosphere Secretariat, U.S. Department of State, SA-44C, 1st Fl., Washington, DC 20522-4401. TEL 202-776-8318. FAX 202-776-8367. *2247*

U.S. NUCLEAR REGULATORY COMMISSION. WEEKLY INFORMATION REPORT.
U.S. Nuclear Regulatory Commission, Washington, DC 20555-0001. URL: http://www.nrc.gov. Available only online. *2705*

U.S. OFFICE OF THE FEDERAL REGISTER. WEEKLY COMPILATION OF PRESIDENTIAL DOCUMENTS.
U.S. Office of the Federal Register, National Archives and Records Administration, Eighth St. and Pennsylvania Ave., N.W., Washington, DC 20408. TEL 202-523-5230.
Vendor(s): Information Access Co. *6198*

UNITED STATES LAW WEEK.
The Bureau of National Affairs, Inc., 1231 25th St., N.W., Washington, DC 20037. TEL 202-452-4200. FAX 202-822-8092. URL: http://www.bna.com/. Vendor(s): Lexis-Nexis (USLW), West Group. *4037*

UNITED STATES PATENTS QUARTERLY.
The Bureau of National Affairs, Inc., 1231 25th St., N.W., Washington, DC 20037. TEL 202-452-4200. FAX 202-822-8092. URL: http://www.bna.com/ Vendor(s): Knight-Ridder Information, Inc. (Patlaw, File 243), Questel Orbit Inc. *5591*

UNITED STATES TAX COURT REPORTS.
U.S. Tax Court, 400 Second St., N.W., Washington, DC 20217. TEL 202-783-3238. FAX 202-606-8704.
Vendor(s): West Group. *1637*

UNITS.
National Apartment Association, 201 N. Union St., No. 200, Alexandria, VA 22314. TEL 703-518-6141. FAX 703-518-6191.
Vendor(s): Information Access Co. *3761*

UNIVERSIDAD DE ZULIA. FACULTAD DE INGENIERIA. REVISTA TECNICA.
Universidad del Zulia, Facultad de Ingenieria, Apdo. 10-482, Correo Bella Vista, Maracaibo, Venezuela. TEL 58-61-525732. FAX 58-61-525732. *2744*

UNIVERSIDADE DE SAO PAULO. REVISTA DE FARMACIA E BIOQUIMICA.
Universidade de Sao Paulo, Faculdade de Ciencias Farmaceuticas, C.P. 66083, 05389-970 Sao Paulo, Brazil. TEL 55-11-8137251. FAX 55-11-2128194. *5697*

UNIVERSIDADE DE SAO PAULO. REVISTA DE ODONTOLOGIA.
Universidade de Sao Paulo, Faculdade de Odontologia, Av. Lineu Prestes, 2227, C.P. 8216, 05508-900 Sao Paulo, SP, Brazil. TEL 55-11-8187861. FAX 55-11-8187413. URL: http://www.usp.br/fo. *4872*

UNIVERSITAET DES SAARLANDES. JAHRESBIBLIOGRAPHIE.
Universitaet des Saarlandes, Universitaetsbibliothek, 66123 Saarbruecken, Germany. TEL 49-681-3023010. FAX 49-681-3022796. URL: http://www.uni-sb.de/z-einr/ub/uni-veroeff/jbpub.html. *568*

UNIVERSITAET HOHENHEIM. FORSCHUNGSBERICHT.
Universitaet Hohenheim, Presse und Forschungsinformation, 70593 Stuttgart, Germany. TEL 49-711-459-2001. FAX 49-711-4593289. *6592*

UNIVERSITAS COMENIANA. ACTA MATHEMATICA.
Univerzita Komenskeho, Matematicko-fizikalna Fakulta, Mlynska Dlina, 842 15 Bratislava, Slovakia. TEL 42-7-725741. FAX 42-7-725882. URL: http://www.emis.de/journals/AMUC/__amuc.html. *4613*

UNIVERSITE DE BORDEAUX III. CENTRE DE RECHERCHES SUR L'AMERIQUE ANGLOPHONE. ANNALES.
Maison des Sciences de l'Homme d'Aquitaine, Esplanade des Antilles, Domaine Universitaire, 33405 Talence Cedex, France. TEL 56-84-68-00. FAX 56-84-68-10. *4482*

UNIVERSITY DAILY KANSAN.
University Daily Kansan, 119 Stauffer-Flint Hall, Lawrence, KS 66045-0001. TEL 913-864-4358. FAX 913-864-5261. URL: http://www.kansan.com. *1976*

UNIVERSITY LAW REVIEW PROJECT.
URL: http://diglib.stanford.edu/lawcgi/join/add.cgi. Available only online. *4057*

UNIVERSITY OF BALTIMORE LAW REVIEW.
University of Baltimore School of Law, Business Editor, 1420 N. Charles St., Baltimore, MD 21201. TEL 410-837-4490.
Vendor(s): West Group. *4038*

UNIVERSITY OF CALGARY GAZETTE.
University of Calgary, Public Affairs, 2500 University Dr., N.W., Calgary, Alta. T2N 1N4, Canada. TEL 403-220-3500. FAX 403-282-8413. *1976*

UNIVERSITY OF CALIFORNIA. DIVISION OF LIBRARY AUTOMATION. TECHNICAL REPORTS.
University of California, Division of Library Automation, 300 Lakeside Dr., 8th Fl., Oakland, CA 94612-3550. TEL 510-987-0564. URL: http://ftp.dla.ucop.edu/pub/techreport/. *4234*

UNIVERSITY OF CALIFORNIA. INSTITUTE OF GOVERNMENTAL STUDIES LIBRARY. ACCESSIONS LIST.
University of California at Berkeley, Institute of Governmental Studies, 109 Moses Hall, No. 2370, Berkeley, CA 94720-2370. TEL 510-643-2370. FAX 510-643-0866. URL: http://www.garnet.berkeley.edu:80/~igs/. *5977*

UNIVERSITY OF CALIFORNIA AT BERKELEY WELLNESS LETTER.
Health Letter Associates, Box 412, Prince St. Sta., New York, NY 10012. TEL 212-505-2255. FAX 212-505-5462.
Vendor(s): Information Access Co., UMI. *5791*

UNIVERSITY OF CHICAGO LAW REVIEW.
University of Chicago, Law School, 1111 E. 60th St., Chicago, IL 60637. TEL 312-702-9832. FAX 312-702-0730.
Vendor(s): Lexis-Nexis. *4038*

UNIVERSITY OF CHICAGO LEGAL FORUM.
University of Chicago, Law School, 1111 E. 60th St., Chicago, IL 60637. TEL 312-702-9832. FAX 312-702-0730.
Vendor(s): West Group. *4038*

UNIVERSITY OF COLORADO LAW REVIEW.
University of Colorado Law Review, 290 Fleming Law Bldg., Campus Box 401, Boulder, CO 80309-0401. TEL 303-492-6145. FAX 303-492-1200. URL: http://stripe.colorado.edu/~cololrev/home.html.
Vendor(s): Lexis-Nexis, West Group. *4039*

UNIVERSITY OF DAYTON LAW REVIEW.
University of Dayton, Law School, 300 College Park, Dayton, OH 45469-1350. TEL 513-229-3642.
Vendor(s): Lexis-Nexis, West Group. *4039*

UNIVERSITY OF ILLINOIS LAW REVIEW.
University of Illinois at Urbana-Champaign, College of Law, Champaign, IL 61820. TEL 217-333-6756.
Vendor(s): West Group. *4039*

UNIVERSITY OF IOWA. LIBRARIES. NEWSLETTER.
University of Iowa Libraries, Iowa City, IA 52242. TEL 319-335-5871. URL: http://www.lib.uiowa.edu/lib/newsletter.html. *4220*

UNIVERSITY OF KANSAS LAW REVIEW.
University of Kansas, School of Law, Rm. 510, Green Hall, Lawrence, KS 66045. TEL 913-864-3463. FAX 913-864-3680.
Vendor(s): Lexis-Nexis, West Group. *4039*

UNIVERSITY OF MANCHESTER. DEPARTMENT OF COMPUTER SCIENCE. TECHNICAL REPORT SERIES.
University of Manchester, Department of Computer Science, Oxford Rd., Manchester M13 9PL, England. TEL 44-161-275-6130. FAX 44-161-275-6236. URL: http://www.cs.man.ac.uk/csonly/cstechrep/index.html. *2159*

UNIVERSITY OF NEW BRUNSWICK LAW JOURNAL.
University of New Brunswick, Faculty of Law, P.O. Box 4400, Fredericton, NB E3B 5A3, Canada. TEL 506-453-4657. FAX 506-453-5186.
Vendor(s): West Group. *4039*

UNIVERSITY OF PENNSYLVANIA JOURNAL OF INTERNATIONAL ECONOMIC LAW.
University of Pennsylvania, Law School, 3400 Chestnut St., Philadelphia, PA 19104-6204. TEL 215-898-6869. FAX 215-573-2025.
Vendor(s): Lexis-Nexis, West Group. *4128*

UNIVERSITY OF PENNSYLVANIA LAW REVIEW.
University of Pennsylvania Law Review, 3400 Chestnut St., Philadelphia, PA 19104-6204. TEL 215-898-7060. FAX 215-573-2005.
Vendor(s): Lexis-Nexis. *4039*

UNIVERSITY OF PITTSBURGH LAW REVIEW.
University of Pittsburgh, School of Law, Pittsburgh, PA 15260. TEL 412-648-1354.
Vendor(s): Lexis-Nexis, West Group. *4039*

UNIVERSITY OF RICHMOND LAW REVIEW.
University of Richmond, T.C. Williams School of Law, Richmond, VA 23173. TEL 804-289-8216. FAX 804-289-8683.
Vendor(s): West Group. *4040*

UNIVERSITY OF SAN FRANCISCO LAW REVIEW.
University of San Francisco, School of Law, Kendrick Hall, 2130 Fulton St., San Francisco, CA 94117. TEL 415-666-6154. FAX 415-666-6433.
Vendor(s): Lexis-Nexis, West Group. *4040*

UNIVERSITY OF TORONTO. INSTITUTE FOR POLICY ANALYSIS. WORKING PAPER SERIES.
University of Toronto, Institute for Policy Analysis, 150 St. George St., Toronto, ON M5S 3G7, Canada. TEL 416-978-8623. FAX 416-978-6713. URL: http://www.chass.utoronto.ca:8080/ecipa/wpa.html. Available only online. *1009*

UNIVERSITY OF TORONTO BULLETIN.
University of Toronto, Department of Public Affairs, 21 King's College Circle, Toronto, ON M5S 3J3, Canada. TEL 416-978-7016. FAX 416-978-7430. *1977*

UNIX NEWS.
12 Sutton Row, 4th Fl., London W1V 5FH, England. TEL 44-171-867-9880.
Vendor(s): Information Access Co. *2160*

UNIX REVIEW.
Miller Freeman, Inc., 600 Harrison St., San Francisco, CA 94107. TEL 415-905-2200. FAX 415-905-2232.
Vendor(s): Information Access Co., UMI. *2146*

UNIX UPDATE.
Worldwide Videotex, Box 3273, Boynton Beach, FL 33424-3273. TEL 407-738-2276.
Vendor(s): Information Access Co. *2220*

UNO MAS MAGAZINE.
Jim Saah, Ed. & Pub., Box 1832, Silver Spring, MD 20915. TEL 301-946-5232. FAX 301-770-3250. URL: http://www.dallas.net/homes/gregp/unomas.html. *4364*

UPDATE WEEKLY MAC.
URL: http://www.webcom.com/level6/
Available only online. *2220*

UPSIDE.
Upside Publishing Company, 2015 Pioneer Ct., San Mateo, CA 94403-1736. TEL 415-377-0950. FAX 415-377-1961. URL: http://www.upside.com.
Vendor(s): UMI. *1412*

UPSTATE NEW YORK BUSINESS DIRECTORY.
American Business Directories, 5711 S. 86th Circle, Box 27347, Omaha, NE 68127. TEL 402-593-4600. FAX 402-331-5481. *1720*

URBAN ABSTRACTS.
London Research Centre, Research Library, 81 Black Prince Rd., London SE1 7SZ, England. TEL 44-171-627-9666. FAX 44-171-627-9674.
Vendor(s): European Space Agency. *6208*

URBAN DESIGN INTERNATIONAL.
Thomson Professional, 2-6 Boundary Row, London SE1 8HN, England. TEL 44-171-8650066. FAX 44-171-5229623. URL: http://udi.thomsonprofessional.com. *3762*

URBAN DESIRES.
54 W. 21st St., Ste. 903, New York, NY 10010. URL: http://www.desires.com.
Available only online. *471*

URBAN POLICY & RESEARCH.
Urban Policy and Research, Landscape, Environment and Policy, RMIT, P.O. Box 2476V, Melbourne, Vic. 3001, Australia. TEL 61-3-4293316. FAX 61-3-6601855. URL: http://www.arts.unimelb.edu.au/projects/upr/. *3763*

URBAN STUDIES.
Carfax Publishing Co., P.O. Box 25, Abingdon, Oxon OX14 3UE, England. TEL 44-1235-401000. FAX 44-1235-401550.
Vendor(s): Information Access Co. *3763*

URBAN TRANSPORT NEWS.
Business Publishers, Inc., 951 Pershing Dr., Silver Spring, MD 20910-4464. TEL 301-587-6300. FAX 301-585-9075.
Vendor(s): Information Access Co., NewsNet (TS10). *7046*

URETHANES TECHNOLOGY.
Crain Communications Ltd., Newgarden House, 78 Hatton Garden, London EC1N 8JQ, England. TEL 44-171-457-1400. FAX 44-171-457-1440. URL: http://www.crain.co.uk.
Vendor(s): Information Access Co. *6505*

URNER BARRY'S PRICE-CURRENT.
Urner Barry Publications, Inc., Box 389, Toms River, NJ 08754. TEL 908-240-5330. FAX 908-341-0891. URL: http://www.urnerbarry.com. *291*

DER UROLOGE. SECTION A.
Springer-Verlag, Heidelberger Platz 3, 14197 Berlin, Germany. TEL 49-30-82787-0. FAX 49-30-82787448. URL: http://link.springer.de. *5166*

DER UROLOGE. SECTION B.
Springer-Verlag, Heidelberger Platz 3, 14197 Berlin, Germany. TEL 49-30-82787-0. FAX 49-30-82787448. URL: http://link.springer.de. *5166*

UROLOGY INTERNATIONAL.
Complete Medical Communications Ltd., C M C House, 19 King Edward St., Macclesfield, Ches. SK10 1AQ, England. TEL 44-1625-619855. FAX 44-1625-619812. URL: http://www.urol-int.org. *5166*

UROLOGY TIMES.
Advanstar Communications, Inc., 7500 Old Oak Blvd., Cleveland, OH 44130. TEL 216-826-2839. FAX 216-891-2726.
Vendor(s): Information Access Co., Knight-Ridder Information, Inc. *5167*

USED EQUIPMENT DIRECTORY.
Penton Publishing Co. (Hasbrouck Heights), 611 Rte. 46 W., Hasbrouck Heights, NJ 07604. TEL 201-393-9558. FAX 201-393-9553. *4553*

USED EQUIPMENT WORLD.
Used Equipment World, Inc., 100 Wall St., New York, NY 10005. TEL 212-558-6800. FAX 212-747-0077. *4757*

USPEKHI FIZICHESKIKH NAUK.
Uspekhi Fizicheskikh Nauk, Leninskii prospekt, 15, 117071 Moscow, Russia. TEL 7-095-9550325. FAX 7-095-1358860. URL: http://urn.ioc.ac.ru. *5832*

UTAH BUSINESS DIRECTORY.
American Business Directories, 5711 S. 86th Circle, Box 27347, Omaha, NE 68127. TEL 402-593-4600. FAX 402-331-5481. *1720*

UTAH LAW REVIEW.
University of Utah, College of Law, Salt Lake City, UT 84112. TEL 801-581-6833.
Vendor(s): West Group. *4041*

UTAH STATE DIGEST.
Division of Administrative Rules, Box 141007, Salt Lake City, UT 84114-1007. TEL 801-538-3218. FAX 801-538-3844. URL: http://www.its.state.ut.us/bbs.htm. *6226*

UTILITY ENVIRONMENT REPORT.
McGraw-Hill, Inc., Energy & Business Newsletters, 1221 Ave. of the Americas, 36th Fl., New York, NY 10020. TEL 212-512-6410.
Vendor(s): Knight-Ridder Information, Inc. (UER), Dow Jones News Retrieval (UER), Lexis-Nexis (UER), NewsNet (EV42). *2849*

UTILITY REPORTER - FUELS ENERGY & POWER.
Merton Allen Associates, InfoTeam Inc., Box 15640, Plantation, FL 33318-5640. TEL 954-473-9560. FAX 954-473-0544.
Vendor(s): Data-Star, Information Access Co., NewsNet (EY12), UMI. *2680*

UTTERANTS...
Global Graphics, Box 822, Mountain View, CA 94042-0822. URL: http://www.globalgraphics.com/Zines/Utterants/Utterants.html.
Available only online. *4483*

V A R BUSINESS.
C M P Publications, Inc., 600 Community Dr., Manhasset, NY 11030-3847. TEL 516-562-6700. FAX 516-562-8585.
Vendor(s): Information Access Co. *2092*

V G.
Verdens Gang A-S, Akersgt. 55, P.O. Box 1185 Sentrum, N-0107 Oslo, Norway. TEL 47-22-00-00-00. FAX 47-22-42-67-80. *3345*

V H L FAMILY FORUM.
V H L Family Alliance, 171 Clinton Rd., Brookline, MA 02146. TEL 617-232-5946. FAX 617-734-8233. URL: http://neurosurgery.mgh.harvard.edu/vhl-fa. *5101*

THE V L D B JOURNAL.
Springer-Verlag, Heidelberger Platz 3, Berlin 14197, Germany. TEL 49-30-82787-0. FAX 49-30-82787448. URL: http://science.springer.de/vldb/vldb.html. *2167*

V L S I DESIGN.
Gordon and Breach - Harwood Academic, Amsteldisk 166, 1st Fl., 1079 LH Amsterdam, Netherlands. URL: http://www.gbhap.com/VLSI_Design. *2116*

V T A C GUIDE TO UNIVERSITY AND T A F E COURSES.
Victorian Tertiary Admissions Centre, 40 Park St., S. Melbourne, Vic. 3205, Australia. TEL 61-3-96907977. *2528*

SERIALS AVAILABLE ONLINE

VAARD I NORDEN.
Sykepleiernes Samarbeid i Norden, P.O. Box 2681, St. Hanshaugen, N-131 Oslo 1, Norway. TEL 47-22-04-33-04. FAX 47-22-38-02-30. *4951*

VACCINE.
Elsevier Science Ltd., Oxford Fulfilment Centre, P.O. Box 800, Kidlington, Oxford OX5 1DX, England. TEL 44-1865-843000. FAX 44-1865-843010. URL: http://www.elsevier.nl/. *4801*

VACCINE WEEKLY.
Charles W. Henderson, Ed. & Pub., Box 5528, Atlanta, GA 31107-0528. TEL 404-377-8895. FAX 404-378-4511.
Vendor(s): Information Access Co. *5697*

VADEMECUM DEUTSCHER LEHR- UND FORSCHUNGSSTAETTEN. STAETTEN DER FORSCHUNG.
Dr. Josef Raabe Verlags GmbH, Postfach 103922, 70034 Stuttgart, Germany. TEL 49-711-62900-0. FAX 49-711-6290010. URL: http://www.raabe.de/.
Vendor(s): STN International. *6582*

VAESTRA SVERIGES AFFAERER & FOERETAG.
Vaestra Sveriges Affaerer & Foeretag, P.O. Box 411, S-401 26 Goeteborg, Sweden. TEL 46-031-624060. FAX 46-031-624066. *1553*

VAIL - BEAVER CREEK MAGAZINE.
Box 4328, Steamboat Springs, CO 80477. TEL 970-476-6600. FAX 970-476-6152. URL: http://www.vailweb.com. *3388*

VALPARAISO UNIVERSITY LAW REVIEW.
Valparaiso University, School of Law, Valparaiso, IN 46383. TEL 219-465-7807. FAX 219-465-7872.
Vendor(s): West Group. *4041*

VANCOUVER ECHO.
Highland Echo Publishing, 3355 Grandview Hwy., Vancouver, BC V5M 1Z5, Canada. URL: http://www.vannet.com/vanecho. *3267*

VANDERBILT JOURNAL OF TRANSNATIONAL LAW.
Vanderbilt University, School of Law, Nashville, TN 37240. TEL 615-322-2284. FAX 615-343-6023.
Vendor(s): Lexis-Nexis, West Group. *4128*

VANDERBILT LAW REVIEW.
Vanderbilt University, School of Law, Nashville, TN 37240. TEL 615-322-4766. FAX 615-343-6023.
Vendor(s): Lexis-Nexis, West Group. *4041*

VANGUARD (MOBILE).
University of South Alabama, University Board of Publications, c/o Student Media Manager Loran Lewis, Drawer U-25100, Mobile, AL 36688. TEL 334-460-6442. FAX 334-414-8293. URL: http://www.usouthal.edu/ *1978*

THE VEGAN NEWS.
Vegan Action, Box 4353, Berkeley, CA 94704. TEL 510-654-6297. FAX 510-595-7569. URL: http://www.vegan.org. *5483*

VEGETARIAN TIMES.
Cowles Enthusiast Media, Healthy Lifestyles Group, 4 High Ridge Park, Stamford, CT 06905. TEL 203-321-1755. FAX 203-322-1966.
Vendor(s): Information Access Co. *5483*

VENDING: THE INTERNATIONAL MARKET.
Euromonitor, 60-61 Britton St., London EC1M 5NA, England. TEL 44-171-251-8024. FAX 44-171-608-3149. URL: http://www.euromonitor.com.
Vendor(s): Data-Star, Knight-Ridder Information, Inc. *1553*

VENEZUELA ANALITICA.
Venezuela Analitica Editores, URL: http://www.internet.ve/analitica.
Available only online. *5978*

VENTURE CAPITAL JOURNAL.
Securities Data Publishing, 40 W. 57th St., 11th Fl., New York, NY 10019. TEL 212-765-5311. FAX 212-765-6123.
Vendor(s): Information Access Co. *1414*

VERBAENDE, BEHOERDEN, ORGANISATIONEN DER WIRTSCHAFT.
Verlag Hoppenstedt GmbH, Havelstr. 9, 64295 Darmstadt, Germany. TEL 49-6151-380-0. FAX 49-6151-380-360.
Vendor(s): GBI. *1294*

VERBOSITY MAGAZINE.
1350 King College Rd., Bristol, TN 37620. URL: http://verbosity.wiw.org.
Available only online. *3388*

VERMONT BUSINESS DIRECTORY.
American Business Directories, 5711 S. 86th Circle, Box 27347, Omaha, NE 68127. TEL 402-593-4600. FAX 402-331-5481. *1720*

VERMONT BUSINESS MAGAZINE.
Lake Iroquois Publishing, Inc., 2 Church St., Burlington, VT 05401. TEL 802-863-8038. FAX 802-863-8069.
Vendor(s): Knight-Ridder Information, Inc., UMI. *1010*

VERSICHERUNGSRECHT.
Verlag Versicherungswirtschaft e.V., Klosestr. 20-24, 76137 Karlsruhe, Germany. TEL 49-721-3509126. FAX 49-721-31833. *3836*

VERTICAL FILE INDEX.
H.W. Wilson Co., 950 University Ave., Bronx, NY 10452. TEL 718-588-8400. FAX 718-590-1617.
Vendor(s): Wilsonline (File VFI). *27*

VERZEICHNIS AUSLAENDISCHER ZEITSCHRIFTEN IN SCHWEIZERISCHEN BIBLIOTHEKEN.
Schweizerische Landesbibliothek, Hallwylstr. 15, CH-3003 Bern, Switzerland. TEL 41-31-3228911. FAX 41-31-3228463. URL: http://www.snl.ch/. *569*

VET ON-LINE.
URL: http://www.priory.com/journals/vet.htm.
Available only online. *7280*

VETERINARY BIOTECHNOLOGY NEWSLETTER.
Office International des Epizooties, 12 rue de Prony, 75017 Paris, France. TEL 33-1-44151888. FAX 33-1-42670987. URL: http://www.oie.org.
Available only online. *7282*

VETERINARY BULLETIN.
CAB International, Wallingford, Oxon. OX10 8DE, England. TEL 44-1491-832111. FAX 44-1491-826090. URL: http://www.cabi.org.
Vendor(s): DIMDI, European Space Agency, Knight-Ridder Information, Inc., STN International. *7286*

VIBRANT LIFE.
Review and Herald Publishing Association, 55 W. Oak Ridge Dr., Hagerstown, MD 21740. TEL 301-791-7000.
Vendor(s): Information Access Co. *5792*

VICE.
Vice Publishing, Inc., Box 20281, New York, NY 10011-0003. TEL 212-727-2787. FAX 212-727-3190. *471*

VICNET ZINE.
VicNet - Victoria's Network, 328 Swanston St., Melbourne, Vic. 3000, Australia. URL: http://www.vicnet.net.au/vicnet/zine.
Available only online. *2140*

VICTORIAN REPORTS.
Butterworths, Division of Reed International Books Australia Pty. Ltd. 271-273 Lane Cove Rd., North Ryde, N.S.W. 2113, Australia. TEL 61-2-93354444. FAX 61-2-93354655.
Vendor(s): Info-One International Pty Ltd. *4042*

VICTORIAN STUDIES.
Indiana University Press, 601 N. Morton, Bloomington, IN 47404. TEL 812-855-9449. FAX 812-855-8507.
Vendor(s): Information Access Co., UMI. *3797*

VIDEO EYEBALL MAGAZINE.
122 Montclair Ave., Boston, MA 02131-1344. URL: http://www.tiac.net/users/videoeye. *5347*

VIDEO MAGAZINE.
Hachette Filipacchi Magazines, Inc., 1633 Broadway, 43rd. Fl., New York, NY 10019. TEL 212-767-6000. FAX 212-767-5619.
Vendor(s): Information Access Co. *2069*

VIDEO REVIEW.
Media Works Group Inc., P.O. Box 2047, Larchmont, NY 10538-8247. TEL 914-576-8800. FAX 914-576-8841.
Vendor(s): Information Access Co., UMI. *5347*

VIDEO STORE.
Advanstar Communications, Inc., 7500 Old Oak Blvd., Cleveland, OH 44130. TEL 216-243-8100.
Vendor(s): Information Access Co., Knight-Ridder Information, Inc. *2070*

VIDEO TECHNOLOGY NEWS.
Phillips Business information, Inc., 1201 Seven Locks Rd., Potomac, MD 20854. TEL 301-424-3338. FAX 301-309-3847.
Vendor(s): Data-Star, Information Access Co., Knight-Ridder Information, Inc., NewsNet (PB39). *2070*

VIDEO WEEK.
Warren Publishing, Inc., 2115 Ward Ct., N.W., Washington, DC 20037. TEL 202-872-9200. FAX 202-293-3435.
Vendor(s): Information Access Co., NewsNet (EL01). *2070*

VIDEOAGE.
Triangle Media Group, Inc., 202 Lord Anson Dr., Raleigh, NC 27610. TEL 919-231-9245. FAX 919-231-8006. *2070*

VIDEOLOG.
Trade Service Corporation, 10996 Torreyana Rd., San Diego, CA 92121. TEL 619-457-5920. FAX 619-457-1320. *2014*

VIDEOMAKER.
Videomaker Inc., Box 4591, Chico, CA 95927. TEL 916-891-8410. FAX 916-891-8443. URL: http://www.videomaker.com.
Vendor(s): CompuServe, Inc. (71161,1722). *2070*

VIDEOS FOR BUSINESS AND TRAINING.
Gale Research, 835 Penobscot Bldg., 645 Griswold St., Detroit, MI 48226-4094. TEL 313-961-2242. FAX 800-414-5043.
Vendor(s): Human Resources Information Network (Video). *2070*

VIDERE.
M I T Press, 5 Cambridge Center, Cambridge, MA 02142. TEL 617-253-2889. FAX 617-577-1545. URL: http://www-mit.edu.
Available only online. *2125*

THE VIETNAM BUSINESS JOURNAL.
Viam Communications Group Ltd., 114 E. 32nd St., Ste. 1010, New York, NY 10016. TEL 212-725-1717. URL: http://www.viam.com.
Vendor(s): Dow Jones News Retrieval. *1010*

VIETNAM JOURNAL OF MATHEMATICS.
Springer-Verlag Singapore, No. 04-01, Cencon, One Tannery Rd., Singapore 347729, Singapore. TEL 65-8-420112. FAX 65-8-420107. *4615*

THE VIEW (FEDERAL WAY).
1089 S.W. 330 Ct., Federal Way, WA 98023. URL: http://www.the-view.com.
Available only online. *2180*

VILLAGE VOICE.
V V Publishing Corporation, 36 Cooper Sq., New York, NY 10003. TEL 212-475-3300. FAX 212-475-8944. URL: http://www.villagevoice.com/'voice/.
Vendor(s): Dow Jones News Retrieval, Lexis-Nexis. *3389*

VILLANOVA LAW REVIEW.
Villanova University Law School, 299 N. Spring Mill Rd., Villanova, PA 19085. TEL 215-645-7053. URL: http://vls.law.vill.edu/academic/jd/jounals/law-reveiw/.
Vendor(s): West Group. *4042*

VIRCHOWS ARCHIV.
Springer-Verlag, Heidelberger Platz 3, 14197 Berlin, Germany. TEL 49-30-82787-0. FAX 49-30-82787448. URL: http://link.springer.de. *633*

VIRGIN MEAT.
Steve Blum, Ed. & Pub., 2325 West Ave., K-15, Lancaster, CA 93536. TEL 805-722-1758. URL: http://members.aol.com/virginmeat/magazine/gothic.html. *4484*

VIRGINIA BUSINESS DIRECTORY.
American Business Directories, 5711 S. 86th Circle, Box 27347, Omaha, NE 68127. TEL 402-593-4600. FAX 402-331-5481. *1721*

VIRGINIA ENVIRONMENTAL LAW JOURNAL.
Virginia Environmental Law Journal, University of Virginia, School of Law, Charlottesville, VA 22903. TEL 804-924-3683. FAX 804-924-7536.
Vendor(s): West Group. *4043*

VIRGINIA JOURNAL OF INTERNATIONAL LAW.
Virginia Journal of International Law Association, University of Virginia, School of Law, 580 Massie Rd., Charlottesville, VA 22903. TEL 804-924-3415. FAX 804-924-3237.
Vendor(s): Lexis-Nexis, West Group. *4128*

VIRGINIA LAW REVIEW.
Virginia Law Review Association, University of Virginia, School of Law, 580 Massie Rd., VA 22903-1789. TEL 804-924-3079. FAX 804-982-2818.
Vendor(s): National Data Corp., West Group. *4043*

VIRGINIA MAGAZINE OF HISTORY AND BIOGRAPHY.
Virginia Historical Society, Box 7311, Richmond, VA 23221. TEL 804-358-4901. FAX 804-355-2399.
Vendor(s): UMI. *3651*

VIRGINIA POLYTECHNIC INSTITUTE AND STATE UNIVERSITY. VIRGINIA AGRICULTURAL EXPERIMENT STATION. INFORMATION SERIES.
Virginia Polytechnic Institute and State University, Virginia Agricultural Experiment Station, College of Agriculture and Life Sciences, Blacksburg, VA 24061-0402. TEL 540-231-6986. FAX 540-231-4163. URL: http://www.web.vaes.vt.edu/VAES/Publications/vaesnumpubs.html.
Available only online. *163*

VIRGINIA TAX REVIEW.
Virginia Tax Review Association, University of Virginia, School of Law, Charlottesville, VA 22901. TEL 804-924-4726. FAX 804-924-7536.
Vendor(s): West Group. *1637*

VIROLOGY.
Academic Press, Inc., Journal Division, 525 B St., Ste. 1900, San Diego, CA 92101-4495. TEL 619-230-1840. FAX 619-688-6800. URL: http://www.apnet.com/www/journal/vy.htm; http://www.idealibrary.com/ *795*

VIROLOGY AND AIDS ABSTRACTS.
Cambridge Scientific Abstracts, 7200 Wisconsin Ave., 6th Fl., Bethesda, MD 20814. TEL 301-961-6750. FAX 301-961-6720. URL: http://www.csa.com.
Vendor(s): Knight-Ridder Information, Inc. (File no.76/LIFE SCIENCES COLLECTION), STN International (LIFESCI). *4789*

VIRTUAL FLYSHOP.
Fly Fisherman Magazine, 223 Linden, Ste. 203, Fort Collins, CO 80525. URL: http://www.flyshop.com.
Available only online. *6887*

VIRTUAL PHYSICS.
URL: http://www.tp.umu.se/vp.html.
Available only online. *5832*

VIRTUAL PROTOTYPING JOURNAL.
M C B University Press Ltd., 60-62 Toller Ln., Bradford, W. Yorks BD8 9BY, England. TEL 44-1274-777700. FAX 44-1274-785200. URL: http://www.mcb.co.uk. *2806*

VIRTUALBUSINESS NEWS.
URL: http://www.virtualbusiness.net/vbnews/
Available only online. *1649*

VISION.
Search Internet Development Services, P.O. Box 27550, Dubai, United Arab Emirates. URL: http://www.careweb.com.
Available only online. *3368*

VISION QUEST.
Visionary Publishing, 10 Gilmore St., No. 3, Cambridge, MA 02139-3754.
Available only online. *3093*

VISIONS OF GLORY MAGAZINE.
B B C of Vanderfrift, Inc., Box 178, Vandergrift, PA 15690-0178. TEL 412-568-1566. URL: http://www.vog.org.
Available only online. *6446*

THE VISUAL COMPUTER.
Springer-Verlag, Heidelberger Platz 3, 14197 Berlin, Germany. TEL 49-30-82787-0. FAX 49-30-82787448. URL: http://link.springer.de. *2125*

VISUAL DEVELOPER.
14455 N. Hayden Rd., Ste. 220, Scottsdale, AZ 85260-6949. URL: http://www.coriolis.com/site/msie/comment.htm. *2147*

VITAL SIGNS (CAMBRIDGE).
International Physicians for the Prevention of Nuclear War, 126 Rogers St., Cambridge, MA 02142. TEL 617-868-5050. FAX 617-868-2560. URL: http://www.healthnet.org/ippnw/. *6253*

VITAL SPEECHES OF THE DAY.
City News Publishing Co. Inc., Box 1247, Mt. Pleasant, SC 29465-1247. TEL 803-881-8733. FAX 803-881-4007.
Vendor(s): Information Access Co., UMI. *3882*

VITAMINS AND DIETARY SUPPLEMENTS: THE INTERNATIONAL MARKET.
Euromonitor, 60-61 Britton St., London EC1M 5NA, England. TEL 44-171-251-8024. FAX 44-171-608-3149. URL: http://www.euromonitor.com.
Vendor(s): Data-Star, Knight-Ridder Information, Inc. *5698*

VITIS - VITICULTURE AND OENOLOGY ABSTRACTS.
Bundesanstalt fuer Zuechtungsforschung an Kulturpflanzen, Institut fuer Rebenzuechtung Geilweilerhof, 76833 Siebeldingen, Germany. TEL 49-63-45410. FAX 49-63-4541177.
Vendor(s): DIMDI, Knight-Ridder Information, Inc., STN International. *185*

VODOHOSPODARSKY CASOPIS.
Slovenska Akademia Vied, Ustav Hydrologie, Racianska 75, P.O. Box 94, 830 08 Bratislava, Slovakia. TEL 421-7-253000. FAX 421-7-259404. URL: http://www.savba.sk/logos/journals/ap. *2398*

VOGUE.
Conde Nast Publications Ltd., Vogue House, Hanover Sq., London W1R OAD, England. TEL 44-171-499-9080. FAX 44-171-493-1345. URL: http://www.condenast.co.uk/vogue. *1928*

VOICE TECHNOLOGY & SERVICES NEWS.
Phillips Business Information, Inc., 1201 Seven Locks Rd., Potomac, MD 20854. TEL 301-424-3338. FAX 301-309-3847.
Vendor(s): Data-Star, Information Access Co., Knight-Ridder Information, Inc., NewsNet. *2008*

VOLUNTEERS WHO PRODUCE BOOKS.
U.S. Library of Congress, National Library Service for the Blind and Physically Handicapped, Washington, DC 20542. TEL 202-707-5100. FAX 202-707-0712. URL: http://www.lcweb.loc.gov/nls. *3475*

VOTING RECORD: SENATE NATIONAL SECURITY INDEX.
Council for a Livable World, 110 Maryland Ave., N.E., Washington, DC 20002. TEL 202-543-4100. URL: http://www.clw.org/pub/clw/. *5978*

VOX M E D A L.
Dalhousie University, Dalhousie Medical Alumni Association, Dalhousie University, First Floor, Tupper Bldg., Halifax, NS B3H 4H7, Canada. TEL 902-494-8800. FAX 902-494-2033. URL: http://www.medicine.dal.ca. *1978*

W A A C NEWSLETTER.
Western Association for Art Conservation, 5905 Wilshire Blvd., Los Angeles, CA 90036. TEL 602-433-0461. *472*

THE W A W L I PAPERS.
19530 Pacific Hwy. S., Ste. 200, Seattle, WA 98188.
Available only online. *6793*

W C E L NEWS.
West Coast Environmental Law Research Foundation, 1001-207 W. Hastings, Vancouver, BC V6B 1H7, Canada. TEL 604-684-7378. FAX 604-684-1312. URL: http://vcn.bc.ca/wcel. *2957*

W C E R HIGHLIGHTS.
Wisconsin Center for Education Research, University of Wisconsin at Madison, 1025 W. Johnston St., Rm. 785, Madison, WI 53706. TEL 608-263-8814. FAX 608-263-6448. URL: http://www.wcer.wisc.edu. *2579*

W G S NEWSLETTER.
Working Group on Software, c/o Mr. Ruth Kool, Secy., Eindhoven University of Technology, Dept. of Mathematics and Computing Science, P.O. Box 513, 5600 MB Eindhoven, Netherlands. FAX 31-40-2465995. *2220*

W H A M! ALERT.
URL: http://www.echonyc.com/~wham/.
Available only online. *7310*

W H Y.
World Hunger Year, 505 Eighth Ave., 21st Fl., New York, NY 10018-6582. TEL 212-629-8850. FAX 212-465-9274. URL: http://www.iglou.com/why/. *6693*

W I N NEWS.
Women's International Network, 187 Grant St., Lexington, MA 02173-2140. TEL 617-862-9431.
Vendor(s): Information Access Co., UMI. *7348*

W R R I NEWS.
University of North Carolina, Water Resources Research Institute, Box 7912, Raleigh, NC 27695-7912. TEL 919-515-2815. FAX 919-515-7802. URL: http://wwwz.ncsu.edu/ncsu/cil/wrri/.
Vendor(s): MediaStream. *7302*

THE WALKER MARKET LETTER.
TEL 303-980-1168. URL: http://www.lowrisk.com.
Available only online. *1414*

WALL STREET & TECHNOLOGY.
United News & Media, One Penn Plaza, New York, NY 10119. TEL 212-869-1300.
Vendor(s): Information Access Co., UMI. *1176*

WALL STREET JOURNAL (EASTERN EDITION).
Dow Jones & Co., Inc., 200 Liberty St., New York, NY 10281. TEL 212-416-2000. URL: http://www.wsj.com.
Vendor(s): Dow Jones News Retrieval. *1172*

THE WALL STREET JOURNAL INDEX.
U M I, 300 N. Zeeb Rd., Ann Arbor, MI 48106. TEL 313-761-4700. FAX 800-864-0019. *1172*

WALL STREET TRANSCRIPT.
Wall Street Transcript Corp., 100 Wall St., New York, NY 10005. TEL 212-747-9500.
Vendor(s): Information Access Co., MediaStream. *1414*

WALT DISNEY WORLD (YEAR).
Hearst Corporation, Walt Disney World, 250 W. 55th St., 11th Fl., New York, NY 10019. TEL 212-903-5190. *7249*

WARD'S AUTO WORLD.
Ward's Communications, 3000 Town Center, Ste. 2750, Southfield, MI 48075-1212. TEL 810-357-0800. FAX 810-357-0810. URL: http://www.wardsauto.com.
Vendor(s): Information Access Co., UMI. *7121*

WARFIELD'S BUSINESS RECORD.
11 E. Saratoga St., Baltimore, MD 21202. TEL 410-752-3849. FAX 410-332-0698.
Vendor(s): Lexis-Nexis, UMI. *1294*

WARNING LETTER BULLETIN.
Washington Information Source, 6506 Old Stage Rd., Ste. 100, Rockville, MD 20852-4326. TEL 301-770-5553.
Vendor(s): Information Access Co. *4758*

WARREN'S CABLE REGULATION MONITOR.
Warren Publishing, Inc., 2115 Ward Ct., N.W., Washington, DC 20037. TEL 202-872-9200. FAX 202-293-3435. *2064*

WARSAW VOICE.
Warsaw Voice S.A., Ksiecia Janusza 64, 01-452 Warsaw, Poland. TEL 48-22-366377. FAX 48-22-371995.
Vendor(s): Lexis-Nexis. *3349*

SERIALS AVAILABLE ONLINE

WASHED - UPDATE.
Box 2598, Seal Beach, CA 90740. URL: http://us.imdb.com/washed-update.html; http://www.bulmash.com/washed.
Available only online. *2065*

WASHINGTON AND LEE LAW REVIEW.
Washington and Lee University, School of Law, Lewis Hall, Lexington, VA 24450-1799. TEL 703-463-8566. FAX 703-463-8488.
Vendor(s): Lexis-Nexis, UMI, West Group. *4044*

WASHINGTON BUSINESS DIRECTORY.
American Business Directories, 5711 S. 86th Circle, Box 27347, Omaha, NE 68127. TEL 402-593-4600. FAX 402-331-5481. *1721*

WASHINGTON BUSINESS JOURNAL.
American City Business Journals, Inc. (Arlington), 2000 14th St., N. Ste. 500, Arlington, VA 22201. TEL 703-875-2200. FAX 703-875-2231. *1011*

WASHINGTON C E O.
Fivash Publishing Group, 2505 Second Ave., Ste. 602, Seattle, WA 98121. TEL 206-441-8415. FAX 206-441-8325. URL: http://fivash.com. *1512*

WASHINGTON D.C. AREA BUSINESS DIRECTORY.
American Business Directories, 5711 S. 86th Circle, Box 27347, Omaha, NE 68127. TEL 402-593-4600. FAX 402-331-5481. *1721*

WASHINGTON D.C. COMPUTER CURRENTS.
Computer Currents Publishing, Inc., 5720 Hollis St., Emeryville, CA 94608. TEL 510-547-6800. FAX 510-547-4613. URL: http://www.currents.net. *2128*

WASHINGTON DRUG LETTER (WASHINGTON, 1979).
Washington Business Information, Inc., 1117 N. 19th St., Arlington, VA 22209. TEL 703-247-3434. FAX 703-247-3421.
Vendor(s): Data-Star, Ovid Technologies, Inc. (DIOG). *5698*

WASHINGTON INTERNATIONAL BUSINESS REPORT.
International Business-Government Counsellors Inc., 818 Connecticut Ave. N.W., 12th Fl., Washington, DC 20006-2702. TEL 202-872-8181. FAX 202-872-8696. *1351*

WASHINGTON LAW REVIEW.
Washington Law Review Association, University of Washington, School of Law, 1100 N.E. Campus Pkwy., Seattle, WA 98105-6617. TEL 206-543-4069. FAX 206-543-5671. URL: http://www.law.washington.edu/~wlr/.
Vendor(s): Lexis-Nexis, West Group. *4044*

THE WASHINGTON MONTHLY.
Washington Monthly Co., 1611 Connecticut Ave., N.W., Washington, DC 20009. TEL 202-462-0128. FAX 202-332-8413. URL: http://www.enews.com/magazines/wash_month.
Vendor(s): Information Access Co., Knight-Ridder Information, Inc., UMI. *5979*

THE WASHINGTON POST INDEX.
U M I, 300 N. Zeeb Rd., Ann Arbor, MI 48106. TEL 313-761-4700. FAX 800-864-0019. URL: http://www.umi.com. *3885*

WASHINGTON QUARTERLY.
M I T Press, 5 Cambridge Center, Cambridge, MA 02142. TEL 617-253-2889. FAX 617-577-1545. URL: http://www-mitpress.mit.edu.
Vendor(s): Information Access Co., Lexis-Nexis. *6043*

WASHINGTON REPORT ON MIDDLE EAST AFFAIRS.
American Educational Trust (A E T), Box 53062, Washington, DC 20009. TEL 202-939-6050. FAX 202-265-4574. URL: http://washington-report.org. *6043*

WASHINGTON SUMMARY.
American Bar Association, Governmental Affairs Office, 740 15th St., Washington, DC 20005-1009. TEL 202-662-1016. URL: http://www.abanet.org/govaffairs. *4057*

THE WASHINGTON TIMES INDEX.
U M I, 300 N. Zeeb Rd., Ann Arbor, MI 48106. TEL 313-761-4700. FAX 800-864-0019. URL: http://www.umi.com. *3885*

WASHINGTON TRADE DAILY.
Trade Reports International Group, 2104 National Press Bldg., Washington, DC 20045. TEL 301-946-0817. FAX 301-946-2631.
Vendor(s): NewsNet. *1351*

WASHINGTON UNIVERSITY LAW QUARTERLY.
Washington University, School of Law, St. Louis, MO 63130. TEL 314-935-6498. FAX 314-935-6493.
Vendor(s): Lexis-Nexis, West Group. *4044*

WASHINGTONIAN.
Washington Magazine Inc., 1828 L St., N.W., Ste. 200, Washington, DC 20036. TEL 202-296-3600.
Vendor(s): Lexis-Nexis. *3389*

WASTE L.A. COMIC BOOK.
Box 90701, Santa Barbara, CA 93190-0701. URL: http://www.west.net/~wastela/. *3680*

WASTE MANAGEMENT GUIDE.
The Bureau of National Affairs, Inc., 1231 25th St., N.W., Washington, DC 20037. TEL 202-452-4200. FAX 202-822-8092. URL: http://www.bna.com/
Vendor(s): Human Resources Information Network (CDD, HDD). *1770*

WASTE TREATMENT TECHNOLOGY NEWS.
Business Communications Co., Inc. (Norwalk), 25 Van Zant St., Norwalk, CT 06855. TEL 203-853-4266. FAX 203-853-0348.
Vendor(s): Information Access Co., NewsNet (EV26). *2992*

WATER ENGINEERING AND MANAGEMENT.
Scranton Gillette Communications, Inc., 380 E. Northwest Hwy., Des Plaines, IL 60016-2282. TEL 847-391-1000. FAX 847-390-0408.
Vendor(s): UMI. *7303*

WATER QUALITY INTERNATIONAL.
Elsevier Science Ltd., Pergamon, P.O. Box 800, Kidlington, Oxford OX5 1DX, England. TEL 44-1865-843000. FAX 44-1865-843010. URL: http://www.elsevier.nl/. *2973*

WATER RESEARCH IN AUSTRALIA: CURRENT PROJECTS.
Department of Primary Industries and Energy, G.P.O. Box 858, Canberra, A.C.T. 2601, Australia. FAX 062-724526. *7305*

WATER RESOURCES ABSTRACTS (BETHESDA).
Cambridge Scientific Abstracts, 7200 Wisconsin Ave., 6th Fl., Bethesda, MD 20814. TEL 301-961-6750. FAX 301-961-6720. URL: http://www.csa.com.
Vendor(s): Knight-Ridder Information, Inc. (File no.117). *7308*

WATER TECHNOLOGY NEWS.
Business Communications Co., Inc. (Norwalk), 25 Van Zant St., Norwalk, CT 06855. TEL 203-853-4266. FAX 203-853-0348.
Vendor(s): Information Access Co. *2992*

WATERMARKS.
University of Texas at Austin, Center for Research in Water Resources, J.J. Pickle Research Campus, Austin, TX 78712. TEL 512-471-3131. URL: http://www.ce.utexas.edu/centers/crwr/watermarks/watermarks.html.
Available only online. *7306*

WAVES IN RANDOM MEDIA.
I O P Publishing Ltd., Dirac House, Temple Back, Bristol BS1 6BE, England. TEL 44-117-929-7481. FAX 44-117-929-4318. URL: http://www.iop.org. *5833*

WAYNE LAW REVIEW.
Wayne State University Law School, 468 W. Ferry, Detroit, MI 48202. TEL 313-577-3939. FAX 313-577-5498.
Vendor(s): Lexis-Nexis, West Group. *4045*

WEATHERWISE.
Heldref Publications, 1319 Eighteenth St., N.W., Washington, DC 20036-1802. TEL 202-296-6267. FAX 202-296-5149. URL: http://www.heldref.org/ww/ww.html.
Vendor(s): Information Access Co., UMI. *5245*

THE WEB DEVELOPER'S JOURNAL.
Markland Communities, Inc., National Computer Tectonics, Rte. 1, Box 80, Burbank, SD 57010. URL: http://nctweb.com/webdev.
Available only online. *2140*

WEB FINANCE.
Investment Dealers' Digest, URL: http://nestegg.iddis.com/webfinance.
Available only online. *1173*

WEB INFORMANT (PORT WASHINGTON).
938 Port Washington Blvd., Port Washington, NY 11050. TEL 516-944-3407. URL: http://www.webinformant.com.
Available only online. *2140*

WEB REVIEW.
URL: http://www.webreview.com.
Available only online. *2140*

WEB SOLUTIONS.
I S - O O P Group, 175 Osborn Ave., New Haven, CT 06511. URL: http://www.online-magazine.com.
Available only online. *2140*

WEB SURFER TRAVEL JOURNAL.
109 Breckenridge Rd., Franklin, TN 37067. URL: http://www.edge.edge.net/~dphillip.
Available only online. *7249*

WEB TECHNIQUES.
Miller Freeman, Inc., 600 Harrison St., San Francisco, CA 94107. TEL 415-905-2200. FAX 415-905-2233. URL: http://www.webtechniques.com. *2141*

WEB TIMES.
516 Centennial Pkwy., Delta, BC V4L 1L1, Canada. URL: http://www.webtimes.com. *2141*

WEB WEEK.
Mecklermedia Corporation, 20 Ketchum St., Westport, CT 06880. TEL 203-226-6957. FAX 203-454-8540. URL: http://pubs.iworld.com/ww-online/. *2141*

WEB - ZINE.
URL: http://www.nmsu.edu/~czimmerm/Web-Zine/.
Available only online. *2141*

WEBDESIGN & REVIEW.
Design & Publishing Center, 15 Southgate, Harrisonburg, VA 22801. URL: http://www.graphic-design.com/WEB/.
Available only online. *2141*

WEBGEIST.
Bismarck State College, 1500 Edwards Ave., Bismarck, ND 58501. URL: http://www.bsc.nodak.edu/English/webgeist/webgeist.htm.
Available only online. *4486*

WEBSIGHT.
Navigate Media Inc., 9520 Jefferson Blvd., Culver City, CA 90232. URL: http://websight.com. *2141*

WEED ABSTRACTS.
CAB International, Wallingford, Oxon OX10 8DE, England. TEL 44-1491-832111. FAX 44-1491-826090. URL: http://www.cabi.org.
Vendor(s): DIMDI, European Space Agency, Knight-Ridder Information, Inc., STN International. *185*

THE WEEK IN GERMANY.
German Information Center, 950 Third Ave., New York, NY 10022. TEL 212-888-9840. FAX 212-752-6691. URL: http://www.germany-info.org. *3292*

WEEKEND WEB PICKS.
URL: http://www.netogether.com/picks.html.
Available only online. *2141*

WEEKLY BOOK NEWSLETTER.
D.W. Thorpe, A member of the Reed Elsevier plc group, 18 Salmon St., Port Melbourne, Vic. 3027, Australia. TEL 03-9245-7370. FAX 03-9245-7395. URL: http://www.reed-elsevier.com. *6286*

WEEKLY BOOKMARK STANDARD.
118 Augusta Ave., Ste. 111, DeKalb, IL 60115. URL: http://www.weeklyb.com/.
Available only online. *3389*

WEEKLY CONGRESSIONAL MONITOR.
Congressional Quarterly Inc., 1414 22nd St., N.W., Washington, DC 20037. TEL 800-432-2250. FAX 202-728-1863. *5979*

SERIALS AVAILABLE ONLINE

WEEKLY CRIMINAL BULLETIN.
Canada Law Book Inc., 240 Edward St., Aurora, ON L4G 3S9, Canada. TEL 905-841-6472. FAX 905-841-5085. *4095*

WEEKLY ECONOMIC UPDATE.
Green Mountain Asset Management Corp., URL: http://www.stockresearch.com/
Available only online. *1414*

WEEKLY EPIDEMIOLOGICAL RECORD.
World Health Organization, Distribution and Sales, CH-1211 Geneva 27, Switzerland. TEL 41-22-791-2476. FAX 41-22-791-4857. URL: http://www.who.ch/wer/wer__home.html. *6254*

WEEKLY LAW REPORTS.
Incorporated Council of Law Reporting for England and Wales, 3 Stone Bldgs., Lincoln's Inn, London WC2A 3XN, England. TEL 44-171-242-6471. FAX 44-171-831-5247.
Vendor(s): Lexis-Nexis. *4045*

WEEKLY NEWS UPDATE ON THE AMERICAS.
Nicaragua Solidarity Network, 339 Lafayette St., New York, NY 10012. TEL 212-674-9499. FAX 212-674-9139. URL: http://home.earthlink.net/~dbwilson/wnuhome.html. *3268*

WEEKLY OF BUSINESS AVIATION.
McGraw-Hill Companies, Aviation Week Group (Washington), 1200 G St., N.W., Ste. 200, Washington, DC 20005. TEL 202-383-2350.
Vendor(s): Dow Jones News Retrieval (BA), Knight-Ridder Information, Inc. (File no.624/McGRAW-HILL PUBLICATIONS ONLINE), Lexis-Nexis (WBA), NewsNet (AE20). *7079*

WEEKLY PHARMACY REPORTS: THE GREEN SHEET.
F-D-C Reports, Inc., 5550 Friendship Blvd., Ste. One, Chevy Chase, MD 20815. FAX 301-664-7238.
Vendor(s): Lexis-Nexis. *5698*

WEEKLY PLANET.
Arcadia Studios, URL: http://www.arcadiastudios.com.
Available only online. *2164*

WEEKLY REVIEW.
Louisiana News Bureau, Inc., Box 44212, Baton Rouge, LA 70804. TEL 504-342-1240.
Available only online. *6200*

THE WEEKLY STANDARD.
William Kristol, Ed. & Pub, 1150 17th St., N.W., 5th Fl., Washington, DC 20036. TEL 202-293-4900. FAX 202-293-4901.
Vendor(s): Lexis-Nexis. *5979*

THE WEEKLY WORLD CRUZ.
URL: http://www.cruzio.com/~djj/wwc/wwc.html. *3389*

WEIDWERK.
Oesterreichischer Jagd- und Fischereiverlag der J F B GmbH, Wickenburggasse 3, A-1080 Vienna, Austria. TEL 43-1-40516360. FAX 43-1-405163636. URL: http://www.weidwerk.co.at/weidwerk/. *6793*

WEIGHT WATCHERS MAGAZINE.
Weight Watchers-Twenty-First Corporation, 360 Lexington Ave., New York, NY 10017. TEL 212-370-0644. FAX 212-687-4398.
Vendor(s): Information Access Co. *5484*

WELARA JOURNAL.
Welara Pony Society, Box 401, Yucca Valley, CA 92286. TEL 760-364-2048. FAX 760-364-2048. *6858*

WELDING ABSTRACTS.
T W I - The Welding Institute, Abington Hall, Abington, Cambridge CB1 6AL. TEL 44-1223-891162. FAX 44-1223-892588. URL: http://www.twi.co.uk/infserv/weldas.html.
Vendor(s): FIZ Technik, Questel Orbit Inc., Telesystemes - Questel. *5221*

WELDING REVIEW INTERNATIONAL.
Argus Business Media Ltd., Queensway House, 2 Queensway, Redhill, Surrey RH1 1QS, England. TEL 44-1737-768611. FAX 44-1737-761989.
Vendor(s): Information Access Co. *5225*

THE WELL-CONNECTED ATTORNEY.
LawyerNet, 3780 S. Broadway, Englewood, CO 80110. TEL 303-761-6067. URL: http://www.lawyernet.com/members/jimfesq/wca/wcaweb.html.
Available only online. *4045*

WENATCHEE BUSINESS JOURNAL.
Wenatchee Business Journal Inc., 304 S. Mission St., Wenatchee, WA 98801-3044. TEL 509-663-6730.
Vendor(s): UMI. *1011*

WER BAUT MASCHINEN IN DEUTSCHLAND.
Verlag Hoppenstedt GmbH, Havelstr. 9, 64295 Darmstadt, Germany. TEL 49-6151-380-0. FAX 49-6151-380-360. *2903*

WER LIEFERT WAS?
Wer Liefert Was? GmbH, Normannenweg 16-20, 20537 Hamburg, Germany. TEL 49-40-25440-0. FAX 49-40-25440100. URL: http://www.wlwonline.de.
Vendor(s): FIZ Technik, Knight-Ridder Information, Inc., Lexis-Nexis. *1721*

WEST EUROPEAN POLITICS.
Frank Cass, Newbury House, 890-900 Eastern Ave., Newbury Park, Ilford, Essex 1G2 7HH. TEL 44-181-599-8866. FAX 44-181-599-0954. URL: http://www.frankcass.com.
Vendor(s): Information Access Co. *6043*

WEST VIRGINIA BUSINESS DIRECTORY.
American Business Directories, 5711 S. 86th Circle, Box 27347, Omaha, NE 68127. TEL 402-593-4600. FAX 402-331-5481. *1722*

WESTCHESTER COUNTY BUSINESS JOURNAL.
Westfair Communications, Inc., 108 Corporate Park Dr., Ste. 105, White Plains, NY 10604-3805. TEL 914-694-3600. FAX 914-694-3699.
Vendor(s): Lexis-Nexis, UMI. *1295*

WESTERN AUSTRALIA REPORTS.
L B C Information Services, 50 Waterloo Rd., N. Ryde, N.S.W. 2113, Australia. TEL 61-2-99366444. FAX 61-2-98889706.
Vendor(s): Info-One International Pty Ltd. *4140*

WESTERN ECONOMIC DEVELOPMENTS.
Federal Reserve Bank of San Francisco, Box 7702, San Francisco, CA 94120. TEL 415-974-3230. FAX 415-974-3341. URL: http://www.frbsf.org. *1295*

WESTERN GROWER AND SHIPPER.
Western Grower and Shipper Publishing Co., Box 2130, Newport Beach, CA 92658. TEL 714-863-1000. FAX 714-863-9028.
Vendor(s): Knight-Ridder Information, Inc. *250*

WESTERN JOURNAL OF COMMUNICATION.
Western States Communication Association, c/o Connie J. Conlee, WSCA Executive Director, Department of Speech Communication, California State University, Fresno, Fresno, CA 93740-0046.
Vendor(s): UMI. *4314*

WESTERN JOURNAL OF MEDICINE.
Carden Jennings Publishing Co., Ltd., 1224 W. Main St., Ste. 200, Charlottesville, VA 22903-2858. TEL 804-979-4913. FAX 804-979-4025.
Vendor(s): Information Access Co. *4758*

WESTERN WEEKLY REPORTS.
Carswell, One Corporate Plaza, 2075 Kennedy Rd., Scarborough, ON M1T 3V4, Canada. TEL 416-609-8000. FAX 416-298-5094.
Vendor(s): QL Systems Ltd. *4045*

WESTPREUSSEN - JAHRBUCH.
Westpreussen-Verlag Muenster, Norbertstr. 29, 48151 Muenster, Germany. TEL 49-251-523424. FAX 49-251-533830. *3612*

WHARF RATS NEWSLETTER.
Wharf Rats, 748 Sunset Blvd., Hayward, CA 94541. URL: http://www.hooked.net/~wharfrat/wr__newsl.html. *5444*

WHAT IS ENLIGHTENMENT?
Moksha Foundation, Box 2360, Lenox, MA 01240. URL: http://www.moksha.org/wie/. *5462*

WHAT'S ON SATELLITE.
Design Publishers, 800 Siesta Way, Sonoma, CA 95476-4413. TEL 707-939-9306. URL: http://www.satnews.com. *2008*

WHEAT, BARLEY AND TRITICALE ABSTRACTS.
CAB International, Wallingford, Oxon. OX10 8DE, England. TEL 44-1491-832111. FAX 44-1491-826090. URL: http://www.cabi.org.
Vendor(s): DIMDI, European Space Agency, Knight-Ridder Information, Inc., STN International. *186*

WHITAKER'S BOOKS IN PRINT.
J. Whitaker & Sons Ltd., 12 Dyott St., London WC1A 1DF, England. TEL 44-171-420-6000. FAX 44-171-836-2909.
Vendor(s): Knight-Ridder Information, Inc. (File no.430). *570*

WHITE COUNTY HERITAGE.
White County Historical Society, Box 537, Searcy, AR 72145. TEL 501-268-8726. *3652*

WHO OWNS WHOM. AUSTRALASIA AND FAR EAST.
Dun & Bradstreet Ltd., Holmers Farm Way, High Wycombe, Bucks. HP12 4UL, England. TEL 44-1494-422000. FAX 44-1494-422260. *1722*

WHO OWNS WHOM. CONTINENTAL EUROPE.
Dun & Bradstreet Ltd., Holmers Farm Way, High Wycombe, Bucks. HP12 4UL, England. TEL 44-1494-422000. FAX 44-1494-422260. *1512*

WHO OWNS WHOM. NORTH AMERICA.
Dun & Bradstreet Ltd., Holmers Farm Way, High Wycombe, Bucks. HP12 4UL, England. TEL 44-1494-422000. FAX 44-1494-422260. *1554*

WHO OWNS WHOM. UNITED KINGDOM AND REPUBLIC OF IRELAND.
Dun & Bradstreet Ltd., Holmers Farm Way, High Wycombe, Bucks. HP12 4UL, England. TEL 44-1494-422000. FAX 44-1494-422260. *1722*

THE WHOLE INTERNET CATALOGUE.
Global Network Navigator, 2200 Aol Way, Dulles, VA 20166. TEL 510-883-7220. URL: http://gnn.com/wic/index.html.
Available only online. *2141*

WHO'S WHO AMONG BLACK AMERICANS.
Gale Research, 835 Penobscot Bldg., 645 Griswold St., Detroit, MI 48226-4094. TEL 313-961-2242. FAX 800-414-5043.
Vendor(s): Lexis-Nexis. *578*

WHO'S WHO AMONG HISPANIC AMERICANS.
Gale Research, 835 Penobscot Bldg., 645 Griswold St., Detroit, MI 48226-4094. TEL 313-961-2242. FAX 800-414-5043.
Vendor(s): Lexis-Nexis. *578*

WHO'S WHO IN AMERICA.
Marquis Who's Who, A Division of Reed Elsevier Inc., 121 Chanlon Rd., New Providence, NJ 07974. TEL 908-464-6800. FAX 908-665-6688. URL: http://www.reedref.com.
Vendor(s): Knight-Ridder Information, Inc. (File no.234). *578*

WHO'S WHO IN AMERICAN ART.
R.R. Bowker, A Division of Reed Elsevier Inc., 121 Chanlon Rd., New Providence, NJ 07974. TEL 908-464-6800. FAX 908-665-6688. URL: http://www.reedref.com.
Vendor(s): Knight-Ridder Information, Inc. (File no.236). *578*

WHO'S WHO IN AMERICAN POLITICS.
R.R. Bowker, A Division of Reed Elsevier Inc., 121 Chanlon Rd., New Providence, NJ 07974. TEL 908-464-6800. FAX 908-665-6688. URL: http://www.reedref.com.
Vendor(s): Knight-Ridder Information, Inc. (File no.236). *578*

WHO'S WHO IN TECHNOLOGY.
Gale Research, 835 Penobscot Bldg., 645 Griswold St., Detroit, MI 48226-4094. TEL 313-961-2242. FAX 800-414-5043.
Vendor(s): Lexis-Nexis, Questel Orbit Inc. (WHOTECH). *579*

WICHITA BUSINESS JOURNAL.
American City Business Journals, Inc. (Wichita), 110 S. Main St., Ste. 200, Wichita, KS 67202-3745. TEL 316-267-6406. FAX 316-267-8570.
Vendor(s): Lexis-Nexis. *1012*

WIDE ANGLE (BALTIMORE).
Johns Hopkins University Press, Journals Publishing Division, 2715 N. Charles St., Baltimore, MD 21218. TEL 410-516-6987. FAX 410-516-6968. URL: http://muse.jhu.edu. *5348*

WIDE AWAKE.
URL: http://wideawake.org.
Available only online. *3389*

WILDERNESS AND ENVIRONMENTAL MEDICINE.
Chapman & Hall, Journals Department 2-6 Boundary Row, London SE1 8HN, England. TEL 44-171-8650066. FAX 44-171-5229623. URL: http://www.chaphall.com/chaphall/journals.html. *5133*

WILDERNESS RECORD.
California Wilderness Coalition, 2655 Portage Bay E., Ste. 5, Davis, CA 95616. TEL 916-758-0380. FAX 916-758-0382. URL: http://www.dcn.davis.ca.us/~cwc. *2249*

WILDLIFE RESEARCH.
C.S.I.R.O. Publishing, 150 Oxford St., Collingwood, Vic. 3066, Australia. TEL 61-3-96627622. FAX 61-3-96627611. URL: http://www.publish.csiro.au/journals/wr. *2249*

WILLIAM AND MARY QUARTERLY.
Omohundro Institute of Early American History and Culture, Box 8781, Williamsburg, VA 23187. TEL 757-221-1120. FAX 757-221-1047. URL: http://www.jstor.org/fcgi-bin/jstor/listjournal.fcg/00435597?configjstor. *3652*

WILLIAM MITCHELL LAW REVIEW.
William Mitchell College of Law, 875 Summit Ave., St. Paul, MN 55105. TEL 612-290-6450. FAX 612-290-6450.
Vendor(s): Lexis-Nexis, West Group. *4046*

WILSON ABSTRACTS.
H.W. Wilson Co., 950 University Ave., Bronx, NY 10452. TEL 718-588-8400. FAX 718-590-1617.
Vendor(s): Knight-Ridder Information, Inc., OCLC, Ovid Technologies, Inc., Wilsonline (File ART). *476*

WILSON APPLIED SCIENCE AND TECHNOLOGY ABSTRACTS.
H.W. Wilson Co., 950 University Ave., Bronx, NY 10452. TEL 718-588-8400. FAX 718-590-1617.
Vendor(s): Knight-Ridder Information, Inc., OCLC, Ovid Technologies, Inc., Wilsonline (AST). *2753*

WILSON BULLETIN.
Wilson Ornithological Society, c/o Charles R. Blem, Ed., Department of Biology, Virginia Commonwealth University, Richmond, VA 23289-2012. TEL 804-367-1562. FAX 804-367-0503. URL: http://www.ummx.lsa.umich.edu/birds/bulletin.html.
Vendor(s): Information Access Co. *810*

WILSON BUSINESS ABSTRACTS.
H.W. Wilson Co., 950 University Ave., Bronx, NY 10452. TEL 718-588-8400. FAX 718-590-1617.
Vendor(s): Knight-Ridder Information, Inc., OCLC, Ovid Technologies, Inc., Wilsonline (File WBA). *1078*

WILSON EDUCATION ABSTRACTS.
H.W. Wilson Co., 950 University Ave., Bronx, NY 10452. TEL 718-588-8400. FAX 718-590-1617.
Vendor(s): Knight-Ridder Information, Inc., OCLC, Ovid Technologies, Inc., Wilsonline (File EDI). *2505*

WILSON GENERAL SCIENCE ABSTRACTS.
H.W. Wilson Co., 950 University Ave., Bronx, NY 10452. TEL 718-588-8400. FAX 718-590-1617.
Vendor(s): OCLC, Wilsonline (File GSI). *6592*

WILSON HUMANITIES ABSTRACTS.
H.W. Wilson Co., 950 University Ave., Bronx, NY 10452. TEL 718-588-8400. FAX 718-590-1617.
Vendor(s): Knight-Ridder Information, Inc., OCLC, Ovid Technologies, Inc. (WHUM), Wilsonline (File HUM). *3799*

WILSON QUARTERLY.
Woodrow Wilson International Center for Scholars, 901 D St., S.W., Ste. 704, Washington, DC 20024-2518.
Vendor(s): Information Access Co., UMI. *4366*

WILSON SOCIAL SCIENCES ABSTRACTS.
H.W. Wilson Co., 950 University Ave., Bronx, NY 10452. TEL 718-588-8400. FAX 718-590-1617.
Vendor(s): Knight-Ridder Information, Inc., OCLC, UMI (PROQUEST), Wilsonline (File SSA). *6651*

WINDOW (RESEDA).
Armenian Church Research & Analysis Group, c/o Armenian National Commission, 104 N. Belmont St., Ste. 208, Glendale, CA 91206-4492. TEL 818-881-5734. *6500*

WINDOWS DEVELOPER'S JOURNAL.
Miller Freeman, Inc. (Lawrence), 1601 W. 23rd St., Ste. 200, Lawrence, KS 66046. TEL 913-841-1631. FAX 913-841-2624. URL: http://www.wdj.com.
Vendor(s): Information Access Co. *2147*

WINDOWS JOURNAL.
Wugnet Publications, Inc., Box 1967, Media, PA 19063. TEL 215-565-1861. FAX 215-565-7106.
Vendor(s): CompuServe, Inc. *2092*

WINDOWS MAGAZINE.
C M P Publications, Inc. (Jericho), 1 Jericho Plaza, 3rd Fl., Jericho, NY 11753. TEL 516-733-6700. FAX 516-733-8390. URL: http://www.winmag.com. *2092*

WINDOWS SOURCES.
Ziff-Davis Publishing Co., One Park Ave., New York, NY 10016. TEL 212-503-3500. FAX 212-503-4141. URL: http://www.zdnet.com/wsources/
Vendor(s): Information Access Co. *2092*

WINDSCRIPT.
Saskatchewan Writers Guild, 1925 7th Ave., Regina, SK S4P 2M4, Canada. FAX 306-565-8554. URL: http://www.sasknet.com/~skwriter.
Available only online. *4488*

WINE & DINE E-ZINE.
Jubilee Cottage, Upper Nyland, Gillingham, Dorset SP8 5SH, England. URL: http://www.winedine.co.uk.
Available only online. *3738*

WINE ON LINE.
Enterprises Publishing, 400 E. 59th St., Ste. 9F, New York, NY 10022. TEL 212-755-4363. FAX 212-755-4365. *529*

WINE: THE INTERNATIONAL MARKET.
Euromonitor, 60-61 Britton St., London EC1M 5NA, England. TEL 44-171-251-8024. FAX 44-171-608-3149. URL: http://www.euromonitor.com.
Vendor(s): Data-Star, Knight-Ridder Information, Inc. *529*

WING.
Koku Shinbunsha, Kanda Kitamura Bldg., 30 Kanda Higashi-Konya-cho, Chiyoda-ku, Tokyo 101, Japan. TEL 03-3258-9840. FAX 03-3258-5044.
Vendor(s): NewsNet (AE06). *82*

WING NEWSLETTER.
Koku Shinbunsha, Kanda Kitamura Bldg., 30 Kanda Higashi-Konya-cho, Chiyoda-ku, Tokyo 101, Japan. TEL 03-3258-0880. FAX 03-3258-5004.
Vendor(s): Data-Star, Knight-Ridder Information, Inc., NewsNet. *82*

WINNIPEG SUN.
Winnipeg Sun, 1700 Church Ave., Winnipeg, MB R2X 3A2, Canada. TEL 204-694-2022. FAX 204-694-2347. URL: http://www.winnipeg.freenet.mb.ca/wpg-sun. *3267*

WIRE.
1011 Main St., No. 9, Woburn, MA 01801. URL: http://members.aol.com/wirezine. *5444*

WIRELESS DATA NEWS.
Phillips Business Information, Inc., 1201 Seven Locks Rd., Potomac, MD 20854. TEL 301-424-3338. FAX 301-309-3847.
Vendor(s): Information Access Co. *2171*

WIRTSCHAFTSWOCHE.
Verlagsgruppe Handelsblatt GmbH, Kasernenstr. 67, 40213 Duesseldorf, Germany. TEL 49-211-887-0. FAX 49-211-374955. *1295*

WISCONSIN BUSINESS DIRECTORY.
American Business Directories, 5711 S. 86th Circle, Box 27347, Omaha, NE 68127. TEL 402-593-4600. FAX 402-331-5481. *1723*

WISCONSIN JEWISH CHRONICLE.
Milwaukee Jewish Federation, Inc., 1360 N. Prospect Ave., Milwaukee, WI 53202. TEL 414-271-2992. FAX 414-271-0487. *3050*

WISCONSIN LAW REVIEW.
University of Wisconsin at Madison, Law School, 975 Bascom Mall, Madison, WI 53706-1399. TEL 608-262-5815. FAX 608-262-5485.
Vendor(s): Lexis-Nexis, West Group. *4046*

WITTGENSTEIN STUDIES.
Springer-Verlag, Sachsensplatz 4-6, A-1201 Vienna, Austria. TEL 43-1-3302415. FAX 43-1-3302426. *5758*

DIE WOCHE.
Die Woche Zeitungsverlag GmbH, Van-der-Smissen-Str. 3, 22767 Hamburg, Germany. TEL 49-40-3803503. FAX 49-40-38035339.
Vendor(s): Lexis-Nexis. *3292*

WOMAN MOTORIST.
TEL 805-641-2400. FAX 805-641-2444. URL: http://www.womanmotorist.com.
Available only online. *7122*

WOMAN POET.
Women-in-Literature, Inc., Box 60550, Reno, NV 89506. TEL 702-972-1671. FAX 415-474-6484. URL: http://www.vaes.vt.edu/VAES/Publications/vaesnumpubs.html.
Available only online. *4527*

WOMAN'S DAY.
Hachette Filipacchi Magazines, Inc., 1633 Broadway, 42nd Fl., New York, NY 10009. TEL 212-767-6000.
Vendor(s): Information Access Co., UMI. *3689*

WOMEN AND ENVIRONMENTS.
Weed Foundation, 736 Bathurst St., Toronto, ON M5S 2R4, Canada. TEL 416-516-2600. FAX 416-516-6214. URL: http://www.web.net/~weed/.
Vendor(s): UMI. *7348*

WOMEN AND LANGUAGE.
George Mason University, Communication Department, 4400 University Dr., Fairfax, VA 22030-4444. TEL 703-993-1099. FAX 703-993-1096.
Vendor(s): Information Access Co. *4314*

WOMEN & PERFORMANCE.
Women & Performance Project, 721 Broadway, 6th Fl., New York, NY 10003. TEL 212-998-1625. URL: http://www.echonyc.com/~women. *7018*

WOMEN OF ACHIEVEMENT AND HERSTORY.
Box 6185, Hot Springs, AR 71902. URL: http://www.imageworld.com/istuber.html.
Available only online. *7338*

WOMEN ONLINE.
URL: http://www.women-online.com.
Available only online. *7338*

WOMEN STUDIES ABSTRACTS.
Transaction Publishers, Transaction Periodicals Consortium, Department 3092, Rutgers University, New Brunswick, NJ 08903. TEL 908-445-2280. FAX 908-445-3138. *7350*

WOMEN'S ENVIRONMENT AND DEVELOPMENT ORGANIZATION NEWS & VIEWS.
Women's Environment and Development Organization (WEDO), 355 Lexington Ave., 3rd fl., New York, NY 10017-6603. TEL 212-973-0325. FAX 212-973-0335. URL: http://www.wedo.org. *7338*

WOMEN'S HEALTH WEEKLY.
Charles W. Henderson, Ed. & Pub., Box 5528, Atlanta, GA 31107-0528. TEL 404-377-8895. FAX 404-378-4511. URL: http://www.newsfile.com. *7311*

THE WOMEN'S REVIEW OF BOOKS.
Wellesley College, Center for Research on Women, Wellesley, MA 02181. TEL 617-283-2087. FAX 617-283-3645. URL: http://www.wellesley.edu/WCW/CRW/WROB/welcome.html.
Vendor(s): UMI. *4366*

WOMEN'S SPORTS AND FITNESS.
Sports & Fitness Publishing, 2025 Pearl St., Boulder, CO 80302. TEL 303-440-5111. FAX 303-440-3313.
Vendor(s): Information Access Co., UMI. *6794*

WOMEN'S STUDIES (NEW YORK).
Gordon and Breach - Harwood Academic, Amsteldisk 166, 1st Fl., 1079 LH Amsterdam, Netherlands.
Vendor(s): Information Access Co. *7349*

WOMEN'S WEAR DAILY.
Fairchild Publications, Fashion & Merchandising Group 7 W. 34th St., New York, NY 10001. TEL 212-630-4000. FAX 212-630-3566.
Vendor(s): Information Access Co., Knight-Ridder Information, Inc., Lexis-Nexis. *1919*

WOOD & WOOD PRODUCTS.
Vance Publishing Corporation (Lincolnshire), Box 1414, Lincolnshire, IL 60069-1414. TEL 708-634-2600. FAX 708-634-4379.
Vendor(s): Information Access Co. *3176*

WOOD BASED PANELS INTERNATIONAL.
Miller Freeman plc, Sovereign Way, Tonbridge, Kent TN9 1RW, England. TEL 44-1732-364422. FAX 44-1732-361534.
Vendor(s): Information Access Co. *3176*

WOOD TECHNOLOGY.
Miller Freeman, Inc., 600 Harrison St., San Francisco, CA 94107. TEL 415-905-2200. FAX 415-905-2232.
Vendor(s): Knight-Ridder Information, Inc., UMI. *3177*

WOODWORKERS WEST.
Goldman Communications, Box 66751, Los Angeles, CA 90066. TEL 310-398-5931. URL: http://www.woodwest.com/wood/ *927*

WOOLGATHERINGS.
URL: http://gpu.srv.ualberta.ca/~dmerriam/hooked.html.
Available only online. *3680*

WORD (NEW YORK, 1996).
c/o ICon, 1700 Broadway, 9th Fl., New York, NY 10019. FAX 212-459-1741. URL: http://www.word.com.
Available only online. *4366*

THE WORD DETECTIVE.
Box 6437, FDR St., New York, NY 10150. URL: http://www.word-detective.com. *4314*

WORD FOR TODAY.
URL: http://www.cforc.com/theword.
Available only online. *6447*

WORDPERFECT FOR WINDOWS MAGAZINE.
Ivy International Communications, Inc., 270 W. Center St., Orem, UT 84057. TEL 801-228-9626. FAX 801-227-3478. URL: http://www.wpmag.com.
Vendor(s): CompuServe, Inc. *2220*

WORDPERFECT MAGAZINE.
Ivy International Communications, Inc., 270 W. Center St., Orem, UT 84057. TEL 801-228-9626. FAX 801-227-3478. URL: http://www.wpmag.com. *2220*

WORK ALERT.
C C H Australia Ltd., P.O. Box 230, North Ryde, N.S.W. 2113, Australia. TEL 61-1-300300224. FAX 61-1-300306224. *1458*

WORK AND OCCUPATIONS.
Sage Publications, Inc., 2455 Teller Rd., Thousand Oaks, CA 91320. TEL 805-499-0721. FAX 805-499-0871. URL: http://www.sagepub.com.
Vendor(s): UMI. *6738*

WORKBENCH.
August Houme Publishing Co., 2200 Grand Ave., Des Moines, IA 50312-5306. TEL 515-282-7000. FAX 515-282-6741.
Vendor(s): Information Access Co., Knight-Ridder Information, Inc., UMI. *3769*

WORKERS NEWS.
Socialist Equality Party, P.O. Box 367, Bankestown, N.S.W. 2200, Australia. TEL 61-2-97903511. FAX 61-2-97903501. URL: http://www.workersnews.flex.com.au. *3901*

WORKFORCE.
A C C Communications, Inc., Box 2440, Costa Mesa, CA 92628. TEL 714-751-1883. FAX 714-751-4106. URL: http://www.HRHQ.com/.
Vendor(s): Information Access Co., UMI. *1577*

WORKGROUP COMPUTING REPORT.
Patricia Seybold Group, 85 Devonshire St., 5th Fl., Boston, MA 02109-3504.
Vendor(s): Information Access Co., NewsNet. *2177*

WORKING WOMAN.
MacDonald Communications Corp., 135 W. 50th St., Ste. 16, New York, NY 10020. TEL 212-445-6100.
Vendor(s): Information Access Co., Knight-Ridder Information, Inc. *7339*

WORKLIFE REPORT.
I R Research Services, P.O. Box 1092, Kingston, ON K7L 4Y5, Canada. TEL 613-542-5596.
Vendor(s): UMI. *1459*

WORKPLACE SUBSTANCE ABUSE ADVISOR.
L R P Publications, 747 Dresher Rd., Box 908, Horsham, PA 19044-0980. TEL 215-784-0941. FAX 215-784-9639. URL: http://www.lrp.com.
Vendor(s): Human Resources Information Network (CDD, HDD). *2307*

WORLD ACCOUNTING REPORT.
Financial Times Professional Publishing, Newsletters Maple House, 149 Tottenham Court Rd., London W1P 9LL, England. TEL 44-171-896-2222. FAX 44-171-896-2276.
Vendor(s): Data-Star, Information Access Co., Lexis-Nexis (WAR). *1100*

WORLD AFFAIRS (WASHINGTON).
Heldref Publications, 1319 Eighteenth St., N.W., Washington, DC 20036-1802. TEL 202-296-6267. FAX 202-296-5149.
Vendor(s): Information Access Co., UMI. *6044*

WORLD AFFAIRS REPORT.
California Institute of International Studies, Hoover Institution, Stanford, CA 94305-6010. TEL 415-322-2026. FAX 415-723-1687. URL: http://www-leland.stanford.sdn/group/ciis.
Available only online. *6044*

WORLD AGRICULTURAL ECONOMICS AND RURAL SOCIOLOGY ABSTRACTS.
CAB International, Wallingford, Oxon. OX10 8DE, England. TEL 44-1491-832111. FAX 44-1491-826090. URL: http://www.cabi.org.
Vendor(s): DIMDI, European Space Agency, Knight-Ridder Information, Inc., STN International. *186*

WORLD AGRICULTURAL PRODUCTION.
U.S. Department of Agriculture, Foreign Agricultural Service, Information Division, Rm. 5920-S, Washington, DC 20250-1000. TEL 202-720-7937.
Vendor(s): Information Access Co. *165*

WORLD AGRICULTURAL SUPPLY AND DEMAND ESTIMATES.
U.S. Department of Agriculture, World Agricultural Outlook Board, 14th St. and Independence Ave., S.W., Rm. 5143-S, Washington, DC 20250-3800. TEL 202-250-3800.
Vendor(s): Knight-Ridder Information, Inc. *204*

WORLD AIRLINE NEWS.
Phillips Business Information, Inc., 1201 Seven Locks Rd., Potomac, MD 20854. TEL 301-424-3338. FAX 301-309-3847.
Vendor(s): Information Access Co., NewsNet (AE31). *7079*

WORLD AIRPORT WEEK.
Phillips Business Information, Inc., 1201 Seven Locks Rd., Potomac, MD 20854. TEL 301-424-3338. FAX 301-309-3847.
Vendor(s): Information Access Co., NewsNet. *7079*

WORLD BANK RESEARCH OBSERVER.
World Bank, 1818 H St., N.W., Washington, DC 20433. TEL 202-473-1155. FAX 202-522-2627.
Vendor(s): Knight-Ridder Information, Inc., UMI. *1173*

WORLD CERAMICS ABSTRACTS.
Ceram Research Ltd., Queens Rd., Penkhull, Stoke-on-Trent, Staffs. ST4 7LQ, England.
Vendor(s): Questel Orbit Inc. *1736*

WORLD COTTON SITUATION.
U.S. Department of Agriculture, Foreign Agricultural Service, Information Division, Rm. 5920-S, Washington, DC 20250-1000. TEL 202-720-7937.
Vendor(s): Information Access Co. *250*

WORLD DEBT TABLES.
World Bank, 1818 H St., N.W., Washington, DC 20433. TEL 202-473-1155. FAX 202-522-2627.
Vendor(s): GSI-ECO. *1371*

WORLD DIRECTORY OF HUMAN RIGHTS RESEARCH AND TRAINING INSTITUTIONS.
UNESCO Publishing, 7 Place de Fontenoy, 75352 Paris 07 SP, France. TEL 33-1-45684300. FAX 33-1-45685741. URL: http://www.unesco.org/publications. *1723*

WORLD DRUG MARKET MANUAL.
IMSWORLD Publications Ltd., 7 Harewood Ave., London NW1 6JB, England. TEL 0171-393-5000. FAX 0171-393-5900. *5698*

WORLD ECONOMIC OUTLOOK.
International Monetary Fund, Publication Services, 700 19th St., N.W., Washington, DC 20431. TEL 202-623-7430. FAX 202-623-7201.
Vendor(s): Information Access Co. *1295*

WORLD FACTBOOK.
U.S. National Technical Information Service, 5285 Port Royal Rd., Springfield, VA 22161. TEL 703-482-0623.
Vendor(s): Lexis-Nexis. *6044*

WORLD FOOD REGULATION REVIEW.
B N A International, Inc., Heron House, 10 Dean Farrar St., London SW1H 0DX, England. TEL 44-171-222-8831. FAX 44-171-222-0294. URL: http://www.bna.com. *3131*

WORLD GAS INTELLIGENCE.
Energy Intelligence Group, 575 Broadway, 4th Fl., New York, NY 10012-3230. TEL 212-941-5500. FAX 212-941-5508. URL: http://www.energyintel.com. *5627*

WORLD HEALTH.
World Health Organization, Distribution and Sales, CH-1211 Geneva 27, Switzerland. TEL 41-22-791-2476. FAX 41-22-791-4857. URL: http://www.who.ch.
Vendor(s): Information Access Co., Knight-Ridder Information, Inc., UMI. *6254*

WORLD HEALTH ORGANIZATION. BULLETIN.
World Health Organization, Distribution and Sales, CH-1211 Geneva 27, Switzerland. TEL 41-22-791-2476. FAX 41-22-791-4857. URL: http://www.who.ch.
Vendor(s): Information Access Co. *4759*

WORLD HOSPITALS AND HEALTH SERVICES.
International Hospital Federation, 4 Abbots Pl., London NW6 4NP, England. TEL 0171-372-7181. FAX 0171-328-7433. URL: http://www.powertek.co.uk/ihf. *3720*

WORLD INFORMATION REPORT.
UNESCO Publishing, 7 Place de Fontenoy, 75352 Paris 07 SP, France. TEL 33-1-45684300. FAX 33-1-45685741. URL: http://www.unesco.org/cii/wirerpt/vers-web.htm. *4223*

WORLD INSURANCE REPORT.
Financial Times Financial Publishing, Maple House, 149 Tottenham Ct. Rd., London W1P 9LL, England. TEL 44-171-896-2314. FAX 44-171-896-2319.
Vendor(s): Information Access Co. *3837*

WORLD INTELLECTUAL PROPERTY REPORT.
B N A International, Inc., Heron House, 10 Dean Farrar St., London SW1H 0DX, England. TEL 44-171-222-8831. FAX 44-171-222-0294. URL: http://www.bna.com. *5592*

WORLD JOURNAL OF SURGERY.
Springer-Verlag, Medical Journals, 175 Fifth Ave., New York, NY 10010. TEL 212-460-1500. FAX 212-473-6272. URL: http://www.springer-ny.com. *5157*

WORLD LITERATURE TODAY.
110 Monnet Hall, University of Oklahoma, Norman, OK 73019-0375. TEL 405-325-4531. FAX 405-325-7495.
Vendor(s): Information Access Co., UMI. *4488*

WORLD MEDIA. BROADCASTING NEWS.
B B C Worldwide Monitoring, Caversham Park, Reading, Berks. RG4 8TZ, England. TEL 44-118-946-9289. FAX 44-118-946-3823. URL: http://www.monitor.bbc.co.uk.
Vendor(s): Data-Star, Lexis-Nexis. *2030*

10226   SERIALS AVAILABLE ONLINE

WORLD NUCLEAR PERFORMANCE.
McGraw-Hill Companies, Energy & Business Newsletters, 1221 Ave. of the Americas, 36th Fl., New York, NY 10020. TEL 212-512-6410. *2705*

WORLD OF WORK.
International Labour Office, Bureau of Public Information, CH-1211 Geneva 22, Switzerland. TEL 41-22-799-7912. FAX 41-22-799-8577. URL: http://www.ilo.org. *6695*

WORLD OIL.
Gulf Publishing Co., Box 2608, Houston, TX 77252-2608. TEL 713-529-4301. FAX 713-520-4433. URL: http//www.gulfpub.com.
Vendor(s): Information Access Co. *5627*

WORLD POLICY GUIDE.
Financial Times Financial Publishing, Maple House, 149 Tottenham Court Rd., London W1P 9LL, England. TEL 44-171-896-2314. FAX 44-171-896-2319. *3837*

WORLD POLICY JOURNAL.
World Policy Institute, 65 Fifth Ave., Ste. 413, New York, NY 10003-3003. TEL 212-229-5808. FAX 212-229-5579. URL: http://worldpolicy.org/
Vendor(s): Information Access Co., UMI. *6044*

WORLD POLITICS (BALTIMORE).
Johns Hopkins University Press, Journals Publishing Division, 2715 N. Charles St., Baltimore, MD 21218-4319. TEL 410-516-6987. FAX 410-516-6968. URL: http://muse.jhu.edu.
Vendor(s): Information Access Co. *6044*

WORLD POPULATION PROFILE.
U.S. Bureau of the Census, Customer Services, Washington, DC 20233. TEL 310-457-4100. FAX 301-457-4714. URL: http://www.census.gov/. *6060*

WORLD POWER SYSTEMS INTELLIGENCE.
Forecast International Inc. - D M S, 22 Commerce Rd., Newtown, CT 06470-1643. TEL 203-426-0800. FAX 203-426-0233.
Vendor(s): Knight-Ridder Information, Inc. *2681*

WORLD PRESS REVIEW.
Stanley Foundation (New York), 200 Madison Ave., Ste. 2104, New York, NY 10016. TEL 212-889-5155. FAX 212-889-5634.
Vendor(s): Information Access Co., UMI. *4367*

WORLD PUBLISHING MONITOR.
Pira International, Randalls Rd., Leatherhead, Surrey KT22 7RU, England. TEL 44-1372-802050. FAX 44-1372-802239. URL: http://www.pira.co.uk/.
Vendor(s): Data-Star, FIZ Technik, Knight-Ridder Information, Inc., Questel Orbit Inc., STN International. *2096*

WORLD SECURITIES LAW REPORT.
B N A International, Inc., Heron House, 10 Dean Farrar St., London SW1H 0DX, England. TEL 44-171-222-8831. FAX 44-171-222-0294. URL: http://www.bna.com. *1415*

WORLD SURFACE COATING ABSTRACTS.
Paint Research Association, 8 Waldgreave Rd., Teddington, Middlesex TW11 8LD, England. TEL 44-181-977-4427. FAX 44-181-943-4705.
Vendor(s): Questel Orbit Inc. (WSCA). *5557*

WORLD TEXTILE ABSTRACTS.
Elsevier Science Ltd., P.O. Box 800, Kidlington, Oxford OX5 1DX, England. TEL 44-1865-843000. FAX 44-1865-843010. URL: http://www.elsevier.nl/.
Vendor(s): Knight-Ridder Information, Inc. (File no.67), Questel Orbit Inc. (WTA). *7000*

WORLD TRADE.
Freedom Magazines, Inc., 17702 Cowan, Ste. 100, Irvine, CA 92714-6035. TEL 714-798-3500.
Vendor(s): UMI. *1352*

WORLD TRANSLATIONS INDEX.
International Translations Centre (ITC), Schutterveld 2, 2611 WE Delft, Netherlands. TEL 31-15-2142242. FAX 31-15-2158535.
Vendor(s): European Space Agency (File no.33/WTI), Knight-Ridder Information, Inc. (File no.295). *6593*

WORLD TUNNELLING.
Mining Journal Ltd., 60 Worship St., London EC2A 2HD, England. TEL 44-171-216-6060. FAX 44-171-216-6050.
Vendor(s): Information Access Co. *2801*

WORLD WASTES.
Intertec Publishing Corp. (Atlanta), 6151 Powers Ferry Rd., N.W., Atlanta, GA 30339-2941. TEL 770-955-2500. FAX 770-955-0400.
Vendor(s): Information Access Co., UMI. *2992*

WORLD WATCH.
Worldwatch Institute, 1776 Massachusetts Ave., N.W., Washington, DC 20036. TEL 202-452-1999. FAX 202-296-7365. URL: http://www.worldwatch.org.
Vendor(s): Information Access Co., UMI. *2958*

THE WORLD WIDE MIRROR.
3036 Lake Lansing Rd., Ste. 255, East Lansing, MI 48823. URL: http://www.paranoia.com/'kafka/mirror.html.
Available only online. *5981*

WORLD WIDE WEB JOURNAL.
O'Reilly & Associates, 103 Morris St., Ste. A, Sebastopol, CA 95472. TEL 707-829-0515. FAX 707-829-0104. URL: http://www.w3.org/pub/www/journal. *2141*

WORLDCASTS: PRODUCT EDITION.
Information Access Company, 362 Lakeside Dr., Foster City, CA 94404. TEL 415-378-5200. FAX 415-358-4759.
Vendor(s): Data-Star, Knight-Ridder Information, Inc. *1078*

WORLDCASTS: REGIONAL EDITION.
Information Access Company, 362 Lakeside Dr., Foster City, CA 94404. TEL 415-378-5200. FAX 415-358-4759.
Vendor(s): Data-Star, Knight-Ridder Information, Inc. *1078*

THE WORLDPAPER.
World Times, Inc., 210 World Trade Center, Boston, MA 02210. TEL 617-439-5400. FAX 617-439-5415.
Vendor(s): Lexis-Nexis. *6045*

WORLDPROFIT ONLINE MAGAZINE.
Worldprofit, Inc., 9010 - 106 Ave., Ste. 208, Edmonton, AB T5H 4K3, Canada. TEL 403-425-2466. URL: http://www.worldprofit.com.
Available only online. *1013*

WORLDSCOPE COMPANY DATABASE.
Worldscope-Disclosure Partners, 1000 Lafayette Blvd., Bridgeport, CT 06604. TEL 203-330-5000. FAX 203-330-5001.
Vendor(s): Dow Jones News Retrieval, Lexis-Nexis, OCLC. *1415*

WORLDVIEWS.
DataCenter, 464 19th St., Oakland, CA 94612-2297. TEL 510-835-4692. FAX 510-835-3017. URL: http://www.igc.apc.org/worldviews/
Vendor(s): Knight-Ridder Information, Inc. *1371*

WORLDWIDE BIOTECH.
Worldwide Videotex, Box 3273, Boynton Beach, FL 33424-3273. TEL 407-738-2276.
Vendor(s): Data-Star, Information Access Co., Knight-Ridder Information, Inc. *688*

WORLDWIDE COMPUTER PRODUCTS NEWS.
M2 Communications Ltd., P.O. Box 475, Coventry CV1 2ZW, England. TEL 44-1203-634700. FAX 44-1203-634144. URL: http://www.m2.com.
Available only online. *2092*

WORLDWIDE DATABASES.
Worldwide Videotex, Box 3273, Boynton Beach, FL 33424-3273. TEL 407-738-2276.
Vendor(s): Data-Star, Information Access Co., Knight-Ridder Information, Inc., NewsNet (PB44). *2168*

WORLDWIDE ENERGY.
Worldwide Videotex, Box 3273, Boynton Beach, FL 33424-3273. TEL 407-738-2276.
Vendor(s): Information Access Co., NewsNet (EY63). *2681*

WORLDWIDE TELECOM.
Worldwide Videotex, Box 3273, Boynton Beach, FL 33424-3273. TEL 407-738-2276.
Vendor(s): Data-Star, Information Access Co., Knight-Ridder Information, Inc., NewsNet (TE19). *2042*

WORLDWIDE VIDEOTEX UPDATE.
Worldwide Videotex, Box 3273, Boynton Beach, FL 33424-3273. TEL 407-738-2276.
Vendor(s): Data-Star, Information Access Co., Knight-Ridder Information, Inc., NewsNet (PB08). *2018*

WRESTLING U.S.A. MAGAZINE.
109 Apple House Ln., Missoula, MT 59802-3324. TEL 406-549-4448. FAX 406-549-4879. URL: http://www.wrestlingusa.com. *6795*

THE WRITER.
Writer, Inc., 120 Boylston St., Boston, MA 02116. TEL 617-423-3157.
Vendor(s): Information Access Co., UMI. *4488*

WRITER & CLIENT NEWSLETTER.
Box 5652, Glendale, AZ 85312-5652. URL: http://www.primenet.com/~essncom/writer.html. *1013*

WRITER'S CAROUSEL.
Writer's Center, 4508 Walsh St., Bethesda, MD 20815. TEL 301-654-8664. *4489*

WRITER'S DIGEST.
F & W Publications, Inc., 1507 Dana Ave., Cincinnati, OH 45207. TEL 513-531-2222.
Vendor(s): Information Access Co., UMI. *3882*

WWWIZ.
17971 Sky Park Circle, Bldg. 33B, Irvine, CA 92614. URL: http://wwwiz.com. *2141*

WWWVOICE HUMOR ZINE THING.
URL: http://www.wwwvoice.com/.
Available only online. *4367*

WYOMING BUSINESS DIRECTORY.
American Business Directories, 5711 S. 86th Circle, Box 27347, Omaha, NE 68127. TEL 402-593-4600. FAX 402-331-5481. *1724*

WYOMING LABOR FORCE TRENDS.
Wyoming Department of Employment, Research & Planning Division, Box 2760, Casper, WY 82602. TEL 307-438-3808. FAX 307-473-3834. URL: http://wyjobs.state.wy.us/mi/rphome.htm. *1459*

X MAGAZINE.
Jeff Hansen, Ed. & Pub., Box 1077, Royal Oak, MI 48068-1077. URL: http://www.msen.com/nxmag. *5445*

X XCITE.
URL: http://www.nrg.com.au/xxcite/index.html.
Available only online. *7339*

X Y Z Z Y NEWS.
URL: http://www.users.interport.net/~eileen/design/xyzzynews.html.
Available only online. *4538*

XANDER MELLISH.
URL: http://www.xmel.com/
Available only online. *4538*

Y O! (YOUTH OUTLOOK).
Pacific News Service, 450 Mission St., Rm. 204, San Francisco, CA 94105. TEL 415-243-4304. URL: http://www.pacificnews.org/yo/ *1894*

YACHTING.
Times Mirror Magazines, Inc. (Greenwich), 20 Elm St., Greenwich, CT 06830. TEL 203-625-4480. FAX 203-625-4481. URL: http://www.yachtingmag.com.
Vendor(s): Information Access Co. *6847*

YAHOO! INTERNET LIFE.
Ziff-Davis Publishing Co., One Park Ave., New York, NY 10016. TEL 212-503-4804. FAX 212-503-5699. URL: http://www.zdnet.com/zdil. *2141*

YALE JOURNAL OF BIOLOGY AND MEDICINE.
Yale Journal of Biology and Medicine, Inc., 333 Cedar St., New Haven, CT 06510. TEL 203-785-4251. FAX 203-785-6309. URL: http://www.med.yale.edu/yjbm/welcome.html. *4760*

YALE JOURNAL OF CRITICISM.
Johns Hopkins University Press, Journals Publishing Division, 2715 N. Charles St., Baltimore, MD 21218-4319. TEL 410-516-6987. FAX 410-516-6968. URL: http://muse.jhu.edu. *4491*

YALE JOURNAL OF INTERNATIONAL LAW.
Yale Journal of International Law, Inc., Yale Law School, Box 208215, New Haven, CT 06520-8215. TEL 203-432-4884. FAX 203-432-2592. *4129*

YALE JOURNAL ON REGULATION.
Yale University, School of Law, Box 208215, New Haven, CT 06520. TEL 203-432-7652. FAX 203-432-2592.
Vendor(s): West Group. *4048*

YALE LAW JOURNAL.
Yale Journal Co. Inc., Box 208215, New Haven, CT 06520-8215. TEL 203-432-1666. FAX 203-432-7482.
Vendor(s): Information Access Co., Lexis-Nexis. *4048*

YEAR 2000 ANNOUNCEMENT LIST.
Tenagra Corporation, 1100 Hercules, Ste. 120, Houston, TX 77058. URL: http://www.year2000.com/.
Available only online. *2092*

YEAR BOOK OF DERMATOLOGIC SURGERY.
Mosby - Year Book, Inc. (Chicago), 161 N. Clark St., Chicago, IL 60601. TEL 312-726-9733.
Vendor(s): Ovid Technologies, Inc. *4882*

YEARBOOK OF EXPERTS, AUTHORITIES & SPOKESPERSONS.
Broadcast Interview Source, 2233 Wisconsin Ave., N.W., Washington, DC 20007. TEL 202-333-4904. FAX 202-342-5411. URL: http://www.yearbooknews.com. *2065*

YEAR BOOK OF PLASTIC, RECONSTRUCTIVE, AND AESTHETIC SURGERY.
Mosby - Year Book, Inc., Continuity Division, 200 N. LaSalle, Chicago, IL 60601. TEL 312-726-9733. FAX 312-726-6075.
Vendor(s): Ovid Technologies, Inc. *5157*

YELLOW PAGES & DIRECTORY REPORT.
Cowles - SIMBA Information, 11 Riverbend Dr. S., Box 4949, Stamford, CT 06907-0949. TEL 203-358-9900. FAX 203-358-5811. URL: http://www.simbanet.com.
Vendor(s): Information Access Co.. *1724*

YGDRASIL.
Yggdrasil Press, 1001-257 Lisgar St., Ottawa, ON K2P 0C4, Canada. TEL 613-233-8353. URL: http://www.synapse.net/~kgerken.
Available only online. *4527*

YINGSHI WENXUE.
Shandong Sheng Yingshi Zhizuo Zhongxin, No. 55, Wenhua Donglu, Jinan, Shandong 250014, People's Republic of China. TEL 86-0531-657715. *4492*

YOUNG CONSERVATIVE LETTER.
341 S. College Rd., No. 11-174, Wilmington, NC 28403. URL: http://members.aol.com/khgwin/ycletter.html.
Available only online. *5981*

YOUR CHURCH.
Christianity Today, Inc., 465 Gundersen Dr., Carol Stream, IL 60188-2498. TEL 630-260-6200. FAX 630-260-0114. URL: http://www.christianity.net/yc. *6383*

YOUR FINANCIAL FUTURE.
Standard & Poor's, 25 Broadway, New York, NY 10004. TEL 212-208-8000. URL: http://users.penn.com/~pneal/index.html. *1416*

YOUR HEALTH & FITNESS.
General Learning Communications, Health Communications Group, 900 kokie Blvd., Ste. 200, Northbrook, IL 60062-4028. TEL 847-205-3000. FAX 847-564-8197. *5793*

YOUTH MARKETS ALERT.
E P M Communications, 160 Mercer St., 3rd Fl., New York, NY 10012-3212. TEL 212-941-0099. FAX 212-941-1622.
Vendor(s): Information Access Co., Knight-Ridder Information, Inc., Lexis-Nexis (AD12). *1554*

YOUTH RESEARCH NEWS.
Youth Research Centre, Faculty of Education, University of Melbourne, Parkville, Vic. 3052, Australia. TEL 61-3-93448251. FAX 61-3-93448256. URL: http://yarn.insted.univelb.edu.au/yarn/yrc-home.html. *1895*

Z.
Seksuaalinen Tasavertaisuus ry, Hietalahdenkatu 2 B 16, FIN-00180 Helsinki, Finland. TEL 358-9-612-3244. FAX 358-9-612-3266. URL: http://www.seta.fi/z. *3702*

Z D NET ANCHORDESK.
Ziff - Davis Publications, Inc., 2300 130th Ave., N.E., Ste.1-101, Bellevue, WA 98005. URL: http://www.anchordesk.com.
Available only online. *2092*

Z V E I ELEKTRO UND ELEKTRONIK - EINKAUFSFUEHRER.
Verlag W. Sachon, Schloss Mindelburg, 87714 Mindelheim, Germany. TEL 49-8261-999-0. FAX 49-8261-999-180. URL: http://www.sachon.de.
Vendor(s): Data-Star, FIZ Technik. *2806*

ZANY ZINE.
2-421 Girja Bhavan, Bhaudaji Rd., Matunga, Maharashtra, Mumbai 400 019, India. URL: http://www.geocities.com/southbeach/4195.
Available only online. *2141*

ZEITSCHRIFT FUER ANGEWANDTE MATHEMATIK UND PHYSIK.
Birkhaeuser Verlag, P.O. Box 133, CH-4010 Basel, Switzerland. TEL 41-61-2050730. FAX 41-61-2050791. *4616*

ZEITSCHRIFT FUER LEBENSMITTEL-UNTERSUCHUNG UND -FORSCHUNG A.
Springer-Verlag, Heidelberger Platz 3, 14197 Berlin, Germany. TEL 49-30-82787-0. FAX 49-30-82787448. URL: http://link.springer.de. *3133*

ZEITSCHRIFTEN - DATENBANK (Z D B).
Deutsches Bibliotheksinstitut, Abt. 1 - Publikationen, Alt-Moabit 101A, 10559 Berlin, Germany. TEL 49-30-39077-0. FAX 49-30-39077100. *4223*

ZENTRALBLATT FUER DIDAKTIK DER MATHEMATIK.
Fachinformationszentrum Karlsruhe, Gesellschaft fuer wissenschaftlich-technische Information mbH, 76344 Eggenstein-Leopoldshafen, Germany. TEL 07247-808-333. FAX 07247-808-135.
Vendor(s): STN International. *4616*

ZENTRALBLATT FUER MATHEMATIK UND IHRE GRENZGEBIETE.
Springer-Verlag, Heidelberger Platz 3, 14197 Berlin, Germany. TEL 49-30-82787-0. FAX 49-30-82787448. URL: http://www.emis.de/cgi-bin/math.
Vendor(s): STN International (MATH). *4618*

ZERO HORA.
Zero Hora Editora Jornalistica S.A., Av. Ipiranga 1075, 90169-900 Porto Alegre, RS, Brazil. TEL 55-51-2184400. FAX 55-51-2184580. URL: http://www.RBS.com.br. *3258*

ZHONGGUO FALU NIANJIAN.
Zhongguo Faxuehui, Zhongguo Falu Nianjian Bianjibu, No. 6 Nandajie, Xizhimen, Beijing 100035, People's Republic of China. TEL 010-6038971. FAX 010-6032251.
Available only online. *4050*

ZHONGGUO SHENGWUXUE WENZHAI.
Zhongguo Kexueyuan, Shanghai Wenxian Qingbao Zhongxin, 319 Yueyang Lu, Shanghai 200031, People's Republic of China. TEL 0086-021-4336650. FAX 0086-021-4718906. *645*

ZHONGGUO XINLI WEISHENG ZAZHI.
Beijing Yike Daxue, Jingshen Weisheng Yanjiusuo, 38 Huayuan Beilu, Beijing 100083, People's Republic of China. TEL 861-2010890. FAX 861-2027314.
Vendor(s): Knight-Ridder Information, Inc. *6160*

ZHONGGUO YANGFENG.
Zhongguo Nongye Kexueyuan, Yangfeng Yanjiusuo, Xiangshan, Beijing 100093, People's Republic of China. TEL 81-10-6259-1473. FAX 86-10-6259-1620.
Vendor(s): Knight-Ridder Information, Inc. *166*

ZINES ZINES EVERYWHERE.
URL: http://thetransom.com/chip/zines.
Available only online. *4368*

ZIPZAP.
URL: http://www.dnai.com/~zipzap.
Available only online. *4493*

ZOO BIOLOGY.
John Wiley & Sons, Inc., Journals, 605 Third Ave., New York, NY 10158. TEL 212-850-6645. FAX 212-850-6021. URL: http://www.wiley.co.uk. *854*

ZOOCRIADEROS.
Centro de Investigacion y Reproduccion de Especies Silvestres, Apdo. Postal 397, Merida 5101, Venezuela. TEL 58-74-712939. URL: http://www.ciens.ula.ve/~cires. *854*

ZOOLOGICAL RECORD.
BIOSIS, 2100 Arch St., Philadelphia, PA 19103-1399. TEL 215-587-4847. FAX 215-587-2016. URL: http://www.biosis.org.
Vendor(s): Knight-Ridder Information, Inc. (File no.185). *645*

ZOOMORPHOLOGY.
Springer-Verlag, Heidelberger Platz 3, 14197 Berlin, Germany. TEL 49-30-82787-0. FAX 49-30-82787448. URL: http://link.springer.de. *634*

ZUZU'S PETALS QUARTERLY ONLINE.
TEL 610-740-1645. URL: http://ourworld.compuserve.com/homepages/anomalous/zuzushm.htm. *4493*

1A: THE PICKS OF THE WEEK!
18 Schoolstraat, 1650 Beersel, Belgium. TEL 32-2-378-17-66. URL: http://laselection.home.ml.org.
Available only online. *3255*

1ST STEPS: DAILY MARKETING AND DESIGN.
Internet Business Network, 346 Starling Rd., Mill Valley, CA 94941. FAX 415-383-8676. URL: http://www.interbiznet.com/normad.html.
Available only online. *1554*

1ST STEPS IN THE HUNT.
Internet Business Network, 346 Starling Rd., Mill Valley, CA 94941. TEL 415-380-8244. FAX 415-383-8676. URL: http://www.interbiznet.com/hunt.
Available only online. *5518*

2 X S.
Box 392, Ector, TX 75439. URL: http://www.netexas.net/rglaser/2xs/.
Available only online. *2119*

4 1 1 NEWSLETTER.
C C M I, 11300 Rockville Pike, Ste. 1100, Rockville, MD 20852-3030. TEL 301-816-8950. FAX 301-816-8945.
Vendor(s): Data-Star (PTBN), Knight-Ridder Information, Inc. (File no.636), NewsNet (TE95). *2042*

8 TRACK MIND.
8 - T M Publications, 1521 10th Ave., S.W., Hickory, NC 28602. URL: http://www.pobox.com/~abbot/8track/. *5446*

13(F) INSTITUTIONAL PORTFOLIOS.
C D A Investment Technologies, Inc., 1355 Piccard Dr., Rockville, MD 20850. FAX 301-590-1329. *1416*

13(F) INSTITUTIONAL STOCK HOLDINGS.
C D A Investment Technologies, Inc., 1355 Piccard Dr., Rockville, MD 20850. FAX 301-590-1329. *1416*

15 CREDIBILITY STREET.
Wright Hall, Smith College, Northampton, MA 01063. URL: http://www.smith.edu/15cst.
Available only online. *475*

20-20 INSIGHT.
Mercury Capital Management, 2010 Corporate Ridge, Ste. 700, McLean, VA 22102. URL: http://www.2020insight/cp. *1416*

21ST, THE V X M NETWORK.
V X M Technologies, Inc., Box 41, Boston, MA 02199. URL: http://www.vxm.com.
Available only online. *2093*

10228 SERIALS AVAILABLE ONLINE

181.4 DEGREES FROM THE NORM!
C D Universe, Commonwealth Network, Welch 3256 Bergman, Ames, IA 50013. URL: http://www.181-4.com/dftn/
Available only online. *5446*

360 DEGREES: THE MAGAZINE WITH EVERY ANGLE.
360 Degree Exchange, Inc., Box 25356, Washington, DC 20007. TEL 202-628-1836. FAX 202-628-1843. URL: http://www.360.org. *1897*

4080 HIP HOP MAGAZINE.
4080 Publishing, 2550 Shattuck, Ste. 107, Berkeley, CA 94704. TEL 510-848-4080. FAX 510-848-2499. URL: http://www.4080.com. *5446*

Vendor Listing/Serials Online

AUSINET
Information Management Group, 310 Ferntree Gully Rd., Clayton, Vic. 3168, Australia Tel: 554 8433
  A B I X: Australasian Business Intelligence.
  The Age.
  Australian Education Index.
  The Business Who's Who of Australia.

BELINDIS (Subsidiary of: Belgian Ministry of Economic Affairs)
Data Processing Centre, 30 rue de Mot, 1040 Brussels, Belgium Tel: 32-22336737 Telex: 23509 energi B
Fax: 32-22304619.
  Bibliotheque Africaine. Liste des Acquisitions. (AFLI)
  I N I S Atomindex.
  Recueil des Brevets d'Invention.

BUREAU OF NATIONAL AFFAIRS
Book Div., 1250 23rd St., NW, Washington, DC 20037. Tel: 202-452-4132 Telex: 892692
Fax: 202-452-4062.
  B N A's Banking Report.
  Daily Labor Report.
  Daily Tax Report.
  S E C News Digest.
  Securities Regulation & Law Report.

CEDOCAR
26 Bd. Victor, 75996 Paris Armees, France Tel: 33-145523456 Telex: 202778 F
Fax: 33-145524993.
  Alloys Index.
  Computer & Control Abstracts.
  Electrical & Electronics Abstracts.
  Engineering Index Annual.
  Engineering Index Monthly.
  Government Reports Announcements & Index.
  Key Abstracts - Business Automation.
  Metals Abstracts.
  Metals Abstracts Index.
  Nonferrous Metals Alert.
  Physics Abstracts.
  Polymers, Ceramics, Composites Alert.

CISTI (Subsidiary of: National Research Council of Canada)
Montreal Rd., Bldg. M55, Ottawa, ON K1A 0S2, Canada Tel: 800-668-1222 Telex: 0533115
Fax: 613-954-8244.
  Alloys Index.
  Bibliography of Agriculture.
  CAB International. Bureau of Nutrition. Annotated Bibliographies.
  Canadian Theses.
  Canadiana on Microfiche.
  Canadiana Pre-1901.
  Current Index to Journals in Education.
  Engineering Index Monthly.
  Food Science and Technology Abstracts.
  Forest Products Abstracts.
  Forestry Abstracts.
  Government Reports Announcements & Index.
  Helminthological Abstracts.
  I N I S Atomindex.
  International Biodeterioration & Biodegradation.
  Merck Index: An Encyclopedia of Chemicals and Drugs.
  Metals Abstracts.
  Metals Abstracts Index.
  Nematological Abstracts.
  Nonferrous Metals Alert.
  Nutrition Abstracts and Reviews. Series B: Livestock Feeds and Feeding.
  Polymers, Ceramics, Composites Alert.
  Romulus.
  Soils and Fertilizers.
  Steels Alert.

CREDOC
34 rue de la Montagne, BP 11, 1000 Brussels, Belgium Tel: 33 (2) 513 9213 Telex: 63129 CREDOC B
Fax: 32-25130911.
  Steels Alert.

CANADIAN CENTRE FOR OCCUPATIONAL HEALTH AND SAFETY
250 Main St., Hamilton, ON L8N 1H6, Canada Tel: 905-572-2981
Fax: 905-572-2206.
  N I O S H T I C.
  R T E C S.

CENTRAL INSTITUTE FOR SCIENTIFIC AND TECHNICAL INFORMATION
52 A.G. Nasser, Sofia 1040, Bulgaria Tel: 71-91-91 Telex: 22404
  Country Report. Albania.
  Physical Therapy.

CHEMICAL INFORMATION SYSTEMS (Subsidiary of: Fein-Marquart Assocs., Inc.)
810 Gleneagles Ct., Baltimore, MD 21286. Tel: 410-321-8440 Telex: 9103801738
Fax: 301-296-0712.
  R T E C S.

COMMISSION OF THE EUROPEAN COMMUNITIES
Rue de la Loi 200, 1049 Brussels, Belgium Tel: 322-235-00-01
Fax: 322-2360624.
  Directory of Community Legislation in Force.
  Eurostatistics Data for Short Term Economic Analysis.
  S C A D Bulletin.

COMPUSERVE, INC.
5000 Arlington Centre Blvd., Columbus, OH 43220. Tel: 800-848-8990
Fax: 614-457-0348.
  Annual Survey of Manufactures.
  Biomedical Market Newsletter.
  BioVenture View.
  Blood Weekly.
  Boston Business Journal.
  Cancer Weekly Plus.
  Corporate Report Minnesota.
  Cowles - SIMBA Media Daily.
  Current Business Reports: Monthly Retail Trade: Sales and Inventories.
  Current Governments Reports: City Employment.
  Current Governments Reports: County Government Employment.
  Current Governments Reports: Government Finances.
  Current Governments Reports: Public Employment.
  Current Population Reports: Series P-70. Household Economic Studies.
  Econews.
  Foreign Trade Reports. U.S. Export and Import Merchandise Trade and Supplement.
  Hogan's Alley. (FUNFOR)
  International Product Alert.
  Japanese Journal of Ophthalmology.
  Journal of Aquaculture and Aquatic Sciences.
  Law and Order.
  Market: Africa - Mid-East.
  Market: Europe.
  Market: Latin America.
  Micro M D Newsletter.
  Minneapolis - St. Paul CityBusiness.
  Mother Jones.
  MusiCopyright Intelligence.
  One to One (Fresno).
  P C Week.
  P C World. (GO PWOFORUM)
  Peterson's Guide to Four-Year Colleges (Year). (PCG)
  Peterson's Guide to Two-Year Colleges (Year). (PCG)
  Philadelphia Business Journal.
  Product Alert.
  Reflector Newsletter.
  Sacramento Business Journal.

The Scientist.
Screen Digest.
Software Catalog: Microcomputers.
Sports Illustrated.
Tomorrow's Morning.
Tomorrow's Morning Classroom Edition.
Tuberculosis & Airborne Disease Weekly.
Twin Cities Reader.
Videomaker.
Windows Journal.
WordPerfect for Windows Magazine.

CONTEXT LTD.
Tranley Hse., Tranley Mews, Fleet Rd., London NW1 2QW, United Kingdom Tel: 071-267-7055 Fax: 071-267-2745.
Bulletin of Northern Ireland Law.
Times Law Reports.

DAFA DATA AB
Box 34101, 100 26 Stockholm, Sweden Tel: 46-8-738-4480
Nytt Juridiskt Arkiv. Avd. 1 - Raettsfall fraan Hoegsta Domstolen.

D I M D I (Subsidiary of: Deutsches Institut fuer Medizinische Dokumentation und Information)
Box 42 05 60, Weisshausstrasse 27, D-5000 Cologne, Germany Tel: (49) 221-4721-1, (42) 221-4724-270 Telex: 88 81 364 dim D Fax: (49) 221411429.
A S F A Aquaculture Abstracts.
Abstracts on Hygiene and Communicable Diseases.
Agricultural Engineering Abstracts.
Agrindex.
Agroforestry Abstracts.
AIDS Newsletter.
Animal Breeding Abstracts.
Animal Disease Occurrence.
Aquatic Sciences & Fisheries Abstracts. Part 1: Biological Sciences and Living Resources.
Aquatic Sciences & Fisheries Abstracts. Part 2: Ocean Technology, Policy and Non-living Resources.
Aquatic Sciences & Fisheries Abstracts. Part 3: Aquatic Pollution and Environmental Quality.
Biocontrol News and Information.
Biological Abstracts.
Biological Abstracts - R R M.
Bulletin of Entomological Research.
CAB International. Bureau of Nutrition. Annotated Bibliographies.
Cotton and Tropical Fibres.
Crop Physiology Abstracts.
Dairy Science Abstracts.
Environment Abstracts.
Excerpta Medica Abstract Journals.
Excerpta Medica. Section 1: Anatomy, Anthropology, Embryology & Histology.
Excerpta Medica. Section 2: Physiology.
Excerpta Medica. Section 3: Endocrinology.
Excerpta Medica. Section 4: Microbiology: Bacteriology, Mycology, Parasitology and Virology.
Excerpta Medica. Section 5: General Pathology and Pathological Anatomy.
Excerpta Medica. Section 6: Internal Medicine.
Excerpta Medica. Section 7: Pediatrics and Pediatric Surgery.
Excerpta Medica. Section 8: Neurology and Neurosurgery.
Excerpta Medica. Section 9: Surgery.
Excerpta Medica. Section 10: Obstetrics and Gynecology.
Excerpta Medica. Section 11: Otorhinolaryngology.
Excerpta Medica. Section 12: Ophthalmology.
Excerpta Medica. Section 13: Dermatology and Venereology.
Excerpta Medica. Section 14: Radiology.
Excerpta Medica. Section 15: Chest Diseases, Thoracic Surgery and Tuberculosis.
Excerpta Medica. Section 16: Cancer.
Excerpta Medica. Section 17: Public Health, Social Medicine and Epidemiology.
Excerpta Medica. Section 18: Cardiovascular Diseases and Cardiovascular Surgery.
Excerpta Medica. Section 19: Rehabilitation and Physical Medicine.
Excerpta Medica. Section 20: Gerontology and Geriatrics.
Excerpta Medica. Section 21: Developmental Biology and Teratology.
Excerpta Medica. Section 22: Human Genetics.
Excerpta Medica. Section 23: Nuclear Medicine.
Excerpta Medica. Section 24: Anesthesiology.
Excerpta Medica. Section 25: Hematology.
Excerpta Medica. Section 26: Immunology, Serology and Transplantation.
Excerpta Medica. Section 27: Biophysics, Bio-Engineering and Medical Instrumentation.
Excerpta Medica. Section 28: Urology and Nephrology.
Excerpta Medica. Section 29: Clinical and Experimental Biochemistry.
Excerpta Medica. Section 30: Clinical and Experimental Pharmacology.
Excerpta Medica. Section 31: Arthritis and Rheumatism.
Excerpta Medica. Section 32: Psychiatry.
Excerpta Medica. Section 33: Orthopedic Surgery.
Excerpta Medica. Section 35: Occupational Health and Industrial Medicine.
Excerpta Medica. Section 36: Health Policy, Economics and Management.
Excerpta Medica. Section 38: Adverse Reactions Titles.
Excerpta Medica. Section 40: Drug Dependence, Alcohol Abuse and Alcoholism.
Excerpta Medica. Section 46: Environmental Health and Pollution Control.
Excerpta Medica. Section 48: Gastroenterology.
Excerpta Medica. Section 49: Forensic Science Abstracts.
Excerpta Medica. Section 50: Epilepsy Abstracts.
Excerpta Medica. Section 52: Toxicology.
Field Crop Abstracts.
Food Science and Technology Abstracts.
Forest Products Abstracts.
Forestry Abstracts.
Grasslands and Forage Abstracts.
Helminthological Abstracts.
Horticultural Abstracts.
Hospital and Health Administration Index.
Index of Current Research on Pigs.
Index of Fungi.
Index to Scientific Book Contents. (ISTP&B Search)
Index Veterinarius.
Informationsdienst Krankenhauswesen.
Informationsdienst Praxisbezogener Literatur im Weinbau.
International Biodeterioration & Biodegradation.
International Pharmaceutical Abstracts.
Irrigation and Drainage Abstracts.
Leisure, Recreation and Tourism Abstracts.
Maize Abstracts.
Medical Science Research.
Nematological Abstracts.
Nutrition Abstracts and Reviews. Series A: Human and Experimental.
Nutrition Abstracts and Reviews. Series B: Livestock Feeds and Feeding.
Ornamental Horticulture.
Packaging Science and Technology Abstracts.
Pig News & Information.
Plant Breeding Abstracts.
Plant Growth Regulator Abstracts.
Potato Abstracts.
Poultry Abstracts.
Protozoological Abstracts.
Psychological Abstracts.
Review of Agricultural Entomology.
Review of Medical and Veterinary Entomology.
Review of Medical and Veterinary Mycology.
Review of Plant Pathology.
Rice Abstracts.
Rural Development Abstracts.
Salud Publica de Mexico.
Schrifttums fuer den Bereich Haushalt und Verbauch. Bibliographie.
Science Citation Index.
Seed Abstracts.
Small Animals.
Social Sciences Citation Index.
Sociological Abstracts. (SA63)
Soils and Fertilizers.
Soils and Fertilizers - Abstracts of World Literature.
Sorghum and Millets.
Soyabean Abstracts.
Tropical Diseases Bulletin.
Tropical Oil Seeds.
Veterinary Bulletin.
Vitis - Viticulture and Oenology Abstracts.
Weed Abstracts.
Wheat, Barley and Triticale Abstracts.
World Agricultural Economics and Rural Sociology Abstracts.

DATA ARKIV AB
PO Box 12079, 102 22 Stockholm, Sweden Tel: 46 (8) 16 52 20
Japanese Journal of Ophthalmology.
Technology Access Report.

DATA-STAR
114 Jermyn St., Plaza Suite, London SW1Y 6HJ, United Kingdom Tel: 44-71-930-5503, 44-71-930-2581
Radio Suisse AG, Laupenstr. 18A, CH-3008 Berne, Switzerland Tel: 41-31-509500 Fax: 41-31-509675.
A B B Review.
A B C der Deutschen Wirtschaft - Quellenwerk fur Einkauf-verkauf.
A B C Europ Production.
A B E C O R Country Reports.
A B I - INFORM. (INFO)
A H F S Drug Information. (DIFT)
A S S I A: Applied Social Sciences Index & Abstracts. (ASSI)
Abstracts in BioCommerce. (CELL)
Abstracts on Hygiene and Communicable Diseases.
Adhesives Abstracts.
Agricultural Supply Industry.
Agroforestry Abstracts.
Agrow.
AIDS Weekly Plus. (PTS NEWSLETTER DATABASE)
Air Fresheners and Insecticides: The International Market.
Air Safety Week.
Air - Water Pollution Report.
Airline Business.
Airline Financial News.
Alcoholism & Drug Abuse Weekly.
Alloys Index. (META)
American Banker. (BANK)
American Doctoral Dissertations.
Analgesics: The International Market.
Analytical Abstracts. (ANAB)
Animal Pharm.
Annuaire Telexport.
Applied Genetics News.
Asbestos & Lead Abatement Report.
Asset Sales Report.
Audio: The International Market.
Audio Week.
Audiotex Update.
Automotives: The International Market.
Autoparts Report.
B D I Deutschland Liefert.
B T Today.
Baby Care Products: The International Market.
Baby Foods: The International Market.
Bakery Products: The International Market.
Bank Automation News.
Bank Mutual Fund Report.
Barclays Country Reports.
Barclays Economic Review.
Bath and Shower Products: The International Market.
Battery & E V Technology News.
Beer: The International Market.
BioCommerce Financial Abstracts. (CELL)
Biological Abstracts.
Biological Abstracts - R R M.
Biomedical Market Newsletter.
Biotech Business.
BioVenture View.
Blood Weekly.
Books: The International Market.
Boston Business Journal.
Breakfast Cereals: The International Market.
Business Computing Brief.
Business Law Europe.
Business Travel News.
Buyouts Newsletter.
C F O Alert (Weekly).
Canadian Index.
Cancer Weekly Plus.
Canned Foods: The International Market.
Car Aftermarket: The International Market.
Car Rental: The International Market.
Card News.
Chem-Facts: Ethylene & Propylene.
Chem-Facts: European Review.
Chem-Facts: France.
Chem-Facts: Germany.
Chem-Facts: P V C.
Chem-Facts: Polyethylene.
Chem-Facts: Polypropylene.
Chem-Facts: Styrenics.
Chem-Facts: United Kingdom.
Chemical Hazards in Industry. (CSNB)

Chemical Monitor.
Chemical Plant File.
Chilled and Delicatessen Foods: The International Market.
Cleaning Appliances: The International Market.
Clinica.
Coal U.K.
Communications Daily.
CommunicationsWeek International.
Commuter - Regional Airline News.
The Composites and Adhesives Newsletter.
Computer & Control Abstracts.
Computer Database. (CMPT)
Computer Fraud & Security.
Computer Protocols.
Confectionery: The International Market.
Consumer Catering: The International Market.
Corporate Report Minnesota.
Cosmetic Insider's Report.
Cough and Cold Remedies: The International Market.
Country Forecasts (Syracuse). (FSRI)
Credit and Charge Cards: The International Market.
Cumulative Index to Nursing & Allied Health Literature. (NAHL)
Current Biotechnology. (CUBI)
The Cyprus Review.
C2C Abstracts: Japan - Analytical Chemistry. (JPTC)
C2C Abstracts: Japan - Ceramics. (JPTC)
C2C Abstracts: Japan - Chemical Engineering. (JPTC)
C2C Abstracts: Japan - Crystallography. (JPTC)
C2C Abstracts: Japan - Hydrocarbons. (JPTC)
C2C Abstracts: Japan - Inorganic Chemistry. (JPTC)
C2C Abstracts: Japan - Materials Science. (JPTC)
C2C Abstracts: Japan - Metals. (JPTC)
C2C Abstracts: Japan - Organic Chemistry. (JPTC)
C2C Abstracts: Japan - Physical Chemistry. (JPTC)
C2C Abstracts: Japan - Plastics. (JPTC)
C2C Abstracts: Japan - Polymer Chemistry. (JPTC)
C2C Abstracts: Japan - Surface Chemistry. (JPTC)
C2C Abstracts: Japan - Textiles. (JPTC)
C2C Currents: Japan - Chemistry. (JPTC)
C2C Currents: Japan - Computers. (JPTC)
C2C Currents: Japan - Electronics. (JPTC)
C2C Currents: Japan - Materials. (JPTC)
D I Y: The International Market.
Dairy Products: The International Market.
Deodorants: The International Market.
Development Business.
Devices & Diagnostics Letter.
Digestive Remedies: The International Market.
Disposable Paper Products: The International Market.
Dissertation Abstracts International. Section A: Humanities and Social Sciences.
Dissertation Abstracts International. Section B: Physical Sciences and Engineering.
Dissertation Abstracts International. Section C: Worldwide.
Dissertation Abstracts on Disc.
E C Energy Monthly.
East Europe & the Republics: A Political Risk Annual. (FSRI)
East European Energy Report.
East European Markets.
Einkaufs 1x1 der Deutschen Industrie.
Electrical & Electronics Abstracts.
Energy Conservation News.
Energy Daily.
Energy Economist.
Engineering Index Annual.
Engineering Index Monthly.
Entertainment Software: The International Market.
Environment Abstracts. (ENVN/Enviroline)
Environment Abstracts Annual. (ENVN/Enviroline)
Environment Week.
Environmental Problems & Remediation.
European Energy Report.
Eventline.
Excerpta Medica Abstract Journals.
Excerpta Medica. Section 1: Anatomy, Anthropology, Embryology & Histology.
Excerpta Medica. Section 2: Physiology.
Excerpta Medica. Section 3: Endocrinology.
Excerpta Medica. Section 4: Microbiology: Bacteriology, Mycology, Parasitology and Virology.
Excerpta Medica. Section 5: General Pathology and Pathological Anatomy.
Excerpta Medica. Section 6: Internal Medicine.
Excerpta Medica. Section 7: Pediatrics and Pediatric Surgery.
Excerpta Medica. Section 8: Neurology and Neurosurgery.
Excerpta Medica. Section 9: Surgery.
Excerpta Medica. Section 10: Obstetrics and Gynecology.
Excerpta Medica. Section 11: Otorhinolaryngology.
Excerpta Medica. Section 12: Ophthalmology.
Excerpta Medica. Section 13: Dermatology and Venereology.
Excerpta Medica. Section 14: Radiology.
Excerpta Medica. Section 15: Chest Diseases, Thoracic Surgery and Tuberculosis.
Excerpta Medica. Section 16: Cancer.
Excerpta Medica. Section 17: Public Health, Social Medicine and Epidemiology.
Excerpta Medica. Section 18: Cardiovascular Diseases and Cardiovascular Surgery.
Excerpta Medica. Section 19: Rehabilitation and Physical Medicine.
Excerpta Medica. Section 20: Gerontology and Geriatrics.
Excerpta Medica. Section 21: Developmental Biology and Teratology.
Excerpta Medica. Section 22: Human Genetics.
Excerpta Medica. Section 23: Nuclear Medicine.
Excerpta Medica. Section 24: Anesthesiology.
Excerpta Medica. Section 25: Hematology.
Excerpta Medica. Section 26: Immunology, Serology and Transplantation.
Excerpta Medica. Section 27: Biophysics, Bio-Engineering and Medical Instrumentation.
Excerpta Medica. Section 28: Urology and Nephrology.
Excerpta Medica. Section 29: Clinical and Experimental Biochemistry.
Excerpta Medica. Section 30: Clinical and Experimental Pharmacology.
Excerpta Medica. Section 31: Arthritis and Rheumatism.
Excerpta Medica. Section 32: Psychiatry.
Excerpta Medica. Section 33: Orthopedic Surgery.
Excerpta Medica. Section 35: Occupational Health and Industrial Medicine.
Excerpta Medica. Section 36: Health Policy, Economics and Management.
Excerpta Medica. Section 38: Adverse Reactions Titles.
Excerpta Medica. Section 40: Drug Dependence, Alcohol Abuse and Alcoholism.
Excerpta Medica. Section 46: Environmental Health and Pollution Control.
Excerpta Medica. Section 48: Gastroenterology.
Excerpta Medica. Section 49: Forensic Science Abstracts.
Excerpta Medica. Section 50: Epilepsy Abstracts.
Excerpta Medica. Section 52: Toxicology.
Eyewear: The International Market.
F D A Medical Bulletin.
Fast Food: The International Market.
Financial Regulation Report.
Financial Technology Insight.
Financial World.
Firmen der Neuen Bundeslaender.
Flight International.
Food and Drug Letter.
Food Chemical News.
Food Retailers: The International Market.
Food Science and Technology Abstracts. (FSTA)
Foreign Policy Bulletin.
Frozen Food: The International Market.
Fruit and Vegetables: The International Market.
Fruit Juices: The International Market.
The G M P Letter.
G P. (GPGP)
Gale Directory of Databases.
Gardening: The International Market.
Genesis Report - Dx.
Genesis Report - Rx.
Global Environmental Change.
Global Private Power.
Government Reports Announcements & Index.
Ground Water Monitor. (PTBN)
Hair Care Products: The International Market.
Handbuch der Grossunternehmen.
Harvard Business Review. (HBRO)
Hazards in the Office. (CSNB)
Haznews. (PTBN,PTSP)
Health Index. (HLTH)
Health News Daily. (HNDO)
Health Policy & Biomedical Research: The Blue Sheet. (FDCR)
Health Service Abstracts.
Helicopter News.
High Tech Ceramics News.
High Tech Separations News.
Holland Exports.
Household Cleaning Agents: The International Market.
Housewares: The International Market.
Hypermarkets and Superstores: The International Market.
I E A Oil Market Report.
I S D N News.
Ice Cream, Yoghurts and Chilled Desserts: The International Market.
Imaging Abstracts. (PIRA)
Imaging Update.
Improved Recovery Week.
In-Car Entertainment: The International Market.
Industrial Health & Hazards Update.
Industrial Specialties News.
Industries in Transition.
Information Management Report. (PTBN)
Innovator's Digest.
Inpharma Weekly. (PHD,IPHC,IPHA,IPZZ)
Integrated Circuits International.
International Coal Report.
International Country Risk Guide.
International Gas Report.
International Packaging Abstracts.
International Pharmaceutical Abstracts. (IPAB)
International Product Alert.
International Solar Energy Intelligence Report.
International Tax Report.
International Tradeshow Directory.
Item Processing Report.
Key Abstracts - Business Automation.
L A N Product News.
Laboratory Hazards Bulletin. (CSNB)
Large Kitchen Appliances: The International Market.
Large Mixed Retailers: The International Market.
Life Sciences & Biotechnology Update.
M I R A Automobile Abstracts.
Mail Order and Home Shopping: The International Market.
Mainframe Computing.
Make-Up and Colour Cosmetics: The International Market.
Management and Marketing Abstracts.
Management Contents. (MGMT)
Management Matters.
Manufacturing Automation.
Market: Africa - Mid-East.
Market: Asia Pacific.
Market Direction Reports.
Market: Europe.
Market: Latin America.
Market Research Abstracts.
Martindale: the Extra Pharmacopoeia.
Meat and Poultry: The International Market.
Medeconomics.
Media Monitor.
Medical Devices, Diagnostics & Instrumentation Reports: The Gray Sheet. (FDCR)
Medical Science Research.
Medical Textiles.
Medical Waste News.
Medicated Skincare: The International Market.
Membrane & Separation Technology News.
Men's Toiletries: The International Market.
Metals Abstracts. (META)
Metals Abstracts Index. (META)
Meyler's Side Effects of Drugs. (SEDB)
Military & Commercial Fiber Business.
Mineral Water: The International Market.
Minneapolis - St. Paul CityBusiness.
Mittelstaendische Unternehmen.
Mobile Communications Report.
Modem User News.
Money Laundering Alert.
N D A Pipeline. (NDAP)
N T I S Bibliographic Data Base.
National Report on Computers and Health.
Nederlands A B C Dienstverleners.
Nederlands A B C voor Handel en Industrie.
Networks Update.
New Product Launch Letter.
New Trade Names in the Rubber and Plastics Industries.
Nonferrous Metals Alert. (MBUS)
Nonprescription Pharmaceuticals and Nutritionals: The Tan Sheet. (FDCR)
Nonwovens Abstracts.
North Sea Letter.
North Sea Rig Forecast.
Octane Week.
Oils and Fats: The International Market.
Online Libraries and Microcomputers.
Online Newsletter.
Optical Materials and Engineering News.
Oral Hygiene Products: The International Market.
P A I S International in Print. (PAIS)

10232 VENDOR LISTING/SERIALS ONLINE

P C Business Products.
The P R S Group. Country Reports: World Service. (FSRI)
The P R S Group. Country Reports: Algeria.
The P R S Group. Country Reports: Argentina.
The P R S Group. Country Reports: Bolivia.
The P R S Group. Country Reports: Brazil.
The P R S Group. Country Reports: Bulgaria.
The P R S Group. Country Reports: Cameroon.
The P R S Group. Country Reports: Chile.
The P R S Group. Country Reports: China.
The P R S Group. Country Reports: Colombia.
The P R S Group. Country Reports: Congo (Kinshasa).
The P R S Group. Country Reports: Costa Rica.
The P R S Group. Country Reports: Cote d'Ivoire.
The P R S Group. Country Reports: Czech Republic.
The P R S Group. Country Reports: Dominican Republic.
The P R S Group. Country Reports: Ecuador.
The P R S Group. Country Reports: Egypt.
The P R S Group. Country Reports: El Salvador.
The P R S Group. Country Reports: Gabon.
The P R S Group. Country Reports: Guatemala.
The P R S Group. Country Reports: Guinea.
The P R S Group. Country Reports: Haiti.
The P R S Group. Country Reports: Honduras.
The P R S Group. Country Reports: Hong Kong.
The P R S Group. Country Reports: Hungary.
The P R S Group. Country Reports: India.
The P R S Group. Country Reports: Indonesia.
The P R S Group. Country Reports: Iran.
The P R S Group. Country Reports: Iraq.
The P R S Group. Country Reports: Israel.
The P R S Group. Country Reports: Jamaica.
The P R S Group. Country Reports: Kenya.
The P R S Group. Country Reports: Kuwait.
The P R S Group. Country Reports: Libya.
The P R S Group. Country Reports: Malaysia.
The P R S Group. Country Reports: Mexico.
The P R S Group. Country Reports: Morocco.
The P R S Group. Country Reports: Nicaragua.
The P R S Group. Country Reports: Nigeria.
The P R S Group. Country Reports: Oman.
The P R S Group. Country Reports: Pakistan.
The P R S Group. Country Reports: Panama.
The P R S Group. Country Reports: Peru.
The P R S Group. Country Reports: Philippines.
The P R S Group. Country Reports: Poland.
The P R S Group. Country Reports: Romania.
The P R S Group. Country Reports: Russia.
The P R S Group. Country Reports: Saudi Arabia.
The P R S Group. Country Reports: Singapore.
The P R S Group. Country Reports: South Africa.
The P R S Group. Country Reports: South Korea.
The P R S Group. Country Reports: Sri Lanka.
The P R S Group. Country Reports: Sudan.
The P R S Group. Country Reports: Syria.
The P R S Group. Country Reports: Taiwan.
The P R S Group. Country Reports: Thailand.
The P R S Group. Country Reports: Tunisia.
The P R S Group. Country Reports: Turkey.
The P R S Group. Country Reports: Ukraine.
The P R S Group. Country Reports: United Arab Emirates.
The P R S Group. Country Reports: Uruguay.
The P R S Group. Country Reports: Venezuela.
The P R S Group. Country Reports: Vietnam.
The P R S Group. Country Reports: Zambia.
The P R S Group. Country Reports: Zimbabwe.
The P R S Group. Executive Reports: Australia.
The P R S Group. Executive Reports: Austria.
The P R S Group. Executive Reports: Belgium.
The P R S Group. Executive Reports: Canada.
The P R S Group. Executive Reports: Denmark.
The P R S Group. Executive Reports: Finland.
The P R S Group. Executive Reports: France.
The P R S Group. Executive Reports: Germany.
The P R S Group. Executive Reports: Greece.
The P R S Group. Executive Reports: Ireland.
The P R S Group. Executive Reports: Italy.
The P R S Group. Executive Reports: Japan.
The P R S Group. Executive Reports: Netherlands.
The P R S Group. Executive Reports: New Zealand.
The P R S Group. Executive Reports: Norway.
The P R S Group. Executive Reports: Portugal.
The P R S Group. Executive Reports: Puerto Rico.
The P R S Group. Executive Reports: Spain.
The P R S Group. Executive Reports: Sweden.
The P R S Group. Executive Reports: United Kingdom.
The P R S Group. Executive Reports: United States.
Packaging Science and Technology Abstracts.
Paperbase Abstracts.
Pasta Products: The International Market.
Perfumes and Fragrances: The International Market.
Personal Care Appliances: The International Market.
Personal Computer Markets.
Pesticide & Toxic Chemical News.
The Pesticide Manual.
Pet Foods and Products: The International Market.
Pharma Marketletter.
Pharmaceutical Approvals Monthly. (FDCR)
Pharmacies and Drugstores: The International Market.
Pharmaprojects Magazine.
Philadelphia Business Journal.
Photography: The International Market.
Physics Abstracts.
Political Risk Yearbook. (FSRI)
Political Risk Yearbook. Volume 1: North & Central America. (FSRI)
Political Risk Yearbook. Volume 2: Middle East & North Africa. (FSRI)
Political Risk Yearbook. Volume 3: South America. (FSRI)
Political Risk Yearbook. Volume 4: Sub-Saharan Africa. (FSRI)
Political Risk Yearbook. Volume 5: Asia & the Pacific. (FSRI)
Political Risk Yearbook. Volume 6: Europe. (FSRI)
Pollution Abstracts. (POLL)
Polymers, Ceramics, Composites Alert. (MBUS)
Power in Asia.
Power in Europe.
Power in Latin America.
Power U K.
Predicasts Basebook.
Predicasts F & S Index Europe.
Predicasts F & S Index International.
Predicasts F & S Index United States.
Predicasts Forecasts. (PTFC)
Predicasts Overview of Markets and Technology.
Prepared Soups: The International Market.
Prescription Pharmaceuticals and Biotechnology: The Pink Sheet. (FDCR)
Printing Abstracts.
Process and Chemical Engineering. (CEAB)
Product Alert.
Productivity Software.
Psychological Abstracts. (PSYC)
R A P R A Abstracts.
R & D Focus.
R T E C S.
Reactions Weekly. (READ, REAC, REAA, REZZ)
Renewable Energy Report.
Retail Stationery: The International Market.
S M T Trends.
Sacramento Business Journal.
Salud Publica de Mexico.
Savoury Snacks: The International Market.
Science Citation Index.
Screen Digest.
Scrip - World Pharmaceutical News. (PHIN)
Sensor Business Digest.
Sensor Review.
Service Stations: The International Market.
Shopper Report.
Side Effects of Drugs Annual. (SEDB)
Skin Care: The International Market.
Small Kitchen Appliances: The International Market.
Social Sciences Citation Index.
Sociological Abstracts. (SOCA)
Soft Drinks: The International Market.
Space Business News.
Spirits: The International Market.
Sport Thesaurus.
SportSearch.
Steels Alert. (MBUS)
Summary of World Broadcasts. Part 1: Former U S S R (Daily).
Summary of World Broadcasts. Part 1: Former U S S R (Weekly Economic Report).
Summary of World Broadcasts. Part 2: Central Europe, the Balkans (Daily).
Summary of World Broadcasts. Part 2: Central Europe, the Balkans (Weekly Economic Report)
Summary of World Broadcasts. Part 3: Asia - Pacific (Daily).
Summary of World Broadcasts. Part 3: Asia - Pacific (Weekly Economic Report).
Summary of World Broadcasts. Part 4: Middle East (Daily).
Summary of World Broadcasts. Part 4: Middle East (Weekly Economic Report).
Summary of World Broadcasts. Part 5: Africa, Latin America and the Caribbean (Daily).
Summary of World Broadcasts. Part 5: Africa, Latin America and the Caribbean (Weekly Economic Report).
Sun Care: The International Market.
Superconductor Week.
Sweet & Savoury Biscuits: The International Market.
Technology Alert.
Technology Transfer Week.
Tele-Service News.
Telecom Markets.
Television and Video: The International Market.
Textile and Fabric Washing Products: The International Market.
Theoretical Chemical Engineering.
Toiletries, Fragrances and Skin Care: The Rose Sheet. (FDCR)
Tour & Travel News - T T G North America.
Toys and Games: The International Market.
Travel and Tourism: The International Market.
Tuberculosis & Airborne Disease Weekly.
Turing Institute Abstracts in Artificial Intelligence.
Twin Cities Reader.
U K Gas Report.
Utility Reporter - Fuels Energy & Power.
Vending: The International Market.
Video Technology News.
Vitamins and Dietary Supplements: The International Market.
Voice Technology & Services News.
Washington Drug Letter (Washington, 1979).
Wine: The International Market.
Wing Newsletter.
World Accounting Report.
World Media. Broadcasting News.
World Publishing Monitor.
Worldcasts: Product Edition.
Worldcasts: Regional Edition.
Worldwide Biotech.
Worldwide Databases.
Worldwide Telecom.
Worldwide Videotex Update.
Z V E I Elektro und Elektronik - Einkaufsfuehrer.
4 1 1 Newsletter. (PTBN)

DOW JONES NEWS RETRIEVAL
PO Box 300, Princeton, NJ 08540. Tel: 609-452-1511
Fax: 609-520-4775.
A B A Banking Journal.
Administrative Science Quarterly.
Aerospace Daily.
Aerospace Propulsion. (ASR)
Air Conditioning, Heating & Refrigeration News.
Airports.
American Demographics.
Architectural Record. (ARCH)
Arizona Business Gazette.
Aviation Daily.
Aviation Europe. (AE)
Aviation Week & Space Technology.
Barron's.
Biomedical Market Newsletter.
BioVenture View.
Blood Weekly.
Boston Business Journal.
Building Supply Business.
Business America.
Business Dateline.
Business Week.
Byte.
Cancer Weekly Plus.
Chemical Engineering. (CE)
Coal Tech International. (CSL)
Coal Week. (COW)
Coal Week International. (CWI)
Composites Industry Monthly.
Corporate Report Minnesota.
Data Communications.
E N R. (ENR)
Electric Utility Week. (EUW)
Electric Utility Week's Demand-Side Report. (DSR)
Electrical World. (EWL)
Emerging & Special Situations. (ESS)
Far Eastern Economic Review.
Federal Technology Report. (TTR)
Forbes.
Foster Natural Gas Report.
Genesis Report - Dx.
Genesis Report - Rx.
Hazardous Waste Business. (HWB)
Independent Power Report. (COG)
Industrial Energy Bulletin.
Industrial Specialties News.

Inside Energy with Federal Lands. *(IE)*
Inside F E R C. *(FERC)*
Inside F E R C's Gas Market Report. *(GSMR)*
Inside N R C. *(NRC)*
Integrated Waste Management.
International Product Alert.
L A N Times. *(LNTM)*
Life Sciences & Biotechnology Update.
McGraw-Hill's Biotechnology Newswatch. *(BIO)*
Metals Week. *(MW)*
Minneapolis - St. Paul CityBusiness.
Modern Plastics. *(MP)*
Money Laundering Alert.
Northeast Power Report. *(NEPR)*
NuclearFuel. *(NUF)*
Nucleonics Week. *(NUC)*
Octane Week.
Online Libraries and Microcomputers.
Online Newsletter.
Peterson's Guide to Four-Year Colleges (Year). *(SCHOOL)*
Peterson's Guide to Two-Year Colleges (Year). *(SCHOOL)*
Philadelphia Business Journal.
The Physician and Sportsmedicine.
Platt's International Petrochemical Report.
Platt's Oilgram News. *(PON)*
Platt's Oilgram Price Report. *(POP)*
Postgraduate Medicine. *(PGM)*
Power (New York). *(PWR)*
Product Alert.
The Review of Banking and Financial Services. *(RBFS)*
The Review of Securities & Commodities Regulation. *(RSCR)*
Sacramento Business Journal.
Securities Week. *(SW)*
Southeast Power Report. *(SEPR)*
Time.
Tuberculosis & Airborne Disease Weekly.
Twin Cities Reader.
Utility Environment Report. *(UER)*
The Vietnam Business Journal.
Village Voice.
Wall Street Journal (Eastern Edition).
Weekly of Business Aviation. *(BA)*
Worldscope Company Database.

EUROPEAN SPACE AGENCY
Via Galileo Galilei, I-00044 Frascati (Rome), Italy
Tel: 39-6-941801   Telex: 610637 ESRIN1
A B I - INFORM. *(File no.30)*
A S F A Aquaculture Abstracts.
A S F A Marine Biotechnology Abstracts.
Aerospace Daily. *(File no.72/AEROSPACE DAILY)*
Agricultural Engineering Abstracts. *(File nos.16 & 124/CAB)*
Agrindex. *(File no.29/AGRIS)*
Agroforestry Abstracts.
Alloys Index. *(File no.3)*
Aluminium Industry Abstracts. *(File no.9/ALUMINUM)*
Animal Breeding Abstracts.
Animal Disease Occurrence.
Apicultural Abstracts. *(File nos.16 & 124/CAB)*
Aqualine Abstracts.
Aquatic Sciences & Fisheries Abstracts. Part 1: Biological Sciences and Living Resources.
Aquatic Sciences & Fisheries Abstracts. Part 2: Ocean Technology, Policy and Non-living Resources.
Aquatic Sciences & Fisheries Abstracts. Part 3: Aquatic Pollution and Environmental Quality.
Biocontrol News and Information.
BioVenture View.
The Bowker Annual Library and Book Trade Almanac.
Bulletin of Entomological Research.
CAB International. Bureau of Nutrition. Annotated Bibliographies.
Computer & Control Abstracts. *(File no.8/INSPEC)*
Convergence: International Congress on Transportation Electronics. Proceedings.
Cotton and Tropical Fibres. *(File nos.16 & 124/CAB)*
Crop Physiology Abstracts.
Current Index to Statistics.
Current Mathematical Publications.
C2C Abstracts: Japan - Analytical Chemistry. *(File no.241)*
C2C Abstracts: Japan - Ceramics. *(File no.241)*
C2C Abstracts: Japan - Chemical Engineering. *(File no.241)*
C2C Abstracts: Japan - Crystallography. *(File no.241)*
C2C Abstracts: Japan - Hydrocarbons. *(File no.241)*
C2C Abstracts: Japan - Inorganic Chemistry. *(File no.241)*
C2C Abstracts: Japan - Materials Science. *(File no.241)*
C2C Abstracts: Japan - Metals. *(File no.241)*
C2C Abstracts: Japan - Organic Chemistry. *(File no.241)*
C2C Abstracts: Japan - Physical Chemistry. *(File no.241)*
C2C Abstracts: Japan - Plastics. *(File no.241)*
C2C Abstracts: Japan - Polymer Chemistry. *(File no.241)*
C2C Abstracts: Japan - Surface Chemistry. *(File no.241)*
C2C Abstracts: Japan - Textiles. *(File no.241)*
C2C Currents: Japan - Chemistry. *(File no.241)*
C2C Currents: Japan - Computers. *(File no.241)*
C2C Currents: Japan - Electronics. *(File no.241)*
C2C Currents: Japan - Materials. *(File no.241)*
Dairy Science Abstracts.
Diffusion Express. *(File no.27)*
E U D I S E D - European Educational Research Yearbook. *(File no.24/EUDISED R&D)*
Electrical & Electronics Abstracts.
Engineered Materials Abstracts. *(File no.134)*
Engineering Index Annual.
Engineering Index Monthly.
Environment Abstracts Annual. *(File no.11/ENVIROLINE and File no.109/Acid Rain Abstracts)*
Eventline.
F R A N C I S. 522: Histoire des Sciences et de Techniques.
Field Crop Abstracts.
Fluid Abstracts: Civil Engineering. *(File no.48/FLUIDEX)*
Fluid Abstracts: Process Engineering. *(File no.48/FLUIDEX)*
Forest Products Abstracts. *(File nos.16 & 124/CAB)*
Forestry. *(File nos.16 & 124/CAB)*
Forestry Abstracts.
Government Reports Announcements & Index.
Grasslands and Forage Abstracts.
Helminthological Abstracts. *(File nos.16 & 124/CAB)*
Horticultural Abstracts.
I M M Abstracts and Index. *(IMMAGE)*
I N I S Atomindex. *(File no.28/INIS)*
Index of Current Research on Pigs.
Index of Fungi.
Index Veterinarius.
Information Eaux. *(File no.73/AFEE)*
International Biodeterioration & Biodegradation. *(File nos.16 & 124/CAB)*
International Labour Documentation. *(File no.53/LABORDOC)*
Irrigation and Drainage Abstracts.
Key Abstracts - Business Automation.
Leisure, Recreation and Tourism Abstracts.
M I R A Automobile Abstracts.
M I R A Automotive Business News.
Maize Abstracts.
Maritime Information Review.
Mathematical Reviews. *(File no.80/MATHSCI)*
Mechanical Engineering Abstracts. *(File no.10/ISMEC)*
Metals Abstracts. *(File no.3/METADEX)*
Metals Abstracts Index. *(File no.3/METADEX)*
N A T O Advanced Science Institutes Series A: Life Sciences. *(File no.128)*
N A T O Advanced Science Institutes Series B: Physics. *(File no.128)*
N A T O Advanced Science Institutes Series C: Mathematical and Physical Sciences. *(File no.128)*
N A T O Advanced Science Institutes Series D: Behavioural and Social Sciences. *(File no.128)*
N A T O Advanced Science Institutes Series E: Applied Sciences. *(File no.128)*
N A T O Advanced Science Institutes Series F: Computer and Systems Sciences. *(File no.128)*
N A T O Advanced Science Institutes Series G: Ecological Sciences. *(File no.128)*
N A T O Advanced Science Institutes Series H: Cell Biology. *(File no.128)*
N I O S H T I C.
Nematological Abstracts. *(File nos.16 & 124/CAB)*
New Trade Names in the Rubber and Plastics Industries.
Nonferrous Metals Alert. *(File no.111)*
Nutrition Abstracts and Reviews. Series A: Human and Experimental.
Nutrition Abstracts and Reviews. Series B: Livestock Feeds and Feeding. *(File nos.16 & 124/CAB)*
Oceanic Abstracts. *(File no.17/OCEANIC)*
Online Libraries and Microcomputers.
Online Newsletter.
Ornamental Horticulture.
P A S C A L. E 11: Physique Atomique et Moleculaire. Plasmas. *(File no.14)*
P A S C A L. E 12: Etat Condense. *(File no.14)*
P A S C A L. E 13: Structure des Liquides et des Solides - Cristallographie. *(File no.14)*
P A S C A L. E 18: Chromatographie. *(File no.14)*
P A S C A L. E 20: Electronique et Telecommunications. *(File no.14)*
P A S C A L. E 27: Methodes de Formation et Traitement des Images. *(File no.14)*
P A S C A L. E 30: Microscopie Electronique et Diffraction Electronique. *(File no.14)*
P A S C A L. E 32: Metrologie et Appareillage en Physique et Physicochimie. *(File no.14)*
P A S C A L. E 33. Informatique.
P A S C A L. E 34. Robotique, Automatique et Automatisation des Processus Industriels. *(File no.14)*
P A S C A L. E 36: Pollution de l'Eau, de l'Air et du Sol - Dechets - Bruit. *(File no.14)*
P A S C A L. E 48: Environnement Cosmique Terrestre, Astronomie et Geologie Extraterrestre. *(File no.14)*
P A S C A L. E 49: Meteorologie, Glaciologie, Physique des Oceans. *(File no.14)*
P A S C A L. E 58: Genetique. *(File no.14)*
P A S C A L. E 61: Microbiologie: Bacteriologie, Virologie, Mycologie, Protozoaires Pathogenes. *(File no.14)*
P A S C A L. E 62: Immunologie. *(File no.14)*
P A S C A L. E 63: Toxicologie. *(File no.14)*
P A S C A L. E 64: Endocrinologie Humaine et Experimentale. Endocrinopathies. *(File no.14)*
P A S C A L. E 65: Psychologie, Psychopathologie, Psychiatrie. *(File no.14)*
P A S C A L. E 68: Genetique Humaine.
P A S C A L. E 71: Ophtalmologie. *(File no.14)*
P A S C A L. E 72: Otorhinolaryngologie. Stomatologie. Pathologie Cervicofaciale. *(File no.14)*
P A S C A L. E 73: Dermatologie. Maladies Sexuellement Transmissibles. *(File no.14)*
P A S C A L. E 74: Pneumologie. *(File no.14)*
P A S C A L. E 75: Cardiologie et Appareil Circulatoire. *(File no.14)*
P A S C A L. E 76: Gastroenterologie, Foie, Pancreas, Abdomen. *(File no.14)*
P A S C A L. E 77: Nephrologie. Voies Urinaires. *(File no.14)*
P A S C A L. E 78: Neurologie. *(File no.14)*
P A S C A L. E 79: Pathologie et Physiologie Osteoarticulaires. *(File no.14)*
P A S C A L. E 80: Hematologie. *(File no.14)*
P A S C A L. E 82: Gynecologie, Obstetrique, Andrologie. *(File no.14)*
P A S C A L. E 83: Anesthesie et Reanimation. *(File no.14)*
P A S C A L. E 84: Genie Biomedical. Informatique Biomedicale. *(File no.14)*
P A S C A L. E 89: Cancer. *(File no.14)*
P A S C A L. F 10: Mecanique, Acoustique et Transfert de Chaleur. *(File no.14)*
P A S C A L. F 16: Chimie Analytique, Minerale et Organique. *(File no.14)*
P A S C A L. F 17: Chimie Generale, Minerale et Organique. *(File no.14)*
P A S C A L. F 23: Genie Chimique. Industries Chimique et Parachimique. *(File no.14)*
P A S C A L. F 24: Polymeres - Peintures - Bois. *(File no.14)*
P A S C A L. F 40: Mineralogie. Geochimie. Geologie Extraterrestre. *(File no.14)*
P A S C A L. F 41: Gisements Metalliques et Non Metalliques. *(File no.14)*
P A S C A L. F 42: Roches Cristallines. *(File no.14)*
P A S C A L. F 43: Roches Sedimentaires. Geologie Marine. *(File no.14)*
P A S C A L. F 44: Stratigraphie, Geologie Regionale, Geologie Generale. *(File no.14)*
P A S C A L. F 45: Tectonique, Geophysique Interne. *(File no.14)*
P A S C A L. F 46: Hydrologie. Geologie de l'Ingenieur. Formations Superficielles. *(File no.14)*
P A S C A L. F 47: Paleontologie. *(File no.14)*
P A S C A L. F 52: Biochimie - Biophysique - Moleculaire - Biologie Moleculaire et Cellulaire. *(File no.14)*

VENDOR LISTING/SERIALS ONLINE

P A S C A L. F 53: Anatomie et Physiologie des Vertebres. *(File no.14)*
P A S C A L. F 54: Reproduction des Vertebres, Embryologie des Vertebres et des Invertebres. *(File no.14)*
P A S C A L. F 55: Biologie Vegetale. *(File no.14)*
P A S C A L. F 56: Ecologie Animale, Vegetale et Microbienne. Ethologie Animale. *(File no.14)*
P A S C A L. F 70: Pharmacologie. Traitements Medicamenteux. *(File no.14)*
P A S C A L. T 205: Sciences de l'Information. Documentation. *(File no.14)*
P A S C A L. T 215: Biotechnologies. *(File no.14)*
P A S C A L. T 230: Energie. *(File no.14)*
P A S C A L. T 235: Medecine Tropicale. *(File no.14)*
P A S C A L. T 240: Metaux - Metallurgie. *(File no.14)*
P A S C A L. T 260: Zoologie Fondamentale et Appliquee des Invertebres. *(File no.14)*
P A S C A L. T 280: Sciences Agronomiques et Forestieres: Productions Vegetales. *(File no.14)*
P A S C A L. T 295: Batiment. Travaux Publics. *(File no.14)*
P A S C A L V.4 Sciences de la Terre. *(File no.14)*
Physics Abstracts.
Pig News & Information.
Plant Breeding Abstracts.
Plant Growth Regulator Abstracts.
Pollution Abstracts. *(File no.18/POLLUTION)*
Polymers, Ceramics, Composites Alert. *(File no.111)*
Potato Abstracts.
Poultry Abstracts.
Protozoological Abstracts.
R A P R A Abstracts.
Recherche en Matiere d'Economie des Transports. *(File no.74/TRANSDOC Subfile: RESEARCH)*
Review of Agricultural Entomology.
Review of Medical and Veterinary Entomology.
Review of Medical and Veterinary Mycology.
Review of Plant Pathology.
Rice Abstracts.
Rural Development Abstracts.
S A E Technical Papers.
S T A R.
Safety and Health at Work. *(File no.40/CISDOC)*
Securite et Sante au Travail.
Seed Abstracts.
Small Animals.
Soils and Fertilizers.
Sorghum and Millets.
Soyabean Abstracts.
Stapp Car Crash Conference. Proceedings.
Steels Alert. *(File no.111)*
Tropical Oil Seeds.
Urban Abstracts.
Veterinary Bulletin.
Weed Abstracts.
Wheat, Barley and Triticale Abstracts.
World Agricultural Economics and Rural Sociology Abstracts.
World Translations Index. *(File no.33/WTI)*

F I Z TECHNIK
Ostbahnhofstrasse 13, D-6000 Frankfurt 60, Germany Tel: (069) 4308-1
Fax: 49-494308200.
A B C der Deutschen Wirtschaft - Quellenwerk fur Einkauf-verkauf.
A B C Europ Production.
Alloys Index. *(META)*
B D I Deutschland Liefert.
Cardiovascular and Interventional Radiology.
Computer & Control Abstracts.
Convergence: International Congress on Transportation Electronics. Proceedings.
D K I Literatur-Schnelldienst Kunststoffe Kautschuk Fasern.
Einkaufs 1x1 der Deutschen Industrie.
Electrical & Electronics Abstracts.
Imaging Abstracts.
International Packaging Abstracts.
Key Abstracts - Business Automation.
Metals Abstracts. *(META)*
Metals Abstracts Index. *(META)*
Nonwovens Abstracts.
Packaging Science and Technology Abstracts.
Paperbase Abstracts.
Physics Abstracts.
Printing Abstracts.
Process and Chemical Engineering. *(DECHEMA)*
Der Radiologe.
S A E Technical Papers.
Stapp Car Crash Conference. Proceedings.

Theoretical Chemical Engineering. *(DECHEMA)*
Welding Abstracts.
Wer Liefert Was?
World Publishing Monitor.
Z V E I Elektro und Elektronik - Einkaufsfuehrer.

G B I (GESELLSCHAFT FUER BETRIEBSWIRTSCHAFTLICHE INFORMATION MBH)
Freischuetzstrasse 96, 81927 Munich, Germany
Tel: 089-9570064
Fax: 089-954229.
Hamburger Wirtschaft.
Handbuch der Grossunternehmen.
Management and Marketing Abstracts.
Mittelstaendische Unternehmen.
Moskovskie Novosti.
Seibt Industriekatalog.
Seibt Medizinische Technik.
Seibt Oberflaechentechnik.
Verbaende, Behoerden, Organisationen der Wirtschaft.

GSI-ECO
45 rue de la Procession, 75015 Paris, France Tel: 45-66-78-89 Telex: 250 682 F
Fax: 47-34-46-92.
France. Conseil National du Credit. Statistiques Mensuelles.
France. Conseil National du Credit. Statistiques Trimestrielles.
Statistical Office of the European Communities. Energy Statistics Monthly Bulletin.
World Debt Tables.

HELSINKI SCHOOL OF ECONOMICS
Runeberginkatu 22-24, SF-00100 Helsinki, Finland
Tel: 358-0-43131 Telex: 122220 econ sf
Fax: 358-0-4313539.
Kauppalehti.
Scanp.

HUMAN RESOURCE INFORMATION NETWORK
(Subsidiary of: Executive Telecom System, Inc.)
9585 Valparaiso Ct., College Park N., Indianapolis, IN 46268. Tel: 317-872-2045
Fax: 317-872-2059.
AIDS Policy and Law. *(CDD, HDD)*
Asbestos & Lead Abatement Report.
B N A Pension & Benefits Reporter. *(CDD, HDD)*
B N A Policy and Practice Series. *(BPP)*
B N A Policy and Practice Series. Compensation.
B N A Policy and Practice Series. Fair Employment Practices.
B N A Policy and Practice Series. Labor Relations.
B N A Policy and Practice Series. Personnel Management.
B N A's Americans with Disabilities Act Manual and Cases. *(ADAM)*
B N A's Banking Report. *(CDD,HDD)*
B N A's Collective Bargaining Bulletin. *(File DD)*
B N A's Employee Relations Weekly. *(Files CDD, HDD)*
B N A's Medicare Report. *(File DD)*
B N A's SafetyNet. *(CDD, HDD)*
B N A's Workers' Compensation Report. *(File DD)*
Bulletin to Management. *(CDD, HDD)*
Business Dateline.
Chemical Regulation Reporter. *(File DD)*
Collective Bargaining Negotiations & Contracts.
Compensation & Benefits Software Census.
Construction Labor Report. *(File DD)*
Consultants and Consulting Organizations Directory. *(CCOD)*
Corporate Jobs Outlook!
Daily Labor Report. *(CDD, HDD)*
Daily Report for Executives. *(CDD, HDD)*
Employment Guide. *(EMPG, CDD, HDD)*
Employment Information in the Mathematical Sciences.
Environment Reporter.
Fair Employment Practices Summary of Latest Developments. *(CDD, HDD)*
Government Employee Relations Report. *(CDD, HDD)*
H R Magazine.
Harvard Business Review.
Human Resource Executive.
Individual Employment Rights. *(CDD, HDD)*
Industrial Health & Hazards Update.
International Labour Documentation.

Labor - Management Relations Analysis - News and Background Information. *(File DD)*
Labor Relations Reference Manual. *(Files BOARDS, COURTS)*
Labor Relations Reporter. Labor Arbitration and Dispute Settlements. *(File LAR)*
Labor Relations Week. *(CDD, HDD)*
Management Matters.
National Report on Work & Family.
Occupational Safety & Health Reporter. *(CDD, HDD)*
Payroll Administration Guide. *(File DD)*
Payroll Administration Guide Newsletter. *(File DD)*
Personnel Software Census.
Right-to-Know Planning Guide (Series). *(File DD)*
Right-to-Know Planning Guide Newsletter. *(File DD)*
Tax Management Weekly Report. *(File DD)*
Toxics Law Reporter. *(CDD, HDD)*
Training.
Training and Development Organizations Directory. *(TDOD)*
Union Labor Report.
Union Labor Report Weekly Newsletter. *(CDD, HDD)*
Videos for Business and Training. *(Video)*
Waste Management Guide. *(CDD, HDD)*
Workplace Substance Abuse Advisor. *(CDD, HDD)*

IBFD PUBNS. BV
Sarphattistraat 602, P.O. Box 20237, 1000 HE Amsterdam, Netherlands Tel: 31-0-20-6467726
Telex: 13217 intax nl
Fax: 31-0-20-6228658.
Tax News Service.
Tax Treaties Data Base on C D - R O M.

IST-INFORMATHEQUE, INC.
1611 Cremazie Blvd., E., Montreal, PQ H2M 2P2, Canada Tel: 514-383-1611
Fax: 514-383-7233.
Canadian Index.
Point de Repere.
Safety and Health at Work.
Securite et Sante au Travail.

INFO-ONE INTERNATIONAL PTY LTD.
Level 3, 2 Elizabeth Plaza, North Sydney, NSW 2060, Australia Tel: 02-959-5075
Fax: 02-929-5127.
Industrial Reports.
Local Government and Environmental Reports of Australia.
New South Wales Law Reports.
Tasmanian Reports.
Victorian Reports.
Western Australia Reports.

INFORMATION ACCESS CO. (Subsidiary of: The Thomson Corp.)
362 Lakeside Dr., Foster City, CA 94404. Tel: 415-378-5000
Fax: 800-676-2345.
A B A Banking Journal.
A N Q: A Quarterly Journal of Short Articles, Notes and Reviews.
A P S News Service.
About Marketing to Women.
Academic Index.
Academy of Management. Journal.
Academy of Management Executive.
Academy of Management Review.
Accent on Living.
Accounting and Finance.
Accounting Today.
Acknowledge the Window Letter.
Across the Board.
Adhesives Age.
Administration & Society.
Administrative Science Quarterly.
Adolescence (San Diego).
Advanced Imaging.
Advanced Intelligent Network News.
Advanced Management Journal.
Advanced Materials & Processes.
Advertising Age.
Adweek (New York).
Adweek: Midwest.
Adweek: Southwest.
Africa Today.
African Affairs.
African American Review.
Afterimage.
Aftermarket Business.

Age and Ageing.
Agency Sales.
AgExporter.
Agra Europe.
Agricultural History.
Agricultural Research.
AIDS Weekly Plus.
Air Cargo Report.
Air Cargo World.
Air Conditioning, Heating & Refrigeration News.
Air Safety Week.
Air Transport World.
Air - Water Pollution Report.
Aircraft Value Newsletter.
Airline Business.
Airline Financial News.
Alaska Business Monthly.
Alcohol Health & Research World.
Alcohol Outlook.
Alcoholism & Drug Abuse Weekly.
Aluminium Today.
America.
American Antiquity.
American Artist.
American Banker.
American Banker's Washington Watch.
American Behavioral Scientist.
American Business Law Journal.
American City & County.
American Criminal Law Review.
American Demographics.
American Dietetic Association. Journal.
American Druggist.
American Economist.
American Family Physician.
American Fitness.
American Forests.
American Health.
American Heritage.
American Imago.
American Indian Quarterly.
American Journal of Agricultural Economics.
American Journal of Community Psychology.
American Journal of Drug and Alcohol Abuse.
American Journal of Economics and Sociology.
American Journal of Law & Medicine.
American Journal of Mathematics.
American Journal of Ophthalmology.
American Journal of Philology.
American Journal of Psychology.
American Journal of Sports Medicine.
American Journalism Review.
American Libraries.
American Marketplace.
American Medical News.
American Metal Market.
American Midland Naturalist.
American Music.
American Oriental Society. Journal.
American Paint & Coatings Journal.
American Philosophical Quarterly.
American Photo.
American Planning Association. Journal.
American Poetry Review.
American Political Science Review.
American Printer.
American Record Guide.
American Rehabilitation.
American Review of Public Administration.
American School & University.
American Scientist.
American Shipper.
American Spectator.
American Theatre.
American Visions.
Americas.
America's Community Banker.
America's Network.
The Amicus Journal.
Amusement Business.
Annual Review of Genetics.
Annual Review of Microbiology.
Annual Review of Psychology.
Annual Review of Sociology.
Antioch Review.
Antiquity.
Antitrust Law Journal.
Antiviral Agents Bulletin.
Apparel Industry Magazine.
Appliance.
Appliance Manufacturer.
Applied Economics.
Applied Genetics News.
Appraisal Journal.
Arab Studies Quarterly.
Architecture.
Archives of Dermatology.
Archives of Environmental Health.
Archives of Family Medicine.
Archives of General Psychiatry.
Archives of Internal Medicine.
Archives of Neurology.
Archives of Ophthalmology.
Archives of Otolaryngology - Head & Neck Surgery.
Archives of Pediatrics & Adolescent Medicine.
Archives of Sexual Behavior.
Archives of Surgery.
Argumentation & Advocacy.
Arkansas Business and Economic Review.
Armed Forces and Society.
Art Bulletin.
Art in America.
Art Journal (Year).
Artforum.
Arthritis Today.
Arts Education Policy Review.
Asbestos & Lead Abatement Report.
Asian Folklore Studies.
Asian Survey.
Assembly (Carol Stream).
Asset Sales Report.
Association for Computing Machinery. Communications.
Association Management.
Astronomy.
Atlanta Business Chronicle.
Atlantic Economic Journal.
The Atlantic Monthly.
Atlantic Trade Report & Global Defense Industry.
Audio (New York).
Audio Week.
Audiotex Update.
Audubon.
Automatic I D News.
Automobile.
Automotive Engineering Magazine.
Automotive Industries.
Automotive News.
Autoparts Report.
AutoWeek.
AZ B - Arizona Business.
The B B I Newsletter.
B C Business.
B M J.
The Back Letter.
Back Stage.
Backpacker.
Bakery Production and Marketing.
Baltimore Business Journal.
Bank Automation News.
Bank Loan Report.
Bank Network News.
Bank Technology News.
Banking Strategies.
Battery & E V Technology News.
Beauty Counter.
Behavioral Health Management.
Behavioral Health Treatment.
Belles Lettres (North Potomac).
Berkeley Journal of Employment and Labor Law.
Best's Review. Life - Health Insurance Edition.
Best's Review. Property - Casualty Insurance Edition.
Better Homes and Gardens.
Better Nutrition.
Beverage Industry.
Beverage World (English Edition).
Bicycling.
Billboard (New York).
Biological Bulletin.
Biomedical Market Newsletter.
BioPharm.
BioScience.
Biotech Business.
BioVenture View.
The Black Collegian.
Black Enterprise.
Blood Weekly.
Boating.
Boating Industry.
Bobbin.
The Bond Buyer.
The Botanical Review.
Boys' Life (Inkprint Edition).
Brandweek.
The British Journal for the Philosophy of Science.
The British Journal of Aesthetics.
The British Journal of Criminology.
British Journal of Political Science.
British Journal of Psychology.
British Plastics and Rubber Magazine.
Broadband Networking News.
Broadcasting & Cable.
Brookings Review.
Brown University Child and Adolescent Behavior Letter.
Brown University Digest of Addiction Theory & Application.
Brown University Long-Term Care Quality Advisor.
Building Supply Business.
Buildings.
Bulletin of Economic Research.
Bulletin of the Atomic Scientists.
Business America.
Business and Commercial Aviation.
Business and Health.
Business and Society.
Business and Society Review.
Business and the Environment.
Business Communication Quarterly.
Business Communications Review.
Business Computing Brief.
Business Credit.
Business Economics.
Business Europa.
Business First (Buffalo).
Business Forum (Los Angeles).
Business History.
Business History Review.
Business Insurance.
The Business Journal (Lima).
Business Journal (Phoenix).
Business Journal (Portland).
Business Journal Serving Greater Milwaukee.
Business Law Europe.
Business Lawyer.
Business Mailers Review.
Business Marketing.
Business North Carolina.
Business Perspectives.
Business Quarterly.
Business Travel News.
Buyouts Newsletter.
C A - A Cancer Journal for Clinicians.
C A D - C A M Update.
C - C Plus Plus.
C D A Investnet Insiders' Chronicle.
C D Computing News.
C D - R O M Databases.
C D - R O M Professional.
C M A Magazine.
C Q Researcher.
C T D News.
C 4 I News.
Cable - Telco Report.
Cablefax.
CADALYST.
California Business.
California Law Review.
California Management Review.
California Planning and Development Report.
California Public Finance.
Callaloo.
Campaign.
Campaigns and Elections.
Camping Magazine.
Canadian Banker.
Canadian Business.
Canadian Chemical News.
Canadian Dimension.
Canadian Geographic.
Canadian Historical Review.
Canadian Journal of Criminology.
Canadian Journal of History.
Canadian Machinery & Metalworking.
Canadian Manager.
Canadian Mining Journal.
Canadian Packaging.
Canadian Public Administration.
The Canadian Review of Sociology and Anthropology.
Cancer Weekly Plus.
Candy Industry.
Car and Driver.
Card Fax.
Card News.
Caribbean Update.
Carpet & Floorcoverings Review.
Catalog Age.
Ceramic Industry.
Ceramics Monthly.
Chain Store Age.
Change (Washington).
Chatelaine (English Edition).
Chemical Marketing Reporter.
Chemical Monitor.
Chemical Week.
Chemist & Druggist.
Chest.
Chicago (Year).
Chicago Review.
Chief Executive Magazine.

Child Health Alert.
Childhood Education.
Children Today.
Children's Business.
Chilton's Automotive Marketing.
Chilton's Distribution.
Chilton's Food Engineering.
Chilton's Food Engineering International.
Chilton's Motor Age.
China Business Review.
Christian Century.
Christianity Today.
Cincinnati Business Courier.
Cineaste.
Classical Antiquity.
The Classical Quarterly.
The Clearing House.
Clinical Diabetes.
Coach and Athletic Director.
Coatings.
College Literature.
Colonial Homes.
Colorado Business.
Columbia Journal of World Business.
Columbia Journalism Review.
Commentary.
Commonweal.
Communication World.
Communications Business & Finance.
Communications Daily.
Communications International.
Communications News.
Communications Standards News.
CommunicationsWeek.
CommunicationsWeek International.
Community and Worker Right-to-Know News.
Community Pharmacy.
Commuter - Regional Airline News.
Commuter Regional Airline News International.
Compensation and Benefits Review.
The Composites and Adhesives Newsletter.
Composites Industry Monthly.
Composites News: InfraStructure.
Computer Aided Design Report.
Computer-Aided Engineering (Cleveland).
Computer Audit Update.
Computer Business Review.
Computer Dealer News.
Computer Fraud & Security.
Computer Gaming World.
Computer Graphics World.
Computer Industry Report.
Computer Protocols.
Computer Publishing & Advertising Report.
Computer Reseller News.
Computer Retail Week.
Computer Shopper.
Computer Weekly.
Computer Workstations.
Computergram International.
Computers in Libraries.
Computing Canada.
Concrete Products.
Congressional Quarterly Service. Weekly Report.
Congressional Research Report.
Construction Review.
Consumer Reports.
Consumer Reports on Health.
Consumer Reports Travel Letter.
Consumers Digest.
Consumer's Research Magazine.
Contemporary Economic Policy.
Contemporary Literature.
The Contemporary Review.
Contracting Business.
Control and Instrumentation.
Controller's Cost Report.
Convenience Store News.
The Cornell Hotel & Restaurant Administration Quarterly.
Corporate Board.
Corporate Cashflow.
Corporate E F T Report.
Corporate Money.
Corporate Report Minnesota.
Corrections Today.
Cosmetic Insider's Report.
Cosmetic World News.
Cosmetics and Toiletries.
Cosmetics International.
Cosmopolitan.
Cotton: Review of the World Situation.
Country Forecast. United Kingdom.
Country Forecasts (Syracuse).
Country Journal.
Country Music.
Countryside and Small Stock Journal.
Courier (Paris).

Cowles - SIMBA Media Daily.
The Cowles - SIMBA Report on Directory Publishing.
Crain's Chicago Business.
Crain's Cleveland Business.
Crain's Detroit Business.
Crain's New York Business.
Creativity.
Credit Card Management.
Credit Card News.
Credit Union Accountant.
Credit Union Executive.
Criminal Justice Ethics.
Criticism.
Critique: Studies in Modern Fiction.
Cruising World.
Current Health 2.
Custom Builder.
Cycle World.
D B M S.
D I Y Week.
D N R.
Daedalus.
Daily Oil Bulletin.
Dairy Foods.
Dairy Markets Weekly.
Dance Magazine.
Data Storage Report.
Database (Wilton).
Datamation.
Dealer Business.
DealerNews.
Debit Card News.
Defense Counsel Journal.
Defense Daily.
Defense Electronics.
Defense Week.
The Denver Business Journal.
Dermatology Times.
Diabetes.
Diabetes Forecast.
Diesel Progress Engines & Drives.
Differences.
Digital Age.
Digital Media: A Seybold Report.
Digital Systems Report.
Direct Marketing.
Directors & Boards.
Discount Store News.
Do-It-Yourself Retailing.
Document Imaging Report.
Dollars & Sense.
Doors and Hardware.
Down Beat.
Downstream Trends.
Dr. Dobb's Journal.
Drug and Cosmetic Industry.
Drug Detection Report.
Drug Resistance Weekly.
Drug Store News.
Drug Topics.
E & P Environment.
E C Energy Monthly.
E D I News.
E D N Magazine.
E D P Weekly.
E F T Report.
E L H.
E M M S.
E N R.
Early American Homes.
Early Music.
East Europe Agriculture & Food.
East European Insurance Report.
East European Markets.
East European Politics & Societies.
East European Quarterly.
Ebony.
Eco-Log Week.
Ecological Monographs.
The Ecologist.
Ecology.
Economic Commentary.
Economic Geography.
Economic Indicators (Washington).
Economic Inquiry.
Economic Journal.
Economic Perspectives (Chicago).
Economic Record.
Economic Review.
The Economist.
Ecumenical Review.
Editor & Publisher - the Fourth Estate.
Education Technology News.
Educational Leadership.
Educational Marketer.
Electric Light and Power.
Electrical Construction & Maintenance.

Electro Manufacturing.
Electronic Advertising & Marketplace Report.
Electronic Business Today.
Electronic Buyers' News.
Electronic Chemicals News.
Electronic Design.
Electronic Engineering Times.
Electronic Information Report.
Electronic Learning.
Electronic Materials and Packaging.
Electronic Materials Technology News.
Electronic Media.
Electronic News.
Electronics Now.
Electronics Times.
Electronics Weekly.
Employee Relations.
Employee Relations Law Journal.
Energy & Environment.
Energy Business Review.
Energy Conservation News.
Energy Daily.
Energy Journal.
Energy Report.
Energy User News.
The Engineer.
Engineering & Mining Journal.
Engineering Economist.
English Historical Review.
English Language Notes.
Enhanced Energy Recovery News.
Enterprise Systems Journal.
Entertainment Marketing Letter.
Entertainment Weekly.
Entrepreneurship: Theory and Practice.
Environment.
Environment Business.
Environment Watch: Latin America.
Environment Watch: West Europe.
Environment Week.
Environmental Action.
Environmental Business Journal.
Environmental Law (Portland).
Environmental Nutrition.
Environmental Problems & Remediation.
Environmental Remediation Technology.
Environmental Solutions.
Equipment and Materials Update.
Esquire.
Essays in Literature.
Essence (New York).
ETC.
Ethnology.
Eurofood.
Euromarketing.
Euromoney.
Europe.
Europe - Asia Studies.
European Adhesives & Sealants.
European Cosmetic Markets.
European Energy Report.
European Media Business & Finance.
European Polymers Paint Colour Journal.
European Power News.
European Rubber Journal.
Evans-Novak Political Report.
Evolution.
Exceptional Children.
Exceptional Parent.
Executive Female.
Executive Health's Good Health Report.
The Explicator.
Extrapolation.
F B I Law Enforcement Bulletin.
F C C Report.
F D A Consumer.
F D A Enforcement Report.
F D A Medical Bulletin.
Facts on File World News Digest with Index.
Family Circle.
The Family Handyman.
The Fate of the Arabian Peninsula.
Faulkner & Gray's Medicine and Health.
Federal & State Insurance Week.
Federal Computer Market Report.
Federal Probation.
Federal Reserve Bank of Richmond. Economic Quarterly.
Federal Reserve Bank of St. Louis. Review.
Federal Reserve Bulletin.
Feminist Studies.
Fertilizer International.
Fiber Optics News.
Field & Stream.
Film Comment.
Film Quarterly.
Finance and Development.
Finance East Europe.

Financial Executive.
Financial Management.
Financial Market Trends.
Financial Planning (New York).
Financial Post.
Financial Review (Statesboro).
Financial Technology Insight.
Financial Times World Tax Report.
Financial World.
Flame Retardancy News.
Flight International.
Flooring.
Florida Trend.
Flower and Garden.
Flying.
Folio (Stamford).
Food & Beverage Marketing.
Food & Drink Weekly.
Food & Drug Packaging.
Food Chemical News.
Food, Cosmetics and Drugs Packaging.
Food in Canada.
Food Ingredient News.
The Food Institute Report.
Food Labeling and Nutrition News.
Food Manufacture International.
Food Nutrition and Agriculture.
Food Processing.
Food Trade Review.
The Foodservice Distributor.
Footwear News.
Forbes.
Foreign Affairs.
Foreign Policy (Washington).
Foundry Management & Technology.
Free Inquiry.
Frohlinger's Marketing Report.
Frontiers (W. Hollywood).
Frozen and Chilled Foods.
Frozen Food Age.
Frozen Food Digest.
Fund Raising Management.
Fusion Power Report.
Futures (Cedar Falls).
The Futurist.
G R I D.
G U I Program News.
Gas Market Trends.
Genesis Report - Dx.
Genesis Report - Rx.
Geo Info Systems.
The Geographical Journal.
Geographical Magazine.
Geographical Review.
George Wells' Washington Beverage Insight.
Georgia Trend.
Geriatrics.
Getting Results...for the Hands-On Manager.
Gifts & Decorative Accessories.
Glass (Redhill).
Glass International.
Global Environmental Change Report.
Global Positioning & Navigation News.
Golf Magazine (New York).
Good Housekeeping.
Government Computer News.
Government Finance Review.
Graphic Arts Monthly.
Greece and Rome.
Grocery Headquarters.
Ground Water.
Ground Water Monitor.
Group & Organization Management.
Growth and Change.
Guarantor (New York).
Guitar Player.
H F N.
H P Professional.
H R Focus.
H R Magazine.
Harper's Bazaar.
Harper's Magazine.
Harvard Health Letter.
Harvard Heart Letter.
Harvard Mental Health Letter.
Harvard Theological Review.
Harvard Women's Health Watch.
Hastings Center Report.
Hawaii Business.
Hazardous Waste News.
HazMat Transport News.
Haznews.
Health (San Francisco).
Health Alliance Alert.
Health & Social Work.
Health Care Financing Review.
Health Care Management Review.
Health Industry Today.

Health Legislation.
Health Management Technology.
Health Plan Business Advisor.
Health Services Research.
Healthcare Financial Management.
Healthcare P R & Marketing News.
Healthcare Technology & Business Opportunities.
HealthFacts.
Heating - Piping - Air Conditioning.
Hecate.
Helicopter News.
The Hemingway Review.
Hewlett-Packard Journal.
High Tech Ceramics News.
High Tech Separations News.
High Yield Report.
Hispanic.
The Historian (East Lansing).
Historical Journal of Film, Radio and Television.
History and Theory.
History Today.
Hollywood Reporter.
Home Fashions Magazine.
Home Office Computing.
Horn Book Magazine.
Horticulture.
Hospital & Health Services Administration.
Hospital Materials Management.
Hospitality Design.
Hospitals and Health Networks.
Hot Rod.
Hotel and Motel Management.
House Beautiful.
Housewares.
Human Biology (Detroit).
Human Ecology (New York).
Human Factors.
Human Life Review.
Human Relations.
Human Resource Planning.
Human Rights Quarterly.
The Humanist.
Hydraulics & Pneumatics.
Hydrocarbon Processing.
Hypatia.
I B T.
I D C Japan Report.
I D - The Voice of Foodservice Distribution.
I S D N News.
Imaging Update.
Implement & Tractor.
Improved Recovery Week.
In Vivo.
Inc.
Indiana Business Magazine.
Indianapolis Business Journal.
Industrial and Labor Relations Review.
Industrial Distribution.
Industrial Environment.
Industrial Health & Hazards Update.
Industrial Management.
Industrial Paint & Powder.
Industrial Relations Journal.
Industrial Specialties News.
Industries in Transition.
Industry Week.
Infection Control Weekly.
The Information Advisor. (Trade & Industry Index)
Information & Interactive Services Report.
Information Law Alert.
Information Outlook.
Information Technology and Libraries.
Information Today.
Information Week.
InfoWorld.
Ink & Print International.
Innovator's Digest.
Inside D O T & Transportation Week.
Inside M S.
Insight on the News.
Institutional Investor.
Instructor.
Insurance Accountant.
Insurance Regulator.
Integrated Circuits International.
Interactive Content.
Interactive Home.
Interactive Video News.
Interior Design.
Interiors: For the Contract Design Professional.
Internal Auditor.
International Banking Regulator.
International Bulletin of Missionary Research.
International Coal Report.
International Food Manufacture.
International Gas Report.
International Journal of Advertising.
International Journal of Comparative Sociology.

International Journal of Manpower.
International Journal of Operations and Production Management.
International Journal of Physical Distribution & Logistics Management.
International Journal of Public Administration.
International Journal of Purchasing & Materials Management.
International Journal of Quality & Reliability Management.
International Journal of Retail & Distribution Management.
International Labour Review.
International Migration Review.
International Monetary Fund. Staff Papers.
International Organization.
International Product Alert.
International Review of Mission.
International Security.
International Small Business Journal.
International Solar Energy Intelligence Report.
International Studies of Management and Organization.
International Trade Finance.
International Trade Forum.
International Wildlife.
Internetwork.
Interview (New York).
Investment Dealers' Digest.
Issues in Law and Medicine.
Issues in Science and Technology.
Item Processing Report.
J A M A: The Journal of the American Medical Association.
J C T: Journal of Coatings Technology.
J E I.
Jet.
Jewelers' Circular Keystone.
Journal for the Scientific Study of Religion.
Journal of Abnormal Child Psychology.
Journal of Accountancy.
Journal of Advertising.
Journal of Advertising Research.
Journal of African History.
Journal of American Ethnic History.
Journal of Asian and African Studies.
The Journal of Business (Chicago).
Journal of Business Administration.
Journal of Business Communication.
Journal of Business Ethics.
Journal of Business Strategy.
Journal of Cognitive Neuroscience.
Journal of Common Market Studies.
Journal of Community Health.
Journal of Comparative Family Studies.
Journal of Consumer Policy.
Journal of Consumer Research.
The Journal of Credit & Risk Management.
Journal of Criminal Law & Criminology.
The Journal of Development Studies.
Journal of Electronic Defense.
Journal of English and Germanic Philology.
Journal of Environmental Health.
Journal of European Industrial Training.
Journal of European Studies.
Journal of Experimental Psychology: General.
Journal of Family History.
Journal of Family Practice.
Journal of Finance.
Journal of Financial Research.
The Journal of General Psychology.
The Journal of Genetic Psychology.
Journal of Health Care Finance.
Journal of Health Care Marketing.
Journal of Higher Education.
Journal of Human Resources.
Journal of Industrial Economics.
Journal of Interamerican Studies and World Affairs.
Journal of Interdisciplinary History.
Journal of International Affairs.
Journal of International Business Studies.
Journal of Latin American Studies.
Journal of Leisure Research.
Journal of Management.
Journal of Management Studies.
Journal of Managerial Issues.
Journal of Managerial Psychology.
Journal of Marketing.
Journal of Marketing Research.
Journal of Money, Credit & Banking.
Journal of Musicology.
Journal of Negro Education.
Journal of Negro History.
Journal of Occupational and Organizational Psychology.
Journal of Palestine Studies.
Journal of Parapsychology.

Journal of Physical Education, Recreation and Dance.
Journal of Popular Film and Television.
Journal of Portfolio Management.
Journal of Post Keynesian Economics.
Journal of Property Management.
Journal of Psychology: Interdisciplinary & Applied.
Journal of Public Policy & Marketing.
Journal of Rehabilitation.
Journal of Retail Banking.
Journal of Retailing.
Journal of Risk and Insurance.
Journal of School Health.
Journal of Small Business Management.
Journal of Social History.
Journal of Social Issues.
The Journal of Social Psychology.
The Journal of Socio-Economics.
Journal of Soil and Water Conservation.
Journal of Southeast Asian Studies.
Journal of Sport Behavior.
Journal of Systems Management.
Journal of Theological Studies.
Journal of Youth and Adolescence.
Judaism.
The Kansas City Business Journal.
Kiplinger's Personal Finance Magazine.
L A N Product News.
L D C Debt Report.
Labor Studies Journal.
Ladies Home Journal (Inkprint Edition).
Lagniappe Letter.
Lagniappe Quarterly Monitor.
Lambda Book Report.
The Lancet.
Land Economics.
Land Mobile Radio News.
Latin American Research Review.
LatinFinance.
Law and Policy in International Business.
Law Office Technology Review.
Leather.
Legal Publisher.
Liability Week.
Library Software Review.
Library Technology Reports.
Library Trends.
Licensing Letter.
Life.
Life Sciences & Biotechnology Update.
Literary Review.
Livestock, Dairy and Poultry Situation & Outlook.
Lloyds Bank Annual Review.
Local Competition Report.
Lodging Hospitality.
Logistics and Transportation Review.
Logistics Management.
Long Island Business News.
Los Angeles.
Los Angeles Business Journal.
M E L U S.
M I S Quarterly.
M L N.
M L O.
McCall's.
Machine Design.
The McKinsey Quarterly.
Maclean's.
MacUser.
MacWEEK.
MacWorld.
The Magazine Antiques.
Mainframe Computing.
Making the Rounds in Health, Faith and Ethics.
Manage.
Managed Care Outlook.
Managed Care Week.
Managed Healthcare News.
Management Accounting.
Management Decision.
Management International Review.
Management Matters.
Management Quarterly.
Management Review.
Managing Office Technology.
Manitoba Business Magazine.
Manufacturing Automation.
Manufacturing Chemist.
Manufacturing News.
Marine Fisheries Review.
Market: Africa - Mid-East.
Market: Asia Pacific.
Market: Europe.
Market: Latin America.
Market Research Society. Journal.
Marketing.
Marketing Computers.
Marketing News.

The Masthead.
Material Handling Engineering.
Mechanical Engineering.
Med Ad News.
Media Industry Newsletter.
MediaWeek.
Medical Device Approval Letter.
Medical Economics.
Medical Marketing & Media.
Medical Outcomes and Guidelines Alert.
Medical Textiles.
Medical Update.
Medical Utilization Management.
Medical Waste News.
Medium Aevum.
Meetings and Conventions.
Membrane & Separation Technology News.
Memphis Business Journal.
Menopause News.
Men's Health.
Mergers & Acquisitions.
Mergers & Acquisitions Report.
Mergers and Restructurings.
Metal Center News.
Metal Heat Treating.
Metallurgia: The Journal of Metals Technology, Metal Forming and Thermal Processing.
Metals Industry News.
Metropolitan Home.
Metropolitan Life Insurance Company. Statistical Bulletin S B.
Mexican Studies.
Mexico Business Monthly.
Michigan C P A.
Michigan Law Review.
Microprocessor Report.
Microsoft Systems Journal.
Microwave Journal (International Edition).
The Middle East.
Middle East Economic Digest.
Middle Eastern Studies.
Midrange Systems.
Midwest Quarterly.
Migration World.
The Milbank Quarterly.
Military Robotics Newsletter.
Milling & Baking News.
Mind.
The Mineralogical Record.
Mining Magazine.
Minority Markets Alert.
The Mississippi Quarterly.
Mobile Communications.
Mobile Communications Report.
Mobile Phone News.
Mobile Satellite News (Potomac).
Model Railroader.
Modem User News.
Modern Brewery Age.
Modern Casting.
Modern Healthcare (Year).
Modern Language Quarterly.
Modern Machine Shop.
Modern Materials Handling.
Modern Maturity.
Modern Paint and Coatings.
Modern Power Systems.
Modern Tire Dealer.
Money (New York).
Money Laundering Alert.
Montana Business Quarterly.
Monthly Labor Review.
Monthly Review.
Mortgage-Backed Securities Letter.
Mortgage Banking.
The Mortgage Marketplace.
Mosaic (Winnipeg, 1967).
Mother Earth News.
Mother Jones.
Mothering.
Motor Boating & Sailing.
Motor Trend.
Mpls. - St. Paul Magazine.
Multichannel News.
Multimedia Entertainment & Technology Report.
Multimedia Monitor.
Multimedia Publisher.
Multimedia Week.
Multinational Monitor.
Municipal and Industrial Water and Pollution Control.
Music and Letters.
Music & Media.
Music Trades.
Music Week.
N A B E Outlook & Policy Survey.
N A C L A Report on the Americas.
N C A H F Newsletter.

N E A Today.
N T I S Alerts: Foreign Technology.
N T T Topics.
The Nation.
National Catholic Reporter.
National Civic Review.
National Fisherman.
National Forum (Auburn).
National Home Center News.
National Institute Economic Review.
The National Interest.
National Parks.
National Petroleum News.
National Productivity Review.
National Real Estate Investor.
National Report on Computers and Health.
National Review.
National Tax Journal.
National Underwriter. Life and Health - Health & Financial Services Edition.
National Underwriter. Property & Casualty - Risk & Benefits Management Edition.
National Wildlife.
Nation's Business.
Nation's Cities Weekly.
Nation's Restaurant News.
Natural Health.
Natural History.
Network Briefing.
Network Computing (Manhasset).
Network V A R.
Networks Update.
New England Economic Review.
New Jersey Industry Environmental Alert.
The New Leader.
New Literary History.
New Materials - Japan.
New Media Markets.
New Mexico Business Journal.
New Orleans Magazine.
New Perspectives Quarterly.
New Product News.
The New Republic.
New Scientist.
New Statesman.
New Steel.
New Technology Week.
New York Magazine.
News Photographer.
NewsInc.
Nieman Reports.
Nineteenth-Century Literature (Berkeley).
19th-Century Music.
Nitrogen.
Non-Foods Merchandising.
Nonwovens Industry.
The North American Review.
North Sea Letter.
North Sea Rig Forecast.
The Northern Miner.
NotiSur.
Nuclear Waste News.
Nursing Homes.
Nutrition Action Healthletter.
Nutrition Forum.
Nutrition Health Review.
Nutrition Research Newsletter.
Nutrition Today.
O E C D Economic Outlook.
O E C D Economic Studies.
O E C D Economic Surveys: Austria.
O E C D Economic Surveys: Canada.
O E C D Economic Surveys: Denmark.
O E C D Economic Surveys: Iceland.
O E C D Economic Surveys: Spain.
O E C D Economic Surveys: United States.
O E C D Observer.
Occupational Hazards.
Occupational Health & Safety Letter.
Occupational Outlook Quarterly.
Oceania.
Oceanus.
Octane Week.
Off Road.
Offshore (Tulsa).
The Ohio C P A Journal.
Oil & Gas Interests Newsletter.
Oil & Gas Journal.
Oil Market Trends.
Oil Spill Intelligence Report.
Omni.
Online (Wilton).
Online Libraries and Microcomputers.
Online Newsletter.
Online Product News.
Opera News.
Operations in Oil Diplomacy.
Ophthalmology Times.

Optical Materials and Engineering News.
Optical Memory News.
Optimum.
Orbis.
Oregon Business Magazine.
Organic Gardening.
Organization Studies.
Organizational Dynamics.
Orlando Business Journal.
Ostomy Quarterly.
The Other Side (Philadelphia).
Outdoor Life.
Outlook (Redwood City).
Oxford Bulletin of Economics and Statistics.
Oxford Economic Papers.
Oxy-Fuel News.
P C Business Products.
P C - Computing.
P C Magazine (U.K.).
P C S Week.
P C User.
P C Week.
P C World.
P S: Political Science & Politics.
P T N.
Pacific Affairs.
Pacific Historical Review.
Packaging Digest.
Packaging Technology and Engineering.
Packaging Week.
Paint and Ink International.
Palaestra.
Paper & Pulp Europe.
Paper, Film and Foil Converter.
Paperboard Packaging.
Papers on Language and Literature.
Parabola.
Paraplegia News.
Parents.
Parks and Recreation.
Parliamentary Affairs.
Party & Paper Retailer.
Patient Care.
Pediatrics for Parents.
Pensions & Investments.
People Weekly.
People's Medical Society Newsletter.
Performing Arts and Entertainment in Canada.
Performing Arts Journal.
Periscope (Great Neck).
Personal Computer Markets.
Personnel Psychology.
Personnel Review.
Perspectives of New Music.
Pest Control.
Pesticide & Toxic Chemical News.
Pet Product News.
Petersen's Photographic.
Petroleum Economist.
Petroleum Independent.
Pharma Marketletter.
Pharmaceutical Executive.
Pharmaceutical Manufacturing Review.
Phi Delta Kappan.
Philadelphia Business Journal.
Philological Quarterly.
Philosophy East and West.
Photonics Spectra.
The Physician and Sportsmedicine.
Physician Executive.
Physician Manager.
Physiological Reviews.
Pipeline & Gas Journal.
Pipeline Industry (Tulsa).
Pit & Quarry.
Pittsburgh Business Times - Journal.
Plant Engineering.
Plants, Sites & Parks.
Plastics and Rubber Asia.
Plastics Engineering.
Plastics News.
Plastics Technology.
Plastics World.
Playboy.
Playthings.
Ploughshares.
Poetry (Chicago).
Policy Review.
Policy Studies Journal.
Political Risk Letter.
Polymer Engineering and Science.
Popular Mechanics.
Popular Photography.
Popular Science.
Population and Development Review.
Postgraduate Medicine.
Potentials in Marketing.
Power Engineering.
Power in Asia.
Power in Europe.
The Practical Accountant.
Precision Toolmaker.
Premiere (New York).
Prepared Foods.
Prepress Commentary.
Prevention.
Print.
Printing Impressions.
Printing News - East.
The Prison Journal.
Private Placement Reporter.
Privatisation International.
Pro Sound News Europe.
Process Engineering.
Product Alert.
Productivity Software.
Professional Builder.
Progressive (Madison).
Progressive Grocer.
Promo.
The Psychological Record.
Psychology Today.
Public Administration.
Public Administration Review.
Public Broadcasting Report.
Public Finance Quarterly.
Public Health Reports.
Public Interest.
Public Management.
The Public Manager.
Public Personnel Management.
Public Relations News.
Public Relations Quarterly.
Public Relations Review.
Public Roads.
Public Utilities Fortnightly.
Public Welfare.
Public Works.
Publishers Weekly.
Publishing Technology Review.
Publius.
Puget Sound Business Journal.
Pulp and Paper.
Pulp & Paper Canada.
Pulp & Paper International.
Purchasing (Newton).
Quarterly Journal of Business and Economics.
Quarterly Journal of Economics.
The Quarterly Review of Economics and Finance.
Quick Frozen Foods International.
Quill (Greencastle).
R & D Management.
R B O C Update.
R N.
R Q.
R V Business.
Railway Age.
Rapid Prototyping Report.
Re-Drawing the Islamic Map.
Real Estate Economics.
Real Estate Today.
Real Estate Weekly.
Reason.
Records Management Quarterly.
Redbook.
Regional Studies.
Regulatory Compliance Watch.
Release 1.0.
Religious Studies.
Renaissance Quarterly.
Report on A T & T.
Report on Defense Plant Waste.
Report on I B M.
Report on Microsoft.
Research Alert (New York).
Research & Development.
Research in African Literatures.
Research Quarterly for Exercise and Sport.
Resource (St. Joseph).
Response T V.
Restaurant Business.
Restaurant Hospitality.
Restaurants and Institutions.
Retail Store Image.
Review of Black Political Economy.
Review of Business.
The Review of Contemporary Fiction.
Review of English Studies.
Review of Financial Economics.
The Review of Metaphysics.
Review of Social Economy.
Reviews in American History.
Risk Management.
Road & Track.
Romance Philology.
Romanic Review.
Rubber & Plastics News.
Rubber & Plastics News II.
Rubber Trends.
Rubber World.
Runner's World.
Russia.
S M T Trends.
S T N.
Sacramento Business Journal.
St. Louis Journalism Review.
Sales & Marketing Management.
Salmagundi.
San Antonio Business Journal.
San Diego Business Journal.
San Francisco Business Times.
Sarasota Magazine.
Saskatchewan Business.
Satellite Communications.
Satellite News.
Satellite Week.
Saturday Evening Post.
Saturday Night.
Scandinavian Studies (Provo).
Scholastic Update.
School Arts.
School Planning and Management.
Science.
Science News.
Science World.
The Sciences.
Scientific American.
Screen Digest.
Screen Finance.
Security Management.
Semiconductor Industry & Business Survey Newsletter.
Sensor Business Digest.
Seventeen.
Sex Roles.
Seybold Report on Desktop Publishing.
Seybold Report on Publishing Systems.
Shoot.
Shooting Industry.
Shopper Report.
Shopping Center World.
Sierra.
Situation & Outlook Report. Agricultural Exports.
Situation & Outlook Report. Fruit & Tree Nuts.
Situation & Outlook Report. Sugar & Sweetener.
Situation & Outlook Report. Tobacco.
Situation & Outlook Report. Vegetables & Specialties.
Skeptical Inquirer.
Skiing.
Skin Diver Magazine.
Sky & Telescope.
Sludge Newsletter.
Smithsonian.
Soap, Cosmetics, Chemical Specialties.
Soap, Perfumery & Cosmetics.
Social Forces.
Social Justice.
Social Policy.
Social Problems.
Social Research.
The Social Science Journal.
Social Security Bulletin.
The Social Studies.
Social Work.
Society.
Society of Research Administrators. Journal.
Sociological Perspectives.
Sociology.
Sociology of Religion.
Soft.letter.
Software Futures.
Software Industry Report.
Software Magazine.
Solid State Technology.
Solid Waste Report.
SourceMex.
South African Food & Beverage Manufacturing Review.
South Dakota Business Review.
South Florida Business Journal.
Southern California Business.
Southern Economic Journal.
The Southern Review.
Southwest Journal of Business and Economics.
Southwest Review.
Space Business News.
Special Delivery.
Speciality Chemicals.
Spectrum (Lexington).
Sport.
Sporting Goods Business.
The Sporting News.
Sports Afield.

Sports Illustrated.
SportStyle.
Stamps.
State Legislatures.
State Telephone Regulation Report.
Stereo Review.
Stores.
Strategic Balance in the Middle East.
Strategy & Leadership.
Studies in American Fiction.
Studies in English Literature 1500-1900.
Studies in Family Planning.
Studies in Short Fiction.
Studies in the Novel.
Style (DeKalb).
Substance Abuse Report.
Success Magazine.
Successful Farming.
Sulphur.
Sunset.
Superconductor Week.
Supermarket Business.
Supermarket News.
Survey of Current Business.
Sussex Past and Present.
The Swedish Economy.
Swiss Business.
Symposium.
Systems & Network Management Report.
T A J A.
T C I.
T D R.
T H E Journal.
T R Wireless News.
Tampa Bay Business Journal.
Tape - Disc Business.
Target Marketing.
The Tax Adviser.
The Tax Executive.
Tea and Coffee Trade Journal.
Teaching Children Mathematics.
Technical Communication.
Technology Alert.
Technology and Learning.
Technology Transfer Week.
Teen.
Telco Business Report.
Telco Competition Report.
Tele-Service News.
Telecom Markets.
Telecommunications (North American Edition).
Telecommunications Reports.
Telecommunications Reports International.
Telecommuting Review.
Teleconnect.
Telemarketing.
Telephone I P News.
Telephony.
Television Digest with Consumer Electronics.
Texas Business Review.
Textile World.
Theatre Journal (Baltimore).
Theatre Research International.
Theological Studies.
Time.
Tire Business.
Today's Homeowner.
Tooling & Production.
Total Health.
Tour & Travel News - T T G North America.
Town and Country.
Traffic World.
Trailer Boats.
Trailer Life.
Training.
Training & Development.
Trains.
Transpacific.
Transportation & Distribution.
Transportation Journal.
Travel Agent.
Travel Holiday.
Travel Trade Gazette Europa.
Travel Trade Gazette U K & Ireland.
Travel Weekly.
Treasury Manager's Report.
Trial.
TriQuarterly.
Trusts and Estates (Atlanta).
Tuberculosis & Airborne Disease Weekly.
Tufts University Health and Nutrition Letter.
Twentieth Century Literature.
U K Venture Capital Journal.
U N Chronicle.
U S A Today.
U S Banker.
U S Catholic.
U S News & World Report.
U S Oil Week.
U S Rail News.
Underground Construction.
U.S. Centers for Disease Control. Morbidity and Mortality Weekly Report.
U.S. Department of Agriculture. Situation & Outlook Report. Agriculture and Trade: Former U S S R.
U.S. Department of State Dispatch.
U.S. Office of the Federal Register. Weekly Compilation of Presidential Documents.
Units.
University of California at Berkeley Wellness Letter.
UNIX News.
UNIX Review.
UNIX Update.
Urban Studies.
Urban Transport News.
Urethanes Technology.
Urology Times.
Utility Reporter - Fuels Energy & Power.
V A R Business.
Vaccine Weekly.
Vegetarian Times.
Venture Capital Journal.
Vibrant Life.
Victorian Studies.
Video Magazine.
Video Review.
Video Store.
Video Technology News.
Video Week.
Vital Speeches of the Day.
Voice Technology & Services News.
W I N News.
Wall Street & Technology.
Wall Street Transcript.
Ward's Auto World.
Warning Letter Bulletin.
The Washington Monthly.
Washington Quarterly.
Waste Treatment Technology News.
Water Technology News.
Weatherwise.
Weight Watchers Magazine.
Welding Review International.
West European Politics.
Western Journal of Medicine.
Wilson Bulletin.
Wilson Quarterly.
Windows Developer's Journal.
Windows Sources.
Wireless Data News.
Woman's Day.
Women and Language.
Women's Sports and Fitness.
Women's Studies (New York).
Women's Wear Daily.
Wood & Wood Products.
Wood Based Panels International.
Workbench.
Workforce.
Workgroup Computing Report.
Working Woman.
World Accounting Report.
World Affairs (Washington).
World Agricultural Production.
World Airline News.
World Airport Week.
World Cotton Situation.
World Economic Outlook.
World Health.
World Health Organization. Bulletin.
World Insurance Report.
World Literature Today.
World Oil.
World Policy Journal.
World Politics (Baltimore).
World Press Review.
World Tunnelling.
World Wastes.
World Watch.
Worldwide Biotech.
Worldwide Databases.
Worldwide Energy.
Worldwide Telecom.
Worldwide Videotex Update.
The Writer.
Writer's Digest.
Yachting.
Yale Law Journal.
Yellow Pages & Directory Report.
Youth Markets Alert.

INFORMATION INTELLIGENCE, INC.
P.O. Box 31098, Phoenix, AZ 85046. Tel: 602-996-2283
  Southwest Review.

JICST
c/o U S A C O Corp., Tsutsumi Bldg., 13-12 Shimbashi 1-chome, Minato-ku, Tokyo 105, Japan Shirobu-Shushuka, 5-2 Nagatacho 2-chome, Chiyoda-ku, Tokyo 100, Japan Tel: 813-581-6411 Telex: 02223604 J
  Brain and Nerve.
  Current Bibliography on Science and Technology: Chemistry and Chemical Engineering (Foreign).
  Current Bibliography on Science and Technology: Chemistry and Chemical Engineering (Japanese).
  Current Bibliography on Science and Technology: Civil Engineering and Architecture.
  Current Bibliography on Science and Technology: Earth Science, Mining and Metallurgy.
  Current Bibliography on Science and Technology: Electronics and Electrical Engineering.
  Current Bibliography on Science and Technology: Energy.
  Current Bibliography on Science and Technology: Environmental Pollution.
  Current Bibliography on Science and Technology: Life Sciences.
  Current Bibliography on Science and Technology: Management Science and Systems Engineering.
  Current Bibliography on Science and Technology: Mechanical Engineering.
  Current Bibliography on Science and Technology: Nuclear Engineering.
  Current Bibliography on Science and Technology: Pure and Applied Physics.
  Current Science and Technology Research in Japan.
  Excerpta Medica Abstract Journals.
  Excerpta Medica. Section 1: Anatomy, Anthropology, Embryology & Histology.
  Excerpta Medica. Section 2: Physiology.
  Excerpta Medica. Section 3: Endocrinology.
  Excerpta Medica. Section 4: Microbiology: Bacteriology, Mycology, Parasitology and Virology.
  Excerpta Medica. Section 5: General Pathology and Pathological Anatomy.
  Excerpta Medica. Section 6: Internal Medicine.
  Excerpta Medica. Section 7: Pediatrics and Pediatric Surgery.
  Excerpta Medica. Section 8: Neurology and Neurosurgery.
  Excerpta Medica. Section 9: Surgery.
  Excerpta Medica. Section 10: Obstetrics and Gynecology.
  Excerpta Medica. Section 11: Otorhinolaryngology.
  Excerpta Medica. Section 12: Ophthalmology.
  Excerpta Medica. Section 13: Dermatology and Venereology.
  Excerpta Medica. Section 14: Radiology.
  Excerpta Medica. Section 15: Chest Diseases, Thoracic Surgery and Tuberculosis.
  Excerpta Medica. Section 16: Cancer.
  Excerpta Medica. Section 17: Public Health, Social Medicine and Epidemiology.
  Excerpta Medica. Section 18: Cardiovascular Diseases and Cardiovascular Surgery.
  Excerpta Medica. Section 19: Rehabilitation and Physical Medicine.
  Excerpta Medica. Section 20: Gerontology and Geriatrics.
  Excerpta Medica. Section 21: Developmental Biology and Teratology.
  Excerpta Medica. Section 22: Human Genetics.
  Excerpta Medica. Section 23: Nuclear Medicine.
  Excerpta Medica. Section 24: Anesthesiology.
  Excerpta Medica. Section 25: Hematology.
  Excerpta Medica. Section 26: Immunology, Serology and Transplantation.
  Excerpta Medica. Section 27: Biophysics, Bio-Engineering and Medical Instrumentation.
  Excerpta Medica. Section 28: Urology and Nephrology.
  Excerpta Medica. Section 29: Clinical and Experimental Biochemistry.
  Excerpta Medica. Section 30: Clinical and Experimental Pharmacology.
  Excerpta Medica. Section 31: Arthritis and Rheumatism.
  Excerpta Medica. Section 32: Psychiatry.
  Excerpta Medica. Section 33: Orthopedic Surgery.
  Excerpta Medica. Section 35: Occupational Health and Industrial Medicine.

Excerpta Medica. Section 36: Health Policy, Economics and Management.
Excerpta Medica. Section 38: Adverse Reactions Titles.
Excerpta Medica. Section 40: Drug Dependence, Alcohol Abuse and Alcoholism.
Excerpta Medica. Section 46: Environmental Health and Pollution Control.
Excerpta Medica. Section 48: Gastroenterology.
Excerpta Medica. Section 49: Forensic Science Abstracts.
Excerpta Medica. Section 50: Epilepsy Abstracts.
Excerpta Medica. Section 52: Toxicology.
Government Reports Announcements & Index.
I to Cho.
Industrial Health.
Iwate Medical University School of Liberal Arts & Sciences. Annual Report. *(JOIS-III)*
J I C S T Online Information System.
Japan Society for Simulation Technology. Journal. *(JOIS)*
Japanese Journal of Clinical Oncology.
Japanese Journal of Ophthalmology.
Jibi Inkoka, Tokeibu Geka.
Kokyu to Junkan.
Neurological Surgery.
Nippon Medical School. Journal.
Rigaku Ryoho Janaru.
Rihabiriteshon Igaku.
Seicho.
Seishin Igaku.

KIWINET
P.O. Box 12-264, Wellington, New Zealand Tel: 64-4-474-3182
Fax: 64-4-474-3042.
A B I X: Australasian Business Intelligence.
Index New Zealand.
LINX Database.
National Business Review.

KNIGHT-RIDDER INFORMATION, INC.
2440 El Camino Real, Mountain View, CA 94040.
Tel: 415-254-7000
Fax: 415-254-8000.
A B A Banking Journal. *(File no.648)*
A B B Review.
A B E C O R Country Reports.
A B I - INFORM. *(File no.15)*
A C M Guide to Computing Literature.
A H F S Drug Information. *(File no.229)*
A S F A Aquaculture Abstracts. *(File no.44)*
A S F A Marine Biotechnology Abstracts. *(File nos.44 and 76)*
Abstracts in BioCommerce. *(file no.286)*
Abstracts in New Technologies and Engineering. *(File no.142)*
Academic Index. *(File no.88)*
Academy of Marketing Science. Journal.
Accounting and Tax Index. *(File no. 485)*
Adhesives Abstracts.
Administrative Science Quarterly.
Adweek (Los Angeles). *(File no.648)*
Adweek (New York). *(File no.648)*
Aerospace Daily. *(File nos.624,648)*
Aerospace Propulsion. *(ASP)*
Aftermarket Business.
Agricultural & Environmental Biotechnology Abstracts. *(File no. 76/Life Sciences Collection)*
Agricultural Engineering Abstracts.
Agricultural Supply Industry. *(File no.129)*
Agrindex. *(File no.203)*
Agroforestry Abstracts.
Agrow. *(File No.129)*
AIDS Weekly Plus. *(File no.636)*
Air Conditioning, Heating & Refrigeration News. *(File no.648)*
Air Fresheners and Insecticides: The International Market.
Air Safety Week.
Air Transport World.
Air - Water Pollution Report.
Airline Financial News.
Airports. *(File no.624/McGRAW-HILL PUBLICATIONS ONLINE)*
Alaska Business Monthly.
Alaska Journal of Commerce & Pacific Rim Reporter.
Alcoholism & Drug Abuse Weekly.
Alloys Index. *(File no.32/METADEX)*
Aluminium Industry Abstracts. *(File no.33)*
America at Work.
America: History and Life. Article Abstracts and Citations of Reviews and Dissertations Covering the United States and Canada. *(File no.38)*

American Banker. *(File no.625)*
American Banker Index.
American Banker's Washington Watch.
American Doctoral Dissertations. *(File no. 35)*
American Fitness. *(File no.149)*
American Heritage.
American Libraries.
American Library Directory. *(File no.460)*
American Men and Women of Science. *(File no.236)*
American Metal Market.
American Review of Public Administration.
American Statistics Index. *(File no.102)*
America's Network.
America's Network Directory.
Amusement Business.
Analgesics: The International Market.
Analytical Abstracts. *(File no.305)*
Animal Behavior Abstracts. *(File no.76/LIFE SCIENCES COLLECTION)*
Animal Breeding Abstracts.
Animal Disease Occurrence.
Animal Pharm. *(File No.129)*
Annual Survey of Manufactures.
Annual World Bank Conference on Development Economics.
Apicultural Abstracts.
Apparel Industry Magazine.
Appliance Manufacturer.
Applied Genetics News.
Applied Science & Technology Index.
Aquatic Sciences & Fisheries Abstracts. Part 1: Biological Sciences and Living Resources. *(File no.44)*
Aquatic Sciences & Fisheries Abstracts. Part 2: Ocean Technology, Policy and Non-living Resources. *(File no.44)*
Aquatic Sciences & Fisheries Abstracts. Part 3: Aquatic Pollution and Environmental Quality. *(File no.44)*
Architectural Publications Index. *(File no.179)*
Architectural Record. *(AR)*
Archives of Dermatology.
Archives of Family Medicine.
Archives of General Psychiatry.
Archives of Internal Medicine.
Archives of Neurology.
Archives of Ophthalmology.
Archives of Otolaryngology - Head & Neck Surgery.
Archives of Pediatrics & Adolescent Medicine.
Archives of Surgery.
Arizona Business Gazette.
Arkansas Business and Economic Review.
Art Index.
Artbibliographies Modern. *(File no.56)*
Arts & Humanities Citation Index. *(File no.439)*
Asbestos & Lead Abatement Report.
Asset Sales Report.
Atlanta Business Chronicle.
Atlantic.
Atlantic Economic Journal.
Audio: The International Market.
Audio Week.
Audiocassette & C D Finder. *(File no.46)*
Audiotex Update.
Australian Journal of Dairy Technology.
Automotive Industries.
Automotives: The International Market.
Autoparts Report.
Avery Index to Architectural Periodicals.
Aviation Daily. *(File no.624/McGRAW-HILL PUBLICATIONS ONLINE)*
Aviation Europe. *(AE)*
Aviation Week & Space Technology. *(File no.624/ McGRAW-HILL PUBLICATIONS ONLINE)*
The B B I Newsletter.
B C Business.
B H A. *(File no.191, Art Literature International)*
B L A S T.
B M T Abstracts. *(TRIS, File No. 63)*
B N A Policy and Practice Series. Fair Employment Practices.
B T Today.
Baby Care Products: The International Market.
Baby Foods: The International Market.
Bakery Production and Marketing.
Bakery Products: The International Market.
Baltimore Business Journal.
Bank Automation News.
Bank Mutual Fund Report.
Barclays Country Reports.
Barclays Economic Review.
Bath and Shower Products: The International Market.
Battery & E V Technology News.
Beer: The International Market.

Beilsteins Handbuch der Organischen Chemie. Supplement. *(File no.390)*
Best's Review. Life - Health Insurance Edition.
Best's Review. Property - Casualty Insurance Edition.
Beverage World (English Edition).
Bibliography and Index of Geology.
Bibliography of Bioethics.
Bibliography of Economic Geology. *(File no.58)*
Billboard (New York).
BioCommerce Financial Abstracts. *(File no.286)*
Biocontrol News and Information.
Biography and Genealogy Master Index. *(File nos.287,288)*
Biography Index.
Biological Abstracts. *(File nos.5 & 55)*
Biological Abstracts - R R M. *(File nos.5 & 55)*
Biological & Agricultural Index.
Biomedical Market Newsletter.
Biotech Business.
Biotechnology Abstracts. *(File no.357)*
BioVenture View. *(File no.636)*
Black Newspaper Index.
Blood Weekly.
Boating.
The Bond Buyer. *(File no.626)*
Book Publishing Report.
Book Review Index. *(File no.137)*
Book World.
Books in Print. *(File no.470)*
Books in Print Supplement. *(File no.470)*
Books Out-of-Print. *(File no.470)*
Books: The International Market.
Boston Business Journal.
The Boston Globe Index. *(File no. 484)*
The Bowker Annual Library and Book Trade Almanac.
Brands and Their Companies.
Brandweek. *(File no.648)*
Breakfast Cereals: The International Market.
British Education Index. *(File no.121)*
Broadcasting & Cable.
Building Supply Business.
Buildings.
Bulletin of Entomological Research.
Business America.
Business and Commercial Aviation.
Business Asia.
Business China.
Business Dateline.
Business Digest of Delaware Valley.
Business Eastern Europe.
Business Europe.
Business First (Buffalo).
Business History Review.
Business Index. *(File no.148)*
Business Journal (Phoenix).
Business Latin America.
Business North Carolina.
Business Periodicals Index.
Business Quarterly.
Business Travel News.
Business Week. *(File no.624/McGRAW-HILL PUBLICATIONS ONLINE)*
Buyouts Newsletter.
Byte. *(File no.624/McGRAW-HILL PUBLICATIONS ONLINE)*
C D Computing News.
C D - R O M Databases.
C D - R O M World.
C F O Alert (Weekly).
C S A Neurosciences Abstracts. *(File no.76/LIFE SCIENCES COLLECTION)*
CAB International. Bureau of Nutrition. Annotated Bibliographies.
Calcium and Calcified Tissue Abstracts. *(File no.76/LIFE SCIENCES COLLECTION)*
California Business.
Canadian Index. *(File no.262)*
Canadian Speeches: Issues of the Day.
Cancer Weekly Plus.
Candy Industry.
Canned Foods: The International Market.
Capital District Business Review.
Car Aftermarket: The International Market.
Car and Driver.
Car Rental: The International Market.
Card News.
Central New York Business Journal.
Ceramic Abstracts. *(File no.335)*
Chem-Facts: Ethylene & Propylene.
Chem-Facts: European Review.
Chem-Facts: France.
Chem-Facts: Germany.
Chem-Facts: P V C.
Chem-Facts: Polypropylene.
Chem-Facts: Styrenics.
Chem-Facts: United Kingdom.

Chemical Engineering. *(File no.624/McGRAW-HILL PUBLICATIONS ONLINE)*
Chemical Hazards in Industry. *(File no.317)*
Chemical Marketing Reporter.
Chemical Monitor.
Chemical Plant File.
Chemoreception Abstracts. *(File no.76/LIFE SCIENCES COLLECTION)*
Children Today.
Children's Books in Print. *(File no.470)*
Chilled and Delicatessen Foods: The International Market.
Chilton's Automotive Marketing.
Chilton's Distribution.
Chilton's Food Engineering.
Chilton's Food Engineering International.
Chilton's Hardware Age.
Chilton's Jewelers' Circular-Keystone.
Chilton's Motor Age.
China Business Review.
China Today (British Edition).
Ching Feng.
Christian Science Monitor.
Christian Science Monitor Index.
Cleaning Appliances: The International Market.
Clinica. *(File No. 129)*
Coal Tech International. *(File no.624/McGRAW-HILL PUBLICATIONS ONLINE)*
Coal U.K.
Coal Week. *(File no.624/McGRAW-HILL PUBLICATIONS ONLINE)*
Coal Week International. *(File no.624/McGRAW-HILL PUBLICATIONS ONLINE)*
Colorado Business.
Columbus Business Journal.
Commerce Business Daily. *(File nos.194 & 195)*
Communication World.
Communications Daily.
Communications News.
CommunicationsWeek International.
Commuter - Regional Airline News.
Companies and Their Brands.
Compensation and Benefits Review.
The Composites and Adhesives Newsletter.
Composites Industry Monthly.
Computer-Aided Engineering (Cleveland).
Computer & Control Abstracts.
Computer Book Review.
Computer Database. *(File no.275)*
Computer Design.
Computer Fraud & Security.
Computer Graphics World.
Computer Protocols.
Computerworld. *(File no.674)*
Computing Reviews.
Confectionery: The International Market.
Conference Papers Annual Index. *(File no. 77)*
Conference Papers Index. *(File no.77)*
Construction Review.
Consumer Catering: The International Market.
Consumer Reports. *(File no.646)*
Consumer Reports on Health. *(File no.646)*
Consumer Reports Travel Letter. *(File no.646)*
Corporate Detroit Magazine.
Corporate E F T Report.
Corporate Report Minnesota.
Cosmetic Insider's Report.
Cotton and Tropical Fibres.
Cough and Cold Remedies: The International Market.
Country Forecast. Algeria.
Country Forecast. Argentina.
Country Forecast. Asia - Pacific.
Country Forecast. Australia.
Country Forecast. Austria.
Country Forecast. Belgium.
Country Forecast. Brazil.
Country Forecast. Bulgaria.
Country Forecast. Canada.
Country Forecast. Chile.
Country Forecast. China.
Country Forecast. Colombia.
Country Forecast. Czech Republic.
Country Forecast. Denmark.
Country Forecast. Eastern Europe and the Former Soviet Union.
Country Forecast. Ecuador.
Country Forecast. Egypt.
Country Forecast. Europe.
Country Forecast. Finland.
Country Forecast. France.
Country Forecast. Germany.
Country Forecast. Global Outlook.
Country Forecast. Greece.
Country Forecast. Hong Kong.
Country Forecast. Hungary.
Country Forecast. India.
Country Forecast. Indonesia.

Country Forecast. Iran.
Country Forecast. Iraq.
Country Forecast. Ireland.
Country Forecast. Israel.
Country Forecast. Italy.
Country Forecast. Japan.
Country Forecast. Latin America.
Country Forecast. Malaysia.
Country Forecast. Mexico.
Country Forecast. Middle East and North Africa.
Country Forecast. Netherlands.
Country Forecast. New Zealand.
Country Forecast. Nigeria.
Country Forecast. Norway.
Country Forecast. Pakistan.
Country Forecast. Peru.
Country Forecast. Philippines.
Country Forecast. Poland.
Country Forecast. Portugal.
Country Forecast. Romania.
Country Forecast. Russia.
Country Forecast. Saudi Arabia.
Country Forecast. Singapore.
Country Forecast. Slovakia.
Country Forecast. South Africa.
Country Forecast. South Korea.
Country Forecast. Spain.
Country Forecast. Sri Lanka.
Country Forecast. Sub-Saharan Africa.
Country Forecast. Sweden.
Country Forecast. Switzerland.
Country Forecast. Taiwan.
Country Forecast. Thailand.
Country Forecast. Turkey.
Country Forecast. United Kingdom.
Country Forecast. United States of America.
Country Forecast. Venezuela.
Country Forecast. Vietnam.
Country Forecasts (New York).
Country Forecasts (Syracuse).
Country Profile. Albania.
Country Profile. Algeria.
Country Profile. Angola.
Country Profile. Argentina.
Country Profile. Australia.
Country Profile. Austria.
Country Profile. Azerbaijan.
Country Profile. Bahrain, Qatar.
Country Profile. Baltic Republics: Lithuania, Latvia, Estonia.
Country Profile. Bangladesh.
Country Profile. Belgium, Luxembourg.
Country Profile. Belize, Bahamas, Bermuda.
Country Profile. Bolivia.
Country Profile. Bosnia-Hercegovina, Croatia.
Country Profile. Botswana, Lesotho.
Country Profile. Brazil.
Country Profile. Bulgaria.
Country Profile. Cambodia, Laos.
Country Profile. Cameroon, Central African Republic, Chad.
Country Profile. Canada.
Country Profile. Chile.
Country Profile. China, Mongolia.
Country Profile. Colombia.
Country Profile. Congo.
Country Profile. Costa Rica.
Country Profile. Cote d'Ivoire, Mali.
Country Profile. Cuba.
Country Profile. Cyprus, Malta.
Country Profile. Czech Republic.
Country Profile. Denmark, Iceland.
Country Profile. Dominican Republic, Haiti, Puerto Rico.
Country Profile. Ecuador.
Country Profile. Egypt.
Country Profile. Ethiopia, Eritrea, Somalia, Djibouti.
Country Profile. Finland.
Country Profile. France.
Country Profile. Gabon, Equatorial Guinea.
Country Profile. Georgia, Armenia.
Country Profile. Germany.
Country Profile. Ghana.
Country Profile. Greece.
Country Profile. Guatemala, El Salvador.
Country Profile. Guinea, Sierra Leone, Liberia.
Country Profile. Guyana, Windward and Leeward Islands.
Country Profile. Hong Kong, Macau.
Country Profile. Hungary.
Country Profile. India, Nepal.
Country Profile. Indonesia.
Country Profile. Iran.
Country Profile. Iraq.
Country Profile. Ireland.
Country Profile. Israel, the Occupied Territories.
Country Profile. Italy.

Country Profile. Jamaica, Barbados.
Country Profile. Japan.
Country Profile. Jordan.
Country Profile. Kazakhstan.
Country Profile. Kenya.
Country Profile. Kuwait.
Country Profile. Lebanon.
Country Profile. Libya.
Country Profile. Macedonia, Serbia-Montenegro.
Country Profile. Madagascar.
Country Profile. Malawi.
Country Profile. Malaysia, Brunei.
Country Profile. Mauritius, Seychelles.
Country Profile. Mexico.
Country Profile. Morocco.
Country Profile. Mozambique.
Country Profile. Myanmar.
Country Profile. Namibia, Swaziland.
Country Profile. Netherlands.
Country Profile. New Zealand.
Country Profile. Nicaragua, Honduras.
Country Profile. Niger, Burkina Faso.
Country Profile. Nigeria.
Country Profile. Norway.
Country Profile. Oman.
Country Profile. Pacific Islands: Fiji, Solomon Islands, Western Samoa, Vanuatu, Tonga and New Caledonia.
Country Profile. Pakistan, Afghanistan.
Country Profile. Panama.
Country Profile. Papua New Guinea.
Country Profile. Peru.
Country Profile. Philippines.
Country Profile. Poland.
Country Profile. Portugal.
Country Profile. Romania.
Country Profile. Russia.
Country Profile. Rwanda, Burundi.
Country Profile. Sao Tome and Principe, Guinea-Bissau, Cape Verde.
Country Profile. Saudi Arabia.
Country Profile. Senegal.
Country Profile. Singapore.
Country Profile. Slovakia.
Country Profile. Slovenia.
Country Profile. South Africa.
Country Profile. South Korea, North Korea.
Country Profile. Spain.
Country Profile. Sri Lanka.
Country Profile. Sudan.
Country Profile. Sweden.
Country Profile. Switzerland.
Country Profile. Syria.
Country Profile. Taiwan.
Country Profile. Tanzania, Comoros.
Country Profile. Thailand.
Country Profile. The Gambia, Mauritania.
Country Profile. Togo, Benin.
Country Profile. Trinidad and Tobago, Suriname, Netherlands Antilles, Aruba.
Country Profile. Tunisia.
Country Profile. Turkey.
Country Profile. Uganda.
Country Profile. Ukraine.
Country Profile. United Arab Emirates.
Country Profile. United Kingdom.
Country Profile. United States of America.
Country Profile. Uruguay, Paraguay.
Country Profile. Venezuela.
Country Profile. Yemen.
Country Profile. Zaire.
Country Profile. Zambia.
Country Profile. Zimbabwe.
Country Profiles.
Country Report. Albania.
Country Report. Algeria.
Country Report. Angola.
Country Report. Argentina.
Country Report. Australia.
Country Report. Austria.
Country Report. Bahrain, Qatar.
Country Report. Baltic Republics: Lithuania, Latvia, Estonia.
Country Report. Bangladesh.
Country Report. Belgium, Luxembourg.
Country Report. Bolivia.
Country Report. Bosnia-Hercegovina, Croatia and Slovenia.
Country Report. Brazil.
Country Report. Bulgaria.
Country Report. Cambodia, Laos.
Country Report. Cameroon, C.A.R., Chad.
Country Report. Canada.
Country Report. Chile.
Country Report. China, Mongolia.
Country Report. Colombia.
Country Report. Congo, Sao Tome and Principe, Guinea-Bissau, Cape Verde.

Country Report. Costa Rica.
Country Report. Cote d'Ivoire, Mali.
Country Report. Cuba, Dominican Republic, Haiti, Puerto Rico.
Country Report. Cyprus, Malta.
Country Report. Czech Republic.
Country Report. Denmark, Iceland.
Country Report. Ecuador.
Country Report. Egypt.
Country Report. Ethiopia, Eritrea, Somalia, Djibouti.
Country Report. Finland.
Country Report. France.
Country Report. Gabon, Equatorial Guinea.
Country Report. Germany.
Country Report. Ghana.
Country Report. Greece.
Country Report. Guatemala, El Salvador.
Country Report. Guinea, Sierra Leone, Liberia.
Country Report. Hong Kong, Macau.
Country Report. Hungary.
Country Report. India, Nepal.
Country Report. Indonesia.
Country Report. Iran.
Country Report. Iraq.
Country Report. Ireland.
Country Report. Israel, the Occupied Territories.
Country Report. Italy.
Country Report. Jamaica, Belize, Bahamas, Bermuda, Barbados.
Country Report. Japan.
Country Report. Jordan.
Country Report. Kazakhstan.
Country Report. Kenya.
Country Report. Kuwait.
Country Report. Lebanon.
Country Report. Libya.
Country Report. Malaysia, Brunei.
Country Report. Mauritius, Madagascar, Seychelles.
Country Report. Mexico.
Country Report. Morocco.
Country Report. Mozambique, Malawi.
Country Report. Netherlands.
Country Report. New Zealand.
Country Report. Nicaragua, Honduras.
Country Report. Nigeria.
Country Report. Norway.
Country Report. Oman, Yemen.
Country Report. Pacific Islands: Papua New Guinea, Fiji, Solomon Islands, Western Samoa, Vanuatu, Tonga.
Country Report. Pakistan, Afghanistan.
Country Report. Panama.
Country Report. Peru.
Country Report. Philippines.
Country Report. Poland.
Country Report. Portugal.
Country Report. Romania.
Country Report. Russia.
Country Report. Saudi Arabia.
Country Report. Senegal, The Gambia, Mauritania.
Country Report. Singapore.
Country Report. Slovakia.
Country Report. South Africa.
Country Report. South Korea, North Korea.
Country Report. Spain.
Country Report. Sri Lanka.
Country Report. Sudan.
Country Report. Sweden.
Country Report. Switzerland.
Country Report. Syria.
Country Report. Taiwan.
Country Report. Tanzania, Comoros.
Country Report. Thailand.
Country Report. Togo, Benin.
Country Report. Trinidad & Tobago, Guyana, Windward & Leeward Islands, Suriname, Netherlands Antilles, Aruba.
Country Report. Tunisia.
Country Report. Turkey.
Country Report. Uganda, Rwanda, Burundi.
Country Report. Ukraine.
Country Report. United Arab Emirates.
Country Report. United Kingdom.
Country Report. United States of America.
Country Report. Uruguay, Paraguay.
Country Report. Venezuela.
Country Report. Zambia, Zaire.
Country Report. Zimbabwe.
Country Reports.
Courier (Paris).
The Cowles - SIMBA Report on Directory Publishing. (File no.636)
Crain's Chicago Business.
Crain's Cleveland Business.
Crain's Detroit Business.
Crain's New York Business.
Credit and Charge Cards: The International Market.
Criminal Justice Periodical Index. (File no. 171)
Crop Physiology Abstracts.
Current Biotechnology. (File no.358)
Current Business Reports: Monthly Retail Trade: Sales and Inventories.
Current Contents: Agriculture, Biology & Environmental Sciences. (File no.440)
Current Contents: Arts & Humanities. (File no.440)
Current Contents: Clinical Medicine. (File no.440)
Current Contents: Engineering, Computing & Technology. (File no.440)
Current Contents: Life Sciences. (File no.440)
Current Contents: Physical, Chemical & Earth Sciences. (File no.440)
Current Contents: Social & Behavioral Sciences. (File no.440)
Current Governments Reports: City Employment.
Current Governments Reports: County Government Employment.
Current Governments Reports: Government Finances.
Current Governments Reports: Public Employment.
Current Index to Journals in Education. (File no.1/ERIC)
Current Index to Statistics.
Current Law Index.
Current Mathematical Publications.
Current Population Reports: Series P-70. Household Economic Studies.
Current Research in Library & Information Science. (File no.61)
The Cyprus Review.
C2C Abstracts: Japan - Analytical Chemistry. (File no.582)
C2C Abstracts: Japan - Ceramics. (File no.582)
C2C Abstracts: Japan - Chemical Engineering. (File no.582)
C2C Abstracts: Japan - Crystallography. (File no.582)
C2C Abstracts: Japan - Hydrocarbons. (File no.582)
C2C Abstracts: Japan - Inorganic Chemistry. (File no.582)
C2C Abstracts: Japan - Materials Science. (File no.582)
C2C Abstracts: Japan - Metals. (File no.582)
C2C Abstracts: Japan - Organic Chemistry. (File no.582)
C2C Abstracts: Japan - Physical Chemistry. (File no.582)
C2C Abstracts: Japan - Plastics. (File no.582)
C2C Abstracts: Japan - Polymer Chemistry. (File no.582)
C2C Abstracts: Japan - Surface Chemistry. (File no.582)
C2C Abstracts: Japan - Textiles. (File no.582)
C2C Currents: Japan - Chemistry. (File no.582)
C2C Currents: Japan - Computers. (File no.582)
C2C Currents: Japan - Electronics. (File no.582)
C2C Currents: Japan - Materials. (File no.582)
D I Y: The International Market.
D N R.
Dairy Foods.
Dairy Products: The International Market.
Dairy Science Abstracts.
Data Communications. (File no.624/McGRAW-HILL PUBLICATIONS ONLINE)
Data Storage Report.
Datamation.
Datapro Directory of Microcomputer Software.
Datapro Directory of Software.
Dealerscope Consumer Electronics Marketplace.
Defense Daily.
Defense Electronics.
Denver Post Index.
Deodorants: The International Market.
Dermatology Times.
Detroit News Index.
Development Business.
Devices & Diagnostics Letter.
Digestive Remedies: The International Market.
Directories in Print.
Directory of Biomedical and Health Care Grants.
Directory of Corporate Affiliations. (File no.513, Corporate Affiliations)
Directory of Grants in the Humanities.
Directory of Research Grants.
Discount Store News.
Discover (Burbank).
Disposable Paper Products: The International Market.
Dissertation Abstracts International. Section A: Humanities and Social Sciences. (File no.35)
Dissertation Abstracts International. Section B: Physical Sciences and Engineering. (File no.35)
Dissertation Abstracts International. Section C: Worldwide. (File no.35)
Dissertation Abstracts on Disc.
Drug and Cosmetic Industry.
Drug Data Report.
Drug News & Perspectives.
Dutchess County Historical Society. Yearbook.
E C Energy Monthly.
E D N Magazine.
E F T Report.
E N R. (File no.624/McGRAW-HILL PUBLICATIONS ONLINE)
East European Energy Report.
EcoCentral.
Ecological Abstracts. (File no.292)
Ecology Abstracts. (File no.76/LIFE SCIENCES COLLECTION)
Economic Indicators (Washington).
Economic Inquiry.
Educational Marketer.
Electric Utility Week. (File no.624/McGRAW-HILL PUBLICATIONS ONLINE)
Electric Utility Week's Demand-Side Report. (DSR)
Electrical & Electronics Abstracts.
Electrical World. (EW)
Electronic Business Today.
Electronic Design.
Electronic Information Report.
Electronic Learning.
Electronic News.
Emerging & Special Situations. (ESS)
Employee Relations Law Journal.
Encyclopedia of Associations. (File no.114)
Energy Conservation News.
Energy Daily.
Energy Data Base.
Energy Economist.
Energy Research Abstracts.
Energy User News.
Engineered Materials Abstracts. (File no.293)
Engineering Index Annual. (File no.8)
Engineering Index Monthly. (File no.8)
Entertainment Software: The International Market.
Entomology Abstracts. (File no.76/LIFE SCIENCES COLLECTION)
Environment Abstracts.
Environment Abstracts Annual. (File no.40)
Environment Week.
Environmental Periodicals Bibliography. (File no.68)
Euromoney.
European Energy Report.
Eventline.
Excerpta Medica Abstract Journals.
Excerpta Medica. Section 1: Anatomy, Anthropology, Embryology & Histology.
Excerpta Medica. Section 2: Physiology.
Excerpta Medica. Section 3: Endocrinology.
Excerpta Medica. Section 4: Microbiology: Bacteriology, Mycology, Parasitology and Virology.
Excerpta Medica. Section 5: General Pathology and Pathological Anatomy.
Excerpta Medica. Section 6: Internal Medicine.
Excerpta Medica. Section 7: Pediatrics and Pediatric Surgery.
Excerpta Medica. Section 8: Neurology and Neurosurgery.
Excerpta Medica. Section 9: Surgery.
Excerpta Medica. Section 10: Obstetrics and Gynecology.
Excerpta Medica. Section 11: Otorhinolaryngology.
Excerpta Medica. Section 12: Ophthalmology.
Excerpta Medica. Section 13: Dermatology and Venereology.
Excerpta Medica. Section 14: Radiology.
Excerpta Medica. Section 15: Chest Diseases, Thoracic Surgery and Tuberculosis.
Excerpta Medica. Section 16: Cancer.
Excerpta Medica. Section 17: Public Health, Social Medicine and Epidemiology.
Excerpta Medica. Section 18: Cardiovascular Diseases and Cardiovascular Surgery.
Excerpta Medica. Section 19: Rehabilitation and Physical Medicine.
Excerpta Medica. Section 20: Gerontology and Geriatrics.
Excerpta Medica. Section 21: Developmental Biology and Teratology.
Excerpta Medica. Section 22: Human Genetics.
Excerpta Medica. Section 23: Nuclear Medicine.
Excerpta Medica. Section 24: Anesthesiology.
Excerpta Medica. Section 25: Hematology.

VENDOR LISTING/SERIALS ONLINE

Excerpta Medica. Section 26: Immunology, Serology and Transplantation.
Excerpta Medica. Section 27: Biophysics, Bio-Engineering and Medical Instrumentation.
Excerpta Medica. Section 28: Urology and Nephrology.
Excerpta Medica. Section 29: Clinical and Experimental Biochemistry.
Excerpta Medica. Section 30: Clinical and Experimental Pharmacology.
Excerpta Medica. Section 31: Arthritis and Rheumatism.
Excerpta Medica. Section 32: Psychiatry.
Excerpta Medica. Section 33: Orthopedic Surgery.
Excerpta Medica. Section 35: Occupational Health and Industrial Medicine.
Excerpta Medica. Section 36: Health Policy, Economics and Management.
Excerpta Medica. Section 38: Adverse Reactions Titles.
Excerpta Medica. Section 40: Drug Dependence, Alcohol Abuse and Alcoholism.
Excerpta Medica. Section 46: Environmental Health and Pollution Control.
Excerpta Medica. Section 48: Gastroenterology.
Excerpta Medica. Section 49: Forensic Science Abstracts.
Excerpta Medica. Section 50: Epilepsy Abstracts.
Excerpta Medica. Section 52: Toxicology.
Executive Report.
Eyewear: The International Market.
F C C Report.
F D A Consumer.
F D A Medical Bulletin.
Facts on File World News Digest with Index. *(File no.264)*
Family Relations.
Fast Food: The International Market.
Federal Register. *(File no.669)*
Federal Research in Progress Database. *(File nos.265,266)*
Federal Reserve Bank of New York. Economic Policy Review.
Federal Reserve Bulletin.
Federal Technology Report. *(TTR)*
Fiber Optics News.
Field Crop Abstracts.
Film & Video Finder. *(File no.46)*
Financial Executive.
Financial Technology Insight.
Financial Times World Tax Report.
Financial World.
Financing Operations. Africa.
Financing Operations. Argentina.
Financing Operations. Australia.
Financing Operations. Belgium.
Financing Operations. Brazil.
Financing Operations. Canada.
Financing Operations. Chile.
Financing Operations. Colombia.
Financing Operations. Costa Rica.
Financing Operations. Czech Republic.
Financing Operations. El Salvador.
Financing Operations. France.
Financing Operations. Germany.
Financing Operations. Greece.
Financing Operations. Guatemala.
Financing Operations. Honduras.
Financing Operations. Hong Kong.
Financing Operations. Hungary.
Financing Operations. India.
Financing Operations. Italy.
Financing Operations. Japan.
Financing Operations. Malaysia.
Financing Operations. Mexico.
Financing Operations. Netherlands.
Financing Operations. Nicaragua.
Financing Operations. Nigeria.
Financing Operations. Norway.
Financing Operations. Panama.
Financing Operations. Philippines.
Financing Operations. Poland.
Financing Operations. Russia.
Financing Operations. Saudi Arabia.
Financing Operations. Singapore.
Financing Operations. South Africa.
Financing Operations. South Korea.
Financing Operations. Spain.
Financing Operations. Sweden.
Financing Operations. Switzerland.
Financing Operations. Taiwan.
Financing Operations. Thailand.
Financing Operations. United Kingdom.
Financing Operations. United States of America.
Financing Operations. Venezuela.
Findex (Year). *(File no.196)*
Firmen der Neuen Bundeslaender.
Florida Trend.

Flower and Garden.
Flower & Garden Crafts Edition.
Fluid Abstracts: Civil Engineering. *(File no.96/FLUIDEX)*
Fluid Abstracts: Process Engineering. *(File no.96/FLUIDEX)*
Flying.
Folio (Stamford).
Food and Drug Letter.
Food Chemical News.
Food, Cosmetics and Drugs Packaging.
Food Retailers: The International Market.
Food Science and Technology Abstracts. *(File no.51)*
Foods Adlibra. *(File no.79)*
Foods Adlibra Beverage Edition. *(File no.79)*
Foods Adlibra Foodservice Edition. *(File no.79)*
Foods Adlibra Seafood Edition. *(File no.79)*
Foods Adlibra Snack & Confections Edition. *(File no.79)*
Footwear News.
Forbes.
Foreign Policy Bulletin.
Foreign Trade Reports. U.S. Export and Import Merchandise Trade and Supplement.
Forest Products Abstracts.
Forestry Abstracts.
Forthcoming Books. *(File no.470)*
Foundation Directory.
Foundation Grants Index.
Foundation Grants Index Quarterly.
Foundry Management & Technology.
Freshwater Fisheries Laboratory Pitlochry. Annual Review.
Frozen Food: The International Market.
Fruit and Vegetables: The International Market.
Fruit Juices: The International Market.
Fund Raising Management.
Fusion Power Report.
Futurescope. *(File no. 192)*
The Futurist.
The G M P Letter.
Gale Directory of Publications and Broadcast Media.
Gardening: The International Market.
Genesis Report - Dx.
Genesis Report - Rx.
Genetics Abstracts. *(File no.76/LIFE SCIENCES COLLECTION)*
Geographical Abstracts: Human Geography. *(File no.292)*
Geographical Abstracts: Physical Geography. *(File no.292)*
Geological Abstracts. *(File no.292)*
Geological Society of India. Journal. *(File no.89)*
Georgia Trend.
Geoscience Documentation. *(File no.58)*
Geotitles. *(File no.58)*
Gifts & Decorative Accessories.
Global Environmental Change.
Global Private Power.
Government Computer News.
Government Product News.
Government Reports Announcements & Index. *(File no.6)*
Government Research Directory.
Grand Rapids Business Journal.
Graphic Arts Monthly.
Grasslands and Forage Abstracts.
Great Britain. H.M.S.O. Books in Print.
Great Britain. H.M.S.O. Daily List.
Great Britain. H.M.S.O. Monthly Catalogue.
Great Britain. H.M.S.O. Publications Catalogue.
Great Britain. H.M.S.O. Statutory Instruments List.
Great Britain. Stationery Office. Annual Catalogue.
Great Britian. H.M.S.O. Committee Reports Index.
Ground Water Monitor.
Guns & Ammo.
H F N.
Hair Care Products: The International Market.
Handbook on Injectable Drugs. *(File no.229)*
Handbuch der Grossunternehmen.
Hangzhou Daxue Xuebao (Ziran Kexue Ban).
Harvard Business Review. *(File no.122)*
Hawaii Business.
Hazardous Waste Business. *(HWB)*
Hazardous Waste News.
Hazards in the Office. *(File no. 317)*
Haznews. *(File nos.636 & 16)*
Health Alliance Alert.
Health Devices Alerts. *(File no.198)*
Health Devices Sourcebook. *(File no.188)*
Health Index. *(File no.149)*
Health Management Technology.
Health News Daily. *(File no.43)*
Health Policy & Biomedical Research: The Blue Sheet. *(File no.187)*
Healthcare Financial Management.

Healthcare Technology & Business Opportunities.
Helicopter News.
Helminthological Abstracts.
Hewlett-Packard Journal.
High Tech Ceramics News.
High Tech Separations News.
High Yield Report.
Historical Abstracts. Part A: Modern History Abstracts, 1450-1914. *(File no.39)*
Historical Abstracts. Part B: Twentieth Century Abstracts, 1914 to the Present. *(File no.39)*
Historical Abstracts. Part B: Twentieth Century Abstracts, 1914 to the Present. Annual Index. *(File no.39)*
Horticultural Abstracts.
Hospitalis.
Hospitals and Health Networks.
Hot Rod.
Hotel and Motel Management.
Household Cleaning Agents: The International Market.
Housewares: The International Market.
Houston Business Journal.
Houston Post Index.
Huadong Ligong Daxue Xuebao.
Hydraulics & Pneumatics.
Hydrotitles. *(File no.58)*
Hypatia. *(File no.57)*
Hypermarkets and Superstores: The International Market.
I D - The Voice of Foodservice Distribution.
I E A Oil Market Report.
I I E Solutions.
I S D N News.
Ice Cream, Yoghurts and Chilled Desserts: The International Market.
Imaging Abstracts. *(F248)*
Imaging Update.
Immunology Abstracts. *(File no.76/LIFE SCIENCES COLLECTION)*
Improved Recovery Week.
In-Car Entertainment: The International Market.
Inc.
Independent Power Report. *(File no.624/McGRAW-HILL PUBLICATIONS ONLINE)*
Index Medicus. *(File nos.154 & 155/MEDLINE)*
Index of Current Research on Pigs.
Index of Economic Articles in Journals and Collective Volumes. *(File no.139)*
Index of Fungi.
Index to Dental Literature. *(File nos.154 & 155/MEDLINE)*
Index Veterinarius.
Indiana Business Magazine.
Industrial and Labor Relations Review.
Industrial Distribution.
Industrial Energy Bulletin. *(File no.624/McGRAW-HILL PUBLICATIONS ONLINE)*
Industrial Health.
Industrial Paint & Powder.
Industrial Researcher.
Industrial Specialties News.
Industries in Transition.
Industry Week.
Information Management Report. *(File no.636)*
Information Science Abstracts. *(File no.202)*
Informationsdienst Praxisbezogener Literatur im Weinbau.
Inpharma Weekly. *(File no.428,429)*
Inside Energy with Federal Lands. *(File no.624/McGRAW-HILL PUBLICATIONS ONLINE)*
Inside F E R C. *(File no.624/McGRAW-HILL PUBLICATIONS ONLINE)*
Inside F E R C's Gas Market Report. *(File no.624/McGRAW-HILL PUBLICATIONS ONLINE)*
Inside N R C. *(File no.624/McGRAW-HILL PUBLICATIONS ONLINE)*
Institute of Paper Science and Technology. Abstract Bulletin. *(File nos.240 & 840/PAPERCHEM)*
Instrumentation and Control Systems.
Insurance Periodicals Index. *(File no.169)*
Integrated Circuits International.
Integrated Waste Management. *(File no. 624/McGRAW-HILL PUBLICATIONS ONLINE)*
International Biodeterioration & Biodegradation.
International Brands and Their Companies.
International Coal Report.
International Country Risk Guide.
International Defense Review.
International Development Abstracts. *(File no.292)*
International Gas Report.
International Journal of Purchasing & Materials Management.
International Journal of Supercomputer Applications and High-Performance Computing.

International Nursing Index. *(File nos.154 & 155/MEDLINE)*
International Packaging Abstracts.
International Pharmaceutical Abstracts. *(File no.74)*
International Product Alert. *(File no. 9)*
International Research Centers Directory.
International Solar Energy Intelligence Report.
International Tradeshow Directory.
Investing, Licensing and Trading. Americas.
Investing, Licensing and Trading. Argentina.
Investing, Licensing and Trading. Asia.
Investing, Licensing and Trading. Australia.
Investing, Licensing and Trading. Austria.
Investing, Licensing and Trading. Belgium.
Investing, Licensing and Trading. Brazil.
Investing, Licensing and Trading. Britain.
Investing, Licensing and Trading. Canada.
Investing, Licensing and Trading. Central America.
Investing, Licensing and Trading. Chile.
Investing, Licensing and Trading. China.
Investing, Licensing and Trading. Colombia.
Investing, Licensing and Trading. Czech Republic.
Investing, Licensing and Trading. Denmark.
Investing, Licensing and Trading. Ecuador.
Investing, Licensing and Trading. Egypt.
Investing, Licensing and Trading. Finland.
Investing, Licensing and Trading. France.
Investing, Licensing and Trading. Germany.
Investing, Licensing and Trading. Global Edition.
Investing, Licensing and Trading. Greece.
Investing, Licensing and Trading. Hong Kong.
Investing, Licensing and Trading. Hungary.
Investing, Licensing and Trading. India.
Investing, Licensing and Trading. Indonesia.
Investing, Licensing and Trading. Ireland.
Investing, Licensing and Trading. Israel.
Investing, Licensing and Trading. Italy.
Investing, Licensing and Trading. Japan.
Investing, Licensing and Trading. Kenya.
Investing, Licensing and Trading. Luxembourg.
Investing, Licensing and Trading. Malaysia.
Investing, Licensing and Trading. Mexico.
Investing, Licensing and Trading. Middle East - Africa.
Investing, Licensing and Trading. Netherlands.
Investing, Licensing and Trading. New Zealand.
Investing, Licensing and Trading. Nigeria.
Investing, Licensing and Trading. Norway.
Investing, Licensing and Trading. Pakistan.
Investing, Licensing and Trading. Panama.
Investing, Licensing and Trading. Peru.
Investing, Licensing and Trading. Philippines.
Investing, Licensing and Trading. Poland.
Investing, Licensing and Trading. Portugal.
Investing, Licensing and Trading. Puerto Rico.
Investing, Licensing and Trading. Russia.
Investing, Licensing and Trading. Saudi Arabia.
Investing, Licensing and Trading. Singapore.
Investing, Licensing and Trading. Slovakia.
Investing, Licensing and Trading. South Africa.
Investing, Licensing and Trading. South Korea.
Investing, Licensing and Trading. Spain.
Investing, Licensing and Trading. Sweden.
Investing, Licensing and Trading. Switzerland.
Investing, Licensing and Trading. Taiwan.
Investing, Licensing and Trading. Thailand.
Investing, Licensing and Trading. Turkey.
Investing, Licensing and Trading. United States of America.
Investing, Licensing and Trading. Uruguay.
Investing, Licensing and Trading. Venezuela.
Investing, Licensing and Trading. Vietnam.
Irrigation and Drainage Abstracts.
Item Processing Report.
J A M A: The Journal of the American Medical Association.
Jane's Defence Weekly.
Jane's Intelligence Review.
Journal of Commerce and Commercial.
Journal of Consumer Research.
Journal of Economic Literature. *(Economic Literature Index File no. 139)*
Journal of Interactive Marketing.
Journal of Marriage and the Family.
Journal of Mormon History. *(File nos.38,39)*
Journal of Near Eastern Studies.
Journal of Psychology and Theology.
Journal of Retailing.
Journal of Risk and Insurance.
Journal of Systems Management.
Journal of Technology Transfer.
Kentucky Business Ledger.
Key Abstracts - Business Automation.
Kiplinger's Personal Finance Magazine.
Kompass Sverige.
L A N Product News.
L A N Times. *(LAN)*
L D C Debt Report.
L I S A: Library & Information Science Abstracts. *(File no.61/LISA)*
Labor Relations Reporter. *(File no. 244, Laborlaw)*
Labor Relations Reporter. Fair Employment Practices.
Labor Relations Reporter. Labor Arbitration and Dispute Settlements. *(Files 243, 244)*
Labor Relations Reporter. Wages and Hours.
Laboratory Hazards Bulletin. *(File no.317)*
Ladies Home Journal (Inkprint Edition).
Lagniappe Letter.
Land Mobile Radio News.
Large Kitchen Appliances: The International Market.
Large Mixed Retailers: The International Market.
Law Office Technology Review.
LegalTrac. *(File no.150)*
Leisure, Recreation and Tourism Abstracts.
Life.
Life Sciences & Biotechnology Update.
Linguistics and Language Behavior Abstracts. *(File no.36)*
Livestock, Dairy and Poultry Situation & Outlook.
Lodging Hospitality.
The Los Angeles Times Index.
Louisville Magazine.
McGraw-Hill's Biotechnology Newswatch. *(File no.624/McGRAW-HILL PUBLICATIONS ONLINE)*
Machine Design.
Magazine Index. *(File no.47)*
Magill's Cinema Annual.
Mail Order and Home Shopping: The International Market.
Mainframe Computing.
Maize Abstracts.
Make-Up and Colour Cosmetics: The International Market.
Management Contents. *(File no.75)*
Managing Office Technology.
Manufacturing Automation.
Market: Africa - Mid-East.
Market: Asia Pacific.
Market Direction Reports.
Market: Europe.
Market: Latin America.
Market Research Abstracts.
Martindale: the Extra Pharmacopoeia. *(File no.141)*
Maryland Business & Living.
Masters Abstracts International. *(File no.35)*
Materials Business Information. *(File no.269)*
Materials Information Translations Service.
Mathematical Reviews.
Meat and Poultry: The International Market.
Mechanical Engineering Abstracts. *(File no.14)*
MediaWeek.
Medical and Health Care Books and Serials in Print.
Medical & Pharmaceutical Biotechnology Abstracts. *(File no.76/LIFE SCIENCES COLLECTION)*
Medical Devices, Diagnostics & Instrumentation Reports: The Gray Sheet. *(File no.187)*
Medical Economics.
Medical Outcomes and Guidelines Alert.
Medical Textiles.
Medical Utilization Management.
Medical Waste News.
Medicated Skincare: The International Market.
Membrane & Separation Technology News.
Memphis Business Journal.
Men's Toiletries: The International Market.
Mercer Business Magazine.
Merck Index: An Encyclopedia of Chemicals and Drugs.
Metals Abstracts. *(File no.32/METADEX)*
Metals Abstracts Index. *(File no.32/METADEX)*
Metals Week. *(File no.624/McGRAW-HILL PUBLICATIONS ONLINE)*
Meteorological and Geoastrophysical Abstracts. *(File no.29)*
Meyler's Side Effects of Drugs. *(File no.70/SEDBASE)*
Microbiology Abstracts: Section A. Industrial & Applied Microbiology. *(File no.76/LIFE SCIENCES COLLECTION)*
Microbiology Abstracts: Section B. Bacteriology. *(File no.76/LIFE SCIENCES COLLECTION)*
Microbiology Abstracts: Section C. Algology, Mycology and Protozoology. *(File no.76/LIFE SCIENCES COLLECTION)*
Microcomputer Abstracts. *(File no.233)*
Middle East: Abstracts and Index. *(File no.248)*
Military & Commercial Fiber Business.
Military Robotics Newsletter. *(NL0650)*
Military Specifications and Standards Services Numeric Index.
Million Dollar Directory. *(File no.517)*
Mineral Water: The International Market.
Minneapolis - St. Paul CityBusiness.
Minority Markets Alert.
Mittelstaendische Unternehmen.
Mobile Communications Report.
Modem User News.
Modern Bride.
Modern Plastics. *(MP)*
Modern Tire Dealer.
Money (New York).
Money Laundering Alert.
Monthly Catalog of United States Government Publications. *(File no.66)*
Monthly Labor Review.
Moskovskie Novosti.
Mother Jones.
Motor Trend.
Mount Sinai Journal of Medicine.
Multimedia Monitor.
N C J R S Document Retrieval Index.
N I O S H T I C.
N T I S Bibliographic Data Base.
Nanjing Huagong Daxue Xuebao.
National Agricultural Statistics Service. Cattle on Feed.
National Newspaper Index. *(File no.111)*
National Petroleum News.
National Report on Computers and Health.
National Review.
Natural History.
Nematological Abstracts.
Network World. *(File no.674)*
Networks Update.
New Hampshire Business Review.
The New Leader.
New Mexico Business Journal.
New Orleans CityBusiness.
The New Republic.
New Steel.
New Trade Names in the Rubber and Plastics Industries.
Newsletters in Print. *(File no.469)*
Nonferrous Metals Alert. *(File no.269)*
Nonprescription Pharmaceuticals and Nutritionals: The Tan Sheet. *(File no.187)*
Nonwovens Abstracts.
North Sea Letter.
North Sea Rig Forecast.
Northeast Power Report. *(NPR)*
NotiSur.
NuclearFuel. *(File no.624/McGRAW-HILL PUBLICATIONS ONLINE)*
Nucleic Acids Abstracts. *(File no.76/LIFE SCIENCES COLLECTION)*
Nucleonics Week. *(File no.624/McGRAW-HILL PUBLICATIONS ONLINE)*
Nursing Homes.
Nutrition Abstracts and Reviews. Series A: Human and Experimental.
Nutrition Abstracts and Reviews. Series B: Livestock Feeds and Feeding.
Occupational Safety & Health Reporter. *(Laborlaw, File no.244)*
Oceanic Abstracts. *(File no.28)*
Octane Week.
Oils and Fats: The International Market.
Oncogenes and Growth Factors Abstracts. *(File no.76)*
Online Libraries and Microcomputers.
Online Newsletter.
Ophthalmology Times.
Optical Materials and Engineering News.
Oral Hygiene Products: The International Market.
Orange County Business Journal.
Ornamental Horticulture.
Outdoor Life.
Outlook (Year) Proceedings.
P A I S International in Print. *(File no.49/PAIS)*
P A S C A L. E 11: Physique Atomique et Moleculaire. Plasmas. *(File no.144)*
P A S C A L. E 12: Etat Condense. *(File no.144)*
P A S C A L. E 13: Structure des Liquides et des Solides - Cristallographie. *(File no.144)*
P A S C A L. E 18: Chromatographie. *(File no.144)*
P A S C A L. E 20: Electronique et Telecommunications. *(File no.144)*
P A S C A L. E 27: Methodes de Formation et Traitement des Images. *(File no.144)*
P A S C A L. E 30: Microscopie Electronique et Diffraction Electronique. *(File no.144)*
P A S C A L. E 32: Metrologie et Appareillage en Physique et Physicochimie. *(File no.144)*
P A S C A L. E 33. Informatique.

VENDOR LISTING/SERIALS ONLINE

P A S C A L. E 34. Robotique, Automatique et Automatisation des Processus Industriels. (File no.144)
P A S C A L. E 36: Pollution de l'Eau, de l'Air et du Sol - Dechets - Bruit. (File no.144)
P A S C A L. E 48: Environnement Cosmique Terrestre, Astronomie et Geologie Extraterrestre. (File no.144)
P A S C A L. E 49: Meteorologie, Glaciologie, Physique des Oceans. (File no.144)
P A S C A L. E 58: Genetique. (File no.144)
P A S C A L. E 61: Microbiologie: Bacteriologie, Virologie, Mycologie, Protozoaires Pathogenes. (File no. 144)
P A S C A L. E 62: Immunologie. (File no.144)
P A S C A L. E 63: Toxicologie. (File no.144)
P A S C A L. E 64: Endocrinologie Humaine et Experimentale. Endocrinopathies (File no.144)
P A S C A L. E 65: Psychologie, Psychopathologie, Psychiatrie. (File no.144)
P A S C A L. E 68: Genetique Humaine.
P A S C A L. E 71: Ophtalmologie. (File no. 144)
P A S C A L. E 72: Otorhinolaryngologie. Stomatologie. Pathologie Cervicofaciale. (File no.144)
P A S C A L. E 73: Dermatologie. Maladies Sexuellement Transmissibles. (File no.144)
P A S C A L. E 74: Pneumologie. (File no.144)
P A S C A L. E 75: Cardiologie et Appareil Circulatoire. (File no.144)
P A S C A L. E 76: Gastroenterologie, Foie, Pancreas, Abdomen. (File no.144)
P A S C A L. E 77: Nephrologie. Voies Urinaires. (File no.144)
P A S C A L. E 78: Neurologie. (File no.144)
P A S C A L. E 79: Pathologie et Physiologie Osteoarticulaires. (File no.144)
P A S C A L. E 80: Hematologie. (File no.144)
P A S C A L. E 82: Gynecologie, Obstetrique, Andrologie. (File no.144)
P A S C A L. E 83: Anesthesie et Reanimation. (File no.144)
P A S C A L. E 84: Genie Biomedical. Informatique Biomedicale. (File no.144)
P A S C A L. E 89: Cancer. (File no.144)
P A S C A L. F 10: Mecanique, Acoustique et Transfert de Chaleur. (File no.144)
P A S C A L. F 16: Chimie Analytique, Minerale et Organique. (File no.144)
P A S C A L. F 17: Chimie Generale, Minerale et Organique. (File no.144)
P A S C A L. F 23: Genie Chimique. Industries Chimique et Parachimique. (File no.144)
P A S C A L. F 24: Polymeres - Peintures - Bois. (File no.144)
P A S C A L. F 40: Mineralogie. Geochimie. Geologie Extraterrestre. (File no.144)
P A S C A L. F 41: Gisements Metalliques et Non Metalliques. (File no.144)
P A S C A L. F 42: Roches Cristallines. (File no.144)
P A S C A L. F 43: Roches Sedimentaires. Geologie Marine. (File no.144)
P A S C A L. F 44: Stratigraphie, Geologie Regionale, Geologie Generale. (File no.144)
P A S C A L. F 45: Tectonique, Geophysique Interne. (File no.144)
P A S C A L. F 46: Hydrologie. Geologie de l'Ingenieur. Formations Superficielles. (File no.144)
P A S C A L. F 47: Paleontologie. (File no.144)
P A S C A L. F 52: Biochimie - Biophysique - Moleculaire - Biologie Moleculaire et Cellulaire. (File no.144)
P A S C A L. F 53: Anatomie et Physiologie des Vertebres. (File no.144)
P A S C A L. F 54: Reproduction des Vertebres, Embryologie des Vertebres et des Invertebres. (File no.144)
P A S C A L. F 55: Biologie Vegetale. (File no.144)
P A S C A L. F 56: Ecologie Animale, Vegetale et Microbienne. Ethologie Animale. (File no.144)
P A S C A L. F 70: Pharmacologie. Traitements Medicamenteux. (File no.144)
P A S C A L. T 205: Sciences de l'Information. Documentation. (File no.144)
P A S C A L. T 215: Biotechnologies. (File no.144)
P A S C A L. T 230: Energie. (File no.144)
P A S C A L. T 235: Medecine Tropicale. (File no.144)
P A S C A L. T 240: Metaux - Metallurgie. (File no.144)
P A S C A L. T 260: Zoologie Fondamentale et Appliquee des Invertebres. (File no.144)
P A S C A L. T 280: Sciences Agronomiques et Forestieres: Productions Vegetales. (File no.144)
P A S C A L. T 295: Batiment. Travaux Publics. (File no.144)
P A S C A L V.4 Sciences de la Terre. (File no.144)
P C Business Products.
P C Magazin.
P N I. (File no.42)
Pacific Business News.
Packaging Science and Technology Abstracts. (File no.252)
Paperbase Abstracts.
Paperboard Packaging.
Pasta Products: The International Market.
Patents Abstracts.
Perfumes and Fragrances: The International Market.
Periodical Abstracts.
Personal Care Appliances: The International Market.
Personalist Forum.
Pesticide & Toxic Chemical News.
The Pesticide Manual. (File no.306)
Pet Foods and Products: The International Market.
Petersen's Photographic.
Peterson's Graduate and Professional Programs: An Overview (Year) (Book 1). (File no.273)
Peterson's Graduate And Professional Programs: Business, Education, Health, Information Studies, Law, and Social Work (Year) (Book 6). (File no.273)
Peterson's Graduate and Professional Programs: Engineering and Applied Sciences (Year) (Book 5). (File no.273)
Peterson's Graduate and Professional Programs: The Biological Sciences (Year) (Book 3). (File no.273)
Peterson's Graduate and Professional Programs: The Humanities, Arts, and Social Sciences (Year) (Book 2). (File no.273)
Peterson's Graduate and Professional Programs: The Physical Sciences, Mathematics, and Agricultural Sciences (Year) (Book 4). (File no.273)
Peterson's Guide to Four-Year Colleges (Year). (File no.214)
Peterson's Guide to Two-Year Colleges (Year). (File no.214)
Petroleum Abstracts. (File no. 87,987)
Petroleum - Energy Business News Index.
Pharmaceutical Approvals Monthly. (File no.187)
Pharmacies and Drugstores: The International Market.
Pharmacoeconomics and Outcomes News.
Pharmaprojects Magazine.
Philadelphia Business Journal.
Philosopher's Index. (File no.57)
Photography: The International Market.
The Physician and Sportsmedicine.
Physics Abstracts.
Pig News & Information.
Plant Breeding Abstracts.
Plant Engineering.
Plant Growth Regulator Abstracts.
Platt's International Petrochemical Report. (File no.624/McGRAW-HILL PUBLICATIONS ONLINE)
Platt's Oilgram News. (File no.624/McGRAW-HILL PUBLICATIONS ONLINE)
Platt's Oilgram Price Report. (File no.624/McGRAW-HILL PUBLICATIONS ONLINE)
Playthings.
Pollution Abstracts. (File no.41)
Polymers, Ceramics, Composites Alert. (File no.269)
Popular Photography.
Popular Science.
Postgraduate Medicine. (PGM)
Potato Abstracts.
Poultry Abstracts.
Power (New York). (POW)
Power in Asia.
Power in Europe.
Power in Latin America.
Power U K.
Predicasts Basebook.
Predicasts F & S Index Europe.
Predicasts F & S Index International.
Predicasts F & S Index of Corporate Change.
Predicasts F & S Index United States.
Predicasts Forecasts.
Predicasts Overview of Markets and Technology.
Prepared Soups: The International Market.
Prescription Pharmaceuticals and Biotechnology: The Pink Sheet. (File no.187)
Printing Abstracts.
Private Placement Reporter.
Process and Chemical Engineering. (File no.315)
Product Alert. (File no. 636)
Productivity Software.
Professional Update.
Progressive Grocer.
Protozoological Abstracts.
Psychological Abstracts. (File no.11/PsycINFO)
Psychology Today.
Publishers Directory.
Publishers, Distributors & Wholesalers of the United States. (File no.450)
Puget Sound Business Journal.
Quill (Greencastle).
R A P R A Abstracts.
R & D Focus.
R T E C S. (File no.336)
Reactions Weekly. (File no.428,429)
Religion in Eastern Europe.
Renewable Energy Report.
Research Alert (New York).
Research & Development.
Research Centers Directory.
Research Services Directory.
Resources in Education.
Retail Stationery: The International Market.
Review of Agricultural Entomology.
The Review of Banking and Financial Services. (BFS)
Review of Medical and Veterinary Entomology.
Review of Medical and Veterinary Mycology.
Review of Plant Pathology.
The Review of Securities & Commodities Regulation. (SCR)
Rice Abstracts.
Rural Development Abstracts.
Rural Libraries.
S M T Trends.
S T A R. (File no.108)
S T N.
Sacramento Business Journal.
St. Louis Business Journal.
Sales and Marketing Management.
Salud Publica de Mexico.
San Diego Business Journal.
Saturday Evening Post.
Savoury Snacks: The International Market.
Scholastic Choices.
Scholastic Update.
School Planning and Management.
Schweizerische Zeitschrift fuer Volkswirtschaft und Statistik.
Science Citation Index. (Files nos.34,432,433,434/SCISEARCH)
Scouting.
Scrip - World Pharmaceutical News. (File No. 129)
Searchable Physics Information Notices. (File no.62/SPIN)
Securities Week. (File no.624/McGRAW-HILL PUBLICATIONS ONLINE)
Seed Abstracts.
Sensor Business Digest.
Sensor Review.
Service Stations: The International Market.
Shopper Report.
Side Effects of Drugs Annual. (File no.70/SEDBASE)
Situation & Outlook Report. Agricultural Income & Finance.
Situation & Outlook Report. Fruit & Tree Nuts.
Situation & Outlook Report. Sugar & Sweetener.
Situation & Outlook Report. Tobacco.
Situation & Outlook Report. Vegetables & Specialties.
Skin Care: The International Market.
Skin Diver Magazine.
Small Animals.
Small Kitchen Appliances: The International Market.
Smithsonian.
Social Sciences Citation Index. (File no.7/SOCIAL SCISEARCH)
Sociological Abstracts. (File no.37)
Soft Drinks: The International Market.
Software Catalog: Microcomputers.
Software Encyclopedia. (File no.278)
Soils and Fertilizers.
Sorghum and Millets.
SourceMex.
Southeast Power Report. (SPR)
Southern Social Studies Journal.
Soyabean Abstracts.
Space Business News.
Spirits: The International Market.
Sport Thesaurus.
Sports Illustrated.

SportSearch.
SportStyle.
Standard & Poor's Corporation Records. *(File no.133/Corporate Descriptions)*
Standard & Poor's Corporation Records. Daily News Section. *(File no.133)*
State Tax Notes.
Steels Alert. *(File no.269)*
Stereo Review.
Subject Guide to Books in Print. *(File no.470)*
Sun Care: The International Market.
Sunset.
Superconductor Week.
Supermarket News.
Survey of Current Business.
Sweet & Savoury Biscuits: The International Market.
T R I S Electronic Bibliographic Data Base. *(File no. 63)*
The Tax Directory.
Tax Management Estates, Gifts and Trusts Journal. *(Files 15, 485)*
Tax Management International Journal. *(Files 15, 485)*
Tax Notes.
Tax Notes International.
Technical Literature Abstracts.
Technical Literature Abstracts: Catalysts - Zeolites.
Technical Literature Abstracts: Fuel Reformulation.
Technical Literature Abstracts: Oilfield Chemicals.
Technical Literature Abstracts: Tribology.
Technology Access Report.
Technology and Learning.
Technology Review.
Technology Transfer Week.
Teen.
Tekstilec.
Telco Business Report.
Tele-Service News.
Television and Video: The International Market.
Textile and Fabric Washing Products: The International Market.
Textile Technology Digest. *(File no.119)*
Theology.
Theoretical Chemical Engineering. *(File no. 315)*
Tin International.
Toiletries, Fragrances and Skin Care: The Rose Sheet. *(File no.187)*
Tooling & Production.
Tour & Travel News - T T G North America.
Toxicology Abstracts. *(File no.76/LIFE SCIENCES COLLECTION)*
Toys and Games: The International Market.
Trade & Industry Index. *(File no.148)*
Transit Research Abstracts. *(File no.63)*
Transportation & Distribution.
Travel and Tourism: The International Market.
Tree Physiology.
Tropical Oil Seeds.
Tuberculosis & Airborne Disease Weekly.
Twin Cities Reader.
U K Gas Report.
U S A Today.
U S News & World Report.
U S Oil Week.
Ulrich's International Periodicals Directory. *(File no.480)*
Ulrich's Update. *(File no.480)*
U.S. Department of Agriculture. Agricultural Outlook.
U.S. Department of Agriculture. Agricultural Statistics Board Report: Agricultural Prices.
U.S. Department of Agriculture. Agricultural Statistics Board Report: Crop Production.
U.S. Department of Agriculture. Situation & Outlook Report. Agriculture and Trade: Former U S S R.
U.S. Department of State. Key Officers of Foreign Service Posts.
U.S. Department of State Dispatch.
U.S. Energy Information Administration. Quarterly Coal Report.
United States Patents Quarterly. *(Patlaw, File 243)*
Urology Times.
Utility Environment Report. *(UER)*
Vending: The International Market.
Vermont Business Magazine.
Veterinary Bulletin.
Video Store.
Video Technology News.
Virology and AIDS Abstracts. *(File no.76/LIFE SCIENCES COLLECTION)*
Vitamins and Dietary Supplements: The International Market.
Vitis - Viticulture and Oenology Abstracts.

Voice Technology & Services News.
The Washington Monthly.
Water Resources Abstracts (Bethesda). *(File no.117)*
Weed Abstracts.
Weekly of Business Aviation. *(File no.624/McGRAW-HILL PUBLICATIONS ONLINE)*
Wer Liefert Was?
Western Grower and Shipper.
Wheat, Barley and Triticale Abstracts.
Whitaker's Books in Print. *(File no.430)*
Who's Who in America. *(File no.234)*
Who's Who in American Art. *(File no.236)*
Who's Who in American Politics. *(File no.236)*
Wilson Abstracts.
Wilson Applied Science and Technology Abstracts.
Wilson Business Abstracts.
Wilson Education Abstracts.
Wilson Humanities Abstracts.
Wilson Social Sciences Abstracts.
Wine: The International Market.
Wing Newsletter.
Women's Wear Daily.
Wood Technology.
Workbench.
Working Woman.
World Agricultural Economics and Rural Sociology Abstracts.
World Agricultural Supply and Demand Estimates.
World Bank Research Observer.
World Health.
World Power Systems Intelligence.
World Publishing Monitor.
World Textile Abstracts. *(File no.67)*
World Translations Index. *(File no.295)*
Worldcasts: Product Edition.
Worldcasts: Regional Edition.
WorldViews.
Worldwide Biotech.
Worldwide Databases.
Worldwide Telecom.
Worldwide Videotex Update.
Youth Markets Alert.
Zhongguo Xinli Weisheng Zazhi.
Zhongguo Yangfeng.
Zoological Record. *(File no.185)*
4 1 1 Newsletter. *(File no.636)*

LEXIS-NEXIS (A member of the Reed Elsevier plc group)
9443 Springboro Pike, Miamisburg, OH 45342.
Fax: 513-865-1211.
A B A Banking Journal.
A B A Journal.
A B I - INFORM. *(ABI)*
A H F S Drug Information.
Abya Yala News.
Advertising Age. *(ADAGE)*
Adweek (New York).
Aerospace America. *(AEROAM)*
Aerospace Daily. *(AIRDLY)*
Aerospace Propulsion. *(AERPRO)*
Affirmative Action - E E O Personnel Update.
Airports.
Alaska Business Monthly.
Albany Law Review.
All England Law Reports.
Almanac of Famous People.
Alternatives to the High Cost of Litigation.
American Banker.
American Banker's Washington Watch.
American College of Surgeons. Journal.
American Demographics.
American Family Physician.
American Journal of Cardiology.
American Journal of International Law.
American Journal of Law & Medicine.
The American Journal of Medicine.
American Journal of Surgery.
American Journal of Tax Policy.
The American Lawyer.
American Maritime Cases.
American University Law Review.
Americans with Disabilities Act Update.
Annals of Neurology.
Annals of Plastic Surgery.
Annals of Thoracic Surgery.
Antitrust.
Antitrust & Trade Regulation Report. *(TRADRG)*
Antitrust Freedom of Information Log.
Antitrust Law Journal.
Antitrust Litigation Reporter.
Archives of Pathology & Laboratory Medicine.
Arizona Business Gazette.
Arthritis and Rheumatism.
Asian Journal of Surgery.
Asian Studies Center Backgrounder.

AsianWeek. *(Ethnic Newswatch)*
Asset Sales Report.
Automotive Industries.
AutoWeek.
Aviation Daily. *(AVDLY)*
Aviation Europe. *(AVEUR)*
Aviation Week & Space Technology.
B L A S T.
B N A Pension & Benefits Reporter. *(PENSN)*
B N A's Banking Report. *(BNABNK)*
B N A's Health Care Policy Report. *(file BNAHCP)*
B N A's Health Law Reporter. *(file BNAHLR)*
B N A's Medicare Report. *(File BNAHMED)*
B N A's Patent, Trademark & Copyright Journal.
Backgrounder.
Backgrounder Update.
Bakery Production and Marketing.
Bank Mutual Fund Report.
Banking Policy Report.
Banking Strategies.
Beverage World (English Edition).
Biomedical Market Newsletter.
Blood.
The Bond Buyer.
Books in Print. *(BIP)*
Boston University Law Review.
Brazil Report.
Brief (Chicago).
British Journal of Surgery.
Broadcasting & Cable.
Brooklyn Law Review.
Bulletin on the Rheumatic Diseases.
Business China.
Business Computing Brief.
Business Dateline.
Business Eastern Europe.
Business - Education Insider.
Business Europe.
Business First (Buffalo).
Business in Broward.
Business Index.
Business Insurance.
Business Latin America.
Business Law Europe.
Business Lawyer. *(BUSLAW)*
Business Mexico.
Business North Carolina.
Business Week.
Byte.
C F O Alert (Weekly).
C I S Index to Publications of the United States Congress.
C I S Legislative Histories Annual.
Calgary Herald.
Canada - United States Law Journal.
Caribbean & Central America Report.
Case Western Reserve Journal of International Law.
Case Western Reserve Law Review.
Catholic University Law Review.
Chemical Engineering. *(CHEMEN)*
Chemical Regulation Reporter. *(BNA-CHEM)*
Chemical Week.
Chicago Enterprise.
Chilton's Automotive Marketing.
Chilton's Distribution.
Chilton's Food Engineering.
Chilton's Motor Age.
Clinical Laser Monthly.
Clinical Orthopaedics and Related Research.
Clinical Pediatrics.
Coal Age.
Coal Tech International. *(SYNFLS)*
Coal U.K.
Coal Week. *(COALWK)*
Coal Week International. *(COALIN)*
Colorado Business.
Columbia Law Review.
Communication World.
Communications Daily.
Communications International.
CommunicationsWeek International.
Computer Industry Forecasts.
Computer Lawyer.
Computerworld.
Consumer Reports.
Contemporary Musicians.
Contraceptive Technology Update.
Cornell International Law Journal.
Cornell Journal of Law and Public Policy.
Cornell Law Review.
Corporate E F T Report.
Corporate Legal Times. *(CORPLT)*
Corporate Report Minnesota.
Cosmetics International.
Country Forecast. Algeria.
Country Forecast. Argentina.
Country Forecast. Asia - Pacific.

VENDOR LISTING/SERIALS ONLINE

Country Forecast. Australia.
Country Forecast. Austria.
Country Forecast. Belgium.
Country Forecast. Brazil.
Country Forecast. Bulgaria.
Country Forecast. Canada.
Country Forecast. Chile.
Country Forecast. China.
Country Forecast. Colombia.
Country Forecast. Czech Republic.
Country Forecast. Denmark.
Country Forecast. Eastern Europe and the Former Soviet Union.
Country Forecast. Ecuador.
Country Forecast. Egypt.
Country Forecast. Europe.
Country Forecast. Finland.
Country Forecast. France.
Country Forecast. Germany.
Country Forecast. Global Outlook.
Country Forecast. Greece.
Country Forecast. Hong Kong.
Country Forecast. Hungary.
Country Forecast. India.
Country Forecast. Indonesia.
Country Forecast. Iran.
Country Forecast. Iraq.
Country Forecast. Ireland.
Country Forecast. Israel.
Country Forecast. Italy.
Country Forecast. Japan.
Country Forecast. Latin America.
Country Forecast. Malaysia.
Country Forecast. Mexico.
Country Forecast. Middle East and North Africa.
Country Forecast. Netherlands.
Country Forecast. New Zealand.
Country Forecast. Nigeria.
Country Forecast. Norway.
Country Forecast. Pakistan.
Country Forecast. Peru.
Country Forecast. Philippines.
Country Forecast. Poland.
Country Forecast. Portugal.
Country Forecast. Romania.
Country Forecast. Russia.
Country Forecast. Saudi Arabia.
Country Forecast. Singapore.
Country Forecast. Slovakia.
Country Forecast. South Africa.
Country Forecast. South Korea.
Country Forecast. Spain.
Country Forecast. Sri Lanka.
Country Forecast. Sub-Saharan Africa.
Country Forecast. Sweden.
Country Forecast. Switzerland.
Country Forecast. Taiwan.
Country Forecast. Thailand.
Country Forecast. Turkey.
Country Forecast. United Kingdom.
Country Forecast. United States of America.
Country Forecast. Venezuela.
Country Forecast. Vietnam.
Country Forecasts (New York).
Country Profile. Albania.
Country Profile. Algeria.
Country Profile. Angola.
Country Profile. Argentina.
Country Profile. Australia.
Country Profile. Austria.
Country Profile. Azerbaijan.
Country Profile. Bahrain, Qatar.
Country Profile. Baltic Republics: Lithuania, Latvia, Estonia.
Country Profile. Bangladesh.
Country Profile. Belgium, Luxembourg.
Country Profile. Belize, Bahamas, Bermuda.
Country Profile. Bolivia.
Country Profile. Bosnia-Hercegovina, Croatia.
Country Profile. Botswana, Lesotho.
Country Profile. Brazil.
Country Profile. Bulgaria.
Country Profile. Cambodia, Laos.
Country Profile. Cameroon, Central African Republic, Chad.
Country Profile. Canada.
Country Profile. Chile.
Country Profile. China, Mongolia.
Country Profile. Colombia.
Country Profile. Congo.
Country Profile. Costa Rica.
Country Profile. Cote d'Ivoire, Mali.
Country Profile. Cuba.
Country Profile. Cyprus, Malta.
Country Profile. Czech Republic.
Country Profile. Denmark, Iceland.
Country Profile. Dominican Republic, Haiti, Puerto Rico.
Country Profile. Ecuador.
Country Profile. Egypt.
Country Profile. Ethiopia, Eritrea, Somalia, Djibouti.
Country Profile. Finland.
Country Profile. France.
Country Profile. Gabon, Equatorial Guinea.
Country Profile. Georgia, Armenia.
Country Profile. Germany.
Country Profile. Ghana.
Country Profile. Greece.
Country Profile. Guatemala, El Salvador.
Country Profile. Guinea, Sierra Leone, Liberia.
Country Profile. Guyana, Windward and Leeward Islands.
Country Profile. Hong Kong, Macau.
Country Profile. Hungary.
Country Profile. India, Nepal.
Country Profile. Indonesia.
Country Profile. Iran.
Country Profile. Iraq.
Country Profile. Ireland.
Country Profile. Israel, the Occupied Territories.
Country Profile. Italy.
Country Profile. Jamaica, Barbados.
Country Profile. Japan.
Country Profile. Jordan.
Country Profile. Kazakhstan.
Country Profile. Kenya.
Country Profile. Kuwait.
Country Profile. Lebanon.
Country Profile. Libya.
Country Profile. Macedonia, Serbia-Montenegro.
Country Profile. Madagascar.
Country Profile. Malawi.
Country Profile. Malaysia, Brunei.
Country Profile. Mauritius, Seychelles.
Country Profile. Mexico.
Country Profile. Morocco.
Country Profile. Mozambique.
Country Profile. Myanmar.
Country Profile. Namibia, Swaziland.
Country Profile. Netherlands.
Country Profile. New Zealand.
Country Profile. Nicaragua, Honduras.
Country Profile. Niger, Burkina Faso.
Country Profile. Nigeria.
Country Profile. Norway.
Country Profile. Oman.
Country Profile. Pacific Islands: Fiji, Solomon Islands, Western Samoa, Vanuatu, Tonga and New Caledonia.
Country Profile. Pakistan, Afghanistan.
Country Profile. Panama.
Country Profile. Papua New Guinea.
Country Profile. Peru.
Country Profile. Philippines.
Country Profile. Poland.
Country Profile. Portugal.
Country Profile. Romania.
Country Profile. Russia.
Country Profile. Rwanda, Burundi.
Country Profile. Sao Tome and Principe, Guinea-Bissau, Cape Verde.
Country Profile. Saudi Arabia.
Country Profile. Senegal.
Country Profile. Singapore.
Country Profile. Slovakia.
Country Profile. Slovenia.
Country Profile. South Africa.
Country Profile. South Korea, North Korea.
Country Profile. Spain.
Country Profile. Sri Lanka.
Country Profile. Sudan.
Country Profile. Sweden.
Country Profile. Switzerland.
Country Profile. Syria.
Country Profile. Taiwan.
Country Profile. Tanzania, Comoros.
Country Profile. Thailand.
Country Profile. The Gambia, Mauritania.
Country Profile. Togo, Benin.
Country Profile. Trinidad and Tobago, Suriname, Netherlands Antilles, Aruba.
Country Profile. Tunisia.
Country Profile. Turkey.
Country Profile. Uganda.
Country Profile. Ukraine.
Country Profile. United Arab Emirates.
Country Profile. United Kingdom.
Country Profile. United States of America.
Country Profile. Uruguay, Paraguay.
Country Profile. Venezuela.
Country Profile. Yemen.
Country Profile. Zaire.
Country Profile. Zambia.
Country Profile. Zimbabwe.
Country Profiles.
Country Report. Algeria.
Country Report. Angola.
Country Report. Argentina.
Country Report. Australia.
Country Report. Austria.
Country Report. Bahrain, Qatar.
Country Report. Baltic Republics: Lithuania, Latvia, Estonia.
Country Report. Bangladesh.
Country Report. Belgium, Luxembourg.
Country Report. Bolivia.
Country Report. Bosnia-Hercegovina, Croatia and Slovenia.
Country Report. Brazil.
Country Report. Bulgaria.
Country Report. Cambodia, Laos.
Country Report. Cameroon, C.A.R., Chad.
Country Report. Canada.
Country Report. Chile.
Country Report. China, Mongolia.
Country Report. Colombia.
Country Report. Congo, Sao Tome and Principe, Guinea-Bissau, Cape Verde.
Country Report. Costa Rica.
Country Report. Cote d'Ivoire, Mali.
Country Report. Cuba, Dominican Republic, Haiti, Puerto Rico.
Country Report. Cyprus, Malta.
Country Report. Czech Republic.
Country Report. Denmark, Iceland.
Country Report. Ecuador.
Country Report. Egypt.
Country Report. Ethiopia, Eritrea, Somalia, Djibouti.
Country Report. Finland.
Country Report. France.
Country Report. Gabon, Equatorial Guinea.
Country Report. Germany.
Country Report. Ghana.
Country Report. Greece.
Country Report. Guatemala, El Salvador.
Country Report. Guinea, Sierra Leone, Liberia.
Country Report. Hong Kong, Macau.
Country Report. Hungary.
Country Report. India, Nepal.
Country Report. Indonesia.
Country Report. Iran.
Country Report. Iraq.
Country Report. Ireland.
Country Report. Israel, the Occupied Territories.
Country Report. Italy.
Country Report. Jamaica, Belize, Bahamas, Bermuda, Barbados.
Country Report. Japan.
Country Report. Jordan.
Country Report. Kazakhstan.
Country Report. Kenya.
Country Report. Kuwait.
Country Report. Lebanon.
Country Report. Libya.
Country Report. Malaysia, Brunei.
Country Report. Mauritius, Madagascar, Seychelles.
Country Report. Mexico.
Country Report. Morocco.
Country Report. Mozambique, Malawi.
Country Report. Netherlands.
Country Report. New Zealand.
Country Report. Nicaragua, Honduras.
Country Report. Nigeria.
Country Report. Norway.
Country Report. Oman, Yemen.
Country Report. Pacific Islands: Papua New Guinea, Fiji, Solomon Islands, Western Samoa, Vanuatu, Tonga.
Country Report. Pakistan, Afghanistan.
Country Report. Panama.
Country Report. Peru.
Country Report. Philippines.
Country Report. Poland.
Country Report. Portugal.
Country Report. Romania.
Country Report. Russia.
Country Report. Saudi Arabia.
Country Report. Senegal, The Gambia, Mauritania.
Country Report. Singapore.
Country Report. Slovakia.
Country Report. South Africa.
Country Report. South Korea, North Korea.
Country Report. Spain.
Country Report. Sri Lanka.
Country Report. Sudan.
Country Report. Sweden.
Country Report. Switzerland.
Country Report. Syria.
Country Report. Taiwan.
Country Report. Tanzania, Comoros.

Country Report. Thailand.
Country Report. Togo, Benin.
Country Report. Trinidad & Tobago, Guyana, Windward & Leeward Islands, Suriname, Netherlands Antilles, Aruba.
Country Report. Tunisia.
Country Report. Turkey.
Country Report. Uganda, Rwanda, Burundi.
Country Report. Ukraine.
Country Report. United Arab Emirates.
Country Report. United Kingdom.
Country Report. United States of America.
Country Report. Uruguay, Paraguay.
Country Report. Venezuela.
Country Report. Zambia, Zaire.
Country Report. Zimbabwe.
Country Reports.
Country Risk Service.
Country Risk Service. Algeria.
Country Risk Service. Angola.
Country Risk Service. Argentina.
Country Risk Service. Australia.
Country Risk Service. Bangladesh.
Country Risk Service. Bolivia.
Country Risk Service. Brazil.
Country Risk Service. Bulgaria.
Country Risk Service. Cameroon.
Country Risk Service. Chile.
Country Risk Service. China.
Country Risk Service. Colombia.
Country Risk Service. Congo.
Country Risk Service. Costa Rica.
Country Risk Service. Cote d'Ivoire.
Country Risk Service. Cyprus.
Country Risk Service. Czech Republic.
Country Risk Service. Dominican Republic.
Country Risk Service. Ecuador.
Country Risk Service. Egypt.
Country Risk Service. El Salvador.
Country Risk Service. Former Yugoslav Republics: Serbia, Montenegro, Macedonia.
Country Risk Service. Gabon.
Country Risk Service. Ghana.
Country Risk Service. Greece.
Country Risk Service. Guatemala.
Country Risk Service. Honduras.
Country Risk Service. Hong Kong.
Country Risk Service. Hungary.
Country Risk Service. India.
Country Risk Service. Indonesia.
Country Risk Service. Iran.
Country Risk Service. Iraq.
Country Risk Service. Israel.
Country Risk Service. Jamaica.
Country Risk Service. Jordan.
Country Risk Service. Kazakhstan.
Country Risk Service. Kenya.
Country Risk Service. Kuwait.
Country Risk Service. Libya.
Country Risk Service. Malawi.
Country Risk Service. Malaysia.
Country Risk Service. Mexico.
Country Risk Service. Morocco.
Country Risk Service. Namibia.
Country Risk Service. New Zealand.
Country Risk Service. Nicaragua.
Country Risk Service. Nigeria.
Country Risk Service. Pakistan.
Country Risk Service. Panama.
Country Risk Service. Papua New Guinea.
Country Risk Service. Paraguay.
Country Risk Service. Peru.
Country Risk Service. Philippines.
Country Risk Service. Poland.
Country Risk Service. Portugal.
Country Risk Service. Romania.
Country Risk Service. Russia.
Country Risk Service. Saudi Arabia.
Country Risk Service. Senegal.
Country Risk Service. Singapore.
Country Risk Service. Slovenia.
Country Risk Service. South Africa.
Country Risk Service. South Korea.
Country Risk Service. Spain.
Country Risk Service. Sri Lanka.
Country Risk Service. Sudan.
Country Risk Service. Syria.
Country Risk Service. Taiwan.
Country Risk Service. Thailand.
Country Risk Service. The Baltic Republics: Latvia, Estonia, Lithuania.
Country Risk Service. Trinidad and Tobago.
Country Risk Service. Tunisia.
Country Risk Service. Turkey.
Country Risk Service. Ukraine.
Country Risk Service. United Arab Emirates.
Country Risk Service. Uruguay.
Country Risk Service. Venezuela.
Country Risk Service. Yemen.
Country Risk Service. Zaire.
Country Risk Service. Zambia.
Country Risk Service. Zimbabwe.
Crain's Chicago Business. (CHIBUS)
Crain's Cleveland Business.
Crain's Detroit Business.
Crain's New York Business. (NYBUS)
Credit Card Management.
Criminal Appeal Reports.
Critical Issues.
Current Digest of the Post-Soviet Press.
Current Law Index.
D B.
D M News.
Daily Labor Report. (DLABRT)
Daily Report for Executives. (DREXEC)
Daily Tax Report. (BNADTR)
Dairy Foods.
Data Communications.
Defense & Foreign Affairs Strategic Policy.
Defense Electronics.
Defense Week.
Delaware Journal of Corporate Law.
Denver University Law Review.
Dickinson Law Review.
Direct Marketing.
Directory of Corporate Affiliations.
Directory of Healthcare Group Purchasing Organizations.
Directory of Hospital Personnel.
Discount Store News.
Discover (Burbank).
Drug Store News.
Duke Law Journal.
E C Energy Monthly.
E F T Report.
E N R. (ENR)
East Asian Business Intelligence.
East Asian Executive Reports.
East Europe & the Republics: A Political Risk Annual. (IBCRPT)
East European Energy Report.
East European Markets.
EcoCentral.
The Economist.
Electric Utility Week. (ELUTL)
Electrical World. (ELECWD)
Electronic Design.
Electronic Media.
Employee Health and Fitness.
Energy Daily.
Energy Economist.
Energy User News.
Engineering & Mining Journal.
Entertainment Law Reporter.
Environment Abstracts.
Environment Reporter. (ENVREP)
Environment Week.
Environmental Law (Portland).
Environmental Law Reporter.
Estate Planner's Alert.
Estate Planning (New York). (TAXRIA-Library)
European Energy Report.
Executive Memorandum.
Executive Report.
Executive Speaker.
The Expert and the Law.
F T C Freedom of Information Log.
F T C Watch.
Facts on File World News Digest with Index.
Family Law Reports.
Federal Contracts Report. (FDCONT)
Federal Law-Related Careers Directory.
Federal Register.
Federal Reserve Bulletin.
Federal Sentencing Reporter.
Federal Tax Coordinator 2d.
Federal Technology Report. (FEDTEC)
Financial Regulation Report.
Financial Times World Tax Report.
Financial World.
Financing Operations. Africa.
Financing Operations. Argentina.
Financing Operations. Australia.
Financing Operations. Belgium.
Financing Operations. Brazil.
Financing Operations. Canada.
Financing Operations. Chile.
Financing Operations. Colombia.
Financing Operations. Costa Rica.
Financing Operations. Czech Republic.
Financing Operations. El Salvador.
Financing Operations. France.
Financing Operations. Germany.
Financing Operations. Greece.
Financing Operations. Guatemala.
Financing Operations. Honduras.
Financing Operations. Hong Kong.
Financing Operations. Hungary.
Financing Operations. India.
Financing Operations. Italy.
Financing Operations. Japan.
Financing Operations. Malaysia.
Financing Operations. Mexico.
Financing Operations. Netherlands.
Financing Operations. Nicaragua.
Financing Operations. Nigeria.
Financing Operations. Norway.
Financing Operations. Panama.
Financing Operations. Philippines.
Financing Operations. Poland.
Financing Operations. Russia.
Financing Operations. Saudi Arabia.
Financing Operations. Singapore.
Financing Operations. South Africa.
Financing Operations. South Korea.
Financing Operations. Spain.
Financing Operations. Sweden.
Financing Operations. Switzerland.
Financing Operations. Taiwan.
Financing Operations. Thailand.
Financing Operations. United Kingdom.
Financing Operations. United States of America.
Financing Operations. Venezuela.
Flight International.
Florida Trend.
Food & Beverage Marketing.
Food & Drink Weekly.
Food in Canada.
Food Manufacture International.
Food Trade Review.
Footwear News.
Forbes.
Fordham Law Review.
Foreign Affairs.
Forensic Services Directory.
Foster Natural Gas Report.
Genesis Report - Dx.
Genesis Report - Rx.
George Mason Law Review.
George Washington Journal of International Law and Economics.
George Washington Law Review.
Georgetown Law Journal.
Georgia Journal of International and Comparative Law.
Georgia Trend.
Global Company Handbook.
Global Private Power.
Governing.
Government Employee Relations Report. (GOVEMP)
Graphic Arts Monthly.
Grocery Headquarters.
Guardian Weekly.
H F N.
Harvard Business Review.
Harvard Law Review. (Lexis)
Harvard Women's Law Journal.
Hastings Law Journal.
Hawaii Business.
Hazardous Waste Business. (HWB)
Health Matrix: Journal of Law-Medicine.
Health Policy & Biomedical Research: The Blue Sheet.
Heritage Foundation. Issue Bulletins.
Heritage Lectures.
High Yield Report.
Hofstra Law Review.
Hollywood Reporter.
Hospital Admitting Monthly.
Hospital Employee Health.
Hospital Infection Control.
Hospital Payment and Information Management.
Hospital Peer Review.
Hospital Risk Management.
Hospitals and Health Networks.
Houston Business Journal.
Howard Law Journal.
Hungarian Observer.
I D - The Voice of Foodservice Distribution.
I E A Oil Market Report.
Illinois Legal Times.
Improved Recovery Week.
Inc.
Independent Power Report. (IPR)
Index to Legal Periodicals & Books.
Indiana Business Magazine.
Indiana Law Journal.
Individual Employment Rights. (File LRRIER, IERNEW)
Industrial and Labor Relations Review.
Industrial Cases Reports.
Industrial Energy Bulletin.
Industrial Relations Law Reports.

Industry Week.
Information Today.
Informe Latinoamericano.
InfoWorld.
Inside D O T & Transportation Week.
Inside Energy with Federal Lands. *(INERGY)*
Inside F E R C. *(INFERC)*
Inside F E R C's Gas Market Report. *(GASMKT)*
Inside N R C. *(INNRC)*
Insurance Periodicals Index.
Integrated Waste Management.
International Coal Report.
International Country Risk Guide.
International Defense Review.
International Environment Reporter. *(File INTENV)*
International Gas Report.
International Lawyer.
International Legal Materials.
International Market Alert.
International Securities Regulation Report.
International Tax Report.
International Trade Reporter. *(INTRAD)*
International Tradeshow Directory.
Investing, Licensing and Trading. Americas.
Investing, Licensing and Trading. Argentina.
Investing, Licensing and Trading. Asia.
Investing, Licensing and Trading. Australia.
Investing, Licensing and Trading. Austria.
Investing, Licensing and Trading. Belgium.
Investing, Licensing and Trading. Brazil.
Investing, Licensing and Trading. Britain.
Investing, Licensing and Trading. Canada.
Investing, Licensing and Trading. Central America.
Investing, Licensing and Trading. Chile.
Investing, Licensing and Trading. China.
Investing, Licensing and Trading. Colombia.
Investing, Licensing and Trading. Czech Republic.
Investing, Licensing and Trading. Denmark.
Investing, Licensing and Trading. Ecuador.
Investing, Licensing and Trading. Egypt.
Investing, Licensing and Trading. Finland.
Investing, Licensing and Trading. France.
Investing, Licensing and Trading. Germany.
Investing, Licensing and Trading. Global Edition.
Investing, Licensing and Trading. Greece.
Investing, Licensing and Trading. Hong Kong.
Investing, Licensing and Trading. Hungary.
Investing, Licensing and Trading. India.
Investing, Licensing and Trading. Indonesia.
Investing, Licensing and Trading. Ireland.
Investing, Licensing and Trading. Israel.
Investing, Licensing and Trading. Italy.
Investing, Licensing and Trading. Japan.
Investing, Licensing and Trading. Kenya.
Investing, Licensing and Trading. Luxembourg.
Investing, Licensing and Trading. Malaysia.
Investing, Licensing and Trading. Mexico.
Investing, Licensing and Trading. Middle East - Africa.
Investing, Licensing and Trading. Netherlands.
Investing, Licensing and Trading. New Zealand.
Investing, Licensing and Trading. Nigeria.
Investing, Licensing and Trading. Norway.
Investing, Licensing and Trading. Pakistan.
Investing, Licensing and Trading. Panama.
Investing, Licensing and Trading. Peru.
Investing, Licensing and Trading. Philippines.
Investing, Licensing and Trading. Poland.
Investing, Licensing and Trading. Portugal.
Investing, Licensing and Trading. Puerto Rico.
Investing, Licensing and Trading. Russia.
Investing, Licensing and Trading. Saudi Arabia.
Investing, Licensing and Trading. Singapore.
Investing, Licensing and Trading. Slovakia.
Investing, Licensing and Trading. South Africa.
Investing, Licensing and Trading. South Korea.
Investing, Licensing and Trading. Spain.
Investing, Licensing and Trading. Sweden.
Investing, Licensing and Trading. Switzerland.
Investing, Licensing and Trading. Taiwan.
Investing, Licensing and Trading. Thailand.
Investing, Licensing and Trading. Turkey.
Investing, Licensing and Trading. United States of America.
Investing, Licensing and Trading. Uruguay.
Investing, Licensing and Trading. Venezuela.
Investing, Licensing and Trading. Vietnam.
Investor's Daily.
Iowa Law Review.
Jack O'Dwyer's Newsletter.
The Jerusalem Post.
The Jerusalem Post (Edition Francaise).
The Jerusalem Post (International Edition).
John Marshall Law Review.
Joint Commission Perspectives.
Journal of Advertising.
Journal of Blacks in Higher Education.
Journal of Commerce and Commercial.

Journal of Consumer Research.
Journal of International Taxation.
Journal of Law & Commerce.
Journal of Marketing.
Journal of Marketing Research.
Journal of Partnership Taxation. *(TAXRIA-Library)*
Journal of Pediatric Surgery.
Journal of Portfolio Management.
The Journal of Taxation. *(TAXRIA-Library)*
Konzerne in Schaubildern.
L A N Times. *(LANTME)*
L D C Debt Report.
Labor Relations Reference Manual. *(File LRRM)*
Labor Relations Reporter.
Labor Relations Reporter. Labor Arbitration and Dispute Settlements.
Lagniappe Letter.
Las Vegas Business Press.
Latin American Economy and Business.
Latin American Informes Especiales.
Latin American Regional Reports - Andean Group.
Latin American Special Reports.
Latin American Weekly Report.
Law Practice Management.
Legal Times.
LegalTrac. *(LGLIND)*
Life.
Life Sciences & Biotechnology Update.
Link-Up.
Los Angeles.
Louisiana Law Review.
Louisville Magazine.
McGraw-Hill's Biotechnology Newswatch. *(BIOTEC)*
Maclean's.
MacWEEK.
Magazine Index.
Maine Law Review.
Major 20th-Century Writers. *(GALBIO)*
Managerial Law.
Manitoba Business Magazine.
Marine Log.
Market Research Europe.
Marketing News.
Martindale-Hubbell Law Directory.
Massachusetts Lawyer Weekly.
Mealey's Daubert Report. *(MEALEY)*
Mealey's Emerging Insurance Disputes. *(MEALEY)*
Mealey's Emerging Toxic Torts. *(MEALEY)*
Mealey's Insurance Law Weekly. *(MEALEY)*
Mealey's Insurance Supplement. *(MEALEY)*
Mealey's International Arbitration Report. *(MEALEY)*
Mealey's Litigation Report: Asbestos. *(MEALEY)*
Mealey's Litigation Report: Bad Faith. *(MEALEY)*
Mealey's Litigation Report: Biotechnology. *(MEALEY)*
Mealey's Litigation Report: Breast Implants. *(MEALEY)*
Mealey's Litigation Report: Drugs and Medical Devices. *(MEALEY)*
Mealey's Litigation Report: Insurance. *(MEALEY)*
Mealey's Litigation Report: Insurance Fraud. *(MEALEY)*
Mealey's Litigation Report: Insurance Insolvency. *(MEALEY)*
Mealey's Litigation Report: Intellectual Property. *(MEALEY)*
Mealey's Litigation Report: Latex. *(MEALEY)*
Mealey's Litigation Report: Lead. *(MEALEY)*
Mealey's Litigation Report: Patents. *(MEALEY)*
Mealey's Litigation Report: Pedicle Screws. *(MEALEY)*
Mealey's Litigation Report: Reinsurance. *(MEALEY)*
Mealey's Litigation Report: Superfund. *(MEALEY)*
Mealey's Litigation Report: Tobacco. *(MEALEY)*
Mechanical Engineering.
MediaWeek.
Medical Devices, Diagnostics & Instrumentation Reports: The Gray Sheet.
Medical Marketing & Media.
Melbourne University Law Review.
Memphis Business Journal.
Metals Week. *(METLWK)*
Metropolitan News - Enterprise. *(METNWS)*
Mexico & N A F T A Report.
Michigan Citizen. *(ETHNIC NEWSWATCH)*
Michigan Law Review.
Michigan Lawyers Weekly.
Middle East Business Intelligence.
Middle East Executive Reports.
Military Law Review.
Mining Annual Review.
Mining Magazine.
Minneapolis - St. Paul CityBusiness.
Minnesota Law Review.
Minority Markets Alert.

Modern Brewery Age.
Modern Plastics. *(MODPLA)*
Money (New York).
Money Laundering Alert.
Nashville Business Journal.
National Association of Insurance Commissioners. Proceedings.
National Cancer Institute. Journal.
National Directory of Law Enforcement Administrators and Correctional Institutions.
National Law Journal.
National Newspaper Index.
Nebraska Law Review.
Network World.
Nevada Lawyer.
New England Law Review.
New Jersey Business.
New Jersey Law Journal.
New Law Journal.
New Mexico Law Review.
New Orleans CityBusiness.
New Product News.
New Technology Week.
New York Law Journal.
The New York Times.
New York University Law Review.
Newsmakers.
Newsweek.
The Nikkei Weekly.
Nonprescription Pharmaceuticals and Nutritionals: The Tan Sheet.
North Carolina Journal of International Law and Commercial Regulation.
North Carolina Law Review.
North Sea Letter.
North Sea Rig Forecast.
Northern Ontario Business.
Northwestern University Law Review.
NotiSur.
Nuclear News.
NuclearFuel. *(NUFUEL)*
Nucleonics Week. *(NUWEEK)*
O'Dwyer's P R Services Report.
Offshore (Tulsa).
Ohio Northern University Law Review.
Ohio State Law Journal.
Oil & Gas Journal.
Oregon Law Review.
Oregon State Bar Bulletin.
The P R S Group. Country Reports: World Service. *(IBCRPT)*
The P R S Group. Country Reports: Algeria.
The P R S Group. Country Reports: Argentina.
The P R S Group. Country Reports: Bolivia.
The P R S Group. Country Reports: Brazil.
The P R S Group. Country Reports: Bulgaria.
The P R S Group. Country Reports: Cameroon.
The P R S Group. Country Reports: Chile.
The P R S Group. Country Reports: China.
The P R S Group. Country Reports: Colombia.
The P R S Group. Country Reports: Congo (Kinshasa).
The P R S Group. Country Reports: Costa Rica.
The P R S Group. Country Reports: Cote d'Ivoire.
The P R S Group. Country Reports: Czech Republic.
The P R S Group. Country Reports: Dominican Republic.
The P R S Group. Country Reports: Ecuador.
The P R S Group. Country Reports: Egypt.
The P R S Group. Country Reports: El Salvador.
The P R S Group. Country Reports: Gabon.
The P R S Group. Country Reports: Guatemala.
The P R S Group. Country Reports: Guinea.
The P R S Group. Country Reports: Haiti.
The P R S Group. Country Reports: Honduras.
The P R S Group. Country Reports: Hong Kong.
The P R S Group. Country Reports: Hungary.
The P R S Group. Country Reports: India.
The P R S Group. Country Reports: Indonesia.
The P R S Group. Country Reports: Iran.
The P R S Group. Country Reports: Iraq.
The P R S Group. Country Reports: Israel.
The P R S Group. Country Reports: Jamaica.
The P R S Group. Country Reports: Kenya.
The P R S Group. Country Reports: Kuwait.
The P R S Group. Country Reports: Libya.
The P R S Group. Country Reports: Malaysia.
The P R S Group. Country Reports: Mexico.
The P R S Group. Country Reports: Morocco.
The P R S Group. Country Reports: Nicaragua.
The P R S Group. Country Reports: Nigeria.
The P R S Group. Country Reports: Oman.
The P R S Group. Country Reports: Pakistan.
The P R S Group. Country Reports: Panama.
The P R S Group. Country Reports: Peru.
The P R S Group. Country Reports: Philippines.
The P R S Group. Country Reports: Poland.

The P R S Group. Country Reports: Romania.
The P R S Group. Country Reports: Russia.
The P R S Group. Country Reports: Saudi Arabia.
The P R S Group. Country Reports: Singapore.
The P R S Group. Country Reports: South Africa.
The P R S Group. Country Reports: South Korea.
The P R S Group. Country Reports: Sri Lanka.
The P R S Group. Country Reports: Sudan.
The P R S Group. Country Reports: Syria.
The P R S Group. Country Reports: Taiwan.
The P R S Group. Country Reports: Thailand.
The P R S Group. Country Reports: Tunisia.
The P R S Group. Country Reports: Turkey.
The P R S Group. Country Reports: Ukraine.
The P R S Group. Country Reports: United Arab Emirates.
The P R S Group. Country Reports: Uruguay.
The P R S Group. Country Reports: Venezuela.
The P R S Group. Country Reports: Vietnam.
The P R S Group. Country Reports: Zambia.
The P R S Group. Country Reports: Zimbabwe.
The P R S Group. Executive Reports: Australia.
The P R S Group. Executive Reports: Austria.
The P R S Group. Executive Reports: Belgium.
The P R S Group. Executive Reports: Canada.
The P R S Group. Executive Reports: Denmark.
The P R S Group. Executive Reports: Finland.
The P R S Group. Executive Reports: France.
The P R S Group. Executive Reports: Germany.
The P R S Group. Executive Reports: Greece.
The P R S Group. Executive Reports: Ireland.
The P R S Group. Executive Reports: Italy.
The P R S Group. Executive Reports: Japan.
The P R S Group. Executive Reports: Netherlands.
The P R S Group. Executive Reports: New Zealand.
The P R S Group. Executive Reports: Norway.
The P R S Group. Executive Reports: Portugal.
The P R S Group. Executive Reports: Puerto Rico.
The P R S Group. Executive Reports: Spain.
The P R S Group. Executive Reports: Sweden.
The P R S Group. Executive Reports: United Kingdom.
The P R S Group. Executive Reports: United States.
Pacific Business News.
Pacific Law Journal.
Pediatrics (English Edition).
Pensions & Investments. (PENINV)
People Weekly.
Pharmaceutical Approvals Monthly.
Philadelphia Business Journal.
Platt's International Petrochemical Report.
Platt's Oilgram News. (PONEWS)
Platt's Oilgram Price Report. (PPRICE)
Policy Review.
Political Finance & Lobby Reporter.
Political Risk Yearbook.
Political Risk Yearbook. Volume 1: North & Central America.
Political Risk Yearbook. Volume 2: Middle East & North Africa.
Political Risk Yearbook. Volume 3: South America.
Political Risk Yearbook. Volume 4: Sub-Saharan Africa.
Political Risk Yearbook. Volume 5: Asia & the Pacific.
Political Risk Yearbook. Volume 6: Europe.
Power (New York). (POWER)
Power in Asia.
Power in Europe.
Power in Latin America.
Power U K.
Prepared Foods.
Prescription Pharmaceuticals and Biotechnology: The Pink Sheet.
Private Placement Reporter.
Progress in Cardiovascular Diseases.
Progressive Grocer.
Property, Planning and Compensation Reports.
Public Health Reports.
Public Perspective. (PUBPER)
Public Pulse.
Public Utilities Fortnightly.
Public Utilities Reports.
Publishers, Distributors & Wholesalers of the United States. (PDW)
Pulp and Paper.
Pulp & Paper International.
Religious Leaders of America.
Renewable Energy Report.
Research Alert (New York).
The Review of Banking and Financial Services. (RBFS)

The Review of Securities & Commodities Regulation. (RSCR)
Road Traffic Reports.
Roll Call.
Russia and Commonwealth Business Law Report.
Sacramento Business Journal.
St. Louis Commerce.
St. Thomas Law Review.
Same-Day Surgery.
San Diego Daily Transcript.
Sarasota Magazine.
Screen Finance.
Seattle University Law Review.
Securities Regulation & Law Report. (SECREG)
Securities Week. (SECWK)
Seminars in Hematology.
Sexually Transmitted Diseases.
Soap, Cosmetics, Chemical Specialties.
SourceMex.
South Carolina Law Review.
Southern Cone Report.
Southern Illinois University Law Journal.
The Sporting News.
Sports Illustrated.
Standard & Poor's Corporation Records.
Standard Directory of Advertisers (Business Classifications Edition).
Stanford Law Review.
State Tax Notes.
Stores.
Suffolk Transnational Law Review.
Summary of World Broadcasts. Part 1: Former U S S R (Daily).
Summary of World Broadcasts. Part 1: Former U S S R (Weekly Economic Report).
Summary of World Broadcasts. Part 2: Central Europe, the Balkans (Daily).
Summary of World Broadcasts. Part 2: Central Europe, the Balkans (Weekly Economic Report)
Summary of World Broadcasts. Part 3: Asia - Pacific (Daily).
Summary of World Broadcasts. Part 3: Asia - Pacific (Weekly Economic Report).
Summary of World Broadcasts. Part 4: Middle East (Daily).
Summary of World Broadcasts. Part 4: Middle East (Weekly Economic Report).
Summary of World Broadcasts. Part 5: Africa, Latin America and the Caribbean (Daily).
Summary of World Broadcasts. Part 5: Africa, Latin America and the Caribbean (Weekly Economic Report).
Supermarket Business.
Supermarket News.
Talking Points.
The Tax Directory.
Tax Lawyer.
Tax News Service.
Tax Notes.
Tax Notes International.
Tax Treaties Data Base on C D - R O M.
Taxation for Accountants.
Taxation for Lawyers.
Tea and Coffee Trade Journal.
Telecom Markets.
Texas Law Review.
Texas Lawyer.
Time.
Toiletries, Fragrances and Skin Care: The Rose Sheet.
Tort & Insurance Law Journal.
Toxics Law Reporter. (File TOXICS)
Triangle Business Journal.
Tulane Environmental Law Journal.
Tulane European and Civil Law Forum.
Tulane Law Review.
Tulane Maritime Law Journal.
Twin Cities Reader.
U C Davis Law Review.
U C L A Law Review.
U K Gas Report.
U S A Today.
U S Banker.
U S News & World Report.
Ulrich's International Periodicals Directory. (ULRICHS)
Ulrich's Update. (ULRICHS)
U.S. Department of Agriculture. Economic Research Service. Food Review.
United States Law Week. (USLW)
University of Chicago Law Review.
University of Colorado Law Review.
University of Dayton Law Review.
University of Kansas Law Review.
University of Pennsylvania Journal of International Economic Law.
University of Pennsylvania Law Review.

University of Pittsburgh Law Review.
University of San Francisco Law Review.
Utility Environment Report. (UER)
Vanderbilt Journal of Transnational Law.
Vanderbilt Law Review.
Village Voice.
Virginia Journal of International Law.
Warfield's Business Record.
Warsaw Voice.
Washington and Lee Law Review.
Washington Law Review.
Washington Quarterly.
Washington University Law Quarterly.
Washingtonian.
Wayne Law Review.
Weekly Law Reports.
Weekly of Business Aviation. (WBA)
Weekly Pharmacy Reports: The Green Sheet.
The Weekly Standard.
Wer Liefert Was?
Westchester County Business Journal.
Who's Who Among Black Americans.
Who's Who Among Hispanic Americans.
Who's Who in Technology.
Wichita Business Journal.
William Mitchell Law Review.
Wisconsin Law Review.
Die Woche.
Women's Wear Daily.
World Accounting Report. (WAR)
World Factbook.
World Media. Broadcasting News.
The WorldPaper.
Worldscope Company Database.
Yale Law Journal.
Youth Markets Alert. (AD12)

LOGIN INFORMATION SERVICES
360 N. Robert St., Ste. 711, Saint Paul, MN 55101. Tel: 612-222-6506 Fax: 612-222-6577.
American City & County.
Governing.

MEDIASTREAM (Subsidiary of: Knight-Ridder, Inc.)
2005 Market St., Ste. 1020, Philadelphia, PA 19103. Tel: 215-587-4410 Fax: 215-587-2148.
Arizona Business Gazette.
Campaign.
Discover (Burbank).
The Economist.
Entertainment Weekly.
Journal of Commerce and Commercial.
Marketing.
Money (New York).
New Scientist.
News Library News.
People Weekly.
Sports Illustrated.
Time.
U S A Today.
W R R I News.
Wall Street Transcript.

NATIONAL DATA CORP.
2 National Data Plaza, Corporate Sq., Atlanta, GA 30329. Tel: 404-728-2000
Boston Business Journal.
Brooklyn Journal of International Law.
Capital University Law Review.
International Financial Statistics.
Virginia Law Review.

NATIONAL LIBRARY OF MEDICINE
8600 Rockville Pike, Bethesda, MD 20209. Tel: 301-496-6193 Fax: 301-496-4000.
Bibliography of Bioethics.
Bibliography of the History of Medicine.
Hospital and Health Administration Index.
Index Medicus.
Index to Dental Literature.
International Nursing Index.
International Pharmaceutical Abstracts.
Issues in Law and Medicine.
Journal of Magnetic Resonance Imaging.
List of Serials Indexed for Online Users.
N I O S H T I C.
Ongoing Current Bibliography of Plastic & Reconstructive Surgery.
Population Index.
Psychopharmacology Bulletin.
R T E C S.

10252 VENDOR LISTING/SERIALS ONLINE

NEWSNET (Subsidiary of: Subs. of Independent Pubns.)

945 Haverford Rd., Bryn Mawr, PA 19010. Tel: 610-527-8030
Fax: 610-527-0338.

Access Reports. *(GT10)*
Advanced Intelligent Network News. *(TE15)*
Aerospace Daily. *(AE29)*
Aerospace Propulsion. *(AE34)*
Affirmative Action - E E O Personnel Update.
Africa News Online.
Aging Research & Training News.
AIDS Weekly Plus. *(HH14)*
Air Cargo Report.
Air Safety Week. *(AE16)*
Air - Water Pollution Report. *(EV10)*
Aircraft Value Newsletter.
Airline Financial News. *(AE25)*
Airports. *(AE21)*
American Banker. *(FI10)*
American Banker's Washington Watch. *(FI05)*
American Marketplace. *(AD13)*
Americans with Disabilities Act Update.
Applied Genetics News. *(BT03)*
Architectural Record. *(BC13)*
Asbestos & Lead Abatement Report. *(EV27)*
Asset Sales Report. *(FI33)*
Audio Week. *(EC93)*
Audiotex Update. *(TE16)*
Autoparts Report. *(AU09)*
Aviation Daily. *(AE28)*
Aviation Europe. *(AE35)*
Aviation Week & Space Technology. *(AE30)*
B T Today. *(TE40)*
Bank Automation News.
Bank Mergers & Acquisitions. *(FI59)*
Bank Mutual Fund Report.
Bank Network News. *(FI71)*
Bank Technology News. *(FI70)*
Battery & E V Technology News. *(RD30)*
Biotech Business. *(BT06)*
Blood Weekly.
The Bond Buyer. *(FI08)*
Book Publishing Report. *(PB19)*
Boot Cove Economic Forecast. *(IV29)*
Bowne Digest for Corporate & Securities Lawyers. *(LA11)*
Broadband Networking News. *(TE51)*
Business Travel News. *(TR08)*
Business Week. *(GB55)*
Byte. *(EC34)*
C A D - C A M Update. *(MG15)*
C D Computing News. *(EC67)*
C D - R O M Databases. *(EC71)*
C D - R O M World.
C F O Alert (Weekly).
Cable - Telco Report. *(TE106)*
California Planning and Development Report. *(EV23)*
California Public Finance. *(FI65)*
Campus Crime.
Cancer Weekly Plus. *(HH15)*
Card Fax. *(FI67)*
Card News. *(FI24)*
Cellular Sales & Marketing. *(TE72)*
Chemical Engineering. *(CH19)*
Chemical Monitor. *(CH15)*
Chief Executive Officers Newsletter.
Child Protection Report.
Coal Tech International. *(EY76)*
Coal Week. *(EY77)*
Coal Week International. *(EY78)*
Commerce Business Daily.
Communications Daily. *(TE01)*
CommunicationsWeek. *(TE23)*
CommunicationsWeek International. *(TE28)*
Commuter - Regional Airline News. *(AE25)*
Commuter Regional Airline News International. *(AE26)*
Composites Industry Monthly.
Computer Protocols. *(EC74)*
Computer Reseller News. *(EC07)*
Computergram International. *(EC72)*
Computers in Libraries.
Congressional Activities. *(GT20)*
Construction Claims Citator. *(BC12)*
Construction Claims Monthly.
Construction Claims Training Guide.
Construction Injury Liability Monthly.
Corporate E F T Report. *(FI12)*
Country Forecasts (Syracuse). *(IT933)*
Cowles - SIMBA Media Daily.
The Cowles - SIMBA Report on Directory Publishing. *(PB30)*
Credit Card Management.

Credit Risk Management. *(FI57)*
Daily Report for Executives.
Daily Tax Report.
Data Communications. *(TE37)*
Defense Daily. *(DE01)*
Defense Week. *(DE16)*
Digest of Activities of Congress.
Document Imaging Report. *(EC02)*
E & P Environment.
E D I News. *(TE80)*
E F T Report. *(FI11)*
E M F Keeptrack.
E M M S. *(EC32)*
E N R. *(BC06)*
EcoCentral.
Economic Opportunity Report.
Editors Only. *(PB13)*
Education Daily. *(ED08)*
Education Technology News.
Educational Marketer. *(PB20)*
Electric Utility Week. *(EY65)*
Electric Utility Week's Demand-Side Report. *(EY87)*
Electrical World. *(EY03)*
Electro Manufacturing.
Electronic Buyers' News. *(EC12)*
Electronic Engineering Times. *(EC14)*
Electronic Information Report. *(PB22)*
Electronic Materials Technology News. *(ML04)*
Electronic Messaging News. *(TE05)*
Electronic World News. *(EC13)*
Emergency Preparedness News. *(GT34)*
Emerging & Special Situations. *(FI16)*
Employment Opportunities (Englewood).
Energy Conservation News. *(EY59)*
Energy Daily. *(EY57)*
Energy Design Update. *(BC08)*
Enhanced Energy Recovery News. *(EY60)*
Environment Watch: Latin America. *(EV44)*
Environment Week. *(EV25)*
Environmental Health Letter.
Environmental Problems & Remediation.
Equipment and Materials Update.
The Exporter. *(IT04)*
F C C Report. *(TE52)*
F T C Watch. *(GT17)*
Fair Employment Report.
Faulkner & Gray's Medicine and Health. *(HH21)*
Federal & State Insurance Week. *(IN04)*
Federal Contract Disputes.
Federal Grants & Contracts Weekly. *(GT37)*
Federal Research Report. *(RD10)*
Federal Technology Report. *(RD46)*
Fiber Optics News. *(TE29)*
Financial Advertising Review.
Flame Retardancy News. *(RD40)*
Food & Drink Weekly. *(FB03)*
Food Chemical News. *(FB07)*
For Your Eyes Only. *(DE15)*
Fusion Power Report. *(EY46)*
George Wells' Washington Beverage Insight.
Global Environmental Change.
Global Positioning & Navigation News. *(DE24)*
Golob's Oil Pollution Bulletin. *(EV05)*
Ground Water Monitor. *(EV18)*
Hazardous Materials Intelligence Report.
Hazardous Materials Transportation. *(EV35)*
Hazardous Waste Business. *(EV41)*
Hazardous Waste News. *(CH10)*
HazMat Transport News. *(CH14)*
Headway. *(PO05)*
Health Alliance Alert. *(HH23)*
Health Care Strategic Management.
Health Grants & Contracts Weekly. *(HH10)*
Health Industry Today.
Health Legislation. *(HH22)*
Health Network Letter.
Health News Daily. *(HH01)*
Health Plan Business Advisor. *(HH16)*
Healthcare Advertising Review.
Helicopter News. *(AE12)*
Heller Report on Education Technology and Telecommunications Markets. *(ED11)*
High Tech Ceramics News. *(ML05)*
High Tech Separations News. *(BT04)*
High Yield Report.
Hospital Materials Management.
Hospital Payment and Information Management.
Hotline (Falls Church). *(PO01)*
I B T. *(IT92)*
I S D N News. *(TE90)*
Ice Cream Reporter. *(FB04)*
Imaging Update. *(EC05)*
Independent Power Report. *(EY67)*
Industrial Energy Bulletin. *(EY68)*
Industrial Health & Hazards Update. *(LA04)*
Industries in Transition. *(GB46)*
Information & Interactive Services Report. *(TE41)*

The Information Freeway Report.
The Information Report. *(IT08)*
Information Week. *(TE34)*
Innovator's Digest. *(RD09)*
Inside D O T & Transportation Week. *(GT41)*
Inside Energy with Federal Lands. *(EY69)*
Inside F E R C. *(EY70)*
Inside F E R C's Gas Market Report. *(EY66)*
Inside N R C. *(EY71)*
Integrated Waste Management. *(EV40)*
Interactive Home.
Interactive Video News. *(AD07)*
International Banking Regulator. *(IT36)*
International Counterterrorism & Security.
The International Information Report. *(IT75)*
International Market Alert. *(FI58)*
International Product Alert. *(AD25)*
International Solar Energy Intelligence Report.
Item Processing Report. *(EC19)*
J E I Report.
Japan - U S Business Report.
Kane's Beverage Week. *(FB06)*
L A N Product News. *(EC99)*
L A N Times. *(EC42)*
L D C Debt Report. *(FI42)*
Land Mobile Radio News. *(TE13)*
Land Use Law Report. *(EV02)*
Law Office Technology Review. *(LA15)*
Lawyers' Micro Users Group Newsletter. *(LA05)*
Legal Publisher.
Legislative Network for Nurses.
Liability Week.
Life Sciences & Biotechnology Update.
Limited Partnership Investment Review.
Local Competition Report.
M P T Review. *(IV48)*
McGraw-Hill's Biotechnology Newswatch. *(BT08)*
Mainframe Computing. *(EC87)*
Managed Care Outlook. *(HH12)*
Management Matters. *(MT11)*
Manufacturing Automation. *(MG17)*
Market: Asia Pacific.
Market: Europe.
Market: Latin America.
Media Industry Newsletter. *(PB14)*
Medical Outcomes and Guidelines Alert.
Medical Utilization Management.
Medical Waste News. *(EV30)*
Membrane & Separation Technology News. *(BT05)*
Mental Health Law Reporter.
Mental Health Report.
Mergers and Restructurings.
Metals Week. *(ML01)*
Micro M D Newsletter.
Military & Commercial Fiber Business. *(DE06)*
Military Robotics Newsletter. *(DE14)*
Mobile Communications Report. *(TE32)*
Mobile Phone News. *(TE25)*
Mobile Satellite News (Potomac). *(TE27)*
Modem User News. *(EC97)*
Modern Plastics. *(CH23)*
Multimedia Monitor. *(EC70)*
Networks Update. *(EC95)*
New Technology Week. *(RD23)*
NewsNet Action Letter. *(PB99)*
Noise Regulation Report. *(EV19)*
Northeast Power Report. *(EY88)*
Northern Ireland News Service. *(IT74)*
NotiSur.
Nuclear Waste News. *(EV03)*
NuclearFuel. *(EY72)*
Nucleonics Week. *(EY73)*
Occupational Health & Safety Letter.
Oil Price Information Service. *(EY02)*
Oil Spill U S Law Report. *(EV06)*
Older Americans Report.
Online Libraries and Microcomputers. *(PB42)*
Online Newsletter. *(PB41)*
Online Product News. *(TE27)*
Optical Materials and Engineering News. *(RD37)*
Optical Memory News. *(EC50)*
Origins, C N S Documentary Service. *(CN03)*
Oxy-Fuel News.
P C Business Products. *(EC94)*
P C S Week. *(TE12)*
Pesticide & Toxic Chemical News. *(CH18)*
Photobulletin. *(PB26)*
Photobulletin Daily.
Photomarket. *(PB17)*
PhotoStockNotes. *(PB12)*
The Physician and Sportsmedicine. *(ME05)*
Plastics Business News. *(CH17)*
Platt's International Petrochemical Report. *(CH20)*
Platt's Oilgram News. *(EY74)*
Platt's Oilgram Price Report. *(EY75)*
Political Finance & Lobby Reporter. *(PO02)*

ULRICH'S INTERNATIONAL PERIODICALS DIRECTORY 1998

Political Risk Letter. *(IT29)*
Postgraduate Medicine. *(ME06)*
Power (New York). *(EY84)*
Privacy Journal.
Private Placement Reporter. *(FI61)*
Product Alert. *(AD24)*
Product Safety Letter. *(GB52)*
Productivity Software. *(EC80)*
Profiles in Healthcare Marketing.
Public Broadcasting Report. *(PB04)*
R T C Watch. *(FI03)*
RateGram. *(IV61)*
Regulatory Compliance Watch. *(FI04)*
Report on A T & T. *(TE50)*
Report on Corporate Educational Support.
Report on Defense Plant Waste. *(EV28)*
Report on Disability Programs.
Report on Education of the Disadvantaged.
Report on Healthcare Management Solutions.
Report on Literacy Program. *(ED10)*
Report on Preschool Programs.
Report on School-Age Child Care.
The Review of Banking and Financial Services. *(FI17)*
The Review of Securities & Commodities Regulation. *(FI20)*
Robotronics Age Newsletter. *(EC16)*
S E C News Digest. *(EV96)*
S M T Trends. *(MG18)*
Satellite Industry Directory. *(TE83E)*
Satellite News. *(TE03)*
Satellite Week. *(AE01)*
Securities Week. *(FI27)*
Security Intelligence. *(IT64)*
Semiconductor Industry & Business Survey Newsletter. *(EC35)*
Sensor Business Digest. *(MG16)*
Sludge Newsletter. *(CH13)*
Small Business Tax Review. *(TX15)*
Solid Waste Report. *(EV20)*
SourceMex. *(IT99)*
Southeast Power Report. *(EY89)*
Space Business News. *(AE11)*
Space Calendar. *(AE04)*
Space Fax Daily. *(AE07)*
Space R & D Alert.
Speednews. *(AE15)*
Standard & Poor's Corporation Records.
State & Local Communications Report. *(TE59)*
State Tax Review.
State Telephone Regulation Report. *(TE47)*
Superconductor Week.
T R Wireless News. *(TE45)*
Tax Management Weekly Report.
Technology Access Report. *(RD38)*
Technology Alert. *(RD09)*
Technology Transfer Week. *(DE17)*
Telco Business Report. *(TE49)*
Telco Competition Report. *(TE62)*
Tele-Service News. *(TE21)*
Telecommunications Reports. *(TE11)*
Telecommunications Reports International. *(TE14)*
Telephone Industry Directory. *(TE83E)*
Television Digest with Consumer Electronics. *(PB01)*
Tobacco Industry Litigation Reporter.
Tour & Travel News - T T G North America. *(TR09)*
Tuberculosis & Airborne Disease Weekly.
U S Oil Week. *(EY55)*
U S Rail News. *(TS11)*
U.S. Centers for Disease Control. Morbidity and Mortality Weekly Report.
Urban Transport News. *(TS10)*
Utility Environment Report. *(EV42)*
Utility Reporter - Fuels Energy & Power. *(EY12)*
Video Technology News. *(PB39)*
Video Week. *(EL01)*
Voice Technology & Services News.
Washington Trade Daily.
Waste Treatment Technology News. *(EV26)*
Weekly of Business Aviation. *(AE20)*
Wing. *(AE06)*
Wing Newsletter.
Workgroup Computing Report.
World Airline News. *(AE31)*
World Airport Week.
Worldwide Databases. *(PB44)*
Worldwide Energy. *(EY63)*
Worldwide Telecom. *(TE19)*
Worldwide Videotex Update. *(PB08)*
4 1 1 Newsletter. *(TE95)*

OCLC ONLINE COMPUTER LIBRARY CTR., INC.
6565 Frantz Rd., Dublin, OH 43017-0702. Tel: 614-764-6000 Telex: 810-339-2026
Fax: 614-764-6096.
American Doctoral Dissertations. *(EPIC)*
Applied Physics Letters.
Applied Science & Technology Index.
Art Index.
Bibliography and Index of Geology. *(EPIC and First Search)*
Biography Index.
Biological & Agricultural Index.
Biology Digest.
Book Review Digest.
Business Periodicals Index.
Consumers Index.
Current Opinion in Anaesthesiology.
Current Opinion in Biotechnology.
Current Opinion in Cardiology.
Current Opinion in Cell Biology.
Current Opinion in Critical Care.
Current Opinion in Dermatology.
Current Opinion in Endocrinology & Diabetes.
Current Opinion in Gastroenterology.
Current Opinion in Genetics & Development.
Current Opinion in Hematology.
Current Opinion in Immunology.
Current Opinion in Infectious Diseases.
Current Opinion in Lipidology.
Current Opinion in Nephrology & Hypertension.
Current Opinion in Neurobiology.
Current Opinion in Neurology.
Current Opinion in Obstetrics & Gynecology.
Current Opinion in Oncology.
Current Opinion in Ophthalmology.
Current Opinion in Orthopedics.
Current Opinion in Otolaryngology & Head and Neck Surgery.
Current Opinion in Pediatrics.
Current Opinion in Periodontology.
Current Opinion in Psychiatry.
Current Opinion in Pulmonary Medicine.
Current Opinion in Rheumatology.
Current Opinion in Structural Biology.
Current Opinion in Surgical Infections.
Current Opinion in Urology.
Dissertation Abstracts International. Section A: Humanities and Social Sciences. *(EPIC)*
Dissertation Abstracts International. Section B: Physical Sciences and Engineering. *(EPIC)*
Dissertation Abstracts International. Section C: Worldwide. *(EPIC)*
Dissertation Abstracts on Disc. *(ERIC)*
Education Index.
Electronics Letters.
Electronics Letters Online.
General Science Index.
Humanities Index.
Immunology Today.
Index to Legal Periodicals & Books.
Institute of Electrical and Electronics Engineers. Proceedings.
Journal of Applied Physiology.
Library Literature.
Masters Abstracts International. *(EPIC)*
A Matter of Fact: Statements Containing Statistics on Current Social, Economic and Political Issues.
The Online Journal of Current Clinical Trials.
Online Journal of Knowledge Synthesis for Nursing.
P A I S International in Print.
Physical Review Letters.
R I L M Abstracts of Music Literature.
Readers' Guide Abstracts.
Readers' Guide to Periodical Literature.
Social Sciences Index.
Sociological Abstracts.
Wilson Abstracts.
Wilson Applied Science and Technology Abstracts.
Wilson Business Abstracts.
Wilson Education Abstracts.
Wilson General Science Abstracts.
Wilson Humanities Abstracts.
Wilson Social Sciences Abstracts.
Worldscope Company Database.

OFICINA ESPANOLA DE PATENTES Y MARCAS
Panama 1, 28071 Madrid, Spain Tel: 349-53-00
Telex: 47020 RPI-E
Fax: 457-22-80.
Boletin Oficial de la Propiedad Industrial. 1: Marcas y Otros Signos Distintivos.
Boletin Oficial de la Propiedad Industrial. 2: Patentes y Modelos de Utilidad.
Boletin Oficial de la Propiedad Industrial. 3: Modelos y Dibujos Industriales y Artisticos.
Boletin Oficial de la Propiedad Industrial. 4: Resumenes de Patentes.

OVID TECHNOLOGIES, INC.
333 Seventh Ave., New York, NY 10001. Tel: 212-563-3006
Fax: 212-563-3784.
A B A Banking Journal. *(TSAP)*
A B I - INFORM. *(INFO)*
A H F S Drug Information. *(DIFT)*
Academic Abstracts C D - R O M.
Academic Index. *(ACAD)*
Administrative Science Quarterly.
Adweek (Los Angeles). *(TSAP)*
Adweek (New York). *(TSAP)*
Aerospace Daily. *(TSAP)*
Age and Ageing.
Agricultural Supply Industry. *(PHIN)*
Agroforestry Abstracts.
Agrow. *(PHIN,PHIC,PHID)*
Air Conditioning, Heating & Refrigeration News. *(TSAP)*
Alcoholism & Drug Abuse Weekly.
American Academy of Child and Adolescent Psychiatry. Journal.
American Banker.
American College of Cardiology. Journal.
American Doctoral Dissertations.
American Family Physician.
American Geriatrics Society. Journal.
American Heart Journal.
American Journal of Cardiology.
The American Journal of Medicine.
American Journal of Obstetrics and Gynecology.
American Journal of Physical Medicine and Rehabilitation.
American Journal of Psychiatry.
American Journal of Public Health.
American Journal of Surgery.
Anesthesia and Analgesia.
Anesthesiology.
Animal Pharm. *(PHIN,PHIC,PHID)*
Annals of Internal Medicine.
Annals of Neurology.
Annals of the Rheumatic Diseases.
Applied Science & Technology Index.
Archives of Disease in Childhood.
Archives of Disease in Childhood. Fetal and Neonatal Edition.
Art Index.
Arthritis and Rheumatism.
Arts & Humanities Citation Index. *(AHCI)*
B L A S T.
B M J.
Biological Abstracts. *(BIOL)*
Biological Abstracts - R R M. *(BIOL)*
Biological & Agricultural Index.
Blood.
Blood Weekly.
Books in Print. *(BBIP)*
Books in Print Supplement. *(BBIP)*
Books Out-of-Print. *(BBIP)*
The Bowker Annual Library and Book Trade Almanac. *(BBIP)*
Brandweek. *(TSAP)*
British Journal of Obstetrics & Gynaecology.
British Journal of Rheumatology.
British Journal of Surgery.
British Journal of Urology.
Business Index.
Business Periodicals Index.
C M A J.
C N S: The Journal for Advanced Nursing Practice.
CAB International. Bureau of Nutrition. Annotated Bibliographies.
Cancer Weekly Plus.
Cardiology Clinics.
Children's Books in Print. *(BBIP)*
Ching Feng.
Circulation (Dallas). *(JWAT)*
Circulation Research.
Clinica. *(PHIN,PHIC,PHID)*
Clinical Diabetes.
Clinical Orthopaedics and Related Research.
Clinical Pediatrics.
Clinical Pharmacology & Therapeutics.
Compumath Citation Index.
Computer Database. *(CMPT)*
Critical Care Medicine.
Cumulative Book Index.
Cumulative Index to Nursing & Allied Health Literature. *(NAHL)*
Current Advances in Applied Microbiology & Biotechnology. *(CABS)*
Current Advances in Cancer Research. *(CABS)*

VENDOR LISTING/SERIALS ONLINE

Current Advances in Cell & Developmental Biology. *(CABS)*
Current Advances in Clinical Chemistry. *(CABS)*
Current Advances in Ecological and Environmental Sciences. *(CABS)*
Current Advances in Endocrinology & Metabolism. *(CABS)*
Current Advances in Genetics and Molecular Biology. *(CABS)*
Current Advances in Immunology & Infectious Diseases. *(CABS)*
Current Advances in Neuroscience. *(CABS)*
Current Advances in Plant Science. *(CABS)*
Current Advances in Protein Biochemistry. *(CABS)*
Current Advances in Toxicology. *(CABS)*
Current Awareness in Biological Sciences. *(CABS)*
Current Awareness in Health Education.
Current Contents: Agriculture, Biology & Environmental Sciences. *(CTOC,CBIB,AGRI)*
Current Contents: Arts & Humanities. *(CTOC,CBIB,ARTS)*
Current Contents: Clinical Medicine. *(CTOC,CBIB,CLIN)*
Current Contents: Engineering, Computing & Technology. *(CTOC,CBIB,ENGI)*
Current Contents: Life Sciences. *(CTOC,CBIB,LIFE)*
Current Contents: Physical, Chemical & Earth Sciences. *(CTOC,CBIB,PHYS)*
Current Contents: Social & Behavioral Sciences. *(CTOC,CBIB,BEHA)*
Current Index to Journals in Education.
Current Index to Statistics. *(MATH)*
Current Law Index.
Current Mathematical Publications.
Current Research in Library & Information Science. *(LISA)*
The Cyprus Review.
Devices & Diagnostics Letter. *(DIOG)*
Diabetes.
Diabetes Care.
Diseases of the Colon and Rectum.
Dissertation Abstracts International. Section A: Humanities and Social Sciences. *(DISS)*
Dissertation Abstracts International. Section B: Physical Sciences and Engineering. *(DISS)*
Dissertation Abstracts International. Section C: Worldwide. *(DISS)*
Dissertation Abstracts on Disc. *(DISS)*
Ear and Hearing.
Emergency Medicine Reports.
Engineering Index Annual. *(COMP)*
Engineering Index Monthly. *(COMP)*
Excerpta Medica Abstract Journals.
Excerpta Medica. Section 1: Anatomy, Anthropology, Embryology & Histology.
Excerpta Medica. Section 2: Physiology.
Excerpta Medica. Section 3: Endocrinology.
Excerpta Medica. Section 4: Microbiology: Bacteriology, Mycology, Parasitology and Virology.
Excerpta Medica. Section 5: General Pathology and Pathological Anatomy.
Excerpta Medica. Section 6: Internal Medicine.
Excerpta Medica. Section 7: Pediatrics and Pediatric Surgery.
Excerpta Medica. Section 8: Neurology and Neurosurgery.
Excerpta Medica. Section 9: Surgery.
Excerpta Medica. Section 10: Obstetrics and Gynecology.
Excerpta Medica. Section 11: Otorhinolaryngology.
Excerpta Medica. Section 12: Ophthalmology.
Excerpta Medica. Section 13: Dermatology and Venereology.
Excerpta Medica. Section 14: Radiology.
Excerpta Medica. Section 15: Chest Diseases, Thoracic Surgery and Tuberculosis.
Excerpta Medica. Section 16: Cancer.
Excerpta Medica. Section 17: Public Health, Social Medicine and Epidemiology.
Excerpta Medica. Section 18: Cardiovascular Diseases and Cardiovascular Surgery.
Excerpta Medica. Section 19: Rehabilitation and Physical Medicine.
Excerpta Medica. Section 20: Gerontology and Geriatrics.
Excerpta Medica. Section 21: Developmental Biology and Teratology.
Excerpta Medica. Section 22: Human Genetics.
Excerpta Medica. Section 23: Nuclear Medicine.
Excerpta Medica. Section 24: Anesthesiology.
Excerpta Medica. Section 25: Hematology.
Excerpta Medica. Section 26: Immunology, Serology and Transplantation.
Excerpta Medica. Section 27: Biophysics, Bio-Engineering and Medical Instrumentation.
Excerpta Medica. Section 28: Urology and Nephrology.
Excerpta Medica. Section 29: Clinical and Experimental Biochemistry.
Excerpta Medica. Section 30: Clinical and Experimental Pharmacology.
Excerpta Medica. Section 31: Arthritis and Rheumatism.
Excerpta Medica. Section 32: Psychiatry.
Excerpta Medica. Section 33: Orthopedic Surgery.
Excerpta Medica. Section 35: Occupational Health and Industrial Medicine.
Excerpta Medica. Section 36: Health Policy, Economics and Management.
Excerpta Medica. Section 38: Adverse Reactions Titles.
Excerpta Medica. Section 40: Drug Dependence, Alcohol Abuse and Alcoholism.
Excerpta Medica. Section 46: Environmental Health and Pollution Control.
Excerpta Medica. Section 48: Gastroenterology.
Excerpta Medica. Section 49: Forensic Science Abstracts.
Excerpta Medica. Section 50: Epilepsy Abstracts.
Excerpta Medica. Section 52: Toxicology.
F D A Enforcement Report. *(DIOG)*
F D A Medical Bulletin. *(DIOG)*
Family Relations.
Federal Applied Technology Database.
Federal Register. *(DIOG)*
Food and Drug Letter. *(DIOG)*
Foot & Ankle International.
Foreign Policy Bulletin.
Forest Products Abstracts. *(CABA)*
Forestry Abstracts. *(CABA)*
Forthcoming Books. *(BBIP)*
The G M P Letter. *(DIOG)*
Gastroenterology.
Gastroenterology Nursing.
Government Reports Announcements & Index.
Grasslands and Forage Abstracts.
Gut.
Handbook on Injectable Drugs. *(DIFT)*
Harvard Business Review. *(HBRO)*
Health Index. *(HEAL)*
Health Policy & Biomedical Research: The Blue Sheet. *(FDCR)*
Heart.
Heart & Lung.
Helminthological Abstracts. *(VETR)*
Humanities Index. *(WHUM)*
Index Medicus. *(MESH, MESZ)*
Index to Dental Literature. *(MESH, MESZ)*
Index to Legal Periodicals & Books.
Injury Prevention.
International Biodeterioration & Biodegradation.
International Nursing Index.
International Pharmaceutical Abstracts. *(IPAB)*
J A M A: The Journal of the American Medical Association. *(JWAR)*
The Journal of Allergy and Clinical Immunology.
Journal of Bone and Joint Surgery: American Volume.
Journal of Clinical Pathology.
Journal of Clinical Psychopharmacology.
Journal of Family History.
Journal of Family Issues.
Journal of Infectious Diseases. *(JWAT)*
The Journal of Laboratory and Clinical Medicine.
Journal of Nervous and Mental Disease.
Journal of Neurology, Neurosurgery and Psychiatry.
Journal of Occupational and Environmental Medicine.
Journal of Orthopaedic and Sports Physical Therapy.
The Journal of Pediatrics.
Journal of Psychology and Theology.
Journal of Technology Transfer.
Journal of Trauma - Injury, Infection and Critical Care.
Journal of Urology.
L I S A: Library & Information Science Abstracts. *(LISA)*
Laboratory Investigation.
The Lancet.
LegalTrac. *(LAWS)*
Magazine Article Summaries. *(PMRO)*
Magazine Index. *(MAGS)*
Management Contents. *(MGMT)*
Masters Abstracts International.
Mathematical Reviews. *(MATH)*
Medical and Health Care Books and Serials in Print. *(BBIP,ULRI)*
Medical Devices, Diagnostics & Instrumentation Reports: The Gray Sheet. *(FDCR)*
Medical Science Research.
Medicine (Baltimore).
Medicine and Science in Sports and Exercise.
Merck Index: An Encyclopedia of Chemicals and Drugs. *(MRCK)*
Meyler's Side Effects of Drugs.
Molecular Pathology.
Monthly Catalog of United States Government Publications.
N T I S Bibliographic Data Base.
National Cancer Institute. Journal.
National Newspaper Index. *(NOOZ)*
Nematological Abstracts. *(CABA)*
Neurology.
Neurosurgery (Baltimore).
New England Journal of Medicine. *(NEJM)*
Nutrition Abstracts and Reviews. Series B: Livestock Feeds and Feeding. *(VETR)*
Obstetrical & Gynecological Survey.
Obstetrics and Gynecology.
Outlook (Year) Proceedings.
P A I S International in Print.
P N I. *(PNII)*
The Pediatric Infectious Disease Journal.
Pediatric Research.
Pediatrics (English Edition).
Peterson's Guide to Two-Year Colleges (Year). *(PETE)*
Pharmaceutical Approvals Monthly. *(FDCR)*
Pharmaprojects Magazine.
Philosophical Forum.
Physical Therapy.
Plastic and Reconstructive Surgery.
Predicasts F & S Index Europe. *(PTSI)*
Predicasts F & S Index International. *(PTSI)*
Predicasts F & S Index of Corporate Change. *(PTSI)*
Predicasts F & S Index United States. *(PTSI)*
Predicasts Overview of Markets and Technology. *(PTSP)*
Prescription Pharmaceuticals and Biotechnology: The Pink Sheet. *(FDCR)*
Psychological Abstracts.
Psychosomatic Medicine.
Quarterly Journal of Medicine.
Radiologic Clinics of North America.
Religion in Eastern Europe.
Resources in Education.
Respiratory Medicine.
Salud Publica de Mexico.
Science. *(SCIE)*
Scientific American. *(SAMM)*
Scientific American Medicine. *(SAMM)*
Scrip - World Pharmaceutical News. *(PHIN,PHIC,PHID)*
Seminars in Neurology.
Seminars in Respiratory and Critical Care Medicine.
Sexually Transmitted Diseases.
Sexually Transmitted Infections.
Shonika.
Side Effects of Drugs Annual.
Social Sciences Citation Index. *(SSCI)*
Social Work Abstracts. *(SWAB)*
Sociological Abstracts. *(SOCA)*
Soil Science.
Soils and Fertilizers.
Southern Social Studies Journal.
Sport Thesaurus.
SportSearch. *(SFDB)*
Stroke.
Subject Guide to Books in Print. *(BBIP)*
Thorax.
Toiletries, Fragrances and Skin Care: The Rose Sheet. *(FDCR)*
Trade & Industry Index. *(TSAP)*
Transplantation.
Tuberculosis & Airborne Disease Weekly.
Ulrich's International Periodicals Directory. *(ULRI)*
Ulrich's Update. *(ULRI)*
U.S. Centers for Disease Control. Morbidity and Mortality Weekly Report.
Washington Drug Letter (Washington, 1979). *(DIOG)*
Wilson Abstracts.
Wilson Applied Science and Technology Abstracts.
Wilson Business Abstracts.
Wilson Education Abstracts.
Wilson Humanities Abstracts. *(WHUM)*
Year Book of Dermatologic Surgery.
Year Book of Plastic, Reconstructive, and Aesthetic Surgery.

PETROSCAN (Subsidiary of: United
Communications Group)
One Central Plaza, 11300 Rockville Pike, Suite
1100, Rockville, MD 20852. Tel: 301-816-8950
Fax: 301-816-8945.
   American Petroleum Institute. Division of
     Statistics. Weekly Statistical Bulletin.
   U.S. Energy Information Administration. Weekly
     Petroleum Status Report.

QL SYSTEMS, LTD.
1819 Granville St., Ste. 300, Halifax, NS B3J 1X8,
Canada
275 Sparks St., Ste. 901, St. Andrews Tower,
Ottawa, ON K1R 7X9, Tel: 613-238-3499
   A S T I S Bibliography.
   A S T I S Current Awareness Bulletin.
   A S T I S Occasional Publications.
   Alberta Reports.
   Canadian Foreign Relations.
   Canadian Index.
   Coal Highlights.
   International Bibliography of the Social Sciences.
     Economics.
   International Bibliography of the Social Sciences.
     Social and Cultural Anthropology.
   Manitoba Reports.
   National Reporter.
   New Brunswick Reports.
   Newfoundland & Prince Edward Island Reports.
   Nova Scotia Reports.
   Ontario. Labour Relations Board. Reports. A
     Monthly Series of Decisions.
   Ontario Appeal Cases.
   Ontario Reports.
   Polar and Glaciological Abstracts.
   Saskatchewan Reports.
   Tax Profile.
   Western Weekly Reports.

QUESTEL ORBIT INC.
8000 Westpark Dr., McLean, VA 22102. Tel: 703-
442-0900
Fax: 703-983-4632.
   A B I - INFORM. *(INFO)*
   Adhesives Abstracts.
   Aerospace Engineering Magazine.
   Agriculture and Environment for Developing
     Countries. *(TROPAG)*
   Alloys Index. *(MDEX)*
   Analytical Abstracts. *(ANAB)*
   Antarctic Bibliography. *(COLD)*
   Aqualine Abstracts. *(AQUA)*
   Automotive Engineering Magazine.
   Bibliography and Index of Geology. *(GEOR)*
   Bibliography on Cold Regions Science &
     Technology. *(COLD)*
   Biotechnology Abstracts. *(BIOT)*
   The Bowker Annual Library and Book Trade
     Almanac.
   Ceramic Abstracts. *(CERM)*
   Chem-Facts: Polyethylene.
   Chem-Facts: Polypropylene.
   Chemical Hazards in Industry. *(CSNS)*
   Computer & Control Abstracts.
   Convergence: International Congress on
     Transportation Electronics. Proceedings.
   Corptech Directory of Technology Companies.
     (CORP)
   Current Index to Journals in Education. *(ERIC)*
   Current Research in Britain. Biological Sciences.
     (CRIB)
   Current Research in Britain. Humanities. *(CRIB)*
   Current Research in Britain. Physical Sciences.
     (CRIB)
   C2C Abstracts: Japan - Analytical Chemistry.
     (JTEC)
   C2C Abstracts: Japan - Ceramics. *(JTEC)*
   C2C Abstracts: Japan - Chemical Engineering.
     (JTEC)
   C2C Abstracts: Japan - Crystallography. *(JTEC)*
   C2C Abstracts: Japan - Hydrocarbons. *(JTEC)*
   C2C Abstracts: Japan - Inorganic Chemistry.
     (JTEC)
   C2C Abstracts: Japan - Materials Science. *(JTEC)*
   C2C Abstracts: Japan - Metals. *(JTEC)*
   C2C Abstracts: Japan - Organic Chemistry.
     (JTEC)
   C2C Abstracts: Japan - Physical Chemistry.
     (JTEC)
   C2C Abstracts: Japan - Plastics. *(JTEC)*
   C2C Abstracts: Japan - Polymer Chemistry.
     (JTEC)
   C2C Abstracts: Japan - Surface Chemistry.
     (JTEC)
   C2C Abstracts: Japan - Textiles. *(JTEC)*
   C2C Currents: Japan - Chemistry. *(JTEC)*
   C2C Currents: Japan - Computers. *(JTEC)*
   C2C Currents: Japan - Electronics. *(JTEC)*
   C2C Currents: Japan - Materials. *(JTEC)*
   Ecological Abstracts. *(GEOB)*
   Electrical & Electronics Abstracts.
   Engineered Materials Abstracts. *(EMAB)*
   Engineering Index Annual.
   Engineering Index Monthly.
   Environment Abstracts Annual. *(Enviroline)*
   Food Science and Technology Abstracts. *(FSTA)*
   Gale Directory of Databases.
   Geographical Abstracts: Human Geography.
     (GEOB)
   Geographical Abstracts: Physical Geography.
     (GEOB)
   Geological Abstracts. *(GEOB)*
   Government Reports Announcements & Index.
     (NTIS)
   Health and Safety Science Abstracts. *(ORBIT)*
   Imaging Abstracts. *(PIRA/IMAB)*
   Index to Scientific & Technical Proceedings.
   International Development Abstracts.
   International Journal of Rock Mechanics & Mining
     Sciences. *(GEOM)*
   International Labour Documentation. *(LDOC)*
   International Packaging Abstracts. *(PIRA)*
   International Petroleum Abstracts. *(IPAB)*
   Key Abstracts - Business Automation.
   L I S A: Library & Information Science Abstracts.
     (LISA)
   Laboratory Hazards Bulletin. *(CSNB)*
   Metals Abstracts. *(MDEX)*
   Metals Abstracts Index. *(MDEX)*
   Million Dollar Directory.
   N T I S Bibliographic Data Base.
   New Trade Names in the Rubber and Plastics
     Industries. *(RAPRA)*
   Nonferrous Metals Alert. *(MABU)*
   Nonwovens Abstracts.
   Off-Highway Engineering.
   P N I.
   Packaging Science and Technology Abstracts.
   Paperbase Abstracts. *(PIRA)*
   Patents Abstracts.
   Petroleum Abstracts. *(TULSA)*
   Petroleum - Energy Business News Index. *(ABIZ)*
   Physics Abstracts.
   Polymers, Ceramics, Composites Alert. *(MABU)*
   Printing Abstracts. *(PIRA)*
   Process and Chemical Engineering. *(CEAB)*
   Professional Update.
   Psychological Abstracts.
   R A P R A Abstracts. *(RAPRA)*
   Reference Book of Corporate Managements.
     (RBCM)
   S A E Handbook.
   S A E Technical Literature Abstracts.
   S A E Technical Papers.
   Safety and Health at Work.
   Science Citation Index.
   Securite et Sante au Travail.
   Stapp Car Crash Conference. Proceedings.
   Steels Alert. *(MABU)*
   Synthetic Methods of Organic Chemistry.
   Technical Literature Abstracts. *(APILIT)*
   Technical Literature Abstracts: Catalysts -
     Zeolites. *(APILIT)*
   Technical Literature Abstracts: Fuel
     Reformulation. *(APILIT)*
   Technical Literature Abstracts: Oilfield Chemicals.
     (APILIT)
   Technical Literature Abstracts: Tribology. *(APILIT)*
   Theoretical Chemical Engineering. *(CEAB)*
   United States Patents Quarterly.
   Welding Abstracts.
   Who's Who in Technology. *(WHOTECH)*
   World Ceramics Abstracts.
   World Publishing Monitor.
   World Surface Coating Abstracts. *(WSCA)*
   World Textile Abstracts. *(WTA)*

REED INFORMATION SERVICES LTD. (Subsidiary of:
Reed Elsevier plc group)
Windsor Ct., East Grinstead Hse., East Grinstead,
West Sussex RH19 1XA, United Kingdom Tel:
0342-326972 Telex: 95127 INFSER G
Fax: 0342-335612.
   British Exports.
   Chemical Plant File.
   Dial Electrical - Electronics.
   Dial Engineering.
   Directory of Directors.
   Kelly's Directory.
   Kelly's Link.
   Kelly's Oil & Gas Directory.
   Kompass United Kingdom.
   U K Industrial Trade Names.

RESEARCH INSTITUTE OF AMERICA (Subsidiary of:
Div. of International Thomson Organization, Inc.)
90 Fifth Ave., New York, NY 10011. Tel: 212-
645-4800
   Federal Tax Regulations.

**RESEARCH LIBRARIES GROUP INFORMATION
NETWORK**
1200 Villa St., Mountain View, CA 94041-1100.
Tel: 415-691-2211
Fax: 415-964-0943.
   Anthropological Literature.
   Avery Index to Architectural Periodicals.

REUTERS, LTD.
85 Fleet St., London EC4P 4AJ, United Kingdom
Tel: 44-71-250-1122
Fax: 44-71-510-6227.
   Airline Business.
   Summary of World Broadcasts. Part 1: Former U
     S S R (Daily).
   Summary of World Broadcasts. Part 1: Former U
     S S R (Weekly Economic Report).
   Summary of World Broadcasts. Part 2: Central
     Europe, the Balkans (Daily).
   Summary of World Broadcasts. Part 2: Central
     Europe, the Balkans (Weekly Economic Report).
   Summary of World Broadcasts. Part 3: Asia -
     Pacific (Daily).
   Summary of World Broadcasts. Part 3: Asia -
     Pacific (Weekly Economic Report).
   Summary of World Broadcasts. Part 4: Middle
     East (Daily).
   Summary of World Broadcasts. Part 4: Middle
     East (Weekly Economic Report).
   Summary of World Broadcasts. Part 5: Africa,
     Latin America and the Caribbean (Daily).
   Summary of World Broadcasts. Part 5: Africa,
     Latin America and the Caribbean (Weekly
     Economic Report).

S T N INTERNATIONAL
c/o Chemical Abstracts Service, 2540 Olentengy
River Rd., Box 3012, Columbus, OH 43210. Tel:
614-447-3700 Telex: 6842086 CHMAB
Fax: 614-447-3751.
   A B I - INFORM. *(STN)*
   A O A C International. Journal. *(CJAOAC)*
   A S F A Aquaculture Abstracts. *(AQUASCI)*
   A S F A Marine Biotechnology Abstracts.
   Accounts of Chemical Research. *(CJACS)*
   Adhesives Abstracts.
   Agricultural & Environmental Biotechnology
     Abstracts. *(LIFESCI)*
   Agricultural Engineering Abstracts.
   Agroforestry Abstracts.
   Alloys Index.
   American Chemical Society. Journal. *(CJACS)*
   American Doctoral Dissertations.
   The Analyst. *(CJRSC)*
   Analytica Chimica Acta.
   Analytical Abstracts. *(ANABSTR)*
   Analytical Chemistry. *(CJACS)*
   Angewandte Chemie. *(CJVCH)*
   Animal Behavior Abstracts. *(LIFESCI)*
   Applied Catalysis A: General.
   Aquatic Sciences & Fisheries Abstracts. Part 1:
     Biological Sciences and Living Resources.
     (AQUASCI)
   Aquatic Sciences & Fisheries Abstracts. Part 2:
     Ocean Technology, Policy and Non-living
     Resources. *(AQUASCI)*
   Aquatic Sciences & Fisheries Abstracts. Part 3:
     Aquatic Pollution and Environmental Quality.
     (AQUASCI)
   Bibliography and Index of Geology. *(GeoRef)*
   Biochemistry. *(CJACS)*
   Biocontrol News and Information.
   Biological Abstracts. *(BIOSIS)*
   Biological Abstracts - R R M. *(BIOSIS)*
   Biopolymers. *(CJWILEY)*
   C S A Neurosciences Abstracts. *(LIFESCI)*
   Calcium and Calcified Tissue Abstracts. *(LIFESCI)*
   Carbohydrate Research.
   Ceramic Abstracts. *(CERAB)*
   Chem Sources International.
   Chem Sources U S A.
   Chemical Abstracts.
   Chemical Abstracts - Applied Chemistry and
     Chemical Engineering Sections. *(CA)*
   Chemical Abstracts - Biochemistry Sections. *(CA)*

VENDOR LISTING/SERIALS ONLINE

Chemical Abstracts - Macromolecular Sections. *(CA)*
Chemical Abstracts - Organic Chemistry Sections. *(CA)*
Chemical Abstracts - Physical, Inorganic and Analytical Chemistry Sections. *(CA)*
Chemical Communications. *(CJRSC)*
Chemical Hazards in Industry. *(CSNB)*
Chemical Research in Toxicology.
Chemical Reviews. *(CJACS)*
Chemoreception Abstracts. *(LIFESCI)*
Computer & Control Abstracts.
Computer and Information Systems Abstracts Journal.
Conference Papers Annual Index. *(CONFSCI)*
Conference Papers Index. *(CONFSCI)*
Crop Physiology Abstracts.
D K I Literatur-Schnelldienst Kunststoffe Kautschuk Fasern.
Dalton Transactions. *(CJRSC)*
Dissertation Abstracts International. Section A: Humanities and Social Sciences.
Dissertation Abstracts International. Section B: Physical Sciences and Engineering.
Dissertation Abstracts International. Section C: Worldwide.
Dissertation Abstracts on Disc.
Ecology Abstracts.
Electrical & Electronics Abstracts.
Electronics and Communications Abstracts Journal. *(ELCOM)*
Energy & Fuels. *(CJACS)*
Energy Data Base.
Energy Research Abstracts. *(ENERGY)*
Engineered Materials Abstracts. *(EMA)*
Engineering Index Annual.
Engineering Index Monthly. *(COMPENDEX)*
Entomology Abstracts. *(LIFESCI)*
Environmental Science & Technology (Washington). *(CJACS)*
Faraday Discussions. *(CJRSC)*
Faraday Transactions. *(CJRSC)*
Field Crop Abstracts.
Food Science and Technology Abstracts.
Genetics Abstracts. *(LIFESCI)*
Government Reports Announcements & Index. *(NTIS)*
Grasslands and Forage Abstracts.
Hazards in the Office. *(CSNB)*
Horticultural Abstracts.
I N I S Atomindex. *(ENERGY)*
Imaging Abstracts. *(PIRA)*
Immunology Abstracts. *(LIFESCI)*
Index Medicus. *(MEDLINE)*
Index of Current Research on Pigs.
Index of Fungi.
Index to Dental Literature. *(MEDLINE)*
Index Veterinarius.
Industrial & Engineering Chemistry Research. *(CJACS)*
Informationsdienst Praxisbezogener Literatur im Weinbau.
Inorganic Chemistry. *(CJACS)*
Institute of Paper Science and Technology. Abstract Bulletin. *(PAPERCHEM2)*
International Nursing Index. *(MEDLINE)*
International Packaging Abstracts.
Irrigation and Drainage Abstracts.
Journal of Agricultural and Food Chemistry. *(CJACS)*
Journal of Analytical Atomic Spectrometry. *(CJRSC)*
Journal of Applied Polymer Science. *(CJWILEY)*
Journal of Chemical and Engineering Data. *(CJACS)*
Journal of Chemical Information and Computer Sciences. *(CJACS)*
Journal of Chemical Research. *(CJRSC)*
Journal of Medicinal Chemistry. *(CJACS)*
Journal of Organic Chemistry (Washington). *(CJACS)*
Journal of Organometallic Chemistry.
Journal of Physical Chemistry. *(CJACS)*
Journal of Polymer Science. Part A: Polymer Chemistry. *(CJWILEY)*
Journal of Polymer Science. Part B: Polymer Physics. *(CJWILEY)*
Journal of Polymer Science. Symposia Proceedings.
Key Abstracts - Business Automation.
Laboratory Hazards Bulletin. *(CSNB)*
Langmuir. *(CJACS)*
Leisure, Recreation and Tourism Abstracts.
Macromolecules. *(CJACS)*
Maize Abstracts.
Masters Abstracts International.
Mechanical Engineering Abstracts. *(ISMEC)*
Medical & Pharmaceutical Biotechnology Abstracts. *(LIFESCI)*
Merck Index: An Encyclopedia of Chemicals and Drugs.
Metals Abstracts. *(METADEX)*
Metals Abstracts Index. *(METADEX)*
Microbiology Abstracts: Section A. Industrial & Applied Microbiology. *(LIFESCI)*
Microbiology Abstracts: Section B. Bacteriology. *(LIFESCI)*
Microbiology Abstracts: Section C. Algology, Mycology and Protozoology. *(LIFESCI)*
N T I S Bibliographic Data Base.
New Trade Names in the Rubber and Plastics Industries.
Nonferrous Metals Alert. *(MATBUS)*
Nonwovens Abstracts.
Nucleic Acids Abstracts. *(LIFESCI)*
Nutrition Abstracts and Reviews. Series A: Human and Experimental.
Oceanic Abstracts. *(OCEAN)*
Oncogenes and Growth Factors Abstracts. *(LIFESCI)*
Organometallics. *(CJACS)*
Ornamental Horticulture.
P N I.
Packaging Science and Technology Abstracts.
Paperbase Abstracts.
Patents Abstracts.
Pharmaprojects Magazine.
Physics Abstracts.
Pig News & Information.
Plant Breeding Abstracts.
Plant Growth Regulator Abstracts.
Pollution Abstracts. *(POLLUAB)*
Polymers, Ceramics, Composites Alert. *(MATBUS)*
Potato Abstracts.
Poultry Abstracts.
Printing Abstracts.
Process and Chemical Engineering. *(CEABA)*
Protozoological Abstracts.
R T E C S.
Review of Agricultural Entomology.
Review of Medical and Veterinary Entomology.
Review of Medical and Veterinary Mycology.
Review of Plant Pathology.
Rice Abstracts.
Royal Society of Chemistry. Journal: Perkin Transactions 1. *(CJRSC)*
Royal Society of Chemistry. Journal: Perkin Transactions 2. *(CJRSC)*
Rural Development Abstracts.
Seed Abstracts.
Small Animals.
Solid State and Superconductivity Abstracts. *(SOLIDSTATE)*
Sorghum and Millets.
Soyabean Abstracts.
Steels Alert. *(MATBUS)*
Technical Literature Abstracts. *(APILIT)*
Technical Literature Abstracts: Catalysts - Zeolites.
Technical Literature Abstracts: Fuel Reformulation. *(APILIT)*
Technical Literature Abstracts: Oilfield Chemicals. *(APILIT)*
Technical Literature Abstracts: Tribology. *(APILIT)*
Theoretical Chemical Engineering. *(CEABA)*
Toxicology Abstracts. *(LIFESCI)*
Tropical Oil Seeds.
Vademecum Deutscher Lehr- und Forschungsstaetten. Staetten der Forschung.
Veterinary Bulletin.
Virology and AIDS Abstracts. *(LIFESCI)*
Vitis - Viticulture and Oenology Abstracts.
Weed Abstracts.
Wheat, Barley and Triticale Abstracts.
World Agricultural Economics and Rural Sociology Abstracts.
World Publishing Monitor.
Zentralblatt fuer Didaktik der Mathematik.
Zentralblatt fuer Mathematik und Ihre Grenzgebiete. *(MATH)*

SOURCE TELECOMPUTING CORP.
1616 Anderson Rd., McLean, VA 22102.
E R I C Clearinghouse on Urban Education. Digest.

SOUTHAM ELECTRONIC PUBLISHING
1450 Don Mills Rd., Don Mills, ON M3B 2X7, Canada Tel: 416-442-2198
Fax: 416-445-3508.
Les Affaires.
Calgary Herald.
Canadian Forest Industries.
Canadian Mining Journal.
Canadian Trade Index.
Canadian Underwriter.
Daily Oil Bulletin.
Le Devoir.
Eco-Log Week.
Financial Post.
Financial Post Directory of Directors.
Gazette.
Inter-Corporate Ownership.
Maclean's.
The Northern Miner.
Pulp & Paper Canada.

TELESYSTEMES-QUESTEL
83-85 blvd. Vincent Auriol, Paris 75013, France
Tel: 33-144236464 Telex: 204594 TELQUES F
Fax: 33-144236465.
Aqualine Abstracts.
B H A.
Bases.
Bibliographie Geographique Internationale. F R A N C I S. 531.
Bibliography of Bioethics. *(BIOETHICS)*
Bulletin Signaletique des Telecommunications.
Catalogue Afnor (Normes Francaises).
Diffusion Express. *(Base EDF.DOC)*
F R A N C I S. 519: Philosophie.
F R A N C I S. 520: Sciences de l'Education.
F R A N C I S. 521: Sociologie.
F R A N C I S. 522: Histoire des Sciences et de Techniques.
F R A N C I S. 523: Histoire et Sciences de la Litterature.
F R A N C I S. 524: Sciences du Langage.
F R A N C I S. 525: Prehistoire et Protohistoire.
F R A N C I S. 526: Art et Archeologie.
F R A N C I S. 527: Histoire et Sciences des Religions.
F R A N C I S. 528: Bibliographie Internationale de Science Administrative.
F R A N C I S. 529: Ethnologie.
F R A N C I S. 603: Informatique et Sciences Juridiques.
F R A N C I S. 617: E C O D O C.
F R A N C I S. 731: Economie de l'Energie.
Gale Directory of Databases.
Merck Index: An Encyclopedia of Chemicals and Drugs.
Le Monde.
N I O S H T I C.
P A S C A L. E 11: Physique Atomique et Moleculaire. Plasmas.
P A S C A L. E 12: Etat Condense.
P A S C A L. E 13: Structure des Liquides et des Solides - Cristallographie.
P A S C A L. E 18: Chromatographie.
P A S C A L. E 20: Electronique et Telecommunications.
P A S C A L. E 27: Methodes de Formation et Traitement des Images.
P A S C A L. E 30: Microscopie Electronique et Diffraction Electronique.
P A S C A L. E 32: Metrologie et Appareillage en Physique et Physicochimie.
P A S C A L. E 33. Informatique.
P A S C A L. E 34. Robotique, Automatique et Automatisation des Processus Industriels.
P A S C A L. E 36: Pollution de l'Eau, de l'Air et du Sol - Dechets - Bruit.
P A S C A L. E 48: Environnement Cosmique Terrestre, Astronomie et Geologie Extraterrestre.
P A S C A L. E 49: Meteorologie, Glaciologie, Physique des Oceans.
P A S C A L. E 58: Genetique.
P A S C A L. E 61: Microbiologie: Bacteriologie, Virologie, Mycologie, Protozoaires Pathogenes.
P A S C A L. E 62: Immunologie.
P A S C A L. E 63: Toxicologie.
P A S C A L. E 64: Endocrinologie Humaine et Experimentale. Endocrinopathies.
P A S C A L. E 65: Psychologie, Psychopathologie, Psychiatrie.
P A S C A L. E 68: Genetique Humaine.
P A S C A L. E 71: Ophtalmologie.
P A S C A L. E 72: Otorhinolaryngologie. Stomatologie. Pathologie Cervicofaciale.
P A S C A L. E 73: Dermatologie. Maladies Sexuellement Transmissibles.
P A S C A L. E 74: Pneumologie.
P A S C A L. E 75: Cardiologie et Appareil Circulatoire.
P A S C A L. E 76: Gastroenterologie. Foie, Pancreas, Abdomen.
P A S C A L. E 77: Nephrologie. Voies Urinaires.
P A S C A L. E 78: Neurologie.

P A S C A L. E 79: Pathologie et Physiologie Osteoarticulaires.
P A S C A L. E 80: Hematologie.
P A S C A L. E 82: Gynecologie, Obstetrique, Andrologie.
P A S C A L. E 83: Anesthesie et Reanimation.
P A S C A L. E 84: Genie Biomedical. Informatique Biomedicale.
P A S C A L. E 89: Cancer.
P A S C A L. F 10: Mecanique, Acoustique et Transfert de Chaleur.
P A S C A L. F 16: Chimie Analytique, Minerale et Organique.
P A S C A L. F 17: Chimie Generale, Minerale et Organique.
P A S C A L. F 23: Genie Chimique. Industries Chimique et Parachimique.
P A S C A L. F 24: Polymeres - Peintures - Bois.
P A S C A L. F 40: Mineralogie. Geochimie. Geologie Extraterrestre.
P A S C A L. F 41: Gisements Metalliques et Non Metalliques.
P A S C A L. F 42: Roches Cristallines.
P A S C A L. F 43: Roches Sedimentaires. Geologie Marine.
P A S C A L. F 44: Stratigraphie, Geologie Regionale, Geologie Generale.
P A S C A L. F 45: Tectonique, Geophysique Interne.
P A S C A L. F 46: Hydrologie. Geologie de l'Ingenieur. Formations Superficielles.
P A S C A L. F 47: Paleontologie.
P A S C A L. F 52: Biochimie - Biophysique - Moleculaire - Biologie Moleculaire et Cellulaire.
P A S C A L. F 53: Anatomie et Physiologie des Vertebres.
P A S C A L. F 54: Reproduction des Vertebres, Embryologie des Vertebres et des Invertebres.
P A S C A L. F 55: Biologie Vegetale.
P A S C A L. F 56: Ecologie Animale, Vegetale et Microbienne. Ethologie Animale.
P A S C A L. F 70: Pharmacologie. Traitements Medicamenteux.
P A S C A L. T 205: Sciences de l'Information. Documentation.
P A S C A L. T 215: Biotechnologies.
P A S C A L. T 230: Energie.
P A S C A L. T 235: Medecine Tropicale.
P A S C A L. T 240: Metaux - Metallurgie.
P A S C A L. T 260: Zoologie Fondamentale et Appliquee des Invertebres.
P A S C A L. T 280: Sciences Agronomiques et Forestieres: Productions Vegetales.
P A S C A L. T 295: Batiment. Travaux Publics.
P A S C A L V.4 Sciences de la Terre.
Patents Abstracts.
Petroleum - Energy Business News Index.
R A P R A Abstracts.
Safety and Health at Work.
Securite et Sante au Travail.
Technical Literature Abstracts.
Technical Literature Abstracts: Catalysts - Zeolites.
Technical Literature Abstracts: Fuel Reformulation.
Technical Literature Abstracts: Oilfield Chemicals.
Technical Literature Abstracts: Tribology.
Travail et Emploi.
Welding Abstracts.

UMI
300 N. Zeeb Rd., Ann Arbor, MI 48106. Tel: 313-761-4700
Fax: 313-761-1203.
A B A Bank Compliance.
A B A Banking Journal.
A B A Journal.
A B I - INFORM.
A C A Journal.
A C A News.
A G A Gas Energy Review.
Academy of Management. Journal.
Academy of Management Executive.
Academy of Management Review.
Accent on Living.
Accountancy.
Accounting and Finance.
Accounting and Tax Index.
Accounting Education News.
Accounting Historians Journal.
Accounting Technology.
Accounting Today.
Across the Board.
Adhesives Age.
Administrative Science Quarterly.
Adolescence (San Diego).
Advanced Management Journal.

Africa Today.
African American Review.
African Arts.
Agency Sales.
Agri Finance.
Agri Marketing.
Agricultural Research.
Air Transport World.
Airfinance Journal.
Alaska Journal of Commerce & Pacific Rim Reporter.
Alcohol Health & Research World.
America.
American Advertising.
American Agent and Broker.
American Banker Index.
American City & County.
American Craft.
American Demographics.
American Dietetic Association. Journal.
American Doctoral Dissertations.
American Economist.
American Enterprise.
American Fitness.
American Forests.
American Gas.
American Historical Review.
American Journal of Agricultural Economics.
American Journal of Economics and Sociology.
American Journal of Nursing.
American Journal of Psychiatry.
American Journal of Psychotherapy.
American Journal of Public Health.
American Journal of Sports Medicine.
American Legion Magazine.
American Music Teacher.
American Oriental Society. Journal.
American Planning Association. Journal.
American Poetry Review.
American Political Science Review.
American Printer.
American Record Guide.
American Rehabilitation.
American Review of Public Administration.
American Rifleman.
American Society for Information Science. Bulletin.
American Society of C L U & Ch F C. Journal.
American Sociological Review.
American Theatre.
American Visions.
Americas.
America's Community Banker.
The Amicus Journal.
Annual Review of Psychology.
Annual Review of Sociology.
Antioch Review.
Apparel Industry Magazine.
Appliance Manufacturer.
Appraisal Journal.
Arab Studies Quarterly.
Architectural Review.
Argumentation & Advocacy.
Arkansas Business and Economic Review.
Armed Forces and Society.
Armed Forces Comptroller.
Arms Control Today.
Art Bulletin.
Art in America.
Art Journal (Year).
Arts Education Policy Review.
Asia - Pacific Journal of Management.
Asiamoney.
Asian Business.
Asian Survey.
Asset Finance and Leasing Digest.
Association for Computing Machinery. Communications.
Association Management.
Astronomy.
Attorney - C P A.
Audubon.
Austin Business Journal.
Australian Accountant.
Australian Economic Review.
Australian Tax Forum.
Automotive Manufacturing and Production.
AZ B - Arizona Business.
B M J.
Backpacker.
Bank Loan Report.
Bank News.
Bank of Canada. Review.
Bank Operations Bulletin.
Bank Personnel News.
Bank Systems & Technology.
Bank Technology News.
The Banker.

Bankers Research.
Banking Strategies.
Banking World.
Barclays Economic Review.
Behavioral Health Management.
Benefits Quarterly.
Best's Review. Life - Health Insurance Edition.
Best's Review. Property - Casualty Insurance Edition.
Better Homes and Gardens.
Better Nutrition.
Beverage World (English Edition).
Bicycling.
BioCycle.
Biological Bulletin.
BioScience.
Birmingham Business.
The Black Collegian.
Black Enterprise.
Black Scholar.
Boating.
Bobbin.
Boston Business Journal.
British Journal of Psychology.
Brookings Review.
Brunswick Business Journal.
Buildings.
Bukkyo Daigaku Shinrigaku Kenkyujo Kiyo.
Bulletin of the Atomic Scientists.
Business America.
Business Credit.
Business Economics.
Business Forum (Los Angeles).
Business History Review.
Business in Broward.
Business Journal of Upper East Tennessee and Southwest Virginia.
Business Journal Serving Greater Milwaukee.
Business Korea.
Business Mexico.
Business North Carolina.
Business People Magazine.
Business Quarterly.
Business Times.
C D - R O M Professional.
C F O.
C P A Client Bulletin.
C P A Letter.
California Management Review.
Campaigns and Elections.
Canadian Banker.
Canadian Geographic.
Canadian Journal of Administrative Sciences.
Canadian Journal of Criminology.
Canadian Journal of History.
Canadian Literature.
Canadian Manager.
Canadian Shareowner.
Canadian Treasury Management Review.
Canadian Underwriter.
Capacity Management Review.
Car and Driver.
Career Development Quarterly.
Catalog Age.
Cato Journal.
Cellular Business.
Central European.
Central New York Business Journal.
Central Penn Business Journal.
Ceramics Monthly.
Chain Store Age.
Chartered Property and Casualty Underwriters Society. Journal.
Chemical Marketing Reporter.
Childhood Education.
Children Today.
China Business Review.
The China Quarterly.
Christian Century.
Christianity Today.
The Chronicle of Higher Education.
Church History.
Cineaste.
Club Management.
Coast Business.
Colorado Springs Business Journal.
Columbia Journalism Review.
Commonweal.
Communication Education.
Communication Monographs.
Communication Quarterly.
Communication Studies.
Communication World.
Communications and the Law.
Communications International.
Comparative Drama.
Comparative Economic Studies.
Comparative Literature.

Compensation and Benefits Review.
Computer Security Journal.
Computer Technology Review.
Computers in Libraries.
Construction Review.
Consultants News.
Consumer Policy Review.
Consumer's Research Magazine.
Contemporary Literature.
Contemporary Sociology.
Controllers Update.
The Cornell Hotel & Restaurant Administration Quarterly.
Corporate Cashflow.
Corporate Detroit Magazine.
Corporate Growth Report.
Corporate Location.
Corporate Report Minnesota.
Corporate Report Ventures.
Corporate Report Wisconsin.
Corrections Today.
Cost Engineering (Morgantown).
Cost Management Update.
Credit Card Management.
Credit Card News.
Credit Control.
Credit Union Management.
Credit World.
Crime & Delinquency.
Criminology.
Critical Studies in Mass Communication.
Criticism.
Critique: Studies in Modern Fiction.
Current Health 2.
Cycle World.
D B.
Dance Magazine.
Database (Wilton).
Dayton Business Reporter.
Debit Card News.
Delaware Business Review.
Dental Economics.
Detroiter.
Diogenes (English Edition).
Direct Marketing.
Directors & Boards.
Disclosure (Chicago).
Down Beat.
Drug and Cosmetic Industry.
Drug Topics.
Duluthian.
E B Quarterly.
Early American Literature.
Earth Island Journal.
East Asian Executive Reports.
East European Quarterly.
Eastern Economic Journal.
Ebony.
Ecological Monographs.
Ecology.
Economic Commentary.
Economic Development Review.
Economic Geography.
Economic Perspectives (Chicago).
Economic Record.
Economic Review.
Economist.
Ecumenical Review.
Edmonton Chamber of Commerce. Commerce News.
Educational Leadership.
Educational Record.
Educational Studies.
Ekistics.
Electric Perspectives.
The Electricity Journal.
Electronic Learning.
Employee Benefit Plan Review.
Engineering Economist.
Enterprise (New York).
Entrepreneurship: Theory and Practice.
Environment.
Environmental Action.
Environmental Problems & Remediation.
Equal Opportunities Review.
Equipment and Materials Update.
Equipment Leasing Today.
Essays in Literature.
ETC.
Ethnology.
Euromoney.
The European Business Journal.
European Industrial Relations Review.
Euroweek.
Exceptional Children.
Exceptional Parent.
Executive Accountant.
Executive Excellence.

Executive Report.
Executive Speeches.
The Explicator.
F B I Law Enforcement Bulletin.
F D A Consumer.
Facilities Design and Management.
Fairfield County Business Journal.
Families in Society.
The Family Handyman.
Family Planning Perspectives.
Family Relations.
Federal Reserve Bank of Minneapolis. Quarterly Review.
Federal Reserve Bank of New York. Economic Policy Review.
Federal Reserve Bank of Philadelphia. Business Review.
Federal Reserve Bank of St. Louis. Review.
Federal Reserve Bank of San Francisco. Economic Review.
Federal Reserve Bulletin.
Fedgazette: Federal Reserve Bank of Minneapolis Regional Business & Economics Newspaper.
Feminist Studies.
Field & Stream.
Film Comment.
Finance and Development.
Financial Analysts Journal.
Financial Executive.
Financial Management.
Financial Market Trends.
Financial Markets, Institutions and Instruments.
Financial World.
Fiscal Studies.
Fleet Equipment.
Florida Trend.
Flower and Garden.
Flying.
Focus (New York, 1950).
Folio (Stamford).
Foreign Affairs.
Foreign Policy (Washington).
Forest Products Journal.
Franchising World.
Free Inquiry.
French Historical Studies.
Frontiers: a Journal of Women Studies.
Frontiers of Health Services Management.
Frozen Food Age.
Fund Raising Management.
The Futurist.
The Geographical Journal.
Geographical Review.
Georgia Trend.
Geriatrics.
Germanic Review.
The Gerontologist.
Getting Results...for the Hands-On Manager.
Global Investor.
Government Executive.
Grand Rapids Business Journal.
Greek, Roman and Byzantine Studies.
Ground Water.
Growth and Change.
H R Focus.
H R Magazine.
Harford Business Ledger.
Harper's Magazine.
Harvard Educational Review.
Harvard Journal of Law and Public Policy.
Hastings Center Report.
Hawaii Business.
Health (San Francisco).
Health Affairs.
Health & Social Work.
Health Care Financing Review.
Health Care Management Review.
Health Care Strategic Management.
Health Care Supervisor.
Health Industry Today.
Health Management Technology.
Health Services Research.
Health Systems Review.
Healthcare Executive.
Healthcare Financial Management.
Healthcare Forum Journal.
Hecate.
The Herald.
Hispanic Review.
The Historian (East Lansing).
History and Theory.
History Today.
Home Office Computing.
Hoosier Banker.
Horticulture.
Hospital & Health Services Administration.
Hospital Materials Management.
Hospital Materiel Management Quarterly.

Hospitals and Health Networks.
Human Biology (Detroit).
Human Relations.
Human Resource Planning.
Human Systems Management.
The Humanist.
Hypatia.
I I E Solutions.
I N F O R Journal.
I P A Review.
Incentive.
Independent Banker.
Independent Energy.
Indiana Business Magazine.
Indiana Business Review.
Indiana Journal of Commerce and Industry.
Indianapolis Business Journal.
Industrial Health & Hazards Update.
Industrial Management.
Industry Week.
Information Technology and Libraries.
Information Today.
InfoWorld.
Innovator's Digest.
Insurance and Technology.
Insurance Brokers' Monthly and Insurance Adviser.
Internal Auditor.
International Bulletin of Missionary Research.
International Business.
International Commercial Litigation (London, 1990).
International Financial Law Review.
International Insurance Monitor.
International Journal of Government Auditing.
International Journal of Purchasing & Materials Management.
International Journal of Social Psychiatry.
International Labour Review.
International Migration Review.
International Monetary Fund. Staff Papers.
International Review of Mission.
International Small Business Journal.
International Studies of Management and Organization.
International Tax Report.
International Tax Review.
International Trade Forum.
Interpreter (Nashville).
Investment Dealers' Digest.
Issues in Science and Technology.
J E I.
Japan Quarterly.
Jet.
Journal for Quality and Participation.
Journal for the Scientific Study of Religion.
Journal of Accountancy.
Journal of Accounting Literature.
Journal of Advertising.
Journal of Advertising Research.
Journal of Agricultural Lending.
Journal of American Culture.
Journal of American History.
Journal of Asian Studies.
Journal of Bank Cost & Management Accounting.
Journal of Broadcasting and Electronic Media.
Journal of Business (Spokane).
Journal of Business Communication.
Journal of Business Ethics.
Journal of Business Forecasting Methods and Systems.
Journal of Business Logistics.
Journal of Business Strategy.
Journal of Career Planning & Employment.
Journal of Chemical Education.
Journal of Clinical Psychology.
Journal of Communication.
Journal of Comparative Family Studies.
Journal of Counseling & Development.
The Journal of Credit & Risk Management.
Journal of Criminal Law & Criminology.
The Journal of Development Studies.
Journal of Education for Business.
Journal of Environmental Health.
Journal of European Studies.
Journal of Financial Planning Today.
The Journal of General Psychology.
The Journal of Genetic Psychology.
Journal of Health and Social Behavior.
Journal of Health Care Finance.
Journal of Health Care Marketing.
Journal of Higher Education.
Journal of Human Resources.
Journal of Insurance Regulation.
Journal of Interamerican Studies and World Affairs.
Journal of International Affairs.
Journal of International Business Studies.

Journal of Leisure Research.
Journal of Macromarketing.
Journal of Management Accounting Research.
Journal of Management Consulting.
Journal of Management Information Systems.
Journal of Manufacturing Systems.
Journal of Marital and Family Therapy.
Journal of Marketing.
Journal of Marriage and the Family.
Journal of Medical Ethics.
Journal of Negro Education.
Journal of Parapsychology.
Journal of Physical Education, Recreation and Dance.
Journal of Popular Culture.
Journal of Popular Film and Television.
Journal of Post Keynesian Economics.
Journal of Property Management.
Journal of Public Policy & Marketing.
Journal of Rehabilitation.
Journal of Rehabilitation Research and Development.
Journal of Religious Thought.
Journal of School Health.
Journal of Sex Research.
Journal of Small Business Management.
Journal of Social History.
Journal of Social Issues.
The Journal of Social Psychology.
Journal of Soil and Water Conservation.
Journal of Sport Behavior.
Journal of Systems Management.
Journal of Travel Research.
Journal of Women's History.
Journal of Youth and Adolescence.
Journalism and Mass Communication Educator.
Journalism History.
Journals of Gerontology. Series A: Biological Sciences & Medical Sciences.
Journals of Gerontology. Series B: Psychological Sciences & Social Sciences.
Judaism.
Kentucky Banker.
The Kentucky Manufacturer.
Kexue (Shanghai).
Kiplinger's Personal Finance Magazine.
Kyklos.
L I M R A's MarketFacts.
Lafayette Business Digest.
Lakewood Report on Positive Employee Practices.
Lambda Book Report.
The Lancet.
Lane Report.
Las Vegas Business Press.
Latin American Research Review.
Legal Assistant Today.
Library Administrator's Digest.
Life.
Life Sciences & Biotechnology Update.
Link-Up.
Literary Review.
Lodging Hospitality.
Logistics and Transportation Review.
Los Angeles.
Louisville Magazine.
M E L U S.
M I S Quarterly.
Machine Design.
The McKinsey Quarterly.
Maclean's.
MacWorld.
Maine Times.
Manage.
Management Accounting.
Management Accounting.
Management International Review.
Management Quarterly.
Management Review.
Management Services.
Management Today.
Managing Intellectual Property.
Managing Office Technology.
Manufacturing Engineering.
Marketing Management.
Marketing News.
Marketing Research.
Marketing Week.
Marketplace Magazine.
Massachusetts C P A Review.
Massachusetts Review.
Material Handling Engineering.
Mechanical Engineering.
MediaWeek.
Medical Letter on Drugs and Therapeutics (English Edition).
Medical Marketing & Media.
Medium Aevum.
Memphis Business Journal.

Men's Health.
Mercer Business Magazine.
Mergers & Acquisitions.
Mergers & Acquisitions Report.
Metropolitan Home.
Michigan C P A.
Mid-America Commerce & Industry.
Mid-American Journal of Business.
Middle East Executive Reports.
Middle East Journal.
Middle Eastern Studies.
Middlesex Magazine.
Midwest Quarterly.
Migration World.
The Mineralogical Record.
The Mississippi Quarterly.
Modern Drama.
Modern Maturity.
Modern Paint and Coatings.
Money (New York).
Montana Business Quarterly.
Monthly Labor Review.
Monthly Review.
Mortgage-Backed Securities Letter.
Mother Earth News.
Mpls. - St. Paul Magazine.
Multinational Business Review.
N C A H F Newsletter.
N E A Today.
N P News.
Nashville Business Journal.
National Civic Review.
National Contract Management Journal.
National Forum (Auburn).
National Institute Economic Review.
National Journal.
National Mortgage News.
National Parks.
National Public Accountant.
National Real Estate Investor.
National Underwriter. Life and Health - Health & Financial Services Edition.
National Underwriter. Property & Casualty - Risk & Benefits Management Edition.
Nation's Business.
Nation's Restaurant News.
Natural History.
Network World.
New Accountant.
New Hampshire Business Review.
New Jersey Business.
New Mexico Business Journal.
New Orleans CityBusiness.
New Orleans Magazine.
New Perspectives Quarterly.
The New Republic.
New Statesman.
New York Review of Books.
New York State Conservationist.
The New York Times.
New Zealand Manufacturer (Wellington, 1992).
News Photographer.
Newspaper Research Journal.
Nieman Reports.
Nonprofit World.
The North American Review.
Northern Ontario Business.
Novel: A Forum on Fiction.
Nursing Homes.
Nutrition Action Healthletter.
Nutrition Reviews.
O E C D Economic Outlook.
O E C D Observer.
Occupational Hazards.
Occupational Health & Safety.
Occupational Outlook Quarterly.
Oceania.
The Ohio C P A Journal.
Oil and Gas Investor.
Oil & Gas Journal.
Opera News.
Orange County Business Journal.
Organic Gardening.
Organization Studies.
Organizational Dynamics.
Origination News Monthly.
Outdoor Life.
Outlook.
Outstate Business.
P M L A.
Pacific Affairs.
Papers on Language and Literature.
Paris Review.
Parks and Recreation.
Patient Care.
Payment Systems Worldwide.
Payments System Report.
Peacekeeping & International Relations.

Pennsylvania Business and Technology.
Pennsylvania C P A Journal.
People Weekly.
Performing Arts and Entertainment in Canada.
Periodical Abstracts.
Personnel Psychology.
Pharmaceutical Executive.
Phi Delta Kappan.
Philadelphia Business Journal.
Philosophy and Public Affairs.
Pittsburgh Business Times - Journal.
Ploughshares.
Plymouth County Business Review.
Policy Studies Journal.
Political Science Quarterly.
Popular Photography.
Popular Science.
The Practical Accountant.
The Practical Lawyer.
The Practical Litigator.
The Practical Real Estate Lawyer.
The Practical Tax Lawyer.
Practicing C P A.
Presidential Studies Quarterly.
Prevention.
Printed Circuit Design.
Production and Inventory Management Journal.
Professional Safety.
Progressive (Madison).
Progressive Grocer.
The Psychological Record.
Psychology Today.
Public Administration Quarterly.
Public Administration Review.
Public Budgeting and Finance.
Public Health Reports.
Public Interest.
Public Management.
Public Productivity and Management Review.
Public Relations Quarterly.
Public Roads.
Public Utilities Fortnightly.
Public Welfare.
Pueblo Business Journal.
Pulp and Paper.
Quality Progress.
R N.
Railway Age.
Real Estate Finance.
Real Estate Finance Today.
Real Estate Issues.
Real Property, Probate and Trust Journal.
Records Management Quarterly.
Renaissance Quarterly.
Research in African Literatures.
Research Quarterly for Exercise and Sport.
Restaurant Business.
Restaurant Hospitality.
Review of Black Political Economy.
Review of Business.
The Review of Contemporary Fiction.
Review of Educational Research.
Review of Public Personnel Administration.
Risk Management.
Road & Track.
Rough Notes.
Royal Anthropological Institute. Journal.
Runner's World.
Rural Telecommunications.
Russian and East European Finance and Trade.
Russian Social Science Review.
St. Louis Commerce.
Sales & Marketing Management.
Sales and Marketing Management.
Salmagundi.
San Diego Business Journal.
Satellite Communications.
Saturday Evening Post.
Saturday Night.
Savannah Business Journal.
Scholastic Update.
Science.
Science & Society.
Science News.
The Sciences.
Secured Lender.
Security Management.
The Service Industries Journal.
Sexually Transmitted Infections.
Shakespeare Quarterly.
Sierra.
Skiing.
Sky & Telescope.
Sloan Management Review.
Small Business News - Akron.
Small Business News - Cleveland.
Social Forces.
Social Policy.

VENDOR LISTING/SERIALS ONLINE

Social Problems.
Social Research.
Social Sciences Index. (PROQUEST)
Social Security Bulletin.
The Social Studies.
Social Work.
Society of Research Administrators. Journal.
Sociology.
Sociology of Education.
Sociology of Religion.
Software Magazine.
South African Food & Beverage Manufacturing Review.
South Dakota Business Review.
Southern California Business.
The Southern Review.
Southwest Review.
Spectrum (Lexington).
Sporting Goods Business.
The Sporting News.
Sports Illustrated.
Springfield Business Journal.
Stamps.
Standard Federal Tax Reports.
The State Journal.
State Tax Review.
Stereo Review.
Studies in English Literature 1500-1900.
Studies in Philology.
Studies in Short Fiction.
Studies in the Novel.
Style (DeKalb).
Successful Farming.
Successful Meetings.
Suicide and Life-Threatening Behavior.
Survey of Current Business.
T C I.
The Tax Adviser.
The Tax Executive.
Tax Management Compensation Planning Journal.
Tax Management Estates, Gifts and Trusts Journal.
Tax Management Financial Planning Journal.
Tax Management International Journal.
Tax Management Memorandum.
Tax Management Real Estate Journal.
Taxes (Riverwoods).
Teachers College Record.
Technical Communication.
Technology Alert.
Technology and Learning.
Technology Review.
Telecommunications (North American Edition).
Telecommunications Americas.
Telecommunications International.
Telephony.
Telesis (Ottawa).
Texas Banking.
Texas Monthly.
Textile World.
Theological Studies.
Time.
Times (Bethlehem).
Today's Homeowner.
Toledo Business Journal.
Total Health.
Trailer Boats.
Training.
Transmission and Distribution.
Transportation & Distribution.
Transportation Journal.
TriQuarterly.
Trust Letter.
Trustee.
Trusts and Estates (Atlanta).
Tufts University Health and Nutrition Letter.
Twentieth Century Literature.
U N Chronicle.
U S A Today.
U S Banker.
U S News & World Report.
Unitas.
University of California at Berkeley Wellness Letter.
UNIX Review.
Upside.
Utility Reporter - Fuels Energy & Power.
Vermont Business Magazine.
Victorian Studies.
Video Review.
Virginia Magazine of History and Biography.
Vital Speeches of the Day.
W I N News.
Wall Street & Technology.
Ward's Auto World.
Warfield's Business Record.
Washington and Lee Law Review.
The Washington Monthly.
Water Engineering and Management.
Weatherwise.
Wenatchee Business Journal.
Westchester County Business Journal.
Western Journal of Communication.
Wilson Quarterly.
Wilson Social Sciences Abstracts. (PROQUEST)
Woman's Day.
Women and Environments.
The Women's Review of Books.
Women's Sports and Fitness.
Wood Technology.
Work and Occupations.
Workbench.
Workforce.
Worklife Report.
World Affairs (Washington).
World Bank Research Observer.
World Health.
World Literature Today.
World Policy Journal.
World Press Review.
World Trade.
World Wastes.
World Watch.
The Writer.
Writer's Digest.

UNITED COMMUNICATIONS GROUP
One Central Plaza, 11300 Rockville Pike, Ste. 1100, Rockville, MD 20852. Tel: 301-816-8950 Fax: 301-816-8945.
Commerce Business Daily. (CBD OnLine)
Oil Price Information Service. (PETROSCAN)

WEST GROUP
620 Opperman Dr., Eagan, MN 55123. Tel: 612-687-7000
A B A Journal.
Alabama Law Review.
Alabama Lawyer.
Albany Law Review.
Alternatives to the High Cost of Litigation.
American Criminal Law Review. (ACRIMLREV)
American Indian Law Review.
American Journal of Law & Medicine.
American Journal of Legal History.
American Journal of Tax Policy.
American University Law Review.
Americans with Disabilities Cases. (FLB-CS, MLRR-CS)
Antitrust. (ANTITR)
Antitrust & Trade Regulation Report. (BNA-ATRR)
Antitrust Law Journal. (ANTITRLJ)
Arizona State Law Journal.
Army Lawyer.
B L A S T.
B N A Pension & Benefits Reporter. (BNA-PEN)
B N A's Americans with Disabilities Act Manual and Cases. (FLB-CS, MLRR-CS)
B N A's Banking Report. (BNA-BNK)
B N A's Patent, Trademark & Copyright Journal. (BNA-PTCJ)
Beverly Hills Bar Association Journal.
Boston College Law Review.
Boston University International Law Journal.
Boston University Law Review.
Brief (Chicago). (BRIEF)
Brigham Young University Law Review.
Brooklyn Journal of International Law.
Buffalo Law Review.
Business Lawyer. (BUSLAW)
C B A Record.
Campbell Law Review.
Capital University Law Review.
Chemical Regulation Reporter.
Chicago - Kent Law Review.
Chicano - Latino Law Review.
Cincinnati Law Review.
Cleveland State Law Review.
Collective Bargaining Negotiations & Contracts.
Columbia Journal of Law and Social Problems.
Columbia Journal of Transnational Law.
Columbia Law Review.
Computer Counsel.
Computer Lawyer.
Connecticut Law Review.
Constitutional Commentary.
Cornell International Law Journal.
Cornell Journal of Law and Public Policy.
Cornell Law Review.
Corporate Legal Times. (CORPLT)
Creighton Law Review.
Criminal Justice Abstracts.
Cumberland Law Review.
Current Law Index.
Daily Environment Report. (file BNA-DEN)
Daily Labor Report. (BNA-DLR)
Daily Report for Executives. (BNA-DER)
Daily Tax Report. (BNA-DTR)
De Paul Business Law Journal.
Defense Counsel Journal.
Delaware Journal of Corporate Law.
Denver Journal of International Law and Policy.
Denver University Law Review.
Dickinson Journal of International Law.
Dickinson Law Review.
Drake Law Review.
Duke Law Journal.
Duquesne Law Review.
East Asian Executive Reports.
Emory International Law Review.
Emory Law Journal.
Energy Law Journal.
Entertainment & Sports Law Review.
Entertainment Law Reporter.
Environment Reporter. (BNA-ER)
Environmental Law (Portland).
Environmental Law Reporter.
Estate Planning (New York). (WGL-ESTPLN)
Family Advocate. (FAMADVO)
Family Law Quarterly. (FAMLQ)
Federal Contracts Report.
Federal Lawyer.
Federal Register.
Federal Sentencing Reporter.
Fletcher Forum of World Affairs.
Florida Bar Journal.
Florida Law Review.
Florida State University Law Review.
Fordham Intellectual Property, Media & Entertainment Law Journal.
Fordham International Law Journal.
Fordham Law Review.
Fordham Urban Law Journal.
Forensic Services Directory.
George Mason Law Review.
George Washington Journal of International Law and Economics.
George Washington Law Review.
Georgetown Immigration Law Journal.
Georgetown International Environmental Law Review.
Georgetown Law Journal.
Georgia Journal of International and Comparative Law.
Georgia Law Review.
Golden Gate University Law Review.
Government Employee Relations Report.
Hamline Law Review.
Harvard Civil Rights - Civil Liberties Law Review.
Harvard Environmental Law Review.
Harvard International Law Journal.
Harvard Journal of Law and Public Policy.
Harvard Journal on Legislation.
Harvard Law Review.
Harvard Women's Law Journal.
Hastings Communications and Entertainment Law Journal (Comm - Ent).
Hastings Constitutional Law Quarterly.
Hastings International and Comparative Law Review.
Hastings Law Journal.
Hastings Women's Law Journal.
Hofstra Labor Law Journal.
Hofstra Law Review.
Houston Journal of International Law.
Houston Law Review.
Howard Law Journal.
Human Rights. (HUMRT)
Idaho Law Review.
Illinois Legal Times.
Index to Legal Periodicals & Books.
Indiana Law Journal.
Indiana Law Review.
Individual Employment Rights. (File FLB-CS, LRR-IERN)
Industrial and Labor Relations Review.
Insurance Periodicals Index.
Inter-American Law Review.
International Journal of Forensic Document Examiners.
International Lawyer.
International Trade Reporter. (BNA-ITR)
Iowa Law Review.
Issues in Law and Medicine.
John Marshall Law Review.
Journal of Air Law and Commerce.
Journal of Corporation Law.
Journal of Criminal Law & Criminology.
Journal of Energy, Natural Resources and Environmental Law.

Journal of Law & Commerce.
Journal of Partnership Taxation. *(WGL-JPTAX)*
The Journal of Taxation. *(WGL-JTAX)*
Judicature.
Judicial Conduct Reporter.
Kentucky Law Journal.
Labor - Management Relations Analysis - News and Background Information. *(File LLR-NEWS)*
Labor Relations Reference Manual. *(File FLB-CS, MLR-CS)*
Labor Relations Reporter.
Labor Relations Reporter. Fair Employment Practices.
Labor Relations Reporter. Labor Arbitration and Dispute Settlements. *(File LRR-LA)*
Labor Relations Reporter. Wages and Hours.
Law & Business Directory of Corporate Counsel.
Law and Policy in International Business.
Law Office Technology Review.
Law Practice Management.
LegalTrac. *(LRI)*
Litigation.
Louisiana Law Review.
Loyola Law Review.
Loyola of Los Angeles International and Comparative Law Journal.
Maine Law Review.
Marquette Law Review.
Maryland Law Review.
Mealey's Daubert Report.
Mealey's Emerging Insurance Disputes.
Mealey's Emerging Toxic Torts.
Mealey's Insurance Law Weekly.
Mealey's Insurance Supplement.
Mealey's International Arbitration Report.
Mealey's Litigation Report: Asbestos.
Mealey's Litigation Report: Bad Faith.
Mealey's Litigation Report: Biotechnology.
Mealey's Litigation Report: Breast Implants.
Mealey's Litigation Report: Drugs and Medical Devices.
Mealey's Litigation Report: Insurance.
Mealey's Litigation Report: Insurance Fraud.
Mealey's Litigation Report: Insurance Insolvency.
Mealey's Litigation Report: Intellectual Property.
Mealey's Litigation Report: Latex.
Mealey's Litigation Report: Lead.
Mealey's Litigation Report: Patents.
Mealey's Litigation Report: Pedicle Screws.
Mealey's Litigation Report: Reinsurance.
Mealey's Litigation Report: Superfund.
Mealey's Litigation Report: Tobacco.
Melbourne University Law Review.
Mercer Law Review.
Michigan Bar Journal.
Michigan Law Review.
Middle East Executive Reports.
Military Law Review.
Minnesota Law Review.
Mississippi College Law Review.
Mississippi Law Journal.
Missouri Law Review.
Natural Resources & Environment.
Nebraska Law Review.
Nevada Lawyer.
New England Law Review.
New Jersey Lawyer (New Brunswick).
New Mexico Law Review.
New York State Bar Journal. *(NYSTBJ)*
New York University Law Review.
North Carolina Journal of International Law and Commercial Regulation.
North Carolina Law Review.
Northern Kentucky Law Review.
Northwestern Journal of International Law & Business.
Northwestern University Law Review.
Notre Dame Law Review.
Nova Law Review.
Ohio Northern University Law Review.
Ohio State Journal on Dispute Resolution.
Ohio State Law Journal.
Oklahoma City University Law Review.
Oklahoma Law Review.
Oregon Law Review.
Oregon State Bar Bulletin.
Pacific Law Journal.
Pepperdine Law Review.
Preview of United States Supreme Court Cases.
Probate & Property.
Public Contract Law Journal.
Public Utilities Fortnightly.
Public Utilities Reports.
Quinnipiac Law Review.
Real Property, Probate and Trust Journal.
Risk: Health, Safety & Environment.
S E C Docket.
S E C News Digest.
Saint Louis University Law Journal.
St. Thomas Law Review.
Santa Clara Law Review.
Seattle University Law Review.
Securities Regulation & Law Report. *(BNA-SRLR)*
Seton Hall Legislative Journal.
South Carolina Law Review.
South Dakota Law Review.
South Texas Law Review.
Southern Illinois University Law Journal.
Southwestern Law Journal.
Stanford Journal of International Law.
Stanford Law & Policy Review.
Stanford Law Review.
State Capitals. Civil Rights.
State Capitals. Environmental Regulation.
State Capitals. Insurance Regulation.
State Capitals. Public Utilities.
State Capitals. Taxation and Revenue Policies.
State Capitals. Taxes - Property.
Stetson Law Review.
Suffolk Transnational Law Review.
Suffolk University Law Review.
Syracuse Journal of International Law & Commerce.
Tax Lawyer.
Tax Management Compensation Planning. *(File TM-CP, TM-CP-OLD, TM-CPJ)*
Tax Management Compensation Planning Journal. *(File TM-CPJ)*
Tax Management Estates, Gifts and Trusts. *(Files TM-EGT, TM-EGT-OLD, TM-EGTJ)*
Tax Management Estates, Gifts and Trusts Journal. *(File TM-EGTJ)*
Tax Management Foreign Income Portfolios. *(File TM-FOR)*
Tax Management Memorandum. *(File TM-TMM)*
Tax Management Real Estate. *(Files TM-RE, TM-RE-OLD, TM-REJ)*
Tax Management Real Estate Journal. *(File TM-REJ)*
Tax Management U S Income. *(Files TM-US, TM-US-OLD, TM-TMWR)*
Tax Management Weekly Report. *(File TM-TMWR)*
Temple Law Review.
Tennessee Bar Journal.
Tennessee Law Review.
Texas Journal of Women and the Law.
Texas Tech Law Review.
Thurgood Marshall Law Review.
Tort & Insurance Law Journal.
Transportation Law Journal.
Tulane Environmental Law Journal.
Tulane European and Civil Law Forum.
Tulane Law Review.
Tulane Maritime Law Journal.
Tulsa Law Journal.
U C Davis Law Review.
United States Law Week.
United States Tax Court Reports.
University of Baltimore Law Review.
University of Chicago Legal Forum.
University of Colorado Law Review.
University of Dayton Law Review.
University of Illinois Law Review.
University of Kansas Law Review.
University of New Brunswick Law Journal.
University of Pennsylvania Journal of International Economic Law.
University of Pittsburgh Law Review.
University of Richmond Law Review.
University of San Francisco Law Review.
Utah Law Review.
Valparaiso University Law Review.
Vanderbilt Journal of Transnational Law.
Vanderbilt Law Review.
Villanova Law Review.
Virginia Environmental Law Journal.
Virginia Journal of International Law.
Virginia Law Review.
Virginia Tax Review.
Washington and Lee Law Review.
Washington Law Review.
Washington University Law Quarterly.
Wayne Law Review.
William Mitchell Law Review.
Wisconsin Law Review.
Yale Journal on Regulation.

WILSONLINE (Subsidiary of: H. W. Wilson Co.)
950 University Ave., Bronx, NY 10452. Tel: 718-588-8400
Fax: 718-538-2746.
Albany Law Review.
Applied Science & Technology Index. *(AST)*
Art Index. *(File ART)*
Bibliographic Index. *(BIB)*
Biography Index. *(File BIO)*
Biological & Agricultural Index.
Book Review Digest. *(File BRD)*
Business Periodicals Index. *(File BPI)*
China Business Review.
Cumulative Book Index. *(File CBI)*
Education Index. *(File EDI)*
Essay and General Literature Index. *(File EGL)*
General Science Index. *(File GSI)*
Humanities Index. *(File HUM)*
I R S Publications.
Index to Legal Periodicals & Books. *(File ILP)*
Industrial and Labor Relations Review.
Library Literature. *(File LIB)*
New York Law Journal.
Ohio State Journal on Dispute Resolution.
Ohio State Law Journal.
Readers' Guide Abstracts. *(File RDG)*
Readers' Guide to Periodical Literature. *(File RDG)*
Rural Libraries.
Social Sciences Index.
Vertical File Index. *(File VFI)*
Wilson Abstracts. *(File ART)*
Wilson Applied Science and Technology Abstracts. *(AST)*
Wilson Business Abstracts. *(File WBA)*
Wilson Education Abstracts. *(File EDI)*
Wilson General Science Abstracts. *(File GSI)*
Wilson Humanities Abstracts. *(File HUM)*
Wilson Social Sciences Abstracts. *(File SSA)*

Index to Publications of International Organizations

This index is divided into four sections: publications of international organizations, of international congresses, of the European Communities, and of the United Nations. Numbers refer to the page in the Classified List of Serials where the full entry appears.

INTERNATIONAL ORGANIZATIONS

A C A R T S O D Monograph Series. (African Centre for Applied Research and Training in Social Development) 1353

A C A R T S O D Newsletter. (African Centre for Applied Research and Training in Social Development) 1353

A D B Review. (Asian Development Bank) 1353

A P O Annual Report. (Asian Productivity Organization) 1578

A P O News. (Asian Productivity Organization) 1578

A S A I H L Seminar Reports. (Association of Southeast Asian Institutions of Higher Learning) 2530

A S E A N Economic Info View. (Association of South East Asian Nations) 1353

A S I F A News. (Association Internationale du Film d'Animation) 5322

A T A - I A T A Reservations Interline Message Procedures - Passenger. 7061

Academy of European Law. Collected Courses/Academie de Droit Europeen. Recueil des Cours. 4104

Across the Oceans. 2398

Acta Astronautica. 52

Acta Colloquii Didactici Classici. 4236

Acta Crystallographica. Section A: Foundations of Crystallography. 1800

Acta Crystallographica. Section B: Structural Science. 1800

Acta Crystallographica. Section C: Crystal Structure Communications. 1801

Acta Crystallographica. Section D: Biological Crystallography. 1801

Acta Cytologica. 735

Acta Geneticae Medicae et Gemellologiae: Twin Research. 4630

Acta Haematologica. 4915

Acta Horticulturae. 3179

Acta Musicologica. 5370

Acta Oncologica. 4969

Acta Radiologica. 5102

The Adelphi Papers. 6003

Advances in Limnology/Ergebnisse der Limnologie. 2392

Advances in Space Research. 52

Aerospace U F O News. 54

Africa Media Monograph Series. 3868

Africa Media Review. 1981

African Development Bank. Report by the Board of Directors/Banque Africaine de Developpement. Rapport du Conseil d'Administration. 1353

African Development Fund. Annual Report/Fonds Africain de Developpement. Rapport Annuel. 1353

African Journal of Plant Protection/Revue Africaine de la Protection des Vegetaux. 211

African Livestock Research. 267

African News Sheet. 3807

African Tax Systems. 1598

Africom. 1981

Afro Asian Economic Review. 1354

Afro-Asian Publications. 3524

Agroforestry Systems. 94

Air Waybill Handbook. 7062

Airline Advertising Project. 31

Airline Coding Directory. 7063

Airline Economic Results and Prospects. 7063

Airport Handling Manual. 7064

Al-Akademiyyah Al-Arabiyyah Lil-Eloum Wa Al-Tehnologia Wa Al-Naql Al-Bahri. Mjallaht/Arab Academy for Science and Technology and Maritime Transport. Journal. 6510

Alcoholism. 2298

Allergy & Clinical Immunology International. 4791

Aluminium Industry Abstracts. 5216

America Cooperativa. 1204

Americas. 3772

Amnesty International Report. 6004

Amphibia Reptilia. 825

Anales Galdosianos. 4374

Analytical and Quantitative Cytology and Histology. 736

Analytical Cellular Pathology. 736

Anatomia, Histologia, Embryologia. 7265

Anciens Pays et Assemblees d'Etats. 5891

Andrologia. 4637

Anesthesia and Analgesia. 4803

Animals International. 301

Annals of Glaciology. 2330

Annals of Oncology. 4970

Annals of Public and Cooperative Economics. 1204

L'Annee Hippique. 6848

L'Annee Philologique. 1909

Annotated Bibliography of Literature on Cooperative Movements in South-East Asia. 532

Annuaire des Arachnologistes Mondiaux. 746

Annuaire des Centres de Recherche Demographique/Directory of Demographic Research Centers. 6046

Annuaire Economique des Pays Membres de l'Organisation de l'Unite Africaine/Economic Yearbook of Member States of the Organization of African Unity. 1221

Annual Bibliography of the History of the Printed Book and Library. 6087

Annual Report on International Statistics. 6892

Annual Report on the Results of Treatment in Gynecological Cancer. 4970

Anthos. 392

Antiviral Research. 780

Anuario Estadistico Centroamericano de Comercio Exterior. 1016

Anuario Interamericano de Derechos Humanos/Inter-American Yearbook on Human Rights. 4105

Apiacta. 99

Applied Geochemistry. 2331

Applied Numerical Mathematics. 4619

Aqua. 7287

Aquatic Mammals. 827

Arab Journal of Language Studies/Al-Majallah al-'Arabiyyah lil-Dirasat al-Lughawiyyah. 4242

Arab League Educational, Scientific, and Cultural Organization. Information Newsletter. 2421

Arab Petroleum. 5595

Arab Struggle. 3654

Archiv fuer Rechts- und Sozialphilosophie/Archives de Philosophie du Droit et de Philosophie Sociale/Archives for Philosophy of Law and Social Philosophy. 5718

Archiv fuer Rechts- und Sozialphilosophie. Beihefte. 5718

Archiv fuer Religionspsychologie. 6321

Artificial Intelligence Communications. 2098

Asia - Pacific Scouting. 1838

Asia - Pacific Tax Bulletin. 1599

Asian and Pacific Council. Food and Fertilizer Technology Center. Extension - Technical Bulletin. 100

Asian and Pacific Labour. 3887

Asian Development Bank. Annual Report. 1103

Asian Development Bank. Board of Governors. Summary of Proceedings. 1354

Asian Development Bank. Key Indicators of Developing Asian and Pacific Countries. 1104

Asian Development Bank. Statistical Report Series. 1016

Asian Institute of Technology. Annual Research and Activities Report. 6955

Asian News Sheet. 3807

Asociacion. 1838

Asociacion Interamericana de Bibliotecarios, Documentalistas y Especialistas en Informacion Agricola. Boletin Especial. 100

Asociacion Interamericana de Bibliotecarios, Documentalistas y Especialistas en Informacion Agricola. Boletin Informativo. 4161

Association Internationale d'Etudes du Sud-Est Europeen. Bulletin. 3550

Association Internationale d'Etudes Patristiques. Bulletin d'Information et de Liaison. 6321

Association Internationale de Geodesie. Commission des Marees Terrestres. Marees Terrestres Bulletin d'Information. 2378

Association Internationale de Signalisation Maritime. Bulletin/I A L A Bulletin. 7145

Association Internationale pour l'Histoire du Verre. Bulletin. 1725

Association of Commonwealth Universities. Annual Report of the Council Together with the Accounts of the Association. 2532

Association of Institutes for European Studies. Annuaire. 3551

Association of Institutes for European Studies. Year-Book. 3551

Association of Southeast Asian Institutions of Higher Learning. Newsletter. 2532

Atherosclerosis. 4811

Atlantic Series. 6005

Audiology and Neuro-Otology. 5020

Automatic Identification in the Airline Industry Handbook. 7065

Automatica. 2106

Automation in Construction. 2106

Aviation Regulatory Watch Group Reports. 7065

B I C - Code. (Bureau International des Containers) 5542

B I R D. (Base d'Information Robert-Debre) 1861

B S P Data Interchange Specifications Handbook. 1105

Babel. 4243

Bank for International Settlements. Annual Report. 1108

Bank Settlement Plan Quick Reference Handbook. 1110

Beche-de-Mer. 3062

Behavioral Ecology. 588

Benelux Economic Union. Conseil Central de l'Economie. Rapport du Secretaire sur l'Activite du Conseil. 1579

Benelux Publikatieblad/Bulletin Benelux. 6165

Bibliographie de la Philosophie/Bibliography of Philosophy. 5760

Bibliographie Internationale de l'Humanisme et de la Renaissance. 3798

Bibliography on Irrigation, Drainage, River Training and Flood Control/Bibliographie de la C I I D. Irrigation, Drainage et Maitrise des Crues. 7307

Bibliography on Soilless Culture. 170

Biochemical Education. 652

Biochemistry and Molecular Biology International. 653

Biofactors. 654

Biology and Fertility of Soils. 216

Biology International: I U B S Newsmagazine. (International Union of Biological Sciences) 592

Biorheology. 674

Blutalkohol. 2299

Boletim Tecnico Interamericano de Formacion Profesional. 2596

Boreas. 2332

Brahmavidya. 6488

Brain Pathology. 5055

Building and Wood. 3887

Building Research and Information. 871

Bulletin de l'O I V. 518

Bulletin de Philosophie Medievale. 5720

Bulletin du Bibliophile. 6266

Bulletin Eucarpia. 697

Bulletin for International Fiscal Documentation. 1601

Bulletin G C I D. (Greek National Committee) 7288

Bulletin of Volcanology. 2379

Bureau International des Societes Gerant les Droits d'Enregistrement et de Reproduction Mecanique. Bulletin. 6075

C A R A P H I N News. (Caribbean Animal and Plant Health Information Network) 106

C C I A Background Information. (World Council of Churches, Commission of the Churches on International Affairs) 6326

C D - Info. (Christian Democrat International) 5896

C E R N Courier. 5850

C E R N - H E R A Reports. 5851

C E R N Reports. 5851

C E R N School of Computing. Proceedings. 6593

C E R N School of Physics. Proceedings. 5851

C I A T in Perspective. (Centro Internacional de Agricultura Tropical) 106

C.I.C.A.E. Bulletin d'Information. (Confederation Internationale des Cinemas d'Art et d'Essai) 5325

C I L E C T News. (Centre International de Liaison des Ecoles de Cinema et de Television) 2045

C I N T E R F O R Estudios y Monografias. (Centro Interamericano de Investigacion y Documentacion sobre Formacion Profesional) 2597

C I R A Bulletin. (Centre International de Recherches sur l'Anarchisme) 5896

C.I.R.P. Annals. 2881

C I S Steel Information. (Commonwealth of Independent States) 5187

C M A S Bulletin d'Information/C M A S Newsletter. (Confederation Mondiale des Activites) 2400

C M I News Letter. (Comite Maritime International) 7147

C M I Year Book. (Comite Maritime International) 7147

C O D E S R I A Book Series. (Council for the Development of Economic and Social Research in Africa (CODESRIA)) 5896

C O N C A W E Review. 2909

C O S P A R Information Bulletin. (Committee on Space Research) 60

CAB International. Abstract Journal. 3167

CAB International. Bureau of Nutrition. Annotated Bibliographies. 5484

Cahiers de Droit Fiscal International. 4107

Cahiers Ligures de Prehistoire et de Protohistoire. 357

Capture Section Reports. 3063

Cardiovascular Drugs and Therapy. 4813

Cardiovascular Surgery. 4813

Cargo Agent's Handbook. 7066

Cargo Community Systems Directory and Guidelines. 7066

Cargo Interchange Message Procedures Manual. 7066

Cargo Services Conference Resolutions Manual. 7066

Cargo Tariff Coordinating Conferences Resolutions Manual. 7066

Cargo Today. 7050

Catalogo de Publicaciones Latinoamericanas sobre Formacion Profesional. 2597

Catalogus Musicus. 5381

Catalogus Translationem et Commentatorium. 4495

Cellular Engineering. 646

Central and East European Tax Directory. 1603

Centre International de Documentation Arachnologique. Liste des Travaux Arachnologiques. 638

Centro de Estudios Monetarios Latinoamericanos. Ensayos. 1120

Centro Interamericano de Investigacion y Documentacion sobre Formacion Profesional. Informes. 2598

Centro Interamericano de Investigacion y Documentacion sobre Formacion Profesional. Serie Bibliografica. 2598

Centro Latinoamericano de Economia Humana. Cuadernos. 6607

Chaine/Keten. 302

Chemical Geology. 2312

Chemistry International. 1745

Chemoreception Abstracts. 1782

Child Abuse & Neglect. 1840

Children in the Tropics. 1842

Child's Nervous System. 5058

Chronica Horticulturae. 3185

Chronicle of Parliamentary Elections and Developments. 5900

Chronobiologia. 596

Chronobiology International. 596

Ciencia Interamericana. 6519

Ciguatera. 3064

Clinical Hemorheology. 4917

Coal Highlights. 2661

Coastline. 2401

Colecciones Basicas C I N T E R F O R. 2598

Collection of Documents for the Study of International Non-Governmental Relations. 4108

Colombo Plan Bureau. The Colombo Plan Council Report. 1355

Colombo Plan for Co-operative Economic and Social Development in Asia and the Pacific. Consultative Committee. Proceedings and Conclusions. 1355

Colombo Plan for Co-operative Economic and Social Development in Asia and the Pacific. Development Perspectives. Country Issues Papers by Member Governments to the Consultative Committee. 1355

Colombo Plan Newsletter. 1355

Comite Consultatif pour la Masse et les Grandeurs Apparentees. 5249

Comite International de Cooperation dans les Recherches Nationales en Demographie. Actes des Seminaires. 6048

Comite International de Dachau. Bulletin. 3559

Comite International des Poids et Mesures. Comite Consultatif d'Electricite. (Rapport et Annexes). 5249

Comite International des Poids et Mesures. Comite Consultatif de Photometrie et Radiometrie. (Rapport et Annexes). 5249

Comite International des Poids et Mesures. Comite Consultatif de Thermometrie. Rapports et Annexes. 5249

Comite International des Poids et Mesures. Comite Consultatif des Unites (Rapport et Annexes). 5249

Comite International des Poids et Mesures. Comite Consultatif pour la Definition de la Seconde. (Rapport et Annexes). 5249

Comite International des Poids et Mesures. Comite Consultatif pour la Definition du Metre (Rapport et Annexes). 5249

Comite International des Poids et Mesures. Comite Consultatif pour les Etalons des Mesure des Rayonnements Ionisants (Rapport et Annexes). 5249

Comite International des Poids et Mesures. Proces-Verbaux des Seances. 5250

Comite International des Poids et Mesures. Systeme International d'Unites. 5250

Commission for the Geological Map of the World. Bulletin. 2335

Commonwealth Judicial Journal. 4109

Commonwealth Universities Yearbook. 2537

Communication World. 1470

Comparative History of Literatures in European Languages/Histoire Comparee des Litteratures en Langues Europeennes. 4392

Comparative Labor Law Journal. 1424

Compendium of Tourism Statistics. 7253

Competition Policy in O E C D Countries. 1356

Composers of the Americas/Compositores de America. 5385

CompStat Symposium. Proceedings. (Computational Statistics) 6907

Computers & Geosciences. 2328

Computers & Security. 2149

Confederacion Latinoamericana de Asociaciones Cristianas de Jovenes. Carta. 6331

Conference de la Haye de Droit International Prive. Actes et Documents/Hague Conference on Private International Law. Proceedings. 4110

Conference Generale des Poids et Mesures. Comptes Rendus des Seances. 5250

Conscience et Liberte. 5989

Consejo Superior Universitario Centroamericano. Actas de la Reunion Ordinaria. 2537

Consumer Policy in O E C D Countries. 1211

Contemporary Philosophy. 5722

The Controller. 62

Convenios Centroamericanos de Integration Economica. 1356

Convergence: International Congress on Transportation Electronics. Proceedings. 7096

Cooperative Press in South-East Asia. 3871

Cooperative Trade Directory for Southeast Asia. 1205

Coral Reefs. 2401

Corporate Air Travel Survey. 7067

Cotton: Review of the World Situation. 6985

Cotton: World Statistics. 6999

Cross-Cultural Psychology Bulletin. 6106

Crude Steel Production. 5217

Current Dialogue. 6333

Dangerous Goods Training Programme. 7067

Democratic Journalist. 3871

Dento-Maxillo-Facial Radiology. Supplement. 5105

Dentomaxillofacial Radiology. 5105

Dermatologic Surgery. 5140

Desert Locust Control Organization for Eastern Africa. Annual Report. 221

Development (London). 1357

Development, Genes and Evolution. 598

Developmental and Comparative Immunology. 4794

Diabetes Research and Clinical Practice. 4885

Dialogues et Cultures. 4252

Diamond World Review. 3863

Directory of the National Productivity Organizations in A P O Member Countries. 1583

Disease Information. 7269

Division d'Aide et de Cooperation Francaise. Bulletin Trimestriel de Statistique. 1035

Document World. 4231

Documenta Ophthalmologica. 4992

Documentacion de la Seguridad Social Americana. 3814

Documentation Bulletin for South-East Asia. 546

Droit Nucleaire. 2695

Drug and Alcohol Dependence. 2300

E B U Technical Review. (European Broadcasting Union) 1988

E C M T Statistical Report on Road Accidents. (European Council of Ministers of Transport) 7050

E C S L News. (European Centre for Space) 63

E F I L Latest Edition. (European Federation for Intercultural Learning) 2564

E I Monthly Monitor. (Education International) 2433

E P P O Bulletin. (European and Mediterranean Plant Protection Organization) 222

E S A Bulletin. (European Space Agency) 63

E S A - I R S News & Views. (European Space Agency) 4231

E S A R B I C A Journal. (International Council on Archives, Eastern and Southern Africa Regional Branch) 4176

E S O M A R Directory (Year). (European Society for Opinion and Marketing Research) 1525

Earth Observation Quarterly. 64

Earthquake Engineering and Structural Dynamics. 2783

Ecological Economics. 2915

Ecology and Farming. 113

Economics and Development Resource Center. Report Series. 1129

Economie Familiale/Home Economics. 3683

Ecumenical Letter on Evangelism. 6336

Ecumenical Review. 6336

Education in O E C D Countries: Compendium of Statistical Information. 2437

Education International Quarterly Magazine. 2437

Educational and Vocational Guidance - Bulletin A I O S P, I A E V G, I V S B B. (Association Internationale d'Orientation Scolaire et Professionnelle) 5508

Electrochimica Acta. 1805

Electroencephalography and Clinical Neurophysiology Including Evoked Potentials and Electromyography and Motor Control. 5062

Electroencephalography and Clinical Neurophysiology. Supplements. 5062

Electromyography and Motor Control. 5062

Elements de Bibliographie sur les Pays du Sahel/Elements for a Bibliography on the Sahelian Countries. 547

Encyclopedia of World Problems and Human Potential. 6012

Energy Policies of I E A Countries. 2667

Energy Statistics of O E C D Countries. 2683

Enfant en Milieu Tropical. 1845

Environment Newsletter. 2919

Environmental Monitor. 2923

Environmental Policy and Law. 2924

Environmental Policy and Law Papers. 2924

Environmental Review. 2925

Epilepsia. 5063

Episodes (Nottingham). 2339

Erosion Control. 2229

Estadistica. 6910

Estadisticas Macroeconomicas de Centroamerica. 1037

Estudios de la Seguridad Social. 3815

Europastimme. 6013

The European Accounting Review. 1089

European Archives of Oto-Rhino-Laryngology. 5021

European Association for Animal Production. Publications. 275

European Bibliography of Slavic and East European Slavonic Studies/Bibliographie Europeene des Travaux sur l'ex-URSS et l'Europe de l'Est/Europaeische Bibliographie Oesteuropastudien. 3520

European Centre for Medium-Range Weather Forecasts. Technical Report. 5230

European Child & Adolescent Psychiatry. 5063

European Community Shipowners' Associations. Annual Report. 7149

European Conference on Controlled Fusion and Plasma Physics. Proceedings. 5851

European Court of Human Rights. Publications. Series A: Judgments and Decisions/Cour Europeenne des Droits de l'Homme. Publications. Serie A: Arrets et Decisions. 5990

European Economic Review. 962

European Federation of Finance House Associations. Annual Report. 1130

European Federation of Finance House Associations. Newsletter. 1130

European Free Trade Association. Annual Report. 1323

European Geophysical Society Series on Hydrological Sciences. 2393

European Journal of Biochemistry. 659

European Journal of Cancer. 4977

European Journal of Cancer. Part B: Oral Oncology. 4977

European Journal of Clinical Investigation. 4665

European Journal of Clinical Investigation. Supplement. 4665

European Journal of Human Genetics. 766

European Journal of Obstetrics & Gynecology and Reproductive Biology. 4956

European Journal of Pharmaceutical Sciences. 5660

European Journal of Political Research. 5925

European Journal of Population/Revue Europeenne de Demographie. 6065

European Journal of Prosthodontics and Restorative Dentistry. 4857

European Journal of Radiology. 5106

European Journal of Surgical Oncology. 4978

European League for Economic Cooperation. Publications. 1359

European League for Economic Cooperation. Report of the Secretary General on the Activities of E.L.E.C. 1359

The European Legacy. 5726

European Materials Research Society. Monographs. 2858

European Neuropsychopharmacology. 5064

European Organisation for Civil Aviation Equipment. General Assembly. Annual Report. 64

European Organization for Nuclear Research. List of Scientific Publications/Conseil Europeen pour la Recherche Nucleaire. Liste des Publications Scientifiques. 5834

European Organization for Research on Treatment of Cancer. Monograph Series. 4978

European Quality. 6959

European Radiology. 5106

The European Respiratory Journal. 5118

European Southern Observatory. Annual Report. 494

European Space Agency. Scientific and Technical Memoranda. 64

European Space Agency. Scientific and Technical Reports. 64

European Tax Handbook. 1607

European Taxation. 1607

European Taxation Data Base on C D - R O M. 1607

European Water Pollution Control. 2968

Europhysics Conference Abstracts. 5834

EUROSIM - Simulation News Europe. 2151

Evoked Potentials. 5064

Expression. 7319

Extensions and Corrections to the U D C. 4177

Eye to Eye. 4993

F A N S Facts Sheet. (Future Air Navigation Systems) 64

F E B S Letters. (Federation of European Biochemical Societies) 660

F E M S. Immunology and Medical Microbiology. (Federation of European Microbiological Societies) 784

F E M S. Microbiology. (Federation of European Microbiological Societies) 784

F E M S. Microbiology Ecology. (Federation of European Microbiological Societies) 784

F E M S. Microbiology Letters. (Federation of European Microbiological Societies) 784

F E M S. Microbiology Reviews. (Federation of European Microbiological Societies) 784

F I A F Classification Scheme for Literature on Film and Television. (International Federation of Film Archives (F I A F)) 5331

F I D Directory. (Federation Internationale d'Information et de Documentation) 4177

F I D News Bulletin. (Federation Internationale d'Information et de Documentation) 4177

F I F A Handbook. (Federation Internationale de Football Association) 6803

F I F A Magazine. 6803

F I F A News. 6803

F I F A Olympic Football Tournament. (Federation Internationale de Football Association) 6803

F I F A Technical Reports. (Federation Internationale de Football Association) 6803

F I F A U-17 World Championship. (Federation Internationale de Football Association) 6803

F I F A World Cup. 6803

F I F A World Youth Championship. 6803

F I O D S Revue. (Federation Internationale des Organisations de Donneurs de Sang Benevoles) 4816

F I S Bulletin. (International Ski Federation) 6868

Facts & Figures. 2669

Faith and Order Papers. 6338

Federacion Panamericana de Asociaciones de Facultades de Medicina. Boletin. 4667

Federation Internationale de Gymnastique. Bulletin. 6760

Federation Internationale de Rugby Amateur. Annuaire. 6803

Federation Internationale Motocycliste. Annuaire. 6827

Financial Market Trends. 1135

Financing and External Debt of Developing Countries. 1360

Fish Aggregating Devices. 3065

Fisheries Education and Training. 3066

Fisheries Newsletter. 3066

Flash. 3890

Flashes from the Trade Unions. 3890

Fluoride. 4779

Folia Linguistica. 4257

Folia Phoniatrica et Logopaedica. 5021

Fontes Artis Musicae. 5447

Fred och Frihet. 6015

Free Labour World. 3890

Fundamenta Informaticae. 4620

Futures Bulletin. 6615

Futuribles. 6711

Futurology. 6960

Fuzzy Sets and Systems. 4574

Garden to Kitchen Newsletter. 5473

General Relativity and Gravitation. 5804

General Treaty for Central American Economic Integration. Permanent Secretariat. Newsletter. 1360

Genetic Counseling. 768

Geneva Papers on Risk and Insurance - Issues and Practice. 3816

Geneva Papers on Risk and Insurance Theory. 3817

Geographical Distribution of Financial Flows to Aid Recipients. Disbursements - Commitments - Country Indicators/Repartition Geographique des Ressources Financieres Allouees aux Pays Beneficiaires de l'Aide. Versements - Engagements - Indicateurs par Pays. 1360

Geophysical Prospecting. 2382

Geothermics. 2315

Giornale Storico della Lunigiana e del Territorio Lucense. 3569

The Global Tenant. 3747

Gold (Year). 5301

Gold Institute. International Conference on Gold & Silver in Medicine. Proceedings. 5301

Gold News/Nouvelles de l'Or. 5301

Greenhouse Issues. 2968

Grotiana. 3957

Guide to Health Services of the World. 3708

Guide to the European V A T Directives. 1611

Guides to European Taxation: Taxation & Investment in Central and East European Countries. 1612

Guides to European Taxation: Taxation of Companies in Europe. 1612

Guides to European Taxation: Taxation of Individuals in Europe. 1612

Guides to European Taxation: Taxation of Patent Royalties, Dividends, Interest in Europe. 1612

Guides to European Taxation: Taxation of Private Investment Income. 1612

Guides to European Taxation: Value Added Taxation in Europe. 1612

Gynecological Endocrinology. 4888

Haemophilia. 4919

Haemophilia. Supplement. 4919

Handbook on the 1989 Double Taxation Convention Between the Federal Republic of Germany and the United States of America. 1612

Health Policy. 6237

Hegel - Studien Beihefte. 5729

Higher Education Management. 2543

Higher Education Policy. 2543

Histopathology. 4979

History of European Ideas. 5729

Homeostasis. 5068

Horticultural Research International. 3194

Hospital Management International. 3713

Human Rights Bulletin (New York). 5992

Hydrographic Journal. 2316

Hydrographic Society. International Headquarters. Special Publications. 7294

Hydrological Sciences Journal/Journal des Sciences Hydrologiques. 2394

Hypertension in Pregnancy. 4818

I A B S E Report. (International Association for Bridge and Structural Engineering) 2786

I A G A News. (International Association of Geomagnetism and Aeronomy) 2383

I A J R C Journal. (International Association of Jazz Record Collectors) 5399

I A L News. (International Association of Laryngectomees) 2584

I A M C R Newsletter. (International Association for Mass Communications Research) 1991

I A S A Journal. (International Association of Sound Archives) 6744

I A S L Newsletter. (International Association of School Librarianship) 4181

I A T A Airport and En-Route Aviation Charges Manual. (International Air Transport Association) 7071

I A T A Annual Report. (International Air Transport Association) 7071

I A T A City Code Directory. (International Air Transport Association) 7071

I A T A - I A L Air Distances. (International Air Transport Association) 7071

I A T A List of Ticket and Airport Taxes and Fees. (International Air Transport Association) 7071

I A T A Review. (International Air Transport Association) 7071

I A W A Journal. (International Association of Wood Anatomists) 708

I B N S Journal. (International Bank Note Society) 5465

I C A C Recorder. (International Cotton Advisory Committee) 6987

I C A Regional Bulletin. (International Cooperative Alliance) 1206

I C A S A L S Newsletter. (International Center for Arid and Semiarid Land Studies) 123

I C A S E - L A R C Interdisciplinary Series in Science. (Institute for Computer Applications in Science and Engineering, Langley Research Center) 6531

I C C O Annual Report. (International Cocoa Organization) 3112

I C C O Cocoa Newsletter. (International Cocoa Organization) 3112

I C C O Quarterly Bulletin of Cocoa Statistics. (International Cocoa Organization) 3112

I C C O World Cocoa Directory. (International Cocoa Organization) 3112

I C E L References. (International Council of Environmental Law) 2962

I C E M Review. (International Council for Educational Media) 2449

I C E S Cooperative Research Report/Rapport des Recherches Collectives. (International Council for the Exploration of the Sea) 3069

I C E S Fisheries Statistics/Bulletin Statistique des Peches Maritimes. 3083

I C E S Journal of Marine Science. (International Council for the Exploration of the Sea) 2404

I C E S Oceanographic Data Lists and Inventories. 2404

I C H A Buyers' Guide to Manufacturers (Year). (International Cargo Handling Co-ordination Association) 7152

I C H S Information Bulletin. (International Council of Homehelp Services) 4934

I C I D Journal. (International Commission on Irrigation and Drainage) 123

I C J Review. (International Commission of Jurists) 4115

I C M A Newsletter. (International City - County Management Association) 6216

I C O M News. (International Council of Museums) 5355

I C S U Newsletter. (International Council of Scientific Unions) 6532

I D F Directory. (International Diabetes Federation) 4889

I D O C Internazionale. (International Documentation and Communication Center) 6650

I E A Coal Research. Newsletter. (International Energy Agency) 2670

I E A Coal Research. Perspectives. (International Energy Agency) 2670

I E A Coal Research. Profiles. (International Energy Agency) 2670

I E C Bulletin. (International Electrotechnical Commission) 2826

I E C Catalogue of Publications. (International Electrotechnical Commission) 2639

I E E E International Conference on Acoustics, Speech and Signal Processing. Proceedings. 2827

I E E E International Symposium on Electrical Insulation. I E E E Conference Record. 2827

I E S A Information. (International Society for Electrosleep and Electroanaesthesia) 5068

I F A P Newsletter. (International Federation of Agricultural Producers) 123

I F H O H Journal. (International Federation of the Hard of Hearing) 3463

I F L A Directory. (International Federation of Library Associations and Institutions) 4182

I F L A Journal. (International Federation of Library Associations and Institutions) 4182

I F L A Publications. (International Federation of Library Associations and Institutions) 4182

I F L Nieuws. (International Friendship League) 1932

I G F - Journal. (International Graphical Federation) 6080

I H F Management Handbooks. (International Hospital Federation) 3714

I I A S A Annual Report. (International Institute for Applied Systems Analysis) 2182

I I R A Bulletin. (International Industrial Relations Association) 1433

I L C A Annual Report and Programme Highlights. (International Livestock Centre for Africa) 277

I L C A Newsletter. (International Livestock Centre for Africa) 277

I L C A Proceedings. (International Livestock Centre for Africa) 277

I L C A Research Report. (International Livestock Centre for Africa) 277

I L G A Bulletin. (International Lesbian and Gay Association) 3696

I M F News. (International Metalworkers Federation) 5193

INDEX TO PUBLICATIONS OF INTERNATIONAL ORGANIZATIONS

I M U Canberra Circular. (International Mathematical Union) 4576

I O J Newsletter. (International Organization of Journalists) 3874

I P D Cahier/P A I D Reports. (Institut Panafricain pour le Developpement) 1361

I P I Report. (International Press Institute) 3874

I P S F News Bulletin. (International Pharmaceutical Students Federation) 5665

I P T C Spectrum. (International Press Telecommunications Council) 2034

I R R I Program Report. (International Rice Research Institute) 263

I S B N Newsletter. (International Standard Book Number) 6273

I S M S Newsletter. (International Society for Mushroom Science) 708

I S O Bulletin (English Edition). (International Organization for Standardization) 5251

I S O Memento. (International Organization for Standardization) 5251

I S O News. (International Society of Organbuilders) 5399

I S P R S Journal of Photogrammetry and Remote Sensing. (International Society for Photogrammetry and Remote Sensing) 3409

I S S A. Social Security Documentation. Caribbean Series. (International Social Security Association) 3818

I S S A Committee on Provident Funds. Reports. (International Social Security Association) 3818

I S T A News Bulletin. (International Seed Testing Association) 227

I S U Constitution. (International Skating Union) 6764

I S U Regulations. (International Skating Union) 6764

I T C Journal. 3409

I T M F Country Statements. (International Textile Manufacturers Federation) 6987

I T M F Directory. (International Textile Manufacturers Federation) 6988

I T U Review. (International Typographical Union) 3891

I U F R O World Congress. Congress Reports. (International Union of Forest Research Organizations) 3155

I U F R O World Series. (International Union of Forestry Research Organizations) 3155

I U G G Year Book. (International Union of Geodesy and Geophysics) 2383

I U O M A Magazine. (International Union of Mail Artists) 445

I U S Newsletter. (International Union of Students) 2544

I U S S P Newsletter/U I E S P Bulletin de Liaison. (International Union for the Scientific Study of Population) 6051

I U S S P Papers/U I E S P Documents de l'Union. (International Union for the Scientific Study of Population) 6051

I U S Women's Newsletter. (International Union of Students) 7323

I W G I A Documents. (International Work Group for Indigenous Affairs) 319

Ice. 2351

Immunology Letters. 4796

Implant. 4994

Index of African Social Science Periodical Articles. 6650

Index to Plant Chromosome Numbers. 708

Indigenous Affairs. 319

Indologica Taurinensia. 5528

Industrial Policy in O E C D Countries. 1264

Inform Quarterly Newsletter. 4904

Information and Management. 2166

Information Bulletin for Catholic Rural Organizations. 125

Information, Computer and Communications Policy. 1993

Information Europe. 4184

Information Technology Catalogue. 7072

Information Technology Outlook/Perspectives des Technologies de l'Information. 4232

Informations Recentes sur les Comptes Nationaux des Pays en Developpement/Latest Information on National Accounts of Developing Countries. 1362

Ingenieria Sanitaria. 6239

Innovation and Employment. 5510

Inspel. 4185

Institut de Droit International. Annuaire. 4116

Institut International du Froid. Bulletin/International Institute of Refrigeration. Bulletin. 3480

Institut International du Froid. Comptes Rendus de Reunions de Commissions/International Institute of Refrigeration. Proceedings of Commission Meetings. 3480

Institut Panafricain pour le Developpement. Travaux d'Etudiants. Bulletin Analytique. 1362

Institut Panafricain pour le Developpement. Travaux Manuscrits. 196

Institut Syndical Europeen. Nouvelles. 1436

Institut Syndical Europeen. Rapport d'Activites. 1436

Instituto Interamericano del Nino. Boletin. 1847

Instituto Panamericano de Geografia e Historia. Boletin Aereo. 5170

Integrated Coastal Fisheries Management Project Technical Document. 3070

Intensive Care Medicine. 4685

Inter American Press Association. Freedom of the Press Annual Report. 5934

Inter-American Center of Tax Administrators. Informativo - Newsletter. 1614

Interamerican Children's Institute. Report of the General Director. 6670

Inter-American Commission of Women. News Bulletin. 7323

Inter-American Commission of Women. Noticiero. 7323

Inter-American Council for Education, Science, and Culture. Final Report. 2451

Inter-American Council of Commerce and Production. Uruguayan Section. Publicaciones. 1362

Inter-American Development Bank. Annual Report. 1146

Inter-American Economic and Social Council. Final Report of the Annual Meeting at the Ministerial Level. 3632

Inter-American Review of Bibliography/Revista Interamericana de Bibliografia. 552

Inter-American Tropical Tuna Commission. Annual Report/Comision Interamericana del Atun Tropical. Informe Anual. 3070

Inter-American Tropical Tuna Commission. Bulletin/Comision Interamericana del Atun Tropical. Boletin. 3071

Inter-American Tropical Tuna Commission. Data Report. 3071

InterMedia. 2052

International Abstracts in Operations Research. 2094

International Academy of Legal Medicine and Social Medicine. Newsletter. 4904

International Air Transport Association. Annual General Meeting. Reports and Proceedings. 7072

International Air Transport Association. List of Operators at Each Airport. 7072

International Angiology. 4818

International Arthurian Society. Bibliographical Bulletin/Societe Internationale Arthurienne. Bulletin Bibliographique. 4496

International Association for Byzantine Studies. Bulletin d'Information et de Coordination. 3575

International Association for Educational and Vocational Information. Studies and Reports. 2451

International Association for Media and History. Newsletter. 5336

International Association for Shell and Spatial Structures. Journal. 2788

International Association for the Exchange of Students for Technical Experience. Annual Report. 2565

International Association for the Physical Science of the Ocean. Proces-Verbaux. 2405

International Association of Agricultural Information Specialists. Quarterly Bulletin. 4186

International Association of Engineering Geology. Bulletin. 2352

International Association of Geodesy. Central Bureau for Satellite Geodesy. Bibliography. 3428

International Association of Geodesy. Central Bureau for Satellite Geodesy. Information Bulletin. 3410

International Association of Geodesy Symposia. 2383

International Association of Hydrogeologists. Memoires. 2395

International Association of Law Libraries. Directory. 4186

International Association of Liberal Religious Women. Newsletter. 6345

International Association of Literary Critics. Revue. 6274

International Association of Theoretical and Applied Limnology. Communications/Internationale Vereinigung fuer Theoretische und Angewandte Limnologie. Mitteilungen. 2395

International Association of Theoretical and Applied Limnology. Proceedings/Internationale Vereinigung fuer Theoretische und Angewandte Limnologie. Verhandlungen. 2395

International Astronomical Union. Transactions. 496

International Baccalaureate Organisation. Annual Report. 1957

International Badminton Federation. Annual Statute Book. 6765

International Bibliography of Historical Demography/Bibliographie Internationale de la Demographie Historique. 6066

International Bibliography of the Forensic Sciences. 4780

International Brain Research Organization Monograph Series. 5069

International Bureau of Fiscal Documentation. Annual Report. 1614

International Business Lawyer. 4116

International Cataloguing and Bibliographic Control. 4186

International Centre for Settlement of Investment Disputes. Annual Report. 1389

International Child Health: A Digest of Current Information. 5032

International Children's Centre. Paris. Report of the Director-General to the Executive Board. 6714

International Civil Defence Journal/Revue Internationale de Protection Civile/Revista Internacional de Proteccion Civil. 1898

International College of Dentists. European Section. Newsletter. 4859

International Commission for Uniform Methods of Sugar Analysis. Report of the Proceedings of the Session (Year). 3114

International Commission on Irrigation and Drainage. Congress Reports. 2873

International Commission on Irrigation and Drainage. Report. 7295

International Commission on Large Dams. Bulletin. 2788

International Commission on Radiological Protection. Annals. 5107

International Committee for Historical Science. Bulletin d'Information. 3501

International Committee of the Red Cross. Annual Report - Rapport d'Activite - Informe de Actividad. 6671

International Committee on Urgent Anthropological and Ethnological Research. Bulletin. 320

International Confederation of Free Trade Unions. World Congress Reports. 3892

International Confederation of Societies of Authors and Composers. 5586

International Conference on Data Processing in the Field of Social Security. Reports. 3821

International Congress on Combustion Engines. Proceedings. 2887

International Congress Science Series. 5170

International Cooperative Alliance. Cooperative Series. 1207

International Cotton Industry Statistics. 7000

International Council of Scientific Unions. Year Book. 6534

International Customs Journal/Bulletin International des Douanes. 1614

International Dairy Federation. Bulletin/Federation Internationale de Laiterie. Bulletin. 255

International Dairy Federation. Catalogue of I D F Publications/Federation Internationale Laitiere. Catalogue des Publications. 176

International Dairy Federation. International Standard/ Federation Internationale de Laiterie. Norme Internationale. 255

International Dental Journal. 4859

International Directory of Film and T V Documentation Collections. 5337

International Directory of Prisoners Aid Agencies. 2269

International Earth Rotation Service. Annual Report. 496

International Earth Rotation Service. Monthly Bulletin. 496

International Egg Commission. Broadsheet. 3114

International Egg Commission. Market Review Situation & Outlook Report. 3114

International Egg Commission. Monthly Chick Placement Bulletin. 3114

International Egg Commission. Monthly News Letter. 3114

International Electrotechnical Commission. Yearbook - Annuaire. 2835

International Energy Agency. Greenhouse Gas R & D Programme. Annual Report. 2969

International Energy Agency. Greenhouse Gas R & D Programme. Proceedings. 2969

International Energy Agency. Greenhouse R&D Programme. Public Summary Reports. 2969

International Federation for Housing and Planning. Directory. 3750

International Federation of Commercial Clerical, Professional and Technical Employees. Newsletter. 3892

International Federation of Journalists and Travel Writers. Official List/Repertoire Officiel. 7212

International Federation of Medical Students' Associations. Newsletter. 4685

International FilmArchive C D - R O M. 5349

International Fiscal Association. Yearbook. 4118

International Grains Council. Food Aid Shipments. 3114

International Grains Council. Grain Market Report. 196

International Grains Council. Ocean Freight Rates. 7153

International Grains Council. Report for Fiscal Year. 264

International Grains Council. World Grain Statistics (Year). 176

International Graphical Federation. Report of Activities. 3892

International Gravimetrique Bureau. Bulletin d'Information. 2384

International Guide to Mergers and Acquisitions. 1614

The International Guide to Partnerships. 1614

International Handbook of Universities and Other Institutions of Higher Education. 2545

International Handbook on Commercial Arbitration. 4118

International Humanist News. 5731

International Hydrographic Bulletin. 2406

International Hydrographic Organization. Yearbook. 2406

International Hydrographic Review. 2406

International Index to Film Periodicals. 5349

International Institute for Land Reclamation and Improvement. Annual Report. 229

International Institute for Land Reclamation and Improvement. Bibliography. 176

International Institute for Land Reclamation and Improvement. Publication. 229

International Institute of Administrative Sciences Monographs. 6179

International Institute of Seismology and Earthquake Engineering. Bulletin. 2384

International Institute of Seismology and Earthquake Engineering. Individual Studies by Participants at I I S E E. 2384

International Institute of Seismology and Earthquake Engineering. Year Book. 2384

International Institute on the Prevention and Treatment of Dependencies. Selected Papers. 2302

International Iron and Steel Institute. Report of Conference Proceedings. 5195

International Journal for Consumer Safety. 2256

International Journal for the Advancement of Counselling. 2451

International Journal of Angiology. 4818

International Journal of Biometeorology. 5235

International Journal of Cancer. 4979

International Journal of Continuing Engineering Education. 2726

International Journal of Dermatology. 4879

International Journal of Developmental Neuroscience. 5069

International Journal of Early Childhood. 1848

International Journal of Environment and Pollution. 2969

International Journal of Fertility and Women's Medicine. 4686

International Journal of Food Microbiology. 787

International Journal of Government Auditing. 6179

International Journal of Group Tensions. 6118

International Journal of Gynecology and Obstetrics. 4960

International Journal of Hospitality Management. 3730

International Journal of Hydrogen Energy. 2672

International Journal of Industrial Ergonomics. 2726

International Journal of Legal Information. 4186

International Journal of Leprosy and Other Mycobacterial Diseases. 4838

International Journal of Occupational Medicine, Immunology and Toxicology. 5492

International Journal of Oral & Maxillofacial Surgery. 4860

International Journal of Physical Education/ Internationale Zeitschrift fuer Sportpaedagogik. 2606

International Journal of Prosthodontics. 4860

International Journal of Psycho-Analysis. 6118

International Journal of Psychology/Journal International de Psychologie. 6118

International Journal of Psychophysiology. 6119

International Journal of Speleology. 2352

International Journal of Sport Psychology. 5129

International Journal of Systematic Bacteriology. 787

International Journal of the Classical Tradition. 1904

International Journal of University Adult Education. 2511

The International Journal on Hydropower & Dams. 2693

International Linguistic Association. Monograph. 4265

International Linguistic Association. Special Publications. 4265

International Narcotics Control Board. Psychotropic Substances. 5831

International Narcotics Control Board. Report for (Year). 5668

International Navigation Association. Proceedings of Annual Meeting. 70

International Navigation Association Newsletter. 7073

International Newsletter on Chemical Education. 1753

International Nursing Review. 4935

International Ocean Institute. Occasional Papers. 2406

International Office of Cocoa, Chocolate and Sugar Confectionery. Annual Statistical Bulletin. 3137

International Oil Scouts Association. Official Publication. 5606

International Organization. 6020

International Organization for Migration. Annual Report. 6052

International Orthopaedics. 5008

International Pacific Halibut Commission (U.S. and Canada). Annual Report. 3071

International Pacific Halibut Commission (U.S. and Canada). Scientific Reports. 3071

International Peace Research Newsletter. 6020

International Peace Update. 6020

International Peat Journal. 5304

International Peat Society. Bulletin/Internationale Moor- und Torf-Gesellschaft. Mitteilungen. 5304

International Pediatric Association. Proceedings of Congress. 5032

International Pharmacy Journal. 5668

International Political Science Abstracts/Documentation Politique Internationale. 5985

International Political Science Association. World Congress. 5934

International Political Science Review/Revue Internationale de Science Politique. 6021

International Population Conference. Proceedings. 6052

International Prisoners Aid Association. Newsletter. 6671

International Psychologist. 6119

International Railway Statistics. 7053

International Rayon and Synthetic Fibres Committee. Statistical Yearbook. 7000

International Rehabilitation Review. 4687

International Rescue Committee. Annual Report. 6671

International Review for Business Education/Revue Internationale pour l'Enseignement Commercial/Internationale Zeitschrift fuer Kaufmaennisches Bildungswesen/Rivista Internazionale per la Cultura Commerciale/Revista Internacional para la Ensenanza Comercial. 973

International Review of Administrative Sciences. 6180

International Review of Mission. 6345

International Review of Social History. 3501

International Review of the Red Cross. 4120

International Rubber Digest. 6502

International Scheduled and Charter Freight Forecast. 7073

International Scheduled Passenger Forecast. 7073

International Seismological Centre. Bulletin. 2384

International Silk Association. Monthly Newsletter. 6989

International Skating Union. Ice Dancing Regulations. 6766

International Social Security Association. Studies and Research. 3821

International Social Security Review. 3822

International Social Work. 6671

International Society for Labor Law and Social Security. Bulletin. 1437

International Society for Mushroom Science. Symposia Proceedings. 709

International Society for Respiratory Protection. Journal. 5119

International Society of Criminology. Bulletin. 2270

International Society of Plant Morphologists. Yearbook. 709

International Society of Soil Science. Bulletin. 230

International Statistical Handbook of Urban Public Transport/Recueil International de Statistiques des Transports Publics Urbains/Internationales Statistik-Handbuch fuer den Oeffentlichen Stadtverkehr. 7053

International Statistical Review. 6918

International Studies Notes. 6021

International Sugar Organization. Statistical Bulletin. 3133

International Surgery. 5144

International Symposium on Canine Heartworm Disease. Proceedings. 7272

International Textile Machinery Shipment Statistics. 7000

International Textile Manufacturing. 6990

International Tin Research Institute. Annual Report. 5195

International Transactions in Operational Research. 2085

International U S Surgeon. 5144

International Union for Inland Navigation. Annual Report. 7031

International Union for Vacuum Science, Technique and Applications. News Bulletin. 5807

International Union of Alpine Associations. Bulletin/Union Internationale des Associations d'Alpinisme. Bulletin. 7212

International Union of Crystallography. Abstracts of the Triennial Congress. 1802

International Union of Food, Agricultural, Hotel, Restaurant, Catering, Tobacco and Allied Workers' Associations. News Bulletin. 3892

International V A T Monitor. 1615

International Whaling Commission. Annual Report. 3071

International Women's News. 7323

Der Internationalen Gesellschaft fuer Geschichte der Pharmazie. Veroeffentlichungen. Neue Folge. 5668

Internationale Gesellschaft fuer Urheberrecht. Yearbook. 5586

Internationale Seilbahn-Rundschau/International Aerial Lift Review. 7031

Internationale Stiftung Mozarteum. Mitteilungen. 5402

Inter-Parliamentary Bulletin. 6022

Inter-Parliamentary Union. Series: "Reports and Documents". 5935

Intervirology. 787

Invertebrate Reproduction and Development. 755

Iron Production. 5219

Islamic Academy of Sciences. Journal. 6535

Isotope and Radiation Research. 5108

J A R Amendment Service to Regulatory Documents. 7073

Jazzforschung/Jazz Research. 5403

Jazzmen's Reference Book. 5403

Joint Aviation Authorities. Certification Information - Procedures. 7074

Joint Aviation Authorities. General Information - Procedures. Information Leaflets. 7074

Joint Aviation Authorities. Maintenance Information - Procedures. 7074

Joint Aviation Authorities. Notice of Proposed Amendment Scheme. 7074

Joint Aviation Authorities. Regulatory Documents. 7074

Journal of Adolescent and Adult Literacy. 2454

Journal of Applied Crystallography. 1802

Journal of Applied Electrochemistry. 1805

Journal of Biomechanics. 4692

Journal of Bronchology. 5120

The Journal of Cardiovascular Surgery. 4820

Journal of Cerebral Blood Flow and Metabolism. 5072

Journal of Coastal Conservation. 2406

Journal of Communication. 1996

Journal of Cranio-Maxillo-Facial Surgery. 5144

Journal of Cryptology. 4582

Journal of Energy and Natural Resources Law. 3969

Journal of Environmental Pathology, Toxicology and Oncology. 2979

Journal of Film Preservation. 5337

Journal of Geochemical Exploration. 2317

Journal of Geodesy. 2385

Journal of Glaciology. 2353

The Journal of Heart and Lung Transplantation. 5145

Journal of Hepatology. 4913

Journal of Hydraulic Research. 2873

Journal of Hypertension. 4820

Journal of Hypertension. Supplement. 4820

Journal of Logic, Language and Information. 4268

Journal of Magnetism and Magnetic Materials. 5810

Journal of Marine Systems. 2407

Journal of Medical & Veterinary Mycology. 4839

Journal of Medical and Veterinary Mycology. Supplement. 4839

Journal of Molecular and Cellular Cardiology. 4821

Journal of Near-Death Studies. 6128

INDEX TO PUBLICATIONS OF INTERNATIONAL ORGANIZATIONS

Journal of Neurochemistry. 664

Journal of Neuroimmunology. 5075

Journal of Neurology/Zeitschrift fuer Neurologie. 5075

Journal of Oral Pathology & Medicine. 4862

Journal of Orofacial Pain. 4862

Journal of Psychosomatic Obstetrics and Gynaecology. 4962

Journal of Reproductive Immunology. 4799

Journal of Rural Cooperation. 1207

The Journal of Sports Medicine and Physical Fitness. 5130

Journal of Structural Learning. 6132

Journal of Systems Architecture. 2189

Journal of Terramechanics. 7032

Journal of the Fantastic in the Arts. 4532

Journal of the Neurological Sciences. 5078

The Journal of Trace Elements in Experimental Medicine. 4899

Journal of Traffic Medicine. 5011

Journal of Tropical Ecology. 2939

Journal of Wind Engineering and Industrial Aerodynamics. 2891

Justice. 3972

Kidney International. 5163

Kidney International. Supplement. 5163

Knowledge Organization. 4190

Labor (Year). 1440

Labor Press and Information. 3893

Labour Market and Social Policy Occasional Papers. 1443

Leben und Umwelt. 2235

Leonardo: Art Science and Technology. 452

Leonardo Music Journal. 5407

Lethaia. 5560

La Lettre de l'O I V. 524

Linguistic Bibliography/Bibliographie Linguistique. 4318

Live Reef Fish. 3073

Livestock Production Science. 281

Log of the Star Class. 6840

Lotus. 4431

Lung Cancer. 4982

Lymphology. 4890

Marketing and Research Today. 1539

Materials Characterization. 5200

Mathematical and Computer Modelling. 4589

Mathematics and Computers in Simulation. 2152

Maturitas. 3441

Ma'yanot. 3027

Measurement. 5252

Meat Balances in O E C D Countries. 178

Mechanism and Machine Theory. 2894

Medailles. 3671

Media Development. 1998

Medical & Biological Engineering & Computing. 648

Medical and Pediatric Oncology. 4982

Medical and Pediatric Oncology. Supplement. 4982

The Messianic Jew (and Hebrew Christian). 6355

Metabolic, Pediatric and Systemic Ophthalmology. 4996

Metrologia. 5252

Microgravity News from E S A. 74

Microtables Imports - Exports of O E C D Countries. 1342

Microwave Power Symposium. Proceedings. 2840

Migration News. 6054

Mileage Manual. 7075

The Military Balance. 5276

Milk and Milk Products Balances in O E C D Countries. 178

Ministerial Formation. 6355

Multilateral Interline Traffic Agreements Manual. 7075

Mushroom Science. 715

Music in the Media - I M Z Bulletin. 5413

Musikforum - Referate und Informationen des Deutschen Musikrates. 5417

Muslim World. 5945

N A T O Advanced Science Institutes Series. Partnership Sub-Series 1: Disarmament Technologies. (North Atlantic Treaty Organization) 5278

N A T O Advanced Science Institutes Series. Partnership Sub-Series 3: High Technologies. (North Atlantic Treaty Organization) 6967

N A T O Advanced Science Institutes Series. Partnership Sub-Series 4: Science and Technology Policy. (North Atlantic Treaty Organization) 6547

N A T O Advanced Science Institutes Series A: Life Sciences. (North Atlantic Treaty Organization) 615

N A T O Advanced Science Institutes Series B: Physics. (North Atlantic Treaty Organization) 5815

N A T O Advanced Science Institutes Series C: Mathematical and Physical Sciences. (North Atlantic Treaty Organization) 4594

N A T O Advanced Science Institutes Series D: Behavioural and Social Sciences. (North Atlantic Treaty Organization) 6137

N A T O Advanced Science Institutes Series E: Applied Sciences. (North Atlantic Treaty Organization) 6967

N A T O Advanced Science Institutes Series F: Computer and Systems Sciences. (North Atlantic Treaty Organization) 2157

N A T O Advanced Science Institutes Series G: Ecological Sciences. (North Atlantic Treaty Organization) 2943

N A T O Advanced Science Institutes Series H: Cell Biology. (North Atlantic Treaty Organization) 743

N A T O Basic Documents/O T A N Documents Fondamentaux. (North Atlantic Treaty Organization) 6027

N A T O Data. (North Atlantic Treaty Organization) 5278

N A T O Final Communiques/O T A N Communiques. (North Atlantic Treaty Organization) 6027

N A T O Handbook. (North Atlantic Treaty Organization) 6027

N A T O Review. (North Atlantic Treaty Organization) 5946

N A T O Scientific Publications. Newsletter. (North Atlantic Treaty Organization) 6547

N E A Issue Brief. (Nuclear Energy Agency) 2700

N E A Newsletter. (Nuclear Energy Agency) 2700

Narcotic Drugs: Estimated World Requirements for (Year). 5702

National Accounts of O E C D Countries. Volume 1 Main Aggregates. 1059

National Accounts of O E C D Countries. Volume 2 Detailed Tables. 1059

Natural Hazards. 2319

Naturism. 7223

Neohelicon. 4439

Nestor. 390

Neural Networks. 2103

Neuroendocrinology. 4891

Neuroscience. 5086

News from I C S I D. (International Centre for Settlement of Investment Disputes) 1400

News from O E C D. 1273

Nonrenewable Resources. 5311

Nonviolence Training in Africa. 5996

Nordisk Statistisk Aarsbok/Yearbook of Nordic Statistics. 6929

Nordisk Statistisk Skriftserie/Statistical Reports of the Nordic Countries. 6929

North Atlantic Report. 7075

North Atlantic Treaty Organization. Facts and Figures/Alliance Atlantique. Structure, Faits et Chiffres. 6029

North Pacific Anadromous Fish Commission. Annual Report. 3075

Noticias de Galapagos. 6555

Nuclear Law Bulletin. 2701

Nuclear Waste Bulletin/Bulletin sur les Dechets Nucleaires. 2987

Numen. 6359

Numen Supplements. 6359

Nutricion en Salud Publica. 6258

O A P E C Monthly Bulletin. (Organization of Arab Petroleum Exporting Countries) 5613

O A S. General Secretariat. Annual Report. (Organization of American States) 3640

O E C D Agricultural Policies, Markets and Trade. Monitoring and Outlook. (Organization for Economic Cooperation and Development) 1623

O E C D Catalogue of Publications. (Organization for Economic Cooperation and Development) 559

O E C D Coal Information. (Organization for Economic Cooperation and Development) 5312

O E C D Code of Liberalization of Capital Movements/O C D E Code de la Liberation des Mouvements de Capitaux. 1159

O E C D Development Centre Seminars. 1365

O E C D Development Centre Studies. 1365

O E C D Development Cooperation. 1365

O E C D Economic Outlook. 1274

O E C D Economic Outlook Historical Statistics. 1061

O E C D Economic Studies. 1274

O E C D Economic Surveys. 1274

O E C D Economic Surveys: Australia. 1274

O E C D Economic Surveys: Austria. 1274

O E C D Economic Surveys: Belgium - Luxembourg. 1274

O E C D Economic Surveys: Canada. 1274

O E C D Economic Surveys: Denmark. 1274

O E C D Economic Surveys: Finland. 1274

O E C D Economic Surveys: France. 1274

O E C D Economic Surveys: Germany. 1274

O E C D Economic Surveys: Greece. 1274

O E C D Economic Surveys: Hungary. 1274

O E C D Economic Surveys: Iceland. 1274

O E C D Economic Surveys: Ireland. 1274

O E C D Economic Surveys: Italy. 1274

O E C D Economic Surveys: Japan. 1274

O E C D Economic Surveys: Mexico. 1274

O E C D Economic Surveys: Netherlands. 1275

O E C D Economic Surveys: New Zealand. 1275

O E C D Economic Surveys: Norway. 1275

O E C D Economic Surveys: Poland. 1275

O E C D Economic Surveys: Portugal. 1275

O E C D Economic Surveys: Spain. 1275

O E C D Economic Surveys: Sweden. 1275

O E C D Economic Surveys: Switzerland. 1275

O E C D Economic Surveys: The Czech Republic. 1275

O E C D Economic Surveys: Turkey. 1275

O E C D Economic Surveys: United Kingdom. 1275

O E C D Economic Surveys: United States. 1275

O E C D Employment Outlook. 1275

O E C D Environmental Data Compendium. 2962

O E C D External Debt Statistics. 1061

O E C D Financial Statistics/Statistiques Financieres de l'O C D E. 1061

O E C D Financial Statistics. Part 1: Monthly Financial Statistics. 1061

O E C D Financial Statistics. Part 2: Financial Accounts. 1061

O E C D Financial Statistics. Part 3: Non-Financial Enterprises Financial Statements. 1061

O E C D Food Consumption Statistics. 3133

O E C D Foreign Trade by Commodities. Series C. 1061

O E C D Indicators of Industrial Activity. 1061

O E C D Industrial Structure Statistics. 1061

O E C D Iron and Steel Industry. 5206

O E C D Labour Force Statistics/O C D E Statistiques de la Population Active. 1448

O E C D Liaison Bulletin Between Research and Training Institutes. 1592

O E C D Library Special Annotated Bibliography: Automation/O C D E Bibliotheque Bibliographie Speciale Analytique: Automation. 2095

O E C D Main Economic Indicators/O C D E Principaux Indicateurs Economiques. 1275

O E C D Main Economic Indicators. Historical Statistics/O C D E Principaux Indicateurs Economiques. Statistiques Retrospectives. 1061

O E C D Main Science and Technology Indicators/O C D E Principaux Indicateurs de la Science et de la Technologie. 6969

O E C D Maritime Transport Committee. Maritime Transport. 7160

O E C D Monthly Statistics of Foreign Trade Series A/O C D E Statistiques Mensuel du Commerce Exterieur. 1061

O E C D Nuclear Energy Agency. Nuclear Energy Data. 2702

O E C D Nuclear Energy Agency Activities in (Year). 2702

O E C D Observer. 1275

O E C D Oil and Gas Information/O C D E Donnees sur le Petrole et sur le Gaz. 5630

O E C D Oil, Gas, Coal & Electricity. Quarterly Statistics/O C D E Statistiques Trimestrielles. Electricite, Charbon, Gaz & Petrole. (Organization for Economic Cooperation and Development) 5631

O E C D Oil Information. 5613

O E C D Oil Statistics. Supply and Disposal. 5631

O E C D Quarterly Labour Force Statistics/O C D E Statistiques Trimestrielles de la Population Active. 1448

O E C D Quarterly National Accounts/O C D E Bulletin des Comptes Nationaux Trimestriels. 1623

O E C D Social Policy Studies Series. 6186

O E C D Steel Market in (Year) and Outlook for (Year). (Organization for Economic Cooperation and Development) 1061

O E C D World Energy Statistics. 2685

O I E Bulletin. (Office International des Epizooties) 7275

O I E C Bulletin. (Office International de l'Enseignement Catholique) 2468

O I E Revue Scientifique et Technique/O I E Scientific and Technical Review. (Office International des Epizooties) 7275

O P E C Review. (Organization of the Petroleum Exporting Countries) 5613

Ocean Yearbook. 2412

Oceanic Fisheries Programme Technical Report. 3075

Ocular Immunology and Inflammation. 4997

Odonto-Stomatologie Tropicale/Tropical Dental Journal. 4865

Oecologia. 618

Oekologie und Landbau. 142

Office International de la Vigne et du Vin. Reglements de la C E E. 525

Oil and Arab Cooperation. 5614

Olympic Review (Year). 6774

Onoma. 4286

Ophthalmic Genetics. 4998

Options Mediterraneennes. Serie A: Seminaires Mediterraneens. 143

Orbis. 4287

Orbis Geographicus. 3416

Orbit. 5000

Organization for Economic Cooperation and Development. Activities: Report by the Secretary General. 1365

Organization of African Unity. Scientific Technical and Research Commission. Publication. 6557

Organization of American States. Department of Cultural Affairs. Manuales del Bibliotecario. 4205

Organization of American States. Department of Scientific Affairs. Report of Activities. 6557

Organization of American States. Department of Scientific Affairs. Serie de Biologia: Monografias. 618

Organization of American States. Department of Scientific Affairs. Serie de Fisica: Monografias. 5817

Organization of American States. Department of Scientific Affairs. Serie de Matematica: Monografias. 4596

Organization of American States. Department of Scientific Affairs. Serie de Quimica: Monografias. 1761

Organization of American States. General Assembly. Actas y Documentos. 6031

Organization of American States. Official Records. Indice y Lista General. 3641

Organization of Arab Petroleum Exporting Countries. Secretary General's Annual Report. 5616

Organization of the Petroleum Exporting Countries. Annual Report. 5617

Organization of the Petroleum Exporting Countries. Annual Statistical Bulletin. 5631

Oriens. 5534

Origins of Life and Evolution of the Biosphere. 619

Osteoporosis International. 4725

P C R Information. (Programme to Combat Racism) 5997

P E B Exchange. (Programme on Educational Building) 2576

P E N International. Bulletin of Selected Books. 4446

P T T I Studies. (Postal Telegraph and Telephone International) 2020

Pacific AIDS Alert Bulletin. 4841

Pacific Diet Advisory Leaflet. 5481

Pacific Islands Nutrition. 5481

Pacific Salmon Commission. Annual Report. 3075

Pain. 5089

Pan American Federation of Engineering Societies. Bulletin. 2735

Pan American Institute of Geography and History. Commission on Geophysics. Boletin. 2387

Parlements et Francophonie. 4352

Participation. 5953

Passenger and Cargo Services News - Insight. 7076

Passenger Reservations Manual. 7076

Passenger Services Conference Resolutions Manual. 7076

Passenger Tariff Coordinating Conferences Resolutions Manual. 7076

Pathophysiology. 820

Pattern Recognition Letters. 2125

Patterns in Reconciliation. 5997

Peace and Security. 6032

Peace Courier. 6032

Pearl Oyster. 3075

Pediatric Allergy and Immunology. 5036

Pediatric Allergy and Immunology. Supplementum. 5036

Pediatric Nephrology. 5164

Pediatric Neurosurgery. 5089

Pedofauna. 238

People. 858

Permanent International Altaistic Conference (PIAC). Newsletter. 5536

Permanent International Association of Navigation Congresses. Bulletin. 7161

Personality and Individual Differences. 6140

Perspectives Economiques de l'O E C D. 991

Pest Advisory Leaflet. 238

Pharmacology and Therapeutics. 5687

Philosophical Problems Today/Problemes Philosophiques d'Aujourd'hui. 5743

Phlebology. 4823

Phonetica. 4288

Phycologia. 719

Physica A - Statistical and Theoretical Physics. 5818

Physica B - Physics of Condensed Matter. 5818

Physica C - Superconductivity. 5818

Physica D - Nonlinear Phenomena. 5818

Physics and Chemistry of Minerals. 5313

Phytochemistry. 720

Phytomorphology. 720

Phytopathological Papers. 721

Planetary and Space Science. 499

Plant Molecular Biology. 620

Plant Tissue Culture and Biotechnology. 723

Police Chief. 2276

Politique du Tourisme et Tourisme International dans les Pays de l'O C D E. 7229

Precambrian Research. 2364

Preparing for the Future: E S A Technology Quarterly. 76

Principles of Cargo Handling and Perishable Cargo Handling Guide. 7077

Promotion & Education. 6247

Prospect. 3757

Prosthetics and Orthotics International. 5015

Psychiatric Rehabilitation Journal. 6143

Psychoneuroendocrinology. 5094

Psychotherapy and Psychosomatics. 5094

Public Transport International. 7037

Pulp and Paper Industry in O E C D Member Countries/Industrie des Pates et Papiers dans les Pays Membres de l'O C D E. 5571

Purchasing Power Parities and Real Expenditures/Parites de Pouvoir d'Achat et Depenses Reelles. 1285

Pure and Applied Chemistry. 1764

Quarantine Advisory Leaflet. 241

Quarterly Bulletin on Solar Activity. 503

Quaternary International. 2365

Quaternary Perspective. 2365

R I. 5997

R I L M Abstracts of Music Literature. (Repertoire International de Litterature Musicale) 5449

The Radio Science Bulletin. 2028

Radiotherapy and Oncology. 5114

Rail International/Schienen der Welt. 7130

Reaching for the Skies. 77

The Reading Professor. 2553

Reading Research Quarterly. 2476

Reading Teacher. 2616

Recherche en Matiere d'Economie des Transports/Research on Transport Economics. 7037

Reformation Review. 6364

Reformed World. 6439

Regards sur l'Etain. 5208

Regional Tuna Bulletin. 3076

Regnum Vegetabile. 725

Regulatory Affairs Review. 7078

Rejuvenation. 3443

Reliability Engineering and System Safety. 2738

Repertoire International des Medievistes. 3594

Repertorium Plantarum Succulentarum. 725

Report on the Situation on Human Rights in the Republic of Guatemala. 5998

Resuscitation. 5122

Revenue Accounting Manual. 7078

Revenue Statistics of O E C D Member Countries. 1066

Review of Fisheries in O E C D Countries. 3077

Review of Income and Wealth. 1461

Review of International Cooperation. 6034

Review of Population Reviews. 6057

Reviews of Manpower and Social Policies. 1452

Reviews of National Policies for Education. 2577

Reviews of National Science and Technology Policy. 6972

Revista Geofisica. 2388

Revista Geografica. 3420

Revista Interamericana de Planificacion. 3758

Revista Latinoamericana de Quimica. 1765

Revue de Bio-Mathematique/Biomathematics. 4601

Revue Informatique et Statistique dans les Sciences Humaines. 2090

Revue Internationale de Police Criminelle. 2279

Risk Book Series. 6368

Rivista di Studi Liguri/Revue d'Etudes Ligures. 3596

The Rotarian. 1936

Rubber Statistical Bulletin. 6506

S A B R A O Journal. (Society for the Advancement of Breeding Researches in Asia and Oceania) 150

S P C Agricultural News. (South Pacific Commission) 150

S P R E P Environmental Case Studies. (South Pacific Regional Environment Programme) 2950

S P R E P Fact Sheet. (South Pacific Regional Environment Programme) 2950

S P R E P Meeting Reports. (South Pacific Regional Environmental Programme) 2950

S P R E P Occasional Papers. 2950

S P R E P Topic Review. 2950

S P R E P Training Reports. 2950

S T I Review. (Science Technology Industry) 6972

Salar. 3077

Samaritan. 6370

Scandinavian Cardiovascular Journal. 5153

Scandinavian Cardiovascular Journal. Supplementum. 5153

Scandinavian Journal of History. 3511

Scandinavian Journal of Rheumatology. 5128

Scandinavian Journal of Rheumatology. Supplement. 5128

Scandinavian Journal of Social Medicine. 4743

Scandinavian Journal of Social Medicine. Supplement. 4743

Scientia Horticulturae. 3204

Secondary Aluminium. 5316

Secretaria Permanente del Tratado General de Integracion Economica Centroamericana. Boletin Estadistico. 5968

Secretaria Permanente del Tratado General de Integracion Economica Centroamericana. Boletin Informativo. 1368

Secretaria Permanente del Tratado General de Integracion Economica Centroamericana. Cuadernos. 1346

Security Dialogue. 5968

Sedimentology. 2368

Seed Science and Technology. 726

Sennacieca Revuo. 6036

Series Estadisticas Seleccionadas de Centroamerica y Panama. 1067

Share International. 5460

Shock. 4745

Short-Term Economic Indicators Central and Eastern Europe. 1288

Signal Processing. 2146

Signal Processing: Image Communication. 2171

Simulation Practice and Theory. 2153

Situation et Statistiques Mondiales du Secteur Viticole. 531

Skeletal Radiology. 5115

Small Ruminant Research. 289

Social Anthropology. 329

Social Networks. 6637

Societe Francaise de Psycho-Prophylaxie Obstetricale. Bulletin Officiel. 4967

Socio-Economic Differential Mortality in Industrialized Societies. 6058

INDEX TO PUBLICATIONS OF INTERNATIONAL ORGANIZATIONS

Sociologia Ruralis. 6730

Soil and Tillage Research. 153

Solar Energy. 2706

Sols Africains/African Soils. 245

Solubility Data Series. 1767

Sources of Contemporary Jewish Thought/Mekevot. 4360

South Pacific Commission. Annual Report. 6037

South Pacific Commission. Handbook. 1368

South Pacific Commission. Report of Meetings. 1289

South Pacific Commission. Statistical Bulletin. 6941

South Pacific Commission. Technical Paper. 6974

South Pacific Conference. Report. 6037

South Pacific Economies: Statistical Summary. 1071

South Pacific Epidemiological and Health Information Service Annual Report. 6258

South Pacific Foods Leaflet. 3128

Southeast Asian Archives. 3539

Speakers' Papers: Speeches from the Gold and Silver Institutes' (Year) Annual Meeting. 5316

Species. 2245

Speech Communication. 4300

Speleological Abstracts/Bulletin Bibliographique Speleologique. 2328

Spinal Cord. 5099

Sport International. 6784

Standard Schedules Information Manual. 7078

Statistical Theory and Method Abstracts. 4617

Statistical Trends in Transport. 7058

Statistics on Insurance. 3840

Steel Statistical Yearbook (Year). 5220

Steel Statistics of Developing Countries. 5221

Stereotactic and Functional Neurosurgery. 5154

Stochastic Processes and Their Applications. 4608

Strategic Survey. 6038

Structure Reports. Section A: Metals and Inorganic Compounds. 1803

Structure Reports. Section B: Organic Compounds. 1803

Studi Genuensi. 384

Studies in Conservation. 467

Studies in Social History. 6640

Summary of Airport Capacities. 7078

Supplementary Service to European Taxation. 1629

Survey of Remittances of Foreign Balances. 7078

Surveys in Geophysics. 2390

Systems Research. 2159

T U I A F P W Information. (Trade Union International of Agricultural, Forestry and Plantation Workers) 3898

Tax - Benefit Position of Production Workers/Situation des Ouvriers au Regard de l'Impot et des Transferts Sociaux. 1630

Tax News Service. 1632

Tax Treaties Data Base on C D - R O M. 1633

Tax Treatment of Cross-Border Donations. 1633

Tax Treatment of Transfer Pricing. 1634

Taxation & Investment in Canada. 1634

Taxation & Investment in Mexico. 1634

Taxation & Investment in South Africa. 1634

Taxation & Investment in the Caribbean. 1634

Taxation & Investment in the People's Republic of China. 1634

Taxation in Latin America. 1634

Taxes and Investment in Asia and the Pacific. 1635

Taxon. 730

Teachers of the World. 2487

Technology and Health Care. 4750

Terminologies Nouvelles. 4307

Terra et Aqua. 7168

Terra Nova. 2323

Terra Una. 6376

Textes et Etudes du Moyen Age. 3607

Theatre en Pologne/Theatre in Poland. 7016

Theosophist. 5755

Thrombosis and Haemostasis. 4824

Ticketing Handbook. 7078

Torah Education. 6410

Tourism Policy and International Tourism in O E C D Countries. 7240

Toxicon. 5696

Trade Unions International of Agricultural, Forestry and Plantation Workers. Bulletin. 3164

Traditional Marine Resource Management and Knowledge. 3080

Translatio. 4308

Transnational Associations/Associations Transnationales. 6039

Transport Museums. 7042

Transport Workers of the World. 3899

Travel Agent's Handbook. 7242

Travel and Tourism Barometer. 7256

Trends in Biochemical Sciences. 672

Trends in Biochemical Sciences (Reference Edition). 672

Trends in Pharmacological Sciences. 5696

Trends in Pharmacological Sciences (Reference Edition). 5696

Trochus. 3080

Tropical Ecology. 731

Tubercle and Lung Disease. 5123

Tunnelling and Underground Space Technology. 2743

Typographical Journal. 3899

U I A Newsletter. (Union Internationale des Architectes) 416

U I C C International Calendar of Meetings on Cancer. (Union Internationale Contre le Cancer) 5172

U I C C International Directory of Cancer Institutes and Organizations. (Union Internationale Contre le Cancer) 4988

U I S Bulletin. (Union Internationale de Speleologie) 2373

U I T B B Bulletin. (Trade Unions International of Workers of the Building, Wood and Building Materials Industries) 3900

U I T Journal. (Union International de Tir) 6792

U I T P Biblio-Express. (International Union of Public Transport) 7059

U L D Control Manual. 7079

U L D Technical Manual. (Unit Load Devices) 7079

Uganda Freshwater Fisheries Research Organization. Annual Report. 3080

Ultrasound in Medicine & Biology. 630

Ultrasound in Obstetrics & Gynecology. 4968

Uniform Law Review. 4127

Union of European Football Associations. Handbook of U E F A. 6821

United States Board on Books for Young People. Newsletter. 6286

United Towns News Newsletter. 6226

University and College Entrance: The Official Guide. 2560

Uranium: Resources, Production and Demand/Uranium: Ressources, Production et Demande. 5318

Veterinary Biotechnology Newsletter. 7282

Veterinary Dermatology. 7282

Vetus Testamentum. 6380

Voice of Silence Newsletter. 3465

Volunteer. 3048

Vox Sanguinis. 4802

Vsemirnoe Profsoyuznoe Dvizhenie. 3901

W A Y Forum. (World Assembly of Youth) 1892

W F D Y News. (World Federation of Democratic Youth) 1892

W I Z O Review (English Edition). (Women's International Zionist Organization) 7336

W T O News. (World Tourism Organization) 7249

Water Quality International. 2973

Water Research. 7304

Water Science and Technology. 7305

Welding in the World/Soudage dans le Monde. 5225

What is the I B A C. (International Business Aviation Council) 82

White Ribbon Bulletin. 2306

Who's Who in Cargo Handling. 7170

Women's News. 7338

Women's World. 7339

Wood Science and Technology. 3177

Work Accomplished by the Inter-American Juridical Committee during Its Meeting. 4047

Workshop of Peace/Muntada al-Salaam. 2567

World Air Transport Statistics. 7060

World Alliance of Y M C A's Directory. 1938

World Animal Health in (Year). 7285

INDEX TO PUBLICATIONS OF INTERNATIONAL ORGANIZATIONS

INTERNATIONAL CONGRESS PROCEEDINGS

World Conservation. (International Union for Conservation of Nature and Natural Resources) 2250

World Council of Churches. Office of Education. Education Newsletter. 6383

World Development Report. 1371

World Directory of Mathematicians. 4615

World Disasters Report. 6254

World Economic Outlook. 1295

World Farmers' Times. 165

World Federation of Teachers' Unions. Information Letter. 2494

World Highways/Routes du Monde. 7144

World Hockey. 6794

World Hospitals and Health Services. 3720

World Industrial Robots. 2208

World Journal of Surgery. 5157

World List of Universities, Other Institutions of Higher Education and University Organisations/Liste Mondiale des Universites. 2529

World Methodist Historical Society. Historical Bulletin. 6447

World Mine Production of Gold. 5319

World Mining Congress. Report. 5319

The World of Music. 5445

World Press Freedom Review. 3882

World S F Newsletter. 4538

World Scout Organization Report. 1859

World Scouting News/Bulletin du Scoutisme Mondial. 1859

World Steel in Figures (Year). 5221

World Steel Statistics Monthly. 5221

World Student News. 2494

World Transport Statistics/Statistiques Mondiales de Transport. 7061

World Youth/Jeunesse du Monde/Juventud del Mundo. 1894

World Zionist Press Service. 3324

Y M C A World. (Young Men's Christian Association) 1859

Yearbook Commercial Arbitration. 4129

Yearbook for Traditional Music. 5445

Yearbook of International Organizations/Annuaire des Organisations Internationales. 6045

Yearbook of Tourism Statistics. 7257

Youthlink. 1895

Zahlentafeln der Physikalisch-Chemischen Untersuchungen des Rheinwassers/Tableaux Numeriques des Analyses Physico-Chimiques des Eaux du Rhin. 2974

Zeitschrift fuer Fremdenverkehr/Revue de Tourisme/Tourist Review. 7251

Zeitschrift fuer Lebensmittel-Untersuchung und -Forschung A. 3133

Zhenshchiny Mira. 7340

Zionist Literature. 6291

Zshurnalist. 3883

Acoustical Imaging. 5871

Acta Endocrinologica Panamericana. 4882

Acta I M E K O. (International Measurement Confederation (IMEKO)) 5248

Acta Medica et Sociologica. 6699

Acta Medicinae Legalis et Socialis. 4903

Advances in Natural and Technological Hazards Research. 6227

Afro-Asian Peoples' Conference. Proceedings. 3524

Afro-Asian Peoples' Solidarity Organization. Council. Documents of the Session. 3524

Applications of Fibonacci Numbers. 4561

Archivum. 4160

Asian Pacific Congress of Cardiology. Symposia. 4810

Assemblee de l'Union de l'Europe Occidentale. Lettre de l'Assemblee. 4105

Association Internationale pour l'Histoire du Verre. Annales des Congres. 1725

Baptist World Alliance. Congress Reports. 6415

Bayesian Statistics. 6900

Biometeorology. 5227

Brown Boveri Symposia. Proceedings. 2810

Caribbean Congress of Labour. Report. 3888

Carnegie-Rochester Conference Series on Public Policy. 947

Carotenoids Other Than Vitamin A. 656

Chemistry of Natural Products. 1814

Clinical Neurosurgery: Proceedings. 5059

Colloques Internationaux d'Histoire Maritime. Travaux. 7148

Colloquium on the Law of Outer Space. Proceedings. 62

Colombo Plan for Co-operative Economic and Social Development in Asia and the Pacific. Consultative Committee. Proceedings and Conclusions. 1355

Commonwealth Magistrates' Conference. Report. 3933

Comparative Education Society in Europe. Proceedings of the General Meeting. 2430

Computational Acoustics. 5838

Computational Intelligence. 2099

Conference de la Haye de Droit International Prive. Actes et Documents/Hague Conference on Private International Law. Proceedings. 4110

Conference Internationale sur les Phenomenes d'Ionisation dans les Gaz. Comptes Rendus. 1827

Conferencia de Facultades Latinoamericanas de Derecho. (Documentos Oficiales). 3934

Congres International d'Histoire des Sciences. Actes. 6520

Congreso Latinoamericano de Siderurgia. Memoria Tecnica. 5188

Congresos Indigenistas Interamericanos. Actas. 313

Congress in Park and Recreation Administration. Programme. 5168

Congress in Park and Recreation Administration. Reports. 6866

Congress of Local and Regional Authorities of Europe. Official Reports of Debates. 6170

Congress of Local and Regional Authorities of Europe. Texts Adopted. 6170

Congresso Europeo di Storia Ospitaliera. Atti. 3705

Congresso Latinoamericano de Hidraulica (Papers). 7289

Coordination Chemistry. 1747

Council for the Social Sciences in East Africa. Social Science Conference. Proceedings. 6609

Council of American Building Officials. One and Two Family Dwelling Code. 883

Credit Communal de Belgique. Collection Histoire. Series in 8. 3561

Developments in Biological Standardization. 5250

Developments in Hematology and Immunology. 4918

E A P R Abstracts of Conference Papers. (European Association for Potato Research) 222

E S O M A R Marketing Research Congress. (European Society for Opinion and Marketing Research) 1525

Educator. 2583

Electra. 2816

Electrochemical Society. Proceedings. 1804

European Association for Personnel Management. Congress Reports. 1565

European Association for Research on Plant Breeding. Report of the Congress. 702

European Brewery Convention. Proceedings of the International Congress. 520

European Civil Aviation Conference (Report of Session) 7067

European Congress of Anaesthesiology. Proceedings. 4805

European Congress of Cardiology. Proceedings. 4816

European Congress on Electron Microscopy. 796

European Grassland Federation. Proceedings of the General Meeting. 223

European League for Economic Cooperation. Reports of the International Congress. 1359

European Materials Research Society. Symposia Proceedings. 2858

European Ophthalmological Society. Congress Acta. 4993

European Organization for Quality. Conference Proceedings. 6959

F E M S Symposium. (Federation of European Microbiological Societies) 784

F I P Notes. 2784

Falk Symposium. 4666

Federation Internationale des Producteurs de Jus de Fruits. Compte-Rendu du Congres/International Federation of Fruit Juice Producers. Proceedings of Congress. 520

Federation Internationale des Producteurs de Jus de Fruits. Rapport Annuel d'Activite. 3103

Financial and Monetary Policy Studies. 1134

Fordham Corporate Law Institute (Proceedings). 4080

Hybrid Microelectronics Symposium. (Papers). 2639

INDEX TO PUBLICATIONS OF INTERNATIONAL ORGANIZATIONS

I A B S E Congress Report. (International Association for Bridge and Structural Engineering) 2786

I A T A Annual Report. (International Air Transport Association) 7071

I B B Y Congress Proceedings. (International Board on Books for Young People) 6273

I C C A Congress Series. (International Council for Commercial Arbitration) 4081

I C E S Marine Science Symposia/Actes du Symposium. (International Council for the Exploration of the Sea) 3069

I C H P E R - S D Congress Proceedings. (International Council on Health, Physical Education, Recreation, Sport and Dance) 5784

I E E E International Conference on Communications. Conference Record. 1992

I E E E International Conference on Innovative Systems in Silicon. 2100

I E E E International Conference on Systems, Man, and Cybernetics. Conference Proceedings. 2161

I E E E International Symposium on Circuits and Systems. Proceedings. 2640

I F A C Workshop Series. (International Federation of Automatic Control) 2885

I F A Congress Seminar Series. (International Fiscal Association) 1613

I F L A Annual. (International Federation of Library Associations and Institutions) 4182

I N S E R M Symposia. (Institut National de la Sante et de la Recherche Medicale) 4681

I S O S C Proceedings. (International Society for Soilless Culture) 3195

I S S X Proceedings. (International Society for the Study of Xenobiotics) 4681

Index to Malaysian Conferences/Indeks Persidangan Malaysia. 5173

Information Network and Data Communication. 2134

Inter-African Conference on Co-Operative Societies Meeting. Reunion. 1207

Inter-African Conference on Food and Nutrition. Programa e Informacoes. 5474

Inter-African Conference on Food and Nutrition. Report. 5474

Inter-African Conference on Industrial Commercial and Agricultural Education Meeting. 2565

Inter-African Conference on Medical Co-Operation. Meeting. 4685

Inter-African Conference on Social Science Meeting. 6619

Inter-African Conference on the Treatment of Offenders. Meetings. Reunion. 2269

Inter-African Forestry Conference. Conference Forestiere Interafricaine (Communications). 3155

Inter-African Labour Conference Reports, Recommendations and Conclusions. 1436

Inter-American Commission of Women. Special Assembly. Final Act/Comision Interamericana de Mujeres. Asamblea Extrarodinaria. Acta Final. 5993

Inter-American Development Bank. Board of Governors. Proceedings of the Meeting. 1146

International Academy of Legal Medicine and Social Medicine. Congress Reports. 4904

International Air Safety Seminar Proceedings. 69

International Association for Cereal Science and Technology. Congress Proceedings. 3114

International Association for Classical Archaeology. Proceedings of Congress. 367

International Association for Cross-Cultural Psychology. International Conference. Selected Papers. 6117

International Association for Dental Research. Abstracts of the General Meeting. 4780

International Association for Hydraulic Research. Congress Proceedings. 2873

International Association for Scientific Study of Mental Deficiency. Proceedings of International Congress. 5069

International Association of Hail Insurers. Congress Report. 3821

International Association of Logopedics and Phoniatrics. Reports of Congress. 5069

International Association of Meteorology and Atmospheric Physics. Report of Proceedings of General Assembly. 5235

International Association of Milk Control Agencies. Proceedings of Annual Meetings. 255

International Association of Museums of Arms and Military History. Congress Reports. 5356

International Association of Performing Arts Libraries and Museums. Congress Proceedings. 447

International Association of Physical Education and Sports for Girls and Women. Proceedings of the International Congress. 6765

International Association of Plant Breeders for the Protection of Plant Varieties. Congress Reports. 709

International Association of State Lotteries. (Reports of Congress). 1614

International Association of Workers for Troubled Children and Youth. Congress Reports. 2585

International Astronomical Union. General Assembly. Highlights. 495

International Astronomical Union. Proceedings of Symposia. 496

International Astronomical Union. Transactions. 496

International Basketball Federation. Official Report of the World Congress. 6809

International Beekeeping Congress. Reports. 127

International Biodeterioration Symposium. Proceedings. 683

International Biophysics Congress. Abstracts. 642

International Bridge Conference. Proceedings. 2788

International Ceramic Congress. Proceedings. 1731

International Commission of Sugar Technology. Proceedings of the General Assembly. 3114

International Commission on Irrigation and Drainage. Congress Reports. 2873

International Commission on Large Dams. Transactions. 2788

International Comparative Literature Association. Proceedings of the Congress. 4417

International Confederation for Agricultural Credit. Assembly and Congress Reports. 196

International Confederation of Free Trade Unions. World Congress Reports. 3892

International Confederation of Midwives. Congress Reports. 4959

International Conference of Agricultural Economists. Proceedings. 196

International Conference of Building Officials. Analysis of Revisions to the (Year) Uniform Codes. 898

International Conference of Building Officials. Building Department Administration. 898

International Conference of Building Officials. Code Changes Committee. Annual Report. 898

International Conference of Building Officials. Dwelling Construction under the Uniform Building Code. 898

International Conference of Building Officials. Plan Review Manual. 898

International Conference of Building Officials. Uniform Code for the Abatement of Dangerous Buildings. 899

International Conference of Building Officials. Uniform Fire Code. 899

International Conference of Building Officials. Uniform Housing Code. 899

International Conference of Building Officials. Uniform Mechanical Code. 899

International Conference of Ethiopian Studies. Proceedings. 3526

International Conference of Social Security Actuaries and Statisticians. Reports. 3821

International Conference on Acoustics. Reports. 5872

International Conference on Asphalt Pavements. Proceedings. 7138

International Conference on Basement Tectonics. Proceedings. 2317

International Conference on Chemical Vapor Deposition. Proceedings. 1752

International Conference on Cloud Physics. Proceedings. 5235

International Conference on Computer Communications. (Proceedings). 2170

International Conference on Computing Fixed Points with Applications. Proceedings. 4578

International Conference on Cosmic Rays. (Proceedings). 5852

International Conference on Large High Voltage Electric Systems. Proceedings. 2835

International Conference on Lead. Proceedings. 5195

International Conference on Lighthouses and Other Aids to Navigation. Reports. 7153

International Conference on Liquefied Natural Gas. Papers. 5606

International Conference on Noise Control Engineering. Proceedings. 2969

International Conference on Piagetian Theory and the Helping Professions. Proceedings. 2451

International Conference on Port and Ocean Engineering under Arctic Conditions. Proceedings. 2725

International Conference on Pressure Surges. Proceedings. 2887

International Conference on Social Welfare. Conference Proceedings. 6671

International Conference on the Physics of Electronic and Atomic Collisions. Abstracts of Contributed Papers and Invited Papers. 5852

International Conference on Vehicle Structural Mechanics. Proceedings. 7103

International Congress Calendar. 5170

International Congress for Analytical Psychology. Proceedings. 6117

International Congress for Byzantine Studies. Acts/ Congres International des Etudes Byzantines. Actes. 3575

International Congress for Cybernetics. Proceedings/Congres International de Cybernetique. Actes. 2162

International Congress for Papyrology. Proceedings. 367

International Congress for Stereology. Proceedings. 2859

International Congress for the Study of Pre-Columbian Cultures of the Lesser Antilles. Proceedings. 320

International Congress of Angiology. Proceedings. 4818

International Congress of Electroencephalography and Clinical Neurophysiology (Proceedings). 5069

International Congress of Entomology. 755

International Congress of Hematology. Proceedings. 4920

International Congress of Histochemistry and Cytochemistry. Proceedings. 661

International Congress of Home Economics. Report. 3686

International Congress of Linguists. Proceedings. 4264

International Congress of Occupational Therapy. Proceedings. 5492

International Congress of Ophthalmology. Abstracts. 4994

International Congress of Parasitology. Proceedings. 837

International Congress of Pharmaceutical Sciences. Proceedings. 5667

International Congress of Primatology. Proceedings. 320

International Congress of Psychology. Proceedings. 6118

International Congress of Radiology. (Reports). 5107

International Congress of Sugarcane Technologists. Proceedings. 3114

International Congress of Verdi Studies. Proceedings. 5401

International Congress on Alcoholism and Drug Dependence. Proceedings. 2302

International Congress on Animal Reproduction. Proceedings. 7272

International Congress on Canned Foods. Texts of Papers Presented and Resolutions/Congres International de la Conserve. Textes des Communications. 3114

International Congress on Metallic Corrosion. (Proceedings). 5195

International Congress on Technology and Technology Exchange. Proceedings. 2725

International Congress on the History of Art. Proceedings. 448

International Congress Series. 6534

International Congresses on Tropical Medicine and Malaria. (Proceedings). 4838

International Council of Homehelp Services. Reports of Congress. 4935

International Council of Onomastic Sciences. Congress Proceedings. 4264

International Economic Association. Proceedings of the Conferences and Congresses. 973

International Electron Devices Meeting. I E D M Technical Digest. 2643

International Eucharist Congress. Proceedings. 6465

International Federation for Information and Documentation. Proceedings of Congress. 4186

International Federation for Psychotherapy. Congress Reports. 5069

International Federation of Agricultural Producers. General Conference Proceedings. 127

International Federation of Asian and Western Pacific Contractors' Associations. Proceedings of the Annual Convention. 5170

International Federation of Catholic Universities. General Assembly. Report. 2545

International Federation of Medical Students' Associations. Minutes and Reports of the General Assembly. 4685

International Federation of Operational Research Societies. Airline Group. Proceedings. 7073

International Federation of Prestressing. Congress Proceedings. 2788

International Federation of Prestressing. Recommendations. 2788

International Federation of Prestressing. Special Reports. 2788

International Forum on Traffic Records Systems Proceedings. 7138

International Foundry Congress. Papers and Communications. 5195

International Gas Union. Proceedings of World Gas Conferences. 5606

International Grassland Congress. Proceedings. 229

International Hop Growers Convention. Report of Congress. 264

International Horticultural Congress. Proceedings. 3195

International Humanist and Ethical Union. Proceedings of the Congress. 5731

International Hydrographic Conference. Reports of Proceedings. 2406

International Institute for Beet Research. Congress Proceedings. 229

International Institute of Administrative Sciences. Reports of the International Congress. 6179

International Institute of Ibero-American Literature. Congress Proceedings. Memoria. 4417

International Institute of Philosophy. Actes. 5731

International Institute of Public Finance. Papers and Proceedings. 1614

International Institute of Synthetic Rubber Producers. Annual Meeting Proceedings. 6502

International Joint Conference on Artificial Intelligence. Advance Papers of the Conference. 2100

International Joint Conference on Artificial Intelligence. Proceedings. 2101

International Journal of Psycho-Analysis. 6118

International Literary and Artistic Association. Proceedings and Reports of Congress. 3781

International Meeting of Animal Nutrition Experts. Proceedings. 279

International Metalworkers' Congress. Reports. 5195

International Mineralogical Association. Proceedings of Meetings. 5304

International Navigation Congress. Papers. 7153

International Navigation Congress. Proceedings. 7153

International Ocean Institute. Pacem in Maribus. Proceedings. 2406

International Olympic Academy. Report of the Sessions. 6765

International Organization for Cooperation in Health Care. General Assembly. Report. 4687

International Organization of Citrus Virologists. Proceedings of the Conference. 3195

International Ornithological Congress. Proceedings. 804

International Orthopaedics. 5008

International Pediatric Association. Proceedings of Congress. 5032

International Philatelic Federation. General Assembly. Proces-Verbal. 5708

International Political Science Association. World Congress. 5934

International Population Conference. Proceedings. 6052

International Potash Institute. Colloquium. Proceedings. 230

International Potash Institute. Congress Proceedings. 230

International Publishers Association. Proceedings of Congress. 6274

International Road Congresses. Proceedings. 7138

International Satellite Symposium on Acute Renal Failure. Proceedings. 5162

International School of Physics "Enrico Fermi". Proceedings. 5807

International Seaweed Symposium. Proceedings. 709

International Sedimentological Congress. Guidebook. 2352

International Skating Union. Minutes of Congress. 6766

International Social Security Association. Reports of the General Assemblies of the I S S A. 3821

International Society for Labour Law and Social Legislation. Proceedings of Congress. 3965

International Society for Mushroom Science. Symposia Proceedings. 709

International Society for Rock Mechanics. Congress. Proceedings. 2789

International Society for Soil Mechanics and Foundation Engineering. Proceedings. 2789

International Society for Terrain-Vehicle Systems. Proceedings of International Conference. 2789

International Society of Blood Transfusion. Proceedings of the Congress. 4920

International Society of Urology. Reports of Congress. 5162

International Society on Optics within Life Sciences. Series (Proceedings). 606

International Statistical Institute. Bulletin. Proceedings of the Biennial Sessions. 6918

International Studies. Nordic Seminar on Human Rights. Proceedings. 3965

International Sweetener Association. Conference Proceedings. 3115

International Symposium on Atherosclerosis. Proceedings. 4819

International Symposium on Canine Heartworm Disease. Proceedings. 7272

International Symposium on Capillary Chromatography and Electrophoresis. Proceedings. 1791

International Symposium on Chemical Reaction Engineering. Proceedings. 2766

INDEX TO PUBLICATIONS OF INTERNATIONAL ORGANIZATIONS

International Symposium on Concrete Roads. Reports. 2789

International Symposium on Crop Protection. Proceedings. 230

International Symposium on Fault-Tolerant Computing. Digest of Papers. 2085

International Symposium on Rarefied Gas Dynamics. Proceedings. 5807

International Symposium on Regional Development. Papers and Proceedings. 3750

International Symposium on Subscriber Loop and Services. Proceedings. 2836

International Symposium on the Aerodynamics and Ventilation of Vehicle Tunnels. Proceedings. 2789

International Symposium on the Chemistry of Cement. Proceedings. 1753

International Television Symposium and Technical Exhibition, Montreux. Symposium Record. 2052

International Thermal Spraying Conference. Preprint of Papers. 5222

International Trade Conference of Workers of the Building, Wood and Building Materials Industries. (Brochure). 899

International U V - E B Processing Conference and Exhibition. Proceedings. 1753

International Union Against Cancer. Proceedings of Congress. 4980

International Union Against Tuberculosis and Lung Disease. Conference Proceedings. 5119

International Union for Conservation of Nature and Natural Resources. Proceedings of the General Assembly. 2233

International Union of Anthropological and Ethnological Sciences Newsletter. 320

International Union of Biological Sciences. General Assemblies. Proceedings. 606

International Union of Crystallography. Abstracts of the Triennial Congress. 1802

International Union of Food, Agricultural, Hotel, Restaurant, Catering, Tobacco and Allied Workers' Associations. Meeting of the Executive Committee. I. Documents of the Secretariat. II. Summary Report. 3892

International Union of Geodesy and Geophysics. Proceedings of the General Assembly. 2384

International Union of Latin Notaries. Proceedings of Congress. 6180

International Union of Prehistoric and Protohistoric Sciences. Congress. Bulletin. 320

International Union of Producers and Distributors of Electrical Energy. Congress Proceedings. 2836

International Union of Public Transport. Reports of the Congresses. 7031

International Union of Radio Science. Proceedings of General Assemblies. 2025

International Water Conference. Proceedings. 7295

International Workshop on H D T V. Proceedings. 2016

Internationaler Weltkongress der U F O-Forscher. Dokumentarbericht. 71

Inter-Parliamentary Union. Summary Records of the Inter-Parliamentary Conferences. 6022

Istituto Internazionale di Studi Liguri. Collezione di Monografie Preistoriche e Archeologiche. 368

Jet Cutting Technology. 2889

Journees Biochimiques Latines. Rapports. 665

Kongres ha-Tsiyoni. Hahlatot/World Zionist Organization. Zionist Congress. 5938

Kongresa Libro. 5170

Macromolecular Chemistry. 1818

Mathematics and Computers in Simulation. 2152

Medical Virology. 4840

Mikroelektronik. 2647

Mushroom Science. 715

N A D C A International Die Casting Congress. Transactions. (North American Die Casting Association) 2867

N A T O Annual Economic Colloquia. Proceedings. (North Atlantic Treaty Organization) 1342

N A T O Challenges of Modern Society. (North Atlantic Treaty Organization) 2943

Nobel Symposium Series. 3787

North Atlantic Treaty Organization. Expert Panel on Air Pollution Modeling. Proceedings. 2971

Open Door International for the Emancipation of the Woman Worker. Report of Congress. 1449

Organization of American States. Permanent Council. Decisions Taken at Meetings (Cumulated Edition). 3641

Pacific Science Association. Congress and Inter-Congress Proceedings. 6558

Pain Research and Clinical Management. 4726

Parapsychology Foundation. Proceedings of International Conferences. 5577

Perugia Quadrennial International Conferences on Cancer. Proceedings. 4985

Photochemistry. 1833

Progress in Protozoology. 847

Rencontres de Philosophie Medievale. 5747

Rubber Research Institute of Malaysia. Rubber Growers' Conference - Proceedings. 6504

Scandinavian Conference on Artificial Intelligence. 2104

Societe d'Ergonomie de Langue Francaise. Actes du Congres. 6154

Soil & Environment. 2952

Studies in Logic and the Foundations of Mathematics. 4608

Surfactants in Solution. 2774

Symposia Foundation Merieux. 4749

Symposium (International) on Combustion. 1835

Teletraffic Science and Engineering. 2018

Trade Unions International of Chemical, Oil and Allied Workers. International Trade Conference. Documents. 3899

TropMed Seminars on Tropical Medicine. Proceedings. 4844

UNESCO. Records of the General Conference. Proceedings. 6040

UNESCO. Records of the General Conference. Resolutions. 6040

United Nations Issues Conference. Report. 6041

United Nations of the Next Decade Conference. Report. 6041

United Schools International. Documents of the Biennial Conference. 2567

Vetus Testamentum. Supplements. 6380

Water Supply. 7306

Wenner Gren Center International Symposium Series. 6583

World Association for Educational Research. Congress Reports. 2494

World Buiatrics Congress. 7285

World Conference on Animal Production. Proceedings. 293

World Congress of the W F D. Proceedings. (World Federation of the Deaf) 3466

World Congress on Fertility and Sterility. Proceedings. 633

World Congress on the Prevention of Occupational Accidents and Diseases. Proceedings. 5501

World Congresses on Information Processing. Proceedings. 4222

World Council of Churches. General Assembly. Assembly - Reports. 6383

World Council of Churches. Minutes and Reports of the Central Committee Meeting. 6383

World Council of Service Clubs. Minutes of the General Meeting. 6695

World Energy Conference. Plenary Conferences. Transactions. 2681

World Federation for Mental Health. Annual Report. 6159

World Movement of Mothers. Reports of Meetings. 6695

World Muslim Conference. Proceedings. 6401

World Union of Jewish Studies. 3050

World Zionist Organization. General Council. Addresses, Debates, Resolutions. 5981

World's Poultry Science Association. Proceedings of World's Poultry Congress. 293

World's Woman's Christian Temperance Union. Triennial Report. 2307

EUROPEAN COMMUNITIES

A C P - E C Council of Ministers. Annual Report (Year) 1353

Agricultural Markets: Prices. 188

Agricultural Statistics Series No.2: Animal Production. 168

Basic Statistics of the European Union. 6900

Biblio Europe. 4163

Biomedical & Health Research. 4646

Biomedical and Health Research Series. 4646

Bulletin d'Information Sportive/Sports Information Bulletin. 6754

Bulletin of European Studies on Time. 6703

Bulletin of the European Communities and Supplements. 1227

Bulletin of the European Union. 1227

C E E International. Droit et Affaires. (Communaute Economique Europeenne) 4107

C O M Documents. 6007

Commission of the European Communities. Collection of Agreements. 1320

Commission of the European Communities. Community Law. 4109

Commission of the European Communities. Directorate of Taxation. Inventory of Taxes. 1604

Commission of the European Communities. Operation of Nuclear Power Stations. 2695

Commission of the European Communities. Report on Competition Policy. 1581

Commission of the European Communities. Report on the Social Developments. 6608

Commission of the European Communities. Trade Union Information Bulletin. 3888

Completing the Internal Market of the European Community: 1992 Legislation - Business. 4109

Completing the Internal Market of the European Community: 1992 Legislation - Financial Services and Capital Movements. 4109

Completing the Internal Market of the European Community: 1992 Legislation. 4109

Completing the Internal Market of the European Community: 1992 Legislation - Transport, Customs & Travel. 4109

Completing the Internal Market of the European Community: 1992 Legislation - Technical Standards. 4110

Completing the Internal Market of the European Community: 1992 Legislation - Veterinary & Phytosanitary Controls. 4110

Council of Europe. Committee of Independent Experts on the European Social Charter. Conclusions. 6662

Council of Europe. Documentation Section. Biblio Bulletin. Series: Legal Affairs. 4052

Council of Europe. Documentation Section. Biblio Bulletin. Series: Political, Economic and Social Affairs. 5983

Council of Europe. European Treaty Series. 4110

Council of Europe. Parliamentary Assembly. Documents: Working Papers. 4110

Council of Europe. Parliamentary Assembly. Official Report of Debates. 4110

Council of Europe. Parliamentary Assembly. Orders of the Day, Minutes of Proceedings. 4110

Council of Europe. Parliamentary Assembly. Texts Adopted by the Assembly. 4110

Council of Europe. Standing Committee on the European Convention on Establishment (Individuals). Periodical Report. 5989

Council of Europe. Study Series: Local and Regional Authorities in Europe. 6213

Council of Europe. Symposium on Legal Processing. Proceedings. 4068

Council of the European Communities. Review of the Council's Work. 1232

Courier. Africa - Caribbean - Pacific - European Union. 1356

Crop Production Half-Yearly Statistics. 172

Current Topics in Veterinary Medicine and Animal Science. 7268

Debates of the European Parliament. 4110

Demographic Statistics (Year). 6048

Developments in Clinical Biochemistry. 658

Developments in Pharmacology. 5655

Developments in the European Communities. Report. 1251

Directory of Community Legislation in Force. 3940

Directory of European Community Trade and Professional Associations/Repertoire des Organisations Professionnelles de la Communaute Europeenne/Verzeichnis der Verbaende in der Europaeischen Gemeinschaft. 1668

Dossier Europa. 5922

E C H O News. (European Community Humanitarian Office) 1358

E C S C Financial Report. (European Coal and Steel Community) 1607

E F News. (European Foundation for the Improvement of Living and Working Conditions) 6610

E I B - Information. (European Investment Bank) 1382

E L F. (European Labour Forum) 6012

E P News. (Spanish edition: Tribuna del Parlamento Europeo) 4111

E U D I S E D - European Educational Research Yearbook. (European Documentation and Information System for Education) 2499

E U Magazin. (Europaeische Union) 5922

Earnings - Industry and Services. 1035

Energy in Europe. 2666

Environmental Research Newsletter. 2925

Erasmus Newsletter. 2540

Eur-Op News. 6013

Euro Abstracts. 6981

Euro Courses. Advanced Scientific Techniques. 6959

Euro Courses. Chemical and Environmental Sciences. 2927

Euro Courses. Computer and Information Science. 2081

Euro Courses. Environmental Impact Assessment. 2927

Euro Courses. Environmental Management. 2927

Euro Courses. Health Physics and Radiation Protection. 2696

Euro Courses. Mechanical and Materials Science. 2858

Euro Courses. Nuclear Science and Technology. 2696

Euro Courses. Reliability and Risk Analysis. 6959

Euro Courses. Remote Sensing. 6959

Euro Courses. Technological Innovation. 6959

Euro-Guide Yearbook of the Institutions of the European Union and of the Other European Organizations/Annuaire des Institutions de l'Union Europeenne et des Autres Organisations Europeennes/Jahrbuch der Institutionen der Europaeischen Union und der Anderen Europaeischen Organisationen. 6173

Euro - Who's Who. 573

Eurocat. 6173

Eurolink Age Bulletin. 3435

Europa Transport. 7027

Europa van Morgen. 6013

Europe. 1258

Europe Information Development. 1359

European Access. 962

European Aspects, Law Series. 3947

European Aspects, Social Studies Series. 6709

European Co-Operation. 4112

European Coal and Steel Community. Consultative Committee. Yearbook. 1359

European Commission. Directory. 4112

European Commission. Joint Research Center. Annual Report. 2696

European Commission. Tacis Programme. Contract Information Update. 1359

European Commission of Human Rights. Decisions and Reports. 5990

European Communities. Court of Justice and Court of First Instance. Proceedings. 4131

European Communities. Court of Justice and Court of First Instance. Reports of Cases before the Court. 4112

European Communities. Diario Oficial. 6173

European Communities. Economic and Social Committee. Bulletin. 962

European Communities. Economic and Social Committee. Commission Documents. 962

European Communities. Economic and Social Consultative Assembly. Annual Report. 962

European Community Humanitarian Office. Annual Report. 1359

European Convention on Human Rights. Yearbook. 5990

European Court of Human Rights. Publications. Series B: Pleadings, Oral Arguments and Documents/Cour Europeenne des Droits de l'Homme. Publications. Serie B: Memoires, Plaidoiries et Documents. 5990

European Economy. Series A: Recent Economic Trends. 1258

European Economy. Series B: Business and Consumer Survey Results. 1258

European File. 1323

European Foundation for the Improvement of Living and Working Conditions. Annual Report. 6709

European Investment Bank. Annual Report. 1131

European Parliament. Bulletin. 6014

European Parliament. Christian-Democratic Group. Report on the Activities. 5925

European Participation Monitor. 6612

European Regional Planning Study Series. 6214

European Savings Bank. Report. 1131

European Yearbook/Annuaire Europeen. 4113

Eurostat. Rapid Reports. Environment. 2962

Eurostat. Rapid Reports. Services and Transports. 7050

Eurostat. Statistics in Focus. Agriculture, Forestry and Fisheries. 173

Eurostat. Statistics in Focus. Economy and Finance. 1037

Eurostat. Statistics in Focus. Energy and Industry. 1037

Eurostat. Statistics in Focus. External Trade. 1037

Eurostat. Statistics in Focus. Population and Social Conditions. 1037

Eurostat. Statistics in Focus. Regions. 1037

Eurostat. Statistics in Focus. Research and Development. 1037

Eurostat. Statistik Kurzgefasst. Bevoelkerung und Soziale Bedingungen. 1037

Eurostat. Statistik Kurzgefasst. Energie und Industrie. 1037

Eurostat. Statistik Kurzgefasst. Forschung und Entwicklung. 1037

Eurostat. Statistik Kurzgefasst. Land- und Forstwirtschaft, Fischerei. 174

Eurostat. Statistik Kurzgefasst. Wirtschaft und Finanzen. 1037

Eurostat. Statistiques en Bref. Agriculture, Sylviculture et Peche. 174

Eurostat. Statistiques en Bref. Economie et Finances. 1038

Eurostat. Statistiques en Bref. Energie et Industrie. 1038

Eurostat. Statistiques en Bref. Population et Conditions Sociales. 1038

Eurostat. Statistiques en Bref. Recherche et Developpement. 1038

Eurostat Catalogue. 6270

Eurostatistics Data for Short Term Economic Analysis. 1038

Eurozoom. 1989

Evropa. 6014

External Trade: Nomenclature of Goods/Commerce Exterieur: Nomenclature des Pays. 1325

Frontier-Free Europe. 1327

General Report on the Activities of the European Communities. 1262

Green Europe. 121

I & T Magazine. (Industrie et Telecoms) 1992

I & T Magazine News Review. 1992

Industrial Trends. 1048

Info - C (English Edition). 2256

Info Phare. 1362

Information Service of the European Communities. Newsletter on the Common Agricultural Policy. 196

Innovation and Technology Transfer. 6018

Ispra Courses on Energy Systems and Technology. 2698

Ispra Courses on Nuclear Engineering and Technology Series. 2698

Janus. 1438

Local and Regional Authorities in Europe. Study Series. 6217

Mines Safety and Health Commission. Report/Organe Permanent pour la Securite dans les Mines de Houille. Rapport. 5309

Nature and Environment Series. 2238

Naturopa. 2239

Nouvelles Universitaires Europeenes/European University News. 2468

O J C D. (Official Journal of the European Communities) 6030

O J Index. (Official Journal of the European Communities) 6030

Official Journal of the European Communities. C Series: Information and Notices (English Edition). 6030

Official Journal of the European Communities. L & C: Legislation and Competition. 6030

Panorama of E U Industry. 1344

Perspectives. 1161

Practical Guide to the Use of the European Communities' Scheme of Generalized Tariff Preferences. 1345

Prison Information Bulletin. 2277

Progress in Coal Steel and Related Social Research. 5321

Recent Demographic Developments in Europe and North America. 6056

Recent Publications on the European Union Received by the Library/Publicaciones Recientes sobre la Union Europea Recibidas por la Biblioteca/Nye Publikationer om den Europaeiske Union Modtaget af Biblioteket/Neuerscheinungen ueber die Europaeische Union Eingegangen in der Bibliothek/ Publications Recentes sur l'Union Europeenne Recues par la Bibliotheque/Pubblicazioni Recenti sull'Unione Europea Recevute della Biblioteca. 5986

Recherches Universitaires sur l'Integration Europeenne/University Research on European Integration. 5986

Results of the Business Survey Carried Out Among Managements in the Community. 1594

S C A D Bulletin. (Systeme Communautaire d'Acces a la Documentation) 4056

Sardius. 5986

Sigma. 6936

Social Europe. 6687

Statistical Office of the European Communities. Agricultural Prices. 183

Statistical Office of the European Communities. Bulletin of Energy Prices. 2685

Statistical Office of the European Communities. Energy Statistics. Yearbook. 2685

Statistical Office of the European Communities. Energy Statistics Monthly Bulletin. 2685

Statistical Office of the European Communities. National Accounts Yearbook. 1072

Statistical Office of the European Communities. Statistical Studies and Surveys. 1072

Statistical Office of the European Communities. Statistical Yearbook. Agriculture. 183

Statistical Office of the European Communities. Transport, Communications, Tourisme - Annuaire Statistique. 7057

Terminologie et Traduction. 4307

Vocational Training. 5516

Vocational Training Information Bulletin. 5516

World Patent Information. 5592

UNITED NATIONS

A B C Human Rights Teaching. 2563

A C E I D Newsletter. (Asian Centre of Educational Innovation for Development) 2563

A F R O Technical Papers. 6227

A F R O Technical Report Series. 6227

Accident - Incident Reporting A D R E P. 7047

Adult Education Information Notes. 2506

Advances in Materials Technology: Monitor. 2851

Aeronautical Information Services Provided by States/ Services d'Information Aeronautique Assures par les Etats/Aeronavigatsionnoe Informatsionnoe Obsluzhivanie, Predostavlyaemoe Gosudarstvami/ Servicios de Informacion Aeronautica Suministrados por los Estados. 7061

African Journal of Science and Technology. Series A. Technology. 6954

African Journal of Science and Technology. Series B. Basic Sciences. 6510

African Journal of Science and Technology. Series C. General. 6510

African Population Newsletter (Bilingual Edition). 6046

Agricultural Review for Europe. 188

Agricultural Taxation Studies. 188

Agricultural Trade in Europe. 188

Agrindex. 93

Agro-Chemicals News in Brief. 212

AIDS - S T D Health Promotion Exchange. 4832

Aircraft Accident Digest. 56

Aircraft Type Designators/Indicatifs de Type d'Aeronef/ Designadores de Tipos de Aeronave. 56

Airport Characteristics Data Bank. Volume 1 - Summary and Explanation. 7063

Airport Characteristics Data Bank. Volume 2 - Indian Ocean Region. 7063

Airport Characteristics Data Bank. Volume 3 - Caribbean and South American Regions. 7063

Airport Characteristics Data Bank. Volume 4 - European Region. 7064

Airport Characteristics Data Bank. Volume 5 - Middle East and Asia Regions. 7064

Airport Characteristics Data Bank. Volume 6 - North Atlantic, North American and Pacific Regions. 7064

Alpha (Year): Current Research in Literacy. 2420

Americans for the Universalaty of UNESCO Newsletter. 6004

Animal Health Yearbook. 7265

Animal Production and Health Newsletter. 5103

Annotated Accessions List of Studies and Reports in the Field of Science Statistics. 532

Annual Bulletin of Coal Statistics for Europe and North America. 5319

Annual Bulletin of Electric Energy Statistics for Europe. 2681

Annual Bulletin of Gas Statistics for Europe/Bulletin Annuel de Statistiques de Gaz pour l'Europe. 5628

Annual Bulletin of General Energy Statistics for Europe. 2681

Annual Bulletin of Housing and Building Statistics for Europe. 919

Annual Bulletin of Steel Statistics for Europe. 5216

Annual Bulletin of Trade in Chemical Products. 1578

Annual Bulletin of Transport Statistics for Europe. 7047

Annual Report on Development Assistance to Mauritius. 1354

Annual World Bank Conference on Development Economics. 932

Anuario Estadistico de America Latina y el Caribe/ Statistical Yearbook for Latin America and the Caribbean. 6892

Anuario Hidrologico del Istmo Centroamericano. 2392

Art. 423

Asia - Pacific Development Journal. 1222

Asia - Pacific Fishery Commission. Report. 3062

Asia - Pacific in Figures. 6894

Asia - Pacific Population Journal. 6046

Asian Bibliography. 3519

Asian - Pacific Book Development. 6261

Asian - Pacific Cultural Centre for Unesco. Organization and Activities. 5521

Asian Pacific Culture. 5521

Asian Research Trends. 5521

Atlas of Mineral Resources of the E S C A P Region. 5294

B F H I News. (Baby-Friendly Hospital Initiative) 6655

B I B E Quarterly Bulletin. 2496

Basic Facts about the United Nations. 6006

Bold. 3433

Boletin de Arte. 432

Bollettino per le Farmacodipendenze e l'Alcoolismo. 2299

Border Epidemiological Bulletin/Boletin Epidemiologico Fronterizo. 6229

Border Health/Salud Fronteriza. 6229

Bulletin of Labour Statistics. 1026

Bulletin on Ageing. 3433

Bulletin on Narcotics. 2300

C C I V S News. (Coordinating Committee for International Voluntary Service) 6657

C E P A L Review. (Comision Economica para America Latina y el Caribe) 1228

C I F A Technical Papers. (Committee for Inland Fisheries of Africa) 3062

C I N D A. 5834

Canadian Commission for UNESCO. Report of the Secretary General/Commission Canadienne pour l'UNESCO. Rapport du Secretaire General. 6007

Canadian Commission for UNESCO. Secretary General's Letter/Commission Canadienne pour l'UNESCO. Lettre du Secretaire General. 2427

Caribbean Documentation Centre. Current Awareness Bulletin. 542

Catalogue of I L O Publications in Print. 1029

Catalonia Cultura. 3359

Census of Motor Traffic on Main International Traffic Arteries. 7137

Centro Latinoamericano de Demografia. Boletin Demografico. 6048

Centro Latinoamericano de Demografia. Notas de Poblacion. 6048

Centro Latinoamericano de Demografia. Serie A/Latin American Demographic Centre. Serie A. 6048

Centro Latinoamericano de Demografia. Serie C/Latin American Demographic Centre. Serie C. 6048

Centro Latinoamericano de Demografia. Serie D/Latin American Demographic Centre. Serie D. 6048

Centro Latinoamericano de Demografia. Serie OI: Publicaciones Conjuntas con Instituciones Nacionales de Paises de America Latina. 6048

Centro Pan-Americano de Febre Aftosa. Boletin. 6231

Cereal Policies Review. 261

Ceres. 108

Chemical Industry in (Year) - Annual Review. 1581

Children First! 6660

Civil Aviation Statistics of the World (Year). 7050

Codes and Abbreviations for the Use of the International Telecommunications Services. 2033

Comision Economica para America Latina y el Caribe. Desarrollo Productivo. 1356

Comision Economica para America Latina y el Caribe. Serie Financiamiento del Desarrollo. 1356

Comision Economica para America Latina y el Caribe. Serie INFOPLAN. 1356

Comision Economica para America Latina y el Caribe. Serie Reformas de Politica Publica. 1231

Commodity Trade Statistics. 1032

Composition of the W M O. (World Meteorological Organization) 5229

Confluence. 7289

Connect. 2911

Copyright Bulletin. 3936

Copyright Laws and Treaties of the World. 5582

Copyright Series. 5582

O Correio da UNESCO. 2431

The Cost of Social Security. 6662

Courier (Paris). 6010

Cuadernos de la C E P A L. 1206

Cultures of Peace Series. 6609

D O C P A L Resumenes sobre Poblacion en America Latina/D O C P A L Latin American Population Abstracts. 6064

Demographic Handbook for Africa/Guide Demographie de l'Afrique. 6048

Demographic Yearbook. 6048

Desertification Control Bulletin. 2313

Designators for Aircraft Operating Agencies, Aeronautical Authorities and Services. 63

Development Business. 1321

Development Business. 1357

Development Forum. 1357

Development Information Abstracts/Bulletin Analytique sur le Developpement/Resumenes de Informacion sobre el Desarrollo. 1034

Diogenes (English Edition). 6708

Direction of Trade Statistics. 1035

Directory of On-Going Research in Cancer Epidemiology. 4977

Disarmament. 5267

Disarmament Newsletter. 5922

Disarmament Times. 5922

Disaster Preparedness and Mitigation in the Americas. 6232

E D I Development Policy Case Series. (Economic Development Institute) 955

E S C A P Energy News. (United Nations Economic and Social Commission for Asia and the Pacific) 2663

E S C W A Population Bulletin. (Economic and Social Commission for Western Asia) 6049

Earth Sciences Series. 2314

East-West Investment News. 1383

Economic and Social Commission for Asia and the Pacific. Annual Report. 1358

Economic and Social Commission for Asia and the Pacific. Annual Report. Supplement. 1358

Economic and Social Survey of Asia and the Pacific. 1253

Economic Bulletin for Europe (Annual). 1254

Economic Commission for Europe. Annual Report. 957

Economic Survey of Europe. 1254

Economic Survey of Latin America and the Caribbean. 1254

Educacion Medica y Salud. 2523

Education in Asia and the Pacific: Reviews, Reports and Notes. 2437

Educational Building Digest. 892

Educational Innovation and Information. 2564

Educational Studies and Documents Series. 2440

Electric Power in Asia and the Pacific. 2817

Emergency Response Guidance for Aircraft Incidents Involving Dangerous Goods. 7067

Emerging Stock Markets Factbook. 1129

Encyclopedie Berbere. 2656

Energy Balances and Electricity Profiles. 2689

Energy Database UNESCO - Iseek. 2686

Energy Statistics and Balances of Non-O E C D Countries. 2689

Energy Statistics Yearbook. 2683

Enfants du Monde. 6664

Environmentally Sustainable Development Proceedings Series. 1359

Epidemiological Surveillance of Rabies for the Americas. 7269

Estudios e Informes de la C E P A L/C E P A L Studies and Reports. 1359

European Civil Aviation Conference (Report of Session). 7067

Everyone's United Nations. 6014

ExtraMED. 4778

F A O Agricultural Services Bulletin. (Food and Agriculture Organization of the United Nations) 192

F A O Animal Production and Health Papers. (Food and Agriculture Organization of the United Nations) 275

F A O Commodity Review and Outlook. (Food and Agriculture Organization of the United Nations) 192

F A O Documentation - Current Bibliography. 3082

F A O Economic and Social Development Paper. (Food and Agriculture Organization of the United Nations) 963

F A O Fertilizer and Plant Nutrition Bulletin. (Food and Agriculture Organization of the United Nations) 192

INDEX TO PUBLICATIONS OF INTERNATIONAL ORGANIZATIONS

F A O Fertilizer Yearbook. 223

F A O Fisheries Circulars. 3065

F A O Fisheries Reports. 3065

F A O Fisheries Series. 3065

F A O Fisheries Technical Paper. 3065

F A O Food and Nutrition Series. (Food and Agriculture Organization of the United Nations) 5472

F A O Irrigation and Drainage Papers. (Food and Agriculture Organization of the United Nations) 7293

F A O Land and Development Series. (Food and Agriculture Organization of the United Nations (Rome)) 115

F A O Legislative Study. 115

F A O Plant Protection Bulletin (Multilingual Edition). 703

F A O Production Yearbook. (Food and Agriculture Organization of the United Nations) 192

F A O Quarterly Bulletin of Statistics/Bulletin Trimestriel F A O de Statistiques/Boletin Trimestral F A O de Estadisticas. 174

F A O Regional Conference for Africa. Report. 115

F A O Regional Conference for Asia and the Pacific. Report. 115

F A O Regional Conference for Europe. Report. (Food and Agriculture Organization of the United Nations) 115

F A O Regional Conference for Latin America and the Caribbean. Report. 115

F A O Regional Conference for the Near East. Report. (Food and Agriculture Organization of the United Nations) 115

F A O Soils Bulletin. (Food and Agriculture Organization of the United Nations) 223

F A O Terminology Bulletin. 115

F A O Yearbook, Trade. 193

F I P L V World News. (Federation Internationale des Professeurs de Langues Vivantes) 2443

Farm Management Notes for Asia and the Far East. 193

The Farnatchi Series. 2603

Fertilizer Trade Information Monthly Bulletin. 224

Finance and Development. 1133

First Call for Children. 6665

Flora, Fauna y Areas Silvestres. 6526

Food and Agricultural Legislation. 3952

Food and Agriculture Organization of the United Nations. Asia and Pacific Plant Protection Commission. Quarterly Newsletter. 225

Food and Agriculture Organization of the United Nations. Asia and Pacific Plant Protection Commission. Technical Document. 225

Food and Agriculture Organization of the United Nations. Asia and the Pacific Commission on Agricultural Statistics. Periodic Report. 174

Food and Agriculture Organization of the United Nations. Basic Texts. 119

Food and Agriculture Organization of the United Nations. European Inland Fisheries Advisory Commission. Occasional Papers. 3068

Food and Agriculture Organization of the United Nations. European Inland Fisheries Advisory Commission. Technical Papers. 3068

Food and Agriculture Organization of the United Nations. World Soil Resources Reports. 225

Food and Agriculture Organization of the United Nations Conference. Report. 119

Food and Nutrition Bulletin. 5473

Food Irradiation Newsletter. 3106

Food Nutrition and Agriculture/Alimentation Nutrition et Agriculture/Alimentacion Nutricion y Agricultura. 5473

Foreign Trade Statistics of Africa. Series A: Direction of Trade. 1040

Foreign Trade Statistics of Africa. Series C: Summary Tables/Statistiques Africaines du Commerce Exterieur. Serie C: Tableaux Recapitulatifs. 1040

Foreign Trade Statistics of Asia and the Pacific. 1040

Fuentes UNESCO. 6614

Fundamentals of Educational Planning. 2564

G A T T Activities. (General Agreement on Tariffs and Trade) 1327

G A T T Focus. (General Agreement on Tariffs and Trade) 1327

G E S A M P Reports and Studies. (Joint Group of Experts on the Scientific Aspects of Marine Environmental Protection) 2968

General Agreement on Tariffs and Trade. Basic Instruments and Selected Documents Series. Supplement. 1327

General Agreement on Tariffs and Trade. International Trade. 1327

General Fisheries Council for the Mediterranean. Reports of the Sessions. 3068

General Fisheries Council for the Mediterranean. Studies and Reviews. 3068

General History of Africa. 3526

General History of the Caribbean. 3627

General Information Program - U N I S I S T Newsletter. 4179

Geological Correlation. 2343

Global Population Policy Database (Year). 6050

Guide to National Bibliographical Information Centres. 4180

Guide to Sources of International Population Assistance. 6050

Guide to U N C T A D Publications. 1044

Handbook of State Trading Organizations of Developing Countries/Repertoire des Organismes de Commerce d'Etat des Pays en Developpement/Repertorio de las Organizaciones Comerciales Estatales de Paises en Desarrollo/Dalil al-Hay'at al-Tiganiyya al-Hukumiyya fi al-Buldan an-Namiya. 1045

High Frequency Broadcasting Schedule. 2024

Higher Education in Europe. 2543

History of Civilizations of Central Asia. 3534

History of Humanity. 6616

How to Do Business with the United Nations. 969

Human Factors Digest. 68

Human Rights Bulletin. 5992

Human Rights Newsletter. 5992

Human Settlements Basic Statistics/Statistiques de Base Etablissements Humains/Estadisticas Basicas de Asentamientos Humanos. 3766

I A E A Bulletin. (International Atomic Energy Agency) 2697

I A E A Library Film Catalog. (International Atomic Energy Agency) 2697

I A E A Technical Documents Series. (International Atomic Energy Agency) 2697

I A R C Biennial Report. (International Agency for Research on Cancer) 4979

I A R C Monographs on the Evaluation of Carcinogenic Risk of Chemicals to Humans. (International Agency for Research on Cancer) 4979

I A R C Scientific Publications. (International Agency for Research on Cancer) 4979

I A R C Technical Reports. (International Agency for Research on Cancer) 4979

I B E Studies Series. (International Bureau of Education) 2564

I C A O Abbreviations and Codes. (International Civil Aviation Organization) 7071

I C A O Circulars. (International Civil Aviation Organization) 7071

The I C A O Financial Regulations. (International Civil Aviation Organization) 7071

I C A O Journal. (International Civil Aviation Organization) 68

I C A O Publications and Audio Visual Training Aids Catalogue. (International Civil Aviation Organization) 7052

I C A O Publications Regulations. (International Civil Aviation Organization) 7071

I C T P Series in Theoretical Physics. (International Centre for Theoretical Physics) 5805

I F A D Update. (International Fund for Agricultural Development) 1361

I F C Discussion Paper. (International Finance Corporation) 1361

I I E P Occasional Papers. (International Institute for Educational Planning) 2564

I I E P Research Reports. (International Institute for Educational Planning) 2564

I I E P Seminar Papers. (International Institute for Educational Planning) 2564

I I E P Studies Series. (International Institute for Educational Planning) 2564

I L C A Proceedings. (International Livestock Centre for Africa) 277

I L O Committee on Salaried Employees and Professional Workers. Report. (International Labour Office) 1433

I L O Joint Committee on the Public Service. Report. (International Labour Office) 1433

I L O Judgements of the Administrative Tribunal. (International Labour Office) 3961

I L O Metal Trades Committee. Report. (International Labour Office) 1433

I L O Multinational Enterprises Programme. Working Paper. (International Labour Office) 1263

I L O Training Papers in Population and Family Welfare Education in the Worksetting. (International Labour Office) 1433

I L P E S Cuadernos. (Instituto Latinoamericano y del Caribe de Planificacion Economica y Social) 1460

I M F Survey. (International Monetary Fund) 1046

I M O News. (International Maritime Organization) 7152

I M S Newsletter. (International Marine Science) 2405

I N I S Atomindex. (International Atomic Energy Agency) 5835

I N I S Newsletter. 4182

I N I S Reference Series. 4182

I N S T R A W News. (International Research and Training Institute for the Advancement of Women) 7323

I T U Newsletter. (International Telecommunication Union) 1993

I T U Statistical Yearbook/Annuaire Statistique des l'U I T. (International Telecommunication Union) 1993

ILOLEX C D - R O M. (International Labour Office) 1434

Improve Your Construction Business Series. 1434

Index Translationum. 4226

Indicators for the Telegram Retransmission System (TRS) - Telex Identification Codes. 2034

Industrial Development News for Asia and the Pacific. 1362

Industrial Property and Copyright. 5585

Industrial Property, Statistics B. Part 1 - Patents/ Propriete Industrielle, Statistiques B. Partie 1 - Brevets. 5593

Industrial Property, Statistics B. Part 2 - Trademarks and Service Marks, Utility Models, Industrial Designs, Varieties of Plants, Microorganisms/ Propriete Industrielle, Statistiques B. Partie 2 - Marques de Produits et des Services, Modeles d'Utilite, Dessins et Modeles Industriels, Obtentions Vegetales, Micro-organismes. 5593

Industry and Environment. 2933

Infoterra Programme Activity Centre. Exchange of Environmental Experience Series. 2934

Inpaz en las Americas. (Instituto Panamericano de Proteccion de Alimentos y Zoonosis) 7271

Insect and Pest Control Newsletter. 2766

Instituto de Nutricion de Centro America y Panama (INCAP). Informe Anual. 5474

Instituto Panamericano de Proteccion de Alimentos y Zoonosis. Publicacion Tecnica. 7272

Intergovernmental Oceanographic Commission. Technical Series. 2405

International Accounting and Reporting Issues. 1091

International Administration. 4116

International Atomic Energy Agency. Annual Report. 2698

International Atomic Energy Agency. Legal Series. 3964

International Atomic Energy Agency. Nuclear Power Reactors in the World. 2698

International Atomic Energy Agency. Panel Proceedings Series. 2698

International Atomic Energy Agency. Proceedings Series. 2698

International Atomic Energy Agency. Safety Series. 6239

International Atomic Energy Agency. Technical Directories. 2698

International Atomic Energy Agency. Technical Report Series. 2698

International Award for Literacy Research/Prix International de Recherche en Alphabetisation/ Premio Internacional a la Investigacion en Alfabetizacion. 2451

International Bulletin on Atomic and Molecular Data for Fusion. 2698

International Catalogue of Occupational Safety and Health Films. 5502

International Centre for Theoretical Physics. Annual Report. 5806

International Civil Aviation Organization. Aeronautical Agreements and Arrangements. Annual Supplement. 7072

International Civil Aviation Organization. Aeronautical Chart Catalogue. 7072

International Civil Aviation Organization. Air Navigation Plan. Africa - Indian Ocean Region. 69

International Civil Aviation Organization. Air Navigation Plan. Caribbean and South American Regions. 69

International Civil Aviation Organization. Air Navigation Plan. Middle East and Asia Regions. 69

International Civil Aviation Organization. Air Navigation Plan. North Atlantic, North American and Pacific Regions. 69

International Civil Aviation Organization. Aircraft Operations. 7072

International Civil Aviation Organization. Annexes to the Convention on Civil Aviation. 7072

International Civil Aviation Organization. Assembly. Minutes of the Plenary Meetings. 7072

International Civil Aviation Organization. Assembly. Report and Minutes of the Administrative Commission. 7072

International Civil Aviation Organization. Assembly. Report and Minutes of the Economic Commission. 7072

International Civil Aviation Organization. Assembly. Report and Minutes of the Legal Commission. 7072

International Civil Aviation Organization. Assembly. Report of the Technical Commission. 70

International Civil Aviation Organization. Assembly. Reports and Minutes of the Executive Committee. 7072

International Civil Aviation Organization. Assembly. Resolutions. 7072

International Civil Aviation Organization. Committee on Aviation Environmental Protection. Report of the Meeting. 70

International Civil Aviation Organization. Conventions. 7072

International Civil Aviation Organization. Council. Annual Report. 7072

International Civil Aviation Organization. Council to Contracting States on Charges for Airports and Air Navigation Systems. Statements. 70

International Civil Aviation Organization. Digests of Statistics. Series AF. Airport and Route Facilities. Financial Data and Summary Traffic Data/ Organisation de l'Aviation Civile. Recueil de Statistiques. Serie AF. Installations et Services d'Aeroport et de Route. Donnes Financieres et Statistiques de Traffic Sommaires/ Mezhdunarodnaya Organizatsiya Grazhdanskoi Aviatsii. Statisticheski Sbornik. Seriya AF. Aeroportnoe i Marshrutnoe Oborudovanie. Finansovye Izlozheniya Dannykh po Perenozhkam/ Organizacion de Aviacion Civil Internacional. Compendio Estadistico. Serie AF. Instalaciones y Servicios de Aeropuerto y en Ruta. Datos Financieros y Resumen de Datos de Trafico. 7053

International Civil Aviation Organization. Digests of Statistics. Series AT. Airport Traffic. 7053

International Civil Aviation Organization. Digests of Statistics. Series F. Financial Data - Commercial Air Carriers. 7053

International Civil Aviation Organization. Digests of Statistics. Series FP. Fleet - Personnel - Commercial Air Carriers. 7053

International Civil Aviation Organization. Digests of Statistics. Series OFOD. On-Flight Origin and Destination/Organisation de l'Aviation Civile Internationale. Receuil de Statistiques. Serie OFOD. Origine et Destination par Vol/Mezhdunarodnaya Organizatsiya Grazhdanskoi Aviatsii. Statisticeski Sbornik. Seriya OFOD. Nasalny i Konesny Punkty Poleta/Organizacion de Aviacion Civil Internacional. Compendio Estadistico. Serie OFOD. Origen y Destino por Vuelo. 7053

International Civil Aviation Organization. Digests of Statistics. Series R. Civil Aircraft on Register. 7053

International Civil Aviation Organization. Digests of Statistics. Series TF. Traffic by Flight Stage. 7053

International Civil Aviation Organization. Digests of Statistics. Series T. Traffic, Commercial Air Traffic. 7053

International Civil Aviation Organization. Legal Committee. Minutes and Documents (of Sessions). 7073

International Civil Aviation Organization. Location Indicators. 70

International Civil Aviation Organization. Protocols. 7073

International Civil Aviation Organization. Report of the Air Navigation Conference. 7073

International Civil Aviation Organization. Rules of the Air and Air Traffic Services. 7073

International Civil Aviation Organization. Special Committee for the Monitoring and Co-ordination of Development and Transition Planning for the Future Air Navigation System (FANS - Phase II). Report of the Meeting. 70

International Civil Aviation Organization. Visual Aids Panel. Report of the Meeting. 7073

International Conference on Education. Final Report/ Conference International de l'Education. Rapport Final. 2451

International Construction Management Series. 1436

International Court of Justice. Bibliography/Cour Internationale de Justice. Bibliographie. (International Court of Justice) 4054

International Court of Justice. Yearbook. 4117

International Designs Bulletin. 5586

International Digest of Health Legislation. 6240

International Directory of New and Renewable Energy Information Sources and Research Centres. 2672

International Directory of Sources. Infoterra. 2934

International Energy Agency. Energy Prices and Taxes. 2672

International Finance Corporation. Report. 1147

International Financial Statistics. 1048

International Financial Statistics Yearbook. 1048

International Frequency List/Liste Internationale des Frequences/Lista Internacional de Frecuencias. 2052

International Frequency List. Preface. 2052

International Institute for Labour Studies. Research Series. 1436

International Journal of Global Energy Issues. 2672

International Labour Conference. Reports to the Conference and Record of Proceedings. 1437

International Labour Documentation. 1048

International Labour Office. Official Bulletin. Series A. 1437

International Labour Office. Official Bulletin. Series B. 1437

INDEX TO PUBLICATIONS OF INTERNATIONAL ORGANIZATIONS

International Labour Review. 1437

International Maritime Organization. International Code for the Construction and Equipment of Ships Carrying Liquefied Gases in Bulk. 7153

International Maritime Organization. Testing and Evaluation of Life-Saving Appliances. 7153

International Markets for Meat. 279

International Monetary Fund. Annual Report of the Executive Board. 1147

International Monetary Fund. Annual Report on Exchange Arrangements and Exchange Restrictions. 1147

International Monetary Fund. Balance of Payments Statistics Yearbook. 1048

International Monetary Fund. Government Finance Statistics Yearbook. 1048

International Monetary Fund. Occasional Papers. 1147

International Monetary Fund. Pamphlet Series. 1147

International Monetary Fund. Selected Decisions of the International Monetary Fund and Selected Documents. 1147

International Monetary Fund. Staff Papers. 1147

International Monetary Fund. Summary Proceedings of the Annual Meeting of the Board of Governors. 1147

International Monetary Fund. World Economic and Financial Surveys. 1147

International Narcotics Control Board. Psychotropic Substances. 5831

International Narcotics Control Board. Report for (Year). 5668

International Radio Consultative Committee. Plenary Assembly. Proceedings. 2025

International Review of Criminal Policy. 2270

International Review of Education/Internationale Zeitschrift fuer Erziehungswissenschaft/Revue Internationale de Pedagogie. 2452

International Rice Commission. Newsletter. 230

International SafetyNet Manual. 1995

International Social Science Journal. 6620

International Telecommunication Union. Booklets. 1995

International Telecommunication Union. Central Library. List of Periodicals/Union Internationales des Telecommunications. Bibliotheque Centrale. Liste des Periodiques/Union Internacional de Telcommunicaciones. Biblioteca Central. Lista de Revistas. 2012

International Telecommunication Union. Central Library. List of Recent Acquisitions/Union Internationale des Telecommunications. Bibliotheque Centrale. Liste des Acquisitions Recentes/Union Internacional de Telecomunicaciones. Biblioteca Central. Lista de Adquisiciones Recientes. 2012

International Telecommunication Union. List of Annuals/Union Internationale des Telecommunications. Listes des Publications Annuelles/Union Internacional de Telecomunicaciones. Lista de Publicaciones Anuales. 2012

International Telecommunication Union. List of Telegraph Offices Open for International Service. 2035

International Telecommunication Union. Operational Bulletin. 2035

International Telecommunication Union. Report on the Activities. 2035

International Telecommunication Union. Seminars. 1995

International Telegraph and Telephone Consultative Committee. Plans. 2035

International Telegraph and Telephone Consultative Committee. Plenary Assembly. Proceedings. 2035

International Trade Forum. 1332

International Trade Statistics Yearbook. 1048

International Travel and Health: Vaccination Requirements and Health Advice. 6240

International Yearbook of Industrial Statistics. 1049

Inventory of Population Projects in Developing Countries Around the World. 6052

Joint F A O - W H O Codex Alimentarius Commission. Report of the Session. 6241

Journal of Development Planning. 1364

Korea Journal. 3332

Korean Social Science Journal. 6624

L I L A C S - C D - R O M. (Literatura Latinoamericana y del Caribe en Ciencias de la Salud) 4781

Labour Education. 1442

Labour-Management Relations Series. 1442

Land Reform, Land Settlement and Cooperatives. 197

Lead and Zinc Statistics. 5219

Lifelong Education Network. 2460

List of Cables Forming the World Submarine Network. 2035

List of E C A Documents Issued/Liste des Documents Publies par la C E A. 1364

List of International Telephone Routes. 2035

Litani. 5275

Management Development Series. 1493

Manufacture of Narcotic Drugs and Psychotropic Substances under International Control. 2304

Market Trends & Prospects for Chemical Products. 1759

MARPOL 73 - 78 Amendments. 2236

Marques Internationales. 5587

Meetings on Atomic Energy. 5171

Memory of Peoples Series. 3505

Migrant Pest Newsletter. 235

Monitoring Information Summary. 2026

Monographs on Oceanographic Methodology Series. 2410

Museum Internacional. 5360

Museum International. 5360

Museum International (French edition). 5360

Museums and Monuments Series. 5361

Mutation Breeding Newsletter. 235

N A T I S - News. (National Information System) 4200

Narcotic Drugs: Estimated World Requirements for (Year). 5702

Natural Resources Research. 2320

Nature and Resources (English Edition). 2238

Nature et Faune. 2239

Navtex Manual. 1999

New Acquisitions in the U N E C A Library. 558

New Trends in Biology Teaching Series. 616

New Trends in Chemistry Teaching Series. 1761

New Trends in Integrated Science Teaching. 2613

New Trends in Physics Teaching Series. 5816

News from I C T P. (International Centre for Theoretical Physics) 5816

Nomenclature des Stations de Radiocommunications Spatiales et des Stations de Radioastronomie/List of Space Radiocommunication Stations and Radioastronomy Station/Nomenclator de las Estaciones de Radiocomunicacion Espacial y de las Estaciones de Radioastronomia. 2026

Nomenclature des Voies de Telecommunication Utilisees pour la Transmission des Telegrammes/List of Telecommunication Channels Used for the Transmission of Telegrams/Nomenclator de las Vias de Telecomunicacion Empleadas para la Transmision de Telegramas. 2037

Notas sobre la Economia y el Desarrollo. 1273

Nuclear Data Newsletter. 2700

Nuclear Fusion/Fusion Nucleaire. 5854

Objective: Justice. 5996

Occupational Safety and Health Series. 5497

Operational Hydrology Report. 2397

Our Planet. 2946

P C T Gazette. (Patent Cooperation Treaty) 5593

Palestine Refugees Today. 6681

Pan American Journal of Public Health. 6246

Peace and Conflict Issues Series. 6032

Periodicals of Asia and the Pacific. 3429

Permanent Missions to the United Nations. 6032

Personnel des Nations Unies et des Agences Specialisees en Republique de Rwanda. 1366

Perspectives. 2472

Pesticide Residues in Food. 6246

Plant Variety Protection. 240

Population Bulletin of the United Nations. 6055

Population Education Accessions List. 2502

Population Headliners. 6056

Population Studies. 6056

Populi. 6056

Prices of Agricultural Products and Selected Inputs in Europe and North America. 200

Professional Training Series. 5997

The Progress of Nations. 6682

La Propriete Industrielle et le Droit d'Auteur. 5589

Prospects. 2474

Rapport Annuel sur l'Assistance au Developpement: Rwanda. 1366

Rapport Annuel sur la Cooperation au Developpement - Burundi. 1366

Recommendations on the Safe Use of Pesticides in Ships. 2980

Refugee Survey Quarterly. 6070

Refugees Magazine. 6034

Regional Development Dialogue. 1367

Regional Development Studies. 1367

Regional Differences in Fares, Rates and Costs for International Air Transport (Year). 7077

Repindex. 2963

Report on Development Assistance to Ethiopia. 1367

Report on Development Cooperation to the Democratic Republic of the Sudan. 1367

Report on the World Health Situation. 6248

Reports and Papers on Mass Communications Series. 2002

Review of Maritime Transport. 7163

Revista Internacional de Ciencias Sociales. 6633

Revista Internacional del Trabajo. 1452

Revue de Coree. 5536

Revue Internationale des Sciences Sociales. 6633

Revue Internationale du Travail. 1452

Rural Progress. 1367

Safety and Health at Work. 5503

Securite et Sante au Travail. 5503

Selective Inventory of Social Science Information and Documentation Services. 6634

Ship Safety and Pollution Prevention - Ship Management and Port State Control. 2981

Siren. 2415

Sister Communities Health Profiles of the U S - Mexico Border/Perfiles de Salud de las Comunidades Hermanas de la Frontera Mexico - Estados Unidos. 6258

Small Industry Bulletin for Asia and the Pacific. 1507

Social Development Newsletter. 6728

Social Indicators of Development (Year). 1368

Soils Newsletter. 245

Solas - International Convention for the Safety of Life at Sea. Amendments. 2981

Sources. 6037

State of Food and Agriculture. 155

The State of the World's Children. 6690

State of World Population. 6058

Statistical Indicators for Asia and the Pacific. 1072

Statistical Indicators of Short Term Economic Changes in E.C.E. Countries. 1290

Statistical Information Bulletin for Africa/Bulletin d'Information Statistique pour l'Afrique. 1072

Statistical Yearbook for Asia and the Pacific/Annuaire Statistique pour l'Asie et le Pacifique. 1072

Statistics of Road Traffic Accidents in Europe and North America. 7058

Statistics of World Trade in Steel. 5220

The Steel Market and Prospects. 5211

Studies and Reports in Hydrology Series. 2397

Studies and Surveys in Comparative Education. 2567

Studies in Mathematics Education Series. 2567

Studies in the Processing, Marketing and Distribution of Commodities. 1550

Study Abroad/Etudes a l'Etranger/Estudios en el Extranjero. 2567

Survey of Economic and Social Conditions in Africa. 1368

Surveys of International Air Transport Fares and Rates. 7078

Table of International Telex Relations and Traffic. 2039

Technical Instructions for the Safe Transport of Dangerous Goods by Air. 7078

Technical Papers in Hydrology Series. 2398

Tiger Paper. 2246

Timber Bulletin. 3175

Tisnet Trade and Investment Information Bulletin. 1411

Tots: Quaderns d'Educacio Ambiental. 2954

Trade and Development Report and Overview. 1349

Trade Policy Review. 1349

Transnational Corporations. 1349

Transnational Corporations and Transborder Data Flows. 1204

Transport & Communications Bulletin for Asia & the Pacific. 7041

Trends in Developing Economies (Year). 1369

Tsetse and Trypanosomiasis Information Quarterly. 645

Tungsten Statistics. 5221

U I E Handbooks. (Unesco Institute for Education) 2489

U I E Studies in Education. (Unesco Institute for Education) 2489

U I E Studies Series. (Unesco Institute for Education) 2489

U I P - Berichte/U I E Reports/Dossiers I U E. (UNESCO Institut fuer Paedagogik) 2489

U N A New Z. (United Nations Association of New Zealand) 5975

U N B I S Plus on C D - R O M. (United Nations Bibliographic Information System) 5986

U N C H S (Habitat) Shelter Bulletin. (United Nations Centre for Human Settlements (Habitat)) 3761

U N C H S Habitat News. (United Nations Centre for Human Settlements (Habitat)) 3761

U N C R D Annual Report. (United Nations Centre for Regional Development) 1369

U N C R D Newsletter. (United Nations Centre for Regional Development) 1369

U N C T A D Bulletin. (United Nations Conference on Trade and Development) 1350

U N C T A D Commodity Yearbook. (United Nations Conference on Trade and Development) 1076

U N C T A D Review. (United Nations Conference on Trade and Development) 1350

U N Chronicle. 6040

U N D O C: Current Index. (United Nations Documents) 5986

U N I C E F Policy Review Series. (United Nations Children's Fund) 6692

U N I D I R Newsletter/Lettre de L'U N I D I R. (United Nations Institute for Disarmament Research) 6040

U N I D O Links. (United Nations Industrial Development Organization) 1369

U N R I S D Social Development News. (United Nations Research Institute for Social Development) 6643

Unasylva. 3164

UNESCO. Centro de Documentacion Cultural, Havana. Informaciones Trimestrales. 3794

UNESCO. Comision Nacional Cubana. Boletin. 3794

UNESCO. Principal Regional Office for Asia and the Pacific. Abstract Bibliography Series on Population Education. 2505

UNESCO. Records of the General Conference. Proceedings. 6040

UNESCO. Records of the General Conference. Resolutions. 6040

UNESCO. Regional Office for Science and Technology for Latin America and the Caribbean. Boletin. 6979

UNESCO. Report of the Director-General on the Activities of the Organization. 6040

UNESCO. Scientific Maps and Atlases and Other Related Publications. 566

UNESCO. Statistics on Science and Technology/Statistiques Relatives aux Science et a la Technologie/Estadisticas Relativas a la Ciencia y a la Tecnologia. 6592

UNESCO. Studies on Books and Reading. 6286

UNESCO Asia Bunka News Bulletin. 3330

UNESCO Asian Fiction Series. 4481

UNESCO Association - U S A Newsletter. 6040

UNESCO Australia. 1369

UNESCO Collection of Representative Works Series/Collection UNESCO d'Oeuvres Representatives. 4481

UNESCO Databases. 566

UNESCO List of Documents and Publications. 2505

UNESCO Nairobi Bulletin. 6580

UNESCO Reports in Marine Science. 631

UNESCO: Resolutions and Decisions 1987-1996. 6643

UNESCO Statistical Reports and Studies Series. 6950

UNESCO Statistical Yearbook. 6950

UNESCO World Heritage Desk Diary (Year). 3516

Union Postale. 2021

Union Postale Universelle. Actes. 2021

Union Postale Universelle. Statistique des Services Postaux. 2021

United Nations. Conference on Trade and Development. Trade and Development Board. Official Records. 1369

United Nations. Conference on Trade and Development. Trade and Development Board. Official Records. Supplements. 6041

United Nations. Department of International Economic and Social Affairs. Statistical Office. Construction Statistic Yearbook. 923

United Nations. Department of Public Information. Programme Update. 6041

United Nations. Development Programme. Compendium of Approved Projects. 1369

United Nations. Division of Narcotic Drugs. Information Letter. 2306

United Nations. Economic and Social Commission for Asia and the Pacific. Asian Population Studies Series. 6059

United Nations. Economic and Social Commission for Asia and the Pacific. Development Papers. 2247

United Nations. Economic and Social Commission for Asia and the Pacific. Mineral Resources Development Series. 5317

United Nations. Economic and Social Commission for Asia and the Pacific. Water Resources Series. 7300

United Nations. Economic and Social Council. Annexes. 1007

United Nations. Economic and Social Council. Index to Proceedings. 5986

United Nations. Economic and Social Council. Official Records. 6041

United Nations. Economic Commission for Asia and the Pacific. Energy Resources Development Series. 2679

United Nations. Economic Commission for Europe. Economic Studies. 1293

United Nations. Economic Commission for Europe. Statistical Journal. 6950

United Nations. General Assembly. Annexes. 1007

United Nations. General Assembly. Index to Proceedings. 5986

United Nations. General Assembly. Official Records. 1007

United Nations. General Assembly. Provisional Records. 1007

United Nations. International Law Commission Yearbook. 4127

United Nations. Multilateral Treaties Deposited with the Secretary-General. 4127

United Nations. National Accounts Statistics. Analysis of Main Aggregates. 1076

United Nations. National Accounts Statistics. Government Accounts and Tables. 1076

United Nations. National Accounts Statistics. Main Aggregates and Detailed Tables. 1076

United Nations. Population and Vital Statistics Report. 6073

United Nations. Security Council. Index to Proceedings. 5986

United Nations. Security Council. Official Records. 6041

United Nations. Security Council. Official Records. Supplement. 6041

United Nations. Statistical Yearbook. 6950

United Nations. Treaty Series. 4127

United Nations. Treaty Series. Cumulative Index. 4057

United Nations. Trusteeship Council. Index to Proceedings. 5986

United Nations. Trusteeship Council. Official Records. 6041

United Nations. Trusteeship Council. Official Records. Annexes - Sessional Fascicle. 6041

United Nations. Trusteeship Council. Official Records. Resolutions. 6041

United Nations. Trusteeship Council. Official Records. Supplements. 6041

United Nations. Trusteeship Council. Official Records. Verbatim Records of Plenary Meetings. 6041

United Nations. Yearbook. 6041

United Nations Association of the Republic of China News Letter. 6041

The United Nations Blue Books Series. 6041

United Nations Children's Fund. Annual Report. 6692

United Nations Children's Fund. Programme Division. Staff Working Papers Series. 6692

United Nations Commission on International Trade Law. Report on the Work of Its Session. 4127

United Nations Commission on International Trade Law. Yearbook. 4127

United Nations Conference on the Standardization of Geographical Names. Report. 3424

United Nations Conference on Trade and Development: Proceedings. 1350

United Nations Congress on the Prevention of Crime and the Treatment of Offenders. Report. 2281

United Nations Disarmament Yearbook. 5288

United Nations Economic and Social Commission for Asia and the Pacific. Statistical Newsletter. 1076

United Nations Economic and Social Council. Disarmament Study Series. 5288

United Nations Economic and Social Council. Official Records. Supplements and Special Supplements. 1007

United Nations Economic and Social Council. Resolutions and Decisions. 1007

United Nations Economic and Social Council. Summary Records of Plenary Meetings. 1007

United Nations Economic Commission for Africa. Annual Report. 1369

United Nations Economic Commission for Africa. Biennial Report of the Executive Secretary. 1369

United Nations Economic Commission for Africa. Statistical Newsletter. 1076

United Nations Economic Commission for Europe. Discussion Papers. 1293

United Nations Environment Programme. Governing Council. Report on the Work of its Session. 2955

United Nations Environment Programme. The State of the Environment; Report of the Executive Director. 2955

United Nations Interregional Crime and Justice Research Institute. Issues and Reports Series/ Institute Interregional de Recherche des Nations Unies sur la Criminalite et la Justice. Themes et Rapports Serie. 2281

United Nations Interregional Crime and Justice Research Institute. Publication. 2281

United Nations Juridical Yearbook. 4127

United Nations Law Report. 4127

United Nations Library. Monthly Bibliography. Part 1: Books, Official Documents, Serials. 5986

United Nations Library. Monthly Bibliography. Part 2: Selected Articles. 5987

United Nations Population Fund. Annual Report. 6059

United Nations Population Fund. Annual Review of Population Law. 6059

United Nations Publications. 5976

United Nations Regional Cartographic Conference for Asia and the Pacific. Report. 3424

United Nations Regional Cartographic Conference for the Americas. Report. 3424

United Nations Resolutions. Series 2. Resolutions and Decisions of the Security Council. 4127

United Nations Review. 6041

United Nations Statistical Office. Monthly Bulletin of Statistics. 6950

United Nations University. Work in Progress. 1369

Urban Age. 1370

Vigilancia Epidemiologica de la Rabia para las Americas. 7284

W H O Food Additives Series. (World Health Organization) 3130

W H O Technical Report Series. (World Health Organization) 4757

W M O Bulletin. (World Meteorological Organization) 5245

Waste Management Research Abstracts. 6259

Water Resources Journal. 7305

Weekly Epidemiological Record. 6254

World Animal Review. 293

World Bank. Annual Report. 1370

World Bank. E D I Development Study. (Economic Development Institute) 1370

World Bank. Global Environment Facility Paper. 1370

World Bank. Publications Update. 1370

The World Bank and the Environment. 1352

World Bank Atlas. 1370

World Bank Country Study. 1371

World Bank Discussion Paper. 1371

The World Bank Economic Review. 1295

World Bank Policy Paper. 1371

World Bank Policy Research Bulletin. 1371

World Bank Regional and Sectoral Studies. 1371

World Bank Research Observer. 1173

World Bank Research Program. 1078

World Bank Technical Paper. 1371

World Biodiversity Database Series. 2323

World Cartography. 3426

World Data (Year). 1295

World Debt Tables. 1371

World Directory of Human Rights Research and Training Institutions. 1723

World Directory of Medical Schools. 2528

World Directory of Schools of Public Health. 2528

World Economic Outlook. 1295

World Education Report. 2494

World Engineering Industries and Automation. 2870

World Food Programme Journal. 5484

World Guide to Higher Education. 2562

World Health. 6254

World Health Forum. 4759

World Health Organization. Bulletin. 4759

World Health Organization. Handbook of Resolutions and Decisions of the World Health Assembly and the Executive Board. 6254

World Health Organization. Regional Office for Africa. Report of the Regional Committee. 6254

World Health Organization. Regional Office for Africa. Report of the Regional Director. 6254

World Health Organization. Regional Office for the Eastern Mediterranean. Annual Report of the Regional Director. 6254

INDEX TO PUBLICATIONS OF INTERNATIONAL ORGANIZATIONS 10287

World Health Organization. Regional Office for the Western Pacific. Annual Report of the Regional Director to the Regional Committee for the Western Pacific. 6254

The World Health Report. 6254

World Health Statistics Annual. 6259

World Health Statistics Quarterly/Rapport Trimestriel de Sanitares Mondiales. 6259

World Heritage Series. 3517

World Information Report. 4223

World Investment Report. 1415

World List of Social Science Periodicals. 6651

World Market for Dairy Products. 165

World Media Handbook. 2009

World Meteorological Congress. Proceedings. 5246

World Meteorological Organization. Abridged Final Reports of Sessions of Technical Commissions. 5246

World Meteorological Organization. Annual Report. 5246

World Meteorological Organization. Basic Documents. 5246

World Meteorological Organization. Commission for Aeronautical Meteorology. Abridged Final Report of the (No.) Session. 5246

World Meteorological Organization. Commission for Agricultural Meteorology. Abridged Final Report of the (No.) Session. 5246

World Meteorological Organization. Commission for Basic Systems. Abridged Final Report of the (No.) Session. 5246

World Meteorological Organization. Commission for Hydrology. Abridged Final Report of the (No.) Session. 5246

World Meteorological Organization. Commission for Instruments and Methods of Observation. Abridged Final Report of the (No.) Session. 5246

World Meteorological Organization. Commission for Marine Meteorology. Abridged Final Report of the (No.) Session. 5246

World Meteorological Organization. Congress. Abridged Report with Resolutions. 5246

World Meteorological Organization. Executive Council Session. Abridged Final Reports with Resolutions. 5246

World Meteorological Organization. Regional Association I (Africa). Abridged Final Report of the (No.) Session. 5247

World Meteorological Organization. Regional Association II (Asia). Abridged Final Report of the (No.) Session. 5247

World Meteorological Organization. Regional Association III (South America). Abridged Final Report of the (No.) Session. 5247

World Meteorological Organization. Regional Association IV (North America and Central America). Abridged Final Report of the (No.) Session. 5247

World Meteorological Organization. Regional Association V (South West Pacific). Abridged Final Report of the (No.) Session. 5247

World Meteorological Organization. Reports on Marine Science Affairs. 2417

World Meteorological Organization. Special Environmental Reports. 2958

World Meteorological Organization. Technical Notes. 5247

World Meteorological Organization. Weather Reporting. Volume A: Observing Stations. 5247

World Meteorological Organization. Weather Reporting. Volume B: Data Processing. 5247

World Meteorological Organization. Weather Reporting. Volume C1: Catalogue of Meteorological Bulletins. 5247

World Meteorological Organization. Weather Reporting. Volume C2: Transmissions. 5247

World Meteorological Organization. Weather Reporting. Volume D: Information for Shipping. 5247

The World of Civil Aviation. 7079

World of Work. 6695

World Patent Information. 5592

World Population Projections. 6074

World Science Report. 6584

World Trade Annual. 1078

World Trade Annual Supplement. 1078

World Weather Watch Planning Reports. 5247

Yearbook of Forest Products/Annuaire des Produits Forestiers/Anuario de Productos Forestales. 3177

Year Book of Labour Statistics/Annuaire des Statistiques du Travail/Anuario de Estadisticas del Trabajo. 1078

Yearbook on Human Rights. 6003

Your United Nations. 3518

Controlled Circulation Serials

A A A A S F NEWS.
American Association for Accreditation of Ambulatory Surgery Facilities, 1202 Allanson Rd., Mundelein, IL 60060. TEL 708-949-6058.
circ. 500. *5133*

A A A TODAY MAGAZINE.
Automobile Club Publications, 1000 AAA Dr., Heathrow, FL 32746-5063. TEL 407-444-8200.
circ. 1,700,000. *7080*

A A A TRAVELER (FLORHAM PARK).
New Jersey Automobile Club, 1 Hanover Rd., Florham Park, NJ 07932. TEL 201-377-7200. FAX 201-377-2979.
circ. 185,000. *7181*

A A B BULLETIN.
American Association of Bioanalysts, 917 Locust St., Ste. 1100, St. Louis, MO 63101-1413. TEL 314-241-1445.
circ. 1,700. *4893*

A A C E BONUS BRIEFS.
American Association for Career Education, 2900 Amby Pl., Hermosa Beach, CA 90254-2216. TEL 310-376-7378. FAX 310-374-1360.
circ. 500. *5503*

A A C E DISTINGUISHED MEMBER SERIES.
American Association for Career Education, 2900 Amby Pl., Hermosa Beach, CA 90254-2216. TEL 310-376-7378. FAX 310-374-1360.
circ. 500. *5503*

A A G BIJDRAGEN.
Landbouwuniversiteit Wageningen, Vakgroep Agrarische Geschiedenis, Hollandseweg 1, 6706 KN Wageningen, Netherlands. TEL 31-8370-84027.
circ. 1,100. *3545*

A A I S VIEWPOINT.
American Association of Insurance Services, 1035 S. York Rd., Bensenville, IL 60106. TEL 708-595-3225. FAX 708-595-4647.
circ. 1,500. *3806*

A A L C REPORTER.
African-American Labor Center, A F L - C I O, 1925 K St., Ste. 300, Washington, DC 20006. TEL 202-778-4600. FAX 202-778-4601.
circ. 3,500. *3885*

A A MAGAZINE.
V N U Business Publications BV, VNU House, 32-34 Broadwick St., London W1A 2HG, England. TEL 44-171-439-4242. FAX 44-171-437-7001.
circ. 62,202. *1079*

A A P A NEWS.
American Academy of Physician Assistants, 950 N. Washington St., Alexandria, VA 22314-1552. TEL 703-836-2272. FAX 703-684-1924.
circ. 22,000. *4628*

A A P S NEWSLETTER.
American Association of Pharmaceutical Scientists, 1650 King St., 2nd Fl., Alexandria, VA 22314-2747. TEL 703-548-3000. FAX 703-684-7349.
circ. 7,000. *5644*

A A R N NEWSLETTER.
Alberta Association of Registered Nurses, 11620-168 St., Edmonton, AB T5M 4A6, Canada. TEL 403-451-0043. FAX 403-452-3276.
circ. 24,000. *4927*

A B C COLOR.
A B C Color, Yegros 745, CC 1241, Asuncion, Paraguay. TEL 595-21-491-160. FAX 595-21-493-059. *3347*

A B C DIALOGUE.
Association of Bridal Consultants, 200 Chestnutland Rd., New Milford, CT 06776-2521. TEL 860-355-0464. FAX 860-354-1404.
circ. 1,700. *4624*

A B D.
Air Service Directory, Inc., 105 Calvert St., Harrison, NY 10528-3138. TEL 914-835-7200.
circ. 20,500. *51*

A B E S P BOLETIM.
Associacao Brasileira de Endodontia, Seccao Sao Paulo, Praca Amadeu Amaral 47-8, Sao Paulo, SP, Brazil.
circ. 2,500. *4848*

A B Q CORRESPONDENT.
A B Q Communications Corporation, Box 1432, Corrales, NM 87048. TEL 505-897-0822. FAX 505-898-6525.
circ. 100. *6953*

A C A D I A QUARTERLY.
Association for Computer Aided Design in Architecture, c/o Skip Van Wyk, Ed., School of Architecture & Planning, Univ. of New Mexico, Albuquerque, NM 87131. TEL 505-277-2903.
circ. 280. *418*

A C J S PROGRAM BOOK.
Academy of Criminal Justice Sciences, 402 Nunn Hall, Northern Kentucky University, Highland Heights, KY 41099-5998. TEL 606-572-5434. FAX 606-572-6665.
circ. 2,000. *2529*

A C M S I G P L A N NOTICES.
Association for Computing Machinery, Special Interest Group on Programming Languages, 1515 Broadway, 17th Fl., New York, NY 10036. TEL 212-869-7440. FAX 212-302-5826.
circ. 11,600. *2141*

A C O G NEWSLETTER.
American College of Obstetricians and Gynecologists, 409 12th St., S.W., Washington, DC 20024. TEL 202-863-2423. FAX 202-479-6826.
circ. 35,000. *4951*

A C S A NEWS.
Association of Collegiate Schools of Architecture, Inc., 1735 New York Ave., N.W., Washington, DC 20006. TEL 202-785-2324. FAX 202-628-0448.
circ. 3,800. *391*

A D L LAW ENFORCEMENT BULLETIN.
Anti-Defamation League, 823 United Nations Plaza, New York, NY 10017. TEL 212-490-2525.
circ. 5,000. *3902*

A D N O C NEWS.
Abu Dhabi National Oil Company, Public Relations Department, P.O. Box 898, Abu Dhabi, United Arab Emirates. TEL 666000. FAX 655745.
circ. 3,500. *5594*

A E A ADVOCATE.
Arizona Education Association, 100 W. Clarendon, Ste. 1600, Phoenix, AZ 85013-3511. TEL 602-264-1774. FAX 602-240-6887.
circ. 30,000. *2418*

A E R REPORT.
Association for Education and Rehabilitation of the Blind and Visually Impaired, Box 22397, Alexandria, VA 22304-9239. TEL 703-548-1884. *3467*

A F F I LETTER.
American Frozen Food Institute, 2000 Corporate Ridge., Ste. 1000, McLean, VA 22102. TEL 703-821-0770. FAX 703-821-1350.
circ. 1,300. *3094*

A G E REFDEX.
Geotechnical Engineering International Resources Center, c/o Asian Institute of Technology, Box 2754, Bangkok 10501, Thailand. TEL 66-2-524-5862. FAX 66-2-516-2126.
circ. 300. *2324*

A G M A ZINE.
American Guild of Musical Artists, 1727 Broadway, New York, NY 10019-5284.
circ. 6,000. *5369*

CONTROLLED CIRCULATION SERIALS

A G NEWS.
Associated Grocers of Colorado Inc., 707 17th St., Ste. 2800, Denver, CO 80202-3428.
circ. 2,000. *3139*

A H & M A'S REGISTER (YEAR).
American Hotel & Motel Association, 1201 New York Ave., N.W., Washington, DC 20005-3931. TEL 202-289-3100. FAX 202-289-3199.
circ. 12,000. *3722*

A I A - D C NEWS.
American Institute of Architects, Washington Chapter, 1777 Church St., N.W., Washington, DC 20036. TEL 202-667-1798. FAX 202-667-4327.
circ. 1,500. *391*

A I ARCHITECT.
American Institute of Architects Press, 1735 New York Ave., N.W., Washington, DC 20006. TEL 202-626-7465.
circ. 56,000. *391*

A I C NEWS.
American Institute for Conservation of Historic and Artistic Works, 1717 K St., N.W., Ste. 301, Washington, DC 20006. TEL 202-452-9545. FAX 202-452-9328.
circ. 3,000. *419*

A I D - AUSLAENDER IN DEUTSCHLAND.
Isoplan Institut, Martin-Luther-Str. 20, 66111 Saarbruecken, Germany. TEL 49-681-936460. FAX 49-681-9364611.
circ. 33,000. *6046*

A I D RESEARCH AND DEVELOPMENT ABSTRACTS.
U.S. Agency for International Development, Policy Directorate, POL-CDIE-DI, Dept. of State, Washington, DC 20523-1802. TEL 202-875-4818. FAX 703-351-4039.
circ. 5,000. *1015*

A I M C FORUM.
Association of Internal Management Consultants, 7960 Soquel Dr., Ste. B296, Aptos, CA 95003-3945. TEL 408-662-9890. FAX 408-662-9855.
circ. 500. *1462*

A I M INTERNATIONAL.
Africa Inland Mission International, Box 178, Pearl River, NY 10965. TEL 914-735-4014. FAX 914-735-1814.
circ. 30,000. *6318*

A I S NEWSLETTER.
American Indian Society of Washington D.C., Box 6431, Falls Church, VA 22040-6531. TEL 804-448-3707. FAX 804-448-2493.
circ. 500. *2992*

A L E B C I; BOLETIN INFORMATIVO.
Asociacion Latinoamericana de Escuelas de Bibliotecologia y Ciencias de la Informacion, Escuela de Bibliotecologia, Centro Regional de Veraguas, Santiago de Veraguas, Panama. FAX 984056.
circ. 500. *4154*

A L I S A.
Australian Clearing House for Library & Information Science, Library, St. Bernards Rd., Magill, S.A. 5072, Australia. TEL 61-8-3024766. FAX 61-8-3024695.
circ. 32. *4223*

A L S A R.
Ediciones Anel, San Vicente Ferrer 13, Granada, Spain.
circ. 25,000. *85*

A L T A CAPITAL COMMENT.
American Land Title Association, 1828 L St. N.W., Washington, DC 20036-5182. TEL 202-296-3671.
circ. 4,300. *6293*

A M.
Editora Ave Maria Ltda, Rua Martins Francisco 646, Caixa Postal, 615, 01000 Sao Paulo, Brazil.
circ. 50,000. *6448*

A M A - AGRICULTURAL MECHANIZATION IN ASIA, AFRICA AND LATIN AMERICA.
Shin-Norinsha Co., Ltd., 7, 2-chome, Kanda Nishiki-cho, Chiyoda-ku, Tokyo 101, Japan. TEL 03-3291-3674. FAX 03-3291-5717.
circ. 15,000. *204*

A M A MANAGEMENT BRIEFINGS.
American Management Association, 1601 Broadway, New York, NY 10019. TEL 212-586-8100. *1462*

A M A VICTORIA BRANCH NEWS.
Australian Medical Association, Victoria Branch, 293 Royal Parade, Parkville, Vic. 3052, Australia. FAX 03-347-9871. *4629*

A M MAGAZINE.
Aston Martin Owners' Club Ltd., 1A High St., Sutton, Nr. Ely, Cambs. CB6 2RB. FAX 44-1376-551431.
circ. 4,200. *7080*

A M O A LOCATION.
Amusement and Music Operators Association, 401 N. Michigan Ave., Chicago, IL 60611. TEL 312-245-1021. FAX 312-321-6869.
circ. 2,000. *5369*

A N S A JOURNAL.
Association of Nurses in Substance Abuse, 18 St. Johns St., Bury St. Edmunds, Suffolk IP33 1SJ, England. TEL 0284-762377. FAX 0284-724374.
circ. 400. *4927*

A O.
Stichting I V I O, Postbus 37, 8200 AA Lelystad, Netherlands. TEL 31-320-244244. FAX 31-320-249094.
circ. 4,000. *3338*

A P C O BULLETIN.
Association of Public-Safety Communications Officials International, Inc., 2040 S. Ridgewood Ave., Daytona Beach, FL 32119-8437. TEL 904-322-2500. FAX 904-322-2501.
circ. 12,500. *6227*

A P F NEWS.
Association of Professional Foresters, 7-9 West St., Belford, Northumber. NE70 7QA, England. TEL 44-1668-213937. FAX 44-1668-213555.
circ. 1,400. *3146*

A P F REPORTER.
Alicia Patterson Foundation, 1730 Pennsylvania Ave., N.W., Ste. 850, Washington, DC 20006. TEL 202-393-5995. FAX 301-951-8512.
circ. 3,200. *3868*

A P I NEWSBRIEFS.
American Prepaid Legal Services Institute, 541 N. Fairbanks Court, Chicago, IL 60611. TEL 312-988-5751. FAX 312-988-5032.
circ. 650. *3903*

A P N Y NEWSLETTER.
Advertising Photographers of New York, 27 W. 20th St., Rm. 601, New York, NY 10011. TEL 212-807-0399. FAX 212-727-8120.
circ. 1,000. *5761*

A P R O DIRECTORY.
B M I Publications Ltd., Suffolk House, George St., Croydon, Surrey CR9 1SR, England. TEL 44-181-649-7233. FAX 44-649-7234.
circ. 1,000. *7182*

A PLUS ARCHITECTURE.
Centre d'Information de l'Architecture, de l'Urbanisme et du Design, Chaussee de Ruisbroek 83, 1190 Brussels, Belgium. TEL 32-2-3322472. FAX 32-2-3322208.
circ. 13,200. *391*

A R D R I NEWS.
University of Fort Hare, Agricultural and Rural Development Research Institute, Private Bag X1314, Alice 5700, South Africa. TEL 0404-31154. FAX 0404-31730.
circ. 1,000. *85*

A R I D O NEWSLETTER.
Association of Registered Interior Designers of Ontario (ARIDO), 717 Church St., Toronto, ON M4W 2M5, Canada. TEL 416-921-2127. FAX 416-921-3660.
circ. 2,200. *3840*

A S A EXPO GUIDE AND MEMBERSHIP DIRECTORY (YEARS).
American Sportfishing Association, 1033 N. Fairfax St., Ste. 200, Alexandria, VA 22314-1540. TEL 703-519-9691. FAX 703-519-1872.
circ. 10,000. *3059*

A S A NEWS.
American Supply Association, 222 Merchandise Mart Pl., Ste. 1360, Chicago, IL 60654-1202. TEL 312-464-0090. FAX 312-464-0091.
circ. 22,000. *3475*

A S B A TODAY.
American Small Businesses Association, Box 3323, Oakton, VA 22124. TEL 202-628-6316.
circ. 65,000. *1639*

A S C C A NEWS.
Societa Editoriale Farmaceutica s.r.l., Via Ausonio 12, 20123 Milan, Italy. TEL 39-2-89404545. FAX 39-2-89401168.
circ. 4,000. *2965*

A S D A TODAY.
American Society for Dental Aesthetics, 635 Madison Ave., New York, NY 10022. TEL 212-371-4575.
circ. 3,000. *4849*

A S H R M FORUM.
American Hospital Association, One North Franklin, Chicago, IL 60606. TEL 312-422-3989. FAX 312-422-4580.
circ. 3,000. *3702*

A S I D REPORT.
American Society of Interior Designers, 608 Massachusetts Ave., N.E., Washington, DC 20002-6006. TEL 202-546-3480. FAX 202-546-3240.
circ. 35,000. *3840*

A S M A NEWS.
American Sports Medicine Association, Board of Certification, 660 W. Duarte Rd., Arcadia, CA 91007. TEL 818-445-1978. FAX 818-574-1999.
circ. 3,500. *6747*

A S P A FLASH.
International Business Ventures Corp., Box 42450, Phoenix, AZ 85080-2450. TEL 602-272-2900. FAX 602-269-1843.
circ. 195. *7081*

A S T R NEWSLETTER.
American Society for Theatre Research, c/o P.T. Dircks, Ed., C.W. Post College, Dept. of English, Greenvale, NY 11548. TEL 516-299-2391.
circ. 600. *7000*

A S U NATIONAL.
Australian Services Union, National Executive, 2nd Fl., 116-124 Queensberry St., Carlton South, Vic. 3053, Australia. TEL 03-348-1788. FAX 03-349-1108.
circ. 190,000. *3886*

A S VORORT.
Verlag Glueckauf GmbH, Postfach 185620, 45206 Essen, Germany. TEL 49-2054-92412023. FAX 49-2054-924129. *5293*

A T.
Svenska Arkitekters Riksfoerbund (SAR), Norrlandsgatan 18, S-111 43 Stockholm, Sweden. TEL 46-8-679-27-60. FAX 46-8-611-49-30.
circ. 5,500. *391*

A T F ANNUAL REPORT.
Australian Teachers Union, c/o Australian Educators Union, 220 Clavendon St., E. Melbourne, Vic. 3002, Australia. TEL 03-254-1800. FAX 03-254-1805. *2418*

A T I P.
Association Technique de l'Industrie Papetiere, 154 bd. Haussmann, 75008 Paris, France. FAX 33-1-45-63-53-09.
circ. 1,850. *5565*

A T L REPORT.
Association of Teachers and Lecturers, 7 Northumberland St., London WC2N 5DA, England. TEL 44-171-930-6441. FAX 44-171-930-1359.
circ. 161,000. *2418*

A U T BULLETIN.
Association of University Teachers, United House, 9 Pembridge Rd., London W11 3JY, England. TEL 0171-221-4370. FAX 0171-727-6547.
circ. 40,000. *2530*

CONTROLLED CIRCULATION SERIALS 10291

A U T UPDATE.
Association of University Teachers, United House, 9 Pembridge Rd., London W11 3JY, England. TEL 44-171-221-4370. FAX 44-171-727-6547.
circ. 40,000. *2530*

A U T WOMAN.
Association of University Teachers, United House, 9 Pembridge Rd., London W11 3JY, England. TEL 44-171-221-4370. FAX 44-171-727-6547.
circ. 40,000. *2530*

A W H P ACTION.
Association for Worksite Health Promotion, 60 Revere Dr., Ste. 500, Northbrook, IL 60062-1577. TEL 847-480-9574. FAX 847-480-9282.
circ. 3,000. *5777*

A W S C P A. NEWSLETTER.
American Women's Society of Certified Public Accountants, 401 N. Michigan Ave., Chicago, IL 60611. TEL 312-644-6610.
circ. 5,000. *1079*

AAKA SKIDOR.
Hummelgren & Almebaeck Foerlag AB, P.O. Box 8014, S-104 20 Stockholm, Sweden. TEL 46-8-650-05-25. FAX 46-8-650-04-07.
circ. 56,000. *6859*

AANDRIJVEN & BESTUREN.
Samsom Bedrijfsinformatie B.V., Postbus 4, 2400 MA Alphen aan den Rijn, Netherlands. TEL 31-1720-66359. FAX 31-172-440681.
circ. 7,500. *2776*

ABBEY.
White Urp Press, 5360 Fallriver Row Ct., Columbia, MD 21044.
circ. 200. *4501*

ABERDEEN PAPERS IN ACCOUNTANCY AND FINANCE.
University of Aberdeen, Department of Accountancy, Edward Wright Bldg., Dunbar St., Aberdeen AB24 3QY, Scotland. TEL 44-1224-272205. FAX 44-1224-272214.
circ. 200. *1079*

ABERDEEN PETROLEUM REPORT.
Aberdeen Petroleum Publishing Ltd., 35 Huntly St., Aberdeen AB10 1TJ, Scotland. TEL 44-1224-644725. FAX 44-1224-647574. *5594*

ABOVE & BEYOND.
Box 2348, Yellow Knife, NT X1A 2P7, Canada. TEL 403-873-2299. FAX 403-873-2295.
circ. 28,200. *2993*

ABSTRACT OF STATISTICS FOR TAMIL NADU.
Director of Statistics, Madras 600006, India. *6890*

ABU DHABI. DA'IRAT AL-TAKHTIT. AL-NASHRAH AL-SANAWIYYAH LI-AS'AR AL-TAJZI'AH.
Planning Administration, Statistical Department, P.O. Box 12, Abu Dhabi, United Arab Emirates.
TEL 727200.
circ. 500. *1015*

ABU DHABI. DA'IRAT AL-TAKHTIT. AL-NASHRAH AL-SHAHRIYYAH LI-AS'AR AL-TAJZI'AH.
Planning Administration, Statistical Department, P.O. Box 12, Abu Dhabi, United Arab Emirates.
TEL 727200. *1015*

ABU DHABI. FOREIGN TRADE STATISTICS.
Government of Abu Dhabi, P.O. Box 255, Abu Dhabi, United Arab Emirates. TEL 720700. *1015*

ABU DHABI CHAMBER OF COMMERCE AND INDUSTRY. ANNUAL REPORT.
Abu Dhabi Chamber of Commerce and Industry, P.O. Box 662, Abu Dhabi, United Arab Emirates. TEL 2-214000. FAX 2-215867.
circ. 500. *1176*

ACADEMIA.
Oesterreichischer Cartell-Verband, Lerchenfelderstr. 14, A-1080 Vienna, Austria. FAX 43-1-405162230.
circ. 20,000. *4321*

ACADEMIA CAMPINENSE DE LETRAS. PUBLICACOES.
Academia Campinense de Letras, Rua Marechal Deodoro, 525, 13020-000 Campinas SP, Brazil.
circ. 200. *4369*

ACADEMIA CHILENA DE LA HISTORIA. BOLETIN.
Academia Chilena de la Historia, Clasificador 245, Correo Central, Santiago, Chile. TEL 6399323.
circ. 350. *3614*

ACADEMIA DE CIENCIAS DE CUBA. INSTITUTO DE GEOLOGIA. SERIE GEOLOGICA.
Academia de Ciencias de Cuba, Instituto de Geologia, Calzada no. 851, Esq. a Calle 4, Havana 4, Cuba. *2329*

ACADEMIC FILE INTERNATIONAL NEWS & PHOTO SYNDICATION.
Eastern Art Publishing Group, 27 Wallorton Gardens, London SL14 8DX, England. TEL 44-81-392-1122. FAX 44-81-392-1422. *419*

ACADEMIC TEXT REVIEW.
Kay Ward & Associates, 2666 Shrewsbury Rd., Columbus, OH 43221. TEL 614-325-5735. FAX 614-459-9273.
circ. 5,000. *6260*

THE ACADEMY.
United States Sports Academy, One Academy Dr., Daphne, AL 36526. TEL 205-626-3303. FAX 205-626-3874.
circ. 10,000. *6747*

ACADEMY OF MANAGEMENT NEWSLETTER.
Academy of Management (Monroe), c/o Lawrence R. Jauch, Ed., Northeast Louisiana Univ., ADMN-3-17, Monroe, LA 71209-8813. TEL 318-342-1210. FAX 318-342-1209.
circ. 10,000. *1463*

ACADEMY REPORTER.
American Pharmaceutical Association, 2215 Constitution Ave., N.W., Washington, DC 20037. TEL 202-628-4410.
circ. 23,000. *5644*

ACCENT.
I O G T - N T O, U N F, Birger Jarlsgatan 25, Box 1747, S-111 87 Stockholm, Sweden. TEL 46-8-789-49-50. FAX 46-8-20-43-54.
circ. 50,271. *2296*

ACCESS (MELBOURNE).
Arts Access Society, Inc., 109-111 Sturt St., S. Melbourne, Vic. 3205, Australia. TEL 61-3-96998299. FAX 61-3-96998868.
circ. 1,500. *3452*

ACCOMMODATOR.
Motels Ontario, 347 Pido Rd., Unit 2, R.R. 6, Peterborough, ON K9J 6X7, Canada. TEL 705-745-4982. FAX 705-745-4983.
circ. 1,300. *3722*

ACCOUNTANCY S A.
South African Institute of Chartered Accountants, P.O. Box 59875, Kengray 2100, South Africa. TEL 27-11-622-6655. FAX 27-11-622-3321.
circ. 22,244. *1080*

THE ACCOUNTANT.
Institute of Certified Public Accountants of Kenya, P.O. Box 59963, Nairobi, Kenya. TEL 254-2-224629. FAX 254-2-211563.
circ. 18,000. *1080*

ACCOUNTING PROFESSIONALS PRODUCT NEWS.
Accounting Professional Product News, Inc., 4210 W. Vickery Blvd., Ft. Worth, TX 76107. TEL 817-738-3371. FAX 817-731-9704.
circ. 40,000. *1082*

ACCREDITATION COUNCIL FOR ACCOUNTANCY AND TAXATION. ACTION LETTER.
Accreditation Council for Accountancy and Taxation, 1010 N. Fairfax St., Alexandria, VA 22314-1574. TEL 703-549-6400. FAX 703-549-2984.
circ. 6,000. *1082*

ACERVO.
Arquivo Nacional, Rua Azeredo Coutinho 77, 20230-170 Rio de Janeiro, Brazil.
circ. 2,000. *3615*

ACHETEURS.
Edipresse, 16 rue Guillaume Tell, 75017 Paris, France. TEL 1-47 66 00 05. FAX 47-66-46-94.
circ. 4,478. *1514*

ACHIEVEMENT.
Response Publishing Group plc, 41-45 Goswell Rd., London EC1V 7EH, England. TEL 44-171-490-0550.
circ. 10,220. *1314*

ACKNOWLEDGE.
Austin College, 900 N. Grand Ave., Ste. 6H, Sherman, TX 75090-4440. TEL 903-813-2386. FAX 903-813-2415.
circ. 13,500. *1938*

ACQUA ARIA.
Editrice Arti Poligrafiche Europee, Via Casella 16, 20156 Milan, Italy. TEL 39-2-392281. FAX 39-2-39214341.
circ. 4,854. *2904*

ACQUISITION COLUMBUS.
Acquisition Columbus, 2910 Brookdown Dr., Columbus, OH 43235-2704. TEL 614-841-0085. *6294*

ACTA ACADEMIAE AGRICULTURAE AC TECHNICAE OLSTENENSIS. AEDIFICATIO ET MECHANICA.
Wydawnictwo A R T Olsztyn, Blok 12, 10-957 Olsztyn-Kortowo, Poland. TEL 48-89-5273310.
circ. 140. *2879*

ACTA ACADEMIAE AGRICULTURAE AC TECHNICAE OLSTENENSIS. AGRICULTURA.
Wydawnictwo A R T Olsztyn, Blok 12, 10-957 Olsztyn-Kortowo, Poland. TEL 48-89-5273310.
circ. 180. *211*

ACTA ACADEMIAE AGRICULTURAE AC TECHNICAE OLSTENENSIS. GEODAESIA ET RURIS REGULATIO.
Wydawnictwo A R T Olsztyn, Blok 12, 10-957 Olsztyn-Kortowo, Poland. TEL 48-89-5273310.
circ. 140. *86*

ACTA ACADEMIAE AGRICULTURAE AC TECHNICAE OLSTENENSIS. OECONOMICA.
Wydawnictwo A R T Olsztyn, Blok 12, 10-957 Olsztyn-Kortowo, Poland. TEL 48-89-5273310.
circ. 130. *186*

ACTA ACADEMIAE AGRICULTURAE AC TECHNICAE OLSTENENSIS. PROTECTIO AQUARUM ET PISCATORIA.
Wydawnictwo A R T Olsztyn, Blok 12, 10-957 Olsztyn-Kortowo, Poland. TEL 48-89-5273310.
circ. 130. *7286*

ACTA ACADEMIAE AGRICULTURAE AC TECHNICAE OLSTENENSIS. TECHNOLOGIA ALIMENTORUM.
Wydawnictwo A R T Olsztyn, Blok 12, 10-957 Olsztyn-Kortowo, Poland. TEL 48-89-5273310.
circ. 130. *3094*

ACTA ACADEMIAE AGRICULTURAE AC TECHNICAE OLSTENENSIS. VETERINARIA.
Wydawnictwo A R T Olsztyn, Blok 12, 10-957 Olsztyn-Kortowo, Poland. TEL 48-89-5273310.
circ. 130. *7263*

ACTA ACADEMIAE AGRICULTURAE AC TECHNICAE OLSTENENSIS. ZOOTECHNICA.
Wydawnictwo A R T Olsztyn, Blok 12, 10-957 Olsztyn-Kortowo, Poland. TEL 48-89-5273310.
circ. 130. *260*

ACTA BIOLOGICA VENEZUELICA.
Universidad Central de Venezuela, Instituto de Zoologia Tropical, Facultad de Ciencias, Apdo. 47058, Caracas 1041-A, Venezuela. FAX 58-2-6052136.
circ. 1,500. *582*

ACTA BIOQUIMICA CLINICA LATINOAMERICANA.
Federacion Bioquimica de la Provincia de Buenos Aires, Calle 6, No. 1344, 1900 La Plata, Buenos Aires, Argentina. TEL 021-38821-42797. FAX 54-21-254224.
circ. 3,000. *649*

ACTA GASTROENTEROLOGICA LATINOAMERICANA.
Juncal 2134, Planta Baja B 1125, Buenos Aires, Argentina. TEL 541-8250050. FAX 541-8222139.
circ. 3,500. *4907*

ACTA GEOLOGICA HISPANICA.
Universidad de Barcelona, Biblioteca Facultat de Geologia, Marti Franques s-n, 08028 Barcelona, Spain. TEL 34-3-4021420. FAX 34-3-4021421.
circ. 600. *2329*

10292 CONTROLLED CIRCULATION SERIALS

ACTA MEDICA ET BIOLOGICA.
Niigata Daigaku, Igakubu, Ichiban-cho, Asahimachi-dori, Niigata 951, Japan.
circ. 600. *4631*

ACTA MEDICA OKAYAMA.
Okayama Daigaku, Igakubu, 2-5-1 Shikata-cho, Okayama-shi, Okayama-ken 700, Japan. TEL 81-86-223-7151. FAX 81-86-225-6295.
circ. 600. *4631*

ACTA OCEANOGRAFICA DEL PACIFICO.
Instituto Oceanografico de la Armada, Av. 25 de Julio, Via al Puerto Maritimo, P.O. Box 5940, Guayaquil, Ecuador. TEL 593-4-480033. FAX 593-4-484723.
circ. 3,000. *2398*

ACTA ORDINIS FRATRUM MINORUM.
Ordo Fratrum Minorum, Curia Generalis, Via S. Maria Mediatrice, 25, I-00165 Rome, Italy. TEL 39-6-684919. FAX 39-6-6380292. *6448*

ACTA PEDIATRICA ESPANOLA.
San Martin de Porres 26, 28035 Madrid, Spain. TEL 34-3-2090255. FAX 34-3-2020643.
circ. 8,000. *5027*

ACTUALITE CHIMIQUE.
Societe Francaise de Chimie, 250 rue Saint Jacques, 75005 Paris, France. TEL 33-1-40467160. FAX 33-1-40467161.
circ. 2,378. *1737*

AD FUNDUM.
Uitgeverij Lakerveld B.V., Mangaanstraat 86, Postbus 43250, 2504 AG The Hague, Netherlands. TEL 31-70-3218218. FAX 31-70-3298744.
circ. 3,000. *513*

AD MARGINEM.
Universitaet zu Koeln, Institut fuer Musikalische Volkskunde, Gronewaldstr. 2, 50931 Cologne, Germany. TEL 49-221-470-5269. *5370*

AD VERBUM.
Confederacion Argentina de Sordomudos, Av. Pedro Medrano 1352, Buenos Aires, Argentina.
circ. 5,000. *3460*

ADAM.
Foerster-Verlag, Schaefergasse 27, 60313 Frankfurt a.M., Germany. TEL 49-69-831022. FAX 49-69-845991.
circ. 31,000. *3690*

ADAY.
Mindanao State University, Mamitua Saber Research Center, P.O. Box 5594, Iligan City 9200, Philippines.
circ. 500. *4371*

ADDICTION RESEARCH FOUNDATION OF ONTARIO. ANNUAL REPORT.
Addiction Research Foundation of Ontario, Subscription - Public Affairs Department, 33 Russell St., Toronto, ON M5S 2S1, Canada. TEL 416-595-6054. FAX 416-595-6881.
circ. 2,000. *2297*

ADHESIVE TRENDS.
Adhesive Manufacturers Association, 401 N. Michigan Ave., Chicago, IL 60611-4267. TEL 312-644-6610. FAX 312-527-6783.
circ. 300. *6501*

ADHESIVES AGE DIRECTORY.
Intertec Publishing (Atlanta), 6151 Powers Ferry Rd., N.W., Atlanta, GA 30339-2941. TEL 770-955-2500. FAX 770-955-0476.
circ. 26,262. *2754*

ADIRONDAC.
Adirondack Mountain Club, Inc., 814 Goggins Rd., Lake George, NY 12845-4117. TEL 518-668-4447. FAX 518-668-3746.
circ. 14,000. *6859*

ADLINE.
Adline Publishing Ltd., 361-363 Moseley Rd., Birmingham B12 9DE, England. TEL 0121-446-4466. FAX 0121-446-4462.
circ. 11,225. *29*

ADMARINE.
Compass Rose Ltd., 92 The Avenue, Sunbury-on-Thames, Middlesex TW16 5EX, England.
circ. 20,000. *6835*

ADOBE MAGAZINE.
Adobe Systems, 411 First Ave., S., Seattle, WA 98104. TEL 206-622-5500. FAX 206-343-3273.
circ. 23,361. *2208*

ADOPTALK.
North American Council on Adoptable Children (NACAC), 970 Raymond Ave., No. 106, St. Paul, MN 55114-1149. TEL 612-644-3036. FAX 612-644-9848.
circ. 8,000. *6652*

ADVANCE (LIBERTY).
Target Marketing, Inc., 1 Liberty Bell Circle, Ste. 200, Liberty, MO 64068. TEL 816-781-7557. FAX 816-792-3892.
circ. 250,000. *5503*

ADVANCE FOR MANAGERS OF RESPIRATORY CARE.
Merion Publications, 650 Park Ave., Box 61556, King of Prussia, PA 19406-0956. TEL 610-265-7812. FAX 610-962-0639.
circ. 18,500. *5117*

ADVANCE NEWS JOURNAL.
Advance Publishing Company, 1101 N. Cage, Twin Palm Plaza, Ste. C1, Pharr, TX 78577. TEL 210-783-0036.
circ. 3,500. *930*

ADVANCE - TITAN.
Advance - Titan, 800 Algoma Blvd., Oshkosh, WI 54901. TEL 414-424-3048. FAX 414-424-0866.
circ. 9,000. *1938*

ADVANCED COMPOSITES MANUFACTURING CENTRE NEWSLETTER.
Advanced Composites Manufacturing Centre, University of Plymouth, School of Manufacturing, Materials and Mechanical Engineering, Drake Circus, Plymouth, Devon PL4 8AA, England. TEL 44-1752-232650. FAX 44-1752-232638.
circ. 4,600. *5875*

ADVANCES IN PSYCHIATRIC TREATMENT.
Royal College of Psychiatrists, 17 Belgrave Sq., London SW1X 8PG, England. TEL 44-171-235-2351. FAX 44-171-245-1231.
circ. 1,200. *5049*

ADVANCES IN THERAPY.
Health Communications Inc., 20 Highland Ave., Metuchen, NJ 08840. TEL 908-548-9130. FAX 908-548-8555.
circ. 3,500. *5645*

ADVENTURE ANNUAL.
Mountain Travel - Sobek, 6420 Fairmount Ave., El Cerrito, CA 94530. TEL 510-527-8100. FAX 510-525-7710.
circ. 100,000. *7182*

ADVERTENTIEBLAD.
B. V. Rotadruk, Postbus 16, Axel, Netherlands. *30*

ADVERTISING AGE'S CREATIVITY.
Crain Communications, Inc. (New York), 220 E. 42nd St., New York, NY 10017-5806. TEL 212-210-0100. FAX 212-210-0111.
circ. 30,000. *30*

THE ADVISOR.
Carter Spencer Publishing Ltd., Chancery Ct., Lincoln Rd., High Wycombe, Bucks. HP12 3RE, England. TEL 44-1494-442424. FAX 44-1494-472790.
circ. 3,500. *211*

ADVOCATE (PANHANDLE).
Peace Farm, HCR2 Box 25, Panhandle, TX 79068. TEL 806-335-1715. FAX 806-335-1715.
circ. 400. *5888*

ADVOCATE (ST. PAUL).
Minnesota Education Association, 41 Sherburne Ave., St. Paul, MN 55103. TEL 612-227-9541. FAX 612-227-4868.
circ. 46,000. *2420*

ADVOKATEN.
Danske Advokatsamfund, Kronprinsessegade 28, 1306 Copenhagen K, Denmark. TEL 45-33-96-97-98. FAX 45-33-32-18-31.
circ. 5,800. *3906*

AEROGRAM.
Cranfield University, College of Aeronautics, Cranfield, Beds. MK43 0AL, England. TEL 44-1234-750111. FAX 44-1234-751640.
circ. 3,000. *52*

AEROLOGICAL DATA OF JAPAN.
Kishocho, 3-4, Otemachi 1-chome, Chiyoda-ku, Tokyo 100, Japan. *5226*

AEROMEXICO PREMIER.
Impresiones Aereas, S.A. de C.V., Arquimedes 5, Col. Polanco, 11560 Mexico DF, Mexico.
circ. 32,000. *7257*

AERONAUTICA AND AIR LABEL COLLECTOR.
Aeronautica & Air Label Collectors Club, Box 1239, Elgin, IL 60121-1239. TEL 847-468-0840. *5703*

AERONAUTICAL SATELLITE NEWS.
Inmarsat, 99 City Rd., London EC1Y 1AX, England. TEL 0171-728-1449. FAX 0171-728-1344.
circ. 13,000. *53*

AEROSPACE ASIA - PACIFIC.
Miller Freeman Pte. Ltd., 100 Beach Rd., 26-00 Shaw Towers, Singapore 0718, Singapore. TEL 294-3366. FAX 298-5534.
circ. 11,375. *53*

AEROSPACE NEWS.
Aerospace Industries Association of Canada, 60 Queen St., Ste. 1200, Ottawa, ON K1P 5Y7, Canada. TEL 613-232-4297. FAX 613-232-1142.
circ. 2,400. *54*

AEROSPACE PRODUCTS.
Phillips Publishing International Inc., 1201 Seven Locks Rd., Ste. 300, Potomac, MD 20854. TEL 301-340-1520. *54*

AEROSPACE REVIEW.
Smiths Industries Aerospace, 765 Finchley Rd., London NW11 8DS, England. TEL 44-181-458-3232. FAX 44-181-209-0526.
circ. 6,500. *54*

AERSCEALA.
Aer Lingus, Communications Department, Dublin Airport PA6, Dublin, Ireland. TEL 353-1-7052326.
circ. 9,500. *55*

AERZTE ZEITUNG.
Aerzte Zeitung Verlagsgesellschaft mbH, Am Forsthaus Gravenbruch 5, 63263 Neu-Isenburg, Germany. TEL 49-6102-5060. FAX 49-6102-58740.
circ. 65,000. *4633*

AERZTLICHER RATGEBER FUER WERDENDE UND JUNGE MUETTER.
Wort und Bild Verlag Konradshoehe GmbH, Konradshoehe, 82065 Baierbrunn, Germany. TEL 089-74433-0. FAX 089-74433155.
circ. 240,000. *4952*

AFFILIATED WAREHOUSE COMPANIES DIRECTORY.
Affiliated Warehouse Companies, Inc., Box 295, Hazlet, NJ 07730. TEL 908-739-2323.
circ. 16,000. *1650*

AFFILIATES DIRECTORY.
C B I Employee Relocation Council, Centre Point, 103 New Oxford St., London WC1A 1DU, England. TEL 44-171-379-7400. FAX 44-171-240-8287.
circ. 2,000. *1562*

AFFIRMATIVE ACTION REGISTER.
Joyce R. Green, Ed. & Pub., 8356 Olive Blvd., St. Louis, MO 63132. TEL 314-991-1335. FAX 314-997-1788.
circ. 60,000. *5503*

AFINIDAD.
Instituto Quimico de Sarria, Asociacion de Quimicos, Via Augusta 390, 08017 Barcelona, Spain. TEL 34-3-2804276. FAX 34-3-2804276.
circ. 2,500. *1738*

AFRICA HEALTH.
F S G Communications Ltd., Vine House, Fair Green, Reach, Cambridge CB5 0JD, England. TEL 44-1638-743633. FAX 44-1638-743998.
circ. 5,000. *4633*

AFRICA LINK.
Africa Regional Secretariat, Planned Parenthood Federation, Madison Insurance House, Upper Mill, P.O. Box 30234, Nairobi, Kenya. TEL 254-2-720280. FAX 254-2-726596.
circ. 3,000. *856*

AFRICA PRODUCT DIGEST.
Reed Business Information South Africa (Pty.) Ltd., P.O. Box 653207, Benmore 2010, South Africa. TEL 27-11-784-1110. FAX 27-11-883-4729.
circ. 10,000. *1314*

AFRICAN AMERICAN REVIEW.
Indiana State University, Department of English, Terre Haute, IN 47809. TEL 812-237-2968. FAX 812-237-3156.
circ. 298. *2993*

AFRICAN BOOK PUBLISHING RECORD.
Hans Zell Publishers, P.O. Box 56, Oxford OX1 2SJ, England. TEL 44-1865-511428. FAX 44-1865-311534.
circ. 800. *6288*

AFRICAN PRINTER.
Coast Graphix Inc., P.O. Box 751119, Gardenview 2047, South Africa. TEL 27-11-6224800. FAX 27-11-6222480.
circ. 8,000. *6074*

AFRICANA LIBRARIES NEWSLETTER.
c/o Joseph J. Lauer, Ed., Africana Bibliographer, Michigan State University Libraries, E. Lansing, MI 48824-1048. TEL 517-355-2366. FAX 517-336-1445.
circ. 600. *4157*

THE AFTERNOON DESPATCH & COURIER.
Courier Publications Pvt. Ltd., Afternoon House, 6, Nanabhai Lane, Fort, Bombay 400 001, India. TEL 2871616. FAX 2870371.
circ. 500. *3306*

AFTERNOON ON SUNDAY.
Courier Publications Pvt. Ltd., Afternoon House, 6 Nanabhai Lane, Fort, Bombay 400 001, India. TEL 2871616. FAX 2870371.
circ. 1,000. *3306*

AG RETAILER MAGAZINE.
Doane Agricultural Service Co., 11701 Borman Dr., Ste. 100, Saint Louis, MO 63146-4199. TEL 314-569-2700. FAX 314-569-1083.
circ. 21,966. *211*

AGENDA (MEMPHIS).
Towery Publishing, Inc., 1835 Union Ave., No. 142, Memphis, TN 38104. TEL 901-725-2400. FAX 901-725-2401.
circ. 20,000. *1176*

AGENDA (NEW YORK, 1991).
Scholastic Inc., 555 Broadway, New York, NY 10012-3999. TEL 212-343-6100.
circ. 250,000. *2420*

AGENT DE VIAJES AL DIA.
Pepperdine Enterprises, 1367 Tadsworth Terr., Heathrow, FL 32746. TEL 407-333-3393. FAX 407-333-3533.
circ. 6,156. *7183*

AGENT ORANGE REVIEW.
U.S. Department of Veterans Affairs, Environmental Agents Service - 131, V.A. Headquarters, 810 Vermont Ave., N.W., Washington, DC 20420. TEL 202-273-8580. *3907*

AGFOCUS.
Cornell Cooperative Extension, 420 E. Main St., Batavia, NY 14020. TEL 716-343-3040. FAX 716-439-8455.
circ. 1,000. *87*

AGGIORNAMENTI DI TERAPIA OFTALMOLOGICA.
Farmigea S.p.A., Via Carmignani, 2, 56127 Pisa, Italy. TEL 39-50-544000. FAX 39-50-544304.
circ. 7,200. *4989*

AGORA.
Lakehead University, Student Union, Thunder Bay, ON P7B 5E1, Canada. TEL 807-343-8193. FAX 807-343-8192.
circ. 2,000. *1938*

AGRARTECHNIK (WUERZBURG).
B L V Verlagsgesellschaft mbH, Lothstr. 29, 80797 Munich, Germany. TEL 49-89-12705-0. FAX 49-89-12705354.
circ. 13,308. *88*

AGRI DERGISI.
Turk Algoloji Derneginin, Istanbul Tip Fakultesi, Agri Merkezi, Capa Klinikleri, 34390 Istanbul, Turkey. TEL 90-212-6350135. FAX 90-212-6310541.
circ. 500. *5050*

AGRIBUSINESS DAIRYMAN.
Agribusiness Publications, 612 N St., Sanger, CA 93657. TEL 309-875-4585. FAX 309-875-4587.
circ. 10,000. *251*

AGRIBUSINESS FRESH FRUIT AND RAISIN NEWS.
Agribusiness Publications, 612 N St., Sanger, CA 93657. TEL 209-875-4585. FAX 209-875-4587.
circ. 10,000. *211*

AGRICULTURA EM SAO PAULO.
Instituto de Economia Agricola, Av. Miguel Estefano, 3900, Caixa Postal 6802, 04301-903 Sao Paulo, Brazil. FAX 55-11-2764062. *187*

AGRICULTURA TECNICA EN MEXICO.
Instituto Nacional de Investigaciones Forestales, Agricolas y Pecuarias, Vocalia Division Agricola, Apdo. Postal 6-882, 06600 Mexico, D.F., Mexico.
circ. 1,000. *90*

AGRICULTURAL EDUCATORS DIRECTORY.
Charles M. Henry Printing Co., Box 68, Greensburg, PA 15601. TEL 412-834-7600. FAX 412-836-7759.
circ. 12,000. *90*

AGRICULTURAL ENGINEERING IN SOUTH AFRICA.
South African Institute of Agricultural Engineers, P.O. Box 912 719, Silverton 0127, South Africa. TEL 27-12-8041540. FAX 27-12-8040753.
circ. 600. *204*

AGRICULTURAL FINANCE REVIEW.
Cornell University, Department of Agricultural Resource and Managerial Economics, 357 Warren Hall, Ithaca, NY 14853-7801. TEL 607-255-4534. FAX 607-255-1589.
circ. 900. *188*

AGRICULTURAL FINANCIAL STATISTICS.
Statistics Canada, Circulation Management, Jean Talon Bldg., 2-C12, Tunney's Pasture, Ottawa, ON K1A 0T6, Canada. TEL 613-951-7277. FAX 613-951-1584.
circ. 400. *167*

AGRICULTURAL STATISTICS OF SABAH.
Department of Agriculture, Statistics Unit, 88632 Kota Kinabalu, Sabah, Malaysia. TEL 088-55155. FAX 088-239046.
circ. 500. *168*

AGRO-NOUVELLES.
Order of Agrologists of Quebec, 1259 Berri St., Ste. 710, Montreal, PQ H2L 4C7, Canada. TEL 514-844-3833. FAX 514-844-7462. *94*

AGRO SUR.
Universidad Austral de Chile, Facultad de Ciencias Agrarias, Casilla 567, Valdivia, Chile. TEL 56-63-221660. FAX 56-63-221460.
circ. 250. *94*

AGROBOREALIS.
University of Alaska at Fairbanks, Agricultural and Forestry Experiment Station, Fairbanks, AK 99775. TEL 907-474-7653.
circ. 4,000. *94*

AGROCIENCIA.
Colegio de Postgraduados, Instituto de Estudios, Investigaciones y Servicio Agripefor Chapingo S.C., Cerro del Vigilante 166, Col. Romero de Terrenos, 04310 Mexico DF, Mexico. TEL 915-5-541304.
circ. 1,500. *94*

AGROCIENCIA. MATEMATICAS APLICADAS, ESTADISTICA Y COMPUTACION.
Colegio de Postgraduados, Instituto de Estudios, Investigaciones y Servicio Agripefor Chapingo S.C., Cerro del Vigilante 166, Col. Romero de Terrenos, 04310 Mexico DF, Mexico. TEL 915-5-54-14-03.
circ. 1,500. *188*

AGROCIENCIA. PROTECCION VEGETAL.
Colegio de Postgraduados, Instituto de Estudios, Investigaciones y Servicio Agripefor Chapingo S.C., Cerro del Vigilante 166, Col. Romero de Terrenos, 04310 Mexico DF, Mexico. TEL 915-5-54-14-03.
circ. 1,500. *212*

AGROFORESTRY TODAY.
International Centre for Research in Agroforestry, P.O. Box 30677, Nairobi, Kenya. TEL 254-2-521450. FAX 254-2-521001.
circ. 6,000. *95*

AGWAY COOPERATOR.
Agway Inc., Box 4741, Syracuse, NY 13221. TEL 315-479-6117. FAX 315-449-6041.
circ. 50,000. *96*

AICHI MEDICAL UNIVERSITY ASSOCIATION. JOURNAL.
Aichi Medical University Association, 21, Yazakokarimata, Nagakutecho, Aichi-gun, Aichi-ken 480-11, Japan. TEL 81-561-62-3311. FAX 81-561-62-3348.
circ. 1,700. *4634*

AIDS BOOK REVIEW JOURNAL.
University of Illinois at Chicago, Library, Box 8198, Chicago, IL 60680-8198. TEL 312-996-2730. FAX 312-413-0424.
circ. 2,000. *4830*

AIDS READER.
S C P Communications, Inc., 134 W. 29th St., New York, NY 10001-5304.
circ. 27,000. *4831*

AIR CADET.
Headquarters Air Cadets, R.A.F. Cranwell, Sleaford, Lincolnshire NG34 8HB, England. TEL 44-1400-261201. FAX 44-1400-261201.
circ. 38,000. *1862*

AIR CHINA.
Regie Club International, Cromwell House, 136 Cromwell Rd., London SW7 4HA, England. TEL 44-71-244-6565.
circ. 60,000. *7257*

AIR CONDITIONING & REFRIGERATION NEWS.
Faversham House Group Ltd., 232a Addington Rd., South Croydon, Surrey CR2 8LE, England. TEL 44-181-651-7100. FAX 44-181-651-7117.
circ. 10,249. *3476*

AIR MARKET NEWS.
General Publications, Inc., Box 480, Hatch, NM 87937-0480. TEL 505-267-1030. FAX 505-267-1920.
circ. 18,500. *55*

AIR QUALITY DATA FOR ARIZONA.
Department of Health Services, Bureau of Air Quality Control, 1740 W. Adams St., Phoenix, AZ 85007. TEL 602-255-1142. *2905*

AIR TRAFFIC MANAGEMENT.
Euromoney Aviation Group, Playhouse Yard, Nestor House, London EC4V 5EX, England. TEL 44-171-779-8866. FAX 44-171-779-8867.
circ. 4,449. *7062*

AIR TRANSPORT WORLD.
Penton Publishing Co. (Stamford), 600 Summer St., Box 1361, Stamford, CT 06904. TEL 203-348-7531. FAX 203-348-4023.
circ. 40,100. *56*

AIR UNIVERSITY LIBRARY INDEX TO MILITARY PERIODICALS.
U.S. Air Force, Air University Library, Maxwell AFB, AL 36112-6424. TEL 334-953-2504. FAX 334-953-1192.
circ. 1,500. *5292*

AIRBORNE LOG.
Lockheed Martin, 542642 LOCKHEED MARA, 86 S. Cobb Dr., Marietta, GA 30063-0244. TEL 770-494-2406. FAX 770-494-4809.
circ. 30,000. *56*

AIRCRAFT ECONOMICS.
Euromoney Aviation Group, Playhouse Yard, Nestor House, London EC4V 5EX, England. TEL 44-171-779-8866. FAX 44-171-779-8867.
circ. 4,000. *7062*

10294 CONTROLLED CIRCULATION SERIALS

AIRCRAFT MAINTENANCE TECHNOLOGY.
Johnson Hill Press, Inc., 1233 Janesville Ave., Fort Atkinson, WI 53538. TEL 920-563-6388. FAX 920-563-1701.
circ. 41,000. *7062*

AIRCRAFT TECHNOLOGY ENGINEERING & MAINTENANCE.
Aviation Industry Press, 31 Palace St., London SW1E 5HW, England. TEL 44-171-828-4376. FAX 44-171-828-9154.
circ. 10,000. *56*

AIRFINANCE JOURNAL.
Euromoney Aviation Group, Playhouse Yard, Nestor House, London EC4V 5EX, England. TEL 44-171-779-8941. FAX 44-171-779-8525.
circ. 900. *7063*

AIRLINE MAINTENANCE WORLD.
A M W Publishing Ltd., 40 Chomham Rd., Sunningdale, Berks. SI5 ODX, England. TEL 44-1344-784866. FAX 44-1344-874543.
circ. 12,708. *7063*

AIRPORT DEVELOPMENT AND CIVIL AVIATION FOR CHINA.
Sterling Publications Ltd., 86-88 Edgware Rd., London W2 2YW, England. TEL 44-171-915-9600. FAX 44-171-915-9619.
circ. 10,000. *7064*

AIRPORT PRESS.
Box 300879, J.F.K. Sta., Jamaica, NY 11430. TEL 718-244-6788. FAX 718-995-3432.
circ. 43,000. *7064*

AIRPORT REPORT.
American Association of Airport Executives, 4212 King St., Alexandria, VA 22302. TEL 703-824-0504. FAX 703-820-1395. *7064*

AIRPORT TECHNOLOGY INTERNATIONAL.
Sterling Publications Ltd., 86-88 Edgware Rd., London W2 2YW, England. TEL 44-171-915-9600. FAX 44-171-915-9619.
circ. 10,000. *7064*

AITIA MAGAZINE.
State University of New York at Farmingdale, Center for Philosophy, Law, Citizenship, Knapp Hall 15, Farmingdale, NY 11735. TEL 516-420-2050. FAX 516-420-2698.
circ. 3,000. *3771*

AIXTRA.
I B M Corporation (Roanoke), 5 W. Kirwood Blvd., MS 01-04-60, Roanoke, TX 76299. TEL 817-962-6551. FAX 817-962-7218.
circ. 40,000. *2072*

AJMAN.
Ajman Chamber of Commerce and Industry, P.O. Box 662, Ajman, United Arab Emirates. TEL 422177.
circ. 1,000. *1176*

AKADEMIA ROLNICZO-TECHNICZNA IM. M. OCZAPOWSKIEGO. HUMANISTYKA I PRZYRODOZNAWSTWO.
Wydawnictwo A R T Olsztyn, Blok 12, 10-957 Olsztyn-Kortowo, Poland. TEL 48-89-5273310.
circ. 190. *3771*

AKAROA MAIL.
Akaroa Mail and Banks Peninsula Advertiser, P.O. Box 9, Akaroa, New Zealand. TEL 64-3-3277-622.
circ. 6,500. *3339*

AKHBAR AL-BUTRUL WAL-SINA'A.
Ministry of Petroleum and Mineral Wealth, P.O. Box 59, Abu Dhabi, United Arab Emirates. TEL 651810. FAX 663414.
circ. 2,000. *5594*

AKKAS DAILY.
Akkas Daily, 1-1, Khetra Das Lane, West Bengal 700012, India. TEL 91-33-261187. FAX 91-33-269644.
circ. 44,000. *3306*

AKRON.
University of Akron, Office of the Alumni Association, Akron, OH 44325-2602. TEL 216-972-7270. FAX 216-972-5335.
circ. 85,000. *1939*

AKTUEL ELEKTRONIK.
Teknisk Forlag A-S, Skelbaekgade 4, DK-1780 Copenhagen V, Denmark. TEL 45-31-21-68-01. FAX 45-31-21-04-01.
circ. 19,820. *2808*

AKTUELLT MAALERI.
Maalarmaestarnas Riksoferening, P.O. Box 16286, S-103 25 Stockholm, Sweden.
circ. 2,681. *5550*

ALABAMA CATTLEMAN.
Alabama Cattleman's Association, 201 S. Bainbridge St., Box 2499, Montgomery, AL 36102-2499. FAX 334-834-6326.
circ. 17,000. *267*

ALABAMA'S HEALTH.
Department of Public Health, 434 Monroe St., Montgomery, AL 36130-3017. TEL 334-613-5300. FAX 334-240-3097.
circ. 3,250. *6227*

ALABAMA'S TREASURED FORESTS.
Alabama Forestry Commission, Box 302550, Montgomery, AL 36130-2550. TEL 334-240-9355. FAX 334-240-9390.
circ. 10,000. *3146*

AL-AKADEMIYYAH AL-ARABIYYAH LIL-ELOUM WA AL-TEHNOLOGIA WA AL-NAQL AL-BAHRI. MJALLHAT.
Arab Academy for Science & Technology & Maritime Transport, P.O. Box 1029, Alexandria, Egypt. TEL 203-5862325. FAX 203-5801937.
circ. 3,000. *6510*

ALASKA AIRLINES MAGAZINE.
Paradigm Communications Group, 2701 First Ave., Ste. 250, Seattle, WA 98121. TEL 206-441-5871. FAX 206-448-6939.
circ. 50,000. *7257*

ALASKA HOUSING FINANCE CORPORATION. ANNUAL REPORT.
Alaska Housing Finance Corporation, 520 E. 34th Ave., Anchorage, AK 99503. TEL 907-561-1900. FAX 907-561-0364.
circ. 2,500. *3740*

ALASKA LIBRARY DIRECTORY.
Alaska Library Association (Fairbanks), c/o AKLA Exec. Sec., Box 81084, Fairbanks, AK 99708. TEL 907-479-5196. *4157*

ALBA POMPEIA.
Comune di Alba, Museo Civico "Federico Eusebio", Via Paruzza 1-a, 12051 Alba, Italy. TEL 39-173-290092. FAX 39-173-362075.
circ. 500. *346*

THE ALBANY REPORT.
Sawchuk, Brown Associates, 41 State St., Albany, NY 12207. TEL 518-462-0318. FAX 518-462-0688.
circ. 1,200. *1220*

ALBERTA AGRICULTURE. ANNUAL REPORT.
Department of Agriculture, Publishing Branch, 7000 113th St., Edmonton, AB T6H 5T6, Canada. TEL 403-427-2121. FAX 403-427-2861. *97*

ALBERTA AGROLOGIST.
Alberta Institute of Agrologists, 8506 - 104 St., Edmonton, AB T6E 4G4, Canada. TEL 403-432-0663. FAX 403-439-8414.
circ. 1,300. *97*

ALBERTA ASSOCIATION OF COLLEGE LIBRARIANS. NEWSLETTER.
Alberta Association of College Librarians, Canadian Union College Library, 50 Ramona Dr., College Heights, AB T4L 2B7, Canada. FAX 403-782-3977.
circ. 100. *4157*

ALBERTA SWEETGRASS.
Aboriginal Multi-Media Society of Canada, 15001-112 Ave., N.W., Edmonton AB T5M 2V6, Canada. TEL 403-455-2945. FAX 403-455-7639.
circ. 7,000. *2995*

ALBRIGHTIAN.
Albright College, Albrightian, Box 15234, Reading, PA 19612-5234.
circ. 1,600. *1939*

ALDERLEA MAGAZINE.
Value Plus Magazine Ltd., 105 Kenneth St., Duncan, BC V9L 1N5, Canada. TEL 604-746-6463. FAX 604-746-7445.
circ. 14,500. *3258*

ALDRICHIMICA ACTA.
Aldrich Chemical Company, Inc., 1001 W. St. Paul Ave., Milwaukee, WI 53233. TEL 414-298-7907. FAX 414-273-4979.
circ. 200,000. *1811*

ALE STREET NEWS.
Tuscarora Inc., Box 1125, Maywood, NJ 07607. TEL 201-368-9100. FAX 201-368-9101.
circ. 100,000. *513*

ALERE FLAMMAM.
Comando Scuola di Guerra, 00053 Civitavecchia, Italy. TEL 0766-30051. FAX 0766-500680.
circ. 900. *5258*

ALERGIA.
Sociedad Mexicana de Alergia e Inmunologia, A.C., Fuente Emperador 6, 53950 Huixquilucan, Edo. de Mexico, Mexico. TEL 52-5-2511844. FAX 52-5-2513975.
circ. 3,000. *4790*

ALERT DIVER.
Divers Alert Network, 3100 Tower Blvd., Ste. 1300, Durham, NC 27707-2563. TEL 919-684-2948. FAX 919-490-6630.
circ. 127,000. *6748*

ALIMENTOS BALANCEADOS PARA ANIMALES.
Watt Publishing Co., 122 S. Wesley Ave., Mt. Morris, IL 61054. TEL 815-734-4171. FAX 815-734-4201.
circ. 9,000. *260*

ALL ABOUT KIDS.
All About Kids, 1077 Celestial St., Ste. 101, Cincinnati, OH 45202. TEL 513-684-0501. FAX 513-684-0507.
circ. 50,000. *1837*

ALL ABOUT TOWN.
Spencer Group Media Pty. Ltd., Level 1, 10 Nash St., Perth, W.A. 6000, Australia. TEL 61-9-2211344. FAX 61-9-2211348.
circ. 16,000. *3722*

I ALLAGHI.
E. Karelli & Co., Kazani Str. 4, Iraklion 71202, Crete, Greece. TEL 30-81-280022. FAX 30-81-243370.
circ. 3,100. *3303*

ALLEGHENY COUNTY MEDICAL SOCIETY. BULLETIN.
Allegheny County Medical Society, 713 Ridge Ave., Pittsburgh, PA 15212. TEL 412-321-5030. FAX 412-321-5323.
circ. 3,700. *4634*

ALLEGRO.
Associated Musicians of Greater New York, AFM, Local 802, 322 W. 48th St., 5th Fl., New York, NY 10036. TEL 212-245-4802. FAX 212-245-6255.
circ. 15,000. *3886*

ALLERGIE KONKRET.
Vereinigte Verlagsanstalten GmbH, Hoeherweg 278, 40231 Duesseldorf, Germany. TEL 49-211-7357-0. FAX 49-211-7357223.
circ. 30,000. *4790*

ALLGEMEINER HOCHSCHUL-ANZEIGER.
Frankfurter Allgemeine Zeitung GmbH, Hellerhofstr. 2-4, 60327 Frankfurt a.M., Germany. TEL 49-69-75911639. FAX 49-69-75912330.
circ. 300,000. *5503*

ALLIANCE (OTTAWA).
Public Service Alliance of Canada, 233 Gilmour St., Ottawa, ON K2P 0P1, Canada. TEL 613-560-4200. FAX 613-236-1654.
circ. 130,000. *3886*

ALLT OM HUSVAGN OCH CAMPING.
Caravan Press AB, P.O. Box 1263, S-171 24 Solna, Sweden. TEL 46-8-730-54-85. FAX 46-8-735-57-10.
circ. 23,700. *6859*

ALLT OM M C.
Albinsson & Sjoeberg, P.O. Box 529, S-371 23 Karlskrona, Sweden. TEL 46-455-3353-30. FAX 46-455-311715.
circ. 30,300. *6823*

ALLURE.
Target s.r.l., Via Bondi 23, 2, 40138 Bologna, Italy. TEL 39-51-342426. FAX 39-51-345554.
circ. 35,000. *509*

ALPHA PSI OMEGA: PLAYBILL.
Alpha Psi Omega National Theatre Honorary, c/o Wabash College, Crawfordsville, IN 47933. TEL 317-361-6394. FAX 317-361-6341.
circ. 7,000. *7001*

ALPINO.
Associazione Nazionale Alpini, Via Marsala 9, 20121 Milan, Italy. TEL 02-6552692. FAX 02-6592364.
circ. 370,000. *3325*

ALT OM DATA.
Audio Media A-S, St. Kongensgade 72, DK-1264 Copenhagen K, Denmark. TEL 45-33-91-28-33. FAX 45-33-91-01-21.
circ. 40,000. *2171*

ALUMINIUM NEWS.
Promech Publishing, P.O. Box 85502, Emmarentia 2029, South Africa. TEL 27-11-7811401. FAX 27-11-7811403.
circ. 4,000. *5185*

ALUMNI COMPANION.
University of New Hampshire, Alumni Association, Elliott Alumni Center, 9 Edgewood Rd., Durham, NH 03824. TEL 603-862-2040. FAX 603-862-4126.
circ. 75,000. *1939*

ALUMNI NEWS (GREENSBORO).
University of North Carolina at Greensboro, Alumni Association, Greensboro, NC 27412-5001. TEL 910-334-5921. FAX 910-334-4055.
circ. 4,000. *1939*

ALUMNI NEWS (ST. LOUIS).
School of the Art Institute of Chicago, 37 S. Wabash, Chicago, IL 60603. FAX 312-263-0141.
circ. 12,000. *1939*

ALUMNI U B C CHRONICLE.
University of British Columbia, Alumni Association, Cecil Green Park, 6251 Cecil Green Park Rd., Vancouver, BC V6T 1Z1, Canada. TEL 604-882-3313. FAX 604-822-8928.
circ. 120,000. *1939*

AMATEUR ATHLETE.
Eliot Wineberg, Ed. & Pub., 7840 N. Lincoln Ave., Skokie, IL 60077. TEL 847-675-0200. FAX 847-675-2903.
circ. 55,000. *6748*

AMATEUR DANCERS.
United States Amateur Ballroom Dancers Association, Inc., 1427 Gibsonwood Rd., Baltimore, MD 21228. TEL 410-747-7855. FAX 410-747-7955.
circ. 13,667. *2290*

AMATEUR THEATRE YEARBOOK.
Platform Publications Ltd., 83 George St., London W1H 5PL, England. TEL 44-171-486-1732. FAX 44-171-224-2215.
circ. 2,000. *7001*

AMBULATORY PEDIATRIC ASSOCIATION. NEWSLETTER.
Ambulatory Pediatric Association, Department of Pediatrics, c/o Dr. Paul Darden II, Dept. of Pediatrics, MUSC, 171 Ashley Ave., Charleston, SC 29425-0793. TEL 803-792-2979. FAX 803-792-2588.
circ. 1,500. *5027*

AMERICA COOPERATIVA.
Organization of the Cooperatives of America, Carrera 11 No. 86-32 Ofc. 101, 241263 Bogota, D.E., Colombia. TEL 2181295. FAX 057-1-610-19-12.
circ. 5,000. *1204*

AMERICAN.
American University, Office of University Publications, Washington, DC 20016-8121. TEL 202-885-5970. FAX 202-885-5949.
circ. 65,000. *1939*

AMERICAN ACADEMY OF CLINICAL SEXOLOGISTS. BULLETIN.
American Academy of Clinical Sexologists, 1929 18th St., N.W., Ste. 1166, Washington, DC 20008. FAX 407-628-5293.
circ. 1,000. *5050*

AMERICAN ACADEMY OF ORTHOPAEDIC SURGEONS. BULLETIN.
American Academy of Orthopaedic Surgeons, 6300 N. River Rd., Rosemont, IL 60018. TEL 847-384-4130. FAX 847-823-8033.
circ. 25,000. *5003*

AMERICAN ACADEMY OF OSTEOPATHY YEARBOOK.
American Academy of Osteopathy, 3500 DePauw Blvd., Ste. 1080, Indianapolis, IN 46268-1136. TEL 317-879-1881. FAX 317-879-0563.
circ. 1,600. *4826*

AMERICAN ASSOCIATION OF BIOANALYSTS. PROFICIENCY TESTING SERVICE. TEST OF THE MONTH.
American Association of Bioanalysts, 917 Locust St., Ste. 1100, St. Louis, MO 63101-1413. TEL 314-241-1445.
circ. 4,500. *4894*

AMERICAN ASSOCIATION OF DENTAL EDITORS. NEWSLETTER.
American Association of Dental Editors, 1100 Lake St., Ste. 240, Oak Park, IL 60301. TEL 708-445-0322. FAX 708-445-0321.
circ. 325. *3868*

AMERICAN ASSOCIATION OF DENTAL EXAMINERS. BOARD BULLETIN.
American Association of Dental Examiners, 211 E. Chicago Ave., Ste. 760, Chicago, IL 60611. TEL 312-440-7464. FAX 312-440-3525.
circ. 1,100. *4849*

AMERICAN ASSOCIATION OF STATE HIGHWAY AND TRANSPORTATION OFFICIALS. SUB-COMMITTEE ON COMPUTER TECHNOLOGY. NATIONAL CONFERENCE. PROCEEDINGS.
American Association of State Highway and Transportation Officials, 444 N. Capitol St., N.W., Ste. 225, Washington, DC 20001. TEL 202-624-5800. FAX 202-624-5806. *7123*

AMERICAN ASSOCIATION OF TISSUE BANKS NEWSLETTER.
American Association of Tissue Banks, 1350 Beverly Rd., Ste. 220A, McLean, VA 22101. TEL 703-827-9582. FAX 703-356-2198.
circ. 1,000. *4635*

AMERICAN ASSOCIATION OF WOMEN DENTISTS. CHRONICLE.
American Association of Women Dentists, 401 N. Michigan Ave., Chicago, IL 60611-4267. TEL 312-644-6610. FAX 312-527-6640.
circ. 2,200. *4849*

AMERICAN BIBLE SOCIETY RECORD.
American Bible Society, 1865 Broadway, New York, NY 10023. TEL 212-408-1344. FAX 212-408-1456.
circ. 240,000. *6319*

AMERICAN BICYCLIST.
Willow Publishing, 400 Skokie Blvd., Northbrook, IL 60062-2816. TEL 847-291-1117. FAX 847-559-4444.
circ. 12,500. *6823*

AMERICAN BIG TWIN DEALER.
Advanstar Communications, Inc. (Santa Ana), 201 Sandpointe Ave., Ste. 600, Santa Ana, CA 92707-5761. TEL 714-513-8400. FAX 714-513-8414.
circ. 6,000. *6823*

AMERICAN BIOTECHNOLOGY LABORATORY.
International Scientific Communications, Inc., 30 Controls Dr., Box 870, Shelton, CT 06484-0870. TEL 203-926-9300. FAX 203-926-9310.
circ. 70,016. *677*

AMERICAN BREWERIANA JOURNAL.
American Breweriana Association, Inc., Box 11157, Pueblo, CO 81001. TEL 719-544-9267.
circ. 3,300. *3662*

AMERICAN BRUSSELS GRIFFON ASSOCIATION. BULLETIN.
American Brussels Griffon Association, c/o Mrs. Ann Catterson, Ed., 8004 Santa Rita St., Corona, CA 91719. FAX 818-444-3063.
circ. 120. *5633*

AMERICAN BUILDER MAGAZINE.
Transcontinental Publishing Inc., Box 45454, Phoenix, AZ 85064-5454. TEL 602-331-8900. FAX 602-331-8448. *861*

AMERICAN CLINICAL LABORATORY.
International Scientific Communications, Inc., 30 Controls Dr., Box 870, Shelton, CT 06484-0870. TEL 203-926-9300. FAX 203-926-9310.
circ. 62,050. *4894*

AMERICAN COLLEGE OF CARDIOLOGY SCIENTIFIC SESSION NEWS.
American College of Cardiology, 9111 Old Georgetown Rd., Bethesda, MD 20814. TEL 301-897-5400. FAX 301-897-9745.
circ. 41,000. *4809*

AMERICAN COLLEGE OF SURGEONS. BULLETIN.
American College of Surgeons, Communications Department, 55 E. Erie St., Chicago, IL 60611-2797. TEL 312-664-4050. FAX 312-440-7014.
circ. 67,257. *5134*

AMERICAN COMPOSERS ALLIANCE BULLETIN.
American Composers Alliance, 170 W. 74th St., New York, NY 10023. TEL 212-362-8900. FAX 212-362-8902. *5371*

AMERICAN CONTRACT BRIDGE LEAGUE. BULLETIN.
American Contract Bridge League, 2990 Airways Blvd., Memphis, TN 38116-3847. TEL 901-332-5586. FAX 901-398-7754.
circ. 147,050. *6748*

AMERICAN CONTRACTOR.
Transcontinental Publishing Inc., Box 45454, Phoenix, AZ 85064-5454. TEL 602-331-8900. FAX 602-331-8448. *861*

THE AMERICAN DREAM.
Yorktown Publishing, 125 Union Pl., Lynbrook, NY 11563-4116. TEL 914-962-2565.
circ. 11,350. *3852*

AMERICAN DROP-SHIPPERS DIRECTORY.
World Wide Trade Service, Box 283, Medina, WA 98039.
circ. 8,500. *1514*

AMERICAN ECONOMIC DEVELOPMENT COUNCIL. COUNCIL NEWS.
American Economic Development Council, 9801 W. Higgins, Ste. 540, Rosemont, IL 60018-4726. TEL 847-692-9944. FAX 847-696-2990.
circ. 2,700. *1220*

AMERICAN FAMILY PHYSICIAN.
American Academy of Family Physicians, 8880 Ward Pkwy., Kansas City, MO 64114. TEL 816-333-9700. FAX 816-333-0303.
circ. 150,000. *4635*

AMERICAN FOREIGN LAW ASSOCIATION NEWSLETTER.
American Foreign Law Association, c/o James R. Maxeiner, Ed., 111 White Plains Post Rd., Bronxville, NY 10708.
circ. 600. *4104*

AMERICAN FROZEN FOOD INSTITUTE. MEMBERSHIP DIRECTORY AND BUYER'S GUIDE.
American Frozen Food Institute, 2000 Corporate Ridge, Ste. 1000, McLean, VA 22102. TEL 703-821-0770. FAX 703-821-1350.
circ. 3,500. *3096*

AMERICAN INDIAN REPORT.
Falmouth Institute, Inc., 3702 Pender Dr., Ste. 300, Fairfax, VA 22030-6066. TEL 703-641-9100. FAX 703-641-1558.
circ. 7,000. *2996*

10296 CONTROLLED CIRCULATION SERIALS

AMERICAN INSTITUTE FOR CANCER RESEARCH NEWSLETTER.
American Institute for Cancer Research (AICR), 1759 R St., N.W., Washington, DC 20009. TEL 202-328-7744. FAX 202-328-7226.
circ. 1,500,000. *4970*

AMERICAN INSTITUTE OF PHYSICS. CENTER FOR HISTORY OF PHYSICS. NEWSLETTER.
American Institute of Physics, Center for History of Physics, One Physics Ellipse, College Park, MD 20740. TEL 301-209-3165. FAX 301-209-0882.
circ. 6,000. *5796*

THE AMERICAN JOURNAL OF ANESTHESIOLOGY.
Quadrant HealthCom, 105 Raider Blvd., Belle Mead, NJ 08502-1510. TEL 908-874-0707. FAX 908-874-5611.
circ. 18,045. *4802*

AMERICAN LABORATORY.
International Scientific Communications, Inc., 30 Controls Dr., Box 870, Shelton, CT 06484-0870. TEL 203-926-9300. FAX 203-926-9310.
circ. 135,000. *1787*

AMERICAN LEGACY.
American Heritage, 60 Fifth Ave., New York, NY 10011. TEL 212-620-1833. FAX 212-620-2332.
circ. 515,000. *2996*

AMERICAN LUTHERIE.
Guild of American Luthiers, 8222 S. Park, Tacoma, WA 98408. TEL 206-472-7853.
circ. 3,000. *5371*

AMERICAN MACHINIST.
Penton Publishing Co., 1100 Superior Ave., Cleveland, OH 44114-2543. TEL 216-696-7000. FAX 216-696-0177.
circ. 82,000. *1578*

AMERICAN NOTARY.
American Society of Notaries, Box 5707, Tallhassee, FL 32314-5707. TEL 904-671-5164. FAX 904-671-5165.
circ. 22,000. *3910*

AMERICAN PRINTER.
Intertec Publishing Corp. (Overland Park), 9800 Metcalf Ave., Overland Park, KS 66202. TEL 312-726-2802. FAX 312-726-3091.
circ. 87,780. *6074*

AMERICAN RED ANGUS.
Red Angus Association of America, 4201 I-35 North, Denton, TX 76207. TEL 817-387-3502. FAX 817-383-4036.
circ. 8,000. *268*

AMERICAN ROMANIAN ACADEMY OF ARTS AND SCIENCES. JOURNAL.
A R A Publications, Department of French and Italian, University of California, Sproul Hall, Davis, CA 95616. TEL 916-758-7720.
circ. 400. *2531*

AMERICAN SMALL FARM.
Magnet Communications, Inc., 21822 Sherman Way, Ste. 200, Canoga Park, CA 91303-1942. TEL 818-727-2236. FAX 818-727-1358.
circ. 65,000. *98*

AMERICAN TOWMAN.
American Towman Network, 246 Third Ave., Westwood, NJ 07675-2106. TEL 201-612-1300.
circ. 15,900. *7082*

AMERICAN TRUST FOR THE BRITISH LIBRARY. NEWSLETTER.
British Library, Humanities and Social Sciences, Great Russell St., London WC1B 3DG, England. TEL 44-171-412-7538. FAX 44-171-412-7563.
4158

AMERICA'S DRIVING FORCE.
American Graphics Group, LLC, 1709 Hillyer Robinson Pkwy., Oxford, AL 36203. TEL 205-236-3788. FAX 205-236-3756.
circ. 175,000. *7172*

AMERON NEWS.
Ameron, 245 S. Los Robles Ave., Pasadena, CA 91101. FAX 818-683-4060.
circ. 10,000. *6954*

AMI DES JARDINS ET DE LA MAISON.
Bayard Presse, 3 rue Bayard, 75393 Paris Cedex 08, France. TEL 33-1-44356060. FAX 33-1-44356091.
circ. 153,809. *3181*

AMICI.
American Friends of the Vatican Library, 157 Lakeshore Rd., Grosse Pointe Farms, MI 48236. TEL 313-885-8855.
circ. 1,500. *6449*

AMITYVILLE HISTORICAL SOCIETY DISPATCH.
Amityville Historical Society, Box 764, Amityville, NY 11701. TEL 516-598-1486.
circ. 500. *3616*

AMOCO ROADSMART.
Aegis Group - Publishers, 30400 Van Dyke Ave., Warren, MI 48093. TEL 810-574-9100.
circ. 1,000,000. *7184*

AMOCO TRAVELER.
Amoco Enterprises, Inc., 200 E. Randolph Dr., Chicago, IL 60601. TEL 212-303-6987. FAX 312-856-2379.
circ. 75,000. *7184*

AN PHOBLACHT.
58 Parnell Sq., Dublin 1, Ireland. TEL 01-8733839. FAX 01-8733074.
circ. 30,000. *3322*

ANAIS HIDROGRAFICOS.
Ministerio da Marinha, Diretoria de Hidrografia e Navegacao, Rio de Janeiro, Brazil. *7287*

ANALECTA VATICANO-BELGICA. DEUXIEME SERIE. SECTION A: NONCIATURE DE FLANDRE.
N.V. Brepols, Steenweg op Tielen 68, 2300 Turnhout, Belgium. TEL 32-14-402500. FAX 32-14-428919. *6450*

ANALECTA VATICANO-BELGICA. DEUXIEME SERIE. SECTION B: NONCIATURE DE COLOGNE.
N.V. Brepols, Steenweg op Tielen 68, 2300 Turnhout, Belgium. TEL 32-14-402500. FAX 32-14-428919. *6450*

ANALECTA VATICANO-BELGICA. DEUXIEME SERIE. SECTION C: NONCIATURE DE BRUXELLES.
N.V. Brepols, Steenweg op Tielen 68, 2300 Turnhout, Belgium. TEL 32-14-402500. FAX 32-14-428919. *6450*

ANALECTA VATICANO-BELGICA. PREMIERE SERIE: DOCUMENTS RELATIFS AUX ANCIENS DIOCESES DE CAMBRAI, LIEGE, THEROUANNE ET TOURNAI.
N.V. Brepols, Steenweg op Tielen 68, 2300 Turnhout, Belgium. TEL 32-14-402500. FAX 32-14-428919. *6450*

ANALES DE LA LEGISLACION ARGENTINA.
Ediciones la Ley S.A., 1471 Tucuman, 1050 Buenos Aires, Argentina. TEL 541-495481. FAX 541-4760953.
circ. 11,000. *3910*

ANALOG DIALOGUE.
Analog Devices, Inc., 1 Technology Way, Box 9106, Norwood, MA 02062-9106. TEL 617-461-3392. FAX 617-326-8703.
circ. 100,000. *2114*

ANALYSE.
Nederlandse Vereniging van BioMedische Laboratoriummedewerkers, Wilhelminapark 52, 3581 NM Utrecht, Netherlands. TEL 31-30-2522881. FAX 31-30-2541814.
circ. 3,500. *4894*

ANDAR PER CERAMICHE NEL MONDO.
Via Statutaria 46-C, 42013 Casalgrande, Reggio Emilia, Italy. TEL 0522-846239. FAX 0522-841063.
circ. 8,000. *1725*

ANDEAN PAST.
Cornell University, Latin American Studies Program, Ithaca, NY 14853. TEL 607-255-2245. FAX 607-255-8919.
circ. 50. *348*

ANGLIA FARMER AND CONTRACTOR.
B C Publications, 16C Market Pl., Diss, Norfolk IP22 3AB, England. TEL 44-1379-644200. FAX 44-1379-650480.
circ. 7,600. *98*

ANGLO-AMERICAN FORUM.
Peter Lang GmbH Europaeischer Verlag der Wissenschaften, Eschborner Landstr. 42-50, 60489 Frankfurt a.M., Germany. TEL 49-69-7807050. FAX 49-69-78070550.
circ. 200. *4375*

ANGLO-NORDIC TIMES INTERNATIONAL.
Peregrine Publishing & Trojan Graphics Co. Ltd., Yorksville, 86A Kingsley Park Terrace, Kingsley Park, Northampton, Northants NN2 7HJ, England. TEL 44-1604-713777. FAX 44-1604-717999.
circ. 5,300. *1314*

ANGOLA. SECRETARIA PROVINCIAL DE SAUDE, TRABALHO. PREVIDENCIA E ASSISTENCIA. SINTESE DA ACTIVIDADE DOS SERVICOS E ORGANISMOS.
Secretaria Provincial de Saude, Trabalho, Previdencia e Assistencia, Luanda, Angola. *6228*

ANIMALDOM.
Pennsylvania S.P.C.A., 350 E. Erie Ave., Philadelphia, PA 19134. TEL 215-426-6300.
circ. 42,000. *5633*

ANIMALS' VOICE.
Ontario S P C A, 16640 Yonge St., Newmarket, ON L3Y 4V8, Canada. TEL 905-898-7122. FAX 905-853-8643.
circ. 50,000. *301*

ANNALI ITALIANI DI DERMATOLOGIA CLINICA E SPERIMENTALE.
Pensiero Scientifico Editore s.r.l., Via Bradano 3-C, 00199 Rome, Italy. TEL 06-86207158. FAX 06-86207160.
circ. 1,200. *4875*

ANNALS OF OPHTHALMOLOGY - GLAUCOMA.
American Society of Contemporary Medicine, Surgery, and Ophthalmology, 4711 Golf Rd., Ste. 408, Skokie, IL 60076-1242. TEL 847-568-1500. FAX 847-568-1527.
circ. 1,800. *4990*

ANNALS OF SAUDI MEDICINE.
King Faisal Specialist Hospital and Research Centre, P.O. Box 3354, Riyadh 11211, Saudi Arabia. TEL 966-1-4647272. FAX 966-1-4427237.
circ. 17,000. *4638*

ANNUAIRE DE L'AFRIQUE DU NORD.
C N R S Editions, 20-22 rue St. Amand, 75015 Paris, France. FAX 45-33-92-13.
circ. 1,500. *6603*

ANNUAIRE DE L'ALIMENTATION ANIMALE.
Gedeon Marketing Eurl, B.P. 16, 29560 Telgruc-sur-Mer, France. TEL 33-2-98273766. FAX 33-2-98273765.
circ. 2,500. *260*

ANNUAIRE DE LEGISLATION FRANCAISE ET ETRANGERE.
C N R S Editions, 20-22 rue St. Amand, 75105 Paris, France. TEL 45-33-16-00. FAX 45-33-92-13.
circ. 1,250. *3911*

ANNUAIRE FRANCAIS DE DROIT INTERNATIONAL.
C N R S Editions, 20-22 rue St. Amand, 75015 Paris, France. TEL 45-33-16-00. FAX 45-33-92-13.
circ. 1,500. *4105*

ANNUAL AUSTRALIAN NOTICES TO MARINERS.
Hydrographic Office R A N, Locked Bag 8801, Wollongong, N.S.W. 2521. FAX 61-42-218599.
circ. 3,200. *7145*

ANNUAL EDUCATIONAL SUMMARY, NEW YORK STATE.
Education Department, Information, Reporting & Technology Services, Education Bldg. Annex, Rm. 962, Albany, NY 12234. TEL 518-474-7082. FAX 518-474-4351. *2421*

ANNUAL NEW MEXICO WATER CONFERENCE. PROCEEDINGS.
New Mexico Water Resources Research Institute, Box 30001, Dept. 3167, New Mexico State University, Las Cruces, NM 88003-0001. TEL 505-646-4337. FAX 505-646-6418.
circ. 500. *7287*

CONTROLLED CIRCULATION SERIALS   10297

ANNUAL SUMMARY OF PROGRESS IN GRAVITATION SCIENCES.
Minas Ensanian Corporation, Box 98, Eldred, PA 16731. TEL 814-225-3296.
circ. 100. *5797*

ANRITSU TECHNICAL BULLETIN.
Anritsu Corporation, 10-27, Minamiazabu 5-chome, Minato-ku, Tokyo 106, Japan.
circ. 5,000. *2808*

ANTIK & AUKTION.
Aller Specialtidningar AB, Landskronavaegen 23, S-251 85 Helsingborg, Sweden. TEL 46-42-173500. FAX 46-42-173600.
circ. 50,600. *336*

ANTIOCH NEW ENGLAND NOTES.
Antioch New England Graduate School, 40 Avon St., Keene, NH 03431-3516. TEL 603-357-3122. FAX 603-357-0718.
circ. 6,800. *2531*

ANTIQUES AND ART AROUND FLORIDA.
Antiques and Art Around Publishing, Inc., Box 2481, Fort Lauderdale, FL 33303-2481. TEL 954-768-9430. FAX 954-768-0621.
circ. 60,000. *337*

ANTIQUES & COLLECTIBLES MAGAZINE.
Antiques & Collectibles, Inc., Box 33, Westbury, NY 11590. TEL 516-334-9650. FAX 516-334-5740.
circ. 5,000. *337*

ANTIQUES FOLIO.
Antiques & General Advertising, 24 Comely Bank, Edinburgh EH14 1AL, Scotland. TEL 44-131-332-4481.
circ. 5,000. *337*

ANTITRUST LAW NEWSLETTER.
Illinois State Bar Association, Illinois Bar Center, Springfield, IL 62701. TEL 217-525-1760. FAX 217-525-0712.
circ. 350. *3911*

ANUARIO INDIGENISTA.
Instituto Indigenista Interamericano, Apdo. Postal 20315, 01001 Mexico DF, Mexico. TEL 525-5680819. FAX 525-6521274. *310*

APARTMENT OWNER.
Apartment Association, 14550 Archwood St., Van Nuys, CA 91405. TEL 818-374-3240. FAX 818-781-6018.
circ. 3,000. *6294*

L'APICOLTORE MODERNO.
Universita di Torino, Osservatorio di Apicoltura, Via Leonardo da Vinci 44, 10095 Grugliasco TO, Italy. TEL 39-11-4033893. FAX 39-11-4033894.
circ. 1,500. *99*

APOGEE.
High Point College, High Point, NC 27262. TEL 919-841-9000.
circ. 400. *4376*

APOTEKSASSISTENTEN.
Danske Apotekstekenikeres Forening, Skt. Peders Str. 36, DK-1453 Copenhagen K, Denmark. TEL 45-33-12-06-00. FAX 45-33-14-06-66.
circ. 6,269. *5647*

APOTHECARY.
Health Care Marketing Services, H C M S Inc., Box AP, Los Altos, CA 94023-0179. TEL 415-941-3955. FAX 415-941-2303.
circ. 65,000. *5647*

APOTHEEKMANAGEMENT.
Mediselect B.V., Postbus 28091, 3828 ZH Hoogland, Netherlands. TEL 31-33-4808020. FAX 31-33-4805881.
circ. 2,300. *5647*

APPAREL INDUSTRY.
Yaffa Publishing Group, 17-21 Bellevue St., Surry Hills, N.S.W. 2010, Australia. TEL 61-2-92812333. FAX 61-2-92812750.
circ. 3,367. *1912*

APPAREL INDUSTRY MAGAZINE.
Shore-Varrone, Inc., 6255 Barfield Rd. N.E., Ste. 200, Atlanta, GA 30328-4300. TEL 404-252-8831. FAX 404-252-4436.
circ. 18,600. *1912*

APPLELAND BULLETIN.
Wenatchee Area Genealogical Society, Box 5280, Wenatchee, WA 98807-5280. TEL 509-664-5989.
circ. 212. *3212*

APPLICATOR.
Sealant, Waterproofing and Restoration Institute, 2841 Main St., Kansas City, MO 64108. TEL 816-472-7974. FAX 816-472-7765.
circ. 800. *861*

APPROACH.
Takenaka Corporation, 1-13, 4-chome, Hon-machi, Chuo-ku, Osaka 541, Japan. TEL 06-252-1201. FAX 06-271-0398.
circ. 10,000. *392*

APUNTES DE INGENIERIA.
Pontificia Universidad Catolica de Chile, Escuela de Ingenieria, Casilla 306, Correo 22, Santiago, Chile. TEL 562-552-2375. FAX 562-552-4054.
circ. 1,000. *2710*

AQUATICS INTERNATIONAL.
Intertec Publishing Corp. (Atlanta), 6151 Powers Ferry Rd., N.W., Atlanta, GA 30339-2941. TEL 770-955-2500. FAX 770-955-0400.
circ. 30,120. *6749*

AQUI.
Asociacion Aqui - Avance, Casilla 10937, La Paz, Bolivia. TEL 34-35-24. FAX 35-24-55.
circ. 5,000. *3256*

AQUI (PHOENIX).
Wilcox Graphics, c/o Owens and Associates, 6530 N. 16th St., Ste. 101, Phoenix, AZ 85016-1311. TEL 602-230-2424. FAX 602-274-5130.
circ. 10,000. *2997*

AQUILO. SERIE BOTANICA.
Societas Amicorum Naturae Ouluensis, Department of Botany, University of Oulu, Linnanmaa, FIN-90570 Oulu, Finland. TEL 358-8-553-1546. FAX 358-981-553-1500.
circ. 305. *692*

L'AQUILON.
P.O. Box 1325, Yellowknife, NT X1A 2N9, Canada. TEL 403-873-6603. FAX 403-873-2158.
circ. 1,000. *3258*

AQUINIAN.
Saint Thomas University, Student Union Bldg., Rm. 32, Fredericton, NB E3B 5G3, Canada, Canada. TEL 506-460-0300. FAX 506-453-4538.
circ. 4,400. *1939*

ARAL DIREKT.
Vereinigte Verlagsanstalten GmbH, Hoeherweg 278, 40231 Duesseldorf, Germany. TEL 49-211-7357-0. FAX 49-211-7357223.
circ. 30,000. *5595*

ARAMCO WORLD.
Aramco Services Company, Box 2106, Houston, TX 77252-2106. TEL 713-423-4426. FAX 713-432-5536.
circ. 180,000. *3654*

ARBEJDSMARKEDSPOLITISK AGENDA.
Dansk Arbejdsgiverforening, 113 Vester Voldgade, DK-1790 Copenhagen V, Denmark. TEL 45-33-93-40-00. FAX 45-33-12-29-76.
circ. 4,500. *1418*

ARBETAREN.
Sveriges Arbetares Centralorganisation, P.O. Box 6507, S-113 83 Stockholm, Sweden. TEL 46-8-16-08-90. FAX 46-8-673-03-45.
circ. 3,000. *3361*

ARBETSLEDAREN.
Sveriges Arbetsledarefoerbund (SALF), P.O. Box 12069, 102 22 Stockholm 12, Sweden. FAX 08-539968.
circ. 93,000. *3886*

ARBITRO.
Federazione Italiana Giuoco Calcio, Via Gregorio Allegri 14, 00198 Rome, Italy.
circ. 20,000. *6798*

ARCHAEOLOGICAL REPORTS (DURHAM).
University of Durham, Department of Archaeology, South Rd., Durham DH1 3LE, England. FAX 44-191-374-3719.
circ. 200. *349*

ARCHAEOLOGICAL REVIEW FROM CAMBRIDGE.
c/o Department of Archaeology, Downing St., Cambridge CB2 3D2, England. TEL 44-1223-333520. FAX 44-1223-333503.
circ. 200. *350*

ARCHAEONAUTICA.
C N R S Editions, 20-22 rue St. Amand, 75105 Paris, France. TEL 45-33-16-00. FAX 45-33-92-13.
circ. 1,250. *351*

ARCHITECT & SPECIFIERN BUILDING.
A A A M S A, P.O. Box 15852, Verwoerdburg 0140, South Africa.
circ. 7,000. *862*

ARCHITECT, BUILDER, CONTRACTOR & DEVELOPER.
Ascent Publishing Ltd., 91-93 High St., Bromsgrove, Worcs. B61 8AQ, England. TEL 44-1527-836600. FAX 44-1527-574388.
circ. 24,344. *862*

ARCHITECTS CATALOG.
Architects Catalog, Inc., 1305 Post Rd., Ste. 305, Fairfield, CT 06430-6016. TEL 203-256-1600. FAX 203-254-8166.
circ. 40,000. *1652*

ARCHITECTS' GUIDE TO GLASS, METAL & GLAZING.
U S Glass Publications, Inc., Box 569, Garrisonville, VA 22463. TEL 540-720-5584. FAX 540-720-5687.
circ. 21,000. *393*

ARCHITECTURAL LIGHTING.
Miller Freeman Inc. (New York), One Penn Plaza, New York, NY 10119. TEL 212-714-1300. FAX 212-714-1313.
circ. 35,000. *394*

ARCHITECTURAL SPECIFIER.
Century Communications Corp., 6201 Howard St., Niles, IL 60714. TEL 847-647-1200. FAX 847-649-7055.
circ. 25,000. *394*

ARCHIV FUER STENOGRAFIE, TEXTVERARBEITUNG, BUEROTECHNIK.
Forschungs- und Ausbildungsstaette fuer Kurzschrift und Maschinenschreiben in Bayreuth e.V., Bernecker Str. 11, 95448 Bayreuth, Germany. TEL 49-921-23445. FAX 49-921-23445.
circ. 400. *2594*

ARCHIVES HERALDIQUES SUISSES.
Societe Suisse d'Heraldique, c/o Dr. Guenter Mattern, Ed., Sichternstr. 35, CH-4410 Liestal, Switzerland. TEL 41-61-921-16-44. FAX 41-61-921-10-81.
circ. 800. *3212*

ARCHIVES OF HISTOLOGY AND CYTOLOGY.
Japan Society of Histological Documentation, c/o Department of Anatomy, Niigata University School of Medicine, Asahimachi, Niigata, Japan. FAX 025-224-1767.
circ. 700. *736*

ARCHIVES OF NATURAL HISTORY.
Society for the History of Natural History, c/o The Natural History Museum, Cromwell Rd., London SW7 5BD, England.
circ. 850. *6512*

ARCHIVES PARLEMENTAIRES DE 1787 A 1860.
C N R S Editions, 20-22 rue St. Amand, 75015 Paris, France. TEL 45-33-16-00. FAX 45-33-92-13.
circ. 1,500. *5892*

ARCHIVES SOCIETY OF ALBERTA. NEWSLETTER.
Archives Society of Alberta, P.O. Box 21080, Dominion Postal Outlet, Calgary, AB T2P 4H5, Canada. FAX 403-244-5173.
circ. 300. *4159*

ARCHIVOS ARGENTINOS DE DERMATOLOGIA.
Parana 731 2o. A, 1017 Buenos Aires, Argentina. TEL 54-1-3732458.
circ. 1,600. *4875*

ARENA (EDINBURGH).
Scottish Sports Council, Caledonia House, South Gyle, Edinburgh EH12 9DQ, Scotland. TEL 0131-317-7200. FAX 0131-317-7202.
circ. 2,000. *6749*

CONTROLLED CIRCULATION SERIALS

ARENA DI POLA.
Libero Comune di Pola in Esilio, Via Mazzini 7, 34170 Gorizia, Italy. TEL 39-481-533911.
circ. 3,500. *3325*

ARGUS (SAN FRANCISCO).
American Academy of Ophthalmology, Box 7424, San Francisco, CA 94120-7424. TEL 415-561-8500. FAX 415-561-8567.
circ. 21,000. *4990*

ARGUS DES METAUX.
Editions Montmartre, 142 rue Momtmartre, 75002 Paris, France. TEL 33-1-40268321. FAX 33-1-40399752.
circ. 300. *5186*

ARI.
Nihon Arirui Kenkyukai, c/o Shiraume Gakuen Tanki Daigaku, 1-830, Ogawa-cho, Kodaira-shi, Tokyo 187, Japan. TEL 81-423-42-2311.
circ. 140. *747*

ARID LANDS NEWSLETTER.
University of Arizona, Office of Arid Lands Studies, 1955 E. Sixth St., Tucson, AZ 85719. TEL 520-621-8584. FAX 520-621-3816.
circ. 2,500. *2906*

ARION.
Boston University, 10 Lenox St., Brookline, MA 02146. TEL 617-353-6480. FAX 617-353-5905.
circ. 800. *1900*

ARIZONA. DEPARTMENT OF HEALTH SERVICES. ANNUAL REPORT.
Department of Health Services, 1740 W. Adams St., Phoenix, AZ 85007. TEL 602-542-1001. FAX 602-542-1062.
circ. 500. *6228*

ARIZONA A A A HIGHROADS.
Arizona Automobile Association, Box 33119, 3144 N. 7th Ave., Phoenix, AZ 85013. TEL 602-274-1116. FAX 602-277-1194.
circ. 295,000. *7184*

ARIZONA COMMISSION ON THE ARTS. REPORT TO THE GOVERNOR (YEAR).
Commission on the Arts, 417 W. Roosevelt St., Phoenix, AZ 85003. TEL 602-255-5882. FAX 602-256-0282.
circ. 1,500. *423*

ARIZONA GROCER.
Arizona Grocers Publishing Co., 120 E. Pierce, Phoenix, AZ 85004. TEL 602-252-9761. FAX 602-252-9021.
circ. 2,300. *3139*

ARIZONA PHILATELIST.
Arizona Federation of Stamp Clubs, Inc., 25050 S. Drifter Dr., Sun Lakes, AZ 85248-7717. TEL 602-802-0822.
circ. 500. *5703*

ARIZONA STATE UNIVERSITY ANTHROPOLOGICAL RESEARCH PAPERS.
Arizona State University, Department of Anthropology, Tempe, AZ 85287-2402. TEL 602-965-7596. FAX 602-965-7671.
circ. 750. *310*

THE ARK.
Rare Breeds Survival Trust, National Agricultural Centre, Kenilworth, Warwickshire CV8 2LG, England. TEL 44-1203-696551. FAX 44-1203-696706.
circ. 10,000. *2223*

ARKANSAS. AGRICULTURAL EXPERIMENT STATION. RESEARCH BULLETIN.
Agricultural Experiment Station, Agricultural Publications, 110 Agriculture Bldg., 1 University of Arkansas, Division of Agriculture, Fayetteville, AR 72701-1201. TEL 501-575-5647. FAX 501-575-7531.
circ. 1,200. *169*

ARKANSAS. EMPLOYMENT SECURITY DEPARTMENT. ANNUAL REPORT.
Department of Labor, Employment Security Department, Box 2981, Little Rock, AR 72203. TEL 501-682-3119. *5504*

ARKANSAS EPISCOPALIAN.
Episcopal Diocese of Arkansas, Box 164668, Little Rock, AR 72216-4668. TEL 501-372-2168.
circ. 8,000. *6413*

ARKANSAS OIL AND GAS STATISTICAL BULLETIN.
Oil and Gas Commission, Box 1472, El Dorado, AR 71731-1472. TEL 501-862-4965. FAX 501-862-8823.
circ. 350. *5628*

ARKITEKTUR.
Arkitektur Foerlag AB, P.O. Box 1742, S-111 87 Stockholm, Sweden. TEL 46-8-679-61-05. FAX 46-8-611-52-70.
circ. 6,200. *396*

ARMY CHAPLAINCY.
U.S. Army Chaplain Center and School, ATSC-CMT-PAO, Jackson, SC 29207. TEL 803-751-8070. FAX 803-751-3647.
circ. 6,000. *5259*

ARMY FAMILIES JOURNAL.
Method Publishing Co. Ltd., Sutherland Press House, Golspie, Sutherland KW10 6RA, Scotland. TEL 44-1408-633871. FAX 44-1408-633876.
circ. 60,000. *7313*

ARMY RESERVE MAGAZINE.
U.S. Army Reserve, 1815 N. Ft. Myer Dr., Rm. 204, Arlington, VA 22209-1805. TEL 703-696-6212. FAX 703-696 5300.
circ. 665,000. *5260*

AROGYA.
Kasturba Medical College Trust, Manipal, Department of Clinical Biochemistry, Editor - Arogyal, Manipal - 576 119, India. TEL 20060.
circ. 1,000. *5778*

AROUND & ABOUT K S U.
Kentucky State University, Office of Publicity Relations, Hume Hall, Frankfort, KY 40601. TEL 502-227-6688.
circ. 450. *1940*

ARQUIVOS DE GASTROENTEROLOGIA.
Instituto Brasileiro de Estudos e Pesquisas de Gastroenterologia, Rua Dr. Seng 320, 01331-020 Sao Paulo SP, Brazil. TEL 55-11-2882119. FAX 55-11-2892768.
circ. 5,000. *4908*

ARROWHEAD.
Society of Archer-Antiquaries, c/o Doug Elmy, 61 Lambert Rd., Bridlington, Yorks YO16 5RD, England. TEL 44-1262-601604. *6749*

ARROZ EN LAS AMERICAS.
Centro Internacional de Agricultura Tropical, Apdo. Aereo 6713, Cali, Colombia. TEL 57-2-4450000. FAX 57-2-4450073.
circ. 1,000. *260*

ARS DECORATIVA.
Iparmuveszeti Muzeum, Hopp Ferenc Keletazsiai Muveszeti Muzeum, Ulloi ut 33-37, 1091 Budapest 9, Hungary. TEL 36-1-2175222. FAX 36-1-2175838.
circ. 1,000. *5350*

ARS LYRICA: JOURNAL OF LYRICA.
Lyrica Society for Word-Music Relations, 90 Church St., Guilford, CT 06437. TEL 203-453-1503. FAX 860-832-2522.
circ. 250. *5373*

ART BUSINESS TODAY.
Fine Art Trade Guild, 16-18 Empress Pl., London SW6 1TT, England. TEL 44-171-381-6616. FAX 44-171-381-2596.
circ. 8,580. *424*

ART ISSUES.
Foundation for Advanced Critical Studies, Inc., 8721 Santa Monica Blvd., Ste. 6, W. Hollywood, CA 90069. TEL 213-876-4508. FAX 213-876-5061.
circ. 8,000. *425*

ART MATERIALS TODAY.
F & W Publications, Inc., 1507 Dana Ave., Cincinnati, OH 45207. TEL 513-531-2222. FAX 513-531-1843.
circ. 5,000. *425*

ART ON SCREEN.
Program for Art on Film, 200 Willoughby Ave., Brooklyn, NY 11205-3817.
circ. 11,000. *5323*

ART WORKERS GUILD. ANNUAL REPORT.
Art Workers Guild, 6 Queen Sq., London WC1N 3AR, England.
circ. 400. *427*

ARTEFACT.
Archaeological and Anthropological Society of Victoria, G.P.O. 328C, Melbourne, Vic. 3001, Australia. TEL 61-3-95230549.
circ. 450. *353*

ARTS ALIVE!
Admar Associates - Theatrical Faces Inc., 548 N. New St., Bethlehem, PA 18018. TEL 215-758-8211. FAX 215-691-0234.
circ. 15,000. *7002*

ARTS & LEISURE TIMES.
Kevin Browne, Ed. & Pub., 2446 E. 65th St., Brooklyn, NY 11234. TEL 718-763-7034. FAX 718-763-7035.
circ. 212,000. *4147*

ARTS EN AUTO.
Wegener Tijdschriften Groep B.V., Postbus 1860, 1110 CD Diemen, Netherlands. TEL 31-20-6603422. FAX 31-20-6005850.
circ. 61,650. *7082*

ARTS ET INDUSTRIES.
Societe des Anciens Eleves de l'Ecole Nationale Superieure des Arts et Industries de Strasbourg, 56 bd. d'Anvers, 67000 Strasbourg, France. TEL 33-3-88604571. FAX 33-3-88606702.
circ. 3,000. *2711*

ARTWORKER.
Queensland Artworkers Alliance Inc., 497 Adelaide St., Brisbane, Qld., 4000, Australia. TEL 61-7-38322230. FAX 61-7-38322231.
circ. 1,000. *430*

ARZTRECHT.
Verlag fuer Arztrecht, Schinnrainstr. 15, 76227 Karlshue, Germany. TEL 0721-402904. *4641*

ASAHI EVENING NEWS.
Asahi Shimbun Publishing Co., 5-3-2, Tsukiji, Chuo-ku, Tokyo 104-11, Japan. TEL 03-5540-7641. FAX 03-3542-6172.
circ. 38,800. *3329*

ASBESTOS WORKER.
International Association of Asbestos Workers, Machinists Bldg., 1776 Massachusetts Ave. N.W., Ste. 301, Washington, DC 20036. TEL 202-785-2388. *3887*

ASEGURADORES.
Colegios de Mediadores de Seguros Titulados, Consejo General, Nunez de Balboa 116, 28006 Madrid, Spain. TEL 34-1-5622703. FAX 34-1-5622702.
circ. 18,439. *3807*

ASEPSIS.
Ad-Com Inc. Publishing, 2003 E. Lamar Blvd., Arlington, TX 76006. FAX 817-261-1399.
circ. 30,000. *4642*

ASHEVILLE REPORT.
Asheville Area Chamber of Commerce, Box 1010, Asheville, NC 28802. TEL 704-258-6131. FAX 704-251-0926.
circ. 2,500. *1178*

ASIA PACIFIC CHEMICALS.
Reed Business Information, Quadrant House, The Quadrant, Sutton, Surrey SM2 5AS, England. TEL 44-181-652-8146. FAX 44-181-652-8918.
circ. 7,514. *1739*

ASIA - PACIFIC FISHERY COMMISSION. REPORT.
Asia - Pacific Fishery Commission, c/o Secretary, F A O Regional Office for Asia and the Pacific, Maliwan Mansion, 39 Phra Athit Rd., Bangkok 10200, Thailand. FAX 662-2800-445.
circ. 1,000. *3062*

ASIA PACIFIC FOODSERVICE PRODUCT NEWS.
Young - Conway Publications, 1101 Richmond Ave., Ste. 201, Point Pleasant Beach, NJ 08742-3049.
circ. 47,724. *3723*

ASIA - PACIFIC I.T. TIMES.
R M Technology Media Pte. Ltd., 1 North Bridge Rd., 24-06 High St. Ctr., Singapore 0617, Singapore. TEL 65-3340393. FAX 65-3343097. circ. 21,468. *2153*

ASIA - PACIFIC SATELLITE.
Icom Publications Ltd., Chancery House, St. Nicholas Way, Sutton, Surrey SM1 1JB, England. TEL 44-181-642-1117. FAX 44-181-642-1941. circ. 7,503. *2043*

ASIA TRAVEL TRADE.
Eastern Publishing Ltd., 87-88 Amoy St., 3rd Fl., Singapore 069906, Singapore. TEL 65-220-0552. FAX 65-226-6096. *7184*

ASIAN ADVERTISING AND MARKETING.
Travel & Trade Publishing (Asia) Ltd., 3201 Bank of America, Central, Hong Kong, People's Republic of China. TEL 890-30677. FAX 895-2378. *31*

ASIAN AND PACIFIC COUNCIL. FOOD AND FERTILIZER TECHNOLOGY CENTER. EXTENSION - TECHNICAL BULLETIN.
Asian and Pacific Council, Food and Fertilizer Technology Center, 14 Wenchow St., 5th Fl., Taipei, Taiwan, Republic of China. FAX 02-362-0478. circ. 4,300. *100*

ASIAN AVIATION.
Asian Aviation Publications Pte. Ltd., 2 Leng Kee Rd., No. 04-01, Thye Hong Centre, Singapore 159086, Singapore. TEL 65-474-7088. FAX 65-479-6668. circ. 10,951. *57*

ASIAN ELECTRICITY.
Reed Business Information, Quadrant House, The Quadrant, Sutton, Surrey SM2 5AS, England. TEL 44-181-652-8773. FAX 44-181-652-8986. circ. 6,567. *2809*

ASIAN HOSPITAL.
Health Asia Communications, Ltd., G.P.O. Box 1099, Hong Kong, People's Republic of China. TEL 852-2869-4933. FAX 852-2525-6086. circ. 38,361. *3703*

ASIAN JOURNAL OF SURGERY.
Asian Surgical Association, Queen Mary Hospital, Hong Kong, People's Republic of China. TEL 852-2855-4621. FAX 852-2855-9950. circ. 1,800. *5136*

ASIAN MANAGER.
Asian Institute of Management, Joseph McMicking Campus, 123 Paseo de Roxas, Makati, Metro Manila, Philippines. TEL 63-2-892-4011. FAX 63-2-817-9240. circ. 22,850. *1465*

ASIAN MEETINGS AND INCENTIVES.
Travel & Trade Publishing (Asia) Ltd., 3201 Bank of America, Central, Hong Kong, People's Republic of China. TEL 890-3067. FAX 895-2378. circ. 12,000. *5167*

ASIAN PLASTICS NEWS.
E M A P Maclaren Ltd., 19 Scarbrook Rd., Croydon, Surrey CR9 1QH, England. TEL 0181-688-7788. FAX 0181-668-8375. circ. 9,877. *5876*

ASIAN POWER.
Icom Publications Ltd., Chancery House, St. Nicholas Way, Sutton, Surrey SM1 1JB, England. TEL 44-181-642-1117. FAX 44-181-642-1941. circ. 8,572. *2809*

ASIAN TRADER.
Asian Trade Publications Ltd., Garavi Gujarat House, 1-2 Silex St., London SE1 0DW, England. TEL 44-171-928-1234. FAX 44-171-261-0055. circ. 45,713. *1653*

ASPHALT.
Asphalt Institute, Box 14052, Lexington, KY 40512-4052. FAX 606-288-4999. circ. 16,000. *7136*

ASPHALT CONTRACTOR.
Group III Communications, 204 W. Kansas Ave., No. 103, Independence, MO 64050-3714. TEL 816-254-8735. FAX 816-254-2128. circ. 10,000. *862*

ASSISTANT LIBRARIAN.
Association of Assistant Librarians, c/o 7 Ridgmount St., London VC1E 7AE, England. TEL 44-1553-772568. circ. 10,500. *4161*

ASSOCIACAO PAULISTA DE CIRURGIOES DENTISTAS. JOURNAL.
Associacao Paulista de Cirurgioes Dentistas, Rua Humaita 389, 01321 Sao Paulo, SP, Brazil. circ. 23,500. *4851*

ASSOCIATED ACCOUNTING FIRMS INTERNATIONAL NEWSLETTER.
Associated Accounting Firms International, 1000 Connecticut Ave., N.W. , Ste. 1006, Washington, DC 20036-5302. TEL 202-463-7900. FAX 202-296-0741. circ. 3,500. *1083*

ASSOCIATED SCIENTIFIC AND TECHNICAL SOCIETIES OF SOUTH AFRICA. ANNUAL PROCEEDINGS.
Associated Scientific and Technical Societies of South Africa, P.O. Box 93480, Yeoville 2143, South Africa. TEL 27-11-4871512. FAX 27-11-6481876. *6513*

ASSOCIATION FOR PSYCHOANALYTIC MEDICINE. BULLETIN.
Association for Psychoanalytic Medicine, 252 W. 85 St., New York, NY 10024. TEL 212-595-7441. circ. 1,500. *6095*

ASSOCIATION NATIONALE DES COMMUNAUTES EDUCATIVES. BULLETIN HEBDOMADAIRE D'INFORMATIONS.
Association Nationale des Communautes Educatives, 145 bd. de Magenta, 75010 Paris, France. TEL 33-1-44635115. FAX 33-1-42855614. *2422*

ASSOCIATION NATIONALE DES COMMUNAUTES EDUCATIVES. BULLETIN MENSUEL D'INFORMATIONS.
Association Nationale des Communautes Educatives, 145 bd. de Magenta, 75010 Paris, France. TEL 33-1-44635115. FAX 33-1-42855614. *2422*

ASSOCIATION OF AMERICAN LAW SCHOOLS. NEWSLETTER.
Association of American Law Schools, 1201 Connecticut Ave., N.W., Ste. 800, Washington, DC 20036. TEL 202-296-8851. *3914*

ASSOCIATION OF AMERICAN UNIVERSITY PRESSES DIRECTORY.
Association of American University Presses, Inc., 584 Broadway, Ste. 410, New York, NY 10012. TEL 212-941-6610. *6261*

ASSOCIATION OF BEHAVIORAL HEALTH MANAGEMENT NEWSLETTER.
Association of Behavioral Health Management, 60 Revere Dr., Ste. 500, Northbrook, IL 60062. TEL 847-480-9626. circ. 1,300. *6229*

ASSOCIATION OF CARIBBEAN UNIVERSITY RESEARCH AND INSTITUTIONAL LIBRARIES. CARTA INFORMATIVA DE A C U R I L.
Association of Caribbean University Research and Institutional Libraries, Box 23317, San Juan, PR 00931. TEL 787-764-0000. FAX 787-765-5685. *4161*

ASSOCIATION OF LIFE INSURANCE MEDICAL DIRECTORS OF AMERICA. TRANSACTIONS.
Association of Life Insurance Medical Directors of America, Southeastern Head Office, Metropolitan Plaza, Tampa, FL 33607. circ. 1,000. *3808*

ASSOCIATION OF NEW BRUNSWICK LAND SURVEYORS. ANNUAL REPORT.
Association of New Brunswick Land Surveyors, 535 Beaverbrook Ct. No. 120, Fredericton, NB E3B 1X6, Canada. TEL 506-458-8266. FAX 506-458-8267. circ. 250. *6294*

ASSOCIATION OF PAEDIATRIC CHARTERED PHYSIOTHERAPISTS. JOURNAL.
Association of Paediatric Chartered Physiotherapists, 14 Bedford Row, London WC1R 4ED, England. TEL 44-171-242-1941. FAX 44-171-831-4509. circ. 1,300. *5042*

ASSOCIATION OF STEEL DISTRIBUTORS. NEWS AND VIEWS.
Association of Steel Distributors, 401 N. Michigan Ave., Chicago, IL 60611-4267. TEL 312-644-6610. FAX 312-321-6774. circ. 300. *5186*

ASSOCIAZIONE LAICA.
Endas Regionale Lazio, 238 Via Cavour, 00184 Rome, Italy. TEL 39-6-4741057. circ. 10,000. *3325*

ASSURANTIE MAGAZINE.
Samsom BedrijfsInformatie B.V., Postbus 4, 2400 MA Alphen aan den Rijn, Netherlands. TEL 31-172-466775. FAX 31-172-440681. circ. 28,393. *3808*

ASSYRIAN STAR.
Assyrian-American National Federation, c/o Jatrum Zaia, Box 192, Turlock, CA 95380. TEL 408-723-1646. circ. 1,500. *2998*

ASTROPHILE.
Space Topics Study Unit, Box 522579, Marathon Shores, FL 33052-2579. TEL 305-289-1847. circ. 1,000. *5703*

ASU HYVIN.
Kauppiaitten Kustannus Oy, Kanavakatu 3.B, FIN-00160 Helsinki, Finland. TEL 358-0-228821. circ. 29,414. *927*

AT RANDOM.
Random House, 201 E. 50th St., New York, NY 10022. TEL 212-940-7315. FAX 212-572-4949. circ. 100,000. *6261*

AT THE PARK.
Yellow Dot Publishing, Box 597783, Chicago, IL 60659-7783. TEL 773-465-4880. FAX 773-465-0084. circ. 18,000. *4147*

ATENEA.
Universidad de Puerto Rico, Faculty of Arts and Sciences, Mayaguez Campus, Mayaguez, PR 00681. FAX 787-834-3031. circ. 800. *4324*

ATHLETIC BUSINESS.
Athletic Business Publications, Inc., 1846 Hoffman St., Madison, WI 53704. TEL 608-249-0186. FAX 608-249-1153. circ. 41,452. *6749*

ATHLETIC MANAGEMENT.
College Athletic Administrator, Inc., 438 W. State St., Ithaca, NY 14850-5220. TEL 607-272-0265. FAX 607-272-2015. circ. 30,000. *2569*

ATLANTA BABY.
4330 Georgetown Sq. II, No. 506, Atlanta, GA 30338-6217. TEL 770-454-7599. FAX 770-454-7699. circ. 30,000. *1838*

ATLANTA N O W NEWS.
National Organization for Women, Atlanta Chapter, Box 8556, Atlanta, GA 30306-0556. TEL 404-523-1227. FAX 404-688-0869. circ. 700. *7313*

ATLANTA PARENT.
Atlanta Parent, Inc., 4330 Georgetown Sq., Ste. 506, Atlanta, GA 30338. TEL 770-454-7599. FAX 770-454-7699. circ. 70,000. *1838*

ATLANTA SMALL BUSINESS MONTHLY.
Media 3 Publications, Inc., 4721 Chamblee Dunwoody Rd., 100-B, Atlanta, GA 30338-6000. TEL 404-394-2811. FAX 404-394-2719. circ. 25,000. *1639*

ATLANTIC BUSINESS REPORT.
A B J Publishing Inc., 599 Main St., Ste. 203, Moncton, NB E1C 1C8, Canada. TEL 506-857-9696. FAX 506-859-7395. circ. 14,000. *7145*

ATLANTIC INFLIGHT.
Hang Gliding Association of Newfoundland, 16 Woodbine Ave., Corner Brook, NF A2H 3N8, Canada. TEL 709-785-2697. circ. 35. *58*

CONTROLLED CIRCULATION SERIALS

ATLAS HISTORIQUE DES VILLES DE FRANCE.
C N R S Editions, 20-22 rue St. Amand, 75015 Paris, France. TEL 45-33-16-00. FAX 45-33-92-13.
circ. 1,500. *3551*

ATMA JAYA RESEARCH CENTRE. SOCIO-RELIGIOUS RESEARCH REPORT.
Atma Jaya Research Centre, Jalan Jenderal Sudirman 51, P.O. Box 2639, Jakarta 10001, Indonesia. *6321*

ATOMIC DATA AND NUCLEAR DATA TABLES.
Academic Press, Inc., Journal Division, 525 B. St., Ste. 1900, San Diego, CA 92101-4495. TEL 619-230-1840. FAX 619-699-6800. *5850*

ATTUALITA ITALIA - AUSTRALIA.
Italian - Australian Chamber of Commerce, Via Barberini 86, 00187 Rome, Italy. TEL 39-6-4743565. FAX 39-6-4817813.
circ. 80,000. *1178*

AUCTUS.
Medical University of South Carolina, Office of Development, 171 Ashley Ave., Charleston, SC 29425. TEL 803-792-4275.
circ. 20,000. *1940*

AUDACITY.
Forbes, Inc., 60 Fifth Ave., New York, NY 10011. TEL 212-620-2200.
circ. 100,000. *934*

AUDIO-DIGEST GASTROENTEROLOGY.
Audio-Digest Foundation, 1577 E. Chevy Chase Dr., Glendale, CA 91206. TEL 213-245-8505. FAX 818-240-7379. *4908*

AUDIO-DIGEST INTERNAL MEDICINE.
Audio-Digest Foundation, 1577 E. Chevy Chase Dr., Glendale, CA 91206. TEL 213-245-8505. FAX 818-240-7379. *4924*

AUDIO-DIGEST OBSTETRICS - GYNECOLOGY.
Audio-Digest Foundation, 1577 E. Chevy Chase Dr., Glendale, CA 91206. TEL 213-245-8505. FAX 818-240-7379. *4953*

AUDIO-DIGEST OPHTHALMOLOGY.
Audio-Digest Foundation, 1577 E. Chevy Chase Dr., Glendale, CA 91206. TEL 213-245-8505. FAX 818-240-7379. *4990*

AUDIO-DIGEST ORTHOPAEDICS.
Audio-Digest Foundation, 1577 E. Chevy Chase Dr., Glendale, CA 91206. TEL 213-245-8505. FAX 818-240-7379. *5005*

AUDIO-DIGEST UROLOGY.
Audio-Digest Foundation, 1577 E. Chevy Chase Dr., Glendale, CA 91206. TEL 213-245-8505. FAX 818-240-7379. *5159*

AUGSBURGER ALLGEMEINE.
Presse Druck- und Verlagsgesellschaft mbH, Curt-Frenzel-Str. 2, 86167 Augsburg, Germany. TEL 49-821-777-0. FAX 49-821-704471.
circ. 368,649. *3282*

AURA WEALTH NEWSLETTER.
Aura Publishing Co., 441 Central Ave., Box 1367, Scarsdale, NY 10538. TEL 914-834-2322. FAX 914-833-0930.
circ. 300. *1222*

AURORA.
Northern Lights Library System, Postal Bag 8, Elk Point, AB T0A 1A0, Canada. TEL 403-724-2596. FAX 403-724-2597.
circ. 700. *4161*

DIE AUSLESE.
Dr. Krueger Verlag, Am Schiessberg 19, 35745 Herborn, Germany. TEL 49-2772-2427. FAX 49-2772-2420.
circ. 26,000. *6322*

AUSTIN GREENSHEET.
Gordon Publications (Austin), Box 140721, Austin, TX 78714-0721. TEL 512-454-1003. FAX 512-454-2442. *2252*

AUSTIN HEALTH & FITNESS.
Metro Publishing, Box 2534, Cedar Park, TX 78630. TEL 512-918-8190. FAX 512-331-9271.
circ. 50,000. *5778*

AUSTIN HOME FINDER.
Southeast Publishing Ventures, 528 East Blvd., Charlotte, NC 28203-5110.
circ. 25,000. *6295*

AUSTIN HOMES & GARDENS.
Publications & Communications, Inc., 12416 Hymeadow, Austin, TX 78750-1896. TEL 512-250-9023. FAX 512-331-3900.
circ. 25,000. *3841*

AUSTIN LAWYERS JOURNAL.
Travis County Bar Association, 700 Lavaca, Ste. 602, Austin, TX 78701. TEL 512-472-0279. FAX 512-473-2720.
circ. 3,200. *3914*

AUSTRALIAN ABORIGINAL STUDIES.
Australian Institute of Aboriginal and Torres Strait Islander Studies, P.O. Box 553, Canberra, A.C.T. 2601, Australia. TEL 61-6-2461111. FAX 61-6-2497310. *311*

AUSTRALIAN BALLET NEWS.
Australian Ballet Foundation, 2 Kavanagh St., Southbank, Vic. 3006, Australia. TEL 61-3-96848600. FAX 61-3-96867081.
circ. 28,000. *2290*

AUSTRALIAN BUILDING NEWS.
Sydney Building Information Centre Ltd., 525 Elizabeth St., Surry Hills, N.S.W. 2010, Australia. TEL 02-318-2988. FAX 02-319-1890.
circ. 17,656. *863*

AUSTRALIAN CITRUS NEWS.
Australian Citrus Growers' Federation, Rm. 107, 10th Fl., 118 King William St., Adelaide. S.A. 5000, Australia. TEL 61-8-2124245. FAX 61-8-2313413.
circ. 3,000. *3182*

AUSTRALIAN DEFENCE FORCE JOURNAL.
Department of Defence, B-4-26, Canberra, A.C.T. 2600, Australia. TEL 61-6-2652682. FAX 61-6-2656972.
circ. 17,500. *5260*

AUSTRALIAN ENTOMOLOGIST.
Entomological Society of Queensland, P.O. Box 537, Indooroopilly, Qld. 4068, Australia.
circ. 500. *747*

AUSTRALIAN HISTORICAL STUDIES.
University of Melbourne, Department of History, Parkville, Vic. 3052, Australia. TEL 61-3-9344-5963. FAX 61-3-9344-7894.
circ. 1,500. *3489*

AUSTRALIAN JOURNAL OF PHYSIOTHERAPY.
Australian Physiotherapy Association, P.o. Box 6465, Melbourne, Vic. 3004, Australia. TEL 61-3-95349400. FAX 61-3-95349199.
circ. 8,760. *5042*

AUSTRALIAN JUNIOR CHAMBER.
Australian Junior Chamber, 6 Thesiger Court, Deakin, A.C.T. 2600, Australia. TEL 61-6-281-1066. FAX 61-6-281-4709.
circ. 3,000. *1929*

AUSTRALIAN LAWYER.
Law Institute of Victoria, 470 Bourke St., Melbourne, Vic. 3000, Australia. TEL 61-3-96079339. FAX 61-3-96079451.
circ. 33,266. *3915*

AUSTRALIAN NINETEENTH CENTURY LITERATURE IN PRINT.
Mulini Press, P.O. Box 82, Jamison Centre, A.C.T. 2614, Australia. TEL 61-6-2512519.
circ. 430. *4494*

AUSTRALIAN NUGGET JOURNAL.
Goldcorp Australia, 300 Hay St., E. Perth, W.A. 6004, Australia. TEL 61-9-4217222. FAX 61-9-2213812.
circ. 3,500. *5295*

AUSTRALIAN PARKS & RECREATION.
Royal Australian Institute of Parks & Recreation, Bldg. E, National Exhibition Centre, Flemington Rd., Lyneham, A.C.T. 2602, Australia. TEL 61-06-241-4371. FAX 61-06-241-5817.
circ. 1,800. *2223*

AUSTRALIAN PRESCRIBER.
Commonwealth Department of Health and Family Services, P.O. Box 100, Woden, A.C.T. 2606, Australia. TEL 61-6-289-7038.
circ. 60,000. *5649*

AUSTRALIAN PRIVATE DOCTOR.
Private Doctors of Australia Ltd., 194 Derby St., Penrith, N.S.W. 2750, Australia. TEL 61-47-322977. FAX 61-47-323762.
circ. 2,500. *4643*

AUSTRALIAN SCIENCE TEACHERS' JOURNAL.
Australian Science Teachers Association, P.O. Box 82, Bentleigh, Vic. 82, Australia. TEL 61-3-95922266. FAX 61-3-95923439.
circ. 6,000. *2595*

AUSTRALIAN SERVICE STATION & CONVENIENCE STORE NEWS.
Berg Bennett & Associates Pty. Ltd., 1-109 Lousa Rd., Birchgrove, N.S.W. 2041, Australia. TEL 61-2-95551355. FAX 61-2-95551434.
circ. 10,458. *7082*

AUSTRALIAN SOCIETY FOR THE HISTORY OF MEDICINE. OCCASIONAL PAPERS.
Australian Society for the History of Medicine, P.O. Box 130, Northbridge, W.A. 6865, Australia. TEL 61-9-4441677. FAX 61-9-2421201.
circ. 350. *4643*

AUSTRALIAN STOCK HORSE JOURNAL.
P.O. Box 288, Scone, N.S.W. 2337, Australia. TEL 61-65-451122. FAX 61-65-452165.
circ. 6,500. *6848*

AUSTRALIAN TRADER.
Exportrad Pty. Ltd., 115-117 Cooper St, Surry Hills, N.S.W. 2010, Australia.
circ. 5,500. *1316*

AUSTRALIAN WINE RESEARCH INSTITUTE TECHNICAL REVIEW.
Australian Wine Research Institute, P.O. Box 197, Glen Osmond, S.A. 5064, Australia. TEL 61-8-83036600. FAX 61-8-83036601.
circ. 925. *515*

AUTO C A D WORLD.
Publications & Communications, Inc., 12416 Hymeadow, Austin, TX 78750-1896. TEL 512-250-9023. FAX 512-331-3900.
circ. 29,000. *2131*

AUTO IMPACT.
Kempec Publications, Inc., 19 Maple Way, Mountain Lakes, NJ 07046-1423. TEL 201-785-0764. FAX 201-785-0753.
circ. 3,830. *7083*

AUTO-JOURNAL.
Societe EDP, 8-10, rue Pierre Brossolette, 92300 Levallois Perret, France. FAX 40-87-42-37.
circ. 267,000. *7083*

AUTO MERCHANDISING NEWS.
Mortimer Communications, Inc., Box 1185, Fairfield, CT 06430. TEL 203-384-9323. FAX 203-375-1463.
circ. 23,224. *7084*

AUTO RENTAL NEWS.
Bobit Publishing Company, 2512 Artesia Blvd., Redondo Beach, CA 90278-3210. TEL 310-376-8788. FAX 310-376-9043.
circ. 16,500. *1516*

AUTO REVISTA.
Revista Communications, Inc., 14330 Midway Rd., Ste. 202, Dallas, TX 75244-3514. TEL 214-386-0040. FAX 214-386-4255.
circ. 41,000. *7084*

AUTOCCASION.
Maxipress S.A., 52 rue Broodcoorens, 1310 La Hulpe, Belgium. TEL 32-2-6520020. FAX 32-2-6521129.
circ. 35,000. *7085*

AUTOFACHMANN.
Vogel Verlag und Druck GmbH & Co. KG, Max-Planck-Str. 7-9, 97082 Wuerzburg, Germany. TEL 49-931-418-2145. FAX 49-931-4182905.
circ. 81,723. *7085*

AUTOKOMPAS.
Auto Vakbladen Uitgeverij bv, Postbus 100, 4920 AC Made, Netherlands. TEL 31-162-687600. FAX 31-162-687444.
circ. 22,000. *7086*

AUTOMATISERING GIDS.
Ten Hagen & Stam b.v., Postbus 34, 2501 AG The Hague, Netherlands. TEL 31-70-3045700. FAX 31-70-3045812.
circ. 27,550. *2073*

AUTOMOBIL-INDUSTRIE.
Vogel Verlag und Druck GmbH & Co. KG, Max-Planck-Str. 7-9, 97082 Wuerzburg, Germany. TEL 49-931-4182145. FAX 49-931-4182905.
circ. 9,789. *7086*

AUTOMOBILES CLASSIQUES.
Excelsior Publications, 1 rue du colonel Pierre Avia, 75503 Paris Cedex 15, France. TEL 46-48-48-48. FAX 46-48-48-09.
circ. 25,383. *7087*

AUTOMOTIVE & TRANSPORTATION INTERIORS.
Shore-Varrone, Inc., 6255 Barfield Rd. N.E., Ste. 200, Atlanta, GA 30328-4300. TEL 404-252-8831. FAX 404-252-4436.
circ. 12,444. *7087*

AUTOMOTIVE BODY REPAIR NEWS.
Chilton Co., 201 King of Prussia Rd., Radnor, PA 19089. TEL 610-964-4000. FAX 610-964-4981.
circ. 60,000. *7087*

AUTOMOTIVE ENGINEER.
Institute of Automotive Mechanical Engineers (Inc.), 227 Great North Rd., Five Dock, N.S.W. 2046, Australia. TEL 61-2-97134711. FAX 61-2-97132671.
circ. 26,846. *7087*

AUTOMOTIVE FLEET.
Bobit Publishing Company, 2512 Artesia Blvd., Redondo Beach, CA 90278-3210. TEL 310-376-8788. FAX 310-376-9043.
circ. 22,000. *7088*

AUTOMOTIVE INTERNATIONAL.
Leading Edge Publishing, 2 Oxted Chambers, 185-187 Station St. E., Oxted, Surrey RH8 0QE, England. TEL 44-181-687-2340. FAX 44-181-646-7926.
circ. 17,500. *7088*

AUTOMOTIVE MANAGEMENT.
1 Oxted Chambers, 185-187 Station Rd. E., Oxted, Surrey RH8 0QE, England. TEL 44-1883-732000. FAX 44-1883-730933.
circ. 19,971. *7088*

AUTOMOTIVE MANAGEMENT INFORMATION SYSTEMS COUNCIL NEWSLETTER.
Automotive Management Information Systems Council, Box 13966, Durham, NC 27709-3966. TEL 201-569-8500.
circ. 150. *1554*

AUTOMOTIVE MANUFACTURING INTERNATIONAL.
Sterling Publications Ltd., 86-88 Edgware Rd., London W2 2YW, England. TEL 44-171-915-9600. FAX 44-171-915-9619.
circ. 10,000. *7088*

AUTOMOTIVE REBUILDER.
Babcox Publications, 11 S. Forge St., Box 1810, Akron, OH 44309-1810. TEL 216-535-6117. FAX 216-535-0874.
circ. 23,000. *7089*

AUTOMOTIVE SERVICES RETAILER.
Graphic Concepts, Inc., 1801 Rockville Pike, Ste. 330, Rockville, MD 20852. TEL 301-984-7333. FAX 301-984-7340.
circ. 15,000. *7089*

AUTOMOTIVE TECHNOLOGY INTERNATIONAL.
Sterling Publications Ltd., 86-88 Edgware Rd., London W2 2YW, England. TEL 44-171-915-9600. FAX 44-171-915-9619.
circ. 10,000. *7089*

AUTOMOVIL DE VENEZUELA.
Ortiz y Asociados, s.r.l., Av. Caurimare, Qta. Expo., Colinas de Bello Monte, Caracas, Venezuela. TEL 58-2-751-1355. FAX 58-2-751-11-22.
circ. 7,500. *7089*

AUTOPART.
M & M Publications, P.O. Box 8859, Johannesburg 2000, South Africa. TEL 27-11-880-5790. FAX 27-11-880-5789.
7089

AUTOPISTA.
Luike - Motorpress, C. Ancora 40, 28045 Madrid, Spain. TEL 34-1-3470100. FAX 34-1-3470135.
circ. 90,000. *7089*

AUTOSPORT.
Medipress Sociedade Editora de Publicacoes, Lda., Av. Infante D. Henrique 334, 1800 Lisbon, Portugal. TEL 351-1-8520756. FAX 351-1-8518990.
circ. 75,000. *7090*

AVENTURA LIFESTYLES.
G S & J Publishing, Inc., 5212 N.W. 54th Ave., Pompano Beach, FL 33073-3755. TEL 305-977-5901.
circ. 15,000. *3369*

AVIATION INDUSTRY DEVELOPMENT.
Sterling Publications Ltd., 86-88 Edgware Rd., London W2 2YW, England. TEL 44-171-915-9600. FAX 44-171-915-9619.
circ. 10,000. *58*

AVIATION INTERNATIONAL NEWS.
Convention News Co., Inc., 21 Cross Ave., Midland Park, NJ 07432. TEL 201-444-5075. FAX 201-444-4647.
circ. 31,000. *7065*

AVIATION MAINTENANCE.
Phillips Business Information, Inc., 1201 Seven Locks Rd., Potomac, MD 20854. TEL 301-424-3338. FAX 301-309-3487.
circ. 37,488. *59*

AVIATION SECURITY INTERNATIONAL.
Halldale Publishing & Media Ltd., 84 Alexandra Rd., Farnborough, Hants GU14 6DD, England. TEL 44-1252-517974. FAX 44-1252-512714.
circ. 7,000. *7065*

AVICULTURA PROFESIONAL.
Avicultura Profesional, Inc., 184 Hickory Poin Dr., Athens, GA 30605. TEL 706-549-4092. FAX 706-543-1854.
circ. 7,500. *270*

AVIFAUNISTISCHER INFORMATIONSDIENST BAYERN.
Ornithologische Gesellschaft in Bayern e.V., c/o Institut fuer Vogelkunde, Am Kreuzweiher 3, 91746 Weidenbach, Germany. TEL 49-9826-9730. FAX 49-9826-1610.
circ. 1,150. *800*

AVIONICS.
Phillips Business Information, Inc., 1201 Seven Locks Rd., Potomac, MD 20854. TEL 301-424-3338. FAX 301-309-3847. *59*

AYIN L'TZION.
Zionist Organization of America, 4 E. 34 St., New York, NY 10016. TEL 212-481-1500.
circ. 2,500. *2999*

AYK AKTIV.
Vereinigte Verlagsanstalten GmbH, Hoeherweg 278, 40231 Duesseldorf, Germany. TEL 49-211-7357-0. FAX 49-211-7357223.
circ. 100,000. *504*

AYLESFORD CARMELITE NEWSLETTER.
Lay Carmelite Office, 8501 Bailey Road, Darien, IL 60561. TEL 630-969-5050. FAX 630-969-5536.
circ. 12,000. *6452*

AZ B - ARIZONA BUSINESS.
Arizona State University, Center for Business Research, College of Business, Box 874406, Tempe, AZ 85287-4406. TEL 602-965-3961. FAX 602-965-5458.
circ. 630. *935*

AZIONE COOPERATIVA.
Comitato Regionale Lombardo delle Cooperative, Via Palmanova 22, 20132 Milan, Italy. TEL 2845-6208.
circ. 10,000. *6655*

B A P C O NEWS.
Bahrain Petroleum Co. B.S.C., P.O. Box 25149, Awali, Bahrain. TEL 755047. FAX 755999.
circ. 1,000. *5596*

B A R GIORNALE.
Agepe Gruppo Editoriale, Via Domenico Trentacoste, 9, 20134 Milan, Italy. TEL 02-215621. FAX 02-2640330.
circ. 246,244. *3723*

B & P A.
Murray State University, College of Business and Public Affairs, Murray, KY 42071. TEL 502-762-4188. FAX 502-762-3482.
circ. 1,000. *935*

B B B - BAUMASCHINE - BAUGERAET - BAUSTELLE.
Technopress Fachzeitschriften Verlagsgesellschaft mbH, Iglaseegasse 21-23, Postfach 176, A-1191 Vienna, Austria. TEL 43-1-3207427. FAX 43-1-327427.
circ. 15,000. *863*

B B W REPORT.
Vereinigte Verlagsanstalten GmbH, Hoeherweg 278, 40231 Duesseldorf, Germany. TEL 49-211-7357-0. FAX 49-211-7357223.
circ. 45,000. *6210*

B C & T NEWS.
Bakery, Confectionery and Tobacco Workers International Union, 10401 Connecticut Ave., Kensington, MD 20895. TEL 301-933-8600. FAX 301-946-8452.
circ. 135,000. *3887*

B C BUSINESS.
Canada Wide Magazines & Communications Ltd., 4180 Lougheed Hwy., 4th Fl., Burnaby, BC V5C 6A7, Canada. TEL 604-299-7311.
circ. 13,000. *935*

B C DAIRY DIRECTORY.
RR 1, Boothe Rd., Naramata, BC, V0H 1N0, Canada. TEL 250-496-5707. FAX 250-496-5132.
circ. 1,600. *1654*

B C L A REPORTER.
British Columbia Library Association, 6545 Bonsor Ave., Ste. 110, Burnaby, BC V5H 1H3, Canada. TEL 604-430-9633. FAX 604-430-8595.
circ. 810. *4162*

BCTC - CAMRASO - FOCUS.
British Carpet Technical Centre, Cleaning & Maintenance Research & Services Organization, Wira House, West Park, Ring Rd., Leeds LS16 6QL, England. TEL 44-113-259-1999. FAX 44-113-278-0306.
circ. 300. *6984*

B F L R ARBEITSPAPIERE.
Bundesforschungsanstalt fuer Landeskunde und Raumordnung, Am Michaelshof 8, 53177 Bonn, Germany. TEL 49-288-826-0. FAX 49-228-826266.
circ. 200. *3741*

B G F BULLETIN.
Banana Growers Federation Co-operative Ltd., P.O. Box 31, Murwillumbah, N.S.W. 2484, Australia. TEL 066-722488. FAX 066-724868.
circ. 2,000. *215*

B.G. RUDOLPH LECTURES IN JUDAIC STUDIES.
Syracuse University, Jewish Studies Program, Syracuse, NY 13244-1170. TEL 315-443-3861. FAX 315-443-5390.
circ. 500. *6402*

B I F U REPORT.
Banking Insurance & Finance Union, Sheffield House, 1B Amity Grove, Raynes Park, London SW20 0LG, England. TEL 44-181-946-9151. FAX 44-181-879-3728.
circ. 112,000. *1105*

B L E S M A G.
M & B (Felstead) Ltd., 185-187 High Rd., Chadwell Heath, Essex RM6 6NA, England. TEL 44-181-590-1124. FAX 44-181-599-2932.
circ. 11,000. *6655*

10302 CONTROLLED CIRCULATION SERIALS

B L Z.
G E W - Gewerkschaft Erziehung und Wissenschaft, Loeningstr. 35, 28195 Bremen, Germany. TEL 49-421-33764-0. FAX 49-421-3376430.
circ. 4,500. *2595*

B M A NEWS REVIEW.
B M J Publishing Group, B.M.A. House, Tavistock Sq., London WC1H 9JP, England. TEL 44-171-783-6122. FAX 44-171-383-6566.
circ. 106,000. *4644*

B M MAGAZINE.
British Museum Society, Great Russell St., London WC1B 3DG, England. TEL 44-171-323-8605. FAX 44-171-323-8614.
circ. 12,500. *5351*

B M T NEWS.
British Maritime Technology Ltd., Orlando House, 1 Waldegrove Rd., Teddington, Mddx. TW11 8LZ, England.
circ. 7,000. *7146*

B-MEN.
Blk Publishing Company, Box 83912, Los Angeles, CA 90083-0912. TEL 310-410-0808. FAX 310-410-9250.
circ. 12,000. *3691*

B N A C COMMUNICATOR.
B N A Communications, Inc., 9439 Key West Ave., Rockville, MD 20850-3396. TEL 301-948-0540. FAX 301-948-2085.
circ. 230,000. *936*

B P I STATISTICAL HANDBOOK.
British Phonographic Industry, 25 Savile Row, London W1X 1AA, England. TEL 44-171-287-4422. FAX 44-171-287-2252.
circ. 1,000. *5446*

B P I - THE BUSINESS OF PHOTOGRAPHY & IMAGING.
Market Link House, Tye Green, Elsenham, Bishops Stratford, Herts. CM22 6DY, England. TEL 0279-647555. FAX 0279-815300.
circ. 6,500. *5762*

B S A A (YEAR) THAILAND SHIPPING HANDBOOK.
Cosmic Group of Companies, 4th Fl., Phyathai Bldg., 31 Phyathai Rd., Rajthevi, Bangkok 10400, Thailand. TEL 245-3850. FAX 246-4737.
circ. 5,000. *7146*

B T A HOTLINE.
Business Technology Association, 12411 Wornall Rd., Kansas City, MO 64145. TEL 816-941-3100. FAX 816-941-8034.
circ. 4,000. *1554*

B T A SOLUTIONS.
Business Technology Association, 12411 Wornall Rd., Kansas City, MO 64145-1166. TEL 816-941-3100. FAX 816-941-8034.
circ. 10,000. *1554*

B T B INFORMATIONEN.
Vereinigte Verlagsanstalten GmbH, Hoeherweg 278, 40231 Duesseldorf, Germany. TEL 49-211-7357-0. FAX 49-211-7357223.
circ. 12,091. *6955*

B T T G INDEPENDENT.
British Textile Technology Group, Wira House, West Park Ring Rd., Leeds LS16 6QL, England. TEL 44-113-259-1999. FAX 44-113-278-0306.
circ. 1,500. *6984*

B V A BULLETIN.
Blinded Veterans Association, National Board of Directors, 477 H St. N.W., Washington, DC 20001. TEL 202-371-8880. FAX 202-371-8258.
circ. 21,200. *3468*

BABSON BULLETIN.
Babson College, Babson Park, MA 02157-0310. TEL 617-239-5256. FAX 617-239-5989.
circ. 31,000. *1940*

BABY AND CHILD CARE QUICK REFERENCE ENCYCLOPEDIA.
Family Communications, Inc., 37 Hanna Ave., Toronto, ON M6K 1X1, Canada. TEL 416-537-2604. FAX 416-538-1794.
circ. 100,000. *7313*

BABY MAGAZINE INFANT CARE GUIDE.
Baby Magazine, 124 E. 40th St., Ste. 1101, New York, NY 10016. TEL 212-986-1422.
circ. 3,700,000. *5028*

BABY SHOP.
Spindle Publishing Co., 4136 Library Rd., Pittsburgh, PA 15234-1300. TEL 412-531-9742. FAX 412-531-2004.
circ. 10,000. *3448*

BADEN-WUERTTEMBERGISCHE BIOGRAPHIEN.
Kommission fuer Geschichtliche Landeskunde in Baden-Wuerttemberg, Eugenstr. 7, 70182 Stuttgart, Germany.
circ. 800. *571*

BAECKER-WERK.
Baecker - Innung Nuernberg, Ostendstr. 149-151, 90482 Nuernberg, Germany.
circ. 3,000. *3134*

BAEDER JOURNAL.
Oesterreichischer Baederverband, Rosenhuegelstr. 198, A-1238 Vienna, Austria. TEL 43-3339-7346. FAX 43-3339-7346.
circ. 200. *1466*

BAELDER.
Coxland Press, c/o 60 Elmhurst Rd., Reading, Berks. RG1 5HY, England. TEL 44-118-954-2058. FAX 44-118-954-2058. *5455*

BAENDER, BLECHE, ROHRE.
Vogel Verlag und Druck GmbH & Co. KG, Max-Planck-Str. 7-9, 97082 Wuerzburg, Germany. TEL 49-931-4182145. FAX 49-931-4182905.
circ. 10,030. *5186*

DET BAESTA.
Reader's Digest AB, P.O. Box 25, 164 93 Kista, Sweden. TEL 46-8-752-03-60. FAX 46-8-752-87-01.
circ. 169,500. *3361*

BAGER OG KONDITOR.
B K D Service A-S, Bjaerregaardsvej 16, DK-2500 Valby, Denmark. TEL 45-36-17-23-00. FAX 45-36-17-27-72.
circ. 2,768. *3134*

BAHAMAS. CHAMBER OF COMMERCE. ANNUAL DIRECTORY.
Chamber of Commerce, Attn: Executive Dir., P.O. Box N665, Nassau, Bahamas. TEL 242-322-2145. FAX 242-322-4649.
circ. 10,000. *1179*

BAIQIUEN YIKE DAXUE XUEBAO.
Baiqiu'en Yike Daxue, Xuebao Bianjibu, 86, Xinmin Dajie, Changchun, Jilin 130021, People's Republic of China. TEL 86-431-5645911. FAX 86-431-644739.
circ. 1,000. *4645*

BAKING AND CONFECTIONERY EUROPE.
Sterling Publications Ltd., 86-88 Edgware Rd., London W2 2YW, England. TEL 44-171-915-9600. FAX 44-171-915-9619.
circ. 10,000. *3134*

BAKING BUYER.
Sosland Publishing Company, 4800 Main St., Ste. 100, Kansas City, MO 64112-2513. TEL 816-756-1000. FAX 816-756-0494.
circ. 30,000. *3134*

BALAIR - C T A YELLOW WINGS.
Airpage AG, Haldenstr. 65, CH-8045 Zurich, Switzerland. TEL 01-451-2920. FAX 01-451-2961.
circ. 150,000. *7258*

BALDE BRANCO.
Cooperativa Central de Laticinios do Estado de Sao Paulo, Rua Gomes Cardim 532, 03050 Sao Paulo, SP, Brazil.
circ. 30,000. *252*

BALLET-HOO.
Royal Winnipeg Ballet, Communications Department, 380 Graham Ave., Winnipeg, MB R3C 4K2, Canada. TEL 204-956-0183. FAX 204-943-1994.
circ. 53,000. *2290*

BALNEOLOGIA POLSKA.
Polskie Towarzystwo Balneoklimatologii, Bioklimatologii i Medycyny Fizykalnej, Ul. Mickiewicza 16, 87-720 Ciechocinek, Poland. TEL 48-54-833211. FAX 48-54-837220.
circ. 700. *4645*

BALTIMORE COUNTY MUSTER.
Sons of the American Revolution, Maryland Society, 10605 Lakespring Way, Hunt Valley, MD 21030-2818. TEL 410-628-2490.
circ. 150. *3618*

BALTIMORE'S CHILD.
11 Dutton Ct., Baltimore, MD 21228. TEL 410-367-5883. FAX 410-719-9342.
circ. 70,000. *1838*

BANCA Y COMERCIO.
Escuela Bancaria y Comercial, Paseo de la Reforma 202, Mexico 06600 D.F., Mexico. FAX 905-546-0326.
circ. 6,500. *1105*

BANCO DO BRASIL. BOLETIM DE INFORMACAO AO PESSOAL.
Banco do Brasil S.A., Departamento Geral de Selecao e Desenvolvimento do Pessoal, Setor Bancarlo Sul, Lote 23, Bloco C, C.P. 562, Brasilia, D.F., Brazil.
circ. 100,000. *1107*

BANDARI.
Kenya Ports Authority, P.O. Box 95009, Mombasa, Kenya. FAX 254-11-311867.
circ. 12,000. *7023*

BANDERSNATCH.
Lewis Carroll Society, 69 Ashby Rd., Woodville, Swadlincote, Derbyshire DE11 7BZ, England.
circ. 350. *4379*

BANGLADESH JOURNAL OF FOREST SCIENCE.
Bangladesh Forest Research Institute, Chittagong 4000, Bangladesh. TEL 880-31-681586. FAX 880-31-681566.
circ. 1,000. *3147*

BANK CREDIT ANALYST.
B C A Publications Ltd., 1002 Sherbrooke St. W. 16th Fl., Montreal, PQ H3A 3L6, Canada. TEL 514-499-9706. FAX 514-499-9709. *1374*

BANK FOR INTERNATIONAL SETTLEMENTS. ANNUAL REPORT.
Bank for International Settlements, 7 Centralbahnstr., Case Postale 262, CH-4002 Basel, Switzerland. *1108*

BANK INVESTMENT REPRESENTATIVE.
Quantum Communications, Inc., 40 W. 57th St., 11th Fl., New York, NY 10019-4001.
circ. 31,209. *1108*

BANK NEGARA MALAYSIA. ANNUAL REPORT.
Bank Negara Malaysia, P.O. Box 10922, Jalan Dato'Onn, 50480 Kuala Lumpur, Malaysia. TEL 2988044. FAX 2912990. *1224*

BANK NEGARA MALAYSIA. BULLETIN EKONOMI SUKU TAHUNAN.
Bank Negara Malaysia, P.O. Box 10922, Jalan Dato'Onn, 50480 Kuala Lumpur, Malaysia. TEL 03-2988044. FAX 03-2912990. *1224*

BANK NEGARA MALAYSIA. STATISTICAL BULLETIN.
Bank Negara Malaysia, P.O. Box 10922, Jalan Dato'onn, 50480 Kuala Lumpur, Malaysia. TEL 2988044. FAX 2912990. *1023*

BANK OF JAMAICA. ECONOMIC STATISTICS.
Bank of Jamaica, P.O. Box 621, King St., Kingston, Jamaica, W.I. TEL 809-922-0750. FAX 809-967-4265.
circ. 1,200. *1023*

BANK SYSTEMS & TECHNOLOGY.
Miller Freeman Inc. (New York), One Penn Plaza, New York, NY 10119. TEL 212-714-1300. FAX 212-302-6273.
circ. 23,400. *1111*

BANKGESELLSCHAFT BERLIN. DEVISENBRIEF.
Bankgesellschaft Berlin AG, Alexanderplatz 2, 10178 Berlin, Germany. TEL 49-30-245500. FAX 49-30-24566333.
circ. 4,600. *1225*

ULRICH'S INTERNATIONAL PERIODICALS DIRECTORY 1998

BANKGESELLSCHAFT BERLIN. UNTERNEHMERBRIEF.
Bankgesellschaft Berlin AG, Alexanderplatz 2, 10178 Berlin, Germany. TEL 49-30-245500. FAX 49-30-24566333.
circ. 1,500. *1225*

BAOBAB.
Alin - Arid Lands Information Network, Casier Postal 3, Dakar-Fann, Senegal. TEL 221-251808. FAX 221-254521.
circ. 200. *1355*

BAPTIST PROGRESS.
Baptist Missionary Association of Texas, Box 2085, Waxahachie, TX 75165. TEL 214-923-0756. FAX 214-923-2679.
circ. 12,000. *6415*

BAPTIST PUBLIC RELATIONS ASSOCIATION NEWSLETTER.
Baptist Public Relations Association, Box 270187, Nashville, TN 37227-0187. TEL 615-227-7836. *6415*

BAPTIST UNION OF WESTERN CANADA. YEARBOOK.
Baptist Union of Western Canada, 605, 999 8 St., S.W., Calgary, AB T2R 1J5, Canada. TEL 403-228-9559. FAX 403-228-9048.
circ. 700. *6415*

BARCHE E CATALOGO.
Gruppo Editoriale Commerciale, Via G. Galilei, 6, 20124 Milan, Italy. TEL 02-29097-1. FAX 02-29097-209.
circ. 26,000. *6836*

BARCLAYS PREMIER WORLD MAGAZINE.
The Publishing Team, Exmouth House, 3-11 Pine St., London EC1R 0JH, England. TEL 44-171-923-5400. FAX 44-171-923-5401.
circ. 70,000. *1115*

BARCOS.
Editorial Barcos S.R.L., Blanco Encalada 121, 1642 San Isidro, B.A., Argentina. TEL 54-1-7354404. FAX 54-1-7354407.
circ. 8,000. *6836*

BARNARDO NEWS.
Barnardo's, Tanners Ln., Barkingside, Ilford, Essex IG6 1QG, England. TEL 44-181-550-8822. FAX 44-181-550-0429.
circ. 6,400. *6656*

BARS AND STRIPES.
Detroit Police Lieutenants & Sergeants Association, 28 W. Adams St., No. 1308, Detroit, MI 48226.
circ. 2,900. *2262*

BARTENDER.
Foley Publishing Corp., Box 158, Liberty Corner, NJ 07938. TEL 908-766-6006. FAX 908-766-6607.
circ. 130,703. *515*

BARTER COMMUNIQUE.
Full Circle Marketing Corp., Box 2527, Sarasota, FL 34230-2527. TEL 941-349-3300. FAX 941-365-6642.
circ. 52,000. *1654*

BARTON SCOPE.
Barton College, Box 5000, College Station, Wilson, NC 27893. TEL 919-399-6529. FAX 919-399-0893.
circ. 17,500. *1941*

BASEBALL HOBBY NEWS.
4540 Kearny Villa Rd., Ste. 215, San Diego, CA 92123. TEL 619-565-2848. FAX 619-565-6608.
circ. 91,000. *6799*

BASILICATA.
Basilicata Editrice, Via Ridola 20, Casella Postale 70, Matera 75100, Italy.
circ. 10,000. *5894*

BASSE NORMANDIE AUTOMOBILE.
Chambre Syndicale Nationale du Commerce et de la Reparation Automobile, Secteur Regional Basse-Normandie, 4 rue Pasteur, B.P. No. 7, 14011 Caen Cedex, France.
circ. 1,000. *7091*

BATTELLE SOLUTIONS UPDATE.
Battelle Memorial Institute, Communications Office, Attn: Harriet A. Craig, Ed., 505 King Ave., Columbus, OH 43201. TEL 614-424-5336. FAX 614-424-3889.
circ. 50,000. *6955*

BATTLER COLUMNS.
Alderson-Broaddus College, Philippi, WV 26416. TEL 304-457-1700. FAX 304-457-1700.
circ. 1,200. *1941*

BAUEN.
Fachschriften Verlag GmbH, Hoehenstr. 17, 70736 Fellbach, Germany. TEL 49-711-5206-256. FAX 49-711-5281424.
circ. 76,253. *865*

DAS BAUZENTRUM.
Verlag das Beispiel GmbH, Spreestr. 9, 64295 Darmstadt, Germany. TEL 49-6151-33557. FAX 49-6151-313089.
circ. 40,000. *398*

BAY AREA BABY.
Bay Area Publishing Group Inc., 401 Alberto Way, Ste. A, Los Gatos, CA 95032-5404. TEL 408-358-1414. FAX 408-356-4903.
circ. 60,000. *1838*

BAY AREA REPORTER.
Benro Enterprises, Inc., 395 Ninth St., San Francisco, CA 94103-3831. TEL 415-861-5019.
circ. 37,500. *3691*

BAYERISCH-SCHWAEBISCHE WIRTSCHAFT.
Industrie- und Handelskammer fuer Augsburg und Schwaben, Stettenstr. 1-3, 86150 Augsburg, Germany. TEL 49-821-3162-0. FAX 49-821-3162180.
circ. 87,500. *1179*

BAYERISCHES LANDESAMT FUER WASSERWIRTSCHAFT. INFORMATIONSBERICHTE.
Bayerisches Landesamt fuer Wasserwirtschaft, Lazarettstr. 67, 80636 Munich, Germany. TEL 49-89-12101203.
circ. 1,000. *7288*

BAYLOR DENTAL JOURNAL.
Baylor College of Dentistry, Office of Institutional Advancement, 3302 Gaston Ave., Dallas, TX 75246. TEL 214-828-8214. FAX 214-828-8906.
circ. 7,000. *4851*

BAYOU BENGAL.
Louisiana State University at Eunice, Box 1129, Eunice, LA 70535. TEL 318-457-7311. FAX 318-546-6620.
circ. 1,000. *1941*

DE BAZUIN.
Stichting De Bazuin, Simon Stevinweg 17, 5223 AX 's Hertogenbosch, Netherlands. TEL 31-73-6220269. FAX 31-73-6219150.
circ. 6,000. *6322*

BEACON (GEORGIA).
Georgia Southern University, Department of Foreign Languages, Box 8081, Statesboro, GA 30460. TEL 912-681-5278. FAX 912-681-062.
circ. 1,100. *2424*

THE BEACON REVIEW.
Century Publications, Inc., 1805 S. Bellaire, Ste. 235, Denver, CO 80222. TEL 303-692-8940.
circ. 30,000. *3433*

BEAN PROGRAM ANNUAL REPORT.
Centro Internacional de Agricultura Tropical, Apdo. Aereo 6713, Cali, Colombia. TEL 57-2-4450000. FAX 57-2-4450073.
circ. 600. *101*

BEAUTIFUL BRITISH COLUMBIA TRAVELLER.
Beautiful British Columbia Magazine Ltd., 929 Ellery St., Victoria, BC V9A 7B4, Canada. TEL 250-384-5456. FAX 250-384-2812.
circ. 118,000. *7186*

BEAUTY.
H.J. Pichler Verlagsgesellschaft, Muthgasse 109, Postfach 16, A-1195 Vienna, Austria. TEL 43-1-31851510. FAX 43-1-375736.
circ. 80,000. *504*

BEAUTY COUNTER.
Miller Freeman plc, Sovereign Way, Tonbridge, Kent TN9 1RW, England. TEL 44-1732-364422. FAX 44-1732-361534.
circ. 13,813. *509*

BEAUTY INC.
Beauty & Barber Supply Institute, Inc., 11811 N. Tatum Blvd., Ste. 1085, Phoeniz, AZ 85028-1625. TEL 602-404-1800. FAX 602-404-8900.
circ. 5,000. *504*

BEAUTY MAGAZINE.
Cosmetics Communications Ltd., 335 Linen Hall, 162-168 Regent St., London W1R 5TB, England. TEL 44-171-434-1530. FAX 44-171-437-0915.
circ. 13,200. *509*

BEBIDAS MEXICANAS.
Alfa Editores Tecnicos S.A., Libertad No. 107-402, 03660 Mexico DF, Mexico. TEL 525-579-3333. FAX 525-532-9504.
circ. 5,000. *515*

BEDFORD INSTITUTE OF OCEANOGRAPHY. SCIENCE REVIEW.
Department of Fisheries and Oceans, Bedford Institute of Oceanography, Dartmouth, N.S. B2Y 4A2, Canada. TEL 902-426-4093. FAX 902-426-2256.
circ. 5,000. *2399*

BEER CANS & BREWERY COLLECTIBLES.
Beer Can Collectors of America, 747 Merus Ct., Fenton, MO 63026-2092. TEL 314-343-6486.
circ. 4,000. *3663*

BEERMAT MAGAZINE.
British Beer-mat Collectors Society (BBCS), c/o Tony Matthews, Hon. Sec., 69 Dunnington Ave., Kidderminster, Worcs. DY10 2YT, England.
circ. 500. *3663*

BEGEGNUNG (BONN).
Varus Verlag Birgit Laube, Koenigswintererstr. 552, 53227 Bonn, Germany. TEL 0228-440015. FAX 0228-440017.
circ. 12,000. *2563*

BEGONIAN.
American Begonia Society, Box 471651, San Francisco, CA 94147-1651. TEL 817-728-3485.
circ. 2,000. *3182*

BEIERSDORF JOURNAL.
Beiersdorf AG, Unnastr. 48, 20253 Hamburg, Germany. FAX 49-40-5696143. *1579*

BEITRAEGE ZUR RHEINKUNDE.
Rhein-Museum e.V., Charlottenstr. 53a, 56077 Koblenz-Ehrenbreitstein, Germany. TEL 49-261-703450. FAX 49-261-703450.
circ. 800. *3552*

BEITRAEGE ZUR ZEITGESCHICHTE OBEROESTERREICHS.
Oberoesterreichisches Landesarchiv, Anzengruberstr. 19, A-4020 Linz, Austria. TEL 43-732-6555230. FAX 43-732-655523-4619.
circ. 500. *3552*

HET BELANG VAN LIMBURG.
Concentra Uitgeversmaatschappij, Herckenrodesingel 10, 3500 Hasselt, Belgium. TEL 32-11-878111. FAX 32-11-878204.
circ. 110,688. *3254*

BELGIAN BUSINESS & INDUSTRIE.
Business & Industrie, Research Park Zellik, De Haak, 1731 Zellik (Brussels). TEL 32-2-4675740. FAX 32-2-4675969.
circ. 31,500. *1579*

BELOIT MAGAZINE.
Beloit College, 700 College St., Beloit, WI 53511. TEL 608-363-2828. FAX 608-363-2870.
circ. 20,000. *1941*

BELSER KUNST KATALOG.
Belser Verlag, Pfizerstr. 5-7, 70184 Stuttgart, Germany. TEL 49-711-2191410. FAX 49-711-2191413.
circ. 60,000. *5351*

CONTROLLED CIRCULATION SERIALS

BELSER KUNST QUARTAL.
Belser Verlag, Pfizerstr. 5-7, 70184 Stuttgart, Germany. TEL 49-711-2191410. FAX 49-711-2191413.
circ. 33,000. *5351*

BERGEN COUNTY DENTAL SOCIETY. NEWSLETTER.
Bergen County Dental Society, 1060 Main St., River Edge, NJ 07661.
circ. 700. *4851*

BERKELEY MONTHLY.
Klaber Publishing Corp., 1301 59th St., Emeryville, CA 94608-2115. TEL 510-658-9811. FAX 510-658-9902.
circ. 75,000. *4325*

BERLINER AERZTEBLATT.
CB Verlag Carl Boldt, Baseler Str. 80, 12205 Berlin, Germany. TEL 49-30-8337087. FAX 49-30-8339125.
circ. 18,500. *4646*

BERLINGSKE TIDENDE.
Berlingske Dagblade, Pilestraede 34, DK-1147 Copenhagen K, Denmark. TEL 45-33-75-75-00. FAX 45-33-75-20-72.
circ. 156,000. *3274*

BERMUDA SHORTS.
Bermuda Department of Tourism, 310 Madison Ave., Ste. 201, New York, NY 10017. TEL 212-818-9800.
circ. 6,000. *7187*

BERNAN GOVERNMENT PUBLICATIONS NEWS.
Bernan Associates, 4611-F Assembly Dr., Lanham, MD 20706-4391. TEL 301-459-7666. FAX 301-459-0056.
circ. 10,200. *4163*

BESCHAFFUNGSDIENST GALABAU.
Rolf Soll Verlag GmbH, Postfach 650680, 22366 Hamburg, Germany. TEL 49-40-6068820. FAX 49-40-60688288.
circ. 9,200. *3183*

BEST READ GUIDE.
Box 1958, 77 Finlay Rd., Orleans, MA 02653. TEL 508-240-1212. FAX 508-240-2912. *7188*

BEST WISHES.
Family Communications, Inc., 37 Hanna Ave., Toronto, ON M6K 1X1, Canada.
circ. 170,000. *1839*

BETA PHI MU NEWSLETTER.
Beta Phi Mu, International Library and Information Science Honor Society, c/o School of Library and Information Studies, Florida State University, Tallahassee, FL 32306-2048. TEL 904-644-3907. FAX 904-644-3253.
circ. 20,000. *4163*

BETA THETA PI.
Beta Theta Pi Fraternity, Box 6277, Oxford, OH 45056-6277. TEL 513-523-7591. FAX 513-523-2381.
circ. 93,000. *1941*

BETHANY MAGAZINE.
Bethany College, 421 N. First, Lindsborg, KS 67456-1897. TEL 913-227-3311.
circ. 7,500. *1941*

BETHEL FOCUS.
Bethel College (St. Paul), 3900 Bethel Dr., St. Paul, MN 55112. TEL 612-638-6083. FAX 612-638-6003.
circ. 35,000. *1941*

BETON.
FeBe - Federation de l'Industrie du Beton, Bd. Aug. Reyers 207-209, 1030 Brussels, Belgium. TEL 32-2-7358015. FAX 32-2-7347794.
circ. 8,500. *867*

BETRIEBLICHE AUSBILDUNGSPRAXIS.
Verlag und Vertriebsgesellschaft mbH, Breite Str. 69, Postfach 8232, 40211 Duesseldorf, Germany.
circ. 1,800. *5186*

DER BETRIEBSLEITER.
Verlag fuer Technik und Wirtschaft GmbH & Co., Lise-Meitner-Str. 2, 55129 Mainz, Germany. TEL 49-6131-992-0. FAX 49-6131-992100.
circ. 17,000. *1466*

BETRIEBSSTATISTIK.
Bundesministerium fuer Wirtschaftliche Angelegenheiten, Bundeslastverteiler, Dienststelle Statistik, Marc-Aurel-Str. 4, Postfach 1457, A-1011 Vienna, Austria. TEL 43-1-531132004. FAX 43-1-531132092.
circ. 400. *2682*

BETTER ROADS.
Gras Industries Inc., Box 558, Park Ridge, IL 60068. TEL 312-693-7710. FAX 847-696-3445. *2778*

BETWEEN THE LEAVES.
Queensland Forest Service, G.P.O. Box 944, Brisbane, Qld. 4001, Australia. TEL 07-234-0157.
circ. 5,000. *3148*

BEVERAGE & FOOD DYNAMICS.
Hunter Publishing Limited Partnership, 2101 S. Arlington Heights Rd., Ste. 150, Arlington Heights, IL 60005. TEL 847-427-9512. FAX 847-427-2097.
circ. 75,000. *515*

BEVERAGE WORLD EN ESPANOL.
Strategic Business Communications, 226 W. 26th St., New York, NY 10011. TEL 212-822-5930. FAX 212-822-5931.
circ. 10,600. *516*

BEVERLY HILLS (213).
Baker Newspaper Group, Inc. (Beverly Hills), 9777 Wilshire Blvd., Ste. 707, Beverly Hills, CA 90212. TEL 213-275-8850.
circ. 50,000. *3370*

BEYOND COMPUTING.
International Business Machines (IBM) Corporation, 590 Madison Ave., New York, NY 10022. TEL 212-745-6326. FAX 212-745-6058.
circ. 150,000. *2073*

BEYOND P E.
209 E. 59th St., Apt. 4F, New York, NY 10022-1412. TEL 212-779-0294. FAX 212-779-1526.
circ. 80,000. *5779*

BEYOND WORDS.
Wycliffe Bible Translators Australia, Graham Rd., Kangaroo Ground, Vic. 3097, Australia. TEL 61-3-97122777. FAX 61-3-97122799.
circ. 10,000. *6323*

BEZPIECZENSTWO PRACY.
Centralny Instytut Ochrony Pracy, Ul. Czerniakowska 16, 00-701 Warsaw, Poland. TEL 48-22-6233695. FAX 48-22-6233693.
circ. 5,800. *5487*

BHABHA ATOMIC RESEARCH CENTRE. NUCLEAR PHYSICS DIVISION. ANNUAL REPORT.
Bhabha Atomic Research Centre, Trombay, Bombay 400085, India. *5850*

BIBEL UND GEMEINDE.
Bibelbund e.V., Narzissenweg 11, 35447 Reiskirchen, Germany. TEL 49-228-638784. FAX 49-228-638784.
circ. 3,500. *6323*

BIBLIOEXPORT.
Association for the Export of Canadian Books, 504-1 Nicholas St., Ottawa, ON K1N 7B7, Canada. TEL 613-562-2324. FAX 613-562-2329.
circ. 1,290. *6263*

BIBLIOGRAFIA VENEZOLANA.
Instituto Autonomo Biblioteca Nacional, Oficina de Information, Apdo. 80593, Prados del Este, Caracas 1080-A, Venezuela. TEL 943-1361. FAX 941-5219.
circ. 1,500. *4163*

BIBLIOGRAPHIA SCIENTIAE NATURALIS HELVETICA.
Schweizerische Landesbibliothek, Hallwylstr. 15, CH-3003 Bern, Switzerland. TEL 41-31-3228911. FAX 41-31-3228463.
circ. 800. *6588*

BIBLIOGRAPHICAL SOCIETY OF CANADA. BULLETIN.
Bibliographical Society of Canada, P.O. Box 575, Sta. "P", Toronto, ON M5S 2T1, Canada.
circ. 400. *536*

BIBLIOGRAPHIE ANNUELLE DE L'HISTOIRE DE FRANCE.
C N R S Editions, 20-22 rue St. Amand, 75015 Paris, France. TEL 45-33-16-00. FAX 45-33-92-13.
circ. 1,500. *3519*

BIBLIOGRAPHIE ZUR GESCHICHTE OBEROESTERREICHS.
Oberoesterreichisches Landesarchiv, Anzengruberstr. 19, A-4020 Linz, Austria. TEL 43-732-6555230. FAX 43-732-655523-4619.
circ. 500. *3553*

BIBLIOGRAPHY ON SMOKING AND HEALTH.
U.S. Centers for Disease Control, National Center for Chronic Disease Prevention and Health Promotion, 4770 Buford Hwy., N.E., MS K-50, Atlanta, GA 30341-3724. TEL 404-488-5705. FAX 404-488-5939. *5793*

BIBLIOTECA "JOSE ARTIGAS". BOLETIN - JUNTA DE VECINOS.
Biblioteca "Jose Artigas", 25 de Mayo 609, Montevideo, Uruguay.
circ. 300. *538*

BIBLIOTEKSBLADET.
Sveriges Allmaenna Biblioteksfoerening, P.O. Box 3127, S-103 62 Stockholm, Sweden. TEL 46-8-723-00-82. FAX 46-8-723-00-83.
circ. 4,918. *4164*

BIBLIOTEKSPRESSEN.
Bibliotekspressen, Lindevangs Alle 2, DK-2000 Frederiksberg, Denmark. TEL 45-38-88-17-70. FAX 45-38-88-31-01.
circ. 6,251. *4164*

BICYCLE RETAILER AND INDUSTRY NEWS.
JayWalker Publication, 502 W. Cordova Rd., Santa Fe, NM 87501-4144. FAX 505-988-7224.
circ. 14,000. *6824*

BIENVENIDOS A MIAMI.
Welcome Publications, Inc., Box 630518, Miami, FL 33163. TEL 305-944-9444.
circ. 20,000. *7258*

BIG APPLE PARENTS' PAPER.
Family Communications, 36 E. 12th St., 4th Fl., New York, NY 10003-4604. TEL 212-533-2277. FAX 212-475-6186.
circ. 62,000. *1839*

BIJBEL EN WETENSCHAP.
Stichting Bijbel en Wetenschap, Postbus 957, 3800 AZ Amersfoort, Netherlands. TEL 31-33-4621732.
circ. 3,500. *6325*

BIJNOR TIMES.
Ram Ganga Prakshan, Bijnor Times Rd., Uttar Pradesh 246701, India. TEL 01342-62602.
circ. 52,000. *3308*

BILLINGTON'S STOCK FOCUS II.
Billington Publications Inc., 1660 Benson Rd., Pt. Roberts, WA 98281. TEL 360-945-1491. FAX 800-721-5726.
circ. 200,000. *1375*

BILLY JAMES HARGIS' CHRISTIAN CRUSADE.
Church of Christian Crusade, Box 977, Tulsa, OK 74102. TEL 417-451-4234. FAX 501-438-6054.
circ. 35,000. *6325*

BILSPORT.
Albinsson & Sjoeberg, P.O. Box 529, S-371 23 Karlskrona, Sweden. TEL 46-455-3353-25. FAX 46-455-311715.
circ. 55,200. *7091*

BILSPORT SPECIAL.
Albinsson & Sjoeberg, P.O. Box 529, S-371 23 Karlskrona, Sweden. TEL 46-0455-335325. FAX 46-0455-311715.
circ. 14,700. *6752*

BINDEN EN BOUWEN.
Sint-Bernardinuscollege, Akerstraat 95, Heerlen, Netherlands.
circ. 2,000. *1942*

BINGO NEWS & GAMING HI-LITES.
Bingo Hi-Lites Ltd., 101, 10171 Saskatchewan Dr., Box 106, Edmonton, AB T6E 4R5, Canada. TEL 403-986-5088. FAX 403-986-5089.
circ. 25,000. *2252*

BIOCELL.
Centro Regional de Investigaciones Cientificas y Tecnologicas, Casilla de Correo 131, 5500 Mendoza, Argentina. TEL 54-61-205020 ext. 2670. FAX 54-61-380232.
circ. 300. *796*

BIOCONNECTION.
Michigan Biotechnology Institute, 3900 Collins Rd., Box 27609, Lansing, MI 48909. TEL 517-337-3181. FAX 517-337-2122.
circ. 2,500. *678*

BIOLOGIA OGGI.
Associazione Nazionale Laureati in Scienze Biologiche, Via Guglielmo degli Ubertini, 64, 00176 Rome, Italy. TEL 39-6-21707494.
circ. 1,000. *590*

BIOLOGIA PESQUERA.
Universidad Catolica de la Santisima Concepcion, Casilla 297, Concepcion, Chile. TEL 56-41-246175. FAX 56-41-245908. *3062*

BIOLOGISCHE ARBEITSSTOFF TOLERANZ WERTE UND EXPOSITIONSAEQUIVALENTE FUER KREBSERZEUGENDE ARBEITSSTOFFE.
V C H Verlagsgesellschaft mbH, Postfach 101161, 69451 Weinheim, Germany. TEL 06201-606-0. FAX 06201-606328.
circ. 600. *5487*

IL BIOLOGO.
Associazione Nazionale Laureati in Scienze Biologiche, Via Guglielmo degli Ubertini 64, 00176 Rome, Italy. TEL 39-6-21707494.
circ. 1,000. *591*

BIOMEDICAL AND ENVIRONMENTAL SCIENCES.
Zhongguo Yufang Yixue Kexueyuan, 27 Nanwei Rd., Beijing 100050, People's Republic of China. TEL 86-10-6317-3957. FAX 86-10-6317-0892.
circ. 200. *4646*

BIOMEDICAL TECHNOLOGY MANAGEMENT.
Second Source Publications, Inc., 10 Risho Ave., East Providence, RI 02914-1215. TEL 401-434-1050. FAX 401-434-1090.
circ. 12,500. *4647*

BIOMETEOROLOGY BULLETIN.
International Society of Biometeorology, c/o Dr. Paul Beggs, School of Earth Sciences, Macquarie University, N.S.W. 2109, Australia. *5227*

BIOTECH BUYER'S GUIDE.
American Chemical Society, 1155 16th St., N.W., Washington, DC 20036. TEL 800-227-5558. FAX 202-872-4615.
circ. 65,000. *679*

BIOTECH PRODUCTS INTERNATIONAL.
Pan European Publishing Co., Rue Verte 216, 1030 Brussels, Belgium. TEL 32-2-2402611. FAX 32-2-2427111.
circ. 30,020. *679*

BIRMINGHAM & WARWICKSHIRE ARCHAEOLOGICAL SOCIETY. TRANSACTIONS.
Birmingham & Warwickshire Archaeological Society, Birmingham & Midland Institute, Margaret Street, Birmingham B3 3BS, England.
circ. 350. *355*

BIRMINGHAM BAR ASSOCIATION. BULLETIN.
Birmingham Bar Association, 2021 Second Ave. N., Birmingham, AL 35203-3703. TEL 205-251-8006.
circ. 1,600. *3920*

BIZ (ST. LOUIS).
American City Business Journals, Inc. (St. Louis), 1 Metropolitan Sq., Ste. 2170, St. Louis, MO 63102. TEL 314-421-6200.
circ. 70,000. *3370*

BIZZ - MISSETS ZAKENBLAD.
Misset, Postbus 4, 7000 BA Doetinchem, Netherlands. TEL 31-314-349371. FAX 31-314-363638.
circ. 205,640. *937*

BLACK EMPLOYMENT AND EDUCATION.
Hamdani, Inc., 2625 Piedmont Rd., Ste. 56-282, Atlanta, GA 30324. TEL 404-469-5891.
circ. 120,000. *3000*

BLACK SPOTS.
Black Spots Publishing, 1283 S. LaBrea Ave., Ste. 304, Los Angeles, CA 90019. TEL 213-938-0101.
circ. 10,000. *3001*

BLACKPOOL HOTEL & GUEST HOUSE ASSOCIATION. JOURNAL.
Blackpool Hotel and Guest House Association Ltd., 87a Coronation St., Blackpool FY1 4PD, Lancasterhire, England. *3723*

BLAETTERTEIG.
Media Austria, Postfach 95, A-1013 Vienna, Austria. TEL 43-1-3665512.
circ. 2,000. *3870*

BLAKES REPORT ON INTELLECTUAL PROPERTY.
Blake, Cassels & Graydon, Box 25, Commerce Court West, Toronto, Ont. M5L 1A9, Canada. TEL 416-863-5840. FAX 416-863-2653.
circ. 5,500. *3920*

BLESK.
Na Florenci 19, 112 86 Prague 1, Czech Republic. TEL 42-2-282-2870. FAX 42-2-232-3630.
circ. 485,000. *3273*

BLICKPUNKT SCHULE.
Hessischer Philologenverband, Schlichterstr. 18, 65185 Wiesbaden, Germany. TEL 0611-307445. FAX 0611-376905.
circ. 6,000. *2425*

BLOCH-ALMANACH.
Ernst-Bloch-Archiv, Bismarckstr. 44-48, 67012 Ludwigshafen, Germany. TEL 0621-5042592. FAX 0621-5042450.
circ. 500. *4325*

BLOMSTER.
Blomster ApS, P.O. Box 39, Oesterled 28, DK-4300 Holbaek, Denmark. TEL 45-53-45-10-24. FAX 45-53-45-08-17.
circ. 2,200. *3208*

BLOMSTER-BRANSCHEN.
Blomster-Branschen i Bromma AB, P.O. Box 808, S-161 24 Bromma, Sweden. TEL 46-8-25-97-31. FAX 46-8-634-4-47.
circ. 3,000. *3208*

BLUE BOOK OF BRITISH BROADCASTING.
Tellex Monitors Ltd., Communications House, 210 Old St., London EC1V 9UN, England. TEL 44-171-566-3100. FAX 44-171-566-3152.
circ. 500. *1655*

BLUE GRASS ROOTS.
Kentucky Genealogical Society, Box 153, Frankfort, KY 40602.
circ. 2,200. *3214*

BLUE PITCHER.
Unicorn Press, Inc., 200 E. Bessemer Ave., Greensboro, NC 27401-1416. TEL 919-852-0281.
circ. 1,000. *4504*

BLUELINE (POTSDAM).
Potsdam College, English Department, Potsdam, NY 13676. TEL 315-267-2005. FAX 315-267-3256.
circ. 400. *4382*

BLUEPRINT (NOTTINGHAM).
Boots Co., plc., 1 Thane Rd. W., Nottingham NG2 3AA, England. TEL 44-115-959-2365. FAX 44-115-959-5684.
circ. 63,000. *1563*

BLUEPRINT (WINFRITH).
Dorset Police, Force Headquarters, Winfrith, Nr. Dorchester DT2 8DZ, England. FAX 44-1929-463755.
circ. 4,000. *2262*

BLUEPRINT FOR SOCIAL JUSTICE.
Twomey Center for Peace through Justice, Loyola University, Box 12, New Orleans, LA 70118. TEL 504-861-5830. FAX 504-861-5833.
circ. 3,500. *5988*

BLUES AT THE FOUNDATION.
Blues Foundation, 49 Union Ave., Memphis, TN 38103-2420. TEL 901-527-2583. FAX 901-529-4030.
circ. 3,000. *5377*

BOATING BUSINESS.
Rushton Marine Press Ltd., Woodside, Burnhams Rd., Little Bookham, Leatherhead, Surrey KT23 3BA, England. TEL 44-1372-453316. FAX 44-1372-459974.
circ. 6,500. *6836*

BOBBIN.
Bobbin Publishing, Inc., 1110 Shop Rd., Box 1986, Columbia, SC 29202. TEL 803-771-7500. FAX 803-799-1461.
circ. 18,752. *1913*

LA BOBINA.
Bobbin Publishing, Inc., 1110 Shop Rd., Box 1986, Columbia, SC 29202. TEL 803-771-7500. FAX 803-799-1461.
circ. 13,345. *1913*

BODY POSITIVE.
Body Positive, New York, 19 Fulton St., Ste. 308B, New York, NY 10038. TEL 212-566-7333. FAX 212-566-4539.
circ. 10,000. *4833*

BODYSHOP BUSINESS.
Babcox Publications, 11 S. Forge St., Box 1810, Akron, OH 44309-1810. TEL 216-535-6117. FAX 216-535-0874.
circ. 58,057. *7091*

BODYSHOP MAGAZINE.
Christopher Mann, Ed. & Pub., Juniper Court, Boxwell Rd., Berkhamsted, Herts. HP4 3ET, England. TEL 44-1442-876686. FAX 44-1442-870740.
circ. 13,000. *7092*

BOERN & UNGE.
Fagbladet Boern og Unge, Blegdamsvej 124, 4, DK-2100 Copenhagen Oe, Denmark. TEL 47-35-43-21-43. FAX 47-35-43-22-99.
circ. 56,158. *2425*

BOERNETEATERAVISEN.
Teatercentrum i Danmark, Frederiksborggade 20, DK-1360 Copenhagen K, Denmark. TEL 45-33-15-69-00. FAX 45-33-13-14-39.
circ. 14,000. *7003*

BOGAZICI JOURNAL: REVIEW OF SOCIAL, ECONOMIC AND ADMINISTRATIVE STUDIES.
Bogazici Universitesi, Bebek, 80815 Istanbul, Turkey. TEL 90-212-2631500. FAX 90-212-2651479.
circ. 150. *6605*

BOGG.
Bogg Publications, 422 N. Cleveland St., Arlington, VA 22201. TEL 703-243-6019.
circ. 850. *4504*

BOLETIM U E R J.
Universidade do Estado do Rio de Janeiro, R. Sao Francisco Xavier, 524 sala T-01, CEP 20550 Maracana, Rio de Janeiro, Brazil.
circ. 2,000. *2425*

BOLETIN DE ARQUEOLOGIA MEDIEVAL.
Asociacion Espanola de Arqueologia Medieval, Apdo. Postal 50449, Breton de los Herreros 59, 30 Izq., 28003 Madrid, Spain.
circ. 613. *355*

BOLETIN DE SEGUROS.
Superintendencia de Bancos, Avda. 12 de Octubre 1561, Apdo. de Correos 17-17-770, Quito, Ecuador. FAX 563-652. *3810*

BOLETIN HIDROLOGICO.
Instituto Costarricense de Electricidad (ICE), Apdo. 10032, 1000 San Jose, Costa Rica. TEL 506-2-207531. FAX 506-2-208204. *2393*

BOLETIN I I E.
Instituto de Investigaciones Electricas, Division de Informacion Tecnologica y Desarrollo Profesional, Liebnitz 14, 3 piso, Col. Anzures, Del. M. Hidalgo, 11590 Mexico, D.F., Mexico. FAX 73-189-854.
circ. 5,500. *2810*

BOLETIN INDUSTRIAL.
Editorial Nova, S.A. de C.V., Goldsmith 37-401, Col. Polanco, 11550 Mexico, D.F., Mexico. TEL 52-5-2806080. FAX 52-5-2803194.
circ. 36,000. *1580*

BOLETIN OFICIAL ECLESIASTICO DEL ARZOBISPADO CASTRENSE DE ESPANA.
Arzobispado Castrense de Orpana, C. Nuncio 13, 28005 Madrid, Spain. TEL 34-1-366-8228. FAX 34-1-366-8225.
circ. 700. *6325*

BOLLETTINO BIBLIOGRAFICO E RASSEGNA ARCHIVISTICA E DI STUDI STORICI DELLA SARDEGNA.
C V E C Edizioni, Via Tocmino 33, Cagliari, Italy. TEL 39-70-276220.
circ. 1,000. *3519*

BOMBUS.
Verein fuer Naturwissenschaftliche Heimatforschung zu Hamburg e.V., Zoologisches Institut und Museum, Martin-Luther-King-Platz 3, 20146 Hamburg, Germany.
circ. 300. *748*

BOND.
Lutheran Brotherhood, 625 Fourth Ave. S., Minneapolis, MN 55415. TEL 612-340-7000.
circ. 700,000. *6416*

BONDINGS.
New Ways Ministry, 4012 29th St., Mt. Rainier, MD 20712. TEL 301-277-5674. FAX 301-864-6948.
circ. 3,200. *3692*

BONNER JAPANFORSCHUNGEN.
Bonner Verein zur Foerderung der Japanforschung, Regina-Pacis-Weg 7, 53113 Bonn, Germany. TEL 0228-737223. FAX 0228-737020.
circ. 500. *5523*

BONNER UMWELT ZEITUNG.
Oekozentrum Bonn e.V., Heerstr. 20a, 53111 Bonn, Germany. TEL 0228-692220. FAX 0228-631124.
circ. 10,000. *2908*

THE BOOK ARTS CLASSIFIED.
Box 77167, Washington, DC 20013. FAX 800-538-7549.
circ. 5,000. *6264*

BOOK OF BRITISH EXCELLENCE.
Custom Publishing Company Ltd., 45 Station Rd., Redhill, Surrey RH1 1QH, England. TEL 44-1737-767213. FAX 44-1737-771662.
circ. 150,000. *867*

BOOKENDS.
Friends of the Reading-Berks Public Libraries, 245 Kohler Rd., Kutztown, PA 19530. TEL 610-683-5508.
circ. 3,000. *4166*

BOOKMARK.
B.C. Teachers' Federation, 100-550 W. 6th Ave., Vancouver, BC V5Z 4P2, Canada. TEL 604-871-1848. FAX 604-871-2291.
circ. 1,000. *2425*

BOOKMARK (MOSCOW, IDAHO).
University of Idaho Library, Moscow, ID 83844. TEL 208-885-6584. FAX 208-885-6817.
circ. 1,100. *4166*

BOOKS AND LIBRARIES AT THE UNIVERSITY OF KANSAS.
University of Kansas Libraries, Lawrence, KS 66045. TEL 913-864-4334. *4166*

BOOSEY AND HAWKES NEWSLETTER.
Boosey and Hawkes, Inc., 35 E. 21st St., New York, NY 10010-6212. TEL 212-228-3300. FAX 212-473-5730.
circ. 12,000. *5378*

BOPUXUE ZAZHI.
Zhongguo Kexueyuan, Wuhan Wuli Yanjiusuo, P.O. Box 71010, Xiaohongshan, Wuchang-qu, Wuhan, Hubei 430071, People's Republic of China. TEL 86-27-786-7791. FAX 86-27-788-5291.
circ. 200. *5859*

BORAX PIONEER.
U.S. Borax, Inc., 26877 Torney Rd., Valencia, CA 91355.
circ. 6,000. *1740*

BORD IASCAIGH MHARA. TUARASCAIL AGUS CUNTAISI.
Irish Sea Fisheries Board, P.O. Box 12, Crofton Rd., Dun Laoghaire, Co. Dublin, Ireland. TEL 01-2841544. FAX 01-2841123.
circ. 3,500. *3062*

BORDER - LINES.
400 Dovercourt Rd., Toronto, ON M6J 3E7, Canada. TEL 416-534-3224. FAX 416-534-2301.
circ. 1,000. *432*

BORTHWICK INSTITUTE OF HISTORICAL RESEARCH. BORTHWICK PAPERS.
St. Anthony's Press, St. Anthony's Hall, York YO1 2PW, England. TEL 44-1904-642315.
circ. 350. *3554*

BOSCH TECHNISCHE BERICHTE.
Robert Bosch GmbH, Abteilung BFV21, Postfach 106050, 70049 Stuttgart, Germany. *2810*

BOSHI KAGAKU RYOHO.
Boshi Kagaku Ryoho Kenkyujo, 55-12, Ikebukuro 2-chome, Toshima-ku, Tokyo 171, Japan. TEL 81-3-3980-6139.
circ. 250. *5028*

BOSO NO KONCHU.
Chibaken Konchu Danwakai, c/o Mr. Yasutoshi Matsui, 3-102, 427-5 Nedo, Kashiwa-shi, Chiba-ken 277, Japan.
circ. 200. *748*

THE BOTANICA.
Delhi University Botanical Society, Department of Botany, University of Delhi, Delhi 110007, India.
circ. 500. *695*

BOTANICAL SURVEY OF INDIA. BULLETIN.
Botanical Survey of India, c/o Ministry of the Environment and Forests, Paryavaran Bhavan, C G O Complex Phase II, Lodi Rd., New Delhi 110 002, India. TEL 436-3951.
circ. 250. *696*

DE BOUWADVISEUR.
Samsom Bedrijfsinformatie B.V., Postbus 4, 2400 MA Alphen aan den Rijn, Netherlands. TEL 31-172-466775. FAX 31-172-440681.
circ. 4,660. *867*

BOUWREVUE.
Misset, Postbus 4, 7000 BA Doetinchem, Netherlands. TEL 31-314-349371. FAX 31-314-363638.
circ. 14,000. *868*

BOWLING PROPRIETOR.
Bowling Proprietors' Association of America, Box 5802, Arlington, TX 76005. TEL 817-649-5105. FAX 817-633-2940.
circ. 4,500. *6800*

BRACTON LAW JOURNAL.
University of Exeter, Faculty of Law, Amory Bldg., Exeter EX4 4RJ, England. TEL 44-1392-263384.
circ. 600. *3921*

BRADEA.
Herbarium Bradeanum, C.P. 15005, 20031-040 Rio de Janeiro, RJ, Brazil.
circ. 400. *697*

BRAILLE TECHNICAL TABLES BANK CATALOG.
National Braille Association, Inc., 3 Townline Cir., Rochester, NY 14623. TEL 716-427-8260. *3468*

BRAINSCAN.
Elsevier Science B.V., P.O. Box 211, 1000 AE Amsterdam, Netherlands. TEL 31-20-4853911. FAX 31-20-4853598. *5056*

BRANCHING OUT.
Baltimore County Public Library, 320 York Rd., Towson, MD 21204. TEL 301-296-8500. FAX 301-296-3139.
circ. 1,000. *4166*

BRANCHLINE.
Bytown Railway Society, Box 141, Sta. A, Ottawa, ON K1N 8V1, Canada. TEL 613-745-1201.
circ. 70. *7124*

BRANCHLINES.
Fine Gael Party, Fine Gael Press Rooms, Leinster House, Dublin 2, Ireland. TEL 353-1-6789030. FAX 353-1-6785806.
circ. 17,000. *5895*

BRANDING IRON.
The Branding Iron, 12436 Landale St., Studio City, CA 91604. TEL 818-761-1415.
circ. 750. *3619*

BRAVE NEW WORLD.
Metropolis Group, 5th Fl., Julco House, 26-28 Great Portland St., London W1N 6AS, England. TEL 44-181-559-2015. FAX 44-181-505-2267.
circ. 30,000. *5324*

BRAZIL. DEPARTAMENTO NACIONAL DA PRODUCAO MINERAL. RELATORIO ANUAL DE ATIVIDADES E PROGRAMACAO.
Departamento Nacional da Producao Mineral, Setor Autarquia Norte, Quadra 1, Bloco B, 70040-200 Brasilia D.F., Brazil. TEL 55-61-224-2670. FAX 55-61-2258274.
circ. 150. *5296*

BRAZIL. SERVICO NACIONAL DE APRENDIZAGEM COMERCIAL. BOLETIM TECNICO.
Servico Nacional de Aprendizagem Comercial, Rua Dona Mariana, 48, 7 andar, Botafogo, 22280 Rio de Janeiro RJ, Brazil. TEL 55-21-5375898. FAX 55-21-2860645.
circ. 2,700. *2425*

BRAZILIAN JOURNAL OF EPILEPSY AND CLINICAL NEUROPHYSIOLOGY.
Liga Brasileira de Epilepsia, Av. Ipiranga 6690, Sala 322, 90610-000 Porto Alegre RS, Brazil. TEL 55-51-3394936. FAX 55-51-3394936.
circ. 700. *5056*

THE BREEZE (MATHISTON).
Wood Junior College, Box 289, Mathiston, MO 39752.
circ. 1,200. *1942*

BRENNSTOFFSTATISTIK.
Bundesministerium fuer Wirtschaftliche Angelegenheiten, Bundeslastverteiler, Dienststelle Statistik, Marc-Aurel-Str. 4, Postfach 1457, A-1011 Vienna, Austria. TEL 43-1-531132004. FAX 43-1-531132092.
circ. 400. *2682*

BREW-INFO.
European Brewery Convention, P.O. Box 510, 2380 BB Zoeterwoude, Netherlands. TEL 31-71-456047. FAX 31-71-410013.
circ. 400. *517*

BREWING AND MALTING BARLEY RESEARCH INSTITUTE. ANNUAL REPORT.
Brewing and Malting Barley Research Institute, 206-167 Lombard Ave., Winnipeg, MB R3B 0T6, Canada. TEL 204-942-1407.
circ. 700. *518*

THE BRIDGE (INDIANAPOLIS).
Indiana Historical Society, 315 W. Ohio St., Indianapolis, IN 46202. TEL 317-233-3156. FAX 317-233-3109.
circ. 11,000. *3619*

BRIDGE S A.
South African Bridge Federation, P.O. Box 890347, Lyndhurst 2106, South Africa. TEL 27-11-3374030. FAX 27-11-4406435.
circ. 2,500. *6753*

BRIEFING ON BRITAIN.
Invest in Britain Bureau, 1 Victoria St., London SW1H 0ET, England. TEL 44-171-215-5638. FAX 44-171-215-5651.
circ. 13,750. *1377*

BRITAIN THE PREFERRED LOCATION.
Invest in Britain Bureau, 1 Victoria St., London SW1H 0ET, England. TEL 44-171-215-5638. FAX 44-171-215-5651.
circ. 11,500. *1377*

BRITISH AIRWAYS EXECUTIVE.
British Airways PLC., Box 10, Heathrow Airport, Middlesex TW6 2JA, England.
circ. 110,000. *7065*

CONTROLLED CIRCULATION SERIALS 10307

BRITISH ARACHNOLOGICAL SOCIETY. BULLETIN.
British Arachnological Society, c/o Dr. P. Merrett, Ed., 6 Hillcrest, Swanage, Dorset BH19 2HS, England.
circ. 700. *829*

BRITISH CACTUS & SUCCULENT JOURNAL.
British Cactus & Succulent Society, 71 Lakes Ln., Newport Pagnell, Bucks. MK16 8HT, England. TEL 44-1908-611650.
circ. 5,600. *697*

BRITISH COLUMBIA. HOUSING MANAGEMENT COMMISSION. ANNUAL REPORT.
B.C. Housing Management Commission, Ste. 1701, 4330 Kingsway, Burnaby, BC V5H 4G7, Canada. TEL 604-433-1711. FAX 604-433-3295.
circ. 1,500. *3742*

BRITISH COLUMBIA. LAW REFORM COMMISSION. ANNUAL REPORT.
Law Reform Commission, 126-800 Hornby St., Vancouver, BC V6Z 2C5, Canada. TEL 604-660-2366. FAX 604-660-2378.
circ. 2,000. *3921*

BRITISH COLUMBIA. MINISTRY OF EDUCATION. ANNUAL REPORT.
Ministry of Education, Parliament Bldgs., Victoria, BC V8V 2M4, Canada. TEL 604-356-2500. FAX 604-356-5945.
circ. 6,000. *2425*

BRITISH COLUMBIA AGRI DIGEST.
BC Interior Agri Publications, RR 2, Chase, BC V0E 1M0, Canada. TEL 250-679-5362. FAX 250-679-5362.
circ. 7,500. *104*

BRITISH COLUMBIA ORCHARDIST.
Box 423, Salmon Arm, BC V1E 4N6, Canada. TEL 604-833-0071. FAX 604-833-0622.
circ. 2,728. *3184*

BRITISH ELECTROTECHNICAL APPROVALS BOARD. ANNUAL LIST OF APPROVED ELECTROTECHNICAL EQUIPMENT.
B E A B, Mark House, the Green, 9-11 Queen's Rd., Hersham, Walton-on-Thames, Surrey KT12 5NA, England. TEL 44-1932-244401. FAX 44-1932-226603.
circ. 10,000. *6955*

BRITISH EXPORTS.
Kompass, Part of the Reed Elsevier group, Windsor Ct., E. Grinstead House, E. Grinstead, W. Sussex RH19 1XD, England. TEL 44-1342-326972. FAX 44-1342-335747.
circ. 40,000. *1657*

BRITISH-ISRAEL TRADE.
British-Israel Chamber of Commerce, 14-15 Rodmarton St., London W1H 3FW, England. TEL 071-486-2371. FAX 071-224-1783.
circ. 2,800. *1180*

BRITISH JOURNAL OF INTENSIVE CARE.
Greycoat Publishing, 1 Harley St., London W1N 1DA, England. TEL 44-171-637-1828. FAX 44-171-631-3020.
circ. 13,878. *4649*

BRITISH JOURNAL OF RUSSIAN PHILATELY.
Postbus 16636, 1001 RC Amsterdam, Netherlands.
circ. 250. *5704*

BRITISH JOURNAL OF THEATRE NURSING.
National Association of Theatre Nurses, 22 Mount Parade, Harrogate HG1 1BX, England. TEL 44-1423-508079. FAX 44-1423-531613.
circ. 8,000. *4929*

BRITISH LIBRARY. NEWSPAPER LIBRARY. NEWSLETTER.
British Library, Newspaper Library, Colindale Ave., London NW9 5HE, England. TEL 44-171-412-7353. FAX 44-171-412-7379.
circ. 2,000. *4167*

BRITISH LIBRARY NEWS.
British Library, Document Supply Centre, Boston Spa, Wetherby, W. Yorks. LS23 7BQ, England. TEL 44-1937-546054. FAX 44-1937-546571.
circ. 8,000. *4167*

BRITISH NATURISM.
Central Council for British Naturism, Assurance House, 30-32 Wycliffe Rd., Northampton NN1 5JF, England. TEL 01604-20361. FAX 01604-230176.
circ. 11,000. *5779*

BRITISH RACING NEWS.
British Racing & Sports Car Club, Brands Hatch Circuit, Fawkham, Dartford, Kent DA3 8NH, England.
circ. 4,500. *6754*

BRITISH SOCIETY OF DOWSERS. JOURNAL.
British Society of Dowsers, Sycamore Barn, Hastingleigh, Ashford, Kent TN25 5HW, England. TEL 01233-750253.
circ. 1,250. *5575*

BRNENSKY VECERNIK.
Brnensky Vecernik s.r.o., Jakubske Nam. 7, 664 83 Brno, Czech Republic. TEL 42-5-42321227. FAX 42-5-42215150.
circ. 15,000. *3273*

BROADCAST TECHNOLOGY.
Diversified Publications Ltd., 6 Farmer's Lane, Box 420, Bolton, ON L7E 5T3, Canada. TEL 905-857-6076.
circ. 6,500. *1983*

BROADCASTING & CABLE INTERNATIONAL.
Cahners Publishing Company (New York), Division of Reed Elsevier Inc., 245 W. 17th St., New York, NY 10011. TEL 212-337-6940. FAX 212-337-7028.
circ. 13,600. *2044*

BROADCASTING AND TELECOMMUNICATIONS FOR CHINA.
Sterling Publications Ltd., 86-88 Edgware Rd., London W2 2YW, England. TEL 44-171-915-9600. FAX 44-171-915-9619.
circ. 10,000. *1983*

BROKEN SPOKE.
Calgary Sports Car Club, P.O. Box 61143 Kensington Postal Stn., Calgary, AB T2N 4S6, Canada. TEL 403-285-1177. FAX 403-289-7256.
circ. 200. *7092*

BRONTE SOCIETY TRANSACTIONS.
Bronte Society, c/o Publications Secretary, Bronte Parsonage Museum, Haworth, Keighley, W. Yorks. BD22 8DR, England. TEL 44-1535-642323. FAX 44-1535-647131.
circ. 3,500. *4383*

BROTHERHOOD.
National Federation of Temple Brotherhoods, 838 Fifth Ave., New York, NY 10021. TEL 212-570-0707. FAX 212-570-0960.
circ. 60,000. *6402*

BROTS DE COLLCEROLA.
C.E.A. Aliga de Vallvidrera, Mont d'Orsa 17, 08017 Barcelona, Spain.
circ. 150. *1930*

BROWARD TIMES.
Broward Times, Inc., 11905 W. Sample Rd., Coral Springs, FL 33065-3164. TEL 954-345-1822. FAX 954-346-6377.
circ. 25,000. *3001*

BRUCE TRAIL NEWS.
Trail News Inc., 17 Marlborough Ave., Toronto, Ont. M5R 1X5, Canada. TEL 416-964-7281.
circ. 10,000. *6863*

BRUG.
Publicarto N.V., Langestraat 170, B-1150 Brussels, Belgium. TEL 32-2-7790000. FAX 32-2-7791616.
circ. 41,236. *2426*

BRUNSWICKAN.
University of New Brunswick, Student Union, P.O. Box 4400, Fredericton, NB E3B 5A3, Canada. TEL 506-453-4983. FAX 506-458-4958.
circ. 10,000. *1943*

BUCH UND BIBLIOTHEK.
Bock und Herchen Verlag, Postfach 1145, 53581 Bad Honnef, Germany. TEL 49-2224-5443. FAX 49-2224-78310.
circ. 7,200. *4167*

BUCHKULTUR.
Buchkultur Verlagsgesellschaft mbH, Waehringerstr. 104, A-1180 Vienna, Austria. TEL 01-4794642-0. FAX 01-479464210.
circ. 14,500. *4326*

BUDAPEST STUDIES IN ARABIC.
Eotvos Lorand University, Chair for Arabic Studies, Muzeum kit. 4-b, 1088 Budapest, Hungary.
circ. 600. *4246*

BUDAPESTI KOZGAZDASAGTUDOMANYI EGYETEM OKTATOINAK SZAKIRODALMI MUNKASSAGA.
Budapesti Kozgazdasagtudomanyi Egyetem, Fovam Ter 8, II-268, 1093 Budapest IX, Hungary. TEL 2179-377. FAX 2174-910.
circ. 300. *1025*

BUDDHISTISCHE MONATSBLAETTER.
Buddhistische Gesellschaft e.V., Beisserstr. 23, 22337 Hamburg, Germany. TEL 49-40-6313696. FAX 49-40-6313690.
circ. 560. *6388*

BUEHNE.
Orac Zeitschriftenverlag GmbH, Brunner Feldstr. 45, A-2380 Perchtoldsdorf, Austria. TEL 43-1-8696536. FAX 43-1-8696536.
circ. 103,800. *7003*

BUFFALO.
Girl Guides of Canada, Manitoba Council, 872 St. James St., Winnipeg, MB R3G 3J7, Canada. TEL 204-774-1939. FAX 204-774-9271.
circ. 1,474. *1839*

BUILD.
28 Lower Baggot St., Dublin 2, Ireland. TEL 766102. FAX 619781.
circ. 4,400. *868*

BUILDER (COLUMBUS).
Midland Mutual Life Insurance Company, 250 E. Broad St., Columbus, OH 43215. TEL 614-228-2001.
circ. 1,300. *3810*

BUILDER PROFILE.
Progressive Publishing, Inc., Box 354, Bloomingdale, IL 60108. TEL 630-582-8888. FAX 630-582-8895.
circ. 7,500. *869*

BUILDERS' MERCHANT NEWS.
B & M Publications (London) Ltd., P.O. Box 13, Hereford House, Bridle Path, Croydon, Surrey CR9 4NL, England. TEL 44-181-680-4200. FAX 44-181-681-5049.
circ. 7,591. *869*

BUILDING & CONSTRUCTION NEWS.
Al Hilal Publishing & Marketing Group, P.O. Box 224, Manama, Bahrain. TEL 973-293131. FAX 973-293400.
circ. 7,175. *869*

BUILDING & REMODELING NEWS.
S R Sound Inc., 600C Lake St., Ramsey, NJ 07446-1245. TEL 201-327-1600. FAX 201-327-3185.
circ. 75,000. *870*

BUILDING CONSTRUCTION NEWS.
Builders Exchange, Inc., 981 Keynote Circle, Cleveland, OH 44131-1842. *870*

BUILDING FOR LEISURE.
Stable Publishing, 19-21 High St., Sutton, Surrey SM1 1DJ, England. TEL 081-770-1080. FAX 081-643-9846.
circ. 12,000. *870*

BUILDING INDUSTRIES FEDERATION. ANNUAL REPORT.
Building Industries Federation, Attn.: Information Services Manager, 14 Alexandra Ave., Halfway House 1685, South Africa. TEL 27-11-8051985. FAX 27-11-3151644.
circ. 6,000. *870*

BUILDING INSPECTORS' ASSOCIATION OF NOVA SCOTIA. REPORTER.
Building Inspectors' Association of Nova Scotia, 2543 Barrington St., Halifax, NS B3K 2X2, Canada.
circ. 250. *871*

CONTROLLED CIRCULATION SERIALS

BUILDING OKLAHOMA.
Oklahoma Retailer Publishing Co., Inc., 4500 N. Sewell, Ste. 12, Oklahoma City, OK 73118. TEL 405-528-0903.
circ. 3,000. *871*

BUILDING PRODUCTS.
Hanley-Wood Inc., One Thomas Circle, Ste. 600, Washington, DC 20006. TEL 202-736-3301. FAX 202-785-1974.
circ. 80,000. *871*

BUILDINGS.
Stamats Communications, Inc., Box 1888, Cedar Rapids, IA 52406-1888. TEL 319-364-6167. FAX 319-364-4278.
circ. 56,600. *872*

BULL & BEAR FINANCIAL NEWSPAPER.
Box 917179, Longwood, FL 32791. TEL 407-682-6170.
circ. 10,000. *1377*

THE BULL BULLETIN.
c/o Industrial Controls Consulting, Inc., 104 S. Main St., Ste. 320, Fond du Lac, WI 54935. TEL 414-929-6544. FAX 414-929-9344.
circ. 4,000. *2107*

THE BULLETIN.
Ackroyd Publications, 1038 ch. de Waterloo, 1180 Brussels, Belgium. TEL 32-2-3739909. FAX 32-2-3759822.
circ. 16,000. *3254*

BULLETIN OF CONCERNED ASIAN SCHOLARS.
Bulletin of Concerned Asian Scholars, Inc., 464 19th St., Oakland, CA 94612-2297. TEL 510-451-1742. FAX 510-835-3017.
circ. 300. *6007*

BULLETIN OF TROPICAL MEDICINE AND INTERNATIONAL HEALTH.
Royal Society of Tropical Medicine and Hygiene, Manson House, 26 Portland Pl., London W1N 4EY, England. TEL 44-171-580-2127. FAX 44-171-436-1389.
circ. 2,500. *4833*

BULLETIN OF ZOO MANAGEMENT.
Royal Zoological Society of South Australia, Inc., Zoological Gardens, Frome Road, Adelaide, S.A. 5000, Australia.
circ. 250. *830*

BULLPEN.
Babe Ruth League, 1770 Brunswick Ave., Box 5000, Trenton, NJ 08638. TEL 609-695-1434. FAX 609-695-2505.
circ. 32,000. *6801*

THE BULLRUSH.
Innes Clan Society, 129 Ravenna Dr., Long Beach, CA 90803. TEL 310-438-6331.
circ. 300. *3215*

BUNDESGESETZBLATT FUER DIE REPUBLIK OESTERREICH.
Oesterreichische Staatsdruckerei, Rennweg 12a, A-1037 Vienna, Austria. TEL 01-79789307. FAX 01-79789419.
circ. 10,000. *4069*

DER BUNDESWEHRBEAMTE.
Vereinigte Verlagsanstalten GmbH, Hoeherweg 278, 40231 Duesseldorf, Germany. TEL 49-211-7357-0. FAX 49-211-7357223.
circ. 23,565. *5262*

BURRELLE'S CLIPPING ANALYST.
Burrelle's Press Clipping Service, 75 E. Northfield Rd., Livingston, NJ 07039. TEL 201-992-6600. FAX 201-992-5122.
circ. 5,000. *32*

BUS & COACH BUYER.
Bus & Coach Buyer Ltd., The Publishing Centre, 1 Woolram Wygate, Spalding, Lincs. PE11 1NU, England. TEL 44-1775-711777. FAX 44-1775-711737.
circ. 6,405. *7024*

BUS FAYRE.
Autobus Review Publications Ltd., 42 Coniston Ave., Queensbury, Bradford, W. Yorks. BD13 2JD, England. TEL 44-1274-881640.
circ. 2,000. *7024*

BUS TOURS MAGAZINE.
National Bus Trader, Inc., 9698 Judson Rd., Polo, IL 61064. TEL 815-946-2341. FAX 815-946-2347.
circ. 7,200. *7025*

BUSINESS AND HEALTH.
Medical Economics Publishing Co., Inc., 5 Paragon Dr., Montvale, NJ 07645. TEL 201-358-7208. FAX 201-573-1045.
circ. 38,000. *3811*

BUSINESS & TEACHER DIRECTORY (YEAR).
Society of Decorative Painters, 303 N. McLean Blvd., Wichita, KS 67203-5916. TEL 316-283-9665. FAX 316-283-5048.
circ. 4,000. *478*

BUSINESS DIGEST OF GREATER BURLINGTON.
Mill Publishing, Inc., 1233 Shelburne Rd., E-5, S. Burlington, VT 05403. TEL 802-862-4109. FAX 802-862-9322.
circ. 5,800. *940*

BUSINESS DIGEST OF GREATER WATERBURY.
Four Stars Publishing Co., Inc., Box 9018, 197 Tranquility Rd., Middlebury, CT 06702-2230. TEL 203-754-9922. FAX 203-754-5192.
circ. 6,300. *940*

BUSINESS DIRECTORY.
Mt. Diablo Peace Center, 65 Eckley Lane, Walnut Creek, CA 94596. TEL 415-933-7850. FAX 284-5357.
circ. 5,000. *1209*

BUSINESS EXECUTIVE.
Business Executive Inc., 466 Speers Rd., Ste. 220, Oakville ON L6K 3W9, Canada. TEL 905-845-8300. FAX 905-845-9086.
circ. 30,000. *1640*

BUSINESS FORUM (LOS ANGELES).
California State University, Los Angeles, School of Business & Economics, 5151 State University Dr., Los Angeles, CA 90032-8120. TEL 213-343-2806. FAX 213-343-5263.
circ. 1,000. *941*

BUSINESS FOUNDATION. BUSINESS & PLEASURE. A GENERAL GUIDE TO POLAND.
Business Foundation Co. Ltd., Ul. Krucza 38-42, 00-512 Warsaw, Poland. TEL 48-22-219993. FAX 48-22-219761.
circ. 20,000. *7189*

BUSINESS FOUNDATION. POLAND. INNOVATION, RESEARCH & DEVELOPMENT.
Business Foundation Co. Ltd., Ul. Krucza 38-42, 00-512 Warsaw, Poland. TEL 48-22-219993. FAX 48-22-219761.
circ. 4,000. *1657*

BUSINESS FOUNDATION BOOK. GENERAL TRADE INDEX & BUSINESS GUIDE.
Business Foundation Co. Ltd., Ul. Krucza 38-42, 00-512 Warsaw, Poland. TEL 48-22-219993. FAX 48-22-219761.
circ. 20,000. *1657*

BUSINESS GAZETTE.
Datateam Publishing Ltd., Attn: Rob Foreman, Fairmeadow, Maidstone, Kent ME14 IN9, England. TEL 01622-687031. FAX 01622-757646.
circ. 15,000. *1468*

BUSINESS GEOGRAPHICS.
G I S World, Inc., 155 E. Boardwalk Dr., Ste. 250, Ft. Collins, CO 80525. TEL 970-223-4848. FAX 970-223-5700.
circ. 22,120. *3397*

BUSINESS INSIGHT (RICHLAND).
B C O Marketing Communications, Inc., Box 347, Richland, MI 49083-0347. TEL 616-629-3131. FAX 616-629-0803.
circ. 8,692. *1640*

BUSINESS JOURNAL (PORTLAND).
American City Business Journals, Inc. (Portland), Box 14490, Portland, OR 97214. TEL 503-274-8733. FAX 503-227-2650.
circ. 4,100. *1227*

THE BUSINESS JOURNAL (SAN JOSE).
American City Business Journals, Inc. (Austin), 505 Powell St., Austin, TX 78703-5121. TEL 408-295-3800. FAX 408-295-5028.
circ. 2,800. *942*

BUSINESS MARKET NEWS.
Hemsing Advertising, 755 W. Big Beaver Rd., Ste. 416, Troy, MI 48084-4903. TEL 810-362-0448. FAX 810-362-3884. *942*

BUSINESS MARKETING.
Crain Communications, Inc. (Chicago), 740 Rush St., Chicago, IL 60611-2590. TEL 312-649-5260. FAX 312-649-5228.
circ. 47,853. *1517*

BUSINESS MEMO FROM BELGIUM.
Embassy of Belgium, Investments Office, 3330 Garfield St. N.W., Washington, DC 20008. TEL 202-625-5888. FAX 202-625-7567.
circ. 50,000. *1180*

BUSINESS MONEY.
Business Money Ltd., Srobe House, 10 Leigh Rd., Somerset BA16 0HA. TEL 44-1458-841112. FAX 44-1458-841286.
circ. 7,000. *1117*

BUSINESS NEWS (SOUTH WALES EDITION).
Euro Publications Ltd., Euro House, 14 Pearl St., Cardiff CF2 1HD, Wales.
circ. 5,000. *1227*

BUSINESS NEWS (WEST OF ENGLAND EDITION).
Euro Publications Ltd., Euro House, 14 Pearl St., Cardiff CF2 1HD, Wales.
circ. 5,000. *1227*

BUSINESS NEWS (WESTFORD).
U.S. Business Council for Southeastern Europe, 7 Broadway, No. 1028, New York, NY 10004-1004. TEL 212-439-9025. FAX 908-439-9105.
circ. 300. *942*

BUSINESS OPPORTUNITIES JOURNAL.
Business Service Corporation, Box 60762, San Diego, CA 92166. TEL 619-223-5661. FAX 619-223-1705.
circ. 25,000. *1377*

BUSINESS PHILADELPHIA.
Penn Communications Group, Inc., 260 S. Broad St., Philadelphia, PA 19102. TEL 215-735-6969. FAX 215-735-6965.
circ. 29,000. *1180*

BUSINESS SPACE REGISTER.
Business Space Registers Ltd., The Foremans Centre, High St., Headcorn, Kent TN27 9NE, England. TEL 44-1622-891589. FAX 44-1622-891590.
circ. 25,000. *6296*

BUSINESS SYSTEMS MAGAZINE.
Corry Publishing, 2840 W. 21st St., Erie, PA 16506-2970. TEL 814-838-0025. FAX 814-838-0035.
circ. 30,000. *1555*

BUSINESS TO BUSINESS.
Bracebridge Examiner Ltd., 16 Manitoba St., Box 1049, Bracebridge, Ont. P0B 1C0, Canada. TEL 705-645-8771. FAX 705-645-1718.
circ. 6,034. *944*

BUSINESS TRENDS ASIA REPORT: INDONESIA.
M P R C (Asia) Sdn. Berhad, P.O. Box 10706, 50722 Kuala Lumpur, Malaysia. TEL 60-3-2217762. FAX 60-3-7564478. *1228*

BUSINESSMATTERS.
G M C Publications Ltd., 166 High St., Lewes, E. Sussex BN7 1XU, England. TEL 01273-477374. FAX 01273-486300.
circ. 30,000. *1468*

BUSKONTAKT INTERNATIONAL.
Huss-Verlag GmbH; Joseph-Dollinger-Bogen 5, 80807 Munich, Germany. TEL 49-89-32391-0. FAX 49-89-32391416.
circ. 7,000. *7189*

BUTLER ALUMNI QUARTERLY.
Butler University, 4600 Sunset Ave., Indianapolis, IN 46208. TEL 317-283-9426.
circ. 24,000. *1943*

BUTLER AVIATION'S ECHELON.
Halsey Publishing Co., 438 Main St., Buffalo, NY 14202-3207. TEL 305-893-1520. *7065*

BUTLER COLLEGIAN.
Butler University, Journalism Department, 4600 Sunset Blvd., Indianapolis, IN 46208-3485. TEL 317-283-9358. FAX 317-283-9930.
circ. 3,000. *1943*

BUVISINDI.
Rannsoknastofnun Landbunadarins, Keldnaholti, IS-112 Reykjavik, Iceland. TEL 354-577-1010. FAX 354-577-1020.
circ. 600. *105*

BYG-TEK & BYGGERI.
Odsgard ApS, Hovedvejen 182, DK-2600 Glostrup, Denmark. TEL 45-43-45-34-91. FAX 45-43-43-13-28.
circ. 26,000. *873*

BYGG & JAERNHANDELN.
Bygg och Jaernhandelns Foerlag, P.O. Box 24143, S-104 51 Stockholm, Sweden. TEL 46-8-663-69-05. FAX 46-8-661-54-20.
circ. 3,400. *1519*

BYGG & TEKNIK.
Foerlags AB Bygg & Teknik, P.O. Box 19099, S-104 32 Stockholm, Sweden. TEL 46-8-612-17-50. FAX 46-8-612-54-81.
circ. 6,595. *873*

BYGGEINDUSTRIEN.
Teknisk Forlag A-S, Skelbaekgade 4, DK-1780 Copenhagen V, Denmark. TEL 45-31-21-68-01. FAX 45-31-21004-01.
circ. 2,793. *873*

BYGGFAKTA PROJEKTNYTT.
Byggfakta AB, S-827 81 Ljusdal, Sweden. TEL 46-651-194-00.
circ. 22,400. *873*

BYWAYS (FAIRFAX).
Patriot Marketing Group, Patriot Sq., 10527-C Braddock Rd., Fairfax, VA 22032. TEL 703-503-3613. FAX 703-250-1477.
circ. 48,000. *7190*

C A - A CANCER JOURNAL FOR CLINICIANS.
Lippincott - Raven Publishers, 227 E. Washington Sq., Philadelphia, PA 19106. TEL 215-238-4200.
circ. 300,000. *4972*

C A D - C A M & INDUSTRIAL SOFTWARE GUIDE.
Business & Management Editions Brussels s.p.r.l., Rue Stephanie, 17, 1020 Brussels, Belgium. TEL 32-2-4266115. FAX 32-2-4258226.
circ. 25,000. *2120*

C A D - C A M REPORT.
Dressler Verlag GmbH, Gaisbergstr. 55, 69115 Heidelberg, Germany. TEL 06221-91130. FAX 06221-911321.
circ. 19,700. *2120*

C A M M A C SOUTHERN ONTARIO REGION NEWSLETTER.
Canadian Amateur Musicians, Southern Ontario Region, 283 Bogert Ave., Toronto, ON M2N 1L4, Canada. TEL 416-250-8527.
circ. 470. *5379*

C A M MAGAZINE.
Construction Association of Michigan, 1625 S. Woodward Ave., Box 3204, Bloomfield Hill, MI 48302-3204. TEL 810-972-1000. FAX 810-972-1001.
circ. 4,200. *873*

C A S BULLETIN.
Catholic Archives Society, c/o P. Bracken, 43 Garthland Dr., Glasgow G31 2RE, Scotland.
circ. 280. *6453*

C B REPORT.
Higher Education Coordinating Board, Box 12788, Capitol Sta., Austin, TX 78711. TEL 512-483-6111. FAX 512-483-6127.
circ. 1,000. *2534*

C. BREWER TODAY.
C. Brewer & Co. Ltd., Box 1826, Honolulu, HI 96805. TEL 808-536-4461.
circ. 2,000. *1580*

C D N L A O NEWSLETTER.
National Diet Library, 1-10-1, Nagata-cho, Chiyoda-ku, Tokyo 100, Japan. TEL 81-3-3581-2331. FAX 81-3-3597-9104.
circ. 950. *4168*

C D SICHERHEITS-MANAGEMENT.
Richard Boorberg Verlag (Stuttgart), Scharrstr. 2, 70563 Stuttgart, Germany. TEL 0711-73850. FAX 0711-7352244.
circ. 14,000. *2285*

C F A DIGEST.
Association for Investment Management and Research, Box 3668, Charlottesville, VA 22903. TEL 804-977-3668. FAX 804-980-9755.
circ. 19,000. *1117*

C - F A R NEWSLETTER.
Citizens for Foreign Aid Reform Inc., Box 332, Stn. B, Etobicoke, Ont. M9W 5L3, Canada. TEL 905-897-7221. FAX 905-277-3914.
circ. 1,500. *1355*

C F B COMOX TOTEM TIMES.
C F B Comox Totem Times, Lazo, BC V0R 2K0, Canada. TEL 604-339-2541. FAX 604-339-5209.
circ. 2,600. *5262*

C H A C INFO.
Catholic Health Association of Canada, 1247 Kilborn Pl., Ottawa, ON K1H 6K9, Canada. TEL 613-731-7148. FAX 613-731-7797.
circ. 1,240. *3705*

C H A I LIGHTS.
Concern for Helping Animals in Israel, Box 3341, Alexandria, VA 22302. TEL 703-658-9650. FAX 703-941-6132.
circ. 3,000. *301*

C H I L D NEWSLETTER.
C H I L D, Inc., Box 2604, Sioux City, IA 51106. TEL 712-948-3500. FAX 712-948-3500.
circ. 440. *1839*

C I A T IN PERSPECTIVE.
Centro Internacional de Agricultura Tropical, Apdo. Aereo 6713, Cali, Colombia. TEL 57-2-4450000. FAX 57-2-4450073.
circ. 3,500. *106*

C I I T ACTIVITIES.
Chemical Industry Institute of Toxicology, Box 12137, 6 Davis Dr., Research Triangle Park, NC 27709-2178. TEL 919-558-1200. *2975*

C I I T IMPACT.
Chemical Industry Institute of Toxicology, Box 12137, 6 Davis Dr., Research Triangle Park, NC 27709-2178. TEL 919-558-1200. *2975*

C I L E C T NEWS.
Centre International de Liaison des Ecoles de Cinema et de Television, CILECT Secretariat, Rue Theresienne, 8, 1000 Brussels, Belgium. TEL 32-2-5119839. FAX 32-2-5110035.
circ. 400. *2045*

C I M NOTES.
Cleveland Institute of Music, 11021 E. Boulevard, Cleveland, OH 44106. TEL 216-791-5000. FAX 216-791-3063.
circ. 12,000. *5380*

C I O CANADA.
Laurentian Technomedia Inc., 501 Oakdale Rd., North York ON M3N 1W7, Canada. TEL 416-746-7360. FAX 416-746-1421.
circ. 7,600. *2126*

C I R I A REPORT.
Construction Industry Research and Information Association, 6 Storey's Gate, Westminster, London SW1P 3AU, England. TEL 44-171-222-8891. FAX 44-171-222-1708.
circ. 500. *2778*

C I S NEWS.
Chemical Information Systems, Inc., 810 Glen Eagles Ct., Ste. 300, Baltimore, MD 21286-2203. TEL 410-321-8440. FAX 410-296-0712.
circ. 2,500. *1799*

C I U S NEWSLETTER.
Canadian Institute of Ukrainian Studies, 352 Athabasca Hall, University of Alberta, Edmonton, AB T6G 2E8, Canada. TEL 403-492-2972. FAX 403-492-4967.
circ. 5,500. *3002*

C K OF A JOURNAL.
Catholic Knights of America, 1850 Dalton Ave., Cincinnati, OH 45214. TEL 513-721-0781. FAX 513-721-0783.
circ. 9,600. *1930*

C L R.
Medical Economics Publishing Co., Inc., Five Paragon Dr., Montvale, NJ 07645. TEL 201-358-7200. FAX 201-573-0344.
circ. 59,000. *4895*

C M B E S - S C G B NEWSLETTER.
Canadian Medical and Biological Engineering Society Inc., Rm. 382, Bldg. M-55, National Research Council, Ottawa, ON K1A 0R8, Canada. TEL 613-993-1686. FAX 613-954-2216. *4650*

C N C AND SOFTWARE GUIDE.
Gardner Publications, Inc., 6915 Valley Ave., Cincinnati, OH 45244-3029. TEL 513-527-8800. FAX 513-527-8801.
circ. 70,000. *4555*

C N S FOCUS.
Cargo Network Services, 300 Garden City Plaza, Ste. 312, Garden City, NY 11530-3325. TEL 516-747-3312. FAX 516-747-3331.
circ. 7,000. *7066*

C O M D A KEY.
Canadian Office Machine Dealers Association, 3464 Kingston Rd., Ste. 204, Scarborough, ON M1M 1R5, Canada. TEL 416-261-1607. FAX 416-261-1679.
circ. 1,837. *1555*

C O P A CONVERSATION.
Canadian Office Products Association, 1243 Islington Ave., Ste. 911, Toronto, ON M8X 1Y9, Canada. TEL 416-239-2737. FAX 416-239-1553.
circ. 4,900. *1555*

C P A C MONITOR.
Center for Process Analytical Chemistry, Box 351700, University of Washington, Seattle, WA 98195-1700. TEL 206-685-2326. FAX 206-543-6506.
circ. 1,800. *1789*

C P A CLIENT BULLETIN.
American Institute of Certified Public Accountants, Harborside Financial Ctr., 201 Plaza Three, Jersey City, NJ 07311-3881. TEL 201-938-3201. FAX 201-938-3329.
circ. 950,000. *1086*

C Q RADIO AMATEUR.
Cetisa - Boixareu S.A., Concepcion Arenal 5, 08027 Barcelona, Spain. TEL 34-3-3527061. FAX 34-3-3492350.
circ. 11,500. *2810*

C R E DOC.
Association of European Universities (CRE), 10 rue du Conseil General, CH-1211 Geneva 4, Switzerland. TEL 41-22-3292644. FAX 41-22-3292821.
circ. 1,300. *2534*

C R R I ROAD ABSTRACTS.
Central Road Research Institute, P.O. Central Road Research Institute, New Delhi 110020, India. TEL 6832274. *2747*

C S A MAGAZIN.
Centrum fuer Selbst Aktivierung e.V., Limesstr. 16, 61389 Schmitten, Germany. TEL 49-6082-970-0. FAX 49-6082-970113.
circ. 5,000. *5455*

C S A NEWS.
Council of Supervisors and Administrators of the City of New York, Local 1, American Federation of School Administrators, AFL-CIO, 16 Court St., 4th Fl., Brooklyn, NY 11241. TEL 718-852-3000. FAX 718-403-0278.
circ. 11,000. *2569*

10310 CONTROLLED CIRCULATION SERIALS

C S E A ANNUAL REPORT.
California Society of Enrolled Agents, 3200 Ramos Circle, Sacramento, CA 95827. TEL 916-366-6646. FAX 916-366-6674.
circ. 3,500. *1602*

C S S P CONGRESSIONAL SOURCEBOOK.
Capitol Advantage, Inc., 1155 16th St., N.W., Washington, DC 20036.
circ. 500. *6167*

C S S P NEWS.
Council of Scientific Society Presidents, 1155 16th St., N.W., Washington, DC 20036. TEL 202-872-4452. FAX 202-872-4079.
circ. 1,500. *6517*

C T E.
David Sheppard & Associates, 35 Picadilly, London W1V 1PB, England. TEL 44-171-734-6143. FAX 44-171-734-1737.
circ. 1,400. *2045*

C W A NEWS.
Communications Workers of America, 501 Third St., N.W., Washington, DC 20001. TEL 202-434-1100. FAX 202-434-1482.
circ. 520,000. *3887*

C W R U: THE MAGAZINE OF CASE WESTERN RESERVE UNIVERSITY.
Case Western Reserve University, 10900 Euclid Ave., Cleveland, OH 44106. TEL 216-368-6265. FAX 216-368-4835.
circ. 92,000. *1943*

CABLE WORLD.
Cowles Business Media (Denver), 1905 Sherman St., Denver, CO 80203. TEL 303-837-0900.
circ. 20,000. *2046*

CACHE CITIZEN.
Utah State University, Department of Communications, Box 703, Logan, UT 84321. TEL 801-750-3292.
circ. 18,000. *3371*

CADERNOS DO PATRIMONIO CULTURAL.
Secretaria Municipal de Cultura, Departamento Geral do Patrimonio Cultural, Rua Afonso Cavalcanti, 455, sala 207, 20211-110 Cidade Nova, Rio de Janeiro RJ, Brazil. TEL 55-21-2734095. FAX 55-21-5032158.
circ. 1,000. *6606*

CAFE REVIEW.
c/o Yes Books, 20 Danforth St., Portland, ME 04101. TEL 207-775-3233.
circ. 400. *4384*

CAHIERS DE L'UNIVERSITE DE PERPIGNAN.
Presses Universitaires de Perpignan, 52 av. de Villeneuve, 66860 Perpignan Cedex, France. TEL 33-4-68662000. FAX 33-4-68662019.
circ. 300. *4385*

CAHIERS DE NUTRITION ET DE DIETETIQUE.
Masson - Periodiques, 120 bd. St. Germain, 75006 Paris, France. TEL 33-1-40466200. FAX 33-1-40466201.
circ. 3,500. *5470*

CAHIERS DE PALEOANTHROPOLOGIE.
C N R S Editions, 20-22 rue St. Amand, 75015 Paris, France. TEL 45-33-16-00. FAX 45-33-92-13.
circ. 1,250. *5558*

CAHIERS DE PALEONTOLOGIE.
C N R S Editions, 20-22 rue St. Amand, 75015 Paris, France. TEL 45-33-16-00. FAX 45-33-92-13.
circ. 1,500. *5558*

CAHIERS DE PALEONTOLOGIE EST-AFRICAINE.
C N R S Editions, 20-22 rue St. Amand, 75015 Paris, France. TEL 45-33-16-00. FAX 45-33-92-13.
circ. 1,500. *5558*

CAHIERS NEPALAIS.
C N R S Editions, 20-22 rue St. Amand, 75015 Paris, France. TEL 45-33-16-00. FAX 45-33-92-13.
circ. 1,500. *5897*

THE CAIRN.
Whyte Museum of the Canadian Rockies, 111 Bear St., P.O. Box 160, Banff, AB T0L 0C0, Canada. TEL 403-762-2291. FAX 403-762-8919.
circ. 2,500. *5352*

CALIFORNIA. DEPARTMENT OF WATER RESOURCES. BULLETIN.
Department of Water Resources, Box 924836, Sacramento, CA 94236-0001. TEL 916-445-9248.
7288

CALIFORNIA. TEACHER'S RETIREMENT BOARD. STATE TEACHER'S RETIREMENT SYSTEM; ANNUAL REPORT TO THE GOVERNOR AND THE LEGISLATURE.
Teacher's Retirement Board, Box 15275, Sacramento, CA 95851-0275. TEL 916-229-3700.
circ. 1,500. *2569*

CALIFORNIA ACCOUNTANCY ACT WITH RULES AND REGULATIONS.
Department of Consumer Affairs, Board of Accountancy, 2000 Evergreen St., Ste. 250, Sacramento, CA 95815-3832. TEL 916-263-3680. FAX 916-263-3975.
circ. 45,000. *1086*

CALIFORNIA COOPERATIVE OCEANIC FISHERIES INVESTIGATIONS REPORTS.
California Cooperative Oceanic Fisheries Investigations, Scripps Institution of Oceanography, University of California, La Jolla, CA 92093-0227. TEL 619-534-4236. FAX 619-534-6500.
circ. 1,200. *3063*

CALIFORNIA EDUCATOR.
California Teachers Association, 1705 Murchison Dr., Burlingame, CA 94010-4583. TEL 415-697-1400. FAX 415-697-0786.
circ. 277,000. *2534*

CALIFORNIA FAMILY PHYSICIAN.
California Academy of Family Physicians, 114 Sansome St., Ste. 1305, San Francisco, CA 94104-3824. TEL 415-394-9121. FAX 415-394-9119.
circ. 6,900. *4650*

CALIFORNIA PRUNE NEWS.
California Prune Board, 5990 Stoneridge Dr., Ste. 101, Pleasanton, CA 94588-3234. TEL 510-734-0150. FAX 510-734-0525.
circ. 1,750. *218*

CALIFORNIA SCHOOL EMPLOYEE.
California School Employees Association, Box 640, San Jose, CA 95106. TEL 408-263-8000. FAX 408-954-0948.
circ. 106,000. *2569*

CALIFORNIA TEACHER.
California Federation of Teachers, One Kaiser Plaza, Ste. 1440, Oakland, CA 94612. TEL 510-832-8812. FAX 510-832-5044.
circ. 45,000. *2427*

CALIFORNIA WATER ENVIRONMENT ASSOCIATION. BULLETIN.
California Water Environment Association, 7677 Oakport St., Ste. 525, Oakland, CA 94621-1935. FAX 510-382-7810.
circ. 7,000. *7289*

CALL NUMBER.
University of North Texas, School of Library and Information Sciences, N.T. Box 13796, Denton, TX 76203. TEL 817-565-2445. FAX 817-565-3101.
circ. 3,000. *4169*

CALL OF THE LOON.
Ontario Federation of Anglers & Hunters, 4601 Guthrie Dr., P.O. Box 2800, Peterborough, ON K9J 8L5, Canada. TEL 705-748-6324. FAX 705-748-9577.
circ. 1,300. *2225*

CALL TO ACTION.
Board of Education, 5057 Woodward, Detroit, MI 48202. TEL 313-494-1000.
circ. 22,000. *2427*

CALORIE CONTROL COMMENTARY.
Calorie Control Council, 5775 Peachtree-Dunwoody Rd., Ste. 500-G, Atlanta, GA 30342. TEL 404-252-3663. FAX 404-252-0774.
circ. 12,000. *5471*

CAMARA DE COMERCIO HISPANO-SUECA DE MADRID. INFO.
Camara de Comercio Hispano-Sueca de Madrid, Caracas, 23, 28010 Madrid, Spain.
circ. 500. *1181*

CAMARA DE COMERCIO URUGUAYO - BRITANICA. BOLETIN INFORMATIVO.
Camara de Comercio Uruguayo - Britanica, Av. Libertador Brig. Gral. Lavalleja, P. 2, Of. 201, 11000 Montevideo, Uruguay. TEL 5982-98-0349. FAX 5982-90-0936.
circ. 150. *945*

CAMARA NACIONAL DE LA INDUSTRIA DE TRANSFORMACION. BOLETIN INFORMATIVO.
Camara Nacional de la Industria de Transformacion, Apdo. Postal 60-468, Av. San Antonio 256, 03849 Mexico, D.F., Mexico. TEL 5-563-3500. *1580*

CAMBRIDGE TIMES.
240 Holiday Inn Dr., Cambridge, ON, Canada. TEL 519-651-2390. FAX 519-651-2358.
circ. 31,400. *3259*

CAMPBELL'S LIST.
Campbell's List, Inc., Campbell Bldg., 100 E. Ventris Ave., Maitland, FL 32751. TEL 407-644-8298. FAX 407-740-6494.
circ. 10,000. *3927*

CAMPESINO.
Editora Dosmil, Carrera 39 A No 15-11, Bogota D.E., Colombia.
circ. 70,000. *3272*

CAMPING AND R V MAGAZINE.
Box 458, Washburn, WI 54891-0458. TEL 715-373-5556. FAX 715-373-5003.
circ. 4,000. *6864*

CAMPUS ACTIVITIES PROGRAMMING.
National Association for Campus Activities, 13 Harbison Way, Columbia, SC 29212-3401. TEL 803-732-6222. FAX 803-749-1047.
circ. 6,500. *2534*

CAMPUS LE MAG.
Rayonnement 5, 4 rue Barthelemy, 92120 Montrouge, France. TEL 33-1-42539089. FAX 33-1-42537875.
circ. 150,000. *1866*

CAMPUS LEADER.
University of Manila, 546 Dr. M.V. de los Santos St., Sampaloc, Manila D-403, Philippines.
circ. 8,000. *2427*

CAMROSE BOOSTER.
Camrose Booster Ltd., 4925 48th St., Camrose, AB T4V 1L7, Canada. TEL 403-672-3142. FAX 403-672-2518.
circ. 12,548. *3259*

CAN MAKERS REPORT.
Can Makers Information Service, 1 Chelsea Manor Gardens, London SW3 5PN, England. TEL 44-171-351-2400. FAX 44-171-352-6246.
circ. 3,000. *518*

CAN TECHNOLOGY INTERNATIONAL.
Trend Publishing Inc., 625 N. Michigan Ave., Ste. 2500, Chicago, IL 60611-3109. TEL 312-654-2300. FAX 312-654-2323.
circ. 1,500. *5542*

CANADA. GRAIN COMMISSION. CORPORATE SERVICES. EXPORTS OF CANADIAN GRAIN AND WHEAT FLOUR.
Grain Commission, Corporate Services, 700-303 Main St., Winnipeg, MB R3C 3G8, Canada. TEL 204-983-2793.
circ. 250. *171*

CANADIAN ART.
Canadian Art Foundation, 70 The Esplanade, 2nd Fl., Toronto, ON M5E 1R2, Canada. TEL 416-368-8854. FAX 416-368-6135.
circ. 4,000. *434*

CANADIAN ASSOCIATION FOR LABORATORY ANIMAL SCIENCE NEWSLETTER.
Canadian Association for Laboratory Animal Science (CALAS), c/o Dr. Donald G. McKay, Biosciences Animal Service, University of Alberta, Edmonton, AB T6G 2E9, Canada.
circ. 1,000. *4895*

CANADIAN ASSOCIATION OF SLAVISTS NEWSLETTER.
Canadian Association of Slavists, c/o Gust Olson, University of Alberta, 347 Arts Building, Edmonton, AB T6G 2E6, Canada. TEL 403-492-2566. FAX 403-492-2715.
circ. 400. *3774*

CANADIAN BIOTECH RESEARCH.
Canadian Biotechnology News Service, 20 Stone Park Lane, Nepean, ON K2H 9P4, Canada. TEL 613-726-0115. FAX 613-726-7344.
circ. 3,000. *681*

CANADIAN ELECTRONICS.
Action Communications Inc., 135 Spy Court, Markham, ON L3R 5H6, Canada. TEL 905-477-3222. FAX 905-477-4320.
circ. 22,000. *2811*

CANADIAN ELECTRONICS ANNUAL BUYER'S GUIDE.
Action Communications Inc., 135 Spy Court, Markham, ON L3R 5H6, Canada. TEL 905-477-3222. FAX 905-477-4320.
circ. 22,000. *2811*

CANADIAN ENVIRONMENTAL PROTECTION.
Baum Publications Ltd., 1625 Ingleton Ave., Burnaby, BC V5C 4L8, Canada. TEL 604-291-9900. FAX 604-291-1906.
circ. 23,393. *2910*

CANADIAN EQUESTRIAN FEDERATION. BULLETIN.
Canadian Equestrian Federation, 1600 James Naismith Dr., Ottawa, ON K1B 4S8, Canada. TEL 613-748-5632. FAX 613-747-2920.
circ. 10,000. *6849*

CANADIAN FACILITY MANAGEMENT & DESIGN.
C F M Communications, 62 Olsen Dr., Don Mills, ON M3A 3J3, Canada. TEL 416-447-3417. FAX 416-447-4410.
circ. 6,000. *3842*

CANADIAN FRUITGROWER.
N C C Publishing, 222 Argyle Ave., Delhi, ON N4B 2Y2, Canada. TEL 519-582-2510. FAX 519-582-4040.
circ. 4,000. *3184*

CANADIAN HEALTHCARE BUSINESS NEWS.
B C S Communications Ltd., 101 Thorncliff Park Dr., Toronto, ON M4H 1M2, Canada. TEL 416-421-7944. FAX 416-421-0966.
circ. 5,000. *5042*

CANADIAN HOME ECONOMICS JOURNAL.
Canadian Home Economics Association, Burnside Bldg., Ste. 901, 901 - 151 Slater St., Ottawa, ON K1P 5H3, Canada. TEL 613-238-8817. FAX 613-238-1677.
circ. 2,800. *3682*

CANADIAN INDEPENDENT ADJUSTER.
Journal Management, 55 Queen St., E., Toronto, ON M5C 1R6, Canada.
circ. 3,400. *3812*

CANADIAN JOURNAL OF ALLERGY AND CLINICAL IMMUNOLOGY.
Medicopea International Inc., 3333 Cote Vertu Blvd., Ste. 300, St. Laurent, PQ H4R 2N1, Canada. TEL 514-333-4561. FAX 514-336-1129.
circ. 3,600. *4792*

CANADIAN JOURNAL OF CARDIOLOGY.
Pulsus Group Inc., 2902 S. Sheridan Way, Oakville, ON L6J 7L6, Canada. TEL 905-829-4770. FAX 905-829-4799.
circ. 16,000. *4811*

CANADIAN JOURNAL OF CLINICAL PHARMACOLOGY.
Pulsus Group Inc., 2902 S. Sheridan Way, Oakville, ON L6J 7L6, Canada. TEL 905-829-4770. FAX 905-829-4799.
circ. 18,000. *5651*

CANADIAN JOURNAL OF DERMATOLOGY.
Rodar Publishing Inc., 8102 Trans Canada Hwy., St. Laurent, PQ H4S 1Z4, Canada. TEL 514-333-5350.
circ. 9,640. *4875*

CANADIAN JOURNAL OF DIABETES CARE.
Canadian Diabetes Association, 15 Toronto St., Ste. 800, Toronto, ON M5C 2E3, Canada. TEL 416-363-3373. FAX 416-363-3393.
circ. 7,000. *4883*

CANADIAN JOURNAL OF GASTROENTEROLOGY.
Pulsus Group Inc., 2902 S. Sheridan Way, Oakville, ON L6J 7L6, Canada. TEL 905-829-4770. FAX 905-829-4799.
circ. 16,000. *4908*

CANADIAN JOURNAL OF INFECTION CONTROL.
Pulsus Group Inc., 2902 S. Sheridan Way, Oakville, ON L6J 7L6, Canada. TEL 905-829-4770. FAX 905-829-4799.
circ. 3,000. *4833*

CANADIAN JOURNAL OF NETHERLANDIC STUDIES.
Canadian Association for the Advancement of Netherlandic Studies, Department of French, University of Windsor, Windsor, ON N9B 3P4, Canada. TEL 519-253-4232. FAX 519-971-3648.
circ. 300. *4386*

CANADIAN JOURNAL OF OB-GYN & WOMEN'S HEALTH CARE.
Rodar Publishing Inc., 8102 Trans Canada Hwy., St. Laurent, PQ H4S 1Z4, Canada. TEL 514-333-5350.
circ. 17,000. *4954*

CANADIAN JOURNAL OF OCCUPATIONAL THERAPY.
Canadian Association of Occupational Therapists, CTTC Ste. 3400, 1125 Colonel By-drive, Ottawa, ON K1S 5R1, Canada. TEL 613-523-2268. FAX 613-523-2552.
circ. 6,172. *5042*

CANADIAN JOURNAL OF PEDIATRICS.
Rodar Publishing Inc., 8102 Trans Canada Hwy., St. Laurent, PQ H4S 1Z4, Canada. TEL 514-333-5350. FAX 514-457-2679.
circ. 15,800. *5029*

CANADIAN LEATHERCRAFT.
Canadian Society of Creative Leathercraft, c/o Lois MacPherson, 1506 - 205 Queen Mary Dr., Oakville, ON L6K 3K8, Canada.
circ. 90. *478*

CANADIAN METEOROLOGICAL AND OCEANOGRAPHIC SOCIETY. ANNUAL CONGRESS.
Canadian Meteorological and Oceanographic Society, Ste. 112, McDonald Bldg., 150 Louis Pasteur, Ottawa, ON K1N 6N5, Canada. TEL 613-562-5616. FAX 613-562-5615.
circ. 850. *5228*

CANADIAN MUSEUM OF FLIGHT & TRANSPORTATION. MUSEUM NEWSLETTER.
Canadian Museum of Flight & Transportation, Unit 200, 5333 216th St. Langley Airport, Langley, BC V3A 4R1, Canada. TEL 604-532-0035. FAX 604-532-0056.
circ. 2,000. *5352*

CANADIAN MUSIC TRADE.
Norris - Whitney Communications Inc., 23 Hannover Dr., No. 7, St. Catharines, ON L2W 1A3, Canada. TEL 905-641-3471. FAX 905-641-1648.
circ. 3,000. *5381*

CANADIAN MUSLIM.
Ottawa Muslim Association, P.O. Box 2952, Sta. D, Ottawa, Ont. 51P 5W9, Canada. TEL 613-725-0004.
circ. 2,000. *6396*

CANADIAN OCCUPATIONAL SAFETY.
Clifford Elliot & Associates Ltd., 3228 South Service Rd., Burlington, ON L7N 3H8, Canada. TEL 905-634-2100. FAX 905-634-2238.
circ. 12,000. *1469*

CANADIAN PHILATELIST.
Philaprint Ltd., Box 100, First Canadian Pl., Toronto, ON M5X 1B2, Canada. TEL 519-846-9954.
circ. 7,000. *5705*

CANADIAN PLASTICS.
Southam Magazine Group, 1450 Don Mills Rd., Don Mills, ON M3B 2X7, Canada. TEL 416-445-6641. FAX 416-442-2213.
circ. 10,188. *5876*

CANADIAN PROCESS EQUIPMENT & CONTROL NEWS.
Canadian Process Equipment & Control News Ltd., 343 Eglinton Ave. E., Toronto, ON M4P 1L7, Canada. TEL 416-481-6483. FAX 416-481-6436.
circ. 25,118. *946*

CANADIAN PROFESSIONAL SALES ASSOCIATION. CONTACT.
Canadian Professional Sales Association, 145 Wellington St. W., Ste. 310, Toronto, ON M5J 1H8, Canada. TEL 416-408-2685. FAX 416-408-2684.
circ. 30,000. *1520*

CANADIAN PROPERTY MANAGEMENT.
MediaEdge Communications Inc., 5255 Yonge St., Ste. 1000, North York, ON M2N 6P4, Canada. TEL 416-512-8186. FAX 416-512-8344.
circ. 14,210. *6297*

CANADIAN RAIL.
Canadian Railroad Historical Association, Box 22, Sta. B, Montreal, PQ H3B 3J5, Canada.
circ. 1,100. *7124*

CANADIAN REALTOR NEWS.
The Canadian Real Estate Association, 344 Slater St., Ste. 1600, Canada Building, Ottawa, ON K1R 7Y3, Canada. TEL 613-237-7111. FAX 613-234-2567.
circ. 72,000. *6297*

CANADIAN SAILOR.
Seafarers International Union of Canada, 1333 rue St-Jacques, Montreal, Que. H3C 4K2, Canada. FAX 514-931-3667.
circ. 5,000. *5262*

CANADIAN SOCIETY FOR MECHANICAL ENGINEERING. TRANSACTIONS.
Canadian Society for Mechanical Engineering, McGill University, Rm. 454 Thomas Workman Engineering Bldg., 817 Sherbrooke St. W., Montreal, PQ H3A 2K6, Canada. TEL 514-398-6311. FAX 514-398-4476.
circ. 350. *2881*

CANADIAN SPORTSCARD COLLECTOR.
Trajan Publishing Corp., 103 Lakeshore Rd., Ste. 202, St. Catharines, ON L2N 2T6, Canada. TEL 905-646-7744. FAX 905-646-0995.
circ. 150. *3664*

CANADIAN TRAVEL PRESS.
Baxter Publishing Co., 310 Dupont St., Toronto, ON M5R 1V9, Canada. TEL 416-968-7252. FAX 416-968-2377.
circ. 14,300. *7191*

CANADIAN WOOD PRODUCTS.
J C F T Forest Communications, 1 rue Pacifique, Ste-Anne-de-Bellevue, PQ H9X 1C5, Canada. TEL 514-457-2211.
circ. 7,000. *3170*

CANCER CONTROL.
Moffitt Cancer Center, 12902 Magnolia Dr., Tampa, FL 33612. TEL 813-632-1349. FAX 813-632-1380.
circ. 25,000. *4973*

CANCER RESEARCH CAMPAIGN. ANNUAL REVIEW.
Cancer Research Campaign, Cambridge House, 6-10 Cambridge Terr., Regent's Park, London NW1 4JL, England. TEL 071-224-1333. *4974*

CANINE COURIER.
United States Police Canine Association, Inc., Rte. 2, Box 221 J, Angier, NC 27501. TEL 919-639-0490. FAX 919-639-6091.
circ. 3,000. *5635*

CANOE FOCUS.
British Canoe Union, Adbolton Ln., W. Bridgford, Nottingham NG2 5AS, England. TEL 0115-9821100. FAX 0115-9821797.
circ. 23,000. *6837*

CANOMA.
Canadian Permanent Committee on Geographical Names, Secretariat CPCGN - Geographical Names, 634 - 615 Booth St., Ottawa, ON K1A 0E9, Canada. TEL 613-992-3892. FAX 613-943-8282.
circ. 500. *3398*

CONTROLLED CIRCULATION SERIALS

CANTEEN NEWS.
Sterling Media, P.O. Box 670, Seven Hills, N.S.W. 2147, Australia. TEL 61-2-98387233. FAX 61-2-96742004.
circ. 10,000. *2570*

CANTERAS Y EXPLOTACIONES.
Miller Freeman, S.A., Maria Auxiliadora 5, 28040 Madrid, Spain. TEL 1-450-88-37. FAX 1-450-94-29.
circ. 10,273. *5297*

CAPE COD LIFE.
Cape Cod Life, Inc., Box 1385, Pocasset, MA 02559-1385. TEL 508-564-4466. FAX 508-564-4470.
circ. 3,694. *3371*

CAPITAL GAY.
Stonewall Press Ltd., 1 Tavistock Chambers, Bloomsbury Way, London WC1A 2SE, England. TEL 0171-242-2750. FAX 0171-242-3334.
circ. 21,586. *3692*

CAPITAL MAGAZINE.
Cappub, Inc., 300 Mill St., Vienna, VA 22180-4524. FAX 703-938-4562.
circ. 70,000. *7191*

CAPITAL NURSING.
District of Columbia Nurses Association, 5100 Wisconsin Ave., N.W., Ste. 306, Washington, DC 20016. TEL 202-244-2705. FAX 202-362-8285.
circ. 15,000. *4930*

CAPITAL REGION U S A.
Phoenix Publishing & Media Ltd., 18-20 Scrutton St., London EC2A 4RJ, England. TEL 44-171-247-0537. FAX 44-171-377-2741.
circ. 140,000. *7191*

CAPITAL SPORTS FOCUS.
Capital Sports Focus, Inc., 124 E. Diamond Ave., Ste. 7, Gaithersburg, MD 20877-3072. TEL 301-670-6717. FAX 301-670-9043.
circ. 100,000. *6755*

CAPITAL XTRA.
Pink Triangle Press (Ottawa), 177 Nepean St., Ste. 506, Ottawa, ON K2P 0B4, Canada. TEL 613-237-7133. FAX 613-237-6651.
circ. 17,000. *3692*

CAPTION.
National Captioning Institute, Inc., 1900 Gallows Rd., Ste. 3000, Vienna, VA 22182-3865. FAX 703-998-2450.
circ. 100,000. *2047*

CARD PLAYER.
3140 S. Polaris Ave., Las Vegas, NV 89102. TEL 702-871-1720. FAX 702-871-2674.
circ. 40,000. *6755*

CARDIOVASCULARIA.
M M V Medizin Verlag, Neumarkter Str. 18, 81673 Munich, Germany. TEL 49-89-43189647. FAX 49-89-43189633.
circ. 55,000. *4813*

CAREER SUCCESS.
Target Marketing, Inc., 1 Liberty Bell Circle, Ste. 200, Liberty, MO 64068. TEL 816-781-7557. FAX 816-792-3892.
circ. 400,000. *5506*

CAREERS & COLLEGES.
E.M. Guild, Inc., 989 Ave. of the Americas, 6th Fl., New York, NY 10018. TEL 212-563-4688. FAX 212-967-2531.
circ. 500,000. *5506*

CAREERS & MAJORS.
Oxendine Publishing, Inc., Box 14081, Gainesville, FL 32604-2081. TEL 352-373-6907. FAX 352-373-8120.
circ. 18,000. *5506*

CAREERS UNLIMITED.
Target Marketing, Inc., 5 Victory Ln., Ste. 101, Liberty, MO 64068. TEL 816-781-7557. FAX 816-792-3892.
circ. 200,000. *5262*

CARGO CLAN.
Emphasis HK Ltd., 505-508 Westlands Centre, 20 Westlands Rd., Quarry Bay, Hong Kong, People's Republic of China. TEL 25161000. FAX 25613306.
circ. 10,000. *7147*

CARGOVISION.
K L M Royal Dutch Airlines, Information and Documentation Department, Postbus 7700, 1117 ZL Schiphol, Netherlands. TEL 31-20-6494545. FAX 31-20-6439261.
circ. 40,000. *7066*

CARIBBEAN UPDATE.
Kal Wagenheim, Ed. & Pub., 52 Maple Ave., Maplewood, NJ 07040. TEL 201-762-1565. FAX 201-762-9585. *1318*

CARIBBEAN WEEK.
Caribbean Communications Inc., Lefferts Pl., River Rd., St. Michael, Barbados, W.I. TEL 246-436-1902.
circ. 26,400. *3391*

CARING TIMES.
Hawker Publications, 13 Park House, 140 Battersea Park Rd., London SW11 4NB, England. TEL 0171-720-2108. FAX 0171-498-3023.
circ. 16,500. *6658*

CARING TODAY.
Vivien Shepherd, Ed. & Pub., 1 Ewood Ct., Hebden Bridge, W. Yorks. HX7 5QX, England. TEL 44-1422-882467. FAX 44-1422-885160.
circ. 12,500. *6658*

CARNEGIE MUSEUM OF NATURAL HISTORY. BULLETIN.
Carnegie Museum of Natural History, Office of Scientific Publications, 4400 Forbes Ave., Pittsburgh, PA 15213-4080. TEL 412-622-3287. FAX 412-622-8837. *6518*

CARNETEC.
Marketing and Technology Group, Inc., 1415 N. Dayton St., Chicago, IL 60622. TEL 312-266-3311. FAX 312-266-3363.
circ. 4,400. *3098*

CAROLINA STYLE.
Carolina Style, Inc., 6404 Serena Ct., Wilmington, NC 28405-4773. TEL 919-341-3033.
circ. 100,000. *3371*

THE CARPENTER.
United Brotherhood of Carpenters and Joiners of America, 101 Constitution Ave., N.W., Washington, DC 20001. TEL 202-546-6206. FAX 202-547-8979.
circ. 500,000. *924*

CARPET CUSHION COUNCIL. FACT SHEET.
Carpet Cushion Council, Box 546, Riverside, CT 06878. TEL 203-637-1312. FAX 203-698-1022.
circ. 3,000. *3853*

CARROSSERIE.
Nederlandse Vereniging van Ondernemers in het Carrosseriebedrijf, Postbus 299, 2170 AG Sassenheim, Netherlands. TEL 31-252-265222. FAX 31-252-265255.
circ. 3,100. *7094*

CARSON - NEWMAN STUDIES.
Carson - Newman College, Jefferson City, TN 37760. TEL 423-471-3275. FAX 423-471-3502.
circ. 600. *2535*

CASA STILE.
Agenzia Gestione Periodici, Via D. Trentacoste 9, 20134 Milan, Italy. TEL 39-2-215621. FAX 39-2-2640330.
circ. 12,000. *3842*

CASE ALUMNUS.
Case Western Reserve University, Case Alumni Association, Crawford Hall 107, 10900 Euclid Ave., Cleveland, OH 44106-7073. TEL 216-231-4567. FAX 216-368-4714.
circ. 16,000. *1944*

CASHEW BULLETIN.
Cashew Export Promotion Council of India, Chittoor Rd., Cochin 682 016, India. TEL 91-484-361459.
circ. 700. *3098*

CASHFLOW.
MarketLynx, 462 Boston St., Topsfield, MA 01983. TEL 508-887-7900. *1641*

CASINO GAMES MAGAZINE.
Compass International, Inc., 1009 Nawkee Dr., Ste. 711, North Las Vegas, NV 89031-1425. TEL 702-399-3998. FAX 702-399-3997.
circ. 150,000. *6755*

CASSIOPEIA.
Canadian Astronomical Society, c/o Dept. of Mathematics, Physics & Engineering, Mount Royal College, 4825 Richard Rd., S.W., Calgary, AB T3E 6K6, Canada. TEL 403-240-6029. FAX 430-240-6664.
circ. 400. *492*

CASTING DESIGN & APPLICATION.
Penton Publishing Co., 1100 Superior Ave., Cleveland, OH 44114. TEL 216-696-7000.
circ. 22,000. *5188*

CASUALTY SIMULATION.
Casualties Union, P.O. Box 707A, Friend St., London ECIV 7NE. TEL 44-171-2786264.
circ. 2,000. *6230*

CAT FANCIERS' ASSOCIATION. ANNUAL YEARBOOK.
Cat Fanciers' Association, Inc., 1805 Atlantic Ave., Box 1005, Manasquan, NJ 08736-1005. TEL 908-528-9797. FAX 908-528-7391.
circ. 7,500. *5635*

CATALOGO MOTORISTICO.
Azienda Cataloghi Italiani s.a.s., Via B. Crespi, 30-2, 20159 Milan, Italy. TEL 39-2-606052. FAX 39-2-606487.
circ. 35,000. *7094*

CATALYST (MELBOURNE).
Royal Melbourne Institute of Technology, Student Union, P.O. Box 12387, A'Beckett St., Melbourne, Vic. 8006, Australia. TEL 61-3-96602884. FAX 61-3-96603705.
circ. 10,000. *1944*

CATALYST (WASHINGTON).
National Crime Prevention Council, 1700 K St., N.W., 2nd Fl., Washington, DC 20006-3817. TEL 202-466-6272. FAX 202-296-1356.
circ. 15,000. *2263*

CATALYST: RESEARCH AT THE UNIVERSITY OF CALGARY.
University of Calgary, Research Services, Public Affairs, 2500 University Drive N.W., Calgary, AB T2N 1N4, Canada. TEL 403-220-3783. FAX 403-282-8413.
circ. 3,000. *6518*

LA CATASTROPHE.
Wreck & Crash Mail Society, 132 Livingston Pl. W., Metairie, LA 70005. TEL 504-835-2856.
circ. 80. *2019*

CATERING BUTCHER.
9 Vermont Pl., Tongwell, Milton Keynes, Bucks. MK15 8JA. TEL 01908-613323. FAX 01908-210656.
circ. 16,065. *3098*

CATERING INDUSTRY EMPLOYEE.
Hotel Employees & Restaurant Employees International Union, A F L - C I O, 1219 28th St., N.W., Washington, DC 20007-3316. TEL 202-393-4373. FAX 202-965-2958.
circ. 250,000. *3888*

CATERVEG MAGAZINE.
Caterveg Association for Vegetarian Catering, Caterveg House, 15 The Old Stables, E. Langton, Leics. LE16 7TW, England. TEL 44-1858-545733. FAX 44-1858-545419.
circ. 40,000. *3724*

CATHEDRAL.
Cathedral Church of St. John the Divine, 1047 Amsterdam Ave. at 112th St., New York, NY 10025. TEL 212-932-7336. FAX 212-932-7348.
circ. 13,000. *3870*

THE CATHOLIC.
Incorporated Catholic Truth Society, 192 Vauxhall Bridge Rd., London SW1V 1PD, England. TEL 0171-834 4392. FAX 0171-630-1124.
circ. 25,000. *6454*

CATHOLIC ARCHDIOCESE OF LOUISVILLE. RECORD.
Catholic Archdiocese of Louisville, 1200 S. Shelby St., Louisville, KY 40203-2600. TEL 502-587-1327.
circ. 61,700. *6454*

CATHOLIC BOOK PUBLISHERS ASSOCIATION DIRECTORY.
Catholic Book Publishers Association, 2 Park Ave., Ste. 206, Manhasset, NY 11030-2442. TEL 516-869-0122. FAX 516-627-1381.
circ. 2,200. *6267*

CATHOLIC FORESTER.
Catholic Order of Foresters, 355 Shuman Blvd., Box 3012, Naperville, IL 60566-7012. TEL 708-983-4900. FAX 708-983-4057.
circ. 100,000. *3371*

CATHOLIC NEAR EAST MAGAZINE.
Cathoilc Near East Welfare Association, 1011 First Ave., New York, NY 10022-4195. TEL 212-826-1480. FAX 212-826-8979.
circ. 100,000. *6456*

CATHOLIC UNIVERSITY MEDICAL COLLEGE JOURNAL.
Catholic University, Graduate School, c/o Catholic Medical College, 505 Banpo-dong, Kangnam-gu, Seoul 135, S. Korea. TEL 02-593-5141. FAX 02-532-3112.
circ. 1,000. *4652*

CATHOLIC WORKMAN.
Box 47, New Prague, MN 56071. TEL 612-758-2229. FAX 612-758-6221.
circ. 8,500. *6457*

CATNAP.
Narcolepsy Association (U.K.), 1 Brook St., Stoke-on-Trent ST4 1JN, England. TEL 44-1782-416417. FAX 44-1782-416417.
circ. 800. *5057*

CATS.
Our Dogs Publishing Co. Ltd., 5 James Leigh St., Manchester M1 6EX, England. TEL 44-161-237-1272. FAX 44-161-236-5534.
circ. 7,000. *5636*

CAVALLO MAGAZINE.
Solitaire S.p.A., Via Enrico Mattei 106, 40138 Bologna, Italy. TEL 39-51-536496. FAX 39-51-536497.
circ. 26,322. *302*

CE B I T NEWS.
Portman Communications Ltd., 52 Foundling Ct., London WC1N 1AN, England. TEL 44-171-837-0815. FAX 44-171-278-9917.
circ. 50,000. *2126*

CEDARVILLE TORCH.
Cedarville College, Box 601, Cedarville, OH 45314. TEL 937-766-7808. FAX 937-766-2760.
circ. 60,000. *1944*

CENTENNIAL STATE LIBRARIES.
State Library, Department of Education, 201 E. Colfax Ave., Rm. 309, Denver, CO 80203. TEL 303-866-6732. FAX 303-866-6940.
circ. 3,500. *4170*

CENTER NEWS.
Memorial Sloan-Kettering Cancer Center, Department of Public Affairs, 1275 York Ave., New York, NY 10021. TEL 212-639-3573. FAX 212-639-3576.
circ. 250,000. *4975*

CENTOOTTO A.
Gruppo Editoriale Faenza Editrice S.p.A., Via Pier. de Crescenzi 44, 48018 Faenza RA, Italy. TEL 39-546-663688. FAX 39-546-660440.
circ. 4,000. *1930*

CENTRAL BANK OF BARBADOS. BALANCE OF PAYMENTS.
Central Bank of Barbados, Research Department, P.O. Box 1016, Spry St., Bridgetown, Barbados, W.I. TEL 246-436-6870. FAX 246-427-1431.
circ. 2,000. *1030*

CENTRAL COUNCIL FOR EDUCATION AND TRAINING IN SOCIAL WORK. REPORT OF COUNCIL MEETING.
Central Council for Education and Training in Social Work, Derbyshire House, St. Chad's St., London WC1H 8AD, England. TEL 44-171-278-2455. FAX 44-171-278-2934. *6658*

CENTRAL FLORIDA FAMILY JOURNAL.
Family Journal Publications, Inc., Box 1100, Orlando, FL 32802-1100. TEL 407-774-9863. FAX 407-788-2099.
circ. 56,312. *1840*

CENTRAL INSTITUTE FOR THE DEAF. NEWS NOTES.
Central Institute for the Deaf, 818 S. Euclid Ave., St. Louis, MO 63110. TEL 314-977-0243. FAX 314-977-0090.
circ. 18,000. *3461*

CENTRAL PENN BUSINESS JOURNAL.
Journal Publications, Inc., 409 S. Second St., Ste. 3D, Harrisburg, PA 17104-1612. TEL 717-236-4300. FAX 717-236-6803.
circ. 16,000. *947*

CENTRAL RAILWAY CHRONICLE.
Central Railway Club of Buffalo, 960 French St., Buffalo, NY 14227-3632. TEL 716-825-0248.
circ. 295. *7124*

CENTRAL ROAD RESEARCH INSTITUTE, NEW DELHI. ROAD RESEARCH PAPER.
Central Road Research Institute, P.O. Central Road Research Institute, New Delhi 110020, India. TEL 6832274. *7137*

CENTRAL SERICULTURAL RESEARCH AND TRAINING INSTITUTE. ANNUAL REPORT.
Central Sericultural Research and Training Institute, Manandavadi Rd., Srirampura, Mysore 570008, India. FAX 91-821-520845.
circ. 300. *107*

CENTRE FOR CONFLICT RESOLUTION. ANNUAL REPORT.
Centre for Conflict Resolution, c/o University of Cape Town, Rondebosch 7700, South Africa. TEL 27-21-6502503. FAX 27-21-6852142.
circ. 2,200. *6704*

CENTRE FOR PLANT BREEDING AND REPRODUCTION RESEARCH. ANNUAL REPORT.
C P R O - D L O, Postbus 16, 6700 AA Wageningen, Netherlands. TEL 31-317-477017. FAX 31-317-418094.
circ. 3,100. *218*

CENTRE NATIONAL DE DOCUMENTATION SCIENTIFIQUE ET TECHNIQUE. RAPPORT D'ACTIVITE.
Centre National de Documentation Scientifique et Technique, 4 Bd. de l'Empereur, B-1000 Brussels, Belgium.
circ. 1,000. *6956*

CENTRE NATIONAL DE LA RECHERCHE SCIENTIFIQUE. ANNUAIRE EUROPEEN D'ADMINISTRATION PUBLIQUE.
C N R S Editions, 20-22 rue St. Amand, 75015 Paris, France. TEL 45-33-16-00. FAX 45-33-92-13.
circ. 1,500. *6168*

CENTREPOINT.
Christian Centre Party, 157 Vicarage Rd., London E10 5DU, England. TEL 44-181-539-3876. *5899*

CERAMIC TECHNOLOGY INTERNATIONAL.
Sterling Publications Ltd., 86-88 Edgware Rd., London W2 2YW, England. TEL 44-171-915-9600. FAX 44-171-915-9619.
circ. 10,000. *1727*

CEREAL RUST BULLETIN.
U.S. Department of Agriculture, Agricultural Research Service (St. Paul), 1551 Lindig St., St. Paul, MN 55108. TEL 612-625-6299. FAX 612-649-5054.
circ. 500. *218*

CERTIFICATION NEWS.
Institute for Certification of Computing Professionals, 2200 E. Devon Ave., Ste. 247, Des Plaines, IL 60018-4503. TEL 847-299-4227. FAX 847-299-4280.
circ. 25,000. *2126*

CERTIFIED LETTER.
Institute of Certified Professional Managers, James Madison University, Harrisonburg, VA 27807. TEL 703-568-3247. FAX 703-568-3587.
circ. 5,300. *1469*

CERVEZA Y MALTA.
Asociacion Espanola de Tecnicos de Cerveza y Malta, Ramirez de Prado, 8-1o F, 28045 Madrid, Spain. TEL 34-1-5277255. FAX 34-1-5285507.
circ. 1,500. *518*

C'EST POUR QUAND.
Family Communications, Inc., 37 Hanna Ave., Toronto, ON M6K 1X1, Canada.
circ. 52,000. *1840*

CHAMBER NEWS.
Greater Hartsville Chamber of Commerce, Box 578, Hartsville, SC 29551. TEL 803-332-6401. FAX 803-332-8017.
circ. 600. *1182*

CHAMBRE DE COMMERCE, D'AGRICULTURE, D'INDUSTRIE ET D'ARTISANAT DU NIGER. WEEKLY BULLETIN.
Chambre de Commerce, d'Agriculture, d'Industrie et d'Artisanat du Niger, B.P. 209, Niamey, Niger.
circ. 170. *1183*

CHAMPLAIN SOCIETY, TORONTO. REPORT.
Champlain Society, P.O. Box 60, 260 Adelaide St. E., Toronto, ON M5A 1N1, Canada. TEL 416-482-9635. FAX 416-482-9341.
circ. 930. *3491*

CHANCE.
Unicum Verlag GmbH, Willy-Brandt-Platz 5-7, 44787 Bochum, Germany. TEL 49-234-96151-0. FAX 49-234-60256.
circ. 333,000. *1945*

CHANGING MEDICAL MARKETS.
Theta Corporation, 2433 Main St., Ste. 1, Rocky Hall, CT 06067-2539. *4652*

CHANNEL (MADISON).
Department of Public Instruction, Division for Library Services, 125 S. Webster St., 5th Fl., Box 7841, Madison, WI 53707. TEL 608-266-9679. FAX 608-267-1052.
circ. 3,600. *4170*

CHANNEL (SUNNYVALE).
Mathews & Clark Communications, 710 Lakeway, Ste. 170, Sunnyvale, CA 94086. TEL 408-736-1120. FAX 408-736-7880.
circ. 8,500. *2626*

THE CHANTICLEER.
Jacksonville State University, Communications Board, Jacksonville, AL 36265. TEL 205-782-5701. FAX 205-782-5445.
circ. 7,000. *1945*

CHAPLIN.
FilmhusFoerlaget AB, P.O. Box 27126, S-102 52 Stockholm, Sweden. TEL 46-8-665-11-00. FAX 46-8-662-26-84.
circ. 5,200. *5326*

CHARAKTER.
Charakter Medien Verlag GmbH, Lotzestr. 29, 37083 Goettingen, Germany. TEL 0551-507510. FAX 0551-73047.
circ. 14,700. *3283*

CHARETTE.
American Institute of Architecture Students, 1735 New York Ave., N.W., Washington, DC 20006. TEL 202-626-7472. FAX 202-626-7414.
circ. 8,000. *2428*

CHARITABLE BUSINESS.
Momentum Media Management, 4040 Creditview Rd., Unit 11, Box 1800, Mississauga, ON L5C 3Y8, Canada. TEL 905-813-7100. FAX 905-813-7117.
circ. 11,100. *947*

CHARTER INDUSTRY.
Charter Industry Services, Inc., 43 Kindred St., Stuart, FL 34994. TEL 407-288-1066.
circ. 750. *6838*

CONTROLLED CIRCULATION SERIALS

CHARTERED ACCOUNTANT.
Institute of Chartered Accountants of India, Indraprastha Marg, P.O. Box 7100, New Delhi 2, India. TEL 91-11-3312055.
circ. 75,000. *1087*

CHARTERED BANKER.
Financial & Business Publications, 4 Cavendish Sq., London W1M 9HA, England. TEL 44-171-637-1115. FAX 44-171-637-1117.
circ. 44,700. *1120*

CHARTERED BUILDING PROFESSIONAL.
Australian Institute of Building, 217 Northbourne Ave., Turner, A.C.T. 2601, Australia. TEL 61-62-477433. FAX 61-62-489030.
circ. 3,000. *876*

CHARTERED INSTITUTE OF PUBLIC FINANCE AND ACCOUNTANCY. CONFERENCE HANDBOOK.
Chartered Institute of Public Finance and Accountancy, 3 Robert St., London WC2N 6BH, England. TEL 44-171-543-5600. FAX 44-171-543-5700. *1087*

CHARTERED INSURANCE INSTITUTE. SOCIETY OF FELLOWS. JOURNAL.
Chartered Insurance Institute, Society of Fellows, 20 Aldermanbury, London EC2V 7HY, England. TEL 44-181-898-8464. FAX 44-171-726-0131.
circ. 18,000. *3812*

CHAT.
I P C Magazines, King's Reach Tower, Stamford St., London SE1 9LS, England. TEL 44-171-261-5000. FAX 44-1444-4488. *7314*

CHECKOUT.
Checkout Publications Ltd., 22 Crofton Rd., Dunlaoire, Co. Dublin, Ireland. TEL 353-1-2808415. FAX 353-1-2808309.
circ. 5,500. *1520*

CHECKOUT FRESH.
Reed Business Publishing Group, Quadrant House, The Quadrant, Sutton, Surrey SM2 5AS, England. TEL 0181-652-3258. FAX 0181-652-8925.
circ. 12,500. *3139*

CHEERS.
Hunter Publishing Limited Partnership, 2101 S. Arlington Heights Rd., Ste. 150, Arlington Heights, IL 60005. TEL 847-427-9512. FAX 847-427-2097.
circ. 92,000. *3724*

CHEMICAL DISTILLATIONS.
Cyrus J. Lawrence, Inc., 1290 Ave. of the Americas, New York, NY 10104. TEL 212-468-5000. *1742*

CHEMICAL INDUSTRY MONITOR.
Cyrus J. Lawrence, Inc., 1290 Ave. of the Americas, New York, NY 10104. TEL 212-468-5000. *1742*

CHEMICAL PROCESSING.
Putman Publishing Co., 301 E. Erie St., Chicago, IL 60611. TEL 312-644-2020. FAX 312-644-1131.
circ. 80,042. *2759*

CHEMICAL PROCESSING DEVELOPMENT ASIA.
Sterling Publications Ltd., 86-88 Edgware Rd., London W2 2YW, England. TEL 44-171-915-9600. FAX 44-171-915-9619.
circ. 10,000. *2760*

CHEMICAL PROCESSING FOR CHINA.
Sterling Publications Ltd., 86-88 Edgware Rd., London W2 2YW, England. TEL 44-171-915-9600. FAX 44-171-915-9619.
circ. 10,000. *2760*

CHEMICAL TECHNOLOGY EUROPE.
V C H Verlagsgesellschaft mbH, Postfach 101161, 69451 Weinheim, Germany. TEL 49-6201-606147. FAX 49-6201-606117.
circ. 30,000. *2760*

CHEMICALS, ADHESIVES AND PHARMACEUTICALS (YEAR).
Reed Business Information South Africa (Pty.) Ltd., P.O. Box 653207, Benmore 2010, South Africa. TEL 27-11-784-1110. FAX 27-11-883-4729. *2760*

CHEMIE-ANLAGEN UND VERFAHREN.
Konradin Verlag Robert Kohlhammer GmbH, Ernst-Mey-Str. 8, 70771 Leinfelden-Echterdingen, Germany. TEL 49-711-7594-0. FAX 49-711-7594390.
circ. 25,487. *2760*

CHEMISCHE RUNDSCHAU.
Vogt-Schild AG, Zuchwilerstr. 21, CH-4501 Solothurn, Switzerland. TEL 065-247247. FAX 065-247235.
circ. 18,500. *1744*

CHEMIST & DRUGSTORE NEWS.
India Publications Co., Denabank House, 2nd Fl., 31 Hamam St., Bombay 1, India. *5652*

CHESHIRE SMILE INTERNATIONAL.
Leonard Cheshire Foundation, 26-29 Maunsel St., London SW1P 2QN, England. TEL 0171-828-1822. FAX 0171-976-5704.
circ. 8,000. *3466*

CHESTER DISTRICT GENEALOGICAL SOCIETY. BULLETIN.
Chester District Genealogical Society, Box 336, Richburg, SC 29729.
circ. 150. *3216*

CHEVRE.
Societe de Presse et d'Edition Ovine et Caprine (S.P.E.O.C.), 19 quai de Juillet, B.P. 18, 14005 Caen Cedex, France. TEL 33-2-31357704. FAX 33-2-31822963.
circ. 4,500. *274*

IL CHI E' DELL'I C T.
Editrice il Grogiolo S.r.l., Piazza Sant Agostino 22, 20123 Milan, Italy. TEL 39-2-48009805. FAX 39-2-48009749.
circ. 5,850. *2074*

CHIANG MAI MEDICAL BULLETIN.
Chiang Mai University, Faculty of Medicine, 110 Intavaroros Street, Chiang Mai 50002, Thailand. TEL 52-221122. FAX 53-217144.
circ. 1,000. *4653*

CHIBA DAIGAKU KOGAKUBU KENKYU HOKOKU.
Chiba Daigaku Kogakubu, 1-33 Yayoicho, Chiba 280, Japan. TEL 0472-51-1111. FAX 0472-51-7337.
circ. 550. *2712*

CHICAGO GENEALOGIST.
Chicago Genealogical Society, Box 1160, Chicago, IL 60690.
circ. 1,000. *3216*

CHICAGO JEWISH STAR.
Box 268, Skokie, IL 60076-0268. TEL 847-674-7827. FAX 847-674-0014.
circ. 24,000. *3005*

CHICAGO MARKET.
Bolger Publications Inc., 3301 Como Ave., S.E., Minneapolis, MN 55414. TEL 612-645-6311. FAX 612-645-1750.
circ. 26,000. *3448*

CHICAGO PARENT MAGAZINE.
Wednesday Journal Inc., 141 S. Oak Park Ave., Oak Park, IL 60302-2901. TEL 708-386-5555. FAX 708-524-0447.
circ. 85,000. *1840*

CHICAGO PURCHASOR.
Purchasing Management Association of Chicago, 2250 E. Devon Ave., Ste. 236, Des Plaines, IL 60018-4509.
circ. 5,000. *1520*

CHICAGO READER.
Chicago Reader Inc., 11 E. Illinois, Chicago, IL 60611. TEL 312-828-0350. FAX 312-828-0305.
circ. 137,000. *3371*

CHIEF INFORMATION OFFICER JOURNAL.
Faulkner & Gray, Inc. (New York), 11 Penn Plaza, 17th Fl., New York, NY 10001. TEL 212-967-7000. FAX 212-967-7155.
circ. 8,095. *2181*

CHIEFTAIN.
Black Hawk College, Quad Cities Campus, 6600 34th Ave., Moline, IL 61265. FAX 309-792-5976.
circ. 3,000. *1945*

CHILD MAGAZINE'S GUIDE TO BABY PRODUCTS.
New York Times Company, Magazine Group, 110 Fifth Ave., New York, NY 10011. TEL 212-463-1600. FAX 212-463-1383.
circ. 600,000. *1841*

CHILD MAGAZINE'S GUIDE TO HAVING A BABY.
New York Times Company, Magazine Group, 110 Fifth Ave., New York, NY 10011. TEL 212-463-1600. FAX 212-463-1553.
circ. 1,200,000. *1841*

CHILD SAFETY REVIEW.
Child Accident Prevention Trust, Clerks Ct., 4th Fl., 18-20 Farringdon Ln., London EC1R 3AU, England. TEL 44-171-636-3828.
circ. 500. *1841*

CHILDBIRTH INSTRUCTOR.
Cradle Publishing, Inc., 124 E. 40th St., Rm. 1101, New York, NY 10016-1723. TEL 212-986-1422. FAX 212-986-0816.
circ. 10,000. *4954*

CHILDREN'S COURT OF NEW SOUTH WALES INFORMATION BULLETIN.
Judicial Commission of New South Wales, Level 5, 301 George St., Sydney, N.S.W. 2000, Australia. TEL 61-2-92994421. FAX 61-2-92903194.
circ. 350. *4088*

CHILDREN'S HEALTH CARE.
Lawrence Erlbaum Associates, Inc., 10 Industrial Dr., Mahwah, NJ 07430-2262. TEL 201-236-9500. FAX 201-236-0072.
circ. 4,000. *6660*

CHILDREN'S MONITOR.
Child Welfare League of America, Inc., 440 First St., N.W., 3rd Fl., Washington, DC 20001. TEL 202-638-2952. FAX 202-638-4004. *4100*

CHILE. SERVICIO NACIONAL DE PESCA. ANUARIO ESTADISTICO DE PESCA.
Servicio Nacional de Pesca, Departamento Sistemas de Informacion y Estadisticas Pesqueras, Yungay 1731 4o piso, Valparaiso, Chile. FAX 56-32-259564. *3063*

CHILEAN NEWS.
Anglo-Chilean Society, 12 Devonshire St., London W1N 2DS, England. TEL 44-171-580-1271.
circ. 600. *6008*

CHILTON'S MOTOR AGE.
Chilton Co., 201 King of Prussia Rd., Radnor, PA 19089. TEL 610-964-4390. FAX 610-964-4251.
circ. 146,400. *7095*

CHILTON'S PRODUCT DESIGN AND DEVELOPMENT.
Chilton Co., One Chilton Way, Radnor, PA 19089. TEL 610-964-4351.
circ. 168,000. *2712*

CHILTON'S REVIEW OF OPTOMETRY.
Chilton Co., Chilton Way, Radnor, PA 19089. TEL 610-964-4370.
circ. 34,024. *4991*

THE CHIMES (LA MIRADA).
Biola University, 13800 Biola Ave., La Mirada, CA 90639. TEL 310-903-4879.
circ. 2,000. *1945*

CHINAMAC JOURNAL.
Adsale Publishing Company, 4-F, Stanhope House, 734 King's Rd., North Point, Hong Kong, People's Republic of China. TEL 852-2811-8897. FAX 852-2516-5119.
circ. 22,000. *4542*

CHIP.
Vogel Publishing Sp. z o.o., Plac Czerwony 1-3-5, 53-661 Wroclaw, Poland. TEL 48-71-734475. FAX 48-71-557361.
circ. 75,000. *2074*

CHIP.
Soft-Press, P.O. Box 596-2, 254205 Kiev, Ukraine. TEL 38-44-2940289. FAX 38-44-2940375.
circ. 10,000. *2074*

CHIP.
Vogel Publishing Srl., B-dul Victoriei 6, 2200 Brasov, Rumania. TEL 40-68-150886. FAX 40-68-153108.
circ. 13,500. *2074*

CHIP.
Vogel Publishing Ltd. Sti, Peker Sokak, Akyildiz Apt. No.26, Levent, Istanbul, Turkey. TEL 90-212-2834244. FAX 90-212-2695021.
circ. 20,000. *2074*

CHIP.
Vogel Verlag und Druck GmbH & Co. KG, Max-Planck-Str. 7-9, 97082 Wuerzburg, Germany. TEL 49-931-4182335. FAX 49-931-4182905.
circ. 227,888. *2187*

CHIPS FROM THE FORESTERS TREE.
Catholic Association of Foresters, 347 Commonwealth Ave., Boston, MA 02115. TEL 617-536-8221. FAX 617-536-2819.
circ. 5,500. *3149*

CHIPS-O-WOOD.
Wood Junior College, Alumni Development, Box 289, Mathiston, MS 39752. TEL 601-263-5352.
circ. 7,000. *1945*

THE CHIROPRACTIC JOURNAL.
2950 N. Dobson Rd., Ste. 1, Chandler, AZ 85224-1800. TEL 602-786-9235. FAX 602-732-9313.
circ. 60,000. *4826*

CHIROPRACTIC PRODUCTS.
Novicom, Inc., 20000 Mariner Ave., Ste. 480, Torrance, CA 90503. TEL 310-793-4141. FAX 310-793-4138.
circ. 35,059. *4826*

CHIZU.
Nihon Kokusai Chizu Gakkai, 9-6 Aobadai 4-chome, Meguro-ku, Tokyo 153, Japan. *3398*

CHIZU NO TOMO.
Japan Map Association, Shinsen Bldg., 8-2 Shinsen-cho, Shibuya, Tokyo 150, Japan. FAX 03-3461-0244. *3398*

CHLODNICTWO.
Wydawnictwo Czasopism i Ksiazek Technicznych SIGMA - NOT, Ul. Ratuszowa 11, P.O. Box 1004, 00-950 Warsaw, Poland. TEL 48-22-180918. FAX 48-22-192187.
circ. 1,050. *3477*

CHOCOLATE AND NUT WORLD.
Lott Publishing Co., Box 9669, Marina Del Rey, CA 90295-2069. TEL 310-397-4217.
circ. 3,000. *3136*

CHONGQING HUANJING KEXUE.
Chongqing Huanjing Kexue Xuehui, 212 Renmin Lu, Chongqing, Sichuan 630015, People's Republic of China. TEL 86-811-3868871. FAX 86-811-3850021.
circ. 5,000. *2910*

CHRISTCHURCH MAIL.
1st Fl., Paxus House, Cnr. Tuam & High Sts., Christchurch, Canterbury, New Zealand. TEL 03-366-1622. FAX 03-365-6623.
circ. 124,000. *3339*

CHRISTIAN MEDICAL COLLEGE VELLORE ALUMNI JOURNAL.
Christian Medical College, Alumni Association, Vellore 632 002, Tamil Nadu, India. TEL 91-416-22603. FAX 91-416-32788.
circ. 2,000. *4653*

CHRISTIANS IN CRISIS.
Christian Forum Research Foundation, 1111 Fairgrounds Rd., Grand Rapids, MN 55744. TEL 218-326-2688.
circ. 1,500. *6330*

CHRONICA DERMATOLOGICA.
Istituto Dermopatico dell'Immacolata, Via Monti di Creta, 104, 00167 Rome, Italy. FAX 39-6-66464437.
circ. 7,000. *4876*

CHRONICLE (GRAYSLAKE).
College of Lake County, 19351 W. Washington, Grayslake, IL 60030. TEL 708-223-3634. FAX 708-223-9371.
circ. 3,750. *1945*

CHRONICLE (HEMPSTEAD).
Hofstra University, 203 Student Center, Hempstead, NY 11550. TEL 516-463-6965.
circ. 11,000. *1945*

CHRYSLER CAR ENTHUSIAST ENGINES ETC. MAGAZINE.
R H O Publications, 1580 Hampton Rd., Bensalem, PA 19020-4610. TEL 215-639-4456.
circ. 60,000. *7095*

CHUGOKU ELECTRIC POWER CO. TECHNICAL LABORATORY. REPORT.
Chugoku Electric Power Co., Inc., Technical Research Center, 4-32, Ozu 4-chome, Hiroshima-shi, Hiroshima-ken 730, Japan. *2811*

CHURCH BUSINESS. PRODUCTS & TECHNOLOGY.
Momentum Media Management, 4040 Creditview Rd., Unit 11, Box 1800, Mississauga, ON L5C 3Y8, Canada. TEL 905-813-7100. FAX 905-813-7117.
circ. 12,400. *6330*

CHURCH HERITAGE.
Church Records and Historical Society (NSW), P.O. Box 2395, North Parramatta, N.S.W. 2151, Australia. TEL 61-2-96833147. FAX 61-2-96833147.
circ. 50. *6419*

CHURCH MUSIC QUARTERLY.
Royal School of Church Music, Cleveland Lodge, Westhumble, Dorking RH5 6BW, England. TEL 44-181-341-6408. FAX 44-181-340-0021.
circ. 13,700. *5383*

CHURCHES PURCHASING SCHEME.
Ecclesiastical Insurance Office, Desk Top Publishing Unit, Beaufort House, Brunswick Rd., Gloucester GL1 1JZ, England. TEL 0452-383080. FAX 0452-383621.
circ. 32,500. *948*

CIAO.
Ciao Publishing Co., 1081 Bas l'Assomption Nord, Ville de l'Assomption, Que. J0K 1G0, Canada. FAX 514-589-4485.
circ. 40,000. *3005*

CIENCIA BIOLOGICA: BIOLOGIA MOLECULAR E CELULAR.
Universidade de Coimbra, Departamento de Zoologia, Coimbra, Portugal. TEL 351-39-34729. FAX 351-39-26798.
circ. 600. *830*

CIENCIA MEDICA.
Alpe Editores, S.A., Pedro Rico, 27, 28029 Madrid, Spain. TEL 34-1-7338811. FAX 34-1-3159652.
circ. 8,000. *4654*

CIENCIA PHARMACEUTICA.
Alpe Editores, S.A., Pedro Rico, 27, 28029 Madrid, Spain. TEL 34-1-7338892. FAX 34-1-3159652.
circ. 6,000. *5653*

CIENCIA RURAL.
Universidade Federal de Santa Maria, Centro de Ciencias Rurais, Campus Universitario, 97119-900 Santa Maria, Rio Grande do Sul, Brazil. TEL 55-55-226-2698.
circ. 1,200. *108*

CINDERELLA PHILATELIST.
Cinderella Stamp Club, c/o L.N. Williams, 44 The Ridgeway, London NW11 8QS, England.
circ. 800. *5705*

CINE-OJA.
Sociedad Civil Cine al Dia, Apdo. 50446, Sabana Grande, Caracas, Venezuela.
circ. 2,500. *5326*

CINEMATOGRAPH.
San Francisco Cinematheque, 480 Potrero, San Francisco, CA 94110. TEL 415-558-8129. FAX 415-558-0455.
circ. 1,800. *5328*

CINFOLINK ANNUAL REVIEW OF INFORMATION SERVICES IN CHINA.
Cinfolink Services, 85 Roe Ave., Toronto, ON M5M 2H6, Canada. TEL 416-485-8063.
circ. 150. *1660*

CIRCLE (PORTLAND).
Circle Forum, Box 176, Portland, OR 97207. *4506*

CIRCUIT RIDER (NASHVILLE).
United Methodist Publishing House, 201 Eighth Ave. S., Box 801, Nashville, TN 37202. TEL 615-749-6319. FAX 615-749-6079.
circ. 40,000. *6419*

CIRCUITS ASSEMBLY.
Miller Freeman, Inc., 600 Harrison St., San Francisco, CA 94107. TEL 415-905-2200. FAX 415-905-2232.
circ. 40,000. *2626*

CIRCULATION MANAGEMENT.
Cowles Business Media, 11 River Bend Dr., S., Box 4949, Stamford, CT 06907-0949. TEL 203-358-9900. FAX 203-358-5811.
circ. 10,000. *6268*

CIRUGIA DEL URUGUAY.
Sociedad de Cirugia del Uruguay, Casilla de Correos 10972, Montevideo, Uruguay.
circ. 1,000. *5138*

CITY & COUNTRY CLUB LIFE.
Club Publications, 665 La Villa Dr., Miami Springs, FL 33166. TEL 305-887-1701. FAX 305-885-1923.
circ. 26,000. *3371*

CITY CLUB GADFLY.
City Club of New York, 33 W. 42nd St., New York, NY 10036. TEL 212-921-9870.
circ. 2,500. *6212*

THE CITY JOURNAL.
Manhattan Institute, Inc., 52 Vanderbilt Ave., New York, NY 10017-3808. TEL 212-599-7000. FAX 212-599-3494.
circ. 2,000. *5900*

CITY LIMITS.
City Limits Community Information Service, Inc., 120 Wall St., 20th Fl., New York, NY 10005-4001. TEL 212-479-3344. FAX 212-344-6457.
circ. 1,000. *6607*

CITY LINE NEWS.
City Line News, Box 569, Bala Cynwyd, PA 19004. TEL 610-667-6623. FAX 610-667-6624.
circ. 32,000. *1231*

CITY TREES.
Society of Municipal Arborists, Wellesley Park and Tree Division, 56 Woodlawn Ave., Wellesley Hills, MA 02181. TEL 617-235-7600. FAX 617-431-7569.
circ. 400. *3149*

CITYSIDE.
University of Regina, School of Journalism and Communications, Regina, SK S4S 0A2, Canada. TEL 306-584-5051. FAX 306-585-4867.
circ. 1,000. *1945*

CIUDADANO.
Fundacion Ciudadano, C. Atocha 26, 28012 Madrid, Spain. TEL 34-1-3691285. FAX 34-1-3690827.
circ. 70,000. *2253*

CIVIL AVIATION TRAINING.
Halldale Publishing & Media Ltd., 84 Alexandra Rd., Farnborough, Hants GU14 6DD, England. TEL 44-1252-517974. FAX 44-1252-512714.
circ. 12,000. *7066*

CIVIL ENGINEERING CONTRACTOR.
Brooke Pattrick (Pty) Ltd., P.O. Box 422, Bedfordview 2008, South Africa. TEL 27-11-6224666. FAX 27-11-6167196.
circ. 4,500. *2779*

CIVIL LIBERTIES REPORTER.
American Civil Liberties Union of New Jersey, 2 Washington Place, Newark, NJ 07102. TEL 201-642-2084.
circ. 6,600. *4059*

CIVIL SERVICE PENSIONER.
Civil Service Pensioners Alliance, 7 The Beeches, Shaw Hill, Melksham, Wilts. SN12 8EW, England. TEL 01225-702416.
circ. 59,000. *3434*

CIVITAN MAGAZINE.
Civitan International, Box 130744, Birmingham, AL 35213-0744. TEL 205-591-8910. FAX 205-592-6307.
circ. 37,000. *1930*

CLAMAVI.
Stichting Mensen in Nood - Caritas Nederland, Postbus 1041, 5200 BA 's-Hertogenbosch, Netherlands. TEL 31-73-6456789. FAX 31-73-6456700.
circ. 250,000. *6660*

CLAN MCLAREN SOCIETY, U S A. QUARTERLY.
Clan McLaren Society, U S A, 5843 Royalcrest, Dallas, TX 75230.
circ. 145. *3217*

CLAN ROSS NEWSLETTER.
Clan Ross Association of the United States, Inc., Box 235, Montezuma, NC 28653-9999. TEL 912-727-2560.
circ. 400. *3005*

CLARIN INTERNACIONAL.
Arte Grafico Editorial Argentino S.A., Piedras 1743, Buenos Aires, Argentina. *3249*

CLARION ALUMNI NEWS.
Clarion University, 974 E. Wood St., Clarion, PA 16214. TEL 814-226-2334.
circ. 27,000. *1946*

CLARK UNIVERSITY NEWS.
Clark University, 950 Main St., Worcester, MA 01610. TEL 508-793-7441. FAX 508-794-7565.
circ. 25,000. *1946*

CLASS.
Class Editori, Via Burigozzo 5, 20122 Milan, Italy. TEL 39-2-582191. FAX 39-2-58317429.
circ. 90,000. *1564*

CLASSICUM.
Classical Association of New South Wales, c/o H. Tarrant, Ed., Dept. of Classics, University of Newcastle, N.S.W. 2308, Australia. FAX 61-49-21-6947.
circ. 300. *1902*

CLEANING MANAGEMENT.
National Trade Publications, Inc., 13 Century Hill, Latham, NY 12110-2197. TEL 518-783-1281. FAX 518-783-1386.
circ. 42,000. *876*

CLEANROOMS.
PennWell Publishing Co., Box 1260, Tulsa, OK 74101. TEL 918-835-3161. FAX 918-832-9295.
circ. 42,000. *2875*

CLEMSON UNIVERSITY. DEPARTMENT OF FOREST RESOURCES. FORESTRY BULLETIN.
Clemson University, Department of Forest Resources, Clemson, SC 29634-1003. TEL 803-656-3302.
circ. 500. *3149*

CLEMSON UNIVERSITY. WATER RESOURCES CENTER. REPORT.
Clemson University, Water Resources Center, Strom Thurmond Institute, Clemson, SC 29634-5203. TEL 864-656-0225. FAX 864-656-4780.
circ. 200. *7289*

CLEMSON WORLD.
Clemson University, Office of Publication & Marketing Services, 103 Fike, Clemson, SC 29634-5608. TEL 864-656-2467. FAX 864-656-5004.
circ. 75,000. *1946*

CLEVEDON PORTISHEAD NEALSEA ADMAG.
Admag Newspapers, 11 Beacons Field Rd., Weston-super-Mare, Avon BS23 1YE, England. TEL 44-1934-417921. FAX 44-1934-635031.
circ. 80,000. *3294*

CLIENT DIRECTORY AND AGENCY LIST.
International Federation of Advertising Agencies, 1450 E. American Ln., Ste. 1400, Schaumburg, IL 60173-4973. TEL 847-330-6344. FAX 847-517-4459.
circ. 100. *33*

CLIENT - SERVER COMPUTING.
Sentry Publishing Company, Inc., 1 Research Dr., Ste. 400B, Westborough, MA 01581-3907. TEL 508-366-2031.
circ. 90,000. *1555*

CLIK.
Clik, 20 Lower Spadina Ave., Toronto, ON M5V 2Z1, Canada. TEL 416-367-2545. FAX 416-367-0382.
circ. 2,500. *1867*

CLINICA CARDIOVASCULAR.
Alpe Editores, S.A., Pedro Rico, 27, 28029 Madrid, Spain. TEL 34-1-7338811. FAX 34-1-3159652.
circ. 6,500. *4814*

CLINICAL CONGRESS NEWS.
Cambridge Medical Publications Ltd., Wicker House, High St., Worthing, W. Sussex BN11 1DJ, England. TEL 01903-205884. FAX 01903-234862. *4655*

CLINICAL LABORATORY INTERNATIONAL.
Pan European Publishing Co., Rue Verte 216, 1030 Brussels, Belgium. TEL 32-2-2402611. FAX 32-2-2427111.
circ. 30,002. *4896*

CLINICAL SYMPOSIA.
Ciba Geigy Corporation, 556 Morris Ave., Summit, NJ 07901. TEL 908-277-4478. FAX 908-277-4478.
circ. 161,000. *4656*

CLINICIAN REVIEWS.
Clinicians Publishing Group, 4 Brighton Rd., Clifton, NJ 07012. TEL 201-916-1000. FAX 201-916-0021.
circ. 52,000. *4656*

CLUB DIRECTOR.
National Club Association, One Lafayette Center, 1120 20th St., N.W., Ste. 725, Washington, DC 20036. TEL 202-822-9822. FAX 202-822-9808.
circ. 8,500. *1930*

CLUB LIVING.
Club Living, Inc., 16 Copper Beech Cir., White Plains, NY 10605-4702.
circ. 51,000. *6756*

CLUB MANAGEMENT IN AUSTRALIA.
Club Managers' Association Australia, 2A Lord St., Botany, N.S.W. 2019, Australia. TEL 02-316-6788. FAX 02-316-6244. *1470*

CLUB MIRROR.
Quantam Publishing Ltd., 29-31 Lower Coombe St., Croydon CR9 0LX, England. TEL 0181-681-2099. FAX 0181-681-2389.
circ. 25,855. *1930*

COACH OPERATORS HANDBOOK.
E M A P - Response Publishing Ltd., Wentworth House, Wentworth St., Peterborough, Cambs. PE1 2DS, England. TEL 01733-63100. FAX 01733-62656.
circ. 4,500. *7026*

COACHING DIGEST.
American Baseball Coaches Association, 108 S. University Ave., Ste. 3, Mt. Pleasant, MI 48858-2327. TEL 517-775-3300. FAX 517-775-3600.
circ. 6,000. *6801*

COAL AGE.
Intertec Publishing Corp., 9800 Metcalf Ave., Overland Park, KS 66212-2215. TEL 913-341-1300. FAX 913-967-1898.
circ. 18,623. *5298*

COASTGUARD.
Department of Transport, H.M. Coastguard, Rm. S13-03 2, Marsham St., London SW1P 3EB, England. TEL 0171-276-5082. FAX 0171-276-6080.
circ. 16,000. *7148*

COCOA GROWERS BULLETIN.
Cadbury Ltd., Bournville, Birmingham B30 2LU, England.
circ. 1,500. *219*

CODE AUTHORITY.
Underwriters Laboratories Inc., Corporate Communications, 333 Pfingsten Rd., Northbrook, IL 60062-2096. TEL 847-272-8800. FAX 847-272-8129.
circ. 40,000. *2713*

COFFEE MAZDOOR SAHAKARI.
All India Coffee Workers Cooperative Societies Federation Ltd., 10 U.B. Bungalow Rd., Jawahar Nagar, Delhi 7, India. *3100*

COGENERATION AND RESOURCE RECOVERY.
Cogeneration and Small Power, 3 Fairway Ln., Old Tappan, NJ 07675-7017. TEL 703-759-5060. FAX 703-759-0232.
circ. 1,500. *2687*

COIFFURE.
Samsom Bedrijfsinformatie B.V., Postbus 4, 2400 MA Alphen aan den Rijn, Netherlands. TEL 31-172-466775. FAX 31-172-440681.
circ. 4,430. *505*

COLD FACTS.
Cryogenic Society of America, c/o Huget Advertising, Inc., 1033 South Blvd., Ste. 13, Oak Park, IL 60302. TEL 708-383-6220. FAX 708-383-9337.
circ. 3,000. *5840*

COLD SPRING HARBOR LABORATORY. ABSTRACTS OF PAPERS PRESENTED AT MEETINGS.
Cold Spring Harbor Laboratory Press, Publications Department, Box 100, Cold Spring Harbor, NY 11724. TEL 800-843-4388. FAX 516-349-1946. *596*

COLD SPRING HARBOR LABORATORY. ANNUAL REPORT.
Cold Spring Harbor Laboratory Press, Publications Department, Box 100, Cold Spring Harbor, NY 11724. TEL 800-843-4388. FAX 516-349-1946. *596*

COLLAGE (CLAREMONT).
Claremont Colleges, 175 E. 8th St., Claremont, CA 91711. TEL 909-624-1887.
circ. 6,000. *1946*

THE COLLECTOR.
Barrington Publications, 54 Uxbridge Rd., London W12 8LP, England.
circ. 18,500. *339*

COLLEGE AND UNIVERSITY ADMISSIONS AND ENROLLMENT, NEW YORK STATE.
Education Department, Post-Secondary Policy Analysis, Cultural Education Bldg., Rm. 5B44, Albany, NY 12230. TEL 518-474-3874. *2536*

COLLEGE AND UNIVERSITY DEGREES CONFERRED, NEW YORK STATE.
Education Department, Post Secondary Policy Analysis, Cultural Education Bldg., Rm. 5B44, Albany, NY 12230. TEL 518-474-3874. *2536*

COLLEGE AND UNIVERSITY EMPLOYEES, NEW YORK STATE.
Education Department, Office of Post-Secondary Policy Analysis, c/o James J. Brady, Chief, Bureau of Post-Secondary Statistical Service, Rm. 5B44 CEC, Albany, NY 12230. TEL 518-474-3874. *2536*

COLLEGE OF PSYCHOLOGISTS OF ONTARIO. BULLETIN.
College of Psychologists of Ontario, 1246 Yonge St., Ste. 201, Toronto, ON M4T 1W5, Canada. TEL 416-961-8817. FAX 416-961-2635.
circ. 2,400. *6104*

COLLEGE OUTLOOK.
Townsend Outlook Publishing, 20 E. Gregory, Kansas City, MO 64114. TEL 816-361-0616. FAX 816-361-0616. *5507*

COLLEGE UNION & ON-CAMPUS HOSPITALITY.
Executive Business Media, Inc., 825 Old Country Rd., Box 1500, Westbury, NY 11590. TEL 516-334-3030.
circ. 11,000. *1946*

COLLEGIAN (ELYRIA).
Lorain County Community College, Student Activities Office, 1005 N. Abbe Rd., Elyria, OH 44035. TEL 216-365-5122. *1946*

COLLOQUIUM.
University of Alberta, c/o Dean of Engineering, 5-1 Mechanical Engineering Bldg., Edmonton, AB T6G 2H1, Canada. TEL 403-492-4514. FAX 403-492-0500.
circ. 11,600. *2881*

COLOMBO PLAN NEWSLETTER.
Colombo Plan Bureau, 12 Melbourne Ave., P.O. Box 596, Colombo 4, Sri Lanka. TEL 94-1-581813. FAX 94-1-581754.
circ. 2,500. *1355*

COLOR PUBLISHING.
PennWell Publishing Co. (Nashua), 10 Tara Blvd., 5th Fl., Nashua, NH 03062-2801. TEL 603-891-9168. FAX 603-891-0539.
circ. 24,000. *6268*

COLORADO MEDICINE.
Colorado Medical Society, 7800 E. Dorado Pl., Englewood, CO 80111. TEL 303-779-5455. FAX 303-771-8657.
circ. 5,500. *4657*

COLOUR.
Ulick Publishing Co., 150 Houston St., Ste. 308, Batavia, IL 60510-1953. TEL 708-406-8330.
circ. 80,000. *6268*

COLUMBAN MISSION.
Columban Fathers, St. Columbans, NE 68056. FAX 402-291-8693.
circ. 100,000. *6459*

COLUMBIA COLLEGE TODAY.
Columbia University, Columbia College, Office of Alumni Affairs, 475 Riverside Dr., Rm. 917, New York, NY 10115. TEL 212-870-2752. FAX 212-870-2747.
circ. 46,000. *1947*

COLUMBIA REVIEW.
Columbia University, Columbia Review, 101 Ferris Booth Hall, New York, NY 10027. TEL 212-854-3611.
circ. 500. *4391*

COLUMBUS C.E.O.
Metropolitan C.E.O., 911 E. 86th St., Ste. 100, Indianapolis, IN 46240-1840. TEL 317-257-8000. FAX 317-257-1482.
circ. 25,000. *1470*

COLUMNS (SEATTLE).
University of Washington Alumni Association, 1415 N.E. 45th St., Seattle, WA 98105. TEL 206-543-0540. FAX 206-685-0611.
circ. 170,000. *1947*

COMBAT CREW.
U.S. Air Force Strategic Air Command, c/o Superintendent of Documents, Box 371954, Pittsburgh, PA 15250-7954. *5263*

COMBONI MISSIONS.
Comboni Missionaries of the Heart of Jesus, 8108 Beechmont Ave., Cincinnati, OH 45255. TEL 513-474-4997. FAX 513-474-0382.
circ. 25,000. *6459*

COMEDIA.
Commissariaat voor de Media, Postbus 1426, 1200 BK Hilversum, Netherlands. TEL 31-35-6721721. FAX 31-35-6721722. *2047*

COMERCIO HISPANO BRITANICO.
Spanish Chamber of Commerce in Great Britain, 5 Cavendish Sq., London W1M 0DP, England. TEL 44-171-637-9061. FAX 44-171-436-7188.
circ. 1,500. *1184*

COMERCIO Y PRODUCCION.
Chamber of Commerce of Puerto Rico, Box 3789, San Juan, PR 00904.
circ. 1,500. *1184*

COMICS RETAILER.
Krause Publications, Inc., 700 E. State St., Iola, WI 54990. TEL 715-445-2214. FAX 715-445-4087.
circ. 6,768. *1641*

COMISION ECONOMICA PARA AMERICA LATINA Y EL CARIBE. SERIE REFORMAS DE POLITICA PUBLICA.
Comision Economica para America Latina y el Caribe, Edificio Naciones Unidas, Av. Dag Hammarskjold, Casilla 197-D, Santiago, Chile. *1231*

COMMAND.
Officers' Christian Fellowship of the United States of America, Box 1177, Englewood, CO 80150-1177. TEL 303-761-1984. FAX 303-761-6226.
circ. 10,000. *5263*

THE COMMERCIAL IMAGE.
P T N Publishing Corp., 445 Broad Hollow Rd., Ste. 21, Melville, NY 11747-4722. TEL 516-845-2700. FAX 516-845-7109.
circ. 25,000. *5763*

COMMERCIAL INVESTMENT REAL ESTATE JOURNAL.
Commercial Investment Real Estate Institute, 430 N. Michigan Ave., Ste. 600, Chicago, IL 60611-4092. TEL 312-321-4470. FAX 312-321-4530.
circ. 10,000. *6298*

COMMERCIAL NEWS U S A.
U.S. Department of Commerce, International Trade Administration, Rm. 1310, Washington, DC 20230. TEL 202-482-4918. FAX 202-482-5362. *1320*

COMMERCIAL PROPERTY NEWS.
Miller Freeman Inc. (New York), One Penn Plaza, New York, NY 10119. TEL 212-714-1300. FAX 212-714-1313.
circ. 35,521. *6298*

COMMERZBANK JOURNAL.
Commerzbank AG, Neue-Mainzer-Str. 32-36, 60311 Frankfurt a.M., Germany. TEL 49-69-1362-0. FAX 49-69-13629336.
circ. 260,000. *1122*

COMMISSION ON PRESERVATION AND ACCESS ANNUAL REPORT.
Commission on Preservation & Access, 1400 16th St., N.W., Ste. 740, Washington, DC 20036-2217. TEL 202-939-3400. FAX 202-939-3407.
circ. 2,500. *4171*

COMMISSION ON PRESERVATION AND ACCESS NEWSLETTER.
Commission on Preservation and Access, 1400 16th St., N.W., Ste. 740, Washington, DC 20036-2217. TEL 202-939-3400. FAX 202-939-3407.
circ. 2,000. *4172*

COMMON GROUND MAGAZINE.
356 Dupont St., Toronto, ON M5R 1V9, Canada. TEL 416-964-0528.
circ. 50,000. *5456*

COMMONWEALTH LAW BULLETIN.
Commonwealth Secretariat, Legal and Constitutional Affairs Division, Marlborough House, Pall Mall, London S1Y 5HX, England. TEL 44-171-747-6389. FAX 44-171-930-0827.
circ. 1,700. *4059*

COMMUNICATIO.
Unisa Press, Periodicals, P.O. Box 392, Pretoria 0001, South Africa. TEL 27-12-4296565. FAX 27-12-4293346.
circ. 1,800. *1984*

COMMUNICATION RESEARCH TRENDS.
Centre for the Study of Communication and Culture, Xavier Hall 325, St. Louis University, Box 59607, St. Louis, MO 63156-0907. TEL 314-977-7290. FAX 314-977-7296.
circ. 600. *1985*

COMMUNICATIONS INDUSTRIES REPORT.
International Communications Industries Association, 11242 Waples Mill Rd., Ste. 200, Fairfax, VA 22030-6079. TEL 703-273-7200. FAX 703-278-8082.
circ. 15,000. *1986*

COMMUNIQUE (ITHACA).
Cornell University, Office of University Development, 55 Brown Rd., Ithaca, NY 14850-1266. TEL 607-254-7111. FAX 607-254-7167.
circ. 17,000. *1947*

COMMUNITY NURSE.
Macmillan Magazines Ltd., Porters South, 4-6 Crinan St., London N1 9XW, England. TEL 44-171-833-4000. FAX 44-171-843-4640.
circ. 14,659. *4657*

COMMUNITY PHARMACY.
Miller Freeman plc, Sovereign Way, Tonbridge, Kent TN9 1RW, England. TEL 44-1732-364422. FAX 44-1732-361534.
circ. 13,813. *5654*

COMMUNITY SERVICE NEWSLETTER.
Community Service, Inc., Box 243, Yellow Springs, OH 45387. TEL 513-767-2161.
circ. 350. *6705*

COMMUNITY TRANSPORTATION REPORTER.
Community Transportation Association of America, 1440 New York Ave., N.W., Ste. 440, Washington, DC 20005. TEL 202-628-1480. FAX 202-737-9197.
circ. 10,000. *7026*

COMPANY.
3441 N. Ashland Ave., Chicago, IL 60657. TEL 773-281-1534. FAX 773-281-2667.
circ. 124,000. *6460*

COMPANY DIGEST.
Piton Publishing House Ltd., 79-81 High St., Godalming, Surrey GU7 1AW, England. TEL 44-1483-425454. FAX 44-1483-414262.
circ. 11,200. *949*

COMPETITION ANGLER.
2160 Renwick Dr., Poland, OH 44514. TEL 330-757-8171.
circ. 500. *6865*

COMPETITIONS AND FINANCIAL OPPORTUNITIES FOR ARTISTS.
Queensland Artworkers Alliance Inc., 497 Adelaide St., Brisbane, Qld. 4000, Australia. TEL 48-7-38322230. FAX 61-7-38322231. *436*

COMPILER.
Illinois Criminal Justice Information Authority, 120 S. Riverside Plaza, Rm. 1016, Chicago, IL 60606-3997. TEL 312-793-8550. FAX 312-793-8422.
circ. 9,000. *2264*

COMPLIANCE MAGAZINE.
I H S Publishing Group, Inc., 17730 W. Peterson Rd., Libertyville, IL 60048-0159. TEL 847-362-8711. FAX 847-362-3484.
circ. 60,000. *5488*

COMPONENTS IN ELECTRONICS.
T A S Publishing Ltd., 80 Highgate Rd., London NW5 1PB, England. TEL 0171-267-9521. FAX 0171-485-9030.
circ. 18,292. *2627*

COMPOSANTS INSTRUMENTATION ELECTRONIQUES.
Editions Elsevier - Thomas, 128 rue d'Aguesseau, 92100 Boulogne-Billancourt, France. TEL 33-1-41104070. FAX 33-1-48251400.
circ. 25,010. *2627*

COMPRESSED AIR.
Compressed Air Magazine Co., 253 E. Washington Ave., Washington, NJ 07882. TEL 908-850-7840. FAX 908-689-3095.
circ. 140,000. *2881*

COMPUTABLE.
V N U Business Publications B.V., Postbus 9194, 1006 CC Amsterdam, Netherlands. TEL 31-20-4875487. FAX 31-20-4875700.
circ. 69,870. *2172*

COMPUTER-AIDED ENGINEERING (CLEVELAND).
Penton Publishing Co., 1100 Superior Ave., Cleveland, OH 44114-2543. TEL 216-696-7000. FAX 216-696-8765.
circ. 60,000. *2802*

COMPUTER DESIGN.
PennWell Publishing Co. (Nashua), Advanced Technology Group, 10 Tara Blvd., 5th Fl., Nashua, NH 03062-2801. TEL 603-891-9111. FAX 603-891-0514.
circ. 106,000. *2121*

COMPUTER GRAPHICS.
Technews (Pty) Ltd., P.O. Box 626, Kloof 3640, South Africa. TEL 27-31-7640593. FAX 27-31-7640386.
circ. 4,685. *2121*

COMPUTER LAW ASSOCIATION BULLETIN.
Computer Law Association Inc., 3028 Javier Rd., Ste. 500 E, Fairfax, VA 22031. TEL 703-560-7747. FAX 703-207-7028.
circ. 1,300. *4067*

COMPUTER RESELLER NEWS.
C M P Publications, Inc., 600 Community Dr., Manhasset, NY 11030. TEL 516-562-5000. FAX 516-733-6916.
circ. 104,000. *2147*

CONTROLLED CIRCULATION SERIALS

COMPUTER SERVICES AND SOFTWARE ASSOCIATION. REFERENCE BOOK AND BUYERS' GUIDE.
Sterling Publications Ltd., 86-88 Edgware Rd., London W2 2YW, England. TEL 44-171-915-9600. FAX 44-171-915-9619.
circ. 6,000. *2077*

COMPUTER SOURCES.
Asian Sources Media Group, 1038 Leigh Ave., Ste. 100, San Jose, CA 95126-4155. TEL 408-295-5900. FAX 408-295-4595.
circ. 30,000. *2129*

COMPUTEREPORT.
Virginia Commonwealth University, Academic Computing, 1015 Floyd Ave., Box 174, Richmond, VA 23284. TEL 804-786-4719. *2077*

COMPUTERLAND MAGAZINE.
ComputerLand Corporation, 5964 W. Las Positas, Pleasanton, CA 94588-8575. TEL 510-734-4087. FAX 510-734-4802.
circ. 270,000. *1199*

COMPUTERWORLD.
I D G Danmark A-S, Carl Jacobsensvej 25, DK-2500 Valby, Denmark. TEL 45-36-19-91-00. FAX 45-36-44-20-33.
circ. 26,000. *2078*

COMPUTERWORLD HONG KONG.
I D G Communications (HK) Ltd., Mount Parker House, Ste. 1011-15, 1111 King's Rd., Quarry Bay, Hong Kong, People's Republic of China. TEL 852-2861-3238. FAX 852-2861-0953.
circ. 11,500. *2127*

COMPUTERWORLD SINGAPORE.
I D G Communications (S) Pte. Ltd., 80 Masire Pasade Rd., 13-09 Parkway Parade, Singapore 1544, Singapore. TEL 65-345-8383. FAX 65-345-7097.
circ. 24,793. *2127*

CONCATENATION.
5 Charlieville Rd., North Heath, Kent DA8 1HJ, England.
circ. 3,000. *4529*

CONCATENATOR.
Western Indexing, 404-1020 Pembroke St., Victoria, BC V8T 4Z6, Canada. TEL 250-920-3528, 250-920-3528.
circ. 600. *4230*

CONCORDIA ALUMNI NEWS.
Concordia College, 901 S. Eighth St., Moorhead, MN 56562. TEL 218-299-4000. FAX 218-299-3646.
circ. 34,000. *1947*

CONCORDIA TORCH.
Concordia Mutual Life Association, 3041 Woodcreek Dr., Downers Grove, IL 60515. TEL 708-971-8000. FAX 708-971-9332.
circ. 10,000. *3813*

THE CONCRETE PRODUCER.
Aberdeen Group, 426 S. Westgate St., Addison, IL 60101. TEL 630-543-0870. FAX 630-543-3112.
circ. 15,500. *877*

THE CONDENSER.
Tongaat-Hulett Group Ltd., P.O. Box 3, Tongaat 4400, Natal, South Africa. TEL 27-322-21000. FAX 27-322-21094.
circ. 14,000. *949*

CONFISERIE.
Editions de la Confiserie, 103 rue LaFayette, 75481 Paris Cedex 10, France. TEL 33-1-42851820. FAX 33-1-40160145.
circ. 4,000. *3136*

CONGREGATIONAL BIBLE REVIVAL NEWS.
Congregational Bible Churches International, Box 47311, Wichita, KS 67201-7311. TEL 316-832-0554.
circ. 1,000. *6420*

CONGRESOS CONVENCIONES E INCENTIVOS.
Princesa 1, Torre de Madrid, planta 13-2, 28008 Madrid, Spain. TEL 91-548-09-73. FAX 91-5479813.
circ. 6,000. *5168*

CONNECTICUT CONSTRUCTION HIGHLIGHTS OF THE WEEK.
Connecticut Construction Industries Association, Inc., 912 Silas Deane Hwy., Wethersfield, CT 06109. TEL 860-529-6855. FAX 860-563-0616.
circ. 650. *878*

CONNECTICUT FAMILY.
Family Publishing Group, Inc., 141 Halstead Ave., Ste. 3D, Mamaroneck, NY 10543-2652. TEL 914-381-7474.
circ. 35,000. *1843*

CONNECTICUT GOVERNMENT.
University of Connecticut, Institute of Public Service, Storrs, CT 06269-4014. TEL 203-486-2828.
6170

CONNECTICUT STATE DENTAL ASSOCIATION. JOURNAL.
Connecticut State Dental Association, 62 Russ St., Hartford, CT 06106. TEL 860-659-2623. FAX 860-244-8287.
circ. 2,700. *4853*

CONNECTION (FALLS CHURCH).
National Association of Plumbing - Heating - Cooling Contractors, 180 S. Washington St., Falls Church, VA 22046-1148. TEL 703-237-8100. FAX 703-237-7442.
circ. 7,000. *3477*

CONNECTIONS.
Chartered Institute of Marketing, Moor Hall, Cookham, Maidenhead, Berkshire SL6 9QH, England. TEL 44-1628-427500. FAX 44-1628-427499.
circ. 25,000. *1521*

CONNECTIONS.
Muscular Dystrophy Association of Canada, 2345 Yonge St., 9th Fl., Toronto, ON M4P 2E5, Canada. TEL 416-488-0030. FAX 416-488-7523.
circ. 16,000. *5125*

CONNECTIVITY.
Taylor Associates, P.O. Box 13281, London N3 3TD, England. TEL 44-70-500-40035. FAX 44-70-500-28485.
circ. 10,000. *2196*

CONNSTRUCTION MAGAZINE.
McHugh Design, 62 LaSalle Rd., Ste. 211, W. Hartford, CT 06107. TEL 203-523-7518. FAX 203-231-8808.
circ. 7,000. *878*

CONSERVER.
British Trust for Conservation Volunteers, 36 St. Mary's St., Wallingford, Oxon. OX10 0EU, England. TEL 44-1491-839766. FAX 44-1491-839646.
circ. 20,000. *2227*

CONSTRUCTION (GUILFORD).
H E S, Inc., 26 Long Hill Rd., Box 362, Guilford, CT 06437-0362. TEL 203-453-3717. FAX 203-453-3717.
circ. 6,900. *878*

CONSTRUCTION ALBERTA NEWS.
Construction Alberta News Ltd., 10536 106th St., Edmonton, AB T5H 2X8, Canada. TEL 403-424-1146. FAX 403-425-5886.
circ. 4,125. *878*

CONSTRUCTION DIGEST.
Construction Magazine Group Inc., Box 6132, Indianapolis, IN 46206-6132. TEL 317-329-3100. FAX 317-329-3110.
circ. 11,276. *879*

CONSTRUCTION EQUIPMENT OPERATION AND MAINTENANCE.
Construction Publications, Inc., Box 1689, Cedar Rapids, IA 52406. TEL 319-366-1597. FAX 319-362-8808.
circ. 64,200. *880*

CONSTRUCTIONEER.
H E S, Inc., 26 Long Hill Rd., Box 362, Guilford, CT 06437. TEL 203-453-3717. FAX 203-453-4390.
circ. 15,000. *924*

CONSTRUIRE.
Association de la Construction du Quebec, 4970 Place de la Savane, Montreal, PQ H4P 1Z6, Canada. TEL 514-739-2381. FAX 514-739-8933.
circ. 18,683. *882*

CONSULTING ENGINEERS OF BRITISH COLUMBIA. COMMENTARY.
Consulting Engineers of British Columbia, 514-409 Granville St., Vancouver, BC V6C 1T2, Canada. TEL 604-687-2811. FAX 604-688-7110.
circ. 2,000. *2714*

CONSUMER CHOICE.
Consumers Association of Ireland Ltd., 45 Upper Mount St., Dublin 2, Ireland. TEL 353-1-6612090. FAX 353-1-6612464.
circ. 11,000. *2253*

CONTACT (QUEBEC).
Service des Communications, Universite Laval, Pavillon Alphonse Desjardins, Local 3577, Laval University, Quebec, PQ G1K 7P4, Canada. TEL 418-656-2571. FAX 418-656-2809.
circ. 118,000. *3260*

CONTACT MAGAZINE.
British Chiropractic Association, Gillets Farm House, Woodville, Stour Provost, Dorset SP8 5LX, England. TEL 44-1747-838553. FAX 44-1747-838039.
circ. 1,000. *4827*

CONTEMPORARY SURGERY.
Bobit Publishing Company, 2512 Artesia Blvd., Redondo Beach, CA 90278-3210. TEL 310-376-8788. FAX 310-376-9043.
circ. 50,000. *5139*

CONTINGENCIES.
American Academy of Actuaries, 1100 17th St., N.W., 7 Fl., Washington, DC 20036. TEL 202-223-8196. FAX 202-872-1948.
circ. 22,000. *3813*

CONTRACT FURNISHING DIRECTORY.
British Contract Furnishing Association, Ste. 214, Business Design Centre, 52 Upper St., London N1 0QH, England. TEL 0171-226-6641. FAX 0171-228-6190.
circ. 3,000. *3853*

CONTRACTING BUSINESS.
Penton Publishing Co., 1100 Superior Ave., Cleveland, OH 44114-2543. TEL 216-696-7000. FAX 216-696-7932.
circ. 52,600. *3477*

CONTRACTORS GUIDE.
Century Communications Corp., 6201 W. Howard St., Niles, IL 60714-3435. TEL 847-647-1200. FAX 847-647-7055.
circ. 32,000. *882*

CONVENIENCE STORE DECISIONS.
Donohue - Meehan Publishing Company (Bensalem), 2 Greenwood Sq., Ste. 410, 3331 Street Rd., Bensalem, PA 19020-2023. TEL 215-245-4555. FAX 215-245-4060.
circ. 42,000. *3139*

CONVENIENCE STORE NEWS.
Macfadden Publishing, Macfadden Trade Publications, 233 Park Ave. S., 6th Fl., New York, NY 10003. TEL 212-780-2300. FAX 212-228-3142.
circ. 5,512. *3140*

CONVENTIONS & MEETINGS CANADA.
Effective Communications Ltd., 5762 Highway 7, Ste. 207, Markham, ON L3P 1A8, Canada. TEL 905-471-1550. FAX 905-471-1552.
circ. 10,416. *5168*

CONVENTIONSOUTH.
Covey Communications Corp., Box 2267, Gulf Shores, AL 36547. TEL 334-968-5300. FAX 334-968-4532.
circ. 10,000. *5168*

CONVERTER.
Faversham House Group Ltd., Faversham House, 232a Addington Rd., South Croydon, Surrey CR2 8LE, England. TEL 44-181-651-7100. FAX 44-181-651-7117.
circ. 3,780. *5566*

COOLEY BENCHMARK.
Thomas M. Cooley Law School, Box 13038, Lansing, MI 48901. TEL 517-371-5140. FAX 517-334-5718.
circ. 10,000. *3936*

COOP - ZEITUNG.
Coop Schweiz, Thiersteineralle 12, Postfach 2550, CH-4002 Basel, Switzerland. TEL 41-61-3367118. FAX 41-61-3367072.
circ. 1,031,921. *1205*

COOPER HELLER RESEARCH. NEWSLETTER.
Cooper Heller Research, Inc., 622 S. 42nd St., Philadelphia, PA 19104. TEL 215-823-5490.
4230

COOPERAZIONE ITALIANA.
Editrice Cooperativa, Via G. Tomassetti 12, 00161 Rome, Italy. TEL 6-8844942. FAX 6-84439406.
circ. 20,000. *1206*

COPPER TOPICS.
Copper Development Association Inc., 260 Madison Ave., New York, NY 10016-2401. TEL 212-251-7200. FAX 203-251-7234.
circ. 35,000. *5189*

COR ET VASA.
Praha Publishing Ltd., Anglicka 19, 120 00 Prague 2, Czech Republic. TEL 42-2-66312615. FAX 42-2-24247568. *4814*

COREL MAGAZINE.
Omray Inc., 9801 Anderson Mill Rd., Ste. 207, Austin, TX 78750. TEL 512-250-1700. FAX 512-219-3156.
circ. 7,000. *2122*

CORN FARMER.
Meredith Corporation, 1716 Locust St., Des Moines, IA 50336. TEL 515-284-2700.
circ. 68,000. *220*

CORNELL FOCUS.
Cornell University, Agricultural Experiment Station, 1150 Comstock Hall, College of Agriculture & Life Sciences, Ithaca, NY 14853. TEL 607-255-1876. FAX 607-255-9873.
circ. 5,000. *109*

CORNELL UNIVERSITY. NEW YORK STATE COLLEGE OF AGRICULTURE AND LIFE SCIENCES. BIOMETRICS UNIT. ANNUAL REPORT.
New York State College of Agriculture and Life Sciences, Department of Plant Breeding and Biometry, Cornell University, 436 Warren Hall, Ithaca, NY 14853. TEL 607-255-5488. FAX 607-255-4698. *597*

CORNHUSKER FAMILY PHYSICIAN.
Nebraska Academy of Family Physicians, 7101 Newport Ave., No. 201, Omaha, NE 68152-2158. TEL 402-572-3530. FAX 402-572-3532.
circ. 3,000. *4658*

CORNISH METHODIST HISTORICAL ASSOCIATION JOURNAL.
c/o Barrie S. May, Pelmear Villa, Carharrack, Redruth, Cornwall TR16 5RB, England. TEL 01209-820381.
circ. 300. *6420*

CORPORATE COMPUTING.
Ziff-Davis Publishing (San Francisco), 50 Beale St., 14th Fl., San Francisco, CA 94105-1813. TEL 415-578-7600. FAX 415-578-7799.
circ. 155,000. *1200*

CORPORATE CRUISE NEWS.
Landry & Kling, Inc., 1390 S. Dixie Hwy., Ste. 1207, Coral Gables, FL 33146-2943. TEL 305-661-1880. *7194*

CORPORATE DETROIT MAGAZINE.
Corporate Detroit, Inc., 19512 Livernois Ave., Detroit, MI 48221-1766. TEL 313-872-6000. FAX 313-872-6009.
circ. 27,000. *950*

CORPORATE EVENT SERVICES.
Showcase Publications Ltd., 38c The Broadway, London N8 9SU, England. TEL 44-181-348-2332. FAX 44-181-340-3750.
circ. 14,000. *5169*

CORPORATE REPORT MINNESOTA.
American City Business Journals, Inc. (Austin), 505 Powell St., Austin, TX 78703-5121.
circ. 1,491. *1471*

CORPORATE UNIVERSITY REVIEW.
Enterprise Communications Inc., 1483 Chain Bridge Rd., Ste. 202, McLean, VA 22101. TEL 703-448-0336. FAX 703-448-0270.
circ. 17,000. *1564*

CORPORATION OF BRITISH COLUMBIA LAND SURVEYORS. REPORT OF PROCEEDINGS.
Corporation of British Columbia Land Surveyors, 895 Fort St., Ste. 306, Victoria, BC V8W 1H7, Canada. TEL 250-382-4323. FAX 250-382-5092.
circ. 500. *3399*

CORPUS CHRISTI BAY AREA BUSINESS.
Woolford Publishing, 711 N. Carancahua St., Ste. 500, Corpus Christi, TX 78475-1301. TEL 512-883-8833. FAX 512-883-4329.
circ. 6,500. *951*

CORPUS CHRISTI MARINER NEWS.
Box 1960, Corpus Christi, TX 78403. TEL 512-882-7262.
circ. 50. *7148*

CORPUS DES LUTHISTES FRANCAIS.
C N R S Editions, 20-22 rue St. Amand, 75015 Paris, France. TEL 45-33-16-00. FAX 45-33-92-13.
circ. 1,500. *5386*

CORPUS VITREARUM.
C N R S Editions, 20-22 rue St. Amand, 75015 Paris, France. TEL 45-33-16-00. FAX 45-33-92-13.
circ. 1,500. *436*

CORRECTIONS FORUM.
Corrections Forum, 320 Broadway, Bethpage, NY 11714. TEL 516-942-3601. FAX 516-942-5968.
circ. 12,000. *2264*

CORREIO AGRICOLA.
Bayer Portugal S A R L, Apdo. 3306, 1308 Lisbon, Portugal. TEL 417-21-21. FAX 417-20-64. *220*

CORREIO POPULAR.
Correio Popular S.A., Rua Conceicao, 124 (Centro), 13010-902 Campinas SP, Brazil. TEL 55-192-328588. FAX 55-192-318152.
circ. 1,000. *3257*

CORRESPONDENT (APPLETON).
Aid Association for Lutherans, 4321 N. Ballard Rd., Appleton, WI 54919. TEL 414-734-5721. FAX 414-730-4818.
circ. 920,000. *3813*

COSMETIC DERMATOLOGY.
Quadrant HealthCom, 105 Raider Blvd., Belle Mead, NJ 08502-1510. TEL 908-874-0707. FAX 908-874-5611.
circ. 13,403. *4876*

COSMETIC NEWS.
Sepem s.r.l., Via Grado 9, 20125 Milan, Italy. TEL 39-2-26825553. FAX 39-2-26823952.
circ. 3,000. *510*

THE COTTAGE GARDENER.
Cottage Garden Society, c/o Clive Lane, Sec., Hurstfield House, 244 Edleston Rd., Crewe, Ches. CW2 7EJ, England. TEL 44-1270-250776. FAX 44-1270-250118.
circ. 5,500. *3185*

COTTAGE LIFE.
Quarto Communications, 111 Queen St. E., Ste. 408, Toronto, ON M5C 1S2, Canada. TEL 416-360-6880. FAX 416-360-6814.
circ. 14,000. *3260*

COUNCIL OF JEWISH THEATRES NEWSLETTER.
National Foundation for Jewish Culture, 330 Seventh Ave., 21st Fl., New York, NY 10001. TEL 212-629-0500. FAX 212-629-0508.
circ. 350. *7004*

COUNTERMAN.
Babcox Publications, 11 S. Forge St., Box 1810, Akron, OH 44309-1810. TEL 216-535-6617. FAX 216-535-0874.
circ. 50,500. *7096*

COUNTY NEWS.
National Association of Counties, 440 First St., N.W., Washington, DC 20001. TEL 202-393-6226. FAX 202-393-2630.
circ. 27,000. *6213*

THE COURIER.
Union Society, King's Walk, Newcastle-upon-Tyne NE1 8QB, England. TEL 44-191-232-4050. FAX 44-191-222-1876.
circ. 3,000. *1947*

COURIER (LEXINGTON).
National Tour Association, Inc., 546 E. Main St., Lexington, KY 40508-2342. TEL 606-253-1036. FAX 606-231-9837.
circ. 5,200. *7194*

COURT NEWS.
Judicial Council of California, Administrative Office of the California Courts, 303 Second St., S. Twr., San Francisco, CA 94107-1366. FAX 415-396-9367.
circ. 3,800. *4131*

COWARD FAMILY NEWSLETTER.
2140 Marion St., Birmingham, AL 35226-3012. TEL 205-822-2446.
circ. 300. *3218*

CRAFTRENDS.
P J S Publications, Inc., 2 News Plaza, Box 1790, Peoria, IL 61656-3435. TEL 309-682-6626. FAX 309-682-7394.
circ. 31,472. *479*

CRESCENDO.
Toronto Musicians' Association, 101 Thorncliffe Park Dr., Toronto, Ont. M4H 1M2, Canada. TEL 416-421-1020. FAX 416-421-7011.
circ. 4,000. *5387*

CRESCENDO (INTERLOCHEN).
Interlochen Center for the Arts, Interlochen Arts Camp, Box 199, Interlochen, MI 49643. TEL 616-276-7200. FAX 616-276-6321.
circ. 58,000. *2431*

CRIME LABORATORY DIGEST.
U.S. Federal Bureau of Investigation Laboratory, FSRTC, F B I Academy, Quantico, VA 22135. TEL 703-640-1531.
circ. 4,000. *4903*

CRITERION (RIVERSIDE).
Riverside County Publishing Co., 7190 Jurupa Ave., Riverside, CA 92504-1016.
circ. 2,000. *1948*

CRITICA.
Universidad Nacional Autonoma de Mexico, Instituto de Investigaciones Filosoficas, Apdo. Postal 70-447, Mexico, D.F., Mexico. FAX 525-7244777.
circ. 800. *5722*

CRITICAL SURVEY.
Berghahn Books Inc., 165 Taber Ave., Providence, RI 02906. TEL 401-861-9330. FAX 401-521-0046.
circ. 700. *4330*

CROP PROTECTION COURIER (INTERNATIONAL).
Bayer AG, Abteilung Publikationen, 51368 Leverkusen, Germany. TEL 49-214-3062875. FAX 49-214-3071985.
circ. 33,500. *220*

CROSSTALK.
Zuerichsee Zeitschriftenverlag, Seestr. 86, CH-8712 Staefa, Switzerland. TEL 01-9285611. FAX 01-9285600.
circ. 70,000. *7258*

CROWN JOURNAL.
Higgs and Hill plc., Crown House, Kingston Rd., New Malden, Surrey KT3 3ST, England. TEL 44-181-942-8921. FAX 44-181-949-9280.
circ. 10,000. *883*

CROYDON AIRPORT SOCIETY JOURNAL.
Croydon Airport Society, 193 Commonside E., Mitcham, Surrey CR4 1HB, England. TEL 44-181-648-3906. FAX 44-181-770-4750.
circ. 800. *62*

CRUISE AND VACATION VIEWS.
Orban Communications, Inc., 25 Washington St., 4th Fl., Morristown, NJ 07960. TEL 201-650-2442. FAX 201-605-2722.
circ. 35,000. *7194*

10320 CONTROLLED CIRCULATION SERIALS

CRUISE ENTERTAINMENT MAGAZINE.
Tony Rome Enterprises, Inc., 660 Livernois, Ferndale, MI 48220. TEL 248-545-9040. FAX 248-545-1073.
circ. 5,000. *3693*

CRUISING ASSOCIATION. HANDBOOK.
Cruising Association, C A House, 1 Northey St., Limestone Basin, London E14 8BT, England. TEL 44-171-537-2828. FAX 44-171-537-2266.
circ. 5,000. *6838*

CRUISING ASSOCIATION. MAGAZINE.
Cruising Association, C A House, 1 Northey St., Limestone Basin, London E14 8BT, England. TEL 44-171-537-2828. FAX 44-171-537-2266.
circ. 5,000. *6838*

CUADERNOS DE ECONOMIA.
Pontificia Universidad Catolica de Chile, Instituto de Economia, Casilla 76, Correo 17, Santiago, Chile. TEL 56-2-6864314. FAX 56-2-5521310. *952*

CUADERNOS DE NUTRICION.
Cuadernos de Nutricion, A.C., Altata 51, P.B., Col. Hipodromo Condesa, 06170 Mexico, D.F., Mexico. TEL 52-5-5151939. FAX 52-5-2726207.
circ. 10,000. *5471*

CUADERNOS DE SEGURIDAD.
Estudios Tecnicos, S.A., Avda. Industria, 32, Edif. 2, 28108 Alcobendas (Madrid), Spain. TEL 34-1-6615189. FAX 34-1-6616884.
circ. 3,833. *2286*

CUBA. OFICINA DE LA PROPIEDAD INDUSTRIAL. BOLETIN OFICIAL.
Oficina de la Propiedad Industrial, Picota no. 15 e Luz y Acosta, Havana Vieja, 10100 Havana 1, Cuba. TEL 537-610185. FAX 537-335610.
circ. 200. *5583*

CULTURAL J B M.
Editora de Publicacoes Cientificas Ltda., Rua Major Suckow, 30, 20911-160 Rio de Janeiro RJ, Brazil. TEL 55-21-2013722.
circ. 60,000. *3257*

CURRENT CANADIAN BOOKS.
John Coutts Library Services Ltd., 6900 Kinsmen, P.O. Box 1000, Niagara Falls, ON L2E 7E7, Canada. TEL 905-356-6382. FAX 905-356-5064.
circ. 100. *6269*

CURRENT SAUCE.
Northwestern State University of Louisiana, Student Publications, NSU Box 5306, Natchitoches, LA 71497. TEL 318-357-5213. FAX 318-357-6564.
circ. 3,500. *1948*

CURRENTS & EDDIES.
Connecticut River Watershed Council, Inc., 1 Ferry St., Easthampton, MA 01027-1244. TEL 413-529-9500. FAX 413-529-9501.
circ. 2,000. *2227*

CURTIS LINE.
Curtis Circulation Co., 730 River Rd., New Milford, NJ 07646-3048. TEL 201-634-7400. FAX 201-634-7499.
circ. 2,400. *6269*

CUSTOM BUILDER.
Gruner & Jahr U.S.A. Publishing, 110 Fifth Ave., New York, NY 10011-5601. TEL 207-828-4470. FAX 207-828-4478.
circ. 30,000. *883*

CUSTOM BUILDERS AND THEIR COMMUNITIES.
Living Partners Ltd., 5501 LBJ Freeway, Ste. 300, Dallas, TX 75240. TEL 214-239-2399. FAX 214-239-7850.
circ. 40,000. *883*

CUSTOM HOMES BOOK OF PLANS.
Custom Publishing Company Ltd., 45 Station Rd., Redhill, Surrey RH1 1QH, England. TEL 44-1737-767213. FAX 44-1737-771662.
circ. 40,000. *401*

CUSTOM TAILOR.
Custom Tailors and Designers Association of America, Inc., Box 53052, Washington, DC 20009-9052. TEL 212-661-1960.
circ. 1,000. *1914*

CUSTOM WOODWORKING BUSINESS.
Vance Publishing Corporation (Lincolnshire), Box 1414, Lincolnshire, IL 60069-1414. TEL 708-634-2600. FAX 708-634-4379.
circ. 60,000. *924*

CYBIUM.
Societe Francaise d'Ichtyologie, 43 rue Cuvier, 75231 Paris Cedex 05, France. TEL 33-1-40793749. FAX 33-1-40793771.
circ. 550. *3064*

CYSTISK FIBROSE.
Landsforeningen til Bekaempelse af Cystisk Fibrose, Hyrdebakken 246, DK-8800 Viborg, Denmark. TEL 45-86-67-44-22. FAX 45-86-67-66-66.
circ. 1,800. *4659*

D B B REGIONALMAGAZIN.
Vereinigte Verlagsanstalten GmbH, Hoeherweg 278, 40231 Duesseldorf, Germany. TEL 49-211-7357-0. FAX 49-211-7357223.
circ. 40,000. *6213*

D B M S.
Miller Freeman Inc. (San Mateo), 411 Borel Ave. Ste. 100, San Mateo, CA 74402. TEL 415-358-9500. FAX 415-358-9855.
circ. 56,360. *2210*

D B Z.
Paul Parey Zeitschriftenverlag GmbH, Erich-Kaestner-Str. 2, 56379 Singhofen, Germany. TEL 49-2604-978601. FAX 49-2604-978610.
circ. 45,000. *5706*

D E C PROFESSIONNEL.
Presse Professionnelle SNC, 45 rue de Henri-de-Regnier, Versailles, France. TEL 39-53-95-26. FAX 39-02-39-71.
circ. 7,500. *2079*

D E C U S MAGAZINE.
Digital Equipment Computer Users Society, Communications Organization, 334 South St., SHR3-1 - T25, Shrewsbury, MA 01545. TEL 508-841-3584. FAX 508-841-3357.
circ. 25,000. *2079*

D E R - DEPONIE ENTSORGUNG RECYCLING.
Verlag Binkert AG, Postfach 32, CH-5080 Laufenburg, Switzerland. TEL 41-62-8697272. FAX 41-62-8697333.
circ. 5,200. *2984*

D F W PEOPLE - THE AIRPORT NEWSPAPER.
Wood Publications, Inc., 400 Fuller-Wiser, Ste. 125, Euless, TX 76039. TEL 817-540-4666. FAX 817-685-7562.
circ. 13,000. *7067*

D G A A E NACHRICHTEN.
Deutsche Gesellschaft fuer Allgemeine und Angewandte Entomologie, Schwabenheimerstr. 101, 69221 Dossenheim, Germany. TEL 49-621-85238. FAX 49-621-861222.
circ. 800. *749*

D H LAWRENCE REVIEW.
Southwest Texas State University, Department of English, San Marcos, TX 78666. TEL 512-245-7682.
circ. 850. *4395*

D-I-Y RADIO.
Radio Society of Great Britain, Lambda House, Cranborne Rd., Potters Bar, Herts EN6 3JE, England. TEL 44-1707-659015. FAX 44-1707-645105.
circ. 10,000. *2023*

D I Y SUPERSTORE.
Faversham House Group Ltd., Faversham House, 232a Addington Rd., South Croydon, Surrey CR2 8LE, England. TEL 44-181-651-7100. FAX 44-181-651-7117.
circ. 4,631. *3768*

D J K - AKTIV.
Deutsche Jugendkraft e.V., Niederwerrnerstr. 191, 97424 Schweinfurt, Germany. TEL 49-9721-81357. FAX 49-9721-83220.
circ. 2,500. *6757*

D M E COMMUNICAZIONE.
Deus Editore s.r.l., Via Breno 1, 20139 Milan, Italy.
circ. 7,467. *1523*

D M NEWS.
D M News Corp., 100 Sixth Ave., 6th Fl., New York, NY 10013-1689. TEL 212-741-2095. FAX 212-633-9367.
circ. 31,000. *1523*

D M REVIEW.
Powell Publishing, Inc., 617 S. 94th St., West Allis, WI 52314-1222. TEL 414-771-7687. FAX 414-771-8058.
circ. 59,308. *2165*

D N V FORUM.
D N V Corporate Communications, Det Norske Veritas, N-1322 Hovik, Norway.
circ. 15,000. *2781*

D R C MISSISSIPPI NEWSLETTER.
Delta Resources Committee, Inc., 300 N. Edison St., Box 584, Greenville, MS 38702. TEL 601-335-3121. FAX 601-335-3123.
circ. 1,500. *6421*

D R D O NEWSLETTER.
Defence Research & Development Organization, Metcalfe House, New Delhi 110 054, India. TEL 91-11-2932252. FAX 91-11-2919151.
circ. 1,900. *5920*

D S S NEWSLETTER.
Department of Social Services, Public Information Office, 1510 Guilford Ave., Baltimore, MD 21202. TEL 301-361-2002. FAX 301-361-3150.
circ. 4,000. *6662*

D S W R.
Verlag C.H. Beck, 80791 Munich, Germany. TEL 49-89-38189-338. FAX 49-89-38189-398.
circ. 35,900. *2173*

DAG OG TID.
Pilestredet 8, N-0180 Oslo, Norway. TEL 47-22-33-00-97. FAX 47-22-41-42-10.
circ. 6,011. *3342*

DAILY CAMPUS (DALLAS).
Student Media Company, Inc., 3140 Dyer St., Dallas, TX 75275. TEL 214-768-4555. FAX 214-768-4573.
circ. 4,500. *1948*

DAILY INQILAB.
Inqilab Enterprise & Publications Ltd., 2-1 R.K. Mission Rd., Dhaka 1203, Bangladesh. TEL 880-2-868440. FAX 880-2-833122.
circ. 5,000. *3254*

DAILY OTHER.
MacMurray College, Journalism Program, Jacksonville, IL 62650. TEL 217-479-7049.
circ. 700. *1949*

DAILY PURBANCHAL.
Purbanchal Publishers, 38 Iqbal Nagar, Khulna 9100, Bangladesh. TEL 880-41-22251. FAX 880-2-839209.
circ. 3,000. *3254*

DAILY TIMES.
Daily Times of Nigeria Ltd., Publications Division, New Isheri Rd., P.M.B. 21340, Agidingbi, Ikeja, Lagos State, Nigeria. TEL 234-1-4900840. FAX 234-1-6421333.
circ. 250,000. *3340*

DAILY TRADE NEWS.
Korea Foreign Trade Association, 159-1 Samsung-dong, Dang-nam-ku, Seoul 135-729, S. Korea. TEL 02-551-5441. FAX 02-551-5400.
circ. 20,000. *1321*

DAINIK MEILLAT.
Daily Meillat, 28 Toyenbee Circular Rd., Motijheel Commercial Area, Dhaka 1000, Bangladesh. TEL 880-2-240026. FAX 880-2-863797.
circ. 10,000. *3254*

DAIRY FIELD.
Stagnito Publishing Company, 1935 Shermer Rd., Ste. 100, Northbrook, IL 60062. TEL 847-205-5660. FAX 847-205-5680.
circ. 18,000. *253*

DAIRY WORLD.
Independent Buyers Association Inc., 27 Providence Rd., Millbury, MA 01527. TEL 508-865-2507.
circ. 41,250. *254*

DALLAS - FORT WORTH HOME BUYER'S GUIDE.
Home Buyer's Guide (Dallas), 5501 LBJ Frwy., Ste. 300, Dallas, TX 75240-6202. TEL 214-239-2399.
circ. 75,000. *6299*

DANCE EAST.
B C Publications, 16C Market Pl., Diss, Norfolk IP22 3AB, England. TEL 44-1379-644200. FAX 44-1379-650480.
circ. 2,500. *2292*

DANCE RESEARCH.
Oxford University Press, Academic Division, Great Clarendon St., Oxford OX2 6DP, England. TEL 44-1865-267907. FAX 44-1865-267485.
circ. 650. *2292*

DANGEROUS PROPERTIES OF INDUSTRIAL MATERIALS REPORT.
Van Nostrand Reinhold, 115 Fifth Ave., New York, NY 10003. TEL 212-254-3232. FAX 212-673-1239.
circ. 2,000. *5489*

DANSK LANDBRUG.
Vest Media A-S, Storegade 28, Skansen, 6800 Varde, Denmark. TEL 75 22 44 00. FAX 75-22-44-77.
circ. 126,495. *111*

DANSK SMEDE-TIDENDE.
Dansk Smedemesterforening, Box 161, Magnoliavej 2, DK-5250 Odense SV, Denmark. TEL 45-66-17-33-12. FAX 45-66-17-36-12.
circ. 3,700. *5189*

DANSK V V S.
Danish National Federation of Master Plumbers, Heating and Ventilation Installation Contractors, 75 Hoejnaesvej, 2610 Roedovre, Denmark. FAX 45-36-41-17-25.
circ. 14,200. *3478*

DANSKE MALERMESTRE.
Danske Malermestre, Snaregade 12, DK-1205 Copenhagen K, Denmark. TEL 45-33-93-36-00. FAX 45-33-93-42-10.
circ. 3,200. *5551*

DANSKE PIONEER.
Bertelsen Publishing Co., 1582 Glen Lake Rd., Hoffman Estates, IL 60195. TEL 847-882-2552. FAX 847-882-7082.
circ. 3,400. *3007*

DANSKE VOGNMAEND.
Danske Vognmaend Hovedorganisationen, Gammeltorv 18, 1457 Copenhagen K, Denmark. TEL 33-13-88-00. FAX 33-32-57-07.
circ. 6,900. *7173*

DATA NEWS.
Diligentia Business Press N.V., 42 av. du Houx, 1170 Brussels, Belgium. TEL 32-2-6781611. FAX 32-2-6603600.
circ. 23,400. *2015*

DATACOM.
E M A P Business Communications, E M A P Computing, Greater London House, Hampstead Rd., London NW1 7QZ, England. TEL 44-171-388-2430. FAX 44-171-388-2480.
circ. 21,000. *2132*

DATAPACK.
Quest Magazines Ltd., Publishing House, 652 Victoria Rd., South Ruislip, Mddx. HA4 0SX, England. TEL 44-181-842-1010. FAX 44-181-841-2557.
circ. 3,000. *1663*

DATATID.
Fasit Forlag AS, P.O. Box 2739 Stanshaugen, N-0131 Oslo, Norway. TEL 47-22-03-22-20. FAX 47-22-03-22-21.
circ. 22,000. *2080*

DATAWEEK.
Technews (Pty) Ltd., P.O. Box 626, Kloof 3640, South Africa. TEL 27-31-7640593. FAX 27-31-7640386.
circ. 5,306. *6957*

DATELINE WINNIPEG.
Better Business Bureau of Winnipeg & Manitoba, 301-365 Hargrave St., Winnipeg, MB R3B 2K3, Canada. TEL 204-942-7166. FAX 204-943-1489.
circ. 2,000. *953*

DATENSCHUTZ NACHRICHTEN.
Deutsche Vereinigung fuer Datenschutz, Reuterstr. 44, 53113 Bonn, Germany. TEL 49-228-222498.
circ. 500. *2149*

DATENSCHUTZ UND INFORMATIONSRECHT.
Oesterreichische Gesellschaft fuer Datenschutz, Sautergasse 20, A-1170 Vienna, Austria. TEL 43-1-4897893. FAX 43-1-4897891310.
circ. 800. *2149*

DAVID DAVIES MEMORIAL INSTITUTE OF INTERNATIONAL STUDIES. OCCASIONAL PAPER.
David Davies Memorial Institute of International Studies, 2 Chadwick St., London SW1P 2EP, England. TEL 44-171-222-4063. FAX 44-171-233-2863.
circ. 1,000. *6011*

DAYTON BUSINESS REPORTER.
Hannover Publishing Co., Inc., 6356 Far Hills Ave., Dayton, OH 45459-2782. TEL 937-291-1100. FAX 937-436-3426.
circ. 10,000. *953*

DE VERE HOTELS MAGAZINE.
Media Partners CPR, Northern Rock House, 20 Market Pl., Guisborough, Cleveland TS14 6HF, England. TEL 44-1287-639111. FAX 44-1287-637201.
circ. 30,000. *3724*

DEALER BUSINESS.
Ward's Communications, 3000 Town Center, Ste. 2750, Southfield, MI 48075-1212. TEL 810-357-0800. FAX 810-357-0810.
circ. 33,501. *7096*

DEALERNEWS.
Advanstar Communications, Inc., 7500 Old Oak Blvd., Cleveland, OH 44130. TEL 216-826-2839. FAX 216-891-2726.
circ. 14,203. *6827*

DEALERS' CHOICE.
Texas Automobile Dealers Association, 1108 Lavaca St., Box 1028, Austin, TX 78767-1028. TEL 512-476-2686. FAX 512-476-2179.
circ. 1,800. *7096*

DEEPWATER.
Greater Baton Rouge Port Commission, Box 380, Pt. Allen, LA 70767. TEL 504-342-1660. FAX 504-342-1666.
circ. 1,000. *7148*

DEFENCE SYSTEMS INTERNATIONAL.
Sterling Publications Ltd., 86-88 Edgware Rd., London W2 2YW, England. TEL 44-171-915-9600. FAX 44-171-915-9619.
circ. 12,500. *5265*

DEFENSE INDUSTRY & AEROSPACE REPORT.
Business Communications Group, P.O. Box 250, Mawson, A.C.T. 2607, Australia. TEL 61-6-2864605. FAX 61-6-2863441.
circ. 6,000. *5266*

DEFENSE TRANSPORTATION JOURNAL.
National Defense Transportation Association, 50 South Pickett St., No. 220, Alexandria, VA 22304-3008. TEL 703-751-5011. FAX 703-823-8761.
circ. 8,500. *7026*

DEGREES NORTH (LEEDS).
University of Leeds, Alumni Office, 18 Blenheim Terrace, Leeds LS2 9HD, England. TEL 44-113-233-6109. FAX 44-113-233-4029.
circ. 55,000. *1949*

DEHI RAZAKAR.
National Farm Guide Council of Pakistan, c/o Shabaz A. Raheem, Ed., 405 Ferozepur Rd., Lahore 54600, Pakistan. TEL 92-42-5864155. FAX 92-42-5864155. *111*

DEKE QUARTERLY.
Delta Kappa Epsilon Fraternity, Inc., 35 McKinley Place, Grosse Pte Farms, MI 48236. TEL 313-886-2400. FAX 313-8862227.
circ. 25,000. *1931*

DEL CONDOMINIUM LIFE.
Del Property Management Inc., 4800 Dufferin St., Downsview, ON M3H 5S9, Canada. TEL 416-736-2552. FAX 416-661-8923.
circ. 25,000. *3844*

DELAWARE BEVERAGE MONTHLY.
Melton Communications Inc., 1518 N. Van Buren St., Wilmington, DE 19806. TEL 302-655-2800. FAX 302-655-2805.
circ. 1,800. *519*

DELEGATES.
Blenheim, Blenheim House, 630 Chiswick High Rd., London W4 5BG, England. TEL 44-181-742-2828. FAX 44-181-742-0387.
circ. 17,307. *5169*

DELTA EPSILON SIGMA JOURNAL.
Delta Epsilon Sigma National Scholastic Honor Society, c/o George Herndl, Ed., Belmont Abbey College, Belmont, NC 28012. TEL 704-825-5026. FAX 305-899-3026.
circ. 20,000. *1950*

DELTA OPTIMIST.
Today Publishing Ltd., 5485 48th Ave., Delta, BC V4K 1X2, Canada. TEL 604-946-4451. FAX 604-946-5680.
circ. 15,000. *3260*

DELUXE.
Maxwell Custom Publishing, 1999 Shepard Rd., St. Paul, MN 55116. TEL 612-690-7200. FAX 612-690-7357. *1127*

DENKMALPFLEGE IN SACHSEN-ANHALT.
Verlag fuer Bauwesen GmbH, Am Friedrichshain 22, 10407 Berlin, Germany. TEL 49-30-42151-0. FAX 49-30-42151468.
circ. 1,000. *438*

DENKMALPFLEGE INFORMATIONEN.
Bayerisches Landesamt fuer Denkmalpflege, Hofgraben 4, 80539 Munich, Germany. TEL 49-89-2114-213. FAX 49-89-2114-300.
circ. 3,000. *6171*

DENTAL ASSISTANT JOURNAL.
American Dental Assistants Association, 203 N. La Salle St., Ste. 1320, Chicago, IL 60601-1225. TEL 312-541-1550. FAX 312-541-1496.
circ. 15,000. *4854*

DENTAL ECONOMICS.
PennWell Publishing Co., Dental Economics Division, Box 3408, Tulsa, OK 74101. TEL 918-835-3161. FAX 918-831-9804.
circ. 110,531. *4854*

DENTAL HEALTH.
British Dental Hygienists' Association, St. Luke, Maywood, Portsmouth Rd., Camberley, Surrey GU15 1LH, England. TEL 44-1276-677156. FAX 44-1276-671072.
circ. 2,500. *4854*

DENTAL PRODUCTS REPORT.
Medical Economics Publishing Co., Inc., 5 Paragon Dr., Montvale, NJ 07645. TEL 201-358-7246. FAX 201-573-0344.
circ. 147,801. *4855*

DENTISTRY IN SOUTH DAKOTA.
South Dakota Dental Association, 330 S. Poplar Ave., Box 1194, Pierre, SD 57501-1194. TEL 605-224-9133. FAX 605-224-9168.
circ. 530. *4856*

DENTISTRY TODAY.
Dentistry Today, Inc., 26 Park St., Montclair, NJ 07042. TEL 201-783-3190. FAX 201-783-6835.
circ. 147,000. *4856*

DENVER HOUSING GUIDE.
Baker Publications, 14406 E. Evans Ave., Ste. 200, Aurora, CO 80014-1479. TEL 303-695-8440. FAX 303-695-8449.
circ. 70,000. *6299*

DEPARTMENT STORE WORKERS' UNION. LOCAL 1-S NEWS.
Department Store Workers' Union, Local 1- S, Retail, Wholesale and Dept. Store Union, A F L - C I O, 140 W. 31st St., New York, NY 10001.
circ. 10,000. *3889*

DESARROLLO NACIONAL.
Intercontinental Media, P.O. Box 3410, Milford, CT 06460. TEL 203-874-1401. FAX 203-222-8793.
circ. 22,000. *2781*

CONTROLLED CIRCULATION SERIALS

DESERT AIRMAN.
Territorial Newspapers, P.O. Box 27087, Tucson, AZ 85726-7087. TEL 602-297-1107. FAX 602-297-6253.
circ. 11,500. *5267*

DESERT MOBILE HOME NEWS.
Box 3386, Palm Desert, CA 92261. TEL 619-568-6633. FAX 619-568-0603.
circ. 10,000. *3372*

DESIGN - BUILD BUSINESS.
McKellar Publications, Inc., 333 E. Glenoaks Blvd., Ste. 204, Glendale, CA 91207-2074. TEL 818-241-0250. FAX 818-241-4406.
circ. 60,000. *884*

DESIGN COST & DATA.
L M Rector Corporation, 8602 N. 40th St., Tampa, FL 33604. TEL 813-989-9300. FAX 813-980-3982.
circ. 12,500. *401*

DESIGN NEWS O E M - SUPPLIERS SPECIAL ISSUE.
Cahners Publishing Company (Newton), Division of Reed Elsevier Inc., 275 Washington St., Newton, MA 02158-1630. TEL 617-964-3030. FAX 617-558-4470. *4543*

DESIGN PRODUCT NEWS.
Action Communications Inc., 135 Spy Court, Markham, ON L3R 5H6, Canada. TEL 905-477-3222. FAX 905-477-4320.
circ. 19,020. *2715*

DESIGNS.
Association Communication Innovation Designs 4, 85 St. Paul St. W., Montreal, PQ H2Y 3V4, Canada. TEL 514-842-4436. FAX 514-848-9730.
circ. 13,900. *3844*

DESKTOP PUBLISHING TODAY.
Andrew Bond, Ed. & Pub., Vine House, East St., Harrietsham, Maidstone, Kent ME17 1HJ, England. TEL 01732-359990. FAX 01732-770049.
circ. 10,500. *6292*

DESTINATION CALGARY AND AREA.
Calgary Convention & Visitors Bureau, 237 Eighth Ave., S.E., Ste. 200, Calgary, AB T2G 0K8, Canada. TEL 403-750-8510. FAX 403-262-3809.
circ. 1,100. *7195*

DEUCE.
University of Central England, Students' Union, Perry Barr, Birmingham B42 2SU, England. TEL 44-121-356-8164. FAX 44-121-344-3670.
circ. 4,000. *1950*

DEUTSCHE EINHEITSVERFAHREN ZUR WASSER-, ABWASSER- UND SCHLAMMUNTERSUCHUNG.
V C H Verlagsgesellschaft mbH, Postfach 101161, 69451 Weinheim, Germany. TEL 49-6201-606-0. FAX 49-6201-606328.
circ. 5,500. *2967*

DEUTSCHE MILCHWIRTSCHAFT.
Verlag Th. Mann, Nordring 10, 45894 Gelsenkirchen, Germany. TEL 49-209-9304184. FAX 49-209-9304185.
circ. 3,481. *254*

DEUTSCHE POSTZEITUNG.
Vereinigte Verlagsanstalten GmbH, Hoeherweg 278, 40231 Duesseldorf, Germany. TEL 49-211-7357-0. FAX 49-211-7357223.
circ. 45,000. *2019*

DEUTSCHER RAT FUER LANDESPFLEGE. SCHRIFTENREIHE.
Deutscher Rat fuer Landespflege, Konstantinstr. 110, 53179 Bonn, Germany. TEL 0228-331097. FAX 0228-334727.
circ. 2,000. *2912*

DEUTSCHES DISCOTHEKEN JAHRBUCH.
Verlag Disco Post GmbH, Oststr. 2, 56424 Staudt, Germany. TEL 49-2602-70044. FAX 49-2602-69939.
circ. 10,000. *1931*

DEUTSCHES INSTITUT FUER WIRTSCHAFTSFORSCHUNG. ECONOMIC BULLETIN.
Deutsches Institut fuer Wirtschaftsforschung, Koenigin-Luise-Str. 5, 14195 Berlin, Germany. TEL 49-30-897890. FAX 49-30-89789200.
circ. 400. *1251*

DEUTSCHES SOLDATENJAHRBUCH.
Schild-Verlag GmbH, Henschelstr. 7, 81249 Munich, Germany. TEL 49-89-8641189. FAX 49-89-8632310.
circ. 7,000. *5267*

DEUTSCHES STEUERRECHT.
Verlag C.H. Beck, 80791 Munich, Germany. TEL 49-89-38189-338. FAX 49-89-38189-398.
circ. 25,135. *1606*

DEVELOPER.
Kwazulu Finance and Investment Corporation Ltd., P.O. Box 2801, Durban 4000, South Africa. TEL 27-31-9078612. FAX 27-31-9073292.
circ. 10,000. *1128*

THE DEVELOPER.
Foundation for African Development, P.O. Box 16206, Kampala, Uganda. TEL 256-41-231824. FAX 256-41-251243.
circ. 2,000. *1357*

DEVELOPMENT OF LATIN AMERICA.
Sterling Publications Ltd., 86-88 Edgware Rd., London W2 2YW, England. TEL 44-171-915-9600. FAX 44-171-915-9619.
circ. 10,000. *1321*

DIA CUATRO QUE FUERA...
Junta Central de Fiestas de Moros y Cristianos, Palacio Municipal, Villena, Alicante, Spain. *6758*

DIABETES.
Finnish Diabetes Association, Kirjoniementie 15, 33680 Tampere, Finland. TEL 358-3-28-60-111. FAX 358-3-3600-462.
circ. 50,000. *4884*

DIABETES PATH FINDER.
American Diabetes Association, Washington Affiliate, Inc., 557 Roy St., Lower Lever, Seattle, WA 98109. TEL 206-282-4616. FAX 206-282-4729.
circ. 15,000. *4885*

DIABETES SELF-MANAGEMENT.
R.A. Rapaport Publishing, Inc., 150 W. 22nd St., New York, NY 10011. TEL 212-989-0200. FAX 212-989-4786.
circ. 30,000. *4885*

DIABETES UND STOFFWECHSEL.
Verlag Kirchheim und Co. GmbH, Kaiserstr. 41, 55116 Mainz, Germany. TEL 49-6131-96070-0. FAX 49-6131-9607070.
circ. 13,000. *4885*

DIABLO.
Diablo Publications, 2520 Camino Diablo, Walnut Creek, CA 94596. TEL 510-943-1111. FAX 510-943-1045.
circ. 50,000. *3373*

DIAKONIESCHWESTER.
Ev. Diakonieverein e.V., Glockenstr. 8, 14163 Berlin, Germany. TEL 030-8018091. FAX 030-8022452.
circ. 3,500. *6334*

DIAL ELECTRICAL - ELECTRONICS.
Dial Industry Publications, Windsor Ct., Grinstead House, E. Grinstead, W. Sussex RH19 1XA, England. TEL 44-1342-326972. FAX 44-1342-335247.
circ. 15,000. *2628*

DIAL ENGINEERING.
Dial Industry Publications, Windsor Ct., East Grinstead House, E. Grinstead, W. Sussex RH19 1XA, England. TEL 44-1342-326972. FAX 44-1342-335747.
circ. 18,000. *2857*

DIALOGO SOCIAL.
Centro de Capacitacion Social, Apdo. 9a-192, Calle 66AE, Carasquilla, Panama. TEL 29-1542.
circ. 7,800. *6707*

DIANNAO KAIFA YU YINGYONG.
Beifang Zidong Kongzhi Jishu Yanjiusuo, P.O. Box 8, Qi Xian (County), Shanxi 030900, People's Republic of China. TEL 86-351-7043553. FAX 86-351-7042975.
circ. 500. *2080*

DIBEVO VAKBLAD.
Landelijke Organisatie DIBEVO, Postbus 94, 3800 AB Amersfoort, Netherlands. TEL 31-33-550433. FAX 31-33-552835.
circ. 5,770. *5636*

AL-DIBLOMASI.
Ministry of Foreign Affairs, Department of Legal Affairs and Studies, P.O. Box 1, Abu Dhabi, United Arab Emirates. TEL 652200. FAX 668015.
circ. 500. *6011*

DICKINSON COUNTY HERITAGE CENTER. GAZETTE.
Dickinson County Heritage Center, 412 S. Campbell St., Abilene, KS 67410-2905. TEL 913-263-2681.
circ. 600. *3624*

DICTUM.
New Jersey State Bar Association, One Constitution Sq., New Brunswick, NJ 08901-1500. TEL 908-249-5000. FAX 908-828-0034.
circ. 3,000. *3939*

DIENST LANDBOUWKUNDIG ONDERZOEK. STARING CENTRUM, INSTITUUT VOOR ONDERZOEK VAN HET LANDELIJK GEBIED. JAARBOEK.
Dienst Landbouwkundig Onderzoek, Staring Centrum, Instituut voor Onderzoek van het Landelijk Gebied, P.O. Box 125, 6700 AC Wageningen, Netherlands. TEL 31-317-474200. FAX 31-317-424812.
circ. 2,500. *2912*

DIER - EN - ARTS.
Transmondial B.V., Waalreseweg 17, 5554 HA Valkenswaard, Netherlands. TEL 31-40-2030535. FAX 31-40-2030535.
circ. 3,200. *7269*

DIESEL & GAS TURBINE WORLDWIDE.
Diesel & Gas Turbine Publications, 13555 Bishop's Court, Brookfield, WI 53005-6286. TEL 414-784-9177. FAX 414-784-8133.
circ. 21,000. *2882*

A DIFFERENT LIGHT REVIEW.
A Different Light Bookstores, 151 W. 19th St., New York, NY 10011. TEL 212-989-4850. FAX 212-989-2158.
circ. 60,000. *3693*

DIGEST OF LABOUR CASES.
V. Subramanian, Ed. & Pub., 337 Thambu Chetty St., Madras 600001, India.
circ. 280. *3940*

DIGITAL TECHNICAL JOURNAL.
Digital Equipment Corporation, Ak02-3-B3, 50 Nagog Park, Acton, MA 01720-9843. TEL 508-264-7549. FAX 508-264-7493.
circ. 15,000. *2115*

DIGNITY - U S A.
Dignity - U S A, 1500 Massachusetts Ave. N.W., Ste. 11, Washington, DC 20005. TEL 219-484-6492.
circ. 500. *3693*

DIMENSIONAL STONE MAGAZINE.
Dimensional Stone Institute, Inc., 6300 Variel Ave., Ste. I, Woodland Hills, CA 91367-2513. TEL 818-704-5555. FAX 818-704-6500.
circ. 15,000. *884*

DIN FASTIGHET.
Tjaellden-Gruppen AB, P.O. Box 64, S-164 94 Kista, Sweden. TEL 46-8-632-94-50. FAX 46-8-632-00-61.
circ. 95,000. *3745*

DIOGENES (ENGLISH EDITION).
Berghahn Books Inc., 165 Taber Ave., Providence, RI 02906. TEL 401-861-9330. FAX 401-521-0046.
circ. 600. *6708*

DIPLOMAT.
Diplomatist Associates Ltd., 58 Theobalds Rd., London, England. TEL 44-171-405-4878. FAX 44-171-831-0667.
circ. 3,000. *6011*

DIPLOMATE.
American Board of Professional Psychology, 2100 E. Broadway, Ste. 313, Columbia, MO 65201-6082. TEL 573-875-1267. FAX 573-443-1199.
circ. 3,000. *6108*

DIPLOMATISCHER PRESSEDIENST.
Diplomatischer Pressedienst, Neustiftgasse 104, A-1070 Vienna, Austria. TEL 43-1-5268080. FAX 43-1-5261810.
circ. 5,000. *6011*

DIRASAT. HUMAN AND SOCIAL SCIENCES.
University of Jordan, Deanship of Academic Research, Amman, Jordan. TEL 962-6-843555. FAX 962-6-840263.
circ. 1,000. *3777*

DIRASAT. NATURAL AND ENGINEERING SCIENCES.
University of Jordan, Deanship of Academic Research, Amman, Jordan. TEL 962-6-843555. FAX 962-6-840263.
circ. 1,000. *6522*

DIRECT FROM MIDREX.
Midrex Direct Reduction Corporation, Charlotte Plaza, Charlotte, NC 28244. TEL 704-373-1600. FAX 704-373-1611.
circ. 2,500. *5189*

DIRECT MARKETING NEWS.
C D M N Publishing, 1200 Markham Rd., Ste. 301, Scarborough, ON M1H 3C3, Canada. TEL 416-439-4083. FAX 416-439-4086.
circ. 7,000. *1524*

DIRECT RESPONSE.
Brainstorm Publishing Co., 4 Market Pl., Hertford, Herts. SG14 1EB, England. TEL 01992-501177. FAX 01992-500387.
circ. 7,400. *1524*

DIRECTIONS.
New Zealand Automobile Association, 342 Lambton Quay, P.O. Box 1, Wellington, New Zealand. TEL 64-4-4738738. FAX 64-4-4712080.
circ. 520,747. *3339*

DIRECTIONS FOR UTAH LIBRARIES.
Department of Community and Economic Development, State Library Division, 2150 S. 300 W., Ste. 16, Salt Lake City, UT 84115. TEL 801-468-6740. FAX 801-468-6767.
circ. 1,900. *4174*

DIRECTOR.
N F D A Publications, Inc., 11121 W. Oklahoma Ave., Box 27641, Milwaukee, WI 53227-0641. TEL 414-541-2500. FAX 414-541-1909.
circ. 275. *3178*

DIRECTOR OF SELECTIVE SERVICE. ANNUAL REPORT.
U.S. Selective Service System, 1515 Wilson Blvd., Arlington, VA 22209. TEL 703-235-2053. *5267*

DIRECTORIO DE LA INDUSTRIA CARNICA.
Alfa Editores Tecnicos S.A., Libertad No. 107-402, 03660 Mexico DF, Mexico. TEL 525-579-3333. FAX 525-532-9504.
circ. 5,000. *1664*

DIRECTORIO DE LA INDUSTRIA MEXICANA DE BEBIDAS.
Alfa Editores Tecnicos S.A., Libertad No. 107-402, 03660 Mexico DF, Mexico. TEL 525-579-3333. FAX 525-532-9504.
circ. 5,000. *1664*

DIRECTORIO DE LACTEOS MEXICANOS.
Alfa Editores Tecnicos S.A., Libertad No. 107-402, 03660 Mexico DF, Mexico. TEL 525-579-3333. FAX 525-532-9504.
circ. 5,000. *1664*

DIRECTORIO HISPANO.
685 S. Hwy. 427, Longwood, FL 32750-6403. TEL 407-767-0070. FAX 407-767-5478.
circ. 50,000. *1665*

DIRECTORIO INDUSTRIAL Y COMERCIAL.
Legis S.A., Av. Eldorado 81-10, Apdo. Aereo 98888, Bogota, Colombia. TEL 91-263-2990. FAX 91-410-0628.
circ. 50,000. *1665*

DIRECTORIO INTERNACIONAL DE LA INDUSTRIA PESQUERA Y LA AQUACULTURA.
Alfa Editores Tecnicos S.A., Libertad No. 107-402, 03660 Mexico DF, Mexico. TEL 525-579-3333. FAX 525-5329504.
circ. 5,000. *1665*

DIRECTORY IN RUSSIAN OF BRITISH FIRMS INTERESTED IN TRADE WITH THE F S U.
Exact Communications Ltd., 90 Moorsom St., Birmingham B6 4NT, England. TEL 44-121-333-4644. FAX 44-121-333-5823. *1321*

DIRECTORY OF FIRMS.
Structural Engineers Trading Organisation Ltd., 11 Upper Belgrave St., London SW1X 8BH, England. TEL 44-171-235-4535. FAX 44-171-235-4294.
circ. 5,000. *1668*

DIRECTORY OF FLORIDA INDUSTRIES.
Harris InfoSource International, 2057-2 Aurora Rd., Twinsburg, OH 44087-1999. TEL 216-425-9000. FAX 216-425-7150.
circ. 5,000. *1668*

DIRECTORY OF FULBRIGHT ALUMNI.
United States Educational Foundation in India, Fulbright House, 12 Hailey Rd., New Delhi 110001, India. *2539*

DIREKT-KONTAKT BETRIEBSBEDARF.
Konradin Verlag Robert Kohlhammer GmbH, Ernst-Mey-Str. 8, 70771 Leinfelden-Echterdingen, Germany. TEL 49-711-7594-0. FAX 49-711-7594390.
circ. 25,000. *1524*

DISABILITY TIMES.
Disability Times Ltd., 84 Claverton St., Pimlico, London SW1V 3AX, England. TEL 44-171-233-7970. FAX 44-171-233-7970.
circ. 19,500. *3454*

DISASTER RECOVERY JOURNAL.
Systems Support, Inc., Box 510110, St. Louis, MO 63151. TEL 314-894-0276. FAX 314-894-7474.
circ. 47,000. *1556*

DISCO POST.
Verlag Disco Post GmbH, Oststr. 2, 56424 Staudt, Germany. TEL 49-2602-70044. FAX 49-2602-69939.
circ. 20,000. *1931*

DISCOVER F M A.
Fabricators and Manufacturers Association International (FMA), 833 Featherstone Rd., Rockford, IL 61107. TEL 815-399-8775. FAX 815-399-7679.
circ. 2,500. *5190*

DISCOVER NORTH AMERICA TRAVEL TRADE DIRECTORY.
Phoenix Publishing & Media Ltd., 18-20 Scrutton St., London EC2A 4RJ, England. TEL 44-171-247-0537. FAX 44-171-377-2741.
circ. 10,000. *7196*

DISPATCHER (COLUMBUS).
Nebraska Public Power District, Box 499, Columbus, NE 68602-0499. TEL 402-563-5811. FAX 402-563-5166.
circ. 3,500. *2815*

DISPLAY & DESIGN IDEAS.
Shore-Varrone, Inc., 6255 Barfield Rd. N.E., Ste. 200, Atlanta, GA 30328-4300. TEL 404-252-8831. FAX 404-252-4436.
circ. 18,039. *3844*

DISTRIBUTION.
D M G Trinity Publishing Ltd., Queensway House, 2 Queensway, Redhill, Surrey RH1 1QS, England. TEL 44-1737-7681. FAX 44-1737-760510.
circ. 14,000. *7027*

DISTRIBUTION BUSINESS.
Landor Industrial Services Publications Ltd., Quadrant House, 250 Kennington Ln., London SE11 5RD, England. TEL 44-171-735-4502. FAX 44-171-587-0497.
circ. 11,500. *1474*

DISTRIBUTION OF HIGH SCHOOL GRADUATES AND COLLEGE GOING RATE, NEW YORK STATE.
Education Department, Information, Reporting & Technology Services, Education Bldg. Annex, Rm. 962, Albany, NY 12234. TEL 518-474-7082. FAX 518-474-4351. *2498*

DIVERSION (NEW YORK).
Hearst Business Communications, 1790 Broadway, Ste. 6, New York, NY 10019-1412. TEL 212-969-7500. FAX 212-969-7557.
circ. 179,000. *4148*

DOBOKU GAKKAISHI.
Japan Society of Civil Engineers, Yotsuya 1-chome, Shinjuku-ku, Tokyo 160, Japan. *2782*

DOCTOR JAZZ MAGAZINE.
Vijverweg 4, 5461 AL Veghel, Netherlands. TEL 31-413-363542. FAX 31-413-363542.
circ. 850. *5389*

DOCTOR - PATIENT STUDIES.
University of Chicago, Center for Clinical Medical Ethics, MC 6098, 5811 S. Maryland, Chicago, IL 60637. TEL 312-702-3742. FAX 312-702-0090.
circ. 600. *4662*

DOCTOR'S REVIEW.
Parkhurst Publishing, 400 McGill St., 3rd Fl., Montreal, PQ H2Y 2G1, Canada. FAX 514-397-0228.
circ. 36,220. *7196*

DOCTOR'S SHOPPER.
Marketing Communications, Inc., 1086 Remsen Ave., Brooklyn, NY 11236. TEL 718-257-8484. FAX 718-257-8845.
circ. 208,000. *4662*

DOCUMENT PROCESSING TECHNOLOGY.
R B Publishing Company, 2701 E. Washington Ave., Madison, WI 53704. TEL 608-241-8777. FAX 608-241-8666.
circ. 10,000. *6076*

DOCUMENTATIE REVUE.
Misset, Postbus 4, 7000 BA Doetinchem, Netherlands. TEL 31-8340-49911. FAX 31-8340-43839.
circ. 15,000. *1524*

DOLLARSENSE.
E.F. Baumer & Company, 401 Shatto Pl., Ste. 105, Los Angeles, CA 90020. TEL 213-386-2111. FAX 213-386-6470.
circ. 800,000. *1128*

DOMINICAN REPUBLIC. CENTRO NACIONAL DE INVESTIGACIONES AGROPECUARIAS. LABORATORIO DE SANIDAD VEGETAL. SANIDAD VEGETAL.
Centro Nacional de Investigaciones Agropecuarias, Laboratorio de Sanidad Vegetal, San Cristobal, Dominican Republic. *701*

THE DOOR.
Oxford Diocesan Publications Ltd., Diocesan Church House, North Hinksey, Oxford OX2 0NB, England. TEL 44-1865-244566. FAX 44-1865-790470.
circ. 53,000. *6422*

THE DOOR-TO-DOOR MAKETING HANDBOOK.
Association of Household Distributors Ltd., 36 Frogmore St., Tring, Hants. HP23 5AU, England. TEL 44-1442-890991. FAX 44-1442-890992.
circ. 3,000. *35*

DOORKIJK.
Katholiek Vrouwengilde Nederland, Bisonspoor 1204, 3605 KZ Maarssen, Netherlands. TEL 03465-73670.
circ. 500. *2715*

DOORS AND HARDWARE.
Door and Hardware Institute, 14170 Newbrook Dr., Chantilly, VA 20151. TEL 703-222-2010. FAX 703-222-2410.
circ. 11,000. *927*

DOSSIER EUROPA.
Commissione Europea, Rappresentanza in Italia, Via Poli 29, 00187 Rome, Italy. TEL 39-6-6991160. FAX 39-6-6793652.
circ. 5,000. *5922*

DOTS AND DASHES.
Morse Telegraph Club, Inc., 415 S. Rife St., Dillon, MT 59725. TEL 406-683-2798. FAX 406-683-2332.
circ. 2,500. *2033*

DOTS AND TAPS.
Canadian National Institute for the Blind, National Office, 1929 Bayview Ave., Toronto, ON M4G 3E8, Canada. TEL 416-480-7417. FAX 416-480-7699.
circ. 310. *3469*

10324 CONTROLLED CIRCULATION SERIALS

DOWN THE ROAD.
Mike Byrnes & Associates, Box 8866, Corpus Christi, TX 78468-8866. TEL 512-980-8337. FAX 512-980-0781.
circ. 350. *5508*

DREAMIN'
Hood County News, Box 879, Granbury, TX 76408. TEL 817-573-7066.
circ. 10,000. *3373*

DRILLING CONTRACTOR.
Drilling Contractor Publications, Inc., Box 4287, Houston, TX 77210. TEL 713-578-7171. FAX 713-578-0589.
circ. 36,000. *5599*

DROIT INTERNATIONAL PRIVE.
C N R S Editions, 20-22 rue St. Amand, 75015 Paris, France. TEL 45-33-16-00. FAX 45-33-92-13.
circ. 1,500. *4111*

DROVERS JOURNAL.
Vance Publishing Corporation (Lenexa), 10901 W. 84th Terr., Ste. 200, Lenexa, KS 66214-1631. TEL 913-438-8700. FAX 913-438-0695.
circ. 90,965. *275*

DRUM! (SAN JOSE).
1275 Lincoln Ave., No. 13, San Jose, CA 95125. TEL 408-971-9794. FAX 408-971-0382.
circ. 30,000. *5389*

DRURY MIRROR.
Drury College, 900 N. Benton, Springfield, MO 65802. TEL 417-865-8731. FAX 416-865-3138.
circ. 1,000. *1950*

DUBAI EXTERNAL TRADE STATISTICS.
Central Accounting Administration, Statistics Section, P.O. Box 516, Dubai, United Arab Emirates. TEL 531074. FAX 531959.
circ. 500. *1035*

DUCA POST.
Duca Community Credit Union Ltd., Box 1100, Willowdale, ON M2N 5W5, Canada. TEL 416-223-8502. FAX 416-223-2575.
circ. 11,000. *1128*

DUMBO.
Ehapa Verlag GmbH, Im Riedenberg 54, 70771 Leinfelden-Echterdingen, Germany. TEL 0711-79711. FAX 0711-7971239.
circ. 120,000. *1870*

DURBAN MUSEUM NOVITATES.
Durban Natural Science Museum, P.O. Box 4085, Durban 4000, South Africa. TEL 27-31-3006211. FAX 27-31-3006302.
circ. 280. *832*

DYNA.
Universidad Nacional de Colombia, Facultad Nacional de Minas, Apdo. Aereo 1027, Medellin, Colombia. TEL 57-2344503. FAX 57-2341002.
circ. 1,500. *2715*

DYNAMIC BUSINESS.
S M C Business Councils, 1400 S. Braddock Ave., Pittsburgh, PA 15218-1264. TEL 412-371-1500. FAX 412-371-0460.
circ. 10,000. *1641*

E A A REVIEW.
Edinburgh Architectural Association, 15 Rutland Sq., Edinburgh EH1 2BE, Scotland. FAX 031-228-2188.
circ. 1,200. *402*

E.A.S.L. NEWSLETTER.
Florida Bar, 650 Apalachee Pkwy., Tallahassee, FL 32399-2300. TEL 904-561-5624.
circ. 745. *3943*

E C S C FINANCIAL REPORT.
Commission of the European Communities, L-2985 Luxembourg, Luxembourg. *1607*

E D N MAGAZINE.
Cahners Publishing Company (Newton), Division of Reed Elsevier Inc., 275 Washington St., Newton, MA 02158-1630. TEL 617-558-4454. FAX 617-558-4470.
circ. 164,800. *2629*

E D V UND KOMMUNIKATION FUER DAS HANDWERK.
Gruber und Fischer Verlagsgesellschaft mbH, Kapellenstr. 46, 76596 Forbach, Germany. TEL 49-7220-213. FAX 49-7220-215.
circ. 40,000. *3768*

E I.
Huethig GmbH, Paul-Gerhardt-Allee 46, 81245 Munich, Germany. TEL 49-89-83948-0. FAX 49-89-8394848.
circ. 16,859. *2630*

E N B NEWS.
English National Board for Nursing, Midwifery, and Health Visiting, Victory House, 170 Tottenham Ct. Rd., London W1P 0HA, England. TEL 44-171-388-3131. FAX 44-171-383-4031.
circ. 19,000. *4932*

E O NEWS SETTIMANALE.
Gruppo Editoriale Jackson S.p.A., Via M. Gorki 69, 20092 Cinisello B. (MI), Italy. TEL 39-2-66034271. FAX 39-2-66034270.
circ. 9,216. *2630*

E P & T.
Lakeview Publications Inc., 1200 Aerowood Dr., 27, Mississauga, ON L4W 2S7, Canada. TEL 905-624-8100. FAX 905-624-1760.
circ. 24,002. *2630*

E P & T'S ELECTROSOURCE PRODUCT REFERENCE GUIDE & TELEPHONE DIRECTORY.
Lakeview Publications Inc., 1200 Aerowood Dr., 27, Mississauga, ON L4W 2S7, Canada. TEL 905-624-8100. FAX 905-624-1760.
circ. 24,002. *2630*

E P E.
Engineers' and Managers' Association, Flaxman House, Gogmore Ln., Chertsey, Surrey KT16 9JS, England. TEL 44-1932-577041. FAX 44-1932-564205.
circ. 30,184. *2716*

E P E JOURNAL.
E P E Association, Secretariat S R B E, Av. de la Plaine 2, 1050 Brussels, Belgium. TEL 32-2-6292819. FAX 32-2-6293620.
circ. 3,100. *2630*

E P MAGAZINE.
N Z C C A, P.O. Box 3278, Wellington, New Zealand. TEL 04-237-4753.
circ. 250. *6759*

E-QUAD NEWS.
Princeton University, School of Engineering and Applied Science, C218 Engineering Quadrangle, Princeton, NJ 08544-5263. TEL 609-258-3617. FAX 609-258-6744.
circ. 12,300. *2716*

E R A TECHNOLOGY NEWS.
E R A Technology Ltd., Cleeve Rd., Leatherhead, Surrey KT22 7SA, England. TEL 44-1372-367000. FAX 44-1372-367099.
circ. 900. *1525*

E R S BULLETIN.
Educational Research Service, 2000 Clarendon Blvd., Arlington, VA 22201-2908. TEL 703-243-2100. FAX 703-243-8316.
circ. 2,700. *2571*

E S E NOTES.
University of North Carolina at Chapel Hill, School of Public Health, CB 7400, Chapel Hill, NC 27599-7400. TEL 919-966-1024. FAX 919-966-2583.
circ. 3,000. *2914*

E S S EMPLOYMENT OPPORTUNITIES.
National Society of Fund Raising Executives, 1101 King St., Ste. 700, Alexandria, VA 22314. TEL 703-684-0410. FAX 703-684-0540.
circ. 16,000. *5508*

E.T.N. REVUE DE L'ENTRETIEN DES TEXTILES ET NETTOYAGE.
Centre Technique de la Teinture et du Nettoyage (CTTN), Chemin des Mouilles, B.P. 41, 69131 Ecully Cedex, France. FAX 78-43-34-12. *6985*

EARLY CHILDHOOD TEACHER.
Scholastic Inc., 555 Broadway, New York, NY 10012-3999. TEL 212-343-6100.
circ. 60,000. *2434*

EARLY CHINA.
University of California at Berkeley, Institute of East Asian Studies, 2223 Fulton St., Berkeley, CA 94720-2318. TEL 510-643-6325. FAX 510-643-7062.
circ. 250. *3533*

EARLY INTERVENTION.
Illinois Public Health Association, 223 S. Third St., Springfield, IL 62701. TEL 217-522-5687.
circ. 4,300. *2583*

EARTH (LOS ANGELES).
Shepherd Media Group, Box 6789, Los Angeles, CA 90022. TEL 310-463-4043. FAX 310-699-0491.
circ. 5,200. *892*

EARTH AND MINERAL SCIENCES.
Pennsylvania State University, College of Earth & Mineral Sciences, 116 Deike Bldg., University Park, PA 16802. TEL 814-863-4667.
circ. 18,000. *2313*

EAST BAY LABOR JOURNAL.
Alameda County Central Labor Council, 7992 Capwell Dr., Oakland, CA 94621. TEL 510-632-4242. FAX 510-632-3993.
circ. 6,000. *3889*

EAST CAROLINIAN.
East Carolina University, Student Publications Bldg.-ECU, Greenville, NC 27858-4353. TEL 919-328-6366. FAX 919-328-6558.
circ. 12,000. *1950*

THE EAST YORK OBSERVER.
Centennial College, P.O. Box 631, Stn. A, Scarborough, ON M1K 5E9, Canada. TEL 416-289-5107. FAX 416-289-5111.
circ. 3,000. *3260*

EAST YORKSHIRE LOCAL HISTORY SOCIETY. BULLETIN.
East Yorkshire Local History Society, Beverley Library, Champney Rd., Beverley, N. Humber. HU17 9BQ, England. TEL 01482-864108. FAX 01482-881084.
circ. 420. *3563*

EASTBOURNIAN.
Eastbourne College, Eastbourne, Sussex, England.
circ. 1,200. *1950*

EASTERN AFTERMARKET JOURNAL.
Stan Hubsher, Ed. & Pub., 8211 Horseshoe Bay Rd., Boynton Beach, FL 33437. TEL 561-733-8761. FAX 561-233-8694.
circ. 10,105. *7097*

EASTERN AIR EASTERN.
Regie Club International, Cromwell House, 136 Cromwell Rd., London SW7 4HA, England. TEL 44-71-244-6565. FAX 44-71-3670-3727.
circ. 60,000. *7258*

EASTERN CHALLENGE.
International Missions, Inc., Box 14866, Reading, PA 19612-4866. TEL 610-375-0300. FAX 610-375-6862.
circ. 22,000. *6422*

EASTERN MASSACHUSETTS REGIONAL LIBRARY SYSTEM. EASTERN REGION NEWS.
Eastern Massachusetts Regional Library System, Boston Public Library, Copley Square, Boston, MA 02117. TEL 617-536-4010. FAX 617-267-0364.
circ. 2,400. *4176*

EASY LIVING MAGAZINE.
Eagle Promotions Ltd., Ste. 201, 20039 96th Ave., Langley, BC V1M 3C6, Canada. TEL 604-882-9380. FAX 604-882-9349.
circ. 150,000. *3260*

ECHO (SKOKIE).
United Order True Sisters, Inc., c/o Mrs. Joanne F. Caldara, Ed., 212 Fifth Ave., New York, NY 10016. TEL 212-679-6790.
circ. 12,000. *1931*

ECHO DE FRONTENAC.
5040 boul. Veterans, Lac Megantic, PQ G6B 2G5, Canada. TEL 819-583-1630. FAX 819-583-1124.
circ. 4,394. *3260*

L'ECHO DU TRANSPORT.
Editions Bomart Ltee., 7493 TransCanada Hwy., Ste. 103, St. Laurent, PQ H4T 1T3, Canada. TEL 514-337-9043. FAX 514-337-1862.
circ. 19,517. *7174*

ECO (MOUNT KISCO).
Eco, Inc., 420 Lexington Ave., New York, NY 10170-0002. TEL 914-242-0140. FAX 914-242-0046.
circ. 80,000. *955*

ECO DEGLI ORATORI E DEI CIRCOLI GIOVANILI.
Fondazione Oratori Milanesi, Via S. Antonio 5, 20122 Milan, Italy. TEL 02-58304383. FAX 02-58304003.
circ. 1,100. *1844*

ECONEWS.
Northcoast Environmental Center, Inc., 879 Ninth St., Arcata, CA 95521. TEL 707-822-6918. FAX 707-822-0827.
circ. 2,300. *2916*

ECONOMIA.
Yokohama Kokuritsu Daigaku, 156 Tokiwadai, Hodogaya-ku, Yokohama 240, Japan.
circ. 1,800. *956*

ECONOMIA.
Italienische Handelskammer fuer Deutschland, Bockenheimer Landstr. 59, 60325 Frankfurt a.M., Germany. TEL 49-69-97145210. FAX 49-69-97145299.
circ. 3,000. *1186*

ECONOMIA CAFETERA.
Federacion Nacional de Cafeteros de Colombia, Calle 73 No. 8-13, piso 10 B, Bogota D.E., Colombia. TEL 57-1-3451088. FAX 57-1-2171021.
circ. 8,000. *192*

ECONOMIA GUIPUZCOANA.
Camara Oficial de Comercio, Industria y Navegacion de Guipuzcoa, Ramon Maria Lili, 6, San Sebastian, Spain. TEL 43-27-2100. FAX 43-29-3105.
circ. 12,000. *1186*

ECOS.
Editorial Sucre, Monzon a Barcenas No. 135, Caracas, Venezuela.
circ. 18,000. *6664*

ECOTROPICA. ECOSISTEMAS TROPICALES.
Universidad de Bogota Jorge Tadeo Lozano, Museo del Mar, Carrera 4, No. 22-61, Bogota, Colombia. TEL 57-1-3426581. FAX 57-1-2826197.
circ. 1,200. *2402*

THE EDGE (SOUTHAMPTON).
Southampton University, Students Union, University Rd., Highfield, Southampton SO17 1BJ, England. TEL 44-1703-595230. FAX 44-1703-595252.
circ. 3,000. *5390*

EDISI CHUSUS BULLETIN KOPERASI.
Department of Cooperatives, Directorate General of the Institutional Promotion for Cooperatives - Direktorat Bina Penyuluhan Koperasi, Jalan H.R. Rasuna Said Kav. 3-5, Jakarta 12940, Indonesia. TEL 5204382.
circ. 7,500. *1256*

EDIT.
Literaturverein Edit Efau e.V., Kochstr. 132, 04277 Leipzig, Germany. TEL 49-341-3080117. FAX 49-341-3080113.
circ. 700. *4508*

EL EDITOR (LUBBOCK).
El Editor Newspapers, 1502 Ave. M, Lubbock, TX 79401. TEL 806-763-3841. FAX 806-741-1110.
circ. 15,000. *3009*

EDITORIAL PACE.
Derus Media Service, Inc., 500 N. Dearborn, Chicago, IL 60610. TEL 312-644-4360.
circ. 10,000. *3872*

EDMONTON CHAMBER OF COMMERCE. COMMERCE NEWS.
Edmonton Chamber of Commerce, Suite 600, 10123-99 St., Edmonton, AB T5J 3G9, Canada. TEL 403-426-4620. FAX 403-424-7946.
circ. 54,000. *1186*

EDPLAY.
Fahy - Williams Publishing, Inc., Box 1080, Geneva, NY 14456-8080. TEL 315-789-0458.
circ. 7,000. *3449*

EDUCACAO E SOCIEDADE.
Centro de Estudos de Educacao e Sociedade, Caixa Postal 6022, 13083-790 Campinas SP, Brazil. TEL 55-19-2391598.
circ. 100. *2435*

EDUCACION Y CIENCIAS HUMANAS.
Universidad Simon Rodriguez, Decanato de Postgrado, Calle 5 entre 7ma. y 8va. Transversal, Edif. El Caney, La Urbina, Caracas, Venezuela. TEL 58-2-2422622. FAX 58-2-2436346.
circ. 500. *2435*

EDUCATION.
S. Kumar and Associates, Mass Communications Division, 32 Sarojini Debi Ln., Maqboolganj, Lucknow 226 078, Uttar Pradesh, India. TEL 91-52-224-1010.
circ. 2,000. *2436*

EDUCATION AND HEALTH.
Schools Health Education Unit, University of Exeter, School of Education, Heavitree Rd., Exeter EX1 2LU, England. TEL 44-1392-264722. FAX 44-1392-264761.
circ. 5,250. *2571*

EDUCATION EQUIPMENT.
Nexus Media Ltd., Warick House, Swanley, Kent BR8 8HY, England.
circ. 13,394. *2571*

EDUCATION FORUM.
Ontario Secondary School Teachers' Federation, 60 Mobile Dr., Toronto, ON M4A 2P3, Canada. TEL 416-751-8300. FAX 416-751-3394.
circ. 46,000. *2437*

EDUCATION QUARTERLY.
University of the Philippines, College of Education, Diliman, Quezon City, Philippines. *2438*

EDUCATION REPORTER.
Education Writers Association, 1331 H St., N.W., Ste. 307, Washington, DC 20005. TEL 202-637-9700. FAX 202-637-9707.
circ. 850. *2438*

EDUCATION SAN DIEGO COUNTY.
Department of Education, Superintendent of Schools, 6401 Linda Vista Rd., San Diego, CA 92111. TEL 619-292-3500.
circ. 13,000. *2438*

EDUCATION STATISTICS, NEW YORK STATE.
Education Department, Information, Reporting & Technology Services, Education Bldg. Annex, Rm. 962, Albany, NY 12234. TEL 518-474-7082. FAX 518-474-4351. *2499*

EDUCATION TODAY.
Ontario Public School Board's Association, 439 University Ave., Ste. 1850, Toronto, ON M5G 1Y8, Canada. TEL 416-340-2540. FAX 416-340-7571.
circ. 500. *2571*

EDUCATIONAL DEALER.
Fahy - Williams Publishing, Inc., Box 1080, Geneva, NY 14456-8080. TEL 315-789-0458.
circ. 13,712. *1675*

EDUCATIONAL FACILITY PLANNER.
Council of Educational Facility Planners, 8687 E. Via de Ventura, Ste. 311, Scottsdale, AZ 85258-3347. TEL 602-948-2337. *2439*

EFFEKTIVT LANDBRUG.
Teknisk Forlag A-S, Skelbaekgade 4, DK-1780 Copenhagen V, Denmark. TEL 45-31-21-68-01. FAX 45-31-21-04-01.
circ. 30,997. *113*

EIGEN AARD.
Publicarto N.V., Langestraat 170, B-1150 Brussels 15, Belgium. TEL 32-2-7790000. FAX 32-2-7791616.
circ. 148,464. *7317*

EILBOTE.
Eilbote Boomgaarden Verlag GmbH, Winsener Landstr. 7, OT Luhdorf, 21423 Winsen-Luhe, Germany. TEL 49-4171-76074. FAX 49-4171-74984.
circ. 8,500. *205*

EISENBAHNER RUNDSCHAU.
Vereinigte Verlagsanstalten GmbH, Hoeherweg 278, 40231 Duesseldorf, Germany. TEL 49-211-7357-0. FAX 49-211-7357223.
circ. 96,000. *7125*

EKSPRESS - ZAKON.
Izdatel'stvo I N F R A - M, Dmitrovskoe shosse, 107, 127247 Moscow, Russia. TEL 7-095-4855779. FAX 7-095-4855318.
circ. 3,000. *1607*

EL.
Svenska Elverksfoereningen, P.O. Box 3192, S-103 63 Stockholm, Sweden. TEL 08-791 69 00. *2816*

THE ELECTRICAL DISTRIBUTOR.
National Association of Electrical Distributors, 45 Danbury Rd., Wilton, CT 06897. TEL 203-761-4900. FAX 203-762-0324.
circ. 29,000. *2818*

ELECTRICAL EQUIPMENT REPRESENTATIVES ASSOCIATION. DIRECTORY.
Electrical Equipment Representatives Association, c/o John S. McDermott, Ed., Box 419264, Kansas City, MO 64141-6264. TEL 816-753-0210. FAX 816-753-1954.
circ. 1,000. *2818*

ELECTRICAL NEWS.
Box 660760, Arcadia, CA 91006. TEL 818-446-8652. FAX 818-447-6047.
circ. 30,000. *2818*

ELECTRICAL UNION WORLD.
International Brotherhood of Electrical Workers, A F L - C I O, Local Union No. 3, 158-11 Harry Van Arsdale Jr. Ave., Flushing, NY 11365. TEL 718-591-4000. FAX 718-380-8998.
circ. 50,000. *3889*

ELECTRICAL WORLD DIRECTORY OF ELECTRIC UTILITIES IN CANADA.
McGraw-Hill Companies, 1221 Ave. of the Americas, New York, NY 10020. *2688*

ELECTRICITE DE FRANCE. STATISTIQUES DE LA PRODUCTION ET DE LA CONSOMMATION.
Electricite de France, Direction de la Production et du Transport, Departement Statistiques, 6 rue de Messine, 75008 Paris, France. *2749*

ELECTRICITY INTERNATIONAL.
Icom Publications Ltd., Chancery House, St. Nicholas Way, Sutton, Surrey SM1 1JB, England. TEL 44-181-642-1117. FAX 44-181-642-1941.
circ. 11,300. *2820*

ELECTRICITY TODAY.
Canadian Electricity Forum, 345 Kingston Rd., Ste. 101, Pickering, ON L1V 1A1, Canada. TEL 905-509-4447. FAX 905-509-4451.
circ. 12,500. *2820*

ELECTROCHEMISTRY AND INDUSTRIAL PHYSICAL CHEMISTRY.
Electrochemical Society of Japan, Shin-yurakucho Bldg., 1-12-1 Yuraku-cho, Chiyoda-ku, Tokyo 100, Japan. TEL 81-3-3214-6001. FAX 81-3-3287-0037.
circ. 2,500. *1805*

ELECTRONIC BUSINESS ASIA.
Cahners Publishing Company (Newton), Division of Reed Elsevier Inc., 275 Washington St., Newton, MA 02158-1630. TEL 617-964-3030. FAX 617-558-4506.
circ. 31,500. *2631*

ELECTRONIC BUSINESS TODAY.
Cahners Publishing Company (Newton), Division of Reed Elsevier Inc., 275 Washington St., Newton, MA 02158-1630. TEL 617-964-3030. FAX 617-558-4470.
circ. 73,000. *2631*

10326 CONTROLLED CIRCULATION SERIALS

ELECTRONIC DISTRIBUTION TODAY.
Custom Media, Inc., 7912 Country Ln., Chagrin Falls, OH 44023. TEL 216-543-9451. FAX 216-543-9764.
circ. 6,894. *2631*

THE ELECTRONIC EDGE.
R.R. Bowker Electronic Publishing, A Division of Reed Elsevier Inc., 121 Chanlon Rd., New Providence, NJ 07974. TEL 908-665-2810. FAX 908-665-3575.
circ. 12,000. *2211*

ELECTRONIC ENGINEERING TIMES.
C M P Publications, Inc., 600 Community Dr., Manhasset, NY 11030. TEL 516-562-5000. FAX 516-562-5325.
circ. 125,000. *2632*

ELECTRONIC EQUIPMENT NEWS - THE INDUSTRIAL BUYER.
Southam Magazine Group, 1450 Don Mills Rd., Don Mills, ON M3B 2X7, Canada. TEL 416-445-6641. FAX 415-442-2261.
circ. 23,262. *2632*

ELECTRONIC GREEN JOURNAL.
University of Idaho Library, University of Idaho Library, Moscow, ID 83844. TEL 208-885-6631. FAX 208-885-6817.
circ. 2,000. *2917*

ELECTRONIC PRODUCT DESIGN.
I M L Group plc, Blair House, High St., Tonbridge, Kent TN9 1BQ, England. TEL 01732-359990. FAX 01732-77049.
circ. 24,500. *2820*

ELECTRONIC PRODUCT NEWS.
Pan European Publishing Co., Rue Verte 216, 1030 Brussels, Belgium. TEL 32-2-2402611. FAX 32-2-2427111.
circ. 60,007. *2633*

ELECTRONIC PRODUCTION.
Inside Communications Ltd., 9 White Lion St., London N1, England. TEL 44-171-837-8727.
circ. 13,000. *2633*

ELECTRONIC PRODUCTS.
Hearst Business Publishing UTP Division, 645 Stewart Ave., Garden City, NY 11530. TEL 516-227-1300. FAX 516-227-1444.
circ. 124,126. *2633*

ELECTRONIC PUBLISHING.
PennWell Publishing Co. (Nashua), 10 Tara Blvd., 5th Fl., Nashua, NH 03062-2801. TEL 603-891-9159. FAX 603-891-0539.
circ. 52,500. *6292*

ELECTRONIC WORLD NEWS.
C M P Publications, Inc., 600 Community Dr., Manhasset, NY 11030. TEL 516-562-5000.
circ. 32,000. *2633*

ELECTRONICS COOLING.
Flomerics Ltd., c/o Livewire Public Relations, 13 Uxbridge Rd., Kingston upon Thames, Surrey KT1 2LH. TEL 44-181-547-3418. FAX 44-181-547-3419.
circ. 10,000. *2634*

ELECTRONICS MANUFACTURING INTERNATIONAL.
Pan European Publishing Co., Rue Verte 216, 1030 Brussels, Belgium. TEL 32-2-2402611. FAX 32-2-2427111.
circ. 30,016. *2634*

ELECTRONIQUE INTERNATIONAL HEBDO.
Groupe Tests, Immeuble Europaris, 26 rue d'Oradour sur Glane, 75504 Paris Cedex 15, France. TEL 1-44-25-30-60. FAX 1-45-57-80-57.
circ. 15,202. *2635*

ELECTROSONIC WORLD.
Electrosonic Limited, Hawley Mill, Hawley Rd., Dartford, Kent DA2 7SY, England. TEL 44-1322-222211. FAX 44-1322-282282.
circ. 80,000. *1989*

ELEKTRIKERN.
Svenska Elektrikerfoerbundet, P.O. Box 1123, S-111 81 Stockholm, Sweden. TEL 46-8-402-14-00. FAX 46-8-402-14-28.
circ. 32,327. *2821*

ELEKTRISCHE ENERGIE TECHNIK.
Huethig GmbH, Postfach 102869, 69018 Heidelberg, Germany. TEL 49-6221-489232. FAX 49-6221-489482.
circ. 8,449. *2821*

ELEKTRO RADIO HANDEL.
Erb Verlag GmbH, Eichenstr. 38, A-1120 Vienna, Austria.
circ. 9,000. *2024*

ELEKTROHAENDLER.
Verlag Technik GmbH, Am Friedrichshain 22, 10407 Berlin, Germany. TEL 49-30-42151274. FAX 49-30-42151232.
circ. 37,000. *2822*

ELEKTROMARKT.
Vogel Verlag und Druck GmbH & Co. KG, Max-Planck-Str. 7-9, 97082 Wuerzburg, Germany. TEL 49-931-4182145. FAX 49-931-4182905.
circ. 19,005. *2635*

ELEKTRONICA REVUE.
Misset, Postbus 4, 7000 BA Doetinchem, Netherlands. TEL 31-8340-49911. FAX 31-8340-43839. *2635*

ELEKTRONIK NYT.
Teknisk Forlag A - S, Skelbaekgade 4, DK-1717 Copenhagen V, Denmark. TEL 45-31-21-68-01. FAX 45-31-21-04-01.
circ. 14,288. *2636*

ELEKTRONIKA UMACHSHAVIM.
Tzavta Publishing, P.O. Box 18287, Tel Aviv 61181, Israel. TEL 03-5622076. FAX 3-5618549.
circ. 8,500. *2081*

ELEKTRONIKK BRANSJEN.
Elektronikk Forbundet, Brynsengvn. 2, P.O. Box 6322, Etterstad, N-0604 Oslo, Norway. TEL 47-22-72-21-40. FAX 47-22-72-21-21.
circ. 2,900. *2636*

ELEKTRONIKPRAXIS.
Vogel Verlag und Druck GmbH & Co. KG, Max-Planck-Str. 7-9, 97082 Wuerzburg, Germany. TEL 49-931-4182145. FAX 49-931-4182905.
circ. 35,928. *2636*

ELEKTRONIKSCHAU.
Erb Verlag GmbH, Eichenstr. 38, A-1120 Vienna, Austria.
circ. 16,000. *2049*

ELEKTROTECHNIK.
Vogel Verlag und Druck GmbH & Co. KG, Max-Planck-Str. 7-9, 97082 Wuerzburg, Germany. TEL 49-931-4182145. FAX 49-931-4182905.
circ. 25,146. *2822*

ELETTRONICA OGGI.
Gruppo Editoriale Jackson S.p.A., Via M. Corki 69, 20092 Cinisello B. (MI), Italy. TEL 39-2-660341. FAX 39-2-66034270.
circ. 8,546. *2637*

ELEVATOR CONSTRUCTOR.
International Union of Elevator Constructor Companies, Clark Bldg., Ste. 310, Columbia, MD 21044. TEL 410-997-9000. FAX 410-997-0243.
circ. 17,500. *892*

ELISABETHBUEHNE MAGAZIN.
Elisabethbuehne Salzburg, Im Petersbrunnhof, Erzabt-Klotz-Str. 22, A-5020 Salzburg, Austria. TEL 43-662-8580-0. FAX 43-662-858033.
circ. 22,000. *7006*

THE ELIZABETHAN REVIEW.
84-35 62 Dr., Ste. T-41, Mioole Village, NY 11379. TEL 718-458-5675. FAX 718-457-6602.
circ. 500. *3564*

ELLIS COUSINS NEWSLETTER.
Ellis Publishers Inc., 1201 Maple St., Friona, TX 68935. TEL 806-247-3053.
circ. 700. *3220*

ELMHURST COLLEGE MAGAZINE.
Elmhurst College, 190 Prospect Ave., Elmhurst, IL 60126. TEL 630-617-3033. FAX 630-617-3282.
circ. 30,000. *1951*

ELTEKNIK.
Teknisk Forlag A-S, Skelbaekgade 4, DK-1780 Copenhagen V, Denmark. TEL 31-216801. FAX 31-212396.
circ. 5,159. *2823*

EMAJL, KERAMIKA, STAKLO.
Udruzenje Emajliraca Jugoslavije, Srebrnjak 169, 41000 Zagreb, Croatia.
circ. 1,000. *1728*

EMERGENCY MEDICINE NEWS.
Lippincott - Raven Publishers, 227 E. Washington Sq., Philadelphia, PA 19106. TEL 215-238-4200. FAX 215-238-4227. *4664*

EMIGRATE.
Outbound Newspapers, 1 Commercial Rd., Eastbourne, E. Sussex BN21 3XQ, England. TEL 44-1323-412001. FAX 44-1323-649249.
circ. 100,000. *7197*

EMORY MAGAZINE.
Emory University, Office of University Periodicals, 1655 N. Decatur Rd., Atlanta, GA 30322. TEL 404-727-7872. FAX 404-727-0169.
circ. 78,000. *1951*

EMPIRE STATE FOOD SERVICE NEWS.
Wood Publishing, Box 89, Skaneateles, NY 13152-0089. TEL 315-685-3300.
circ. 15,000. *3725*

EMPIRE STATE MASON.
Grand Lodge Free and Accepted Masons of the State of New York, Committee on Publications, 37 Oliver St., Lockport, NY 14094-4615. TEL 716-434-4946. FAX 716-434-4946.
circ. 120,000. *1931*

EMPIRISCHE SOZIALFORSCHUNG.
Campus Verlag, Heerstr. 149, 60488 Frankfurt a.M., Germany. TEL 49-69-9765160. FAX 49-69-97651678.
circ. 800. *6611*

EMPLOI PLUS.
D G R Publication, 125 Principale N. St., Ste. 013, L'Annonciation, Quebec, PQ J0T 1T0, Canada. TEL 819-275-3293.
circ. 500. *4401*

EMPLOYMENT LAW REPORTS.
Round Hall Sweet & Maxwell, 4 Upper Ormond Quay, Dublin 7, Ireland. TEL 353-1-8730101. FAX 353-1-8720078.
circ. 400. *3945*

EMPLOYMENT OUTLOOK SURVEY.
Manpower Temporary Services, International Headquarters, 5301 N. Ironwood Rd., Milwaukee, WI 53217. TEL 414-961-1000. FAX 414-961-2124.
circ. 40,000. *1429*

EMPURIES.
Departament de Cultura, Museu d'Arqueologia de Catalunya, Passeig de Santa Madrona, 39-41, Parque de Montjuich, 08038 Barcelona, Spain. TEL 34-3-4232149. FAX 34-3-4254244. *361*

ENCOUNTER (JOLIET).
College of St. Francis, Journalism - Communications Department, 500 N. Wilcox, Joliet, IL 60435. TEL 815-740-3461. FAX 815-740-4285.
circ. 1,200. *1951*

ENCYCLOPAEDIA OF POLISH INDUSTRY.
Sterling Publications Ltd., 86-88 Edgware Rd., London W2 2YW, England. TEL 44-171-915-9600. FAX 44-171-915-9619.
circ. 10,000. *1323*

ENDUSTRI MUHENDISLIGI DERGISI.
Chamber of Mechanical Engineers, Sumer Sokak, 36-1-A Demirtepe, 06440 Ankara, Turkey. TEL 90-4-2313164. FAX 90-4-2313165.
circ. 5,000. *2883*

ENERGIA Y MEDIO AMBIENTE.
Sociedad de la Energia y el Medio Ambiente de Madrid, Princesa 5, 28008 Madrid, Spain. TEL 34-1-5599179. FAX 34-1-5597344.
circ. 8,500. *2664*

ENERGIE UND CHARAKTER.
Gottschedstr. 2, 13357 Berlin, Germany. TEL 030-4653882. FAX 030-6223140.
circ. 1,000. *6109*

ENERGIEONDERZOEK CENTRUM NEDERLAND. JAARVERSLAG.
Energieonderzoek Centrum Nederland, Postbus 1, 1755 ZG Petten, Netherlands. TEL 331-224-564949. FAX 31-224-5464480.
circ. 4,000. *2664*

ENERGIEWENDE.
Oesterreichisches Oekologie Institut, Seidengasse 13, A-1070 Vienna, Austria. TEL 43-1-5236105-0. FAX 43-1-5235843.
circ. 1,700. *2664*

ENERGY IN THE NEWS.
New York Mercantile Exchange, Corporate Communications Department, One North End Ave., World Financial Center, New York, NY 10282-1101. TEL 212-299-2777. FAX 212-301-4700.
circ. 12,000. *1211*

ENERGY NEWS EXCHANGE.
Kentucky Utilities Company, One Quality St., Lexington, KY 40507. TEL 606-255-2100. FAX 606-288-1165.
circ. 3,000. *2667*

ENERGYWISE.
Energy Publications, Livanos House, Granhams Rd., Great Shelford, Cambridgeshire CB2 5LQ, England. TEL 44-12223-844040. FAX 44-1223-843208.
circ. 12,600. *2668*

ENGINE REPAIR AND REMANUFACTURE.
R G O Exhibitions and Publications Ltd., Oakapple Cottage, Furnace Ln., Broad Oak Brede, Rye, E. Sussex TN31 6ES, England. TEL 44-1424-882702. FAX 44-1424-882702.
circ. 1,400. *7027*

ENGINEER.
Association of Professional Engineers of Nova Scotia, 1355 Barrington St., Box 129, Halifax, NS B3J 2M4, Canada. TEL 902-429-2250. FAX 902-423-9769.
circ. 4,500. *2716*

ENGINEER - I.M.E. NEWS.
Institution of Mechanical Engineers (India), Janmabhoomi Chambers, 3rd Fl., 29 W. Hirachand Marg, Ballard Estate, Mumbai 400 038, India. TEL 91-22-2692885. FAX 91-22-2614815.
circ. 38,000. *2883*

ENGINEERED SYSTEMS.
Business News Publishing Co., 755 W. Big Beaver Rd., Ste. 1000, Troy, MI 48084. TEL 810-362-3700. FAX 810-362-0317.
circ. 57,518. *3478*

ENGINEERING & MINING JOURNAL.
Intertec Publishing Corp., 29 N. Wacker Dr., Chicago, IL 60606. TEL 312-726-2802. FAX 312-726-4103.
circ. 22,892. *5299*

ENGINEERING CAPACITY.
Construction Publications Ltd., 2-6 Boundary Row, London SE1 8HN, England. TEL 44-171-410-6611. FAX 44-171-522-9646.
circ. 10,136. *2717*

ENGINEER'S DIGEST (SOLON).
Huebcore Communications, Inc., 29100 Aurora Rd., Ste. 200, Solon, OH 44139. TEL 216-248-1125. FAX 216-248-0187.
circ. 123,754. *2718*

ENGINEERS NEWS.
International Union of Operating Engineers, Local No. 3, 1620 S. Loop Rd., Alameda, CA 94502. TEL 510-748-7400. FAX 510-748-7401.
circ. 35,000. *3889*

ENGINEERS NEWS REPORT.
International Union of Operating Engineers, Local 428, 1426 N. First St., Phoenix, AZ 85004. TEL 602-254-5266. FAX 602-257-8674.
circ. 3,500. *2784*

ENJINIASU.
Union of Japanese Scientists and Engineers, 5-10-11 Sendagaya, Shibuya-ku, Tokyo 151, Japan. TEL 03-5379-1227. FAX 03-3225-1813.
circ. 11,000. *2719*

ENTELECHY.
Flat Earth Media, 1791 Ninth Ave., San Francisco, CA 94122. TEL 415-731-4146.
circ. 1,000,000. *4402*

ENTERPRISE SYSTEMS JOURNAL.
Cardinal Business Media, Inc., 12225 Greenville Ave., Ste. 700, Dallas, TX 75243-9338. TEL 972-669-9000. FAX 972-669-9909.
circ. 83,500. *2174*

ENTERTAINMENT, ARTS & SPORTS LAW.
New York State Bar Association, Entertainment, Arts & Sports Law Section, 1 Elk St., Albany, NY 12207-1096. TEL 518-463-3200. FAX 518-463-8844.
circ. 1,450. *3945*

ENTERTAINMENT TODAY.
Best Publishing Inc., 801 S. Main St., Ste. L, Burbank, CA 91506. TEL 818-566-4030. FAX 818-566-4295.
circ. 205,000. *3373*

ENVIRON.
Wary Canary Press, Box 2204, Ft. Collins, CO 80522. TEL 303-224-0083.
circ. 2,000. *2917*

ENVIRONMENT NEWSLETTER.
South Pacific Regional Environment Programme, P.O. Box 240, Apia, Western Samoa. TEL 685-21929. FAX 685-20231.
circ. 1,000. *2919*

ENVIRONMENTAL AND URBAN ISSUES.
Florida Atlantic University - Florida International University, Joint Center for Environmental and Urban Problems, 220 S.E. Second Ave., Ste. 709, Ft. Lauderdale, FL 33301. TEL 305-355-5255. FAX 305-760-5666.
circ. 3,800. *2920*

ENVIRONMENTAL CAREERS BULLETIN.
11693 San Vicente Blvd., Ste. 327, Los Angeles, CA 90049. TEL 310-399-3533. FAX 310-399-8763.
circ. 30,000. *2920*

ENVIRONMENTAL CAREERS ORGANIZATION. CONNECTIONS.
Environmental Careers Organization, Inc., 286 Congress St., 3rd Fl., Boston, MA 02210-1009. TEL 617-426-4375. FAX 617-423-0998.
circ. 15,000. *2920*

ENVIRONMENTAL ENGINEER.
American Academy of Environmental Engineers, 130 Holiday Ct., Ste. 100, Annapolis, MD 21401. TEL 410-266-3311. FAX 410-266-7653. *2921*

ENVIRONMENTAL RESEARCH IN JAPAN.
Environment Agency, 1-2-2 Kasumigaseki, Chiyoda-ku, Tokyo 100, Japan. TEL 03-3580-1703. FAX 03-3580-3542.
circ. 320. *2925*

ENVIRONMENTAL RESEARCH NEWSLETTER.
Environment Institute, Joint Research Centre, 21020 Ispra, Italy. TEL 39-332-789981. FAX 39-332-785631.
circ. 5,000. *2925*

ENVIRONMENTAL TECHNOLOGY.
Hunter Publishing Limited Partnership, 2101 S. Arlington Heights Rd., Ste. 150, Arlington Heights, IL 60005. TEL 847-427-9512. FAX 847-427-2097.
circ. 65,000. *2926*

ENVIRONMENTAL TESTING AND ANALYSIS.
Target Group, Box 5244, Glendale, CA 91221-1081. TEL 818-842-4777. FAX 818-842-0578.
circ. 20,000. *2926*

EQUIPMENT TODAY.
Johnson Hill Press, Inc., 1233 Janesville Ave., Ft. Atkinson, WI 53538. TEL 920-563-6388. FAX 920-563-1699.
circ. 81,000. *893*

EQUITY NEWS.
Dick Moore & Associates, Inc., Box 21216, Saint Paul, MN 55121-0216. TEL 212-719-9570.
circ. 36,500. *7006*

ERGOTHERAPIE.
Ergotherapeutinnen Verband Schweiz, Stauffacherstr. 96, CH-8026 Zurich, Switzerland. TEL 41-1-2425464. FAX 41-1-2915440.
circ. 5,000. *2583*

ERICH MARIA REMARQUE JAHRBUCH.
Erich Maria Remarque Archiv, Markt 6, 49069 Osnabrueck, Germany. TEL 49-541-9692430. FAX 49-541-9692431.
circ. 500. *4402*

EROSION CONTROL.
Forester Communications, Inc., 5638 Hollister Ave., Ste. 301, Goleta, CA 93117-3474. TEL 805-681-1300. FAX 805-681-1312.
circ. 20,000. *2229*

ERYTHROPOIESIS.
Adis International Ltd., Chowley Oak Ln., Tattenhall, Chester, Ches. CH3 9GA, England. TEL 44-1829-771155. FAX 44-1829-770330.
circ. 9,000. *4918*

ESCUELA NACIONAL DE INTELIGENCIA. REVISTA.
Escuela Nacional de Inteligencia, C. Libertad 1235, 1012 Buenos Aires, Argentina. TEL 54-1-812-4930. FAX 54-1-812-9230.
circ. 2,500. *5267*

ESHER AND LEATHERHEAD COURIER.
Surrey Advertiser Group, 134 High St., Esher, Surrey KT10 9QJ, England. TEL 01372-463553. FAX 01372-469045.
circ. 34,000. *3296*

ESOTERIK HEUTE.
Gesellschaft zur Pflege, Verbreitung und Erforschung Esoterische Grenzwissenschaften, Wartholzstr. 12, A-2651 Reichenau, Austria. TEL 43-2666-2967. FAX 43-2666-29674.
circ. 14,000. *5575*

ESPACE ET MILIEUX.
C N R S Editions, 20-22 rue St. Amand, 75015 Paris, France. TEL 45-33-16-00. FAX 45-33-92-13.
circ. 1,500. *3401*

ESPACES TROPICAUX.
Centre de Recherches sur les Espaces Tropicaux, Universite Michel de Montaigne, Esplanade des Antilles, 33405 Talence Cedex, France. TEL 33-5-56845050. FAX 33-5-56845128.
circ. 400. *3401*

ESSEX FAMILY HISTORIAN.
Essex Society for Family History, The Old Granary, Justice Wood, Polstead, Suffolk CO6 5DH, England. TEL 44-1787-211361.
circ. 2,000. *3220*

ESTACION EXPERIMENTAL REGION AGROPECUARIA PERGAMINO. INFORME TECNICO.
Instituto Nacional de Tecnologia Agropecuaria, Estacion Experimental Regional Agropecuaria Pergamino, C.C.31, 2700 Pergamino, Argentina.
circ. 2,000. *114*

ESTADIO.
Editores Nacionales, Aguirre 730 y Boyaca, Casilla 1239, Guayaquil, Ecuador. TEL 593-4-327200. FAX 593-4-320499.
circ. 30,000. *6760*

ESTATISTICA BRASILEIRA DE ENERGIA.
Conselho Mundial da Energia, Comite Nacional Brasileiro, Rua Real Grandeza, 219, 22283-900 Rio de Janeiro RJ, Brazil. TEL 55-21-246-8593. FAX 55-21-226-0508.
circ. 1,000. *2683*

ESTIA.
7 Anthimou Gazi, Athens 105 61, Greece. TEL 30-1-322-0481. FAX 30-1-324-3071.
circ. 5,000. *3303*

ESTRATEGIA FINANCIERA.
Grupo Especial Directivos, C. Orense 39 2o D, 28020 Madrid, Spain. TEL 34-1-5566411. FAX 34-1-5554118.
circ. 8,000. *1130*

10328 CONTROLLED CIRCULATION SERIALS

ESTUDIOS OCEANOLOGICOS.
Universidad de Antofagasta, Facultad de Recursos del Mar, Casilla 170, Antofagasta, Chile. FAX 56-55-247542.
circ. 600. *2402*

ESTUDOS AFRO-ASIATICOS.
Sociedade Brasileira de Instrucao, Centro de Estudos Afro-Asiaticos, Rua da Assembleia, 10 Conj. 501, 20011-000 Rio de Janeiro, Brazil. TEL 55-21-5312636. FAX 55-21-5312155.
circ. 1,000. *6612*

ESTUDOS LEOPOLDENSES.
Unisinos, Av. Unisinos, 950, 93022-000 Sao Leopoldo RS, Brazil. TEL 55-51-5920333 ext. 1951. FAX 55-51-5921035.
circ. 1,400. *2927*

ETAT-KALKULATOR.
Creativ Collection Verlag GmbH, Basler Landstr. 61, 79111 Freiburg, Germany. TEL 49-761-42606. FAX 49-761-42608.
circ. 5,000. *35*

ETELA - POHJANMAA.
Ilkka Oy, PL 10, Koulukatu 10, FIN-60101 Seinajoki, Finland. TEL 964-4186711. FAX 964-4144905.
circ. 9,203. *3277*

ETHNICITY & DISEASE.
International Society on Hypertension in Blacks, 2045 Manchester St., N.E., Atlanta, GA 30324-4110. TEL 404-875-6263. FAX 404-875-6334.
circ. 150. *4665*

ETUDES CELTIQUES.
C N R S Editions, 20-22 rue St. Amand, 75015 Paris, France. TEL 45-33-16-00. FAX 45-33-92-13.
circ. 1,250. *4256*

ETUDES D'HISTOIRE DE L'ART.
N.V. Brepols, Steenweg op Tielen 68, 2300 Turnhout, Belgium. TEL 32-14-402500. FAX 32-14-428919. *440*

ETUDES D'HISTOIRE ECONOMIQUE ET SOCIALE.
N.V. Brepols, Steenweg op Tielen 68, 2300 Turnhout, Belgium. TEL 32-14-402500. FAX 32-14-428919. *1303*

ETUDES DE PHILOLOGIE, D'ARCHEOLOGIE ET D'HISTOIRE ANCIENNE.
N.V. Brepols, Steenweg op Tielen 68, 2300 Turnhout, Belgium. TEL 32-14-402500. FAX 32-14-428919. *4256*

ETUDES ET GESTION DES SOLS.
Association Francaise pour l'Etude du Sol, 2 rue Le Notre, 49045 Angers Cedex 01, France. TEL 33-2-41225421. FAX 33-2-41731557.
circ. 1,300. *222*

EURO-JAPANESE JOURNAL.
Anglo-Japanese Economic Institute, Morley House, Rm. 1-6, 2nd Fl., 314-322 Regent St., London W1R 5AD, England. TEL 44-171-637-7872. FAX 44-171-636-3614.
circ. 1,000. *1323*

EUROPE TODAY.
Greater Europe Mission, 18950 Base Camp Rd., Monument, CO 80132-8009. TEL 719-488-8008. FAX 719-488-8018.
circ. 30,000. *6337*

EUROPEAN CLINICAL LABORATORY.
International Scientific Communications, Inc., 30 Controls Dr., Box 870, Shelton, CT 06484-0870. TEL 203-926-9300. FAX 203-926-9310.
circ. 32,801. *4897*

EUROPEAN COAL AND STEEL COMMUNITY. CONSULTATIVE COMMITTEE. YEARBOOK.
European Coal and Steel Community, Consultative Committee, Secretariat, B.P. 1907, L-2920 Luxembourg, Luxembourg. FAX 430134455.
circ. 1,170. *1359*

EUROPEAN COFFEE REPORT.
European Coffee Federation, Boudewijnlaan 21, B-1000 Brussels, Belgium. TEL 02-2035141. FAX 02-2033244.
circ. 2,500. *3102*

EUROPEAN COMMUNICATIONS.
Harrington Kilbridge plc, The Publishing House, Highbury Station Rd., Islington, London N1 1SE, England. TEL 44-171-226-2222. FAX 44-171-226-1255.
circ. 15,048. *2034*

EUROPEAN CORPORATE LAWYER.
Legalease, 28-33 Cato St., London W1H 5HS, England. TEL 44-171-396-9309. FAX 44-171-396-9301.
circ. 5,500. *4080*

EUROPEAN FEDERATION OF FINANCE HOUSE ASSOCIATIONS. ANNUAL REPORT.
European Federation of Finance House Associations, 267 av. de Tervuren, 1150 Brussels, Belgium. FAX 32-2-7780579. *1130*

EUROPEAN FEDERATION OF FINANCE HOUSE ASSOCIATIONS. NEWSLETTER.
European Federation of Finance House Associations, 267 av. de Tervuren, 1150 Brussels, Belgium. FAX 32-2-7780579. *1130*

EUROPEAN JUDAISM.
Berghahn Books Inc., 165 Taber Ave., Providence, RI 02906. TEL 401-861-9330. FAX 401-521-0046.
circ. 500. *6404*

EUROPEAN MEDIA ART FESTIVAL.
International Experimental Film Workshop, Postfach 1861, 49008 Osnabrueck, Germany. TEL 49-541-21658. FAX 49-541-28327.
circ. 1,000. *5330*

EUROPEAN PATTERN BOOK.
Weatherbys, Sanders Rd., Wellingborough, Northants. NN8 4BX, England. TEL 44-1933-440077. FAX 44-1933-440807.
circ. 5,000. *6851*

EUROPEAN PLASTICS NEWS.
E M A P Maclaren Ltd., 19 Scarbrook Rd., Croydon, Surrey CR9 1HQ, England. TEL 0181-688-7788. FAX 0181-688-8375.
circ. 24,051. *5877*

THE EUROPEAN SCREEN PRINTER MAGAZINE.
Federation of European Screen Printers Association, 7A West St., Reigate, Surrey RH2 9BL, England. TEL 44-1737-240788. FAX 44-1737-240770.
circ. 4,500. *6077*

EUROPEAN SEMICONDUCTOR.
Angel Business Communications Ltd., Kingsland House, 361-373 City Rd., London EC1V 1LR, England. TEL 44-171-417-7400. FAX 44-171-417-7500.
circ. 10,125. *2637*

EUROPETROLEUM.
Aberdeen Petroleum Publishing Ltd., 35 Huntly St., Aberdeen AB10 1TJ, Scotland. TEL 44-1224-644725. FAX 44-1224-647574. *5601*

EUROSHELL CLUB NEWS.
Vereinigte Verlagsanstalten GmbH, Hoeherweg 278, 40231 Duesseldorf, Germany. TEL 49-211-7357-0. FAX 49-211-7357223.
circ. 250,000. *7098*

EUROSUD.
Centro Studi Comunita Europee, c/o Eurocampus, Strata Prov. Bitonto, Km. 2.200, S. Spirito, 70032 Bitonto, Italy.
circ. 1,800. *6014*

L'EVENEMENT IMMOBILIER.
Editions Dupuis, S.A., 52 rue Destree, B-6001 Marcinelle, Belgium. TEL 32-71-600500. FAX 32-71-600599.
circ. 30,000. *963*

EVERY WEDNESDAY.
Afro-American Co. of Baltimore City, 2519 N. Charles St., Baltimore, MD 21218. TEL 410-554-8200. FAX 410-554-8213.
circ. 15,000. *3011*

EXCALIBUR.
Excalibur Publications Inc., 4700 Keele St., Downsview, ON M3J 1P3, Canada. TEL 416-736-5239. FAX 416-736-5841.
circ. 17,000. *1951*

EXCEPTIONAL PARENT.
Psy-Ed. Corp., 555 Kinderkamack Rd., Oradell, NJ 07649-1517. TEL 201-489-0871. FAX 201-489-1240.
circ. 33,000. *1845*

EXCLAIMER.
University Outreach & Extension, 817 Clark Hall, Columbia, MO 65211. TEL 573-882-0604. FAX 573-882-2595.
circ. 10,000. *2541*

EXCURSIONS EN AUTOCAR.
Publicom Inc., C.P. 365, Place d'Armes, Montreal, PQ H2Y 3H1, Canada. TEL 514-274-0004. FAX 514-274-5884.
circ. 6,447. *7198*

EXECUTIVE ENGINEER.
Institution of Incorporated Executive Engineers, Wix Hill House, W. Horsley, Surrey KT24 6DZ, England. TEL 44-1483-222383. FAX 44-1483-211109.
circ. 4,000. *2720*

EXECUTIVE LIVING.
Mid-Yorkshire Chamber of Commerce and Industry, Commerce House, Wakefield Rd., Huddersfield, W. Yorks. HD5 9AA, England. TEL 44-1484-426591. FAX 44-1484-514199.
circ. 19,000. *3844*

EXECUTIVE NORTH EAST.
Executive North East Magazine, 30 Queen St., Redcar, Cleveland TS10 1BD, England. TEL 0642-477155. FAX 0642-477143.
circ. 10,000. *1258*

EXECUTIVE TRAVEL.
Reed Travel Group (London), Part of the Reed Elsevier Group Church St., Dunstable, Beds LU5 4HB, England. TEL 44-1582-695498. FAX 44-1582-695095.
circ. 43,000. *7198*

EXETER BULLETIN.
Phillips Exeter Academy, 20 Main St., Exeter, NH 03833-2460. TEL 603-778-3450. FAX 603-778-4397.
circ. 26,500. *1951*

EXISTENZANALYSE.
Gesellschaft fuer Logotherapie und Existenzanalyse, Ed.-Suess-Gasse 10, A-1150 Vienna, Austria. TEL 43-1-9859566. FAX 43-2-9824845.
circ. 1,850. *5064*

EXPANSION MANAGEMENT.
New Hope Communications, Inc., 1301 Spruce St., Boulder, CO 80302-4832. TEL 303-939-8440. FAX 303-939-8640.
circ. 40,000. *1477*

EXPAT INVESTOR.
Tolley Publishing Co. Ltd., Tolley House, 2 Addiscombe Rd., Croydon, Surrey CR9 5AF, England. TEL 44-181-686-9141. FAX 44-181-760-0588.
circ. 30,000. *1131*

EXPECTATIONS.
Braille Institute of America, Inc., 741 N. Vermont Ave., Los Angeles, CA 90029. TEL 213-663-1111.
circ. 3,000. *3470*

EXPECTING.
Family Communications, Inc., 37 Hanna Ave., Toronto, ON M6K 1X1, Canada. TEL 416-537-2604. FAX 416-538-1794.
circ. 145,000. *1845*

EXPECTING.
Gruner & Jahr U.S.A. Publishing, 110 Fifth Ave., New York, NY 10011. TEL 212-499-2000.
circ. 1,300,000. *4956*

L'EXPEDITEUR.
Editions Bomart Ltee., 7493 Transcanada Hwy., Ste. 103, St. Laurent, PQ H4T 1T3, Canada. TEL 514-337-9043. FAX 514-337-1862.
circ. 9,900. *7028*

EXPERIENCED LIVING.
Paxton Media Group, 119 Riverbend Dr., Box 4810, Sevierville, TN 37864. TEL 423-428-0746. FAX 423-428-3502.
circ. 11,000. *3435*

EXPLOITANT AGRICOLE DU GARD.
L'Exploitant Agricole, 7 rue Bernard Aton, B. P. 144, 30011 Nimes Cedex, France. TEL 33-4-66670812. FAX 33-4-66216824.
circ. 2,200. *114*

EXPLORER (NOTRE DAME).
Explorer Publications Co., Box 210, Notre Dame, IN 46556. TEL 219-277-3465.
circ. 50. *4405*

EXPLORER NEWS.
Barossa News Pty. Ltd., 27 Murray St., Tanunda, S.A. 5352, Australia. TEL 61-85-632041. FAX 61-85-633655.
circ. 30,000. *7199*

EXPO (KANSAS CITY).
Atwood Convention Publishing, 11600 College Blvd., Overland Park, KS 66210. TEL 913-469-1185. FAX 913-469-0806.
circ. 7,500. *1477*

EXPORT COURIER.
Stokes & Lindley-Jones Ltd., 36 Stonehills House, Welwyn Garden City, Herts AL8 6NA, England. TEL 44-1707-326688. FAX 44-1707-323447.
circ. 9,500. *1324*

EXPORT - IMPORT NEWS.
India - International News Service, 12 India Exchange Place, Calcutta 700 001, India. *1324*

EXPRESS.
Mediamark Publishing International Ltd., 35 Gresse St., Rathbone Pl., London W1P 1PN, England. TEL 44-171-580-3105. FAX 44-171-580-1695.
circ. 50,000. *1990*

L'EXPRESS.
Case Postale 561, CH-2001 Neuchatel, Switzerland. TEL 038-256501. FAX 038-247736.
circ. 33,428. *3363*

EXPRESSION.
Redwood Publishing Ltd., 101 Bayham St., London NW1 0AG, England. TEL 0171-331-8000. FAX 0171-331-8001.
circ. 300,500. *3296*

EXTENSAO EM MINAS GERAIS.
Empresa de Assistencia Tecnica e Extensao Rural do Estado de Minas Gerais, Assessoria de Relacoes Publicas & Impresa, Av. Raja Gabaglia 1626, 1 andar, 30350-540 Belo Horizonte MG, Brazil. TEL 55-31-349-8000. FAX 55-31-349-8250.
circ. 4,500. *114*

EXTRA EQUITY FOR HOMEBUYERS.
Smart Marketing, Home & Land Publishing, Inc., RR 6 Box 284, Okatie, SC 29910-9806. TEL 203-225-0855. FAX 203-259-0724.
circ. 250,000. *6300*

EYELINE.
Eyeline Publishing Ltd., c/o Academy of the Arts - Visual Arts, Park Rd., Kelvin Grove, Qld. 4059, Australia. TEL 61-7-38645521. FAX 61-7-38643974.
circ. 2,000. *440*

F A P I G.
First Atomic Power Industry Group, Nissho-Iwai Bldg. 3rd Fl., 2-4-5 Akasaka, Minato-ku, Tokyo 107, Japan. TEL 81-3-3588-4231. FAX 81-3-3588-4232.
circ. 2,000. *2696*

F E B S LETTERS.
Elsevier Science B.V., P.O. Box 211, 1000 AE Amsterdam, Netherlands. TEL 31-20-4853911. FAX 31-20-4853598. *660*

F F I - PUBLICATIONS.
Norwegian Defence Research Establishment, Box 25, N-2007 Kjeller, Norway. FAX 63-807159. *6526*

F I Z CHEMIE AKTUELL.
Fachinformationszentrum Chemie, Franklinstr. 11, 10587 Berlin, Germany. TEL 49-30-39977111. FAX 49-30-39977134.
circ. 2,200. *1784*

F K T.
Huethig GmbH, Postfach 102869, 69018 Heidelberg, Germany. TEL 49-6221-489411. FAX 49-6221-489323.
circ. 3,000. *5331*

F L I C C NEWSLETTER.
U.S. Library of Congress, Federal Library and Information Center Committee, Washington, DC 20540. TEL 202-707-4800. FAX 202-707-4818. *4177*

F M T.
Verlag fuer Technik und Handwerk GmbH, Robert-Bosch-Str. 4, 76532 Baden-Baden, Germany. TEL 49-7221-5087-0. FAX 49-7221-508752.
circ. 43,000. *3667*

F N V - MAGAZINE (WOERDEN).
F N V Dienstenbond, Postbus 550, 3440 AN Woerden, Netherlands. TEL 31-3480-87788. FAX 31-3480-31498.
circ. 92,000. *3890*

F P A NEWS.
Dorcom International Ltd., 700 Lawrence Ave. W., Ste. 435, Toronto, ON M6A 3B4, Canada.
circ. 400. *3872*

F P A P ANNUAL REPORT.
Family Planning Association of Pakistan, 3-A Temple Rd., Lahore, Pakistan.
circ. 1,000. *857*

F P S MEMBERSHIP DIRECTORY AND ANNUAL REPORT.
Fluid Power Society, 2433 N. Mayfair Rd., Ste. 111, Milwaukee, WI 53226. TEL 414-257-0910. FAX 414-257-4092.
circ. 3,000. *5844*

F U: NACHRICHTEN.
Freie Universitaet Berlin, Kaiserswertherstr. 16-18, 14195 Berlin, Germany. TEL 030-83873180. FAX 030-83873187.
circ. 20,000. *1951*

F W'S CORPORATE FINANCE.
Financial World Partners, 1328 Broadway, New York, NY 10001. TEL 212-594-5030. FAX 212-629-0026.
circ. 60,000. *1132*

FAAGLAR I NORRKOEPINGSTRAKTEN.
Faagelfoereningen i Norrkoeping (FiNk), c/o Juhani Vuorinen, ed., Bergslagsgatan 37, SE-602 18 Norrkoeping, Sweden. TEL 45-11-121-682. FAX 46-11-121-682.
circ. 350. *803*

FABRICATION & GLAZING INDUSTRIES.
T B B Publications Ltd., 4 Simon Campion Ct., High St., Epping, Essex CM16 4AU, England. TEL 01992-560215. FAX 01992-560216.
circ. 8,329. *1728*

FABRICNEWS.
Arthur J. Imparato Associates, 80 Park Ave., New York, NY 10016. TEL 213-274-6752.
circ. 9,500. *6986*

FACETS OF FRESHWATER.
Freshwater Foundation, 2500 Shadywood Rd., Navarre, MN 55331. TEL 612-471-9773. FAX 617-471-7685. *7293*

FACHBUCHVERZEICHNIS WIRTSCHAFTSWISSENSCHAFTEN.
Rossipaul Kommunikation GmbH, Menzingerstr. 37, 80638 Munich, Germany. TEL 49-89-179106-0. FAX 49-89-17910622.
circ. 25,000. *1038*

FACILITIES.
Bedrock Communications, Inc., 650 First Ave., 7th Fl., New York, NY 10016-3240. TEL 212-532-4150. FAX 212-213-6382.
circ. 30,000. *1477*

FACTS.
African Oxygen Ltd., Box 5404, Johannesburg 2000, South Africa. TEL 27-11-490-0400. FAX 27-11-493-8828.
circ. 8,500. *2720*

FACTS & FIGURES.
Organization of the Petroleum Exporting Countries, Information Department, Obere Donaustr. 93, A-1020 Vienna, Austria. TEL 43-1-21112. FAX 43-1-2149827.
circ. 6,000. *2669*

FAITH AND MISSION.
Southeastern Baptist Theological Seminary, Inc., Wake Forest, NC 27587. TEL 919-556-3101. FAX 919-556-0998.
circ. 1,000. *6425*

FAITH FOR DAILY LIVING.
Faith for Daily Living Foundation, P.O. Box 3737, Durban, Natal, South Africa.
circ. 120,000. *6490*

FAKTA.
A-Lehdet Oy, Hitsaajankatu 7, FIN-00081 A-Lehdet, Finland. TEL 358-9-75961. FAX 358-9-783526.
circ. 22,176. *964*

FAMILIEN.
Hjemmet Mortensens Forlag AS, Soerkedalsveien 10 A, N-0369 Oslo, Norway. TEL 47-2-961-500. FAX 47-2-961-382.
circ. 162,778. *3342*

FAMILY ALMANAC.
Creative Comics Syndicate, 1608 South Dakota, Sioux Falls, SD 57105.
circ. 40,000. *1527*

FAMILY BACKTRACKING.
Puget Sound Genealogical Society, Box 601, Tracyton, WA 98393-0601. TEL 206-871-0202.
circ. 300. *3220*

FAMILY LAW REVIEW.
New York State Bar Association, Family Law Section, 1 Elk St., Albany, NY 12207-1096. TEL 518-463-3200. FAX 518-463-8844.
circ. 3,850. *4101*

FAMILY MEDICINE.
Medpress, Tubs Hill House, 8th Fl., London Rd., Sevenoaks, Kent TN13 1BL, England. TEL 44-1732-464190. FAX 44-1732-464939.
circ. 25,000. *5031*

FAMILY TIMES (WILMINGTON).
Family Times, Inc., 1900 Superfine Ln., No. 6, Wilmington, DE 19802. TEL 302-575-0935. FAX 302-575-0933.
circ. 35,000. *1845*

FAMILY TRAVELERS.
7101 Loch Lomond Dr., Bethesda, MD 20817-4759. TEL 301-986-1227.
circ. 10,000. *7199*

FANLIGHT NEWS.
Fanlight Productions, 47 Halifax St., Boston, MA 02130. TEL 617-524-0980. FAX 617-524-8838.
circ. 15,000. *4667*

FARM BUREAU PRESS.
Arkansas Farm Bureau Federation, 10720 Kanis Road, Little Rock, AR 72211. TEL 501-224-4400. FAX 501-228-1557.
circ. 203,000. *116*

FARM EQUIPMENT.
Johnson Hill Press, Inc., 1233 Janesville Ave., Ft. Atkinson, WI 53538. TEL 920-563-6388. FAX 920-563-1701.
circ. 13,500. *205*

FARM INDUSTRY NEWS.
Intertec Publishing Corp., Webb Division, 7900 International Dr., Ste. 300, Minneapolis, MN 55425. TEL 612-851-4684. FAX 612-851-4601.
circ. 257,000. *116*

FARM SUPPLY RETAILING.
Pro Group, Inc., Box 6585, Englewood, CO 80155. TEL 303-792-3000. FAX 303-792-5589.
circ. 22,000. *262*

FARMACI.
Danmarks Apotekerforening, Bredgade 54, 1260 Copenhagen K, Denmark. TEL 45-33-76-76-00. FAX 45-33-76-76-99.
circ. 2,400. *5662*

10330 CONTROLLED CIRCULATION SERIALS

FARMERS AND CONSUMERS MARKET BULLETIN.
Department of Agriculture, 19 Martin Luther King Jr. Dr., Rm. 226, Capitol Sq., Atlanta, GA 30334-4250. TEL 404-656-3722. FAX 404-651-7957.
circ. 250,000. *117*

FARMING.
Farming Magazine, 43 So. Water St. E., Fort Atkinson, WI 53508. TEL 414-563-9500.
circ. 600,000. *193*

FARMING AHEAD.
Kondinin Group, P.O. Box 913, Cloverdale, W.A. 6105, Australia. TEL 61-9-4783343. FAX 61-9-4783353.
circ. 29,000. *117*

FARMING BUSINESS.
Genus Ltd., Westmere Dr., Crewe, Ches. CW1 1ZY, England. TEL 44-1270-536536. FAX 44-1270-536601.
circ. 40,000. *254*

FARMIS - REPTILEN.
Farmaceutiska Studentkaaren, P.O. Box 8036, S-750 08 Uppsala, Sweden.
circ. 1,200. *5662*

EL FARO.
Associated Collectors of El Salvador, c/o Jeff Brasor, Ed., Box 173, Coconut Creek, FL 33097.
circ. 100. *5706*

FARUMASHIA.
Pharmaceutical Society of Japan, 12-15, Shibuya 2-chome, Shibuya-ku, Tokyo 150, Japan.
circ. 22,000. *5662*

FASTENER TECHNOLOGY INTERNATIONAL.
Initial Publications Inc., 3869 Darrow Rd., Ste. 109, Stow, OH 44224. TEL 216-686-9544. FAX 216-686-9563.
circ. 13,000. *928*

FATIMA FINDINGS.
Reparation Society of the Immaculate Heart of Mary, Inc., Fatima House, 8006 Caliburn Ct., Pasadena, MD 21122-6478. TEL 410-360-1817.
circ. 4,000. *6490*

FAX PLUS.
Montreal Children's Hospital, 2300 Tupper St., Ste. E-203, Montreal, PQ H3H 1P3, Canada. TEL 514-934-4307.
circ. 1,200. *3707*

FEATURE.
Feature Publishing Ltd., Maison Astral, 2100 Rue Ste-Catherine Ouest, Bureau 900, Montreal, PQ H3H 2T3. TEL 514-939-5024. FAX 514-939-1515.
circ. 290,000. *2050*

FEDERAL CIVILIAN WORK FORCE STATISTICS. PAY STRUCTURE OF THE FEDERAL CIVIL SERVICE.
U.S. Office of Personnel Management, Personnel Systems and Oversight Group, Office of Workforce Information, Washington, DC 20415. TEL 703-487-4650. FAX 202-606-1719.
circ. 900. *1038*

FEDERAL CIVILIAN WORK FORCE STATISTICS. WORK YEARS AND PERSONNEL COSTS. EXECUTIVE BRANCH, UNITED STATES GOVERNMENT.
U.S. Office of Personnel Management, Personnel Systems and Oversight Group, Office of Workforce Information, 1900 E St., N.W., Washington, DC 20415. TEL 703-487-4650.
circ. 400. *1039*

FEDERAL CIVILIAN WORKFORCE STATISTICS. EMPLOYMENT AND TRENDS.
U.S. Office of Personnel Management, Personnel Systems and Oversight Group, Office of Workforce Information, 1900 E St., N.W., Washington, DC 20415. TEL 202-606-1178.
circ. 950. *1039*

FEDERAL PHYSICIAN.
Federal Physicians Association, Box 45150, Washington, DC 20026. TEL 703-455-5947. FAX 703-455-8282.
circ. 1,000. *6233*

FEDERATION.
Federation of Worker Writers & Community Publishers, c/o 60 Upper Valley Rd., Sheffield S8 9HB, England. TEL 44-1782-822327.
circ. 1,500. *3872*

FEDERATION INTERNATIONALE DE RUGBY AMATEUR. ANNUAIRE.
International Amateur Rugby Federation, 9 rue de Liege, 75009 Paris, France. FAX 45-26-19-19.
circ. 700. *6803*

FEDERATION JAZZ.
Federation of Jazz Societies, 2787 Del Monte St., W. Sacramento, CA 95691. TEL 916-372-5277. FAX 916-372-3479.
circ. 800. *5392*

FEDERATION NEWS (WILTON).
Forefront Publishing Group, 5 River Rd., Ste. 113, Wilton, CT 06897-4069. TEL 203-834-0631. FAX 203-834-0940.
circ. 10,750. *5142*

FEDERATION OF KENYA EMPLOYERS. NEWSLETTER.
Federation of Kenya Employers, P.O. Box 48311, Nairobi, Kenya. TEL 254-2-721929. FAX 254-2-721990.
circ. 3,000. *1430*

FEED AND GRAIN.
Johnson Hill Press, Inc., 1233 Janesville Ave., Ft. Atkinson, WI 53538. TEL 920-563-6388. FAX 920-563-1702.
circ. 19,000. *262*

FEED INTERNATIONAL.
Watt Publishing Co., 122 S. Wesley Ave., Mt. Morris, IL 61054. TEL 815-734-4171. FAX 815-734-4201.
circ. 20,605. *262*

FEED LEGISLATION.
H G M Publications, Abney House, School Ln., Baslow, Bakewell, Derbyshire DE45 1RZ, England. TEL 44-1246-582470. FAX 44-1246-582425.
circ. 600. *262*

FEED-LOT.
Feed-Lot Magazine, Box 850, Dighton, KS 67839-0850. TEL 316-397-2838. FAX 316-397-2839.
circ. 9,042. *276*

FEED MANAGEMENT.
Watt Publishing Co., 122 S. Wesley Ave., Mt. Morris, IL 61054. TEL 815-734-4171. FAX 815-734-4201.
circ. 20,182. *262*

FELIX LETTER.
Clara Felix, Ed. & Pub., Box 7094, Berkeley, CA 94707. TEL 510-526-6268.
circ. 1,500. *5473*

FEMINA.
Edipresse Publications SA, Av. de la Gare 33, CH-1001 Lausanne, Switzerland. TEL 41-21-3494848. FAX 41-21-3494859.
circ. 223,075. *7319*

FENESTRATION.
Ashlee Publishing Co., Inc., 18 E. 41st St., Phse., New York, NY 10017-6222. TEL 212-376-7722. FAX 212-376-7723.
circ. 14,000. *893*

FERRETECNIC - F Y T.
Publitecnic S.A., Calle 4, no. 188, Apdo. Postal 74-290, 09070 Mexico DF, Mexico. TEL 685-28-19. FAX 6706318.
circ. 10,000. *5190*

FERRUM MAGAZINE.
Ferrum College, Ferrum, VA 24088. TEL 540-365-4216. FAX 540-365-4203.
circ. 14,000. *1952*

FESTIVALMAGAZIN.
Verein Berner Tanztage, Postfach 317, CH-3000 Bern 14, Switzerland. TEL 41-31-3760303. FAX 41-31-3710333.
circ. 10,000. *2293*

FIDELITY FOCUS.
Fidelity Investments, 82 Devonshire St., R20E, Boston, MA 02109. *1384*

FIFTH ESTATE.
Fifth Estate Newspaper, 4632 Second Ave., Detroit, MI 48201. TEL 313-831-6800.
circ. 5,000. *4334*

FIJI. OFFICE OF THE OMBUDSMAN. ANNUAL REPORT OF THE OMBUDSMAN.
Office of the Ombudsman, Suva, Fiji. TEL 679-211652. FAX 679-314756.
circ. 200. *3950*

FILM BILL.
Film Bill, Inc., 250 W. 54 St., New York, NY 10019. TEL 212-977-4140. FAX 212-977-4404.
circ. 500,000. *5332*

FILM CLIPS.
San Jose Convention and Visitors Bureau, Film and Video Commission, 333 W. San Carlos St., Ste. 1000, San Jose, CA 95110-2720. TEL 408-295-9600. FAX 408-295-3937.
circ. 3,975. *5332*

FILTRATION NEWS.
Eagle Publications, Inc., 42400 Nine Mile Rd., Ste. B, Novi, MI 48375. TEL 810-347-3490. FAX 810-347-3492.
circ. 26,000. *2928*

FINANCE DIRECTOR INTERNATIONAL.
Sterling Publications Ltd., 86-88 Edgware Rd., London W2 2YW, England. TEL 44-171-915-9600. FAX 44-171-915-9619.
circ. 10,000. *1133*

FINANCIAL ADVISER (LONDON).
Financial Times Business Information, Magazines 2 Greystoke Pl., Fetter Ln., London EC4A 1ND, England. TEL 0171-405-6969. FAX 0171-405-5276. *1384*

FINANCIAL INSTITUTIONS DIRECTORY OF NEW ENGLAND.
Shawmut Bank, N.A., Correspondent Banking Group, One Federal St., Boston, MA 02211. TEL 617-292-3823. FAX 617-292-4417. *1134*

FINANSTIDNINGEN.
Sveriges Finansnyheter AB, P.O. Box 70347, S-107 23 Stockholm, Sweden. TEL 46-8-677-4500. FAX 46-8-14-99-30.
circ. 250. *1141*

FINANZA MARKETING E PRODUZIONE.
E G E A s.p.a., Via Sarfatti 25, 20136 Milan, Italy. TEL 39-2-58363726. FAX 39-2-58363793.
circ. 3,000. *1478*

DER FINANZBERATER.
Akademie fuer Finanz-Marketing, Postfach 102143, 40745 Langenfeld, Germany. TEL 02173-23048. FAX 02173-235754.
circ. 18,000. *1141*

FINE ART TRADE GUILD. DIRECTORY.
Fine Art Trade Guild, 16-18 Empress Pl., London SW6 1TT, England. TEL 0171-381-6616. FAX 0171-381-2596.
circ. 1,800. *441*

FINE FOODS.
Griffin Publishing Company, Inc., 1099 Hingham St., Rockland, MA 02370. TEL 617-878-5300. FAX 617-871-4721.
circ. 14,500. *3104*

FINLAND FOLIO.
Consulate General of Finland, 866 UN Plaza, Ste. 250, New York, NY 10017. TEL 212-750-4400. FAX 212-750-441.
circ. 6,500. *3011*

FIRE MARSHALS ASSOCIATION OF NORTH AMERICA. DIRECTORY.
Fire Marshals Association of North America, NFPA, Baterymarch Park, Quincy, MA 02269-9101. TEL 617-770-3000.
circ. 1,400. *3054*

FIRE NEWS.
National Fire Protection Association, 1 Batterymarch Park, Quincy, MA 02269. TEL 617-770-3500.
circ. 67,000. *3054*

FIRES & FIREPLACES.
Carter Spencer Publishing Ltd., Chancery Ct., Lincoln Rd., High Wycombe, Bucks. HP12 3RE, England. TEL 44-1494-442424. FAX 44-1494-472790.
circ. 10,000. *3855*

FIRST CALL FOR CHILDREN.
United Nations Children's Fund (UNICEF), UNICEF House, 3 United Nations Plaza, New York, NY 10017. TEL 212-326-7787. FAX 212-326-7768.
circ. 65,000. *6665*

FIRST-TIME PARENTS.
K-III Communications Corp., 745 Fifth Ave., New York, NY 10151. TEL 212-745-0100.
circ. 500,000. *1846*

FIRUDO BAIOROJISUTO.
Gunma Yagai Seibutsu Gakkai, c/o Mr. S. Saito, Gunma Pref. Women's University, 1395 Kaminote, Tamamuramachi, Sawa-gun, Gunma-ken 370-11, Japan. TEL 0270-65-8511. FAX 0270-65-9538.
circ. 500. *601*

FISH.
Institute of Fisheries Management, 22 Rushworth Ave., W. Bridgford, Notts. NG7 7LF, England. TEL 0115-982-2317. FAX 0115-982-6150.
circ. 1,500. *3065*

FISH AND GAME FINDER.
Fish and Game Finder Magazines, 41 W. Michigan, Orlando, FL 32806. TEL 407-425-0045. FAX 407-425-1529.
circ. 720,000. *6868*

FISHERMAN.
Fisherman Publishing Society, 111 Victoria Dr., No. 160, Vancouver, BC V5L 4C4, Canada. TEL 604-255-1366. FAX 604-255-3162.
circ. 10,500. *3067*

FISHING BOAT WORLD.
Baird Publications Pty. Ltd., 10 Oxford St., South Yarra, Vic. 3141, Australia. TEL 61-3-98268741. FAX 61-3-98270704.
circ. 4,000. *3067*

FISHING TACKLE TRADE NEWS.
Outdoor Group, Down East Enterprise, Box 370, Camden, ME 04843-0370. TEL 360-693-4721. FAX 360-693-3997.
circ. 21,500. *6869*

FISKERITIDSKRIFT FOER FINLAND.
Kalatalouden Keskusliitto, Koydenpunojankatu 7 B 23, FIN-00180 Helsinki, Finland. TEL 358-9-640126. FAX 358-9-608309.
circ. 4,878. *3067*

FITECH INTERNATIONAL.
Argus Business Media Ltd., Queensway House, 2 Queensway, Redhill, Surrey RH1 1QS, England. TEL 44-1737-768611. FAX 44-1737-761685.
3056

FITOTERAPIA.
IdB Holding, Viale Ortles 12, 20139 Milan, Italy. TEL 39-2-57496442. FAX 39-2-57496443.
circ. 4,200. *703*

FJARMALATIDINDI.
Sedlabanki Islands, Kalkofnsvegur 1, IS-150 Reykjavik, Iceland. TEL 354-569-9600. FAX 354-569-9608.
circ. 2,200. *1141*

FL A C S.
American Chemical Society, Florida Section, c/o Harold Van Wart, Department of Chemistry, Florida State University, Tallahassee, FL 32306.
circ. 2,350. *1749*

FLASCHENPOST.
Lotharstr. 65, 47048 Duisburg, Germany. TEL 49-203-3792397. FAX 49-203-3793333.
circ. 1,000. *1990*

FLASH POINT.
Tile Heritage Foundation, Box 1850, Healdsburg, CA 95448. TEL 707-431-8453. FAX 707-431-8455.
340

FLAX CRAFT.
Virginia Handy, Ed. & Pub., 3503 Edwards Rd., Sodus, MI 49126-9707. TEL 616-944-5719. FAX 616-944-5719.
circ. 50. *480*

FLEET EQUIPMENT.
Maple Publishing, 134 W. Slade St., Palatine, IL 60067. TEL 847-359-6100. FAX 847-359-6420.
circ. 63,000. *7174*

FLEET NORTH.
Tweedprint Ltd., 97 Heaton St., Standish, Wigan, Lancashire WN6 0DA, England. TEL 0257-427332. FAX 0257-422054.
circ. 17,100. *7100*

FLEET OPERATORS HANDBOOK.
E M A P - Response Publishing Ltd., Wentworth House, Wentworth St., Peterborough, Cambs. PE1 1DS, England. TEL 01733-63100. FAX 01733-67367.
circ. 10,000. *7100*

FLEET OWNER.
Intertec Publishing Corp. (White Plains), 707 Westchester Ave., Ste. 101, White Plains, NY 10604-3102. TEL 914-949-8500. FAX 914-287-6752.
circ. 100,150. *7174*

FLEETLINE.
Historic Commercial Vehicle Association Co-Op, G.P.O. Box 1010, Sydney, N.S.W. 1043, Australia. FAX 61-2-8914947.
circ. 500. *7028*

FLEISCH UND FEINKOST.
Verband Schweizer Metzgermeister, Postfach 284, CH-8028 Zurich, Switzerland. TEL 01-2527766. FAX 01-262874.
circ. 4,938. *3104*

DIE FLEISCHMEHL-INDUSTRIE.
Wirtschaftsdienst der Fleischmehl-Industrie GmbH, Kaiserstr. 9, 53113 Bonn, Germany. TEL 49-228-212185. FAX 49-228-212198.
circ. 500. *2984*

FLIGHTPATH.
Kingsclere Publications Ltd., Furlongs House, Peasemore, Newbury, Berks RG16 0JE, England. TEL 0635-247770. FAX 0635-247272.
circ. 10,000. *7258*

FLIPPING FLIPPINS.
Nova A. Lemons, Ed. & Pub., 12206 Brisbane Ave., Dallas, TX 75234-6528. TEL 972-241-2739. FAX 972-620-1416.
circ. 65. *3222*

FLORACULTURE INTERNATIONAL.
International Horticulture Publications, Box 9, 335 N. River St., Batavia, IL 61510-0009. TEL 708-208-9080. FAX 708-208-9350.
circ. 11,200. *3187*

FLORIDA AND THE OTHER FORTY-NINE.
Department of Commerce, Bureau of Economic Analysis, 107 W. Gaines St., Tallahassee, FL 32399-2000. TEL 904-487-2971. *1040*

FLORIDA COUNTY COMPARISONS.
Department of Commerce, Bureau of Economic Analysis, 107 W. Gaines St., Tallahassee, FL 32399-2000. TEL 904-487-2971. *1040*

FLORIDA COUNTY PROFILES.
Department of Commerce, Bureau of Economic Analysis, 107 W. Gaines St., Tallahassee, FL 32399-2000. TEL 904-487-2971. *1187*

FLORIDA FORUM.
F R S A, Drawer 4850, Winter Park, FL 32793. TEL 407-671-3772. FAX 407-679-0010.
circ. 9,200. *894*

FLORIDA GOLF REPORTER.
Golf Reporter Enterprises Inc., Box 951422, Lake Mary, FL 32795-1422. FAX 407-767-5748.
circ. 20,000. *6804*

FLORIDA INDEPENDENT ACCOUNTANT.
Florida Association of Independent Accountants, Box 13089, Tallahassee, FL 32317. TEL 904-878-3134. FAX 904-878-1291.
circ. 900. *1090*

FLORIDA LIBRARIES.
Florida Library Association, 1133 W. Morse Blvd., No. 201, Winter Park, FL 32789-3788. TEL 407-647-8839. FAX 407-629-2502.
circ. 1,300. *4178*

FLORIDA MARKET BULLETIN.
Department of Agriculture and Consumer Services, 545 E. Tennessee St., Tallahassee, FL 32308.
circ. 30,000. *118*

FLORIDA PUBLIC DOCUMENTS.
State Library, Documents Section, Tallahassee, FL 32399. TEL 904-487-2651. *6174*

FLORIDA RURAL ELECTRIC NEWS.
Florida Rural Electric Cooperatives Association, Box 590, Tallahassee, FL 32302. FAX 904-656-5485.
circ. 9,000. *2824*

FLORIDA SPECIFIER.
National Technical Communications Co., Inc., Box 2027, Winter Park, FL 32790. TEL 407-671-7777. FAX 407-671-7757.
circ. 15,000. *2928*

FLORIDA TRUCK NEWS.
Florida Trucking Association, Inc., 350 E. College Ave., Tallahassee, FL 32301. TEL 904-222-9900. FAX 904-222-9363.
circ. 2,300. *7174*

THE FLUE CURED TOBACCO FARMER.
SpecComm International, Inc., 3000 Highwoods Blvd., Raleigh, NC 27604-1029. TEL 919-872-5040. FAX 919-876-6531.
circ. 22,000. *7019*

FLUID POWER HANDBOOK & DIRECTORY.
Penton Publishing Co., 1100 Superior Ave., Cleveland, OH 44114-2543. TEL 216-696-7000. FAX 216-696-8765.
circ. 36,000. *2858*

FLYDOSCOPE.
Luxair, L-2987 Luxembourg, Luxembourg. TEL 4798-4282. FAX 4798-4289.
circ. 160,000. *7258*

FLYING DUTCHMAN.
Media Partners, P.O. Box 2215, 1180 EE Amstelveen, Netherlands. TEL 31-20-5473600. FAX 31-20-6475121.
circ. 100,000. *7259*

FLYNYTT.
Norsk Aero Klubb, Tollbugaten 3, N-0152 Oslo, Norway. TEL 47-23-10-29-00. FAX 47-23-10-29-01.
circ. 10,000. *66*

FLYV.
Danish General Aviation ApS, Lufthavnsvej 28, DK-4000 Roskilde, Denmark. TEL 45-31-35-45-00. FAX 45-31-35-97-68.
circ. 8,500. *66*

FOCUS (NEW YORK, 1978).
State University of New York, Health Science Center at Brooklyn, 450 Clarkson Ave., Brooklyn, NY 11203. *4668*

FOCUS (WESTFIELD).
Westfield State College, Public Affairs Office, Western Ave., Westfield, MA 01086. TEL 413-572-5208. FAX 413-572-4843.
circ. 22,000. *1952*

FOCUS ON FOOD & BEVERAGE.
Food Processing Machinery and Supplies Association, 200 Daingerfield Rd., Alexandria, VA 22314. TEL 703-684-1080. FAX 703-548-6563.
circ. 3,000. *3104*

FOCUS ON H M A T.
National Asphalt Pavement Association, N.A.P.A. Bldg. 5100 Forbes Blvd., Lanham, MD 20706-4413. TEL 301-731-4748. FAX 301-731-4621.
circ. 20,000. *7138*

FOCUS ON MISSIONS.
Fellowship of Missions, 140 Jacaveline Dr., Berea, OH 44017-2730. TEL 216-243-0156.
circ. 23,000. *6426*

10332 CONTROLLED CIRCULATION SERIALS

FOCUS ON N A R I.
National Association of the Remodeling Industry, 4900 Seminary Rd., Ste. 320, Alexandria, VA 22311-1811. TEL 703-575-1121.
circ. 7,500. *894*

FOCUS ON PAKISTAN.
Pakistan Tourism Development Corporation Ltd., House No. 170, Street 36, F-10-1, P.O. Box 1465, Islambad 44000, Pakistan. TEL 92-51-294550. FAX 92-51-294540.
circ. 5,000. *7200*

FOCUS ON THE FAMILY.
Focus on the Family, Inc., 8605 Explorer Dr., Colorado Springs, CO 80920-1051. TEL 719-531-3400. FAX 719-531-3499.
circ. 2,000,000. *6339*

FOCUS ON WOMEN.
Campbell Communications Inc., 1218 Langley St., 3rd Fl., Victoria, BC V8W 1W2, Canada. TEL 604-388-7231. FAX 604-383-1140.
circ. 35,000. *7320*

FOCUS PLUS.
Society of Teachers in Business Education, 28 Norlands Crescent, Chislehurst, Kent BR7 5RN, England. TEL 44-181-402-3569.
circ. 1,800. *2603*

FOCUS WEST (PHOENIX).
Valley National Corporation, Communication Services (4-646), Box 71, Phoenix, AZ 85001. TEL 602-221-4840. FAX 602-221-4899.
circ. 9,500. *1141*

FOERDERUNGSDIENST.
Bundesministerium fuer Land- und Forstwirtschaft, Stubenring 1, A-1010 Vienna, Austria. TEL 43-1-711006710. FAX 43-1-711002127.
circ. 3,500. *119*

FOERSAAKRINGSTIDNINGEN.
Sveriges Foersaekringsfoerbund, P.O. Box 1436, S-111 84 Stockholm, Sweden. TEL 46-8-783-71-50. FAX 46-8-723-03-08.
circ. 3,500. *3816*

FOERSVARSFORSKNINGSREFERAT.
Foersvarets Forskningsanstalt (FOA), Centralkansliet, 172 90 Sundbyberg, Sweden.
circ. 950. *1899*

FOLK DANCE PROBLEM SOLVER.
Society of Folk Dance Historians, 2100 Rio Grande, Austin, TX 78705-5513. TEL 512-478-9676. FAX 512-478-8900.
circ. 350. *2293*

FOLK OG FRITID.
Folkeligt Oplysnings Forbund, Moellevej 9, DK-5683 Haarby, Denmark.
circ. 7,500. *2444*

FOLKEVIRKE.
Folkevirke, Niels Hemmingsensgade 10, 3. sal, DK-1153 Copenhagen K, Denmark. TEL 45-33-32-83-01. FAX 45-33-32-83-11.
circ. 2,000. *4334*

FOLKLIVSSTUDIER.
Svenska Litteratursaellskapet i Finland, Marieg. 8, 00170 Helsinki 17, Finland. FAX 358-0-632820.
317

FOMRHI QUARTERLY.
Fellowship of Makers and Researchers of Historical Instruments, c/o Jeremy Montagu, 171 Iffley Rd., Oxford OX4 1EL, England.
circ. 700. *5394*

FOOD AND AGRICULTURAL EXPORT DIRECTORY.
U.S. Department of Agriculture, Foreign Agricultural Service, Information Division, Rm. 5920-S, Washington, DC 20250-1000. TEL 202-720-7937.
circ. 10,000. *193*

FOOD AND AGRICULTURE ORGANIZATION OF THE UNITED NATIONS. ASIA AND PACIFIC PLANT PROTECTION COMMISSION. TECHNICAL DOCUMENT.
Food and Agriculture Organization of the United Nations, Regional Office for Asia and the Pacific, Maliwan Mansion, Phra Atit Rd., Bangkok 10200, Thailand.
circ. 500. *225*

FOOD & BEVERAGE MARKETING.
Charleson Publishing Co., 445 Broadhollow Rd., Melville, NY 11747-3601.
circ. 20,219. *3104*

FOOD & BEVERAGE MONITOR.
Donaldson, Lufkin & Jenrette, 140 Broadway, New York, NY 10005. TEL 212-504-4209. *1384*

FOOD & BEVERAGE SPOTLIGHT.
Donaldson, Lufkin & Jenrette, 140 Broadway, New York, NY 10005. TEL 212-504-4209. *1384*

FOOD, DRUG, COSMETIC, AND MEDICAL DEVICE LAW DIGEST.
New York State Bar Association, Food, Drug and Cosmetic Law Section, One Elk St., Albany, NY 12207. TEL 518-463-3200. FAX 518-463-8844.
circ. 400. *3952*

FOOD PROCESSING.
Putman Publishing Co., 301 E. Erie St., Chicago, IL 60611. TEL 312-644-2020.
circ. 75,000. *3107*

FOOD SCIENCE AND TECHNOLOGY TODAY.
Institute of Food Science and Technology, 210 Shepherd's Bush Rd., London W6 7NJ, England. TEL 44-171-603-6317. FAX 44-171-602-9936.
circ. 3,500. *3108*

FOOD TECHNOLOGY FOR CHINA.
Sterling Publications Ltd., 86-88 Edgware Rd., London W2 2YW, England. TEL 44-171-915-9600. FAX 44-171-915-9619.
circ. 10,000. *3109*

FOOD TECHNOLOGY INTERNATIONAL EUROPE.
Sterling Publications Ltd., 86-88 Edgware Rd., London W2 2YW, England. TEL 44-171-915-9600. FAX 44-171-915-9619.
circ. 10,000. *3109*

THE FOODSERVICE DISTRIBUTOR.
Penton Publishing Co., 1100 Superior Ave., Cleveland, OH 44114-2543. TEL 216-696-7000. FAX 216-696-8765.
circ. 38,946. *3110*

FOODSERVICE EAST.
Newbury Street Group, Inc., 76 Summer St., Boston, MA 02110. TEL 617-695-9080.
circ. 23,000. *3110*

FOODSERVICE PRODUCT NEWS.
Young - Conway Publications, 1101 Richmond Ave., Ste. 201, Point Pleasant Beach, NJ 08742-3049.
circ. 135,050. *3726*

FOODWATCH UPDATE.
Agriculture Council of America, 11020 King St., Ste. 205, Overland Park, KS 66210-1201. TEL 202-682-9200. FAX 202-289-6648.
circ. 10,000. *2255*

FOOTBALL REFEREE.
Referees' Association, 15 Penrith Ave., Whitefield, Manchester M45 6UJ, England. TEL 44-161-773-5917. FAX 44-161-773-5917.
circ. 8,000. *6804*

FOOTPRINTS (PLAINVIEW).
Wayland Baptist University, 1900 W. 7th St., Plainview, TX 79072. TEL 806-296-4844. FAX 806-296-4580.
circ. 12,000. *1952*

FOOTWEAR BUSINESS INTERNATIONAL.
S A T R A Footwear Technology Centre, SATRA House, Rockingham Rd., Kettering, Northants NN16 9JH, England. TEL 01536-410000. FAX 01536-410626.
circ. 1,500. *6595*

FOOTWEAR PLUS.
Earnshaw Publications, Inc., 225 W. 34th St., Ste. 1212, New York, NY 10001. TEL 212-563-2742.
circ. 18,000. *6595*

FOR THE RECORD (VALLEY FORGE).
Great Valley Publishing, Box 2224, Valley Forge, PA 19482. TEL 610-917-9300. FAX 610-917-9186.
circ. 45,000. *4668*

FOR YOU.
Heinrich Bauer Verlag, Burchardstr. 11, 20095 Hamburg, Germany. TEL 49-40-30193040. FAX 49-40-335923.
circ. 1,000,000. *7320*

FORBES A S A P.
Forbes, Inc., 60 Fifth Ave., New York, NY 10011. TEL 212-620-2200.
circ. 760,000. *1201*

FORCES.
Societe d'Edition de la Revue Forces, 500 rue Sherbrooke Oeust, Bur. 430, Montreal, Que. H3A 3C6, Canada. TEL 514-286-7600. *3261*

FORCES NEWS.
Mandrake Associates Ltd., 6 North Brink, Wisbech, Cambs PE13 1JR, England. TEL 01945-65177. FAX 01945-64712.
circ. 35,000. *1141*

FORD MAGAZIN.
Vereinigte Verlagsanstalten GmbH, Hoeherweg 278, 40231 Duesseldorf, Germany. TEL 49-211-7357-0. FAX 49-211-7357223.
circ. 250,000. *7100*

FORD REPORT.
Vereinigte Verlagsanstalten GmbH, Hoeherweg 278, 40231 Duesseldorf, Germany. TEL 49-211-7357-0. FAX 49-211-7357223.
circ. 60,000. *7100*

FOREIGN SERVICE.
Diplomatist Associates Ltd., 58 Theobalds Rd., London WC1X 8SF, England. TEL 44-171-405-4874. FAX 44-171-831-0667.
circ. 3,000. *6015*

FOREST RESEARCH BIENNIAL REPORT.
Forest Research Centre, P.O. Box 1407, 90008 Sandakan, Sabah, Malaysia. TEL 089-531522. FAX 089-531068. *3152*

FORESTRY AND FOREST PRODUCTS INTERNATIONAL.
Sterling Publications Ltd., 86-88 Edgware Rd., London W2 2YW, England. TEL 44-171-915-9600. FAX 44-171-915-9619.
circ. 10,000. *3152*

FORGING.
Penton Publishing Co., 1100 Superior Ave., Cleveland, OH 44114-2534. TEL 216-696-7000. FAX 216-696-7658.
circ. 5,000. *5191*

FORM & FUNCTION.
U S G Corporation, 125 S. Franklin St., Chicago, IL 60606-4678. TEL 312-606-4181. FAX 312-606-5566.
circ. 130,000. *403*

FORMACIO.
Editorial Interpress S.L., Benedicto Mateo 8-10 bajos, 08034 Barcelona, Spain. TEL 34-3-2800522. FAX 34-3-2054620.
circ. 20,000. *894*

FORMAT.
Stilt Press, c/o Alan & Joan Tucker, The Bookshop, Station Rd., Stroud GL5 3AP, England. TEL 44-1453-764738. FAX 44-1453-766899.
circ. 150. *4509*

FORSCHUNGSGEMEINSCHAFT EISENHUETTENSCHLACKEN. SCHRIFTENREIHE.
Forschungsgemeinschaft Eisenhuettenschlacken, Bliersheimerstr. 62, 47229 Duisburg, Germany. TEL 49-2065-9945-0. FAX 49-2065-994510.
circ. 2,000. *2984*

FORSIKRING.
Forlaget Forsikring, Amaliegade 10, DK-1256 Copenhagen K, Denmark. TEL 45-33-13 75 55. FAX 45-33-33-02-71.
circ. 3,000. *3816*

FORTSCHRITTE DER MEDIZIN.
Urban und Vogel, Lindwurmstr. 95, 80337 Munich, Germany. TEL 49-89-53292-0. FAX 49-89-53292-100.
circ. 47,000. *4669*

FORUM.
National Funeral Directors' Association of Southern Africa, P.O. Box 9, Simontown 7995, South Africa. TEL 27-21-967493. FAX 27-21-967493.
circ. 800. *3178*

FORUM.
Office of Court Administration, Vela St., Stop 35 1-2, Hato Rey Station, P.O. Box 190917, San Juan, PR 00919-0917. TEL 787-754-6634.
circ. 600. *3953*

FORUM (SYRACUSE).
Independent Insurance Agents Association of New York State, Inc., Box 9001, Mt. Vernon, NY 10552. TEL 914-699-2020. FAX 914-664-1503.
circ. 3,000. *3816*

FORUM (VANCOUVER).
Association of British Columbia Professional Foresters, 1201-1130 W. Pender St., Vancouver, BC V6E 4A4, Canada. TEL 604-687-8027. FAX 604-687-3264.
circ. 3,500. *3153*

FORUM DR. MED.
Medizinische Fachzeitschriften GmbH, Rosenbergstr. 18, A-2464 Goettlesbrunn, Austria. TEL 43-2162-8735. FAX 43-2162-87354.
circ. 28,500. *4669*

FORUM FOR READING.
University of Pittsburgh, School of Education, 5T01 Forbes Quadrangle, Pittsburgh, PA 15260.
circ. 650. *2603*

FORVM.
Museumstr. 5, A-1070 Vienna, Austria. FAX 938368.
circ. 25,000. *4334*

FOTBALL.
Hjemmet Mortensens Forlag AS, Soerkedalsveien 10 A, N-0369 Oslo, Norway. TEL 47-2-961-500. FAX 47-2-961-382.
circ. 86,354. *6804*

FOTO - VENTAS.
Fopren S.L., Caspe 54 5o, 08010 Barcelona, Spain. TEL 93-301-28-89. FAX 93-412-53-75.
circ. 5,000. *5765*

FOTO VIDEO AUDIO NEWS (DUTCH EDITION).
Mema N.V., Wielewaalstraat 20, 2610 Wilrijk, Belgium. TEL 32-3-4480827. FAX 32-3-4480832.
circ. 6,000. *5765*

FOUNDERS HALL.
St. Michael's College, Winooski Park, Colchester, VT 05439. TEL 802-654-2535. FAX 802-654-2592.
circ. 200,000. *1952*

FOUNDRY DATABOOK & CATALOG FILE.
Penton Publishing Co., 1100 Superior Ave., Cleveland, OH 44114-2543. TEL 216-696-7000. FAX 216-696-8765.
circ. 24,000. *5191*

FOUNDRY MANAGEMENT & TECHNOLOGY.
Penton Publishing Co., 1100 Superior Ave., Cleveland, OH 44114-2543. TEL 216-696-7000. FAX 216-696-8765.
circ. 22,000. *5191*

FRACHT UND MATERIALFLUSS.
Konradin Verlag Robert Kohlhammer GmbH, Ernst-Mey-Str. 8, 70771 Leinfelden-Echterdingen, Germany. TEL 49-711-7594-0. FAX 49-711-7594-390.
circ. 16,333. *7028*

FRAENKISCHES VOLKSBLATT.
Volksblatt Verlagsgesellschaft mbH, Juliuspromenade 64, 97070 Wuerzburg, Germany. TEL 0931-3091-0. FAX 0931-13270. *3284*

FRANCE. COMMISSION CENTRALE POUR LA NAVIGATION DU RHIN. RAPPORT ANNUEL.
Commission Centrale pour la Navigation du Rhin, Palais du Rhin, 67082 Strasbourg Cedex, France. TEL 33-3-88522010. FAX 33-3-88321072.
circ. 500. *7150*

FRANCE. CONSEIL NATIONAL DU CREDIT. STATISTIQUES MENSUELLES.
Banque de France, Service de l'Information, 48, rue Croix des Petits Champs, 75001 Paris, France. TEL 1-42-92-39-08. FAX 1-42-92-39-40. *1040*

FRANCE. CONSEIL NATIONAL DU CREDIT. STATISTIQUES TRIMESTRIELLES.
Banque de France, Service de l'Information, 48, Croix des Petits Champs, 75001 Paris, France. TEL 1-42-92-39-08. FAX 1-42-92-39-40. *1040*

FRANCE AVIATION.
Societe d'Informations et d'Editions Aeronautiques, 25 bd. de Vaugirard, 75757 Paris Cedex 15, France. TEL 43-23-05-02. FAX 43-23-94-02.
circ. 65,000. *66*

FRANCE MAGAZINE.
French Embassy, 4101 Reservoir Rd., N.W., Washington, DC 20007. TEL 202-944-6069. FAX 202-944-6072.
circ. 40,000. *3279*

FRANCE PAYS-BAS.
Nederlands - Franse Kamer van Koophandel, Postbus 90852, 2509 LW The Hague, Netherlands. TEL 31-70-3820551. FAX 31-70-3477975.
circ. 2,500. *1187*

FRANKLIN MINT ALMANAC.
Franklin Mint, Franklin Center, PA 19091. TEL 610-459-6000. FAX 610-459-6880.
circ. 2,100. *5464*

FRAUENSOLIDARITAET.
Frauensolidaritaet, Berggasse 7, A-1090 Vienna, Austria. TEL 43-1-3174020-0. FAX 43-1-3174020355.
circ. 1,500. *7343*

FREE STATE EDUCATIONAL NEWS.
Ficksburg Press (Pty) Ltd., P.O. Box 521, Bloemfontein 9300, South Africa.
circ. 1,000. *2445*

FREEDOM TO READ FOUNDATION NEWS.
Freedom to Read Foundation, 50 E. Huron St., Chicago, IL 60611. TEL 312-280-4226. FAX 312-280-4227. *4179*

FREEDOM WRITER.
Institute for First Amendment Studies, Inc., Box 589, Great Barrington, MA 01230. TEL 413-528-3800. FAX 413-528-4466.
circ. 54,000. *5991*

FREETHOUGHT TODAY.
Freedom from Religion Foundation, Box 750, Madison, WI 53701. TEL 608-256-5800. FAX 608-256-1116.
circ. 400. *6340*

FREIE FAHRT.
Auto-, Motor- und Radfahrerbund Oesterreichs, Mariahilferstr. 180, A-1150 Vienna, Austria. TEL 43-1-89121257. FAX 43-1-89121227.
circ. 400,000. *7100*

FREIGHT.
Freight Transport Association Ltd., Hermes House, St. John's Rd., Tunbridge Wells, Kent TN4 9UZ, England. TEL 01892-26171. FAX 01892-34989.
circ. 14,989. *7028*

FREIGHT & TRADING WEEKLY.
Travel and Trade Publishing (Pty) Ltd., P.O. Box 662, Auckland Park 2006, South Africa. TEL 27-11-7263036. FAX 27-11-7263994.
circ. 3,493. *965*

FREIHEIT DER WISSENSCHAFT.
Vereinigte Verlagsanstalten GmbH, Hoeherweg 278, 40231 Duesseldorf, Germany. TEL 49-211-7357-0. FAX 49-211-7357223.
circ. 11,000. *6527*

FREIZEIT UND SPORT.
Otto Hoffmanns Verlag GmbH, Arnulfstr. 10, 80335 Munich, Germany. TEL 49-89-545845-0. FAX 49-89-54584520.
circ. 2,100,000. *4148*

FREIZEITPLANER NIEDERRHEIN.
Vereinigte Verlagsanstalten GmbH, Hoeherweg 278, 40231 Duesseldorf, Germany. TEL 49-211-7357-0. FAX 49-211-7357223.
circ. 25,000. *7205*

FREMANTLE PORT NEWS.
Fremantle Port Authority, P.O. Box 95, Fremantle, W.A. 6160, Australia. TEL 61-9-430-3438. FAX 61-9-430-4112.
circ. 3,000. *7150*

FREMDSPRACHE DEUTSCH.
Klett Edition Deutsch, Kuehbachstr. 11, 81543 Munich, Germany. TEL 089-623084-0. FAX 089-650256.
circ. 6,500. *4258*

FRENCH - AMERICAN NEWS.
French - American Chamber of Commerce, 1350 Ave. of the Americas, 6th Fl., New York, NY 10019-4702. TEL 212-765-4460. FAX 212-765-4650.
circ. 650. *1187*

FRESHWATER.
Marine Museum Great Lakes - Kingston, 55 Ontario St., Kingston, ON K7L 2Y2, Canada. TEL 613-542-2261. FAX 613-542-0043.
circ. 600. *7150*

FRIENDLY EXCHANGE.
Aegis Group - Publishers, 30400 Van Dyke Ave., Warren, MI 48093. TEL 810-574-9100.
circ. 6,000,000. *3374*

FRIHET.
Frihets Media Ekonomisk Foerening, P.O. Box 11544, 100 61 Stockholm, Sweden. TEL 46-8-714-48-00. FAX 46-8-714-95-08.
circ. 32,500. *5928*

FROBBER.
FROBCO, c/o Embarcadero Venture, Box 2600, Menlo Park, CA 94026-2600.
circ. 200. *2188*

FRONTIERES.
Universite de Quebec a Montreal, Service des Publications, Centre d'Etudes sur la Mort, Box 8888, Succ. A, Montreal, PQ H3C 3P8, Canada. TEL 514-987-8537. FAX 514-987-0307.
circ. 1,500. *6112*

FRONTPAGE.
Newspaper Guild of New York, A F L - C I O, C L C, 133 W. 44th St., New York, NY 10036. TEL 212-575-1580.
circ. 3,800. *3890*

FRUIT PROCESSING.
Verlag Fluessiges Obst GmbH, Diezer Str. 5, 56370 Schoenborn, Germany. TEL 49-6486-8016. FAX 49-6486-6220.
circ. 3,758. *520*

FUELING INDIANA.
Indiana Oil Marketers Association, Inc., 101 W. Washington St., Ste. 1338, Indianapolis, IN 46204-3413. TEL 317-633-4662. FAX 317-630-1827.
circ. 1,000. *5601*

FUER SIE PRIVAT.
V S R W Verlag, Annabergerstr. 283, 53175 Bonn, Germany. TEL 49-228-95124-0. FAX 49-228-9512490.
circ. 9,500. *1610*

FUJIAN LINXUEYUAN XUEBAO.
Fujian Linxueyuan, Xiqin, Nanping, Fujian 353001, People's Republic of China. TEL 86-599-8508080. FAX 86-599-8508194.
circ. 400. *3154*

FULCRUM.
University of the Witwatersrand, Johannesburg, Student Engineers Council, CM 1124-1125, P.O. Box WITS, Johannesburg 2050, South Africa. FAX 27-11-716-5467.
circ. 3,000. *2720*

FULCRUM.
Deep Foundations Institute, 120 Charlotte Pl., 3rd Fl., Englewood Cliffs, NJ 07632-2607. TEL 201-567-4232. FAX 201-567-4436.
circ. 1,000. *2785*

FUNE TO KISHO.
Nihon Kisho Kyokai, Senpaku Bunkai, 9-2, Kanda Nishikicho 2-chome, Chiyoda-ku, Tokyo 102, Japan. TEL 81-3-3295-1525. FAX 81-3-3295-1097.
5231

10334 CONTROLLED CIRCULATION SERIALS

FURNISHING.
Times House, Station Approach, Ruislip, Mddx. HA4 8NB, England. TEL 01895-677677. FAX 01895-676027.
circ. 10,552. *3856*

FUTURES (CEDAR FALLS).
Oster Communications, Inc., 219 Parkade, Cedar Falls, IA 50613. TEL 319-277-1271. FAX 319-277-5803.
circ. 62,000. *1385*

FUTURES (EAST LANSING).
Michigan State University, Agricultural Experiment Station, 310 Agriculture Hall, East Lansing, MI 48824-1039. TEL 517-432-1555. FAX 517-355-1804.
circ. 5,000. *120*

G A P P MAGAZIN.
Varus Verlag Birgit Laube, Koenigswintererstr. 552, 53227 Bonn, Germany. TEL 0228-440015. FAX 0228-440017.
circ. 4,000. *2564*

G E I C O DIRECT.
Maxwell Custom Publishing, 1999 Shepard Rd., St. Paul, MN 55666. TEL 612-690-7200. FAX 612-690-7357. *3816*

G E S BOLETIN DE INFORMACION.
General Espanola de Seguros, Plaza de las Cortes, 2, Madrid 28014, Spain.
circ. 1,500. *3816*

G E W LEHRERKALENDER N R W.
Vereinigte Verlagsanstalten GmbH, Hoeherweg 278, 40231 Duesseldorf, Germany. TEL 49-211-7357-0. FAX 49-211-7357223.
circ. 50,000. *2445*

G F A NEWS.
Georgia Forestry Association, Inc., 500 Pinnacle Way, Ste. 505, Norcross, GA 30071-3634. TEL 770-416-7621. FAX 770-840-8961.
circ. 4,800. *3154*

G F W C OF MINNESOTA NEWS.
General Federation of Women's Clubs of Minnesota, Inc., 5701 Normandale Rd., Ste. 345, Minneapolis, MN 55424. TEL 612-920-2057.
circ. 3,900. *1932*

G I S ASIA - PACIFIC.
Pearson Professional, 159 Telok Ayer St., Singapore 068614, Singapore. TEL 65-6-257-2519. FAX 65-6-357-2518.
circ. 8,000. *3429*

G I S EUROPE.
GeoInformation International, 307 Cambridge Science Pk., Milton Rd., Cambridge CB4 4ZD, England. TEL 44-1223-423020. FAX 44-1223-425787.
circ. 9,350. *3429*

G I S NEWSLETTER.
Geoscience Information Society, c/o American Geological Institute, 4220 King St., Alexandria, VA 22302.
circ. 300. *2314*

G L A FACHBERICHTE.
Bayerisches Geologisches Landesamt, Hessstr. 128, 80797 Munich, Germany. TEL 089-12132600. FAX 089-12132647.
circ. 1,000. *2929*

G M B DIRECT.
General, Municipal, Boilermakers and Allied Trades Union, 22-24 Worple Rd., Wimledon, London SW19 4DD, England. TEL 44-181-947-3131.
circ. 80,000. *3890*

G M I ALUMNI NEWS.
G M I Engineering & Management Institute, 1700 W. Third Ave., Flint, MI 48504-4898. TEL 810-762-9824. FAX 810-762-7435.
circ. 21,000. *1953*

G R I D.
Gas Research Institute, Member Relations and Communications, 8600 W. Bryn Mawr Ave., Chicago, IL 60631. TEL 773-399-8100. FAX 773-399-8170.
circ. 11,000. *5601*

G S B CHICAGO.
University of Chicago, Graduate School of Business, 5801 Ellis Ave., Chicago, IL 60637. TEL 312-702-1234.
circ. 35,000. *966*

G T E AUTOMATIC ELECTRIC WORLD-WIDE COMMUNICATIONS JOURNAL.
G T E Communications Systems, 333 E. First St., Cenoa, IL 60135-1015.
circ. 9,000. *2015*

G V B NIEUWS.
Geementevervoerbedryf Amsterdam, Prins Hendrikkade 108-114, 1011 AK Amsterdam, Netherlands. TEL 31-20-5514351. FAX 31-20-5514527.
circ. 60,000. *7029*

GAAF GOED.
Uitgeverij Cobbenhage B.V., Treubstraat 1N, Postbus 1890, 2280 DW Rijswijk. TEL 31-70-3995108. FAX 31-70-3902488.
circ. 2,600. *3856*

GACETA MEDICA.
Laboratorios Chalver de Colombia Ltda., Av. 68 No. 40-21 Sur, Bogota, Colombia. TEL 571-7100477. FAX 571-2303573.
circ. 10,000. *4670*

GALLIA. SUPPLEMENT.
C N R S Editions, 20-22 rue St. Amand, 75015 Paris, France. TEL 45-33-16-00. FAX 45-33-92-13.
circ. 1,500. *363*

GALLIA PREHISTOIRE. SUPPLEMENT.
C N R S Editions, 20-22 rue St. Amand, 75015 Paris, France. TEL 45-33-16-00. FAX 45-33-92-13.
circ. 1,500. *363*

GALWAY ADVERTISER.
Galway Advertiser Ltd., 2-3 Church Ln., Galway, Ireland. TEL 091-67077. FAX 091-67079.
circ. 33,000. *3322*

GARAGE & SERVICE STATION NEWS.
Garage & Service Station News Publishing Co., No. 204, 260 Raymur Ave., Vancouver 6, B.C., Canada. *7100*

GARAGE TRADER.
Main Stream Publications, 139 Thomas St., Portadown, Co. Armagh BT62 3BE, N. Ireland. TEL 44-1762-334272. FAX 44-1762-351046.
circ. 10,214. *7100*

THE GARDEN DESIGN JOURNAL.
Society of Garden Designers, 6 Borough Rd., Kingston-upon-Thames, Surrey KT2 6BD, England. TEL 44-181-974-9483.
circ. 700. *3189*

GARDEN NEWSLETTER.
Friends of the Georgia State Botanical Garden, 2450 S. Milledge Ave., Athens, GA 30605. TEL 706-542-1244. FAX 706-542-3091.
circ. 1,900. *3189*

GARDEN PESKEM.
University of Queensland, Gatton College, Lawes (via Gatton), Qld. 4343, Australia. TEL 074-601-291. FAX 074-601-283.
circ. 300. *3189*

GARDEN SUPPLY RETAILER GREEN BOOK.
Chilton Co., 201 King of Prussia Rd., Radnor, PA 19089. TEL 610-964-4275.
circ. 27,000. *3189*

GARRISON.
Land Force Central Area, P.O. Box 17, 5775 Yonge St., Toronto, ON M5R 2T1, Canada. TEL 416-733-4781. FAX 416-733-5315.
circ. 11,000. *5269*

GARTENKURIER.
Bernhard Thalacker Verlag GmbH, Postfach 8364, 38133 Braunschweig, Germany. TEL 49-531-380040. FAX 49-531-3800425.
circ. 129,662. *3190*

GARUDA MAGAZINE.
Aerospace Communications Pte. Ltd., 14 Shaw Rd., No. 04-03, BTC Bldg., Singapore 1336, Singapore. TEL 65-344-6465. FAX 65-345-9919.
circ. 75,000. *7259*

GAS APPLIANCES.
Carter Spencer Publishing Ltd., Chancery Ct., Lincoln Rd., High Wycombe, Bucks. HP12 3RE, England. TEL 44-1494-442424. FAX 44-1494-472790.
circ. 30,000. *5602*

GAS INDUSTRIES MAGAZINE.
Gas Industries Inc., Box 558, Park Ridge, IL 60068. TEL 312-693-3682. FAX 847-696-3445.
circ. 11,000. *5602*

GASNYTT.
Svenska Gasfoereningen, Sct. Eriksgatan 44, P.O. Box 49134, S-100 29 Stockholm, Sweden. TEL 46-8-692-1845. FAX 46-8-654-46-15.
circ. 2,500. *5603*

GATEWAY.
University of Alberta, Students Union, Students' Union Building, Edmonton, AB T6G 2J7, Canada. TEL 403-492-5168. FAX 403-492-4643.
circ. 12,000. *1953*

GAZETA DE TRANSILVANIA.
Gazeta de Transilvania, S.A., Mihail Sadoveanu St., 3, 2200 Brasov, Rumania. TEL 40-68-142029. FAX 40-68-152927.
circ. 10,000. *3351*

GAZETA KRAKOWSKA.
Wydawnictwo Gazeta Krakowska Spolka z o.o., Ul. Warnenczyka 14, 30-510 Krakow, Poland. TEL 48-12-563796. FAX 48-12-236557.
circ. 120. *3348*

GAZETA LEKARSKA.
Naczelna Izba Lekarska w Warszawie, Ul. Grojecka 65A, 02-094 Warsaw, Poland. TEL 48-22-6250121. FAX 48-22-6296333.
circ. 125,000. *4670*

GAZETTE DES COMMUNES, DES DEPARTEMENTS, DES REGIONS.
Groupe Moniteur, 17 rue d'Uzes, 75002 Paris, France. FAX 33-1-42333819.
circ. 20,079. *1479*

GAZETTE DES FEMMES.
Conseil du Statut de la Femme, 8 rue Cook, 3e Etage, Bur. 300, Quebec, PQ G1R 5J7, Canada. TEL 418-643-4326. FAX 418-643-8926.
circ. 17,000. *7321*

GAZZETTINO AGRICOLO (PARMA).
Unione Provinciale Agricoltori di Parma, Piazzale A. Barezzi 3, 43100 Parma, Italy. TEL 22-546.
circ. 6,500. *120*

GEGENSCHEIN.
Gegenschein Press, 421 Hudson St., Ste. 220, New York, NY 10014. TEL 212-989-7845. FAX 212-627-1797.
circ. 100. *4408*

GEMS OF GENEALOGY.
Bay Area Genealogical Society, Inc., c/o Lisa Youngblood, Box 283, Green Bay, WI 54305-0283. TEL 414-494-9286.
circ. 80. *3223*

THE GEN.
PowerGen plc, Westwood Business Park, Westwood Way, Coventry CV4 8LG, England. TEL 44-1203-424862. FAX 44-1203-425292.
circ. 16,000. *2689*

GENDER AND DEVELOPMENT DIRECTORY. AUSTRALIA.
Australian Development Studies Network, National Centre for Development Studies, Australian National University, Canberra, A.C.T. 0200, Australia. TEL 61-6-2492466. FAX 61-6-2572886.
circ. 2,000. *7344*

GENERAL-ANZEIGER.
Bonner Zeitungsdruckerei und Verlagsanstalt H. Neusser GmbH, Justus-von-Liebig-Str. 15, 53121 Bonn, Germany. TEL 49-228-6688-0. FAX 49-228-6688178.
circ. 93,674. *3285*

GENERATIONS (WAYZATA).
National Ataxia Foundation, 750 Twelve Oaks Center, 15500 Wayzata Blvd., Wayzata, MN 55391. TEL 612-473-7666. FAX 612-473-9289.
circ. 9,000. *5066*

GENETICS NEWSLETTER.
South African Genetic Society, c/o Department of Genetics, University of Stellenbosch, Stellenbosch, South Africa. *769*

GENEVE LE MENSUEL.
Promoedition SA, 2 rue Bovy-Lysberg, Case postale 5615, CH-1211 Geneva 11, Switzerland. TEL 41-22-8279100. FAX 41-22-3215513.
circ. 15,000. *3363*

GENGO TO KYOIKU NO KENKYU.
Saitama Daigaku Kyoiku Gakubu, Kyoiku Gakubu, Takenaga Laboratory, 255, Shimo Okubo, Urawa-shi 338, Japan. TEL 048-858-3175. FAX 048-858-3690. *2603*

GENRE MAGAZINE.
7080 Hollywood Blvd., Ste. 1104, Hollywood, CA 90028. TEL 213-467-8300. FAX 213-467-8365.
circ. 20,000. *5176*

IL-GENS.
Media Centre, National Rd., Blata L-Bajda HMR 02, Malta. TEL 356-246677. FAX 356-234057.
circ. 12,000. *3334*

GEOFISICA INTERNACIONAL.
Universidad Nacional Autonoma de Mexico, Instituto de Geofisica, Circuito Exterior, Ciudad Universitaria, Mexico 20, D.F., Mexico. TEL 52-5-622-4113. FAX 52-5-550-2486.
circ. 1,200. *2381*

GEOLOGIA COLOMBIANA.
Universidad Nacional de Colombia, Departamento de Geociencias, Apdo. Aereo 14490, Bogota D.C., Colombia. TEL 3681227. FAX 3681326.
circ. 1,000. *2342*

GEOMINAS.
Universidad de Oriente, Escuela de Ciencias de la Tierra, c/o Comision de Publicaciones, La Sabanita, Ciudad Bolivar, 8001, Venezuela. FAX 58-85-26678. *2315*

GEORGESON REPORT.
Georgeson & Company Inc., 88 Pine St., New York, NY 10005. FAX 212-440-9014.
circ. 8,000. *1386*

GEORGIA ADVOCATE.
University of Georgia Law School Association, University of Georgia School of Law, Athens, GA 30602. TEL 706-542-5172. FAX 706-542-5556.
circ. 7,500. *1953*

GEORGIA ALUMNI RECORD.
University of Georgia Alumni Society, Alumni House, Athens, GA 30602-4370. TEL 706-542-3354. FAX 706-542-9492.
circ. 25,000. *1953*

GEORGIA ANCHORAGE.
Georgia Ports Authority, Box 2406, Savannah, GA 31402. TEL 912-964-3811. FAX 912-964-3921.
circ. 13,000. *7151*

GEORGIA COURTS JOURNAL.
Administrative Office of the Courts, 244 Washington St., S.W., Ste. 550, Atlanta, GA 30334. TEL 404-656-5171. FAX 404-651-6449.
circ. 3,000. *4132*

GEORGIA FORESTRY.
Forestry Commission, Forest Education Department, Box 819, Macon, GA 31298. TEL 912-751-3534. FAX 912-751-3465.
circ. 8,000. *3154*

GEORGIA HUMANITIES.
Georgia Humanities Council, 50 Hurt Plaza, S.E., Ste. 1565, Atlanta, GA 30303-2915. TEL 404-523-6220. FAX 404-523-5702.
circ. 11,000. *3779*

GEORGIA JOURNAL - LIVING.
Grimes Publications, Inc., Box 1266, Athens, GA 30603. TEL 404-354-0463. FAX 404-354-6824.
circ. 14,000. *3374*

GEORGIA STATE UNIVERSITY SIGNAL.
Georgia State University, Box 1862, University Plaza, Atlanta, GA 30303. TEL 404-651-2242. FAX 404-651-1045.
circ. 15,000. *1953*

GEORGIA STRAIGHT.
Vancouver Free Press Publishing Corp., 1770 Burrard St., 2nd Fl., Vancouver, BC V6J 3G7, Canada. TEL 604-730-7000. FAX 604-730-7010.
circ. 97,000. *3261*

GEORGIA TREND.
Grimes Publications, Inc., Box 1266, Athens, GA 30603. TEL 404-354-0463. FAX 404-354-6824.
circ. 39,400. *1142*

GEORGIA VITAL STATISTICS REPORT.
Department of Human Resources, Division of Public Health, 2 Peachtree St., S.W., Ste. 3-522, Atlanta, GA 30303-3186. TEL 404-657-6300.
circ. 650. *6065*

GEOSUR.
Asociacion Sudamericana de Estudios Geopoliticos e Internacionales, Casilla de Correo 18112, 11400 Montevideo, Uruguay. TEL 598-2-692953. FAX 598-2-961923.
circ. 1,500. *6016*

GERIATRIC CONSULTANT.
Medical Publishing Enterprises, 15-22 Fair Lawn Ave., Fair Lawn, NJ 07410. TEL 201-796-6500.
circ. 97,500. *3435*

GERIATRIKA.
Alpe Editores, S.A., Pedro Rico, 27, 28029 Madrid, Spain. TEL 34-1-7338811. FAX 34-1-3159652.
circ. 7,000. *3436*

GESAMTSTATISTIK DER KRAFTFAHRTVERSICHERUNG.
Verband der Haftpflicht- , Unfall- und Kraftverkehrsversicherer e.V., Glockengiesserwall 1, 20095 Hamburg, Germany. TEL 49-40-33449-0. FAX 49-40-33449500. *3838*

GESELLSCHAFT FUER BIBLIOTHEKSWESEN UND DOKUMENTATION DES LANDBAUES. MITTEILUNGEN.
Gesellschaft fuer Bibliothekswesen und Dokumentation des Landbaues, Engesserstr. 20, 76131 Karlsruhe, Germany. TEL 49-721-6625148. FAX 49-721-6625111.
circ. 150. *175*

GESELLSCHAFT FUER LOGOTHERAPIE UND EXISTENZANALYSE. TAGUNGSBERICHTE.
Gesellschaft fuer Logotherapie und Existenzanalyse, Ed.-Suess-Gasse 10, A-1150 Vienna, Austria. TEL 43-1-9859566. FAX 43-1-9824845.
circ. 2,000. *5066*

GESTION HOSPITALARIA.
Alpe Editores, S.A., Pedro Rico, 27, 28029 Madrid, Spain. TEL 34-1-7338811. FAX 34-1-3159652.
circ. 6,500. *3707*

GESUNDES TIROL.
Ablinger und Garber, Johannesfeldstr. 2, A-6111 Volders, Austria. TEL 05224-57367. FAX 05224-5736717.
circ. 80,000. *4672*

GET KINKY.
Contact Advertising, 2010 St. Lucie Blvd., Ft. Pierce, FL 34946. TEL 561-464-5447. FAX 561-466-7294.
circ. 30,000. *5177*

GETTING ABOUT BRITAIN.
Drumport Ltd., 21 Church Walk, Thames Ditton, Surrey KT7 ONP, England. TEL 44-81-398-8332. FAX 44-81-398-8322.
circ. 47,000. *7206*

GEWAESSERSCHUTZBERICHT.
Bundesministerium fuer Land- und Forstwirtschaft, Stubenring 1, A-1012 Vienna, Austria. TEL 43-1-714095021. FAX 43-1-711002127.
circ. 2,500. *7293*

GHANA. NATIONAL COUNCIL ON WOMEN AND DEVELOPMENT. ANNUAL REPORT.
National Council on Women and Development, Box M. 53, Accra, Ghana. TEL 233-21-229119.
circ. 3,000. *7321*

GHAQDA BIBLJOTEKARJI.
Library Association, c/o University Library, Msida MSD 06, Malta. TEL 356-32902412.
circ. 100. *4179*

GIFTWARE NEWS.
Talcott Communications Corporation, 521 Fifth Ave., Ste. 1721, New York, NY 10175, TEL 212-292-4520, 212-292-4522.
circ. 42,400. *3449*

GIGAJOULE.
Sasol Heating Fuels, P.O. Box 4211, Randburg 2125, South Africa. TEL 27-11-889-7600.
circ. 3,500. *2670*

GINTONG BUTIL.
National Food Authority, E. Rodriguez Sr. Ave., Quezon City, Philippines. FAX 7121364.
circ. 10,000. *263*

GIORNALE.
Europea di Edizioni S.p.A., Via G. Negri 4, 20123 Milan, Italy.
circ. 300,000. *3326*

GIORNALE DELLO SPETTACOLO.
Gestioni Editoriali A G I S, Via di Villa Patrizi 10, 00161 Rome, Italy. TEL 39-6-4402704. FAX 39-6-4404257.
circ. 13,000. *2294*

GIRL SCOUT LEADER.
Girl Scouts of the U.S.A., 420 Fifth Ave., New York, NY 10018-2798. TEL 212-852-8000. FAX 212-852-6511.
circ. 800,000. *1846*

GLASGOW UNIVERSITY STUDENTS' HANDBOOK.
Students Representative Council, John McIntyre Bldg., The University, Glasgow G12 8QQ, Scotland. TEL 041-339-8541. FAX 041-337-3557.
circ. 8,000. *2446*

GLASS & PORSELEN.
A-S Ursus Forlag og Pressbyraa, Odins gt. 26, 0266 Oslo, Norway. TEL 47-22-43-40-60. FAX 47-22-43-61-43.
circ. 3,000. *1730*

GLASS PRODUCTION TECHNOLOGY INTERNATIONAL.
Sterling Publications Ltd., 86-88 Edgware Rd., London W2 2YW, England. TEL 44-171-915-9600. FAX 44-171-915-9619.
circ. 6,000. *1730*

GLEN BURNIELAND.
9195-H Hitching Post Ln., Laurel, MD 20723. TEL 301-604-8236. FAX 202-835-9608.
circ. 600. *4336*

GLENMARY CHALLENGE.
Glenmary Home Missioners, Box 465618, Cincinnati, OH 45246-5618. TEL 513-874-8900. FAX 513-874-1690.
circ. 100,000. *6340*

GLOBAL CHANGE NEWSLETTER.
Royal Swedish Academy of Science, International Geosphere-Biosphere Programme, P.O. Box 50005, S-104 05 Stockholm, Sweden. TEL 46-8-16-46-48. FAX 46-8-16-45-05.
circ. 10,000. *2349*

GLOBAL CONTACT.
E P S, P.O. Box 40, 4273 ZG Hank, Netherlands. TEL 31-162-403350. FAX 31-162-403802.
circ. 3,000. *4993*

GLOBAL MANAGEMENT.
Sterling Publications Ltd., 86-88 Edgware Rd., London W2 2YW, England. TEL 44-171-915-9600. FAX 44-171-915-9619.
circ. 15,000. *1479*

GLOBAL RISK MANAGER (YEAR).
Regent Publications Ltd., Hadleigh Business Centre, 351 London Rd., Hadleigh, Essex SS7 2BT, England. TEL 44-1702-551556. FAX 44-1702-551511.
circ. 18,000. *3817*

GLOBAL STAMP NEWS.
Brandewie Inc., 110 N. Ohio Ave., Box 97, Sidney, OH 45365. TEL 513-492-3183. FAX 513-492-6514.
circ. 20,000. *5707*

10336 CONTROLLED CIRCULATION SERIALS

GLOBAL VILLAGE VOICE.
Canadian Catholic Organization for Development and Peace, 420 - 10 St. Mary St., Toronto, ON M4Y 1P9, Canada. TEL 416-922-1592. FAX 416-922-0957.
circ. 45,000. *1360*

GO!
Shell South Africa (Pty) Ltd., P.O. Box 2231, Cape Town 8000, South Africa. TEL 021-408-4911. FAX 021-253807.
circ. 1,500. *7101*

GO WEST.
Motor Transport Publishers Inc., 2200 Mill Rd., Alexandria, VA 22314-4686. TEL 916-852-5700. FAX 916-852-5707.
circ. 36,144. *7174*

GOING PLACES.
Intercontinental Church Society, 175 Tower Bridge Rd., London SE1 2AQ, England. TEL 071-407-4588. FAX 071-378-0541.
circ. 5,000. *6341*

GOING PLACES (MINOT).
Box 1427, Minot, ND 58702-1427. TEL 701-839-0809. FAX 701-852-0408.
circ. 40,000. *7207*

GOLD BULLETIN.
World Gold Council, Kings House, 10 Haymarket, London SW1Y 4BP, England.
circ. 5,500. *5218*

GOLDA MEIR LIBRARY NEWSLETTER.
University of Wisconsin at Milwaukee, Golda Meir Library, 2311 E. Hartford Ave., Box 604, Milwaukee, WI 53201. TEL 414-229-4786. FAX 414-229-4380.
circ. 4,000. *4180*

GOLDEN GATER.
San Francisco State University, 1600 Holloway Ave., San Francisco, CA 94132. TEL 415-338-3123. FAX 415-338-3111.
circ. 10,000. *1954*

GOLF INDUSTRY.
Sterling Southeast, Inc., 3301 Ponce De Leon Blvd., No.300, Coral Gables, FL 33134-7273. TEL 305-893-8771. FAX 305-893-8783.
circ. 16,692. *6806*

GOLF MARKET TODAY.
National Golf Foundation, 1150 S. U.S. Hwy. One, Jupiter, FL 33477. TEL 561-744-6006. FAX 561-744-6107.
circ. 9,000. *6807*

GOLF VACATIONS.
Pacom Publications Pte. Ltd., 190 Middle Rd. 14-07, Fortune Centre, Singapore 0718, Singapore. TEL 65-3370255. FAX 65-3394857.
circ. 15,000. *6807*

GONGYE JIANZHU.
Yejin-bu, Jianzhu Yanjiu Zongyuan, 33 Xitucheng Lu, Haidian-qu, Beijing 100088, People's Republic of China. TEL 86-10-6222-5599. FAX 86-10-6222-5938.
circ. 8,000. *895*

GOOD MOTORING.
Good Motoring (Publishers) Ltd., c/o Guild of Experienced Motorists, Station Rd., Forest Row, E. Sussex RH18 5EN, England. TEL 44-1342-825676. FAX 44-1342-824847.
circ. 53,000. *7101*

GOOD NEWS (BIRMINGHAM).
Additional Curates Society for England and Wales, Gordon Browning House, 8 Spitfire Rd., Birmingham B24 9PB, England. TEL 44-121-382-5533. FAX 44-121-382-6999.
circ. 20,000. *6341*

THE GOOD NEWS LETTER (WASHINGTON, 1972).
National Institute for the Word of God, 487 Michigan Ave., N.E., Washington, DC 20017. TEL 202-529-0001. FAX 202-636-4460.
circ. 2,500. *6464*

GOPHER OVERSEA'R.
Veterans of Foreign Wars of the United States, Department of Minnesota, Veterans Service Bldg., St. Paul, MN 55155. TEL 612-291-1757. FAX 612-291-2753.
circ. 85,000. *5269*

THE GOSPEL HERALD AND SUNDAY SCHOOL TIMES.
Union Gospel Press, Box 6059, Cleveland, OH 44101. TEL 216-749-2100. FAX 216-459-1337.
circ. 50,000. *6341*

GOSPEL OUTREACH.
Concordia Gospel Outreach, Box 201, St. Louis, MO 63166-0201. TEL 314-268-1363. FAX 314-268-1329.
circ. 8,500. *6341*

GOSS AND CRESTED CHINA.
Milestone Publications, 62 Murray Rd., Horndean, Waterlooville, Hants PO8 9JL, England. TEL 44-1705-597440. FAX 44-1705-591975.
circ. 1,000. *340*

GOURMET RETAILER.
Sterling Southeast Inc., 3301 Ponce De Leon Blvd. No.300, Coral Gables, FL 33134-7273. TEL 305-893-8771.
circ. 17,389. *3111*

GOVERNMENT BUSINESS.
Momentum Media Management, 4040 Creditview Rd., Unit 11, Box 1800, Mississauga, ON L5C 3Y8, Canada. TEL 905-813-7100. FAX 905-813-7117.
circ. 19,000. *1528*

GOVERNMENT COMPUTER MAGAZINE.
557 Cambridge St., S., Ste. 202, Ottawa, ON K1S 4J4, Canada. TEL 613-237-4862. FAX 613-237-4232.
circ. 13,000. *2174*

GOVERNMENT COMPUTING AND INFORMATION MANAGEMENT.
Government Group Publications, Southbank House, Black Prince Rd., London SE1 7SJ, England. TEL 0171-582-9191. FAX 0171-587-1810.
circ. 11,445. *6209*

GOVERNMENT INFORMATION AND IMAGING TECHNOLOGY.
1224 Daleview Dr., McLean, VA 22102-1539. TEL 301-445-4405. FAX 301-445-5722.
circ. 34,000. *2067*

GOVERNMENT PRODUCT NEWS.
Penton Publishing Co., 1100 Superior Ave., Cleveland, OH 44114-2543. TEL 216-696-7000. FAX 216-696-7658.
circ. 85,000. *6176*

GOVERNMENT PURCHASING GUIDE.
Moorshead Magazines Ltd., 10 Gateway Blvd., Ste. 490, North York, ON M3C 3T4, Canada. TEL 416-696-5488. FAX 416-696-7395.
circ. 17,000. *6176*

GOVERNMENT TECHNOLOGY.
9719 Lincoln Village Dr., No. 500, Sacramento, CA 95827-3303. TEL 916-363-5000. FAX 916-363-5197.
circ. 60,000. *6209*

GRACE TIDINGS.
Grace University, Ninth & William, Omaha, NE 68108-3600. TEL 402-449-2800. FAX 402-341-9587.
circ. 19,000. *1954*

GRAFISK FAKTORSTIDNING.
Grafiska Faktors- och Tjaenstemannafoerbundet, Sankt Eriksgatan 26 III, P.O. Box 12069, S-102 22 Stockholm, Sweden. TEL 46-8-6935597.
circ. 3,500. *6078*

GRAFISKT FORUM.
Grafiska Foeretagens Service AB, P.O. Box 16383, Blasieholmsgatan 4 A, S-103 27 Stockholm, Sweden. TEL 46-8-762-68-00. FAX 46-8-611-61-02.
circ. 4,200. *6078*

GRAND TIMES.
Grand Times Publishing, Inc., 403 Village Dr., El Cerrito, CA 94530-3355. TEL 510-527-4337.
circ. 45,000. *3437*

GRANDE DISTRIBUZIONE E DISTRIBUZIONE ORGANIZZATA.
Agepe Gruppo Editoriale, Via D. Trentacoste 9, 20134 Milan, Italy. TEL 02-215621. FAX 02-2640330.
circ. 41,500. *967*

GRANDS NOTABLES DU PREMIER EMPIRE.
C N R S Editions, 20-22 rue St. Amand, 75015 Paris, France. TEL 45-33-16-00. FAX 45-33-92-13.
circ. 1,500. *574*

GRANITE STATE LIBRARIES.
New Hampshire State Library, Department of Cultural Affairs, 20 Park St., Concord, NH 03301-6314. TEL 603-271-2393. FAX 603-271-6826.
circ. 2,500. *4180*

GRAPHIC ARTS MONTHLY.
Cahners Publishing Company (New York), Division of Reed Elsevier Inc., 245 W. 17th St., New York, NY 10011. TEL 212-463-6836. FAX 212-463-6530.
circ. 85,000. *6079*

GRAPHIC DESIGN: U S A.
Kaye Publishing Corporation, 1556 3rd Ave. Ste. 405, New York, NY 10128-3106. TEL 212-534-5003. FAX 212-534-4415.
circ. 30,186. *6079*

GRAPHIC NEWS.
Printing Industry of Minnesota, Inc., 2829 University Ave., S.E., Ste. 750, Minneapolis, MN 55414-3230. TEL 612-379-6003. FAX 612-379-6030.
circ. 5,000. *6079*

GRAPHICS UPDATE.
Printing Association of Florida, Inc., Box 170010, Hialeah, FL 33017-0010. TEL 305-558-4855. FAX 305-823-8965.
circ. 10,000. *6079*

GRAPHICUS.
Associazione Culturale Progresso Grafico, Via Morgari 36/B, 10125 Turin, Italy. TEL 39-11-6690577. FAX 39-11-6689200.
circ. 6,500. *6079*

GRAPHIX DIRECT RESPONSE.
Graphix Publications (Pty) Ltd., P.O. Box 751119, Gardenview 2047, South Africa. TEL 27-11-6224800. FAX 27-11-6222480.
circ. 3,300. *6079*

GRASSY KNOLL GAZETTE.
Cutler Designs, Box 1465, Manchester, MA 01944. TEL 508-526-1521.
circ. 250. *2268*

GRAVES FAMILY NEWSLETTER.
Graves Family Association, 261 South St., Wrentham, MA 02093-1504. TEL 508-384-8084.
circ. 90. *3225*

GRAVURE ENVIRONMENTAL NEWSLETTER.
Gravure Association of America, Inc., 1200A Scottsville Rd., Rochester, NY 14624-5703. TEL 716-436-2150. FAX 716-436-7689.
circ. 1,400. *6079*

GRAYBAR OUTLOOK.
Graybar Electric Co., Box 7231, St. Louis, MO 63177. TEL 314-512-9200. *2825*

GREAT BRITAIN. NATURAL ENVIRONMENT RESEARCH COUNCIL. BRITISH GEOLOGICAL SURVEY. UNITED KINGDOM OFFSHORE REGIONAL REPORTS.
Natural Environment Research Council, British Geological Survey, Kingsley Dunham Centre, Keyworth, Nottingham NG12 5GG, England. TEL 44-115-936-3100. FAX 44-115-936-3200.
circ. 1,000. *2349*

GREAT BRITAIN. OVERSEAS DEVELOPMENT ADMINISTRATION. REPORT ON RESEARCH AND DEVELOPMENT.
Overseas Development Administration, Abercrombie House, Library, Eaglesham Rd., E. Kilbride, Glasgow G75 8EA, Scotland. *1360*

GREAT EXPECTATIONS.
Professional Publishing Associates, 269 Richmond St. W., Toronto, ON M5V 1X1, Canada. TEL 416-596-8680. FAX 416-596-1991.
circ. 200,000. *4958*

GREAT LAKES GETAWAY.
Camden Publications, 331 E. Bell St., Box 8, Camden, MI 49232-0008. TEL 517-368-0365. FAX 517-368-5131.
circ. 130,000. *7207*

GREAT LAKES PILOT NEWS.
1219 Van Dusen, Ann Arbor, MI 48103. TEL 313-439-8847. FAX 313-769-6471.
circ. 13,000. *66*

GREATER WASHINGTON BOARD OF TRADE NEWS.
Greater Washington Board of Trade, 1129 20th St., N.W., Washington, DC 20036. TEL 202-857-5900. FAX 202-223-2648.
circ. 5,875. *1212*

GREATER WASHINGTON BOARD OF TRADE PROGRESS REPORT.
Greater Washington Board of Trade, 1129 20th St., N.W., Ste. 200, Washington, DC 20036. TEL 202-857-5900. FAX 202-223-2648.
circ. 6,700. *1188*

THE GREEN BOOK: ENVIRONMENTAL RESOURCE DIRECTORY.
Green Book, Inc., 711 Atlantic Ave., Boston, MA 02111-2809. TEL 508-474-5000. FAX 508-474-5054.
circ. 120,000. *2930*

GREEN PAGES.
Murdoch, Walrath & Holmes, 1130 K St., Ste. 210, Sacramento, CA 95814. TEL 916-441-3883.
circ. 6,000. *1683*

GREENHOUSE PRODUCT NEWS.
Scranton Gillette Communications, Inc., 380 E. Northwest Hwy., Des Plaines, IL 60016-2282. TEL 847-391-1000. FAX 847-390-0408.
circ. 20,500. *3210*

GREYHOUND ADVISER.
Greyhound Racing Control Board (Victoria), 438-442 William St., West Melbourne, Vic. 3003, Australia. TEL 61-3-93263422. FAX 61-3-93263415.
circ. 6,000. *5638*

GROCERS REPORT.
Supermarket Productions, Box 6124, San Rafael, CA 94903-0124. TEL 415-479-0211.
circ. 15,000. *3142*

GROCERY DISTRIBUTION.
Trend Publishing, Inc., 625 N. Michigan Ave., Ste. 1500, Chicago, IL 60611. TEL 312-654-2300. FAX 312-654-2323.
circ. 15,000. *3142*

GROENE MARKT.
M'Xpress vof, P.O. Box 66, 5258 ZH Berlicum, Netherlands. TEL 31-73-5034347. FAX 31-73-5034347.
circ. 2,500. *3191*

GROUND SUPPORT EQUIPMENT TODAY.
General Publications, Inc., Box 480, Hatch, NM 87937-0480. TEL 505-267-1030. FAX 505-267-1920.
circ. 14,000. *66*

GROUNDS MAINTENANCE.
Intertec Publishing Corp., 9800 Metcalf, Overland Park, KS 66212-2215. TEL 913-341-1300. FAX 913-967-1898.
circ. 45,521. *3192*

GROUNDSMAN.
Adam Publishing Ltd., 42 West End Ave., Pinner, Mddx. HA5 1BJ, England. TEL 44-181-868-3600. FAX 44-181-429-2374.
circ. 6,000. *6870*

GROUP CIRCLE.
American Group Psychotherapy Association, 25 E. 21st St., 6th Fl., New York, NY 10010. TEL 212-477-2677. FAX 212-979-6627.
circ. 4,000. *6113*

GROUP TRAVEL LEADER.
Group Travel Leader, Inc., 130 N. Broadway St., Lexington, KY 40507-1227. TEL 606-253-0455. FAX 606-253-0499.
circ. 30,000. *7208*

GROWTH AND CHANGE.
Blackwell Publishers, 238 Main St., Cambridge, MA 02141. TEL 617-547-7110. FAX 617-547-0789.
circ. 150. *1585*

GRUE MAGAZINE.
Hell's Kitchen Productions, Inc., Box 370, Times Sq. Sta., New York, NY 10108-0370. TEL 212-245-2329.
circ. 2,000. *4531*

GUIA AUTOMOTRIZ DE VENEZUELA.
Ortiz y Asociados, s.r.l., Av. Caurimare, Qta. Expo., Colinas de Bello Monte, Caracas, Venezuela. TEL 7511355. FAX 582-7511122.
circ. 8,000. *7101*

THE GUIDE (PEACHTREE CITY).
Print Graphics Services, Inc., Box 2752, Peachtree City, GA 30269. TEL 770-631-9159. FAX 770-631-8852.
circ. 40,000. *3375*

GUIDE DE L'INGENIERIE.
Genie Industriel Multimedia, 9 rue Denis Poisson, 75017 Paris, France. TEL 40-63-12-12. FAX 40-68-12-29. *2721*

GUIDE TO EATING ONTARIO SPORT FISH.
Ministry of Environment and Energy, Communications Branch, 125 Resources Rd., Etobicoke, ON M9P 3V6, Canada. TEL 416-235-6220. FAX 416-235-6235.
circ. 300,000. *3069*

GUIDELINES LETTER.
Guidelines, Box 456, Orinda, CA 94563. TEL 510-299-1323. FAX 510-299-0181.
circ. 3,000. *404*

GUILD NEWS.
Graphic Artists Guild, 11 W. 20th St., 8th Fl., New York, NY 10011-3704. TEL 212-463-7730. FAX 212-463-8779.
circ. 5,000. *444*

GULDSMEDEBLADET.
Guldsmedefagets Faellesraad, Ryvangs Alle 26, DK-2100 Copenhagen Oe, Denmark. TEL 45-39-29-52-11. FAX 45-39-27-08-11.
circ. 1,400. *3864*

GULF COAST GOLFER.
Golfer Magazines, Inc., 9182 Old Katy Rd., Ste. 212, Houston, TX 77055. TEL 713-464-0308. FAX 713-464-0129.
circ. 35,000. *6808*

GULF CONSTRUCTION & SAUDI ARABIA REVIEW.
Al Hilal Publishing & Marketing Group, P.O. Box 224, Manama, Bahrain. TEL 973-293131. FAX 973-293400.
circ. 10,200. *895*

GUYANA. NATIONAL INSURANCE BOARD. ANNUAL REPORT: GUYANA NATIONAL INSURANCE SCHEME.
National Insurance Board, Brickdam and Winter Place, Georgetown, Guyana. TEL 592-02-66797. FAX 592-02-52273.
circ. 300. *3838*

H.
Quest, 430 S. Broadway, Denver, CO 80209. TEL 303-722-5965. FAX 303-695-1183.
circ. 7,500. *3695*

THE H E D U BULLETIN.
University of Botswana, Higher Education Development Unit, Private Bag 0022, Gaborone, Botswana. TEL 267-351151. FAX 267-356591.
circ. 800. *2543*

H I V O S MAGAZINE.
Humanistisch Instituut voor Ontwikkelingssamenwerking, Raamweg 16, 2596 HL The Hague, Netherlands. TEL 31-701-3636907. FAX 31-70-3617447.
circ. 9,000. *1360*

H M K KURIER - STIMME DER MAERTYRER.
Hilfsaktion Maertyrerkirche e.V., Postfach 1160, 88683 Uhldingen, Germany. TEL 49-7556-92110. FAX 49-7556-921130.
circ. 38,000. *6342*

H N O AKTUELL.
Dr. R. Kaden Verlag, Poststr. 24-26, 69115 Heidelberg, Germany. TEL 49-6221-10313. FAX 49-6221-29910.
circ. 4,000. *5022*

H P A C TECHLIT SELECTOR.
Penton Publishing Co., 1100 Superior Ave., Cleveland, OH 44114-2543. TEL 216-696-7000. FAX 216-696-8765.
circ. 52,000. *2884*

H R A I NEWS.
Heating, Refrigerating and Air Conditioning Institute of Canada, 5045 Orbitor Dr., Bldg. 11, Ste. 300, Mississauga, ON L4W 4Y4, Canada. TEL 905-602-4700. FAX 905-602-1197.
circ. 1,200. *3479*

H R D I ADVISORY.
Human Resources Development Institute, 815 16th St., N.W., Washington, DC 20006. TEL 202-638-3912.
circ. 2,700. *1432*

H S R C - R G N IN FOCUS.
Human Sciences Research Council, Private Bag X41, Pretoria 0001, South Africa.
circ. 4,000. *6615*

H XTRA.
Two Queens, Inc., 19 W. 21st St., Ste. 504, New York, NY 10010. TEL 212-627-0747. FAX 212-627-5280.
circ. 30,000. *4149*

HABIT.
Mentor Communications ab, P.O. Box 27817, S-115 93 Stockholm, Sweden. TEL 46-8-6704128. FAX 46-8-6616455.
circ. 8,049. *1923*

HABITAT (NEW YORK CITY EDITION).
Carol Group Ltd., 928 Broadway, New York, NY 10010. TEL 212-505-2030. FAX 212-254-6795.
circ. 10,000. *6302*

HABITAT (REGIONAL EDITION).
Carol Group Ltd., 928 Broadway, Ste. 1105, New York, NY 10010. TEL 212-505-2030. FAX 212-254-6795.
circ. 8,000. *6302*

HAFLINGERSPORT.
Reitclub St. Erhard, Haymogasse 19, A-1238 Vienna, Austria. TEL 01-8827224.
circ. 1,500. *6851*

HAFRANNSOKNIR.
Hafrannsoknastofnunin, Skulagata 4, P.O. Box 1390, 121 Reykjavik, Iceland. TEL 354-552-0240.
circ. 420. *3069*

AL-HAHOMA.
Hashomar Hatzair Israel, 7 Bezalel Yaffe St., Tel Aviv 65204, Israel. TEL 972-3-5255666. FAX 972-3-5255667.
circ. 5,000. *5931*

HAIYANG YUYE.
Zhongguo Shuichan Kexue Yanjiuyuan, Donghai Shuichan Yanjiusuo, 300 Jungong Lu, Shanghai 200090, People's Republic of China. TEL 86-21-5434690. FAX 86-21-5432926.
circ. 500. *3069*

HALLASCHKA.
Brueckenhofstr. 84, 34132 Kassel, Germany.
circ. 50. *4337*

HAMBURG AFRICAN STUDIES.
Institut fuer Afrika-Kunde, Neuer Jungfernstieg 21, 20354 Hamburg, Germany. TEL 49-40-3562523. FAX 49-40-3562511.
circ. 300. *5931*

HAMBURGER NOTIZEN.
Vereinigte Verlagsanstalten GmbH, Hoeherweg 278, 40231 Duesseldorf, Germany. TEL 49-211-7357-0. FAX 49-211-7357223.
circ. 12,000. *6215*

HAMILTON ALUMNI REVIEW.
Hamilton College, Trustees of Hamilton College, 198 College Hill Rd., Anderson-Connell Alumni Center, Clinton, NY 13323. TEL 315-859-4680. FAX 315-859-4035.
circ. 19,000. *1954*

CONTROLLED CIRCULATION SERIALS

HANDBUCH KULTURMANAGEMENT.
Dr. Josef Raabe Verlags GmbH, Postfach 103922, 70034 Stuttgart, Germany. TEL 49-711-62900-0. FAX 49-711-6290010.
circ. 2,500. *1480*

HANDELSBESTYREREN.
Handelsbestyrerforbundet, Arbeidersamfundets Plass 1, 0181 Oslo, Norway. TEL 02-20-52-40. FAX 47-2-113194.
circ. 1,450. *1480*

HANDLING AND PACKAGING PRODUCT INFORMATION CARDS.
D M G Trinity Publishing Ltd., Queensway House, 2 Queensway, Redhill, Surrey RH1 1QS, England. TEL 44-1737-768611. FAX 44-1737-761941.
circ. 21,500. *5544*

AL-HARAKAH.
Islamic Party of Malaysia, 28A Jalan Pahang Barat, Off Jalan Pahang, 53000 Kuala Lumpur, Malaysia. TEL 603-4213343. FAX 603-4212422.
circ. 50,000. *5931*

HARDWARE AGE "WHO MAKES IT" BUYERS' GUIDE.
Chilton Co., Chilton Way, Radnor, PA 19089. TEL 215-964-4269. *1684*

HARDWARE AND GARDEN REVIEW.
Faversham House Group Ltd., Faversham House, 232a Addington Rd., South Croydon, Surrey CR2 8LE, England. TEL 44-181-651-7100. FAX 44-181-651-7117.
circ. 14,970. *928*

HARDWARE TRADE.
Screened Porch Publishing Co., 10510 France Ave. S., No. 225, Bloomington, MN 55431-3538. TEL 612-944-3172.
circ. 17,242. *928*

HARDWOOD FLOORS.
Athletic Business Publications, Inc., 1846 Hoffman St., Madison, WI 53704. TEL 608-249-0186. FAX 608-249-1153.
circ. 24,153. *925*

HARSTAD TIDENDE.
Harstad Tidende A-S, P.O. Box 85, Storgaten 11, Harstad, N-9401 Troms, Norway. TEL 47-770-18000. FAX 47-770-18005.
circ. 16,448. *3343*

I T T HARTFORD AGENT.
Hartford, Hartford Plaza, Hartford, CT 06115. TEL 860-547-4959. FAX 860-547-3799.
circ. 14,000. *3817*

HARTFORD DENTAL SOCIETY NEWSLETTER.
Hartford Dental Society, 230 Scarborough St., Hartford, CT 06105. TEL 203-523-8657. FAX 203-523-8657.
circ. 600. *4858*

HARVARD DENTAL BULLETIN.
Harvard School of Dental Medicine, 188 Longwood Ave., Boston, MA 02115. TEL 617-432-1533. FAX 617-432-4266.
circ. 2,500. *4858*

HARVARD UNIVERSITY. GRADUATE SCHOOL OF EDUCATION. BULLETIN.
Harvard University, Graduate School of Education, Appian Way, Cambridge, MA 02138. TEL 617-495-3615.
circ. 20,500. *2447*

HARYANA HEALTH JOURNAL.
State Health Education Bureau, Directorate of Health Services, 36 Madhaya Marg, Sector 7C, Chandigarh, Haryana, India. *6235*

HASSADEH.
G.K. Hassadeh Monthly Review Ltd., 8 Shaul Hamelech St., P.O. Box 40044, 61400 Tel Aviv, Israel. 972-3-6929978. FAX 972-3-6929979.
circ. 8,000. *122*

HAUSAPOTHEKE.
Otto Hoffmanns Verlag GmbH, Arnulfstr. 10, 80335 Munich, Germany. TEL 49-89-545845-0. FAX 49-89-54584520.
circ. 2,100,000. *5665*

HAUSARZT SACHSEN-ANHALT.
B M V - Berliner Medizinische Verlagsanstalt GmbH, Lietzenburgerstr. 97, 10719 Berlin, Germany. TEL 49-30-886749-0. FAX 49-30-88674999.
circ. 2,000. *4675*

DAS HAUSBAU MAGAZIN.
Fachschriften Verlag GmbH, Hoehenstr. 17, 70736 Fellbach, Germany. TEL 49-711-5206-256. FAX 49-711-5281424.
circ. 74,062. *896*

HAUSMEISTER UND HAUSVERWALTUNG.
Rolf Soll Verlag GmbH, Postfach 650680, 22366 Hamburg, Germany. TEL 49-40-6068820. FAX 49-40-60688288.
circ. 15,000. *3748*

HAVEN.
Det Danske Haveselskab, Jaegersborgvej 47, DK-2800 Lyngby, Denmark. TEL 45-93-60-00. FAX 45-93-51-44.
circ. 74,000. *3192*

HAWAII. OFFICE OF THE OMBUDSMAN. REPORT.
Office of the Ombudsman, Kekuanaoa Bldg., 4th Fl., 465 S. King St., Honolulu, HI 96813. TEL 808-587-0770. FAX 808-587-0773. *6215*

HAWAII DENTAL JOURNAL.
Hawaii Dental Association, 1000 Bishop St., Ste. 805, Honolulu, HI 96813. TEL 808-536-2135. FAX 808-536-2137.
circ. 950. *4858*

HAWAII HEALTH MESSENGER.
Department of Health, Communication Office, Box 3378, Honolulu, HI 96801. TEL 808-586-4442. FAX 808-586-4444.
circ. 5,500. *6235*

HAWAII HOSPITALITY.
Rainbow Pacific Publishing Co., Ltd., 1188 Bishop St., Ste. 1512, Honolulu, HI 96813. TEL 808-521-8877. FAX 808-521-8876.
circ. 3,800. *3726*

HAWAII HOTEL NETWORK.
Network Media, Box 88377, Honolulu, HI 96830-8377. TEL 808-955-2378.
circ. 70,000. *7259*

HAWAIIAN ACQUISITION LIST.
University of Hawaii Library, Hawaiian Collection, 2550 the Mall, Honolulu, HI 96822. TEL 808-956-7923. FAX 808-956-5968.
circ. 180. *550*

HAWAIIAN JOURNAL OF HISTORY.
Hawaiian Historical Society, 560 Kawaiahao St., Honolulu, HI 96813. TEL 808-537-6271.
circ. 2,000. *3542*

HAYNES ALLOYS DIGEST.
Haynes International, Inc., 1020 W. Park Ave., Box 9013, Kokomo, IN 46904-9013. TEL 317-456-6000. FAX 317-456-6905.
circ. 11,000. *5222*

HAZARDOUS SUBSTANCES & PUBLIC HEALTH.
U.S. Department of Health and Human Services, Agency for Toxic Substances and Disease Registry, 1600 Clifton Rd., N.E., Mail Stop E-33, Atlanta, GA 30333. TEL 404-639-0540. FAX 404-639-6208.
circ. 10,000. *2985*

HAZELDEN VOICE.
Hazelden Foundation, Box 11, Center City, MN 55012-0011. TEL 612-213-4455. FAX 612-257-1055.
circ. 60,000. *2301*

HE LINES.
Streamline Fashion Publishing Ltd., 6-8 Vestry St., 2nd Fl., London N1 7RE, England. TEL 0171-490-0745. FAX 0171-490-0709.
circ. 10,000. *1915*

HEADLINER.
Kempec Publications, Inc., 19 Maple Way, Mountain Lakes, NJ 07046-1423. TEL 201-785-0764. FAX 201-785-0447.
circ. 2,300. *7101*

HEADLINES.
J R Publishing, Inc. (Boston), 13432 Third Ave., N.E., Brandenton, FL 34202-2729.
circ. 135,000. *4675*

HEADLINES (LONDON).
Newspaper Society, Bloomsbury House, 74-77 Gt. Russell St., London WC1B 3DA, England. TEL 44-171-636-7014. FAX 44-171-631-5119.
circ. 8,000. *3873*

HEALTH AND PHYSICAL EDUCATION.
Taishukan Publishing Co. Ltd., 3-24 Kanda Nishikicho, Chiyoda-ku, Tokyo 101, Japan. FAX 81-3-3295-4108.
circ. 5,000. *2447*

HEALTH & SAFETY NEWSLINE.
Engineering Employers' Federation, Broadway House, Tothill St., London SW1H 9NQ, England. TEL 0171-222-7777. FAX 0171-222-2782.
circ. 8,000. *6236*

HEALTH & SAFETY RESOURCE.
Ontario Natural Resource Safety Association, 690 Mc Keown Ave., P.O. Box 2050, North Bay, ON P1B 9P1, Canada. TEL 705-472-4120. FAX 705-474-5800.
circ. 10,000. *3154*

HEALTH JOURNAL.
Madison Publishing, 263 Summer St., Boston, MA 02210. TEL 617-428-4600. FAX 617-428-4626.
circ. 1,108,229. *5783*

HEALTH LAW BULLETIN.
Institute of Government - North Carolina, UNC - Knapp Bldg. CB3330, Chapel Hill, NC 27599-3330. TEL 919-966-4119. FAX 919-962-2707.
circ. 500. *6236*

HEALTH LAW REVIEW.
Health Law Institute, 457 Law Centre, University of Alberta, Edmonton, AB T6G 2H5, Canada. TEL 403-492-8343. FAX 403-492-9575.
circ. 1,000. *3959*

HEALTH PROMOTION IN CANADA.
Health Canada, Ottawa, ON K1A 1B4, Canada. TEL 613-954-8842. FAX 613-990-7097.
circ. 14,000. *6237*

HEALTH SYSTEMS REVIEW.
F A H S Review, Inc., 1405 N. Pierce St., Ste. 308, Little Rock, AR 72207. TEL 501-661-9555. FAX 501-663-4903.
circ. 60,000. *3709*

HEALTHCARE NEW ORLEANS.
CityBusiness - New Orleans Publishing Group, 111 Veterans Blvd., Rm. 1810, Metairie, LA 70005. TEL 504-834-9292. FAX 504-837-2258.
circ. 25,000. *5783*

HEARING CONCERN.
British Association of the Hard of Hearing, 7-11 Armstrong Rd., London W3 7JL, England. TEL 44-181-743-1110. FAX 44-181-742-9043.
circ. 6,000. *3463*

HEARING JOURNAL.
Hearing Journal, c/o Jerry Laux, Box 188, Harvard, MA 01451-0188. TEL 508-456-4180. FAX 508-456-3159.
circ. 22,000. *3463*

HEARTBEAT (NASHVILLE).
Free Will Baptist Foreign Missions, Box 5002, Antioch, TN 37011-5002. TEL 615-731-6812. FAX 615-731-5345.
circ. 45,000. *6427*

HEARTH & HOME.
Village West Publishing, Box 2008, Laconia, NH 03247-2008. TEL 603-528-4285. FAX 603-524-0643.
circ. 19,000. *2670*

HEARTLAND.
Susquehanna Radio Corp., 8120 Knue Rd., Indianapolis, IN 46250. TEL 317-842-9550. FAX 317-577-3361.
circ. 108,872. *2024*

HEARTLAND RETAILER.
Podany Printing Co., 10310 Ellison Circle, Omaha, NE 68134. TEL 402-496-0717. FAX 402-496-0678.
circ. 14,500. *3479*

HEARTLAND U S A.
U S T Publishing, 1 Sound Shore Dr., Ste. 3, Greenwich, CT 06830-7251. TEL 203-622-3456. FAX 203-863-5393.
circ. 950,000. *5177*

HEAT ENGINEERING.
Foster Wheeler Corp., Perryville Corporate Park, Clinton, NJ 08809-4000. TEL 908-730-4000. FAX 908-730-5315.
circ. 15,000. *2721*

HEATHROW FLIGHT GUIDE.
Mediamark Publishing International Ltd., 35 Gresse St., Rathbone Pl., London W1P 1PN, England. TEL 44-171-580-3105. FAX 44-171-580-1695.
circ. 120,000. *7071*

HEATHROW VILLAGER.
Town Crier Printing & Publisher, 260 Kingston Rd., Staines, Middlesex TW18 1PS, England. TEL 44-1784-453196.
circ. 30,369. *3297*

HEATING AND VENTILATING REVIEW.
Faversham House Group Ltd., Faversham House, 232a Addington Rd., South Croydon, Surrey CR2 8LE, England. TEL 44-181-651-7100. FAX 44-181-651-7117.
circ. 23,265. *3479*

HEATING - PIPING - AIR CONDITIONING.
Penton Publishing Co., 1100 Superior Ave., Cleveland, OH 44114-2543. TEL 216-969-7000. FAX 216-696-8765.
circ. 52,000. *3479*

HEBEI CAIKUAI.
Hebei Sheng Caizheng Ting, Fu 9, Kangle Jie, Shijiazhuang, Hebei 050051, People's Republic of China. TEL 744621. *1090*

HEBEI FAXUE.
Hebei Sheng Zhengfa Guanli Ganbu Xueyuan, Wuqi Lu, Shijiazhuang, Hebei 050061, People's Republic of China. TEL 86-311-6839147.
circ. 5,000. *3959*

HEBREW UNIVERSITY OF JERUSALEM. AUTHORITY FOR RESEARCH AND DEVELOPMENT. CURRENT RESEARCH.
Hebrew University of Jerusalem, Authority for Research and Development, Jerusalem 91904, Israel. TEL 972-2-6586633. FAX 972-2-5664740.
6616

HEILMITTEL AUS DER NATUR.
Otto Hoffmanns Verlag GmbH, Arnulfstr. 10, 80335 Munich, Germany. TEL 49-89-545845-0. FAX 49-89-54584520.
circ. 2,100,000. *296*

HELICE.
Mexican Air Line Pilots Association, c/o Capt. J.J. Castillo A., Av. Palomas 110, Lomas de Sotelo, Mexico 10, D.F., Mexico. FAX 52-5-202-25-73.
circ. 2,000. *67*

HELLENIC VETERINARY MEDICAL SOCIETY. BULLETIN.
Hellenic Veterinary Medical Society, P.O. Box 18281, 116 10 Athens, Greece.
circ. 1,000. *7270*

HELLO ISRAEL.
Tourguide Ltd., P.O. Box 3656, Tel Aviv 61036, Israel. TEL 972-3-490930. FAX 972-3-497640.
circ. 15,000. *7209*

HELSINGIN KAUPUNGIN TIETOKESKUKSEN NELJANNESVUOSIJULUAISU. KVARTTI.
Helsingin Kaupungin Tietokeskus, P.O. Box 303, FIN-00171 Helsinki, Finland. FAX 358-0-169-3777.
circ. 800. *6915*

HEMVAERNET.
Riksshemvaernsraadet (RiksHvr), S-107 87 Stockholm, Sweden. TEL 46-8-788-97-19. FAX 46-8-664-57-90.
circ. 130,000. *5270*

HERALDO DE SALTILLO.
Cia. Editora de Coahuila, Abasolo 228, 25000 Saltillo, Coahuila, Mexico. TEL 52-84-142250. FAX 52-84-148874.
circ. 5,000. *3335*

HERE AND NOW.
Institute of Psychological Research, Inc., 34 Fleury St. W., Montreal, PQ H3L 1S9, Canada. TEL 514-382-3000. FAX 514-382-3007.
circ. 2,000. *6114*

HERON.
Technische Universititeit Delft, Faculty of Civil Engineering, c/o J.G.M van Mier, P.O. Box 5048, 2600 GA Delft, Netherlands. TEL 31-15-2784568. FAX 31-15-2786993.
circ. 2,000. *2786*

HEWLETT-PACKARD JOURNAL.
Hewlett Packard Co. (Palo Alto), 3000 Hanover St., Palo Alto, CA 94304. TEL 415-857-2387. FAX 415-857-2157.
circ. 130,000. *2188*

HI CLASS LIVING.
M N R Promotions, Inc., 111 Charlotte Pl., Englewood Cliffs, NJ 07632. TEL 201-871-2221. FAX 201-871-2223.
circ. 15,000. *3375*

HIFI & VIDEO MARKT.
S Z V Spezial Zeitschriftengesellschaft mbH, Schmiedberg 4, 86415 Mering, Germany. TEL 49-8233-4117. FAX 49-8233-30206.
circ. 13,466. *2639*

HIGH-PERFORMANCE COMPOSITES.
Ray Publishing, 4891 Independence St., Ste. 270, Wheat Ridge, CO 80033-6714. TEL 303-292-4080. FAX 302-292-4181. *5877*

HILDEBRANDT REPORT.
Hildebrandt, Inc. (Somerville), 50 Division St., Somerville, NJ 08876-2900. TEL 908-725-1600. FAX 908-725-9764.
circ. 5,000. *3959*

HILLSDALE MAGAZINE.
Hillsdale College, 38 E. College St., Hillsdale, MI 49242. TEL 517-437-7341. FAX 517-437-0160.
circ. 24,000. *1955*

HILLTOP.
Howard University, 2251 Sherman Ave., N.W., Washington, DC 20059. TEL 202-806-6866.
circ. 10,000. *1955*

HINDUSTAN CHAMBER REVIEW.
Hindustan Chamber of Commerce, 8 Kondi Chetty St., Madras 600 001, India. TEL 583134. FAX 568063. *1188*

HINE'S DIRECTORY OF INSURANCE ADJUSTERS.
Hine's, Inc., Box 143, Geneva, IL 60134-0143. TEL 630-365-1630.
circ. 6,000. *3817*

HINE'S INSURANCE COUNSEL.
Hine's, Inc., Box 143, Geneva, IL 60134. TEL 630-365-1630.
circ. 7,000. *3959*

HIPPOCRATES.
Health Publishing Group, 2 Embarcadero Center, Ste. 600, San Francisco, CA 94111. TEL 415-248-2700. FAX 415-248-2779.
circ. 130,000. *4679*

HIROSHIMA IGAKU.
Hiroshima Igakkai, 1-1-1 Kannonhon-machi, Nishi-ku, Hiroshima 733, Japan. TEL 082-232-7211. FAX 082-293-3363.
circ. 5,800. *4679*

HIROSHIMA UNIVERSITY. RESEARCH INSTITUTE FOR RADIATION BIOLOGY AND MEDICINE. PROCEEDINGS.
Hiroshima University, Research Institute for Radiation Biology and Medicine, Kasumi, Hiroshima 734, Japan.
circ. 450. *5106*

HISPANIC YELLOW PAGES (MCLEAN).
Vega and Associates, 2071 Chain Bridge Rd., Ste. 50, Vienna, VA 22182-2622. TEL 703-903-9779. FAX 703-903-9788.
circ. 100,000. *1685*

HISTORIC NANTUCKET.
Nantucket Historical Association, Box 1016, Nantucket, MA 02554. TEL 508-228-1894. FAX 508-228-5618.
circ. 2,875. *3630*

HISTORICAL GEOGRAPHY RESEARCH PAPER SERIES.
Historical Geography Research Group, Department of Geography, University of Edinburgh, Drummond St., Edinburgh EH8 9XP, Scotland. TEL 44-131-650-2559. FAX 44-131-650-2524.
circ. 450. *3408*

HISTORISCHE TATSACHEN.
Verlag fuer Volkstum und Zeitgeschichtsforschung, Winterbergstr. 32, 32602 Vlotho, Germany. TEL 49-5733-2157. FAX 49-5733-4419.
circ. 10,000. *3572*

HISTORY OF ANTHROPOLOGY NEWSLETTER.
c/o George W. Stocking, 1126 E. 59th St., University of Chicago, Dept. of Anthropology, Chicago, IL 60637. TEL 312-702-7702. FAX 312-702-4503.
circ. 300. *318*

HITACHI ZOSEN TECHNICAL REVIEW.
Hitachi Zosen Corporation, Technical Research Institute, 3-22, Sakurajima 1-chome, Konohana-ku, Osaka-shi, Osaka 554, Japan. FAX 81-6-465-4040.
circ. 2,800. *2722*

HITSAUSTEKNIIKKA - SVETSTEKNIK.
Suomen Hitsausteknillinen Yhdistys, Makelankatu 36A, 00510 Helsinki, Finland. TEL 358-773-21-99. FAX 358-773-26-61.
circ. 5,500. *5222*

HIV FUNDING WATCH.
Texas Department of Health, Funding Information Center, 1100 W. 49th St., Austin, TX 78756-3199. TEL 512-458-7684. FAX 512-458-7683. *6238*

HJELPEPLEIEREN.
Norsk Hjelpepleierforbund, P.O. Box 151, Brun, N-0611 Oslo 1, Norway. FAX 645602.
circ. 48,000. *4933*

HOGAR.
Editores Nacionales, Aguirre 730 y Boyaca, Casilla 1239, Guayaquil, Ecuador. TEL 593-4-327200. FAX 593-4-320499.
circ. 35,000. *7322*

HOGARAMA.
J S A Publishing, 2601 Ocean Park Blvd., Ste. 200, Santa Monica, CA 90405. TEL 310-399-9000. FAX 310-399-1722.
circ. 1,200,000. *3685*

HOJA DEL LUNES DE ORENSE.
Region, Cardenal Quiroga 11 y 15, Orense, Spain.
3359

HOKKAIDO UNIVERSITY. ECONOMIC JOURNAL.
Hokkaido University, Faculty of Economics, North 9, West 7, Kita-ku, Sapporo 060, Japan. TEL 81-11-706-4112. FAX 81-11-706-4947.
circ. 560. *968*

HOKKAIDO UNIVERSITY. FACULTY OF SCIENCE. JOURNAL. SERIES 4: GEOLOGY AND MINERALOGY.
Hokkaido University, Faculty of Science, Nishi-8-chome, Kita-10-jo, Kita-ku, Sapporo 060, Japan. TEL 011-706-3225. FAX 011-716-0394.
circ. 850. *2350*

HOLD PUSTEN.
Norsk Radiografforbund, Lakkegt. 19-21, N-0187 Oslo, Norway. TEL 47-22-11-72-79. FAX 47-22-17-52-04.
circ. 1,465. *5106*

HOLLAND HERALD.
Media Partners International, P.O. Box 2215, 1180 EE Amstelveen, Netherlands. TEL 31-20-5473600. FAX 31-20-6475121.
circ. 170,000. *7259*

HOLSTEIN FRIESIAN JOURNAL.
Holstein Friesian Society of Great Britain & Ireland, Scotsbridge House, Rickmansworth, Herts. WD3 3BB, England. TEL 44-1923-494600. FAX 44-1923-770003.
circ. 14,500. *255*

HOME & AWAY (MINNESOTA EDITION).
American Automobile Association, Minnesota State Automobile Association, Seven Travelers Trail, Burnsville, MN 55337. TEL 612-707-4430. FAX 612-707-4762.
circ. 212,000. *7210*

10340 CONTROLLED CIRCULATION SERIALS

HOME AND COMMUNITY HEALTHCARE.
Sterling Publications Ltd., 86-88 Edgware Rd., London W2 2YW, England. TEL 44-171-915-9600. FAX 44-171-915-9619.
circ. 10,000. *4934*

HOME BUILDER MAGAZINE.
Work-4 Projects Ltd., 4819 St. Charles Blvd., Pierrefonds, PQ H9H 3C7, Canada. TEL 514-620-2200. FAX 514-620-6300.
circ. 25,138. *896*

HOME ECONOMICS NEWS.
Institute of Home Economics, 21 Portland Pl., London W1N 3AF, England. TEL 44-171-436-5677.
circ. 1,700. *3685*

HOMEBRIGHT MAGAZINE.
Media Partners CPR, Northern Rock House, 20 Market Pl., Guisborough, Cleveland TS14 6HF, England. TEL 44-1287-639111. FAX 44-1287-637201.
circ. 2,000,000. *2689*

HOMEMAKERS'S MAGAZINE.
Telemedia Procom Inc., 25 Sheppard Ave. W., Ste. 100, North York, ON M2N 6S7, Canada. TEL 416-733-7600. FAX 416-733-8683.
circ. 1,600,000. *3685*

HOMES MAGAZINE.
Homes Publishing Group, 178 Main St., Unionville, ON L3R 2G9, Canada. TEL 905-479-4663. FAX 905-479-4482.
circ. 100,000. *6302*

HOMEWORLD BUSINESS.
I C D Publications, 1393 Veterans Hwy, Ste. 214 N, Hauppauge, NY 11788. TEL 516-979-7878. FAX 516-979-8182.
circ. 12,800. *3857*

HONG KONG APPAREL.
Hong Kong Trade Development Council, 36-39th Fl., Office Tower, Convention Plaza, 1 Harbour Rd., Wanchai, Hong Kong, People's Republic of China. TEL 584-4333. FAX 824-0249.
circ. 30,000. *1915*

HONG KONG EXTERNAL TRADE.
Census and Statistics Department, Wanchai Tower, 12 Harbour Rd., Central, Hong Kong, People's Republic of China. TEL 852-2598-8197. FAX 852-2598-7482.
circ. 700. *1046*

HONG KONG TOYS.
Hong Kong Trade Development Council, 36-39th Fl., Office Tower, Convention Plaza, 1 Harbour Rd., Wanchai, Hong Kong, People's Republic of China. TEL 2584-4333. FAX 2824-0249.
circ. 40,000. *3450*

HONOURABLE ARTILLERY COMPANY JOURNAL.
Honourable Artillery Company, Armoury House, London, EC1Y 2BQ, England. FAX 0171-628-0949.
circ. 2,800. *5270*

HOPPENSTEDT BOERSENFUEHRER.
Verlag Hoppenstedt GmbH, Havelstr. 9, 64295 Darmstadt, Germany. TEL 49-6151-380-0. FAX 49-6151-380-360.
circ. 3,000. *1144*

HORA DE CIERRE.
Inter American Press Association, 2911 N.W. 39th St., Miami, FL 33142. TEL 305-634-2465. FAX 305-635-2272.
circ. 15,000. *3873*

HORECA NEDERLAND VISIE.
Horeca Nederland, Postbus 566, 3440 AN Woerden, Netherlands. TEL 31-3480-66842. FAX 31-3480-24061.
circ. 15,750. *3727*

HORIZON AIR MAGAZINE.
Paradigm Communications Group, 2701 First Ave., Ste. 250, Seattle, WA 98121. TEL 206-441-5871. FAX 206-448-6939.
circ. 25,000. *7259*

HORIZONTES (SAN FRANCISCO).
Horizontes, Passaic County C.C., 1 College Blvd., Paterson, NJ 07505. TEL 415-641-6051. FAX 415-282-3320.
circ. 19,700. *3016*

HORSE BRASS.
National Horse Brass Society, 69 West Chiltern, Woodcote, Reading RG8 OSG, England. TEL 44-1491-680484.
circ. 500. *3669*

HORSE CENTS.
Canadian Thoroughbred Horse Society, Alberta Division, P.O. Box 172, Etobicoke, ON M9W 5L1, Canada. TEL 403-266-2248. FAX 403-233-8085.
circ. 500. *6852*

HORT EXPO NORTHWEST.
Columbia Publishing and Design, 2520 W. Washington, Ste. 2, Box 9036, Yakima, WA 98909-0036. TEL 509-248-2452. FAX 509-248-4056.
circ. 10,796. *227*

HOSHASEN EIKYO KENKYUJO HAPPYO RONBUN MOKUROKU.
Radiation Effects Research Foundation, 5-2, Hijiyama Park, Minami-ku, Hiroshima-shi, Hiroshima-ken 732, Japan. FAX 81-82-263-7279. *4780*

HOSIERY STATISTICS.
National Association of Hosiery Manufacturers, 200 N. Sharon Amity Rd., Charlotte, NC 28211. TEL 704-365-0913. FAX 704-362-2056.
circ. 1,000. *1920*

HOSPICE TODAY.
Hospice of the Florida Suncoast, 300 E. Bay Dr., Largo, FL 34640. TEL 813-586-4432. FAX 813-586-5213.
circ. 65,000. *6669*

EL HOSPITAL (CINCINNATI).
Salud Publications International Inc., 2724 Erie Ave., Ste. B, Cincinnati, OH 45208-2125. TEL 513-533-5470. FAX 513-533-5474.
circ. 15,500. *4680*

HOSPITAL & HEALTHCARE NEWS.
H. Robert Jacobs Publishing Co., Inc., 2022 E. Allegheny Ave., Philadelphia, PA 19134. TEL 215-739-2033. FAX 215-426-4438.
circ. 46,700. *3711*

HOSPITAL BLUE BOOK (OFFICIAL SOUTHERN EDITION).
Billian Publishing, Inc., 2100 Powers Ferry Rd., Ste. 300, Atlanta, GA 30339. TEL 404-955-5656. FAX 404-952-0669.
circ. 10,654. *3712*

HOSPITAL BUSINESS.
Momentum Media Management, 4040 Creditview Rd., Unit 11, Box 1800, Mississauga, ON L5C 3Y8, Canada. TEL 905-813-7100. FAX 905-813-7117.
circ. 8,700. *3712*

HOSPITAL DEVELOPMENT.
Wilmington Business Publishing, Apex House, London Rd., Northfleet, Kent DA11 9JA, England. TEL 44-1322-277788. FAX 44-1474-569418.
circ. 8,635. *3712*

HOSPITAL FOOD SERVICE.
American Hospital Association, One North Franklin, Chicago, IL 60606. TEL 312-422-3873. FAX 312-422-4579.
circ. 1,700. *5474*

HOSPITAL MANAGEMENT INTERNATIONAL.
Sterling Publications Ltd., 86-88 Edgware Rd., London W2 2YW, England. TEL 44-171-915-9600. FAX 44-171-915-9619.
circ. 10,000. *3713*

HOSPITAL MEDICINE.
Quadrant HealthCom, 105 Raider Blvd., Belle Mead, NJ 08502-1510. TEL 908-874-0707. FAX 908-874-5611.
circ. 34,000. *4680*

HOSPITAL NEWS.
14 Crestview Dr., Box 1018, Westborough, MA 01581-6018. TEL 508-366-2225. FAX 508-366-5030.
circ. 28,000. *3713*

HOSPITALIS.
Hospitalis Verlag AG, Hermetschloostr. 73, Postfach 1632, CH-8048 Zurich, Switzerland. TEL 41-1-4330080. FAX 41-1-4330242.
circ. 11,200. *3714*

HOSPITALITY AND HOTELIER INTERNATIONAL.
Sterling Publications Ltd., 86-88 Edgware Rd., London W2 2YW, England. TEL 44-171-915-9600. FAX 44-171-915-9619.
circ. 10,000. *3727*

HOSPITALITY & TOURISM EDUCATOR.
Council on Hotel, Restaurant and Institutional Education, 1200 17th St., Washington, DC 20036-3047. TEL 202-331-5990. FAX 202-785-2511.
circ. 2,000. *2510*

HOSPITALITY INDUSTRY INTERNATIONAL.
B M I Publications Ltd., Suffolk House, George St., Croydon, Surrey CR9 1SR, England. TEL 44-181-649-7233. FAX 44-181-649-7234.
circ. 25,000. *3727*

HOT SHOTS.
Sunshine Publishing Co., 7060 Convoy Ct., San Diego, CA 92111. FAX 619-278-9081.
circ. 45,000. *3696*

HOTEL BUSINESS.
I C D Publications, 1393 Veterans Hwy., Ste. 214 N., Hauppauge, NY 11788. TEL 516-979-7878.
circ. 45,000. *3728*

HOTEL INC. HOTEL PROPRIETOR.
Manor Publishing Ltd., Unit 7, Edison Rd., Highfield Industrial Estate, Hampden Park, Eastbourne, E. Sussex BN23 6PT, England. TEL 44-1323-507474. FAX 44-1323-509306.
circ. 8,000. *3728*

HOTEL UND GASTGEWERBE.
S H Z Fachverlag AG, Alte Landstr. 43, CH-8700 Kuesnacht, Switzerland. TEL 01-9108022. FAX 01-9105155.
circ. 10,000. *3728*

HOTELNEWS.
Equipotel Feiras Edicoes e Promocoes Ltda., Rua Afonso Celso 797, 04119-060 Sao Paolo SP, Brazil. TEL 55-11-5745166. FAX 55-11-5495049.
circ. 18,000. *3729*

HOUSE BUILDER.
Housebuilder Publications Ltd., 82 New Cavendish St., London W1M 8AD, England. TEL 44-171-580-5588. FAX 44-171-323-0890.
circ. 18,134. *896*

HOUSE EAR INSTITUTE. REVIEW.
House Ear Institute, 2100 W. Third St., 5th Fl., Los Angeles, CA 90057. TEL 213-484-2642. FAX 213-483-8789.
circ. 22,000. *5022*

HOUSE, HOME & GARDEN.
Berkeley House Enterprises, Inc., 809 Virginia Ave., Martinsburg, WV 25401. TEL 304-267-2673. FAX 304-262-4585.
circ. 15,000. *3375*

HOUSEWARES FOCUS.
Faversham House Group Ltd., Faversham House, 232a Addington Rd., South Croydon, Surrey CR2 8LE, England. TEL 44-181-651-7100. FAX 44-181-651-7117.
circ. 4,825. *3857*

HOUSING IN SOUTHERN AFRICA.
Unified Communications C.C., P.O. Box 344, Westhoven 2142, South Africa. TEL 27-11-477-9760. FAX 27-11-673-6218.
circ. 4,000. *3749*

HOUSING POLICY DEBATE.
Federal National Mortgage Association, 3900 Wisconsin Ave., N.W., Washington, DC 20016-2899. TEL 202-752-4422. FAX 202-752-4933.
circ. 4,000. *3749*

HOUSING RESEARCH REVIEW.
Scottish Homes, Thistle House, 91 Haymarket Terrace, Edinburgh EH12 5HE, Scotland. TEL 44-131-313-0044. FAX 44-131-313-1115.
circ. 4,500. *3749*

HOUSING RESEARCH SUMMARY.
Joseph Rowntree Foundation, The Homestead, 40 Water End, York YO3 6LP, England. TEL 44-1904-629241. FAX 44-1904-620072.
circ. 3,000. *3749*

HOUSTON FIRE FIGHTER.
Houston Professional Firefighters Association, 1907 Freeman St., Houston, TX 77009. TEL 713-223-9166. FAX 713-237-0912.
circ. 4,000. *3056*

HET HOUTBLAD.
Het Houtblad B.V., Postbus 1375, 1300 BJ Almere, Netherlands. TEL 31-36-5327331. FAX 31-36-5329708.
circ. 18,500. *925*

HOW TO START YOUR OWN BUSINESS WITH 2000 TO 5000 DOLLARS.
Royal University, Ltd., 6 Lower Hatch St., Dublin 2, Ireland. FAX 353-1-6686632.
circ. 20. *1643*

HOWARD UNIVERSITY MAGAZINE.
Howard University, Department of Publications, Arrupe House, 1400 Shepherd St., N.E., Washington, DC 20017. TEL 202-806-0970. FAX 202-806-4577.
circ. 10,000. *2544*

HUAXIA KAOGU.
Henan Sheng Wenwu Yanjiusuo, No. 9, Longhai Bei 3 Jie, Zhengzhou, Henan 450004, People's Republic of China. TEL 6252066.
circ. 5,000. *365*

HUDIKSVALLS TIDNING.
Hudiksvalls-Tidningens Tryckeri AB, Vaestra Tullgatan 18, P.O. Box 1201, S-824 15 Hudiksvall, Sweden. TEL 46-650-154-00. FAX 46-650-355-30.
circ. 17,000. *3362*

HUDSON GAZETTE.
397 Main Rd., Hudson, PQ J0P 1H0, Canada. TEL 514-458-5482. FAX 514-458-3337.
circ. 1,115. *3262*

HUDSON VALLEY MAGAZINE.
Suburban Publishing Co., 40 Garden St., Poughkeepsie, NY 12601-3106. TEL 914-485-7844. FAX 914-485-5975.
circ. 4,000. *3375*

HULLFIRE.
Hull University, Students' Union, University House, Cottingham Rd., Hull, North Humberside HU6 7RX, England. TEL 44-1482-466269. FAX 44-1482-466280.
circ. 8,000. *1955*

HUMAN GENOME NEWS.
Human Genome Management Information System, Oak Ridge National Laboratory, 1060 Commerce Park, Oak Ridge, TN 37830. TEL 423-576-6669. FAX 423-574-9888.
circ. 14,300. *770*

HUMAN GENOME PROGRAM REPORT.
U.S. Department of Energy, Human Genome Program, Office of Health and Environmental Research, ER-72 GTN, Washington, DC 20585. TEL 301-903-6488. FAX 301-903-5051.
circ. 12,300. *770*

HUMAN RESOURCE MANAGER.
Thorpe Park, Peterborough, Cambs. PE3 6JY, England. TEL 44-1733-555777. FAX 44-1733-312347.
circ. 6,000. *1568*

HUMAN RESOURCE PROFESSIONAL.
Faulkner & Gray, Inc. (New York), 11 Penn Plaza, 17th Fl., New York, NY 10001. TEL 212-967-7000. FAX 212-967-7155.
circ. 1,147. *1568*

HUMANES LEBEN - HUMANES STERBEN.
Gesellschaft fuer Humanes Sterben e.V., Postfach 110529, 86030 Augsburg, Germany. TEL 49-821-502350. FAX 49-821-5023555.
circ. 40,000. *4681*

HUMPHREYS COLLEGE QUARTERLY NEWS BULLETIN.
Humphreys College, 6650 Inglewood Ave., Stockton, CA 95207. TEL 209-478-0800. FAX 209-478-8721.
circ. 20,000. *1956*

THE HUNTED NEWS.
The Subourbon Press, Box 9101, Warwick, RI 02889. TEL 401-739-2279.
circ. 250. *4415*

HUNTER EDUCATION INSTRUCTOR.
Outdoor Empire Publishing, Inc., 511 Eastlake Ave. E., Box 19000, Seattle, WA 98109. TEL 206-624-3845.
circ. 11,000. *6871*

HUNTING REVIEW.
Hunting Group Management Services Ltd., 3 Cockspur St., London SW1Y 5BQ, England. TEL 44-171-321-0123. FAX 44-171-839-2072.
circ. 14,000. *5604*

HUSTON VOICE.
811 Westheimee, Ste. 105, Houston, TX 77006. TEL 713-529-8490. FAX 713-529-9531.
circ. 10,000. *3696*

HYDRA NACHTEXPRESS.
Hydra e.V., Koepenickerstr. 187-188, 10997 Berlin, Germany.
circ. 2,000. *7323*

HYDRAULICS & PNEUMATICS.
Penton Publishing Co., 1100 Superior Ave., Cleveland, OH 44114-2543. TEL 216-696-7000. FAX 216-696-8765.
circ. 52,000. *2872*

HYDROCARBON TECHNOLOGY INTERNATIONAL.
Sterling Publications Ltd., 86-88 Edgware Rd., London W2 2YW, England. TEL 44-171-915-9600. FAX 44-171-915-9619.
circ. 10,000. *5605*

HYDROPNEUMA.
F I M O P - C C I B, 500 Louisalaan, 1050 Brussels, Belgium. TEL 32-2-6407735. FAX 32-2-6408480.
circ. 10,000. *2876*

HYVA ATERIA.
A-Lehdet Oy, Hitsaajankatu 7, FIN-00081 A-Lehdet, Helsinki, Finland. TEL 358-0-75961. FAX 358-0-7596373.
circ. 20,000. *3729*

I A C P - B J A POLICY ISSUES.
International Association of Chiefs of Police, Inc., 515 N. Washington St., Ste. 400, Alexandria, VA 22314-2340. TEL 703-243-6500. *2268*

I A C P TRAINING KEY.
International Association of Chiefs of Police, Inc., 515 N. Washington St., Ste. 400, Alexandria, VA 22314-2340. TEL 703-243-6500. *2268*

I A C V B NEWS.
International Association of Convention and Visitor Bureaus, 2000 L St., N.W., Ste. 702, Washington, DC 20036-4990. TEL 202-296-7888. FAX 202-296-7889.
circ. 19,000. *5170*

I A E A NEWSBRIEFS.
International Atomic Energy Agency, Division of Public Information, Wagramstr. 5, Postfach 100, A-1400 Vienna, Austria. TEL 43-1-23601286. FAX 43-1-2307610.
circ. 8,500. *2697*

I A E A TECHNICAL DOCUMENTS SERIES.
International Atomic Energy Agency, Wagramerstr. 5, P.O. Box 100, A-1400 Vienna, Austria. TEL 43-1-2060-22529. FAX 43-1-2060-29302.
circ. 200. *2697*

I A O STRAIGHT TALK.
International Association for Orthodontics, 1100 Lake St., Ste. 240, Oak Park, IL 60301-1035. TEL 708-445-0320. FAX 708-445-0321.
circ. 2,100. *4859*

I A P I BUSINESS READERSHIP SURVEY.
I A P I, 8 Upper Fitzwilliam St., Dublin 2, Ireland. TEL 353-1-6765991. FAX 353-1-6614589.
circ. 200. *37*

I A T A ANNUAL REPORT.
International Air Transport Association, 2000 Peel St., Montreal, PQ H3A 2R4, Canada. TEL 514-844-6311. FAX 514-844-3788. *7071*

I A T A REVIEW.
International Air Transport Association, 2000 Peel St., Montreal, PQ H3A 2R4, Canada. TEL 514-844-6311. FAX 514-844-3788. *7071*

I B E C - E S R I BUSINESS FORECAST.
Irish Business and Employers Confederation, Confederation House, 84-86 Lower Baggot St., Dublin 2, Ireland. TEL 353-1-6601011. FAX 353-1-6601717. *1586*

I B E C NEWS.
Irish Business and Employers Confederation, Confederation House, 84-86 Lower Baggot St., Dublin 2, Ireland. TEL 353-1-6601011. FAX 353-1-6601717. *1586*

I B M NIEUWS.
I B M Nederland N.V., Johan Huizingalaan 765, P.O. Box 9999, 1000 AG Amsterdam, Netherlands. TEL 31-20-5133813. FAX 31-20-6177600.
circ. 15,000. *2109*

I B M - READ ME.
I B M United Kingdom Ltd., P.O. Box 41, North Harbour, Portsmouth PO6 3AU, England. TEL 44-1705-563799. FAX 44-1705-385081.
circ. 29,000. *2083*

I B W A NEWS.
International Bottled Water Association, 113 N. Henry St., Alexandria, VA 22314. TEL 703-683-5213. FAX 703-683-4074.
circ. 2,500. *521*

I B W A TECHNICAL BULLETIN.
International Bottled Water Association, 113 N. Henry St., Alexandria, VA 22314. TEL 703-683-5213. FAX 703-683-4074.
circ. 2,500. *521*

I C A N COMMUNICATE.
Invalid Children's Aid Nationwide, Barbican City Gate, 1-3 Dufferin St., London EC1Y 8NA, England. TEL 44-171-374-4422. FAX 44-171-374-2762.
circ. 1,500. *2585*

I C A NEWSLETTER.
International Communication Association, 8140 Burnet Rd., Box 9589, Austin, TX 78766. TEL 512-454-8299. FAX 512-454-4221. *1992*

I C A S A L S NEWSLETTER.
International Center for Arid and Semiarid Land Studies, Texas Tech Univ., Box 41036, Lubbock, TX 79409-1036. TEL 806-742-2218. FAX 806-742-1954.
circ. 3,000. *123*

I C A S A NEWS.
International Consortium for Agricultural Systems Applications (ICASA), 2500 Dole St., Krauss 22, Honolulu, HI 96822. TEL 808-956-8858. FAX 808-956-3421.
circ. 300. *227*

I C M R BULLETIN.
Indian Council of Medical Research, Division of Publication & Information, P.O. Box 4911, Ansari Nagar, New Delhi 110 029, India. TEL 91-11-6963980. FAX 91-11-6868662.
circ. 7,200. *4681*

I C S C RESEARCH QUARTERLY.
International Council of Shopping Centers, 665 Fifth Ave., New York, NY 10022. TEL 212-421-8181. FAX 212-486-0849.
circ. 9,000. *6302*

I.D.
Conseil National des Ingenieurs et des Scientifiques de France, 7 rue Lamennais, 75008 Paris, France. TEL 33-1-44136688. FAX 33-1-42898250.
circ. 5,000. *2722*

I E E - AUTOMATISIERUNG UND DATENTECHNIK.
Huethig GmbH, Postfach 102869, 69018 Heidelberg, Germany. TEL 49-6221-489232. FAX 49-6221-489482.
circ. 20,000. *2826*

I E E E SPECTRUM.
Institute of Electrical and Electronics Engineers, Inc., 345 E. 47th St., New York, NY 10017-2394. TEL 732-981-0060. FAX 732-981-9667.
circ. 300,000. *2829*

I E N - EUROPE.
I E N Europe N.V., Rue Verte 216, 1030 Brussels, Belgium. TEL 32-2-2402611. FAX 32-2-2427111.
circ. 50,008. *2876*

CONTROLLED CIRCULATION SERIALS

I E S E REVISTA.
Estudios y Ediciones I E S E S.L., Juan de Alos 43, 08034 Barcelona, Spain. TEL 34-3-2044000. FAX 34-3-2801177.
circ. 15,834. *969*

I F M A WORLD.
International Foodservice Manufacturers Association, 180 N. Stetson Ave., Ste. 4400, Chicago, IL 60601. TEL 312-540-4400. *3112*

I F S NEWSLETTER.
Institute for Fusion Studies, University of Texas, Austin, TX 78712. TEL 512-471-4378.
circ. 400. *2697*

I G A B NEWSLETTER.
International Group of Agencies and Bureaus, 6845 Parkdale Pl., Ste. A, Indianapolis, IN 46254. TEL 317-297-0872. FAX 317-387-3387.
circ. 300. *1993*

I G B P GLOBAL CHANGE REPORT.
Royal Swedish Academy of Sciences, International Geosphere-Biosphere Programme, P.O. Box 50005, S-104 05 Stockholm, Sweden. TEL 46-8-16-64-48. FAX 46-8-16-64-05.
circ. 5,000. *2350*

I G C C NEWSLETTER.
Institute on Global Conflict and Cooperation, University of California, 9500 Gilman Dr., La Jolla, CA 92093-0518. TEL 619-534-1979. FAX 619-534-7655.
circ. 8,000. *6017*

I G C C POLICY BRIEFS.
Institute on Global Conflict and Cooperation, University of California, 9500 Gilman Dr., La Jolla, CA 92093-0518. TEL 619-534-1979. FAX 619-534-7655.
circ. 1,000. *6018*

I G C C POLICY PAPERS.
Institute on Global Conflict and Cooperation, University of California, 9500 Gilman Dr., La Jolla, CA 92093-0518. TEL 619-534-1979. FAX 619-534-7655.
circ. 750. *6018*

I H A BULLETIN.
Independent Healthcare Association, 22 Little Russell St., London WC1A 2HT, England. TEL 0171-430-0537. FAX 0171-242-2681. *3714*

I H K REPORT SUEDHESSEN.
Eduard Roether KG, Postfach 101205, 64212 Darmstadt, Germany. TEL 49-6151-3001-0. FAX 49-6151-314026.
circ. 41,500. *1189*

I L A REPORTER.
Illinois Library Association, 33 W. Grand Ave No. 301, Chicago, IL 60610. TEL 312-644-1896. FAX 312-644-1899.
circ. 4,400. *4182*

I LAISVE.
Friends of the Lithuanian Front, 1634-49th Ave., Cicero, IL 60650. *3016*

I LOVE NEW YORK: THE FINGER LAKES TRAVEL GUIDE.
Finger Lakes Association, Inc., 309 Lake Street, Penn Yan, NY 14527. TEL 315-536-7488. FAX 315-536-1237.
circ. 65,000. *7211*

I M S NEWSLETTER.
UNESCO, SC-IOC-MRI, 1 rue Miollis, 75732 Paris Cedex 15, France. TEL 33-1-45684300. FAX 33-1-45685741.
circ. 5,000. *2405*

I N D A C MAGAZINE.
Indianapolis Athletic Club, 350 North Meridian St., Indianapolis, IN 46204. TEL 317-634-4331. FAX 317-686-4155.
circ. 3,500. *1932*

I N E M BULLETIN.
International Network for Environmental Management, Bahnhofstr. 36, 22880 Wedel, Germany. TEL 04103-84019. FAX 04103-13699.
circ. 4,000. *2932*

I N F O.
Tulsa City-County Library System, Business and Technology Dept., 400 Civic Center, Tulsa, OK 74103. TEL 918-596-7988. FAX 918-596-7895.
circ. 1,400. *4225*

I N T I X NEWSLETTER.
International Ticketing Association, 250 W. 57th St., Ste. 722, New York, NY 10107. TEL 212-581-0600. FAX 212-581-0885.
circ. 1,400. *1529*

I O M NEWS.
International Organization for Migration, 17 route des Morillons, P.O. Box 71, CH-1211 Geneva 19, Switzerland. TEL 41-22-7179242. *6051*

I P A AKTUELL.
A. Bernecker Verlag, Unter dem Schoeneberg 1, 34212 Melsungen, Germany. TEL 49-5661-731-0. FAX 49-5661-73189.
circ. 54,500. *2268*

I P A S E BIBLIOTECA INFORMA.
Instituto de Previdencia e Assistencia dos Servidores do Estado, Divisao de Relacoes Publicas, Biblioteca, Rua Pedro Lessa 36, 13 Andar, Rio de Janeiro, G B, Brazil.
circ. 400. *4226*

I P O ANNUAL PROGRESS REPORT.
I P O, Centrum voor Onderzoek naar Mens - Systeem Interactie, P.O. Box 513, 5600 MB Eindhoven, Netherlands. TEL 31-40-2435200. FAX 31-40-2431930.
circ. 1,500. *4262*

I P P F MEDICAL BULLETIN.
International Planned Parenthood Federation, Regent's College, Inner Circle, Regent's Park, London NW1 4NS, England. TEL 44-171-486-0741. FAX 44-171-487-7950.
circ. 30,000. *6051*

I P P F OPEN FILE.
International Planned Parenthood Federation, Regent's College, Inner Circle, Regent's Park, London NW1 4NS, England. TEL 44-171-486-0741. FAX 44-171-487-7950.
circ. 2,500. *6051*

I P P F PLANNED PARENTHOOD CHALLENGES.
International Planned Parenthood Federation, Regent's College, Inner Circle, Regent's Park, London SW1 4NS, England. TEL 44-171-486-0741. FAX 44-171-487-7950. *6051*

I-PUNKT.
Echter Wuerzburg, Fraenkische Gesellschaftsdruckerei und Verlag GmbH, Postfach 5560, 97005 Wuerzburg, Germany. TEL 49-931-6671-171. *1433*

I.Q.S.
Institut Quimic de Sarria, 08017 Barcelona, Spain. FAX 2056266. *1751*

I S C T S - WORLD SOCIETY OF CARDIO-THORACIC SURGEONS. ANNUAL MEETING.
I S C T S - World Society of Cardio-Thoracic Surgeons, I.P.O. Box 5048, Tokyo 100-31, Japan. TEL 81-3-5660-3230. FAX 81-3-5800-5090.
circ. 500. *4818*

I S P NEWS.
M I S Training Institute Press, Inc., 498 Concord St., Framingham, MA 01701. TEL 508-879-7999.
circ. 25,000. *2286*

I S S A JOURNAL.
Information Systems Security Association, 1926 Waukegan Rd., Ste. 1, Glenview, IL 60025-1770. TEL 847-699-6441. FAX 847-699-6369. *2150*

I S S A TODAY.
International Sanitary Supply Association, Inc., 7373 N. Lincoln Ave., Lincolnwood, IL 60646. TEL 847-982-0800. FAX 847-982-1012.
circ. 4,100. *6238*

I T A A MEMBERSHIP DIRECTORY.
Information Technology Association of America, Publications Dept., 1616 N. Ft. Myer Dr., Ste. 1300, Arlington, VA 22209-9998. TEL 410-543-0475. FAX 410-543-2921.
circ. 10,000. *2174*

I T E M.
R & B Enterprises (West Conshohocken), 20 Clipper Rd., West Conshohocken, PA 19428. TEL 610-825-1960. FAX 610-825-1684.
circ. 24,325. *2833*

I T R.
Technopress Fachzeitschriften Verlagsgesellschaft mbH, Iglaseegasse 21-23, Postfach 176, A-1191 Vienna, Austria. TEL 43-1-322551. FAX 43-1-3207427.
circ. 15,000. *7175*

IBARAKI DAIGAKU KYOIKUGAKUBU KIYO. SHIZEN KAGAKU.
Ibaraki Daigaku, Kyoikugakubu, 1-1, Bunkyo 2-chome, Mito-shi, Ibaraki-ken 310, Japan. TEL 81-29-228-8282. FAX 81-29-228-8329.
circ. 300. *6532*

IBERIAN STUDIES.
University of Keele, Centre for Iberian Studies, Keele, Staffs. ST5 5BG, England. TEL 44-1782-621111. FAX 44-1782-613847.
circ. 300. *6617*

ICE CREAM.
Ice Cream Alliance, 5 Pelham Ct., Pelham Rd., Nottingham NG5 1AP, England. TEL 44-115-985-8505. FAX 44-115-985-7985.
circ. 1,250. *3136*

ICONO PERPETUO SOCORRO.
Editorial Perpetuo Socorro, Covarrubias, 19, 28010 Madrid, Spain. TEL 34-1-4455126. FAX 34-1-4455127.
circ. 12,500. *6344*

IDAHO. DEPARTMENT OF FISH AND GAME. FEDERAL AID INVESTIGATION PROJECTS. PROGRESS REPORTS AND PUBLICATIONS.
Department of Fish and Game, Box 25, Boise, ID 83707. TEL 208-334-3746. FAX 208-334-2148. *2232*

IDAHO BUREAU OF LAND MANAGEMENT TECHNICAL BULLETIN.
U.S. Bureau of Land Management, Idaho State Office, 1387 S. Vinnell Way, Boise, ID 83709. TEL 208-373-3827. FAX 208-373-3805.
circ. 200. *2232*

IDAHO CITIES.
Association of Idaho Cities, 3314 Grace St., Boise, ID 83703. TEL 208-344-8594. FAX 208-344-8677.
circ. 2,250. *6216*

IDEAS FOR BETTER LIVING.
Boulevard Associates, Inc., 724 E. Woodrow Ave., Columbus, OH 43207-2057. TEL 614-449-0133. FAX 614-449-0135.
circ. 250,000. *3686*

ILLINOIS. HOUSING DEVELOPMENT AUTHORITY. ANNUAL REPORT.
Housing Development Authority, 401 N. Michigan Ave., Chicago, IL 60611. TEL 312-836-5200. FAX 312-836-5249.
circ. 5,000. *3749*

ILLINOIS BROKER.
Broker Publishing, Inc., 16921 E. Pallisades Blvd., Ste. 109, Fountain Hills, AZ 85268. TEL 602-816-1400. FAX 602-816-1292.
circ. 61,000. *3818*

ILLINOIS BUSINESS.
Progressive Publishing, Inc., Box 354, Bloomingdale, IL 60108. TEL 630-582-8888. FAX 630-582-8895.
circ. 25,000. *1189*

ILLINOIS DEER & TURKEY SHOW PREVIEW.
Target Communications Corp., 7626 W. Donges Bay Rd., Mequon, WI 53097-3400. TEL 414-242-3990. FAX 414-242-7391.
circ. 20,000. *6872*

ILLINOIS DENTAL NEWS.
Illinois State Dental Society, 1010 S. Second St., Springfield, IL 62705. TEL 217-525-1406. FAX 217-525-8872.
circ. 6,300. *4859*

ILLINOIS POLICE ASSOCIATION. OFFICIAL JOURNAL.
Illinois Police Association, 220 Yosemite Cir. N., Minneapolis, MN 55422-5032.
circ. 17,000. *2269*

ILLINOIS QUARTERLY.
University of Illinois at Urbana-Champaign, Alumni Association, University of Illinois, 1401 W. Green St., Urbana, IL 61801. TEL 217-337-1471. FAX 217-333-7803.
circ. 87,000. *1956*

ILLINOIS TECHNOGRAPH.
Illini Media Co., 57 E. Green St., Champaign, IL 61820. TEL 217-333-3733. FAX 217-244-6616.
circ. 4,500. *2723*

ILLINOIS WILDLIFE.
Illinois Wildlife Federation, 123 S. Chicago, Rossville, IL 60963. TEL 217-748-6365. FAX 217-748-6304.
circ. 12,500. *2233*

ILMAILU.
Suomen Ilmailuliitto, Malmi Airport, 00700 Helsinki 70, Finland. TEL 358-0-35093444. FAX 358-0-35093440.
circ. 10,600. *69*

IMAGE DE LA MAURICIE.
Publicite G.M. Inc., 564 Blvd. des Prairies, Cap-de-la-Madeleine, Que. G8T 1K9, Canada. TEL 819-378-2176.
circ. 10,000. *2256*

IMAGING BUSINESS.
Phillips Business Information, Inc., 1201 Seven Locks Rd., Potomac, MD 20854. TEL 301-424-3338. FAX 301-309-3847. *2123*

IMPACT (AUSTIN).
Department of Mental Health and Mental Retardation, Public Information Office, Box 12668, Austin, TX 78711. TEL 512-206-4540. FAX 512-206-5054.
circ. 23,000. *5068*

IMPACT (NORTH YORK).
Seneca College, Student Federation Council, 1750 Finch Ave. E., North York, ON M2J 2X5, Canada. TEL 416-491-5050. FAX 416-756-2765.
circ. 5,000. *1956*

IMPERIAL CANCER RESEARCH FUND. SCIENTIFIC REPORT.
Imperial Cancer Research Fund, Lincoln's Inn Fields, London WC2A 3PX, England. TEL 44-171-269-3206. FAX 44-171-269-3084.
circ. 1,500. *4979*

IMPORT AUTOMOTIVE PARTS & ACCESORIES.
Meyers Publishing Corp., 6211 Van Nuys Blvd., Van Nuys, CA 91401. TEL 818-785-3900. FAX 818-785-4397.
circ. 35,000. *7102*

IMPULSO.
Universidade Metodista de Piracicaba, Rodovia do Acucar, Km. 156, 13400-911 Piracicaba, Sao Paulo, Brazil. TEL 55-19-4221515. FAX 55-19-4222500.
circ. 700. *6618*

IN CONTACT.
British Red Cross Society, 9 Grosvenor Cresc., London SW1X 7EJ, England. TEL 44-171-235-5454. FAX 44-171-245-6315.
circ. 41,000. *6670*

THE IN-HOUSE LAWYER.
Legalease, 28-33 Cato St., London W1H 5HS, England. TEL 44-171-396-5606. FAX 44-171-396-9301.
circ. 5,500. *3962*

IN OLTRE.
Schena Editore, Viale le Stazione 177, 72015 Fasano (BR), Italy. TEL 080-71-46-81. FAX 80714690.
circ. 1,000. *4415*

IN ONTARIO.
Insurance Institute of Ontario, 18 King St., E., 6th Fl., Toronto, ON M5C 1C4, Canada. TEL 416-362-8586. FAX 416-362-1126.
circ. 15,000. *3818*

IN OTHER WORDS.
Wycliffe Bible Translators, Inc., Box 2727, Huntington Beach, CA 92647. TEL 714-969-4600. FAX 714-969-4661.
circ. 300,000. *6344*

IN THE DRIVER'S SEAT.
Ontario Safety League, 21 Four Seasons Place, Etobicoke, ON M9B 6J8, Canada. TEL 416-620-1720. *7102*

INCENTIVE & MEETINGS ASIA.
Miller Freeman Pte. Ltd., 100 Beach Rd., 26-00 Shaw Towers, Singapore 189702, Singapore. TEL 65-294-3366. FAX 65-298-5534.
circ. 10,808. *5170*

INCENTIVE TAXATION.
Center for the Study of Economics, 2000 Century Plaza (238), Columbia, MD 21044. TEL 410-740-1177. FAX 410-740-3279.
circ. 4,500. *3749*

INDEPENDENT BOOKSELLING TODAY!
Paz & Associates, 2106 20th Ave. S., Nashville, TN 37212-4312. TEL 800-260-8605. FAX 615-298-9864.
circ. 400. *6273*

INDEPENDENT BUSINESS.
Group IV Communications, Inc., 125 Auburn Ct., Ste. 100, Thousand Oaks, CA 91362-3617. TEL 805-496-6156. FAX 805-496-5469.
circ. 600,000. *971*

INDEPENDENT GASOLINE MARKETING.
Society of Independent Gasoline Marketers of America, 11911 Freedom Dr., No. 590, Reston, VA 20190-5602. TEL 703-709-7000. FAX 703-709-7007.
circ. 5,500. *5605*

INDEPENDENT HEALTH FACILITIES.
Sterling Publications Ltd., 86-88 Edgware Rd., London W2 2YW, England. TEL 44-171-915-9600. FAX 44-171-915-9619.
circ. 10,000. *3714*

INDEX NEW ZEALAND.
National Library of New Zealand, P.O. Box 1467, Wellington, New Zealand. TEL 64-4-4743098. FAX 64-4-4753124.
circ. 400. *15*

INDEX TO PHILIPPINE PERIODICALS.
University of the Philippines Diliman, University Library, Gonzalez Hall, Diliman, Quezon City 1101, Philippines. TEL 632-9205301. FAX 632-9292180.
circ. 93. *551*

INDIA. CENTRAL VIGILANCE COMMISSION. REPORT.
Central Vigilance Commission, No.3, Dr. Rajendra Prasad Road, New Delhi, India. *6178*

INDIA. DEPARTMENT OF SPACE. ANNUAL REPORT.
Department of Space, Antariksh Bhavan, New Bel Rd., Bangalore 560094, India. TEL 080-3334474. FAX 080-3332253.
circ. 5,000. *69*

INDIA. MINISTRY OF EDUCATION AND SOCIAL WELFARE. DEPARTMENT OF SOCIAL WELFARE. DOCUMENTATION SERVICE BULLETIN.
Ministry of Education and Social Welfare, Department of Social Welfare, Shastri Bhavan, New Delhi 110001, India. *6650*

INDIA. MINISTRY OF EDUCATION AND SOCIAL WELFARE. PROVISIONAL STATISTICS OF EDUCATION IN THE STATES.
Ministry of Education and Social Welfare, Department of Education, Shastri Bhavan, New Delhi 110001, India. *2501*

INDIA. MINISTRY OF FINANCE. FINANCE LIBRARY. WEEKLY BULLETIN.
Ministry of Finance, Finance Library, North Block, New Delhi 110001, India. TEL 3013852. *1145*

INDIAN CHEMICALS AND PHARMACEUTICALS STATISTICS.
Ministry of Chemicals and Fertilizers, Economics and Statistics Division, New Delhi, India. *5701*

INDIAN CRUSADER.
American Indian Liberation Crusade, Inc., 4009 Halldale Ave., Los Angeles, CA 90062. TEL 213-299-1810.
circ. 4,000. *3017*

INDIAN EDUCATION ABSTRACTS.
Ministry of Education and Social Welfare, Department of Education, Shastri Bhavan, New Dehli 110001, India. *2501*

INDIAN FERTILISER STATISTICS.
Ministry of Chemicals and Fertilisers, Economics and Statistics Division, New Delhi, India. *176*

INDIAN INSTITUTE OF TROPICAL METEOROLOGY. ANNUAL REPORT.
Indian Institute of Tropical Meteorology, Dr. Homi Bhabha Rd., Pashan, Pune 411 008, India. *5234*

INDIAN JOURNAL OF MEDICAL RESEARCH. SECTION A: INFECTIOUS DISEASES.
Indian Council of Medical Research, Division of Publication & Information, P.O. Box 4911, Ansari Nagar, New Delhi 110 029, India. TEL 91-11-6963980. FAX 91-11-6868662.
circ. 700. *4683*

INDIAN PETROLEUM AND NATURAL GAS STATISTICS.
Ministry of Petroleum & Chemicals, Department of Petroleum & Natural Gas, Economics and Statistics Division, Shastri Bhawan, New Delhi 110 001, India. FAX 66235. *5630*

INDIAN VACUUM SOCIETY. BULLETIN.
Indian Vacuum Society, c/o Technical Physics & Prototype Engineering Division, Bhabha Atomic Research Centre, Mumbai 400 085, India. TEL 91-22-556-3060. FAX 91-22-556-0750.
circ. 800. *5806*

INDIANA CONSTRUCTOR.
I B J Corp., 431 N. Pennsylvania St., Indianapolis, IN 46204. TEL 317-634-6200. FAX 317-263-5060.
circ. 3,500. *897*

INDIANA CONTRACTOR.
Indiana Association of Plumbing - Heating - Cooling Contractors, Inc., Box 40963, Indianapolis, IN 46240. TEL 317-575-9292. FAX 317-575-9378.
circ. 5,579. *3480*

INDIANA MUSICATOR.
Indiana Music Educators Association, Ball State University, School of Music, Muncie, IN 47306. TEL 765-285-5496. FAX 765-285-1139.
circ. 2,000. *5400*

INDIANA PUBLISHER.
Hoosier State Press Association, Inc., 300 Consolidated Building, 1 Virginia Ave., Ste. 701, Indianapolis, IN 46204-3616. TEL 317-637-3966. FAX 317-624-4428. *3874*

INDIANA TIMETRIP.
Department of Commerce, Division of Tourism, 1 N. Capitol, Ste. 700, Indianapolis, IN 46204. TEL 317-232-8800.
circ. 250,000. *3631*

INDIANA UNIVERSITY. SCHOOL OF LIBRARY & INFORMATION SCIENCES. ALUMNI NEWSLETTER.
Indiana University, Alumni Association, 1000 E. 17th St., Bloomington, IN 47408. TEL 812-855-5844. FAX 812-855-4228.
circ. 3,800. *4183*

INDIANAPOLIS C.E.O.
Metropolitan C.E.O., 911 E. 86th St., Ste. 100, Indianapolis, IN 46240-1840. TEL 317-257-8000. FAX 317-257-1482.
circ. 30,000. *1482*

INDO - U S BUSINESS.
Indo-American Chamber of Commerce, Vulcan Insurance Bldg., Veer Nariman Rd., Churchgate, Bombay 400 020, India.
circ. 1,800. *1189*

INDOCHINA NEWSLETTER.
Asia Resource Center, 2161 Massachusetts Ave., Cambridge, MA 02140. TEL 617-497-5273. FAX 617-354-2832.
circ. 1,000. *6018*

INDONESIA. DIREKTORAT PERUMAHAN RAKJAT. LAPORAN KERDJA.
Direktorat Perumahan Rakjat, Jalan Wijaya I-68, Kebayoran Baru, Jakarta, Indonesia. *3749*

INDOOR COMFORT NEWS.
Institute of Heating & Air Conditioning Industries, 454 W. Broadway, Glendale, CA 91204. TEL 818-551-1555. FAX 818-551-1115.
circ. 20,000. *3480*

INDRESCO INC. MARION DIVISION. NEWS AND REVIEW.
Indresco Inc., Marion Division, 617 W. Center St., Box 505, Marion, OH 43302. TEL 614-383-5211. FAX 614-382-2052.
circ. 7,500. *4545*

INDRETNINGSHAANDBOGEN.
NOVA Kommunikation A-S, P.O. Box 146, DK-3450 Alleroed, Denmark. TEL 45-48-17-00-78. FAX 45-48-17-13-65.
circ. 12,000. *1687*

INDUSTRIA ALIMENTARIA.
Alfa Editores Tecnicos S.A., Libertad No. 107-402, 03660 Mexico DF, Mexico. TEL 525-579-3333. FAX 525-532-9504.
circ. 5,000. *3113*

INDUSTRIA ALIMENTICIA.
Stagnito Publishing Company, 1935 Shermer Rd., Ste. 100, Northbrook, IL 60062. TEL 847-205-5660. FAX 847-205-5680.
circ. 20,000. *3113*

INDUSTRIA INTERNACIONAL.
Publicaciones Internacionales S.A., Paseo de Castellana 210, 28046 Madrid, Spain. TEL 1-457-08-06. FAX 1-457-29-38.
circ. 6,000. *1586*

INDUSTRIA PORCINA.
Watt Publishing Co., 122 S. Wesley Ave., Mt. Morris, IL 61054. TEL 815-734-4171. FAX 815-734-4201.
circ. 8,842. *278*

INDUSTRIA TURISTICA.
Charles Francis Publications, Inc., Box 52-1898, Miami, FL 33152-1898. TEL 305-592-3168.
circ. 6,000. *7212*

INDUSTRIAL AND LABOR RELATIONS REVIEW.
Cornell University, New York State School of Industrial and Labor Relations, Ithaca, NY 14853-3901. TEL 607-255-2732. FAX 607-255-8016.
circ. 400. *1435*

INDUSTRIAL COMPUTING.
E M A P Business & Computer Publications Ltd., 33-39 Bowling Green Ln., London EC1R 0DA, England. TEL 44-171-837-1212. FAX 44-171-278-4008.
circ. 15,002. *2084*

INDUSTRIAL COMPUTING.
I S A Services, Inc., 67 Alexander Dr., Box 12277, Research Triangle Park, NC 27709. TEL 919-549-8411. FAX 919-832-0237.
circ. 40,000. *2109*

INDUSTRIAL DIAMOND REVIEW.
De Beers Industrial Diamond Division (UK), Charters, Sunninghill, Ascot, Berks. SL5 9PX, England. TEL 44-1344-23456. FAX 44-1344-28188.
circ. 10,000. *6962*

INDUSTRIAL ENVIRONMENTAL MANAGEMENT.
Faversham House Group Ltd., Faversham House, 232a Addington Rd., South Croydon, Surrey CR2 8LE, England. TEL 44-181-651-7100. FAX 44-181-651-7117.
circ. 8,128. *2986*

INDUSTRIAL HEATING.
Business News Publishing Company, 755 W. Big Beaver Rd., Ste. 1000, Troy, MI 48084. TEL 810-362-3700. FAX 810-362-0317.
circ. 22,500. *2876*

INDUSTRIAL LOCOMOTIVE.
Industrial Locomotive Society, Byfield, Wreford's Ln., Exeter, Devon EX4 5BR, England. TEL 01793-692588.
circ. 350. *7126*

INDUSTRIAL NOTTINGHAMSHIRE.
Nottinghamshire Chamber of Commerce and Industry, 395 Mansfield Rd., Nottingham NG5 2DL, England. TEL 0602-624624. FAX 0602-605981.
circ. 2,500. *1189*

INDUSTRIAL PROGRESS.
Donnelly Marketing, 1717 Park St., Ste. 250, Naperville, IL 60563-8479.
circ. 60,000. *6962*

INDUSTRIAL PUERTO RICO.
Antilles Publishing, 721 Hernandez St., Miramar Towers, Apt. 12B, Santurce 00908, PR 00901.
circ. 7,500. *1587*

INDUSTRIAL SYSTEMS.
Business & Management Editions Brussels s.p.r.l., Rue Stephanie, 17, 1020 Brussels, Belgium. TEL 32-2-4266115. FAX 32-2-4258226.
circ. 20,000. *2876*

INDUSTRIAL TEACHER EDUCATION DIRECTORY.
National Association of Industrial and Technical Teacher Educators, Dept. of Industrial Technology, University of Northern Iowa, Cedar Falls, IA 50615-0178. TEL 319-273-2753. FAX 319-273-5818.
circ. 3,800. *2545*

INDUSTRIAL WOODWORKER.
Willowe Magazines Ltd., 47-49 Cinque Ports St., Rye, E. Sussex TN31 7AN, England. TEL 44-1797-227300. FAX 44-1797-222445.
circ. 13,000. *925*

INDUSTRIE MEISTER.
Vogel Verlag und Druck GmbH & Co. KG, Max-Planck-Str. 7-9, 97082 Wuerzburg, Germany. TEL 49-931-4182145. FAX 49-931-4182905.
circ. 15,922. *1587*

INDUSTRY WEEK.
Penton Publishing Co., 1100 Superior Ave., Cleveland, OH 44114-2543. TEL 216-696-7000. FAX 216-969-7670.
circ. 233,000. *1482*

INDY'S CHILD.
Indy's Child, Inc., 6502 E. Westfield Blvd., Indianapolis, IN 46220-1110. TEL 317-843-1494. FAX 317-574-3233.
circ. 70,000. *1847*

INFARMA.
Conselho Federal de Farmacia, SBS Quadra 01, Bloco K, 70093-900 Brasilia D.F., Brazil. TEL 061-224-68-49. FAX 061-224-68-25.
circ. 10,000. *5667*

INFECTIONS IN MEDICINE.
S C P Communications, Inc., 134 W. 29th St., New York, NY 10001-5304. TEL 212-714-1740.
circ. 36,000. *4837*

INFIRMIERE DU QUEBEC.
Ordre des Infirmieres et Infirmiers du Quebec, 4200 Dorchester Blvd. W., Montreal, PQ H3Z 1V4, Canada. TEL 514-935-2501. FAX 514-935-2055.
circ. 61,803. *4934*

INFO MAGAZINE.
Union Pacific Railroad, Employee Communications Department, 1416 Dodge St., Omaha, NE 68179.
circ. 78,000. *7126*

INFOPACK E & E.
Ediciones Press Graph, S.L., C. Mallorca 219 5o 2o, 08008 Barcelona, Spain. TEL 34-3-3237554. FAX 34-3-3237463.
circ. 7,000. *5544*

INFORM-ACTION.
Manitoba Teachers Society, 191 Harcourt St., Winnipeg, MB R3J 3H2, Canada. TEL 204-888-7961. FAX 204-831-0877.
circ. 1,850. *4263*

INFORMAL LOGIC.
Department of Philosophy, University of Windsor, Windsor, ON N9B 3P4, Canada. TEL 519-253-4232. FAX 519-973-7050.
circ. 300. *5731*

INFORMATICA 70.
Editrice il Crogiolo S.r.l., Piazza Sant Agostino 22, 20123 Milan, Italy. TEL 39-2-48009805. FAX 39-2-48009749.
circ. 4,875. *4231*

INFORMATION DISPLAY.
Society for Information Display, 1526 Brookhollow Dr., Ste. 82, Santa Ana, CA 92705-5421. TEL 714-545-1526. FAX 714-545-1547.
circ. 10,000. *4232*

INFORMATION FUER DIE TRUPPE.
Bundesministerium der Verteidigung, Fue SI 4, Postfach 1328, 53003 Bonn, Germany. *5271*

INFORMATION LEGISLATIVE SERVICE.
Pennsylvania School Boards Association, 774 Limekiln Rd., New Cumberland, PA 17070-2398. TEL 717-774-2331. FAX 717-774-0718.
circ. 11,300. *2450*

INFORMATION RESOURCES MANAGEMENT JOURNAL.
Idea Group Publishing, 1331 E. Chocolate Ave., Hershey, PA 17033-1117. TEL 717-541-9150. FAX 717-541-9159.
circ. 500. *1482*

INFORMATION TECHNOLOGY REVIEW.
Price Waterhouse, 32 London Bridge St., London SE1 9SY, England. TEL 44-171-939-6283. FAX 44-171-403-5265.
circ. 25,000. *2170*

INFORMATION TECHNOLOGY SOLUTIONS EUROPE.
Sterling Publications Ltd., 86-88 Edgware Rd., London W2 2YW, England. TEL 44-171-915-9600. FAX 44-171-915-9619.
circ. 15,000. *2175*

INFORMATIONEN UND BERICHTE.
Braunschweigisches Landesmuseum, Burgplatz 1, 38100 Braunschweig, Germany. TEL 49-531-4842602. FAX 49-531-4842607.
circ. 1,000. *366*

INFORMATIONSDIENST PRAXISBEZOGENER LITERATUR IM WEINBAU.
Bundesanstalt fuer Zuechtungsforschung an Kulturpflanzen, Institut fuer Rebenzuechtung Geilweilerhof, 76833 Siebeldingen, Germany. TEL 49-6345-41-0. FAX 49-6345-41177.
circ. 150. *176*

L'INFORMATORE AGRARIO.
Edizione L' Informatore Agrario s.r.l., Lungadige Galtarossa 23-E, 37123 Verona, Italy. TEL 39-45-597855. FAX 39-45-597510.
circ. 40,111. *125*

INFORMATORE DI VETERINARIA E ZOOTECNIA.
Organizzazione Editoriale Medico Farmaceutica, Via Edolo 42, 20125 Milan, Italy. TEL 39-2-675051. FAX 39-2-67505223.
circ. 45,000. *7271*

INFORME DE OPERACION DE LAS PRINCIPALES EMPRESAS PRODUCTORAS Y DISTRIBUIDORAS DE ENERGIA ELECTRICA DE COSTA RICA.
Instituto Costarricense de Electricidad (ICE), Apdo. 10032, 1000 San Jose, Costa Rica. TEL 506-2-207741. FAX 506-2-208204. *2834*

INFRASTRUCTURE FINANCE.
Institutional Investor, Inc., 488 Madison Ave., New York, NY 10022. TEL 212-224-3570. FAX 212-224-3592.
circ. 16,000. *1362*

INGENIERIA CIVIL.
Obsidiana Editores, S.A., Czda. de Tlalpan 2365, Col. Ciudad Jardin, 04370 Mexico DF, Mexico. TEL 6899133.
circ. 3,900. *2787*

INGENIERIA DE COSTOS.
D'Pastrana Editores, S.A., Kepler 147-A, Mexico 5, D.F., Mexico.
circ. 5,000. *1483*

INGENIEUR ET INDUSTRIE.
Association pour la Promotion des Publications Scientifiques (APPS), 26 av. de l'Amarante, B-1020 Brussels, Belgium. TEL 32-2-268-29-33. FAX 32-2-268-25-14.
circ. 20,000. *2724*

INGENJOEREN.
Ingenjoersfoerbundet, P.O. Box 302 25, S-104 25 Stockholm, Sweden.
circ. 8,700. *2724*

INITIATIVE.
German British Chamber of Industry and Commerce, 16 Buckingham Gate, London SW1E 6LB, England. TEL 071-233-5656. FAX 071-233-7835.
circ. 4,000. *1330*

INJECTION MOLDING.
55 Madison St., Ste 770, Denver, CO 80206. TEL 303-321-2322. FAX 303-321-3552.
circ. 37,500. *5878*

INLAND.
Inland Steel Flat Product Co., 30 W. Monroe St., Chicago, IL 60603. TEL 312-346-0300.
circ. 12,000. *3376*

INNER CIRCLE LETTER.
Nelson Newsletter Publishing Corp., Box 41630, Tucson, AZ 85717-1630. TEL 520-629-0434. FAX 520-629-0387. *3669*

INNIS HERALD.
University of Toronto, Innis College Student Society, 2 Sussex Ave., Toronto, ON M5S 1A1, Canada. TEL 416-978-4748. FAX 416-978-5503.
circ. 1,500. *1956*

INNISFAIL BOOSTER.
4932 49th St., Innisfail, AB T4G 1N2, Canada. TEL 403-227-3477.
circ. 7,500. *3262*

INNOMINATE.
Sydney University Medical Society, Blackburn Bldg. D06, University of Sydney, Sydney, N.S.W. 2006, Australia. TEL 61-2-9351-2635. FAX 61-2-9351-6198.
circ. 800. *1956*

INNOVATOR (ANN ARBOR).
University of Michigan, School of Education, E. & S. University Aves., Ann Arbor, MI 48109. TEL 313-763-4880. FAX 313-763-4062.
circ. 49,000. *1957*

INSIDE (ALBANY).
New York State Bar Association, Corporate Counsel Section, 1 Elk St., Albany, NY 12207-1096. TEL 518-463-3200. FAX 518-463-8844.
circ. 1,100. *4082*

INSIDE E S F.
State University of New York at Syracuse, College of Environmental Science and Forestry, Office of News and Publications, 122 Bray Hall, One Forestry Dr., Syracuse, NY 13210. TEL 315-470-6644. FAX 315-470-6651.
circ. 18,000. *3155*

INSIDE THE VATICAN.
Urbi et Orbi Communications, 3050 Gap Knob Rd., New Hope, KY 40052. TEL 502-325-3061. FAX 502-325-3091.
circ. 15,000. *6465*

INSIDE TRACKS.
93 Goulding Ave., North York, ON M2M 1L3, Canada. TEL 416-229-9213.
circ. 5,000. *5400*

INSIDE TUCSON BUSINESS.
Territorial Newspapers, P.O. Box 27087, Tucson, AZ 85726-7087. TEL 520-294-1200. FAX 520-294-4040.
circ. 8,000. *972*

INSIDER (SKOKIE).
Michiana Ventures, Inc., 4124 Oakton St., Skokie, IL 60076. TEL 847-673-3703. FAX 847-329-0358.
circ. 1,018,350. *1957*

INSIEME.
Publications Ensemble Inc., 4358 rue Charleroi, Montreal-Nord, PQ H1H 1T3, Canada. TEL 514-328-2062. FAX 514-328-6562.
circ. 20,000. *3018*

INSIGHT (AKRON).
Akron - Summit County Public Library, 55 S. Main St., Akron, OH 44326. TEL 330-643-9000.
circ. 2,000. *4185*

INSIGHT (CHICAGO).
Illinois C P A Society, 222 S. Riverside Plaza, 16th Fl., Chicago, IL 60606. TEL 312-993-0393. FAX 312-993-7713.
circ. 26,000. *1091*

INSIGHT (SPRINGFIELD).
State Library, 300 S. Second St., Springfield, IL 62701. TEL 217-785-6925. FAX 217-785-4324.
circ. 3,900. *4185*

INSIGHTS (WASHINGTON, 1988).
Library of Congress Professional Association, Library of Congress, Washington, DC 20540. TEL 202-707-3635.
circ. 2,200. *4185*

INSTALLATIONS NYT.
Teknisk Forlag A - S, Skelbaekgade 4, DK-1780 Copenhagen V, Denmark. TEL 45-31-21-68-01. FAX 45-31-21-04-01.
circ. 8,838. *2834*

INSTANT MAGAZINE.
Instant Entertainment, Box 2224, Woburn, MA 01888-0324. TEL 617-246-0334. FAX 617-246-0587.
circ. 10,000. *5400*

INSTITUT CATHOLIQUE DE PARIS. ANNUAIRE.
Institut Catholique de Paris, 21 rue d'Assas, 75270 Paris Cedex 06, France. TEL 44-39-52-00. FAX 45-44-27-14. *6465*

INSTITUT FUER AFRIKA-KUNDE. ARBEITEN.
Institut fuer Afrika-Kunde, Neuer Jungfernstieg 21, 20354 Hamburg, Germany. TEL 49-40-3562523. FAX 49-40-3562511.
circ. 250. *5934*

INSTITUT FUER ALLGEMEINE BOTANIK UND BOTANISCHER GARTEN. MITTEILUNGEN.
Universitaet Hamburg, Institut fuer Allgemeine Botanik und Botanischer Garten, Ohnhorststr. 18, 22609 Hamburg, Germany. FAX 49-40-82282254.
circ. 550. *709*

INSTITUT FUER SCHWEIZERISCHES ARBEITSRECHT. MITTEILUNGEN.
Staempfli AG, Hallerstr. 7-9, CH-3012 Bern, Switzerland. TEL 41-31-3006666. FAX 41-31-3006699.
circ. 400. *1436*

INSTITUT FUER VERKEHRSWESEN. MITTEILUNGEN.
Universitaet fuer Bodenkultur, Institut fuer Verkehrswesen, Peter-Jordan-Str. 82, A-1190 Vienna, Austria. TEL 43-1-476545300. FAX 43-1-476545344.
circ. 400. *7030*

INSTITUT FUER WISSENSCHAFT UND KUNST. MITTEILUNGEN.
Institut fuer Wissenschaft und Kunst, Berggasse 17-1, A-1090 Vienna, Austria.
circ. 2,000. *2545*

INSTITUT GEOGRAPHIQUE NATIONAL. BULLETIN D'INFORMATION.
Institut Geographique National, Service de la Documentation Geographique, 136 bis, rue de Grenelle, 75700 Paris, France. TEL 43-98-80-00. *3428*

INSTITUT HISTORIQUE BELGE DE ROME. BULLETIN.
N.V. Brepols, Steenweg op Tielen 68, 2300 Turnhout, Belgium. TEL 32-14-402500. FAX 32-14-428919. *3575*

INSTITUT INTERNATIONAL J. MARITAIN. NOTES ET DOCUMENTS.
Institut International Jacques Maritain, Via Quintino Sella, 33, 00187 Rome, Italy. TEL 39-6-4874336. FAX 39-6-4825188.
circ. 2,000. *5934*

INSTITUTA ET MONUMENTA. SERIE II: INSTITUTA.
Fondazione "Claudio Monteverdi", Via Pallavicino 7, 26100 Cremona, Italy. TEL 39-372-26580.
circ. 500. *5400*

INSTITUTE FOR INTEGRATED AGRICULTURAL DEVELOPMENT. RESEARCH REPORT.
Institute for Integrated Agricultural Development, Department of Agriculture Energy & Minerals, RMB 1145, Chiltern Valley Rd., Rutherglen, Vic. 3685, Australia. TEL 61-60-304500. FAX 61-60-304600.
circ. 1,000. *126*

INSTITUTE FOR SOCIAL RESEARCH NEWSLETTER.
Institute for Social Research, York University, 4700 Keele St., North York, ON M3J 1P3, Canada. TEL 416-736-5061. FAX 416-736-5749.
circ. 2,600. *6619*

INSTITUTE OF ELECTROLYSIS. LIST OF QUALIFIED OPERATORS. SYLLABUS PROSPECTUS.
Institute of Electrolysis, 251 Seymour Grove, Manchester M16 0DS, England. *506*

INSTITUTE OF ENERGY. JOURNAL.
Institute of Energy, 18 Devonshire St., London W1N 2AU, England. TEL 071-580-0008. FAX 071-580-4420.
circ. 2,500. *2671*

INSTITUTE OF ENGINEERS & TECHNICIANS JOURNAL.
Deeson Editorial Services Ltd., Ewell House, Graveney Rd., Faversham, Kent ME13 8UP, England. TEL 44-1795-535468. FAX 44-1795-535469.
circ. 6,500. *2885*

INSTITUTE OF MODERN RUSSIAN CULTURE NEWSLETTER.
Institute of Modern Russian Culture, Box 4353, University of Southern California, Los Angeles, CA 90089-4353. TEL 213-740-2735. FAX 213-740-8550.
circ. 1,000. *3018*

INSTITUTO BRASIL - ESTADOS UNIDOS. BOLETIM.
Instituto Brasil - Estados Unidos, Av. N.S. de Copacabana, 690 - 11 andar, 22050-000 Rio de Janeiro, RJ, Brazil. TEL 55-21-2558332. FAX 55-21-2559355.
circ. 10,000. *2451*

INSTITUTO BUTANTAN. MEMORIAS.
Instituto Butantan, Av. Vital Brasil 1500, 05503-900 Sao Paulo, Brazil. TEL 55-11-8137222. FAX 55-11-8151505.
circ. 800. *837*

INSTITUTO DE ECONOMIA AGRICOLA. INFORMACOES ECONOMICAS.
Instituto de Economia Agricola, Av. Miguel Stefano, 3900, Caixa Postal 6802, 04301-903 Sao Paulo, SP, Brazil. FAX 55-11-2764062. *196*

INSTITUTO DE INVESTIGACION TEXTIL Y DE COOPERACION INDUSTRIAL. BOLETIN INTEXTER.
Instituto de Investigacion Textil y de Cooperacion Industrial, Colon 15, 08222 Terrassa, Spain. TEL 34-3-7398277. FAX 34-3-7398272.
circ. 1,000. *6989*

INSTITUTO NACIONAL DE ENFERMEDADES RESPIRATORIAS. REVISTA.
Instituto Nacional de Enfermedades Respiratorias, Clz. Tlalpan 4502, Col. Seccion XVI, 14082 Mexico DF, Mexico. TEL 52-5-6663187. FAX 52-5-6663187.
circ. 3,000. *5119*

INSTITUTO POLITECNICO NACIONAL. ESCUELA NACIONAL DE CIENCIAS BIOLOGICAS. ANALES.
Instituto Politecnico Nacional, Escuela Nacional de Ciencias Biologicas, Carpio y Plan de Ayala, Col. Santo Tomas, Apdo. Postal 42-186, 11340, Mexico, D.F., Mexico. FAX 52-5-3963503.
circ. 1,000. *606*

INSTYTUT TRANSPORTU SAMOCHODOWEGO. ZESZYTY NAUKOWE.
Instytut Transportu Samochodowego, Ul. Jagiellonska 80, Warsaw, Poland. TEL 48-22-113231. FAX 48-22-110906. *7030*

INSURANCE DIRECTORY OF NEW ZEALAND.
Mercantile Gazette Marketing, P.O. Box 20-034, Christchurch 5, New Zealand.
circ. 3,050. *3819*

INSURANCE FIELD.
Insurance Field Company, Box 948, Northbrook, IL 60062. TEL 847-498-0100. FAX 847-498-6695.
circ. 3,000. *3819*

INSURANCE TIMES.
20 Park Plz., Ste. 1101, Boston, MA 02116-4303. TEL 617-292-7117. FAX 617-292-0111.
circ. 5,000. *3821*

INTEGRATED SYSTEM DESIGN.
The Verecom Group, 5150 El Camino Real, Ste. D-31, Los Altos, CA 94022-1527. TEL 415-903-0140. FAX 415-903-0151.
circ. 55,000. *2109*

INTENSIVE CARING UNLIMITED.
Intensive Caring Unlimited (ICU), 571 Creek Rd., Ivyland, PA 18974. TEL 215-629-0449.
circ. 3,000. *1847*

INTER - MECANIQUE DU BATIMENT.
Corporation des Maitres Mecaniciens en Tuyauterie du Quebec, 8175 bd. Saint-Laurent, Montreal, PQ H2P 2M1, Canada. TEL 514-382-2668. FAX 514-382-1566.
circ. 6,450. *3481*

INTERACTIVITY.
Miller Freeman, Inc. (San Mateo), 411 Borel Ave., Ste. 100, San Mateo, CA 94402. TEL 415-358-9500. FAX 415-655-4360.
circ. 55,000. *2123*

INTERCHANGE (PORTLAND).
Oregon Educational Media Association, Box 1759, Roseburg, OR 97470. TEL 541-839-6557. FAX 541-440-4118.
circ. 700. *2451*

INTERCHANGE CUSTOMER NEWSLETTER.
Nebraska Public Power District, Box 499, Columbus, NE 68601-0499. TEL 402-563-5811. FAX 402-563-5511.
circ. 5,000. *3376*

INTERFACE (STORRS).
University of Connecticut, Center for Instructional Media & Technology, UCIMT, U-1, 249 Glenbrook Rd., Storrs, CT 06269-2001. TEL 203-486-2530. FAX 203-486-1766.
circ. 7,000. *1994*

INTERIEUR.
NOVA Kommunikation A-S, Box 146, Solvang 23, DK-3450 Alleroed, Denmark. TEL 45-48-17-00-78. FAX 45-48-17-13-65.
circ. 7,176. *3847*

INTERIOR DECORATORS' HANDBOOK.
Columbia Communications, Inc., 2125 Center Ave., Ste. 305, Fort Lee, NJ 07024-5859. TEL 212-532-9290. FAX 212-779-8345.
circ. 20,000. *3847*

INTERIORSCAPE.
Brantwood Publications, Inc., 3023 Eastland Blvd., Ste. 103, Clearwater, FL 34621-4106. TEL 813-796-3877.
circ. 7,500. *3847*

INTERMEDIAIR.
V N U Business Publications B.V., Postbus 9194, 1006 CC Amsterdam, Netherlands. TEL 31-206175137.
circ. 195,000. *1146*

THE INTERMOUNTAIN RETAILER.
Utah Food Industry Association, 1578 W. 1700 S., Ste. 200, Salt Lake City, UT 84104. TEL 801-973-9517. FAX 801-972-8712.
circ. 1,000. *3142*

INTERNAL MEDICINE WORLD REPORT.
Medical World Business Press, Inc., 241 Forsgate Dr., CN 505, Jamesburg, NJ 08831. TEL 908-656-1140. FAX 908-656-1142.
circ. 105,000. *4925*

THE INTERNATIONAL (LONDON, 1988).
Financial Times Business Information, Magazines 2 Greystoke Pl., Fetter Ln., London EC4A 1ND, England. TEL 0171-405-6969. FAX 0171-405-5276.
circ. 35,000. *1389*

INTERNATIONAL ACADEMY FOR THE STUDY OF TOURISM. NEWSLETTER.
Tourism Center, 116 Classroom Office Bldg., University of Minnesota, St. Paul, MN 55108. TEL 612-624-4947. FAX 612-624-4264.
circ. 150. *7212*

INTERNATIONAL ARTHURIAN SOCIETY. NEWSLETTER.
International Arthurian Society, North American Branch, Sothern Methodist University, Dallas, TX 75275-0432. TEL 214-768-2949. FAX 214-768-4129. *4417*

INTERNATIONAL ASSOCIATION OF EDUCATORS FOR WORLD PEACE. CIRCULATION NEWSLETTER.
Peace Progress Press, Box 3282, Mastin Lake Sta., Huntsville, AL 35810-0282. TEL 205-534-5501. FAX 205-536-1018.
circ. 10,000. *2565*

INTERNATIONAL ASSOCIATION OF METEOROLOGY AND ATMOSPHERIC PHYSICS. REPORT OF PROCEEDINGS OF GENERAL ASSEMBLY.
International Association of Meteorology and Atmospheric Physics, c/o Prof. Roland List, Department of Physics, University of Toronto, Toronto, ON M5S 1A7, Canada. TEL 416-978-2982. FAX 416-978-8905. *5235*

INTERNATIONAL ASSOCIATION OF MILK CONTROL AGENCIES. PROCEEDINGS OF ANNUAL MEETINGS.
International Association of Milk Control Agencies, c/o Lyle Newcomb, New York Int'l Dept. of Agriculture and Markets, 1 Winners Circle, Albany, NY 12235. TEL 518-457-5731. FAX 518-485-5816. *255*

INTERNATIONAL ASSOCIATION OF MUSEUMS OF ARMS AND MILITARY HISTORY. CONGRESS REPORTS.
International Association of Museums of Arms and Military History, c/o Markku Melkko, P.O. Box 266, FIN-00171 Helsinki, Finland. FAX 358-0-1616390. *5356*

INTERNATIONAL ASSOCIATION OF PHYSICAL EDUCATION AND SPORTS FOR GIRLS AND WOMEN. PROCEEDINGS OF THE INTERNATIONAL CONGRESS.
Japan Association of Physical Education for Women and Girls, 6-102 O.M.Y.C., 3-1 Jinen-cho Yoyogi, Shibuya-ku, Tokyo, Japan. *6765*

INTERNATIONAL BAR NEWS.
International Bar Association, 2 Harewood Pl., Hanover Sq., London W1R 9HB, England. TEL 44-71-629-1206. FAX 44-71-409-0456.
circ. 16,000. *4116*

INTERNATIONAL BASKETBALL FEDERATION. OFFICIAL REPORT OF THE WORLD CONGRESS.
International Basketball Federation, Postfach 700607, 81306 Munich, Germany. TEL 49-89-7481580. FAX 49-89-74815833.
circ. 300. *6809*

INTERNATIONAL BIODETERIORATION & BIODEGRADATION.
Elsevier Science Ltd., P.O. Box 800, Kidlington, Oxford OX5 1DX, England. TEL 44-1865-843000. FAX 44-1865-843010. *683*

INTERNATIONAL BIOTECHNOLOGY LABORATORY.
International Scientific Communications, Inc., 30 Controls Dr., Box 870, Shelton, CT 06484-0870. TEL 203-926-9300. FAX 203-926-9310.
circ. 37,000. *684*

INTERNATIONAL BOWLING INDUSTRY.
Crown Publications, 660 Hampshire Rd., No. 200, Westlake Village, CA 91361-2504. TEL 805-371-7877. FAX 805-371-7885.
circ. 10,750. *6809*

INTERNATIONAL CABLE.
Phillips Business Information, Inc., 1201 Seven Locks Rd., Potomac, MD 20854. TEL 301-424-3338. FAX 301-309-3847. *2052*

INTERNATIONAL COMMISSION FOR THE CONSERVATION OF ATLANTIC TUNAS. COLLECTIVE VOLUME OF SCIENTIFIC PAPERS.
International Commission for the Conservation of Atlantic Tunas, Estebanez Calderon 3 8l, 28020 Madrid, Spain. TEL 34-1-5793352. FAX 34-1-5715299. *3071*

INTERNATIONAL COMMISSION FOR THE CONSERVATION OF ATLANTIC TUNAS. DATA RECORD.
International Commission for the Conservation of Atlantic Tunas, Estebanez Calderon 3 8l, 28020 Madrid, Spain. TEL 34-1-5793352. FAX 34-1-5725299. *3071*

INTERNATIONAL COMMISSION FOR THE CONSERVATION OF ATLANTIC TUNAS. STATISTICAL BULLETIN.
International Commission for the Conservation of Atlantic Tunas, Estebanez Calderon, 3 8l, 28020 Madrid, Spain. TEL 34-1-5793352. FAX 34-1-5715299. *3083*

INTERNATIONAL COMMISSION ON IRRIGATION AND DRAINAGE. REPORT.
International Commission on Irrigation and Drainage, 48 Nyaya Marg, Chanakyapuri, New Delhi 110021, India. TEL 3016837.
circ. 1,000. *7295*

INTERNATIONAL COMMUNICATOR.
Academy of Dentistry International, 5125 MacArthur Blvd., N.W., Ste. 50, Washington, DC 20016-3315. TEL 202-364-8349. FAX 202-364-8349.
circ. 2,000. *4859*

INTERNATIONAL CONFERENCE ON LASERS. PROCEEDINGS (YEAR).
STS Press, Box 245, McLean, VA 22101. TEL 703-642-5835. FAX 703-642-5838.
circ. 300. *5861*

INTERNATIONAL CONGRESS FOR STEREOLOGY. PROCEEDINGS.
International Society for Stereology, c/o Dr. Aurora Astudillo, Sec.-Treas., Tatiana, Univ. de Oviedo, Ed. Quimicas, Julian Claveria s-n, 33006 Oviedo, Spain. TEL 34-85-103658.
circ. 480. *2859*

INTERNATIONAL CONGRESS OF HEMATOLOGY. PROCEEDINGS.
International Society of Hematology, c/o Dr. Robert Kyle, Mayo Clinic, Rochester, MN 55905.
circ. 2,000. *4920*

INTERNATIONAL CONGRESS OF OPHTHALMOLOGY. ABSTRACTS.
International Federation of Ophthalmological Societies, c/o Dr. Bruce E. Spivey, Northwestern Healthcare Network, 980 N. Michigan Ave., Ste. 1500, Chicago, IL 60611.
circ. 8,500. *4994*

INTERNATIONAL CRANES.
K H L International Ltd., Southfields, Southview Rd., Wadhurst, E. Sussex TN5 6TP, England. TEL 44-1892-784088. FAX 44-1892-784086.
circ. 14,200. *2859*

INTERNATIONAL DESALINATION AND WATER REUSE QUARTERLY.
Lineal Publishing Co., 10842 Pine Bark Ln., Boca Raton, FL 33428-2852. TEL 561-451-9429. FAX 561-451-9435.
circ. 8,146. *7295*

INTERNATIONAL DEVELOPMENT POLICIES.
Commonwealth Secretariat, Marlborough House, Pall Mall, London SW1Y 5HX, England. TEL 44-171-839-3411. FAX 44-171-747-6235.
circ. 350. *1363*

INTERNATIONAL DIABETES DIGEST.
F S G Communications Ltd., Vine House, Fair Green, Reach, Cambridge CB5 OJD, England. TEL 44-1638-743633. FAX 44-1638-743998.
circ. 5,000. *4889*

INTERNATIONAL ENVIRONMENTAL TECHNOLOGY.
International Labmate Ltd., 12 Alban Park, Hatfield Rd., St. Albans, Herts. AL4 OJJ, England. TEL 44-1727-858840. FAX 44-1727-840310.
circ. 51,072. *2969*

INTERNATIONAL FEDERATION FOR HOUSING AND PLANNING. DIRECTORY.
International Federation for Housing and Planning, Wassenaarseweg 43, 2596 CG The Hague, Netherlands.
circ. 1,500. *3750*

INTERNATIONAL FIBER JOURNAL.
International Medic Group, Inc., 1515 Mockingbird Lane, Ste. 210, Charlotte, NC 28209-4628. TEL 704-565-5175. FAX 704-565-5177. circ. 8,450. *6989*

INTERNATIONAL FINANCIER.
International Society of Financiers, Box 18508, Asheville, NC 28814. TEL 704-252-5907. FAX 704-251-5061. circ. 500. *1147*

INTERNATIONAL FIRE FIGHTER.
International Association of Fire Fighters, 1750 New York Ave., N.W., Washington, DC 20006-5301. TEL 202-737-8484. FAX 202-737-8418. circ. 195,000. *3056*

INTERNATIONAL FOOD INGREDIENTS.
Miller Freeman plc, Miller Freeman House, 30 Calderwood St., London SE18 6QH, England. TEL 44-181-855-7777. FAX 44-181-316-3206. circ. 8,500. *3114*

INTERNATIONAL GRAVIMETRIQUE BUREAU. BULLETIN D'INFORMATION.
Bureau Gravimetric International, 18 av. Edouard Belin, 31401 Toulouse Cedex 04, France. TEL 33-5-61332980. FAX 33-5-61253098. circ. 350. *2384*

INTERNATIONAL HOSPITAL EQUIPMENT.
Pan European Publishing Co., Rue Verte 216, 1030 Brussels, Belgium. TEL 32-2-2402611. FAX 32-2-2427111. circ. 30,004. *4685*

INTERNATIONAL INSTITUTE OF SEISMOLOGY AND EARTHQUAKE ENGINEERING. YEAR BOOK.
International Institute of Seismology and Earthquake Engineering, Building Research Institute-Ministry of Construction, 1 Tatehare, Tsukuba-city, Ibaraki Prefecture 305, Japan. TEL 81-298-64-2151. FAX 81-298-64-2989. *2384*

INTERNATIONAL JOURNAL OF CIRCUMPOLAR HEALTH.
Institute for Arctic Medicine, Aapistie 1, FIN-90220 Oulu, Finland. TEL 358-8-537-6201. FAX 358-8-537-6203. circ. 1,600. *4686*

INTERNATIONAL JOURNAL OF EDUCOLOGY.
Educology Research Associates, P.O. Box 216, Terrigal, N.S.W. 2260, Australia. TEL 61-43-653120. FAX 61-43-652871. circ. 1,500. *2510*

INTERNATIONAL JOURNAL OF FOOD SCIENCES AND NUTRITION.
Carfax Publishing Co., P.O. Box 25, Abingdon, Oxon. OX14 3UE, England. TEL 44-1235-401000. FAX 44-1235-401550. circ. 1,000. *5475*

INTERNATIONAL JOURNAL OF INTENSIVE CARE.
Greycoat Publishing, 1 Harley St., London W1N 1DA, England. TEL 44-171-637-1828. FAX 44-171-637-3020. circ. 25,868. *4686*

INTERNATIONAL JOURNAL OF THE SOCIOLOGY OF LANGUAGE.
Walter de Gruyter und Co., Mouton de Gruyter, Genthiner Str. 13, 10785 Berlin, Germany. TEL 49-30-26005-0. FAX 49-30-26005251. circ. 900. *4265*

INTERNATIONAL LABORATORY.
International Scientific Communications, Inc., 30 Controls Dr., Box 870, Shelton, CT 06484-0870. TEL 203-926-9300. FAX 203-926-9310. circ. 52,503. *1791*

INTERNATIONAL LAW PRACTICUM.
New York State Bar Association, International Law and Practice Section, 1 Elk St., Albany, NY 12207-1096. TEL 518-463-3200. FAX 518-463-8844. circ. 2,000. *4119*

INTERNATIONAL LEADS.
American Library Association, International Relations Round Table, 50 E. Huron St., Chicago, IL 60611. TEL 312-944-6780. FAX 312-280-3256. circ. 900. *4187*

INTERNATIONAL MARKETING.
Quest Magazines Ltd., Publishing House, 652 Victoria Rd., South Ruislip, Mddx. HA4 0SX, England. TEL 44-181-842-1010. FAX 44-181-841-2557. circ. 5,000. *1531*

THE INTERNATIONAL PRESS DIRECTORY.
The Magazine Business Ltd., 8 Tottenham Mews, London W1P 9PJ, England. TEL 44-171-436-5211. FAX 44-171-436-5290. circ. 12,500. *6274*

INTERNATIONAL RELATIONS.
David Davies Memorial Institute of International Studies, 2 Chadwick St., London SW1P 2EP, England. TEL 44-171-222-4063. FAX 44-171-233-2863. circ. 1,000. *6021*

INTERNATIONAL REVIEW OF WORLD TRADE.
Sterling Publications Ltd., 86-88 Edgware Rd., London W2 2YW, England. TEL 44-171-915-9600. FAX 44-171-915-9619. circ. 20,000. *1331*

INTERNATIONAL SADDLERY AND APPAREL JOURNAL.
EEMG, Inc, Box 3039, Berea, KY 40403-3039. FAX 606-986-1770. circ. 6,863. *6853*

INTERNATIONAL SHIPPING REVIEW.
Contract Communications Ltd., Nestor House, Playhouse Yard, London EC4V 5EX, England. TEL 44-171-779-8714. FAX 44-171-779-8760. circ. 8,000. *7153*

INTERNATIONAL SKYLINE.
I.S.P. of Canada, 3738 - 39th Ave. W., Vancouver, BC V6N 3A7, Canada. circ. 18,750. *1995*

INTERNATIONAL SOCIETY FOR BRITISH GENEALOGY AND FAMILY HISTORY. NEWSLETTER.
International Society for British Genealogy and Family History, Box 3115, Salt Lake City, UT 84110-3115. TEL 801-272-2178. circ. 1,100. *3228*

INTERNATIONAL SOCIETY OF BLOOD TRANSFUSION. PROCEEDINGS OF THE CONGRESS.
Societe Internationale de Transfusion Sanguine, c/o C N T S, B.P. 100, 91943 Les Ulis Cedex, France. TEL 69-07-20-40. FAX 69-07-41-85. *4920*

INTERNATIONAL SOCIETY OF WEIGHING AND MEASUREMENT. MEMBERSHIP DIRECTORY & PRODUCT GUIDE.
International Society of Weighing and Measurement, 10 Kimball St., W., Winder, GA 30680. TEL 770-868-5300. FAX 770-868-5301. circ. 1,400. *5251*

INTERNATIONAL THEATRE INSTITUTE OF THE UNITED STATES. NEWSLETTER.
International Theatre Institute of the United States, Inc., 47 Great Jones St., New York, NY 10012-1114. TEL 212-254-4141. FAX 212-254-6814. circ. 1,500. *7007*

INTERNATIONAL TRANSPORT WORKERS' FEDERATION REPORT ON ACTIVITIES.
International Transport Workers' Federation, 49-60 Borough Rd., London SE1 1DS, England. circ. 500. *3892*

INTERNATIONAL TURFGRASS BULLETIN.
Sports Turf Research Institute, St. Ives Estate, Bingley, W. Yorkshire BD16 1AU, England. TEL 44-1274-565131. FAX 44-1274-561891. circ. 5,500. *6766*

INTERNATIONALES JAHRBUCH FUER RECHTSPHILOSOPHIE UND GESETZGEBUNG.
Manzsche Verlags- und Universitaetsbuchhandlung GmbH, Kohlmarkt 16, A-1014 Vienna, Austria. TEL 43-1-531610. FAX 43-1-53161181. circ. 500. *3965*

INTERNETWORK.
Cardinal Business Media, Inc., 1300 Virginia Dr., Ste. 400, Fort Washington, PA 19034. TEL 215-643-8000. FAX 215-643-3901. circ. 80,000. *2136*

INTERPLANETARY NEWS.
Interplanetary Space Travel Research Association (United Kingdom), 21 Hargwyne St., Stockwell, London SW9 9RQ, England. *71*

INTERPRETER (NASHVILLE).
United Methodist Communications, 810 12th Ave. S., Nashville, TN 37203-4744. TEL 615-742-5400. FAX 615-742-5460. circ. 264,903. *6429*

INTER-SOCIETY COLOR COUNCIL NEWS.
Inter-Society Color Council, c/o Danny C. Rich, Sec., Datacolor Int'l, 5 Princess Rd., Lawrenceville, NJ 08648. TEL 609-895-7427. FAX 609-895-7461. circ. 1,000. *5862*

INTERVAL.
Interval International, 6262 Sunset Dr., Penthouse 1, South Miami, FL 33143. TEL 305-666-1861. FAX 305-668-3408. circ. 500,000. *7213*

INTERVUE.
Intergraph Corporation, LR24C2, Huntsville, AL 35894. TEL 205-730-8172. FAX 205-730-9508. circ. 60,000. *2127*

INTO VIEW.
Youth for Christ, P.O. Box 5254, Halesowen, W. Midlands B63 3DG, England. TEL 44-121-550-8055. FAX 44-121-550-9979. circ. 6,000. *1874*

INTRODUCTION TO GRAVITATION CHEMISTRY.
Ensanian Physicochemical Institute, Box 98, Eldred, PA 16731. TEL 814-225-3296. circ. 100. *1753*

INTRON - CANADIAN MOLECULAR BIOLOGY.
Canadian Biotechnology News Service, 340 Richmond Rd., Box 67039, Ottawa, ON K2A 0E8, Canada. TEL 613-726-0115. FAX 613-726-7344. circ. 6,000. *684*

INUIT ART QUARTERLY.
Inuit Art Foundation, 2081 Merivale Rd., Nepean, ON K2G 1G9, Canada. TEL 613-224-8189. FAX 613-224-2907. circ. 1,862. *448*

INVEST IN BRITAIN ANNUAL REPORT.
Invest in Britain Bureau, 1 Victoria St., London SW1H 0ET, England. TEL 44-171-215-2501. FAX 44-171-215-5651. circ. 6,000. *974*

INVESTIGACION Y EDUCACION EN ENFERMERIA.
Universidad de Antioquia, Facultad de Enfermeria, Apdo. Aereo 1226, Carrera 53, no. 62-65, Medellin, Colombia. TEL 574-5106335. FAX 574-2110058. circ. 1,000. *4935*

INVESTIR.
Societe d'Information Economique et Financiere, Investir Publications, 48 rue Notre-Dame des Victoires, 75002 Paris, France. TEL 1-44-88-48-00. FAX 1-44-88-48-01. circ. 120,000. *1148*

INVESTMENT MANAGEMENT.
Mitre House Publishing Ltd., The Clifton Centre, 110 Clifton St., London EC2A 4HD, England. TEL 071-729-6644. circ. 8,000. *1148*

THE INVESTMENT REPORTER.
Share Holder Communication Systems, 4600 Campus Dr., Ste. 205, Newport Beach, CA 92660-1801. TEL 714-724-0444. circ. 36,204. *1391*

IOWA. DEPARTMENT OF EMPLOYMENT SERVICES. ANNUAL REPORT.
Department of Employment Services, 1000 E. Grand Ave., Des Moines, IA 50319. TEL 515-281-3201. circ. 2,000. *1438*

IOWA ACADEMY OF SCIENCE. JOURNAL.
Allen Press, 175 Baker Hall, University of Northern Iowa, Cedar Falls, IA 50614. TEL 319-273-2021. circ. 2,100. *6535*

CONTROLLED CIRCULATION SERIALS

IOWA AGRICULTURE AND HOME ECONOMICS EXPERIMENT STATION. RESEARCH BULLETIN.
Iowa State University of Science and Technology, 304 Curtiss Hall, Ames, IA 50011. TEL 515-294-5616. FAX 515-294-8662. *127*

IOWA CITY MAGAZINE.
Iowa City Magazine Publishing, Inc., Box 2672, Iowa City, IA 52244-2672. TEL 319-354-7738. FAX 319-354-7738.
circ. 15,000. *3376*

IOWA STATER.
Iowa State University, Ames, IA 50011. TEL 515-294-3129. FAX 515-294-9748.
circ. 135,000. *1957*

IOWA TRUCKING LIFELINER.
Iowa Motor Truck Association, Capital Center One, 600 E. Court, Ste. D, Des Moines, IA 50309-2020. TEL 515-244-5193. FAX 515-244-2204.
circ. 3,187. *7175*

IRAN. MINISTRY OF ECONOMY. INTERNAL WHOLESALE TRADE STATISTICS.
Ministry of Finance and Economic Affairs, Bureau of Statistics, Teheran, Iran. *1049*

IRAN. MINISTRY OF ECONOMY. INTERNATIONAL TRADE STATISTICS.
Ministry of Finance and Economic Affairs, Bureau of Statistics, Teheran, Iran. *1049*

IRELAND. DEPARTMENT OF SOCIAL WELFARE. STATISTICAL INFORMATION ON SOCIAL WELFARE.
Department of Social Welfare, Statistics Unit, Store St., 4th Fl., Dublin 1, Ireland. TEL 353-1-8748444. FAX 353-1-87043868.
circ. 1,300. *6671*

IRIS YEAR BOOK.
British Iris Society, Copper Beeches, N. End Ln., Downe, Orpington, Kent BR6 7HG, England. TEL 01689-853646.
circ. 800. *3195*

IRISH AMERICAN POST.
Irish American Post Ltd., 301 N. Water St., 3rd Floor, Milwaukee, WI 53202-5713. TEL 414-273-8132. FAX 414-273-8196.
circ. 25,000. *3019*

IRISH BANK OFFICIALS ASSOCIATION NEWSHEET.
Irish Bank Officials Association, 93 St. Stephen's Green, Dublin 2, Ireland. TEL 353-1-8722255. FAX 353-1-4780567.
circ. 11,000. *1148*

IRISH COLLEGE OF OPHTHALMOLOGISTS. YEARBOOK.
Irish College of Ophthalmologists, 10 Hagans Ct., Lad Ln., Dublin 2, Ireland. TEL 353-1-6785974. FAX 353-1-6785047.
circ. 450. *4995*

IRISH COMPANY REPORTING.
University of Ulster, School of Management, Coleraine BT52 1SA, N. Ireland. TEL 44-1232-365131. FAX 44-1232-366805.
circ. 100. *1092*

IRISH COOPERATIVE ORGANIZATION SOCIETY. ANNUAL REPORT.
Irish Cooperative Organization Society Ltd., Plunkett House, 84 Merrion Sq., Dublin 2, Ireland. TEL 353-1-6764783. FAX 353-1-6624502. *128*

IRISH IN BRITAIN DIRECTORY.
Brent Irish Advisory Service, Premier House, 313 Kilburn Lane, London W9 3EG, England. TEL 44-181-968-6914. FAX 44-181-960-5636.
circ. 10,000. *3019*

IRISH MEDICAL TIMES.
Medical Publications Ltd., 30 Lancaster Gate, London W2 3LP, England. *4688*

IRISH MOTOR INDUSTRY.
Jude Publications Ltd., Jude House, Tara St., Dublin 2, Ireland. TEL 01-6713500. FAX 01-6713074.
circ. 2,500. *7103*

IRON MOUNTAIN REVIEW.
Emory & Henry College, Box 64, Emory, VA 24327. TEL 540-944-4121. FAX 540-944-6934.
circ. 450. *4418*

AL-ISLAM.
c/o Jamiat Ahl-e-Hadith, 106 Ravi Rd., Lahore, Pakistan. FAX 042-54072.
circ. 4,000. *6397*

ISRAEL. GOVERNMENT PRESS OFFICE. DAILY NEWS AND EDITORIAL SURVEY.
Government Press Office, Agron House, 37 Hillel St., Jerusalem 94581, Israel. *3324*

ISRAEL. KNESSET. HA-VA'ADA LE-INYANEI BIKORET HA-MEDINA. SIKUMEHA VE-HATSA'OTEHA SHEL HA-VA'ADA LE-INYANEI BIKORET HA-MEDINA LE-DIN VE-KHESHBON SHEL MEVAKER HA-MEDINA.
Knesset, Jerusalem, Israel. *6216*

ISRAEL. KNESSET. VA'ADAT HA-KESAFIM MISPARIM AL VA'ADAT HA-KESAFIM.
Knesset, Jerusalem, Israel. *1616*

ISRAEL SOCIAL SCIENCE RESEARCH.
Hubert H. Humphrey Institute for Social Research, Ben-Gurion University of the Negev, P.O. Box 653, Beer-Sheva 84105, Israel. TEL 972-7-6461112. FAX 972-7-6472938.
circ. 750. *6620*

ISRAELI MAP COLLECTORS SOCIETY. JOURNAL.
Israeli Map Collectors Society, 4 Brenner St., Jerusalem 92103, Israel. TEL 972-2-5611687.
circ. 100. *3669*

ISSUES (SAN FRANCISCO).
A Messianic Jewish Perspective, Box 424885, San Francisco, CA 94142-4885. TEL 415-864-2600. FAX 415-552-8325.
circ. 40,000. *6492*

ISTITUTO RICERCHE PESCA MARITTIMA. QUADERNI.
Istituto Ricerche sulla Pesca Marittima, Molo Mandracchio, 60100 Ancona, Italy. TEL 39-71-5314. FAX 39-71-55313.
circ. 500. *3071*

ISTITUTO STORICO ARTISTICO ORVIETANO. BOLLETTINO.
Istituto Storico Artistico Orvietano, Piazza Febei N.1, 05018 Orvieto, Italy. *3576*

ITALIAN JOURNAL OF ZOOLOGY.
Mucchi Editore s.r.l., Via Emilia Est. 1527, 41100 Modena, Italy. TEL 39-59-374094. FAX 39-59-282628.
circ. 500. *838*

ITALIC HANDWRITING NEWSLETTER.
Continuing Education Press, 1633 S.W. Park, Box 1491, Portland, OR 97207. TEL 503-725-4846. FAX 503-725-4840.
circ. 15,000. *2606*

ITHACA COLLEGE QUARTERLY.
Ithaca College, Alumni Hall, Ithaca, NY 14850. TEL 607-274-3830. FAX 607-274-1490.
circ. 40,000. *1957*

ITINERA GEOBOTANICA.
Universidad de Leon, Secretariado de Publicaciones, Campus de Verganza, s-n, 24007 Leon, Spain. TEL 34-87-291558. FAX 34-87-291558.
circ. 1,000. *709*

IVY LEAF.
Alpha Kappa Alpha Sorority, Inc., 5656 S. Stony Island Ave., Chicago, IL 60637. *1957*

IWATE MEDICAL UNIVERSITY SCHOOL OF LIBERAL ARTS & SCIENCES. ANNUAL REPORT.
Iwate Ika Daigaku Kyoyobu, 16-1, 3-chome, Honcho-dori, Morioka-shi, Iwate-ken 020, Japan. TEL 0196-51-5111. FAX 0196-25-5816.
circ. 330. *6536*

IZOTOPTECHNIKA, DIAGNOSZTIKA.
Izotop Intezet Kft., P.O. Box 77, 1525 Budapest, Hungary. TEL 361-169-9499. FAX 361-169-5087.
circ. 350. *1753*

J A M I F.
Association des Medecins Israelites de France, 11 ave. de la Republique, 94260 Fresnes, France.
circ. 8,500. *4689*

J L B SMITH INSTITUTE OF ICHTHYOLOGY. ICHTHYOLOGICAL BULLETIN.
J L B Smith Institute of Ichthyology, Private Bag 1015, Grahamstown 6140, South Africa. TEL 27-461-311002. FAX 27-461-22403.
circ. 1,000. *838*

J L B SMITH INSTITUTE OF ICHTHYOLOGY. SPECIAL PUBLICATION.
J L B Smith Institute of Ichthyology, Private Bag 1015, Grahamstown 6140, South Africa. TEL 27-461-27124. FAX 27-461-22403.
circ. 1,000. *838*

J U MAGAZINE.
Jacksonville University, 2800 University Blvd. N., Jacksonville, FL 32211. TEL 904-745-7045. FAX 904-775-7047.
circ. 17,000. *1957*

J. WAYNE AND ELSIE M. GUNN CENTER FOR THE STUDY OF SCIENCE FICTION NEWSLETTER.
J. Wayne and Elsie M. Gunn Center for the Study of Science Fiction, University of Kansas, English Department, Lawrence, KS 66045. TEL 913-864-3380. FAX 913-864-4298.
circ. 1,200. *4532*

JAARBOEK NUMAGA.
Vereniging Numaga, P.O. Box 1359, 6501 BJ Nijmegen, Netherlands.
circ. 1,300. *3576*

JACKSON BUSINESS JOURNAL.
Box 12727, Jackson, MS 39236-2727. TEL 601-956-0756. FAX 601-956-4047.
circ. 4,007. *974*

JACKSONVILLE MEDICINE.
Duval County Medical Society, 515 Lomax St., Jacksonville, FL 32204. TEL 904-355-6561. FAX 904-353-5848.
circ. 1,800. *4689*

JAEGER.
Jaegerne, Danmarks Jaegerforbund, Hoejnaesvej 56, DK-2610 Roedovre, Denmark. TEL 45-38 33 29 11. FAX 45-31-19-02-41. *6872*

DER JAEGER IN BADEN-WUERTTEMBERG.
Dr. Neinhaus Verlag AG, Wollgrasweg 31, 70599 Stuttgart, Germany. TEL 49-711-4512768. FAX 49-456603.
circ. 30,000. *6872*

JAHRBUCH FUER GLOCKENKUNDE.
Deutsches Glockenmuseum auf Burg Greifenstein e.V., Talstr. 19, 35753 Greifenstein, Germany. TEL 49-6449-6460.
circ. 600. *5356*

JAMAICAN GEOGRAPHER.
Jamaican Geographical Society, c/o Geography Dept., University of the West Indies, Kingston 7, Jamaica, W.I. TEL 809-927-2129. FAX 809-977-6029.
circ. 350. *3411*

JAMAICAN HISTORICAL REVIEW.
Jamaican Historical Society, P.O. Box 105, Kingston 977-5448, Jamaica, W.I. TEL 809-968-7280. FAX 809-926-2217.
circ. 1,000. *3632*

JAMESTOWN COLLEGE. ALUMNI & FRIENDS.
6093 College Lane, Jamestown, ND 58405. TEL 701-252-3467. FAX 701-253-4318.
circ. 12,000. *1957*

JAMI'AT AL-AZHAR. KULLIYYAT AL-LUGHAH AL-ARABIYYAH BIL-ZAGAZIG. MAJALLAH.
Jami'at al-Azhar, Kulliyyat al-Lughah al-Arabiyyah bil-Zagazig, Zagazig, Egypt. TEL 02-055-324114. FAX 02-055-330204. *4266*

JANA SANGH PATRIKA.
Bharatiya Janasangh Kerala Pradesh, M.G. Road, Cochin 11, India. *5936*

JAPAN. FORESTRY AND FOREST PRODUCTS RESEARCH INSTITUTE. ANNUAL REPORT.
Kyushu Research Center, Forestry and Forest Products Research Institute, 4-11-16 Kurokami, Kumamoto 860, Japan. TEL 096-343-3168. FAX 096-344-5054.
circ. 700. *3156*

JAPANESE BULLETIN OF ARTS THERAPY.
Societe Japonaise de Psychopathologie de l'Expression, c/o Neuropsychiatric Research Institute, 91 Bentencho, Shinjuku-ku, Tokyo 162, Japan. TEL 81-3-3260-9171. FAX 81-3-3260-9191.
circ. 4,500. *449*

JAPANESE GUIDE TO HAWAII.
Stone Publishing Company, Box 8983, Honolulu, HI 96830. TEL 808-531-2637.
circ. 45,000. *7213*

JAPANESE JOURNAL OF EDUCATIONAL PSYCHOLOGY.
Japanese Association of Educational Psychology, c/o Faculty of Education, University of Tokyo, 7-3-1 Hongo, Bunkyo-ku, Tokyo 113, Japan. *6120*

JAPANESE JOURNAL OF ORAL AND MAXILLOFACIAL SURGERY.
Japanese Society of Oral and Maxillofacial Surgeons, 1-15-2-502 Nakasato, Kita-ku, Tokyo 114, Japan.
circ. 2,500. *4860*

JAPANESE JOURNAL OF TOXICOLOGY AND ENVIRONMENTAL HEALTH.
Pharmaceutical Society of Japan, 12-15, Shibuya 2-chome, Shibuya-ku, Tokyo 150, Japan.
circ. 1,700. *2979*

JAPANESE TELEPHONE DIRECTORY AND GUIDE OF SOUTHERN CALIFORNIA.
Japan Publicity, 19300 S. Hamilton Ave., Ste. 110, Gardena, CA 90248-4408. TEL 310-515-7100. FAX 310-515-7188.
circ. 65,000. *1690*

JAYCEES MAGAZINE.
United States Jaycees, 4 W. 21st St., Box 7, Tulsa, OK 74102-0007. TEL 918-584-2481. FAX 918-584-4422.
circ. 140,000. *1933*

JAZZ.
Hochuli AG, Box 4132, Mutteuz, Switzerland.
circ. 10,000. *5402*

JEG ARBEJDER MED.
Dansk Historisk Haandbogsforlag ApS, Buddingevej 87 A, DK-2800 Lyngby, Denmark. TEL 45-93-48-00. FAX 45-93-47-47.
circ. 2,400. *3229*

JEOPARDY.
College Hall 132, Western Washington University, Bellingham, WA 98225. TEL 360-650-3118.
circ. 1,200. *4419*

THE JERSEY.
Jersey Cattle Society of the United Kingdom, Scotsbridge House, Scots Hill, Rickmannsworth, Herts WD3 3BB, England. TEL 44-1923-897063. FAX 44-1923-897691.
circ. 1,000. *279*

JERSEY AT HOME.
Royal Jersey Agricultural and Horticultural Society, Springfield, St. Helier, Jersey JE2 4LF, Channel Islands. TEL 44-1534-866555. FAX 44-1534-865619.
circ. 2,000. *256*

JERSEY EVENING POST.
P.O. Box 582, Jersey JE4 8XQ, Channel Islands. TEL 44-1534-611611. FAX 44-1534-611622.
circ. 25,000. *3368*

JERSEY JAZZ.
New Jersey Jazz Society, Box 410, Brookside, NJ 07926. TEL 201-543-2039.
circ. 1,500. *5404*

JESSE MEYERS' BEVERAGE DIGEST.
Beverage Digest Company, LLC, Box 621, Bedford Hills, NY 10507-0621. *522*

JEWELLERY NEWS ASIA (CHINESE EDITION).
Miller Freeman Asia Ltd., 102-5 Stanhope House, 738 King's Rd., Quarry Bay, Hong Kong, People's Republic of China. TEL 852-2805-5661. FAX 852-2960-0977.
circ. 9,000. *3865*

JEWELLERY TIME.
Ink Link Publications, Box 46-218, Herne Bay, Auckland, New Zealand. TEL 64-9-3781222. FAX 64-9-3781270.
circ. 1,200. *3865*

THE JEWELRY APPRAISER.
National Association of Jewelry Appraisers, Box 6558, Annapolis, MD 21401-0558. TEL 301-261-8270.
circ. 700. *3865*

JEWISH CIVIC PRESS.
924 Valmont St., New Orleans, LA 70115. TEL 504-895-8784.
circ. 5,845. *3020*

JEWISH JOURNAL (DEERFIELD BEACH).
Newspaper Network, 601 Fairway Dr., Deerfield Beach, FL 33441. TEL 305-698-6397. FAX 305-429-1207.
circ. 56,000. *3021*

JEWISH SPORTS & FITNESS.
Jewish Sports Congress, P.O. Box 234549, Great Neck, NY 11023-4549. TEL 516-482-5550. FAX 516-482-5583.
circ. 250,000. *5785*

JEWISH STAR (SAN FRANCISCO).
Fraternal Media, 109 Minna St., Ste. 323, San Francisco, CA 94105-3701. TEL 415-421-4874. FAX 415-398-7983.
circ. 3,000. *3022*

JEWISH VEGETARIAN NEWSLETTER.
Jewish Vegetarians of North America, 6938 Reliance Rd., Federalsburg, MD 21632. TEL 410-754-5550.
circ. 520. *5475*

THE JEWISH VOICE (PROVIDENCE).
Jewish Federation of Rhode Island, 130 Sessions St., Providence, RI 02906. TEL 401-421-4111. FAX 401-331-7961.
circ. 7,500. *3022*

JEWS FOR JESUS NEWSLETTER.
Jews for Jesus, 60 Haight St., San Francisco, CA 94102. TEL 415-864-2600. FAX 415-552-8325.
circ. 135,000. *6492*

JIANGSU GAOJIAO.
Jiangsu Sheng Gaodeng Jiaoyu Xuehui, 207 Shanghai Rd., Nanjing, Jiangsu 210024, People's Republic of China. TEL 86-25-6638659. FAX 86-25-7714402.
circ. 5,000. *2546*

JIDOSHA HOYU SHARYOSU.
Jidosha Kensa Toroku Kyoryokukai, Toranomon Kiyoshi Bldg., 3-10, 4-chome, Toranomon, Minato-ku, Tokyo 105, Japan. TEL 81-3-3432-5611. FAX 81-3-3432-1044.
circ. 1,500. *6921*

JIEGOU GONGCHENGSHI.
Tongji Chubanshe, 1239 Siping Rd., Shanghai 200092, People's Republic of China. TEL 86-21-6502-5080.
circ. 2,000. *2789*

JINKO KOKYU.
Nihon Kokyurhyohou Igakkai, Fukushima Kenritsu Ika Daigaku Masuikagaku Kyoshitsu, 1, Hikarigaoka, Fukushima-shi, Fukushima-ken 960-12, Japan. TEL 81-245-48-0828. FAX 81-245-48-0828.
circ. 1,350. *5119*

JOB PRATIQUE MAGAZINE.
23 rue des Appenins, 75017 Paris, France. TEL 33-1-42285900. FAX 33-1-42282458.
circ. 11,000. *5511*

JOB SHOP TECHNOLOGY.
Edwards Publishing, 16 Waterbury Rd., Box 7193, Prospect, CT 06712-1237. TEL 203-758-4474. FAX 203-758-4475.
circ. 100,000. *1588*

JOBMART.
American Planning Association, 122 S. Michigan Ave., Ste. 1600, Chicago, IL 60603-6107. TEL 312-431-9100. FAX 312-431-9985.
circ. 5,500. *5511*

JOHN & MABLE RINGLING MUSEUM OF ART.
John and Mable Ringling Museum of Art Foundation, 5401 Bay Shore Rd., Sarasota, FL 34243-2161. TEL 813-359-5700. FAX 813-359-5745.
circ. 5,000. *5356*

JOHNS HOPKINS A P L TECHNICAL DIGEST.
Johns Hopkins University, Applied Physics Laboratory, Johns Hopkins Rd., Laurel, MD 20723. TEL 301-953-5625. FAX 301-953-1093.
circ. 5,800. *5808*

JOINT GOVERNMENTAL SALARY AND BENEFITS SURVEY: ARIZONA.
Department of Administration, Personnel Division, 1831 W. Jefferson, Phoenix, AZ 85007-3204. TEL 602-542-5250. *1052*

JORDANS JOURNAL.
Jordan Publishing Ltd., 21 St. Thomas St., Bristol BS1 6JS, England. TEL 0117-923-0600. FAX 0117-923-0063.
circ. 7,200. *975*

JOSLYN NEWS.
Joslyn Art Museum, 2200 Dodge St., Omaha, NE 68102. TEL 402-342-3300. FAX 402-342-2376.
circ. 7,500. *5356*

JOURNAL DE L'ILE DE LA REUNION.
Ste. France Antilles, 42 rue Alexis-de-Villeneuve, B.P. 166, 97463 Saint-Denis, Reunion. TEL 21-32-64. FAX 262-20-08-37.
circ. 26,000. *3248*

JOURNAL DES PAYS D'EN HAUT.
Les Publications Laurentiennes, P.O. Box 1890, 1012 rue Valiquette, Ste. Adele PQ J0R 1L0, Canada. TEL 514-229-6664. FAX 514-229-6063.
circ. 17,000. *3262*

JOURNAL DU BARREAU.
Barreau du Quebec, Maison du Barreau, 445 St-Laurent Blvd., Montreal, PQ H2Y 3T8, Canada. TEL 514-954-3440. FAX 514-954-3477.
circ. 21,800. *3968*

JOURNAL HOLDINGS IN THE NATIONAL CAPITAL AREA.
Interlibrary Users Association, c/o Barbara Kopp, P R C Inc., 1500 PRC Dr., McLean, VA 22102. TEL 703-556-1166. FAX 703-556-1174.
circ. 250. *4226*

JOURNAL INDUSTRIEL DU QUEBEC.
Info-Industriel Inc., 2370 E. Boul. Henri-Bourassa, Montreal, Que. H2B 1T6, Canada. TEL 514-388-8801. FAX 514-388-7871.
circ. 25,000. *900*

JOURNAL OF AFFORDABLE HOUSING AND COMMUNITY DEVELOPMENT LAW.
American Bar Association, 750 N. Lake Shore Dr., Chicago, IL 60611. TEL 312-988-5522. FAX 312-988-5568.
circ. 1,300. *3751*

JOURNAL OF ATHLETIC TRAINING.
National Athletic Trainers Association, Inc., 2952 N. Stemmons Fwy., Dallas, TX 75247. TEL 800-879-6282. FAX 214-637-2206.
circ. 21,000. *5130*

JOURNAL OF CELLULOSE SCIENCE AND TECHNOLOGY.
Guangzhou Research Institute of Chemistry, P.O. Box 1122, Wushan, Guangzhou, Guangdong Province 510650, People's Republic of China. TEL 86-20-705360. FAX 86-20-7705319.
circ. 1,000. *5567*

JOURNAL OF COLLEGE AND UNIVERSITY STUDENT HOUSING.
Association of College and University Housing Officers' International, 364 West Lane Ave., Ste. C, Columbus, OH 43201-1062. TEL 614-292-0099. FAX 614-292-3205.
circ. 3,000. *2546*

JOURNAL OF COMPUTER INFORMATION SYSTEMS.
International Association for Computer Information Systems, 217 College of Business, Oklahoma State University, Stillwater, OK 74078. TEL 405-744-8632. FAX 405-744-5180.
circ. 1,000. *2156*

CONTROLLED CIRCULATION SERIALS

JOURNAL OF COMPUTING IN TEACHER EDUCATION.
International Society for Technology in Education, 1787 Agate St., Eugene, OR 97403-1923. TEL 541-346-4414.
circ. 2,500. *2518*

JOURNAL OF COOPERATIVE EDUCATION.
Cooperative Education Association, Inc., 8640 Giulford Rd., Ste. 215, Columbia, MD 21046-2615. TEL 410-290-3666. FAX 410-290-7084.
circ. 3,000. *2455*

JOURNAL OF CYTOLOGY AND GENETICS.
Society of Cytologists and Geneticists, Department of Botany, Bangalore University, Bangalore 560 056, India. TEL 91-81-3355036.
circ. 350. *772*

JOURNAL OF DATABASE MANAGEMENT.
Idea Group Publishing, 1331 E. Chocolate Ave., Hershey, PA 17033-1751. TEL 717-541-9150. FAX 717-541-9159.
circ. 300. *2167*

JOURNAL OF ELECTROTOPOGRAPHY.
Electrotopograph Corporation, Box 98, Eldred, PA 16731. TEL 814-225-3296.
circ. 1,000. *5809*

JOURNAL OF EUROPEAN BUSINESS.
Faulkner & Gray, Inc. (New York), 11 Penn Plaza, 17th Fl., New York, NY 10001. TEL 212-967-7000. FAX 212-967-7155.
circ. 6,202. *977*

JOURNAL OF FAMILY LIFE.
72 Philip St., Albany, NY 12202. TEL 518-432-1578. FAX 518-462-6836.
circ. 4,000. *6716*

JOURNAL OF FINANCIAL PLANNING TODAY.
New Directions Publications, Inc., Box 6097, W. Palm Beach, FL 33405. TEL 407-434-0100. FAX 407-641-4801.
circ. 500. *1150*

JOURNAL OF GENERAL ORTHODONTICS.
International Association for Orthodontics, 1100 Lake St., Ste. 240, Oak Park, IL 60301-1035. TEL 708-445-0320. FAX 708-445-0321.
circ. 3,800. *4861*

JOURNAL OF GENETICS & BREEDING.
Istituto Sperimentale per la Cerealicoltura, Via Cassia, 176, 00191 Rome, Italy. TEL 39-6-3295705. FAX 39-6-36306022.
circ. 300. *130*

JOURNAL OF HOUSING RESEARCH.
Federal National Mortgage Association, 3900 Wisconsin Ave., N.W., Washington, DC 20016-2899. TEL 202-752-4422. FAX 202-752-4933.
circ. 3,200. *3751*

JOURNAL OF INDO-EUROPEAN STUDIES.
Institute for the Study of Man, 1133 13th St., N.W., No. C-2, Washington, DC 20005. TEL 202-371-2700. FAX 202-371-1523.
circ. 80. *6622*

JOURNAL OF INTERNATIONAL MARKETING & MARKETING RESEARCH.
European Marketing Association, 18 St. Peters Steps, Brixham, Devon, England. *1534*

JOURNAL OF KANSAS PHARMACY.
Kansas Pharmacists Association, 1308 SW. 10th Ave., Topeka, KS 66604-1299. TEL 913-232-0439. FAX 913-232-3764.
circ. 1,200. *5671*

JOURNAL OF MICROWAVE POWER AND ELECTROMAGNETIC ENERGY.
International Microwave Power Institute, 10210 Leatherleaf Ct., Manassas, VA 20111-4245. TEL 703-257-1415.
circ. 1,000. *2837*

JOURNAL OF MIND AND BEHAVIOR.
Institute of Mind & Behavior, Box 522, Village Sta., New York, NY 10014. TEL 212-595-4853.
circ. 1,097. *6128*

JOURNAL OF MYOCARDIAL ISCHEMIA.
P R R, Inc., 17 Prospect St., Huntington, NY 11743. TEL 516-424-8900. FAX 516-424-8503.
circ. 27,833. *4821*

JOURNAL OF N I H RESEARCH.
William M. Miller, 1444 I St., NW, Ste. 1000, Washington, DC 20005. TEL 202-785-5333. FAX 202-872-7738.
circ. 28,774. *4697*

JOURNAL OF NUCLEAR AGRICULTURE AND BIOLOGY.
Indian Society for Nuclear Techniques in Agriculture and Biology, Nuclear Research Laboratory, Indian Agricultural Research Institute, New Delhi 110012, India.
circ. 400. *232*

JOURNAL OF ORTHOPAEDIC SURGERY.
Hong Kong University Press, 139 Pokfulam Rd., Hong Kong, People's Republic of China. TEL 852-2550-2703. FAX 852-2875-0734.
circ. 2,000. *5010*

JOURNAL OF PARK AND RECREATION ADMINISTRATION.
Sagamore Publishing Inc., 804 Neil St., Ste. 100, Champaign, IL 61820. TEL 217-359-5940. FAX 217-359-5975.
circ. 720. *6873*

JOURNAL OF PLANAR CHROMATOGRAPHY - MODERN T L C.
Research Institute for Medicinal Plants, Lupaszigeti st. 4, P.O. Box 11, 2011 Budakalasz, Hungary. TEL 36-1-1688042. FAX 36-26-340426.
circ. 220. *1793*

JOURNAL OF POPULATION AND HEALTH STUDIES.
Korea Institute for Population and Health, SAN 42-14 Bulgwang-Dong, Eunpyung-Ku, Seoul 122, S. Korea. *857*

JOURNAL OF SPORTS PHILATELY.
Sports Philatelists International, c/o Margaret A. Jones, 5310 Lindenwood Ave., St.Louis, MO 63109-1758. TEL 314-352-0888.
circ. 500. *5708*

JOURNAL OF TAIWAN MUSEUM.
Taiwan Provincial Museum, 2 Siangyang Rd., Taipei, Taiwan 100, Republic of China. TEL 886-2-397-9396. FAX 886-2-397-9514.
circ. 1,000. *5356*

JOURNAL OF TOSOH RESEARCH.
Tosoh Corporation, 4560 Tonda, Shinnanyo-shi, Yamaguchi-ken 746, Japan. FAX 81-834-62-1748.
circ. 750. *2767*

JOURNAL OF TRANSPORTATION MEDICINE.
Japanese Association of Transportation Medicine, c/o Business Center for Academic Societies Japan, 5-16-9 Honkomagome, Bunkyo-ku, Tokyo 113, Japan. TEL 03-5814-5811. FAX 03-5814-5822.
circ. 600. *5011*

JOURNALIST'S HANDBOOK.
Carrick Media, 2-7 Galt House, 31 Bank St., Irvine KA12 OLL, Scotland. TEL 44-1294-311322.
circ. 2,600. *3876*

JOURNALS OF DISSENT AND SOCIAL CHANGE.
California State University, Sacramento, Library, 2000 Jed Smith Dr., Sacramento, CA 95819. TEL 916-278-6466. *6740*

JOURNEE VINICOLE.
Promovin, B.P. 1064, 34007 Montpellier Cedex 1, France. TEL 04-67-07-91-01. FAX 04-67-47-93-63.
circ. 15,900. *523*

JUDARNA I F.D. SOVJET.
Svenska Kommitten foer Judarna i f.d. Sovjet, P.O. Box 5053, S-102 42 Stockholm, Sweden. TEL 46-8-664-53-38. FAX 46-8-664-05-91.
circ. 2,600. *5994*

THE JUDICIAL REVIEW.
Judicial Commission of New South Wales, Level 5, 201 George St., Sydney, N.S.W. 2000, Australia. TEL 61-2-92994421. FAX 61-2-92903194.
circ. 500. *4133*

JUDO.
Judo Magazine B.V., Blokhoeve 5, 3438 LC Nieuwegein, Netherlands. TEL 31-23-325260. FAX 31-23-342721.
circ. 60,000. *6767*

JUNIOR STATEMENT.
Junior Statesmen of America, 60 E. Third Ave., Ste. 320, San Mateo, CA 94401. TEL 415-347-1600. FAX 415-347-7200.
circ. 20,000. *1876*

JUNTENDO MEDICAL JOURNAL.
Juntendo Medical Society, 2-1-1 Hongo, Bunkyo-ku, Tokyo 113, Japan. FAX 91-3-3814-9100.
circ. 3,550. *4699*

JURBOOK.
Varus Verlag Birgit Laube, Koenigswintererstr. 552, 53227 Bonn, Germany. TEL 0228-440015. FAX 0228-440017.
circ. 18,000. *4054*

JURISTISCHE SCHULUNG.
Verlag C.H. Beck, 80791 Munich, Germany. TEL 49-89-38189-338. FAX 49-89-38189-398.
circ. 24,738. *3972*

JUS-EXTRA.
Oesterreichische Staatsdruckerei, Rennweg 12a, A-1037 Vienna, Austria. TEL 01-79789307. FAX 01-79789419.
circ. 1,250. *4071*

K.A.C.B. AUTO REVUE.
Koninklijke Automobiel Club van Belgie, 53 rue d'Arlon, B-1040 Brussels, Belgium. TEL 32-2-2870911. FAX 32-2-2307584.
circ. 40,000. *7104*

K C M S BULLETIN.
Medical Society County of Kings, Inc., 1313 Bedford Ave., Brooklyn, NY 11216. TEL 718-467-9000. FAX 718-778-0380.
circ. 2,800. *4699*

K F Z BETRIEB AKTUELLE WOCHENZEITUNG.
Vogel Verlag und Druck GmbH & Co. KG, Max-Planck-Str. 7-9, 97082 Wuerzburg, Germany. TEL 49-931-4182145. FAX 49-931-4182905.
circ. 37,231. *7104*

K F Z BETRIEB UNTERNEHMERMAGAZIN.
Vogel Verlag und Druck GmbH & Co. KG, Max-Planck-Str. 7-9, 97082 Wuerzburg, Germany. TEL 49-931-4182145. FAX 49-931-4182905.
circ. 38,298. *7104*

K MITTEILUNGEN.
Gesamtverband Kunststoffverarbeitende Industrie e.V., Froschpfort 16, 56410 Montabaur, Germany. FAX 49-2602-4308.
circ. 3,000. *5879*

K N A G NIEUWS.
Koninklijk Nederlands Aardrijkskundig Genootschap, P.O. Box 80123, 3508 TC Utrecht, Netherlands. TEL 31-30-532757. FAX 31-30-535523.
circ. 4,300. *3412*

K O A DIRECTORY ROAD ATLAS AND CAMPING GUIDE.
Meredith Corporation, 1716 Locust St., Des Moines, IA 50336. TEL 515-284-3412. FAX 515-284-2700.
circ. 1,900,000. *1690*

K: REVISTA DE POESIA.
Lubio Cardozo y Juan Pinto, Eds. & Pubs., Apartado 410, Herida, Venezuela. *4512*

K W S NEWSLETTER.
Kenya Wildlife Service, Nairobi Education Centre, P.O. Box 40241, Nairobi, Kenya. TEL 254-2-501081. FAX 254-2-505866.
circ. 2,000. *2234*

KABAR.
Australia Indonesia Association of New South Wales, G.P.O. Box 802, Sydney, N.S.W. 2001, Australia. TEL 61-2-635-4186.
circ. 150. *6024*

KACHERE TEXTS.
University of Malawi, Chancellor College, P.O. Box 280, Zomba, Malawi. TEL 265-50-522549. FAX 265-50-522046.
circ. 500. *6350*

KAERNTER BAUER.
Kammer fuer Land- und Forstwirtschaft Kaernten, Museumgasse 5, A-9020 Klagenfurt, Austria. TEL 43-463-5850. FAX 43-463-5850389.
circ. 30,000. *131*

KAGAKU GIJUTSU BUNKEN TOYAMA.
Kagaku Gijutsu Bunken Riyo Shikokai, c/o Toyama Prefectural Library, 206-3 Chayamachi, Toyama 930-01, Japan.
circ. 500. *6981*

KAGOSHIMA UNIVERSITY. RESEARCH CENTER FOR THE SOUTH PACIFIC. OCCASIONAL PAPERS.
Kagoshima University, Research Center for the South Pacific, 1-21-24, Korimoto, Kagoshima 890, Japan. TEL 81-99-285-7394. FAX 81-99-256-9358.
circ. 700. *6539*

KAI TIAKI: NURSING NEW ZEALAND.
New Zealand Nurses' Organisation, P.O. Box 2128, Wellington, New Zealand. TEL 64-4-385-0847. FAX 64-4-382-9993.
circ. 24,000. *4939*

KAKU YUUGOU KAGAKU KENKYUSHO NYUSU.
Kaku Yuugou Kagaku Kenkyusho, Furocho, Chikusa-ku, Nagoya-shi, Aichi-ken 464-01, Japan. TEL 81-52-789-4551. FAX 81-52-789-4200.
circ. 2,650. *5853*

KALAMAZOO COLLEGE QUARTERLY.
Kalamazoo College, 1200 Academy St., Kalamazoo, MI 49006-3295. TEL 616-377-7304. FAX 616-337-7305.
circ. 15,500. *1958*

KALASTAJA.
Kalatalouden Keskusliitto, Koydenpunojankatu 7 B 23, FIN-00180 Helsinki, Finland. TEL 358-9-640-126. FAX 358-9-608-309.
circ. 9,636. *3072*

KALEIDOSCOPE (BIRMINGHAM).
University of Alabama at Birmingham, Box 76, University Center, Birmingham, AL 35294-1150. TEL 205-934-3354.
circ. 8,000. *1958*

KALEVA.
Sanomalehti Kaleva, P.O. Box 70, FIN-90101 Oulu, Finland. TEL 358-8-5377245. FAX 358-8-5377248.
circ. 83,867. *3278*

KALOKAGATHIA.
Magyar Testnevelesi Egyetem, Alkotas u. 44, 1123 Budapest, Hungary. TEL 36-1-1564-444. FAX 36-1-1566-337.
circ. 300. *6767*

KAN ANDERS.
Kan Anders, Werkgemeenschap voor Pacifisme, Ekologie en Socialisme, Vlamingstraat 82, 2611 LA Delft, Netherlands. TEL 31-15-2121694.
circ. 900. *6024*

KANAGAWA-KEN HAKUBUTSUKAN KYOKAI KAIHO.
Kanagawa-ken Hakubutsukan Kyokai, 5-60 Minami-Nakadori, Naka-ku, Yokohama-shi, Kanagawa-ken 231, Japan. TEL 045-201-0926. FAX 045-201-7364. *5357*

KANSAS. DEPARTMENT OF HEALTH AND ENVIRONMENT. ANNUAL SUMMARY OF VITAL STATISTICS.
Department of Health and Environment, Center for Health and Environmental Statistics, 900 S.W. Jackson, Topeka, KS 66612-1290. TEL 913-296-5640. FAX 913-296-7025.
circ. 1,000. *6053*

KANSAS. LEGISLATIVE RESEARCH DEPARTMENT. REPORT ON KANSAS LEGISLATIVE INTERIM STUDIES.
Legislative Research Department, Topeka, KS 66612. TEL 913-296-3181. *5938*

KANSAS RESTAURANT.
Kansas Restaurant Association, 359 S. Hydraulic, Wichita, KS 67211. TEL 316-267-8383.
circ. 1,500. *3731*

KANSAS WILDFLOWER SOCIETY NEWSLETTER.
Hall Publishing Co., Washburn University, Topeka, KS 66621. TEL 913-231-1010. FAX 913-233-2780.
circ. 550. *3197*

KANTINEN.
Kantineledernes Landsklub, Kolleruplund 63, 2665 Vallensbaek Strand, Denmark. FAX 45-43-54-34-52.
circ. 4,347. *1933*

KAPPA ALPHA PSI JOURNAL.
McQuiddy Publishing Co., 2320 N. Broad St., Philadelphia, PA 19132. TEL 215-228-7184.
circ. 16,000. *1933*

KAPPA DELTA EPSILON CURRENT.
Kappa Delta Epsilon, c/o Toni Gorrell, Ed., 201 Suelynn Dr., Normal, IL 61761. TEL 309-438-2164. FAX 309-438-8659.
circ. 1,500. *1958*

KAPPA TAU ALPHA. NEWSLETTER.
Kappa Tau Alpha, U M School of Journalism, Columbia, MO 65211. TEL 573-882-7685. FAX 573-882-4823.
circ. 500. *3876*

KARAYOLLARI TEKNIK BULTENI.
General Directorate of Highways, Ankara, Turkey.
circ. 3,000. *2792*

DER KARTOFFELBAU.
Verlag Th. Mann, Nordring 10, 45894 Gelsenkirchen, Germany. TEL 49-209-9304184. FAX 49-209-9304185.
circ. 5,491. *233*

KATES KIN.
1395 Main St., Box 8, Rarden, OH 45671. TEL 614-372-6705.
circ. 800. *3229*

KATORIKKU KENKYU.
Sophia University, Theological Society, Kamishakujii 4-32-11, Nerima-ku, Tokyo 177, Japan. TEL 81-3-5991-0343. FAX 81-3-5991-6928.
circ. 1,000. *6467*

KAUPPAKAMARILEHTI.
Keskuskauppakamari, P.O. Box 1000, FIN-00101 Helsinki 10, Finland. TEL 358-9-696969. FAX 358-9-650303.
circ. 20,000. *1191*

KEADILAN.
Islamic University of Indonesia, Faculty of Law, Jalan Taman Siswa 158, Yogyakarta 55151, Indonesia. TEL 2978.
circ. 2,500. *3973*

KEEP ON TRUCKIN' NEWS.
Mid-West Truckers Association, Inc., 2727 N. Dirksen Parkway, Springfield, IL 62702. TEL 217-525-0310. FAX 217-525-0342.
circ. 3,500. *7175*

KEHITTYVAE KAUPPA.
Kauppiaitten Kustannus Oy, Kanavakatu 3.B, FIN-00160 Helsinki, Finland. TEL 358-0-228821.
circ. 21,368. *1536*

KEIRYO KOKUGO GAKU.
Keiryo Kokugo Gakkai, c/o Tokyo Joshi Daigaku, Zenpukuji 2-6-1, Suginami-ku, Tokyo 167, Japan. TEL 81-3-3395-1211.
circ. 600. *4270*

KEIZAIGAKU KENKYU.
Keizai Riron Gakkai, c/o Rikkyo Daigaku Keizaigakubu, 3 Ikebukuro, Toshima-ku, Tokyo 171, Japan. *979*

KEIZAIGAKU RONSHU.
University of Tokyo Press, 3-1 Hongo 7-chome, Bunkyo-ku, Tokyo 113, Japan. *979*

KELLY'S LINK.
Kelly's Directories, Part of the Reed Elsevier group, Windsor Court, E. Grinstead House, E. Grinstead, W. Sussex RH19 1XB, England. TEL 01342-326972. FAX 01342-335747.
circ. 50,000. *1690*

KELLY'S OIL & GAS DIRECTORY.
Kelly's Directories, Part of the Reed Elsevier group, Windsor Court, E. Grinstead House, E. Grinstead, W. Sussex RH19 1XB, England. TEL 01342-326972. FAX 01342-335747.
circ. 7,000. *1690*

KEMPER MAGAZINE.
Kemper Insurance Cos., Corporate Marketing, F-3, 1 Kemper Dr., Long Grove, IL 60049-0001. FAX 847-320-4270.
circ. 13,600. *3823*

KENKALUSIKKA.
Suomen Kenkakauppiaiden Liitto r.y., Fredrikinkatu 67 E 42, FIN-00100 Helsinki 10, Finland. TEL 358-0-409-932. FAX 358-0-409-563.
circ. 1,296. *6595*

KENTUCKY COUNCIL ON HIGHER EDUCATION. COUNCIL ACTIONS.
Kentucky Council on Higher Education, 1050 U.S. 127 S., Ste. 101, Frankfort, KY 40601-4395. TEL 502-564-3553. FAX 502-564-2063.
circ. 1,200. *2547*

KENTUCKY NURSE.
Kentucky Nurses Association, Box 2616, Louisville, KY 40201. TEL 502-637-2546. FAX 502-637-8236.
circ. 28,000. *4939*

KENTUCKY TEACHER.
Department of Education, Office of Communication Services, 1919 Capital Plaza Tower, Frankfort, KY 40601. TEL 502-564-3421. FAX 502-564-6470.
circ. 50,000. *2458*

KENYA SOCIETY FOR THE BLIND. ANNUAL REPORT AND ACCOUNTS.
Kenya Society for the Blind, P.O. Box 46656, Nairobi, Kenya. TEL 254-2-503757.
circ. 2,000. *3471*

KERALA SABHA.
Better Life Movement, Better Life Center, Aloor, Kallettumkara, Kerala 680 683, India.
circ. 2,000. *6493*

KESHEV.
Bar-Ilan University, Institute of Holocaust Research, Ramat Gan 52100, Israel.
circ. 1,000. *3579*

KEY - A GUIDE TO COLLEGE AND CAREERS.
Target Marketing, Inc., 5 Victory Ln., Ste. 101, Liberty, MO 64068. TEL 816-781-7557. FAX 816-792-3892.
circ. 1,400,000. *2525*

KHADYA VIGYAN.
Central Food Technological Research Institute, Mysore 570 013, India.
circ. 1,500. *3117*

KIDS WORLD MAGAZINE.
M2 Communications, 93 Lombard Ave., Ste. 108, Winnipeg, MB R3B 3B1, Canada. TEL 204-985-8160. FAX 204-943-8991.
circ. 225,000. *1876*

DER KIESELSTEIN.
Bundesvereinigung Stotterer-Selbsthilfe e.V., Gereonswall 112, 50670 Cologne, Germany. TEL 49-221-1391106. FAX 49-221-1391370.
circ. 1,300. *2586*

KINDAI.
Kindai-Eiga Corp., Owaricho Bldg., 2F, 6-8-3 Ginza, Chuo-ku, Tokyo 104, Japan. TEL 81-3-5568-2811. FAX 81-3-5568-2818. *5338*

KINGSMAN.
City University of New York, Brooklyn College, c/o Michael Golub, Box 23-0200, Brooklyn, NY 11223. TEL 718-376-1429.
circ. 20,000. *1958*

KINO JOURNAL FRANKFURT.
Presse Verlagsgesellschaft fuer Zeitschriften und Neue Medien mbH, Ludwigstr. 37, 60327 Frankfurt a.M., Germany. TEL 49-69-97460-0. FAX 49-69-97460400.
circ. 22,000. *5338*

KIRJASTOLEHTI.
Suomen Kirjastoseura, Kansakoulukatu 10 A 19, SF-00100 Helsinki, Finland. TEL 358-0-694-1856. FAX 358-0-694-1859.
circ. 6,748. *4190*

KIRKLAND LAKE GAZETTE.
1 Duncan Ave., Kirkland Lake, ON P2N 2N8, Canada. TEL 705-568-NEWS. FAX 705-568-4444.
circ. 7,479. *3262*

CONTROLLED CIRCULATION SERIALS

KNOX COUNTY ILLINOIS GENEALOGICAL SOCIETY. QUARTERLY.
Knox County Illinois Genealogical Society, Box 13, Galesburg, IL 61402-0013.
circ. 280. *3230*

DER KNUEPFTEPPICH.
Panorama Verlags- und Werbegesellschaft mbH, Sudbrackstr. 14-18, 33611 Bielefeld, Germany. TEL 49-521-585540. FAX 49-521-585371.
circ. 4,000. *3847*

KOBE UNIVERSITY. SCHOOL OF BUSINESS ADMINISTRATION. ANNALS.
Kobe Daigaku, School of Business Administration, Rokkodai-cho, Nada-ku, Kobe-shi, Hyogo-ken 657, Japan. FAX 81-78-881-8100. *1490*

KOEBENHAVNS HAVNEBLAD.
Faellesrepraesentationen for Funktionaerer ved Koebenhavns Havnevaesen, Nordre Toldbod 7, Postboks 2083, 1013 Copenhagen K, Denmark. TEL 33 14 43 40, local 310. FAX 33-93-23-40.
circ. 4,400. *7155*

KOEBENHAVNS UNIVERSITET. GEOLOGISK CENTRALINSTITUT. AARSBERETNING.
Koebenhavns Universitet, Geologisk Institut, Oester Voldgade 10, DK-1350 Copenhagen K, Denmark. TEL 33-11-22-32.
circ. 525. *2355*

KOEDBRANCHEN.
Danske Slagtermestres Landsforening, P.O. Box 709, Poppelvej 83, DK-5230 Odense M, Denmark. TEL 45-66-12-87-30. FAX 45-66-12-87-94.
circ. 2,425. *3118*

KOKURITSU KAGAKU HAKUBUTSUKAN SENPO.
Monbusho, Kokuritsu Kagaku Hakubutsukan, 7-20 Ueno Koen, Taito-ku, Tokyo 110, Japan.
circ. 1,000. *6541*

KOKURITSU KOKKAI TOSHOKAN GEPPO.
National Diet Library, 1-10-1 Nagata-cho, Chiyoda-ku, Tokyo 100, Japan. TEL 81-3-3581-2331. FAX 81-3-3597-9104.
circ. 4,000. *4190*

KOKUSAIHO GAIKO ZASSHI.
Kokusaiho Gakkai, c/o Faculty of Law, University of Tokyo, 3-1, Hongo 7-chome, Bunkyo-ku, Tokyo, Japan. TEL 03-3812-2111.
circ. 800. *4121*

KOLDFAX.
Air-Conditioning and Refrigeration Institute, 4301 Fairfax Dr., Ste. 425, Arlington, VA 22203-1627. TEL 703-524-8800. FAX 703-528-3816. *3481*

KOLEINU.
Habonim-Dror Organisation, 523 Finchley Rd., London NW3 7BD, England. TEL 44-171-4359033. FAX 44-171-4314503.
circ. 1,500. *6406*

KOLONITRAEDGAARDEN.
Svenska Foerbundet foer Kolonitraedgaardar och Fritidsbyar, Aasoegatan 149, S-116 32 Stockholm, Sweden. TEL 46-8-743-00-90. FAX 46-8-40-38-98.
circ. 29,300. *3197*

KOMMUNALES ECHO RHEINLAND-PFALZ.
Vereinigte Verlagsanstalten GmbH, Hoeherweg 278, 40231 Duesseldorf, Germany. TEL 49-211-7357-0. FAX 49-211-7357223.
circ. 5,500. *6675*

KOMPETENZ.
Vereinigte Verlagsanstalten GmbH, Hoeherweg 278, 40231 Duesseldorf, Germany. TEL 49-211-7357-0. FAX 49-211-7357223.
circ. 10,000. *1202*

KONCAR STRUCNE INFORMACIJE.
S O U R Rade Koncar, O O U R Elektrotehnicki Institut, Bastijanova ul. bb, 41001 Zagreb, Croatia. TEL 041-312222. FAX 041-334170.
circ. 2,500. *2838*

KONEVIESTI.
Viestilehdet Oy, Revontulentie 8b, 02100 Espoo 10, Finland. TEL 90-131151. FAX 0-131-15209.
circ. 53,500. *4546*

KONJUNKTURNI BAROMETAR.
Zavod za Trzisna Istrazivanja, Mose Pijade 8-I, 11001 Belgrade, Yugoslavia. *1589*

KONSTRUKTIONSPRAXIS.
Vogel Verlag und Druck GmbH & Co. KG, Max-Planck-Str. 7-9, 97082 Wuerzburg, Germany. TEL 49-931-4182145. FAX 49-931-4182905.
circ. 26,918. *2864*

KONTROLLE.
Konradin Verlag Robert Kohlhammer GmbH, Ernst-Mey-Str. 8, 70771 Leinfelden-Echterdingen, Germany. TEL 49-711-7594-0. FAX 49-711-7594-390.
circ. 20,525. *2730*

KOOTENAY BUSINESS JOURNAL.
Catalyst Communications Inc., 2F-601 Front St., Nelson, BC V1L 5P5, Canada. TEL 604-352-6397. FAX 604-352-2588.
circ. 6,500. *981*

KOREA FORUM.
Korea-Verband im Asienhaus, Bullmannaue 11, 45327 Essen, Germany. TEL 0201-8303812.
circ. 600. *5531*

KOSMETISCHE MEDIZIN.
B M V - Berliner Medizinische Verlagsanstalt GmbH, Lietzenburgerstr. 97, 10719 Berlin, Germany. TEL 49-30-886749-0. FAX 49-30-88674999.
circ. 4,360. *4701*

KOSMOS.
International Society for Astrological Research, Inc., Box 38613, Los Angeles, CA 90038-0613. TEL 805-525-0461. FAX 805-525-0461.
circ. 1,000. *486*

KOSMOS.
Deutsche Verlags-Anstalt GmbH, Postfach 106012, 70049 Stuttgart, Germany. TEL 49-711-2631-0. FAX 49-711-2631110.
circ. 71,201. *6542*

KOTI.
Maa- ja Kotitalousnaisten Keskus, Lonnrotinkatu 13, SF-00120 Helsinki, Finland. TEL 90-680-700. FAX 90-680-70270.
circ. 25,365. *3686*

KRASNAPOLSKY GROUP NEWS.
Grand Hotel Krasnapolsky N.V., Dam 9, 1012 JS Amsterdam, Netherlands. TEL 31-20-5549111. FAX 31-20-6228607.
circ. 12,000. *7260*

KRISTDEMOKRATEN.
Samhaellsgemenskaps Foerlags AB, P.O. Box 19098, S-104 32 Stockholm, Sweden. TEL 46-8-15-05-45. FAX 46-8-612-79-53.
circ. 9,700. *5939*

KRISTELIGT DAGBLAD.
Fanoegade 15, DK-2100 Copenhagen Oe, Denmark. TEL 45-39-27-12-35. FAX 45-39-27-15-25.
circ. 15,662. *3275*

KRITERION.
Universitaet Salzburg, Institut fuer Philosophie, Franziskanergasse 1, A-5020 Salzburg, Austria. FAX 43-662-8044629.
circ. 500. *5735*

KROPPSOEVING.
Landslaget Fysisk Fostring i Skolen, Moellegt. 10, N-3111 Toensberg, N-3111 Toensberg, Norway. TEL 47-33-31-53-00. FAX 47-33-31-52-66.
circ. 2,700. *2459*

KUENSTLER JAHRBUCH.
Verlag Disco Post GmbH, Oststr. 2, 56424 Staudt, Germany. TEL 49-2602-70044. FAX 49-2602-69939.
circ. 10,000. *1693*

KUKHOEBO.
National Assembly, c/o Secretary-General, 1-1 Yeoidodong, Yeongdungpo-ku, Seoul, S. Korea. TEL 788-2058. FAX 788-3348.
circ. 5,500. *5939*

KULDE SKANDINAVIA.
Skarland Press A-S, P.O. Box 5042 Maj., N-0301 Oslo, Norway. TEL 47-22-59-88-00. FAX 47-22-69-36-50.
circ. 5,284. *3482*

KULTUR NEWS.
Kulturring in Berlin e.V., Friedrichstr. 120, 10117 Berlin, Germany. TEL 49-30-2826343. FAX 49-30-2826343.
circ. 1,500. *451*

KULTUR UND TECHNIK.
Verlag C.H. Beck, 80791 Munich, Germany. TEL 49-89-38189-338. FAX 49-89-38189398.
circ. 12,551. *5357*

KUNSTHISTORISCHES INSTITUT IN FLORENZ. MITTEILUNGEN.
Kunsthistorisches Institut in Florenz, Via G. Giusti 44, 50121 Florence, Italy. TEL 39-55-2491147. FAX 39-55-2491155.
circ. 900. *451*

KURIER WILENSKI.
Parliament of the Republic of Lithuania, Laisves 60, Vilnius 2056, Lithuania. TEL 42-79-01. FAX 42-72-65.
circ. 20,000. *3025*

KURSKONTAKTE.
Flurweg 4, 83646 Bad Toelz, Germany. TEL 49-8041-5439. FAX 49-8041-73814.
circ. 15,500. *5458*

KUSPI.
Turun Hammaslaaketieteenkandidaattiseura, Lemminkaisenkatu 2, 20520 Turku 52, Finland.
circ. 2,600. *4863*

KUTLWANO.
Department of Information and Broadcasting, Private Bag 0060, Gaborone, Botswana. TEL 267-32541. FAX 267-352971.
circ. 24,000. *5939*

KUWAIT BULLETIN OF MARINE SCIENCE.
Kuwait Institute for Scientific Research, Mariculture and Fisheries Department, P.O. Box 1638, Salmiya, Kuwait. TEL 965-575-1984. FAX 965-571-1293.
circ. 700. *3072*

KVINNER I BEVEGELSE.
Norges Husmorforbund, Akersgate 16, N-0158 Oslo, Norway. TEL 47-22-47-83-80. FAX 47-22-47-83-99.
circ. 19,718. *7324*

KWANSEI GAKUIN DAIGAKU RIGAKUBU TSUSHIN.
Kwansei Gakuin University, School of Science, 1-155 Uegahara-ichiban-cho, Nishinomiya-shi, Hyogo-ken 662, Japan. TEL 0798-53-6111. FAX 0798-51-0914.
circ. 1,200. *1958*

KWIETNIK.
Proszynski i S-ka S.A., Ul. Rozana 34, 02-569 Warsaw, Poland. TEL 48-22-451256. FAX 48-22-452736. *3197*

KYOIKU HYORON.
Japan Teachers' Union, Nihon Kyoiku-Kaikan, 2-6-2 Hitotsubashi, Kanda, Chiyoda-ku, Tokyo, Japan.
circ. 20,000. *2459*

KYOTO UNIVERSITY. FACULTY OF ENGINEERING. MEMOIRS.
Kyoto University, Faculty of Engineering, Yoshida Hon-machi, Sakyo-ku, Kyoto 606, Japan. *2730*

KYOTO UNIVERSITY. INSTITUTE FOR VIRUS RESEARCH. ANNUAL REPORT.
Kyoto University Press, Yoshida-Hon-cho, Sakyo-ku, Kyoto 606, Japan. *789*

KYOTO UNIVERSITY. RESEARCH REACTOR INSTITUTE. TECHNICAL REPORT.
Kyoto University, Research Reactor Institute, Kumatori-cho, Sennani-gun, Osaka 590-04, Japan. TEL 81-724-51-2310. FAX 81-724-51-2600.
circ. 500. *2699*

KYRKOFOERFATTNINGAR.
Verbum Foerlag AB, P.O. Box 15169, S-104 65 Stockholm, Sweden. TEL 46-8-743-65-00. FAX 46-8-641-45-85.
circ. 2,000. *6352*

KYUSHU NEURO-PSYCHIATRY.
Kyushu Association of Neuro-Psychiatry, c/o Department of Neuro-Psychiatry, Faculty of Medicine, Kyushu University, Maidashi, Higashi-ku, Fukuoka 812-82, Japan. TEL 81-92-641-1151. FAX 81-92-632-3558.
circ. 1,100. *5078*

L A N A NYT.
Lokalhistoriske Arkiver i Nordjyllands Amt, c/o Lokalhistorisk Arkiv for Aalborg Kommune, Arkivstraede 1, P.O. Box 1353, DK-9100 Aalborg, Denmark. TEL 45-98-12-85-77. FAX 45-98-10-22-48.
circ. 800. *3580*

L AE S.
Aarhus Universitet, Institut for Nordisk Sprog og Litteratur, Niels Juelsgade 84, DK-8200 Aarhus N, Denmark. TEL 45-89-42-11-11. FAX 45-86-10-43-07.
circ. 700. *4424*

L & D - LIEFERANTEN UND DIENSTLEISTER FUER VERLAGE UND AGENTUREN.
Presse Fachverlag, Eidelstedter Weg 22, 20255 Hamburg, Germany. TEL 49-40-565031. FAX 49-40-5602920.
circ. 3,800. *6081*

L.G. ARGOMENTI.
Comune di Genova, Civiche Biblioteche, Via Archimede, 44, 16142 Genoa, Italy. TEL 39-10-509181.
circ. 1,500. *4342*

L M S.
George Warman Publications (Pty.) Ltd., P.O. Box 704, Cape Town 8000, South Africa. TEL 27-21-245320. FAX 27-21-261332.
circ. 5,500. *4899*

L T U MAGAZIN.
Westend GmbH, Westendstr. 1, 45143 Essen, Germany. TEL 49-201-1882269. FAX 49-201-1882235.
circ. 400,000. *7260*

L V P C NEWSLETTER.
Lehigh Valley Planning Commission, 961 Marcon Blvd., Ste. 310, Allentown, PA 18103-9397. TEL 215-264-4544.
circ. 1,600. *3752*

LAB PRODUCTS INTERNATIONAL.
Pan European Publishing Co., Rue Verte 216, 1030 Brussels, Belgium. TEL 32-2-2402611. FAX 32-2-242711.
circ. 49,750. *4899*

LAB 2000.
Ediciones Mayo, S.A., Muntaner 374, 4o, 08006 Barcelona, Spain. TEL 34-3-2090255. FAX 34-3-2020643.
circ. 5,000. *6543*

LABMEDICA INTERNATIONAL.
Globetech Publishing, 8 Cannon Rd., Wilton, CT 06897. TEL 203-762-3432. FAX 203-762-8640.
circ. 26,000. *4899*

LABO.
Verlag Hoppenstedt GmbH, Havelstr. 9, 64295 Darmstadt, Germany. TEL 49-6151-380-0. FAX 49-6151-380-360.
circ. 20,000. *4899*

LABOR AND EMPLOYMENT UPDATE.
Reed McClure, 3600 Columbia Center, 701 Fifth Ave., Seattle, WA 98104-7081. TEL 206-292-4900. FAX 206-223-0152.
circ. 4,400. *1440*

LABOR FORCE AND NONAGRICULTURAL EMPLOYMENT ESTIMATES.
Department of Employment Security, 500 James Robertson Pkwy., 11th Fl., Nashville, TN 37245-1000. TEL 615-741-1729. *1054*

LABOR LEADER.
San Diego-Imperial Counties Labor Council, 4265 Fairmount Ave., San Diego, CA 92105-1265.
circ. 33,000. *3893*

LABOR VOICE.
Australian Labor Party, Western Australia Branch, 2nd Fl., Labor Centre, 82 Beaufort St., Perth, W.A. 6000, Australia. FAX 09-2279585.
circ. 10,000. *5939*

LABORATORIET.
Institutet foer Biomedicinsk Laboratorievetenskap, Adolf Fredriks Kyrkogata 11, S-111 37 Stockholm, Sweden. TEL 46-8-240131. FAX 46-8-240124.
circ. 12,428. *4899*

LABORATORY PRODUCT NEWS.
Southam Magazine Group, 1450 Don Mills Rd., Don Mills, ON M3B 2X7, Canada. TEL 416-445-6641. FAX 416-442-2213.
circ. 20,000. *4900*

LABORPRAXIS.
Vogel Verlag und Druck GmbH & Co. KG, Max-Planck-Str. 7-9, 97082 Wuerzburg, Germany. TEL 49-931-4182145. FAX 49-931-4182905.
circ. 25,000. *4900*

LACTEOS Y CARNICOS MEXICANOS.
Alfa Editores Tecnicos S.A., Libertad No. 107-402, 03660 Mexico DF, Mexico. TEL 525-579-3333. FAX 525-5329504.
circ. 5,000. *3118*

LADUE PUBLIC SCHOOLS BULLETIN.
Ladue Board of Education, c/o Elizabeth Schwartz, Ed., School District of the City of Ladue, 9703 Conway Rd., St. Louis, MO 63124. TEL 314-994-7080. FAX 314-994-0441.
circ. 12,000. *2459*

LAGOS EDUCATION REVIEW.
Joja Educational Research and Publishers Limited, 13 B Ikorodu Rd., Maryland, P.M.B. 21526, Ikeja, Lagos State, Nigeria. TEL 234-64-933866.
circ. 3,000. *2459*

LAHN-DILL-ANZEIGER.
Anzeigenblatt Verlag Lahn-Dill, Elsa-Brandstroem-Str. 18, 35578 Wetzlar, Germany. TEL 49-6441-959277. FAX 49-6441-75166.
circ. 384,628. *3287*

LAKE BIWA STUDY MONOGRAPHS.
Lake Biwa Research Institute, 1-10, Uchide-hama, Otsu-shi, Shiga-ken 520, Japan. TEL 81-775-26-4800. FAX 81-775-26-4803.
circ. 600. *2396*

LAMAZE PARENTS' MAGAZINE.
Lamaze Publishing Co., 372 Danbury Rd., Wilton, CT 06897-2523. TEL 203-834-2711. FAX 203-761-8696.
circ. 2,400,000. *4962*

LAMAZEBABY.
Lamaze Publishing Co., 372 Danbury Rd., Wilton, CT 06897-2523. TEL 203-834-2711. FAX 203-761-8696.
circ. 1,800,000. *4962*

LAMP (NEW YORK).
Exxon Corporation, 5959 Las Colinas Blvd., Irving, TX 75039-2298. TEL 214-444-1116. FAX 214-444-1139.
circ. 680,000. *5609*

LAMPA I ISKRA BOZA.
Lampa i Iskra Boza, Ul. Przasnyska 18 m.20, 01-756 Warsaw, Poland.
circ. 1,000. *4424*

LANCASHIRE CONSTABULARY JOURNAL.
Lancashire Constabulary, County Police Headquarters, P.O. Box 77, Hutton, Preston PR4 5SB, England. TEL 44-1772-618444. FAX 44-1772-618356.
circ. 4,000. *2272*

LANCE.
University of Windsor, Student Media Corp, Windsor, ON N9B 3P4, Canada. TEL 519-253-4232. FAX 519-971-3624.
circ. 10,000. *1958*

LAND AND LIBERTY.
Henry George Foundation of Great Britain Ltd., 177 Vauxhall Bridge Rd., London SW1V 1EU, England. TEL 44-171-834-4266. FAX 44-171-834-4979.
circ. 2,000. *6304*

LAND & WATER.
V N U Business Publications B.V., Postbus 9194, 1006 CC Amsterdam, Netherlands. TEL 31-20-4875515. FAX 31-20-4875735.
circ. 11,000. *2793*

LAND LINE MAGAZINE.
Owner-Operator Independent Drivers Association of America, Box L, Grain Valley, MO 64029. TEL 816-229-5791. FAX 816-229-0518.
circ. 107,000. *7175*

LANDESBIBLIOGRAPHIE VON BADEN-WUERTTEMBERG.
Kommission fuer Geschichtliche Landeskunde in Baden-Wuerttemberg, Eugenstr. 7, 70182 Stuttgart, Germany.
circ. 800. *3521*

LANDESVERSICHERUNGSANSTALT WUERTTEMBERG. MITTEILUNGEN.
W. Kohlhammer GmbH, Hessbruehlstr. 69, 70565 Stuttgart, Germany. TEL 49-711-7863-1. FAX 49-711-7863263. *6675*

LANDMAN.
American Association of Professional Landmen, 4100 Fossil Creek Blvd., Fort Worth, TX 76137-2791. TEL 817-847-7700.
circ. 10,000. *5609*

LANGUAGE AND CULTURE.
Hokkaido University, Institute of Language and Culture Studies, Nishi 8, Kita 17, Kita-ku, Sapporo 060, Japan. TEL 81-11-706-8572. FAX 81-11-736-2861.
circ. 400. *4272*

LANGUAGE QUARTERLY.
University of South Florida, College of Arts & Sciences, 4202 E. Fowler Ave., CPR 107, Tampa, FL 33620-5550. TEL 813-974-5618. FAX 813-974-5618.
circ. 500. *4273*

LASER APPLICAZIONI INDUSTRIALI, TECNOLOGIE, MERCATI.
Gruppo Editoriale Jackson S.p.A., Via M. Gorkí 69, 20092 Cinisello B. (MI), Italy. TEL 39-2-660327. FAX 39-2-66034333.
circ. 18,800. *5864*

LASTBILEN.
Aakerifoerlaget AB, P.O. Box 508, 182 15 Danderyd, Sweden. TEL 46-08-753-54-40. FAX 46-08-755-88-95.
circ. 16,500. *7175*

LASTEBILEN.
Norges Lastebileier-Forbund, Th. Meyersgt. 72, P.O. Box 4658 Sofienberg, N-0506 Oslo, Norway. TEL 47-22-11-01-55. FAX 47-22-20-56-15.
circ. 13,000. *7175*

LATEINAMERIKA JAHRBUCH (YEAR).
Vervuert Verlag GmbH, Wielandstr. 40, 60318 Frankfurt a.M., Germany. TEL 49-69-5974617. FAX 49-69-5978743.
circ. 200. *4342*

LATIN AMERICA - CHICAGO.
University of Chicago, Center for Latin American Studies, 5848 S. University Ave., Chicago, IL 60637. TEL 312-702-8420. FAX 312-702-1755.
circ. 1,500. *3026*

LAUREL OF PHI KAPPA TAU.
Phi Kappa Tau Foundation, 14 N. Campus Ave., Oxford, OH 45056-0030. TEL 513-523-1778. FAX 513-524-4812.
circ. 50,000. *1958*

LAW ENFORCEMENT PRODUCT NEWS.
General Communications, Inc., 100 Garfield St., Denver, CO 80206-5550. TEL 303-322-6400. FAX 303-322-0627.
circ. 40,000. *2272*

LAW OF THE SEA INSTITUTE. OCCASIONAL PAPER.
Law of the Sea Institute, University of Hawaii - Manoa, Richardson School of Law, 2515 Dole St., Honolulu, HI 96822. TEL 808-956-3300. FAX 808-956-3307.
circ. 500. *4142*

LAW QUADRANGLE NOTES.
University of Michigan, Law School, Hutchins Hall, Ann Arbor, MI 18109. TEL 313-647-3589. FAX 313-764-8309.
circ. 22,500. *1959*

LAW TECHNOLOGY JOURNAL.
University of Warwick, CTI Law Technology Centre, Coventry CV4 7AL, England. TEL 44-1203-523294. FAX 44-1203-524105.
circ. 600. *4068*

LAWN & GARDEN TRADE.
2585 Skymark Ave., Ste. 306, Mississauga, ON L4W 4L5, Canada. TEL 905-624-8218. FAX 905-624-6764.
circ. 14,000. *1537*

THE LAWYERS WEEKLY.
Butterworths Canada Ltd., Part of the Reed Elsevier group, 75 Clegg Rd., Markham, ON L6G 1A1, Canada. TEL 905-479-2665. FAX 905-479-3758.
circ. 16,000. *3980*

LEADER (STOCKPORT).
Covenanters, 11-33 Lower Hillgate, Stockport, Ches. SK1 1JQ, England. TEL 0161-474-1262. FAX 0161-474-1300.
circ. 4,300. *6352*

LEADER MAGAZINE.
Active Parenting Publishers, 810 Franklin Court, Ste. B, Marietta, GA 30067-8943. TEL 770-429-0565. FAX 770-429-0334.
circ. 55,000. *1850*

LEADERS.
Leaders Magazine, Inc., 59 E. 54th St., New York, NY 10022. TEL 212-758-0740. FAX 212-593-5194.
circ. 33,000. *1340*

LEADING LIGHT.
Wellington Maritime Museum, P.O. Box 893, Wellington, New Zealand. TEL 64-4-4728904. FAX 64-4-4711373.
circ. 800. *5357*

LEAN TRIMMINGS.
National Meat Association, 1970 Broadway, Ste. 825, Oakland, CA 94612. TEL 510-763-1533. FAX 510-763-6186.
circ. 1,400. *280*

LEBENSBAUM.
Markgrafenstr. 21, 91438 Bad Windsheim, Germany. TEL 09841-2974.
circ. 300. *2235*

LEBENSMITTEL PRAXIS.
Lebensmittel Praxis Verlag Neuwied GmbH, Postfach 1861, 56508 Neuwied, Germany. TEL 02631-879-0. FAX 02631-879175. *3143*

DER LEBENSMITTELKAUFMANN.
Oesterreichischer Wirtschaftsverlag, Nikolsdorfergasse 7-11, A-1051 Vienna, Austria. TEL 0222-555585.
circ. 21,200. *3143*

LEBLANC BELL.
G. Leblanc Corporation, P.O. Box 1415, Kenosha, WI 53141-1415. TEL 414-658-1644. FAX 414-658-2824.
circ. 40,000. *5407*

THE LECTURER.
N A T F H E - The University and College Lecturers' Union, 27 Britannia St., London WC1X 9JP, England. TEL 0171-837-3636. FAX 0171-837-4403.
circ. 72,000. *2511*

LEE HOWARD NEWSLETTER.
Selective Books, Inc., Box 1140, Clearwater, FL 34617. TEL 813-447-0100.
circ. 5,500. *6276*

LEEDS ON.
Leeds City Council, City Hall, Leeds, Yorkshire LS1 3AD, England.
circ. 50,000. *4150*

LEGAL EXECUTIVE.
Institute of Legal Executives, Kempston Manor, Kempston, Bedford, England. TEL 01234-840022. FAX 01234-841999.
circ. 19,997. *3981*

LEGAL MANAGEMENT.
Association of Legal Administrators, 175 E. Hawthorn Pkwy., Ste. 325, Vernon Hills, IL 60061-1428. TEL 847-247-5574. FAX 847-816-1213.
circ. 25,000. *3981*

LEGIS-MATE.
National Diet Library, 1-10-1 Nagata-cho, Chiyoda-ku, Tokyo 100, Japan. TEL 81-3-3581-2331. FAX 81-3-3597-9104.
circ. 1,700. *4192*

LEHEL AKTUELL.
S P D - Ortsverein Lehel, c/o Dr. Thomas Lange, Knobelstr. 30, 80538 Munich, Germany. TEL 49-89-222918. FAX 49-89-222918.
circ. 7,200. *5940*

LEHIGH ALUMNI BULLETIN.
Lehigh University, Alumni Association, 436 Broadhead Ave., Bethlehem, PA 18015. TEL 610-758-4838. FAX 610-758-4708.
circ. 50,000. *1959*

LEHRER UND SCHULE HEUTE.
Saarlaendischer Lehrerinnen- und Lehrerverband, Lisdorferstr. 21b, 66740 Saarlouis, Germany. TEL 49-6831-49440. FAX 49-6831-46601.
circ. 3,000. *2574*

LEHRMITTEL AKTUELL - LEHRMITTEL COMPUTER.
Westermann Schulbuchverlag GmbH, Postfach 4938, 38039 Braunschweig, Germany. TEL 49-531-708375. FAX 49-531-708127.
circ. 38,404. *2574*

LEICHHARDT HISTORICAL JOURNAL.
9 The Avenue, Balmain E., N.S.W. 2041, Australia. TEL 61-2-98108560.
circ. 300. *3543*

LEIPURI.
Suomen Leipuriliitto r.y., P.O. Box 115, SF-00241 Helsinki, Finland. TEL 358-0-14887304. FAX 358-0-14887301.
circ. 1,600. *3137*

LEIPZIGER WIRTSCHAFT.
Schluetersche GmbH und Co. KG, Hans-Boeckler-Allee 7, 30173 Hannover, Germany. TEL 49-511-8550-0. FAX 49-511-8550402.
circ. 38,000. *1191*

LEISURE WORLD GOLDEN RAIN NEWS.
Golden Rain Foundation, Box 2338, Seal Beach, CA 90740-1338. TEL 562-430-0534. FAX 562-598-1617.
circ. 2,392. *3440*

LEISUREJET.
B B B Publishing Ltd., 34 Hereford Rd., London W2 5AJ, England. TEL 44-171-229-6632. FAX 44-171-727-0986.
circ. 200,000. *7260*

LEISUREWAYS ONTARIO MAGAZINE.
Canada Wide Magazines & Communications Ltd., 4180 Lougheed Hwy., Ste. 401, Burnaby, BC V5C 6A7, Canada. TEL 604-299-7311. FAX 604-299-9188.
circ. 665,000. *3263*

LENNOX NEWS.
Lennox International Inc., Office of Government and Public Relations, Box 799900, Dallas, TX 75379-9900. TEL 214-497-5258. FAX 214-497-5292.
circ. 15,000. *3482*

LESBIAN NEWS.
Box 55, Torrance, CA 90507. TEL 310-787-8658. FAX 310-787-1965.
circ. 27,000. *3697*

LESBIAN REVIEW OF BOOKS.
Box 6369, Altadena, CA 91003. TEL 818-398-4200. FAX 818-398-4200.
circ. 2,000. *4425*

LESOTHO. MINISTRY OF NATURAL RESOURCES. HYDROLOGICAL YEARBOOK.
Ministry of Natural Resources, Department of Water Affairs, P.O. Box MS 772, Maseru 100, Lesotho. FAX 266-310437. *2396*

LETRAS DE DEUSTO.
Universidad de Deusto, Facultad de la Filosofia y Letras, Departamento de Publicaciones, Apdo. 1, 48080 Bilbao, Spain. TEL 34-4-4453100. FAX 34-4-445-8916.
circ. 750. *3785*

LET'S PLAY HOCKEY.
Let's Play, Inc., 2721 E. 42nd St., Minneapolis, MN 55406. TEL 612-729-0023. FAX 612-729-0259.
circ. 13,500. *6769*

LET'S TALK FAMILIES!
Family Service Canada, 600-220 Laurier Ave., W., Ottawa, ON K1P 5Z9, Canada. TEL 613-230-9960. FAX 613-230-5884.
circ. 4,000. *6675*

LA LETTRE D'ACTIVITES EN PAYS BASQUE.
Bayonne and Basque country's Chamber of Commerce, 50-51 allees Marines, B.P. 215, 64102 Bayonne Cedex, France. TEL 33-5-59465999. FAX 33-5-59594279.
circ. 11,000. *1191*

LETTRE D'INFORMATION METAUX.
Editions Montmartre, 142 rue Montmartre, 75002 Paris, France. TEL 33-1-40268321. FAX 33-1-40399752.
circ. 500. *5199*

LEUKEMIA SOCIETY OF AMERICA. NEWSLINE.
Leukemia Society of America, Inc., 600 Third Ave., 4th Fl., New York, NY 10016. TEL 212-573-8484. FAX 212-856-9686.
circ. 77,000. *4982*

LEVNEDSMIDDELBLADET - SUPERMARKEDET.
Visholm Media AS, Sydvestvej 49, P.O. Box 221, DK-2600 Glostrup, Denmark.
circ. 3,000. *3143*

LEXICON VEVY EUROPE SKIN CARE INSTANT REPORTS.
Vevy Europe S.p.A., Casella Postale 81570, 16131 Genoa, Italy. TEL 39-10-5221515. FAX 39-10-5221530.
circ. 12,900. *4879*

LEXINGTON THEOLOGICAL QUARTERLY.
Lexington Theological Seminary, 631 S. Limestone St., Lexington, KY 40508. FAX 606-281-6042.
circ. 2,300. *6353*

LEY.
Ediciones la Ley S.A., 1471 Tucuman, 1050 Buenos Aires, Argentina. TEL 541-495481. FAX 541-4760953.
circ. 12,000. *3983*

LIANGSHI WENTI YANJIU.
Sichuan Liangshi Jingji Xuehui, 67 Dajie, Chengdu, Sichuan 610012, People's Republic of China. TEL 86-28-6671208. FAX 86-28-6661969.
circ. 230. *3118*

LIBERAL REVIEW.
Liberal Party, 88-1 Rosmead Place, Colombo 7, Sri Lanka. TEL 582779. FAX 588875.
circ. 1,000. *5940*

LIBRA.
Chartered Accountant Students' Society of London (CASSL), Friendly House, 52 Tabernacle St., London EC2A 4NB, England. TEL 44-171-250-3072. FAX 44-171-253-4630.
circ. 6,500. *1094*

LIBRARY ASSOCIATION RECORD.
Library Association, 7 Ridgmount St., London WC1E 7AE, England. TEL 44-171-636-7543. FAX 44-171-436-7218.
circ. 28,000. *4194*

LIBRARY DEVELOPMENTS.
Texas State Library, Library Development Division, Box 12927, Austin, TX 78711. TEL 512-463-5465. FAX 512-463-8006.
circ. 1,000. *4194*

LIBRARY MATTERS.
Queens Borough Public Library, 89-11 Merrick Blvd., Jamaica, NY 11432. TEL 718-990-0705. FAX 718-291-2695.
circ. 20,000. *4195*

DAS LIEBHABERORCHESTE.
Bund Deutscher Liebhaberorchester e.V., Schlegelstr. 14, 90491 Nuernberg, Germany. TEL 49-911-591309. FAX 49-911-594836.
circ. 4,700. *5407*

LIFE LINES.
Monumental Life Insurance Company, 2 E. Chase St., Baltimore, MD 21202. TEL 301-685-2900. FAX 301-347-8666.
circ. 850. *3824*

LIFT.
Association for Spina Bifida and Hydrocephalus, 42 Park Rd., Peterborough, Cambs. PE1 2UQ, England. TEL 01733-555988. FAX 01733-555985.
circ. 1,000. *3455*

LIGHT (WASHINGTON).
A F L - C I O, Utility Workers Union of America, 815 Sixteenth St., N.W., Washington, DC 20006. TEL 202-347-8105. FAX 202-347-4872.
circ. 65,000. *1443*

LIGHT (WHEATON).
Christian Blind Mission International Inc., Box 19000, Greenville, SC 29602-9000. TEL 803-239-0065. FAX 803-239-0069.
circ. 38,000. *3471*

LIJECNICKI VJESNIK.
Zbor Lijecnika Hrvatske, Subiceva 9, 41000 Zagreb, Croatia. TEL 041-440-621.
circ. 7,400. *4703*

LIJFBLAD.
Mediselect B.V., Postbus 28091, 3828 ZH Hoogland, Netherlands. TEL 31-33-4808020. FAX 31-33-4805881.
circ. 10,000. *5676*

LIMITED EDITION.
Oxford County Newspapers, Newspaper House, Osney Mead, Oxford OX2 0EJ, England. TEL 01865-244988. FAX 01865-243382.
circ. 30,000. *3298*

LINGUISTIC CIRCLE OF MANITOBA AND NORTH DAKOTA. PROCEEDINGS.
University of North Dakota, Box 7128, Grand Forks, ND 58202-7128. TEL 701-777-2714. FAX 701-777-3650.
circ. 500. *4427*

LINKAGE.
National Diet Library, Information Processing Division, 1-10-1 Nagata-cho, Chiyoda-ku, Tokyo 100, Japan. TEL 81-3-3581-2331. FAX 81-3-3581-3292.
circ. 1,000. *2086*

LINKING LIBRARIES.
Rochester Regional Library Council, Box 66160, Fairport, NY 14450-6160. TEL 716-223-7570. FAX 716-223-7712.
circ. 1,050. *4196*

LINKING RING.
International Brotherhood of Magicians, 348 S. Wilshire Ln., Arlington Heights, IL 60004. TEL 847-577-7337. FAX 847-577-9363.
circ. 14,000. *3670*

LITERACY ADVOCATE.
Laubach Literacy International, 1320 Jamesville Ave., Box 131, Syracuse, NY 13210. TEL 315-422-9121.
circ. 20,000. *2511*

THE LITERARIAN.
Mercantile Library Association of the City of New York, 17 E. 47th St., New York, NY 10017. TEL 212-755-6711.
circ. 600. *4196*

LITERARY ONOMASTICS STUDIES.
State University of New York at Brockport, State University College, Brockport, Brockport, NY 14420. TEL 719-395-2269. *4428*

LITERATURNACHRICHTEN - AFRIKA - ASIEN - LATEINAMERIKA.
Gesellschaft zur Foerderung der Literatur aus Afrika, Asien und Lateinamerika e.V., Reineckstr. 3, 60313 Frankfurt a.M., Germany. TEL 49-69-2102247. FAX 49-69-2102277.
circ. 2,900. *4429*

LITHO WEEK.
Haymarket Publishing Ltd., 174 Hammersmith Rd., London W6 7JP, England. TEL 44-171-413-4328. FAX 44-171-413-4013.
circ. 12,832. *6081*

THE LITTLE SHIP.
Little Ship Club, Bell Wharf Ln., Upper Thames St., London EC4R 3TB, England. TEL 44-171-236-7729. FAX 44-171-236-9100.
circ. 2,000. *6840*

LIVE RAIL.
Southern Electric Group, 12 Dorchester Gardens, Grand Ave., Worthing, W. Sussex BN11 5AY, England. TEL 44-1903-501029. FAX 44-1903-501029.
circ. 750. *7128*

LIVER UPDATE.
American Liver Foundation, 1425 Pompton Ave., Cedar Grove, NJ 07009-1043. TEL 201-256-2550.
circ. 70,000. *4913*

LIVING LIGHT.
United States Catholic Conference, Office for Publishing and Promotion Services, 3211 Fourth St., N.E., Washington, DC 20017-1194. TEL 202-541-3453. FAX 202-541-3089.
circ. 1,200. *6469*

LIVING MUSIC.
Living Music Foundation, Inc., Box 173, Desert Hot Springs, CA 92240-8463. TEL 619-595-7838.
circ. 300. *5408*

LIVINGRIGHT.
American Cancer Society, Inc., Florida Division, 3709 W. Jetton Ave., Tampa, FL 33629. TEL 813-253-0541. FAX 813-254-5857.
circ. 350,000. *4982*

LIVINGSTON COUNTY AGRICULTURAL NEWS.
Cooperative Extension Association of Livingston County, Agricultural Division, 158 S. Main St., Mount Morris, NY 14510. TEL 716-658-4110. FAX 716-658-4707.
circ. 250. *134*

LIVSMEDELSTEKNIK.
Stiftelsen Svensk Livsmedelsteknik, Katarinavaegen 20, 116 45 Stockholm, Sweden. FAX 46-8-640-80-45.
circ. 2,300. *3119*

LLOYDS BANK ANNUAL REVIEW.
Lloyds Bank plc., Economics Department, P.O. Box 19, Hays Lane House, 1 Hays Ln., London SE1 2HA, England. TEL 44-171-407-1000. FAX 44-171-357-4378. *1153*

LLOYD'S SHIPPING CONNECTIONS.
L L P Limited, Sheepen Pl., Colchester, Essex CO3 3LP, England. TEL 44-1206-772277. FAX 44-1206-772118.
circ. 1,000. *1694*

LOCAL AUTHORITY WASTE & ENVIRONMENT.
Faversham House Group Ltd., Faversham House, 232a Addington Rd., South Croydon, Surrey CR2 8LE, England. TEL 44-181-651-7100. FAX 44-181-651-7117.
circ. 5,813. *2987*

LOCAL GOVERNMENT EXECUTIVE.
Tempus House of Publishers, Fourways House, 57 Hilton St., Manchester M1 2EJ, England. TEL 44-161-237-1007. FAX 44-161-237-1006.
circ. 4,200. *6218*

LOCAL GOVERNMENT FINANCES IN MARYLAND.
Department of Fiscal Services, 90 State Circle, Annapolis, MD 21401. TEL 410-841-3710. FAX 410-841-3722. *1619*

LOCAL GOVERNMENT MANAGEMENT.
Institute of Municipal Management, P.O. Box 418, S. Melbourne, Vic. 3205, Australia. TEL 61-3-96459044. FAX 61-3-96901377.
circ. 4,500. *6218*

LOCAL 1010 STEELWORKER.
U S W A Local 1010, 3703 Euclid Ave., E. Chicago, IN 46312. TEL 219-398-3100. FAX 219-397-5968.
circ. 23,000. *3893*

LOCATION UPDATE.
Location Update, Inc., 7021 Hayvenhurst Ave., 205, Van Nuys, CA 91406-3802. TEL 213-461-8887. FAX 213-469-3711.
circ. 30,000. *5339*

LOCATOR OF USED MACHINERY, EQUIPMENT & PLANT SERVICES.
Machinery Information Systems, Inc., 1110 Spring St., Silver Spring, MD 20910. TEL 301-585-9498. FAX 301-585-9460. *4546*

LOCOMOTIVE JOURNAL.
Associated Society of Locomotive Engineers and Firemen, 9 Arkwright Rd., Hampstead, London NW3 6AB, England.
circ. 17,000. *7128*

LODGING.
American Hotel Association Directory Corp., 1201 New York Ave., N.W., Ste. 600, Washington, DC 20005-3931. TEL 202-289-3100. FAX 202-289-3199.
circ. 45,000. *3731*

LODGING HOSPITALITY.
Penton Publishing Co., 1100 Superior Ave., Cleveland, OH 44114-2543. TEL 216-696-7000. FAX 216-696-8765.
circ. 49,000. *3732*

LOGISTICA MANAGEMENT.
Edizioni Ritman s.r.l., Via Varesina 76, 20156 Milan, Italy. TEL 39-2-38008859. FAX 39-2-38008828.
circ. 5,269. *1491*

LOGISTICS FOCUS.
Institute of Logistics, Douglas House, Queen's Sq., Corby, Northants. NN17 1PL, England. TEL 44-1536-205500. FAX 44-1536-400979.
circ. 13,000. *1214*

LOGISTICS NEWS.
Bolton Publications (Pty) Ltd., P.O. Box 966, Parklands 2121, South Africa. TEL 27-11-8803520. FAX 27-11-8806574.
circ. 3,408. *7033*

LOGISTICS TECHNOLOGY INTERNATIONAL.
Sterling Publications Ltd., 86-88 Edgware Rd., London W2 2YW, England. TEL 44-171-915-9600. FAX 44-171-915-9619.
circ. 10,000. *2878*

LONDON ACCOUNTANT.
Angel Business Communications Ltd., Kingsland House, 361-373 City Rd., London EC1V 1LR, England. TEL 44-171-417-7400. FAX 44-171-417-7500.
circ. 21,041. *1094*

LONDON COLLEGE OF MUSIC MAGAZINE.
London College of Music, Thames Valley University, St. Mary's Rd., Ealing, London W5 5RF, England. TEL 44-181-231-2364. FAX 44-181-231-2433. *5408*

LONDON PORTRAIT.
I P C Magazines, Specialist Magazine Group King's Reach Tower, Stamford St., London SE1 9LS, England. TEL 44-171-261-5000. FAX 44-1444-445599.
circ. 90,000. *3298*

LONG ISLAND PARENTING NEWS.
R D M Publishing Corporation, Box 214, Island Park, NY 11558. TEL 516-889-5510. FAX 516-889-5513.
circ. 55,000. *1851*

LONGWOOD GRADUATE PROGRAM SEMINARS.
University of Delaware, College of Agricultural Sciences, 153 Townsend Hall, Newark, DE 19717-1303. TEL 302-451-2517. FAX 302-292-3651.
circ. 800. *713*

LOOKOUT (NEW YORK).
Seamen's Church Institute of New York and New Jersey, 241 Water St., New York, NY 10038. TEL 212-349-9090. FAX 212-349-8342.
circ. 10,000. *6676*

LOSINKA.
Losinka, Letchika Babushkina ul., 1, 129344 Moscow, Russia.
circ. 15,000. *6219*

LOST TREASURE.
Lost Treasure, Inc., Box 451589, Grove, OK 74345. TEL 918-786-2182. FAX 918-786-2192. circ. 45,832. *3670*

LOUGHTON REVIEW.
Monkswood Press, Caxton House, Old Station Rd., Loughton, Essex IG10 4PE, England. TEL 0181-502-0236. FAX 0181-508-2834. circ. 17,700. *39*

LOUISIANA AGRICULTURE.
Louisiana State University, Agricultural Center, Box 25100, Baton Rouge, LA 70894-5100. TEL 504-388-2263. FAX 504-388-4524. circ. 5,000. *134*

LOUISIANA BUSINESS SURVEY.
University of New Orleans, Lake Front, Division of Business and Economic Research, Lake Front, New Orleans, LA 70148. TEL 504-286-6248. FAX 504-286-6094. circ. 9,000. *1269*

LOUISIANA STATE UNIVERSITY. LIBRARY LECTURES.
Louisiana State University, Library, Baton Rouge, LA 70803-7507. TEL 504-388-2217. FAX 504-388-6825. *4196*

LOUISIANA WATER RESOURCES RESEARCH INSTITUTE. ANNUAL REPORT.
Louisiana Water Resources Research Institute, 3418 Ceba Bldg., Louisiana State University, Baton Rouge, LA 70803. FAX 504-388-5990. *7296*

LOURDES - ROSEN.
Deutscher Lourdes-Verein, Schwalbengasse 10, 50667 Cologne, Germany. TEL 0221-2576246. FAX 0221-2576189. circ. 25,000. *6469*

LOW BIDDER.
Associated General Contractors of America, N.Y. State Chapter, 1900 Western Ave., Albany, NY 12203. TEL 518-456-1134. FAX 518-456-1198. circ. 1,700. *7139*

LOYOLA MAGAZINE.
Loyola University Chicago, 820 N. Michigan Ave., Chicago, IL 60611. TEL 312-915-6407. FAX 312-915-7742. circ. 93,000. *1959*

LUBRICANTS WORLD.
Hart Publications, Inc., 4545 Post Oak Pl., Ste. 210, Houston, TX 77027. TEL 713-993-9320. circ. 10,000. *5609*

LUCKY MEE FAMILY ASSOCIATION. YEARBOOK.
Lucky Mee Family Association, Drawer 4487, El Paso, TX 79914. TEL 915-751-7233. circ. 180. *3231*

LUMPEN MAGAZINE.
Lumpen Media Group, 2558 W. Armitage Ave., Chicago, IL 60647. TEL 773-227-2072. FAX 773-227-2072. circ. 22,500. *5942*

LUNDIAN.
M. Arthur Diakite, P.O. Box 722, S-220 07 Lund, Sweden. TEL 46-111322. FAX 46-111322. circ. 10,000. *3362*

LUREN.
Scandinavian Philatelic Library of Southern California, Box 310, Claremont, CA 91711. TEL 909-626-1764. circ. 300. *5709*

LUSAKA CITY LIBRARY. ANNUAL REPORT.
Lusaka City Library, P.O. Box 31304, Katondo Rd., Lusaka, Zambia. TEL 227282. circ. 150. *4196*

LUSORAMA.
Verlag Teo Ferrer de Mesquita, Postfach 100839, 60008 Frankfurt a.M., Germany. TEL 49-69-282647. FAX 49-69-287363. circ. 800. *4279*

LUTHERAN JOURNAL.
MacAlester Park Publishing Co., Inc., 7317 Cahill Rd., Edina, MN 55439. TEL 612-941-6830. FAX 612-941-3010. circ. 125,000. *6432*

LUXE.
Style Communications Inc., 1448 Lawrence Ave. E., Ste. 302, Toronto, ON M4A 4V6, Canada. TEL 416-755-5199. FAX 416-755-9123. circ. 10,500. *3866*

LUXEMBOURG. MINISTERE DES FINANCES. BUDGET DE L'ETAT.
Ministere des Finances, 3 rue de la Congregation, L-1352 Luxembourg, Luxembourg. *1619*

LYCOMING COUNTY HISTORICAL SOCIETY JOURNAL.
Lycoming County Historical Society, 858 W. Fourth St., Williamsport, PA 17701. TEL 717-326-3326. FAX 717-326-3689. circ. 1,200. *3636*

M A R G I N.
Mulini Press, P.O. Box 82, Jamison Centre, A.C.T. 2614, Australia. TEL 61-6-2512519. circ. 200. *4431*

M.A.S.H. MAGAZINE.
Banzai Productions, Postbus 5050, 3502 JB Utrecht, Netherlands. TEL 31-30-2942988. circ. 1,100. *6769*

M A S T.
R B Publishing Company, 2701 E. Washington Ave., Madison, WI 57304-5002. TEL 604-241-8777. FAX 608-241-8666. circ. 36,000. *2019*

M & T - METALLHANDWERK & TECHNIK.
Charles Coleman Verlag GmbH & Co. KG, Wahmstr. 56, 23552 Luebeck, Germany. TEL 49-451-79933-0. FAX 49-451-7993399. *902*

M B.
Bitaon Publishing Co. Ltd., 15 Rambam St., P.O. Box 1480, Tel Aviv 61014, Israel. TEL 972-3-5164461. FAX 972-3-5164435. circ. 4,000. *3324*

M C C NEWS.
Manhattan Christian College, c/o Laurin Hill, Dir. of Alumni and Public Relations, 1415 Anderson, Manhattan, KS 66502-4081. TEL 913-539-3571. FAX 913-539-0832. circ. 15,000. *1960*

M E M C O NEWS.
Miller Electric Manufacturing Co., 1635 W. Spencer, Box 1079, Appleton, WI 54911. TEL 414-735-4249. FAX 414-735-4013. circ. 44,000. *5223*

M E T E M - INTERNATIONAL SOCIETY OF TORONTO FOR HUNGARIAN CHURCH HISTORY. NEWSLETTER.
M E T E M - International Society of Toronto for Hungarian Church History, Regis College, 15 St. Mary St., Toronto, ON M4Y 2R5, Canada. TEL 416-922-2476. FAX 416-922-2898. *3582*

M F D REGISTER.
Milwaukee Fire Department Athletic Association, 711 W. Wells St., Milwaukee, WI 53233. TEL 414-276-5656. *6243*

M H L S NEWS.
Mid-Hudson Library System, 103 Market St., Poughkeepsie, NY 12601. TEL 914-471-6060. FAX 914-454-5940. circ. 1,100. *4197*

M H - R V BUILDERS NEWS.
Dan Kamrow & Associates, Inc., Box 72367, Roselle, IL 60172. TEL 747-891-8872. circ. 9,000. *902*

M I Z - MATERIALIEN UND INFORMATIONEN ZUR ZEIT.
Alibri Verlag, Postfach 167, 63703 Aschaffenburg, Germany. TEL 49-6021-15744. FAX 49-6021-15744. circ. 1,200. *4345*

M K - MARKETING Y VENTAS PARA DIRECTIVOS.
Grupo Especial Directivos, C. Orense 39 2o D, 28020 Madrid, Spain. TEL 34-1-5566411. FAX 34-1-5554118. circ. 9,637. *1537*

M L SEIDMAN MEMORIAL TOWN HALL LECTURE SERIES.
Rhodes College, 2000 N. Pkwy., Memphis, TN 38112. TEL 901-726-3818. circ. 600. *5942*

M L T A NEWS.
Modern Language Teachers' Association of New South Wales, c/o School of Modern Languages, Macquarie University, N. Ryde, NSW 2113, Australia. circ. 650. *4279*

M O P S A NEWSLETTER.
Missouri Political Science Association, c/o George Connor, Sect.-Treas., Dept. of Political Science, Southwest Missouri State University, Springfield, MO 65804. TEL 417-836-6956. circ. 80. *5942*

M P R C REPORT ON FINANCE, COMMERCE, INDUSTRY: INDONESIA.
M P R C (Asia) Sdn. Berhad, P.O. Box 10706, 50722 Kuala Lumpur, Malaysia. TEL 60-3-2217762. FAX 60-3-7564478. *1269*

M P R C REPORT ON FINANCE, COMMERCE, INDUSTRY: SINGAPORE.
M P R C (Asia) Sdn. Berhad, P.O. Box 10706, 50722 Kuala Lumpur, Malaysia. TEL 60-3-2217762. FAX 60-3-7564478. *1269*

M P R C REPORT ON FINANCE, COMMERCE, INDUSTRY: SOUTH EAST ASIA.
M P R C (Asia) Sdn. Berhad, P.O. Box 10706, 50722 Kuala Lumpur, Malaysia. TEL 60-3-2217762. FAX 60-3-7564478. *1269*

M P R C REPORT ON FINANCE, COMMERCE, INDUSTRY: THAILAND.
M P R C (Asia) Sdn. Berhad, P.O. Box 10706, 50722 Kuala Lumpur, Malaysia. TEL 60-2-2217762. FAX 60-3-7564478. *1269*

M P T - METALLURGICAL PLANT AND TECHNOLOGY INTERNATIONAL.
Verlag Stahleisen GmbH, Sohnstr. 65, 40237 Duesseldorf, Germany. TEL 49-211-6707-0. FAX 49-211-6707-517. circ. 10,000. *5199*

M S C KONTAKTE.
Birkenverlag der Herz-Jesu-Missionare, Postfach 1146, 83381 Freilassing, Germany. TEL 49-8654-9324. FAX 49-8654-67606. circ. 8,000. *6469*

M S L A JOURNAL.
Manitoba School Library Association, c/o Manitoba Teachers' Society, 191 Harcourt St., Winnipeg, Man. R3J 3H2, Canada. TEL 204-888-7961. circ. 250. *2610*

M S U ALUMNI MAGAZINE.
Michigan State University, Alumni Association, Rm. 108, Student Union, E. Lansing, MI 48824-1029. TEL 517-355-8314. FAX 517-355-5265. circ. 44,000. *1960*

M S U MATHEMATICS NEWSLETTER.
Montana State University, Mathematical Sciences Department, Bozeman, MT 59717. TEL 406-994-3601. *4587*

M S U U NEWSLETTER: GLEANINGS.
Ministerial Sisterhood Unitarian Universalist, c/o Universalist Unitarian Church, 740 E. Main St., Santa Paula, CA 93060. TEL 805-525-8859. circ. 300. *6493*

M S W MANAGEMENT.
Forester Communications, Inc., 5638 Hollister Ave., Ste. 301, Goleta, CA 93117-3474. TEL 805-681-1300. FAX 805-681-1312. circ. 24,000. *2987*

M T I REPORTER.
Madison Teachers, Inc., 821 Williamson St., Madison, WI 53703. TEL 608-257-0491. *2461*

M T S ECHO.
Manitoba Telephone System, 489 Empress St., Winnipeg, MB R3C 3V6, Canada. TEL 204-941-8256. FAX 204-775-0718. circ. 6,000. *2036*

M T TODAY.
Valley Forge Press, 1288 Valley Forge Rd., Box 1135, Valley Forge, PA 19482. TEL 610-935-3302. FAX 215-935-3072.
circ. 60,000. *4901*

M T U FOCUS.
Motoren- und Turbinen-Union Muenchen GmbH, Postfach 500640, 80976 Munich, Germany. TEL 49-89-14894332. FAX 49-89-14892172.
circ. 3,000. *73*

M UND A - MESSEPLANER INTERNATIONAL.
M und A Verlag fuer Messen, Ausstellungen und Kongresse GmbH, Postfach 101528, 60015 Frankfurt a.M., Germany. TEL 49-69-759502. FAX 49-69-75951280.
circ. 8,098. *1694*

M UND A REPORT.
M und A Verlag fuer Messen, Ausstellungen und Kongresse GmbH, Postfach 101528, 60015 Frankfurt a.M., Germany. TEL 49-69-759502. FAX 49-69-75951280.
circ. 12,515. *39*

MAANEDSBLADET PRESS.
Maanedsbladet Press, Studiestraede 24, 1, DK-1455 Copenhagen K, Denmark. TEL 45-33-11-58-11. FAX 45-33-11-68-66.
circ. 9,082. *3275*

MAANEDSMAGASINET ERHVERV - NORDJYLLAND.
Sct. Thoegersvej 8, P.O. Box 30, 7770 Vestervig, Denmark. FAX 97-94-14-10.
circ. 16,600. *1492*

MCALLEN NEWS JOURNAL.
Advance Publishing Company, 1101 N. Cage, Twin Palm Plaza, Ste. C1, Pharr, TX 78577. TEL 210-783-0036.
circ. 1,000. *983*

MACCABI WORLD UNION. NEWSLETTER.
Maccabi World Union, Kfar Hamaccabiah, Israel.
circ. 500. *6770*

MACHINE DESIGN.
Penton Publishing Co., 1100 Superior Ave., Cleveland, OH 44114-2543. TEL 216-696-7000. FAX 216-696-8765.
circ. 180,000. *2892*

MACHINE DYNAMICS PROBLEMS.
Wydawnictwo M E T, c/o Mieczyslaw Pekalak, Ul. Piekalkiewicza 5 m.6, 00-710 Warsaw, Poland. TEL 48-22-490195. FAX 48-22-490306.
circ. 300. *2892*

MACHINE TOOL SELECTOR.
Nexus Media Ltd., Nexus House, Azalea Dr., Swanley, Kent BR8 8HY, England. TEL 44-1322-660070. FAX 44-1322-337633.
circ. 18,634. *4547*

MACHINERY & EQUIPMENT M R O.
Southam Magazine Group, 1450 Don Mills Rd., Don Mills, ON M3B 2X7, Canada. TEL 416-445-6641. FAX 416-442-2214.
circ. 21,511. *4547*

MACHINIST.
International Association of Machinists and Aerospace Workers, 900 Machinists Pl., Upper Marboro, MD 20772. TEL 301-967-4500.
circ. 700,000. *3894*

THE MCKINSEY QUARTERLY.
McKinsey & Co. Inc., 55 E. 52nd St., New York, NY 10022. TEL 212-446-7000. *1492*

MACUSER.
Ziff-Davis Publishing (San Francisco), 50 Beale St., 14th Fl., San Francisco, CA 94105-1813. TEL 415-378-5600.
circ. 311,253. *2198*

MADAME.
Magazinpresse Verlag GmbH, Elisenstr. 3, 80335 Munich, Germany. TEL 089-55135-0. FAX 089-55135299.
circ. 110,079. *7326*

MADAMINA!
Music Associates of America, 224 King St., Englewood, NJ 07631. TEL 201-569-2898. FAX 201-569-7023.
circ. 5,000. *5409*

MADENCILIK.
Turk Muhendis ve Mimar Odalari Birligi, Maden Muhendisleri Odasi, Selanik Cad. 19-3, 06650 Ankara, Turkey. TEL 4-1251080. FAX 4-1175290.
circ. 5,000. *5306*

MAERKISCHE ZEITUNG.
Landsmannschaft Berlin-Mark Brandenburg, Landesverband Berlin, Stresemannstr. 90, 10117 Berlin, Germany. TEL 2611046.
circ. 8,500. *5943*

DAS MAGAZIN.
Das Magazin Verlagsgesellschaft mbH, Brunnenstr. 4, 10119 Berlin, Germany. TEL 49-30-443375-0. FAX 49-30-44337522.
circ. 92,000. *3287*

MAGAZIN FESTSPIELE.
W i W Verlags GmbH, Walfischgasse 14, A-1010 Vienna, Austria. TEL 01-5129230. FAX 01-5139469.
circ. 80,000. *7008*

MAGAZINE & BOOKSELLER.
North American Publishing Co. (New York), 322 Eighth Ave., 3rd Fl., New York, NY 10001. TEL 212-620-7330. FAX 212-620-7335.
circ. 19,000. *6277*

THE MAGAZINE HANDBOOK (YEAR).
Periodical Publishers Association, Queens House, 28 Kingsway, London WC2B 6JR, England. TEL 44-171-404-4166. FAX 44-171-404-4167.
circ. 6,000. *39*

MAGAZINE NEWS.
Periodical Publishers Association, Queens House, 28 Kingsway, London WC2B 6JR, England. TEL 44-171-404-4166. FAX 44-171-404-4167.
circ. 10,194. *39*

"MAGISCHE" WELT.
Verlag W. Geissler-Werry, In den Benden 13, 52355 Dueren, Germany. TEL 02421-51667.
circ. 1,600. *3670*

THE MAGISTRATE.
Digma Publications (Pty) Ltd., 270 Main St., Waterkloof, Pretoria 0181, South Africa. TEL 27-12-346-3840. FAX 27-12-346-3845.
circ. 1,900. *3986*

MAGNET MARKETING.
Graham Communications, 40 Oval Rd., Quincy, MA 02170. TEL 617-328-0069. FAX 617-471-1504.
circ. 3,500. *1537*

MAGNOLIA (WINSTON-SALEM).
Southern Garden History Society, c/o Old Salem, Inc., Drawer F, Salem Sta., Winston-Salem, NC 27108. TEL 910-724-3125. FAX 910-721-7335.
circ. 600. *3198*

MAHARASHTRA BHUGOLSHASTRA SANSHODHAN PATRIKA.
Maharashtra Bhugolshastra Parishad, Kala Basant Sahakari Grih. Sanstha, 808, Shivajinagar, Bhandarkar Rd., Prabhat Lane 15, Pune 411 004, India. TEL 91-212-352017.
circ. 1,000. *3413*

MAHARASHTRA STATE BUDGET IN BRIEF.
Directorate of Economics and Statistics, MHADA Bldg., Kalanagar, Bandra (E), Bombay 400051, India. *1619*

MAIDSTONE STAR.
Star Publishing Ltd., Maidstone Press Centre, Bank St., Maidstone, Kent ME1 1PZ, England. TEL 44-1622-678556. FAX 44-1622-675071.
circ. 40,350. *3298*

MAILOUT.
Mailout Trust, Kirklees Media Centre, 7 Northumberland St., Huddersfield HD1 1RL, England. TEL 44-1484-469009. FAX 44-1484-469009.
circ. 7,500. *453*

MAINE APPRISE.
Maine Secondary School Principals' Association, Box 2468, Augusta, ME 04338-2468. FAX 207-622-1513.
circ. 480. *2574*

MAINE POTATO NEWS.
Northeast Publishing Company, Box 510, Presque Isle, ME 04769. TEL 207-764-7033. FAX 207-764-4499.
circ. 6,000. *234*

MAINE TRAILS.
Maine Better Transportation Association, 146 State St., Augusta, ME 04330. TEL 207-622-0526. FAX 207-623-2928.
circ. 1,200. *2793*

MAINTENANCE TECHNOLOGY.
Applied Technology Publications, Inc., 1300 S. Grove Ave., Barrington, IL 60010. TEL 708-382-8100. FAX 708-304-8603.
circ. 72,000. *6966*

LE MAITRE IMPRIMEUR.
Association des Arts Graphiques du Quebec, Inc., 65, rue de Castelnau Ouest, Bureau 101, Montreal, PQ H2R 2W3, Canada. TEL 514-274-7446. FAX 514-274-7482.
circ. 3,959. *6081*

MAJALLAT AL-SHURTAH.
Royal Oman Police, Directorate of Public Relations, P.O. Box 2, 113 Muscat, Sultanate of Oman. TEL 968-569216. FAX 968-563352.
circ. 9,000. *2272*

MAKEDONSKI JAZIK.
Institut za Makedonski Jazik, Skopje, P.O. Box 434, 91000 Skopje, Macedonia.
circ. 1,000. *4280*

MAKERERE UNIVERSITY. ALBERT COOK LIBRARY. LIBRARY BULLETIN AND ACCESSION LIST.
Makerere University, Albert Cook Library, Makerere Medical School, Box 7072, Kampala, Uganda.
4227

MAKKAL KURAL.
Newsmen Associates Ltd., 1, First Main Rd., United India Colony, Kodambakkam, Madras 600 024, India. TEL 044-4831188. FAX 044-4832833.
circ. 1,900. *3314*

MALAWI. NATIONAL LIBRARY SERVICE BOARD. ANNUAL REPORT.
National Library Service Board, P.O. Box 30314, Lilongwe 3, Malawi. TEL 265-783700. FAX 265-783560.
circ. 300. *4197*

MALAWI. NATIONAL LIBRARY SERVICE BOARD. STAFF NEWSLETTER.
National Library Service Board, P.O. Box 30314, Lilongwe 3, Malawi. TEL 265-783700. FAX 265-783560.
circ. 400. *4197*

MALAYSIAN AGRICULTURAL JOURNAL.
Ministry of Agriculture, Publications Officer, Wisma Tani, Jalan Mahameru, 50624 Kuala Lumpur, Malaysia.
circ. 1,500. *135*

MAMAMIA.
Randersackererstr. 81, 97074 Nuernberg, Germany. TEL 49-931-15729. FAX 49-931-3552512.
circ. 10,000. *1879*

MAMMALIA.
Museum National d'Histoire Naturelle, Mammiferes et Oiseaux, 55 rue Buffon, 75005 Paris, France. TEL 33-1-40793069. FAX 33-1-40793063.
circ. 670. *842*

MANAGED CARE.
Stezzi Communications, Inc., 301 Oxford Valley Rd., Ste. 1105A, Yardley, PA 19067. TEL 215-321-6663. FAX 215-321-6670.
circ. 80,000. *4705*

MANAGEMENT.
Jemma Publications Ltd., Marino House, 53 Glasthule Rd., Sandycove, Co. Dublin, Ireland. TEL 01-800000. FAX 01-844041.
circ. 8,000. *1492*

MANAGEMENT ACCOUNTER.
Society of Management Accountants of Alberta, 1800-125 Ninth Ave., S.E., Calgary, AB T2G 0P6, Canada. TEL 403-269-5341. FAX 403-262-5477.
circ. 7,000. *1094*

CONTROLLED CIRCULATION SERIALS

MANAGEMENT BRIEFS.
Clinical Laboratory Management Association, 989 Old Eagle School Rd., Ste. 815, Wayne, PA 19087-1704. TEL 610-647-8970. FAX 610-889-9731.
circ. 8,500. *4901*

MANAGEMENT CONSULTANTS NEWS.
Prime Marketing Publications Ltd., Witton House, Lower Rd., Chorleywood, Hertfordshire WD3 5LB, England. TEL 44-1923-285323. FAX 44-1923-285819.
circ. 11,000. *1493*

MANAGEMENT FORUM.
International Management Council, 430 S. 20th St., No. 3, Omaha, NE 68102. TEL 402-345-1904. FAX 402-345-4480.
circ. 6,000. *1493*

MANAGEMENT OF THE CALIFORNIA STATE WATER PROJECT.
Department of Water Resources, Box 942836, Sacramento, CA 94236-0001. TEL 916-445-9248.
7296

MANAGEMENT UPDATE (DENVER).
Medical Group Management Association, 104 Inverness Terrace E., Englewood, CO 80112. TEL 303-799-1111.
circ. 22,000. *4705*

MANAGERSEMINARE.
ManagerSeminare Gerhard May Verlags GmbH, Endenicherstr. 282, 53121 Bonn, Germany. TEL 49-228-97791-0. FAX 49-228-616164.
circ. 48,000. *1495*

MANAGING.
Sterling Publications Ltd., 86-88 Edgware Rd., London W2 2YW, England. TEL 44-171-915-9600. FAX 44-171-915-9619.
circ. 10,000. *1495*

MANAGING AUTOMATION.
Thomas Publishing Company, Five Penn Plaza, New York, NY 10001. TEL 212-629-0500. FAX 212-629-1551.
circ. 104,000. *2110*

MANAGING OFFICE TECHNOLOGY.
Penton Publishing Co., 1100 Superior Ave., Cleveland, OH 44114-2543. TEL 216-696-7000. FAX 216-696-7648.
circ. 110,000. *1558*

MANHATTAN ARTS INTERNATIONAL.
200 E. 72nd St., Ste. 26L, New York, NY 10021. TEL 212-472-1660. FAX 212-794-0324.
circ. 40,000. *454*

MANIPULACION DE MATERIALES EN LA INDUSTRIA.
Publicaciones Internacionales S.A., P. Castellana, 210, 28046 Madrid, Spain.
circ. 2,000. *902*

MANITOBA MUSEUM OF MAN AND NATURE. ANNUAL REPORT.
Manitoba Museum of Man and Nature, 190 Rupert Ave., Winnipeg, MB R3B 0N2, Canada. TEL 204-956-2830. FAX 204-942-3679.
circ. 3,000. *5358*

MANITOBAN.
University of Manitoba, Students' Union, University Centre, Rm. 312, Winnipeg, MB R3T 2N2, Canada. TEL 204-474-6535. FAX 204-269-1299.
circ. 13,000. *1960*

MANUFACTURED HOME MERCHANDISER.
R L D Group, Inc., 203 N. Wabash, Ste. 800, Chicago, IL 60601-2476. TEL 312-236-3528.
circ. 15,000. *3753*

MANUFACTURING & PROCESS AUTOMATION.
Kerrwil Publications Ltd., 395 Matheson Blvd. E., Mississauga, ON L4Z 2H2, Canada. TEL 905-890-1846. FAX 905-890-5769.
circ. 21,000. *2110*

MANUFACTURING COMPUTER SOLUTIONS.
Findlay Publications Ltd., Hadlow House, 9 High St., Green St. Green, Orpington, Kent BR6 6BG, England. TEL 44-1689-854754. FAX 44-1689-860041.
circ. 54,000. *2806*

MANUFACTURING MANAGEMENT.
Industrial Trade Journals Ltd., 8th Fl., Tubs Hill House, London Rd., Sevenoaks, Kent TN13 1BL, England. TEL 01732-464154. FAX 01732-464454.
circ. 20,688. *2878*

MANUFACTURING SYSTEMS.
Hitchcock Publishing, 191 S. Gary Ave., Carol Stream, IL 60188-2292. TEL 708-665-1000. FAX 708-462-2225.
circ. 115,000. *1590*

MAPFRE SEGURIDAD.
Editorial Mapfre, Ctra. Majadahonda a Pozuelo km. 3500, 28220 Majadahonda (Madrid), Spain. TEL 626-55-17. FAX 626-21-42.
circ. 21,226. *5494*

MAPLE LEAVES.
Canadian Philatelic Society of Great Britain, c/o David F. Sessions, Ed., 31 Eastergate Green, Rustington, Littlehampton, W. Sussex BN16 3EN, England. TEL 44-1903-787867.
circ. 500. *5709*

MAPPING AWARENESS.
GeoInformation International, 307 Cambridge Science Park, Milton Rd., Cambridge CB4 4ZD, England. TEL 44-1223-423020. FAX 44-1223-425787.
circ. 5,750. *3430*

MAQUINAS & METAIS.
Aranda Editora Ltda., Al. Olga 315, Perdizes, 01155-900 Sao Paulo, SP, Brazil. TEL 55-11-8264511. FAX 55-11-669585.
circ. 15,000. *4548*

MAR.
Liga Maritima de Chile, Errazurriz 471, Casilla 117-V, Valparaiso, Chile. TEL 255179.
circ. 2,000. *7156*

MARANATHA.
South African Union Conference of Seventh-Day Adventists, P.O. Box 468, Bloemfontein 9300, South Africa. TEL 27-51-4478271. FAX 27-51-4488059.
circ. 13,008. *6493*

MARCA.
Recoletos Cia. Editorial, C. Recoletos 1, 28001 Madrid, Spain. TEL 337-32-20. FAX 337-37-71.
circ. 741,000. *6770*

MARGARET SHAW LECTURES.
South African Museum, P.O. Box 61, Cape Town 8000, South Africa. TEL 27-21-243330. FAX 27-21-246716.
circ. 450. *372*

MARI - PAPEL.
Latin Press Inc., Apdo. Postal 67252, Medellin, Colombia. TEL 57-4-2627037. FAX 57-4-2628005.
circ. 3,000. *5568*

MARINA DOCK AGE.
Preston Publications, Inc., 7800 N. Merrimac Ave., Box 48312, Niles, IL 60714-3426. TEL 847-967-1810. FAX 947-965-0056.
circ. 18,000. *6840*

MARINA OPERATOR INTERNATIONAL.
Rushton Marine Press Ltd., Woodside, Burnhams Rd., Little Bookham, Leatherhead, Surrey KT23 3BA, England. TEL 44-1372-453316. FAX 44-1372-459974.
circ. 7,500. *7157*

MARITIME TRANSPORT INTERNATIONAL.
Sterling Publications Ltd., 86-88 Edgware Rd., London W2 2YW, England. TEL 44-171-915-9600. FAX 44-171-915-9619.
circ. 10,000. *7158*

MARKEE.
B C Holding & Markee Limited, 3650 N. Federal Hwy, Lighthouse Point, FL 33064-6649. TEL 407-324-1733. FAX 407-324-1766.
circ. 18,500. *5339*

MARKET CONNECTION.
Last Mountain Times Ltd., 103 First Ave. W., Nokomis, SK S0G 3R0, Canada. TEL 306-528-2020. FAX 306-528-2090.
circ. 6,410. *3263*

MARKETEER.
c/o J. Cook, Ed., 1602 E. Glen Ave., Peoria, IL 61614.
circ. 2,000. *1538*

THE MARKETER.
Oklahoma Petroleum Marketers Association, 5115 N. Western, Oklahoma City, OK 73118. TEL 405-842-6625. FAX 405-842-9564.
circ. 1,300. *5609*

MARKETING HIGHER EDUCATION NEWSLETTER.
Topor & Associates, 655 Castro St., Ste. 8, Mountain View, CA 94041-2000. TEL 415-961-6121.
circ. 700. *2548*

MARKETPLACE MAGAZINE.
A D D Inc., 211 N. Lynndale Dr., Ste. 8, Appleton, WI 54913-1897. TEL 414-735-5969. FAX 414-735-5970.
circ. 16,000. *984*

MARMARA UNIVERSITY. FACULTY OF DENTISTRY. JOURNAL.
Marmara University, Faculty of Dentistry, Buyukciftlik Sok. No. 6, 80200 Nisantasi - Istanbul, Turkey. TEL 90-212-2483127. FAX 90-212-2465247.
circ. 1,200. *4863*

MARQUETTE TRIBUNE.
Marquette University, 1131 W. Wisconsin Ave., Milwaukee, WI 53233. TEL 414-288-7057. FAX 414-288-1979.
circ. 7,500. *1960*

MARTLET.
Martlet Publishing Society, P.O. Box 3035, Victoria, BC V8W 3P3, Canada. TEL 250-721-8360. FAX 250-472-4556.
circ. 10,000. *1960*

MARYLAND. STATE HIGHWAY ADMINISTRATION. TRAFFIC TRENDS.
State Highway Administration, Department of Transportation, 707 Calvert St., Baltimore, MD 21203. TEL 140-545-5511. FAX 410-545-1023.
circ. 200. *7139*

MARYLAND BIRDLIFE.
Maryland Ornithological Society, Inc., Patuxent Wildlife Research, Laurel, MD 20708-4015. TEL 301-497-5641. FAX 301-497-5624.
circ. 2,200. *806*

MARYLAND MEDICAL JOURNAL.
Medical and Chirurgical Faculty of Maryland, 1211 Cathedral St, Baltimore, MD 21201. TEL 410-539-0872. FAX 410-547-0915.
circ. 7,500. *4705*

MARYLAND MUSIC EDUCATOR.
Maryland Music Educators Association, 11021 Old Princess Anne Rd., Princess Anne, MD 21853-4654. TEL 410-651-9359. FAX 410-651-9359.
circ. 1,400. *5409*

MARYLAND P T A BULLETIN.
Maryland Congress of Parents and Teachers, 3121 Saint Paul St., Ste. 25, Baltimore, MD 21218-3857. TEL 301-685-0865. *2462*

MASCHINEN ANLAGEN VERFAHREN.
Konradin Verlag Robert Kohlhammer GmbH, Ernst-Mey-Str. 8, 70771 Leinfelden-Echterdingen, Germany. TEL 49-711-7594-0. FAX 49-711-7594-390.
circ. 18,134. *1496*

MASCHINENMARKT.
Vogel Verlag und Druck GmbH & Co. KG, Max-Planck-Str. 7-9, 97082 Wuerzburg, Germany. TEL 49-931-4182145. FAX 49-931-4182905.
circ. 50,310. *4548*

MASKIN - AKTUELT.
Teknisk Forlag A-S, Skelbaekgade 4, DK-1717 Copenhagen V, Denmark. TEL 45-31-21-68-01. FAX 45-31-21-04-01.
circ. 20,430. *5199*

MASKINBEFAELET.
Svenska Maskinbefaelsfoerbundet, P.O. Box 12100, S-102 23 Stockholm, Sweden. TEL 46-8-693-56-21. FAX 46-8-651-08-48.
circ. 4,200. *7158*

MASKINMESTEREN.
Maskinmestrenes Forening, Sankt Annae Plads 16, DK-1250 Copenhagen K, Denmark. TEL 45-33-13-16-22. FAX 45-33-13-02-60.
circ. 10,500. *4548*

MASKINSTATIONEN OG LANDBRUGSLEDEREN.
I-S Moeller, L.P. Bechs Vej 29, DK-8240 Risskov, Denmark. TEL 45-86-17-77-58. FAX 45-86-17-46-80.
circ. 4,200. *208*

MASONIC WORLD.
Publishers, Inc., 500 Temple Ave., Detroit, MI 48201. TEL 313-831-6250.
circ. 12,000. *1934*

MASSACHUSETTS COLLEGE OF PHARMACY. BULLETIN.
Massachusetts College of Pharmacy and Allied Health Sciences, 179 Longwood Ave., Boston, MA 02115. TEL 617-732-2800. FAX 617-732-2801.
circ. 8,000. *5677*

MASSACHUSETTS STATE LABOR COUNCIL A F L - C I O NEWSLETTER.
Massachusetts State Labor Council, A F L - C I O, 8 Beacon St., 3rd Fl., Boston, MA 02108. TEL 617-227-8260. FAX 617-227-2010.
circ. 8,000. *3894*

MASTER LOCK NEWS TODAY.
Master Lock Co., 2600 N. 32nd St., Milwaukee, WI 53210. TEL 414-444-2800. FAX 414-449-3193.
circ. 1,900. *928*

MASTER, MATE & PILOT.
International Organization of Masters, Mates & Pilots, 700 Maritime Blvd., Linthicum Heights, MD 21090. TEL 410-850-8700. FAX 410-850-0973.
circ. 13,000. *3894*

MASTER PLUMBER OF SOUTH AUSTRALIA.
Master Plumbers & Mechanical Services Association, 219 Henley Rd., Torrensville, S.A. 5031, Australia.
circ. 550. *3482*

MASTERSTROKE.
Mediamark Publishing International Ltd., 35 Gresse St., Rathbone Pl., London W1P 1PN, England. TEL 44-171-580-3105. FAX 44-171-580-1695.
circ. 31,278. *6810*

MASTHEAD.
North Island Sound Ltd., 1606 Sedlescomb Dr., Unit 8, Mississauga, ON L4X 1M6, Canada. TEL 905-625-7070. FAX 905-625-4856.
circ. 4,504. *6277*

MATCH NEWS.
Match International Centre, 1102-200 Elgin St., Ottawa, ON K2P 1L5, Canada. TEL 613-238-1312. FAX 613-238-6867.
circ. 5,000. *7326*

MATEMATICA APLICADA E COMPUTACIONAL.
Birkhauser Boston, 675 Massachusetts Ave., Cambridge, MA 02139. TEL 617-876-2333. FAX 617-876-1272.
circ. 700. *4622*

MATERIAL HANDLING ENGINEERING.
Penton Publishing Co., 1100 Superior Ave., Cleveland, OH 44114-2543. TEL 216-696-7000. FAX 216-696-8765.
circ. 101,447. *4548*

MATERIAL HANDLING ENGINEERING HANDBOOK AND DIRECTORY.
Penton Publishing Co., 1100 Superior Ave., Cleveland, OH 44114-2543. TEL 216-696-7000. FAX 216-696-8765.
circ. 113,000. *4548*

MATERIALS HANDLING NEWS.
Nexus Media Ltd., Nexus House, Azalea Dr., Swanley, Kent BR8 8HY, England. TEL 44-1322-660070. FAX 44-1322-667633.
circ. 20,096. *4549*

MATERIALS ON ASIA - ACCESSION LIST AND REVIEW.
National Diet Library, 1-10-1 Nagata-cho, Chiyoda-ku, Tokyo 100, Japan. TEL 81-3-3581-2331. FAX 81-3-3597-9104.
circ. 490. *556*

MATHEMATECH.
Parrish Platt International, Great Percy House, 26 Great Percy St., London WC1X 9QP, England. TEL 0171-278-3650. FAX 0171-278-3659.
circ. 27,000. *4588*

MATHEMATICAL LOG.
Mu Alpha Theta, 601 Elm St., Rm. 423, Norman, OK 73019. TEL 405-325-4489.
circ. 25,000. *4589*

MATHEMATICS TEACHING.
Association of Teachers of Mathematics, 7 Shaftesbury St., Derby DE23 8YB, England. TEL 44-1332-346599. FAX 44-1332-204357.
circ. 3,800. *4592*

MATHILDA AND TERENCE KENNEDY INSTITUTE OF RHEUMATOLOGY. ANNUAL REPORT.
Mathilda and Terence Kennedy Institute of Rheumatology, 1 Aspenlea Rd., Hammersmith, London W6 8LH, England. TEL 44-181-383-4444. FAX 44-181-383-4499.
circ. 1,000. *5126*

MATHITIKI ESTIA.
Ministry of Education and Culture, Pagkyprion Gymnasion, P.O. Box 1034, 1500 Nicosia, Cyprus. TEL 357-2-430670. FAX 357-2-430915.
circ. 1,000. *1879*

MATTER.
G L M Publications, 10 Bank St., Ste. 1200, White Plains, NY 10606-1952. *482*

MATURE AMERICAN.
Alternative Publications, Inc., 1123 N. Water St., Milwaukee, WI 53202. TEL 414-276-2222. FAX 414-276-3312.
circ. 32,000. *3441*

MAXINE'S PAGES.
Crystal Rain Research Agency, Box 792, Franklin, GA 30217-0792. TEL 706-846-9332.
circ. 137. *5944*

MAY TRENDS.
George S. May International Company, Management Consultants, 303 S. Northwest Hwy., Park Ridge, IL 60068-4265. TEL 847-825-8806. FAX 847-825-8806.
circ. 30,000. *1645*

MAYO AGRICOLA.
Distrito de Riego No. 38, Rio Mayo, Pesquera y Jimenez, Navojoa, Sonora, Mexico. *136*

MAYO ALUMNI.
Mayo Foundation, Mayo Clinic, Rochester, MN 55905.
circ. 14,000. *4705*

ME.
Tradeka Oy, Hameentie 19, P.O. Box 72, FIN-00501 Helsinki, Finland. TEL 358-0-733-2204. FAX 385-0-733-2120.
circ. 340,000. *1207*

MECHANICAL BUYER AND SPECIFIER - H V A C - REFRIGERATION.
Nytek Publishing Inc., 130 Belfield Rd., Etobicoke, ON M9W 1G1, Canada. TEL 416-242-8088. FAX 416-242-8085.
circ. 8,041. *3482*

MECHANICAL BUYER AND SPECIFIER - PLUMBING, PIPING AND HEATING.
Nytek Publishing Inc., 130 Belfield Rd., Etobicoke, ON M9W 1G1, Canada. TEL 416-242-8088. FAX 416-242-8085.
circ. 13,020. *3482*

MECHANIKA TEORETYCZNA I STOSOWANA.
Polskie Towarzystwo Mechaniki Teoretycznej i Stosowanej, Palac Kultury, p.309, 00-901 Warsaw, Poland.
circ. 400. *2867*

MEDBOOK.
Varus Verlag Birgit Laube, Koenigswintererstr. 552, 53227 Bonn, Germany. TEL 0228-440015. FAX 0228-440017.
circ. 16,000. *4782*

LE MEDECIN DU QUEBEC.
Federation des Medecins Omnipraticiens du Quebec, 1440 rue St.Catherine Ouest, Ste. 1000, Montreal, PQ H3G 1R8, Canada. TEL 514-878-1911. FAX 514-878-4455.
circ. 17,700. *4706*

MEDIA MOVES.
Two-Ten Communications Ltd., Communications House, 210 Old St., London EC1V 9UN, England. TEL 44-171-490-8111. FAX 44-171-490-1255.
circ. 5,000. *3876*

MEDIA NEWS.
Ming Chuan University, No. 250 Chung Shan N. Rd., Sec. 5, Taipei, Taiwan, Republic of China. TEL 02-882-4564. FAX 02-881-8675.
circ. 7,000. *1998*

MEDICAL DEVICE & DIAGNOSTIC INDUSTRY.
Canon Communications UC, 3340 Ocean Park Blvd., Ste. 1000, Santa Monica, CA 90405-3207. TEL 310-392-5509. FAX 310-392-4920.
circ. 48,000. *3804*

MEDICAL EXPRESS REPORTS.
Cambridge Medical Publications Ltd., Wicker House, High St., Worthing, W. Sussex BN11 1DJ, England. TEL 01903-205884. FAX 01903-234862. *4708*

MEDICAL FOCUS.
Beta Verlag GmbH, Postfach 140121, 53056 Bonn, Germany. TEL 49-228-91937-0. FAX 49-228-252067.
circ. 17,000. *6244*

MEDICAL FORUM REPORTER.
Cambridge Medical Publications Ltd., Wicker House, High St., Worthing, W. Sussex BN11 1DJ, England. TEL 01903-205884. FAX 01903-234862. *4708*

MEDICAL IMAGING (PORTSMOUTH).
Second Source Publications, Inc., 10 Risho Ave., East Providence, RI 02914-1215. TEL 401-434-1050. FAX 401-434-1090.
circ. 17,000. *4709*

MEDICAL IMAGING INTERNATIONAL.
Globetech Publishing, 8 Cannon Rd., Wilton, CT 06897. TEL 203-762-3432. FAX 203-762-8640.
circ. 26,000. *4709*

MEDICAL MANUFACTURING INTERNATIONAL.
Sterling Publications Ltd., 86-88 Edgware Rd., London W2 2YW, England. TEL 44-171-915-9600. FAX 44-171-915-9619.
circ. 10,000. *5677*

MEDICAL MARKETING & MEDIA.
C P S Communications, Inc., 7200 W. Camino Real, Ste. 215, Boca Raton, FL 33433. TEL 407-368-9301. FAX 407-368-7870.
circ. 12,800. *5677*

MEDICAL MEETINGS.
60 Main St., Maynard, MA 01754. TEL 847-427-9512. FAX 847-427-2097.
circ. 14,000. *5171*

MEDICAL PLASTICS AND BIOMATERIALS.
Canon Communications UC, 3340 Ocean Park Blvd., Ste. 1000, Santa Monica, CA 90405-3216. TEL 310-392-5509. FAX 310-392-4920.
circ. 10,000. *4710*

MEDICAL PRODUCT MANUFACTURING NEWS.
Canon Communications UC, 3340 Ocean Park Blvd., Ste. 1000, Santa Monica, CA 90405-3207. TEL 310-392-5509. FAX 310-392-4920.
circ. 38,000. *3804*

MEDICAL PROTECTION SOCIETY. ANNUAL REPORT.
Medical Protection Society Ltd., 50 Hallam St., London W1N 6DE, England. TEL 44-171-637-0541. FAX 44-171-636-0690.
circ. 135,000. *4710*

MEDICAL RECORD RISKS: CLAIMS & LITIGATION.
Cox Publications, Box 20316, Billings, MT 59104-0316. TEL 406-256-2248. FAX 406-256-7550. *3825*

MEDICAL RESEARCH COUNCIL NEWSLETTER.
Medical Research Council of Canada, 1600 Scott St., Tower B, Ottawa, ON K1A 0W9, Canada. TEL 613-954-1806. FAX 613-954-6653.
circ. 4,500. *4710*

MEDICAL RESEARCH COUNCIL OF CANADA. REPORT OF THE PRESIDENT.
Medical Research Council of Canada, 1600 Scott St., Tower B, Ottawa, ON K1A 0W9, Canada. TEL 613-954-1806. FAX 613-954-6653.
circ. 2,300. *4710*

MEDICAL RESEARCH FUNDING BULLETIN.
Science Support Center, Box 7507, New York, NY 10150. TEL 212-371-3398.
circ. 3,100. *4710*

MEDICAL SCIENCES BULLETIN.
Pharmaceutical Information Associates, Ltd., 2761 Trenton Rd., Levittown, PA 19056. TEL 215-949-0490. FAX 215-949-2594.
circ. 30,000. *5677*

MEDICAL SCIENTIFIC UPDATE.
National Jewish Center for Immunology and Respiratory Medicine, 1400 Jackson St., Denver, CO 80206. TEL 303-388-4461. FAX 303-398-1125.
circ. 26,000. *5120*

MEDICAL SOCIETY OF LONDON. TRANSACTIONS.
Medical Society of London, 11 Chandos St., Cavendish Sq., London W1N 0EB, England. TEL 44-171-580-1043. FAX 44-171-580-5793.
circ. 550. *4711*

MEDICAL TRIBUNE.
Medical Tribune, Inc., 100 Ave. of the Americas, 9th Fl., New York, NY 10013-1606. TEL 212-674-8500. FAX 212-529-8490.
circ. 130,000. *4711*

MEDICAMUNDI.
Philips Medical Systems International B.V., P.O. Box 10000, 5680 DA Best, Netherlands. TEL 31-40-2763856. FAX 31-40-2762019.
circ. 12,000. *5111*

MEDICINA DE LA EMPRESA.
Sociedad Catalana de Seguridad y Medicina del Trabajo, Tapineria, 10 pral., 08002 Barcelona, Spain. *5494*

MEDICINE INTERNATIONAL (MIDDLE EASTERN EDITION).
The Medicine Group (Journals) Ltd., Publishing House, 62 Stert St., Abingdon, Oxon OX14 3UQ, England. TEL 44-1235-555770. FAX 44-1235-554691.
circ. 20,000. *4713*

MEDICINE NORTH AMERICA.
C M E Publishing, 400 McGill St., 3rd Fl., Montreal, PQ H2Y 2G1, Canada. TEL 514-397-9393.
circ. 30,500. *4713*

MEDICINE NORTHWEST.
University of Washington, School of Medicine, Mail Stop SC-60, Seattle, WA 98195. TEL 206-685-0381.
circ. 17,000. *4713*

MEDICINE ON THE MIDWAY.
University of Chicago Hospitals, Office of Public Affairs, 5841 S. Maryland Ave., Mail Code 6063, Chicago, IL 60637. TEL 312-702-7322. FAX 312-702-3171.
circ. 14,000. *1960*

MEDICO-LEGAL SOCIETY OF VICTORIA. PROCEEDINGS.
Medico-Legal Society of Victoria, 3 Berkeley St., Hawthorn, Vic. 3122, Australia.
circ. 600. *4063*

MEDITERRANEA. SERIE DE ESTUDIOS BIOLOGICOS.
Universidad de Alicante, Facultad de Ciencias, Apdo. 99, 03080 Alicante, Spain. TEL 96-590-3400. FAX 96-590-3464.
circ. 600. *842*

MEDIUM.
Saskatchewan Teachers' Federation, 2317 Arlington Ave., Saskatoon, SK S7J 2H8, Canada. TEL 306-373-1660.
circ. 400. *4198*

MEDIZINISCHE KLINIK.
Urban und Vogel, Lindwurmstr. 95, 80337 Munich, Germany. TEL 49-89-53292-0. FAX 49-89-53292-100.
circ. 10,000. *4715*

MEDLEMSTIDNINGEN INDUSTRIFACKET.
Industrifacket, P.O. Box 1120, S-111 81 Stockholm, Sweden. TEL 46-8-786-85-95. FAX 46-8-21-28-72.
circ. 125,000. *3894*

MEETING NEWS.
Miller Freeman Inc. (New York), One Penn Plaza, New York, NY 10119. TEL 212-714-1300. FAX 708-647-5972.
circ. 60,100. *5171*

MEETINGS AND CONVENTIONS ASIA PACIFIC.
Venture Asia Publishing, 10 Craig Rd., Singapore 089670, Singapore. TEL 65-223-2911. FAX 65-223-0811.
circ. 12,059. *5171*

MEETINGS MONTHLY, NEWS BULLETIN.
Publicom Inc., C.P. 365, Place d'Armes, Montreal, PQ H2Y 3H1, Canada. TEL 514-274-0004. FAX 514-274-5884.
circ. 12,703. *5171*

MEGAPHONE (CANTON).
Culver-Stockton College, Attn.: Steve Wiegenstein, Canton, MO 63435. TEL 217-231-6380. FAX 217-231-6611.
circ. 1,000. *1961*

MELANGES DE SCIENCE RELIGIEUSE.
Institut Catholique de Lille, 60 bd. Vauban, B.P. 109, 59016 Lille Cedex, France. TEL 33-3-20134089. FAX 33-3-20134090.
circ. 500. *6470*

MELLIAND TEXTILBERICHTE.
Melliand Textilberichte GmbH, Mainzer Landstr. 251, 60326 Frankfurt a.M., Germany. TEL 49-69-75951651. FAX 49-69-75951650.
circ. 7,000. *6991*

MEMISA MEDISCH.
Memisa Medicus Mundi, Eendrachtsweg 48, 3012 LD Rotterdam, Netherlands. FAX 31-10-4047319.
circ. 4,000. *4715*

MEMO TO THE PRESIDENT.
American Association of State Colleges and Universities, One Dupont Circle, N.W., Ste. 700, Washington, DC 20036. TEL 202-293-7070. FAX 202-296-5819. *2549*

MENDEL.
Mendelian Society of India, 194-B, S.K. Puri, Patna 800001, India. TEL 91-612-233741.
circ. 750. *773*

MENNINGER PERSPECTIVE.
Menninger Foundation, Box 829, Topeka, KS 66601-0829. TEL 913-350-5841. FAX 913-271-9723.
circ. 66,000. *5079*

MENORCA, DIARIO INSULAR.
Editorial Menorca, S.A., Avda. Central 5, 07714 Mahon, Baleares, Spain. TEL 971-35-16-00. FAX 971-35-38-35.
circ. 326. *3359*

MENSA BULLETIN.
American Mensa Ltd. (Fort Worth), 201 Main St., Ste. 1101, Fort Worth, TX 76102-3115. TEL 817-332-2600.
circ. 49,000. *1934*

MENTAL HEALTH MATTERS.
Northern Ireland Association for Mental Health, 80 University St., Belfast BT7 1HE, N. Ireland. FAX 0232-234940.
circ. 1,500. *6135*

MENTAL HEALTH MATTERS.
Canadian Mental Health Association, 2160 Yonge St., 3rd Fl., Toronto, ON M4S 2Z3, Canada. TEL 416-484-7750. FAX 416-484-4617.
circ. 1,500. *6135*

MERKBLAETTER GEFAEHRLICHE ARBEITSSTOFFE.
Ecomed Verlagsgesellschaft AG & Co. KG, Rudolf-Diesel-Str. 3, 86899 Landsberg, Germany. TEL 49-8191-125-0. FAX 49-8191-125492.
circ. 10,500. *5494*

MERTON MESSENGER.
Merton Council, Civic Centre, London Rd., Morden, Surrey SM4 5DX, England. TEL 44-181-345-3366. FAX 44-181-545-4054.
circ. 80,000. *3298*

MESECHABE: THE JOURNAL OF SURREGIONALISM.
Center for Gulf South History and Culture, Inc., 1539 Crete St., New Orleans, LA 70119-3006. TEL 504-944-4823.
circ. 1,000. *5737*

MESSAGES.
Society for Environmental Graphic Design, 401 F St., N.W., Ste. 333, Washington, DC 20001. TEL 202-638-5555. FAX 202-638-0891.
circ. 1,500. *6081*

MESSENGER.
Southeast Asia Union Mission of Seventh-Day Adventists, 251 Upper Serangoon Rd., Singapore, Singapore.
circ. 2,000. *6494*

METAL CENTER NEWS.
Hitchcock Publishing, 191 S. Gary Ave., Carol Stream, IL 60188. TEL 708-665-1000. FAX 708-462-2225.
circ. 12,600. *5201*

METAL FORMING.
Precision Metal Forming Association, 27027 Chardon Rd., Richmond Hts., OH 44143. TEL 216-585-8800. FAX 216-585-2126.
circ. 60,000. *5202*

METAL HEAT TREATING.
Penton Publishing Co., 1100 Superior Ave., Cleveland, OH 44114-2543. TEL 216-696-7000.
circ. 16,000. *5202*

METALES Y METALURGIA.
Tecnipublicaciones, S.A., C. Albacete 5, 28027 Madrid, Spain. TEL 34-1-3261440. FAX 34-1-3262407.
circ. 5,000. *5202*

METALWORKING PRODUCTION & PURCHASING.
Action Communications Inc., 135 Spy Court, Markham, ON L3R 5H6, Canada. TEL 905-477-3222. FAX 905-477-4320.
circ. 18,000. *5204*

METHODIST COLLEGE TODAY.
Methodist College, 5400 Ramsey St., Fayetteville, NC 28311. TEL 910-630-7043. FAX 910-630-2123.
circ. 15,000. *1961*

METMENYS.
A M & M Publications, 306 55th Place, Downers Grove, IL 60516. TEL 630-852-3887.
circ. 1,000. *4434*

METRIC REPORTER.
American National Metric Council, 4340 East-West Hwy., Ste. 401, Bethesda, MD 20814. TEL 301-718-6508. FAX 301-656-0989.
circ. 5,000. *5252*

METRO (REDONDO BEACH).
Bobit Publishing Company, 2512 Artesia Blvd., Redondo Beach, CA 90278-3210. TEL 310-376-8788. FAX 310-376-9043.
circ. 17,500. *7034*

METROKIDS.
KidStuff Publication, Inc., 1080 N. Delaware Ave., Ste. 702, Philadelphia, PA 19125-4330. TEL 215-551-3200. FAX 215-551-3203.
circ. 75,000. *1851*

METROPOLITAN NASHVILLE BOARD OF EDUCATION. NEWS AND VIEWS.
Metropolitan Nashville Board of Education, 2601 Bransford Ave., Nashville, TN 37204. TEL 615-259-8400.
circ. 7,500. *2463*

METROSPORTS MAGAZINE.
Tate House Enterprises, Inc., 27 W. 24th St., New York, NY 10010. TEL 212-627-7040. FAX 212-627-7446.
circ. 170,000. *6770*

MEXICAN AMERICAN GROCERS ASSOCIATION. MAGAZINE.
Mexican American Grocers Association, 405 N. San Fernando Rd., Los Angeles, CA 90031. TEL 213-227-1565. FAX 213-227-6935.
circ. 12,500. *3143*

MEXICO BUSINESS MONTHLY.
Kal Wagenheim, Ed. & Pub., 52 Maple Ave., Maplewood, NJ 07040. TEL 201-762-1565. FAX 201-762-9585. *1342*

MEXICO CITY DAILY BULLETIN.
Edit, S.A., Gomez Farias 41, Col. San Rafael, 06470 Mexico, D.F., Mexico. TEL 52-5-5465115. FAX 52-5-5356060.
circ. 10,000. *7218*

MICHIGAN. DEPARTMENT OF STATE POLICE. ANNUAL REPORT.
Department of State Police, 714 S. Harrison Rd., East Lansing, MI 48823. TEL 517-332-2521. *2273*

MICHIGAN. STATE COURT ADMINISTRATOR. ANNUAL REPORT.
State Court Administrative Office, Box 30048, Lansing, MI 48909. TEL 517-373-0130. FAX 517-373-8922.
circ. 1,500. *4055*

MICHIGAN AIRPORT DIRECTORY.
Aeronautics Commission, 2700 E. Airport Service Dr., Capital City Airport, Lansing, MI 48906. TEL 517-335-8521. FAX 517-321-6422.
circ. 8,000. *7075*

MICHIGAN ASSOCIATION OF SECONDARY SCHOOL PRINCIPALS' BULLETIN.
Michigan Association of Secondary School Principals, 418 Erickson Hall, Michigan State University, E. Lansing, MI 48823. *2463*

MICHIGAN AVIATION.
Aeronautics Commission, 2700 E. Airport Service Dr., Capital City Airport, Lansing, MI 48906. TEL 517-335-9283. FAX 517-321-6422.
circ. 17,000. *74*

MICHIGAN DEER & TURKEY SHOW PREVIEW.
Target Communications Corp., 7626 W. Donges Bay Rd., Mequon, WI 53097-3400. TEL 414-242-3990. FAX 414-242-7391.
circ. 20,000. *6874*

MICHIGAN FOOD NEWS.
Michigan Grocers Association, 221 N. Walnut St., Lansing, MI 48933. TEL 517-372-6800. FAX 517-372-3002.
circ. 9,000. *3120*

MICHIGAN JOURNAL OF POLITICAL SCIENCE.
University of Michigan, Michigan Journal of Political Science, 5620 Haven Hall, Ann Arbor, MI 48109-1045. TEL 313-764-6386.
circ. 1,000. *5944*

MICHIGAN LUTHERAN.
Lutheran Church - Missouri Synod, Michigan District, 3773 Geddes Road, Ann Arbor, MI 48105. TEL 313-665-3791. FAX 313-665-0255.
circ. 76,000. *6433*

MICHIGAN STATE UNIVERSITY. AGRICULTURAL ECONOMICS REPORT.
Michigan State University, Department of Agricultural Economics, Reference Rm., East Lansing, MI 48824-1039. TEL 517-355-6650. FAX 517-432-1800.
circ. 90. *198*

MICHIGAN STATE UNIVERSITY. LIBRARY. AFRICANA: SELECT RECENT ACQUISITIONS.
Michigan State University Libraries, East Lansing, MI 48824-1048. TEL 517-355-2366. FAX 517-432-1445.
circ. 200. *556*

MICRO.
Canon Communications, Inc., 3340 Ocean Park Blvd., Ste. 1000, Santa Monica, CA 90405-3207. TEL 310-392-5509. FAX 310-392-4920.
circ. 23,000. *2646*

MICROWAVES & R F PRODUCT EXTRA.
Penton Publishing Co. (Hasbrouck Heights), 611 Rte. 46 W., Hasbrouck Heights, NJ 07604. TEL 201-393-6060.
circ. 40,000. *2840*

MID-AMERICA BANNER.
Mid-America Machine Dealers Association, 40625 N. Sunset Dr., Antioch, IL 60002. TEL 847-395-6922. FAX 847-395-6922.
circ. 1,000. *1591*

MID-AMERICA COMMERCE & INDUSTRY.
M A C I Inc., 1824 Cheyenne Rd., Topeka, KS 66604. TEL 913-272-5280.
circ. 9,483. *1271*

MID-AMERICAN REVIEW.
Bowling Green State University, Department of English, Bowling Green State University, Bowling Green, OH 43403. TEL 419-372-2725.
circ. 1,000. *4346*

MIDDLE ATLANTIC PERSPECTIVE.
Middle Atlantic Region, N N - L M, New York Academy of Medicine, 1216 Fifth Ave., New York, NY 10029. TEL 212-822-7396. FAX 212-534-7042.
circ. 1,800. *4716*

MIDDLE EAST EXPATRIATE.
Al Hilal Publishing & Marketing Group, P.O. Box 224, Manama, Bahrain. TEL 973-293131. FAX 973-293400.
circ. 16,200. *3336*

MIDDLE EAST SATELLITE TODAY.
Icom Publications Ltd., Chancery House, St. Nicholas Way, Sutton, Surrey SM1 1JB, England. TEL 44-181-642-1117. FAX 44-181-642-1941.
circ. 6,034. *2054*

MIDDLE EAST TRADE.
Middle East Trade Publications Ltd., 21 Newman St., London W1P 3HB, England. TEL 44-171-636-2911. FAX 44-171-637-5733.
circ. 15,320. *1342*

MIDRANGE SYSTEMS.
Cardinal Business Media, Inc., 1300 Virginia Dr., Ste. 400, Fort Washington, PA 19034-3225. TEL 215-643-8000. FAX 215-643-3901.
circ. 50,000. *2193*

MIDWEST AUTOMOTIVE & AUTOBODY NEWS.
Automotive Publishing Co., 2900 W. Peterson Ave., Chicago, IL 60659. TEL 312-764-1640.
circ. 11,562. *7106*

MIDWEST EXPRESS MAGAZINE.
Paradigm Communications Group, 2701 First Ave., Ste. 250, Seattle, WA 98121. TEL 206-441-5871. FAX 206-448-6939.
circ. 30,000. *7260*

MIDWEST GAS NEWS.
Gas Digest, 11246 S. Post Oak, Ste. 206, Houston, TX 77035-5741. TEL 713-723-7456.
circ. 2,000. *5610*

MIDWEST MOTORIST.
Automobile Club of Missouri, 12901 North Forty Dr., St. Louis, MO 63141. TEL 314-523-7350.
circ. 420,000. *7106*

MIDWESTERN DENTIST.
Greater Kansas City Dental Society, 5907 Raytown Trafficway, Kansas City, MO 64133. TEL 816-737-5353.
circ. 800. *4864*

MIE UNIVERSITY. FACULTY OF FISHERIES. JOURNAL.
Mie Daigaku, Suisan Gakubu, 2-80 Edobashi, Tsu-shi, Mie-ken 514, Japan. *3073*

MIKRO P C.
Oy Talentum Ab, P.O. Box 920, FIN-00101 Helsinki, Finland. TEL 358-9-148-801. FAX 358-9-685-6605.
circ. 59,090. *2199*

MILITARY ADVOCATE.
Judge Advocates Association, 1815 H St. N.W., Ste. 408, Washington, DC 20006-3697. TEL 202-628-0979. FAX 202-775-0295.
circ. 700. *4143*

MILITARY & AEROSPACE ELECTRONICS.
PennWell Publishing Co. (Nashua), 10 Tara Blvd., 5th Fl., Nashua, NH 03062-2801. TEL 603-891-0123. FAX 603-891-0574.
circ. 48,000. *74*

MILITARY CLUB & HOSPITALITY.
Executive Business Media, Inc., 825 Old Country Rd., Box 1500, Westbury, NY 11590. TEL 516-334-3030.
circ. 11,000. *3120*

MILITARY EXCHANGE MAGAZINE.
Downey Communications, Inc., 4800 Montgomery Lane, Ste. 710, Bethesda, MD 20814-5341. TEL 301-718-7600. FAX 301-718-7604.
circ. 10,000. *5276*

MILITARY GROCER.
Downey Communications, Inc., 4800 Montgomery Ln., Ste. 710, Bethesda, MD 20814-5341. TEL 301-718-7600. FAX 301-718-7604.
circ. 9,500. *3143*

MILITARY HISTORY JOURNAL.
South African National Museum of Military History, P.O. Box 52090, Saxonwold 2132, South Africa. TEL 27-11-6465513. FAX 27-11-6465256.
circ. 750. *5277*

MILITARY MARKET.
Army Times Publishing Co., 6883 Commercial Dr., Springfield, VA 22159. TEL 703-750-8676.
circ. 12,000. *5277*

MILITARY REVIEW.
U.S. Army Command and General Staff College, 290 Grant Ave., Bldg. 77, Ft. Leavenworth, KS 66027-1254. TEL 913-684-9327. FAX 913-684-9328.
circ. 12,500. *5277*

MILK BULLETIN.
Scottish Milk Marketing Board, Underwood Rd., Paisley, Renfrewshire PA3 1TJ, Scotland. FAX 041-889-1225.
circ. 3,200. *257*

MILL NECK MANOR BULLETIN.
Mill Neck Foundation, Frost Mill Rd., Box 100, Mill Neck, NY 11765. TEL 516-922-4100. FAX 516-922-3759.
circ. 76,000. *3464*

MILTON KEYNES CITIZEN.
Napier House, Auckland Park, Bletchley, Milton Keynes, Bucks. MK1 1BU, England. TEL 01908-374033. FAX 01908-371115.
circ. 89,700. *3299*

MINAMI TAIHEIYO KENKYU.
Kagoshima University, Research Center for the South Pacific, 1-21-24, Korimoto, Kagoshima 890, Japan. TEL 81-99-285-7394. FAX 81-99-256-9358.
circ. 700. *6545*

MINBAR AL-TAMRID.
Ministry of Health, School of Nursing, P.O. Box 3798, Abu Dhabi, United Arab Emirates. TEL 668591. FAX 665472.
circ. 1,000. *4940*

MINDANAO ART & CULTURE.
Mindanao State University, Mamitua Saber Research Center, P.O. Box 5594, Iligan City 9200, Philippines.
circ. 500. *3089*

MINI DATA REPORT.
Siemens, S.A., Calle Orense No. 2, Madrid 20, Spain. *2193*

MINILAB DEVELOPMENTS.
Professional & Trade Publications Ltd., 46 Ford End, Woodford Green, Essex IG8 0EG, England. TEL 0181-506-1011.
circ. 5,000. *5769*

MINING MIRROR.
Brooke Pattrick (Pty) Ltd., P.O. Box 422, Bedfordview 2008, South Africa. TEL 27-11-6224666. FAX 27-11-6167196.
circ. 5,348. *5310*

MINING NEWS.
Chamber of Mines of South Africa, P.O. Box 809, Johannesburg 2000, South Africa. TEL 27-11-4987100. FAX 27-11-8368070. *5310*

MINISTERIALTIDENDE FOR KONGERIGET DANMARK.
Justisministeriet, Sekretariatet for Retsinformation, Axeltorv 6, 5. sal, DK-1609 Copenhagen V, Denmark. TEL 45-33-32-52-22. FAX 45-33-91-28-01.
circ. 2,007. *6184*

MINNEAPOLIS LABOR REVIEW.
Minneapolis Central Labor Union Council, 312 Central Ave., Rm. 526, Minneapolis, MN 55414. TEL 612-379-4206. FAX 612-379-1307.
circ. 50,000. *3894*

MINNEAPOLIS - ST. PAUL CITYBUSINESS.
American City Business Journals, Inc. (Austin), 505 Powell St., Austin, TX 78703-5121.
circ. 6,000. *985*

MINNESOTA AGRICULTURAL ECONOMIST.
University of Minnesota, Department of Applied Economics, 1994 Buford Ave., St. Paul, MN 55108. TEL 612-625-1705. FAX 612-625-6245.
circ. 4,000. *199*

MINNESOTA MEDICINE.
Minnesota Medical Association, 3433 Broadway St., N.E., Ste. 300, Minneapolis, MN 55413-1761. TEL 612-378-1875. FAX 612-378-3875.
circ. 10,000. *4717*

MINNESOTA P - H - C CONTRACTOR MAGAZINE.
Minnesota Master Plumber Publishing Co., Inc., c/o Paula Shelander, Ed., 8085 Wayzata Blvd., no. 109, Minneapolis, MN 55426-1456. TEL 612-546-4448. FAX 612-546-4507.
circ. 2,500. *3482*

MINNESOTA SCIENCE.
University of Minnesota, Agricultural Experiment Station, 405 Coffey Hall, St. Paul, MN 55108. TEL 612-625-7290.
circ. 24,000. *6545*

MINNESOTA SPORTS.
Skyway News, 33 S. Fifth St., Ste. 800, Minneapolis, MN 55402-1050. TEL 612-375-9222. FAX 612-375-9208.
circ. 40,000. *6770*

MINORITY M B A.
Peterson's Magazine Group, 202 Carnegie Center, Box 2123, Princeton, NJ 08543-2123. TEL 609-243-9111.
circ. 20,000. *5513*

MINOTAUR.
Minotaur Press, P.O. Box 4705, Burlingame, CA 94011-4705.
circ. 150. *4514*

MINZU YANJIU (BEIJING, 1979).
Zhongguo Shehui Kexueyuan, Minzu Yanjiusuo, 27 Baishiqiao Lu, Beijing 100081, People's Republic of China. TEL 8022288.
circ. 5,000. *5533*

MIRACULOUS MEDAL.
Central Association of the Miraculous Medal, 475 E. Chelten Ave., Philadelphia, PA 19144. TEL 215-848-1010.
circ. 340,000. *6494*

MIRROR.
Graphic Corporation, Graphic Rd., P.O. Box 742, Accra, Ghana. FAX 233-21-669886.
circ. 126,000. *3293*

MIRROR AND PROBE.
Dental Students' Association, University of Sri Lanka, University Park, Peradeniya, Sri Lanka. *4864*

MISSET BULK.
Misset, Postbus 4, 7000 BA Doetinchem, Netherlands. TEL 31-314-349371. FAX 31-314-363638.
circ. 6,040. *7034*

MISSIONHURST.
Missionhurst, Inc., 4651 N. 25th St., Arlington, VA 22207-3500. TEL 703-528-3800. FAX 703-522-7864.
circ. 80,000. *6471*

MISSISSIPPI CONGRESS OF PARENTS AND TEACHERS. PROCEEDINGS.
Mississippi Congress of Parents and Teachers, Box 1937, Jackson, MS 39215-1937. TEL 601-352-7383. *2574*

MISSISSIPPI CONGRESS OF PARENTS AND TEACHERS. YEARBOOK.
Mississippi Congress of Parents and Teachers, Box 1937, Jackson, MS 39215-1937. TEL 601-352-7383. *2574*

MISSISSIPPI UNITED METHODIST ADVOCATE.
United Methodist Church, Mississippi Conference, Box 1093, Jackson, MS 39215. TEL 601-354-0515.
circ. 15,000. *6434*

MISSOURI. DIVISION OF HIGHWAY SAFETY (YEAR). HIGHWAY SAFETY PLAN.
Division of Highway Safety, Box 104808, Jefferson City, MO 65110-4808. TEL 314-751-4161. FAX 314-634-5977.
circ. 50. *7139*

MISSOURI PIPELINE.
Missouri Petroleum Marketers Association, 238 E. High St., Jefferson City, MO 65101. TEL 314-635-7117. FAX 314-635-3575.
circ. 1,400. *5610*

MISSOURI'S NEW AND EXPANDING INDUSTRY.
Department of Economic Development, Box 118, Jefferson City, MO 65102. TEL 573-751-9072. FAX 573-751-7385.
circ. 400. *1591*

MITRE.
Bishop's University, Student's Representative Council, c/o Box 2133, Lennoxville, PQ J1M 1Z7, Canada. TEL 819-569-9551. *4346*

MITSUBISHI DENSEN KOGYO JIHO.
Mitsubishi Cable Industries, Ltd., Patent & Technology Administration Department, OAP Tower, 25Fl., 1-8-30, Temmabashi, Kita-ku, Osaka-shi, Osaka 530, Japan. TEL 81-6-881-5209. FAX 81-6-881-5223.
circ. 6,500. *2840*

MITTEILEN.
Evangelisch-Lutherisches Missionswerk in Niedersachsen, Georg-Haccius-Str. 9, 29320 Hermannsburg, Germany. TEL 49-5052-69233. FAX 49-5052-69222.
circ. 17,000. *6434*

MITTEILUNGEN DER AERZTEKAMMER FUER WIEN - WIENER ARZT.
Aerztekammer fuer Wien, Weihburggasse 10-12, A-1010 Vienna, Austria. TEL 43-1-51501223. FAX 43-1-51501289.
circ. 12,000. *4717*

MITTELFRAENKISCHE WIRTSCHAFT.
Hofmann Druck Nuernberg, Postfach 120260, 90109 Nuernberg, Germany. TEL 49-911-5203-0. FAX 49-911-5203148.
circ. 70,000. *1192*

HAMIZRAH HEHADASH.
Magnes Press, Hebrew University, Jerusalem, P.O. Box 7695, Jerusalem 91076, Israel. TEL 972-2-5660341. FAX 972-2-5633370.
circ. 2,500. *5533*

MIZZOU MAGAZINE.
Publications & Alumni Communication, 407 D.W. Renolds Alumni & Visitor Center, Columbia, MO 65211. TEL 573-882-7357. FAX 573-882-7290.
circ. 125,000. *1962*

MOBILE.
Verlag Herder GmbH und Co. KG, Hermann-Herder-Str. 4, 79104 Freiburg, Germany. TEL 49-761-2717-438. FAX 49-761-2717426.
circ. 320,000. *1880*

MOBILE & SATELLITE SINGLE MARKET REVIEW.
Kline Publishing Ltd., 4-6 Station Parade, Balham High Rd., London SW12 9AD, England. TEL 081-673-7783. FAX 081-675-6466.
circ. 22,000. *1999*

MOBILE ELECTRONICS RETAILER.
Bobit Publishing Company, 2512 Artesia Blvd., Redondo Beach, CA 90278-3210. TEL 213-376-8788. FAX 213-376-9043.
circ. 23,000. *1999*

MOBILE PRODUCT ASIA.
Phillips Business Information, Inc., 1201 Seven Locks Rd., Potomac, MD 20854. TEL 301-340-1520. FAX 301-424-4297. *2036*

MOBILE PRODUCT EUROPE.
Phillips Business Information, Inc., 1201 Seven Locks Rd., Potomac, MD 20854. TEL 301-340-1520. FAX 301-424-4297. *2036*

MODEL ROCKET NEWS.
Estes Industries, 1295 H St., Penrose, CO 81240. TEL 719-372-6565. FAX 719-372-3419. *3672*

MODERATOR.
Mt. Marty College, 1105 W. 8th St., Yankton, SD 57078. TEL 605-668-1543.
circ. 1,000. *1962*

MODERN BAKING.
Donohue - Meehan Publishing Company (Des Plaines), 2700 River Rd., Des Plaines, IL 60018. TEL 847-299-4430. FAX 847-296-5936.
circ. 27,000. *3137*

MODERN FARMING.
Massey Ferguson, P.O. Box 62, Floor 10, Coventry CV4 9GF, England. TEL 44-1203-851221. FAX 44-1203-851182.
circ. 17,130. *137*

MODERN FOOD MANUFACTURING AND MARKETING.
E.W. Williams Publications Co., 2125 Center Ave., Ste. 305, Fort Lee, NJ 07024-5859. TEL 201-592-7007. FAX 201-592-7171.
circ. 10,000. *3120*

MODERN HEALTHCARE (YEAR).
Crain Communications, Inc. (Chicago), 740 N. Rush St., Chicago, IL 60611-2590. TEL 312-649-5341. FAX 312-280-3189.
circ. 86,915. *3717*

MODERN MEDIA.
Eiken Chemical Co. Ltd., 5-26-20 Oji, Kita-ku, Tokyo 114, Japan. TEL 81-3-3913-6231. FAX 81-3-3914-7027. *790*

MODERN REPROGRAPHICS.
Marion Street Press, Inc., Box 2249, Oak Park, IL 60303-2249. TEL 708-445-9454. FAX 708-445-9477.
circ. 8,000. *6081*

MODERNA.
Hispanic Publishing Corp., 98 San Jacinto Blvd., Ste. 1150, Austin, TX 78701-4039. TEL 512-476-5599.
circ. 150,000. *3029*

MOEBEL-KULTUR.
Ferdinand Holzmann Verlag GmbH, Mexikoring 37, 22297 Hamburg, Germany. TEL 040-632018-0. FAX 040-6307510. *3859*

MOEBELMARKT.
Verlag Matthias Ritthammer GmbH, Andernacherstr. 5a, 90019 Nuernberg, Germany. TEL 49-911-955780. FAX 49-911-9557811.
circ. 12,800. *3859*

MOISTURE MANAGER.
Munters Ltd., Blackstone Rd., Huntingdon, Cambs. PE18 6EF, England. TEL 44-1480-432243. FAX 44-1480-413147.
circ. 12,500. *2942*

MONDO ECONOMICO.
Societa Editoriale Media Economici Seme S.p.A., Via P. Lomazzo, 52, 20154 Milan, Italy. TEL 39-2-331211. FAX 39-2-316905.
circ. 25,744. *1271*

MONITEUR DES TRAVAUX PUBLICS ET DU BATIMENT.
Groupe Moniteur, 17 rue d'Uzes, 75002 Paris, France. FAX 33-1-42333819.
circ. 76,054. *2794*

MONITORE DIOCESANO.
Curia Vescovile, 93100 Caltanissetta, Italy.
circ. 450. *6471*

MONKEY.
Japan Monkey Centre, Kanrin Inuyama 26, Aichi 484, Japan. TEL 81-568-61-2327. FAX 81-568-62-6823.
circ. 2,000. *843*

MONOCLE.
Piton Publishing House Ltd., 79-81 High St., Godalming, Surrey GU7 1AW, England. TEL 44-1483-425454. FAX 44-1483-414262.
circ. 10,500. *4151*

MONTANA.
Montana Historical Society, 225 N. Roberts St., Box 201201, Helena, MT 59620-1201. TEL 406-444-4708. FAX 406-444-2696.
circ. 10,000. *3638*

MONTANA FARM BUREAU SPOKESMAN.
Montana Farm Bureau Federation, 502 S. 19th, Bozeman, MT 59718. TEL 406-587-3153. FAX 406-587-0319.
circ. 7,000. *137*

MONTANA VITAL STATISTICS.
Department of Public Health and Human Services, Vital Statistics Bureau, 111 N. Sanders, Helena, MT 59604. TEL 406-444-2614. FAX 406-444-2606.
circ. 850. *6257*

MONTHLY BREWING INDUSTRY COMMENTARY.
Cyrus J. Lawrence, Inc., 1290 Ave. of the Americas, New York, NY 10104. TEL 212-468-5000. *1271*

MONTREAL BUSINESS MAGAZINE.
275 St. Jacques St. W., Ste. 43, Montreal, PQ H2Y 1M9, Canada. TEL 514-286-8038. FAX 514-287-7346.
circ. 16,500. *986*

MONTREAL SCOPE.
Metro Plaza Ltd., Rm. 232, 1253 McGill College, Montreal, PQ H3B 2Y5, Canada. TEL 514-933-3333. FAX 514-931-9581.
circ. 40,000. *3263*

MOOREA.
Irish Garden Plant Society, c/o National Botanical Gardens, Glasnevin, Dublin 9, Ireland. FAX 353-1-337329.
circ. 800. *3199*

MORE THAN MONEY.
Impact Project, 2244 Alder St., Eugene, OR 97405-8900. TEL 541-343-2420.
circ. 1,000. *1398*

MORGUNBLADID.
Arvakur h.f., Kringlan 1, 103-Reykjavik, Iceland. TEL 354-569-1100. FAX 354-569-1181.
circ. 53,276. *3306*

MORNING STAR.
Morning Star Ltd., 1-3 Ardleigh Rd., London N1 4HS, England. TEL 44-171-254-0033. FAX 44-171-254-5950.
circ. 10,000. *3299*

MOTHERING.
Mothering Magazine, Box 1690, Santa Fe, NM 87504. FAX 505-986-8335.
circ. 7,322. *7310*

MOTO MAGAZYN.
Proszynski i S-ka, S.A., Ul. Rozana 34, 02-569 Warsaw, Poland. TEL 48-22-451256. FAX 48-22-452736.
circ. 145,000. *7106*

MOTOR.
Forlaget Motor ApS, Firskovvej 32, P.O. Box 500, DK-2800, Lyngby. TEL 45-45-27-07-07. FAX 45-45-27-09-93.
circ. 205,000. *7107*

MOTOR.
Hearst Business Publishing, 645 Stewart Ave., Garden City, NY 11530. TEL 516-227-1370. FAX 516-227-1405.
circ. 140,000. *7107*

MOTOR CARAVANNER.
Motor Caravanners' Club, 71 Cricklewood Broadway, London NW2 3JR, England. *6874*

MOTOR CLUB NEWS.
Motor Club of America, c/o Marlene Timm, Ed., 484 Central Ave., Newark, NJ 07107.
circ. 130,000. *7222*

MOTOR FREIGHT CONTROLLER.
American Trucking Associations, 2200 Mill Rd., Alexandria, VA 22304. TEL 703-838-1915. FAX 703-836-6070.
circ. 1,100. *7176*

MOTOR - MAGASINET.
Dansk Auto Media A-S, Hoejvangen 23, P.O. Box 159, DK-3480 Fredensborg, Denmark. TEL 45-48-48-51-00. FAX 45-48-48-20-15.
circ. 15,200. *7108*

MOTOR TRADER.
Reed Business Information, Quadrant House, The Quadrant, Sutton, Surrey SM2 5AS, England. TEL 44-181-652-3276. FAX 44-181-652-8982.
circ. 25,263. *7108*

MOTOR TRANSPORT.
Reed Business Information, Quadrant House, The Quadrant, Sutton, Surrey SM2 5AS, England. TEL 44-181-652-3284. FAX 44-181-652-8957.
circ. 28,766. *7176*

MOTORCYCLE INDUSTRY MAGAZINE.
Industry Shopper Publishing, Inc., Box 160, Gardnerville, NV 89410-0160. TEL 702-782-0222. FAX 702-782-0266.
circ. 13,200. *6830*

MOTORCYCLE PRODUCT NEWS.
M H West, Inc., 3000 Town Ctr., Ste. 2750, Southfield, MI 48075-1212. TEL 818-997-0664. FAX 818-997-1058.
circ. 12,951. *6830*

MOTORING.
Western India Automobile Association, 76 Veer Nariman Rd., Churchgate, Bombay 20, India.
circ. 30,000. *7109*

MOTORING & LEISURE.
Civil Service Motoring Association Ltd., Britannia House, 21 Station St., Brighton BN1 4DE, England. TEL 44-1273-744751. FAX 44-1273-323990.
circ. 320,242. *7109*

MOTORRAD NEWS.
Syburger Verlag GmbH, Hertingerstr. 60, 59423 Unna, Germany. TEL 49-2303-98550. FAX 49-2303-98559.
circ. 80,000. *6831*

MOUNTAIN CONSTRUCTOR & RECLAMATIONIST.
Phoenix Publishing Corporation, Box 6048, Denver, CO 80206-0048. TEL 303-988-2784.
circ. 11,201. *904*

MOUNTAIN TRAVEL - SOBEK, THE ADVENTURE COMPANY.
Mountain Travel - Sobek, 6420 Fairmount Ave., El Cerrito, CA 94530.
circ. 160,000. *7222*

MOUNTAIN XPRESS.
Mountain Xpress, Inc., Box 144, Asheville, NC 28802. TEL 704-251-1333. FAX 704-251-1311.
circ. 18,000. *3379*

MOVIE (YEAR).
Greater Union Organization, 49 Market St., Sydney, N.S.W. 2000, Australia. TEL 61-2-93736600. FAX 61-2-92675277.
circ. 20,000. *5340*

MOVIMENTO ANAGRAFE DITTE.
Camera di Commercio Industria, Artigianato e Agricoltura di Pesaro e Urbino, Corso XI Settembre, 116, 61100 Pesaro, Italy. TEL 0721-3571. FAX 0721-31015.
circ. 720. *1192*

MOVIMIENTO DE ROCK.
Zona 10, S.A., C. Bruc 65, 3o 2a, 08009 Barcelona, Spain. TEL 34-3-4883609. FAX 34-3-4876665.
circ. 25,000. *5411*

MOVIN' OUT.
118 1-2 Franklin St., Box 97, Slippery Rock, PA 16057. TEL 412-794-6857. FAX 412-794-1314.
circ. 42,000. *7176*

MRS. EAGLE.
Fraternal Order of Eagles, Box 25916, Milwaukee, WI 53225-0916. TEL 414-781-7585. FAX 414-781-5046.
circ. 350,000. *1934*

MUHENDIS VE MAKINA.
Chamber of Mechanical Engineers, Sumer Sokak, 36-1-A Demirtepe, 06440 Ankara, Turkey. TEL 90-4-2313159. FAX 90-4-2313165.
circ. 30,000. *2894*

MULTI-HOUSING NEWS.
Miller Freeman Inc. (New York), One Penn Plaza, New York, NY 10119. TEL 212-869-1300. FAX 212-944-7164.
circ. 28,300. *905*

MULTICULTURAL PUBLISHING AND EDUCATION COUNCIL. NEWSLETTER.
Multicultural Publishing and Education Council, c/o Rennie Mau, President, 2280 Grass Valley Hwy., No.181, Auburn, CA 95603. TEL 916-889-4438. FAX 916-888-0690.
circ. 1,500. *6278*

MUNDI MEDICINA.
Holy Cross Monastery, Box 99, West Park, NY 12493. TEL 914-384-6660. FAX 914-384-6031.
circ. 6,500. *6356*

EL MUNDO.
Alameda Publishing, 630 20th St., Oakland, CA 94612. TEL 510-763-1120. FAX 510-763-9670.
circ. 30,000. *3030*

MUNDO DEL PERRO.
Moreno Marin s.l., Calle San Romualdo 26, 28037 Madrid, Spain. TEL 34-1-3044634. FAX 34-1-3046783.
circ. 30,000. *5639*

MUNDO NEGRO.
Misioneros Combonianos, Congregacion Misionera, Arturo Soria, 101, 28043 Madrid, Spain. TEL 91-4152412. FAX 91-5192550.
circ. 100,000. *6356*

MUNICIPAL ASSOCIATION OF TASMANIA. SESSION. MINUTES OF PROCEEDINGS.
Municipal Association of Tasmania, 34 Patrick St., Hobart, Tas. 7000, Australia. TEL 002-310666. FAX 002-240086.
circ. 200. *6220*

MUNICIPAL ATTORNEY.
National Institute of Municipal Law Officers, 3554 Chain Bridge Rd., Ste. 205, Fairfax, VA 22030-2709.
circ. 2,500. *3992*

MUNICIPAL ENGINEER.
Brooke Pattrick (Pty) Ltd., P.O. Box 422, Bedfordview 2008, South Africa. TEL 27-11-6224666. FAX 27-11-6167196.
circ. 4,357. *2794*

MUNRO EAGLE.
Clan Munro Association U S A, Inc., 11 Las Huertas Ridge Rd., Placitas, NM 87043.
circ. 600. *3233*

MURMUR.
Cambridge University Medical Society, Department of Anatomy, Cambridge University, Cambridge CB2 9DT, England. TEL 44-1223-60160.
circ. 750. *4718*

MUSEO CIVICO DI STORIA NATURALE DI TRIESTE. ATTI.
Tipografia Villaggio del Fanciullo, Via Conconello 16, Opicina, 34016 Trieste, Italy. TEL 39-40-301821. FAX 39-40-302563.
circ. 400. *6546*

MUSEO CIVICO DI STORIA NATURALE DI VENEZIA. BOLLETTINO.
Museo Civico di Storia Naturale di Venezia, Fontego dei Turchi, S. Croce 1730, 30135 Venice, Italy. TEL 39-41-721852. FAX 39-41-5242592.
circ. 1,000. *615*

CONTROLLED CIRCULATION SERIALS

MUSEUM OF THE FUR TRADE QUARTERLY.
Museum of the Fur Trade, HC-74, Box 18, Chadron, NE 69337. TEL 308-432-3843.
circ. 3,000. *3638*

MUSHROOM JOURNAL.
Mushroom Growers' Association, 2 St. Pauls St., Stamford, Lincs. PE9 2BE, England.
circ. 1,000. *3199*

MUSIC CRITICS ASSOCIATION. NEWSLETTER.
Music Critics Association, 7 Pine Ct., Westfield, NJ 07090. TEL 908-233-8468. FAX 908-233-8468.
circ. 1,000. *5412*

MUSIC FROM CHINA. NEWS.
Music from China, 170 Park Row, Ste. 12-D, New York, NY 10038. TEL 212-962-5698.
circ. 1,200. *5412*

MUSICAL HERITAGE REVIEW MAGAZINE.
Musical Heritage Society, 1710 Highway 35, Ocean, NJ 07712. TEL 201-531-7000. *5415*

MUSICAL MERCHANDISE REVIEW.
Larkin-Pluznick-Larkin, Inc., 100 Wells Ave., Box 9103, Newton, MA 02159-9103. TEL 617-964-5100. FAX 617-964-2752.
circ. 12,000. *5415*

MUSIKK - KULTUR.
Musikk - Kultur AS, P.O. Box 210, N-4301 Sandnes, Norway. TEL 47-51-68-62-00. FAX 47-51-68-62-01.
circ. 5,000. *5417*

MUTUALITE.
Association Internationale des Societes d'Assurance Mutuelle, 114 rue la Boetie, 75008 Paris, France. FAX 33-1-42560449.
circ. 2,500. *3826*

MUZIEKHANDEL.
Nederlandse Muziek Federatie - N M F, Eikbosserweg 181, 1213 RX Hilversum, Netherlands. TEL 31-35-6248104. FAX 31-35-6214220.
circ. 500. *5418*

MY CAREER.
Department of Labour, Private Bag X117, Pretoria 0001, South Africa. TEL 27-12-3106358. FAX 27-12-3222839.
circ. 45,000. *5513*

MYCOPHILE.
North American Mycological Association, 3556 Oakwood, Ann Arbor, MI 48104-5213. TEL 313-971-2522.
circ. 2,000. *715*

MYCOTAXON.
Mycotaxon Ltd., Box 264, Ithaca, NY 14851. TEL 607-273-4357. FAX 607-273-4357.
circ. 650. *716*

MYSTIC TRAVELER.
Traveler Publications, Inc., 174 Bellevue Ave., Ste. 205, Newport, RI 02840. TEL 401-847-0226. FAX 401-847-5267.
circ. 40,000. *7222*

N A A C NEWSLETTER.
Huts Corner, Tilford Rd., Hindhead, Surrey GU26 6SF, England. TEL 44-1428-605360. FAX 44-1428-606531.
circ. 600. *137*

N A A F I NEWS.
Navy, Army & Air Force Institutes, HQ N A A F I, London Rd., Amesbury, Wilts SP4 7EN, England. TEL 0980-627043. FAX 0980-627155.
circ. 11,000. *5278*

N A B P NEWSLETTER.
National Association of Boards of Pharmacy, 700 Busse Hwy., Park Ridge, IL 60068-2402. TEL 708-698-6227.
circ. 1,800. *5679*

N A C R C BULLETIN.
National Association of County Recorders and Clerks, c/o National Association of Counties, 440 First St., N.W., 8th Fl., Washington, DC 20001. TEL 202-393-6226.
circ. 900. *6184*

N A C W P I JOURNAL.
Simpson Publishing Co., c/o Richard K. Weerts, Ed., Division of Fine Arts, Truman State University, Kirksville, MO 63501. TEL 816-785-4442. FAX 816-785-7463.
circ. 6,000. *5418*

N A E B BULLETIN.
National Association of Educational Buyers, 450 Wireless Blvd., Hauppauge, NY 11788-3934. TEL 516-273-2600. FAX 516-273-2305. *2612*

N A E I R ADVANTAGE.
National Association for the Exchange of Industrial Resources, 560 McClure St., Box 8076, Galesburg, IL 61402. TEL 309-343-0704. FAX 309-343-0862.
circ. 38,000. *6677*

N A M A JOURNAL.
National Account Management Association, 150 N. Wacker Dr., Ste. 960, Chicago, IL 60606-1607. TEL 312-251-3131. FAX 312-251-3132.
circ. 2,000. *1542*

N A P O PROBATION DIRECTORY.
Owen Wells Publishing Company, 23 Eaton Rd., Ilkley, W. Yorks LS29 9PU, England. TEL 44-1943-602270. FAX 44-1943-816732.
circ. 9,000. *6677*

N A P R A REVIEW.
New Age Publishing & Retailing Alliance, Box 9, Eastsound, WA 98245. TEL 360-376-2702. FAX 360-376-2704.
circ. 10,500. *5458*

N A R F REHABILITATION REPORT.
National Association of Rehabilitation Facilities, Box 17675, Washington, DC 20041. TEL 703-648-9300. FAX 703-648-0346.
circ. 2,000. *5044*

N A R I REMODELER'S JOURNAL.
National Association of the Remodeling Industry, 4900 Deminary Rd., Ste. 320, Alexandria, VA 22311-1811. TEL 703-575-1100. FAX 703-575-1121.
circ. 7,500. *905*

N B I A NEWSLETTER.
New Brunswick Institute of Agrologists, P.O. Box 20280, Fredericton, NB E3B 4Z7, Canada. TEL 506-452-3260. FAX 506-452-3316.
circ. 200. *137*

N B T A NEWS.
New Brunswick Teachers' Association, Box 752, Fredericton, NB E3B 5R6, Canada. TEL 506-452-8921. FAX 506-453-9795.
circ. 8,200. *2464*

N C G A NEWS.
Northern California Golf Association, 3200 Lopez Rd., Box NCGA, Pebble Beach, CA 93953. TEL 408-625-4653. FAX 408-625-0150.
circ. 150,000. *6772*

N E C RESEARCH AND DEVELOPMENT.
N E C Creative Ltd., 29-11, Shiba 5-chome, Minato-ku, Tokyo 108, Japan.
circ. 5,000. *2840*

N E F E DIGEST.
National Endowment for Financial Education, 4695 S. Monaco St., Denver, CO 80237-3403. TEL 303-220-1200. FAX 303-220-1810.
circ. 70,000. *1156*

N I C SENTINEL.
North Idaho College, 1000 W. Garden, Coeur D. Alene, ID 83814. TEL 208-769-3388.
circ. 2,300. *1962*

N N F A TODAY.
National Nutritional Foods Association, 3931 MacArthur Blvd., Ste. 101, Newport Beach, CA 92660-3021. TEL 714-622-6272. FAX 714-622-6266. *5478*

N N O MAGAZINE.
Noord - Nederlands Orkest, Emmaplein 2, P.O. Box 818, 9700 AV Groningen, Netherlands. TEL 31-50-3126200. FAX 31-50-3138164.
circ. 3,500. *5479*

N NOTICIAS.
National Association of Hispanic Journalists, 1193 National Press Bldg., 529 14th St., N.W., Washington, DC 20045. TEL 202-662-7145. FAX 202-662-7144.
circ. 2,500. *3877*

N & M.
Norges Naturvernforbund, Postboks 2113 Grunerlokka, N-0505 Oslo, Norway. TEL 47-22-715520. FAX 47-22-715640.
circ. 27,000. *2943*

N R R I NOW.
University of Minnesota, Duluth, Natural Resources Research Institute, 5013 Miller Trunk Hwy., Duluth, MN 55811. TEL 218-720-4280. FAX 218-720-4219.
circ. 2,500. *2319*

N S D C A TIMES.
National Square Dance Campers Association, P.O. Box 18, Lower Waterford, VT 05848-0018. TEL 802-748-9478. FAX 802-748-4742.
circ. 5,000. *2294*

N S G A RETAIL FOCUS.
National Sporting Goods Association, 1699 Wall St., Mt. Prospect, IL 60056-5780. TEL 847-439-4000. FAX 847-439-0111. *1543*

N S R A NEWS.
Nuclear Safety Research Association, 1-2-2 Uchisaiwai-cho, Chiyoda-ku, Tokyo 107, Japan. TEL 03-3503-5785.
circ. 1,500. *2700*

N S S R A NEWSLETTER.
National Ski & Snowboard Retailers Association, 1699 Wall St., Mt. Prospect, IL 60056. TEL 847-439-4293. FAX 847-439-0111.
circ. 500. *1543*

N.S.W. MASTER PLUMBER.
Master Plumbers and Mechanical Contractors Association of New South Wales, P.O. Box 65, Haberfield, N.S.W. 2045, Australia. TEL 61-2-97977055. FAX 61-2-97995841.
circ. 1,600. *3482*

N V V K INFO.
Uitgeverij Kluwer B.V., Postbus 23, 7400 GA Deventer, Netherlands. TEL 31-570-633155. FAX 31-570-633834.
circ. 1,500. *5495*

N W D A EXECUTIVE NEWSLETTER.
National Wholesale Druggists' Association, Box 2219, Reston, VA 22090. TEL 703-787-0000. FAX 703-787-6930.
circ. 2,300. *5679*

N Y C - ON STAGE.
c/o Theatre Development Fund, 1501 Broadway, Rm. 2110, New York, NY 10036. TEL 212-221-0885. FAX 212-768-1563. *7009*

N.Y. REAL PROPERTY LAW JOURNAL.
New York State Bar Association, Real Property Section, 1 Elk St., Albany, NY 12207-1096. TEL 518-463-3200. FAX 518-463-8844.
circ. 4,800. *6306*

N Y S S A SPHERE.
New York State Society of Anesthesiologists, Inc., 360 Lexington Ave., Ste. 1800, New York, NY 10017. TEL 212-867-7140. FAX 212-867-7153.
circ. 3,200. *4806*

N Y U PHYSICIAN.
New York University School of Medicine, 550 First Ave., New York, NY 10016. FAX 212-263-8425.
circ. 18,000. *1962*

NACION.
Estudios y Publicaciones Economicas y Sociales, S.A., Cerrada de Eugenia, 25, Col. del Valle, Delegacion Benito Juarez, Apartado Postal 32-470, CP 03100 Mexico DF, Mexico. TEL 536-18-31. FAX 525-687-2922.
circ. 15,000. *5946*

NADI ABU DHABI AL-SIYAHI.
Nadi Abu Dhabi al-Siyahi, P.O. Box 28, Abu Dhabi, United Arab Emirates. TEL 724954.
circ. 1,000. *1934*

NADI AL-WASL.
Nadi al-Wasl, P.O. Box 3888, Dubai, United Arab Emirates. TEL 374487.
circ. 500. *1934*

NAERINGSMIDDELINDUSTRIEN.
Skarland Press A-S, P.O. Box 5042 Maj., N-0301 Oslo, Norway. TEL 47-22-59-88-00. FAX 47-22-69-36-50.
circ. 3,909. *3121*

NAGOYA MATHEMATICAL JOURNAL.
Nagoya Daigaku, Daigakuin Tagensurikagaku Kenkyuka, Chikusa-ku, Nagoya 464-01, Japan. FAX 81-52-789-2829.
circ. 1,250. *4594*

NAILPRO.
Creative Age Publications, Inc., 7628 Densmore Ave., Van Nuys, CA 91406-2042. TEL 818-782-7328. FAX 818-782-7450.
circ. 48,118. *512*

NAMO BUDDHA NEWSLETTER.
Namo Buddha Seminar, Maytrees, Aylesbury Rd., Monks Risborough, Bucks. HP27 0JT; England. TEL 08444-3642.
circ. 2,000. *6389*

NARA IGAKU ZASSHI.
Nara Igakkai, Nara Medical University, Kashihara 634, Nara, Japan. TEL 81-7442-2-3051. FAX 81-7442-5-7308.
circ. 1,200. *4719*

NAROD POLSKI.
Polish Roman Catholic Union of America, 984 N. Milwaukee Ave., Chicago, IL 60622. TEL 312-278-3210. FAX 312-278-4595.
circ. 30,000. *3030*

NASHVILLE SCENE.
209 Tenth Ave. S., Ste. 222, Nashville, TN 37203-4101. TEL 615-244-7989. FAX 615-244-8578.
circ. 50,000. *5419*

NASSAU COUNTY DENTAL SOCIETY. NEWSLETTER.
Nassau County Dental Society Headquarters, 377 Oak St., No. 205, Garden City, NY 11530-6543. TEL 516-764-9620. FAX 516-227-1114.
circ. 2,000. *4864*

NATCHEZ TRACE TRAVELER.
Natchez Trace Genealogical Society, Box 420, Florence, AL 35631-0420.
circ. 150. *3233*

NATIONAL ASSOCIATION OF BEVERAGE RETAILERS. NEWS AND VIEWS.
National Association of Beverage Retailers, 5101 River Rd., Ste. 108, Bethesda, MD 20816. TEL 301-656-1494. FAX 301-656-7539.
circ. 15,000. *525*

NATIONAL ASSOCIATION OF RAILROAD PASSENGERS NEWS.
National Association of Railroad Passengers, 900 Second St., N.E., Ste. 308, Washington, DC 20002-3557. TEL 202-408-8362. FAX 202-408-8287.
circ. 2,300. *7129*

NATIONAL ASSOCIATION OF STATE PARK DIRECTORS. ANNUAL INFORMATION EXCHANGE.
National Association of State Park Directors, c/o Ney C. Landrum, Exec. Dir., 126 Mill Branch Rd, Tallahassee, FL 32312.
circ. 400. *2237*

NATIONAL ASSOCIATION OF WOMEN ARTISTS. ANNUAL EXHIBITION CATALOG.
National Association of Women Artists, 41 Union Sq., W., Rm. 906, New York, NY 10003. TEL 212-675-1616. FAX 212-675-1616.
circ. 1,000. *456*

NATIONAL BOTANIC RESEARCH INSTITUTE, LUCKNOW. PROGRESS REPORT.
National Botanical Research Institute, Lucknow, Lucknow 226001, India. TEL 91-522-282849. FAX 91-522-282849.
circ. 500. *716*

NATIONAL BOTANICAL INSTITUTE. REVIEW.
National Botanical Institute (Claremont), Private Bag X7, Claremont 7735, South Africa. TEL 27-21-762-1166. FAX 27-21-762-3229.
circ. 500. *716*

NATIONAL BRAILLE ASSOCIATION. GENERAL INTEREST CATALOG.
National Braille Association, Inc., 3 Townline Cir., Rochester, NY 14623. TEL 716-427-8260. *3472*

NATIONAL BRAILLE ASSOCIATION. MUSIC CATALOG.
National Braille Association, Inc., 3 Townline Cir., Rochester, NY 14623. TEL 716-427-8260. *3472*

NATIONAL BRAILLE ASSOCIATION. TEXTBOOK CATALOG.
National Braille Association, Inc., 3 Townline Cir., Rochester, NY 14623. TEL 716-427-8260. *3472*

NATIONAL BUSINESS BULLETIN.
National Business Magazines, 361 Riley St., Surry Hills, N.S.W. 2010, Australia. TEL 61-2-2125588. FAX 61-2-2122709.
circ. 41,989. *986*

NATIONAL CENTRE FOR OCCUPATIONAL HEALTH. ANNUAL REPORT.
Department of Health, National Centre for Occupational Health, P.O. Box 4788, Johannesburg 2000, South Africa. FAX 27-11-720-6608.
circ. 400. *5495*

NATIONAL CLOTHESLINE.
B P S Communications, Box 340, Willow Grove, PA 19090-0340. TEL 215-830-8467. FAX 215-830-8490.
circ. 38,000. *1911*

NATIONAL CONFERENCE OF APPELLATE COURT CLERKS. NEWSLETTER.
National Conference of Appellate Court Clerks, National Center for State Courts, 300 Newport Ave., Williamsburg, VA 23187-8798. TEL 757-253-2000.
circ. 225. *4135*

NATIONAL CONFERENCE OF STATE SOCIAL SECURITY ADMINISTRATORS. PROCEEDINGS.
National Conference of State Social Security Administrators, c/o Social Security Division, c/o Jim Larche, Deputy Dir., Employee Retirement System of Georgia, Two Northside 75, Ste. 300, Atlanta, GA 30318. TEL 404-352-6400. *6678*

NATIONAL COUNCIL OF ELECTED COUNTY EXECUTIVES.
Griffin Media Group, 640 W. 231 St., Apt. 7B, Bronx, NY 10463-3258. TEL 212-481-4188. FAX 212-481-7239.
circ. 2,500. *6185*

NATIONAL COUNCIL OF TEACHERS OF MATHEMATICS. YEARBOOK.
National Council of Teachers of Mathematics, 1906 Association Dr., Reston, VA 22091. TEL 703-620-9840. FAX 703-476-2970. *4594*

NATIONAL COUNCIL OF THE PAPER INDUSTRY FOR AIR AND STREAM IMPROVEMENT. TECHNICAL BULLETIN.
National Council of the Paper Industry for Air and Stream Improvement, Inc., Box 13318, Research Triangle Park, NC 27709-3318.
circ. 1,500. *2971*

NATIONAL DAIRY COUNCIL OF CANADA. DIRECTION.
National Dairy Council of Canada, 221 Laurier Ave., E., Ottawa, ON K1N 6P1, Canada. TEL 613-238-4116. FAX 613-238-6247.
circ. 1,500. *257*

NATIONAL DEVELOPMENT.
Intercontinental Media, 25 Sylvan Rd. S., Ste. R, Box 3410, Milford, CT 06460. TEL 203-226-7463. FAX 203-222-8793.
circ. 22,000. *2794*

NATIONAL DEVELOPMENT FINANCE CORPORATION. QUARTERLY REVIEW.
National Development Finance Corporation, Finance and Trade Center, 2nd Fl., Shahrah-e Faisal, Karachi, Pakistan. FAX 525310.
circ. 1,200. *1272*

NATIONAL DIET LIBRARY. BOOKS ON JAPAN IN WESTERN LANGUAGES RECENTLY ACQUIRED.
National Diet Library, 1-10-1 Nagata-cho, Chiyoda-ku, Tokyo 100, Japan. TEL 81-3-3581-2331. FAX 81-3-3597-9104.
circ. 800. *557*

NATIONAL DIET LIBRARY. NEWSLETTER.
National Diet Library, 1-10-1 Nagata-cho, Chiyoda-ku, Tokyo 100, Japan. TEL 81-3-3581-2331. FAX 81-3-3597-9104.
circ. 1,000. *4201*

NATIONAL DIET LIBRARY. REFERENCE.
National Diet Library, 1-10-1 Nagata-cho, Chiyoda-ku, Tokyo 100, Japan. TEL 81-3-3581-2331. FAX 81-3-3597-9104.
circ. 1,700. *3994*

NATIONAL DIRECTORY OF CHIROPRACTIC.
National Directory of Chiropractic Foundation, Box 10056, Olathe, KS 66051. FAX 913-780-0658.
circ. 31,000. *1700*

NATIONAL FEDERATION OF FRUIT & POTATO TRADES. FEDERATION NEWS.
National Federation of Fruit and Potato Trades Ltd., 103-107 Market Towers, 1 Nine Elms Ln., London SW8 5NQ, England. *138*

NATIONAL FORUM (AUBURN).
Honor Society of Phi Kappa Phi (Auburn), c/o Dr. James P. Kaetz, Ed., 129 Quad Center, Mell St., Auburn, AL 36849-5306. TEL 334-844-5200. FAX 334-844-5994.
circ. 120,000. *1963*

NATIONAL FOUNDATION FOR ADVANCEMENT IN THE ARTS. ANNUAL REPORT.
National Foundation for Advancement in the Arts, 800 Brickell Ave. No. 5, Miami, FL 33131-2944. TEL 305-377-1140. FAX 305-377-1149.
circ. 1,000. *457*

NATIONAL HOG FARMER.
Intertec Publishing Corp., Webb Division, 7900 International Dr., Ste. 300, Minneapolis, MN 55425. TEL 612-851-4710. FAX 612-851-4601.
circ. 88,373. *283*

NATIONAL HOUSING REGISTER.
William D. Diemer, Ed. & Pub., 27239 Meadowbrook Dr., Davis, CA 95616-5049. TEL 916-757-6403. FAX 916-753-1768.
circ. 50. *6306*

NATIONAL INDUSTRIAL NEWS.
Brymell Publications, Inc., 801 York Mills Rd., Ste. 201, Don Mills, ON M3B 1X7, Canada. TEL 416-446-1404. FAX 416-446-0502.
circ. 24,500. *1591*

NATIONAL INDUSTRIAL TRANSPORTATION LEAGUE. NOTICE.
National Industrial Transportation League, 1700 N. Moore St., Ste. 1900, Arlington, VA 22209-1904. TEL 703-524-5011. FAX 703-524-5017.
circ. 2,000. *7035*

NATIONAL INSTITUTE FOR EDUCATIONAL RESEARCH. RESEARCH BULLETIN.
National Institute for Educational Research, 6-5-22 Shimo-Meguro, Meguro-ku, Tokyo 153, Japan. *2465*

NATIONAL INSTITUTE OF MATERIALS AND CHEMICAL RESEARCH. JOURNAL.
National Institute of Materials and Chemical Research, Ibaraki 305, Japan. TEL 81-298-54-4410. FAX 81-298-54-4422.
circ. 2,700. *1760*

NATIONAL INSTITUTE OF WATER AND ATMOSPHERIC RESEARCH. BIODIVERSITY MEMOIRS.
National Institute of Water and Atmospheric Research Ltd., P.O. Box 14-901, Kilbirnie, Wellington, New Zealand. TEL 64-4-3860388. FAX 64-4-3862153.
circ. 500. *2410*

NATIONAL INVESTMENT BANK, GHANA. ANNUAL REPORT.
National Investment Bank, 37 Kwame Nkrumah Ave., P.O. Box 3726, Accra, Ghana. *1157*

NATIONAL MISSING PERSONS REPORT.
Search Reports, Inc., 345 Boulevard, Hasbrouck Heights, NJ 07604. TEL 201-288-4445. FAX 201-288-8055.
circ. 45,000. *2274*

NATIONAL MUSEUM OF THE PHILIPPINES. ANNUAL REPORT.
National Museum of the Philippines, Padre Burgos St., Manila, Philippines. TEL 632-527-12-15. FAX 632-530-0229.
circ. 500. *5362*

NATIONAL NEWSBYTES NEWSLETTER.
Association for Women in Computing, 41 Sutter St., Ste. 1006, San Francisco, CA 94104. TEL 415-905-4663.
circ. 1,500. *2128*

NATIONAL POLICE REVIEW.
National Police Officers Association, 7811 Old Tree Run, Louisville, KY 40222-4694. TEL 502-425-9215.
circ. 22,500. *2274*

THE NATIONAL PROVISIONER.
Stagnito Publishing Company, 1935 Shermer Rd., Ste. 100, Northbrook, IL 60062. TEL 847-205-5660. FAX 847-205-5680.
circ. 18,500. *3121*

NATIONAL RETIREMENT QUARTERLY.
Pierce Publications, 3 Northender Rd., Gatley, Ches. SK8 4NR, England. TEL 44-161-491-6000. FAX 44-161-491-1557.
circ. 20,000. *3299*

NATIONAL SAFETY.
Safety First Association, 7 Pitcairn Rd., Blairgowrie, Johannesburg 2194, South Africa. TEL 27-11-7827698.
circ. 3,200. *6245*

NATIONAL SECURITY REVIEW.
National Defense College of the Philippines, Logcom Area, Camp Aguinaldo, Quezon City, Philippines.
circ. 500. *5946*

NATIONALLY COORDINATED PROGRAM OF HIGHWAY RESEARCH, DEVELOPMENT, AND TECHNOLOGY.
U.S. Federal Highway Administration, Office of Highway Information Management, Department of Transportation, 400 Seventh St., S.W., Washington, DC 20590. TEL 703-285-2101. FAX 703-285-2379.
circ. 1,500. *7139*

NATUN THIKANA.
71-4 Dr. Nilmani Sarkar St., Calcutta 50, India.
4348

NATUR.
Natur Media GmbH, Belfortstr. 6-8, 81667 Munich, Germany.
circ. 120,696. *716*

NATURAL CHOICE MAGAZINE.
Media Partners CPR, Northern Rock House, 20 Market Pl., Guisborough, Cleveland TS14 6HF, England. TEL 44-1287-639111. FAX 44-1287-637201.
circ. 150,000. *5787*

NATURAL FOOD TRADER.
I B T M Ltd., Queensway House, 2 Queensway, Redhill, Surrey RH1 1QS, England. TEL 0737-768611. FAX 0737-760425.
circ. 4,500. *5478*

NATURAL FOODS MERCHANDISER.
New Hope Communications, Inc., 1301 Spruce St., Boulder, CO 80302-4832. TEL 303-939-8440. FAX 303-939-9559.
circ. 14,000. *1543*

NATURAL GAS FUELS.
R P Publishing, Inc., 1290 Broadway, Ste. 700, Denver, CO 80203-5607. TEL 303-863-0521. FAX 303-863-1722.
circ. 8,000. *7035*

NATURAL HISTORY MUSEUM AND INSTITUTE, CHIBA. ANNUAL REPORT.
Natural History Museum and Institute, Chiba, 955-2 Aoba-cho, Chuo-ku, Chiba 260, Japan. TEL 81-43-265-3111. FAX 81-43-266-2481.
circ. 1,000. *5363*

NATURAL HISTORY MUSEUM AND INSTITUTE, CHIBA. BULLETIN. HUMANITIES.
Natural History Museum and Institute, Chiba, 955-2 Aoba-cho, Chuo-ku, Chiba 260, Japan. TEL 81-43-265-3111. FAX 81-43-266-2481.
circ. 1,500. *3537*

NATURAL HISTORY MUSEUM AND INSTITUTE, CHIBA. JOURNAL.
Natural History Museum and Institute, Chiba, 955-2 Aoba-cho, Chuo-ku, Chiba 260, Japan. TEL 81-43-265-3111. FAX 81-43-266-2481.
circ. 1,500. *6550*

NATURAL HISTORY MUSEUM AND INSTITUTE, CHIBA. JOURNAL. SPECIAL ISSUE.
Natural History Museum and Institute, Chiba, 955-2 Aoba-cho, Chuo-ku, Chiba 260, Japan. TEL 81-43-265-3111. FAX 81-43-266-2481.
circ. 1,500. *616*

NATURAL HISTORY RESEARCH.
Natural History Museum and Institute, Chiba, 955-2 Aoba-cho, Chuo-ku, Chiba 260, Japan. TEL 81-43-265-3111. FAX 81-43-266-2481.
circ. 1,500. *6550*

NATURAL HISTORY RESEARCH. SPECIAL ISSUE.
Natural History Museum and Institute, Chiba, 955-2 Aoba-cho, Chuo-ku, Chiba 260, Japan. TEL 81-43-265-3111. FAX 81-43-266-2481.
circ. 1,500. *616*

NATURAL WORLD.
R S N C - The Wildlife Trusts Partnership, 20 Upper Ground, London SE1 9PF, England. TEL 44-171-805-5555. FAX 44-171-805-5565.
circ. 154,200. *2238*

NATURFREUNDE.
Naturfreunde Bundesgruppe Deutschland e.V., Postfach 600441, 70304 Stuttgart, Germany. TEL 49-711-40954-0. FAX 49-711-409544.
circ. 70,000. *6875*

NATURSCHUTZ HEUTE.
Naturschutzbund Deutschland e.V., Postfach 301054, 53190 Bonn, Germany. TEL 49-228-9756141. FAX 49-228-9756194.
circ. 180,000. *2239*

NAVAL AVIATION NEWS.
U.S. Department of the Navy, Naval Historical Center, Bldg. 157-1 WNY, Washington, DC 20374-5059. TEL 202-433-4407. FAX 202-433-2343.
circ. 30,000. *75*

NAVAL WAR COLLEGE REVIEW.
U.S. Naval War College, 686 Cushing Rd., Code 32, Newport, RI 02841-1207. TEL 401-841-2236. FAX 401-841-3579.
circ. 9,500. *5279*

NAVY CHAPLAIN.
U.S. Navy, Bureau of Naval Personnel, Washington, DC 20370. TEL 804-444-7665. FAX 804-445-1006.
circ. 4,200. *5279*

NAWPA PACHA.
Institute of Andean Studies, Box 9307, Berkeley, CA 94709. TEL 510-525-7816.
circ. 550. *374*

NAZARETH.
Via Filitteria 10, 06049 Spoleto, Italy.
circ. 2,000. *6357*

NEAR WEST GAZETTE.
Near West Gazette, Inc., 1335 W. Harrison St., Chicago, IL 60607-3318. TEL 312-243-4288. FAX 312-243-4270.
circ. 15,000. *3380*

NEBELSPALTER.
Reinhardt AG, CH-4012 Basel, Switzerland. TEL 41-61-2646480. FAX 41-61-2646488.
circ. 38,864. *4348*

NEBRASKA. DEPARTMENT OF ROADS. TRAFFIC ANALYSIS UNIT. CONTINUOUS TRAFFIC COUNT DATA AND TRAFFIC CHARACTERISTICS ON NEBRASKA STREETS AND HIGHWAYS.
Department of Roads, Transportation Planning Division, 1500 Nebraska Hwy. 2, Box 94759, Lincoln, NE 68509-4759. TEL 402-471-4567. FAX 402-479-4325. *7139*

NEBRASKA. DEPARTMENT OF SOCIAL SERVICES. ANNUAL REPORT.
Department of Social Services, Research and Finance Division, Box 95026, 301 Centennial Mall So., Lincoln, NE 68509. FAX 402-471-9455.
circ. 500. *6678*

NEBRASKA HIGHWAY PROGRAM.
Nebraska Department of Roads, 1500 NE Hwy. 2, Box 94759, Lincoln, NE 68509-4759. TEL 402-479-4512. FAX 402-479-4325.
circ. 3,850. *7139*

NEBRASKA MORTAR AND PESTLE.
Nebraska Pharmacists Association, Inc., 6221 S. 58th St., Ste. A, Lincoln, NE 68516-3679. TEL 402-420-1500. FAX 402-420-1406.
circ. 1,250. *5680*

NEBRASKA MUSIC EDUCATOR.
Nebraska Music Educators Association, Box 83046, Lincoln, NE 68501-3046. TEL 402-435-6913. FAX 402-474-3250.
circ. 1,650. *5419*

NEBRASKA RETAILER.
Nebraska Retail Grocers Association, 5533 S. 27th St., Ste. 104, Lincoln, NE 68512-1611.
circ. 500. *1543*

NEDERDUITSE GEREFORMEERDE KERK VAN NATAL GEMEENTE VRYHEID. MAANDBRIEF.
Nederduitse Gereformeerde Kerk van Natal Gemeentevryheid, Smalstraat 82, Vryheid, Natal, South Africa.
circ. 600. *6435*

NEDERDUITSE GEREFORMEERDE TEOLOGIESE TYDSKRIF.
Nederduitse Gereformeerde Kerk Uitgewers, P.O. Box 4539, Cape Town, South Africa. TEL 27-21-215540. FAX 27-21-4191865.
circ. 1,800. *6435*

NEDERLANDS ELEKTRONICA- EN RADIOGENOOTSCHAP. TIJDSCHRIFT.
Nederlands Elektronica- en Radiogenootschap, Box 39, Leidschendam, Netherlands. TEL 31-70-3325112. FAX 31-70-3326477.
circ. 900. *2000*

NEEDLE'S EYE.
Union Special Corp., 1 Union Special Plaza, Huntley, IL 60142. TEL 847-669-4334. FAX 847-669-3534.
circ. 26,300. *1917*

NEERLANDIA.
Algemeen Nederlands Verbond, J. van Nassaustraat 109, 2596 BS The Hague, Netherlands. TEL 31-70-3245514. FAX 31-70-3246186.
circ. 3,000. *4348*

NEIGHBOR.
309 W. 43rd St., Ste. 103, Sioux Falls, SD 57105-6805. TEL 605-335-7300. FAX 605-335-8141.
circ. 29,000. *138*

NEIGHBORLINE.
University of Dayton, Dayton, OH 45469. TEL 513-229-4639.
circ. 900. *6678*

NEMATOLOGIA MEDITERRANEA.
Istituto di Nematologia Agraria, Via G. Amendola, 165-A, 70126 Bari, Italy. TEL 39-80-5484186. FAX 39-80-5484165.
circ. 300. *236*

NEPHROLOGY NEWS & ISSUES.
Nephrology News & Issues, Inc., 15150 N. Hayden Rd., Ste. 101, Scottsdale, AZ 85260-2514. TEL 602-443-4635. FAX 602-443-4528.
circ. 13,400. *5164*

NEPSZABADSAG.
Nepszabadsag, Ltd., Becsi ut, 1034 Budapest, Hungary. TEL 36-1-2501680. FAX 36-1-2500250.
circ. 300,000. *3305*

NEPSZAVA (BUDAPEST EDITION).
Torokvesz ut 30-A, 1022 Budapest, Hungary. TEL 361-202-7788. FAX 361-202-7798.
circ. 120,000. *3305*

CONTROLLED CIRCULATION SERIALS 10367

NET FRIEND NEWS.
American Tennis Federation, 200 Castlewood Dr., North Palm Beach, FL 33408. TEL 407-848-1026. FAX 407-863-8984.
circ. 200. *6812*

NETNEWS MAGAZINE.
T D A Group, 289 S. San Antonio Rd., Ste. 204, Los Altos, CA 94022. TEL 415-948-3140. FAX 415-948-4280.
circ. 250,000. *2137*

NETWARE CONNECTION.
NetWare Users International, Inc., 1555 N. Technology Way, Orem, UT 84057. TEL 801-221-9634.
circ. 140,000. *2137*

NETWORK.
Canadian Controlled Media Communications, 287 MacPherson Ave., Toronto, ON M4V 1A4, Canada. TEL 416-928-2909. FAX 416-966-1181.
circ. 80,000. *3263*

NETWORK (ATLANTA).
Presbyterian Church in America, Mission to the World, Box 29765, Atlanta, GA 30359. TEL 404-320-3373. FAX 404-325-5974.
circ. 88,000. *6357*

NETWORK (DURHAM).
Family Health International, Research Triangle Park Branch, Box 13950, Durham, NC 27709. FAX 919-544-7040.
circ. 65,000. *858*

NETWORK (ROCKVILLE).
National School Public Relations Association, 15948 Derwood Rd., Rockville, MD 20855-2123. TEL 301-519-0496. FAX 301-519-0494. *41*

NETWORK COMPUTING (MANHASSET).
C M P Publications, Inc., 600 Community Dr., Manhasset, NY 11030. TEL 516-562-5000. FAX 516-365-4601.
circ. 175,425. *2138*

NETWORK WORLD.
Network World Inc., 161 Worcester Rd., 5th Fl., Framingham, MA 01701. TEL 508-875-6400. FAX 508-879-3167.
circ. 150,210. *2138*

NETWORKING.
B M I Publications Ltd., Suffolk House, George St., Croydon, Surrey CR9 1SR, England. TEL 44-181-649-7233. FAX 44-181-649-7234.
circ. 27,000. *7223*

NETWORKING NEWSPAPER.
Networking Newspaper for Women, Inc., Box 906, Remsenburg, NY 11960-0906. TEL 516-287-4845. FAX 516-283-3197. *7329*

NEUE ARGUMENTE.
Arbeitsgemeinschaft Nein zur Atomenergie, Ja zur Umwelt, Postfach 27, A-2103 Langenzersdorf, Austria. TEL 43-2244-30542. FAX 43-2244-30542.
circ. 8,500. *2944*

NEUE JURISTISCHE WOCHENSCHRIFT.
Verlag C.H. Beck, 80791 Munich, Germany. TEL 49-89-38189-338. FAX 49-89-38189-398.
circ. 55,858. *3995*

NEUMATICOS Y ACCESSORIOS.
General de Ediciones Especializadas, S.L., C. Juan de Olias, 11 y 13, 28020 Madrid, Spain. TEL 34-1-5719676. FAX 34-1-5210695.
circ. 3,000. *6503*

NEUROLOGICAL INSTITUTE. BULLETIN.
Kyushu Daigaku, Igakubu, 1-1, Maidashi 3-chome, Higashi-ku, Fukuoka-shi, Fukuoka-ken 812-82, Japan. TEL 81-92-641-1151. FAX 81-92-642-5545. *5083*

NEUROLOGY REVIEWS.
Partners in Medical Communication, 4 Brighton Rd., Clifton, NJ 07012. TEL 201-913-1000. FAX 201-916-0021. *5084*

NEVADA STATE MUSEUM NEWSLETTER.
Nevada State Museum, Publications Office, 600 S. Carson St., Carson City, NV 89701. TEL 702-687-4811 ext.221.
circ. 1,100. *5363*

NEW ACCOUNTANT.
Real Estate News Corp., 3525 W. Petersen Ave., Chicago, IL 60659.
circ. 64,632. *1095*

NEW AGE RETAILER.
Continuity Publishing, Inc., 1300 N. State St., Ste. 105, Bellingham, WA 98225-4730. TEL 360-676-0789. FAX 360-676-0932.
circ. 5,800. *5459*

NEW BOOKS ON FAMILY PLANNING.
National Institute of Health and Family Welfare, New Mehrauli Rd., Munirka, New Delhi 110067, India.
circ. 1,250. *859*

NEW BRUNSWICK. DEPARTMENT OF ADVANCED EDUCATION AND LABOUR. ANNUAL REPORT.
Department of Advanced Education and Labour, P.O. Box 6000, Fredericton, NB E3B 5H1, Canada. TEL 506-453-2568. FAX 506-453-3806.
circ. 700. *1446*

NEW BRUNSWICK GOVERNMENT DOCUMENTS. ANNUAL CATALOGUE.
Legislative Assembly, Legislative Library, 766 King St., P.O. Box 6000, Fredericton, NB E3B 5H1, Canada. TEL 506-453-2338. FAX 506-444-5889.
circ. 200. *6206*

NEW CANTERBURY LITERARY SOCIETY NEWS.
Norman T. Gates, Ed. & Pub., 520 Woodland Ave., Haddonfield, NJ 08033.
circ. 125. *4439*

NEW CITY.
New City Press, Box 332, Manila, Philippines. FAX 02-623956.
circ. 10,000. *6358*

NEW CONVERSATIONS.
United Church Board for Homeland Ministries, 700 Prospect Ave., Cleveland, OH 44115-1100. TEL 216-736-3277. FAX 216-736-3263.
circ. 1,500. *6358*

NEW DETROIT, INC. ANNUAL REPORT.
New Detroit, Inc., 2900 Penobscot Bldg., 645 Griswold St., Detroit, MI 48226-4234. TEL 313-496-2000. FAX 313-496-2071.
circ. 10,000. *6679*

NEW ELECTRONIC PRODUCTS JAPAN.
Incom Co., Ltd., 23-6, Sekiguchi 1-chome, Bunkyo-ku, Tokyo 112, Japan. *2841*

NEW ELECTRONICS.
Findlay Publications Ltd., Franks Hall, Franks Ln., Horton Kirby, Kent DA4 9LL, England. TEL 44-1322-222222. FAX 44-1322-289577.
circ. 25,055. *2647*

NEW ENGLAND ECONOMIC INDICATORS.
Federal Reserve Bank of Boston, Research Department, 600 Atlantic Ave., Boston, MA 02106. TEL 617-973-3397. FAX 617-973-4292.
circ. 6,000. *1273*

NEW ENGLAND PRINTER AND PUBLISHER.
Pine Printing Industries of New England, 10 Tech Circle, Box 2009, Natick, MA 01760-0015. TEL 508-655-8700. FAX 508-655-2586.
circ. 680. *6081*

NEW ENGLAND PROGRESS.
178 Forbes Rd., Ste. 218, Braintree, MA 01701. TEL 617-843-3800. FAX 617-843-1178.
circ. 3,600. *3482*

NEW ENGLAND SKIERS' GUIDE.
Ski Racing International, Box 1125, Waitsfield, VT 05673-1125. TEL 802-496-7700. FAX 802-496-7704.
circ. 90,000. *6875*

NEW EQUIPMENT DIGEST.
Penton Publishing Co., 1100 Superior Ave., Cleveland, OH 44114-2543. TEL 216-696-7000. FAX 216-696-8765.
circ. 209,041. *6968*

NEW EQUIPMENT NEWS.
Canadian Engineering Publications Ltd., 204 Richmond St. W., Ste. 415, Toronto, ON M5V 1V6, Canada. TEL 416-599-3737. FAX 416-599-3730.
circ. 23,000. *6968*

NEW ERA MAGAZINE.
New Era Magazine, 22031 Bushard St., Huntington Beach, CA 92646-8490. TEL 714-962-1351. FAX 714-962-1354.
circ. 19,615. *1911*

NEW HAMPSHIRE QUARTER NOTES.
New Hampshire Music Educators Association, Rt. 5, Box 307, Penacook, NH 03303. TEL 603-648-2692.
circ. 800. *5420*

NEW HAVEN COLONY HISTORICAL SOCIETY. JOURNAL.
New Haven Colony Historical Society, 114 Whitney Ave., New Haven, CT 06510. TEL 203-562-4183.
circ. 1,200. *3639*

NEW HOLLAND NEWS.
New Holland, Inc., Box 1895, New Holland, PA 17557. TEL 717-354-1121.
circ. 400,000. *139*

NEW HOMES MAGAZINE.
New Homes, Inc., 7643 W. 85th St., Bloomington, MN 55438-1308. FAX 612-933-6310.
circ. 60,000. *6307*

NEW HOMES REGISTER.
Bartow Communications, Inc., 1568 Spring Hill Rd., Ste. 301, McLean, VA 22102. TEL 703-734-7001. FAX 703-734-7005.
circ. 20,000. *6307*

NEW JERSEY AVIATION NEWS.
Department of Transportation, Division of Aeronautics, 1035 Parkway Ave., CN 610, Trenton, NJ 08625-0610. TEL 609-530-2915. FAX 609-530-5719.
circ. 14,000. *75*

NEW JERSEY FAMILY.
104 LaBarre Ave., Trenton, NJ 08618. TEL 609-695-5646.
circ. 30,000. *1881*

NEW JERSEY LEAGUE NEWS.
New Jersey Community & Savings League Bankers League, 411 North Ave. E., Cranford, NJ 07016. TEL 908-272-8500. FAX 908-272-6626.
circ. 1,200. *1158*

NEW JERSEY MOTOR TRUCK ASSOCIATION. BULLETIN.
New Jersey Motor Truck Association, 160 Tices Ln., E. Brunswick, NJ 08816. TEL 908-254-5000. FAX 908-613-1745.
circ. 2,100. *7177*

NEW JERSEY SPEECH AND HEARING ASSOCIATION. JOURNAL.
New Jersey Speech and Hearing Association, c/o Auriemma, 6 Crest Ln., Warren, NJ 07059-5110.
circ. 1,100. *4721*

NEW JERSEY STATE BAR ASSOCIATION. CERTIFIED TRIAL ATTORNEYS SECTION. NEWSLETTER.
New Jersey State Bar Association, 1 Constitution Sq., New Brunswick, NJ 08901-1500. TEL 908-249-5000. FAX 908-828-0034.
circ. 400. *4136*

NEW JERSEY STATE BAR ASSOCIATION. CORPORATE AND BUSINESS LAW SECTION. NEWSLETTER.
New Jersey State Bar Association, 1 Constitution Sq., New Brunswick, NJ 08901-1500. TEL 908-249-5000. FAX 908-828-0034.
circ. 1,300. *4084*

NEW METHODS.
New Methods Co., Box 22605, San Francisco, CA 94122-0605. TEL 415-664-3469.
circ. 5,600. *7275*

NEW MOTHER.
Professional Publishing Associates, 269 Richmond St. W., Toronto, ON M5V 1X1, Canada. TEL 416-596-8680. FAX 416-596-1991.
circ. 160,000. *1852*

NEW MUSIC NEWS.
Contemporary Music Centre, 95 Lower Baggot St., Dublin 2, Ireland. TEL 353-1-6612105. FAX 353-1-6762639.
circ. 3,500. *5420*

10368 CONTROLLED CIRCULATION SERIALS

NEW ON THE CHARTS.
Music Business Reference, Inc., 70 Laurel Pl., New Rochelle, NY 10801. TEL 914-632-3349. FAX 914-633-7690.
circ. 2,500. *5420*

NEW PAGES.
New Pages Press, Box 438, Grand Blanc, MI 48439. TEL 313-743-8055. FAX 313-743-2730.
circ. 5,000. *6278*

NEW RESOURCES.
State Library, 1500 Senate St., Box 11469, Columbia, SC 29211. TEL 803-734-8666. FAX 803-734-8676.
circ. 575. *558*

NEW STAMPS GAZETTE.
Shield Stamp Company, Box 2977, Grand Central Sta., New York, NY 10163. TEL 212-629-7979. FAX 212-629-3350.
circ. 15,000. *5709*

NEW STEEL.
Chilton Publishing Company, 191 S. Gary Ave., Carol Stream, IL 60188. TEL 630-462-2285.
circ. 24,000. *5205*

NEW TECH TIMES.
New York City Technical College, 300 Jay St, Rm. A310, Brooklyn, NY 11201. TEL 718-260-5453. FAX 718-260-5455.
circ. 8,000. *1963*

NEW UNIVERSITY.
University of California, Irvine, 3100 Gateway Commons, Irvine, CA 92717. TEL 714-856-4285. FAX 714-856-4287.
circ. 13,000. *1963*

THE NEW VISION.
P.O. Box 9815, Kampala, Uganda. TEL 256-41-235846. FAX 256-41-235221.
circ. 37,000. *3367*

NEW WORLD HEALTH (YEAR).
Sterling Publications Ltd., 86-88 Edgware Rd., London W2 2YW, England. TEL 44-171-915-9600. FAX 44-171-915-9619.
circ. 10,000. *4721*

NEW WORLD TRANSPORT.
Sterling Publications Ltd., 86-88 Edgware Rd., London W2 2YW, England. TEL 44-171-915-9600. FAX 44-171-915-9619.
circ. 10,000. *7035*

NEW WORLD WATER.
Sterling Publications Ltd., 86-88 Edgware Rd., London W2 2YW, England. TEL 44-171-915-9600. FAX 44-171-915-9619.
circ. 10,000. *7298*

NEW YORK (STATE). CRIME VICTIMS BOARD. REPORT.
Crime Victims Board, 845 Central Ave., Rm. 107, Albany, NY 12206-1588. TEL 578-457-8066. FAX 578-457-8658.
circ. 2,000. *2274*

NEW YORK (STATE). DEPARTMENT OF LABOR. OPERATIONS - EMPLOYMENT SERVICE AND UNEMPLOYMENT INSURANCE.
Department of Labor, Division of Research and Statistics, 1 Main St., 9th Fl., Brooklyn, NY 11201. TEL 718-797-7703. *1447*

NEW YORK (STATE). INSURANCE DEPARTMENT. BULLETIN.
Insurance Department, Research Bureau, 160 W. Broadway, 21st Fl., New York, NY 10013. TEL 212-602-0473. FAX 212-602-0437.
circ. 5,000. *3828*

NEW YORK AGRICULTURAL STATISTICS.
Department of Agriculture and Markets, 1 Winner's Cir., Albany, NY 12235-0001. FAX 518-453-6564.
circ. 2,800. *179*

NEW YORK AUTO REPAIR NEWS.
Van Allen Publishing Co., Box 354, Hicksville, NY 11802. TEL 516-422-5521.
circ. 11,300. *7110*

NEW YORK CITY BALLET NEWS.
New York City Ballet Guild, New York City Ballet, Inc., New York State Theater, 20 Lincoln Center, New York, NY 10023. TEL 212-870-5677. FAX 212-870-4244.
circ. 6,000. *2295*

NEW YORK HOLSTEIN NEWS.
New York Holstein Association, Box 190, Ithaca, NY 14851. TEL 607-273-7591. FAX 607-273-7612.
circ. 4,300. *258*

NEW YORK INTERNATIONAL LAW REVIEW.
New York State Bar Association, International Law and Practice Section, 1 Elk St., Albany, NY 12207-1096. TEL 518-463-3200. FAX 518-463-8844.
circ. 2,000. *4123*

NEW YORK LOTTERY PLAYERS MONTHLY.
2150 Goodlette Rd., Ste. 200, Naples, FL 34102. TEL 941-643-3085. *6773*

NEW YORK STATE BAR ASSOCIATION. ANTITRUST LAW SECTION SYMPOSIUM.
New York State Bar Association, Antitrust Law Section, 1 Elk St., Albany, NY 12207. TEL 518-463-3200. FAX 518-463-8844.
circ. 675. *3998*

NEW YORK STATE BAR ASSOCIATION. BUSINESS LAW SECTION. PROCEEDINGS OF THE ANNUAL MEETING.
New York State Bar Association, Business Law Section, One Elk St., Albany, NY 12207. TEL 518-463-3200. FAX 518-487-5699.
circ. 5,000. *4084*

NEW YORK STATE BAR ASSOCIATION. ENVIRONMENTAL LAW SECTION JOURNAL.
New York State Bar Association, Environmental Law Section, 1 Elk St., Albany, NY 12207-1096. TEL 518-463-3200. FAX 518-463-8844.
circ. 1,700. *2944*

NEW YORK STATE BAR ASSOCIATION. LABOR AND EMPLOYMENT LAW SECTION. NEWSLETTER.
New York State Bar Association, Labor and Employment Law Section, 1 Elk St., Albany, NY 12207-1096. TEL 518-463-3200. FAX 518-463-8844.
circ. 2,000. *1447*

NEW YORK STATE BAR JOURNAL.
New York State Bar Association, One Marine Midland Plaza, Binghamton, NY 13902. FAX 607-772-6093.
circ. 59,000. *3998*

THE NEW YORK STATE TROOPER.
State Police, Public Security Bldg., State Campus, Albany, NY 12226. FAX 518-485-7818.
circ. 14,000. *2275*

NEW ZEALAND. CENTRAL ADVISORY COMMITTEE ON THE APPOINTMENTS AND PROMOTION OF PRIMARY TEACHERS. REPORT TO THE MINISTER OF EDUCATION.
Government Printing Office, Private Bag, Wellington, New Zealand. *2467*

NEW ZEALAND CHILDCARE ASSOCIATION. REPORT TO ANNUAL CONFERENCE.
New Zealand Childcare Association, P.O. Box 11-863, Wellington, New Zealand.
circ. 800. *1852*

NEW ZEALAND DAIRY BOARD. ANNUAL REPORT AND STATEMENT OF ACCOUNTS.
New Zealand Dairy Board, P.O. Box 417, Wellington, New Zealand. FAX 64-4-4723691.
circ. 50,000. *258*

NEW ZEALAND HEALTH INFORMATION SERVICE. CANCER: NEW REGISTRATIONS AND DEATHS.
New Zealand Health Information Service, Ministry of Health, Level 11, Ballantrae House, 192-194 Willis St., P.O. Box 5013, Wellington, New Zealand. TEL 64-4-8012700. FAX 64-4-8012769. *4783*

NEW ZEALAND HEALTH INFORMATION SERVICE. FETAL AND INFANT DEATHS.
New Zealand Health Information Service, Ministry of Health, Level 11, Ballantrae House, 192-194 Willis St., P.O. Box 5013, Wellington, New Zealand. TEL 64-4-8012700. FAX 64-4-8012769. *6069*

NEW ZEALAND HEALTH INFORMATION SERVICE. MENTAL HEALTH DATA.
New Zealand Health Information Service, Ministry of Health, Level 11, Ballantrae House, 192-194 Willis St., P.O. Box 5013, Wellington, New Zealand. TEL 64-4-8012700. FAX 64-4-8012769. *4783*

NEW ZEALAND HEALTH INFORMATION SERVICE. MORTALITY AND DEMOGRAPHIC DATA.
New Zealand Health Information Service, Ministry of Health, Level 11, Ballantrae House, 192-194 Willis St., P.O. Box 5013, Wellington, New Zealand. TEL 64-4-8012700. FAX 64-4-8012769. *6069*

NEW ZEALAND INSTITUTE OF VALUERS. LIBRARY CATALOGUE.
New Zealand Institute of Valuers, P.O. Box 27-146, Wellington, New Zealand. TEL 64-4-3858436. FAX 64-4-3829214.
circ. 2,200. *6317*

NEW ZEALAND INSTITUTE OF VALUERS. PROPERTY DIGEST.
New Zealand Institute of Valuers, P.O. Box 27-146, Wellington, New Zealand. TEL 64-4-3858436. FAX 64-4-3829214.
circ. 2,400. *6307*

NEW ZEALAND INTERNATIONAL REVIEW.
New Zealand Institute of International Affairs, P.O. Box 600, Wellington 2, New Zealand. TEL 64-4-4715356. FAX 64-4-4731-261.
circ. 1,500. *6028*

NEW ZEALAND JOURNAL OF PHYSIOTHERAPY.
New Zealand Society of Physiotherapists (Inc.), P.O. Box 27386, Wellington, New Zealand. TEL 64-4-8016500. FAX 64-4-48015571.
circ. 1,500. *5045*

NEW ZEALAND JOURNAL OF PSYCHOLOGY.
New Zealand Psychological Society, c/o Business Manager, P.O. Box 4092, Wellington, New Zealand. TEL 64-4-8015414. FAX 64-4-8015366.
circ. 900. *6138*

NEW ZEALAND JOURNAL OF SPORTS MEDICINE.
Sports Medicine New Zealand, 96 Anzac Ave., P.O. Box 6398, Dunedin, New Zealand. TEL 64-3-4777887. FAX 64-3-4777882.
circ. 1,000. *5131*

NEW ZEALAND MANUFACTURER (WELLINGTON, 1992).
New Zealand Manufacturers Federation, 3 Church St., P.O. Box 11-543, Wellington 1, New Zealand. TEL 64-4-4733000. FAX 64-4-4733004.
circ. 3,000. *988*

NEW ZEALAND MARINE SCIENCES SOCIETY REVIEW.
New Zealand Marine Sciences Society, P.O. Box 434, Cambridge, New Zealand. TEL 64-7-8567020. FAX 64-7-8560151.
circ. 300. *617*

NEW ZEALAND PLUMBING REVIEW.
Akron Consolidated Ltd., Box 51-182, Auckland 6, New Zealand.
circ. 1,250. *3482*

NEW ZEALAND R S A REVIEW.
New Zealand Returned Services Association, 181-183 Willis St., P.O. Box 27248, Wellington, New Zealand. TEL 64-4-3847994. FAX 64-4-3853325.
circ. 101,000. *6679*

NEWFOUNDLAND ANCESTOR.
Newfoundland and Labrador Genealogical Society Inc., Colonial Bldg., Military Rd., St. John's, NF A1C 2C9, Canada. TEL 709-754-9525.
circ. 1,100. *3234*

NEWMEDIA.
HyperMedia Communications, Inc., 901 Mariners Island, Ste. 365, San Mateo, CA 94404. TEL 415-573-5170. FAX 415-573-5131.
circ. 40,000. *2055*

NEWPORT BEACH (714).
Baker Communications, Inc., 901 Dover Dr., Ste. 231, Newport Beach, CA 92660. TEL 714-722-1286. FAX 714-722-6632.
circ. 50,000. *3381*

NEWPORT NAVALOG.
Edward A. Sherman Publishing Co., 101 Malbone Rd., Box 420, Newport, RI 02840. FAX 401-849-3300.
circ. 7,200. *5280*

NEWS ABOUT LIBRARY SERVICES FOR THE BLIND AND PHYSICALLY HANDICAPPED.
State Library, 1500 Senate St., Box 11469, Columbia, SC 29211. TEL 803-737-9970.
circ. 7,200. *3456*

NEWS & VIEWS OF LOCAL 23.
United Food and Commercial Workers, Local 23, 951 Penn Ave., Pittsburgh, PA 15222. TEL 412-261-0301. FAX 412-261-4429.
circ. 23,000. *3895*

NEWS FOR SOUTH CAROLINA LIBRARIES.
State Library, 1500 Senate St., Box 11469, Columbia, SC 29211. TEL 803-734-8666. FAX 803-734-8676.
circ. 1,800. *4203*

NEWS FROM HOPE COLLEGE.
Hope College, 141 E. 12th St., Holland, MI 49423. TEL 616-395-7860. FAX 616-395-7991.
circ. 40,000. *1963*

NEWS IN HEADACHE.
Cambridge Medical Publications Ltd., Wicker House, High St., Worthing, W. Sussex BN11 1DJ, England. TEL 01903-205884. FAX 01903-234862. *5087*

NEWS OF NORWAY.
Royal Norwegian Embassy, 2720-34th St., N.W., Washington, DC 20008. TEL 202-333-6000. FAX 202-337-0870.
circ. 19,000. *3033*

NEWSLETTER FROM DICK B. ON THE SPIRITUAL ROOTS OF ALCOHOLICS ANONYMOUS.
Good Book Publishing Co., Box 959, Kihei, HI 96753-0959. TEL 808-874-4876. FAX 808-874-4876.
circ. 800. *2304*

NEWSLINE (JEFFERSON CITY).
Missouri State Library, Box 387, Jefferson City, MO 65102-0387. TEL 573-751-3615. FAX 573-751-3612.
circ. 4,250. *4203*

NEWSOUTH JAPANESE MAGAZINE.
Print Graphics Services, Inc., Box 2752, Peachtree City, GA 30269. TEL 770-631-9159. FAX 770-631-8852.
circ. 40,000. *3381*

NEXUS (BOULDER).
1680 Sixth St., Ste. 6, Boulder, CO 80302. TEL 303-442-6662. FAX 303-442-7596.
circ. 54,000. *298*

NICARAGUA UPDATE.
Nicaragua Solidarity Campaign, 129 Seven Sisters Rd., London N7 7QG, England. TEL 44-171-272-9619. FAX 44-171-272-5476.
circ. 1,750. *5948*

NICHOLS NEWS.
Nichols College, Box 5000, Dudley, MA 01571. TEL 508-943-1560.
circ. 10,000. *1963*

NIEDERRHEIN TENNIS.
Vereinigte Verlagsanstalten GmbH, Hoeherweg 278, 40231 Duesseldorf, Germany. TEL 49-211-7357-0. FAX 49-211-7357223.
circ. 23,091. *6812*

NIEDERSAECHSISCHE GEMEINDE.
Niedersaechsischer Staedte-und Gemeindebund, Seelhorststr. 18, 30175 Hannover, Germany. TEL 0511-280720. FAX 0511-854107.
circ. 12,700. *6222*

NIEDERSAECHSISCHE RUNDSCHAU.
Vereinigte Verlagsanstalten GmbH, Hoeherweg 278, 40231 Duesseldorf, Germany. TEL 49-211-7357-0. FAX 49-211-7357223.
circ. 5,000. *6679*

NIET ZO BENAUWD.
Stichting Familieclub Johannes van der Linden, Salomeschouw 61, 2726 JP Zoetermeer, Netherlands. TEL 31-79-3411955.
circ. 150. *3234*

NIGERIA INDUSTRIAL DIRECTORY.
Malthouse Press Ltd., 8 Amore St. (off Toyin St.), P.O. Box 8917, Ikeja, Lagos State, Nigeria.
circ. 5,000. *1703*

NIGHTLIFE (LOS ANGELES).
Data-Boy Enterprises, Inc., 6363 Santa Monica Blvd., Ste. 200, Los Angeles, CA 90038-1619. TEL 213-656-2960. FAX 213-656-7312.
circ. 44,000. *3698*

NIHON DAIGAKU RIKOGAKU KENKYUJO SHOHO.
Nihon Daigaku, Rikogaku Kenkyujo, 1-8 Kanda Surugadai, Chiyoda-ku, Tokyo 101, Japan. *6968*

NIHON DAIGAKU RIKOGAKUBU GAKUJUTSU KOENKAI KOEN RONBUNSHU.
Nihon Daigaku, Rikogakubu Rikogaku Kenkyujo, 1-8 Kanda Surugadai, Chiyoda-ku, Tokyo 101, Japan. *6968*

NIHON FUJIN KAGAKUSHA NO KAI NYUSU.
Nihon Fujin Kagakusha no Kai, Toho Daigaku Rigakubu, 2-2-1, Miyama, Funabashi-shi, Chiba-ken 274, Japan. TEL 81-474-70-1335.
circ. 1,000. *7329*

NIHON GAISHO GAKKAI ZASSHI.
Nihon Gaisho Gakkai, Teikyo Daigaku Kyumei Kyukyu Senta, 11-1, Kaga 2-chome, Itabashi-ku, Tokyo 173, Japan. TEL 81-3-3964-1211. FAX 81-3-5375-0854.
circ. 1,200. *5012*

NIHON KOTSU KEITAI KEISOKU GAKKAI ZASSHI.
Nihon Kotsu Keitai Gakkai, Niigata Daigaku Igakubu Seikei Gekagaku Kyoshitsu, Asahimachi Dori 1 Bancho, Niigata-shi, Niigata-ken 951, Japan. TEL 81-25-223-6161. FAX 81-25-229-1675.
circ. 1,000. *5012*

NIHON SHINSEIJI GAKKAI ZASSHI.
Nihon Shinseiji Gakkai, c/o Toho University, School of Medicine, Department of Neonatology, 6-11-1 Ohmorinishi, Ohta-ku, Tokyo 143, Japan. TEL 81-3-3762-0841. FAX 81-3-3762-0842.
circ. 4,000. *5035*

NIHON SUPINDORU GIHO.
Nihon Supindoru Seizo K.K., 2-30, Shioe 4-chome, Amagasaki-shi, Hyogo-ken 661, Japan. TEL 81-06-499-4304. FAX 81-06-499-5631.
circ. 1,000. *2895*

NIKKEI ELECTRONICS ASIA.
Nikkei Business Publications, Inc., Nikkei Business Publications Asia, Ltd., Unit 1404, East Point Centre (New Wing), 533 Hennessy Rd., Causeway Bay, Hong Kong, People's Republic of China. TEL 852-2575-8301. FAX 852-2574-8175.
circ. 28,068. *2647*

NIKKEI MEDICAL.
Nikkei Business Publications, Inc., 2-7-6 Hirakawa-cho, Chiyoda-ku, Tokyo 102, Japan. TEL 03-5210-8502. FAX 03-5210-8119.
circ. 104,000. *4722*

NIMBUS.
Societa Meteorologica Subalpina, V. Gioberti 88, 10128 Turin, Italy. TEL 39-11-591145. FAX 39-11-5683190.
circ. 500. *5240*

NIPPON BIYO GEKA GAKKAISHI.
Nippon Biyo Geka Gakkai, 12-5, Shinbashi 1-chome, Minato-ku, Tokyo 105, Japan. TEL 03-3573-2111. FAX 03-3573-2114.
circ. 400. *5149*

NIPPON JUI CHIKUSAN DAIGAKU KENKYU HOKOKU.
Nippon Jui Chikusan Daigaku, 1-7-1 Kyonan-cho, Musashino-shi, Tokyo 180, Japan. TEL 422-31-4151. FAX 422-33-2035.
circ. 500. *7275*

NIPPON MEDICAL SCHOOL. JOURNAL.
Nippon Medical School, Medical Association, 1-1-5 Sendagi, Bunkyo-ku, Tokyo 113, Japan. TEL 81-3-3822-2131. FAX 81-3-3822-3759.
circ. 2,850. *4722*

NONESUCH.
University of Bristol, Information Office, Senate House, Tyndall Ave., Bristol BS8 1TH, England. TEL 44-117-9287777. FAX 44-117-9292396.
circ. 45,000. *1963*

NONPUBLIC SCHOOL ENROLLMENT AND STAFF, NEW YORK STATE.
Education Department, Information, Reporting & Technology Services, Education Bldg. Annex, Rm. 962, Albany, NY 12234. TEL 518-474-7082. FAX 518-474-4351. *2467*

NONSOLOBUS.
Azienda Trasporti Area Fiorentina, Viale dei Mille 115, 50131 Florence, Italy. TEL 39-55-5650241. FAX 39-55-5650243.
circ. 4,000. *7035*

NONVIOLENT SANCTIONS.
Albert Einstein Institution, 50 Church St., 3rd Fl., Cambridge, MA 02138-3726. TEL 617-876-0311. FAX 617-876-0837.
circ. 800. *5949*

NOR MARMARA.
Solakzade Sok. No. 5, Istanbul. TEL 90-212-2491989. FAX 90-212-2444736.
circ. 1,700. *3366*

NORD-EMBALLAGE.
AB Thorsten Fahlskog, P.O. Box 25, S-162 11 Vaellingby, Sweden. TEL 46-8-870280. FAX 46-8-874815.
circ. 3,800. *5546*

NOR'EASTER (DULUTH).
Lake Superior Marine Museum Association, Box 177, Duluth, MN 55802. TEL 218-727-2497. FAX 218-720-5270.
circ. 600. *3639*

NOR'EASTER LEADERSHIP NEWS.
Presbyterian Church (U.S.A.), Synod of the Northeast, 3049 E. Genesee St., Syracuse, NY 13224. TEL 315-446-5990. FAX 315-446-5708.
circ. 20,000. *6435*

NORFOLK SOUTHERN WORLD.
Norfolk Southern Corporation, Public Relations Department, 3 Commercial Pl., Norfolk, VA 23510. TEL 804-629-2707. FAX 804-629-2822.
circ. 47,000. *7129*

NORGES TEKNISK-NATURVITENSKAPELIGE UNIVERSITET. VITENSKAPSMUSEET. RAPPORT. BOTANISK SERIE.
Norwegian University of Science and Technology, Museum of Natural History and Archaeology, N-7004 Trondheim, Norway. TEL 47-73-59-22-60. FAX 47-73-59-22-49.
circ. 275. *717*

NORSK IDRETT.
Norsk Idrettsforbund, N-1351 Rud, Norway.
circ. 13,000. *6773*

NORSK SKOLEBLAD.
Norsk Laererlag, Rosenkrantzgt. 15, N-0160 Oslo, Norway. TEL 47-22-00-20-00. FAX 47-22-00-21-90.
circ. 69,830. *2468*

NORSK V V S.
Skarland Press A-S, P.O. Box 5042 Maj., N-0301 Oslo, Norway. TEL 47-22-59-88-oo. FAX 47-22-69-36-50.
circ. 4,894. *3482*

NORSKE TANNLEGEFORENINGS TIDENDE.
Norske Tannlegeforening, P.O. Box 3063 Elisenberg, 0207 Oslo, Norway. TEL 47-22-54-74-00. FAX 47-22-55-11-09.
circ. 5,200. *4865*

NORTE.
Frente de Afirmacion Hispanista A.C., Lago Como 201, 11320 Mexico DF, Mexico. TEL 525-5963328. FAX 525-5962426.
circ. 3,000. *4442*

NORTH AMERICAN ASSOCIATION OF SUMMER SESSIONS. NEWSLETTER.
North American Association of Summer Sessions, 43 Belanger Dr., Dover, NH 03820-4602. *2576*

NORTH AMERICAN FARM EQUIPMENT JOURNAL.
G J P Enterprises Inc., 101 W. 29th St., Ste. 102, Box 1210, Marshfield, WI 54449. TEL 715-389-2234. FAX 715-389-2380.
circ. 6,050. *208*

10370 CONTROLLED CIRCULATION SERIALS

NORTH AMERICAN MEAT PROCESSORS ASSOCIATION. NEWSFAX.
National Association of Meat Purveyors, 1920 Association Dr., Ste. 400, Reston, VA 20191-1547. TEL 703-758-1900. FAX 703-758-8001.
circ. 420. *3122*

NORTH AMERICAN MISSIONS.
Association of North American Missions, 3859 Nottingham Dr., Sarasota, FL 34235. TEL 941-955-8529. FAX 941-951-0805.
circ. 5,000. *6435*

NORTH CAROLINA. SECRETARY OF STATE. DIRECTORY OF STATE AND COUNTY OFFICIALS.
Secretary of State, 300 N. Salisbury St., Raleigh, NC 27603-5909. TEL 919-733-7355.
circ. 10,000. *6186*

NORTH CAROLINA DENTAL REVIEW.
University of North Carolina, School of Dentistry, Brauer Hall, Rm. 410, CB 7450, Chapel Hill, NC 27599-7450. TEL 919-966-2730. FAX 919-966-4049.
circ. 6,200. *4865*

NORTH CAROLINA LAWYER.
North Carolina Bar Association, Box 3688, Cary, NC 27519-3688. TEL 919-677-0561. FAX 919-677-0761.
circ. 11,000. *4000*

NORTH CAROLINA MANUAL.
Secretary of State, 300 N. Salisbury St., Raleigh, NC 27603-5909. TEL 919-733-7355.
circ. 5,000. *6186*

NORTH CAROLINA PLUMBING - HEATING - COOLING FORUM.
North Carolina Association of Plumbing - Heating - Cooling Contractors, Inc., 413 Glenwood Ave., Raleigh, NC 27603. TEL 919-833-0372. FAX 919-833-0921.
circ. 4,000. *3482*

NORTH CAROLINA SEED LAW.
Department of Agriculture, Box 27647, Raleigh, NC 27611. TEL 919-733-7125. *141*

NORTH CAROLINA STATE UNIVERSITY. COLLEGE OF FOREST RESOURCES. TECHNICAL REPORT.
North Carolina State University, College of Forest Resources, Raleigh, NC 27695.
circ. 75. *3159*

NORTH CENTRAL OPTOMETRIC VIEWPOINT.
R.C. Publications, Inc. (Brookfield), Box 604, Brookfield, WI 53008-0604. TEL 414-789-2749. FAX 414-789-9458.
circ. 26,200. *4997*

NORTH COUNTRY FARM NEWS.
Clinton County Cooperative Extension, 6064 State Rte. 22, Ste. 5, Plattsburgh, NY 12901-6222.
circ. 900. *141*

NORTH DAKOTA. JUDICIAL SYSTEM. ANNUAL REPORT.
Judicial System, Office of State Court Administrator, State Capitol, Bismarck, ND 58505. TEL 701-328-4216. FAX 701-328-4480.
circ. 1,000. *4055*

NORTH DAKOTA'S HIGHWAY SAFETY PLAN.
Department of Transportation, Driver's License and Traffic Safety, Traffic Safety Programs Section, 608 E. Blvd. Ave., Bismarck, ND 58505-0700. TEL 701-224-2600. FAX 701-224-4545.
circ. 150. *7140*

NORTH GEORGIA JOURNAL.
Legacy Communications, Inc., P.O. Box 127, Roswell, GA 30077-0127. TEL 770-642-5569. FAX 770-642-6598.
circ. 2,451. *7224*

NORTH LOUISIANA HISTORICAL ASSOCIATION. JOURNAL.
North Louisiana Historical Association, Box 6701, Shreveport, LA 71136. TEL 318-797-5337.
circ. 500. *3640*

NORTH TEXAS GOLFER.
Golfer Magazines, Inc., 9182 Old Katy Rd., Ste. 212, Houston, TX 77055. TEL 713-464-0308. FAX 713-464-0129.
circ. 31,000. *6812*

NORTH THOMPSON TIMES.
Rubicon Publishing Inc., RR 1, Box 1102, Clearwater, BC V0E 1N0, Canada. TEL 604-674-3343. FAX 604-674-3777.
circ. 1,903. *3264*

NORTH WIND.
Northern Michigan University, Marquette, MI 49855. TEL 906-227-2545. *1963*

NORTHEAST DIRECTORY OF TRANSPORTATION SERVICES.
Northeast Journal of Transportation, 31 Fargo St., S. Boston, MA 02127. TEL 617-695-1660. FAX 617-695-1665. *1703*

NORTHEASTERN UNIVERSITY MAGAZINE.
Northeastern University, Office of University Relations, 360 Huntington Ave., 598 CP, Boston, MA 02115. TEL 617-373-5444. FAX 617-373-5430.
circ. 140,000. *1964*

NORTHERN ARIZONA GENEALOGICAL SOCIETY. BULLETIN.
Northern Arizona Genealogical Society, Box 695, Prescott, AZ 86302.
circ. 200. *3234*

NORTHERN AUTOMOTIVE NEWS.
13304 Stone Rd., Minnetonka, MN 55305. TEL 612-544-6805.
circ. 7,000. *7111*

NORTHERN IRELAND TRADE DIRECTORY.
Business to Business Publications, The King Bldg., Ste. 11, 152 Albertbridge Rd., Belfast BT5 4GS, N. Ireland. TEL 44-1232-455775. FAX 44-1232-461924.
circ. 5,000. *1703*

NORTHERN MOSAIC.
Thunder Bay Multicultural Association, 17 N. Court St., Thunder Bay, ON P7A 4T4, Canada. TEL 807-345-0551. FAX 807-345-0173.
circ. 600. *3033*

NORTHERN NEW ENGLAND REVIEW.
Franklin Pierce College, Box 60, Rindge, NH 03461. TEL 603-899-4089. FAX 603-899-6448.
circ. 600. *4442*

NORTHERN ONTARIO BUSINESS.
Laurentian Publishing Co., 158 Elgin St., Sudbury, ON P3E 3N5, Canada. TEL 705-673-5705. FAX 705-673-9542.
circ. 10,000. *989*

NORTHWEST ASSOCIATION OF SCHOOLS AND COLLEGES. CONVENTION PROCEEDINGS.
Northwest Association of Schools and Colleges, Boise State University, 1910 Unicersity Dr., Boise, ID 83725-1060. TEL 208-334-3210. FAX 208-334-3228. *2551*

NORTHWEST ASSOCIATION OF SCHOOLS AND COLLEGES. NEWSLETTER.
Northwest Association of Schools and Colleges, Boise State University, 1910 University Dr., Boise, ID 83725-1060. TEL 208-334-3210. FAX 208-334-3228. *2468*

NORTHWEST HOSPITALITY NEWS.
Blue Chip Publishing, Box 21027, Salem, OR 97307-1027. TEL 503-390-8343. FAX 503-390-8344.
circ. 25,000. *3733*

NORTH WEST LABOUR HISTORY.
North West Labour History, 81 Parrin Ln., Winton, Eeeles, Manchester M30 8AY, England. TEL 44-161-789-6118.
circ. 1,000. *3588*

NORTHWEST PASSAGES.
Northwest Airlines, Inc., 5101 Northwest Dr., St. Paul, MN 55111-3034. TEL 612-726-7357. FAX 612-726-3942.
circ. 56,000. *7075*

NORTHWESTERN PERSPECTIVE.
Northwestern University, 555 Clark St., Evanston, IL 60208-1230. TEL 847-491-5000. FAX 847-491-2376.
circ. 95,624. *1964*

NORTHWESTERN UNIVERSITY. MATERIALS RESEARCH CENTER. ANNUAL TECHNICAL REPORT.
Northwestern University, Materials Research Center, 2145 Sheridan Rd., Evanston, IL 60208-3116. TEL 708-491-3606. FAX 312-491-4181. *2868*

NORWEB MAGAZINE.
Media Partners CPR, Northern Rock House, 20 Market Pl., Guisborough, Cleveland TS14 6HF, England. TEL 44-1287-639111. FAX 44-1287-637201.
circ. 1,800,000. *2690*

NORWEGIAN OFFSHORE INDEX.
Selvig Publishing A-S, P.O. Box 9070 Groenland, 0133 Oslo, Norway. TEL 22-364440. FAX 22-360550. *5630*

NOS MAISONS FAMILIALES DE VACANCES.
Federation des Maisons Familiales de Vacances, 28 place St-Georges, 75442 Paris 9, France. *7224*

NOSTALGIA MOTOR MAGAZINE.
Albinsson & Sjoeberg, P.O. Box 529, S-371 23 Karlskrona, Sweden. TEL 46-455-335325. FAX 46-455-311715.
circ. 18,700. *342*

NOSTRE TOR.
Famija Albeisa - Ente Morale, Via Pierino Belli 6, 12051 Alba CN, Italy. TEL 39-173-441742.
circ. 2,250. *3787*

NOTAS.
Vervuert Verlag GmbH, Wielandstr. 40, 60318 Frankfurt a.M., Germany. TEL 49-69-5974617. FAX 49-69-5978743.
circ. 750. *4350*

NOTI S A I.
Sociedad Antioquena de Ingenieros y Arquitectos, Calle 71, No. 65-100, Apdo. Aereo 4754, Medellin, Colombia. TEL 257-3900. FAX 255-4584.
circ. 2,500. *2734*

NOTIZIARIO MOTORISTICO.
Azienda Cataloghi Italiani s.a.s., Via B. Crespi, 30-2, 20159 Milan, Italy. TEL 39-2-606052. FAX 39-2-606487.
circ. 18,072. *7111*

NOTRE DAME MAGAZINE.
University of Notre Dame, Notre Dame Magazine, Main Bldg., Rm. 415, Notre Dame, IN 46556. TEL 219-631-6767. FAX 219-631-6767.
circ. 135,000. *1964*

NOTRE DAME REPORT.
University of Notre Dame, Office of the Provost, Notre Dame, IN 46556. TEL 219-631-5337.
circ. 1,600. *1964*

NOUVEAU GLOSSAIRE NAUTIQUE D'AUGUSTIN JAL.
C N R S Editions, 20-22 rue St. Amand, 75015 Paris, France. TEL 45-33-16-00. FAX 45-33-92-13.
circ. 1,250. *2411*

NOVA SCOTIA. DEPARTMENT OF ECONOMIC DEVELOPMENT. ANNUAL REPORT.
Department of Economic Development, P.O. Box 519, Halifax, NS B3J 2R7, Canada. TEL 902-424-8922. FAX 902-424-5739.
circ. 300. *6186*

NOVAS DE ALEGRIA.
Casa Publicadora das Assembleias de Deus, Av. Alm. Gago Coutinho 158, 1700 Lisbon, Portugal.
circ. 10,400. *6495*

NOVYI ZHURNAL.
New Review Inc., 611 Broadway, Ste. 842, New York, NY 10012-2608. TEL 212-353-1478.
circ. 1,300. *3034*

NOW HEAR THIS - U S S CALLAWAY NEWSLETTER.
5319 Manning Pl., N.W., Washington, DC 20013-5311. TEL 202-363-3663.
circ. 387. *5280*

NUCLEAR FORUM.
British Nuclear Industry Forum, 22 Buckingham Gate, London SW1E 6LB, England. TEL 071-828-0116. FAX 071-828-0110.
circ. 7,000. *2701*

NUCLEAR INDIA.
Department of Atomic Energy, Publications Officer, Chhatrapati Shivaji Maharaj Marg, Bombay 400039, India.
circ. 5,000. *2701*

THE NUCLEUS (HARVARD).
American Chemical Society, Inc., Northeastern Section, 19 Mill Rd., Harvard, MA 01451. TEL 508-456-8622.
circ. 5,000. *1761*

NUEVA CARDIOLOGIA.
Obsidiana Editores, S.A., Czda. de Tlalpan 2365, Col. Ciudad Jardin, 04370 Mexico DF, Mexico. TEL 6899133.
circ. 570. *4822*

NUEVA LENTE.
Miguel J. Goni Fernandez, Ed. & Pub., Ardemans 64, Madrid, Spain.
circ. 10,000. *5769*

NUEVO SIGLO.
7137 N. Armenia Ave., Ste. B, Tampa, FL 33604-5250. TEL 813-932-7181. FAX 813-877-6444.
circ. 18,000. *3034*

NUMARK NEWS.
Numark Ltd., Numark House, 5-6 Fairway Ct., Amber Close, Tamworth Business Park, Tamworth, Staffs B77 4RP, England. TEL 44-1827-69269. FAX 44-1827-62369.
circ. 6,000. *5681*

NUMBER ONE.
Volunteer State Community College, Humanities Division, 1480 Nashville Pike, Gallatin, TN 37066. TEL 615-452-8600.
circ. 2,000. *4516*

THE NUMISMATIST.
American Numismatic Association, 818 N. Cascade Ave., Colorado Springs, CO 80903-3279. TEL 719-632-2646. FAX 719-634-4085.
circ. 25,000. *5467*

NUORTEN SARKA.
Suomen 4H-Liitto, Bulevardi 28, 00120 Helsinki 12, Finland. TEL 358-0-645133.
circ. 28,500. *142*

LE NURB.
Brunel University, Union of Brunel Students, Cleveland Rd., Uxbridge, Middlesex UB8 3PH, England. TEL 44-1895-462232. FAX 44-1895-810477.
circ. 7,000. *1964*

NURSCENE.
Manitoba Association of Registered Nurses, 647 Broadway, Winnipeg, MB R3C 0X2, Canada. TEL 204-774-3477. FAX 204-775-6052.
circ. 11,000. *4942*

NURSING (YEAR) CAREER DIRECTORY.
Springhouse Corporation, 1111 Bethlehem Pike, Box 908, Springhouse, PA 19477-0908. TEL 215-646-8700. FAX 215-646-4399.
circ. 100,000. *1703*

NURSING AND ALLIED HEALTHWEEK.
Nurseweek Publishing, Inc., 1156 Aster Ave., Ste. C, Sunnyvale, CA 94086-6801. TEL 408-249-5877. FAX 408-249-8021.
circ. 100,000. *4943*

NURSING B C.
Registered Nurses Association of British Columbia, 2855 Arbutus St, Vancouver, BC V6J 3Y8, Canada. TEL 604-736-7331. FAX 604-738-2272.
circ. 35,000. *4943*

NURSING IN CRITICAL CARE.
Greycoat Publishing, 1 Harley St., London W1N 1DA, England. TEL 44-171-637-1828.
circ. 1,100. *4944*

NURSING MANAGEMENT.
Springhouse Corporation, 1111 Bethlehem Pike, Box 908, Springhouse, PA 19477. TEL 215-646-8700.
circ. 135,000. *4944*

NUSLECA.
Nusleca Publications, Shripney Works, Bognor Regis, W. Sussex PO22 9NQ, England. FAX 0243-868052.
circ. 5,000. *3482*

NUTRICION CLINICA.
Alpe Editores, S.A., Pedro Rico, 27, 28029 Madrid, Spain. TEL 34-1-7338811. FAX 34-1-3159652.
circ. 5,000. *5478*

NUTRITION FORUM.
Canadian Society for Nutritional Sciences, Department of Foods and Nutrition, University of Manitoba, Winnipeg, MB R3T 2N2, Canada. TEL 613-993-4484. *5479*

NUTRITION HEALTH REVIEW.
Vegetus Publications, Box 406, Haverford, PA 19041. TEL 610-896-1853. FAX 610-896-1857.
circ. 280,800. *5479*

NUTRITION NEWS IN ZAMBIA.
National Food and Nutrition Commission, P.O. Box 32669, Lusaka, Zambia.
circ. 5,000. *3122*

NUX.
University of Natal, Students Representative Council, P.O. Box 375, Pietermaritzburg, Natal, South Africa.
circ. 2,500. *1964*

NWY NEWS.
British Gas Wales, Public Relations Dept., Helmont House, Churchill Way, Cardiff CF1 4NB, Wales. TEL 0222-239290. FAX 0222-290738.
circ. 6,500. *5613*

NY TEKNIK.
Ingenjoersfoerlaget AB, S-106 12 Stockholm, Sweden. TEL 46-8-796-6650. FAX 46-8-789-6224.
circ. 133,956. *2734*

NYE FAMILY NEWSLETTER.
Nye Family of America Association, Box 134, E. Sandwich, MA 02537. TEL 508-888-2368.
circ. 2,400. *3235*

O A N DIGGER.
Oregon Association of Nurserymen, 2780 S.E. Harrison, Ste. 102, Milwaukie, OR 97222. TEL 503-653-8733. FAX 503-653-1528.
circ. 4,710. *3200*

O A N DIRECTORY & BUYER'S GUIDE.
Oregon Association of Nurserymen, 2780 S.E. Harrison, Ste. 102, Milwaukie, OR 97222. TEL 503-653-8733. FAX 503-653-1528.
circ. 6,500. *1703*

O B G MANAGEMENT.
Dowden Publishing Company, 110 Summit Ave., Montvale, NJ 07645. TEL 201-391-9100. FAX 201-391-2778.
circ. 34,500. *4964*

O C D DIAMOND.
American Cyanamid Co., Organic Chemical Division, Bound Brook, NJ 08805. TEL 908-831-2000.
circ. 6,500. *6969*

O D I INDEX TO DEVELOPMENT LITERATURE.
Overseas Development Institute, Regent's College, Inner Circle, Regent's Park, London NW1 4NS, England. TEL 44-171-487-7413. FAX 44-171-487-7590.
circ. 200. *1061*

O D I NATURAL RESOURCE PERSPECTIVES.
Overseas Development Institute, Regent's College, Inner Circle, Regent's Park, London NW1 4NS, England. TEL 0171-487-7413. FAX 0171-487-7590.
circ. 6,000. *1365*

O E M DESIGN.
Wilmington Business Publishing, Apex House, London Rd., Northfleet, Kent DA11 9JA, England. TEL 44-1322-277788. FAX 44-1474-569418.
circ. 30,500. *2735*

O P A NEWSGRAM.
Oregon Psychological Association, 147 S.E. 102nd Ave., Portland, OR 97216-2703.
circ. 700. *6138*

O P M A OVERSEAS MEDIA GUIDE.
Overseas Press and Media Association, c/o Sinclairs, 32 Queen Anne St., London W1M 9LB, England.
circ. 5,000. *1704*

O P S E U NEWS.
Ontario Public Service Employees Union, 100 Lesmill Rd., North York, ON M3B 3P8, Canada. TEL 416-443-8888. FAX 416-443-1762.
circ. 20,000. *1448*

O P T I M A NEWSLETTER.
Organization for the Phyto-Taxonomic Investigation of the Mediterranean Area, Departamento Biologia Vegetal, Universidad Politecnica de Madrid, Ciudad Universitaria, 28040 Madrid, Spain. TEL 34-15445800. FAX 34-13365656.
circ. 900. *718*

O R INSIGHT.
Operational Research Society, Seymour House, 12 Edward St., Birmingham B1 2RX, England. TEL 44-121-233-9300. FAX 44-121-233-0321.
circ. 3,000. *2469*

THE O S L A CONNECTION.
Ontario Association of Speech - Language Pathologists and Audiologists, 410 Jarvis St., Toronto, ON M4Y 2G6, Canada. TEL 416-920-3676. FAX 416-920-6214.
circ. 1,450. *2588*

O S M T ADVOCATE.
Ontario Society of Medical Technologists, 234 Eglinton Ave. E., Ste. 402, Toronto, ON M4P 1K5, Canada.
circ. 4,000. *4901*

OAKLAND UNIVERSITY MAGAZINE.
Oakland University, Publications Department, 109 N. Foundation Hall, Rochester, MI 48309-4401. TEL 248-370-3184. FAX 248-370-3182.
circ. 40,000. *1964*

OASIS (LONDON, 1986).
WaterAid, Prince Consort House, 27-29 Albert Embankment, London SE1 7UB, England. TEL 44-171-793-4500. FAX 44-171-793-4545.
circ. 85,000. *1365*

OB-GYN NEWS.
International Medical News Group, 12230 Wilkins Ave., Rockville, MD 20852. TEL 301-816-8700.
circ. 31,000. *4964*

OBEROESTERREICHER-LEBENSBILDER ZUR GESCHICHTE OBEROESTERREICHS.
Oberoesterreichisches Landesarchiv, Anzengruberstr. 19, A-4020 Linz, Austria. TEL 43-732-6555230. FAX 43-732-655523-4619.
circ. 500. *3588*

OBEROESTERREICHISCHES LANDESARCHIV. MITTEILUNGEN.
Oberoesterreichisches Landesarchiv, Anzengruberstr. 19, A-4020 Linz, Austria. TEL 43-732-6555230. FAX 43-732-655523-4619.
circ. 500. *3589*

OBERWEIS REPORT: A MONTHLY REVIEW.
Oberweis Asset Management, Inc., 951 Ice Cream Dr., Ste. 200, North Aurora, IL 60542-1472. FAX 630-896-5282.
circ. 4,000. *1159*

OBLATES.
Missionary Association of Mary Immaculate, 15 S. 59th St., Belleville, IL 62223-4694. TEL 618-398-4848.
circ. 500,000. *6359*

OBSERVER (ANCHORAGE).
Regional Citizens' Advisory Council of Prince William Sound, 750 W. Second Ave., No. 100, Anchorage, AK 99501-2167. TEL 907-277-7222. FAX 907-277-4523.
circ. 30,000. *2971*

OBSERVER (FT. LAUDERDALE).
Broward Community College Board of Trustees, 225 E. Las Olas Blvd., Ft. Lauderdale, FL 33301. TEL 305-973-2237. FAX 305-968-2448.
circ. 10,000. *1964*

10372 CONTROLLED CIRCULATION SERIALS

OCCASIONAL PAPERS IN ENTOMOLOGY.
Department of Food and Agriculture, Division of Plant Industry, 1220 N St., Sacramento, CA 95814. TEL 916-445-5421.
circ. 200. *759*

OCCUPATIONAL HAZARDS.
Penton Publishing Co., 1100 Superior Ave., Cleveland, OH 44114-2543. TEL 216-696-7000. FAX 216-696-8765.
circ. 60,000. *5496*

OCEAN DRILLING PROGRAM. PROCEEDINGS. INITIAL REPORTS.
Texas A&M University, Ocean Drilling Program, 1000 Discovery Dr., College Station, TX 77845-9547. TEL 409-845-2016. FAX 409-845-4857.
circ. 1,550. *2411*

OCEAN DRILLING PROGRAM. SCIENTIFIC RESULTS. PROCEEDINGS. SCIENTIFIC RESULTS.
Texas A&M University, Ocean Drilling Program, 1000 Discovery Dr., College Station, TX 77845-9547. TEL 409-845-2016. FAX 409-845-4857.
circ. 1,550. *2411*

OCEAN REALM.
Friends of the Sea, Inc., 4067 Broadway, San Antonio, TX 78209. TEL 210-824-8099. FAX 210-820-3522.
circ. 2,543. *2240*

OCEAN VOICE.
International Maritime Satellite Organization, 99 City Rd., London EC1Y 4AX, England. TEL 0171-728-1000. FAX 0171-728-1044.
circ. 18,684. *7160*

OCEANOGRAPHIC RESEARCH INSTITUTE. INVESTIGATIONAL REPORT.
Oceanographic Research Institute, P.O. Box 10712, Marine Parade, Durban 4056, South Africa. TEL 27-31-373536. FAX 27-31-372132.
circ. 400. *846*

THE OCTAGON.
American Chemical Society, Lehigh Valley Section, 744 N. Broad St., Allentown, PA 18104. TEL 610-770-7348. FAX 610-770-7348.
circ. 1,000. *1761*

ODINI.
Likuni Press and Publishing House, P.O. Box 133, Lilongwe, Malawi. TEL 265-721388. FAX 265-721141.
circ. 12,000. *6473*

ODONTOLOGO.
Asociacion Odontologica Panamena, Apdo. 6777, Zona 5, Panama, Panama. TEL 507-269-1603. FAX 507-269-3749.
circ. 1,000. *4866*

DER OEFFENTLICHE DIENST AN RHEIN UND RUHR.
Vereinigte Verlagsanstalten GmbH, Hoeherweg 278, 40231 Duesseldorf, Germany. TEL 49-211-7357-0. FAX 49-211-7357223.
circ. 116,000. *6222*

DER OEFFENTLICHE DIENST IN BRANDENBURG.
Vereinigte Verlagsanstalten GmbH, Hoeherweg 278, 40231 Duesseldorf, Germany. TEL 49-211-7357-0. FAX 49-211-7357223.
circ. 10,000. *6222*

OESTERREICHISCHE BAUERNZEITUNG.
Baeuerlicher Presseverein, Castellezgasse 20-1, A-1020 Vienna, Austria.
circ. 16,000. *142*

OESTERREICHISCHE BLASMUSIK.
Tuba Musikverlag, Steinamangererstr. 187, A-7400 Oberwart, Austria. TEL 43-3352-33392. FAX 43-3352-34130.
circ. 9,500. *5421*

OESTERREICHISCHE FREIBERUFS TIERARZT.
Ostag Werbung und Verlag, Wickenburggasse 17, A-1082 Vienna, Austria. TEL 43-1-4027573. FAX 43-1-4088292.
circ. 3,100. *7275*

OESTERREICHISCHE INSTALLATEURZEITUNG.
Verlag Piletzky, Nikolsdorfergasse 7, A-1050 Vienna, Austria.
circ. 4,600. *3482*

OESTERREICHISCHER WALDBERICHT.
Bundesministerium fuer Land- und Forstwirtschaft, Stubenring 1, A-1012 Vienna, Austria. TEL 43-1-213237304. FAX 43-1-711002127.
circ. 3,600. *3159*

OESTERREICHISCHES JUGENDROTKREUZ. ARBEITSBLAETTER.
Oesterreichisches Jugendrotkreuz, Wiedner Hauptstr. 32, A-1041 Vienna 4, Austria. FAX 43-1-58900179.
circ. 10,000. *6680*

OESTERREICHISCHES STAATSARCHIV. MITTEILUNGEN.
Verlag Ferdinand Berger und Soehne GmbH, Wienerstr. 21-23, A-3580 Horn, Austria. TEL 43-2982-4161232. FAX 43-2982-2317235.
circ. 500. *3589*

OFF DUTY AMERICA.
Off Duty Enterprises, 3303 Harbor Blvd., Ste. C-2, Costa Mesa, CA 92626. TEL 714-549-7172. FAX 714-549-4222.
circ. 400,000. *5280*

OFFICE EQUIPMENT NEWS.
Wilmington Business Publishing, Apex House, London Rd., Northfleet, Kent DA11 9JA, England. TEL 44-1322-277788. FAX 44-1474-569418.
circ. 55,236. *1559*

OFFICE WORLD NEWS.
B U S Publications, 366 Ramtown Greenville Rd., Howell, NJ 07731-2789. TEL 908-785-1616. FAX 908-785-1347.
circ. 37,000. *1559*

OFFICERS CALL.
National Officers Association, Box 4975, Reston, VA 20195-1464. TEL 703-438-3060. FAX 703-438-3072.
circ. 24,000. *5280*

OFFICIAL BRITISH THEATRE DIRECTORY SEATING PLAN GUIDE.
Richmond House Publishing Company Ltd., Douglas House, 3 Richmond Bldgs., London W1V 5AE, England. TEL 44-171-437-9556. FAX 44-171-287-3463.
circ. 3,000. *7010*

OFFICIAL GUIDE TO HOUSTON.
Desert Publications, Inc., 303 N. Indian Canyon Dr., Box 2724, Palm Springs, CA 92262. TEL 619-325-2333. FAX 619-325-7008.
circ. 600,000. *7226*

OFFICIAL MOTOR SHIPPERS GUIDE.
Official Motor Freight Guide, Inc., 1700 W. Cortland St., Chicago, IL 60622-1150. TEL 312-278-2454. FAX 312-489-0482.
circ. 1,767. *7177*

OFFICIAL VISITORS GUIDE.
Orlando - Orange County Convention and Visitors Bureau, Inc., 6700 Forum Dr., Ste. 100, Orlando, FL 32821-8087. TEL 407-363-5800. FAX 407-370-5018.
circ. 1,200,000. *7226*

OFFSHORE (TULSA).
PennWell Publishing Co., Box 1260, Tulsa, OK 74101. TEL 918-835-3161. FAX 918-832-9295.
circ. 35,500. *5613*

OFFSHORE FINANCIAL REVIEW.
Financial Times Business Information, Magazines 2 Greystoke Pl., Fetter Ln., London EC4A 1ND, England. TEL 0171-405-6969. FAX 0171-405-5726. *1400*

OFFSHORE VISIE.
Uitgeverij Tridens, Postbus 526, 1970 AM IJmuiden, Netherlands. TEL 31-255-530577. FAX 31-255-536068.
circ. 3,500. *5614*

OHIO A F L - C I O NEWS AND VIEWS.
Ohio A F L - C I O, 271 E. State St., Columbus, OH 43215. TEL 614-224-8271. FAX 614-224-2671.
circ. 11,500. *3895*

OHIO BEVERAGE JOURNAL.
Midwest Beverage Publications, Inc., 3 12th St., Wheeling, WV 26003. TEL 304-232-7620. FAX 304-233-1236.
circ. 7,125. *525*

OHIO CONTRACTOR.
Triad, Inc., 6525 Busch Blvd., Columbus, OH 43229. TEL 614-846-8761. FAX 614-846-8763.
circ. 5,500. *7140*

OHIO DEER & TURKEY SHOW PREVIEW.
Target Communications Corp., 7626 W. Donges Bay Rd., Mequon, WI 53097-3400. TEL 414-242-3990. FAX 414-242-7391.
circ. 20,000. *6877*

OHIO ENGINEER.
Ohio Society of Professional Engineers, 445 King Ave., Columbus, OH 43201. TEL 614-424-6640. FAX 614-421-1257.
circ. 4,000. *2735*

THE OHIO FAMILY PHYSICIAN.
Ohio Academy of Family Physicians, 4075 N. High St., Columbus, OH 43214. TEL 614-267-7867.
circ. 4,000. *4724*

OHIO GENEALOGICAL SOCIETY. WOOD COUNTY CHAPTER. NEWSLETTER.
Ohio Genealogical Society, Wood County Chapter, Box 722, Bowling Green, OH 43402. TEL 419-352-4940.
circ. 150. *3235*

OHIO GRANGER.
Ohio State Grange, 1031 E. Broad St., Columbus, OH 43205. TEL 614-258-9569.
circ. 14,500. *142*

OHIO NURSES REVIEW.
Ohio Nurses Association, 4000 E. Main St., Columbus, OH 43213-2983. TEL 614-237-5414. FAX 614-237-6074.
circ. 10,000. *4945*

OHIO STATE LANTERN.
Ohio State University, School of Journalism, 242 W. 18th Ave., Columbus, OH 43210. TEL 614-292-2031. FAX 614-292-3722.
circ. 30,000. *1964*

OHIO STATE UNIVERSITY. COLLEGE OF MEDICINE. JOURNAL.
Ohio State University, College of Medicine, 370 W. 9th Ave., Columbus, OH 43210-1238. TEL 614-292-5671. FAX 614-292-1544.
circ. 19,000. *4724*

OHIO STATE UNIVERSITY. SCHOOL OF PUBLIC ADMINISTRATION. WORKING PAPER SERIES.
Ohio State University, Administrative Science Research, 1775 College Rd., Columbus, OH 42310. TEL 614-422-8696. *6187*

OIL CAN.
Illinois Petroleum Marketers Association, Box 12020, Springfield, IL 62791-2020. TEL 217-544-4609. FAX 217-789-0222.
circ. 1,250. *5615*

OIL, GAS & PETROCHEM EQUIPMENT.
PennWell Publishing Co., Box 1260, Tulsa, OK 74101. TEL 918-835-3161. FAX 918-832-9295.
circ. 36,000. *5615*

OILSEEDS AND INDUSTRIAL CROPS.
Processors & Growers Research Organisation, 34 Cavendish Rd., London NW6 7XP, England. TEL 0181-459-5330.
circ. 12,000. *142*

OKLAHOMA. CONSERVATION COMMISSION. BIENNIAL REPORT.
Conservation Commission, 2800 Lincoln, Ste. 160, Oklahoma City, OK 73105. TEL 405-521-2384.
circ. 175. *2240*

OKLAHOMA DAILY.
University of Oklahoma, Student Publication Board, 860 Van Vleet, Norman, OK 73019. TEL 405-325-2521. FAX 405-325-7517.
circ. 13,500. *1965*

OKLAHOMA FARM BUREAU JOURNAL.
Oklahoma Farm Bureau, 2501 N. Stiles, Oklahoma City, OK 73105. TEL 405-273-4200. FAX 405-523-2326.
circ. 112,000. *142*

OKLAHOMA SCHOOL BOARD JOURNAL.
Oklahoma State School Boards Association, 2801 N. Lincoln Blvd., Oklahoma City, OK 73105. TEL 405-528-3571. FAX 405-528-5695.
circ. 4,600. *2469*

OLD BEN NEWS.
Newsvendors' Benevolent Institution, P.O. Box 306, Dunmow, Essex CM6 1HY, England.
circ. 46,000. *1215*

OLD YORK ROAD HISTORICAL SOCIETY BULLETIN.
Old York Road Historical Society, c/o Jenkintown Library, York and Vista Rds., Jenkintown, PA 19046. TEL 215-884-0593.
circ. 265. *3641*

ON COURT.
Fourhand II, Inc., 1200 Sheppard Ave. E., Ste. 400, Willowdale, Ont. M2K 2S5, Canada. TEL 416-497-1370. FAX 416-494-5343.
circ. 50,000. *6813*

ON THE MARK.
Underwriters Laboratories Inc., Corporate Communications, 333 Pfingsten Rd., Northbrook, IL 60062-2096. TEL 847-272-8800. FAX 847-272-8129.
circ. 80,000. *1499*

ON THE TOWN.
On the Town Publications Inc., 705 Bagley Ave., S.E., Ste. 102, Grand Rapids, MI 49506-3001. TEL 616-451-0361. FAX 616-454-4666.
circ. 35,000. *3381*

ON TRACK (WASHINGTON).
National Railroad Construction and Maintenance Association, Inc., 122 C St., NW., Ste. 850, Washington, DC 20001-2109. FAX 202-638-1045.
circ. 1,500. *7129*

ON WALL STREET.
Securities Data Publishing, 40 W. 57th St., 11th Fl., New York, NY 10019. TEL 212-765-5311. FAX 212-765-6123.
circ. 90,000. *1400*

ONCOLOGIA.
Alpe Editores, S.A., Pedro Rico, 27, 28029 Madrid, Spain. TEL 34-1-7338811. FAX 34-1-3159652.
circ. 6,000. *4984*

ONCOLOGY.
P R R, Inc., 17 Prospect St., Huntington, NY 11743. TEL 516-424-8900. FAX 516-424-8503.
circ. 26,265. *4984*

ONCOLOGY NEWS INTERNATIONAL.
17 Prospect St., Huntington, NY 11743. TEL 516-424-8900. FAX 516-424-8503.
circ. 26,722. *4984*

ONDERSTEPOORT JOURNAL OF VETERINARY RESEARCH.
Agricultural Research Council, Onderstepoort Veterinary Institute, Private Bag X5, Onderstepoort 0110, South Africa. TEL 27-12-5299101. FAX 27-12-5299318.
circ. 600. *7276*

ONSEI GENGO IGAKU.
Nihon Onsei Gengo Igakkai, Hakuo Bldg., 5F, 2-3-10 Kohraku, Bunkyo-ku, Tokyo 112, Japan. FAX 03-5684-5954.
circ. 1,850. *5024*

ONTARIO BEEF.
Ontario Cattlemen's Association, 130 Malcolm Rd., Guelph, ON N1K 1B1, Canada. TEL 519-824-0334. FAX 519-824-9101.
circ. 20,931. *284*

ONTARIO GOLF NEWS.
Ontario Golf News Inc., 2 Billingham Rd., Ste. 400, Toronto, ON M9B 6E1, Canada. TEL 416-232-2380. FAX 416-232-9291.
circ. 40,000. *6813*

ONTARIO GOVERNMENT LIBRARIES COUNCIL. EXCHANGE.
Ontario Government Libraries Council, 77 Wellesley St., W., 4th Fl., Ferguson Block, Toronto, ON M7A 1N3, Canada. TEL 416-327-2535. FAX 416-327-2530.
circ. 110. *4205*

ONTARIO GRAPE GROWER.
Ontario Grape Growers' Marketing Board, Box 100, Vineland, ON L0R 2E0, Canada. TEL 905-688-0990. FAX 905-688-3211.
circ. 8,000. *237*

ONTARIO MUSEUM ANNUAL.
Ontario Museum Association, George Brown House, 50 Baldwin St., Toronto, ON M5T 1L4, Canada. TEL 416-348-8672. FAX 416-348-0438.
circ. 1,500. *5364*

ONTARIO ROYAL BOTANICAL GARDENS. TECHNICAL BULLETIN.
Royal Botanical Gardens, Box 399, Hamilton, ON L8N 3H8, Canada. TEL 905-527-1158. FAX 905-577-0375.
circ. 1,000. *718*

ONTARION.
Ontarion, Inc., University of Guelph, University Centre, Rm. 264, Guelph, ON N1G 2W1, Canada. TEL 519-824-4120. FAX 519-824-7838.
circ. 12,000. *1965*

ONZE VOGELS.
Nederlandse Bond van Vogelliefhebbers, Postbox 74, 4600 AB Bergen Op Zoom, Netherlands. TEL 31-1640-35007. FAX 31-1640-39020.
circ. 43,000. *807*

OP CIT.
Waterstone's Publications, 26 Exeter St., Boston, MA 02116. TEL 617-859-8030. FAX 617-437-0997.
circ. 25,000. *4351*

OP OOGHOOGTE.
Stichting Oogzorg Himalaya, Postbus 174, 2110 AD Aerdenhout, Netherlands. TEL 31-23-5290073. FAX 31-23-5286922.
circ. 20,000. *4997*

OPEN DEUR.
Boekencentrum B.V., Postbus 29, 2700 AA Zoetermeer, Netherlands. TEL 31-79-615481. FAX 31-79-615489. *6436*

OPERNWELT.
Friedrich Kulturzeitschriftenverlag, Luetzowplatz 7, 10785 Berlin, Germany. TEL 49-30-254495-0. FAX 49-30-25449512.
circ. 10,000. *5422*

LA OPINION.
Avda. 4, 16-12, Cucuta, N. de S., Colombia. TEL 75-719999. FAX 75-717869.
circ. 1,500. *3272*

OPINION.
Opinion Publications, Box 681, Cape May Court House, NJ 08210-0681.
circ. 3,700. *5740*

OPPORTUNITIES FOR THEATRE STAFF & OTHER SPECIALISTS.
Newton Mann Ltd., Stretton Rd., Tansley Matlock, Derbyshire DE4 5GE, England. TEL 44-1629-583941. FAX 44-1629-580479.
circ. 5,000. *4945*

OPPORTUNITIES IN OPTIONS.
Box 2126, Malibu, CA 90265. FAX 310-456-3840.
circ. 5,000. *1400*

OPPORTUNITY MAGAZINE.
Ashlee Publishing, 18 E. 41st St., New York, NY 10017. TEL 212-376-7722. FAX 212-376-7723.
1544

OPTICAL PRISM.
VezCom Inc., 31 Hastings Dr., Unionville, ON L3R 4Y5, Canada. TEL 905-475-9343. FAX 905-477-2821.
circ. 7,368. *4999*

OPTIMUM.
Canada Communication Group, Publishing Division, Ottawa, ON K1A 0S9, Canada. TEL 819-956-4802.
circ. 1,200. *1499*

OPTIONS.
International Institute for Applied Systems Analysis, A-2361 Laxenburg, Austria. TEL 43-2236-807-0. FAX 43-2236-73149.
circ. 8,000. *2185*

OPTO & LASER EUROPE.
I O P Publishing Ltd., Dirac House, Temple Back, Bristol BS1 6BE, England. TEL 44-117-929-7481. FAX 44-117-929-4318.
circ. 25,000. *5868*

OPUNTIA.
Speirs Publishing, P.O. Box 6830, Calgary, AB T2P 2E7, Canada.
circ. 100. *4534*

OPUS DEI AWARENESS NETWORK.
Opus Dei Awareness Network, Inc., Box 4333, Pittsfield, MA 01202. TEL 413-499-7168. FAX 413-499-7860. *6474*

ORANGE SEED TECHNICAL BULLETIN.
Department of State, Division of Library and Information Services, R.A. Gray Bldg., Tallahassee, FL 32399-0250. TEL 904-487-2651. FAX 904-488-2746.
circ. 1,200. *4205*

ORBIT MAGAZINE.
Popular Amusement, Inc., 919 S. Main, No. 2001, Royal Oak, MI 48067. TEL 810-541-3900. FAX 810-541-4054.
circ. 55,000. *4151*

ORD & BILD.
Stiftelsen Ord & Bild, Box 12034, S-402 41 Goeteborg, Sweden. TEL 46-31-775-90-95. FAX 46-31-775-00-15.
circ. 8,000. *4351*

OREGON BUSINESS NETWORK NEWS.
Oregon Business Network, Box 5488, Portland, OR 97219. TEL 503-244-2689. FAX 503-618-8771.
circ. 21,000. *990*

OREGON PUBLISHER.
Oregon Newspaper Publishers Association, 7150 S.W. Hampton St., Ste. 111, Portland, OR 97223. TEL 503-624-6397. FAX 503-639-9009.
circ. 600. *6279*

OREGON PURCHASOR.
Purchasing Management Association of Oregon, c/o Decorators West, Box 25191, Portland, OR 97225-0191. TEL 503-245-2296.
circ. 2,200. *1544*

OREGON QUARTERLY.
University of Oregon, 5228 University of Oregon, Eugene, OR 97403-5228. TEL 503-346-5047. FAX 503-346-5571.
circ. 100,000. *1965*

OREGON WHEAT.
Oregon Wheat Growers League, 202 S.E. Dorion, Box 400, Pendleton, OR 97801. TEL 503-276-7330. FAX 503-276-1723.
circ. 6,050. *265*

ORGAN CLUB JOURNAL.
Organ Club, c/o Philip Weston, Gen. Sec., 36 Fortismere Ave., London N10 3BL, England. *5423*

ORGANIC CONSUMER REPORT.
Eden Ranch, Box 370, Topanga, CA 90290. TEL 213-455-2065. *5481*

ORGANICA.
Organica Press, 4419 N. Manhattan Ave., Tampa, FL 33614. TEL 813-877-4186. FAX 813-876-8166.
circ. 200,000. *4445*

ORIENTAL COLLEGE MAGAZINE.
Punjab University, Oriental College, Lahore, Pakistan. TEL 311496.
circ. 500. *4445*

ORION (CHICO).
California State University, Chico, College of Communication, Department of Journalism, Chico, CA 95929-0600. TEL 916-898-5625. FAX 916-898-4839.
circ. 10,000. *1965*

ORITA.
University of Ibadan, Department of Religious Studies, Ibadan, Oyo State, Nigeria.
circ. 500. *6360*

CONTROLLED CIRCULATION SERIALS

ORIZZONTE SICILIA.
Banca Popolare Sant'Angelo, Via Ruggiero VII, no.78, 90141 Palermo, Italy. TEL 39-91-332922. FAX 39-91-584923. *1276*

ORNIS FENNICA.
Finnish Ornithological Society, University of Helsinki, Department of Ecology and Systematics, Division of Population Biology, P.O. Box 17, SF-00014 Helsinki, Finland. TEL 358-81-5531214. FAX 358-81-5531227.
circ. 1,100. *807*

THE OSWEGONIAN.
State University of New York, Oswego, 15B Hewitt Union, Oswego, NY 13126. TEL 315-341-3600. FAX 315-341-3542.
circ. 6,000. *1965*

OTECHESTVENNAYA GEOLOGIYA.
Ts N I G R I, Varshavskoe Shosse, 129B, 113545 Moscow, Russia. TEL 7-095-3152847. FAX 7-095-3152701.
circ. 1,500. *2363*

OTIS RUSH.
S A Publishing Ventures and Futures, P.O. Box 8091, Hindley St., Concord, N.S.W. 2137, Australia. TEL 61-8-82117505. FAX 61-8-82117323.
circ. 450. *4516*

OTTERBEIN MISCELLANY.
Otterbein College, Westerville, OH 43081. TEL 614-890-3000.
circ. 300. *4351*

OUR HERITAGE.
Genealogical Society of Van Zandt County, Box 716, Canton, TX 75103-0716. TEL 903-567-5012.
circ. 425. *3236*

OUR PAPER.
Grain Dealers Mutual Insurance Co., 1752 N. Meridian St., Box 1747, Indianapolis, IN 46206. TEL 317-923-2453.
circ. 2,500. *3829*

OUR VOICE (CLEVELAND).
American Mutual Life Association, 19424 S. Waterloo Rd., Cleveland, OH 44119-3250.
circ. 8,500. *3829*

OUT AND ABOUT SMITH MOUNTAIN LAKE.
Rte. 1, Box 437, Moneta, VA 24121. TEL 703-297-6444.
circ. 40,000. *7226*

OUTDOOR OKLAHOMA.
Department of Wildlife Conservation, 1801 N. Lincoln, Oklahoma City, OK 73105. TEL 405-521-3855. FAX 405-521-6535.
circ. 21,500. *2241*

OUTDOOR RETAILER.
Pacifica Publishing Corporation, 310 Broadway, Laguna Beach, CA 92651. TEL 714-376-8155. FAX 714-497-2093.
circ. 16,191. *1544*

OUTDOOR TRADE AND INDUSTRY.
97 Front St., Whickham, Newcastle-upon-Tyne NE16 4JL, England. *6878*

OUTERWEAR.
Creative Marketing Plus, 19 W. 21st St., Ste. 403, New York, NY 10010. TEL 212-727-1210.
circ. 16,000. *1918*

OUTLOOK.
General Conference of the New Church, c/o G.S. Kuphal, 20 Red Barn Rd., Brightlingsea, Colchester, Essex CO7 0SH, England. TEL 44-1206-302932.
circ. 2,000. *6495*

OUTLOOK (WAKE FOREST).
Southeastern Baptist Theological Seminary, Inc., Wake Forest, NC 27587. TEL 919-556-3101. FAX 919-556-8550.
circ. 13,000. *6436*

OUTLOOK MAGAZINE.
Summer and Casual Furniture Manufacturers Association, 223 S. Wrenn St., HP-7, High Point, NC 27261. TEL 910-884-5000. FAX 910-884-5303.
circ. 7,000. *3860*

OUTREACH (NEW YORK).
Armenian Apostolic Church of America, 138 E. 39th St., New York, NY 10016. TEL 212-689-7810. FAX 212-689-7168.
circ. 10,500. *6495*

OUTYOUTH.
Lesbian and Gay Community Services Center, Youth Enrichment Program, 208 W. 13th St., New York, NY 10011.
circ. 2,000. *3699*

OVERALL THERE IS A SMELL OF FRIED ONIONS.
P.O. Box 73, West PDO, Nottingham NG7 4DG, England. TEL 44-115-953-8333. FAX 44-115-953-8333.
circ. 5,000. *5341*

OVERSEAS TRADE.
Brass Tacks Publishing, 143 Charing Cross Rd., London WC2E OEE, England. TEL 44-171-478-4700. FAX 44-171-478-4701.
circ. 30,762. *1344*

OVERTURE.
Winnipeg Symphony Orchestra, 101-555 Main St., Winnipeg, MB R3B 1C3, Canada. TEL 204-949-3950. FAX 204-956-4271.
circ. 14,000. *5424*

OVERVIEW (WOODRIDGE).
Overview Ltd., Box 211, Woodridge, NJ 07075.
circ. 450. *4516*

OXFORD REVIEW.
Oxford Books, Inc., 360 Pharr Rd., N.E., Atlanta, GA 30305. TEL 404-262-3333.
circ. 227,000. *4352*

OXFORDSHIRE LOCAL HISTORY.
Oxfordshire Local History Association, c/o Dr. F.B. Atlins, 8 Thornbury Rd., Eynsham, Oxon OX8 1PW, England.
circ. 300. *3590*

OXYGEN.
Oxygen Editions, 535 Geary St., Ste. 1010, San Francisco, CA 94102-1633. TEL 415-776-9681.
circ. 300. *4446*

P C DISTRIBUTOR.
Empresar Editores Ltda., Carrera 11, No. 94-02, L-123, Bogota, Colombia. TEL 2182730. FAX 610-1958.
circ. 5,000. *2200*

P C I A JOURNAL.
Personal Communications Industry Association, 500 Montgomery St., Ste. 700, Alexandria, VA 22314-1560.
circ. 3,500. *2037*

P C MAGAZINE.
Gruppo Editoriale Jackson S.p.A., Via M. Gorki 69, 20092 Cinisello B. (MI), Italy. TEL 39-2-66034229. FAX 39-2-66034448.
circ. 52,387. *2201*

P C MICRO MAGAZINE.
Ecopress S.A., Rue Gabrielle 114, 1180 Brussels, Belgium. FAX 32-2-3442451.
circ. 15,000. *2201*

P C NETZE.
Datacom Zeitschriften Verlag GmbH, Postfach 1502, 50105 Bergheim, Germany. TEL 49-2271-608-0.
circ. 20,240. *2139*

P C SPECIAL MONTHLY.
Interface Electronic Publisher, Flat 8, 13th Fl., Yeung Yiu Chung no.8, Ind. Bldg., 20 Wang Hoi Rd., Kowloon Bay, Kowloon, Hong Kong. TEL 3-7955582. FAX 3-7952962. *2202*

P C T NEWSLETTER.
World Intellectual Property Organization (WIPO), Publications Sales and Distribution Unit, 34 chemin des Colombettes, CH-1211 Geneva 20, Switzerland. TEL 41-22-730-9618. FAX 41-22-740-1812.
circ. 3,000. *5588*

P C WEEK.
Ziff-Davis Publishing Co., One Park Ave., New York, NY 10016-5146. TEL 212-503-5100.
circ. 128,277. *2202*

P C WEEK ASIA.
Newsources Investments Ltd., 1501 Shiu Lam Bldg., 23 Luard Rd., Wanchai, Hong Kong, People's Republic of China. TEL 852-2528-4808. FAX 852-2865-6832.
circ. 21,429. *2203*

THE P E G G.
Association of Professional Engineers, Geologists & Geophysicists of Alberta, 1500 Scotia Pl., Tower One, 10060 Jasper Ave., Edmonton, AB T5J 4A2, Canada. TEL 403-426-3990. FAX 403-426-1877.
circ. 32,219. *2735*

P E I T F NEWSLETTER.
Prince Edward Island Teachers Federation, P.O. Box 6000, Charlottetown, PE C1A 8B4, Canada. TEL 902-569-4157. FAX 902-569-3682.
circ. 2,400. *2470*

P F I WORLD REPORT.
Prison Fellowship International, Box 17434, Washington, DC 20041. TEL 703-481-0000. FAX 703-481-0003.
circ. 6,500. *6360*

P G A PROFILE.
In Focus Publishing, 52 Mere Green Rd., Sutton Coldfield, W. Midlands B75 5BT, England. TEL 021-323-3073. FAX 021-323-2911.
circ. 5,500. *6813*

P G W NEWSLINE.
Philadelphia Gas Works, 800 W. Montgomery Ave., Philadelphia, PA 19122. TEL 215-684-6564.
circ. 4,500. *5617*

P H - O FORUM.
P H - O Forum, c/o King - Drew Medical Center, Rm. 5101, 12021 S. Wilmington Ave., Los Angeles, CA 90059. TEL 310-668-3850. FAX 310-668-3108.
circ. 2,200. *5035*

P H R RECORD.
Physicians for Human Rights, 100 Boylston St., Ste. 702, Boston, MA 02116-4610. TEL 617-695-0041. FAX 617-695-0307.
circ. 5,000. *6031*

P I M A'S NORTH AMERICAN PAPERMAKER.
Paper Industry Management Association, 1699 Wall St., Ste. 212, Mt. Prospect, IL 60056-5782. TEL 847-956-0250. FAX 847-956-0520.
circ. 42,000. *5568*

P L I WARWICK JOURNAL OF PHILOSOPHY.
University of Warwick, Department of Philosophy, Coventry CV4 7AL, England. TEL 44-1203-523421. FAX 44-1203-523019.
circ. 400. *5740*

P N L A QUARTERLY.
Pacific Northwest Library Association, Mansfield Library, University of Montana, Missoula, MT 59812-1195. TEL 406-243-4335. FAX 406-243-2060.
circ. 800. *4205*

P O B - POINT OF BEGINNING.
Business News Publishing Co., 755 W. Big Beaver, Ste. 1000, Troy, MI 48084. TEL 810-362-3700. FAX 810-362-0317.
circ. 50,450. *2795*

P O N S I REPORT.
American Council of Education, One Dupont Circle, N.W., Ste. 250, Washington, DC 20036-1193. TEL 202-939-9731. FAX 202-775-8578.
circ. 5,000. *2552*

P P O UPDATE.
Lippincott - Raven Publishers, 227 E. Washington Sq., Philadelphia, PA 19106. TEL 215-238-4200. FAX 215-238-4227.
circ. 25,000. *4985*

P S A C UNION UPDATE.
Public Service Alliance of Canada, 233 Gilmour St., Ottawa, ON K2P 0P1, Canada. TEL 613-560-4241. FAX 613-236-1654.
circ. 30,000. *3895*

P S A INDUSTRIAL BULLETIN.
Public Service Association of New South Wales, G.P.O. Box 3365, Sydney, N.S.W. 2001, Australia. TEL 61-2-92901555. FAX 61-2-92621623.
circ. 7,000. *3895*

P S A REPORTER.
Public Service Association of New South Wales, G.P.O. Box 3365, Sydney, N.S.W. 2001, Australia. TEL 61-2-92901555. FAX 61-2-92621623.
circ. 7,000. *3895*

P S B A BULLETIN.
Pennsylvania School Boards Association, 774 Limekiln Rd., New Cumberland, PA 17070-2398. TEL 717-774-2331. FAX 717-774-0718.
circ. 11,300. *2576*

P S I NACHRICHTEN.
Praesent Service Institut, Neusserstr. 111, 40219 Duesseldorf, Germany. TEL 49-211-901910. FAX 49-211-9019125.
circ. 6,500. *42*

P T DISTRIBUTOR.
Penton Publishing Co., 1100 Superior Ave., Cleveland, OH 44114-2543. TEL 216-696-7000. FAX 216-696-8765.
circ. 10,000. *2896*

P T I C BULLETIN.
Patent and Trademark Institute of Canada, Box 1298, Sta. B, Ottawa, ON K1P 5R3, Canada. TEL 613-234-0516. *5588*

P T I NEWSLETTER.
Post-Tensioning Institute, 1717 W. Northern Ave., Ste. 114, Phoenix, AZ 85021. TEL 602-870-7540. FAX 602-870-7541.
circ. 1,200. *411*

P T S NEWS.
Philatelic Traders Society Ltd., British Philatelic Centre, 107 Charterhouse St., London EC1M 6PT, England. TEL 0171-490-1005. FAX 0171-253-0414. *5710*

P T TODAY.
Valley Forge Press, 1288 Valley Forge Rd., Ste. 50, Box 1135, Valley Forge, PA 19482. TEL 610-935-3302. FAX 610-935-3072.
circ. 50,000. *5045*

PAA KRYSS TILL RORS.
Svenska Kryssarklubben, P.O. Box 1189, S-131 27 Nacha Strand, Sweden. TEL 46-8-448-28-80. FAX 46-8-448-28-89.
circ. 34,000. *6842*

PACIFIC COAST NURSERYMAN AND GARDEN SUPPLY DEALER.
Cox Publishing Co., Box 1477, Glendora, CA 91740. TEL 818-914-3916. FAX 818-914-3751.
circ. 10,200. *3202*

PACIFIC ECHO.
Neighbors of Woodcraft, Box 769, Oregon City, OR 97045-0052. TEL 503-224-3525. FAX 503-223-5140.
circ. 10,000. *1935*

PACIFIC HOSTELLER.
Canadian Hostelling Association, B.C. Region, 1515 Discovery St., Vancouver, B.C. V6R 4K5, Canada. TEL 604-224-7177. FAX 604-224-4852.
circ. 10,000. *7227*

PACIFIC RIM MANAGEMENT.
Sterling Publications Ltd., 86-88 Edgware Rd., London W2 2YW, England. TEL 44-171-915-9600. FAX 44-171-915-9619.
circ. 10,000. *1344*

PACK NEWS & MECHANICAL HANDLING NEWS.
Kluwer Business Press, Kouterveldstraat 2, 1831 Diegem, Belgium. TEL 32-2-7231111. FAX 32-2-7231512.
circ. 9,500. *5546*

PACKAGING DIGEST EDICION LATINO AMERICANA.
Cahners Publishing Company (Des Plaines), Division of Reed Elsevier Inc., 1350 E. Touhy Ave., Box 5080, Des Plaines, IL 60018-5080. TEL 847-390-2363. FAX 847-390-2460.
circ. 30,584. *5547*

PACKAGING DIGEST MACHINERY - MATERIALS GUIDE.
Cahners Publishing Company (Des Plaines), Division of Reed Elsevier Inc., 1350 E. Touhy Ave., Box 5080, Des Plaines, IL 60611. TEL 847-635-8800. FAX 847-390-2460.
circ. 109,000. *5547*

PACKAGING DIGEST MARKETPLACE EDITION.
Cahners Publishing Company (Des Plaines), Division of Reed Elsevier Inc., 1350 E. Touhy Ave., Box 5080, Des Plaines, IL 60018-5080. TEL 847-390-2363. FAX 847-635-6858.
circ. 150,000. *5547*

PACKPLAS INTERNATIONAL.
International Printing Communications Ltd., P.O. Box 923, Crownhill Industry, Milton Keynes, Bucks. MK8 0AY, England. TEL 44-1908-561444. FAX 44-1908-569564.
circ. 14,000. *5548*

PADDLER'S PRINT.
Professional Paddlesports Association, Box 248, Butler, KY 41006-0248. TEL 606-472-2205. FAX 606-472-2030.
circ. 750. *6842*

PADOVA ECONOMICA.
Camera di Commercio, Industria, Artigianato e Agricoltura di Padova, Via E. Filiberto 34, Padua, Italy.
circ. 2,000. *1194*

PAEDAGOGISCHE HOCHSCHULE WEINGARTEN. PERSONEN- UND VORLESUNGSVERZEICHNIS.
Paedagogische Hochschule Weingarten, Kirchplatz 2, 88250 Weingarten, Germany. TEL 49-751-501240. FAX 49-751-501200.
circ. 2,500. *1966*

PAGAN DAWN.
Pagan Federation, BM Box 5896, London WC1N 3XX, England. TEL 44-181-891-1302.
circ. 6,000. *6495*

PAINOMAAILMA.
Painomaailma Oy, Loennrotinkatu 11 A, FIN-00120 Helsinki, Finland. TEL 358-9-2287-7242. FAX 358-9-603-914.
circ. 3,000. *6082*

PAINTING AND WALLCOVERING CONTRACTOR.
Finan Publishing Company, Inc., 8730 Big Bend Blvd., St. Louis, MO 63119. TEL 314-961-6644. FAX 314-961-4809.
circ. 31,000. *5554*

EL PAISANO.
Desert Protective Council, Inc., Box 2312, Valley Center, CA 92082-2312. TEL 619-670-7127. FAX 619-749-3485.
circ. 500. *2946*

PAKISTAN. FINANCE DIVISION. SUPPLEMENTARY DEMANDS FOR GRANTS AND APPROPRIATIONS.
Finance Division, Islamabad, Pakistan. *1624*

PAKISTAN. OFFICE OF THE ECONOMIC ADVISER. GOVERNMENT SPONSORED CORPORATIONS AND OTHER INSTITUTIONS.
Office of the Economic Adviser, Islamabad, Pakistan. *1592*

PAKISTAN JOURNAL OF BOTANY.
Pakistan Botanical Society, Dept. of Botany, University of Karachi, Karachi 75270, Pakistan. TEL 92-21-447867. FAX 92-21-466896.
circ. 1,000. *718*

PAKISTAN JOURNAL OF HYDROCARBON RESEARCH.
Hydrocarbon Development Institute of Pakistan, 230 Nizamuddin Rd. F 7-4, P.O. Box 1308, Islamabad, Pakistan. TEL 92-51-823690. FAX 92-51-828773.
circ. 500. *5617*

PAKISTAN JOURNAL OF NEMATOLOGY.
Pakistan Society of Nematologists, National Nematological Research Centre, University of Karachi, Karachi 75270, Pakistan. FAX 92-21-4963373.
circ. 600. *846*

PAKISTAN TEXTILE JOURNAL.
Mazhar Yusuf, Ed. & Pub., 304 Shaheen Centre, Kehkashan, Main Clifton Rd., Karachi, Pakistan. TEL 534792. FAX 572231.
circ. 2,200. *6992*

PALAEONTOLOGIA AFRICANA.
University of the Witwatersrand, Johannesburg, Bernard Price Institute for Palaeontological Research, Wits 2050, South Africa. TEL 27-11-7162870. FAX 27-11-4031423.
circ. 600. *5561*

PALAESTRA.
Via Tiglio S. Biagio, Maddaloni 81024, Italy.
circ. 1,000. *4447*

PALEORIENT.
C N R S Editions, 20-22 rue St. Amand, 75015 Paris, France. TEL 45-33-16-00. FAX 45-33-92-13.
circ. 1,500. *5562*

PALLIATIVE CARE TODAY.
C C T Healthcare Communications Ltd., 50-52 Union St., London SE1 1TD, England. TEL 0171-407-9731. FAX 0171-407-7083.
circ. 8,000. *4985*

PALMER VIDEO MAGAZINE.
Palmer Video Corp., 1767 Morris Ave., Union, NJ 07083. TEL 908-686-3030. FAX 908-686-2151.
circ. 203,915. *2068*

PALMETTO.
Florida Native Plant Society, Box 6116, Spring Hill, FL 34611-6116. TEL 813-856-8202.
circ. 3,500. *3202*

PANGOLIN PAPERS.
Turtle Press, Box 241, Nordland, WA 98358. TEL 360-385-3626.
circ. 500. *4352*

PANNONISCHE FORSCHUNGSSTELLE OBERSCHUETZEN. ARBEITSBERICHTE - MITTEILUNGEN.
Pannonische Forschungsstelle Oberschuetzen, Postfach 12, A-7432 Oberschuetzen, Austria. TEL 43-3353-669340.
circ. 500. *5424*

PAPER AGE.
Global Publications, 77 Waldron Ave., Glen Rock, NJ 07452-2830. TEL 201-666-2262. FAX 201-666-9046.
circ. 31,400. *5568*

PAPER BOOK.
Delta Theta Phi Law Fraternity, International, 666 High St., Ste. 201, Worthington, OH 43085-4135. TEL 614-888-2600. FAX 614-888-7680.
circ. 13,500. *4006*

PAPER, FILM AND FOIL CONVERTER.
Intertec Publishing Corp., 29 N. Wacker Dr., Chicago, IL 60606. TEL 312-726-2802. FAX 312-726-2574.
circ. 39,737. *5548*

PAPER INDUSTRY CHINA.
Sterling Publications Ltd., 86-88 Edgware Rd., London W2 2YW, England. TEL 44-171-915-9600. FAX 44-171-915-9619.
circ. 6,000. *5569*

PAPER INDUSTRY MAGAZINE.
Box 5675, Montgomery, AL 36103-5675. FAX 334-265-4310.
circ. 17,000. *5569*

PAPERWORKER.
United Paperworkers International Union, 3340 Perimeter Hill Dr., Box 1475, Nashville, TN 37202. TEL 615-834-8590. FAX 615-831-6791.
circ. 290,000. *3896*

PAPERWORLD.
American Papermaker, 57 Executive Park South, N.E., No. 3oo, Atlanta, GA 30329-2213. TEL 404-841-3333. FAX 404-841-3332.
circ. 40,000. *5570*

PAPUA NEW GUINEA NATIONAL BIBLIOGRAPHY.
National Library Service, Office of Libraries and Archives, P.O. Box 734, Waigani, N.C.D., Papua New Guinea. FAX 675-3251331.
circ. 280. *560*

PARABAS.
21-B, Quarter-6D, Chittaranjan, West Bengal, India. *4352*

PARENTS NEWS.
10 The Manor Dr., Worcester Park, Surrey KT4 7LG, England. TEL 44-181-337-6337. FAX 44-181-715-2842.
circ. 83,000. *1854*

10376 CONTROLLED CIRCULATION SERIALS

PARIS-ANGLOPHONE.
Anglophone S.A., 32 rue Edouard Vaillant, 93100 Montreuil, France. TEL 33-1-48596658. FAX 33-1-48596668.
circ. 10,000. *1705*

PARISH AND COMMUNITY LIBRARIES NEWS.
Catholic Library Association, Parish Section, Box 16321, St. Paul, MN 55116. FAX 612-690-2131.
circ. 350. *4206*

PARISH MAGAZINE - ARTHUR CONAN DOYLE SOCIETY.
Arthur Conan Doyle Society, c/o Christopher Roden, Ashcroft, 2 Abbotsford Dr., Penyffordd, Ches. CH4 0JG, England. TEL 44-1244-545210.
circ. 350. *4501*

PARK-NICOLLET INSTITUTE FOR RESEARCH AND EDUCATION BULLETIN.
Park Nicollet Medical Center, 5000 W. 39th St, Minneapolis, MN 55416. TEL 612-993-3123.
circ. 11,000. *4727*

PARKING.
National Parking Association, 1112 16th St. N.W., Ste. 300, Washington, DC 20036. TEL 202-296-4336. FAX 202-331-8523.
circ. 5,000. *7112*

PAROISSES ET COMMUNES DE FRANCE.
C N R S Editions, 20-22 rue St. Amand, 75015 Paris, France. TEL 45-33-16-00. FAX 45-33-92-13.
circ. 1,500. *3591*

PARTICIPATION.
International Political Science Association, c/o University College Dublin, Department of Politics, Belfield, Dublin 4, Ireland. TEL 353-1-7068182. FAX 353-1-7061171. *5953*

PASS HERALD LTD.
Crowswest Mall, Blairmore, AB T0K 0E0, Canada. TEL 403-562-2248. FAX 403-562-8379.
circ. 1,255. *3264*

THE PASSING SHOW.
Shubert Archive, 149 W. 45th St., New York, NY 10036. TEL 212-944-3895. FAX 212-944-4139.
circ. 3,000. *7010*

PASSPORT.
Briercrest Family of Schools, 510 College Dr., Caronport, SK S0H 0S0, Canada. TEL 306-756-3200. FAX 306-756-3366.
circ. 27,000. *1966*

PASTE-UP.
Cedar Rapids Stamp Club, Box 2554, Cedar Rapids, IA 52406.
circ. 50. *5710*

PATENT AND TRADEMARK INSTITUTE OF CANADA. ANNUAL PROCEEDINGS.
Patent and Trademark Institute of Canada, Box 1298, Sta. B, Ottawa, ON K1P 5R3, Canada. TEL 613-234-0516. *5588*

PATHWAYS TO HEALTH.
A.R.E. Medical Clinic, 4018 N. 40th St., Phoenix, AZ 85018. TEL 602-955-0551.
circ. 3,500. *5741*

PATINAGRAM.
Potomac Antique Tools and Industries Association, 13004 Clarion Rd., Ft. Washington, MD 20744. TEL 301-292-1606.
circ. 360. *343*

PATOLOGIA.
Obsidiana Editores, S.A., Czda. de Tlalpan 2365, Col. Ciudad Jardin, 04370 Mexico DF, Mexico. TEL 6899133.
circ. 1,370. *619*

PATRE.
Societe de Presse et d'Edition Ovine et Caprine (S.P.E.O.C.), 19 quai de Juillet, B.P. 18, 14005 Caen Cedex, France. TEL 33-2-31357704. FAX 33-2-31822963.
circ. 5,300. *284*

PATRIOT (ASHLAND).
Runaway Publications, Box 1172, Ashland, OR 97520-0040. TEL 503-482-2578.
circ. 100. *4517*

PAVEMENT MAINTENANCE AND RECONSTRUCTION.
Johnson Hill Press, Inc., 1233 Janesville Ave., Ft. Atkinson, WI 53538. TEL 920-563-6388. FAX 920-563-1702.
circ. 20,000. *2795*

PAYLOAD ASIA.
Asian Media Services Ltd., P.O. Box 3580, GPO Hong Kong, Hong Kong, People's Republic of China. TEL 852-893-3676. FAX 852-893-3676.
circ. 12,500. *7076*

PEABODY NEWS.
Johns Hopkins University, Peabody Institute, 1 E. Mt. Vernon Place, Baltimore, MD 21202-2397. TEL 301-659-8163. FAX 301-783-8576.
circ. 25,000. *1966*

PEABODY REFLECTOR.
George Peabody College for Teachers, Alumni Association, Box 161, Nashville, TN 37203. TEL 615-322-2601.
circ. 25,000. *1966*

PEACE CORPS TIMES.
U.S. Peace Corps, 1990 K St., N.W., Washington, DC 20526. TEL 202-254-3371. FAX 202-606-3110.
circ. 19,000. *1366*

THE PEANUT FARMER.
SpecComm International, Inc., 3000 Highwoods Blvd., Ste. 300, Raleigh, NC 27604-1029. TEL 919-872-5040. FAX 919-876-6531.
circ. 20,000. *237*

THE PEANUT GROWER.
Vance Publishing Corporation, Box 83, Tifton, GA 31793. TEL 912-386-8591. FAX 912-386-9772.
circ. 22,500. *237*

PEARLS OF WISDOM.
Summit Lighthouse, Box 5000, Corwin Springs, MT 59030-5000. TEL 406-222-8300. FAX 406-222-8307. *5741*

PEAT ABSTRACTS.
Bord na Mona, Peat Research Centre, Droichead Nua, Co. Kildare, Ireland. TEL 353-45-31201. FAX 353-45-33240.
circ. 210. *5321*

PEDIATRIA MODERNA.
Grupo Editorial Moreira Jr., Rua Henrique Martins 493, 04504 Sao Paulo SP, Brazil. TEL 55-11-8849911. FAX 55-11-8849993.
circ. 12,000. *5036*

PEDIATRICIAN.
Educational Programs, Inc., 261 Old York Rd., Ste. 831, Jenkintown, PA 19046-3255. TEL 215-635-1700.
circ. 10,565. *5038*

PEDIATRIKA.
Alpe Editores, S.A., Pedro Rico, 27, 28029 Madrid, Spain. TEL 34-1-7338811. FAX 34-1-3159652.
circ. 6,500. *5039*

PEDOLOGIST.
Japanese Society of Pedology, c/o National Institute of Agro-Environmental Sciences, 3-1-1 Kannondai, Tsukuba, Ibaraki 305, Japan. TEL 81-298-38-8275. FAX 81-298-38-8199.
circ. 700. *238*

PENMEN'S NEWS LETTER.
Eileen Richardson, Ed. & Pub., 34 Broadway Ave., Ottawa, ON K1S 2V6, Canada. TEL 613-232-3014.
circ. 300. *2472*

PENN LINES.
Pennsylvania Rural Electric Association, Box 1266, 212 Locust St., Harrisburg, PA 17108. TEL 717-233-5704. FAX 717-234-1309.
circ. 176,000. *3382*

PENNSYLVANIA. CRIME COMMISSION. REPORT.
Crime Commission, 1800 Elmerton Ave., 3rd Fl., Harrisburg, PA 17110-9718. TEL 215-834-1164. FAX 215-834-0737.
circ. 40,000. *2275*

PENNSYLVANIA A F L - C I O NEWS.
c/o David H. Wilderman, Dir., 230 State St., Harrisburg, PA 17101. TEL 717-238-9351. FAX 717-238-8541.
circ. 10,000. *3896*

PENNSYLVANIA ECONOMIC REVIEW.
Pennsylvania Economic Association, Economics Dept., Millersville University, Box 1002, Millersville, PA 17551. TEL 717-872-3561. FAX 717-871-2326.
circ. 200. *991*

PENNSYLVANIA LAWYER.
Pennsylvania Bar Association, 100 South St., Harrisburg, PA 17108. TEL 717-238-6715. FAX 717-238-7182.
circ. 30,000. *4007*

PENNSYLVANIA MESSAGE.
Pennsylvania Association for Retarded Citizens, Inc., 2001 N. Front St., Ste. 221, Harrisburg, PA 17102-2104. FAX 717-234-7615.
circ. 8,500. *2588*

PENNSYLVANIA OSTEOPATHIC MEDICAL ASSOCIATION. JOURNAL.
Pennsylvania Osteopathic Medical Association, 1330 Eisenhower Blvd., Harrisburg, PA 17111. TEL 717-939-9318. FAX 717-939-7255.
circ. 3,400. *4728*

PENNSYLVANIA PRINCIPAL.
Pennsylvania Association of Secondary School Principals, 801 N. Second St., Harrisburg, PA 17102-3297. TEL 717-233-3001.
circ. 3,200. *2472*

PENNTRUX.
Pennsylvania Motor Truck Association, 910 Linda Ln, Camp Hill, PA 17011-6401. TEL 717-761-7122. FAX 717-761-8434.
circ. 2,500. *7177*

THE PENSION ACTUARY.
American Society of Pension Actuaries, 4350 N. Fairfax Dr., Ste. 820, Arlington, VA 22203-1619. TEL 703-516-9300. FAX 703-519-9308.
circ. 4,200. *3829*

PEOPLE & THE PLANET.
Planet 21, 1 Woburn Walk, London WC1H 0JJ, England. TEL 44-171-383-4388. FAX 44-171-388-2398.
circ. 20,000. *6055*

PEOPLES SPECTATOR.
2-17 Hollywood Ave., Bondi Junction, N.S.W. 2022, Australia.
circ. 40,000. *3251*

PEPEROMIA AND EXOTIC PLANT SOCIETY. GAZETTE.
Peperomia and Exotic Plant Society, 4278 N. Hazel St., Apt. 8C, Chicago, IL 60613.
circ. 75. *3202*

PEPPER'N SALT.
Standard Schnauzer Club of America, 1884 W. Lake Storey Rd., Galesburg, IL 61401. TEL 309-344-1140.
circ. 600. *5640*

PERCEPTIVE REPORT.
Perceptive Marketers Agency, Ltd., 1100 E. Hector St., Ste. 301, Conshohocken, PA 19428. TEL 610-825-8710. FAX 610-825-9186.
circ. 500. *1544*

PERFORMANCE.
Detroit Symphony Orchestra Hall, 28400 Northwestern Hwy., Ste. 200, Southfield, MI 48034-8347. TEL 313-963-8500. FAX 313-963-3664.
circ. 85,000. *5425*

PERFORMANCE.
Phillips Petroleum Co. UK Ltd., 35 Guildford Rd., Woking, Surrey GU22 7QT, England. TEL 01483-752657. FAX 01483-752607.
circ. 5,000. *5617*

PERFORMER.
National Ballet of Canada, 470 Queens Quay W., Toronto, ON M5V 3KA, Canada. TEL 416-345-9686. FAX 416-345-8323.
circ. 14,000. *2295*

PERFORMING ARTS.
Performing Arts Network, 10350 Santa Monica Blvd., Ste. 350, Los Angeles, CA 90025. TEL 310-839-8000. FAX 310-839-5651.
circ. 700,000. *7010*

CONTROLLED CIRCULATION SERIALS 10377

PERFORMING ARTS BUYERS GUIDE: FOOTNOTES.
Stagestep, 2000 Hamilton St., Ste. C200, Philadelphia, PA 19130. TEL 215-636-9000. FAX 800-877-3342.
circ. 300,000. *2295*

PERFUMERY.
I C O International, 3A Barbanou, P.O. Box 190 25, 117 10 Athens, Greece. TEL 30-1-9017-806. FAX 30-1-9016-663.
circ. 10,000. *512*

LOS PERROS DEL MUNDO.
Publitecnic S.A., Calle 4, no. 188, Apdo. Postal 74-290, 09070 Mexico DF, Mexico. TEL 685-28-19. FAX 67-06318.
circ. 10,000. *5640*

PERSONAL ENGINEERING & INSTRUMENTATION NEWS.
P E C Inc., Box 430, Rye, NH 03870-0430. TEL 603-427-1377. FAX 603-427-1388.
circ. 50,000. *2204*

PERSPECTIVAS EM CIENCIA DA INFORMACAO.
Universidade Federal de Minas Gerais, Escola de Biblioteconomia, Caixa Postal 1606, 30161-970, Belo Horizonte MG, Brazil. TEL 55-31-4995227. FAX 55-31-4995200.
circ. 500. *4206*

PERSPECTIVE (INDIANAPOLIS).
Resort Condominiums International, Inc., Box 80229, Indianapolis, IN 46280-0229. TEL 317-871-9641. FAX 317-871-9507.
circ. 7,000. *6308*

PERSPECTIVES.
Chambre Francaise de Commerce et d'Industrie de Madrid, C. Ruiz de Alarcon, 7, 28014 Madrid, Spain. TEL 34-1-5226742. FAX 34-1-5233642.
circ. 2,200. *1194*

PERSPECTIVES ON MEDICAL RESEARCH.
Medical Research Modernization Committee, Box 2751, New York, NY 10163. TEL 216-832-3904. FAX 216-283-6702.
circ. 1,200. *4901*

PESARO CITTA E CONTA.
Societa Pesarese di Studi Storici, Via Abbati 30, Casella 9, 61100 Pesaro, Italy. TEL 39-721-34411.
circ. 800. *3591*

PESQUISA AGROPECUARIA BRASILEIRA.
Empresa Brasileira de Pesquisa Agropecuaria, Servico de Producao e Informacao, Caixa Postal 040315, 70770-901 Brasilia D.F., Brazil. TEL 55-61-2739616. FAX 55-61-2724168.
circ. 1,600. *145*

PESQUISA MEDICA.
Fundacao Faculdade Federal de Ciencias Medicas de Porto Alegre, Centro Academico XXII de Marco, Rua Sarmento Leite, 245, 90050-170 Porto Alegre RS, Brazil. TEL 55-512-2248822. FAX 55-512-2267913.
circ. 1,000. *4729*

PEST MANAGEMENT.
National Pest Control Association, 8100 Oak St., Dunn Loring, VA 22027. TEL 703-573-8330. FAX 703-573-4116.
circ. 5,500. *759*

PET FOCUS.
Focus Publications, Inc., Box 609, Windham, ME 04038. TEL 207-893-0058. FAX 207-893-1077.
circ. 105,000. *5641*

PET PRODUCT NEWS.
Fancy Publications, 3 Burroughs, Irvine, CA 92618-2804. TEL 714-855-8822. FAX 714-855-3045. *5641*

PET SERVICES JOURNAL.
American Boarding Kennels Association, 4575 Galley Rd., Ste. 400A, Colorado Springs, CO 80915. TEL 719-591-1113. FAX 719-579-0006.
circ. 1,700. *5641*

PETROLEUM MARKETER.
G C I Publishing Co., Inc., 1801 Rockville Pike, Ste. 330, Rockville, MD 20852. TEL 301-984-7333.
circ. 17,000. *5618*

PETS QUARTERLY MAGAZINE.
P Q M, 151 - 8333 Jones Rd., Richmond, BC V6Y 1L5, Canada. TEL 604-244-7450. FAX 604-244-7450.
circ. 31,400. *5641*

PETSPECTIVES.
American Professional Pet Distributors, Inc., c/o Opan Featherson; Royale Kennel, RR 1, Whiting, KS 66552. TEL 612-293-1049.
circ. 1,000. *5641*

PFLANZENSCHUTZ KURIER.
Bayer AG, Geschaeftsbereich Pflanzenschutz, 51368 Leverkusen, Germany.
circ. 168,000. *239*

PHARE.
BFC Bagotville, B.P. 369, Alouette, PQ G0V 1A0, Canada. TEL 418-677-8160. FAX 418-677-8480.
circ. 3,000. *5281*

PHARMA SELECTA.
Stichting Pharma Selecta, Postbus 122, 8430 Oosterwolde, Netherlands. TEL 31-597-646812. FAX 31-597-645174.
circ. 2,800. *5683*

PHARMACEUTICAL MANUFACTURING INTERNATIONAL.
Sterling Publications Ltd., 86-88 Edgware Rd., London W2 2YW, England. TEL 44-171-915-9600. FAX 44-171-915-9619.
circ. 10,000. *5685*

PHARMACEUTICAL MEDICINE (WORTHING).
Cambridge Medical Publications Ltd., Wicker House, High St., Worthing, W. Sussex BN11 1DJ, England. TEL 01903-205884. FAX 01903-234862. *4729*

PHARMACEUTICAL TECHNOLOGY EUROPE - BIOPHARM.
Advanstar Communications, Advanstar House, Park West, Sealand Rd., Chester CH1 4RN, England. TEL 44-1244-378888. FAX 44-1244-370512.
circ. 19,000. *5685*

PHARMACEUTISCH WEEKBLAD.
Koninklijke Nederlandse Maatschappij ter Bevordering der Pharmacie, Alexanderstraat 11, 2514 JL The Hague, Netherlands. TEL 31-70-3624111. FAX 31-70-3106530.
circ. 4,000. *5686*

THE PHARMACIST.
Mediselect B.V., Postbus 28091, 3828 ZH Hoogland, Netherlands. TEL 31-33-4808020. FAX 31-33-4805881. *5686*

PHARMACOTHERAPY.
Pharmacotherapy Publications, Inc., New England Medical Center - Box 806, 750 Washington St., Boston, MA 02111. TEL 617-636-5390. FAX 617-636-5318.
circ. 292. *5688*

PHARMACTUEL.
Association des Pharmaciens des Etablissements de Sante du Quebec, 1470 Peel, Tour B, Bureau 900, Montreal, PQ H3A 1T1, Canada. TEL 514-286-0776. FAX 514-286-1081.
circ. 1,800. *5688*

PHARMACY NEWS.
Rajesh Publications, 1 Ansari Rd., Daryaganj, Dew Delhi 110 002, India.
circ. 12,000. *5688*

PHARMACY PRODUCTS REVIEW.
Cosmetics Communications Ltd., 335 Linen Hall, 162-168 Regent St., London W1R 5TB, England. TEL 44-171-434-1530. FAX 44-171-437-0915.
circ. 15,000. *5688*

PHARMACY TODAY.
American Pharmaceutical Association, 2215 Constitution Ave., N.W., Washington, DC 20037. TEL 202-628-4410. FAX 202-628-5425.
circ. 40,000. *5689*

PHARMACY TODAY.
Miller Freeman Publishers Ltd., Sovereign Way, Tonbridge, Kent TN9 1RW, England. TEL 01732-364422. FAX 01732-361534.
circ. 9,969. *5689*

PHARMACY WEEK.
Pharmacy Week, 7 N. Plackney St., No. 345, Madison, WI 53701-0552. TEL 608-251-1112. FAX 608-251-1155.
circ. 11,500. *5689*

PHI ALPHA DELTA REPORTER.
Phi Alpha Delta, 10722 White Oak Ave., Granda Hills, CA 91344-4698. TEL 818-360-1941. FAX 818-363-5851.
circ. 95,000. *1935*

PHI RHO SIGMA. JOURNAL.
Phi Rho Sigma Medical Society, Box 90264, Indianapolis, IN 46290-0264. TEL 317-255-4379. FAX 317-253-5067.
circ. 16,000. *1966*

PHILADELPHIA MEDICINE.
Philadelphia County Medical Society, 2100 Spring Garden St., Philadelphia, PA 19130. TEL 215-563-5343. FAX 215-563-3627.
circ. 4,300. *4729*

PHILALETHES.
Philalethes Society, Drawer 70, 110 Quince Ave., Highland Springs, VA 23075. TEL 804-737-4498.
circ. 4,800. *1935*

PHILATELIC FOUNDATION QUARTERLY.
Philatelic Foundation, 501 Fifth Ave., No. 1901, New York, NY 10017-6103. TEL 212-867-3699. FAX 212-867-3984.
circ. 1,700. *5711*

PHILIPPINE INSURANCE COMMISSION. ANNUAL REPORT.
Insurance Commission, Insurance Commission Bldg., 1071 United Nations Ave., P.O. Box 3589, Manila, Philippines. TEL 632-523-84-61. FAX 632-522-1434.
circ. 320. *3829*

PHILIPPINES. FOOD AND NUTRITION RESEARCH INSTITUTE. ANNUAL REPORT.
Food and Nutrition Research Institute, Science Complex, Bicutan, Tagig, Metro Manila 1604, Philippines. TEL 837-89-34. FAX 837-89-34. *5481*

PHILIPPINES. NATIONAL MUSEUM PAPERS.
National Museum of the Philippines, Padre Burgos St., Manila, Philippines. TEL 632-527-12-15. FAX 632-530-03-06.
circ. 500. *5364*

THE PHILIPPINES: NEWS AND VIEWS.
Philippine Embassy, 1617 Massachusetts Ave., N.W., Washington, DC 20036. TEL 202-483-1414.
circ. 1,000. *6032*

THE PHILOSOPHER'S STONE.
Winged Feet Productions, 59 Masons Rd., Hemel Hempstead, Herts HP2 4QU, England. TEL 44-1442-391333.
circ. 100. *5577*

PHOENIX (MANCHESTER).
C S U Ltd., Armstrong House, Oxford Rd., Manchester M1 7ED, England. TEL 44-161-236-9816. FAX 44-161-236-8541.
circ. 1,200. *5514*

PHOENIX TIMES.
Sam Weller Associates, 139 Kensington High St., London W8 6SU, England. TEL 44-171-937-0052. FAX 44-171-937-1393.
circ. 3,650. *3178*

PHOENIX: VOICE OF THE SCRAP RECYCLING INDUSTRIES.
Institute of Scrap Recycling Industries, Inc., 1325 G St., Ste. 1000, Washington, DC 20005. TEL 202-737-1770. FAX 202-626-0900.
circ. 45,000. *2946*

PHOTO DISTRICT NEWS.
B P I Communications, Inc. (New York), 1515 Broadway, New York, NY 10036. TEL 212-764-7300. FAX 212-944-1719.
circ. 20,000. *5770*

PHOTO VIDEO AUDIO NEWS (FRENCH EDITION).
Mema N.V., Wielewaalstraat 20, 2610 Wilrijk, Belgium. TEL 32-3-4480827. FAX 32-3-4480832.
circ. 6,000. *5771*

10378 CONTROLLED CIRCULATION SERIALS

PHOTOBULLETIN DAILY.
PhotoSource International, 1910 35th Rd., Pine Lake Farm, Osceola, WI 54020. TEL 715-248-3800. FAX 715-248-7394. *5771*

PHOTOFILE.
Australian Centre for Photography, 257 Oxford St., Paddington, N.S.W. 2021, Australia. TEL 61-2-3321455. FAX 61-2-3316887.
circ. 5,000. *5771*

PHOTOGRAMMETRIC COYOTE.
E. Coyote Enterprises, Inc., Rt. 3, Bldg. 228, Box 1119, Mineral Wells, TX 76067. TEL 817-325-0757.
circ. 10,000. *3417*

PHOTOGRAPHIC JOURNAL.
Royal Photographic Society of Great Britain, Acorn House, 74-94 Cherry Orchard Dr., Croydon CR0 6BA, England. TEL 44-181-681-8339. FAX 44-181-681-1880.
circ. 10,000. *5772*

PHOTOGRAPHICA.
American Photographic Historical Society, 1150 Sixth Ave., 3rd Fl., New York, NY 10036-2701. TEL 212-575-0483.
circ. 500. *5772*

PHOTOGRAPHY.
Devin - Adair Publishers, Inc., Box A, Old Greenwich, CT 06807. TEL 203-531-7755. FAX 203-622-6688.
circ. 4,800. *5772*

PHOTONICS SPECTRA.
Laurin Publishing Co., Inc., Box 4949, Berkshire Common, Pittsfield, MA 01202-4949. TEL 413-499-0514. FAX 413-442-3180.
circ. 85,000. *5869*

PHYSICIANS' DESK REFERENCE.
Medical Economics Publishing Co., Inc., 5 Paragon Dr., Montvale, NJ 07645. TEL 201-358-7200. FAX 201-573-1045.
circ. 485,000. *4729*

PHYSICIANS' DESK REFERENCE FOR NONPRESCRIPTION DRUGS.
Medical Economics Publishing Co., Inc., 5 Paragon Dr., Montvale, NJ 07645. TEL 201-358-7200. FAX 201-573-1045.
circ. 315,000. *4729*

PHYSICIANS LIFESTYLE MAGAZINE.
K & K Publishing, Inc., 19 W. 34th St., Ste. 1010, New York, NY 10001-3006. TEL 212-643-0991. *3382*

PHYTON.
Fundacion Romulo Raggio, Gaspar Campos 861, 1638 Vicente Lopez, Argentina. TEL 54-1-791-0868. FAX 54-1-796-1456.
circ. 750. *720*

PIANO - HARPA.
Odilia Publishing Ltd., Dorneckstr. 105, CH-4143 Dornach, Switzerland. TEL 41-61-7018866. FAX 41-61-7018858.
circ. 1,500. *5426*

PICTOU ADVOCATE.
82 Church St., P.O. Box 1000, Pictou, NS B0K 1H0, Canada. TEL 902-485-8014. FAX 902-752-4816.
circ. 188. *3265*

PIG INDUSTRY.
B C Publications, 16C Market Pl., Diss, Norfolk IP22 3AB, England. TEL 44-1379-644200. FAX 44-1379-650480.
circ. 7,800. *145*

PIG INTERNATIONAL.
Watt Publishing Co., 122 S. Wesley Ave., Mt. Morris, IL 61054. TEL 815-734-4171. FAX 815-734-4201.
circ. 20,000. *285*

THE PILOT LOG.
Pilot International, 244 College Street, Macon, GA 31201. TEL 912-743-7403. FAX 912-743-2173.
circ. 17,500. *1935*

PINELLAS COUNTY REVIEW.
Warfield Media Co., Box 6130, Clearwater, FL 34618-6130. TEL 813-724-1112.
circ. 10,000. *991*

PINKER MODA.
Ediciones Tecnicas Doria, Avda. Puerta del Angel 7, Sobreat. A y B, 08002 Barcelona, Spain. TEL 34-3-3187489. FAX 34-3-3011105.
circ. 12,000. *6992*

PINT - NIEUWS.
Pint, P.O. Box 3757, 1001 AN Amsterdam, Netherlands. TEL 31-252-522909. FAX 31-10-4112879.
circ. 6,500. *526*

THE PIONEER.
Church Army in Australia, 75 Hawkesbury Rd., Wetmead, N.S.W. 2145, Australia. TEL 61-2-6355669.
circ. 4,000. *6437*

PIONIER.
C A M A - Zending, Amersfoortseweg 44, 3951 LC Maarn, Netherlands. TEL 31-343-443392. FAX 31-343-441404.
circ. 5,900. *6437*

PIPE DREAM.
State University of New York at Binghamton, University Union, No.168, Binghamton, NY 13902. TEL 607-777-2515. FAX 607-777-2600.
circ. 9,000. *1967*

THE PIPE SMOKER'S EPHEMERIS.
Tom Dunn, Ed. & Pub., 20-37 120th St., College Point, NY 11356-2128.
circ. 7,500. *7020*

PIPELINES.
Plumbers - Steamfitters U A Local 38, 1621 Market St., San Francisco, CA 94103. TEL 415-626-2000.
circ. 3,000. *3896*

PIRKKA.
Kauppiaitten Kustannus Oy, Kanavakatu 3.B, FIN-00160 Helsinki, Finland. TEL 358-0-1053010. FAX 358-0-105336235.
circ. 2,300,000. *1545*

PITT MAGAZINE.
University of Pittsburgh, Department of University Relations, 400 Craig Hall, Pittsburgh, PA 15260. TEL 412-624-4147. FAX 412-624-1021.
circ. 125,000. *1967*

PITTSBURGH LEGAL JOURNAL (MONTHLY EDITION).
Allegheny County Bar Association, 436 7th Ave., Ste. 400, Pittsburgh, PA 15219-1818. TEL 412-261-6161. FAX 412-261-3622.
circ. 7,900. *4008*

PITTSBURGH MUSICIAN.
Pittsburgh Musicians Union, Local No.60-471, A.F.M., 709 Forbes Ave., Pittsburgh, PA 15219. TEL 412-281-1822.
circ. 1,200. *5426*

PIVOT.
250 Riverside Dr., Apt. No. 23, New York, NY 10025. TEL 212-222-1408.
circ. 1,500. *4518*

PLACE OF GRADUATION.
University of British Columbia, Centre for Health Services and Policy Research, No. 429 - 2194 Health Sciences Mall, Vancouver, BC V6T 1Z3, Canada. TEL 604-822-4810. FAX 604-822-5690.
circ. 200. *4730*

PLAISANCIERS.
970 Montee de Liesse, Ville St-Laurent, PQ H4T 1W7, Canada. TEL 514-856-0788.
circ. 20,000. *6842*

PLAN AND ACTION.
Stichting Mensen in Nood - Caritas Nederland., Postbus 1041, 5200 BA 's-Hertogenbosch, Netherlands. TEL 31-73-6456789. FAX 31-73-6456700.
circ. 2,000. *6681*

PLANNING IN NORTHEASTERN ILLINOIS.
Northeastern Illinois Planning Commission, 222 S. Riverside Plz., Ste. 1800, Chicago, IL 60606-6001. TEL 312-454-0400. FAX 312-454-0411.
circ. 9,500. *3756*

PLANT ENGINEERING PRODUCT SUPPLIER GUIDE.
Cahners Publishing Company (Des Plaines), Division of Reed Elsevier Inc., 1350 E. Touhy Ave., Box 5080, Des Plaines, IL 60018-5080. TEL 847-635-8800. FAX 847-390-2636. *2736*

PLANT EQUIPMENT HIRE & RATE REVIEW.
Brooke Pattrick (Pty) Ltd., P.O. Box 422, Bedfordview 2008, South Africa. TEL 27-11-6224666. FAX 27-11-6167196.
circ. 4,100. *1593*

PLANT GENETIC RESOURCES NEWSLETTER.
International Plant Genetic Resources Institute, Via delle Sette Chiese 142, 00145 Rome, Italy. TEL 39-6-51892233. FAX 39-6-575009.
circ. 5,000. *2242*

PLANTS, SITES & PARKS.
B P I Communications, 49 Music Sq., W., Nashville, TN 37203. TEL 615-329-4940. FAX 615-329-4733.
circ. 40,500. *1593*

PLAST PANORAMA SCANDINAVIA.
Teknisk Forlag A-S, Skelbaekgade 4, DK-1780 Copenhagen V, Denmark. TEL 45-31-21-68-01. FAX 45-31-21-04-01.
circ. 4,447. *5881*

PLASTERER AND CEMENT MASON.
Plasterers & Cement Masons International, 14405 Laurel Pl., Ste. 300, Laurel, MD 20707-6102.
circ. 40,000. *3896*

PLASTICHEM.
Singapore Polytechnic Polymer Society, Dover Rd., Singapore 5, Singapore.
circ. 1,000. *2770*

PLASTICS AND RUBBER WEEKLY.
E M A P Maclaren Ltd., 19 Scarbrook Rd., Croydon, Surrey CR9 1QH, England. TEL 0181-760-9690. FAX 0181-681-1672.
circ. 20,584. *5882*

THE PLASTICS DISTRIBUTOR & FABRICATOR MAGAZINE.
P M D Publishing Inc., 2701 N. Pulaski Rd., Chicago, IL 60639-2119. TEL 773-235-3800. FAX 773-235-7204.
circ. 25,000. *5882*

PLASTICS TECHNOLOGY.
Bill Communications, Inc., 355 Park Ave. S., 5th Fl., New York, NY 10010-1789. TEL 212-592-6200. FAX 212-592-6339.
circ. 48,334. *5883*

PLASTIQUES MODERNES ET ELASTOMERES.
Editions Montmartre, 142 rue Montmartre, 75002 Paris, France. TEL 33-1-40268321. FAX 33-1-40399752.
circ. 5,000. *5884*

PLASTVERARBEITER.
Huethig GmbH, Postfach 102869, 69018 Heidelberg, Germany. TEL 49-6221-489230. FAX 49-6221-489481.
circ. 12,664. *5884*

PLAY GOLF (NEDERLANDSE EDITIE).
Play Golf S.A., Rue du Chatelain 49, 1050 Brussels, Belgium. TEL 32-2-6471750. FAX 32-2-6482989. *6814*

PLAYBACK.
Brunico Communications Inc., 366 Adelaide St. W., Ste. 500, Toronto, ON M5V 1R9, Canada. TEL 416-408-2300. FAX 416-408-0870.
circ. 9,800. *2056*

PLAYBACK (CARLSBAD).
National Association of Music Merchants Inc., 5790 Armada Dr., Carlsbad, CA 92008. TEL 760-438-8001.
circ. 10,500. *5426*

PLAYTIMES.
Playgroup Association of Queensland, 396 Milton Rd., Auchenflower, Qld. 4066, Australia. TEL 61-7-3718253. FAX 61-7-8700569.
circ. 18,000. *1854*

PLAZA DE LA CONSTITUCION.
Ayuntamiento, Plaza de la Constitucion, 28700 San Sebastian de los Reyes, Spain. TEL 1-6526200.
circ. 15,000. *6222*

PLEIN CHANT.
Editions Plein Chant, Bassac, 16120 Chateauneuf-sur-Charente, France. TEL 16-45-81-93-26. FAX 16-45-81-92-83.
circ. 1,000. *4450*

PLUG.
Kunst en Cultuur Noordholland, Postbus 5348, 2000 GH Haarlem, Netherlands. TEL 31-23-5319139. FAX 31-23-5315284.
circ. 35,000. *7011*

PLUMBING ENGINEER.
T M B Publishing, 1884 Techny Ct., Northbrook, IL 60062. TEL 847-564-1127. FAX 847-564-1264.
circ. 23,000. *3483*

PLYMOUTH COUNTY BUSINESS REVIEW.
Plymouth County Development Council, Box 1620, Pembroke, MA 02359. TEL 617-826-3136. FAX 617-826-0444.
circ. 5,000. *1215*

PLYMOUTH COUNTY HEALTH UPDATE.
Larry Fox Associates, Inc., Box 918, Dennis, MA 02638. TEL 508-760-2761. FAX 508-771-3745.
circ. 120,000. *5788*

PNEURAMA.
Promotec s.r.l., Via A.G. Ragazzi 9, 40011 Anzola dell'Emilia (BO), Italy. TEL 39-51-733000. FAX 39-51-731886.
circ. 15,000. *6503*

PODIATRIC PRODUCTS.
Novicom, Inc., 20000 Mariner Ave., Ste. 480, Torrance, CA 90503. TEL 310-793-4141. FAX 310-793-4138.
circ. 13,000. *5014*

PODIATRY TODAY.
Dowden Publishing Company, 110 Summit Ave., Montvale, NJ 07625. TEL 201-391-2778. FAX 202-391-2778.
circ. 16,995. *5014*

POET (MISHAWAKA).
Fine Arts Society, 2314 W. Sixth St., Mishawaka, IN 46544.
circ. 1,000. *4518*

POETRY KANTO.
Kanto Poetry Center, Kanto Gakuin University, Kamariya-cho, Kanazawa-ku, Yokohama 236, Japan. TEL 81-45-781-2001.
circ. 800. *4519*

POETS' ROUNDTABLE.
826 S. Center St., Terre Haute, IN 47807. TEL 812-234-0819.
circ. 2,000. *4520*

THE POET'S VOICE.
Universitaet Salzburg, Institut fuer Anglistik und Amerikanistik, Akademiestr. 24, A-5020 Salzburg, Austria.
circ. 150. *4520*

POINT OF VIEW.
Holt Renfrew & Co., Limited, 50 Bloor St., W., Toronto, Ont. M4W 1A1, Canada. TEL 416-922-2333. FAX 416-922-3240.
circ. 150,000. *1926*

POINTS NORTH.
North Country Reference & Research Resources Council, 7 Commerce Ln., Canton, NY 13617. TEL 315-386-4569. FAX 315-379-9553.
circ. 200. *4206*

POLICE AND SECURITY NEWS.
Days Communications Inc., 1690 Quarry Rd., Box 330, Kulpsville, PA 19443. TEL 215-362-2233. FAX 215-368-9955.
circ. 20,960. *2276*

POLICE MARTIAL ARTS ASSOCIATION NEWS.
Police Martial Arts Association, P.O. Box 7303, Sub 12, Riverview, NB E1B 4T9, Canada. TEL 506-387-5126. FAX 506-387-5126.
circ. 1,000. *2276*

POLICE OFFICERS JOURNAL.
Dale Corporation, 22150 W. Nine Mile Rd., Southfield, MI 48034-6007. TEL 248-204-2244. FAX 248-204-2240.
circ. 5,000. *2276*

POLIMERY W MEDYCYNIE.
Akademia Medyczna we Wroclawiu, Zaklad Chirurgii Eksperymentalnej i Badania Biomaterialow, Ul. Poniatowskiego 2, 50-326 Wroclaw, Poland. TEL 48-71-226310. FAX 48-71-215729.
circ. 200. *1820*

POLISH AMERICAN JOURNAL.
Panagraphics Corporation, 1275 Harlem Rd., Buffalo, NY 14206-1960. TEL 716-893-5771. FAX 716-893-5783.
circ. 3,000. *3036*

POLISH AMERICAN WORLD.
3100 Grand Blvd., Baldwin, NY 11510. TEL 516-223-6514. FAX 516-868-6618.
circ. 10,000. *3036*

POLITISCHES DENKEN JAHRBUCH (YEAR).
Verlag J.B. Metzler, Postfach 103241, 70028 Stuttgart, Germany. TEL 49-711-2194-0. FAX 49-711-2194119.
circ. 450. *4354*

POLLUTION ATMOSPHERIQUE.
Association pour la Prevention de la Pollution Atmospherique, 58 rue du Rocher, 75008 Paris, France. TEL 33-1-42936930. FAX 33-1-42934199.
circ. 2,000. *2971*

POLLUTION ENGINEERING.
Cahners Publishing Company (Des Plaines), Division of Reed Elsevier Inc., 1350 E. Touhy Ave., Box 5080, Des Plaines, IL 60018-5080. TEL 847-390-2611. FAX 847-390-2636.
circ. 58,800. *2971*

POLLUTION PREVENTION IN SOUTH CAROLINA.
Institute of Public Affairs, University of South Carolina, 1422 Carolina Plaza, 937 Assembly St., Columbia, SC 29208. TEL 803-777-8157. FAX 803-777-4575.
circ. 4,778. *2988*

PONDICHERRY INDUSTRIAL PROMOTION, DEVELOPMENT AND INVESTMENT CORPORATION. ANNUAL REPORTS AND ACCOUNTS.
Pondicherry Industrial Promotion, Development and Investment Corporation Ltd., 38 Romain Rolland St, Pondicherry 605001, India. *1215*

POPULAR ASTRONOMY.
Society for Popular Astronomy, 36 Fairway, Keyworth, Nottingham NG12 5DU, England. *499*

POR ESCRITO.
Editorial Unidifusion, Av. Mexico 3150, Monraz, 44670 Guadalajara, Jalisco, Mexico. TEL 3-813-1415. FAX 3-813-1465.
circ. 1,500. *3335*

PORK REPORT.
National Pork Producers Council, Box 10383, Des Moines, IA 50306. TEL 515-223-2600. FAX 513-223-2646.
circ. 109,000. *285*

PORK REPORT.
S P I Marketing Group, 502 45th St. W., 2nd Fl., Saskatoon, SK S7L 6H2, Canada. TEL 306-653-3014. FAX 306-244-2918.
circ. 2,100. *285*

PORN FREE.
Abby Ehmann, Ed. & Pub., Box 1365, Stuyvesant Sta., New York, NY 10009. TEL 212-598-4343.
circ. 500. *5181*

PORT OF BALTIMORE MAGAZINE.
Maryland Port Administration, Media Two, 1031 Cromwell Bridge Rd., Baltimore, MD 21286. TEL 410-828-0120. FAX 410-825-3463.
circ. 11,000. *7161*

PORT OF NEW ORLEANS ANNUAL DIRECTORY.
New Orleans Publishing Group, 111 Vetrans Blvd., Ste. 1810, Metairie, LA 70005. TEL 504-834-9292. FAX 504-837-2258.
circ. 10,300. *7037*

PORT OF ROTTERDAM MAGAZINE (NEDERLANDSE EDITIE).
FHp BV, Keizergracht 743, 1017 DZ Amsterdam, Netherlands. TEL 31-10-4896508.
circ. 16,000. *7162*

PORT PROGRESS NEWS AND EVENTS.
Port of Oakland, 530 Water St., Oakland, CA 94607. TEL 510-272-1100. FAX 510-272-1172.
circ. 15,000. *7162*

PORTLAND ART MUSEUM NEWSLETTER.
Portland Art Museum, 1219 S.W. Park Ave., Portland, OR 97205. TEL 503-226-2811. FAX 503-226-2842.
circ. 20,000. *5364*

PORTSIDE.
Port of Portland, Box 3529, Portland, OR 97208. TEL 503-231-5000.
circ. 10,000. *7162*

PORTUGAL. INSTITUTO NACIONAL DE ESTATISTICA. SERIE ESTATISTICAS REGIONAIS.
Instituto Nacional de Estatistica, Ave. Antonio Jose de Almeida, 1078 Lisbon Codex, Portugal. *6933*

POST EAGLE.
Post Publishing Co. Inc., 800 Van Houten Ave., Clifton, NJ 07013. TEL 201-473-5414. FAX 201-473-3211.
circ. 17,000. *3037*

POST OFFICE XPRESS.
S A Post Office, P.O. Box 9255, Pretoria 0001, South Africa. TEL 27-12-4217714. FAX 27-12-4217606.
circ. 33,000. *2020*

POSTAL HISTORY JOURNAL.
Postal History Society, Inc., c/o Kalman V. Illyefalvi, Sec.-Treas., 8207 Daren Ct., Pikesville, MD 21208. TEL 410-653-0665.
circ. 600. *2020*

POSTGRADUATE DOCTOR: AFRICA.
P M H Publications Ltd., P.O. Box 100, Chichester, W. Sussex PO18 8HD, England. TEL 44-1243-576444. FAX 44-1243-576456.
circ. 13,181. *4731*

POSTGRADUATE DOCTOR: CARIBBEAN.
P M H Publications Ltd., P.O. Box 100, Chichester, W. Sussex PO18 8HD, England. TEL 44-1243-576444. FAX 44-1243-576456.
circ. 3,000. *4731*

POSTGRADUATE DOCTOR: MIDDLE EAST.
P M H Publications Ltd., P.O. Box 100, Chichester, W. Sussex PO18 8HD, England. TEL 44-1243-576444. FAX 44-1243-576456.
circ. 21,413. *4731*

POSTHORN.
Scandinavian Collectors Club, 2316 Lakeview Dr., Fergus Falls, MN 56537-3903. TEL 218-739-3260.
circ. 1,000. *5712*

POSTMASTERS ADVOCATE.
National League of Postmasters, 1023 N. Royal St., Alexandria, VA 22314-1569. TEL 703-548-5922. FAX 703-836-8937.
circ. 23,000. *2021*

POTATO NEWSLETTER.
Department of Agriculture, Plant Industry Branch, Box 6000, Fredericton, NB E3B 5H1, Canada. TEL 506-457-7244. FAX 506-457-7267.
circ. 1,000. *241*

POTOMAC LIFE.
C E R Publications, Box 59508, Potomac, MD 20859. TEL 301-299-5183. FAX 301-299-9886.
circ. 30,000. *3383*

POWDER RIVER BREAKS.
Powder River Basin Resource Council, Box 1178, Douglas, WY 82633. TEL 307-358-5002.
circ. 975. *2947*

POWER DELIVERY PRODUCT NEWS.
PennWell Publishing Co., Box 1260, Tulsa, OK 74112-6619. TEL 918-835-3161. FAX 918-831-9834.
circ. 60,000. *2843*

POWER TECHNOLOGY INTERNATIONAL.
Sterling Publications Ltd., 86-88 Edgware Rd., London W2 2YW, England. TEL 44-171-915-9600. FAX 44-171-915-9619.
circ. 14,000. *2844*

POWER TRANSMISSION DESIGN.
Penton Publishing Co., 1100 Superior Ave., Cleveland, OH 44114-2543. TEL 216-696-7000. FAX 216-696-8765.
circ. 52,000. *2898*

POWER TRANSMISSION DESIGN HANDBOOK.
Penton Publishing Co., 1100 Superior Ave., Cleveland, OH 44114-2543. TEL 216-696-7000. FAX 216-696-8765.
circ. 52,000. *2898*

PRACTICAL DIABETOLOGY.
R.A. Rapaport Publishing, Inc., 150 W. 22nd St., New York, NY 10011. TEL 212-989-0200. FAX 212-989-4786.
circ. 52,000. *4891*

PRACTICAL GASTROENTEROLOGY.
Shugar Publishing, 12 Moniebogue Lane, Westhampton Beach, NY 11978.
circ. 16,000. *4914*

PRACTICAL OPTOMETRY.
Medicopea International Inc., 3333 Cote Vertu Blvd., Ste. 300, St. Laurent, PQ H4R 2N1, Canada. TEL 514-333-4561. FAX 514-336-1129.
circ. 2,300. *5000*

PRACTICING C P A.
American Institute of Certified Public Accountants, Private Companies Practice Section, Harborside Financial Ctr., 201 Plaza Three, Jersey City, NJ 07311-3881. TEL 201-938-3796. FAX 800-329-1112. *1096*

PRAGMA'S PRODUCT PROFILES.
Semaphore Corp., 207 Granada Dr., Aptos, CA 95003. TEL 408-688-9200.
circ. 4,000. *2180*

PRAIRIE HARVESTER.
Prairie Bible Institute, Three Hills, AB T0M 2N0, Canada. TEL 403-443-5511. FAX 403-443-5540.
circ. 13,000. *1967*

PRATTFOLIO.
Pratt Institute, Office of Alumni Resources, Brooklyn, NY 11205.
circ. 27,000. *1967*

PRAXIS COMPUTER.
Deutscher Aerzte-Verlag GmbH, Postfach 400265, 50532 Cologne, Germany. TEL 49-2234-7011-0. FAX 49-2234-7011255.
circ. 40,000. *2089*

PRAXISREPORT PSYCHOLOGISCHE THERAPIEN UND PSYCHOTHERAPIEN.
Psychomedia Verlags GmbH, Postfach 465, 12214 Berlin, Germany. TEL 49-30-4927200. FAX 49-30-7749176.
circ. 500. *6141*

PRE & POST NATAL NEWS.
Professional Publishing Associates, 269 Richmond St. W., Toronto, ON M5V 1X1, Canada. TEL 416-596-8680. FAX 416-596-1991.
circ. 7,000. *4947*

PRE-VUE ENTERTAINMENT MAGAZINE.
National Pre-Vue Network, 7825 Fay Ave., La Jolla, CA 92037. TEL 619-456-5577. FAX 619-542-0114.
circ. 200,000. *5342*

PRENATAL EDUCATOR.
Educational Programs, Inc., 261 Old York Rd., Ste. 831, Jenkintown, PA 19046-3255. TEL 215-635-1700.
circ. 8,540. *4966*

PRESBYTERIAN COLLEGE MAGAZINE.
Presbyterian College, Office of Public Relations, Box 975, Clinton, SC 29325. TEL 864-833-2820. FAX 864-833-8481.
circ. 13,500. *1967*

PRESBYTERIAN SUN.
Synod of the Sun, 920 S. I-35 E., Denton, TX 76205-7898.
circ. 107,000. *6438*

PRESBYTERION.
Covenant Theological Seminary, 12330 Conway Rd., St. Louis, MO 63141. TEL 314-434-4044. FAX 314-434-4819.
circ. 100. *6438*

PRESENTATIONS.
Lakewood Publications Inc., 50 S. Ninth St., Minneapolis, MN 55402. TEL 612-333-0471. FAX 612-333-6526.
circ. 70,000. *43*

PRESERVATION NOTES.
Society for the Preservation of Long Island Antiquities, 93 North Country Rd., Setauket, NY 11733. TEL 516-941-9444. FAX 516-941-9184.
circ. 1,800. *413*

PRESERVATION PERSPECTIVE.
Preservation New Jersey, Inc., 149 Kearny Ave., Perth Amboy, NJ 08861-4700. TEL 908-442-1100. FAX 908-442-2442.
circ. 3,000. *413*

PRESHIPMENT TESTING.
International Safe Transit Association, Box 10744, Chicago, IL 60610-0744. TEL 312-645-0083. FAX 312-645-1078.
circ. 3,200. *5549*

PRESS COUNCIL OF THE REPUBLIC OF CHINA.
National Press Council of the Republic of China, Nanchang Rd. Sec. 1, Lane 9, No. 4, 3rd Fl., Taipei, Taiwan 107, Republic of China.
circ. 4,000. *3879*

PRESS - GRAPH.
Ediciones Press Graph, S.L., C. Mallorca, 219 5o 2o, 08008 Barcelona, Spain. TEL 34-3-3237554. FAX 34-3-3237463.
circ. 8,000. *6083*

PRESSEMARKT EUROPA.
Verband Deutscher Zeitschriften Verleger, Winterstr. 50, 53117 Bonn, Germany. TEL 49-228-3820323. FAX 49-228-312219.
circ. 500. *6280*

PRETTIG WEEKEND.
Ram Press, Heerengracht 4, 1141 TR Monnickendam, Netherlands. TEL 31-299-652337. FAX 31-299-655258.
circ. 25,000. *3338*

PREVIEW (COLLINSVILLE).
Stehman Publications, 300 W. Main St., Collinsville, IL 62234. TEL 618-345-7559. *4868*

PREVIEW THEATER BROCHURE.
American Film Institute, John F. Kennedy Center for the Performing Arts, Washington, DC 20566. TEL 202-828-4000. *5342*

PREVISOES IONOSFERICAS M U F.
Ministerio da Marinha, Diretoria de Armamento e Comunicacoes, Rua 1 de Marco, 118, Rio de Janeiro, RJ, Brazil. FAX 021-216-5048.
circ. 250. *2056*

PRIESTERJAHRHEFT.
Bonifatiuswerk der Deutschen Katholiken e.V., Postfach 1169, 33041 Paderborn, Germany. TEL 49-5251-29960. FAX 49-5251-299688.
circ. 20,000. *6476*

PRIMARY CARE & CANCER.
P R R, Inc., 17 Prospect St., Huntington, NY 11743. TEL 516-424-8900. FAX 516-424-8503.
circ. 70,440. *4985*

PRIMARY SCHOOL MANAGER.
Pitman Publishing, 128 Long Acre, London WC2E 9AN, England. TEL 44-171-447-2000. FAX 44-171-240-5771.
circ. 3,000. *2576*

PRIME TIMES.
Life Newspapers, 709 Enterprise Dr., Oak Brook, IL 60521. TEL 708-368-1100. FAX 708-368-1188.
circ. 55,000. *3443*

PRIME TIMES MAGAZINE.
Grote Publishing, 634 W. Main St., Ste. 207, Madison, WI 53703-2634. TEL 608-257-4640. FAX 608-257-4670.
circ. 80,000. *2258*

PRINCETON ALUMNI WEEKLY.
Princeton Alumni Publications, 194 Nassau St., Princeton, NJ 08542. TEL 609-258-4885. FAX 609-258-2247.
circ. 59,000. *1967*

PRINCIPALS' PERSPECTIVES.
Western Australian Secondary Principals Association, Australind Senior High School, Break O'Day Dr., Australind, W.A. 6230, Australia. TEL 61-97-971800. FAX 61-97-971811.
circ. 300. *2474*

PRINT & GRAPHICS.
East-West Communications, 911 N. Fillmore St., Arlington, VA 22201-2127. TEL 703-525-4800. FAX 703-525-4805.
circ. 20,000. *6083*

PRINT BUYER GUIDE.
Uitgeverij Compres b.v., Postbus 55, 2300 AB Leiden, Netherlands. TEL 31-71-161515. FAX 31-71-121550.
circ. 6,500. *6083*

PRINTER'S NORTHWEST TRADER.
Eagle Newspapers, Inc., Box 450, Woodburn, OR 97071. TEL 800-426-2416. FAX 503-981-1253.
circ. 5,850. *6083*

PRINTING JOURNAL.
East-West Communications, 911 N. Fillmore St., Arlington, VA 22201-2127. TEL 703-525-4800. FAX 703-525-4805.
circ. 18,000. *6084*

PRINTING PRODUCT NEWS.
Manor Publishing Ltd., Unit 7, Edison Rd., Highfield Industrial Estate, Hampden Park, Eastbourne, E. Sussex BN23 6PT, England. TEL 44-1323-507474. FAX 44-1323-509306.
circ. 8,000. *6084*

(YEAR) PRIORITIES AND PROGRESS UNDER THE GREAT LAKES WATER QUALITY AGREEMENT.
International Joint Commission, Great Lakes Regional Office, 100 Ouellette Ave., 8th Fl., Windsor, ON N9A 6T3, Canada. TEL 519-257-6700. FAX 519-257-6740.
circ. 8,000. *7298*

PRISON SERVICE JOURNAL.
H M Prison Service College, Newbold Rd., Rugby, Warwickshire CV23 0TN, England. TEL 44-1759-372447. FAX 44-1759-371206.
circ. 7,000. *2278*

PRISON SERVICE NEWS.
H.M. Prison Service, Rm. 302, Cleland House, Page St., London SW1P 4LN, England. TEL 44-171-217-6575. FAX 44-171-828-8692.
circ. 30,000. *2278*

PRIVATE CARRIER.
National Private Truck Council, 66 Canal Center Plaza, Ste. 600, Alexandria, VA 22314. TEL 703-683-1300. FAX 703-683-1217.
circ. 13,000. *7177*

PRIVATE LINE (ALEXANDRIA).
National Private Truck Council, 66 Canal Center Plaza, Ste. 600, Alexandria, VA 22314. TEL 703-683-1300. FAX 703-683-1217.
circ. 2,500. *7177*

PRO.
Johnson Hill Press, Inc., 1233 Janesville Ave., Ft. Atkinson, WI 53538. TEL 920-563-6388. FAX 920-563-1699.
circ. 47,500. *3203*

PRO MOTION.
Beyond the Byte, c/o Emily Laisy, Ed., 2501 Laurel Brook Rd., Box 388, Fallston, MD 21047-0388. TEL 410-877-3524. FAX 410-877-7064.
circ. 300. *2001*

PRO SHOP EUROPE.
Mark Allen Publishing Ltd., Snow Hill, Dinton, Salisbury, Wiltshire SP3 5HN, England. TEL 01722-716996. FAX 01722-716926.
circ. 6,850. *6815*

PRO ZUKUNFT.
Verlag Julius Beltz GmbH, Werderstr. 10, 69469 Weinheim, Germany. TEL 49-6201-60070. FAX 49-6201-17464.
circ. 1,800. *2948*

PROBABLE LEVELS OF R & D EXPENDITURES: FORECAST AND ANALYSIS.
Battelle Memorial Institute, Columbus Operations, 505 King Ave., Columbus, OH 43201. TEL 614-424-6424. *6970*

PROBE.
Adelaide University Dental Students Society (AUDSS), School of Dentistry, Undergraduate Mailbox, 5th Fl., Dental Hospital, Frome Rd., Adelaide, S.A. 5000, Australia. TEL 618-223-9211. FAX 61-8-232-4061.
circ. 220. *4868*

PROBLEMI DI GESTIONE.
Centro di Formazione e Studi (Formez), Via Campi Flegrei 34, Comprensorio Olivetti, 80072 Arco Felice (NA), Italy. TEL 39-81-5250111. FAX 39-81-8041348.
circ. 7,000. *1501*

PROBLEMY RODZINY.
Towarzystwo Rozwoju Rodziny, Zarzad Glowny, c/o Problemy Rodziny, Redakcja, Ul. Schillera 4-35, 00-248 Warsaw, Poland. TEL 48-2-319310.
circ. 1,200. *6723*

PROCESS HEATING.
Business News Publishing Co., 3150 River Rd., Ste. 101, Des Plaines, IL 60018. TEL 847-297-3450. FAX 847-297-8371.
circ. 26,000. *2878*

PROCESS INDUSTRIES CANADA.
Zanny Publications Ltd., 11966 Woodbine Ave., Gormley, ON L0H 1G0, Canada. TEL 905-887-5048. FAX 905-887-0764.
circ. 24,000. *2772*

PROCESSING.
Putman Publishing Co., 301 E. Erie St., Chicago, IL 60611. TEL 312-644-2020. FAX 312-644-0380.
circ. 105,000. *2772*

PROCESSING TECHNOLOGY FOR CHINA.
Sterling Publications Ltd., 86-88 Edgware Rd., London W2 2YW, England. TEL 44-171-915-9600. FAX 44-171-915-9619.
circ. 10,000. *1593*

PRODUCE MERCHANDISING.
Vance Publishing Corporation (Lenexa), 10901 W. 84th Terr., Lenexa, KS 66214-1631. TEL 913-438-8700. FAX 913-438-0692.
circ. 12,200. *3124*

PRODUCT MANAGEMENT TODAY.
Product Management Today, Inc., 28 Jones Ave., Flourtown, PA 19031. TEL 215-233-9384. FAX 215-233-9320.
circ. 9,600. *1545*

PRODUCTION.
University of British Columbia, Centre for Health Services and Policy Research, No. 429 - 2194 Health Sciences Mall, Vancouver, BC V6T 1Z3, Canada. TEL 604-822-4810. FAX 604-822-5690.
circ. 300. *4733*

PRODUCTION JOURNAL.
Newspaper Society, Bloomsbury House, 74-77 Great Russell St., London WC1B 3DA, England. TEL 44-171-636-7014. FAX 44-171-631-5119.
circ. 3,000. *6084*

PRODUCTRONIC.
Huethig GmbH, Paul-Gerhardt-Allee 46, 81245 Munich, Germany. TEL 49-89-83948-0. FAX 49-89-8394848.
circ. 10,568. *2649*

PRODUITS EQUIPEMENTS INDUSTRIELS.
Editions Elsevier - Thomas, 128 rue d'Aguesseau, 92100 Boulogne-Billancourt, France. TEL 33-1-41104070. FAX 33-1-48251400.
circ. 49,350. *2869*

PRODUITS POUR L'INDUSTRIE QUEBECOISE.
Action Communications Inc., 135 Spy Court, Markham, ON L3R 5H6, Canada. TEL 905-477-3222. FAX 905-477-4320.
circ. 15,050. *6970*

PRODUKTION.
Dansk Landbrugs Grovvareselskab a.m.b.a., Axelborg, DK-1503 Copenhagen V, Denmark. TEL 45-33-15-11-13. FAX 45-33-15-13-56.
circ. 126,000. *200*

PRODUKTIONS NYT.
Christtreu, Strandlodsvei 48, DK-2300 Copenhagen S, Denmark. TEL 45-32-84-48-48. FAX 45-31-58-20-55.
circ. 24,850. *4551*

PROEFTUIN NIEUWS.
Binnenweg 6, 2860 Sint-Ka telijine-Waver, Belgium. TEL 32-15-552771. FAX 32-15-553061.
circ. 4,023. *241*

PROFESSIONAL BOATBUILDER.
WoodenBoat Publications, Inc., Box 78, Brookline, ME 04616. TEL 207-359-4651. FAX 207-359-8920.
circ. 23,000. *6843*

PROFESSIONAL CAR WASHING & DETAILING.
National Trade Publications, Inc., 13 Century Hill, Latham, NY 12110-2197. TEL 518-783-1281. FAX 518-783-1386.
circ. 17,590. *7113*

PROFESSIONAL EDGE.
Association of Professional Engineers of Saskatchewan, 2255 13th Av., Regina, SK S4P 0V6, Canada. TEL 306-525-9547. FAX 306-525-0851.
circ. 4,000. *2737*

PROFESSIONAL FORESTER.
Ontario Professional Foresters Association, 27 West Beaver Creek Rd., Richmond Hill, ON L4B 1M8, Canada. TEL 905-764-2921. FAX 905-764-2921.
circ. 1,300. *3160*

PROFESSIONAL INSTITUTE OF THE PUBLIC SERVICE OF CANADA. COMMUNICATIONS.
Professional Institute of the Public Service of Canada, 53 Auriga Dr., Nepean, Ont. K2E 8C3, Canada. TEL 613-228-6310. FAX 613-228-9048.
circ. 29,000. *6189*

PROFESSIONAL OFFICER.
Federated Union of Managerial and Professional Officers, Terminus House, The High, Harlow, Essex CM20 1TZ, England. TEL 44-1274-434444. FAX 44-1279-451176.
circ. 12,500. *6189*

PROFESSIONAL PILOT MAGAZINE.
Queensmith Communications Corporation, 3014 Colvin St., Alexandria, VA 22314. TEL 703-370-0606. FAX 703-370-7082.
circ. 33,500. *7077*

PROFESSIONAL SURVEYOR.
American Surveyors Publishing Co., 1713 Rosemont Ave., Ste. J, Frederick, MD 21702-4199.
circ. 54,725. *3418*

PROFILE (SKOKIE).
Brunswick Corporation, One N. Field Ct., Lake Forest, IL 60045-4811. TEL 847-735-4457. FAX 847-735-4765.
circ. 30,000. *1594*

PROFOTO.
Professional Photographers of Southern Africa, P.O. Box 47044, Parklands 2121, South Africa.
circ. 3,200. *5774*

PROGNOSTICO.
Instituto de Economia Agricola, Av. Miguel Stefano 3900, Caixa Postal 6802, 04301-9031 Sao Paulo SP, Brazil. FAX 55-11-2764062. *241*

PROGRAM T V.
Oficyna Wydawnicza Press - Media, Ul. Trembeckiego 5, 35-234 Rzeszow, Poland. TEL 48-17-8520570. FAX 48-17-8525555.
circ. 450,000. *2057*

PROGRAMA DE FORRAJES TROPICALES. INFORME BIANUAL.
Centro Internacional de Agricultura Tropical, Apdo. Aereo 6713, Cali, Colombia. TEL 57-2-4450000. FAX 57-2-4450073.
circ. 250. *147*

PROGRAMMA COMUNISTA.
Istituto Programma Comunista, Casella Postale 962, 20100 Milan, Italy.
circ. 2,000. *5961*

PROGRESS IN DERMATOLOGY.
Dermatology Foundation, 1560 Sherman Ave., Ste. 302, Evanston, IL 60201-4802.
circ. 3,000. *4880*

THE PROGRESS OF NATIONS.
United Nations Children's Fund (UNICEF), UNICEF House, 3 United Nations Plaza, New York, NY 10017. TEL 212-326-7000. FAX 212-888-7465.
circ. 71,500. *6682*

PROGRESSIVE GIFTS.
Max Publishing Ltd., United House, North Rd., London N7 9DP, England. TEL 44-171-700-6740. FAX 44-171-609-4222.
circ. 7,500. *3450*

PROGRESSIVE GROCER'S ANNUAL REPORT OF THE GROCERY INDUSTRY.
263 Tresser Blvd., Stamford, CT 06901. TEL 203-325-3500. FAX 203-325-4377.
circ. 70,049. *3144*

PROMAX INTERNATIONAL.
Promotion & Marketing Executives in the Electronic Media, 2029 Century Pk. E., Ste. 555, Los Angeles, CA 90067-2906. TEL 310-788-7600. FAX 310-788-7616.
circ. 2,000. *2057*

PROMPT.
Deutsche Blindenstudienanstalt e.V., Postfach 1160, 35001 Marburg, Germany. TEL 49-6421-606-0.
circ. 70. *3473*

PROP.
Oesterreichischer Aero Club, Prinz-Eugen-Str. 12, A-1040 Vienna, Austria. TEL 01-5051028.
circ. 6,000. *3675*

PROPANE VEHICLE.
R P Publishing, Inc., 1290 Broadway, Ste. 700, Denver, CO 80203-5607. TEL 303-863-0521. FAX 303-863-1722.
circ. 5,000. *7037*

PROPERTY REGISTER.
Tophill Press, 49 High St., Sevenoaks, Kent TN13 1L8, England. TEL 0732-743300. FAX 0732-743006. *6309*

PROSPECT (SUTTON).
Harrington Publications, Rafferty House, 2-4 Sutton Court Rd., Sutton, Surrey SM1 4SS, England. TEL 44-181-770-9340. FAX 44-181-770-9345.
circ. 12,000. *3830*

PROSPEROUS TIMES.
Howard Publications, 417 Fayette St., Hammond, IN 46320. TEL 219-933-3253.
circ. 42,000. *3383*

PROSTHETICS AND ORTHOTICS INTERNATIONAL.
International Society for Prosthetics and Orthotics, Borgervaenget 5, DK-2100 Copenhagen OE, Denmark. TEL 45-31-20-72-60. FAX 45-31-18-16-69.
circ. 3,300. *5015*

PROTEE.
Protee, 555 bd. de l'Universite, Chicoutimi, PQ, Canada. TEL 418-545-5011. FAX 418-545-5012.
circ. 750. *3789*

PROTEIN INFORMATION RESOURCE NEWSLETTER.
National Biomedical Research Foundation, 3900 Reservoir Rd., N.W., Washington, DC 20007. TEL 202-687-2121. FAX 202-687-1662.
circ. 1,000. *621*

PROVEN AND POPULAR HOME PLANS.
Giroux Publishing, 102 Ellis St., Penticton, BC V2A 4L5, Canada. TEL 604-493-0942. FAX 604-493-7526.
circ. 10,000. *909*

CONTROLLED CIRCULATION SERIALS

PROVENCE GENEALOGIE.
Centre Genealogique de Midi-Provence, B.P. 30, 13243 Marseille Cedex 01, France.
circ. 1,300. *3238*

PROVIDERS.
Kenilworth Publishing Inc., 27 W. Beaver Creek, Richmond Hill, ON L4B 1M8, Canada. TEL 905-771-7333. FAX 905-771-7336.
circ. 4,000. *4947*

PROVINCIA NUOVA.
Amministrazione Provinciale, Corso V. Emanuele 17, 26100 Cremona, Italy. TEL 0372-406268. FAX 0372-456744.
circ. 2,000. *6189*

PROVINCIAL JUDGES JOURNAL.
Canadian Association of Provincial Court Judges, P.O. Box 339, Grand Bank, NF A0E 1E0, Canada. TEL 709-832-1450. FAX 709-832-1758.
circ. 1,250. *4011*

PROVINCIAL NEWSLETTER.
British Columbia Registered Music Teachers' Association, 197 Vancouver Ave., Penticton, BC V2A 1A1, Canada. TEL 604-492-8944. FAX 604-493-9130.
circ. 1,000. *5427*

PROYECTOS QUIMICOS.
Tecnipublicaciones, S.A., C. Albacete 5, 28027 Madrid, Spain. TEL 34-1-3261440. FAX 36-1-3262407.
circ. 3,000. *1763*

PRZEGLAD ANTROPOLOGICZNY.
Polskie Towarzystwo Antropologiczne, Ul. Marymoncka 34, 01-813 Warsaw, Poland.
circ. 500. *327*

PRZEMYSLOWY INSTYTUT ELEKTRONIKI. PRACE.
Przemyslowy Instytut Elektroniki, Ul. Dluga 44-50, 00-241 Warsaw, Poland. TEL 48-22-313839. FAX 48-22-313014.
circ. 300. *2650*

PRZEWODNIK KATOLICKI.
Drukarnia i Ksiegarnia Sw. Wojciecha, Pl. Wolnosci 1, 60-967 Poznan, Poland. TEL 48-61-529186. FAX 48-61-523746.
circ. 40,000. *6476*

PSIQUIS.
Alpe Editores, S.A., Pedro Rico, 27, 28029 Madrid, Spain. TEL 34-1-7338811. FAX 34-1-3159652.
circ. 6,000. *5091*

PSYCHIATRIC FORUM.
Department of Mental Health, William S. Hall Psychiatric Institute, Box 202, Columbia, SC 29202. TEL 803-734-7154. FAX 803-734-0791.
circ. 4,000. *5092*

PSYCHIATRIC TIMES.
C M E Inc., 2801 McGraw Ave., Irvine, CA 92614-5835. TEL 714-250-1008. FAX 714-250-0045.
circ. 42,445. *5092*

PSYCHOLOGY BULLETIN.
Psychology Resource Centre, Private Bag X17, Bellville 7535, South Africa. TEL 27-21-959-2283. FAX 27-21-959-3515.
circ. 1,000. *6147*

PUBLIC EDUCATION ALERT.
Public Education Association, 39 W. 32nd St., New York, NY 10001-3803. TEL 212-868-1640. FAX 212-268-7344.
circ. 5,000. *2475*

PUBLIC EMPLOYEE PRESS.
American Federation of State, County & Municipal Employees, A F L - C I O, District Council 37, 125 Barclay St., New York, NY 10007. TEL 212-815-1000. FAX 212-815-7535.
circ. 160,000. *3896*

PUBLIC LIBRARY NEWS.
State Library of New South Wales, Public Libraries Branch, Macquarie St., Sydney, N.S.W. 2000, Australia. TEL 61-2-92301526. FAX 61-2-92239702.
circ. 700. *4207*

PUBLIC PERSPECTIVE.
Roper Center for Public Opinion Research, Box 440, Storrs, CT 06269. TEL 860-486-4440. FAX 860-486-6308.
circ. 3,000. *5962*

PUBLIC SCHOOL ENROLLMENT AND STAFF, NEW YORK STATE.
Education Department, Information, Reporting & Technology Services, Education Bldg. Annex, Rm. 962, Albany, NY 12234. TEL 518-474-7082. FAX 518-474-4351. *2576*

PUBLIC SCHOOL PROFESSIONAL PERSONNEL REPORT, NEW YORK STATE.
Education Department, Information, Reporting & Technology Services, Education Bldg. Annex, Rm. 962, Albany, NY 12234. TEL 518-474-7082. FAX 518-474-4351. *2475*

PUBLIC SECTOR.
Auburn University, Center for Governmental Services, 2232 Haley Center, Auburn University, Auburn, AL 36849. TEL 205-844-1913. FAX 205-844-1919.
circ. 3,000. *6190*

PUBLICITY AND MEDIA RESOURCES FOR PUBLISHERS.
Association of American University Presses, Inc., 584 Broadway, Ste. 410, New York, NY 10012. TEL 212-941-6610. *44*

PUEBLO BUSINESS JOURNAL.
201 W. 8th St., Ste. 408, Box 1544, Pueblo, CO 81002. TEL 719-542-3616. FAX 719-542-4506.
circ. 6,500. *1285*

PUERTO RICO. OFICINA DE PRESUPUESTO Y GERENCIA. PRESUPUESTO (YEARS).
Oficina de Presupuesto, Box 3228, San Juan, PR 00902. TEL 787-725-9420. FAX 787-723-7308. *6191*

PULMONARY REVIEWS.
Partners in Medical Communication, 4 Brighton Rd., Clifton, NJ 07012. TEL 201-916-1000. FAX 201-916-0021. *5121*

PULP AND PAPER.
Miller Freeman, Inc., 600 Harrison St., San Francisco, CA 94107. TEL 415-905-2200. FAX 415-905-2232.
circ. 40,900. *5571*

PULSE (PICO RIVERA).
Southern California Veterinary Medical Association, 8338 Rosemead Blvd., Pico Rivera, CA 90660. TEL 310-948-4979.
circ. 1,100. *7277*

PULSE! (WEST SACRAMENTO).
M T S, Incorporated, Tower Records - Pulse!, 2500 Delmonte St., Bldg. C, W. Sacramento, CA 95691. TEL 916-373-2450. FAX 916-373-2480.
circ. 300,000. *5427*

PULSO.
Universidad Internacional de la Florida, Miami, Programa Centroamericano de Periodismo, Biscayne Blvd. at N.E. 151st St., North Miami, FL 33181. TEL 305-940-5672. FAX 305-956-5498.
circ. 4,500. *3879*

PUNJABI SAHITYA.
c/o H. S. Kalra, Ed., 254 Rowley Gardens, Woodberry Grove, London N4 1HW, England.
circ. 4,000. *4355*

PUPPETRY JOURNAL.
Puppeteers of America, 8005 Swallow Dr., Macedonia, OH 44056.
circ. 2,200. *7011*

PURCHASING TODAY.
National Association of Purchasing Management, 2055 E. Centennial Circle, Tempe, AZ 85285. TEL 602-752-6276. FAX 602-752-7890.
circ. 40,000. *1546*

PURDUE UNIVERSITY. OFFICE OF MANPOWER STUDIES. MANPOWER & TECHNICAL EDUCATION REQUIREMENTS REPORTS.
Purdue University, Office of Manpower Studies, Knoy Hall, W. Lafayette, IN 47907. TEL 317-494-2559. FAX 317-494-0486. *1451*

PURJEHTIJA.
Finnish Yachting Association, Radiokatu 20, SF-00240 Helsinki, Finland. TEL 358-0-1582350. FAX 358-0-1582369.
circ. 31,000. *6843*

PUROSANGUE IN ITALIA.
Associazione Nazionale Allevatori Cavalli Purosangue, Via del Caravaggio 3, 20144 Milan, Italy. TEL 39-2-48012002. FAX 39-2-48194547.
circ. 2,500. *6855*

PURPLE AND GOLD.
Chi Psi Educational Trust, 20180 Governors Hwy., Ste. 303, Olympia Fields, IL 60461-1066.
circ. 17,000. *1935*

PUTTERIDGE BURY MANAGEMENT REVIEW.
University of Luton, Putteridge Bury, Hitchin Rd., Luton, Beds. LU2 8LE, England. TEL 01582-482555. FAX 01582-482689.
circ. 300. *1503*

PYRETHRUM POST.
Pyrethrum Bureau, Pyrethrum Board of Kenya, P.O. Box 420, Nakuru, Kenya. TEL 254-37-211567. FAX 254-37-45274. *670*

Q: THE PHYSICIANS GUIDE TO QUALITY.
Target Marketing, Inc., 5 Victory Ln., Ste. 101, Liberty, MO 64068. TEL 816-781-7557. FAX 816-781-3298.
circ. 60,000. *4734*

QUADERNI DI COOPERAZIONE SANITARIA.
Amici di Raoul Follereau, Via Borselli 4, 40135 Bologna, Italy. TEL 39-51-433402. FAX 39-51-434046.
circ. 2,000. *4842*

QUADERNI DI ECONOMIA E FINANZA.
Banco di Sardegna S.p.A., Servizio Studi, Viale Umberto I, 36, 07100 Sassari, Italy. TEL 39-79-226572. FAX 39-79-226579.
circ. 2,000. *1285*

QUADRANT.
C.G. Jung Foundation for Analytical Psychology, Inc., 28 E. 39th St., New York, NY 10016. TEL 212-697-6430. FAX 201-953-3989.
circ. 2,000. *6149*

QUAKER CAMPUS.
Whittier College, Quaker Campus, Box 8613, Whittier, CA 90608. TEL 310-907-4354. FAX 310-945-5301.
circ. 2,000. *1968*

QUALITY MATTERS.
Mississippi Foundation for Medical Care, 735 Riverside Dr., Box 4665, Jackson, MS 39296-4665. TEL 601-354-0304. FAX 601-948-8917.
circ. 5,000. *4735*

QUALITY OF CARE.
Commission on Quality of Care for the Mentally Disabled, 99 Washington Ave., Ste. 1002, Albany, NY 12210. TEL 518-473-6304. FAX 518-473-6302.
circ. 11,000. *5095*

QUALITY SOURCE.
American Medical Group Association, 1422 Duke St., Alexandria, VA 22314. TEL 703-838-0033. FAX 703-548-1890. *4735*

QUANTUM (NEW YORK).
Springer-Verlag, Science Journals, 175 Fifth Ave., New York, NY 10010. TEL 212-460-1500. FAX 212-473-6272.
circ. 40,000. *6561*

QUARTERLY FORECAST OF JAPANESE ECONOMY.
Japan Center for Economic Research, Nikkei Kayabacho Bldg., 6-1 Nihonbashi Kayabacgi 2-chome, Chuo-ku, Tokyo 103, Japan. TEL 81-3-3639-2801. FAX 81-3-3639-2839. *1594*

QUARTERLY JOURNAL OF TAIWAN LAND CREDIT.
Land Bank of Taiwan, Credit Investigation & Research Department, 46 Kuan Chien Rd., Taipei, Taiwan, Republic of China. TEL 02-3613020. FAX 02-3115782.
circ. 500. *200*

CONTROLLED CIRCULATION SERIALS

QUARTERNOTE.
American Musicians Union, Inc., 8 Tobin Ct., Dumont, NJ 07628. TEL 201-384-5378.
circ. 300. *5428*

QUEBEC HOME & SCHOOL NEWS.
Quebec Federation of Home and School Associations, 3285 Cavendish Blvd., Ste. 562, Montreal, PQ H4B 2L9, Canada. TEL 514-481-5619. FAX 514-481-5610.
circ. 1,350. *2475*

QUEEN'S AWARDS MAGAZINE.
Nexus Media Ltd., Nexus House, Azalea Dr., Swanley, Kent BR8 8HY, England. TEL 44-1322-660070. FAX 44-1322-666408.
circ. 10,000. *1345*

QUEENSLAND FOREST SERVICE. RESEARCH NOTE.
Queensland Forest Service, G.P.O. Box 944, Brisbane, Qld. 4001, Australia. TEL 07-877-9727. FAX 07-371-2217.
circ. 400. *3160*

QUEENSLAND FOREST SERVICE. RESEARCH PAPER.
Queensland Forest Service, G.P.O. Box 944, Brisbane, Qld. 4001, Australia. TEL 07-877 9727. FAX 07-371-2217.
circ. 400. *3160*

QUEENSLAND FRUIT AND VEGETABLE NEWS.
Queensland Fruit and Vegetable Growers, Box 19, Brisbane Market, Brisbane, Qld. 4106, Australia. TEL 61-7-32132464. FAX 61-7-32132438.
circ. 8,000. *3203*

QUEENSLAND TEACHERS' JOURNAL.
Queensland Teachers' Union, P.O. Box 1750, Milton, Qld. 4064, Australia. TEL 61-7-33690088. FAX 61-7-33690022.
circ. 35,000. *2475*

QUERCE.
Collegio alla Querce, Via della Piazzuola 44, 50133 Florence, Italy. TEL 39-55-573621. FAX 39-55-579655.
circ. 2,000. *2475*

QUERSCHNITTE.
Verlag fuer Kultur und Wissenschaft, Friedrichstr. 38, 53111 Bonn, Germany. TEL 49-228-638784. FAX 49-228-638784.
circ. 1,000. *6439*

QUEST.
Meigher Communications, 100 6th Ave., 7th Fl., New York, NY 10013-1689. TEL 212-219-7465. FAX 212-334-1260.
circ. 75,000. *3383*

QUEST (BOSTON).
Church of the Larger Fellowship, Unitarian Universalist, 25 Beacon St., Boston, MA 02108. TEL 617-742-2100. FAX 617-523-4123.
circ. 3,000. *6364*

QUESTE.
Premier Magazines Ltd., Haymarket House, 1 Oxendon St., London SW1Y 4EE, England. TEL 44-171-925-2544. FAX 44-171-839-4491.
circ. 25,000. *7114*

QUICK TOPICS NEWSLETTER.
American Wholesale Marketers Association, 1128 16th St., N.W., Washington, DC 20036. TEL 202-463-2124. FAX 202-467-0559.
circ. 4,200. *3138*

QUIET MIRACLE.
Bible Literature International, 625 E.N. Broadway, Columbus, OH 43214-4133. TEL 614-267-3116. FAX 614-267-7110.
circ. 20,000. *6364*

QUILL & SCROLL.
Quill and Scroll Society, School of Journalism and Mass Communication, Univ. of Iowa, Iowa City, IA 52242. TEL 319-335-5795. FAX 319-335-5210. *3879*

QUINCY BUSINESS NEWS.
John R. Graham, Inc., 40 Oval Rd., Ste. 2, Quincy, MA 02170-3813. TEL 617-328-0069. FAX 617-471-1504.
circ. 2,850. *994*

QUIRK'S MARKETING RESEARCH REVIEW.
Quirk Enterprises, Box 23536, Minneapolis, MN 55423. TEL 612-861-1836. FAX 612-861-8051.
circ. 15,500. *1546*

QUO.
Hachette Filipacchi Revistas, Cardenal Herrera Oria 3, 28034 Madrid, Spain. TEL 34-1-3581122. FAX 34-1-7290150.
circ. 332,000. *3360*

QUOTARIAN.
Quota International, 1420 21st St., N.W., Washington, DC 20036. TEL 202-331-9694.
circ. 14,000. *1935*

R A C JOURNAL.
I I T Research Institute, Reliability Analysis Center, 201 Mill St., Rome, NY 13440. TEL 315-337-0900. FAX 315-337-9932.
circ. 20,000. *2738*

R A C M S A NEWS.
R A C Motor Sports Association Ltd., Motor Sports House, Riverside Park, Colnbrook, Slough SL3 0HG, England. TEL 44-1753-681736. FAX 44-1753-682938.
circ. 32,000. *6777*

R A NEWS.
Recreation Association of the Public Service of Canada, 2451 Riverside Dr., Ottawa, ON K1H 7X7, Canada. TEL 613-733-5100. FAX 613-733-3310.
circ. 40,000. *1935*

R B ELEKTRONICA.
Uitgeverij de Muiderkring B.V., Hogeweyselaan 227, 1382 JL Weesp, Netherlands. TEL 31-2940-15210. FAX 31-2940-12782.
circ. 12,000. *2650*

R E F Z.
Medialog Verlag GbR, Sabelsbergerstr. 9, 80333 Munich, Germany. TEL 49-89-282058. FAX 49-89-2802265.
circ. 19,985. *4012*

R E I D QUARTERLY.
Prudential Insurance Co. of America, Public Relations & Advertising Dept., 5 Plaza, Newark, NJ 07101. TEL 201-877-6000.
circ. 3,000. *3830*

R E R F UPDATE.
Radiation Effects Research Foundation, 5-2 Hijiyama Park, Minami-ku, Hiroshima-shi, Hiroshima-ken 732, Japan. FAX 81-82-263-7279.
5113

R E S.
Tecnipublicaciones S.A., Fernando VI 27-1, 28004 Madrid, Spain. TEL 91-319-7889. FAX 91-410-1069.
circ. 5,000. *1163*

R I A L UPDATE.
Religion in American Life, 2 Queenston Pl., Rm. 200, Princeton, NJ 08540. TEL 609-921-3639. FAX 609-921-0551.
circ. 4,000. *6364*

R I L M ABSTRACTS OF MUSIC LITERATURE.
R I L M Abstracts, City University of New York, 33 W. 42nd St., New York, NY 10036. TEL 212-642-2709. FAX 212-642-1973.
circ. 1,500. *5449*

R I P A REPORT.
Royal Institute of Public Administration, 3 Birdcage Walk, London SW1H 9JH, England. TEL 071-222-2248. FAX 071-222-2249. *6191*

R S E NEWS.
Royal Society of Edinburgh, 22 George St., Edinburgh EH2 2PQ, Scotland. TEL 44-131-225-6057. FAX 44-131-220-6889.
circ. 1,200. *6561*

R S - MAGAZINE.
Computer Publishing Group, 320 Washington St., Brookline, MA 02146-3202. TEL 617-739-7001. FAX 617-739-7003.
circ. 40,000. *2192*

R T.
Allied Healthcare Publications, 4676 Admiralty Way, Ste. 202, Marina Del Rey, CA 90292. TEL 310-306-2206. FAX 310-301-8101.
circ. 20,000. *5122*

R T P VIEWPOINTS.
Research Triangle Park, 2 Hanes Dr., Box 12255, Research Triangle Park, NC 27709. TEL 919-549-8181. FAX 919-549-8246.
circ. 3,500. *6561*

R V BUSINESS.
Affinity Group, Inc., T L Enterprises, 2575 Vista Del Mar Dr., Ventura, CA 93001-3920. TEL 805-667-4100.
circ. 13,510. *6797*

R V NEWS.
D & S Media Enterprises, Inc., 408 E. Southern Ave., Tempe, AZ 85283-5200. TEL 602-784-4060. FAX 602-784-4420.
circ. 13,000. *7037*

R V TIMES.
Sheila Jones Publishing Ltd., 3378 Douglas St., Victoria, BC V8Z 3L3, Canada. TEL 250-475-8860. FAX 250-475-8861.
circ. 50,000. *7230*

RACIAL - ETHNIC DISTRIBUTION OF PUBLIC SCHOOL STUDENTS AND STAFF, NEW YORK STATE.
Education Department, Information, Reporting & Technology Services, Education Bldg. Annex, Rm. 962, Albany, NY 12234. TEL 518-474-7082. FAX 518-474-4351. *2476*

RACQUETTE.
State University of New York, College at Potsdam, 119 Borrington Student Union, Potsdam, NY 13676. TEL 315-267-8451. FAX 315-267-2170.
circ. 3,500. *1968*

RADCLIFFE NEWS.
Radcliffe College, 10 Garden St., Cambridge, MA 02138. TEL 617-495-8608. FAX 617-496-4640.
circ. 50,000. *1968*

RADCLIFFE QUARTERLY.
Radcliffe College, 10 Garden St., Cambridge, MA 02138. TEL 617-495-8608. FAX 617-496-0255.
circ. 35,000. *1968*

RADIATION EFFECTS RESEARCH FOUNDATION. ANNUAL REPORT.
Radiation Effects Research Foundation, 5-2 Hijiyama Park, Minami-ku, Hiroshima-shi, Hiroshima-ken 732, Japan. FAX 81-82-263-7279.
5113

RADIATION EFFECTS RESEARCH FOUNDATION. COMMENTARY AND REVIEW SERIES.
Radiation Effects Research Foundation, 5-2 Hijiyama Park, Minami-ku, Hiroshima-shi, Hiroshima-ken 732, Japan. FAX 81-82-261-7279.
5113

RADIATION EFFECTS RESEARCH FOUNDATION NEWSLETTER.
Radiation Effects Research Foundation, 5-2, Hijiyama Park, Minami-ku, Hiroshima-shi, Hiroshima-ken 732, Japan. FAX 81-82-261-7279.
5113

RADIO CLUB OF AMERICA. PROCEEDINGS.
Radio Club of America, Inc., c/o Gerri Hopkins, 3 Caro St., Red Bank, NJ 07701. TEL 732-842-5070. FAX 732-219-1938.
circ. 1,500. *2027*

RADIO RESOURCE MAGAZINE.
Pandata Corporation, 14 Inverness Dr. E., D-136, Englewood, CO 80112. TEL 303-792-2390. FAX 303-792-2391.
circ. 35,000. *2028*

RADIO - T V INTERVIEW REPORT.
Bradley Communications Corp., Box 1206, Lansdowne, PA 19050. TEL 215-259-1070. FAX 215-284-3704.
circ. 4,000. *44*

RADIO WEEK.
National Association of Broadcasters, 1771 N St., N.W., Washington, DC 20036. TEL 202-429-5350. FAX 202-429-5406. *2028*

10384 CONTROLLED CIRCULATION SERIALS

RADIOBOTE.
F.O. Rothy, Ed. & Pub., A-4360 Grein, Austria.
circ. 150,000. *2028*

RADIUS (ROCKFORD).
Tube and Pipe Association, International (TPA), 833 Featherstone Rd., Rockford, IL 61107. TEL 815-399-8775. FAX 815-399-7679.
circ. 1,200. *5208*

RAIL WHISPERS.
Whisper Publications, Inc., 1865 Palmer Ave., Ste. 202, Larchmont, NY 10538. TEL 914-833-3634. FAX 914-834-7651.
circ. 30,000. *3383*

RAILWAY TECHNOLOGY INTERNATIONAL.
Sterling Publications Ltd., 86-88 Edgware Rd., London W2 2YW, England. TEL 44-171-915-9600. FAX 44-171-915-9619.
circ. 7,250. *7132*

RAILWAYS AFRICA.
Rail-Link C C, P.O. Box 4794, 2125 Randburg, Transvaal, South Africa. TEL 27-11-463-4330. FAX 27-11-463-4224.
circ. 2,500. *7132*

RAILWAYS INSTITUTE MAGAZINE.
Railways Institute Council, P.O. Box 8436, Perth Business Centre, Perth, W.A. 6849, Australia. TEL 61-9-3262461. FAX 61-9-3262754.
circ. 4,000. *7132*

RAINEY TIMES.
Rt. 4, Box 56, Sulphur Springs, TX 75482. TEL 903-885-3523. FAX 903-439-1081.
circ. 300. *3238*

THE RAM PAGE.
Angelo State University, Department of Communication, Drama and Journalism, 2601 W. Ave. N., San Angelo, TX 76909. TEL 915-942-2322. FAX 915-942-2078.
circ. 4,500. *1968*

RANDSE AFRIKAANSE UNIVERSITEIT. JAARBOEK.
Rand Afrikaans University, P.O. Box 524, Auckland Park 2006, South Africa. FAX 27-11-4892790. *2553*

RANSOMER.
Guild of Our Lady of Ransom, 31 Southdown Rd., Wimbledon, London SW20 8QJ, England. TEL 44-181-947-2598. FAX 44-181-944-6208.
circ. 2,000. *6477*

RAPPORT ANNUEL SUR LA COOPERATION AU DEVELOPPEMENT - BURUNDI.
United Nations Development Program, Programme des Nations Unies pour le Developpement au Burundi, c/o Ms. Linda Schrieber, Chief, Documentation and Statistics Office, BPPE, UNDP, New York, NY 10017. *1366*

RARE COIN REVIEW.
Bowers and Merena Galleries, Inc., Box 1224, Wolfeboro, NH 03894. TEL 603-596-5095. FAX 603-569-5319. *5467*

RASSEGNA DELL'IMBALLAGGIO E CONFEZIONAMENTO.
Editrice Arti Poligrafiche Europee, Via Casella 16, 20156 Milan, Italy. TEL 39-2-392281. FAX 39-2-39214341.
circ. 11,797. *5549*

RASSEGNA ECONOMICA (NAPLES).
Banco di Napoli, Direzione Generale, Ufficio Studi, Via Roma 177-178, 80132 Naples, Italy.
circ. 5,350. *1285*

RASSEGNA GRAFICA.
Editrice Arti Poligrafiche Europee, Via Casella, 16, 20156 Milan, Italy. TEL 39-2-392281. FAX 39-2-39214341.
circ. 12,627. *6085*

THE RATTLE.
Theta Chi Funds for Leadership and Education, Inc., 3330 Founders Rd., Indianapolis, IN 46268. TEL 317-824-1881. FAX 317-824-1908.
circ. 32,000. *1968*

RAZZA BOVINA PIEMONTESE.
Associazione Nazionale Allevatori Bovini di Razza Piemontese, Via Valeggio 22, 10128 Turin, Italy. TEL 39-173-750791. FAX 39-173-750915.
circ. 4,000. *287*

REACH (NEW HAVEN).
Religious Education Association, 409 Prospect St., New Haven, CT 06511-2177. TEL 203-865-6142. FAX 203-865-6142.
circ. 1,000. *2476*

READER (SAN DIEGO).
Box 85803, San Diego, CA 92138. TEL 619-235-3000. FAX 619-231-0489.
circ. 131,000. *4356*

READING TIME.
Children's Book Council of Australia, P.O. Box 62, Ashmont, Wagga Wagga, N.S.W. 2650, Australia. FAX 61-69-254907.
circ. 2,200. *4455*

THE READMORE NEWSLETTER.
Readmore Publications, Inc., 22 Cortlandt St., New York, NY 10007-3194. TEL 212-349-5540. FAX 212-571-7328.
circ. 2,500. *4208*

REAL ESTATE BUSINESS.
Realtors National Marketing Institute, Real Estate Brokerage Council, Box 300, Wheaton, IL 60189-0300. TEL 630-752-0500. FAX 630-752-0525.
circ. 40,000. *6309*

REAL ESTATE FORUM.
Real Estate Forum, Inc., 111 Eighth Ave., No. 1511, New York, NY 10011-5201. TEL 212-563-6460. FAX 212-967-1498.
circ. 24,000. *6310*

REAL ESTATE NEWS.
T R E B - R E N Venture, Inc., 15 Kern Rd., Don Mills, ON M3B 3N1, Canada. TEL 416-443-8113. FAX 416-443-9185.
circ. 65,000. *6310*

REAL SOCIEDAD ARQUEOLOGICA. BOLETIN ARQUEOLOGICO.
Real Sociedad Arqueologica Tarraconense, Museo Nacional Arqueologico, Tarragona, Spain.
circ. 1,000. *379*

REALITY (ALEXANDRIA).
Reality Inc., 1 Canyon Dr., Alexandria, VA 22305. TEL 703-836-0565.
circ. 10,000. *6364*

REALTIME.
Australian Council for the Arts, P.O. Box A2246, Sydney S. Post Office, Sydney, N.S.W. 1235, Australia.
circ. 25,000. *7012*

RECAMBIO LIBRE.
General de Ediciones Especializadas, S.L., C. Juan de Olias, 11 y 13, 28020 Madrid, Spain. TEL 34-1-5719676. FAX 34-1-5210695.
circ. 3,000. *7114*

THE RECORD OF SIGMA ALPHA EPSILON.
Sigma Alpha Epsilon National Fraternity, Box 1856, Evanston, IL 60204. TEL 708-475-1856.
circ. 81,000. *1968*

RECORDER (SEARCY).
Alpha Chi National Honor Society, Box 2249, Harding University, Searcy, AR 72149. TEL 501-268-6161.
circ. 7,500. *2554*

RECREATION NEWS.
Icarus Publishers, Inc., Box 32335, Washington, DC 20007-0635. TEL 202-965-6960. FAX 202-965-6964.
circ. 104,000. *7231*

RECYCLAGE MAGAZINE.
Editions Montmartre, 142, rue Montmartre, 75002 Paris, France. TEL 33-1-40268321. FAX 33-1-40399752.
circ. 6,000. *2988*

RECYCLAGE RECUPERATION.
Editions Montmartre, 142 rue Montmartre, 75002 Paris, France. TEL 33-1-40268321. FAX 33-1-40399752.
circ. 6,000. *2989*

RED AND BLACK (WASHINGTON).
Washington & Jefferson College, 60 S. Lincoln St., Washington, PA 15301. TEL 412-222-4400.
circ. 1,500. *1968*

RED MEN MAGAZINE.
Improved Order of Red Men, Box 683, Waco, TX 76703. TEL 817-756-1221. FAX 817-756-4828.
circ. 27,000. *1935*

RED SHIELD NEWS.
Royal Insurance, Corporate Communications Dept., 9300 Arrowpoint Blvd., Charlotte, NC 28217. TEL 704-522-2000. FAX 704-522-2055.
circ. 10,000. *3831*

RED TAPE.
Public Service Association of New South Wales, G.P.O. Box 3365, Sydney, N.S.W. 2001, Australia. TEL 61-2-92901555. FAX 61-2-92621623.
circ. 45,000. *3897*

REDWOOD NEWS.
California Redwood Association, 405 Enfrente Dr., Ste. 200, Novato, CA 94949. TEL 415-382-0662. FAX 415-382-8531.
circ. 30,000. *413*

REFINISHER.
Dulux Australia, P.O. Box 60, Rosebank MDC, Clayton S., Vic. 3169, Australia. TEL 61-2-94763199. FAX 61-2-94765739.
circ. 17,000. *7114*

REFLECTIONS.
Springer-Verlag Hong Kong, Ltd., 701 Mirror Tower, 61 Mody Rd., Tsim Sha Tsui, Kowloon, Hong Kong, People's Republic of China. TEL 852-723-9698. FAX 852-724-2366.
circ. 5,000. *6282*

REFLEX MAGAZINE.
Xelfer, 1011 W. Armour St., Seattle, WA 98119-2234. TEL 206-682-7688. FAX 206-682-6912.
circ. 7,000. *462*

REFRIGERATED AND FROZEN FOODS.
Stagnito Publishing Company, 1935 Shermer Rd., Ste. 100, Northbrook, IL 60062. TEL 847-205-5660. FAX 847-205-5680.
circ. 29,500. *3126*

REGARDS SUR LE COMITE D'ETABLISSEMENT D'ORLY SUD.
Comite d'Etablissement Air France-Orly Sud, Extension Est, Batiment CRP, Aerogare d'Orly Sud, France.
circ. 8,000. *77*

REGENCY INTERNATIONAL DIRECTORY.
Regency International Publications Ltd., 325 Canterbury Road, Densole, Folkestone, Kent CT18 7BB, England. TEL 0303-893488. FAX 0303-893488. *1708*

REGIONAL AIRLINE ASSOCIATION. ANNUAL REPORT.
Regional Airline Association, 1200 19th S., N.W., Ste. 300, Washington, DC 20036. TEL 202-857-1170. FAX 202-429-5113.
circ. 2,700. *7077*

REGIONAL DEVELOPMENT CORPORATION. ANNUAL REPORT.
Regional Development Corporation, P.O. Box 428, Fredericton, N.B. E3B 5R4, Canada. TEL 506-453-2277.
circ. 1,000. *1286*

THE REGIONAL REVIEW.
Yorkshire and Humberside Regional Research Observatory, University of Leeds, School of Geography, Leeds LS2 9JT, England. TEL 44-113-233-3336. FAX 44-113-233-3308.
circ. 150. *6562*

REGIONS BEYOND ADVANCE.
Regions Beyond Missionary Union International, 1431 Stuckert Rd., Warrington, PA 18976-1526. TEL 215-745-0680. FAX 215-742-3031.
circ. 11,400. *6365*

REGISTERED REPRESENTATIVE.
Plaza Communications, Inc., 18818 Teller Ave., No. 280, Irvine, CA 92612-1680. TEL 714-851-2220. FAX 714-851-1636.
circ. 90,000. *1404*

CONTROLLED CIRCULATION SERIALS 10385

REHAB & COMMUNITY CARE MANAGEMENT.
B C S Communications Ltd., 101 Thorncliffe Park Dr., Toronto, ON M4H 1M2, Canada. TEL 416-421-7944. FAX 416-421-0966.
circ. 20,000. *5046*

REIGN OF THE SACRED HEART.
Priests of the Sacred Heart, 6889 S. Lovers Ln., Hales Corners, WI 53130. TEL 414-425-3383. FAX 414-425-5719.
circ. 490,000. *6477*

REINSURANCE REPORTER.
Lincoln National Life Reinsurance Co., One Reinsurance Pl., P.O. Box 7808, Ft. Wayne, IN 46801. FAX 219-455-4124.
circ. 4,400. *3831*

RELAY MAGAZINE.
Florida Municipal Electric Association, Inc., Box 10114, 417 E. College Ave., Tallahassee, FL 32302-2114. TEL 904-224-3314.
circ. 2,200. *2691*

REMOVALS AND STORAGE.
Quarrington-Curtis Ltd., 15-17 Canute Rd., Southampton SO14 3FJ, England. TEL 44-1703-635438. FAX 44-1703-632198.
circ. 1,800. *7038*

RENDER.
Editors West, 10961 Desert Lawn Dr., No. 57, Calimesa, CA 92320. TEL 714-795-4240.
circ. 7,500. *148*

RENEWAL NEWS.
Presbyterian Renewal Publications, Box 429, Black Mountain, NC 28711-0429. TEL 704-669-7373. FAX 704-669-4880.
circ. 14,000. *6440*

RENOVA.
Verlag fuer Bauwesen GmbH, Am Friedrichshain 22, 10407 Berlin, Germany. TEL 49-30-42151388. FAX 49-30-42151232.
circ. 10,000. *910*

RENS OG VASK.
Visholm Media AS, Sydvestvej 49, P.O. Box 221, DK-2600 Glostrup, Denmark.
circ. 3,000. *1911*

RENT I DANMARK.
Forlaget Thorsgaard ApS, Holmensvej 5, P.O. Box 5, 3600 Frederikssund, Denmark. TEL 42-31-21-05. FAX 47-38-36-33.
circ. 7,000. *1504*

RENTAL EQUIPMENT REGISTER.
Miramar Communications Inc., 23815 Stuart Ranch Rd., Box 8987, Malibu, CA 90265-8987. TEL 310-337-9717.
circ. 17,500. *1546*

RENTAL PRODUCT NEWS.
Johnson Hill Press, Inc., 1233 Janesville Ave., Ft. Atkinson, WI 53538. TEL 920-563-6388. FAX 920-563-1699.
circ. 20,500. *1594*

REPORT TO BUSINESS.
Better Business Bureau of Metropolitan New York Inc., 257 Park Ave. S., New York, NY 10010. TEL 212-533-7500. *2258*

THE REPORTER (LITTLE ROCK).
Arkansas School Boards Association, 808 Dr. M.L. King Dr., Little Rock, AR 72202-3646. TEL 501-372-1415. FAX 501-375-2454.
circ. 3,500. *2577*

REPORTER ON HUMAN REPRODUCTION & THE LAW.
Legal-Medical Studies, Inc., Box 8219, Boston, MA 02114. TEL 617-742-7959. *4015*

REPORTERO INDUSTRIAL.
Keller International Publishing Corporation, 150 Great Neck Rd., Great Neck, NY 11021. TEL 516-829-9210. FAX 516-829-7265.
circ. 38,428. *4551*

REPROGRAFIA ACTUAL.
Ediciones Press Graph, S.L., C. Mallorca 219 5o 2o, 08008 Barcelona, Spain. TEL 34-3-3237554. FAX 34-3-3237463.
circ. 2,500. *6085*

RES PUBLICA NOWA.
Batory Press Sp. z o.o., P.O. Box 856, 00-950 Warsaw 1, Poland. TEL 48-22-6298934. FAX 48-22-6273668.
circ. 5,000. *4356*

RESEARCH (SAN FRANCISCO).
Research Holdings Ltd., 2201 Third St., San Francisco, CA 94107. TEL 415-621-0220. FAX 415-621-0735.
circ. 61,500. *1404*

RESEARCH & DEVELOPMENT.
Cahners Publishing Company (Des Plaines), Division of Reed Elsevier Inc., 1350 E. Touhy Ave., Box 5080, Des Plaines, IL 60018-5080. TEL 847-390-2343. FAX 847-390-2618.
circ. 101,600. *6971*

RESEARCH & DEVELOPMENT PRODUCT SOURCE TELEPHONE DIRECTORY.
Cahners Publishing Company (Des Plaines), Division of Reed Elsevier Inc., 1350 E. Touhy Ave., Box 5080, Des Plaines, IL 60018-5080. TEL 847-635-8800. FAX 847-390-2618.
circ. 100,000. *6971*

RESEARCH IN FISHERIES.
University of Washington, School of Fisheries WH-10, Seattle, WA 98195. TEL 206-543-4678. FAX 206-685-7471.
circ. 3,000. *3077*

RESEARCH - PENN STATE.
Pennsylvania State University, Senior Vice President for Research, 320 Kern Bldg., University Park, PA 16802. TEL 814-865-3477. FAX 814-863-4627.
circ. 25,000. *2554*

RESEARCHPLUS.
Market Research Society, 15 Northburgh St., London EC1V 0AH, England. TEL 44-171-490-4911. FAX 44-171-490-0608.
circ. 7,000. *1547*

RESIDENCES.
Marketing U.S.P. Inc., 554 Grosvenor, Westmount, PQ H3Y 2S4, Canada. TEL 514-935-1171. FAX 514-935-4504.
circ. 71,053. *3849*

RESIDENTIAL LIGHTING MAGAZINE.
Vance Publishing Corporation (Lincolnshire), Box 1414, Lincolnshire, IL 60069-1414. TEL 708-634-2600. FAX 708-634-4379.
circ. 11,600. *3860*

RESOURCES (NASHVILLE).
F I S I - Madison Financial, Box 40726, Nashville, TN 37204. TEL 615-371-2658.
circ. 1,200,000. *2258*

RESSOURCE EN SANTE ET EN SECURITE.
Ontario Natural Resource Safety Association, 690 Mc Keown Ave., P.O. Box 2050, North Bay, ON P1B 9P1, Canada. TEL 705-474-SAFE. FAX 705-472-5800.
circ. 10,000. *5498*

RESTAURANT HOSPITALITY.
Penton Publishing Co., 1100 Superior Ave., Cleveland, OH 44114-2543. TEL 216-696-7000. FAX 216-696-8765.
circ. 124,048. *3734*

RESTORATION HERALD.
Christian Restoration Association, 5664 Cheviot Rd., Cincinnati, OH 45247. TEL 513-385-0461.
circ. 4,500. *6367*

RETAIL OBSERVER.
1442 Sierra Creek Way, San Jose, CA 95132. TEL 408-272-8974. FAX 408-272-3344.
circ. 8,500. *3860*

RETAIL PHARMACY.
Sterling Media, P.O. Box 670, Seven Hills, N.S.W. 2147, Australia. TEL 61-2-98388233. FAX 61-2-96742004.
circ. 7,124. *5692*

RETHINKING SCHOOLS.
Rethinking Schools Limited, 1001 E. Keefe Ave., Milwaukee, WI 53212. TEL 414-694-9646. FAX 414-964-7220.
circ. 33,000. *2477*

THE RETIRED OFFICER.
Retired Officers' Association, 201 N. Washington St., Alexandria, VA 22314-2539. TEL 703-838-8115. FAX 703-838-8179.
circ. 389,592. *5283*

RETIREMENT LIFE (WASHINGTON).
National Association of Retired Federal Employees, 1533 New Hampshire Ave., N.W., Washington, DC 20036. TEL 202-234-0832. FAX 202-797-9698.
circ. 1,000. *3444*

REUMATIKERTIDNINGEN.
Riksfoerbundet mot Reumatism, P.O. Box 12851, Alstroemergatan 39, S-112 98 Stockholm, Sweden. TEL 46-8-653-21-00. FAX 46-8-650-64-15.
circ. 53,000. *5126*

REVIEW OF BUSINESS.
St. John's University, College of Business Administration, Bent Hall, 8000 Utopia Pkwy., Jamaica, NY 11439. TEL 718-990-6768. FAX 718-990-1868.
circ. 7,000. *996*

REVIEW OF OPHTHALMOLOGY.
Chilton Co., 201 King of Prussia Rd., Radnor, PA 19089. TEL 610-964-4370. FAX 610-964-2959.
circ. 18,000. *5000*

REVISTA A T E M C O P.
Asociacion Espanola de Tecnicos de Maquinaria para la Construccion, Obras Publicas y Mineria, c/o Cruz del Sur, No. 3 bajo, 28007 Madrid, Spain. TEL 1-574-98-18. FAX 1-573-18-00.
circ. 5,000. *2796*

REVISTA AEREA.
Strato Publishing Co., Inc., 310 E. 44th St., Ste. 1601, New York, NY 10017. TEL 212-370-1740. FAX 212-949-6756.
circ. 10,200. *77*

REVISTA ALENTEJANA.
Casa do Alentejo, Rua das Portas de Santo Antao 58, Lisbon 2, Portugal.
circ. 3,000. *4356*

REVISTA BRASILEIRA DE XADREZ POSTAL.
Clube de Xadrez Epistolar Brasileiro, Caixa Postal 21200, 04602-970 Sao Paulo SP, Brazil. TEL 55-21-535-2938.
circ. 1,950. *6778*

REVISTA CUBANA DE INVESTIGACIONES PESQUERAS. BOLETINES BIBLIOGRAFICOS.
Direccion de Ciencia y Tecnica, Ministerio de la Industria Pesquera, 5ta Avda. y 248 Barlovento, Santa Fe, Playa, Havana, Cuba. FAX 0511345.
circ. 900. *3077*

REVISTA DE ARQUITECTURA.
Sociedad Central de Arquitectos, Montevideo 938, 1019 Buenos Aires, Argentina. TEL 54-1-812-3644. FAX 54-1-953-5508.
circ. 8,000. *414*

REVISTA DE CIENCIA Y TECNOLOGIA.
Universidade Metodista de Piracicaba, Rodovira do Acucar, Km. 156, 13400-911 Piracicaba, Sao Paulo, Brazil. TEL 55-19-4221515. FAX 55-19-4222500.
circ. 900. *6563*

REVISTA DE CIENCIAS FARMACEUTICAS.
Universidade Estadual Paulista, Av. Vicente Ferreira 1278, Caixa Postal 71, 17515-901 Marilia SP, Brazil. TEL 55-144-222504. FAX 55-144-222504. *5693*

REVISTA DE ESTUDIOS SOCIALES.
Centro de Estudios Sociales de la Santa Cruz del Valle de los Caidos, Palacio Real, Bailen s-n, Apdo. de Correas 14158, Madrid 15, Spain.
circ. 2,000. *6725*

REVISTA DE HISTORIA.
Comite Provincial del Partido Comunista de Cuba, Seccion de Investigaciones Historicas, Ave. 20 Aniversario y Plaza de la Revolucion, Holguin, Cuba. TEL 462013.
circ. 3,000. *3510*

10386 CONTROLLED CIRCULATION SERIALS

REVISTA ECONOMICA (LA PLATA).
Universidad Nacional de la Plata, Instituto de Investigaciones Economicas, Calle 48 No. 555, Piso 5, Ofic. 523, 1900 La Plata, Argentina. TEL 54-21-229383.
circ. 1,000. *997*

REVISTA ELECTROTECNICA.
Asociacion Electrotecnia Argentina, Posadas 1659, C.P. 1112 Buenos Aires, Argentina. TEL 804-3454-1532.
circ. 1,600. *2845*

REVISTA IBEROAMERICANA DE MICOLOGIA.
Asociacion Espanola de Micologia, Depto. Inmunologia, Microbiologia y Parasitologia, Universidad del Pais Vasco, Apartado 699, 48080 Bilbao, Spain. TEL 34-4-4648800 ext. 2745. FAX 34-4-4649266.
circ. 850. *4739*

REVISTA LAMAZE PARA PADRES.
Lamaze Publishing Co., 372 Danbury Rd., Wilton, CT 06897-2523. TEL 203-834-2711. FAX 203-761-8696.
circ. 500,000. *4967*

REVISTA TRIMESTRAL DE JURISPRUDENCIA.
Imprensa Nacional, SIG, Quadra 6, Lote 800, Caixa Postal 30000, 70604-900 Brasilia DF, Brazil. TEL 55-61-3139905. FAX 55-61-3139528.
circ. 2,000. *4018*

REVUE ARCHEOLOGIQUE DE L'EST ET DU CENTRE-EST.
C N R S Editions, 20-22 rue St. Amand, 75015 Paris, France. TEL 45-33-16-00. FAX 45-33-92-13.
circ. 1,500. *379*

REVUE ARCHEOLOGIQUE NARBONNAISE.
C N R S Editions, 20-22 rue St. Amand, 75015 Paris, France. TEL 45-33-16-00. FAX 45-33-92-13.
circ. 1,500. *380*

REVUE D'ELEVAGE ET DE MEDECINE VETERINAIRE DES PAYS TROPICAUX.
Expansion Scientifique Francaise, 31 Bd. de la Tour Maubourg, 75343 Paris Cedex 07, France. TEL 33-1-40626400. FAX 33-1-45556920. *7278*

REVUE D'HISTOIRE DES TEXTES.
C N R S Editions, 20-22 rue St. Amand, 75015 Paris, France. TEL 45-33-16-00. FAX 45-33-92-13.
circ. 1,250. *4459*

REVUE DE L'ALIMENTATION ANIMALE.
Gedeon Marketing Eurl, B.P. 16, 29560 Telgruc-sur-Mer, France. TEL 33-2-98273766. FAX 33-2-98273765.
circ. 3,000. *265*

REVUE FRANCAISE DE SERVICE SOCIAL.
Association Nationale des Assistants de Service Social, 15 rue de Bruxelles, 75009 Paris, France. TEL 33-1-45263379. FAX 33-1-42800703.
circ. 2,700. *6684*

REVUE INTERNATIONALE DE CRIMINOLOGIE ET DE POLICE TECHNIQUE.
Marcel Meichtry Editions, Chemin de la Caroline 26, CH-1213 Petit-Lancy, Switzerland. TEL 41-22-8798820. FAX 41-22-8798825.
circ. 1,500. *2279*

REVUE MEDICALE DE BRUXELLES.
Association des Medecins Anciens Etudiants de l'Universite Libre de Bruxelles (A.M.U.B.), Route de Lennik 808, Bte. 612, 1070 Brussels, Belgium. TEL 32-2-555-6062. FAX 32-2-555-6117.
circ. 2,900. *4739*

REVUE OCCASIONS D'AFFAIRES.
Revue Occasions d'Affaires Ltee, 425 St.-Amable St., Ste. 145, Quebec, PQ G1R 5E4, Canada. TEL 418-640-1686. FAX 418-640-1687. *998*

RHEINISCHES ZAHNAERZTEBLATT.
Vereinigte Verlagsanstalten GmbH, Hoeherweg 278, 40231 Duesseldorf, Germany. TEL 49-211-7357-0. FAX 49-211-7357223.
circ. 9,000. *4870*

RHODE ISLAND. OFFICE OF LIBRARY AND INFORMATION SERVICES. NEWSLETTER.
Office of Library and Information Servces, One Capitol Hill, Providence, RI 02908. TEL 401-277-2726. FAX 401-277-4195.
circ. 800. *4210*

THE RHODE ISLAND BUILDER REPORT.
Rhode Island Builders Association, 450 Veterans Memorial Pkwy. No. 301, East Providence, RI 02914-5380. TEL 401-438-7400. FAX 401-438-7446.
circ. 3,400. *911*

RICHMOND AFRO-AMERICAN NEWSPAPER.
Afro-American Co. of Baltimore City, 2519 N. Charles St., Baltimore, MD 21218. TEL 410-554-8200. FAX 804-554-8477.
circ. 30,000. *3039*

RICHTER UND STAATSANWALT IN N R W.
Vereinigte Verlagsanstalten GmbH, Hoeherweg 278, 40231 Duesseldorf, Germany. TEL 49-211-7357-0. FAX 49-211-7357223.
circ. 6,750. *4138*

RIDER UNIVERSITY MAGAZINE.
Rider University, 2083 Lawrenceville Rd., Lawrenceville, NJ 08648-3099. TEL 609-869-5165. FAX 609-895-5440.
circ. 32,500. *1969*

RINKSIDER.
Target Publishing Co., Inc. (Columbus), 2470 E. Main St., Columbus, OH 43209. TEL 614-235-1022. FAX 614-235-3584.
circ. 3,000. *1505*

RIO (SAN ANTONIO).
Paseo del Rio Association of San Antonio, 213 Broadway, Ste. 5, San Antonio, TX 78205-1923. TEL 210-227-4262. FAX 210-212-7602.
circ. 50,000. *1195*

RIO GRANDE DO SUL, BRAZIL. PROCURADORIA GERAL DO ESTADO. REVISTA.
Procuradoria Geral do Estado, Av. Borges Medeiros 1501, 13th, Porto Alegre 90060, Brazil. FAX 0512-255496.
circ. 1,500. *4019*

RIPON MAGAZINE.
Ripon College, Box 248, Ripon, WI 54971. TEL 414-748-8364. FAX 414-748-9262.
circ. 14,000. *1969*

RISCONTROL.
Edition Vega Verlagsgesellschaft mbH, Postfach 11, A-3532 Rastenfeld, Austria. TEL 43-1-8185354. FAX 43-1-5132942.
circ. 7,000. *3831*

RISK MAGAZINE.
I I A Publishing Pty. Ltd., P.O. Box 861, Double Bay, N.S.W. 2028, Australia. TEL 61-2-3287699. FAX 61-2-32887690.
circ. 5,800. *3832*

RISK MANAGEMENT FOR EXECUTIVE WOMEN.
Cox Publications, Box 20316, Billings, MT 59104-0316. TEL 406-256-8822.
circ. 470. *3832*

RIVISTA DELL'ARBITRATO.
Casa Editrice Dott. A. Giuffre, Via Busto Arsizio, 40, 20151 Milan, Italy. TEL 39-2-38089200. FAX 39-2-38009582.
circ. 1,500. *1452*

RIVISTA TECNICA DI CINEMATOGRAFIA.
Edizione Cinemeccanica S.p.A., Viale Campania 23, Milan, Italy. TEL 39-2-718941. FAX 39-2-70100470.
circ. 5,000. *5343*

ROAD AHEAD.
Road Ahead Publishing Co. Pty Ltd., G.P.O. Box 1403, Brisbane, Qld. 4001, Australia. TEL 61-7-33612340. FAX 61-7-32571863.
circ. 665,066. *7114*

ROAD KING.
Hammock Publishing, Inc., 3322 W. End Ave., Ste. 700, Nashville, TN 37203-0076. TEL 615-385-9745. FAX 615-386-9349.
circ. 229,939. *7178*

ROAD PATROL.
Royal Automobile Club of Western Australia, G.P.O. Box C140, Perth, W.A. 6001, Australia. TEL 61-9-4214444. FAX 61-9-2211887.
circ. 361,847. *7115*

ROCAS Y MINERALES.
Editorial Rocas y Minerales, C. Arturo Baldasano, 15 bajo, 28043 Madrid, Spain. TEL 34-1-4151804. FAX 34-1-4151661.
circ. 6,000. *5315*

ROCKEFELLER FOUNDATION. ANNUAL REPORT.
Rockefeller Foundation, 420 Fifth Ave., New York, NY 10018. TEL 212-869-8500. FAX 212-764-3468.
circ. 18,000. *6684*

ROCKET.
Bam Publications, Inc., 3470 Buskirk Ave., Pleasant Hill, CA 94523. TEL 510-934-3700. FAX 510-946-2974.
circ. 70,000. *5431*

ROCKETEER.
Missouri Training Center for Men, Box 7, Moberly, MO 65270. TEL 816-263-3778.
circ. 2,700. *2279*

ROCKY MOUNTAIN COAL MINING INSTITUTE. PROCEEDINGS.
Rocky Mountain Coal Mining Institute, 3000 Youngfield, Ste. 324, Lakewood, CO 80215. TEL 303-238-9099. FAX 303-238-0509.
circ. 1,000. *5315*

ROCKY MOUNTAIN CONSTRUCTION (SOUTH EDITION).
Rocky Mountain Construction Magazine, Inc., Associated Construction Publications, 2403 Champa, Denver, CO 80205-2694. TEL 303-295-0630. FAX 303-295-2159.
circ. 7,800. *911*

ROCZNIK BIBLIOTEKI NARODOWEJ.
Biblioteka Narodowa, Zespol Redakcji Czasopism, Al. Niepodleglosci 213, 00-973 Warsaw, Poland. TEL 48-22-6082252. FAX 48-22-255251.
circ. 600. *4210*

ROEH HACHESHBON.
Institute of Certified Public Accountants in Israel, P.O. Box 29281, 1 Montefiore St., Tel Aviv, Israel. TEL 972-3-5161114. FAX 972-3-5103105.
circ. 2,700. *1098*

ROERFAG.
Skarland Press A-S, P.O. Box 5042 Maj., N-0301 Oslo, Norway. TEL 47-22-59-88-00. FAX 47-22-69-36-50.
circ. 3,842. *3484*

THE ROLL.
Scholar Contemplationis, 3425 Forest Ln., Pfafftown, NC 27040-9545. TEL 910-924-4980.
circ. 600. *5749*

ROLL CALL.
Roll Call, Inc., 900 Second St., N.E., Ste. 107, Washington, DC 20002. TEL 202-289-4900. FAX 202-289-2205.
circ. 12,000. *5966*

ROMA E PROVINCIA ATTRAVERSO LA STATISTICA.
Camera di Commercio Industria Artigianato e Agricoltura di Roma, Via De'Burro 147, 00186 Rome, Italy. *6934*

ROMANIAN JOURNAL OF METEOROLOGY.
National Institute of Meteorology and Hydrology, 97 Bucuresti-Ploiesti Hwy., 71581 Bucharest, Rumania. TEL 40-1-6793240. FAX 40-1-3129843.
circ. 250. *5242*

ROMATOLOJI VE TIBBI REHABILITASYON DERGISI.
Turk Tibbi Rehabilitasyon Kurumu Dernegi, Hacettepe Universitesi, Tip Fakultesi, 06100 Hacettepe - Ankara, Turkey. TEL 90-312-309-4142. FAX 90-312-3105769.
circ. 600. *5128*

ROOFING HOLLAND.
Mandate Publishers BV, Postbus 9198, 1800 GD Alkmaar, Netherlands. TEL 31-2513-20500.
circ. 14,000. *911*

ROSACRUZ.
Supreme Grand Lodge of AMORC, Inc., Rosicrucian Park, San Jose, CA 95191-0001. TEL 408-287-9171.
circ. 17,000. *5749*

THE ROSE.
Royal National Rose Society, Chiswell Green, St. Albans AL2 3NR, England. TEL 44-1727-850461. FAX 44-1727-850360.
circ. 19,000. *3204*

ROSKILL'S METALS DATABOOK.
Roskill Information Services Ltd., 2 Clapham Rd., London SW9 OJA, England. TEL 44-171-582-5155. FAX 44-171-793-0008.
circ. 75. *5315*

ROSSING MAGAZINE.
Rossing Uranium Ltd., Corporate Affairs, P.O. Box 22391, Windhoek 9000, Namibia. TEL 264-61-236760. FAX 264-61-228147.
circ. 4,000. *2243*

ROTOR AND WING INTERNATIONAL.
Phillips Business Information, Inc., 1201 Seven Locks Rd., Potomac, MD 20854. TEL 301-424-3338. FAX 301-309-3847. *77*

ROUND BOBBIN.
Offinger Management Co., P.O. Box 2188, Zanesville, OH 43702-2188. TEL 614-452-4541. FAX 614-452-2552.
circ. 5,400. *5453*

ROUNDUP (EL PASO).
Acme Boot Co., Inc., Box 9216, El Paso, TX 79983-0216. TEL 615-552-2000.
circ. 2,500. *6596*

ROYAL AIR FORCE EDUCATION BULLETIN.
Royal Air Force Training Development and Support Unit, Department of Educational and Training Technology Development, RAF Newton, Nottingham NG13 8HL, England. TEL 0949-20771. FAX 0949-21201.
circ. 1,300. *5284*

ROYAL BANK LETTER.
Royal Bank of Canada, Public Affairs Department, One Place Ville Marie, 7th Fl. W., Box 6001, Montreal, PQ H3C 3A9, Canada. TEL 514-874-2110. FAX 514-874-5891.
circ. 150,000. *1165*

ROYAL CALEDONIAN CURLING CLUB. ANNUAL.
Royal Caledonian Curling Club, Cairnie House, Ave. K, Ingliston Showground, Newbridge, Midlothian EH28 2NB, Scotland. TEL 44-131-333-3003. FAX 44-131-333-3323.
circ. 3,000. *6779*

ROYAL COLLEGE OF ANAESTHETISTS. NEWSLETTER.
Royal College of Anaesthetists, 48-49 Russell Sq., London WC1B 4JY, England. TEL 44-171-813-1900. FAX 44-171-813-1876.
circ. 6,000. *4807*

ROYAL COLLEGE OF PHYSICIANS OF EDINBURGH. PROCEEDINGS.
Royal College of Physicians of Edinburgh, 9 Queen St., Edinburgh EH2 1JQ, Scotland. TEL 0131-225-7324. FAX 0131-220-3939.
circ. 6,100. *4741*

ROYAL COLLEGE OF SPEECH AND LANGUAGE THERAPISTS. BULLETIN.
Royal College of Speech and Language Therapists, 7 Bath Pl., London EC2 3DR, England. TEL 44-171-613-3855. FAX 44-171-613-3854.
circ. 8,000. *2589*

ROYAL INSTITUTION OF GREAT BRITAIN. RECORD.
Royal Institution of Great Britain, 21 Albemarle St., London W1X 4BS, England. TEL 44-171-409-2992.
circ. 3,000. *6563*

ROYAL INSTITUTION OF GREAT BRITAIN. ROYAL INSTITUTION LECTURES.
Royal Institution of Great Britain, 21 Albemarle St., London W1X 4BS, England. TEL 44-171-409-2992.
circ. 4,000. *6563*

ROYAL SOCIETY NEWS.
Royal Society of London, 6 Carlton House Terrace, London SW1Y 5AG, England. TEL 44-171-839-5561. FAX 44-171-976-1837.
circ. 5,000. *6563*

RUBBER & PLASTICS NEWS.
Crain Communications Inc. (Akron), 1725 Merriman Rd., Ste. 300, Akron, OH 44313-5251. TEL 330-836-9180. FAX 330-836-1005.
circ. 16,641. *6504*

RUCH FILOZOFICZNY.
Polskie Towarzystwo Filozoficzne, c/o Uniwersytet Mikolaja Kopernika, Instytut Filozofii, Ul. Podmurna 74, 87-100 Torun, Poland. TEL 48-56-21157. FAX 48-56-21157.
circ. 530. *5749*

RUDY I METALLY.
Ts N I G R I, Varshavskoe Shosse, 129B, 113545 Moscow, Russia. TEL 7-095-3152847. FAX 7-095-3152701.
circ. 500. *5315*

RUNDBRIEF FRAUEN IN DER LITERATURWISSENSCHAFT.
Universitaet Hamburg, Arbeitsstelle fuer Feministische Literaturwissenschaft, Von-Melle-Park 6, 20146 Hamburg, Germany. TEL 49-40-41234818. FAX 49-40-41234785.
circ. 1,000. *4461*

RUNNING & FITNEWS.
American Running and Fitness Association, 4405 East-West Hwy., Ste. 405, Bethesda, MD 20814. TEL 301-913-9517. FAX 301-913-9520.
circ. 20,000. *5789*

THE RUNNING BOARD.
Edmonton Antique Car Club, P.O. Box 102, Edmonton AB T5J 2G9, Canada.
circ. 95. *7115*

RURAL ELECTRIC NEBRASKAN.
Nebraska Rural Electric Association, 800 S. 13th St., Lincoln, NE 68501. TEL 402-475-4988.
circ. 58,000. *2691*

RURAL ROOTS.
Prince Albert Daily Herald, 30-10th St., P.O. Box 550, Prince Albert, SK S6V 5R9, Canada. TEL 306-764-4276. FAX 306-763-3331.
circ. 24,107. *150*

RUSSKOE VOZROZHDENIE.
St. Seraphim Foundation, 887 Stockton Rd., Valley Cottage, NY 10989. TEL 914-268-5548. FAX 914-267-4818.
circ. 1,500. *6393*

RUTGERS MAGAZINE.
Rutgers University, Department of University Communications, Alexander Johnston Hall, New Brunswick, NJ 08903. TEL 908-932-7315. FAX 908-932-8412.
circ. 110,000. *1969*

RX REMEDY.
Rx Remedy, Inc., 120 Post Rd. W., Westport, CT 06880. TEL 203-341-7000. FAX 203-221-4913.
circ. 2,000,000. *3444*

RX UPDATE.
Valley Forge Press, 1288 Valley Forge Rd., Box 1135, Valley Forge, PA 19482. TEL 610-935-3302. FAX 610-935-3072.
circ. 60,000. *5693*

RYERSON MAGAZINE.
Ryerson Polytechnic University, Office of University Advancement, 350 Victoria St., Toronto, ON M5B 2K3, Canada. TEL 416-979-5304. FAX 416-979-5166.
circ. 65,000. *1970*

S A B S CATALOGUE.
South African Bureau of Standards, Private Bag X191, Pretoria 0001, South Africa. TEL 27-12-428-7911. FAX 27-12-344-1568.
circ. 2,000. *5254*

S A CLEANING REVIEW.
George Warman Publications (Pty.) Ltd., P.O. Box 704, Cape Town 8000, South Africa. TEL 27-21-245320. FAX 27-21-261332.
circ. 1,417. *1911*

S A INSTRUMENTATION & CONTROL.
Technews (Pty) Ltd., P.O. Box 626, Kloof 3640, South Africa. TEL 27-31-7640593. FAX 27-31-7640386.
circ. 6,500. *6972*

S A L S IN BRIEF.
Southern Adirondack Library System, 22 Whitney Pl., Saratoga Springs, NY 12866. TEL 518-584-7300.
circ. 425. *4211*

S.A. MARKSMAN.
South African Pistol Association, P.O. Box 73989, Fairland 2030, South Africa.
circ. 500. *6779*

S A R A SCOPE.
Society of American Registered Architects, 1411 London Rd., Duluth, MN 55805. TEL 218-728-4293. FAX 218-728-5361.
circ. 500. *414*

S A T H NEWS.
Society for the Advancement of Travel for the Handicapped, 347 Fifth Ave., Ste. 610, New York, NY 10016. TEL 212-447-7284. FAX 212-725-8253.
circ. 1,000. *7232*

S A W E NEWSLETTER.
Society of Allied Weight Engineers, Inc., 5530 Aztec Dr., La Mesa, CA 91942-2110. TEL 619-465-1367. FAX 619-465-2561.
circ. 1,000. *77*

S C A N.
U.S. National Aeronautics and Space Administration, Scientific and Technical Information Office, 800 Elkridge Landing Rd., Linthicum Heights, MD 21090-2934. *84*

S C O U T.
U S A Volleyball, 3595 E. Fountain Blvd., Ste. I-2, Colorado Springs, CO 80910-1740. TEL 719-637-8300. FAX 719-597-6307. *6816*

S D P M A PETROLEUM JOURNAL.
South Dakota Petroleum Marketers Association, Box 1058, Pierre, SD 57501. TEL 605-224-8606.
circ. 500. *5621*

S D S U MAGAZINE.
San Diego State University, University Communications, 5500 Campanile Dr., San Diego, CA 92182-0763. TEL 619-594-5204. FAX 619-594-5956.
circ. 110,000. *1970*

S E C DOCKET.
U.S. Securities and Exchange Commission, 450 Fifth St., N.W., MISC-11, Washington, DC 20549. TEL 202-272-7460. FAX 202-272-7050.
circ. 12,500. *1405*

S E C E D NEWSLETTER.
Society for Earthquake and Civil Engineering Dynamics, Great George St., London SW1P 3AA, England. TEL 44-171-665-2230.
circ. 400. *2797*

S E C NEWS DIGEST.
U.S. Securities and Exchange Commission, 450 Fifth St., N.W., MISC-11, Washington, DC 20549. TEL 202-272-7460. FAX 202-272-7050. *1405*

S E I U ACTION.
Service Employees International Union, 1313 L St., N.W., Washington, DC 20005. TEL 202-898-3331. FAX 202-898-3491.
circ. 85,000. *3897*

S E I U UPDATE.
Service Employees International Union, 1313 L St., N.W., Washington, DC 20005. TEL 202-898-3200. FAX 202-898-3438.
circ. 50,000. *3897*

S F E P DIRECTORY.
Society of Freelance Editors and Proofreaders, Mermaid House, 1 Mermaid Ct., London SE1 1HR, England. TEL 44-171-403-5141.
circ. 2,500. *6283*

S F WEEKLY.
S F Weekly, 425 Brannan St., San Francisco, CA 94107. TEL 415-541-0700. FAX 415-777-1839.
circ. 100,000. *3384*

S H O T BUSINESS.
National Shooting Sports Foundation, 11 Mile Hill Rd., Newtown, CT 06470-2359. TEL 203-426-1320. FAX 203-426-1087.
circ. 20,000. *6881*

S I G A C T NEWS.
Association for Computing Machinery, Special Interest Group on Automata and Computability Theory, 1515 Broadway, 17th Fl., New York, NY 10036.
circ. 1,588. *2111*

S I G N U M NEWSLETTER.
Association for Computing Machinery, Special Interest Group on Numerical Mathematics, 1515 Broadway, 17th Fl., New York, NY 10036. TEL 212-869-7440.
circ. 1,800. *4624*

S I REVIEW.
Staffing Industry Analysts, Inc., 2235 Grant Rd., No. 3, Los Altos, CA 94024. TEL 415-903-9494. FAX 415-903-9811.
circ. 21,000. *1575*

S K A V - FACHBLATT.
Schweizerischer Verband Christlicher Institutionen, Zaehringerstr. 19, 6000 Lucerne 7, Switzerland.
circ. 1,500. *6684*

S N E S U P BULLETIN.
Syndicat National de l'Enseignement Superieur, 78 rue du Faubourg Saint-Denis, 75010 Paris, France.
2555

S N V BULLETIN.
Schweizerische Normen-Vereinigung, Muehlebachstr. 54, CH-8008 Zurich, Switzerland. TEL 41-1-2545454. FAX 41-1-2545474.
circ. 1,200. *5254*

S O R T BULLETIN.
American Library Association, Staff Organizations Round Table, 50 E. Huron St., Chicago, IL 60611. TEL 312-280-4277. FAX 312-280-3256.
circ. 550. *4211*

S P A B NEWS.
Society for the Protection of Ancient Buildings, 37 Spital Sq., London E1 6DY, England. TEL 44-171-377-1644. FAX 44-171-247-5296.
circ. 5,500. *414*

S P E E A SPOTLITE.
Seattle Professional Engineering Employees Association, 15205 52nd Ave. S., Seattle, WA 98188. TEL 206-433-0995. FAX 206-248-3990.
circ. 18,000. *3897*

S P E REVIEW.
McQuillan Young Communications, 5 Arlington St., London SW1A 1RA, England. TEL 44-171-355-1161. FAX 44-171-355-1171.
circ. 4,000. *5621*

SAAGVERKEN.
Arbor Publishing AB, P.O. Box 26212, S-100 41 Stockholm, Sweden. TEL 46-8-611-60-30. FAX 46-8-679-90-50.
circ. 3,100. *3174*

SAASTOPANKKI.
Saastopankkiliitto, Postilokero 47, SF-00101 Helsinki 10, Finland. FAX 0-1334935.
circ. 27,188. *1165*

SACERDOZIO REGALE.
Centro Sacerdozio Regale, Via Villanova, 14, Casa Betania, 33170 Pordenone, Italy. TEL 39-434-570019.
circ. 3,000. *6369*

SADO MARINE BIOLOGICAL STATION. REPORT.
Niigata Daigaku, Rigakubu Fuzoku Sado Rinkai Jikkenjo, 2-8050 Igarashi, Niigata 950-21, Japan. TEL 0259-75-2012. FAX 0259-75-2012.
circ. 600. *624*

SAFE CYCLING.
Motorcycle Safety Foundation, 2 Jenner St., Ste. 150, Irvine, CA 92718-3812. TEL 714-727-3227. FAX 714-727-4217.
circ. 6,500. *6833*

SAFE DRIVER.
Order of the Road, P.O. Box 227, Forest Row, E. Sussex RH18 5YS, England. TEL 44-1342-826536. FAX 44-1342-824847.
circ. 1,000. *7115*

SAFECO AGENT.
Safeco Corporation, Safeco Plaza, Seattle, WA 98185. TEL 206-545-6009.
circ. 11,000. *3832*

SAFETY & COMPLIANCE NEWS.
National Private Truck Council, 66 Canal Center Plaza, Ste. 600, Alexandria, VA 22314. TEL 703-683-1300. FAX 703-683-1217.
circ. 2,500. *7178*

SAFETY RESOURCES.
Gulf Atlantic Communications Corporation, Inc., Box 407000, Ft. Lauderdale, FL 33340-7000. TEL 954-489-4070. FAX 954-489-4079.
circ. 10,000. *5499*

SAFETY SIGNALS.
Industrial Safety Equipment Association, 1901 N. Moore St., Ste. 808, Arlington, VA 22209. TEL 703-525-1695. FAX 703-528-2148.
circ. 450. *5499*

SAG SERVUS IN WIEN.
Milde Verlag GmbH, Autokaderstr. 29, A-1210 Vienna, Austria. TEL 01-27703. FAX 01-2770326.
circ. 67,000. *3253*

SAGA OF SIGMA TAU GAMMA.
Sigma Tau Gamma Fraternity, Box 54, Warrensburg, MO 64093. TEL 816-747-2222. FAX 816-747-9599.
circ. 28,000. *1970*

SAGGI.
Masson S.p.A., Divisione Periodici, Via Flli. Bressan 2, 20126 Milan, Italy. TEL 39-2-270741. FAX 39-2-27074210.
circ. 1,000. *5097*

SAKHO & TELE.
Association of Electrical Engineers in Finland, Merikasarmink. 7 J 53, SF-00160 Helsinki, Finland. TEL 358-0-171-050. FAX 358-0-657-562.
circ. 4,500. *2845*

SAIL.
K - III Magazine Corp., 84 State St., Boston, MA 02109-2202. TEL 617-720-8600. FAX 617-723-0911.
circ. 5,000. *6843*

ST. ALBERT GAZETTE.
Jamison Newspapers, Inc., 25 Chisholm Ave., Box 263, St. Albert, AB T8N 1N3, Canada. TEL 403-460-5500. FAX 403-460-8220.
circ. 14,000. *3265*

ST. AUSTELL BODMIN AND NEWQUAY PACKET.
Packet Newspapers, Ponsharden, Falmouth, Cornwall TR10 8AP, England. TEL 44-1326-370500. FAX 44-1326-373887.
circ. 23,843. *3300*

ST. DUNSTAN'S ANNUAL REVIEW.
St. Dunstan's for Men and Women Blinded in the Services, P.O. Box 4XB, 12-14 Harcourt St., London W1A 4XB, England. TEL 44-171-723-5021. FAX 44-171-262-6199. *3473*

ST. GALLEN.
Tourist Information St. Gallen, Bahnhofplatz 1a, Postfach, CH-9001 St. Gallen, Switzerland. TEL 41-71-2273737. FAX 41-71-2273767.
circ. 5,500. *7232*

ST. JOSEPH VALLEY RECORD.
Northern Indiana Historical Society, 808 W. Washington, S. Bend, IN 46601. TEL 219-235-9664. FAX 219-235-9059.
circ. 2,500. *3646*

ST. LOUIS POCKET GUIDE.
Land & Sea Publications, 9650 Clayton Rd., St. Louis, MO 63124. TEL 314-991-5222. FAX 314-991-1260.
circ. 800,000. *7232*

SAINT LOUIS UNIVERSITY RESEARCH JOURNAL.
Saint Louis University, Graduate School of Arts and Sciences, Box 71, Baguio City 2600, Philippines.
circ. 1,000. *3791*

SALE AND ALTRINCHAM MESSENGER.
Sale and Altrincham Messenger Ltd., 46 Washway Rd., Sale, Manchester M33 1QZ, England. TEL 44-161-969-8411. FAX 44-161-976-3703.
circ. 54,575. *3300*

SALES AND MARKETING STRATEGIES & NEWS.
Hughes Communications, Inc., 211 W. State St., Box 197, Rockford, IL 61105. TEL 800-435-2937. FAX 815-963-7773.
circ. 62,000. *1548*

SALES PROMOTION.
Clifford Elliot & Associates Ltd., 3228 South Service Rd., Burlington, ON L7N 3H8, Canada. TEL 905-634-2100. FAX 905-634-2238.
circ. 2,000. *1548*

SALESDOCTORS MAGAZINE.
SeaBird Associates, Inc., 5455 N. Federal Hwy., Ste. Q, Boca Raton, FL 33487. TEL 561-997-9345. FAX 561-997-9375.
circ. 21,000. *1548*

SALMANTICENSIS.
Universidad Pontificia, Departamento de Ediciones y Publicaciones, Apdo. de Correos 541, 37080 Salamanca, Spain. TEL 34-23-215140. FAX 34-23-215140.
circ. 2,000. *6479*

SALUS MILITIAE.
Hospital Central de las Fuerzas Armadas, San Martin, Caracas-1060, Venezuela.
circ. 1,000. *4742*

SALUTE.
Military Forces Features, Inc., 169 Lexington Ave., New York, NY 10157-0014. TEL 212-532-0660. FAX 212-779-3080.
circ. 225,000. *3384*

SALVO.
Fort Point and Presidio Historical Association, Box 29163, Presidio of San Francisco, CA 94129. TEL 415-921-8193.
circ. 900. *3646*

SALZBURG ENGLISH AND AMERICAN STUDIES.
Universitaet Salzburg, Institut fuer Anglistik und Amerikanistik, Akademiestr. 24, A-5020 Salzburg, Austria.
circ. 200. *4462*

SAMPLE CASE.
Order of United Commercial Travelers of America, 632 N. Park St., Columbus, OH 43215. TEL 614-228-3276. FAX 614-228-1898.
circ. 160,000. *1936*

SAMVADADHVAM.
Indian Statistical Institute, 203 Barrackpore Trunk Rd., Calcutta 700035, India.
circ. 2,500. *6935*

SAN FRANCISCO BAY VIEW.
Bay View Inc., 2900 Griffith St., San Francisco, CA 94124-3722. TEL 415-671-0449. FAX 415-822-8971.
circ. 20,000. *3040*

SAN FRANCISCO CATHOLIC.
Archdiocese of San Francisco, Catholic Communications Center, 441 Church St., San Francisco, CA 94114. TEL 415-565-3630.
circ. 48,000. *6479*

SAN FRANCISCO DOWNTOWN.
Gordon Media, 215 Leidesdorff, No. 400, San Francisco, CA 94111. TEL 415-362-6641. FAX 415-362-2254.
circ. 35,000. *3384*

SAN FRANCISCO GIFTCENTER AND JEWELRYMART BUYER'S GUIDE.
Bolger Publications Inc., 3301 Como Ave., S.E., Minneapolis, MN 55414. TEL 612-645-6311. FAX 612-645-1750.
circ. 24,000. *3450*

SAN FRANCISCO PENINSULA PARENT.
Peninsula Parent Newspaper Inc., 1480 Rollins Rd., Burlingame, CA 94010-2307. TEL 415-342-9203. FAX 415-342-9276.
circ. 60,000. *1856*

SAN JOSE FILM & VIDEO PRODUCTION BINDER.
San Jose Film & Video Commission, 333 W. San Carlos St., Ste. 1000, San Jose, CA 95110. TEL 408-295-9600. FAX 408-295-3937.
circ. 1,000. *5343*

SANATORIO SAO LUCAS. BOLETIM.
Fundacao para o Progresso da Cirurgia, Rua Pirapitingui 80, Sao Paulo, Brazil.
circ. 2,000. *5152*

SANCHAR.
Sangam Paper Corporation, Sanchar Bldg., Hotgi Rd., Solapur, Maharashtra 413 003, India. TEL 91-22-600481. FAX 91-22-600484.
circ. 543. *3318*

SANDLAPPER.
Sandlapper Society, Inc., Box 1108, Lexington, SC 29071. TEL 803-359-9954. FAX 803-957-8226.
circ. 7,000. *3384*

SANDUQ ABU DHABI LIL-INMA' AL-IQTISADI AL-ARABI. AL-TAQRIR AL-SANAWI.
Abu Dhabi Fund for Arab Economic Development, P.O. Box 814, Abu Dhabi, United Arab Emirates. TEL 725800.
circ. 1,000. *1368*

SANGYO GIJUTSU JOHO YOKKAICHI.
Yokkaichi-shiritsu Toshokan, 2-42 Kubota 1-chome, Yokkaichi-shi, Mie-ken 510, Japan. *6972*

SANKYO RESEARCH LABORATORIES. ANNUAL REPORT.
Sankyo Co., Ltd., Research Institute, 1-2-58 Hiromachi, Shinagawa-ku, Tokyo 140, Japan. TEL 81-3-3492-3131. FAX 81-3-5436-8569. *5693*

SANTO CENACOLO.
Commissariato di Terra Santa, Via dell'Ospizio 15, Pistoia, Italy. TEL 39-573-236740.
circ. 2,900. *6370*

SANYO KASEI NEWS.
Sanyo Chemical Industries Ltd., 11-1 Ikkyo Nomotocho, Higashiyama-ku, Kyoto 605, Japan.
circ. 6,000. *1766*

SAO PAULO (CITY) ARQUIVO MUNICIPAL. REVISTA.
Arquivo Historico do Municipio de Sao Paulo, Rua Roberto Simonsen, 136-B, 01017-020 Sao Paulo, Brazil. TEL 55-11-6045431. FAX 55-11-6041463.
circ. 1,000. *3646*

SARAWAK ELECTRICITY SUPPLY CORPORATION. ANNUAL REPORT.
Sarawak Electricity Supply Corporation, P.O. Box 149, 93700 Kuching, Sarawak, Malaysia. TEL 082-441188. FAX 082-444082.
circ. 2,000. *2846*

SARTRE STUDIES INTERNATIONAL.
Berghahn Books Inc., 165 Taber Ave., Providence, RI 02906. TEL 401-861-9330. FAX 401-521-0046.
circ. 300. *5750*

SASKATCHEWAN. DEPARTMENT OF INDUSTRY AND COMMERCE. INDUSTRIAL BENEFITS FROM RESOURCE DEVELOPMENT.
Government Printing Co., 2005 8th St., Regina, Sask. S4P 3V7, Canada. TEL 306-566-9393. *999*

SASKATCHEWAN BULLETIN.
Saskatchewan Teachers' Federation, 2317 Arlington Ave., Saskatoon, SK S7J 2H8, Canada. TEL 306-373-1660. FAX 306-374-1122.
circ. 22,300. *2479*

SASKATCHEWAN FARM LIFE.
Farm Life Publications, 75 Lenore Dr., No. 4, Saskatoon, SK S7K 7Y1, Canada. TEL 306-242-5723. FAX 306-668-6164.
circ. 160,000. *151*

SASKATCHEWAN MANUFACTURERS GUIDE.
Government Printing Co., 2005 8th St., Regina, Sask. S4P 3V7, Canada. TEL 306-566-9393. *1711*

SASKATCHEWAN RESEARCH COUNCIL. ANNUAL REPORT.
Saskatchewan Research Council, 15 Innovation Blvd., Saskatoon, SK S7N 2X8, Canada. TEL 306-933-5400. FAX 306-933-7446.
circ. 200,000. *6566*

SATVISION MAGAZINE.
Satellite Broadcasting and Communications Association, 225 Reinekers Ln., Ste. 600, Alexandria, VA 22314-2322. TEL 703-549-6990. FAX 703-549-7640.
circ. 10,000. *2058*

SCAN.
Dienst Landbouwkundig Onderzoek, Staring Centrum, Instituut voor Onderzoek van het Landelijk Gebied, P.O. Box 125, 6700 AC Wageningen, Netherlands. TEL 31-317-474200. FAX 31-317-424812.
circ. 2,000. *243*

SCANDINAVIAN JOURNAL OF NUTRITION.
Swedish Nutrition Foundation, Ideon, S-223 70 Lund, Sweden. TEL 46-(0)-46-18-22-80. FAX 46-0-46-18-22-81.
circ. 2,500. *5482*

THE SCANNER.
Rocky Mountain Food Dealers Association, 1370 Pennsylvania St., Ste. 320, Denver, CO 80203-5022. TEL 303-830-7001.
circ. 1,400. *3144*

SCENE (CLEVELAND).
Northeast Scene, Inc., 1375 Euclid Ave., Ste. 312, Cleveland, OH 44115. TEL 216-241-7550. FAX 216-241-6275.
circ. 48,169. *3385*

SCENE (NEW YORK, 1990).
Scene, 240 E. 79th St., Ste. 10D, New York, NY 10021. TEL 212-737-8100.
circ. 1,500,000. *5344*

SCHERZO.
Scherzo Editorial, S.A., Marques de Mondejar, 11 2o D, 28028 Madrid, Spain. TEL 34-3-567622.
circ. 15,000. *5433*

SCHIFFS-INGENIEUR JOURNAL.
Verein der Schiffs-Ingenieur zu Hamburg e.V., Gurlittstr. 32, 20099 Hamburg, Germany. TEL 49-40-2803883. FAX 49-40-2803565.
circ. 1,500. *7164*

SCHOOL ADMINISTRATOR.
American Association of School Administrators, 1801 North Moore St., Arlington, VA 22209. TEL 703-528-0700. FAX 703-528-2146. *2577*

SCHOOL BUS BRIEFS.
Department of Public Instruction, Pupil Transportation Service, 125 S. Webster St., Box 7841, Madison, WI 53707-7841. *7038*

SCHOOL BUS FLEET.
Bobit Publishing Company, 2512 Artesia Blvd., Redondo Beach, CA 90278-3210. TEL 310-376-8788. FAX 310-376-9043.
circ. 20,000. *7038*

SCHOOL BUSINESS MAGAZINE.
Momentum Media Management, 4040 Creditview Rd., Unit 11, Box 1800, Mississauga, ON L5C 3Y8, Canada. TEL 905-813-7100. FAX 905-813-7117.
circ. 10,500. *2577*

SCHOOL LIBRARIES BULLETIN.
Anambra State School Libraries Association, c/o Enugu Campus Library, University of Nigeria, Nsukka, Enugu State, Nigeria.
circ. 250. *4212*

SCHOOL PLANNING AND MANAGEMENT.
Peter Li, Inc., 330 Progress Rd., Dayton, OH 45449. TEL 573-847-5900. FAX 513-847-5910.
circ. 55,000. *2480*

SCHUETTGUT.
Trans Tech Publications, Postfach 1254, 38670 Clausthal-Zellerfeld, Germany. TEL 49-5323-9697-0. FAX 49-5323-969799.
circ. 7,500. *6972*

DER SCHWEIZER TREUHAENDER.
Treuhand-Kammer, Postfach 892, CH-8025 Zurich, Switzerland. TEL 41-1-2677575. FAX 41-1-2677555.
circ. 10,465. *1098*

SCHWEIZERISCHE FEUERWEHR-ZEITUNG.
Schweizerischer Feuerwehrverband, Ensingerstr. 37, CH-3000 Bern 16, Switzerland. TEL 41-31-3528311. FAX 41-31-3523464.
circ. 22,000. *3058*

SCHWEIZERISCHE LEHRERZEITUNG.
Zuerichsee Medien AG, Seestr. 86, CH-7612 Staefa, Switzerland. TEL 01-9285611.
circ. 16,500. *2481*

SCHWIMMBAD UND SAUNA.
Fachschriften Verlag GmbH, Hoehenstr. 17, 70736 Fellbach, Germany. TEL 49-711-5206-256. FAX 49-711-5281424.
circ. 20,187. *912*

SCIENCE TECHNOLOGY JOURNAL.
Institute of Science Technology, Mansell House, 22 Bore St., Lichfield, Staffs. WS13 6LP, England. TEL 44-1543-251346. FAX 44-1543-415804.
circ. 2,000. *6973*

SCIENTIFIC COMPUTING WORLD.
I O P Publishing Ltd., Dirac House, Temple Back, Bristol BS1 6BE, England. TEL 44-117-929-7481. FAX 44-117-927-4318. *2090*

SCOPE.
Verlag Hoppenstedt GmbH, Havelstr. 9, 64295 Darmstadt, Germany. TEL 49-6151-380-0. FAX 49-6151-380-360.
circ. 80,000. *1595*

SCOTTISH LICENSED TRADE NEWS.
Peebles Publishing Group Ltd., Bergius House, Clifton St., Glasgow G3 7LA, Scotland. TEL 44-141-331-1022. FAX 44-141-331-1395.
circ. 16,000. *526*

SCOTTISH LITERARY JOURNAL.
Association for Scottish Literary Studies, Dept. of English, University of Aberdeen, Old Aberdeen AB9 2UB, Scotland. TEL 0224-272634.
circ. 820. *4463*

SCOTTISH MEDICINE.
Hermiston Publications Ltd., 9 Stonelaws, E. Linton, E. Lothian EH40 3DX, Scotland. TEL 44-1620-870612. FAX 44-1620-870313.
circ. 5,000. *4743*

SCOTTISH OPTOMETRIST.
Scottish Committee of Optometrist, c/o 24 Tweed Crescent, Pean Park, Renfred, Scotland. *5001*

SCOTTISH TRAVEL AGENTS NEWS.
S & G Publishing (Scotland) Ltd., 71 Henderson St., Bridge of Allan, Stirling FK9 4HG, Scotland. TEL 44-1786-834238. FAX 44-1786-834295.
circ. 1,000. *7233*

SCOTTSDALE SCENE MAGAZINE.
P H & G, Inc., 4041 N. Central Ave., Ste. A100, Phoenix, AZ 85012-3331. TEL 602-277-7838. FAX 602-277-7857.
circ. 40,000. *3385*

SCREENWRITER.
L S W - Screenwriter Publications, 187 Manygate Ln., Shepperton, Middx. TW17 9ER, England. TEL 44-1932-232952.
circ. 1,250. *5344*

THE SCRIBE.
University of Bridgeport, Student Center, 244 University Ave., Bridgeport, CT 06601. TEL 203-576-4382. FAX 203-576-4485.
circ. 2,500. *1970*

SCRIBES JOURNAL OF LEGAL WRITING.
American Society of Writers on Legal Subjects, Wake Forest University, School of Law, Box 7206, Winston-Salem, NC 27109. TEL 910-759-5440. FAX 910-759-4301.
circ. 3,900. *4023*

SCRINIUM.
Verband Oesterreichischer Archivare, Postfach 164, A-1014 Vienna, Austria. TEL 43-1-79540450. FAX 43-1-79540109. *4213*

SCRIPPS RESEARCH INSTITUTE. SCIENTIFIC REPORT.
Scripps Research Institute, Office of Communications, 10550 N. Torrey Pines Rd., La Jolla, CA 92037. TEL 619-784-8134. FAX 619-784-8118.
circ. 5,000. *4743*

SCRIPTA GEOLOGICA.
Nationaal Natuurhistorisch Museum, Postbus 9517, 2300 RA Leiden, Netherlands.
circ. 575. *2368*

SCROLL OF PHI DELTA THETA.
Phi Delta Theta Fraternity, 2 So. Campus, Oxford, OH 45056. TEL 513-523-6345. FAX 513-523-9200. *1970*

SEA BREEZE.
Wachters' Organic Sea Products Corporation, 360 Shaw Rd., South San Francisco, CA 94080. FAX 415-875-1626.
circ. 50,000. *7233*

SEA MASS TRAVELER.
Traveler Publications, Inc., 174 Bellevue Ave., Ste. 205, Newport, RI 02840. TEL 401-847-0226. FAX 401-847-5267.
circ. 25,000. *7233*

SEARCH (LONDON, 1957).
Muscular Dystrophy Group of Great Britain and Northern Ireland, 7-11 Prescott Pl., London SW4 6BS, England. TEL 0171-720-8055. FAX 0171-498-0670.
circ. 16,000. *3467*

SEARCH (YORK).
Joseph Rowntree Foundation, The Homestead, 40 Water End, York YO3 6LP, England. TEL 44-1904-629241. FAX 44-1904-620072.
circ. 8,500. *6685*

SECRETARESSE.
Kluwer Editorial, Kouterveld 2, B-1831 Diegem, Belgium. TEL 32-2-7231511.
circ. 5,500. *1560*

SECURITY CONCEPTS.
Terra Publishing, Inc., R.D. 1, Box 142, Center St. Ext., Salamanca, NY 14779. TEL 716-945-3488. FAX 716-945-5238.
circ. 21,000. *2288*

SECURITY INDUSTRY.
S P L, Berwick House, 8-10 Knoll Rise, Orpington, Kent BR6 0PS, England. TEL 44-1689-874025. FAX 44-1689-896847.
circ. 6,000. *2288*

SECURITY NEWS (SALAMANCA).
Terra Publishing, Inc., R.D. 1, Box 142, Center St. Ext., Salamanca, NY 14779. TEL 716-945-3488. FAX 716-945-5238.
circ. 21,000. *2289*

SECURITY PULSE.
Canadian Alarm & Security Association, 610 Alden Rd., Ste. 201, Markham, ON L3R 9Z1, Canada. TEL 905-513-0622. FAX 905-513-0624.
circ. 1,500. *2289*

SECURITY SALES.
Bobit Publishing Company, 2512 Artesia Blvd., Redondo Beach, CA 90278-3210. TEL 310-376-8788. FAX 310-376-9043.
circ. 23,500. *929*

SECURITY TECHNOLOGY & DESIGN.
Locksmith Publishing Corp., 850 Busse Hwy., Park Ridge, IL 60068. TEL 847-692-5940. FAX 847-692-4604.
circ. 28,500. *2289*

SEEDS FOR THE PARISH.
Evangelical Lutheran Church in America, 8765 W. Higgins Rd., Chicago, IL 60631-4177. TEL 312-380-2949. FAX 312-380-2406.
circ. 200,000. *6441*

THE SEEING EYE GUIDE.
The Seeing Eye, Inc., Box 375, Morristown, NJ 07963-0375. TEL 201-539-4425. FAX 201-539-0922.
circ. 25,000. *3474*

SEGAVISIONS.
Infotainment World, Inc., 951 Mariners Island Blvd., Ste. 700, San Mateo, CA 94404-1561. TEL 415-349-4300.
circ. 1,000,000. *2119*

SEI MARIANNA IKA DAIGAKU KIYO.
St. Marianna University School of Medicine, 2-16-1 Sugao Miyamae-ku, Kawasaki-shi 216, Japan. TEL 81-44-977-8111. FAX 81-44-977-9835.
circ. 1,000. *2527*

SEIKEI KISHO KANSOKUJO HOKOKU.
Seikei Gakuen Integrated Educational Institute, 3-1, Kichijoji Kita-machi 3-chome, Musashino-shi, Tokyo 180, Japan. FAX 0422-37-3863. *5248*

SEKTOR ERZIEHUNG.
Gewerkschaft Erziehung Basel, Rebgasse 1, Postfach, CH-4005 Basel, Switzerland. TEL 061-6921400.
circ. 1,250. *1856*

SELECCION.
Alpe Editores, S.A., Pedro Rico, 27, 28029 Madrid, Spain. TEL 34-1-7338811. FAX 34-1-3159652.
circ. 5,500. *5132*

SELECTA - MEDIZIN AKTUELL.
Selecta Verlagsgesellschaft mbH, Postfach 4240, 65032 Wiesbaden, Germany. TEL 0611-1705-0. FAX 0611-1705379. *4744*

SELECTED READINGS IN PLASTIC SURGERY.
411 N. Washington Ave., Ste. 6900, Dallas, TX 75246. TEL 214-824-0154. FAX 214-824-0463.
circ. 1,500. *5153*

SELF-EMPLOYED AMERICA.
National Association for the Self-employed, 2121 Precinct Line Rd., Hurst, TX 76054. TEL 817-428-4243. FAX 817-428-4210.
circ. 320,000. *1646*

SELF-STORAGE NOW.
MiniCo, Inc., Publishing Division, 2531 W. Dunlap Ave., Phoenix, AZ 85021. TEL 602-870-1711. FAX 602-8611094.
circ. 30,000. *1216*

SELLING LONG-HAUL.
B M I Publications Ltd., Suffolk House, George St., Croydon, Surrey CR9 1SR, England. TEL 44-181-649-7233. FAX 44-181-649-7234.
circ. 19,000. *7234*

SELVATICA.
2737 Kalmia Ave., Boulder, CO 80304. TEL 303-413-9649.
circ. 5,000. *4358*

SEMAPHORE SIGNAL.
Semaphore Corp., 207 Granada Dr., Aptos, CA 95003. TEL 408-688-9200.
circ. 7,000. *2158*

SEMBRADOR.
Parroquia Santisima Trinidad Rufino, La Misma del Punto (8), Italia 62, Rufino, Argentina. *3249*

SEMINAR HAUSARZTPRAXIS.
B M V - Berliner Medizinische Verlagsanstalt GmbH, Lietzenburgerstr. 97, 10719 Berlin, Germany. TEL 49-30-886749-0. FAX 49-30-88674999.
circ. 27,130. *4744*

SENDTNERA.
Botanische Staatssammlung Muenchen, Menzingerstr. 67, 80638 Munich, Germany. *727*

SENIOR BULLETIN.
Senior Publications Pty Ltd, P.O. Box 37492, Fairie Glen 0043, South Africa. TEL 27-12-9910443. FAX 27-12-9910443.
circ. 15,000. *3444*

SENIOR CITIZENS POST.
Coordinating Council for Senior Citizens, 807 S. Duke St., Durham, NC 27701. TEL 919-688-8247. FAX 919-683-3406.
circ. 1,500. *3444*

SENIOR GROUP TRAVEL.
Senior Travel Publications, Inc., 2 Brentwood Commons, No. 150, Brentwood, TN 37027-4502. TEL 615-371-6181. FAX 615-221-8825.
circ. 11,035. *7234*

SENIOR NEWS.
Box 23307, Waco, TX 76702. TEL 254-399-9811. FAX 254-399-9228.
circ. 185,000. *3445*

SENIOR SUN.
New York State Electric & Gas Corp., 4500 Vestal Parkway E., Binghamton, NY 13903. TEL 607-762-4149. FAX 607-762-4259.
circ. 65,000. *2679*

SENIOR TRAVEL TIPS (SAN RAFAEL).
Senior Marketing Associates, 710 C St., Ste. 200, San Rafael, CA 94901. TEL 415-453-8481. FAX 415-453-8540.
circ. 11,000. *7234*

SENIOR TRAVEL TIPS (SCOTTS VALLEY).
5281 Scotts Valley Dr., Scotts Valley, CA 95066-3514. TEL 408-438-6085. FAX 408-438-4705.
circ. 11,500. *7234*

SENIOR WORLD OF LOS ANGELES COUNTY.
Kendell Communications Inc., 500 Fesler St., Box 13560, El Cajon, CA 92022-3560. TEL 310-820-1125.
circ. 153,000. *3445*

THE SENIORS REVIEW.
11 Bond St., Ste. B2, St. Catharines, ON L2R 4Z4, Canada. TEL 905-687-9861. FAX 905-687-6911.
circ. 40,000. *3445*

SENSHU SHIZEN KAGAKU KIYO.
Senshu Daigaku, Shizen Kagaku Kenkyukai, 1-1 Higashi-Mita 2-chome, Tama-ku, Kawasaki-shi, Kanagawa-ken 214, Japan. TEL 81-44-911-0588. FAX 81-44-911-1243.
circ. 350. *6571*

SENSOR REPORT.
P. Keppler Verlag GmbH und Co. KG, Industriestr. 2, 63150 Heusenstamm, Germany. TEL 49-6104-606208. FAX 49-6104-606323.
circ. 10,000. *3805*

SENSUS WATER JOURNAL.
Sensus Technologies, Inc., 450 N. Gallatin Ave., Box 487, Uniontown, PA 15401. TEL 412-439-7700. FAX 412-430-3959.
circ. 15,000. *7299*

SER PADRES.
Gruner & Jahr U.S.A. Publishing, 110 Fifth Ave., New York, NY 10011. TEL 212-499-2000.
circ. 325,000. *7333*

SERIALS HOLDINGS IN NEWFOUNDLAND LIBRARIES.
Memorial University of Newfoundland Library, Periodicals Division, St. John's, NF A1C 5S7, Canada. TEL 709-753-8425. FAX 709-737-4569. *562*

SERICA.
Silk Association of Great Britain, c/o Rheinbergs Ltd., Morley Rd., Tonbridge TN9 1RN, England. TEL 0732-351357. FAX 0732-770217.
circ. 150. *6993*

SERPENTINE MUSE.
Adventuresses of Sherlock Holmes, c/o Evelyn Herzog, Man. Ed., 360 W. 21st St., New York, NY 10011. TEL 212-527-7789. *4501*

SERVER - PENNSYLVANIA.
Group Publications, Inc., 1816 Brownsville Rd., Pittsburgh, PA 15210-3908. TEL 412-885-7600. FAX 412-885-7617.
circ. 21,000. *3736*

SEVENTY SIX.
Unocal Corporation, Box 7600, Los Angeles, CA 90051. TEL 213-977-6814.
circ. 16,000. *5622*

SEVERN TRENT PLC. ANNUAL REPORT AND ACCOUNTS (YEAR).
Severn Trent Plc., 2297 Coventry Rd., Birmingham B26 3PU, England. TEL 44-121-722-4000.
circ. 130,000. *7299*

SHALE SHAKER.
Oklahoma City Geological Society, Inc., 227-W Park Ave., Oklahoma City, OK 73102. TEL 405-236-8086. FAX 405-236-8085.
circ. 1,250. *2368*

SHALOM.
Jewish Peace Fellowship, Box 271, Nyack, NY 10960. TEL 914-358-4601. FAX 914-358-4924.
circ. 3,000. *5998*

SHARING TIMES.
Christ Truth Ministries, Box 610, Upland, CA 91785. TEL 909-981-2838. FAX 909-981-2839.
circ. 3,500. *6727*

SHARK NEWS.
Nature Conservation Bureau Ltd., 36 Kingfisher Ct., Hambridge Rd., Newbury, Berks. RG14 5SJ, England. TEL 44-1635-550380. FAX 44-1635-550230.
circ. 1,500. *849*

SHELL-VENSTER.
Shell Nederland B.V., Dept. PAC/1, Hofplein 20, Rotterdam, Netherlands.
circ. 51,000. *5622*

THE SHEPHERD COLLEGE PICKET.
Shepherd College, Shepherdstown, WV 25443. TEL 304-876-2511. FAX 304-876-3262.
circ. 4,000. *1971*

SHICHOKAKU KYOIKU.
Japan Audio-Visual Education Association, 1-17-1 Toranomon, Minato-ku, Tokyo 105, Japan. FAX 81-3-3597-0564.
circ. 5,000. *2482*

SHIFT.
Behaviour Publishing Inc., 119 Spadina Ave., Studio 202, Toronto, ON M5V 2L1, Canada. TEL 416-977-7982. FAX 416-977-7983.
circ. 55,000. *6973*

SHINKO PANTEC GIHO.
Shinko Pantec Co. Ltd., 1-4, 1-chome, Murotani, Nishi-ku, Kobe-shi, Hyogo-ken 651-22, Japan. TEL 81-78-992-6525. FAX 81-78-992-6504. *2899*

SHINRIGAKU HYORON.
Kyoto University, Graduate School of Letters, Yoshida Honmachi, Sakyo-ku, Kyoto 606, Japan. FAX 81-75-753-2835.
circ. 900. *6153*

SHIPYARD BULLETIN.
Newport News Shipbuilding, Newport News, VA 23607. TEL 804-380-2342. FAX 804-380-3867.
circ. 30,000. *7166*

SHIPYARD LOG.
Pearl Harbor Naval Shipyard, 401 Ave. E, Ste. 124, Pearl Harbor, HI 96860-5350. TEL 808-474-3214. FAX 808-471-0709.
circ. 3,100. *5285*

SHOCKWAVES.
Shockwaves Publications, Box 93213, Los Angeles, CA 90093-0213. FAX 800-715-4690.
circ. 20,000. *5434*

SHOPPING AND TOURIST GUIDE ZURICH.
Promotion Verlag AG, Mainaustr. 50, Postfach 10, CH-8008 Zurich, Switzerland. TEL 41-1-3835252. FAX 41-1-3835275.
circ. 28,000. *7234*

SHOPTALK (ENGLEWOOD).
American Humane Association, Animal Protection Division, 63 Inverness Dr. E., Englewood, CO 80112-5117. TEL 303-792-9900. FAX 303-792-5333.
circ. 9,300. *304*

SHOWBOAT CENTENNIALS NEWSLETTER.
Showboat Centennials, 76 Glen Dr., Worthington, OH 43085. TEL 614-431-9422.
circ. 160. *6844*

SHUTTLE PLUS.
Sewing Machine Trade Association, 24 Fairlawn Grove, Chiswick, London W4 5EH, England. TEL 44-181-995-0411. FAX 44-181-742-2396.
circ. 3,200. *1918*

SIA.
Samverkande Traefacken, P.O. Box 1138, S-111 81 Stockholm, Sweden. TEL 46-8-23-04-25. FAX 46-8-411-27-42.
circ. 73,000. *3175*

SICHER SCHAFFEN - LAENGER LEBEN.
Landwirtschaftliche Sozialversicherung, Postfach 310110, 86062 Augsburg, Germany. TEL 49-821-4081-0. FAX 49-821-4081115.
circ. 55,000. *6686*

SICHERHEITS-BESCHAFFUNGSDIENST.
Richard Boorberg Verlag (Stuttgart), Scharrstr. 2, 70563 Stuttgart, Germany. TEL 0711-73850. FAX 0711-7352244.
circ. 15,000. *2289*

SIDNEY HAUGHTON MEMORIAL LECTURES.
South African Museum, P.O. Box 61, Cape Town 8000, South Africa. TEL 27-21-243330. FAX 27-21-246716.
circ. 450. *5563*

SIETE DIAS MEDICOS.
Ediciones Mayo, S.A., Muntaner 374, 4o, 08006 Barcelona, Spain. TEL 34-3-2090255. FAX 34-3-2020643.
circ. 30,000. *4745*

SIGN BUILDER ILLUSTRATED.
Journalistic, Inc., 4905 Pine Cone Dr., Ste. 2, Durham, NC 27707. TEL 919-489-1916. FAX 919-489-4767.
circ. 12,000. *45*

SIGNATURE.
Griffin Printing and Lithograph, Co., Inc., 544 W. Colorado St., Glendale, CA 91204-1102. TEL 818-244-2128. FAX 818-242-1172.
circ. 6,500. *6284*

SIGNS OF THE TIMES (CINCINNATI).
S T Publications Inc., 407 Gilbert Ave., Cincinnati, OH 45202. TEL 513-421-2050. FAX 513-421-5144.
circ. 4,219. *45*

SIIRTOLAISUUS.
Siirtolaisuusinstituutti, Piispankatu 3, FIN-20500 Turku, Finland. TEL 358-2-231-75-36. FAX 358-2-233-34-60.
circ. 1,400. *6058*

AL-SIJIL AL-SHAHRI LI-AHDATH AL-ALAM.
Ministry of Information and Culture, Information Department, P.O. Box 17, Abu Dhabi, United Arab Emirates. TEL 453000.
circ. 1,000. *6036*

AL-SIJIL AL-SHAHRI LI-AHDATH DAWLAT AL-IMARAT AL-ARABIYYAH AL-MUTTAHIDAH.
Ministry of Information and Culture, Information Department, P.O. Box 17, Abu Dhabi, United Arab Emirates. TEL 453000.
circ. 1,000. *6193*

SILENT ADVOCATE.
St. Rita School for the Deaf, 1720 Glendale-Milford Rd., Cincinnati, OH 45215. TEL 513-771-7600. FAX 513-326-8264.
circ. 30,000. *3465*

SILHOUETTE.
McMaster Students Union, Rm. 406, Hamilton Hall, 1280 Main St. W., Hamilton, ON L8S 4K1, Canada. TEL 905-525-9140. FAX 905-523-0107.
circ. 11,000. *4359*

SILKROAD.
Emphasis HK Ltd., 505-508 Westlands Centre, 20 Westlands Rd., Quarry Bay, Hong Kong, People's Republic of China. TEL 590-1328. FAX 590-1333.
circ. 46,425. *7261*

LE SILLON ROMAND.
Edipresse Publications SA, Av. de la Gare 33, CH-1001 Lausanne, Switzerland. TEL 41-21-3494545. FAX 41-21-3494079.
circ. 23,675. *153*

SILVER BARON'S MONEY FEVER.
S B Stocks U S A, 1 E. Camelback Rd., Ste. 680, Phoenix, AZ 85012-1051. TEL 602-265-4245. FAX 602-265-2806.
circ. 1,900. *1407*

SILVER CIRCLE.
Home Savings of America, 4900 Rivergrade Rd., Irwindale, CA 91706.
circ. 600,000. *3385*

SIMMENTALER JOURNAL.
Simmentaler Cattle Breeders' Society of S.A., P.O. Box 3868, Bloemfontein 9300, South Africa. TEL 27-51-477696. FAX 27-51-471529.
circ. 1,200. *289*

SIMMONS REVIEW.
Simmons College, 300 The Fenway, Boston, MA 02115. TEL 617-521-2363. FAX 617-521-3193.
circ. 23,000. *1971*

SINGAPORE. HOUSING AND DEVELOPMENT BOARD. ANNUAL REPORT.
Housing and Development Board, 3451 Jalan Bukit Merah, Singapore 0315, Singapore. TEL 65-2739090. *3759*

SINGAPORE. MINISTRY OF THE ENVIRONMENT. ANNUAL REPORT.
Ministry of the Environment, Environment Bldg., 40 Scotts Rd., Singapore 0922, Singapore. TEL 065-7327733. FAX 065-7319866. *2952*

SINGAPORE CONTRACTORS' EQUIPMENT CATALOGUE.
Times Trade Directories Pte. Ltd., Times Centre, One New Industrial Rd., Singapore 536196, Singapore. TEL 65-285-0161. FAX 65-2881186.
circ. 20,000. *1712*

SINGAPORE SOURCE BOOK FOR ARCHITECTS & DESIGNERS.
Times Trade Directories Pte. Ltd., Times Centre, One New Industrial Rd., Singapore 536196, Singapore. TEL 65-2850161. FAX 65-2850161.
circ. 15,000. *1712*

THE SINGER.
Rhinegold Publishing Ltd., 241 Shaftesbury Ave., London WC2H 8EH, England. TEL 44-171-333-1720. FAX 44-171-333-1769.
circ. 8,000. *5435*

SINGLE FILE MAGAZINE.
Single File Magazine, 250 Pearl St., Grand Rapids, MI 49503-2624. TEL 616-774-8100. FAX 616-774-9552.
circ. 35,000. *6599*

SINGLE PARENT.
Parents Without Partners Inc., 401 N. Michigan Ave., Chicago, IL 60611. TEL 312-644-6610. FAX 312-245-1083.
circ. 110,000. *6686*

SIXTEENTH CENTURY JOURNAL.
Sixteenth Century Journal Publishers, Inc., Truman State University, MC 111L, Kirksville, MO 63501. TEL 816-785-4665. FAX 816-785-4181.
circ. 2,500. *3599*

SJOESPORT.
Sjoesport A-S, P.O. Box 576, 5001 Bergen, Norway.
circ. 21,000. *6844*

SJONVARPSVISIR.
Islenska Utvarpsfelagid hf. - Stoed 2, Lynghalsi 5, P.O. Box 10110, IS-130 Reykjavik, Iceland. TEL 354-515-6770. FAX 354-515-6870.
circ. 50,000. *2059*

SKETCH BOOK.
Kappa Pi International Honorary Art Fraternity, 9321 Paul Adrian Dr., Crestwood, MO 63126.
circ. 2,000. *465*

SKI.
Habegger AG Druck und Verlag, Gutenbergstr. 1, CH-4552 Derendingen, Switzerland. TEL 065-411151. FAX 065-422632.
circ. 114,000. *6882*

SKI COST OF DOING BUSINESS SURVEY.
National Ski & Snowboard Retailers Association, 1699 Wall St., Mt. Prospect, IL 60056. TEL 847-439-4293. FAX 847-439-0111.
circ. 400. *6797*

SKI WATCH ATLAS.
C R N International, Inc., One Circular Ave., Hamden, CT 06514. TEL 203-288-2002. FAX 203-281-3291.
circ. 100,000. *6882*

SKIER'S POCKET GUIDE.
Land & Sea Publications, 9650 Clayton Rd., St. Louis, MO 63124. TEL 314-991-5222. FAX 314-991-1260.
circ. 1,100,000. *6882*

SKOGSSPORT.
Svenska Orienteringsfoerbundet, Idrottens Hus, S-123 87 Farsta, Sweden. TEL 46-8-605-60-00. FAX 46-8-605-63-60.
circ. 10,500. *6883*

SKOHANDLAREN.
Skohandlarens Foerlags AB, Surbrunnsgatan 12, S-114 21 Stockholm, Sweden. TEL 46-8-612--83-90. FAX 46-8-612-83-80.
circ. 1,600. *6597*

SKOLEFOKUS.
Laererforbundet, Wergelandsveien 15, N-0167 Oslo, Norway. TEL 47-22-03-00-00. FAX 47-22-42-65-87.
circ. 36,000. *2555*

SKOLVAERLDEN.
Laerarnas Riksfoerbund, P.O. Box 3529, 103 69 Stockholm, Sweden. TEL 46-86-13-27-00. FAX 46-84-411-01-75.
circ. 54,800. *2483*

SKOOP.
Auto Vakbladen Uitgeverij bv, Postbus 100, 4920 AC Made, Netherlands. TEL 31-162-687600. FAX 31-162-687444.
circ. 10,000. *7116*

SKOVEN.
Dansk Skovforening, Amalievej 20, 1875 Frederiksberg C, Denmark. TEL 45-31-244266. FAX 45-33-255082.
circ. 4,678. *3162*

SKUPNOST.
Drustvo Associazione "Skupnost", Via G. Gallina 5, 34122 Trieste, Italy. TEL 39-40-639126.
circ. 5,000. *3042*

SKYE TERRIER CLUB OF AMERICA. BULLETIN.
Skye Terrier Club of America, Box 60366, Harrisburg, PA 17106-0366.
circ. 200. *5642*

SKYPOWER.
Lockheed Martin, 542642 LOCKHEED MARA, 86 S. Cobb Dr., Marietta, GA 30063-0244. TEL 770-494-2406. FAX 770-494-4809.
circ. 30,000. *78*

SLATE.
Slate, 155 King St. E., Kingston, ON K7L 2Z9, Canada. TEL 613-542-3717. FAX 613-542-1447.
circ. 12,100. *466*

SLOOP & RECYCLING.
Misset, Postbus 4, 7000 BA Doetinchem, Netherlands. TEL 31-314-349371. FAX 31-314-363638.
circ. 7,920. *2990*

SMALL BUSINESS ADVOCATE (WASHINGTON).
U.S. Small Business Administration, Office of Advocacy, Mail Code 3114, 409 Third St., S.W., Washington, DC 20416. TEL 202-205-6531. FAX 202-205-6928.
circ. 9,800. *1647*

SMALL BUSINESS BULLETIN (WORCESTER).
Small Business Service Bureau, Inc., Box 1441, 554 Main St., Worcester, MA 01601. TEL 508-756-3513. FAX 508-791-4709.
circ. 35,000. *1647*

SMALL BUSINESS NEWS - AKRON.
Small Business News, Inc. (Akron), 86 W. Bowery St., Akron, OH 44308-1101. TEL 330-535-6397. FAX 330-535-6491.
circ. 18,000. *1647*

SMALL BUSINESS NEWS - CLEVELAND.
Small Business News, Inc. (Cleveland), 14725 Detroit Ave., Ste. 300, Cleveland, OH 44107-4103. TEL 216-228-6397. FAX 216-529-8924.
circ. 29,000. *1647*

SMART CARD NEWS.
Smart Card News Ltd., 40 Arundel Pl., Brighton BN2 1GO, England. TEL 44-1273-302503. FAX 44-1273-300991.
circ. 1,000. *2128*

SNOW.
Delius Klasing Verlag, Postfach 101671, 33516 Bielefeld, Germany. TEL 49-521-559280. FAX 49-521-559113.
circ. 50,000. *6782*

SNOW GOER.
Camar Publications Ltd., 130 Spy Court, Markham, ON L3R 5H6, Canada. TEL 416-485-8440. FAX 416-475-9246.
circ. 150,000. *6883*

SOBER TIMES.
Box 13013, Mill Creek, WA 98082-1013.
circ. 80,000. *2305*

SOBRE LOS DERIVADOS DE LA CANA DE AZUCAR.
Ediciones Cubanas, Obispo No. 527, Apdo. 605, Havana, Cuba.
circ. 1,500. *244*

SOCIAL CARE RESEARCH FINDINGS.
Joseph Rowntree Foundation, The Homestead, 40 Water End, York YO3 6LP, England. TEL 44-1904-629241. FAX 44-1904-620072.
circ. 2,500. *6687*

SOCIAL WORK IN EUROPE.
Russell House Publishing Ltd., 38 Silver St., Lyme Regis, Dorset DT7 3HS, England. TEL 44-1297-443948. FAX 44-1297-443948.
circ. 75. *6688*

SOCIALE DIENST POST.
Sociale Dienst, Vlaardingenlaan 15, 1062 HM Amsterdam, Netherlands. TFL 31-21-3464985. FAX 31-20-3466192.
circ. 75,000. *6689*

SOCIALIST PERSPECTIVE.
Council for Political Studies, 140-20E, South Sinthee Rd., 1st Fl., Calcutta 700 050, India. TEL 91-33-557-5351.
circ. 1,000. *5969*

SOCIEDAD ARGENTINA DE ESTUDIOS GEOGRAFICOS. BOLETIN.
Sociedad Argentina de Estudios Geograficos - GAEA, Rodriquez Pena 158, 4, 1020 Buenos Aires, Argentina. TEL 541-40-2076. *3421*

SOCIEDAD ESPANOLA DE CERAMICA Y VIDRIO. BOLETIN.
Sociedad Espanola de Ceramica y Vidrio, Ctra. Antigua de Valencia, km. 24300, 28500 Arganda del Rey (Madrid), Spain. TEL 34-1-871-18-00. FAX 34-1-870-05-50.
circ. 1,500. *1733*

SOCIEDAD MATEMATICA MEXICANA. BOLETIN.
Sociedad Matematica Mexicana, Apdo. Postal 14-170, 07000 Mexico, D.F., Mexico. TEL 525-747-7103. FAX 525-747-7104.
circ. 900. *4606*

SOCIEDADE DE MEDICINA E CIRURGIA DE SAO JOSE DO RIO PRETO. REVISTA.
Sociedade de Medicina e Cirurgia de Sao Jose do Rio Preto, Rua Spinola s-n, Sao Jose da Rio Preto 15100, Brazil. *5154*

SOCIETA ECONOMICA DI CHIAVARI. ATTI.
Publipress, Via M. Vattuone 157-1, 16039 Sestri Levante (GE), Italy. *6689*

SOCIETE GEOGRAPHIQUE DE LIEGE. BULLETIN.
Societe Geographique de Liege, Sart Tilman B11, 4000 Liege, Belgium. TEL 32-41-665324. FAX 32-41-665700.
circ. 650. *3422*

SOCIETE HISTORIQUE NICOLAS DENYS. REVUE D'HISTOIRE.
Societe Historique Nicolas Denys, Centre Universitaire, Shippagan, NB E0B 2P0, Canada.
circ. 800. *3647*

SOCIETE J.K. HUYSMANS. BULLETIN.
Societe J.K. Huysmans, 22 rue Guynemer, 75006 Paris, France. FAX 33-1-42840587.
circ. 600. *4359*

SOCIETE NATIONALE DES CHEMINS DE FER BELGES. RAPPORT ANNUEL.
Societe Nationale des Chemins de Fer Belges, Fonsnylaan 47B, Bureau 40-231, B-1060 Brussels, Belgium. *7133*

SOCIETY FOR THE ADVANCEMENT OF SCANDINAVIAN STUDY. NEWS AND NOTES.
Ohio State University, Department of German, 314 Cunz Hall, 1841 Millikin Rd., Columbus, OH 43210. TEL 614-292-8687.
circ. 700. *6639*

SOCIETY OF ARCHER-ANTIQUARIES. JOURNAL.
Society of Archer-Antiquaries, c/o Doug Elmy, 61 Lambert Rd., Bridlington, Yorks YO16 5RD, England. TEL 44-1262-601604. *6782*

SOCIETY OF DEPRECIATION PROFESSIONALS. JOURNAL.
Society of Depreciation Professionals, 5505 Connecticut Ave. N.W., No. 280, Washington, DC 20015-2601. TEL 202-362-0680. FAX 202-866-2283.
circ. 400. *1099*

SOCIETY OF FEDERAL LINGUISTS. NEWSLETTER.
Society of Federal Linguists, Inc., Box 7765, Washington, DC 20044.
circ. 150. *4299*

SOCIETY OF PHOTOGRAPHER AND ARTIST REPRESENTATIVES. NEWSLETTER.
Society of Photographer and Artist Representatives, 60 E. 42nd St., No. 1166, New York, NY 10165-0006. TEL 212-779-7464. *5775*

SOCIETY OF PROFESSORS OF EDUCATION. OCCASIONAL PAPERS.
Society of Professors of Education, c/o Dr. Dalton B. Curtis, Jr., Southeast Missouri State University, One University Plz., Cape Girardeau, MO 63701. TEL 615-974-2201. FAX 615-974-8718. *2483*

SOCIETY OF TELECOM EXECUTIVES. REVIEW.
Society of Telecom Executives, 75-79 York Rd., London SE1 7AQ, England. TEL 44-171-928-9951. FAX 44-171-928-5440.
circ. 24,000. *2003*

SOCIOECONOMIC NEWSLETTER.
Institute for Socioeconomic Studies, Airport Rd., White Plains, NY 10604. TEL 914-428-7400.
circ. 17,500. *6730*

SOFTWARE MAGAZINE.
Sentry Publishing Company, Inc., 1 Research Dr., Ste. 400B, Westborough, MA 01581-3907. TEL 508-366-2031. FAX 508-836-4732.
circ. 91,000. *2218*

SOIL SCIENCE ALERT.
Elsevier Science B.V., P.O. Box 211, 1000 AE Amsterdam, Netherlands. TEL 31-20-4853911. FAX 31-20-4853598. *2328*

SOJOURNS.
Journal Communications, Inc., 1749 Mallory Ln., Ste.110, Brentwood, TN 37027. TEL 615-371-0010. FAX 615-371-0258.
circ. 3,000,000. *7235*

SOKOL POLSKI.
Polish Falcons of America, 615 Iron City Dr., Pittsburgh, PA 15205-4397. TEL 412-922-2244. FAX 412-922-5029.
circ. 15,300. *1936*

EL SOL (SALINAS).
Sol de Salinas Inc., 230 Capitol St., Box 1610, Salinas, CA 93902-1610. TEL 408-757-8118. FAX 408-757-1006.
circ. 14,000. *3043*

SOL DE PARRAL.
Sol de Parral, S.A., Colegio No. 20, 33800 Hgo. del Parral, Chihuahua, Mexico. TEL 2-52-50. FAX 2-53-40.
circ. 5,400. *3335*

EL SOL DE TEXAS.
Organizacion Editorial Hispana, Inc., Box 803402, Dallas, TX 75380-3402. TEL 214-386-9120. FAX 214-386-7125.
circ. 26,000. *3043*

SOLDIERS.
U.S. Department of the Army, Cameron Sta., Alexandria, VA 22304-5050. TEL 703-274-6671. FAX 703-274-1896.
circ. 250,000. *5286*

LE SOLEIL DE COLOMBIE-BRITANNIQUE.
1177 W. Hastings St., No. 2405, Vancouver, BC V6E 2K3, Canada. TEL 604-609-6611. FAX 604-609-6612.
circ. 2,800. *3266*

SOLID FUEL REVIEW.
Carter Spencer Publishing Ltd., Chancery Ct., Lincoln Rd., High Wycombe, Bucks HP12 3RE, England. TEL 44-1494-442424. FAX 44-1494-472790.
circ. 7,000. *2679*

SOLID WASTE TECHNOLOGIES.
Hunter Publishing Limited Partnership, 2101 S. Arlington Heights Rd., Ste 150, Arlington Heights, IL 60005. TEL 847-427-9512. FAX 847-427-2097.
circ. 33,090. *2679*

SOMMETS.
Universite de Sherbrooke, Pavillon J.S. Bourque, 2500 bd. de l'Universite, Sherbrooke, PQ J1K 2R1, Canada. TEL 819-821-7388. FAX 819-821-7900.
circ. 55,000. *1971*

SONG OF ZION.
Jackman Music Corp., Box 1900, Orem, UT 84059-5900. TEL 801-225-0859. FAX 801-225-0851.
circ. 17,000. *5436*

SONNTAGSANZEIGER.
Power Print Druck und Verlags KG, Holtenklinkerstr. 88-92, Postfach 800806, 21029 Hamburg Bergedorf, Germany. TEL 49-40-724040-0.
circ. 3,200. *3290*

SONS OF ITALY NEWS.
Order of the Sons of Italy in America, Grand Lodge of Massachusetts, 93 Concord Ave., Belmont, MA 02178-4042.
circ. 17,500. *1936*

SOPHIA.
Melkite Diocese of Newton, Sophia Editorial Office, 11245 Rye St., N. Hollywood, CA 91602-2022. TEL 818-761-2034. FAX 818-761-2922.
circ. 13,500. *6480*

SOTAINVALIDI.
Sotainvalidien Veljesliitto, Kasarmikatu 34 A, FIN-00130 Helsinki, Finland. TEL 358-9-478-500. FAX 358-9-4785-0100.
circ. 51,000. *6690*

SOTILASAIKAKAUSLEHTI.
Upseeriliitto Ry, Luotsikatu 7 A 2, FIN-00160 Helsinki, Finland. TEL 358-0-6689-4016. FAX 358-0-6689-4020.
circ. 6,200. *5286*

SOUND AND VIBRATION.
Acoustical Publications, Inc., Box 40416, Bay Village, OH 44140. TEL 216-835-0101. FAX 216-835-9303.
circ. 21,000. *2900*

SOUNDINGS FROM AROUND THE WORLD.
World Neighbors, Inc., 4127 N.W. 122nd St., Oklahoma City, OK 73120-8869. TEL 405-752-9700. FAX 405-752-9393.
circ. 1,700. *6037*

THE SOURCE (PRINCETON).
Construction Financial Management Association, 707 State Rd., Ste. 223, Princeton, NJ 08540-1413. TEL 609-683-5000. FAX 609-683-4821.
circ. 5,500. *1712*

SOURCES.
Fine Arts Trade Guild, 16-18 Empress Pl., London SW6 1TT, England. TEL 44-171-381-6616. FAX 44-171-381-2596.
circ. 2,000. *484*

SOURCES D'HISTOIRE MEDIEVALE.
C N R S Editions, 20-22 rue St. Amand, 75015 Paris, France. TEL 45-33-16-00. FAX 45-33-92-13.
circ. 1,250. *3602*

SOUTH AFRICA. DEPARTMENT OF AGRICULTURE. DIRECTORATE OF AGRICULTURAL STATISTICS. ABSTRACT OF AGRICULTURAL STATISTICS.
Department of Agriculture, Directorate Agricultural Statistics, Private Bag X144, Pretoria 0001, South Africa. *183*

SOUTH AFRICA. DEPARTMENT OF AGRICULTURE. DIRECTORATE OF AGRICULTURAL STATISTICS. TRENDS IN THE AGRICULTURAL SECTOR.
Department of Agriculture, Directorate of Agricultural Statistics, Private Bag X144, Pretoria 0001, South Africa. *202*

SOUTH AFRICA. DEPARTMENT OF AGRICULTURE. OFFICIAL LIST OF PROFESSIONAL RESEARCH WORKERS, LECTURING STAFF AND EXTENSION WORKERS IN THE AGRICULTURAL FIELD.
Department of Agriculture, Private Bag X144, Pretoria 0001, South Africa. TEL 27-12-3197141. FAX 27-12-3232516. *154*

SOUTH AFRICA. DEPARTMENT OF LAND AFFAIRS. DIRECTORATE OF SURVEYS AND LAND INFORMATION. ANNUAL REPORT OF THE CHIEF SURVEYOR-GENERAL.
Department of Land Affairs, Directorate of Surveys and Land Information, Rhodes Ave., Mowbray 7705, South Africa. TEL 27-21-6854070. FAX 27-21-6891351.
circ. 400. *2798*

SOUTH AFRICA. NATIONAL PARKS BOARD. ANNUAL REPORT.
National Parks Board, P.O. Box 787, Pretoria 0001, South Africa. TEL 27-12-343-9770. FAX 27-12-343-9958. *2244*

SOUTH AFRICAN ASSOCIATION FOR MARINE BIOLOGICAL RESEARCH. BULLETIN.
South African Association for Marine Biological Research, P.O. Box 10712, Marine Parade 4056, South Africa. TEL 27-31-373536. FAX 27-31-372132.
circ. 450. *628*

SOUTH AFRICAN DRAUGHTSMAN.
South African Institute of Draughtsmen, P.O. Box 30, Bergvliet 7864, South Africa. TEL 27-21-750156. FAX 27-21-750156.
circ. 3,000. *6974*

SOUTH AFRICAN EXPORTERS.
Reed Business Information South Africa (Pty.) Ltd., P.O. Box 653207, Benmore 2010, South Africa. TEL 27-11-784-1110. FAX 27-11-883-4729.
circ. 14,000. *1347*

SOUTH AFRICAN JOURNAL OF AGRICULTURAL EXTENSION.
South African Society for Agricultural Extension, University of Pretoria, Pretoria 0002, South Africa. TEL 27-12-420-3247. FAX 27-12-342-2713. *154*

SOUTH AFRICAN JOURNAL OF OCCUPATIONAL THERAPY.
South African Association of Occupational Therapists, P.O. Box 145, Rondebosch 7700, South Africa. TEL 27-2241-42244. FAX 27-2241-42244.
circ. 900. *4747*

SOUTH AFRICAN JOURNAL OF SURVEYING AND MAPPING.
South African Council for Professional Land Surveyors and Technical Surveyors, P.O. Box 62041, Marshalltown 2107, South Africa. TEL 27-11-8346431. FAX 27-11-836-8657.
circ. 2,000. *2798*

SOUTH AFRICAN LAPIDARY MAGAZINE.
Federation of South African Gem & Mineralogical Societies, P.O. Box 28744, Sunnyside 0132, South Africa. TEL 27-12-44-4620.
circ. 600. *2322*

SOUTH AFRICAN MECHANICAL ENGINEER.
Promech Publishing, P.O. Box 85502, Emmarentia 2029, South Africa. TEL 27-11-7811401. FAX 27-11-7811403.
circ. 4,310. *2900*

SOUTH AFRICAN MUSEUM. ANNALS.
South African Museum, P.O. Box 61, Cape Town 8000, South Africa. TEL 27-21-243330. FAX 27-21-246716.
circ. 450. *628*

SOUTH AFRICAN MUSIC TEACHER.
South African Society of Music Teachers, P.O. Box 20032, Noordbrug 2522, South Africa. TEL 27-148-299-1699. FAX 27-148-2991707.
circ. 1,600. *5437*

SOUTH AFRICAN TRANSPORT.
Bolton Publications (Pty) Ltd., P.O. Box 966, Parklands 2121, South Africa. TEL 27-11-8803520. FAX 27-11-8806574.
circ. 5,039. *7039*

SOUTH AUSTRALIAN BUILDER.
Master Builders Association of South Australia, 47 South Terrace, Adelaide, S.A. 5000, Australia.
circ. 2,000. *913*

SOUTH AUSTRALIAN TENNIS NEWS.
South Australia Hard Court Tennis League, P.O. Box 202, Goodwood, S.A. 5034, Australia. TEL 61-8-2932347. FAX 61-8-2938024.
circ. 7,000. *6817*

SOUTH BUCKS STAR.
Bucks Free Press Group, Gomm Rd., High Wycombe, Bucks. HP13 7DW, England. TEL 44-1494-521212. FAX 44-1494-441977.
circ. 84,000. *3300*

SOUTH CAROLINA. MARINE RESOURCES DIVISION. TECHNICAL REPORT.
Department of Natural Resources, Marine Resources Division, Box 12559, Charleston, SC 29422-2559. TEL 803-762-5026. FAX 803-762-5110.
circ. 100. *2415*

SOUTH CAROLINA LAWYER.
South Carolina Bar, Box 608, Columbia, SC 29202-0608. TEL 803-799-6653. FAX 803-799-4118.
circ. 9,200. *4026*

SOUTH CAROLINA MEDICAL ASSOCIATION. JOURNAL.
South Carolina Medical Association, Box 11188, Columbia, SC 29211. TEL 803-798-6207. FAX 803-772-6783.
circ. 5,300. *4747*

SOUTH CAROLINA RULES AND REGULATIONS FOR HUNTING AND FISHING LICENSES.
Atlantic Publication Group, Inc., Box 61719, Charleston, SC 29419-1719. TEL 803-747-0025. FAX 803-744-0816.
circ. 400,000. *6883*

SOUTH CAROLINA STATE LIBRARY. ANNUAL REPORT.
State Library, 1500 Senate St., Box 11469, Columbia, SC 29211. TEL 803-734-8666. FAX 803-734-8676.
circ. 500. *4215*

SOUTH CAROLINA Y F AND F F A.
South Carolina Young Farmers and Future Farmers, 914A Rutledge Bldg., 1429 Senate St., Columbia, SC 29201. TEL 803-734-8426. FAX 803-734-3525.
circ. 8,000. *154*

SOUTH DAKOTA ACADEMY OF SCIENCE. PROCEEDINGS.
South Dakota Academy of Science, 414 E. Clark St., Vermillion, SD 57069. TEL 605-677-6176.
circ. 350. *6575*

SOUTH DAKOTA GEOLOGICAL SURVEY. BULLETIN.
Geological Survey, Science Center University, 414 E. Clark, Vermillion, SD 57069. TEL 605-677-5227. FAX 605-677-5895. *2370*

SOUTH DAKOTA GEOLOGICAL SURVEY. CIRCULAR.
Geological Survey, Science Center University, 414 East Clark, Vermillion, SD 57069. TEL 605-677-5227. FAX 605-677-5895. *2370*

SOUTH DAKOTA GEOLOGICAL SURVEY. REPORTS OF INVESTIGATION.
Geological Survey, Science Center University, 414 East Clark, Vermillion, SD 57069. TEL 605-677-5227. FAX 605-677-5895. *2370*

SOUTH DAKOTA JOURNAL OF MEDICINE.
South Dakota State Medical Association, 1323 S. Minnesota Ave., Sioux Falls, SD 57105. TEL 605-336-1965. FAX 605-336-0270.
circ. 1,800. *4747*

SOUTH DAKOTAN.
University of South Dakota Alumni Association, University of South Dakota, 414 E. Clark St., Vermillion, SD 57069. TEL 605-677-6714. FAX 605-677-6717.
circ. 34,000. *1971*

SOUTH FLORIDA PARENTING.
Ken Roberts, Ed. & Pub., 8323 N.W. 12th St., Ste. 212, Miami, FL 33126-1840. TEL 305-448-6003. FAX 305-448-6290.
circ. 100,000. *1857*

CONTROLLED CIRCULATION SERIALS

SOUTH FLORIDA'S HAUT DECOR.
Florida Media Affiliates, Inc., 800 Douglas Rd., Ste. 500, Coral Gables, FL 33134. TEL 305-445-4500. FAX 305-445-4600.
circ. 52,600. *3850*

SOUTHAMPTON CITY NEWS.
Southampton City Council, Civic Centre, Southampton SO14 7NG, England. TEL 44-1703-832000. FAX 44-1703-234537.
circ. 93,000. *6194*

SOUTH EAST EUROPEAN MONITOR.
9-12 Goldegasse, A-1040 Vienna, Austria. TEL 43-1-5055680. FAX 43-1-5055680.
circ. 1,500. *3602*

SOUTHEAST TRAVEL PROFESSIONAL.
Florida Travel Professional, 1200 N.W. 78th Ave., No. 216, Miami, FL 33126-1817. TEL 305-592-6133. FAX 305-592-9741.
circ. 10,000. *7235*

SOUTHEASTERNER.
University of Kentucky, Southeast Community College, Cumberland, KY 40823. TEL 606-589-2145.
circ. 3,500. *3880*

SOUTHERN AFRICA'S TRAVEL NEWS WEEKLY.
Travel and Trade Publishing (Pty) Ltd., P.O. Box 662, Auckland Park 2006, South Africa. TEL 27-11-7263036. FAX 27-11-7263994.
circ. 5,670. *7235*

SOUTHERN CALIFORNIA BUSINESS.
Los Angeles Area Chamber of Commerce, 350 S. Bixel St., Los Angeles, CA 90017. TEL 213-580-7571. FAX 213-580-7586.
circ. 10,000. *1196*

SOUTHERN CALIFORNIA GUIDE.
Westworld Publishing Corp., 11385 Exposition Bl., No. 102, Los Angeles, CA 90064. TEL 310-391-8255.
circ. 37,000. *7235*

SOUTHERN EXPOSURE (CARBONDALE).
Southern Illinois University at Carbondale, Library Affairs, Carbondale, IL 62901. TEL 618-453-2516.
circ. 404. *4215*

SOUTHERN ILLINOIS UNIVERSITY AT EDWARDSVILLE. REGIONAL RESEARCH AND DEVELOPMENT SERVICES. REPORT: PRIVATE SECTOR INVESTMENTS.
Southern Illinois University at Edwardsville, Regional Research and Development Services, Campus Box 1456, Edwardsville, IL 62026-1456. TEL 618-692-3500. FAX 618-692-2886.
circ. 100. *3759*

SOUTHERN LANDSCAPE & TURF.
Brantwood Publications, Inc., 3023 Eastland Blvd., Ste. 103, Clearwater, FL 34621-4106. TEL 813-796-3877.
circ. 18,000. *3205*

SOUTHERN METHODIST UNIVERSITY SCHOOL OF LAW. BRIEF.
Southern Methodist University, School of Law, Dallas, TX 75275. TEL 214-768-3341. FAX 214-768-4330.
circ. 9,000. *4026*

SOUTHERN MOTOR CARGO.
Southern Motor Cargo, Inc., Box 40169, Memphis, TN 38174. TEL 901-276-5424. FAX 901-276-5400.
circ. 50,000. *7178*

SOUTHERN PACIFIC BULLETIN.
Southern Pacific Lines, Southern Pacific Bldg., One Market Plaza, San Francisco, CA 94105. TEL 415-541-1656.
circ. 45,000. *7133*

SOUTHWEST BAPTIST UNIVERSITY OMNIBUS.
Southwest Baptist University, 623 Pike St., Bolivar, MO 65613. TEL 417-326-5281. FAX 417-326-1833.
circ. 1,800. *1971*

SOUTHWEST BOOSTER.
30-4th Ave. N.W., Swift Current, SK S9H 3X4, Canada. TEL 306-773-9321. FAX 306-773-9136.
circ. 19,100. *3266*

SOUTHWEST CONTRACTOR.
McGraw-Hill Companies, Southwest Contractor, 2050 E. University, Phoenix, AZ 85034. TEL 602-258-1641.
circ. 5,600. *913*

SOU'WESTER (EDWARDSVILLE).
Southern Illinois University at Edwardsville, Edwardsville, IL 62026. TEL 618-692-3190.
circ. 300. *4470*

SOVEREIGN.
Sovereign Magazine Ltd., 45 Blondvil St., Coventry CV3 5QX, England. TEL 44-1203-505339. FAX 44-1203-503135.
circ. 108,000. *7116*

THE SOWER.
Bible Society of South Africa, P.O. Box 6215, Roggebaai, Cape Town 8012, South Africa. FAX 27-21-419-4846.
circ. 68,000. *6372*

SOWITIMES.
Studenteninformationsverein Public Media, Stifterstr. 20, A-4100 Ottensheim, Austria. TEL 04234-4547.
circ. 12,000. *2556*

SOZIALES SEMINAR INFORMATIONEN.
Akademie Franz-Hitze-Haus, Kardinal-von-Galen-Ring 50, 48149 Muenster, Germany. TEL 49-251-9818-0. FAX 49-251-9818480.
circ. 6,000. *6481*

SPA DESTINATIONS.
Spa Management Corp., C.P. 365, Place d'Armes, Montreal, PQ H2Y 3H1, Canada. TEL 514-274-0004. FAX 514-274-5884.
circ. 20,000. *7235*

SPACE BUSINESS NEWS.
Phillips Business Information, Inc., 1201 Seven Locks Rd., Potomac, MD 20854. TEL 301-424-3338. FAX 301-309-3847. *79*

SPARE TIME.
Kipen Publishing Corporation, 5810 W. Oklahoma Ave., Milwaukee, WI 53219. TEL 414-543-8110. FAX 414-543-9767.
circ. 301,000. *1408*

SPAREBANKBLADET.
Sparebankforeningens Publikasjoner AS, P.O. Box 6772, St. Olavs Plass, N-0130 Oslo, Norway. TEL 47-22-11-00-75. FAX 47-22-36-25-33.
circ. 7,500. *1167*

SPAREN - BAUEN - WOHNEN.
Orac Zeitschriftenverlag GmbH, Brunner Feldstr. 45, A-2380 Perchtoldsdorf, Austria. TEL 43-1-8696536. FAX 43-1-8696536.
circ. 908,000. *1167*

SPEAK OUT!
Trinity College London, 16 Park Crescent, London W1N 4AP, England. TEL 44-171-323-2328. FAX 44-171-323-5201.
circ. 2,000. *2590*

SPEAK UP!
Bible Holiness Movement, P.O. Box 223, Stn. A, Vancouver, BC V6C 2M3, Canada. TEL 250-498-3895.
circ. 1,500. *5971*

SPECIAL LIBRARIES ASSOCIATION. SOCIAL SCIENCE DIVISION. BULLETIN.
Special Libraries Association, Social Science Division, Stanford Law Library, Stanford, CA 94605-8612. TEL 415-425-0804.
circ. 800. *4215*

LO SPECIALISTA.
Ansid - Edit s.r.l., Viale Monte Ceneri 58, 20155 Milan, Italy. TEL 39-2-33003971. FAX 39-2-39215800.
circ. 18,000. *7116*

SPECIALIZATION UPDATE.
American Bar Association, Standing Committee on Specialization, 541 N. Fairbanks Ct., Chicago, IL 60611. TEL 312-988-5753. FAX 312-988-5032.
circ. 700. *4027*

SPECTROSCOPY EUROPE.
I M Publications, 6 Charlton Mill, Charlton, Chichester, W. Sussex PO18 0HY, England. TEL 49-1243-811334. FAX 49-1243-811711.
circ. 21,000. *1796*

SPECTRUM.
Tzavta Publishing, P.O. Box 18287, Tel Aviv 61181, Israel. TEL 3-5622076. FAX 3-5618549.
circ. 4,000. *5870*

SPEIDEREN.
Norges Speiderforbund, Oevre Vollgate 9, N-0158 Oslo, Norway. TEL 47-22-42-26-60. FAX 47-22-42-07-04.
circ. 40,000. *1887*

SPHINCTER.
University of Liverpool, Medical School, Royal Liverpool Hospital, Box 147, Liverpool L69 3BX, England.
circ. 900. *4747*

SPICAE.
C N R S Editions, 20-22 rue St. Amand, 75015 Paris, France. TEL 45-33-16-00. FAX 45-33-92-13.
circ. 1,500. *4300*

SPIEL UND THEATER.
Deutscher Theaterverlag GmbH, Postfach 100261, 69496 Weinheim, Germany. TEL 06201-51061. FAX 06201-507082. *7013*

SPIELPLAN.
Orac Zeitschriftenverlag GmbH, Brunner Feldstr. 45, A-2380 Perchtoldsdorf, Austria. TEL 43-1-8696536. FAX 43-1-8696536.
circ. 20,000. *7013*

SPIRIT (METAIRIE).
Volunteers of America, 110 S. Union St., No. 2510, Alexandria, VA 22314-3324.
circ. 23,000. *6690*

THE SPIRITUAL HEALER.
Harry Edwards Spiritual Healing Sanctuary Trust, Burrows Lea, Shere, Guildford, Surrey GU5 9QG, England. TEL 44-1483-202054.
circ. 7,250. *5461*

SPOLETIUM.
Accademia Spoletina, Palazzo Mauri, Via Brignone 14, 06049 Spoleto (PG), Italy. TEL 0743-221203.
circ. 1,500. *3793*

SPORTFISKE.
Sveriges Sportfiske- och Fiskevaardsfoerbund Sportfiskarna, P.O. Box 104, S-443 22 Lerum, Sweden.
circ. 60,000. *6884*

SPORTING SCENE.
Sporting Scene, 22 Maberley Cres., West Hill, Ont. M1C 3K8, Canada. TEL 416-284-0304. FAX 416-284-1299.
circ. 19,800. *6786*

SPORTING TIMES (CALGARY).
Quicksilver Communications, Box 42001, Acadia Postal Outlet, Calgary, AB T2J 7A6, Canada. TEL 403-255-8067.
circ. 2,000. *6786*

SPORTS TREND.
Shore-Varrone, Inc., 6255 Barfield Rd. N.E., Ste. 200, Atlanta, GA 30328-4300. TEL 404-252-8831. FAX 404-252-4436.
circ. 29,102. *6787*

SPORTSFISKEREN.
Danmarks Sportsfiskerforbund, Worsaaesgade 1, DK-7100 Vejle, Denmark. TEL 64-75-82-06-99.
circ. 20,637. *3079*

SPORTSTYLE.
Fairchild Fashion & Merchandising Group, 7 W. 34th St., New York, NY 10001. TEL 212-630-4870. FAX 212-630-4879.
circ. 23,500. *6788*

SPRINGFIELD PUBLIC SCHOOLS. NEWS AND VIEWS.
Springfield Public Schools, Board of Education, 940 N. Jefferson, Springfield, MO 65802.
circ. 50,000. *2484*

SPRINGHILLIAN.
Spring Hill College, 4000 Dauphin St., Mobile, AL 36608. TEL 334-380-3850. FAX 334-460-2185.
circ. 2,100. *1972*

SPRINGS.
Spring Manufacturers Institute, Inc., 2001 Midwest Rd., Ste. 106, Oak Brook, IL 60521-1335. TEL 630-495-8588. FAX 630-495-8595.
circ. 7,000. *2900*

SPRINKLER AGE.
American Fire Sprinkler Association, 12959 Jupiter Rd., Ste. 142, Dallas, TX 75238. TEL 214-349-5965. FAX 214-343-8898.
circ. 3,900. *3058*

SPRINKLER BULLETIN.
Mather and Platt Ltd., Park Works, Manchester M10 6BA, England.
circ. 10,000. *3834*

SQUILLA.
Francescani di Recco, Via S. Francesco 4, 16036 Recco GE, Italy. TEL 39-185-720215. FAX 39-185-770529.
circ. 6,000. *6481*

SRPSKO BRATSTVO.
1 Secroft Cres., North York, ON M3N 1R5, Canada. TEL 416-769-7181. FAX 416-850-4401.
circ. 2,200. *3044*

STACKHOUSE - ROOSTER BLUES NEWSLETTER.
Stackhouse - Rooster Blues Records, 232 Sunflower Ave., Clarksdale, MS 38614. TEL 601-627-2209. FAX 601-627-9861.
circ. 10,000. *5438*

STADT DUISBURG. WAHLEN (YEAR).
Amt fuer Statistik, Stadtforschung und Europaangelegenheiten, Der Oberstadtdirektor, 47049 Duisburg, Germany. TEL 49-203-2833085. FAX 49-203-2834404.
circ. 350. *6207*

STADT UND GEMEINDE.
Verlag Otto Schwartz und Co., Annastr. 7, 37075 Goettingen, Germany. TEL 49-551-31051. FAX 49-551-372812.
circ. 7,000. *6194*

STADTGEMEINDE DEUTSCHLANDSBERG. MITTEILUNGEN.
Stadtgemeinde Deutschlandsberg, Hauptplatz 35, A-8530 Deutschlandsberg, Austria. TEL 03462-2011253. FAX 03462-2011262.
circ. 3,600. *3253*

STAFFROOM GUIDE TO SCHOOL JOURNEYS.
E M A P - Response Publishing Ltd., Wentworth House, Wentworth St., Peterborough, Cambs. PE1 1DS, England. TEL 01733-63100. FAX 01733-62656.
circ. 5,000. *2578*

STAGE.
Lusaka Theatre Club (Co-Op) Ltd., P.O. Box 30615, Lusaka, Zambia.
circ. 300. *7013*

STAINLESS STEEL.
Southern Africa Stainless Steel Development Association, P.O. Box 4479, Rivonia 2128, South Africa. TEL 27-11-803-5610. FAX 27-11-803-2011.
circ. 7,623. *5211*

STAINLESS STEEL BUYER'S GUIDE (YEAR).
Southern Africa Stainless Steel Development Association, P.O. Box 4479, Rivonia 2128, South Africa. TEL 27-11-803-5610. FAX 27-11-803-2011.
circ. 3,010. *5211*

STAMP LOVER.
National Philatelic Society, 107 Charterhouse St., London EC1M 6PT, England. TEL 44-171-336-0882.
circ. 1,500. *5713*

STAND BY.
International Brotherhood of Electrical Workers Local Union 369, Box 36275, Louisville, KY 40233. TEL 502-368-2568. FAX 502-368-1270.
circ. 2,000. *3898*

STAND BY.
Sociale Dienst, Vlaardingenlaan 15, 1062 HM Amsterdam, Netherlands. TEL 31-20-3464988. FAX 31-20-3466192.
circ. 2,900. *6690*

THE STANDARD.
170-176 Koroit St., Warrnambool, Vic. 3280, Australia. TEL 61-03-55631800. FAX 61-03-55631880.
circ. 146. *3252*

STANDARD & POOR'S CORPORATION RECORDS.
Standard & Poor's, 25 Broadway, New York, NY 10004. TEL 212-208-8000. FAX 212-412-0459. *1408*

STANDBEIN SPIELBEIN.
Szenario Verlag, Friesenstr. 6, 31134 Hildesheim, Germany. TEL 49-5121-33001. FAX 49-5121-34929.
circ. 1,000. *5366*

STANFORD.
Stanford Alumni Association, Bowman Alumni House, Stanford, CA 94305. TEL 415-723-2021. FAX 415-725-8676.
circ. 100,000. *1972*

STAR CARRIER.
National Star Route Mail Contractors Association, 324 E. Capitol St., Washington, DC 20003. TEL 202-543-1661. FAX 202-543-8863.
circ. 5,000. *2021*

THE STARK REPORT.
International Traders Research, 1020 Prospect St., Ste. 405, La Jolla, CA 92037. TEL 619-459-0818. FAX 619-459-0819.
circ. 250. *1409*

STATE & LOCAL LAW NEWS.
American Bar Association, State and Local Government Law Section, 750 N. Lake Shore Dr., Chicago, IL 60611. TEL 312-988-6083. FAX 312-988-6081.
circ. 6,400. *6225*

STATE BAR OF NEW MEXICO. BAR BULLETIN.
State Bar of New Mexico, 5121 Masthead St., N.E., Albuquerque, NM 87109-4367.
circ. 4,700. *4028*

STATE DIRECTORY OF KENTUCKY.
Directories, Inc., Box 187, Pewee Valley, KY 40056. TEL 502-241-8256.
circ. 5,000. *6196*

STATE GEOLOGISTS JOURNAL.
Association of American State Geologists, c/o Ohio Geological Survey, 4383 Fountain Sq. Dr., Columbus, OH 43224-1362. TEL 614-265-6576. FAX 614-447-1918.
circ. 200. *2371*

THE STATE OF THE MARKET.
Chartered Institute of Marketing, Moor Hall, Cookham, Maidenhead, Berkshire SL6 9QH, England. TEL 44-1628-427500. FAX 44-1628-427499.
circ. 25,000. *1290*

STATE OF THE UNION.
Union League Club of Chicago, 65 W. Jackson Blvd., Chicago, IL 60604. TEL 312-427-7800.
circ. 4,800. *1937*

STATE PEACE OFFICERS JOURNAL.
North American Publishing Company, Box 130155, Houston, TX 77219-0155. TEL 713-526-6425.
circ. 20,000. *2280*

STATE PLANNING NEWSLETTER.
Office of State Planning, 116 W. Jones St., Raleigh, NC 27603-8003. TEL 919-733-4131. FAX 919-715-3562.
circ. 2,700. *6942*

STATE UNIVERSITY OF NEW YORK AT ALBANY. ALBANY.
State University of New York at Albany, Office of University Relations, AD233, Albany, NY 12222. TEL 518-442-3070.
circ. 70,000. *1972*

STATION REPORTER.
Alfers Advertising & Publishing Inc., 5121 Sackville St., Ste. 601, Halifax, NS B3J 1K1, Canada. TEL 902-423-6788. FAX 902-423-3354.
circ. 4,800. *7117*

STATIONERY UPDATE.
Datateam Publishing Ltd., Fair Meadow, Maidstone, Kent ME14 1NG, England. TEL 44-1622-687031. FAX 44-1622-757646.
circ. 6,000. *1561*

STATISTICAL NOTES OF JAPAN.
International Statistical Affairs Division, Statistical Standards Department, Statistics Bureau, Management and Coordination Agency, 19-1 Wakamatsu-cho, Shinjuku-ku, Tokyo, Japan. FAX 81-3-5273-1181.
circ. 550. *6943*

STATISTICAL REPORT ON VISITOR ARRIVALS TO INDONESIA.
Department of Tourism, Post, and Telecommunications, Jalan Kebon Sirih, No.36, Jakarta, Indonesia. TEL 021-347611. FAX 021-375409.
circ. 500. *7256*

STATISTISK AARBOG FOR HOVEDSTADSREGIONEN.
Hovedstadsregionens Statistikkontor, Vester Voldgade 87, 4, DK-1552 Copenhagen, Denmark. TEL 45-33-66-24-24. FAX 45-33-91-05-02.
circ. 1,000. *6946*

STAVANGER AFTENBLAD.
P.O. Box 229, N-4001 Stavanger, Norway. TEL 47-51-50-00-00. FAX 47-51-89-32-23.
circ. 71,771. *3345*

STEEL TECHNOLOGY INTERNATIONAL.
Sterling Publications Ltd., 86-88 Edgware Rd., London W2 2YW, England. TEL 44-171-915-9600. FAX 44-171-915-9619.
circ. 10,000. *5212*

STEN.
Sveriges Stenindustrifoerbund, P.O. Box 106, S-121 22 Johanneshov, Sweden. TEL 46-08-81-86-00. FAX 46-08-81-86-02.
circ. 8,800. *914*

STENOGRAFISK TIDSSKRIFT.
Dansk Stenografisk Forening, Grumstrupsalle 4, DK-8660 Skanderborg, Denmark. TEL 75-571073. *1561*

STEVENS INDICATOR.
Stevens Alumni Association, Castle Point, Hoboken, NJ 07030. TEL 201-216-5161. FAX 201-216-5374.
circ. 21,000. *1972*

STILL WATERS NEWSLETTER.
Still Waters Foundation, Inc., 615 Stafford Ln., Pensacola, FL 32506. TEL 904-455-9511.
circ. 2,000. *5752*

STIRPES.
Texas State Genealogical Society, 204 Glentower, San Antonio, TX 78213. TEL 210-341-8372. FAX 210-341-7529.
circ. 850. *3242*

STITCHES.
Stitches Publishing Inc., 16787 Warden Ave., R.R. 3, Newmarket, ON L3Y 4W1, Canada. TEL 905-853-1884. FAX 905-853-6565.
circ. 44,000. *4748*

STNEWS.
Chemical Abstracts Service, 240 Olentangy River Rd., Box 3012, Columbus, OH 43210-0012. TEL 614-447-3600. FAX 614-447-3713. *1786*

STOCKTON NEWS.
Stockton Borough Council, P.O. Box 11, Municipal Bldgs., Church Rd., Stockton-on-Tees TS18 1LD, England. TEL 44-1642-393020. FAX 44-1642-393026.
circ. 75,000. *6225*

STORE EQUIPMENT AND DESIGN.
S E D Publishing, Box 578249, Chicago, IL 60657-8429. TEL 312-281-4441. FAX 312-281-8275.
circ. 20,000. *3144*

CONTROLLED CIRCULATION SERIALS

STRADA MAESTRA.
Leopoldo Fusconi Editore, Piazza Roosevelt 4, 40123 Bologna, Italy. TEL 39-51-228148. FAX 39-51-220825.
circ. 500. *3513*

STRAHLENTELEX MIT ELEKTROSMOG-REPORT.
Rauxeler Weg 6, 13507 Berlin, Germany. TEL 49-30-4352840. FAX 49-30-4352840.
circ. 1,200. *2981*

STRATTON MAGAZINE.
Lee A. Romano, Associates, Inc., Box 141, Dorset, VT 05251. TEL 802-867-0242. FAX 802-867-0102.
circ. 20,000. *3386*

STRAZ.
Polish National Union of America, 1004 Pittston Ave., Scranton, PA 18505. TEL 717-344-1513. FAX 717-961-5961.
circ. 10,000. *3044*

STREIFE.
Vereinigte Verlagsanstalten GmbH, Hoeherweg 278, 40231 Duesseldorf, Germany. TEL 49-211-7357-0. FAX 49-211-7357223.
circ. 24,000. *2280*

STRITCH M.D.
Loyola University Chicago, Stritch School of Medicine, 2160 S. First Ave., Maywood, IL 60153. TEL 708-216-6700. FAX 708-216-8199.
circ. 6,500. *1972*

STROKE NEWS.
Stroke Association, CHSA House, Whitecross St., London EC1Y 8JJ, England. TEL 44-171-490-7999. FAX 44-171-490-2686.
circ. 29,000. *5047*

STUD. MED.
Danish Medical Students Association, Blegdamsvej 3, DK-2200 Copenhagen N, Denmark.
circ. 5,000. *4748*

STUDENT B M J (SOUTH AFRICAN EDITION).
George Warman Publications (Pty.) Ltd., P.O. Box 704, Cape Town 8000, South Africa. TEL 27-21-245320. FAX 27-21-261332. *4748*

STUDENT MAGAZINE (COSTA MESA).
Box 1641, Costa Mesa, CA 92628-1641. TEL 714-548-9116.
circ. 20,000. *1973*

STUDIA PHONOLOGICA.
Kyoto University, Institution for Phonetic Sciences, c/o Mr. Shuji Doshita, Kyoto Daigaku Kogakubu Johokagakka, Yoshida Honmachi, Sakyo-ku, Kyoto 606, Japan. FAX 81-75-753-5977.
circ. 1,000. *4303*

STUDIE O RUKOPISECH.
Archiv Akademie Ved Ceske Republiky, V Zamcich 56-76, 181 00 Prague 8, Czech Republic. TEL 42-2-8541765. FAX 42-2-8541560.
circ. 300. *3605*

STUDIEN VON ZEITFRAGEN.
Peter Spengler Verlag, Postfach 101920, 60019 Frankfurt a.M., Germany. TEL 49-69-5963690. FAX 49-69-5974213.
circ. 100. *3514*

STUDIES IN AVIAN BIOLOGY.
Cooper Ornithological Society, Inc. (Riverside), Department of Biology, University of California at Riverside, Riverside, CA 92521. FAX 909-787-4286.
circ. 1,000. *809*

STUDIES IN ENGLISH LITERATURE.
English Literary Society of Japan, 501 Kenkyusha Bldg., 9 Surugadai 2-chome, Kanda, Chiyoda-ku, Tokyo 101, Japan. TEL 03-3293-7528. FAX 03-3233-3398.
circ. 3,800. *4473*

STUDIO MAGAZINE.
E M A P Alpha, 150 rue Gallieni, 92100 Boulogne-Billancourt, France.
circ. 96,000. *5346*

STUDIO ONE.
College of Saint Benedict, St. Joseph, MN 56374.
circ. 700. *4524*

STYLE (EDITION FRANCAISE).
N.V. Trends Magazines, Bd. Louis Schmidt 97, 1040 Brussels, Belgium. TEL 32-2-7321860. FAX 32-2-7344018. *3255*

STYLE (NEDERLANDSE EDITIE).
N.V. Trends Magazines, Bd. Louis Schmidt 97, 1040 Brussels, Belgium. TEL 32-2-7321860. FAX 32-2-7344018. *3255*

SUB-POSTMASTER.
National Federation of Sub-Postmasters, Evelyn House, 22 Windlesham Gardens, Shoreham-By-Sea, Sussex, England. TEL 44-1273-452324. FAX 44-1273-465403.
circ. 21,000. *2021*

SUBCONSCIOUS SOUP.
Scott Clark, Ed. & Pub., 103 Nicholas Ct., Kissimmee, FL 34758-3115. TEL 407-932-4597.
circ. 1,000. *4524*

SUBTERRANEAN SOCIOLOGY NEWSLETTER.
Subterranean Sociological Association, Department of Sociology, Eastern Michigan University, Ypsilanti, MI 48197. TEL 517-522-3551.
circ. 600. *6735*

SUBURBAN REAL ESTATE NEWS (MAINE).
Suburban Publishing Corp., 10 First Ave., Box 6039, Peabody, MA 01961-6039. TEL 508-532-5880. FAX 508-532-4250.
circ. 35,000. *6313*

SUBURBAN REAL ESTATE NEWS (NORTH OF BOSTON).
Suburban Publishing Co., 10 First Ave., Box 6039, Peabody, MA 01961-6039. TEL 508-532-5880. FAX 508-532-4250.
circ. 35,000. *6313*

SUBURBAN REAL ESTATE NEWS (SOUTH OF BOSTON).
Suburban Publishing Corp., 10 First Ave., Box 6039, Peabody, MA 01961-6039. TEL 508-532-5880. FAX 508-532-4250.
circ. 35,000. *6313*

SUBURBAN REAL ESTATE NEWS (WEST OF BOSTON).
Suburban Publishing Corp., 10 First Ave., Box 6039, Peabody, MA 01961-6039. TEL 508-532-5880. FAX 508-532-4250.
circ. 35,000. *6313*

SUD OUEST.
8 rue de Cheverus, 33094 Bordeaux Cedex, France. TEL 33-5-56003333. FAX 33-5-56003622.
circ. 347,772. *3281*

SUEDWEST PRESSE.
Neue Pressegesellschaft, Frauenstr. 77, 89073 Ulm, Germany. TEL 49-731-156500. FAX 49-731-156308.
circ. 130,000. *3291*

SUGAR MILLING RESEARCH INSTITUTE. ANNUAL REPORT.
Sugar Milling Research Institute, University of Natal, Durban 4041, South Africa. TEL 27-31-2616882. FAX 27-31-2616886.
circ. 400. *3128*

SUGAR TECHNOLOGISTS' ASSOCIATION OF TRINIDAD AND TOBAGO. PROCEEDINGS.
Sugar Manufacturers' Association of Trindad & Tobago, Suite 402, 4th Level, Mecalfab's Building, 92 Queen St., Port-of-Spain, Trinidad & Tobago, W.I. *3128*

SUGARBEET GROWER.
Sugar Publications, 503 Broadway, Fargo, ND 58102. TEL 701-237-5747. FAX 701-235-0140.
circ. 12,800. *246*

SUI YUAN WEN HSIEN.
Association of Fellow Provincials of Sui Yuan, 101 Fourth St., Chung Yang Rd., Hsin Tien, Taipei Hsien, Taiwan 23127, Republic of China. TEL 886-2-219-6633.
circ. 1,500. *3044*

SULPHUR IN AGRICULTURE.
Sulphur Institute, 1140 Connecticut Ave., N.W., Ste. 612, Washington, DC 20036. TEL 202-331-9660. FAX 202-293-2940.
circ. 3,000. *155*

SUMMARY OF STATE LAWS AND REGULATIONS RELATING TO DISTILLED SPIRITS.
Distilled Spirits Council of the United States, Inc., Legal Division, 1250 Eye St., N.W., Ste. 900, Washington, DC 20005. TEL 202-682-8825. FAX 202-682-8888. *527*

SUMMER POCKET GUIDE.
Land & Sea Publications, 9650 Clayton Rd., St. Louis, MO 63124. TEL 314-991-5222. FAX 314-991-1260.
circ. 500,000. *7236*

SUN-DIAMOND GROWER.
Sun-Diamond Growers of California, Box 1727, Stockton, CA 95201. TEL 209-467-6219. FAX 209-467-6357.
circ. 12,000. *3128*

SUNEXPERT.
Computer Publishing Group, 320 Washington St., Brookline, MA 02146-3202. TEL 617-739-7001. FAX 617-739-7003.
circ. 69,000. *2193*

SUNNHETSBLADET.
Norsk Bokforlag A-S, Grensevn 91, N-0663 Oslo, Norway. TEL 47-22-28-52-20. FAX 47-22-29-85-11.
circ. 11,000. *5791*

SUO.
Helsinki University, Department of Forest Ecology, P.O. Box 24, FIN-00014 Helsinki, Finland. FAX 358-9-191-7605.
circ. 700. *3163*

SUOMEN KALASTUSLEHTI.
Kalatalouden Keskusliitto, Koydenpunojankatu 7 B 23, FIN-00180 Helsinki, Finland. TEL 358-9-640-126. FAX 358-9-608-309.
circ. 4,392. *3079*

SUOMEN LAAKARILEHTI.
Suomen Laakariliitto, Makelankatu 2, 00500 Helsinki, Finland. TEL 358-90-393-0795.
circ. 21,500. *4749*

SUOMEN LEHDISTO.
Sanomalehtien Liitto, Lonnrotinkatu 11, FIN-00120 Helsinki, Finland. TEL 358-9-2287-7300. FAX 358-9-607-989.
circ. 3,376. *3881*

SUOMI - U S A.
Suomi-Amerikka Yhdistysten Liitto, Mechelininkatu 10A, FIN-00100 Helsinki, Finland. TEL 358-9-440711. FAX 358-9-408974.
circ. 30,275. *6038*

SUPERCONDUCTOR INDUSTRY.
WestTech, Box 411433, San Fransisco, CA 94141. FAX 415-837-0327.
circ. 7,000. *2847*

SUR IN ENGLISH.
Prensa Malaguena, S.A., Ave. Dr. Maranon 48, 29009 Malaga, Spain. TEL 34-52-649600. FAX 34-52-611256.
circ. 50,000. *3360*

SURFACE COATINGS AUSTRALIA.
Surface Coatings Association Australia Inc., 443 High St., Prahran, Vic. 3181, Australia. TEL 61-3-95106238. FAX 61-3-95296069.
circ. 1,350. *5555*

SURGICAL UPDATE.
American Association of Oral and Maxillofacial Surgeons, 9700 W. Bryn Mawr Ave., Rosemont, IL 60018. TEL 708-678-6200. FAX 708-678-6286.
circ. 150,000. *4871*

SURPLUS RECORD.
Surplus Record, Inc., 20 N. Wacker Dr., Chicago, IL 60606. TEL 312-372-9077. FAX 312-372-6537.
circ. 70,000. *4552*

SVENSK JAKT.
Svenska Jaegarefoerbundet, P.O. Box 1, S-163 21 Spaanga, Sweden. TEL 46-8-795-33-00. FAX 46-8-761-20-15.
circ. 173,400. *6885*

SVENSK PAPPERSTIDNING - NORDISK CELLULOSA.
Arbor Publishing AB, P.O. Box 26212, S-100 41 Stockholm, Sweden. TEL 46-8-611-60-30. FAX 46-8-679-90-50.
circ. 7,687. *5572*

SVENSK SJOEFARTS TIDNING.
Sveriges Redarefoerening, Box 53090, S-400 14 Goeteborg, Sweden. TEL 46-31-10-53-80. FAX 46-31-711-54-18.
circ. 7,300. *7167*

SVENSK TENNIS.
I C A Foerlaget AB, Storagatan 41, S-721 85 Vaesteraas, Sweden. TEL 46-21-19-40-00. FAX 46-21-19-42-42.
circ. 73,500. *6819*

SVENSK VAEGTIDNING.
Svenska Vaegfoereningens Foerlags AB, Wallingatan 33, S-111 24 Stockholm, Sweden. TEL 46-8-23-17-35. FAX 46-8-7918158.
circ. 3,000. *2799*

SVENSK VETERINAERTIDNING.
Sveriges Veterinaerfoerbund, P.O. Box 12 709, S-112 94 Stockholm, Sweden. TEL 08-654-2480. FAX 08-6517082.
circ. 2,600. *7279*

SVERIGES NATUR.
Svenska Naturskyddsfoereningen, P.O. Box 4625, S-116 91 Stockholm, Sweden. TEL 08-7026500. FAX 08-702-2702.
circ. 150,200. *2245*

SVETSAREN.
Esab AB, Marketing Communications, P.O. Box 8004, S-402 77 Goeteborg, Sweden. FAX 46-31-509-390.
circ. 1,600. *5224*

SVOBODA'S HOME & SMALL BUSINESS.
American Business Communicators, 3553 W.Peterson Ave., Ste. 40, Chicago, IL 60659. TEL 773-588-4410. FAX 773-588-4415.
circ. 29,500. *1648*

SVOBODNE SLOVO.
Melantrich, Inc., Vaclavske nam. 36, 112 12 Prague 1, Czech Republic. TEL 420-2-24227258. FAX 420-2-24229477.
circ. 155,000. *3274*

SWAMP GAS JOURNAL.
Ufology Research of Manitoba, Box 1918, Winnipeg General Post Office, Winnipeg, MB R3C 3R2, Canada. TEL 204-269-7553.
circ. 250. *80*

SWANSEA GEOGRAPHER.
University College of Swansea, Department of Geography, Singleton Park, Swansea, Glam. SA2 8PP, Wales. FAX 44-1792-205556.
circ. 200. *3423*

SWARTHMORE COLLEGE PHOENIX.
Swarthmore College, Swarthmore, PA 19081. TEL 610-328-8173. FAX 610-328-8674.
circ. 2,700. *1973*

SWATCHES.
National Association of Decorative Fabric Distributors, 3008 Millwood Ave., Columbia, SC 29205. TEL 803-252-5646.
circ. 17,000. *6994*

SWEET'S CANADIAN CONSTRUCTION CATALOGUE.
McGraw-Hill Information Systems Company of Canada, 270 Yorkland Blvd., North York, ON M2J 1R8, Canada. TEL 416-496-3100. FAX 416-496-3123.
circ. 7,000. *915*

SWEET'S CATALOG FILE FOR THE CIVIL ENGINEERING & RETROFIT MARKET.
Sweet's Catalog Files, 1221 Ave. of the Americas, New York, NY 10020. TEL 212-512-4450. FAX 212-512-2348.
circ. 15,000. *2799*

SWEET'S CATALOG FILE FOR THE ELECTRICAL ENGINEERING AND RETROFIT MARKET.
Sweet's Catalog Files, 1221 Ave. of the Americas, New York, NY 10020. TEL 212-512-4450. FAX 212-512-2348.
circ. 15,000. *2847*

SWEET'S CONTRACT INTERIORS FILE.
Sweet's Catalog Files, 1221 Ave. of the Americas, New York, NY 10020. TEL 212-512-4450. FAX 212-512-2348.
circ. 10,000. *3850*

SWEET'S GENERAL BUILDING AND RENOVATION FILE.
Sweet's Catalog Files, 1221 Ave. of the Americas, New York, NY 10020. TEL 212-512-4450. FAX 212-512-2348.
circ. 25,000. *915*

SWEET'S HOMEBUILDING & REMODELING FILE.
Sweet's Catalog Files, 1221 Ave. of the Americas, New York, NY 10020. TEL 212-512-4450. FAX 212-512-2348.
circ. 29,000. *915*

SWEET'S INDUSTRIAL CONSTRUCTION AND RENOVATION FILE.
Sweet's Catalog Files, 1221 Ave. of the Americas, New York, NY 10020. TEL 212-512-4450. FAX 212-512-2348.
circ. 25,000. *915*

SWEET'S INTERNATIONAL BUILDING PRODUCTS CATALOG FILE.
Sweet's Catalog Files, 1221 Ave. of the Americas, New York, NY 10020. TEL 212-512-4450. FAX 212-512-2348. *915*

SWEET'S INTERNATIONAL PRODUCTLINE.
Sweet's Catalog Files, 1221 Ave. of the Americas, New York, NY 10020. TEL 212-512-4750. FAX 212-512-4302. *915*

SWEET'S LIGHT SOURCE.
Sweet's Catalog Files, 1221 Ave. of the Americas, New York, NY 10020. TEL 212-512-4450. FAX 212-512-2348.
circ. 21,000. *915*

SWEET'S MECHANICAL ENGINEERING AND RETROFIT FILE.
Sweet's Catalog Files, 1221 Ave. of the Americas, New York, NY 10020. TEL 212-512-4450. FAX 212-512-2348.
circ. 15,000. *2901*

SWEET'S PRODUCTLINE.
Sweet's Catalog Files, 1221 Ave. of the Americas, New York, NY 10020. TEL 212-512-4750. FAX 212-512-4302.
circ. 25,000. *915*

SWENSON CENTER NEWS.
Swenson Swedish Immigration Research Center, Augustana College, 639 38th St., Rock Island, IL 61201-2273. TEL 309-794-7204. FAX 309-794-7443.
circ. 4,500. *3045*

SWIFT CURRENT SUN.
55 1st Ave. N.E., Swift Current, SK S9H 2A9, Canada. TEL 306-773-3116. FAX 306-773-2653.
circ. 20,032. *3266*

SWINGER'S TODAY.
Contact Advertising, 2010 St. Lucie Blvd., Ft. Pierce, FL 34946. TEL 561-464-5447. FAX 561-466-7294.
circ. 15,000. *5182*

SWINGERS UPDATE.
Contact Advertising, 2010 St. Lucie Blvd., Ft. Pierce, FL 34946. TEL 561-464-5447. FAX 561-466-7294.
circ. 22,000. *5182*

SWINGING TIMES.
Contact Advertising, 2010 St. Lucie Blvd., Ft. Pierce, FL 34946. TEL 561-464-5447. FAX 561-466-7294.
circ. 50,000. *5182*

SWISS SURGERY.
Hans Huber AG, Laenggassstr. 76, CH-3000 Bern 9, Switzerland. TEL 41-31-3004500. FAX 41-31-3004590.
circ. 2,000. *5156*

SYMANTEC.
Symantec Corporation, 10201 Torre Ave., Cupertino, CA 95014-2132. TEL 408-253-9600. FAX 408-253-3968.
circ. 650,000. *2219*

SYMBIOSE.
Vereinigte Verlagsanstalten GmbH, Hoeherweg 278, 40231 Duesseldorf, Germany. TEL 49-211-7357-0. FAX 49-211-7357223.
circ. 50,000. *5695*

SYMPATICO NETLIFE.
Telemedia Communications Inc., 25 Sheppard Ave. W., Ste. 100, Toronto, ON M2N 6S7, Canada. TEL 416-733-7600. FAX 416-733-8272.
circ. 193,000. *3760*

SYNAPSE (BOSTON).
Unitarian Universalist Association, 25 Beacon St., Boston, MA 02108-2800. TEL 617-742-2100. FAX 617-367-3237.
circ. 10,500. *4361*

SYNCOPATED PERFS.
Greater Cincinnati Philatelic Society, 6508 Craigland Ct., Cincinnati, OH 45230-2821. TEL 513-231-4208. FAX 513-231-9430.
circ. 150. *5714*

SYNDICAT NATIONAL DES ARCHITECTES D'INTERIEUR. BULLETIN.
Syndicat National des Architectes d'Interieur, 57, Bd. Richard Lenoir, 75011 Paris, France.
circ. 650. *416*

SYSTEMS CONTRACTOR NEWS.
Miller Freeman P S N Inc., 460 Park Ave. South, 9th Fl., New York, NY 10016-7315. TEL 212-378-0400. FAX 212-378-2160.
circ. 14,000. *2653*

SZABADSAG.
Szabadsag Ltd., Str. Napoca Nr. 16, P.O. Box 340, 3400 Cluj, Rumania. TEL 40-64-198985. FAX 42-64-196207.
circ. 500. *3351*

SZIVARVANY.
Framo Publishing, 561 W. Diversey Pkwy., Chicago, IL 60614. TEL 312-477-1485. FAX 312-477-2698.
circ. 1,200. *3045*

T A M BULLETIN.
Travelling Art Mail, c/o T A M, Postbus 10388, 5000 JJ Tilburg, Netherlands. TEL 31-13-5366103. *468*

T & A M REPORT.
University of Illinois at Urbana-Champaign, Department of Theoretical and Applied Mechanics, 216 Talbot Laboratory, Urbana, IL 61801. TEL 217-333-2322.
circ. 65. *2870*

T C U MAGAZINE.
Texas Christian University, Box 298940, Ft. Worth, TX 76129. TEL 817-921-7807. FAX 817-921-7110.
circ. 51,000. *1973*

T E A M HORIZONS.
Evangelical Alliance Mission, Box 969, Wheaton, IL 60189-0969. TEL 708-653-1826. FAX 708-653-1826.
circ. 45,000. *6376*

T G.
Ediciones Sohail, Velazquez 21, 28001 Madrid, Spain. TEL 1-275-38-28.
circ. 10,000. *468*

T H E JOURNAL.
Ed Warnshius Ltd., 150 El Camino Real, Ste. 112, Tustin, CA 92780. TEL 714-730-4011. FAX 714-730-3739.
circ. 160,000. *2519*

T H - TRANSPORT OCH HANTERING.
T.H. Foerlag, Box 3427, S-103 68 Stockholm, Sweden. TEL 46-8-23-03-70. FAX 46-8-10-46-18.
circ. 3,400. *7039*

T I A NEWS.
Sosland Publishing Company, 4800 Main St., Ste. 100, Kansas City, MO 64112-2513. TEL 816-756-1000. FAX 816-756-0484.
circ. 2,500. *3138*

10398 CONTROLLED CIRCULATION SERIALS

T I F F A FREIGHT FORWARDING HANDBOOK.
Cosmic Group of Companies, 4th Fl., Phyathai Bldg., 31 Phyathai Rd., Rajthevi, Bangkok 10400, Thailand. TEL 245-3850. FAX 246-4737.
circ. 5,000. *7167*

T M A GUIDE TO TOBACCO TAXES.
Tobacco Merchants Association of the United States, Inc., 231 Clarksville Rd., Ste. 6, Box 8019, Princeton, NJ 08543-8019. TEL 609-275-4900. FAX 609-275-8379. *7020*

T M A LEAF BULLETIN.
Tobacco Merchants Association of the United States, Inc., 231 Clarksville Rd., Ste. 6, Box 8019, Princeton, NJ 08543-8019. TEL 609-275-4900. FAX 609-275-8379. *7020*

T M A TOBACCO BAROMETER.
Tobacco Merchants Association of the United States, Inc., 231 Clarksville Rd., Ste. 6, Box 8019, Princeton, NJ 08543-8019. TEL 609-275-4900. FAX 609-275-8379. *7021*

T M A TOBACCO BAROMETER: SMOKING, CHEWING, SNUFF.
Tobacco Merchants Association of the United States, Inc., 231 Clarksville Rd., Ste. 6, Box 8019, Princeton, NJ 08543-8019. TEL 609-275-4900. FAX 609-275-8379. *7021*

T M A TOBACCO TRADE BAROMETER.
Tobacco Merchants Association of the United States, Inc., 231 Clarksville Rd., Ste. 6, Box 8019, Princeton, NJ 08543-8019. TEL 609-275-4900. FAX 609-275-8379. *7021*

T N SERRURERIE - MIROITERIE.
28 rue Andre Bonnenfant, 78100 Saint-Germain en Laye, France. TEL 39-73-50-31. FAX 39-73-53-31.
circ. 6,000. *929*

T N T MAGAZINE.
14-15 Child's Pl., Earls Ct., London SW5 9RX, England. TEL 44-171-373-3377. FAX 44-171-341-6600.
circ. 69,504. *3301*

T.P.L. NEWS.
Toronto Public Library, 281 Front St. E., Toronto, Ont. M5A 4L2, Canada. TEL 416-393-7565. FAX 416-393-7782.
circ. 900. *4216*

T R I P SOUTH.
Browning Publications, 3103 Medlock Bridge Rd., Norcross, GA 30071. TEL 770-825-0220. FAX 770-825-0880.
circ. 60,782. *7236*

T S I JOURNAL OF PARTICLE INSTRUMENTATION.
T S I Incorporated, 500 Cardigan Rd., Box 64394, St. Paul, MN 55164. TEL 612-490-2833. FAX 612-490-3860.
circ. 9,000. *2901*

T S S A REPORT.
Tackle & Shooting Sports Agents Association, 1033 N. Fairfax St., Ste. 200, Alexandria, VA 22314-1540. TEL 708-381-3032. FAX 708-381-9518.
circ. 400. *1005*

T T G ASIA HOTEL GUIDE.
Miller Freeman Pte. Ltd., 100 Beach Rd., 26-00 Shaw Towers, Singapore 0718, Singapore. TEL 65-2943366. FAX 65-2985534.
circ. 60,608. *7236*

T T R A NEWS.
University of Utah, 10200 W. 44th Ave., No. 304, Wheat Ridge, CO 80033. TEL 303-422-6557. FAX 303-422-8894.
circ. 900. *7236*

T U C NEWS.
Trades Union Congress of Ghana, Hall of Trade Unions, P.O. Box 701, Accra, Ghana.
circ. 10,000. *3898*

T U SPEKTRUM.
Technische Universitaet Chemnitz - Zwickau, 09107 Chemnitz, Germany. TEL 49-371-5311424. FAX 49-371-5311651.
circ. 4,000. *2742*

T V NEWS.
80 Eighth Ave., Ste. 315, New York, NY 10011. TEL 212-243-6800. FAX 212-243-7457.
circ. 331,000. *2061*

T V 7 JOURS.
Trustar Ltd., 2020 rue Universite, 20th Fl., Montreal, PQ H3A 2A5, Canada. TEL 514-383-3400. FAX 514-383-1766.
circ. 255. *2061*

T V TODAY.
National Association of Broadcasters, 1771 N St., N.W., Washington, DC 20036. TEL 202-429-5350. FAX 202-429-5406. *2061*

T W I C E.
Cahners Publishing Company (New York), Division of Reed Elsevier Inc., 249 W. 17th St., New York, NY 10011. TEL 212-645-0067. FAX 212-337-7066.
circ. 31,700. *2653*

TABI TO TETSUDO.
Tetsudo Journal Sha, Iidabashi 4-8-6, Chiyoda-ku, Tokyo, Japan. TEL 81-3-3264-1891. FAX 81-3-3265-3597.
circ. 120,000. *7237*

TACOMA - PIERCE COUNTY CHAMBER OF COMMERCE UPDATE.
Tacoma-Pierce County Chamber of Commerce, 950 Pacific Ave., Ste. 300, Box 1933, Tacoma, WA 98401. TEL 206-627-2175. FAX 206-597-7305.
circ. 3,500. *1196*

TAGEBLATT.
Editpress, 44 rue du Canal, P.O. Box 147, L-4050 Esch - Alzette, Luxembourg. TEL 00352-547131. FAX 00352-547130.
circ. 29,000. *3333*

TAHITI BEACH PRESS.
Tahiti Publications Touristiques, P.O. Box 887, Papeete 98713, Tahiti. TEL 689-426850. FAX 689-423356.
circ. 2,700. *7237*

TAIEI TOSHI NEWS.
Invest in Britain Bureau, 1 Victoria St., London SW1H OET, England. TEL 44-171-215-5638. FAX 44-171-215-5651.
circ. 11,300. *1410*

TAITO.
Kasi- ja Taideteollisuusliitto, P.O. Box 186, Kalevankatu 61, FIN-00181 Helsinki, Finland. TEL 358-9-694-0012. FAX 358-9-694-0067.
circ. 10. *484*

TAIWAN HAIXIA.
Guojia Haiyang-ju, Disan Haiyang Yanjiusuo, P.O. Box 0570, Xiamen, Fujian 361005, People's Republic of China. TEL 0592-2085880. FAX 0592-2086646.
circ. 1,000. *2415*

TAKAHE.
Takahe Collective Trust, P.O. Box 13-335, Christchurch 1, New Zealand. TEL 64-3-3598133.
circ. 340. *4476*

TAKE OFF.
Skandinavisk Bladforlag A-S, Frederiksberg Alle 3, DK-1621 Copenhagen V, Denmark. TEL 45-31-23-80-99. FAX 45-31-23-70-42.
circ. 6,000. *7237*

TALKING PICTURES.
Valis Books, 3 Glengarry Rd., E. Dulwich, London SE22 8PZ, England. TEL 44-181-693-2134. FAX 44-171-737-4720.
circ. 500. *5346*

TALKING POINT.
Trinity College London, 16 Park Crescent, London W1N 4AP, England. TEL 44-171-323-2328. FAX 44-171-323-5201.
circ. 6,000. *2620*

TALKING TO THE BOSS.
4556 Oakton St., No.200, Skokie, IL 60076-3144. TEL 708-933-9659. FAX 708-933-9667.
circ. 15,000. *1005*

TAMKANG JOURNAL OF MATHEMATICS.
Tamkang University Press, Tamsui, Taipei, Taiwan 25137, Republic of China. TEL 886-2-621-5656. FAX 886-2-620-2613.
circ. 300. *4610*

TAMPA BAY FAMILY JOURNAL.
Family Journal Publications, Inc., Box 1100, Orlando, FL 32802-1100. TEL 813-289-4060. FAX 813-289-4585.
circ. 25,000. *1857*

TANNING TRENDS.
Tanning Trends Inc., 3101 Page Ave., Jackson, MI 49203. TEL 517-784-1772. FAX 517-787-3940.
circ. 20,000. *1648*

TANZANIA. BUREAU OF STANDARDS. DIRECTOR'S ANNUAL REPORT.
Bureau of Standards, P.O. Box 9524, Dar es Salaam, Tanzania. TEL 255-51-43298. FAX 255-51-43298. *5255*

TAOS MAGAZINE.
Whitney Publishing Co., Inc., Box 1380, Taos, NM 87571. TEL 505-758-5404.
circ. 8,500. *7256*

TAPOVAN PRASAD.
Chinmaya Mission, No. 2, 13th Ave., Harrington Rd., Madras 600031, Tamil Nadu, India. TEL 8265641.
circ. 5,000. *6395*

TARGET THE FAMILY.
Gruner & Jahr U.S.A. Publishing, 110 Fifth Ave., New York, NY 10011. TEL 212-463-1000. FAX 212-463-1908.
circ. 1,000,000. *3387*

TASMANIA. DEPARTMENT OF PRIMARY INDUSTRY AND FISHERIES. MARINE RESOURCES DIVISION. TECHNICAL REPORT.
Department of Primary Industry and Fisheries, Marine Resources Division, P.O. Box 619F, Hobart, Tas. 7001, Australia. TEL 61-3-6227727. FAX 61-02-278035.
circ. 400. *3080*

TASMANIAN BUSINESS REPORTER.
Tasmanian Chamber of Commerce and Industry, G.P.O. Box 793H, Hobart, Tas. 7001, Australia. TEL 61-3-62345933. FAX 61-3-62311278.
circ. 16,400. *1196*

TASMANIAN EDUCATION REVIEW.
Australian Education Union, Tasmanian Branch, 32 Patrick St., Hobart, Tas., Australia. TEL 61-3-62349500. FAX 61-2-62343052.
circ. 6,400. *3898*

TATER NEWS.
National Potato Promotion Board, 7555 E. Hampden Ave., No. 412, Denver, CO 80231-4835. TEL 303-758-7783. FAX 303-756-9256.
circ. 17,000. *247*

TAX NOTES.
Tax Analysts, 6830 N. Fairfax Dr., Arlington, VA 22213. TEL 703-533-4400. FAX 703-533-4444. *1633*

TAXATION IN AUSTRALIA (BLUE EDITION).
Taxation Institute of Australia, 7th Fl., 64 Castlereagh St., Sydney, N.S.W. 2000, Australia. TEL 61-2-92323422. FAX 61-2-92216953.
circ. 10,000. *1634*

TAYLOR.
Taylor University, 500 W. Reade Ave., Upland, IN 46989. TEL 765-998-2751. FAX 765-998-4910.
circ. 23,500. *2557*

TEACHER IN ZIMBABWE.
Zimbabwe Publishing House, P.O. Box 350, Harare, Zimbabwe. TEL 263-4-497548. FAX 263-4-497554.
circ. 60,000. *2487*

TEACHERS' MONEY MATTERS.
Teachers' Money Matters Ltd., 70 Scriven Rd., Bailieboro, Ont. K0L 1B0, Canada. TEL 705-939-1203. FAX 705-939-1179.
circ. 33,000. *1169*

CONTROLLED CIRCULATION SERIALS

TEACHING EDUCATION.
University of South Carolina, College of Education, Columbia, SC 29208. TEL 803-777-6301. FAX 803-777-3090.
circ. 1,200. *2487*

TEAM (LONDON).
22-24 Worple Rd., Wimbledon, London SW19 4DD, England. TEL 081-947-3131. FAX 081-944-6552.
circ. 40,000. *3736*

TEAM REHAB REPORT.
Miramar Communications Inc., 23815 Stuart Ranch Rd., Box 8987, Malibu, CA 90265-8987. TEL 310-317-4522. FAX 310-317-9644.
circ. 12,000. *3458*

TEAM WORK SERVICE UND GESUNDHEIT.
Vereinigte Verlagsanstalten GmbH, Hoeherweg 278, 40231 Duesseldorf, Germany. TEL 49-211-7357-0. FAX 49-211-7357223.
circ. 50,000. *6251*

TECAGRI NEWS.
Clark Consulting International, Inc., Box 600, Dundee, IL 60118-0600. TEL 847-836-5100. FAX 847-836-5140.
circ. 90,000. *210*

TECH CENTER NEWS.
Springer Publishing Inc., 31201 Chicago Rd. S., Warren, MI 48093. TEL 810-939-6800. FAX 810-939-5850.
circ. 15,000. *7118*

TECH DIRECTIONS.
Prakken Publications, Inc., Box 8623, Ann Arbor, MI 48107. TEL 313-769-1211. FAX 313-769-8383.
circ. 44,000. *2621*

TECHNICAL EDUCATION NEWS.
Glencoe - McGraw-Hill, 1221 Ave. of the Americas, New York, NY 10020. TEL 212-512-4736. FAX 212-512-6904.
circ. 47,000. *2621*

TECHNION - ISRAEL INSTITUTE OF TECHNOLOGY. PRESIDENT'S REPORT.
Technion - Israel Institute of Technology, Division of Public Affairs, Haifa 3200, Israel.
circ. 30,000. *6975*

TECHNISCH WEEKBLAD.
V N U Business Publications B.V., P.O. Box 90162, 1006 BD Amsterdam, Netherlands. TEL 31-20-4875459. FAX 31-20-4875731.
circ. 24,241. *2742*

TECHNISCHE REVUE.
Misset, Postbus 4, 7000 BA Doetinchem, Netherlands. TEL 31-314-349371. FAX 31-314-363638.
circ. 30,660. *6975*

TECHNOLOGY FOCUS.
Defence Research & Development Organization, Metcalfe House, New Delhi 110 054, India. TEL 91-11-239975. FAX 91-11-2919151.
circ. 2,500. *5287*

TECHNOLOGY FOR ALASKAN TRANSPORTATION.
Alaska Transportation Technology Transfer Program, DOT & PF T2 Program, 2301 Peger Rd., Fairbanks, AK 99709-5399. TEL 907-451-5320. FAX 907-451-2313.
circ. 2,400. *7040*

TECHNOLOGY IN EDUCATION.
B & S Publications, 3 Crescent Terr., Cheltenham, Glos. GL50 3PE, England. TEL 44-1242-510760. FAX 44-1242-22626.
circ. 8,000. *6977*

TECNICA E INVENCION.
Princesa 14, 28008 Madrid, Spain. TEL 2414800.
circ. 3,000. *5590*

EL TECOLOTE.
Accion Latina, 766 Valencia St., San Francisco, CA 94110. TEL 415-252-5957. FAX 415-252-5701.
circ. 10,000. *3045*

TED SLANKER'S MARKET UPDATE.
Ted E. Slanker, Jr., Ed. & Pub., R.R. 2, Box 175, Powderly, TX 75473-9740. TEL 903-732-4653. FAX 903-732-4151.
circ. 10,650. *1411*

TEE TO GREEN.
Custom Publishing Company Ltd., 45 Station Rd., Redhill, Surrey RH1 1QU, England. TEL 44-1737-767213. FAX 44-1737-771662.
circ. 11,100. *4153*

TEESWATER SHEEP BREEDERS' ASSOCIATION. ANNUAL FLOCK BOOK.
Teeswater Sheep Breeders' Association, 1 The Mount, Leyburn, N. Yorks DL8 5JA, England. TEL 44-1969-23432.
circ. 140. *290*

TEKNISK NYT.
Teknisk Forlag A-S, Skelbaekgade 4, DK-1780 Copenhagen V, Denmark. TEL 45-31-21-68-01. FAX 45-31-21-04-01.
circ. 18,522. *2742*

TEKSTIILIOPETTAJA.
Tekstiiliopettajaliitto, Mannerheimintie 132 B 31, SF-00270 Helsinki, Finland.
circ. 1,500. *3689*

TELECOMMAGAZINE.
V N U Business Publications B.V., Postbus 9194, 1006 CC Amsterdam, Netherlands. TEL 31-20-4875487. FAX 31-20-4875727.
circ. 17,000. *2171*

TELECOMMS ABSTRACTS.
Techgnosis Ltd., Blade House, Battersea Rd., Stockport, Cheshire SK4 3AE, England. TEL 44-161-442-2639. FAX 44-161-443-1162. *2096*

TELECOMMUNICATION AUTHORITY OF SINGAPORE. SINGAPORE TELECOM ANNUAL REPORT.
Telecommunication Authority of Singapore, 35 Robinson Rd., TAS Bldg., Singapore 0106, Singapore. TEL 65-323-3888. FAX 65-323-0941. *2040*

TELECOMMUNICATIONS AMERICAS.
Portland House, Stag Pl., London SW1E 5XT, England. TEL 44-171-957-0030. FAX 44-171-957-0031.
circ. 54,050. *2040*

TELEPHONY.
Telephony Publishing, One I B M Plaza, Chicago, IL 60611. TEL 312-595-1080.
circ. 48,307. *2041*

TELESIS (OTTAWA).
Bell-Northern Research Ltd., 3500 Carling Ave., Ottawa, ON K1Y 4H7, Canada. TEL 613-765-2520. FAX 613-763-2008.
circ. 35,000. *2041*

TELEVISION BROADCAST.
Miller Freeman P S N Inc., 460 Park Ave. South, 9th Fl., New York, NY 10016-7315. TEL 212-378-0400. FAX 212-378-2160.
circ. 30,800. *2063*

TELEVISION BUYER.
E M A P Media, 33-39 Bowling Green Ln., London WC1R 0DA, England. FAX 44-171-833-4519.
circ. 7,927. *2063*

TELEVISION INTERNATIONAL MAGAZINE.
Television International Publications Ltd., Box 2430, Hollywood, CA 90028. TEL 213-462-1099.
circ. 14,000. *2063*

TELLING IT LIKE IT IS.
Transportation Communications International Union, 3 Research Pl., Rockville, MD 20850. TEL 301-948-4910. FAX 301-948-1369.
circ. 2,200. *7134*

TENNESSEE. DEPARTMENT OF SAFETY. ANNUAL REPORT.
Department of Safety, 1150 Foster Ave., Nashville, TN 37249-1000. TEL 615-251-5313. FAX 615-251-5242.
circ. 500. *7141*

TENNESSEE DEER & TURKEY SHOW & PREVIEW.
Target Communications Corp., 7626 W. Donges Bay Rd., Mequon, WI 53097-3400. TEL 414-242-3990. FAX 414-242-7391.
circ. 15,000. *6885*

TENNESSEE LAW ENFORCEMENT JOURNAL.
Tennessee Law Enforcement Officers Association, c/o Lt. J.P. Ruff, Box 139, Ellendale, TN 38029-0139. FAX 612-541-0435.
circ. 3,000. *2281*

TENNESSEE PARENT - TEACHER BULLETIN.
Tennessee Congress of Parents and Teachers, 1905 Acklen Ave., Nashville, TN 37212. TEL 615-383-9740.
circ. 1,400. *2487*

TENNESSEE SCHOOL BOARD BULLETIN.
Tennessee School Boards Association, 500 13th Ave. North, Nashville, TN 37203-2830. FAX 615-741-2824.
circ. 1,800. *2579*

TENNESSEE TRUCKING NEWS.
Tennessee Trucking Association, 1415 Murgreesboro Rd., Ste. 672, Nashville, TN 37217. TEL 615-360-9200. FAX 615-361-3137.
circ. 1,000. *7178*

TENNIS U S T A.
New York Times Magazine Group, Sports - Leisure Division, 5520 Park Ave., Box 395, Trumbull, CT 06611. TEL 203-373-7155. FAX 203-371-2199.
circ. 440,000. *6820*

TENSOR.
Tensor Society, Kawaguchi Sutikenkyujo - Kawaguchi Institute of Mathematical Sciences, 7-15, Matsu-ga-oka 2-chome, Chigasaki-shi, Kanagawa-ken 253, Japan.
circ. 600. *4610*

TENTH TIMES.
Texas Dental Association, Tenth District Dental Society, 3303 Northland, No. 313, Austin, TX 78731. TEL 512-452-9296.
circ. 450. *4871*

TERMALISMO - BALNEARIOS.
Editorial J.S. Publicaciones Especiales, Santa Susana 55, 5o 1 y 2, 28033 Madrid, Spain. TEL 1-7633401.
circ. 20,000. *3485*

TERRAIN.
Ecology Center, 2530 San Pablo Ave., Berkeley, CA 94702. TEL 510-548-2220.
circ. 3,000. *2953*

TERRATECH.
Vereinigte Fachverlage GmbH, Lise-Meitner-Str. 2, 55129 Mainz, Germany. TEL 49-6131-992146. FAX 49-6131-992100.
circ. 2,500. *2953*

TEXAS AGRINEWS.
Big River Press, Inc., 1217 N. Conway, Box 353, Mission, TX 78572. TEL 210-585-4893. FAX 210-585-2304.
circ. 9,379. *157*

TEXAS BICYCLIST.
Yellow Jersey Enterprises, 12814 Azalea Creek Trail, Houston, TX 77095-4209. TEL 713-782-1661.
circ. 45,000. *6834*

TEXAS CIVIL ENGINEER.
American Society of Civil Engineers, Texas Section, 3501 Manor Rd., Austin, TX 78723. TEL 512-472-8905. FAX 512-472-2934.
circ. 5,750. *2799*

TEXAS DIRECTOR.
Rector - Duncan & Associates, Box 14667, Austin, TX 78761. TEL 512-454-5262. FAX 512-451-9556.
circ. 1,000. *3179*

TEXAS HIGHER EDUCATION COORDINATING BOARD. C B POLICY PAPER.
Texas Higher Education Coordinating Board, Box 12788, Capitol Sta., Austin, TX 78711. TEL 512-483-6111. FAX 512-483-6127. *2557*

TEXAS HIGHER EDUCATION COORDINATING BOARD. C B STUDY PAPER.
Texas Higher Education Coordinating Board, Box 12788, Capitol Sta., Austin, TX 78711. TEL 512-483-6111. FAX 512-483-6127. *2557*

10400 CONTROLLED CIRCULATION SERIALS

TEXAS HIGHER EDUCATION COORDINATING BOARD. STATUS REPORT ON HIGHER EDUCATION AND STATISTICAL REPORT.
Texas Higher Education Coordinating Board, Box 12788, Capitol Sta., Austin, TX 78711. TEL 512-483-6111. FAX 512-483-6127.
circ. 1,000. *2557*

TEXAS INSTRUMENTS TECHNICAL JOURNAL.
Texas Instruments, Box 650311, Mail Sta. 3940, Dallas, TX 75265. TEL 214-917-3906. FAX 214-917-3850.
circ. 12,300. *2742*

TEXAS LEGION TIMES.
Adcraft Agency, Box 337, Jacksboro, TX 76458-0337. TEL 817-567-6622. FAX 817-567-6372.
circ. 100,500. *1937*

TEXAS PETROLEUM AND C-STORE JOURNAL.
Texas Oil Marketers Association, 701 W. 15th St., Austin, TX 78701. TEL 512-476-9547. FAX 512-477-4239.
circ. 1,200. *5624*

TEXAS PROPANE.
Texas Propane Gas Association, Box 140735, Austin, TX 78714-0735. TEL 512-836-8620. FAX 512-834-0758.
circ. 1,250. *5624*

TEXAS PUBLIC LIBRARY DIRECTORY.
Texas State Library, Library Development Division, Box 12927, Austin, TX 78711. TEL 512-463-5465. FAX 512-463-8800.
circ. 500. *4217*

TEXAS PUBLIC LIBRARY STATISTICS.
Texas State Library, Library Development Division, Box 12927, Austin, TX 78711. TEL 512-463-5465.
circ. 500. *4228*

TEXAS PUBLIC LIBRARY SUMMARY.
Texas State Library, Library Development Division, Box 12927, Austin, TX 78711. TEL 512-463-5465.
circ. 500. *4228*

TEXAS TOUR AND MEETING GUIDE.
Publishing Partnership, Box 1569, Austin, TX 78767. TEL 512-320-6900. FAX 512-476-9007.
circ. 52,355. *7237*

TEXTIEL BEHEER.
Stichting Vakblad Textielreiniging, Postbus 10, 4060 GA Ophmert, Netherlands. FAX 31-34-4651525.
circ. 1,000. *1911*

TEXTILE TECHNOLOGY FOR CHINA.
Sterling Publications Ltd., 86-88 Edgware Rd., London W2 2YW, England. TEL 44-171-915-9600. FAX 44-171-915-9619.
circ. 10,000. *6997*

TEXTILE TECHNOLOGY INTERNATIONAL.
Sterling Publications Ltd., 86-88 Edgware Rd., London W2 2YW, England. TEL 44-171-915-9600. FAX 44-171-915-9619.
circ. 10,000. *6997*

TEXTILE WORLD.
Intertec Publishing Corp., Textile Publications, P.O. Box 12901, Overland Park, KS 66282-2901.
circ. 32,164. *6997*

THAI CHAMBER OF COMMERCE. DIRECTORY (YEAR).
Cosmic Group of Companies, 4th Fl., Phyathai Bldg., 31 Phyathai Rd., Rajthevi, Bangkok 10400, Thailand. TEL 662-2453850. FAX 662-2461710.
circ. 5,000. *1196*

THAI FURNITURE INDUSTRIES ASSOCIATION DIRECTORY.
Cosmic Group of Companies, 4th Fl., Phyathai Bldg., 31 Phyathai Rd., Rajthevi, Bangkok 10400, Thailand. TEL 245-3850. FAX 246-4737.
circ. 5,000. *1716*

THAI-KOREAN CHAMBER OF COMMERCE HANDBOOK & DIRECTORY.
Cosmic Group of Companies, 4th Fl., Phyathai Bldg., 31 Phyathai Rd., Rajthevi, Bangkok 10400, Thailand. TEL 662-2453850. FAX 662-2461710.
circ. 2,000. *1196*

THAILAND SHOWCASE.
Cosmic Group of Companies, 4th Fl., Phyathai Bldg., 31 Phyathai Rd., Rajthevi, Bangkok 10400, Thailand. TEL 245-3850. FAX 246-4737.
circ. 10,000. *1348*

THAQAFA WA FANN.
Cultural Foundation, Culture and Arts Department, P.O. Box 2380, Abu Dhabi, United Arab Emirates. TEL 215300. FAX 336059.
circ. 500. *469*

THAT'S MY BABY.
That's My Baby, Inc., Box 1156, Lake Oswego, OR 97035. TEL 503-620-9132. FAX 503-620-3800.
circ. 500,000. *1858*

THEATER HEUTE.
Friedrich Kulturzeitschriftenverlag, Luetzowplatz 7, 10785 Berlin, Germany. TEL 49-30-254495-0. FAX 49-30-25449512.
circ. 20,000. *7015*

THEMIS.
Zeta Tau Alpha, International Office, 3450 Founders Rd., Indianapolis, IN 46268. TEL 317-872-0540. FAX 371-876-3948.
circ. 65,000. *1974*

THEOLOGIA REFORMATA.
Drukkerij Oosterbaan en Le Cointre B.V., Postbus 25, 4460 AA Goes, Netherlands. TEL 08380-17091.
circ. 750. *6444*

THEOLOGICA XAVERIANA.
Pontificia Universidad Javeriana, Facultad de Teologia, Apdo. Aereo 54953, Carrera 10, No. 65-48, Bogota 2 D.E., Colombia. TEL 57-1-2124846. FAX 57-1-2123360. *6482*

THEOLOGY AND CULTURE NEWSLETTER.
Andover Newton Theological School, 210 Herrick Rd., Newton Centre, MA 02159. TEL 617-964-1100. FAX 508-771-7919.
circ. 3,100. *6378*

THEORIA.
Berghahn Books Inc., 165 Taber Ave., Providence, RI 02906. TEL 401-861-9330. FAX 401-521-0046.
circ. 150. *3794*

THE THIRD ALTERNATIVE.
T T A Press, 5 Martins Ln., Witcham, Ely, Cambs. CB6 2LB, England. TEL 44-1353-777931.
circ. 2,000. *4537*

THIRD DEGREE.
University of Regina, Communications Office, Regina, SK S4S 0A2, Canada. TEL 306-585-4403. FAX 306-585-4997.
circ. 27,000. *1974*

THOMIST.
Thomist Press, 487 Michigan Ave., N.E., Washington, DC 20017. TEL 202-529-5300. FAX 202-636-4460.
circ. 1,000. *6483*

THOROUGHBRED RACING ASSOCIATIONS. DIRECTORY AND RECORD BOOK.
Thoroughbred Racing Associations, 420 Fair Hill Dr., No. 1, Elkton, MD 21921-2573. FAX 410-398-1366.
circ. 3,000. *6857*

THYSSEN AKTUELL.
Vereinigte Verlagsanstalten GmbH, Hoeherweg 278, 40231 Duesseldorf, Germany. TEL 49-211-7357-0. FAX 49-211-7357223.
circ. 132,000. *5213*

TIDEWATER PARENT.
Windmill Publishing, Inc., 2753 Atwoodtown Rd., Virginia Beach, VA 23456. TEL 757-426-2595. FAX 757-426-5299.
circ. 40,000. *1858*

TIDSKRIFTET SYKEPLEIEN.
Norsk Sykepleierforbund, P.O. Box 2633, St. Hanshaugen, N-0131 Oslo, Norway. TEL 47-22-04-33-04. FAX 47-22-38-35-36.
circ. 59,161. *4950*

TIEFKUEHL-REPORT.
Dr. Vollmer GmbH, Siegfriedstr. 5, 63785 Obernburg a.M., Germany. TEL 06022-1604. FAX 06022-7696.
circ. 7,500. *3485*

TIEMPO LATINO.
Tiempo Latino News, 3288 21st St., Box 9, San Francisco, CA 94110. TEL 415-821-4452. FAX 415-642-1065.
circ. 35,000. *3046*

TIERRA ADENTRO.
Instituto de Investigaciones Agropecuarias, Casilla 469, Correo 3, Santiago, Chile. TEL 56-2-5417223. FAX 56-2-5417667.
circ. 5,000. *158*

TIETOVERKKO.
Oy Talentum Ab, P.O. Box 920, FIN-00101 Helsinki, Finland. TEL 358-0-148-801. FAX 358-0-6856512.
circ. 12,819. *2140*

TIETOVIIKKO.
Oy Talentum Ab, P.O. Box 920, FIN-00101 Helsinki, Finland. TEL 358-9-148-801. FAX 358-9-685-6605.
circ. 27,304. *2091*

TIJDSCHRIFT VOOR CRIMINOLOGIE.
Gouda Quint B.V., Postbus 1148, 6801 MK Arnhem, Netherlands.
circ. 600. *2281*

TILBURY TIMES.
Phoenix Media Group, P.O. Box 490, 9 Prospect St., Tilbury, ON N0P 2L0, Canada. TEL 519-682-0411. FAX 519-682-3633.
circ. 288. *3266*

TIMBER - WEST.
Timber - West Publications, Inc., Box 610, Edmonds, WA 98020. TEL 206-778-3388. FAX 206-771-3623.
circ. 10,500. *3175*

TIMBROSCOPIE.
Le Particulier Editions, 21 bd. Montmartre, 75080 Paris Cedex 02, France. TEL 33-1-40207020. FAX 33-1-40207042.
circ. 53,772. *5714*

TIMES BUSINESS DIRECTORY OF SINGAPORE.
Times Trade Directories Pte. Ltd., Times Centre, One New Industrial Rd., Singapore 536196, Singapore. TEL 65-2848844. FAX 65-2850161.
circ. 25,000. *1716*

TIMES GUIDE TO COMPUTERS.
Times Trade Directories Pte. Ltd., Times Centre, One New Industrial Rd., Singapore 536196, Singapore. TEL 65-2848844. FAX 65-2850161.
circ. 30,000. *1717*

TIPSICO BULLETIN.
Tipsico Coin Co., Box 1128, 2141 Broadway, N. Bend, OR 97459. TEL 541-756-7111.
circ. 1,000. *5467*

TIRE RETREADING - REPAIR JOURNAL.
Tire Industry Publication Service, Inc., Box 37203, Louisville, KY 40233-7203. TEL 502-968-8900. FAX 502-964-7859.
circ. 2,650. *6505*

TOAR.
Hebrew University of Jerusalem, Department of Alumni Affairs and New Leadership, Jerusalem, Israel.
circ. 60,000. *1974*

TOBACCO ASSOCIATES. ANNUAL REPORT.
Tobacco Associates, Inc., 1306 Annapolis Dr., Ste. 102, Raleigh, NC 27608. TEL 919-821-7670. FAX 919-821-7674.
circ. 7,500. *7021*

TOBAKSHANDLAREN.
Tobaks- & Servicehandelns Riksfoerbund, Instrumentvaegen 10, P.O. Box 9025, S-126 09 Haegersten, Sweden. TEL 46-8-681-03-20. FAX 46-8-19-95-26.
circ. 1,700. *7022*

TODAY'S ARIZONA WOMAN (SCOTTSDALE).
Publishers West, Inc., 4425 N. Saddlebag Trail, Scottsdale, AZ 85251-3419. TEL 602-945-5000. FAX 602-941-5196.
circ. 50,000. *7334*

TODAY'S ARIZONA WOMAN (TUCSON EDITION).
Publishers West, Inc. (Tucson), 4725 E. Sunrise Dr., Ste. 406, Tucson, AZ 85718-4534. TEL 602-795-6202. FAX 602-795-6305.
circ. 20,000. *7334*

TODAY'S ASTROLOGER.
American Federation of Astrologers, Inc., 6535 S. Rural Rd., Box 22040, Tempe, AZ 85285. TEL 602-838-1751. FAX 602-838-8293.
circ. 2,700. *487*

TODAY'S CHICAGO WOMAN.
Leigh Communications, Inc., 150 E. Huron St., Ste. 1225, Chicago, IL 60611-2912. TEL 312-951-7600. FAX 312-951-9083.
circ. 100,000. *7334*

TODAY'S DISTRIBUTOR.
Johnson Hill Press, Inc., 1233 Janesville Ave., Ft. Atkinson, WI 53538. TEL 920-563-6388. FAX 920-563-1702.
circ. 42,000. *1552*

TODAY'S HEALTH CARE.
Transcontinental Publishing Inc., Box 45454, Phoenix, AZ 85064-5454. TEL 602-331-8900. FAX 602-331-8448. *4752*

TODAY'S HOSPITAL GIFT SHOP BUSINESS.
Nason & Associates, Box 8204, Asheville, NC 28814. TEL 704-298-1322. FAX 704-298-1312.
circ. 8,000. *1552*

TODAY'S PARENT.
Professional Publishing Associates, 269 Richmond St. W., Toronto, ON M5V 1X1, Canada. TEL 416-596-8680. FAX 416-596-1991.
circ. 50,000. *1858*

TODAY'S REFINERY.
Percy Publishing Company, Inc., 170 King St., Box 287, Chappaqua, NY 10514. TEL 914-238-0205. FAX 914-238-0210.
circ. 10,406. *5625*

TOELEVEREN & UITBESTEDEN.
Misset, Postbus 4, 7000 BA Doetinchem, Netherlands. TEL 31-314-349371. FAX 31-314-363638.
circ. 12,370. *4553*

TOHKAI SEIKEI GEKA GAISHO KENKYU KAISHI.
Tohkai Seikei Geka Gaisho Kenkyukai, Gifu Kenritsu Tajimi Byoin Seikei Geka, 5-161, Maebatacho, Tajimi-shi, Gifu-ken 507, Japan. TEL 81-572-22-5311. FAX 81-572-25-1246.
circ. 1,000. *5017*

TOHKAI SEKITSUI GEKA.
Tohkai Sekitsui Geka Kenkyukai, Gifu Kenritsu Tajimi Byoin, 5-161, Maebatacho, Tajimi-shi, Gifuken 507, Japan. TEL 81-572-22-5311. FAX 81-572-25-1246.
circ. 600. *5017*

TOHOKU DAIGAKU SOZAI KOGAKU KENKYUJO IHO.
Tohoku Daigaku, Sozai Kogaku Kenkyujo, 1-1 Katahira 2-chome, Aoba-ku, Sendai 980-77, Japan. TEL 81-22-217-5166. FAX 81-22-217-5211.
5214

TOHOKU KOGYO DAIGAKU KIYO, 1. RIKOGAKU HEN.
Tohoku Kogyo Daigaku, 35-1 Kasumi-cho, Yagiyama, Taihaku-ku, Sendai-shi, Miyagi-ken 982, Japan.
circ. 730. *2743*

TOHOKU NO NOGYO KISHO.
Nihon Nogyo Kisho Gakkai, Tohoku Shibu, Norin Suisansho Tohoku Nogyo Shikenjo, 4 Akahira, Shimokuriyagawa, Morioka-shi, Iwate-ken 020-01, Japan. TEL 81-196-43-3461. FAX 81-196-41-7794.
circ. 300. *5244*

TOKYO DAIGAKU TEOIN SENTA DAYORI.
Tokyo Daigaku, Teoin Senta, 11-16, Yayoi 2-chome, Bunkyo-ku, Tokyo 113, Japan. TEL 81-3-3812-2111. FAX 81-3-3815-8389.
circ. 500. *5843*

TOKYO JOSHI IKA DAIGAKU ZASSHI.
Tokyo Joshi Ika Daigaku Gakkai, c/o Library, 8-1 Kawada-cho, Shinjuku-ku, Tokyo 162, Japan. TEL 81-3-3353-8111.
circ. 1,750. *4753*

TOLEDO MEDICINE.
Academy of Medicine of Toledo and Lucas County, 4428 Secor Rd., Toledo, OH 43623. TEL 419-473-3200. FAX 419-475-6744.
circ. 1,500. *4753*

TOLSTOY FOUNDATION NEWS.
Tolstoy Foundation, Inc., 104 Lake Rd., Valley Cottage, NY 10989-2459. TEL 212-677-7770. FAX 914-268-6937.
circ. 10,000. *6692*

TOMATO MAGAZINE.
Columbia Publishing and Design, 2520 W. Washington, Ste. 2, Box 9036, Yakima, WA 98909-0036. TEL 509-248-2452. FAX 509-248-4056.
circ. 4,000. *247*

TOOWOOMBA AND GOLDEN WEST VISITORS' GUIDE.
Toowoomba and Golden West Regional Tourist Association Ltd., P.O. Box 3090, Toowoomba, Qld. 4350, Australia. TEL 61-76-321988. FAX 61-76-324404. *7239*

TOP BUSINESS.
Verlag Moderne Industrie, Justus-von-Liebig-Str. 1, 86899 Landsberg, Germany. TEL 49-8191-125-0. FAX 49-89-8191-125312. *1510*

TOP HOTEL.
Freizeit Verlag Landsberg GmbH, Celsiusstr. 6, 86899 Landsberg, Germany. TEL 49-8191-3049. FAX 49-8191-47685.
circ. 18,828. *3736*

TOP RAIL.
B L A Group Ltd., 5-8 Hardwick St., London EC1R 4RB, England. TEL 44-171-278-7603. FAX 44-171-278-6246.
circ. 200,000. *7239*

TOP SOCIETY.
National Merchant Buying Society, 3 Chancery Place, Millstone Ln., Leicester LE1 5JN, England. TEL 44-116-253-0531. FAX 44-116-251-7589.
circ. 2,500. *916*

TOPICS IN PEDIATRICS.
Minneapolis Children's Medical Center, 2525 Chicago Ave., S., Minneapolis, MN 55404. TEL 612-863-6222. FAX 612-863-6674.
circ. 10,000. *5041*

TOPLINE.
McCollum-Spielman Worldwide, Inc., 235 Great Neck Rd., Great Neck, NY 11021. TEL 516-482-0310. FAX 516-482-3228.
circ. 5,000. *1552*

TORCH (CHICAGO).
International Association of Torch Clubs, c/o R. Patrrick Deans, Ed., Strickland & Jones, PC, 749 Boush St., Norfolk, VA 23510-1517. TEL 757-627-7672. FAX 757-623-9740.
circ. 2,850. *1937*

TORCH & TREFOIL.
Alpha Phi Omega, 14901 E. 42nd St., Independence, MO 64108. TEL 816-471-8667.
circ. 17,000. *1974*

TORONTO COMPUTES.
ConText Publishing Inc., 99 Atlantic Ave., No. 408, Toronto, Ont. M4G 3J8, Canada. TEL 416-588-6818.
circ. 95,000. *2091*

TORONTO GARDENS.
Bayview Media Inc., 1560 Bayview Ave., Ste. 302A, Toronto, ON M4G 3B8, Canada. TEL 416-481-1955. FAX 416-481-2819.
circ. 50,000. *3206*

TORONTO STOCK EXCHANGE REVIEW.
Toronto Stock Exchange, 2 First Canadian Place, Toronto, ON M5X 1J2, Canada. TEL 416-947-4222. FAX 416-947-4585.
circ. 1,150. *1411*

TOSCANA LIONS.
Lions International, Distretto 108, Via Valdelsa 23, 53011 Castellina in Chianti, Italy. TEL 39-577-740374.
circ. 3,500. *1937*

TOSHOKAN KYORYOKU TSUSHIN.
National Diet Library, 1-10-1 Nagata-cho, Chiyoda-ku, Tokyo 100, Japan. TEL 81-3-3581-2331. FAX 81-3-3597-9104.
circ. 4,500. *4217*

TOTALISATOR AGENCY BOARD. HALF YEAR REPORT.
Totalisator Agency Board, 106-110 Jackson St., Petone, New Zealand. TEL 644-576-6999. FAX 644-576-6942.
circ. 1,600. *6198*

TOUCHLINE.
Soccer Association for Youth U S A, 4050 Executive Park Dr., Ste. 100, Cincinnati, OH 45241-2020. TEL 513-769-3800. FAX 513-769-0500.
circ. 100,000. *6820*

TOUCHSTONE (SPRING).
Touchstone Press, Box 8308, Spring, TX 77387-8308.
circ. 500. *4525*

TOUR T T - REVUE.
Verband Oeffentlicher Verkehr, Daehlhoelzliweg 12, CH-3000 Bern 6, Switzerland. *7040*

TOURS ON MOTORCOACH.
Publicom Inc., C.P. 365, Place d'Armes, Montreal, PQ H2Y 3H1, Canada. TEL 514-274-0004. FAX 514-274-5884.
circ. 13,302. *7241*

TOW TIMES.
T T Publications, Inc., 203 State Rd. 434, W., Winter Springs, FL 32708-2598. TEL 407-327-4817. FAX 407-327-2603.
circ. 30,000. *7179*

TOWN AND COUNTRY FARMER.
Town and Country Farmer Publications Pty. Ltd., P.O. Box 798, Benalla, Vic. 3672, Australia. TEL 61-57-641348. FAX 61-57-641349.
circ. 18,000. *158*

TOWN HALL.
Informed Publications Ltd., 95 Ditchling Rd., Brighton, Sussex BN1 4SE, England. TEL 44-1273-277110. FAX 44-1273-623338.
circ. 1,000. *6225*

TOXICOLOGIC PATHOLOGY.
Society of Toxicologic Pathologists, c/o Dr. Carl L. Alden, Ed., G.D. Searle & Co., 4901 Searle Pky., Skokie, IL 60077. TEL 847-982-7379. FAX 847-982-7374.
circ. 845. *2981*

TOYAMA DAIGAKU KYOIKUGAKUBU KIYO, A. BUNKAKEI.
Toyama Daigaku, Kyoikugakubu, 3190 Gofuku, Toyama-shi, Toyama-ken 930, Japan. TEL 0764-41-1271. FAX 0764-32-4212. *4479*

TOYAMA DAIGAKU KYOIKUGAKUBU KIYO, B. RIKAKEI.
Toyama Daigaku, Kyoikugakubu, 3190 Gofuku, Toyama-shi, Toyama-ken 930, Japan. TEL 0764-41-1271. FAX 0764-32-4212. *6580*

TOYOTA.
Toyota Motor Corporation, International Public Affairs Division, 4-18, Koraku 1-chome, Bunkyo-ku, Tokyo 112, Japan. TEL 03-3817-9930. FAX 03-3817-9017.
circ. 30,000. *7119*

TOYOTA ENGINE TECHNOLOGY.
Toyota Motor Corporation, International Public Affairs Division, 4-18, Koraku 1-chome, Bunkyo-ku, Tokyo 112, Japan. TEL 03-3817-9930. FAX 03-3817-9017.
circ. 20,000. *7119*

TRACES OF INDIANA AND MIDWESTERN HISTORY.
Indiana Historical Society, 315 W. Ohio, Indianapolis, IN 46202-3299. TEL 317-232-1878. FAX 317-233-3109.
circ. 11,000. *3649*

TRACK AND TIRE.
29829 Greenfield Rd., Ste. 101, Southfield, MI 48076-2201. TEL 800-872-2574. FAX 313-557-4156.
circ. 30,100. *916*

TRADE CHRONICLE.
Chronicle Publications, P.O. Box 5257, Iftikhar Chambers, Altaf Hussain Rd., Karachi 74000, Pakistan. TEL 92-21-218129. FAX 92-21-219190.
circ. 5,500. *1597*

TRADERS MAGAZINE.
Securities Data Publishing, 40 W. 57th St., 11th Fl., New York, NY 10106. TEL 212-765-5311. FAX 212-765-6123.
circ. 4,000. *1170*

TRADEWINDS.
Portuguese UK Chamber of Commerce, 22-25a Sackville St., 4th Fl., London W1X 1DE, England. TEL 44-171-494-1844. FAX 44-171-494-1822.
circ. 2,000. *1349*

TRADITIONS.
University of Connecticut, 1266 Storrs Rd., Storrs, CT 06269-5144. TEL 860-486-3530. FAX 860-486-2063.
circ. 120,000. *1974*

TRAGER INSTITUTE NEWSLETTER.
Trager Institute, 21 Locust Ave., Mill Valley, CA 94941-2805. TEL 415-388-2688. FAX 415-388-2710.
circ. 2,000. *5047*

TRAILER.
Foerlags AB Albinsson & Sjoeberg, P.O. Box 529, S-371 23 Karlskrona, Sweden. TEL 46-455-335325. FAX 46-455-311715.
circ. 29,200. *7119*

TRAILER-BODY BUILDERS.
Tunnell Publications, Inc., Box 66010, Houston, TX 77266. TEL 713-523-8124. FAX 713-523-8384.
circ. 14,000. *7179*

TRAILS.
Texas State Library and Archives Commission, Box 12927, Austin, TX 78711. TEL 512-463-5514. FAX 512-463-5436.
circ. 2,500. *4217*

TRAIN COLLECTORS QUARTERLY.
Train Collectors Association, Box 619, Willow Street, PA 17584. TEL 717-687-8623.
circ. 28,200. *3679*

TRAINING AKTUELL.
ManagerSeminare Gerhard May Verlags GmbH, Endenicherstr. 282, 53121 Bonn, Germany. TEL 49-228-97791-0. FAX 49-228-616164.
circ. 1,300. *1510*

TRAINING AND CONDITIONING.
Mag, Inc., 438 W. State St., Ithaca, NY 14850. TEL 607-272-0265. FAX 607-272-2015.
circ. 23,295. *6791*

TRANS WORLD RADIO.
Trans World Radio, Box 8700, Cary, NC 27512-8700. TEL 919-460-3700. FAX 919-460-3702.
circ. 45,000. *6379*

TRANSAT.
Inmarsat, 99 City Rd., London EC1Y 1AX, England. TEL 44-171-728-1450. FAX 44-171-728-1344.
circ. 18,000. *2007*

TRANSCEND.
Transcend Publications, 4 Daniels Farm Rd., Ste. 134, Trumbull, CT 06611.
circ. 15,000. *3046*

TRANSCULTURAL PSYCHIATRY.
Sage Publications Ltd., 6 Bonhill St., London EC2A 4PU, England. TEL 44-171-374-0645. FAX 44-171-374-8741.
circ. 600. *5100*

TRANSILVANIA.
Casa de Presa si Editura Cultura Nationala, Str. Dr. Ion Ratiu nr.2, 2400 Sibiu, Rumania. TEL 40-24-69213377.
circ. 1,000. *6379*

TRANSITIONS.
Center for Population Options, 1025 Vermont Ave., N.W., Ste. 200, Washington, DC 20005. TEL 202-347-5700. FAX 202-347-2263.
circ. 5,000. *1858*

TRANSMISSION AND DISTRIBUTION.
Intertec Publishing Corp., 9800 Metcalf, Overland Park, KS 66212-2215. TEL 913-341-1300. FAX 913-967-1904.
circ. 36,400. *2848*

TRANSMISSION & DISTRIBUTION INTERNATIONAL.
Intertec Publishing Corp., 9800 Metcalf Ave., Overland Park, KS 66212-2215. TEL 913-341-1300. FAX 913-967-1898.
circ. 17,000. *2848*

TRANSPONDER.
Terra Publishing, Inc., R.D. 1, Box 142, Center St. Ext., Salamanca, NY 14779. TEL 716-945-3488. FAX 716-945-5238.
circ. 14,500. *2064*

TRANSPORT MANAGEMENT.
Institute of Transport Administration, 32 Palmerston Rd., Southampton SO14 1LL, England. FAX 44-1703-634165.
circ. 3,500. *7042*

TRANSPORTARBETAREN.
Svenska Transportarbetarefoerbundet, P.O. Box 714, S-101 33 Stockholm, Sweden. TEL 46-8-723-77-00. FAX 46-8-723-00-76.
circ. 71,300. *7043*

TRANSPORTATION & DISTRIBUTION.
Penton Publishing Co., 1100 Superior Ave., Cleveland, OH 44114-2543. TEL 216-696-7000. FAX 216-696-8765.
circ. 74,138. *7043*

TRANSPORTATION FOR CHINA.
Sterling Publications Ltd., 86-88 Edgware Rd., London W2 2YW, England. TEL 44-171-915-9600. FAX 44-171-915-9619.
circ. 10,000. *7043*

TRANSPORTRECHT.
Luchterhand Verlag (Kriftel), Gutenbergstr. 8, 65830 Kriftel, Germany. TEL 49-6192-408233. FAX 49-6192-408248.
circ. 1,100. *7045*

TRAVEL AGENT.
Universal Media, Inc., 801 Second Ave., New York, NY 10017. TEL 212-370-5050. FAX 212-370-4491.
circ. 53,503. *7242*

TRAVEL COUNSELOR MAGAZINE.
Miller Freeman Inc. (New York), One Penn Plaza, New York, NY 10119. TEL 212-714-1300. FAX 212-714-1313.
circ. 28,000. *7242*

TRAVEL COURIER.
Baxter Publishing Co., 310 Dupont St., Toronto, ON M5R 1V9, Canada. TEL 416-968-7252. FAX 416-968-2377.
circ. 10,000. *7243*

TRAVEL DIRECTORY (YEAR).
Interasia Publications, Ltd., No. 11-01 Fortune Centre, 190 Middle Rd., Singapore 0718, Singapore. TEL 3397622. FAX 3398521.
circ. 3,700. *7243*

TRAVEL ON SASKATCHEWAN HIGHWAYS.
Department of Highways and Transportation, 1855 Victoria Ave., Regina, SK S4P 3V5, Canada. TEL 306-787-8334. FAX 306-787-1007.
circ. 300. *7142*

TRAVEL RETAILER INTERNATIONAL.
Euromoney Publications plc., Nestor House, Playhouse Yard, London EC4V 5EX, England. TEL 44-171-799-8935. FAX 44-171-779-8541.
circ. 5,000. *1552*

TRAVEL TRADE REPORT.
Travel Press, Asia Bldg., 12th Fl., 294-1 Phya Thai Rd., Bangkok 10400, Thailand. TEL 66-2-216-7252. FAX 66-2-216-6599.
circ. 12,600. *7244*

TRAVELAGE EAST.
Reed Travel Group, Part of the Reed Elsevier group 500 Plaza Dr., Secaucus, NJ 07096. TEL 201-902-2021. FAX 201-902-1967.
circ. 23,400. *7244*

TRAVELAGE MID-AMERICA.
Reed Travel Group, Part of the Reed Elsevier group 500 Plaza Dr., Secaucus, NJ 07096. TEL 201-902-2021. FAX 201-902-1967.
circ. 17,600. *7244*

TRAVELAGE WEST.
Reed Travel Group, Part of the Reed Elsevier group 500 Plaza Dr., Secaucus, NJ 07096. TEL 201-902-2021. FAX 201-902-1967.
circ. 31,000. *7245*

TRAX D J MUSIC GUIDE.
American Trax D Js, 111 N. La Cienega Blvd., Beverly Hills, CA 90211-2206. TEL 310-659-7852. FAX 310-659-7856.
circ. 1,000. *5441*

TREASURY & RISK MANAGEMENT.
C F O Publishing Corporation, 253 Summer St., Boston, MA 02210. TEL 617-345-9700. FAX 617-951-4090.
circ. 46,000. *1411*

TREASURYLOG.
Go Public Relations, Badnerstr. 3-21, A-2500 Baden, Austria.
circ. 14,000. *1170*

TREE - RING BULLETIN.
Tree - Ring Society, University of Arizona, Tree - Ring Laboratory, Tucson, AZ 85721. TEL 520-621-1608. FAX 520-621-8229.
circ. 350. *730*

TRENDS (DUESSELDORF).
Vereinigte Verlagsanstalten GmbH, Hoehenweg 278, 40231 Duesseldorf, Germany. TEL 49-211-7357-0. FAX 49-211-7357223.
circ. 400,000. *3867*

TRENDS (LIBERTY).
Target Marketing, Inc., 1 Liberty Bell Circle, Ste. 200, Liberty, MO 64068. TEL 816-781-7557. FAX 816-792-3892.
circ. 100,000. *5516*

TRENDS MAGAZINE.
Netmar Publications Inc., 1383 Confederation St., Sarnia, ON N7S 5P1, Canada. TEL 519-336-1100. FAX 519-336-1833.
circ. 5,000. *1006*

TRI-CITY NEWS.
Meadowridge Publications, 1405 Broadway, Port Coquitlam, BC V3C 5W9, Canada. TEL 604-525-6397. FAX 604-944-0703.
circ. 45,458. *3266*

TRI-STATE REAL ESTATE JOURNAL.
Adler Group, Inc., 4002 Lincoln Drive West, Ste. G, Marlton, NJ 08053. TEL 609-988-0092. FAX 609-988-0093.
circ. 7,000. *6314*

TRIBULUS.
Cultural Foundation, Emirates Natural History Group, P.O. Box 2380, Abu Dhabi, United Arab Emirates. TEL 212900. FAX 336059.
circ. 500. *6580*

TRIBUNAL DE JUSTICA DO ESTADO DO RIO GRANDE DO SUL. REVISTA DE JURISPRUDENCIA.
Tribuna de Justica, Praca Marechal Deodoro, 55, 5o andar, 90010-908 Porto Alegre RS, Brazil. TEL 55-51-2282444 ext. 1550.
circ. 4,650. *4035*

TRIBUNE BUSINESS WEEKLY.
South Bend Tribune, 225 W. Colfax, South Bend, IN 46626. TEL 219-235-6474. FAX 219-239-2646.
circ. 8,000. *1007*

TRIBUS.
Linden-Museum Stuttgart-Staatliches Museum fuer Voelkerkunde, Hegelplatz 1, 70174 Stuttgart, Germany. TEL 49-711-2022400. FAX 49-711-2022590.
circ. 800. *332*

CONTROLLED CIRCULATION SERIALS 10403

TRIBUTE.
Tribute Publishing, Inc., 900 A Don Mills Rd., Ste. 1000, Don Mills, ON M3C 1V6, Canada. TEL 416-445-0544. FAX 416-445-2894.
circ. 600,000. *5346*

TRINITY REVIEW.
Trinity Foundation, Box 1666, Hobbs, NM 88241-1666. TEL 505-392-7274. FAX 505-392-7274.
circ. 3,000. *5756*

TRITON MUSEUM OF ART. MEMBERS' BULLETIN.
Triton Museum of Art, 1505 Warburton Ave., Santa Clara, CA 95050. TEL 408-247-3754. FAX 408-247-3796.
circ. 1,500. *5367*

TRIVIZIER.
V B M, Mesdagstraat 118, 2596 XZ The Hague, Netherlands. TEL 31-70-3242125. FAX 31-70-3282000.
circ. 26,000. *5288*

TROPICAL AGRICULTURIST.
Department of Agriculture, No. 1, Sarasavi Mawatha, P.O. Box 05, Peradeniya, Sri Lanka. TEL 94-8-88136. FAX 94-8-88030.
circ. 850. *159*

TROPICAL FRESHWATER BIOLOGY.
Idodo Umeh Publishers Ltd., 52 Ewah Rd., P.O. Box 3441, Benin City, Edo State, Nigeria. TEL 234-52-254404.
circ. 200. *3080*

TROPICAL MEDICINE AND HYGIENE NEWS.
American Society of Tropical Medicine and Hygiene (Washington), 6436 31st St., N.W., Washington, DC 20015. TEL 202-364-5969. FAX 202-369-5969.
circ. 3,500. *4844*

TRUCK AND COMMERCIAL VEHICLE INTERNATIONAL.
Sterling Publications Ltd., 86-88 Edgware Rd., London W2 2YW, England. TEL 44-171-915-9600. FAX 44-171-915-9619.
circ. 15,000. *7179*

TRUCK SALES & LEASING MAGAZINE.
Newport Communications East, Inc., 600 Reisterstown Rd., Ste. 404, Baltimore, MD 21208-5107. TEL 410-486-7430. FAX 410-786-7478.
circ. 22,000. *7180*

TRUCKER'S CONNECTION.
5960 Crooked Creek Rd., Ste. 15, Norcross, GA 30092. TEL 404-416-0927. FAX 404-416-1734.
circ. 170,081. *7180*

TRUCKERS - U S A.
Horizon Media, Box 3168, Tuscaloosa, AL 35403-3168. TEL 205-758-3070.
circ. 100,000. *7180*

TRUCKING TIMES.
Herrmeyer Publishing, 2413 Center St., Box 707, Cedar Falls, IA 50613. TEL 319-277-8332. FAX 319-277-8950.
circ. 13,800. *7180*

TRUSTEE QUARTERLY.
Association of Community College Trustees, 1740 N St., N.W., Washington, DC 20036. TEL 202-775-4667.
circ. 7,000. *2558*

TRYBUNA.
Ad Novum, Ul. Miedziana 11, 00-835 Warsaw, Poland. TEL 48-2-625-3015. FAX 48-22-204100.
circ. 100,000. *3349*

TRZISTE STOKE I STOCHIH PROIZODA.
Zavod za Trzisna Istrazivanja, Mose Pijade 8-I, 11001 Belgrade, Yugoslavia. *184*

TSUSHIN KOGYO.
Tsushin Kikai Kogyokai, Sankei Bldg. Annex, 7-2, Ote-machi 1-chome, Chiyoda-ku, Tokyo 100, Japan. TEL 81-3-3231-3156. FAX 81-3-3231-3110.
2041

TUCSON WEEKLY.
Tucson Weekly, Inc., Box 2429, Tucson, AZ 85702. TEL 520-795-2143. FAX 520-792-2096.
circ. 50,000. *4363*

TUFTS MEDICINE.
Tufts University, School of Medicine, 136 Harrison Ave., Boston, MA 02111. TEL 617-636-5705. FAX 617-636-8075.
circ. 12,500. *4754*

TUG WORLD NEWSLETTER.
Thomas Reed Publications Ltd., 38 S. John St., London EC1M 4AY, England.
circ. 2,500. *7168*

TULANE MEDICINE.
Tulane University, Office of University Publications, 300 Hebert Hall, New Orleans, LA 70118-5698. TEL 504-865-5714. FAX 504-865-5621.
circ. 18,500. *4754*

TULANIAN.
Tulane University, University Relations, Hebert Hall, Rm. 300, New Orleans, LA 70118. TEL 504-865-5714. FAX 504-865-5621.
circ. 75,000. *1975*

TURBULENCE.
Wydawnictwo Politechniki Czestochowskiej, Ul. Dabrowskiego 69, 42-200 Czestochowa, Poland. TEL 48-34-250974. FAX 48-34-612385.
circ. 500. *5255*

TURKEY. DEVLET ISTATISTIK ENSTITUSU. TOPTAN FIYAT ISTATISTIKLERI.
Devlet Istatistik Enstitusu, Necatibey Caddesi No. 114, 06100 Ankara, Turkey. TEL 90-312-4185027. FAX 90-312-4170432.
circ. 500. *1075*

TURNBERRY.
G S & J Publishing, Inc., 5212 N.W. 54th Ave., Pompano Beach, FL 33073-3755. TEL 305-977-5901.
circ. 5,000. *469*

TUTTI AL BAR.
Tuttopress Editrice s.r.l., Via Cagliero, 21, 20125 Milan, Italy. TEL 39-2-6682834. FAX 39-2-6072185.
circ. 170,000. *3737*

TWIN CITIES VISITOR.
Skyway Publications, 15 S. Fifth St., Ste. 800, Minneapolis, MN 55402-1050. TEL 512-375-9222. FAX 512-375-9208.
circ. 30,000. *7246*

TWINS.
Twins Magazine, Inc., 6740 Antioch, Ste.155, Merriam, KS 66204. TEL 913-722-1090. FAX 913-722-1767.
circ. 17,000. *1858*

TWO - TEN TODAY.
56 Main St., Waterdown, MA 02172. TEL 617-923-4500. FAX 617-926-6037.
circ. 12,000. *6597*

TY I SZKOLA.
Atest - Studio Sp. z o.o., Ul. Narutowicza 128, 90-145 Lodz, Poland. TEL 48-42-783925. FAX 48-42-406032. *2489*

TYLER JUNIOR COLLEGE NEWS.
Tyler Junior College, Box 9020, Tyler, TX 75711. TEL 214-510-2335. FAX 903-510-2708.
circ. 3,500. *1975*

U A P D REPORT.
Union of American Physicians and Dentists, 1330 Broadway, Ste. 730, Oakland, CA 94612. TEL 510-839-0193. FAX 510-763-8756.
circ. 3,000. *3899*

U B S INTERNATIONAL FINANCE.
Union Bank of Switzerland, Bahnhofstr. 45, CH-8021 Zurich, Switzerland. TEL 41-1-2346544. FAX 41-1-2346190.
circ. 25,000. *1170*

U D I DATAGRAM.
Utility Data Institute, 1200 G St., N.W., Ste. 250, Washington, DC 20005. TEL 202-942-8788. FAX 202-942-8789. *2691*

U F C W ACTION.
United Food and Commercial Workers International Union, 1775 K St., N.W., Washington, DC 20006. TEL 202-223-3111. FAX 202-466-1562.
circ. 1,300,000. *3899*

U K PRODUCT REVIEW.
Macmillan Magazines Ltd., Porters South, 4-6 Crinan St., London N1 9XW, England. TEL 44-171-833-4000. FAX 44-171-843-4640.
circ. 15,000. *672*

U M D S DIVISION OF PUBLIC HEALTH SCIENCES. ANNUAL REPORT.
United Medical and Dental Schools, Division of Public Health Sciences, Lambeth Palace Rd., London SE1 7EH, England. TEL 44-171-928-9292. FAX 44-171-928-1468.
circ. 500. *4754*

U N E NEWS.
University of New England, Distance Eduction Centre, Armidale, N.S.W. 2351, Australia. FAX 61-67-711644.
circ. 10,000. *2558*

U N I D O LINKS.
United Nations Industrial Development Organization, Box 300, A-1400 Vienna, Austria. TEL 43-1-211-31-5538. FAX 43-1-209-2669.
circ. 12,000. *1369*

U OF L.
University of Louisville, Alumni Association, 19 Development and University Relations Bldg., University of Louisville, Louisville, KY 40292. TEL 502-852-6171. FAX 502-852-7658.
circ. 85,000. *1975*

U P E N.
University of Port Elizabeth, P.O. Box 1600, Port Elizabeth 6000, South Africa. TEL 27-41-5042173. FAX 27-41-5042574.
circ. 3,000. *1975*

U S A AND EUROPE IN BUSINESS.
Sterling Publications Ltd., 86-88 Edgware Rd., London W2 2YW, England. TEL 44-171-915-9600. FAX 44-171-915-9619.
circ. 17,500. *1350*

U S A RICE QUARTERLY.
U S A Rice Federation, 6699 Rookin, Box 740123, Houston, TX 77274. TEL 713-270-6699. FAX 713-270-9021.
circ. 16,000. *248*

U S B E: FOR MEMBERS ONLY.
United States Book Exchange, Periodicals and Serials Division, 2969 W. 25th St., Cleveland, OH 44113.
circ. 2,100. *4218*

U S - CHINA REVIEW.
U S - China Peoples Friendship Association, 122 W. 27th St., 10th Fl., New York, NY 10001-6227. TEL 212-736-7355.
circ. 17,000. *6040*

U S GLASS, METAL & GLAZING.
Key Communications, Inc., Box 569, Garrissonville, VA 22463. TEL 540-720-5584. FAX 540-720-5687.
circ. 20,000. *916*

U S TECH.
Mid-Atlantic Tech Publications, Inc., Box 957, Valley Forge, PA 19482. TEL 610-783-6100. FAX 610-783-0317.
circ. 50,000. *2654*

U T A INTERNATIONAL.
G I T Verlag GmbH, Roesslerstr. 90, 64293 Darmstadt, Germany. TEL 49-6151-8090-0. FAX 49-6151-8090144.
circ. 41,000. *2955*

U: THE NATIONAL COLLEGE MAGAZINE.
American Collegiate Network, 1800 Century Park E., Ste. 820, Los Angeles, CA 90067-1511. TEL 310-551-1381. FAX 310-551-1659.
circ. 1,500,000. *2558*

UGEMAGASINET INDUSTRIEN.
Dansk Industri (DI), DK-1787 Copenhagen V, Denmark. TEL 45-33-77-33-77. FAX 45-33-77-37-70.
circ. 14,600. *1597*

UHREN KATALOG.
Heel Verlag GmbH, Wintermuehlenhof, 53639 Koenigswinter, Germany. TEL 49-2223-9230-0. FAX 49-2223-923026.
circ. 55,000. *3867*

CONTROLLED CIRCULATION SERIALS

ULTIMO.
Akzente Salzburg, Nonntaler Hauptstr. 1, A-5020 Salzburg, Austria. TEL 0662-849291. FAX 0662-84929122.
circ. 30,000. *3253*

ULUSAL CERRAHI DERGISI.
Turkish Surgical Society, Guzelbahce Sok. 35-7, 80200 Nisantasi - Istanbul, Turkey. TEL 90-212-2475295. FAX 90-212-2470835.
circ. 1,000. *5156*

UMWELT JOURNAL.
Journal Verlag, Dietrichgasse 24b-18, A-1030 Vienna, Austria. TEL 43-1-7155827-0.
circ. 24,000. *2955*

UMWELTMAGAZIN.
Vogel Verlag und Druck GmbH & Co. KG, Max-Planck-Str. 7-9, 97082 Wuerzburg, Germany. TEL 49-931-4182145. FAX 49-931-4182905.
circ. 20,000. *2955*

UNDERGROUND LAMP POST.
Henry A. Pohs, Ed. & Pub., 4537 Quitman St., Denver, CO 80212. TEL 303-455-3922.
circ. 450. *344*

UNDERHOOD SERVICE.
Babcox Publications, 11 S. Forge St., Akron, OH 44304. TEL 216-536-6117. FAX 216-535-0874.
circ. 40,000. *7120*

UNDERNEATH IT ALL.
Associated Utility Contractors of Maryland, 2913 Crabapple Lane, Ellicott City, MD 21042. TEL 410-750-2554. FAX 410-750-7668.
circ. 3,000. *2744*

UNDERWATER MAGAZINE.
Doyle Publishing Co., 5222 FM 1960 W., Ste. 112, Houston, TX 77069. TEL 713-440-0278. FAX 713-580-4433.
circ. 15,000. *1553*

UNDZER VEG.
Achdut Ha-Avoda-Poale Zion of Canada, 272 Codsell Ave., Downsview, Ont. M3H 3X2, Canada.
circ. 4,000. *3047*

UNI-INFO.
Carl von Ossietzky Universitaet Oldenburg, Ammerlaender Heerstr. 114, 26129 Oldenburg, Germany. TEL 49-441-7982417. FAX 49-441-7982435.
circ. 4,500. *1975*

UNICUM.
Unicum Verlag GmbH, Willy-Brandt-Platz 5-7, 44787 Bochum, Germany. TEL 49-234-96151-0. FAX 49-234-60256.
circ. 333,000. *1975*

DIE UNIE.
Suid-Afrikaanse Onderwysersunie, P.O. Box 196, Cape Town 8000, South Africa. TEL 27-21-461-6340. FAX 27-21-461-9238.
circ. 7,055. *2490*

UNIFICATION.
Unification Printers & Publishers Pty. Ltd., 12 Vernon St., Strathfield, N.S.W. 2135, Australia. TEL 61-2-746-8789. FAX 61-2-7642058.
circ. 4,300. *3047*

UNION ELECTRIC NEWS.
Union Electric Company, 1901 Chouteau Ave, Box 149, St. Louis, MO 63166. TEL 314-554-3120.
circ. 10,100. *2692*

UNION MATEMATICA ARGENTINA. REVISTA.
Union Matematica Argentina, Ciudad Universitaria, 5000 Cordoba, Argentina. TEL 54-51-334051. FAX 54-51-334054.
circ. 2,000. *4612*

UNION MATTERS.
Saskatchewan Government Employees' Union, 1440 Broadway Ave., Regina, Sask. S4P 1E2, Canada. TEL 306-522-8571. FAX 306-352-1969.
circ. 17,500. *3900*

UNION MEDICALE BALKANIQUE. ARCHIVES.
Union Medicale Balkanique, Str. Gabriel Peri Nr. 1, Bucharest, Rumania.
circ. 2,000. *4755*

UNION SIGNAL.
National Woman's Christian Temperance Union, 1730 Chicago Ave., Evanston, IL 60201. TEL 847-864-1396.
circ. 10,000. *2306*

UNIONE MATEMATICA ITALIANA. NOTIZIARIO.
Unione Matematica Italiana, Piazza Porta San Donato 5, 40126 Bologna, Italy. TEL 39-51-243190. FAX 39-51-243190.
circ. 3,000. *4613*

UNITA.
Unita S.p.A., Via d'Aracoeli 13, 20162 Milan, Italy.
circ. 400,000. *5976*

UNITED ARAB EMIRATES. AL-MASRAF AL-MARKAZI. AL-MULHIQ AL-IHSA'I.
Central Bank, P.O. Box 854, Abu Dhabi, United Arab Emirates. TEL 652220. FAX 668483.
circ. 500. *1076*

UNITED ARAB EMIRATES. AL-MASRAF AL-MARKAZI. AL-NASHRAH AL-IQTISADIYYAH.
Central Bank, P.O. Box 854, Abu Dhabi, United Arab Emirates. TEL 652220. FAX 668483. *1171*

UNITED ARAB EMIRATES. AL-MASRAF AL-MARKAZI. AL-TAQRIR AL-SANAWI.
Central Bank, P.O. Box 854, Abu Dhabi, United Arab Emirates. TEL 652220. FAX 668483. *1636*

UNITED ARAB EMIRATES. WIZARAT AL-SIHHAH. IDARAT AL-TIBB AL-WAQA'I. AL-TAQRIR AL-SANAWI.
Wizarat al-Sihhah, Idarat al-Tibb al-Waqa'i, P.O. Box 344, Abu Dhabi, United Arab Emirates. TEL 333485.
circ. 1,000. *6252*

UNITED ARAB EMIRATES. WIZARAT AL-TARBIYYAH WAL-TA'LIM. AL-TAQRIR AL-SANAWI.
Wizarat al-Tarbiyyah wal-Ta'lim, Idarat al-I'lam al-Tarbawi, P.O. Box 259, Abu Dhabi, United Arab Emirates. TEL 213800.
circ. 1,000. *2579*

UNITED NATIONS CHILDREN'S FUND. ANNUAL REPORT.
United Nations Children's Fund (UNICEF), UNICEF House, 3 United Nations, New York, NY 10017. TEL 212-326-7000. FAX 212-888-7465.
circ. 66,650. *6692*

U.S. CENTERS FOR DISEASE CONTROL. ABORTION SURVEILLANCE REPORT.
U.S. Centers for Disease Control, 1600 Clifton Rd., Atlanta, GA 30333. TEL 404-639-3311. *859*

U.S. CHAMBER OF COMMERCE. ASSOCIATION AGENDA.
U.S. Chamber of Commerce, 1615 H St., N.W., Washington, DC 20062. TEL 202-463-5560. FAX 202-463-3190.
circ. 1,200. *1197*

U.S. COAST GUARD. ENVIRONMENTAL PROTECTION NEWSLETTER.
U.S. Coast Guard, 2100 Second St., S.W., Washington, DC 20593. TEL 202-267-1054. *2955*

U.S. FOREST SERVICE. GENERAL TECHNICAL REPORT N C.
U.S. Forest Service, North Central Forest Experiment Sta., 1992 Folwell Ave., St. Paul, MN 55108. TEL 612-649-5000. FAX 612-649-5285.
circ. 1,000. *3165*

U.S. FOREST SERVICE. NORTH CENTRAL FOREST EXPERIMENT STATION. LIST OF PUBLICATIONS.
U.S. Forest Service, North Central Forest Experiment Sta., 1992 Folwell Ave., St. Paul, MN 55108. TEL 612-649-5000. FAX 612-649-5285.
circ. 1,500. *3168*

U.S. FOREST SERVICE. RESEARCH NOTE N C.
U.S. Forest Service, North Central Forest Experiment Sta., 1992 Folwell Ave., St. Paul, MN 55108. TEL 612-649-5000. FAX 612-649-5285.
circ. 2,000. *3165*

U.S. FOREST SERVICE. RESEARCH PAPER N C.
U.S. Forest Service, North Central Forest Experiment Sta., 1992 Folwell Ave., St. Paul, MN 55108. TEL 612-649-5000. FAX 612-649-5285.
circ. 2,000. *3165*

U.S. FOREST SERVICE. RESOURCE BULLETIN N C.
U.S. Forest Service, North Central Forest Experiment Sta., 1992 Folwell Ave., MN 55108. TEL 612-649-5000. FAX 612-649-5285.
circ. 2,000. *3165*

U.S. NATIONAL ENDOWMENT FOR THE ARTS. ANNUAL REPORT.
U.S. National Endowment for the Arts, Public Information Office, 1100 Pennsylvania Ave., N.W., Washington, DC 20506. TEL 202-682-5400.
circ. 4,000. *470*

U.S. SMALL BUSINESS ADMINISTRATION. ANNUAL REPORT.
U.S. Small Business Administration, c/o John Ward, Ed., MC-3114, 409 Third St., S.W., Washington, DC 20416. TEL 202-205-6740.
circ. 2,000. *1648*

U.S. SURGEON GENERAL. REPORT.
U.S. Centers for Disease Control, National Center for Chronic Disease Prevention and Health Promotion, 4770 Buford Hwy., N.E., MS K-50, Atlanta, GA 30341-3724. TEL 404-488-5705. FAX 404-488-5939. *2306*

UNITED STATES AMATEUR BOXING. ANNUAL GUIDE.
United States Amateur Boxing (U S A Boxing), Inc., One Olympic Plaza, Colorado Springs, CO 80909. TEL 719-578-4506. *6792*

UNITED STATES PILOTS ASSOCIATION NEWS.
United States Pilots Association, 483 S. Kirkwood Rd., Ste. 10, St. Louis, MO 63122. TEL 314-849-8772.
circ. 200. *81*

UNITED WAY CANADA. DIRECTORY.
United Way of Canada, 56 Sparks St., Ste. 404, Ottawa, ON K1P 5A9, Canada. TEL 613-236-7041. *6692*

UNITS.
National Apartment Association, 201 N. Union St., No. 200, Alexandria, VA 22314. TEL 703-518-6141. FAX 703-518-6191.
circ. 37,000. *3761*

UNIVERSAL MESSAGE.
Islamic Research Academy, D-35, Block 5, Federal 'B' Area, Karachi 75950, Pakistan. TEL 92-21-6349840. FAX 92-21-422827.
circ. 1,000. *6401*

UNIVERSAL POST.
Charlton Allison Publishing, Universal Post, 2 Ashwood Terrace, Sunderland, Tyne & Wcar SR2 7NB, England.
circ. 5,000. *1976*

UNIVERSIDAD AUTONOMA DE SANTO DOMINGO. BIBLIOTECA CENTRAL. BOLETIN DE ADQUISICIONES.
Universidad Autonoma de Santo Domingo, Biblioteca Central, Santo Domingo, Dominican Republic. *568*

UNIVERSIDAD COMPLUTENSE DE MADRID. REVISTA MATEMATICA.
Universidad Complutense de Madrid, Servicio de Publicaciones, Isaac Peral s-n, Ciudad Universitaria, 28040 Madrid, Spain. TEL 34-1-3946934. FAX 34-1-3946954. *4613*

UNIVERSIDAD DE ORIENTE. INSTITUTO OCEANOGRAFICO BIBLIOTECA. BOLETIN BIBLIOGRAFICO.
Universidad de Oriente, Instituto Oceanografico de Venezuela, Apdo. Postal 94, Cumana, Sucre, Venezuela.
circ. 1,000. *2328*

UNIVERSIDAD NACIONAL AUTONOMA DE MEXICO. SEMINARIO DE INVESTIGACIONES BIBLIOTECOLOGICA. PUBLICACIONES. SERIE B. BIBLIOGRAFIA.
Universidad Nacional Autonoma de Mexico, Seminario de Investigaciones Bibliotecologicas, Ciudad Universitaria, 04510 Mexico D.F., Mexico. *568*

UNIVERSIDADE DE SAO PAULO. ESCOLA DE ENFERMAGEM. REVISTA.
Universidade de Sao Paulo, Escola de Enfermagem, Av. Dr. Eneas de Carvalho Aguiar, 419, SP, Caixa Postal 5751, 05403 Sao Paolo, Brazil. TEL 55-11-8528922 ext. 7524. FAX 55-11-2808213.
circ. 1,000. *4950*

UNIVERSIDADE ESTADUAL PAULISTA. REVISTA DE ODONTOLOGIA.
Universidade Estadual Paulista, Av. Vicente Ferreira, 1278, Caixa Postal 71, 17515-901 Marilia SP, Brazil. TEL 55-144-222504. FAX 55-144-222504.
circ. 1,000. *4872*

UNIVERSIDADE FEDERAL DO CEARA. CENTRO DE CIENCIAS DA SAUDE. REVISTA DE MEDICINA.
Universidade Federal do Ceara, Centro de Ciencias da Saude, Rua Alexandre Barauna 949, Caixa Postal 3170, 60430 Fortaleza, Ceara, Brazil. TEL 085-243-9002. FAX 085-243-90-10.
circ. 2,000. *4755*

UNIVERSIDADE FEDERAL DO RIO DE JANEIRO. FACULDADE DE ODONTOLOGIA. ANAIS.
Universidade Federal do Rio de Janeiro, Faculdade de Odontologia, Ilha da Cidade Universitaria, Rio de Janeiro, Brazil. *4872*

UNIVERSIDADE FEDERAL DO RIO DE JANEIRO. INSTITUTO DE MATEMATICA. ESTUDOS E COMUNICACOES.
Universidade Federal do Rio de Janeiro, Instituto de Matematica, C.P. 68530, 21945-970 Rio de Janeiro, RJ, Brazil. TEL 55-21-5900940. FAX 55-21-2901095. *4613*

UNIVERSIDADE FEDERAL DO RIO DE JANEIRO. INSTITUTO DE MATEMATICA. MEMORIAS DE MATEMATICA.
Universidade Federal do Rio de Janeiro, Instituto de Matematica, C.P. 68530, 21945-970 Rio de Janeiro, RJ, Brazil. TEL 55-21-5900940. FAX 55-21-2901095. *4618*

UNIVERSITAET LEIPZIG.
Leipziger Universitaetsverlag GmbH, Augustusplatz 10, 04109 Leipzig, Germany. TEL 49-341-2619964. FAX 49-341-9730099.
circ. 9,000. *1976*

UNIVERSITAETSBIBLIOTHEK GIESSEN. HANDSCHRIFTENKATALOGE.
Universitaetsbibliothek Giessen, Otto-Behaghel-Str. 8, 35394 Giessen, Germany. TEL 49-641-9914001. FAX 49-641-9914009.
circ. 500. *568*

UNIVERSITAS. CIENCIA.
Universidade Federal da Bahia, Centro Editorial e Didatico, Rua Augusto Viana s-n, Canela, 40000 Salvador, Bahia, Brazil. TEL 071-245-2811.
circ. 500. *6581*

UNIVERSITAS. CULTURA.
Universidade Federal da Bahia, Centro Editorial e Didatico, Rua Augusto Viana s-n, Canela, 40000 Salvador, Bahia, Brazil. TEL 071-245-2811.
circ. 500. *3795*

UNIVERSITAT DE BARCELONA. BIBLIOTECA. MEMORIA ANUAL.
Universitat de Barcelona, Biblioteca, Gran via de les Corts Catalanes, 585, 08007 Barcelona, Spain. *4219*

UNIVERSITE DE BRETAGNE OCCIDENTALE. GUIDE DE L'ETUDIANT.
Universite de Bretagne Occidentale, 3 rue des Archives, 29285 Brest Cedex, France. TEL 33-2-98016020. FAX 33-2-98016001. *2490*

UNIVERSITE DE MONCTON. REVUE.
Universite de Moncton, Moncton, NB E1A 3E9, Canada. TEL 506-858-4062. FAX 506-858-4103.
circ. 650. *3267*

UNIVERSITEIT UTRECHT. UNIVERSITEIT MEDIA BULLETIN.
Universiteit Utrecht, Afdeling In- en Externe Betrekkingen, Heidelberglaan 8, 3584 CS Utrecht, Netherlands. TEL 31-30-2533550. FAX 31-30-2521818.
circ. 900. *2559*

UNIVERSITY OF ALASKA MUSEUM. ANNUAL REPORT.
University of Alaska Museum, 907 Yukon Dr., Fairbanks, AK 99775-1200. TEL 907-474-7505. FAX 907-474-5469. *5367*

UNIVERSITY OF ALBERTA. CENTRE FOR CRIMINOLOGICAL RESEARCH. DISCUSSION PAPERS.
University of Alberta, Department of Sociology, Centre for Criminological Research, Edmonton, AB T6G 2H4, Canada. TEL 403-492-3322. FAX 403-492-7196.
circ. 150. *2282*

UNIVERSITY OF ALLAHABAD. EDUCATION DEPARTMENT. RESEARCHES AND STUDIES.
University of Allahabad, Education Department, Allahabad 211002, Uttar Pradesh, India. *2490*

UNIVERSITY OF CALIFORNIA. SEISMOGRAPHIC STATIONS. BULLETIN.
University of California at Berkeley, Seismographic Station, 475 Earth Sciences Bldg., Berkeley, CA 94720. TEL 415-642-3977. FAX 643-5811.
circ. 450. *2392*

UNIVERSITY OF CALIFORNIA, SANTA CRUZ. INSTITUTE FOR MARINE SCIENCES. SPECIAL PUBLICATION.
University of California, Santa Cruz, Institute of Marine Sciences, Santa Cruz, CA 95064. TEL 408-429-2464. FAX 408-429-0146.
circ. 500. *2416*

UNIVERSITY OF CAPE TOWN. RESEARCH REPORT.
University of Cape Town, Research Support Services, Private Bag, Rondebosch 7700, South Africa. TEL 27-21-6502433. FAX 27-21-6897781.
circ. 600. *2560*

UNIVERSITY OF DELAWARE. STUDENT CENTER. REVIEW.
University of Delaware, Student Center, B-1 Student Ctr., Newark, DE 19716. TEL 302-451-2771. FAX 032-451-1396.
circ. 15,000. *1976*

UNIVERSITY OF DENVER JOURNAL.
University of Denver, Office of Communications, Denver, CO 80208. TEL 303-871-2711. FAX 303-871-3827.
circ. 70,000. *1976*

UNIVERSITY OF GEORGIA. COLLEGE OF AGRICULTURE EXPERIMENT STATIONS. BULLETIN.
University of Georgia, College of Agriculture Experiment Stations, Connor Hall, Athens, GA 30602. TEL 404-542-3621. *161*

UNIVERSITY OF GEORGIA. COLLEGE OF AGRICULTURE EXPERIMENT STATIONS. RESEARCH REPORTS.
University of Georgia, College of Agriculture Experiment Stations, Connor Hall, Athens, GA 30602. TEL 404-542-3621.
circ. 1,500. *161*

UNIVERSITY OF HARTFORD STUDIES IN LITERATURE.
University of Hartford, English Department, 200 Bloomfield Ave., W. Hartford, CT 06117. TEL 203-243-4574.
circ. 500. *4482*

UNIVERSITY OF HAWAII. WATER RESOURCES RESEARCH CENTER. ANNUAL REPORT.
University of Hawaii, Water Resources Research Center, 2540 Dole St., Holmes Hall 283, Honolulu, HI 96822. TEL 808-956-7847. FAX 808-956-5044.
circ. 500. *7301*

UNIVERSITY OF HAWAII. WATER RESOURCES RESEARCH CENTER. TECHNICAL REPORT.
University of Hawaii, Water Resources Research Center, 2540 Dole St., Honolulu, HI 96822. TEL 808-956-7847. FAX 808-956-5044.
circ. 300. *7301*

UNIVERSITY OF ILLINOIS AT CHICAGO. COLLEGE OF DENTISTRY. ALUMNI REPORT.
University of Illinois at Chicago, College of Dentistry, 801 S. Paulina St., Chicago, IL 60612-7211. TEL 312-996-8495. FAX 312-996-1022.
circ. 5,500. *1977*

UNIVERSITY OF ILLINOIS AT URBANA-CHAMPAIGN. DEPARTMENT OF AGRICULTURAL ECONOMICS. LEASE SHARES AND FARM RETURNS.
University of Illinois at Urbana-Champaign, Department of Agricultural Economics, Urbana, IL 61801. TEL 217-333-2638. *203*

UNIVERSITY OF ILLINOIS AT URBANA-CHAMPAIGN. SCHOOL OF ART AND DESIGN. NEWSLETTER.
University of Illinois at Urbana-Champaign, Continuing Education and Public Service-Visual Arts, 123 Fine and Applied Arts Bldg., Champaign, IL 61820. TEL 217-333-2439. FAX 217-244-7388.
circ. 6,000. *471*

UNIVERSITY OF KANSAS. NATURAL HISTORY MUSEUM. SCIENTIFIC PAPERS.
University of Kansas, Natural History Museum, Lawrence, KS 66045. TEL 913-864-3347. FAX 913-864-5321.
circ. 900. *6581*

UNIVERSITY OF LONDON. ROYAL POSTGRADUATE MEDICAL SCHOOL. ANNUAL REPORT.
University of London, Royal Postgraduate Medical School, Hammersmith Hospital, Du Cane Rd., London W12 0NN, England. TEL 44-181-383-3201. FAX 44-181-383-3203.
circ. 6,000. *4756*

UNIVERSITY OF MANCHESTER. DEPARTMENT OF COMPUTER SCIENCE. TECHNICAL REPORT SERIES.
University of Manchester, Department of Computer Science, Oxford Rd., Manchester M13 9PL, England. TEL 44-161-275-6130. FAX 44-161-275-6236.
circ. 100. *2159*

UNIVERSITY OF MANILA LAW GAZETTE.
University of Manila, 546 Dr. M.V. de los Santos St., Sampaloc, Manila D-403, Philippines.
circ. 500. *4039*

UNIVERSITY OF NEVADA. BASQUE STUDIES PROGRAM NEWSLETTER.
University of Nevada, Basque Studies Program, Getchell Library, Reno, NV 89557-0012. TEL 702-784-4854. FAX 702-784-1355.
circ. 8,500. *3047*

UNIVERSITY OF NEWCASTLE. DEPARTMENT OF ELECTRICAL AND COMPUTER ENGINEERING. TECHNICAL REPORT EE.
University of Newcastle, Department of Electrical and Computer Engineering, Callaghan, N.S.W. 2308, Australia. TEL 61-49-216026. FAX 61-49-216993.
circ. 800. *2849*

UNIVERSITY OF OCCUPATIONAL AND ENVIRONMENTAL HEALTH. JOURNAL.
University of Occupational and Environmental Health, Japan, Iseigaoka 1-1, Yahatanishi-ku, Kita-Kyushu 807, Japan. FAX 093-692-4876.
circ. 900. *5501*

UNIVERSITY OF OXFORD. SCHOOL OF GEOGRAPHY. RESEARCH PAPERS.
University of Oxford, School of Geography, Mansfield Rd., Oxford OX1 3TB, England. TEL 44-1865-271919. FAX 44-1865-271929.
circ. 300. *3425*

UNIVERSITY OF PORT ELIZABETH. INSTITUTE FOR DEVELOPMENT PLANNING AND RESEARCH. ANNUAL REPORT.
University of Port Elizabeth, Institute for Development Planning and Research, P.O. Box 1600, Port Elizabeth 6000, South Africa. TEL 27-41-5042336. FAX 27-41-531769.
circ. 400. *1370*

UNIVERSITY OF RHODE ISLAND. LIBRARY. LIBRARY LETTER.
University of Rhode Island, Association of Friends of the Library, Kingston, RI 02881. *4220*

UNIVERSITY OF SINGAPORE. HISTORY SOCIETY. JOURNAL.
National University of Singapore, History Department, Kent Ridge, Singapore 0511, Singapore. TEL 772-3839.
circ. 500. *3540*

10406 CONTROLLED CIRCULATION SERIALS

UNIVERSITY OF SYDNEY. DEPARTMENT OF ECONOMICS. WORKING PAPERS IN ECONOMICS.
University of Sydney, Department of Economics, Room 324 Merewether Bldg., City Rd., Sydney, N.S.W. 2006, Australia. TEL 61-2-513074. FAX 61-2-5521118.
circ. 200. *1009*

UNIVERSITY OF THE PHILIPPINES. INSTITUTE OF LIBRARY SCIENCE. NEWSLETTER.
University of the Philippines, Institute of Library Science, U.P. Diliman, Quezon City 1101, Philippines. TEL 63-2-920-5303. FAX 63-2-922-4714.
circ. 1,200. *4221*

UNIVERSITY OF THE PUNJAB. INSTITUTE OF GEOLOGY. GEOLOGICAL BULLETIN.
University of the Punjab, Institute of Geology, Qaid-E-Azam Campus, Lahore, Pakistan. TEL 92-42-5866809. *2374*

UNIVERSITY OF TOKYO. INSTITUTE OF APPLIED MICROBIOLOGY. REPORTS.
University of Tokyo, Institute of Applied Microbiology, 1-1-1 Yayoi, Bunkyo-ku, Tokyo 113, Japan. *645*

UNIVERSITY OF WALES AT ABERYSTWYTH. LIBRARY REPORT.
University of Wales at Aberystwyth, Library, Aberystwyth, Dyfed SY23 3DZ, Wales.
circ. 100. *4221*

UNIVERSITY OF WASHINGTON DAILY.
University of Washington, Board of Student Publications, 144 Communications, Box 353720, Seattle, WA 98195. TEL 206-543-7666. FAX 206-543-2345.
circ. 18,000. *1977*

UNIVERSITY OF WATERLOO. GAZETTE.
University of Waterloo, Internal Communications Department, Waterloo, ON N2L 3G1, Canada. TEL 519-885-1211. FAX 519-746-8652.
circ. 10,000. *2491*

UNIVERSITY OF WATERLOO COURIER.
University of Waterloo, Waterloo, Ont. N2L 3G1, Canada. TEL 519-885-1211.
circ. 50,000. *1977*

UNIVERSITY OF WISCONSIN AT MADISON. COLLEGE OF ENGINEERING. ANNUAL REPORT.
University of Wisconsin at Madison, College of Engineering, 215 N. Randall Ave., Madison, WI 53706-1688. TEL 608-263-5988. FAX 608-263-9259.
circ. 6,500. *2744*

UNIX REVIEW.
Miller Freeman, Inc., 600 Harrison St., San Francisco, CA 94107. TEL 415-905-2200. FAX 415-905-2232.
circ. 80,000. *2146*

UNMUZZLED OX.
Unmuzzled Ox Foundation, Ltd., 105 Hudson St., New York, NY 10013. TEL 212-226-7170.
circ. 20,000. *4526*

UP TO DATE.
Mediamark Publishing International Ltd., 35 Gresse St., Rathbone Pl., London W1P 1PN, England. TEL 44-171-580-3105. FAX 44-171-580-1695.
circ. 650,000. *2041*

UP WITH PEOPLE REPORTS.
Up with People, Inc., 1 International Ct., Broomfield, CO 80021-9806. TEL 303-438-7391. FAX 303-438-7302.
circ. 60,000. *2567*

UPDATE (SOUTH AFRICAN EDITION).
George Warman Publications (Pty.) Ltd., P.O. Box 704, Cape Town 8000, South Africa. TEL 27-21-245320. FAX 27-21-261332.
circ. 7,050. *4756*

UPPER CASE.
National Life Insurance Company of Vermont, Montpelier, VT 05604. TEL 802-229-3333.
circ. 3,000. *3836*

UPPER TRIAD.
Upper Triad Association, Inc., Box 2248, Leesburg, VA 20177. TEL 703-443-8289. FAX 703-443-8294.
circ. 2,000. *5757*

UPSOUTH.
Upsouth, Inc., 3627 Hammett Hill Rd., Bowling Green, KY 42101. TEL 502-843-8018.
circ. 75. *4483*

UROLOGIA.
Libreria Editrice Canova, Viale della Liberazione 40, 31030 Dosson di Casier (Treviso), Italy. TEL 39-422-322393. FAX 39-422-322305.
circ. 1,300. *5166*

UROLOGY INTERNATIONAL.
Complete Medical Communications Ltd., C M C House, 19 King Edward St., Macclesfield, Ches. SK10 1AQ, England. TEL 44-1625-619855. FAX 44-1625-619812.
circ. 24,000. *5166*

USED EQUIPMENT DIRECTORY.
Penton Publishing Co. (Hasbrouck Heights), 611 Rte. 46 W., Hasbrouck Heights, NJ 07604. TEL 201-393-9558. FAX 201-393-9553.
circ. 75,000. *4553*

UTAH NURSE.
Utah Nurses Association, 455 E. 400 South, Ste. 50, Salt Lake City, UT 84111. TEL 801-322-3439. FAX 801-322-3430.
circ. 19,000. *4950*

UTAH STATE UNIVERSITY MAGAZINE.
Utah State University, Information Services, Logan, UT 84322-0500. TEL 801-797-1353. FAX 801-797-1250.
circ. 60,000. *1978*

UTILITIES FOR CHINA.
Sterling Publications Ltd., 86-88 Edgware Rd., London W2 2YW, England. TEL 44-171-915-9600. FAX 44-171-915-9619.
circ. 10,000. *2680*

UTILITY CONSTRUCTION AND MAINTENANCE.
Practical Communications, Inc., Box 183, Cary, IL 60013-0183. TEL 847-639-2200. FAX 847-639-9542.
circ. 25,500. *917*

UTILITY FINANCE.
O X E R A Press, Blue Boar Ct., Alfred St., Oxford OX1 4EH, England. TEL 44-1865-251142. FAX 44-1865-201080.
circ. 1,000. *2680*

UTTAR BHARAT BHOOGOL PATRIKA.
Uttar Bharat Parishad, Department of Geography, University of Gorakhpur, Gorakhpur 273 009, India. TEL 91-551-200091. FAX 91-551-208026. *3426*

UTTAR BHARAT TIMES.
Paresh Kumar Kashyap, Ed. & Pub., Court Rd., Bijnor 246 701, U.P., India. TEL 01342-62664.
circ. 2,200. *3321*

V.C.F. NEWSLETTER.
Veterinary Christian Fellowship, 112 Lenthay Rd., Sherborne, Dorset DT9 6AG, England. TEL 01935-812872.
circ. 420. *7280*

V C OE ZEITUNG.
Verkehrsclub Oesterreich, Dingelstedtgasse 15, A-1150 Vienna, Austria. TEL 43-1-8932697. FAX 43-1-8932431.
circ. 22,000. *7046*

V D E W DIE OEFFENTLICHE ELEKTRIZITAETSVERSORGUNG.
Vereinigung Deutscher Elektrizitaetswerke e.V., Stresemannallee 23, 60596 Frankfurt a.M., Germany. FAX 069-6304339. *2849*

V F A PROFIL.
Profil Verlag GmbH, Scheideweg 160B, 26127 Oldenburg, Germany. TEL 49-441-93023-0. FAX 49-441-9302320.
circ. 36,000. *416*

V F W AUXILIARY.
Veterans of Foreign Wars of the United States, Ladies Auxiliary, 406 W. 34th St., Kansas City, MO 64111. TEL 816-561-8655. FAX 816-931-4753.
circ. 775,000. *1937*

V H W MITTEILUNGEN.
Vereinigte Verlagsanstalten GmbH, Hoeherweg 278, 40231 Duesseldorf, Germany. TEL 49-211-7357-0. FAX 49-211-7357223.
circ. 5,000. *2492*

V O B S MAGAZIN.
Vereinigte Verlagsanstalten GmbH, Hoeherweg 278, 40231 Duesseldorf, Germany. TEL 49-211-7357-0. FAX 49-211-7357223.
circ. 40,000. *6693*

V S D A VOICE.
Video Software Dealers Association, 16530 Ventura Blvd., Encino, CA 91436-4551. TEL 609-231-7800. FAX 609-231-9791.
circ. 5,000. *2069*

V V S.
Teknisk Forlag A-S, Skelbaekgade 4, DK-1780 Copenhagen V, Denmark. TEL 45-31-21-68-01. FAX 45-31-21-04-01.
circ. 4,876. *3485*

THE V W AUTOIST.
Volkswagen Club of America, Box 154, N. Aurora, IL 60542-0154. TEL 708-896-2803.
circ. 2,000. *7120*

VAART BLAD.
Norges Kooperative Landsforening, Kirkegt. 4, 0107 Oslo 1, Norway. TEL 22-89-95-00. FAX 22-41-11-38.
circ. 253,355. *1208*

VAART VERN.
Krigsskoleutdannede Offiserers Landsforening, P.O. Box 7207, Ho, N-0307 Oslo 3, Norway. TEL 02-52-15-46. FAX 02-69-56-08.
circ. 2,000. *5289*

VACATION INDUSTRY REVIEW.
Interval International, 6262 Sunset Dr., Penthouse 1, S. Miami, FL 33143. TEL 305-666-1861. FAX 305-668-3408.
circ. 15,000. *7247*

VAESTRA SVERIGES AFFAERER & FOERETAG.
Vaestra Sveriges Affaerer & Foeretag, P.O. Box 411, S-401 26 Goeteborg, Sweden. TEL 46-031-624060. FAX 46-031-624066.
circ. 7,530. *1553*

VAEXTSKYDDSKURIREN.
Bayer (Sverige) AB, Agro-Kemi, P.O. Box 50113, S-202 11 Malmoe, Sweden.
circ. 40,000. *248*

VAKBLAD MIX.
M'Xpress vof, P.O. Box 66, 5258 ZH Berlicum, Netherlands. TEL 31-73-5034347. FAX 31-73-5034347.
circ. 2,000. *3769*

VALLEYKIDS PARENT NEWS.
227 N. Second St., Geneva, IL 60134-1436. TEL 708-208-7221. FAX 708-208-7257.
circ. 60,000. *1858*

VALOER.
Foereningen Valoer, Konstvetenskapliga Institutionen, Slottet, Soedra tornet, inngaang HO, S-752 37 Uppsala, Sweden. TEL 46-18-18-28-88. FAX 46-18-18-28-92.
circ. 50. *471*

VANGUARD (LA HABRA).
Alpha Beta Company, 777 S. Harbor Blvd., La Habra, CA 90631. TEL 714-738-2000.
circ. 34,000. *3130*

VANTAGE.
Signature Group, 200 N. Martingale Rd., Schaumburg, IL 60173-2096. TEL 847-605-3000.
circ. 340,000. *3446*

EL VAQUERO.
Glendale Community College, 1500 N. Verdugo Rd., Glendale, CA 91208-2894. TEL 818-240-1000. FAX 818-549-9436.
circ. 3,500. *1978*

VARME OG SANITETS NYT.
Christtreu, Strandlodsvei 48, DK-2300 Copenhagen S, Denmark. TEL 32-844848. FAX 31-582055.
circ. 12,456. *3485*

VARSITY.
S R C Press, University of Cape Town, Rondebosch 7700, South Africa. TEL 021 698531.
circ. 7,500. *1978*

VASAMA.
Sahkoalojen Ammattiliitto ry., P.O. Box 747, 33101 Tampere, Finland. TEL 358-3-2520-111. FAX 358-3-2520-210.
circ. 31,238. *3900*

VASTGOEDMARKT.
Ten Hagen & Stam b.v., Postbus 34, 2501 AG The Hague, Netherlands. TEL 31-70-3045700. FAX 31-70-3045812.
circ. 7,955. *917*

VATTEN.
Foereningen foer Vatten, Avd. VA-teknik, LTH, Box 118, S-221 00 Lund, Sweden. TEL 46-47-222-8996. FAX 46-46-222-42-24.
circ. 1,200. *7301*

VECINOS DEL VALLE.
Daily News, 21221 Oxnard St., Woodland Hills, CA 91367. TEL 818-713-3229. FAX 818-713-3024.
circ. 48,000. *3047*

THE VEGAN NEWS.
Vegan Action, Box 4353, Berkeley, CA 94704. TEL 510-654-6297. FAX 510-595-7569.
circ. 10,000. *5483*

THE VEGAS CONNECTION.
Contact Advertising, 2010 St. Lucie Blvd., Ft. Pierce, FL 34946. TEL 561-464-5447. FAX 561-464-5447.
circ. 6,000. *5182*

VEILIG VLIEGEN.
Koninklijke Luchtmacht, Afdeling Bedrijfsveiligheid Koninklijke Luchtmachtstaf, Binckhorstlaan 135, Postbus 20703, 2500 ES The Hague, Netherlands. TEL 70-3492358. FAX 70-3492500.
circ. 5,000. *81*

VEN'D'EST.
Editions Cooperatives du Ven'd'Est, Ltee., P.O. Box 266, Bathhurst, NB E2A 3Z2, Canada. TEL 506-548-4907. FAX 506-545-6299.
circ. 4,500. *3267*

VENEZUELA. OFICINA CENTRAL DE ESTADISTICA E INFORMATICA. ENCUESTA CUALITATIVA.
Oficina Central de Estadistica e Informatica, Apdo. de Correos 4593, Carmelitas, Caracas 1010A, Venezuela. TEL 58-2-782-11-33. FAX 58-2-781-13-80. *1077*

VEREIN ZUM SCHUTZ DER BERGWELT. JAHRBUCH.
Verein zum Schutz der Bergwelt e.V., Praterinsel 5, 80538 Munich, Germany. TEL 49-89-479053. FAX 49-89-479053. *2247*

VERKEHRSBLATT.
Verkehrsblatt Verlag Borgmann GmbH, Hohe Str. 39, 44139 Dortmund, Germany. TEL 49-231-128047. FAX 49-231-125640.
circ. 10,000. *7143*

VERKO.
Verko Maskinkontakt AB, Datavaegen 12 a, S-436 32 Askim, Sweden. TEL 031-680000. FAX 031-680009.
circ. 4,466. *2903*

VERMILION STANDARD.
4917 50 Ave., Box 750, Vermilion, AB T0B 4M0, Canada. TEL 403-853-5344. FAX 403-853-5203.
circ. 82. *3267*

VERMONT. COMMISSIONER OF BANKING INSURANCE AND SECURITIES. ANNUAL REPORT OF THE BANK COMMISSIONER.
Department of Banking Insurance and Securities, Division of Banking, 89 Main St., Drawer 20, Montpelier, VT 05620. TEL 802-828-3301.
circ. 1,700. *1172*

VERMONT DEPARTMENT OF LIBRARIES NEWS.
Department of Libraries, Pavilion Office Bldg., 109 State St., Montpelier, VT 05609.
circ. 2,000. *4221*

VERMONT ECONOMIC DEVELOPMENT AUTHORITY. ANNUAL REPORT.
Economic Development Authority, 58 E. State St., Montpelier, VT 05602-3043. TEL 802-223-7226. FAX 802-223-4205.
circ. 400. *1597*

VERMONT PARENT AND CHILD MAGAZINE.
Box 545, Montpelier, VT 05601-0545. TEL 802-425-3835.
circ. 25,000. *1859*

VERMONT PHILATELIST.
Vermont Philatelic Society, 18 Fuller St., Montpelier, VT 05602. *5714*

VERMONT VACATION.
Travel Routes, Inc., Box 949, Chester, VT 05143-0949. FAX 802-257-0848.
circ. 150,000. *7247*

VERNISSAGE.
Vereinigte Verlagsanstalten GmbH, Hoeherweg 278, 40231 Duesseldorf, Germany. TEL 49-211-7357-0. FAX 49-211-7357223.
circ. 27,000. *471*

VERPACKUNGS-RUNDSCHAU.
P. Keppler Verlag GmbH und Co. KG, Industriestr. 2, 63150 Heusenstamm, Germany. TEL 49-6104-606207. FAX 49-6104-606323.
circ. 12,000. *5549*

VERSES.
Cader Publishing, Ltd., 36915 Ryan Rd., Sterling Heights, MI 48310. TEL 810-795-3635. FAX 810-795-9875.
circ. 5,000. *4484*

VERWARMING EN VENTILATIE.
Vereniging van Nederlandse Installatiebedrijven (VNI), Postbus 7272, 2701 AG Zoetermeer, Netherlands.
circ. 4,000. *3485*

VERZEICHNIS DER KONSULARISCHEN VERTRETUNGEN IN OESTERREICH.
Bundesministerium fuer Auswaertige Angelegenheiten, Ballhausplatz 2, A-1014 Vienna, Austria. *6042*

VESAK.
Australian Buddhist Mission Inc., 16 Woodhouse Drive, Ambarvale, N.S.W. 2560, Australia. TEL 61-46-267420. FAX 61-2-4494657.
circ. 2,000. *6390*

VESTKUSTEN.
Vestkusten, 237 Ricardo Rd., Mill Valley, CA 94941-2517. TEL 415-381-5149. FAX 415-381-9664.
circ. 2,100. *3048*

VETERANPOSTEN.
Sveriges Paensionaers Foerbund - S P F, P.O. Box 22574, S-104 22 Stockholm, Sweden. TEL 46-8-692-32-50. FAX 46-8-651-15053.
circ. 149,400. *6693*

VETERANS' BULLETIN.
Georgia Department of Veterans Service, Floyd Veterans Bldg., 970 East, Atlanta, GA 30334. TEL 404-656-5933. FAX 404-656-5934.
circ. 2,400. *1937*

VETERINARY FORUM.
Forum Publications, Inc., 500 Executive Blvd., Ossining, NY 10562. FAX 914-762-8820.
circ. 45,000. *7282*

VETS HELPING VETS.
USVMI, Golden Triangle Sales, 3738 E. First St., Fort Worth, TX 76111. TEL 817-834-7573.
circ. 10,000. *5289*

VIA FEDEX.
The Wells Group, 430 First Ave. N., Ste. 550, Minneapolis, MN 55401-1735. TEL 612-338-8300. FAX 612-338-6546.
circ. 330,000. *2007*

VIA INTERNATIONAL PORT OF NEW YORK - NEW JERSEY.
Port Authority of New York and New Jersey, One World Trade Ctr., Rm. 34E, New York, NY 10048. TEL 212-435-6614. FAX 212-435-6032.
circ. 30,000. *7169*

VIA SATELLITE.
Phillips Business Information, Inc., 1201 Seven Locks Rd., Potomac, MD 20854. TEL 301-424-3338. FAX 301-340-0542. *2008*

VIBORG STIFTS FOLKEBLAD.
Viborg Stifts Folkeblad, Sct. Mathiasgade 7, DK-8800 Viborg, Denmark. TEL 45-89-27-63-00. FAX 45-86-62-22-20.
circ. 12,720. *3275*

VICTORIAN REAL ESTATE JOURNAL.
Real Estate Institute of Victoria Ltd., P.O. Box 443, Camberwell, Vic. 3124, Australia. TEL 61-3-92056666. FAX 61-3-92056699.
circ. 2,500. *6315*

VIDA RELIGIOSA.
Misioneros Hijos del Inmaculado Corazon de Maria (Claretianos), Buen Suceso, 22, 28008 Madrid, Spain. TEL 34-1-5482101. FAX 34-1-5401226.
circ. 10,000. *6484*

VIDEO RETAILER SHOWCASE.
Tel-Aire Publications, Inc., 3105 E. Carpenter Frwy., Irving, TX 75062. TEL 214-438-4111. FAX 214-579-7483.
circ. 19,500. *2070*

VIE DE L'AUTO.
Elvea - La Vie de l'Auto, B.P. 88, 77303 Fontainbleau Cedex, France. TEL 33-1-60715555. FAX 33-1-60722237.
circ. 68,500. *344*

VIE DE LA MOTO.
Elvea - La Vie de l'Auto, B.P. 88, 77303 Fontainbleau Cedex, France. TEL 33-1-60715555. FAX 33-1-60722237.
circ. 43,000. *344*

VIE ET SANTE.
Editions Vie et Sante, 60 av. Emile Zola, 77192 Dammarie les Lys Cedex, France. FAX 64-87-00-66.
circ. 40,000. *5792*

VIE SOCIALE.
Centre d'Etudes, de Documentation, d'Information et d'Action Sociales (CEDIAS), 5 rue Las-Cases, 75007 Paris, France. TEL 33-1-45516610. FAX 33-1-44180181.
circ. 1,750. *6738*

VIEWPOINT (LONDON, 1965).
Delane Press, 157 Vicarage Rd., London E1O 5DU, England. TEL 44-181-539-3876. *5978*

VIEWPOINTS.
Bowthorpe plc., Gatwick Rd., Crawley, W. Sussex RH10 2RZ, England. TEL 44-1293-528888. FAX 44-1293-541905.
circ. 7,000. *3302*

VIHERPIHA.
A-Lehdet Oy, Hitsaajankatu 7, FIN-00081 A-Lehdet, Finland. TEL 358-0-786858.
circ. 37,419. *3207*

VIKING SOCIETY FOR NORTHERN RESEARCH. SAGA BOOK.
Viking Society for Northern Research, c/o Dept. of Scandinavian Studies, University College, London WC1E 6BT, England. TEL 44-171-380-7176. FAX 44-171-380-7750.
circ. 650. *3611*

VIM & VIGOR.
McMurry Publishing, 1010 E. Missouri Ave., Phoenix, AZ 85014-2601. FAX 602-395-5853.
circ. 950,000. *5792*

VINTAGE NORTHWEST.
Box 193, Bothell, WA 98011.
circ. 500. *4484*

VINTNERS WORLD.
Jemma Publications Ltd., Marino House, 53 Glasthule Rd., Sandycove, Co. Dublin, Ireland. TEL 2800000. FAX 2801818.
circ. 7,500. *528*

VIRGIN ISLANDS (U.S.). DEPARTMENT OF LABOR. BUREAU OF LABOR STATISTICS. LABOR MARKET REVIEW.
Department of Labor, Bureau of Labor Statistics, P.O. Box 3359, Charlotte Amalie, St. Thomas, VI 00803. TEL 809-776-3700. FAX 809-774-5908.
circ. 900. *1457*

VIRGINIA MARITIMER.
Port Authority, 600 World Trade Center, Norfolk, VA 23510. TEL 804-683-8000. FAX 804-683-2897.
circ. 9,500. *7169*

VIRGINIA P H C IMAGE.
Virginia Association of Plumbing - Heating - Cooling Contractors, 1001 E. Broad St., Ste. 225, Richmond, VA 23219-1928. TEL 804-644-5826. FAX 804-643-5927.
circ. 6,000. *3485*

VIRGINIA POLYTECHNIC INSTITUTE AND STATE UNIVERSITY. DEPARTMENT OF GEOLOGICAL SCIENCES. GEOLOGICAL GUIDEBOOKS.
Virginia Polytechnic Institute and State University, Department of Geological Sciences, 4044 Derring Hall, Blacksburg, VA 24061. TEL 703-231-6521.
2375

VIRGINIA SCHOOL BOARDS ASSOCIATION NEWSLETTER.
Virginia School Boards Association, 2320 Hunters Way, Ste. B, Charlottesville, VA 22911-7931. TEL 804-295-8722. FAX 804-295-8785.
circ. 2,300. *3485*

VIRKSOMHEDS NYT.
Christtreu, Strandlodsvej 48, DK-2300 Copenhagen S, Denmark. TEL 32-844848. FAX 31-582055.
circ. 16,954. *7046*

VISION (STAMFORD).
Keep America Beautiful, Inc., 1010 Washington Blvd., 7th Fl., Stamford, CT 06901-2202. TEL 203-323-8987.
circ. 2,000. *2957*

VISION OF REALITY.
Piranesi Ltd., Bogisiceva 11, 61000 Ljubljana, Slovenia. TEL 386-61-223-039. FAX 386-61-221-226.
circ. 2,000. *417*

VISIONS (ALHAMBRA).
California School of Professional Psychology, 1000 S. Fremont Ave., Alhambra, CA 91803-1360. TEL 818-293-1848. FAX 818-284-1712.
circ. 8,000. *6158*

VISIONS: AN ART QUARTERLY.
L A Artcore, 420 E. Third St., Ste. 110, Los Angeles, CA 90013-1644. TEL 213-628-6164. FAX 213-620-1277.
circ. 12,000. *471*

EL VISITANTE DE PUERTO RICO.
Puerto Rican Catholic Conference, Box 41305, Minillas Sta., San Juan, PR 00940-1305. TEL 787-728-3710. FAX 787-728-3656.
circ. 59,500. *6485*

VISTA MAGAZINE.
Horizon, 999 Ponce de Leon Blvd., Ste. 600, Coral Gables, FL 33134. TEL 305-442-2462. FAX 305-443-7650.
circ. 1,100,000. *7248*

VISTA U S A.
Aegis Group - Publishers, 30400 Van Dyke Ave., Warren, MI 48093. TEL 810-574-9100.
circ. 400,000. *7248*

VITA IN CAMPAGNA.
Edizioni L' Informatore Agrario S.r.l., Lungadige Galtarossa 23-E, 37133 Verona, Italy. TEL 39-45-597855. FAX 39-45-597510.
circ. 80,073. *3207*

VITA TRENTINA.
Vita Trentina Editrice - Coop., s.r.l., Via S. Giovanni Bosco, 5, 38100 Trento, Italy. TEL 39-461-272666. FAX 39-461-272655.
circ. 15,000. *3328*

VITALITY.
Vitality, Inc., 8080 N. Central, LB 78, Dallas, TX 75206. TEL 214-691-1480.
circ. 2,500,000. *5792*

VITALITY MAGAZINE.
356 Dupont St., Toronto, ON M5R 1V9, Canada. TEL 416-964-0528.
circ. 40,000. *299*

VIVRE ENSEMBLE.
Union Nationale des Associations de Parents et Amis de Personnes Handicapees Mentales, 15 rue Coysevox, 75018 Paris, France.
circ. 75,250. *2592*

VOCE SERAFICA DELLA SARDEGNA.
Frati Minori Cappuccini di Sardegna, Via S. Ignazio da Laconi 94, 09123 Cagliari, Italy. TEL 39-70-660303. FAX 39-70-655583.
circ. 3,000. *6485*

VOETBAL TOTAAL.
Koninklijke Nederlandsche Voetbalbond, P.O. Box 515, 3700 AM Zeist, Netherlands. TEL 31-3439-9211. FAX 31-3439-1397.
circ. 30,500. *6821*

VOICE (ALBANY).
United University Professions, 159 Wolf Rd., Albany, NY 12205. TEL 518-458-7935. FAX 518-459-3242.
circ. 20,000. *2562*

VOICE (FT. LAUDERDALE).
Cary - Joy Communications, 1405 S.E. First St., Ft. Lauderdale, FL 33301. TEL 954-463-5556. FAX 954-463-2674.
circ. 70,000. *5047*

VOICE OF SILENCE NEWSLETTER.
World Federation of the Deaf, 120 via Gregoria VII, Rome 00165, Italy.
circ. 500. *3465*

THE VOICE OF WALDEN.
Walden Forever Wild, Inc., Box 275, Concord, MA 01742. TEL 508-429-2839. FAX 860-487-1629.
2248

VOIES DE LA CREATION THEATRALE.
C N R S Editions, 20-22 rue St. Amand, 75015 Paris, France. TEL 45-33-16-00. FAX 45-33-92-13.
circ. 1,500. *7017*

VOIX SEPHARADE.
Communaute Sepharade du Quebec, 4735 Chemin de la Cote Ste. Catherine, Montreal, PQ H3W 1M1, Canada. TEL 514-733-4998. FAX 514-733-3158.
circ. 6,000. *3048*

VOLKSDANS.
Landelijk Centrum voor Amateurdans, Postbus 452, 3500 AL Utrecht, Netherlands. TEL 31-30-334255. FAX 31-30-332721.
circ. 1,850. *3093*

THE VOLUME FRAMER.
Vic Faulkner Associates, 45 Longfield Dr., Amersham., Bucks. HP6 5H6, England. TEL 44-1494-791451. FAX 44-1494-778224.
circ. 5,000. *472*

THE VOLUNTEER LIBRARIAN.
Association of Private Libraries, c/o Sophie Mitrisin, 66 Frankfort St., Apt. 2G, New York, NY 10038-1622. TEL 212-732-4461. *4221*

VORSCHAU.
Forschungsgesellschaft fuer Wohnen, Bauen und Planen, Loewengasse 47, A-1030 Vienna, Austria. TEL 43-1-71262510. FAX 43-1-712625121. *917*

VORTEX.
American Chemical Society, California Section, 2140 Shattuck Ave., Rm. 1101, Berkeley, CA 94704. TEL 415-848-0512.
circ. 3,500. *1770*

VOX ME D A L.
Dalhousie University, Dalhousie Medical Alumni Association, Dalhousie University, First Floor, Tupper Bldg., Halifax, NS B3H 4H7, Canada. TEL 902-494-8800. FAX 902-494-2033.
circ. 6,700. *1978*

VOXAIR.
Canadian Forces Base Winnipeg, Westwin, MB R3J 0T0, Canada. TEL 204-889-3963. FAX 204-885-4176.
circ. 3,600. *5290*

LA VOZ (SEATTLE).
Concilio for the Spanish Speaking, 157 Yesler Way., Ste. 400, Seattle, WA 98104-2572. TEL 206-461-4891. FAX 206-461-4893.
circ. 14,000. *3048*

VYZIVA A POTRAVINY.
Spolecnost pro Vyzivu, Sobeslavska 40, 130 00 Prague 3, Czech Republic. TEL 42-2-67311280. FAX 42-2-67310515.
circ. 5,500. *5484*

VYZOV.
Permskii Gorispolkom, Upravlenie Vnutrennikh Del, Ul. Druzhby 34, 614600 Perm, Russia. TEL 48-39-24. FAX 32-52-19.
circ. 50,000. *6002*

W B F IN ACTION.
Workmen's Benefit Fund of the United States of America, 99 N. Broadway, Hicksville, NY 11801-2905. TEL 516-938-6060.
circ. 15,000. *3836*

W C E R HIGHLIGHTS.
Wisconsin Center for Education Research, University of Wisconsin at Madison, 1025 W. Johnston St., Rm. 785, Madison, WI 53706. TEL 608-263-8814. FAX 608-263-6448.
circ. 9,300. *2579*

W D A JOURNAL.
Wisconsin Dental Association, 111 E. Wisconsin Ave., Ste. 1300, Milwaukee, Milwaukee, WI 53202. TEL 414-276-4520. FAX 414-276-8431.
circ. 3,100. *4873*

W E R A BROCHURE.
Western English Retailers Association, 451 E. 58th Ave., Box 087, Denver, CO 80216. TEL 303-298-7882. FAX 303-292-3468.
circ. 1,000. *1919*

W E R A SPECIAL NEWSLETTER.
Western English Retailers Association, 451 E. 58th Ave., Box 087, Denver, CO 80216. TEL 303-298-7882. FAX 303-292-3468.
circ. 300. *1919*

W E S A NEWSLETTER.
Wisconsin Electronic Sales and Service Association, Box 531, Butler, WI 53007-0531. TEL 414-246-6495.
circ. 250. *1649*

W N C BUSINESS JOURNAL.
Nason & Associates, Box 8204, Asheville, NC 28814. TEL 704-298-1322. FAX 704-298-1312.
circ. 19,000. *1011*

W P A NEWS.
Western Publications Association, 823 Rim Crest Dr., Westlake Village, CA 91361. TEL 805-495-1863. FAX 805-497-1849.
circ. 2,200. *6286*

W U U A NEWSLETTER.
World Union for a Universal Alphabet, Box 252, Cincinnati, OH 45201-0252. TEL 513-574-7638.
circ. 650. *2008*

DIE WAAGE.
Gruenenthal GmbH, 52220 Stolberg, Germany. TEL 02402-103345. FAX 02402-103520.
circ. 30,000. *3292*

WAGES AND BENEFITS.
Employee Futures Research, Box 15236, Colorado Springs, CO 80935-5236.
circ. 700. *2579*

WAGONER JOURNAL.
Northwest Genealogical Society, Box 6, Alliance, NE 69301.
circ. 300. *3245*

WAKE FOREST LAW REVIEW.
Wake Forest Law Review Association, Inc., Wake Forest University, Winston-Salem, NC 27109. TEL 919-759-5439. FAX 919-759-4496.
circ. 1,500. *4044*

WALDVIERTEL UND GOLF.
Orac Zeitschriftenverlag GmbH, Brunner Feldstr. 45, A-2380 Perchtoldsdorf, Austria. TEL 43-1-8696536. FAX 43-1-8696536.
circ. 50,000. *6888*

WALL STREET & TECHNOLOGY.
United News & Media, One Penn Plaza, New York, NY 10119. TEL 212-869-1300.
circ. 25,200. *1176*

WALLACES FARMER.
Farm Progress Companies, 191 S. Gary Ave., Carol Stream, IL 60188. TEL 630-690-5600. FAX 630-462-2869.
circ. 80,000. *164*

WANASAN.
Royal Forest Department, Vanasarn Forest Journal Office, Bangkok, Thailand.
circ. 5,400. *3166*

WASHINGTON (STATE). DEPARTMENT OF REVENUE. RESEARCH DIVISION. COMPARATIVE STATE - LOCAL TAXES.
Department of Revenue, Research Division, Box 47459, Olympia, WA 98504-7459. TEL 360-753-2087. FAX 360-664-0972. *1637*

WASHINGTON (STATE). DEPARTMENT OF REVENUE. RESEARCH DIVISION. PROPERTY TAX STATISTICS.
Department of Revenue, Research Division, Box 47459, Olympia, WA 98504-7459. TEL 360-753-2087. FAX 360-664-0972. *1077*

WASHINGTON (STATE) RESEARCH COUNCIL. NOTEBOOK.
Washington Research Council, 1301 Fifth Ave., Ste. 350, Seattle, WA 98101-2603. TEL 206-357-6643. FAX 206-754-2193.
circ. 2,500. *6200*

WASHINGTON CRIME NEWS SERVICES CALENDAR OF EVENTS.
Washington Crime News Services, 3918 Prosperity Ave., Ste. 318, Fairfax, VA 22031-3304. TEL 703-573-1600. FAX 703-573-1604. *5172*

WASHINGTON OPERA MAGAZINE.
Washington Opera Guild, Kennedy Center, Washington, DC 20566. TEL 202-416-7850. FAX 202-416-7857.
circ. 60,000. *5444*

WASHINGTON REAL ESTATE NEWS.
Department of Licensing, Real Estate Division, Box 9015, Olympia, WA 98507. TEL 206-753-3194. FAX 206-586-0998.
circ. 60,000. *6315*

WASHINGTON UNIVERSITY MAGAZINE AND ALUMNI NEWS.
Washington University, Office of Publications, Campus Box 1086, One Brookings Dr., St. Louis, MO 63130-4899. TEL 314-935-5248. FAX 314-935-8533.
circ. 113,000. *1979*

WASHINGTON'S HILL RAG.
Fagon Publishing Group, 224 Seventh St., S.E., Ste. 300, Washington, DC 20003. TEL 202-543-8300.
circ. 20,000. *3389*

WASTE MAGAZIN.
Bohmann Druck und Verlag GmbH & Co. KG, Leberstr. 122, A-1110 Vienna, Austria. TEL 43-1-74095-0. FAX 43-1-74095183.
circ. 8,000. *2991*

THE WASTE MANAGER.
Environmental Services Association, 154 Buckingham Palace Rd., London SWIW 9TR, England. TEL 44-171-824-8882. FAX 44-171-824-8753.
circ. 4,200. *2991*

WATCH MAGAZINE.
Watch Magazines Inc., 245-401 Richmond St. W., Toronto, ON M5V 1X3, Canada. TEL 416-595-1313. FAX 416-595-1312.
circ. 75,000. *1893*

WATER AND WASTE TREATMENT.
Faversham House Group Ltd., Faversham House, 232a Addington Rd., South Croydon, Surrey CR2 8LE, England. TEL 44-181-651-7100. FAX 44-181-651-7117.
circ. 8,506. *7303*

WATER CONDITIONING AND PURIFICATION.
Publicom Inc., 2800 E. Ft. Lowell Rd., Tucson, AZ 85716-1518. FAX 520-323-7412.
circ. 18,537. *7303*

WATER FLYING.
Seaplane Pilots Association, 421 Aviation Way, Frederick, MD 21701. TEL 301-695-2083. FAX 301-695-2375.
circ. 7,000. *82*

WATER PRODUCTS.
Faversham House Group Ltd., Faversham House, 232a Addington Rd., South Croydon, Surrey CR2 8LE, England. TEL 44-181-651-7100. FAX 44-181-651-7117. *7304*

WATER SEWAGE AND EFFLUENT.
Brooke Pattrick (Pty) Ltd., P.O. Box 422, Bedfordview 2008, South Africa. TEL 27-11-6224666. FAX 27-11-6167196.
circ. 3,210. *7306*

WATER SKIER.
American Water Ski Association, 799 Overlook Dr., Winter Haven, FL 33884. TEL 914-324-4341. FAX 914-325-8259.
circ. 30,000. *6888*

WATER TECHNOLOGY.
National Trade Publications, Inc., 13 Century Hill, Latham, NY 12110-2197. TEL 518-783-1281. FAX 518-783-1386.
circ. 18,000. *7306*

WATERWORLD.
PennWell Publishing Co., Box 1260, Tulsa, OK 74101. TEL 918-835-3161. FAX 918-832-9295.
circ. 65,000. *7306*

AL-WATHA'IQ AL-FILASTINIYYAH.
Cultural Foundation, Centre for Documentation and Research, P.O. Box 2380, Abu Dhabi, United Arab Emirates. TEL 212900. FAX 541595.
circ. 1,000. *3661*

WATT.
Gruppo Editoriale Jackson S.p.A., Via M. Gorki 69, 20092 Cinisello B. (MI), Italy. TEL 39-2-6607214. FAX 39-2-66034270.
circ. 9,804. *2849*

WAYN-E-GRAM MAGAZINE.
Continental Grain Company, Wayne Feed Division, 10 S. Riverside Plaza, Chicago, IL 60606-3708. TEL 312-930-1050. FAX 312-466-6614.
circ. 2,500. *266*

WAYNE STATE MAGAZINE.
Wayne State University, Alumni Association, Office of Alumni Relations, Detroit, MI 48202. TEL 313-577-2300. FAX 313-577-2302.
circ. 13,500. *1979*

WE ARE ONE WORLD.
Kindernothilfe e.V., Duesseldorfer Landstr. 180, 47249 Duisburg, Germany. TEL 49-203-7789-0. FAX 49-203-7789118.
circ. 14,000. *1893*

WE PROCEEDED ON.
Lewis and Clark Trail Heritage Foundation, Inc., Box 3434, Great Falls, MT 59403. TEL 406-453-2826.
circ. 1,500. *3651*

WEBMASTER.
Box 9208, Framingham, MA 01701-9208. *2141*

WEDDING BELLS MAGAZINE.
50 Wellington St., E., 2nd Fl., Toronto, ON M5E 1C8, Canada. TEL 416-862-8479. FAX 416-862-2184.
circ. 104,000. *4627*

WEEKEND SPARK.
Rowland B. Martyn, Ed. & Pub., 7 Lamina Sankoh St., Freetown, Sierra Leone. TEL 232-22-263285.
circ. 20,000. *3354*

WEEKLY NEWS UPDATE ON THE AMERICAS.
Nicaragua Solidarity Network, 339 Lafayette St., New York, NY 10012. TEL 212-674-9499. FAX 212-674-9139.
circ. 140. *3268*

WEEKLY PETROLEUM ARGUS.
Petroleum Argus Ltd., 93 Shepperton Rd., London N1 3DF, England. TEL 0171-359-8792. FAX 0171-226-0695. *5626*

WEHRMEDIZINISCHE MONATSSCHRIFT.
Beta Verlag GmbH, Postfach 140121, 53056 Bonn, Germany. TEL 49-228-91937-0. FAX 49-228-252067.
circ. 5,173. *4758*

WEHRTECHNISCHER REPORT.
Report Verlag GmbH, Stuttgarterstr. 18-24, 60329 Frankfurt a.M., Germany. TEL 49-69-2600-0. FAX 49-69-2600609.
circ. 7,000. *5290*

WELCOME BACK STUDENT MAGAZINE.
Kingston Publications, P.O. Box 1352, Kingston, ON K7L 5C6, Canada. TEL 613-549-8442.
circ. 18,000. *1979*

WELCOME HOME MAGAZINE.
James F. & Mary Sweeney, Eds. & Pubs., 5944 S. Kipling St., Ste. 204, Littleton, CO 80127-2590. TEL 303-972-2584. FAX 303-972-2261.
circ. 31,000. *3389*

THE WELDER.
Esab Group (UK) Ltd., Hertford Rd., Waltham Cross, Herts. EN8 7RP, England. TEL 44-1992-768815.
circ. 15,500. *5224*

WELDING DESIGN AND FABRICATION.
Penton Publishing Co., 1100 Superior Ave., Cleveland, OH 44114-2543. TEL 216-696-7000. FAX 216-696-8765.
circ. 40,000. *5224*

WELDING RESEARCH ABROAD.
Welding Research Council, 345 E. 47th St., New York, NY 10017. TEL 212-705-7956.
circ. 800. *5225*

WELDING RESEARCH COUNCIL BULLETIN.
Welding Research Council, 345 E. 47th St., New York, NY 10017. TEL 212-705-7956.
circ. 900. *5225*

WELFARE BULLETIN.
Center on Social Welfare Policy and Law, 275 Seventh Ave., Ste. 1205, New York, NY 10001-6708. TEL 212-633-6967. FAX 212-633-6371.
circ. 600. *4057*

WELL SERVICING.
Workover-Well Servicing Publications, Inc., 6060 N. Central Expy., Ste. 428, Dallas, TX 75206. TEL 214-692-0771. FAX 214-692-0162.
circ. 10,000. *5627*

WELLINGTON REGIONAL EMPLOYERS ASSOCIATION NEWSLETTER.
Wellington Regional Employers Association (Inc.), Federation House, 6th Floor, Box 1087, 95-99 Molesworth St., Wellington, New Zealand. TEL 64-4-737224. FAX 374501. *1457*

WELSH FARMER.
Farmers' Union of Wales, Llys Amaeth, Queens Sq., Aberystwyth, Dyfed, Wales. TEL 44-1970-612755. FAX 44-1225-774660.
circ. 16,000. *164*

WER - WAS - WO.
Studentenwerk Goettingen, Platz der Goettinger Sieben 4, 37073 Goettingen, Germany. TEL 49-551-390. FAX 49-551-395186.
circ. 12,500. *1979*

WE'RE NEXT.
Box GG, Jal, NM 88252. TEL 505-395-2053.
circ. 200,000. *1893*

WERELD.
Communicatie A B P - U S Z O, Oude Lindestraat 70, 6401 JS Heerlen, Netherlands. TEL 31-45-5798100. FAX 31-45-5792194.
circ. 50,000. *3339*

WERTPAPIER.
Deutsche Schutzvereinigung fuer Wertpapierbesitz e.V., Humboldtstr. 9, 40237 Dusseldorf, Germany.
circ. 34,000. *1414*

WESLEYAN WORLD.
Wesleyan World Missions, 6060 Castleway West Dr., Box 50434, Box 50434, IN 46250-0434. TEL 317-595-4172. FAX 317-841-1125.
circ. 36,000. *6382*

WESPENNEST.
Rembrandtstr. 31-9, A-1020 Vienna, Austria. TEL 43-1-3326691. FAX 43-1-3332970.
circ. 5,000. *4366*

10410 CONTROLLED CIRCULATION SERIALS

WEST CENTRAL BUSINESS JOURNAL.
Ronald Freed, Ed. & Pub., Box 388, Lima, OH 45802-0388. TEL 419-991-6839. FAX 419-991-4762.
circ. 10,000. *1011*

WEST COAST LIFESTYLE MAGAZINE.
W. Bill Golding, Ed. & Pub., 14148 Burbank Blvd., Spt. 7, Van Nuys, CA 91401-4943. TEL 818-780-8400. FAX 818-780-8979.
circ. 70,000. *3389*

WEST COAST PEDDLER.
Box 5134, Whittier, CA 90607. TEL 310-698-1718. FAX 310-698-1500. *344*

WEST VIRGINIA. COMMISSION ON AGING. ANNUAL PROGRESS REPORT.
Commission on Aging, State Capitol, Charleston, WV 25305. TEL 304-348-3317.
circ. 500. *3447*

WEST VIRGINIA FOURTH ESTATESMAN.
West Virginia University, School of Journalism, 112 Martin Hall, Box 6010, Morgantown, WV 26506-6010. TEL 304-293-3505. FAX 304-293-3027.
circ. 3,500. *1979*

WESTCHESTER FAMILY.
Family Publishing Group, Inc., 141 Halstead Ave., Ste. 3D, Mamaroneck, NY 10543-2652. TEL 914-381-7474.
circ. 60,000. *1859*

WESTENDER.
108-110 Camden High St., London NW1 0LU, England. TEL 44-171-485-6050.
circ. 40,000. *3302*

WESTERN ALUMNI GAZETTE.
University of Western Ontario, Department of Communications and Public Affairs, London, ON N6A 5B9, Canada. TEL 519-679-2111. FAX 519-661-3921.
circ. 130,000. *1979*

WESTERN ASSOCIATION NEWS.
Schneider Publishing Company, Box 5657, Santa Monica, CA 90409-5657. TEL 213-458-3777. FAX 213-458-3770. *1512*

WESTERN ASSOCIATION OF GRADUATE SCHOOLS. PROCEEDINGS OF THE ANNUAL MEETING.
Western Association of Graduate Schools, University of Wyoming, The Graduate School, Box 3018, Laramie, WY 82071-3108. TEL 307-766-2287. FAX 307-766-4042.
circ. 500. *2562*

WESTERN AUSTRALIA. DEPARTMENT OF TRANSPORT. ANNUAL REPORT.
Department of Transport, 136-138 Stirling Highway, Nedlands, W.A. 6009, Australia. FAX 61-9-3865119.
circ. 600. *7047*

WESTERN AUSTRALIA. FAMILY AND CHILDREN'S SERVICES. ANNUAL REPORT.
Family and Children's Services, 189 Royal St., E. Perth, W.A. 6004, Australia. TEL 61-9-2222555. FAX 61-9-2222776.
circ. 2,000. *6694*

WESTERN AUSTRALIAN COASTAL SHIPPING COMMISSION. ANNUAL REPORT.
Coastal Shipping Commission, P.O. Box 394, Fremantle, Australia. *7170*

WESTERN BEEF PRODUCER.
Western Farmer-Stockman Magazines, Box 2160, Spokane, WA 99210-1615. TEL 509-459-5361. FAX 509-459-5102.
circ. 34,404. *292*

WESTERN CANADA HIGHWAY NEWS MAGAZINE.
Craig Kelman & Associates Ltd., 3C - 2020 Portage Ave., Winnipeg, MB R3J 0K4, Canada. TEL 204-885-7798. FAX 204-889-3576.
circ. 4,500. *7181*

WESTERN CAVER.
Western Australian Speleological Group, P.O. Box 67, Nedlands, W.A. 6909, Australia. TEL.61-9-3465550.
circ. 200. *2376*

WESTERN CHECKOUT.
Sunset Publishing Corp., 80 Willow Rd., Menlo Park, CA 94025-3691. TEL 415-321-3600. FAX 415-328-6215.
circ. 9,000. *3145*

WESTERN CLEANER AND LAUNDERER.
Wakefield Publishing Co., 3236 Estado St., Pasadena, CA 91107-2916. TEL 818-793-2911. FAX 818-793-5540.
circ. 15,000. *1911*

WESTERN HOG JOURNAL.
Alberta Pork Producers Development Corp., 10319 Princess Elizabeth Ave., Edmonton, AB T5G 0Y5, Canada. TEL 403-474-8288. FAX 403-471-8065.
circ. 9,559. *292*

WESTERN HOSPITALITY NEWS.
Ishcom Publications, 2065 Dundas St. E., Ste. 201, Mississauga, ON L4X 2W1, Canada. TEL 905-206-0150. FAX 905-206-9972.
circ. 13,500. *3737*

WESTERN POWER CORPORATION. ANNUAL REPORT.
Western Power Corporation, Perth, W.A., Australia. TEL 61-9-325-4597. FAX 61-9-326-4984.
circ. 4,000. *2681*

WESTERN ROOFING - INSULATION - SIDING.
Dodson Publications Inc., 546 Court St., Reno, NV 89501-1711. TEL 702-333-1080. FAX 702-333-1081.
circ. 20,000. *918*

WESTERN SHOW NEWS.
Bolger Publications Inc., 3301 Como Ave., S.E., Minneapolis, MN 55414. TEL 612-645-6311. FAX 612-645-1750.
circ. 30,000. *3451*

WESTERN VIKING.
Western Viking Inc., 2405 N.W. Market St., Ste. 202, Seattle, WA 98107. TEL 206-784-4617. FAX 206-784-4856.
circ. 3,000. *3049*

WESTMINSTER MAGAZINE.
Westminster College, Office of Communication Services, New Wilmington, PA 16172. TEL 412-946-7226. FAX 412-946-7187.
circ. 20,225. *1979*

WESTMOUNT EXAMINER.
210 Victoria St., Westmount, PQ H3Z 2M4, Canada. TEL 514-484-5610. FAX 514-484-6028.
circ. 8,000. *3267*

WESTON-SUPER-MARE ADMAG.
Admag Newspapers, 11 Beacons Field Rd., Weston-super-Mare, Avon BS23 1YE, England. TEL 44-1934-417921. FAX 44-1934-635031.
circ. 80,000. *3302*

WETLANDS INTERNATIONAL.
International Waterfowl and Wetlands Research, Slimbridge, Gloucester GL2 7BX, England. TEL 44-1453-890624. FAX 44-1453-890697.
circ. 1,700. *853*

WHAT! A MAGAZINE.
What! Publishers Inc., 108-93 Lombard Ave., Winnipeg, MB R3B 3B1, Canada. TEL 204-985-8160. FAX 204-943-8991.
circ. 200,000. *3267*

WHAT'S NEW IN COMMUNICATIONS.
Westwick-Farrow Pty. Ltd., Crn. Fox Valley Rd. and Kogle St., Wahroonga. N.S.W. 2076, Australia. TEL 61-2-94872700. FAX 61-2-94891265.
circ. 7,200. *2008*

WHAT'S NEW IN ELECTRONICS.
Westwick-Farrow Pty. Ltd., Cnr. Fox Valley Rd. and Kogle St., Wahroonga, N.S.W. 2076, Australia. TEL 61-2-94872700. FAX 61-2-94891265.
circ. 9,200. *2654*

WHAT'S NEW IN PROCESS ENGINEERING.
Westwick-Farrow Pty. Ltd., Cnr. Fox Valley Rd. and Kogle St., Wahroonga, N.S.W. 2076, Australia. TEL 61-2-94872700. FAX 61-2-94891265.
circ. 9,200. *2745*

WHAT'S NEW IN RADIO COMMUNICATIONS.
Westwick-Farrow Pty. Ltd., Cnr. Fox Valley Rd. and Kiogle St., Wahroonga, N.S.W. 2076, Australia. TEL 61-2-94872700. FAX 61-2-94891265.
circ. 5,200. *2030*

WHAT'S NEW IN SCIENTIFIC & LABORATORY TECHNOLOGY.
Westwick-Farrow Pty. Ltd., Cnr. Fox Valley Rd. and Kiogle St., Wahroonga, N.S.W. 2076, Australia. TEL 61-2-94872700. FAX 61-2-94891265.
circ. 7,200. *6980*

THE WHEEL EXTENDED.
Toyota Motor Corporation, International Public Affairs Division, 1-4-18, Koraku, Bunkyo-ku, Tokyo 112, Japan. TEL 03-3817-9930. FAX 03-3817-9017.
circ. 11,000. *7121*

WHERE ATLANTA.
Where Atlanta, 180 Allen Rd., 302 N. Bldg., Atlanta, GA 30328. TEL 404-843-9800. FAX 404-843-9070.
circ. 52,000. *7261*

WHERE BALTIMORE.
Where Magazines International (Baltimore), 516 N. Charles St., Ste. 300, Baltimore, MD 21201. TEL 410-539-4373. FAX 410-539-4381.
circ. 30,000. *7250*

WHERE BOSTON.
Where Magazines International (Boston), 120 Boylston St., Fl. 3, Boston, MA 02116-4611. TEL 617-482-6777. FAX 617-482-3337.
circ. 60,000. *7262*

WHERE CALGARY.
Key West Publishers Ltd., 125 Ninth Ave. S.E., Ste. 250, Calgary, AB T2G 0P6, Canada. TEL 403-299-1888. FAX 403-299-1899.
circ. 18,900. *7262*

WHERE CHICAGO.
Where Magazines International (Chicago), 1165 N. Clark St., Chicago, IL 60610-2845. TEL 312-642-1896. FAX 312-642-5467.
circ. 100,000. *7262*

WHERE EDMONTON.
Where Magazines International (Edmonton), 9343-50th St., Unit 4, Edmonton, AB T6B 2L5, Canada. TEL 403-465-3362. FAX 403-448-0424.
circ. 40,000. *7250*

WHERE HALIFAX.
Metro-Guide Publishing, Box 14, 5475 Spring Garden Rd., Halifax, NS B3J 3T2, Canada. TEL 902-420-9943. FAX 902-429-9058.
circ. 24,000. *7262*

WHERE LOS ANGELES.
Where Magazines International (Los Angeles), 3733 Motor Ave., Ste. 301, Los Angeles, CA 90034-6403. TEL 310-280-2880. FAX 310-836-1803.
circ. 50,000. *7262*

WHERE NEW ORLEANS.
V.I.P., 621 Decatur St., 2nd Fl., New Orleans, LA 70130. TEL 504-522-6468. FAX 504-522-0018.
circ. 70,000. *7262*

WHERE NEW YORK.
Where Magazines International (New York), 475 Park Ave. S., Fl. 2100, New York, NY 10016-6901. TEL 212-725-8100. FAX 212-725-3412.
circ. 119,000. *7262*

WHERE OTTAWA - HULL.
Capital Publishers, 400 Cumberland St., Ottawa, ON K1N 8X3, Canada. TEL 613-241-7888. FAX 613-241-3112.
circ. 32,000. *7262*

WHERE PARIS.
Where Magazines International, 6 rue de Ponthieu, 75008 Paris, France. TEL 33-1-53838940. FAX 33-1-53838950.
circ. 40,000. *7262*

WHERE ROCKY MOUNTAINS.
R M V Publications Ltd., Ste. 250, One Palliser Sq., 125 Ninth Ave. S.E., Calgary, AB T2G 0P6, Canada. TEL 403-299-1888. FAX 403-299-1899.
circ. 187,500. *7250*

WHERE ST. LOUIS.
Where Magazines International (St. Louis), 1750 S. Brentwood Blvd., Ste. 311, St. Louis, MO 63144. TEL 314-968-4940. FAX 314-968-0813.
circ. 33,000. *7262*

WHERE SAN FRANCISCO.
Where Magazines International (San Francisco), 74 New Montgomery St., Ste. 320, San Francisco, CA 94105. TEL 415-546-6101. FAX 415-546-6108.
circ. 57,000. *7262*

WHERE SEATTLE.
Where Magazines International (Seattle), 2505 Third Ave., Ste. 305, Seattle, WA 98121. TEL 206-728-2624. FAX 206-728-1423.
circ. 33,000. *7250*

WHERE TORONTO.
Key Publishers Co. Ltd., 6 Church St., Toronto, ON M5E 1M1, Canada. TEL 416-364-3333. FAX 416-594-3375.
circ. 79,000. *7262*

WHERE TWIN CITIES.
Minnesota Monthly Publications, 10 S. Fifth St., Ste. 1000, Minneapolis, MN 55402-1011. TEL 612-339-1619. FAX 612-371-5801.
circ. 30,000. *7262*

WHERE VANCOUVER.
Where Canada, Inc., The Sixth Estate, 2208 Spruce St., Vancouver, BC V6H 2P3, Canada. TEL 604-736-5586. FAX 604-736-3465.
circ. 50,000. *7262*

WHERE VICTORIA.
Key Pacific Publishers Co. Ltd., 1001 Wharf St., 3rd Fl., Victoria, BC V8W 1T6, Canada. TEL 604-388-4324. FAX 604-388-6166.
circ. 22,000. *7262*

WHERE VIENNA.
Orac Zeitschriftenverlag GmbH, Brunner Feldstr. 45, A-2380 Perchtoldsdorf, Austria. TEL 43-1-8696536. FAX 43-1-8696536.
circ. 57,000. *7250*

WHERE WASHINGTON, D.C.
Where Magazines International (Washington, DC), 1225 19th St., N.W., Washington, DC 20036. TEL 202-463-4550. FAX 202-463-4553.
circ. 90,000. *7262*

WHERE WINNIPEG.
Where Magazines International, Fanfare Communications, 128 James Ave., Ste. 300, Winnipeg, MB R3B 0N8, Canada. TEL 204-943-4439. FAX 204-947-5463.
circ. 32,000. *7262*

WHICH AIRLINE? AND BUSINESS TRAVEL UPDATE.
B M I Publications Ltd., Suffolk House, George St., Croydon, Surrey CR9 1SR, England. TEL 44-181-649-7233. FAX 44-181-649-7234.
circ. 45,000. *7250*

THE WHITE PAPER.
Association of Certified Fraud Examiners, 716 West Ave., Austin, TX 78701. TEL 512-478-9070. FAX 512-478-9297.
circ. 14,000. *2289*

THE WHOLESALER.
T M B Publishing, 1838 Techny Ct., Northbrook, IL 60082. TEL 847-564-1127. FAX 847-564-1127.
circ. 32,000. *3486*

WHO'S WHO IN CARGO HANDLING.
International Cargo Handling Coordination Association, 71 Bondway, London SW8 1SH, England. TEL 0171-793-1022. FAX 0171-820-1703. *7170*

WHO'S WHO IN ECONOMIC DEVELOPMENT.
American Economic Development Council, 9801 W. Higgins, Ste. 540, Rosemont, IL 60018-4726. TEL 847-692-9944. FAX 847-696-2990.
circ. 2,700. *578*

WHO'S WHO IN RECREATION.
Society of Recreation Executives, Box 520, Gonzale, FL 32560-0520. TEL 904-477-7992. FAX 904-479-8393.
circ. 4,100. *579*

WIADOMOSCI RATUSZOWE.
Urzad Miejski w Cieszynie, Rynek 1, 43-400 Cieszyn, Poland. TEL 48-33-520701. FAX 48-33-511643.
circ. 3,000. *6226*

WIDERHAKEN.
Projektwerkstatt Saasen, Ludwigstr. 11, 35447 Reiskirchen, Germany. TEL 49-6401-903283.
circ. 3,000. *2958*

WILDLANDS NEWS.
Plymouth County Wildlands Trust, Box 2282, Duxbury, MA 02331. TEL 617-934-9018.
circ. 1,300. *2249*

WILDLIFE RESCUE.
Wildlife Rescue Association of British Columbia, 5216 Glencarin Dr., Burnaby, BC V5B 3C1, Canada. TEL 604-526-7275. FAX 604-524-2890.
circ. 2,000. *2249*

WILLIAMS ALUMNI REVIEW.
Williams College, Society of Alumni, Mears House, 75 Park St., Box 38, Williamstown, MA 01267. TEL 413-597-4151. FAX 413-597-4158.
circ. 29,000. *1980*

WILTSHIRE GAZETTE AND HERALD.
Media in Wessex, 100 Victoria Rd., Swindon, Wilts. SN1 3BE, England. TEL 44-1793-528144. FAX 44-1793-542434.
circ. 24,000. *3302*

WINDSPEAKER.
Aboriginal Multi-Media Society of Alberta, 15001 112th Ave., Edmonton, AB T5M 2V6, Canada. TEL 403-455-2700. FAX 403-455-7639.
circ. 3,000. *3050*

WINDY CITY TIMES.
Sentury Publications, Inc., 325 W. Huron St., Ste. 510, Chicago, IL 60610-3617. TEL 312-935-1970. FAX 312-935-1853.
circ. 24,000. *3701*

WINGED HEAD.
Pittsburgh Athletic Association, 4215 Fifth Ave., Pittsburgh, PA 15213. TEL 412-621-2400. FAX 412-321-4541.
circ. 3,500. *1938*

THE WINNING EDGE.
Transportation Communications International Union, 3 Research Pl., Rockville, MD 20850. TEL 301-948-4910. FAX 301-948-1369.
circ. 2,200. *3901*

WIRELESS BUSINESS & TECHNOLOGY.
Phillips Business Information, Inc., 1201 Seven Locks Rd., Potomac, MD 20854. TEL 301-424-3338. FAX 301-309-3847. *2042*

WIRELESS: FOR THE CORPORATE USER.
Wireless Publishing Co., 3 Wing Dr., Ste. 240, Cedar Knolls, NJ 07927. TEL 973-285-1500. FAX 973-285-1519.
circ. 34,000. *2008*

WIRELINE (DALLAS).
American Orthodontic Society, 11884 Greenville Ave., No. 112, Dallas, TX 75243-3537. TEL 972-234-4000. FAX 972-234-4290.
circ. 15,000. *4873*

WIRTSCHAFT NORDHESSEN.
Industrie- und Handelskammer Kassel, Kurfuerstenstr. 9, 34117 Kassel, Germany. TEL 49-561-78910. FAX 49-561-7891290.
circ. 50,000. *1198*

WIRTSCHAFT UND WEITERBILDUNG.
Max Schimmel Verlag GmbH, Im Kreuz 9, 97076 Wuerzburg, Germany. TEL 49-931-2791510. FAX 49-931-2791511.
circ. 30,000. *2514*

WISCONSIN ARCHITECT.
Wisconsin Architect, Inc., 321 S. Hamilton St., Madison, WI 53703-3606. TEL 608-257-8477.
circ. 3,700. *417*

THE WISCONSIN C P A.
Wisconsin Institute of Certified Public Accountants, 235 N. Executive Dr., Brookfield, WI 53008-1010. TEL 414-785-0445. FAX 414-785-0838.
circ. 8,100. *1100*

WISCONSIN DEER & TURKEY SHOW PREVIEW.
Target Communications Corp., 7626 W. Donges Bay Rd., Mequon, WI 53092-3400. TEL 414-242-3990. FAX 414-242-7391.
circ. 25,000. *6889*

WISCONSIN PASTORAL HANDBOOK.
Milwaukee Catholic Press Apostolate, Inc., 3501 S. Lake Dr., Box 07913, Milwaukee, WI 53207-7913. TEL 414-769-3472.
circ. 2,300. *6486*

WISCONSIN SCHOOL NEWS.
Wisconsin Association of School Boards, 122 W. Washington Ave., Madison, WI 53703. TEL 608-257-2622. FAX 608-257-8386.
circ. 5,700. *2580*

WITNESS (FARMINGTON HILLS).
Oakland Community College, 27055 Orchard Lake Rd., Farmington Hills, MI 48334. TEL 810-471-7740.
circ. 1,500. *4366*

WOLKENRIDDER.
K L M Royal Dutch Airlines, Public Relations Bureau, Postbus 7700, 1117 ZR Schiphol Airport, Netherlands. TEL 31-20-6491126. FAX 31-20-6488200.
circ. 42,000. *7250*

WOMAN ACTIVIST.
Woman Activist, Inc., 2310 Barbour Rd., Falls Church, VA 22043.
circ. 600. *6002*

WOMAN'S VOICE.
Shelby J. Hoon, Ed. & Pub., Box 454, Kent, OH 44240-0454. TEL 216-673-2990. FAX 216-673-6141.
circ. 20,000. *7337*

WOMEN IN THE ARTS.
National Museum of Women in the Arts, 1250 New York Ave. N.W., Washington, DC 20005-3920. TEL 202-783-5000. FAX 202-393-3234.
circ. 60,000. *473*

WOMENPOLICE.
R.R. 1, Box 149, Deer Isle, ME 04627. TEL 207-348-6976. FAX 207-348-6171.
circ. 3,500. *2282*

WOMEN'S CONTACT BULLETIN.
Public Service Association of New South Wales, G.P.O. Box 3365, Sydney, N.S.W. 2001, Australia. TEL 61-2-92901555. FAX 61-2-92621623.
circ. 9,000. *3901*

WOMEN'S DIGEST.
Women's Digest, Inc., 5111-6 Baymeadows Rd., Ste. 200, Jacksonville, FL 32217. TEL 904-992-7228. FAX 904-992-7230.
circ. 72,500. *7338*

WOMEN'S ENVIRONMENT AND DEVELOPMENT ORGANIZATION NEWS & VIEWS.
Women's Environment and Development Organization (WEDO), 355 Lexington Ave., 3rd fl., New York, NY 10017-6603. TEL 212-973-0325. FAX 212-973-0335.
circ. 20,000. *7338*

WOMEN'S HEALTH NEWSLETTER.
Women's Health, 52 Featherstone St., London EC1Y 8RT, England. TEL 44-171-251-6580. FAX 44-171-608-0928.
circ. 600. *7311*

WOMEN'S HISTORY CATALOG.
National Women's History Project, 7738 Bell Rd., Windsor, CA 95492. TEL 707-838-6000. FAX 707-838-0478.
circ. 250,000. *7349*

WOMEN'S STUDIES QUARTERLY.
Feminist Press at the City University of New York, 311 E. 94th St., New York, NY 10128-5603. TEL 212-360-5790. FAX 212-348-1241.
circ. 3,000. *7349*

WOMEN'S VIEW.
Smith Family, 16 Larkin St., Camperdown, N.S.W. 2050, Australia. TEL 61-2-95504422. FAX 61-2-95576436.
circ. 27,000. *7339*

10412 CONTROLLED CIRCULATION SERIALS

WOMEN'S WORLD.
Jewish Women International, 1828 L St., N.W., Ste. 250, Washington, DC 20036. TEL 202-857-1320. FAX 202-857-1380.
circ. 60,000. *7339*

WOOD DIGEST.
Johnson Hill Press, Inc., 1233 Janesville Ave., Ft. Atkinson, WI 53538. TEL 920-563-6388. FAX 920-563-1702.
circ. 52,000. *3177*

WOOD TECHNOLOGY.
Miller Freeman, Inc., 600 Harrison St., San Francisco, CA 94107. TEL 415-905-2200. FAX 415-905-2232.
circ. 20,600. *3177*

WOODMEN.
Woodmen of the World Life Insurance Society, c/o Billie Jo Foust, Asst. Ed., 1700 Farnam St., Omaha, NE 68102. TEL 402-342-1890. FAX 402-271-7269.
circ. 508,000. *3837*

WOODWORKING.
Action Communications Inc., 135 Spy Court, Markham, ON L3R 5H6, Canada. TEL 905-477-3222. FAX 905-477-4320.
circ. 11,000. *927*

WOOL NEWS.
Wool & Woollens Export Promotion Council, 612-714 Ashoka Estate, 24 Barakhamba Rd., New Delhi 110001, India. TEL 91-11-3315512. FAX 91-11-3314626.
circ. 1,000. *6998*

WOOL SACK.
Mid-States Wool Growers Cooperative, Box 328, Brookings, SD 57006. TEL 605-692-2324. FAX 605-692-8182.
circ. 18,000. *6998*

WORCESTER BUSINESS JOURNAL.
Worcester Publishing Ltd., 172 Shrewsbury St., Worcester, MA 01604. TEL 508-755-8004. FAX 508-755-8860. *1219*

THE WORD.
Three R Publications, 13 Bevington Rd., Oxford OX2 6NB, England. TEL 44-1865-57411.
circ. 10,000. *3302*

WORD (CINCINNATI).
Word Publications, Inc., 6895 Farmbrook, Cincinnati, OH 45230. TEL 513-231-9673.
circ. 50,000. *4366*

WORD IN LIFE.
Australian Catholic University, P.O. Box 256, Dickson, A.C.T. 2602, Australia. TEL 61-6-62091184. FAX 61-6-62091148.
circ. 800. *6486*

WORD OF LIFE QUARTERLY.
Word of Life Fellowship, Rte. 9, Schroon Lake, NY 12870. TEL 518-532-7111. FAX 518-532-7421.
circ. 50,000. *6383*

WORD OF MOUTH (SAN FRANCISCO).
c/o Delta Dental Plan of CA, Box 7736, San Francisco, CA 94120. TEL 415-972-8300.
circ. 9,000. *4873*

WORDPERFECT REPORT.
WordPerfect Corporation, 1555 N. Technology Way, Orem, UT 84057. TEL 801-225-5000. FAX 801-222-5077.
circ. 2,000,000. *1204*

WORKBOAT INTERNATIONAL.
Rushton Marine Press Ltd., Woodside, Burnhams Rd., Little Bookham, Leatherhead, Surrey KT23 3BA, England. TEL 44-1372-453316. FAX 44-1372-459974.
circ. 7,108. *7170*

WORKERS EDUCATION JOURNAL.
Central Board for Workers Education, 1400 West High Court, Gokulpeth, Nagpur 440010, India.
circ. 2,000. *2514*

WORKING MOMS AND DADS.
Corporate Marketing and Publishing Inc., Box 12217, Tucson, AZ 85732-2217. TEL 520-790-4044.
circ. 10,000. *1859*

THE WORKMEN'S CIRCLE - ARBITER RING CALL.
Workmen's Circle, 45 E. 33 St., New York, NY 10016. TEL 212-898-6800. FAX 212-532-7518.
circ. 30,000. *3050*

THE WORLD & I.
News World Communications, Inc., 3600 New York Ave., N.E., Washington, DC 20002. TEL 202-635-4000. FAX 202-269-9353.
circ. 3,523. *3390*

WORLD BROADCAST NEWS.
Intertec Publishing Corp., 9800 Metcalf, Overland Park, KS 66212-2215. TEL 913-341-1300. FAX 913-967-1898.
circ. 12,500. *2065*

WORLD CRUISE INDUSTRY REVIEW.
Sterling Publications Ltd., 86-88 Edgware Rd., London W2 2YW, England. TEL 44-171-915-9600. FAX 44-171-915-9619.
circ. 7,000. *7170*

WORLD EXPRO.
Sterling Publications Ltd., 86-88 Edgware Rd., London W2 2YW, England. TEL 44-171-915-9600. FAX 44-171-915-9619.
circ. 15,000. *5627*

WORLD FEDERATION FOR MENTAL HEALTH. ANNUAL REPORT.
World Federation for Mental Health, Sheppard & Enoch Pratt Hospital, Box 6815, Baltimore, MD 21285-6815. TEL 410-938-3180. FAX 410-938-3183.
circ. 4,000. *6159*

WORLD GAMING AND LEISURE INDUSTRY REVIEW.
Sterling Publications Ltd., 86-88 Edgware Rd., London W2 2YW, England. TEL 44-171-915-9600. FAX 44-171-915-9619.
circ. 10,000. *4153*

WORLD INDUSTRIAL REPORTER.
Keller International Publishing Corporation, 150 Great Neck Rd., Great Neck, NY 11021. TEL 516-829-9210. FAX 516-829-7265.
circ. 40,093. *4554*

WORLD M & A NETWORK.
International Executive Reports, Ltd., 717 D St., N.W., Ste. 300, Washington, DC 20004-2807. TEL 202-628-7767. FAX 202-628-6618.
circ. 15,000. *1013*

WORLD OF CHABAD.
Lubavitch British Columbia, 5750 Oak St., Vancouver, BC V6M 2V9, Canada. TEL 604-266-1313. FAX 604-263-7934.
circ. 6,000. *3050*

WORLD OUTLOOK.
Baptist Men's Movement, Kingsley, Pontesbury, Shrewsbury, Shrops. SY5 0QH, England. TEL 44-1442-865245. FAX 44-1442-873830.
circ. 1,200. *6447*

WORLD PEACEMAKERS QUARTERLY.
World Peacemakers Inc., 11427 Scottsbury Terr., Germantown, MD 20876-6010. TEL 202-265-7582.
circ. 1,000. *5981*

WORLD PULP AND PAPER TECHNOLOGY.
Sterling Publications Ltd., 86-88 Edgware Rd., London W2 2YW, England. TEL 44-171-915-9600. FAX 44-171-915-9619.
circ. 10,000. *5573*

WORLD STUDENT NEWS.
International Union of Students, 17th November St., P.O. Box 58, 11001 Prague 01, Czech Republic. *2494*

WORLD SUPERYACHT REVIEW.
Sterling Publications Ltd., 86-88 Edgware Rd., London W2 2YW, England. TEL 44-171-915-9600. FAX 44-171-915-9619.
circ. 10,000. *7170*

WORLD VISION.
World Vision, Inc., Box 9716, Federal Way, WA 98063-9716. TEL 206-815-1000. FAX 206-815-3445.
circ. 100,651. *6447*

WORLD WATER AND ENVIRONMENTAL ENGINEERING.
Faversham House Group Ltd., Faversham House, 232a Addington Rd., South Croydon, Surrey CR2 8LE, England. TEL 44-181-651-7100. FAX 44-181-651-7117.
circ. 9,997. *7307*

WORLD WIDE BARACA - PHILATHEA NEWS.
World Wide Baraca-Philathea Union, Tower House, 610 S. Harlem Ave., Freeport, IL 91032-4833.
circ. 600. *6383*

WORLD'S CHILDREN.
Save the Children Fund, Mary Datchelor House, 17 Grove Ln., London SE5 8RD, England. TEL 44-171-703-5400. FAX 44-171-703-2278.
circ. 200,000. *1859*

WORTHING GUARDIAN.
Worthing Guardian Series, 56a Chapel Rd., Worthing, W. Sussex BN11 0HJ, England. TEL 44-1903-209025. FAX 44-1903-201481.
circ. 102,000. *3302*

WRITERS GUILD OF AMERICA, EAST. NEWSLETTER.
Writers Guild of America, East, Inc., 555 W. 57th St., New York, NY 10019. TEL 212-767-7800. FAX 212-582-1909.
circ. 3,500. *4489*

WRITER'S N W.
Media Weavers, 24450 N.W Hansen Rd., Hillsboro, OR 97124. TEL 503-621-3911.
circ. 75,000. *6287*

THE WRITING INSTRUCTOR.
T W I (The Writing Instructor), University of Southern California, THH 440 - MC 0354, Los Angeles, CA 90089-0354. TEL 213-740-3744. FAX 213-741-0377.
circ. 1,000. *4489*

WUQUF.
Edition Wuquf, Postfach 130662, 20106 Hamburg, Germany.
circ. 300. *3530*

WYOMING. DEPARTMENT OF ADMINISTRATION AND INFORMATION. STATE LIBRARY. ANNUAL REPORT DIGEST.
Department of Administration and Information, State Library, Supreme Court Bldg., Cheyenne, WY 82002. TEL 307-777-7281. FAX 307-777-6289. *6201*

WYOMING AGRICULTURE.
Wyoming Farm Bureau Federation, 406 S. 21st St., Box 1348, Laramie, WY 82070. TEL 307-745-4835. FAX 307-721-7790.
circ. 8,000. *165*

WYOMING MINERAL YEARBOOK.
Department of Commerce, Division of Economic and Community Development, 1601 Yellowstone Rd., Cheyenne, WY 82002. TEL 307-777-7284. FAX 307-777-5840.
circ. 1,000. *2376*

WYOMING RURAL ELECTRIC NEWS.
Wyoming Rural Electric Association, Box 380, Casper, WY 82602. TEL 307-234-6152. FAX 307-234-4115.
circ. 31,400. *2692*

X C.
B L A Group Ltd., 5-8 Hardwick St., London EC1R 4RB, England. TEL 44-171-278-7711. FAX 44-171-278-6246.
circ. 100,000. *4154*

X S.
Gold Coast Publishing, Box 14426, Ft. Lauderdale, FL 33302. TEL 305-356-4943. FAX 305-356-4949.
circ. 45,000. *3390*

XAVIER REVIEW.
Xavier University of Louisiana, Box 110C, New Orleans, LA 70125. TEL 504-483-7304. FAX 504-486-2385.
circ. 300. *4490*

XEROX DISCLOSURE JOURNAL.
Xerox Corporation, Xerox Square 05B, Rochester, NY 14644. TEL 716-423-3255.
circ. 500. *5592*

XIANDAI FAXUE.
Xiandai Faxue Zazhishe, Chongqing, Sichuan 630031, People's Republic of China. TEL 0811-9861199.
circ. 50,000. *4047*

XIN SHIXUE.
Xin Shixue Zazhishe, P.O. Box 1-44, Nan-kang, Taipei, Taiwan 11529, Republic of China. TEL 886-2-7829555. FAX 886-2-7868834.
circ. 300. *3541*

XIUCI XUEXI.
Fudan University Press, 220 Handan Rd., Shanghai 200433, People's Republic of China. TEL 86-21-5492222. FAX 86-21-5491875.
circ. 300. *4315*

XTRA!
Pink Triangle Press (Toronto), 491 Church St., Ste. 200, Toronto, ON M4Y 2C6, Canada. TEL 416-925-6665. FAX 416-925-6674.
circ. 37,000. *3701*

Y A B A FRAMEWORK.
Young American Bowling Alliance, 5301 S. 76th St., Greendale, WI 53129. TEL 414-421-4700. FAX 414-421-1301.
circ. 25,000. *6823*

YALE UNIVERSITY. ECONOMIC GROWTH CENTER. THREE YEAR REPORT.
Yale University, Economic Growth Center, Box 208269, New Haven, CT 06520-8269. TEL 203-432-3610. FAX 203-432-3898. *1013*

YAMAGUCHI UNIVERSITY. SCHOOL OF MEDICINE. BULLETIN.
Yamaguchi Daigaku, Igakubu, Kogushi, Ube-shi 755, Japan. *4760*

YARD AND GARDEN.
Johnson Hill Press, Inc., 1233 Janesville Ave., Ft. Atkinson, WI 53538. TEL 920-563-6388. FAX 920-563-6388.
circ. 26,000. *3207*

YEON-GU WEOLBO.
Jeon la Bug-do Gyo Yug Yeon Gu Won, Jeon Ju, S. Korea.
circ. 2,500. *2494*

YINGSHI WENXUE.
Shandong Sheng Yingshi Zhizuo Zhongxin, No. 55, Wenhua Donglu, Jinan, Shandong 250014, People's Republic of China. TEL 86-0531-657715.
circ. 8,000. *4492*

YIQI YIBIAO XUEBAO.
Yiqi Yibiao Xuebao Bianjibu, 25 Xi Binghe Lu, Andingmenwai, Beijing 100011, People's Republic of China. TEL 86-10-6422-6664. FAX 86-10-6422-6687. *3805*

YORK JOURNAL OF CONVOCATION.
Convocation of York, c/o Synodal Secretary, Church House, West Walls, Carlishe CA3 8UE, England.
circ. 400. *6383*

YOU AND YOUR BUSINESS.
Thomas J. Martin, Ed. & Pub., 16 Fox LN, Locust Valley, NY 11560-1119. TEL 516-681-2111. *1649*

YOUNG ARCHAEOLOGIST.
Council for British Archaeology, Bowes Morell House, 111 Walmgate, York YO1 2UA, England. TEL 44-1904-671417. FAX 44-1904-671384.
circ. 1,400. *389*

YOUNG ISRAEL VIEWPOINT.
National Council of Young Israel, 3 W. 16th St, New York, NY 10011. TEL 212-929-1525. FAX 212-727-9526.
circ. 30,000. *5981*

YOUNG MEN'S INSTITUTE. INSTITUTE JOURNAL.
Young Men's Institute, 50 Oak St., San Francisco, CA 94102. TEL 415-621-4948. FAX 415-621-0963.
circ. 4,500. *6383*

YOUNG PEOPLE NOW.
National Youth Agency, 17-23 Albion St., Leicester LE1 6GD, England. TEL 44-116-285-6789. FAX 44-116-247-1043.
circ. 5,000. *6695*

YOUNG TELEGRAPH.
Two-Can Publishing, 346 Old St., London EC1V 9NQ, England. TEL 44-171-684-4000. FAX 44-171-613-3372.
circ. 1,300,000. *1895*

YOUR BABY.
Professional Publishing Associates, 269 Richmond St. W., Toronto, ON M5V 1X1, Canada. TEL 416-596-8680. FAX 416-596-1991.
circ. 190,000. *1860*

YOUR CHURCH.
Christianity Today, Inc., 465 Gundersen Dr., Carol Stream, IL 60188-2498. TEL 630-260-6200. FAX 630-260-0114.
circ. 157,026. *6383*

YOUR HEALTH.
British Columbia Lung Association, 2675 Oak St., Vancouver, BC V6H 2K2, Canada. TEL 604-731-5864. FAX 604-731-5810.
circ. 19,500. *4760*

YOUR ILLINOIS F F A.
Illinois F F A, Box 50, Roanoke, IL 61561. TEL 309-923-7413. FAX 309-923-7618.
circ. 17,000. *165*

YUCA BOLETIN INFORMATIVO.
Centro Internacional de Agricultura Tropical, Apdo. Aereo 6713, Cali, Colombia. TEL 57-2-4450000. FAX 57-2-4450073.
circ. 2,200. *165*

Z A B S REVIEW.
Bureau of Standards, P.O. Box RW 50259, Lusaka, Zambia. TEL 260-1-227171.
circ. 500. *5256*

Z F K - ZEITUNG FUER KOMMUNALE WIRTSCHAFT.
Sigillum-Verlag GmbH, Brohlerstr. 13, 50968 Koeln, Germany. TEL 49-221-3770207. FAX 49-221-3770266.
circ. 20,000. *3764*

Z M P D KWARTALNY BIULETYN INFORMACYJNY.
Zrzeszenie Miedzynarodowych Przewoznikow Drogowych, Grojecka 17, 02-021 Warsaw, Poland. *7181*

ZAHN MAGAZIN.
Quintessenz Verlags GmbH, Ifenpfad 2-4, 12107 Berlin, Germany. TEL 49-30-74006-0. FAX 49-30-7415080.
circ. 48,000. *4873*

ZAJEDNICAR.
Croatian Fraternal Union of America, 100 Delaney Dr., Pittsburgh, PA 15235. TEL 412-351-3909. FAX 412-823-1594.
circ. 40,000. *3051*

ZAKENAUTO.
Misset, Postbus 4, 7000 BA Doetinchem, Netherlands. TEL 31-8340-49911. FAX 31-8340-43839.
circ. 174,000. *7122*

ZAMBIA. MINISTRY OF AGRICULTURE AND WATER DEVELOPMENT. LAND USE BRANCH. SOIL SURVEY REPORT.
Ministry of Agriculture and Water Development, Land Use Branch, c/o Soil Survey Unit, Mount Makulu Research Station, Private Bag 7, Chilanga, Zambia. TEL 260-1-278087. *250*

ZAMBIA LAW JOURNAL.
University of Zambia, School of Law, P.O. Box 32379, Lusaka, Zambia. TEL 260-1-293580. FAX 260-1-253952.
circ. 500. *4049*

ZDANIE.
Oficyna Cracovia, Ul. Miodowa 41, 31-052 Krakow, Poland. TEL 48-12-222289. FAX 48-12-222289.
circ. 1,000. *5981*

ZEITBUEHNE.
Magazin-Verlag Zachl, Lederergasse 67, A-4021 Linz, Austria. TEL 49-7252-67133. FAX 49-7252-68228.
circ. 10,000. *1296*

ZEITSCHRIFT FUER VERKEHRSERZIEHUNG.
Rot-Gelb-Gruen Lehrmittel GmbH, Theodor-Heuss-Str. 3, 38102 Braunschweig, Germany. TEL 0531-809070. FAX 0531-8090721.
circ. 5,000. *7144*

ZERO ONE.
Zero One Publications, 39 Minford Gardens, W. Kensington, London W14 0AP, England.
circ. 600. *3303*

ZGODA.
Polish National Alliance of North America, 6100 N. Cicero Ave., Chicago, IL 60646-4385. TEL 312-286-0500. FAX 312-286-0842.
circ. 72,200. *3051*

ZHIYE YU JIANKANG.
Tianjin Institute of Industrial Hygiene and Occupational Diseases, 221 Ma Chang Rd., Hexi District, Tianjin 300204, People's Republic of China. TEL 3283432.
circ. 100,000. *6255*

ZHIYIN.
Hubei Sheng Funu Lianhehui, Shuiguo Hu, Wuhan, Hubei 430071, People's Republic of China. TEL 7811030. FAX 7811223.
circ. 690,485. *7340*

ZHONGGUO FANGZHI.
China National Textile Council, General Office, Rm. 302, 105 Jiangxi Zhonglu, Shanghai 200002, People's Republic of China. TEL 3233411.
circ. 20,000. *6999*

ZHONGHUA LAODONG WEISHENG ZHIYEBING ZAZHI.
Tianjin Institute of Industrial Hygiene and Occupational Diseases, 211 Ma Chang Rd., Hexi District, Tianjin 300204, People's Republic of China. TEL 86-22-3280264.
circ. 400. *5502*

ZHONGWEN XINXI.
Zhongguo Zhongwen Xinxi Xuehui, P.O. Box 263, Chendu Keji Daxue - Chengdu University of Science and Technology, Chengdu, Sichuan Province, People's Republic of China. TEL 028-581554.
circ. 5,000. *4223*

ZIMBABWE. COTTON RESEARCH INSTITUTE. ANNUAL REPORT.
Ministry of Lands, Agriculture and Rural Resettlement, Research and Specialist Services, P.O. Box 8108, Causeway, Zimbabwe.
circ. 300. *251*

ZIMBABWE RESEARCH INDEX.
Scientific Liaison Office, P.O. Box CY 294, Causeway, Harare, Zimbabwe. TEL 263-4-700573. FAX 263-4-728799.
circ. 500. *6593*

ZINBVN.
Kyoto University, Institute for Research in Humanities, Ushinomiya-cho, Yoshida, Sakyo-ku, Kyoto 606, Japan. *3798*

THE ZONTIAN.
Zonta International, 557 W. Randolph St., Chicago, IL 60661-2206. TEL 312-930-5848. FAX 312-930-0951.
circ. 36,000. *7340*

ZUERCHER OBERLAENDER.
Zuercher Oberlaender, Rapperswilerstr. 1, CH-8620 Wetzikon, Switzerland. TEL 01-9333333. FAX 01-9323232.
circ. 800. *3364*

ZUKUENFTE.
Klartext Verlag, Dickmannstr. 2-4, 45143 Essen, Germany. TEL 49-201-8620628. FAX 49-201-8620622.
circ. 2,000. *6980*

2 X 4.
Editions C.R. Inc., P.O. Box 1010, Victoriaville, PQ G6P 8Y1, Canada. TEL 819-752-4243. FAX 819-758-8812.
circ. 7,959. *3177*

4 WHEEL DRIVE.
Albinsson & Sjoeberg, P.O. Box 529, S-371 23 Karlskrona, Sweden. TEL 46-455-335325. FAX 46-455-311715.
circ. 21,800. *7122*

10414 CONTROLLED CIRCULATION SERIALS

7 DIES.
Premsa Andorrana S.A., Ave. Riberaygua 39, Andorra la Vella, Spain. TEL 34-376-863770. FAX 34-376-863800.
circ. 20,000. *3360*

20 - 20.
Canadian Table Tennis Association, 1600 James Naismith Dr., Gloucester, ON K1B 5N4, Canada. TEL 613-748-5675. FAX 613-748-5705.
circ. 3,000. *6823*

33 METALPRODUCING.
Penton Publishing, 1100 Superior Ave., Cleveland, OH 44114. TEL 216-696-7000. FAX 216-696-1267.
circ. 22,000. *5216*

40 PLUS.
Trustar Ltd., 2020 Universite, 20th Fl., Montreal, PQ H3A 2A5, Canada. TEL 514-383-3400. FAX 514-383-1766.
circ. 600. *3447*

THE 170 NEWS.
International Cessna 170 Association Inc., Box 1667, Lebanon, MO 65536-1667. TEL 417-532-4847. FAX 417-532-4847.
circ. 1,550. *1938*

1590 BROADCASTER.
1590 Broadcasting Corp., 502 W. Hollis St., Box 548, Nashua, NH 03061. TEL 603-889-1590. FAX 603-883-4344.
circ. 63,500. *2065*

U.S. Newspapers User's Guide

This User's Guide refers exclusively to the U.S. Newspaper Section of Volume 5, which contains a comprehensive listing of general-interest daily and weekly newspapers published in the United States. *Subject-oriented newspapers* from the United States, and *all* newspapers from the rest of the world are subject-classified are listed in the CLASSIFIED LIST OF SERIALS, Volumes 1-3 of **Ulrich's**.

This volume is arranged in several sections: DAILY NEWSPAPERS, detailed citations of daily newspapers filed alphabetically by state, city, and newspaper name; WEEKLY NEWSPAPERS, detailed citations of weekly newspapers filed alphabetically by state, city, and name; TITLE INDEX; DAILY NEWSPAPERS INDEX, WEEKLY NEWSPAPERS INDEX, GEOGRAPHIC INDEX, and CESSATIONS INDEX.

This User's Guide is separated into three divisions for ease of use: I) Section Descriptions, II) Full Entry Content Description, and III) Alphabetizing Rules for Main Entry Title.

Section Descriptions

DAILY NEWSPAPERS

This section comprises active U.S. general-interest newspapers that are published four or more days per week. All titles are active and are arranged alphabetically by state, city, and newspaper name. A (▼) appears in front of new titles that began publication in 1995, 1996 or 1997.

WEEKLY NEWSPAPERS

This section comprises active U.S. general-interest newspapers that are published three or less days per week. All titles are active and are arranged alphabetically by state, city, and newspaper name. A (▼) appears in front of new titles that began 1995, 1996 or 1997.

TITLE INDEX

The TITLE INDEX is a major point of access to the newspapers contained in Volume 5 of **Ulrich's**. Only U.S.-based general-interest daily and weekly newspaper titles listed in Volume 5 are included in this index; the titles of other types of serials, as well as titles of subject-specific newspapers from the U.S. and all categories of newspapers from the rest of the world, can be found in the main TITLE INDEX in Volume 4 of **Ulrich's**.

The TITLE INDEX lists all current and ceased newspapers in this directory. The city and state of publication appear in parentheses next to the newspaper title. Boldface type indicates the page number where the complete entry can be found in Volume 5.

Prior to using the TITLE INDEX, a user should become familiar with title alphabetizing rules as described in the "Alphabetizing Rules for Main Entry Title" paragraphs of this User's Guide on p. liii. Newspapers with identical titles are sorted alphabetically by their two-letter state abbreviation. A (▼) appears in front of titles that began publication in 1995, 1996 or 1997. A dagger (†) appears in front of titles known to have ceased publication. No page references are listed for ceased titles, as full entries for such titles do not appear in this directory.

DAILY NEWSPAPER INDEX

The DAILY NEWSPAPER INDEX is a subset of the TITLE INDEX. Daily newspapers are segregated and listed alphabetically by title. The city and state of publication appear in parentheses next to the daily newspaper title. **Boldface** type indicates the page number where the complete entry can be found in Volume 5. Newspapers with identical titles are sorted alphabetically by their two-letter state abbreviation. A (▼) appears in front of titles that began publication in 1995, 1996 or 1997. A dagger (†) appears in front of titles known to have ceased publication. No page references are listed for ceased titles, as full entries for such titles do not appear in this directory.

WEEKLY NEWSPAPER INDEX

The WEEKLY NEWSPAPER INDEX is a subset of the TITLE INDEX. Weekly newspapers are segregated and listed alphabetically by title. The city and state of publication appear in parentheses next to the weekly newspaper title. **Boldface** type indicates the page number where the complete entry can be found in Volume 5. Newspapers with identical titles are sorted alphabetically by their two-letter state abbreviation. A (▼) appears in front of titles that began publication in 1995, 1996 or 1997. A dagger (†) appears in front of titles known to have ceased publication. No page references are listed for ceased titles, as full entries for such titles do not appear in this directory.

GEOGRAPHIC INDEX

All daily and weekly newspaper titles are sorted alphabetically by state. The city name appears in parentheses following each title. **Boldface** type indicates the page number where the complete entry will be found in Volume 5. A (▼) appears in front of titles that began publication in 1995, 1996 or 1997. A dagger (†) appears in front of titles known to have ceased publication. No page references are listed for ceased titles, as full entries for such titles do not appear in this directory.

CESSATION INDEX

In this section, titles of newspapers known to have ceased publication are listed alphabetically by title. The city name appears in parentheses following each title. No page references are listed, as full citations for these titles do not appear in this directory.

Full Entry Content Description

Basic Information
The following items are mandatory for listing and appear in all entries: country code, main entry title, frequency of publication, address, and owner name. Other items listed are not mandatory and are also briefly described below.

Country Code
The country code is centered in the top line over each entry. The only country code appearing is "US" which is the country code for the United States.

ISSN
The ISSN for the main entry title is printed immediately following the country code. Not all publications have been assigned an ISSN, and lack of a number does not render a publication ineligible for listing.

Title Information
The main title is printed in boldfaced, uppercased lettering as the first item of an entry. Titles are listed alphabetically within their respective states and cities. Former titles, if known, are given at the end of an entry; they are preceded by a boldfaced notation "**Formerly:**."

A (▼) printed before the title indicates that the title began publishing in 1995, 1996 or 1997.

Year First Published
The year first published is given if provided by the publisher.

Frequency
The frequency of a publication is given in abbreviated form such as "d." for daily, "w." for weekly. For newspapers published less than seven days per week, the days of the week the newspaper is published are given, if known. Abbreviations for frequency notations are listed in the "General Abbreviations" on p. liv.

Price
The price is listed in U.S. dollars. The price may be given for annual subscriptions, per copy, per month, in state, out of county, and so forth. There may be several price structures, depending on the information received from the publisher.

Address, Telephone and Fax Numbers, E-mail and Web Site Addresses
The location address, telephone and fax number, e-mail address and Uniform Resource Locator (URL), if available, are listed in each entry.

Owner Information
The name of the owner of a newspaper is listed. Usually the owner address, telephone, and fax number are also listed. Occasionally there will be more than one owner listed. The owner address may differ from the location address. This information is preceded by the boldfaced notation "**Owner(s):**."

Editor
One name is given, preceded by the notation "Ed." This person may be the Editor-in-Chief, the Managing Editor, or another high-ranking editor. Advanced degrees and titles are omitted; the absence of a title does not mean the editor does not have one.

Publisher
One name is given preceded by the notation "Pub." Advanced degrees and titles are omitted; the absence of a title does not mean the publisher does not have one.

Advertising
If advertising is accepted or included, and no advertising contact name or advertising rate have been provided by the publisher, the abbreviation "adv." prints in the entry.

USER'S GUIDE   liii

Advertising Rate and Contact Name

When provided by the publisher, an advertising contact name and/or display rate are listed. The name is preceded by the words "adv. contact:." The price is preceded by the words "adv. rate:."

Special Features

A listing of special features may include such items as book reviews or photos.

Publication Size

If known, the trim size of the newspaper is listed. The size, such as "tabloid" will be preceded by the words "pub. size:."

Circulation

All circulation figures used are approximate. Circulation is given only if provided by the publisher. Various types of circulations may be noted, such as "paid," "free," or "controlled." There may be more than one circulation figure and more than one type of circulation listed. If the type of circulation is not known, only the circulation figure will be listed. All circulation data are preceded by the notation 'circ." If the circulation figures are known to pertain to either Sunday, evening, or morning circulation, or a combination thereof, such information is noted.

Wire Services

If a newspaper is known to use one or more news or photo wire services, abbreviations or names of the services are listed in the entry. Such information is preceded by the boldfaced words "**Wire Service(s):**." Abbreviations for wire services used are listed in the "General Abbreviations" on p. liv.

Alphabetizing Rules for Main Entry Title

Titles are filed in strict alphabetical order, without regard to acronyms, abbreviations, or spaces; for example:

> *Saint Louis* before *St. Louis*
>
> *Newport Daily News* before *New Rochelle Standard-Star*
>
> *St. Louis News* between *Stillwater Gazette* and *Stockton Record.*

Hyphenated titles will sort before unhyphenated titles; for example:

> *News-Tribune* before *News Advance* and *News Tribune*

Articles at the beginning of titles are omitted, or are bypassed in filing.

In an index, when two or more titles with the same name are listed, the titles will sort alphabetically on the two-letter state abbreviations.

SAMPLE ENTRY

❶ ALASKA
❷ KODIAK
        ❸ US   **❹** ISSN 0740-2112

❺ KODIAK DAILY MIRROR.   **❻** 1940 **❼** Mon.-Fri. **❽** $.50 newsstand; $8/mo. local.
❾ 1419 Selig St., Kodiak, AK 99615. **❿** TEL 907-486-3227; **⓫** FAX 907-486-3088.
⓬ E-mail: nfreeman@dailymirror.com; URL: http://www.nfreeman@dailymirror.com
⓭ Owner(s): Kodiak Publishing Co., Inc., 1419 Selig St., Kodiak, AK 99615, TEL 907-486-3227;
⓮ Ed. Andy Hall; **⓯** Pub. Nancy Freeman; **⓰** adv. contact: Amy Willis. **⓱** adv. rate: $12.50/SAU;
⓲ photos; **⓳** pub. size: tabloid; **⓴** circ. evening, 3,000 (paid); Sun. 3,000 (paid).
㉑ Wire service(s): AP.
        ㉒ Formerly: Kodiak Mirror

KEY

❶ State
❷ City
❸ Country Code
❹ ISSN
❺ Title
❻ First Published
❼ Frequency
❽ Price
❾ Address
❿ Telephone
⓫ Fax
⓬ E-mail; URL
⓭ Owner(s)
⓮ Editor
⓯ Publisher
⓰ Advertising Contact
⓱ Advertising Rate
⓲ Special Features
⓳ Publication Size
⓴ Circulation
㉑ Wire Service(s)
㉒ Former Title(s)

Abbreviations
General Abbreviations and Special Symbols

3/m.	3 times per month	CST	Chicago Sun Times
3/yr.	3 times per year	Ct.	Court
a.	annual	CT-NYT	Chicago Tribune-New York Times
abstr.	abstracts	Ctr.	Center
adv.	advertising	CUP	Canadian United Press
Affs.	Affairs	cy.	county
aft.	afternoon	d.	daily
AP	Associated Press	Dec.	December
API	Allied Press International	deliv.	delivery
approx.	approximately	Dept.	Department
Apr.	April	Dgn.	Design
Assn.	Association	Dir.	Director
Asst.	Assistant	DJ	Dow Jones
Aug.	August	Dr.	Drive
Ave.	Avenue	E.	East
Bd.	Board	ea.	each
Bhd.	Brotherhood	Ed.	Editor
bi-m.	every 2 months	Ent.	Entertainment
bi-w.	biweekly	ERR	Editorial Research Reports
bibl.	bibliography	exc.	except
Bldg.	Building	Expy.	Expressway
Blvd.	Boulevard	Feb.	February
BPS	Black Press Service	FIELD	Field News Service (formerly Chicago Daily News Sun Times)
BUP	British United Press		
BW	Business Wire	Fl.	Floor
c/o	care of	fortn.	fortnightly
CanP	Canadian Press	Fri.	Friday
CaNS	Catholic News Service	Ft.	Fort
CEO	Chief Executive Officer	Fwy.	Freeway
CFO	Chief Financial Officer	Gen.	General
CiNS	City News Service	GNS	Gannett News Service
Cir.	Circle	Govt.	Government
circ.	circulation	GrNS	Graham News Service
Clas.	Classified	HHS	Hearst Headline Service
CN	Capital News	Hwy.	Highway
CNS	Copley News Service	in.	inch
col.	column	Int'l.	International
Comns.	Comminications	IPN	International Photo News
Comp.	Composer	irreg.	irregularly
contr.	controlled	ITNA	Independent Television News Association, Inc.
COO	Chief Operating Officer		
Coord.	Coordinator	Jan.	January
CQ	Congressional Quarterly Service	Jct.	Junction
CSM	Christian Science Monitor	Jul.	July

Jun.	June	q.	quarterly
KNS	Knight News Service	qtr.	quarter
KNT	Knight News-Tribune News Service	Rd.	Road
KR	Knight-Ridder	rec.	recording
LAT-WP	Los Angeles Times-Washington Post News Service	rev.	review
		R.D.	Rural Delivery
LDE	London Daily News	Rels.	Relations
lit.	literature	Rm.	Room
Ln.	Lane	RN	Reuters News Agency
LT	Times of London	Rte.	Route
m.	monthly	s-a.	twice annually
Mar.	March	s-m.	twice monthly
MG	Manchester Guardian	s-w.	twice weekly
Mgmt.	Management	S.	South
Mgr.	Manager	Sat.	Saturday
Mktg.	marketing	SAU	Standard Advertising Unit
Mng.	Managing	SC	Southern News Service
MNS	Massachusetts News Service	Sep.	September
mo.	month	SHNA	Scripps-Howard Newspaper Alliance
Mon.	Monday	sing.	single
morn.	morning	Sq.	Square
mult.	multiple	St.	Street
N	National News Service	Sta.	Station
N.	North	Ste.	Suite
Nat'l.	National	Sun.	Sunday
NEA	Newspaper Enterprises Association	Supvr.	Supervisor
NENS	New England News Service	Svcs.	Services
NNS	Newhouse News Service	Terr.	Terrace
Nov.	November	Thu.	Thursday
NWS	National Weather Service	Tpke.	Turnpike
NYT	New York Times	Tue.	Tuesday
Oct.	October	UPI	United Press International
ONS	Ottawa News Service	W.	West
P	Pacific News Service	w.	weekly
Pbcty.	Publicity	wd.	word
pg.	page	Wed.	Wednesday
Pk.	Park	WIP	Washington International Report
Pkwy.	Parkway	wk.	week
Pl.	Place	WN	World News
Plz.	Plaza	WNS	Women's News Service
Pres.	President	WWD	Women's Wear Daily
Prod.	product	yr.	year
Prodn.	production	†	denotes ceased title
Promo.	promotion	▼	denotes newly published title
pub.	publication		
Publ.	Publisher		

United States Abbreviations

AK	Alaska	NY	New York
AL	Alabama	OH	Ohio
AR	Arkansas	OK	Oklahoma
AZ	Arizona	OR	Oregon
CA	California	PA	Pennsylvania
CO	Colorado	RI	Rhode Island
CT	Connecticut	SC	South Carolina
DC	District of Columbia	SD	South Dakota
DE	Delaware	TN	Tennessee
FL	Florida	TX	Texas
GA	Georgia	UT	Utah
HI	Hawaii	VA	Virginia
IA	Iowa	VT	Vermont
ID	Idaho	WA	Washington
IL	Illinois	WI	Wisconsin
IN	Indiana	WV	West Virginia
KS	Kansas	WY	Wyoming
KY	Kentucky		
LA	Louisiana		
MA	Massachusetts		
MD	Maryland	**Canadian Province Abbreviations**	
ME	Maine		
MI	Michigan	AB	Alberta
MN	Minnesota	BC	British Columbia
MO	Missouri	MB	Manitoba
MS	Mississippi	NB	New Brunswick
MT	Montana	NF	Newfoundland
NC	North Carolina	NS	Nova Scotia
ND	North Dakota	NT	NW Territory
NE	Nebraska	ON	Ontario
NH	New Hampshire	PE	Prince Edward Island
NJ	New Jersey	PQ	Quebec
NM	New Mexico	SK	Saskatchewan
NV	Nevada	YT	Yukon Territory

Daily Newspapers

ALABAMA

ALEXANDER CITY

US ISSN 0738-5110
ALEXANDER CITY OUTLOOK. 1892. Tue.-Sun. $.50/day newsstand; $1.25/Sun.; $97.50/yr. in cy.; $103/yr. out of cy. 548 Cherokee Rd., Alexander City, AL 35010. TEL 205-234-4281; FAX 205-234-6550. **Owner(s):** Tallapoosa Publishers, Inc., P.O. Box 999, Alexander City, AL 35010. TEL 205-234-4281; Ed. K.A. Turner; Pub. Bruce Wallace; adv. contact: Billy McGhee. photos; pub. size: broadsheet; circ. morning 6,200(paid); Sun. 6,200(paid). **Wire Service(s):** AP.

ANDALUSIA

US
ANDALUSIA STAR NEWS. Tue.-Sat. $.50 newsstand; $21/3 mos. in cy.; $24/3 mos. out of cy. 207 Dunson St., Andalusia, AL 36420. TEL 334-222-2402; FAX 334-222-6597. **Owner(s):** Boone Newspapers, Inc., P.O. Box 2370, Tuscaloosa, AL 35403. TEL 407-338-3298; Ed. Greg Mc Cord; Pub. Bill Beckner; adv. contact: Ruck Ashworth. pub. size: broadsheet; circ. morning 4,000(paid).

ANNISTON

US
ANNISTON STAR. 1883. d. $.50/day newsstand; $1/Sun.; $10/mo. carrier. 216 W. Tenth St., Anniston, AL 36201. TEL 205-236-1551; FAX 205-231-0027. **Owner(s):** Consolidated Publishing Co., 216 W. Tenth St., Anniston, AL 36201. TEL 205-236-1551; FAX 205-231-0027; Ed. H. Brandt Ayers; Pub. H. Brandt Ayers; adv. contact: Ken Warren. photos; bk.rev.; pub. size: broadsheet; circ. evening 31,500(paid); Sun. 35,000(paid). **Wire Service(s):** AP, NYT, KRT.

ATHENS

US ISSN 0739-1307
NEWS-COURIER. 1880. Tue.-Fri. & Sun. $.35/day newsstand; $1/Sun.; $50/yr.; $26.50/26 wks. Houston & Green Sts., Athens, AL 35611. TEL 205-232-2720; FAX 205-233-7753. **Owner(s):** News-Courier, Inc., P.O. Drawer 190, Cullman, AL 35056. TEL 205-232-2720; Ed. Sonny Turner; Pub. Robert Bryan; adv. contact: Linda Williams. adv.: $5.70/SAU local; $7.70/SAU national. photos; pub. size: broadsheet; circ. morning 8,479(paid); Sun. 8,479(paid). **Wire Service(s):** AP.

BIRMINGHAM

US ISSN 0899-0050
BIRMINGHAM NEWS. 1888. d. $.35/day newsstand; $1.25/Sun.; $123.60/yr. local; $248.40/yr. out of state. 2200 Fourth Ave., N., Birmingham, AL 35203. TEL 205-325-2237; FAX 205-325-3217; E-mail: rogernelson@earthlink.net. **Owner(s):** Newhouse Newspapers, 1101 Connecticut Ave., N.W., Washington, DC 20036. TEL 202-383-7800; Ed. James E. Jacobson; Pub. Victor H. Hanson, II; adv. contact: Roger Nelson. photos; bk.rev.; pub. size: broadsheet; circ. morning 181,620(paid); Sun. 205,245(paid). **Wire Service(s):** AP, NNS, KNS, CSM.

US ISSN 1040-1571
BIRMINGHAM POST-HERALD. 1870. Mon.-Fri. $.35 newsstand; $54/yr. 2200 Fourth Ave., N., Birmingham, AL 35203. TEL 205-325-2214; FAX 205-325-2410; E-mail: postherald@aol.com; URL: http://www.postherald.com. **Owner(s):** Scripps-Howard, 312 Walnut St., 26th Fl., Cincinnati, OH 45202. TEL 513-977-3000; Ed. Jim Willis. adv. contact: Tom Lager. photos; bk.rev.; pub. size: broadsheet; circ. evening 31,000(paid). **Wire Service(s):** AP, SHNS, NYT.

CULLMAN

US
CULLMAN TIMES. 1901. d. $.35/day newsstand; $1/Sun.; $52/yr. in cy.; $80.88/yr. out of cy.; $46.80/yr. senior citizens. 300 Fourth Ave., S.E., Cullman, AL 35055. TEL 205-734-2131; FAX 205-737-1020. **Owner(s):** Robert Bryan, 300 Fourth Ave., S.E., Cullman, AL 35055. TEL 205-734-2131; FAX 205-737-1020; Ed. David Poynor; Pub. Robert Bryan; adv. contact: Robert Camp. pub. size: broadsheet; circ. morning 11,759(paid); Sun. 12,939(paid). **Wire Service(s):** AP.

DECATUR
US
DECATUR DAILY. 1912. d. $.25/day newsstand; $1.25/Sun.; $108/yr. 201 First Ave., S.E., Decatur, AL 35601. TEL 205-353-4612; FAX 205-340-2392. **Owner(s):** Tennessee Valley Printing Co., Inc., 201 First Ave., S.E., Decatur, GA 35601. TEL 205-353-4612; Ed. Barrett C. Shelton, Jr.; photos; bk.rev.; pub. size: broadsheet; circ. evening 31,000(paid); Sun. 32,000(paid). **Wire Service(s):** AP, NYT, SHNA.

DOTHAN
US
DOTHAN EAGLE. d. $.50/day newsstand; $1.25/Sun.; $129.60/yr. 227 N. Oates, Dothan, AL 36302. TEL 334-792-3141; FAX 334-712-7975. **Owner(s):** Thomson Newspapers, Inc., One Station Pl., Stamford, CT 06902. TEL 203-428-2500; Ed. Terry Conner; Pub. Stanley Warren; adv. contact: Rick Chapman. photos; pub. size: standard; circ. evening 38,000(paid); Sun. 40,000(paid). **Wire Service(s):** AP.

ENTERPRISE
US
ENTERPRISE LEDGER. 1898. Sun.-Fri. $.50/day newsstand; $1.25/Sun.; $123/yr. 106 N. Edwards St., Enterprise, AL 36330. TEL 205-347-9533; FAX 205-347-0825. **Owner(s):** Thomson Newspapers, Inc., 3150 Des Plaines Ave., Des Plaines, IL 60014. TEL 708-299-5544; Pub. Rick Martin; adv.; pub. size: broadsheet; circ. morning 9,471(paid); Sun. 10,800(paid).

FLORENCE
US ISSN 0743-1511
TIMES DAILY. 1869. d. $.50/day newsstand; $1.25/Sun.; $135/yr. 219 W. Tennessee St., Florence, AL 35630. TEL 205-766-3434; FAX 205-740-4717; E-mail: timesdly@timesdaily.com; URL: http://www.timesdaily.com/tdnewspa.html. **Owner(s):** New York Times Co., The, 229 W. 43rd St., New York, NY 10036. TEL 212-556-1234; Ed. Kathy Silverberg; Pub. Frank Helldermann; pub. size: broadsheet; circ. morning 34,000(paid); Sun. 36,000(paid). **Wire Service(s):** UPI.

FORT PAYNE
US
TIMES-JOURNAL, THE. 1879. Tue.-Sat. $.50/day newsstand; $.75/Sat. & Sun.; $60/yr. 811 Greenhill Blvd., Fort Payne, AL 35967. TEL 205-845-2550; FAX 205-845-7459. **Owner(s):** Southern Newspapers, Inc., 1050 Wilcrest Dr., Houston, TX 77042. TEL 713-266-5481; Ed. William Bynum; Pub. Ben Shurett; adv. contact: Sharon Beene. pub. size: broadsheet; circ. evening 6,500(paid). **Wire Service(s):** AP.

GADSDEN
US
GADSDEN TIMES. 1867. d. $.50/day newsstand; $1.25/Sun.; $8.41/mo. 401 Locust, Gadsden, AL 35901. TEL 205-549-2000; FAX 205-549-2105. **Owner(s):** New York Times Co., The, 229 W. 43rd St., New York, NY 10036. TEL 212-556-1234; Pub. Roger Hawkins; pub. size: broadsheet; circ. morning 30,000(paid); evening 30,637; Sun. 33,005. **Wire Service(s):** AP, NYT.

HUNTSVILLE
US
HUNTSVILLE TIMES, THE. 1910. d. $.25/day newsstand; $1.25/Sun. newsstand; $10.50/mo. carrier; $126/yr.; $72/yr. Sun. 2317 S. Memorial Pkwy., Huntsville, AL 35801. TEL 205-532-4000; FAX 205-532-4420; E-mail: jdestel@travellers.com; URL: http://www.htimes.com. **Owner(s):** Newhouse Newspapers, 1101 Connecticut Ave., N.W., Ste. 300, Washington, DC 20036. TEL 202-383-7800; Ed. Melinda Joiner. adv. contact: William Joyner, Jr. photos; bk.rev.; pub. size: broadsheet; circ. evening 60,000(paid); Sun. 83,000(paid). **Wire Service(s):** AP, LAT-WP, NNS, KR.

JASPER
US ISSN 0893-0759
JASPER DAILY MOUNTAIN EAGLE. 1872. Sun.-Fri. $.35/day newsstand; $.75/Sun.; $9/mo.; $108/yr. 1301 Viking Dr., Jasper, AL 35501. TEL 205-221-2840; FAX 205-221-6203. **Owner(s):** Cleveland Newspapers, Inc., Cleveland, TN; Ed. Steve Cox; Pub. R. Douglas Pearson, Jr.; adv.; photos; bk.rev.; pub. size: broadsheet; circ. evening 14,200(controlled & paid); Sun. 149,000(controlled & paid). **Wire Service(s):** AP.

LANETT
US
VALLEY TIMES-NEWS. 1950. Mon.-Fri. $.50 newsstand; $5.50/mo. 220 N. 12th St., Lanett, AL 36863. TEL 334-644-1101; FAX 334-644-5587. **Owner(s):** Valley Newspapers, Inc., 220 N. 12th St., Lanett, AL 36863. TEL 334-644-1101; Ed. Cy Wood; Pub. Cy Wood; adv. contact: Bridge Turner. adv.: $6.75/SAU. pub. size: broadsheet; circ. evening 15,000(free & paid). **Wire Service(s):** AP.
Formerly: Lanett Valley Times-News.

MOBILE
US
MOBILE REGISTER, THE. 1932. d. $.50/day newsstand; $1/Sun.; $9.95/mo. carrier. 304 Government St., Mobile, AL 36602. TEL 334-433-1551; FAX 334-434-8662; E-mail: mobile.eds@dibbs.com; URL: http://www.mobileregister.com. **Owner(s):** Newhouse Publishing, Inc., Syracuse, NY 13321; Ed. Mike Marshall; Pub. Howard Bronson; adv. contact: Larry Wooley. photos; pub. size: broadsheet; circ. morning 110,000(paid); Sun. 128,000(paid). **Wire Service(s):** CST, NNS, AP, LAT-WP, SHNA, KNT.

MONTGOMERY
US ISSN 0892-4457
MONTGOMERY ADVERTISER. 1827. d. $.50/day newsstand; $1.25/Sun. 200 Washington Ave., Montgomery, AL 36101-1000. TEL 334-262-1611; FAX 334-261-1505. **Owner(s):** Gannett Company, Inc., 1100 Wilson Blvd., Arlington, VA 22340. TEL 703-284-6000; Ed. Jim Tharpe; Pub. Thomas A. Bookstaver; adv. contact: Leo Pieri. photos; bk.rev.; pub. size: broadsheet; circ. morning 65,000(paid); Sun. 85,000(paid). **Wire Service(s):** AP, KR, SHNA.
Formerly: Advertiser, The.

OPELIKA
US ISSN 1044-7539
OPELIKA-AUBURN NEWS. 1903. Sun.-Fri. $.35/day newsstand; $1/Sun.; $107.25/yr. 3505 Pepperell Pkwy., Opelika, AL 36801. TEL 334-749-6271; FAX 334-749-1228. **Owner(s):** Thomson Newspapers, Inc., 3150 Des Plaines Ave., Des Plaines, IL 60018. TEL 708-299-5544; Ed. Phil Lucas; Pub. Steven McPhaul; adv. contact: Jack Nolan. pub. size: broadsheet; circ. morning 14,000(paid); Sun. 15,800(paid). **Wire Service(s):** AP.

SCOTTSBORO
US
DAILY SENTINEL, THE. 1887. Tue.-Fri. & Sun. $.50/day newsstand; $.75/Sun.; $69/yr. 701 Veterans Hwy., Scottsboro, AL 35768. TEL 205-259-1020; FAX 205-259-2709. **Owner(s):** Scottsboro Newspapers, Inc., 701 Veterans Hwy., Scottsboro, AL 35768. TEL 205-259-1020; Ed. William Bynum; Pub. Anita F. Bynum; photos; bk.rev.; pub. size: broadsheet; circ. evening 7,000(paid); Sun. 7,500(paid).

SELMA
US ISSN 1043-9129
SELMA TIMES-JOURNAL. 1827. Mon.-Fri. & Sun. $.50/day newsstand; $1.25/Sun.; $10.75/mo. carrier; $32.35/3 mos. carrier; $64.50/6 mos. carrier; $125/yr. carrier. 1018 Water Ave., Selma, AL 36701. TEL 334-875-2110; FAX 334-872-4588. **Owner(s):** Selma Newspapers, Inc., 1018 Water Ave., Selma, AL 36701. TEL 205-875-2110; Ed. Chuck Chandler; Pub. E. Wilson Koeppel; adv. contact: Buddy Hensen. photos; bk.rev.; pub. size: broadsheet; circ. morning 9,257(paid); Sun. 9,798(paid). **Wire Service(s):** AP.

TALLADEGA
US ISSN 1059-6461
DAILY HOME. 1867. Tue.-Sun. $12/mo. 4 Sylacauga Hwy., Talladega, AL 35160. TEL 205-362-1000; FAX 205-249-4315. **Owner(s):** Consolidated Publishing Co., P.O. Box 977, Talladega, AL 35161. TEL 205-362-1000; Ed. Carol Pappas; Pub. Ed Fowler, Jr.; adv. contact: Pam Carden. pub. size: standard; circ. evening 11,000(free & paid); Sun. 41,400(free & paid). **Wire Service(s):** AP.

DAILY NEWSPAPERS

TROY

US   ISSN 1044-0070

MESSENGER, THE. 1866. Tue.-Fri. & Sun. $.50/day newsstand; $1/Sun.; $84/yr. 918 S. Brundidge St., Troy, AL 36081. TEL 334-566-4270; FAX 334-566-4281; E-mail: troymssngr@aol.com. **Owner(s):** Troy Publications, Inc., P.O. Box 727, Troy, AL 36081. TEL 205-566-4281; Ed. Chris Day; Pub. Rick Reynolds; adv. contact: DeeDee Carter. pub. size: broadsheet; circ. morning 5,000(paid); Sun. 5,000(paid).

Formerly: Troy Messenger.

TUSCALOOSA

US

TUSCALOOSA NEWS, THE. 1818. d. $.50/day newsstand; $1.50/Sun.; $11.25/mo.; $135/yr. 2001 Sixth St., Tuscaloosa, AL 35402. TEL 205-345-0505; FAX 205-349-0802. **Owner(s):** New York Times Co., The, 229 W. 43rd St., New York, NY 10036. TEL 212-556-1234; Ed. Ben Windham; Pub. Ron Sawyer; adv. contact: Grady Smith. pub. size: broadsheet; circ. morning 40,316(paid); Sun. 40,929(paid). **Wire Service(s):** AP, NYT.

ALASKA

ANCHORAGE

US   ISSN 0194-6870

ANCHORAGE DAILY NEWS. 1946. d. $.50/day newsstand; $1.50/Sun.; $12.50/mo. Sun. mailed; $30/mo. mailed; $135/yr. carrier. 1001 Northway Dr., Anchorage, AK 99508. TEL 907-257-4200; FAX 907-258-2157; E-mail: 74220.2560@compuserve.com; URL: http://www.adn.com/. **Owner(s):** McClatchy Newspapers, P.O. Box 15779, Sacramento, CA 95852. TEL 916-321-1000; FAX 916-321-1869; Ed. Patrick Dougherty; Pub. Fuller A. Cowell; adv. contact: Dave Kuta. bk.rev.; pub. size: broadsheet; circ. morning 82,310(paid); Sun. 92,728(paid). **Wire Service(s):** Cox, AP, SHNA.

FAIRBANKS

US   ISSN 8750-5495

FAIRBANKS DAILY NEWS-MINER. 1903. d. $.75/day newsstand; $1.50/Sun.; $25.50/mo. in state mailed; $27.75/mo. out of state mailed; $221/yr. in state mailed. 200 N. Cushman St., Fairbanks, AK 99701. TEL 907-456-6661; FAX 907-452-7917. **Owner(s):** Media News Group, 4888 Loop Central Dr., Ste. 525, Houston, TX 77081-2211. TEL 713-295-3800; Ed. Kelly Bostian; Pub. Paul J. Massey; adv. contact: Marilyn Romano. pub. size: broadsheet; circ. morning 20,000(paid); Sun. 25,000(paid). **Wire Service(s):** AP, NYT, McClatchey.

JUNEAU

US

JUNEAU EMPIRE. 1912. Sun.-Fri. $.50/day newsstand; $1.25/Sun.; $52.50/3 mo. 2nd class; $49.50/mo. 1st class. 3100 Channel Dr., Juneau, AK 99801. TEL 907-586-3740; FAX 907-586-3740. **Owner(s):** Morris Communications, 3100 Channel Dr., Juneau, AK 99801. TEL 907-586-3740; Ed. Suzanne Downing; Pub. John A. Winters; adv. contact: Robin H. Paul. pub. size: broadsheet; circ. evening 7,500(paid). **Wire Service(s):** AP, KR, LAT-WP.

KENAI

US

PENINSULA CLARION. 1970. Mon.-Fri. $.50 newsstand; $78/yr. 150 Trading Bay Rd., Kenai, AK 99611. TEL 907-283-7551; FAX 907-283-3299. **Owner(s):** William Morris, III, P.O. Box 3009, Kenai, AK 99611. TEL 907-283-7551; Ed. Lori Evans; Pub. William Morris, III; adv. contact: Michelle Glaves. pub. size: tabloid; circ. morning 5,500(paid). **Wire Service(s):** AP.

KETCHIKAN

US

KETCHIKAN DAILY NEWS. 1936. Mon.-Sat. $.75/day newsstand; $1.50/Sat.; $115/yr. local. 501 Dock St., Ketchikan, AK 99901. TEL 907-225-3157; FAX 907-225-1096. **Owner(s):** Pioneer Printing Co., 501 Dock St., Ketchikan, AK 99901. TEL 907-225-3157; Ed. Belinda Chase; Pub. Tena Williams; adv.; pub. size: broadsheet; circ. 5,823(paid). **Wire Service(s):** AP.

Formerly: Ketchikan Log.

KODIAK

US

ISSN 0740-2112

KODIAK DAILY MIRROR. 1940. Mon.-Fri. $.50 newsstand; $8/mo. local. 1419 Selig St., Kodiak, AK 99615. TEL 907-486-3227; FAX 907-486-3088. **Owner(s):** Kodiak Publishing Co., Inc., 1419 Selig St., Kodiak, AK 99615. TEL 907-486-3227; Ed. Cecil Ranney; Pub. Nancy Freeman; adv. contact: Laurie Skonberg. photos; pub. size: tabloid; circ. evening 3,000(paid). **Wire Service(s):** AP.

SITKA

US

DAILY SITKA SENTINEL. 1939. Mon.-Fri. $.50 newsstand; $80/yr. local. 112 Barracks St., Sitka, AK 99835. TEL 907-747-3219; FAX 907-747-8898. **Owner(s):** Verstovia Corp., 112 Barracks St., Sitka, AK 99835. TEL 907-747-3219; Ed. Thad Poulson; Pub. Thad Poulson; adv. contact: Catherine Bagley. pub. size: broadsheet; circ. evening 2,965(paid). **Wire Service(s):** AP.

AMERICAN SAMOA

PAGO PAGO

US

SAMOA NEWS. 1969. Mon.-Fri. $200/yr. in country; $400/yr. out of country. P.O. Box 909, Pago Pago, AS 96799. TEL 684-633-5599; FAX 684-633-4864. **Owner(s):** Samoa News, P.O. Box 999, Pago Pago, AS 96799; Pub. Lewis Wolman; adv.; photos; bk.rev.; pub. size: tabloid; circ. morning 3,500(paid). **Wire Service(s):** AP, PAC News.

ARIZONA

BISBEE

US

BISBEE DAILY REVIEW. Sun.-Fri. $.50/day newsstand; $1.25/Sun.; $111.60/yr. 12 Main St., Bisbee, AZ 85603-0127. TEL 520-432-2231; FAX 520-432-2356. **Owner(s):** Wick Communications, Inc., 333 Wilcox Dr., Ste. 302, Sierra Vista, AZ 85635. TEL 520-458-0200; Ed. John Moeur; Pub. Walter Wick; adv.; photos; bk.rev.; pub. size: broadsheet; circ. 2,200(paid).

BULLHEAD CITY

US   ISSN 1061-8589

MOHAVE VALLEY DAILY NEWS. 1926. Sun.-Fri. $.50 newsstand; $21.39/3 mos. home deliv.; $35.09/6 mos. senior citizens. P.O. Box 21209, Bullhead City, AZ 86439-8589. TEL 520-763-2505; FAX 520-763-7820. **Owner(s):** Brehm Communications, Inc., 17065 Via del Campo, Ste. 200, San Diego, CA 92127. TEL 619-451-6200; Ed. Darryle Purcell; Pub. Martin Cody; adv. contact: Steve Paterson. photos; bk.rev.; pub. size: broadsheet; circ. morning 9,200(paid); Sun. 8,500(paid). **Wire Service(s):** AP.

Formerly: Bullhead City Mohave Valley News.

CASA GRANDE

US

CASA GRANDE DISPATCH. 1912. Mon.-Sat. $.50 newsstand; $175/yr. in state; $195/yr. out of state. 200 W. Second St., Casa Grande, AZ 85222. TEL 520-836-7461. **Owner(s):** Casa Grande Valley Newspapers, Inc., Box 15002, Casa Grande, AZ 85230-5002. TEL 602-836-7461; Ed. Donovan Kramer, Jr.; Pub. Donovan M. Kramer, Sr.; adv. contact: Kara Cooper. pub. size: broadsheet; circ. evening 9,027(paid). **Wire Service(s):** AP.

CHANDLER

US

CHANDLER ARIZONAN TRIBUNE. d. $.50/day newsstand; $1.75/Sun.; $96/yr. 25 S. Arizona Pl., Ste. 565, Chandler, AZ 85225. TEL 602-821-7474; FAX 602-821-7480. **Owner(s):** Thomson Newspapers, Inc., Metro Centre, One Station Pl., 6th Fl., Stamford, CT 06902. TEL 203-425-2500; FAX 203-425-2516; Ed. Hal DeKeyser. adv.; photos; bk.rev.; pub. size: broadsheet.

US

GILBERT TRIBUNE. d. $.50/day newsstand; $1.75/Sun.; $96/yr. 25 S. Arizona Pl., Chandler, AZ 85225. TEL 602-821-7474; FAX 602-821-7480. **Owner(s):** Thomson Newspapers, Inc., Metro Centre, One Station Pl., 6th Fl., Stamford, CT 06902. TEL 203-425-2500; FAX 203-425-2516; Ed. Jeff Bruce. adv. contact: Ed Moss. photos; bk.rev.; pub. size: broadsheet; **Wire Service(s):** AP, LAT-WP, SHNS, NYT.

US   ISSN 0746-1445

TRIBUNE. 1912. d. $.50/day newsstand; $1.75/Sun.; $10/mo. carrier. 25 S. Arizona Pl., Ste. 565, Chandler, AZ 85225. TEL 602-821-7474; FAX 602-821-7480. **Owner(s):** Thomson Newspapers, Inc., 3150 Des Plaines Ave., Des Plaines, IL 60018. TEL 708-299-5544; Ed. Jim Repley; Pub. Karren Whittmer; adv. contact: Diane Snoble. photos; pub. size: broadsheet; circ. morning 12,000(paid); Sun. 11,000(paid). **Wire Service(s):** AP, LAT-WP, NYT.
   Formerly: Chandler Arizonan Tribune.

DOUGLAS

US

DAILY DISPATCH. 1902. Tue.-Fri. & Sun. $.35/day newsstand; $.50/Sun.; $72/yr. 530 11th St., Douglas, AZ 85607. TEL 520-364-3424; FAX 520-364-6750. **Owner(s):** Wick Communications, Inc., 333 W. Wilcox Dr., Ste. 302, Sierra Vista, AZ 85635. TEL 602-458-0200; Ed. Sharilyn Cox; Pub. Sharilyn Cox; adv.; pub. size: broadsheet; circ. evening 16,800(free & paid); Sun. 5,900(free & paid). **Wire Service(s):** AP.
   Formerly: Douglas Dispatch.

FLAGSTAFF

US   ISSN 1054-9536

ARIZONA DAILY SUN. 1883. d. $.50/day newsstand; $1.25/Sun.; $216/yr. 417 W. Santa Fe Ave., Flagstaff, AZ 86001. TEL 602-774-4545; FAX 602-773-1934. **Owner(s):** Flagstaff Publishing Co., P.O. Box 1849, Flagstaff, AZ 86002. TEL 602-774-4545; Ed. Randy Wilson; Pub. Don Rowley; adv. contact: Theresa Givens. photos; pub. size: broadsheet; circ. evening 13,222(paid); Sun. 14,792(paid). **Wire Service(s):** AP.

KINGMAN

US

KINGMAN DAILY MINER. 1883. Sun.-Fri. $.50/day newsstand; $1/Fri. & Sun.; $6.50/mo. 3015 Stockton Hill Rd., Kingman, AZ 86401. TEL 520-753-6397; FAX 520-753-5661. **Owner(s):** Western Newspapers, Inc., P.O. Box 3909, Yuma, AZ 85365. TEL 602-753-6397; Ed. Tim Wiederaenders; Pub. Kit K. Atwell; adv.; pub. size: broadsheet; circ. evening 8,600(paid); Sun. 9,000(paid). **Wire Service(s):** AP.

LAKE HAVASU CITY

US   ISSN 1068-1884

LAKE HAVASU CITY HERALD. 1964. Tue.-Fri & Sun. $.50/day newsstand; $.75/Sun.; $73.50/yr. in cy.; $132/yr. out of cy. 2225 W. Acoma Blvd., Lake Havasu City, AZ 86403. TEL 520-855-2197; FAX 520-855-2637. **Owner(s):** Wick Communications, Inc., 333 W. Wilcox Dr., Ste. 302, Sierra Vista, AZ 85365. TEL 520-458-0200; FAX 520-458-6166; Western Newspaper, 290 S. First Ave., Ste. 4, Yuma, AZ 85364; Ed. Stan Usinowicz; Pub. Mike Quinn; pub. size: standard; circ. 13,500(paid).

US   ISSN 1068-1876

TODAY'S NEWS-HERALD. 1980. Tue.-Fri. & Sun. $.50/day newsstand; $.75/Sun.; $73.50/yr. in state; $132/yr. out of state. 2225 W. Acoma Blvd., Lake Havasu City, AZ 86403. TEL 520-855-6397; FAX 520-855-2637. **Owner(s):** Wick Communications, Inc., 333 W. Wilcox Dr., Ste. 302, Sierra Vista, AZ 85635. Western Newspapers, Inc., 290 S. First Ave., Ste. 4, Yuma, AZ 85364. TEL 520-783-3311; Ed. Stan Usinowicz; Pub. Michael Quinn; adv. contact: Steven Stevens. pub. size: broadsheet; circ. morning 10,000(paid); Sun. 12,000(paid). **Wire Service(s):** AP.
   Formerly: Lake Havasu City/Today's Daily News; Today's Daily News-Herald.

MESA

US

MESA TRIBUNE. d. $.50/day newsstand; $1.75/Sun.; $96/yr. 120 W. First Ave., Mesa, AZ 85210. TEL 602-898-6500; FAX 602-898-6362; E-mail: coxtrib@prodigy.com. **Owner(s):** Thomson Newspapers, Inc., Metro Centre, One Station Pl., 6th Fl., Stamford, CT 06902. TEL 203-425-2500; FAX 203-425-2516; Ed. Jeff Bruce. adv. contact: Ed Moss. photos; bk.rev.; pub. size: broadsheet; circ. morning 112,963(paid); Sun. 114,007(paid). **Wire Service(s):** AP, LAT-WP, SHNS, NYT.

PHOENIX

US   ISSN 0892-8711

ARIZONA REPUBLIC. 1889. d. $.50/day newsstand; $2/Sun.; $3.50/wk. 200 E. Van Buren St., Phoenix, AZ 85004. TEL 602-271-8000; FAX 602-271-8044. **Owner(s):** Phoenix Newspapers, Inc., P.O. Box 1950, Phoenix, AZ 85001. TEL 602-271-8000; Pub. John Oppedahl; adv. contact: Jeanne Bonham. photos; bk.rev.; pub. size: standard; circ. morning 399,830(paid); Sun. 597,255(paid). **Wire Service(s):** AP, NYT, LAT-WP, KR.

PRESCOTT

US

DAILY COURIER, THE. 1882. Sun.-Fri. $.50/day newsstand; $1.25/Sun.; $9.11/mo. home deliv. 147 N. Cortez, Prescott, AZ 86301. TEL 520-445-3333. **Owner(s):** Prescott Newspapers, Inc., 147 N. Cortez, Prescott, AZ 86301. TEL 520-445-3333; Ed. Jim Garner; Pub. Robert D. Gilliland; adv. contact: Pam Hood. adv.: $12.46/SAU Mon.-Fri.; $13.68/SAU Sun. photos; bk.rev.; pub. size: broadsheet; circ. evening 17,789(paid); Sun. 20,001(paid). **Wire Service(s):** AP, LAT-WP.
   Formerly: Courier.

SCOTTSDALE

US   ISSN 0888-0271

SCOTTSDALE PROGRESS TRIBUNE. 1948. d. $.35/day newsstand; $1.50/Sun.; $1.85/home deliv. 7525 E. Camelback Rd., Ste. 100, Scottsdale, AZ 85251. TEL 602-941-2300; FAX 602-970-2360. **Owner(s):** Thomson Newspapers, Inc., Metro Centre, One Station Pl., 6th Fl., Stamford, CT 06902. TEL 203-425-2500; FAX 203-425-2516; Ed. Hal DeKeyser. adv. contact: Ed Moss. photos; bk.rev.; pub. size: broadsheet; circ. evening 15,545(paid). **Wire Service(s):** AP, LAT-WP, SHNS, NYT.

SIERRA VISTA

US   ISSN 8750-3891

SIERRA VISTA HERALD. 1956. Sun.-Fri. $.50/day newsstand; $1.25 Sun.; $8.80/mo. home deliv. 102 Fab Ave., Sierra Vista, AZ 85635. TEL 520-458-9440; FAX 520-459-0120. **Owner(s):** Wick Communications, Inc., 333 W. Wilcox Dr., Ste. 302, Sierra Vista, AZ 85635. TEL 520-458-0200; Pub. Bob Wick; adv. contact: Dennis Benth. photos; bk.rev.; pub. size: standard; circ. evening 10,500(paid); Sun. 18,000(paid). **Wire Service(s):** AP.

SUN CITY

US

DAILY NEWS-SUN. 1957. Mon.-Sat. $.50 newsstand; $91.20/yr. home deliv.; $135/yr. mailed. 10102 Santa Fe Dr., Sun City, AZ 85351. TEL 602-977-8351; FAX 602-876-3695. **Owner(s):** Ottaway Newspapers, Inc., P.O. Box 401, Campbell Hall, NY 10916. TEL 914-294-8181; Ed. Maryanne Leyshon; Pub. Sam L. Marocco; adv. contact: Jan McKinney. adv.: $12.15/SAU. pub. size: broadsheet; circ. evening 21,200(paid). **Wire Service(s):** AP, ONS.

TEMPE

US   ISSN 0744-2092

TEMPE DAILY NEWS TRIBUNE. 1887. d. $.50/day newsstand; $1.75/Sun.; $10/mo. carrier. 51 W. Third St., Ste. 106, Tempe, AZ 85281. TEL 602-898-5680; FAX 602-968-8030. **Owner(s):** Thomson Newspapers, Inc., Metro Centre, One Station Pl., Stamford, CT 06902. TEL 203-425-2500; FAX 203-425-2616; Ed. Jim Ripley. adv.; pub. size: broadsheet; circ. morning 10,401(paid). **Wire Service(s):** AP, SHNA, LAT-WP, CNS.

TUCSON

US

ARIZONA DAILY STAR. 1877. d. $.50/day newsstand; $1.50/Sun.; $2.90/wk.; $150.80/yr.; $299/yr. mailed. 4850 S. Park Ave., Tucson, AZ 85714-1637. TEL 520-573-4220; FAX 520-573-4107. **Owner(s):** Star Publishing Co., 4850 S. Park Ave., Tucson, AZ 85714. TEL 602-573-4220; Ed. Bobbie Jo Buel; Pub. Michael E. Pulitzer; adv. contact: Paul Ingegneri. pub. size: broadsheet; circ. morning 98,793(paid); Sun. 174,987(paid). **Wire Service(s):** AP, NYT, KR.

DAILY NEWSPAPERS

TUCSON CITIZEN. 1870. Mon.-Sat. $.35 newsstand; $3.50/wk.; $6.50/mo.; $78/yr. mailed; $182/yr. out of city. 4850 S. Park Ave., Tucson, AZ 85714. TEL 602-573-4561; FAX 602-573-4569; E-mail: tcnew@aol.com. **Owner(s):** Gannett Company, Inc., 1100 Wilson Blvd., Arlington, VA 22234. TEL 703-284-6000; Ed. Michael Limou; Pub. C. Donald Hatfield; adv. contact: Paul Ingegneri. photos; bk.rev.; pub. size: broadsheet; circ. evening 60,000(paid). **Wire Service(s):** AP, LAT-WP, GNS.

YUMA
US   ISSN 1048-2237

YUMA DAILY SUN. 1872. d. $.50/day newsstand; $1.25/Sun.; $9.50/mo. 2055 S. Arizona Ave., Yuma, AZ 85364. TEL 602-783-3333; FAX 602-343-1009; E-mail: yumasun@primenet.com; URL: http://www.yumasun.com. **Owner(s):** Thomson Newspapers, Inc., 3150 Des Plaines Ave., Des Plaines, IL 60018. TEL 708-299-5544; Ed. Terry L. Ross; Pub. Sam Pepper; adv. contact: Jerry Collins. photos; pub. size: broadsheet; circ. evening 20,613(paid); Sun. 24,464(paid). **Wire Service(s):** AP.

ARKANSAS

ARKADELPHIA
US

ARKADELPHIA DAILY SIFTINGS HERALD. 1886. Mon.-Fri. $.50 newsstand; $60/yr. in town; $66/yr. rural. 205 S. 26th St., Arkadelphia, AR 71923. TEL 501-246-5525; FAX 501-246-6556. **Owner(s):** Stephens Group, Inc., P.O. Box 1359, Fort Smith, AR 72910. TEL 501-785-7810; Ed. Steve Fellers; Pub. Judith Collis; adv. contact: Lois Baker. pub. size: broadsheet; circ. evening 3,200(paid). **Wire Service(s):** AP.

BATESVILLE
US   ISSN 1076-4801

BATESVILLE GUARD. 1876. Mon.-Fri. $.35 newsstand; $42/yr. 258 W. Main St., Batesville, AR 72501. TEL 501-793-2383; FAX 501-793-9268; E-mail: batguard@intellinet.com. **Owner(s):** Batesville Guard-Record Co., Inc., 258 W. Main St., Batesville, AR 72501. TEL 501-793-2383; FAX 501-793-9268; Ed. Debbie Miller; Pub. Pat Jones; adv. contact: Mike Smith. pub. size: standard; circ. evening 10,000(paid). **Wire Service(s):** AP.

BENTON
US

BENTON COURIER. 1876. Mon.-Fri. $.50 newsstand; $6.25/mo.; $75/yr. mailed in state. 321 N. Market, Benton, AR 72015. TEL 501-315-8228; FAX 501-315-1230. **Owner(s):** Hollinger International, Inc., 401 N. Wabash, Chicago, IL 60611. TEL 312-321-3000; Ed. Steven Brawner; Pub. Rebecca H. Winburn; adv. contact: Marvin Newman. photos; bk.rev.; pub. size: broadsheet; circ. evening 10,000(paid). **Wire Service(s):** AP.

BENTONVILLE
US

BENTON COUNTY DAILY RECORD. 1886. d. $.25/day newsstand; $1/Sun.; $72/yr. mailed. 104 S.W. A St., Bentonville, AR 72712. TEL 501-271-3700; FAX 501-273-7777; E-mail: compub@95aol.com. **Owner(s):** Community Publishers, Inc., P.O. Box 1049, Bentonville, AR 72712. TEL 501-271-3700; Ed. Kent Marts; Pub. Mike Brown; adv.; photos; bk.rev.; pub. size: broadsheet; circ. morning 9,500(paid); Sun. 10,500(paid). **Wire Service(s):** AP.

BLYTHEVILLE
US

COURIER NEWS. 1903. Sun.-Fri. $.50/day newsstand; $.50/Sun.; $7.95/mo. carrier; $87/yr.; $29.70/3 mos. mailed. 900 N. Broadway & Moultrie, Blytheville, AR 72316. TEL 501-763-4461; FAX 501-763-6874. **Owner(s):** Tennyson Publishing, N. Broadway & Moultrie, Blytheville, AR 72316; Ed. Cynthia Jarden; Pub. David Tennyson; pub. size: broadsheet; circ. evening 5,500(paid); Sun. 5,500(paid). **Wire Service(s):** AP, NYT.

CAMDEN
US

CAMDEN NEWS. 1921. Mon.-Fri. $.50 newsstand; $75/yr. home deliv.; $90/yr. mail deliv.; $98/yr. out of cy. 113 Madison Ave., Camden, AR 71701. TEL 501-836-8192; FAX 501-837-1414. **Owner(s):** Camden News Publishing Co., 113 Madison Ave., Camden, AR 71701. TEL 501-836-8192; FAX 501-837-1414; Ed. Jim Edwards; Pub. Walter E. Hussman, Jr.; adv. contact: Sue Parnell. adv.: $7.50/SAU. photos; bk.rev.; pub. size: broadsheet; circ. evening 5,000(paid). **Wire Service(s):** AP.

CONWAY
US

LOG CABIN DEMOCRAT. 1879. Sun.-Fri. $.50/day newsstand; $1/Sun.; $112/yr. out of cy. 1058 Front St., Conway, AR 72032. TEL 501-327-6621; FAX 501-327-6787. **Owner(s):** Morris Communications, P.O. Box 936, Augusta, GA 30903. TEL 706-724-0851; Ed. David Keith; Pub. Mike Hengel; photos; pub. size: broadsheet; circ. evening 11,000(paid); Sun. 13,000(paid). **Wire Service(s):** AP.

DE QUEEN
US

DE QUEEN DAILY CITIZEN. 1933. Mon.-Fri. $.35 newsstand; $84/yr. 404 De Queen Ave., De Queen, AR 71832. TEL 501-642-2111; FAX 501-642-3138. **Owner(s):** De Queen Bee Co., P.O. Box 1000, De Queen, AR 71832. TEL 501-642-2111; Ed. Billy Ray McKelvy; Pub. Ray Kimball; adv. contact: Gail Mitchell. photos; pub. size: broadsheet; circ. evening 2,646(paid). **Wire Service(s):** AP, NEA.

EL DORADO
US

EL DORADO NEWS-TIMES. 1888. d. $.50/day newsstand; $1/Sun.; $24.75/3 mos. 111 N. Madison, El Dorado, AR 71730. TEL 501-862-6611; FAX 501-862-0054. **Owner(s):** Walter E. Husman Jr., 111 N. Madison, El Dorado, AR 71730. TEL 501-862-6611; Ed. George Arnold; Pub. Walter E. Hussman, Jr.; adv. contact: Karen Williams. pub. size: broadsheet; circ. morning 11,800(paid); Sun. 12,050(paid). **Wire Service(s):** AP.

FAYETTEVILLE
US   ISSN 1066-3355

NORTHWEST ARKANSAS TIMES. 1867. d. $.25/day newsstand; $1/Sun.; $72/yr. 212 N. East Ave., Fayetteville, AR 72701. TEL 501-442-1710; FAX 501-442-5477. **Owner(s):** American Publishing Co., 606 N. Van Buren, P.O. Box 520, Marion, IL 62959. TEL 618-993-1711; Pub. Randy Cope; adv. contact: Kaye Hunton. pub. size: broadsheet; circ. morning 14,368(paid); Sun. 14,195(paid). **Wire Service(s):** AP.
Formerly: Fayetteville Arkansas Times.

FORREST CITY
US

FORREST CITY TIMES-HERALD. 1875. Mon.-Fri. $.50 newsstand; $5/mo. in cy; $5.40/mo. out of cy.; $82.50/yr. local; $105/yr. elsewhere. 222 N. Izard St., Forrest City, AR 72335. TEL 501-633-3130; FAX 501-633-0599; E-mail: fctimes@intellinet.com. **Owner(s):** Times-Herald Publishing Co., Inc., P.O. Box 1699, Forrest City, AR 72335. TEL 501-633-3130; Ed. Kersh Hall; Pub. Trent Bonner McCollum; adv. contact: Jim Wirski. pub. size: broadsheet; circ. evening 4,750(paid). **Wire Service(s):** AP.

FORT SMITH
US

SOUTHWEST TIMES RECORD. 1832. d. $8/mo. 920 Rogers Ave., Fort Smith, AR 72901. TEL 501-785-7700; FAX 501-785-7741. **Owner(s):** Stephens Group, Inc., 920 Rogers Ave., Fort Smith, AR 72901. TEL 501-785-7700; Ed. Jerry Huff; Pub. Gene Kincy; adv. contact: Ronnie Bell. pub. size: broadsheet; circ. morning 43,000(paid); Sun. 45,700(paid). **Wire Service(s):** AP.
Formerly: Fort Smith Southwest Times Record.

HARRISON
US   ISSN 1074-0384

HARRISON DAILY TIMES. 1876. Sun.-Fri. $.50/day newsstand; $1/Sun.; $79.50/yr. local; $96/yr. out of state. 111 W. Rush Ave., Harrison, AR 72601. TEL 501-741-2325; FAX 501-741-5632. **Owner(s):** American Publishing Co., 606 N. Van Buren, P.O. Box 520, Marion, IL 62959. TEL 618-993-1711; Ed. Dwain Lair; Pub. Jeff Christenson; adv. contact: Michelle Kennedy. pub. size: standard; circ. evening 11,500(paid); 12,000(paid). **Wire Service(s):** AP.

HELENA

HELENA WEST HELENA DAILY WORLD. 1871. Sun.-Fri. $.50 newsstand; $78/yr. carrier; $84/yr. mailed. 417 York St., Helena, AR 72342. TEL 501-338-9181; FAX 501-338-9184. **Owner(s):** American Publishing Co., 606 N. Van Buren, P.O. Box 520, Marion, IL 62959. TEL 618-993-1711; Ed. Larry Binz; Pub. Ed Trainor; adv. contact: Ann Puckett. photos; bk.rev.; pub. size: broadsheet; circ. evening 7,200(paid). **Wire Service(s):** AP.
Formerly: Helena Daily World.

HOPE

HOPE STAR, THE. 1899. Mon.-Fri. $.50 newsstand; $69/yr. 522 W. Third St., Hope, AR 71801. TEL 501-777-8841; FAX 501-771-3311; E-mail: hopestar@hope.cleaf.com. **Owner(s):** Phillips Media, 215 Mountain Dr., Ste. 101, Destin, FL 32541. TEL 904-837-4040; Ed. Pat Harris; Pub. Ronnie Cupstid; adv. contact: Richard Haycox. pub. size: broadsheet; circ. evening 5,068(paid). **Wire Service(s):** AP.

HOT SPRINGS

SENTINEL-RECORD, THE. 1876. d. $9.50/mo. 300 Spring, Hot Springs, AR 71901. TEL 501-623-7711; FAX 501-623-2984; E-mail: hotsr@direclnx.com. **Owner(s):** Sentinel-Record, Inc., P.O. Box 580, Hot Springs, AR 71902. TEL 501-623-7711; FAX 501-623-2984; Pub. Walter E. Hussman, Jr.; adv. contact: F.E. Emerson. adv.: $17/SAU. bk.rev.; pub. size: broadsheet; circ. morning 17,406(paid); Sun. 19,069(paid). **Wire Service(s):** AP.

JACKSONVILLE

US ISSN 8750-7501
JACKSONVILLE PATRIOT. 1957. Mon.-Fri. $.25 newsstand; $29/yr. in cy.; $51/yr. out of cy.; $76/yr. out of state. 1108 B Main St., Jacksonville, AR 72076. TEL 501-982-6506; FAX 501-985-2054. **Owner(s):** Magie Enterprises, Inc., 903 S. Pine, P.O. Box 1058, Cabot, AR 72023. TEL 501-843-3534; Ed. Jon Parham; Pub. Mark Magie; adv. contact: Susie Magie. photos; pub. size: broadsheet; circ. evening 2,350(paid).
Formerly: Jacksonville Daily News.

JONESBORO

US
JONESBORO SUN. 1903. d. $.35/day newsstand; $1/yr. Sun.; $8.50/mo. 518 Carson St., Jonesboro, AR 72401. TEL 501-935-5525; FAX 501-935-5823. **Owner(s):** Troutt Bros. Inc., 518 Carson, Jonesboro, AR 72401. TEL 501-935-5525; Ed. John Troutt, Jr.; Pub. John Troutt; adv. contact: Jerry P. Donohue. pub. size: broadsheet; circ. morning 27,077(paid); Sun. 30,209(paid). **Wire Service(s):** AP.

LITTLE ROCK

US ISSN 1060-4332
ARKANSAS DEMOCRAT-GAZETTE. 1870. d. $.50/day newsstand; $1.25/Sun.; $10.75/mo. Capitol Ave. & Scott St., Little Rock, AR 72201. TEL 501-378-3400; FAX 501-372-3908; E-mail: news@ardemgaz.com; URL: http://www.ardemgaz.com. **Owner(s):** Little Rock Newspapers, Inc., P.O. Box 2221, Little Rock, AR 72203. TEL 501-378-3400; Ed. Robert Lutgen; Pub. Walter Hussman, Jr.; adv. contact: John Mobbs. pub. size: broadsheet; circ. morning 181,126(paid); Sun. 299,172(paid). **Wire Service(s):** AP, TPNS, SHNA, NYT, KR, LAT-WP.

MAGNOLIA

US
BANNER-NEWS. 1878. d. $1.50 newsstand; $78/yr. 134 S. Washington, Magnolia, AR 71753. TEL 501-234-5130; FAX 501-234-2551. **Owner(s):** Banner-News Publishing Co., P.O. Box 100, Magnolia, AR 71753. TEL 501-234-5130; FAX 501-234-2551; Ed. Melissa Butler; Pub. Walter E. Hussman Jr.; adv. contact: Susan Gill. photos; pub. size: broadsheet; circ. evening 5,000(paid). **Wire Service(s):** AP.
Formerly: Magnolia Banner-News.

MALVERN

US
MALVERN DAILY RECORD. 1916. Mon.-Fri. $6.50/mo.; $78/yr.; $78/yr. mailed out of town. 219 Locust St., Malvern, AR 72104. TEL 501-337-7523; FAX 501-337-1226. **Owner(s):** American Publishing Co., 606 N. Van Buren, P.O. Box 520, Marion, IL 62959. TEL 618-993-1711; Ed. Cleo Beard; Pub. Ron Causey; adv.; photos; pub. size: standard; circ. evening 5,178(paid). **Wire Service(s):** AP.

MOUNTAIN HOME

US ISSN 0745-7707
BAXTER BULLETIN. 1901. Mon.-Sat. $.50 newsstand; $68.64/yr. 16 W. Sixth St., Mountain Home, AR 72653. TEL 501-425-3133; FAX 501-425-5091; E-mail: bulletin@mtnhome.com. **Owner(s):** Gannett Company, Inc., P.O. Box 1688, Greenville, SC 29602; Ed. Linda Leicht; Pub. Betty Barker Smith; adv.; photos; bk.rev.; pub. size: broadsheet; circ. morning 9,900(paid). **Wire Service(s):** AP.
Formerly: Mountain Home Baxter Bulletin.

US
DAILY NEWS. 1985. Mon.-Sat. $.35/day newsstand; $.50/Sun.; $55/yr. local. Hwy. 62, E., Mountain Home, AR 72653. TEL 501-425-6301; FAX 501-424-4488. **Owner(s):** Rupert & Sandra Phillips, 2720 Prosperity Ave., Fairfax, VA 22034-1000. TEL 703-560-4000; Ed. Joe Dobson; Pub. Chuck Pullins; adv. contact: Chuck Pullins. photos; bk.rev.; pub. size: broadsheet; circ. evening 2,000(paid); Sun. 2,000(paid). **Wire Service(s):** AP.
Formerly: North Arkansas View-Daily News.

NEWPORT

US
NEWPORT DAILY INDEPENDENT. 1901. Mon.-Fri. $.50 newsstand; $6.75/mo. carrier; $41.50/6 mos. carrier. 2408 Hwy. 367, N., Newport, AR 72112. TEL 501-523-5855; FAX 501-523-6540. **Owner(s):** American Publishing Co., 606 N. Van Buren, P.O. Box 520, Marion, IL 62959. TEL 618-993-1711; Ed. Patricia Mays; Pub. John Reynolds; adv. contact: John Reynolds. photos; pub. size: broadsheet; circ. evening 3,202(paid). **Wire Service(s):** AP.

PARAGOULD

US
PARAGOULD DAILY PRESS. 1883. Tue.-Sun. $69/yr. 1401 W. Hunt St., Paragould, AR 72450. TEL 501-239-8562; FAX 501-239-8565. **Owner(s):** Paxton Media Group, Inc., P.O. Box 2300, Paducah, KY 42002. TEL 502-443-1771; Ed. Sharon Knight; Pub. Dina Mason; adv. contact: Donna Estes. adv.: $6.50/SAU. pub. size: broadsheet; circ. morning 6,500(paid); 16,500(controlled & free). **Wire Service(s):** AP.

PINE BLUFF

US
PINE BLUFF COMMERCIAL. 1881. d. $.50/day newsstand; $1/Sun.; $7.50/mo. 300 Beech St., Pine Bluff, AR 71601. TEL 501-534-3400; FAX 501-543-1455. **Owner(s):** Stephens Group, Inc., P.O. Box 1359, Fort Smith, AR 72902. TEL 501-785-7700; Ed. Byron Tate; Pub. Charles Berry; adv.; photos; bk.rev.; pub. size: broadsheet; circ. morning 20,000(paid); Sun. 20,000(paid). **Wire Service(s):** AP, KR.

RUSSELLVILLE

US ISSN 1075-1866
COURIER, THE. 1874. Tue.-Sun. $.50/day newsstand; $1/Sun.; $8.25/mo. 201 E. Second St., Russellville, AR 72811. TEL 501-968-5252; FAX 501-968-4037. **Owner(s):** Paducah Newspapers, Inc., 408 Kentucky Ave., Paducah, KY 42002. Ed. Bill Newsom; Pub. Craig Martin; adv.; photos; bk.rev.; pub. size: broadsheet; circ. evening 11,862(paid); Sun. 14,846(paid). **Wire Service(s):** AP.

SEARCY

US ISSN 0747-0401
DAILY CITIZEN. 1854. Sun.-Fri. $.50/day newsstand; $1/Sun.; $7.75/mo. 3000 E. Race Ave., Searcy, AR 72143. TEL 501-268-8621; FAX 501-268-6277. **Owner(s):** Paxton Media Group, Inc., P.O. Box 2300, Paducah, KY 42002. TEL 502-443-1771; FAX 502-442-8188; Ed. Tommy Jackson. adv. contact: Nick Coltharp. photos; bk.rev.; pub. size: broadsheet; circ. morning 6,350(paid); Sun. 10,000(paid). **Wire Service(s):** AP.

SPRINGDALE
US ISSN 1053-9689
MORNING NEWS OF NORTHWEST ARKANSAS. 1886. d. $.25/day newsstand; $1/Sun.; $72/yr. local. 2560 Lowell Rd., Springdale, AR 72765. TEL 501-751-6200; FAX 501-872-5055. **Owner(s):** Don Rey Media Group, P.O. Box 1350, Fort Smith, AR 72902. TEL 501-785-7801; Ed. Rusty Turner; Pub. Tom Stallbaumer; adv. contact: Kent Eikenberry. pub. size: broadsheet; circ. morning 35,000(paid); Sun. 37,000(paid). **Wire Service(s):** AP, LAT-WP, Bloomberg News Service.
Formerly: Morning News & Northwest Arkansas Morning News.

STUTTGART
US
STUTTGART DAILY LEADER. 1889. Mon.-Fri. $.50 newsstand; $57/yr. in cy.; $78/yr. out of cy. 111 W. Sixth St., Stuttgart, AR 72160. TEL 501-673-8533; FAX 501-673-3671. **Owner(s):** American Publishing Co., 606 N. Van Buren, P.O. Box 520, Marion, IL 62959. TEL 618-993-1711; Ed. Rene' Hunter; Pub. Bill Park; adv.; photos; pub. size: broadsheet; circ. evening 4,500(paid). **Wire Service(s):** AP.

WEST MEMPHIS
US
EVENING TIMES. 1931. Mon.-Fri. $.50 newsstand; $66/yr. in cy.; $72/yr. out of cy. 111 E. Bond St., West Memphis, AR 72301. TEL 501-735-1010; FAX 501-735-1020. **Owner(s):** West Memphis Evening Times, 111 E. Bond St., West Memphis, AR 72301. TEL 501-735-1010; Pub. Alexander P. Coulter; adv. contact: Bob Bruce. pub. size: broadsheet; circ. evening 9,547(paid). **Wire Service(s):** AP.
Formerly: West Memphis Evening Times.

CALIFORNIA

ANTIOCH
US
LEDGER DISPATCH & SUNDAY TIMES, THE. 1870. d. $.50/day newsstand; $1.50/Sun.; $9.80/mo. 1650 Cavallo Rd., Antioch, CA 94509. TEL 510-757-2525; FAX 510-706-2305. **Owner(s):** Knight-Ridder, Inc., One Herald Plz., Miami, FL 33132. TEL 305-376-3800; FAX 305-376-3875; Ed. Gene Williams; Pub. George E. Riggs; adv.; photos; bk.rev.; pub. size: standard; circ. evening 22,000(paid); Sun. 40,000(paid). **Wire Service(s):** AP, McClatchy, NYT.
Formerly: Daily Ledger-Post Dispatch.

AUBURN
US
AUBURN JOURNAL. 1856. Sun.-Fri. $.50/day newsstand; $.75/Sun.; $77.22/yr. carrier; $19.31/3 mos. senior citizens. 1030 High St., Auburn, CA 95603. TEL 916-885-5656; FAX 916-887-1231. **Owner(s):** Brehm Communications, Inc., 17065 Via del Campo, Ste. 200, San Diego, CA 92127. TEL 619-451-6200; Ed. Deric Rothe; Pub. Scott Little; adv. contact: Rhonda Blocker. pub. size: broadsheet; circ. morning 15,500(paid); Sun. 15,000(paid). **Wire Service(s):** AP.

BAKERSFIELD
US ISSN 0276-5837
BAKERSFIELD CALIFORNIAN. 1866. d. $.50/day newsstand; $1.25/Sun; $12.50/mo.; $8/mo. Sat. & Sun. 1707 Eye St., Bakersfield, CA 93301. TEL 805-395-7500; FAX 805-395-7519. **Owner(s):** Bakersfield Californian Corp., 1707 Eye St., Bakersfield, CA 93301. TEL 805-395-7519; Ed. Mike Jenner; Pub. Ginger Moorhouse; photos; bk.rev.; pub. size: broadsheet; circ. morning 85,000(paid); Sun. 91,000(paid). **Wire Service(s):** AP.

BANNING
US ISSN 0747-1521
BANNING RECORD GAZETTE. 1908. Mon.-Fri. $.35 newsstand; $5.75/mo. 218 N. Murray St., Banning, CA 92220. TEL 909-849-4586; FAX 909-849-2437. **Owner(s):** Century Group, 218 N. Murray St., Banning, CA 92220. TEL 714-849-4586; Ed. Conny Israelson; Pub. Ken Smith;.adv. contact: Dale Cross. pub. size: broadsheet; circ. evening 18,400(paid). **Wire Service(s):** AP.

BARSTOW
US
DESERT DISPATCH. 1910. Mon.-Sun. $.25/day newsstand; $.75/Sat.; $1.35/Sun.; $8.46/mo. 130 Coolwater Ln., Barstow, CA 92311. TEL 619-256-2257; FAX 619-256-0685. **Owner(s):** Freedom Communications, Inc., 1055 N. Main St., Ste. 901, Irvine, CA 92701. TEL 714-542-4415; Ed. Merrill McCarty; Pub. Tom Porter; pub. size: broadsheet; circ. evening 8,000(paid). **Wire Service(s):** AP.
Formerly: Barstow Desert Dispatch.

BENICIA
US
BENICIA HERALD. 1877. Tue.-Fri. & Sun. $.50 newsstand; $4.50/mo. carrier. 820 First St., Benicia, CA 94520. TEL 707-745-0733; FAX 707-557-6380. **Owner(s):** Gibson Publications, Inc., 820 First St., Benicia, CA 94510. TEL 707-745-0733; FAX 707-557-6380; Pub. David L. Payne; adv. contact: Pam Pope. photos; bk.rev.; pub. size: broadsheet; circ. morning 10,000(paid).

CAMARILLO
US
CAMARILLO STAR. 1926. d. $.35/day newsstand; $1.50/Sun. 2245 Ventura Blvd., Camarillo, CA 93010. TEL 805-987-5001; FAX 805-482-8631. **Owner(s):** Scripps Howard, 312 Walnut St., 28th Fl., Cincinnati, OH 45202. TEL 513-977-3000; Pub. Howard Beck; pub. size: broadsheet; circ. morning 11,500(paid); Sun. 11,800(paid). **Wire Service(s):** AP.
Formerly: Camarillo Star-Free Press.

CHICO
US ISSN 0746-5548
CHICO ENTERPRISE-RECORD. 1853. d. $.50/day newsstand; $1/Sun.; $8.58/mo. in town; $9.12/yr. motor carrier. 400 E. Park Ave., Chico, CA 95928. TEL 916-891-1234; FAX 916-342-3617. **Owner(s):** Stephens Group, Inc., P.O. Box 1350, Fort Smith, AR 72902. TEL 501-785-7815; Ed. Jack Winning; Pub. James Dimmitt; adv.; pub. size: broadsheet; circ. morning 31,000(paid); Sun. 32,000(paid). **Wire Service(s):** AP.

COSTA MESA
US
DAILY PILOT, THE. 1907. Mon.-Sat. $.25 newsstand; $8.50/mo. mailed out of state. 330 W. Bay St., Costa Mesa, CA 92627. TEL 714-642-4321; FAX 714-646-4170. **Owner(s):** Times Mirror Co., Times Mirror Sq., 220 W. First St., Los Angeles, CA 90053. TEL 213-237-3700; Ed. Steve Marble; Pub. Tom Johnson; adv.; pub. size: broadsheet; circ. 48,700(paid). **Wire Service(s):** AP.
Formerly: Orange Coast Daily Pilot.

CRESCENT CITY
US ISSN 1056-9510
DEL NORTE TRIPLICATE. 1879. Tue.-Sat. $.35/day newsstand; $.50/Sat.; $54/yr. carrier. 312 H St., Crescent City, CA 95531. TEL 707-464-2141; FAX 707-464-5102. **Owner(s):** Western Communications, Inc., 1526 N.W. Hill St., Crescent City, CA 95531. TEL 707-464-2141; Ed. John Pritchett; Pub. Geoffrey T. White; adv. contact: Patty Leonard. photos; pub. size: boadsheet; circ. morning 5,900(paid). **Wire Service(s):** AP.

DANVILLE
US
SAN RAMON VALLEY TIMES, THE. 1945. Sun.-Fri. $.50/day newsstand; $1.25/Sun.; $10.99/mo. carrier; $6.98/mo. Sun. 524 Hartz Ave., Danville, CA 94526. TEL 510-837-4267; FAX 510-837-4334. **Owner(s):** Knight-Ridder, Inc., One Herald Plz., Miami, FL 33132. TEL 305-376-3800; FAX 305-376-3875; Ed. Karen Magnuson; Pub. David Rounds; adv. contact: Wendy Davidson. photos; pub. size: broadsheet; circ. morning 40,000(paid); Sun. 45,000(paid). **Wire Service(s):** AP.

DAVIS
US
DAVIS ENTERPRISE. 1897. Sun.-Fri. $.50 newsstand; $6.44/4 wks. 315 G St., Davis, CA 95616. TEL 916-756-0800; FAX 916-756-1668; E-mail: editor@davis.com; URL: http://www.davisenterprise.com. **Owner(s):** McNaughton Newspapers, 315 G St., P.O. Box 1078, Davis, CA 95617. TEL 916-756-0800; Ed. Debbie Davis; Pub. Burt McNaughton; adv. contact: Donna Okinga. pub. size: broadsheet; circ. evening 10,000(paid); Sun. 11,000(paid). **Wire Service(s):** AP, NYT.

EL CAJON
US ISSN 0898-1817
DAILY CALIFORNIAN, THE. 1892. d. $.25/day newsstand; $.50/Sat. or Sun.; $24.94/3 mos.; $48/6 mos.; $83.46/yr. 1000 Pioneer Way, El Cajon, CA 92020. TEL 619-442-4404; FAX 619-447-6165. **Owner(s):** Central Valley Publishing, 1000 Pioneer Way, El Cajon, CA 92020. TEL 619-442-4404; Ed. Della Elliott; Pub. Joe Browning; pub. size: broadsheet; circ. evening 16,500(paid); Sun. 26,500(paid). **Wire Service(s):** AP.
Formerly: Californian, The.

EL CENTRO

US   ISSN 1072-9283
IMPERIAL VALLEY PRESS. 1901. Sun.-Fri. $1/day newsstand; $1/Sun.; $8/mo. home deliv.; $10/mo. in cy. mailed; $13/mo. out of cy. mailed. 205 N. Eighth St., El Centro, CA 92243. TEL 619-337-3400; FAX 619-353-3003. **Owner(s):** Associated Desert Newspapers, 205 N. Eighth St., El Centro, CA 92243. TEL 619-337-3400; FAX 619-353-3003; Ed. E. Mayer Maloney, Jr.; Pub. E. Mayer Maloney, Jr.; adv. contact: John Yanni. bk.rev.; pub. size: broadsheet; circ. evening 18,500(paid); Sun. 19,000(paid). **Wire Service(s):** AP.
    Formerly: Brawley News.

ESCONDIDO

US   ISSN 1059-5694
NORTH COUNTY TIMES. 1986. d. $.35/day newsstand; $1.25/Sun.; $9.80/4 wks. 207 E. Pennsylvania Ave., Escondido, CA 92025. TEL 619-433-7333; FAX 619-745-3769. **Owner(s):** South Coast Newspapers, 1722 S. Hill St., Oceanside, CA 92054. TEL 619-433-7333; Ed. W. Russel Harris; Pub. Richard High; adv.; pub. size: broadsheet; circ. evening 98,000(paid); Sun. 98,000(paid). **Wire Service(s):** AP.
    Formerly: Times Advocate.

EUREKA

US
TIMES-STANDARD. 1854. d. $11/mo. 930 Sixth St., Eureka, CA 95501. TEL 707-441-0500; FAX 707-441-0565. **Owner(s):** Media News Group, 4888 Loop Central Dr., Ste. 525, Houston, TX 77081. TEL 713-295-3800; Ed. Rex Wilson; Pub. Stephen J. Sosinski; adv. contact: Gary Siegel. pub. size: broadsheet; circ. evening 21,300(paid); Sun. 24,885(paid). **Wire Service(s):** AP.

FAIRFIELD

US   ISSN 0746-5858
DAILY REPUBLIC. 1855. d. $.35/day newsstand; $1.25/Sun.; $9.65/mo. home deliv. 1250 Texas St., Fairfield, CA 94533. TEL 707-425-4646; FAX 707-425-5924. **Owner(s):** McNaughton Newspapers, 315 G St., P.O. Box 1078, Davis, CA 95617. TEL 916-756-0800; Ed. Bill Buchanan; Pub. Foy McNaughton; pub. size: broadsheet; circ. morning 21,147(paid); Sun. 22,865(paid). **Wire Service(s):** AP.

FREMONT

US
ARGUS, THE. 1960. d. $.50/day newsstand; $1.25/Sun.; $3.25/wk .deliv. 39737 Paseo Padre Bldg., Fremont, CA 94538. TEL 510-353-7012; FAX 510-353-7029. **Owner(s):** Ang Newspapers, P.O. Box 1350, Oakland, CA 94604-1350. TEL 510-763-1120; Ed. Chris Forsyth; Pub. Peter Bernhard; adv. contact: Lynn Marleau. pub. size: broadsheet; circ. morning 33,939(paid). **Wire Service(s):** AP, LAT-WP, CNS, SHNA, NYT.

FRESNO

US   ISSN 0889-6070
FRESNO BEE, THE. 1922. d. $11.45/mo; $148.19/yr. 1626 E St., Fresno, CA 93786. TEL 209-441-6111; FAX 209-441-6436. **Owner(s):** McClatchy Newspapers, P.O. Box 15779, Sacramento, CA 95852. TEL 916-446-9211; Pub. Robert Weil; photos; pub. size: standard; circ. morning 154,644(paid); Sun. 192,262(paid). **Wire Service(s):** AP, NYT, McClatchy, RN, KR, SHNA.

GILROY

US
DISPATCH, THE. 1868. Mon.-Fri. $.50 newsstand; $25/3 mos. carrier; $42.22/3 mos. mailed local; $39/3 mos. mailed elsewhere. 6400 Monterey St., Gilroy, CA 95020. TEL 408-842-6400; FAX 408-842-7105. **Owner(s):** U.S. Media Group, P.O. Box 227, Crystal City, MO 63019; Pub. Leroy Gorrell; adv. contact: Cindy Courter. photos; pub. size: broadsheet; circ. morning 5,671(paid). **Wire Service(s):** AP, McClatchy News Service.

GLENDALE

US   ISSN 0746-3340
GLENDALE NEWS-PRESS. 1905. Mon.-Sat. $.25 newsstand; $7.50/mo. 425 W. Broadway, Ste. 300, Glendale, CA 91204-1269. TEL 818-241-4141; FAX 818-241-1975. **Owner(s):** Times-Mirror Co., Times-Mirror Sq., Los Angeles, CA 90053. TEL 213-237-3700; Ed. William Lobdell. adv. contact: Willa Robinson. photos; bk.rev.; pub. size: broadsheet; circ. morning 10,409(paid). **Wire Service(s):** AP, CINS.

GRASS VALLEY

US
UNION, THE. 1864. Mon.-Sat. $.50 newsstand; $8/mo.; $10.19/mo. mailed. 11464 Sutton Way, Grass Valley, CA 95945. TEL 916-273-9561; FAX 916-273-1854; E-mail: mail@theunion.com; URL: http://www.theunion.com. **Owner(s):** Nevada County Publishing Co., 131 S. Cedar, Nevada, MO 64772. TEL 417-667-8121; Ed. John Seelmyer. adv. contact: Matt Bodourian. photos; bk.rev.; pub. size: broadsheet; circ. evening 17,500(paid). **Wire Service(s):** AP.

HANFORD

US
HANFORD SENTINEL, THE. 1886. d. $9.50/mo. carrier; $10/mo. motor rte. 300 W. Sixth St., Hanford, CA 93230. TEL 209-582-0471; FAX 209-582-8631. **Owner(s):** Scripps League Newspapers, Inc., P.O. Box 16B, Charlottesville, VA 22901; Ed. Leah Leach; Pub. Neil Williams; adv. contact: Bob Rankin. photos; bk.rev.; pub. size: broadsheet; circ. evening 14,375(paid); Sun. 14,640(paid). **Wire Service(s):** AP.

HAYWARD

US
DAILY REVIEW. 1892. d. $.50/day newsstand; $1.25/Sun; $10.84/mo. 116 W. Winton Ave., Hayward, CA 94544. TEL 510-783-6111; FAX 510-293-2490. **Owner(s):** Alameda Publishing Corp., 116 W. Winton Ave., Hayward, CA 94544. TEL 510-783-6111; Pub. Roger Grossman; adv.; photos; pub. size: broadsheet; circ. morning 41,900(paid); Sun. 50,500(paid). **Wire Service(s):** AP, LAT-WP, NYT, SHNA.

HOLLISTER

US
FREE LANCE. 1873. d. $.50 newsstand; $75/yr. 350 Sixth St., Hollister, CA 95023. TEL 408-637-5566; FAX 408-637-4104. **Owner(s):** U.S. Media Group, P.O. Box 227, Crystal City, MO 63019; Ed. Mark Paxton; Pub. Michael Eastman; adv. contact: Brenda Weatherly. photos; bk.rev.; pub. size: broadsheet; circ. morning 4,600(paid). **Wire Service(s):** AP, McClatchy.

LAKEPORT

US   ISSN 0746-4304
LAKE COUNTY RECORD-BEE. 1878. Tue.-Sat. $.50 newsstand; $57.80/yr. 2150 S. Main St., Lakeport, CA 95453. TEL 707-263-5636; FAX 707-263-0600. **Owner(s):** Lake County Publishing, 2150 S. Main, P.O. Box 849, Lakeport, CA 95453. TEL 707-263-5636; Ed. Thomas Monigan; Pub. Tim Timmons; adv. contact: Debbie Geissler. photos; pub. size: standard; circ. morning 9,010(paid).

LODI

US
LODI NEWS-SENTINEL. 1881. Mon.-Sat. $.35 newsstand; $6.75/mo. 125 N. Church St., Lodi, CA 95240. TEL 209-369-2761. **Owner(s):** Lodi News-Sentinel, P.O. Box 1360, Lodi, CA 95241. TEL 209-369-2761; Ed. Marty Weybret. adv. contact: Chuck Higgs. pub. size: broadsheet; circ. morning 18,000(free). **Wire Service(s):** AP, SJNS.

LOMPOC

US
LOMPOC RECORD. 1875. Sun.-Fri. $.50/day newsstand; $1/Sun.; $7.35/mo. 115 N. H St., Lompoc, CA 93436. TEL 805-736-2313; FAX 805-736-5654. **Owner(s):** Donrey Media Group, P.O. Box 17017, Fort Smith, AR 72902. TEL 501-785-7810; Ed. Rita Henning; Pub. Ron Hoffer; adv. contact: Dick Bausman. pub. size: broadsheet; circ. evening 7,945(paid); Sun. 8,158(paid). **Wire Service(s):** AP.

LONG BEACH

US
PRESS-TELEGRAM. 1897. d. $.25/day newsstand; $1.25/Sun.; $2.25/wk. home deliv. 604 Pine Ave., Long Beach, CA 90844-0001. TEL 310-435-1161; FAX 310-437-7892; E-mail: ptweb@ptconnect.infi.net; URL: http://www.ptconnect.com. **Owner(s):** Knight-Ridder, Inc., One Herald Plz., Miami, FL 33132. TEL 305-376-3800; FAX 305-376-3875; Ed. Rich Archbold; Pub. Rick Sadowski; adv.; pub. size: broadsheet; circ. morning 132,000(paid); Sun. 153,000(paid). **Wire Service(s):** AP, NYT, KR.

LOS ANGELES

US
LOS ANGELES BULLETIN. Mon.-Fri. $.25 newsstand; $20/mo. mailed; $170/yr. mailed. 210 S. Spring St., Los Angeles, CA 90012-3710. TEL 213-628-4384; FAX 213-687-3886. **Owner(s):** Metropolitan News Co., 210 S. Spring St., Los Angeles, CA 90012-3710. TEL 213-628-4384; FAX 213-687-3886; Ed. Roger M. Grace. Pub. Roger M. Grace; adv.; photos; bk.rev.; pub. size: tabloid; circ. morning 1,700(paid). **Wire Service(s):** AP.

DAILY NEWSPAPERS

LOS ANGELES
US ISSN 0458-3035
LOS ANGELES TIMES. 1881. d. $.50 newsstand; $4.04/wk. Times Mirror Sq., Los Angeles, CA 90053. TEL 213-237-5000; FAX 213-237-4712; E-mail: letters@latimes.com; URL: http://www.latimes.com/. **Owner(s):** Times-Mirror Co., Times Mirror Sq., Los Angeles, CA 90053. TEL 213-237-3700; Ed. Michael Parks; Pub. Richard Schlosberg III; adv. contact: Lawrence M. Kline. photos; bk.rev.; pub. size: broadsheet; circ. morning 1,021,121(paid); Sun. 1,391,076(paid). **Wire Service(s):** AP, DJ, RN, UPI, LAT-WP, CSM, CiNS.

MADERA
US ISSN 8750-9571
MADERA TRIBUNE. 1885. Mon.-Sat. $.50 newsstand; $75/yr. home deliv.; $114/yr. mailed. 100 E. Seventh St., Madera, CA 93638. TEL 209-674-2424; FAX 209-673-6526. **Owner(s):** U.S. Media Group, P.O. Box 227, Crystal City, MO 63019; Ed. Robert Adams; Pub. Fred Ward; adv. contact: Armida Roberts. pub. size: broadsheet; circ. evening 9,900(paid). **Wire Service(s):** AP.

MANTECA
US ISSN 0745-2748
MANTECA BULLETIN. 1908. d. $.50 newsstand; $9.50/mo. carrier; $98/yr. mailed. 531 E. Yosemite Ave., Manteca, CA 95336. TEL 209-239-3531; FAX 209-239-1801. **Owner(s):** Morris Communications, P.O. Box 936, Augusta, GA 30903. TEL 706-724-0851; Ed. Karen Hodges; Pub. Darrel Phillips; adv. contact: Rita Hill. pub. size: broadsheet; circ. morning 7,500(paid); Sun. 7,500(paid). **Wire Service(s):** AP.

MARYSVILLE
US
APPEAL-DEMOCRAT. 1860. d. $.50/day newsstand; $1/Sun. 1530 Ellis Lake Dr., Marysville, CA 95901. TEL 916-741-2345; FAX 916-741-1195; E-mail: appeal@syix.com. **Owner(s):** Freedom Communications, Inc., 17666 Fitch St., Irvine, CA 92714. TEL 716-553-9292; Ed. Julie Shirley; Pub. Robert Hardie; pub. size: broadsheet; circ. evening 26,555(paid); Sun. 26,555(paid). **Wire Service(s):** AP, NYT, KR.
Formerly: Yuba-Sutter Appeal Democrat.

MERCED
US
MERCED SUN-STAR. 1869. Mon.-Sat. $.50/day newsstand; $1/Sat. 3033 N. G St., Merced, CA 95340. TEL 209-722-1511; FAX 209-384-2226. **Owner(s):** U.S. Media Group, P.O. Box 227, Crystal City, MO 63019; Ed. Norman Martin, Jr.; Pub. Tom Schmitt; adv. contact: Debbie Geissler. pub. size: broadsheet; circ. morning 21,000(paid). **Wire Service(s):** AP.

MODESTO
US
MODESTO BEE, THE. 1884. d. $.50 newsstand; $11.26/mo. 1325 H St., Modesto, CA 95354. TEL 209-578-2000; FAX 209-578-2207; E-mail: eelamont@aol.com; URL: http://www.modbee.com. **Owner(s):** McClatchy Newspapers, P.O. Box 15779, Sacramento, CA 95852. TEL 916-446-9211; Ed. Mark Vasche; Pub. Orage Quarles III; adv.; photos; bk.rev.; pub. size: broadsheet; circ. morning 85,000(paid); Sun. 94,000(paid). **Wire Service(s):** AP, NYT, LAT-WP, McClatchy, KR.

MONTEREY
US ISSN 0889-3101
MONTEREY COUNTY HERALD, THE. 1922. d. $.50/day newsstand; $1.50/Sun.; $14/mo. carrier; $23/mo. mailed. 8 Upper Ragsdale Dr., Monterey, CA 93940. TEL 408-372-3311; FAX 408-372-8401; E-mail: herald@ix.netcom.com. **Owner(s):** Scripps Howard, 312 Walnut St., 28th Fl., Cincinatti, OH 45202. TEL 513-977-3000; Ed. J. Bruce Baumann. adv. contact: Jay Palmquist. pub. size: broadsheet; circ. morning 36,000(paid); Sun. 39,000(paid). **Wire Service(s):** AP, LAT-WP, CSM.
Formerly: Monterey Peninsula Herald, The.

MOORPARK
US
MOORPARK STAR. 1983. d. $.25/day newsstand; $1.50/Sun. 530 Moorpark Ave., Ste. 180, Moorpark, CA 93021. TEL 805-523-7440; FAX 805-523-7816; E-mail: vcstar@aol.com. **Owner(s):** Scripps-Howard, 312 Walnut St., 28th Fl., Cincinnati, OH 45202. TEL 513-977-3000; Ed. Tim Gallagher; Pub. John Wilcox; adv. contact: P. Birmingham. pub. size: broadsheet; circ. morning 2,000(free & paid).
Formerly: Moorpark News-Mirror.

NAPA
US
NAPA VALLEY REGISTER. 1863. d. $.50/day newsstand; $1.25/Sun. 1615 Second St., Napa, CA 94559. TEL 707-226-3711; FAX 707-224-3963. **Owner(s):** Napa Valley Publishing Co., 1615 Second St., Napa, CA 94559. TEL 707-224-3963; Ed. Marilee Talley; Pub. Michael Giangreco; adv. contact: Sandy Aimo. pub. size: broadsheet; circ. evening 21,600(paid). **Wire Service(s):** AP.
Formerly: Napa Register.

NOVATO
US ISSN 0891-5164
MARIN INDEPENDENT JOURNAL. 1861. d. $.35/day newsstand; $1/Sun.; $18.02/8 wks. home deliv. 150 Alameda Del Prado, Novato, CA 94948-6150. TEL 415-883-8600; FAX 415-883-5458; E-mail: ij@well.com. **Owner(s):** Gannett Company, Inc., 1100 Wilson Blvd., Arlington, VA 22340. TEL 703-284-6000; Pub. Phyllis Pfeiffer; pub. size: broadsheet; circ. evening 37,350(paid); Sun. 41,540(paid). **Wire Service(s):** AP, GNS.

OAKLAND
US
ALAMEDA TIMES STAR. 1872. d. $.50/day newsstand; $1.25/Sun.; $3.25/wk. 66 Jack London Sq., Oakland, CA 94607. TEL 510-208-6333; FAX 510-748-0437. **Owner(s):** Alameda Newspaper Grp., 66 Jack London Sq., Oakland, CA 94607. TEL 510-208-6333; Ed. Thomas Tuttle; Pub. Thomas Tuttle; pub. size: broadsheet; circ. morning 6,908(paid). **Wire Service(s):** UPI, NYT, CNS, AP.

US ISSN 0745-3841
OAKLAND TRIBUNE, THE. 1874. d. $.50/day newsstand; $1.50/Sun. 66 Jack London Sq., Oakland, CA 94607. TEL 510-208-6300; FAX 510-208-6477. **Owner(s):** Alameda Newspaper Group, San Francisco, CA; Ed. Nancy Conway; Pub. Scott McKibben; pub. size: broadsheet; circ. morning 75,480(paid); Sun. 73,000(paid). **Wire Service(s):** AP.
Formerly: Tribune, The.

ONTARIO
US
INLAND VALLEY DAILY BULLETIN. 1885. d. $.35/day newsstand; $1/Sun.; $10.36/4 wks. 2041 E. Fourth St., Ontario, CA 91761. TEL 909-987-6397; FAX 909-948-9038. **Owner(s):** Stephens Group, Inc., P.O. Box 1359, Fort Smith, AR 72901. TEL 501-785-7810; Pub. Mike Ferguson; adv. contact: John Souza. bk.rev.; pub. size: broadsheet; circ. morning 82,600(free & paid); Sun. 86,000(free & paid). **Wire Service(s):** AP, KNS.
Formerly: Progress Bulletin Daily Report.

OROVILLE
US
OROVILLE MERCURY-REGISTER. 1873. Mon.-Sat. $.50 newsstand; $8.04/mo. carrier. 2081 Second St., Oroville, CA 95965. TEL 916-533-3131; FAX 916-533-3127. **Owner(s):** Donrey Media Group, P.O. Box 17017, Fort Smith, AR 72901. TEL 501-785-7810; Ed. Roger H. Aylworth; Pub. John Fenrich; adv. contact: Milt Moore. pub. size: broadsheet; circ. evening 7,800(paid). **Wire Service(s):** AP.

PALMDALE
US ISSN 0744-5830
ANTELOPE VALLEY PRESS. 1915. Tue.-Sun. $.50/day newsstand; $1.25/Sun.; $124.95/yr. 37404 N. Sierra Hwy., Palmdale, CA 93550. TEL 805-273-2700; FAX 805-947-4870; E-mail: editor@avpress.com; URL: http://www.avpress.com. **Owner(s):** Antelope Valley Newspapers, Inc., P.O. Box 880, Palmdale, CA 93550. TEL 805-273-2700; Ed. Vern Lawson. adv.; photos; bk.rev.; pub. size: broadsheet; circ. morning 56,276(paid); Sun. 58,775(paid). **Wire Service(s):** NYT, AP.

PALM SPRINGS
US
DESERT SUN, THE. 1927. d. $.50/day newsstand; $.75/Sat.; $1/Sun. 750 N. Gene Autry Trail, Palm Springs, CA 92262. TEL 619-322-8889; FAX 619-778-4654; E-mail: pssun@aol.com; 74111.2461@compuserve.com; URL: http://www.desert-sun.com. **Owner(s):** Gannett Company, Inc., 1100 Wilson Blvd., Arlington, VA 22234. TEL 703-284-6000; Ed. Keith Carter; Pub. Robert Dickey; adv.; photos; bk.rev.; pub. size: broadsheet; circ. morning 59,479(paid); Sun. 63,268(paid). **Wire Service(s):** AP, GNS, NYT.

PALO ALTO
US
▼**PALO ALTO DAILY NEWS.** 1995. d. free. 329 Alma St., Palo Alto, CA 94301. TEL 415-327-6397; FAX 415-327-0676. **Owner(s):** Priceless LLC, 329 Alma St., Palo Alto, CA 94301. TEL 415-327-6397; FAX 415-327-0676; Ed. David Price; Pub. David Price; adv. contact: James Pavelich. photos; pub. size: tabloid; circ. morning 15,000(free).

PASADENA
US ISSN 1069-2827
PASADENA STAR-NEWS, THE. 1886. d. $.25/day newsstand; $1/Sun. 911 E. Colorado Blvd., Pasadena, CA 91109. TEL 818-578-6300; FAX 818-792-9413. **Owner(s):** Media News, Inc., Denver, CO; Ed. Lawrence Wilson; Pub. Ike Massey; pub. size: broadsheet; circ. morning 42,800(paid); Sun. 42,800(paid). **Wire Service(s):** AP, NYT.
Formerly: Star-News.

PASO ROBLES
US
COUNTRY NEWS-PRESS. 1886. Mon.-Fri. $.35 newsstand; $6.50/mo. cy.; $78/yr. cy. 1414 Park St., Paso Robles, CA 93446. TEL 805-237-6060; FAX 805-237-6066. **Owner(s):** US Media Group, 1400 W. Main St., Festus, MO 63028. TEL 314-937-5200; Pub. Keith Berwick; adv. contact: Tim Halbin. adv.: $7.95/SAU. pub. size: standard; circ. evening 4,983(paid). **Wire Service(s):** AP, CNS, NEA.

US
NEWS PRESS, THE. 1986. Tue.-Sat. $.50 newsstand; $87/yr. 1414 Park St., Paso Robles, CA 93446. TEL 805-237-6060; FAX 805-237-6066. **Owner(s):** U.S. Media Group, P.O. Box 227, Crystal City, MO 63019; Ed. Pat Cavanaugh; Pub. Pat Cavanaugh; adv. contact: Karen Sorenson. photos; bk.rev.; pub. size: broadsheet; circ. evening 5,000(paid). **Wire Service(s):** AP, CNS, CN.
Formerly: Paso Robles Press; The Daily Press.

PLACERVILLE
US
MOUNTAIN DEMOCRAT. 1851. Wed.-Fri. & Mon. $.50 newsstand; $68/yr. in cy. 1360 Broadway, Placerville, CA 95667. TEL 916-622-1255; FAX 916-622-7894; E-mail: mtdemo@calweb.com; URL: http://www.mtdemocrat.com. **Owner(s):** Mother Lode Printing & Publishing Co., 1360 Broadway, Placerville, CA 95667. TEL 916-622-1255; Ed. Michael Raffety; Pub. James Webb; adv. contact: A. Felcher. photos; bk.rev.; pub. size: broadsheet; circ. morning 13,093(paid). **Wire Service(s):** NYT.
Formerly: Mountain Democrat & Placerville Times.

PLEASANTON
US ISSN 8750-9946
TRI-VALLEY HERALD. 1874. d. $.50/day newsstand; $1.25/Sun. 4770 Willow Rd., Pleasanton, CA 94588. TEL 510-734-8600; FAX 510-416-4850. **Owner(s):** Alameda Publishing Corp., P.O. Box 5050, Hayward, CA 94540. TEL 510-783-6111; Ed. Steve Waterhouse; Pub. Peter Bernhard; adv. contact: Jennine Loumena. photos; bk.rev.; pub. size: standard; circ. morning 38,000(paid); Sun. 38,000(paid). **Wire Service(s):** AP.

US
VALLEY TIMES. d. $.50 newsstand; $53.50/yr. 127 Spring St., Pleasanton, CA 94566. TEL 510-462-4160; FAX 510-847-2189; E-mail: valleytims@aol.com. **Owner(s):** Knight-Ridder, Inc., One Herald Plz., Miami, FL 33132. TEL 305-376-3800; FAX 305-376-3875; Ed. Karen Magnuson; Pub. George Riggs; adv. contact: Wendy Davidson. bk.rev.; pub. size: broadsheet; circ. evening 38,500(paid); Sun. 40,000(paid). **Wire Service(s):** AP, NYT, LAT-WP, McClatchy.

PORTERVILLE
US
PORTERVILLE RECORDER. 1908. Mon.-Sat. $.50/day newsstand; $.75/Sat.; $87/yr. 115 E. Oak Ave., Porterville, CA 93257. TEL 209-784-5000; FAX 209-784-1689. **Owner(s):** Freedom Communications, Inc., 1766 Fitch, Irvine, CA 92714-6022. TEL 714-253-2303; FAX 714-474-7675; Ed. Rick Elkins; Pub. James L. Lyons; adv. contact: Jonell Webb. photos; pub. size: broadsheet; circ. evening 13,000(paid). **Wire Service(s):** AP.

RED BLUFF
US
RED BLUFF DAILY NEWS. 1885. Mon.-Sat. $.50 newsstand; $89.40/yr. deliv. 545 Diamond Ave., Red Bluff, CA 96080. TEL 916-527-2151; FAX 916-527-3719. **Owner(s):** Donrey Media Group, P.O. Box 17017, Fort Smith, AR 72901. TEL 501-785-7810; Ed. Bill Goodyear; Pub. Mel Wagner; adv. contact: Jean Hanson. pub. size: standard; circ. evening 9,000(paid). **Wire Service(s):** AP.

REDDING
US
RECORD SEARCHLIGHT. 1938. d. $.50/day newsstand; $1.50/Sun. 1101 Twin View Blvd., Redding, CA 96003. TEL 916-243-2424; FAX 916-225-8236; E-mail: recsrch@snowcrest.net; URL: http://www.redding.com/. **Owner(s):** John P. Scripps Newspapers, Inc., 306 Scripps Bldg., 525 C St., San Diego, CA 92101. TEL 714-233-7231; Ed. Tom King; Pub. Tom King; adv. contact: Chris Howard. photos; bk.rev.; pub. size: broadsheet; circ. morning 40,000(paid); Sun. 41,000(paid). **Wire Service(s):** AP.
Formerly: Redding Record Searchlight.

REDLANDS
US
REDLANDS DAILY FACTS. 1890. Sun.-Fri. $.35/day newsstand; $1/Sun.; $1.61/wk. carrier. 700 Brookside Ave., Redlands, CA 92373. TEL 909-793-3221; FAX 909-793-9588. **Owner(s):** Stephens Group, Inc., P.O. Box 1359, Fort Smith, AR 72902; Ed. Carl Baker; Pub. Toebe Bush; adv. contact: Dave Berkowitz. pub. size: broadsheet; circ. evening 8,750(paid); Sun. 8,750(paid). **Wire Service(s):** AP.

RICHMOND
US ISSN 0746-6323
WEST COUNTY TIMES. 1899. d. $.50/day newsstand; $1.50/Sun.; $10.99/mo. home deliv. 4301 Lakeside Dr., Richmond, CA 94806. TEL 510-262-2770; FAX 510-262-2776; E-mail: wctimes@aol.com. **Owner(s):** Knight Ridder, Inc., One Herald Plz., Miami, FL 33132. TEL 305-376-3800; Ed. Anthony Marquez. pub. size: broadsheet; circ. morning 34,797(paid); Sun. 35,244(paid). **Wire Service(s):** AP, NYT, LAT-WP.

RIDGECREST
US ISSN 1076-0059
DAILY INDEPENDENT, THE. 1928. Tue.-Fri. & Sun. $.25/day newsstand; $1/Sun.; $7/mo. carrier; $6/mo. senior citizens. 224 E. Ridgecrest Blvd., Ridgecrest, CA 93555. TEL 619-375-4481; FAX 614-375-4880. **Owner(s):** Swift Newspapers, Inc., 1802 N. Carson St., Ste. 100, Carson City, NV 89706; Ed. Scott Farwell; Pub. W. Les Hill; adv. contact: Matthew Hill. pub. size: broadsheet; circ. evening 9,000(paid); Sun. 9,200(paid). **Wire Service(s):** AP.

RIVERSIDE
US
PRESS-ENTERPRISE, THE. 1878. d. $.25/day newsstand; $1/Sun.; $2.40/wk. 3512 14th St., Riverside, CA 92501. TEL 909-684-1200; FAX 909-782-7634. **Owner(s):** Press-Enterprise Co., 3512 14th St., Riverside, CA 92501. TEL 909-684-1200; FAX 909-782-6034; A.H. Belo Corp., 400 S. Record, Dallas, TX 75202. TEL 214-977-6606; Ed. Mel Opotowsky. adv. contact: David Cornwall. photos; pub. size: broadsheet; circ. morning 164,028(paid); Sun. 171,139(paid). **Wire Service(s):** NYT, AP, KR.

DAILY NEWSPAPERS

SACRAMENTO
US ISSN 0890-5738
SACRAMENTO BEE. 1857. d. $.50/day newsstand; $1.25/Sun.; $11.25/mo. carrier. 2100 Q St., Sacramento, CA 95816-6816. TEL 916-321-1000; FAX 916-321-1109; E-mail: sacbeeedit@netcom.com; URL: http://www.sacbee.com. **Owner(s):** McClatchy Newspapers, P.O. Box 15779, Sacramento, CA 95852. TEL 916-321-1850; Ed. Rick Rodriguez; Pub. James McClatchy; adv. contact: Gene Grant. photos; bk.rev.; pub. size: broadsheet; circ. morning 279,942(paid); Sun. 350,361(paid). **Wire Service(s):** AP, NYT, LAT-WP, SHNA.

SALINAS
US
CALIFORNIAN, THE. 1872. Mon.-Sat. $.35/day newsstand; $1/Sat.; $11/mo. in cy.; $13/mo. out of cy. 123 W. Alisal St., Salinas, CA 93901. TEL 408-424-2221; FAX 408-754-4293; E-mail: valleynews@aol.com. **Owner(s):** Gannett Company, Inc., 1100 Wilson Blvd., Arlington, VA 22234. TEL 703-284-6000; Pub. Michael Chihak; adv. contact: Robert Aguilar. pub. size: broadsheet; circ. morning 20,951(paid). **Wire Service(s):** AP, GNS, NYT.

SAN BERNARDINO
US
SAN BERNARDINO COUNTY SUN. 1894. d. $.50/day newsstand; $1.50/Sun. 399 N. D St., San Bernardino, CA 92401. TEL 909-889-9666; FAX 909-885-8741. **Owner(s):** Gannett Company, Inc., 1100 Wilson Blvd., Arlington, VA 22234. TEL 703-284-6000; Ed. Catherine Hamm; Pub. Brooks Johnson; adv. contact: Robert Balzer. photos; pub. size: broadsheet; circ. morning 96,000(paid); Sun. 105,000(paid). **Wire Service(s):** AP, GNS, NYT.

SAN DIEGO
US
SAN DIEGO UNION-TRIBUNE. 1868. d. $.35/day newsstand; $1.50/Sun.; $10.50/mo. 350 Camino De La Reina, San Diego, CA 92108. TEL 619-299-3131; FAX 619-293-2148; E-mail: ellen.bevier@uniontrib.com; URL: http://www.uniontrib.com/. **Owner(s):** Union-Tribune Publishing Co., 350 Camino De La Reina, San Diego, CA 92108. TEL 619-299-3131; Ed. Karin Winner; Pub. Helen K. Copley; adv.; photos; bk.rev.; pub. size: broadsheet; circ. morning 380,500(paid); Sun. 455,600(paid). **Wire Service(s):** AP, UPI, CNS, DJ, RN, KR, NYT, BPI, CSM, CT-NYT.
Formerly: San Diego Union.

SAN FRANCISCO
US
SAN FRANCISCO CHRONICLE. 1865. d. $.50 newsstand; $14.40/4 wks. 901 Mission St., San Francisco, CA 94103-2988. TEL 415-777-1111; FAX 415-896-1107; E-mail: chronletters@sfgate.com; URL: http://www.sfgate.com/. **Owner(s):** Chronicle Publishing Co., 901 Mission St., San Francisco, CA 94103. TEL 415-777-1111; Ed. Jerry Roberts. adv. contact: Bart Green. photos; bk.rev.; pub. size: broadsheet; circ. morning 493,942(paid); Sun. 646,171(paid). **Wire Service(s):** AP, NYT, RN, LAT-WP.

US
SAN FRANCISCO EXAMINER. 1865. d. $.25/day newsstand; $1.50/Sun.; $12/4 wks.; $6.60/4 wks. Sun. only. 110 Fifth St., San Francisco, CA 94103. TEL 415-777-2424; FAX 415-777-2525; E-mail: letters@examiner.com; URL: http://www.sfgate.com/ examiner. **Owner(s):** Hearst Corp., 959 Eighth Ave., New York, NY 10019. TEL 212-262-5700; Pub. Lee Guittar; adv. contact: Bart Green. photos; bk.rev.; pub. size: standard; circ. evening 125,000(paid); Sun. 646,171(paid). **Wire Service(s):** AP, CDN, CSM, CT, KR, RN.

SAN JACINTO
US
HEMET NEWS, THE. 1893. d. $.25/day newsstand; $.50/Sun.; $19.47/13 wks. home deliv.; $64.65/yr. 474 W. Esplanade Ave., San Jacinto, CA 92583. TEL 909-487-2275; FAX 909-487-2250. **Owner(s):** Stephens Group, Inc., P.O. Box 1359, Fort Smith, AR 72902. TEL 501-785-7810; Ed. Craig Shultz; Pub. Jim Fredericks; adv. contact: Manny Padilla. pub. size: broadsheet; circ. morning 12,500(paid). **Wire Service(s):** AP.

SAN JOSE
US ISSN 0747-2099
SAN JOSE MERCURY NEWS. 1851. d. $.35/day newsstand; $1.35/Sun.; $11.95/mo. home deliv. 750 Ridder Park Dr., San Jose, CA 95190. TEL 408-920-5000; FAX 408-298-1966; E-mail: jceppos@sjmercury.com; URL: http://www.sjmercury.com/. **Owner(s):** Knight-Ridder, Inc., One Herald Plz., Miami, FL 33132-1693. TEL 305-376-3800; FAX 305-376-3875; Ed. Rob Elder; Pub. Jay Harris; adv. contact: Steve Weaver. photos; bk.rev.; pub. size: broadsheet; circ. morning 285,000(paid); Sun. 360,000(paid). **Wire Service(s):** AP, NYT, LAT-WP, KR.

SAN LUIS OBISPO
US
SAN LUIS OBISPO COUNTY TELEGRAM-TRIBUNE. 1869. Mon.-Sat. $.50/day newsstand; $1/Sat.; $11.75/mo. 3825 S. Higuera St., San Luis Obispo, CA 93401. TEL 805-781-7800; FAX 805-781-7870; E-mail: slott@scripps.com; URL: http://www.sanluisobispo.com. **Owner(s):** John P. Scripps Newspapers, Inc., 306 Scripps Bldg., 525 C St., San Diego, CA 92101. TEL 714-233-7231; Ed. John T. Moore. adv. contact: Butch Hughes. photos; bk.rev.; pub. size: broadsheet; circ. morning 35,000. **Wire Service(s):** AP, MMS, SHNS.

SAN MATEO
US
SAN MATEO COUNTY TIMES. 1889. Mon.-Sat. $.50/day newsstand; $.75/Sat.; $7.50/mo. 1080 S. Amphlett Blvd., San Mateo, CA 94402. TEL 415-348-4321; FAX 415-348-4476; E-mail: editor@smctimes.com. **Owner(s):** Alameda Publishing Corp., 116 W. Winton Ave., Hayward, CA 94544. TEL 510-783-6111; Pub. Roger Grossman; adv. contact: Robert Miller. photos; bk.rev.; pub. size: broadsheet; circ. evening 32,000(paid). **Wire Service(s):** AP, NYT, SHNA, McClatchy, Cox.
Formerly: San Mateo Times.

SAN PEDRO
US ISSN 0747-4180
NEWS-PILOT, THE. 1928. Mon.-Sat. $.25 newsstand; $6.50/mo. 362 W. Seventh St., San Pedro, CA 90731. TEL 310-832-0221; FAX 310-833-1540; E-mail: newspilot@aol.com. **Owner(s):** Copley Press, Inc., 7776 Ivanhoe Ave., La Jolla, CA 92037; Ed. Phillip F. Sanfield; Pub. Tom Wafer; adv. contact: Charlie Mc Manis. pub. size: broadsheet; circ. morning 13,925(paid). **Wire Service(s):** AP, CNS.
Formerly: San Pedro News-Pilot.

SANTA ANA
US ISSN 0886-4934
ORANGE COUNTY REGISTER, THE. 1905. d. $.25/day newsstand; $1.25/Sun.; $9.96/4 wks.; $5.56/Sat. & Sun. only. 625 N. Grand Ave., Santa Ana, CA 92701. TEL 714-835-1234; FAX 714-543-3904; E-mail: rworld@link.freedom.com; URL: http://www.ocregister.com. **Owner(s):** Freedom Communications, Inc., 1055 N. Main St., Ste. 901, Irvine, CA 92701. TEL 714-542-4415; Pub. R. David Threshie, Jr.; photos; bk.rev.; pub. size: broadsheet; circ. morning 353,812(paid); Sun. 415,553(paid). **Wire Service(s):** AP, NYT, KR, RN, SHNA.

SANTA BARBARA
US
SANTA BARBARA NEWS PRESS. 1855. d. $.50/day newsstand; $1/Sun.; $2.79/wk.; $133.35/yr. 715 Ana Capa, Santa Barbara, CA 93101. TEL 805-564-5200; FAX 805-564-5136. **Owner(s):** New York Times Co., The, 229 W. 43rd St., New York, NY 10036. TEL 212-556-1234; Ed. Tom Bolton; Pub. Steven Ainsley; adv. contact: Lynn Randolph. pub. size: broadsheet; circ. morning 53,000(paid); Sun. 58,000(paid). **Wire Service(s):** AP, NYT, KRS.

SANTA CRUZ
US
SANTA CRUZ COUNTY SENTINEL. 1856. d. $.50/day newsstand; $1.50/Sun.; $21.39/8 wks. carrier. 207 Church St., Santa Cruz, CA 95060. TEL 408-423-4242; FAX 408-429-9620; E-mail: sented@cruzio.com; URL: http://www.cruzio.com/bus/news/sentinel.html. **Owner(s):** Ottaway Newspapers, Inc., P.O. Box 401, Campbell Hall, NY 10916. TEL 914-294-8181; Ed. Tom Honig; Pub. David B. Regan; adv. contact: Karen Carnot. pub. size: broadsheet; circ. morning 27,860(paid); Sun. 30,021(paid). **Wire Service(s):** AP, McClatchy, ONS, NYT.
Formerly: Santa Cruz Sentinel.

SANTA MARIA
US ISSN 0745-6166
SANTA MARIA TIMES. 1882. d. $.50/day newsstand; $1/Sun.; $9.50/mo. mailed; $10.25/mo. in state; $11.25/mo. out of state. 3200 Skyway Dr., Santa Maria, CA 93455. TEL 805-925-2691; FAX 805-928-5657. **Owner(s):** Pulitzer Community Newspapers, Inc., St. Louis, MO; Ed. Wayne Agner; Pub. John Shields; adv. contact: Tobey Anglin. photos; bk.rev.; pub. size: broadsheet; circ. evening 22,500(paid); Sun. 24,100(paid). **Wire Service(s):** AP, CNS, SHNA, McClatchy.

SANTA MONICA
US   ISSN 0898-5375
OUTLOOK, THE. 1875. Mon.-Sat. $.25 newsstand; $6.50/mo. carrier. 1920 Colorado Ave., Santa Monica, CA 90404. TEL 310-829-6811; FAX 310-453-3085. **Owner(s):** Copley Los Angeles Newspapers, 5215 Torrance Blvd., Torrance, CA 90509; Ed. Lou Brancaccio; Pub. Thomas Wafer; adv. contact: Janice Sheldon. photos; pub. size: broadsheet; circ. morning 25,000(paid). **Wire Service(s):** AP, NYT, CNS, McClatchy, Cox, CiNS.

SANTA ROSA
US
SANTA ROSA PRESS DEMOCRAT. 1857. d. $3/wk. 427 Mendocino Ave., Santa Rosa, CA 95401. TEL 707-546-2020; FAX 707-546-7538. **Owner(s):** New York Times Co., The, 229 W. 43rd St., New York, NY 10036. TEL 212-556-1234; Ed. Peter Golis; Pub. Michael J. Parman; adv. contact: Ken Svanum. bk.rev.; pub. size: standard; circ. morning 98,000(paid); Sun. 103,000(paid). **Wire Service(s):** AP, NYT, CNS, LAT-WP.

SIMI VALLEY
US
SIMI VALLEY STAR. 1912. d. $.35/day newsstand; $1.50/Sun.; $98/yr. local. 888 Easy St., Simi Valley, CA 93065. TEL 805-526-6211; FAX 805-526-0479. **Owner(s):** John P. Scripps Newspapers, Inc., 888 Easy St., Simi Valley, CA 92065. TEL 805-526-6211; Ed. Michael Hoffman; Pub. John Wilcox; adv. contact: Pepper Aarvold. pub. size: broadsheet; circ. evening 16,562(controlled & paid); Sun. 17,161(controlled & paid). **Wire Service(s):** AP.
Formerly: Simi Valley Enterprise.

SONORA
US
UNION DEMOCRAT, THE. 1854. Mon.-Fri. $.50 newsstand; $6/mo. carrier. 84 S. Washington St., Sonora, CA 95370. TEL 209-532-7151; FAX 209-532-5139. **Owner(s):** Union Democrat Corp., 84 S. Washington St., Sonora, CA 95370. TEL 209-532-7151; Ed. Buzz Eggleston; Pub. Harvey C. McGee; adv. contact: Bud Vogel. pub. size: broadsheet; circ. evening 13,800(paid). **Wire Service(s):** AP.

SOUTH LAKE TAHOE
US   ISSN 8750-3948
TAHOE DAILY TRIBUNE. 1958. Mon.-Fri. $.50/day newsstand; $1/Fri.; $90/yr. 3079 Harrison Ave., South Lake Tahoe, CA 96150. TEL 916-541-3880; FAX 916-541-0373; E-mail: tribune@tahoe.com; URL: http://www.tahoe.com. **Owner(s):** Tahoe Daily Tribune Inc., P.O. Box 1358, South Lake Tahoe, CA 96156. TEL 916-541-3880; Ed. Claire Fortier; Pub. Loren C. Abbott; adv. contact: Larry Womack. photos; pub. size: broadsheet; circ. morning 10,000(paid). **Wire Service(s):** AP.

STOCKTON
US
RECORD, THE. 1895. d. $.35/day newsstand; $1.25/Sun.; $11.31/mo. carrier. 530 E. Market St., Stockton, CA 95202. TEL 209-943-6397; FAX 209-546-8288. **Owner(s):** Omaha World-Herald Co., World-Herald Sq., 1334 Dodge St., Omaha, NE 68102. TEL 402-444-1000; Ed. Jim Gold; Pub. Terry Kroeger; adv. contact: Dave Windgarden. photos; bk.rev.; pub. size: broadsheet; circ. morning 55,078(paid); Sun. 68,741(paid). **Wire Service(s):** AP, NYT.
Formerly: Stockton Record.

TAFT
US
DAILY MIDWAY DRILLER. 1910. Mon.-Fri. $.35 newsstand; $5.90/mo. in cy. 800 Center St., Taft, CA 93268. TEL 805-763-3171; FAX 805-763-5638. **Owner(s):** Midway Driller, Inc., 800 Center St., Taft, CA 93268. TEL 805-763-3171; FAX 805-763-5638; Ed. Dave Hook; Pub. Dorthy M. Parsons; adv.; photos; pub. size: broadsheet; circ. evening 4,700(paid). **Wire Service(s):** AP.
Formerly: Taft Daily Midway Driller.

TEMECULA
US   ISSN 1045-5868
CALIFORNIAN, THE. 1976. d. $.25/day newsstand; $1/Sun.; $17.51/13 wks. home deliv. 28765 Single Oak Dr., Ste. 100, Temecula, CA 92590. TEL 909-676-4315; FAX 909-699-1467. **Owner(s):** North County Times, Escondido, CA; Ed. Kathy Day; Pub. Linda Wunerlich; adv.; photos; pub. size: broadsheet; circ. morning 14,500(paid); Sun. 14,500(paid). **Wire Service(s):** AP.

THOUSAND OAKS
US
THOUSAND OAKS STAR. 1954. d. $.25/day newsstand; $1.50/Sun. 2595 E. Thousand Oaks Blvd., Thousand Oaks, CA 91362. TEL 805-496-3211; FAX 805-379-3251. **Owner(s):** Scripps-Howard, 312 Walnut St., 28th Fl., Cincinatti, OH 45202. TEL 513-977-3000; Ed. John Wilcox; Pub. John Wilcox; adv. contact: Steve McConnell. pub. size: broadsheet; circ. morning 100,000(paid); Sun. 22,537(paid). **Wire Service(s):** AP, SH.
Formerly: Thousand Oaks News-Chronicle.

TORRANCE
US
DAILY BREEZE. 1895. d. $.25/day newsstand; $1.25/Sun.; $8/mo.; $96/yr. 5215 Torrance Blvd., Torrance, CA 90503. TEL 310-540-5511; FAX 310-540-6272. **Owner(s):** Copley Los Angeles Newspapers, 5215 Torrance Blvd., Torrance, CA 90509; Ed. Jean Adelsman; Pub. Thomas J. Wafer, Jr.; pub. size: broadsheet; circ. morning 80,800(paid); Sun. 118,903(paid). **Wire Service(s):** AP, CNS, NYT.

TRACY
US
TRACY PRESS. 1896. Mon.-Sat. $.25 newsstand; $36/yr. carrier. 145 W. Tenth St., Tracy, CA 95376. TEL 209-835-3030; FAX 209-835-0655. **Owner(s):** Tom, Bob, & Sam Matthews, P.O. Box 419, Tracy, CA 95378. TEL 209-835-3030; FAX 209-835-0655; Ed. Sam Matthews; Pub. Robert S. Matthews; adv. contact: Diane Lopez. pub. size: broadsheet; circ. morning 11,000(paid). **Wire Service(s):** AP, NYT.

TULARE
US
TULARE ADVANCE-REGISTER. 1882. Mon.-Sat. $.50 newsstand; $7.75/mo. 388 E. Cross Ave., Tulare, CA 93274. TEL 209-688-0521; FAX 209-688-7503. **Owner(s):** Gannett Company, Inc., 1100 Wilson Blvd., Arlington, VA 22234. TEL 703-284-6000; Ed. Steve Fountain; Pub. Amy L. Pack; adv. contact: David Dakin. photos; pub. size: broadsheet; circ. evening 9,000(paid). **Wire Service(s):** AP, SHNA, GNS.
Formerly: Advance-Register.

TURLOCK
US
TURLOCK JOURNAL. 1904. Mon.-Sat. $.50/day newsstand; $.75/Sat. 138 S. Center St., Turlock, CA 95380. TEL 209-634-9141; FAX 209-632-8813. **Owner(s):** Central Valley Publishing Co., P.O. Box 227, Crystal City, MO 63019; Ed. Doane Yawger; Pub. Wolf Rosenberg; adv. contact: Darryl Clayman. pub. size: broadsheet; circ. evening 7,461(paid). **Wire Service(s):** AP.
Formerly: Turlock Daily Journal.

UKIAH
US
UKIAH DAILY JOURNAL. 1862. Sun.-Fri. $.50/day newsstand; $1/Sun.; $7.50/mo.; $90/yr. carrier. 590 S. School St., Ukiah, CA 95482. TEL 707-468-0123; FAX 707-468-5780. **Owner(s):** Stephens Group, Inc., P.O. Box 1359, Fort Smith, AR 72901; Ed. Robb Hicken; Pub. Dennis Wilson; adv. contact: John Speck. pub. size: broadsheet; circ. evening 7,609(paid); Sun. 7,727(paid). **Wire Service(s):** AP.

VACAVILLE
US   ISSN 0746-4193
REPORTER, THE. 1883. d. $.50/day newsstand; $1.25/Sun.; $20/2 mos. 916 Cotting Ln., Vacaville, CA 95688. TEL 707-448-6401; FAX 707-447-8411. **Owner(s):** John Rico Publishing Co., Inc., 318 Main St., Vacaville, CA 95688. TEL 707-448-6401; Ed. Diane Barney; Pub. Richard Rico; adv. contact: Debbie Tavy. photos; pub. size: broadsheet; circ. morning 21,500(paid); Sun. 22,500(paid). **Wire Service(s):** AP.

DAILY NEWSPAPERS

ASPEN, CO   10427

VALENCIA
US
SIGNAL, THE. 1919. d. $.50/day newsstand; $1.75/Sun.; $78/yr. carrier; $150/yr. mailed. 24000 Creekside Rd., Valencia, CA 91355. TEL 805-259-1234; FAX 805-254-8068. **Owner(s):** Morris Communications, P.O. Box 8167, Savannah, GA 31412. TEL 912-233-1281; Ed. Tim Whyte; Pub. Darell Phillips; adv. contact: Ethel Nakutin. photos; bk.rev.; pub. size: broadsheet; circ. morning 44,000(paid); Sun. 44,000(paid). **Wire Service(s):** AP.
Formerly: Newhall Signal & Saugus Enterprise.

VALLEJO
US
VALLEJO TIMES-HERALD. 1875. d. $.50/day newsstand; $1/Sun.; $8.58/mo. 440 Curtola Pkwy., Vallejo, CA 94590. TEL 707-644-1141; FAX 707-643-5217. **Owner(s):** Stephens Group, Inc., P.O. Box 1359, Fort Smith, AR 72902. TEL 501-785-7810; Ed. Joe Lowell; Pub. David Stringer; adv.; pub. size: broadsheet; circ. morning 23,000(paid); Sun. 24,000(paid). **Wire Service(s):** AP, TP.

VENTURA
US
VENTURA COUNTY STAR. 1883. d. $.35/day newsstand; $1.50/Sun.; $9/mo. carrier; $15.90/mo. mailed. 5250 Ralson St., Ventura, CA 93003. TEL 805-650-2900; FAX 805-650-2950; E-mail: vcstar@aol.com. **Owner(s):** John P. Scripps Newspapers, Inc., 525 C St., Ste. 306, San Diego, CA 92101; Ed. Joe Howry; Pub. John Wilcox; adv. contact: P. Birmingham. photos; bk.rev.; pub. size: broadsheet; circ. morning 97,000(paid); Sun. 104,000(paid). **Wire Service(s):** AP, NYT, MNS, SHNA.
Formerly: Ventura County Star-Free Press.

VICTORVILLE
US   ISSN 1042-8496
DAILY PRESS. 1937. d. $.35/day newsstand; $1.25/Sun.; $4/wk. carrier; $240.76/yr. 13891 Park Ave., Victorville, CA 92392-1389. TEL 760-241-7744; FAX 760-241-1860; E-mail: rmm@vvdailypress.com. **Owner(s):** Freedom Communications, Inc., P.O. Box 19549, Irvine, CA 92713-9549. TEL 714-553-9292; Pub. Tom Portor; adv. contact: Ray Marien. photos; bk.rev.; pub. size: broadsheet; circ. morning 27,000(paid); Sun. 39,000(paid). **Wire Service(s):** AP.
Formerly: Victor Valley Daily Press.

VISALIA
US
VISALIA TIMES-DELTA. 1859. Mon.-Sat. $.50/day newsstand, $1/Sat.; $11.30/mo. home deliv. 330 N. West St., Visalia, CA 93291. TEL 209-734-5821; FAX 209-734-5843. **Owner(s):** Gannett Company, Inc., 1100 Wilson Blvd., Arlington, VA 22234. TEL 703-284-6000; Ed. Tom Bray; Pub. Amy L. Pack; adv. contact: David Dakin. pub. size: broadsheet; circ. morning 24,000(paid). **Wire Service(s):** AP, GNS.

WALNUT CREEK
US   ISSN 0192-0235
CONTRA COSTA TIMES. 1911. d. $.50 newsstand; $11.85/mo. 2640 Shadelands Dr., Walnut Creek, CA 94598. TEL 510-935-2525; FAX 510-977-8410. **Owner(s):** Knight-Ridder, Inc., One Herald Plz., Miami, FL 94598. TEL 305-376-3800; FAX 305-376-3875; Ed. Saundra Keyes; Pub. George E. Riggs; adv.; pub. size: broadsheet; circ. morning 97,500(paid); Sun. 107,221(paid). **Wire Service(s):** AP, McClatchy, NYT, LAT-WP, SHNA.

WATSONVILLE
US
REGISTER-PAJARONIAN. 1868. Mon.-Sat. $.35/day newsstand; $.50/Sat.; $7.25/mo. carrier; $10.55/mo. mailed. 1000 Main St., Watsonville, CA 95076. TEL 408-761-7300; FAX 408-722-8386; E-mail: pajaro@cruzio.com. **Owner(s):** News Media Corp., 211 Hwy. 38 E., P.O. Box 46, Rochelle, IL. TEL 815-562-2061; Pub. Douglas Leifheit; adv. contact: Nancy Moors. photos; bk.rev.; pub. size: broadsheet; circ. evening 11,000(paid). **Wire Service(s):** AP, LAT-WP, SHNA.
Formerly: Watsonville Register-Pajaronian.

WEST COVINA
US   ISSN 8755-9595
SAN GABRIEL VALLEY TRIBUNE. 1955. d. $.25/day newsstand; $1/Sun.; $2.75/wk.; $143/yr. 1210 Azusa Canyon Rd., West Covina, CA 91790. TEL 818-962-8811; FAX 818-856-2758; E-mail: tribune@earthlin.com. **Owner(s):** Media News Group, 4888 Loop Center Dr., Ste. 525, Houston, TX 77081. TEL 713-295-3800; Pub. Ike Massey; adv.; photos; bk.rev.; pub. size: broadsheet; circ. morning 57,903(paid); Sun. 59,380(paid). **Wire Service(s):** AP, NYT, Scripps-McClatchy.

WHITTIER
US   ISSN 1069-2819
WHITTIER DAILY NEWS. 1900. d. $.25/day newsstand; $1/Sun.; $1.65/wk. 7612 Greenleaf Ave., Whittier, CA 90602. TEL 310-698-0955; FAX 310-698-0450. **Owner(s):** Media News Group, 4888 Loop Central Dr., Houston, TX 77081. TEL 713-295-3800; Ed. Bill Bell; Pub. Bill Bell; pub. size: broadsheet; circ. evening 17,000(paid). **Wire Service(s):** AP, CiNS, DJ, KR, NYT.

WOODLAND
US   ISSN 0747-1890
DAILY DEMOCRAT. 1857. Mon.-Sat. $.50 newsstand; $7.50/mo. home deliv. 711 Main St., Woodland, CA 95776. TEL 916-662-5421; FAX 916-662-1288. **Owner(s):** Donrey Media Group, P.O. Box 17017, Fort Smith, AR 72901. TEL 501-785-7810; Ed. Jim Smith; Pub. Ron Rhea; adv. contact: Neill Rabon. pub. size: broadsheet; circ. evening 10,800(paid). **Wire Service(s):** AP.

WOODLAND HILLS
US
DAILY NEWS. 1911. d. $.25/day newsstand; $1/Sun.; $14.84/2 mos. 21221 Oxnard St., Woodland Hills, CA 91367. TEL 818-713-3000; FAX 818-713-3545. **Owner(s):** Jack Kent Cooke, Inc., 21221 Oxnard St., Woodland Hills, CA 91367. TEL 818-713-3131; Ed. Ron Kaye; Pub. Larry Beasley; adv. contact: Kevin E. Drolet. pub. size: broadsheet; circ. morning 212,252(paid); Sun. 227,054(paid).

YREKA
US
SISKIYOU DAILY NEWS. 1941. Mon.-Fri. $.50 newsstand; $70/yr. 309 S. Broadway, Yreka, CA 96097. TEL 916-842-5777; FAX 916-842-6787. **Owner(s):** American Publishing Co., 606 N. Van Buren, P.O. Box 520, Marion, IL 62959. TEL 618-993-1711; Ed. Darren Bensen. adv.; photos; pub. size: broadsheet; circ. evening 6,100(paid). **Wire Service(s):** AP.

COLORADO

ALAMOSA
US   ISSN 1047-1170
VALLEY COURIER. 1925. Tue.-Sat. $.50 newsstand; $7.90/mo. 401-407 State St., Alamosa, CO 81101. TEL 719-589-2553; FAX 719-589-6573. **Owner(s):** News Media Corp., Rochelle, IL. TEL 815-562-2061; Ed. Greg Johnson; Pub. Keith R. Cerny; adv. contact: Keith R. Cerny. adv.: $8.65/SAU. photos; pub. size: standard; circ. evening 5,150(paid). **Wire Service(s):** AP.

ASPEN
US
ASPEN DAILY NEWS. 1978. Mon.-Sat. free. 517 E. Hopkins, Aspen, CO 81611. TEL 970-925-2220; FAX 970-920-2118; E-mail: aspnews@sopris.net. **Owner(s):** David Danforth, 517 E. Hopkins, Aspen, CO 81611. TEL 303-925-2220; Ed. Ben Gagnen; Pub. David Danforth; adv. contact: Brigitte Center. photos; bk.rev.; pub. size: tabloid; circ. morning 12,500(free). **Wire Service(s):** AP.

US
ASPEN TIMES, THE. 1881. Mon.-Fri. free/Mon.-Thu. newsstand; $.25/Fri.; $32/yr. 310 E. Main St., Aspen, CO 81611. TEL 970-925-3414; FAX 970-925-6240; E-mail: aspenonline@infosphere.com; URL: http://www.aspenonline.com/clients/aspenonline/directory/times. **Owner(s):** Full Court Press, Ltd., 310 E. Main St., Aspen, CO 81611. TEL 970-925-3414; FAX 970-925-6240; Ed. Andy Stone; Pub. Michael McVoy; adv. contact: Chris Cheo. photos; bk.rev.; pub. size: tabloid; circ. morning 12,500(free & paid); Sun. 11,000(free & paid). **Wire Service(s):** AP.
Formerly: Aspen Times & Times Daily.

DAILY NEWSPAPERS

AVON
US
VAIL DAILY. 1981. d. free; $30/yr. mailed. 40780 US Hwy. 6 & 24, Avon, CO 81620. TEL 970-476-0555; FAX 970-949-7096; E-mail: vdail@vail.net; URL: http://www.vaildaily.com/vail. Owner(s): Swift Publications, Reno, NV; Ed. Rob Spencer; Pub. Bob Brown; adv. contact: Michael Bennett. photos; pub. size: tabloid; circ. morning 12,000(free). **Wire Service(s):** AP.

BOULDER
US ISSN 0746-8733
DAILY CAMERA. 1891. d. $.25/day newsstand; $.75/Sun.; $29.25/13 wks. 1048 Pearl St., Boulder, CO 80302. TEL 303-442-1202; FAX 303-449-9358; E-mail: news@dailycamera.com. Owner(s): Knight-Ridder, Inc., One Herald Plz., Miami, FL 33132. TEL 305-376-3800; FAX 305-376-3875; Ed. Barrie Hartman; Pub. Harold Higgins; adv. contact: Bill Sabo. pub. size: broadsheet; circ. morning 35,000(paid); Sun. 43,000(paid). **Wire Service(s):** AP, LAT-WP, KNT, NYT.
Formerly: Boulder Daily Camera.

CANON CITY
US ISSN 1054-3457
DAILY RECORD. 1896. Mon.-Sat. $.35 newsstand; $7/mo.; $7.25/mo. motor rte. 701 S. Ninth St., Canon City, CO 81212. TEL 719-275-7565; FAX 719-275-1353. Owner(s): Royal Gorge Publishing Co., 523 Main St., Canon City, CO 81212. TEL 719-275-7565; Ed. Troy Schwindt; Pub. Ed Lehman; adv. contact: Terri Holloway. pub. size: broadsheet; circ. evening 8,794(paid). **Wire Service(s):** AP.
Formerly: Canon City Daily Record.

COLORADO SPRINGS
US
GAZETTE, THE. 1872. d. $.50/day newsstand; $1/Sun.; $9.50/mo. home deliv. 30 S. Prospect St., Colorado Springs, CO 80903. TEL 719-632-5511; FAX 719-636-0202; E-mail: gazette@usa.net; URL: http://usa.net/gazette. Owner(s): Freedom Communications, Inc., 17666 Fitch St., Irvine, CA 92614. TEL 714-553-9292; Ed. Terri Fleming; Pub. N. Christian Anderson III; bk.rev.; pub. size: broadsheet; circ. morning 103,945(paid); Sun. 123,051(paid). **Wire Service(s):** AP, KNT, NYT, SHNA, NNS.
Formerly: Colorado Springs Gazette Telegraph.

CRAIG
US
NORTHWEST COLORADO DAILY PRESS. 1965. Mon.-Sat. $.25 newsstand; $5.50/mo. home deliv. 466 Yampa Ave., Craig, CO 81625. TEL 970-824-7031; FAX 970-824-6810. Owner(s): WorldWest Limited Liability Co., 609 New Hampshire, P.O. Box 688, Lawrence, KS 66044. TEL 913-843-1000; Ed. Jim Files; Pub. Bill Muldoon; adv. contact: Bill Muldoon. photos; pub. size: tabloid; circ. evening 3,500(paid). **Wire Service(s):** AP.

DENVER
US
DENVER POST. 1895. d. $.25/day newsstand; $1/Sun.; $7.25/mo. 1560 Broadway, Denver, CO 80202. TEL 303-820-1010; FAX 303-820-1369; E-mail: newsroom@denverpost.com; URL: http://www.denverpost.com. Owner(s): Media News Group, 4888 Loop Central Dr., Ste. 525, Houston, TX 77081. TEL 713-295-3800; Ed. Dennis Britton; Pub. Ryan McKibben; adv. contact: Allen J. Walters. photos; pub. size: broadsheet; circ. morning 316,027(paid); Sun. 456,057(paid). **Wire Service(s):** AP, LAT-WP, KR, UPI, DJ, NYT.

US
ROCKY MOUNTAIN NEWS. 1859. d. $.35/day newsstand; $.75/Sun.; $12.80/mo. 400 W. Colfax Ave., Denver, CO 80204. TEL 303-892-5000; FAX 303-892-5249; E-mail: newsdesk@denver-rmn.com; URL: http://www.denver-rmn.com. Owner(s): Scripps-Howard, 312 Walnut St., 28th Fl., Cincinnatti, OH 45202. TEL 513-977-3000; Ed. John Temple; Pub. Larry D. Strutton; adv. contact: Jerry Dunning. pub. size: tabloid; circ. morning 331,044(paid); Sun. 446,866(paid). **Wire Service(s):** AP, SHN, NEA.

DURANGO
US
DURANGO HERALD. 1881. Tue.-Sun. $.35/day newsstand; $1/Sun. 1275 Main Ave., Durango, CO 81301. TEL 970-247-3504; FAX 970-259-5011; E-mail: herald@frontier.net. Owner(s): Durango Herald Inc., P.O. Drawer A, Durango, CO 81302. TEL 303-247-3504; Ed. Dave Stats; Pub. Richard G. Ballantine; adv. contact: Sharon Hermes. pub. size: broadsheet; circ. morning 10,000(paid); Sun. 10,672(paid). **Wire Service(s):** AP.

FORT COLLINS
US ISSN 0164-9167
FORT COLLINS COLORADOAN. 1873. d. $.35/day newsstand; $1/Sun.; $32.50/13 wks. carrier. 1212 Riverside Ave., Fort Collins, CO 80524. TEL 970-224-7730; FAX 970-224-7899; E-mail: editor@fortnet.org; URL: http://www.fortnet.org/coloradoan/home.html. Owner(s): Gannett Company, Inc., 1100 Wilson Blvd., Arlington, VA 22234. TEL 703-284-6000; Pub. Dorothy Bland; adv. contact: Pamela Browning. photos; bk.rev.; pub. size: broadsheet; circ. morning 23,500(paid); Sun. 35,000(paid). **Wire Service(s):** AP, GNS, LAT-WP.

FORT MORGAN
US
FORT MORGAN TIMES, THE. 1884. Mon.-Sat. $.50 newsstand; $130/yr. 329 Main St., Fort Morgan, CO 80701-4000. TEL 970-867-5651; FAX 970-867-7448. Owner(s): Media News Group, 309 S. Broad St., Woodbury, NJ 08096. TEL 609-845-3300; Ed. Bill Spencer; Pub. Robert W. Spencer, Jr.; adv. contact: Timi McCormick. photos; pub. size: broadsheet; circ. evening 5,182(paid). **Wire Service(s):** AP.

FRISCO
US
SUMMIT DAILY NEWS. 1989. d. free in area; $2/Sun. mailed only. 40 W. Main St., Frisco, CO 80443. TEL 970-668-3998; FAX 970-668-3859. Owner(s): Eagle-Summit Publishing Co., P.O. Box 81, Vail, CO 81658. TEL 303-476-0555; Pub. Bob Brown; adv. contact: Ned Basworth. pub. size: tabloid; circ. morning 8,000(free); Sun. 8,000(free). **Wire Service(s):** AP.

GLENWOOD SPRINGS
US
GLENWOOD POST. 1890. Mon.-Sat. $.35 newsstand; $102/yr. carrier. 2014 Grand Ave., Glenwood Springs, CO 81601. TEL 970-945-8515; FAX 970-945-4487; E-mail: glenpost@rof.net; URL: http://www.glenwoodpost.com. Owner(s): Morris Communications, P.O. Box 936, Augusta, GA 30903. TEL 706-724-0851; Ed. Dennis Webb; Pub. Gary Dickson; adv. contact: Bob Zanella. bk.rev.; pub. size: broadsheet; circ. evening 5,100(paid). **Wire Service(s):** AP.

GRAND JUNCTION
US
DAILY SENTINEL, THE. 1893. d. $.35/day newsstand; $1/Sun.; $2.75/wk. carrier. 734 S. Seventh St., Grand Junction, CO 81501-7786. TEL 970-256-4256; FAX 970-241-6860. Owner(s): Cox Enterprises, Inc., 1400 Lake Hearn Dr., N.E., Atlanta, GA 30319. TEL 404-843-5000; Ed. Dennis Herzog; Pub. George Orbanek; adv. contact: Dennis Mitchell. pub. size: broadsheet; circ. evening 35,000(paid); Sun. 30,000(paid). **Wire Service(s):** AP, Cox, SHNA, LAT-WP.

GREELEY
US
GREELEY TRIBUNE. 1870. d. $.50/day newsstand; $.75/Sun.; $9.25/mo. local; $9.25/mo. mailed. 501 Eighth Ave., Greeley, CO 80631. TEL 303-352-0211; FAX 303-356-5780. Owner(s): Swift Publications, 501 Eighth Ave., Greeley, CO 80631. TEL 303-352-0211; Ed. Chris Cobler; Pub. David Trussell; adv. contact: George Snyder. photos; bk.rev.; pub. size: broadsheet; circ. evening 24,000(paid); Sun. 24,500(paid). **Wire Service(s):** AP, LAT-WP.

GUNNISON
US ISSN 0892-1113
GUNNISON COUNTRY TIMES. 1880. Mon.-Fri. $.25 newsstand; $48/yr. 218 N. Wisconsin, Gunnison, CO 81230. TEL 970-641-1414; FAX 970-641-6515; E-mail: streed@frontier.net; URL: http://www.gunnisontimes.com/current/news.html. Owner(s): Ventana Publishing Co., 283 S. Fir St., Telluride, CO 81435. TEL 970-728-0788; Ed. Steve Reed. adv. contact: Patti Daniel. pub. size: tabloid; circ. 3,500(paid). **Wire Service(s):** AP.

DAILY NEWSPAPERS

LA JUNTA
US   ISSN 1056-4616
LA JUNTA TRIBUNE-DEMOCRAT. 1897. Mon.-Fri. $.25 newsstand; $51/yr. carrier mailed in city; $57/yr. carrier mailed in 810 zip code; $79.50/yr. elsewhere. 422 Colorado Ave., La Junta, CO 81050. TEL 719-384-4475; FAX 719-384-5999. **Owner(s):** La Junta Democrat Publishing Co., Inc., P.O. Box 480, La Junta, CO 81050. TEL 719-384-4475; Ed. Wanda Lowe; Pub. John Lowe; adv. contact: Shelley Noe. photos; pub. size: tabloid; circ. evening 3,787(paid). **Wire Service(s):** AP.

LAMAR
US
LAMAR DAILY NEWS. 1907. Tue.-Fri. & Sun. $.50 newsstand; $84/yr. local; $116/yr. tri-state; $126/yr. elsewhere. 310 S. Fifth St., Lamar, CO 81052-1217. TEL 719-336-2266; FAX 719-336-2526; E-mail: ldnews@iquana.ruralnet.net. **Owner(s):** Media News Group, 309 S. Broad St., Woodbury, NJ 08096. TEL 609-845-3300; Ed. Ava Betz; Pub. Tom Betz; pub. size: broadsheet; circ. evening 2,650(paid); Sun. 2,700(paid). **Wire Service(s):** AP.

LONGMONT
US
DAILY TIMES-CALL. 1871. d. $.25/day newsstand; $.75/Sun.; $8.70/mo. local; $9/mo. in cy.; $12/mo. mailed. 350 Terry St., Longmont, CO 80501. TEL 303-776-2244; FAX 303-678-8615; E-mail: tcedit@frll.com; URL: http://www.longmontfyi.com. **Owner(s):** Times-Call Publishing Corp., P.O. Box 299, Longmont, CO 80502. TEL 303-776-2244; FAX 303-678-8615; Ed. Curt Anderson; Pub. Edward Lehman; adv. contact: Linda Szaloczi. photos; pub. size: broadsheet; circ. evening 21,000(paid); Sun. 23,000(paid). **Wire Service(s):** AP, LAT-WP.
Formerly: Longmont Daily Times-Call.

LOVELAND
US
LOVELAND DAILY REPORTER-HERALD. 1880. Mon.-Sat. $.35 newsstand; $.50/Sat.; $93/yr. in town; $96/yr. motor rte. 201 E. Fifth St., Loveland, CO 80537. TEL 970-669-5050; FAX 970-667-1111; E-mail: news@reporter-herald.com; URL: http://www.lovelandfyi.com. **Owner(s):** Loveland Publishing Co., 201 E. Fifth St., Loveland, CO 80537. TEL 970-669-5050; Ed. Ken Amundson; Pub. Edward Lehman; adv. contact: Sally Lee. photos; bk.rev.; pub. size: broadsheet; circ. evening 17,500(paid). **Wire Service(s):** AP, LAT-WP.

MONTROSE
US
MONTROSE DAILY PRESS. 1908. Mon.-Fri. $.35 newsstand; $60/yr. in state; $72/yr. out of state. 535 S. First St., Montrose, CO 81401. TEL 970-249-3444; FAX 970-249-3331. **Owner(s):** Wick Communications, Inc., 333 W. Wilcox Dr., Ste. 302, Sierra Vista, AZ 85635. TEL 520-458-0200; FAX 520-458-6166; Ed. Richard E. Day; Pub. Steven Woody; pub. size: broadsheet; circ. evening 7,500(paid). **Wire Service(s):** AP.

US
▼**MONTROSE MORNING SUN.** 1996. Mon.-Fri. free. 120 N. Selig Ave., Montrose, CO 81401. TEL 970-240-4900; FAX 970-240-1842. **Owner(s):** D.P. Newspaper LLC, 120 N. Selig Ave., Montrose, CO 81401. TEL 970-240-4900; Ed. Gary Taylor; Pub. Mike Ritchey; adv. contact: Jean Burkholder. pub. size: standard.

PUEBLO
US   ISSN 0747-3559
PUEBLO CHIEFTAIN. 1873. d. $.25/day newsstand; $.75/Sun.; $9/mo. 825 W. Sixth St., Pueblo, CO 81003. TEL 719-544-3520; FAX 719-546-3235. **Owner(s):** Star Journal Publishing Corp., Inc., P.O. Box 4040, Pueblo, CO 81003. TEL 719-544-3520; Ed. Robert H. Rawlings; Pub. Robert H. Rawlings; adv. contact: Jack Wyss. photos; pub. size: broadsheet; circ. morning 51,000(paid); Sun. 56,500(paid). **Wire Service(s):** AP.

ROCKY FORD
US
ROCKY FORD DAILY GAZETTE. 1907. Mon.-Fri. $.25 newsstand; $40/yr. carrier; $60/yr. mailed. 912 Elm Ave., Rocky Ford, CO 81067. TEL 719-254-3351; FAX 719-254-3354. **Owner(s):** Rocky Ford Publishing Co., 912 Elm Ave., Rocky Ford, CO 81067. TEL 303-254-3351; Ed. J.R. Thompson; Pub. Anne M. Thompson; adv. contact: Laura Thompson. photos; pub. size: broadsheet; circ. evening 3,304(paid).

SALIDA
US
MOUNTAIN MAIL. 1880. Mon.-Fri. $.25 newsstand; $48/yr. 125-129 E. Second St., Salida, CO 81201. TEL 719-539-6691; FAX 719-539-6630; E-mail: mtnmail@rmii.com; URL: http://www.peaksnewsnet.com. **Owner(s):** Arkansas Valley Publishing Co., P.O. Box 189, Salida, CO 81201. TEL 719-539-6691; FAX 719-539-6630; Ed. Merle Baranczyk; Pub. Merle Baranczyk; adv. contact: Vickie Vigil. photos; bk.rev.; pub. size: tabloid; circ. morning 3,200(paid).

STEAMBOAT SPRINGS
US
STEAMBOAT TODAY. 1989. Mon.-Fri. free. 1041 Lincoln Ave., Steamboat Springs, CO 80477. TEL 970-879-1505; FAX 970-879-2888; E-mail: jbone@rmii.com. **Owner(s):** WorldWest Limited Liability Co., 609 New Hampshire, P.O. Box 688, Lawrence, KS 66044. TEL 913-843-1000; Ed. Tom Ross; Pub. Suzanne Antinora; adv. contact: Sandy Lettunich. pub. size: tabloid; circ. morning 5,000(free). **Wire Service(s):** AP.

STERLING
US
STERLING JOURNAL-ADVOCATE. 1885. Mon.-Sat. $.50 newsstand; $77/yr. motor rte. 504 N. Third St., Sterling, CO 80751. TEL 970-522-1990; FAX 970-522-2320; E-mail: journal@sosinc.net. **Owner(s):** Media News Group, 309 S. Broad St., Woodbury, NJ 08096. TEL 609-845-3300; Pub. Bill Muldoon; adv. contact: Doug Knight. bk.rev.; pub. size: broadsheet; circ. evening 5,875(paid). **Wire Service(s):** AP.

TELLURIDE
US
TELLURIDE DAILY PLANET. 1993. Mon.-Fri. free. 283 S. Fir St., Telluride, CO 81435. TEL 970-728-9788; FAX 970-728-9793; E-mail: tdplanet@aol.com; URL: http://www.telluridegateway.com/current/news.html. **Owner(s):** Ventana Publishing Co., 283 S. Fir St., Telluride, CO 81435. TEL 970-728-9788; FAX 970-728-9793; Ed. Bob Beer; Pub. Tony Daranyi; adv. contact: John Dourlet. photos; bk.rev.; pub. size: tabloid; circ. morning 4,500(free).

TRINIDAD
US
CHRONICLE NEWS, THE. 1876. Mon.-Fri. $.25 newsstand; $42/yr. local. 200 W. Church St., Trinidad, CO 81082. TEL 719-846-3311; FAX 719-846-3612. **Owner(s):** Lake Charles American Press, 327 Board St., Lake Charles, LA 70601. TEL 318-439-2781; Ed. Cosette Henritze. pub. size: broadsheet; circ. evening 4,000(paid). **Wire Service(s):** AP.
Formerly: Trinidad Chronicle News.

CONNECTICUT

BRIDGEPORT
US
CONNECTICUT POST. 1883. d. $.50/day newsstand; $1.75/Sun.; $234/yr. 410 State St., Bridgeport, CT 06604. TEL 203-333-0161; FAX 203-366-3373; E-mail: edit@snet.net. **Owner(s):** Thomson Newspapers, Inc., 3150 Des Plaines Ave., Des Plaines, IL 60018. TEL 708-299-5544; Ed. Michael Daly; Pub. Robert Laska; adv. contact: Brenda MacDonald. pub. size: broadsheet; circ. morning 75,000(paid); Sun. 92,455(paid). **Wire Service(s):** AP, UPI, KR.
Formerly: Bridgeport Post Telegram.

BRISTOL
US   ISSN 0891-5563
BRISTOL PRESS, THE. 1871. d. $42.25/3 mos. in area; $65/3 mos. out of area. 99 Main St., Bristol, CT 06010. TEL 860-584-0501; FAX 860-585-9283. **Owner(s):** Journal Register Co., 50 W. State St., 12th Fl., Trenton, NJ 08608. TEL 609-396-2200; Ed. John Desanto; Pub. Michael Vanacore; pub. size: broadsheet; circ. evening 20,484(paid). **Wire Service(s):** AP.

DANBURY
US   ISSN 1044-4106
NEWS-TIMES, THE. 1883. d. $.50/day newsstand; $1.50/Sun.; $3.60/wk. carrier. 333 Main St., Danbury, CT 06810-5868. TEL 203-744-5100; FAX 203-792-8730. **Owner(s):** Ottaway Newspapers, Inc., P.O. Box 401, Campbell Hall, NY 10916. TEL 914-294-8181; Ed. Paul Steinmetz, Jr.; Pub. Wayne J. Shepperd; adv. contact: Richard Steel. adv.: $20.82/SAU daily; $24.13/SAU Sun. photos; bk.rev.; pub. size: broadsheet; circ. morning 36,618(paid); Sun. 43,654(paid). **Wire Service(s):** AP, ONS, KRTN.

GREENWICH

US   ISSN 0279-5213
GREENWICH TIME. 1861. d. $.50/day newsstand; $1.50/Sun. 20 E. Elm, Greenwich, CT 06830. TEL 203-625-4400; FAX 203-964-4419. **Owner(s):** Southern Connecticut Newspapers, Inc., 75 Tresser Blvd., P.O. Box 9307, Stamford, CT 06901. TEL 203-964-2200; Ed. Joseph Pisani; Pub. William J. Rowe; adv.; pub. size: broadsheet; circ. evening 13,407(paid); Sun. 14,300(paid). **Wire Service(s):** AP, LAT-WP, KR, CT-NYT, UPI Photo.

HARTFORD

US   ISSN 1047-4153
HARTFORD COURANT. 1764. d. $.50/day newsstand; $1.50/Sun.; $3.90/wk.; $50.70/13 wks. 285 Broad St., Hartford, CT 06115-2510. TEL 860-241-6200; FAX 860-241-3865. **Owner(s):** Times Mirror Co., Times Mirror Sq., 220 W. First St., Los Angeles, CA 90012. TEL 213-237-3700; Ed. Clifford L. Teutsch; Pub. Michael E. Waller; adv. contact: Kathleen Coddington. pub. size: broadsheet; circ. morning 209,785(paid); Sun. 307,219(paid). **Wire Service(s):** AP, KR, LAT-WP, DJ, RN, Bloomberg Business News.

MANCHESTER

US
JOURNAL INQUIRER. 1968. Mon.-Sat. $.50 newsstand; $124.80/yr. carrier. 306 Progress Dr., Manchester, CT 06040. TEL 860-646-0500; FAX 860-646-9867; E-mail: journalinq@aol.com; URL: http://www.journalinquirer.com. **Owner(s):** Journal Publishing Co., 306 Progress Dr., Manchester, CT 06040. TEL 203-643-8111; Ed. Chris Powell; Pub. Elizabeth S. Ellis; adv. contact: Bill Sybert. pub. size: tabloid; circ. evening 50,000(paid). **Wire Service(s):** AP.
Formerly: Manchester Journal Inquirer.

MERIDEN

US
RECORD-JOURNAL. 1867. d. $4/wk. 11 Crown St., Meriden, CT 06450-5788. TEL 203-235-1661; FAX 203-639-0210. **Owner(s):** Record-Journal Publishing Co., 11 Crown St., Meriden, CT 06450. TEL 203-235-1661; Ed. Donald Schiller; Pub. Eliot C. White; adv. contact: Michael F. Killian. photos; bk.rev.; pub. size: broadsheet; circ. morning 29,350(paid); Sun. 30,068(paid). **Wire Service(s):** AP.

MIDDLETOWN

US
MIDDLETOWN PRESS. 1884. d. $.50/day newsstand; $.50/Sun. $169/yr. home deliv. 2 Main St., Middletown, CT 06457. TEL 860-347-3331; FAX 860-347-3380. **Owner(s):** Journal Register Co., 50 W. State St., 12th Fl., Trenton, NJ 08608. TEL 609-396-2200; Ed. Karen Avitabile; Pub. Gerald Garcia; adv. contact: Jamie M. Tomasic. photos; bk.rev.; pub. size: standard; circ. morning 12,161(paid). **Wire Service(s):** UPI, NYT, LAT-WP.

NAUGATUCK

US
NAUGATUCK DAILY NEWS. 1885. Mon.-Sat. $.50 newsstand; $93.60/yr. carrier; $120/yr. mailed. 71 Weid Dr., Naugatuck, CT 06770. TEL 203-729-2228; FAX 203-729-9099. **Owner(s):** American Publishing Co., 606 N. Van Buren, P.O. Box 520, Marion, IL 62959. TEL 618-993-1711; Ed. Mary Ellen Godin; Pub. Ronald Waer; pub. size: broadsheet; circ. evening 5,250(paid). **Wire Service(s):** AP.

NEW BRITAIN

US
HERALD, THE. 1880. d. $.50/day newsstand; $.50/Sun.; $138.60/yr. One Herald Sq., New Britain, CT 06050-2050. TEL 860-225-4601; FAX 860-225-4601. **Owner(s):** Journal Register Co., 50 W. State St., 12th Fl., Trenton, NJ 08608. TEL 609-396-2200; Pub. Jerald Garcia; adv. contact: Michael Moses. photos; bk.rev.; pub. size: broadsheet; circ. evening 33,252(paid). **Wire Service(s):** AP.

NEW HAVEN

US
NEW HAVEN REGISTER. 1812. d. $.50/day newsstand; $1.50/Sun.; $3.50/wk. 40 Sargent Dr., New Haven, CT 06511. TEL 203-789-5211; FAX 203-789-5309. **Owner(s):** E.M. Warburg/Pincus & Co., 40 Sargent Dr., New Haven, CT 06511; Ed. David Funkhouser; Pub. William Rush; adv.; photos; pub. size: standard; circ. morning 100,410(paid); Sun. 120,109(paid). **Wire Service(s):** AP, LAT-WP, KR.

NEW LONDON

US   ISSN 0744-0499
DAY, THE. 1881. d. $.50/day newsstand; $1/Sun.; $3.10/wk. carrier; $15.38/mo. mailed; $12.40/4 wks. motor rte. 47 Eugene O'Neill Dr., New London, CT 06320. TEL 203-442-2200; FAX 203-447-1683. **Owner(s):** Day Publishing Co., The, P.O. Box 1231, New London, CT 06320. TEL 203-442-2200; FAX 203-447-1683; Ed. Lance Johnson; Pub. Reid MacCluggage; adv.; photos; bk.rev.; pub. size: broadsheet; circ. morning 42,366(paid); Sun. 48,713(paid). **Wire Service(s):** AP, NYT, KNT.
Formerly: New London Day.

NORWALK

US
HOUR, THE. 1871. Mon.-Sat. $.50/day newsstand; $.75/Sat.; $117.60/yr. in cy.; $173/yr. out of cy. 346 Main Ave., Norwalk, CT 06851. TEL 203-846-3281; FAX 203-840-1802. **Owner(s):** Estate of Nellie Thomas, 346 Main Ave., Norwalk, CT 06851. TEL 203-846-3281; Ed. Mark Allison; Pub. B.J. Frazier; adv. contact: Thomas Kies. photos; pub. size: standard; circ. evening 21,500(paid). **Wire Service(s):** AP.
Formerly: Norwalk Hour.

NORWICH

US
NORWICH BULLETIN. 1791. d. $.50/day newsstand; $1/Sun.; $2.75/wk. home deliv. 66 Franklin St., Norwich, CT 06360. TEL 860-887-9211; FAX 860-887-9666; E-mail: norbull@q.continuum.net; URL: http://www.ctonline.com/ctonline/nbulletin.html. **Owner(s):** Gannett Company, Inc., 1100 Wilson Blvd, Arlington, VA 22234; Pub. David Whitehead; adv.; bk.rev.; pub. size: broadsheet; circ. morning 32,841(paid); Sun. 38,409(paid). **Wire Service(s):** AP, GNS.

STAMFORD

US   ISSN 0279-5167
ADVOCATE, THE. 1829. d. $.50/day newsstand; $1.50/Sun.; $3/wk. 75 Tresser Blvd., Stamford, CT 06904. TEL 203-964-2200; FAX 203-964-2345. **Owner(s):** Times-Mirror Co., Times-Mirror Sq., 220 W. First St., Los Angeles, CA 90053. TEL 213-237-3700; Ed. Deirdre Channing; Pub. William J. Rowe; pub. size: broadsheet; circ. evening 31,000(paid); Sun. 42,000(paid). **Wire Service(s):** AP.

TORRINGTON

US   ISSN 0746-8180
REGISTER CITIZEN. 1874. d. $.50/day newsstand; $1.25/Sun.; $3.20/wk.; $12.80/4 wks. 190 Water St., Torrington, CT 06790-0058. TEL 860-489-3121; FAX 860-489-6790. **Owner(s):** Journal Register Co., 50 W. State St., 12th Fl., Trenton, NJ 08608. TEL 609-396-2200; Ed. Ann Karoyli; Pub. William Murray; adv. contact: Jan Russo. pub. size: broadsheet; circ. morning 16,585(paid). **Wire Service(s):** AP, NYT.

WATERBURY

US
WATERBURY REPUBLICAN-AMERICAN. 1990. d. $.50/day newsstand; $1.50/Sun.; $2/wk. 389 Meadow St., Waterbury, CT 06722-2090. TEL 203-574-3636; FAX 203-596-9277. **Owner(s):** Rebublican-American, Inc., P.O. Box 2090, Waterbury, CT 06722-2090. TEL 203-574-3636; Ed. Robert D. Veillette; Pub. William J. Pape, II; adv. contact: Patrick Cox. pub. size: broadsheet; circ. morning 59,709(paid); Sun. 74,000(paid). **Wire Service(s):** AP.

DAILY NEWSPAPERS   CRYSTAL RIVER, FL   10431

WILLIMANTIC

US

CHRONICLE, THE. 1876. Mon.-Sat. $.50 newsstand; $2.10/wk. carrier. One Chronicle Rd., Willimantic, CT 06226. TEL 860-423-8466; FAX 860-423-2641. **Owner(s):** Lucy Crosby, One Chronicle Rd., Willimantic, CT 06226. TEL 860-423-8466; Ed. Ron Robillard. adv. contact: Walter Riley. pub. size: broadsheet; circ. evening 13,000(paid). **Wire Service(s):** AP.

Formerly: Willimantic Chronicle.

DELAWARE

DOVER

US   ISSN 0745-8096

DELAWARE STATE NEWS. 1953. d. $.50/day newsstand; $1.50/Sun.; $2.50/wk. Webbs Ln. & New Burton Rd., Dover, DE 19901. TEL 302-674-3600; FAX 302-741-8232. **Owner(s):** Independent Newspapers, Inc., 8015 N. 54th St., Scottsdale, AZ 85253. TEL 602-997-5811; Pub. Tammy Brittingham; Ed. Michael Pelrine; Pub. Tammy Brittingham; adv. contact: Helen Downing. photos; pub. size: broadsheet; circ. morning 25,000(paid); Sun. 38,000(paid). **Wire Service(s):** SHNA, KNT, LAT-WP.

NEW CASTLE

US   ISSN 1042-4121

NEWS JOURNAL, THE. 1880. d. $3.35/wk. home deliv. 950 W. Basin Rd., New Castle, DE 19720. TEL 302-324-2500; FAX 302-324-2557; E-mail: jrowley@wilmingt.gannett.com. **Owner(s):** Gannett Company, Inc., 1100 Wilson Blvd., Arlington, VA 22234. TEL 703-248-6000; Ed. E. J. Mitchell; Pub. W. Curtis Riddle; adv. contact: Sam Martin. photos; bk.rev.; pub. size: broadsheet; circ. morning 125,000(paid); Sun. 151,000(paid). **Wire Service(s):** AP, LAT-WP, GNS, Baltimore Sun, SHNS.

REHOBOTH BEACH

US

DAILY WHALE, THE. 1975. d. $.50/day newsstand; $1.25/Sun.; $130/yr. home deliv. Rte. 1, Midway Shopping Ctr., Rehoboth Beach, DE 19971. TEL 302-645-2265; FAX 302-645-2267. **Owner(s):** Independent Newspapers, Inc., P.O. Box 7001, Dover, DE 19903. TEL 302-674-4750; FAX 302-674-5910; Ed. Gwen Guerke; Pub. Tamra Brittingham; adv. contact: Darel LaPrede. photos; pub. size: broadsheet; circ. morning 5,500(free & paid); Sun. 35,000(free & paid). **Wire Service(s):** KR, SHNA, LAT-WP.

DISTRICT OF COLUMBIA

WASHINGTON

US   ISSN 0190-8286

WASHINGTON POST, THE. 1877. d. $.25/day newsstand; $1.50/Sun; $132.60/yr. 1150 15th St., N.W., Washington, DC 20071. TEL 202-334-7973; FAX 202-334-5609. **Owner(s):** Washington Post, The, 1150 15th St., N.W., Washington, DC 20071. TEL 202-334-6000; Ed. Robert Kaiser; Pub. Donald E. Graham; adv.; photos; bk.rev.; pub. size: broadsheet; circ. morning 834,641(paid); Sun. 1,140,564(paid). **Wire Service(s):** AP, UPI, CT, NYNS, CDN, LAT-WP.

US   ISSN 0732-8494

WASHINGTON TIMES. 1982. d. $.25/day newsstand; $1/Sun.; $2/wk. local. 3600 New York Ave., N.E., Washington, DC 20002. TEL 202-636-3000; FAX 202-269-3419. **Owner(s):** News World Communications, Inc., 401 Fifth Ave., New York, NY 10016. TEL 212-532-8300; Ed. Josette Shiner. adv.; photos; bk.rev.; pub. size: broadsheet; circ. morning 100,000(paid); Sun. 85,000(paid). **Wire Service(s):** AP, AFP, RN, LDE.

FLORIDA

BOCA RATON

US

BOCA RATON NEWS. 1958. d. $.25/day newsstand; $.75/Sun.; $1.48/wk. 33 S.E. Third St., Boca Raton, FL 33432. TEL 407-338-4910; FAX 407-338-4944. **Owner(s):** Knight-Ridder, Inc., One Herald Plz., Miami, FL 33132. TEL 305-376-3800; FAX 305-376-3875; Ed. Phyllis Gilchrist; Pub. Roger Coover; adv. contact: Lesli Monahan. photos; bk.rev.; pub. size: broadsheet; circ. morning 16,000(paid); Sun. 20,000(paid). **Wire Service(s):** AP, KNT, LAT-WP.

Formerly: The News.

BRADENTON

US

BRADENTON HERALD, THE. 1922. d. $.35/day newsstand; $1/Sun.; $135.20/yr. 102 Manatee Ave., W., Bradenton, FL 34205. TEL 941-748-0411; FAX 941-745-7094. **Owner(s):** Knight-Ridder, Inc., One Herald Plz., Miami, FL 33132. TEL 305-376-3800; FAX 305-376-3875; Ed. Bruce Lind; Pub. Craig Wells; adv. contact: Bruce Faulmann. photos; bk.rev.; pub. size: broadsheet; circ. morning 43,194(paid); Sun. 55,149(paid). **Wire Service(s):** AP, KR, KNT.

BROOKSVILLE

US

HERNANDO TODAY. 1987. Mon.-Sat. $.25 newsstand; $49.40/yr. 15299 Cortez Blvd., Brooksville, FL 34613-6095. TEL 904-544-5295; FAX 904-799-3688. **Owner(s):** Media General, Inc., P.O. Box 85333, Richmond, VA 23293-0001. TEL 804-649-6000; Ed. Robert Nolte. adv.; photos; bk.rev.; pub. size: broadsheet; circ. morning 25,600(free & paid). **Wire Service(s):** AP.

CAPE CORAL

US   ISSN 0747-4199

CAPE CORAL DAILY BREEZE, THE. 1963. Mon.-Sat. $.25 day newsstand; $45/yr. 2510 Del Prado Blvd., Cape Coral, FL 33904. TEL 941-574-1110; FAX 941-574-5693. **Owner(s):** Breeze Corp., P.O. Box 846, Cape Coral, FL 33904. TEL 941-574-1110; Pub. Harry Pappas; adv.; photos; pub. size: broadsheet; circ. evening 10,000(free & paid). **Wire Service(s):** AP.

Formerly: Daily Breeze, The.

CHARLOTTE HARBOR

US   ISSN 1044-0399

CHARLOTTE SUN HERALD. 1893. d. $.50/day newsstand; $1.50/Sun.; $32.37/3 mos.; $104.96/yr. 23170 Harbor View Rd., Charlotte Harbor, FL 33980. TEL 941-629-2855; FAX 941-629-2085; E-mail: chared@aol.com; URL: http://www.charlotte-florida.com. **Owner(s):** Sun Coast Media Group, 23170 Harbor View Rd., Charlotte Harbor, FL 33980. TEL 941-629-2855; Ed. Jeff Dunn-Rankin; Pub. Derrick Dunn-Rankin; adv. contact: Jim Leatham. pub. size: broadsheet; circ. evening 27,824(paid); Sun. 33,472. **Wire Service(s):** AP, Pix Stocks.

Formerly: Charlotte Herald-News.

CRYSTAL RIVER

US

CITRUS COUNTY CHRONICLE. 1890. d. $.25/day newsstand; $.75/Sun.; $89/yr. 1624 N. Meadowcrest Blvd., Crystal River, FL 34429. TEL 904-726-1441; FAX 904-563-5665; E-mail: citrus@infi.net; URL: http://www.chronicle-online.com. **Owner(s):** LCNI-Landmark Community Newspaper, P.O. Box 549, Shelbyville, KY 40066. TEL 502-633-4334; Ed. Ken Melton; Pub. Gerard Mulligan; adv. contact: Dale Bowen. photos; bk.rev.; pub. size: broadsheet; circ. morning 22,000(paid); Sun. 25,000(paid). **Wire Service(s):** AP, KR, N, LAT-WP.

DAYTONA BEACH

US

NEWS-JOURNAL, THE. 1904. d. $.35/day newsstand; $1/Sun.; $11.03/mo.; $132.29/yr. 901 Sixth St., Daytona Beach, FL 32117. TEL 904-252-1511; FAX 904-258-0221; E-mail: +cook@n-jcenter.com. **Owner(s):** News-Journal Corp., 901 Sixth St., Daytona Beach, FL 32117. TEL 904-252-1511; FAX 904-736-2714; Ed. Donald Lindley; Pub. Tippen Davidson; adv. contact: Kathy Coughlin. adv.: $44.10/SAU daily; $48.90/SAU Sun. photos; pub. size: broadsheet; circ. morning 99,556(paid); Sun. 117,571(paid). **Wire Service(s):** AP, NYT.
   Formerly: Daytona Beach News-Journal, The.

ENGLEWOOD

US

ENGLEWOOD SUN HERALD. d. $.50/day newsstand; $1/Sun.; $18.50/3 mos. carrier in cy.; $26.50/3 mos. carrier Charlotte & Englewood cys. 167 W. Dearborn St., Englewood, FL 34223. TEL 941-474-5521; FAX 941-426-3576. **Owner(s):** Sun Coast Media Group, 23170 Harbor View Rd., Charlotte Harbor, FL 33980. TEL 941-629-2855; FAX 941-629-2085; Ed. Chris Porter; Pub. Derek Dunn-Rankin; adv. contact: Lang Capasso. photos; bk.rev.; pub. size: broadsheet; circ. morning 35,000(paid); Sun. 40,000(paid). **Wire Service(s):** AP, KRTN.
   Formerly: Englewood Sun-Times.

FORT LAUDERDALE

US   ISSN 0744-8139

SUN-SENTINEL. 1911. d. $.35/day newsstand; $1/Sun.; $2.45/wk. 200 E. Las Olas Blvd., Fort Lauderdale, FL 33301-2293. TEL 954-356-4000; FAX 954-356-4500. **Owner(s):** Tribune Co., 435 N. Michigan Ave., Chicago, IL 60601; Ed. Ellen Soeteber; Pub. Scott C. Smith; adv.; photos; bk.rev.; pub. size: broadsheet; circ. morning 264,300(paid); Sun. 366,200(paid). **Wire Service(s):** AP, RN, LAT-WP, KRT, DJ, NYT, CQ.

FORT MYERS

US

NEWS-PRESS, THE. 1884. d. $.50/day newsstand; $1.50/Sun.; $13.70/mo. 2442 Martin Luther King, Jr. Blvd., Fort Myers, FL 33901-2442. TEL 941-335-0200; FAX 941-334-0708. **Owner(s):** Gannett Company, Inc., 1100 Wilson Blvd., Arlington, VA 22209. TEL 703-284-6000; Ed. Vickie Kilgore; Pub. Frederick Jacobi; adv.; photos; bk.rev.; pub. size: broadsheet; circ. morning 90,000(paid); Sun. 140,000(paid). **Wire Service(s):** AP, GNS, KRT.
   Formerly: Fort Myers News-Press.

FORT PIERCE

US

TRIBUNE, THE. 1903. d. $.25/day newsstand; $.75/Sun.; $1.60/wk. 600 Edwards Rd., Fort Pierce, FL 34982. TEL 561-461-2050; FAX 561-461-4447. **Owner(s):** Freedom Communications, Inc., 17666 Fitch, Irvine, CA 92714. TEL 714-553-9292; Ed. Harold Muddiman; Pub. Maureen Saltzer; adv.; pub. size: standard; circ. morning 32,298(paid); Sun. 35,097(paid). **Wire Service(s):** UPI, AP.

FORT WALTON BEACH

US

NORTHWEST FLORIDA DAILY NEWS. 1946. d. $.50/day newsstand; $1.25/Sun.; $11.50/mo. 200 Racetrack Rd., N.W., Fort Walton Beach, FL 32547. TEL 904-863-1111; FAX 904-862-5230. **Owner(s):** Freedom Communications, Inc., 17666 Fitch, Irvine, CA 92714. TEL 714-553-9292; Ed. Tom Conner; Pub. Marvin DeBolt; adv. contact: Sam Childs. photos; pub. size: broadsheet; circ. morning 38,000(paid); Sun. 50,000(paid). **Wire Service(s):** AP, KRTN.

GAINESVILLE

US   ISSN 0163-4925

GAINESVILLE SUN, THE. 1876. d. $.50/day newsstand; $1.25/Sun.; $151.58/yr. 2700 S.W. 13th St., Gainesville, FL 32608. TEL 904-378-1411; FAX 904-338-3128. **Owner(s):** New York Times Co., The, 229 W. 43rd St., New York, NY 10036. TEL 212-556-1234; Ed. Curt Pierson; Pub. John W. Fitzwater; adv. contact: David Minnich. photos; bk.rev.; pub. size: broadsheet; circ. morning 55,972(paid); Sun. 61,389(paid). **Wire Service(s):** AP, NYT.

JACKSONVILLE

US   ISSN 0704-2325

FLORIDA TIMES-UNION. 1864. d. $.50/day newsstand; $1.50/Sun.; $234/yr.; $134.16/yr. Sat. & Sun. One Riverside Ave., Jacksonville, FL 32202-4904. TEL 904-359-4111; FAX 904-359-4624; E-mail: scheski@tu.infi.net; URL: http://www.times-union.com. **Owner(s):** Florida Times-Union, One Riverside Ave., Jacksonville, FL 32202-4904. TEL 904-359-4111; Ed. Mary Kress; Pub. Carl N. Cannon; adv.; photos; bk.rev.; pub. size: broadsheet; circ. morning 190,900(paid); Sun. 247,900(paid). **Wire Service(s):** AP, NYT, LAT-WP, KNS, DJ.

KEY WEST

US

KEY WEST CITIZEN. 1881. Sun.-Fri. $.50/day newsstand; $1/Sun.; $99.51/yr. carrier; $138.24/yr. elsewhere. 3420 Northside Dr., Key West, FL 33040. TEL 305-294-6641; FAX 305-294-0768. **Owner(s):** Thomson Newspapers, Inc., 3150 Des Plaines Ave., Des Plaines, IL 60018. TEL 708-299-5544; Ed. Bernie Hunt; Pub. William Barry; adv. contact: Randy Erickson. bk.rev.; pub. size: standard; circ. morning 10,940(paid); Sun. 11,470(paid). **Wire Service(s):** AP.

LAKE CITY

US

LAKE CITY REPORTER. 1874. Mon.-Sat. $.25 newsstand; $83.46/yr. 126 E. Duval St., Lake City, FL 32055. TEL 904-752-1293; FAX 904-752-9400. **Owner(s):** New York Times Co., The, 229 W. 43rd St., New York, NY 10036. TEL 212-556-1234; Ed. Tommy Hornsby; Pub. Don L. Caldwell; adv. contact: Andy Caldwell. pub. size: broadsheet; circ. evening 10,500(paid). **Wire Service(s):** AP, NYT.

LAKELAND

US   ISSN 0163-0288

LEDGER, THE. 1924. d. $.50/day newsstand; $1/Sun.; $10.60/4 wks.; $137.80/yr. 401 S. Missouri Ave., Lakeland, FL 33801. TEL 941-687-7000; FAX 941-687-7090; E-mail: info@tsolv.com; URL: http://www.lakeland.tsolv.com. **Owner(s):** New York Times Co., The, 229 W. 43rd St., New York, NY 10036. TEL 212-556-1234; Ed. Hunter George; Pub. Don Whitworth; adv. contact: Steve Schmidt. pub. size: broadsheet; circ. morning 78,200(paid); Sun. 96,000(paid). **Wire Service(s):** AP, NYT, KNT.

LEESBURG

US

DAILY COMMERCIAL. 1875. d. $.25/day newsstand; $1/Sun. 212 E. Main St., Leesburg, FL 34748. TEL 352-365-8212; FAX 352-365-1951. **Owner(s):** Better Built Media Group, Inc., P.O. Box 490007, Leesburg, FL 34749; Ed. John Pastor; Pub. Jim Perry; adv. contact: Carmen Cullen. photos; bk.rev.; pub. size: broadsheet; circ. morning 34,782(paid); Sun. 37,654(paid). **Wire Service(s):** AP.

MARIANNA

US

JACKSON COUNTY FLORIDAN. 1927. Tue.-Fri. & Sun. $.35/day newsstand; $.75/Sun.; $97.80/yr. 4403 Constitution Ln., Marianna, FL 32446. TEL 904-526-3614; FAX 904-482-4478. **Owner(s):** Thomson Newspapers, Inc., One Thorn Run Ctr., Ste. 500, Coraopolis, PA 15108. TEL 412-262-7870; Ed. Judy Green; Pub. Jane Benton; adv. contact: Valeria Roberts. pub. size: broadsheet; circ. evening 6,500(paid); Sun. 7,000(paid). **Wire Service(s):** AP.

MELBOURNE

US   ISSN 1051-8304

FLORIDA TODAY. 1966. d. $.50 newsstand; $13.78/mo. One Gannett Plz., Melbourne, FL 32940. TEL 407-242-3500; FAX 407-242-6620; E-mail: 71333.1616@compuserve.com; URL: http://www.flatoday.com/space. **Owner(s):** Gannett Company, Inc., 1100 Wilson Blvd., Arlington, VA 22209. TEL 703-284-6000; Ed. Melinda Meers; Pub. Michael J. Coleman; adv. contact: Mike Jung. photos; bk.rev.; pub. size: broadsheet; circ. morning 98,377(paid); Sun. 124,839(paid). **Wire Service(s):** AP, GNS.

MIAMI

US

MIAMI HERALD. 1910. d. $.35/day newsstand; $1/Sun.; $152.30/yr. in cy.; $157.10/yr. east & west coast. One Herald Plz., Miami, FL 33132-1693. TEL 305-350-2111; FAX 305-376-2072; E-mail: 74763.3324@compuserve.com; URL: http://www.herald.com/. **Owner(s):** Knight-Ridder, Inc., One Herald Plz., Miami, FL 33132. TEL 305-376-3800; Ed. Larry Olmstead; Pub. David Lawrence, Jr.; adv.; photos; bk.rev.; pub. size: broadsheet; circ. morning 425,304(paid); Sun. 532,158(paid). **Wire Service(s):** AP, UPI, LAT-WP, KNT, TD.

DAILY NEWSPAPERS

NAPLES

US

NAPLES DAILY NEWS. 1923. d. $.50/day newsstand; $1.50/Sun.; $183.38/yr. in state; $173/yr. mailed. 1075 Central Ave., Naples, FL 34102. TEL 941-263-4770; FAX 813-263-4816. **Owner(s):** Scripps-Howard, 1100 Central Trust Tower, Cincinnati, OH 45202. TEL 513-977-3000; Ed. Phil Lewis; Pub. Corbin Wyant; pub. size: broadsheet; circ. morning 57,000(paid); Sun. 71,000(paid).
Formerly: Naples News.

NEW SMYRNA

US

NEW SMYRNA BEACH OBSERVER. 1913. Tue.-Sat. $.50 newsstand; $19.82/3 mos. 823 S. Dixie Fwy., New Smyrna, FL 32168. TEL 904-427-1000; FAX 904-428-1265. **Owner(s):** American Publishing Co., 606 N. Van Buren, Marion, IL 62959. TEL 618-993-1711; Ed. Jim Jones; Pub. George Sample; adv.; photos; bk.rev.; pub. size: broadsheet; circ. morning 4,300(paid). **Wire Service(s):** AP.

US

OBSERVER, THE. 1913. Tue.-Sat. $.50 newsstand; $72.34/yr. 823 S. Dixie Fwy., New Smyrna, FL 32168. TEL 904-427-1000; FAX 904-428-1265. **Owner(s):** American Publishing Co., 606 N. Van Buren, Marion, IL 62959. TEL 618-993-1711; Ed. Jim Jones; Pub. George Sample; adv. contact: Jamie Smith. photos; bk.rev.; pub. size: broadsheet; circ. morning 10,000(paid). **Wire Service(s):** AP.

NORTH PORT

US

NORTH PORT SUN HERALD. d. $.50/day newsstand; $.1.25/Sun. 13644 S. Tamiami Trail, North Port, FL 34287. TEL 941-426-9544; FAX 941-423-2318. **Owner(s):** Sun Coast Media Group, 23170 Harbor View Rd., Charlotte Harbor, FL 33980. TEL 941-629-2855; FAX 941-629-2085; Ed. Marshall Grove; Pub. Derek Dunn-Rankin; adv.; photos; pub. size: broadsheet; circ. morning 7,000(paid).
Formerly: North Port Sun Times.

OCALA

US ISSN 0163-3201

OCALA STAR BANNER. 1866. d. $.50/day newsstand; $.75/Sat.; $1.25/Sun. 2121 S.W. 19th Ave., Rd., Ocala, FL 34474. TEL 352-867-4010; FAX 352-867-4018. **Owner(s):** New York Times Co., The, 229 W. 43rd St., New York, NY 10036. TEL 212-556-1234; Ed. Jay McKenzie; Pub. Charles Stout; adv. contact: Bob Gruber. photos; bk.rev.; pub. size: broadsheet; circ. morning 50,000(paid); Sun. 54,000(paid). **Wire Service(s):** AP, NYT, SHNA, KR, LAT-WP.

OKEECHOBEE

US

DAILY OKEECHOBEE NEWS, THE. 1910. d. $.50/day newsstand; $.75/Sun.; $9.01/mo. in cy.; $17.23/mo. out of cy. 107 S.W. 17th St., Ste. D, Okeechobee, FL 34974. TEL 813-763-3134; FAX 813-763-5901. **Owner(s):** Independent Newspapers, Inc., P.O. Box 7001, Dover, DE 19903. TEL 302-674-4750; Ed. Katrina Elsken; Pub. Richard Hitt; adv. contact: Judy Kasten. photos; pub. size: broadsheet; circ. morning 6,000(paid); Sun. 6,000(paid). **Wire Service(s):** AP.
Formerly: Okeechobee News.

ORLANDO

US ISSN 0744-6055

ORLANDO SENTINEL. 1876. d. $.50/day newsstand; $1.50/Sun.; $3.85/wk. in cy.; $196/yr. in cy. 633 N. Orange Ave., Orlando, FL 32801. TEL 407-420-5000; FAX 407-420-5758. **Owner(s):** Tribune Co., 435 N. Michigan Ave., Chicago, IL 60611. TEL 312-222-3394; Ed. Jane Healy; Pub. John Puerner; adv. contact: William E. Steiger. photos; pub. size: broadsheet; circ. morning 273,761(paid); Sun. 376,003(paid). **Wire Service(s):** AP, KRTN, LAT-WP, NYT, DJ, SHNA, RN.

PALATKA

US ISSN 0163-5050

DAILY NEWS. 1885. Mon.-Fri. $.50 newsstand; $82.58/yr. 1825 St. Johns Ave., Palatka, FL 32177. TEL 904-328-2721; FAX 904-325-0663. **Owner(s):** New York Times Co., The, 229 W. 43rd St., New York, NY 10036. TEL 212-556-1234; Ed. Rick Moore; Pub. Robert R. Starr; adv. contact: Bruce Davis. photos; pub. size: broadsheet; circ. evening 12,200(paid). **Wire Service(s):** AP.

PALM BEACH

US

PALM BEACH DAILY NEWS. 1897. d.: Sep.-May; Sun.-Thu.: June-Sep. $.25/day newsstand; $.50/Sun.; $1.60/wk. 265 Royal Poinciana Way, Palm Beach, FL 33480. TEL 407-820-3860; FAX 407-655-4594; E-mail: zfzt92@prodigy.com. **Owner(s):** Palm Beach Newspapers, Inc., 2751 S. Dixie, P.O. Drawer T, West Palm Beach, FL 33405. TEL 407-833-7411; Ed. Linda Rawls; Pub. Joyce Harr; adv. contact: Toni Richardson. adv.: $32.50/SAU Sun.; $28.90/SAU daily. photos; bk.rev.; pub. size: standard; circ. morning 9,200(paid); Sun. 10,900(paid).

PANAMA CITY

US

NEWS HERALD, THE. 1970. d. $.50/day newsstand; $1.25/Sun.; $106.50/yr. 501 W. 11th St., Panama City, FL 32401. TEL 904-763-7621; FAX 904-763-4636. **Owner(s):** Freedom Communications, Inc., 1055 N. Main St., Ste. 901, Santa Ana, CA 92701. TEL 714-542-4415; Ed. Steve Bornhoft; Pub. Karen Hanes; adv. contact: Ken Carpenter. photos; pub. size: standard; circ. morning 37,470(paid); Sun. 43,087(paid). **Wire Service(s):** AP, KR.

PENSACOLA

US

PENSACOLA NEWS JOURNAL. 1889. d. $.50/day newsstand; $1.50/Sun.; $13/mo. home deliv. 101 E. Romana St., Pensacola, FL 32501. TEL 904-435-8500; FAX 904-435-8633; E-mail: pns@gulfsurf.infi.net; URL: http://www.gulfcoastgateway.com. **Owner(s):** Gannett Company, Inc., 1100 Wilson Blvd., Arlington, VA 22234. TEL 703-284-6000; Ed. Mike Ryan; Pub. Denise H. Bannister; adv. contact: John DiMambro. photos; pub. size: broadsheet; circ. morning 63,871(paid); Sun. 82,729(paid). **Wire Service(s):** AP, GNS, KR.

SANFORD

US ISSN 0893-3642

SANFORD HERALD. 1908. Tue.-Fri. & Sun. $.50/day newsstand; $.75/Sun.; $83.46/yr. 300 N. French Ave., Sanford, FL 32771. TEL 407-322-2611; FAX 407-323-9408. **Owner(s):** Martinsville Bulletin, P.O. Box 1667, Sanford, FL 32772. TEL 407-322-2611; Ed. Lacy Loar. pub. size: standard; circ. evening 7,465(paid). **Wire Service(s):** AP.

SARASOTA

US

SARASOTA HERALD TRIBUNE. 1925. d. $.50/day newsstand; $1.25/Sun. 801 S. Tamiami Trail, Sarasota, FL 34236. TEL 941-953-7755; FAX 941-957-5276. **Owner(s):** New York Times Co., The, 229 W. 43rd St., New York, NY 10036. TEL 212-556-1234; Ed. Waldo Proffitt; Pub. Lynn O. Matthews; adv.; photos; bk.rev.; pub. size: broadsheet; circ. morning 115,000(paid); Sun. 160,000(paid). **Wire Service(s):** AP, NYT, LAT-WP.

ST. AUGUSTINE

US ISSN 1041-1577

ST. AUGUSTINE RECORD. 1894. d. $.50/day newsstand; $1/Sun.; $7/mo. 158 Cordova St., St. Augustine, FL 32084. TEL 904-829-6562; FAX 904-829-6664; E-mail: record@aug.com; URL: http://staugustine.com. **Owner(s):** Morris Communications, P.O. Box 936, Augusta, GA 30903. TEL 706-724-0851; FAX 706-722-0011; Pub. Ronnie Hughes; adv. contact: Grover Ford. photos; bk.rev.; pub. size: broadsheet; circ. evening 15,000(paid); Sun. 180,000. **Wire Service(s):** AP, KR, LAT-WP.

ST. PETERSBURG

US

ST. PETERSBURG TIMES. 1884. d. $.25/day newsstand; $1/Sun.; $29.90/3 mos. home deliv. 490 First Ave., S., St. Petersburg, FL 33701-1121. TEL 813-893-8111; FAX 813-893-8673; E-mail: lacorty@sptimes.com; URL: http://www.sptimes.com. **Owner(s):** Times Publishing Co., P.O. Box 1121, St. Petersburg, FL 33731. TEL 813-893-8111; Ed. Neil Brown; Pub. Judith Roales; adv. contact: Richard Reeves. photos; bk.rev.; pub. size: broadsheet; circ. morning 364,810(paid); Sun. 462,103(paid). **Wire Service(s):** AP, NYT, LAT-WP, RN.

DAILY NEWSPAPERS

STUART
US
STUART NEWS. 1913. d. $.50/day newsstand; $1/Sun.; $9.49/mo.; $212/yr. 1939 S. Federal Hwy., Stuart, FL 34994. TEL 561-287-1550; FAX 561-221-4246. **Owner(s):** Scripps-Howard, 312 Walnut St., Cincinnati, OH 45202. TEL 513-977-3000; Ed. Nancy Smith. adv. contact: Greg Anderson. photos; bk.rev.; pub. size: broadsheet; circ. morning 39,104(paid); Sun. 47,214(paid). **Wire Service(s):** AP, NYT, SHNS.

TALLAHASSEE
US ISSN 0738-5153
TALLAHASSEE DEMOCRAT. 1905. d. $.50/day newsstand; $1.25/Sun.; $154.44/yr. 277 N. Magnolia Dr., Tallahassee, FL 32302. TEL 904-599-2100; FAX 904-599-2295; E-mail: telltdo@tdo.infi.net; URL: http://www.tdo.com. **Owner(s):** Knight-Ridder, Inc., One Herald Plz., Miami, FL 33132. TEL 305-376-3800; FAX 305-376-3875; Ed. Bob Shaw; Pub. J. Carrol Dadisman; adv.; pub. size: broadsheet; circ. morning 45,020(paid); Sun. 53,234(paid). **Wire Service(s):** KR, AP, LAT-WP.

TAMPA
US ISSN 1042-3761
TAMPA TRIBUNE, THE. 1895. d. $.25/day newsstand; $.75/Sun.; $138.45/yr. home deliv. 202 S. Parker St., Tampa, FL 33606. TEL 813-259-7711; FAX 813-259-7773; E-mail: pbreckenridge@tboweb.com; URL: http://www.tampatrib.com/. **Owner(s):** Media General, Inc., 333 E. Grace St., Richmond, VA 23219. TEL 804-649-6671; Ed. Bruce Witwer; Pub. Reid Ashe; adv. contact: Tony DiSalvo. photos; bk.rev.; pub. size: broadsheet; circ. morning 265,988(paid); Sun. 360,251(paid). **Wire Service(s):** AP, AP Wire Photo.

VERO BEACH
US
PRESS-JOURNAL. 1919. d. $.50/day newsstand; $1/Sun.; $112/yr. carrier. 1801 S. U.S. Hwy. 1, Vero Beach, FL 32960. TEL 561-562-2315; FAX 561-562-7210. **Owner(s):** Scripps-Howard, 312 Walnut St., 28th Fl., Cincinnati, OH 45202; Ed. Larry Reisman; Pub. Darryl Hicks; adv.; photos; pub. size: broadsheet; circ. morning 49,500(paid); Sun. 41,500(paid). **Wire Service(s):** AP, UPI.
Formerly: Vero Beach Press-Journal.

WEST PALM BEACH
US
PALM BEACH POST. 1923. d. $.50/day newsstand; $1/Sun.; $2.55/wk. 2751 S. Dixie Hwy., West Palm Beach, FL 33405. TEL 561-820-4400; FAX 561-820-4445. **Owner(s):** Cox Enterprises, Inc., P.O. Box 4689, Atlanta, GA 30302. TEL 404-526-5537; Ed. Tom O'Hara; Pub. Tom Giuffrida; adv. contact: Van Esselstyn. photos; bk.rev.; pub. size: broadsheet; circ. morning 173,000(paid); Sun. 222,000(paid). **Wire Service(s):** AP, RN, LAT-WP, NYT, Cox.

WINTER HAVEN
US
NEWS CHIEF. 1879. d. $.25/day newsstand; $.50/Sun.; $92.60/yr. 650 Sixth St. S.W., Winter Haven, FL 33880. TEL 941-294-7731; FAX 941-294-2008. **Owner(s):** Morris Communications, P.O. Box 936, Augusta, GA 30903. TEL 706-724-0851; Pub. Wayne Ezell; adv. contact: Al Koerner. bk.rev.; pub. size: standard; circ. evening 14,161(paid); Sun. 14,161(paid). **Wire Service(s):** AP.

GEORGIA

ALBANY
US
ALBANY HERALD, THE. 1891. d. $.50/day newsstand; $1.25/Sun.; $144/yr. 126 N. Washington St., Albany, GA 31701. TEL 912-888-9300; FAX 912-888-9357. **Owner(s):** Gray Communications Systems, Inc., P.O. Box 48, Albany, GA 31703. TEL 912-888-9300; Pub. Thomas J. Stultz; adv.; photos; bk.rev.; pub. size: standard; circ. morning 34,000(paid); Sun. 40,000(paid). **Wire Service(s):** AP.

AMERICUS
US
AMERICUS TIMES-RECORDER. 1879. Mon.-Sat. $.50 newsstand; $93/yr. 1612 Vienna Rd., Americus, GA 31709. TEL 912-924-2751; FAX 912-928-6344. **Owner(s):** Thomson Newspapers, Inc., Metro Centre, One Station Pl., Stamford, CT 06902. TEL 203-425-2500; FAX 203-425-2516; Ed. Beth Alston; Pub. Daryl Henning; adv. contact: Jeff Masters. photos; pub. size: broadsheet; circ. evening 7,400(paid). **Wire Service(s):** AP, AP Photo.

ATHENS
US ISSN 0898-3712
ATHENS BANNER HERALD. 1965. d. $.25/day newsstand; $1/Sun.; $8.67/mo. carrier; $106/yr. One Press Pl., Athens, GA 30601. TEL 706-549-0123; FAX 706-543-5234. **Owner(s):** Morris Communications, P.O. Box 136, Augusta, GA 30913. TEL 706-724-0851; Ed. Les Simpson; Pub. Jeff Wilson; adv.; photos; pub. size: broadsheet; circ. evening 13,282(paid); Sun. 37,000(paid). **Wire Service(s):** AP, NYT, LAT-WP.

US ISSN 0898-3712
ATHENS DAILY NEWS. 1965. d. $.50/day newsstand; $1.50/Sun.; $8.67/mo. One Press Pl., Athens, GA 30601. TEL 706-549-0123; FAX 706-208-2246; E-mail: 76735.26@compuserve.com; URL: http://www.athensnewspapers.com. **Owner(s):** Morris Communications, P.O. Box 936, Augusta, GA. TEL 706-724-0851; Ed. Les Simpson; Pub. Jeff Wilson; adv.; photos; bk.rev.; pub. size: broadsheet; circ. morning 31,070(paid); Sun. 36,000(paid). **Wire Service(s):** AP, KR, LAT-WP.

ATLANTA
US ISSN 0093-1179
ATLANTA JOURNAL-CONSTITUTION. 1883. d. $.50/day newsstand; $2/Sun.; $149.19/yr. 72 Marietta St., Atlanta, GA 30303. TEL 404-526-5151; FAX 404-526-5746; E-mail: constitution@ajc.com. **Owner(s):** Cox Enterprises, Inc., P.O. Box 105357, Atlanta, GA 30348. TEL 404-843-5000; Ed. John Walter; Pub. Roger Kintzel; adv. contact: Roy Sheppard. photos; bk.rev.; pub. size: broadsheet; circ. morning 308,984(paid); evening 161,393(paid); Sun. 715,397(paid). **Wire Service(s):** AP, UPI, LAT-WP.

AUGUSTA
US ISSN 0747-1343
AUGUSTA CHRONICLE, THE. 1785. d. $.50/day newsstand; $1.25/Sun.; $11/mo. home deliv. 725 Broad St., Augusta, GA 30901. TEL 706-724-0851; FAX 706-722-7403. **Owner(s):** Southeastern Newspapers Corp., P.O. Box 1928, Augusta, GA 30903-1928. TEL 706-724-0851; Ed. John Fish; Pub. William S. Morris, III; adv. contact: Ron Tennant. pub. size: broadsheet; circ. morning 78,000(paid); Sun. 102,000(paid). **Wire Service(s):** AP, NYT, LAT-WP.

BRUNSWICK
US
BRUNSWICK NEWS, THE. 1902. Mon.-Sat. $.35 newsstand; $5/mo. local; $7/mo. out of state. 3011 Altama Ave., Brunswick, GA 31520-1557. TEL 912-265-8320; FAX 912-264-4973. **Owner(s):** Brunswick News Publishing Co., P.O. Box 1557, Brunswick, GA 31521-1557. TEL 912-265-8320; FAX 912-264-4973; Ed. Hank Rowland. adv. contact: Ron Maulden. photos; bk.rev.; pub. size: standard; circ. morning 16,356(paid). **Wire Service(s):** AP.

US
GEORGIA TIMES-UNION. d. $.50/day newsstand; $1/Sun.; $2.99/wk. deliv.; $155.48/yr. 3675 Community Rd., Brunswick, GA 31520. TEL 912-264-0720; FAX 912-264-1407. **Owner(s):** Billy Morris, Augusta, GA; Ed. Joe Adams; Pub. Carl N. Cannon; adv.; pub. size: broadsheet; circ. morning 20,000(paid); Sun. 7,500(paid).
Formerly: Florida Times Union - Georgia Edition.

CARROLLTON
US ISSN 1049-9458
TIMES-GEORGIAN. 1872. Tue.-Sun. $.50/day newsstand; $1/Sun.; $90/yr. carrier. 901 Hays Mill Rd., Carrollton, GA 30117. TEL 770-834-6631; FAX 770-834-9991. **Owner(s):** Paxton Media Group, Inc., P.O. Box 2300, Paducah, KY 42002. TEL 502-443-1771; Ed. Bruce Browning; Pub. Dawn Weatherly; pub. size: broadsheet; circ. morning 13,000(paid). **Wire Service(s):** AP.

CARTERSVILLE
US ISSN 1049-6750
CARTERSVILLE DAILY TRIBUNE NEWS. 1946. Sun.-Fri. $.50/day newsstand; $1/Sun.; $71/yr. 251 S. Tennessee, Cartersville, GA 30120. TEL 770-382-4545; FAX 770-382-2711. **Owner(s):** Cleveland Newspapers, Inc., Cleveland, TN; Ed. Jim Jaquish; Pub. Charles E. Hurley; adv.: $8.22/SAU. photos; bk.rev.; pub. size: broadsheet; circ. evening 10,000(paid). **Wire Service(s):** AP.

DAILY NEWSPAPERS

US

DAILY TRIBUNE NEWS. Sun.-Fri. $.50 newsstand; $19.50/3 mos.; $35.50/6 mos.; $75/yr. 251 S. Tennessee St., Cartersville, GA 30120. TEL 770-382-4545; FAX 770-382-2711. **Owner(s):** Cleveland Newspapers, Inc., Cleveland, OH; Ed. Jim Jaquish; Pub. Charles Hurley; adv. contact: Jennifer Moates. photos; bk.rev.; pub. size: broadsheet; circ. evening 10,500(paid).

COLUMBUS

US   ISSN 8750-8389

COLUMBUS LEDGER-ENQUIRER. 1886. d. $.50 newsstand; $3.25/wk. 17 W. 12th St., Columbus, GA 31902. TEL 706-324-5526; FAX 706-376-6336; E-mail: leonline@leo.infi.net; URL: http://www.l-e-o.com. **Owner(s):** Knight-Ridder, Inc., One Herald Plz., Miami, FL 33132. TEL 305-376-3800; FAX 305-376-3875; Pub. John F. Greenman; adv.; photos; bk.rev.; pub. size: broadsheet; circ. evening 53,511(paid); Sun. 67,659(paid). **Wire Service(s):** AP, KNS, NYT.

CONYERS

US   ISSN 1050-1401

ROCKDALE CITIZEN. 1909. Mon.-Fri. $60/yr. 969 S. Main St., Conyers, GA 30207. TEL 770-483-7108. **Owner(s):** Gray Communications Systems, Inc., P.O. Box 48, Albany, GA 31703. TEL 912-888-9300; Ed. Fred Turner; Pub. Richard T. Rae; photos; bk.rev.; pub. size: broadsheet; circ. 11,500(paid).

CORDELE

US

CORDELE DISPATCH. 1908. Mon.-Fri. $.50/newsstand; $84/yr. carrier. 306 13th Ave., W., Cordele, GA 31015. TEL 912-273-2277; FAX 912-273-7239. **Owner(s):** Thomson Newspapers, Inc., 3150 Des Plaines Ave., Des Plaines, IL 60018. TEL 708-299-5544; Ed. Bill Rungy; Pub. Darryl Henning; adv. contact: Jeff Masters. pub. size: broadsheet; circ. evening 6,143(free). **Wire Service(s):** AP.

DALTON

US

DAILY CITIZEN NEWS. 1800. d. $.50/day newsstand; $1/Sun.; $10.50/mo. 308 S. Thornton Ave., Dalton, GA 30720. TEL 706-278-1011; FAX 706-275-6641. **Owner(s):** Thomson Newspapers, Inc., 3150 Des Plaines Ave., Des Plaines, IL 60018. TEL 708-299-5544; Pub. Ken Fortenberry; pub. size: broadsheet; circ. morning 14,500(paid). **Wire Service(s):** AP.
Formerly: Dalton Daily Citizen News.

DOUGLASVILLE

US

DOUGLAS COUNTY SENTINEL. 1902. Tue.-Sat. $.25 newsstand; $50/yr. carrier. 6405 Fairburn Rd., Douglasville, GA 30134. TEL 770-942-6571; FAX 770-949-7556. **Owner(s):** Paxton Media Group, Inc., P.O. Box 2300, Paducah, KY 42002. TEL 502-443-1771; Ed. Bill Fordham; Pub. Dawn Wetherby; adv. contact: Susan Hopkins. pub. size: broadsheet; circ. evening 11,000(paid). **Wire Service(s):** AP.

DUBLIN

US

COURIER HERALD, THE. 1913. Mon.-Sat. $.50 newsstand; $76/yr. 115 S. Jefferson St., Dublin, GA 31040. TEL 912-272-5522; FAX 912-272-2189. **Owner(s):** DuBose Porter, 115 S. Jefferson St., Dublin, GA 31021. TEL 912-272-5522; Griffin Lovett, 115 S. Jefferson St., Dublin, GA 31201; Ed. Rodney Manley; Pub. Griffin Lovett; adv. contact: Marsha Green. pub. size: broadsheet; circ. evening 13,600(paid). **Wire Service(s):** AP.
Formerly: Dublin Courier Herald.

GAINESVILLE

US

TIMES, THE. 1947. d. $.35/day newsstand; $1.50/Sun.; $37.70/13 wks. home deliv. 345 Green St., N.W., Gainesville, GA 30501. TEL 770-532-1234; FAX 770-532-0457; E-mail: 102432.3532@compuserve.com. **Owner(s):** Gannett Company, Inc., 1100 Wilson Blvd., Arlington, VA 22234. TEL 703-284-6000; Ed. John R. Vardeman; Pub. Sandra S. Bailey; adv. contact: Brenda Bohn. pub. size: broadsheet; circ. evening 18,000(paid); Sun. 21,005(paid). **Wire Service(s):** AP.

GRIFFIN

US   ISSN 0746-3324

GRIFFIN DAILY NEWS. d. $.50/day newsstand; $1/Sun.; $9.75/mo. home deliv. 323 E. Solomon St., Griffin, GA 30223. TEL 770-227-3276; FAX 770-412-1678; E-mail: editor@griffin-news.com; URL: http://www.griffin-news.com. **Owner(s):** Thomson Newspapers, Inc., 3150 Des Plaines Ave., Des Plaines, IL 60018. TEL 704-299-5544; Ed. Michelle Phillips; Pub. Tom Overton; adv. contact: Jeff Jones. pub. size: broadsheet; circ. morning 13,000(paid); Sun. 15,000(paid).

JONESBORO

US

CLAYTON NEWS DAILY. 1971. Mon.-Sat. $.50 newsstand; $7/mo. 138 Church St., Jonesboro, GA 30236. TEL 770-478-5753; FAX 770-473-9032. **Owner(s):** Southern Crescent Publishers, 138 Church St., Jonesboro, GA 30236. TEL 770-478-5753; Ed. Tom Kerlin; Pub. Neely Young; adv. contact: Colleen Mitchell. pub. size: broadsheet; circ. evening 25,000(paid). **Wire Service(s):** UPI.

LA GRANGE

US

LA GRANGE DAILY NEWS. Mon.-Sat. $.50 newsstand; $7.75/mo. home deliv. 105 Ashton St., La Grange, GA 30240. TEL 706-884-7311; FAX 706-884-8712. **Owner(s):** Mid-South Acquisition Co., Inc., P.O. Box 929, La Grange, GA 30241. TEL 706-884-7311; Ed. C. Lee West; Pub. Louis Harvath, III; adv. contact: Jeniifer Bell. pub. size: broadsheet; circ. evening 15,000(paid). **Wire Service(s):** AP.

LAWRENCEVILLE

US

GWINNETT DAILY POST. 1970. Tue.-Sun. $.50 newsstand; $64.95/yr. in cy. 166 Buford Dr., Lawrenceville, GA 30245. TEL 770-963-9205; FAX 770-339-8081. **Owner(s):** Gray Communications Systems, Inc., P.O. Box 603, Lawrenceville, GA 30246. TEL 770-963-9205; FAX 770-338-7353; Ed. Howard Reed; Pub. Richard T. Rae; adv. contact: Joel Jenkins. bk.rev.; pub. size: standard; circ. morning 45,000(paid).
Formerly: Gwinnett Post-Tribune; Gwinnett Home Weekly.

MACON

US   ISSN 1054-2485

MACON TELEGRAPH. 1826. d. $.50/day newsstand; $1.50/Sun. 120 Broadway, Macon, GA 31201. TEL 912-744-4200; FAX 912-744-4385; E-mail: metro@mto.infi.net; URL: http://www.macontel.com. **Owner(s):** Knight-Ridder, Inc., One Herald Plz., Miami, FL 33132. TEL 305-376-3800; FAX 305-376-3875; Ed. Cecil Bently; Pub. Carol Hudler; adv. contact: Pete Herschberger. photos; bk.rev.; pub. size: broadsheet; circ. morning 75,000(paid); Sun. 102,000(paid). **Wire Service(s):** AP, NYT, KRN.

MARIETTA

US   ISSN 8750-4618

MARIETTA DAILY JOURNAL. 1867. d. $.25 newsstand; $10.50/mo. 580 Fairground St., Marietta, GA 30060. TEL 770-428-9411; FAX 770-422-9533. **Owner(s):** Otis A. Brumby, Jr., Marietta, GA 30060; Pub. Otis Brumby; pub. size: broadsheet; circ. morning 30,000(paid); Sun. 35,000(paid). **Wire Service(s):** AP, SHNA.

MILLEDGEVILLE

US

UNION-RECORDER. 1820. Tue.-Sat. $.50 newsstand; $79.30/yr. One Union-Recorder Plz., Garrett Way, Milledgeville, GA 31061-0520. TEL 912-452-0567; FAX 912-453-1449. **Owner(s):** Knight-Ridder, Inc., One Herald Plz., Miami, FL 33132-1693. TEL 305-376-3800; FAX 305-376-3875; Ed. Debra Evans; Pub. Susan L. Patterson; adv.; photos; bk.rev.; pub. size: broadsheet; circ. morning 9,200(paid). **Wire Service(s):** AP, KR.

MOULTRIE

US

OBSERVER, THE. 1894. Mon.-Sat. $.50 newsstand; $92.46/yr. 25 N. Main St., Moultrie, GA 31768. TEL 912-985-4545; FAX 912-985-3569. **Owner(s):** Gannett Company, Inc., 1100 Wilson Blvd., Arlington, VA 22340. TEL 703-284-6000; Ed. Dwain Walden; Pub. Michael Bortvit; adv. contact: Michael Bortvit. photos; pub. size: broadsheet; circ. morning 8,000(paid). **Wire Service(s):** AP, GNS.
Formerly: Moultrie Observer.

ROME

US   ISSN 1060-4049

ROME NEWS-TRIBUNE. 1838. Sun.-Fri. $.50/day newsstand; $1.50/Sun.; $74/yr. in cy.; $140/yr. out of state. 305 E. Sixth Ave., Rome, GA 30161. TEL 706-291-6397; FAX 706-232-9632. **Owner(s):** News Publishing Co., P.O. Box 1633, Rome, GA 30162. TEL 706-290-5330; Ed. David Williams; Pub. B.H. Mooney, III; adv.; pub. size: broadsheet; circ. evening 24,500(paid); Sun. 24,500(paid). **Wire Service(s):** AP.

SAVANNAH

US

SAVANNAH MORNING NEWS. 1850. d. $.50/day newsstand; $1.50/Sun.; $120/yr. 111 W. Bay St., Savannah, GA 31401. TEL 912-236-9511; FAX 912-234-6522. **Owner(s):** Southeastern Newspapers Corp., GA; Ed. Don Suwyn; Pub. Frank Anderson; adv. contact: Don Bailey. pub. size: broadsheet; circ. morning 75,900(paid); evening 15,360(paid); Sun. 84,399(paid). **Wire Service(s):** AP, NEA, LAT-WP.

Formerly: Savannah News/Evening Press.

STATESBORO

US   ISSN 0746-4665

STATESBORO HERALD. 1937. d. $.50/day newsstand; $.75/Sun.; $10.55/4 wks.; $31.57/13 wks.; $60.39/26 wks.; $118.03/yr. One Herald Sq., Statesboro, GA 30458. TEL 912-764-9031; FAX 912-489-8181. **Owner(s):** Morris Communications, P.O. Box 936, Augusta, GA. TEL 706-724-0851; Pub. Randy Morton; adv. contact: Jan Milton. pub. size: broadsheet; circ. morning 8,000(paid); Sun. 8,000(paid). **Wire Service(s):** UPI.

THOMASVILLE

US   ISSN 0746-4894

THOMASVILLE TIMES-ENTERPRISE. 1889. Tue.-Sun. $2.20/wk. 106 South St., Thomasville, GA 31792. TEL 912-226-2400; FAX 912-228-5863. **Owner(s):** Thomson Newspapers, Inc., Metro Centre, One Station Pl., 6th Fl., Stamford, CT 06902. TEL 203-425-2500; FAX 203-425-2516; Pub. Wallace Goodman; adv. contact: Norman Bankston. pub. size: broadsheet; circ. morning 10,343(paid). **Wire Service(s):** AP.

TIFTON

US   ISSN 1065-2884

TIFTON GAZETTE. 1888. Mon.-Sat. $.50 newsstand; $8.40/mo. 211 N. Tift Ave., Tifton, GA 31794. TEL 912-382-4321; FAX 912-387-7322. **Owner(s):** Thomson Newspapers, Inc., Metro Centre, One Station Plaza, 6th fl., Stamford, CT 06902. TEL 203-425-2500; FAX 203-425-2516; Ed. James S. McKee; Pub. James S. McKee; adv. contact: Randy Cox. bk.rev.; pub. size: broadsheet; circ. morning 9,431(paid). **Wire Service(s):** AP.

VALDOSTA

US

VALDOSTA DAILY TIMES. 1867. d. $.50/day newsstand; $1/Sun.; $2.65/wk. 201 N. Troup St., Valdosta, GA 31601. TEL 912-244-1880; FAX 912-244-2560. **Owner(s):** Thomson Newspapers, Inc., Metro Centre, One Station Pl. 6th Fl., Stamford, CT 06902. TEL 203-425-2500; FAX 203-425-2516; Ed. Gerald Guys; Pub. Bob Morrell; adv. contact: Larry Boatwright. pub. size: broadsheet; circ. morning 21,147(paid); Sun. 21,147(paid). **Wire Service(s):** AP.

WARNER ROBINS

US

DAILY SUN, THE. 1949. Sun.-Fri. $.35/day newsstand; $1/Sun.; $8.67/mo. carrier; $11/mo. mailed. 1553 Watson Blvd., Warner Robins, GA 31093. TEL 912-923-6432; FAX 912-328-7682; E-mail: talktous@dailysun.com. **Owner(s):** Newspaper Holdings, Inc., 269 W. Main St., 6th Fl., Lexington, KY 40507. TEL 606-388-2644; FAX 606-225-8115; Ed. Robin Booker; Pub. William Chiusano; adv. contact: Doug Allan. photos; bk.rev.; pub. size: broadsheet; circ. evening 9,500(paid); Sun. 10,000(paid). **Wire Service(s):** AP.

Formerly: Daily/Sunday Sun, The.

WAYCROSS

US

WAYCROSS JOURNAL HERALD. 1914. Mon.-Sat. $.35 newsstand; $8/mo.; $96/yr. in city. 400 Isabella St., Waycross, GA 31501. TEL 912-283-2244; FAX 912-283-2815. **Owner(s):** Journal Herald Co., Inc., P.O. Box 219, Waycross, GA 31501. TEL 912-283-2244; Ed. Jack Williams, III; Pub. Roger L. Williams; adv. contact: David Tanner. pub. size: broadsheet; circ. evening 13,500(paid). Wire Service(s): AP.

GUAM

AGANA

US   ISSN 0196-2485

PACIFIC DAILY NEWS. 1944. d. P.O. Box DN, Agana, GU 96910. TEL 671-477-9712; FAX 671-472-1512. **Owner(s):** Pacific Daily News, Agana, GU; Ed. Joseph A. Novotny; Pub. Lee P. Webber; adv.; photos; pub. size: tabloid; circ. morning 25,232(paid); Sun. 22,981(paid). **Wire Service(s):** AP, GNS, LAT-WP.

HAWAII

HILO

US

HAWAII TRIBUNE-HERALD. 1923. Sun.-Fri. $.50/day newsstand; $1/Sun.; $9/mo. 355 Kinoole St., Hilo, HI 96720. TEL 808-935-6621; FAX 808-961-3680. **Owner(s):** Don Rey Media Group, P.O. Box 17017, Fort Smith, AR 72917. TEL 502-785-7810; Pub. Jim D. Wilson; adv. contact: Renee Carpenter. pub. size: broadsheet; circ. morning 19,688(paid); Sun. 23,888(paid). **Wire Service(s):** AP.

HONOLULU

US   ISSN 1072-7191

HONOLULU ADVERTISER. 1856. d. $.50/day newsstand; $1.50/Sun.; $26.80/4 wks. airmail. 605 Kapiolani Blvd., Honolulu, HI 96813. TEL 808-525-8000; FAX 808-525-8037. **Owner(s):** Gannett Company, Inc., 1100 Wilson Blvd., Arlington, VA 22234. TEL 703-284-6000; Ed. Jim Gatti; Pub. Larry Fuller; adv.; photos; pub. size: broadsheet; circ. morning 192,000(paid); Sun. 198,000(paid). **Wire Service(s):** AP, LAT-WP, KR.

US

HONOLULU STAR-BULLETIN. 1882. d. $.50 newsstand; $7.50/4 wks. daily; $13.50/4 wks. daily & Sun. 605 Kapiolani Blvd., Honolulu, HI 96813. TEL 808-525-8640; FAX 808-523-8509; E-mail: davids@aloha.net; URL: http://www.starbulletin.com. **Owner(s):** Liberty Newspaper LLP, Honolulu, HI 96813; Ed. David Shapiro; Pub. John M. Flanagan; adv. contact: Howard Griffin. bk.rev.; pub. size: broadsheet; circ. evening 80,069(paid). **Wire Service(s):** AP, NYT, RN, SHNA, NNS.

KAILUA KONA

US   ISSN 0744-4591

WEST HAWAII TODAY. 1968. Sun.-Fri. $7.75/mo. carrier. 75-5580 Kuakini Hwy., Kailua Kona, HI 96745-0789. TEL 808-329-9311; FAX 808-329-4860; E-mail: wht@1lhawaii.net; URL: http://www.ihawaii.net/~wht. **Owner(s):** Stephens Group, Inc., P.O. Box 17017, Fort Smith, AR 72917-7017. TEL 501-785-7810; Ed. Reed Flickinger; Pub. Richard Asbach; adv. contact: Deborah Ward. pub. size: tabloid; circ. morning 13,000(paid); Sun. 13,800(paid). **Wire Service(s):** AP.

LIHUE

US

ISLAND TIMES. 1902. Sun.-Fri. $.50/day newsstand; $.75/Sun.; $7.75/mo. 3137 Kuhio Hwy., Lihue, HI 96766. TEL 808-245-3681; FAX 808-245-5286. **Owner(s):** Pulitzer Publishing Co., 900 N. Tucker Blvd., St. Louis, MO 63101. TEL 313-340-8000; Ed. Rita DeSilva; Pub. Roy Callaway; adv. contact: Christin Myreall. pub. size: standard; circ. morning 10,000(paid); Sun. 10,000(paid). **Wire Service(s):** AP.

Formerly: Garden Island Times.

DAILY NEWSPAPERS

WAILUKU
US
MAUI NEWS. 1900. Sun.-Fri. $.50/day newsstand; $1.50/Sun.; $90/yr. in cy. 100 Mahalani St., Wailuku, HI 96793. TEL 808-244-3981; FAX 808-242-9087; E-mail: mauinews@maui.net; URL: http://www.maui.net/~mauinews/news.html. **Owner(s):** Maui Publishing Co., Ltd., P.O. Box 550, Wailuku, HI 96793. TEL 808-244-3981; Ed. Dave Hoff; Pub. Richard Kameron; adv.; photos; pub. size: broadsheet; circ. morning 20,300(paid); Sun. 27,000(paid). **Wire Service(s):** AP.

IDAHO

BLACKFOOT
US   ISSN 0893-3812
BLACKFOOT MORNING NEWS. 1904. Mon.-Sat. $.50 newsstand; $86.20/yr. in cy.; $97.45/yr. mailed. 34 N. Ash, Blackfoot, ID 83221. TEL 208-785-1100; FAX 208-785-4239. **Owner(s):** American Publishing Co., 606 N. Van Buren, P.O. Box 520, Marion, IL 62959. TEL 618-993-1711; Ed. Michael O'Donnell; Pub. Kaye Moses; adv. contact: Leslie Bare. photos; bk.rev.; pub. size: broadsheet; circ. morning 5,000(paid). **Wire Service(s):** AP.

BOISE
US
IDAHO STATESMAN, THE. 1864. d. $.50/day newsstand; $1.50/Sun.; $13/4 wks. 1200 N. Curtis Rd., Boise, ID 83706. TEL 208-377-6200; FAX 208-377-6309; E-mail: news@idstates.com. **Owner(s):** Gannett Company, Inc., 1100 Wilson Blvd., Arlington, VA 22234. TEL 703-248-6000; Ed. Karen Baker; Pub. Pamela Meals; adv.; photos; bk.rev.; pub. size: broadsheet; circ. morning 65,975(paid); Sun. 87,819(paid). **Wire Service(s):** AP, GNS, NYT.

BURLEY
US
SOUTH IDAHO PRESS. 1904. Sun.-Fri. $.50 newsstand; $8.20/mo. 230 E. Main St., Burley, ID 83318. TEL 208-678-2201; FAX 208-678-0412; E-mail: sip@cyberway.net; URL: http://www.cyberhighway.net/~sip. **Owner(s):** Community Newspaper Holdings, Inc., 269 W. Main St., 6th Fl., Lexington, KY 40507. TEL 606-388-2644; FAX 606-225-8115; Ed. Kart Miller; Pub. Jay Lenkersdorfer; pub. size: broadsheet; circ. evening 5,500(paid); Sun. 5,200(paid). **Wire Service(s):** AP.
Formerly: Burley South Idaho Press.

COEUR D'ALENE
US   ISSN 1041-2883
COEUR D'ALENE PRESS. 1892. d. $.50/day newsstand; $1/Sun.; $11.50/mo. carrier. 201 Second St., Coeur d'Alene, ID 83814. TEL 208-664-8176; FAX 208-664-0212. **Owner(s):** Hagadone Corp., 201 Second St., Coeur d'Alene, ID 83814. TEL 208-667-3431; Ed. Mike Feiler; Pub. Jim Thompson; adv. contact: Paul Burke. pub. size: broadsheet; circ. morning 15,000(paid); Sun. 30,000(paid). **Wire Service(s):** AP.

IDAHO FALLS
US
IDAHO FALLS POST REGISTER. 1881. d. $.50/day newsstand; $1.50/Sun., $9.50/mo. 333 Northgate Mile, Idaho Falls, ID 83401. TEL 208-522-1800; FAX 208-529-9683; E-mail: mchan@idahonews.com; URL: http://www.idahonews.com. **Owner(s):** Post Co., The, P.O. Box 1800, Idaho Falls, ID 83403. TEL 208-522-1800; Ed. Jerry M. Brady; Pub. Jerry M. Brady; adv. contact: David Gilchrist. photos; bk.rev.; pub. size: broadsheet; circ. evening 29,000(paid); Sun. 30,000(paid). **Wire Service(s):** AP, KR.

KELLOGG
US   ISSN 1044-9553
SHOSHONE NEWS-PRESS. 1926. Tue.-Sun. $.50 newsstand; $9.25/mo. 401 Main St., Kellogg, ID 83837. TEL 208-783-1107; FAX 208-784-6791. **Owner(s):** Hagadone Corp., 401 Main St., Kellogg, ID 83837. TEL 208-667-3431; Ed. Judy Binkley; Pub. Dan Drewery; pub. size: standard; circ. morning 5,100(paid). **Wire Service(s):** AP.
Formerly: Shoshone County News-Press.

LEWISTON
US   ISSN 0892-2586
LEWISTON MORNING TRIBUNE. 1892. d. $.50/day newsstand; $1.25/Sun.; $126/yr. local; $138/yr. motor rte.; $156/yr. mailed. 505 C St., Lewiston, ID 83501. TEL 208-743-9411; FAX 208-746-1185; E-mail: city@lmtribune.com; URL: http://www.lmtribune.com. **Owner(s):** Tribune Publishing Co., 505 C St., P.O. Box 957, Lewiston, ID 83501. TEL 208-743-9411; Ed. Paul Emerson; Pub. A.L. Alford; adv. contact: Rob Minervini. pub. size: broadsheet; circ. morning 26,500(paid); Sun. 28,500(paid). **Wire Service(s):** AP, NYT.

MOSCOW
US
MOSCOW/PULLMAN DAILY NEWS. 1981. Mon.-Sat. $.50/day newsstand; $1/Sat.; $12.25/mo. mailed. 409 S. Jackson, Moscow, ID 83843. TEL 208-882-5561; FAX 208-883-8205; E-mail: editor@moscow.com; URL: http://www.dnews.com. **Owner(s):** Kearns-Tribune Corp., 143 S. Main St., Salt Lake City, UT 84111. TEL 801-237-2031; News Review Publishing Co., 505 C. St., Lewiston, ID 83501. TEL 800-745-9411; Ed. Rick Hoover; Pub. Mark Trahant; adv. contact: Randy Pressnall. pub. size: broadsheet; circ. evening 8,900(paid). **Wire Service(s):** AP, KRTN.
Formerly: Daily News.

NAMPA
US
IDAHO PRESS-TRIBUNE. 1883. d. $.50/day newsstand; $1/Sun.; $9/mo. 1618 N. Midland St., Nampa, ID 83651. TEL 208-467-9251; FAX 208-467-9562; E-mail: vholbrook@idahopress.com; URL: http://www.idahopress.com. **Owner(s):** Swift-Pioneer Newspapers, 221 First Ave., W., Ste. 405, Seattle, WA 98119. TEL 206-284-4424; Ed. Vickie Holbrook; Pub. Jim Barnes; adv. contact: Carolyn Sinnard. photos; bk.rev.; pub. size: broadsheet; circ. evening 21,000(paid); Sun. 21,000(paid). **Wire Service(s):** AP.

POCATELLO
US
IDAHO STATE JOURNAL. 1893. Sun.-Fri. $.50/day newsstand; $1.25/Sun.; $9/mo. in city; $9.75/mo. rural. 305 S. Arthur Ave., Pocatello, ID 83204. TEL 208-232-4161; FAX 208-233-8007. **Owner(s):** Idaho State Publishing, Inc., Pocatello, ID 83204; Ed. Donald H. Black; Pub. Donald J. Byrne; adv. contact: Leonard Martin. photos; pub. size: broadsheet; circ. evening 20,000(paid); Sun. 22,500(paid). **Wire Service(s):** AP.

SANDPOINT
US   ISSN 1047-6822
BONNER COUNTY DAILY BEE. 1965. Tue.-Sun. $.50/day newsstand; $1.25/Sun.; $10.25/mo. in city; $10.75/mo. motor rte. 310 Church St., Sandpoint, ID 83864. TEL 208-263-9534; FAX 208-263-9091. **Owner(s):** Hagadone Corp., P.O. Box 1178, Coeur D Alene, ID 83814. TEL 208-667-3431; Ed. Bill Buley; Pub. Joe Grimes; adv. contact: Herb Offermann. photos; bk.rev.; pub. size: broadsheet; circ. evening 6,800(paid); Sun. 32,000(paid). **Wire Service(s):** AP.
Formerly: Sandpoint Daily Bee.

TWIN FALLS
US
TWIN FALLS TIMES-NEWS. 1905. d. $.50/day newsstand; $1.50/Sun.; $3.50/wk. home deliv. 132 Third St., W., Twin Falls, ID 83301. TEL 208-733-0931. **Owner(s):** Howard Publications, Inc., P.O. Box 570, Oceanside, CA 92049. TEL 714-433-5771; Ed. Clark Walworth; Pub. Stephen Hartgen; adv. contact: Pete York. photos; bk.rev.; pub. size: broadsheet; circ. morning 23,500(paid); Sun. 24,000(paid). **Wire Service(s):** LAT-WP, KR, AP.

ILLINOIS

ALTON
US
TELEGRAPH, THE. 1836. d. $.50/day newsstand; $1.50/Sun.; $3.25/wk; $13/4 wks. 111 E. Broadway, Alton, IL 62002. TEL 618-463-2500; FAX 618-463-9829. **Owner(s):** Journal Register Co., 50 W. State St., 12th Fl., Trenton, NJ 08608. TEL 609-396-2200; Ed. Rick Jarvis; Pub. Thomas Rice; pub. size: broadsheet; circ. morning 34,500(paid); Sun. 36,500(paid). **Wire Service(s):** AP.

ARLINGTON HEIGHTS
US
DAILY HERALD. 1872. d. $.50/day newsstand; $1.50/Sun.; $197.60/yr. carrier. 155 E. Algonquin Rd., Arlington Heights, IL 60005. TEL 847-427-4300; FAX 847-427-1301. **Owner(s):** Paddock Publications, P.O. Box 280, Arlington Heights, IL 60006. TEL 708-870-3600; Ed. John Lampinen. adv. contact: Jim Walsh. pub. size: broadsheet; circ. morning 125,000(paid); Sun. 119,838(paid). **Wire Service(s):** UPI, AP.
Formerly: Hanover Park Daily Herald.

AURORA

US

BEACON NEWS. 1846. d. $.35/day newsstand; $1/Sun.; $120/yr. 101 S. River St., Aurora, IL 60506. TEL 708-844-5844; FAX 708-844-5818. **Owner(s):** Copley Press, Inc., 7776 Ivanhoe St., LaJolla, CA 92037. TEL 619-454-0411. Ed. Mike Chapin. photos; pub. size: broadsheet; circ. evening 40,000(paid). **Wire Service(s):** AP.

BELLEVILLE

US ISSN 8750-1058

BELLEVILLE NEWS-DEMOCRAT. 1858. d. $.50/day newsstand; $1.25/Sun.; $2.10/wk. daily; $2/wk. weekends; $3.25/wk. home deliv. 120 S. Illinois St., Belleville, IL 62220. TEL 618-234-1000; FAX 618-234-5521; E-mail: garyccb@aol.com. **Owner(s):** Knight-Ridder, Inc., One Herald Plz., Miami, FL 33132. TEL 305-376-3800; FAX 305-376-3875; Ed. Greg Edwards; Pub. Gary Berkley; adv.; pub. size: broadsheet; circ. morning 51,000(paid); Sun. 62,000(paid). **Wire Service(s):** AP, NYT, CSM.

BELVIDERE

US

BELVIDERE DAILY REPUBLICAN. 1894. Mon.-Sat. $.35 newsstand; $7/mo. local. 401 Whitney Blvd., Belvidere, IL 61008. TEL 815-544-9811; FAX 815-544-6334; E-mail: realibertry@aol.com; URL: http://www.members.gnn.com/lpahl/bdr.htm. **Owner(s):** Belvidere Daily Republican, 401 Whitney Blvd., Belvidere, IL 61008. TEL 815-544-9811; FAX 815-544-6334; Ed. Kathy Sterbencz. adv. contact: Sheri Aspenson. photos; bk.rev.; pub. size: broadsheet; circ. evening 5,100(paid). **Wire Service(s):** AP.

BENTON

US

EVENING NEWS. Sat.-Thu. $.50/newsstand; $116/yr. in cy.; $136/yr. out of state. 111-115 E. Church St., Benton, IL 62812. TEL 618-438-5611; FAX 618-435-2413. **Owner(s):** American Publishing Co., 606 N. Van Buren, Marion, IL 62959. TEL 618-993-1711; adv. contact: Terra Kerkemeyer. pub. size: broadsheet; circ. morning 4,800(paid); Sun. 4,800(paid).
Formerly: Benton Evening News.

BLOOMINGTON

US

PANTAGRAPH, THE. 1837. d. $.50/day newsstand; $1.25/Sun.; $175.25/carrier; $180/yr. motor rte. 301 W. Washington, Bloomington, IL 61701. TEL 309-829-9411; FAX 309-829-9104; E-mail: pantagra@pantagraph.com; URL: http://www.pantagraph.com. **Owner(s):** Chronicle Publishing Co., 901 Mission St., San Francisco, CA 94103; Ed. Jan Dennis; Pub. Donald R. Scagg; adv. contact: John Hoffman. bk.rev.; pub. size: broadsheet; circ. morning 49,600(paid); Sun. 53,500(paid). **Wire Service(s):** AP, LAT-WP, SH, Smithsonian.

CANTON

US

DAILY LEDGER. 1849. Mon.-Sat. $.50 newsstand; $99/yr. in cy.; $125.05/yr. out of cy. 53 W. Elm, Canton, IL 61520. TEL 309-647-5100; FAX 309-647-4665. **Owner(s):** American Publishing Co., 606 N. Van Buren, Marion, IL 62959. TEL 618-993-1711; Ed. Linda Woods; Pub. Scott Koon; adv. contact: Jackie Caulkins. photos; pub. size: broadsheet; circ. evening 6,000(paid). **Wire Service(s):** AP.

CARBONDALE

US

SOUTHERN ILLINOISAN. 1947. d. $.50/day newsstand; $1.50/Sun.; $11.80/4 wks. local. 710 N. Illinois Ave., Carbondale, IL 62901. TEL 618-529-5454; FAX 618-457-2935; E-mail: fiexpress@aol.com. **Owner(s):** Lee Enterprises, Inc., 130 E. Second St., Davenport, IA 52801. TEL 319-383-2202; Ed. Carl Rexroad; Pub. Richard Johnston; adv. contact: Jeff Barr. photos; bk.rev.; pub. size: broadsheet; circ. morning 30,000(paid); Sun. 36,000(paid). **Wire Service(s):** AP.

CARMI

US

CARMI TIMES. 1950. Mon.-Sat. $.50 newsstand; $103.40/yr. in cy. 323-325 E. Main St., Carmi, IL 62821. TEL 618-382-4176; FAX 618-384-2163. **Owner(s):** American Publishing Co., 606 N. Van Buren, Marion, IL 62959. TEL 618-993-1711; Pub. Barry C. Cleveland; pub. size: broadsheet; circ. evening 3,800(paid). **Wire Service(s):** AP.

CENTRALIA

US

CENTRALIA SENTINEL. 1863. Sun.-Fri. $.35/day newsstand; $1/Sun.; $85.80/ carrier; $105/yr. mailed in area; $105yr. mailed out of area. 232 E. Broadway, Centralia, IL 62801. TEL 618-532-5604; FAX 618-532-1212. **Owner(s):** Centralia Press, Ltd., P.O. Box 627, Centralia, IL 62801. TEL 618-532-5604; FAX 618-532-1212; Ed. Mark Hodapp; Pub. John Perine; adv.; photos; pub. size: broadsheet; circ. morning 16,250(paid); Sun. 17,100(paid). **Wire Service(s):** AP, LAT-WP.
Formerly: Centralia Evening & Sunday Sentinel.

CHAMPAIGN

US ISSN 1042-3354

CHAMPAIGN NEWS GAZETTE. 1852. d. $.35/day newsstand; $1.50/Sun.; $163.80/yr. home deliv. 15 Main St., Champaign, IL 61820. TEL 217-351-5252; FAX 217-351-5291; E-mail: Mcdonald@news-gazette.com; URL: http://www.news-gazette.com. **Owner(s):** Professional Impressions Media Group, 15 Main St., P.O. Box 677, Champaign, IL 61824. TEL 217-351-5252; Ed. Dan Corkery; Pub. Marajen Stevick Chinigo; adv. contact: Sue Trippiedi. pub. size: broadsheet; circ. evening 45,375(paid); Sun. 52,514(paid). **Wire Service(s):** AP, NYT.

CHARLESTON

US

CHARLESTON TIMES-COURIER. 1840. Mon.-Sat. $.50/day newsstand; $.75/Sat.; $2.20/wk.; $28/13 wks. mailed. 307 Sixth St., Charleston, IL 61920. TEL 217-345-7085; FAX 217-345-7090. **Owner(s):** Howard Publications, Inc., P.O. Box 570, Oceanside, CA; Ed. Bill Lair. adv. contact: Robert Yamamoto. pub. size: broadsheet; circ. morning 7,741(paid). **Wire Service(s):** AP.
Formerly: Charleston Coles County Daily.

CHICAGO

US ISSN 0745-7014

CHICAGO DEFENDER. 1905. Mon.-Thu. & Sat. $.35/day newsstand; $.50/Sat.; $55.47/6 mos.; $112.84/yr. 2400 S. Michigan Ave., Chicago, IL 60616. TEL 312-225-2400; FAX 312-225-9231. **Owner(s):** Sengstackes Enterprises, 2400 S. Michigan Ave., Chicago, IL 60616. TEL 312-225-2400; Ed. John H. Sengstacke; Pub. Frederick D. Sengstacke; adv.; photos; pub. size: tabloid; circ. morning 18,000(paid). **Wire Service(s):** AP.

US

CHICAGO SUN TIMES. 1948. d. $.35/day newsstand; $1.25/Sun.; $3.50/wk. carrier. 401 N. Wabash Ave., Chicago, IL 60611. TEL 312-321-3000; FAX 312-321-3084; E-mail: metro@suntimes.com; URL: http://www.suntimes.com/. **Owner(s):** American Publishing Co., 606 N. Van Buren, Marion, IL 62959. TEL 618-993-1711; Ed. Nigel Wade; Pub. F. David Radler; adv. contact: Mike Beatty. photos; bk.rev.; pub. size: tabloid; circ. morning 501,115(paid); Sun. 469,161(paid). **Wire Service(s):** AP, DJ, LAT-WP, RN, GNS.

US

CHICAGO TRIBUNE. 1847. d. $.50/day newsstand; $1.75/Sun.; $3.80/wk. 435 N. Michigan Ave., Chicago, IL 60611-4041. TEL 312-222-3920; FAX 312-222-3093; E-mail: prjeff@aol.com; URL: http://www.chicago.tribune.com. **Owner(s):** Tribune Co., 435 N. Michigan Ave., Chicago, IL 60611-4041. TEL 312-222-3232; Ed. Ann Marie Lipinski; Pub. Scott C. Smith; adv.; photos; bk.rev.; pub. size: broadsheet; circ. morning 667,908(paid); Sun. 1,066,393(paid). **Wire Service(s):** AP, RN, KR.

CLINTON

US

CLINTON DAILY JOURNAL. 1905. Mon.-Fri. $.50 newsstand; $92/yr. Rte. 54, W., Clinton, IL 61727. TEL 217-935-3171; FAX 217-935-6086. **Owner(s):** New Media Corp., 401 N. Main, Rochelle, IL 61068. TEL 815-562-4171; Ed. Bob Loeschner; Pub. Terrie L. Baker; adv.; photos; pub. size: broadsheet; circ. evening 3,760(paid). **Wire Service(s):** AP.

CRYSTAL LAKE

US ISSN 8750-0396

NORTHWEST HERALD. 1875. d. $.50/day newsstand; $1.25/Sun.; $2.90/wk. home deliv. 7717 S. Rte. 31, Crystal Lake, IL 60014. TEL 815-459-4040; FAX 815-459-5640. **Owner(s):** B.F. Shaw Printing Co., 444 Pine Hill Drive, Dixon, IL 61021; Ed. Cliff Ward; Pub. Robert A. Shaw; adv. contact: Chris Golbeck. pub. size: broadsheet; circ. morning 32,969(paid); Sun. 35,107(paid). **Wire Service(s):** AP.

DAILY NEWSPAPERS

DANVILLE
US

COMMERCIAL-NEWS. 1866. d. $.35/day newsstand; $1.25/Sun.; $104.25/6 mos.; $200.50/yr. 17 W. North St., Danville, IL 61832. TEL 217-446-1000; FAX 217-446-9825. **Owner(s):** Gannett Company, Inc., 1100 Wilson Blvd., Arlington, VA 22340; Ed. Denise Richter; Pub. Charles E. Morris; adv. contact: Carol Nichols. photos; pub. size: broadsheet; circ. evening 19,999(paid); Sun. 22,325(paid). **Wire Service(s):** AP, GNS.
Formerly: Danville Commercial-News.

DECATUR
US

HERALD & REVIEW. 1873. d. $.50/day newsstand; $1.75/Sun.; $14.40/4 wks. 601 E. William, Decatur, IL 62523. TEL 217-429-5151; FAX 217-421-7965. **Owner(s):** Lee Enterprises, Inc., 215 N. Main Street, Davenport, IA 52801. TEL 319-383-2202; Ed. George T. Althoff; Pub. Charles V. Pittman; pub. size: broadsheet; circ. morning 44,000(paid); Sun. 55,000(paid). **Wire Service(s):** AP, KR.

DE KALB
US

DAILY CHRONICLE. 1879. Sun.-Fri. $.50/day newsstand; $1/Sun.; $9/mo. cy.; $9.75/ out of cy. 1586 Barber Green Rd., De Kalb, IL 60115. TEL 815-756-4841; FAX 815-756-2079. **Owner(s):** Northern Illinois Publishing Co., 1586 Barber Greene Rd., De Kalb, IL 60115. TEL 815-756-4841; Ed. John Secor. adv. contact: Reino Rippi. pub. size: broadsheet; circ. evening 12,599(paid); Sun. 12,825(paid). **Wire Service(s):** AP.

DES PLAINES
US

DES PLAINES JOURNAL. 1933. Wed.-Sat. & Mon. $.50 newsstand; $25/yr. in city; $26/yr. out of city. 622 Graceland Ave., Des Plaines, IL 60016. TEL 847-299-5511; FAX 847-298-8549. **Owner(s):** Des Plaines Journal, Inc., 622 Graceland Ave., Des Plaines, IL 60016. TEL 708-299-5511; Ed. Todd C. Wessell; Pub. Richard C. Wessell, Sr.; adv.; pub. size: standard; circ. evening 12,000(paid).

DIXON
US ISSN 0889-4612

TELEGRAPH, THE. 1851. Mon.-Sat. $.50/day newsstand; $1/Sat.; $98/yr. 113 Peoria Ave., Dixon, IL 61021-0409. TEL 815-284-2222; FAX 815-284-2870. **Owner(s):** B.F. Shaw Printing Co., P.O. Box 409, Dixon, IL 61021-0409. TEL 815-284-2222; FAX 815-284-2870; Ed. Ken Brown; Pub. William E. Shaw; adv.; pub. size: broadsheet; circ. evening 10,300(paid). **Wire Service(s):** AP, CNS.
Formerly: Dixon Telegraph.

DU QUOIN
US

DU QUOIN EVENING CALL. 1895. d. $.50/newsstand; $102/yr. mailed in cy.; $104/yr. mailed out of cy. 9 N. Division St., Du Quoin, IL 62832. TEL 618-542-2133; FAX 618-542-2726; E-mail: dqedit@ampub.com; URL: http://www.ampub.com/~duquoin/call.html. **Owner(s):** American Publishing Co., 606 N. Van Buren, Marion, IL 62959. TEL 618-993-1711; Ed. John Croessman; Pub. Steve Fisher; adv. contact: Doris Hottes. photos; pub. size: broadsheet; circ. evening 4,800(paid). **Wire Service(s):** AP.

EDWARDSVILLE
US ISSN 1074-1860

EDWARDSVILLE INTELLIGENCER. 1862. Mon.-Sat. $.50/day newsstand; $.75/Sat.; $1.50/wk. carrier. 117 N. Second St., Edwardsville, IL 62025. TEL 618-656-4700; FAX 618-656-7618; E-mail: mminton@edwpub.com; URL: http://www.edwpub.com. **Owner(s):** Hearst Corp., 959 Eighth Ave., New York, NY 10019; Pub. Bruce Coury; adv. contact: Shelley Loftus. photos; pub. size: broadsheet; circ. evening 7,200(paid). **Wire Service(s):** AP.

EFFINGHAM
US

EFFINGHAM DAILY NEWS. 1899. Mon.-Sat. $.50 newsstand; $7.40/mo.; $78/yr. 201 N. Banker St., Effingham, IL 62401. TEL 217-347-7151; FAX 217-342-9315. **Owner(s):** Community Newspaper Holdings, 269 W. Main St., Lexington, KY 40507; Ed. Susan Duncan; Pub. Paul E. Semple; adv. contact: Carl A. Thoele. pub. size: broadsheet; circ. morning 13,000(paid); evening 13,000(paid). **Wire Service(s):** AP.

ELDORADO
US

ELDORADO DAILY JOURNAL. 1911. Mon.-Sat. $.50 newsstand; $2.10/wk.; $54/6 mos.; $104/yr. 1200 Locust St., Eldorado, IL 62930. TEL 618-273-3379; FAX 618-273-3738. **Owner(s):** American Publishing Co., 606 N. Van Buren, Marion, IL 62959. TEL 618-993-1711; Ed. Scott Hines; Pub. George Wilson; pub. size: broadsheet; circ. evening 7,200(paid). **Wire Service(s):** AP.

ELGIN
US

COURIER-NEWS, THE. 1874. d. $.35/day newsstand; $1/Sun.; $102.90/yr. 300 Lake St., Elgin, IL 60120. TEL 847-888-7800; FAX 847-888-7836. **Owner(s):** Copley Press, Inc., 7776 Ivanhoe Ave., La Jolla, CA 92037. TEL 619-454-0411; Ed. Mike Bailey; Pub. Art Wible; pub. size: standard; circ. evening 25,000(paid); Sun. 28,000(paid). **Wire Service(s):** AP, CNS, NYT.
Formerly: Daily Courier-News.

FLORA
US

DAILY CLAY COUNTY ADVOCATE-PRESS. 1886. Mon.-Fri. $.50 newsstand; $7.50/yr. in cy.; $84.50/yr. out of cy. 105 W. North Ave., Flora, IL 62839. TEL 618-662-2108. **Owner(s):** American Publishing Co., 606 N. Van Buren, Marion, IL 62959. TEL 618-993-1711; Pub. J.L. Thatcher; adv. contact: Bonnie Thatcher. pub. size: broadsheet; circ. evening 3,500(paid). **Wire Service(s):** AP.

FREEPORT
US

FREEPORT JOURNAL-STANDARD. 1847. Mon.-Sat. $.50/day newsstand; $1/Sat.; $131/yr. carrier. 27 S. State Ave., Freeport, IL 61032. TEL 815-232-1171; FAX 615-232-3601. **Owner(s):** Howard Publications, Inc., 1722 S. Hill, Oceanside, CA 92054. TEL 619-433-7333; Ed. Jeff Rogers; Pub. Gary Quinn; adv.: $12/SAU. photos; pub. size: broadsheet; circ. evening 17,000(paid). **Wire Service(s):** AP.

GALESBURG
US

REGISTER-MAIL. 1872. Mon.-Sat. $.50 newsstand; $84.25/yr. carrier; $103.92/yr. in state; $153/yr. out of state. 140 S. Prairie St., Galesburg, IL 61401-0310. TEL 309-343-7181; FAX 309-343-2382. **Owner(s):** Copley Press, Inc., 7776 Ivanhoe Ave., La Jolla, CA 92037. TEL 619-454-0411; Pub. Don Cooper; adv. contact: Doris Medhurst. pub. size: broadsheet; circ. evening 19,000(paid). **Wire Service(s):** AP.

GENEVA
US

KANE COUNTY CHRONICLE. 1881. Tue.-Sat. $.50 newsstand; $68.85/yr. 1000 Randall Rd., Geneva, IL 60134. TEL 630-232-9222; FAX 630-232-4962; E-mail: kcchronl@aol.com. **Owner(s):** B.F. Shaw Printing Co., 444 Pine Hill Dr., P.O. Box 409, Dixon, IL 61021. TEL 815-284-2222; FAX 815-284-2870; Ed. David Heun; Pub. Roger F. Coleman; adv. contact: Jim Holm. photos; pub. size: broadsheet; circ. 15,000(paid). **Wire Service(s):** AP.

HARRISBURG
US

HARRISBURG DAILY REGISTER. 1915. Mon.-Sat. $.50/day newsstand; $104/yr. in cy.; $112/yr. out of cy.; $125/yr. in state; $135/yr. out of state. 35 S. Vine St., Harrisburg, IL 62946. TEL 618-253-7146; FAX 618-252-0863; E-mail: gwilson@ampub.com; URL: http://www.dailyregister.com. **Owner(s):** American Publishing Co., 606 N. Van Buren, Marion, IL 62959. TEL 618-993-1711; Ed. Lee Smith; Pub. George Wilson; adv. contact: Sally Wofford. pub. size: broadsheet; circ. evening 6,200(paid). **Wire Service(s):** AP.

JACKSONVILLE

US

JACKSONVILLE JOURNAL-COURIER. 1830. d. $.50/day newsstand; $1.50/Sun.; $3.00/wk. carrier; $156/yr. mailed. 235 W. State St., Jacksonville, IL 62651-1048. TEL 217-245-6121; FAX 217-245-1226. **Owner(s):** Illinois Freedom Newspapers, Inc., 235 W. State St., Jacksonville, IL 62651-1048. TEL 217-245-6121; FAX 217-245-1226; Ed. Ted Roth; Pub. John R. Power; adv. contact: Randy Lohrenz. photos; bk.rev.; pub. size: broadsheet; circ. morning 14,500(paid); Sun. 14,500(paid). **Wire Service(s):** AP.

JOLIET

US

HERALD-NEWS, THE. 1839. d. $.35/day newsstand; $1.25/Sun.; $2.50/wk. home deliv.; $3.50/wk. mailed. 300 Caterpillar Dr., Joliet, IL 60436. TEL 815-729-6069; FAX 815-729-6063. **Owner(s):** Copley Press, Inc., 7776 Ivanhoe Ave., La Jolla, CA 92037. TEL 619-454-0411; adv. contact: Cory Bollinger. photos; bk.rev.; pub. size: broadsheet; circ. morning 49,750(paid); Sun. 50,130(paid). **Wire Service(s):** AP, CNS, SHNA.
Formerly: Joliet Herald-News.

KANKAKEE

US

DAILY JOURNAL. 1903. Sun.-Fri. $.50/day newsstand; $1.50/Sun.; $4.70/2 wks. carrier; $117/yr. 7 cys.; $170/yr. out of state. 8 Dearborn Sq., Kankakee, IL 60901. TEL 815-937-3300; FAX 815-937-3301. **Owner(s):** Small Newspaper Group, 8 Dearborn Sq., Kankakee, IL 60901. TEL 815-937-3300; Ed. Phil Angelo; Pub. Jean Alice Small; adv. contact: Pam Dunlap. photos; pub. size: broadsheet; circ. evening 22,850(paid); Sun. 33,223(paid). **Wire Service(s):** AP.

KEWANEE

US

KEWANEE STAR-COURIER. 1893. Mon.-Sat. $.50 newsstand; $110/yr. local. 105 E. Central Blvd., Kewanee, IL 61443. TEL 309-852-2181; FAX 309-852-0010; E-mail: strcurgr@*courier.com. **Owner(s):** Lee Enterprises, Inc., 215 N. Main St., Davenport, IA 52801. TEL 319-383-2202; Ed. Anita Bird. pub. size: broadsheet; circ. evening 6,986(paid). **Wire Service(s):** AP.

LA SALLE

US

NEWS-TRIBUNE. 1891. Mon.-Sat. $.50 newsstand; $84/yr. 426 Second St., La Salle, IL 61301-2366. TEL 815-223-3200; FAX 815-223-2543. **Owner(s):** Daily News-Tribune, Inc., 426 Second St., La Salle, IL 61301-2366. TEL 815-223-3200; Ed. Linda Kleezewski; Pub. Peter Miller, III; adv. contact: Bob Vickery. photos; bk.rev.; pub. size: broadsheet; circ. evening 19,550(paid). **Wire Service(s):** AP.

LAWRENCEVILLE

US

LAWRENCEVILLE DAILY RECORD. 1847. Mon.-Fri. $.25 newsstand; $59/yr. 1209 State St., Lawrenceville, IL 62439. TEL 618-943-2331; FAX 618-943-3976. **Owner(s):** Larry R. Lewis, 1209 State St., Lawrenceville, IL 62439. TEL 618-943-2331; Ed. Michael Van Dorn; Pub. Larry R. Lewis; adv. contact: Sandie Stafford. pub. size: broadsheet; circ. evening 4,500(paid). **Wire Service(s):** AP.

LINCOLN

US

LINCOLN COURIER. Mon.-Sat. $.35 newsstand; $2.35/wk. in cy. 601 Pulaski St., Lincoln, IL 62656. TEL 217-732-2101; FAX 217-732-7039; E-mail: courier@abelink.com. **Owner(s):** Copley Press, Inc., 7776 Ivanhoe, La Jolla, CA 92037. TEL 619-454-0411; Ed. Jeff Nelson; Pub. Patrick Coburn; adv. contact: Karen Harges. pub. size: broadsheet; circ. evening 7,200(paid). **Wire Service(s):** AP.
Formerly: Courier, The.

LITCHFIELD

US

LITCHFIELD NEWS-HERALD. 1856. Mon.-Fri. $.30 newsstand. 112 E. Ryder St., Litchfield, IL 62056. TEL 217-324-2121; FAX 217-324-2122. **Owner(s):** Litchfield News-Herald, Inc., P.O. Box 160, Litchfield, IL 62056. TEL 217-324-2121; Ed. Micki Romanus; Pub. John C. Hanafin; adv. contact: Fred W. Jones. pub. size: broadsheet; circ. evening 5,800(paid). **Wire Service(s):** AP.

MACOMB

US

MACOMB JOURNAL. 1855. d. $.35/day newsstand; $.75/Sun.; $1.90/wk. carrier. 128 N. Lafayette, Macomb, IL 61455. TEL 309-833-2114; FAX 309-833-2346. **Owner(s):** Newspaper Holdings, Inc, 269 W. Main St., 6th. Fl., Lexington, KY. TEL 606-388-2644; Ed. Tom Martin. adv. contact: Lisa Havens. adv.: $10.38/SAU. photos; bk.rev.; pub. size: broadsheet; circ. evening 7,000(paid); Sun. 7,500(paid). **Wire Service(s):** AP.

MARION

US

MARION DAILY REPUBLICAN. 1914. Mon.-Sat. $.50/day newsstand; $1/Sun.; $9.70/mo. carrier. 502 W. Jackson St., Marion, IL 62959. TEL 618-993-2626; FAX 618-993-8326. **Owner(s):** American Publishing Co., 606 N. Van Buren, Marion, IL 62959. TEL 618-993-1711; Ed. Richard Darby; Pub. Sam Shelton; adv. contact: Michelle Bean. photos; pub. size: broadsheet; circ. evening 4,600(paid). **Wire Service(s):** AP.

MATTOON

US

MATTOON JOURNAL GAZETTE. 1905. Mon.-Sat. $.50/day newsstand; $.75/Sat.; $114.40/yr. 100 Broadway, Mattoon, IL 61938. TEL 217-235-5656; FAX 217-235-1925. **Owner(s):** Howard Publications, Inc., 1715 S. Freeman, Oceanside, CA 92054. TEL 619-433-5771; Pub. William Hamel, Jr.; adv. contact: Robert Yamamoto. photos; bk.rev.; pub. size: broadsheet; circ. morning 11,921(paid). **Wire Service(s):** AP.

MOLINE

US

ROCK ISLAND ARGUS & THE DISPATCH. 1878. d. $.50/day; $1.50/Sun.; $2.70/wk. home deliv.; $39/12wks. mail. 1720 Fifth Ave., Moline, IL 61265. TEL 309-764-4344; FAX 309-797-0311. **Owner(s):** Moline Dispatch Publishing, 1720 Fifth Ave., Moline, IL 61265. TEL 309-764-4344; Ed. Russell Scott; Pub. Gerald J. Taylor; photos; bk.rev.; pub. size: broadsheet; circ. evening 43,296(paid); Sun. 53,341(paid). **Wire Service(s):** UPI, KNT.
Formerly: Rock Island Argus Dispatch, The.

MONMOUTH

US

DAILY REVIEW ATLAS. 5924. Mon.-Sat. $.50 newsstand; $23.50/3 mos. carrier; $45.82/yr. 400 S. Main St., Monmouth, IL 61462. TEL 309-734-3176; FAX 309-734-7649. **Owner(s):** American Publishing Co., 606 N. Van Buren, Marion, IL 62959. TEL 618-993-1700; Pub. Scott Champion; adv.; pub. size: broadsheet; circ. evening 3,600(paid). **Wire Service(s):** AP.

MORRIS

US

MORRIS DAILY HERALD. 1891. Mon.-Fri. $.50 newsstand; $75/yr. local. 1804 N. Division St., Morris, IL 60450. TEL 815-942-3221; FAX 815-942-0988. **Owner(s):** B.F. Shaw Printing Co., 113 Peoria Ave., Dixon, IL 61021. TEL 815-284-2222; Pub. Timothy J. West; adv.; photos; pub. size: broadsheet; circ. evening 7,900(paid). **Wire Service(s):** AP.
Formerly: Morris Herald.

MT. CARMEL

US

MOUNT CARMEL DAILY REPUBLICAN-REGISTER. 1839. Mon.-Fri. $.50 newsstand; $57.90/yr. in cy. 115-117 E. Fourth St., Mt. Carmel, IL 62863. TEL 618-262-5144; FAX 618-263-4437. **Owner(s):** Brehm Communications, Inc., 17065 Via del Campo, Ste. 100, San Diego, CA 92198. TEL 619-451-6200; FAX 619-451-3814; Ed. Phil Gower; Pub. Jack Rodgers; adv. contact: Sally Voigt. bk.rev.; pub. size: broadsheet; circ. evening 4,600(paid). **Wire Service(s):** AP.

MT. VERNON

US

REGISTER-NEWS. 1871. Mon.-Sat. $.35 newsstand; $7.50/mo. home deliv. 118 N. Ninth St., Mt. Vernon, IL 62864. TEL 618-242-0113; FAX 618-242-8286. **Owner(s):** Hollinger International, Inc., 401 N. Wabash, Chicago, IL 60611. TEL 312-321-3000; Ed. Terry Geese; Pub. Charles E. Dietz; adv. contact: Sara Sledge. pub. size: broadsheet; circ. evening 11,900(paid). **Wire Service(s):** AP.

DAILY NEWSPAPERS

OLNEY
US

OLNEY DAILY MAIL. 1898. Mon.-Sat. $.50 newsstand; $90/yr. 206 Whittle Ave., Olney, IL 62450-0340. TEL 618-393-2931; FAX 618-392-2953. **Owner(s):** American Publishing Co., 606 N. Van Buren, Marion, IL 62959. TEL 618-993-1711; Ed. Perry Dable; Pub. Steve Raymond; adv. contact: Carol Lydle. photos; pub. size: broadsheet; circ. evening 5,000(paid). **Wire Service(s):** API.

OTTAWA
US

DAILY TIMES. 1844. Mon.-Sat. $.50 newsstand; $92/yr. in city. 110 W. Jefferson St., Ottawa, IL 61350. TEL 815-433-2000; FAX 815-433-1639. **Owner(s):** Ottawa Publishing Co., 110 W. Jefferson St., Ottawa, IL 61350. TEL 815-433-2000; Ed. Lonny Cain. adv. contact: Joan Heyers. photos; pub. size: broadsheet; circ. evening 12,473(paid). **Wire Service(s):** AP.

PARIS
US

PARIS BEACON NEWS. 1848. Mon.-Sat. $.40 newsstand; $78/yr. carrier. 218 N. Main St., Paris, IL 61944. TEL 217-465-6424; FAX 217-463-1232. **Owner(s):** Ned Jenison, 218 N. Main St., Paris, IL 61944. TEL 217-465-6424; Ed. Nancy Garrett; Pub. Ned Jenison; adv.; pub. size: broadsheet; circ. evening 7,300(paid). **Wire Service(s):** AP.

PAXTON
US

PAXTON DAILY RECORD. 1865. Mon.-Fri. $.25 newsstand; $54/yr. in cy.; $80/yr. elsewhere. 218 N. Market St., Paxton, IL 60957. TEL 217-379-2356; FAX 217-379-3104. **Owner(s):** Paxton Printing Co., 218 N. Market St., Paxton, IL 60957. TEL 217-379-4313; Ed. Bob Maney; Pub. Paul E. Anderson; adv. contact: Toni Swan. pub. size: broadsheet; circ. evening 1,550(paid).

PEKIN
US ISSN 0745-7863

PEKIN DAILY TIMES. 1880. Mon.-Sat. $.50 newsstand; $1.75/wk. 20 S. Fourth St., Pekin, IL 61554. TEL 309-346-1111; FAX 309-346-9815. **Owner(s):** Howard Publications, Inc., P.O. Box 570, Oceanside, CA 92049; Pub. David Simpson; adv. contact: Eleanor Gibbons. pub. size: broadsheet; circ. evening 15,472(paid). **Wire Service(s):** AP.

PEORIA
US

PEORIA JOURNAL STAR. 1855. d. $.50/day newsstand; $1.50/Sun.; $200.20/yr. One News Plz., Peoria, IL 61643. TEL 309-686-3020; FAX 309-686-3265. **Owner(s):** Copley Press, Inc., 7776 Ivanhoe Ave., La Jolla, CA 92037. TEL 619-454-0411; Ed. Jack Brimeyer; Pub. John McConnell; adv. contact: Carl Arrenius. photos; bk.rev.; pub. size: broadsheet; circ. morning 76,895(paid); Sun. 105,974(paid). **Wire Service(s):** AP, KNT, NWS.

PONTIAC
US

PONTIAC DAILY LEADER. 1880. Mon.-Sat. $.50 newsstand; $2.05/wk. 318 N. Main St., Pontiac, IL 61764. TEL 815-842-1153; FAX 815-842-4388; E-mail: pontiacdl@aol.com. **Owner(s):** American Publishing Co., 606 N. Van Buren, Marion, IL 62959. TEL 618-933-1711; Ed. Pat Graziano; Pub. R.A. Westerfield; adv.; bk.rev.; pub. size: broadsheet; circ. evening 6,200(paid). **Wire Service(s):** AP.

QUINCY
US ISSN 0746-6358

QUINCY HERALD-WHIG. 1835. d. $.50/day newsstand; $1.25/Sun.; $128.05/yr. 130 S. Fifth St., Quincy, IL 62301. TEL 217-223-5100; FAX 217-223-9757; E-mail: whig@bcl.net; URL: http://www.bcl.net/~whig/. **Owner(s):** Quincy Newspapers, Inc., 130 S. Fifth St., Quincy, IL 62301; Ed. Michael Hilfrink; Pub. Thomas A. Oakley; adv. contact: Mel Evanoff. pub. size: broadsheet; circ. evening 25,300(paid); Sun. 30,145(paid). **Wire Service(s):** AP.

ROBINSON
US

ROBINSON DAILY NEWS. 1919. Mon.-Sat. $.35 newsstand; $71/yr. 302 S. Cross St., Robinson, IL 62454. TEL 618-544-2101; FAX 618-544-9533. **Owner(s):** Robinson Daily News, Inc., P.O. Box 639, Robinson, IL 62454; Ed. Byron Tracy; Pub. Larry H. Lewis; adv. contact: Wally Dean. photos; bk.rev.; pub. size: broadsheet; circ. evening 7,100(paid). **Wire Service(s):** AP, CNS.

ROCKFORD
US

REGISTER STAR. 1888. d. $.50/day newsstand; $1.50/Sun.; $182/yr. carrier; $195/yr. motor rte. 99 E. State St., Rockford, IL 61104-1004. TEL 815-987-1200; FAX 815-987-1365. **Owner(s):** Gannett Company, Inc., 1100 Wilson Blvd., Arlington, VA 22234. TEL 703-284-6000; Pub. Mary P. Stier; adv.; pub. size: broadsheet; circ. morning 79,000(paid); Sun. 90,000(paid). **Wire Service(s):** AP, GNS, TP.

SHELBYVILLE
US

SHELBYVILLE DAILY UNION. 1887. Mon.-Fri. $.25 newsstand; $1.25/wk. carrier; $50/yr. carrier. 100 W. Main St., Shelbyville, IL 62565. TEL 217-774-2161; FAX 217-774-5732. **Owner(s):** George Frazier, 100 W. Main St., Shelbyville, IL 62565; Ed. George Frazier; Pub. George Frazier; adv.; pub. size: broadsheet; circ. evening 5,000(paid). **Wire Service(s):** AP.
Formerly: Shelbyville Union.

SPRINGFIELD
US

STATE JOURNAL-REGISTER. 1831. d. $.50/day newsstand; $1.50/Sun.; $3/wk. carrier; $3.22/wk. in state mailed; $3.85/wk. out of state mailed; $139.36/yr. in state. One Copley Plz., Springfield, IL 62705-0219. TEL 217-788-1300; FAX 217-788-1551. **Owner(s):** Copley Press, Inc., 7776 Ivanhoe Ave., La Jolla, CA 92037. TEL 619-454-0411; Ed. Barry Locher; Pub. Patrick Coburn; adv. contact: Gary Kreppert. photos; bk.rev.; pub. size: broadsheet; circ. morning 68,048(paid); Sun. 77,270(paid). **Wire Service(s):** AP, CNS, NYT, SHNA.

STERLING
US

DAILY GAZETTE. 1854. d. $.50/day newsstand; $1/Sun.; $105/yr. home deliv. 312 Second Ave., Sterling, IL 61081. TEL 815-625-3600; FAX 815-625-9390. **Owner(s):** Shaw Newspaper Co., Peoria St., Dixon, IL 61021. TEL 815-664-4321; Ed. Jonie Larson; Pub. William E. Shaw; adv.; photos; pub. size: broadsheet; circ. evening 15,000(paid); Sun. 15,000(paid). **Wire Service(s):** AP, SHNA.
Formerly: Sterling Daily Gazette.

STREATOR
US ISSN 0745-5542

STREATOR TIMES-PRESS. 1927. Mon.-Sat. $.50 newsstand; $82/yr. 115 Oak St., Streator, IL 61364. TEL 815-673-3771; FAX 815-672-9332. **Owner(s):** Small Newspaper Group, Kankakee, IL 60901; Ed. James Russell. adv.; photos; pub. size: broadsheet; circ. evening 8,600(free & paid). **Wire Service(s):** AP.

TAYLORVILLE
US

TAYLORVILLE BREEZE-COURIER. 1894. Sun.-Fri. $.50/day newsstand; $1/Sun.; $6.85/mo. home deliv. 212 S. Main St., Taylorville, IL 62568. TEL 217-824-2233; FAX 217-824-2026. **Owner(s):** James Frank Cooper, P.O. Box 440, Taylorville, IL 62568. TEL 217-824-2233; FAX 217-824-2026; Ed. J. Robert Cooper; Pub. James F. Cooper; adv. contact: Jospeh Dorr. adv.: $7.50/SAU. photos; bk.rev.; pub. size: broadsheet; circ. evening 14,484(free & paid); Sun. 69,960(free & paid). **Wire Service(s):** AP.

TINLEY PARK
US ISSN 1070-2040

DAILY SOUTHTOWN. 1906. d. $.35/day newsstand; $1.50/Sun.; $116/yr. carrier. 6901 W. 159th St., Tinley Park, IL 60477. TEL 708-633-6777; FAX 708-633-5999. **Owner(s):** American Publishing Co., 606 N. Van Buren, Marion, IL 62959. TEL 618-993-1711; Ed. Michael J. Kelley; Pub. Norman A. Rosinski; adv.; pub. size: broadsheet; circ. evening 55,813(paid); Sun. 62,322(paid). **Wire Service(s):** AP.
Formerly: Southtown Economist.

WATSEKA

US

IROQUOIS COUNTY TIMES REPUBLIC. 1870. Mon.-Fri. $.50 newsstand; $72.50/yr. in cy. mailed; $91/yr. carrier. 1492 E. Walnut St., Watseka, IL 60970. TEL 815-432-5227; FAX 815-432-5159. **Owner(s):** Twin States Publishing Co., Inc., 1492 E. Walnut St., Watseka, IL 60970. TEL 815-432-5227; Ed. Carla Waters; Pub. Bette Schmid; adv.; pub. size: tabloid; circ. evening 2,865(paid). **Wire Service(s):** AP.
 Formerly: Watseka Iroquois County Daily Times Republic.

WAUKEGAN

US

NEWS-SUN, THE. 1892. Mon.-Sat. $.35/day newsstand; $1/Sat.; $2.30/wk. 100 W. Madison St., Waukegan, IL 60085. TEL 708-336-7000; FAX 708-249-7202. **Owner(s):** Copley Press, Inc., 7776 Ivanhoe Ave., La Jolla, CA 92037. TEL 619-454-0411; Ed. Chris Adams. adv.; pub. size: broadsheet; circ. evening 40,000(paid). **Wire Service(s):** AP, CNS, SHNA, NYT.

WEST FRANKFORT

US

DAILY AMERICAN. 1916. Mon.-Sat. $.50/day newsstand; $.75/Sat.; $114/yr. home deliv. 111 S. Emma St., West Frankfort, IL 62896. TEL 618-932-2146; FAX 618-937-6006. **Owner(s):** American Publishing Co., 606 N. Van Buren, Marion, IL 62959. TEL 618-993-1711; Ed. Bob Ellis; Pub. G. David Green; adv. contact: Diann Walthes. pub. size: broadsheet; circ. evening 4,100(paid). **Wire Service(s):** AP.
 Formerly: West Frankfort Daily American.

BEDFORD

US

TIMES-MAIL. 1884. Mon.-Sat. $.50 newsstand; $11.75/mo. home deliv.; $141/yr. 813 16th St., Bedford, IN 47421. TEL 812-275-3355; FAX 812-275-4191; E-mail: tmnews@tmnews.com; URL: http://www.tmnews.com. **Owner(s):** Schurz Communications, Inc., South Bend, IN 46626. TEL 219-233-6161; Ed. Carol Johnson; Pub. Scott C. Schurz; adv. contact: Ellen Ware. pub. size: broadsheet; circ. evening 15,000(paid). **Wire Service(s):** AP.

BLOOMFIELD

US

EVENING WORLD. 1930. Mon.-Fri. $.35 newsstand; $6.25/mo. carrier. 29-31 W. Main St., Bloomfield, IN 47424. TEL 812-384-3501; FAX 812-384-3741. **Owner(s):** William C. Miles, P.O. Box 311, Bloomfield, IN 47424. TEL 812-384-3501; Ed. Gayle Robbins; Pub. William C. Miles; adv.; pub. size: broadsheet; circ. evening 3,800(paid). **Wire Service(s):** AP.

BLOOMINGTON

US ISSN 1044-4246

HERALD-TIMES. 1877. d. $.50/day newsstand; $1.50/Sun.; $11.95/mo. 1900 S. Walnut St., Bloomington, IN 47401. TEL 812-332-4401; FAX 812-331-4383. **Owner(s):** Schurz Communications, Inc., 225 W. Colfax Ave., South Bend, IN 46626. TEL 219-287-1001; Ed. Bob Zaltsberg; Pub. Scott C. Schurz; adv.; pub. size: broadsheet; circ. morning 30,940(paid); Sun. 45,000(paid). **Wire Service(s):** AP, NYT.

INDIANA

ANDERSON

US

HERALD BULLETIN. 1868. d. $.50/day newsstand; $1.50/Sun.; $3/wk. carrier deliv. 1133 Jackson St., Anderson, IN 46016. TEL 317-622-1212; FAX 317-640-4815; E-mail: thb@indy.net; URL: http://www.indol.com/tp.html. **Owner(s):** Thomson Newspapers, Inc., Metro Centren Ctr., Ste. 500, One Station Pl., 6th fl., Stamford, CT 06902. TEL 203-425-2516; Ed. John Irby; Pub. John Irby; adv.; pub. size: broadsheet; circ. morning 35,000(paid); Sun. 37,000(paid). **Wire Service(s):** AP.
 Formerly: Anderson Herald Bulletin.

AUBURN

US

EVENING STAR. 1871. Mon.-Sat. $.50/day newsstand; $.75/Sat.; $62.40/6 mos. home deliv. 118 W. Ninth St., Auburn, IN 46706. TEL 219-925-2611; FAX 219-925-2625. **Owner(s):** Kendallville Publishing Co., 112 N. Main St., Kendallville, IN 46755. TEL 219-347-0400; Ed. David Kurtz; Pub. Jim Claymore; adv. contact: Martin Alexander. pub. size: broadsheet; circ. evening 9,000(paid). **Wire Service(s):** AP.
 Formerly: Auburn Evening Star.

BLUFFTON

US

BLUFFTON NEWS-BANNER. 1929. Mon.-Sat. $.50 newsstand; $110/yr. carrier; $135/yr. mailed. 125 N. Johnson St., Bluffton, IN 46714. TEL 219-824-0224; FAX 219-824-0700; E-mail: newsbanner@ssi.parlorcity.com. **Owner(s):** News-Banner, P. O. Box 436, Bluffton, IN 46714. TEL 219-824-0224; FAX 219-824-0700; Ed. Joel Smekens; Pub. James C. Barbieri; adv. contact: Connie Edington. photos; pub. size: broadsheet; circ. evening 5,700(paid). **Wire Service(s):** AP.

BRAZIL

US

BRAZIL TIMES. 9888. Mon.-Sat. $.50 newsstand; $84/yr. motor rte. in state; $78/yr. in state mailed. 100 N. Meridian, Brazil, IN 47834. TEL 812-446-2216; FAX 812-446-0938; E-mail: btimes@indiana.net. **Owner(s):** Nixon Newspapers, Inc., P.O. Box 1149, Peru, IN 46970. TEL 317-473-3091; FAX 317-473-8428; Ed. James Dressler; Pub. William Harper; adv.; photos; bk.rev.; pub. size: broadsheet; circ. evening 5,300(paid). **Wire Service(s):** AP.

CHESTERTON

US

CHESTERTON TRIBUNE. 1884. Mon.-Fri. $.50 newsstand; $6/mo. carrier; $8/mo. mailed. 193 S. Calumet Rd., Chesterton, IN 46304. TEL 219-926-1131. E-mail: chestertontrib@niia.net. **Owner(s):** Warren Canright, 193 S. Calumet Rd., Chesterton, IN 46304. TEL 219-926-1131; Ed. David Canright; Pub. Warren Canright; adv. contact: Bill Mathe. pub. size: broadsheet; circ. evening 5,200(paid).

CLINTON

US

DAILY CLINTONIAN. 1912. Mon.-Fri. $.50 newsstand; $82/yr. in cy.; $86/yr. out of cy. 422 S. Main St., Clinton, IN 47842-2414. TEL 765-832-2443. E-mail: gbcarey@aol.com. **Owner(s):** Clinton Color Crafters, Inc., 422 S. Main St., Clinton, IN 47842. TEL 765-832-2443; Ed. George L. Carey; Pub. George L. Carey; adv. contact: Bob Bartlett. photos; pub. size: broadsheet; circ. evening 5,483(paid). **Wire Service(s):** AP, PhotoStream.
 Formerly: Clinton Daily Clintonian.

COLUMBIA CITY

US ISSN 0746-9950

POST & MAIL, THE. 1853. Mon.-Sat. $.50 newsstand; $115.10/yr. carrier home deliv.; $125/yr. motor rte. & mailed. 116 N. Chauncey St., Columbia City, IN 46725-2002. TEL 219-244-5153; FAX 219-244-7598. **Owner(s):** American Publishing Co., 606 N. Van Buren, Marion, IL 62959. TEL 618-993-1711; Ed. Marilee Kreps; Pub. Doug Caldwell; adv. contact: Rick Kreps. pub. size: broadsheet; circ. evening 4,700(paid). **Wire Service(s):** AP.

COLUMBUS

US

REPUBLIC, THE. 1872. d. $.50/day newsstand; $1.50/Sun.; $10.50/mo. home deliv. 333 Second St., Columbus, IN 47201. TEL 812-372-7811; FAX 812-379-5711. **Owner(s):** Home News Enterprises, 333 Second St., Columbus, IN 47201. TEL 812-372-7811; Ed. J.K. Murphy; Pub. Don R. Bucknam; adv. contact: Pamela Wells-Lego. pub. size: broadsheet; circ. morning 22,000(paid); Sun. 26,000(paid). **Wire Service(s):** AP, KR, SHNA, NEA.
 Formerly: Columbus Republic.

CONNERSVILLE

US

CONNERSVILLE NEWS-EXAMINER. 1888. Mon.-Sat. $.50 newsstand; $8/mo. home deliv. in town; $8.25/mo. in cy; $5.50/wk. subscription. 406 Central Ave., Connersville, IN 47331. TEL 317-825-0585; FAX 317-825-4599. **Owner(s):** Nixon Newspapers, Inc., 33 W. Third St., Peru, IN 46970. TEL 317-473-3091; Ed. Bob Powers. adv. contact: Diane Howell. pub. size: broadsheet; circ. evening 9,200(paid). **Wire Service(s):** AP, NEA.

DAILY NEWSPAPERS

CRAWFORDSVILLE

US

CRAWFORDSVILLE JOURNAL REVIEW. 1841. Mon.-Sat. $.50/day newsstand; $1/Sat.; $7.75/mo. carrier; $7.75/mo. motor rte. 119 N. Green St., Crawfordsville, IN 47933. TEL 765-362-1200; FAX 765-364-5424; E-mail: jreview@link2000.net. **Owner(s):** Freedom Communications, Inc., 17666 Fitch, Irvine, CA 92713. TEL 714-553-9292; FAX 765-364-5424; Ed. Gaildene Hamilton; Pub. James J. McMillen; adv. contact: Randy List. photos; bk.rev.; pub. size: broadsheet; circ. morning 10,700(paid). **Wire Service(s):** AP, KTR.

DECATUR

US   ISSN 0894-2307

DECATUR DAILY DEMOCRAT. 1857. Mon.-Sat. $.50 newsstand; $104/yr. carrier. 141 S. Second St., Decatur, IN 46733. TEL 219-724-2121; FAX 219-724-7981. **Owner(s):** American Publishing Co., 606N. Van Buren, Marion, IL 62959. TEL 618-993-1711; Ed. Bob Shraluka. adv. contact: Ron Platt. pub. size: broadsheet; circ. evening 6,100(paid). **Wire Service(s):** AP.
Formerly: Decatur Democart.

ELKHART

US   ISSN 0746-7516

ELKHART TRUTH, THE. 1889. d. $.50/day newsstand; $1.25/Sun.; $119.70/yr. home deliv.; $128.25/yr. motor rte. 421 S. Second St., Elkhart, IN 46516. TEL 219-294-1661; FAX 219-294-4014. **Owner(s):** Truth Publishing Co., 421 S. Second St., Elkhart, IN 46516. TEL 219-294-1661; Ed. Terry Greenberg; Pub. Anthony Biggs; adv.; pub. size: broadsheet; circ. evening 30,000(paid); Sun. 31,000(paid). **Wire Service(s):** AP, SHNA.

ELWOOD

US

CALL-LEADER. 1891. Mon.-Sat. $.35 newsstand; $105/yr. out of cy. mailed. 317 S. Anderson St., Elwood, IN 46036. TEL 317-552-3355; FAX 317-552-3358. **Owner(s):** Elwood Publishing Co., Inc., 317 S. Anderson St., Elwood, IN 46036. TEL 317-552-3355; Ed. Sandy Burton; Pub. Robert Nash; adv. contact: Robert Nash. pub. size: broadsheet; circ. evening 4,000(paid). **Wire Service(s):** AP.

EVANSVILLE

US

EVANSVILLE COURIER. 1845. d. $.50/day newsstand; $2/Sun.; $15.75/mo. carrier; $16.40/mo. motor rte. 300 Walnut St., Evansville, IN 47713. TEL 812-424-7711; FAX 812-422-8196; E-mail: courier@evansville.net; URL: http://www.evansville.net. **Owner(s):** Scripps-Howard, 312 Walnut St., 28th Fl., Cincinnati, OH 45202. TEL 513-977-3000; Ed. Vince Vawter. adv. contact: Jack Pate. photos; pub. size: broadsheet; circ. morning 61,930(paid); evening 25,940(paid); Sun. 115,282(paid). **Wire Service(s):** AP, NYT, SHNA, LAT-WP.

US   ISSN 0896-6249

EVANSVILLE PRESS. 1906. Mon.-Sat. $.50 newsstand; $9.35/mo.; $112.20/yr. carrier. 300 E. Walnut St., Evansville, IN 47713. TEL 812-464-7614; FAX 812-464-7641. **Owner(s):** Hartmann Publishing Co., 300 E. Walnut St., Evansville, IN 47713. TEL 812-464-7614; Ed. Bob Gustin. adv. contact: Jack Pate. pub. size: broadsheet; circ. evening 23,000(paid). **Wire Service(s):** KNT, AP.

FISHER

US

DAILY LEDGER. 1888. Mon.-Sat. $.35 newsstand; $86/yr. motor rte; $80/yr. carrier. 13095 Publishers Dr., Fisher, IN 46030. TEL 317-598-6397; FAX 317-598-6340. **Owner(s):** Central Newspapers, Inc., 135 N. Pennsylvania St., Ste. 1200, Indianapolis, IN 46204-2400. TEL 317-231-9200; Pub. David A. Lewis; adv.; photos; pub. size: broadsheet; circ. evening 10,000(paid). **Wire Service(s):** AP.
Formerly: Noblesville Daily Ledger.

FORT WAYNE

US

FORT WAYNE NEWS-SENTINEL. 1918. Mon.-Sat. $.50 newsstand; $1.45/wk. carrier. 600 W. Main St., Fort Wayne, IN 46802. TEL 219-461-8439; FAX 219-461-8817; E-mail: aseditor@fortwayne.infi.net; URL: http://www.fortwayne.com. **Owner(s):** Knight-Ridder, Inc., One Herald Plz., Miami, FL 33132. TEL 305-376-3800; FAX 305-376-3875; Ed. Richard Battin; Pub. Ms. Scott McGehee; adv. contact: Lisa Goodman. photos; bk.rev.; pub. size: broadsheet; circ. evening 57,000(paid). **Wire Service(s):** AP, KR.

US   ISSN 0734-3701

JOURNAL-GAZETTE, THE. d. $.50/day newsstand; $1.75/Sun. 600 W. Main St., Fort Wayne, IN 46802. TEL 219-461-8333; FAX 219-461-8648. **Owner(s):** Journal Gazette Co., The, 600 W. Main St., Fort Wayne, IN 46802. TEL 219-461-8333; Ed. Sherry Skufca; Pub. Julie Inskeep Walda; adv. contact: Lisa Goodman. photos; bk.rev.; pub. size: broadsheet; circ. morning 62,000(paid); Sun. 136,000(paid). **Wire Service(s):** AP, LAT-WP, SHNA,.
Formerly: fort wayne journal-gazette.

FRANKFORT

US

FRANKFORT TIMES. 1885. Mon.-Sat. $.50 newsstand; $8/mo. carrier. 251 E. Clinton St., Frankfort, IN 46041. TEL 765-659-4622; FAX 765-654-7031. **Owner(s):** Nixon Newspapers, Inc., P.O. Box 1149, Peru, IN 46970. TEL 765-473-3091; Ed. Howard W. Hewitt; Pub. Mark Ingels; adv. contact: Greg Ludlow. pub. size: standard; circ. evening 7,600(paid). **Wire Service(s):** AP.

FRANKLIN

US

DAILY JOURNAL. 1962. Mon.-Sat. $.50/day newsstand; $.75/Sat.; $6.50/mo. carrier; $7.50/mo. motor rte 2575 N. Morton St., Franklin, IN 46131. TEL 317-736-7101; FAX 317-736-2713. **Owner(s):** Home News Enterprises, 333 Second St., Columbus, IN 47201. TEL 812-372-7811; Ed. Jeff Owen; Pub. Howard Herron; adv. contact: J. Fred Mattingly. pub. size: broadsheet; circ. morning 17,500(paid). **Wire Service(s):** AP, SHNA.

GARY

US   ISSN 8750-3492

POST-TRIBUNE. 1907. d. $.50/day newsstand; $1.50/Sun.; $2.80/wk. carrier. 1065 Broadway, Gary, IN 46402. TEL 219-881-3000; FAX 219-881-3232. **Owner(s):** Knight-Ridder, Inc., One Herald Plz., Miami, FL 33132. TEL 305-376-3800; FAX 305-376-3875; Ed. Kay Manning; Pub. Scott Bosley; adv. contact: Larry Leibengood. photos; pub. size: broadsheet; circ. morning 67,228(paid); Sun. 76,210(paid). **Wire Service(s):** AP, LAT-WP, KRI.

GOSHEN

US   ISSN 8750-3867

GOSHEN NEWS, THE. 1837. Mon.-Sat. $.50 newsstand; $93/yr. 114 S. Main St., Goshen, IN 46526. TEL 219-533-2151; FAX 219-533-0839; E-mail: goshennews@tln.net; URL: http://www.tln.net/news/current. **Owner(s):** News Printing Co., Inc., P.O. Box 569, Goshen, IN 46526-0569. TEL 219-533-2151; Ed. Gerald Hertzler; Pub. John W. Gemmer; adv. contact: James Young. pub. size: broadsheet; circ. evening 18,000(paid). **Wire Service(s):** AP.

GREENCASTLE

US

BANNER-GRAPHIC. 1918. Mon.-Sat. $.50 newsstand; $92/yr. in state. 100 N. Jackson St., Greencastle, IN 46135. TEL 317-653-5151; FAX 317-653-2063. **Owner(s):** Truth Publishing Co., 421 S. Second St., Elkhart, IN 46516. TEL 219-294-1661; Ed. Eric Bernsee; Pub. Steve Hendershot; adv. contact: Steve Hendershot. pub. size: broadsheet; circ. morning 6,500(paid). **Wire Service(s):** AP.

GREENFIELD

US

DAILY REPORTER. 1908. Mon.-Sat. $.50 newsstand; $7.50/mo. 22 W. New Rd., Greenfield, IN 46140. TEL 317-462-5528; FAX 317-467-6009. **Owner(s):** Home News Enterprises, 333 Second St., Columbus, IN 47201. TEL 812-372-7811; Ed. Dave Scott; Pub. Randall Shields; adv. contact: Dave McCammon. photos; bk.rev.; pub. size: broadsheet; circ. evening 8,970(paid). **Wire Service(s):** AP.

GREENSBURG

US

GREENSBURG DAILY NEWS. 1894. Mon.-Sat. $.50 newsstand; $117/yr. carrier; $130.20/yr. mailed. 135 S. Franklin St., Greensburg, IN 47240. TEL 812-663-3111; FAX 812-663-2985; E-mail: gedit00@gpbx.mail.net. **Owner(s):** Thomson Newspapers, Inc., Metro Centre, One Station Pl., 6th Fl., Stamford, CT 06902. TEL 203-425-2500; FAX 203-425-2516; Ed. Jeffrey Ensweller; Pub. Phillip Hart; adv. contact: Mona Deiwert. pub. size: broadsheet; circ. evening 6,600(paid). **Wire Service(s):** AP.

HARTFORD CITY
US
NEWS-TIMES. 1892. Mon.-Thu. & Sat. $.50 newsstand; $2.20/wk. home deliv.; $125/yr. mailed. 123 S. Jefferson St., Hartford City, IN 47348. TEL 317-348-0110; FAX 317-348-0112. **Owner(s):** Thomson Newspapers, Inc., Metro Centre, One Station Pl., 6th Fl., Stamford, CT 06902. TEL 203-425-2500; Ed. Brian Logan; Pub. James Carroll; adv. contact: Holly Kolb. pub. size: broadsheet; circ. evening 2,231(paid). **Wire Service(s):** AP.

HUNTINGTON
US
HERALD-PRESS. 1848. Sun.-Fri. $.50/day newsstand, $1.50/Sun.; $93.60/yr. carrier; $101/yr. motor rte.; $127.40/yr. mailed. 7 N. Jefferson, Huntington, IN 46750-0860. TEL 219-356-6700; FAX 219-356-9026. **Owner(s):** Huntington Newspapers, Inc., P.O. Box 860, Huntington, IN 46750-0860. TEL 219-356-6700; FAX 219-356-9026; Ed. Michael V. Perkins. adv. contact: Claude Good. pub. size: broadsheet; circ. morning 8,000(paid); Sun. 10,000(paid). **Wire Service(s):** AP.
Formerly: Huntington Herald-Press.

INDIANAPOLIS
US
INDIANAPOLIS NEWS. 1869. Mon.-Sat. $.50 newsstand. 307 N. Pennsylvania St., Indianapolis, IN 46204. TEL 317-633-1240; FAX 317-633-1038. **Owner(s):** Central Newspapers, Inc., 135 N. Pennsylvania Ave., Ste. 1200, Indianapolis, IN 46280. TEL 317-231-9200; Ed. Ted Daniels; Pub. Eugene S. Pulliam; adv. contact: Kimberly Parker. photos; bk.rev.; pub. size: broadsheet; circ. evening 58,000(paid). **Wire Service(s):** AP, CNS, LAT-WP, SHNA, NYT.

US
INDIANAPOLIS STAR. 1903. d. $.50/day newsstand; $1.80/Sun.; $3.60/wk. carrier; $171.60/yr. carrier. 307 N. Pennsylvania St., Indianapolis, IN 46204-1899. TEL 317-633-1240; FAX 317-633-9423; E-mail: fcaperton@starnews.com. **Owner(s):** Central Newspapers, Inc., 135 N. Pennsylvania Ave., Indianapolis, IN 46204. TEL 317-231-9200; Ed. Ted Daniels; Pub. Eugene S. Pulliam; adv. contact: Kimberly Parker. photos; bk.rev.; pub. size: broadsheet; circ. morning 229,876(paid); Sun. 404,469(paid). **Wire Service(s):** AP, SHNA, NYT, KNT, LAT-WP.

JASPER
US
HERALD, THE. 1895. Mon.-Sat. $.50 newsstand; $8.50/mo. carrier; $8.75/mo. motor rte. 216 E. Fourth St., Jasper, IN 47546. TEL 812-482-2424; FAX 812-482-4104. **Owner(s):** Jasper Herald Co., 216 Fourth St., Jasper, IN 47546. TEL 812-482-2424; Ed. Fred Smith. adv. contact: Don Schreve. pub. size: tabloid; circ. evening 13,000(paid). **Wire Service(s):** AP.

JEFFERSONVILLE
US
JEFFERSONVILLE EVENING NEWS. 1872. Mon.-Sat. $.50 newsstand; $7.80/mo. home deliv. 221 Spring St., Jeffersonville, IN 47131. TEL 812-283-6636; FAX 812-284-7081; E-mail: jlg@iglou.com. **Owner(s):** Community Newspaper Holdings, Inc., 269 W. Main St., 6th Fl., Lexington, KY 40507; Ed. John L. Gilkey. adv.; bk.rev.; pub. size: broadsheet; circ. evening 10,800(paid). **Wire Service(s):** AP.

KENDALLVILLE
US ISSN 8750-0876
KENDALLVILLE NEWS-SUN. Mon.-Sat. $.50/day newsstand; $.75/Sat.; $119.60/yr. carrier; $135.95/yr. motor rte.; $163/yr. out of state. 102 N. Main St., Kendallville, IN 46755. TEL 219-347-0400; FAX 219-347-2693. **Owner(s):** Kendallville Publishing Co., P.O. Box 39, Kendallville, IN 46755. TEL 219-347-0400; FAX 219-347-2693; Ed. James Kroemer; Pub. James D. Kroemer; adv. contact: Martin Alexander. photos; bk.rev.; pub. size: broadsheet; circ. evening 8,000(paid).

KOKOMO
US ISSN 0746-2034
KOKOMO TRIBUNE, THE. 1850. d. $.50/day newsstand; $1.50/Sun.; $3/wk.; $13/mo. 300 N. Union St., Kokomo, IN 46904. TEL 317-459-3121; FAX 317-456-3815; E-mail: ktonline@aol.com; URL: http://www.members.aol.com/ktonline/. **Owner(s):** Thomson Newspapers, Inc., Metro Centre, One Station Pl., 6th Fl., Stamford, CT 06902. TEL 203-425-2500; Ed. John C. Wiles; Pub. Wayne Lowman; adv. contact: Jeff Pizzano. pub. size: broadsheet; circ. evening 29,000(paid); Sun. 30,000(paid). **Wire Service(s):** AP.

LAFAYETTE
US
JOURNAL & COURIER. 1829. d. $.50/day newsstand; $1.50/Sun.; $3.25/wk. 217 N. Sixth St., Lafayette, IN 47901-1420. TEL 317-423-5511; FAX 317-423-2613; E-mail: postmaster@jandc.mdn.com; URL: http://www.jconline.com. **Owner(s):** Gannett Company, Inc., 1100 Wilson Blvd., Arlington, VA 22234. TEL 703-284-6000; Ed. Carol Bangert; Pub. Richard L. Holtz; adv. contact: Ted Taylor. photos; pub. size: broadsheet; circ. morning 38,172(paid); Sun. 44,892(paid). **Wire Service(s):** AP, GNS, LAT-WP.

LA PORTE
US
LA PORTE HERALD-ARGUS. 1880. Mon.-Sat. $.50 newsstand; $93.60/yr. 701 State St., La Porte, IN 46350. TEL 219-362-2161; FAX 219-362-2166. **Owner(s):** Small Newspaper Group, 701 State St., La Porte, IN 46350-3328. TEL 219-362-2161; FAX 219-362-2166; Ed. Mark Johnson; Pub. Clem Otolski; adv. contact: Carol Kuta. photos; bk.rev.; pub. size: broadsheet; circ. evening 13,199(paid). **Wire Service(s):** AP, SHNS.

LEBANON
US
REPORTER, THE. 1891. Mon.-Sat. $.50 newsstand. 117 E. Washington St., Lebanon, IN 46052. TEL 317-482-4650; FAX 317-482-4652. **Owner(s):** Lebanon Newspapers, Inc., 117 E. Washington St., Lebanon, IN 46052. TEL 317-482-4650; adv.; photos; pub. size: broadsheet; circ. evening 7,400(paid). **Wire Service(s):** AP.
Formerly: Lebanon Reporter.

LINTON
US
LINTON DAILY CITIZEN. 1900. Mon.-Fri. $.75 newsstand; $84/yr. 79 S. Main St., Linton, IN 47441. TEL 812-847-4487; FAX 812-847-9513. **Owner(s):** Thomson Newspapers, Inc., Metro Centre, One Station Pl., 6th Fl., Stamford, CT 06902. TEL 203-425-2500; FAX 203-425-2516; Ed. Heather Atkinson; Pub. L.W. McCall; adv. contact: Tina Cunningham. pub. size: broadsheet; circ. evening 9,500(paid). **Wire Service(s):** AP.

LOGANSPORT
US
PHAROS-TRIBUNE. 1844. Sun.-Fri. $.50/day newsstand; $1.25/Sun.; $137.80/yr. carrier; $179.40/yr. in state mailed; $192.40/yr. out of state mailed. 517 E. Broadway, Logansport, IN 46947. TEL 219-722-5000; FAX 219-722-5238. **Owner(s):** Thomson Newspapers, Inc., Metro Centre, One Station Pl., 6th Fl., Stamford, CT 06902. TEL 203-425-2500; FAX 203-425-2516; Ed. Dave Kitchel; Pub. Mark Cohen; adv. contact: Robin McCloskey. photos; bk.rev.; pub. size: broadsheet; circ. evening 14,499(paid); Sun. 15,233(paid). **Wire Service(s):** AP,KR.

MADISON
US
MADISON COURIER. 1837. Mon.-Sat. $.50 newsstand; $67.10/yr. carrier; $82/yr. IN & KY; $88/yr. out of area. 310 Courier Sq., Madison, IN 47250. TEL 812-265-3641. **Owner(s):** Madison Courier, Inc., 310 Courier Sq., Madison, IN 47250. TEL 812-265-3641; Ed. Graham Taylor; Pub. Jane W. Jacobs; adv. contact: Ron Wehner. photos; bk.rev.; pub. size: broadsheet; circ. evening 9,800(paid). **Wire Service(s):** AP.

MARION
US
CHRONICLE-TRIBUNE. 1886. d. $.35/day newsstand; $1.50/Sun.; $11.60/4 wks. 610 S. Adams St., Marion, IN 46953. TEL 317-664-5111; FAX 317-664-6292. **Owner(s):** Gannett Company, Inc., 1100 Wilson Blvd., Arlington, VA 22234. TEL 703-284-6000; Ed. Randolph Brandt; Pub. Victor W. Hussey; adv. contact: Mike Casuscelli. pub. size: broadsheet; circ. morning 20,812(paid); Sun. 25,050(paid).
Formerly: Marion Chronicle-Tribune.

DAILY NEWSPAPERS

MARTINSVILLE
US
MARTINSVILLE DAILY REPORTER. 1889. Mon.-Sat. $.50 newsstand; $1.65/wk.; $7.15/mo.; $76.50/yr. 60 S. Jefferson, Martinsville, IN 46151. TEL 317-342-3311; FAX 317-342-1446. **Owner(s):** Robert Kendall, 1290 E. Jackson, Martinsville, IN 46151; Dorothy Kendall, 1290 E. Jackson, Martinsville, IN 46151; Mark Kendall, P.O. Box 1636, Lawrenceville, NJ 08648; Harriet Tackitt, P.O. Box 1636, Lawrenceville, NJ 08648; Wendell & Kay Holt, 1290 E. Jackson, Martinsville, IN 46151. TEL 317-342-3527; Robert Adams, E. High St., Mooresville, IN 46158; Ed. Bette Nunn; Pub. Mr. Kay Selch; adv. contact: Mr. Kay Selch. pub. size: broadsheet; circ. evening 8,450(paid). **Wire Service(s):** UPI.

MICHIGAN CITY
US   ISSN 1047-6016
MICHIGAN CITY NEWS-DISPATCH. 1881. d. $.50/day newsstand; $1/Sun.; $10.25/mo. mailed; $10.55/mo. motor rte.; $129/yr. in state mailed; $171/yr. out of state mailed. 121 W. Michigan Blvd., Michigan City, IN 46360. TEL 219-874-7211; FAX 219-872-8511. **Owner(s):** Nixon Newspapers, Inc., 33 W. Third St., Peru, IN 46970. TEL 317-473-3091; Ed. Dave Hawk; Pub. Don Manaher; adv. contact: Kurt Struss. photos; pub. size: broadsheet; circ. morning 15,000(paid); Sun. 15,500(paid). **Wire Service(s):** AP.

MONTICELLO
US
HERALD-JOURNAL, THE. 1862. Mon.-Sat. $.50 newsstand; $9/mo. 114 S. Main St., Monticello, IN 47960. TEL 219-583-5121; FAX 219-583-4241. **Owner(s):** Home News Enterprises, P.O. Box 3011, Columbus, IN 47202. TEL 812-379-5658; Ed. Larry Magrath; Pub. Don Hurd; adv. contact: Kevin Lashbrook. pub. size: broadsheet; circ. evening 6,000(paid). **Wire Service(s):** UPI.

MUNCIE
US
STAR PRESS, THE. 1904. Mon.-Sat. $.50 newsstand; $83.20/yr. carrier. 125 S. High St., Muncie, IN 47305. TEL 317-747-5754; FAX 317-747-5748. **Owner(s):** Muncie Newspapers, Inc., Muncie, IN 47307; Ed. Brian Walker; Pub. Henry Bird; adv. contact: Karen Schumen. photos; bk.rev.; pub. size: broadsheet; circ. morning 36,600(paid); Sun. 41,000(paid). **Wire Service(s):** AP, KR, SHNA.
Formerly: Muncie Star & Evening Press.

MUNSTER
US
TIMES, THE. 1906. d. $.50/day newsstand; $1.50/Sun.; $2.75/wk. 601 45th St., Munster, IN 46321. TEL 219-933-3223; FAX 219-933-3249. **Owner(s):** Howard Publications, Inc., P.O. Box 570, Oceanside, CA 92049. TEL 619-433-5771; Pub. William Howard; adv. contact: Joseph Pepe. photos; bk.rev.; pub. size: broadsheet; circ. morning 81,000(paid); Sun. 88,000(paid). **Wire Service(s):** AP, NYT, CNS.

NEW ALBANY
US
LEDGER TRIBUNE, THE. 1845. Sun.-Fri. $.50/day newsstand; $1.25/Sun.; $117/yr. 303 Scribner Dr., New Albany, IN 47150. TEL 812-944-6481; FAX 812-949-6585; E-mail: editor@tribnews.com; URL: http://www.tribnews.com. **Owner(s):** American Publishing Co., 606 N. Van Buren, Marion, IL 62959. TEL 618-993-1711; Ed. W. Curt Vincent; Pub. Russ Maroney; adv.; photos; pub. size: broadsheet; circ. evening 12,500(paid); Sun. 12,500(paid). **Wire Service(s):** AP.
Formerly: Ledger.

NEW CASTLE
US
NEW CASTLE COURIER-TIMES. 1841. Mon.-Sat. $.50 newsstand; $130/yr. carrier; $156/yr. mailed. 201 S. 14th St., New Castle, IN 47362. TEL 317-529-1111; FAX 317-529-1731. **Owner(s):** Nixon Newspapers, Inc., 33 W. Third St., Peru, IN 46970; Ed. Phil Beebe; Pub. J. Wesley Rowe, Jr.; adv. contact: Tina West. photos; pub. size: broadsheet; circ. evening 12,000(paid). **Wire Service(s):** AP.

PERU
US
PERU TRIBUNE. 1921. Mon.-Sat. $.50 newsstand; $9.50/mo. mailed. 26 W. Third St., Peru, IN 46970. TEL 317-473-6641; FAX 317-472-4438. **Owner(s):** Nixon Newspapers, Inc., 33 W. Third St., Peru, IN 46970. TEL 317-473-3091; Ed. Andrew Tallackson; Pub. James L. Widner; adv.; photos; pub. size: broadsheet; circ. morning 7,700(paid). **Wire Service(s):** AP.
Formerly: Peru Daily Tribune.

PLYMOUTH
US
PILOT-NEWS. 1851. Mon.-Sat. $.35 newsstand; $78/yr. carrier; $84/yr. motor rte.; $102/yr. mail. 217-223 N. Center St., Plymouth, IN 46563. TEL 219-936-3101; FAX 219-936-3844. **Owner(s):** Community Newspaper Holdings, Lexington, KY; Ed. Joe Beach. pub. size: broadsheet; circ. evening 6,800(paid). **Wire Service(s):** AP.

PORTLAND
US   ISSN 0010-3101
PORTLAND COMMERCIAL REVIEW. 1871. d. $.50 newsstand; $74/yr. 309 W. Main St., Portland, IN 47371. TEL 219-726-8141; FAX 219-726-8143; E-mail: comrevjay@aol.com. **Owner(s):** Graphic Printing Co., Inc., 309 W. Main St, P.O. Box 1049, Portland, IN 47371. TEL 219-726-8141; Ed. Jack C. Ronald; Pub. Jack C. Ronald; adv. contact: Don Gillespie. adv.: $5.45/SAU. pub. size: broadsheet; circ. evening 6,100(paid). **Wire Service(s):** AP.

PRINCETON
US
PRINCETON DAILY CLARION. 1846. Mon.-Fri. $.50 newsstand; $58/yr. 100 N. Gibson, Princeton, IN 47670. TEL 812-385-2525; FAX 812-386-6199. **Owner(s):** Brehm Communications, Inc., 17065 Via del Campo, Ste. 200, San Diego, CA 92197. TEL 619-451-6200; Ed. Andrea Culberth; Pub. Gary Blackburn; adv.; photos; pub. size: broadsheet; circ. morning 6,700(paid). **Wire Service(s):** AP.

RENSSELAER
US
RENSSELAER REPUBLICAN. 1865. Mon.-Sat. $.50 newsstand; $105/yr. home deliv. 117 N. Van Rensselaer St., Rensselaer, IN 47978. TEL 219-866-5111; FAX 219-866-3775. **Owner(s):** Kankakee Publishing Co., P.O. Box 298, Rensselaer, IN 47978; Ed. William Kaye. adv. contact: Frank Copley. photos; bk.rev.; pub. size: broadsheet; circ. evening 3,600(paid). **Wire Service(s):** AP.

RICHMOND
US
RICHMOND PALLADIUM-ITEM. 1831. d. $.35/day newsstand; $1.50/Sun.; $19.50/13 wks. Sun. only; $39.00/13 wks. daily;. 1175 N. A St., Richmond, IN 47374. TEL 317-962-1575; FAX 317-966-6377. **Owner(s):** Gannett Company, Inc., 1100 Wilson Blvd., Arlington, VA 22234. TEL 703-284-6000; adv. contact: Al Bonner. pub. size: broadsheet; circ. evening 19,403(paid); Sun. 24,094(paid). **Wire Service(s):** AP, GNS.

ROCHESTER
US
ROCHESTER SENTINEL, THE. 1858. Mon.-Sat. $.50 newsstand; $93/yr. local; $123/yr. out of state. 118 E. Eighth St., Rochester, IN 46975-0260. TEL 219-223-2111; FAX 219-223-5782; E-mail: raincreek@aol.com. **Owner(s):** Sentinel Corp., 118 E. Eighth St., Rochester, IN 46975. TEL 219-223-2111; FAX 219-223-5782; Ed. W.S. Wilson; Pub. Sarah O. Wilson; adv. contact: Ryan N. Showley. photos; pub. size: broadsheet; circ. evening 4,845(paid). **Wire Service(s):** AP.

RUSHVILLE
US   ISSN 8756-6443
RUSHVILLE REPUBLICAN. 1840. Mon.-Sat. $.50 newsstand; $8.05/mo. carrier. 219 N. Perkins St., Rushville, IN 46173. TEL 317-932-2222; FAX 317-932-4358. **Owner(s):** Thomson Newspapers, Inc., Metro Centre, One Station Pl., 6th Fl., Stamford, CT 06902. TEL 203-425-2500; FAX 203-425-2516; Ed. Don Krause; Pub. Norman D. Voiles; adv. contact: Marilyn Land. pub. size: broadsheet; circ. evening 4,150(paid). **Wire Service(s):** AP.

SEYMOUR

US

TRIBUNE, THE. 1879. Mon.-Sat. $.50 newsstand; $112.25/yr. in state mailed; $123.65/yr. out of state. 1215 E. Tipton, Seymour, IN 47274. TEL 812-522-4871; FAX 812-522-7691. **Owner(s):** Freedom Communications, Inc., 17666 Fitch, Irvine, CA 92714. TEL 714-553-9292; Ed. Dan Davis; Pub. Tim Timmons; adv. contact: Jeanne Piersall. photos; bk.rev.; pub. size: broadsheet; circ. evening 9,687(paid). **Wire Service(s):** AP.

Formerly: Seymour Tribune.

SHELBYVILLE

US

SHELBYVILLE NEWS. 1948. Mon.-Sat. $.50 newsstand; $45/6 mos. home deliv. 123 E. Washington, Shelbyville, IN 46176. TEL 317-398-6631; FAX 317-398-0194. **Owner(s):** Shelbyville Newspapers, Inc., 123 E. Washington St., Shelbyville, IN 46176. TEL 317-398-6631; Ed. Scarlett Syse; Pub. John C. Deprez, Jr.; adv. contact: Dee Bonner. bk.rev.; pub. size: broadsheet; circ. evening 11,500(paid). **Wire Service(s):** AP, SHNA, NEA, RN, NYT.

SOUTH BEND

US

SOUTH BEND TRIBUNE. 1872. d. $.50/day newsstand; $1.50/Sun.; $126/yr. carrier; $135/yr. motor rte. 225 W. Colfax Ave., South Bend, IN 46626. TEL 219-235-6161; FAX 219-236-1765. **Owner(s):** Schurz Communications, Inc., 225 W. Colfax Ave., South Bend, IN 46626. TEL 219-235-6161; Ed. Tim Harmon; Pub. Todd Schurz; adv. contact: Carol A. Smith. photos; bk.rev.; pub. size: broadsheet; circ. evening 80,000(paid); Sun. 114,000(paid). **Wire Service(s):** AP, NYT, SH.

SPENCER

US   **ISSN 0745-7227**

SPENCER EVENING WORLD. 1927. Mon.-Fri. $.30 newsstand; $48/yr. 114 E. Franklin St., Spencer, IN 47460. TEL 812-829-2255; FAX 812-829-4666. **Owner(s):** Spencer Evening World, Inc., P.O. Box 226, Spencer, IN 47460. TEL 812-829-2255; FAX 812-829-4666; Ed. Tom Douglas; Pub. John A. Gillaspy; adv.: $4.45/SAU. photos; pub. size: broadsheet; circ. evening 3,600(paid).

SULLIVAN

US

SULLIVAN DAILY TIMES. 1905. Mon.-Fri. $.30 newsstand; $42/yr. in cy; $48/yr. out of cy. 115 W. Jackson, Sullivan, IN 47882. TEL 812-268-6356; FAX 812-268-3110. **Owner(s):** Pierce Oil Co., Inc., P.O. Box 130, Sullivan, IN 47882. TEL 812-268-6356; Ed. Tom P. Gettinger; Pub. Nancy Pierce Gettinger; adv. contact: Dena Ridge. pub. size: broadsheet; circ. evening 5,000(paid). **Wire Service(s):** AP.

TERRE HAUTE

US

TRIBUNE-STAR. 1894. d. $.50/day newsstand; $1.50/Sun.; $156/yr. home deliv. 721 Wabash Ave., Terre Haute, IN 47807. TEL 812-231-4200; FAX 812-231-4234. **Owner(s):** Thomson Newspapers, Inc., Metro Centre, One Station Pl., 6th Fl., Stamford, CT 06902. TEL 203-425-2500; FAX 203-425-2516; Ed. David Cox; Pub. Jack Meany; adv. contact: Rick Schmidt. bk.rev.; pub. size: broadsheet; circ. morning 36,000(paid); Sun. 43,000(paid). **Wire Service(s):** AP.

TIPTON

US   **ISSN 0746-0619**

TIPTON TRIBUNE. Mon.-Sat. $.35 newsstand; $64.80/yr. in town; $75.60/yr. motor rte.; $85/yr. mailed. 110 W. Madison, Tipton, IN 46072. TEL 317-675-2115; FAX 317-675-4147. **Owner(s):** Elwood Publishing Co., Inc., 317 S. Anderson St., Elwood, IN 46036. TEL 317-552-3355; Ed. E. Neil Johnson; Pub. Robert L. Nash; adv. contact: Jay Puterbaugh. pub. size: broadsheet; circ. evening 4,000(paid). **Wire Service(s):** AP.

VALPARAISO

US

VALPARAISO VIDETTE-TIMES. 1927. d. $.50/day newsstand; $1.75/Sun.; $9.40/mo. carrier. 1111 Glendale Blvd., Valparaiso, IN 46383. TEL 219-462-5151; FAX 219-465-7298. **Owner(s):** Howard Publications, 601 45th, Munster, IN 46321. TEL 219-933-3329; Ed. Don Asher; Pub. Jack Palmer; adv. contact: Marc Leuthart. photos; bk.rev.; pub. size: broadsheet; circ. evening 90,000(paid); Sun. 90,000(paid). **Wire Service(s):** AP, TN, SHNA.

Formerly: Valparaiso Vidette-Messenger.

VINCENNES

US   **ISSN 1072-3609**

VINCENNES SUN-COMMERCIAL. 1804. Sun.-Fri. $.50/day newsstand; $1.50/Sun.; $78.80/yr. home deliv.; $98.80/yr motor rte. 702 Main St., Vincennes, IN 47591. TEL 812-886-9955; FAX 812-885-2235. **Owner(s):** Central Newspapers, Inc., 135 N. Pennsylvania, Indianapolis, IN 46204. TEL 317-231-9200; Ed. Lloyd Pletsch; Pub. Michael E. Quayle; adv. contact: Vickie Palmer. pub. size: broadsheet; circ. evening 15,000(paid); Sun. 16,000(paid). **Wire Service(s):** AP.

WABASH

US

WABASH PLAIN DEALER. 1859. Mon.-Sat. $.50 newsstand; $6.25/mo. carrier; $6.65/mo. motor rte. 123 W. Canal St., Wabash, IN 46992. TEL 219-563-2131; FAX 219-563-0816; E-mail: wapd@holli.com; URL: http://207.2.127.1:80/newswave. **Owner(s):** Nixon Newspapers, Inc., 33 W. Third St., Peru, IN 46970. TEL 219-563-7414; Ed. Roy Church; Pub. Jim Widner; adv.; pub. size: broadsheet; circ. evening 7,500(paid). **Wire Service(s):** UPI.

WARSAW

US

TIMES-UNION. 1854. Mon.-Sat. $.50 newsstand; $8.10/mo. motor rte.; $10/mo. local mailed; $11/mo. elsewhere. Times Bldg., Warsaw, IN 46581-1448. TEL 219-267-3111. E-mail: news@timeswrsw.com; URL: http://www.timeswrsw.com. **Owner(s):** Reub Williams & Sons, Inc., P.O. Box 1448, Warsaw, IN 46581-1448. TEL 219-267-3111; Ed. Norman Hagg; Pub. M.R. Williams; adv. contact: Bill Hays. photos; pub. size: broadsheet; circ. evening 14,500(paid). **Wire Service(s):** AP, NYT.

WASHINGTON

US

WASHINGTON TIMES-HERALD. 1867. Mon.-Sat. $.50 newsstand; $81/yr. 102 E. Van Trees St., Washington, IN 47501. TEL 812-254-0480; FAX 812-254-7517; E-mail: mmaust@dmtrc.net. **Owner(s):** Stephens Group, Inc., P.O. Box 1359, Fort Smith, AR 72901. TEL 501-785-7810; Ed. Melody Maust; Pub. Lars Purdue; adv. contact: Don Brown. photos; bk.rev.; pub. size: standard; circ. evening 10,200(paid). **Wire Service(s):** AP.

WINCHESTER

US

NEWS-GAZETTE, THE. 1847. Mon.-Sat. $.50 newsstand; $106.20/yr. in cy.; $112/yr. in cy. mailed; $112/yr. out of cy. mailed. 224 W. Franklin St., Winchester, IN 47394. TEL 317-584-4501; FAX 317-584-3066. **Owner(s):** Whitewater Publishing Co., Frankfort, IL; Ed. Michael Buckmaster; Pub. Jack J. Armstrong; adv.; photos; pub. size: broadsheet; circ. evening 5,000(paid). **Wire Service(s):** AP.

IOWA

AMES

US   **ISSN 0893-7915**

DAILY TRIBUNE, THE. 1867. Mon.-Sat. $.50/day newsstand; $1/Sat.; $121.70/yr. carrier in cy.; $159.10/yr. mailed in cy.; $210.15/yr. mailed out of cy. 317 Fifth St., Ames, IA 50010. TEL 515-232-2160; FAX 515-232-2364. **Owner(s):** Daily Tribune, Inc., 317 Fifth. St., P.O. Box 380, Ames, IA 50010. TEL 515-232-2160; Ed. Jeff Bruner; Pub. Gary G. Gerlach; adv. contact: Jeannette Frankl. photos; pub. size: broadsheet; circ. evening 10,000(paid). **Wire Service(s):** AP, NYT.

Formerly: Ames Daily Tribune.

ATLANTIC

US   **ISSN 8756-6400**

ATLANTIC NEWS-TELEGRAPH. 1871. Mon.-Sat. $.50 newsstand; $25/3 mos.; $91/yr. 410 Walnut St., Atlantic, IA 50022. TEL 712-243-2624; FAX 712-243-4988. **Owner(s):** Community Media Group, West Frankfort, IL 62959. TEL 618-937-3246; Pub. Ken Lingen; adv.; photos; pub. size: broadsheet; circ. evening 4,800(paid). **Wire Service(s):** AP.

DAILY NEWSPAPERS

BOONE

US   ISSN 1050-4087
BOONE NEWS-REPUBLICAN. 1865. Mon.-Fri. $.50 newsstand; $75/yr. carrier in town; $90/yr. motor in cy.; $95/yr. in cy. mailed. 812 Keeler St., Boone, IA 50036. TEL 515-432-1234; FAX 515-432-7811. **Owner(s):** Schaub Publishing, Inc., 812 Keeler St., P.O. Box 100, Boone, IA 50036-0100. TEL 515-432-1234; FAX 515-432-7811; Ed. James A. Bachtell; Pub. R.C. Schaub; adv. contact: Susan E. Tolan. pub. size: broadsheet; circ. evening 3,600(paid). **Wire Service(s):** AP.

BURLINGTON

US   ISSN 1073-9297
HAWK EYE, THE. 1837. d. $.50/day newsstand; $1.25/Sun.; $10.50/mo. 800 S. Main St., Burlington, IA 52601. TEL 319-754-8461; FAX 319-754-6824. **Owner(s):** Burlington Hawk Eye Co., P.O. Box 10, Burlington, IA 52601. TEL 319-754-8461; FAX 319-754-6824; Ed. Dale Alison; Pub. Bill Mertens; adv. contact: Nelson Showalter. photos; pub. size: broadsheet; circ. morning 18,153(paid); Sun. 20,400(paid). **Wire Service(s):** AP.

CARROLL

US
DAILY TIMES HERALD. 1928. Mon.-Fri. $.50 newsstand; $78/yr. 508 N. Court St., Carroll, IA 51401. TEL 712-792-3573; FAX 712-792-5218. **Owner(s):** James B. & Ann Wilson, 508 N. Court St., Carroll, IA 51401. TEL 712-792-3573; Ed. James B. Wilson; Pub. James B. Wilson; adv. contact: Debra Lucht. pub. size: broadsheet; circ. evening 6,500(paid). **Wire Service(s):** AP.
Formerly: Carroll Daily Times Herald.

CEDAR RAPIDS

US   ISSN 1066-0291
CEDAR RAPIDS GAZETTE. 1883. d. $.50/day newsstand; $.75/Sat.; $1.75/Sun.; $197/yr. carrier. 500 Third Ave., S.E., Cedar Rapids, IA 52401-1608. TEL 319-398-8211; FAX 319-398-5846; E-mail: gazette@infi.net; URL: http://www.fyiowa.com/gazette. **Owner(s):** Gazette Co., The, 500 Third Ave., S.E., Cedar Rapids, IA 52401. TEL 319-398-8211; Ed. Mark Bowden; Pub. Joseph Hladky, III; adv.: $43.89/SAU daily; $48.75/SAU Sun. photos; bk.rev.; pub. size: broadsheet; circ. morning 68,727(paid); Sun. 84,307(paid). **Wire Service(s):** AP, LAT-WP.

CENTERVILLE

US
AD EXPRESS & DAILY IOWEGIAN. 1883. Mon.-Fri. $.50 newsstand; $49/yr. local; $61/yr. out of state. 105 N. Main St., Centerville, IA 52544. TEL 515-856-6336; FAX 515-856-8118. **Owner(s):** Appanoose Publishing Co., Inc., 105 N. Main St., Centeville, IA 52544; Ed. Steve Dunn; Pub. John C. Arnold; adv. contact: Cindy Briggs. pub. size: broadsheet; circ. morning 3,100(paid).

CHARLES CITY

US   ISSN 1049-7242
CHARLES CITY PRESS. 1896. Mon.-Sat. $.50 newsstand; $88.50/yr. 801 Riverside, Charles City, IA 50616. TEL 515-228-3211; FAX 515-228-2641. **Owner(s):** American Publishing Co., 606 N. Van Buren, Marion, IL 62959. TEL 618-993-1711; Ed. Mark Wicks; Pub. Gene A. Hall; adv. contact: Rich Gifford. pub. size: broadsheet; circ. evening 3,100(paid). **Wire Service(s):** AP.

CHEROKEE

US   ISSN 0747-4776
CHEROKEE DAILY TIMES. 1870. Tue.-Sat. $.50 newsstand; $65/yr. in cy.; $80/yr. out of cy. 111 S. Second St., Cherokee, IA 51012. TEL 712-225-5111; FAX 712-225-2910. **Owner(s):** Edwards Publications, P.O. Box 1193, Seneca, SC 29769; Ed. Jeff Lundquist; Pub. Marcella Brown; adv. contact: Marcella Brown. pub. size: broadsheet; circ. morning 3,200(paid). **Wire Service(s):** AP.
Formerly: Cherokee County's Daily Times.

CLINTON

US
CLINTON HERALD. 1856. Mon.-Sat. $.50 newsstand; $80/yr. 221 Sixth Ave., S., Clinton, IA 52732. TEL 319-242-7101; FAX 319-242-7147. **Owner(s):** Donrey Media Group, P.O. Box 1359, Fort Smith, AR 72902. TEL 501-785-7196; Pub. Jack Dermody; adv. contact: Gary Bicker. photos; pub. size: broadsheet; circ. evening 18,000(paid). Wire Service(s): AP.

COUNCIL BLUFFS

US   ISSN 1046-1833
DAILY NONPAREIL. 1857. d. $.35/day newsstand; $1.25/Sun.; $1.90/wk.; $93.60/yr. 117 Pearl St., Council Bluffs, IA 51503. TEL 712-328-1811; FAX 712-328-1597. **Owner(s):** Media News Group, 1560 Broadway, Ste. 1485, Denver, CO 80202. TEL 303-820-1952; Ed. Jon Leu; Pub. Joseph Craig; adv. contact: Denny Koenders. photos; pub. size: broadsheet; circ. evening 17,800(paid); Sun. 19,500(paid). **Wire Service(s):** AP.

CRESTON

US
CRESTON NEWS ADVERTISER. 1881. Mon.-Fri. $.50 newsstand; $122.50/yr. 503 W. Adams St., Creston, IA 50801. TEL 515-182-2141; FAX 515-782-6628; E-mail: cna@creston.heartland.net. **Owner(s):** Shaw Newspaper Co., 444 Pine Hill Dr., Dixon, IL 61021. TEL 815-284-4000; Ed. Jeff Young; Pub. Arvid Huisman; adv. contact: Roger Lanning. adv.: $7.26/SAU. photos; pub. size: broadsheet; circ. evening 5,602(paid). **Wire Service(s):** AP.

DAVENPORT

US   ISSN 1064-2986
QUAD-CITY TIMES. 1855. d. $.50/day newsstand; $2/Sun.; $3.95/wk. carrier; $4.90/wk. out of state. 500 E. Third St., Davenport, IA 52801. TEL 319-383-2200; FAX 319-383-2370. **Owner(s):** Lee Enterprises, Inc., 130 E. Second St., Davenport, IA 52801. TEL 319-383-2100; Ed. Daniel K. Hayes; Pub. Beth Colby Clark; adv.; photos; bk.rev.; pub. size: broadsheet; circ. morning 54,000(paid); Sun. 83,000(paid). **Wire Service(s):** AP.

DES MOINES

US
DES MOINES REGISTER. 1849. d. $.35/day newsstand; $1.50/Sun.; $1.75/wk. home deliv. 715 Locust, Des Moines, IA 50309. TEL 515-284-8281; FAX 515-284-8287. **Owner(s):** Gannett Company, Inc., 1100 Wilson Blvd., Arlington, VA 22209. TEL 703-284-6000; Pub. Barbara A. Henry; adv.; photos; bk.rev.; pub. size: broadsheet; circ. morning 117,442(paid); Sun. 294,794(paid). **Wire Service(s):** AP, CDN, DJ, LAT-WP, GNS.

DUBUQUE

US
TELEGRAPH HERALD. 1836. d. $.50/day newsstand; $1.50/Sun.; $3.25/wk. home deliv. 801 Bluff St., Dubuque, IA 52001. TEL 319-588-5611; FAX 319-588-5739; E-mail: thonline@wcinet.com; URL: http://www.thonline.com. **Owner(s):** Woodward Communications, Inc., P.O. Box 688, Dubuque, IA 52004-0688. TEL 319-588-5611; Ed. Soren Nielson; Pub. Tom Yunt; adv. contact: Don Hansen. pub. size: broadsheet; circ. morning 34,025(paid); Sun. 39,020(paid). **Wire Service(s):** KR.

ESTHERVILLE

US   ISSN 0747-0754
ESTHERVILLE DAILY NEWS. 1902. Mon.-Sat. $.35 newsstand; $16/3 mos.; $60/yr. 10 N. Seventh St., Estherville, IA 51334. TEL 712-362-2622; FAX 712-362-2624. **Owner(s):** Ogden Newspapers, Inc., 1500 Main St., Wheeling, WV 26003; Ed. Ron Menendez; Pub. Ron Menendez; adv.; pub. size: broadsheet; circ. morning 2,300(paid).

FAIRFIELD

US   ISSN 1061-4508
FAIRFIELD DAILY LEDGER. 1849. Mon.-Fri. $.50 newsstand; $74/yr. in cy. mailed; $99/yr. out of state. 112 E. Broadway, Fairfield, IA 52556. TEL 515-472-4129; FAX 515-472-1916. **Owner(s):** Inland Industries, Inc., P.O. Box 15999, Shawnee Mission, KS 66285; Ed. William Draper; Pub. Jeff Wilson; adv. contact: Gene Luedtke. pub. size: broadsheet; circ. evening 5,000(paid). **Wire Service(s):** AP.

FORT DODGE

US   ISSN 0740-6991
FORT DODGE MESSENGER. 1855. d. $.50/day newsstand; $1/Sun.; $104.50/yr. 713 Central Ave., Fort Dodge, IA 50501. TEL 515-573-2141; FAX 515-573-2148. **Owner(s):** Ogden Newspapers, Inc., 1500 Main St., Wheeling, WV 26003. TEL 304-233-0100; Ed. Mark Smidt; Pub. Larry D. Bushman; adv. contact: Tim Craig. photos; bk.rev.; pub. size: standard; circ. morning 23,000(paid); Sun. 23,000(paid). **Wire Service(s):** AP.

10448 FORT MADISON, IA **DAILY NEWSPAPERS**

FORT MADISON
US   ISSN 0746-4266
FORT MADISON DAILY DEMOCRAT. 1869. Mon-Fri. $.50 newsstand; $68.25/yr. local. 1226 Ave. H, Fort Madison, IA 52627. TEL 319-372-6421; FAX 319-372-3867. **Owner(s):** Brehm Communications, Inc., P.O. Box 28429, San Diego, CA 92128. TEL 619-451-6200; Ed. Robin Delaney. adv. contact: Danna Cambel. photos; pub. size: broadsheet; circ. evening 7,500(paid). **Wire Service(s):** AP.

IOWA CITY
US
IOWA CITY PRESS-CITIZEN. 1841. Mon.-Sat. $.35/day newsstand; $.75/Sat.; $9/mo. carrier. 1725 N. Dodge St., Iowa City, IA 52245. TEL 319-337-3181; FAX 319-339-7342; E-mail: cwanninger@aol.com. **Owner(s):** Gannett Company, Inc., 1100 Wilson Blvd., Arlington, VA 22234. TEL 703-284-6000; Ed. Mike Beck; Pub. Charles T. Wanninger; adv.; photos; bk.rev.; pub. size: broadsheet; circ. evening 16,500(paid). **Wire Service(s):** AP, GNS.

KEOKUK
US
KEOKUK DAILY GATE CITY. 1847. Mon.-Fri. $.50 newsstand; free/Wed.; $83.20/yr. in town; $88.40/yr. elsewhere. 1016 Main St., Keokuk, IA 52632-0430. TEL 319-524-8300; FAX 319-524-4363. **Owner(s):** Brehm Communications, Inc., P.O. Box 28429, San Diego, CA 92128. TEL 619-451-6200; Ed. Jeff Hanan; Pub. William D. DeLost; adv. contact: Wes Grooms. adv.: $8.80/SAU. photos; bk.rev.; pub. size: broadsheet; circ. evening 6,600(paid). **Wire Service(s):** AP.

LE MARS
US
LE MARS DAILY SENTINEL. 1870. Mon.-Fri. $.50 newsstand; $96/yr. in cy.; $114/yr. in state; $182/yr. out of state. 41 First Ave., N.E., Le Mars, IA 51031. TEL 712-546-7031; FAX 712-546-7035. **Owner(s):** U.S. Media Group, P.O. Box 227, Crystal City, MO 63019. TEL 501-423-6688; Ed. John Buntsma; Pub. Kevin Hook; adv. contact: Kevin Hook. photos; bk.rev.; pub. size: broadsheet; circ. evening 5,500(paid). **Wire Service(s):** AP.

MARSHALLTOWN
US
MARSHALLTOWN TIMES-REPUBLICAN. 1858. d. $.50/day newsstand; $.75/Sun.; $85/yr. 135 W. Main St., Marshalltown, IA 50158. TEL 515-753-6611; FAX 515-753-7221; E-mail: timesr@mrshlnet.com; URL: http://www.oweb.com/times-republican. **Owner(s):** Ogden Newspapers, Inc., 1500 Main St., Wheeling, WV 26003. TEL 304-233-0100; Ed. Jim Stern; Pub. Mike Schlesinger; adv. contact: Reed Riskedahl. photos; bk.rev.; pub. size: broadsheet; circ. evening 12,500(paid); Sun. 12,500(paid). **Wire Service(s):** AP.

MASON CITY
US
GLOBE-GAZETTE. 1893. d. $.50/day newsstand; $1.50/Sun.; $187/yr. 300 N. Washington, Mason City, IA 50401-3222. TEL 515-421-0524; FAX 515-421-0516. **Owner(s):** Lee Enterprises, Inc., 215 N. Main St., Davenport, IA 52801. TEL 319-383-2202; Ed. Bob Stenson; Pub. Howard Query; adv. contact: Kristie Grooms. photos; pub. size: broadsheet; circ. morning 20,000(paid); Sun. 23,000(paid). **Wire Service(s):** AP, NYT.

MT. PLEASANT
US
MOUNT PLEASANT NEWS. 1978. Mon.-Fri. $.50 newsstand; $73/yr. 215 W. Monroe, Mt. Pleasant, IA 52641. TEL 319-385-3131. E-mail: mpnew@se-iowa.net. **Owner(s):** Mount Pleasant News, Inc., 215 W. Monroe St., Mt. Pleasant, IA 52641. TEL 319-385-3131; Ed. John Stoca; Pub. Emery Styron; adv.; photos; pub. size: broadsheet; circ. evening 3,500(paid). **Wire Service(s):** AP.

MUSCATINE
US
MUSCATINE JOURNAL. 1888. Mon.-Sat. $.50 newsstand; $121.75/yr. in cy. 301 E. Third St., Muscatine, IA 52761. TEL 319-263-2331; FAX 319-262-8042; E-mail: musjournal@aol.com. **Owner(s):** Lee Enterprises, Inc., 215 N. Main St., Davenport, IA 52801. TEL 319-383-2108; Ed. Jeff Techlenberger; Pub. Mark S. Roby; adv.; pub. size: broadsheet; circ. evening 10,000(paid). **Wire Service(s):** AP.

NEWTON
US   ISSN 1040-1539
NEWTON DAILY NEWS. 1902. Mon.-Fri. $.50 newsstand; $70/yr. 200 First Ave., E., Newton, IA 50208. TEL 515-792-3121; FAX 515-792-5505. **Owner(s):** B.F. Shaw Printing Co., 444 Pine Hill Dr., Dixon, IL 61021. TEL 815-284-2222; FAX 815-254-9290; Ed. Pete Hussmann; Pub. Joe McDermott; adv. contact: Annette West. photos; pub. size: broadsheet; circ. evening 7,500(paid). **Wire Service(s):** UPI.

OELWEIN
US   ISSN 1074-4487
OELWEIN DAILY REGISTER. 1881. Mon.-Sat. $.50/day newsstand; $1/Sat.; $99/yr. mailed; $124.80/yr. deliv. 25 First St., S.E., Oelwein, IA 50662. TEL 319-283-2144; FAX 319-283-3268. **Owner(s):** Oelwein Publications, P.O. Box 1193, Seneca, SC 29769; Ed. James A. Morrison; Pub. Jody Perrotto; adv. contact: Martin VanEe. photos; pub. size: broadsheet; circ. evening 6,500(paid). **Wire Service(s):** AP.

OSKALOOSA
US   ISSN 0898-2066
OSKALOOSA HERALD. 1850. Mon.-Sat. $.50 newsstand; $66/yr. in cy. 1901 A Ave., W., Oskaloosa, IA 52577. TEL 515-672-2581; FAX 515-672-2294. **Owner(s):** Donrey Media Group, P.O. Box 17017, Fort Smith, AR 72902. TEL 501-785-7802; Ed. Kimberly Walker; Pub. Keith Ponder; adv.; photos; pub. size: broadsheet; circ. evening 4,500(paid).

OTTUMWA
US   ISSN 0886-4209
OTTUMWA COURIER. 1848. Mon.-Sat. $.50 newsstand; $10.25/4 wks. carrier in cy. 213 E. Second St., Ottumwa, IA 52501. TEL 515-684-4611; FAX 515-684-7834. **Owner(s):** Lee Enterprises, Inc., 215 Main St., Ste. 400, Davenport, IA 52801. TEL 319-383-2100; Ed. Russell Cunningham, Jr.; Pub. Martha Wells; adv.; photos; pub. size: broadsheet; circ. morning 19,400(paid). **Wire Service(s):** AP.

SHENANDOAH
US
VALLEY NEWS TODAY-DAILY SENTINEL. 1993. Tue.-Sat. $.50 newsstand; $24/3 mos.; $44/6 mos.; $76/yr. 702 W. Sheridan St., Shenandoah, IA 51601. TEL 712-246-3097; FAX 712-246-3099. **Owner(s):** Knowles Publishing Corp., 702 W. Sheridan St., Shenandoah, IA 51601; Ed. Julia Dinvelle; Pub. Gregg Knowles; adv.; photos; pub. size: tabloid; circ. evening 3,500(paid). **Wire Service(s):** Iowa Media Link.
 Formerly: Valley News Today, Shenandoah Evening Sentinel.

SIOUX CITY
US
SIOUX CITY JOURNAL, THE. 1854. d. $.50/day newsstand; $1.50/Sun.; $12.25/mo. carrier; $49/4 mos. mailed. Sixth & Pavonia Sts., Sioux City, IA 51102. TEL 712-279-5072; FAX 712-279-5059. **Owner(s):** Hagadone Corp., P.O. Box C-6200, Coer d'Alene, ID 83814-1937. TEL 208-667-3431; Ed. Karen Luken; Pub. Tom Kurdy; photos; pub. size: broadsheet; circ. morning 50,000(paid); Sun. 50,000(paid). **Wire Service(s):** AP.

SPENCER
US   ISSN 0746-0872
SPENCER DAILY REPORTER. 1875. Tue.-Sat. $.75 newsstand; $65/yr. carrier. 416 First Ave., W., Spencer, IA 51301. TEL 712-262-6610; FAX 712-262-3044. **Owner(s):** Edwards Publications, P.O. Box 1193, Seneca, SC 29679. TEL 803-882-3272; Ed. Cynthia Kingsley; Pub. Joni Weerheim; adv. contact: Chris Swanson. pub. size: broadsheet; circ. morning 4,300(paid). **Wire Service(s):** AP.

STORM LAKE
US   ISSN 0893-8555
STORM LAKE PILOT TRIBUNE. 1870. Tue.-Sat. $.50 newsstand; $50/yr. 111 W. Seventh St., Storm Lake, IA 50588. TEL 712-732-3130; FAX 712-732-3152. **Owner(s):** Edwards Publications, P.O. Box 1193, Seneca, SC 29679. TEL 803-882-3272; Ed. Dana Larsen; Pub. Robert L. Madsen; adv.; photos; bk.rev.; pub. size: broadsheet; circ. morning 4,625(paid). **Wire Service(s):** AP.

DAILY NEWSPAPERS

VINTON
US
CEDAR VALLEY DAILY TIMES. 1889. Mon.-Fri. $.50 newsstand; $49/yr. out of town mailed; $60/yr. in town carrier. 108 E. Fifth St., Vinton, IA 52349. TEL 319-472-2311; FAX 319-472-4811. **Owner(s):** Mid-America Publishing Corp, 108 Third St., Ste. 350, Des Moines, IA 50309. TEL 515-282-8220; Ed. Daniel Adix; Pub. Doug Lindner; adv. contact: Kathy Mahr. photos; bk.rev.; pub. size: broadsheet; circ. evening 3,500(paid). **Wire Service(s):** LAT-WP.
Formerly: Vinton Cedar Valley Daily Times.

WASHINGTON
US   ISSN 0894-2552
WASHINGTON EVENING JOURNAL. 1893. Mon.-Fri. $.50 newsstand; $8.25/mo. carrier; $7.75/mo. in cy. mailed; $9.90/mo. in state mailed; $32.50/3 mos. elsewhere. 111 N. Marion Ave., Washington, IA 52353. TEL 319-653-2191. **Owner(s):** Washington Publishing Co., Inc., 111 N. Marion Ave., Washington, IA 52353. TEL 319-653-2191; Ed. Brooks Taylor; Pub. Darwin Sherman; adv. contact: Arnold Smith. bk.rev.; pub. size: broadsheet; circ. evening 14,200(paid). **Wire Service(s):** AP.

WATERLOO
US
WATERLOO COURIER. 1859. Sun.-Fri. $.50/day newsstand; $1.50/Sun.; $156/yr. 501 Commercial St., Waterloo, IA 50701. TEL 319-291-1400; FAX 319-234-6405. **Owner(s):** Howard Publications, Inc., 501 Commercial St., Waterloo, IA 50701. TEL 319-291-1400; Ed. Nancy Raffensperger; Pub. James Lewis; adv. contact: David E. Tansey. photos; bk.rev.; pub. size: broadsheet; circ. evening 47,837(paid). **Wire Service(s):** AP, LAT-WP, SHNA, KNT, NEA.

WEBSTER CITY
US
DAILY FREEMAN JOURNAL. 1857. Mon.-Fri. $.35 newsstand; $59.80/yr. 720 Second St., Webster City, IA 50595. TEL 515-832-4350; FAX 515-832-2314. **Owner(s):** Ogden Newspapers, Inc., 1500 Main St., Wheeling, WV 26003; Ed. Lori Niles; Pub. Mike Fertig; adv.; pub. size: broadsheet; circ. evening 4,000(paid).
Formerly: Webster City Freeman Journal.

KANSAS

ABILENE
US
ABILENE REFLECTOR-CHRONICLE. 1872. Mon.-Sat. $.50 newsstand; $6.50/mo.; $75/yr. in cy.; $85/yr. out of cy.; $102/yr. out of state. 303 N. Broadway, Abilene, KS 67410. TEL 913-263-1000; FAX 913-263-1645. **Owner(s):** Reflector-Chronicle Publishing Corp., 303 N. Broadway, Abilene, KS 67410. TEL 913-263-1000; FAX 913-263-1645; Ed. Dave Bergmeier; Pub. Vivien L. Sadowski; adv.; photos; bk.rev.; pub. size: broadsheet; circ. evening 4,500(paid). **Wire Service(s):** AP.

ARKANSAS CITY
US   ISSN 0888-8485
ARKANSAS CITY TRAVELER. 1873. Mon.-Sat. $.50 newsstand; $68.81/yr. carrier. 200 E. Fifth Ave., Arkansas City, KS 67005. TEL 316-442-4200; FAX 316-442-7483. **Owner(s):** Morris Communications, P.O. Box 936, Augusta, GA 30903. TEL 706-724-0851; Ed. Rick Horn; Pub. Kim Benedict; adv. contact: Lisa Fooese. pub. size: broadsheet; circ. evening 6,700(paid). **Wire Service(s):** AP.

ATCHISON
US
ATCHISON DAILY GLOBE. 1877. Mon.-Sat. $.50 newsstand; $8/mo. carrier; $110.40/yr. mailed. 1015 Main St., Atchison, KS 66002. TEL 913-367-0583; FAX 913-367-7531; E-mail: aglobe@microworld.net. **Owner(s):** American Publishing Co., 606 N. Van Buren, Marion, IL 62959. TEL 618-993-1711; Ed. Jim Headley; Pub. Stan Wilson; adv.: $8.55/SAU. photos; pub. size: broadsheet; circ. evening 8,651(free & paid). **Wire Service(s):** AP.

AUGUSTA
US
AUGUSTA DAILY GAZETTE. 1893. Mon.-Fri. $.50 newsstand; $70/yr. in cy.; $80.96/yr. out of cy.; $122.26/yr. elsewhere. 204 E. Fifth St., Augusta, KS 67010-0009. TEL 316-775-2218; FAX 316-775-3220. **Owner(s):** American Publishing Co., 606 N. Van Buren, Marion, IL 62959. TEL 618-993-1711; Ed. Michael McDermott; Pub. Carter J. Zerbe; adv.; pub. size: broadsheet; circ. evening 7,900(paid). **Wire Service(s):** AP.

BELOIT
US   ISSN 8750-1791
BELOIT DAILY CALL. 1901. Mon.-Fri. $.50 newsstand; $63.60/yr. 122 Court St., Beloit, KS 67420. TEL 913-738-3537; FAX 913-738-6442. **Owner(s):** Beloit Newspapers, Inc., P.O. Box 366, Beloit, KS 67420. TEL 913-738-3757; Ed. Larry Hiatt; Pub. Larry Hiatt; adv. contact: Robert Milburn. photos; bk.rev.; pub. size: broadsheet; circ. evening 2,500(paid). **Wire Service(s):** AP.
Formerly: Beloit Daily Call & Posts.

CHANUTE
US
CHANUTE TRIBUNE. 1892. Mon.-Sat. $.50 newsstand; $70.20/yr. 15 N. Evergreen, Chanute, KS 66720. TEL 316-431-4100; FAX 316-431-4100. **Owner(s):** Harris Enterprises, P.O. Box 190, Hutchinson, KS 67504. TEL 316-694-5830; Ed. Thomas N. Bell; Pub. Thomas N. Bell; adv. contact: Joanne Johnson. photos; bk.rev.; pub. size: broadsheet; circ. evening 4,900(paid). **Wire Service(s):** AP.

CLAY CENTER
US
CLAY CENTER DISPATCH. 1873. Mon.-Fri. $.35 newsstand; $61/yr. carrier; $69.50/yr. in state mailed; $78.75/yr. out of state mailed. 805 Fifth St., Clay Center, KS 67432. TEL 913-632-2127. **Owner(s):** Clay Center Publishing Co., P.O. Box 519, Clay Center, KS 67432. TEL 913-632-2127; Ed. Ned Valentine. adv. contact: Ken Knepper. pub. size: broadsheet; circ. evening 3,500(paid).

COFFEYVILLE
US   ISSN 0746-8202
COFFEYVILLE JOURNAL, THE. 1892. Tue.-Fri. & Sun. $.35/day newsstand; $.75/Sun.; $74/yr. Eighth & Elm Sts., Coffeyville, KS 67337. TEL 316-251-3300; FAX 316-251-1905. **Owner(s):** Murphy McGinnis Media, Inc., 130 W. Superior St., Duluth, MN 55802. TEL 218-723-8000; FAX 218-723-8980; Ed. Tim Flowers; Pub. Mike Thornberry; adv. contact: Chris Zimmerman. photos; pub. size: broadsheet; circ. evening 6,700(paid); Sun. 7,200(paid). **Wire Service(s):** AP.

COLBY
US
COLBY FREE PRESS. 1888. Mon.-Thu. & Sat. $.50 newsstand; $55/yr. 155 W. Fifth St., Colby, KS 67701. TEL 913-462-3963; FAX 913-462-7749. **Owner(s):** Haynes Publishing, Oberlin, KS; Pub. Patty Decker; adv. contact: Patty Decker. pub. size: broadsheet; circ. morning 2,500(paid); 2,255(paid). **Wire Service(s):** AP.

COLUMBUS
US   ISSN 8756-6044
COLUMBUS DAILY ADVOCATE. 1874. Mon.-Fri. $.25 newsstand; $36/yr. carrier. 215 S. Kansas, Columbus, KS 66725. TEL 316-429-2773; FAX 316-429-3223. **Owner(s):** Columbus Communications Inc., P.O. Box 231, Columbus, KS 66725. TEL 316-429-2773; Ed. Jay M. Lacy; Pub. J.L. Nichols; adv. contact: Micki Murdock. photos; pub. size: broadsheet; circ. evening 2,537(paid). **Wire Service(s):** AP.

CONCORDIA
US
CONCORDIA BLADE-EMPIRE. 1902. Mon.-Fri. $.50 newsstand; $56.13/yr. trade area; $63.57/yr. carrier; $68.84/yr. outside of area; $65/yr. out of state. 510 Washington, Concordia, KS 66901. TEL 913-243-2424; FAX 913-243-4407. **Owner(s):** Blade-Empire Publishing Co., Inc., P.O. Box 309, Concordia, KS 66901. TEL 913-243-2424; Ed. Jim Lowell; Pub. Brad Lowell; adv. contact: Joni Regnier. photos; bk.rev.; pub. size: broadsheet; circ. evening 3,100(paid). **Wire Service(s):** AP.

COUNCIL GROVE
US
COUNCIL GROVE REPUBLICAN. 1872. Mon.-Fri. $.25 newsstand; $51/yr. carrier in town. 208 W. Main St., Council Grove, KS 66846. TEL 316-767-5123. **Owner(s):** Council Grove Publishing Co., Inc., 208 W. Main St., Council Grove, KS 66846. TEL 316-767-5123; Ed. Craig A. McNeal; Pub. Craig A. McNeal; adv. contact: Don A. McNeal. pub. size: broadsheet; circ. evening 2,450(paid). **Wire Service(s):** AP.

DERBY
US
DAILY REPORTER, THE. 1922. Mon.-Fri. $.50 newsstand; $78/yr. carrier; $81/yr. mailed. 201 S. Baltimore, Derby, KS 67037. TEL 316-788-2835; FAX 316-788-0854. **Owner(s):** American Publishing Co., 606 N. Van Buren, Marion, IL 62959. TEL 618-993-1711; Ed. Randy Fogg; Pub. Jim Stephenson; adv.; photos; bk.rev.; pub. size: standard; circ. evening 1,800(paid). **Wire Service(s):** AP.

DODGE CITY

US ISSN 0889-3489
DODGE CITY DAILY GLOBE. 1911. Mon.-Sat. $.50 newsstand; $104/yr. 705 Second Ave., Dodge City, KS 67801. TEL 316-225-4151; FAX 316-225-4154. **Owner(s):** Morris Communications, P.O. Box 936, Augusta, GA 30903. TEL 706-724-0851; Ed. Gary Reber; Pub. Terry Cochran; adv. contact: Linda Irsik. photos; pub. size: broadsheet; circ. morning 9,300(paid). **Wire Service(s):** AP.

EL DORADO

US ISSN 1053-9999
EL DORADO TIMES. 1919. Mon.-Sat. $.50 newsstand; $86.75/yr. 114 N. Vine, El Dorado, KS 67042. TEL 316-321-1120; FAX 316-321-7722; E-mail: eldtimes@southwind.net; URL: http://www.southwind.net/~eldtimes. **Owner(s):** American Publishing Co., 606 N. Van Buren, Marion, IL 62959. TEL 618-993-1711; Pub. Guy P. Russell; adv.; pub. size: broadsheet; circ. evening 4,800(paid). **Wire Service(s):** AP.

EMPORIA

US
EMPORIA GAZETTE. 1890. Mon.-Sat. $.35/day newsstand; $.50/Sat.; $69/yr. 517 Merchant St., Emporia, KS 66801. TEL 316-342-4800; FAX 316-342-8108; E-mail: egazette@cadvantage.com; URL: http://www.emporiagazette.com. **Owner(s):** White Corp., Inc., 517 Merchant St., Emporia, KS 66801. TEL 316-342-4800; FAX 316-342-4800; Ed. Patrick Kelley; Pub. Paul David Walker; adv. contact: Bruce Knaak. photos; bk.rev.; pub. size: broadsheet; circ. evening 10,000(paid). **Wire Service(s):** AP, NYT.

FORT SCOTT

US ISSN 8755-3171
FORT SCOTT TRIBUNE, THE. 1884. Mon.-Sat. $.35/newsstand; $69.85/yr. 6 E. Wall St., Fort Scott, KS 66701. TEL 316-223-1460; FAX 316-223-1469. **Owner(s):** Frank E. Emery, 6 E. Wall St., Fort Scott, KS 66701. TEL 316-223-1462; FAX 316-223-1469; Ed. Melinda Rhodes; Pub. Frank E. Emery; adv. contact: Kathy Freener. photos; pub. size: broadsheet; circ. evening 4,452(paid). **Wire Service(s):** AP.

GARDEN CITY

US
GARDEN CITY TELEGRAM. 1929. Mon.-Sat. $.50 newsstand; $.75/Sat.; $79.58/yr. carrier. 310 N. Seventh St., Garden City, KS 67846. TEL 316-275-8500; FAX 316-275-5165. **Owner(s):** Harris Enterprises, P.O. Box 190, Hutchinson, KS 67504. TEL 316-662-3311; Affiliates Profit Sharing Trust, P.O. Box 190, Hutchinson, KS 67504. TEL 316-662-3311; Ed. Carol Crupper; Pub. James E. Bloom; adv. contact: Darla Craig. photos; pub. size: broadsheet; circ. evening 11,408(paid). **Wire Service(s):** AP, HNS.

GOODLAND

US ISSN 0893-0562
GOODLAND DAILY NEWS. 1932. Mon.-Fri. $.50 newsstand; $59.64/yr. local; $78/yr. elsewhere. 1205 Main St., Goodland, KS 67735-0500. TEL 913-899-2338; FAX 913-899-6186. **Owner(s):** Haynes Publishing, Oberlin, KS; Ed. Peter Liwoski; Pub. Jim Davidson; adv. contact: Karen Porter. photos; pub. size: standard; circ. evening 2,493(paid). **Wire Service(s):** AP.

GREAT BEND

US ISSN 0891-7078
GREAT BEND TRIBUNE. 1876. d. $.50/day newsstand; $1/Sun.; $25.54/3 mos. in city carrier; $91.93/yr. carrier; $24.45/3 mos. mailed; $97.50/yr. mailed. 2012 Forest Ave., Great Bend, KS 67530. TEL 316-792-1211; FAX 316-792-3441. **Owner(s):** Morris Newspaper Corp., P.O. Box 8167, Savannah, GA 31412. TEL 912-233-1281; Ed. Daren Watkins; Pub. Tom Larimer; adv.; photos; bk.rev.; pub. size: broadsheet; circ. evening 8,500(paid); Sun. 9,500(paid). **Wire Service(s):** AP.

HAYS

US
HAYS DAILY NEWS. 1929. Sun.-Fri. $.50/day newsstand; $1/Sun.; $98/yr. carrier. 507 Main St., Hays, KS 67601. TEL 913-628-1081; FAX 913-628-8186; E-mail: classad@dailynews.net. **Owner(s):** News Publishing Co., 507 Main St., P.O. Box 857, Hays, KS 67601. TEL 913-628-1081; FAX 913-628-8186; Ed. Greg Halling; Pub. Jim Hitch; adv. contact: Michael H. Haas. pub. size: standard; circ. evening 13,304(paid); Sun. 14,380(paid). **Wire Service(s):** AP.

HIAWATHA

US
HIAWATHA DAILY WORLD. 1908. Mon.-Fri. $.50 newsstand; $51.21/yr. carrier; $62.80/yr. out of cy. mailed. 607 Utah St., Hiawatha, KS 66434. TEL 913-742-2111; FAX 913-742-2276. **Owner(s):** Cleveland Newspapers, Inc., P.O. Box 3600, Cleveland, TN 37320; Ed. Deb Rosenberger; Pub. Barry Stokes; adv. contact: Barry Stokes. pub. size: broadsheet; circ. evening 2,800(paid).

HUTCHINSON

US
HUTCHINSON NEWS. 1872. d. $.50/day newsstand; $1.25/Sun.; $150.24/yr. 300 W. Second, Hutchinson, KS 67501-0190. TEL 316-694-5700; FAX 316-662-4186. **Owner(s):** Hutchinson Publishing Co., 300 W. Second, Hutchinson, KS 67501. TEL 316-694-5700; FAX 316-662-4186; Ed. Bruce Buchanan; Pub. Bruce Buchanan; adv.; photos; pub. size: broadsheet; circ. morning 37,940(paid); Sun. 41,325(paid). **Wire Service(s):** AP, NYT, LAT-WP.

INDEPENDENCE

US
INDEPENDENCE DAILY REPORTER. 1881. d. $.50/day newsstand; $1/Sun.; $81.95/yr. 320 N. Sixth St., Independence, KS 67301. TEL 316-331-3550; FAX 316-331-3550. **Owner(s):** Reporter Publishing Co., Inc., P.O. Box 869, Independence, KS 67301. TEL 316-331-3550; FAX 316-331-3550; Ed. Georgia High; Pub. Herbert A. Meyer, III; adv. contact: Steve McBride. photos; pub. size: broadsheet; circ. evening 7,675(free & paid); Sun. 7,675(free & paid). **Wire Service(s):** AP.

IOLA

US
IOLA REGISTER. 1867. Mon.-Sat. $.50 newsstand; $18.81/3 mos. 302 S. Washington, Iola, KS 66749. TEL 316-365-2111; FAX 316-365-6289; E-mail: register@midusa.net. **Owner(s):** Mickey Lynn, 302 S. Washington, Iola, KS 66749; Ed. Emerson Lynn; Pub. Emerson Lynn; adv. contact: Jack Hastings. photos; bk.rev.; pub. size: broadsheet; circ. evening 4,200(paid). **Wire Service(s):** AP.

JUNCTION CITY

US
JUNCTION CITY DAILY UNION. 1861. d. $.35/day newsstand; $1/Sun.; $6.50/mo. 222 W. Sixth St., Junction City, KS 66441. TEL 913-762-5000; FAX 913-762-4614. **Owner(s):** Montgomery Communications, Inc., 222 W. Sixth St., Junction City, KS 66441. TEL 913-762-5000; FAX 913-762-4584; Ed. Ron Hosie; Pub. John G. Montgomery; adv. contact: Steve Stevens. adv.: $8.85/SAU. photos; pub. size: broadsheet; circ. evening 7,249(paid); Sun. 8,047(paid). **Wire Service(s):** AP, CNS.

KANSAS CITY

US
KANSAS CITY KANSAN. 1921. Tue.-Fri. & Sun. $.35/day newsstand; $1/Sun.; $67.35/yr. carrier; $53.05/yr. senior citizens. 901 N. Eighth St., Kansas City, KS 66101. TEL 913-371-4300; FAX 913-342-8620. **Owner(s):** Inland Industries, Inc., 105th & Santa Fe, Shawnee, KS 66215. TEL 913-492-9050; Ed. Patrick Lowry; Pub. William E. Epperheimer; adv. contact: Patrick E. Lowry. photos; bk.rev.; pub. size: broadsheet; circ. evening 14,941(paid); Sun. 17,039(paid). **Wire Service(s):** AP.

LARNED

US ISSN 0888-1189
TILLER & TOILER. 1879. Mon.-Fri. $.50 newsstand; $52.95/yr. 115 W. Fifth St., Larned, KS 67550. TEL 316-285-3111; FAX 316-285-6062. **Owner(s):** Star Communications, Inc., 115 W. Fifth St., Larned, KS 67550; Ed. Dennis Martin. adv. contact: Dennis Martin. pub. size: broadsheet; circ. evening 3,000(paid). **Wire Service(s):** AP. **Formerly:** Larned Tiller & Toiler.

DAILY NEWSPAPERS

LAWRENCE
US
JOURNAL-WORLD, THE. 1854. d. $.50/day newsstand; $1/Sun.; $129.96/yr. 609 New Hampshire St., Lawrence, KS 66044. TEL 913-843-1000; FAX 913-843-1922; E-mail: rgage@ljworld.com; URL: http://www.ljworld.com/. **Owner(s):** World Co., 609 New Hampshire St., Lawrence, KS 66044. TEL 913-843-1000; FAX 913-832-7207; Ed. Roger Verdon; Pub. Dolph C. Simons, Jr.; adv. contact: Tom Fisher. photos; bk.rev.; pub. size: broadsheet; circ. morning 17,946(paid); Sun. 18,992(paid). **Wire Service(s):** AP, NYT, LAT-WP, KR.

LEAVENWORTH
US
LEAVENWORTH TIMES. 1857. Sun.-Fri. $.50/day newsstand; $1/Sun.; $106.36/yr. 422 Seneca St., Leavenworth, KS 66048. TEL 913-682-0305; FAX 913-682-1114. **Owner(s):** American Publishing Co., 606 N. Van Buren, Marion, IL 62959. TEL 618-993-1711; Ed. Cathy Trowbridge; Pub. Tom Throne; adv. contact: Bev Schultz. photos; bk.rev.; pub. size: broadsheet; circ. evening 9,200(paid); Sun. 9,900(paid). **Wire Service(s):** AP.

LIBERAL
US   ISSN 0745-8916
LIBERAL SOUTHWEST DAILY TIMES. 1886. Sun.-Fri. $.50/day newsstand; $1/Sun.; $99/yr. 16 S. Kansas, Liberal, KS 67901. TEL 316-624-2541; FAX 316-624-0735. **Owner(s):** Liberal Newspapers, Inc., P.O. Box 889, Liberal, KS 67905-0889. TEL 316-624-2541; FAX 316-624-0735; Pub. Jeff Burkhead; adv. contact: Mitch Bettis. photos; pub. size: broadsheet; circ. evening 5,323(paid); Sun. 7,653(paid). **Wire Service(s):** AP.

LYONS
US   ISSN 1040-1504
LYONS DAILY NEWS. 1906. Mon.-Fri. $.35 newsstand; $38/yr. 210 W. Commercial, Lyons, KS 67554. TEL 316-257-2368; FAX 316-257-2369. **Owner(s):** Lyons Publishing Co., Inc., 210 W. Commercial, Lyons, KS 67554. TEL 316-257-2368; Ed. John L. Sayler; Pub. Paul E. Jones; adv. contact: Paul E. Jones. photos; pub. size: broadsheet; circ. evening 2,407(paid). **Wire Service(s):** AP.

MANHATTAN
US
MANHATTAN MERCURY. 1884. Sun.-Fri. $.35/day newsstand; $.75/Sun.; $96/yr. in cy.; $117.15/yr. out of cy. Fifth & Osage, Manhattan, KS 66502. TEL 913-776-8805; FAX 913-776-2200. **Owner(s):** Seaton Publishing Co., P.O. Box 787, Manhattan, KS 66502; Pub. Edward Seaton; adv. contact: Steve Stallwitz. pub. size: broadsheet; circ. evening 12,850(paid); Sun. 14,000(paid). **Wire Service(s):** AP, NYT, LAT-WP.

MCPHERSON
US
MCPHERSON SENTINEL. 1887. Mon.-Sat. $.50 newsstand; $8.40/mo.; $91.60/yr. 301 S. Main, McPherson, KS 67460. TEL 316-241-2422; FAX 316-241-2425. **Owner(s):** American Publishing Co., 606 N. Van Buren, Marion, IL 62959. TEL 618-993-1711; FAX 618-997-4018; Pub. Gary Mehl; adv.: $8.25/SAU. pub. size: broadsheet; circ. evening 5,700(paid). **Wire Service(s):** AP.

NEWTON
US
NEWTON KANSAN. 1872. Mon.-Sat. $.50 newsstand; $7.50/4 wks. 121 W. Sixth, Newton, KS 67114. TEL 316-283-1500; FAX 316-283-2471; E-mail: nkansan@southwind.net; URL: http://www.southwind.net/nkansan. **Owner(s):** Morris Communications, P.O. Box 936, Augusta, GA 30903. TEL 706-724-0851; Ed. Connie White; Pub. Douglas J. Anstaett; adv. contact: Dennis Garrison. photos; bk.rev.; pub. size: broadsheet; circ. evening 7,705(paid). **Wire Service(s):** AP.

NORTON
US
NORTON DAILY TELEGRAM. 1906. Mon.-Fri. $.25 newsstand; $44.27/yr. local; $52.70/yr. mailed. 215 S. Kansas, Norton, KS 67654. TEL 913-877-3361; FAX 913-877-3732. **Owner(s):** Richard D. Boyd, 215 S. Kansas, Norton, KS 67654. TEL 913-877-3361; Ed. Richard D. Boyd; Pub. Richard D. Boyd; adv. contact: Victor Randolph. photos; pub. size: broadsheet; circ. evening 2,000(paid). **Wire Service(s):** AP.

OLATHE
US   ISSN 0886-9871
OLATHE DAILY NEWS. 1960. Mon.-Sat. $.35/day newsstand; $1/Sat.; $7.31/mo. 514 S. Kansas, Olathe, KS 66061. TEL 913-764-2211; FAX 913-764-2251. **Owner(s):** Keltatim Inc., 514 S. Kansas, Olathe, KS 66061. TEL 913-764-2211; Ed. Jack Kurtz; Pub. Tim O'Donnell; adv. contact: Rick Brown. photos; pub. size: broadsheet; circ. morning 10,275(paid). **Wire Service(s):** AP.

OTTAWA
US
OTTAWA HERALD. 1896. Mon.-Sat. $.50 newsstand; $75.30/yr. local; $110.16/yr. out of area. 104 S. Cedar, Ottawa, KS 66067. TEL 913-242-4700; FAX 913-242-9420. **Owner(s):** Harris Enterprises, First National Bank Bldg., Hutchinson, KS 67501. TEL 316-694-5880; Ed. Jay Bemis; Pub. John D. Montgomery; adv. contact: Tom Love. photos; bk.rev.; pub. size: broadsheet; circ. evening 6,100(paid). **Wire Service(s):** AP.

PARSONS
US
PARSONS SUN. 1871. Mon.-Sat. $.50 newsstand; $78.30/yr. 220 S. 18th St., Parsons, KS 67357-0836. TEL 316-421-2000; FAX 316-421-2217; E-mail: annc/oparsons@hays.dailynews.net. **Owner(s):** Parsons Publishing Co., 220 S. 18th St., Parsons, KS 67357. TEL 316-421-2000; Ed. Jim Cook; Pub. Ann K. Charles; adv. contact: Carolyn Kennett. photos; pub. size: broadsheet; circ. evening 7,000(paid). **Wire Service(s):** AP, Harris.

PITTSBURG
US
PITTSBURG MORNING SUN. 1887. d. $.50/day newsstand; $1/Sun.; $98.08/yr. 701 N. Locust, Pittsburg, KS 66762. TEL 316-231-2600; FAX 316-231-0645. **Owner(s):** Morris Communications, P.O. Box 936, Augusta, GA 30903. TEL 706-724-0851; Ed. Tom Epling; Pub. Tom H. Collinson; adv.; pub. size: broadsheet; circ. morning 12,000(paid); Sun. 12,000(paid). **Wire Service(s):** AP.

PRATT
US   ISSN 1048-3675
PRATT TRIBUNE. 1917. Mon.-Fri. $.50 newsstand; $80/yr. in trade zone; $90/yr. elsewhere. 320 S. Main St., Pratt, KS 67124. TEL 316-672-5511; FAX 316-672-5514. **Owner(s):** Murphy McGinnis Media, Inc., 130 W. Superior St., Duluth, MN 55802. TEL 218-723-8000; FAX 218-723-8980; Ed. Conrad Easterday; Pub. Jim Phillips; adv. contact: Jim Phillips. pub. size: broadsheet; circ. morning 2,700(paid). **Wire Service(s):** AP.

RUSSELL
US
RUSSELL DAILY NEWS. 1947. Mon.-Sat. $.50 newsstand; $78/yr. 802 N. Maple St., Russell, KS 67665. TEL 913-483-2116; FAX 913-483-4012. **Owner(s):** Russell Publishing, Inc., P.O. Box 513, Russell, KS 67665. TEL 913-483-2116; Ed. Jim Joule; Pub. Allan D. Evans; adv. contact: Cindy Reed. pub. size: broadsheet; circ. evening 3,900(paid).

SALINA
US
SALINA JOURNAL. 1871. d. $.50/day newsstand; $1.50/Sun.; $15/mo. carrier; $16/mo. motor rte.; $16.50/mo. in state; $22/mo. out of state. 333 S. Fourth St., Salina, KS 67401. TEL 913-823-6363; FAX 913-827-6363. **Owner(s):** Harris Publications, 300 W. Second, Hutchinson, KS 67501. TEL 316-694-5700; FAX 316-662-4186; Ed. Scott Seirer; Pub. Harris Rayl; adv. contact: Jeanny Sharp. photos; pub. size: broadsheet; circ. morning 33,600(controlled & paid); Sun. 33,000(controlled & paid). **Wire Service(s):** AP.

TOPEKA

US ISSN 1067-1994
CAPITAL-JOURNAL. 1879. d. $.50/day newsstand; $1.50/Sun.; $156/yr. carrier; $53/3 mos. mailed. 616 S.E. Jefferson St., Topeka, KS 66607. TEL 913-295-1111; FAX 913-295-1216. **Owner(s):** Morris Communications, P.O. Box 936, Augusta, GA 30903. TEL 706-724-0851; Pub. John Goosen; adv. contact: Ron Burns. photos; bk.rev.; pub. size: broadsheet; circ. morning 66,000(paid); Sun. 73,000(paid). **Wire Service(s):** AP, LAT-WP.

WELLINGTON

US
WELLINGTON DAILY NEWS. 1901. Mon.-Wed. & Fri. $.50 newsstand; $54/yr. in city; $67/yr. out of city; $110/yr. out of state. 113 W. Harvey, Wellington, KS 67152-0368. TEL 316-326-3326; FAX 316-326-3290. **Owner(s):** Jack C. Mitchell, 22 Pinecrest, Wellington, KS 67152. TEL 316-326-3326; Ed. Janet Johnson; Pub. Jack C. Mitchell; adv. contact: Bill Newlland. photos; pub. size: broadsheet; circ. evening 3,800(paid). **Wire Service(s):** AP.
Formerly: Wellington Daily News Evening Paper.

WICHITA

US ISSN 1046-3127
WICHITA EAGLE. 1872. d. $.50/day newsstand; $1.50/Sun.; $3.69/wk. 825 E. Douglas, Wichita, KS 67201. TEL 316-268-6000; FAX 316-268-6627. **Owner(s):** Knight-Ridder, Inc., One Herald Plz., Miami, FL 33132. TEL 305-376-3800; FAX 305-376-3875; Ed. Rick Thimes. adv. contact: Ron Davidson. photos; bk.rev.; pub. size: broadsheet; circ. morning 93,016(paid); Sun. 170,000(paid). **Wire Service(s):** NYT, AP, KR, LAT-WP, CNS.

WINFIELD

US ISSN 0889-6747
WINFIELD DAILY COURIER. 1887. Mon.-Sat. $.50 newsstand; $60.75/yr. 201 E. Ninth St., Winfield, KS 67156. TEL 316-221-1050; FAX 316-221-1101; E-mail: courier@horizon.hit.net; URL: http://www.hit.net:80/courier. **Owner(s):** Winfield Publishing Co., Inc., 201 E. Ninth St., Winfield, KS 67156. TEL 816-647-2121; FAX 816-647-2122; Ed. Tod Megredy; Pub. F.D. Seaton; adv. contact: Lloyd Craig. pub. size: tabloid; circ. evening 6,000(paid). **Wire Service(s):** AP.

KENTUCKY

ASHLAND

US
DAILY INDEPENDENT, THE. 1896. d. $.50/day newsstand; $1.25/Sun.; $166.40/yr. carrier; $154.40/yr. mailed. 224 17th St., Ashland, KY 41101. TEL 606-329-1717; FAX 606-324-8434. **Owner(s):** Ottaway Newspapers, Inc., P.O. Box 401, Campbell Hall, NY 10916. TEL 914-294-8181; Ed. Mike Reliford; Pub. John W. Del Santo; adv.; photos; bk.rev.; pub. size: broadsheet; circ. evening 24,889(paid); Sun. 26,933(paid). **Wire Service(s):** AP, ONS, SHNA.

BOWLING GREEN

US
DAILY NEWS. 1854. Sun.-Fri. $.50/day newsstand; $1.25/Sun.; $2.30/wk. 813 College, Bowling Green, KY 42101. TEL 502-781-1700; FAX 502-781-0726; E-mail: dnews@bgn.mindspring.com; URL: http://www.bowlinggreen.ky.net/dailynews. **Owner(s):** News Publishing Co., 813 College, Bowling Green, KY 42101. TEL 502-781-1700; FAX 502-781-0726; Pub. John B. Gaines; adv. contact: Roger Jones. photos; bk.rev.; pub. size: broadsheet; circ. evening 21,479(paid); Sun. 25,780(paid). **Wire Service(s):** AP.
Formerly: Park City Daily News.

CORBIN

US
CORBIN TIMES-TRIBUNE. 1892. Mon.-Sat. $.50 newsstand; $102/yr. 201 N. Kentucky, Corbin, KY 40701. TEL 606-528-2464; FAX 606-528-9850. **Owner(s):** American Publishing Co., 606 N. Van Buren, Marion, IL 62959. TEL 618-993-1711; Ed. Cheryl Meadows; Pub. Rochelle Stidham; adv. contact: Shirley Clark. pub. size: broadsheet; circ. evening 7,500(paid). **Wire Service(s):** AP.

COVINGTON

US
KENTUCKY POST, THE. 1890. Mon.-Sat. $.35/day newsstand; $.75/Sat.; $8.95/mo. 421 Madison Ave., Covington, KY 41011. TEL 606-292-2600; FAX 606-291-2525; E-mail: kypost@fuse.net; URL: http://www.kypost.com. **Owner(s):** Scripps Howard, 312 Walnut St., 28th Fl., Cincinnati, OH 45202. TEL 513-977-3000; Ed. Robert Kraft. adv.; pub. size: broadsheet; circ. evening 38,147(paid). **Wire Service(s):** AP.
Formerly: Covington Kentucky Post.

DANVILLE

US ISSN 0889-0056
ADVOCATE-MESSENGER. 1865. Sun.-Fri. $.50/day newsstand; $1.50/Sun.; $109.20/yr. local; $133.20/yr. in state; $142/yr. out of state. 330 S. Fourth St., Danville, KY 40422. TEL 606-236-2551; FAX 606-236-9566; E-mail: advocate@amnews.com; URL: http://www.amnews.com. **Owner(s):** Schurz Communications, Inc., 223 W. Colfax, South Bend, IN 46601; Ed. John T. Davis; Pub. Mary Schurz; adv. contact: Mike Elliott. photos; bk.rev.; pub. size: broadsheet; circ. evening 13,000(paid); Sun. 13,000(paid). **Wire Service(s):** AP.

ELIZABETHTOWN

US
NEWS-ENTERPRISE. 1974. Sun.-Fri. $.50/day newsstand; $1/Sun.; $105/yr. in cy.; $150/yr. in state. 408 W. Dixie Ave., Elizabethtown, KY 42701. TEL 502-769-2312; FAX 502-769-6965; E-mail: etown@infi.net; URL: http://www.newsenterpriseonline.com. **Owner(s):** Landmark Communications, Inc., 150 W. Brambleton Ave., Norfolk, VA 23510; Ed. David Greer; Pub. Mike Anders; adv. contact: Debbie Crawford. pub. size: broadsheet; circ. morning 16,100(paid); Sun. 20,000(paid). **Wire Service(s):** AP.

FRANKFORT

US
STATE JOURNAL. Sun.-Fri. $.50/day newsstand; $1.25/Sun.; $9.25/mo. Wilkinson Blvd., Frankfort, KY 40601. TEL 502-227-4556; FAX 502-227-2831. **Owner(s):** Ann Dix Maenza & Troy Dix, P.O. Box 168, Frankfort, KY 40601. TEL 502-227-4556; Ed. Carl West; Pub. Albert Dix; adv. contact: Lloyd Lynch. pub. size: broadsheet; circ. evening 10,500(paid); Sun. 12,500(paid).

GLASGOW

US
GLASGOW DAILY TIMES. 1889. Sun.-Fri. $.50/day newsstand; $1/Sun.; $72/yr. 100 Commerce Dr., Glasgow, KY 42141. TEL 502-678-5171; FAX 502-678-5052. **Owner(s):** Stephens Group, Inc., P.O. Box 1359, Fort Smith, AR 72902. TEL 501-785-7801; Ed. Joel Wilson; Pub. William Tinsley; adv. contact: Harold Spear. photos; pub. size: broadsheet; circ. evening 10,000(paid); Sun. 10,000(paid).

HARLAN

US
HARLAN DAILY ENTERPRISE. 1901. Mon.-Sat. $.50 newsstand; $93/yr. carrier; $126/yr. mailed. 1548 S. US Hwy. 421, Harlan, KY 40831. TEL 606-573-4510; FAX 606-573-0042. **Owner(s):** American Publishing Co., 606 N. Van Buren, Marion, IL 62959. TEL 618-993-1711; Pub. James Kirby; adv. contact: Wilene Miniard. photos; pub. size: broadsheet; circ. evening 6,766(paid). **Wire Service(s):** AP.

HENDERSON

US
HENDERSON GLEANER. 1884. Tue.-Sun. $.50/day newsstand; $1.50/Sun.; $10.50/mo. in cy.; $11.50/mo. in state; $12.50/mo. out of state. 455 Klutey Park Plz., Henderson, KY 42420. TEL 502-827-2000; FAX 502-827-2765. **Owner(s):** A.H. Belo Corp., 400 S. Record, Dallas, TX 75202. TEL 214-977-6606; Ed. David Dixon; Pub. Steve Austin; adv. contact: Nancy Pippin. pub. size: broadsheet; circ. morning 11,500(paid); Sun. 14,000(paid). **Wire Service(s):** AP.

HOPKINSVILLE

US
KENTUCKY NEW ERA. 1869. Mon.-Sat. $.50 newsstand; $8/mo. home deliv.; $12/mo. mailed. 1618 E. Ninth St., Hopkinsville, KY 42240. TEL 502-886-4444. **Owner(s):** Kentucky New Era, Inc., 1618 E. Ninth St., Hopkinsville, KY 42440. TEL 502-886-4444; Ed. Mike Herndon; Pub. Robert C. Carter; adv. contact: Taylor Hayes. photos; bk.rev.; pub. size: broadsheet; circ. evening 15,134(paid). **Wire Service(s):** AP.

DAILY NEWSPAPERS

LEXINGTON
US   ISSN 0745-4260
LEXINGTON HERALD-LEADER. 1888. d. $.50/day newsstand; $1.75/Sun.; $18.85/mo. carrier. 100 Midland Ave., Lexington, KY 40508. TEL 606-231-3100; FAX 606-231-3454. **Owner(s):** Knight-Ridder, Inc., One Herald Plz., Miami, FL 33132. TEL 305-376-3800; FAX 305-376-3875; Ed. David Holwerk; Pub. Timothy M. Kelly; adv. contact: Larry Brooks. photos; pub. size: broadsheet; circ. morning 126,000(paid); Sun. 165,000(paid). **Wire Service(s):** AP, KNS, NYT.

LOUISVILLE
US
COURIER-JOURNAL, THE. 1868. d. $.50/day newsstand; $1.50/Sun.; $15/mo. carrier; $15.50/mo. motor rte. 525 W. Broadway, Louisville, KY 40202. TEL 502-582-4011; FAX 502-582-4075; E-mail: cjletter@louisvil.gannett.com; URL: http://www.courier-journal.com. **Owner(s):** Gannett Company, Inc., 1100 Wilson Blvd., Arlington, VA 22209. TEL 703-284-6000; Ed. Debbie Henley; Pub. Edward E. Manassah; adv.; pub. size: broadsheet; circ. morning 239,907(paid); Sun. 330,022(paid). **Wire Service(s):** AP, NYT, LAT-WP, DJ.

MADISONVILLE
US
MESSENGER, THE. 1917. Tue.-Sun. $.50 newsstand; $70/yr. 221 S. Main, Madisonville, KY 42431. TEL 502-821-6833; FAX 502-821-6855. **Owner(s):** Paxton Media Group, Inc., P.O. Box 2300, Paducah, KY 42002. TEL 502-443-1771; Ed. Tom Clinton; Pub. Bob Morris; adv. contact: Beth Baggerly. photos; pub. size: broadsheet; circ. evening 11,322(paid). **Wire Service(s):** AP. **Formerly:** Madisonville Messenger.

MAYFIELD
US
MAYFIELD MESSENGER. 1900. Mon.-Sat. $.50 newsstand; $5/mo. 201 N. Eighth St., Mayfield, KY 42066. TEL 502-247-5223; FAX 502-247-6336. **Owner(s):** Messenger Newspapers, Inc., P.O. Box 709, Mayfield, KY 42066. TEL 502-247-5223; Ed. Mike Turley; Pub. Eric Hoffman; adv.; pub. size: broadsheet; circ. evening 7,600(controlled & paid). **Wire Service(s):** AP.

MAYSVILLE
US
LEDGER-INDEPENDENT. 1968. Mon.-Sat. $.50 newsstand; $2.25/wk. 41-43 W. Second St., Maysville, KY 41056. TEL 606-564-9091; FAX 606-564-6893; E-mail: ponto@mau-uky.campus.mcl.net; URL: http://www.trib.com/maysville. **Owner(s):** Howard Publications, Inc., 1715 S. Beeman St., P.O. Box 570, Oceanside, CA 92079. TEL 619-433-5771; Pub. Robert Hendrickson; adv. contact: Patty Moore. pub. size: broadsheet; circ. morning 9,400(paid). **Wire Service(s):** AP.

MIDDLESBORO
US   ISSN 1041-7095
MIDDLESBORO DAILY NEWS. 1911. Mon.-Sat. $.50 newsstand; $7.75/mo. carrier; $108/yr. in state; $108/yr. out of state. 120 N. 11th St., Middlesboro, KY 40965. TEL 606-248-1010; FAX 606-248-7614. **Owner(s):** American Publishing Co., 606 N. Van Buren, Marion, IL 62959. TEL 618-993-1711; Ed. Ray Short; Pub. J.T. Hurst; adv. contact: Pat Cheek. photos; bk.rev.; pub. size: broadsheet; circ. evening 7,600(paid). **Wire Service(s):** AP.

MURRAY
US
MURRAY LEDGER & TIMES. 1879. Mon.-Sat. $.50 newsstand; $72/yr. Whitnell & Glendale, Murray, KY 42071. TEL 502-753-1916; FAX 502-753-1927. **Owner(s):** Murray Newspapers, Inc., P.O. Box 1040, Murray, KY 42071. TEL 502-753-1916; Ed. Walter Apperson; Pub. Walter Apperson; adv. contact: Mary Ann Orr. bk.rev.; pub. size: broadsheet; circ. evening 8,400(paid). **Wire Service(s):** AP.

OWENSBORO
US
OWENSBORO MESSENGER-INQUIRER. 1874. d. $.50/day newsstand; $1.50/Sun.; $140.75/yr. 1401 Frederica St., Owensboro, KY 42301. TEL 502-926-0123; FAX 502-686-7868. **Owner(s):** A.H. Belo Corp., 400 S. Record, Dallas, TX 75202. TEL 214-977-6606; Ed. Bob Ashley; Pub. Robert Mong; adv. contact: Frank Leto. photos; bk.rev.; pub. size: broadsheet; circ. morning 32,518(paid); Sun. 34,189(paid). **Wire Service(s):** AP, LAT-WP, KR.

PADUCAH
US   ISSN 1050-0030
PADUCAH SUN, THE. 1929. d. $.50/day newsstand; $1.25/Sun.; $11.40/mo. carrier; $12.25/mo. in region mailed; $15/mo. elsewhere mailed. 408 Kentucky Ave., Paducah, KY 42003. TEL 502-443-1771; FAX 502-442-7859. **Owner(s):** Paxton Media Group, Inc., P.O. Box 2300, Paducah, KY 42002. TEL 502-443-1771; FAX 502-442-8188; Ed. Jim Paxton; Pub. Fred Paxton; adv.; photos; bk.rev.; pub. size: broadsheet; circ. morning 30,570(paid); Sun. 33,042(paid). **Wire Service(s):** AP, NYT.

RICHMOND
US
RICHMOND REGISTER. 1917. d. $.50/day newsstand; $.75/Sun.; $114/yr. carrier; $108/yr. in cy. mailed; $120/yr. out of cy. 380 Big Hill Ave., Richmond, KY 40475. TEL 606-623-1669; FAX 606-623-2337. **Owner(s):** American Publishing Co., 606 N. Van Buren, Marion, IL 62959. TEL 618-993-1711; Ed. Gary Moyers; Pub. James Kerby; adv. contact: Teresa Senters. pub. size: broadsheet; circ. evening 9,300(paid); Sun. 9,300. **Wire Service(s):** AP.

SOMERSET
US   ISSN 0899-1839
COMMONWEALTH JOURNAL. 1895. Sun.-Fri. $.50/day newsstand; $1/Sun.; $83.80/yr. 110-112 E. Mount Vernon St., Somerset, KY 42501. TEL 606-678-8191; FAX 606-679-9225. **Owner(s):** Media General, Inc., 333 E. Grace St., Richmond, VA 23219. TEL 804-649-6000; FAX 804-775-8090; Ed. James T. Stratton; Pub. James T. Stratton; adv. contact: Kathy Patscheck. photos; bk.rev.; pub. size: broadsheet; circ. evening 8,300(paid); Sun. 8,300(paid). **Wire Service(s):** AP.

WINCHESTER
US
WINCHESTER SUN. 1878. Mon.-Sat. $.50 newsstand; $96/yr. 20 Wall St., Winchester, KY 40392-4300. TEL 606-744-3123; FAX 606-745-0638. **Owner(s):** Winchester Sun Co., Inc., 20 Wall St., Winchester, KY 40391. TEL 606-744-3123; Ed. William S. Blakeman; Pub. Betty Berryman; adv. contact: Ann Laurence. photos; bk.rev.; pub. size: broadsheet; circ. evening 12,500(free & paid). **Wire Service(s):** AP.

LOUISIANA

ABBEVILLE
US
ABBEVILLE MERIDIONAL. 1857. Tue.-Fri. & Sun. $.50/day newsstand; $.75/Sun.; $60.96/yr. 318 N. Main St., Abbeville, LA 70510. TEL 318-893-4223; FAX 318-898-9022. **Owner(s):** Louisiana State Newspapers, 666 Jefferson, Lafayette, LA 70501. TEL 318-233-6400; Ed. William Weathers; Pub. David Clevenger; adv.; photos; pub. size: broadsheet; circ. morning 5,200(controlled & paid); Sun. 6,000(controlled & paid). **Wire Service(s):** AP.

ALEXANDRIA
US
ALEXANDRIA DAILY TOWN TALK. 1883. d. $.50/day newsstand; $1/Sun.; $12/mo.; $144/yr. 1201 Third St., Alexandria, LA 71301. TEL 318-487-6397; FAX 318-487-6315. **Owner(s):** Central Newspapers, Inc., 135 N. Pennsylvania Ave., Indianapolis, IN 45204. TEL 317-231-9200; Ed. James R. Butler; Pub. John E. Newhouse, III; adv. contact: Bill Hertzler. photos; bk.rev.; pub. size: broadsheet; circ. morning 39,000(paid); Sun. 43,000(paid). **Wire Service(s):** AP, NYT, SHNS.

BASTROP
US
BASTROP DAILY ENTERPRISE. 1899. Mon.-Fri. $.50 newsstand; $55/yr. carrier; $60/yr. in state mailed; $81.25/yr. out of state mailed. 119 E. Hickory, Bastrop, LA 71220. TEL 318-281-4421; FAX 318-283-1699. **Owner(s):** Smith Newspapers, Inc., P.O. Box 27, Fort Payne, AL 35967. TEL 205-845-5510; Ed. Bill Wirner; Pub. Wally Gallian; adv. contact: Lynn Hilton. photos; pub. size: broadsheet; circ. evening 6,200(paid). **Wire Service(s):** AP.

BATON ROUGE

ADVOCATE, THE. 1842. d. $.50 newsstand; $1.25/Sun.; $2.76/wk. 525 Lafayette St., Baton Rouge, LA 70802. TEL 504-383-1111; FAX 504-388-0323. **Owner(s):** Capital City Press, 525 Lafayette St., Baton Rouge, LA 70802. TEL 504-383-1111; adv. contact: Mike Nola. photos; bk.rev.; pub. size: broadsheet; circ. morning 110,000(paid); Sun. 141,000(paid). **Wire Service(s):** AP, WP-LAT, KR.
Formerly: State Times/Morning Advocate.

BOGALUSA

US

BOGALUSA DAILY NEWS & SUNDAY NEWS. 1927. Sun.-Fri. $.50/day newsstand; $1/Sun.; $115/yr. in state mailed; $120/yr. out of state. 525 Ave. V, Bogalusa, LA 70427. TEL 504-732-2565; FAX 504-732-4006. **Owner(s):** Pontchartrain Newspapers, Inc., P.O. Box 820, Bogalusa, LA 70429. TEL 504-732-2565; Ed. Lou Major, Jr.; Pub. Lou Major, Sr.; adv. contact: Linda Clements. pub. size: broadsheet; circ. evening 8,000(paid); Sun. 9,000(paid). **Wire Service(s):** UPI.

CROWLEY

US

CROWLEY POST-SIGNAL. 1974. Tue.-Fri. & Sun. $.50/day newsstand; $.75/Sun.; $62.40/yr. carrier; $74.88/yr. in state mailed; $84/yr. out of state. 602 N. Parkerson Ave, Crowley, LA 70526. TEL 318-783-3450; FAX 318-788-0949. **Owner(s):** Moody Co., First National Bank Towers, Lafayette, LA 70501; Ed. Harold Gonzales; Pub. Milo A. Nickel; adv. contact: Glen Boudreaux. photos; pub. size: broadsheet; circ. evening 5,800(paid); Sun. 7,100(paid). **Wire Service(s):** AP.

DE RIDDER

US

BEAUREGARD DAILY NEWS. Tue.-Fri. & Sun. $.25/day newsstand; $.75/Sun.; $52/yr. 903 W. First St., De Ridder, LA 70634. TEL 318-462-0616; FAX 318-463-5347. **Owner(s):** Erban Wise, Sulphur, LA; Ed. Bob Houston; Pub. Erban Wise; adv. contact: Beaux Victor. pub. size: broadsheet; circ. morning 13,800(paid).
Formerly: De Ridder Beauregard Daily News.

FRANKLIN

US

FRANKLIN BANNER-TRIBUNE. 1884. Mon.-Fri. $.25 newsstand; $45.76/yr. carrier; $93.60/yr. elsewhere mailed. 115 Wilson St., Franklin, LA 70538. TEL 318-828-3706; FAX 318-828-2874. **Owner(s):** Morgan City Newspapers, Inc., Morgan City, LA; Ed. Vanesa Phitchett; Pub. Allan R. Von Werder; adv.; photos; bk.rev.; pub. size: broadsheet; circ. evening 3,750(paid). **Wire Service(s):** AP.

HAMMOND

US   ISSN 1049-3395

HAMMOND DAILY STAR. 1959. Sun.-Fri. $.50/day newsstand; $1/Sun.; $8/mo. carrier. 725 S. Morrison Blvd., Hammond, LA 70403. TEL 504-345-2333; FAX 504-542-0242. **Owner(s):** Nixon Newspapers, Inc., 33 W. Third St., P.O. Box 1149, Peru, IN 46970; Ed. Lil Mirando; Pub. David K. Frazer; adv. contact: Liz Black. pub. size: broadsheet; circ. evening 12,766(paid); Sun. 14,227(paid). **Wire Service(s):** AP.

HOUMA

US

COURIER, THE. 1878. Sun.-Fri. $.50/day newsstand; $1/Sun.; $105/yr. carrier; $120/yr. elsewhere mailed. 3030 Barrow St., Houma, LA 70360. TEL 504-879-1557; FAX 504-857-2244. **Owner(s):** New York Times Co., The, 229 W. 43rd St., New York, NY 10036. TEL 212-556-1234; Pub. Miles Forrest; adv. contact: Lisa Ferrell. photos; bk.rev.; pub. size: broadsheet; circ. evening 22,000(paid); Sun. 25,000(paid). **Wire Service(s):** AP, NYT.
Formerly: Houma Daily Courier.

JENNINGS

US

JENNINGS DAILY NEWS. 1896. Tue.-Fri. & Sun. $.50/day newsstand; $.75/Sun.; $6/mo.; $18/3 mos.; $36/6 mos.; $72/yr. 238 Market St., Jennings, LA 70546. TEL 318-824-3011; FAX 318-824-3019. **Owner(s):** Newspaper Service Co., Inc., c/o R.H. Fackelman, P.O. Drawer 12428, Panama City, FL 32401; Ed. Jack Givo; Pub. Marc Richard; adv. contact: Donna Smith. pub. size: broadsheet; circ. evening 5,800(paid); Sun. 5,800(paid). **Wire Service(s):** AP.

LAFAYETTE

US

LAFAYETTE ADVERTISER. 1894. d. $.50/day newsstand; $1/Sun.; $14/mo. home deliv.; $168/yr. 221 Jefferson St., Lafayette, LA 70501. TEL 318-289-6300; FAX 318-233-5340. **Owner(s):** Thomson Newspapers, Inc., Metro Centre, One Station Pl., 6th Fl., Stamford, CT 06902. TEL 203-425-2500; FAX 203-425-2516; Ed. Lou Zeigler; Pub. John E. Miller; adv. contact: Johnny Meche. photos; pub. size: broadsheet; circ. morning 38,000(paid); Sun. 44,000(paid).

LAKE CHARLES

US   ISSN 0739-1196

LAKE CHARLES AMERICAN PRESS. 1895. d. $.50/day newsstand; $1/Sun.; $12/mo. 4900 Hwy. 90, E., Lake Charles, LA 70615. TEL 318-433-3000; FAX 318-494-4008. **Owner(s):** Shearman Corp., 4900 Hwy. 90, E., Lake Charles, LA 70601. TEL 318-433-3000; FAX 318-494-4008; Ed. Bret Downer. adv.; photos; bk.rev.; pub. size: broadsheet; circ. morning 37,391(paid); Sun. 42,119(paid). **Wire Service(s):** AP.

LEESVILLE

US   ISSN 1069-3548

LEESVILLE DAILY LEADER. 1870. Tue.-Fri. & Sun. $.25/day newsstand; $.75/Sun.; $52/yr. carrier; $75/yr. out of parish mailed; $85/yr. out of state mailed. 206 E. Texas St., Leesville, LA 71446. TEL 318-239-3444; FAX 318-238-1152. **Owner(s):** News Leader, Inc., P.O. Box 1999, Sulphur, LA 70664. TEL 318-238-9788; Ed. Shannon Duhon; Pub. Erbon Wise; adv. contact: William Holliday. photos; bk.rev.; pub. size: broadsheet; circ. morning 9,000(paid); Sun. 13,800(paid). **Wire Service(s):** AP.

MINDEN

US

MINDEN PRESS-HERALD. 1849. Mon.-Fri. $.50 newsstand; $84/yr. carrier; $96/yr. in parish mailed; $108/yr. out of parish mailed. 203 Gleason St., Minden, LA 71055. TEL 318-377-1866; FAX 318-377-1895. **Owner(s):** Specht Newspapers, Inc., P.O. Box 1339, Minden, LA 71058. TEL 318-377-1866; adv. contact: John Emory. pub. size: broadsheet; circ. evening 5,200(paid). **Wire Service(s):** AP.

MONROE

US

NEWS-STAR, THE. d. $.50/day newsstand; $1.50/Sun.; $13.25/mo.; $159/yr. 411 N. Fourth St., Monroe, LA 71201. TEL 318-322-5161; FAX 318-362-0273. **Owner(s):** Gannett Company, Inc., 1100 Wilson Blvd., Arlington, VA 22340. TEL 703-284-6000; Ed. Reed Eckhart; Pub. Ed Major; adv.; photos; bk.rev.; pub. size: broadsheet; circ. morning 40,000(paid); Sun. 50,000(paid). **Wire Service(s):** AP.
Formerly: The New Star.

MORGAN CITY

US

DAILY REVIEW, THE. 1872. Mon.-Fri. $.50 newsstand; $52/yr. carrier; $104/yr. mailed. 1014 Front St., Morgan City, LA 70380-0948. TEL 504-384-8370; FAX 504-384-4255; E-mail: reviewApetro.net; URL: http://www.daily-review.com. **Owner(s):** Morgan City Newspapers, Inc., 1014 Front St., Morgan City, LA 70381. TEL 504-384-8370; FAX 504-384-4255; Ed. Steve Shirley; Pub. Doyle E. Shirley; adv. contact: Steve Shirley. adv.: $6.30/SAU. photos; bk.rev.; pub. size: broadsheet; circ. evening 6,242(paid). **Wire Service(s):** AP.

NATCHITOCHES

US

NATCHITOCHES TIMES. Tue.-Fri. & Sun. $.50 newsstand; $65/yr. in cy.; $130/yr. out of cy. 904 Hwy. 1, S., Natchitoches, LA 71457. TEL 318-352-3618; FAX 318-352-7842. **Owner(s):** Lovan B. & Patricia W. Thomas, P.O. Box 448, Natchitoches, LA 71458. TEL 318-352-3618; Ed. Carolyn Roy; Pub. Lovan B. Thomas; adv. contact: Charles Norman. pub. size: broadsheet; circ. 8,100(paid).

DAILY NEWSPAPERS

NEW IBERIA
US

DAILY IBERIAN. 1893. d. $.50/day newsstand; $1/Sun.; $104/yr. home deliv.; $134.52/yr. mailed. 926 E. Main St., New Iberia, LA 70560. TEL 318-365-6773; FAX 318-367-9640. **Owner(s):** Wick Communications, Inc., 333 W. Wilcox Dr., Ste. 302, Sierra Vista, AZ 85635; Ed. James Smith; Pub. Will Chapman; adv. contact: Rachel Lemoine. photos; bk.rev.; pub. size: broadsheet; circ. evening 16,500(free & paid); Sun. 17,000(paid). **Wire Service(s):** AP.

NEW ORLEANS
US ISSN 1055-3053

TIMES-PICAYUNE. 1837. d. $.50/day newsstand; $1.50/Sun.; $6.20/mo. daily; $7/mo. Sun.; $11/mo. daily & Sun. deliv. 3800 Howard Ave., New Orleans, LA 70140. TEL 504-826-3279; FAX 504-826-3007; E-mail: ldennery@aol.com; URL: http://www.neworleans.net/. **Owner(s):** Newhouse Newspapers, 140 E. 45th St., New York, NY 10017. TEL 212-697-8020; Ed. Dan Shea; Pub. Ashton Phelps, Jr.; adv. contact: Robert G. O'Neill. photos; pub. size: broadsheet; circ. morning 270,228(paid); Sun. 319,119(paid). **Wire Service(s):** AP, CDN, ANS, CNS, DJ.

OPELOUSAS
US

DAILY WORLD. 1940. Sun.-Fri. $.50/day newsstand; $.75/Sun.; $96/yr. carrier; $114/yr. in or out of state mailed. 2781 I49 Service Rd., S., Opelousas, LA 70570-1179. TEL 318-942-4971; FAX 318-948-6572. **Owner(s):** New York Times Co., The, 229 W. 43rd St., New York, NY 10036. TEL 212-556-1234; Ed. Harlan Kirgan; Pub. Chris Bond; adv. contact: Bill Brownley. pub. size: broadsheet; circ. evening 12,650(paid); Sun. 14,000(paid). **Wire Service(s):** NYT.

RUSTON
US ISSN 0891-8708

RUSTON DAILY LEADER. 1894. Sun.-Fri. $.50/day newsstand; $.75/Sun.; $6/mo. carrier; $7.25/mo. in parish mailed; $8/mo. out of parish. 208 W. Park Ave., Ruston, LA 71270. TEL 318-255-4353; FAX 318-255-4006. **Owner(s):** Ruston Newspapers, Inc., P.O. Box 520, Ruston, LA 71273. TEL 318-255-4353; Ed. Jeff Benson; Pub. Rick Hohlt; adv. contact: Jeanie McCartney. photos; pub. size: broadsheet; circ. evening 6,800(paid); Sun. 7,000(paid). **Wire Service(s):** AP.

SHREVEPORT
US

TIMES, THE. 1871. d. $.40/day newsstand; $1.50/Sun.; $13.25/mo. carrier; $21/mo. mailed. 222 Lake St., Shreveport, LA 71101. TEL 318-459-3200; FAX 318-459-3301. **Owner(s):** Gannett Company, Inc., 1100 Wilson Blvd., Arlington, VA 22234. TEL 703-284-6000; Ed. Mike Whitehead; Pub. Mike Craft; adv. contact: Carol Hahn. pub. size: broadsheet; circ. morning 79,903(paid); Sun. 99,936(paid). **Wire Service(s):** AP, SC, GNS.

SLIDELL
US

SLIDELL SENTRY-NEWS. 1965. Tue.-Sun. $.50/day newsstand; $1/Sun.; $101/yr.; $121.28/yr. mailed. 3648 Pontchartrain Dr., Slidell, LA 70458. TEL 504-643-4918; FAX 504-643-4966; E-mail: sentry@neosoft.com; URL: http://www.tamnet.com. **Owner(s):** Wick Communications, Inc., 333 W. Wilcox Dr., Ste. 302, Sierra Vista, AZ 85635; Ed. Kevin Chiri; Pub. Terry Maddox; adv.; photos; bk.rev.; pub. size: broadsheet; circ. morning 27,704(free & paid); Sun. 27,650(free & paid). **Wire Service(s):** AP.

SULPHUR
US

SOUTHWEST DAILY NEWS. 1930. d. $.25 newsstand; $36/yr. 716 E. Napoleon, Sulphur, LA 70663. TEL 318-527-7075; FAX 318-528-3044. **Owner(s):** News Leader, Inc., P.O. Box 1999, Sulphur, LA 70664-1999. TEL 318-527-7075; FAX 318-528-3044; Ed. O. Hayes; Pub. E.W. Wise; adv. contact: Susan Peveto. bk.rev.; pub. size: broadsheet; circ. morning 16,000(paid). **Wire Service(s):** AP, NEA.
Formerly: Southwest Builder News.

THIBODAUX
US

DAILY COMET. 1889. Mon.-Fri. $.50 newsstand; $79/yr. carrier. 705 W. Fifth St., Thibodaux, LA 70301. TEL 504-447-4055; FAX 504-448-7606. **Owner(s):** New York Times Co., The, 229 W. 43rd St., New York, NY 10036; Ed. Colley Charpentier; Pub. Gary Palmer; adv. contact: Alan Rini. pub. size: broadsheet; circ. evening 12,400(paid). **Wire Service(s):** AP.

MAINE

AUGUSTA
US ISSN 0745-2039

KENNEBEC JOURNAL. 1825. d. $.50/day newsstand; $1.25/Sun.; $148/yr. carrier; $165/yr. in state mailed; $254.40/yr. out of state. 274 Western Ave., Augusta, ME 04330. TEL 207-623-3811; FAX 207-623-2167. **Owner(s):** Guy Gannett Communications, One City Ctr., Portland, ME 04101. TEL 800-442-6036; Ed. Davis Rawson. adv.; photos; pub. size: broadsheet; circ. morning 17,700(paid); Sun. 15,037(paid). **Wire Service(s):** AP.

BANGOR
US ISSN 0892-8738

BANGOR DAILY NEWS. 1889. Mon.-Sat. $.60/day newsstand; $1.50/Sat.; $2.60/wk. carrier. 491 Main St., Bangor, ME 04401. TEL 207-990-8000; FAX 207-941-9476; E-mail: bangornews@aol.com. **Owner(s):** Bangor Publishing Co., 491 Main St., Bangor, ME 04401; Pub. Richard J. Warren; adv. contact: Wayne Lawton. photos; pub. size: standard; circ. morning 75,142(paid). **Wire Service(s):** AP, UPI, NYT.

BIDDEFORD
US

JOURNAL TRIBUNE. 1884. Mon.-Sat. $.75 newsstand; $130/yr. carrier; $135.20/yr. motor rte.; $175/yr. mailed. Alfred Rd., Rte. 111, Biddeford, ME 04005. TEL 207-282-1535; FAX 207-282-3138. **Owner(s):** Community Newspaper Co., 82 Devonshire St., Boston, MA 02109. TEL 508-728-6553; Ed. Robert Saunders; Pub. Dennis J. Flaherty; adv.; pub. size: broadsheet; circ. evening 14,766(paid). **Wire Service(s):** AP, SHNA, KR.

BRUNSWICK
US ISSN 0747-1300

TIMES-RECORD. 1967. Mon.-Fri. $.50/day newsstand; $.75/Fri.; $98.30/yr. junior carrier; $105.30/yr. motor rte.; $115.50/yr. in area mailed; $124.70/yr. out of area mailed. 6 Industry Rd., Brunswick, ME 04011. TEL 207-729-3311; FAX 207-729-5728. **Owner(s):** Brunswick Publishing Co., P.O. Box 10, Brunswick, ME 04011. TEL 207-729-3311; FAX 207-721-5728; Ed. Martin McKenna; Pub. Campbell B. Niven; adv. contact: John Bamford. photos; bk.rev.; pub. size: broadsheet; circ. evening 13,500(paid). **Wire Service(s):** AP, NYT.

LEWISTON
US

SUN-JOURNAL. 1893. d. $.50 newsstand; $1.50/Sun.; $164.42/yr. carrier. 104 Park St., Lewiston, ME 04243-4400. TEL 207-784-5411; FAX 207-777-3436. **Owner(s):** Lewiston Daily Sun, Inc., 104 Park St., Lewiston, ME 04240-4400. TEL 207-784-5411; Ed. Rex Rhoades; Pub. James Costello, Sr.; adv. contact: Steve Costello. photos; bk.rev.; pub. size: broadsheet; circ. morning 38,900(paid); Sun. 42,098(paid). **Wire Service(s):** AP, KR,.

PORTLAND
US

PORTLAND PRESS HERALD. 1921. d. $.60/day newsstand; $1.75/Sun.; $149.95/yr. carrier; $304/yr. in state mailed; $401/yr. out of state. 390 Congress St., Portland, ME 04101. TEL 207-791-6310; FAX 207-791-6920; E-mail: joem@portland.com; URL: http://www.portland.com/. **Owner(s):** Guy Gannett Communications, One City Ctr., Portland, ME 04101; Ed. Jeannine Guttman; Pub. Madeleine G. Corson; adv. contact: Mandy Schumaker. photos; bk.rev.; pub. size: broadsheet; circ. morning 70,000(paid); Sun. 140,000(paid). **Wire Service(s):** AP.

WATERVILLE

US

CENTRAL MAINE MORNING SENTINEL. 1904. d. $.50/day newsstand; $.75/Sat.; $1.25/Sun.; $163.80/yr. carrier; $165/yr. in state mailed; $250.40/yr. out of state mailed. 31 Front St., Waterville, ME 04901. TEL 207-873-3341; FAX 207-861-9222. **Owner(s):** Guy Gannett Communications, One City Ctr., Portland, ME 04101. TEL 800-442-6036; Ed. Timothy Allen. adv. contact: Kurt Vantosky. photos; pub. size: broadsheet; circ. morning 22,397(paid); Sun. 18,900(paid). **Wire Service(s):** AP, UPI.
Formerly: Waterville Central Maine.

MARYLAND

ANNAPOLIS

US

CAPITAL, THE. 1727. d. $.35/day newsstand, $.79/Sun.; $2.55/wk. carrier; $45.50/13 wks. mailed. 2000 Capital Dr., Annapolis, MD 21401. TEL 410-268-5000; FAX 410-280-5953. **Owner(s):** Capital-Gazette Newspapers, 2000 Capital Dr., Annapolis, MD 21401. TEL 410-268-5000; Ed. Thomas Marquardt. adv.; photos; pub. size: broadsheet; circ. evening 48,000(paid); Sun. 50,000(paid). **Wire Service(s):** AP, KR.
Formerly: Annapolis Capital.

BALTIMORE

US

BALTIMORE SUN. 1837. d. $.50/day newsstand; $1.50/Sun.; $13.67/mo. carrier; $14.75/mo. mailed. 501 N. Calvert St., Baltimore, MD 21278. TEL 410-332-6000; FAX 410-752-6049. **Owner(s):** Times-Mirror Co., Times-Mirror Sq., Los Angeles, CA 90053. TEL 310-972-7000; Ed. Bill Marimow; Pub. Mary E. Junck; adv.; photos; bk.rev.; pub. size: broadsheet; circ. morning 337,292(paid); Sun. 488,562(paid). **Wire Service(s):** AP, RN, KNT, NYT, DJ, LAT-WP.

CAMBRIDGE

US

DAILY BANNER. 1897. Mon.-Fri. $.35 newsstand; $78/yr. carrier; $95/yr. mailed. 1000 Goodwill Rd., Cambridge, MD 21613. TEL 410-228-3131; FAX 410-228-6547; E-mail: dafb@aol.com. **Owner(s):** Independent Newspapers, Inc., P.O. Box 7001, Dover, DE 19903. TEL 302-674-3600; Ed. Debra Bierbaum; Pub. Joe Smyth; adv. contact: Jane Bird. photos; bk.rev.; pub. size: broadsheet; circ. evening 6,705(paid). **Wire Service(s):** LAT-WP.

CUMBERLAND

US

CUMBERLAND TIMES-NEWS. 1869. d. $.50/day newsstand; $1.25/Sun.; $2.75/wk. home deliv. 19 Baltimore St., Cumberland, MD 21502. TEL 301-722-4600; FAX 301-722-4870; E-mail: lwhite@miworld.net; URL: http://www.times-news.com. **Owner(s):** Thomson Newspapers, Inc., Metro Centre, One Station Plz., 6th Fl., Stamford, CT 06902. TEL 203-425-2500; Ed. Lance White; Pub. Donald F. Miller; adv. contact: Stephen Stouffer. photos; bk.rev.; pub. size: broadsheet; circ. morning 31,800(paid); Sun. 33,923(paid). **Wire Service(s):** AP.

EASTON

US   ISSN 1065-2345

STAR-DEMOCRAT, THE. 1799. Sun.-Fri. $.50/day newsstand; $1.25/Sun.; $92.40/yr. in cy.; $96.60/yr. out of cy.; $136.50/yr. out of state. 29088 Airpark Dr., Easton, MD 21601-0600. TEL 410-822-1500; FAX 410-820-6519; E-mail: mail@stardem.com. **Owner(s):** Whitney-Conn, P.O. Box 600, Easton, MD 21601-0600. TEL 410-822-1500; Ed. Barbara Sauers; Pub. Larry Effingham; adv.; photos; bk.rev.; pub. size: broadsheet; circ. morning 17,500(paid); Sun. 18,000(paid). **Wire Service(s):** AP.

ELKTON

US   ISSN 1046-2058

CECIL WHIG. 1841. Mon.-Fri. $.40 newsstand; $68.25/yr. carrier. 601 Bridge St., Elkton, MD 21921. TEL 410-398-3311; FAX 410-398-4044. **Owner(s):** Chesapeake Publishing Corp., Airport Industrial Park, Easton, MD 21601. TEL 410-822-1500; Ed. Terry Peddicord; Pub. Tom Bradlee; adv. contact: Tina Winmill. pub. size: broadsheet; circ. morning 17,000(paid). **Wire Service(s):** AP.

FREDERICK

US

FREDERICK POST, THE. 1910. Mon.-Sat. $.50/newsstand; $94.45/yr. home delivery. 200 E. Patrick St., Frederick, MD 21701-5632. TEL 301-662-1177; FAX 301-662-1615. **Owner(s):** Great Southern Printing & Mfg. Co., 200 E. Patrick St., Frederick, MD 21701. TEL 301-662-1177; Ed. Mike Powell; Pub. George B. Delaplaine; adv. contact: Jim Enright. pub. size: broadsheet; circ. morning 34,000(paid). **Wire Service(s):** AP.

US

NEWS, THE. 1883. Mon.-Sat. $.50 newsstand; $94.45/yr. home deliv. 200 E. Patrick St., Frederick, MD 21701-5632. TEL 301-662-1177; FAX 301-662-8299. **Owner(s):** Great Southern Printing & Mfg., 200 E. Patrick St., Frederick, MD 21701-5632. TEL 301-662-1177; FAX 301-662-1615; Ed. Michael Powell; Pub. George Delaplaine; adv. contact: Jim Enright. pub. size: broadsheet; circ. evening 15,425(paid). **Wire Service(s):** AP.

HAGERSTOWN

US

DAILY MAIL, THE. d. $.50/day newsstand; $1.25/Sun.; $10.50/mo. carrier; $11.29/mo. motor rte. 100 Summit Ave., Hagerstown, MD 21740. TEL 301-833-5131; FAX 301-714-0245. **Owner(s):** Schurz Communications, Inc., 225 W. Colfax Ave., South Bend, IN 46626. TEL 219-233-6161; Ed. Linda Duffield; Pub. John League; adv.; photos; pub. size: broadsheet; circ. morning 38,022; evening 18,000(paid). **Wire Service(s):** AP, UPI.

US

HERALD-MAIL, THE. 1828. d. $.50/day newsstand; $1.25/Sun.; $10.50/mo. carrier; $11.29/mo. motor rte. 100 Summit Ave., Hagerstown, MD 21740. TEL 301-733-5131; FAX 301-714-0245; E-mail: news@herald-mail.com; URL: http://www.herald-mail.com. **Owner(s):** Schurz Communications, Inc., 225 W. Colfax Ave., South Bend, IN 46626. TEL 219-233-6161; Ed. Linda Duffield; Pub. John League; adv.; photos; bk.rev.; pub. size: broadsheet; circ. morning 38,022(paid); Sun. 41,000(paid). **Wire Service(s):** AP, KR.
Formerly: The Herald.

LANHAM

US

PRINCE GEORGES JOURNAL. 1975. d. $.25/newsstand; $65/yr. 9410 Annapolis Rd., Lanham, MD 20706. TEL 301-459-3131; FAX 301-731-8363. **Owner(s):** Journal Newspapers, Inc., 2720 Prosperity Ave., Fairfax, VA 22034-1000. TEL 703-560-4000; Ed. Lon Slepicka; Pub. Ryan Phillips; adv.; photos; pub. size: broadsheet; circ. morning 32,253(paid). **Wire Service(s):** AP.

ROCKVILLE

US   ISSN 0162-2080

MONTGOMERY JOURNAL, THE. 1973. d. $.25/day newsstand; $21/3 mos. carrier; $39/6 mos.; $72/yr.; $62/yr senior citizens & military. One Research Ct., Rockville, MD 20850. TEL 301-670-1400; FAX 301-670-1421. **Owner(s):** Journal Newspapers, Inc., 2720 Prosperity Ave., Fairfax, VA 22034. TEL 703-560-4000; Ed. Julie Rasicot; Pub. Ryan E. Phillips; adv. contact: Kenneth Courter. photos; pub. size: broadsheet; circ. morning 29,378(paid). **Wire Service(s):** AP.

SALISBURY

US

DAILY TIMES. 1886. d. $.50/day newsstand; $1.25/Sun.; $2.90/wk. carrier; $150.70/yr. P.O. Box 1937, Salisbury, MD 21802-1937. TEL 410-749-7171; FAX 410-543-8736; E-mail: toadvine@shore.intercom.net; URL: http://www.intercom.net/dailytimes. **Owner(s):** Thomson Newspapers, Inc., 65 Queen St., W., Toronto, ON M5H 2M8, Canada; Ed. Gary Groffman; Pub. Keith Blevins; adv. contact: Meredith White. pub. size: broadsheet; circ. morning 28,000(paid); Sun. 34,215(paid). **Wire Service(s):** AP.

WESTMINSTER

US

CARROLL COUNTY SUN. 1984. Sun.-Fri. $.50/day newsstand; $1.50/Sun.; $12.95/mo. 15 E. Main St., Winchester Exchange, Westminster, MD 21157. TEL 410-751-7900; FAX 410-751-7916. **Owner(s):** Times-Mirror Co., Times-Mirror Sq., 220 W. First St., Los Angeles, CA 90053. TEL 213-237-3700; pub. size: broadsheet; circ. morning 5,000(paid); evening 7,000(paid); Sun. 22,740(paid). **Wire Service(s):** AP, Sun, LAT-WP, RN, NYT.

DAILY NEWSPAPERS

CARROLL COUNTY TIMES. US ISSN 0746-7494. 1911. d. $.50/day newsstand; $1/Sun.; $105/yr. 201 Railroad Ave., Westminster, MD 21157. TEL 410-848-4400; FAX 410-857-8749; E-mail: carolcyt@cct.infi.net; URL: http://www.infi.net/carrollcounty. **Owner(s):** Landmark Community Newspapers, Inc., P.O. Box 549, Shelbyville, KY 40065. TEL 502-633-4334; Ed. David Ammenheuser. adv. contact: Charles Baker. photos; bk.rev.; pub. size: broadsheet; circ. morning 23,400(paid); Sun. 23,400(paid). **Wire Service(s):** AP, SHNA, GNS.

MASSACHUSETTS

ATHOL

ATHOL DAILY NEWS. US. 1934. Mon.-Sat. $.40 newsstand; $2.10/wk. carrier; $93/yr. office paid; $144/yr. mailed. 225 Exchange St., Athol, MA 01331. TEL 508-249-3535; FAX 508-249-9630. **Owner(s):** Athol Press, Inc., 225 Exchange St., Athol, MA 01331. TEL 508-249-3535; Ed. Cynthia Jack; Pub. Richard J. Chase, Jr.; adv. contact: Dan Mahoney. photos; bk.rev.; pub. size: broadsheet; circ. evening 6,000(paid). **Wire Service(s):** AP.

ATTLEBORO

SUN CHRONICLE. US ISSN 1053-7805. 1973. d. $.50/day newsstand; $1.50/Sun.; $3.50/wk. carrier; $17/mo. mailed. 34 S. Main, Attleboro, MA 02703. TEL 508-222-7000; FAX 508-226-5851. **Owner(s):** United Communications Corp., 715 58th St., Kenosha, WI 53410. TEL 414-657-1000; Ed. Ned Bristol; Pub. Paul Rixon; adv. contact: Paul Morrissey. pub. size: broadsheet; circ. evening 25,000(paid); Sun. 25,000(paid). **Wire Service(s):** AP.

BEVERLY

SALEM EVENING NEWS. US. 1893. Mon.-Sat. $.50 day newsstand; $2.20/wk. carrier; $14.75/mo. mailed. 32 Dunham Rd., Beverly, MA 01915. TEL 508-922-1234; FAX 508-922-4330. **Owner(s):** Ottaway Newspapers, Inc., P.O. Box 401, Campbell Hall, NY 10916. TEL 914-294-8181; Ed. David Marcus; Pub. John Kinney; pub. size: broadsheet; circ. evening 36,474(paid). **Wire Service(s):** AP, ONS.
Formerly: Beverly Times.

BOSTON

BOSTON GLOBE. US ISSN 0743-1791. 1872. d. $.50/day newsstand; $1.50/Sun.; $4.50/wk. in city; $27/mo. in state; $35.50/mo. elsewhere. 135 Morrissey Blvd., Boston, MA 02107. TEL 617-929-2000; FAX 617-929-3192. **Owner(s):** New York Times Co., The, 229 W. 43rd St., New York, NY 10036. TEL 212-556-1234; Ed. Gregory Moore; Pub. Benjamin B. Taylor; adv. contact: Robert Manning. pub. size: broadsheet; circ. morning 486,403(paid); Sun. 777,902(paid). **Wire Service(s):** AP, UPI, LAT-WP, KNT, RN.

BOSTON HERALD. US ISSN 0738-5854. 1982. d. $.50/day newsstand; $1.50/Sun.; $3.30/wk. One Herald Sq., Boston, MA 02106-2096. TEL 617-426-3000; FAX 617-542-1315. **Owner(s):** Patrick J. Purcell, One Herald Sq., Boston, MA 02106-2096. TEL 617-426-3000; Ed. Kevin Covey; Pub. Patrick J. Purcell; adv. contact: Sean Butler. photos; bk.rev.; pub. size: tabloid; circ. morning 320,000(paid); Sun. 227,040(paid). **Wire Service(s):** AP, RN, SHNA, GNS, DJ, LT, NWS, LAT-WP, CNS, CN.

BROCKTON

ENTERPRISE, THE. US ISSN 0279-4683. 1880. d. $.50/day newsstand; $1.25/Sun.; $3.05/wk. carrier. 60 Main St., Brockton, MA 02401. TEL 508-586-6200; FAX 508-586-6506. **Owner(s):** Newspaper Media Corp., 60 Main St., P.O. Box 1450, Brockton, MA 02401. TEL 508-586-6200; Pub. James F. Plugh; bk.rev.; pub. size: broadsheet; circ. evening 50,000(paid); Sun. 62,000(paid). **Wire Service(s):** AP, LAT-WP, SHNA.

DEDHAM

DAILY TRANSCRIPT. US ISSN 1068-1914. 1973. Mon.-Fri. $.50 day newsstand; $91/yr. carrier; $100/yr. mailed. 254 Second Ave., Dedham, MA 02194. TEL 617-433-7800; FAX 617-326-9675. **Owner(s):** Fidelity Investments, 82 Devonshire St., Boston, MA 02019. TEL 617-728-6488; Ed. Joseph Gibbs; Pub. Asa Cole; adv.; pub. size: standard; circ. evening 8,000(paid). **Wire Service(s):** AP.

FALL RIVER

HERALD NEWS, THE. US. 1872. d. $.50/day newsstand, $1.75/Sun.; $3.70/wk. $192.40/yr. carrier; $286/yr. mailed. 207 Pocasset St., Fall River, MA 02722. TEL 508-676-8211; FAX 508-676-2566. **Owner(s):** Northeast Publishing, Inc., 207 Pocasset St., Fall River, MA 02722. TEL 508-676-8211; Ed. Paul Palange; Pub. Tracy R. Greene; adv.; photos; pub. size: broadsheet; circ. evening 33,767(paid); Sun. 37,084(paid). **Wire Service(s):** AP.
Formerly: Fall River Herald News.

FITCHBURG

SENTINEL & ENTERPRISE. US ISSN 1049-1155. 1838. d. $.50/day newsstand; $.75/Sun.; $2.75/wk. 808 Main St., Fitchburg, MA 01420. TEL 508-343-6911; FAX 508-342-1158. **Owner(s):** Media News Group, 4888 Loop Central Dr., Ste. 525, Houston, TX 77081. TEL 713-295-3800; Ed. Michael Cleveland; Pub. William A. White; adv. contact: Janet Banville. photos; bk.rev.; pub. size: broadsheet; circ. evening 20,000(paid); Sun. 21,000(paid). **Wire Service(s):** AP.

FRAMINGHAM

MIDDLESEX NEWS. US. 1897. d. $.50/day newsstand; $1.50/Sun.; $171.60/yr. carrier; $241.80/yr. mailed. 33 New York Ave., Framingham, MA 01701. TEL 508-626-3800; FAX 508-626-4400. **Owner(s):** Fidelity Investments, 82 Devonshire St., Boston, MA 02019. TEL 617-728-6488; Pub. Kirk Davis; adv. contact: Shawn Burke. pub. size: broadsheet; circ. morning 2,000(paid); evening 35,500(paid); Sun. 45,174(paid). **Wire Service(s):** AP, RN.

NEWS-TRIBUNE. US. 1882. Mon.-Fri. $.50 day newsstand; $2/wk. home deliv.; $110/yr. mailed. 33 New York Ave., Framingham, MA 01701. TEL 617-398-8001; FAX 617-398-8010. **Owner(s):** Community Newspaper Co., 254 Second Ave., Needham, MA 02194. TEL 617-433-7800; Ed. Ellen Ishkanian. adv. contact: Mark Oliveri. pub. size: tabloid; circ. evening 8,831(paid). **Wire Service(s):** AP.

GARDNER

GARDNER NEWS. US ISSN 0740-0837. 1869. Mon.-Sat. $.50/newsstand; $128.40/yr. carrier & motor rte.; $168/yr. mailed. 309 Central St., Gardner, MA 01440. TEL 508-632-8000; FAX 508-630-2231. **Owner(s):** Gardner News, Inc., The, 309 Central St., Gardner, MA 01440. TEL 508-632-8000; Ed. Scott Campbell; Pub. Alberta Bell; adv. contact: Donna Watson. photos; bk.rev.; pub. size: broadsheet; circ. evening 8,000(paid). **Wire Service(s):** AP.

GLOUCESTER

GLOUCESTER DAILY TIMES. US. 1856. Mon.-Sat. $.50 newsstand; $165/yr. Whittemore St., Gloucester, MA 01930. TEL 508-283-7000; FAX 508-281-5748. **Owner(s):** Essex County Newspapers, Inc., Whittemore St., Gloucester, MA 01930. TEL 508-283-7000; Ed. Meredith Fine; Pub. John Kinney; adv.; pub. size: broadsheet; circ. evening 14,000(paid). **Wire Service(s):** AP, ONS.

GREENFIELD

RECORDER, THE. US. 1792. Mon.-Sat. $.50/day newsstand; $2.10/wk. carrier; $12/mo. mailed. 14 Hope St., Greenfield, MA 01301. TEL 413-772-0261; FAX 413-774-5020. **Owner(s):** Newspapers of New England, Inc., P.O. Box 273, Greenfield, MA 01302. TEL 413-772-0261; Ed. Tim Blagg; Pub. Kay Berenson; adv. contact: Rich Fahey. pub. size: broadsheet; circ. morning 15,169(paid); evening 15,300(paid). **Wire Service(s):** AP, LAT-WP.

HAVERHILL

HAVERHILL GAZETTE. US. 1821. Mon.-Sat. $.35 newsstand; $2.40/wk. carrier; $12/mo. mailed. W. Lowell Ave., Haverhill, MA 01832. TEL 508-374-0321; FAX 508-374-9631; E-mail: hgazette@aol.com; URL: http://www.hgazette.com. **Owner(s):** Pulitzer Publishing Co., 900 N. Tucker Blvd., St. Louis, MO 63101. TEL 313-340-8000; Ed. Robert Gates. adv.; pub. size: broadsheet; circ. evening 10,357(paid). **Wire Service(s):** UPI, AP.

HYANNIS

CAPE COD TIMES. US ISSN 0747-1467. 1936. d. $.50/day newsstand; $1.75/Sun.; $182/yr. 319 Main St., Hyannis, MA 02601. TEL 508-775-1200; FAX 508-775-7337. **Owner(s):** Ottaway Newspapers, Inc., P.O. Box 401, Campbell Hall, NY 10916. TEL 914-294-8181; Ed. Alicia Blaisdell-Bannon; Pub. John Wilcox; adv.; photos; bk.rev.; pub. size: standard; circ. morning 44,000(paid); Sun. 55,000(paid). **Wire Service(s):** AP, NYT, ONS, WP.

LOWELL

US

LOWELL SUN. 1878. d. $.50/day newsstand, $1.50/Sun.; $3.50/wk. carrier. 15 Kearney Sq., Lowell, MA 01852. TEL 508-458-7100; FAX 508-970-4600. **Owner(s):** Lowell Sun Publishing Co., 15 Kearney Sq., Lowell, MA 01852. TEL 508-458-7100; FAX 508-970-4700; Ed. Malcolm Gibson; Pub. John H. Costello, Jr.; adv.: $23.80/SAU. photos; bk.rev.; pub. size: broadsheet; circ. evening 52,673(paid); Sun: 56,033(paid). **Wire Service(s):** AP, NYT, CHR, SHNA, LAT-WP, Cox, CNS, NEA.

LYNN

US   ISSN 8750-8249

DAILY EVENING ITEM. 1877. Mon.-Sat. $.50 day newsstand; $120/yr. home deliv. 38 Exchange St., Lynn, MA 01901. TEL 617-593-7700; FAX 617-595-0035; E-mail: lynnitem@shore.net. **Owner(s):** Peter Gamage, P.O. Box 951, Lynn, MA 01903. TEL 617-593-7700; FAX 617-595-0035; Ed. Allan T. Kort; Pub. Brian C. Thayer; adv. contact: Kevin J. Kelly. photos; bk.rev.; pub. size: broadsheet; circ. evening 21,548(paid). **Wire Service(s):** AP, NEA, SHNA, CNS, United Media.

MALDEN

US

MALDEN EVENING NEWS. Mon.-Fri. $.35 newsstand; $1.85/wk. 277 Commercial St., Malden, MA 02148. TEL 617-321-8000; FAX 617-321-8008. **Owner(s):** Eastern Middlesex Press Publications, Inc., 277 Commercial St., Malden, MA 02148; Ed. Stephen Freker; Pub. Daniel Horgan; adv.; pub. size: broadsheet; circ. evening 14,000. **Wire Service(s):** UPI.

US

MEDFORD DAILY MERCURY. 1908. Mon.-Fri. $.35 newsstand; $1.85/wk. carrier; $200/yr. mailed. 277 Commercial St., Malden, MA 02148. TEL 617-321-8000; FAX 617-321-8008; E-mail: newsmerc@user1.channel1.com. **Owner(s):** Eastern Middlesex Press Publications, Inc., 277 Commercial St., Malden, MA 02148; Ed. Stephan Freker; Pub. Daniel Horganb; adv.; pub. size: broadsheet; circ. evening 14,000(paid). **Wire Service(s):** UPI.
Formerly: Daily News-Mercury, The.

MILFORD

US

MILFORD DAILY NEWS. 1887. d. $.50 newsstand; $140.40/yr. home deliv.; $175/yr. mailed. 159 S. Main St., Milford, MA 01757. TEL 508-473-1111; FAX 508-478-8769. **Owner(s):** Community Newspaper Co., 82 Devinshire St., Boston, MA 02109. TEL 508-728-6553; Ed. Nicholas·J. Tosches; Pub. Thomas C. Sawyer, Sr.; adv. contact: Richard Rae. pub. size: broadsheet; circ. evening 15,000(paid). Wire Service(s): AP.

NEW BEDFORD

US   ISSN 0745-3574

STANDARD-TIMES, THE. 1850. d. $.50/day newsstand; $1.65/Sun.; $202/yr. mail. 25 Elm St., New Bedford, MA 02740. TEL 508-997-7411; FAX 508-997-7491; E-mail: newsroom@s-t.com; URL: http://www.s-t.com/. **Owner(s):** Ottoway Newspapers, Inc., P.O. Box 401, Campbell Hall, NY 10916. TEL 914-294-8181; Ed. Dave Humphrey; Pub. William T. Kennedy; adv. contact: Coralia Merritt. photos; bk.rev.; pub. size: broadsheet; circ. evening 43,448(paid); Sun. 48,992(paid). **Wire Service(s):** AP, DJ, ONS, NYT.
Formerly: New Bedford Standard-Times.

NEWBURYPORT

US

DAILY NEWS OF NEWBURYPORT, THE. 1793. Mon.-Sat. $.50 newsstand; $9/mo. carrier; $14.75/mo. mailed. 23 Liberty St., Newburyport, MA 01950. TEL 508-462-6666; FAX 508-465-8505. **Owner(s):** Ottaway Newspapers, Inc., P.O. Box 401, Campbell Hall, NY 10916. TEL 914-294-8181; Ed. Calhoun Kleen; Pub. John Kinney; adv. contact: Mike Eramo. pub. size: broadsheet; circ. evening 14,000(paid). **Wire Service(s):** UPI, ONS.
Formerly: Newburyport Daily News.

NORTH ADAMS

US

TRANSCRIPT, THE. 1896. Mon.-Sat. $.50 newsstand; $116.40/yr. carrier. American Legion Dr., North Adams, MA 01247. TEL 413-663-3741; FAX 413-662-2792. **Owner(s):** New England Newspapers, Inc., 23 Exchange St., Pawtucket, RI 02860. TEL 401-722-4000; Ed. David Nahan; Pub. David Nahan; adv. contact: Sharon Oakes. pub. size: broadsheet; circ. morning 8,500(paid). **Wire Service(s):** AP.

NORTHAMPTON

US   ISSN 0739-3504

DAILY HAMPSHIRE GAZETTE. 1786. Mon.-Sat. $.50 newsstand; $2.70/wk.; $128.50/yr. 115 Conz St., Northampton, MA 01060. TEL 413-584-5000; FAX 413-585-5222; E-mail: gazette@crocker.com. **Owner(s):** H.S. Gere & Sons, Inc., 115 Conz St., Northampton, MA 01060. TEL 413-584-5000; Ed. Lou Groccia; Pub. Peter L. DeRose; adv. contact: John Ebbets. pub. size: broadsheet; circ. evening 23,000(paid). Wire Service(s): AP, CSM, LAT-WP.

NORTH ANDOVER

US

EAGLE TRIBUNE, THE. 1868. d. $.50/day newsstand, $1.50/weekend; $3.50/wk. carrier; $182/yr. carrier; $250/yr. mailed. 100 Turnpike St., North Andover, MA 01845. TEL 508-685-1000; FAX 508-687-6045; E-mail: dwarner@eagletribune.com. **Owner(s):** Eagle Tribune Publishing Co., 100 Turnpike St., North Andover, MA 01845. TEL 508-685-1000; Ed. Dan J. Warner, Sr.; Pub. Irving E. Rogers, Jr.; adv. contact: V.S. Cottone. photos; pub. size: broadsheet; circ. evening 55,754(paid). **Wire Service(s):** AP, SHNA.

PITTSFIELD

US   ISSN 0895-8793

BERKSHIRE EAGLE. 1789. d. $.50/day newsstand; $1.50/Sun.; $150.60/yr. carrier; $219.60/yr. mailed. 75 S. Church St., Pittsfield, MA 01201. TEL 413-447-7311; FAX 413-499-3419; E-mail: eagle@berkshire.net. **Owner(s):** New England Newspapers, Inc., 23 Exchange St., Pawtucket, RI 02860. TEL 401-722-4000; Ed. David Scribner; Pub. Martin Longeveld; adv. contact: John Gallacher. photos; pub. size: broadsheet; circ. morning 30,500(paid); Sun. 34,000(paid). **Wire Service(s):** AP, NYT.

QUINCY

US   ISSN 0889-2253

PATRIOT LEDGER. 1837. Mon.-Sat. $.75/day newsstand; $1/Sat.; $1.50/Sat. deliv.; $3/wk. deliv.; $6/wk mailed in US. 400 Crown Colony Dr., Quincy, MA 02169. TEL 617-786-7000; FAX 617-786-7025. **Owner(s):** George W. Prescott Publishing Co., Inc., 400 Crown Colony Dr., Quincy, MA 02169. TEL 617-786-7000; Ed. Terry Ryan; Pub. K. Prescott Low; adv.; pub. size: broadsheet; circ. evening 87,374(paid). **Wire Service(s):** AP, NYT, CSM.

READING

US

DAILY TIMES & CHRONICLE. Mon.-Fri. $.50 newsstand; $152.75/yr. in cy.; $178.75/yr. out of cy. 531 Main St., Reading, MA 01867. TEL 617-944-2200; FAX 617-942-0884. **Owner(s):** Haggerty Family, One Arrow Dr., Woburn, MA 01801. TEL 617-933-3700; Pub. Peter Haggerty; adv. contact: Judy McCoy. pub. size: broadsheet; circ. morning 41,774(paid).
Formerly: Reading Times & Chronicle.

SOUTHBRIDGE

US

NEWS, THE. 1923. Mon.-Fri. $.45 newsstand; $80/yr. carrier; $120/yr. mailed; $156/yr. out of cy. 25 Elm St., Southbridge, MA 01550. TEL 508-764-4325; FAX 508-764-6743. **Owner(s):** Stonebridge Press, Inc., 25 Elm St., Southbridge, MA 01501. TEL 508-764-4325; Ed. Joe Capillo; Pub. Loren F. Ghiglione; adv.; photos; pub. size: broadsheet; circ. evening 5,300(paid). **Wire Service(s):** AP.

SPRINGFIELD

US   ISSN 0894-2765

UNION-NEWS. d. $.50/day newsstand; $1.50/Sun.; $156/yr. daily; $78/yr. Sun. 1860 Main St., Springfield, MA 01101. TEL 413-788-1000; FAX 413-788-1301. **Owner(s):** Republican Co., 1860 Main St., Springfield, MA 01103. TEL 413-788-1000; Pub. David Starr; adv. contact: Dwight Brouillard. pub. size: standard; circ. morning 115,000(paid); Sun. 160,000(paid). **Wire Service(s):** AP, UPI.

TAUNTON

US

TAUNTON DAILY GAZETTE. 1848. Mon.-Sat. $.50 newsstand; $2.55/wk. 5 Cohannet, Taunton, MA 02780. TEL 508-880-9000; FAX 508-880-9049. **Owner(s):** Journal Register Co., 50 W. State St., Trenton, NJ 08608. TEL 609-396-2200; Ed. Eva T. Gaffney; Pub. Tracy Greene; adv. contact: Margaret G. Vieira. bk.rev.; pub. size: broadsheet; circ. evening 15,570(paid). Wire Service(s): AP.

DAILY NEWSPAPERS

WAKEFIELD
US

WAKEFIELD ITEM. 1894. Mon.-Fri. $.35 newsstand; $11.50/mo. 26 Albion St., Wakefield, MA 01880. TEL 617-245-0080; FAX 617-246-0061. **Owner(s):** Wakefield Item Co., Inc., 26 Albion St., Wakefield, MA 01880. TEL 617-245-0080; Ed. Peter Rossi; Pub. Robert P. Dolbeare; adv. contact: Maryann Atherton. pub. size: broadsheet; circ. evening 5,100(paid). **Wire Service(s):** AP.

WESTFIELD
US

WESTFIELD EVENING NEWS. 1932. Mon.-Sat. $.50 newsstand; $125/yr. 62-64 School St., Westfield, MA 01085. TEL 413-562-4181; FAX 413-562-4185. **Owner(s):** Westfield News Publishing Co., P.O. Box 930, Westfield, MA 01086-0930. TEL 413-562-4181; Ed. Hope Murray; Pub. E. Carol Mazza; adv.; photos; pub. size: broadsheet; circ. evening 5,500(paid). **Wire Service(s):** UPI.

WOBURN
US

DAILY TIMES CHRONICLE. 1901. Mon.-Fri. $.50 newsstand; $2.25/wk. One Arrow Dr., Woburn, MA 01801. TEL 617-933-3700; FAX 617-932-3321. **Owner(s):** Woburn Daily Times, Inc., One Arrow Dr., Woburn, MA 01801. TEL 617-933-3700; FAX 617-932-3321; Ed. James Haggerty, III; Pub. Peter Haggerty; adv. contact: Thomas R. Kirk. photos; pub. size: broadsheet; circ. evening 14,000(free & paid). **Wire Service(s):** AP.

WORCESTER
US   ISSN 1050-4184

TELEGRAM & GAZETTE. 1989. d. $.50/day newsstand; $1.50/Sun.; $3.10/wk. P.O. Box 15012, Worcester, MA 01615-0012. TEL 508-793-9100; FAX 508-793-9281; E-mail: people@telegram.infi.net; URL: http://www.telegram.com. **Owner(s):** Chronicle Publishing Co., 901 Mission St., San Francisco, CA 94103. TEL 415-777-1111; Ed. Harry T. Whitin; Pub. Bruce S. Bennett; adv.; photos; pub. size: broadsheet; circ. morning 115,129(paid); Sun. 140,000(paid). **Wire Service(s):** AP, NYT.

MICHIGAN

ADRIAN
US

DAILY TELEGRAPH. 1892. d. $.50/day newsstand; $1.25/Sun.; $156/yr. motor rte.; $165/yr. mailed. 133 N. Winter St., Adrian, MI 49221. TEL 517-265-5111; FAX 517-263-4152. **Owner(s):** Independent Media Group, 321 Frenette, Chippewa Falls, WI 54729. TEL 715-723-5515; Ed. Robert Jodon; Pub. Steven Staloch; adv. contact: M. Mickelwright. photos; pub. size: broadsheet; circ. evening 18,000(paid). **Wire Service(s):** AP.
    Formerly: Adrian Daily Telegram.

ALBION
US   ISSN 8750-9008

ALBION RECORDER. 1908. Mon.-Sat. $.50 newsstand; $8.50/mo. in area; $9.50/mo. out of area. 111 W. Center St., Albion, MI 49224. TEL 517-629-3984; FAX 517-629-5790. **Owner(s):** Calhoun Communications, 111 W. Center St., Albion, MI 49224. TEL 517-629-3984; Ed. Stacy Henson; Pub. Richard Milliman, II; adv.; photos; pub. size: broadsheet; circ. morning 19,400(paid). **Wire Service(s):** AP.

ALPENA
US

ALPENA NEWS. 1899. Mon.-Sat. $.35/day newsstand; $.75/Sat.; $101.40/yr. in cy.; $160/yr. out of area mailed. 130 Park Pl., Alpena, MI 49707. TEL 517-354-3111; FAX 517-354-2096; E-mail: alpenanews@oweb.com; URL: http://www.oweb.com/upnorth/. **Owner(s):** Ogden Newspapers, Inc., 1500 Main St., Wheeling, WV 26003. TEL 304-233-0100; FAX 304-233-0327; Ed. William B. Speer, Jr.; Pub. William B. Speer, Jr.; adv. contact: John Jackowiak. pub. size: broadsheet; circ. evening 13,000(paid). **Wire Service(s):** AP.

ANN ARBOR
US

ANN ARBOR NEWS. 1835. d. $.35/day newsstand; $1.25/Sun.; $144/yr.; $72/6 mos. 340 E. Huron St., Ann Arbor, MI 48104-1147. TEL 313-994-6876; FAX 313-994-6702. **Owner(s):** Newhouse Newspapers, 140 E. 45th St., New York, NY 10017. TEL 212-697-8020; Ed. Ed Petykiewicz; Pub. Dave Wierman; adv. contact: Joe Grech. photos; bk.rev.; pub. size: broadsheet; circ. evening 58,144(paid); Sun. 77,981(paid). **Wire Service(s):** AP, LAT-WP, NYT, NNS.

BAD AXE
US

HURON DAILY TRIBUNE. 1876. Sun.-Fri. $.50 newsstand; $108/yr. in cy.; $120/yr. in cy. mailed; $132/yr. out of cy. mailed. 211 N. Heisterman, Bad Axe, MI 48413. TEL 517-269-6461; FAX 517-269-9893; E-mail: tribune@hdt.com; URL: http://www.hdtinfo.com. **Owner(s):** Hearst Corp., 959 Eighth Ave., New York, NY 10019; Ed. Mark Ranzenberger; Pub. H. Allen Wamsley; adv. contact: Vickie Yaroch. photos; bk.rev.; pub. size: broadsheet; circ. morning 10,000(paid); Sun. 20,000(paid). **Wire Service(s):** AP.

BATTLE CREEK
US

BATTLE CREEK ENQUIRER. 1900. d. $.50/day newsstand; $1.50/Sun.; $3/wk. local; $3.25/wk. out of area. 155 W. Van Buren St., Battle Creek, MI 49017. TEL 616-964-7161; FAX 616-964-0299. **Owner(s):** Gannett Company, Inc., 1100 Wilson Blvd., Arlington, VA 22234. TEL 703-284-6000; Pub. Randy N. Miller; adv. contact: Heather Lipp. pub. size: broadsheet; circ. evening 28,000(paid); Sun. 38,000(paid). **Wire Service(s):** AP, GNS.

BAY CITY
US

BAY CITY TIMES. d. $.35/day newsstand; $1.25/Sun.; $10.50/mo. carrier; $135/yr. motor rte. 311 Fifth St., Bay City, MI 48708. TEL 517-894-9630; FAX 517-893-0649; E-mail: newsroom@bctimes.com. **Owner(s):** Advance Publications, Inc., 950 Fingerboard Rd., Staten Island, NY 10305. TEL 718-981-1234; FAX 718-981-1456; Ed. Paul Keep; Pub. Kevin Dykema; adv. contact: Archie Duncan. photos; pub. size: standard; circ. morning 39,719(paid); Sun. 52,085(paid). **Wire Service(s):** AP, NYT.

BIG RAPIDS
US   ISSN 8750-5533

BIG RAPIDS PIONEER. 1862. Mon.-Sat. $.50 newsstand; $89.75/yr. 502 N. State, Big Rapids, MI 49307. TEL 616-796-4831; FAX 616-796-1152. **Owner(s):** Conine Publishing Co., Inc., 502 N. State, Big Rapids, MI 49307. TEL 616-796-4831; FAX 616-796-1152; Ed. Judy Hale; Pub. John A. Batdorff, II; adv. contact: Denise Clasen. photos; pub. size: broadsheet; circ. morning 5,900(paid). **Wire Service(s):** UPI, AP.
    Formerly: Pioneer, The.

CADILLAC
US   ISSN 0745-3655

CADILLAC EVENING NEWS. 1872. Mon.-Sat. $.50 newsstand; $108.11/yr. 130 N. Mitchell, Cadillac, MI 49601-0640. TEL 616-775-6565; FAX 616-775-8790. **Owner(s):** Thomas C. Huckle, 130 N. Mitchell, Cadillac, MI 49601-0640. TEL 616-775-6565; Ed. Matt Seward; Pub. Thomas C. Huckle; adv. contact: Chris Huckle. pub. size: broadsheet; circ. morning 10,500(paid). **Wire Service(s):** AP.

CHEBOYGAN
US

CHEBOYGAN DAILY TRIBUNE. 1875. Mon.-Fri. $.50 newsstand; $103/yr. 308 N. Main St., Cheboygan, MI 49721. TEL 616-627-7144; FAX 616-627-5331. **Owner(s):** American Publishing Co., 606 N. Van Buren, Marion, IL 62959. TEL 618-993-1711; Ed. Denis Mansfield; Pub. Roy S. Trahan, II; adv. contact: Roy S. Trahan, II. pub. size: broadsheet; circ. morning 5,000(paid). **Wire Service(s):** UPI.

COLDWATER
US   ISSN 0745-6794

DAILY REPORTER, THE. 1896. Mon.-Sat. $.50 newsstand; $77/yr.; $82.50 motor rte.; $144/yr. mailed. 15 W. Pearl St., Coldwater, MI 49036. TEL 517-278-2318; FAX 517-278-6041. **Owner(s):** Independent Media Group, 321 Frenette, Chippewa Falls, WI 54729. TEL 715-723-5515; Ed. Michelle Reen. adv. contact: Becky Coulter. bk.rev.; pub. size: broadsheet; circ. evening 6,300(paid). **Wire Service(s):** AP.

DETROIT

DETROIT FREE PRESS. 1831. d. $.35/day newsstand; $1.50/Sun.; $2.50/wk. 321 Lafayette, Detroit, MI 48226. TEL 313-222-6400; FAX 313-222-5981; E-mail: 72662.1736@compuserve.com; URL: gopher://gopher.det-freepress.com:9002/. **Owner(s):** Knight-Ridder, Inc., One Herald Plz., Miami, FL 33132. TEL 305-376-3800; FAX 305-376-3875; Pub. Heath Meriwether; adv.; photos; bk.rev.; pub. size: broadsheet; circ. morning 531,825(paid); Sun. 1,107,645(paid). **Wire Service(s):** AP, UPI, KR, NYT.

US ISSN 1055-2758

US ISSN 1055-2715
DETROIT NEWS. d. $.35/day newsstand; $1.50/Sun.; $117/yr. home deliv.; $494/yr. mailed in state; $530.40/yr. mailed out of state. 615 W. Lafayette, Detroit, MI 48226. TEL 313-222-6400; FAX 313-222-2335. **Owner(s):** Gannett Company, Inc., 1100 Wilson Blvd., Arlington, VA 22340. TEL 703-284-6000; Ed. Robert H. Giles; Pub. Robert H. Giles; adv.; pub. size: broadsheet; circ. evening 237,000(paid); Sun. 789,660(paid). **Wire Service(s):** AP, UPI, DJ, NYT.

DOWAGIAC
US
DOWAGIAC DAILY NEWS. 1897. Mon.-Fri. $.50 newsstand; $6/mo. carrier. 205 Spaulding St., Dowagiac, MI 49047. TEL 616-782-2101; FAX 616-782-5290. **Owner(s):** Boone/Narragansett Publishers, 205 Spaulding St., Dowagiac, MI 49047. TEL 616-782-2101; Ed. John Eby. adv. contact: Diana Kingsley. pub. size: broadsheet; circ. evening 3,187(paid). **Wire Service(s):** UPI.

ESCANABA
US
DAILY PRESS, THE. Mon.-Sat. $.50 newsstand; $139.50/yr. home deliv. 600 Lundington St., Escanaba, MI 49829. TEL 906-786-2021; FAX 906-786-3752. **Owner(s):** Ogden Newspapers, Inc., 1500 Main St., Wheeling, WV 26033. TEL 304-233-0100; Ed. Peggy Bryson; Pub. Robert Gregg; adv. contact: Jodi Olsen. pub. size: broadsheet; circ. evening 12,700(paid).

FLINT
US
FLINT JOURNAL. 1913. d. $.50/day newsstand; $1.50/Sun.; $10.40/mo. carrier; $11.40/mo. motor rte. 200 E. First St., Flint, MI 48502. TEL 810-766-6100; FAX 810-766-7518. **Owner(s):** Booth Newspapers, Inc., P.O. Box 2168, Grand Rapids, MI 49507. TEL 616-459-1400; Ed. Tom Lindley; Pub. Roger D. Samuel; adv. contact: Thomas Eason. bk.rev.; pub. size: broadsheet; circ. evening 921,000(paid); Sun. 113,722(paid). **Wire Service(s):** UPI, LAT-WP, NYT.

GRAND HAVEN
US
GRAND HAVEN TRIBUNE. 1885. Mon.-Sat. $.50 newsstand; $2.00/wk. carrier; $2.10/wk. motor rte. 101 N. Third St., Grand Haven, MI 49417. TEL 616-842-6400; FAX 616-842-9584. **Owner(s):** Grand Haven Publishing Corp., 101 N. Third St., Grand Haven, MI 49417. TEL 616-842-6400; Ed. Fred Vandenbrand; Pub. Lee Carter; adv. contact: Paul Bedient. photos; pub. size: broadsheet; circ. evening 11,500(paid). **Wire Service(s):** AP.

GRAND RAPIDS
US
GRAND RAPIDS PRESS, THE. 1892. d. $.50/day newsstand, $1.50/Sun.; $12/mo. carrier; $13 mo. motor rte. 155 Michigan, N.W., Grand Rapids, MI 49503. TEL 616-222-5640; FAX 616-222-5276. **Owner(s):** Advance Publications, Inc., 950 Fingerboard Rd., Staten Island, NY 10305. TEL 718-981-1234; Ed. Michael Lloyd; Pub. Danny R. Gaydou; adv. contact: Steven Westphal. pub. size: broadsheet; circ. evening 144,625(paid); Sun. 194,876(paid). **Wire Service(s):** AP, NYT, NNS.

GREENVILLE
US ISSN 0899-6342
DAILY NEWS. 1856. Mon.-Sat. $102/yr. out of state. 109 N. Lafayette, Greenville, MI 48838. TEL 616-754-9301; FAX 616-754-8559. **Owner(s):** John Stafford, 109 N. Lafayette St., Greenville, MI 48838. TEL 616-754-9301; Ed. Alan Blanchard; Pub. John Stafford; adv. contact: Brette Mathis. pub. size: broadsheet; circ. evening 8,468(paid). **Wire Service(s):** UPI.

HILLSDALE
US
HILLSDALE DAILY NEWS. 1909. Mon.-Sat. $83.70/yr. carrier; $144/yr. mailed. 33 McCollum, Hillsdale, MI 49242-1630. TEL 517-437-7351; FAX 517-437-3963; E-mail: hillsdnews@dmci.net. **Owner(s):** Morris Communications, P.O. Box 936, Augusta, GA 30903. TEL 706-724-0851; Ed. Marilynn Fryer; Pub. William K. Turner; adv. contact: Judy Gabriele. pub. size: broadsheet; circ. evening 7,800(paid). **Wire Service(s):** AP.

HOLLAND
US ISSN 1050-4044
HOLLAND SENTINEL. 1896. d. $.50/day newsstand; $1.25/Sun.; $120/yr. 54 W. Eighth, Holland, MI 49423. TEL 616-392-2311; FAX 616-392-3526; E-mail: rwallace@sentinel.com; URL: http://www.sentinelnet.com. **Owner(s):** Morris Communications, P.O. Box 936, Augusta, GA 30903. TEL 706-724-0851; Ed. David Stacks; Pub. Ron Wallace; adv. contact: Susan Temple. photos; bk.rev.; pub. size: broadsheet; circ. morning 20,000(paid); Sun. 20,000(paid). **Wire Service(s):** AP.

HOUGHTON
US
DAILY MINING GAZETTE. 1858. Mon.-Sat. $.50 newsstand; $2.35/wk. carrier; $10.20/mo. motor rte. 206 Shelden Ave., Houghton, MI 49931. TEL 906-482-1500; FAX 906-482-2726. **Owner(s):** Ogden Newspapers, Inc., 1500 Main St., Wheeling, WV 26033. TEL 304-233-0100; Ed. Cyndi Perkins; Pub. Brian McMillan; adv. contact: Karen Callaway. pub. size: broadsheet; circ. evening 13,000(paid). **Wire Service(s):** AP.

IONIA
US ISSN 0745-2128
IONIA SENTINEL-STANDARD. 1866. Mon.-Sat. $.50 newsstand; $99/yr. 114 N. Depot, Ionia, MI 48846. TEL 616-527-2100; FAX 616-527-6860. **Owner(s):** American Publishing Co., 606 N. Van Buren, Marion, IL 62959. TEL 618-993-1711; Ed. Brian P. Abbott; Pub. Jan Anderson; adv.; pub. size: broadsheet; circ. morning 4,082(paid). **Wire Service(s):** AP.

IRON MOUNTAIN
US
DAILY NEWS. 1921. Mon.-Sat. $.50 newsstand; $147/yr. mailed. 215 E. Ludington St., Iron Mountain, MI 49801. TEL 906-774-2772; FAX 906-774-7660; E-mail: dnews@up.lib.mi.us. **Owner(s):** Ogden Newspapers, Inc., 1500 Main St., Wheeling, WV 26033. TEL 304-233-0100; Ed. Blaine Hyska; Pub. Robert Johnson; adv.; photos; bk.rev.; pub. size: broadsheet; circ. evening 11,500(paid). **Wire Service(s):** AP.

IRONWOOD
US
IRONWOOD DAILY GLOBE. 1919. Mon.-Sat. $.50 newsstand; $9.80/mo. carrier; $11.50/mo. motor rte.; $13.50/mo. mailed. 118 E. McLeod Ave., Ironwood, MI 49938. TEL 906-932-2211; FAX 906-932-5358. **Owner(s):** Globe Publishing Co., 118 E. McLeod Ave., Ironwood, MI 49938. TEL 906-932-2211; Ed. Andrew Hill. adv. contact: Gary Mecum. pub. size: broadsheet; circ. evening 8,500(paid). **Wire Service(s):** AP.

JACKSON
US
JACKSON CITIZEN PATRIOT. 1837. d. $.50/day newsstand; $1.50/Sun.; $1.90/wk.; $8.55/mo. 214 S. Jackson St., Jackson, MI 49201-2282. TEL 517-787-2300; FAX 517-787-9711; E-mail: jcpnews@catpat.com. **Owner(s):** Newhouse Newspapers, 140 E. 45th St., 36th Fl., New York, NY 10017. TEL 212-697-8020; Ed. Sandra D. Petykiewicz; Pub. F.T. Weaver; adv. contact: Jerry C. Gerdes. photos; bk.rev.; pub. size: broadsheet; circ. evening 38,003(paid); Sun. 42,002(paid). **Wire Service(s):** NNS, AP, SHNA.

KALAMAZOO

US

KALAMAZOO GAZETTE. 1847. d. $.50/day newsstand, $1.25/Sun; $11.30/mo. motor rte.; $19.75/mo. mailed. 401 S. Burdick, Kalamazoo, MI 49007. TEL 616-345-3511; FAX 616-388-8447. **Owner(s):** Newhouse Newspapers, 1101 Connecticut Ave., N.W., Washington, DC 20036. TEL 202-383-7800; Pub. George Arwady; adv. contact: Jim Coppinger. pub. size: standard; circ. evening 66,000(paid); Sun. 82,000(paid). **Wire Service(s):** AP, UPI, LAT-WP, NNS.

LANSING

US ISSN 0274-9742

LANSING STATE JOURNAL. 1855. d. $.35/day newsstand; $1.50/Sun.; $3.25/wk. carrier or motor rte. 120 E. Lenawee, Lansing, MI 48919. TEL 517-377-1000; FAX 517-377-1298. **Owner(s):** Gannett Company, Inc., 1000 Wilson Blvd., Arlington, VA 22234. TEL 703-284-6000; Ed. Roni Rucker-Waters; Pub. Gary Suisman; adv. contact: Stan Howard. photos; bk.rev.; pub. size: standard; circ. morning 71,000(paid); Sun. 96,619(paid). **Wire Service(s):** AP, GNS.

LUDINGTON

US

LUDINGTON DAILY NEWS. 1873. d. $.50 newsstand; $92.90/yr. 202 N. Rath Ave., Ludington, MI 49431-1663. TEL 616-845-5181; FAX 616-843-4011. **Owner(s):** David R. Jackson, P.O. Box 340, Ludington, MI 49431-0340. TEL 616-845-5181; Ed. Steve Begnoche; Pub. David R. Jackson; adv.; photos; bk.rev.; pub. size: broadsheet; circ. evening 8,300(paid). **Wire Service(s):** AP.

MANISTEE

US

MANISTEE NEWS-ADVOCATE. 1894. Mon.-Sat. $.50 newssstand; $25/3 mos. in cy.; $28/3 mos. mailed in state; $37/3 mos. mailed out of state. 75 Maple St., Manistee, MI 49660-1554. TEL 616-723-3593; FAX 616-723-4733. **Owner(s):** J.B. Publishing Co., 75 Maple St., Manistee, MI 49660-1554. TEL 616-723-3593; FAX 616-723-4733; Ed. Phil Watson; Pub. Jack Batdorff; adv. contact: Marilyn Barker. pub. size: broadsheet; circ. morning 5,200(paid). **Wire Service(s):** AP.

MARQUETTE

US ISSN 0898-4964

MINING JOURNAL. 1846. d. $.50/day newsstand, $1/Sun.; $2.50/wk. carrier; $2.65/wk. motor rte.; $2.85/wk. mailed. 249 W. Washington St., Marquette, MI 49855. TEL 906-228-2500; FAX 906-228-5556. **Owner(s):** Ogden Newspapers, Inc., 1500 Main St., Wheeling, WV 26033. TEL 304-233-0100; Ed. Dave Edwards; Pub. James Reeves; adv. contact: Willie Peterson. pub. size: standard; circ. evening 20,200(paid); Sun. 21,600(paid). **Wire Service(s):** AP.

MARSHALL

US

MARSHALL CHRONICLE. 1879. Mon.-Sat. $.50 newsstand; $80./yr. mailed in cy.; $100yr. mailed out of cy. 115 S. Grand, Marshall, MI 49068. TEL 616-781-3943; FAX 616-781-4012. **Owner(s):** Milliman Communications, Inc., P.O. Box 160, Mason, MI 49068. TEL 517-676-9300; Pub. Dirk Milliman; adv.; photos; bk.rev.; pub. size: broadsheet; circ. evening 2,000(paid). **Wire Service(s):** UPI.

MIDLAND

US

MIDLAND DAILY NEWS. 1930. d. $.50/day newsstand; $1.25/Sun.; $2.65/wk. carrier; $12.50/mo. mailed local; $13.50/mo. mailed out of state. 124 S. McDonald, Midland, MI 48640. TEL 517-835-7171; FAX 517-835-6991; E-mail: gordon.hall@mdn.net. **Owner(s):** Hearst Corp., 959 Eighth Ave., New York, NY 10019; Ed. Ralph Wirtz; Pub. Gordon Hall; pub. size: broadsheet; circ. evening 17,165(paid); Sun. 18,000(paid). **Wire Service(s):** AP.

MONROE

US

MONROE EVENING NEWS. 1825. d. $.50/day newsstand; $1.25/Sun.; $3/wk. carrier. 20 W. First St., Monroe, MI 48161. TEL 313-242-1100; FAX 313-242-3175. **Owner(s):** Monroe Publishing Co., Inc., 20 W. First St., Monroe, MI 48161. TEL 313-242-1100; Ed. Stephen Gray; Pub. Grattan Gray; adv. contact: A. David Trewin. adv.: $15.84/SAU. photos; bk.rev.; pub. size: broadsheet; circ. evening 23,600(paid); Sun. 25,000(paid). **Wire Service(s):** AP.

MT. CLEMENS

US ISSN 1071-1406

MACOMB DAILY. 1860. Sun.-Fri. $.50/day newsstand; $1/Sun.; $2.10/wk. carrier; $155/yr. 100 Macomb Daily Dr., Mt. Clemens, MI 48043. TEL 810-469-4510; FAX 810-469-2892; E-mail: edit@macombdaily.com; URL: http://www.macombdaily.com. **Owner(s):** Independent Newspapers, Inc., 100 Macomb Daily Dr., Mt. Clemens, MI 48043. TEL 810-469-4510; Ed. Phil VanHule; Pub. J. Gene Chambers; adv. contact: Mark Lewis. photos; bk.rev.; pub. size: broadsheet; circ. evening 50,000(paid); Sun. 60,000(paid). **Wire Service(s):** AP.

MT. PLEASANT

US

MORNING SUN. 1977. Sun.-Fri. $.50/day newsstand; $1.50/Sun.; $11.27/mo. carrier; $12.35/mo. motor rte. 215 N. Main, Mt. Pleasant, MI 48858. TEL 517-772-2971; FAX 517-773-0382. **Owner(s):** Central Michigan Newspapers, Inc., 215 N. Main, Mt. Pleasant, MI 48858. TEL 517-772-2971; Ed. Rick Mills; Pub. Ray Pike; adv. contact: Cathy Simon. photos; pub. size: broadsheet; circ. morning 11,148(paid); Sun. 12,023(paid). **Wire Service(s):** AP.
  Formerly: Mt. Pleasant/Alma Morning Sun.

MUSKEGON

US

MUSKEGON CHRONICLE, THE. 1857. d. $.50/day newsstand; $1.25/Sun.; $11.50/mo. motor rte.; $12.50 mailed in state; $13.50 mailed out of state. 981 Third St., Muskegon, MI 49440. TEL 616-722-0320; FAX 616-722-2552. **Owner(s):** Booth Newspapers, Inc., P.O. Box 2168, Grand Rapids, MI 49500. TEL 616-459-1400; Ed. D. Gunnar Carlson; Pub. Gary Ostrom; adv. contact: Kevin Newton. pub. size: broadsheet; circ. evening 48,507(paid); Sun. 53,248(paid). **Wire Service(s):** AP, LAT-WP, NNS.

NILES

US

NILES DAILY STAR. 1886. Mon.-Sat. $.50 newsstand; $7/mo. carrier. 217 N. Fourth St., Niles, MI 49120. TEL 616-683-2100; FAX 616-683-2175. **Owner(s):** Boone/Narragansett Publishers, 217 N. Fourth St., Niles, MI 49120; Ed. Jan Griffey; Pub. Doug Phares; adv. contact: Hal Shue. pub. size: broadsheet; circ. evening 5,000(paid). **Wire Service(s):** UPI.

OWOSSO

US

ARGUS-PRESS, THE. 1854. d. $.50/day newsstand; $.75/Sun.; $8.75/mo. carrier & motor rte.; $12.25/mo. mailed. 201 E. Exchange St., Owosso, MI 48867. TEL 517-725-5136; FAX 517-725-6376; E-mail: argus@shianet.com.org; URL: http://www.shianet.org/~argus/. **Owner(s):** Argus-Press Co., 201 E. Exchange St., Owosso, MI 48867. TEL 517-725-5136; Ed. Helene Bough; Pub. Tom Campbell; adv. contact: Mark Ludington. photos; pub. size: broadsheet; circ. evening 12,500(paid); Sun. 12,500(paid). **Wire Service(s):** AP.

PETOSKEY

US

PETOSKEY NEWS-REVIEW. 1875. d. $166.15/yr. 319 State St., Petoskey, MI 49770. TEL 616-347-2544; FAX 616-347-6833. **Owner(s):** Northern Michigan Review, Inc., P.O. Box 528, Petoskey, MI 49770. TEL 616-347-2544; FAX 616-347-6833; Ed. Ken Winter; Pub. Kirk Schaller; adv.; photos; bk.rev.; pub. size: broadsheet; circ. evening 11,245(paid). Wire Service(s): AP.

PONTIAC

US

OAKLAND PRESS, THE. 1821. d. $.35/day newsstand; $1.25/Sun.; $2.30/wk. carrier; $13/mo. mailed in town; $21.67/mo. mailed out of town. 48 W. Huron St., Pontiac, MI 48342. TEL 810-332-8181; FAX 810-332-8885. **Owner(s):** Walt Disney Co., 500 S. Buena Vista St., Burbank, CA 91521. TEL 818-560-5300; Ed. Gary Gilbert; Pub. Dale Duncan; adv.; photos; pub. size: standard; circ. morning 78,000(paid); Sun. 100,000(paid). **Wire Service(s):** AP.

PORT HURON

TIMES HERALD. 1910. d. $.40/day newsstand; $1.50/Sun. 911 Military St., Port Huron, MI 48060. TEL 810-985-7171; FAX 810-989-6294; E-mail: tmshrld@ic.net2. **Owner(s):** Gannett Company, Inc., 1100 Wilson Blvd., Arlington, VA 22234. TEL 703-284-6000; Pub. William Monopoli; adv. contact: Kathy Powell. photos; bk.rev.; pub. size: broadsheet; circ. evening 32,000(paid); Sun. 39,986(paid). **Wire Service(s):** AP, GNS.

ROYAL OAK
US   ISSN 1041-9977

DAILY TRIBUNE, THE. 1902. Sun.-Fri. $.50/day newsstand; $1/Sun.; $2/wk. carrier. 210 E. Third St., Royal Oak, MI 48067. TEL 810-541-3000; FAX 810-541-7903. **Owner(s):** Independent Newspapers, Inc., 100 Macomb Daily Dr., Mount Clemens, MI 48043. TEL 810-469-4510; Ed. Mike Beeson; Pub. R.D. Isham; adv. contact: Matt Fasing. photos; pub. size: broadsheet; circ. evening 22,889(paid); Sun. 26,226(paid). **Wire Service(s):** AP.

SAGINAW
US

SAGINAW NEWS. 1859. d. $.50/day newsstand; $1.50/Sun.; $11.50/mo. carrier; $12.50/mo. motor rte. 203 S. Washington Ave., Saginaw, MI 48607. TEL 517-752-7171; FAX 517-752-3115. **Owner(s):** Booth Newspapers, Inc., P.O. Box 2168, Grand Rapids, MI 49501. TEL 616-459-1400; Ed. Rob Handeyside; Pub. Rex Thatcher; adv. contact: Gene Bobic. photos; pub. size: broadsheet; circ. evening 55,158(paid); Sun. 65,044(paid). **Wire Service(s):** AP.

SAULT STE. MARIE
US

SAULT STE. MARIE EVENING NEWS. 1879. Sun.-Fri. $.50/day newsstand; $1/Sun.; $13/mo. carrier & motor rte.; $45/3 mo. out of area. 109 Arlington St., Sault Ste. Marie, MI 49783. TEL 906-632-2235; FAX 906-632-1222. **Owner(s):** American Publishing Co., 606 N. Van Buren, P.O. Box 520, Marion, IL 62959. TEL 618-993-1711; Ed. Ken Fazzari; Pub. Howard Kaiser; adv. contact: Richard Beadle. photos; pub. size: broadsheet; circ. evening 9,784(paid); Sun. 12,067(paid). **Wire Service(s):** AP.

SOUTH HAVEN
US

SOUTH HAVEN DAILY TRIBUNE. 1899. Mon.-Fri. $.50 newsstand; $82.80/yr. mailed local; $88.80/yr. mailed out of area. 950 Bailey Ave., Ste. 4, South Haven, MI 49090. TEL 616-637-1104; FAX 616-637-8415; E-mail: shaven@accn.org. **Owner(s):** American Publishing Co., 606 N. Van Buren, Marion, IL 62959. TEL 618-993-1711; Ed. Cathy Sisson; Pub. Michael Eastman; adv.; pub. size: broadsheet; circ. morning 2,500(paid). **Wire Service(s):** AP.

ST. JOSEPH
US   ISSN 0387-4400

HERALD-PALLADIUM. 1858. d. $.50/day newsstand; $1.25/Sun.; $135.20/yr. in state mailed. 3450 Hollywood Rd., St. Joseph, MI 49085. TEL 616-429-2400; FAX 616-429-7661. **Owner(s):** Hollinger International, Inc., 401 N. Wabash, Chicago, IL 60611. TEL 312-321-3000; Ed. Steve Pepple; Pub. David Harrison; adv.; photos; pub. size: broadsheet; circ. evening 33,143(paid); Sun. 33,935(paid). **Wire Service(s):** AP.

STURGIS
US   ISSN 0747-3230

STURGIS JOURNAL. 1859. Mon.-Sat. $.50 newsstand; $94.80/yr. carrier; $102/yr. motor rte.; $10/mo. mailed. 209 John St., Sturgis, MI 49091. TEL 616-651-5407; FAX 616-651-2296; E-mail: journal@voyager.net; URL: http://www.sturgisjournal.com. **Owner(s):** Independent Media Group, 160 Pendexter Ave., Watseka, IL 60970; Ed. Candice Phelps; Pub. Rich Piatt; adv.; pub. size: broadsheet; circ. evening 8,200(paid). **Wire Service(s):** AP, GNS.

THREE RIVERS
US

THREE RIVERS COMMERCIAL-NEWS. 1895. Mon.-Sat. $.50 newsstand $7/mo. 124 N. Main St., Three Rivers, MI 49093. TEL 616-279-7488; FAX 616-279-6007. **Owner(s):** Three Rivers Commercial, Inc., 124 N. Main St., Three Rivers, MI 49093. TEL 616-279-7488; Ed. Joseph K. Albertson; Pub. Richard L. Milliman, II; adv.; photos; pub. size: broadsheet; circ. evening 5,000(paid). **Wire Service(s):** AP.

TRAVERSE CITY
US

TRAVERSE CITY RECORD-EAGLE. 1904. d. $.50/day newsstand; $1.50/Sun.; $146.20/yr. in cy. 120 W. Front St., Traverse City, MI 49684. TEL 616-946-2000; FAX 616-946-8273. **Owner(s):** Ottaway Newspapers, Inc., P.O. Box 401, Campbell Hall, NY 10916. TEL 914-294-8181; Ed. John Tune; Pub. Frank B. Senger; adv.; photos; bk.rev.; pub. size: broadsheet; circ. morning 26,000(paid); Sun. 37,000(paid). **Wire Service(s):** AP, DJ, ONS.

MINNESOTA

ALBERT LEA
US   ISSN 1051-7421

ALBERT LEA TRIBUNE. 1897. Sun.-Fri. $.50/day newsstand; $1.25/Sun.; $9.50/mo. carrier. 808 W. Front St., Albert Lea, MN 56007. TEL 507-373-1411; FAX 507-373-0333. **Owner(s):** Boone Newspapers, Inc., P.O. Box 2370, Tuscaloosa, AL 35403. TEL 407-338-3298; Ed. Floyd Jernigan; Pub. Curtis Williams; adv. contact: Neal Ronquist. pub. size: broadsheet; circ. evening 7,300(paid); Sun. 8,500(paid). **Wire Service(s):** AP.

AUSTIN
US   ISSN 0746-9713

AUSTIN DAILY HERALD. Sun.-Fri. $.50/day newsstand, $1.50/Sun.; $10.50/mo. carrier; $12/mo. motor rte. or mailed. 310 Second St., N.E., Austin, MN 55912. TEL 507-433-8851; FAX 507-437-8644. **Owner(s):** Boone Newspapers, Inc., P.O. Box 2370, Tuscaloosa, AL 35403. TEL 407-338-3298; Pub. David Churchill; adv. contact: Eric Bishop. pub. size: broadsheet; circ. evening 8,000(paid); Sun. 8,000(paid). **Wire Service(s):** AP.

BEMIDJI
US   ISSN 0899-1812

PIONEER, THE. 1896. Sun.-Fri. $.50/day newsstand; $.75/Sun.; $8/mo. carrier. 1320 Neilson Ave., S.E., Bemidji, MN 56601. TEL 218-751-3740; FAX 218-751-6914. **Owner(s):** Forum Communications Co., 101 Fifth St., N, Fargo, ND 58102. TEL 701-235-7311; Ed. Brad Swenson. adv. contact: Jeff Halvorsen. photos; pub. size: broadsheet; circ. morning 8,600(paid); Sun. 8,800(paid). **Wire Service(s):** AP.
Formerly: Bemidji Pioneer.

BRAINERD
US

BRAINERD DAILY DISPATCH. 1881. Sun.-Fri. $.50/day newsstand; $1.25/Sun; $102/yr. 506 James St., Brainerd, MN 56401. TEL 218-829-4705; FAX 218-829-7735; E-mail: dailyd@brainerd.net; URL: http://www.brainerddispatch.com. **Owner(s):** Morris Communications, P.O. Box 936, Augusta, GA 30903. TEL 706-721-0851; Ed. Roy Miller; Pub. Terry McCollough; adv. contact: Joe Smart. photos; pub. size: broadsheet; circ. evening 14,108(paid); Sun. 16,943(paid). **Wire Service(s):** AP.

CROOKSTON
US

CROOKSTON DAILY TIMES. 1885. Mon.-Fri. $.50 newsstand; $1.75/wk. carrier; $24/3 mos. mailed in cy.; $35/3 mos. mailed MN, ND, & SD. 124 S. Broadway, Crookston, MN 56716. TEL 218-281-2730; FAX 218-281-7234. **Owner(s):** American Publishing Co., 606 N. Van Buren, Marion, IL 62959. TEL 618-993-1711; Ed. Twylla Attepeter; Pub. Randal Hultgren; adv. contact: Ann-Pell Logue. pub. size: broadsheet; circ. evening 4,600(paid). **Wire Service(s):** AP.

DULUTH
US   ISSN 0896-9418

DULUTH NEWS-TRIBUNE. 1870. d. $.50/day newsstand; $1.50/Sun.; $3.17/wk. carrier. 424 W. First St., Duluth, MN 55802. TEL 218-723-5281; FAX 218-720-4120; E-mail: mnduh@gif.com. **Owner(s):** Knight-Ridder, Inc., One Herald Plz., Miami, FL 33132. TEL 305-376-3800; FAX 305-376-3875; Ed. Craig Gemoules; Pub. Jim Gels; adv.; photos; bk.rev.; pub. size: broadsheet; circ. morning 64,000(paid); Sun. 84,000(paid). **Wire Service(s):** AP.

DAILY NEWSPAPERS

ST. PAUL, MN 10463

FAIRMONT
US ISSN 0893-3804

FAIRMONT SENTINEL. 1874. Mon.-Sat. $.50 newsstand; $67/yr. carrier; $73/yr. mail; $94.95/yr. out of area. 64 Downtown Plz., Fairmont, MN 56031-0681. TEL 507-235-3303; FAX 507-235-3718; E-mail: sentnews@rconnect.com; URL: http://www.oweb.com/sentinel. **Owner(s):** Ogden Newspapers, Inc., 1500 Main St., Wheeling, WV 26033. TEL 304-233-0100; Pub. Gary Andersen; adv. contact: Gary Andersen. pub. size: broadsheet; circ. morning 10,100(paid). **Wire Service(s):** AP.

FARIBAULT
US ISSN 0889-8898

FARIBAULT DAILY NEWS. 1914. Tue.-Sun. $.50 newsstand; $85.25/yr. 514 Central Ave., N., Faribault, MN 55021. TEL 507-334-1853; FAX 507-334-8569. **Owner(s):** Huckle Publishing, Inc., 6291 Peninsula Dr., Traverse City, MI 49684. TEL 616-929-3571; Ed. Lisa Schwarz; Pub. David Balcom; adv. contact: Paula Patton. pub. size: broadsheet; circ. evening 7,800(paid). **Wire Service(s):** AP.

FERGUS FALLS
US

DAILY JOURNAL, THE. 1873. Mon.-Sat. $.75 newsstand; $10/mo. carrier & motor rte.; $10/mo. mailed in cy.; $10/mo. mailed out of cy.; $10/mo. mailed out of state. 914 E. Channing Ave., Fergus Falls, MN 56537. TEL 218-736-7511; FAX 218-736-5919. **Owner(s):** Boone Newspapers, Inc., P.O. Box 2370, Tuscaloosa, AL 35403. TEL 407-338-3298; Ed. Jeff Durham; Pub. James Morgan; adv. contact: Lori Hanson. photos; bk.rev.; pub. size: broadsheet; circ. evening 10,500(paid). **Wire Service(s):** AP.
Formerly: Fergus Falls Daily Journal.

HIBBING
US ISSN 1075-4040

HIBBING DAILY TRIBUNE. 1894. d. $.50/day newsstand; $1.25/Sun.; $2.52/wk. carrier & motor rte. 2142 First Ave., Hibbing, MN 55746. TEL 218-262-1011; FAX 218-262-4318. **Owner(s):** Murphy-McGinnis Media, 1226 Ogden Ave., Superior, WI 54880. TEL 715-394-4411; Ed. Jim Gehrke; Pub. John Murphy; adv. contact: Terry Backstrom. photos; pub. size: broadsheet; circ. evening 9,000(paid); Sun. 18,000(paid). **Wire Service(s):** AP.

INTERNATIONAL FALLS
US

DAILY JOURNAL, THE. 1920. Mon.-Fri. $.50 newsstand; $80.40/yr. carrier. 500 Third St., International Falls, MN 56649. TEL 218-285-7411; FAX 218-285-7206. **Owner(s):** North Star Publishing Co., 500 Third St., International Falls, MN 56649. TEL 218-285-7411; Ed. Tom Klein; Pub. Arlin Albrecht; adv. contact: Harry Swendsen. photos; bk.rev.; pub. size: broadsheet; circ. evening 4,500(paid). **Wire Service(s):** AP.
Formerly: International Falls Daily Journal.

MANKATO
US ISSN 0893-3715

FREE PRESS. 1887. Mon.-Sat. $.50/day newsstand; $2.40/wk. carrier; $2.55/wk. motor rte.; $2.95/wk. mailed. 418 S. Second St., Mankato, MN 56001. TEL 507-625-4451; FAX 507-388-4355; E-mail: freepress@ic.mankato.mn.us; URL: http://www.mankato-freepress.com. **Owner(s):** Ottaway Newspapers, Inc., P.O. Box 401, Campbell Hall, NY 10916. TEL 914-294-8181; Ed. Deb Flemming; Pub. E. Joe Vanderhoof; adv.; pub. size: broadsheet; circ. evening 26,500(paid). **Wire Service(s):** AP, LAT-WP.

MARSHALL
US

MARSHALL INDEPENDENT. 1873. Mon.-Sat. $.50 newsstand; $71.50/yr. local; $96/yr. out of state. 508 W. Main St., Marshall, MN 56258. TEL 507-537-1551. **Owner(s):** Ogden Newspapers, Inc., 1500 Main St., Wheeling, WV 26033. TEL 304-233-0100; Ed. Jim Tate; Pub. Russ Labate; adv. contact: Connie Nuese. pub. size: broadsheet; circ. morning 9,300(paid). **Wire Service(s):** AP.

MINNEAPOLIS
US ISSN 0895-2825

STAR TRIBUNE. 1867. d. $.35/day newsstand; $1.75/Sun.; $6.45/wk.; $335.40/yr. mailed. 425 Portland Ave., Minneapolis, MN 55488. TEL 612-673-4000; FAX 612-673-4359; E-mail: letters@startribune.com; URL: http://www.startribune.com. **Owner(s):** Cowles Media Co., 329 Portland Ave., Minneapolis, MN 55488. TEL 612-673-7100; FAX 612-673-7020; Ed. Pam Fine; Pub. Joel Kramer; adv.; pub. size: standard; circ. morning 388,120(paid); Sun. 682,318(paid). **Wire Service(s):** AP, NYT, LAT-WP, SHNA.

NEW ULM
US

JOURNAL, THE. 1900. d. $.50/day newsstand; $1/Sun.; $7/4 wks. carrier or motor rte. 303 N. Minnesota St., New Ulm, MN 56073-0487. TEL 507-359-2911; FAX 507-359-7362. **Owner(s):** Ogden Newspapers, Inc., 1500 Main St., Wheeling, WV 26003. TEL 304-233-0100; Ed. Kevin Sweeney; Pub. Bruce Fenske; adv. contact: Marian Petersen. pub. size: broadsheet; circ. morning 10,400(paid); Sun. 10,400(paid). **Wire Service(s):** AP.

OWATONNA
US ISSN 0890-2860

OWATONNA PEOPLE'S PRESS. 1874. Tue.-Sun. $.50 newsstand; $96.75/yr. 135 W. Pearl St., Owatonna, MN 55060. TEL 507-451-2840; FAX 507-451-6020. **Owner(s):** Huckle Publishing, Inc., P.O. Box 346, Owatonna, MN 55060. TEL 507-451-2840; Ed. Tom Head; Pub. Ron Eneley; adv. contact: Holly Westercamp. bk.rev.; pub. size: broadsheet; circ. morning 8,000(paid); Sun. 8,000(paid). **Wire Service(s):** AP.

RED WING
US

RED WING REPUBLICAN EAGLE. 1857. Mon.-Sat. $.50 newsstand; $99/yr. carrier; $104/yr. motor rte.; $105/yr. mail. 2760 N. Service Dr., Red Wing, MN 55066-0082. TEL 612-388-8235; FAX 612-388-8912. **Owner(s):** Red Wing Publishing Co., 2760 N. Service Dr., Red Wing, MN 55066. TEL 612-388-3128; FAX 612-388-8912; Ed. James Pumarlo; Pub. Arlin Albrecht; adv. contact: Vickie Winge. photos; bk.rev.; pub. size: broadsheet; circ. morning 8,450(paid). **Wire Service(s):** AP.

ROCHESTER
US

POST-BULLETIN. 1925. Mon.-Sat. $.50/day newsstand; $1.75/Sun.; $37.70/13 wks. in city; $49.95/13 wks. rural deliv. 18 First Ave., S.E., Rochester, MN 55904. TEL 507-285-7600; FAX 507-285-7772. **Owner(s):** Post-Bulletin Co. LLC, 18 First Ave. S.E., Rochester, MN 55904. TEL 507-285-7600; Ed. Jon Losness; Pub. William C. Boyne; adv. contact: Gerry Rhea. photos; bk.rev.; pub. size: broadsheet; circ. evening 40,700(paid). **Wire Service(s):** AP, NYT, KR.
Formerly: Rochester Post-Bulletin.

ST. CLOUD
US ISSN 0899-5028

ST. CLOUD TIMES. 1861. d. $.50/day newsstand; $1.50/Sun.; $42.25/3 mos. carrier; $46.15/3 mos. motor rte.; $52/3 mos. mail in state. 3000 Seventh St. N., St. Cloud, MN 56303. TEL 612-255-8700; FAX 612-255-8704. **Owner(s):** Gannett Company, Inc., 1100 Wilson Blvd., Arlington, VA 22234. TEL 703-284-6000; Ed. John Bodette; Pub. Sonja Sorensen Craig; adv. contact: Rhonda Barlow. pub. size: broadsheet; circ. evening 28,963(paid); Sun. 37,870(paid). **Wire Service(s):** AP, GNS.

STILLWATER
US

STILLWATER GAZETTE. 1870. Mon.-Fri. $.35 newsstand; $103/yr. mailed. 102 S. Second St., Stillwater, MN 55082. TEL 612-439-3130; FAX 612-439-4713. **Owner(s):** American Publishing Co., 606 N. Van Buren, Marion, IL 62959. TEL 618-993-1711; Ed. Chris Baldus; Pub. Mike Mahoney; adv. contact: John Lund. photos; pub. size: broadsheet; circ. evening 4,200(free & paid). **Wire Service(s):** AP.

ST. PAUL
US ISSN 1050-0405

ST. PAUL PIONEER PRESS. 1849. d. $.35/day newsstand; $1.50/Sun.; $3.30/wk. carrier; $4/wk. mail. 345 Cedar St., St. Paul, MN 55101. TEL 612-222-5011. E-mail: lundy@pioneerplanet.infi.net; URL: http://www.pioneerplanet.com. **Owner(s):** Knight-Ridder, Inc., One Herald Plz., Miami, FL 33132. TEL 305-376-3800; FAX 000-376-3875; Ed. Ken Doctor; Pub. Peter Ridder; adv.; bk.rev.; pub. size: broadsheet; circ. morning 212,000(paid); Sun. 276,055(paid).

VIRGINIA

MESABI DAILY NEWS. 1893. d. $.50/day newsstand; $1.50/Sun.; $17.10/6 wks. carrier; $17.70/6 wks. motor rte.; $35.05/13 wks. mailed; $74.10/26 wks. mailed; $148.20/yr. mailed. 704 Seventh Ave. S., Virginia, MN 55792. TEL 218-741-5544; FAX 218-741-1005. **Owner(s):** Mesabi Publishing Co., P.O. Box 956, Virginia, MN 55792. TEL 218-741-5544; Ed. Bill Hanna. adv. contact: Chris Knight. pub. size: broadsheet; circ. morning 12,245(paid); Sun. 22,166(paid). **Wire Service(s):** UPI.

WILLMAR

WEST CENTRAL TRIBUNE. 1895. Mon.-Sat. $.50 newsstand; $99/yr. carrier; $105/yr. mail. 2208 W. Trott Ave., Willmar, MN 56201-0839. TEL 320-235-1150; FAX 320-235-6769. **Owner(s):** Forum Communications Co., Fargo, ND; Ed. Paul E. London; Pub. Paul E. London; adv. contact: Marilyn Birkland. photos; bk.rev.; pub. size: broadsheet; circ. morning 17,500(paid). **Wire Service(s):** AP.

WINONA

US ISSN 0273-9941
WINONA DAILY NEWS. 1855. d. $.50 newsstand; $1.25/Sun.; $155/yr. 601 Franklin St., Winona, MN 55987. TEL 507-453-3500; FAX 507-454-1440. **Owner(s):** Lee Enterprises, Inc., 130 E. Second St., Davenport, IA 52801. TEL 319-383-2202; Ed. Jim Galewski; Pub. Howard Hoffmaster; adv. contact: Mike Corbett. photos; pub. size: standard; circ. morning 14,000(paid); Sun. 14,363(paid). **Wire Service(s):** AP.

WORTHINGTON

WORTHINGTON DAILY GLOBE. 1872. d. $.50 newsstand; $90/yr.; $101/yr. mailed; $111/yr. mailed out of area. 300 11th St., Worthington, MN 56187. TEL 507-376-9711; FAX 507-376-5202. **Owner(s):** Forum Communications Co., P.O. Box 2020, Fargo, ND 58207. TEL 701-223-7311; Ed. Dennis Hall; Pub. Dennis Hall; adv. contact: Denise McMillen. photos; pub. size: broadsheet; circ. morning 13,915(paid). **Wire Service(s):** AP, Thompson News Service.

MISSISSIPPI

BROOKHAVEN

BROOKHAVEN DAILY LEADER. 1883. Mon.-Fri. & Sun. $.50/day newsstand; $1/Sun.; $8/mo.; $96/yr. 128 N. Railroad Ave., Brookhaven, MS 39601. TEL 601-833-6961; FAX 601-833-6714; E-mail: dailyleader.com. **Owner(s):** Southwest Publishers, Inc., P.O. Box 551, Brookhaven, MS 39601. TEL 601-833-6961; Ed. William O. Jacobs; Pub. William O. Jacobs; adv. contact: Natalie Davis. photos; pub. size: broadsheet; circ. evening 7,500(paid); Sun. 7,500(paid). **Wire Service(s):** AP.

CLARKSDALE

CLARKSDALE PRESS REGISTER. 1865. Mon.-Sat. $.50 newsstand; $7/mo.; $77/yr. 123 Second St., Clarksdale, MS 38614. TEL 601-627-2201; FAX 601-624-5125. **Owner(s):** Delta Publishing Co., Inc., 123 Second St., Clarksdale, MS 38614. TEL 601-627-2201; Ed. Clyde K. Burson; Pub. Wyatt Emmerich; adv. contact: Joann Stevens. pub. size: broadsheet; circ. morning 7,675(paid). **Wire Service(s):** AP.

CLEVELAND

CLEVELAND BOLIVAR COMMERCIAL. 1917. Mon.-Fri. $.50 newsstand; $5.50/mo. carrier & motor rte.; $6.50/mo. mailed. 821 N. Chrisman, Cleveland, MS 38732. TEL 601-843-4241; FAX 601-843-1830. **Owner(s):** Walls Newspapers, Inc., P.O. Box 530447, Birmingham, AL 35253. TEL 205-870-1684; Ed. Wayne Nicholas; Pub. Norman Van Liew; adv. contact: Ricky Nobile. photos; pub. size: broadsheet; circ. evening 8,500(paid). **Wire Service(s):** AP.

COLUMBUS

US ISSN 0746-7729
COMMERCIAL DISPATCH, THE. 1879. Sun.-Fri. $.25/day newsstand; $.75/Sun.; $84/yr. 516 Main St., Columbus, MS 39701-0511. TEL 601-328-2427; FAX 601-329-8937; E-mail: letters@cdispatch.com. **Owner(s):** Commercial Dispatch, Inc., 516 Main St., Columbus, OH 39701-0511. TEL 601-328-2427; FAX 601-329-8937; Ed. Birney Imes, III; Pub. Birney Imes; adv. contact: Dianne Medley. photos; bk.rev.; pub. size: broadsheet; circ. evening 14,836(paid); Sun. 15,980(paid). **Wire Service(s):** AP.

CORINTH

DAILY CORINTHIAN. 1895. Tue.-Sun. $.50 newsstand; $24/3 mos. carrier & motor rte.; $45/3 mos. mailed. 1607 S. Harper Rd., Corinth, MS 38834. TEL 601-287-6111; FAX 601-287-3525. **Owner(s):** Paxton Media Group, Inc., P.O. Box 2300, Paducah, KY 42002. TEL 502-443-1771; Ed. Mark Boehler; Pub. Tom Overton; adv. contact: Jim Burnett. pub. size: standard; circ. morning 9,400(paid). **Wire Service(s):** AP.
Formerly: Corinth Daily Corinthian.

GREENVILLE

DELTA DEMOCRAT-TIMES. 1868. Sun.-Fri. $.50/day newsstand; $1/Sun.; $9/mo. 988 N. Broadway, Greenville, MS 38701. TEL 601-335-1155; FAX 601-335-2860. **Owner(s):** Freedom Communications, Inc., 1055 N. Main St., Ste. 901, Santa Ana, CA 92701. TEL 714-542-4415; Pub. Ed Nichols; adv. contact: Jim Kennedy. photos; bk.rev.; pub. size: standard; circ. evening 13,100(paid); Sun. 15,000(paid). **Wire Service(s):** AP.

GREENWOOD

US ISSN 0884-4569
GREENWOOD COMMONWEALTH. 1896. Sun.-Fri. $.50/day newsstand, $1/Sun.; $7.50/mo. carrier city, $8/mo. rural carrier; $27/3 mos. mailed out of area. 329 Hwy. 82 W., Greenwood, MS 38930. TEL 601-453-5312; FAX 601-453-2908. **Owner(s):** Emmerich Newspapers, Inc., P.O. Box 8050, Greenwood, MS 38935-8050. TEL 601-453-5312; FAX 601-453-2908; Ed. Tim Kalich; Pub. Tim Kalich; adv. contact: Larry Alderman. pub. size: broadsheet; circ. evening 8,859(paid); Sun. 9,017(paid). **Wire Service(s):** AP, NYT.

GRENADA

US ISSN 1066-7512
DAILY SENTINEL-STAR, THE. 1854. Mon.-Fri. $.50 newsstand; $5.75/mo. carrier. 158 S. Green St., Grenada, MS 38901. TEL 601-226-4321; FAX 601-226-8310; E-mail: grenada@teclink.net. **Owner(s):** Grenada Newspapers, Inc., P.O. Box 907, Grenada, MS 38902-0907. TEL 601-226-4321; FAX 601-226-8310; Ed. Terri Ferguson; Pub. Joe Lee, III; adv. contact: Jay Lee. photos; pub. size: standard; circ. evening 5,200(paid). **Wire Service(s):** AP.
Formerly: Grenada Daily Sentinel-Star.

GULFPORT

SUN HERALD, THE. 1884. d. $.50/day newsstand; $1.25/Sun.; $11.75/mo. 205 DeBuys Rd., Gulfport, MS 39507. TEL 601-896-2100; FAX 601-896-2104; E-mail: mtonos@sunherald.infi.net; URL: http://www.sunherald.com. **Owner(s):** Knight-Ridder, Inc., One Herald Plz., Miami, FL 33132. TEL 305-376-3800; FAX 305-376-3875; Pub. Roland Weeks; adv. contact: Stone Ellis. bk.rev.; pub. size: broadsheet; circ. morning 49,059(paid); Sun. 54,980(paid). **Wire Service(s):** AP, KR.

HATTIESBURG

HATTIESBURG AMERICAN. 1885. d. $.35/day newsstand; $1.25/Sun.; $11/mo. 825 N. Main St., Hattiesburg, MS 39401. TEL 601-582-4321; FAX 601-583-8244. **Owner(s):** Gannett Company, Inc., 1100 Wilson Blvd., Arlington, VA 22234. TEL 703-284-6000; Ed. Ronnie Agnew; Pub. Leslie J. Hurst; adv. contact: Susanne Pepper. photos; bk.rev.; pub. size: broadsheet; circ. evening 28,000(paid); Sun. 30,000(paid). **Wire Service(s):** AP, GNS.

JACKSON

US ISSN 0744-9526
CLARION-LEDGER, THE. 1837. d. $.50/day newsstand; $1.50/Sun.; $13.50/mo. carrier; $19.50/mo. in state mailed; $21.50/mo. out of state mailed. 201 Congress St., Jackson, MS 39205. TEL 601-961-7175; FAX 601-961-7211. **Owner(s):** Gannett Company, Inc., 1100 Wilson Blvd., Arlington, VA 22234. TEL 703-284-6000; Ed. Margaret Downing; Pub. Richard R. Stone; adv. contact: John Kelly. photos; bk.rev.; pub. size: broadsheet; circ. morning 107,876(paid); Sun. 127,393(paid). **Wire Service(s):** AP, KR, NYT.

DAILY NEWSPAPERS

LAUREL
US
LAUREL LEADER-CALL. 1911. d. $.50/day newsstand; $1/Sun. 130 Beacon St., Laurel, MS 39440. TEL 601-428-0551; FAX 601-426-3550. **Owner(s):** American Publishing Co., 606 N. Van Buren, Marion, IL 62959. TEL 618-993-1711; Ed. Hal Marx; Pub. Paul Barrett; adv. contact: Crystal Dupre. pub. size: broadsheet; circ. evening 10,515(paid). **Wire Service(s):** AP.

MCCOMB
US
MCCOMB ENTERPRISE-JOURNAL. 1889. Sun.-Fri. $.50/day newsstand; $1/Sun.; $8/mo. Oliver Emmerich Dr., McComb, MS 39648. TEL 601-684-2421; FAX 601-684-0836; E-mail: ejournal@telepex.com. **Owner(s):** J.O. Emmerich & Associates, Inc., Oliver Emmerich Dr., McComb, MS 39648. TEL 601-684-2421; FAX 601-684-0836; Ed. Jack Ryan; Pub. Charles M. Dunagin; adv. contact: Deborah W. Best. pub. size: broadsheet; circ. evening 12,000(paid); Sun. 12,000(paid). **Wire Service(s):** AP.

MERIDIAN
US ISSN 1064-9549
MERIDIAN STAR. 1896. d. $.50/day newsstand; $1.25/Sun.; $10.95/mo. carrier & motor rte.; $12.25/mo. mailed in cy.; $14/mo. mailed outside cy. 814 22nd Ave., Meridian, MS 39301. TEL 601-693-1551; FAX 601-485-1275. **Owner(s):** American Publishing Co., 606 N. Van Buren, Marion, IL 62959. TEL 618-993-1711; Ed. David Sullens; Pub. Ed Darling; adv. contact: Gary Peeples. pub. size: standard; circ. evening 21,000(paid); Sun. 23,000(paid). **Wire Service(s):** AP, KR, NEA.

NATCHEZ
US ISSN 0888-8744
NATCHEZ DEMOCRAT. 1865. d. $.50/day newsstand; $1.25/Sun.; $144/yr. carrier. 503 N. Canal St., Natchez, MS 39120. TEL 601-442-9101; FAX 601-442-9101. **Owner(s):** Boone Newspapers, Inc., P.O. Box 2370, Tuscaloosa, AL 35403. TEL 407-338-3298; Ed. Jimmy Sexton; Pub. Kenneth S. Boone; adv. contact: Brian Pierpont. pub. size: broadsheet; circ. morning 13,500(paid); Sun. 14,000(paid). **Wire Service(s):** AP.

OXFORD
US
OXFORD EAGLE. 1867. Mon.-Fri. $.35 newsstand; $5.25/mo. motor rte.; $19.50/3 mos. mailed. 916 Jackson Ave., Oxford, MS 38655. TEL 601-234-4331; FAX 601-234-4351. **Owner(s):** Oxford Eagle, Inc., 916 Jackson Ave., Oxford, MS 38655; Ed. Nina B. Goolsby; Pub. Jesse P. Phillips; adv. contact: Sandra Leake. photos; pub. size: broadsheet; circ. evening 6,000(paid). **Wire Service(s):** AP.

PASCAGOULA
US ISSN 1059-7166
MISSISSIPPI PRESS. 1964. Sun.-Fri. $.25/day newsstand, $1/Sun.; $4.75/mo. Mon.-Fri.; $4.90/mo. Sun.; $8/mo. daily & Sun. 405 Delmas Ave., Pascagoula, MS 39567. TEL 601-934-1408; FAX 601-934-1454. **Owner(s):** Newhouse Newspapers, 140 E. 45th St., 36th Fl., New York, NY 10017. TEL 212-697-8020; Ed. Dan Davis; Pub. Wanda Henry Jacobs; adv.; photos; bk.rev.; pub. size: broadsheet; circ. evening 22,493(paid); Sun. 24,000(paid). **Wire Service(s):** AP, CST, NNS. **Formerly:** Mississippi Press Register.

PICAYUNE
US
PICAYUNE ITEM. 1926. Tue.-Fri. & Sun. $.50/day newsstand; $.75/Sun. 214 N. Curran Ave., Picayune, MS 39466. TEL 601-798-4766; FAX 601-798-8602. **Owner(s):** Stephens Group, Inc., P.O. Box 17017, Fort Smith, AR 72914-7017. TEL 501-785-7810; Ed. Will Sullivan; Pub. Dave Simms; adv. contact: Tom Andrews. pub. size: standard; circ. morning 6,200(paid); Sun. 7,339(paid).

STARKVILLE
US ISSN 1044-3657
STARKVILLE DAILY NEWS. 1901. d. $.50/day newsstand; $1/Sun.; $77/yr. home deliv. 316 University Dr., Starkville, MS 39759. TEL 601-323-1642; FAX 601-323-6586. **Owner(s):** American Publishing Co., 606 N. Van Buren, Marion, IL 62959. TEL 618-993-1711; Ed. Pattye Archer; Pub. Rick Noffsinger; adv. contact: Brian Tarun. pub. size: broadsheet; circ. morning 6,900(paid); Sun. 7,000(paid). **Wire Service(s):** AP.

TUPELO
US ISSN 0744-5431
NORTHEAST MISSISSIPPI DAILY JOURNAL. 1870. d. $.50/day newsstand; $1/Sun; $8.90/mo. carrier. 1655 S. Green St., Tupelo, MS 38801-6557. TEL 601-842-2611; FAX 601-842-2233; E-mail: djuser@djournal.com; URL: http://www.djournal.com. **Owner(s):** Journal Publishing Co., P.O. Box 909, Tupelo, MS 38802. TEL 601-842-2611; FAX 601-842-2233; Ed. Charlotte Wolfe; Pub. Billy Crews; adv. contact: Richard Crenshaw. photos; bk.rev.; pub. size: broadsheet; circ. morning 39,148(paid); Sun. 38,390(paid). **Wire Service(s):** AP, KR.

VICKSBURG
US ISSN 0884-8912
VICKSBURG POST. 1883. d. $.50/day newsstand; $1.25/Sun.; $10.50/mo. home deliv. 1601 N. Frontage Rd., Vicksburg, MS 39180. TEL 601-636-4545; FAX 601-634-0897; E-mail: staff@vicksburgpost.com; URL: http://www.vicksburgpost.com. **Owner(s):** Vicksburg Printing & Publishing Co., 920 South St., Vicksburg, MS 39180. TEL 601-636-4545; FAX 601-634-0897; Ed. Charles D. Mitchell; Pub. Louis P. Cashman, III; adv. contact: David Gills. photos; bk.rev.; pub. size: broadsheet; circ. evening 15,869(paid); Sun. 16,283(paid). **Wire Service(s):** AP. **Formerly:** Vicksburg Evening/Sunday Post.

WEST POINT
US
DAILY TIMES LEADER. 1929. Tue.-Fri. & Sun. $.50 newsstand; $74/yr. carrier. 227 Court West Point, West Point, MS 39773. TEL 601-494-1422; FAX 601-494-1414. **Owner(s):** American Publishing Co., 606 N. Van Buren, Marion, IL 62959. TEL 618-993-1711; Ed. Floyd Ingram; Pub. Rick Noffsinger; adv. contact: Joyce Pierce. pub. size: broadsheet; circ. morning 4,000(paid); Sun. 4,000(paid).

MISSOURI

BLUE SPRINGS
US
BLUE SPRINGS EXAMINER. 1974. Mon.-Sat. $.50/day newsstand; $.75/Sat.; $7.90/yr. carrier. 500 W. R.D. Mize Rd., Blue Springs, MO 64015. TEL 816-229-9161; FAX 816-224-7245. **Owner(s):** Morris Communications, P.O. Box 936, Augusta, GA 30903. TEL 706-724-0851; Ed. Dale Brendel; Pub. Dan Potter; adv.; photos; pub. size: broadsheet; circ. morning 5,500(paid). **Wire Service(s):** AP.

BOONVILLE
US
BOONVILLE DAILY NEWS. 1919. Mon.-Fri. $.50 newsstand; $10.67/mo.; $26.68/3 mos. 412 High St., Boonville, MO 65233. TEL 816-882-5335; FAX 816-882-2256. **Owner(s):** American Publishing Co., 606 N. Van Buren, Marion, IL 62959. TEL 618-993-1711; Ed. Steve Thomas; Pub. Scott J. Jackson; adv. contact: Kim Alberts. pub. size: broadsheet; circ. evening 3,200(paid). **Wire Service(s):** AP.

BROOKFIELD
US
DAILY NEWS-BULLETIN, THE. 1879. Mon.-Fri. $.50 newsstand; $9.07/mo. carrier; $66.70/yr. carrier; $66.70/yr. mailed in cy.; $80.04/yr. mailed out of cy.; $86/yr. outside state. 107-109 N. Main, Brookfield, MO 64628. TEL 816-258-7237; FAX 816-258-7238. **Owner(s):** American Publishing Co., 606 N. Van Buren, Marion, IL 62959. TEL 618-993-1711; Ed. Greg Orear. adv. contact: Carol Moorse. photos; pub. size: broadsheet; circ. evening 3,500(free & paid). **Wire Service(s):** AP.

CAMDENTON
US ISSN 1063-7001
LAKE SUN LEADER. 1879. Mon.-Fri. $.50 newsstand; $91.14/yr. carrier; $96.50/yr. mailed in state; $99/yr. mailed out of state. 450 N. Hwy. 5, Camdenton, MO 65020. TEL 573-346-2132; FAX 573-346-4508; E-mail: newsdude@is.usmo.com; URL: http://www.odd.net/lsl. **Owner(s):** American Publishing Co., 606 N. Van Buren, Marion, IL 62959. TEL 618-993-1711; Ed. Mike Feeback; Pub. Tom Turner; adv. contact: Lisa Miller. pub. size: broadsheet; circ. evening 5,850(paid). **Wire Service(s):** AP. **Formerly:** Reveille, The.

DAILY NEWSPAPERS

CAPE GIRARDEAU

US ISSN 0746-4452
SOUTHEAST MISSOURIAN. 1904. d. $.50/day newsstand; $1.50/Sun. 301 Broadway, Cape Girardeau, MO 63701. TEL 314-335-6611; FAX 314-334-9258. **Owner(s):** Gary Rust, 301 Broadway, Cape Girardeau, MO 63701. TEL 314-335-9258; Ed. Joni Adams; Pub. Wally Lage; adv. contact: Pat Zellmer. pub. size: broadsheet; circ. evening 19,000(paid); Sun. 29,000(paid).

CARTHAGE

US
CARTHAGE PRESS. 1884. Mon.-Sat. $.50 newsstand; $22.33/qtr. 527 S. Main, Carthage, MO 64836. TEL 417-358-2191; FAX 417-358-7428. **Owner(s):** American Publishing Co., 606 N. Van Buren, Marion, IL 62959. TEL 618-993-1711; Ed. Randy Turner; Pub. Jim Farley; adv. contact: Jim Farley. pub. size: standard; circ. evening 5,100(paid). **Wire Service(s):** AP.

CHILLICOTHE

US ISSN 0746-8555
CHILLICOTHE CONSTITUTION-TRIBUNE. 1860. Mon.-Fri. $.50 newsstand; $94.99/yr. in cy.; $100.91/yr. out of cy.; $97.20/yr. out of state. 818 Washington, Chillicothe, MO 64601. TEL 816-646-2411; FAX 816-646-2028; E-mail: constribune@vax2.rainis.net. **Owner(s):** American Publishing Co., 606 N. Van Buren, P.O. Box 520, Marion, IL 62959. TEL 618-993-1711; FAX 618-997-4018; Ed. Charles Haney; Pub. Charles Haney; adv. contact: Rod Dixon. photos; bk.rev.; pub. size: broadsheet; circ. evening 4,700(paid). **Wire Service(s):** AP.

CLINTON

US
CLINTON DAILY DEMOCRAT. 1868. Mon.-Fri. $.50 newsstand; $54/yr. in cy.; $67.39/yr. out of cy.; $68/yr. out of state. 212 S. Washington St., Clinton, MO 64735. TEL 816-885-2281; FAX 816-885-2265. **Owner(s):** Democrat Publishing Co., 212 S. Washington St., Clinton, MO 64735. TEL 816-885-2281; FAX 816-885-2265; Ed. Daniel B. Miles, Jr.; Pub. Kathleen White Miles; adv. contact: Kathleen Miles. pub. size: broadsheet; circ. evening 4,250(paid).

COLUMBIA

US
COLUMBIA DAILY TRIBUNE. 1901. d. $.50/day newsstand; $1/Sun.; $25.95/3 mo.; $49.75/6 mo.; $94/yr. 101 N. Fourth St., Columbia, MO 65201. TEL 314-449-3811; FAX 314-874-6413; E-mail: cdteditr@bigcat.missouri.edu; URL: http://www.trib.net. **Owner(s):** Tribune Publishing Co., 101 N. Fourth St., Columbia, MO 65201. TEL 314-449-3811; Ed. Jim Robertson; Pub. Henry J. Waters, III; adv. contact: Randall McMillan. pub. size: broadsheet; circ. evening 17,868(paid); Sun. 22,307(paid). **Wire Service(s):** AP, KR.

US ISSN 0747-1874
COLUMBIA MISSOURIAN. 1908. Sun.-Fri. $.50/day newsstand; $.75/Sun.; $85/yr. 221 S. Eighth St., Columbia, MO 65201. TEL 573-882-5700; FAX 573-882-5702; E-mail: jourab@muccmail@missouri.edu; URL: http://digmo.org. **Owner(s):** Missourian Publishing Co., P.O. Box 917, Columbia, MO 65205. TEL 314-442-3161; Ed. George Kennedy; Pub. Dean Mills; adv. contact: Jack Swartz. pub. size: broadsheet; circ. morning 5,500(paid); Sun. 26,500(paid). **Wire Service(s):** AP, NYT, SHNA.

DEXTER

US
DAILY STATESMAN. 5000. Tue., Wed., Fri. & Sun. $.50 newsstand; $69/yr. in cy. 133 S. Walnut, Dexter, MO 63841. TEL 573-624-4545; FAX 573-624-7449. **Owner(s):** Rust Communications, P.O. Box 699, Cape Girardeau, MO 63702-0699. TEL 573-335-6611; Ed. Buck Collier; Pub. Barbara Hill; pub. size: broadsheet; circ. evening 5,000(paid).
Formerly: Stoddard County News.

US
DEXTER DAILY STATESMAN. 1898. Tue.-Fri. & Sun. $.50 newsstand; $.75/Sun.; $69/yr. in cy. 33 S. Walnut, Dexter, MO 63841. TEL 573-624-4545; FAX 573-624-7449. **Owner(s):** Rust Communications, P.O. Box 699, Cape Girardeau, MO 63702-0699. TEL 314-335-6611; Ed. Buck Collier; Pub. Barbara Hill; adv. contact: Elaine Pursell. pub. size: broadsheet; circ. evening 5,000(paid); Sun. 5,000(paid). **Wire Service(s):** API.

EXCELSIOR SPRINGS

US
DAILY STANDARD. 1889. Mon.-Fri. $.50 newsstand; $11.75/3 mo. carrier or mail; $14.25/3 mo. in st.; $15.75/3 mo. out of st. 417 Thompson, Excelsior Springs, MO 64024. TEL 816-637-3147; FAX 816-637-8411. **Owner(s):** Facklelman Publishers, LA. TEL 318-824-3011; FAX 318-824-6238; Ed. Gene Hanson; Pub. Jim Bouldin; adv. contact: Brian Rice. photos; bk.rev.; pub. size: broadsheet; circ. evening 3,000(paid). **Wire Service(s):** MissouriLink.
Formerly: Excelsior Springs Daily Standard.

FARMINGTON

US ISSN 1076-5832
PRESS LEADER, THE. 1950. Tue.-Sat. $.50 newsstand; $54/yr. carrier. 218 N. Washington St., Farmington, MO 63640. TEL 573-756-8927; FAX 573-756-9160; E-mail: rdennis@pressleader.com; URL: http://www.pressleader.com. **Owner(s):** American Publishing Co., 606 N. Van Buren, Marion, IL 62959. TEL 618-993-1711; Ed. Tim Kenyon; Pub. Mark Griggs; pub. size: broadsheet; circ. 25,000(paid).
Formerly: Farmington Press Greensheet.

FULTON

US ISSN 8750-6696
FULTON SUN GAZETTE, THE. 1876. Tue.-Fri. & Sun. $.50 newsstand; $61/yr. carrier; $78/yr. mailed in cy; $81.82/yr. mailed in state; $86.32/yr. mailed out of cy & state; $77.68/yr. senior citizens. 115 E. Fifth St., Fulton, MO 65251. TEL 573-642-7272; FAX 573-642-0656. **Owner(s):** Mrs. William H. Weldon, P.O. Box 420, Jefferson City, MO 65101. TEL 573-636-3131; Ed. Rich Gleba; Pub. Mrs. William H. Weldon; adv.; pub. size: broadsheet; circ. morning 5,200(paid); Sun. 5,200(paid). **Wire Service(s):** AP.
Formerly: Fulton Sun, The.

HANNIBAL

US
HANNIBAL COURIER-POST. 1838. Mon.-Sat. $.50 newsstand; $8/mo. carrier & motor rte; $12.50/mo. in state & elsewhere. 200 N. Third St., Hannibal, MO 63401. TEL 573-221-2800; FAX 573-221-1568; E-mail: hep@nemonet.com. **Owner(s):** Morris Communications, P.O. Box 936, Augusta, GA 30903. TEL 706-724-0851; Ed. Jim Whitaker. adv. contact: Bob Hudson. pub. size: standard; circ. morning 10,000(paid). **Wire Service(s):** AP.

HOLLISTER

US
BRANSON DAILY NEWS. 1898. Tue.-Sun. $.50/day newsstand; $1/Sun.; $88/yr. in Stone & Taney cys.; $140/yr. out of area. 200 Industrial Park Dr., Hollister, MO 65672. TEL 417-334-3161; FAX 417-334-4299. **Owner(s):** James Lancaster, P.O. Box 609, Gadsden, AL 35902; Pub. Ted Delaney; adv. contact: Shane Walton. pub. size: broadsheet; circ. morning 11,245(paid); Sun. 12,000(paid).
Formerly: Taney County Republican.

INDEPENDENCE

US
INDEPENDENCE EXAMINER, THE. 1898. Mon.-Sat. $.50 newsstand; $.75/Sat.; $85.88/yr. carrier; $113.28yr. out of town. 410 S. Liberty, Independence, MO 64050. TEL 816-254-8600; FAX 816-836-3805. **Owner(s):** Morris Communications, P.O. Box 936, Augusta, GA 30903. TEL 706-724-0851; Ed. Sheila Davis; Pub. Ben Weir, Jr.; adv. contact: Irene Baltrusaitis. photos; bk.rev.; pub. size: broadsheet; circ. evening 21,087(paid). **Wire Service(s):** AP.

JEFFERSON CITY

US
POST-TRIBUNE. 1865. d. $.50 newsstand; $7.50/mo. 210 Monroe St., Jefferson City, MO 65101. TEL 573-636-3131; FAX 573-636-7035. **Owner(s):** News Tribune Co., P.O. Box 420, Jefferson City, MO 65101. TEL 573-636-3131; FAX 573-636-7035; Ed. Richard McGonegal. adv. contact: Jim Ward. photos; bk.rev.; pub. size: standard; circ. evening 18,000(paid); Sun. 25,500(paid). **Wire Service(s):** AP, CNS, CQ, SHNA, NYT.

DAILY NEWSPAPERS

JOPLIN
US

JOPLIN GLOBE, THE. 1896. d. $.50/day newsstand; $1.50/Sun.; $141.83/yr. home deliv.; $161.76/yr. in state mailed; $175.74/yr. mailed. 117 E. Fourth St., Joplin, MO 64801. TEL 417-623-3480; FAX 417-623-8450. **Owner(s):** Ottaway Newspapers, Inc., P.O. Box 401, Campbell Hall, NY 10916. TEL 914-294-8181; Ed. Thomas P. Murray; Pub. Dan Chiodo; pub. size: broadsheet; circ. morning 36,340(paid); Sun. 45,995(paid). **Wire Service(s):** AP.

KANSAS CITY
US   ISSN 0745-1067

KANSAS CITY STAR. 1880. d. $.50/day newsstand, $1.50/Sun; $12.95/mo. carrier; $19.99/mo. mailed in state. 1729 Grand Blvd., Kansas City, MO 64108. TEL 816-234-4141; FAX 816-234-4926. **Owner(s):** Knight-Ridder, Inc., One Herald Plz., Miami, FL 33132. TEL 305-376-3800; FAX 305-376-3875; Ed. Arthur Brisbane; Pub. Bob Woodworth; adv.; photos; bk.rev.; pub. size: broadsheet; circ. morning 291,000(paid); Sun. 431,616(paid). **Wire Service(s):** NYT, AP, CDN, KR, LATS.

KENNETT
US   ISSN 1047-7160

DAILY DUNKLIN DEMOCRAT. 1888. Tue.-Fri. & Sun. $.50/day newsstand; $.75/Sun.; $6.50/mo. carrier; $72/yr. carrier. 203 First St., Kennett, MO 63857. TEL 573-888-4505; FAX 573-888-5114. **Owner(s):** Delta Publishing Co., Inc., P.O. Box 669, Kennett, MO 63857. TEL 573-888-4505; Ed. Tracy Madden; Pub. Bud Hunt; adv. contact: Terri Coleman. photos; bk.rev.; pub. size: standard; circ. evening 5,200(paid). **Wire Service(s):** AP.

    Formerly: Kennett Daily Dunklin Democrat.

KIRKSVILLE
US

KIRKSVILLE DAILY EXPRESS. 1915. Sun.-Fri. $.50/day newsstand; $.75/Sun. 110 E. McPherson St., Kirksville, MO 63501. TEL 816-665-2808; FAX 816-665-2608. **Owner(s):** American Publishing Co., 606 N. Van Buren, Marion, IL 62959. TEL 618-993-1711; Ed. Judy Tritz; Pub. Larry W. Freels; adv.; photos; bk.rev.; pub. size: broadsheet; circ. evening 7,400(paid); Sun. 7,900(paid). **Wire Service(s):** AP.

LEBANON
US

LEBANON DAILY RECORD. 1934. Sun.-Fri. $.50/day newsstand; $.75/Sun.; $62.50/yr. in cy.; $66.80/yr. neighboring cys.; $118.30/yr. in state; $135.35/yr. out of state. 290 S. Madison, Lebanon, MO 65536. TEL 417-532-9131; FAX 417-532-8140; E-mail: infoline@mail.llion.org; URL: http://www.llion.org/ldr/news.html. **Owner(s):** Dalton Wright, 290 S. Madison, Lebanon, MO 65536. TEL 417-532-9131; Ed. Eric Chrism; Pub. Steve Hilton; adv. contact: Rene Barker. bk.rev.; pub. size: broadsheet; circ. evening 5,281(paid); Sun. 5,642(paid). **Wire Service(s):** AP.

MACON
US

MACON CHRONICLE-HERALD. 1910. Tue.-Fri. $.50 newsstand; $11.51/mo. carrier. 204 W. Bourke, Macon, MO 63552. TEL 816-385-3121; FAX 816-385-3082. **Owner(s):** American Publishing Co., 606 N. Van Buren, Marion, IL 62959. TEL 618-993-1711; Ed. Mark Snow; Pub. Bill Hall; adv. contact: Pat Quinly. pub. size: broadsheet; circ. evening 3,500(free). **Wire Service(s):** AP.

MARSHALL
US

MARSHALL DEMOCRAT-NEWS. 1881. Mon.-Fri. $.50 newsstand; $41.40/yr. in town. 121 N. Lafayette, Marshall, MO 65340. TEL 816-886-2233. **Owner(s):** U.S. Media Group, P.O. Box 227, Crystal City, MO 63019; Ed. Mary Jo Rieth; Pub. Shelly M. Arth; adv.; photos; bk.rev.; pub. size: broadsheet; circ. evening 4,300(paid). **Wire Service(s):** AP.

MARYVILLE
US

MARYVILLE DAILY FORUM. 1869. Tue.-Fri. & Sun. $.50/day newsstand; $.75/Sun.; $7/mo. 111 E. Jenkins, Maryville, MO 64468. TEL 816-562-2424; FAX 816-562-2823; E-mail: dailyforum@msc-net.com. **Owner(s):** Midland Media, Inc., 111 E. Jenkins, Maryville, MO 64468. TEL 816-562-2424; Ed. Steve Woolfolk; Pub. Jerry Pye; adv.; photos; bk.rev.; pub. size: broadsheet; circ. evening 4,225(paid); Sun. 4,361(paid). **Wire Service(s):** AP.

MEXICO
US

MEXICO LEDGER. 1855. d. $.50 day newsstand; $8.50/mo. 300 N. Washington, Ledger Plz., Mexico, MO 65265-0008. TEL 314-581-1111; FAX 314-581-2029. **Owner(s):** Hollinger, Inc.; Ed. Tracey Berry; Pub. Joe May; adv. contact: Martin Keller. photos; bk.rev.; pub. size: broadsheet; circ. evening 9,541(paid). **Wire Service(s):** AP.

MOBERLY
US

MOBERLY MONITOR INDEX. 1869. Sun.-Fri. $.50/day newsstand; $.75/Sun.; $6/mo. carrier or mailed. 218 N. Williams St., Moberly, MO 65270. TEL 816-263-4123; FAX 816-263-3626. **Owner(s):** Stephens Group, Inc., 3600 Wheeler Ave., Fort Smith, AR 72901. TEL 501-785-7827; Ed. Ruth Carr; Pub. Bob Cunningham; adv. contact: Judy Orton. photos; bk.rev.; pub. size: standard; circ. evening 8,100(paid); Sun. 8,595(paid). **Wire Service(s):** AP.

MONETT
US

MONETT TIMES. 1888. Mon.-Fri. $.25 newsstand; $35/yr. carrier; $48/yr. mailed in cy.; $69/yr. out of cy.; $71/yr. out of state. 505 Broadway, Monett, MO 65708. TEL 417-235-3135; FAX 417-235-8852. **Owner(s):** Walls Newspapers, Inc., P.O. Box 530447, Birmingham, AL 35253. TEL 201-870-1684; Ed. Murray Bishoff; Pub. Stephen Crass; adv. contact: Mike Stubbs. pub. size: broadsheet; circ. evening 4,600(paid).

NEOSHO
US

NEOSHO DAILY NEWS. 1905. Sun.-Fri. $.50/day newsstand; $.75/Sun.; $7.50/mo. carrier. 1006 W. Harmony St., Neosho, MO 64850. TEL 417-451-1520; FAX 417-451-6408. **Owner(s):** American Publishing Co., 606 N. Van Buren, Marion, IL 62959. TEL 618-993-1711; Ed. Sherry Langston; Pub. Valerie Praytor; adv. contact: Steve Praytor. pub. size: broadsheet; circ. evening 4,600(paid); Sun. 5,200(paid). **Wire Service(s):** AP.

NEVADA
US   ISSN 1056-3555

DAILY MAIL & SUNDAY HERALD. 1883. Tue.-Fri. & Sun. $.50 newsstand; $9/mo.; $75/yr. 131 S. Cedar St., Nevada, MO 64772. TEL 417-667-3344; FAX 417-667-8121. **Owner(s):** U.S. Media Group, P.O. Box 227, Crystal City, MO 63019. TEL 314-937-5200; FAX 314-937-7947; Ed. Angela H. Cutrer; Pub. Randall E. Batlegler; adv.; photos; bk.rev.; pub. size: broadsheet; circ. evening 4,500(paid); Sun. 4,800(paid). **Wire Service(s):** AP.

PARK HILLS
US

DAILY JOURNAL. Sun.-Fri. $.50/day newsstand, $.75/Sun. 1513 Saint Joe Dr., Park Hills, MO 63601. TEL 573-431-2010; FAX 573-431-7640. **Owner(s):** Pulitzer Publishing Co., 900 N. Tucker Blvd., St. Louis, MO 63101. TEL 313-340-8000; Ed. Joseph Layden; Pub. Ron Weir; pub. size: broadsheet; circ. evening 10,300(paid); Sun. 10,300(paid). **Wire Service(s):** AP.

POPLAR BLUFF
US   ISSN 1061-7116

DAILY AMERICAN REPUBLIC. 1923. Sun.-Fri. $.50/day newsstand; $1/Sun.; $98/yr. carrier; $150/yr. out of state. 208 Poplar St., Poplar Bluff, MO 63901. TEL 573-785-1414; FAX 573-785-2706. **Owner(s):** Butler County Publishing, 208 Poplar St., Poplar Bluff, MO 63901; Ed. Stan Berry; Pub. Don Schrieber; adv. contact: Joe Jordan. pub. size: broadsheet; circ. evening 15,000(paid); Sun. 22,000(paid). **Wire Service(s):** AP.

RICHMOND
US

DAILY NEWS. 1914. Mon.-Fri. $.50 newsstand; $51/yr. in cy.; $57/yr. in state; $57/yr. out of state. 204 W. N. Main St., Richmond, MO 64085. TEL 816-776-5454; FAX 816-637-1639. **Owner(s):** Richmond News, Inc., The, 204 W. N. Main St., P.O. Box 100, Richmond, MO 64085. TEL 816-776-5454; FAX 816-637-1639; Richmond News, Inc., The, 204 W. N. Main St., P.O. Box 100, Richmond,MO 64085; Ed. Randy Roberts; Pub. Chris Sharp; adv. contact: Chris Sharp. adv.: $6.75/SAU. photos; pub. size: broadsheet; circ. evening 12,888(free & paid).

DAILY NEWSPAPERS

ROLLA

US
ROLLA DAILY NEWS. 1942. Sun.-Fri. $.50/day newsstand; $.75/Sun.; $89/yr. carrier; $149.45/yr. out of cy.; $150.80/yr. out of state. 101 W. Seventh St., Rolla, MO 65401. TEL 573-364-2468; FAX 573-341-5847. **Owner(s):** American Publishing Co., 606 N. Van Buren, Marion, IL 62959. TEL 618-993-1711; Ed. R.D. Hohenfeldt; Pub. Stephen E. Sowers; pub. size: standard; circ. evening 5,300(paid); Sun. 6,100(paid). **Wire Service(s):** UPI.

SEDALIA

US ISSN 1061-1762
SEDALIA DEMOCRAT, THE. 1868. d. $.50/day newsstand; $1.25/Sun. 700 S. Massachusetts, Sedalia, MO 65301. TEL 816-826-1000; FAX 816-826-2413. **Owner(s):** Freedom Communications, Inc., 1055 N. Main St., Ste. 901, Irvine, CA 92701. TEL 714-542-4415; Ed. Oliver Wiest; Pub. Frank Lyon; adv. contact: Lisa A. Lynn. pub. size: broadsheet; circ. evening 13,723(paid); Sun. 14,455(paid). **Wire Service(s):** AP, KRT.

SIKESTON

US ISSN 1074-4460
SIKESTON STANDARD DEMOCRAT, THE. 1913. Sun.-Fri. $.50/day newsstand; $1/Sun.; $8.40/mo. carrier; $84/yr. carrier; $102.34/yr. mailed out of state. 205 S. New Madrid, Sikeston, MO 63801. TEL 573-471-1137; FAX 573-471-6277. **Owner(s):** D.A. Publishing LC, 205 S. New Madrid, Sikeston, MO 63801. TEL 573-471-1137; Ed. Jill Bock; Pub. Michael Jensen; adv. contact: Deanna Nelson. pub. size: broadsheet; circ. morning 11,000(paid); Sun. 12,500(paid). **Wire Service(s):** AP.
Formerly: Standard Democrat.

SPRINGFIELD

US ISSN 0893-3448
SPRINGFIELD NEWS-LEADER, THE. 1867. d. $.50/day newsstand; $1.75/Sun.; $13/mo. carrier. 651 Boonville Ave., Springfield, MO 65806. TEL 417-836-1208; FAX 417-836-1147. **Owner(s):** Gannett Company, Inc., 1100 Wilson Blvd., Arlington, VA 22234. TEL 703-284-6000; Ed. Kate Marymont; Pub. Dan A. Martin; adv. contact: Larry Whitaker. pub. size: broadsheet; circ. morning 62,553(paid); Sun. 99,090(paid). **Wire Service(s):** AP, GNS, LAT-WP.

ST. CHARLES

US
COURIER-POST, THE. Mon.-Fri. $.50 newsstand; $55/yr. carrier. 201 N. Main St., Ste. 205, St. Charles, MO 63301. TEL 314-949-6928; FAX 314-949-6973. **Owner(s):** Legal Communications Corp., P.O. Box 88910, St. Louis, MO 63188. TEL 314-421-1880; Pub. Sue Tedesco; pub. size: tabloid; circ. morning 3,700(paid).

ST. JOSEPH

US ISSN 1063-4312
ST. JOSEPH NEWS-PRESS. 1845. d. $.50/day newsstand; $1.25/Sun.; $120.12/yr. carrier. 825 Edmond, St. Joseph, MO 64502. TEL 816-271-8500; FAX 816-271-8692. **Owner(s):** News-Press & Gazette Co., P.O. Box 29, St. Joseph, MO 64502. TEL 816-271-8500; Ed. David R. Bradley, Jr.; Pub. David R. Bradley, Jr.; adv. contact: Ron Ciani. photos; bk.rev.; pub. size: standard; circ. morning 44,841(paid); Sun. 50,165(paid). **Wire Service(s):** AP, NYT.
Formerly: St. Joseph News-Press/Gazette.

ST. LOUIS

US
ST. LOUIS POST-DISPATCH. 1878. d. $.50/day newsstand; $1.25/Sun.; $3.10/wk. carrier. 900 N. Tucker Blvd., St. Louis, MO 63101. TEL 314-340-8901; FAX 314-340-3165. **Owner(s):** Pulitzer Publishing Co., 900 N. Tucker Blvd., St. Louis, MO 63101. TEL 314-340-8000; Ed. Richard Weil, Jr.; Pub. Nicholas G. Penniman, IV; adv.; pub. size: standard; circ. morning 345,700(paid); Sun. 541,991(paid). **Wire Service(s):** AP, CT-NYT, LAT-WP, KR, RN, SHNA.

ST. ROBERT

US
DAILY GUIDE. 1963. Mon.-Fri. $.50 newsstand; $67.35/yr. 108 Holly Dr., St. Robert, MO 65583. TEL 573-336-3711; FAX 573-336-4640. **Owner(s):** American Publishing Co., 606 N. Van Buren, Marion, IL 62959. TEL 618-993-1711; Ed. James Bradley; Pub. Joel Goodrich; adv.; pub. size: broadsheet; circ. evening 2,800(paid). **Wire Service(s):** AP.

TRENTON

US
TRENTON REPUBLICAN TIMES. 1864. Mon.-Fri. $.50 newsstand; $53.36/yr. local. 122 E. Eighth St., Trenton, MO 64683. TEL 816-359-2212; FAX 816-359-4414. **Owner(s):** Wendell J. Lenhart, 514 Town & Country, Trenton, MO 64683. TEL 816-359-2212; Ed. Wendell J. Lenhart; Pub. Wendell J. Lenhart; adv. contact: DeLane Hein. pub. size: broadsheet; circ. evening 3,850(paid). **Wire Service(s):** AP.

WARRENSBURG

US
DAILY STAR-JOURNAL, THE. 1865. Mon.-Fri. $.50 newsstand; $48.22/yr. carrier; $58.75/yr. out of state. 135 E. Market, Warrensburg, MO 64093. TEL 816-747-8123; FAX 816-747-8741. **Owner(s):** Star-Journal Publishing Co., 135 E. Market, Warrensburg, MO 64093. TEL 816-747-8123; Ed. Avis G. Tucker; Pub. Avis G. Tucker; adv. contact: Don Kirkpatrick. photos; bk.rev.; pub. size: broadsheet; circ. evening 5,097(paid). **Wire Service(s):** AP.

WEST PLAINS

US
WEST PLAINS DAILY QUILL. 1902. Mon.-Fri. $.35 newsstand; $5.31/mo. carrier; $6/mo. out of state;. 125 N. Jefferson, West Plains, MO 65775-0110. TEL 417-256-9191; FAX 417-256-9196. **Owner(s):** Quill Press Co., 125 Jefferson, P.O. Box 110, West Plains, MO 65775-0110. TEL 417-256-9191; Ed. Jerry P. Womack; Pub. Frank L. Martin, III; adv. contact: Sunie K. Pace. photos; bk.rev.; pub. size: broadsheet; circ. evening 9,639(paid). **Wire Service(s):** AP.

MONTANA

BILLINGS

US
BILLINGS GAZETTE. 1885. d. $.50/day newsstand; $.75/Sat.; $1.75/Sun.; $18/4 wks. carrier; $22/4 wks. mailed MT, WY, ND. 401 N. Broadway, Billings, MT 59101. TEL 406-657-1200; FAX 406-657-1208; E-mail: bgazette@bsw.infi.net. **Owner(s):** Lee Enterprises, Inc., 215 N. Main St., Davenport, IA 52801. TEL 319-383-2202; Ed. Gerry O'Brien; Pub. Wayne Schile; bk.rev.; pub. size: broadsheet; circ. morning 62,370(paid); Sun. 64,064(paid). **Wire Service(s):** AP, KR.

BOZEMAN

US
BOZEMAN DAILY CHRONICLE. 1883. d. $.50/day newsstand; $1.25/Sun.; $12/mo. carrier; $13/mo. motor rte. 32 S. Rouse, Bozeman, MT 59715. TEL 406-587-4491. **Owner(s):** Big Sky Publishing Co., P.O. Box 1188, Bozeman, MT 59771. TEL 406-587-4491; Ed. Bill Wilke; Pub. Rick Coffman; adv. contact: Mike Smit. pub. size: broadsheet; circ. morning 135,000(paid); Sun. 15,800(paid). **Wire Service(s):** AP, LAT-WP.

BUTTE

US
MONTANA STANDARD. 1876. d. $.50/day newsstand; $1.50/Sun.; $3.50/wk. carrier; $4.20/wk. mailed in state; $4.48/wk. mailed out of state. 25 W. Granite, Butte, MT 59701-9213. TEL 406-496-5500; FAX 406-496-5551. **Owner(s):** Lee Enterprises, Inc., 400 Putnam Bldg., 215 N. Main St., Davenport, IA 52801-1924. TEL 319-383-2100; Ed. Drew Vanfossem; Pub. Norm Lewis; adv. contact: Lori Devoti. pub. size: standard; circ. morning 16,000(paid); Sun. 16,600(paid). **Wire Service(s):** AP, NYT.

GREAT FALLS

US
GREAT FALLS TRIBUNE. 1884. d. $.50/day newsstand; $1.50/Sun.; $3.35/wk. carrier; $14.80/mo. mailed in state. 205 River Dr. S., Great Falls, MT 59405. TEL 406-791-1444; FAX 406-791-1431. **Owner(s):** Great Falls Tribune Co., Div. of Gannett, P.O. Box 5468, Great Falls, MT 59403. TEL 406-791-1444; Ed. Gary Moseman; Pub. Elizabeth Franz; adv. contact: Dave Gould. pub. size: broadsheet; circ. morning 35,000(paid); Sun. 41,000(paid). **Wire Service(s):** AP, NYT, SHNA, GNS.

DAILY NEWSPAPERS

HAMILTON
US
RAVALLI REPUBLIC. 1889. Mon.-Fri. $.50 newsstand; $79/yr. mailed in cy.; $88/yr. mailed out of cy. 232 W. Main St., Hamilton, MT 59840. TEL 406-363-3300; FAX 406-363-1767. **Owner(s):** Pulitzer Community Newspapers, Inc., 900 N. Tucker Blvd., St. Louis, MO 63101. TEL 314-340-3127; Ed. Rob Breeding; Pub. Cindy Petrusaitis; adv.; photos; bk.rev.; pub. size: broadsheet; circ. morning 5,600(paid). **Wire Service(s):** AP.

HAVRE
US
HAVRE DAILY NEWS. 1915. Mon.-Fri. $.50 newsstand; $108/yr. carrier; $156/yr. out of state. 119 Second St., Havre, MT 59501. TEL 406-265-6796; FAX 406-265-6798. **Owner(s):** Pioneer Press, Inc., 3701 W. Lake Ave., Glenview, IL 60025. TEL 847-486-9200; Ed. Steve Miller; Pub. Rick Weaver; adv. contact: Paula Reynolds. pub. size: standard; circ. evening 4,800(paid). **Wire Service(s):** AP.

HELENA
US
INDEPENDENT RECORD. d. $.50/day newsstand; $.75/Fri.; $1.50/Sun.; $12.50/mo. carrier for seniors. 317 Cruse St., Helena, MT 59601. TEL 406-447-4000; FAX 406-447-4052. **Owner(s):** Lee Enterprises, Inc., 120 E. Second St., Davenport, IA 52801. TEL 319-383-2202; Ed. Charles Wood; Pub. Bruce Whittenberg; adv. contact: Tom Zebrun-Gero. pub. size: broadsheet; circ. morning 14,500(paid); Sun. 15,000(paid). **Wire Service(s):** AP, NYT.
  Formerly: Helena Independent Record.

KALISPELL
US
DAILY INTER LAKE, THE. 1891. Sun.-Fri. $.50/day newsstand; $1.50/Sun.; $144/yr. carrier; $150/yr. motor rte.; $200/yr. out of state. 727 E. Idaho St., Kalispell, MT 59901. TEL 406-755-7000; FAX 406-752-6114. **Owner(s):** Hagadone Corp., P.O. Box 1178, Coeur d'Alene, ID 83814. TEL 208-667-3431; Ed. Dan Black; Pub. Ron Peterson; adv.; photos; bk.rev.; pub. size: broadsheet; circ. evening 15,300(paid); Sun. 18,235(paid). **Wire Service(s):** AP.

LIVINGSTON
US
LIVINGSTON ENTERPRISE. 1883. Mon.-Fri. $.50 newsstand; $8/mo. carrier; $8.75/mo. motor rte.; $12/mo. out of state. 401 S. Main, Livingston, MT 59047. TEL 406-222-2000; FAX 406-222-8580. **Owner(s):** Yellowstone Newspapers, 401 S. Main, P.O. Box 665, Livingston, MT 59047. TEL 406-222-2000; Ed. Stephen Matlow; Pub. John Sullivan; adv.; pub. size: broadsheet; circ. evening 3,430(paid). **Wire Service(s):** AP.

MILES CITY
US   ISSN 0891-8988
MILES CITY STAR. 1910. Mon.-Fri. $.50 newsstand; $105/yr. carrier; $130.70/yr. mailed out of cy. 13 N. Sixth St., Miles City, MT 59301. TEL 406-232-0450; FAX 406-232-6687. **Owner(s):** Yellowstone Newspapers, 401 S. Main, P.O. Box 665, Livingston, MT 59047. TEL 406-222-2000; Ed. Marla Prell; Pub. John Watson; adv. contact: Giff Wood. pub. size: broadsheet; circ. evening 4,150(paid). **Wire Service(s):** AP.

MISSOULA
US   ISSN 0746-4495
MISSOULIAN, THE. 1873. d. $.50/day newsstand; $1.50/Sun.; $13.80/4 wks. 500 S. Higgins Ave., Missoula, MT 59801. TEL 406-523-5294; FAX 406-523-5221. **Owner(s):** Lee Enterprises, Inc., 400 Putnam Bldg. , 215 N. Main St., Davenport, IA 52801. TEL 319-383-2100; Ed. Mike McInally; Pub. James E. Bell; adv.; photos; pub. size: broadsheet; circ. morning 31,686(paid); Sun. 38,000(paid). **Wire Service(s):** AP, LAT-WP, KR.

NEBRASKA

ALLIANCE
US
ALLIANCE TIMES-HERALD. 1888. Mon.-Sat. $.50 newsstand; $56/yr. carrier; $76/yr. mailed locally; $88/yr. mailed out of area. 114 E. Fourth, Alliance, NE 69301. TEL 308-762-3060. **Owner(s):** Alliance Publishing Co., P.O. Box G, Alliance, NE 69301. TEL 308-762-3060; Ed. Donna Price; Pub. Fred G. Kuhlman; pub. size: broadsheet; circ. evening 3,559(paid). **Wire Service(s):** AP.

BEATRICE
US
BEATRICE DAILY SUN. 1902. Mon.-Sat. $.50 newsstand; $7.75/mo. carrier NE & KS. 200 N. Seventh St., Beatrice, NE 68310. TEL 402-223-5233; FAX 402-228-3571. **Owner(s):** American Publishing Co., 606 N. Van Buren, Marion, IL 62959. TEL 618-993-1711; Ed. Diane Vicars; Pub. Reg Durant; adv. contact: Ken Lingen. photos; pub. size: broadsheet; circ. evening 10,250(paid). **Wire Service(s):** AP.

COLUMBUS
US
COLUMBUS TELEGRAM. 1879. Sun.-Fri. $.50/day newsstand; $.75/Sun.; $87/yr. carrier; $99/yr. motor rte.; $90/yr. in state mailed; $102/yr. out of state. 1254 27th Ave., Columbus, NE 68601. TEL 402-564-2741; FAX 402-563-7500. **Owner(s):** Omaha World-Herald Co., World-Herald Sq., Columbus, NE 68601. TEL 402-444-1000; Ed. Todd Franko; Pub. Julie Speirs; adv. contact: Jo Sherbo. photos; pub. size: broadsheet; circ. evening 11,100(paid); Sun. 11,700(paid). **Wire Service(s):** AP.

FREMONT
US   ISSN 1049-8338
FREMONT TRIBUNE. 1865. Mon.-Sat. $.35 newsstand; $7/mo. carrier. 135 N. Main St., Fremont, NE 68025. TEL 402-721-5000. **Owner(s):** Independent Media Group, Watseka, IL; Ed. Brent Wasenius; Pub. Jim Holland; adv. contact: Pam Zoucha. bk.rev./; pub. size: broadsheet; circ. evening 11,000(paid). **Wire Service(s):** AP, GNS.

GRAND ISLAND
US   ISSN 1049-3018
GRAND ISLAND INDEPENDENT. 1872. d. $.50/day newsstand; $1/Sun.; $9/mo. carrier. 422 W. First St., Grand Island, NE 68801. TEL 308-382-1000; FAX 308-382-8129. **Owner(s):** Morris Communications, P.O. Box 936, Augusta, GA 30903. TEL 706-724-0851; Ed. Jeff Funk; Pub. Rob Krecklow; adv. contact: Gary Loftus. photos; bk.rev.; pub. size: broadsheet; circ. morning 25,057(paid); Sun. 25,934(paid). **Wire Service(s):** AP, KNT, NEA, SHNA, CQ.

HASTINGS
US
HASTINGS DAILY TRIBUNE. 1905. Mon.-Sat. $.50 newsstand; $84/yr. carrier; $90/yr. motor rte.; $123/yr. mailed out of state. 908-912 W. Second St., Hastings, NE 68901. TEL 402-462-2131; FAX 402-461-4657; E-mail: lhavranek@nebland.cnweb.com; URL: http://www.cnweb.com.tribune. **Owner(s):** Seaton Publishing Co., P.O. Box 788, Hastings, NE 68902. TEL 402-462-2131; Ed. Gary Johansen; Pub. Donald R. Seaton; adv. contact: Ken Gettner. pub. size: broadsheet; circ. evening 15,000(paid). **Wire Service(s):** AP, LAT-WP, SHNA, NEA.

HOLDREGE
US
HOLDREGE DAILY CITIZEN. 1886. Mon.-Fri. $.25 newsstand; $48/yr. carrier. 418 Garfield, Holdrege, NE 68949. TEL 308-995-4441; FAX 308-995-5992. **Owner(s):** Holdrege Daily Citizen, Inc., 418 Garfield, Holdrege, NE 68949; Ed. Tunney Price; Pub. Robert King; adv. contact: Barbara J. Penrod. pub. size: broadsheet; circ. evening 4,000(paid). **Wire Service(s):** AP.

KEARNEY
US
KEARNEY HUB. 1888. Mon.-Sat. $.50/day newsstand; $1/Sat.; $91/yr. carrier; $103/yr. mailed in area; $120/yr. mailed out of area. 13 E. 22nd St., Kearney, NE 68847. TEL 308-237-2152; FAX 308-234-5736. **Owner(s):** Kearney Hub Publishing Co., Inc., 13-15 E. 22nd St., Kearney, NE 68847. TEL 308-237-2152; Ed. Mike Konz. adv. contact: Gine Mortimore. bk.rev./; pub. size: broadsheet; circ. evening 26,424(paid). **Wire Service(s):** AP.
  Formerly: Kearney Saturday A.M. Hub.

KEARNEY, NE   10469

Dailies

ULRICH'S INTERNATIONAL PERIODICALS DIRECTORY 1998

LINCOLN

US ISSN 1054-7983
LINCOLN JOURNAL STAR. 1894. d. $.50/day newsstand; $1.75/Sun.; $136/yr. carrier; $161.20/yr. mailed. 926 P St., Lincoln, NE 68508. TEL 402-475-4200; FAX 402-473-7466. **Owner(s):** Journal-Star Printing Co., P.O. Box 81869, Lincoln, NE 68501. TEL 402-475-7200; Pub. William K. Johnston; adv. contact: Kevin Mowbray. photos; bk.rev.; pub. size: broadsheet; circ. morning 44,144(paid); Sun. 87,148(paid). **Wire Service(s):** AP, UPI.

MCCOOK

US
MCCOOK DAILY GAZETTE. 1911. Mon.-Sat. $.50 newsstand; $69/yr. carrier. W. First & E Sts., McCook, NE 69001. TEL 308-345-4500; FAX 308-345-7881. **Owner(s):** McCook Daily Gazette, Inc., W. First & E. Sts., McCook, NE 69001; Ed. Bruce Crosby; Pub. Gene O. Morris; adv. contact: Butch Mires. pub. size: broadsheet; circ. evening 7,600(paid). **Wire Service(s):** AP.

NEBRASKA CITY

US
NEBRASKA CITY NEWS-PRESS. 1854. Tue.-Sat. $.50 newsstand; $75/yr. carrier; $82/yr. mailed elsewhere. 806 Central Ave., Nebraska City, NE 68410. TEL 402-873-3334; FAX 402-873-5436. **Owner(s):** Midwest Newspapers, Inc., P.O. Box 380, Ames, IA 50010. TEL 515-232-2160; Ed. Carol Anderson; Pub. William Holland; adv. contact: William Holland. pub. size: broadsheet; circ. evening 2,800(paid); Sun. 2,800(paid). **Wire Service(s):** AP.

NORFOLK

US
NORFOLK DAILY NEWS. 1887. Mon.-Sat. $.50 newsstand; $86/yr. carrier; $88/yr. mailed. 525 Norfolk Ave., Norfolk, NE 68701. TEL 402-371-1020; FAX 402-371-5802; E-mail: ndnews@ncfcomm.com; URL: http://www.norfolkne.com/dalynews.htm. **Owner(s):** Huse Publishing Co., Box 977, Norfolk, NE 68702. TEL 402-371-1020; Ed. Kent Warneke; Pub. Jerry Huse; adv. contact: Larry Bartscher. pub. size: broadsheet; circ. evening 22,000(paid). **Wire Service(s):** AP.

NORTH PLATTE

US ISSN 0747-4008
TELEGRAPH, THE. 1881. Tue.-Sun. $.50/day newsstand; $.75/Sat. & Sun.; $104.60/yr. mailed; $115/yr. mailed outside area; $150/yr. mailed out of state. 621 N. Chestnut, North Platte, NE 69101. TEL 308-532-6000; FAX 308-532-9268; E-mail: editor@ns.nque.com; URL: http://www.nptelegraph.com. **Owner(s):** Western Publishing Co., P.O. Box 1228, North Platte, NE 69103. TEL 308-532-6783; Ed. Gary Reber; Pub. Larry Shearer; adv. contact: Dee Klein. pub. size: broadsheet; circ. morning 14,500(paid); Sun. 15,050(paid). **Wire Service(s):** AP.

OMAHA

US ISSN 0276-4962
OMAHA WORLD-HERALD. 1885. d. $.25/day newsstand; $1.25/Sun.; $2/wk. World-Herald Sq., 1334 Dodge St., Omaha, NE 68102. TEL 402-444-1000; FAX 402-445-1299. **Owner(s):** World Newspapers Inc., Landmark Center, 15th Fl., 1299 Farnam St., Omaha, NE 68102. TEL 402-444-1000; Ed. Deanna Sands; Pub. John Gottschalk; adv. contact: Thomas Golden. photos; bk.rev.; pub. size: broadsheet; circ. morning 227,409(paid); Sun. 289,452(paid). **Wire Service(s):** AP, CDN-CST, NYT, LAT-WP.

SCOTTSBLUFF

US
STAR-HERALD. 1903. Tue.-Sun. $.50/day newsstand; $.75/Sat.-Sun.; $97.50/yr. carrier. 1405 Broadway, Scottsbluff, NE 69361. TEL 308-632-0670; FAX 308-635-1258. **Owner(s):** Western Publishing Co., P.O. Box 1228, North Platte, NE 69103. TEL 308-532-6783; Ed. Steve Miller; Pub. Steven Hungerford; adv. contact: Johnny Aguirre. photos; pub. size: broadsheet; circ. morning 16,000(paid); Sun. 16,190(paid). **Wire Service(s):** AP, SHNA.

YORK

US
YORK NEWS-TIMES. 1887. Mon.-Sat. $67.50/yr. mailed in cy.; $77.50/yr. mailed elsewhere. 327 Platte Ave., York, NE 68467. TEL 402-362-4478; FAX 402-362-6748; E-mail: yt5230@ltec.net. **Owner(s):** Morris Communications, P.O. Box 936, Augusta, GA 30903. TEL 706-724-0851; Ed. Kelly Harre; Pub. Dan Collin; adv. contact: David H. Sjuts. pub. size: broadsheet; circ. evening 5,400(paid). **Wire Service(s):** AP.

NEVADA

CARSON CITY

US
NEVADA APPEAL. 1865. d. $.35/day newsstand; $1.25/Sun.; $9/mo. carrier; $96/yr. 200 Bath St., Carson City, NV 89702-2288. TEL 702-882-2111; FAX 702-887-2426. **Owner(s):** Swift Newspapers, Inc., 437 W. Plumb Ln., Reno, NV 89509. TEL 703-333-7676; Ed. Barry Smith; Pub. Jeff Ackerman; adv. contact: Steve Reynolds. pub. size: broadsheet; circ. morning 15,000(paid); Sun. 15,000(paid). **Wire Service(s):** AP.

ELKO

US
ELKO DAILY FREE PRESS. 1883. Mon.-Sat. $.50 newsstand; $93/yr. carrier. 3720 Idaho St., Elko, NV 89801. TEL 702-738-3118; FAX 702-738-2215. **Owner(s):** Rex, Kim & Dan Steninger, 3720 Idaho St., Elko, NV 89801. TEL 702-738-3118; Ed. Dan Steninger; Pub. Rex Steninger; adv. contact: Glennis Bir. photos; pub. size: standard; circ. evening 8,000(paid). **Wire Service(s):** AP.

ELY

US
ELY DAILY TIMES. 1920. Mon-Fri. $.50 newsstand; $6.75/mo. local carrier. 700 Aultman St., Ely, NV 89301. TEL 702-289-4491; FAX 702-289-4566. **Owner(s):** Donrey Media Group, P.O. Box 17017, Fort Smith, AZ 72902. TEL 501-785-7801; Ed. Kent Harper; Pub. George Carnes; adv. contact: Kenneth Kliewer. pub. size: standard; circ. evening 2,600(paid). **Wire Service(s):** AP.

FALLON

US
LAHONTAN VALLEY NEWS. 1912. Mon.-Sat. $.35 newsstand; $74/yr. in cy.; $99/yr. out of cy.; $64/yr. senior citizens. 562 N. Maine St., Fallon, NV 89406. TEL 702-423-6041; FAX 702-423-0474. **Owner(s):** David & Ludie Henley, 562 N. Maine St., Fallon, NV 89406. TEL 702-423-6041; FAX 702-423-0474; Ed. Anne Pershing; Pub. Ludie Henley; adv. contact: Joyce Thompson. photos; bk.rev.; pub. size: broadsheet; circ. morning 5,200(paid). **Wire Service(s):** AP. **Formerly:** Fallon Lahontan Valley News.

LAS VEGAS

US
LAS VEGAS REVIEW-JOURNAL. 1905. d. $.50/day newsstand; $2.50/Sun.; $3/wk. carrier; $156/yr. 1111 W. Bonanza Rd., Las Vegas, NV 89106. TEL 702-383-0211; FAX 702-383-4665. **Owner(s):** Donrey Media Group, P.O. Box 17017, Fort Smith, AR 72902. TEL 501-785-7810; Ed. Tom Mitchell; Pub. Sherman Frederick; adv. contact: Jack Harpster. photos; bk.rev.; pub. size: standard; circ. morning 156,371(paid); Sun. 222,252(paid). **Wire Service(s):** AP, LAT-WP, KR.

US
LAS VEGAS SUN. 1950. d. $.50/day newsstand; $2.50/Sun.; $1.75/wk. carrier. 800 S. Valley View Blvd., Las Vegas, NV 89107. TEL 702-385-3111; FAX 702-383-7264; E-mail: bryan@lvsun.com; URL: http://www.lasvegassun.com. **Owner(s):** Las Vegas Sun, Inc., 800 S. Valley View Blvd., Las Vegas, NV 89107. TEL 702-385-3111; FAX 702-383-7264; Ed. Sandra Thompson; Pub. Barbara Greenspun; pub. size: broadsheet; circ. evening 40,000(paid); Sun. 230,000(paid). **Wire Service(s):** AP.

RENO

US ISSN 0745-1415
RENO GAZETTE-JOURNAL. 1870. d. $.50/day newsstand; $1.50/Sun.; $3.50/wk. carrier; $2.10/Sat. & Sun. carrier. 955 Kuenzli St., Reno, NV 89502. TEL 702-788-6200; FAX 702-788-6458. **Owner(s):** Gannett Company, Inc., 1100 Wilson Blvd., Arlington, VA 22340. TEL 703-284-6000; Ed. Tonia Cunning; Pub. Sue Clark-Johnson; adv. contact: John Zidich. pub. size: standard; circ. morning 6,630(paid); Sun. 84,335(paid). **Wire Service(s):** AP, DJ, NYT, GNS.

DAILY NEWSPAPERS   BRIDGETON, NJ   10471

SPARKS
US
DAILY SPARKS TRIBUNE, THE. 1910. Sun.-Fri. $.35 newsstand; $7.50/mo. carrier. 1002 C St., Sparks, NV 89431-4929. TEL 702-358-8061; FAX 702-359-3837. **Owner(s):** Kearns-Tribune Corp., P.O. Box 887, Sparks, NV 89431. TEL 702-358-8062; FAX 702-358-3837; Ed. Bryan Jacobson; Pub. Linda Brown; adv.; photos; pub. size: broadsheet; circ. evening 7,000(paid); Sun. 10,000(paid). **Wire Service(s):** AP.

WINNEMUCCA
US   ISSN 1082-2976
HUMBOLDT SUN. 1972. Mon.-Fri. $65/yr. in cy.; $85/yr. elsewhere. 1022 S. Grass Valley Rd., Winnemucca, NV 89445. TEL 702-623-5011; FAX 702-623-5243. **Owner(s):** Winnemucca Publishing, Inc., 1022 S. Grass Valley Rd., Winnemucca, NV 89445; Pub. Susan Brockus; adv.; pub. size: broadsheet; circ. 4,500(paid).

NEW HAMPSHIRE

BERLIN
US
BERLIN DAILY SUN. 1992. Mon.-Fri. free newsstand; $220/yr. mailed weekly; $350/yr. mailed daily. 177 Main St., Berlin, NH 03570. TEL 603-752-5858; FAX 603-752-4160; E-mail: bds@moose.mcia.net. **Owner(s):** Country Club News, Inc., Seavey St., Berlin, NH 03860. TEL 603-356-2999; Ed. Rose Dodge; Pub. Mark Guerringue; adv.; pub. size: tabloid; circ. morning 8,000(free). **Wire Service(s):** AP.

US
BERLIN REPORTER, THE. 1897. Mon.-Sat. $.25/day newsstand; $.50/Wed.; $17/3 mos. carrier. 151 Main St., Berlin, NH 03570. TEL 603-752-1200; FAX 603-752-2339. **Owner(s):** Munro Enterprises, Inc., P.O. Box 38, Berlin, NH 03570. TEL 603-752-1200; Ed. Howard James; Pub. Howard James; adv. contact: Julie Hamlin. pub. size: tabloid; circ. morning 6,300(paid).
Formerly: Daily Berlin Reporter, The.

CLAREMONT
US
EAGLE-TIMES. 1892. Sun.-Fri. $.50/day newsstand; $1.25/Sun.; $2.10/wk. carrier; $2.20/wk. motor rte. RFD 2, Box 301, Claremont, NH 03743. TEL 603-543-3100; FAX 603-542-9705. **Owner(s):** Eagle Publications, Inc., RFD 2, Box 301, Claremont, NH 03730. TEL 603-543-3100; FAX 603-542-9705; Ed. Todd Driscoll; Pub. Harvey D. Hill; adv. contact: Roger Carroll. photos; bk.rev.; pub. size: broadsheet; circ. evening 9,600(paid); Sun. 10,420(paid). **Wire Service(s):** AP.

CONCORD
US
CONCORD MONITOR. 1802. d. $.50/day newsstand; $1.50/Sun.; $13.65/mo. One Monitor Dr., Concord, NH 03302-1177. TEL 603-224-5301; FAX 603-228-8238; E-mail: primary@www.cmonitor.com; URL: http://www.cmonitor.com/primary. **Owner(s):** Newspapers of New England, Inc., One Monitor Dr., P.O. Box 1177, Concord, NH 03302-1177. TEL 603-224-5301; Ed. Mike Pride; Pub. Tom C. Brown; adv. contact: Roger Proulx. pub. size: broadsheet; circ. morning 23,000(paid). **Wire Service(s):** AP, LAT-WP.

DOVER
US   ISSN 0892-6026
FOSTER'S DAILY DEMOCRAT. 1873. Mon.-Sat. $.50 newsstand; $105/yr. carrier; $138/yr. mailed in state; $145/yr. mailed out of state. 333 Central Ave., Dover, NH 03820. TEL 603-742-4455; FAX 603-749-7079; E-mail: pkincade@fosters.com; URL: http://www.fosters.com. **Owner(s):** George J. Foster & Co., Inc., 333 Central Ave., Dover, NH 03820. TEL 603-742-4455; Ed. Therece D. Foster; Pub. Robert H. Foster; adv. contact: Wayne Chick. pub. size: broadsheet; circ. evening 32,000(paid). **Wire Service(s):** AP, NYT.

HUDSON
US
TELEGRAPH, THE. 1832. d. $.50/day newsstand; $1.50/Sun.; $2.25/wk.; $156/yr. 17 Executive Dr., Hudson, NH 03051-1008. TEL 603-882-2741; FAX 603-882-5138. **Owner(s):** Independent Publications, Inc., P.O. Box 1008, Nashua, NH 03061. TEL 603-882-2741; Ed. David Solomon; Pub. Terrence Williams; adv. contact: John Vistorino. photos; bk.rev.; pub. size: broadsheet; circ. morning 29,000(paid); Sun. 34,000(paid). **Wire Service(s):** CSM, SHNA, AP.

KEENE
US
KEENE SENTINEL. 1799. d. $.50 newsstand; $1.25/Sun.; $118/yr. carrier/motor rte.; $148/yr. out of cy. mailed. 60 West St., Keene, NH 03431. TEL 603-352-1234; FAX 603-352-0437; E-mail: tfk@keenesentinel.com; URL: http://www.keenesentinel.com. **Owner(s):** Keene Publishing Corp., 60 West St., Keene, NH 03431. TEL 603-352-1234; Ed. James A. Rousmaniere, Jr. ; Pub. Thomas M. Ewing; adv. contact: Colin R. Lyle. photos; bk.rev.; pub. size: broadsheet; circ. evening 15,000(paid); Sun. 14,000(paid). **Wire Service(s):** AP, LAT-WP.

LACONIA
US
CITIZEN, THE. 1925. Mon.-Sat. $.50 newsstand; $99/yr. home deliv. 171 Fair St., Laconia, NH 03246. TEL 603-524-3800; FAX 603-524-6702. **Owner(s):** Robert Foster, Dover, NH. TEL 603-742-4455; adv. contact: Terry Rosseau. pub. size: standard; circ. evening 12,000(paid). **Wire Service(s):** AP.

MANCHESTER
US   ISSN 0745-5798
UNION LEADER/NEW HAMPSHIRE SUNDAY NEWS. 1863. d. $.50/day newsstand; $1.50/Sun.; $140.40/yr.; $80.08/yr. Sun. 100 William Loeb Dr., Manchester, NH 03109-9555. TEL 603-668-4321; FAX 603-624-0727. **Owner(s):** Nackey Loeb, 100 William Loeb Dr., P.O. Box 9555, Manchester, NH 03109-9555. TEL 603-668-4321; Ed. Joseph W. McQuaid; Pub. Nackey Loeb; adv.; pub. size: standard; circ. morning 75,000(paid); Sun. 102,000(paid). **Wire Service(s):** AP.

NORTH CONWAY
US
CONWAY DAILY SUN, THE. 1989. Mon.-Sat. free newsstand; $7/mo. mailed; $220/yr. mailed weekly; $350/yr. mailed daily. 64 Seavey St., North Conway, NH 03860. TEL 603-356-2999; FAX 603-356-8774; E-mail: dailysun@mountwashingtonvalley.com; URL: http://www.mountwashingtonvalley.com. **Owner(s):** Country Club News, Inc., Seavey St., North Conway, NH 03860. TEL 603-356-2999; FAX 603-356-8774; Ed. Adam Hirshan; Pub. Mark Guerringue; adv. contact: Bob Waters. pub. size: broadsheet; circ. morning 15,000(free & paid). **Wire Service(s):** AP.

PORTSMOUTH
US   ISSN 0746-6218
PORTSMOUTH HERALD. 1886. d. $.50/day newsstand; $1.50/Sun.; $2.95/wk. home deliv.; $12.78/mo. mailed; $153.40/yr. 111 Maplewood Ave., Portsmouth, NH 03801. TEL 603-436-1800; FAX 603-427-0550; E-mail: pherald@nh-meseacoast.com; URL: http://www.nh-meseacoast.com. **Owner(s):** Thomson Newspapers, Inc., 3150 Des Plaines Ave., Des Plaines, IL 60018. TEL 708-299-5544; Ed. Sam Pollak. adv. contact: Gloria Bonito. photos; pub. size: broadsheet; circ. morning 15,000(paid); Sun. 18,600(paid). **Wire Service(s):** AP.

WEST LEBANON
US
VALLEY NEWS. 1952. d. $.50/day newsstand; $1.25/Sun. Seven Interchange Dr., West Lebanon, NH 03784. TEL 603-298-8711; FAX 603-298-0212. **Owner(s):** Newspapers of New England, Inc., Concord, NH 03302; Ed. Jim Fox; Pub. John Kuhns; adv.; pub. size: broadsheet; circ. morning 18,500(paid); Sun. 17,000(paid).

NEW JERSEY

BRIDGETON
US
BRIDGETON EVENING NEWS. 1879. Mon.-Sat. $.50 newsstand; $119.60/yr. 100 E. Commerce St., Bridgeton, NJ 08302. TEL 609-451-1000; FAX 609-451-7214. **Owner(s):** Media News Group, 1560 Broadway, Ste. 1485, Denver, CO 80202. TEL 303-820-1952; FAX 303-820-1929; Ed. John Barna; Pub. John M. Ewing; adv. contact: Bernie Heller. photos; pub. size: broadsheet; circ. evening 20,000(paid). **Wire Service(s):** AP.

ULRICH'S INTERNATIONAL PERIODICALS DIRECTORY 1998

10472 BRIDGETON, NJ

DAILY NEWSPAPERS

BRIDGETON

US

MILVILLE NEWS. 1990. Mon.-Sat. $.50 newsstand; $2.30/wk. 100 E. Commerce St., Bridgeton, NJ 08302. TEL 609-327-1100; FAX 609-327-7214. **Owner(s):** Media News Group, 1560 Broadway, Ste. 1485, Denver, CO 80202. TEL 303-820-1952; FAX 303-820-1929; Pub. John M. Ewing; adv. contact: Burnie Heller. pub. size: broadsheet; circ. evening 1,500(paid). **Wire Service(s):** AP.

BRIDGEWATER

US   ISSN 0895-8785

COURIER-NEWS, THE. 1884. d. $.35/day newsstand; $1/Sun.; $2.75/wk. home deliv.; $143/yr. 1201 Rte. 22, W., Bridgewater, NJ 08807. TEL 908-722-8800; FAX 908-707-3272. **Owner(s):** Gannett Company, Inc., 1100 Wilson Blvd., Arlington, VA 22234. TEL 703-284-6000; Ed. Laura Harrigan; Pub. Henry M. Freeman; adv. contact: Al Frattura. photos; bk.rev.; pub. size: standard; circ. morning 50,014(paid); Sun. 52,600(paid). **Wire Service(s):** LAT-WP, GNS, AP.

CHERRY HILL

US

COURIER-POST, THE. 1875. d. $.50/day newsstand, $1.50/Sun.; $302.90/yr. mailed. 301 Cuthbert Blvd., Cherry Hill, NJ 08002. TEL 609-663-6000; FAX 609-663-3190; E-mail: cphotline@aol.com. **Owner(s):** Gannett Company, Inc., 1100 Wilson Blvd., Arlington, VA 22234. TEL 703-284-6000; Pub. Robert T. Collins; adv. contact: John E. Ziomek. bk.rev.; pub. size: broadsheet; circ. morning 96,000(paid); Sun. 101,000(paid). **Wire Service(s):** GNS, AP.

EAST BRUNSWICK

US

HOME NEWS & TRIBUNE, THE. 1879. d. $.35/day newsstand; $.75/Sun.; $2.85/wk. 35 Kennedy Blvd., East Brunswick, NJ 08816-1049. TEL 908-246-5500; FAX 908-937-6046; E-mail: editor@injersey.com; URL: http://www.thnt.com. **Owner(s):** Asbury Park Press Corp., 3601 Hwy. 66, P.O. Box 1550, Neptune, NJ 07753. TEL 908-922-6000; Ed. Richard Hughes; Pub. E. Donald Lass; adv. contact: Robert Waitt. photos; bk.rev.; pub. size: broadsheet; circ. morning 53,084(paid); Sun. 57,000(paid). **Wire Service(s):** AP, LAT-WP, KR.

Formerly: Home News; News Tribune.

HACKENSACK

US

RECORD, THE. 1895. d. $.50/day newsstand; $1.50/Sun. 150 River St., Hackensack, NJ 07601. TEL 201-646-4000; FAX 201-646-4135; E-mail: editor@www.bergen.com; URL: http://www.bergen.com. **Owner(s):** Macromedia Publishing, Inc., 150 River St., Hackensack, NJ 07601. TEL 201-646-4000; Pub. Malcolm Borg; adv. contact: Cosmo DiFiore. photos; bk.rev.; pub. size: broadsheet; circ. morning 161,991(paid); Sun. 222,892(paid). **Wire Service(s):** AP, UPI, LAT-WP, RN.

JERSEY CITY

US

JERSEY JOURNAL, THE. 1879. Mon.-Sat. $.50 newsstand; $1.85/wk. home deliv.; $20/3 mos. home deliv.; $20/mo. mailed. 30 Journal Sq., Jersey City, NJ 07306. TEL 201-863-2000; FAX 201-653-1414. **Owner(s):** Advance Publications, Inc., 950 Fingerboard Rd., Staten Island, NY 10305. TEL 718-981-1234; FAX 718-981-1456; Ed. Judy Locorriere; Pub. Scott Ring; adv.; pub. size: broadsheet; circ. morning 55,000(paid). **Wire Service(s):** AP, KR, CT-NYT.

Formerly: Hudson Dispatch.

NEPTUNE

US

ASBURY PARK PRESS. 1879. d. $.40/day newsstand; $1.50/Sun.; $2.95/wk. 3601 Hwy. 66, Neptune, NJ 07754. TEL 908-922-6000; FAX 908-922-4818; E-mail: editor@injersey.com; URL: http://www.app.com. **Owner(s):** Asbury Park Press Corp., 3601 Hwy. 66, P.O. Box 1550, Neptune, NJ 07754. TEL 908-922-6000; Ed. E. Donald Lass; Pub. Donald Lass; adv.; photos; bk.rev.; pub. size: broadsheet; circ. evening 160,000(paid); Sun. 230,000(paid). **Wire Service(s):** AP, TPS, KR, CSM, RN.

NEWARK

US

STAR-LEDGER. 1938. d. $.35/day newsstand; $1.25/Sun.; $3/wk. home deliv. One Star Ledger Plz., Newark, NJ 07102. TEL 201-877-4141; FAX 201-643-4945; E-mail: jterrito@newhouse.com; URL: http://www.nj.com/interact. **Owner(s):** Advance Publications, Inc., 485 Lexington Ave., New York, NY 10017; Ed. Rick Everett; Pub. Martin Bartner; adv. contact: Mark Herrick. photos; pub. size: broadsheet; circ. morning 433,300(paid); Sun. 641,390(paid). **Wire Service(s):** AP, LAT-WP, RN.

Formerly: Newark Star-Ledger.

NEWTON

US   ISSN 0893-3677

NEW JERSEY HERALD. 1829. Sun.-Fri. $.35/day newsstand; $1/Sun.; $2.15/wk. home deliv.; $98.80/yr. carrier. 2 Spring St., Newton, NJ 07860. TEL 201-383-1500; FAX 201-383-8477; E-mail: comments@njherald.com; URL: http://www.njherald.com. **Owner(s):** New Jersey Herald, P.O. Box 10, Newton, NJ 07860. TEL 201-383-1500; Ed. R. Kent Roeder; Pub. R. Kent Roeder; adv. contact: Dianne Ryan. photos; bk.rev.; pub. size: broadsheet; circ. evening 18,000(paid); Sun. 26,000(paid). **Wire Service(s):** AP.

PARSIPPANY

US

DAILY RECORD. 1900. d. $.25/day newsstand; $1/Sun.; $2.25/wk. 800 Jefferson Rd., Parsippany, NJ 07054-0217. TEL 201-428-6200; FAX 201-428-6666; E-mail: newsroom@gti.net; URL: http://www.adone.com/dailyrecord. **Owner(s):** Goodson Newspaper Group, 1009 Lenox Dr., Lawrenceville, NJ 08648; Ed. Jack Bowie; Pub. Tom Geyer; adv.; pub. size: broadsheet; circ. morning 55,641(paid); Sun. 62,333(paid). **Wire Service(s):** AP, KNT.

PASSAIC

US   ISSN 0895-8807

NORTH JERSEY HERALD & NEWS, THE. 1872. d. $.35/day newsstand; $.50/Sun.; $2.60/wk. home deliv. 988 Main Ave., Passaic, NJ 07055. TEL 201-365-3000; FAX 201-614-0906. **Owner(s):** North Jersey Newspapers Co., 988 Main Ave., Passaic, NJ 07055. TEL 201-365-3000; Ed. Scott West; Pub. Richard Vezza; adv.; photos; pub. size: broadsheet; circ. morning 54,420(paid); Sun. 52,000(paid). **Wire Service(s):** AP, LAT-WP.

Formerly: Paterson Evening News.

PLEASANTVILLE

US

PRESS OF ATLANTIC CITY, THE. 1895. d. $.50/day newsstand; $1.50/Sun.; $3.35/wk. 11 Devins Ln., Pleasantville, NJ 08232-3806. TEL 609-645-1234; FAX 609-272-7224; E-mail: merkoski@globalent.net; URL: http://www.pressplus.com. **Owner(s):** Abarta, Inc., 1000 R.I.D.C. Plz., Pittsburgh, PA 15238. TEL 412-963-6226; Ed. Maryjane Briant; Pub. Robert McCormick; adv.; photos; pub. size: broadsheet; circ. morning 76,228(paid); Sun. 98,070(paid). **Wire Service(s):** AP, UPI, LAT-WP.

SALEM

US   ISSN 0890-9830

TODAY'S SUNBEAM. 1972. Sun.-Fri. $.35/day newsstand; $1/Sun. 93 Fifth St., Salem, NJ 08079. TEL 609-935-1500; FAX 609-845-3139. **Owner(s):** Media News Group, 4888 Loop Central Dr., Ste. 525, Houston, TX 77081. TEL 713-295-3800; Ed. Bill Long; Pub. George Lawson; adv. contact: Ceil Smith. photos; bk.rev.; pub. size: broadsheet; circ. morning 12,000(paid); Sun. 11,800(paid). **Wire Service(s):** AP.

TOMS RIVER

US   ISSN 0746-5416

OCEAN COUNTY'S OBSERVER. 1850. d. $.35/day newsstand; $.75/Sun.; $1.80/wk. carrier. 8 Robbins St., Toms River, NJ 08753. TEL 908-349-3000; FAX 908-349-8636. **Owner(s):** Ocean County Newspapers, Inc., 8 Robbins St., Toms River, NJ 08753. TEL 908-349-3000; Ed. Charles C. Triblehorn. adv. contact: Paul J. Haney. pub. size: broadsheet; circ. morning 20,000(paid); Sun. 18,500(paid). **Wire Service(s):** AP.

TRENTON

US   ISSN 8750-9083

TIMES, THE. d. $.25/day newsstand; $1.25/Sun.; $2.60/wk. carrier; $2.80/wk. motor rte. 500 Perry St., Trenton, NJ 08605. TEL 609-989-5454; FAX 609-394-2819; E-mail: news@njtimes.com. **Owner(s):** Newhouse Newspapers, 140 E. 45th St., New York, NY 10018. TEL 212-697-8020; Ed. Brian Malone; Pub. Richard Bilotti; adv. contact: Sandra Lohr. pub. size: broadsheet; circ. morning 86,772(paid); Sun. 93,423(paid). **Wire Service(s):** AP, LAT-WP, NYT.

Formerly: Trenton Times.

DAILY NEWSPAPERS

US

TRENTONIAN, THE. 1946. d. $.35/day newsstand; $.75/Sun.; $2.30/wk. 600 Perry St., Trenton, NJ 08618-3996. TEL 609-989-7800; FAX 609-393-6072. **Owner(s):** Journal Register Co., 50 W. State St., 12th Fl., Trenton, NJ 08608. TEL 609-396-2200; Ed. Mike Raffaele; Pub. H.L. Schwartz, III; adv.; photos; bk.rev.; pub. size: tabloid; circ. morning 73,352(paid); Sun. 63,000(paid). **Wire Service(s):** KR, AP, SH.

VINELAND
US

DAILY JOURNAL. 1864. Mon.-Sat. $.35 newsstand; $132.60/yr. carrier. 891 E. Oak Rd., Vineland, NJ 08332. TEL 609-825-3456; FAX 609-691-2031. **Owner(s):** Gannett Company, Inc., 1100 Wilson Blvd., Arlington, VA 22234. TEL 703-284-6000; Pub. Albert Dolata; adv. contact: Joe Calchi. pub. size: broadsheet; circ. evening 19,235(paid). **Wire Service(s):** AP.

WILLINGBORO
US

BURLINGTON COUNTY TIMES. 1958. d. $.35/day newsstand; $1.50/Sun.; $2.75/wk. 4282 Rte. 130, Willingboro, NJ 08046. TEL 609-871-8000; FAX 609-871-8000. **Owner(s):** Calkins Newspapers, Inc., 8400 Rte. 13, Levittown, PA 19057. TEL 215-949-4000; Ed. Ron Martin; Pub. Stanley Ellis; adv. contact: Joseph Browne. pub. size: broadsheet; circ. evening 43,080(paid); Sun. 47,795(paid). **Wire Service(s):** AP.

WOODBURY
US

GLOUCESTER COUNTY TIMES. 1897. Sun.-Fri. $.35/day newsstand; $1/Sun.; $2/wk. 309 S. Broad St., Woodbury, NJ 08096. TEL 609-845-3300; FAX 609-845-2132. **Owner(s):** Media News Group, 309 S. Broad St., Woodbury, NJ 08096. TEL 609-845-3300; FAX 609-845-2132; Ed. William Long; Pub. George Lawson; adv.; photos; bk.rev.; pub. size: broadsheet; circ. evening 29,200(paid); Sun. 29,800(paid). **Wire Service(s):** AP.

NEW MEXICO

ALAMOGORDO
US

ALAMOGORDO DAILY NEWS. 1898. Sun.-Fri. $.50 newsstand; $7/mo. 518 24th St., Alamogordo, NM 88310. TEL 505-437-7120. **Owner(s):** Don Rey Media Group, P.O. Box 17017, Fort Smith, AR 72917. TEL 501-785-7800; Pub. Thomas W. Reeves; adv. contact: Mildred House. pub. size: broadsheet; circ. evening 8,706(paid); Sun. 9,652(paid). **Wire Service(s):** AP.

ALBUQUERQUE
US

ALBUQUERQUE JOURNAL. 1880. d. $.50/day newsstand; $1/Sun.; $10.25/mo. carrier. 7777 Jefferson, N.E., Albuquerque, NM 87109-4343. TEL 505-823-7777; FAX 505-823-3994; E-mail: journal@abqjournal.com; URL: http://www.abqjournal.com. **Owner(s):** T.H. Lang, 7777 Jefferson, N.E., Albuquerque, NM 87109-4343. TEL 505-823-7777; Ed. Rod Deckert; Pub. T.H. Lang; adv.; photos; bk.rev.; pub. size: broadsheet; circ. morning 160,325(paid); Sun. 169,072(paid). **Wire Service(s):** AP, CSM, LAT-WP, RN.

US

ALBUQUERQUE TRIBUNE, THE. 1922. Mon.-Sat. $.50 newsstand; $5.25/mo.; $31.50/6 mos. 7777 Jefferson, N.E., Albuquerque, NM 87109. TEL 505-823-7777; FAX 505-823-3689. **Owner(s):** Scripps Howard, 312 Walnut St., 28th Fl., Cincinnati, OH 45202. TEL 513-977-3000; FAX 513-977-3689; Ed. Terri Burke. pub. size: broadsheet; circ. evening 27,000(paid). **Wire Service(s):** AP, SHNA, NYT, LAT-WP.

ARTESIA
US

ARTESIA DAILY PRESS. 1954. Tue.-Fri. & Sun. $.35/day newsstand; $.75/Sun.; $5.75/mo. in town; $19.50/3 mos. 503 W. Main, Artesia, NM 88210. TEL 505-746-3524. **Owner(s):** Valley Newspapers, Inc., P.O. Box 179, Artesia, NM 88211-0190. TEL 505-746-3524; Ed. Darrell Pehr; Pub. Gary Scott; adv.; pub. size: broadsheet; circ. evening 4,000(paid); Sun. 4,200(paid). **Wire Service(s):** AP.

CARLSBAD
US

CARLSBAD CURRENT-ARGUS. 1889. Tue.-Sun. $.50/day newsstand; $1.25/Sun.; $8.75/mo. deliv. in cy. 620 S. Main, Carlsbad, NM 88220-6243. TEL 505-887-5501; FAX 505-885-1066; E-mail: argus@carlsbad.com. **Owner(s):** Omaha World-Herald Co., World-Herald Sq., 1334 Dodge St., Omaha, NE 68102. TEL 402-444-1000; Ed. Eric Fisher; Pub. Sammy Lopez; pub. size: broadsheet; circ. evening 8,800(paid); Sun. 9,000(paid). **Wire Service(s):** AP.
Formerly: Current-Argus.

CLOVIS
US

CLOVIS NEWS JOURNAL. 1929. Sun.-Fri. $7.50/mo. home deliv. 501 Pile St., Clovis, NM 88101. TEL 505-763-3431; FAX 505-762-3879. **Owner(s):** Freedom Communications, Inc., 17666 Fitch, Irvine, CA 92714; Ed. Bob Wright; Pub. Julie Moreno; adv. contact: Candy Duvall. photos; pub. size: broadsheet; circ. evening 10,000(paid); Sun. 12,000(paid). **Wire Service(s):** AP, KR, Freedom.

DEMING
US ISSN 0738-8349

DEMING HEADLIGHT. 1881. Mon.-Fri. $.50 newsstand; $60/yr. mailed. 219 E. Maple, Deming, NM 88030. TEL 505-546-2611; FAX 505-546-8116. **Owner(s):** WorldWest Limited Liability Co., 609 New Hampshire, P.O. Box 688, Lawrence, KS 66044. TEL 913-843-1000; FAX 913-832-7207; Ed. John Brennan; Pub. Tamara M. Montes; adv.; photos; pub. size: tabloid; circ. evening 11,000(free & paid). **Wire Service(s):** AP.

FARMINGTON
US

DAILY TIMES. 1894. d. $.50/day newsstand; $1/Sun.; $88/yr. carrier. 201 N. Allen, Farmington, NM 87401. TEL 505-325-4545; FAX 505-564-4580; E-mail: dtimes@cyberport.com. **Owner(s):** New Mexico Newspapers, Inc., P.O. Box 450, Farmington, NM 87499. TEL 505-325-4545; FAX 505-564-4545; Ed. Mary Busha; Pub. Eliot O'Brien; adv. contact: Dennis Gross. photos; bk.rev.; pub. size: broadsheet; circ. evening 18,706(paid); Sun. 17,401(paid). **Wire Service(s):** AP, NYT.

HOBBS
US

HOBBS DAILY NEWS-SUN. 1937. Sun.-Fri. $.50/day newsstand; $1/Sun. 201 N. Thorp, Hobbs, NM 88240. TEL 505-393-2123; FAX 505-393-5724. **Owner(s):** Sun Publishing Corp., P.O. Box 860, Hobbs, NM 88241. TEL 505-393-2123; Ed. Manny Marquez; Pub. Kathi Bearden; adv. contact: Linda Coenig. photos; pub. size: broadsheet; circ. morning 11,908(paid); Sun. 12,716(paid). **Wire Service(s):** AP,.

LAS CRUCES
US

LAS CRUCES SUN-NEWS. 1937. d. $.50/day newsstand; $1.25/Sun. 256 W. Las Cruces Ave., Las Cruces, NM 88005. TEL 505-541-5400; FAX 505-527-1249. **Owner(s):** Media News Group, 4888 Loop Central Dr., Ste. 575, Houston, TX 77081. TEL 713-295-3800; Ed. Harold R. Cousland; Pub. David McCallum; pub. size: broadsheet; circ. morning 22,500(paid); Sun. 23,500(paid). **Wire Service(s):** AP, NYT.

LAS VEGAS
US

LAS VEGAS DAILY OPTIC. 1879. Mon.-Fri. $59.40/yr. home deliv.; $90/yr. in cy.; $102/yr. out of cy. 614 Lincoln, Las Vegas, NM 87701. TEL 505-425-6796; FAX 505-425-1005. **Owner(s):** Las Vegas Optic, Inc., 614 Lincoln, P.O. Box 2670, Las Vegas, NM 87701. TEL 505-425-6796; FAX 505-425-1005; Pub. Stuart Beck; adv. contact: Anna Huie. photos; bk.rev.; pub. size: broadsheet; circ. evening 6,248(paid). **Wire Service(s):** AP.

LOS ALAMOS
US   ISSN 0893-3456

MONITOR, THE. 1963. Tue.-Fri. & Sun. $.50 newsstand; $66.95/yr. 256 DP Rd., Los Alamos, NM 87544. TEL 505-662-4185; FAX 505-662-4334; E-mail: lamonitr@rt66.com; URL: http://www.rt66.com/lamonitr. **Owner(s):** Landmark Community Newspapers, Inc., P.O. Box 549, Shelbyville, KY 40065. TEL 502-633-4334; Ed. Stephen Shankland. pub. size: broadsheet; circ. evening 5,400(paid); Sun. 5,400(paid). **Wire Service(s):** AP, NYT.
     Formerly: Los Alamos Monitor.

LOVINGTON
US

LOVINGTON DAILY LEADER. 1909. Tue.-Fri. & Sun. $.50 newsstand; $78/yr. in town; $84/yr. in cy.; $90/yr. out of cy. 14 W. Ave. B, Lovington, NM 88260. TEL 505-396-2844; FAX 505-396-5775. **Owner(s):** Wal-Roy Publishing, Inc., P.O. Box 1717, Lovington, NM 88260. TEL 505-396-2844; Ed. John Graham; Pub. John Graham; adv. contact: Joyce Clemens. pub. size: broadsheet; circ. evening 2,100(paid); Sun. 2,400(paid). **Wire Service(s):** AP.

PORTALES
US

PORTALES NEWS-TRIBUNE. 1957. Sun., Tue.-Fri. $.50/day newsstand; $1/Sun.; $69.75/yr. in city; $72/yr. elsewhere. 101 E. First St., Portales, NM 88130. TEL 505-356-4481; FAX 505-356-3630; E-mail: pnt@yucca.net. **Owner(s):** Freedom Communications, Inc., 17666 Fitch, Irvine, CA 92614. TEL 714-553-9292; Ed. Shawn Ankrom; Pub. Lone Beasley; adv. contact: Milly Hillesheim. pub. size: broadsheet; circ. evening 3,200(paid); Sun. 3,400(paid). **Wire Service(s):** AP.

ROSWELL
US

ROSWELL DAILY RECORD. 1891. Sun.-Fri. $.35/day newsstand; $1/Sun.; $6.50/mo. deliv. 2301 N. Main, Roswell, NM 88201-6452. TEL 505-622-7710; FAX 505-625-0421. **Owner(s):** Roswell Daily Record, Inc., 2301 N. Main St., Roswell, NM 88201-6452. TEL 505-622-7710; FAX 505-625-0421; Ed. Mike Bush; Pub. R. Cory Beck; adv. contact: Marion Saint. photos; bk.rev.; pub. size: broadsheet; circ. morning 14,500(paid); Sun. 15,000(paid). **Wire Service(s):** AP.

SANTA FE
US

SANTA FE NEW MEXICAN. 1849. d. $.50/day newsstand; $1/Sun.; $225/yr. 202 E. Marcy St., Santa Fe, NM 87501. TEL 505-983-3303; FAX 505-986-9147; E-mail: newmex@newmexico.com; URL: http://www.sfnewmexican.com. **Owner(s):** Robert McKinney, The New Mexican, Inc., P.O. Box 2048, Santa Fe, NM 87504. TEL 505-986-3000; Ed. Rob Dean. adv. contact: Virginia Sohn-Shahi. pub. size: broadsheet; circ. morning 23,900(paid); Sun. 26,200(paid). **Wire Service(s):** AP, NYT, LAT-WP.

SILVER CITY
US   ISSN 0891-7981

SILVER CITY DAILY PRESS & INDEPENDENT. 1896. Mon.-Sat. $.45 newsstand; $77/yr. in town; $94/yr. out of town. 300 Market St., Silver City, NM 88061. TEL 505-388-1576; FAX 505-388-1196. **Owner(s):** Silver City Daily Press & Independent Pub. Co., P.O. Box 740, Silver City, NM 88061. TEL 505-538-2794; Ed. Bill Archibald; Pub. Betty Jane Ely; adv. contact: Mary Frost. photos; bk.rev.; pub. size: broadsheet; circ. evening 7,800(paid). **Wire Service(s):** AP.

NEW YORK

ALBANY
US

TIMES UNION. 1856. d. $.50/day newsstand; $2/Sun; $3.90/wk. home deliv. News Plz., Albany, NY 12212. TEL 518-454-5694; FAX 518-454-5628; E-mail: tunewsroom@aol.com; URL: http://www.timesunion.com. **Owner(s):** Hearst Corp., 959 Eighth Ave., New York, NY 10019. TEL 212-649-2000; Ed. Harry Rosenfeld; Pub. Timothy O. White; adv. contact: David White. photos; bk.rev.; pub. size: broadsheet; circ. morning 106,000(paid); Sun. 168,000(paid). **Wire Service(s):** AP, LAT-WP, NYT, SHNA, KR, HHS, CNS.

AMSTERDAM
US   ISSN 0739-2540

RECORDER, THE. 1878. d. $.35/day newsstand; $.75/Sun.; $2.50/wk. One Venner Rd., Amsterdam, NY 12010. TEL 518-843-1100; FAX 518-843-1338. **Owner(s):** Wm. J. Kline & Sons, Inc., P.O. Box 640, Amsterdam, NY 12010. TEL 518-843-1100; Ed. Tony Benjamin; Pub. Frank Gappa; adv. contact: Bob Simpson. photos; bk.rev.; pub. size: broadsheet; circ. evening 11,900(paid); Sun. 11,450(paid). **Wire Service(s):** AP, Tribune.

AUBURN
US

CITIZEN, THE. 1816. Sun.-Fri. $.35/day newsstand; $1.25/Sun. 25 Dill St., Auburn, NY 13021. TEL 315-253-5311; FAX 315-253-5311. **Owner(s):** Howard Publications, Inc., P.O. Box 570, Oceanside, CA 92049; Ed. Don Rogers; Pub. Doris Rush; adv. contact: Julie Taulman. pub. size: broadsheet; circ. evening 17,000(paid); Sun. 17,500(paid). **Wire Service(s):** AP, LAT-WP.
     Formerly: Auburn Citizen.

BATAVIA
US

BATAVIA DAILY NEWS. 1878. Mon.-Sat. $.50 newsstand; $109.20/yr. carrier; $116/yr. local motor rte. 2 Apollo Dr., Batavia, NY 14020. TEL 716-343-8000; FAX 716-343-2623. **Owner(s):** Batavia Newspapers Corp., P.O. Box 360, Batavia, NY 14020. TEL 716-343-8000; Ed. Mark Graczyk; Pub. Roger Mosher; pub. size: standard; circ. evening 17,000(paid). **Wire Service(s):** AP.

BROOKLYN
US

BROOKLYN DAILY EAGLE & DAILY BULLETIN. 1955. Mon.-Fri. $.50 newsstand; $90/6 mos.; $150/yr. 125 Montague St., 2nd Fl., Brooklyn, NY 11201. TEL 718-625-7500; FAX 718-624-2716. **Owner(s):** Brooklyn Journal Publications, 125 Montague St., 2nd Fl., Brooklyn, NY 11201. TEL 718-625-7500; FAX 718-624-2716; Ed. Ranaan Geberer; Pub. Dozier Hasty; adv. contact: Pat Higgins. photos; pub. size: tabloid; circ. morning 5,300(paid). **Wire Service(s):** CNS.
     Formerly: Brooklyn Daily Bulletin.

US   ISSN 0746-8865

NEW YORK DAILY CHALLENGE. 1972. Mon.-Fri. $.35 newsstand; $65/yr. 1360 Fulton St., Brooklyn, NY 11216. TEL 718-636-9500; FAX 718-857-9115. **Owner(s):** Tom Watkins, 1360 Fulton St., Brooklyn, NY 11216; Ed. Dawad Phillip; Pub. Tom Watkins; adv. contact: Fred Hudson. pub. size: tabloid; circ. morning 79,000(paid). **Wire Service(s):** API, UPI.

BUFFALO
US   ISSN 0745-2691

BUFFALO NEWS, THE. 1880. d. $.50/day newsstand; $1.75/Sun.; $4/wk. The News Plz., Buffalo, NY 14203. TEL 716-849-4444; FAX 716-856-5150. **Owner(s):** Berkshire Hathaway, Inc., 1440 Kiewit Plz., Omaha, NE 68131. TEL 402-346-1400; FAX 402-346-3375; adv.; photos; bk.rev.; pub. size: broadsheet; circ. evening 284,222(paid); Sun. 365,140(paid). **Wire Service(s):** AP, KR, LAT-WP, RN.

CANANDAIGUA
US

CANANDAIGUA DAILY MESSENGER. 1796. Sun.-Fri. $.50/day newsstand; $1/Sun.; $109.20/yr. in cy. 73 Buffalo St., Canandaigua, NY 14424. TEL 716-394-0770. **Owner(s):** Canandaigua Messenger, Inc., 73 Buffalo St., Canandaigua, NY 14424. TEL 716-394-0770; Ed. Kevin Frisch; Pub. George M. Ewing Jr.; adv. contact: Catherine Gardner. pub. size: broadsheet; circ. evening 14,603(paid); Sun. 14,447(paid). **Wire Service(s):** AP, Data Stream, Photo Stream, SHNA, LAT-WP.

CATSKILL
US

DAILY MAIL. 1879. Mon.-Sat. $.50 newsstand; $104/yr. motor rte.; $155.16/yr. mailed. 30 Church St., Catskill, NY 12414. TEL 518-943-2100; FAX 518-943-2063. **Owner(s):** Johnson Newspaper Corp., 260 Washington St., Watertown, NY 13601. TEL 315-782-1000; Ed. Annabar Jensis; Pub. Anthony Panetta; adv.; pub. size: broadsheet; circ. evening 5,700(paid). **Wire Service(s):** AP.

CORNING
US

LEADER, THE. d. $.50/day newsstand; $1.50/Sun. 34 W. Pulteney St., Corning, NY 14830. TEL 607-936-4651; FAX 607-936-9939. **Owner(s):** Howard Publications, Inc., 1715 S. Freeman St., Oceanside, CA 92054; Ed. Mike Gossie; Pub. William Blake; adv. contact: Rick Emmanuel. pub. size: broadsheet; circ. evening 17,000(paid). **Wire Service(s):** AP.

CORTLAND
US
CORTLAND STANDARD. 1867. Mon.-Sat. $.35 newsstand; $109.20/yr. carrier; $149.50/yr. mailed. 110 Main St., Cortland, NY 13045. TEL 607-756-5665; FAX 607-756-5665. **Owner(s):** Cortland Standard Printing Co., Inc., 110 Main St., Cortland, NY 13045. TEL 607-756-5665; Pub. Kevin Howe; adv. contact: Edward J. Rounds. pub. size: broadsheet; circ. evening 12,500(paid). **Wire Service(s):** AP.

DUNKIRK
US
EVENING-OBSERVER. 1882. d. $.35/day newsstand; $1/Sun.; $105/yr. 8-10 E. Second St., Dunkirk, NY 14048. TEL 716-366-3000; FAX 716-366-3005. **Owner(s):** Ogden Newspapers, Inc., 1500 Main St., Wheeling, WV 26033. TEL 304-233-0100; Ed. Keith Sheldon. adv. contact: Craig Bertoldson. pub. size: broadsheet; circ. evening 14,500(paid); Sun. 14,000(paid). **Wire Service(s):** AP.

ELMIRA
US
STAR-GAZETTE. 1829. d. $.40/day newsstand; $1.50/Sun.; $3.25/wk. carrier; $220.90/yr. in area; $244.92/yr. out of area mailed. 201 Baldwin St., Elmira, NY 14901. TEL 607-734-5151; FAX 607-732-3786; E-mail: sgdata@aol.com; URL: http://www.star-gazette.com. **Owner(s):** Gannett Company, Inc., 1100 Wilson Blvd., Arlington, VA 22234. TEL 703-284-6000; Ed. Charles W. Nutt, Jr.; Pub. Margaret E. Buchanan; adv. contact: Nancy Meyer. photos; pub. size: broadsheet; circ. morning 33,923(paid); Sun. 47,797(paid). **Wire Service(s):** AP, GNS.

GENEVA
US
FINGER LAKES TIMES, THE. 1872. Sun.-Fri. $.50/day newsstand; $1/Sun.; $120/yr. 218 Genesee St., Geneva, NY 14456. TEL 315-789-3333; FAX 315-789-4077. **Owner(s):** Independent Publications, Inc., Bryn Mawr, PA; Ed. Philip Beckley; Pub. George A. Park, Jr.; adv.; photos; pub. size: broadsheet; circ. evening 19,000(paid); Sun. 20,400(paid). **Wire Service(s):** AP, LAT-WP.
Formerly: Geneva Times.

GLENS FALLS
US   ISSN 0897-0505
POST-STAR. 1889. d. $.50/day newsstand; $1.75/Sun.; $3.15/wk. carrier; $3.75/wk. rural deliv.; $5/wk. mailed. Lawrence & Cooper Sts., Glens Falls, NY 12801. TEL 518-792-3131; FAX 518-743-1684; E-mail: poststar@globalone.net; URL: http://www.albany.globalone.net/poststar. **Owner(s):** Howard Publications, Inc., 1715 S. Freeman St., P.O. Box 570, Oceanside, CA 92049. TEL 619-433-5771; Ed. Steve Bennett; Pub. Jim Marshall; adv. contact: Nick Cinmano. pub. size: broadsheet; circ. morning 34,164(paid); Sun. 37,247(paid). **Wire Service(s):** AP.

GLOVERSVILLE
US
LEADER-HERALD, THE. 1887. d. $.50 newsstand; $1/Sun.; $2.45/wk. local; $2.55/wk. rural. 8 E. Fulton St., Gloversville, NY 12078. TEL 518-725-8616; FAX 518-725-7407. **Owner(s):** Ogden Newspapers, Inc., 1500 Main St., Wheeling, WV 26033; Ed. Tom Nevich; Pub. Patricia Beck; bk.rev.; pub. size: broadsheet; circ. morning 15,000(paid); Sun. 15,000(paid). **Wire Service(s):** AP.
Formerly: Gloversville Leader-Herald.

HERKIMER
US
EVENING TELEGRAM. 1898. Mon.-Sat. $.50 newsstand; $2/wk. 111-113 Green St., Herkimer, NY 13350. TEL 315-866-2220; FAX 315-866-5913. **Owner(s):** American Publishing Co., 606 N. Van Buren, Marion, IL 62959. TEL 618-993-1711; Ed. Dan Guzewich; Pub. Beth Brewer; adv. contact: John Snyder. adv.: $9.19/SAU. photos; bk.rev.; pub. size: broadsheet; circ. evening 7,100(paid). **Wire Service(s):** AP.

HORNELL
US
HORNELL EVENING TRIBUNE. 1851. Mon.-Fri. $.50 newsstand. 85 Canisteo St., Hornell, NY 14843. TEL 607-324-1425; FAX 607-324-1753. **Owner(s):** American Publishing Co., 606 N. Van Buren, Marion, IL 62959. TEL 618-993-1711; Ed. Andy Tompson; Pub. Kelly Luvison; adv. contact: John Frungillo. pub. size: broadsheet; circ. morning 10,000(paid). **Wire Service(s):** AP.

HUDSON
US   ISSN 0747-2374
REGISTER-STAR. 1785. Sun.-Fri. $.50/day newsstand; $.75/Sun.; $115/yr. home deliv. 364 Warren St., Hudson, NY 12534. TEL 518-828-1616; FAX 518-828-9437. **Owner(s):** Johnson Newspaper Corp., 260 Washington St., Watertown, NY 13601. TEL 315-782-1000; Ed. Jack Kehrer; Pub. Anthony Pinnetta; adv.; pub. size: broadsheet; circ. evening 6,700(paid); Sun. 15,500(paid). **Wire Service(s):** AP.

ITHACA
US
ITHACA JOURNAL, THE. 1815. Mon.-Sat. $.35/day newsstand; $.50/Sat.; $2.75/wk. home deliv.; $3/wk. motor rte. 123-127 W. State St., Ithaca, NY 14850. TEL 607-272-2321; FAX 607-272-4335. **Owner(s):** Gannett Company, Inc., 1100 Wilson Blvd., Arlington, VA 22234. TEL 703-284-6000; Ed. Ted Haider; Pub. Ellen Leifeld; adv. contact: Carol Becker. bk.rev.; pub. size: broadsheet; circ. morning 19,623(paid). **Wire Service(s):** AP, GNS.

JAMESTOWN
US
POST-JOURNAL, THE. 1826. d. $.35/day newsstand; $1/Sun.; $8.20/mo. motor rte. 15 W. Second St., Jamestown, NY 14701. TEL 716-487-1111; FAX 716-664-3119. **Owner(s):** Ogden Newspapers, Inc., 1500 Main St., Wheeling, WV 26033. TEL 304-233-0100; Ed. Cristie L. Herbst; Pub. Donald L. Meyer; adv. contact: Nancy Philips. pub. size: broadsheet; circ. evening 26,000(paid); Sun. 30,000(paid). **Wire Service(s):** AP.

KINGSTON
US   ISSN 0746-4932
DAILY & SUNDAY FREEMAN. 1871. Sun.-Fri. $.50/day newsstand; $1.50/Sun.; $12.25/mo. carrier; $13.25/mo. motor rte. 79 Hurley Ave., Kingston, NY 12401. TEL 914-331-5000; FAX 914-331-3557. **Owner(s):** Mark Goodson Enterprises Ltd., 79 Hurley Ave., Kingston, NY 12401. TEL 914-331-5000; Ed. Sam Daleo; Pub. Ira Fusfeld; adv. contact: John Martin. photos; pub. size: broadsheet; circ. morning 23,000(paid); Sun. 32,000(paid). **Wire Service(s):** AP.

LITTLE FALLS
US
EVENING TIMES, THE. 1886. Mon.-Sat. $.50 newsstand; $2.25/wk. carrier. 347 S. Second St., Little Falls, NY 13365-1007. TEL 315-823-3680; FAX 315-823-4086. **Owner(s):** Community Newspaper Co., 82 Devonshire St., Boston, MA 02109. TEL 508-728-6553; Ed. Larry Neely; Pub. Donald Paparella; adv. contact: Elaine McEvoy. photos; pub. size: broadsheet; circ. evening 6,740(paid). **Wire Service(s):** AP.
Formerly: Little Falls Evening Times.

LOCKPORT
US
UNION-SUN & JOURNAL. 1821. Mon.-Sat. $.50 newsstand; $2.10/wk. home deliv. 459 S. Transit St., Lockport, NY 14094. TEL 716-439-9222; FAX 716-439-9239; E-mail: journal@localnet.com. **Owner(s):** Community Newspaper Holdings, Inc., 269 W. Main St., 6th Fl., Lexington, KY 40507. TEL 606-388-2644; FAX 606-225-8115; Ed. Daniel Kane; Pub. Daniel M. Caswell; adv. contact: Richard Conley. pub. size: broadsheet; circ. evening 17,200(paid). **Wire Service(s):** AP.
Formerly: Lockport Union-Sun & Journal.

MALONE
US
MALONE TELEGRAM. 1905. Mon.-Sat. $.50 newsstand; $130/yr. in cy.; $145/yr. 387 E. Main St., Malone, NY 12953. TEL 518-483-4700; FAX 518-483-8579. **Owner(s):** Johnson Newspaper Corp., 260 Washington St., Watertown, NY 13601. TEL 315-782-1000; Ed. Tom Graser; Pub. Russell F. Webster; adv.; pub. size: broadsheet; circ. evening 7,000(paid). **Wire Service(s):** AP.

MASSENA

DAILY COURIER OBSERVER, THE. 1891. Tue.-Sat. $.35 newsstand; $98/yr. carrier; $100/yr. motor rte. 56 1/2 Main St., Massena, NY 13662. TEL 315-769-2451; FAX 315-764-0337. **Owner(s):** Johnson Acquisitions Corp., Watertown, NY 13601; Ed. Ryne R. Martin. adv. contact: Mary McGee. pub. size: standard; circ. morning 7,500(paid).

MEDINA

JOURNAL-REGISTER. 1903. Mon.-Fri. $.50 newsstand; $99/yr. mailed. 413 Main St., Medina, NY 14103-1416. TEL 716-798-1400; FAX 716-798-0290. **Owner(s):** Community Newspaper Holdings, Inc., 269 W. Main St. 6th Fl., Lexington, KY 40507. TEL 606-388-2644; FAX 606-225-8115; Ed. Michael Wertman. adv. contact: Greg Kerth. adv.: $9.43/SAU. pub. size: broadsheet; circ. evening 5,000(paid). **Wire Service(s):** AP.

MELVILLE

US   ISSN 0278-5587
NEWSDAY. 1940. d. $.50/day newsstand; $1.50/Sun. 235 Pinelawn Rd., Melville, NY 11747-4250. TEL 516-843-2020; FAX 516-843-2953; E-mail: esgdesk@aol.com; URL: http://www.newsday.com. **Owner(s):** Times-Mirror Co., Times Mirror Sq., 220 W. First St., Los Angeles, CA 90053; Ed. Howard Schneider; Pub. Raymond A. Jansen; adv. contact: John McKeon. pub. size: tabloid; circ. morning 564,754(paid); Sun. 643,421(paid). **Wire Service(s):** AP, DJ, LAT-WP, NWS, RN, CSM.

MIDDLETOWN

TIMES HERALD-RECORD. 1956. d. $.50/day newsstand; $1.50/Sun.; $3.20/wk.; $12.80/mo. 40 Mulberry St., Middletown, NY 10940. TEL 914-341-1100; FAX 914-343-6414. **Owner(s):** Ottaway Newspapers, Inc., P.O. Box 401, Campbell Hall, NY 10916. TEL 914-294-8181; Ed. Jeff Storey; Pub. James A. Moss; adv. contact: Susan Krafve. photos; bk.rev.; pub. size: tabloid; circ. morning 86,310(paid); Sun. 102,040(paid). **Wire Service(s):** AP, NYT, KNT, SHNA.

NEW ROCHELLE

US   ISSN 1060-4553
DAILY ITEM, THE. 1899. d. $.50/day newsstand; $1.50/Sun.; $3.95/wk. 92 North Ave., New Rochelle, NY 10801. TEL 914-637-2200; FAX 914-637-2230. **Owner(s):** Gannett Suburban Newspapers, One Gannett Dr., White Plains, NY 10604. TEL 914-694-5000; Ed. William Carey; Pub. Robert Ritter; adv. contact: Bob Twesten. pub. size: broadsheet; circ. evening 9,200(paid); Sun. 10,300(paid). **Wire Service(s):** AP, GNS.
Formerly: Port Chester Daily Item.

DAILY TIMES, THE. 1925. d. $.50/day newsstand; $1.50/Sun.; $3.45/wk. 92 North Ave., New Rochelle, NY 10801. TEL 914-637-2200; FAX 914-637-2230. **Owner(s):** Gannett Suburban Newspapers, One Gannett Dr., White Plains, NY 10604. TEL 914-694-5000; Ed. William Cary; Pub. Robert Ritter; adv.; pub. size: broadsheet; circ. morning 6,500(paid); Sun. 5,700(paid). **Wire Service(s):** AP, GNS.

US   ISSN 1060-4618
STANDARD-STAR. 1926. d. $.50/day newsstand; $1.50/Sun. $3.45/wk. 92 North Ave., New Rochelle, NY 10801. TEL 914-637-2200; FAX 914-637-2230. **Owner(s):** Gannett Suburban Newspapers, One Gannett Dr., White Plains, NY 10604. TEL 914-694-5000; Ed. William Cary; Pub. Robert Ritter; adv. contact: Bob Twesten. pub. size: broadsheet; circ. morning 10,645(paid); Sun. 11,612(paid). **Wire Service(s):** AP.
Formerly: New Rochelle Standard-Star.

NEW YORK

NEW YORK DAILY NEWS, THE. 1919. d. $.50/day newsstand; $1.50/Sun. 450 W. 33rd St., New York, NY 10001. TEL 212-210-2100; FAX 212-661-4953. **Owner(s):** Mortimer Zuckerman, 450 W. 33rd St., New York, NY 10001; Ed. Pete Hamill; Pub. Mortimer Zuckerman; adv. contact: William D. Holiber. photos; pub. size: tabloid; circ. morning 758,509(paid); Sun. 1,010,504(paid). **Wire Service(s):** AP, RN, CT-NYT.

NEW YORK POST. 1801. d. $.50 newsstand; $178/yr. 1211 Ave. of the Americas, New York, NY 10036-8790. TEL 212-930-8000; FAX 212-930-8540. **Owner(s):** Rupert Murdoch/News Corp., 210 South St., New York, NY 10002; Ed. Marc Kalech; Pub. Martin Singerman; adv. contact: Patrick Judge. pub. size: tabloid; circ. evening 418,255(paid). **Wire Service(s):** AP, CDN, CST, LAT-WP, AF.

US   ISSN 0362-4331
NEW YORK TIMES, THE. 1851. d. $.60/day newsstand in area; $1/day out of area; $2.50/Sun.; $6.70/wk. deliv. 229 W. 43rd St., New York, NY 10036. TEL 212-556-1234; FAX 212-556-7389. **Owner(s):** New York Times Co., The, 229 W. 43rd St., New York, NY 10036. TEL 212-556-1234; Ed. William Keller; Pub. Arthur Ochs Sulzberger, Jr.; adv. contact: Robert Clark. pub. size: broadsheet; circ. morning 1,157,700(paid); Sun. 1,746,900(paid). **Wire Service(s):** AP, RN, TASS, DJ, PR Newswire, NYT.

NIAGARA FALLS

NIAGARA GAZETTE. 1854. d. $.50/day newsstand; $1/Sun.; $3/wk. home deliv. 310 Niagara St., Niagara Falls, NY 14302-0549. TEL 716-282-2311; FAX 716-286-3895. **Owner(s):** Newspaper Holdings, Inc., 269 W. Main St., 6th Fl., Lexington, KY 40507. TEL 606-388-2644; FAX 606-225-8115; Pub. Mark Francis; adv. contact: Michael Kellogg. photos; bk.rev.; pub. size: broadsheet; circ. morning 27,000(paid); Sun. 27,900(paid). **Wire Service(s):** AP, GNS.

NORTH TONAWANDA

TONAWANDA NEWS. 1880. Mon.-Sat. $.35 newsstand; $1.70/wk. 435 River Rd., North Tonawanda, NY 14120. TEL 716-693-1000; FAX 716-693-8573. **Owner(s):** American Publishing Co., 606 N. Van Buren, Marion, IL 62959. TEL 618-993-1711; Ed. Terry Shaw; Pub. Joseph P. Armenia; adv. contact: Frank Skally. pub. size: broadsheet; circ. evening 13,500(paid). **Wire Service(s):** AP.

NORWICH

US   ISSN 0747-0355
EVENING SUN, THE. 1891. Mon.-Fri. $.40 newsstand; $95/yr. carrier; $100/yr. motor rte. 29 Lackawanna Ave., Norwich, NY 13815. TEL 607-334-3276; FAX 607-334-8273. **Owner(s):** Snyder Communication Corp., Mechanic St., Norwich, NY 13815. TEL 607-334-3276; Ed. Jeff Genung. adv. contact: Russ Foote. photos; bk.rev.; pub. size: broadsheet; circ. evening 6,687(paid). **Wire Service(s):** AP.

OGDENSBURG

US   ISSN 0893-5149
JOURNAL, THE. 1830. Mon.-Fri. $.35 newsstand. 308 Isabella, Ogdensburg, NY 13669. TEL 315-393-1000; FAX 315-393-5108. **Owner(s):** Johnson Newspaper Corp., 260 Washington St., Watertown, NY 13601. TEL 315-782-1000; Ed. James Reagen. adv.; pub. size: broadsheet; circ. evening 5,500(paid). **Wire Service(s):** AP.

OLEAN

OLEAN TIMES HERALD. 1860. d. $.50/day newsstand; $1.50/Sun.; $13/mo. carrier; $14.50/mo. 639 Norton Dr., Olean, NY 14760. TEL 716-372-3121; FAX 716-372-0740. **Owner(s):** American Publishing Co., 606 N. Van Buren, Marion, IL 62959. TEL 618-993-1711; Ed. Charles Ward; Pub. Charles Ward; adv. contact: Larry Chiott. pub. size: broadsheet; circ. morning 19,500(paid); Sun. 19,500(paid). **Wire Service(s):** AP, UPI.

ONEIDA

ONEIDA DAILY DISPATCH. 1851. Mon.-Sat. $.40 newsstand; $109.20/yr. carrier; $132.60/yr. mail deliv. 130 Broad St., Oneida, NY 13421. TEL 315-363-5100; FAX 315-363-9832. **Owner(s):** Goodson Newspaper Group, P.O. Box 6490, Trenton, NJ 08648; Ed. Phyllis M. Harris; Pub. Ann Campanie; adv.; pub. size: broadsheet; circ. evening 9,000(paid). **Wire Service(s):** AP.

ONEONTA

DAILY STAR, THE. 1890. Mon.-Sat. $.50 newsstand; $2/wk. carrier; $99/yr. carrier. 102 Chestnut St., Oneonta, NY 13820. TEL 607-432-1000; FAX 607-432-5847. **Owner(s):** Ottaway Newspapers, Inc., P.O. Box 401, Campbell Hall, NY 10916. TEL 914-294-8181; Ed. Carey Brunswick; Pub. Richard J. Anthony; adv. contact: Bill Reeves. photos; pub. size: broadsheet; circ. morning 19,800(paid). **Wire Service(s):** AP, ONS.

OSWEGO

PALLADIUM-TIMES, THE. 1845. Mon.-Sat. $.50 newsstand; $102/yr. home deliv. 140 W. First St., Oswego, NY 13126. TEL 315-343-3800. E-mail: bruce.p@reddragon.com. **Owner(s):** Hollinger, Inc.; Pub. Bruce P. Frassinelli; adv. contact: Jon Spauiding. photos; pub. size: broadsheet; circ. evening 11,124(paid). **Wire Service(s):** AP, SHNA.
Formerly: Oswego Palladium-Times.

DAILY NEWSPAPERS

PLATTSBURGH

US ISSN 1041-4754
PRESS-REPUBLICAN. 1942. d. $.50/day newsstand; $1.75/Sun.; $204/yr. mailed. 170 Margaret St., Plattsburgh, NY 12901. TEL 518-561-2300; FAX 518-561-3362. **Owner(s):** Plattsburgh Publishing Co., 170 Margaret St., Plattsburgh, NY 12901. TEL 518-561-2300; Ed. James D. Dynko; Pub. Brenda J. Tallman; adv. contact: George Rock. bk.rev.; pub. size: broadsheet; circ. morning 24,000(paid); Sun. 25,000(paid). **Wire Service(s):** AP, DJNS, ONS, SHNS.

POUGHKEEPSIE

US
POUGHKEEPSIE JOURNAL. 1785. d. $.50/day newsstand; $1.50/Sun.; $13/mo. home deliv.; $14.50/mo. motor rte. 85 Civic Center Plz., Poughkeepsie, NY 12601. TEL 914-454-2010; FAX 914-437-4902. **Owner(s):** Gannett Company, Inc., 1100 Wilson Blvd., Arlington, VA 22234. TEL 703-284-6000; Ed. Diana Mitsu-Klos; Pub. Richard K. Wager; adv.; photos; bk.rev.; pub. size: broadsheet; circ. morning 45,000(paid); Sun. 62,500(paid). **Wire Service(s):** AP, GNS, KR.

ROCHESTER

US
ROCHESTER DEMOCRAT & CHRONICLE. 1833. d. $.50/day newsstand; $2.05/Sun.; $158.60/yr. 55 Exchange Blvd., Rochester, NY 14614. TEL 716-232-7100; FAX 716-258-9788. **Owner(s):** Gannett Company, Inc., 1100 Wilson Blvd, Arlington, VA 22234. TEL 703-284-6000; Ed. Tom Callinan; Pub. Steven Brandt; adv.; photos; bk.rev.; pub. size: broadsheet; circ. morning 142,649(paid); Sun. 251,307(paid). **Wire Service(s):** AP, LAT-WP, CDN, GNS, CST, RN.

ROME

US
DAILY & SUNDAY SENTINEL. 1865. d. $.50/day newsstand; free/Sun.; $124.80/yr. in cy. carrier deliv.; $130/yr. motor rte.; $143/yr. mailed. 333 W. Dominick St., Rome, NY 13440. TEL 315-337-4000; FAX 315-337-4704. **Owner(s):** Rome Sentinel Co., 333 W. Dominick St., Rome, NY 13440. TEL 315-337-4000; Ed. David G. Swanson; Pub. Stephen B. Waters; adv. contact: Ron O'Neil. photos; pub. size: broadsheet; sun. tabloid; circ. evening 16,745(free & paid); Sun. 26,500(free & paid). **Wire Service(s):** AP.

SALAMANCA

US ISSN 8755-9110
SALAMANCA PRESS. 1867. Mon.-Sat. $.50 newsstand; $8.80/mo. in cy. carrier; $9.20/mo. motor rte. 36-42 River St., Salamanca, NY 14779. TEL 716-945-1644; FAX 716-945-4285. **Owner(s):** American Publishing Co., 606 N. Van Buren, Marion, IL 62959. TEL 618-993-1711; Ed. Kevin Burleson; Pub. Kevin Burleson; adv. contact: Glenda Pearson. pub. size: broadsheet; circ. evening 2,400(paid). **Wire Service(s):** AP.

SARANAC LAKE

US
ADIRONDACK DAILY ENTERPRISE. 1895. Mon.-Sat. $.50/day newsstand; $87/yr. carrier. P.O. Box 318, Saranac Lake, NY 12983. TEL 518-891-2600; FAX 518-891-2756. **Owner(s):** Ogden Newspapers, Inc., 1500 Main St., Wheeling, WV; Ed. John Penny; Pub. Catherine Moore; adv.; photos; bk.rev.; pub. size: broadsheet; circ. evening 6,000(paid). **Wire Service(s):** AP.

SARATOGA SPRINGS

US ISSN 1071-4448
SARATOGIAN, THE. 1855. d. $.50/day newsstand; $1/Sun.; $33.15/3 mos. 20 Lake Ave., Saratoga Springs, NY 12866. TEL 518-584-4242; FAX 518-587-7750; E-mail: saratoga4u@ad.com. **Owner(s):** Gannett Company, Inc., 1100 Wilson Blvd., Arlington, VA 22234. TEL 703-284-6901; Ed. Barbara Lombardo; Pub. Monte I. Trammer; adv. contact: Thomas Claybaugh. photos; pub. size: broadsheet; circ. morning 12,086(paid); Sun. 14,033(paid). **Wire Service(s):** AP, GNS.

SCHENECTADY

US ISSN 1050-0340
DAILY GAZETTE. 1894. d. $.50/day newsstand; $1.75/Sun.; $3.50/wk.; $14/mo. 2345 Maxon Rd., Schenectady, NY 12301-1090. TEL 518-374-4141; FAX 518-395-3089; E-mail: gazette@dailygazette.com; URL: http://www.dailygazette.com. **Owner(s):** Daily Gazette Co., Inc., 2345 Maxon Rd., Schenectady, NY 12301-1090. TEL 518-374-4141; FAX 518-395-3084; Ed. Thomas Woodman; Pub. John E.N. Hume, III; adv. contact: Daniel T. Beck. bk.rev.; pub. size: broadsheet; circ. morning 56,249(paid); Sun. 58,174(paid). **Wire Service(s):** AP, LAT-WP.

STATEN ISLAND

US
STATEN ISLAND ADVANCE. 1886. d. $.50/day newsstand; $1.50/Sun.; $2.25/wk. 950 Fingerboard Rd., Staten Island, NY 10305. TEL 718-981-1234; FAX 718-981-5679. **Owner(s):** Advance Publications, Inc., 950 Fingerboard Rd., Staten Island, NY 10305. TEL 718-981-1235; FAX 718-981-1234; Ed. William Huus; Pub. Richard E. Diamond; adv. contact: Gary Cognetta. photos; bk.rev.; pub. size: broadsheet; circ. evening 80,000(paid); Sun. 91,000(paid). **Wire Service(s):** AP, LAT, NNS.

SYRACUSE

US
HERALD-JOURNAL. 1877. d. $.35/day newsstand; $1.75/Sun.; $3.60/wk. carrier. One Clinton Sq., Syracuse, NY 13221. TEL 315-470-0011; FAX 315-470-3018. **Owner(s):** Advance Publications, Inc., 950 Fingerboard Rd., Staten Island, NY 10305. TEL 718-981-1234; FAX 718-981-1456; Ed. Timothy Atseff; Pub. Stephen A. Rogers; adv. contact: James Kleinklaus. photos; pub. size: broadsheet; circ. evening 82,488(paid); Sun. 226,000(paid). **Wire Service(s):** NNS, KR, AP, NYT, ANS.
Formerly: Syracuse Herald-Journal/American.

WATERTOWN, NY

US
POST-STANDARD. Mon.-Sat. $.35 newsstand; $2.10/wk. carrier; $109.20/yr. carrier. Clinton Sq., Syracuse, NY 13221. TEL 315-470-0011; FAX 315-470-3081. **Owner(s):** Syracuse Newspapers, Inc., Syracuse, NY; Ed. Rosemary Robinson; Pub. Stephen A. Rogers; adv. contact: Klein Klaus. photos; pub. size: broadsheet; circ. morning 89,000(paid). **Wire Service(s):** AP, LAT-WP.

TROY

US
RECORD, THE. 1896. d. $.50/day newsstand; $1.50/Sun.; $3.15/wk. 501 Broadway, Troy, NY 12180-3381. TEL 518-270-1200; FAX 518-270-1202; E-mail: troyrecord@globalone.net; URL: http://www.globalone.net/record/. **Owner(s):** Troy Publishing Co., Inc., 501 Broadway, Troy, NY 12180. TEL 518-270-1200; Ed. Lisa Robert Louis; Pub. Mark Romanow; adv.; bk.rev.; pub. size: broadsheet; circ. morning 30,017(paid); Sun. 33,300(paid). **Wire Service(s):** AP, KR.

UTICA

US
OBSERVER-DISPATCH. 1817. d. $.50/day newsstand; $1.50/Sun.; $3.30/wk. home deliv. 221 Oriskany Plz., Utica, NY 13501. TEL 315-792-5000; FAX 315-792-5033; E-mail: 76275.227@compuserve.com. **Owner(s):** Gannett Company, Inc., 1100 Wilson Blvd., Arlington, VA 22209; Pub. Donna Donovan; adv. contact: Bob Parker. pub. size: standard; circ. morning 60,000(paid); Sun. 68,321(paid). **Wire Service(s):** AP, GNS.

VESTAL

US
PRESS & SUN-BULLETIN. 1822. d. $.35/day newsstand; $1.50/Sun.; $119.60/yr. Mon.-Sat.; $171.60/yr. carrier delivery. 4421 Vestal Pkwy. E., Vestal, NY 13850. TEL 607-798-1234; FAX 607-798-1113. **Owner(s):** Gannett Company, Inc., 1100 Wilson Blvd., Arlington, VA 22234. TEL 703-284-6000; Ed. Barry Rothfeld; Pub. Bernard Griffin; adv.; bk.rev.; pub. size: broadsheet; circ. morning 70,000(paid); Sun. 90,000(paid). **Wire Service(s):** AP, GNS, LAT-WP.
Formerly: Binghamton Press & Sun-Bulletin.

WATERTOWN

US
WATERTOWN DAILY TIMES. 1861. d. $.50/day newsstand; $1.75/Sun.; $3.85/wk. carrier; $4/wk. motor rte. 260 Washington St., Watertown, NY 13601. TEL 315-782-1000; FAX 315-782-2337. **Owner(s):** John B. Johnson, 221 Flower Ave., W., Watertown, NY 13601; Ed. John B. Johnson, Jr.; Pub. John B. Johnson; adv. contact: Robert Cornell. pub. size: broadsheet; circ. evening 36,710(paid); Sun. 42,300(paid). **Wire Service(s):** AP, NYT.

WELLSVILLE

US

WELLSVILLE DAILY REPORTER. 1880. Sun.-Fri. $.50/day newsstand; $1.50/Sun.; $9.75/mo. carrier; $10/mo. motor rte.; $11/mo. mailed in US. 159 N. Main St., Wellsville, NY 14895. TEL 716-593-5300; FAX 716-593-5303. **Owner(s):** American Publishing Co., 606 N. Van Buren, Marion, IL 62959. TEL 618-993-1711; Ed. Neal Simon; Pub. Oak Duke; pub. size: broadsheet; circ. evening 4,000(paid); Sun. 14,000(paid). **Wire Service(s):** AP.

WEST NYACK

US

ROCKLAND JOURNAL-NEWS. 1889. d. $.50/day newsstand; $1.50/Sun.; $3.45/wk. 200 Rte. 303, N., West Nyack, NY 10994. TEL 914-358-2200; FAX 914-578-2477. **Owner(s):** Gannett Company, Inc., 1100 Wilson Blvd., Arlington, VA 22234. TEL 703-284-6000; Ed. Steve Lambert; Pub. Gary Sherlock; adv. contact: Enedina Vega. photos; bk.rev.; pub. size: broadsheet; circ. evening 43,000(paid); Sun. 53,000(paid). **Wire Service(s):** AP, GNS.
Formerly: Journal-News.

WHITE PLAINS

US

REPORTER DISPATCH, THE. 1964. d. $.50/day newsstand; $1.50/Sun.; $3.45/wk. carrier; $288/yr. mailed. One Gannett Dr., White Plains, NY 10604. TEL 914-694-9300; FAX 914-694-5018; E-mail: 73424.1275@compuserve.com. **Owner(s):** Gannett Suburban Newspapers, One Gannet Dr., White Plains, NY 10604. TEL 914-694-5000; Ed. Robert W. Ritter; Pub. Gary F. Sherlock; pub. size: broadsheet; circ. morning 28,115(paid); Sun. 31,468(paid). **Wire Service(s):** AP, GNS, LAT-WP, KR.

US

TARRYTOWN DAILY NEWS. d. $.50/day newsstand; $1.50/Sun.; $3.45/wk. One Gannett Dr., White Plains, NY 10604. TEL 914-694-9300; FAX 914-694-3535. **Owner(s):** Gannett Suburban Newspapers, One Gannett Dr., White Plains, NY 10604. TEL 914-694-5000; Ed. Robert W. Ritter; Pub. Gary Sherlock; adv.; pub. size: broadsheet; circ. morning 3,383(paid); Sun. 4,057(paid). **Wire Service(s):** AP, GNS.

YONKERS

US

HERALD STATESMAN. 1863. d. $.50/day newsstand; $1.50/Sun.; $3.45/wk. carrier. One Odell Plz., Yonkers, NY 10701. TEL 914-965-5000; FAX 914-696-8208; E-mail: 73424.1275@compuserve.com. **Owner(s):** Gannett Suburban Newspapers, One Gannett Dr., White Plains, NY 10604. TEL 914-694-5000; Pub. Gary Sherlock; adv.; pub. size: broadsheet; circ. evening 23,256(paid); Sun. 30,740(paid). **Wire Service(s):** AP, GNS, LAT-WP.

US ISSN 1060-4723

MT. VERNON ARGUS. d. $.50/day newsstand; $1.50/Sun.; $3.45/wk. One Odell Plz., Yonkers, NY 10701. TEL 914-696-8253; FAX 914-696-8208. **Owner(s):** Gannett Suburban Newspapers, One Gannett Dr., White Plains, NY 10604. TEL 914-694-5000; Pub. Gary Sherlock; adv. contact: Bob Twesten. pub. size: broadsheet; circ. morning 14,000(paid); Sun. 10,300(paid). **Wire Service(s):** AP, GNS.
Formerly: Mt. Vernon Daily Argus.

YORKTOWN HEIGHTS

US ISSN 1060-4588

CITIZEN REGISTER. 1839. d. $.50/day newsstand; $1.50/Sun.; $3.45/wk. home deliv.; $2.20/Sun. home deliv. 2 Commerce St., Yorktown Heights, NY 10512. TEL 914-243-3704; FAX 914-243-3703. **Owner(s):** Gannett Suburban Newspapers, One Gannett Dr., White Plains, NY 10604. TEL 914-694-5000; Pub. Gary Sherlock; adv. contact: Susan Butash. pub. size: broadsheet; circ. evening 7,900(paid); Sun. 8,800(paid). **Wire Service(s):** AP, GNS.
Formerly: Ossining Citizen Register.

US

PEEKSKILL STAR. 1920. d. $.50/day newsstand; $1.50/Sun.; $4.50/wk. 2 Commerce St., Yorktown Heights, NY 10512. TEL 914-243-3704; FAX 914-243-3703. **Owner(s):** Gannett Suburban Newspapers, One Gannett Dr., White Plains, NY 10604. TEL 914-694-5000; Pub. Gary Sherlock; adv. contact: Susan Butash. pub. size: broadsheet; circ. evening 12,500(paid); Sun. 13,200(paid). **Wire Service(s):** AP.

NORTH CAROLINA

ASHEBORO

US

ASHEBORO COURIER-TRIBUNE. 1876. Sun.-Fri. $.50/day newsstand; $1/Sun.; $80/yr. carrier; $140/yr. mail. 500 Sunset Ave., Asheboro, NC 27203. TEL 910-625-2102; FAX 910-626-7074; E-mail: ctnet@atomic.net; URL: http://www.atomic.net/ctnet. **Owner(s):** Donrey Media Group, P.O. Box 17017, Fort Smith, AK 72901. TEL 501-785-7810; Ed. Ray Criscoe; Pub. David Renfro; adv. contact: Chris Allen. photos; pub. size: broadsheet; circ. evening 18,500(paid); Sun. 18,500(paid). **Wire Service(s):** AP.

ASHEVILLE

US ISSN 1060-3255

ASHEVILLE CITIZEN-TIMES. 1870. d. $.50/day newsstand; $.75/Sat; $1.50/Sun.; $15.17/mo. 14 O'Henry Ave., Asheville, NC 28801. TEL 704-252-5611; FAX 704-251-0585. **Owner(s):** Gannett Company, Inc., 1100 Wilson Blvd., Arlington, VA 22340; Ed. Ed Dawson; Pub. Virgil L. Smith; adv. contact: Bob Williams. photos; bk.rev.; pub. size: broadsheet; circ. morning 68,454(paid); Sun. 80,412(paid). **Wire Service(s):** AP, AP Leaf Desk; KNS.

BURLINGTON

US

TIMES-NEWS, THE. 1887. d. $.50/day newsstand; $1/Sun.; $9/mo. carrier. 707 S. Main St., Burlington, NC 27215. TEL 910-227-0131; FAX 910-229-2463. **Owner(s):** Freedom Communications, Inc., 17666 Fitch, Irvine, CA 92714. TEL 714-253-9292; FAX 714-474-7675; Ed. John Pea; Pub. J. Stephen Buckley; photos; bk.rev.; pub. size: standard; circ. morning 29,000(paid); Sun. 30,848(paid). **Wire Service(s):** AP.

CHAPEL HILL

US

CHAPEL HILL HERALD. 1988. d. $.50/day newsstand; $1.50/Sun.; $13.50/mo. carrier; $18.05/mo. out of state. 106 Mallette St., Chapel Hill, NC 27516. TEL 919-967-6581; FAX 919-918-1055. **Owner(s):** Durham Herald-Sun Papers, 106 Mallette St., Chapel Hill, NC 27516. TEL 919-967-6581; Ed. William Hawkins; Pub. David Hughey; adv. contact: Zina Almers. pub. size: standard; circ. morning 25,000(paid); Sun. 25,000(paid).

CHARLOTTE

US

CHARLOTTE OBSERVER. 1886. d. $.50/day newsstand; $1.50/Sun.; $2.50/wk. carrier in area. 600 S. Tryon St., Charlotte, NC 28202. TEL 704-358-5000; FAX 704-358-5022; E-mail: gnielson@charlotte.infi.net; URL: http://www.charlotte.com. **Owner(s):** Knight-Ridder, Inc., One Herald Plz., Miami, FL 33132. TEL 305-376-3800; FAX 305-376-3875; Ed. Jennie Buckner; Pub. Rolfe Neill; adv. contact: Maggie Krost. photos; pub. size: broadsheet; circ. morning 235,000(paid); Sun. 301,000(paid). **Wire Service(s):** AP, AP Photo, NYT, LAT-WP.

CLINTON

US

SAMPSON INDEPENDENT, THE. 1929. Sun.-Fri. $.35/day newsstand; $.75/Sun.; $7/mo. home deliv. 303 Elizabeth St., Clinton, NC 28328. TEL 910-592-8137; FAX 910-592-8756. **Owner(s):** Community Newspaper Holdings, Lexington, KY; Ed. Debbie Chiarella. adv. contact: Lisa Hawkins. pub. size: broadsheet; circ. evening 8,200(paid); Sun. 8,700(paid). **Wire Service(s):** AP.
Formerly: Clinton Sampson Independent.

DUNN

US

DUNN DAILY RECORD. 1950. Mon.-Fri. $.50 newsstand; $60/yr. carrier; $100/yr. mailed. 100 W. Broad St., Dunn, NC 28335. TEL 910-891-1234; FAX 910-891-4445; E-mail: record@nceye.net. **Owner(s):** Record Publishing Co., LLC, 100 W. Broad St., Dunn, NC 28335. TEL 910-891-1234; Ed. Lisa Farmer; Pub. Bart Adams; adv.; photos; pub. size: broadsheet; circ. evening 10,185(paid). **Wire Service(s):** AP.

DURHAM

US ISSN 1055-4467

HERALD-SUN, THE. 1889. d. $.50/day newsstand; $1.50/Sun.; $13.50/mo. carrier; $40.50/13 wks. carrier; $60.91/13 wks. in state mailed. 2828 Pickett Rd., Durham, NC 27705. TEL 919-419-6500; FAX 919-419-6889; E-mail: jch@herald-sun.com; URL: http://www.herald-sun.com. **Owner(s):** Durham Herald Co., P.O. Box 2092, Durham, NC 27702. TEL 919-419-6500; Ed. Jon C. Ham; Pub. David Hughey; adv. contact: Gene Bobbitt. bk.rev.; pub. size: broadsheet; circ. morning 56,000(paid); Sun. 64,000(paid). **Wire Service(s):** AP, NYT, SHNA, KR, RN.

EDEN

US ISSN 1067-0874
DAILY NEWS, THE. 1924. Mon.-Fri. $.35 newsstand; $53/yr. home deliv.; $82.50/yr. mailed. 804 Washington St., Eden, NC 27288. TEL 910-623-2155; FAX 910-623-2228. **Owner(s):** Media General, Inc., 333 E. Grace St., Richmond, VA 23219. TEL 804-649-6000; FAX 804-775-8090; Ed. Angela Stadler. adv. contact: Maureen Craig. photos; bk.rev.; pub. size: broadsheet; circ. evening 7,878(paid). **Wire Service(s):** AP.
Formerly: Eden Daily News.

ELIZABETH CITY

US
DAILY ADVANCE. 1911. Sun.-Fri. $.50/day newsstand; $1.25/Sun.; $9.95/mo. carrier. 216 S. Poindexter, Elizabeth City, NC 27909. TEL 919-335-0841; FAX 919-335-4415. **Owner(s):** Cox Enterprises, Inc., P.O. Box 105357, Atlanta, GA 30348; Ed. Julian Eure; Pub. Belinda Gaudet; adv. contact: Frank Paris. photos; pub. size: broadsheet; circ. evening 13,000(paid); Sun. 13,100(paid). **Wire Service(s):** AP.
Formerly: Elizabeth City Daily Advance.

ELIZABETHTOWN

US
BLADEN JOURNAL. 1908. Tue.-Fri. $.50 newsstand; $26/yr. in cy.; $42/yr. out of cy.; $54/yr. out of state. 109 E. Broad St., Elizabethtown, NC 28337. TEL 919-862-4163; FAX 919-862-6602. **Owner(s):** Newspaper Holdings, Inc., 269 W. Main St., 6th Fl., Lexington, KY 40507. TEL 606-388-2644; Ed. Lynn McLamb; Pub. Lynn McLamb; adv.; photos; bk.rev.; pub. size: standard; circ. morning 4,200(paid). **Wire Service(s):** AP.
Formerly: Bladen Daily Journal.

FAYETTEVILLE

US ISSN 1052-9829
FAYETTEVILLE OBSERVER-TIMES. 1816. d. $.50/day newsstand; $1.50/Sun.; $11.75/mo. carrier. 458 Whitfield St., Fayetteville, NC 28306. TEL 910-323-4848; FAX 910-486-3531. **Owner(s):** Fayetteville Publishing Co., 458 Whitfield St., Fayetteville, NC 28306. TEL 919-323-4848; Pub. Ramon L. Yarborough; adv. contact: Ron Watts. pub. size: broadsheet; circ. morning 72,957(paid); Sun. 83,000(paid). **Wire Service(s):** AP, LAT-WP.
Formerly: Fayetteville Observer-Times Morning.

FOREST CITY

US
DAILY COURIER. 1978. Mon.-Fri. $.25 newsstand; $4/mo. 601 Oak St., Forest City, NC 28043. TEL 704-245-6431; FAX 704-248-2790. **Owner(s):** Ron Paris, 601 Oak St., Forest City, NC 28043. TEL 704-245-6431; Bill Blair, 601 Oak St., Forest City, NC 28043. TEL 704-245-6431; FAX 704-248-2790; Ed. Amy Revis; Pub. Ron Paris; adv. contact: Jim Deviney. pub. size: broadsheet; circ. evening 12,500(paid). Wire Service(s): AP.

GASTONIA

US
GASTON GAZETTE. 1880. Mon.-Sun. $.25/day newsstand; $1.25/Sun.; $102/yr. home deliv. 2500 E. Franklin Blvd., Gastonia, NC 28054. TEL 704-864-3291; FAX 704-867-6988; E-mail: gazettenet@aol.com. **Owner(s):** Freedom Communications, Inc., 17666 Fitch, Irvine, CA 92614. TEL 714-553-6000; Ed. Jennie Lambert; Pub. Mike McMillan; adv. contact: Jim Bretzius. photos; bk.rev.; pub. size: broadsheet; circ. morning 43,000(paid); Sun. 46,000(paid). **Wire Service(s):** AP.

GOLDSBORO

US
GOLDSBORO NEWS-ARGUS. 1885. Sun.-Fri. $.50/day newsstand; $1.25/Sun.; $7.75/mo. 310 N. Berkeley Blvd., Goldsboro, NC 27534. TEL 919-778-2211; FAX 919-778-9891. **Owner(s):** Wayne Printing Co., Inc., Goldsboro, NC 27532. TEL 919-778-2211; FAX 919-778-9891; Ed. J. Michael Rouse; Pub. Hal Tanner, Jr.; adv. contact: Nelson Mitchell. photos; bk.rev.; pub. size: broadsheet; circ. evening 22,000(paid); Sun. 25,000(paid). **Wire Service(s):** AP.

GREENSBORO

US ISSN 0747-1858
NEWS & RECORD, THE. 1972. d. $.50/day newsstand, $1.25/Sun.; $2.75/wk. carrier. 200 E. Market St., Greensboro, NC 27401. TEL 910-373-7000; FAX 910-373-7067. **Owner(s):** Landmark Communications, Inc., 150 W. Brambleton Ave., Norfolk, VA 23510. TEL 804-446-2000; Ed. Patrick Yack; Pub. Van King; adv. contact: Kathy Lambeth. photos; bk.rev.; pub. size: broadsheet; circ. morning 93,400(paid); Sun. 120,300(paid). **Wire Service(s):** AP, NYT, LAT-WP.
Formerly: Greensboro Daily News.

GREENVILLE

US ISSN 1060-6130
GREENVILLE DAILY REFLECTOR. 1882. d. $.50/day newsstand; $1.25/Sun.; $115.40/yr. 209 Cotanche St., Greenville, NC 27858. TEL 919-752-6166; FAX 919-752-9583. **Owner(s):** Cox Enterprises, Inc., P.O. Box 105357, Atlanta, GA 30348. TEL 404-843-5000; Pub. David J. Whichard, III; pub. size: broadsheet; circ. morning 18,846(paid); Sun. 21,117. **Wire Service(s):** AP.

HENDERSON

US
DAILY DISPATCH, THE. 1914. Tue.-Sun. $.50/day newsstand; $1/Sun.; $8.50/mo. mailed; $70/yr. 304 S. Chestnut St., Henderson, NC 27536. TEL 919-492-4001; FAX 919-430-0125. **Owner(s):** Paducah Newspapers, Inc., 408 Kentucky Ave., P.O. Box 2300, Paducah, KY 42002. TEL 302-443-1771; Ed. Laverene Jeffries; Pub. Rick Bean; adv. contact: Deborah Tuck. photos; bk.rev.; pub. size: broadsheet; circ. morning 10,500(paid); Sun. 11,000(paid). **Wire Service(s):** AP.
Formerly: Henderson Daily Dispatch.

HENDERSONVILLE

US ISSN 1042-2323
HENDERSONVILLE TIMES-NEWS. 1881. d. $.25/day newsstand; $1/Sun.; $8.25/mo. carrier. 1717 Four Seasons Blvd., Hendersonville, NC 28792. TEL 704-692-0505; FAX 704-692-2319. **Owner(s):** New York Times Co., The, 229 W. 43rd St., New York, NY 10036. TEL 212-556-1234; Pub. Judy Robinette; adv. contact: Mike Sternberg. pub. size: broadsheet; circ. morning 21,397(paid); Sun. 23,000(paid). **Wire Service(s):** AP, NYT.

HICKORY

US ISSN 1061-5628
HICKORY DAILY RECORD. 1915. d. $.50/day newsstand; $1/Sun.; $129.60 mailed. 1100 Park Pl., Hickory, NC 28602. TEL 704-322-4510; FAX 704-328-9378. **Owner(s):** Hickory Publishing Co., Inc., 1100 Park Pl., Hickory, NC 28602. TEL 704-322-4510; Ed. Elizabeth Williams; Pub. Suzanne G. Millholland; adv. contact: David Millholland. pub. size: broadsheet; circ. morning 20,065(paid); Sun. 19,452(paid). **Wire Service(s):** AP.

HIGH POINT

US ISSN 0747-1491
HIGH POINT ENTERPRISE. 1885. d. $.50/day newsstand; $1/Sun.; $7.95/mo. 210 Church Ave., High Point, NC 27262. TEL 910-888-3500; FAX 910-883-7865; E-mail: gbm@hpe.com. **Owner(s):** High Point Enterprises, Inc., 210 Church St., High Point, NC 27262. TEL 910-888-3500; FAX 910-841-5165; Ed. Kenneth Irons; Pub. Joseph P. Rawley; adv. contact: Demi Foust. photos; bk.rev.; pub. size: broadsheet; circ. morning 31,600(paid); Sun. 32,700(paid). **Wire Service(s):** AP, KR.

JACKSONVILLE

US
DAILY NEWS. 1953. d. $.50/day newsstand; $1.25/Sun.; $10/mo. carrier; $25.50/3 mos. carrier. 724 Bell Fork Rd., Jacksonville, NC 28540. TEL 910-353-1171; FAX 910-353-7316. **Owner(s):** Freedom Communications, Inc., 17666 Fitch, Irvine, CA 92614. TEL 714-553-9292; FAX 714-474-7675; Ed. Madison Taylor; Pub. Charles Fischer; adv. contact: W.R. Taylor. photos; bk.rev.; pub. size: broadsheet; circ. morning 23,500(paid); Sun. 25,000(paid). **Wire Service(s):** AP.
Formerly: Jacksonville Daily News.

KANNAPOLIS

US
INDEPENDENT TRIBUNE. 1900. d. $.50/day newsstand; $1/Sun.; $7.80/mo. $93.60/yr. carrier. 924 Cloverleaf Plz., Kannapolis, NC 28023. TEL 704-782-3155; FAX 704-786-0645. **Owner(s):** Media General, Inc., 333 E. Grace St., Richmond, VA 23219. TEL 804-649-6000; FAX 804-775-8090; Ed. Stan Honjacki. adv.; photos; pub. size: broadsheet; circ. evening 27,000(paid); Sun. 14,000(paid). **Wire Service(s):** AP.
Formerly: Concord Tribune.

KINSTON

US

KINSTON DAILY FREE PRESS. 1882. Sun.-Fri. $.50/day newsstand; $1/Sun.; $72/yr. 2103 N. Queen St., Kinston, NC 28501. TEL 919-527-3191; FAX 919-527-1813. **Owner(s):** Freedom Communications, Inc., 17666 Fitch, Irvine, CA 92614. TEL 714-553-9292; Ed. Carolyn Waller; Pub. Vernon DeBolt; adv. contact: Billy Moore. photos; bk.rev.; pub. size: standard; circ. evening 14,500(paid); Sun. 15,500(paid). **Wire Service(s):** AP, KR, SHNA.

LAURINBURG

US

LAURINBURG EXCHANGE. 1899. Mon.-Fri. $.50 newsstand; $58/yr. in cy.; $65/yr. out of cy. 211 Cronly St., Laurinburg, NC 28352. TEL 910-276-2311; FAX 910-276-3815. **Owner(s):** Mid-South Management Co., Inc., 221 Cronly St., Laurinburg, NC 28352. TEL 919-276-2311; Ed. Betsy Shearron; Pub. Mike Milligan; adv.; photos; pub. size: broadsheet; circ. evening 9,400(paid).

LENOIR

US

LENOIR NEWS-TOPIC. 1875. Mon.-Sat. $.50 newsstand; $90/yr. home deliv.; $108/yr. mailed. 123 Pennton Ave., Lenoir, NC 28645. TEL 704-758-7381; FAX 704-754-0110. **Owner(s):** Paxton Media Group, Inc., P.O. Box 2300, Paducah, KY 42002. TEL 502-443-1771; Ed. Richard Tuttell; Pub. Richard Mitchell; adv. contact: Steve Garland. photos; bk.rev.; pub. size: broadsheet; circ. evening 12,300(paid). **Wire Service(s):** AP, NYT.

LEXINGTON

US   ISSN 0163-3090

DISPATCH, THE. 1882. Mon.-Sat. $.50 newsstand; $10/mo. carrier. 30 E. First Ave., Lexington, NC 27292. TEL 910-249-3981; FAX 910-249-0712. **Owner(s):** New York Times Co., The, 229 W. 43rd. St., New York, NY 10036. TEL 212-556-1234; Pub. Joe S. Sink, Jr.; adv. contact: Betty Barnes. pub. size: broadsheet; circ. evening 13,800(paid). **Wire Service(s):** AP, NYT.

Formerly: Lexington Dispatch.

LUMBERTON

US

ROBESONIAN, THE. 1870. Sun.-Sat. $.35/day newsstand; $.75/Sun.; $93/yr. 121 W. Fifth St., Lumberton, NC 28358. TEL 910-739-4322; FAX 910-739-6553. **Owner(s):** Community Newspaper Holdings, 269 W. Main St., Lexington, KY 40507; Ed. Donnie Douglas. adv. contact: Greg Ratliff. photos; bk.rev.; pub. size: broadsheet; circ. evening 13,800(paid); Sun. 15,800(paid). **Wire Service(s):** AP.

MARION

US

MCDOWELL NEWS, THE. 1929. Mon.-Fri. $.50 newsstand; $78/yr. carrier; $91/yr. mailed. 26 N. Logan St., Marion, NC 28752. TEL 704-652-3313; FAX 704-652-4769. **Owner(s):** Media General, Inc., 333 E. Grace St., Richmond, VA 23219. TEL 804-649-6000; FAX 804-775-8090; Ed. Scott Hollifield; Pub. David Setzer; adv. contact: Keith Austin. pub. size: broadsheet; circ. evening 7,200(paid). **Wire Service(s):** AP.

MONROE

US

ENQUIRER-JOURNAL, THE. 1873. Sun.-Fri. $.50/day newsstand; $1/Sun.; $7.40/4 wks. 500 W. Jefferson St., Monroe, NC 28112. TEL 704-289-1541; FAX 704-289-2929. **Owner(s):** Paxton Media Group, Inc., 408 Kentucky Ave., Paducah, KY 40223. TEL 502-575-8600; Ed. Luanne Williams. adv. contact: Dale Morefield. pub. size: standard; circ. evening 13,273(paid); Sun. 15,163(paid). **Wire Service(s):** AP.

MORGANTON

US

NEWS HERALD, THE. 1885. Sun.-Fri. $.50/day newsstand; $.75/Sun.; $7.90/mo. carrier. 301 Collett St., Morganton, NC 28655. TEL 704-437-2161; FAX 704-437-5372. **Owner(s):** Media General, Inc., 333 E. Grace St., Richmond, VA 23219. TEL 804-649-6000; FAX 804-775-8090; Ed. Bill Poteat; Pub. Eugene Willard; adv. contact: Randy Hart. pub. size: broadsheet; circ. evening 12,500(paid); Sun. 13,000(paid). **Wire Service(s):** AP.

Formerly: Morganton News-Herald.

MT. AIRY

US

MOUNT AIRY NEWS. 1880. Sun.-Fri. $.50/day newsstand; $1.25/Sun.; $95.25/yr. carrier; $112.70/yr mailed; $118.80/yr. mailed out of state. 319 Renfro St., Mt. Airy, NC 27030. TEL 910-786-4141; FAX 910-789-2816. **Owner(s):** Mid-South Management Co., Inc.; Ed. Thomas Joyce; Pub. George W. Summerlin; adv. contact: Anthony Summerlin. pub. size: broadsheet; circ. evening 9,500(paid); Sun. 10,000(paid). **Wire Service(s):** AP.

NAGS HEAD

US

VIRGINIAN PILOT. d. $.50/day newsstand; $1.50/Sun.; $32.49/13 wks. 2224 S. Carlton Hwy, Nags Head, NC 27959. TEL 919-441-1620; FAX 919-441-8895. **Owner(s):** Virginian Pilot, The, 150 Brambleton Ave., Norfolk, VA 23510; Ed. Ronald L. Speer. adv. contact: Charles Huff. pub. size: broadsheet; circ. morning 250,000(paid); Sun. 290,000(paid).

NEW BERN

US

SUN-JOURNAL. 1871. d. $.50/day newsstand; $1/Sun.; $78/yr. 226 Pollock St., New Bern, NC 28560. TEL 919-638-8101; FAX 919-638-4664. **Owner(s):** Freedom Communications, Inc., P.O. Box 19549, Irvine, CA 92713. TEL 714-553-9292; Ed. Patrick Holmes; Pub. John Graham; adv. contact: Judy Avery. pub. size: standard; circ. morning 18,000(paid); Sun. 18,000(paid). **Wire Service(s):** AP.

Formerly: New Bern Sun-Journal.

NEWTON

US

OBSERVER NEWS. 1879. Mon.-Fri. $.50 newsstand; $11/ mos.; $20/6 mos.; $38/yr. 309 N. College Ave., Newton, NC 28658. TEL 704-464-0221; FAX 704-464-1267. **Owner(s):** American Publishing Co., 606 N. Van Buren, Marion, IL 62959. TEL 618-993-1711; Ed. Jennifer W. Miller; Pub. Jerry Hodge; adv. contact: Sharon Rhymer. pub. size: broadsheet; circ. evening 4,000(controlled). **Wire Service(s):** AP.

RALEIGH

US

NEWS & OBSERVER. 1865. d. $.50/day newsstand; $1.50/Sun.; $7/mo. Mon.-Sat.; $12/mo. daily & Sun.; $8/mo. Sat. & Sun.; $7/mo. Sun. 215 S. McDowell St., Raleigh, NC 27601. TEL 919-829-4500; FAX 919-829-4529; E-mail: sford@nando.com; URL: http://www.nando.net/nao/. **Owner(s):** McClatchy Newspapers, P.O. Box 15779, Sacramento, CA 95816. TEL 916-321-1000; Ed. Anders Gyllenhaal; Pub. Fred D. Crisp; adv.; photos; bk.rev.; pub. size: broadsheet; circ. morning 149,021(paid); Sun. 198,176(paid). **Wire Service(s):** AP, NYT, KR, LAT-WP, Tribune, Cox, SHNA.

REIDSVILLE

US

REIDSVILLE REVIEW. 1888. Tue.-Fri. & Sun. $.50/day newsstand; $1/Sun.; $1.25/wk.; $68/yr. 1921 Vance St., Reidsville, NC 27320. TEL 910-349-4331; FAX 910-342-2513. **Owner(s):** Media General, Inc., 333 E. Grace St., Richmond, VA 23219. TEL 804-649-6000; FAX 804-775-8090; Ed. Ann Fish; Pub. James M. DeLapp; adv. contact: Teresa Talley. photos; bk.rev.; pub. size: broadsheet; circ. evening 6,600(paid). **Wire Service(s):** UPI.

ROANOKE RAPIDS

US

ROANOKE RAPIDS DAILY & SUNDAY HERALD. 1914. Sun.-Fri. $.50/day newsstand; $1.25/Sun. 916 Roanoke Ave., Roanoke Rapids, NC 27870. TEL 919-537-2505; FAX 919-537-2314. **Owner(s):** Wick Communications, Inc., 333 W, Wilcox Dr., Ste. 302, Sierra Vista, AZ 85635; Ed. Bill Moss; Pub. Steven Woody; adv. contact: Tim Frates. photos; pub. size: broadsheet; circ. morning 13,500(paid). **Wire Service(s):** UPI.

DAILY NEWSPAPERS

ROCKINGHAM

US ISSN 1050-7639
RICHMOND COUNTY DAILY JOURNAL. 1931. Sun.-Fri. $.35/day newsstand; $.50/Sun.; $84/yr. 105 E. Washington St., Rockingham, NC 28379-3639. TEL 910-997-3111; FAX 910-997-4321. **Owner(s):** Community Newspapers, Inc., P.O. Box 792, Athens, GA 30603. TEL 706-548-0010; FAX 706-548-0808; Ed. Bert Unger; Pub. Marvin Enderle; adv. contact: Terri Cooper. adv.: $9.90/SAU. photos. pub. size: broadsheet; circ. evening 8,600(paid); Sun. 8,800(paid). **Wire Service(s):** AP.

ROCKY MOUNT

US ISSN 0738-5137
ROCKY MOUNT TELEGRAM. 1911. d. $.50/day newsstand; $1.25/Sun.; $120/yr. in town; $133.39/yr. out of town. 150 Howard St., Rocky Mount, NC 27804. TEL 919-446-5161; FAX 919-446-4057. **Owner(s):** Cox Enterprises, Inc., P.O. Box 105357, Atlanta, GA 30348; Ed. Jeff Herrin; Pub. Den Dickerson; adv.; bk.rev.; pub. size: broadsheet; circ. evening 15,000(paid); Sun. 17,000(paid). **Wire Service(s):** AP.
Formerly: Rocky Mount Evening Telegram.

SALISBURY

US ISSN 0747-0738
SALISBURY POST. 1905. d. $.50/day newsstand; $1/Sun.; $8/mo. carrier. 131 W. Innes St., Salisbury, NC 28144-0105. TEL 704-633-8950; FAX 704-639-0003. **Owner(s):** Evening Post Publishing Co., 131 W. Innes St., Salisbury, NC 28144. TEL 704-633-8950; FAX 704-633-7373; Ed. Frank Deloache; Pub. Cathy Wilkerson; adv. contact: Steve Johnson. photos; bk.rev.; pub. size: broadsheet; circ. evening 25,409(paid); Sun. 26,399(paid). **Wire Service(s):** AP.

SANFORD

US
SANFORD HERALD, THE. 1930. Mon.-Sat. $.50 newsstand; $60/yr. 208 St. Clair Ct., Sanford, NC 27330. TEL 919-708-9000; FAX 919-708-9001; E-mail: bhorner3@interpath.com. **Owner(s):** Sanford Herald, Inc., 208 St. Clair Ct., Sanford, NC 27330. TEL 919-708-9000; FAX 919-708-9001; Ed. Cornelia Olive; Pub. W.E. Horner, Jr.; adv. contact: James C. Banks. bk.rev.; pub. size: broadsheet; circ. evening 14,706(paid). Wire Service(s): AP.

SHELBY

US ISSN 1043-1950
SHELBY STAR. 1894. d. $.50/day newsstand; $1/Sun.; $10/mo. 315 E. Graham St., Shelby, NC 28150. TEL 704-484-7000; FAX 704-484-0805. **Owner(s):** Thomson Newspapers, Inc., Metro Centre, One Station Pl., 6th Fl., Stamford, CT 06902. TEL 203-428-2500; FAX 203-425-2516; Ed. Roberta Wilson; Pub. R. Keith Walters; adv. contact: Charles Price. bk.rev.; pub. size: standard; circ. evening 17,500(paid); Sun. 17,500(paid). **Wire Service(s):** AP.

STATESVILLE

US ISSN 0745-7804
STATESVILLE RECORD & LANDMARK. 1874. d. $.50/day newsstand; $1/Sun.; $2.10/wk. carrier. 222 E. Broad St., Statesville, NC 28677. TEL 704-873-1451; FAX 704-872-3150. **Owner(s):** Media General, Inc., 333 E. Grace St., Richmond, VA 23219. TEL 804-649-6000; FAX 804-775-8090; Ed. Eric Millsaps. adv. contact: Dwayne Menster. pub. size: broadsheet; circ. evening 16,000(paid); Sun. 17,400(paid). **Wire Service(s):** AP.

TARBORO

US
DAILY SOUTHERNER, THE. 1889. Mon.-Fri. $.50 newsstand; $6.25/mo. carrier; $100/yr. mailed. 504 W. Wilson St., Tarboro, NC 27886. TEL 919-823-3106; FAX 919-823-4599. **Owner(s):** American Publishing Co., 606 N. Van Buren, Marion, IL 62959. TEL 618-993-1711; Ed. Frank Taylor; Pub. Jerome Creech; adv. contact: Ellis W. Hooks. pub. size: broadsheet; circ. evening 6,200(paid). **Wire Service(s):** AP.

TRYON

US
TRYON DAILY BULLETIN. 1928. Mon.-Fri. $.25 newsstand; $35/yr. 106 N. Trade St., Tryon, NC 28782. TEL 704-859-9151; FAX 704-859-5575. **Owner(s):** Tryon Daily Bulletin, Inc., 106 N. Trade St., Tryon, NC 28782. TEL 704-859-9151; FAX 704-859-5575; Ed. Reen Smith; Pub. Jeffrey A. Byrd; adv.; pub. size: broadsheet; circ. morning 4,400(paid).

WASHINGTON

US ISSN 1057-7068
WASHINGTON DAILY NEWS. 1909. d. $.50/day newsstand; $.75/Sun.; $8/mo. carrier; $7.25/mo. senior citizens. 217 N. Market St., Washington, NC 27889. TEL 919-946-2144; FAX 919-946-9797. **Owner(s):** Washington News Publishing Co., P.O. Box 1788, Washington, NC 27889. TEL 919-946-2144; Ed. Mark Inabinatt; Pub. Ashley B. Futrell, Jr.; adv. contact: Eugene E. King. pub. size: broadsheet; circ. morning 10,600(paid); Sun. 10,600(paid). **Wire Service(s):** AP.

WILMINGTON

US
WILMINGTON MORNING STAR. 1867. d. $.50/day newsstand; $1.75/Sun.; $9.95/mo. 1003 S. 17th St., Wilmington, NC 28401-0840. TEL 910-343-2000. E-mail: mseditor@wilmington.net; URL: http://www.wilmington.net/starnews. **Owner(s):** New York Times Co., The, 229 W. 43rd St., New York, NY 10036. TEL 212-556-1234; Ed. John Meyer; Pub. John Lynch; adv. contact: Dan Schuette. photos; bk.rev.; pub. size: broadsheet; circ. morning 53,615(paid); Sun. 65,615(paid). **Wire Service(s):** NYT, AP, KR, LAT-WP.

WILSON

US
WILSON DAILY TIMES. 1902. Mon.-Sat. $.50/day newsstand; $1/Sat.; $7/mo.; $11/mo. in state mailed; $11.50/mo. out of state. 2001 Downing St. Ext., Wilson, NC 27894. TEL 919-243-5151; FAX 919-243-2999. **Owner(s):** Morgan P. & Margaret Dickerman, P.O. Box 2447, Wilson, NC 27894. TEL 919-243-5151; Ed. Hal Tarleton; Pub. Morgan Dickerman; adv. contact: Ray McKeithan. bk.rev.; pub. size: broadsheet; circ. evening 17,000(paid). **Wire Service(s):** AP.

WINSTON-SALEM

US
WINSTON-SALEM JOURNAL. 1897. d. $.50/day newsstand; $1.25/Sun.; $2.50/wk. carrier. 418 N. Marshall St., Winston-Salem, NC 27101. TEL 910-727-7211; FAX 910-727-7245. **Owner(s):** Media General, Inc., 333 E. Grace St., Richmond, VA 23219. TEL 804-649-6671; Ed. Carl Crothers; Pub. Jon Witherspoon; adv. contact: Timothy Maby. photos; bk.rev.; pub. size: broadsheet; circ. morning 93,000(paid); Sun. 108,000(paid). **Wire Service(s):** AP, NYT, LAT-WP.

NORTH DAKOTA

BISMARCK

US ISSN 0745-1091
BISMARCK TRIBUNE. 1873. d. $.50/day newsstand; $.75/Wed.; $1.75/Sun.; $162/yr. carrier. 707 E. Front Ave., Bismarck, ND 58504. TEL 701-223-2500; FAX 701-224-1412; E-mail: bismarcktribune@ndonline.com; URL: http://www.ndonline.com/. **Owner(s):** Lee Enterprises, Inc., 215 N. Main St., Davenport, IA 52801. TEL 319-383-2100; Ed. Kevin Giles; Pub. Margaret Wade; adv. contact: Lani Renneau. pub. size: broadsheet; circ. evening 33,000(paid); Sun. 32,000(paid). **Wire Service(s):** AP, LAT-WP.

DEVIL'S LAKE

US
DEVIL'S LAKE DAILY JOURNAL. 1905. Mon.-Fri. $.50 newsstand; $6.50/mo. home deliv. 516 Fourth St., Devil's Lake, ND 58301. TEL 701-662-2127; FAX 701-662-3115. **Owner(s):** Community Newspaper Holdings, 269W. Main St., Lexington, KY 40507; Ed. Gordon Weixel; Pub. Kathy Svidel; adv. contact: Chris Olsen. photos; pub. size: broadsheet; circ. evening 4,800(paid). **Wire Service(s):** AP.

DICKINSON

US ISSN 1049-6718
DICKINSON PRESS, THE. 1883. Tue.-Sun. $.50/day newsstand; $1/Sun.; $2.38/wk. home deliv.; $9.50/mo. home deliv. 127 W. First St., Dickinson, ND 58601. TEL 701-225-8141; FAX 701-225-4205. **Owner(s):** Forum Communications Co., P.O. Box 2020, Fargo, ND 58207. TEL 701-223-7311; Ed. Sharon Dietz. adv. contact: Erv Barth. photos; pub. size: broadsheet; circ. morning 7,700(paid); Sun. 8,200(paid). **Wire Service(s):** AP.

FARGO

FORUM, THE. 1878. d. $.50/day newsstand; $.75/Sat.; $1.75/Sun.; $171/yr. 101 N. Fifth St., Fargo, ND 58102. TEL 701-235-7311; FAX 701-241-5487; E-mail: pol@pol.org; URL: http://www.pol.org/forum. **Owner(s):** Forum Communications Co., P.O. Box 2020, Fargo, ND 58107. TEL 701-223-7311; Ed. Terry DeVine; Pub. William C. Marcil; adv.; bk.rev.; pub. size: standard; circ. morning 54,714(paid); Sun. 68,911(paid). **Wire Service(s):** AP, FIELD.

US ISSN 0895-1292

GRAND FORKS

GRAND FORKS HERALD. 1876. d. $.50/day newsstand; $.75/Sat.; $1.75/Sun.; $13/4 wks. carrier. 303 Second Ave., N, Grand Forks, ND 58203. TEL 701-780-1100; FAX 701-780-1123; E-mail: gfherald@grandforks.polaristel.net. **Owner(s):** Knight-Ridder, Inc., One Herald Plz., Miami, FL 33132. TEL 305-376-3800; Ed. Jim Durkin; Pub. Michael Maidenberg; adv. contact: Tom Kuchera. photos; bk.rev.; pub. size: broadsheet; circ. morning 40,000(paid); Sun. 40,785(paid). **Wire Service(s):** AP, KR, NYT, Telephoto.

US ISSN 0745-9661

JAMESTOWN

JAMESTOWN SUN, THE. 1925. Mon.-Sat. $.50 newsstand; $8.85/mo. carrier; $93.54/yr. in state. 122 Second St., N.W., Jamestown, ND 58401. TEL 701-252-3120; FAX 701-251-2878. **Owner(s):** American Publishing Co., 606 N. Van Buren, Marion, IL 62959. TEL 618-993-1711; Pub. Bruce Henke; adv. contact: Gene Keller. pub. size: broadsheet; circ. morning 7,300(paid). **Wire Service(s):** AP.

US

MINOT

MINOT DAILY NEWS. d. $.50/day newsstand; $1.50/Sun.; $135/yr. in cy.; $147/yr. out of cy.; $211/yr. out of state. 301 Fourth St., S.E., Minot, ND 58701. TEL 701-857-1900; FAX 701-857-1961. **Owner(s):** Ogden Newspapers, Inc., 1500 Main St., Wheeling, WV 26003. TEL 304-233-0100; Ed. Mark Hanson. adv. contact: Vaughn Kessler. photos; bk.rev.; pub. size: standard; circ. morning 26,000(paid); Sun. 27,000(paid). **Wire Service(s):** AP.

US ISSN 0885-3053

VALLEY CITY

VALLEY CITY TIMES-RECORD. Mon.-Fri. $.50 newsstand; $8.50/mo. carrier; $79.50/yr. carrier. 146 Third St., N.E., Valley City, ND 58072. TEL 701-845-0463; FAX 701-845-0175. **Owner(s):** American Publishing Co., 606 N. Van Buren, Marion, IL 62959. TEL 618-993-1711; Pub. Patrick Kellar; adv. contact: Jan Olafson. adv.: $5.75/SAU. photos; bk.rev.; pub. size: broadsheet; circ. evening 3,400(paid). **Wire Service(s):** AP.

US

WAHPETON

DAILY NEWS. 1880. Tue.-Fri. & Sun. $.50/day newsstand; $.75/Fri.; $1.25/Sun.; $82/yr. 601 Dakota Ave., Wahpeton, ND 58075. TEL 701-642-8585; FAX 701-642-1501. **Owner(s):** Wick Communications, Inc., 333 W. Wilcox Dr., Ste. 302, Sierra Vista, AZ 83635; Ed. Barbara Grant; Pub. Newell C. Grant; adv. contact: Roger Harty. pub. size: broadsheet; circ. morning 5,600(paid). **Wire Service(s):** AP.
Formerly: Wahpeton-Breckenridge Daily News.

US

WILLISTON

WILLISTON HERALD. 1899. Sun.-Fri. $.50/day newsstand; $1/Sun.; $7.85/mo. carrier; $8/mo. motor rte. 14 W. Fourth St., Williston, ND 58801. TEL 701-572-2165; FAX 701-572-1965. **Owner(s):** Wick Communications, Inc., 333 W. Wilcox Dr., Ste. 302, Sierra Vista, AZ 85635. TEL 701-572-2165; FAX 701-572-1965; Ed. Ruth Newman; Pub. Don Mrachek; adv. contact: Brian Standfield. photos; pub. size: standard; circ. evening 6,600(paid); Sun. 6,750(paid). **Wire Service(s):** AP.

US

NORTHERN MARIANA ISLANDS

SAIPAN

MARIANAS VARIETY NEWS & VIEWS. 1972. Mon.-Fri. $.50 newsstand; $72/6 mo.; $144/yr. P.O. Box 231, Saipan, MP 96950. TEL 670-234-6341; FAX 670-234-9271. **Owner(s):** Younis Art Studio, Inc., P.O. Box 231, Saipan, MP 96950. TEL 670-234-6341; FAX 670-234-9271; Pub. Paz Younis; adv.; photos; bk.rev.; pub. size: standard; circ. morning 3,500(free & paid). **Wire Service(s):** Asia Wire.

US

SAIPAN TRIBUNE. 1989. Mon.-Fri. $.35 newsstand. Caller Box AAA-34, Saipan, MP 96950. TEL 670-235-6397; FAX 670-235-3733. **Owner(s):** Pacific Publications & Printing, Inc., Caller Box AAA-34, Saipan, MP 96950. TEL 011-1-670-235-2440; FAX 011-1-670-235-3733; Pub. Mark Broadhurst; adv. contact: Lizette Silva. photos; bk.rev.; pub. size: tabloid; circ. morning 3,500(paid). **Wire Service(s):** AP.

US

OHIO

AKRON

AKRON BEACON JOURNAL. 1839. d. $.35/day newsstand; $1.50/Sun.; $3.40/wk. home deliv.; $44.20/13 wks. 44 E. Exchange St., Akron, OH 44328. TEL 330-996-3000; FAX 330-376-9235. **Owner(s):** Knight-Ridder, Inc., One Herald Plz., Miami, FL 33132; Ed. Dale Allen; Pub. John L. Dotson, Jr.; adv.; photos; bk.rev.; pub. size: broadsheet; circ. morning 114,000(paid); Sun. 223,105(paid). **Wire Service(s):** AP, NYT, KNS, LAT-WP.

US

ALLIANCE

ALLIANCE REVIEW. 1888. Mon.-Sat. $.50 newsstand; $91/yr. carrier. 40 S. Linden Ave., Alliance, OH 44601-0180. TEL 330-821-1300; FAX 330-821-8258. **Owner(s):** Dix Communications Group, 210 E. Liberty St., Wooster, OH 44691; Ed. Michael Patterson; Pub. G. Charles Dix, II; adv. contact: Don Watson. pub. size: broadsheet; circ. evening 12,700. **Wire Service(s):** AP, Pony.

US

ASHLAND

ASHLAND TIMES-GAZETTE. 1850. Mon.-Sat. $.50 newsstand; $7.80/4 wks. in town; $8.00/4 wks. motor rte.; $9.75/4 wks. in cy. mailed; $10/4 wks. out of cy.; $10.50/4 wks. out of state. 40 E. Second St., Ashland, OH 44805. TEL 419-281-0581; FAX 419-281-5591. **Owner(s):** Ashland Publishing Co., 40 E. Second St., Ashland, OH 44805. TEL 419-281-0581; Ed. Mel McKeachie; Pub. William McKinney; adv. contact: Rhonda Geer. pub. size: broadsheet; circ. evening 12,000(paid). **Wire Service(s):** UPI, NYT.

US

ASHTABULA

ASHTABULA STAR-BEACON. 1891. d. $.35/day newsstand; $1/Sun.; $31.20/3 mos. in cy.; $32.50/3 mos. carrier; $34.45/3 mos. motor rte. 4626 Park Ave., Ashtabula, OH 44004. TEL 216-998-2323; FAX 216-992-9655. **Owner(s):** Thomson Newspapers, Inc., Metro Centre, One Station Pl., 6th Fl., Stamford, CT 06902. TEL 203-425-2500; FAX 203-425-2516; Pub. Ed Looman; adv. contact: Vanessa Coper. photos; pub. size: broadsheet; circ. morning 25,000(paid); Sun. 25,000(paid). **Wire Service(s):** UPI.

US

ATHENS

ATHENS MESSENGER, THE. 1905. Sun.-Fri. $.35 newsstand; $114/yr. carrier; $124/yr. mailed in OH. Rte. 33 N. & Johnson Rd., Athens, OH 45701. TEL 614-592-6612; FAX 614-592-4647; E-mail: messenger@seorf.ohiou.edu; URL: http://www.seorf.ohiou.edu/ x005. **Owner(s):** Messenger Publishing Co., Inc., Rt. 33 N. & Johnson Rd., Athens, OH 45201. TEL 614-592-6612; FAX 614-592-4647; Ed. Karl Runser; Pub. G. Kenner Bush; adv. contact: Charles Douglas. bk.rev.; pub. size: broadsheet; circ. evening 14,374(paid); Sun. 17,492(paid). **Wire Service(s):** AP, SHNA.

US ISSN 1064-2005

BELLEFONTAINE

BELLEFONTAINE EXAMINER. 1891. Mon.-Sat. $.50 newsstand; $1.85/wk. 127 E. Chillicothe Ave., Bellefontaine, OH 43311. TEL 937-592-3060; FAX 937-592-4463. **Owner(s):** Hubbard Publishing Co., Inc., P.O. Box 40, Bellefontaine, OH 43311. TEL 937-592-3060; FAX 937-592-4463; Ed. David Wagner; Pub. T.E. Hubbard; adv. contact: Lane Moon. adv.: $10.12/SAU. photos; pub. size: broadsheet; circ. evening 10,345(paid). **Wire Service(s):** AP.

US ISSN 0747-3273

DAILY NEWSPAPERS

BELLEVUE
US

BELLEVUE GAZETTE. 1867. Mon.-Sat. $.50 newsstand; $2/wk. 107 N. Sandusky St., Bellevue, OH 44811. TEL 419-483-4190; FAX 419-483-3737. **Owner(s):** Gazette Printing Co., Inc., 107 N. Sandusky St., Bellevue, OH 44811. TEL 419-483-4190; Ed. Dennis Sabo; Pub. Thomas R. Smith; adv. contact: Rick Miller. pub. size: broadsheet; circ. evening 3,200(paid). **Wire Service(s):** AP.

BOWLING GREEN
US

SENTINEL-TRIBUNE. 1867. Mon.-Sat. $.35 newsstand; $1.75/wk.; $85/yr. 300 E. Poe Rd., Bowling Green, OH 43402. TEL 419-352-4611; FAX 419-354-0314. **Owner(s):** Thomas M. Haswell, P.O. Box 88, Bowling Green, OH 42402. TEL 419-352-4611; FAX 419-354-0314; Ed. David C. Miller; Pub. Thomas M. Haswell; adv. contact: Vicky Graf. photos; pub. size: broadsheet; circ. evening 13,850(paid). **Wire Service(s):** SHNA, AP.

BRYAN
US

BRYAN TIMES. 1949. Mon.-Sat. $.50 newsstand; $86/yr. 127 S. Walnut St., Bryan, OH 43506. TEL 419-636-1111; FAX 419-636-8937. **Owner(s):** Bryan Publishing Co., The, 127 S. Walnut St., Bryan, OH 43506. TEL 419-636-1111; FAX 419-636-8937; Pub. Christopher Cullis; adv. contact: Mary Nickels. pub. size: broadsheet; circ. evening 12,000(paid). Wire Service(s): AP.

BUCYRUS
US

BUCYRUS TELEGRAPH-FORUM. 1923. Mon.-Sat. $.35/day newsstand; $.50/Sat; $104/yr. carrier. 117 W. Rensselaer St., Bucyrus, OH 44820. TEL 419-562-3333; FAX 419-562-9162. **Owner(s):** Thomson Newspapers, Inc., Metro Centre, One Station Pl., 6th Fl., Stamford, CT 06902. TEL 203-425-2500; FAX 203-425-2516; Ed. Don Tudor; Pub. James F. Croneis; adv. contact: Jeanette Parker. photos; bk.rev.; pub. size: broadsheet; circ. evening 21,200(free & paid). **Wire Service(s):** AP.

CAMBRIDGE
US

DAILY JEFFERSONIAN, THE. 1824. Mon.-Sat. $.35 newsstand; $104/yr. 831 Wheeling Ave., Cambridge, OH 43725. TEL 614-439-3531; FAX 614-432-6219. **Owner(s):** Dix Communications Group, 210 E. Liberty St., Wooster, OH 44691. TEL 216-264-3511; Ed. Greg Parks. adv. contact: E. Archibald. pub. size: broadsheet; circ. evening 14,150(paid). **Wire Service(s):** AP.
Formerly: Cambridge Daily Jeffersonian.

CANTON
US ISSN 0745-7575

REPOSITORY, THE. 1815. d. $.35/day newsstand; $1.20/Sun. deliv.; $1.25/Sun.; $2.70/wk. home deliv. 500 Market Ave., S., Canton, OH 44702. TEL 216-454-5611; FAX 216-454-5610. **Owner(s):** Thomson Newspapers, Inc., Metro Centre, One Station Pl., 6th Fl., Stamford, CT 06902. TEL 203-425-2500; FAX 203-425-2516; Ed. David Kaminski; Pub. David Greenfield; adv. contact: Robert Miller. photos; bk.rev.; pub. size: broadsheet; circ. morning 62,500(paid); Sun. 82,000(paid). **Wire Service(s):** AP, NYT.
Formerly: Canton Repository.

CELINA
US

DAILY STANDARD. 1848. Mon.-Sat. $.50 newsstand; $109.20/yr. in cy. 123 E. Market St., Celina, OH 45822. TEL 419-586-2371; FAX 419-586-6271. **Owner(s):** Standard Printing Co., 123 E. Market St., Celina, OH 45822. TEL 419-586-2371; FAX 419-586-6271; Pub. Frank Snyder; adv. contact: John Lake. pub. size: broadsheet; circ. evening 10,300(paid). **Wire Service(s):** AP.
Formerly: Celina Daily Standard.

CHILLICOTHE
US

CHILLICOTHE GAZETTE. 1800. Mon.-Sat. $.35/day newsstand; $.75/Sat.; $156/yr. in state mailed; $171.50/yr. out of state mailed. 50 W. Main St., Chillicothe, OH 45601. TEL 614-773-2111; FAX 614-773-2160. **Owner(s):** Gannett Company, Inc., 1100 Wilson Blvd., Arlington, VA 22340. TEL 703-284-6000; Ed. Chaz Osburn; Pub. Marvin Jones; adv. contact: Ron Clausen. pub. size: broadsheet; circ. evening 17,100(paid). Wire Service(s): AP, GNS.

CINCINNATI
US

CINCINNATI ENQUIRER, THE. 1841. d. $.35/day newsstand; $1.50/Sun.; $15/mo. home deliv. 312 Elm St., Cincinnati, OH 45202. TEL 513-721-2700; FAX 513-768-8079; E-mail: enqedit@aol.com. **Owner(s):** Gannett Company, Inc., 1100 Wilson Blvd., Arlington, VA 22209. TEL 703-284-6000; Ed. Janet Leach; Pub. Harry M. Whipple; adv. contact: David Hunke. photos; pub. size: broadsheet; circ. morning 198,850(paid); Sun. 348,700(paid). **Wire Service(s):** AP, NYT, LAT-WP, KNS, GNS.

US

CINCINNATI POST. 1881. Mon.-Sat. $.35 newsstand; $7.50/mo. carrier OH; $8.95/mo. carrier KY; $281.76/yr. mailed. 125 E. Court St., Cincinnati, OH 45202. TEL 513-352-2000; FAX 513-621-3962. **Owner(s):** Scripps Howard, 312 Walnut St., 28th Fl., Cincinatti, OH 45202. TEL 513-977-3000; Ed. Robert Kraft; Pub. William Burleigh; pub. size: broadsheet; circ. evening 100,000(paid). **Wire Service(s):** AP, SHNA.

CIRCLEVILLE
US

CIRCLEVILLE HERALD. 1883. Mon.-Sat. $.50 newsstand; $96.20/yr. 210 N. Court St., Circleville, OH 43113. TEL 614-474-3131; FAX 614-474-9525. **Owner(s):** Brown Publishing Co., P.O. Box 555, Urbana, OH 43078. TEL 513-652-2100; Ed. Willie Ehrlich; Pub. Timothy C. Kay; adv. contact: Jerry Shasteen. pub. size: broadsheet; circ. evening 8,500(paid). **Wire Service(s):** AP.

CLEVELAND
US

CLEVELAND PLAIN DEALER. 1842. d. $.35/day newsstand; $1/Sun.; $93.60/yr. 1801 Superior Ave., Cleveland, OH 44114. TEL 216-344-4500; FAX 216-999-6354. **Owner(s):** Advance Publications, Inc., 950 Fingerboard Rd., Staten Island, NY 10305. TEL 718-981-1234; FAX 718-981-1456; Ed. Brent Larkin; Pub. Alex Machaskee; adv. contact: Terry Hebert. bk.rev.; pub. size: broadsheet; circ. morning 398,398(paid); Sun. 528,818(paid). **Wire Service(s):** AP, NYT, LAT-WP.

COLUMBUS
US

COLUMBUS DISPATCH. 1871. d. $.35/day newsstand; $1.75/Sun.; $3/wk.; $156/yr. 34 S. Third St., Columbus, OH 43215. TEL 614-461-5000; FAX 614-461-7580; E-mail: letters@cd.columbus.oh.us; URL: http://www.dispatch.com. **Owner(s):** Dispatch Newspapers, Inc., 34 S. Third St., Columbus, OH 43215. TEL 614-461-5000; Ed. Michael Curtin. adv. contact: Timothy Doty. photos; bk.rev.; pub. size: broadsheet; circ. morning 265,000(paid); Sun. 393,250(paid). **Wire Service(s):** AP, LAT-WP, NYT, KNT, SHNA.

US

DAILY REPORTER. 1896. Mon.-Fri. $.50 newsstand; $40/3 mos.; $60/6 mos.; $85/yr.; $135/2 yrs. 329 S. Front St., Columbus, OH 43215. TEL 614-224-4835; FAX 614-224-8649; E-mail: cdr@netwalk.com. **Owner(s):** Calcomco, Inc., 534 Rivard Blvd., Detroit, MI 48230. TEL 313-885-9228; Ed. Chuck Nelson. pub. size: broadsheet; circ. morning 4,800(paid). **Wire Service(s):** UPI.

COSHOCTON
US

COSHOCTON TRIBUNE. 1909. d. $.35/day newsstand; $1/Sun.; $117/yr. 550 Main St., Coshocton, OH 43812. TEL 614-622-1122; FAX 614-622-7341. **Owner(s):** Thomson Newspapers, Inc., Metro Centre, One Station Pl., 6th Fl., Stamford, CT 06902. TEL 203-425-2500; FAX 203-425-2516; Ed. R. Michael Johnson. adv.; photos; pub. size: standard; circ. evening 9,000(paid); Sun. 9,200(paid). **Wire Service(s):** AP.

DAYTON

US
BEAVERCREEK NEWS-CURRENT. 1959. d. $.35 newsstand; $70/yr. mailed. 1350 N. Fairfield Rd., Dayton, OH 45432. TEL 513-426-5263; FAX 513-426-4548. **Owner(s):** Amos Press, Inc., P.O. Box 4129, Sidney, OH 45365. TEL 513-435-7273; Ed. Tom Mitsoff; Pub. Mark Raymond; adv. contact: Ruth Mitsoff. photos; bk.rev.; pub. size: broadsheet; circ. evening 6,000(paid). **Wire Service(s):** AP.
Formerly: Beavercreek Daily News.

US   ISSN 0890-8931
DAYTON DAILY NEWS. 1898. d. $.50/day newsstand; $1.50/Sun.; $3/wk. 45 S. Ludlow St., Dayton, OH 45402. TEL 513-225-2000; FAX 513-225-2489. **Owner(s):** Dayton Newspapers, Inc., Fourth & Ludlow Sts., Dayton, OH 45401. TEL 513-225-2326; Ed. Steve Sidlo; Pub. Brad Tillson; adv.; photos; bk.rev.; pub. size: broadsheet; circ. morning 162,103(paid); Sun. 219,282(paid). **Wire Service(s):** AP.

DEFIANCE

US
CRESCENT-NEWS. 1878. Sun.-Fri. $.50/day newsstand; $1/Sun.; $8.50/mo. deliv. 624 W. Second St., Defiance, OH 43512. TEL 419-784-5441; FAX 419-784-1492. **Owner(s):** Defiance Publishing Co., 624 W. Second St., Defiance, OH 43512. TEL 419-784-5441; Ed. Robert M. Cummins. adv. contact: Mark Ryan. pub. size: broadsheet; circ. evening 17,000(paid); Sun. 17,000(paid). **Wire Service(s):** AP.

DELAWARE

US   ISSN 1064-2013
DELAWARE GAZETTE. 1818. Mon.-Sat. $.50 newsstand; $2.28/wk. carrier; $2.46/wk. motor rte. 18 E. William St., Delaware, OH 43015. TEL 614-363-1161; FAX 614-363-6262; E-mail: addeptAdelgazette.com; HRL: http://www.delgazette.com. **Owner(s):** W.D. Thomson, P.O. Box 100, Delaware, OH 43015. TEL 614-363-1161; FAX 614-363-6262; Ed. Larry Gibbs. adv. contact: Dierdre Warden. adv.: $9.90/SAU. pub. size: broadsheet; circ. evening 8,760(paid). **Wire Service(s):** AP.

DELPHOS

US
DAILY HERALD. 1869. Mon.-Sat. $.50 newsstand; $21/3 mos. in town; $28/3 mos. in cy. mailed; $35/3 mos. out of cy. mailed. 405 N. Main St., Delphos, OH 45833. TEL 419-695-0015; FAX 419-692-7704. **Owner(s):** Delphos Newspapers, 405 N. Main St., Delphos, OH 45833. TEL 419-695-0015; FAX 419-692-7704; Ed. Esther Bielawski; Pub. Marilyn Hoffman; adv. contact: Jane Ricker. photos; bk.rev.; pub. size: broadsheet; circ. evening 4,200(controlled). **Wire Service(s):** UPI.

EAST LIVERPOOL

US
REVIEW, THE. 1879. Mon.-Sat. $.35 newsstand; $2/wk.; $104/yr. 210 E. Fourth Street, East Liverpool, OH 43920. TEL 330-385-4545; FAX 330-385-7114. **Owner(s):** Thomson Newspapers, Inc., 65 Queen St., Toronto, ON M5H 2M8, Canada. TEL 416-864-1710; Ed. Robin Webster; Pub. Charles Govey; adv. contact: Tammie McIntosh. photos; pub. size: broadsheet; circ. morning 11,900(paid). **Wire Service(s):** UPI.
Formerly: The Evening Review.

ELYRIA

US
ELYRIA CHRONICLE-TELEGRAM. 1829. d. $.35/day newsstand; $1/Sun.; $2.60/wk. home deliv. 225 East Ave., Elyria, OH 44035. TEL 216-329-7000; FAX 216-329-7282; E-mail: ect@ohio.net; URL: http://www.ohio.net/~ect. **Owner(s):** Lorain County Printing & Publishing Co., 225 East Ave., Elyria, OH 44035. TEL 216-329-7000; Ed. Arnold Miller; Pub. A.D. Hudnutt; adv. contact: Bill Posey. pub. size: broadsheet; circ. evening 40,000(paid); Sun. 40,000(paid). **Wire Service(s):** AP, KR, LAT-WP, SHNA.

FAIRBORN

US
FAIRBORN DAILY HERALD. Mon.-Sat. $.35 newsstand; $16.90/3 mos. home deliv.; $33/6 mos.; $67/yr.; $27.50/3 mos. mailed; $110/yr. One Herald Sq., Fairborn, OH 45324. TEL 937-878-3993; FAX 937-878-8314. **Owner(s):** Amos Press, Inc., 3085 Woodman Dr., Ste.170, Kettering, OH 45420. TEL 513-294-7000; Ed. Bill Flanagan; Pub. Mark Raymond; adv. contact: Jackie Helter. pub. size: broadsheet; circ. evening 15,300(paid). **Wire Service(s):** UPI.

FINDLAY

US
COURIER, THE. 1836. Mon.-Sat. $.50 newsstand; $104/yr. 701 W. Sandusky St., Findlay, OH 45840. TEL 419-422-5151. **Owner(s):** Findlay Publishing Co., 701 W. Sandusky St., Findlay, OH 45840. TEL 419-422-5151; Ed. Jim Harrold; Pub. Edwin L. Heminger; adv. contact: Roger Powell. photos; pub. size: broadsheet; circ. morning 27,000(paid). **Wire Service(s):** AP.

FOSTORIA

US
REVIEW TIMES. 1860. Mon.-Sat. $.50 newsstand; $1.85/wk. carrier; $2/wk. motor rte. 113 E. Center St., Fostoria, OH 44830. TEL 419-435-6641; FAX 419-435-9073. **Owner(s):** Spenley Newspapers, Inc., 39 S. Fourth St., Newark, OH 43055. TEL 614-345-4000; Ed. Linda Woodland; Pub. Clarence Pennington; adv. contact: Kurt Madden. pub. size: broadsheet; circ. evening 8,000(paid). **Wire Service(s):** AP.

FREMONT

US   ISSN 0746-8148
NEWS-MESSENGER. 1856. Mon.-Sat. $.35 newsstand; $117/yr. 1700 Cedar St., Fremont, OH 43420. TEL 419-332-5511; FAX 419-332-9750. **Owner(s):** Gannett Company, Inc., 1100 Wilson Blvd., Arlington, VA 22209. TEL 703-284-6000; Ed. James F. Daubel; Pub. James F. Daubel; adv. contact: Genia Lovett. photos; bk.rev.; pub. size: broadsheet; circ. evening 14,000(paid). **Wire Service(s):** AP, GNS.
Formerly: Fremone News-Messenger.

GALION

US
GALION INQUIRER. 1877. Mon.-Sat. $.35 newsstand; $2.10/wk.; $109.20/yr. 378 N. Market St., Galion, OH 44833. TEL 419-468-1117; FAX 419-468-7255. **Owner(s):** Inquirer Printing Co., 378 N. Market St., Galion, OH 44833. TEL 419-468-1117; Ed. Brenda Young; Pub. Edgar Koehl, III; adv. contact: Connie Axline. pub. size: broadsheet; circ. evening 5,000(paid). **Wire Service(s):** AP.

GALLIPOLIS

US
GALLIPOLIS DAILY TRIBUNE. 1893. d. $.35/day newsstand; $1/Sun.; $104/yr. 825 Third Ave., Gallipolis, OH 45631. TEL 614-446-2342; FAX 614-446-3008. **Owner(s):** Gannett Company, Inc., 1100 Wilson Blvd., Arlington, VA 22234. TEL 703-284-6000; Ed. Hobart Wilson; Pub. Robert Wingett; adv. contact: Larry L. Boyer. pub. size: broadsheet; circ. evening 6,500(paid); Sun. 13,800(paid). **Wire Service(s):** AP.

GREENFIELD

US
TIMES-GAZETTE. 1932. Mon.-Sat. $.50 newsstand; $55/yr. 345 Jefferson, Greenfield, OH 45123. TEL 513-981-2141; FAX 513-981-2880. **Owner(s):** Brown Publishing Co., P.O. Box 555, Urbana, OH 43078. TEL 513-652-2100; FAX 513-652-2448; Ed. Ray Ryan; Pub. Phil Roberts; adv. contact: Gary Schluep. pub. size: broadsheet; circ. evening 4,500(paid). **Wire Service(s):** AP.
Formerly: greenfield daily times.

GREENVILLE

US
DAILY ADVOCATE. 1883. d. $.50/day newsstand; Sun. free deliv. in Darke Cy.; $2/wk. W. Main & Sycamore, Greenville, OH 45331. TEL 513-548-3151; FAX 513-548-3913. **Owner(s):** Thomson Newspapers, Inc., Metro Centre, One Station Pl., 6th Fl., Stamford, CT 06902. TEL 203-425-2500; FAX 203-425-2516; Ed. Richard Gillette; Pub. Vicky Rifenberg; adv. contact: Mary Kay Boyer. photos; bk.rev.; pub. size: broadsheet; circ. evening 9,000(free & paid); Sun. 26,000. **Wire Service(s):** AP.

US
GREENVILLE DAILY ADVOCATE. 1883. d. $.50 newsstand; $104/yr. home deliv.; $110/yr. out of cy. mailed. 133 W. Main St., Greenville, OH 45331. TEL 937-548-3151; FAX 937-548-3913. **Owner(s):** Thomson Newspapers, Inc., Metro Centre, One Station Pl., 6th Fl., Stamford, CT 06902. TEL 203-425-2500; FAX 203-425-2516; Ed. Richard Gillette; Pub. Vicky Risenberg; adv. contact: Mary Kay Boyer. pub. size: broadsheet; circ. 9,100(paid). **Wire Service(s):** AP.

DAILY NEWSPAPERS

HAMILTON
US

JOURNAL NEWS. 1879. d. $.35/day newsstand; $1.55/Sun.; $2.80/wk. 228 Court St., Hamilton, OH 45011. TEL 513-863-8200; FAX 513-896-9489; E-mail: journal@erinet.com. **Owner(s):** Thomson Newspapers, Inc., Metro Centre, One Station Pl., 6th Fl., Stamford, CT 06902. TEL 203-425-2500; FAX 203-425-2516; Pub. Robert Murphy; adv.; photos; pub. size: broadsheet; circ. morning 27,000; Sun. 29,000(paid). **Wire Service(s):** AP, NYT.
Formerly: Hamilton-Fairfield Journal News.

LIMA
US

LIMA NEWS. 1884. d. $.50/day newsstand; $1.50/Sun.; $11/mo. home deliv. 121 E. High St., Lima, OH 45801. TEL 419-223-1010; FAX 419-229-0426; E-mail: limanews@alpha.wcoil.com; URL: http://www.limanews.com. **Owner(s):** Freedom Communications, Inc., 17666 Fitch, Irvine, CA 92614. TEL 714-553-9292; Ed. Ray Sullivan; Pub. Thomas J. Mullen; adv. contact: Jim Shine. photos; pub. size: broadsheet; circ. evening 44,484(paid); Sun. 50,200(paid). **Wire Service(s):** KNS, AP.

MANSFIELD
US

NEWS JOURNAL. 1933. d. $.50/day newsstand; $1.50/Sun.; $3.25/wk. carrier; $3.35/wk. motor rte.; $169/yr. carrier. 70 W. Fourth St., Mansfield, OH 44903. TEL 419-522-3311; FAX 419-522-2672. **Owner(s):** Thomson Newspapers, Inc., Metro Centre, One Statation Pl., 6th Fl., Stamford, CT 06902. TEL 203-425-2500; FAX 203-425-2516; Ed. Tom Brennan; Pub. Nick Monico; adv. contact: Coreen Fisher. photos; pub. size: broadsheet; circ. evening 40,381(paid); Sun. 54,446(paid). **Wire Service(s):** AP, KR, CSM.
Formerly: Mansfield News Journal.

HILLSBORO
US   ISSN 8750-8168

TIMES GAZETTE, THE. 1818. Mon.-Sat. $.50 newsstand; $96.20/yr. in town; $156/yr. out of cy. 209 S. High St., Hillsboro, OH 45133. TEL 937-393-3456; FAX 937-393-2059. **Owner(s):** Brown Publishing Co., P.O. Box 9239, Cincinnati, OH 45209. TEL 513-871-1202; Ed. Rory Ryan; Pub. Phillip A. Roberts; adv. contact: Sharon Kersey. photos; pub. size: broadsheet; circ. 7,000(paid).
Formerly: Press Gazette, The.

LISBON
US

MORNING JOURNAL. 1852. d. $.35/day newsstand; $.50/Sun. 308 Maple St., Lisbon, OH 44432. TEL 330-424-9541; FAX 330-424-0048. **Owner(s):** Buckeye Publishing Co., Inc., 308 Maple St., P.O. Box 249, Lisbon, OH 44432. TEL 216-424-9541; Ed. Dorma Tolson; Pub. John Blanchflower; adv. contact: Mace Pavelek. photos; pub. size: broadsheet; circ. morning 13,078(paid); Sun. 13,000(paid). **Wire Service(s):** AP.

MARIETTA
US

MARIETTA TIMES. 1864. Mon.-Sat. $.50/day newsstand; $.75/Sat.; $32.50/13 wks. carrier. 700 Channel Ln., Marietta, OH 45750. TEL 614-373-2121; FAX 614-373-6251. **Owner(s):** Gannett Company, Inc., 1100 Wilson Blvd., Arlington, VA 20044. TEL 703-284-6000; Ed. Juli Metzger; Pub. Stephen Reynolds; adv. contact: Kim Wilson. pub. size: broadsheet; circ. evening 13,008(paid). **Wire Service(s):** AP, GNS.

IRONTON
US   ISSN 0279-5124

IRONTON TRIBUNE. 1850. Sun.-Fri. $.50/day newsstand; $1.25/Sun.; $32.85/3 mos. carrier; $131.40/yr. carrier; $156/yr. mailed. 2903 S. Fifth St., Ironton, OH 45638. TEL 614-532-1441; FAX 614-532-1506. **Owner(s):** Ironton Publications, Inc., P.O. Box 647, Ironton, OH 45638. TEL 614-532-1441; Ed. Renee Carey; Pub. Jennifer J. Allen; adv. contact: Brenda Renfroe. pub. size: broadsheet; circ. evening 8,700(paid); Sun. 9,300(paid). **Wire Service(s):** AP.

LOGAN
US

LOGAN DAILY NEWS. 1842. Mon.-Sat. $.50 newsstand; $1.85/wk. city; $1.95/wk. out of city. 72 E. Main St., Logan, OH 43138. TEL 614-385-2107; FAX 614-385-4514. **Owner(s):** Brown Publishing Co., P.O. Box 758, Logan, OH 43138. TEL 614-385-2107; FAX 614-385-4514; Ed. Mark Hartman; Pub. Daniel P. Rodenfels; adv. contact: Keith Conner. photos; pub. size: broadsheet; circ. evening 5,600(paid). **Wire Service(s):** AP.

MARION
US

MARION STAR. 1877. d. $.35/day newsstand; $1.25/Sun.; $2.40/wk. in town; $2.45/wk. in cy. 150 Court St., Marion, OH 43302. TEL 614-387-0400; FAX 614-382-2210. **Owner(s):** Thomson Newspapers, Inc., 65 Queen St., Toronto, ON M5H 2M5, Canada; Ed. Mary Lawrence; Pub. Tim Dowd; adv. contact: Donna Huffman. photos; pub. size: broadsheet; circ. evening 20,000(paid); Sun. 20,000(paid). **Wire Service(s):** AP.
Formerly: The Star.

KENTON
US

KENTON TIMES. 1953. Mon.-Sat. $.50 newsstand; $93.35/yr. 201 E. Columbus, Kenton, OH 43326. TEL 419-674-4066; FAX 419-673-1125. **Owner(s):** Hardin County Publishing Co., 201 E. Columbus St., Kenton, OH 43326. TEL 419-674-4066; FAX 419-673-1125; Ed. Tim Thomas. adv. contact: Jim Grauel. bk.rev.; pub. size: standard; circ. evening 7,100(paid). **Wire Service(s):** AP.

LONDON
US

MADISON PRESS, THE. 1845. Mon.-Fri. $.50 newsstand; $85/yr. carrier. 30 S. Oak St., London, OH 43140-0390. TEL 614-852-1616; FAX 614-852-1620. **Owner(s):** Central Ohio Printing Corp., P.O. Box 390, London, OH 43140-0390. TEL 614-852-1616; Ed. Bill McCullick; Pub. Donald L. Hartley; adv.; photos; pub. size: broadsheet; circ. evening 6,500(paid). **Wire Service(s):** AP.
Formerly: London Madison Press.

MARTINS FERRY
US

TIMES LEADER. 1891. Sun.-Fri. $.35/day newsstand; $1/Sun.; $6.50/mo. carrier. 200 S. Fourth St., Martins Ferry, OH 43935-1925. TEL 614-633-1131; FAX 614-633-1122. **Owner(s):** Ogden Newspapers, Inc., 1500 Main St., Wheeling, WV 26003. TEL 304-233-0100; Ed. Phyliss Sigal; Pub. Alexander F. Marshall, III; adv. contact: Jeff Herr. pub. size: broadsheet; circ. evening 22,000(paid); Sun. 23,000(paid). **Wire Service(s):** AP.

LANCASTER
US

LANCASTER EAGLE-GAZETTE. 1807. d. $.35/day newsstand; $1.25/Sun.; $2.65/wk. carrier. 138 W. Chestnut St., Lancaster, OH 43130. TEL 614-654-1321; FAX 614-654-8271. **Owner(s):** Thomson Newspapers, Inc., Metro Centre, One Station Pl., 6th Fl., Stamford, CT 06902. TEL 203-425-2500; FAX 203-425-2516; Ed. Roy Youst; Pub. Greg Ptacin; adv. contact: Janet Blair. photos; pub. size: broadsheet; circ. evening 18,000(paid); Sun. 10,000. **Wire Service(s):** AP;SHN;Thomson.

LORAIN
US

MORNING JOURNAL. 1921. d. $.50/day newsstand; $1.25/Sun.; $3/wk.; $156/yr. carrier. 1657 Broadway, Lorain, OH 44052. TEL 216-245-6901; FAX 216-245-5637. **Owner(s):** Journal Register Co., 50 W. State St., 12th Fl., Trenton, NJ 08608. TEL 609-396-2200; Ed. Tom Skoch; Pub. Kevin F. Walsh; adv. contact: William Cyran. photos; bk.rev.; pub. size: broadsheet; circ. morning 45,000(paid); Sun. 51,000(paid). **Wire Service(s):** AP, SHNA.

MARYSVILLE
US   ISSN 1069-2207

MARYSVILLE JOURNAL-TRIBUNE. 1843. Mon.-Sat. $89/yr. in state; $90/yr. out of state. 207 N. Main St., Marysville, OH 43040. TEL 937-644-9111; FAX 937-644-9211. **Owner(s):** Mary Elizabeth Behrens, 207 N. Main St., Marysville, OH 43040. TEL 513-644-9111; Ed. Holly Zachariah; Pub. David G. Behrens; adv. contact: Marie Woodford. pub. size: broadsheet; circ. evening 6,200(paid). **Wire Service(s):** AP.

MASSILLON

US

INDEPENDENT, THE. 1863. d. $.35 newsstand; $93.60/yr. carrier. 50 North Ave., N.W., Massillon, OH 44648. TEL 216-833-2631; FAX 216-833-2635; E-mail: indeedit@aol.com. **Owner(s):** Goodson Newspaper Group, 989 Lenox Dr., Trenton, NJ 08648. TEL 609-895-2600; Ed. Kevin D. Coffey; Pub. Jack D. Shores; adv.; photos; bk.rev.; pub. size: broadsheet; circ. evening 15,500(free & paid). **Wire Service(s):** SHNA, AP, American News Service.

MEDINA

US

MEDINA COUNTY GAZETTE. 2832. Mon.-Sat. $.35 newsstand; $72/yr. in cy.; $78/yr. out of cy. t85 W. Liberty St., Medina, OH 44256. TEL 330-725-4166; FAX 330-725-4299. **Owner(s):** Medina County Publications, Inc., 885 W. Liberty St., Medina, OH 44256. TEL 330-725-4166; Ed. Liz Sheaffer; Pub. George Hudnutt; adv. contact: Kris High. photos; pub. size: broadsheet; circ. morning 17,000(paid). **Wire Service(s):** AP.

MIDDLETOWN

US

MIDDLETOWN JOURNAL. 1857. d. $.50/day newsstand; $1.25/Sun.; $2.60/wk.; $10.40/mo.; $135.20/yr. 52 S. Broad, Middletown, OH 45044. TEL 513-422-3611; FAX 513-423-6940; E-mail: news@journalink.com; URL: http://www.journalink.com. **Owner(s):** Thomson Newspapers, Inc., Metro Centre, One Station Pl., 6th Fl., Stamford, CT 06902. TEL 203-425-2500; Ed. Mike Williams; Pub. Carl Esposito; adv. contact: Barb Staples. photos; pub. size: broadsheet; circ. evening 23,100(paid); Sun. 24,400(paid). **Wire Service(s):** AP.

MT. VERNON

US

MOUNT VERNON NEWS. 1837. Mon.-Sat. $.50 newsstand; $6.50/mo. carrier; $9.05/mo. motor rte.; $10.50/mo. in state mailed; $11.45/mo. out of state mailed. 18 E. Vine St., Mt. Vernon, OH 43050. TEL 614-397-5333; FAX 614-397-1321. **Owner(s):** Progressive Communications Corp., 18 E. Vine St., Mt. Vernon, OH 43050. TEL 614-397-5333; Ed. Robert Nitzel; Pub. Kay Culbertson; adv. contact: John Nesbitt. photos; pub. size: broadsheet; circ. evening 10,907(paid). **Wire Service(s):** AP.

NAPOLEON

US

NORTHWEST SIGNAL. 1966. Mon.-Fri. $.50 newsstand; $71.50/yr. in cy.; $90.50/yr. out of state mailed. 595 E. Riverview, Napoleon, OH 43545. TEL 419-592-5055; FAX 419-592-9778. **Owner(s):** James K. Kuser, P.O. Box 567, Napoleon, OH 43545. TEL 419-592-5055; Ed. Paul Miller; Pub. James K. Kuser; adv. contact: Jim Hull. pub. size: broadsheet; circ. morning 5,800(paid). **Wire Service(s):** UPI.
  Formerly: Napoleon Northwest Signal.

NEWARK

US   ISSN 0740-2120

ADVOCATE, THE. 1821. d. $.35/day newsstand; $1/Sun.; $102/yr. in cy.; $114/yr. out of cy. 22 N. First St., Newark, OH 43055. TEL 614-345-4053; FAX 614-345-1634. **Owner(s):** Thomson Newspapers, Inc., Metro Centre, One Station Pl., 6th Fl., Stamford, CT 06902. TEL 203-425-2500; FAX 203-425-2516; Ed. Jerri Kornegay; Pub. Mark D. Richmond; adv. contact: Ronald Frailly. photos; pub. size: broadsheet; circ. evening 24,000(paid); Sun. 24,000(paid). **Wire Service(s):** AP.

NEW PHILADELPHIA

US

TIMES-REPORTER, THE. 1872. d. $.50/day newsstand; $1.50/Sun.; $187.20/yr. in cy. carrier deliv.; $195/yr. in cy. motor rte. 629 Wabash Ave., N.W., New Philadelphia, OH 44663-0667. TEL 330-364-5577; FAX 330-364-8449. **Owner(s):** Journal Register Co., 50 W. State St., Trenton, NJ 08608. TEL 609-396-2200; Ed. Sandra Stewart; Pub. James E. Shrader; adv. contact: Mark Conrad. adv.: $24.96/SAU. photos; pub. size: broadsheet; circ. morning 24,300(paid); Sun. 27,000(paid). **Wire Service(s):** AP, KR.

NORWALK

US   ISSN 0745-4023

NORWALK REFLECTOR. 1830. Mon.-Sat. $.35 newsstand; $91/yr. home deliv.; $110/yr. mailed. 61 E. Monroe St., Norwalk, OH 44857. TEL 419-668-3771; FAX 419-668-2424; E-mail: jrbpub@accnorwalk.com; reflector@nwohio.com. **Owner(s):** Reflector Herald Inc., Norwalk, OH 44857; Ed. Jay Thwaite; Pub. James R. Brown; adv. contact: John Ringenberg. adv.: $10.43/SAU. photos; pub. size: broadsheet; circ. evening 8,970(paid). **Wire Service(s):** AP.

PIQUA

US

PIQUA DAILY CALL. 1883. Mon.-Sat. $.50 newsstand; $109.20/yr. in area; $135/yr. out of area. 310 Spring St., Piqua, OH 45356. TEL 513-773-2721; FAX 513-773-2782. **Owner(s):** Thomson Newspapers, Inc., Metro Centre, One Station Pl., 6th Fl., Stamford, CT 06902. TEL 203-425-2500; FAX 203-425-2516; Ed. Patricia Speelman; Pub. Vicky Rifenberg; adv. contact: Mary Kay Boyer. pub. size: broadsheet; circ. evening 10,000(paid). **Wire Service(s):** AP.

POMEROY

US

DAILY SENTINEL, THE. 1948. Sun.-Fri. $.35/day newsstand; $1/Sun.; $8.70/mo. 111 Court St., Pomeroy, OH 45769-1016. TEL 614-992-2156; FAX 614-992-2157. **Owner(s):** Gannett Company, Inc., 1100 Wilson Blvd., Arlington, VA 22340. TEL 703-284-6000; Ed. Charlene Hoeflich; Pub. Robert L. Wingett; adv. contact: Dave Harris. photos; bk.rev.; pub. size: broadsheet; circ. evening 6,500(paid); Sun. 14,000(paid). **Wire Service(s):** AP.

PORT CLINTON

US

NEWS-HERALD. 1865. Mon.-Sat. $.35 newsstand; $104/yr. 115 W. Second, Port Clinton, OH 43452. TEL 419-734-3141; FAX 419-734-1850. **Owner(s):** Gannett Company, Inc., 1100 Wilson Blvd., Arlington, VA 22234. TEL 703-284-6000; Ed. James Daubel; Pub. James Daubel; adv. contact: David Barth. pub. size: broadsheet; circ. evening 6,500(paid). **Wire Service(s):** AP, GNS.

PORTSMOUTH

US   ISSN 8750-6963

PORTSMOUTH DAILY TIMES. 1852. d. $.50/day newsstand; $1/Sun.; $132.60/yr. in cy.; $153.87/yr. out of cy. 637 Sixth St., Portsmouth, OH 45662. TEL 614-353-3101; FAX 614-353-7280. **Owner(s):** American Publishing Co., 606 N. Van Buren, Marion, IL 62959. TEL 618-993-1711; Ed. Debbie Allard; Pub. William J. Riley; adv. contact: Phil Jackson. pub. size: broadsheet; circ. evening 17,101(paid); Sun. 16,412(paid). **Wire Service(s):** AP.

RAVENNA

US

KENT-RAVENNA RECORD-COURIER. 1830. d. $.50/day newsstand; $1/Sun. 126 N. Chestnut St., Ravenna, OH 44266. TEL 216-296-9657; FAX 216-296-2698; E-mail: rcletters@aol.com; URL: http://www.recordpub.com. **Owner(s):** Record Publishing Co., LLC, 126 N. Chestnut St., P.O. Box 1201, Ravenna, OH 44266. TEL 216-296-9657; FAX 216-296-2698; Ed. Jill Elish; Pub. David Dix; adv. contact: Ron Waite. photos; pub. size: broadsheet; circ. evening 21,500(paid); Sun. 22,500(paid). **Wire Service(s):** AP.

SALEM

US

SALEM NEWS. 1889. Mon.-Sat. $.35 newsstand; $80/yr. 161 N. Lincoln Ave., Salem, OH 44460. TEL 330-332-4601; FAX 330-332-1441. **Owner(s):** Thomson Newspapers, Inc., Metro Centre, One Station Pl., 6th Fl., Stamford, CT 06902. TEL 203-425-2500; FAX 203-425-2516; Ed. J.D. Creer; Pub. Lee Gordon; adv. contact: Jim Williams. photos; bk.rev.; pub. size: broadsheet; circ. evening 11,500(paid). **Wire Service(s):** AP.

SANDUSKY

US

SANDUSKY REGISTER. 1822. d. $.50/day newsstand; $1/Sun.; $2.10/wk. carrier. 314 W. Market St., Sandusky, OH 44870. TEL 419-625-5500; FAX 419-625-3007. **Owner(s):** Sandusky Newspapers, Inc., 314 W. Market St., Sandusky, OH 44870. TEL 419-625-5500; Ed. Eileen Guy; Pub. Jim Hofmann; adv. contact: Walling Gray. pub. size: broadsheet; circ. evening 24,500(paid); Sun. 27,600(paid). **Wire Service(s):** AP.

DAILY NEWSPAPERS

SHELBY
US

SHELBY GLOBE. 1900. Mon.-Sat. $.30 newsstand; $71/yr. local; $95/yr. elsewhere. 37 W. Main St., Shelby, OH 44875-0647. TEL 419-342-4276. **Owner(s):** Shelby Daily Globe, Inc., 37 W. Main St., Shelby, OH 44875-0647. TEL 419-342-4276; Ed. Scott Gove; Pub. Scott Gove; pub. size: broadsheet; circ. evening 4,168(paid). **Wire Service(s):** AP.

SIDNEY
US

SIDNEY DAILY NEWS. 1891. Mon.-Sat. $.50 newsstand; $29.94/3 mos. home deliv.; $37.09/3 mos. students. 911 Vandemark Rd., Sidney, OH 45365-4099. TEL 513-498-8088; FAX 513-498-0893. **Owner(s):** Amos Press, Inc., P.O. Box 4129, Sidney, OH 45365. TEL 513-498-2111; FAX 513-498-0806; Ed. Jeffrey Billiel; Pub. Linda Coffman; adv. contact: Mark Kaufman. adv.: $10.50/SAU. pub. size: broadsheet; circ. evening 13,367(paid). **Wire Service(s):** AP.

SPRINGFIELD
US ISSN 0744-6101

SPRINGFIELD NEWS-SUN. 1817. d. $.50/day newsstand; $1.25/Sun; $3.55/wk. carrier; $184.60/yr. carrier. 202 N. Limestone St., Springfield, OH 45503. TEL 513-328-0300; FAX 513-328-0328. **Owner(s):** Cox Enterprises, Inc., 1400 Lake Hearne Dr., Atlanta, GA 30319. TEL 404-843-5000; Ed. Jack Bianchi; Pub. Charles Rinehart; photos; pub. size: broadsheet; circ. morning 38,227(paid); Sun. 44,905(paid). **Wire Service(s):** AP, KR.

STEUBENVILLE
US ISSN 0890-8656

HERALD-STAR. 1806. d. $.50/day newsstand; $1/Sun.; $2.20/wk. 401 Herald Sq., Steubenville, OH 43952. TEL 614-283-4711; FAX 614-282-4261. **Owner(s):** Ogden Newspapers, Inc., 1500 Main St., Wheeling, WV 26033. TEL 304-233-0100; Ed. Judy McGovern; Pub. Robert Dunn; pub. size: broadsheet; circ. evening 21,416(paid); Sun. 21,905(paid). **Wire Service(s):** AP.
  Formerly: Steubenville Herald-Star.

ST. MARYS
US ISSN 0745-5550

EVENING LEADER, THE. 1905. Mon.-Sat. $.50 newsstand; $2.70/wk. carrier. 102 E. Spring St., St. Marys, OH 45885. TEL 419-394-7414; FAX 419-394-7202. **Owner(s):** American Publishing Co., 606 N. Van Buren, Marion, IL 62959. TEL 618-993-1711; Ed. Jose Nogueras; Pub. David Creech; adv.; pub. size: broadsheet; circ. evening 6,600(paid). **Wire Service(s):** AP.
  Formerly: St. Marys Leader.

TIFFIN
US

ADVERTISER-TRIBUNE. 1832. d. $.50/day newsstand; $1.25/Sun.; $10/mo. carrier; $11.25/mo. motor rte.; $13.75/mo. mailed. 320 Nelson St., Tiffin, OH 44883. TEL 419-448-3200; FAX 419-447-3274. **Owner(s):** Ogden Newspapers, Inc., 1500 Main St., Wheeling, WV 26003. TEL 304-233-0100; Ed. John Kauffman; Pub. David Frisch; adv. contact: Chris Dixon. pub. size: broadsheet; circ. morning 11,000(paid); Sun. 11,600(paid). **Wire Service(s):** AP.
  Formerly: Tiffin Advertiser-Tribune.

TOLEDO
US

TOLEDO BLADE. 1835. d. $.50/day newsstand; $1.50/Sun.; $1.35/wk. Mon.-Sat. 541 Superior St., Toledo, OH 43660. TEL 419-245-6000; FAX 419-245-6439. **Owner(s):** Toledo Blade Co., 541 Superior St., Toledo, OH 43660. TEL 419-245-6000; Ed. John Block; Pub. John Robinson Block; adv. contact: Gerard Grabowski. photos; bk.rev.; pub. size: broadsheet; circ. evening 150,000(paid); Sun. 211,864(paid). **Wire Service(s):** AP, LAT-WP, RN, KNT, NYT, CSM, SHNA.

TROY
US

TROY DAILY NEWS. 1909. d. $.50 newsstand; $2.50/wk. 224 S. Market St., Troy, OH 45373. TEL 513-335-5634; FAX 513-335-3552. **Owner(s):** TDN Publications, 224 S. Market St., Troy, OH 45373. TEL 513-335-5634; Ed. David Lindeman; Pub. Joel H. Walker; adv. contact: Vicki Houston. pub. size: broadsheet; circ. evening 11,087(paid); Sun. 14,000(paid). **Wire Service(s):** AP.

UPPER SANDUSKY
US

UPPER SANDUSKY DAILY CHIEF-UNION. 1936. Mon.-Sat. $.50 newsstand; $92.40/yr. 111 W. Wyandot, Upper Sandusky, OH 43351-0180. TEL 419-294-2331; FAX 419-294-5608. **Owner(s):** Hardin County Publishing Co., 317 S. Anderson St., Elwood, IN 46036. TEL 317-552-3355; Ed. Bette Snyder; Pub. Tom Martin; adv. contact: Tom Martin. pub. size: broadsheet; circ. evening 4,500(paid). **Wire Service(s):** AP.

URBANA
US

URBANA DAILY CITIZEN. 1837. d. $.50 newsstand; $101.40/yr. motor rte.; $124/yr. mailed in cy. 220 E. Court St., Urbana, OH 43078. TEL 513-652-1331; FAX 513-652-1336. **Owner(s):** Brown Publishing Co., 310 Patrick Ave., Urbana, OH 43078. TEL 513-652-2148; Ed. Anthony Conchel; Pub. Linda Anderson; adv. contact: Debby Madison. photos; bk.rev.; pub. size: broadsheet; circ. evening 7,700(paid). **Wire Service(s):** AP.

VAN WERT
US ISSN 8750-1503

TIMES-BULLETIN. 1846. Mon.-Sat. $.50 newsstand; $1.85/wk. in town; $1.95/wk. motor rte. 700 Fox Rd., Van Wert, OH 45891. TEL 419-238-2285; FAX 419-238-0447. **Owner(s):** Brown Publishing Co., P.O. Box 555, Urbana, OH 43078. TEL 513-652-2100; Ed. David Mosier; Pub. L.R. Joseph; adv. contact: Tracy Hoghe. photos; pub. size: broadsheet; circ. evening 6,500(paid). **Wire Service(s):** AP.

WAPAKONETA
US

DAILY NEWS. 1904. Mon.-Sat. $.50 newsstand; $126/yr. in cy.; $165/yr. mailed. 8 Willipie St., Wapakoneta, OH 45895. TEL 419-738-2128; FAX 419-738-5352; E-mail: wapakwdn@brutus.bright.net; URL: http://www.bright.net/~Wapakwdn. **Owner(s):** American Publishing Co., 606 N. Van Buren, P.O. Box 520, Marion, IL 62959. TEL 618-993-1711; Ed. J. Swygart; Pub. Dianna Epperly; adv. contact: Karen Brown. photos; bk.rev.; pub. size: broadsheet; circ. evening 5,300(paid). **Wire Service(s):** AP.
  Formerly: Wapakoneta Daily News.

WARREN
US

TRIBUNE CHRONICLE, THE. d. $.25/day newsstand; $1/Sun.; $2.25/wk. home deliv. 240 Franklin St., S.E., Warren, OH 44482-1431. TEL 330-841-1600; FAX 330-841-1721; E-mail: soravecz@cisnet.com; URL: http://www.cisnet.com/tribune. **Owner(s):** Thomson Newspapers, Inc., Metro Centre, One Station Pl., 6th Fl., Stamnford, CT 06092. TEL 203-425-2500; FAX 203-425-2516; Pub. Steven Roszczyk; adv. contact: Cindy Genge. photos; bk.rev.; pub. size: broadsheet; circ. evening 44,000(paid); Sun. 45,406(paid). **Wire Service(s):** AP, KNT.
  Formerly: Warren Tribune Chronicle.

WASHINGTON COURT HOUSE
US

RECORD HERALD. 1937. Mon.-Sat. $.50 newsstand; $8.10/mo. carrier in town. 138 S. Fayette St., Washington Court House, OH 43160. TEL 614-335-3611; FAX 614-335-5728. **Owner(s):** Brown Publishing Co., P.O. Box 555, Urbana, OH 43078. TEL 513-652-2100; Ed. Margaret Jones; Pub. Jeff Pollard; adv.; photos; bk.rev.; pub. size: broadsheet; circ. evening 6,200(paid). **Wire Service(s):** AP.

WILLOUGHBY
US

NEWS-HERALD. 1879. d. $.50/day newsstand; $1.50/Sun.; $1.75/wk. carrier. 7085 Mentor Ave., Willoughby, OH 44094-7900. TEL 216-951-0000; FAX 216-975-2293. **Owner(s):** State Street Square, 50 W. State, Trenton, NJ 08608-1298. TEL 609-396-2200; Ed. James Collins; Pub. Joe Cocozzo; adv.; pub. size: broadsheet; circ. evening 56,000(paid); Sun. 68,000(paid). **Wire Service(s):** AP, LAT-WP, KR.

WILMINGTON

WILMINGTON NEWS-JOURNAL. 1838. Mon.-Sat. $.50 newsstand; $85/yr. home deliv. 47 S. South St., Wilmington, OH 45177. TEL 513-382-2574; FAX 513-382-4392. **Owner(s):** Brown Publishing Co., 47 S. South St., Wilmington, OH 45177. TEL 513-382-2574; FAX 513-382-4392; Ed. Jay Carey; Pub. Clarence Graham; adv. contact: Rick Irvin. photos; bk.rev.; pub. size: broadsheet; circ. evening 7,500(paid). **Wire Service(s):** AP.

WOOSTER

US ISSN 0892-8215
WOOSTER DAILY RECORD. 1898. d. $.50/day newsstand; $1/Sun.; $8.60/4 wks.; $160/yr. 212 E. Liberty St., Wooster, OH 44691. TEL 216-264-1125; FAX 216-264-3756. **Owner(s):** Wooster Republican Printing Co., 212 E. Liberty St., Wooster, OH 44691. TEL 216-264-1125; Ed. Melody Snure; Pub. R. Victor Dix; adv. contact: Bob Anderson. pub. size: broadsheet; circ. evening 25,695(paid). **Wire Service(s):** AP, NYT.

XENIA

US ISSN 8750-4650
XENIA DAILY GAZETTE. 1868. Mon.-Sat. $.50 newsstand; $98.80/yr. carrier. 37 S. Detroit St., Xenia, OH 45385. TEL 937-372-4444; FAX 937-372-3385. **Owner(s):** Thomson Newspapers, Inc., Metro Centre, One Station Pl., 6th Fl., Stamford, CT 06902. TEL 203-425-2500; FAX 203-425-2516; Ed. Gary Brock; Pub. Terri Dearth; adv. contact: Melissa Monteith. pub. size: broadsheet; circ. evening 10,000(paid). **Wire Service(s):** AP.

YOUNGSTOWN

US ISSN 0890-9857
VINDICATOR, THE. 1869. d. $.25/day newsstand; $.75/Sun.; $2/wk. carrier. 107 Vindicator Sq., Youngstown, OH 44503. TEL 330-747-1471; FAX 330-747-6712; E-mail: pjvindy@aol.com. **Owner(s):** Vindicator Printing Co., P.O. Box 780, Youngstown, OH 44503. TEL 330-747-1471; Ed. Paul C. Jagnow; Pub. Betty H. Brown Jagnow; adv. contact: Bruce Crawford. photos; bk.rev.; pub. size: broadsheet; circ. evening 93,000(paid); Sun. 135,265(paid). **Wire Service(s):** AP, CT-NYT, LAT-WP, KR.

ZANESVILLE

US
TIMES RECORDER, THE. 1864. d. $.35/day newsstand; $1/Sun.; $124.80/yr. 34 S. Fourth St., Zanesville, OH 43701. TEL 614-452-4561; FAX 614-452-0750; E-mail: 75563.306@compuserve.com. **Owner(s):** Thomson Newspapers, Inc., Metro Centre, One Station Pl., 6th Fl., Stamford, CT 06902. TEL 203-425-2500; Ed. Richard Stubbe; Pub. John B. Raytis; adv.; photos; pub. size: broadsheet; circ. morning 24,263(paid); Sun. 23,780(paid). **Wire Service(s):** AP.

OKLAHOMA

ADA

US
ADA EVENING NEWS. 1904. Sun.-Fri. $.50/day newsstand; $1.25/Sun.; $8.20/mo. in city; $8.35/mo. in cy.; $9/mo. elsewhere. 112-120 N. Broadway, Ada, OK 74820. TEL 405-332-4433; FAX 405-332-8734. **Owner(s):** American Publishing Co., 606 N. Van Buren, Marion, IL 62959. TEL 618-993-1711; Ed. Steve Boggs; Pub. Roy Biondi; adv. contact: Rick Cash. pub. size: broadsheet; circ. evening 10,200(paid); Sun. 9,800(paid). **Wire Service(s):** AP, Thomson.

ALTUS

US
ALTUS TIMES. 1900. d. $.50/day newsstand; $1/Sun.; $72/yr. 218 W. Commerce, Altus, OK 73521. TEL 405-482-5709; FAX 405-482-5709. **Owner(s):** Stephens Group, Inc., P.O. Box 17017, Fort Smith, AR 72917. TEL 501-785-7810; Ed. Carol Cole; Pub. Lyle M. Exstrom; adv. contact: Virginia Rezoie. pub. size: broadsheet; circ. evening 5,500(paid); Sun. 6,000(paid). **Wire Service(s):** AP.

ALVA

US
ALVA REVIEW-COURIER. 1893. Sun.-Tue., Thu. & Fri. $.25/day newsstand; $.75/Sun.; $96/yr. in cy.; $132/yr. out of state. 620 Choctaw, Alva, OK 73717. TEL 405-327-2200; FAX 405-327-2454. **Owner(s):** Martin Broadcasting Corp., 620 Choctaw, Alva, OK 73717. TEL 405-327-2200; FAX 405-327-2454; Pub. Lynn L. Martin; adv.; photos; bk.rev.; pub. size: tabloid; circ. morning 2,200(paid); Sun. 2,200(paid). **Wire Service(s):** AP.

ANADARKO

US
ANADARKO DAILY NEWS. 1901. Mon.-Sat. $.50 newsstand; $72/yr. in cy. 117 E. Broadway, Anadarko, OK 73005-0548. TEL 405-247-3331; FAX 405-247-5571. **Owner(s):** Anadarko Publishing Co., 117 E. Broadway, Anadarko, OK 73005. TEL 405-247-3331; Ed. Paula McBride Savage; Pub. Carolyn N. McBride; adv.; bk.rev.; pub. size: broadsheet; circ. evening 5,100(paid). **Wire Service(s):** AP.

ARDMORE

US
DAILY ARDMOREITE. 1893. Sun.-Fri. $.50/day newsstand; $1/Sun.; $60/yr. local. 117 W. Broadway, Ardmore, OK 73401. TEL 405-223-2200; FAX 405-226-2363. **Owner(s):** Morris Communications, P.O. Box 936, Augusta, GA 30903. TEL 706-724-0851; Ed. John Bridwell; Pub. Bill Stauffer; adv. contact: Bryant Pierpont. photos; pub. size: broadsheet; circ. evening 11,432(paid); Sun. 13,985(paid). **Wire Service(s):** AP.

BARTLESVILLE

US ISSN 0883-7015
BARTLESVILLE EXAMINER-ENTERPRISE. 1895. d. $.50/day newsstand; $1/Sun.; $7.75/mo. carrier. 4125 S.E. Nowata Rd., Bartlesville, OK 74006. TEL 918-335-8200; FAX 918-335-3111. **Owner(s):** Stephens Group, Inc., P.O. Box 17017, Fort Smith, AR 72917-0707. TEL 501-785-7810; Ed. Steve Linam; Pub. Joseph Edwards; adv. contact: Donna Silver. pub. size: broadsheet; circ. evening 13,100(paid); Sun. 15,300(paid). **Wire Service(s):** AP.

BLACKWELL

US
BLACKWELL JOURNAL-TRIBUNE. 1893. Tue.-Fri. & Sun. $.50 newsstand; $6/mo. carrier; $10/mo. in state mailed. 113 E. Blackwell St., Blackwell, OK 74631. TEL 405-363-3370; FAX 405-363-4415. **Owner(s):** Stephens Group, Inc., P.O. Box 17017, Fort Smith, AR 72917. TEL 501-785-7810; Ed. Bob William; Pub. Dayle McGaha; adv. contact: Tammy Zeman. pub. size: broadsheet; circ. evening 2,850(paid); Sun. 2,900(paid). **Wire Service(s):** AP.

CHICKASHA

US
CHICKASHA DAILY EXPRESS. 1889. Sun.-Fri. $.50/day newsstand; $1/Sun.; $78/yr. home deliv. 302 N. Third St., Chickasha, OK 73018. TEL 405-224-2600; FAX 405-224-7087. **Owner(s):** Don Rey Media Group, P. O. Box 13597, Fort Smith, AR 72901; Pub. Reg Freemyer; adv. contact: Elaine Johnson. photos; bk.rev.; pub. size: broadsheet; circ. evening 5,500(paid); Sun. 6,400(paid). **Wire Service(s):** AP.

CLAREMORE

US
CLAREMORE PROGRESS. 1893. Tue.-Fri. & Sun. $.50/day newsstand; $1/Sun.; $78/yr. carrier. 315 W. Will Rogers Blvd., Claremore, OK 74017. TEL 918-341-1101; FAX 918-341-1131. **Owner(s):** Stephens Group, Inc., P.O. Box 1359, Ft. Smith, AR 72901. TEL 501-785-7810; Ed. Pat Reeder; Pub. Dave Story; adv. contact: Dave Kucifer. pub. size: broadsheet; circ. evening 6,100(paid); Sun. 7,100(paid). **Wire Service(s):** AP.

DAILY NEWSPAPERS

CLINTON
US
CLINTON DAILY NEWS. 1903. Sun.-Fri. $.50 newsstand; $6.25/mo. home deliv. 522 Avant Ave., Clinton, OK 73601. TEL 405-323-5151; FAX 405-323-5154. **Owner(s):** Clinton Daily News Co., 522 Avant Ave., Clinton, OK 73601. TEL 405-323-5151; FAX 405-323-5154; Ed. Steve Belcher; Pub. Charles E. Engleman; adv. contact: Reba Donleyr. pub. size: broadsheet; circ. evening 5,200(paid). **Wire Service(s):** AP.

CUSHING
US
CUSHING DAILY CITIZEN. 1895. Mon.-Fri. $.50 newsstand; $60/yr. 115 S. Cleveland St., Cushing, OK 74023-1031. TEL 918-225-3333; FAX 918-225-1050; E-mail: dreid@fullnet.net. **Owner(s):** Reid Newspapers, Inc., P.O. Box 1031, Cushing, OK 74023-1031. TEL 918-225-3333; Ed. Terry Hoggett; Pub. David Reid; adv. contact: Brian Hammock. pub. size: broadsheet; circ. morning 3,200(paid). **Wire Service(s):** AP.

DUNCAN
US
DUNCAN BANNER. 1892. Sun.-Fri. $.50/day newsstand; $1/Sun.; $7.25/mo. home deliv. 1001 Elm St., Duncan, OK 73533. TEL 405-255-5354; FAX 405-255-8889. **Owner(s):** Wimberly Investments, Inc., 1001 Elm St., Duncan, OK 73533. TEL 405-255-5354; FAX 405-255-8889; Ed. Larry Gittings; Pub. Alexander J. Hruby; adv. contact: Jill Hunt. adv.: $8.10/SAU. photos; bk.rev.; pub. size: broadsheet; circ. evening 9,146(paid); Sun. 10,654(paid). **Wire Service(s):** AP.

DURANT
US
DURANT DAILY DEMOCRAT. 1900. Sun.-Fri. $.50/day newsstand; $1/Sun.; $7/mo. home deliv.; $84/yr. 200 W. Beech St., Durant, OK 74701. TEL 405-924-4388; FAX 405-924-6026. **Owner(s):** Don Rey Media Group, P.O. Box 17017, Ft. Smith, AR 72917. TEL 501-785-7810; Pub. David Crouch; adv. contact: Paula M. Howell. adv.: $8.80/SAU. pub. size: broadsheet; circ. evening 7,000(paid); Sun. 7,600(paid). **Wire Service(s):** AP.

EDMOND
US
EDMOND EVENING SUN. 1889. Tue.-Fri. & Sun. $.50/day newsstand; $.75/Sun.; $84/yr. home deliv.; $90/yr. mailed. 123 S. Broadway, Edmond, OK 73034. TEL 405-341-2121; FAX 405-340-7363. **Owner(s):** Edmond Publishing Co., Inc., P.O. Box 2470, Edmond, OK 13083. TEL 405-341-2121; FAX 405-340-7363; Ed. Ed Livermore; Pub. Ed Livermore; adv. contact: Marsha Baugus. pub. size: broadsheet; circ. evening 10,000(paid); Sun. 11,000(paid). **Wire Service(s):** AP, NYT.

ELK CITY
US
ELK CITY DAILY NEWS. 1901. Sun.-Fri. $.50 newsstand; $6/mo. home deliv.; $65/yr. 200-206 W. Broadway, Elk City, OK 73644. TEL 405-225-3000; FAX 405-243-2414. **Owner(s):** Larry R. Wade, P.O. Box 1037, Elk City, OK 73648. TEL 405-225-3000; Mary Jane Wade, P.O. Box 1037, Elk City, OK 73648. TEL 405-225-3000; Mary Elizabeth Wade, P.O. Box 1037, Elk City, OK 73648. TEL 405-225-3000; Pub. Larry R. Wade; adv. contact: Sharon Denny. photos; bk.rev.; pub. size: broadsheet; circ. evening 6,176(paid); Sun. 10,795(paid). **Wire Service(s):** AP.

ENID
US
ENID NEWS & EAGLE. 1893. d. $.35/day newsstand; $1.50/Sun.; $10.40/mo. home deliv. 227 W. Broadway, Enid, OK 73701. TEL 405-233-6600; FAX 405-233-7645. **Owner(s):** American Publishing Co., 606 N. VanBuren, Marion, IL 62959. TEL 618-993-1711; FAX 618-997-4018; Ed. Jerry D. Pittman; Pub. Dennis DeRossett; adv.; pub. size: broadsheet; circ. morning 21,190(paid); Sun. 24,040(paid). **Wire Service(s):** AP, Thomson News Service.
  Formerly: Enid Morning News & Enid Daily Eagle.

GROVE
US
▼**GROVE DAILY NEWS.** 1995. Tue.-Sat. $.25 newsstand; $5/mo.; $15/3 mos.; $39/yr. 22 E. Third St., Grove, OK 74344. TEL 918-786-9002; FAX 918-786-6048. **Owner(s):** David Ulrich & Francis Stipe, P.O. Box 335, Grove, OK 74344. TEL 918-786-9002; FAX 918-786-6048; Ed. Bruce Jones; Pub. Francis Stipe; adv. contact: Judi Cole. photos; bk.rev.; pub. size: broadsheet; circ. morning 1,750(paid). **Wire Service(s):** AP.

GUTHRIE
US
GUTHRIE NEWS LEADER. 1889. Sun.-Fri. $.50 newsstand; $5.50/mo.; $66/yr. 107 W. Harrison, Guthrie, OK 73044. TEL 405-282-2222; FAX 405-282-7378. **Owner(s):** Territorial Publishing Co., P.O. Box 2470, Edmond, OK 73083. TEL 405-341-2121; FAX 405-340-7363; Ed. Lisa Shearer; Pub. Ed Livermore; adv.; bk.rev.; pub. size: broadsheet; circ. evening 3,000(paid); Sun. 3,000(paid). **Wire Service(s):** AP.
  Formerly: Guthrie Daily Leader; Logan County News.

GUYMON
US
GUYMON DAILY HERALD. 1890. Mon.-Sat. $.50 newsstand; $6/mo. home deliv.; $72/yr. 515 N. Ellison St., Guymon, OK 73942. TEL 405-338-3355; FAX 405-338-5000. **Owner(s):** Don Rey Media Group, P.O. Box 17017, Fort Smith, AR 72917-7017. TEL 501-785-7810; Ed. Linda Holbert; Pub. William Murphy; adv. contact: Linda O'Leary. photos; bk.rev.; pub. size: broadsheet; circ. evening 4,000(paid). **Wire Service(s):** AP.

HENRYETTA
US
HENRYETTA DAILY FREE-LANCE. 1901. Tue.-Fri. & Sun. $.50 newsstand; $72/yr. carrier; $72/yr. mailed in cy.; $73/yr. out of cy.; $76/yr. out of state. 812 W. Main St., Henryetta, OK 74437. TEL 918-652-3311; FAX 918-652-7347. **Owner(s):** Stephens Group, Inc., P.O. Box 1359, Fort Smith, AR 72901. TEL 501-785-7810; FAX 501-785-9430; Ed. Mr. Chelsea Cook; Pub. Nancy Miller; adv. contact: Bess Standley. adv.: $6.30/SAU. photos; pub. size: broadsheet; circ. evening 2,200(paid); Sun. 2,400(paid). **Wire Service(s):** AP.

HOLDENVILLE
US
HOLDENVILLE DAILY NEWS. 1927. Tue.-Fri. & Sun. $.35 newsstand; $4/mo. carrier; $42/yr. mailed. 112 S. Creek, Holdenville, OK 74848. TEL 405-379-5411; FAX 405-379-5413. **Owner(s):** Francis Stipe Publishing, 112 S. Creek, Holdenville, OK 74888. TEL 405-379-5411; Pub. Dan Corley; adv. contact: Melissa Michom. pub. size: tabloid; circ. morning 2,860(paid).

HUGO
US
HUGO DAILY NEWS. 1907. Mon.-Fri. $.35 newsstand; $6/mo. carrier; $70/yr. in cy. mailed. 128 E. Jackson St., Hugo, OK 74743. TEL 405-326-3311; FAX 405-326-6397; E-mail: sstamper@1starnet.com; URL: http://www.hug.onews.com. **Owner(s):** Hugo Publishing Co., 128 E. Jackson St., Hugo, OK 74743. TEL 405-326-3311; Ed. Pam Proctor; Pub. Stan Stamper; adv. contact: Linda Packard. pub. size: broadsheet; circ. morning 3,015(paid). **Wire Service(s):** AP.

IDABEL
US
MCCURTAIN DAILY GAZETTE. 1906. Tue.-Fri. & Sun. $.25/day newsstand; $.50/Sun.; $4.75/mo. carrier. 107 S. Central St., Idabel, OK 74745. TEL 405-286-3321; FAX 405-286-2208. **Owner(s):** Gwen & Bruce Willingham, 107 S. Central, Idabel, OK 74745. TEL 405-286-3321; Ed. Bruce Willingham; Pub. Bruce Willingham; adv. contact: Margie Jones. photos; pub. size: broadsheet; circ. evening 6,400(paid); Sun. 8,400(paid). **Wire Service(s):** AP.

LAWTON
US
LAWTON CONSTITUTION. 1910. d. $.50/day newsstand; $1/Sun.; $11/mo. carrier. P.O. Box 2069, Lawton, OK 73502. TEL 405-353-0620; FAX 405-585-5140; E-mail: paper@sirinet.net; URL: http://www.lawton-constitution.com. **Owner(s):** Lawton Publishing Co., Inc., P.O. Box 2069, Lawton, OK 73502. TEL 405-353-0620; FAX 405-585-5140; Ed. Dennis A. Lang; Pub. Donald S. Bentley; adv. contact: Mike Owensby. bk.rev.; pub. size: broadsheet; circ. morning 26,000(paid); Sun. 31,000(paid). **Wire Service(s):** AP, NYT, CNS, COX.
  Formerly: The Lawton Consititution/Lawton Morning Press.

MCALESTER

US

NEWS-CAPITAL & DEMOCRAT. Sun.-Fri. $.50/day newsstand; $1/Sun.; $7.50/mo. carrier. 500 S. Second St, McAlester, OK 74501. TEL 918-423-1700; FAX 918-426-3081. **Owner(s):** Newspaper Holdings, Inc., 269 W. Main St., 6th Fl., Lexington, KY 40507. TEL 606-388-2644; FAX 606-225-8115; adv. contact: Janet Grider. pub. size: broadsheet; circ. evening 11,900(paid); Sun. 13,000(paid).
Formerly: McAlester News-Capital & Democrat.

MIAMI

US

MIAMI NEWS-RECORD. 1903. Sun.-Fri. $.50/day newsstand; $1.25/Sun.; $8.50/mo. home deliv.; $10.31/mo. in state mailed. 14 First Ave., N.W., Miami, OK 74354. TEL 918-542-5533; FAX 918-542-1903. **Owner(s):** Boone Newspapers, Inc., P.O. Box 2370, Tuscaloosa, AL 35403. TEL 407-338-3298; Ed. John Fox; Pub. Floyd Jeringan; adv. contact: Chris Rush. pub. size: broadsheet; circ. morning 7,500(paid); Sun. 8,000(paid).

MUSKOGEE

US

MUSKOGEE DAILY PHOENIX & TIMES-DEMOCRAT. 1888. d. $.35/day newsstand; $1.25/Sun.; $11.50/mo. 214 Wall St., Muskogee, OK 74401. TEL 918-684-2875; FAX 918-682-3998. **Owner(s):** Gannett Company, Inc., 1100 Wilson Blvd., Arlington, VA 22234. TEL 703-248-6000; Pub. Lawrence Corvi; adv. contact: Roger Runnels. pub. size: broadsheet; circ. morning 19,700(paid); Sun. 21,300(paid). **Wire Service(s):** UPI, AP.

NORMAN

US

NORMAN TRANSCRIPT. 1889. d. $.50/day newsstand; $1/Sun.; $7/mo. in cy.; $14/mo. elsewhere. 215 E. Comanche, Norman, OK 73069. TEL 405-321-1800; FAX 405-366-3516. **Owner(s):** Stephens Group, Inc., P.O. Box 1359, Fort Smith, AR 72902; Ed. Andy Rieger; Pub. David Stringer; adv. contact: Walt Disney. pub. size: broadsheet; circ. evening 15,000(paid); Sun. 15,500(paid). **Wire Service(s):** AP, KNS.

OKLAHOMA CITY

US

DAILY OKLAHOMAN. 1903. d. $.50/day newsstand; $1.50/Sun.; $14/mo. home deliv. 9000 N. Broadway, Oklahoma City, OK 73114. TEL 405-475-3311; FAX 405-475-3183. **Owner(s):** Oklahoma Publishing Co., 9000 N. Broadway, Oklahoma City, OK 73114. TEL 405-475-3311; Ed. Ed Kelly; Pub. Edward L. Gaylord; adv. contact: David Thompson. bk.rev.; pub. size: broadsheet; circ. morning 214,590(paid); Sun. 321,268(paid). **Wire Service(s):** AP, RN.

OKMULGEE

US

OKMULGEE TIMES. 1903. Tue.-Sun. $.50/day newsstand; $.75/Wed. & Sun.; $6/mo. home deliv.; $23.10/3 mos. mailed; $25.17/3 mos. out of state. 114 E. Seventh, Okmulgee, OK 74447. TEL 918-756-3600; FAX 918-756-8197. **Owner(s):** Stephens Group, Inc., P.O. Box 1359, Fort Smith, AR 72901-7017. TEL 501-785-7810; Pub. Jerry Quinn; adv.; photos; bk.rev.; pub. size: broadsheet; circ. morning 5,750(paid); Sun. 5,800(paid). **Wire Service(s):** AP.

PAULS VALLEY

US

PAULS VALLEY DAILY DEMOCRAT. 1904. Tue.-Fri. & Sun. $.50/day newsstand; $.75/Sun.; $5.50/mo. carrier. 108 S. Willow St., Pauls Valley, OK 73075. TEL 405-238-6464; FAX 405-238-3042. **Owner(s):** Stephens Group, Inc., P.O. Box 1359, Fort Smith, AR 72901. TEL 501-785-7810; Ed. Robert Douchette; Pub. Mary Anne Lynn; adv.; bk.rev.; pub. size: broadsheet; circ. evening 4,000(paid); Sun. 4,200(paid). **Wire Service(s):** AP.
Formerly: Pauls Valley Democrat.

PERRY

US   ISSN 0746-7559

PERRY DAILY JOURNAL. 1893. Mon.-Sat. $.35 newsstand; $6.50/mo. home deliv. 714 Delaware St., Perry, OK 73077. TEL 405-336-2222; FAX 405-336-3222. **Owner(s):** Weatherford News, Inc., P.O. Box 191, Weatherford, OK 73096. TEL 405-772-3301; Ed. Gloria Brown; Pub. Phillip Reid; adv. contact: Vivian McKinnis. pub. size: broadsheet; circ. evening 3,250(paid). **Wire Service(s):** AP.

PONCA CITY

US

PONCA CITY NEWS. 1894. Sun.-Fri. $.35/day newsstand; $1/Sun.; $6.25/mo. carrier. 300 N. Third, Ponca City, OK 74601. TEL 405-765-3311; FAX 405-762-6397. **Owner(s):** Ponca City Publishing Co., Inc., 300 N. Third, Ponca City, OK 74601. TEL 405-765-3311; Ed. Foster Johnson; Pub. Allan W. Muchmore; adv. contact: Everett Lockwood. adv.: $9/SAU. pub. size: standard; circ. evening 11,781(paid); Sun. 13,540(paid). **Wire Service(s):** AP.

POTEAU

US

POTEAU DAILY NEWS & SUN. 1895. Tue.-Sat. $.35/day newsstand; $1/Sat.; $15/3 mos. in cy; $30/6 mos. in cy; $60/yr. in cy. 804 N. Broadway, Poteau, OK 74953. TEL 918-647-3188; FAX 918-647-8198; E-mail: pdn&s@www.clnk.com; URL: http://www.pdns.com. **Owner(s):** LeFlore County Newspapers, P.O. Box 1237, Poteau, OK 74953. TEL 918-647-3188; Ed. Ken Milam; Pub. Wallace S. Burchett; adv. contact: Janet Fox. pub. size: broadsheet; circ. morning 5,000(paid). **Wire Service(s):** AP.

PRYOR

US

PRYOR DAILY TIMES. 1940. Tue.-Fri. & Sun. $.50/day newsstand; $1/Sun.; $6.50/mo. carrier; $78/yr. 105 S. Adair St., Pryor, OK 74361. TEL 918-825-3292; FAX 918-825-1965. **Owner(s):** Pryor Publishing Co., Inc., 105 S. Adair St., Pryor, OK 74361. TEL 918-825-3292; FAX 918-852-3292; Ed. Henry Goodman. adv. contact: Diana Morgan. pub. size: broadsheet; circ. evening 5,800(paid); Sun. 7,200(paid). **Wire Service(s):** AP.

SAPULPA

US

SAPULPA DAILY HERALD. 1914. Sun.-Fri. $.50/day newsstand; $1/Sun.; $75.60/yr. home deliv. 16 S. Park, Sapulpa, OK 74066. TEL 918-224-5185; FAX 918-224-5196. **Owner(s):** Community Newspaper Holdings, Lexington, KY; Ed. Joe Ben Oller. adv. contact: Joanita Brewer. pub. size: broadsheet; circ. evening 7,000(paid); Sun. 7,075(paid). **Wire Service(s):** AP.

SEMINOLE

US

SEMINOLE DAILY PRODUCER. 1927. Tue.-Fri. & Sun. $.35/day newsstand; $.75/Sun.; $6/mo. home deliv. 121 N. Main St., Seminole, OK 74868. TEL 405-382-1100; FAX 405-382-1104. **Owner(s):** Seminole Producer, Inc., P.O. Box 431, Seminole, OK 74818. TEL 405-382-1100; FAX 405-382-1104; Ed. Karen Anson; Pub. Ted Phillips; adv. contact: Jim Keisman. bk.rev.; pub. size: broadsheet; circ. evening 5,400(paid); Sun. 5,400(paid).

SHAWNEE

US

SHAWNEE NEWS-STAR. 1929. Tue.-Sun. $.50/day newsstand; $1/Sun.; $8.25/mo. carrier; $8.75/mo. city carrier; $9.00/mo. motor rte. in state; $10.25/mo. out of state. 215 N. Bell, Shawnee, OK 74801. TEL 405-273-4200; FAX 405-273-4207. **Owner(s):** Morris Communications, P.O. Box 936, Augusta, GA 30903. TEL 706-724-0851; Ed. Mike McCormick; Pub. John Tucker; adv. contact: Sherry Wilkins. photos; pub. size: broadsheet; circ. morning 14,500(paid); Sun. 15,608(paid). **Wire Service(s):** AP..

STILLWATER

US

STILLWATER NEWS-PRESS. 1940. Sun.-Fri. $.50/day newsstand; $1/Sun.; $6.75/mo. in town. 211 W. Ninth St., Stillwater, OK 74074. TEL 405-372-5000; FAX 405-372-3112. **Owner(s):** Stillwater Publishing Co., P.O. Box 2288, Stillwater, OK 74076. TEL 405-372-5000; FAX 405-372-3112; Ed. Lawrence Gibbs; Pub. L.F. Bellatti; adv. contact: Rhesa Funk. photos; pub. size: broadsheet; circ. evening 11,800(paid); Sun. 12,500(paid). **Wire Service(s):** AP, KNT.

DAILY NEWSPAPERS

TAHLEQUAH
US

TAHLEQUAH DAILY PRESS. 1850. Tue.-Fri. & Sun. $.35/day newsstand; $.75/Sun.; $75/yr. carrier; $69/yr. senior citizens carrier. 106 W. Second St., Tahlequah, OK 74464. TEL 918-456-8833; FAX 918-456-2019. **Owner(s):** Indian Nations Communications, Inc., 106 W. Second St., Tahlequah, OK 74464; Ed. Kim Poindexter; Pub. Brad Sugg; adv. contact: Pam Hutson. pub. size: broadsheet; circ. evening 6,800(paid); Sun. 7,100(paid).
Formerly: Tahlequah Star Citizen.

TULSA
US   ISSN 8750-5959

TULSA WORLD. 1905. d. $.50/day newsstand; $1.50/Sun.; $12.10/mo. 318 Main Mall, Tulsa, OK 74103. TEL 918-581-8300; FAX 918-581-8353; E-mail: tulsaworld@mail.webtek.com; URL: http://www.tulsaworld.com. **Owner(s):** World Publishing Co., 318 Main Mall, Tulsa, OK 74103. TEL 918-581-8330; Ed. Susan Ellerbach; Pub. Robert E. Lorton; adv.; photos; bk.rev.; pub. size: broadsheet; circ. morning 170,000(paid); Sun. 240,000(paid). **Wire Service(s):** AP, LAT-WP, KR, NYT, GNS.

VINITA
US

VINITA DAILY JOURNAL. 1907. Mon.-Fri. $.50 newsstand; $6.50/mo. in town; $18/3 mos. in state. 130-40 S. Wilson St., Vinita, OK 74301. TEL 918-256-6422; FAX 918-256-7100. **Owner(s):** Vinita Printing Co., Inc., P.O. Box 328, Vinita, OK 74301. TEL 918-256-6422; Ed. David Burgess; Pub. Phillip Reid; adv. contact: Helen Walker. pub. size: broadsheet; circ. evening 4,250(paid). **Wire Service(s):** UPI.

WEATHERFORD
US

WEATHERFORD DAILY NEWS. 1889. Tue.-Fri. & Sun. $.50/ day newsstand; $.50/Sun.; $58/yr. 118 S. Broadway, Weatherford, OK 73096. TEL 405-772-3301; FAX 405-772-7329; E-mail: wdn@itlnet.net; URL: http://wdn.itlnet.com. **Owner(s):** Weatherford News, Inc., P.O. Box 191, Weatherford, OK 73096. TEL 405-772-3301; Ed. Larry Adler; Pub. Philip Reid; adv. contact: Kristi Regier. photos; bk.rev.; pub. size: broadsheet; circ. evening 4,800(free & paid); Sun. 5,200(free & paid). **Wire Service(s):** AP.

WOODWARD
US   ISSN 0883-8755

WOODWARD NEWS. 1983. Tue.-Sun. $.50 newsstand; $70/yr. 904 Oklahoma Ave., Woodward, OK 73801. TEL 405-256-2200; FAX 405-254-2159. **Owner(s):** American Publishing Co., 606 N. Van Buren, Marion, IL 62959. TEL 618-993-1711; Ed. Joel Kindel; Pub. Gloria Fletcher; adv. contact: Amy Poulson. photos; pub. size: broadsheet; circ. evening 6,500(paid); Sun. 6,500(paid). **Wire Service(s):** AP.

OREGON

ALBANY
US

ALBANY DEMOCRAT-HERALD. 1865. d. $.50/day newsstand; $.75/Sat.; $8.50/mo. 600 Lyon St., S.W., Albany, OR 97321. TEL 503-926-2211; FAX 503-926-5298; E-mail: albanydh@proqxis.com; URL: http://www.mvonlinej.com. **Owner(s):** Walt Disney Co., 500 S. Buena Vista St., Burbank, CA 91521. TEL 818-560-5300; Ed. Graham Kislingbury; Pub. John E. Buchner; adv.: $14.51/SAU. photos; bk.rev.; pub. size: broadsheet; circ. evening 21,745(paid). **Wire Service(s):** AP.

ASHLAND
US

ASHLAND DAILY TIDINGS. 1876. Mon.-Sat. $.50 newsstand; $7.40/mo. home deliv. 1661 Siskiyou Blvd., Ashland, OR 97520. TEL 541-482-3456; FAX 541-482-3688. **Owner(s):** Walt Disney Co., 500 S. Buena Vista St., Burbank, CA 91521. TEL 818-560-5300; Ed. Jeff Keating; Pub. Mike O'Brien; adv. contact: Shawn McDonald. photos; pub. size: broadsheet; circ. evening 6,000(paid). **Wire Service(s):** AP.

ASTORIA
US   ISSN 0739-5078

DAILY ASTORIAN. 1873. Mon.-Fri. $.50 newsstand; $7/mo. carrier; $11/mo. mailed. 949 Exchange St., Astoria, OR 97103. TEL 503-325-3211; FAX 503-325-6573. **Owner(s):** East Oregonian Publishing Co., 1089 Pendleton, Astoria, OR 97801. TEL 503-325-3211; Ed. Laura Sellers-Earl. adv. contact: Dave Gorham. pub. size: broadsheet; circ. evening 10,000(paid). **Wire Service(s):** AP.

BAKER CITY
US

BAKER CITY HERALD. 1870. Mon.-Fri. $.35 newsstand; $87/yr. carrier; $90/yr. motor rte.; $132/yr. mailed. 1915 First St., Baker City, OR 97814-0807. TEL 541-523-3673; FAX 541-523-6426; E-mail: bcherald@triax.com. **Owner(s):** Western Communications, Inc., 1526 N.W. Hill St., Bend, OR 97701. TEL 541-382-1811; Ed. Dean Brickey; Pub. Jack Turner; adv. contact: Lynette Perry. adv.: $5.75/SAU. photos; pub. size: standard; circ. evening 3,273(paid). **Wire Service(s):** AP.

BEND
US

BULLETIN, THE. 1903. Sun.-Fri. $.35/day newsstand; $.50/Fri.; $1.25/Sun.; $9/mo. 1526 N.W. Hill St., Bend, OR 97701. TEL 541-382-1811; FAX 541-385-5802; E-mail: bulletin@bendnet.com; URL: http://www.oregonbusiness.com/newsnet/bulletin.html. **Owner(s):** Western Communications, Inc., 1526 N.W. Hill St., Bend, OR 97701. TEL 541-382-1811; FAX 541-385-5802; Ed. Steve Bagwell; Pub. Gordon Black; adv. contact: Mike Thorpe. photos; bk.rev.; pub. size: standard; circ. evening 27,500(paid); Sun. 28,500(paid). **Wire Service(s):** AP, LAT-WP.

COOS BAY
US

WORLD, THE. 1878. Mon.-Sat. $.50/day newsstand; $.75/Sat.; $7/mo. 350 Commercial, Coos Bay, OR 97420. TEL 503-269-1222; FAX 503-267-0294; E-mail: theworld@ucinet.com. **Owner(s):** Pulitzer Community Newspapers, Inc., 7701 Forsyth Blvd., Ste. 1000, Clayton, MO 63105; Ed. Veronica Combs; Pub. Don Brown; adv. contact: Juan Mejia. pub. size: broadsheet; circ. evening 17,000(paid). **Wire Service(s):** AP, SLNI, NEA.

CORVALLIS
US   ISSN 0746-3995

CORVALLIS GAZETTE-TIMES. 1862. d. $.50/day newsstand; $1.50/Sun.; $11.45/4 wks. home deliv. 600 S.W. Jefferson Ave., Corvallis, OR 97333. TEL 541-753-2641; FAX 541-758-9505; E-mail: gtnews@proaxis.com; URL: http://www.gtconnect.com. **Owner(s):** Lee Enterprises, Inc., 130 E. Second St., Davenport, IA 52801. TEL 319-383-2202; adv. contact: Gene Fulton. photos; bk.rev.; pub. size: broadsheet; circ. morning 15,500(paid); Sun. 17,200(paid). **Wire Service(s):** AP, LAT-WP, KR.

EUGENE
US   ISSN 0739-8557

REGISTER-GUARD. 1867. d. $.50/day newsstand; $.75/Sat.; $1.25/Sun.; $10.50/mo. home deliv. 975 High St., Eugene, OR 97401. TEL 541-485-1234; FAX 541-687-6668. **Owner(s):** Guard Publishing Co., 975 High St., Eugene, OR 97401. TEL 541-343-3878; FAX 541-984-4699; Ed. Jim Godbold; Pub. Alton F. Baker, III; adv. contact: Michael Raz. bk.rev.; pub. size: broadsheet; circ. morning 75,140(paid); Sun. 78,358(paid). **Wire Service(s):** AP, NYT, LAT-WP.

GRANTS PASS
US

GRANTS PASS DAILY COURIER. 1885. Mon.-Sat. $.50 newsstand; $8/mo. 409 S.E. Seventh St., Grants Pass, OR 97526. TEL 541-474-3711; FAX 541-474-3723; E-mail: courier@magik.net. **Owner(s):** Courier Publishing Co., P.O. Box 1468, Grants Pass, OR 97526. TEL 541-474-3700; FAX 541-474-3723; Ed. Dennis Roler; Pub. Dennis Mack; adv. contact: Michele Thomas. pub. size: broadsheet; circ. evening 18,520(paid). **Wire Service(s):** AP.

KLAMATH FALLS
US
HERALD & NEWS. 1906. Sun.-Fri. $.50/day newsstand; $1/Sun.; $8.75/mo. home deliv. 1301 Esplanade, Klamath Falls, OR 97601. TEL 503-885-4410; FAX 503-885-4456; E-mail: handnews@mg1.cdsnet.net; URL: http://www.cdsnet.net/business/herald/news. **Owner(s):** Pioneer Newspapers, Seattle, WA; Ed. Patrick Bushey; Pub. Dwight Tracy; adv. contact: Mike Waltman. pub. size: broadsheet; circ. evening 17,637(paid); Sun. 17,805(paid). **Wire Service(s):** AP.

Formerly: Klamath Falls Herald and News.

LA GRANDE
US
OBSERVER, THE. 1896. Mon.-Sat. $.35 newsstand; $8/mo. carrier; $13/mo. mail. 1406 Fifth St., La Grande, OR 97850. TEL 503-963-3161; FAX 503-963-7804. **Owner(s):** Western Communications, Inc., 1526 N.W. Hill St., Bend, OR 97701. TEL 503-382-1811; FAX 503-385-1811; Ed. Ted Kramer; Pub. Robert K. Moody; adv. contact: Don Powell. photos; bk.rev.; pub. size: broadsheet; circ. evening 7,814(paid). **Wire Service(s):** AP.

MEDFORD
US
MAIL TRIBUNE. 1906. d. $.50/day newsstand; $1.25/Sun.; $134.40/yr. home deliv. 111 N. Fir St., Medford, OR 97501-0229. TEL 541-776-4411; FAX 541-776-4376; E-mail: circ@mailtribune.com; URL: http://www.mailtribune.com. **Owner(s):** Ottaway Newspapers, Inc., P.O. Box 401, Campbell Hall, NY 10916. TEL 914-294-8181; Ed. Julie Wurth; Pub. Gregory Taylor; adv. contact: Teresa Keplinger. photos; bk.rev.; pub. size: broadsheet; circ. morning 32,000(paid); Sun. 38,000(paid). **Wire Service(s):** AP.

Formerly: Medford Mail Tribune.

ONTARIO
US
ARGUS OBSERVER. 1976. Sun.-Fri. $.50/day newsstand; $1.25/Sun.; $8.60/mo. home deliv.; $108.80/yr. home deliv. 1160 S.W. Fourth St., Ontario, OR 97914-0130. TEL 541-889-5387; FAX 541-889-3347. **Owner(s):** Wick Communications, Inc., 333 Wilcox, Ste. 302, Sierra Vista, AZ 85635. TEL 602-458-0200; Ed. Larry Hurrle; Pub. Francis McLean; adv. contact: Linda Warren. photos; bk.rev.; pub. size: broadsheet; circ. evening 7,900(paid); Sun. 9,000(paid). **Wire Service(s):** AP.

PENDLETON
US
EAST OREGONIAN, THE. 1875. Mon.-Sat. $.50 newsstand; $12/mo. 211 S.E. Byers Ave., Pendleton, OR 97801. TEL 541-276-2211; FAX 541-276-8314; E-mail: eastoregonian.com. **Owner(s):** East Oregonian Publishing Co., 211 S.E. Byers Ave., Pendleton, OR 97801. TEL 503-276-2211; Ed. Richard Hensley; Pub. Mark Garber; adv. contact: Christine Moore. pub. size: standard; circ. evening 12,000(paid). **Wire Service(s):** AP.

PORTLAND
US ISSN 8750-1317
OREGONIAN, THE. 1850. d. $.35/day newsstand; $1.50/Sun.; $11/mo. home deliv. 1320 S.W. Broadway, Portland, OR 97201. TEL 503-221-8327; FAX 503-227-5306; E-mail: letters@news.oregonian.com; URL: http://www.oregonian.com. **Owner(s):** Advance Publications, Inc., 950 Fingerboard Rd., Staten Island, NY 10305. TEL 718-981-1234; FAX 718-981-1456; Ed. Peter Bhatia; Pub. Fred A. Stickel; adv.; photos; bk.rev.; pub. size: broadsheet; circ. morning 349,193(paid); Sun. 446,300(paid). **Wire Service(s):** AP, NYT, CNS, LAT-WP, NNS.

ROSEBURG
US
NEWS-REVIEW. 1867. Sun.-Fri. $.35/day newsstand; $1/Sun.; $88.75/yr. home deliv. 345 N.E. Winchester, Roseburg, OR 97470. TEL 541-957-4270; FAX 541-673-5994; E-mail: newsdesk@oregonnews.com; URL: http://www.oregonnews.com. **Owner(s):** Swift Newspapers, Inc., 345 N.E. Winchester, Roseburg, OR 97470. TEL 541-673-5994; Ed. Bart M. Smith; Pub. Ron Stewart; adv. contact: Kelly Gant. photos; pub. size: standard; circ. evening 19,497(paid); Sun. 20,400(paid). **Wire Service(s):** AP.

SALEM
US ISSN 0739-5507
STATESMAN JOURNAL. 1851. d. $.50/day newsstand; $.40/day stores; $1.50/Sun.; $11.50/mo. carrier; $12.25/mo. motor rte. 280 Church St., N.E., Salem, OR 97301. TEL 503-399-6611; FAX 503-399-6706. **Owner(s):** Gannett Company, Inc., 1100 Wilson Blvd., Arlington, VA 22234. TEL 703-284-6000; Pub. Sara Bentley; adv. contact: Frank Bauer. pub. size: broadsheet; circ. morning 60,824(paid); Sun. 71,493(paid). **Wire Service(s):** AP, GNS, LAT-WP.

THE DALLES
US ISSN 0747-3443
THE DALLES DAILY CHRONICLE. 1890. Sun.-Fri. $.50 newsstand; $7/mo. carrier; $7.25/mo. mailed in cy. 414 Federal St., The Dalles, OR 97058. TEL 541-296-2141; FAX 541-298-1365. **Owner(s):** Eagle Newspapers, Inc., 4901 Indian School Rd., P.O. Box 12008, Salem, OR 97309. TEL 503-393-1774; Ed. Dan Spatz; Pub. Marilyn Roth; adv. contact: Skip Tschanz. pub. size: broadsheet; circ. evening 6,100(paid); Sun. 6,100(paid). **Wire Service(s):** AP.

PENNSYLVANIA

ALLENTOWN
US ISSN 0884-5557
MORNING CALL, THE. 1883. d. $.50/day newsstand; $1.75/Sun.; $3.80/wk. 101 N. Sixth St., Allentown, PA 18101. TEL 610-820-6695; FAX 610-770-3766. **Owner(s):** Times-Mirror Co., Times-Mirror Sq., Los Angeles, CA 90053. TEL 213-237-3700; Ed. Raymond Holton; Pub. Gary K. Shorts; adv. contact: Howard Renner. pub. size: broadsheet; circ. morning 131,628(paid); Sun. 186,733(paid). **Wire Service(s):** AP, NYT, LAT-WP, KNT.

ALTOONA
US
ALTOONA MIRROR. 1874. d. $.50/day newsstand; $1.50/Sun.; $108/yr. home deliv. 01 Cayuga Ave., Altoona, PA 16602. TEL 814-946-7411; FAX 814-946-7539. **Owner(s):** Thomson Newspapers, Inc., Metro Centre, One Station Pl., 6th Fl., Stamford, CT 06902. TEL 203-425-2500; Pub. Michael J. Miller; adv.; pub. size: broadsheet; circ. evening 36,292(paid); Sun. 40,997(paid). **Wire Service(s):** AP.

BEAVER
US
BEAVER COUNTY TIMES. 1876. d. $.50/day newsstand; $1.25/Sun.; $2.70/wk. home deliv. 400 Fair Ave., Beaver, PA 15009. TEL 412-775-3200; FAX 412-775-4180; E-mail: bingle@pgh.net; URL: http://www.pgh.net/beaver/. **Owner(s):** Calkins Newspapers, Inc., Levittown, PA 19058; Ed. Dennis D. Dible; Pub. F. Wallace Gordon; adv.; bk.rev.; pub. size: broadsheet; circ. morning 48,000(paid); Sun. 57,000(paid). **Wire Service(s):** AP, KR.

BEDFORD
US ISSN 0744-8457
BEDFORD GAZETTE/GAZETTE SUNDAY. 1805. d. $.35 newsstand; free/Sun. in cy.; $93.50/yr. 424 W. Penn St., Bedford, PA 15522. TEL 814-623-1151; FAX 814-623-5055. **Owner(s):** Edward K. Frear, 424 W. Penn St., Bedford, PA 15522. TEL 814-623-1151; Ed. Edward K. Frear; Pub. Edward K. Frear; adv. contact: Keith Landis. photos; bk.rev.; pub. size: broadsheet; circ. morning 10,145(paid); Sun. 19,100(controlled & free). **Wire Service(s):** AP.

BLOOMSBURG
US
PRESS ENTERPRISE, THE. 1903. d. $.50/day newsstand; $.75/Sat. & Sun.; $121.55/yr. carrier deliv. 3185 Lackawanna Ave., Bloomsburg, PA 17815. TEL 717-784-2121; FAX 717-784-9226. **Owner(s):** Press-Enterprise, Inc., 3185 Lackawanna Ave., Bloomsburg, PA 17815. TEL 717-784-2121; Ed. Dean Kashner; Pub. Paul R. Eyerly, III; adv. contact: Sandy Bower. photos; bk.rev.; pub. size: broadsheet; circ. morning 25,000(paid); Sun. 25,000(paid). **Wire Service(s):** AP, KNT.

BRADFORD
US
BRADFORD ERA, THE. 1877. Mon.-Sat. $.50 newsstand; $12/mo. carrier; $13/mo. motor rte. 43 Main St., Bradford, PA 16701. TEL 814-368-3173; FAX 814-362-6510. **Owner(s):** American Publishing Co., 606 N. Van Buren, Marion, IL 62959. TEL 618-993-1711; Ed. Marty R. Wilder. adv. contact: H.L. Woodruff. pub. size: broadsheet; circ. morning 13,500(paid). **Wire Service(s):** AP.

DAILY NEWSPAPERS

BUTLER
US
BUTLER EAGLE. 1869. Sun.-Fri. $.35/day newsstand; $.75/Sun.; $2.10/wk. 114 W. Diamond St., Butler, PA 16001. TEL 412-282-8000; FAX 412-282-1280. **Owner(s):** Eagle Printing Co., 114 W. Diamond, Butler, PA 16001. TEL 412-282-8000; Ed. Mark Mann; Pub. Vernon L. Wise, Jr.; adv. contact: Arthur Kephart. photos; pub. size: broadsheet; circ. evening 31,032(paid); Sun. 32,500(paid). **Wire Service(s):** AP, NYT.

CARLISLE
US
CARLISLE SENTINEL. 1861. d. $.50/day newsstand; $1/Sun.; $3/wk. 457 E. North St., Carlisle, PA 17013. TEL 717-243-2611; FAX 717-243-3121; E-mail: wanfried@epix.net; URL: http://www.1.trib.com/cumberlink/. **Owner(s):** Howard Publications, Inc., P.O. Box 570, Oceanside, CA 92049. TEL 619-433-5771; Ed. Kurt Wanfried; Pub. Wayne Powell; adv. contact: Steve Crowley. photos; pub. size: broadsheet; circ. evening 16,700(paid); Sun. 17,000(paid). **Wire Service(s):** AP.

CHAMBERSBURG
US
PUBLIC OPINION, THE. 1869. Mon.-Sat. $.35/day newsstand; $.75/Sat.; $2.50/wk. carrier; $25/2 mos. motor rte. & mailed. 77 N. Third St., Chambersburg, PA 17201. TEL 717-264-6161; FAX 717-264-0377. **Owner(s):** Gannett Company, Inc., 1100 Wilson Blvd., Arlington, VA 22234. TEL 703-284-6000; Pub. John W. Mason; adv.; photos; bk.rev.; pub. size: broadsheet; circ. evening 21,500(paid). **Wire Service(s):** AP, GNS, SHNA.

CLIFTON HEIGHTS
US
DELAWARE COUNTY DAILY-SUNDAY TIMES. 1876. Sun.-Fri. $.50/day newsstand; $1.25/Sun.; $3.30/wk. carrier. 500 Mildred Ave., Clifton Heights, PA 19018. TEL 610-622-8800; FAX 610-622-8829. **Owner(s):** Goodson Newspaper Group, Lawrenceville, NJ. TEL 609-895-2600; Ed. Linda DeMeglio; Pub. Frank Gothie; adv.; photos; bk.rev.; pub. size: tabloid; circ. morning 56,000(paid); Sun. 54,000(paid). **Wire Service(s):** AP.

CONNELLSVILLE
US
DAILY COURIER, THE. 1902. Mon.-Sat. $.35 newsstand; $1.80/wk. carrier; $2/wk. motor. rte.; $38.50/3 mos. in cy. mailed. 127 W. Apple St., Connellsville, PA 15425. TEL 412-628-2000; FAX 412-628-5270. **Owner(s):** Thomson Newspapers, Inc., Metro Centre, One Station Pl., 6th Fl., Stamford, CT 06902. TEL 203-425-2500; FAX 203-425-2516; Ed. Shawnee Culbertson. adv. contact: Nancy Henry. photos; bk.rev.; pub. size: broadsheet; circ. evening 12,000(paid). **Wire Service(s):** AP.

CORRY
US
CORRY JOURNAL. Mon.-Sat. $.40 newsstand; $9/mo. home deliv. 28 W. South St., Corry, PA 16407. TEL 814-665-8291; FAX 814-664-2288. **Owner(s):** American Publishing Co., 606 N. Van Buren, Marion, IL 62959. TEL 618-993-1711; Ed. Kevin Downey; Pub. George R. Sample; adv. contact: Linnell Ashby. pub. size: broadsheet; circ. evening 4,353(paid). **Wire Service(s):** AP photo.

DANVILLE
US
DANVILLE NEWS. 1897. Mon.-Sat. $.50 newsstand; $83.20/yr. carrier. 14 E. Mahoning St., Danville, PA 17821. TEL 717-275-3235; FAX 717-275-7624. **Owner(s):** Stauffer Media, Inc., 14 E Mahoning St., Danville, PA 17821; Ed. Holly Brandon. adv. contact: Donna Keefer. pub. size: broadsheet; circ. evening 4,300(paid). **Wire Service(s):** AP.

DOYLESTOWN
US
INTELLIGENCER/RECORD, THE. 1804. Sun-Fri. $.35/day newsstand; $1.50/Sun.; $3.20/wk. carrier; $3.75/wk. motor rte. 333 N. Broad St., Doylestown, PA 18901. TEL 215-345-3000; FAX 215-345-3150. **Owner(s):** Calkins Newspapers, Inc., Rte. 13, Levittown, PA. TEL 215-949-4000; Ed. Joan Bastel; Pub. Charles P. Smith; adv. contact: Rosemary Rocconi. pub. size: broadsheet; circ. morning 45,107(paid); Sun. 50,116(paid). **Wire Service(s):** AP.
Formerly: Doylestown Daily Intelligencer.

DU BOIS
US ISSN 8750-4049
COURIER-EXPRESS. 1879. Sun.-Fri. $.50/day newsstand; $1/Sun.; $102/yr. mailed. 500 Jeffers St., Du Bois, PA 15801-0407. TEL 814-371-4200; FAX 814-371-3241; E-mail: courierexpress@penn.com. **Owner(s):** Independent Publications, Inc., 945 Haverford Rd., Bryn Mawr, PA 19010. TEL 215-527-6330; Ed. Dennis Bonavita; Pub. W. Dock Lias; adv. contact: Linda Smith. photos; pub. size: broadsheet; circ. evening 10,180(paid); Sun. 14,116(paid). **Wire Service(s):** AP, SHNS.

EASTON
US ISSN 1062-3620
EXPRESS-TIMES, THE. 1855. d. $.35/day newsstand; $1/Sun.; $3.10/wk. 30 N. Fourth St., Easton, PA 18042. TEL 610-258-7171; FAX 610-258-7130; E-mail: staff@express-times.com; URL: http://www.express-times.com. **Owner(s):** Media News Group, 4888 Loop Central Dr., Ste. 525, Houston, TX 77081. TEL 713-295-3800; Ed. Joe Owens; Pub. Timothy W. Sowecke; adv. contact: Ernie Reed. pub. size: broadsheet; circ. morning 53,000(paid); Sun. 50,000(paid). **Wire Service(s):** AP, LAT-WP, KR.
Formerly: Express, The.

ELLWOOD CITY
US
ELLWOOD CITY LEDGER. 1920. Mon.-Sat. $.35 newsstand; $1.70/wk. 835 Lawrence Ave., Ellwood City, PA 16117. TEL 412-758-7529. **Owner(s):** Citizens Publishing & Printing Co., P.O. Box 471, Ellwood City, PA 16117. TEL 412-758-5573; Pub. W.R. Kegel; adv. contact: Dom A. Viccari. pub. size: broadsheet; circ. evening 7,300(paid). **Wire Service(s):** AP.

ERIE
US
ERIE DAILY TIMES/SUNDAY TIMES NEWS. 1888. d. $.35/day newsstand; $1.50/Sun. 205 W. 12th St., Erie, PA 16534. TEL 814-870-1600; FAX 814-870-1808. **Owner(s):** Times Publishing Co., 205 W. 12th St., Erie, PA 16534. TEL 814-870-1600; Ed. Jeff Pinski. adv. contact: John Andersen. pub. size: standard; circ. evening 38,585(paid); Sun. 102,298. **Wire Service(s):** AP, KNT, LAT-WP.
Formerly: Daily Times.

US
ERIE MORNING NEWS. 1957. d. $.35/day newsstand; $1.50/Sun.; $78/yr. 205 W. 12th St., Erie, PA 16534. TEL 814-870-1600; FAX 814-870-1808; E-mail: mgmead@ncinter.net; URL: http://www.timesnews.com. **Owner(s):** Times Publishing Co., 205 W. 12th St., Erie, PA 16534. TEL 814-870-1600; Ed. Jeff Pinski; Pub. Michael Mead; adv. contact: John Anderson. photos; pub. size: broadsheet; circ. morning 32,855(paid). **Wire Service(s):** AP, LAT.

GETTYSBURG
US
GETTYSBURG TIMES. 1902. Mon.-Sat. $.35/day newsstand; $72/yr. 1570 Fairfield Rd., Gettysburg, PA 17325. TEL 717-334-1131; FAX 717-334-4243; E-mail: times@cvn.net; URL: http://www1.visitgettysburg.com. **Owner(s):** Times & News Publishing Co., 1570 Fairfield Rd., Gettysburg, PA 17325. TEL 717-334-1131; FAX 717-334-4243; Ed. B.J. Small; Pub. Cynthia Ford; adv.; pub. size: broadsheet; circ. morning 10,000(paid). **Wire Service(s):** AP, SHNA.

GREENSBURG
US
STANDARD-OBSERVER. 1972. Mon.-Sat. $.35 newsstand; $62.40/yr. in state. R.D. 1, Rte. 136, Greensburg, PA 15601. TEL 412-863-3601; FAX 412-523-6805; E-mail: stdobsc@aol.com. **Owner(s):** T-R Printing & Publishing Co., P. O. Box 280, Irwin, PA 15642. TEL 412-863-3601; adv. contact: Dawn Iezzi. pub. size: broadsheet; circ. evening 16,500. **Wire Service(s):** AP.
Formerly: Irwin Standard-Observer.

US
TRIBUNE-REVIEW. 1889. d. $.35/day newsstand; $2.50/wk. 622 Cabin Hill Dr., Greensburg, PA 15601-1692. TEL 412-834-1151. E-mail: letters@tribune-review.com; Url:http://www.tribune-review.com. **Owner(s):** Tribune-Review Publishing Co., P.O. Box 622, Greensburg, PA 15601. TEL 412-834-1151; Pub. Richard M. Scaife; adv.; photos; bk.rev.; pub. size: broadsheet; circ. morning 80,000(paid); Sun. 142,000(paid). **Wire Service(s):** AP, LAT-WP, RN.

GREENVILLE
US
GREENVILLE RECORD-ARGUS. 1848. Mon.-Sat. $.35 newsstand; $88.20/yr. 10 Penn Ave., Greenville, PA 16125. TEL 412-588-5000; FAX 412-588-4691. **Owner(s):** Greenville Newspapers, Inc., P.O. Box 711, Greenville, PA 16125. TEL 412-588-5000; Ed. Betsy Fontaine; Pub. Robert N. Bracey; adv. contact: Steve Gargasz. photos; pub. size: standard; circ. morning 5,400(paid). **Wire Service(s):** AP News, AP laserphoto.

HANOVER
US
EVENING SUN. 1915. d. $.35/day newsstand; $1/Sun.; $2.50/wk. 135 Baltimore St., Hanover, PA 17331. TEL 717-637-3736; FAX 717-637-7730; E-mail: esunl@sun-link.com; URL: http://www.sun-link.com. **Owner(s):** Garden State Newspapers, Inc.; Ed. Stan Hough; Pub. William Burgess; pub. size: broadsheet; circ. evening 21,200(paid); Sun. 21,000(paid). **Wire Service(s):** AP.
Formerly: Hanover Sun.

HARRISBURG
US ISSN 0887-7939
PATRIOT-NEWS. 1854. d. $.50/day newsstand; $1.75/Sun.; $.30/day deliv.; $121.68/yr. 812 Market St., Harrisburg, PA 17101. TEL 717-255-8100; FAX 717-255-8221. **Owner(s):** Advance Publications, Inc., 950 Fingerboard Rd., Staten Island, NY 10305. TEL 718-981-1234; FAX 718-981-1456; Ed. Tom Baden; Pub. Raymond L. Gover; adv. contact: James Stephanak. bk.rev.; pub. size: broadsheet; circ. morning 105,594(paid); Sun. 177,329(paid). **Wire Service(s):** AP, NNS, NYT, LAT-WP, BS, KR.
Formerly: Patriot & Evening News.

HAZLETON
US
HAZLETON STANDARD SPEAKER. 1866. d. $.50 newsstand; $10/mo.; $25/3 mos. 21 N. Wyoming, Hazleton, PA 18201-0578. TEL 717-455-3636; FAX 717-455-4244. **Owner(s):** Hazleton Standard-Speaker, Inc., 21 N. Wyoming St., Hazleton, PA 18201. TEL 717-455-3636; Ed. Ramon Saul; Pub. Paul N. Walser; adv. contact: Gary Yacubek. pub. size: broadsheet; circ. morning 24,000(paid); Sun. 24,000(paid). **Wire Service(s):** AP, CNS.

HONESDALE
US
WAYNE INDEPENDENT, THE. 1878. Tue.-Sat. $.50 newsstand; $120/yr. mailed. 220 Eighth St., Honesdale, PA 18431. TEL 717-253-3055; FAX 717-253-5387. **Owner(s):** American Publishing Co., 606 N. Van Buren, Marion, IL 62959. TEL 618-993-1711; Ed. Paul Quigley; Pub. Donald Doyle; adv. contact: Michelle Hessling. pub. size: broadsheet; circ. evening 6,198(paid). **Wire Service(s):** AP.

HORSHAM
US
RECORD, THE. Sun.-Fri. $.35/day newsstand; $1.40/Sun.; $197/yr. mailed. 145 Easton Rd., Horsham, PA 19044. TEL 215-957-8100; FAX 215-957-8165; E-mail: 75703.3217@compuserve.com. **Owner(s):** Calkins Newspapers, Inc., 8400 Rt. 13, Levittown, PA 19057. TEL 215-949-4000; Ed. Joan Bastel. adv. contact: Rosemary Rocconi. pub. size: broadsheet; circ. morning 45,000(paid); Sun. 50,000(paid).
Formerly: Intelligencer-Record Newspaper.

HUNTINGDON
US
DAILY NEWS. Mon.-Sat. $.50 newsstand; $110/yr. 325 Penn St., Huntingdon, PA 16652. TEL 814-643-4040; FAX 814-643-0376. **Owner(s):** Joseph F. Biddle Publishing Co., Inc., P.O. Box 384, Huntingdon, PA 16652. TEL 814-643-4040; Ed. James D. Hunt; Pub. George Sample, III; adv. contact: Carol Cutshall. pub. size: broadsheet; circ. evening 10,600(paid). **Wire Service(s):** UPI.
Formerly: Huntingdon Daily News.

INDIANA
US
INDIANA GAZETTE. 1890. d. $.50/day newsstand; $1/Sun.; $132.95/yr. carrier. 899 Water St., Indiana, PA 15701. TEL 412-465-5555; FAX 412-349-4550. **Owner(s):** Indiana Printing & Publishing Co., P.O. Box 10, Indiana, PA 15201. TEL 412-465-5555; Ed. Carl Kologie. adv. contact: Carol Harkleroad. photos; bk.rev.; pub. size: standard; circ. evening 20,000(paid); Sun. 10,000(paid). **Wire Service(s):** AP, NYT.

JOHNSTOWN
US
TRIBUNE-DEMOCRAT, THE. 1853. d. $.50/day newsstand; $1.25/Sun. 425 Locust St., Johnstown, PA 15907. TEL 814-532-5050; FAX 814-539-1409. **Owner(s):** Johnstown Tribune Publishing Co., 425 Locust St., Johnston, PA 15907-0340. TEL 814-532-5050; Ed. Larry Hudson; Pub. Pamela J. Mayer; photos; bk.rev.; pub. size: broadsheet; circ. morning 51,581(paid); Sun. 53,799(paid). **Wire Service(s):** AP, KR, GNS.

KANE
US
KANE REPUBLICAN. 1894. Mon.-Sat. $.50 newsstand; $11/mo. carrier; $11.50/mo. motor rte. 200 N. Fraley St., Kane, PA 16735. TEL 814-837-6000; FAX 814-837-2227. **Owner(s):** American Publishing Co., 606 N. Van Buren, Marion, IL 62959. TEL 618-993-1711; Pub. Kay Pearson. adv. contact: Kay Pearson. photos; bk.rev.; pub. size: broadsheet; circ. evening 2,544(paid). **Wire Service(s):** AP.

KITTANNING
US
LEADER TIMES. 1898. Mon.-Sat. $.35 newsstand; $1.75/wk. carrier; $1.90/wk. motor rte.; $82.25/yr. carrier; $89.50/yr. motor rte.; $127.40/yr. 115 N. Grant Ave., Kittanning, PA 16201. TEL 412-543-1303; FAX 412-545-6768. **Owner(s):** Thomson Newspapers, Inc., Metro Centre, One Station Pl., 6th Fl., Stamford, CT 06902. TEL 203-425-2500; FAX 203-425-2516; Ed. Michael O'Hare; Pub. Kristy Green; adv. contact: Barbara Sheasley. photos; pub. size: broadsheet; circ. evening 12,000(paid). **Wire Service(s):** AP.
Formerly: Kittanning Leader Times.

LANCASTER
US
INTELLIGENCER JOURNAL. Mon.-Sat. $.50 newsstand. 8 W. King St., Lancaster, PA 17608. TEL 717-291-8811; FAX 717-399-6506; E-mail: intelj@lancnewsinfi.net. **Owner(s):** Lancaster Newspapers, Inc., 8 King St., Lancaster, PA 17608. TEL 717-291-8811; Ed. Ray Shaw. adv.; pub. size: broadsheet; circ. morning 43,000(paid). **Wire Service(s):** AP, NYT, KR.

US
LANCASTER INTELLIGENCER JOURNAL. 1794. Mon.-Sat. $.50 newsstand; $104.20/yr. 8 W. King St., Lancaster, PA 17608-8622. TEL 717-291-8811; FAX 717-399-6507. **Owner(s):** Lancaster Newspapers, Inc., 8 W. King St., Lancaster, PA 17603. TEL 717-291-8811; Ed. William H. Cody. adv. contact: Harold E. Miller. photos; pub. size: broadsheet; circ. morning 45,000(paid). **Wire Service(s):** AP, NYT, States News Service, Med. Tribune Service.

US
LANCASTER NEW ERA. 1877. Mon.-Sat. $.50/day newsstand; $31.20/3 mos. home deliv. 8 W. King St., Lancaster, PA 17603. TEL 717-291-8600; FAX 717-399-6506; E-mail: newera@lancnews.infi.net; URL: http://www.lancnews.com. **Owner(s):** Lancaster Newspapers, Inc., 8 W. King St., Lancaster, PA 17603. TEL 717-291-8600; Ed. Robert J. Kozak. adv. contact: Harold Miller. pub. size: broadsheet; circ. evening 51,283(paid). **Wire Service(s):** AP, NYT, KR.
Formerly: New Era.

LANSDALE
US ISSN 0890-8443
REPORTER, THE. 1870. Mon.-Sat. $.35 newsstand; $2.50/wk. 307 Derstine Ave., Lansdale, PA 19446. TEL 215-855-8440; FAX 215-368-5367. **Owner(s):** Gannett Company, Inc., 1100 Wilson Blvd., Arlington, VA 22209. TEL 703-284-6000; Ed. Barbara Delp; Pub. Suzanne Bush; adv. contact: Tom Geonnotti. photos; pub. size: broadsheet; circ. evening 114,276(paid). **Wire Service(s):** AP, GNS.

LATROBE
US
LATROBE BULLETIN. 1902. Mon.-Sat. $.25 newsstand; $5.75/mo.; $6/mo. out of cy. 1211 Ligonier St., Latrobe, PA 15650-0111. TEL 412-537-3351; FAX 412-537-0489. **Owner(s):** Latrobe Printing & Publishing Co., 1211 Ligonier St., Latrobe, PA 15650. TEL 412-537-3351; Ed. Marie McCandless. adv. contact: Ken Seremet. pub. size: broadsheet; circ. evening 10,000(paid). **Wire Service(s):** AP.

DAILY NEWSPAPERS

LEBANON
US
LEBANON DAILY NEWS. 1872. d. $.50/day newsstand; $1.50/Sun.; $160.55/yr. carrier. 718 Poplar St., Lebanon, PA 17042. TEL 717-272-5611; FAX 717-274-1608; E-mail: lebnews@leba.net; URL: http://www.leba.net/lebnews. **Owner(s):** Media News Group, 4888 Loop Central Dr., Ste. 525, Houston, TX 77081. TEL 713-295-3800; Ed. Andy Mick; Pub. Blake Sanderson; adv. contact: Karen Williams. photos; pub. size: broadsheet; circ. evening 24,088(paid); Sun. 22,962(paid). **Wire Service(s):** UPI.

LEHIGHTON
US
TIMES NEWS. 1883. Mon.-Sat. $.50 newsstand; $8.75/mo. First & Iron Sts., Lehighton, PA 18235-0239. TEL 610-377-2051; FAX 610-377-5800; E-mail: tnonline@postoffice.ptd.net; URL: http://www.tnonline.com. **Owner(s):** Times News, Inc., 471 Delaware Ave., Palmerton, PA 18071. TEL 610-826-2115; Ed. Bob Urban. adv. contact: Don Reese. photos; pub. size: broadsheet; circ. evening 16,200(paid). **Wire Service(s):** AP.
Formerly: Lehighton Times News.

LEVITTOWN
US
BUCKS COUNTY COURIER TIMES. 1910. Sun.-Fri. $.35/day newsstand; $1.50/Sun.; $3/wk. 8400 Rte. 13, Levittown, PA 19057. TEL 215-949-4010; FAX 215-949-4177. **Owner(s):** Courier Times, Inc., 8400 Rte. 13, Levittown, PA 19057. TEL 215-949-4010; Pub. Arthur E. Mayhew; adv. contact: Tim Birch. photos; pub. size: broadsheet; circ. morning 70,000(paid); Sun. 77,000(paid). **Wire Service(s):** AP.
Formerly: Levittown Bucks County Courier Times.

LEWISTOWN
US
SENTINEL, THE. 1903. Mon.-Sat. $.50 newsstand; $105/yr. carrier. 375 Sixth St., Lewistown, PA 17044. TEL 717-248-6741; FAX 717-248-3481. **Owner(s):** Ogden Newspapers, Inc., 1500 Main St., Wheeling, WV 26003. TEL 304-233-0100; Ed. Brad Siddons; Pub. Bart Leath; adv. contact: Diane Brown. pub. size: broadsheet; circ. 13,000(paid). **Wire Service(s):** AP.
Formerly: Lewistown Sentinel.

LOCK HAVEN
US
EXPRESS. 1882. Mon.-Sat. $.35 newsstand; $1.95/wk. carrier. 9-11 W. Main St., Lock Haven, PA 17745-6791. TEL 717-748-6791; FAX 717-748-1544; E-mail: express@oak.kcsd.k12.pa.us; URL: http://oak.kcsd.k12.pa.us/~express. **Owner(s):** Ogden Newspapers, Inc., 1500 Main St., Wheeling, WV 26033. TEL 304-233-0100; Ed. Robert Sealy; Pub. Charles R. Ryan; adv. contact: Richard Noll. pub. size: broadsheet; circ. evening 11,200(paid). **Wire Service(s):** AP.

MCKEESPORT
US
MCKEESPORT DAILY NEWS. 1884. Mon.-Sat. $.35 newsstand. 409 Walnut St., McKeesport, PA 15132-2613. TEL 412-664-9161; FAX 412-664-3972. **Owner(s):** Daily News Publishing Co., 409 Walnut St., McKeesport, PA 15132. TEL 412-664-9161; FAX 412-664-3972; Ed. Pam Reinsel Cotter; Pub. Patricia M. Miles; adv.; photos; bk.rev.; pub. size: standard; circ. evening 33,000(paid). **Wire Service(s):** AP, LAT-WP.

MEADVILLE
US ISSN 0747-2412
MEADVILLE TRIBUNE, THE. 1884. d. $.35 newsstand; $2.15/wk. 947 Federal Ct., Meadville, PA 16335. TEL 814-724-6370; FAX 814-724-8755. **Owner(s):** Thomson Newspapers, Inc., Metro Centre, One Station Pl., 6th Fl., Stamnford, CT 06902. TEL 203-425-2500; Ed. Hope Stephan; Pub. Jeanne Moore-Yount; adv. contact: Mark Yocum. photos; pub. size: broadsheet; circ. morning 16,600(paid). **Wire Service(s):** AP, SHNA, Thomson News Service.

MILTON
US ISSN 0895-4232
LEWISBURG DAILY JOURNAL. 1906. Mon.-Sat. $.50 newsstand; $1.95/wk.; $93.60/yr. carrier. 21 Arch St., Milton, PA 17847. TEL 717-523-1268; FAX 717-742-9876. **Owner(s):** American Publishing Co., 606 N. Van Buren, Marion, IL 62959. TEL 618-993-1711; Ed. Troy Sellers. adv. contact: Amy Moyer. pub. size: standard; circ. morning 11,300(paid).

US
MILTON DAILY STANDARD. 1890. Mon.-Sat. $.50 newsstand; $1.95/wk.; $93.60/yr. carrier. 21 Arch St., Milton, PA 17847. TEL 717-742-9671; FAX 717-742-9876. **Owner(s):** American Publishing Co., 606 N. Van Buren, Marion, IL 62959. TEL 618-993-1711; Ed. Troy Sellers. adv.; photos; pub. size: broadsheet; circ. evening 2,987(paid). **Wire Service(s):** AP.

MONESSEN
US
VALLEY INDEPENDENT. 1901. Mon.-Sat. $.50 newsstand; $2.45/wk.; $11.05/mo. motor rte. Eastgate 19, Monessen, PA 15062. TEL 412-684-5200; FAX 412-684-8104. **Owner(s):** Thomson Newspapers, Inc., Metro Centre, One Station Pl., 6th Fl., Stamford, CT 06902. TEL 203-425-2500; FAX 203-425-2516; Ed. J. Frank Jawordwski; Pub. Barbara Raitano; adv. contact: John Bennati. pub. size: standard; circ. evening 17,300(paid). **Wire Service(s):** AP.
Formerly: Monessen Valley Independent.

MOON TOWNSHIP
US
ALLEGHENY TIMES. 1986. Sun.-Fri. $.50/day newsstand; $1.25/Sun. 894 Beavergrade Rd., Moon Township, PA 15108. TEL 412-269-1144; FAX 412-269-1151. **Owner(s):** Calkins Newspapers, Inc., Rte. 13, Levittown, PA. TEL 215-949-4000; Ed. Dennis Dible; Pub. F. Wallace Gordon; pub. size: broadsheet; circ. morning 3,500(paid); Sun. 3,500(paid).

NEW CASTLE
US
NEW CASTLE NEWS. 1880. Mon.-Sat. $.35/day newsstand; $.50/Sat.; $2.20/wk. carrier. 27 N. Mercer St., New Castle, PA 16101. TEL 412-654-6651; FAX 412-654-9593. **Owner(s):** Thomson Newspapers, Inc., Metro Centre, One Station Pl., Stamford, CT 06902. TEL 203-425-2500; FAX 203-425-2516; Ed. Tim Kolodziej; Pub. Max Thomson; adv. contact: Chris D'Angelo. photos; pub. size: broadsheet; circ. evening 22,700(paid). **Wire Service(s):** UPI.

NORRISTOWN
US
TIMES HERALD, THE. 1799. d. $.50/day newsstand; $1.25/Sun. $3.15/wk. 410 Markley St., Norristown, PA 19401. TEL 610-272-2500; FAX 610-272-4003. **Owner(s):** Journal Register Co., 50 W. State St., 12th Fl., Trenton, NJ 08608. TEL 609-396-2200; Ed. Dave Gilmartin; Pub. Geoffrey L. Moser; adv.; photos; bk.rev.; pub. size: broadsheet; circ. morning 26,041; Sun. 22,512(paid). **Wire Service(s):** AP, SHNA.
Formerly: Norristown Times Herald.

OIL CITY
US
DERRICK, THE. 1871. Mon.-Sat. $.50 newsstand; $9/mo. carrier; $11/mo. mailed. 1510 W. First St., Oil City, PA 16301. TEL 814-676-7444; FAX 814-676-7444. **Owner(s):** P.C. Boyle, P.O. Box 928, Oil City, PA 16301. TEL 814-676-7444; Ed. Glen Monkern; Pub. P.C. Boyle; adv. contact: Ned Cowart. pub. size: broadsheet; circ. morning 18,732(paid).

US
NEWS-HERALD. 1878. Mon.-Sat. $.50 newsstand; $9.95/4 wks. 1510 W. First St., Oil City, PA 16301. TEL 814-676-7444; FAX 814-677-8347. **Owner(s):** P.C. Boyle, P.O. Box 928, Oil City, PA 16301. TEL 814-676-7444; Ed. James Davis; Pub. P.C. Boyle; adv. contact: Ned Cowart. photos; pub. size: broadsheet; circ. morning 9,000(paid). **Wire Service(s):** AP.
Formerly: Franklin News-Herald.

PHILADELPHIA
US
PHILADELPHIA DAILY NEWS. 1925. Mon.-Sat. $.60 newsstand; $3.60/wk. home deliv. 400 N. Broad St., Philadelphia, PA 19130. TEL 215-854-5900; FAX 215-854-5910; E-mail: dailynews.opinion@phillynews.com; URL: http://www.phillynews.com/. **Owner(s):** Philadelphia Newspapers, Inc., 400 N. Broad St., Philadelphia, PA 19130; Ed. Brian Toolan; Pub. Robert Hall; adv. contact: Mireille Grangenois. pub. size: tabloid; circ. evening 200,000(paid). **Wire Service(s):** KNS, AP, RN.

US ISSN 0885-6613
PHILADELPHIA INQUIRER. 1969. d. $.50/day newsstand; $1.50/Sun.; $4.30/wk. home deliv. 400 N. Broad St., Philadelphia, PA 19130. TEL 215-854-2000; FAX 215-854-5553; E-mail: inquirer@phillynews.com; URL: http://www.phillynews.com/. **Owner(s):** Knight-Ridder, Inc., One Herald Plz., Miami, FL 33132. TEL 305-376-3800; FAX 305-376-3875; Ed. Max King; Pub. Robert Hall; adv. contact: Kathy McKenna. pub. size: broadsheet; circ. morning 446,842(paid); Sun. 901,891(paid). **Wire Service(s):** AP, KNS, LAT-WP.

PHOENIXVILLE
US
PHOENIX, THE. 1888. Mon.-Sat. $.35 newsstand; $2/wk. 225 Bridge St., Phoenixville, PA 19460. TEL 610-933-8926; FAX 610-933-1187. **Owner(s):** Journal Register Co., 50 W. State St., 12th Fl., Trenton, NJ 08608. TEL 609-396-2200; Ed. Lynn Vanderberg; Pub. Chad Beatty; adv. contact: Craig Schwartz. pub. size: broadsheet; circ. evening 7,000(paid); Sun. 7,000(paid). **Wire Service(s):** AP.

PITTSBURGH
US
PITTSBURGH POST-GAZETTE. 1786. d. $.50/day newsstand; $1.50/Sun.; $3/wk. carrier. 34 Blvd. of the Allies, Pittsburgh, PA 15222. TEL 412-263-1100; FAX 412-391-8452. **Owner(s):** William Block, Sr., 541 N. Superior St., Toledo, OH 43660. TEL 419-245-6000; Ed. Madelyn Ross. adv. contact: Robert D. McCray. photos; bk.rev.; pub. size: broadsheet; circ. morning 244,204(paid); Sun. 432,581(paid). **Wire Service(s):** AP, NYT, RN.

POTTSTOWN
US
MERCURY, THE. 1931. d. $.50/day newsstand; $1/Sun. King & Hanover Sts., Pottstown, PA 19464. TEL 610-323-3000; FAX 610-970-4492. **Owner(s):** Peerless Publications, King & Hanover Sts., Pottstown, PA 19464. TEL 610-323-3000; Ed. Andy Hachadorian; Pub. Barry Hopwood; adv. contact: Dennis Pfeiffer. photos; bk.rev.; pub. size: broadsheet; circ. morning 30,000(paid); Sun. 30,000(paid). **Wire Service(s):** AP.

POTTSVILLE
US
POTTSVILLE REPUBLICAN & EVENING HERALD. 1884. Mon.-Sat. (Sat./Sun. combined). $.50/day newsstand; $.75/Sat.; $11/mo. 111-117 Mahantongo St., Pottsville, PA 17901. TEL 717-622-3456; FAX 717-628-6092; E-mail: jkane@pottsville.infi.net; URL: http://www.pottsville.com. **Owner(s):** J.H. Zerbey Newspapers, Inc., 111-117 Mahantongo St., P.O. Box 209, Pottsville, PA 17901. TEL 717-628-6092; Ed. James B. Kane; Pub. Uzal H. Martz, Jr.; adv. contact: Henry H. Nyce. photos; bk.rev.; pub. size: broadsheet; circ. evening 34,500(paid). **Wire Service(s):** AP.

PUNXSUTAWNEY
US
PUNXSUTAWNEY SPIRIT. 1873. Mon.-Sat. $.35 newsstand; $9.50/mo. 510 Pine St., Punxsutawney, PA 15767. TEL 814-938-8740; FAX 814-938-3794. **Owner(s):** American Publishing Co., 606 N. Van Buren, Marion, IL 62959. TEL 618-993-1711; Ed. Wick Divelbiss; Pub. William C. Anderson; adv. contact: Mary Roberts. pub. size: broadsheet; circ. morning 6,600(paid). **Wire Service(s):** AP.

READING
US
READING EAGLE & READING TIMES. 1868. d. $.50 newsstand; $124.80/yr. home deliv.; $78/yr. Sun. only. 345 Penn St., Reading, PA 19601. TEL 215-371-5000; FAX 215-371-5098. **Owner(s):** Reading Eagle Co., 345 Penn St., Reading, PA 19601. TEL 215-371-5000; Ed. Charles M. Gallagher; Pub. William S. Flippin; adv. contact: Walter Woolwine. photos; bk.rev.; pub. size: broadsheet; circ. morning 48,222(paid); evening 21,109(paid); Sun. 103,330(paid). **Wire Service(s):** AP, CNS, KNT, NEA, RN, SHNA.

RIDGWAY
US
RIDGWAY RECORD. 1892. Mon.-Sat. $.50 newsstand; $128/yr. in cy. mailed; $134/yr. out of cy. mailed. 20 Main St., Ridgway, PA 15853-1718. TEL 814-773-3161; FAX 814-776-1086. **Owner(s):** American Publishing Co., 606 N. Van Buren, Marion, IL 62959. TEL 618-993-1711; Ed. Bekki Guildyard; Pub. Joseph C. Piccirillo; adv. contact: Susan Klase. pub. size: broadsheet; circ. evening 3,295(paid). **Wire Service(s):** AP.

SAYRE
US ISSN 0746-4843
EVENING TIMES. 1891. Mon.-Sat. $.50 newsstand; $10/mo. carrier; $11.50/mo. mailed. 201 N. Lehigh Ave., Sayre, PA 18840. TEL 717-888-9643; FAX 717-888-6463. **Owner(s):** American Publishing Co., 606 N. Van Buren, Marion, IL 62959. TEL 618-993-1711; Ed. Steve Piatt; Pub. Ted Mike, Jr.; adv. contact: Vickee Mike. pub. size: broadsheet; circ. evening 9,000(paid). **Wire Service(s):** AP.

SCRANTON
US ISSN 1062-5844
SCRANTON TIMES/SUNDAY TIMES. 1990. d. $.35/day newsstand; $1.50/Sun.; $158.60/yr. 149 Penn Ave. & Spruce St., Scranton, PA 18503. TEL 717-348-9100; FAX 717-348-9135. **Owner(s):** Edward J. Lynett, Jr., P.O. Box 3311, Scranton, PA 18505. TEL 717-348-9100; Ed. Edward J. Lynett, Jr.; Pub. Edward J. Lynett, Jr.; adv. contact: Steve Sauder. photos; pub. size: broadsheet; circ. morning 31,500(paid); evening 40,500(paid); Sun. 86,000(paid). **Wire Service(s):** AP, NYT, KNT.

US
TRIBUNE, THE/SUNDAY TIMES. 1870. d. $.40/day newsstand; $1.50/Sun.; $42.90/13 wks. in city; $44.20/13 wks. motor rte. 149 Penn Ave., Scranton, PA 18505. TEL 717-348-9100; FAX 717-348-9145. **Owner(s):** George V., William R., Edward J., Jr., Lynett, 149 Penn Ave., Scranton, PA 18503. TEL 717-348-9100; Ed. Robert Burke; Pub. Edward J. Lynett, Jr.; adv. contact: Steve Sauder. pub. size: broadsheet; circ. morning 31,200(paid). **Wire Service(s):** AP, NYT, KNT.

SHAMOKIN
US
NEWS-ITEM. 1970. Mon.-Sat. $.50 newsstand; $2.20/wk. carrier. 707 N. Rock St., Shamokin, PA 17872. TEL 717-648-4641; FAX 717-644-0892. **Owner(s):** Scranton Times, 149 Penn Ave., Scranton, PA 18503. TEL 717-348-9101; Ed. M. Philip Yucha. adv. contact: Barbara Freeman. photos; bk.rev.; pub. size: broadsheet; circ. evening 12,655(paid). **Wire Service(s):** AP.

SHARON
US ISSN 0744-7302
HERALD, THE. 1864. d. $.50/day newsstand; $.75/Sun.; $2.15/wk. carrier; $2.25/wk. motor rte. 52 S. Dock St., Sharon, PA 16146. TEL 412-981-6100; FAX 412-981-5116; E-mail: zavinski@pgh.net; URL: http://www.sharon-herald.com. **Owner(s):** Ottaway Newspapers, Inc., P.O. Box 401, Campbell Hall, NY 10916. TEL 914-294-8181; Ed. James A. Raykie, Jr.; Pub. John L. Lima; adv.; bk.rev.; pub. size: broadsheet; circ. evening 25,347(paid); Sun. 24,766(paid). **Wire Service(s):** AP, SHNA.
Formerly: The Sharon Herald.

SOMERSET
US
DAILY AMERICAN. 1929. Mon.-Sat. $.35/day newsstand; $.50/Sat.; $27/3 mos.; $52/6 mos.; $100/yr. 334 W. Main St., Somerset, PA 15501. TEL 814-445-9621; FAX 814-445-2935. **Owner(s):** Somerset Newspapers, Inc., 334 W. Main St., Somerset, PA 15501. TEL 814-445-9621; Ed. James Oliver; Pub. David H. Reiley; adv. contact: Tom Koppenhofer. photos; pub. size: broadsheet; circ. morning 13,605(paid). **Wire Service(s):** AP.

STATE COLLEGE
US
CENTRE DAILY TIMES. 1898. d. $.50/day newsstand; $1.25/Sun. 3400 E. College Ave., State College, PA 16801. TEL 814-238-5000; FAX 814-237-5966. **Owner(s):** Knight-Ridder, Inc., One Herald Plz., Miami, FL 33132. TEL 305-376-3800; Pub. Lou Heldman; adv. contact: Mark Mateer. photos; bk.rev.; pub. size: broadsheet; circ. morning 26,561(paid); Sun. 34,695(paid). **Wire Service(s):** AP, KR, LAT-WP.

ST. MARYS
US
DAILY PRESS, THE. 1910. Mon.-Sat. $.50 newsstand; $128/yr. 245 Brussells St., St. Marys, PA 15857-0353. TEL 814-781-1596; FAX 814-834-7473. **Owner(s):** American Publishing Co., 606 N. Van Buren, Marion, IL 62959. TEL 618-993-1711; Ed. Wayne Bauer; Pub. Val Mahaney; adv. contact: Grace Cutalano. photos; pub. size: broadsheet; circ. evening 5,456(free & paid). **Wire Service(s):** AP.

DAILY NEWSPAPERS

STROUDSBURG
US
POCONO RECORD. 1894. d. $.50/day newsstand; $1.50/Sun., $156.75/yr. carrier; $166.30/yr. motor rte. 511 Lenox St., Stroudsburg, PA 18360. TEL 717-421-3000; FAX 717-424-2625. **Owner(s):** Ottaway Newspapers, Inc., P.O. Box 401, Campbell Hall, NY 10916. TEL 914-294-8181; Ed. William Kline; Pub. Carolynn Allen-Evans; adv.: $13.83/SAU daily; $16.04/SAU Sun. pub. size: broadsheet; circ. morning 22,000(paid); Sun. 26,000(paid). **Wire Service(s):** AP.

SUNBURY
US
DAILY ITEM, THE. 1937. d. $.50/day newsstand; $1.50/Sun.; $135/yr. 200 Market St., Sunbury, PA 17801. TEL 717-286-5671; FAX 717-286-2570. **Owner(s):** Ottaway Newspapers, Inc., P.O. Box 401, Campbell Hall, NY 10916. TEL 914-294-8181; Ed. Leonard Ingrassia; Pub. Donald P. Micozzi; adv. contact: Martin Hughes. photos; pub. size: broadsheet; circ. evening 25,672(paid); Sun. 28,750(paid). **Wire Service(s):** LAT-WP, AP, ONS.

TARENTUM
US
VALLEY NEWS DISPATCH. 1891. d. $.50/day newsstand; $1/Sun.; $3/wk. 210 Fourth Ave., Tarentum, PA 15084. TEL 412-224-4321; FAX 412-226-7787. **Owner(s):** Gannett Company, Inc., 1100 Wilson Blvd., Arlington, VA 22234. TEL 703-284-6000; Pub. Lawrence J. Jock, Jr.; adv. contact: Randy Mooney. pub. size: broadsheet; circ. evening 35,000(paid). **Wire Service(s):** AP, GNS.

TITUSVILLE
US
TITUSVILLE HERALD. 1865. Mon.-Sat. $.50 newsstand; $9.76/mo. carrier & motor rte. 209 W. Spring St., Titusville, PA 16354. TEL 814-827-3634; FAX 814-827-2512. **Owner(s):** American Publishing Co., 606 N. Van Buren, Marion, IL 62959. TEL 618-993-1711; Ed. Gwen Evers; Pub. Michael Sample; adv.; photos; pub. size: broadsheet; circ. morning 5,000(paid). **Wire Service(s):** AP.

TOWANDA
US
DAILY REVIEW & SUNDAY REVIEW. 1880. d. $.50/day newsstand; $1.25/Sun.; $130/yr. carrier; $132.60/yr. motor rte. 116 Main St., Towanda, PA 18848. TEL 717-265-2151; FAX 717-265-4200. **Owner(s):** Towanda Printing Co., 116 Main St., Towanda, PA 18848. TEL 717-265-2151; Ed. Dennis Irvine; Pub. James E. Towner; adv. contact: Tony Mercaldo. pub. size: broadsheet; circ. morning 8,846(paid); Sun. 9,501(paid). **Wire Service(s):** AP.

TYRONE
US
DAILY HERALD, THE. 1857. Mon.-Sat. $.35 newsstand; $92.80/yr.; $113.60/yr. out of town. 1018 Pennsylvania Ave., Tyrone, PA 16686. TEL 814-684-4000; FAX 814-684-4238. **Owner(s):** George Sample, III, 208 Penn St., Huntington, PA 16652. TEL 814-643-4040; Pub. George Sample, III; adv. contact: Deborah Garner. photos; pub. size: broadsheet; circ. evening 4,100(paid). **Wire Service(s):** AP.
Formerly: The Tyrone Daily Herald.

UNIONTOWN
US
HERALD STANDARD. 1888. Sun.-Fri. $.40/day newsstand; $1.25/Sun.; $3/wk. carrier; $3.25/wk. motor rte. 8-18 E. Church St., Uniontown, PA 15401. TEL 412-439-7500; FAX 412-439-7528; E-mail: hsnews@hhs.net-URL: http://www.hsonline.com. **Owner(s):** Shirley Ellis, 8-18 E. Church St., Uniontown, PA 15401. TEL 215-752-6744; Carolyn Smith, 8-18 E. Church St., Uniontown, PA 15401. TEL 215-752-6744; Sandra Hardy, 8-18 E. Church St., Uniontown, PA 15401. TEL 215-752-6744; Ed. Gloria Ruane; Pub. Val J. Laub; adv. contact: Maureen Zorichak. photos; bk.rev.; pub. size: broadsheet; circ. morning 31,098(paid); Sun. 32,986(paid). **Wire Service(s):** AP.

WARREN
US
WARREN TIMES OBSERVER. 1966. Mon.-Sat. $.50 newsstand; $9.50/mo. carrier; $10/mo. motor rte. 205 Pennsylvania Ave., W., Warren, PA 16365. TEL 814-723-8200; FAX 814-723-6922. **Owner(s):** Kevin, Michael & Edward, Sr. Mead, 205 Pennsylvania Ave., W., Warren, PA 16365. TEL 814-723-8200; Ed. Jude Dippold; Pub. Kevin Mead; adv. contact: Dawn Burger. pub. size: broadsheet; circ. morning 13,500(paid). **Wire Service(s):** AP, NYT.

WARRENDALE
US   ISSN 8750-5916
NORTH HILLS NEWS RECORD. 1962. d. $.35/day newsstand; $.75/Sun.; $117/yr. carrier. 137 Commonwealth Dr., Warrendale, PA 15086. TEL 412-772-3900; FAX 412-772-3915; E-mail: metrodesk@newsrecord.com; URL: http://www.nauticom.net/www/nhnr/top.html. **Owner(s):** Gannett Company, Inc., 1100 Wilson Blvd., Arlington, VA 22340. TEL 703-284-6000; Ed. Dave Fritz. adv. contact: Jack Robb. pub. size: broadsheet; circ. morning 25,000. **Wire Service(s):** GNS.

WASHINGTON
US   ISSN 0891-0693
OBSERVER-REPORTER, WASHINGTON COUNTY EDITION. 1808. d. $.50/day newsstand; $1/Sun.; $2.70/wk. carrier; $2.85/wk. motor rte.; $13/mo. motor rte. 122 S. Main St., Washington, PA 15301. TEL 412-222-2200; FAX 412-222-3982. **Owner(s):** Observer Publishing Co., 122 S. Main St., Washington, PA 15301. TEL 412-222-2200; FAX 412-222-3982; Ed. A. Parker Burroughs; Pub. John Northrop; adv. contact: Barry A. Martin. pub. size: broadsheet; circ. morning 40,500(paid); Sun. 41,500(paid). **Wire Service(s):** AP, NYT.

WAYNESBORO
US
RECORD HERALD. 1847. Mon.-Sat. $.50 newsstand; $9.70/mo. carrier; $10.25/mo. motor rte. 30 Walnut St., Waynesboro, PA 17268. TEL 717-762-2151; FAX 717-762-3824. **Owner(s):** American Publishing Co., 606 N. Van Buren, Marion, IL 62959. TEL 618-993-1711; Ed. Sue Ernde; Pub. Pat Patterson; adv.; pub. size: broadsheet; circ. evening 10,200(paid). **Wire Service(s):** AP.
Formerly: Waynesboro Record Herald.

WAYNESBURG
US
OBSERVER-REPORTER. 1808. d. $.50/day newsstand; $1/Sun.; $13/mo. carrier. 32 Church St., Waynesburg, PA 15370. TEL 412-852-2602; FAX 412-852-1497. **Owner(s):** Observer Publishing Co., 122 S. Main St., Washington, PA 15301. TEL 412-222-2200; Ed. Bob Neidbala; Pub. John Northrop; adv.; pub. size: broadsheet; circ. morning 7,500(paid); Sun. 7,500(paid). **Wire Service(s):** AP, NYT.

WEST CHESTER
US   ISSN 0163-3082
DAILY LOCAL NEWS. 1872. d. $.50/day newsstand; $1.50/Sun.; $3.95/wk. deliv. 250 N. Bradford Ave., West Chester, PA 19382-2800. TEL 610-696-1776; FAX 610-430-1180; E-mail: dlnnews@aol.com. **Owner(s):** Journal Register Co., 50 W. State St., 12th Fl., Trenton, NJ 08608. TEL 609-396-2200; Ed. Bruce Mowday; Pub. Richard Stenger; adv. contact: Diane Ryan. photos; pub. size: broadsheet; circ. morning 35,707(paid); Sun. 34,342(paid). **Wire Service(s):** AP, CNS, NEA, SHNA.

WILKES BARRE
US   ISSN 0896-4084
TIMES LEADER, THE. 1810. d. $.35/day newsstand; $1/Sun.; $93.60/yr. 15 N. Main St., Wilkes Barre, PA 18711. TEL 717-829-7100; FAX 717-829-2002. **Owner(s):** Knight-Ridder, Inc., One Herald Plz., Miami, FL 33132. TEL 305-376-3800; FAX 305-376-3875; Ed. Allison Walzer; Pub. Mark Contreras; adv. contact: Dennis Sheely. pub. size: broadsheet; circ. morning 48,000(paid); Sun. 77,705(paid). **Wire Service(s):** AP, KRT.

US   ISSN 0163-4224
WILKES-BARRE CITIZENS' VOICE. 1978. d. $.50/day newsstand; $1/Sun.; $2.40/wk. home deliv. 75 N. Washington St., Wilkes Barre, PA 18711. TEL 717-821-2000; FAX 717-821-2247. **Owner(s):** Citizen's Voice, Inc., 75 N. Washington St., Wilkes Barre, PA 18701. TEL 717-821-2000; Ed. Paul Golias; Pub. Robert Manganiello; adv. contact: Mark Altazilla. bk.rev.; pub. size: tabloid; circ. morning 38,000(paid); Sun. 30,000(paid). **Wire Service(s):** AP, SHNA.

WILLIAMSPORT

US   ISSN 1056-3083
WILLIAMSPORT SUN-GAZETTE. 1801. d. $.35/day newsstand; $1/Sun.; $2/wk. carrier; $2.10/wk. motor rte; $104/yr. 252 W. Fourth St., Williamsport, PA 17701. TEL 717-326-1551; FAX 717-323-0948. **Owner(s):** Ogden Newspapers, Inc., 1500 Main St., Wheeling, WV 26003. TEL 304-233-0100; Ed. Dave Troisi; Pub. Thomas C. Briley; adv. contact: John Yahner. photos; pub. size: broadsheet; circ. evening 33,000(paid); Sun. 42,000(paid). **Wire Service(s):** AP.

YORK

US   ISSN 1043-4313
YORK DAILY RECORD. 1796. Mon-Sat. $.35 newsstand; $10/mo. carrier; $9/mo. motor rte. 122 S. George St., York, PA 17402-1741. TEL 717-771-2000; FAX 717-771-2009; E-mail: news@ydr.com; URL: http://www.ydr.com. **Owner(s):** Buckner News Alliance, 2101 Fourth Ave., Ste. 2300, Seattle, WA 98121. TEL 206-727-2727; Ed. Jim McClure; Pub. Dennis Hetzel; bk.rev.; pub. size: broadsheet; circ. morning 43,000(paid); Sun. 72,000(paid). **Wire Service(s):** AP, KNT.

US
YORK DISPATCH/YORK SUNDAY NEWS. 1876. Sun.-Fri. $.35/day newsstand; $1/Sun.; $9/mo. carrier; $10/mo. motor rte. 205 N. George St., York, PA 17401. TEL 717-854-1575. **Owner(s):** Garden State Newspapers, Inc., Woodbury, NJ; Ed. Deena Gross; Pub. Jim Sneddon; photos; bk.rev.; pub. size: broadsheet; circ. evening 40,000(paid); Sun. 90,000(paid). **Wire Service(s):** NYT, LAT-WP, AP, SHNA, Cox.

RHODE ISLAND

NEWPORT

US   ISSN 1053-2560
NEWPORT DAILY NEWS, THE. 1846. Mon.-Sat. $.50/day newsstand; $.75/Sat.; $114/yr. 101 Malbone Rd., Newport, RI 02840. TEL 401-849-3300; FAX 401-849-3300; E-mail: editor@newportri.com. **Owner(s):** Edward A. Sherman Publishing Co., 101 Malbone Rd., Newport, RI 02840. TEL 401-849-3300; FAX 401-849-3306; Ed. David Offer; Pub. Albert K. Sherman, Jr.; adv.; pub. size: broadsheet; circ. evening 15,176(paid). **Wire Service(s):** AP, Photo Wire, SHNA.

PAWTUCKET

US   ISSN 1060-2747
TIMES, THE. 1885. Mon.-Sat. $.50 newsstand; $2.50/wk. home deliv. 23 Exchange St., Pawtucket, RI 02860. TEL 401-722-4000; FAX 401-727-9252. **Owner(s):** New England Newspapers, Inc., 23 Exchange St., Pawtucket, RI 02860. TEL 401-722-4000; Ed. Karen Hupp; Pub. T. Paul Mahony; adv. contact: Diane McCarthy. photos; bk.rev.; pub. size: broadsheet; circ. evening 24,134(paid). **Wire Service(s):** AP.

PROVIDENCE

US
PROVIDENCE JOURNAL-BULLETIN. 1863. d. $.50/day newsstand; $1.80/Sun. 75 Fountain St., Providence, RI 02902. TEL 401-277-7136; FAX 401-277-7802. **Owner(s):** A.H. Belo Corp., 400 S. Record, Dallas, TX 75202. TEL 214-977-6606; Pub. Stephen Hamblett; adv. contact: Donald Ross. pub. size: broadsheet; circ. morning 173,000(paid); Sun. 254,000(paid). **Wire Service(s):** AP, NYT, LAT-WP, KR.

WESTERLY

US   ISSN 1065-1209
WESTERLY SUN. 1893. Sun.-Fri. $.50/day newsstand; $.75/Sun.; $91/26 wks.; $182/yr. 56 Main St., Westerly, RI 02891. TEL 401-596-7791; FAX 401-348-5080; E-mail: utter02891@aol.com. **Owner(s):** Nicholas C. Utter, 56 Main St., Westerly, RI 02891. TEL 401-596-7791; Robert D. Utter, 56 Main St., Westerly, RI 02891. TEL 401-596-7791; Ed. Donald Lewis; Pub. William E. Sherman; adv. contact: Dan O'Neil. pub. size: broadsheet; circ. morning 12,900(paid); Sun. 13,200(paid). **Wire Service(s):** AP.

WEST WARWICK

US
KENT COUNTY DAILY TIMES. 1892. Mon.-Sat. $.35 newsstand; $1.80/wk. 1353 Main St., West Warwick, RI 02893. TEL 401-821-7400; FAX 401-828-0810. **Owner(s):** Theodore Holmberg, 1353 Main St., West Warwick, RI 02893. TEL 401-821-7400; Ed. Theodore Holmberg; Pub. Theodore Holmberg; adv. contact: Dan O'Neil. photos; bk.rev.; pub. size: standard; circ. evening 10,450(paid). **Wire Service(s):** AP.

WOONSOCKET

US
CALL, THE. 1892. d. $.25/day newsstand; $1.25/Sun.; $2.95/wk. home deliv.; $5/wk. mailed. 75 Main St., Woonsocket, RI 02895. TEL 401-762-3000; FAX 401-765-2834. **Owner(s):** Journal Register Co., 50 W. State St., 12th Fl., Trenton, NJ 08608. TEL 609-396-2200; Ed. Susan Hawrylur; Pub. Daniel Goodrich; adv. contact: Steve Pitochelli. photos; bk.rev.; pub. size: broadsheet; circ. morning 26,600(paid); Sun. 26,600(paid). **Wire Service(s):** AP.
Formerly: Woonsocket Call.

SOUTH CAROLINA

AIKEN

US   ISSN 0893-2557
AIKEN STANDARD. 1867. d. $.25/day newsstand; $.75/Sun.; $102/yr. 326 Rutland Dr., Aiken, SC 29801. TEL 803-648-2311; FAX 803-648-6052. **Owner(s):** Aiken Communications, Inc., 124 Rutland Dr., Aiken, SC 29801. TEL 803-648-2311; Evening Post Publishing Co., Charleston, SC 29801. TEL 803-577-7111; Ed. Jeffrey B. Wallace; Pub. Scott B. Hunter; adv. contact: Steven K. Ranzer. photos; pub. size: broadsheet; circ. evening 15,000(paid); Sun. 15,000(paid). **Wire Service(s):** AP, KR.

ANDERSON

US
ANDERSON INDEPENDENT-MAIL. 1899. d. $.50/day newsstand; $1.50/Sun.; $143.40/yr. 1000 Williamston Rd., Anderson, SC 29621. TEL 864-224-4321; FAX 864-260-1276. **Owner(s):** Harte-Hanks Communications, Inc., P.O. Box 269, San Antonio, TX 78291. TEL 864-344-8000; Ed. John Gouch; Pub. Fred L. Foster; adv. contact: Tony G. Marroni. photos; bk.rev.; pub. size: broadsheet; circ. morning 42,366(paid); Sun. 48,479(paid). **Wire Service(s):** AP, KNT, NYT.

BEAUFORT

US
BEAUFORT GAZETTE. 1897. Sun.-Fri. $.25/day newsstand; $1/Sun.; $94/yr. 1556 Salem Rd., Beaufort, SC 29902-0399. TEL 803-524-3183; FAX 803-524-8728; E-mail: gazette@hargray.com. **Owner(s):** McClatchy Newspapers, 2100 Q. St., P.O. Box 15774, Sacramento, CA 95816. TEL 916-321-1000; Ed. James A. Cato; Pub. John Heath; adv. contact: Ann Robb. photos; pub. size: broadsheet; circ. morning 10,900(paid); Sun. 10,900(paid). **Wire Service(s):** AP.

CHARLESTON

US   ISSN 1061-5105
CHARLESTON POST & COURIER. 1803. d. $.50/day newsstand; $1.25/Sun.; $10.75/mo. carrier. 134 Columbus St., Charleston, SC 29403-4800. TEL 803-577-7111; FAX 803-937-5463. **Owner(s):** Evening Post Publishing Co., 134 Columbus St., Charleston, SC 29403-4800. TEL 803-577-7111; Ed. Barbara Williams; Pub. Ivan V. Anderson; adv.; photos; bk.rev.; pub. size: broadsheet; circ. morning 112,404(paid); Sun. 129,452(paid). **Wire Service(s):** AP, KNS.
Formerly: Evening Post.

COLUMBIA

US
STATE, THE. 1891. d. $.50/day newsstand; $1.50/Sun.; $3.40/wk. carrier. 1401 Shop Rd., Columbia, SC 29201. TEL 803-771-6161; FAX 803-771-8639; E-mail: cyberst@cyberstate.infi.net; URL: http://www.thestate.com. **Owner(s):** Knight-Ridder, Inc., One Herald Plz., Miami, FL 33132. TEL 305-376-3800; FAX 305-376-3875; Ed. Paula Ellis; Pub. Frederick Mott, Jr.; adv. contact: Kelly Mirt. pub. size: broadsheet; circ. morning 135,497(paid); evening 28,003(paid); Sun. 162,173(paid). **Wire Service(s):** AP, UPI, NYT, LAT-WP.

FLORENCE

US
FLORENCE MORNING NEWS. 1922. d. $.50/day newsstand; $1.25/Sun.; $126/yr. 310 S. Dargan St., Florence, SC 29501. TEL 803-317-6397; FAX 803-317-7292. **Owner(s):** Thomson Newspapers, Inc., One Thorn Run Ctr., Ste. 1187, 1187 Thorn Run Rd. Ext., Coraopolis, PA 15108. TEL 412-262-7870; Ed. Frank Sayles, Jr.; Pub. C. Thomas Marschel; adv. contact: David Haddad. photos; bk.rev.; pub. size: broadsheet; circ. morning 33,850(paid); Sun. 34,200(paid). **Wire Service(s):** AP, SHNA, Thomson News Service.

DAILY NEWSPAPERS

GREENVILLE
US
GREENVILLE NEWS. 1875. d. $.50/day newsstand; $1.50/Sun.; $3.41/wk. carrier; $13.50/mo. carrier. 305 S. Main St., Greenville, SC 29601. TEL 864-298-4100; FAX 864-298-4395. **Owner(s):** Gannett Company, Inc., 1100 Wilson Blvd., Arlington, SC 22234. TEL 703-284-6000; Ed. Wanda Lloyd; Pub. Bern Mebane; adv. contact: Mark Johnston. photos; pub. size: broadsheet; circ. morning 112,920(paid); Sun. 142,817(paid). **Wire Service(s):** AP, LAT-WP.

GREENWOOD
US
INDEX-JOURNAL. 1919. Sun.-Fri. $.50/day newsstand; $1.25/Sun.; $105.30.60/yr.; $182.52/yr. mailed. 610 Phoenix St., Greenwood, SC 29646. TEL 864-223-1411; FAX 864-223-7331; E-mail: design@indexjournal.com. **Owner(s):** Eleanor M. Mundy & Judith M. Burns, P.O. Box 1018, Greenwood, SC 29648. TEL 803-223-1411; Pub. Eleanor M. Mundy; adv. contact: Ron Lucas. photos; bk.rev.; pub. size: standard; circ. evening 15,659(paid); Sun. 16,856(paid). **Wire Service(s):** AP.

HILTON HEAD
US
HILTON HEAD ISLAND PACKET. 1970. d. $.25/day newsstand; $1/Sun.; $90/yr. carrier. One Pope Ave., Executive Park, Hilton Head, SC 29928. TEL 803-785-4293; FAX 803-785-9424. **Owner(s):** McClatchy Newspapers, P.O. Box 15774, Sacramento, CA 95816. TEL 916-321-1000; Ed. Janet Smith; Pub. Sara Borton; adv. contact: Phil Porter. photos; bk.rev.; pub. size: broadsheet; circ. morning 14,500(paid); Sun. 17,000(paid). **Wire Service(s):** AP, NYT.

MYRTLE BEACH
US
SUN NEWS, THE. 1935. d. $.50/day newsstand; $1.50/Sun.; $37/13 wks. 914 Frontage Rd., E., Myrtle Beach, SC 29577. TEL 803-626-8555; FAX 803-626-0208. **Owner(s):** Knight-Ridder, Inc., One Herald Plz., Miami, FL 33132. TEL 305-376-3800; FAX 305-376-3875; Ed. John X. Miller; Pub. J. Michael Pate; adv. contact: Philip LaPorte. photos; pub. size: broadsheet; circ. morning 41,430(paid); Sun. 51,766(paid). **Wire Service(s):** AP, NYT, KRN.

ORANGEBURG
US
TIMES & DEMOCRAT, THE. 1881. d. $.35/day newsstand; $1/Sun.; $10/mo. carrier. 1010 Broughton St., S.E., Orangeburg, SC 29115. TEL 803-533-5501; FAX 803-533-5526. **Owner(s):** Howard Publications, Inc., 1715 S. Beeman St., P.O. Box 570, Oceanside, CA 92049. TEL 619-433-5771; Ed. Lee Harter; Pub. Dean B. Livingston; adv. contact: Cathy Hughes. pub. size: broadsheet; circ. morning 19,000(paid); Sun. 18,700(paid). **Wire Service(s):** AP.
Formerly: Orangeburg Times & Democrat.

ROCK HILL
US
HERALD, THE. 1872. d. $.35/day newsstand; $.75/Sun.; $6/mo. 132 W. Main St., Rock Hill, SC 29730. TEL 803-329-4000. **Owner(s):** McClatchy Newspapers, P.O. Box 15774, Sacramento, CA 95852. TEL 916-321-1000; Ed. Terry Plumb; Pub. Jayne Speizer; adv. contact: Andy Bass. photos; pub. size: broadsheet; circ. morning 31,000(paid); Sun. 31,500(paid). **Wire Service(s):** AP, LAT-WP, SHNA.

SPARTANBURG
US ISSN 0740-4743
HERALD-JOURNAL. 1844. d. $.50/day newsstand; $1/Sun.; $9.10/mo. 189 W. Main St., Spartanburg, SC 29306. TEL 864-582-4511; FAX 864-594-6349. **Owner(s):** New York Times Co., The, 229 W. 43rd St., New York, NY 10036. TEL 212-556-1234; Ed. Scott Kearns; Pub. Dave Roberts; adv. contact: Bill Cranford. pub. size: broadsheet; circ. morning 62,000(paid); Sun. 69,000(paid). **Wire Service(s):** AP.

SUMTER
US
ITEM, THE. 1894. d. $.35/day newsstand; $1/Sun.; $86.40/yr. 20 N. Magnolia St., Sumter, SC 29150. TEL 803-775-6331; FAX 803-775-1024. **Owner(s):** Osteen Publishing Co., P.O. Box 1677, Sumter, SC 29151. TEL 803-775-6331; Ed. Hubert D. Osteen, Jr.; Pub. Hubert D. Osteen, Jr.; adv. contact: Kyle Osteen. photos; bk.rev.; pub. size: broadsheet; circ. evening 22,180(paid); Sun. 21,500(paid). **Wire Service(s):** AP.

UNION
US
UNION DAILY TIMES. 1850. Mon.-Sat. $.50 newsstand; $6/mo.; $118.80/yr. mailed. 100 Times Blvd., Union, SC 29379. TEL 864-427-1234; FAX 864-427-1237. **Owner(s):** Mid-South Management Co., Inc., 100 Times Blvd., Union, SC 29379. TEL 864-427-1237; Ed. Graham Williams; Pub. Mike Pippin; adv. contact: Ron Prince. photos; bk.rev.; pub. size: broadsheet; circ. evening 7,000(paid). **Wire Service(s):** AP.

SOUTH DAKOTA

ABERDEEN
US
ABERDEEN AMERICAN NEWS. 1885. d. $.50/day newsstand; $1.50/Sun. 124 S. Second St., Aberdeen, SD 57401. TEL 605-225-4100. **Owner(s):** Knight-Ridder, Inc., One Herald Plz., Miami, FL 33132. TEL 305-350-2871; Ed. Cindy Eikamp; Pub. Billie Smith; adv. contact: Roger Brokke. photos; pub. size: standard; circ. morning 18,305(paid); Sun. 20,239(paid). **Wire Service(s):** AP, KNT.

BROOKINGS
US
BROOKINGS REGISTER. 1879. Mon.-Sat. $.50 newsstand; $84/yr. local; $92/yr. out of area. 312 Fifth St., Brookings, SD 57006-0177. TEL 605-692-6271; FAX 605-692-2979; E-mail: register@brookings.net. **Owner(s):** World Newspaper, Inc., 312 Fifth St., P.O. Box 177, Brookings, SD 57006. TEL 605-692-6271; Ed. Amy G. Dunkle. adv. contact: Phil Dahlmeier. photos; bk.rev.; pub. size: broadsheet; circ. evening 5,900(paid). **Wire Service(s):** AP.

HURON
US
PLAINSMAN, THE. 1886. Tue.-Sun. $.50/day newsstand; $1/Sun.; $8/mo. carrier. 49 E. Third St., Huron, SD 57350. TEL 605-352-6401; FAX 605-352-7754. **Owner(s):** World Newspapers, Inc., World Herald Sq., Omaha, NE 68102. TEL 402-444-1000; Ed. Bette Pore; Pub. Tom Hawley; adv. contact: Peg Mercer. pub. size: broadsheet; circ. morning 10,500(paid); Sun. 10,700(paid). **Wire Service(s):** AP.
Formerly: Huron Daily Plainsman.

MADISON
US
MADISON DAILY LEADER. 1890. Mon.-Fri. $.40 newsstand; $77.87/yr. in town. 214 S. Egan Ave., Madison, SD 57042. TEL 605-256-4555; FAX 605-256-6190. **Owner(s):** Hunter Publishing, Inc., P.O. Box 348, Madison, SD 57042. TEL 605-256-4555; FAX 650-256-6190; Ed. Marcia Schoebert; Pub. Jon M. Hunter; adv. contact: Glennys McCool. photos; bk.rev.; pub. size: broadsheet; circ. evening 3,600(paid). **Wire Service(s):** AP.

MITCHELL
US
DAILY REPUBLIC. 1882. Mon.-Sat. $.50 newsstand; $99/yr. in state mailed. 120 S. Lawler St., Mitchell, SD 57301. TEL 605-996-5514; FAX 605-996-7793. **Owner(s):** Forum Communications Co., P.O. Box 2020, Fargo, ND 58207. TEL 701-223-7311; Ed. Kim Dohrer; Pub. Noel Hamiel; adv. contact: Linda Klein. pub. size: broadsheet; circ. evening 12,000(paid). **Wire Service(s):** AP.

PIERRE
US
CAPITAL JOURNAL. Mon.-Fri. $.50 newsstand; $70/yr. carrier; $84/yr. mailed. 333 N. Dakota, Pierre, SD 57501. TEL 605-224-7301; FAX 605-224-9210. **Owner(s):** Hipple Printing Co., Inc., P.O. Box 878, Pierre, SD 57501. TEL 605-224-7301; FAX 605-225-9210; Ed. Dana Hess; Pub. Terry Hipple; adv.; photos; pub. size: broadsheet; circ. 5,000(paid).

RAPID CITY
US
RAPID CITY JOURNAL. 1878. d. $.60/day newsstand; $1.75/Sun.; $152/yr. 507 Main, Rapid City, SD 57701. TEL 605-394-8300; FAX 605-342-8463. **Owner(s):** Lee Enterprises, Inc., 130 E. Second St., Davenport, IA 52801. TEL 319-383-2100; Ed. Steve Miller; Pub. John Van Strydonck; adv. contact: Brenda Speth. photos; bk.rev.; pub. size: broadsheet; circ. morning 37,981(paid); Sun. 40,400(paid). **Wire Service(s):** AP, NYT.

SIOUX FALLS
US

ARGUS LEADER. 1881. d. $.50/day newsstand, $1.50/Sun.; $169/yr. carrier; $182/yr. motor rte. 200 S. Minnesota Ave., Sioux Falls, SD 57102-5034. TEL 605-331-2200; FAX 605-331-2371. **Owner(s):** Gannett Company, Inc., 1100 Wilson Blvd., Arlington, VA 22234. TEL 703-284-6000; Ed. Pete Ellis; Pub. Arnold Garson; adv. contact: Peter Ricker. photos; bk.rev.; pub. size: broadsheet; circ. morning 50,000(paid); Sun. 74,000(paid). **Wire Service(s):** AP, GNS, KR, LAT-WP.

SPEARFISH
US ISSN 1061-6179

BLACK HILLS PIONEER. 1876. Mon.-Sat. $.50/day newsstand; $.50/Sat.; $7.50/mo. carrier; $7.50/mo. motor rte. 315 Seaton Cir., Spearfish, SD 57783. TEL 605-642-2761; FAX 605-642-8179. **Owner(s):** Seaton Publishing Co., P.O. Box 7, Spearfish, SD 57783. TEL 605-642-2761; Ed. Larry Weiers; Pub. Bill Masterson, Jr.; adv. contact: Hollie Hall. adv.: $7.95/SAU. photos; bk.rev.; pub. size: tabloid; circ. evening 25,000(paid). **Wire Service(s):** AP.
Formerly: Spearfish Daily Queen County Word.

WATERTOWN
US

WATERTOWN PUBLIC OPINION. 1887. Mon.-Sat. $.50 newsstand; $91.80/yr. 120 Third Ave., N.W., Watertown, SD 57201. TEL 605-886-6903; FAX 605-886-4280. **Owner(s):** Watertown Public Opinion Co., Inc., 120 Third Ave., N.W., Watertown, SD 57201. TEL 605-886-6901; FAX 605-886-4280; Ed. Gordon Garnos; Pub. Steve Lowrie; adv. contact: A.W. Johnson. adv.: $15.24/SAU. photos; bk.rev.; pub. size: broadsheet; circ. evening 17,500(paid). **Wire Service(s):** AP.

YANKTON
US

YANKTON DAILY PRESS & DAKOTAN. 1861. Mon.-Sat. $.50 newsstand; $87.15/yr. 319 Walnut St., Yankton, SD 57078. TEL 605-665-7811; FAX 605-665-1721; E-mail: pandd@willinet. **Owner(s):** Morris Communications, P.O. Box 936, Augusta, GA 30903. TEL 706-724-0851; Ed. Kelly Hertz; Pub. Don S. Smith; adv. contact: Christy Orwig. photos; bk.rev.; pub. size: standard; circ. evening 9,851(paid). **Wire Service(s):** AP.

TENNESSEE

ATHENS
US

ATHENS DAILY POST. 1848. Mon.-Fri. $.50 newsstand; $6.50/mo.; $76/yr. 320 S. Jackson, Athens, TN 37303. TEL 423-745-5664; FAX 423-745-8295; E-mail: ralphpa@aol.com. **Owner(s):** Daily Post-Athenian Co., Inc., P.O. Box 340, Athens, TN 37371. TEL 423-745-5664; FAX 423-745-5664; Ed. Doug Headrick; Pub. Ralph C. Baldwin, Jr.; adv. contact: Sara Jane Locke. photos; bk.rev.; pub. size: broadsheet; circ. evening 20,000(free & paid). **Wire Service(s):** AP.

CHATTANOOGA
US

CHATTANOOGA FREE PRESS. 1936. d. $.50/day newsstand; $1.50/Sun.; $2.80/wk. 400 E. 11th St., Chattanooga, TN 37401-1447. TEL 615-756-6900; FAX 615-757-6383. **Owner(s):** Chattanooga Free Press, 400 E. 11th St., Chattanooga, TN 37401-1447. TEL 615-756-6900; Ed. Lee Anderson; Pub. Lee Anderson; adv. contact: Dan Nausley. photos; bk.rev.; pub. size: broadsheet; circ. evening 43,000(paid); Sun. 115,000(paid). **Wire Service(s):** AP.
Formerly: Chattanooga News-Free Press.

US

CHATTANOOGA TIMES. 1869. Mon.-Sat. $.50/day newsstand; $1.50/Sun.; $35/13 wks. home deliv. 100 E. Tenth St., Chattanooga, TN 37402. TEL 423-756-1234; FAX 423-752-3388. **Owner(s):** Times Printing Co., 100 E. Tenth St., Chattanooga, TN 37402. TEL 423-756-1234; Ed. Ron Smith; Pub. Paul Neely; adv.; photos; bk.rev.; pub. size: broadsheet; circ. morning 42,000(paid). **Wire Service(s):** AP, NYT.

CLARKSVILLE
US

LEAF-CHRONICLE, THE. 1808. d. $.50 newsstand; $125/yr. 200 Commerce St., Clarksville, TN 37040. TEL 615-552-1808; FAX 615-648-8001; E-mail: fgeno@aol.com. **Owner(s):** Gannett Company, Inc., 1100 Wilson Blvd., Arlington, VA 22234. TEL 703-284-6000; Pub. F. Gene Washer; adv. contact: Lee Ireland. photos; bk.rev.; pub. size: broadsheet; circ. morning 22,500(paid); Sun. 25,000(paid). **Wire Service(s):** AP.

CLEVELAND
US

CLEVELAND DAILY BANNER. 1854. Sun.-Fri. $.35/day newsstand; $1/Sun.; $6.25/mo. home deliv. 1505 25th St., N.W., Cleveland, TN 37311. TEL 615-472-5041; FAX 615-476-1046. **Owner(s):** Cleveland Newspapers, Inc., 1505 25th St., N.W., Cleveland, TN 37311. TEL 615-472-5041; Ed. Pledger L. Wattenbarger; Pub. Pledger L. Wattenbarger; adv. contact: Jack Bennett. photos; bk.rev.; pub. size: broadsheet; circ. evening 16,152(paid); Sun. 18,054(paid). **Wire Service(s):** AP.

COLUMBIA
US

DAILY HERALD. 1848. Sun.-Fri. $.50/day newsstand; $1/Sun.; $18.75/3 mos.; $75/yr. prepaid. 1115 S. Main St., Columbia, TN 38401. TEL 615-388-6464; FAX 615-388-1003. **Owner(s):** Stephens Group, Inc., P.O. Box 17017, Fort Smith, AR 72902. TEL 501-785-7822; Pub. Mark Palmer; adv. contact: Charles Martin. pub. size: broadsheet; circ. evening 11,567(paid); Sun. 13,344(paid). **Wire Service(s):** AP.

COOKEVILLE
US ISSN 8750-5541

HERALD-CITIZEN. 1903. Sun.-Fri. $.50/day newsstand; $1/Sun.; $70/yr. carrier; $70/yr. in area mailed. 124 S. Dixie, Cookeville, TN 38501. TEL 615-526-9715; FAX 615-526-1209; E-mail: heraldcitizennews@midtenn.net. **Owner(s):** Cleveland Newspapers, Inc., P.O. Box 3600, Cleveland, TN 37320; Ed. Charles Denning; Pub. Bill Shuster; adv. contact: Al Profant. photos; bk.rev.; pub. size: broadsheet; circ. evening 10,944(paid); Sun. 13,059(paid). **Wire Service(s):** AP.

DYERSBURG
US

STATE GAZETTE. 1865. Mon.-Fri. $.50 newsstand; $1/Sunday; $133.20/yr. mailed. 294 Hwy. 51 Bypass, Dyersburg, TN 38024. TEL 901-285-4091; FAX 901-285-9747. **Owner(s):** Paxton Media Group, Inc., P.O. Box 2300, Paducah, KY 42002. TEL 502-443-1771; Pub. Billy R. Smith; adv. contact: Johnny McConnell. photos; bk.rev.; pub. size: broadsheet; circ. evening 8,281(paid); Sun. 7,800(paid). **Wire Service(s):** AP, NYT.

ELIZABETHTON
US

ELIZABETHTON STAR. Sun.-Fri. $.35/day newsstand; $1/Sun.; $68/yr. home deliv.; $99/yr. mailed; $64/yr. senior citizens. 300 Sycamore St., Elizabethton, TN 37643. TEL 423-542-4151; FAX 423-542-2004. **Owner(s):** Frank Robinson, Elizabethton, TN; Ed. John Thompson; Pub. Charles Robinson; adv.; photos; bk.rev.; pub. size: broadsheet; circ. evening 9,000(paid); Sun. 10,500(paid). **Wire Service(s):** AP.

GREENEVILLE
US

GREENEVILLE SUN. 1879. Mon.-Sat. $.50 newsstand; $91.50/yr. carrier. 121 W. Summer St., Greeneville, TN 37743. TEL 423-638-4181; FAX 423-638-3645. **Owner(s):** Greeneville Publishing Co., P.O. Box 1630, Greeneville, TN 37744. TEL 423-638-4181; Ed. Douglas Watson; Pub. John M. Jones, Sr.; adv. contact: John E. Cash. pub. size: broadsheet; circ. evening 16,000(paid). **Wire Service(s):** AP.

JACKSON
US ISSN 0890-9938

JACKSON SUN, THE. 1848. d. $.35/day newsstand; $1.50/Sun.; $12.60/mo. carrier; $25.20/2 mos. in cy. 245 W. Lafayette, Jackson, TN 38301. TEL 901-427-3333; FAX 901-425-9639. **Owner(s):** Gannett Company, Inc., 1100 Wilson Blvd., Arlington, VA 22234. TEL 703-384-6000; Ed. Don Hudson; Pub. Scott M. Brown; adv. contact: Kerry Johnson. pub. size: broadsheet; circ. morning 40,000(paid); Sun. 44,000(paid). **Wire Service(s):** AP, GNS.

DAILY NEWSPAPERS

JOHNSON CITY
US
JOHNSON CITY PRESS. 1934. d. $.35/day newsstand; $1.25/Sun.; $10/mo. carrier; $26/3 mos. 204 W. Main St., Johnson City, TN 37604. TEL 423-929-3111; FAX 423-929-7484. **Owner(s):** Press, Inc., P.O. Box 1717, Johnson City, TN 37605-1717. TEL 423-929-3111; FAX 423-461-9546; Ed. John A. Jones. adv. contact: Frank Hawkins. photos; bk.rev.; pub. size: broadsheet; circ. morning 31,600(paid); Sun. 36,000(paid). **Wire Service(s):** AP, NYT.

KINGSPORT
US
KINGSPORT DAILY NEWS. 1963. Mon.-Fri. $.25 newsstand; $60/yr. local; $90/yr. out of area. 310 E. Sullivan, Kingsport, TN 37660. TEL 423-246-4800; FAX 423-247-2502. **Owner(s):** Daily News of Kingsport, Inc., 310 E. Sullivan, Kingsport, TN 37660. TEL 615-246-4800; Ed. Pete Dykes; Pub. Steve Dykes; adv. contact: Steve Dykes. pub. size: standard; circ. morning 8,000(paid). **Wire Service(s):** RN.

US
KINGSPORT TIMES-NEWS. 1918. d. $.50/day newsstand; $1.25/Sun.; $216/yr. mailed. 701 Lynn Garden Dr., Kingsport, TN 37662. TEL 423-929-2197; FAX 423-392-1392. **Owner(s):** Sandusky Newspapers, Inc., Sandusky, OH; Ed. Ted Como; Pub. Keith Wilson; adv.; photos; bk.rev.; pub. size: broadsheet; circ. evening 46,000(paid); Sun. 48,000(paid). **Wire Service(s):** AP.

KNOXVILLE
US
KNOXVILLE NEWS-SENTINEL. 1886. d. $.50/day newsstand, $2/Sun.; $17.50/mo. deliv. 208 W. Church Ave., Knoxville, TN 37902. TEL 423-523-3131; FAX 423-521-8124; E-mail: kns@knoxnews.com; URL: http://www.knoxnews.com/. **Owner(s):** Scripps-Howard, 312 Walnut St., 28th Fl., Cincinnati, OH 45202. TEL 513-977-3000; Ed. Frank Cagle. adv. contact: Debbie Smiddy. pub. size: broadsheet; circ. morning 123,000(paid); Sun. 184,000(paid). **Wire Service(s):** AP, NYT, SHNA.

LEBANON
US
LEBANON DEMOCRAT, THE. 1888. Mon.-Fri. $.50 newsstand; $12/3 mos. mailed; $44/yr. mailed. 402 N. Cumberland St., Lebanon, TN 37087. TEL 615-444-3952; FAX 615-444-1358. **Owner(s):** Carolton A. Jones Newspapers, Inc., Johnson City, TN 37601; Pub. Sam Hatcher; adv.; pub. size: broadsheet; circ. morning 9,500(paid). **Wire Service(s):** UPI, AP.

MARYVILLE
US
DAILY TIMES. 1883. Mon.-Fri. $.35 newsstand; $85.80/yr. motor rte.; $156/yr. mailed. 307 E. Harper Ave., Maryville, TN 37801. TEL 423-981-1100; FAX 423-981-1175. **Owner(s):** Horvitz Corp., Bellview, WA; Ed. Dean Stone; Pub. F. Max Crotser; adv. contact: Raymond Tuck. photos; pub. size: broadsheet; circ. morning 22,500(paid). **Wire Service(s):** AP. **Formerly:** Morning Daily Times.

MEMPHIS
US ISSN 0745-4856
COMMERCIAL APPEAL, THE. 1841. d. $.50/day newsstand; $2/Sun. 495 Union Ave., Memphis, TN 38103. TEL 901-529-2345; FAX 901-529-2522. **Owner(s):** Scripps-Howard, 312 Walnut St., 28th Fl., Cincinnati, OH 45202. TEL 513-977-3000; Ed. Henry Stokes. adv. contact: David Enstad. photos; pub. size: broadsheet; circ. morning 220,000(paid); Sun. 284,949(paid). **Wire Service(s):** AP, NYT, SHNS, RN, LAT-WP.

MORRISTOWN
US
CITIZEN TRIBUNE. 1966. d. $.50/day newsstand; $1.25/Sun.; $106/yr. carrier. 1609 W. First North St., Morristown, TN 37815. TEL 615-581-5630; FAX 615-586-3061. **Owner(s):** Lakeway Publishers, Inc., P.O. Box 625, Morristown, TN 37815. TEL 615-581-5630; FAX 615-581-3061; Ed. R. Jack Fishman; Pub. R. Jack Fishman; adv. contact: Reece Sexton. bk.rev.; pub. size: broadsheet; circ. evening 20,492(paid); Sun. 24,125(paid). **Wire Service(s):** AP.
Formerly: Morristown Citizen Tribune.

MURFREESBORO
US
MURFREESBORO DAILY NEWS JOURNAL. 1849. d. $.35/day newsstand, $1.25/Sun.; $125/yr. in state. 224 N. Walnut, Murfreesboro, TN 37133. TEL 615-893-5860; FAX 615-896-8702; E-mail: online@dnj.com; URL: http://www.dnj.com. **Owner(s):** Morris Communications, P.O. Box 68, Savanah, GA 31402; Ed. Mike Pirtle; Pub. William Fryar; adv. contact: Paul Mauney. pub. size: standard; circ. evening 17,000(paid); Sun. 21,500(paid). **Wire Service(s):** AP.

NASHVILLE
US
NASHVILLE BANNER. 1876. Mon-Fri. $.50/day newsstand, $88.40/yr home delivery. 1100 Broadway, Nashville, TN 37203-3116. TEL 615-259-8800; FAX 615-259-8890; E-mail: pembry@nashvillebanner.com. **Owner(s):** Nashville Banner, 1100 Broadway, Nashville, TN 37203-3116. TEL 615-259-8800; Ed. Pat Embry; Pub. Irby C. Simpkins; adv.; photos; bk.rev.; pub. size: broadsheet; circ. morning 207,658(paid); evening 46,500(paid); Sun. 292,859(paid). **Wire Service(s):** AP, LAT-WP, KR.

US ISSN 1053-6590
TENNESSEAN, THE. 1812. d. $.35 newsstand; $1.50/Sun.; $3.25/wk. carrier. 1100 Broadway, Nashville, TN 37203. TEL 615-259-8000; FAX 616-259-8093. **Owner(s):** Gannett Company, Inc., 1100 Wilson Blvd., Arlington, VA 22234. TEL 703-284-6000; Ed. David Green; Pub. Craig Moon; adv.; bk.rev.; pub. size: broadsheet; circ. morning 203,805(paid); Sun. 286,956(paid). **Wire Service(s):** NYT, UPI, PS, AP.

OAK RIDGE
US ISSN 0890-6009
OAK RIDGER, THE. 1949. Mon.-Fri. $.50/day newsstand; $1/Fri.; $110/yr. carrier; $144/yr. mailed. 785 Oak Ridge Tpke., Oak Ridge, TN 37830. TEL 423-482-1021; FAX 423-482-7834. **Owner(s):** Morris Communications, P.O. Box 936, Augusta, GA 30903. TEL 706-724-0851; Ed. Ron Bridgeman; Pub. Pete Esser; adv. contact: Tammy Carroll. pub. size: broadsheet; circ. evening 11,000(paid). **Wire Service(s):** AP.

PARIS
US ISSN 0893-3669
PARIS POST-INTELLIGENCER, THE. 1866. Mon.-Fri. $.25 newsstand; $51/yr. carrier; $73.50/yr. mailed. 208 E. Wood St., Paris, TN 38242-0310. TEL 901-642-1162; FAX 901-642-1165; E-mail: parispi@aeneas.net. **Owner(s):** Paris Publishing Co. Inc., 208 E. Wood St., Paris, TN 38242. TEL 901-642-1162; FAX 901-642-1165; Ed. Michael Williams; Pub. Bill Williams; adv. contact: B. Stubblefield. adv.: $6.42/SAU. pub. size: broadsheet; circ. evening 7,986(free & paid). **Wire Service(s):** AP.

SEVIERVILLE
US ISSN 0894-2218
MOUNTAIN PRESS, THE. 1928. d. $.50/day newsstand; $1/Sun.; $9.50/mo. carrier; $8.50/mo. senior citizens. 119 Riverbend Dr., Sevierville, TN 37876. TEL 423-428-0746; FAX 423-453-4913. **Owner(s):** Paxton Media Group, Inc., P.O. Box 2300, Paducah, KY 42002. TEL 502-443-1771; Ed. Anna Garber; Pub. Bob Childress; adv. contact: Don Shwartz. photos; bk.rev.; pub. size: broadsheet; circ. morning 10,000(paid); Sun. 10,000(paid). **Wire Service(s):** AP.

SHELBYVILLE
US
SHELBYVILLE TIMES-GAZETTE. 1874. Mon.-Fri. $34/yr. in cy. 323 E. Depot St., Shelbyville, TN 37160-0380. TEL 615-684-1200; FAX 615-684-3228. **Owner(s):** Shelbyville Publishing Co., Inc., 323 E. Depot St., Shelbyville, TN 37160. TEL 615-684-1200; FAX 615-684-3228; Ed. Mark McGee; Pub. David Segroves; adv. contact: Ruth Coop. photos; pub. size: broadsheet; circ. evening 8,699(paid). **Wire Service(s):** AP.

UNION CITY

US   ISSN 0745-5534
UNION CITY DAILY MESSENGER. 1926. Mon.-Fri. $.50 newsstand; $80/yr. 613 E. Jackson, Union City, TN 38281. TEL 901-885-0744; FAX 901-885-0782. **Owner(s):** David Critchlow, Sr., P.O. Box 430, Union City, TN 38281. TEL 901-885-0744; Scott Critchlow, P.O. Box 430, Union City, TN 38281; David Critchlow, Jr., P.O. Box 430, Union City, TN 38281; Ed. David Critchlow, Jr.; Pub. David Critchlow, Sr.; adv. contact: Gloria Chesteen. photos; bk.rev.; pub. size: broadsheet; circ. evening 8,700(paid). **Wire Service(s):** AP.

TEXAS

ABILENE

US
ABILENE REPORTER-NEWS. 1881. d. $.50/day newsstand; $1.50/Sun.; $14.50/mo. carrier. 101 Cypress St., Abilene, TX 79601. TEL 915-673-4271; FAX 915-673-1901; E-mail: reagan@texnews.com; URL: http://www.texnews.com. **Owner(s):** Harte-Hanks Communications, Inc., P.O. Box 269, San Antonio, TX 78291. TEL 512-344-8000; Ed. Danny Reagan; Pub. Frank Puckett, Jr.; adv.; photos; bk.rev.; pub. size: broadsheet; circ. morning 45,000(paid); Sun. 55,000(paid). **Wire Service(s):** AP, SHNA, KR.

ALICE

US
ALICE ECHO-NEWS. 1896. Sun.-Fri. $.50/day newsstand, $1.50/Sun.; $9/mo. local. 405 E. Main, Alice, TX 78332. TEL 512-664-6588; FAX 512-668-1030. **Owner(s):** Alice Newspapers, Inc., 405 E. Main, Alice, TX 78332. TEL 512-664-6588; Ed. Scott Willey; Pub. Tony Morris; adv.; photos; pub. size: broadsheet; circ. evening 15,000(paid); Sun. 6,000(paid). **Wire Service(s):** AP.

AMARILLO

US
AMARILLO DAILY NEWS/SUNDAY NEWS GLOBE. 1909. d. $.50/day newsstand; $1.25/Sun.; $19.75/mo. carrier; $29.55/3 mos. carrier. 900 S. Harrison St., Amarillo, TX 79101. TEL 806-345-3364; FAX 806-373-0810; E-mail: editor@netjava.com; URL: http://amarillonet.com. **Owner(s):** Morris Communications, P.O. Box 2091, Amarillo, TX 79166-2091. TEL 806-376-4488; Ed. Dennis Spies; Pub. Garet von Netzer; adv. contact: Steve Beasley. photos; bk.rev.; pub. size: broadsheet; circ. morning 44,008(paid); Sun. 76,613(paid). **Wire Service(s):** AP, MNS, KR, LAT-WP.

US
AMARILLO GLOBE TIMES. 1909. d. $.50 newsstand; $9.50/mo. carrier. 900 S. Harrison, Amarillo, TX 79101. TEL 806-376-4488; FAX 806-373-0810. **Owner(s):** Morris Communications, P.O. Box 2091, Amarillo, TX 79166-2091. TEL 806-376-4488; Ed. Dennis Spies; Pub. Garet von Netzer; adv. contact: Steve Beasley. photos; bk.rev.; pub. size: broadsheet; circ. morning 42,499; evening 19,099(paid); Sun. 74,727. **Wire Service(s):** AP, KRT, LAT-WP.

ARLINGTON

US
▼**ARLINGTON MORNING NEWS.** 1996. d. $.25/day newsstand; $.50/Sun. 1112 N. Copeland, Ste. 400, Arlington, TX 76011. TEL 817-461-6397. **Owner(s):** A.H. Belo Corp., 400 S. Record, Dallas, TX 75202. TEL 214-977-6606; Ed. Lawrence Young; Pub. Gary Jacobson; adv. contact: June DeRousse. photos; pub. size: broadsheet; circ. morning 53,039(paid); Sun. 80,188(paid).

US
ARLINGTON STAR TELEGRAM. 1883. d. $.50/day newsstand; $1.25/Sun.; $11.50/mo. carrier. 1111 W. Abram, Arlington, TX 76013. TEL 817-548-5400; FAX 817-261-1193. **Owner(s):** Knight-Ridder, Inc., One Herald Plz., Miami, FL 33132. TEL 305-376-3800; FAX 305-376-3875; Pub. Michael "Mac" Tully; adv. contact: Walter Owen. pub. size: broadsheet; circ. morning 52,000(paid); Sun. 80,000(paid). **Wire Service(s):** AP, RN, NYT.
Formerly: Arlington Citizen-Journal.

ATHENS

US   ISSN 1040-6522
ATHENS DAILY REVIEW. 1885. Sun.-Fri. $.50 newsstand; $6.50/mo. $19.25/3 mos. in cy. 201 S. Prairieville St., Athens, TX 75751. TEL 903-675-5626; FAX 903-675-9450. **Owner(s):** Don Rey Media Group, P.O. Box 17017, Fort Smith, AR 72902. TEL 502-785-7810; Ed. Gene Lehmann; Pub. Dan Dwelle; adv. contact: Dan Youngman. photos; bk.rev.; pub. size: broadsheet; circ. evening 7,000(paid); Sun. 7,050(paid). **Wire Service(s):** AP.

AUSTIN

US   ISSN 0199-8560
AUSTIN AMERICAN-STATESMAN. 1885. d. $.50/day newsstand; $1.50/Sun.; $13.52/mo. carrier. 305 S. Congress Ave., Austin, TX 78704. TEL 512-445-3500; FAX 512-445-3557. **Owner(s):** Cox Enterprises, Inc., 72 Marietta St., N.W., Atlanta, GA 30303. TEL 404-526-5537; Ed. Kathy Warbelow. adv. contact: George Gutierrez. pub. size: broadsheet; circ. morning 182,199(paid); Sun. 271,491(paid). **Wire Service(s):** AP, LAT-WP, NYT, Cox News Line, KNT, FIELD.

BAY CITY

US
DAILY TRIBUNE, THE. 1845. Tue.-Fri. & Sun. $.50 newsstand; $69/yr. carrier in cy.; $17.25/3 mos. out of cy.; $27/3 mos. out of state. 2901 Carey Smith Blvd., Bay City, TX 77414. TEL 409-245-5555; FAX 409-244-5908. **Owner(s):** Bay City Newspapers Inc., P.O. Box 1551, Bay City, TX 77404. TEL 409-245-5555; Ed. Karen Pannell; Pub. Jim Finley; adv. contact: Linda Conrad. pub. size: broadsheet; circ. evening 7,000(paid); Sun. 6,600(paid). **Wire Service(s):** AP.

BAYTOWN

US
BAYTOWN SUN. 1931. Mon.-Sat. $.50/day newsstand, $1/Sat.; $6.75/mo. home deliv.; $9/mo. mailed. 1301 Memorial Dr., Baytown, TX 77520. TEL 713-422-8302; FAX 713-427-6283. **Owner(s):** Southern Newspapers, Inc., P.O. Box 42828, Houston, TX 77242; Ed. David Eldridge; Pub. Gary Dobbs; adv. contact: Penn Neville. pub. size: broadsheet; circ. evening 16,000(paid). **Wire Service(s):** UPI, AP.

BEAUMONT

US   ISSN 0744-1207
BEAUMONT ENTERPRISE. 1880. d. $.50/day newsstand; $1.50/Sun.; $11/mo. home deliv.; $15/mo. mailed. 380 Main St., Beaumont, TX 77701. TEL 409-833-3311; FAX 409-838-2857; E-mail: dpero@ih200.net. **Owner(s):** Hearst Corp., 959 Eighth Ave., New York, NY 10019. TEL 212-262-5700; Ed. Keith Briscoe; Pub. Aubrey L. Webb; adv. contact: Mike Tieman. photos; pub. size: broadsheet; circ. morning 69,000(paid); Sun. 84,000(paid). **Wire Service(s):** AP, HHS, NYT.

BIG SPRING

US   ISSN 0746-6811
BIG SPRING HERALD. 1904. Sun.-Fri. $.50/day newsstand; $1.25/Sun.; $8.65/mo. carrier. 710 Scurry, Big Spring, TX 79720. TEL 915-263-7331; FAX 915-264-7205. **Owner(s):** American Publishing Co., 606 N. Van Buren, Marion, IL 62959. TEL 618-993-1711; Ed. John H. Walker; Pub. Charles Williams; adv. contact: Jim White. photos; bk.rev.; pub. size: broadsheet; circ. evening 7,000(paid); Sun. 8,000(paid). **Wire Service(s):** AP, SHNA.

BONHAM

US
BONHAM DAILY FAVORITE. 1894. Tue.-Fri. & Sun. $.50/day newsstand; $.75/Sun.; $90/yr. carrier; $140/yr. mailed. 314 N. Center St., Bonham, TX 75418. TEL 903-583-2124; FAX 903-583-8321. **Owner(s):** Bonham Publishers, Inc., 314 N. Center St., Bonham, TX 75418. TEL 903-583-2124; FAX 903-583-8321; Ed. John Frair; Pub. John Frair; adv. contact: Elaine Ashlock. pub. size: broadsheet; circ. evening 3,800(paid); Sun. 4,300(paid). **Wire Service(s):** AP.

BORGER

US
BORGER NEWS-HERALD. 1926. Sun.-Fri. $.50/day newsstand; $.75/Sun.; $7/mo. home deliv.; $96/yr. mailed. 207 N. Main St., Borger, TX 79007. TEL 806-273-5611; FAX 806-273-2552. **Owner(s):** Stephens Group, Inc., P.O. Box 1359, Fort Smith, AR 72902; Ed. Laura Frye; Pub. Tom Quinn; adv. contact: Helen Thomas. photos. pub. size: broadsheet; circ. evening 6,725(paid); Sun. 6,900(paid). **Wire Service(s):** AP.

DAILY NEWSPAPERS

BRENHAM
US   ISSN 8750-5800
BRENHAM BANNER-PRESS. 1866. Mon.-Sat. $.50 newsstand; $65/yr. 2000 Stringer, Brenham, TX 77833. TEL 409-836-7956; FAX 409-830-8577. **Owner(s):** Hartman Newspapers, Inc., P.O. Bos 1390, Rosenberg, TX 77471. TEL 713-342-4474; FAX 713-342-3219; Ed. Arthur Hahn; Pub. Charles Moser; adv.; photos; pub. size: broadsheet; circ. evening 6,500(paid). **Wire Service(s):** AP.

BROWNSVILLE
US   ISSN 0894-2064
BROWNSVILLE HERALD. 1892. d. $.50/day newsstand; $1.25/Sun.; $6/mo. carrier; $12/mo. elsewhere. 1135 E. Van Buren, Brownsville, TX 78520. TEL 210-542-4301; FAX 210-542-0840; E-mail: herald@hiline.net. **Owner(s):** Freedom Communications, Inc., P.O. Box 19549, Irvine, CA 92713. TEL 714-553-9292; FAX 714-474-7675; Ed. George Cox; Pub. Douglas Hardie; pub. size: standard; circ. morning 18,640(paid); Sun. 21,200(paid). **Wire Service(s):** AP.

BROWNWOOD
US
BROWNWOOD BULLETIN. 1900. Sun.-Fri. $.50/day newsstand; $1.50/Sun.; $11/mo. local; $16.50/mo. out of state. 700 Carnegie, Brownwood, TX 76801. TEL 915-646-2541; FAX 915-646-6835. **Owner(s):** Boone Newspapers, Inc., P.O. Box 2370, Tuscaloosa, AL 35403. TEL 407-338-3298; Ed. Gene Deason; Pub. Robert W. Brincefield; adv. contact: Bill Crist. photos; bk.rev.; pub. size: broadsheet; circ. evening 9,286(paid); Sun. 11,228(paid). **Wire Service(s):** AP.

BRYAN
US   ISSN 0739-8727
BRYAN COLLEGE STATION EAGLE. 1876. d. $.50 newsstand; $1.25/Sun.; $108/yr. 1729 Briarcrest Dr., Bryan, TX 77802. TEL 409-776-4444; FAX 409-774-0496. **Owner(s):** Eagle Printing Co., P.O. Box 3000, Bryan, TX 77805. TEL 409-776-4444; Ed. Joe Michael Feist; Pub. Donnis Baggett; adv. contact: Carol Hampton. pub. size: broadsheet; circ. morning 24,500(paid); 31,000(paid). **Wire Service(s):** AP.

CLEBURNE
US
TIMES-REVIEW. 1904. Sun.-Fri. $.50/day newsstand; $1/Sun.; $6/mo. carrier; $70/yr. in area; $73/yr. out of area. 108 S. Anglin, Cleburne, TX 76031. TEL 817-645-2441; FAX 817-645-4020. **Owner(s):** Donrey Media Group, P.O. Box 17017, Fort Smith, AK 72902. TEL 501-785-7810; Ed. Rob Fraser; Pub. Bill Rice; adv. contact: Kay Pace. pub. size: broadsheet; circ. evening 10,700(paid); Sun. 11,910(paid). **Wire Service(s):** AP.
Formerly: Cleburne Times-Review.

CLUTE
US
BRAZOSPORT FACTS, THE. 1913. d. $.50/day newsstand; $1.25/Sun.; $8.75/mo. 720 S. Main, Clute, TX 77531. TEL 409-265-7411; FAX 409-265-9052; E-mail: thefacts@sat.net. **Owner(s):** Southern Newspapers, Inc., 720 S. Main, Clute, TX 77531. TEL 409-265-7411; FAX 409-265-9052; Ed. Wanda Garner Cash; Pub. Bill Cornwell; adv. contact: Deana Lesco. photos; bk.rev.; pub. size: broadsheet; circ. evening 19,958(paid); Sun. 21,530(paid). **Wire Service(s):** AP.

CONROE
US
CONROE COURIER, THE. 1892. d. $.50/day newsstand; $1/Sun.; $9.75/mo. carrier. 100 Ave. A, Conroe, TX 77301. TEL 409-756-6671; FAX 409-756-6676. **Owner(s):** Westward Communications, Inc., Dallas, TX; Ed. Jim Fredricks; Pub. Arlena McLaughlin; adv. contact: Brenda Roy. photos; pub. size: broadsheet; circ. morning 13,701(paid); Sun. 14,760(paid). **Wire Service(s):** AP.

CORPUS CHRISTI
US   ISSN 0894-5365
CORPUS CHRISTI CALLER-TIMES. 1883. d. $.50/day newsstand; $2/Sun.; $12.95/mo. carrier. 820 Lower N. Broadway, Corpus Christi, TX 78401. TEL 512-884-2011; FAX 512-886-3732; E-mail: scottr@caller.com; URL: http://www.caller.com. **Owner(s):** Harte-Hanks Communications, Inc., P.O. Box 269, San Antonio, TX 78291. TEL 512-344-8000; Pub. Steve Sullivan; adv. contact: Leslie Wendland. photos; pub. size: broadsheet; circ. morning 67,500(paid); Sun. 96,031(paid). **Wire Service(s):** AP, CT-NYT, KR, NYT.

CORSICANA
US   ISSN 8750-2518
CORSICANA DAILY SUN. 1894. d. $.50/day newsstand; $1/Sun.; $8.75/mo. carrier; $9.50/mo. mailed. 405 E. Collin Ave., Corsicana, TX 75110. TEL 903-872-3931; FAX 903-872-6878. **Owner(s):** American Publishing Co., 606 N. Van Buren, Marion, IL 62959. TEL 618-993-1711; Ed. Rob Ludwig; Pub. Gary Connor; adv. contact: T.C. Hurst. pub. size: broadsheet; circ. evening 7,900(paid); Sun. 8,100(paid). **Wire Service(s):** AP.

DALHART
US
DALHART DAILY TEXAN. 1901. Tue.-Fri. & Sun. $.25 newsstand; $50/yr. out of state; $54.60/yr. home deliv. 410 Denrock, Dalhart, TX 79022. TEL 806-249-4511; FAX 806-249-2395. **Owner(s):** Susan J. & Robert S. Clay, 410 Denrock, Dalhart, TX 79022. TEL 806-249-4511; FAX 806-249-2395; Pub. Robert S. Clay; adv. contact: Pat Warden. bk.rev.; pub. size: broadsheet; circ. evening 2,520(paid); Sun. 2,700(paid). **Wire Service(s):** AP.

DALLAS
US
DALLAS MORNING NEWS, THE. 1885. d. $.75/day newsstand; $1.50/Sun.; $132/yr. home deliv. 400 S. Record, 4th Fl., Dallas, TX 75202. TEL 214-977-8222; FAX 214-977-8019. **Owner(s):** A.H. Belo Corp., 400 S. Record, Dallas, TX 75202. TEL 214-977-6606; Ed. Stuart Wilk; Pub. Burl Osborne; adv. contact: Doug Burke. bk.rev.; pub. size: broadsheet; circ. morning 494,266(paid); Sun. 803,610(paid). **Wire Service(s):** AP, NYT, KNI, AFP.

DEL RIO
US
DEL RIO NEWS-HERALD. 1929. d. $.50/day newsstand; $1.25/Sun; $8/mo.; $46.50/6 mos.; $93/yr. 2205 Bedell Ave., Del Rio, TX 78842-0397. TEL 210-775-1551; FAX 210-774-2610. **Owner(s):** American Publishing Co., 606 N. Van Bruen, Marion, IL 62959. TEL 618-993-1711; Ed. Rosa Delgado; Pub. Joe San Miguel; adv. contact: Janie Sharp. pub. size: broadsheet; circ. evening 6,400(paid); Sun. 6,900(paid). **Wire Service(s):** AP.

DENISON
US
HERALD-DEMOCRAT. 1879. Sun.-Fri. $.50/day newsstand; $1/Sun.; $7.50/mo. carrier; $7.75/mo. mailed. 331 W. Woodard, Denison, TX 75020. TEL 903-465-7171; FAX 903-465-7188. **Owner(s):** Stephens Group, Inc., P.O. Box 17017, Ft. Smith, AR 72917. TEL 501-785-7801; Ed. Steve Martaindale; Pub. John Wright; pub. size: standard; circ. morning 26,700(paid); Sun. 29,600(paid). **Wire Service(s):** AP.
Formerly: Denison Herald; Sherman Democrat.

DENTON
US
DENTON RECORD-CHRONICLE. 1903. d. $.25/day newsstand; $1/Sun.; $8/mo. daily carrier, $4/mo. Sun.; $16/mo. daily mailed, $11/mo. Sun. 314 E. Hickory St., Denton, TX 76201. TEL 817-387-3811; FAX 214-434-2400. **Owner(s):** Denton Publications, Inc., 314 E. Hickory St., P.O. Box 369, Denton, TX 76201. TEL 817-387-3811; Pub. Fred Patterson; adv. contact: Sandra Kelly. pub. size: broadsheet; circ. evening 17,140(paid); Sun. 20,058(paid). **Wire Service(s):** AP.

EDINBURG
US
EDINBURG DAILY REVIEW. 1914. Tue.-Fri. & Sun. $.25 newsstand; $60.13/yr. 215 E. University Ave., Edinburg, TX 78539. TEL 210-383-2705; FAX 210-383-3172. **Owner(s):** Hidalgo Publishing Co., Inc., 215 E. University, Edinburg, TX 78539. TEL 512-383-2705; Ed. Gilbert Tagle; Pub. Pearl A. Mathis; adv.; photos; bk.rev.; pub. size: standard; circ. evening 5,500(paid); Sun. 5,500(paid). **Wire Service(s):** AP.

10504 EL PASO, TX   DAILY NEWSPAPERS

EL PASO

US
EL PASO HERALD-POST. 1881. Mon.-Sat. $.35 newsstand; $5.50/mo. carrier. 300 N. Campbell St., El Paso, TX 79901. TEL 915-546-6100; FAX 915-546-6349. **Owner(s):** Scripps-Howard, 312 Walnut St., 28th Fl., Cincinnati, OH 45202. TEL 513-977-3000; Ed. Georgiana Vines. adv. contact: J. Michael Price. pub. size: broadsheet; circ. evening 21,500(paid). **Wire Service(s):** AP, NYT, SHNS.

US   ISSN 0746-3588
EL PASO TIMES. 1881. d. $.35/day newsstand; $1.50/Sun.; $11.50/mo. carrier;. 300 N. Campbell St., El Paso, TX 79901. TEL 915-546-6100; FAX 915-546-6415. **Owner(s):** Gannett Company, Inc., 1100 Wilson Blvd., Arlington, VA 22234. TEL 703-284-6000; Ed. Paula Moore; Pub. Don Flores; adv. contact: J. Michael Price. pub. size: broadsheet; circ. morning 47,000(paid); Sun. 99,000(paid). **Wire Service(s):** AP, GNS.

ENNIS

US   ISSN 8755-9056
ENNIS DAILY NEWS. 1891. Sun.-Fri. $.25 newsstand; $5/mo. carrier. 213 N. Dallas, Ennis, TX 75119. TEL 214-875-3801; FAX 972-875-9747. **Owner(s):** Fackelman Newspaper Group, Tarpon Springs, FL; Ed. Charles Gentry; Pub. Bart Leath; adv. contact: Roger Gentry. pub. size: broadsheet; circ. evening 4,500(paid); Sun. 4,500(paid). **Wire Service(s):** AP.

FORT WORTH

US   ISSN 0889-0013
FORT WORTH STAR-TELEGRAM. 1906. d. $.50/day newsstand; $1.50/Sun.; $10.95/mo. carrier; $7.95/mo. Sat. & Sun. carrier. 400 W. Seventh St., Fort Worth, TX 76102. TEL 817-390-7400; FAX 817-390-7789. **Owner(s):** Knight-Ridder, Inc., One Herald Plz., Miamia, FL 33132. TEL 305-376-3800; Ed. Michael Blackman; Pub. Wesley Turner; adv. contact: M. "Mac" Tully. bk.rev.; pub. size: broadsheet; circ. morning 256,789(paid). Sun. 350,000(paid). **Wire Service(s):** AP, LAT-WP, KNS, CDN.

GAINESVILLE

US
GAINESVILLE DAILY REGISTER. 1890. Sun.-Fri. $.50/day newsstand; $.75/Sun.; $78/yr. in cy.; $90/yr. out of cy. 306 E. California, Gainesville, TX 76240. TEL 817-665-5511; FAX 817-665-0920. **Owner(s):** Stephens Group, Inc., P.O. Box 1350, Fort Smith, AR 72902. TEL 501-785-7810; Ed. Jerry Prickett; Pub. David Scott; adv. contact: Sandi Clement. pub. size: broadsheet; circ. evening 7,500(paid); Sun. 8,500(paid). **Wire Service(s):** AP.

GALVESTON

US   ISSN 0738-8047
GALVESTON COUNTY DAILY NEWS, THE. 1842. d. $.50/day newsstand; $1.50/Sun.; $12/mo. carrier. 8522 Teichman, Galveston, TX 77553. TEL 409-744-3611; FAX 409-744-6268; E-mail: galvnews@aol.com; URL: http://www.galvnews.com. **Owner(s):** Galveston Newspapers, Inc., P.O. Box 628, Galveston, TX 77553. TEL 409-744-3611; Ed. Heber Taylor; Pub. Dolph Tillotson; adv. contact: Ilana Cowan. pub. size: broadsheet; circ. morning 26,739(paid); Sun. 27,813(paid). **Wire Service(s):** AP.

GREENVILLE

US   ISSN 1042-3710
GREENVILLE HERALD BANNER. 1956. d. $.50/day newsstand; $1/Sun.; $8.50/mo. 2305 King St., Greenville, TX 75401-3299. TEL 903-455-4220; FAX 903-455-6281; E-mail: ghb@topher.net; URL: http://www.neteflex.com/banner. **Owner(s):** American Publishing Co., 606 N. Van Buren, P.O. Box 520, Marion, IL 62959. TEL 618-993-1711; Ed. Melva Geyer; Pub. Ronald W. Sohl; adv. contact: Terri McCreary. photos; bk.rev.; pub. size: broadsheet; circ. morning 96,849(paid); Sun. 10,643(paid). **Wire Service(s):** AP.

HARLINGEN

US
VALLEY MORNING STAR. 1911. d. $.50/day newsstand; $1.25/Sun.; $8.50/mo. 1310 S. Commerce, Harlingen, TX 78550. TEL 210-423-5511; FAX 210-430-6204. **Owner(s):** Freedom Communications, Inc., 17666 Fitch, Irvine, CA 92701. TEL 714-542-4415; Ed. Patrick Canty; Pub. V. Lyle DeBolt; adv.; photos; bk.rev.; pub. size: broadsheet; circ. morning 28,735(paid); Sun. 32,201(paid). **Wire Service(s):** AP.
   Formerly: Harlingen Valley Morning Star.

HENDERSON

US
HENDERSON DAILY NEWS. 1931. Sun.-Fri. $.25/day newsstand; $.75/Sun.; $5.50/mo. carrier. 1711 Hwy. 79 S., Henderson, TX 75654. TEL 903-657-2501; FAX 903-657-2452. **Owner(s):** Henderson Newspapers, Inc., P.O. Box 30, Henderson, TX 75653. TEL 903-657-2501; Ed. Randy Chote; Pub. Noble Welch; adv. contact: William Ashby. pub. size: broadsheet; circ. evening 6,500(paid); Sun. 8,000(paid). **Wire Service(s):** AP.

HEREFORD

US
HEREFORD BRAND. 1901. Tue.-Fri. & Sun. $.50/day newsstand; $.50/Sun.; $52/yr. 313 N. Lee St., Hereford, TX 79045. TEL 806-364-2030; FAX 806-364-8364. **Owner(s):** Roberts Publishing Co., 210 E. Broadway, Andrews, TX 79714; Ed. Tom Wells; Pub. O.G. Nieman; adv. contact: Mauri Montgomery. photos; pub. size: broadsheet; circ. evening 3,700(paid); Sun. 4,600(paid). **Wire Service(s):** AP.

HOUSTON

US
HOUSTON CHRONICLE. 1901. d. $.50/day newsstand; $1.75/Sun.; $11/mo. home deliv. 801 Texas Ave., Houston, TX 77002. TEL 713-220-7171; FAX 713-220-6806; E-mail: hci@chron.com; URL: http://www.chron.com. **Owner(s):** Hearst Corp., 959 Eighth Ave., New York, NY 10019. TEL 212-262-5700; Ed. Tony Pederson; Pub. R.J.V. Johnson; adv.; photos; pub. size: broadsheet; circ. morning 600,000(paid); Sun. 764,443(paid). **Wire Service(s):** AP, NYT, LAT-WP, KNT, SHNA, Cox, NNS.

HUNTSVILLE

US   ISSN 0888-4145
HUNTSVILLE ITEM. 1850. d. $.50/day newsstand; $1/Sun.; $9.95/mo. home deliv. 1409 Tenth St., Huntsville, TX 77340. TEL 409-295-4911; FAX 409-293-3909. **Owner(s):** American Publishing Co., 606 N. Van Buren, P.O. Box 520, Marion, IL 62959. TEL 618-993-1711; Ed. Lisa Trow; Pub. David Lyons; adv. contact: Kelly Lawson. photos; pub. size: broadsheet; circ. morning 6,486(controlled & paid); Sun. 7,648(controlled & paid). **Wire Service(s):** AP.

JACKSONVILLE

US
JACKSONVILLE DAILY PROGRESS. 1910. Sun.-Fri. $.50/day newsstand, $.75/Sun.; $6/mo. home deliv.; $8/mo. in cy. mailed; $9/mo. out of cy. mailed; $6/mo. home deliv. 525 E. Commerce, Jacksonville, TX 75766-0071. TEL 903-586-2236; FAX 903-586-0987. **Owner(s):** Stephens Group, Inc., P.O. Box 1350, Fort Smith, AR 72901. TEL 501-785-7810; Ed. Chris Fletcher; Pub. Robb Grindstaff; adv. contact: James Hutchison. photos; bk.rev.; pub. size: broadsheet; circ. evening 4,953(paid); Sun. 5,137(paid). **Wire Service(s):** AP.

KERRVILLE

US
KERRVILLE DAILY TIMES. 1908. Sun.-Fri. $.50/day newsstand, $1/Sun.; $6.95/mo in area; $8.10/mo. out of area; $9.85/mo. in state; $10.60/mo. out of state. 429 Jefferson St., Kerrville, TX 78028. TEL 210-896-7000; FAX 210-896-1150; E-mail: kdt@ktc.com. **Owner(s):** Southern Newspapers, Inc.; Ed. Clint Schroeder; Pub. Greg Schrader; adv. contact: Dawn Steele. photos; bk.rev.; pub. size: broadsheet; circ. evening 10,000(paid); Sun. 12,000(paid). **Wire Service(s):** AP.

KILGORE

US
KILGORE NEWS HERALD. 1931. Sun.-Fri. $.50/day newsstand; $.75/Sun.; $5.50/mo. carrier. 610 E. Main St., Kilgore, TX 75662. TEL 903-984-2593; FAX 903-984-7462. **Owner(s):** Stephens Group, Inc., P.O. Box 1359, Fort Smith, AR 72902; Ed. Greg A. Collins; Pub. Edward N. Souza; adv. contact: Don Alexander. photos; pub. size: broadsheet; circ. evening 5,000(paid); Sun. 5,500(paid). **Wire Service(s):** AP.

KILLEEN

US
KILLEEN DAILY HERALD. 1890. d. $.50/day newsstand; $1/Sun.; $8.40/mo. home deliv.; $12.10/mo. out of cy. mailed. 1809 Florence Rd., Killeen, TX 76541. TEL 817-634-2125; FAX 817-634-3293. **Owner(s):** F. Mayborn Enterprises, Inc., P.O. Box 614, Temple, TX 76503. TEL 817-778-4444; Pub. Thad Byars; adv. contact: Thad Byars. pub. size: broadsheet; circ. morning 22,000(paid); Sun. 26,000(paid). **Wire Service(s):** AP, SHNA.

LAREDO
US   ISSN 0740-5227
LAREDO MORNING TIMES. 1890. d. $.35/day newsstand; $1/Sun.; $6/mo. carrier. 111 Esperanza Dr., Laredo, TX 78041. TEL 210-728-2500; FAX 210-723-1227; E-mail: times@lmtonline.com; URL: http://lmtonline.com. **Owner(s):** Hearst Corp., 959 Eighth Ave., New York, NY 10019; Ed. Odie Arambula; Pub. Bill Green; adv. contact: Frank Escoredo. pub. size: broadsheet; circ. morning 23,500(paid); Sun. 25,000(paid). **Wire Service(s):** AP.

LONGVIEW
US
LONGVIEW NEWS JOURNAL. 1871. d. $.50/day newsstand; $1/Sun.; $99/yr. carrier; $14/mo. mailed. 320 E. Methvin St., Longview, TX 75601. TEL 903-757-3311; FAX 903-757-3742. **Owner(s):** Longview Newspapers, Inc., P.O. Box 1792, Longview, TX 75606. TEL 903-757-3311; Ed. Pete Litterski; Pub. Bill Martin; adv. contact: Tim Hobbs. pub. size: standard; circ. morning 31,000(paid); Sun. 41,000(paid). **Wire Service(s):** AP, NYT, CNS, SHNA.
Formerly: Daily News.

LUBBOCK
US
LUBBOCK AVALANCHE-JOURNAL. 1904. d. $.50/day newsstand; $1.50/Sun.; $12.15/mo. carrier; $145.80/yr. carrier. 710 Ave. J, Lubbock, TX 79401. TEL 806-762-8844; FAX 806-744-9603. **Owner(s):** Morris Communications, P.O. Box 936, Augusta, GA 30903. TEL 706-724-0851; Ed. Burle Pettit; Pub. David Sharp; adv. contact: Charles Evers. photos; bk.rev.; pub. size: broadsheet; circ. morning 72,500(paid); Sun. 82,300(paid). **Wire Service(s):** AP, KR, LAT-WP, SHNA.

LUFKIN
US
LUFKIN DAILY NEWS. 1906. d. $.50/day newsstand; $1.25/Sun. 300 Ellis, Lufkin, TX 75901. TEL 409-632-6631; FAX 409-632-6655; E-mail: glennm@tcac.com. **Owner(s):** Cox Enterprises, Inc., 72 Marietta St., N.W., Atlanta, GA 30303. TEL 404-843-5000; Ed. Ernie Murray; Pub. Glenn McCutchen; adv.; photos; bk.rev.; pub. size: broadsheet; circ. morning 14,256(free & paid); Sun. 16,520(free & paid). **Wire Service(s):** AP, Cox.

MARSHALL
US
NEWS MESSENGER. Sun.-Fri. $.50/day newsstand; $1/Sun.; $8/mo. home deliv. 309 E. Austin St., Marshall, TX 75670. TEL 903-935-7914; FAX 903-935-6242. **Owner(s):** Cox Newspapers, Inc., P.O. Box 105357, Atlanta, GA 30348; Ed. Shelly Jones; Pub. Phil Latham; adv. contact: Tami Goodell. pub. size: standard; circ. morning 10,000(paid); Sun. 10,500(paid).

MCALLEN
US
MCALLEN MONITOR. 1911. d. $.50/day newsstand, $1.50/Sun.; $8.75/mo. carrier; $15/mo. mailed. 1101 Ash St., McAllen, TX 78501. TEL 210-686-4343; FAX 210-686-4370. **Owner(s):** Freedom Communications, Inc., 1055 N. Main, Ste. 901, Santa Anna, CA 93060; Ed. Paul Binz; Pub. Ray M. Stafford; adv. contact: Abel Fernandez. pub. size: broadsheet; circ. morning 37,823(paid); Sun. 45,034(paid). **Wire Service(s):** AP, KR.

MCKINNEY
US
MCKINNEY COURIER GAZETTE. 1847. Sun.-Fri. $.50/day newsstand; $.50/Sun.; $75/yr. in cy. mailed. 4005 W. University, McKinney, TX 75070. TEL 972-542-2631; FAX 972-548-7527. **Owner(s):** McKinney Newspapers, Inc., P.O. Box 400, McKinney, TX 75069. TEL 972-542-2631; Pub. Jim Robertson; adv. contact: Pete Mulkey. pub. size: broadsheet; circ. evening 8,300(paid); Sun. 8,700(paid). **Wire Service(s):** AP.

MEXIA
US
MEXIA DAILY NEWS. 1872. Tue.-Sat. $.50 newsstand; $83.20/yr. in cy.; $91/yr. out of cy. 214 N. Railroad St., Mexia, TX 76667. TEL 817-562-2868; FAX 817-562-3121. **Owner(s):** American Publishing Co., 606 N. Van Buren, P.O. Box 520, Marion, IL 62959. TEL 618-993-1711; Ed. Robert E. Wright; Pub. Lynette Copley; adv.; photos; bk.rev.; pub. size: broadsheet; circ. evening 3,500(paid). **Wire Service(s):** AP.

MIDLAND
US   ISSN 0890-5932
MIDLAND REPORTER-TELEGRAM. 1929. d. $.50/day newsstand; $1.50/Sun.; $11/mo. home deliv.; $8.50/mo. Fri., Sat. & Sun. 201 E. Illinois, Midland, TX 79701. TEL 915-682-5311; FAX 915-682-3793; E-mail: jpatterson@basinlink.com; URL: http://www.mrt.com. **Owner(s):** Hearst Corp., 1700 Broadway, New York, NY 10019. TEL 212-649-2000; Ed. Gary Ott; Pub. Charles Spence; adv. contact: Sam Bakke. photos; bk.rev.; pub. size: broadsheet; circ. morning 22,000(paid); Sun. 26,550(paid). **Wire Service(s):** AP, LAT-WP, HHS.

MINERAL WELLS
US
MINERAL WELLS INDEX. 1900. Tue.-Fri. & Sun. $.25/day newsstand; $.75/Sun.; $60/yr. carrier; $60/yr. in cy.; $73/yr. out of town. 300 S.E. First St., Mineral Wells, TX 76067. TEL 817-325-4466; FAX 817-325-2020. **Owner(s):** Edward K. Livermore, P.O. Box 370, Mineral Wells, TX 76067. TEL 817-325-4465; Pub. Gary Adkisson; adv. contact: Mary Jo Watson. pub. size: broadsheet; circ. evening 4,750(paid); Sun. 5,000(paid). **Wire Service(s):** AP.

MT. PLEASANT
US
MOUNT PLEASANT DAILY TRIBUNE. 1874. Sun.-Fri. $.50/day newsstand; $1/Sun.; $74/yr. in cy.; $75/yr. out of cy. mailed, $80/yr. out of state mailed. 1705 Industrial Rd., Mt. Pleasant, TX 75455. TEL 903-572-1705; FAX 903-572-1705. **Owner(s):** Palmer Media, Inc., 111 E. Second St., Mt. Pleasant, TX 75455. TEL 214-572-3607; Ed. R.L. Palmer; Pub. R.B. Palmer; adv. contact: Martha McGregor. pub. size: broadsheet; circ. evening 6,500(paid); Sun. 8,000(paid). **Wire Service(s):** AP.

NACOGDOCHES
US
DAILY SENTINEL, THE. 1972. d. $.50/day newsstand; $1.25/Sun.; $8.55/mo. local deliv.; $92.35/yr. 4920 Colonial Dr., Nacogdoches, TX 75961. TEL 409-564-8361; FAX 409-560-4267. **Owner(s):** Cox Publishing Co., P.O. Box 68, Nacogdoches, TX 75963. TEL 409-564-8361; Ed. Robby Goodrich; Pub. Gary Borders; adv. contact: David Lawrence. pub. size: broadsheet; circ. morning 11,000(paid); Sun. 12,500(paid). **Wire Service(s):** AP.
Formerly: Sunday Sentinel.

NEW BRAUNFELS
US
NEW BRAUNFELS HERALD & ZEITUNG. 1852. Tue.-Fri. & Sun. $.50/day newsstand; $1/Sun.; $60/yr. carrier. 707 Landa St., New Braunfels, TX 78130. TEL 210-625-9144; FAX 210-625-1224. **Owner(s):** Southern Newspapers, Inc., 1050 Wilcrest Dr., Houston, TX 77042. TEL 713-266-5481; Ed. Micah Boyd; Pub. Doug Toney; adv. contact: Jason Pochardt. photos; pub. size: broadsheet; circ. evening 8,300(paid); Sun. 10,800(paid). **Wire Service(s):** AP.

ODESSA
US
ODESSA AMERICAN. 1939. d. $.50/day newsstand; $1.50/Sun.; $10,50/mo. carrier; $15.50/mo. mailed. 222 E. Fourth St., Odessa, TX 79761. TEL 915-337-4661; FAX 915-337-6262; E-mail: oa@link.freedom.com; URL: http://www.oaoa.com. **Owner(s):** Freedom Communications, Inc., Box 19549, Irvine, CA 92713. TEL 714-553-9292; Ed. Gary Newsom; Pub. Bill Salter; adv.; photos; pub. size: broadsheet; circ. morning 25,846(paid); Sun. 31,409(paid). **Wire Service(s):** AP.

ORANGE
US   ISSN 0885-8047
ORANGE LEADER. 1875. d. $.35/day newsstand; $1/Sun.; $8.50/mo. home deliv.; $13/mo. mailed. 200 Front Ave., Orange, TX 77630. TEL 409-883-3571; FAX 409-883-6342. **Owner(s):** American Publishing Co., 606 N. Van Buren, P.O. Box 520, Marion, IL 62959. TEL 618-993-1711; Pub. Ken Sury; adv. contact: Ray Trahan. pub. size: broadsheet; circ. evening 10,013(paid); Sun. 12,500(paid). **Wire Service(s):** AP.

PALESTINE

US   ISSN 1053-5748
PALESTINE HERALD-PRESS. 1898. d. $.25/day newsstand, $1/Sun.; $7.25/mo. carrier; $7.25/mo. in cy.; $7.25/mo. out of cy. 519 N. Elm St., Palestine, TX 75801. TEL 903-729-0281; FAX 903-729-0284. **Owner(s):** Patrick Management, P.O. Box 379, Palestine, TX 75802. TEL 903-729-0281; Ed. Bonnie Lasiter; Pub. Larry Mayo; adv. contact: Mike Whitworth. pub. size: broadsheet; circ. evening 96,876(paid); Sun. 10,265(paid). **Wire Service(s):** AP.

PAMPA

US
PAMPA NEWS. 1927. Sun.-Fri. $.50/day newsstand; $1/Sun.; $25.50/3 mos. mailed; $84/yr. carrier. 403 W. Atchison, Pampa, TX 79065. TEL 806-669-2525; FAX 806-669-2520. **Owner(s):** Freedom Communications, Inc., 17666 Fitch, Irvine, CA 92714. TEL 714-553-9292; Ed. Larry D. Hollis; Pub. Wayland Thomas; adv. contact: Rick Clark. pub. size: broadsheet; circ. evening 6,600(paid); Sun. 7,000(paid). **Wire Service(s):** AP.

PARIS

US   ISSN 8756-2081
PARIS NEWS, THE. 1869. Sun.-Fri. $.50/day newsstand; $1.25/Sun.; $8.75/yr. carrier. 5050 S.E. Loop 286, Paris, TX 75460-5050. TEL 903-785-8744; FAX 903-785-1263; E-mail: editor@theparisnews.com; URL: http://theparisnews.com. **Owner(s):** Southern Newspapers, Inc., 1050 Wilcrest Dr., Houston, TX 77042. TEL 713-266-5481; Ed. Bill Hankins; Pub. Michael Graxiola; adv.; photos; bk.rev.; pub. size: broadsheet; circ. evening 13,800(paid); Sun. 15,631(paid). **Wire Service(s):** AP.

PASADENA

US   ISSN 0896-3320
PASADENA CITIZEN. 1947. Tue.-Sun. $.50 newsstand; $7/mo. carrier; $19/3 mos. 102 S. Shaver, Pasadena, TX 77506. TEL 713-477-0221; FAX 713-477-9090. **Owner(s):** Westward Communications, Inc., 5005 LBJ Fwy., Ste. 1040, Dallas, TX 75225. TEL 214-450-1717; Ed. Lisa Bass; Pub. Lonnie Clement; adv.; photos; pub. size: broadsheet; circ. morning 8,000(paid); Sun. 15,000(paid). **Wire Service(s):** AP.

PECOS

US   ISSN 0746-4231
PECOS ENTERPRISE. 1887. Sun.-Fri. $.35/day newsstand; free/Sun.; $7/mo. carrier; $21/3 mos. city deliv.; $25.50/3 mos. mailed. 324 S. Cedar St., Pecos, TX 79772. TEL 915-445-5475; FAX 915-445-4321. **Owner(s):** Buckner News Alliance, 2101 Fourth Ave., Ste. 2300, Seattle, WA 98121. TEL 206-727-2727; Ed. Jon Fulbright; Pub. Mac McKinnon; adv. contact: Christina Bitolas. photos; pub. size: broadsheet; circ. evening 2,550(free & paid); Sun. 4,500(free & paid). **Wire Service(s):** AP.

PLAINVIEW

US
PLAINVIEW DAILY HERALD. 1889. Sun.-Fri. $.50/day newsstand; $1.25/Sun.; $8.25/mo. carrier; $9.50/mo. mailed. 820 Broadway, Plainview, TX 79072. TEL 806-296-1300; FAX 806-296-1315; E-mail: rohyde@lonestarbbs.com; URL: http://www.texasonline.net/pageone.htm. **Owner(s):** Hearst Corp., 1700 Broadway, New York, NY 10019. TEL 212-649-2000; Ed. Danny Andrews; Pub. Rollie D. Hyde; adv. contact: Jeff Noble. photos; pub. size: standard; circ. evening 7,500(paid); Sun. 9,000(paid). **Wire Service(s):** AP, HHS.

PLANO

US   ISSN 0895-4305
PLANO STAR COURIER. 1888. Wed.-Sun. $.50/day newsstand; $1/Sun; $8/mo. 801 E. Plano Pkwy., Plano, TX 75074. TEL 214-424-6565; FAX 214-424-4388; E-mail: editorial@dal.cleaf.com; URL: http://clover.cleaf.com/~hhone/. **Owner(s):** Harte-Hanks Communications, Inc., P.O. Box 269, San Antonio, TX 78291. TEL 512-344-8000; Ed. Tim Watterson; Pub. Beth Roddy; adv. contact: Patty Lucas. pub. size: broadsheet; circ. morning 20,000(paid); Sun. 17,000(paid). **Wire Service(s):** AP.

PORT ARTHUR

US   ISSN 0889-6755
PORT ARTHUR NEWS. 1897. d. $.50/day newsstand, $1/Sun.; $9/mo. carrier. 549 Fourth St., Port Arthur, TX 77640. TEL 409-985-5541; FAX 409-982-4903. **Owner(s):** American Publishing Co., 606 N. Van Buren, P.O. Box 520, Marion, IL 62959. TEL 618-993-1711; Ed. Roger Cowles; Pub. Jeff Jeffus; adv. contact: Horace Fontenot. pub. size: broadsheet; circ. morning 23,000(paid); Sun. 25,000(paid). **Wire Service(s):** Laserphoto, AP, Cox.

ROSENBERG

US
HERALD COASTER. 1892. Sun.-Fri. $.50/day newsstand; $1/Sun.; $5.65/mo. motor rte.; $7/mo. deliv.; $7.25/mo. mailed; $21.75/3 mos. mailed. t902 Fourth St., Rosenberg, TX 77471-5142. TEL 281-342-4474; FAX 281-342-3219. **Owner(s):** Hartman Newspapers, Inc., 1904 Fourth St., Rosenberg, TX 77471. TEL 713-342-4474; FAX 713-342-3219; Ed. Bob Haenel; Pub. Clyde C. King, Jr.; adv. contact: James Moser. photos; bk.rev.; pub. size: broadsheet; circ. evening 9,013(paid); Sun. 9,876(paid). **Wire Service(s):** AP.

SAN ANGELO

US
SAN ANGELO STANDARD-TIMES. 1884. d. $.50/day newsstand; $1.50/Sun.; $155.40/yr. 34 W. Harris Ave., San Angelo, TX 76903. TEL 915-653-1221; FAX 915-658-7341; E-mail: comments@texaswest.com; URL: http://www.texaswest.com. **Owner(s):** San Angelo Standard, Inc., 34 W. Harris, San Angelo, TX 76903. TEL 915-653-1221; Ed. Dennis Ellsworth; Pub. Kevin J. Barry; adv. contact: John Bair. pub. size: broadsheet; circ. morning 32,831(paid); Sun. 39,465(paid). **Wire Service(s):** AP, SHNS.

SAN ANTONIO

US   ISSN 1065-7908
SAN ANTONIO EXPRESS-NEWS. 1865. d. $.50/day newsstand; $1.50/Sun.; $9.75/mo. carrier. Ave. E & Third St., San Antonio, TX 78297. TEL 210-225-7411; FAX 210-250-3105; E-mail: jmoss@express-news.net; URL: http://www.express-news.net. **Owner(s):** Hearst Corp., 1700 Broadway, New York, NY 10019. TEL 212-649-2000; Ed. Lynnell Burkett; Pub. W. Lawrence Walker Jr.; adv.; photos; bk.rev.; pub. size: broadsheet; circ. morning 289,000(paid); Sun. 399,389(paid). **Wire Service(s):** AP, NYT, LAT-WP, SH.

SAN MARCOS

US
SAN MARCOS DAILY RECORD. 1912. Tue.-Fri. & Sun. $.50/day newsstand; $1/Sun.; $6/mo. carrier; $8/mo. mailed. 1910 I-35 S., San Marcos, TX 78666. TEL 512-392-2458; FAX 512-392-1514. **Owner(s):** American Publishing Co., 606 N. Van Buren, P.O. Bos 520, Marion, IL 62959. TEL 618-993-1711; Ed. Rowe Ray; Pub. Guy Trimble; adv. contact: Janice Eaton. pub. size: broadsheet; circ. evening 7,500(paid); Sun. 8,500(paid). **Wire Service(s):** AP.

SEGUIN

US
SEGUIN GAZETTE-ENTERPRISE. 1979. Tue.-Fri. & Sun. $.50/day newsstand; $1/Sun.; $67/yr. carrier; $67/yr. in cy. mailed; $57/yr. senior citizens. 1012 Schriewer Rd., Seguin, TX 78155. TEL 210-379-5402; FAX 210-379-8328. **Owner(s):** Southern Newspapers, Inc., P. O. Box 1200, Seguin, TX 78156-1200. TEL 512-379-5402; Ed. Kathie Ninneman; Pub. Larry Reynolds; pub. size: broadsheet; circ. evening 6,200(paid); Sun. 7,700(paid). **Wire Service(s):** AP.

SNYDER

US
SNYDER DAILY NEWS. 1950. Sun.-Fri. $.50 newsstand; $99/yr. out of town. 3600 College, Snyder, TX 79549. TEL 915-573-5486; FAX 915-573-0044. **Owner(s):** Roy McQueen, P.O. Box 949, Snyder, TX 79550. TEL 915-573-5486; FAX 915-573-0044; Ed. Bill McClellan; Pub. Roy McQueen; adv. contact: Wayne Burney. pub. size: standard; circ. evening 6,000(paid). Sun. 6,000(paid). **Wire Service(s):** AP.

STEPHENVILLE

US
STEPHENVILLE EMPIRE-TRIBUNE. 1870. Sun.-Fri. $.50/day newsstand; $1.50/Sun.; $9/mo. carrier. 590 S. Loop, Stephenville, TX 76401. TEL 817-965-3124; FAX 817-965-4269; E-mail: embtrib@our-town.com. **Owner(s):** Boone Newspapers, Inc., P.O. Box 2370, Tuscaloosa, AL 35403. TEL 407-338-3298; Ed. Jeff Osborne; Pub. Lee Leschper; adv. contact: Jack Mitchell. photos; pub. size: broadsheet; circ. evening 6,000(paid); Sun. 6,200(paid). **Wire Service(s):** AP.

DAILY NEWSPAPERS

SULPHUR SPRINGS
US ISSN 0745-6425
SULPHUR SPRINGS NEWS-TELEGRAM. 1881. Sun.-Fri. $.50/day newsstand; $.75/Fri. & Sun.; $75/yr. in city; $81/yr. out of city; $91/yr. mailed. 401 Church St., Sulphur Springs, TX 75482. TEL 903-885-8663; FAX 903-885-8768. **Owner(s):** Echo Publishing Co., 401 Church St., Sulphur Springs, TX 75482. TEL 903-885-8663; Ed. Bill Lamb; Pub. Scott Keys; adv. contact: Johnie Hardgrave. pub. size: broadsheet; circ. evening 6,900(paid); Sun. 7,100(paid). **Wire Service(s):** AP.

SWEETWATER
US
SWEETWATER REPORTER. 1881. Sun.-Fri. $.50/day newsstand; $.75/Sun.; $72/yr. home deliv. 112 W. Third St., Sweetwater, TX 79556. TEL 915-236-6677; FAX 915-235-4967. **Owner(s):** Stephens Group, Inc., Box 13507, Fort Smith, AR 72902. TEL 501-785-7810; Ed. Don Rogers; Pub. Mike Davis; adv. contact: Janice Briscoe. photos; bk.rev.; pub. size: broadsheet; circ. evening 3,400(paid); Sun. 4,000(paid). **Wire Service(s):** AP.

TAYLOR
US ISSN 1054-3171
TAYLOR DAILY PRESS. 1912. Mon.-Fri. $.50 newsstand; $70/yr. in cy.; $96/yr. out of cy. 211 W. Third St., Taylor, TX 76574. TEL 512-352-8535; FAX 512-352-2227. **Owner(s):** Jim Chiosini, Blackland Publications, P.O. Box 1040, Taylor, TX 76574. TEL 512-352-8535; Ed. Don McAlister; Pub. Robert Swonke; adv. contact: David Ariola. photos; bk.rev.; pub. size: broadsheet; circ. evening 5,300(paid). **Wire Service(s):** AP.

TEMPLE
US
TEMPLE DAILY TELEGRAM. 1907. d. $.50/day newsstand; $1/Sun.; $9/mo. 10 S. Third St., Temple, TX 76501. TEL 817-778-4444; FAX 817-778-4444; E-mail: tdt@vvm.com. **Owner(s):** Frank Mayborn Enterprises, Inc., P.O. Box 6114, Temple, TX 76503-6114. TEL 817-778-4444; FAX 817-778-4444; Ed. Steve Walters; Pub. Sue Mayborn; adv. contact: Gary Garner. photos; bk.rev.; pub. size: broadsheet; circ. morning 25,500(paid); Sun. 28,500(paid). **Wire Service(s):** AP.

TERRELL
US
TERRELL TRIBUNE. 1916. Sun.-Fri. $.50/day newsstand; $.50/Sun.; $6.25/mo. in city; $7.75/mo. motor rte. 1125 S. Virginia St., Terrell, TX 75160. TEL 214-563-6476; FAX 214-563-6478. **Owner(s):** Hartman Newspapers, Inc., P.O. Box 1390, Rosenberg, TX 77471. TEL 713-342-4474; FAX 713-342-3219; Ed. Jim Raynes; Pub. Bill Jordan; pub. size: broadsheet; circ. evening 6,200(paid); Sun. 6,500(paid). **Wire Service(s):** AP.

TEXARKANA
US
TEXARKANA GAZETTE. 1875. d. $.50/day newsstand; $1/Sun.; $119.40/yr.; $129/yr. mailed. 315 Pine St., Texarkana, TX 75501-5655. TEL 903-794-3311; FAX 903-792-7183; E-mail: txargaz@cei.net; URL: http://www.txargaz.com. **Owner(s):** Texarkana Newspapers, Inc., P.O. Box 621, Texarkana, TX 75504. TEL 903-794-3311; Ed. Les Minor; Pub. Walter Hussman, Jr.; adv.; pub. size: broadsheet; circ. morning 32,608(paid); Sun. 36,430(paid). **Wire Service(s):** AP, SHNA, Tribune Media, KR.

TEXAS CITY
US
TEXAS CITY SUN. 1912. d. $.50/day newsstand; $1/Sun.; $9.95/mo. carrier; $14/mo. mailed. 7800 Emmett Lowry Expy., Texas City, TX 77591. TEL 409-945-3441; FAX 409-935-0428. **Owner(s):** Walls Investment Co., Houston, TX. TEL 713-266-5481; Ed. Wendy Mohon; Pub. Les Daughtery, Jr.; adv. contact: Larry Cook. photos; bk.rev.; pub. size: broadsheet; circ. morning 8,800(paid); Sun. 9,100(paid). **Wire Service(s):** AP.

TYLER
US
TYLER MORNING TELEGRAPH. 1877. d. $.25/day newsstand; $.75/Sun.; $6.75/mo. carrier. 410 W. Erwin St., Tyler, TX 75702. TEL 903-597-8111; FAX 903-595-0335. **Owner(s):** T.B. Butler Publishing Co., Inc., P.O. Box 2030, Tyler, TX 75710. TEL 903-597-8111; Ed. Everett Taylor; Pub. Nelson Clyde, III; adv. contact: Nelson Clyde, IV. photos; bk.rev.; pub. size: broadsheet; circ. morning 44,000(paid); Sun. 52,000(paid). **Wire Service(s):** AP, UPI.

VERNON
US ISSN 1046-1426
VERNON DAILY RECORD. 1923. Sun.-Fri. $.50/day newsstand; $.50/Sun. $19.50/3 mos.; $35.60/6 mos.; $63.50/yr. 3214 Wilbarger St., Vernon, TX 76384. TEL 817-552-5454; FAX 817-553-4823. **Owner(s):** Larry L. Crabtree, 3214 Wilbarger St., Vernon, TX 76384. TEL 817-552-5454; Ed. Jimmy Carr; Pub. Larry L. Crabtree; adv. contact: Jim Surber. pub. size: broadsheet; circ. evening 4,900(paid); Sun. 5,200(paid). **Wire Service(s):** AP.

VICTORIA
US
VICTORIA ADVOCATE. 1846. d. $.50/day newsstand; $1/Sun.; $10/mo. carrier. 311 E. Constitution, Victoria, TX 77901. TEL 512-575-1451; FAX 512-574-1220. **Owner(s):** Victoria Advocate Publishing Co., P.O. Box 1518, Victoria, TX 77902. TEL 512-575-1451; Ed. Jim Bishop; Pub. John Roberts; adv. contact: Fred Hornberger. photos; bk.rev.; pub. size: broadsheet; circ. morning 40,000(paid); Sun. 42,000(paid). **Wire Service(s):** AP, LAT-WP.

WACO
US
WACO TRIBUNE HERALD. 1909. d. $.50/day newsstand; $1.25/Sun.; $11.80/mo. carrier. 900 Franklin Ave., Waco, TX 76701. TEL 817-757-5757; FAX 817-757-0302; E-mail: letters@mail.iamerica.net. **Owner(s):** Cox Enterprises, Inc., P.O. Box 105357, Atlanta, GA 30348; Ed. Barbara Elmore; Pub. Dan C. Savage; adv. contact: Tricia Phillips. photos; bk.rev.; pub. size: broadsheet; circ. morning 50,500(paid); Sun. 65,000(paid). **Wire Service(s):** AP, NYT, Cox.

WAXAHACHIE
US ISSN 0896-0291
WAXAHACHIE DAILY LIGHT. 1867. Sun.-Fri. $.50/day newsstand; $1.50/Sun.; $9.50/mo. 200 W. Marvin St., Waxahachie, TX 75165. TEL 214-937-3310; FAX 214-937-1139; E-mail: thelight@hachie.citylimits.net; URL: http://hachi.citylimits.net/thelight. **Owner(s):** Boone Newspapers, Inc., P.O. Box 2370, Tuscaloosa, AL 35403. TEL 407-338-3298; Ed. Scot Walker; Pub. Jimmy Sexton; adv. contact: Don Wilson. pub. size: broadsheet; circ. evening 7,000(paid); Sun. 7,000(paid). **Wire Service(s):** UPI.

WEATHERFORD
US
WEATHERFORD DEMOCRAT. 1895. Sun.-Fri. $.50/day newsstand; $.75/Sun.; $5.75/mo.; $69/yr. 512 Palo Pinto St., Weatherford, TX 76086. TEL 817-594-7447; FAX 817-594-9734. **Owner(s):** Stephens Group, Inc., P.O. Box 1359, Fort Smith, AR 72902. TEL 501-785-7810; Pub. Jane Trimble; adv. contact: Carla Bandera. photos; bk.rev.; pub. size: broadsheet; circ. morning 6,000(paid); Sun. 6,700(paid). **Wire Service(s):** AP.

WICHITA FALLS
US ISSN 0895-6138
TIMES RECORD NEWS. 1907. d. $.50/day newsstand; $1.50/Sun.; $11.55/mo. home deliv. 1301 Lamar St., Wichita Falls, TX 76301. TEL 817-767-8341; FAX 817-767-5201; E-mail: cwilson105@aol.com; URL: http://www.wtr.com. **Owner(s):** Harte-Hanks Communications, Inc., P.O. Box 860248, Plano, TX 85086; Ed. Gary Schneeberger; Pub. Lynn Dickerson; adv. contact: Kevin Davis. pub. size: standard; circ. morning 40,000(paid); Sun. 50,000(paid). **Wire Service(s):** AP, CTG, HHNS, KRNS.

UTAH

LOGAN
US
HERALD JOURNAL, THE. 1931. Sun.-Fri. $.50/day newsstand; $1.25/Sun.; $108/yr. in state; $114/yr. out of state. 75 W. Third, N., Logan, UT 84321. TEL 801-752-2121; FAX 801-753-6642. **Owner(s):** Pioneer Newspapers, Inc., 221 W. First Ave., Ste. 405, Seattle, WA 98119; Ed. Charles McCollum; Pub. Bruce K. Smith; adv. contact: Wayne Ashcroft. pub. size: broadsheet; circ. evening 15,500(paid); Sun. 15,600(paid). **Wire Service(s):** AP, SHNA.

OGDEN

US

STANDARD-EXAMINER. 1888. d. $.50/day newsstand; $1.50/Sun.; $10.25/mo. mailed; $8.75/mo. carrier. 455 23rd St., Ogden, UT 84401. TEL 801-625-4200; FAX 801-625-4299; E-mail: ronthornburg@standard.net. **Owner(s):** Sandusky Newspapers, Inc., 314 W. Market St., Sandusky, OH 44870. TEL 419-625-5500; Ed. Ronald Thornburg; Pub. Scott Trundle; adv. contact: Brad Roghaar. photos; bk.rev.; pub. size: broadsheet; circ. evening 61,000(paid); Sun. 64,000(paid). **Wire Service(s):** AP, SHNA, LAT-WP.

PROVO

US   **ISSN 0891-2777**

DAILY HERALD, THE. 1873. d. $.50/day newsstand; $1.25/Sun.; $9/mo. carrier; $9.25/mo. motor rte. 1555 N. 200 W., Provo, UT 84604-0717. TEL 801-373-5050; FAX 801-373-5489. **Owner(s):** Pulitzer Publishing Co., 900 N. Tucker Blvd., St. Louis, MO 63101. TEL 314-340-8000; Ed. Mike Patrick; Pub. Kirk Parkinson; adv. contact: Mike Stansfield. photos; bk.rev.; pub. size: broadsheet; circ. evening 32,383(paid); Sun. 33,531(paid). **Wire Service(s):** AP.

SALT LAKE CITY

US   **ISSN 0745-4724**

SALT LAKE CITY DESERET NEWS. 1850. d. $.50/day newsstand; $1.50/Sun. 30 E. 100th St., Salt Lake City, UT 84110. TEL 801-237-2100; FAX 801-237-2121. **Owner(s):** Church of Jesus Christ of Latter-Day Saints, P.O. Box 1257, Salt Lake City, UT 84110. TEL 801-237-2175; FAX 801-237-2121; Ed. Don C. Woodward; Pub. William James Mortimer; adv. contact: Edward McCaffrey. photos; bk.rev.; pub. size: broadsheet; circ. evening 63,000(paid); Sun. 69,000(paid). **Wire Service(s):** AP, RN, NYT, SHNA, UPI, LAT-WP.

US   **ISSN 0746-3502**

SALT LAKE TRIBUNE. 1871. d. $.50/day newsstand; $1.75/Sun.; $107/yr. carrier. 143 S. Main St., Salt Lake City, UT 84111. TEL 801-237-2045; FAX 801-521-9418; E-mail: jshelledy@sltrib.com; URL: http://www.sltrib.com/. **Owner(s):** Kearns-Tribune Corp., 143 S. Main, Salt Lake City, UT 84111. TEL 801-237-2031; Ed. James E. Shelledy; Pub. Dominic A. Welch; adv. contact: Ed McAffrey. pub. size: broadsheet; circ. morning 129,000(paid); Sun. 163,000(paid). **Wire Service(s):** NYT, LAT-WP, AP, RN, KR.

ST. GEORGE

US   **ISSN 0745-6611**

SPECTRUM, THE. 1963. d. $.50/day newsstand; $1.50/Sun.; $102/yr. 275 E. St. George Blvd., St. George, UT 84770. TEL 801-674-6200; FAX 801-674-6265; E-mail: rplotnow@aol.com. **Owner(s):** Thomson Newspapers, Inc., Metro Centre, One Station Pl., 6th Fl., Stamford, CT 06902. TEL 203-425-2500; Ed. Linda Lindus; Pub. Roger Plotnow; adv. contact: Jennie Johns. photos; bk.rev.; pub. size: broadsheet; circ. evening 22,000(paid); Sun. 22,200(paid). **Wire Service(s):** AP.

Formerly: The Daily Spectrum.

VERMONT

BARRE

US

TIMES ARGUS. 1897. d. $.50/day newsstand; $1.50/Sun.; $13.20/5 wks. carrier; $15.50/5 wks. motor rte. 540 N. Main St., Barre, VT 05641. TEL 802-479-0191; FAX 802-479-0191. **Owner(s):** Times Argus Assoc. Inc., Barre, VT 00761; Ed. Ann Gibbons; Pub. R. John Mitchell; adv. contact: Glen Dunning. pub. size: broadsheet; circ. evening 12,500(paid); Sun. 13,500(paid). **Wire Service(s):** AP, NYT, KR.

BENNINGTON

US

BENNINGTON BANNER. 1841. Mon.-Sat. $.50/day newsstand; $.75/Sat.; $11/mo. carrier; $13/mo. mailed. 425 Main St., Bennington, VT 05201. TEL 802-447-7567; FAX 802-442-3413. **Owner(s):** New England Newspapers, Inc., 23 Exchange St., Pawtucket, RI 02860. TEL 401-722-4000; Ed. Jim Rogalski; Pub. Jules Molenda; adv. contact: Ed Shepardson. pub. size: broadsheet; circ. morning 8,400(paid). **Wire Service(s):** AP.

BRATTLEBORO

US

BRATTLEBORO REFORMER. 1913. Mon.-Sat. $.50/day newsstand; $.75/Sat.; $115/yr. carrier; $125/yr. mailed in cy.; $150/yr. out of cy. Black Mountain Rd., Brattleboro, VT 05302-0802. TEL 802-254-2311; FAX 802-257-1305. **Owner(s):** New England Newspapers, Inc., 75 S. Church St., P.O. Box 1171, Pittsfield, MA 01201. TEL 413-447-7311; Ed. Glenn Drohan; Pub. Richard Macko; adv. contact: Mark Elliott. photos; bk.rev.; pub. size: broadsheet; circ. morning 11,235(paid). **Wire Service(s):** AP.

BURLINGTON

US

BURLINGTON FREE PRESS. 1827. d. $.50/day newsstand; $1.75/Sun.; $3.25/wk. carrier. 191 College St., Burlington, VT 05401. TEL 802-863-3441; FAX 802-660-1802; E-mail: bfreepress@aol.com. **Owner(s):** Gannett Company, Inc., 1100 Wilson Blvd., Arlington, VA 22234. TEL 703-284-6000; Ed. Mickey Hirten; Pub. James Carey; adv. contact: Mike Ricken. photos; bk.rev.; pub. size: broadsheet; circ. morning 52,800(paid); Sun. 63,500(paid). **Wire Service(s):** AP, GNS, LAT-WP.

NEWPORT

US

NEWPORT DAILY EXPRESS. 1936. d. $.35 newsstand; $102/yr. Hill St., Newport, VT 05855. TEL 802-334-6568; FAX 802-334-8691. **Owner(s):** Pulitzer Community Newspapers, Inc., Pierre LaClede Center, 7701 Forsyth Blvd., Ste.102, St. Louis, MO 63105; Ed. Terry Albee. adv.; photos; pub. size: standard; circ. evening 4,891(paid). **Wire Service(s):** AP.

RUTLAND

US

RUTLAND HERALD. 1794. d. $.50/day newsstand; $1.50/Sun.; $3.05/wk. carrier; $3.45/wk. motor rte. 27 Wales St., Rutland, VT 05701. TEL 802-747-6121; FAX 802-775-2423. **Owner(s):** Herald Association, Inc., 27 Wales St., Rutland, VT 05701. TEL 802-747-6121; FAX 802-775-2423; Ed. John Van Hoesen; Pub. John Mitchell; adv. contact: Glenda Hawley. pub. size: broadsheet; circ. morning 22,321(paid); Sun. 23,881(paid). **Wire Service(s):** AP, NYT.

ST. ALBANS

US

ST. ALBANS MESSENGER. 1861. Mon.-Sat. $.50 newsstand; $2.10/wk. in cy.; $3/wk. out of cy.; $2.30/wk. motor route. 281 N. Main St., St. Albans, VT 05478. TEL 802-524-9771; FAX 802-527-1948. **Owner(s):** Emerson & Cynthia Lynn, French Hill Rd. 1, St. Albans, VT 05478. TEL 802-527-0800; Ed. Emerson Lynn; Pub. Emerson K. Lynn; adv. contact: Jeremy Read. bk.rev.; pub. size: broadsheet; circ. evening 5,000(paid). **Wire Service(s):** AP.

ST. JOHNSBURY

US

CALEDONIAN-RECORD, THE. 1837. Mon.-Sat. $.35 newsstand; $2.10/wk. carrier; $110/yr. mailed. 25 Federal St., St. Johnsbury, VT 05819. TEL 802-748-8121; FAX 802-748-1613. **Owner(s):** Caledonian-Record Publishing Co., Inc., P.O. Box 8, St. Johnsbury, VT 05819. TEL 802-748-8121; Ed. Ellie Dixon; Pub. Mark Smith; adv. contact: Michael Gonyaw. pub. size: broadsheet; circ. evening 11,043(paid). **Wire Service(s):** AP.

Formerly: St. Johnsbury Caledonian-Record.

VIRGIN ISLANDS

ST. CROIX

US

ST. CROIX AVIS. 1844. d. $.50/day newsstand; $.60/Sun. & Mon.; $95/yr. local; $172/yr. out of area. 36 ANB La Grande Princesse, Christiansted, St. Croix, VI 00820. TEL 809-773-2300; FAX 809-773-5511. **Owner(s):** St. Croix Avis, 36 ANB La Princesse, St. Croix, VI 00820. TEL 809-773-2300; Ed. Rena Broadhurst Knight; Pub. Rena Broadhurst Knight; adv. contact: Linda Clark. photos; bk.rev.; pub. size: tabloid; circ. morning 10,500(paid). **Wire Service(s):** AP.

DAILY NEWSPAPERS

ST. THOMAS
US

VIRGIN ISLANDS DAILY NEWS. 1930. d. $.60 newsstand; $254.25/yr. US mainland; $199.25/yr. Puerto Rico. 49 & 52a Estate Thomas, St. Thomas, VI 00801. TEL 809-774-8772; FAX 809-776-0740. **Owner(s):** Daily News Publishing Co., P.O. Box 7760, Charlotte Amalie, St. Thomas, VI; Pub. Ariel Melchior, Jr.; adv.; photos; bk.rev.; pub. size: tabloid; circ. morning 16,623(free & paid). **Wire Service(s):** AP.

VIRGINIA

BRISTOL
US   ISSN 8750-6505

BRISTOL HERALD-COURIER, THE. 1870. d. $.50/day newsstand; $1.25/Sun.; $10.95/mo. carrier; $7/mo. weekend pkge. 320 Morrison Blvd., Bristol, VA 24201. TEL 540-669-2181; FAX 540-669-3696. **Owner(s):** Bristol Newspapers, Inc., 320 Morrison Blvd., Bristol, VA 24201. TEL 703-669-2181; Ed. Brian Reece; Pub. Arthur S. Powers; adv. contact: Joseph Adams. pub. size: broadsheet; circ. morning 47,000(paid); Sun. 47,000(paid). **Wire Service(s):** AP, SHNA, NEA.

CHARLOTTESVILLE
US   ISSN 0746-0430

DAILY PROGRESS. 1892. d. $.50/day newsstand; $1.50/Sun.; $2.80/wk. motor rte.; $145.60/yr. motor rte. 685 W. Rio Rd., Charlottesville, VA 22901. TEL 804-978-7210; FAX 804-978-7214. **Owner(s):** Media General, Inc., 333 E. Grace St., Richmond, VA 23219. TEL 804-649-6000; FAX 804-775-8090; Ed. Wayne Mogielnicki; Pub. Lawrence McConnell; adv. contact: Wanda Brickhead. photos; bk.rev.; pub. size: broadsheet; circ. evening 30,096(paid); Sun. 33,500(paid). **Wire Service(s):** AP, LAT-WP.

COVINGTON
US

VIRGINIAN REVIEW. 1914. Mon.-Sat. $.50 newsstand; $63/yr. 128 N. Maple Ave., Covington, VA 24426-0271. TEL 540-962-2121; FAX 540-962-5072. **Owner(s):** Covington Virginian Inc., 128 N. Maple Ave., Covington, VA 24426. TEL 703-962-2121; FAX 703-962-5072; Ed. Horton P. Beirne; Pub. Horton P. Beirne; adv. contact: Robert Tucker. photos; bk.rev.; pub. size: broadsheet; circ. evening 8,400(paid). **Wire Service(s):** AP.

CULPEPER
US

CULPEPER STAR EXPONENT. 1882. d. $.35/day newsstand; $1/Sun.; $98.80/yr. in cy. 122 W. Spencer St., Culpeper, VA 22701. TEL 540-825-0771; FAX 540-825-0778. **Owner(s):** Media General, Inc., 333 E. Grace St., Richmond, VA 23219. TEL 804-649-6000; FAX 804-775-8090; Pub. Robin L. Quillan; adv. contact: Diane Holt. photos; pub. size: broadsheet; circ. morning 8,010(paid). **Wire Service(s):** AP.

DANVILLE
US   ISSN 0744-3242

DANVILLE REGISTER & BEE. 1848. d. $.50/day newsstand; $1/Sun.; $8.50/mo. carrier; $11/mo. mailed. 700 Monument St., Danville, VA 24541. TEL 804-793-2311; FAX 804-797-2299; E-mail: rbnews@ns.gamewood.net; URL: http://www.gamewood.net/~rbnews. **Owner(s):** Media General, Inc., 333 E. Grace St., Richmond, VA 23219. TEL 804-649-6000; FAX 804-775-8090; Pub. Peter Yates; adv.; photos; bk.rev.; pub. size: broadsheet; circ. morning 24,000(paid); Sun. 29,000(paid). **Wire Service(s):** AP.

FAIRFAX
US   ISSN 0162-2064

ALEXANDRIA JOURNAL. 1938. d. $.25 newsstand; $72/yr. 2720 Prosperity Ave., Fairfax, VA 22034-1000. TEL 703-560-4000; FAX 703-846-8301; E-mail: ryan@jrnl.com; URL: http://www.jrnl.com. **Owner(s):** Journal Newspapers, Inc., 2720 Prosperity Ave., Fairfax, VA 22034-1010. TEL 703-560-4000; FAX 703-846-8301; Ed. Jane Touzalin; Pub. Ryan Phillips; adv.; photos; bk.rev.; pub. size: broadsheet; circ. morning 5,098(paid). **Wire Service(s):** AP.

US   ISSN 0162-2072

ARLINGTON JOURNAL. 1933. d. $.50 newsstand; $72/yr. 2720 Prosperity Ave., Fairfax, VA 22034. TEL 703-560-4000; FAX 703-846-8366; E-mail: ryan@jrnl.com; URL: http://www.jrnl.com. **Owner(s):** Journal Newspapers, Inc., 2720 Prosperity Ave., Fairfax, VA 22034. TEL 703-560-4000; FAX 703-846-8366; Ed. Jane Touzalin; Pub. Ryan Phillips; adv.; photos; bk.rev.; pub. size: broadsheet; circ. morning 9,370(paid). **Wire Service(s):** AP.

US   ISSN 0162-2056

FAIRFAX JOURNAL. 1938. d. $.25 newsstand; $21/3 mos.; $39/6 mos.; $72/yr.; $62/yr. senior citizens & military. 2720 Prosperity Ave., Fairfax, VA 22031. TEL 703-560-4000; FAX 708-846-8366; E-mail: ryan@jrnl.com; URL: http://www.jrnl.com. **Owner(s):** Journal Newspapers, Inc., 2720 Prosperity Ave., Fairfax, VA 22034. TEL 703-560-4000; Ed. Jane Touzalin; Pub. Ryan Phillips; adv. contact: Kenneth Courter. photos; bk.rev.; pub. size: broadsheet; circ. morning 45,088(paid). **Wire Service(s):** AP.

FREDERICKSBURG
US

FREDERICKSBURG FREE LANCE-STAR. 1885. Mon.-Sat. $.35 newsstand; $1/Sat.; $130/yr. mailed in state; $136/yr. mailed out of state. 616 Amelia St., Fredericksburg, VA 22401. TEL 540-374-5000; FAX 540-373-8450. **Owner(s):** Free Lance-Star Publishing Co., 616 Amelia St., Fredericksbrg, VA 22401. TEL 703-374-5000; Ed. Edward W. Jones; Pub. Charles S. Rowe; adv. contact: C. Murphy Street. pub. size: broadsheet; circ. evening 52,000(paid). **Wire Service(s):** AP, KNT.

HARRISONBURG
US

DAILY NEWS-RECORD. 1897. Mon.-Sat. $.35 newsstand; $58/yr. in state; $70/yr. out of state. 231 S. Liberty St., Harrisonburg, VA 22801. TEL 540-574-6200; FAX 540-466-9112. **Owner(s):** Rockingham Publishing Co., Inc., 231 S. Liberty St., Harrisonburg, VA 22801. TEL 540-574-6200; FAX 540-433-9112; Ed. Ken P. Mink; Pub. Harry F. Byrd, Jr.; adv.; bk.rev.; pub. size: broadsheet; circ. morning 32,752(paid). **Wire Service(s):** AP.

HOPEWELL
US

HOPEWELL NEWS. 1926. Mon.-Fri. $.50 newsstand; $6.50/mo. carrier; $9/mo. mailed. 516 E. Randolph Rd., Hopewell, VA 23860. TEL 804-458-8511; FAX 804-458-7556. **Owner(s):** Hopewell Publishing Co., Inc., 206 S. Randolph Rd., Hopewell, VA 23860. TEL 804-458-8511; Ed. Rebecca Isom; Pub. Barney White; adv. contact: Clint Robertson. pub. size: broadsheet; circ. evening 7,800(paid). **Wire Service(s):** UPI.

LYNCHBURG
US

NEWS & ADVANCE. 1866. d. $.50/day newsstand; $1.25/Sun.; $2.70/wk. home deliv. 101 Wyndale Dr., Lynchburg, VA 24501. TEL 804-385-5400; FAX 804-385-5538. **Owner(s):** Media General, Inc., 411 E. Franklin St., Richmond, VA 23219. TEL 804-775-8030; Ed. Joe Stinnett; Pub. Terry Hall; adv. contact: Jo Pearse. photos; bk.rev.; pub. size: broadsheet; circ. morning 44,000(paid); Sun. 45,000(paid). **Wire Service(s):** AP, NYT.

MANASSAS
US   ISSN 0745-6859

JOURNAL MESSENGER. 1869. Mon.-Sat. $.35 newsstand; $52.20/yr. 9009 Church St., Manassas, VA 22110. TEL 703-368-3101; FAX 703-368-9017; E-mail: jm@cais.com. **Owner(s):** Media General, Inc., 333 E. Grace St., Richmond, VA 23219. TEL 804-649-6000; FAX 804-775-8090; Ed. Kathryn McQuaid; Pub. Myron Struck; adv. contact: Craig Bender. pub. size: broadsheet; circ. evening 12,517(paid). **Wire Service(s):** AP.

US

▼**PRINCE WILLIAM JOURNAL.** 1995. Sun.-Fri. $.25 newsstand; $21/3 mos.; $39/6 mos.; $72/yr. 9275 Corporate Cir., Manassas, VA 22110. TEL 703-257-4600; FAX 703-257-4960. **Owner(s):** Journal Newspapers, Inc., 2720 Prosperity Ave., Fairfax, VA 22034. TEL 703-560-4000; Ed. Derald Everhart; Pub. Ryan Phillips; adv. contact: Robin McClure. photos; bk.rev.; pub. size: broadsheet; circ. evening 10,000(paid). **Wire Service(s):** AP.

MARTINSVILLE
US

MARTINSVILLE BULLETIN. Sun.-Fri. $.35/day newsstand; $1/Sun.; $93/yr. carrier; $132/yr. mailed. 204 Broad St., Martinsville, VA 24112. TEL 540-638-8801; FAX 540-638-4153. **Owner(s):** Robert Haskell, 204 Broad St., Martinsville, VA 24112. TEL 703-638-8801; FAX 703-638-4153; Ed. Richard Hammerstrom; Pub. Robert Haskell; adv. contact: Robert Cox. pub. size: broadsheet; circ. evening 18,915(paid); Sun. 20,400(paid). **Wire Service(s):** AP, UPI.

10510 NEWPORT NEWS, VA **DAILY NEWSPAPERS**

NEWPORT NEWS
US

DAILY PRESS, THE. 1896. d. $.50/day newsstand; $1.50/Sun.; $3.05/wk. 7505 Warwick Blvd., Newport News, VA 23607-1517. TEL 757-247-4776; FAX 757-245-8618. **Owner(s):** Tribune Co., 435 N. Michigan Ave., Chicago, IL 60611; Ed. Will Corbin; Pub. Jack W. Davis, Jr.; adv.; photos; bk.rev.; pub. size: broadsheet; circ. morning 97,835(paid); Sun. 118,980(paid). **Wire Service(s):** KNT, AP, NYT, LAT-WP.

Formerly: Newport News Daily Press.

NORFOLK
US   ISSN 0889-6127

VIRGINIAN-PILOT, THE. 1865. d. $.50/day newsstand; $1.25/Sun.; $120/yr. home deliv.; $290/yr. mail deliv. 150 W. Brambleton Ave., Norfolk, VA 23510. TEL 757-446-2000; FAX 757-446-2983. **Owner(s):** Landmark Communications, Inc., 150 W. Brambleton Ave., Norfolk, VA 23510. TEL 757-446-2000; Ed. Dennis Hautrig; Pub. R. Bruce Bradley; adv. contact: Joe Antle. photos; bk.rev.; pub. size: broadsheet; circ. morning 201,232(paid); Sun. 238,655(paid). **Wire Service(s):** AP, LAT-WP, NYT, KR.

PETERSBURG
US

PROGRESS-INDEX. 1865. d. $9.50/mo. carrier; $12.10/mo. mailed in city; $13.50/mo. mailed out of city. 15 Franklin St., Petersburg, VA 23803. TEL 804-732-3456; FAX 804-861-9452. **Owner(s):** Scranton Times, 149 Penn Ave., Scranton, PA 18503. TEL 717-348-9101; Ed. Elizabeth Hedgepeth; Pub. George R. Fain; adv.; bk.rev.; pub. size: broadsheet; circ. evening 19,500(paid); Sun. 20,000(paid). **Wire Service(s):** AP, SHNA.

PULASKI
US

SOUTHWEST TIMES, THE. 1906. Sun.-Fri. $.50/day newsstand; $1/Sun.; $1.80/wk. carrier. 34 Fifth St., N.E., Pulaski, VA 24301. TEL 540-980-5220; FAX 540-980-3618. **Owner(s):** Southwest Publishers LLC, 34 Fifth St., Pulaski, VA 24301. TEL 540-980-5220; FAX 540-980-3618; Ed. Mike Williams; Pub. Syd M. Kibodeaux; adv. contact: Vickie Clay. adv.: $10.30/SAU. photos; pub. size: broadsheet; circ. morning 6,230(paid); Sun. 7,984(paid). **Wire Service(s):** AP.

RICHMOND
US

RICHMOND TIMES-DISPATCH. 1850. d. $.50/day newsstand; $.75/Sat.; $1.75/Sun.; $168/yr. carrier. 333 E. Grace St., Richmond, VA 23219. TEL 804-649-6000; FAX 804-649-6898. **Owner(s):** Media General, Inc., 333 E. Grace St., Richmond, VA 23219. TEL 804-649-6000; FAX 804-649-6898; Ed. Louise Seals; Pub. J. Stewart Bryan III; adv.; photos; bk.rev.; pub. size: broadsheet; circ. morning 209,698(paid); Sun. 244,065(paid). **Wire Service(s):** AP, NYT, LAT-WP.

ROANOKE
US

ROANOKE TIMES, THE. 1886. d. $.50/day newsstand; $1.50/Sun.; $22.40/wk. carrier. 201 W. Campbell Ave., Roanoke, VA 24011. TEL 540-981-3353; FAX 540-981-3318; E-mail: roatimes@infi.net; URL: http://www.infi.net/roatimes/index.html. **Owner(s):** Landmark Communications, Inc., 150 W. Brambleton Ave., P.O. Box 449, Norfolk, VA 23510. TEL 804-446-2000; Ed. Wendy Zomparelli; Pub. Walter Rugaber; adv. contact: Cathy Greenberg. photos; pub. size: broadsheet; circ. morning 115,644(paid); Sun. 126,444(paid). **Wire Service(s):** AP, LAT, WP, NYT, KRT.

Formerly: Roanoke Times & World News.

STAUNTON
US   ISSN 0747-2501

DAILY NEWS LEADER, THE. 1904. d. $.50/day newsstand; $1.25/Sun. 11 N. Central Ave., Staunton, VA 24401. TEL 540-885-7281; FAX 540-885-1094; E-mail: news@newsleader.com; URL: http://www.newleader.com/daily. **Owner(s):** Gannett Company, Inc., 1100 Wilson Blvd., Arlington, VA 22234. TEL 703-284-6000; Ed. Rick Gunter; Pub. Wesley Wampler; adv. contact: Marty White. pub. size: broadsheet; circ. morning 18,200(paid); Sun. 22,500(paid). **Wire Service(s):** AP.

STRASBURG
US

NORTHERN VIRGINIA DAILY. 1932. Mon.-Sat. $.35 newsstand; $59/yr.; $55/yr. home deliv. 152 N. Holliday St., Strasburg, VA 22657. TEL 540-465-5137; FAX 540-465-9388; E-mail: nvd@shentel.net. **Owner(s):** Shenandoah Publishing House, Inc., 152 N. Holliday St., Strasburg, VA 22657. TEL 703-405-5137; FAX 703-405-9388; Ed. Joe Strohmeyer. adv.; photos; pub. size: broadsheet; circ. morning 17,300(paid). **Wire Service(s):** AP.

SUFFOLK
US   ISSN 8750-9598

SUFFOLK NEWS-HERALD. 1873. Tue.-Sun. $.25/day newsstand; $.75/Sun.; $72.60/yr. in state. 130 S. Saratoga St., Suffolk, VA 23434. TEL 757-539-3437; FAX 757-539-8804. **Owner(s):** Media General, Inc., 411 E. Franklin St., Richmond, VA 23219. TEL 804-775-8030; Ed. Tim Copeland; Pub. Gaither Perry; adv. contact: Ernie Chenalt. photos; pub. size: broadsheet; circ. morning 4,200(paid); Sun. 4,300(paid).

WAYNESBORO
US   ISSN 8750-7862

NEWS-VIRGINIAN. 1892. Mon.-Sat. $.50 newsstand; $93.60/yr. mailed. 544 W. Main St., Waynesboro, VA 22980. TEL 540-949-8213; FAX 540-942-4542; E-mail: newsvir@cfw.com. **Owner(s):** Media General, Inc., 333 E. Grace St., Richmond, VA 23219. TEL 804-649-6000; FAX 804-775-8090; Pub. Dale Gerstenslager; adv. contact: Roxanne Viccaro. photos; bk.rev.; pub. size: broadsheet; circ. evening 9,457(paid). **Wire Service(s):** AP.

WINCHESTER
US   ISSN 1064-0665

WINCHESTER STAR. Mon.-Sat. $.25 newsstand; $7/mo. local carrier; $58/yr. local. 2 N. Kent St., Winchester, VA 22601. TEL 540-667-3200; FAX 540-667-0012. **Owner(s):** Thomas T. Byrd, 2 N. Kent St., Winchester, VA 22601. TEL 703-667-3200; FAX 703-667-0012; Ed. Ron Morris; Pub. Thomas T. Byrd; adv. contact: John Parkinson. pub. size: broadsheet; circ. evening 24,000(paid). **Wire Service(s):** AP, NYT.

WOODBRIDGE
US

POTOMAC NEWS. 1959. d. $.35 newsstand; $2.50/wk. 14010 Smoketown Rd., Woodbridge, VA 22193. TEL 703-878-8000; FAX 703-878-8099. **Owner(s):** Media General, Inc., 333 E. Grace St., Richmond, VA 23219. TEL 804-649-6000; FAX 804-775-8090; Ed. Luke West; Pub. Andrew Mick; adv.; bk.rev.; pub. size: broadsheet; circ. evening 30,300(paid). **Wire Service(s):** AP, NYT, GNS.

WASHINGTON

ABERDEEN
US   ISSN 0740-3135

DAILY WORLD, THE. 1890. d. $.50/day newsstand; $1/Sun. 315 S. Michigan St., Aberdeen, WA 98520. TEL 360-532-4000; FAX 360-533-1328. **Owner(s):** Donrey Media Group, P.O. Box 17017, Fort Smith, AR 72902. TEL 501-785-7810; Ed. John C. Hughes; Pub. Ted Dixon; adv. contact: Theresa Wincewicz. photos; bk.rev.; pub. size: broadsheet; circ. evening 17,010(paid); Sun. 17,050(paid). **Wire Service(s):** AP.

BELLEVUE
US

EASTSIDE JOURNAL. 1976. d. $8.50/mo. 1705 132nd St., N.E., Bellevue, WA 98005. TEL 206-455-2222; FAX 206-635-0603. **Owner(s):** Horvitz Newspapers, Inc., P.O. Box 90130, Bellevue, WA 98009; Ed. Tom Wolfe; Pub. Peter Horvitz; adv. contact: Hallie Olsen. pub. size: broadsheet; circ. morning 36,500(controlled & paid); Sun. 37,500(controlled & paid). **Wire Service(s):** AP.

Formerly: Journal American.

BELLINGHAM
US

BELLINGHAM HERALD. 1890. d. $.35/day newsstand; $1.50/Sun. 1155 N. State St., Bellingham, WA 98225. TEL 360-676-2600; FAX 360-647-9260; E-mail: herald@az.com; URL: http://marie.az.com/~herald. **Owner(s):** Gannett Company, Inc., 1100 Wilson Blvd., Arlington, VA 22234. TEL 703-284-6000; Ed. Evan Miller; Pub. Robert Robbins; adv. contact: Kristine Kincaid. pub. size: broadsheet; circ. evening 28,500(paid); Sun. 36,500(paid). **Wire Service(s):** AP, GNS.

DAILY NEWSPAPERS

BREMERTON
US   ISSN 1050-3692

SUN, THE. 1935. d. $.50/day newsstand; $1/Sun.; $11/mo. home deliv.; $132/yr. 545 Fifth St., Bremerton, WA 98337-0053. TEL 360-377-3711; FAX 360-479-7681; E-mail: mikepsun@aol.com. **Owner(s):** Scripps-Howard, 312 Walnut St., 28th Fl., Cincinnati, OH 45202. TEL 513-977-3000; Ed. Mike Phillips; Pub. Elizabeth F. Brenner; adv. contact: John Souza. photos; bk.rev.; pub. size: broadsheet; circ. morning 38,800(paid); Sun. 42,050(paid). **Wire Service(s):** AP, NYT, SHNA.

CENTRALIA
US

CHRONICLE, THE. 1889. Mon.-Sat. $.50 newsstand; $9.25/mo. carrier. 321 N. Pearl St., Centralia, WA 98531. TEL 360-736-3311; FAX 360-736-4796. **Owner(s):** Lafromboise Newspapers, Inc., 321 N. Pearl St., Centralia, WA 98531. TEL 206-736-3311; Ed. Sarah Jenkins; Pub. Dennis R. Waller; adv. contact: Tom May. photos; bk.rev.; pub. size: broadsheet; circ. evening 14,500(paid). **Wire Service(s):** AP.
   Formerly: Daily Chronicle, The.

ELLENSBURG
US

DAILY RECORD. 1909. Mon.-Sat. $.35 newsstand; $8.50/mo. in city; $15/mo. out of city. 401 N. Main St., Ellensburg, WA 98926-0248. TEL 509-925-1414; FAX 509-925-5696. **Owner(s):** Pioneer Newspapers, Inc., 3701 W. Lake Ave., Glenview, IL 60025. TEL 708-846-9200; Ed. Keith Love; Pub. Keith Love; adv. contact: Dave Martin. pub. size: broadsheet; circ. evening 6,000(paid). **Wire Service(s):** AP.
   Formerly: Ellensburg Daily Record.

EVERETT
US

HERALD, THE. 1891. d. $.35/day newsstand; $1.25/Sun.; $9/mo. 1213 California St., Everett, WA 98201. TEL 206-339-3000; FAX 206-339-3049. **Owner(s):** Washington Post Co., 1150 15th St., N.W., Washington, DC 20071. TEL 202-334-7100; Pub. Larry L. Hanson; photos; pub. size: broadsheet; circ. evening 52,254(paid); Sun. 62,430(paid). **Wire Service(s):** AP, NYT, LAT-WP.

KENNEWICK
US

TRI-CITY HERALD. 1947. d. $.50/day newsstand; $1.25/Sun.; $10.75/mo. 107 N. Cascade St., Kennewick, WA 99336. TEL 509-582-1500. E-mail: krobertson@tri-cityherald.com; URL: http://www.tri-cityherald.com. **Owner(s):** McClatchy Newspapers, 2100 Q St., Sacramento, CA 95852. TEL 916-321-1936; Ed. Ken Robertson; Pub. Jack Briggs; adv. contact: Ellen Evans. photos; bk.rev.; pub. size: broadsheet; circ. morning 39,935(paid); Sun. 43,530(paid). **Wire Service(s):** AP, LAT-WP, McClatchy News Service, KR, NYT.
   Formerly: Pasco-Kennewick-Richland Tri-City Herald.

KENT
US

SOUTH COUNTY JOURNAL. d. $.35/day newsstand; $1/Sun.; $9/4 wks.; $114/yr. 600 S. Washington, Kent, WA 98032. TEL 206-872-6600; FAX 206-854-1006; E-mail: valleyedit@aol.com. **Owner(s):** Horvitz Newspapers, Inc., 1705 132nd St., N.E., Belleview, WA 98005. TEL 206-453-4270; Ed. Dave Burch; Pub. John Perry; adv. contact: Mike Steven. pub. size: broadsheet; circ. morning 33,000(paid); Sun. 34,000(paid).
   Formerly: Daily Globe News, Valley Daily News.

LONGVIEW
US   ISSN 0889-0005

DAILY NEWS. 1923. Mon.-Sat. $.50 newsstand; $8/mo. 770 11th Ave., Longview, WA 98632. TEL 360-577-2500; FAX 360-577-2538. **Owner(s):** Westmedia Corp., P.O. Box 189, Longview, WA 98632. TEL 360-577-2500; Ed. Robert Gaston; Pub. Ted M. Natt; adv.; photos; pub. size: broadsheet; circ. evening 26,000(paid). Wire Service(s): AP.

MOSES LAKE
US   ISSN 1041-1658

COLUMBIA BASIN HERALD. Mon.-Fri. $.50 newsstand; $132/yr. in cy.; $138/yr. out of cy. 813 W. Third Ave, Moses Lake, WA 98837. TEL 509-765-4561; FAX 509-765-8659. **Owner(s):** Columbia Basin Publishing Co., P.O. Box 910, Moses Lake, WA 98837. TEL 509-765-4561; Pub. Steve Hill; adv. contact: Steve Hill. pub. size: broadsheet; circ. evening 8,475(paid). **Wire Service(s):** AP.

MT. VERNON
US

SKAGIT VALLEY HERALD. 1884. Mon.-Sat. $.50 newsstand; $8.75/mo. 1000 E. College Way, Mt. Vernon, WA 98273-0578. TEL 360-424-3251; FAX 360-424-5300. **Owner(s):** Skagit Valley Publishing Co., P.O. Box 578, Mt. Vernon, WA 98273. TEL 360-424-3251; FAX 360-424-5300; Pub. L. Stedem Wood; adv.; photos; bk.rev.; pub. size: broadsheet; circ. evening 22,000(paid). **Wire Service(s):** AP.

OLYMPIA
US   ISSN 0746-7575

OLYMPIAN, THE. 1889. d. $.35/day newsstand; $1.50/Sun.; $13.25/mo. carrier; $13.75/mo. motor rte. 1268 E. Fourth Ave., Olympia, WA 98506. TEL 360-754-5400; FAX 360-754-4221; E-mail: olympian@halcyon.com; URL: http://www.halcyon.com/olympian. **Owner(s):** Gannett Company, Inc., 1100 Wilson Blvd., Arlington, VA 22234. TEL 703-284-6000; Pub. Fred Hamilton; adv. contact: Narva Walton. photos; pub. size: broadsheet; circ. morning 36,000(paid); Sun. 45,800(paid). **Wire Service(s):** AP, GNS.

PORT ANGELES
US   ISSN 1050-7000

PENINSULA DAILY NEWS. 1916. d. $.35/day newsstand; $1.25/Sun.; $8.75/mo. carrier; $9.75/mo. motor rte. 305 W. First St., Port Angeles, WA 98362. TEL 360-452-2345; FAX 360-417-3521; E-mail: pdnedit@aol.com. **Owner(s):** Horvitz Newspapers, Inc., P.O. Box 90130, Bellevue, WA 98009; Ed. Frank Ducceschi; Pub. Frank Ducceschi; adv. contact: John Huston. photos; pub. size: broadsheet; circ. morning 15,000(paid); Sun. 17,000(paid). **Wire Service(s):** AP.

SEATTLE
US

SEATTLE DAILY JOURNAL OF COMMERCE. 1893. Mon.-Sat. $1.25 newsstand; $190/yr. 83 Columbia St., Seattle, WA 98104. TEL 206-622-8272; FAX 206-622-8416. **Owner(s):** Daily Journal of Commerce, Inc., 83 Columbia St., Seattle, WA 98111. TEL 206-622-8272; Ed. M. Scott; Pub. Phil Brown; adv. contact: John Mihalyo. adv.: $20/SAU. pub. size: broadsheet; circ. morning 6,544(paid). **Wire Service(s):** AP & Business Wire.

US

SEATTLE POST-INTELLIGENCER. 1863. d. $.50 newsstand; $2/Sun.; $2.65/wk. King, Shuhomish, Pierce & Kitsap cys.; $2.71/wk. elsewhere. 101 Elliott Ave., W., Seattle, WA 98119-4220. TEL 206-448-8000; FAX 206-448-8166. **Owner(s):** Hearst Corp., 959 Eighth Ave., New York, NY 10019. TEL 212-649-2000; Ed. Kenneth Bunting; Pub. J.D. Alexander; adv.; photos; bk.rev.; pub. size: broadsheet; circ. morning 200,000(paid); Sun. 500,000(paid). **Wire Service(s):** AP, COX, NYT, HHS, RN, SHNS.

US   ISSN 0745-9696

SEATTLE TIMES, THE. 1896. d. $.50/day newsstand; $2/Sun. 1120 John St., Seattle, WA 98109. TEL 206-464-2111; FAX 206-464-2261. **Owner(s):** Blethen Corp., P.O. Box 70, Seattle, WA 98111. TEL 206-464-2111; Knight Ridder, Inc., One Herald Plz., Miami, FL 33132. TEL 305-376-3800; FAX 305-376-3875; Ed. Alex MacLeod; Pub. Michael Lemke; adv. contact: Michael Lemke. photos; pub. size: broadsheet; circ. morning 198,385(paid); evening 226,287(paid); Sun. 502,395(paid). **Wire Service(s):** AP, DJ, KNS, LAT-WP, CT-NYT.

SPOKANE
US

SPOKESMAN-REVIEW, THE. 1883. d. $.50/day newsstand; $1.50/Sun.; $12/mo. 999 W. Riverside Ave., Spokane, WA 99201-1010. TEL 509-459-5000; FAX 509-459-5258; E-mail: editor@spokesman.com; URL: http://www.virtuallynw.com. **Owner(s):** Cowles Publishing Co., Review Tower, 999 W. Riverside Ave., Spokane, WA 99201-1010. TEL 509-459-5000; FAX 509-459-5258; Ed. Chris Peck. adv.; pub. size: broadsheet; circ. morning 125,000(paid); Sun. 150,000(paid). **Wire Service(s):** AP, NYT, KR, McClatchy.

SUNNYSIDE

US   ISSN 1046-1612
DAILY SUN-NEWS. 1962. Mon.-Fri. $.35 newsstand; $4/mo. carrier; $48/yr. mailed in cy.; $50/yr. out of cy. 600 S. 6th St., Sunnyside, WA 98944. TEL 509-837-4500; FAX 509-837-6397. **Owner(s):** Eagle Newspapers, Inc., P.O. Box 12008, Salem, OR 97309. TEL 503-393-1774; FAX 503-463-9898; Ed. Olaf Elze; Pub. Tom Lanctot; adv. contact: Bob Dedolph. photos; bk.rev.; pub. size: tabloid; circ. evening 4,033(free & paid).

TACOMA

US   ISSN 1042-3621
NEWS TRIBUNE, THE. 1883. d. $.35/day newsstand; $1.50/Sun.; $10.50/mo carrier. 1950 S. State St., Tacoma, WA 98405-2860. TEL 206-597-8742; FAX 206-597-8274; E-mail: leted@p.tribnet.com; URL: http://www.tribnet.com/. **Owner(s):** McClatchy Newspapers, P.O. Box 15779, Sacramento, CA 95852. TEL 916-321-1000; adv. contact: Cathy Brewis. photos; bk.rev.; pub. size: broadsheet; circ. morning 128,432(paid); Sun. 147,114(paid). **Wire Service(s):** AP, NYT, LAT, KNT, SHNS.
Formerly: The Morning News Tribune.

VANCOUVER

US   ISSN 1043-4151
COLUMBIAN, THE. 1890. Sun.-Fri. $.50/day newsstand; $1.50/Sun.; $10/mo. home deliv.; $11/mo. motor rte.; $20/mo. mailed. 701 W. Eighth St., Vancouver, WA 98660-0180. TEL 360-694-3391; FAX 360-699-6033; E-mail: editors@columbian.com; URL: http://www.columbian.com. **Owner(s):** Scott Campbell, P.O. Box 180, Vancouver, WA 98660. TEL 360-694-3391; FAX 360-699-6033; Ed. Tom Koenninger; Pub. Scott Campbell; adv. contact: Susan Hirtzel. photos; bk.rev.; pub. size: standard; circ. evening 56,500(paid); Sun. 66,000(paid). **Wire Service(s):** AP, LAT-WP.

WALLA WALLA

US
WALLA WALLA UNION-BULLETIN. 1968. Sun.-Fri. $.50/day newsstand; $1/Sun.; $7.50/mo. 112 S. First St., Walla Walla, WA 99362. TEL 509-525-3300; FAX 509-525-1232. **Owner(s):** Seattle Times Co., P.O. Box 1358, Walla Walla, WA 99362. TEL 509-525-3300; Ed. Rick Doyle; Pub. Debbie Frol; adv. contact: Carl Tyler. pub. size: broadsheet; circ. evening 16,000(paid); Sun. 16,300(paid). **Wire Service(s):** LAT-WP.

WENATCHEE

US
WENATCHEE WORLD. 1905. Mon.-Sat. $.50/day newsstand; $1.50/Sun.; $9.50/mo. 14 N. Mission, Wenatchee, WA 98801. TEL 509-663-5161; FAX 509-662-5413. **Owner(s):** World Publishing Co., 14 N. Mission, Wenatchee, WA 98807; Ed. Steve Lachowictz; Pub. Wilfred R. Woods; adv. contact: Jay White. photos; pub. size: broadsheet; circ. evening 30,107(paid); Sun. 33,201(paid). **Wire Service(s):** AP.

YAKIMA

US
YAKIMA HERALD-REPUBLIC. 1903. d. $.50/day newsstand; $1.25/Sun.; $9.50/mo. carrier. 114 N. Fourth St., Yakima, WA 98901. TEL 509-248-1251; FAX 509-577-7766. **Owner(s):** Seattle Times Co., P.O. Box 70, Seattle, WA 98111; Ed. Bob Cryder; Pub. Charles Cochrane, Jr.; adv. contact: Robert Bickler. pub. size: standard; circ. morning 41,500(paid); Sun. 45,000(paid). **Wire Service(s):** UPI, AP, KR.

WEST VIRGINIA

BECKLEY

US   ISSN 0746-6854
REGISTER/HERALD. 1880. d. $.50/day newsstand; $1.25/Sun.; $11.95/mo. carrier. 801 N. Kanawha St., Beckley, WV 25801. TEL 304-255-4400; FAX 304-255-4427; E-mail: news@register-herald.com; URL: http://www.register-herald.com. **Owner(s):** Thomson Newspapers, Inc., 3150 Des Plaines Ave., Des Plaines, IL 60018. TEL 708-299-5544; Ed. Pat Hanna; Pub. Robert R. Hammond; adv. contact: Jack L. Scott. photos; bk.rev.; pub. size: broadsheet; circ. morning 33,500(paid); Sun. 34,500(paid). **Wire Service(s):** AP.

BLUEFIELD

US
BLUEFIELD DAILY TELEGRAPH. 1893. d. $.50/day newsstand; $1.25/Sun.; $11.25/mo. carrier; $13.50/mo. mailed in cy. 928 Bluefield Ave., Bluefield, WV 24701. TEL 304-327-2811; FAX 304-327-6179; E-mail: editor@bdtonline.com; URL: http://www.bdtonline.com. **Owner(s):** Thomson Newspapers, Inc., 3150 Des Plaines Ave., Des Plaines, IL 60018. TEL 708-299-5544; Ed. Tom Colley; Pub. Steve Smith; adv. contact: Terri Hale. pub. size: broadsheet; circ. morning 25,500(paid); Sun. 27,000(paid). **Wire Service(s):** AP.

CHARLESTON

US
CHARLESTON DAILY MAIL. 1920. d. $.50/day newsstand; $1.25/Sun.; $135.20/yr. 1001 E. Virginia St. E., Charleston, WV 25301. TEL 304-348-5140; FAX 304-348-4847. **Owner(s):** Thomson Newspapers, Inc., One Thorn Run Ctr., Ste. 500, 1187 Thorn Run Rd. Ext., Coraopolis, PA 15108. TEL 412-262-7870; Ed. Nanya Friend; Pub. Sam Hindman; adv. contact: Larry Levak. photos; pub. size: broadsheet; circ. evening 46,460(paid); Sun. 105,257(paid). **Wire Service(s):** AP, LAT-WP.

US
CHARLESTON GAZETTE, THE. 1872. d. $.50/day newsstand; $1.25/Sun.; $117/yr. carrier. 1001 Virginia St., E., Charleston, WV 25301. TEL 304-348-5100; FAX 304-348-1233; E-mail: gazette@citymet.met. **Owner(s):** Daily Gazette Co., Inc., 1001 Virginia St., E., Charleston, WV 25301. TEL 304-348-5140; Ed. James A. Haught; Pub. Craig Selby; adv. contact: Larry Levak. photos; bk.rev.; pub. size: broadsheet; circ. morning 51,000(paid); Sun. 103,000(paid). **Wire Service(s):** NYT, AP.

CLARKSBURG

US
CLARKSBURG EXPONENT. 1927. d. $.35/day newsstand; $1/Sun.; $124.80/yr. carrier. 324-326 Hewes Ave., Clarksburg, WV 26301. TEL 304-624-6411; FAX 304-622-3629; E-mail: webmaster@earthlink.net; URL: http://www.cpubco.com. **Owner(s):** Clarksburg Publishing Co., 324 Hewes Ave., P.O. Box 2000, Clarksburg, WV 26301. TEL 304-624-6411; Ed. Robert F. Stealey; Pub. Terry Horne; adv. contact: Jack L. Smith. pub. size: oversize; circ. morning 7,134(paid); Sun. 24,050(paid). **Wire Service(s):** AP.

US
CLARKSBURG TELEGRAM. 1906. d. $.35/day newsstand; $1/Sun.; $140.40/yr. carrier. 324 Hewes Ave., Clarksburg, WV 26301. TEL 304-624-6411; FAX 304-622-3629. **Owner(s):** Cecil Highland, 324 Hewes Ave., Clarksburg, WV 26301. TEL 304-624-6411; Ed. Robert F. Stealey; Pub. Cecil Highland, Jr.; adv. contact: Jack L. Smith. pub. size: broadsheet; circ. evening 14,000(paid); Sun. 24,000(paid).

ELKINS

US
INTER-MOUNTAIN, THE. 1893. Mon.-Sat. $.35/day newsstand; $.50/Sat.; $81/yr. 520 Railroad Ave., Elkins, WV 26241. TEL 304-636-2121; FAX 304-636-8252. **Owner(s):** Ogden Newspapers, Inc., 1500 Main St., Wheeling, WV 26003. TEL 304-233-0100; Ed. Don Smith; Pub. James Hoffman; adv. contact: Michael Duplaga. pub. size: broadsheet; circ. evening 12,700(paid). **Wire Service(s):** AP.

FAIRMONT

US
TIMES WEST VIRGINIAN. 1845. d. $.50/day newsstand; $1.25/Sun.; $162/yr. carrier. Quincy & Ogden Sts., Fairmont, WV 26554. TEL 304-367-2500; FAX 304-367-2569; E-mail: timeswv@timeswv.com; URL: http://www.timeswv.com. **Owner(s):** Thomson Newspapers, Inc., 3150 Des Plaines Ave., Des Plaines, IL 60018. TEL 708-299-5544; Ed. Valerie Nieman; Pub. Frank Wood; adv. contact: William Watkins. pub. size: broadsheet; circ. morning 15,862(paid); Sun. 16,268(paid). **Wire Service(s):** AP.

HUNTINGTON

US
HUNTINGTON HERALD-DISPATCH. 1889. d. $.50/day newsstand; $1.50/Sun.; $14.08/mo. home deliv. 946 Fifth Ave., Huntington, WV 25701. TEL 304-526-4000; FAX 304-526-2857; E-mail: hdnews@ramlink.net. **Owner(s):** Gannett Company, Inc., 1100 Wilson Blvd., Arlington, VA 22234. TEL 703-284-6000; Pub. Nancy C. Monaghan; adv.; pub. size: broadsheet; circ. morning 38,516(paid); Sun. 44,087(paid). **Wire Service(s):** AP, GNS.

DAILY NEWSPAPERS

KEYSER
US
MINERAL DAILY TRIBUNE. Mon.-Sat. $.30 newsstand; $6.19/mo. in cy. carrier; $9.66/mo. other areas. 24 Armstong St., Keyser, WV 26726. TEL 304-788-3333; FAX 304-788-3398. **Owner(s):** James Tetrick, 24 Armstrong, Keyser, WV 26726. TEL 304-788-3333; Ed. Liz Beavers. adv. contact: Robert Tetrick. pub. size: broadsheet; circ. morning 5,200(paid). **Wire Service(s):** AP.

LEWISBURG
US
WEST VIRGINIA DAILY NEWS. Mon.-Fri. $.25 newsstand; $72.08/yr. in state; $70/yr. out of state. 200 S. Court St., Lewisburg, WV 24901-0471. TEL 304-645-1206; FAX 304-645-7104. **Owner(s):** Moffitt Newspapers, Inc., P.O. Box 8565, Roanoke, VA 24014. TEL 703-344-2489; Ed. Tina Alvey; Pub. Frank Spicer; adv. contact: Judy Dowdy. photos; pub. size: broadsheet; circ. evening 4,000(paid).

LOGAN
US   ISSN 0746-0570
LOGAN BANNER. 1888. Sun.-Fri. $.50/day newsstand; $1/Sun.; $84/yr. carrier; $121/yr. mailed. 435 Stratton St., Logan, WV 25601. TEL 304-752-6950; FAX 304-752-1239. **Owner(s):** Logan Media, Inc., 435 Stratton St., Logan, WV 25601. TEL 304-752-6950; Ed. Jack McNelly; Pub. Richard Osbourne; adv. contact: Kathy Chafin. pub. size: broadsheet; circ. morning 10,000(paid); Sun. 10,000(paid). **Wire Service(s):** AP.

MARTINSBURG
US
JOURNAL, THE. 1927. d. $96/yr. local; $102/yr. mailed. 207 W. King St., Martinsburg, WV 25401. TEL 304-263-8931; FAX 304-263-8058. **Owner(s):** Ogden Newspapers, Inc., 1500 Main St., Wheeling, WV 26003. TEL 304-233-0100; Ed. Maria Lorensen. adv. contact: James Connors. pub. size: broadsheet; circ. morning 17,796(paid); Sun. 19,363(paid). **Wire Service(s):** UPI.
Formerly: Evening Journal/Weekend Journal.

MORGANTOWN
US
DOMINION POST, THE. 1873. d. $.50/day newsstand; $1.25/Sun.; $156.36/yr. carrier. 1251 Earl Core Rd., Morgantown, WV 26505-6298. TEL 304-292-6301; FAX 304-291-2326. **Owner(s):** Richard G., John R., David A. Raese, 1251 Earl Core Rd., Morgantown, WV 26505-6298. TEL 304-292-6301; FAX 304-291-2326; Ed. Ralph Brem; Pub. David Raese; adv.; pub. size: broadsheet; circ. morning 20,150(paid); Sun. 27,806(paid). **Wire Service(s):** AP.

MOUNDSVILLE
US
MOUNDSVILLE DAILY ECHO. 1891. d. $.15 newsstand; $35/yr. 713 Lafayette, Moundsville, WV 26041-0369. TEL 304-845-2660; FAX 304-845-2661. **Owner(s):** Charles L. Walton, 713 Lafayette, Moundsville, WV 26041-0369. TEL 304-845-2660; FAX 304-845-2661; Pub. Charles & Marian Walton; adv.; photos; pub. size: broadsheet; circ. evening 4,680(paid). **Wire Service(s):** AP.

PARKERSBURG
US   ISSN 8750-3956
PARKERSBURG SENTINEL. 1875. d. $.50/day newsstand; $1/Sun. 519 Juliana St., Parkersburg, WV 26101. TEL 304-485-1891; FAX 304-422-7134. **Owner(s):** Ogden Newspapers, Inc., 1500 Main St., Wheeling, WV 26003. TEL 304-233-0100; Ed. David Owen; Pub. Ed Kruger; adv. contact: Ed Hoffman. photos; bk.rev.; pub. size: broadsheet; circ. morning 23,400(paid); evening 10,800(paid); Sun. 43,600(paid). **Wire Service(s):** AP.
Formerly: Parkersburg News Sentinel.

POINT PLEASANT
US
POINT PLEASANT REGISTER. Mon.-Sat. $.35 newsstand; $1.70/wk. 200 Main St., Point Pleasant, WV 25550. TEL 304-675-1333; FAX 304-675-5234. **Owner(s):** Ohio Valley Publishing Co., P.O. Box 1688, Greenville, SC 29602; Pub. Robert L. Wingett; adv. contact: Brian Billings. photos; bk.rev.; pub. size: standard; circ. evening 6,000(paid). **Wire Service(s):** AP.

WEIRTON
US
DAILY TIMES. 1928. d. $96.20/yr. 114 Lee Ave., Weirton, WV 26062. TEL 304-748-0606; FAX 304-748-2202. **Owner(s):** Ogden Newspapers, Inc., 1500 Main St., Wheeling, WV 26033. TEL 304-233-0100; Ed. Linda Harris; Pub. Charles Jarvis; photos; pub. size: broadsheet; circ. evening 9,000(paid). **Wire Service(s):** AP, SHNA, Thomson.

WELCH
US
WELCH DAILY NEWS. 1923. Mon.-Fri. $.30 newsstand; $75/yr. 125 Wyoming St., Welch, WV 24801. TEL 304-436-3144; FAX 304-436-3146. **Owner(s):** Jack Moffitt, 125 Wyoming St., Welch, VA 24804. TEL 304-436-3144; Ed. Mary Stillwell; Pub. W.A. Johnson; adv. contact: Vance Hayes. pub. size: broadsheet; circ. morning 6,000(paid). **Wire Service(s):** UPI.

WHEELING
US
INTELLIGENCER, THE. 1852. d. $.50/day newsstand; $1/Sun. 1500 Main St., Wheeling, WV 26003. TEL 304-233-0100; FAX 304-233-5718. **Owner(s):** Ogden Newspapers, Inc., 1500 Main St., Wheeling, WV 26003. TEL 304-233-0100; Ed. Bob Kelly. adv.; pub. size: broadsheet; circ. morning 23,300(paid); Sun. 54,900(paid). **Wire Service(s):** UPI.
Formerly: Morning Intelligencer, The.

US
WHEELING NEWS-REGISTER. 1890. Sun.-Fri. $.50/day newsstand; $.75/Sun.; $8/mo. carrier; $106/yr. Mon.-Sat. mailed; $57/yr. Sun. mailed. 1500 Main St., Wheeling, WV 26003. TEL 304-233-0100; FAX 304-233-0827. **Owner(s):** Ogden Newspapers, Inc., 1500 Main St., Wheeling, WV 26003. TEL 304-233-0100; Pub. G. Ogden Nutting; adv. contact: Perry Nardo. photos; bk.rev.; pub. size: broadsheet; circ. evening 20,859(paid); Sun. 52,442(paid). **Wire Service(s):** AP.

WILLIAMSON
US   ISSN 0883-1602
WILLIAMSON DAILY NEWS. 1904. Mon.-Sat. $.50 newsstand; $37.44/13 wks.; $68.64/26 wks. 100 Block E. Third Ave., Williamson, WV 25661. TEL 304-235-4242; FAX 304-235-0730. **Owner(s):** Williamson Daily News, Inc., Box 1660, Williamson, WV 25661. TEL 304-235-4242; Ed. Terry Richardson; Pub. Sandy Hurley; adv. contact: Lisa Marcum. pub. size: broadsheet; circ. evening 11,000(paid). **Wire Service(s):** AP.

WISCONSIN

ANTIGO
US
ANTIGO DAILY JOURNAL. 1905. Mon.-Sat. $73.95/yr. in cy.; $103.40/yr. mailed. 612 Superior St., Antigo, WI 54409-2086. TEL 715-623-4191; FAX 715-623-4193. **Owner(s):** Berner Bros. Publishing Co., Inc., 612 Superior St., Antigo, WI 54409. TEL 715-623-4191; FAX 715-623-4193; Ed. Fred A. Berner; Pub. Marie F. Berner; adv.; photos; bk.rev.; pub. size: standard; circ. evening 7,000(paid). **Wire Service(s):** AP.

APPLETON
US
POST-CRESCENT, THE. 1853. d. $.50/day newsstand; $1.75/Sun.; $182/yr. carrier; $195/yr. mtr. rte.; $234/yr. mailed. 306 W. Washington St., Appleton, WI 54911. TEL 414-733-4411; FAX 414-733-1945. **Owner(s):** Thomson Newspapers, Inc., 3150 Des Plaines Ave., Des Plaines, IL 60018. TEL 708-299-5544; Ed. William Knutson; Pub. Paul Seveska; adv.; photos; pub. size: broadsheet; circ. evening 61,580(paid); Sun. 80,000(paid). **Wire Service(s):** AP, SHFS, Thomson News Service.

ASHLAND
US   ISSN 1050-4095
DAILY PRESS, THE. 1888. Mon.-Sat. $.50 newsstand; $8.50/mo. carrier. 122 W. Third St., Ashland, WI 54806. TEL 715-682-2313; FAX 715-682-4699; E-mail: ashpress@win.bright.net; URL: http://badger.win.bright.net/~wgcs/ashpress/adphome.htm. **Owner(s):** Murphy McGinnis Media, 625 First Bank Pl., 130 W. Superior St., Duluth, MN 55802. TEL 218-723-8000; FAX 218-723-8980; Pub. John Murphy; adv. contact: Jeff Swiston. photos; bk.rev.; pub. size: broadsheet; circ. morning 7,900(paid). **Wire Service(s):** AP.

DAILY NEWSPAPERS

BARABOO
US

BARABOO NEWS-REPUBLIC. 1855. Fri.-Sat. $.50 newsstand; $.75/Sat.; $9.25/mo. carrier; $98/yr. in state; $144/yr. out of state. 219 First St., Baraboo, WI 53913. TEL 608-356-4808; FAX 608-356-0344. **Owner(s):** Independent Media Group, 321 Frenette, Chippewa Falls, WI 54729. TEL 715-723-5515; Ed. Ken Pritchard; Pub. David W. Gentry; adv. contact: Jay Anderle. photos; pub. size: standard; circ. morning 20,613(paid); evening 4,000(paid); Sun. 20,293(paid). **Wire Service(s):** AP.

BEAVER DAM
US ISSN 0749-1379

BEAVER DAM DAILY CITIZEN. 1856. Mon.-Sat. $123.20/yr.carrier; $126.84/yr. motor rte.; $154/US mailed. 805 Park Ave., Beaver Dam, WI 53916. TEL 414-887-0321; FAX 414-887-8790. **Owner(s):** Citizen Publishing Co., 805 Park Ave., Beaver Dam, WI 53916. TEL 414-887-0321; FAX 414-887-8190; Ed. Jeff Hovind; Pub. James E. Conley; adv. contact: Steve Ciccantelli. pub. size: broadsheet; circ. evening 12,000(paid). **Wire Service(s):** AP, NYT.

BELOIT
US

BELOIT DAILY NEWS. 1892. Mon.-Sat. $.50 newsstand; $10.75/mo. 149 State St., Beloit, WI 53511. TEL 608-365-8811; FAX 608-365-1420. **Owner(s):** Greater Beloit Publishing Co., 149 State St., Beloit, WI 53511. TEL 608-368-8811; Ed. William Barth; Pub. Kent Eymann; adv. contact: John Wingate. pub. size: broadsheet; circ. evening 16,600(paid). **Wire Service(s):** AP.

CHIPPEWA FALLS
US ISSN 8756-2960

CHIPPEWA HERALD-TELEGRAM. 1879. Sat.-Thu. $.50/day newsstand; $1/Sun.; $101/yr. local. 321 Frenette Dr., Chippewa Falls, WI 54729-0069. TEL 715-723-5515; FAX 715-723-9644; E-mail: chiphrld@discover-net.net. **Owner(s):** Independent Media Group, 321 Frenette, Chippewa Falls, WI 54729. TEL 715-723-5515; adv. contact: Andrew Bruns. pub. size: broadsheet; circ. evening 7,500(free & paid); Sun. 20,000(free & paid). **Wire Service(s):** AP.

EAU CLAIRE
US ISSN 0891-0227

LEADER-TELEGRAM. 1881. d. $.50 newsstand; $2.60/wk. 701 S. Farwell, Eau Claire, WI 54701. TEL 715-834-3471; FAX 715-833-9244; E-mail: leadertele@aol.com. **Owner(s):** Eau Claire Press Co., 701 S. Farwell St., Eau Claire, WI 54701. TEL 715-833-9208; Ed. Gene Ringhand; Pub. Charles Graaskamp; adv. contact: Jerry Merryfield. pub. size: standard; circ. morning 36,744(paid); evening 31,771(paid); Sun. 41,496(paid). **Wire Service(s):** AP, NYT, SH.

FOND DU LAC
US

REPORTER, THE. 1870. Sun-Fri. $.50/day newsstand; $1.25/Sun.; $169/yr. 33 W. Second St., Fond Du Lac, WI 54935. TEL 414-922-4600; FAX 414-922-5388; E-mail: mail@thereporter.net. **Owner(s):** Thomson Newspapers, Inc., 65 Queen St., Toronto, ON M5H 2M8, Canada; Ed. Richard Roesgen; Pub. Larry Antony; adv. contact: Doug Rankin. pub. size: broadsheet; circ. evening 21,000(paid); Sun. 22,000(paid). **Wire Service(s):** AP, TNS, SHNA. **Formerly:** Fond Du Lac Reporter.

FORT ATKINSON
US

DAILY JEFFERSON COUNTY UNION. 1870. Mon.-Fri. $.50 newsstand; $70/yr. 28 W. Milwaukee Ave., Fort Atkinson, WI 53538. TEL 414-563-5551; FAX 414-563-7298. **Owner(s):** W.D. Hoard & Sons Co., 28 Milwaukee Ave., W., Fort Atkinson, WI 53538. TEL 414-563-5551; Ed. Christine Spangler; Pub. Brian Knox; adv. contact: Charles Frandson. photos; bk.rev.; pub. size: broadsheet; circ. evening 9,000(paid). **Wire Service(s):** AP.

GREEN BAY
US

GREEN BAY NEWS-CHRONICLE. 1972. Sun.-Fri. $.50 newsstand; $2/wk. 133 S. Monroe, Green Bay, WI 54301. TEL 414-432-2941; FAX 414-432-8581. **Owner(s):** Brown County Publishing Co., P.O. Box 2467, Green Bay, WI 54306. TEL 414-432-2941; Ed. Ronald Poppenhagen; Pub. Frank A. Wood; adv.; pub. size: tabloid, sun.: broadsheet; circ. morning 10,000(paid); Sun. 65,000(free). **Wire Service(s):** UPI, NYT, LAT-WP.

GREEN BAY PRESS-GAZETTE. 1915. d. $.35/day newsstand; $1.50/Sun.; $3.25/wk. 435 E. Walnut St., Green Bay, WI 54301. TEL 414-435-4411; FAX 414-431-8379. **Owner(s):** Gannett Company, Inc., 1100 Wilson Blvd., Arlington, VA 22234. TEL 703-284-6000; Ed. Laurie Holloway; Pub. William T. Nusbaum; adv.; photos; pub. size: broadsheet; circ. evening 61,000(paid); Sun. 86,000(paid). **Wire Service(s):** AP, GNS, KRT.

JANESVILLE
US

JANESVILLE GAZETTE. 1845. d. $.50 newsstand; $176.80/yr. One S. Parker Dr., Janesville, WI 53547. TEL 608-754-3311; FAX 608-754-8038. **Owner(s):** Bliss Communications, Inc., P.O. Box 5001, Janesville, WI 53547-5001. TEL 608-754-3311; FAX 608-754-8038. Ed. Grant Vander Velden; Pub. Sidney H. Bliss; adv.; photos; bk.rev.; pub. size: broadsheet; circ. evening 26,990(paid); Sun. 27,876(paid). **Wire Service(s):** AP.

KENOSHA
US

KENOSHA NEWS. 1894. d. $.50 newsstand; $1.75/Sun., $3.50/wk. 715 58th St., Kenosha, WI 53141. TEL 414-657-1000; FAX 414-657-5101; E-mail: knews1@acronet.net. **Owner(s):** United Communications Corp., 715 58th St., Kenosha, WI 53140. TEL 414-657-1000; Ed. James Meyers; Pub. Howard J. Brown; adv. contact: Frank Misureli. photos; pub. size: broadsheet; circ. evening 31,500(paid); Sun. 31,500(paid). **Wire Service(s):** AP, LAT-WP. **Formerly:** Kenosha Evening News.

LA CROSSE
US ISSN 0745-9793

LA CROSSE TRIBUNE. 1904. d. $.50/day newsstand; $1.75/Sun.; $208/yr. carrier; $221/yr. motor rte. 401 N. Third St., La Crosse, WI 54601. TEL 608-782-9710; FAX 608-782-9723. **Owner(s):** Lee Enterprises, Inc., 130 E. Second St., Davenport, IA 52801. TEL 319-383-2100; Ed. David Stoeffler; Pub. Jim Santori; adv. contact: Tom Kelley. pub. size: broadsheet; circ. morning 35,500(paid); Sun. 42,500(paid). **Wire Service(s):** AP, KR, SHNA.

MADISON
US ISSN 0749-4068

CAPITAL TIMES, THE. 1917. Mon.-Sat. $.50 newsstand; $2.15/wk. carrier; $2.50/wk. mailed. 1901 Fish Hatchery Rd., Madison, WI 53713. TEL 608-252-6400; FAX 608-252-6445; E-mail: tctvoice@captimes.madison.com; URL: http://www.madison.com. **Owner(s):** Capital Times Co., 1901 Fish Hatchery Rd., Madison, WI 53713. TEL 608-252-6200; Ed. Dave Zweifel. pub. size: broadsheet; circ. evening 23,744(paid). Wire Service(s): AP, LAT-WP, SHNA.

WISCONSIN STATE JOURNAL. 1901. d. $.50/day newsstand; $1.75/Sun.; $95/yr.; $163/yr. motor rte. 1901 Fish Hatchery Rd., Madison, WI 53713. TEL 608-252-6100; FAX 608-252-6119. **Owner(s):** Lee Enterprises, Inc., 400 Putnam Bldg., 215 N. Main St., Davenport, IA 52801-1924. TEL 319-383-2100; Ed. Frank Denton; Pub. Phil Blake; adv.; pub. size: broadsheet; circ. morning 90,000(paid); Sun. 180,000(paid). **Wire Service(s):** AP, NYT, KR.

MANITOWOC
US

HERALD-TIMES REPORTER. 1875. d. $.50/day newsstand; $1/Sun.; $144.40/yr. in city. 902 Franklin St., Manitowoc, WI 54220-0790. TEL 414-684-4433; FAX 414-684-4416. **Owner(s):** Thomson Newspapers, Inc., 3150 Des Plaines Ave., Des Plaines, IL 60018. TEL 708-299-5544; pub. size: broadsheet; circ. evening 19,000(paid); Sun. 18,500(paid). **Wire Service(s):** AP. **Formerly:** Manitowoc Herald-Times Reporter.

DAILY NEWSPAPERS

MARINETTE
US
EAGLE-HERALD. 1871. Mon.-Sat. $.50 newsstand; $9.50/mo. 1809 Dunlap Ave., Marinette, WI 54143. TEL 715-735-6611; FAX 715-735-7580. **Owner(s):** Eagle-Herald Publishing LLC, 1809 Dunlap Ave., Marinette, WI 54143; Ed. Terri Lescelius; Pub. Dennis Colling; pub. size: broadsheet; circ. evening 11,500(paid).
Formerly: Marinette Eagle-Star & Menominee Herald Leader.

MARSHFIELD
US
MARSHFIELD NEWS-HERALD. 1927. Mon.-Sat. $.50 newsstand; $.75/weekend; $91/yr. city. 111 W. Third St., Marshfield, WI 54449. TEL 715-384-3131; FAX 715-387-4175. **Owner(s):** Thomson Newspapers, 3150 Des Plaines Ave., Des Plaines, IL 60018. TEL 708-299-5544; Ed. William R. Heath; Pub. Randy Graf; adv. contact: Karen Olson. photos; bk.rev.; pub. size: broadsheet; circ. evening 14,600(paid). Wire Service(s): AP.

MILWAUKEE
US ISSN 1052-4452
MILWAUKEE JOURNAL SENTINEL. 1882. d. $.50/day newsstand; $1.50/Sun. 333 W. State St., Milwaukee, WI 53203. TEL 414-224-2000; FAX 414-224-2047; E-mail: adrep@onwis.com; URL: http://www.onwis.com/. **Owner(s):** Journal Communications, Inc., 333 W. State St., Milwaukee, WI 53203. TEL 414-224-2000; Ed. George Stanley; Pub. Keith Spore; adv.; photos; bk.rev.; pub. size: broadsheet; circ. morning 272,454(paid); Sun. 462,168(paid). **Wire Service(s):** AP, NYT, LAT-WP.
Formerly: Milwaukee Sentinel.

MONROE
US ISSN 1068-5820
MONROE TIMES, THE. 1898. Mon.-Sat. $.50 newsstand; $106.21/yr. 1065 Fourth Ave., W., Monroe, WI 53566. TEL 608-328-4202; FAX 608-328-4217. **Owner(s):** Monroe Publishing LLC, 1065 Fourth Ave., W., Monroe, WI 53566. TEL 608-328-4202; FAX 608-328-4217; Ed. Judie Hintzman. adv.; photos; bk.rev.; pub. size: broadsheet; circ. evening 7,136(paid). **Wire Service(s):** AP.
Formerly: Monroe Evening Times.

OSHKOSH
US
OSHKOSH NORTHWESTERN. 1868. d. $.50/day newsstand; $1.50/Sun. 224 State St., Oshkosh, WI 54902. TEL 414-235-7700; FAX 414-235-1316. **Owner(s):** Oshkosh Northwestern Co., 224 State St., Oshkosh, WI 54901. TEL 414-235-7700; Pub. Russell F. Sprung; pub. size: broadsheet; circ. morning 26,500(paid); Sun. 28,500(paid). **Wire Service(s):** AP.

PORTAGE
US ISSN 0747-2927
DAILY REGISTER, THE. 1886. Mon.-Sat. $.50/day newsstand; $.75/Sat.; $9.25/mo. carrier. 309 DeWitt St., Portage, WI 53901. TEL 608-742-2111; FAX 608-742-8346. **Owner(s):** Independent Media Group, P.O. Box 470, Portage, WI 53901. TEL 608-742-2111; Ed. Tracy Moeller; Pub. David W. Gentry; adv. contact: Tom Dugan. photos; pub. size: broadsheet; circ. morning 5,500(paid); Sun. 5,500(paid). **Wire Service(s):** AP.

RACINE
US ISSN 0746-2867
JOURNAL TIMES. 1857. d. $.50/day newsstand; $1.50/Sun.; $14/mo. carrier. 212 Fourth St., Racine, WI 53403. TEL 414-634-3322; FAX 414-631-1702; E-mail: journaltimes@wi.net; URL: http://www.jtracine.com. **Owner(s):** Lee Enterprises, Inc., 130 E. Second St., Davenport, IA 52801; Ed. Alan Buncher; Pub. Peter Selkowe; pub. size: standard; circ. morning 36,385(paid); Sun. 40,000(paid). **Wire Service(s):** AP, KRTN.

RHINELANDER
US ISSN 0746-5866
RHINELANDER DAILY NEWS. 1882. Sun.-Fri. $.50/day newsstand; $1.25/Sun.; $114/yr. carrier. 314 S. Courtney, Rhinelander, WI 54501. TEL 715-362-6397; FAX 715-365-6367. **Owner(s):** Pultizer Publishing Company, 900 N. Tucker Blvd., St. Louis, MO 63101. TEL 313-340-8000; Ed. Meredith Albright; Pub. Richard W. Timmons; adv. contact: Dennis Piotrowski. pub. size: broadsheet; circ. evening 6,400(paid); Sun. 7,000(paid). **Wire Service(s):** AP.

SHAWANO
US ISSN 0749-7148
SHAWANO LEADER. 1881. Sun.-Fri. $.50/day newsstand; $1/Sun.; $99/yr. carrier; $135/yr. mailed. 1464 E. Green Bay St., Shawano, WI 54166. TEL 715-526-2121; FAX 715-524-3941. **Owner(s):** Independent Media Group, 321 Frenette, Chippewa Falls, WI 54729. TEL 715-723-5515; Ed. Kent Tempas; Pub. Stephen P. Staloch; adv. contact: Patti Peterson. photos; bk.rev.; pub. size: broadsheet; circ. evening 7,500(paid); Sun. 7,500(paid). **Wire Service(s):** AP.

SHEBOYGAN
US ISSN 0749-7121
SHEBOYGAN PRESS, THE. 1907. d. $.50/day newsstand; $1.50/Sun.; $168/yr. carrier; $221/yr. mailed. 632 Center Ave., Sheboygan, WI 53081. TEL 414-457-7711; FAX 414-457-0178. **Owner(s):** Metro Centre, One Station Pl., 6th. Fl., Stamford, CT 06902. TEL 203-425-2500; FAX 203-425-2516; Ed. Bob Joslyn; Pub. David Decker; adv. contact: David Leibelt. pub. size: broadsheet; circ. evening 30,500(paid); Sun. 30,500(paid). **Wire Service(s):** AP, NYT.

STEVENS POINT
US ISSN 0748-6332
STEVENS POINT JOURNAL. 1895. Mon.-Sat. $.50 newsstand; $84.75/yr. carrier. 1200 Third Ct., Stevens Point, WI 54481. TEL 715-344-6100; FAX 715-344-7229. **Owner(s):** Journal Printing Co., 1200 3rd Ct., P.O. Box 7, Stevens Point, WI 54481. TEL 714-344-6100; Ed. Debbie Bradley; Pub. Frank W. Leahy; adv. contact: Ken Brezinski. pub. size: broadsheet; circ. evening 15,000(paid). Wire Service(s): AP, NYT.

SUPERIOR
US
SUPERIOR DAILY TELEGRAM. 1890. Mon.-Sat. $.50/day newsstand; $.75/Sat.; $7/mo. carrier. 1226 Ogden Ave., Superior, WI 54880. TEL 715-394-4411; FAX 715-394-9404. **Owner(s):** Daily Telegram Co., 1226 Ogden Ave., Superior, WI 54880. TEL 715-394-4411; FAX 715-394-9404; Pub. John B. Murphy; adv. contact: Randi Smith. pub. size: broadsheet; circ. evening 10,750(paid). **Wire Service(s):** AP.
Formerly: Superior Evening Telegram.

WATERTOWN
US
WATERTOWN DAILY TIMES. 1895. Mon.-Sat. $.50 newsstand; $100/yr. 115 Main St., Watertown, WI 53094. TEL 414-261-4949; FAX 414-261-5102. **Owner(s):** Times Publishing Co., P.O. Box 140, Watertown, WI 53094. TEL 414-261-4949; Ed. Thomas Schultz; Pub. James M. Clifford; adv. contact: Judy Christian. photos; bk.rev.; pub. size: broadsheet; circ. evening 10,100(paid). **Wire Service(s):** AP.

WAUKESHA
US ISSN 1062-9041
FREEMAN, THE. 1859. Mon.-Sat. $.50/day newsstand; $.75/Sat.; $2.05/wk. carrier; $9.61/mo. motor rte. 801 N. Barstow St., Waukesha, WI 53187-0007. TEL 414-542-2501; FAX 414-542-2015. **Owner(s):** Thomson Newspapers, Inc., Metro Centre, One Station Pl., 6th Fl., Stamford, CT 06902. TEL 203-425-2500; FAX 203-425-2516; Ed. Pete Kennedy; Pub. Patrick Doyle; adv.; photos; pub. size: broadsheet; circ. evening 21,679(paid). **Wire Service(s):** AP, KR.
Formerly: Waukesha Freeman.

WAUSAU
US ISSN 0887-4271
WAUSAU DAILY HERALD. 1907. d. $.35/day newsstand; $1.25/Sun.; $38.35/3 mos.; $40.95/3 mos. motor rte. 800 Scott St., Wausau, WI 54401. TEL 715-842-2101; FAX 715-848-9360. **Owner(s):** Gannett Company, Inc., 1100 Wilson Blvd., Arlington, VA 22234. TEL 703-284-6000; Ed. Jim Herman; Pub. Michael Scobey; adv. contact: Victor Brabender. bk.rev.; pub. size: broadsheet; circ. evening 30,000(paid); Sun. 33,000(paid). **Wire Service(s):** AP, GNS.

WEST BEND

DAILY NEWS. 1855. Mon.-Sat. $.50 newsstand; $9.10/mo. carrier; $9.80/mo. motor rte.; $10.30/mo. mailed. 100 S. Sixth Ave., West Bend, WI 53095. TEL 414-338-0622; FAX 414-338-1984. **Owner(s):** Thomson Newspapers, Inc., Metro Centre, One Station Pl., 6th Fl., Stamford, CT 06902. TEL 203-425-2500; FAX 203-425-2516; Ed. Steve Sandburg. adv. contact: Barbara Swan. pub. size: broadsheet; circ. 11,300(paid).
Formerly: West Bend Daily News.

US ISSN 0899-2444

WISCONSIN RAPIDS

US

DAILY TRIBUNE, THE. 1930. Mon.-Sat. $.50 newsstand; $113.20/yr. carrier; $125.20/yr. motor rte.; $141.40/yr. mailed in area; $177.40/yr. mailed out of area; $142/yr. mailed out of state. 220 First Ave., S., Wisconsin Rapids, WI 54495-8090. TEL 715-423-7200; FAX 715-421-1545. **Owner(s):** Metro Centre, One Station Pl. 6th Fl., Stamford, CT 06902. TEL 203-425-2500; Ed. Tom Enwright; Pub. Randy Graf; adv. contact: Helen Jungwirth. pub. size: broadsheet; circ. evening 14,000(paid). **Wire Service(s):** AP.

WYOMING

CASPER

US

CASPER STAR TRIBUNE. 1891. d. $.50/day newsstand; $1.50/Sun.; $13.80/mo. carrier; $3.20/wk. 170 Star Ln., Casper, WY 82604. TEL 307-266-0500; FAX 307-266-0501. **Owner(s):** Howard Publications, Inc., P.O. Box 570, Oceanside, CA 92049. TEL 619-433-5771; Ed. David Hipschman; Pub. Rob Hurless; adv.; pub. size: broadsheet; circ. morning 31,825(paid); Sun. 35,113(paid). **Wire Service(s):** NYT, AP.

CHEYENNE

US ISSN 8750-0825

WYOMING TRIBUNE-EAGLE. 1867. d. $.50/day newsstand; $1.25/Sun.; $7.25/mo. carrier. 702 W. Lincoln Way, Cheyenne, WY 82001. TEL 307-634-3361; FAX 307-638-7330. **Owner(s):** Cheyenne Newspapers, Inc., 702 W. Lincoln Way, Cheyenne, WY 82001. TEL 307-634-3361; Ed. Mary Woolsey; Pub. L. Michael McCraken; adv. contact: Scott Walker. photos; pub. size: broadsheet; circ. morning 17,000(paid); Sun. 21,000(paid). **Wire Service(s):** AP.
Formerly: Sunday Tribune Eagle.

GILLETTE

US ISSN 0739-4926

NEWS-RECORD. 1904. Sun.-Fri. $.35/day newsstand; $1/Sun.; $102/yr. home deliv. 1201 W. Second St., Gillette, WY 82716. TEL 307-682-9306; FAX 307-686-9306; E-mail: newsrcrd@vcn.com. **Owner(s):** Betty Kennedy, Gillette, WY 82716; Ron & Ann Franscell, Gillette, WY 82716; Ed. Ron Franscell; Pub. Ron Franscell; adv. contact: Gail Muhlbauer. pub. size: broadsheet; circ. evening 7,000(paid); Sun. 7,500(paid). **Wire Service(s):** AP.

LARAMIE

US

LARAMIE DAILY BOOMERANG. 1881. Tue.-Sun. $.35/day newsstand; $.75/Sun.; $39/6 mos. home deliv. 314 S. Fourth St., Laramie, WY 82070-3712. TEL 307-742-2176; FAX 307-721-2973. **Owner(s):** Laramie Newspapers, Inc., 320 E. Grand Ave., Laramie, WY 82070-3712. TEL 307-742-2176; FAX 307-721-2973; Ed. Bob Wilson; Pub. Ron VanEkeren; adv. contact: Sheryn Pulse. photos; bk.rev.; pub. size: broadsheet; circ. morning 6,700(paid); Sun. 6,800(paid). **Wire Service(s):** AP.

RAWLINS

US

DAILY TIMES, THE. 1890. Tue.-Sat. $.50 newsstand; $49/yr. carrier; $59.50/yr. mailed. Sixth & Buffalo, Rawlins, WY 82301-0370. TEL 307-324-3411; FAX 307-324-2797. **Owner(s):** Rawlins Newspapers, Inc., P.O. Box 370, Rawlins, WY 82301-0370. TEL 307-634-3361; Ed. C.H. Bowlus; Pub. David Perry; adv.; photos; bk.rev.; pub. size: tabloid; circ. morning 3,800(paid). **Wire Service(s):** AP.

RIVERTON

US

RIVERTON RANGER. 1953. Mon.-Fri. $60/yr. 421 E. Main St., Riverton, WY 82501. TEL 307-856-2244; FAX 307-856-0189. **Owner(s):** Robert & Steve Peck, 421 E. Main St., Riverton, WY 82501. TEL 307-856-2244; Ed. Dave Perry; Pub. Robert A. Peck; adv. contact: John Birbari. photos; pub. size: broadsheet; circ. evening 7,280(paid). **Wire Service(s):** AP.

ROCK SPRINGS

US ISSN 0893-3650

ROCK SPRINGS DAILY ROCKET-MINER. 1880. Tue.-Sat. $.30 newsstand; $58.20/yr. carrier; $58.60/yr. mailed in state; $62.80/yr. mailed out of state. 215 D St., Rock Springs, WY 82901. TEL 307-362-3736; FAX 307-382-2763. **Owner(s):** Rock Springs Newspapers, Inc., P.O. Box 98, Rock Springs, WY 82902. TEL 307-362-3736; Ed. Bruce Yoder; Pub. Charles Richardson; adv. contact: Garry Gouger. pub. size: broadsheet; circ. morning 7,955(paid). **Wire Service(s):** AP.

SHERIDAN

US

SHERIDAN PRESS. 1886. Mon.-Sat. $.50 newsstand; $77.50/yr.; $90/yr. mailed. 144 Grinnell, Sheridan, WY 82801. TEL 307-672-2431; FAX 307-672-7950. **Owner(s):** Sheridan Press, The, P.O. Box 2006, Sheridan, WY 82801. TEL 307-672-2431; FAX 307-672-7950; Ed. T.D. Dreiling; Pub. Carl Sanders; bk.rev.; pub. size: broadsheet; circ. evening 6,348(paid). **Wire Service(s):** AP.

WORLAND

US

NORTHERN WYOMING DAILY NEWS. 1905. Tue.-Sat. $.50 newsstand; $30.25/6 mos. mail deliv. 201 N. Eighth, Worland, WY 82401. TEL 307-347-3241; FAX 307-347-4267; E-mail: nwdn@trib.com. **Owner(s):** Big Horn Basin Newspapers, Inc., 201 N. Eighth, Worland, WY 82401. TEL 307-347-3241; Ed. Lee Lockhart; Pub. Lee Lockhart; adv.; photos; bk.rev.; pub. size: broadsheet; circ. morning 5,000(paid). **Wire Service(s):** AP.

Weekly Newspapers

ALABAMA

ABBEVILLE
US
ABBEVILLE HERALD. 1941. Thu. $.50 newsstand; $14.58/yr. in cy.; $18.90/yr. in state; $20/yr. out of state. 135 Kirkland St., Abbeville, AL 36310. TEL 334-585-2331; FAX 334-585-2331. **Owner(s):** J. Edward Dodd, III, P.O. Box 609, Abbeville, AL 36310. TEL 205-585-2331; Ed. J. Edward Dodd, III; Pub. J. Edward Dodd, III; adv.; pub. size: tabloid; circ. 2,200(paid).

ALBERTVILLE
US   ISSN 0889-1724
SAND MOUNTAIN REPORTER. 1955. 3/wk.: Tue., Thu., Sat. $.50 newsstand; $25/yr. 3760 U.S. Hwy. 431, Albertville, AL 35950. TEL 205-878-1311; FAX 205-878-2104. **Owner(s):** Sand Mountain Publishing Co., P.O. Box 190, Albertville, AL 35950. TEL 205-878-1311; Pub. Michael J. Hudgins; adv. contact: Debra Hedgepath. pub. size: broadsheet; circ. 13,500(paid).

ALEXANDER CITY
US
DADEVILLE RECORD. 1896. Thu. $.50 newsstand; $20/yr. in cy.; $25/yr. out of cy. 548 Cherokee Rd., Alexander City, AL 35010. TEL 205-234-4281; FAX 205-234-6550. **Owner(s):** Kenneth Boone, P.O. Box 999, Alexander City, AL 35010. TEL 205-234-4281; FAX 205-234-6550; Ed. Janet Goodyear; Pub. Bruce Wallace; adv. contact: Doug Patterson. pub. size: standard; circ. 2,500(paid).

ANDALUSIA
US
COUNTY REPORTER, THE. Thu. $.50 newsstand; $25/yr. 1025 E. Three Notch St., Andalusia, AL 36420. TEL 334-222-1485; FAX 334-222-5567. **Owner(s):** James Walker, 1025 E. Three Notch St., Andalusia, AL 36420. TEL 334-222-1485; Ed. James Walker. adv.; pub. size: broadsheet; circ. 2,500(free & paid).

ARAB
US
ARAB TRIBUNE. 1958. Wed. $.50 newsstand; $15/yr. local; $20/yr. out of area; $25/yr. out of state. 619 S. Brindlee Mountain Pkwy., Arab, AL 35016. TEL 205-586-3188; FAX 205-586-3190. **Owner(s):** Edwin H. Reed, 619 S. Brindlee Mountain Pkwy., Arab, AL 35016. TEL 205-586-3188; FAX 205-586-3190; Ed. David Moore; Pub. Edwin H. Reed; pub. size: broadsheet; circ. 6,500(paid).

ATMORE
US   ISSN 0746-1968
ATMORE ADVANCE. 1927. s-w.: Wed. & Sun. $.50 newsstand; $35/yr. carrier in area; $50/yr. out of state; $32.50/yr. senior citizens. 301 S. Main St., Atmore, AL 36502. TEL 205-368-2123; FAX 205-368-2124. **Owner(s):** Boone Newspapers, Inc., P.O. Box 2370, Tuscaloosa, AL 35403. TEL 407-338-3298; Ed. Michele Gerlach; Pub. Michele Gerlach; adv. contact: Katie Guyton. photos; pub. size: broadsheet; circ. 10,000(free & paid); Sun. 3,800(free & paid).

AUBURN
US
LEE COUNTY EAGLE, THE. 1937. s-w.: Wed. & Sun. $.50 newsstand; $25/yr. home deliv. 122 Tichenor Ave., Auburn, AL 36830. TEL 334-821-7150; FAX 334-887-0037. **Owner(s):** Thomson Newspapers, Inc., Metro Centre, One Station Pl., 6th Fl., Stamford, CT 06902. TEL 203-425-2500; FAX 203-425-2516; Pub. Stanley Warren; adv. contact: Don Norman. pub. size: broadsheet; circ. 20,600(paid).
Formerly: Auburn Bulletin.

BAY MINETTE
US
BALDWIN TIMES. 1890. Thu. $.50 newsstand; $23/yr. local; $26/yr. out of state; $19.95/yr. senior citizens. 329 Courthouse Sq., Bay Minette, AL 36507. TEL 334-937-2511; FAX 334-937-1637. **Owner(s):** Gulf Coast Newspapers, Inc., Alabama Hwy. 59, Robertsdale, AL 36567. TEL 334-947-7712; Pub. Mike Mueck; adv. contact: Mike Mueck. photos; bk.rev.; pub. size: broadsheet; circ. 3,600(paid).

BESSEMER
US
WESTERN STAR. 1984. Wed. $.50 newsstand; $21/yr. local; $17/yr. senior citizens. 1709 Third Ave., Bessemer, AL 35020. TEL 205-424-7827; FAX 205-424-8118. **Owner(s):** Tribble Publications, Inc., Manchester, GA 31816; adv.; pub. size: broadsheet; circ. 7,000(paid).

BIRMINGHAM, AL

BIRMINGHAM

US
ALABAMA MESSENGER. 1959. Sat. $10/yr. mailed. 706 Frank Nelson Bldg., Birmingham, AL 35203. TEL 205-252-3672; FAX 205-252-3679. **Owner(s):** Eleanor Foster, 706 Frank Nelson Bldg., Birmingham, AL 35103. TEL 205-252-3672; Ed. Karen Abercrombie. adv. contact: Traci A. Smeraglia. pub. size: broadsheet; circ. 2,500(paid).

US
BIRMINGHAM WORLD. Thu. $.75 newsstand; $31.20/yr. 407 15th St., N., Birmingham, AL 35203. TEL 205-251-6523; FAX 205-328-6729. **Owner(s):** Birmingham World, Inc., 407 15th St., N., Birmingham, AL 35203. TEL 205-251-6523; Pub. Joe Dickson; adv. contact: Clinton Moon. pub. size: broadsheet; circ. 12,600(paid). **Wire Service(s):** AP, NNS, Newsfinder.

US
COMMUNITY SHOPPER. 1977. m. free direct mail. 9229 Todd Dr., Ste. 205, Birmingham, AL 35206. TEL 205-833-8588; FAX 205-833-8589. **Owner(s):** Jarrell & Associates, Inc., 9229 Todd Dr., Ste. 205, Birmingham, AL 35206. TEL 205-833-8588; FAX 205-833-8589; Pub. Rick Jarrell; pub. size: tabloid; circ. 32,000(free).
Formerly: Shoppers Guide.

US
OVER THE MOUNTAIN JOURNAL. 1980. bi-w.: Thu. free in cy.; $18/yr mailed. 3250 Independence Dr., #5, Birmingham, AL 35209. TEL 205-879-9686; FAX 205-879-4579. **Owner(s):** Maurice G. Wald, III, P.O. Box 20502, Birmingham, AL 35216. TEL 205-879-9686; FAX 205-879-4579; Ed. Cara Morrison; Pub. Maurice G. Wald, III; adv. contact: Jeff Wingo. photos; pub. size: tabloid; circ. 39,600(free & paid).

US
SAMFORD CRIMSON. Wed. $10/yr. in cy.; $12/yr. out of cy. 800 Lake Shore Dr., Birmingham, AL 35209. TEL 205-870-2998; FAX 205-870-2586. **Owner(s):** Cook Publications, Colman, AL; Ed. Robert Strickland. pub. size: tabloid; circ. 4,000(paid).

US
THRIFTY NICKEL. 1982. Thu. free. 619 Robert Jemison Rd., Ste. 200, Birmingham, AL 35209. TEL 205-942-2555; FAX 205-942-5770. **Owner(s):** Rob Puckett, 619 Robert Jemison Rd., Ste. 200, Birmingham, AL 35209. Ed. Rob Puckett. pub. size: tabloid; circ. 70,000(free).

BREWTON

US
BREWTON STANDARD, THE. 1887. s-w.: Wed. & Sun. $.50 newsstand; $35/yr. in state; $40/yr. out of state; $32/yr. senior citizens. 407 St. Nicholas Ave., Brewton, AL 36426. TEL 334-867-4876; FAX 334-867-4877. **Owner(s):** Boone Newspapers, Inc., P.O. Box 2370, Tuscaloosa, AL 35403. TEL 407-338-3298; Ed. Candy Parker; Pub. George Turner; adv. contact: Marilyn Raines. pub. size: broadsheet; circ. 7,400(paid); Sun. 3,800(paid).

BUTLER

US
CHOCTAW ADVOCATE. 1890. Wed. $.50 newsstand; $16/yr. in cy.; $21/yr. out of cy. 210 N. Mulberry Ave., Butler, AL 36904. TEL 205-459-2858; FAX 205-459-3000. **Owner(s):** Choctaw Advocate, Inc., 210 N. Mulberry St., P.O. Box 475, Butler, AL 36904. TEL 205-459-2858; Ed. Tommy J. Campbell; Pub. Tommy J. Campbell; adv. contact: Lee Mosley. photos; bk.rev.; pub. size: standard; circ. 4,600(paid). **Wire Service(s):** AP.
Formerly: Butler Choctaw Advocate.

CAMDEN

US
WILCOX PROGRESSIVE ERA. 1860. w. $.50 newsstand; $14/yr. in cy.; $24/yr. out of cy. P.O. Box 100, Camden, AL 36726. TEL 304-682-4422; FAX 304-682-5163. **Owner(s):** M. Hollis Curl, P.O. Box 100, Camden, AL 36726. TEL 205-682-4422; Ed. M. Hollis Curl; Pub. M. Hollis Curl; adv. contact: Melissa Dove. pub. size: standard; circ. 2,840(paid).

CARROLLTON

US
PICKENS COUNTY HERALD. 1848. Wed. $.50 newsstand; $20/yr. in cy.; $30/yr. out of state. Hwy. 17, Junkin Bldg., Carrollton, AL 35447. TEL 205-367-2217; FAX 207-367-2217. **Owner(s):** Hershel Lake, P.O. Box 390, Carrollton, AL 35447. TEL 205-367-2217; Ed. Doug Sanders; Pub. Doug Sanders; pub. size: standard; circ. 5,000(paid).

CENTRE

US
CHEROKEE COUNTY HERALD. 1938. Wed. $.50 newsstand; $14/yr. in cy.; $22/yr. out of cy. 107 W. First Ave., Centre, AL 35960. TEL 205-927-5037; FAX 205-927-4853. **Owner(s):** B.H. Mooney, III, 107 W. First Ave., Centre, AL 35960. TEL 205-927-5037; FAX 205-927-4853; Ed. Paul W. Dale; Pub. B.H. Mooney; adv. contact: Vickie Robinson. photos; pub. size: broadsheet; circ. 5,150(paid).

CENTREVILLE

US
CENTREVILLE PRESS. 1879. Wed. $.50 newsstand; $19.44/yr. mailed. 119 Court Sq., W., Centreville, AL 35042. TEL 205-926-9769; FAX 205-926-9760. **Owner(s):** Trib Publications, Inc., 119 Court Sq., W., Centreville, AL 35042. TEL 205-926-9769; Ed. Judy M. Farnetti; Pub. Robert Tribble; adv. contact: Judy M. Farnetti. pub. size: broadsheet; circ. 4,200(paid).

CHATOM

US
WASHINGTON COUNTY NEWS. 1892. Wed. $.50 newsstand; $15/yr. 305 Jordan St., Chatom, AL 36518. TEL 334-847-2599; FAX 334-847-3847. **Owner(s):** James A. Specht, P.O. Box 510, Chatom, AL 36518. TEL 334-847-2599; FAX 334-847-3847; Ed. Frank Harwell. adv.; photos; bk.rev.; pub. size: standard; circ. 3,700(paid).
Formerly: Call-News Dispatch.

CLANTON

US
CLANTON ADVERTISER. 1972. 3/wk.: Wed., Fri., Sun. $.75 newsstand; $56/yr. in state; $65/yr. out of state. 1109 Seventh St., N., Clanton, AL 35046. TEL 205-755-5747; FAX 205-755-5857. **Owner(s):** Boone Newspapers, Inc., P.O. Box 2370, Tuscaloosa, AL 35403. TEL 205-752-3381; Pub. Michael Kelly; adv. contact: Dan Cook. pub. size: broadsheet; circ. 135,000(free & paid).

CLAYTON

US
CLAYTON RECORD. Thu. $.50 newsstand; $18/yr. in state; $20/yr. out of state. P.O. Box 69, Clayton, AL 36016. TEL 334-775-3254; FAX 334-775-8554. **Owner(s):** Bertie G. Parish, P.O. Box 69, Clayton, AL 36016. TEL 334-775-3254; Ed. Rebecca Beasley; Pub. Bertie G. Parish; adv.; pub. size: broadsheet; circ. 2,500(paid).

COLUMBIANA

US   ISSN 1063-9489
SHELBY COUNTY REPORTER. 1843. Wed. $.75 newsstand; $30/yr. carrier. Main St., Columbiana, AL 35051. TEL 205-669-3131; FAX 205-669-4217. **Owner(s):** Boone Newspapers, Inc., P.O. Box 2370, Tuscaloosa, AL 35403. TEL 205-752-3381; Ed. Leada L. DeVaney; Pub. Kim N. Price; adv. contact: Kim N. Price. photos; pub. size: broadsheet; circ. 10,235(paid).

CULLMAN

US
CULLMAN TRIBUNE. 1874. Thu. $.50 newsstand; $20/yr. in cy.; $25/yr. out of cy. 219 Second Ave., S.E., Cullman, AL 35055. TEL 205-739-1351; FAX 205-739-4422. **Owner(s):** Delton & Barbara Blalock, P.O. Box 496, Hanceville, AL 35077; Ed. Delton Blalock; Pub. Barbara Blalock; adv. contact: Nina Hurst. photos; bk.rev.; pub. size: broadsheet; circ. 16,000(paid).

DEMOPOLIS

US
DEMOPOLIS TIMES. 1902. s-w.: Sun. & Wed. $.75 newsstand; $40/yr. in cy.; $55/yr. elswhere. 315 E. Jefferson St., Demopolis, AL 36732. TEL 334-289-4017; FAX 334-289-4019. **Owner(s):** Boone Newspapers, Inc., P.O. Box 2370, Tuscaloosa, AL 35403. TEL 205-752-3381; FAX 205-752-3392; Ed. Danny Smith; Pub. Danny Smith; adv.; pub. size: broadsheet; circ. 2,800(paid).

DORA

US
COMMUNITY NEWS, THE. 1968. Wed. $.50 newsstand; $12.50/yr. in state mailed; $17.50/yr. out of state; $9/yr. senior citizens. 6 Midway Plz., Dora, AL 35062. TEL 205-648-3231; FAX 205-648-3246. **Owner(s):** Lee Walls, Birmingham, AL; adv.: $4/SAU. pub. size: broadsheet; circ. 2,000(paid).

WEEKLY NEWSPAPERS

ELBA
US

ELBA CLIPPER, THE. Thu. $.50 newsstand. 417 W. Buford St., Elba, AL 36323. TEL 334-897-2823; FAX 334-897-3434. **Owner(s):** John Ferrin Cox, 417 W. Buford St., Elba, AL 36323. TEL 334-897-2823; Ed. Marvin McIlwain; Pub. John Ferrin Cox; adv.; pub. size: broadsheet; circ. 3,200(paid).

EUFAULA
US

EUFAULA TRIBUNE. 1929. s-w.: Wed. & Sun. $.50 newsstand; $26.50/yr. carrier; $34.95/yr. in state mailed; $49.95/yr. out of state. 514 E. Barbour St., Eufaula, AL 36027. TEL 334-687-3506; FAX 334-687-3229. **Owner(s):** Joel P. Smith, 325 N. Eufaula Ave., Eufaula, AL 36027; Tribune Publishing Co., P.O. Box 628, Eufaula, AL 36072-0628; Ed. Joel P. Smith; Pub. Joel P. Smith; adv.; photos; pub. size: broadsheet; circ. 6,200(paid).

EUTAW
US

GREENE COUNTY INDEPENDENT. 1985. Wed. $.50 newsstand; $16/yr. in cy.; $22/yr. out of cy. 106 Main St., Eutaw, AL 35462. TEL 205-372-2232; FAX 205-372-2232. **Owner(s):** Greene County Independent Newspapers, Inc., 106 Main St., Eutaw, AL 35462. TEL 205-372-2232; Ed. Leewanna Parker; Pub. Betty C. Banks; adv. contact: Betty C. Banks. pub. size: broadsheet; circ. 1,500(paid).

EVERGREEN
US

EVERGREEN COURANT, THE. 1895. Thu. $15/yr. in cy.; $25/yr. out of cy. 204 Rural St., Evergreen, AL 36401. TEL 334-578-1492; FAX 334-578-1496. **Owner(s):** Maurice G. Bozeman, P.O. Box 440, Evergreen, AL 36401. TEL 205-578-1210; Ed. Robert Bozeman, III; Pub. Maurice G. Bozeman; pub. size: standard; circ. 3,800(paid).

FAIRHOPE
US

FAIRHOPE COURIER, THE. 1894. s-w.: Wed. & Sat. $.50 newsstand; $30/yr. carrier; $32.50/yr. out of state mailed; $20.50/yr. senior citizens in cy. mailed; $25.75/yr. senior citizens in state mailed. 325 Fairhope Ave., Fairhope, AL 36532. TEL 334-928-2321; FAX 334-928-9963. **Owner(s):** Gulf Coast Newspapers, Inc., P.O. Box 509, Robertsdale, AL 36567. TEL 334-947-7712; Ed. Sheila Propp; Pub. Dennis Thomas; adv.; bk.rev.; pub. size: broadsheet; circ. 33,900(paid). **Wire Service(s):** AP.

FAYETTE
US

TIMES RECORD. 1977. Wed. $.50 newsstand; $20/yr. in cy.; $22/yr. out of cy. 106 First St., S.E., Fayette, AL 35555. TEL 205-932-6271; FAX 205-932-6998. **Owner(s):** Mid-South Publishing Co., Pulaski, TN; Ed. Michael James; Pub. Horace Moore; adv. contact: Bobbie Cross. photos; pub. size: standard; circ. 5,000(paid).

FLOMATON
US

TRI-CITY LEDGER. 1970. Thu. $.50 newsstand; $25/yr. local; $30/yr. out of cy.; $35/yr. out of state. 20766 Hwy. 31, Flomaton, AL 36441. TEL 334-296-3491; FAX 334-296-0010. **Owner(s):** Tri-City Ledger, P.O. Drawer F, Flomaton, AL 36441. TEL 334-296-3491; Ed. Joe Thomas; Pub. Joe Thomas; adv. contact: Gary Murph. pub. size: broadsheet; circ. 5,500(paid). **Formerly:** Flomaton Tri-City Ledger.

FLORALA
US

FLORALA NEWS, THE. 1900. Thu. $.50 newsstand; $21.60/yr. in state; $20/yr. out of state. 421 S. Fifth St., Florala, AL 36442. TEL 334-858-3342; FAX 334-858-3786. **Owner(s):** Larry Woodham, 421 S. Fifth St., Florala, AL 36442. TEL 334-858-3342; Ed. Lisa Windham; Pub. Gary Woodham; adv.; photos; pub. size: broadsheet; circ. 2,200(paid).

FLORENCE
US

COURIER JOURNAL. 1884. Wed. free direct mail. 116 W. Mobile St., Florence, AL 35630. TEL 205-764-4268; FAX 205-760-9618. **Owner(s):** L & L Services, 301 Montgomery Ave., Sheffield, AL 35660; Ed. Tom Magazzu. adv.; photos; pub. size: tabloid; circ. 61,350(free).

FOLEY
US

ONLOOKER, THE. 1907. s-w.: Wed. & Sat. $.50 newsstand; $30/yr. in state; $32.50/yr. out of state; $25.75/yr. senior citizens in state; $28.50/yr. senior citizens out of state. 217 N. McKenzie St., Foley, AL 36535. TEL 334-943-2151; FAX 334-934-3441. **Owner(s):** Denny Thomas, 217 N. McKenzie St., Foley, AL 36535. TEL 334-943-2151; Pub. Diane Mueck; adv.; pub. size: broadsheet; circ. 5,150(paid).

GARDENDALE
US

NORTH JEFFERSON NEWS. Thu. $.50 newsstand; $18/yr. in cy.; $25/yr. out of cy. 125 Bell St., Gardendale, AL 35071. TEL 205-631-8716; FAX 205-631-9902. **Owner(s):** Robert Bryan, 125 Bell St., Gardendale, AL 35071. TEL 205-734-2131; Ed. Charles Whisenant; Pub. Bob Bryan; adv. contact: Mona Richards. pub. size: broadsheet; circ. 4,500(paid). **Wire Service(s):** AP.

GENEVA
US

GENEVA COUNTY REAPER. 1933. Wed. $.50 newsstand; $19.44/yr. in cy.; $25./yr. out of cy. 803 E. Town Ave., Geneva, AL 36340. TEL 334-684-2280; FAX 334-684-3099. **Owner(s):** David Specht, P.O. Box 160, Geneva, AL 36340. TEL 205-684-2280; Ed. Jay Felsberg; Pub. Moe Pujol; adv. contact: Brenda Pujol. photos; pub. size: broadsheet; circ. 15,000(paid).

GULF SHORES, AL 10519

US

SAMSON LEDGER. 1899. Wed. $.50 newsstand; $18/yr. in cy.; $25/yr. out of cy. 803 E. Town Ave., Geneva, AL 36340. TEL 334-684-2280; FAX 334-684-3099. **Owner(s):** Maurice Pujol, 803 E. Town Ave., Geneva, AL 36340. TEL 334-898-2491; David Specht, P.O. Box 66, Samson, AL 36477. TEL 334-898-2491; Ed. Jay Sellsberg; Pub. Brenda Pujol; adv.; photos; pub. size: standard; circ. 1,500(free & paid).

GEORGIANA
US

BUTLER COUNTY NEWS. 1911. Thu. $13/yr. in cy.; $14/yr. out of cy. 122 Miranda Ave., Georgiana, AL 36033. TEL 334-376-2325; FAX 334-376-9302. **Owner(s):** R.W. Pride, P.O. Box 488, Georgiana, AL 36033. TEL 205-376-2325; Ed. R.W. Pride; Pub. R.W. Pride; adv. contact: Teresa Nicholas. pub. size: standard; circ. 2,500(paid).

GREENSBORO
US

GREENSBORO WATCHMAN, THE. 1876. Thu. $18.50/yr. in cy.; $20.50/yr. in state; $26.50/yr. out of state. 1005 Market St., Greensboro, AL 36744-0550. TEL 334-624-8323. **Owner(s):** E.E. Lowry, Jr., P.O. Drawer 550, Greensboro, AL 36744-0550. TEL 334-624-8323; Ed. Willie L. Arrington. pub. size: broadsheet; circ. 3,100(paid).

GREENVILLE
US

GREENVILLE ADVOCATE, THE. 1865. s-w.: Wed. & Sat. $.75 newsstand; $38/yr. local; $48/yr. elsewhere. 103 Hickory St., Greenville, AL 36037. TEL 334-382-3111; FAX 335-382-7104. **Owner(s):** Greenville Newspapers, P.O. Box 507, Greenville, AL 36037. TEL 334-382-3111; Ed. Greg Fuller; Pub. Todd Carpenter; adv. contact: Susan Rhodes. photos; bk.rev.; pub. size: broadsheet; circ. 5,300(paid).

GROVE HILL
US

CLARKE COUNTY DEMOCRAT. 1856. Thu. $.50 newsstand; $16.05/yr. in cy.; $19.26/yr. out of cy.; $22/yr. out of state; $14.98/yr. senior citizens. 261 N. Jackson, Grove Hill, AL 36451. TEL 334-275-3375; FAX 334-275-3060. **Owner(s):** James A. Cox, 261 N. Jackson, Grove Hill, AL 36451. TEL 205-275-3375; Ed. James A. Cox; Pub. James A. Cox; pub. size: broadsheet; circ. 5,100(paid).

GULF SHORES
US ISSN 1041-2662

ISLANDER, THE. 1977. s-w.: Wed. & Sat. $.50 newsstand; $30/yr. in state; $32.50/yr. out of state; $25.75/yr. senior citizens. 128 Cove Dr., Gulf Shores, AL 36542. TEL 334-968-6414; FAX 334-968-5233. **Owner(s):** Gulf Coast Newspapers, Inc., P.O. Box 509, Robertsdale, AL 36567. TEL 334-947-7712; Pub. Denny Thomas; adv.; pub. size: broadsheet; circ. 6,000(paid).

WEEKLY NEWSPAPERS

GUNTERSVILLE
US
ADVERTISER-GLEAM. 1880. s-w.: Wed. & Sat. $.35 newsstand; $18/yr. in cy.; $33/yr. elsewhere. 2218 Taylor St., Guntersville, AL 35976. TEL 205-582-3232; FAX 205-582-3231. **Owner(s):** Sam Harvey, 2218 Taylor St., Guntersville, AL 35976. TEL 205-582-3232; FAX 205-582-3231; Don Woodward, 2218 Taylor St., Guntersville, AL 35976. TEL 205-582-3232; FAX 205-582-3231; Ed. Sam Harvey. pub. size: broadsheet; circ. 11,934(paid).

HALEYVILLE
US
NORTHWEST ALABAMIAN. 1906. s-w.: Wed. & Sat. $.50 newsstand; $25/yr. in cy.; $28/yr. out of cy. Hwy. 195, Haleyville, AL 35565. TEL 205-486-9461; FAX 205-486-4849. **Owner(s):** Hershel Lake, P.O. Box 430, Haleyville, AL 35565. TEL 205-486-9461; Pub. Horace Moore; adv. contact: Roger Carden. photos; pub. size: broadsheet; circ. 8,600(paid).

HAMILTON
US
JOURNAL RECORD. 1970. s-w.: Wed. & Sat. $.50 newsstand; $27/yr. in cy.; $29.50/yr. adj. cys.; $39/yr. in state; $38/yr. out of state. Hwy. 17, Hamilton, AL 35570. TEL 205-921-3104; FAX 205-921-3105. **Owner(s):** Mid-South Publishing Co., P.O. Box 430, Haleyville, AL 35565. TEL 205-486-9461; FAX 205-486-4849; Ed. Les Walters; Pub. Horace Moore; adv. contact: Cindy Ballard. photos; pub. size: broadsheet; circ. 8,500(paid).

HANCEVILLE
US
HANCEVILLE HERALD. 1977. Wed. $.25 newsstand; $10.80/yr. 111 Commercial St., Hanceville, AL 35077. TEL 205-352-4775. **Owner(s):** Ginger Grantham & Violet Earing, P.O. Box 880, Hanceville, AL 35077. TEL 205-352-4775; Ed. Ginger Grantham. adv.; pub. size: broadsheet; circ. 1,800(paid).

HARTSELLE
US
HARTSELLE ENQUIRER. 1874. Thu. $.50 newsstand; $24/yr. mailed. 407 W. Chestnut St., Hartselle, AL 35640. TEL 205-773-6566; FAX 205-773-1953; E-mail: enquirer@hiwaay.net; URL: http://www.hartselle-enquirer.com. **Owner(s):** Hartselle Enquirer, Inc., P.O. Box 929, Hartselle, AL 35640. TEL 205-773-6566; Ed. Clifton P. Knight; Pub. T. L. Beasley; adv.; photos; pub. size: broadsheet; circ. 7,800(paid).

HEADLAND
US
HEADLAND OBSERVER. 1965. Thu. $.50 newsstand; $15/yr. in cy.; $18/yr. out of cy.; $21/yr. out of state. P.O. Box 707, Headland, AL 36345. TEL 334-693-3326; FAX 334-693-5224. **Owner(s):** Thomson Newspapers, Inc., Metro Centre, One Station Pl., 6th Fl., Stamford, CT 96902. TEL 203-425-2500; Ed. Terry Grimes; Pub. Guy Beasley; adv. contact: Betty Gamble. pub. size: broadsheet; circ. 2,000(paid).

HEFLIN
US
CLEBURNE NEWS. 1906. Thu. $.50 newsstand; $15/yr. local; $20/yr. out of cy. Ross St., Heflin, AL 36264. TEL 205-463-2872; FAX 205-463-2872. **Owner(s):** Consolidated Publishing Co., 216 W. Tenth St., Anniston, AL 36201. TEL 205-236-1551; FAX 205-231-0027; Ed. Kim Sloan; Pub. Ed Fowler; adv.; photos; pub. size: broadsheet; circ. 7,000(paid).

JACKSON
US
SOUTH ALABAMIAN. 1887. Thu. $.50 newsstand; $16/yr. local; $24/yr. out of area. 1064 Coffeeville Rd., Jackson, AL 36545. TEL 334-246-4494; FAX 334-246-7486. **Owner(s):** Michael Breedlove, P.O. Box 68, Jackson, AL 36545. TEL 334-246-4494; Ed. Michael M. Breedlove; Pub. Michael M. Breedlove; adv.; photos; pub. size: broadsheet; circ. 4,700(paid).

JACKSONVILLE
US
JACKSONVILLE NEWS. 1936. Wed. $.50 newsstand; $16/yr. in cy.; $25/yr. outside of cy. 203 S. Pelham Rd., Jacksonville, AL 36265. TEL 205-435-5021; FAX 205-435-1028. **Owner(s):** Consolidated Publishing Co., 216 W. Tenth St., Anniston, AL 36201. TEL 205-236-1551; Ed. P.A. Sanguinetti. adv.; photos; pub. size: broadsheet; circ. 4,000(paid).

LAFAYETTE
US
LAFAYETTE SUN, THE. 1880. Wed. $.25 newsstand; $11.25/yr. in cy.; $12.50/yr. out of cy. 116 Lafayette St., Lafayette, AL 36862. TEL 334-864-8885; FAX 334-864-8310. **Owner(s):** Michael Hand, P.O. Box 378, Lafayette, AL 36862. TEL 334-864-8885; Pub. Michael Hand; adv. contact: Michael Hand. pub. size: broadsheet; circ. 2,800(paid).

LEEDS
US
LEEDS NEWS. 1939. Thu. $.50 newsstand; $18/yr. 720 Parkway Dr., Leeds, AL 35094. TEL 205-699-2214; FAX 205-699-3157. **Owner(s):** Robert Bryan, 300 Fourth Ave., S.E., Cullman, AL 35055. TEL 205-734-2131; Ed. Kimberly Stark; Pub. Robert Bryan; adv. contact: Linda Richey. pub. size: broadsheet; circ. 5,000(paid).

LINDEN
US
DEMOCRAT-REPORTER, THE. 1879. Thu. $.50 newsstand; $20/yr. in cy.; $25/yr. out of cy.; $30/yr. out of state. 108 E. Coats Ave., Linden, AL 36748. TEL 334-295-5224. **Owner(s):** Goodloe Sutton, P.O. Box 480040, Linden, AL 36748. TEL 205-295-5224; Ed. Goodloe Sutton; Pub. Goodloe Sutton; pub. size: broadsheet; circ. 6,580(paid).

LINEVILLE
US ISSN 1053-9123
CLAY TIMES JOURNAL. 1903. Wed. $.50 newsstand; $18/yr. in cy.; $24/yr. out of cy. 60132 Hwy. 49, Lineville, AL 36266-0097. TEL 205-396-5760; FAX 205-396-5760. **Owner(s):** Connie & David Proctor, P.O. Box 97, Lineville, AL 36266. TEL 205-396-5760; Ed. David Proctor. adv. contact: Linda McDonald. photos; bk.rev.; pub. size: standard; circ. 3,600(paid).

LIVINGSTON
US
SUMTER COUNTY RECORD-JOURNAL, THE. 1968. Thu. $15/yr. local; $18/yr. in state; $23/yr. out of state. 200 S. Washington St., Livingston, AL 35470. TEL 205-652-6100; FAX 205-652-4466. **Owner(s):** Tommy McGraw, P.O. Drawer B, Livingston, AL 35470. TEL 205-652-6100; Pub. Tommy McGraw; adv. contact: Judy Johnston. pub. size: broadsheet; circ. 3,600(paid).
Formerly: Sumter County Record.

LUVERNE
US
LUVERNE JOURNAL & NEWS. 1888. Wed. $.50 newsstand; $15/yr. in cy.; $17/yr. out of cy. 506 Forest Ave., Luverne, AL 36049. TEL 334-335-3541; FAX 334-335-3541. **Owner(s):** Alvin Bland, P.O. Box 152, Luverne, AL 36049. TEL 334-335-3541; James Morgan, P.O. Box 152, Luverne, AL 36049. TEL 334-335-3541; Ed. Alvin Bland; Pub. James Morgan; adv. contact: James Morgan. pub. size: broadsheet; circ. 3,500(paid).

MADISON
US ISSN 0889-4205
MADISON COUNTY RECORD. 1967. Wed. $.50 newsstand; $19/yr. in cy.; $40/yr. out of cy. 202 Main St., Madison, AL 35758. TEL 205-772-6677; FAX 205-772-6655. **Owner(s):** MCR, Inc., P.O. Box 859, Madison, AL 35758. TEL 205-772-6677; FAX 205-772-6655; Ed. Joan Diehl; Pub. MCR, Inc.; adv.; photos; pub. size: broadsheet; circ. 12,000(paid).

MARION
US
MARION TIMES-STANDARD. 1839. Wed. $.35 newstand; $16.20/yr. in cy.; $24.30/yr. out of cy.; $30/yr. out of state. 414 Washington St., Marion, AL 36756. TEL 334-683-6318; FAX 334-683-4616. **Owner(s):** Robert Tribble, P.O. Box 418, Marion, AL 36756. TEL 334-683-6318; Pub. Robert Tribble; adv. contact: Lorrie Blankenship. pub. size: standard; circ. 2,100(paid).

MILLBROOK
US
COMMUNITY PRESS, THE. Wed. $.50 newsstand. 83 Deatsville Hwy., Millbrook, AL 36054. TEL 334-285-6000; FAX 334-285-6001. **Owner(s):** Gannett Co., Inc., 1100 Wilson Blvd., Arlington, VA 22234. TEL 703-284-6000; Ed. Steve Sawyer; Pub. Lamar Smitherman; adv. contact: Boyd Smith. pub. size: broadsheet; circ. 2,000(free & paid).

WEEKLY NEWSPAPERS

MILLPORT
US
WEST ALABAMA GAZETTE. 1976. Thu. $.50 newsstand; $15/yr. in cy.; $20/yr. in state; $25/yr. out of state. 30431 Hwy. 17, Millport, AL 35576-0249. TEL 205-662-4296; FAX 205-662-4740. **Owner(s):** Peyton & Barbara Bobo, P.O. Drawer 249, Millport, AL 35576-0249. TEL 205-662-4296; FAX 205-662-4740; Ed. Barbara Bobo; Pub. Peyton Bobo; adv. contact: Barbara Bobo. photos; bk.rev.; pub. size: broadsheet; circ. 4,200(paid).

MOBILE
US
MOBILE BEACON. 1943. Wed. $.25 newsstand; $20/yr. 2311 Costarides, Mobile, AL 36617. TEL 334-479-0629; FAX 334-342-0390. **Owner(s):** Mobile Beacon, P.O. Box 1407, Mobile, AL 36633. TEL 205-479-0629; Ed. Cleretta Blackmon; Pub. Lancie M. Thomas; adv. contact: Cleretta Blackmon. photos; pub. size: broadsheet; circ. 7,000(paid).

MONROEVILLE
US   ISSN 0884-8750
MONROE JOURNAL. 2866. Thu. $.50 newsstand; $23/yr. in cy.; $27.50/yr. in state; $30/yr. out of state. 126 Hines St., Monroeville, AL 36460. TEL 334-575-3282; FAX 334-575-3284; E-mail: monjour@monroeville.gulf.net; URL: http://www.monroeville.gulf.net/email/monjour. **Owner(s):** Bolton Newspapers, Inc., 126 Hines St., Monroeville, AL 36460. TEL 334-575-3282; FAX 334-575-3284; Ed. Marilyn W. Handley; Pub. Bo Bolton; adv. contact: Bo Bolton. photos; pub. size: broadsheet; circ. 7,400(paid).

MONTGOMERY
US
MONTGOMERY INDEPENDENT. 1964. Thu. $.50 newsstand; $24/yr. mailed. 6005-B Monticello Dr., Montgomery, AL 36117. TEL 334-213-7323; FAX 334-271-2143. **Owner(s):** Bob Martin, 6005-B Monticello Dr., Montgomery, AL 36117. TEL 205-213-7323; Ed. Wendi Lewis. pub. size: tabloid; circ. 8,000(paid).

MOULTON
US
MOULTON ADVERTISER. 1828. Thu. $.50 newsstand; $20/yr. in cy.; $30/yr. out of cy. Main St., Moulton, AL 35650. TEL 205-974-1114. **Owner(s):** Slatcon, Inc., P.O. Box 517, Moulton, AL 35650. TEL 205-974-1114; Ed. Luke Slaton; Pub. Luke Slaton; adv. contact: Teresa Woodruff. pub. size: standard; circ. 13,500(paid).

MOUNDVILLE
US
MOUNDVILLE TIMES. 1988. Thu. $.50 newsstand; $14/yr. in cy.; $16/yr. in state; $18/yr. out of state. 520 Market St., Moundville, AL 35474. TEL 205-371-2488; FAX 205-371-9010. **Owner(s):** Larry Taylor, 520 Market St., Moundville, AL 35474. TEL 205-371-9011; FAX 205-371-9010; Ed. Austin Dare; Pub. Larry Taylor; adv.; photos; pub. size: standard; circ. 2,500(free & paid).

ONEONTA
US   ISSN 1056-4205
BLOUNT COUNTIAN, THE. 1894. Wed. $.30 newsstand; $12/yr. in cy.; $15/yr. out of cy.; $20/yr. out of state. 217 Third St., S., Oneonta, AL 35121. TEL 205-625-3231. **Owner(s):** Southern Democrat, Inc., 217 Third St., S., P.O. Box 310, Oneonta, AL 35121. TEL 205-625-3231; Ed. Lisa Ryan; Pub. Molly Howard Ryan; adv. contact: Melanie Skillman. pub. size: broadsheet; circ. 6,660(free & paid).

OPP
US
OPP NEWS. 1901. Thu. $.50 newsstand; $22/yr. in cy.; $27/yr. out of cy.; $32/yr. out of state. 200 W. Covington Ave., Opp, AL 36467. TEL 334-493-3595; FAX 334-493-4901. **Owner(s):** Covington Publishing Corp., P.O. Box 870, Opp, AL 36467. TEL 334-493-3595; Ed. Tracey Nelson; Pub. Randy Pebworth; adv. contact: Jennifer Cosby. pub. size: broadsheet; circ. 5,200(paid).

OZARK
US
SOUTHERN STAR. 1867. Wed. $.50 newsstand; $17.82/yr. in cy.; $19.98/yr. out of cy. P.O. Box 1729, Ozark, AL 36361. TEL 334-774-2715; FAX 334-774-9619. **Owner(s):** Joseph H. Adams, P.O. Box 1729, Ozark, AL 36361. TEL 205-774-2715; Ed. Joseph H. Adams; Pub. Joseph H. Adams; adv. contact: Dot Adams. pub. size: broadsheet; circ. 5,200(paid).

PELL CITY
US
ST. CLAIR NEWS-AEGIS. 1823. Thu. $.50 newsstand; $18/yr. in cy.; $25/yr. out of cy.; $16.20/yr. senior citizens. 1820 Second Ave., N., Pell City, AL 35125. TEL 205-884-2310; FAX 205-884-2312. **Owner(s):** Robert Bryan, 300 Fourth Ave., S.E., Cullman, AL 35055. TEL 205-734-2131; Ed. Gary Hanner. adv. contact: Gary Hanner. pub. size: standard; circ. 7,000(paid). **Wire Service(s):** UPI.

PHENIX CITY
US
PHENIX-CITIZEN. Thu. $20/yr. in state; $25/yr. out of state. 1606 Broad St., Phenix City, AL 36867. TEL 334-298-0679; FAX 334-298-0690. **Owner(s):** Mike Venable & Jill Tigner, 1606 Broad St., Phenix City, AL 36867. TEL 334-298-0679; FAX 334-298-0679; Ed. Mike Venable; Pub. Mike Venable; adv. contact: Jill Tigner. pub. size: broadsheet; circ. 6,000(paid).

PIEDMONT
US   ISSN 0890-6017
PIEDMONT JOURNAL-INDEPENDENT. 1982. Wed. $.25 newsstand; $12.84/yr.; $23.54/2 yrs. 115 N. Center Ave., Piedmont, AL 36272-0213. TEL 205-447-2837; FAX 205-447-2837. **Owner(s):** Consolidated Publishing Co., P.O. Box 189, Anniston, AL 36202. TEL 205-236-1551; Lane Weatherbee, 115 N. Center Ave., Piedmont, AL 36272. TEL 205-447-2837; Ed. Lane Weatherbee; Pub. Lane Weatherbee; adv.; photos; pub. size: standard; circ. 6,600(paid).

PRATTVILLE
US
PRATTVILLE PROGRESS. 1886. s-w.: Wed. & Sat. $.50 newsstand; $24/yr. carrier. 152 W. Third St., Prattville, AL 36067. TEL 344-365-6739; FAX 344-365-1400. **Owner(s):** Multimedia, Inc., P.O. Box 1688, Greenville, SC 24602. TEL 803-298-4373; Ed. Brightman Brock; Pub. Lamar Smitherman; adv. contact: Chris Caver. photos; pub. size: broadsheet; circ. 6,250(paid).

RAINSVILLE
US
WEEKLY POST. 1987. Thu. $15/yr. in area; $25/yr. elsewhere; $10/yr. senior citizens in area. 690 McCurdy Ave., Rainsville, AL 35986-0849. TEL 205-638-4027; FAX 205-638-2329. **Owner(s):** JRT Communications, Inc., 690 McCurdy Ave., Rainville, AL 35986-0849. TEL 205-638-4027; FAX 205-638-2329; Pub. Jerry R. Turner; adv.; photos; pub. size: broadsheet; circ. 4,000(paid).

RED BAY
US
RED BAY NEWS. 1963. Wed. $.50 newsstand; $16/yr. local; $22/yr. elsewhere. 120 Fourth Ave., S.E., Red Bay, AL 35582. TEL 205-356-2148; FAX 205-356-2787. **Owner(s):** Harden Publishers, Inc., P.O. Box 1339, Red Bay, AL 35582. TEL 205-356-2148; FAX 205-356-2787; Ed. Tony Launius; Pub. LaVale Mills; adv. contact: LaVale Mills. photos; pub. size: broadsheet; circ. 4,020(paid). **Wire Service(s):** CNS.

ROANOKE
US
RANDOLPH LEADER. 1892. Wed. $.50 newsstand; $18/yr. local; $24/yr. elsewhere. 524 E. Main St., Roanoke, AL 36274. TEL 334-863-2819; FAX 334-863-4006. **Owner(s):** Randolph Publishers, P.O. Box 1267, Roanoke, AL 36274. TEL 334-863-2819; Ed. John W. Stevenson; Pub. John W. Stevenson; pub. size: standard; circ. 6,200(paid).

ROBERTSDALE
US
INDEPENDENT, THE. 1975. Thu. $.50 newsstand; $23/yr. in state; $26/yr. out of state. P.O. Box 509, Robertsdale, AL 36567. TEL 334-947-7318; FAX 334-947-7652. **Owner(s):** Gulf Coast Newspapers, Inc., P.O. Box 509, Robertsdale, AL 36567. TEL 334-947-7712; Ed. Sheri Killam-Williams; Pub. Diane Mueck; adv.; pub. size: broadsheet; circ. 3,000(paid).

ROGERSVILLE
US
EAST LAUDERDALE NEWS. 1965. Thu. $.25 newsstand; $15/yr. in state; $20/yr. out of state. E. Lee St., Rogersville, AL 35652. TEL 205-247-5565; FAX 205-247-1902. **Owner(s):** James B. & Phyllis D. Cox, P.O. Box 179, Rogersville, AL 35652. TEL 205-247-5565; FAX 205-247-1902; Ed. Phyllis D. Cox. adv.: $8.57/SAU. pub. size: broadsheet; circ. 4,500(paid).

Weeklies

RUSSELLVILLE

US
FRANKLIN COUNTY PLUS. Wed. free. 14131 Hwy. 43, Russellville, AL 35653. TEL 205-332-1881; FAX 205-332-1883. **Owner(s):** Boone Newspapers, Inc., P.O. Box 2320, Tuscaloosa, AL 35403. TEL 205-752-3381; FAX 205-752-3392; Ed. Stanley Allison; Pub. Stanley Allison; adv.; pub. size: broadsheet; circ. 27,000(free).

US
FRANKLIN COUNTY TIMES. 1878. s-w.: Wed. & Sun. $.75 newsstand; $39.95/yr. in cy.; $44.95/yr. out of cy. 1413 Hwy. 43, Russellville, AL 35653. TEL 205-332-1881; FAX 205-332-1883. **Owner(s):** Boone Newspapers, Inc., P.O. Box 2320, Tuscaloosa, AL 35403. TEL 205-752-3381; FAX 205-752-3392; Ed. Stanley Allison; Pub. Stanley Allison; adv.; photos; pub. size: broadsheet; circ. 13,700(paid); Sun. 5,000(paid).

SCOTTSBORO

US
VALLEY SUN, THE. Wed. free. 701 Veterans Hwy., Scottsboro, AL 35768. TEL 205-259-1020; FAX 205-259-2709. **Owner(s):** Scottsboro Newspapers, Inc., P.O. Box 220, Scottsboro, AL 35768. TEL 205-259-1020; Ed. William Bynum; Pub. Anita Bynum; pub. size: broadsheet; circ. 7,200(free). **Wire Service(s):** AP, NEA. **Formerly:** Advertiser-Free Press.

STEVENSON

US
NORTH JACKSON PROGRESS. s-w.: Mon. & Thu. $.50 newsstand; $17/yr. 128 Oak Hill Cir., Stevenson, AL 35772. TEL 205-437-2395; FAX 205-437-2592. **Owner(s):** Larry O. Glass, P.O. Drawer 625, Stevenson, AL 35772. TEL 205-437-2395; Ed. Faye Glass; Pub. Larry O. Glass; adv. contact: Lee Glass. pub. size: standard; circ. 4,800(paid).

SULLIGENT

US
LAMAR LEADER. 1973. Wed. $.50 newsstand; $14/yr. in cy.; $16/yr. adjacent cys.; $17/yr. in state; $20/yr. out of state. 55071 Hwy. 17, Sulligent, AL 35586. TEL 205-698-8148; FAX 205-698-8146. **Owner(s):** Orman & Camille Wilson, 55071 Hwy. 17, Sulligent, AL 35586. TEL 205-698-8148; FAX 205-698-8146; Ed. Don Dollar; Pub. Don Dollar; adv. contact: Don Dollar. pub. size: broadsheet; circ. 3,400(paid).

TALLASSEE

US
TALLASSEE TRIBUNE. 1899. Thu. $.50 newsstand; $18/yr. in cy.; $24/yr. out of state. 301 Gilmer Ave., Tallassee, AL 36078. TEL 334-283-6568; FAX 334-283-6569. **Owner(s):** Jack B. Venable, 301 Gilmer Ave., Tallassee, AL 36078; Ed. Jack B. Venable; Pub. Jack B. Venable; adv. contact: Barbara Morrow. pub. size: broadsheet; circ. 4,200(paid).

THOMASVILLE

US
THOMASVILLE TIMES, THE. Thu. $.50 newsstand. P.O. Box 367, Thomasville, AL 36784. TEL 334-636-2214; FAX 334-636-9822. **Owner(s):** Michael & Linda Breedlove, P.O. Box 367, Thomasville, AL 36784. TEL 334-636-2214; Jim & Suzanne Cox, P.O. Box 367, Thomasville, AL 36784. TEL 334-636-2214; Pub. Michael Breedlove; adv. contact: Tonya Joyce. pub. size: broadsheet; circ. 4,100(free & paid).

TROY

US
TROY PROGRESS. Sun. free. 906-A S. Brundidge St., Troy, AL 36081. TEL 334-566-9401; FAX 334-566-9403. **Owner(s):** Boone Newspapers, Inc., P.O. Box 2370, Tuscaloosa, AL 35403. TEL 205-752-3381; FAX 205-752-3392; Ed. June Treadwell; Pub. Rick Reynolds; adv.; pub. size: broadsheet; circ. Sun. 13,700(free).

TUSCUMBIA

US
COLBERT COUNTY REPORTER. 1911. Tue. $.50 newsstand; $14/yr. in state mailed; $18/yr out of state; $12/yr. senior citizens. 106 W. Fifth St., Tuscumbia, AL 35674. TEL 205-383-8471; FAX 205-383-8476. **Owner(s):** Jim Crawford, Jr., Lawrenceburg, TN 38464. TEL 356-757-2000; Ed. Jim Crawford, Jr.; Pub. Jim Crawford, Jr.; adv. contact: Marcy Hill. pub. size: broadsheet; circ. 6,000(paid).

US
STANDARD & TIMES. 1829. Thu. $.50 newsstand; $14/yr. in cy. 106 W. Fifth St., Tuscumbia, AL 35674. TEL 205-383-8476; FAX 205-383-8476. **Owner(s):** Jim Crawford, Jr., 106 W. Fifth St., Tuscumbia, AL 35674. TEL 205-383-8476; Pub. Jim Crawford, Jr.; adv.; pub. size: broadsheet; circ. 4,500(paid).

TUSKEGEE

US
TUSKEGEE NEWS. 1865. Thu. $.50 newsstand; $22.50/yr. in cy. 120 Eastside St., Tuskegee, AL 36083. TEL 334-727-3020; FAX 334-727-7700. **Owner(s):** Tuskegee Newspapers, Inc., P.O. Box 830060, Tuskegee, AL 36083. TEL 205-727-3020; Ed. Guy Rhodes; Pub. Paul Davis; pub. size: broadsheet; circ. 4,800(paid).

UNION SPRINGS

US
UNION SPRINGS HERALD. 1866. Wed. $.50 newsstand; $17/yr. in state; $21/yr. out of state. 104 E. Conecuh Ave., Union Springs, AL 36089. TEL 334-738-2360; FAX 334-738-2342. **Owner(s):** Terry Everett, 104 E. Conecuh Ave., Union Springs, AL 36089. TEL 334-738-2360; FAX 334-739-2342; Pub. Thomas May; adv. contact: Neal May. pub. size: broadsheet; circ. 2,900(paid).

VERNON

US
LAMAR DEMOCRAT. 1896. Wed. $.50 newsstand; $15/yr. in cy.; $17.50/yr. out of cy.; $25/yr. out of state. 125 First Ave., N.E., Vernon, AL 35592-0587. TEL 205-695-7029; FAX 205-695-9501. **Owner(s):** Rex Rainwater, P.O. Box 587, Vernon, AL 35592. TEL 205-695-7029; Howard Reeves, P.O. Box 587, Vernon, AL 35592. TEL 205-695-7029; Ed. Howard Reeves; Pub. Rex Rainwater; adv.; photos; pub. size: broadsheet; circ. 4,300(paid).

WETUMPKA

US
WETUMPKA HERALD. 1898. Thu. $.50 newsstand; $16/yr. in cy.; $20/yr. in state; $24/yr. out of state. 300 Green St., Wetumpka, AL 36092-0029. TEL 334-567-7811; FAX 334-567-3284. **Owner(s):** Ellen T. Williams, 60 Tankersley Ln., Wetumpka, AL 36092. TEL 334-569-3284; Ed. Gerald M. Williams; Pub. Ellen T. Williams; adv. contact: Gerald M. Williams. photos; bk.rev.; pub. size: standard; circ. 4,156(free & paid).

ALASKA

ANCHORAGE

US
GREAT LANDER BUSH MAILER. 1969. m. free. 3110 Spenard Rd., Anchorage, AK 99503. TEL 907-274-0611; FAX 907-272-2105. **Owner(s):** Anchorage Printing, Inc., 3110 Spenard Rd., Anchorage, AK 99503. TEL 907-272-2213; Ed. Charles Rhodes; Pub. Charles Rhodes; adv. contact: Dennie Ford. pub. size: tabloid; circ. 43,000(free).

US ISSN 0049-4801
TUNDRA TIMES. 1962. bi-w. $1 newsstand; $30/yr.; $20/yr. senior citizens. 1711 E. Lore Rd., Anchorage, AK 99507. TEL 907-349-2512; FAX 907-349-0335. **Owner(s):** Eskimo, Indian, Aleut Publishing Co., P.O. Box 92247, Anchorage, AK 99507. TEL 907-349-2512; FAX 907-349-0335; Ed. Toni Kahklen-Jones; Pub. Toni Kahklen-Jones; adv. contact: Paulette Moreno. photos; bk.rev.; pub. size: tabloid; circ. 3,500(paid).

BARROW

US
ARCTIC SOUNDER, THE. Thu. $.75/newsstand; $45/yr. 2nd class; $90/yr 1st class. 1637 Okpik St., Barrow, AK 99723. TEL 907-852-2531; FAX 907-852-2255. **Owner(s):** Alaska Newspapers, Inc., 336 E. Fifth Ave., Anchorage, AK 99501. TEL 907-272-9830; Ed. Duncan Adams; Pub. Christopher Casati; adv.; pub. size: broadsheet; circ. 2,800(free & paid).

BETHEL

US

TUNDRA DRUMS. 1974. Wed. $.75 newsstand; $45/yr. 660 Third Ave., Bethel, AK 99559. TEL 907-543-3500; FAX 907-543-3312; E-mail: aknewspr@alaska.net; URL: http://alaska.net/~aknewspr/drums/drums.html. **Owner(s):** Alaska Newspapers, Inc., 336 E. Fifth Ave., Anchorage, AK 99501. TEL 907-272-9830; FAX 907-272-9512; Ed. Patty Sullivan; Pub. Chris Casati; adv. contact: Natalie S. Alexie. photos; pub. size: tabloid; circ. 6,300(paid). **Wire Service(s):** AP, CSM.

CORDOVA

US

CORDOVA TIMES. 1914. Thu. $.75 newsstand; $45/yr. mailed 2nd class; $90/yr. 1st class. P.O. Box 200, Cordova, AK 99574-0200. TEL 907-424-7181; FAX 907-424-5799; E-mail: aknewspr@alaska.net; URL: http://alaska.net/~aknewspr/cordova/cordova.html. **Owner(s):** Alaska Newspapers, Inc., 503 E. Fifth Ave., Anchorage, AK 99501. TEL 907-262-9830; Ed. Chris Casati; Pub. Chris Casati; adv. contact: Joy Landaluce. bk.rev.; pub. size: standard; circ. 1,700(paid). **Wire Service(s):** AP.

DELTA JUNCTION

US

DELTA WIND, THE. Wed. $.50 newsstand. P.O. Box 986, Delta Junction, AK 99737. TEL 907-895-5115. **Owner(s):** Loretta Schooley, The Delta Wind, Delta Junction, AK 99737. TEL 907-895-4550; Ed. Loretta Schooley. adv.; pub. size: broadsheet; circ. 1,100(free & paid).

DILLINGHAM

US

BRISTOL BAY TIMES, THE. Thu. $.75 newsstand. P.O. Box 1770, Dillingham, AK 99576. TEL 907-842-5572; FAX 907-842-5562. **Owner(s):** Alaska Newspapers, Inc., 503 E. Fifth Ave., Anchorage, AK 99501. TEL 907-272-9830; Ed. Greg Corr; Pub. Christopher Casati; adv.; pub. size: tabloid; circ. 2,000(free & paid).

DUTCH HARBOR

US

DUTCH HARBOR FISHERMAN, THE. Thu. $.75 newsstand. P.O. Box 920472, Dutch Harbor, AK 99692. TEL 907-581-2092; FAX 907-581-2090. **Owner(s):** Alaska Newspapers, Inc., 336 E. Fifth Ave., Anchorage, AK 99501. TEL 907-272-9830; Ed. Jim Paulin; Pub. Christopher Casati; adv.; pub. size: broadsheet; circ. 1,547(free & paid).

EAGLE RIVER

US

ALASKA STAR. Thu. $.50 newsstand. 16941 N. Eagle River Loop Rd., Eagle River, AK 99577. TEL 907-694-2727; FAX 907-694-1545. **Owner(s):** Star Publishing Co., Inc., 16941 N. Eagle River Loop Rd., Eagle River, AK 99577. TEL 907-694-2727; Ed. Stacy Simonet; Pub. Lee B. Jordan; adv.; pub. size: tabloid; circ. 7,500(free & paid).

HAINES

US

CHILKAT VALLEY NEWS. 1966. Thu. $36/yr. local; $42/yr. in state; $48/yr. mailed 2nd class; $64/yr. local mailed 1st class. Main St., Haines, AK 99827. TEL 907-766-2688. **Owner(s):** Bonnie Hedrick, P.O. Box 630, Haines, AK 99827. TEL 907-766-2688; Ed. Bonnie Hedrick. adv.: $7/SAU. pub. size: tabloid; circ. 1,100(paid).

HOMER

US

HOMER NEWS. 1964. Thu. $.75 newsstand; $35/yr. local; $43/yr. in state; $48/yr. out of state. 3482 Landings St., Homer, AK 99603. TEL 907-235-7767; FAX 907-235-4199; E-mail: hnews@alaska.net; URL: http://www.alaska.netnews. **Owner(s):** Homer News, Inc., 3482 Landings St., Homer, AK 99603. TEL 907-235-7767; Ed. Mark Turner; Pub. Mark Turner; adv. contact: Jane Alberts. adv.: $10.85/SAU. pub. size: tabloid; circ. 7,000(controlled & paid).

JUNEAU

US

CAPITAL CITY WEEKLY. 1980. w. free. 1910 Alex Holden Way, Juneau, AK 99801. TEL 907-789-4144; FAX 907-789-0987; E-mail: capweek@ptialaska.net; URL: http://www.adone.com/capcity. **Owner(s):** Summit Services, Inc., 1910 Alex Holden Way, Juneau, AK 99801; Ed. Vanessa Orr; Pub. Renda Heimbigner; adv. contact: Renda Heimbigner. photos; bk.rev.; pub. size: tabloid; circ. 20,000(free & paid).

NOME

US ISSN 0745-9106

NOME NUGGET. 1900. Thu. $.50 newsstand; $55/yr. in state; $60/yr out of state. 123 Front St., Nome, AK 99762. TEL 907-443-5235. E-mail: nugget@nome.net; URL: http://www.nome.net/NomeNugget. **Owner(s):** Nancy McGuire, P.O. Box 610, Nome, AK 99762. TEL 907-443-5235; Ed. Nancy McGuire; Pub. Nancy McGuire; adv. contact: Michael Price. photos; pub. size: tabloid; circ. 6,000(paid). **Wire Service(s):** AP.

NONE

US

BERING STRAIT RECORD. Thu. $.50 newsstand. 240 E. Front St., None, AK 99762. TEL 907-443-6397; FAX 907-443-5600. **Owner(s):** Alaska Newspapers, Inc., 336 E. Fifth Ave., Anchorage, AK 99501. TEL 907-272-9830; Ed. Mark Gillespie; Pub. Christopher Casati; adv.; pub. size: broadsheet; circ. 2,200(free & paid).

PETERSBURG

US

PETERSBURG PILOT. 1974. Thu. $1 newsstand; $36/yr. in town; $47/yr. out of town; $58/yr. out of state. 212 Harborway, Petersburg, AK 99833. TEL 907-772-9393; FAX 907-772-4871; E-mail: ppub@alaska.net. **Owner(s):** Pilot Publishing, Inc., 212 Harborway, Petersburg, AK 99833. TEL 907-772-9393; FAX 907-772-4871; Ed. Ronald J. Loesch; Pub. Ronald J. Loesch; adv.: $7.50/SAU. pub. size: tabloid; circ. 1,800(paid). **Wire Service(s):** AP.

SEWARD

US

SEWARD PHOENIX LOG. 1966. Thu. $.75 newsstand; $45/yr. 315 Fourth Ave., Seward, AK 99664. TEL 907-224-8070; FAX 907-224-3157; E-mail: aknewspr@alaska.net; URL: http://alaska.net/~aknewspr/seward/seward.html. **Owner(s):** Alaska Newspapers, Inc., 336 E. Fifth Ave., Anchorage, AK 99664. TEL 907-272-9830; FAX 907-272-9512; Ed. Chris Casati; Pub. Chris Casati; adv. contact: Bruce Swanson. photos; pub. size: tabloid; circ. 2,000(free & paid). **Wire Service(s):** AP.

VALDEZ

US

VALDEZ VANGUARD. 1976. Wed. $.75 newsstand; $45/yr. 224 Galena, Valdez, AK 99686. TEL 907-835-2211; FAX 907-835-5101; E-mail: aknewpr@alaska.net; URL: http://alaska.net/~aknewspr/valdez/vanguard.html. **Owner(s):** Alaska Newspapers, Inc., 336 E. Fifth Ave., Anchorage, AK 99501. TEL 907-272-9830; FAX 907-272-9512; Ed. Tony Bickert; Pub. Chris Casati; adv.; photos; bk.rev.; pub. size: tabloid; circ. 1,650(free & paid). **Wire Service(s):** AP.

WASILLA

US

FRONTIERSMAN, THE. 1947. s-w.: Wed. & Fri. $.50 newsstand; $40/yr. in city; $65.60/yr. out of city; $70.60/yr. out of state. 1261 Seward-Meridian, Wasilla, AK 99654. TEL 907-376-5225; FAX 907-352-2277. **Owner(s):** Wick Communications, Inc., 333 W. Wilcox Dr., Ste. 302, Sierra Vista, AZ 85635. TEL 520-728-4488; FAX 520-728-6090; Ed. Vicki Naegele. adv. contact: Jerry Gamb. pub. size: broadsheet; circ. 8,000(paid). **Wire Service(s):** AP Newsfinder.

US

VALLEY SUN. Tue. free. 1261 Seward-Meridian, Wasilla, AK 99654. TEL 907-376-5225; FAX 907-352-2277. **Owner(s):** Wick Communications, Inc., 333 W. Wilcox Dr., Ste. 302, Sierra Vista, AZ 85635. TEL 520-728-4488; FAX 520-728-6090; Ed. Vicki Naegele. adv. contact: Jerry Gamb. pub. size: broadsheet; circ. 8,200(free).

WRANGELL

US

WRANGELL SENTINEL. 1902. Thu. $.75 newsstand; $30/yr. in town; $34/yr. out of town mailed 2nd class; $56/yr. out of town mailed 1st class. 312 Front St., Wrangell, AK 99929.
TEL 907-874-2301; FAX 907-874-2303.
Owner(s): Wrangell Publishing, P.O. Box 798, Wrangell, AK 99929. TEL 907-874-2301; Ed. Jodi Stephens; Pub. Seane Saunders; adv.; photos; bk.rev.; pub. size: tabloid; circ. 1,500(controlled & paid).

ARIZONA

AJO

US

AJO COPPER NEWS. 1916. Wed. $.25 newsstand; $18/6 mos.; $20/yr. 10 Pajaro, Ajo, AZ 85321. TEL 520-387-7688; FAX 520-387-7505.
Owner(s): Gabrielle, Hollister J. & Joseph D. David, P.O. Box 39, Ajo, AZ 85321. TEL 520-387-7688; Ed. Gabrielle David; Pub. Hollister J. David; adv. contact: Michelle Pacheco. photos; pub. size: tabloid; circ. 2,456(paid).

APACHE JUNCTION

US

APACHE JUNCTION INDEPENDENT. 1959. Wed. $.25 newsstand; $20/yr.; $20/3 mos. out of state. 201 W. Apache Trail, Ste. 708, Apache Junction, AZ 85220. TEL 602-982-7799; FAX 602-671-0016. **Owner(s):** INI Holding Co., P.O. Box 7001, Dover, DE 19903. TEL 302-674-4750; Ed. James L. Files. adv.: $16.10/SAU. pub. size: broadsheet; circ. 20,000(free & paid).

US

EAST MESA INDEPENDENT. 1963. Wed. $.25 newsstand; $18/yr.; $20/3 mos. out of state. 201 W. Apache Trail, Ste. 708, Apache Junction, AZ 85220. TEL 602-982-7799; FAX 602-671-0016. **Owner(s):** INI Holding Co., P.O. Box 7001, Dover, DE 19901. TEL 302-674-4750; Ed. Richard Dyer. adv.: $20.72/SAU. photos; pub. size: broadsheet; circ. 37,000(paid).
Formerly: Mesa Independent.

ARIZONA CITY

US

ARIZONA CITY INDEPENDENT. bi-w. $.50 newsstand; $10/yr.; $15/yr. out of state. 13350 S. Sunland Gym Rd., Ste. 1-C, Arizona City, AZ 85223. TEL 520-466-6277; FAX 520-466-6676.
Owner(s): Casa Grande Valley Newspapers, Inc., 200 W. Second St., Casa Grande, AZ 85222. TEL 602-836-7461; Ed. Angela Colhoun. circ. 2,500.

AVONDALE

US

WEST VALLEY VIEW. 1985. Wed. $.50 newsstand; $32/yr. 310 N. Dysart Rd., Avondale, AZ 85323. TEL 602-932-4361; FAX 602-932-4368.
Owner(s): E. Freirich, 310 N. Dysart Rd., Avondale, AZ 85323. TEL 602-932-4361; FAX 602-932-4368; B. Freirich, 310 N. Dysart Rd., Avondale, AZ 85323. TEL 602-932-4361; FAX 602-932-4368; Ed. J. Conway; Pub. E. Freirich; adv.; photos; bk.rev.; pub. size: tabloid; circ. 28,000(free).

BENSON

US

SAN PEDRO VALLEY NEWS-SUN. Wed. $.50/issue; $22/yr. 200 S. Ocotillo, Benson, AZ 85602. TEL 520-586-3382; FAX 520-586-2382.
Owner(s): Wick Communications, Inc., 333 W. Wilcox Dr., Ste. 302, Sierra Vista, AR 85635. TEL 620-458-0200; FAX 620-458-6166; Ed. James Tiffin; Pub. John Toth; adv.; pub. size: broadsheet; circ. 3,200(free & paid).

BISBEE

US

▼**BISBEE NEWS, THE.** 1995. Thu. free newsstand; $30/yr. mailed. 99 Bisbee Rd., Ste. B, Bisbee, AZ 85603. TEL 520-432-4400; FAX 520-432-4441. **Owner(s):** Bisbee Publishing Co., 99 Bisbee Rd., Ste. B, Bisbee, AZ 85603. TEL 520-432-4400; FAX 520-432-4441; Ed. Suzanne Darlington; Pub. Mary Ellen Corbett; adv. contact: Judy Benjamin. adv.: $6/SAU. photos; bk.rev.; pub. size: tabloid; circ. 5,000(free & paid).

US

BISBEE OBSERVER, THE. 1985. Thu. $.50 newsstand; $22/yr. in cy. 7 Bisbee Rd., Bisbee, AZ 85603. TEL 520-432-7254; FAX 520-432-4192; E-mail: bisbeeobserver@theriver.com. **Owner(s):** Robert W. Maguire, 7 Bisbee Rd., Bisbee, AZ 85603. TEL 520-432-7254; FAX 520-432-4192; Pub. Lorraine Marcill; adv. contact: Laura Swan. photos; pub. size: tabloid; circ. 2,400(paid).

BUCKEYE

US

BUCKEYE VALLEY NEWS. Thu. $.40/issue; $14.95/yr. in cy.; $16.95/yr. out of cy. 122 S. Fourth St., Buckeye, AZ 85326.
TEL 602-386-4426; FAX 602-386-4427.
Owner(s): Mark Shepard, 122 S. Fourth St., Buckeye, AZ 85326. TEL 602-386-4426; Pub. Sharon Butler; adv.; pub. size: tabloid; circ. 2,900(free & paid).

BULLHEAD CITY

US

TRI-STATE ADVERTISER. 1955. Tue. free. 1960 Hwy. 95, Ste. 6, Bullhead City, AZ 86442.
TEL 520-758-5868; FAX 520-758-4543.
Owner(s): Associated Desert Shoppers, Inc., 73-400 Hwy. 111, Palm Desert, CA 92260. TEL 760-346-1729; FAX 760-346-7350; Pub. Hal Paradis; adv.; pub. size: tabloid; circ. 12,900(free).

CAVE CREEK

US

DESERT WINDS, THE. Wed. $.50/newsstand; $22.50/yr. 6045 Hidden Valley, Cave Creek, AZ 85331. TEL 602-488-3436;
FAX 602-488-4779. **Owner(s):** Western Newspapers, Inc., 290 S. First Ave., Ste. 4, Yuma, AZ 85364; Ed. James Dir; Pub. Cheryl Lopez; adv.; pub. size: broadsheet; circ. 17,661(free & paid).

[Foothills]

US

FOOTHILLS SENTINEL. Wed. $.50/newsstand; $22.50/yr. 6045 Hidden Valley, Cave Creek, AZ 85331. TEL 602-488-3436;
FAX 602-488-4779. **Owner(s):** Western Newspapers, Inc., 290 S. First Ave., Ste.4, Yuma, AZ 85364; Ed. James Dir; Pub. Cheryl Lopez; adv.; pub. size: broadsheet; circ. 17,661(free & paid).

CHANDLER

US

CHANDLER INDEPENDENT. 1986. Wed. free in area; $18/yr. mailed 3rd class. 325 E. Elliot Rd., Ste 21, Chandler, AZ 85225-1127.
TEL 602-497-0048; FAX 602-926-1019.
Owner(s): Joe Smyth, P.O. Box 12292, Scottsdale, AZ 85268. TEL 602-991-5333; adv.: $13.16/SAU. pub. size: broadsheet; circ. 21,000(free & paid).

CHINO VALLEY

US

CHINO VALLEY REVIEW. Wed. free deliv. 401 W. Palomino, Chino Valley, AZ 86323.
TEL 520-636-1334; FAX 520-636-5276.
Owner(s): Prescott Newspapers, Inc., 147 N. Cortez, Prescott, AZ 86302. TEL 520-445-3333; Ed. Ivan Murray; Pub. Robert D. Gilliland; adv. contact: Jamie Hall. pub. size: broadsheet; circ. 4,000(free).

CLIFTON

US

COPPER ERA. 1899. Wed. $.35 newsstand; $17/yr. in cy.; $23/yr. in state; $28/yr. out of state. One Wards Canyon, Clifton, AZ 85533.
TEL 520-865-3162; FAX 520-428-3110.
Owner(s): Wick Communications, Inc., 333 W. Wilcox Dr., Ste. 302, Sierra Vista, AZ 85635-1357. TEL 520-458-0200; FAX 520-458-6166; Ed. Lawrence Blaskey; Pub. Jim Hornbeck; adv.; photos; pub. size: broadsheet; circ. 3,500(free & paid).

COOLIDGE

US

COOLIDGE EXAMINER. Wed. $.50 newsstand; $35/yr. in state; $45/yr. out of state. 353 W. Central, Coolidge, AZ 85228.
TEL 602-723-5441. **Owner(s):** Casa Grande Valley Newspapers, Inc., P.O. Box 15002, Casa Grande, AZ 85230-5002. TEL 602-836-7461; Ed. Thomas Martinez. adv. contact: Bob Tuley. pub. size: broadsheet; circ. 2,288(paid).

COTTONWOOD

US

COTTONWOOD JOURNAL EXTRA. 1988. Wed. controlled/home deliv. 830 S. Main., Ste. 1E, Cottonwood, AZ 86326. TEL 520-634-8551; FAX 520-282-6888. **Owner(s):** L & L Printing Co., P.O. Box 619, Sedona, AZ 86336. TEL 602-282-6809; FAX 602-282-6011; Ed. Tom Brossart; Pub. Robert Larson, Jr.; adv.; pub. size: broadsheet; circ. 7,250(controlled).

WEEKLY NEWSPAPERS

US
VERDE INDEPENDENT. 1947. s-w.: Wed. & Fri. $42/yr. 116 S. Main St., Cottonwood, AZ 86326. TEL 602-634-2241; FAX 602-634-2312. **Owner(s):** Western Newspapers, Inc., 2055 Arizona Ave., Yuma, AZ 85364. TEL 602-783-3333; Ed. Dan Engler; Pub. Dick Larson; adv.; pub. size: broadsheet; circ. 16,635(free & paid).

EAGAR

US
ROUND VALLEY PAPER, THE. 1988. Wed. $.25 newsstand; $18/yr. in cy; $24/yr. out of state. 150 N. Poverty Flat, Eagar, AZ 85925-0867. TEL 602-333-2033. **Owner(s):** Jacobs Family Trust, The, P.O. Box 867, Eagar, AZ 85925-0867. TEL 602-333-2033; Pub. Dorothy Jacobs; adv.; photos; pub. size: broadsheet; circ. 1,100(free & paid).

ELOY

US
ELOY ENTERPRISE. 1947. Thu. $.50 newsstand; $21/yr. local; $35/yr. out of cy. 710 N. Main St., Eloy, AZ 85231. TEL 520-466-7333. **Owner(s):** Casa Grande Valley Newspapers, Inc., P.O. Box 15002, Casa Grande, AZ 85230-5002. TEL 602-836-7461; Ed. Joe Meahl; Pub. Joe Meahl; adv.; pub. size: broadsheet; circ. 891(paid).

FLORENCE

US
FLORENCE REMINDER & BLADE-TRIBUNE. 1882. Thu. $.50 newsstand; $21/yr. in cy.; $30/yr. out of cy. 224 N. Main St., Florence, AZ 85232. TEL 520-868-5897. **Owner(s):** Casa Grande Valley Newspapers, Inc., 200 W. Second St., Casa Grande, AZ 85222. TEL 602-836-7461; Ed. Mark Cowling; Pub. Donovan Kramer, Sr.; adv.; pub. size: standard; circ. 3,000(paid).

FOUNTAIN HILLS

US
TIMES OF FOUNTAIN HILLS & RIO VERDE. Wed. $.75/newsstand; $26/yr. 16929 E. Enterprise Dr., Fountain Hills, AZ 85269. TEL 602-837-1931; FAX 602-837-1951. **Owner(s):** L. Alan Cruikshank, 16929 E. Enterprise Dr., Fountain Hills, AZ 85269. TEL 602-837-1931; Ed. Michael Scharnow; Pub. L. Alan Cruikshank; adv.: $6.47/SAU. pub. size: broadsheet; circ. 4,300(free & paid).

GLENDALE

US
ARROW, THE. 1987. m. free. 17035 N. 67th Ave., Ste. 2, Glendale, AZ 85308. TEL 602-878-8881; FAX 602-878-8899. **Owner(s):** Phyllis C. & Elwyn W. Brown, 17035 N. 67th Ave., Ste. 2, Glendale, AZ 85308. TEL 602-878-8881; FAX 602-878-8899; Ed. Phyllis C. Brown; Pub. Phyllis C. Brown; adv.; photos; bk.rev.; pub. size: tabloid; circ. 1,800(controlled & paid).

US ISSN 1053-7600
GLENDALE STAR, THE. 1979. Thu. $.50 newsstand; $20/yr. 7122 N. 59th Ave., Glendale, AZ 85301. TEL 602-842-6000; FAX 602-842-6017. **Owner(s):** William V. & Darlene M. Toops, 7122 N. 59th Ave., Glendale, AZ 85301. TEL 602-842-6000; FAX 602-842-6017; Ed. Michael G. Hart; Pub. William V. Toops; adv. contact: William V. Toops. pub. size: tabloid; circ. 10,940(free & paid).

US
PEORIA TIMES. 1952. Fri. $.50 newsstand; $20/yr. 7122 N. 59th Ave., Glendale, AZ 85301. TEL 602-842-6000; FAX 602-842-6017. **Owner(s):** William V. & Darlene M. Toops, 7122 N. 59th Ave., Glendale, AZ 85301. TEL 602-842-6000; FAX 602-842-6017; Ed. Carolyn Dryer. adv. contact: William E. Toops. photos; pub. size: tabloid; circ. 5,203(free & paid).

GLOBE

US
ARIZONA SILVER BELT. 1878. Wed. $.50 newsstand; $24/yr. in cy.; $27/yr. out of cy. 298 N. Pine, Globe, AZ 85501. TEL 520-425-7121; FAX 520-425-7001. **Owner(s):** American Publishing Co., 606 N. Van Buren, P.O. Box 520, Marion, IL 62959. TEL 618-993-1711; Ed. Ellen Kretsch; Pub. Ellen Kretsch; adv. contact: David Andrade. pub. size: broadsheet; circ. 5,400(paid).
Formerly: Globe Arizona Silver Belt.

US
COPPER COUNTRY NEWS. 1984. Tue. free newsstand; $36/yr. 254 N. Broad, Globe, AZ 85501. TEL 520-425-0355; FAX 520-425-6535. **Owner(s):** Guy & Donna L. Anderson, 254 N. Broad, Globe, AZ 85501. TEL 520-425-0355; FAX 520-425-6535; Pub. Donna L. Anderson; adv.; photos; pub. size: tabloid; circ. 8,600(free).

US
SAN CARLOS APACHE MOCCASIN. Tue. $.50 newsstand. 298 N. Pine St., Globe, AZ 85501. TEL 520-425-7121; FAX 520-425-7001. **Owner(s):** American Publishing Co., 606 N. Van Buren, Marion, IL 62959. TEL 618-993-1711; Pub. Ellen Kretsch; adv. contact: David Andrade. pub. size: broadsheet; circ. 2,000(free & paid).

GREEN VALLEY

US
GREEN VALLEY NEWS & SUN. 1964. s-w.: Wed. & Fri. $.50 newsstand; $39/yr. carrier; $55/yr. mailed. 102-42 Loconada, Green Valley, AZ 85614. TEL 520-625-5511; FAX 602-625-1603. **Owner(s):** Wick Communications, Inc., 333 Wilcox Dr., Ste. 302, Sierra Vista, AZ 85635-1756. TEL 520-458-0200; Ed. Kathleen M. Engle; Pub. Frank Newel; adv.; bk.rev.; pub. size: standard; circ. 10,800(paid).

HOLBROOK

US
HOLBROOK TRIBUNE NEWS & SNOWFLAKE HERALD. 1909. s-w.: Wed. & Fri. $.35 newsstand; $24/yr. in cy.; $30/yr. in state; $38/yr. out of state. 200 E. Hopi Dr., Holbrook, AZ 86025. TEL 520-524-6203; FAX 520-524-3541. **Owner(s):** Navajo County Publishers, Inc., 200 E. Hopi Dr., Holbrook, AZ 86025. TEL 520-524-6205; Ed. Francie Payne; Pub. Paul Barger; adv. contact: Matthew Barger. photos; pub. size: broadsheet; circ. 3,476(paid).

LAKE HAVASU CITY

US
LAKE HAVASU CITY ADVERTISER. 1955. w. free. 2099 W. Acoma Blvd., Ste. A, Lake Havasu City, AZ 86403. TEL 520-855-7871; FAX 520-855-8183. **Owner(s):** Associated Desert Shoppers, Inc., 73-400 Hwy. 111, Palm Desert, CA 92260. TEL 760-346-1729; FAX. 760-346-7350; Pub. Hal Paradis; adv.; pub. size: tabloid; circ. 13,700(free).

PAGE

US
LAKE POWELL CHRONICLE. 1965. Wed. $.50 newsstand; $37/yr. in state; $47/yr. out of state. P.O. Box 1716, Page, AZ 86040. TEL 520-645-8888; FAX 520-645-2209. **Owner(s):** Lake Powell Newspapers, Inc., P.O. Box 1716, Page, AZ 86040. TEL 520-645-8888; Ed. David Carkhuff; Pub. Sue Shenniman; pub. size: broadsheet; circ. 3,400(paid).

PARKER

US
PARKER ADVERTISER. 1955. w. free. 1316 Joshua, Ste. A, Parker, AZ 85344. TEL 520-669-9227; FAX 520-669-2410. **Owner(s):** Associated Desert Shoppers, Inc., 73-400 Hwy. 111, Palm Desert, CA 92260. TEL 760-346-1729; Pub. Hal Paradis; adv.; pub. size: tabloid; circ. 7,900(free).

US
PARKER PIONEER. 1954. Wed. $.50 newsstand; $18/yr. local; $22/yr. in state; $32/yr. out of state. 1001 12th St., Parker, AZ 85344. TEL 520-669-2275; FAX 520-669-9624. **Owner(s):** River City Newspapers, LLC, 2225 W. Acoma Blvd., Lake Havasu City, AZ 86403-1756. TEL 520-453-4237; Ed. Joan M. Travis. adv.; pub. size: broadsheet.

PAYSON

US
PAYSON ROUNDUP. 1937. s-w.: Wed. & Fri. $.35 newsstand; $37.50/yr. in state; $44/yr. out of state. 708 N. Beeline Hwy., Payson, AZ 85547. TEL 520-474-5251; FAX 520-474-1897; E-mail: tproundup@aol.com; URL: http://members.aol.com/tproundup/index.html. **Owner(s):** WorldWest Limited Liability Co., 609 New Hampshire, P.O. Box 688, Lawrence, KS 66044. TEL 913-843-1000; Ed. Brian Beck; Pub. Richard Haddad; adv.; photos; bk.rev.; pub. size: standard; circ. 6,200(paid). **Wire Service(s):** AP Newsfinder.
Formerly: Payson Roundup & Rim Country News.

PHOENIX

US ISSN 0279-3962
NEW TIMES. 1970. Thu. free newsstand; $60/yr. mailed. 1201 E. Jefferson, Phoenix, AZ 85034. TEL 602-271-0040; FAX 602-340-8806. **Owner(s):** New Times, Inc., P.O. Box 2510, Phoenix, AZ 85002. TEL 602-271-0040; FAX 602-340-8806; Ed. Jeremy Voas; Pub. Michele Laven; adv. contact: Steve Levin. photos; pub. size: tabloid; circ. 140,000(free).

PRESCOTT VALLEY

US
PRESCOTT VALLEY TRIBUNE, THE. Wed. free deliv.; $.50 newsstand. 8249 E. State Rte. 69, Prescott Valley, AZ 86314. TEL 520-772-2679; FAX 520-772-3393. **Owner(s):** Prescott Newspapers, Inc., 147 N. Cortez, Prescott, AZ 86302. TEL 520-445-3333; Ed. Heidi Dahms; Pub. Robert D. Gilliland; adv. contact: Lee Giffith. pub. size: broadsheet; circ. 10,500(free).

SAFFORD

US
EASTERN ARIZONA COURIER. 1967. Wed. $.50 newsstand; $22/yr. in state; $37/yr. out of state. 301 E. Hwy. 70, Safford, AZ 85546. TEL 520-428-2560; FAX 520-428-5396. **Owner(s):** Wick Communications, Inc., 333 W. Wilcox Dr., Ste. 302, Sierra Vista, AZ 85635. TEL 520-458-0200; FAX 520-458-6166; Ed. Jim Hornbeck; Pub. Jim Hornbeck; adv. contact: Ted Hecht. photos; pub. size: broadsheet; circ. 8,900(free & paid).

SCOTTSDALE

US
GILBERT INDEPENDENT. 1978. Wed. free. 11000 N. Scottsdale Rd., Ste. 210, Scottsdale, AZ 85254. TEL 602-483-0977; FAX 602-948-0496. **Owner(s):** INI Holding Co., P.O. Box 7001, Dover, DE 19901. TEL 302-674-4750; Ed. Jeremy Handel; Pub. Ed Dulin; adv.: $14.56/SAU. pub. size: broadsheet; circ. 16,000(free).

US
PARADISE VALLEY INDEPENDENT. 1982. Wed. $20/yr. 11000 N. Scottsdale Rd., Ste. 210, Scottsdale, AZ 85254. TEL 602-483-0977; FAX 602-948-0496. **Owner(s):** Independent Newspapers, Inc., P.O. Box 7001, Dover, DE 19901. TEL 302-674-4750; FAX 302-674-5910; Ed. Patrick O'Grady. adv.: $12.72/SAU. pub. size: broadsheet; circ. 20,000(controlled & free).

US
TOWN OF PARADISE VALLEY INDEPENDENT. 1985. Wed. $.25 newsstand; $18/yr. 11000 N. Scottsdale Rd., Ste. 210, Scottsdale, AZ 85254. TEL 602-483-0977; FAX 602-948-0496. **Owner(s):** Independent Newspapers, Inc., P.O. Box 7001, Dover, DE 19903. TEL 302-674-4750; FAX 302-674-5910; Ed. Patrick O'Grady. adv.: $9.96/SAU. photos; pub. size: broadsheet; circ. 6,000(controlled & paid).

SEDONA

US
SEDONA RED ROCK NEWS. 1963. s-w.: Wed. & Fri. $.50 newsstand; $30/yr. local; $43/yr. out of town. 298 Van Deren Rd., Sedona, AZ 86336. TEL 520-282-7795; FAX 520-282-6011. **Owner(s):** Larson Publishing, 298 Van Deven Rd., Sedona, AZ 86336. TEL 602-282-7795; Ed. Tom Brossart; Pub. Robert B. Larson; adv.; photos; pub. size: broadsheet; circ. 7,500(paid).

SHOW LOW

US
WAMPUM SAVER. 1975. s-w.: Wed. & Sat. free. 3191 S. White Mountain Rd., Show Low, AZ 85901. TEL 520-537-5721; FAX 520-537-1780. **Owner(s):** White Mountain Publishing Co., P.O. Box 1570, Show Low, AZ 85901. TEL 520-537-5721; Pub. Greg Tock; adv. contact: Greg Tock. pub. size: tabloid; circ. 20,000(free).

US
WHITE MOUNTAIN INDEPENDENT. 1909. s-w.: Tue. & Fri. $.50 newsstand; $32/yr.; $64/2 yrs. in Navajo & Apache cys. 3191 S. White Mountain Rd., Show Low, AZ 85901. TEL 520-537-5721; FAX 520-537-1780. **Owner(s):** White Mountain Publishing Co., P.O. Box 1570, Show Low, AZ 85901. TEL 520-537-5721; Pub. Greg Tock; adv.; photos; bk.rev.; pub. size: broadsheet; circ. morning 7,000(paid).

SUN CITY

US
▼**ARROWHEAD RANCH INDEPENDENT.** 1995. Wed. free home deliv.; $.25 newsstand. 10327 W. Coggins Dr., Sun City, AZ 85351. TEL 602-972-6101; FAX 602-974-6004. **Owner(s):** Independent Newspapers, Inc., P.O. Box 7001, Dover, DE 19903. TEL 302-674-4750; FAX 302-674-5910; Pub. Bret McKeand; adv. contact: Tammi Abrahms. adv.: $10.56/SAU. photos; pub. size: broadsheet; circ. 12,000(free & paid).

US
SUN CITIES INDEPENDENT. 1960. Wed. $.25 newsstand; $20/3 mos.; $40/6 mos.; $80/yr. 10327 W. Coggins Dr., Sun City, AZ 85351. TEL 602-972-6101; FAX 602-974-6004. **Owner(s):** Independent Newspapers, Inc., P.O. Box 7001, Dover, DE 19903. TEL 302-674-4750; FAX 302-674-5910; Ed. Bret McKeand; Pub. Bret McKeand; adv. contact: Bill Siewert. photos; bk.rev.; pub. size: broadsheet; circ. 39,500(paid).

US
SUN CITY/YOUNGTOWN. Wed. free. 10327 W. Coggins Dr., Sun City, AZ 85351. TEL 602-972-6101; FAX 602-974-6004. **Owner(s):** Independent Newspapers, Inc., P.O. Box 7001, Dover, DE 19903. TEL 302-674-4750; FAX 302-674-5910; Ed. Bret McKeand. adv.: $17.36/SAU. pub. size: broadsheet; circ. 25,000(free).

US
SUN CITY WEST. Wed. free. 10327 W. Coggins Dr., Sun City, AZ 85351. TEL 602-972-6101; FAX 602-974-6004. **Owner(s):** Independent Newspapers, Inc., P.O. Box 7001, Dover, DE 19903. TEL 302-674-4750; FAX 302-674-5910; Ed. Bret McKeand; Pub. Bret McKeand; adv.: $13.72/SAU. pub. size: broadsheet; circ. 14,000(free).

TOMBSTONE

US
TOMBSTONE EPITAPH, THE. 1880. m. free; $15/yr. 9 S. Fifth Ave., Tombstone, AZ 85638. TEL 520-457-2211. **Owner(s):** Sara E. Love, 6545 St. Andrew's Dr., Tucson, AZ 85718. TEL 520-297-7919; Wallace E. Clayton, 4610 E. Blue Mountain Dr., Tucson, AZ 85718. TEL 520-299-4657; Rudolf G. Wunderlich, 704 N. Wells St., Chicago, IL 60610; Ed. E. Dean Prichard; Pub. Wallace E. Clayton; adv. contact: Carol Winkelmann. photos; pub. size: tabloid; circ. 8,500(paid).

WICKENBURG

US
WICKENBURG SUN, THE. 1934. Wed. $.50 newsstand; $20/yr. in cy. 180 N. Washington St., Wickenburg. AZ 85390. TEL 520-684-5454; FAX 520-684-3185. **Owner(s):** Brehm Communications, Inc., 17065 Via del Campo, Ste. 200, P.O. Box 28429, San Diego, CA 92127. TEL 619-451-3814; Ed. Philip Swift; Pub. Kevin Cloe; adv.; photos; pub. size: broadsheet; circ. 4,500(paid).

WILLIAMS

US
WILLIAMS GRAND CANYON NEWS. 1889. Wed. $27.50/yr. 118 S. First St., Williams, AZ 86046. TEL 602-635-4426; FAX 602-635-4887. **Owner(s):** Western Newspapers, Inc., 290 S. First Ave., Ste. 4, Yuma, AZ 85364. TEL 602-783-3311; Ed. Jerry Herrmann. adv. contact: Joyce Fuller McNelly. pub. size: broadsheet; circ. 5,000(paid).

WINSLOW

US ISSN 8750-5711
WINSLOW MAIL. 1894. s-w.: Wed & Fri. $.35 newsstand; $24/yr. in cy.; $30/yr. out of cy.; $38/yr. out of state. 208 W. First St., Winslow, AZ 86047. TEL 520-289-2467; FAX 520-524-3541. **Owner(s):** Navajo County Publishers, Inc., 200 E. Hopi Dr., Holbrook, AZ 86025. TEL 520-524-6203; Ed. Francie Paine; Pub. Paul Barger; adv. contact: Manny Maniaci. photos; pub. size: broadsheet; circ. 2,900(free & paid).

ARKANSAS

ATKINS

US
ATKINS CHRONICLE, THE. 1894. Wed. $.50 newsstand; $20/yr. in cy.; $25/yr. in state; $30/yr. out of state. 204 Ave. One, N.E., Atkins, AR 72823. TEL 501-641-7161; FAX 501-641-1604. **Owner(s):** Ginnie & Van Allen Tyson, 584 Murdoch Rd., Atkins, AR 72823. TEL 501-641-2688; FAX 501-641-1604; Ed. Van Allen Tyson; Pub. Ginnie Tyson; adv. contact: Brooka Hamilton. photos; bk.rev.; pub. size: broadsheet; circ. 2,600(paid).

BEEBE

US
BEEBE NEWS. Wed. $.50 newsstand; $25/yr. in cy.; $30/yr. surrounding cys.; $25/yr. out of state. 107 E. Center, Beebe, AR 72012. TEL 501-882-5414; FAX 501-882-3576. **Owner(s):** Lee K. McLane, 107 E. Center, Beebe, AR 72012. TEL 501-882-5414; Ed. Lee K. McLane. photos; bk.rev.; pub. size: broadsheet; circ. 2,500(paid).

WEEKLY NEWSPAPERS

BERRYVILLE

US ISSN 8750-6467
EUREKA SPRINGS TIMES-ECHO. 1879. Thu. $.50 newsstand; $21.50/yr. local; $31.75/yr. out of area. Oakview Dr., 62 Spur, Berryville, AR 72616. TEL 501-423-6636; FAX 501-423-6640. **Owner(s):** U.S. Media Group, P.O. Box 227, Crystal City, MO 63019. TEL 314-937-5200; FAX 314-937-7947; Ed. Ken O'Toole; Pub. Cynthia Chappell; adv. contact: Lance Holman. photos; pub. size: broadsheet; circ. 3,687(paid). **Wire Service(s):** AP.

US
GREEN FOREST TRIBUNE. 1889. Wed. $.50 newsstand; $21/yr. local; $34.75/yr. out of area. Oakview Dr., 62 Spur, Berryville, AR 72616. TEL 501-423-6636; FAX 501-423-6640. **Owner(s):** U.S. Media Group, P.O. Box 227, Crystal City, MO 63019. TEL 314-937-5200; FAX 314-937-7947; Ed. Ken O'Toole; Pub. Cynthia Chappell; adv. contact: Joe Dinsmore. photos; pub. size: broadsheet; circ. 1,537(paid).
Formerly: Green Forest Carroll County Tribune.

US
STAR-PROGRESS, THE. 1873. Thu. $.50 newsstand; $21.50/yr. in cy.; $31.75/yr. out of cy.; $34.75/yr. out of state. Oakview Dr., 62 Spur, Berryville, AR 72616. TEL 501-423-6636; FAX 501-423-6640. **Owner(s):** U.S. Media Group, P.O. Box 227, Crystal City, MO 63019. TEL 314-937-5200; FAX 314-937-7947; Ed. Kim O'Toole; Pub. Cynthia Chapell; adv. contact: Joe Dinsmore. photos; pub. size: broadsheet; circ. 2,851(paid). **Wire Service(s):** AP.

BRINKLEY

US
BRINKLEY ARGUS. 1875. s-w.: Wed. & Fri. $.50 newsstand; $25/yr. in state; $45/yr. out of state. 308 W. Cedar, Brinkley, AR 72021. TEL 501-734-1056; FAX 501-734-2302. **Owner(s):** Franklin & Flora Jane Elledge, 308 W. Cedar, Brinkley, AR 72021. TEL 501-734-1056; Ed. Thomas Jacques. adv.; photos; pub. size: broadsheet; circ. 3,600(paid).

CALICO ROCK

US
WHITE RIVER CURRENT. 1972. Thu. $.50 newsstand; $15/yr. in cy.; $20/yr. out of cy. 105 Garden St., Calico Rock, AR 72519. TEL 501-297-8300; FAX 501-297-8799. **Owner(s):** Jeannie Day, P.O. Box 570, Calico Rock, AR 72519. TEL 501-297-8300; FAX 501-297-8799; Ed. Jeannie Day; Pub. Jeannie Day; adv. contact: Margaret Waters. adv.: $4.50/SAU. photos; bk.rev.; pub. size: broadsheet; circ. 2,200(paid).

CLARKSVILLE

US
JOHNSON COUNTY GRAPHIC. 1877. Wed. $.25 newsstand; $25/yr. 203 E. Cherry, Clarksville, AR 72830. TEL 501-754-2005; FAX 501-754-2098; E-mail: rwylie@cswnet.com; & graphic@cswnet.com; URL: http://www.cswnet.com/ngraphic. **Owner(s):** Johnson County Graphic, Inc., 203 E. Cherry, Clarksville, AR 72830. TEL 501-754-2005; Ed. Margaret Wylie; Pub. Debra Grey; adv. contact: Debra Grey. photos; pub. size: standard; circ. 7,500(paid).

CLINTON

US
CLINTON VAN BUREN COUNTY DEMOCRAT. 1909. Wed. $.50 newsstand; $15/yr. in cy.; $20/yr. in state; $25/yr. out of state. 114 S. Court, Clinton, AR 72031-0119. TEL 501-745-5175; FAX 501-745-8865. **Owner(s):** Jay W. Jackson, P.O. Box 119, Clinton, AR 72031. TEL 501-745-5175; FAX 501-745-8865; Patsy Jackson, P.O. Box 119, Clinton, AR 72031. TEL 501-745-5175; FAX 501-745-8865; Pub. Jay W. Jackson; adv.; pub. size: standard; circ. 4,646(paid).

CROSSETT

US
ASHLEY COUNTY SHOPPERS GUIDE. Mon. free. 102 Pine St., Crossett, AR 71635. TEL 501-364-5186; FAX 501-364-2116. **Owner(s):** Ashley County Publishing Co., 102 Pine St., Crosssett, AR 71635. TEL 501-364-5186; FAX 501-364-2116; Ed. Steve Sanders; Pub. Larry W. Johnson; adv. contact: Charlotte Johnson. pub. size: tabloid; circ. 10,653(free).

US
ASHLEY NEWS OBSERVER. 1907. Wed. $.75 newsstand; $26/yr. in cy.; $42/yr. out of cy. 102 Pine St., Crossett, AR 71635. TEL 501-364-5186; FAX 501-364-2116. **Owner(s):** Ashley County Publishing Co., 102 Pine St., Ashley, AR 71635. TEL 501-364-5186; FAX 501-364-2116; Ed. Larry Wittenbert; Pub. Larry W. Johnson; adv. contact: Charlotte Johnson. photos; pub. size: broadsheet; circ. 5,100(paid).

DE QUEEN

US
DE QUEEN BEE. 1897. Thu. $.35 newsstand; $15/yr. 404 De Queen Ave., De Queen, AR 71832. TEL 501-642-2111; FAX 501-642-3138. **Owner(s):** Ray Kimball, P.O. Box 1000, De Queen, AR 71832. TEL 501-642-2111; Ed. Billy Ray McKelvy; Pub. Ray Kimball; adv. contact: Gail Mitchell. pub. size: broadsheet; circ. 1,500(paid).

DES ARC

US
WHITE RIVER JOURNAL. 1907. Thu. $.30 newsstand; $14/yr. in cy.; $22/yr. out of state. Fifth & Main, Des Arc, AR 72040. TEL 870-256-4254; FAX 870-256-4254. **Owner(s):** White River Journal Corp., Fifth & Main, Des Arc, AR 72040. TEL 870-256-4254; Ed. Dean L. Walls; Pub. Dean L. Walls; adv. contact: Sandy Allred. adv.: $4.50/SAU. pub. size: broadsheet; circ. 2,650(paid).

DUMAS

US
DUMAS CLARION. 1899. Wed. $.35 newsstand; $15/yr. local; $18/yr. out of cy. 136 E. Waterman, Dumas, AR 71639. TEL 501-382-4925; FAX 501-382-6421. **Owner(s):** Clarion Publishing Co., Inc., 136 E. Waterman, Dumas, AR 71639. TEL 501-382-4925; Ed. Terry Hawkins; Pub. Charlotte Schexnayder; adv.; pub. size: broadsheet; circ. 4,200(paid).

ENGLAND

US
ENGLAND DEMOCRAT. Wed. $.30 newsstand; $12/yr. in cy.; $15/yr. out of cy.; $22/yr. out of state. 121 E. Haywood, England, AR 72046. TEL 501-842-3111; FAX 501-842-3081. **Owner(s):** Jerry Jackson, P.O. Drawer 250, England, AR 72046. TEL 501-842-3111; Ed. Jerry Jackson; Pub. Jerry Jackson; pub. size: standard; circ. 1,080(paid).

GENTRY

US
DECATUR HERALD. Wed. $.50 newsstand. Main St., Gentry, AR 72734. TEL 501-736-2822; FAX 501-736-2822. **Owner(s):** Community Publishers, Inc., P.O. Box 1044, Siloam Springs, AR 72761. TEL 501-524-4131; Ed. James Garner. pub. size: broadsheet; circ. 1,050(paid).

US
GENTRY COURIER-JOURNAL. Wed. $.50 newsstand; $18/yr. Main St., Gentry, AR 72734. TEL 501-736-2822. **Owner(s):** Community Publishers, Inc., P.O. Box 1044, Siloam Springs, AR 72761. TEL 501-736-2822; Ed. James Garner. pub. size: broadsheet; circ. 1,050(paid).

GLENWOOD

US
GLENWOOD HERALD. 1926. Thu. $.50 newsstand; $15/yr. local; $30/yr. out of area; $35/yr. out of state. 204 Broadway, Glenwood, AR 71943. TEL 870-356-2111; FAX 870-356-4400. **Owner(s):** Graves Publishing Co., Inc., P.O. Box 297, Nashville, AR 71852. TEL 501-845-2010; Ed. Mike McCoy; Pub. Louie Graves; adv. contact: Theresa Parrish. pub. size: broadsheet; circ. 2,500.

GRAVETTE

US
GRAVETTE NEWS HERALD. 1894. Wed. $.50 newsstand; $16/yr. local; $22/yr. elsewhere. 123 Main St., Gravette, AR 72736. TEL 501-787-5300; FAX 501-787-5300. **Owner(s):** Community Publishers, Inc., P.O. Box 1049, Bentville, AR 72712. TEL 501-787-5300; Ed. Robert D. Evans; Pub. Mike Brown; adv. contact: Linda Milton. pub. size: broadsheet; circ. 2,100(paid).

GREENWOOD

US
GREENWOOD DEMOCRAT. 1882. Wed. $.50 newsstand; $19/yr. in cy.; $26/yr. in state; $29/yr. out of state. 38 Towne Sq., Greenwood, AR 72936. TEL 501-996-4494; FAX 501-996-4122. **Owner(s):** Westward Communications, Inc., 5005 LBJ Fwy., Dallas, TX 75244. TEL 214-450-1717; Ed. C.A. Wells; Pub. C.A. Wells; adv.; pub. size: broadsheet; circ. 2,700(paid).

HARRISBURG

US
MODERN NEWS. 1888. Wed. $.50 newsstand; $16/yr. in cy.; $20/yr. elsewhere. 216 Main St., Harrisburg, AR 72432. TEL 501-578-2121; FAX 501-578-9415. **Owner(s):** Hazel Freeman, P.O. Box 400, Harrisburg, AR 72432. TEL 501-578-2121; FAX 501-578-9415; Ed. Charles D. Nix. pub. size: broadsheet; circ. 2,841(paid).

WEEKLY NEWSPAPERS

HEBER SPRINGS

US ISSN 1050-5105
SUN TIMES. 1888. s-w.: Wed. & Fri. $.50 newsstand; $29/yr. in trade zone; $36/yr. elsewhere. 107-109 N. Fourth St., Heber Springs, AR 72543-0669. TEL 501-362-2425; FAX 501-362-5877; E-mail: suntimes@cswnet.com. **Owner(s):** American Publishing Co., 606 N. Van Buren, Marion, IL 62959. TEL 618-993-1711; Ed. Randy Kemp; Pub. Suzanne Reed; adv.: $7.19/SAU. photos; bk.rev.; pub. size: broadsheet; circ. 4,385(paid).

HOT SPRINGS VILLAGE

US ISSN 0747-2781
LAVILLA NEWS. 1970. s-w: Tue. & Fri. $.50 newsstand; $25/yr. in cy.; $30/yr. out of cy. 121 DeSoto Ctr. Dr., Hot Springs Village, AR 71909. TEL 501-922-1900; FAX 501-922-0958. **Owner(s):** American Publishing Co., 606 Van Buren, Marion, IL 62959. TEL 618-993-1711; Ed. Dottie Stewart; Pub. Randal Hunhoff; adv. contact: Cindy Wagstaff. photos; bk.rev.; pub. size: broadsheet; circ. 6,000(free & paid).

HUNTSVILLE

US
MADISON COUNTY RECORD. 1879. Thu. $.25 newsstand; $16/yr. in cy.; $18/yr. out of cy.; $20/yr. out of state. 201 Church St., Huntsville, AR 72740. TEL 501-738-2141; FAX 501-738-1250. **Owner(s):** Alta Faubus, 201 Church St., Huntsville, AR 72740. TEL 501-738-2141; FAX 501-738-1550; Ed. Carol S. Whittemore; Pub. Alta Faubus; adv.; pub. size: broadsheet; circ. 5,500(paid).

IMBODEN

US
OZARK JOURNAL. 1915. Thu. $.25 newsstand; $10/yr. in state; $14/yr. out of state. 101 Second St., Imboden, AR 72434. TEL 501-869-2220. **Owner(s):** Ozark Journal, Inc., P.O. Box 598, Imboden, AR 72434. TEL 501-869-3159; Ed. Karen Glass; Pub. Bob Glass, Jr.; pub. size: standard; circ. 2,000(paid).

MANSFIELD

US
CITIZEN, THE. 1967. Wed. $.25 newsstand; $12/yr. local; $18/yr. in state. 112 E. Howard St., Mansfield, AR 72944-0036. TEL 501-928-5340; FAX 501-928-5340. **Owner(s):** Waldron Newspapers, Inc., P.O. Box 745, Waldron, AR 72958-0347; Ed. Marty Backus. adv. contact: Vickie Backus. pub. size: broadsheet; circ. 3,000(free & paid).

MARIANNA

US
MARIANNA COURIER INDEX. 1874. Thu. $.50 newsstand; $20/yr. in cy.; $30/yr. in state; $42/yr. out of state. 31 S. Popular St., Marianna, AR 72360. TEL 501-295-2521; FAX 501-295-9662. **Owner(s):** Times-Herald Publishing Co., Inc., P.O. Box 1699, Forrest City, AR 72335. TEL 501-633-3130; Pub. Bonner McCollum; adv. contact: Melinda Burns. pub. size: broadsheet; circ. 2,500(paid).

MARKED TREE

US
TRI-CITY TRIBUNE. 1903. Thu. $.50 newsstand; $21/yr. 18 Elm St., Marked Tree, AR 72365. TEL 500-358-2993; FAX 870-358-4538. **Owner(s):** Tri-City Tribune, Inc., P.O. Box 490, Marked Tree, AR 72365. TEL 870-358-2993; Ed. John Boxley; Pub. John Boxley; adv.; pub. size: broadsheet; circ. 2,400(paid).

MARSHALL

US
MARSHALL MOUNTAIN WAVE. 1890. Thu. $.25 newsstand; $15/yr. in cy.; $17/yr. out of cy.; $22/yr. out of state. 103 E. Main St., Marshall, AR 72650. TEL 501-448-3321; FAX 501-448-5659. **Owner(s):** Marshall Mountain Wave Publishing Co., Inc., 103 E. Main St., Marshall, AR 72650. TEL 501-448-3321; FAX 501-448-5659; Ed. Debbie Horton; Pub. Jim Tilley; adv. contact: Glenda Griffith. pub. size: broadsheet; circ. 4,650(paid).

MCCRORY

US
WOODRUFF COUNTY MONITOR LEADER ADVOCATE. 1990. Wed. $.50 newsstand; $22/yr. in city; $25/yr. out of city. 301 N. Edmonds Ave., McCrory, AR 72101-0898. TEL 501-731-2263; FAX 501-731-5899. **Owner(s):** Elden J. Thompson, Fletcher Lewis, Bill Riddle, 301 N. Edmonds Ave., McCrory, AR 72101-0898. TEL 501-731-2263; FAX 501-731-5899; Ed. Bill Riddle; Pub. Paula Davis; adv.; photos; pub. size: broadsheet; circ. 2,300(paid).
Formerly: Woodruff County Monitor.

MENA

US ISSN 0747-1513
MENA STAR. 1898. Thu. $19/yr. local; $30/yr. elsewhere. 501-07 Mena St., Mena, AR 71953. TEL 501-394-1900; FAX 501-394-1908. **Owner(s):** Waldron Newspapers, Inc., P.O. Box 745, Gadsden, AR 72958-0347; Ed. Barney White; Pub. Barney White; adv. contact: Debbie Frost. pub. size: broadsheet; circ. 3,250(paid). **Wire Service(s):** AP.

MONTICELLO

US
ADVANCE-MONTICELLONIAN. 1870. Wed. $.50 newsstand; $23/yr. in state; $30/yr. out of state. 314 N. Main, Monticello, AR 71655. TEL 501-367-5325; FAX 501-367-6612. **Owner(s):** Smith Newspapers, Inc., P.O. Box 27, Fort Payne, AL 35967; Ed. Betty Evans; Pub. Tom White; adv. contact: Jamey Honeycutt. pub. size: broadsheet; circ. 5,850(paid).

MORRILTON

US
CONWAY COUNTY PETIT JEAN COUNTRY HEADLIGHT. 1874. Wed. $.75 newsstand; $30/yr. in cy. 908 W. Broadway, Morrilton, AR 72110. TEL 501-354-2451; FAX 501-354-4225. **Owner(s):** Clifton T. Wells, 15 Pilot Point, Little Rock, AR 72205. TEL 501-664-4456; FAX 501-354-4225; Eddy Hodge, P.O. Box 621, Morrilton, AR 72110. TEL 501-354-5537; FAX 501-354-4225; Ed. Charlotte Hodge; Pub. Clifton T. Wells; adv. contact: Carol McKuin. pub. size: broadsheet; circ. 6,700(paid).

PERRY COUNTY PETIT JEAN COUNTRY HEADLIGHT.

US
Wed. $.75 newsstand; $27/yr. in cy. 908 W. Broadway, Morrilton, AR 72110. TEL 501-354-2451; FAX 501-354-4225. **Owner(s):** Clifton T. Wells, 15 Pilot Point, Little Rock, AR 72205. TEL 501-664-4456; FAX 501-354-4225; Eddy Hodge, P.O. Box 621, Morrilton, AR 72110. TEL 501-354-5537; FAX 501-354-4225; Ed. Charlotte Hodge; Pub. Clifton T. Wells; adv. contact: Carol McKuin. pub. size: broadsheet; circ. 2,150(paid).

MOUNTAIN VIEW

US
STONE COUNTY CITIZEN. 1986. Tue. $.35 newsstand; $10/yr. in cy.; $20/yr. out of cy. P.O. Box 6, Mountain View, AR 72560. TEL 501-269-8626; FAX 501-269-8634. **Owner(s):** Dennis Brannon, P.O. Box 6, Mountain View, AR 72560. TEL 501-269-8626; Ed. Dennis Brannon; Pub. Dennis Brannon; adv. contact: Ellen Brannon. pub. size: standard; circ. 4,000(free & paid).

US
STONE COUNTY LEADER. 1951. Wed. $16/yr. in cy.; $26/yr. out of cy. 103 W. Main St., Mountain View, AR 72560. TEL 501-269-3841; FAX 501-269-2171. **Owner(s):** Stone County Publishing Co., Inc., P.O. Box 509, Mountain View, AR 72560. TEL 501-269-3841; Ed. James R. Fraser. pub. size: broadsheet; circ. 3,958(paid).

MURFREESBORO

US
MURFREESBORO DIAMOND. 1975. Wed. $.50 newsstand; $15/yr. local; $35/yr. elsewhere. 105 Court St., Murfreesboro, AR 71958. TEL 501-285-2723; FAX 501-285-3820. **Owner(s):** Graves Publishing Co., Inc., P.O. Box 297, Nashville, AR 71852. TEL 501-845-2010; Ed. John L. Balch; Pub. Louie Graves; pub. size: tabloid; circ. 1,800(paid).

NASHVILLE

US
NASHVILLE NEWS. 1878. s-w.: Mon. & Thu. $.50 newsstand; $20/yr. trade area; $40/yr. elsewhere. 418 N. Main, Nashville, AR 71852. TEL 501-845-2010; FAX 501-845-5091. **Owner(s):** Graves Publishing Co., Inc., 418 N. Main, Nashville, AR 71852. TEL 501-845-2010; FAX 501-845-5091; Ed. Louie Graves. adv. contact: Tracy Bailey. pub. size: broadsheet; circ. 5,000(paid). **Wire Service(s):** AP.

NORTH LITTLE ROCK

US
TIMES, THE. 1898. Thu. $.50 newsstand; $16.50/yr. in cy.; $25/yr. in state; $30/yr. out of state. 26th & Willow Sts., North Little Rock, AR 72114. TEL 501-758-2571; FAX 501-758-2597; E-mail: thetimes@lr.cleaf.com. **Owner(s):** David & Kitty Chism, P.O. Box 428, North Little Rock, AR 72115. TEL 501-758-2571; Ed. Kitty Chism; Pub. David Chism; adv. contact: Tom Kennedy. adv.: $10.75/SAU. pub. size: broadsheet; circ. 8,823(free & paid).

WEEKLY NEWSPAPERS

OSCEOLA
US

OSCEOLA TIMES. 1870. Thu. $.50 newsstand; $15/yr. in cy.; $42/yr. out of cy. 112 N. Poplar, Osceola, AR 72370. TEL 501-563-2615; FAX 501-563-2616. **Owner(s):** Tennyson Publishing, Blytheville, AR; Ed. Sandra Brand; Pub. David Tennyson; adv. contact: Kathy Stiles. pub. size: broadsheet; circ. 9,000(paid). **Wire Service(s):** AP.

PARIS
US   ISSN 1071-9709

PARIS EXPRESS. 1880. Wed. $.50 newsstand; $23/yr. local. 22 S. Express St., Paris, AR 72855. TEL 501-963-2901; FAX 501-963-3062. **Owner(s):** Westward Communications, Inc., 5005 LBJ Fwy., Dallas, TX 75244. TEL 214-450-1717; FAX 214-450-1770; Ed. Roger Smith; Pub. Vickey Wiggins; adv. contact: Mary Hill. pub. size: broadsheet; circ. 3,950(paid).

PEA RIDGE
US

TIMES OF NORTHEAST BENTON COUNTY. 1966. Thu. $.50 newsstand; $14-$20/yr. 150 S. Curtis, Pea Ridge, AR 72751. TEL 501-451-1196. **Owner(s):** Mike Freeman, 150 S. Curtis, Pea Ridge, AR 72751. TEL 501-451-1196; Ed. Mike Freeman. adv.; pub. size: broadsheet; circ. 1,700(paid).

PIGGOTT
US

PIGGOTT TIMES, THE. 1967. Wed. $20/yr. in cy.; $25/yr. out of cy.; $30/yr. out of state. 209 W. Main, Piggott, AR 72454. TEL 501-598-2201; FAX 501-598-5189. **Owner(s):** K.M.B. Corp., Rector, AR. TEL 501-598-2201; FAX 501-598-5189; Ed. Ron Kemp; Pub. Ron Kemp; adv. contact: Gayla Johnson. photos; bk.rev.; pub. size: standard; circ. 3,040(paid).

PINE BLUFF
US

PINE BLUFF NEWS. Wed. free. 3900 B. Miramar Dr., Pine Bluff, AR 71603-3718. TEL 501-879-5450; FAX 501-879-5636. **Owner(s):** Community Group Publishing Co., 1301 Maine St., Jacksonville, AR 72076. TEL 501-985-0544; Ed. Tracie Browning; Pub. Brent Leslie; adv. contact: Cindy Lee. pub. size: tabloid; circ. 6,000(free).
Formerly: Pine Bluff Shoppers News.

US   ISSN 0747-1572

WHITE HALL JOURNAL. 1983. Wed. $.50 newsstand; $18/yr. in cy.; $25/yr. elsewhere. 6210 Dollarway Rd., Ste. 2A, Pine Bluff, AR 71602. TEL 501-247-4700; FAX 501-247-4755. **Owner(s):** Forest Communicators, Inc., 6210 Dollarway Rd., Ste. 2A, Pine Bluff, AR 71602. TEL 501-247-4700; Ed. Frank Lightfoot; Pub. Frank Lightfoot; adv. contact: Vicki Kelly. photos; bk.rev.; pub. size: broadsheet; circ. 1,910(paid).

POCAHONTAS
US

POCAHONTAS STAR HERALD. 1880. Thu. $.50 newsstand; $20/yr. in cy.; $30/yr. out of cy. 109 N. Van Bibber St., Pocahontas, AR 72455. TEL 501-892-4451; FAX 501-892-4453. **Owner(s):** J.V. Rockwell, P.O. Box 128, Corning, AR 72422. TEL 501-857-3531; Ed. Kathryn T. Cheyne; Pub. J.V. Rockwell; adv. contact: Anita Murphy. pub. size: broadsheet; circ. 15,000(free & paid).

PRESCOTT
US

NEVADA COUNTY PICAYUNE. 1878. Wed. $.50 newsstand; $12.50/yr. in cy.; $20/yr. in state; $25/yr. out of state. 125 W. Main St., Prescott, AR 71857-0060. TEL 501-887-2002; FAX 501-887-2949. **Owner(s):** John & Betty Ragsdale, P.O. Box 60, Prescott, AR 71857. TEL 501-887-2002; Ed. John R. Ragsdale; Pub. John R. Ragsdale; adv. contact: Ricky Ragsdale. pub. size: broadsheet; circ. 2,500(paid).

SALEM
US

NEWS, THE. Thu. $.50 newsstand; $18/yr. in cy.; $23/yr. out of cy. P.O. Box 248, Salem, AR 72576. TEL 501-895-3207; FAX 501-895-4277. **Owner(s):** Paxton Media Group, Inc., P.O. Box 2300, Paducah, KY 42002. TEL 502-443-1771; Ed. Max Cates. adv. contact: Carolyn Clarke. adv.: $13.80/SAU; $13.80/SAU classified. photos; pub. size: broadsheet; circ. 3,600(paid).
Formerly: Salem Headlight.

SHERIDAN
US

SHERIDAN HEADLIGHT. 1881. Wed. $.50 newsstand; $15/yr. in cy.; $21/yr. out of cy.; $28/yr. elsewhere. 101 E. Center, Sheridan, AR 72150. TEL 501-942-2142; FAX 501-942-2143. **Owner(s):** Melodie Moorehouse, 101 E. Center, Sheridan, AR 72150. TEL 501-942-2142; Ed. Melody Moorehouse; Pub. Melody Moorehouse; adv. contact: Kathie Webb. photos; pub. size: broadsheet; circ. 4,050(paid).

SILOAM SPRINGS
US

HERALD-LEADER. 1892. s-w.: Wed. & Sun. $.50 newsstand; $28/yr. local; $25/yr. out of area. 101 N. Mt. Olive, Siloam Springs, AR 72761. TEL 501-524-5144; FAX 501-524-3612; E-mail: compub95@aol.com; URL: http://nwanews.com/leader.html. **Owner(s):** Community Publishers, Inc., 101 N. Mt. Olive, Siloam Springs, AR 72761. TEL 501-524-5144; Ed. Jamie Jones; Pub. Scott Harrell; adv.; pub. size: broadsheet; circ. 10,000(paid).
Formerly: Siloam Springs Herald & Democrat.

STAR CITY
US

LINCOLN LEDGER. 1876. Wed. $.25 newsstand; $9/yr. in cy.; $12/yr. out of cy.; $15/yr. out of state. 2161 W. Bradley, Star City, AR 71667. TEL 501-628-4161; FAX 501-628-3802. **Owner(s):** Lincoln County Publishing Co., Inc., Town Sq., Star City, AR 71667. TEL 501-628-4161; FAX 501-628-3802; Ed. Joe V. Mason. adv. contact: Rebecca Patrick. pub. size: standard; circ. 2,500(paid).

TRUMANN
US

TRUMANN DEMOCRAT. 1922. Wed. $.50 newsstand; $16/yr. in cy.; $18/yr. out of cy. 200 Hwy. 463, S., Trumann, AR 72472. TEL 501-483-6317; FAX 501-483-6031. **Owner(s):** Charles Nix, Harrisburg, AR; Ed. Joyce Jaynes; Pub. Charles Nix; adv.; pub. size: broadsheet; circ. 2,200(paid).

VAN BUREN
US

ADVERTISER, THE. Wed. & Sat. free. 100 N. 11th St., Van Buren, AR 72956. TEL 501-474-5215; FAX 501-471-5607. **Owner(s):** Van Buren Publishing Co., Inc., 100 N. 11th St., Van Buren, AR 72956. TEL 501-474-5215; FAX 501-471-5607; Ed. Roy Faulkenberry; Pub. Bill Hager; adv. contact: Jim Peoples. pub. size: broadsheet; circ. 13,000(free).

US   ISSN 0885-9086

PRESS ARGUS-COURIER. 1859. s-w.: Wed. & Sat. $.50 newsstand; $35/yr. in area; $44/yr. out of area. 100 N. 11th St., Van Buren, AR 72956. TEL 501-474-5215; FAX 501-471-5607. **Owner(s):** Van Buren Publishing Co., Inc., 100 N. 11th St., Van Buren, AR 72956. TEL 501-474-5215; Ed. Roy Faulkenberry; Pub. Bill Hager; adv. contact: Jim Peoples. photos; pub. size: broadsheet; circ. 7,000(paid).

WALDRON
US

SCOTT COUNTY ADVERTISER. 1987. Wed. free. 10 W. Second St., Waldron, AR 72958-1816. TEL 501-637-4647; FAX 501-928-5340. **Owner(s):** Waldron Newspapers, Inc., P.O. Box 745, Waldron, AR 72958-0347; Ed. Marty Backus. adv. contact: Vickie Backus. pub. size: broadsheet; circ. 4,600(free).

US

TRI-COUNTY TRADER. 1967. Wed. free. P.O. Box 745, Waldron, AR 72944. TEL 501-928-5340; FAX 501-637-4162. **Owner(s):** Waldron Newspapers, Inc., P.O. Box 745, Waldron, AR 72958-0347; Ed. Marty Backus. adv. contact: Vickie Backus. pub. size: broadsheet; circ. 5,000(free).

WALNUT RIDGE
US

TIMES DISPATCH. 1910. Wed. $.50 newsstand; $14/yr. local; $22/yr. elsewhere. 225 W. Main St., Walnut Ridge, AR 72476. TEL 501-886-2464; FAX 501-886-9369. **Owner(s):** Times Dispatch, Inc., 225 W. Main St., Walnut Ridge, AR 72476. TEL 501-886-2464; FAX 501-886-9369; Ed. John A. Bland; Pub. John A. Bland; adv. contact: Janice Hibbard. photos; bk.rev.; pub. size: broadsheet; circ. 6,200(paid).
Formerly: Walnut Ridge Times Dispatch.

WYNNE

US
WYNNE PROGRESS. 1894. Fri. $.50 newsstand. 702 N. Falls Blvd., Wynne, AR 72396. TEL 501-238-2375; FAX 501-238-4655. **Owner(s):** Bonner McCollom, 222 N. Izzard, Forrest City, AR 72335. TEL 501-633-3130; FAX 501-633-0599; David Boger, 1328 Rowena St., Wynne, AR 72396. TEL 501-238-2375; FAX 501-238-4655; Ed. Randy Hogan; Pub. David M. Boger; adv. contact: Brandon Boger. photos; bk.rev.; pub. size: broadsheet; circ. 26,837(free & paid).

YELLVILLE

US
MOUNTAIN ECHO. 1886. Thu. $.50 newsstand; $21.50/yr. in cy.; $28.50/yr. out of cy.; $31.50/yr. out of state. Church St., Hwy. 62, Yellville, AR 72687. TEL 501-449-4257; FAX 501-424-4488. **Owner(s):** Journal Newspapers, Inc., 2720 Prospserity Ave., Fairfax, VA 22034-1000. TEL 703-560-4000; Ed. Ray Dean Davis; Pub. Chuck Pullins; adv.; photos; pub. size: broadsheet; circ. 2,500(paid).
Formerly: Yellville Mountain Echo.

CALIFORNIA

AGOURA HILLS

US
ACORN, THE. 1974. Thu. $.25 newsstand; $42.50/6 mos.; $85/yr. carrier. 30423 Canwood St., Ste. 223, Agoura Hills, CA 91301-4316. TEL 818-706-0266; FAX 818-706-8942; E-mail: jim@acornews.com. **Owner(s):** J. Bee NP Publishing Ltd., 30423 Canwood St., Ste. 223, Agoura Hills, CA 91301-4316. TEL 818-706-0266; FAX 818-706-8942; Ed. Joanna Tobin; Pub. Jim Rule; adv. contact: Steve Holt. photos; pub. size: tabloid; circ. 35,000(paid).

ALTURAS

US
MODOC COUNTY RECORD. 1892. Thu. $.50 newsstand; $20/yr. local; $25/yr. elsewhere. 201 W. Carlos, Alturas, CA 96101. TEL 916-233-2632; FAX 916-233-5113. **Owner(s):** Rick & Jane Holloway, P.O. Box 531, Alturas, CA 96101. TEL 916-233-2632; Ed. Rick Holloway; Pub. Jane Holloway; adv.; photos; pub. size: standard; circ. 4,500(paid).
Formerly: Alturas/Modoc County Record.

ANAHEIM

US
ANAHEIM BULLETIN. 1923. Thu. $.25 newsstand. 1771 S. Lewis St., Anaheim, CA 92805. TEL 714-634-1567; FAX 714-704-3714. **Owner(s):** Freedom Communications, Inc., 17666 Fitch, Irvine, CA 92714. TEL 714-553-9292; Ed. Tonnie Katz. adv.; photos; pub. size: tabloid; circ. 60,000(controlled & free).

US
ANAHEIM HILLS NEWS. 1969. Thu. $39/6 mos. mailed; $78/yr. mailed. 1771 S. Lewis St., Anaheim, CA 92805. TEL 714-634-1567; FAX 714-704-3714. **Owner(s):** Freedom Communications, Inc., 17666 Fitch, Irvine, CA 92714; Pub. R. David Threshie, Jr.; adv.; pub. size: tabloid; circ. 14,000(controlled & free).
Formerly: Anaheim Hills Highlander.

US
BREA PROGRESS. 1922. Thu. $39/6 mos. mailed; $78/yr. mailed. 1771 S. Lewis St., Anaheim, CA 92805. TEL 714-634-1567; FAX 714-704-3714. **Owner(s):** Freedom Communications, Inc., 17666 Fitch, Irvine, CA 92714. TEL 714-253-9292; Ed. Jannlee Watson; Pub. R. David Threshie, Jr.; pub. size: tabloid; circ. 10,000(controlled).
Formerly: Brea News.

US
LA HABRA STAR. 1916. Thu. free newsstand. 1771 S. Lewis St., Anaheim, CA 92805. TEL 714-634-1567; FAX 714-704-3714. **Owner(s):** Freedom Communications, Inc., 17666 Fitch, Irvine, CA 92614. TEL 714-553-9292; Ed. Frank Mickadeit; Pub. R. David Threshie, Jr.; adv. contact: Susan Perretano. pub. size: broadsheet; circ. 44,000(controlled & free). **Wire Service(s):** AP.
Formerly: La Habra Daily Star Progress.

US
PLACENTIA NEWS-TIMES. 1924. Thu. free. 1771 S. Lewis, Anaheim, CA 92805. TEL 714-634-1567; FAX 714-704-3714. **Owner(s):** Freedom Communications, Inc., 17666 Fitch, Irvine, CA 92614. TEL 714-553-9292; Ed. Frank Mickadeit; Pub. R. David Threshie, Jr.; adv.; pub. size: broadsheet; circ. 12,000(controlled).
Formerly: Placentia Highlander News-Time.

ANDERSON

US
VALLEY POST. 1886. Tue. $.25 newsstand; $14/yr. in cy.; $17/yr. out of cy. 2680 Gateway, Anderson, CA 96007. TEL 916-365-2797; FAX 916-365-2829. **Owner(s):** Douglas Hirsch, 2680 Gateway, Anderson, CA 96007. TEL 916-365-2797; Ed. Loretta Carrico; Pub. Douglas Hirsch; adv. contact: Susan Stone. pub. size: broadsheet; circ. 13,000(free & paid).

APPLE VALLEY

US
APPLE VALLEY NEWS. 1965. Fri. free; $19/yr. local mailed; $21/yr. out of area. 19250 Hwy. 18, Apple Valley, CA 92307. TEL 619-244-0021; FAX 619-244-6609. **Owner(s):** Raymond Pryke, 19250 Hwy. 18, Apple Valley, CA 92307. TEL 619-244-0021; FAX 619-244-6609; Ed. Joyce Bohannan; Pub. Jenny Jones; pub. size: broadsheet; circ. 500(free & paid).

ARROYO GRANDE

US
FIVE CITIES TIMES-PRESS-RECORDER. 1887. s-w.: Wed. & Fri. $.50 newsstand; $42/yr. in cy.; $46/yr. in state mailed. 1052 Grand Ave., Arroyo Grande, CA 93421. TEL 805-489-4206; FAX 805-473-0571. **Owner(s):** Dick & Maxine Blankenburg, P.O. Box 460, Arroyo Grande, CA 93421. TEL 805-489-4206; Ed. Dick Blankenburg; Pub. Dick Blankenburg; adv. contact: Cindy Hodgson. photos; pub. size: broadsheet; circ. 18,500(paid).
Formerly: Arroyo Grande Five Cities Times.

ATASCADERO

US
ATASCADERO NEWS. 1916. s-w.: Wed. & Fri. $.50 newsstand; $25/yr. in cy. 5660 El Camino Real, Atascadero, CA 93422. TEL 805-466-2585; FAX 805-466-2714. **Owner(s):** James, Judson & John Porter, P.O. Box 6068, Atascadero, CA 93424. TEL 805-466-2585; Ed. Lon Allan; Pub. James Porter; adv.; photos; pub. size: broadsheet; circ. 8,000(paid).

US
NORTH COUNTY SHOPPING NEWS. Thu. free. 5660 El Camino Real, Atascadero, CA 93422. TEL 805-466-2585; FAX 805-466-2714. **Owner(s):** James, Judson & John Porter, P.O. Box 6068, Atascadero, CA 93424. TEL 805-466-2585; Ed. Lon Allan; Pub. Jack Porter; adv.; pub. size: standard; circ. 2,000(free).

ATWATER

US
CHRONICLE, THE. Wed. free. 927 Atwater Blvd., Atwater, CA 95301. TEL 209-358-6431; FAX 209-357-2968. **Owner(s):** U.S. Media Group, P.O. Box 227, Crystal City, MO 63019; Ed. Kim Yancey; Pub. Tom Schmitt; adv. contact: Cheri Mister. photos; pub. size: broadsheet; circ. 8,000(controlled & paid).

US
SIGNAL, THE. 1911. Wed. free deliv.; $.50 newsstand; $18/yr. in cy. 927 Atwater Blvd., Atwater, CA 95301. TEL 209-358-6431; FAX 209-357-2968. **Owner(s):** U.S. Media Group, P.O. Box 227, Crystal City, MO 63019; Ed. David J. Wickenhauser; Pub. Tom Schmitt; adv. contact: Debbie Geissler. photos; pub. size: broadsheet; circ. 11,500(controlled & paid).
Formerly: Atwater Signal.

AUBURN

US
SENTINEL, THE. 1990. Thu. free newsstand; $25/yr. 1551 Lincoln Way, Auburn, CA 95603. TEL 916-823-2463; FAX 916-823-1309. **Owner(s):** Janice Forbes, 1226 High St., Auburn, CA 95603. TEL 916-823-2463; FAX 916-823-1309; Ed. Jill Rietgens; Pub. Janice Forbes; adv. contact: Grace Handel. photos; pub. size: broadsheet; circ. 10,000(controlled & free).

AVALON

US
AVALON BAY NEWS, THE. 1990. w. $.60 newsstand; $30/yr. 117 Whittley, Avalon, CA 90704-1809. TEL 310-510-1500; FAX 310-510-1371. **Owner(s):** Barbara L. Crow, 117 Whittley, Avalon, CA 90704. TEL 310-510-1500; FAX 310-510-1371; Ed. Barbara L. Crow; Pub. Barbara L. Crow; adv. contact: Barbara L. Crow. photos; pub. size: tabloid; circ. 2,000(free & paid).

US
CATALINA ISLANDER, THE. 1914. Fri. $.50 newsstand; $30/yr. 615 Crescent Ave., Avalon, CA 90704-0428. TEL 310-510-0500; FAX 310-510-2882; E-mail: islander@lightside.com; URL: http://www.catalina.com/islander/. **Owner(s):** West Coast Community Newspapers, Inc., 2841 Loker Ave., E., Carlsbad, CA 92008. TEL 619-431-4850; FAX 619-431-4866; Pub. Sherri Walker; adv. contact: Su Marion. photos; pub. size: tabloid; circ. 6,000(free & paid).

WEEKLY NEWSPAPERS

AVENAL

US

AVENAL PROGRESS. 1986. Wed. free home deliv.; $18/yr. mailed. 524 E. Merced St., Avenal, CA 93204. TEL 209-386-9385; FAX 209-386-4661. **Owner(s):** Pulitzer Publishing Co., 900 N. Tucker Blvd., St. Louis, MO 63101. TEL 313-340-8000; Ed. Arlene Santino; Pub. Dale Anderson; adv.; photos; pub. size: broadsheet; circ. 1,200(controlled & free).

BEAUMONT

US

COMMUNITY ADVISER. 1987. Wed. $.25 newsstand; $15/yr. 795 E. Sixth St., Ste. N, Beaumont, CA 92223. TEL 909-845-9564; FAX 909-845-6713. **Owner(s):** Ken Smith, 795 E. Sixth St., Ste. N, Beaumont, CA 92223. TEL 909-845-9564; FAX 909-845-6713; Ed. Hal Lowe; Pub. Ken Smith; adv.; photos; pub. size: broadsheet; circ. 14,000(free & paid).

BEL TIBURON

US

ARK, THE. 1972. Wed. $.50 newsstand; $31/yr. in area; $41/yr. out of area. 1550 Tiburon Blvd., Bel Tiburon, CA 94920. TEL 510-435-2652; FAX 510-435-0849. **Owner(s):** Barbara Gross, 1550 Tiburon Blvd., Bel Tiburon, CA 94920. TEL 415-435-2652; FAX 415-435-0849; Marilyn Kessler, 1550 Tiburon Blvd., Bel Tiburon, CA 94920. TEL 415-435-2652; FAX 415-435-0849; Steve McNamara, 1550 Tiburon Blvd., Bel Tiburon, CA 94920. TEL 510-435-2652; Ed. Marilyn Kessler; Pub. Barbara Gross; adv. contact: Jack Sweeney. pub. size: tabloid; circ. 3,000(paid).

BERKELEY

US

EAST BAY EXPRESS. 1978. Thu. free; $20/yr. in cy. mailed. 931 Ashby Ave., Berkeley, CA 94709. TEL 510-540-7400; FAX 510-540-7700; E-mail: ebxpress@aol.com. **Owner(s):** Express Publishing Co., Inc., 931 Ashby Ave., Berkeley, CA 94709. TEL 510-540-7400; FAX 510-540-7700; Ed. John Raeside; Pub. Nancy Banks; adv. contact: Julia Sibbet. bk.rev.; pub. size: tabloid; circ. 64,000(free).

BEVERLY HILLS

US

BEVERLY HILLS COURIER. 1965. Fri. $.50 newsstand; $75/yr. in cy. 8840 Olympic Blvd., Beverly Hills, CA 90211. TEL 310-278-1322; FAX 310-271-5118; E-mail: bhcourier@adl.com. **Owner(s):** March Schwartz, 8840 W. Olympic Blvd., Beverly Hills, CA 90211. TEL 310-278-1322; Pub. March Schwartz; adv. contact: Sande Schwartz. photos; pub. size: tabloid; circ. 48,000(paid).

BIG BEAR LAKE

US

BIG BEAR LIFE. 1941. Sat. free. 42007 Fox Farm Rd., Ste. 3, Big Bear Lake, CA 92315. TEL 909-866-3456; FAX 909-866-2302. **Owner(s):** Brehm Communications, Inc., 17065 Via del Campo, Ste. 200, San Diego, CA 92127. TEL 619-451-6200; Ed. John Emig; Pub. Jerry Wright; adv. contact: Doug Moore. adv.: $12.60/SAU. photos; bk.rev.; pub. size: tabloid; circ. 10,000(free).

US ISSN 1073-6867

GRIZZLY, THE. 1941. Wed. $.50 newsstand; $21/yr. in cy.; $30/yr. out of cy.; $39/yr. out of state. 42007 Fox Farm Rd., Ste. 3, Big Bear Lake, CA 92315. TEL 909-866-3456; FAX 909-866-2302. **Owner(s):** Brehm Communications, Inc., 17065 Via del Campo, Ste. 200, San Diego, CA 92127. TEL 619-451-6200; Pub. Jerry Wright; adv. contact: Doug Moore. adv.: $12.60/SAU. photos; bk.rev.; pub. size: broadsheet; circ. 10,000(paid).

BISHOP

US

INYO REGISTER. 1870. 3/wk.: Tue., Thu., Sat. $48/yr. local; $53/yr. out of state. 450 E. Line St., Bishop, CA 93514. TEL 619-873-3535; FAX 619-873-3591. **Owner(s):** Register Review Publishing Co., 450 E. Line St., Bishop, CA 93514. TEL 619-873-3535; Ed. Benett Kessler. pub. size: standard; circ. morning 6,300(paid). **Wire Service(s):** AP.

BLYTHE

US

PALO VERDE VALLEY TIMES. 1924. s-w.: Wed. & Fri. $.50 newsstand; $38/yr. in cy.; $58/yr. out of cy. 231 N. Spring.St., Blythe, CA 92225. TEL 619-922-3181; FAX 619-922-3184. **Owner(s):** Western Newspapers, Inc., P.O. Box 1271, Yuma, AZ 85366. TEL 602-783-3311; Pub. Robin Mauser; adv. contact: Dixie Allison. pub. size: broadsheet; circ. 13,000(free & paid).

BOLINAS

US

COASTAL POST. 1975. m. $20/yr. P.O. Box 31, Bolinas, CA 94924. TEL 415-868-1600; FAX 415-868-0502; E-mail: editor@coastalpost.com; URL: http://www.coastalpost.com. **Owner(s):** Don Deane, P.O. Box 31, Bolinas, CA 94924. TEL 415-868-1600; Ed. Don Deane; Pub. Don Deane; pub. size: tabloid; circ. 12,000(free & paid).

BREA

US

HARTE-HANKS PENNYSAVER. 1962. Wed. free. 2830 Orbiter St., Brea, CA 92621. TEL 714-996-8900; FAX 714-993-4711. **Owner(s):** Harte-Hanks Communications, Inc., P.O. Box 269, San Antonio, TX 78291. TEL 210-829-9000; adv.; pub. size: standard; circ. 4,500,000(free).

BURLINGAME

US

BOUTIQUE & VILLAGER. 1965. Wed. $.25 newsstand; $18/yr. in cy. 824 Cowan Rd., Burlingame, CA 94010. TEL 415-692-9406; FAX 415-692-7587. **Owner(s):** Pan-Asian Venture Capital Corp., 1201 Evans Ave., San Francisco, CA 94124. TEL 415-826-1100; Ed. Marc Burkhardt; Pub. Ted Fang; adv. contact: Larry Boline. photos; pub. size: broadsheet; circ. 13,859(paid).

US

ENQUIRER BULLETIN. 1924. Wed. $18/yr. 824 Cowan Rd., Burlingame, CA 94010. TEL 415-692-9406; FAX 415-692-7587. **Owner(s):** Pan-Asian Venture Capital Corp., 1201 Evans Ave., San Francisco, CA 94124. TEL 415-826-1100; Ed. Ann Sumwalt; Pub. Ted Fang; adv.; photos; bk.rev.; pub. size: broadsheet; circ. 22,600(free).
Formerly: San Carlos/Belmont Enquirer.

US

FOSTER CITY PROGRESS. 1966. Wed. free. 824 Cowan Rd., Burlingame, CA 94010. TEL 415-692-9406; FAX 415-692-7587. **Owner(s):** Pan-Asian Venture Capital Corp., 1201 Evans Ave., San Francisco, CA 94124. TEL 415-826-1100; Ed. Marc Burkhardt; Pub. Ted Fang; adv. contact: Larry Boline. photos; bk.rev.; pub. size: broadsheet; circ. 10,700(controlled & free).

US

MILLBRAE & SAN BRUNO SUN. 1935. Wed. free home deliv.; $.25 newsstand. 824 Cowan Rd., Burlingame, CA 94010. TEL 415-692-9406; FAX 415-692-7587. **Owner(s):** Pan-Asian Venture Capital Corp., 1201 Evans Ave., San Francisco, CA 94124. TEL 415-826-1100; Ed. Mark Burkhardt; Pub. Ted Fang; adv. contact: Larry Boline. pub. size: broadsheet; circ. 19,000(free & paid).
Formerly: Millbrae Sun; Millbrae-San Bruno Sun.

US

PENINSULA INDEPENDENT. 1994. Wed. free. 824 Cowan Rd., Burlingame, CA 94010. TEL 415-692-9406; FAX 415-692-7587. **Owner(s):** Pan-Asian Venture Capital Corp., 1201 Evans Ave., San Francisco, CA 94124. TEL 415-826-1100; Ed. Marc Burkhardt; Pub. Ted Fang; adv. contact: Larry Boline. photos; bk.rev.; pub. size: broadsheet; circ. 43,600(free).

US

SAN MATEO WEEKLY. Wed. & Sat. free. 824 Cowan Rd., Burlingame, CA 94010. TEL 415-692-9406; FAX 415-692-7587. **Owner(s):** Pan-Asian Venture Capital Corp., 1201 Evans Ave., San Francisco, CA 94124. TEL 415-826-1100; Pub. Ted Fang; adv. contact: Larry Boline. photos; bk.rev.; pub. size: broadsheet; circ. 28,800(free).

BURNEY

US

INTERMOUNTAIN NEWS. 1957. Wed. $.75/newsstand; $30/yr. 36965 Main St., Burney, CA 96013. TEL 916-335-4533; FAX 916-335-5335. **Owner(s):** Craig Harrington, 36965 Main St., Burney, CA 96013. TEL 916-335-4533; Pub. Craig Harrington; adv. contact: Craig Harrington. pub. size: standard; circ. 3,335(paid).
Formerly: Burney Intermountain News.

CALIFORNIA CITY

US ISSN 1065-1152

MOJAVE DESERT NEWS, THE. 1938. Thu. $.50 newsstand; $20/yr. in cy.; $29/yr. out of cy.; $35/yr. out of state. 8046 California City Blvd., California City, CA 93505. TEL 619-373-4812; FAX 619-373-2941. **Owner(s):** MOCAL News Corp., 8046 California City Blvd., California City, CA 93505. TEL 619-373-4812; Ed. Connie Baker; Pub. Van Pray; adv. contact: Dale Biggs. photos; bk.rev.; pub. size: standard; circ. 5,650(free & paid).
Formerly: Enterprise, The.

CALISTOGA
US

WEEKLY CALISTOGAN. 1877. Thu. $.50 newsstand; $17.50/yr. in cy.; $23.50/yr. out of cy. 1422 C Lincoln Ave., Calistoga, CA 94515. TEL 707-942-6242; FAX 707-942-4617; E-mail: weeklycal@aol.com; URL: http://www.sonic.net/~johnfr/calistogan. **Owner(s):** Cal Star Publishing, 1422 C Lincoln Ave., P.O. Box 385, Calistoga, CA 94515-0385. TEL 707-942-6242; FAX 707-942-4617; Ed. Pat Hampton; Pub. Bill Brenner; pub. size: broadsheet; circ. 1,000(paid).

CARLSBAD
US

CARLSBAD SUN. 1925. Thu. $.25 newsstand; $50/yr. 3rd class. 2841 Loker Ave., E, Carlsbad, CA 92008. TEL 760-431-4850; FAX 760-431-4888. **Owner(s):** West Coast Community Newspapers, Inc., 2841 Loker Ave., E., Carlsbad, CA 92008. TEL 619-431-4850; FAX 619-431-4888; Pub. Donna Medeiros; adv.; pub. size: broadsheet; circ. 25,500(controlled & paid).
Formerly: Carlsbad Journal.

US ISSN 0191-5584
DEL MAR, SOLANA BEACH, CARMEL VALLEY, RANCHO SANTA FE SUN. 1958. Thu. free. 2841 Loker Ave. E, Carlsbad, CA 92008. TEL 619-792-3820; FAX 619-481-3312. **Owner(s):** West Coast Community Newspapers, Inc., 2841 Loker Ave., E., Carlsbad, CA 92007. TEL 619-431-4850; FAX 619-431-4888; Ed. Brad Falduto; Pub. Joel Zlotnik; adv.; photos; pub. size: broadsheet; circ. 22,706(paid).
Formerly: Del Mar Surfcomber.

CARMEL
US

CARMEL PINE CONE. 1915. Thu. free newsstand; $95/yr. Fourth St. & Mission, S.W., Carmel, CA 93921. TEL 408-624-0162; FAX 408-624-8076. **Owner(s):** Paul Miller, Fourth St. & Mission, S.W., Carmel, CA 93921. TEL 408-624-0162; FAX 408-624-8076; Ed. Paul Wolf; Pub. Paul Miller; bk.rev.; pub. size: tabloid; circ. 16,000(free & paid).

CARMICHAEL
US

CARMICHAEL TIMES. 1981. Tue. $39/yr. 4807-D El Camino Ave., Carmichael, CA 95608. TEL 916-483-0946; FAX 916-483-1902. **Owner(s):** Shirley Turner, P.O. Box 88, Carmichael, CA 95609. TEL 916-483-0946; FAX 916-483-1902; Paul O'Brien, P.O. Box 88, Carmichael, CA 95609. TEL 916-486-2908; FAX 916-483-1902; Ed. Shirley Turner. adv. contact: Shirley Turner. photos; bk.rev.; pub. size: tabloid; circ. 10,000.

CARNELIAN BAY
US

NORTH TAHOE/TRUCKEE WEEK. 1982. bi-w: Thu. free. 5009 N. Lake Blvd., Carnelian Bay, CA 96140. TEL 916-546-5995; FAX 916-546-8113. **Owner(s):** North Tahoe Week Publishing Co., P.O. Box 49, Tahoe Vista, CA 96148. TEL 916-546-5995; FAX 916-546-8113; Pub. Dale Good; adv. contact: Dale Good. pub. size: tabloid; circ. 19,000(free).

CERES
US

CERES COURIER. 1910. s-w.: Wed. & Fri. $.25 newsstand; $30/yr. in cy.; $42/yr. mailed. 2940 Fourth St., Ceres, CA 95307. TEL 209-537-5032. **Owner(s):** Morris Communications, P.O. Box 8167, Savannah, GA 31412. TEL 912-233-1281; Ed. Jeffery Benziger; Pub. Darell Phillips; adv. contact: Bill Sanborn. pub. size: broadsheet; circ. 17,000(free & paid).

CHULA VISTA
US

STAR NEWS, THE. 1820. s-w.: Wed. & Sat. free; $25/deliv.; $45.63/yr. in cy.; $53.10/yr. out of cy. 279 Third Ave., Chula Vista, CA 91910. TEL 619-427-3000; FAX 619-426-6346. **Owner(s):** West Coast Community Newspaper, Inc., 2841 Loker Ave. E, Carsbad, CA 92008. TEL 619-431-4850; Ed. Joe Guerin; Pub. Joe Guerin; adv. contact: Linda Rosas. pub. size: broadsheet; circ. 50,000(paid).
Formerly: Imperial Beach Star News.

CITY OF COMMERCE
US

CITY TERRACE COMET. 1974. Thu. free newsstand; $92/yr. mail deliv. 2500 S. Atlantic Blvd., Bldg. B, City of Commerce, CA 90040-2004. TEL 213-263-5743. **Owner(s):** Eastern Group Publications, Inc., 2500 S. Atlantic Blvd., Bldg. B, City of Commerce, CA 90040. TEL 213-263-5743; Ed. Jonathan Sanchez; Pub. Dolores Sanchez; adv.; photos; bk.rev.; pub. size: standard; circ. 4,528(free & paid). **Wire Service(s):** CNS.

US
EASTSIDE SUN. 1948. Thu. $92/yr. 2500 S. Atlantic Blvd., Bldg. B, City of Commerce, CA 90040. TEL 213-263-5741; FAX 213-263-9161. **Owner(s):** Eastern Group Publications, Inc., 2500 S. Atlantic Blvd., Bldg. B, City of Commerce, CA 90040. TEL 213-263-5743; FAX 213-263-9169; Ed. Dolores Sanchez; Pub. Dolores Sanchez; adv.; bk.rev.; pub. size: standard; circ. 22,000(free & paid). **Wire Service(s):** CNS.

US
NORTHEAST SUN. 1985. Thu. $92.50/yr. 2500 S. Atlantic Blvd., Bldg. B, City of Commerce, CA 90040. TEL 213-263-5743; FAX 213-263-9169. **Owner(s):** Eastern Group Publications, Inc., 2500 S. Atlantic Blvd., Bldg. B, City of Commerce, CA 90040. TEL 213-263-5743; Dolores Sanchez, 2500 S. Atlantic Blvd., Bldg. B, City of Commerce, CA 90040. TEL 213-263-5743; Ed. Jonathan Sanchez; Pub. Dolores Sanchez; adv.; photos; bk.rev.; pub. size: standard; circ. 19,500(controlled & free). **Wire Service(s):** CiNS.

CLAREMONT
US

CLAREMONT COURIER. 1908. s-w.: Wed. & Sat. $.50 newsstand; $34.50/yr. 111 S. College, Claremont, CA 91711. TEL 909-621-4761; FAX 909-621-4072. **Owner(s):** Martin & Janis Weinberger, 111 S. College, Claremont, CA 91711. TEL 909-621-4761; FAX 909-621-4072; Ed. Martin Weinberger; Pub. Martin Weinberger; adv. contact: Phyllis Metzner. photos; pub. size: tabloid; circ. 6,025(paid).

CLEARLAKE
US

CLEAR LAKE OBSERVER-AMERICAN. 1936. s-w.: Wed. & Sat. $.25 newsstand; $19.30/yr. in cy.; $40.22/yr. out of cy. 14913-B Lakeshore Dr., Clearlake, CA 95422. TEL 707-994-6444; FAX 707-994-5335. **Owner(s):** Lake County Publishing, P.O. Box 6328, Clearlake, CA 95422. TEL 707-994-6444; Ed. Debbie Geissler; Pub. Tim Timmons; adv. contact: Debbie Geissler. photos; pub. size: broadsheet; circ. 3,462(paid).

CLOVERDALE
US

CLOVERDALE REVEILLE. 1879. Wed. $.50 newsstand; $18.50/yr. 207 N. Cloverdale Blvd., Cloverdale, CA 95425. TEL 707-894-3339; FAX 707-894-3343. **Owner(s):** Hanchett Publishing, Inc., P.O. Box 157, Cloverdale, CA 95425. TEL 707-894-3339; FAX 707-894-3343; Ed. Bonny J. Hanchett; Pub. Bonny J. Hanchett; adv.; photos; pub. size: broadsheet; circ. 2,500(paid).

CLOVIS
US ISSN 1068-5944

CLOVIS INDEPENDENT. 1906. Fri. $.50 newsstand; $21/yr. 1321 Railroad Ave., Clovis, CA 93612. TEL 209-298-8081; FAX 209-298-0459. **Owner(s):** McClatchy Newspapers, 2100 Q St., Sacramento, CA 95816. TEL 916-321-1000; Ed. Earl Wright, Jr.; Pub. Earl Wright, Jr.; adv. contact: Barbara Parnell. pub. size: broadsheet; circ. 4,000(paid).

COALINGA
US

COALINGA RECORD. 1904. Wed. $.35 newsstand; $18/yr. local; $25/yr. in CA.; $22/yr. out of state. 152 E. Elm, Coalinga, CA 93210. TEL 209-935-2906; FAX 209-935-5257. **Owner(s):** Pulitzer Publishing Co., 900 N. Tucker Blvd., St. Louis, MO 63101. TEL 313-340-8000; Ed. William Howell. adv. contact: Joy Redding. pub. size: standard; circ. 9,000(paid).

COLUSA
US ISSN 0897-8743

COLUSA COUNTY SUN-HERALD. 1862. 3/wk.: Mon., Wed., Fri. $.50 newsstand; $48/yr. home deliv.; $63/yr. mailed out of cy. 825 Bridge St., Colusa, CA 95932. TEL 916-458-2121; FAX 916-458-5711. **Owner(s):** Morris Communications, P.O. Box 89, Colusa, CA 95932. TEL 916-458-2121; Ed. Dirk Damon; Pub. Darell Phillips; adv.; pub. size: broadsheet; circ. 6,500(paid).

COMPTON
US

CARSON BULLETIN. 1980. Wed. $.25 newsstand; $26.60/yr. 349 W. Compton Blvd., Compton, CA 90220. TEL 310-635-6776. **Owner(s):** Rapid Publishing Inc., 349 W. Compton Blvd., Compton, CA 90220. TEL 310-635-6776; Ed. Betty Wilson; Pub. O. Ray Watkins; adv.; photos; bk.rev.; pub. size: broadsheet; circ. 18,000(paid).

WEEKLY NEWSPAPERS

COMPTON

US
COMPTON BULLETIN. 1980. Wed. $.25 newsstand; $25.60/yr. 349 W. Compton Blvd., Compton, CA 90220. TEL 310-635-6776. **Owner(s):** Rapid Publishing Inc., 349 W. Compton Blvd., Compton, CA 90220. TEL 310-635-6776; Ed. Betty Wilson; Pub. O. Ray Watkins; adv.; photos; bk.rev.; pub. size: broadsheet; circ. 22,000(paid).

US
INGLEWOOD TRIBUNE. Wed. $.25 newsstand; $25.60/yr. 349 W. Compton Blvd., Compton, CA 90220. TEL 310-635-6776. **Owner(s):** Rapid Publishing Inc., 349 W. Compton Blvd., Compton, CA 90220. TEL 310-635-6776; Ed. Betty Wilson; Pub. O. Ray Watkins; adv.; photos; bk.rev.; pub. size: broadsheet; circ. 10,000(paid).

US
LYNWOOD JOURNAL. 1980. Wed. $.25 newsstand; $25.60/yr. 349 W. Compton Blvd., Compton, CA 90220. TEL 310-635-6776. **Owner(s):** Rapid Publishing Inc., 349 W. Compton Blvd., Compton, CA 90220. TEL 310-635-6776; Ed. Betty Wilson; Pub. O. Ray Watkins; adv.; pub. size: broadsheet; circ. 15,000(paid).

US
WILMINGTON BEACON. 1980. Wed. $.25 newsstand; $25.60/yr. 349 W. Compton Blvd., Compton, CA 90220. TEL 310-635-6776. **Owner(s):** Rapid Publishing Inc., 349 W. Compton Blvd., Compton, CA 90020. TEL 310-635-6776; Ed. Betty Wilson; Pub. O. Ray Watkins; adv.; photos; bk.rev.; pub. size: broadsheet; circ. 10,000(paid).

CORNING

US
CORNING OBSERVER. 1887. 3/wk.: Mon., Wed., Fri. $.50 newsstand; $36/yr. carrier. 710 Fifth St., Corning, CA 96021. TEL 916-824-5464; FAX 916-824-4804. **Owner(s):** Morris Communications, P.O. Box 1928, Augusta, GA 30903. TEL 706-724-0851; Ed. Michael Griffin; Pub. Darell Phillips; adv.; pub. size: broadsheet; circ. 9,800(paid).
Formerly: Corning Daily Observer.

CORONA

US ISSN 0745-3930
CORONA-NORCO INDEPENDENT. 1887. Fri. $.25 newsstand; $9/yr. in cy.; $25/yr. out of cy. 823 S. Main St., Corona, CA 91720. TEL 909-737-1234; FAX 909-737-1572. **Owner(s):** Press-Enterprise Co., P.O. Box 792, Riverside, CA 92502; Ed. John Orr. adv. contact: Tom Pardis. pub. size: broadsheet; circ. 29,500(paid).

CORONADO

US
CORONADO JOURNAL. 1912. Fri. free; $25/yr. 3rd class; $75/yr. 1st class. 1224 Tenth St., Coronado, CA 92118. TEL 619-435-3141; FAX 619-435-3051. **Owner(s):** West Coast Community Newspapers, Inc., 2841 Loker Ave., E., Carlsbad, CA 92008. TEL 619-431-4850; FAX 619-431-4866; Ed. Heather Mccluskey. pub. size: broadsheet; circ. 11,500(paid).

CORTE MADERA

US
TWIN CITIES TIMES. 1975. Wed. $20/yr. P.O. Box 186, Corte Madera, CA 94925. TEL 415-332-3778; FAX 415-332-8714. **Owner(s):** Paul Anderson, P.O. Box 186, Corte Madera, CA 94925. TEL 313-340-8000; Ed. Billie L. Anderson; Pub. Paul A. Anderson; adv.; pub. size: standard; circ. 6,500(controlled & paid).

CRESTLINE

US
CRESTLINE COURIER-NEWS. 1924. Thu. $.50/newsstand; $19.80/yr. in cy.; $33/yr. out of cy.; $49.50/yr. out of state. Box 3307, Crestline, CA 92325. TEL 909-338-1893; FAX 909-338-4449. **Owner(s):** Desert Community Newspapers, Yucca Valley, CA; Ed. Matthew Proietti. adv. contact: Sue Mosher. adv.: $6.50/SAU. pub. size: standard; circ. 3,500(paid).
Formerly: Mountain Courier-News.

CUPERTINO

US
CUPERTINO COURIER. 1947. Wed. $.50 newsstand; $26/yr. in cy.; $55/yr. out of cy.; $15/yr. senior citizens. 20465 Silverado Ave., Cupertino, CA 95014-4439. TEL 408-255-7500; FAX 408-252-3381. **Owner(s):** Metro Publishing, Inc., 550 S. First St., San Jose, CA 95110; Ed. Mike deGive; Pub. David Cohen; adv. contact: Matt Stegman. photos; pub. size: tabloid; circ. 18,940(free & paid).

DELANO

US
DELANO RECORD. Thu. $.35 newsstand; $19/yr. in cy.; $21/yr. out of cy.; $24/yr. out of state. 1231 Jefferson, Delano, CA 93215. TEL 805-725-0600; FAX 805-725-4373. **Owner(s):** Reed Print, Inc., 5409 Aldrin Ct., Bakersfield, CA 93313; Ed. Bob Schettler; Pub. Robert Reed; adv. contact: Lonnie Lemons. pub. size: broadsheet; circ. 4,650(paid).

US
MARKET SHOPPER, THE. Wed. $.35 newsstand; free in area. 1231 Jefferson, Delano, CA 93215. TEL 805-725-0600; FAX 805-725-4373. **Owner(s):** Reed Print, Inc., 5409 Aldrin Ct., Bakersfield, CA 93313; Ed. Bob Schettler; Pub. Robert Reed; adv. contact: Lonnie Lemons. pub. size: broadsheet; circ. 16,150(free).

DESERT HOT SPRINGS

US
DESERT SENTINEL, THE. 1941. Thu. $.35 newsstand; $19.40/yr. in cy. 13550 Palm Dr., Desert Hot Springs, CA 92240. TEL 619-329-1411; FAX 619-329-3860. **Owner(s):** Gannett Company, Inc., 1100 Wilson Blvd., Arlington, VA 22234. TEL 703-284-6000; Ed. John Waters, Jr.; Pub. Bob Dickey; adv.; photos; pub. size: broadsheet; circ. 2,600(free & paid).

DOWNIEVILLE

US ISSN 0278-4394
MOUNTAIN MESSENGER. 1853. Thu. $.50 newsstand; $17/yr. in cy.; $21/yr. out of cy. 100 Main St., Downieville, CA 95936. TEL 916-289-3262; FAX 916-289-3262. **Owner(s):** Donald S. Russell, Inc., 100 Main St., Downieville, CA 95936-3262. TEL 916-289-3421; James Roos, 100 Main St., Downieville, CA 95936. TEL 510-837-0571; Don Smith, 100 Main St., Downieville, CA 95936; Pub. Donald S. Russell; adv.: $5.50/SAU. bk.rev.; pub. size: broadsheet; circ. 2,680(paid).

EL CENTRO

US
BRAWLEY ADVERTISER. 1955. Wed. free. 1699 W. Main St., Ste. J, El Centro, CA 92243. TEL 760-353-8400; FAX 760-352-0936. **Owner(s):** Associated Desert Shoppers, Inc., 73-400 Hwy. 111, Palm Desert, CA 92260. TEL 760-346-1729; FAX 760-346-7350; Pub. Hal Paradis; adv.; pub. size: tabloid; circ. 6,822(free).

US
CALEXICO ADVERTISER. 1955. w. free. 1699 W. Main St., Ste. J, El Centro, CA 92243. TEL 760-353-8400; FAX 760-352-0936. **Owner(s):** Associated Desert Shoppers, Inc., 73-400 Hwy. 111, Palm Desert, CA 92260. TEL 760-346-1729; FAX 760-346-7350; Pub. Hal Paradis; adv.; pub. size: tabloid; circ. 7,862(free).
Formerly: Imperial Valley Advertiser.

US
EL CENTRO ADVERTISER. 1955. Fri. free. 1699 W. Main St., Ste. J, El Centro, CA 92243. TEL 760-353-8400; FAX 760-352-0936. **Owner(s):** Associated Desert Shoppers, Inc., 73-400 Hwy. 111, El Centro, CA 92260. TEL 760-346-1729; FAX 760-346-7350; Pub. Hal Paradis; adv.; pub. size: tabloid; circ. 18,787(free).

ELK GROVE

US
ELK GROVE CITIZEN. 1903. s-w.: Wed. & Fri. $.35 newsstand; $35/yr. in cy. 8936 Elk Grove Blvd., Elk Grove, CA 95624. TEL 916-685-5533; FAX 916-686-6675. **Owner(s):** Herburger Publications, Inc., 604 N. Lincoln, Galt, CA 95632. TEL 209-745-1551; Ed. Keith Gebers; Pub. Roy E. Herburger; adv. contact: Dean Davy. photos; pub. size: broadsheet; circ. 23,260(paid).

EL MONTE

US
MID VALLEY NEWS. 1966. Wed. free; $30/yr. in cy. mailed. 11001 Valley Mall, Ste. 204, El Monte, CA 91731. TEL 818-443-1753; FAX 818-443-2245. **Owner(s):** Michael DeWeese, 11001 Valley Mall, Ste. 204, El Monte, CA 91731. TEL 818-443-1753; Ed. Michael DeWeese; Pub. Michael DeWeese; adv. contact: Irene Ramirez. pub. size: tabloid; circ. 15,000(free & paid).

EL SEGUNDO

US

EL SEGUNDO HERALD. 1911. Thu. free; $50/yr. in cy. mailed. 312 E. Imperial Ave., El Segundo, CA 90245. TEL 310-322-1830; FAX 310-322-2787. **Owner(s):** El Segundo Herald, Inc., P.O. Box 188, El Segundo, CA 90245. TEL 310-322-1830; Ed. Heidi Maerker; Pub. Michelle Killenger; adv. contact: Michelle Killenger. pub. size: tabloid; circ. 15,000(controlled & free).

ENCINITAS

US

ENCINITAS SUN. 1925. Thu. free; $2.10/mo.; $6.25/3 mos.; $12.50/6 mos.; $75/yr. 1st class. 1139 Second St., Encinitas, CA 92024. TEL 619-634-1534; FAX 619-431-4888. **Owner(s):** West Coast Community Newspapers, Inc., 2841 Loker Ave., E., Carlsbad, CA 92008. TEL 619-431-4850; FAX 619-431-4888; Ed. Joel Zoltnik. adv.; pub. size: broadsheet; circ. 19,479(controlled & paid).
Formerly: Coast Dispatch.

ESCONDIDO

US

ESCONDIDO NEWS-REPORTER. 1983. s-w.: Tue. & Fri. $.50 newsstand; $30/yr. 210 S. Juniper St., Ste. 205A, Escondido, CA 92025. TEL 760-747-8911; FAX 760-747-8912. **Owner(s):** Metropolitan News Co., 210 S. Spring St., Los Angeles, CA 90012-3710. TEL 213-628-4384; FAX 213-687-3886; Ed. Roger M. Grace. adv.; pub. size: standard; circ. 2,000(paid). **Wire Service(s):** AP.

EXETER

US ISSN 1072-1584

EXETER SUN, THE. 1903. Wed. $.50 newsstand; $17/yr. local; $23/yr. elsewhere; $25/yr. out of state. 120 N. E St., Exeter, CA 93221-0007. TEL 209-592-3171; FAX 209-592-4308. **Owner(s):** Mineral King Publishing Co., P.O. Box 7, Exeter, CA 93221-0007. TEL 209-592-3171; FAX 209-592-4308; Ed. Dave Adalian; Pub. Bill Brown; adv. contact: Marilee Stevens. photos; pub. size: broadsheet; circ. 15,000(free & paid).
Formerly: The Sun.

FALLBROOK

US

ENTERPRISE, THE. 1910. Thu. $.50 newsstand; $26/yr. mailed; $30/yr. out of cy. mailed. 232 S. Main St., Fallbrook, CA 92028. TEL 619-728-5511; FAX 619-723-4967. **Owner(s):** South Coast Newspapers, 1722 S. Hill St., Oceanside, CA 92054. TEL 619-433-7333; Ed. Betty Johnston; Pub. G.L. Taylor; adv.; pub. size: standard; circ. 8,000(paid).
Formerly: Enterprise Mountaineer, The.

FILLMORE

US

FILLMORE HERALD. 1907. Thu. $.35 newsstand; $22.51/yr. 606 Sespe Ave., Ste. 106, Fillmore, CA 93016. TEL 805-524-0153. **Owner(s):** Sentinel Media Publications, Inc., P.O. Box 727, Fillmore, CA 93016-0727; Ed. Doug Huff; Pub. Doug Huff; adv. contact: Doug Huff. photos; pub. size: broadsheet; circ. 3,000(controlled & paid).

FOLSOM

US

FOLSOM TELEGRAPH. 1856. Wed. $.50 newsstand; $20/yr. carrier. 49 Natoma St., Ste. E, Folsom, CA 95630. TEL 916-985-2581; FAX 916-985-0720. **Owner(s):** Brehm Communications, Inc., 17065 Via del Campo, Ste. 200, San Diego, CA 92127. TEL 619-451-6200; Ed. Patty McAlpin; Pub. Dave Reese; pub. size: broadsheet; circ. 6,000(paid).

FONTANA

US

FONTANA HERALD NEWS. 1923. Thu. $.50 newsstand; $18/yr. 16920 Spring St., Fontana, CA 92335. TEL 909-822-2231; FAX 909-355-9358. **Owner(s):** Herald News Publishing, Inc., 16920 Spring St., Fontana, CA 92235. TEL 909-822-2231; Ed. Russell Ingold; Pub. Jerry Bean; adv.; photos; pub. size: broadsheet; circ. evening 11,712(free & paid).

FORT BRAGG

US ISSN 0886-8840

FORT BRAGG ADVOCATE-NEWS. 1889. Thu. $.50 newsstand; $20/yr. local. 450 N. Franklin St., Fort Bragg, CA 95437. TEL 707-964-5642; FAX 707-964-0424. **Owner(s):** Stephens Group, Inc., P.O. Box 1359, Fort Smith, AR 72902. TEL 501-785-7801; Ed. Katherine Lee; Pub. Sharon Brewer; adv.: $6.20/SAU. photos; pub. size: broadsheet; circ. 14,009(free & paid).

FORTUNA

US

HUMBOLDT BEACON. 1902. Thu. $.50 newsstand; $10/6 mos. in cy.; $17.50/yr.; $25/yr. in state; $30/yr. out of state. 928 Main St., Fortuna, CA 95540. TEL 707-725-6166; FAX 707-725-4981; E-mail: beacon@humboldt1.com. **Owner(s):** Humboldt Group, The, 928 Main St., Fortuna, CA 95540. TEL 707-725-6166; FAX 707-725-4981; Ed. Jack Hamilton; Pub. Patrick O'Dell; adv.; photos; bk.rev.; pub. size: standard; circ. 8,000(paid).

FRESNO

US

CALIFORNIA ADVOCATE, THE. 1967. Wed. $.50 newsstand; $20/yr. mailed. 1715 East St., Ste. 108, Fresno, CA 93706. TEL 209-268-0941; FAX 209-268-0943. **Owner(s):** Mark Kimber, 1715 East St., Ste. 108, Fresno, CA 93706. TEL 209-268-0941; Ed. Pauline Kimber; Pub. Mark Kimber; adv.; photos; pub. size: broadsheet; circ. 25,000(paid).

GALT

US

GALT HERALD. 1903. Wed. $.35 newsstand; $18/yr. in cy. 604 N. Lincoln Way, Galt, CA 95632. TEL 209-745-1551; FAX 209-745-4492. **Owner(s):** Herburger Publications, Inc., 604 N. Lincoln Way, Galt, CA 95632. TEL 209-745-1551; Ed. Bryan Gold; Pub. Roy Herburger; adv. contact: Dean Davy. photos; pub. size: broadsheet; circ. 9,000(free & paid).

GARDENA

US

GARDENA VALLEY NEWS. 1904. Thu. $.25 newsstand; $12/yr. home deliv.; $47/yr. mailed. 16417 S. Western Ave., Gardena, CA 90247. TEL 310-329-6351; FAX 310-329-7501. **Owner(s):** Don Algie, 16417 S. Western Ave., Gardena, CA 90247. TEL 310-329-6351; Ed. Justin Pecot; Pub. Don Algie; adv. contact: Dan Gagajena. photos; bk.rev.; pub. size: broadsheet; circ. 36,000(free & paid).

GARDEN GROVE

US

ORANGE COUNTY NEWS. 1909. s-w.: Wed. & Fri. $30/yr. in cy. mailed. 9872 Chapman Ave., Ste. 108, Garden Grove, CA 92841. TEL 714-530-7622; FAX 714-530-7142. **Owner(s):** Orange County News Publishing Co., Inc., 9872 Chapman, Ste. 108, Garden Grove, CA 92641. TEL 714-530-7622; Ed. David Roque. adv. contact: Carroll Wilson. photos; pub. size: broadsheet; circ. 34,000(paid).

GLENDALE

US ISSN 0008-0950

CALIFORNIA COURIER. 1958. Thu. $49/yr. P.O. Box 5390, Glendale, CA 91221. TEL 818-409-0949. **Owner(s):** California Courier, P.O. Box 5390, Glendale, CA 91221. TEL 818-409-0949; FAX 818-500-7372; Ed. Harut Sassounian; Pub. Harut Sassounian; adv.; bk.rev.; pub. size: tabloid; circ. 3,000(paid).

GREENFIELD

US

GREENFIELD NEWS. Wed. $.50 newsstand; $22.50/yr. in cy.; $31.50/yr. out of cy. 845 Oak Ave., Greenfield, CA 93927. TEL 408-674-5907. Owner(s): News Media Corp., 211 Hwy. 38, E., Rochelle, IL 61068; Ed. Judith Spitzer; Pub. Daniel Wright; adv. contact: Suzi Taylor. pub. size: broadsheet; circ. 1,665(paid).

GRIDLEY

US

GRIDLEY HERALD, THE. 1880. s-w.: Wed. & Fri. $.50 newsstand; $30/yr. in cy.; $34/yr. out of cy. 630 Washington St., Gridley, CA 95948. TEL 916-846-3661; FAX 916-846-4519. **Owner(s):** Gridley Publishing Co., Inc., P.O. Box 68, Gridley, CA 95948. TEL 916-846-3661; Ed. Scotty Williams; Pub. William D. Burleson; adv. contact: Lisa Beebe. pub. size: broadsheet; circ. 4,000(paid).

HALF MOON BAY

US

HALF MOON BAY REVIEW. 1898. Wed. $.50 newsstand; $21/yr. home deliv.; $23.50/yr. mailed. 714 Kelly Ave., Half Moon Bay, CA 94019. TEL 415-726-4424; FAX 415-726-7054; E-mail: hmbreview@hmbreview.com; URL: http://www.hmbreview.com/. **Owner(s):** Wick Communications, Inc., 333 Wilcox Dr., Ste. 302, Sierra Vista, AZ 85635. TEL 602-458-0200; Ed. Marc DesJardins; Pub. Debra Godshall; adv.; pub. size: broadsheet; circ. 6,200(paid).

WEEKLY NEWSPAPERS

HEALDSBURG

US

HEALDSBURG TRIBUNE. 1856. Wed. $.50 newsstand; $21.50/yr. in cy.; $37.50/yr. out of cy.; $16/yr. senior citizens. 5 Mitchell Ln., Healdsburg, CA 95448. TEL 707-433-4451; FAX 707-431-2623. **Owner(s):** Beverly C. Reeves, 5 Mitchell Ln., Healdburg, CA 95448. TEL 707-433-4451; Ed. Val Hansen; Pub. Beverly Reeves; adv. contact: Kathryn Roth. photos; pub. size: broadsheet; circ. 4,650(paid).

HERMOSA BEACH

US

EASY READER. 1970. Thu. free; $40/yr. in cy. 832 Hermosa Ave., Hermosa Beach, CA 90254. TEL 310-372-4611; FAX 310-318-6292. **Owner(s):** Kevin Cody, 1233 Hermosa Ave., Hermosa Beach, CA 90254. TEL 310-372-4611; Ed. Kevin Cody; Pub. Kevin Cody; adv.; bk.rev.; pub. size: tabloid; circ. 70,000(free).

HESPERIA

US

HESPERIA RESORTER. 1959. Thu. free; $19/yr. mailed local; $21/yr. mailed elsewhere. 16925 Main St., Hesperia, CA 92345. TEL 760-244-0021; FAX 760-244-6609. **Owner(s):** Raymond Pryke, 16925 Main St., Hesperia, CA 92345. TEL 619-244-0021; Ed. Joyce Bohannan; Pub. Jenny Jones; adv. contact: Patricia Thomas. pub. size: broadsheet; circ. 7,000(free & paid).

HILMAR

US

HILMAR TIMES. Thu. $.25 newsstand; $19/yr. in cy. mailed; $23/yr. out of cy. mailed. 8260 Lander, Hilmar, CA 95324. TEL 209-632-4156; FAX 209-358-7108. **Owner(s):** Mid-Valley Publications, Inc., 6950 Gerard, Winton, CA 95388. TEL 209-358-5311; Ed. John Derby; Pub. John Derby; pub. size: broadsheet; circ. 6,000(paid).

HOLLISTER

US

PINNACLE, THE. 1986. Thu. free newsstand; $28/yr. 341 Tres Pinos Rd., Ste. 201, Hollister, CA 95023. TEL 408-637-6300; FAX 408-637-8174. **Owner(s):** K & S Market, Inc., P.O. Box 499, Hollister, CA 95024. TEL 408-637-6300; FAX 408-637-8174; Ed. Marvin Snow; Pub. Frank Klauer; adv. contact: Julie Moshay. photos; pub. size: tabloid; circ. morning 15,235(free & paid).

HOLTVILLE

US

HOLTVILLE TRIBUNE. 1906. Thu. $.50 newsstand; $22.50/yr. in cy.; $26.50/yr. elsewhere. 523 Pine Ave., Holtville, CA 92250. TEL 619-356-2995; FAX 619-356-4915. **Owner(s):** Steve Larson, 523 Pine Ave., Holtville, CA 92250. TEL 619-356-2995; Ed. Steve Larson; Pub. Steve Larson; pub. size: tabloid; circ. 3,000(paid).

HUNTINGTON BEACH

US ISSN 0194-6021

HUNTINGTON BEACH/FOUNTAIN VALLEY INDEPENDENT. 1966. Thu. free. 18682 Beach Blvd., Ste. 160, Huntington Beach, CA 92646. TEL 714-965-3030; FAX 714-965-7174. **Owner(s):** Los Angeles Times, Times Mirror Sq., Los Angeles, CA 90053. TEL 213-237-3700; Ed. Bill Lobdell; Pub. Tom Johnson; adv. contact: Janice Cross. pub. size: tabloid; circ. 65,000(free).

INDIO

US

INDIO POST. 1963. Thu. $.25 newsstand; $25/yr. in cy.; $45/yr. out of cy. 82-632 Hwy. 111, Ste. B, Indio, CA 92201. TEL 760-775-4200; FAX 760-342-7128. **Owner(s):** Desert Sun, The, 750 N. Gene Autry Trail, Palm Springs, CA 92262. TEL 619-322-8889; Ed. Dick Gazi; Pub. Robert Dickey; adv. contact: Jeffrey Levine. photos; pub. size: standard; circ. 30,000(controlled & free).

US

PALM DESERT POST. 1963. Thu. $.25 newsstand; $25/yr. in cy.; $45/yr. mailed. 82-632B Hwy. 111, Indio, CA 92201. TEL 619-775-4200; FAX 619-342-7128. **Owner(s):** Desert Sun, The, 750 N. Gene Autry Trail, Palm Springs, CA 92262. TEL 619-322-8889; Pub. Robert Dickey; adv. contact: Jeffrey Levine. photos; pub. size: standard; circ. 30,000(controlled & free).
Formerly: Desert Sun Community Newspaper, Desert Post; Palm Desert.

IRVINE

US ISSN 0195-4822

IRVINE WORLD NEWS. 1970. Thu. free; $36/6 mos.; $60/yr. 2712 McGaw, Irvine, CA 92614. TEL 714-261-2435; FAX 714-261-2623. **Owner(s):** Irvine Co., The, P.O. Box I, Newport Beach, CA 92663. TEL 714-720-2000; Ed. Don Dennis; Pub. Brien Manning; adv. contact: Jack Eagan. pub. size: tabloid; circ. 49,000(controlled).

JACKSON

US

AMADOR/CALAVARAS LEDGER DISPATCH. 1853. 3/wk.: Mon., Wed. & Fri. $.50 newsstand; $45.05/yr. 10776 Argonaut Ln., Jackson, CA 95642. TEL 209-223-1767; FAX 209-223-1264. **Owner(s):** U.S. Media Group, P.O. Box 227, Crystal City, MO 63019; Ed. Joe Evans; Pub. Randy McCants; adv.; photos; pub. size: broadsheet; circ. morning 14,400(controlled & paid).
Formerly: Amador Ledger.

KERMAN

US

FIREBAUGH/MENDOTA JOURNAL. Wed. $.50 newsstand; $21.55/yr. mailed. 681 S. Madera Ave., Ste. 109, Kerman, CA 93630. TEL 209-846-6689; FAX 209-846-8045. **Owner(s):** KerWest, Inc., 681 S. Madera Ave., Ste. 109, Kerman, CA 93630. TEL 209-846-6689; Ed. Mark Kilen. adv. contact: Merlyn Wilcox. pub. size: broadsheet; circ. 7,700(free).

LAFAYETTE, CA 10535

US

KERMAN NEWS. 1905. Wed. $.50 newsstand; $21.55/yr. 681 S. Madera Ave., Ste. 109, Kerman, CA 93630. TEL 209-846-6689; FAX 209-846-8045. **Owner(s):** KerWest, Inc., P.O. Box 336, Kerman, CA 93630. TEL 209-846-6689; Ed. Mark Kilen. adv. contact: Merlyn Wilcox. pub. size: broadsheet; circ. 2,000(paid).

US

WEST SIDE ADVANCE. 1905. Wed. free; $21.55/yr. in cy. mailed. 681 S. Madera Ave., Ste. 109, Kerman, CA 93630. TEL 209-846-6689; FAX 209-846-8045. **Owner(s):** KerWest, Inc., 681 S. Madera Ave., Ste. 109, Kerman, CA 93630. TEL 209-846-6689; Ed. Mark Kilen. adv. contact: Merlyn Wilcox. pub. size: broadsheet; circ. 2,700(free & paid).

KING CITY

US

KING CITY RUSTLER. 1901. Wed. $.50 newsstand; $25.50/yr. in cy.; $31.50/yr. out of cy. 116 S. Third St., King City, CA 93930. TEL 408-385-4880; FAX 408-385-4799. **Owner(s):** News Media Corp., 211 Hwy. 38, E., Rochelle, IL 61068; Ed. Judith Spitzer; Pub. Daniel Wright; adv. contact: Suzi Taylor. pub. size: broadsheet; circ. 4,486(paid).

US

VISTAS. Wed. free. 116 S. Third St., King City, CA 93930. TEL 408-385-4880; FAX 408-385-4799. **Owner(s):** News Media Corp., 211 Hwy. 38, E., Rochelle, IL 61068; Pub. Daniel Wright; adv. contact: Suzi Taylor. pub. size: broadsheet; circ. 5,400(free).

KINGSBURG

US

KINGSBURG RECORDER. Wed. $.50 newsstand; $20/yr. local; $25/yr. in state; $17/yr. senior citizens. 1467 Marion St., Kingsburg, CA 93631. TEL 209-897-2993; FAX 209-897-4868. **Owner(s):** Community Newspapers, Inc., P.O. Box 100, Selma, CA 93662. TEL 209-896-1976; FAX 209-896-9160; Ed. Tim Sheehan; Pub. Jim Brock; adv.; pub. size: standard; circ. 2,700(paid).

LA CANADA

US

LA CANADA VALLEY SUN. 1946. Thu. $.50 newsstand; $22/yr. in cy. 1061 Valley Sun Ln., La Canada, CA 91011. TEL 818-790-8774; FAX 818-790-5690. **Owner(s):** Gerald A. Bean, 1061 Valley Sun Ln., La Canada, CA 91011. TEL 818-790-8774; FAX 818-790-5690; Pub. Gerald A. Bean; adv. contact: Pat Miller. photos; pub. size: tabloid; circ. 5,900(paid).

LAFAYETTE

US

CONTRA COSTA SUN. 1938. Wed. $.75 newsstand; $30/yr. mailed. 3685 Mt. Diablo Blvd., Ste. 150, Lafayette, CA 94549. TEL 510-284-4444; FAX 510-284-1039. **Owner(s):** Knight-Ridder, Inc., One Herald Plz., Miami, FL 33132-1693. TEL 305-376-3800; FAX 305-376-3875; Ed. Bev Britton; Pub. George Riggs; adv.; photos; pub. size: broadsheet; circ. 8,000(paid).

LAGUNA HILLS

US
LEISURE WORLD NEWS. 1965. Thu. $.50 newsstand; $12/yr. home deliv. 23522 Paseo de Valencia, Laguna Hills, CA 92653. TEL 714-837-5200; FAX 714-837-0106. **Owner(s):** Freedom Communications, Inc., 17666 Fitch, Irvine, CA 92614. TEL 714-553-9292; Ed. Cathy Lawhon. pub. size: tabloid; circ. 11,567(paid).

US
SOUTH COAST SHOPPERS/PENNY SAVERS. 1960. Wed. free. 25201 Paseo de Alicia, Ste. 120, Laguna Hills, CA 92600. TEL 714-996-8900; FAX 714-859-3469. **Owner(s):** Harte-Hanks Communications, Inc., P.O. Box 269, San Antonio, TX 78291. TEL 210-829-9000; adv.; pub. size: tabloid; circ. 4,300,000(free).
Formerly: South Coast Shoppers.

LA JOLLA

US
LA JOLLA LIGHT. 1913. Thu. free home deliv.; $.50 newsstand; $25/yr. 3rd class; $75/yr. 1st class. 450 Pearl St., La Jolla, CA 92037. TEL 619-459-4201; FAX 619-459-5507. **Owner(s):** West Coast Community Newspapers, Inc., 2841 Loker Ave., E., Carlsbad, CA 92008. TEL 619-431-4850; FAX 619-431-4888; Pub. Bonnie Nichols; adv.; pub. size: broadsheet; circ. 24,000(free & paid).

LAKE ARROWHEAD

US
MOUNTAIN NEWS, THE. 1920. Thu. $.50 newsstand; $22.50/yr. in cy.; $55/2 yrs.; $35/yr. out of cy.; $45/yr. out of state. 28200 Hwy. 189, Bldg. 0-1, Ste. 200, Lake Arrowhead, CA 92352. TEL 909-336-3555; FAX 909-337-5275. **Owner(s):** Brehm Communications, Inc., 17065 Via del Campo, Ste. 200, San Diego, CA 92127. TEL 619-451-3814; Ed. Matt Proietti; Pub. Phil Jaffe; adv.; pub. size: broadsheet; circ. 7,500(paid).

LAKE ELSINORE

US
LAKE ELSINORE VALLEY SUN-TRIBUNE. 1886. Thu. $.35 newsstand; $12/yr. in cy. 31900 Mission Trail, Ste. 120, Lake Elsinore, CA 92530. TEL 909-674-1535; FAX 909-674-0280. **Owner(s):** Southwest Riverside County Newspapers, Inc., P.O. Box 2108, Lake Elsinore, CA 92531-2108. TEL 909-674-1535; Ed. Lowanna Maxwell; Pub. Tom Paradis; pub. size: broadsheet; circ. 11,069(paid).

LAKE FOREST

US
ALISO VIEJO NEWS. Thu. free. 22481 Aspan St., Lake Forest, CA 92630. TEL 714-768-3631; FAX 714-454-7354. **Owner(s):** Freedom Communications, Inc., 17666 Fitch, Irvine, CA 92614. TEL 714-553-9292; Ed. Liam Truchard. adv. contact: Sheila Malloy. pub. size: tabloid; circ. 7,247(free).

US
CAPISTRANO VALLEY NEWS. 1972. Thu. free. 22481 Aspan St., Lake Forest, CA 92630. TEL 714-768-3631; FAX 714-454-7354. **Owner(s):** Freedom Communications, Inc., 17666 Fitch, Irvine, CA 92614. TEL 714-835-1234; Ed. Jonathan Volzke. adv.; pub. size: tabloid; circ. 9,200(free).

US
DANA POINT NEWS. Thu. free. 22481 Aspan, Lake Forest, CA 92630. TEL 714-768-3631; FAX 714-830-9504. **Owner(s):** Freedom Communications, Inc., 17666 Fitch, Irvine, CA 92614. TEL 714-553-9292; Ed. Dennis Kaiser. adv.; pub. size: tabloid; circ. 12,300(free).

US
LAGUNA NEWS POST. 1915. Thu. free. 22481 Aspan, Lake Forest, CA 92630. TEL 714-768-3631; FAX 714-454-7354. **Owner(s):** Freedom Communications, Inc., 17666 Fitch, Irvine, CA 92714. TEL 714-553-9292; FAX 714-474-7675; Ed. Cathy Lawhon. adv. contact: Sheila Malloy. photos; pub. size: tabloid; circ. 14,213(free).
Formerly: Laguan Beach News.

US
LAGUNA NIGUEL NEWS. 1972. Thu. free. 22481 Aspan, Lake Forest, CA 92630. TEL 714-768-3631; FAX 714-454-7354. **Owner(s):** Freedom Communications, Inc., 17666 Fitch, Irvine, CA 92614. TEL 714-553-9292; Ed. Cathy Lawhon. adv. contact: Sheila Malloy. photos; pub. size: tabloid; circ. 10,400(free).

US
RANCHO SANTA MARGARITA NEWS. s-w.: Wed. & Fri. free. 22481 Aspan, Lake Forest, CA 92630. TEL 714-768-3631; FAX 714-830-9504. **Owner(s):** Freedom Communications, Inc., 17666 Fitch, Irvine, CA 92614. TEL 714-553-9292; Ed. James Kim. pub. size: tabloid; circ. 7,000(free).

US
SADDLEBACK VALLEY NEWS. s-w.: Wed. & Fri. free. 22481 Aspan St., Lake Forest, CA 92630. TEL 714-768-3631; FAX 714-454-7354. **Owner(s):** Orange County Register, 23811 Via Fabricante, Mission Viejo, CA 92690. TEL 714-768-3631; Ed. Cathy Lawhon. pub. size: tabloid; circ. 57,000(controlled & free).

LAKE ISABELLA

US
KERN VALLEY SUN. 1957. Wed. $.50 newsstand; $18.13/yr. home deliv.; $23.19/yr. local mailed. 6404 Lake Isabella Blvd., Lake Isabella, CA 93240. TEL 619-379-3667; FAX 619-379-4343. **Owner(s):** Wick Communications, Inc., 333 W. Wilcox Dr., Ste. 302, Sierra Vista, AZ 85635. TEL 520-458-0200; FAX 520-458-6166; Ed. Bret Bradigan; Pub. Bret Bradigan; adv.; pub. size: broadsheet; circ. 6,275(paid).

LAMONT

US
LAMONT REPORTER. Wed. free; $19/yr. in cy. mailed; $21/yr. out of cy.; $24/yr. elsewhere. 9717 Main St., Lamont, CA 93241. TEL 805-845-3704; FAX 805-832-0841. **Owner(s):** Reed Print, Inc., 5409 Aldrin Ct., Bakersfield, CA 93313; Ed. Frank W. Reed; Pub. Donald Reed; adv.; pub. size: broadsheet; circ. 8,100(free & paid).

LANCASTER

US
DESERT MAILER NEWS. 1975. Tue. free; $16/yr. mailed. 123 West Ave., Ste. J-5, Lancaster, CA 93534. TEL 805-945-8671; FAX 805-942-6418. **Owner(s):** Hamilton Diversified Services, P.O. Box 179, Pauma Valley, CA 92061. TEL 619-742-1905; FAX 619-742-1894; Pub. James Collins; adv.; photos; pub. size: broadsheet; circ. 10,000(free & paid).

LEMON GROVE

US
LA MESA FORUM. Thu. free. 3434 Grove St., Lemon Grove, CA 91946. TEL 619-469-0101. **Owner(s):** Forum Publications Co., P.O. Box 127, Lemon Grove, CA 91946. TEL 619-469-0101; Ed. Steve Saint; Pub. Steve Saint; pub. size: tabloid; circ. 4,000(paid).

US
LEMON GROVE REVIEW. 1948. s-w.: Tue. & Thu. $.25 newsstand; $18/yr. P.O. Box 127, Lemon Grove, CA 91946. TEL 619-469-0101. **Owner(s):** Forum Publications Co., P.O. Box 127, Lemon Grove, CA 91946. TEL 619-469-0101; Pub. Steve Saint; adv.; bk.rev.; pub. size: tabloid; circ. 2,000(paid).

US
SPRING VALLEY BULLETIN. 1949. s-w.: Tue. & Thu. free; $18/yr. P.O. Box 127, Lemon Grove, CA 91946. TEL 619-469-0101. **Owner(s):** Forum Publications Co., P.O. Box 127, Lemon Grove, CA 91946. TEL 619-469-0101; Pub. Steve Saint; adv.; pub. size: tabloid; circ. 3,000(controlled).

LINDEN

US
LINDEN HERALD. 1959. Thu. $.40 newsstand; $23.50/yr. 4950 N. Bonham, Linden, CA 95236. TEL 209-887-3112; FAX 209-887-3111. **Owner(s):** Brian Reilly, 4950 N. Bonham, Linden, CA 95236-0929. TEL 209-887-3112; Ed. Brian Reilly; Pub. Brian Reilly; adv.; pub. size: broadsheet; circ. 1,200(paid).

LINDSAY

US ISSN 1072-1800
LINDSAY GAZETTE. 1901. Wed. $17/yr. in cy.; $23/yr. out of cy. 136 Honolulu, Lindsay, CA 93247. TEL 209-562-2585; FAX 209-562-2214. **Owner(s):** Mineral King Publishing Co., P.O. Box 308, Lindsay, CA 93247. TEL 209-562-2585; Ed. Bruce Whitworth; Pub. Bill Brown; adv. contact: Marilee Stevens. pub. size: broadsheet; circ. 2,300(paid).

LIVERMORE

US
INDEPENDENT, THE. 1963. Wed. free; $18/yr. 2250 First St., Livermore, CA 94550. TEL 510-447-8700; FAX 510-447-0212; E-mail: editmail@compuserve.com. **Owner(s):** Independent, The, 2250 First St., Livermore, CA 94550. TEL 510-447-8700; FAX 510-447-0212; Ed. Janet Armantrout; Pub. Joan Seppala; adv.; pub. size: standard; circ. 26,200(controlled).

WEEKLY NEWSPAPERS

LOCKEFORD

US
LOCKEFORD-CLEMENTS NEWS. Wed. $13.50/yr. 18540 N. Hwy. 88, Unit 2, Lockeford, CA 95237. TEL 209-727-5776; FAX 209-727-3931. **Owner(s):** Mike Henry, 18540 N. Hwy. 88, Unit 2, Lockeford, CA 95237. TEL 209-727-5776; Ed. Mike Henry; Pub. Mike Henry; adv.; pub. size: tabloid; circ. 2,800(paid).

LONG BEACH

US
DOWNTOWN GAZETTE. 1978. Mon. free. 5225 E. Second St., Long Beach, CA 90803. TEL 562-433-2000; FAX 562-434-8826; E-mail: editor@gazettes.com; URL: http://www.gazettes.com. **Owner(s):** John & Fran Blowitz, 5225 E. Second St., Long Beach, CA 90803. TEL 562-433-2000; FAX 562-434-8826; Ed. Harry Saltzgaver; Pub. Fran Blowitz; adv.; bk.rev.; pub. size: tabloid; circ. 50,000(free).

US
GRUNION GAZETTE. 1978. Thu. free newsstand; $40/yr. 5225 E. Second St., Long Beach, CA 90803. TEL 562-433-2000; FAX 562-434-8826. **Owner(s):** John & Fran Blowitz, 5225 E. Second St., Long Beach, CA 90803. TEL 562-433-2000; FAX 562-434-8826; Pub. Fran Blowitz; adv.; bk.rev.; pub. size: tabloid; circ. 30,000(free).

LOS ALAMITOS

US
NEWS ENTERPRISE, THE. 1923. Thu. $.25 newsstand; $15/yr. mailed local; $25/yr. out of state. 3622 Florista, Los Alamitos, CA 90720. TEL 562-527-8217; FAX 562-493-2310. **Owner(s):** Athena Publishing Corp., 3182 Blume Drive, Los Alamitos, CA 90720. TEL 562-431-1397; Pub. Germaine R. Erskine; adv. contact: Gerry Erskine. photos; pub. size: standard; circ. 30,000(free & paid).
Formerly: Seal Beach, Rossmoor, Los Alamitos, Cypress, & LaPalma News Enterprises.

LOS ALTOS

US   ISSN 8750-4588
LOS ALTOS TOWN CRIER. 1947. Wed. $.50 newsstand; $20/yr. in cy.; $40/yr. out of cy.; $15/yr. senior citizens. 138 Main St., Los Altos, CA 94022. TEL 415-948-9000; FAX 415-948-6647; E-mail: towncrier@losaltosonline.com; URL: http://www.losaltosonline.com. **Owner(s):** Select Communications, Inc., 138 Main St., Los Altos, CA 94022. TEL 415-948-4821; Ed. Bruce Barton; Pub. Paul Nyberg; adv. contact: Susan Glaze. pub. size: tabloid; circ. 16,500(controlled).

LOS ANGELES

US
ALHAMBRA POST ADVOCATE. s-w.: Wed. & Sat. $100/yr. in state. 2621 W. 54th St., Los Angeles, CA 90043. TEL 213-290-3000; FAX 213-291-0219. **Owner(s):** Wave Community Newspapers, Inc., 2621 W. 54th St., Los Angeles, CA 90043. TEL 213-727-1117; Ed. Art Aquilar; Pub. Ric Trent; circ. 25,014(controlled).

US
ARGONAUT, THE. 1971. Thu. $110/yr. 1st class mail. 5355 McConnell Ave., Los Angeles, CA 90066. TEL 310-822-1629; FAX 310-821-8029. **Owner(s):** Argonaut, Inc., 5355 McConnell Ave., Los Angeles, CA 90066. TEL 310-822-1629; Ed. David Asper Johnson; Pub. David Asper Johnson; adv. contact: James Cloud. pub. size: tabloid; circ. 35,000(paid).

US
BELEVEDERE CITIZEN. Wed. free; $125/yr. mailed. 2621 W. 54th St., Los Angeles, CA 90043. TEL 213-290-3000; FAX 213-291-0219. **Owner(s):** Wave Community Newspapers, Inc., 2621 W. 54th St., Los Angeles, CA 90043. TEL 213-727-1117; Pub. Ric Trent; adv. contact: Ric Trent. pub. size: broadsheet; circ. 15,100(free & paid).

US
BELL GARDENS REVIEW. Thu. $78/yr. in state. 2621 W. 54th St., Los Angeles, CA 90043. TEL 213-727-1117; FAX 213-292-8289. **Owner(s):** Wave Community Newspapers, Inc., 2621 W. 54th St., Los Angeles, CA 90043. TEL 213-727-1117; FAX 213-292-8289; Ed. Art Agular; Pub. Ric Trent; circ. 21,662(controlled).

US
BELL MAYWOOD CUDAHY INDUSTRIAL POST. s-w.: Thu. & Sat. $125/yr. in state. 2621 W. 54th St., Los Angeles, CA 90043. TEL 213-290-3000; FAX 213-727-9515. **Owner(s):** Wave Community Newspapers, Inc., 2621 W. 54th St., Los Angeles, CA 90043. TEL 213-727-1117; Ed. Art Auglar; Pub. Ric Trent; pub. size: standard; circ. 21,662(controlled).

US
CARSON WAVE. Wed. $65/6 mos.; $125/yr. 2621 W. 54th St., Los Angeles, CA 90043. TEL 213-290-3000; FAX 213-291-0219. **Owner(s):** Wave Community Newspapers, Inc., 2621 W. 54th St., Los Angeles, CA 90043. TEL 213-727-1117; Pub. Ric Trent; adv.; bk.rev.; pub. size: broadsheet; circ. 14,082(paid).

US
CIVIC CENTER NEWSOURCE. Mon. $.50 newsstand; $30/yr. 210 S. Spring St., Los Angeles, CA 90012-3710. TEL 213-628-4384; FAX 213-687-3886. **Owner(s):** Metropolitan News Co., 210 S. Spring St., Los Angeles, CA 90012-3710. TEL 213-628-4384; FAX 213-687-3886; Ed. Roger M. Grace; Pub. S. John Babigian; pub. size: tabloid; circ. 7,500(paid). **Wire Service(s):** AP.

US
COMPTON WAVE. Wed. $65/6 mos.; $125/yr. 2621 W. 54th St., Los Angeles, CA 90043. TEL 213-290-3000; FAX 213-291-0219. **Owner(s):** Wave Community Newspapers, Inc., 2621 W. 54th St., Los Angeles, CA 90043. TEL 213-727-1117; Pub. Ric Trent; adv.; pub. size: broadsheet; circ. 26,283(paid).

US
CULVER CITY STAR. Wed. free; $78/yr. in state. 2621 W. 54th St., Los Angeles, CA 90043. TEL 213-290-3000; FAX 213-292-8289. **Owner(s):** Wave Community Newspapers, Inc., 2621 W. 54th St., Los Angeles, CA 90043. TEL 213-290-3000; adv. contact: Ric Trent. pub. size: standard; circ. 29,109(free & paid).

US
DOWNEY HERALD AMERICAN. 1953. Thu. $.25 newsstand; $78/yr. in state. 2621 W. 54th St., Los Angeles, CA 90043. TEL 213-290-3000; FAX 213-291-0219. **Owner(s):** Wave Community Newspapers, Inc., 2621 W. 54th St., Los Angeles, CA 90043. TEL 213-727-1117; Ed. Art Aquilar; Pub. Ric Trent; adv. contact: Ric Trent. pub. size: broadsheet; circ. 25,747(paid).

US
EAGLE ROCK SENTINEL. Wed. free deliv.; $125/yr. mailed. 2621 W. 54th St., Los Angeles, CA 90043. TEL 213-290-3000; FAX 213-292-8289. **Owner(s):** Wave Community Newspapers, Inc., 2621 W. 54th St., Los Angeles, CA 90043. TEL 213-727-1711; Ed. Art Aguilar; Pub. Ric Trent; adv.; pub. size: broadsheet; circ. 8,660(paid).

US
EAST L.A./COMMERCE TRIBUNE. Wed. $.25 newsstand; $78/yr. in state. 2621 W. 54th St., Los Angeles, CA 90043. TEL 213-290-3000; FAX 213-291-0219. **Owner(s):** Wave Community Newspapers, Inc., 2621 W. 54th St., Los Angeles, CA 90043. TEL 213-727-1117; Ed. Art Aquilar; Pub. Ric Trent; adv. contact: Tanner Oliver. pub. size: standard; circ. 19,059(paid).

US
EASTSIDE JOURNAL. Wed. $78/yr. in state. 2621 W. 54th St., Los Angeles, CA 90043. TEL 213-290-3000; FAX 213-291-2019. **Owner(s):** Wave Community Newspapers, Inc., 2621 W. 54th St., Los Angeles, CA 90043. TEL 213-727-1117; Pub. C.Z. Wilson; adv. contact: Rick Billings. pub. size: broadsheet; circ. 16,075(paid).

US
EL SERENO STAR. Wed. $78/yr. in state. 2621 W. 54th St., Los Angeles, CA 90043. TEL 213-290-3000; FAX 213-291-0219. **Owner(s):** Wave Community Newspapers, Inc., 2621 W. 54th St., Los Angeles, CA 90043; Pub. C.Z. Wilson; adv. contact: Rick Billings. pub. size: broadsheet; circ. 7,650(paid).

US
HIGHLAND PARK NEWS/HERALD/JOURNAL. 1905. Wed. free; $125/yr. mailed. 2621 W. 54th St., Los Angeles, CA 90043. TEL 213-290-3000; FAX 213-292-8289. **Owner(s):** Wave Community Newspapers, Inc., 2621 W. 54th St., Los Angeles, CA 90043; Ed. Art Aguilar; Pub. Ric Trent; adv. contact: Marty Vasquez. pub. size: broadsheet; circ. 15,250(free & paid).

US
INGLEWOOD/HAWTHORNE WAVE. Wed. free deliv.; $55/6 mo.; $78/yr. in state. 2621 W. 54th St., Los Angeles, CA 90043. TEL 213-290-3000; FAX 213-292-8289. **Owner(s):** Wave Community Newspapers, Inc., 2621 W. 54th St., Los Angeles, CA 90043. TEL 213-727-1117; Pub. Ric Trent; adv. contact: Ric Trent. pub. size: broadsheet; circ. 281,000(controlled & free).

US
JEWISH JOURNAL OF GREATER LOS ANGELES, THE. Fri. $23.50/yr.; $236/yr. out of area. 3660 Wilshire Blvd., Ste. 204, Los Angeles, CA 90010. TEL 213-738-7778; FAX 213-386-9501. **Owner(s):** Ed Brennglass, 3660 Wilshire Blvd., Ste. 204, Los Angeles, CA 90010. TEL 213-738-7778; Ed. Marlene Marks; Pub. Ed Brennglass; circ. 55,000(paid).

LOS ANGELES, CA

Weeklies

L.A. WEEKLY. Thu. free; $1 newsstand Orange cy. 6715 Sunset Blvd., Los Angeles, CA 90028. TEL 213-465-9909; FAX 213-465-3220. **Owner(s):** Stern Publishing, Inc., 667 Madison Ave., New York, NY 10021. TEL 212-308-3336; Ed. Sue Horton; Pub. Michael Sigman; adv. contact: Leslie Prentice. pub. size: broadsheet; circ. 200,000(free & paid).

LINCOLN HEIGHTS BULLETIN-NEWS. Wed. free; $125/yr. mailed. 2621 W. 54th St., Los Angeles, CA 90043. TEL 213-290-3000; FAX 213-291-0219. **Owner(s):** Central News-Wave Publications, 621 West 54th St., Los Angeles, CA 90043; Ed. Art Aguilar; Pub. Ric Trent; adv.; pub. size: broadsheet; circ. 9,125(free & paid).

LOS ANGELES INDEPENDENT. 1935. s-w.: Wed. & Sat. free; $60/yr. in cy. mailed. 4201 Wilshire Blvd., Ste. 600, Los Angeles, CA 90010. TEL 213-932-6397; FAX 213-932-8285. **Owner(s):** National Media, Inc., 4201 Wilshire Blvd., Ste. 600, Los Angeles, CA 90010. TEL 213-932-6397; Ed. Brian Lewis; Pub. Michael Laxineta; adv.; photos; pub. size: broadsheet; circ. 200,000(controlled). **Wire Service(s):** CiNS.

LYNWOOD PRESS. 1922. Wed. free; $125/yr. mailed. 2621 W. 54th St., Los Angeles, CA 90043. TEL 213-290-3000; FAX 213-291-0219. **Owner(s):** Wave Community Newspapers, Inc., 2621 W. 54th St., Los Angeles, CA 90043. TEL 213-290-3000; Pub. Ric Trent; adv. contact: Ric Trent. pub. size: broadsheet; circ. 24,006(controlled).

MESA TRIBUNE WAVE. Wed. free; $125/yr. mailed. 2621 W. 54th St., Los Angeles, CA 90043. TEL 213-290-3000; FAX 213-292-8289. **Owner(s):** Wave Community Newspapers, Inc., 2621 W. 54th St., Los Angeles, CA 90043. TEL 213-290-3000; Pub. Ric Trent; adv. contact: Ric Trent. pub. size: broadsheet; circ. 31,609(controlled).

MONTEBELLO NEWS. Wed. $78/yr. in state. 2621 W. 54th St., Los Angeles, CA 90043. TEL 213-727-1117; FAX 213-291-2019. **Owner(s):** Wave Community Newspapers, Inc, 2621 W. 54th St., Los Angeles, CA 90043. TEL 213-290-3000; FAX 213-291-0219; Pub. Ric Trent; adv.; pub. size: broadsheet; circ. 17,919(paid).

MONTEREY PARK PROGRESS. Wed. $.25 newsstand; $78/yr. in state. 2621 W. 54th St., Los Angeles, CA 90043. TEL 213-290-3000; FAX 213-291-0219. **Owner(s):** Wave Community Newspapers, Inc., 2621 W. 54th St., Los Angeles, CA 90043. TEL 213-290-3000; Ed. Ray Babcock; Pub. Ric Trent; adv. contact: Ric Trent. pub. size: broadsheet; circ. 17,788(paid).

MT. WASHINGTON STAR REVIEW. Wed. $78/yr. in state. 2621 W. 54th St., Los Angeles, CA 90043. TEL 213-290-3000; FAX 213-291-0219. **Owner(s):** Wave Community Newspapers, Inc., 2621 W. 54th St., Los Angeles, CA 90043. TEL 213-727-1117; Pub. C.Z. Wilson; adv. contact: Rick Billings. pub. size: broadsheet; circ. 5,425(paid).

NORWALK HERALD AMERICAN. Thu. $.25 newsstand; $78/yr. in state. 2621 W. 54th St., Los Angeles, CA 90043. TEL 213-290-3000; FAX 213-291-0219. **Owner(s):** Wave Community Newspapers, Inc., 2621 W. 54th St., Los Angeles, CA 90043. TEL 213-290-3000; Ed. Art Aquilar; Pub. Ric Trent; adv. contact: Ric Trent. pub. size: broadsheet; circ. 24,305(paid).

▼**OC WEEKLY.** 1995. w. free. 6715 Sunset Blvd., Los Angeles, CA 90028. TEL 213-465-9909; FAX 213-465-3220. **Owner(s):** Stern Publishing, Inc., 393 Jericho Tpke., Mineola, NY 11501-1205. TEL 516-877-7373; Ed. Sue Horton; Pub. Michael Sigman; pub. size: tabloid; circ. 55,000(free).

PARK LABREA NEWS/BEVERLY PRESS. 1947. Thu. free; $50/yr. mailed. 142 S. Fairfax Ave., Los Angeles, CA 90036. TEL 213-933-5518; FAX 213-933-5812. **Owner(s):** Michael & Karen Villalpando, 142 S. Fairfax Ave., Los Angeles, CA 90036. TEL 213-933-5518; FAX 213-933-5812; Ed. Marianne Love; Pub. Michael Villalpando; adv.; pub. size: tabloid; circ. 13,100(controlled).

PICO RIVERA NEWS. Wed. free; $125/yr. mailed. 2621 W. 54th St., Los Angeles, CA 90043. TEL 213-290-3000; FAX 213-291-0219. **Owner(s):** Wave Community Newspapers, Inc., 262 W. 54th St., Los Angeles, CA 90043. TEL 213-290-3000; Ed. Art Aguilar; Pub. Ric Trent; adv.; pub. size: broadsheet; circ. 15,133(free & paid).

PRESS, THE. Wed. free home deliv.; $100/yr. mailed. 2621 W. 54th St., Los Angeles, CA 90043. TEL 213-290-3000; FAX 213-219-0219. **Owner(s):** Wave Community Newspapers, Inc., 2621 W. 54th St., Los Angeles, CA 90043. TEL 213-727-1711; adv.; pub. size: broadsheet; circ. 12,888(controlled & free). **Wire Service(s):** CNS. **Formerly:** Huntington Park Bulletin.

RIVERSIDE BULLETIN, THE. Thu. $.25 newsstand; $10/yr. 210 S. Spring St., Los Angeles, CA 90012-3710. TEL 213-628-4384; FAX 213-687-3886. **Owner(s):** Metropolitan News Co., 210 S. Spring St., Los Angeles, CA 90012-3710. TEL 213-628-4384; FAX 213-687-3886; Ed. Roger M. Grace; Pub. Roger M. Grace; pub. size: standard; circ. 500(paid). **Wire Service(s):** AP.

SAN BERNARDINO BULLETIN, THE. Tue. $.25 newsstand; $10/yr. 210 S. Spring St., Los Angeles, CA 90012-3710. TEL 213-628-4384; FAX 213-687-3886. **Owner(s):** Metropolitan News Co., 210 S. Spring St., Los Angeles, CA 90012-3710. TEL 213-628-4384; FAX 213-687-3886; Ed. Roger M. Grace; Pub. Roger M. Grace; pub. size: standard; circ. 300(paid). **Wire Service(s):** AP.

SAN GABRIEL PROGRESS. Wed. $78/yr. in state. 2621 W. 54th St., Los Angeles, CA 90043. TEL 213-290-3000; FAX 213-291-0219. **Owner(s):** Wave Community Newspapers, Inc., 2621 W. 54th St., Los Angeles, CA 90043. TEL 213-290-3000; Ed. Ray Babcock; Pub. Ric Trent; adv. contact: Ric Trent. bk.rev.; pub. size: standard; circ. 16,272(paid).

SANTA FE SPRINGS NEWS. Wed. $.25 newsstand; $78/yr. in state. 2621 W. 54th St., Los Angeles, CA 90043. TEL 213-290-3000; FAX 213-291-0219. **Owner(s):** Wave Community Newspapers, Inc., 2621 W. 54th St., Los Angeles, CA 90043. TEL 213-290-3000; Ed. Art Aquilar; Pub. Ric Trent; adv. contact: Ric Trent. bk.rev.; pub. size: standard; circ. 2,530(paid).

SOUTH GATE PRESS. Wed. $78/yr. in state. 2621 W. 54th St., Los Angeles, CA 90043. TEL 213-290-3000; FAX 213-291-0219. **Owner(s):** Wave Community Newspapers, Inc., 2621 W. 54th St., Los Angeles, CA 90043. TEL 213-290-3000; Ed. Dennis Coffeman; Pub. Ric Trent; circ. 23,822(controlled).

SOUTH SAN GABRIEL/ROSEMEAD PROGRESS. Wed. $78/yr. in state. 2621 W. 54th St., Los Angeles, CA 90043. TEL 213-290-3000; FAX 213-291-0219. **Owner(s):** Wave Community Newspapers, Inc., 2621 W. 54th St., Los Angeles, CA 90043. TEL 213-290-3000; Ed. Ray Babcock; Pub. Ric Trent; adv. contact: Ric Trent. bk.rev.; pub. size: standard; circ. 14,447(paid).

SOUTHSIDE JOURNAL. 1923. Wed. free; $78/yr. out of area mailed. 2621 W. 54th St., Los Angeles, CA 90043. TEL 213-290-3000; FAX 213-291-0219. **Owner(s):** Wave Community Newspapers, Inc., 2621 W. 54th St., Los Angeles, CA 90043. TEL 213-290-3000; Pub. C.Z. Wilson; adv. contact: Florence Dinwidd. pub. size: broadsheet; circ. 21,300(free).

SOUTHWEST WAVE/NEWS. 1918. Wed. free in area; $125/yr. mailed. 2621 W. 54th St., Los Angeles, CA 90043. TEL 310-290-3000; FAX 310-292-8289. **Owner(s):** Wave Community Newspapers, Inc., 2621 W. 54th St., Los Angeles, CA 90043. TEL 310-290-3000; Pub. Ric Trent; adv. contact: Ric Trent. pub. size: broadsheet; circ. 30,000(free & paid).

TOPICS SUN WAVE. Wed. free deliv.; $78/yr. in state. 2621 W. 54th St., Los Angeles, CA 90043. TEL 213-290-3000; FAX 213-292-8289. **Owner(s):** Wave Community Newspapers, Inc., 2621 W. 54th St., Los Angeles, CA 90043. TEL 213-290-3000; FAX 213-292-8289; Pub. Ric Trent; adv. contact: Ric Trent. bk.rev.; pub. size: broadsheet; circ. 30,731(controlled).

WESTCHESTER STAR. Wed. $78/yr. in state. 2621 W. 54th St., Los Angeles, CA 90043. TEL 213-290-3000; FAX 213-292-8289. **Owner(s):** Wave Community Newspapers, Inc., 2621 W. 54th St., Los Angeles, CA 90043; Pub. Ric Trent; adv.; pub. size: standard; circ. 9,956(paid).

LOS BANOS

LOS BANOS ENTERPRISE. 1891. s-w.: Wed. & Sat. $.50 newsstand; $17.16/6 mos. in cy.; $30.03/yr. in cy.; $56.84/yr. out of cy. 1253 W. I St., Los Banos, CA 93635. TEL 209-826-3831; FAX 209-826-2005. **Owner(s):** U.S. Media Group, P.O. Box 227, Crystal City, MO 63019; Pub. Rhonda Lowe; adv.; pub. size: broadsheet; circ. 7,000(paid).

WEEKLY NEWSPAPERS

MT. SHASTA, CA   10539

LOS GATOS
US
LOS GATOS WEEKLY-TIMES. 1881. Tue. $.50 newsstand; $26/yr. in city mailed; $52/yr. elsewhere. 245 Almendra Ave., Los Gatos, CA 95030. TEL 408-354-3110; FAX 408-354-3917. **Owner(s):** Metro Newspapers, Inc., 590 S. First St., San Jose, CA 95113. TEL 408-298-8000; Ed. Dale Bryant; Pub. David Cohen; adv.; pub. size: tabloid; circ. 19,000(paid).
Formerly: Los Gatos Times Observer.

MALIBU
US   ISSN 0191-7307
MALIBU SURFSIDE NEWS. 1972. Thu. $25/yr. local; $45/yr. out of state. 28990 Pacific Coast Hwy., Malibu, CA 90265. TEL 310-457-2112; FAX 310-457-9908; E-mail: mailibunews@eworld.com. **Owner(s):** A.C. Soble/Malibu News Enterprises, 28990 Pacific Coast Hwy., Malibu, CA 90265. TEL 310-457-2112; Ed. A.C. Soble; Pub. A.C. Soble; adv. contact: Christine Stoddard. pub. size: tabloid; circ. 13,500(controlled).

US   ISSN 1050-4931
MALIBU TIMES. 1946. Thu. $.25 newsstand; $45/yr. 3864 Las Flores Canyon Rd., Malibu, CA 90265. TEL 310-456-5507; FAX 310-456-8976; E-mail: agyork@malibutimes.com. **Owner(s):** Arnold G. & Karen P. York, P.O. Box 1127, Malibu, CA 90265. TEL 310-456-5507; Ed. Arnold G. York; Pub. Arnold G. York; adv.; photos; bk.rev.; pub. size: broadsheet; circ. 12,500(paid).

MAMMOTH LAKES
US
MAMMOTH TIMES. 1987. Thu. free newsstand; $40/yr. mailed. 452 Old Mammoth Rd., Mammoth Lakes, CA 93546. TEL 619-934-3929; FAX 619-934-3951; E-mail: mamtimes@aol.com. **Owner(s):** New Times Publishing, Inc., 452 Old Mammoth Rd., Mammoth Lakes, CA 93546. TEL 619-934-3929; FAX 619-934-3951; Pub. Wally Hofmann; adv. contact: Greg Myers. photos; pub. size: tabloid; circ. 13,000(free & paid).

US   ISSN 1052-5300
REVIEW HERALD, THE. 1879. Thu. $32.33/yr. local; $46.33/yr. out of state. 1566 Tavern Rd., Mammoth Lakes, CA 93546. TEL 619-934-8544; FAX 619-934-7385. **Owner(s):** Register Review Publishing Co., 450 E. Line St., Bishop, CA 93514. TEL 619-873-3535; Ed. Dave Reynolds. pub. size: broadsheet; circ. 2,500(paid). **Wire Service(s):** AP.
Formerly: Mono Herald & Bridgeport Chronicle.

MANHATTAN BEACH
US
BEACH REPORTER, THE. 1977. Thu. free; $140/yr. in cy. mailed. 500 S. Sepulveda, Ste. 213, Manhattan Beach, CA 90266. TEL 310-374-4040; FAX 310-379-8570. **Owner(s):** National Media, Inc., P.O. Box 383, Manhattan Beach, CA 90266. TEL 310-374-4040; FAX 310-379-8570; Ed. Cara Murphy; Pub. Richard Frank; adv.; pub. size: tabloid; circ. 61,000(controlled).

MARIPOSA
US
MARIPOSA GAZETTE. 1854. Wed. $.30 newsstand; $18.54/yr. in state. 5081 Jones St., Mariposa, CA 95338. TEL 209-966-2500; FAX 209-966-3384. **Owner(s):** C. Ruth & Dalmar J. Campbell, P.O. Box 38, Mariposa, CA 95338. TEL 209-966-2500; FAX 209-966-3384; Ed. Jerry Rankin; Pub. Dalmar J. Campbell; adv.; pub. size: broadsheet; circ. 5,100(paid).

MOUNTAIN LIFE. 1970. Tue. free; $16/yr. in state; $21.45/yr. out of state. 5081 Jones St., Mariposa, CA 95338. TEL 209-966-2500; FAX 209-966-3384. **Owner(s):** C. Ruth & Dalmar J. Campbell, P.O. Box 38, Mariposa, CA 95338. TEL 209-966-2500; Ed. Jerry Rankin; Pub. Dalmar Campbell; adv.; pub. size: tabloid; circ. 12,000(free & paid).

MARTINEZ
US
MARTINEZ NEWS GAZETTE. 1858. 3/wk.: Tue., Thu., Sat. $.25 newsstand; $4/wk. carrier; $7/mo. mailed. 615 Estudillo St., Martinez, CA 94553. TEL 510-228-6400; FAX 510-228-1536. **Owner(s):** Gibson Publications, Inc., 544 Maryland St., Vallejo, CA 94589. TEL 707-643-1706; Ed. Robert V. Osmond; Pub. David Payne; adv. contact: Joel Gordiejew. photos; bk.rev.; pub. size: broadsheet; circ. 35,000(free & paid).

MENDOCINO
US
MENDOCINO BEACON, THE. 1877. Thu. $.50 newsstand; $20/yr. in cy.; $30/yr. out of cy. 45066 Ukiah St., Mendocino, CA 95460. TEL 707-937-5874; FAX 707-937-0825. **Owner(s):** Stephens Group, Inc., P.O. Box 1359, Fort Smith, AR 72902. TEL 501-785-7801; Ed. Kathryn Lee; Pub. Sharon Brewer; adv.: $5.35/SAU. photos; pub. size: standard; circ. 2,400(paid).

MENLO PARK
US   ISSN 0192-0111
COUNTRY ALMANAC. 1923. Wed. $.50 newsstand; $20/yr. in area mailed; $30/yr. elsewhere mailed. 3525 Alameda De Las Pulgas, Menlo Park, CA 94025-6558. TEL 415-854-2626; FAX 415-854-0677. **Owner(s):** Embarcadero Publishing Co., 703 High St., Palo Alto, CA 94302. TEL 415-326-8210; Ed. Richard Hine; Pub. Tom Gibboney; adv. contact: Connie Colton. photos; pub. size: tabloid; circ. 17,500(free & paid).
Formerly: Menlo Park Almanac.

MILL VALLEY
US   ISSN 0048-2641
PACIFIC SUN. 1963. Wed. free; $25/yr. in cy. mailed. 21 Corte Madera Ave., Mill Valley, CA 94941. TEL 415-383-4500; FAX 415-383-4159. **Owner(s):** Pacific Sun Publishing Co., Inc., 21 Corte Madera Ave., Mill Valley, CA 94941. TEL 415-383-4500; Ed. Linda Xiques; Pub. Stephen McNamara; adv. contact: Kathy Clos. pub. size: broadsheet; circ. 44,000(free).

MILPITAS
US
BERRYESSA SUN. 1992. m. $.25 newsstand; $17/yr. 1615A S. Main St., Milpitas, CA 95035. TEL 408-262-2454; FAX 408-263-9710. **Owner(s):** Mort Levine, 1615A S. Main St., Milpitas, CA 95035. TEL 408-262-2454; Ed. Rob Devincenzi; Pub. Mort Levine; adv. contact: Linda Schmitz. pub. size: tabloid; circ. 20,000(paid).

US   ISSN 0745-6212
MILPITAS POST. 1955. Thu. $.50 newsstand; $20/yr. in town; $30/yr. out of town. 1615A S. Main St., Milpitas, CA 95035. TEL 408-262-2454; FAX 408-263-9710. **Owner(s):** Mort Levine, 1615A S. Main St., Milpitas, CA 95035. TEL 408-262-2454; Ed. Rob Devincenzi; Pub. Mort Levine; adv. contact: Linda Schmitz. pub. size: tabloid; circ. 23,000(paid).

MORENO VALLEY
US
VALLEY TIMES, THE. 1952. Thu. $.50 newsstand; $12/yr. 25873 Alessandro Blvd., Moreno Valley, CA 92553. TEL 909-242-7614; FAX 909-247-1920. **Owner(s):** Stephens Group, Inc., P.O. Box 1359, Fort Smith, AK 72902. TEL 501-785-7810; Ed. Larry Venus; Pub. Mel Harkavy; adv. contact: Bob Pay. photos; pub. size: standard; circ. 7,300(paid).
Formerly: Butterfield Express, The.

MORGAN HILL
US
MORGAN HILL TIMES. 1894. s-w.: Tue. & Fri. $.50 newsstand; $34.40/yr. local. 30 E. Third St., Morgan Hill, CA 95037. TEL 408-779-4106; FAX 408-779-3886. **Owner(s):** U.S. Media Group, P.O. Box 227, Crystal City, MO 63019; Ed. Walt Glines; Pub. Paula Mabry; adv. contact: Arlene Hudson. photos; pub. size: broadsheet; circ. 3,800(controlled). **Wire Service(s):** McClatchy News Service, SHNA.

MORRO BAY
US
CENTRAL COAST SUN-BULLETIN. 1931. Wed. $.50 newsstand; $26/yr. home deliv.; $45/yr. mailed. 1149 Market St., Morro Bay, CA 93442. TEL 805-772-7346; FAX 805-772-7044. **Owner(s):** Scripps-Howard, 312 Walnut St., 28th Fl., Cincinnati, OH 45202. TEL 513-977-3000; Ed. Richard Palmer. pub. size: broadsheet; circ. 8,000(paid).

MT. SHASTA
US
MOUNT SHASTA HERALD. 1888. Wed. $.50 newsstand; $22.50/yr. in cy.; $27.50/yr. out of cy. 924B N. Mt. Shasta Blvd., Mt. Shasta, CA 96067-0127. TEL 916-926-5214; FAX 916-926-4166. **Owner(s):** American Publishing Co., 606 N. Van Buren, P.O. Box 520, Marion, IL 62959. TEL 618-993-1711; Ed. Steve Gerace; Pub. Genny Axtman; adv. contact: Genny Axtman. pub. size: standard; circ. 4,200(paid).

Weeklies

10540 NAPA, CA

WEEKLY NEWSPAPERS

NAPA
US
NAPA COUNTY RECORD. 1947. Mon. $20/yr. 1320 Second St., Napa, CA 94559. TEL 707-252-8877. **Owner(s):** David W. Barker, 520 Third St., Napa, CA 94559. TEL 707-252-8877; Ed. Nancy Hutchins; Pub. David W. Barker; adv. contact: David W. Barker. photos; bk.rev.; pub. size: broadsheet; circ. 6,000(controlled & paid).

NEEDLES
US
NEEDLES DESERT STAR. 1888. Wed. $.50 newsstand; $13.95/yr. in city; $19/yr. in cy.; $27/yr. out of cy. 911 Third St., Needles, CA 92363-2935. TEL 619-326-2222; FAX 619-326-3480. **Owner(s):** News West Publishing Co., P.O. Box 28429, San Diego, CA 92198. TEL 619-326-2222; FAX 619-326-6480; Ed. Robin Richards; Pub. Martin Cody; adv.: $10.50/SAU. photos; pub. size: broadsheet; circ. 5,000(paid).

NOVATO
US
NOVATO ADVANCE. 1922. Wed. $3.50/mo. home deliv.; $4/mo. in cy. 1068 Machin Ave., Novato, CA 94945. TEL 415-892-1516; FAX 415-897-0940. **Owner(s):** Scripps Enterprises, P.O. Box 1109, Herndon, VA 22070; Ed. John Jackson; Pub. John Burns; pub. size: standard; circ. 15,000(free & paid).

OAKDALE
US
OAKDALE LEADER. 1894. Wed. $.50 newsstand; $25/yr. in cy.; $32/yr. out of cy.; $20/yr. senior citizens. 122 S. Third Ave., Oakdale, CA 95361. TEL 209-847-3021; FAX 209-847-9750. **Owner(s):** Live Oak Publishing, 122 S. Third Ave., Oakdale, CA 95361; Ed. Steve Breen; Pub. S.L. Cook; adv. contact: Melinda Owens. pub. size: broadsheet; circ. 10,000(free & paid).

OAKLAND
US
BAY AREA PRESS. 1970. bi-w.: Fri. free; $20/yr. mailed. Grand Lake Sta., Oakland, CA 94610. TEL 510-428-2000. **Owner(s):** Oakland Press Publications, P.O. Box 10151, Oakland, CA 94610. TEL 510-547-4000; Ed. George Epstein; Pub. George Epstein; adv.; photos; bk.rev.; pub. size: tabloid; circ. 7,000(free).

US
MONTCLARION. 1943. s-w.: Tue. & Fri. $.50 newsstand; $30/yr. in cy. 5707 Redwood Rd., Oakland, CA 94619. TEL 510-339-4060; FAX 510-339-4066. **Owner(s):** Chip & Mary Brown, 6208 La Salle Ave., Oakland, CA 94611. TEL 510-339-8777; Ed. Chris Treadway; Pub. Chip Brown; adv. contact: Jan Wasserman. photos; bk.rev.; pub. size: broadsheet; circ. 63,000(controlled). **Wire Service(s):** CNS.

US
PIEDMONTER, THE. 1916. w. $.50 newsstand; $30/yr. 5707 Redwood Rd., Oakland, CA 94619-2414. TEL 510-339-4050; FAX 510-339-4066. **Owner(s):** Hills Newspapers, Inc., 6208 LaSalle Ave., Piedmont, CA 94611. TEL 510-339-8777; Ed. Don McConnell. adv. contact: Jan Wasserman. pub. size: standard; circ. 7,000(paid).

OJAI
US
OJAI VALLEY NEWS. 1891. s-w.: Wed. & Fri. $.50 newsstand. 408 Bryant Cir., Ste. A, Ojai, CA 93023. TEL 805-646-1476; FAX 805-646-4281. **Owner(s):** Ren Adam, 408 Bryant Cir., Ste. A, Ojai, CA 93023. TEL 805-646-1476; Ed. Tim Dewar. adv.; photos; pub. size: broadsheet; circ. 11,100(free & paid).

ORLAND
US
ORLAND PRESS-REGISTER. 1868. 3/wk.: Mon., Wed., Fri. $.50/newsstand; $48/yr. carrier; $60/yr. in cy. mailed; $63/yr. out of cy.; $40/yr. senior citizens carrier; $50/yr. in cy.; $55/yr. out of cy. 407 Walker St., Orland, CA 95963. TEL 916-865-4433; FAX 916-865-3110. **Owner(s):** Tri-County Newspapers, Inc., 101 Airport Rd., Willows, CA 95988. TEL 916-865-4433; Ed. Kevin Askeland; Pub. Darryl Phillips; adv. contact: Christine A. Stifter. pub. size: broadsheet; circ. 5,000(paid).

OROVILLE
US
DIGGER SHOPPER & NEWS, THE. 1977. Thu. free. 2057 Mitchell Ave., Oroville, CA 95966. TEL 916-533-2170; FAX 916-533-2181; E-mail: digger@cncnet.com; URL: http://www.oroville-city.com. **Owner(s):** David Miller, 2057 Mitchell Ave., Oroville, CA 95966. TEL 916-533-2170; Pub. David Miller; adv.; pub. size: tabloid; circ. 19,000(free).

PACIFICA
US
PACIFICA TRIBUNE. 1947. Wed. $.50 newsstand; $21/yr. carrier; $24/yr. mailed in cy.; $25/yr. in state; $27/yr. out of state; $18/yr. senior citizens. 59 Aura Vista, Pacifica, CA 94044. TEL 415-359-6666; FAX 415-359-3821; E-mail: pactrib@hax.com; URL: http://www.ci.pacifica.ca.us/tribune. **Owner(s):** Main Street Media, Houston, TX; Ed. Chris Hunter; Pub. Chris Hunter; adv.; photos; pub. size: broadsheet; circ. 10,500(paid).

PACIFIC PALISADES
US
NORTH SHORE SHOPPER. 1928. Thu. free. 839 Via De La Paz, Pacific Palisades, CA 90272. TEL 310-454-1321; FAX 310-454-1078. **Owner(s):** Small Newspaper Group, 8 Dearborn Sq., Kankakee, IL 60901; Ed. Bill Bruns; Pub. Roberta Donohue; adv. contact: Don Oswald. pub. size: tabloid; circ. 17,600(free).

US
PALISADIAN-POST. 1928. Thu. $.50 newsstand; $24/yr. 839 Via De La Paz, Pacific Palisades, CA 90272. TEL 310-454-1321; FAX 310-454-1078. **Owner(s):** Small Newspaper Group, 8 Dearborn Sq., Kankakee, IL 60901; Ed. Bill Bruns; Pub. Roberta Donohue; adv. contact: Don Osward. pub. size: broadsheet; circ. 5,000(paid).

PALM DESERT
US
BLYTHE ADVERTISER. 1955. Tue. free. 73-400 Hwy. 111, Palm Desert, CA 92260. TEL 760-346-1729; FAX 760-346-7350. **Owner(s):** Associated Desert Shoppers, Inc., 73-400 Hwy. 111, Palm Desert, CA 92260. TEL 760-345-1729; Pub. Hal Paradis; adv.; pub. size: tabloid; circ. 7,400(free).

US
DESERT MOBILE HOME NEWS. 1955. w. free. 38-155 Story Creek, Palm Desert, CA 92261. TEL 619-568-6633; FAX 619-568-0603. **Owner(s):** Robert K. & Judith A. Brownell, 38-155 Story Creek, Palm Desert, CA 92261. TEL 619-568-6633; FAX 619-568-6633; Ed. Robert K. Brownell; Pub. Robert K. Brownell; adv. contact: Judith A. Brownell. pub. size: tabloid.

US
EAST RIVERSIDE ADVERTISER. Thu. free. 73-400 Hwy. 111, Palm Desert, CA 92260. TEL 760-346-1729; FAX 760-346-7350. **Owner(s):** Associated Desert Shoppers, Inc., 73-400 Hwy. 111, Palm Desert, CA 92260. TEL 760-346-1729; FAX 760-346-7350; Pub. Hal Paradis; adv.; pub. size: tabloid; circ. 17,000(free).

US
INDIO ADVERTISER. 1955. w. free. 73-400 Hwy. 111, Palm Desert, CA 92260. TEL 760-346-1729; FAX 760-346-7350. **Owner(s):** Associated Desert Shoppers, Inc., 73-400 Hwy. 111, Palm Desert, CA 92260. TEL 760-346-1729; FAX 760-346-7350; Pub. Hal Paradis; adv.; pub. size: tabloid; circ. 15,000(free).

US
MORONGO BASIN. Wed. free. 73-400 Hwy. 111, Palm Desert, CA 92260. TEL 760-346-1729; FAX 760-346-7350. **Owner(s):** Associated Desert Shoppers, Inc., 73-400 Hwy. 111, Palm Desert, CA 92260. TEL 760-346-1729; FAX 760-346-7350; Ed. Hal Parndis; Pub. Hal Parndis; adv.; pub. size: tabloid; circ. 13,900(free).

US
PALM DESERT ADVERTISER. 1955. Thu. free. 73-400 Hwy. 111, Palm Desert, CA 92260. TEL 760-346-1729; FAX 760-346-7350. **Owner(s):** Associated Desert Shoppers, Inc., 73-400 Hwy. 111, Palm Desert, CA 92260. TEL 760-346-1729; FAX 760-346-7350; Pub. Hal Paradis; adv.; pub. size: tabloid; circ. 10,000(free).

US
PALM SPRING ADVERTISER. 1955. w. free. 73-400 Hwy. 111, Palm Desert, CA 92260. TEL 760-346-1729; FAX 760-346-7350. **Owner(s):** Associated Desert Shoppers, Inc., 73-400 Hwy. 111, Palm Desert, CA 92260. TEL 760-346-1729; FAX 760-346-7350; Pub. Hal Paradis; adv.; pub. size: tabloid; circ. 11,250(free).

WEEKLY NEWSPAPERS

PALO ALTO
US   ISSN 0199-1159
PALO ALTO WEEKLY. 1979. s-w.: Wed. & Fri. $.50 newsstand; $40/yr. 703 High St., Palo Alto, CA 94301. TEL 415-326-8210; FAX 415-326-3928; E-mail: editor@paweekly.com. **Owner(s):** Embarcadero Publishing Co., P.O. Box 1610, Palo Alto, CA 94302. TEL 415-326-8210; FAX 415-326-3928; Ed. Paul Gullixson; Pub. Bill Johnson; adv. contact: Franklin Elieh. photos; bk.rev.; pub. size: tabloid; circ. 49,500(controlled & paid).

PALOS VERDES PENINSULA
US
PALOS VERDES PENINSULA NEWS. 1937. s-w.: Thu. & Sat. $.25 newsstand; $41.41/yr. P.O. Box 2609, Palos Verdes Peninsula, CA 90274. TEL 310-377-6877; FAX 310-377-4522. **Owner(s):** National Media, Inc., P.O. Box 2609, Palos Verdes Peninsula, CA 90274. TEL 310-377-6877; Ed. Michelle Fisher. adv.; photos; bk.rev.; pub. size: broadsheet; circ. 19,900(free & paid). **Wire Service(s):** CiNS.

PARADISE
US
PARADISE POST. 1945. 3/wk.: Tue., Thu., Sat. $.50 newsstand; $19.30/6 mos.; $36.50/yr. P.O. Box 70, Paradise, CA 95967. TEL 916-877-4413; FAX 916-877-1326. **Owner(s):** Roland Rebele, P.O. Drawer 70, Paradise, CA 95967. TEL 916-877-4413; Lowel Blankfort, P.O. Box 70, Paradise, CA 95967. TEL 916-877-4413; Ed. Linda Meilink; Pub. Randy Goldberg; adv. contact: Carol Peterson. pub. size: broadsheet; circ. 10,000(paid).

PASADENA
US
PASADENA WEEKLY. 1984. Fri. $65/yr. 50 S. De Lacey Ave., #200, Pasadena, CA 91105-1904. TEL 818-584-1500; FAX 818-795-0149. **Owner(s):** Pasadena Publications, Inc., 50 S. Delacey Ave., Rm. 200, Pasadena, CA 91105-1904. TEL 818-584-1500; FAX 818-795-0149; Ed. Paula Johnson; Pub. Jim Laris; adv. contact: Fred Bankston. pub. size: tabloid; circ. 35,000(controlled & paid).

PETALUMA
US
PETALUMA ARGUS-COURIER. 1855. s-w.: Tue. & Fri. $.50 newsstand; $5/mo. carrier or motor rte.; $7/mo. mailed. 830 Petaluma Blvd., N., Petaluma, CA 94952. TEL 707-762-4541; FAX 707-765-1707. **Owner(s):** Pulitzer Publishing Co., 900 N. Tucker Blvd., St. Louis, MO 63101. TEL 313-340-8000; Ed. Chris Samson; Pub. Dan Zimmerman; adv. contact: Michael Vail. pub. size: broadsheet; circ. 10,000(paid). **Wire Service(s):** AP.

POINT REYES STATION
US
POINT REYES LIGHT. 1948. Thu. $.60 newsstand; $26/yr. in cy.; $29/yr. out of cy. 11431 Hwy. 1, Point Reyes Station, CA 94956. TEL 415-663-8404; FAX 415-663-8458. **Owner(s):** Point Reyes Light, Inc., P.O. Box 210, Point Reyes Station, CA 94956. TEL 415-663-8404; FAX 415-663-8458; Don Schinske, P.O. Box 210, Point Reyes Station, CA 94956. TEL 415-663-8404; FAX 415-663-8458; Ed. David V. Mitchell; Pub. David V. Mitchell; adv. contact: Renee Shannon. pub. size: tabloid; circ. 4,500(paid).

POWAY
US
CORRIDOR NEWS. Thu. $.50 newsstand; $24/yr. in cy. 13247 Poway Rd., Poway, CA 92064. TEL 619-748-2311; FAX 619-748-7695; E-mail: editor@cts.com; URL: http://www.pomeradonews.com. **Owner(s):** Pomerado Publishing Co., Inc., 13247 Poway Rd., Poway, CA 92064. TEL 619-748-2311; FAX 619-748-7695; Ed. Steve Dreyer; Pub. David Calvert; pub. size: broadsheet; circ. 4,750(paid). **Formerly:** Rancho Penasquitos News.

US
POWAY NEWS CHIEFTAIN. 1955. Thu. $.50 newsstand; $18/yr. in cy. 13247 Poway Rd., Poway, CA 92064. TEL 619-748-2311; FAX 619-748-7695; E-mail: editor@cts.com; URL: http://www.pomeradonews.com. **Owner(s):** Pomerado Publishing Co., Inc., 13247 Poway Rd., Poway, CA 92064; Ed. Steve Dreyer; Pub. David Calvert; adv.; photos; pub. size: broadsheet; circ. 13,700(paid).

PRATHER
US
MOUNTAIN PRESS. 1973. Wed. $.25 newsstand; $9.50/yr. in cy.; $12.50/yr. out of cy. 29424 Auberry Rd., Ste. 118, Prather, CA 93651-0097. TEL 209-855-8100. **Owner(s):** Homer Scott, 29424 Auberry Rd., Prather, CA 93651. TEL 209-855-8100; Ed. Alyson Nelson. adv.; photos; bk.rev.; pub. size: tabloid; circ. 2,200(paid).

RAMONA
US
RAMONA SENTINEL. 1886. Thu. $.50 newsstand; $18/yr. in cy.; $25/yr. out of cy. 611 Main St., Ramona, CA 92065. TEL 619-789-1350; FAX 619-789-4057. **Owner(s):** Cameron Publications, Inc., 611 Main St., Romona, CA 92065; Ed. Wayne E. Green; Pub. Jackie A. Green; adv. contact: Carol Kinney. photos; pub. size: broadsheet; circ. 5,500(paid).

REDLANDS
US
REDLANDS ADVERTISER. 1955. Thu. free. 611 W. Redlands Blvd., Redlands, CA 92373. TEL 909-793-3768; FAX 909-793-8998. **Owner(s):** Associated Desert Shoppers, Inc., 73-400 Hwy. 111, Palm Desert, CA 92260. TEL 760-346-1729; FAX 760-346-7350; Pub. Hal Paradis; adv.; pub. size: tabloid; circ. 20,400(free).

REDWOOD CITY
US
REDWOOD CITY TRIBUNE. 1994. s-w.: Wed. & Sat. $.25 newsstand, $18/yr. 2317 Broadway, Ste. 110, Redwood City, CA 94063. TEL 415-367-9834; FAX 415-367-8745. **Owner(s):** Pan-Asian Venture Capital Corp., 1201 Evans Ave., San Francisco, CA 94124. TEL 415-826-1100; Ed. Amy Bell; Pub. Ted Fang; adv. contact: Porter Deese. photos; bk.rev.; pub. size: broadsheet; circ. 27,000(free).

REEDLEY
US
ORANGE COVE MOUNTAIN TIMES. 1984. Wed. $.30 newsstand; $10/yr. local; $13/yr. out of cy. 1130 G St., Reedley, CA 93654. TEL 209-638-2244; FAX 209-638-5021. **Owner(s):** Reedley Exponent, P.O. Box 432, Reedley, CA 93654. TEL 209-638-2244; Ed. Woody Miner; Pub. Fred Hall; adv.; pub. size: broadsheet; circ. 6,000(paid).

US
REEDLEY EXPONENT. 1891. Thu. $.50 newsstand; $17.50/yr. in cy. 1130 G St., Reedley, CA 93654. TEL 209-638-2244; FAX 209-638-5021. **Owner(s):** Reedley Exponent, P.O. Box 432, Reedley, CA 93654; Ed. Budd Brockett; Pub. Fred Hall; adv. contact: Janie Lucio. pub. size: tabloid; circ. 6,300(paid).

RIDGECREST
US
NEWS REVIEW. 1976. Wed. $.35 newsstand; $24/yr. in cy; $25 outside cy. 109 N. Sanders, Ridgecrest, CA 93555. TEL 760-371-4301; FAX 760-371-4304. **Owner(s):** Patricia Farris, 109 N. Sanders, Ridgecrest, CA 93555. TEL 760-371-4301; Pub. Patricia Farris; adv.; photos; bk.rev.; pub. size: tabloid; circ. 13,500(controlled).

US
SWAP SHEET. Thu. free newsstand. 619 W. Ridgecrest Blvd., Ste. D, Ridgecrest, CA 93555. TEL 619-375-5400; FAX 619-375-1901. **Owner(s):** Howard Sutton, 619 W. Ridgecrest Blvd., Ste. D, Ridgecrest, CA 93555. TEL 619-375-1901; Pub. Howard Sutton; adv.; pub. size: standard; circ. 12,000(free).

ROCKLIN
US
PLACER HERALD. 1852. Tue. $.25 newsstand; $15/yr. 5903B Sunset Blvd., Rocklin, CA 95677. TEL 916-624-9713; FAX 916-624-7469. **Owner(s):** Brehm Communications, Inc., 17065 Via del Campo, Ste. 200, San Diego, CA 92127. TEL 619-451-6200; Ed. J.T. Long; Pub. David Reese; adv.; photos; pub. size: broadsheet; circ. 5,500(paid).

ROSAMOND
US
ROSAMOND NEWS. 1988. w. $.50 newsstand; $42/yr. 2654 Diamond St., Rosamond, CA 93560-0848. TEL 805-256-0149; FAX 805-269-2139; E-mail: joycemed@pacbell.net. **Owner(s):** Joyce Media, Inc., 2654 Diamond St., Rosamond, CA 93560-0848. TEL 805-256-0249; FAX 805-269-2139; Ed. Helen Dennis; Pub. John Joyce; adv. contact: Lynne Sickler. photos; bk.rev.; pub. size: tabloid; circ. 3,100(paid). **Wire Service(s):** UPI.

10542 ROSEVILLE, CA — **WEEKLY NEWSPAPERS**

ROSEVILLE

US
ROSEVILLE PRESS-TRIBUNE. 1906. 3/wk.: Tue., Fri., Sun. $.50/day newsstand; $.75/Sun.; $8.75/mo. carrier. 188 Cirby Way, Roseville, CA 95678. TEL 916-786-6500; FAX 916-783-1183. **Owner(s):** Brehm Communications, Inc., 17065 Via del Campo, Ste. 200, San Diego, CA 92198. TEL 619-451-6200; Ed. Richard Walker. adv. contact: Angela Wood. pub. size: broadsheet; circ. 14,000(paid); Sun. 14,600(paid). **Wire Service(s):** CNS.

SACRAMENTO

US
GOLD RIVER NEWS. 1989. s-w. $35/yr. 6231 Center Mall Way, Sacramento, CA 95823-2709. TEL 916-392-5843; FAX 916-392-5843. **Owner(s):** James E. Jones, 6231 Center Mall Way, Sacramento, CA 95823-2709. TEL 916-392-5843; FAX 916-392-5843; Ed. James Jones; Pub. James Jones; adv.; photos; pub. size: tabloid.

US
SACRAMENTO BULLETIN, THE. Tue. $.25 newsstand. 1713 J St., Ste. 202, Sacramento, CA 95814. TEL 916-445-6336; FAX 916-443-5871. **Owner(s):** Metropolitan News Co., 210 S. Spring St., Los Angeles, CA 90012-3710. TEL 213-628-4384; FAX 213-687-3886; Ed. Roger M. Grace; Pub. Roger M. Grace; pub. size: standard; **Wire Service(s):** AP.

SAN BERNARDINO

US
GREEN SHEET, THE. 1955. Tue. free. 345 N. I St., San Bernardino, CA 92410. TEL 909-889-2741; FAX 909-889-8910. **Owner(s):** Associated Desert Shoppers, Inc., 74-300 Hwy. 111, Palm Desert, CA 92260. TEL 760-346-1729; FAX 760-346-7350; Pub. Hal Paradis; adv.; pub. size: standard; circ. 19,800(free).
Formerly: San Bernardino Advertiser.

US
ONTARIO ADVERTISER. 1955. w. free. 345 N. I St., San Bernardino, CA 92410. TEL 909-889-2741; FAX 909-889-8910. **Owner(s):** Associated Desert Shoppers, Inc., 73-400 Hwy. 111, Palm Desert, CA 92260. TEL 760-346-1729; FAX 760-346-7350; Pub. Hal Paradis; adv.; pub. size: tabloid; circ. 22,800(free).

US
RIALTO RECORD. 1879. Thu. free newsstand; $29/yr. mailed in cy. 1809 S. Commer Center W., San Bernardino, CA 92408. TEL 909-381-9898; FAX 909-384-0406. **Owner(s):** Gloria Macias-Harrison, Inland Empire Community Newspapers, 1809 S. Commer Center W., San Bernardino, CA 92408. TEL 909-381-9898; Ed. Syeda Jafri; Pub. Gloria Macias-Harrison; adv.; photos; pub. size: broadsheet; circ. 9,000(paid). **Wire Service(s):** AP.

US
RIVERSIDE ADVERTISER. 1955. Thu. free. 345 N. I St., San Bernardino, CA 92410. TEL 909-889-2741; FAX 909-889-8910. **Owner(s):** Associated Desert Shoppers, Inc., 73-400 Hwy. 111, Palm Desert, CA 92260. TEL 760-346-1729; FAX 760-346-7350; Pub. Hal Paradis; adv.; pub. size: tabloid; circ. 13,400(free).

US
SAN BERNARDINO ADVERTISER. Thu. free. 345 N. I St., San Bernardino, CA 92410. TEL 909-889-2741; FAX 909-889-8910. **Owner(s):** Associated Desert Shoppers, Inc., 73-400 Hwy. 111, Palm Desert, CA 92260. TEL 760-346-1729; FAX 760-346-7350; Pub. Hal Paradis; adv.; pub. size: tabloid; circ. 19,900(free).

US
VICTOR VALLEY ADVERTISER. 1955. w. free. 345 N. I St., San Bernardino, CA 92410. TEL 909-889-2741; FAX 909-889-8910. **Owner(s):** Associated Desert Shoppers, Inc., 73-400 Hwy. 111, Palm Desert, CA 92260. TEL 760-346-1729; FAX 760-346-7350; Pub. Hal Paradis; adv.; pub. size: tabloid; circ. 15,500(free).

US
WEST SAN BERNARDINO ADVERTISER. 1955. Thu. free. 345 N. I St., San Bernardino, CA 92410. TEL 909-889-2741; FAX 909-889-8910. **Owner(s):** Associated Desert Shoppers, Inc., 73-400 Hwy. 111, Palm Desert, CA 92260. TEL 760-346-1729; FAX 760-346-7350; Pub. Hal Paradis; adv.; pub. size: tabloid; circ. 18,300(free).
Formerly: White Sheet.

SAN CLEMENTE

US
POST NEWS. 1986. 3/wk.: Tue., Thu., Fri. $.25 newsstand; $9.75/mo. home deliv. 95 Avenida DelMar, San Clemente, CA 92672. TEL 714-492-5121; FAX 714-492-0401. **Owner(s):** Freedom Communications, Inc., 17666 Fitch, Irvine, CA 92614. TEL 714-553-9292; Ed. Steve Silverman; Pub. David Threshie, Jr.; adv. contact: Michelle Marquis. pub. size: broadsheet; circ. 7,500(paid).
Formerly: San Clemente News.

SAN DIEGO

US
BEACH & BAY PRESS. 1988. Thu. $38.35/yr. 4645 Cass, San Diego, CA 92109. TEL 619-270-3103; FAX 619-270-9325. **Owner(s):** San Diego Community Newspaper Group, P.O. Box 9550, San Diego, CA 92169. TEL 619-270-3103; FAX 619-270-9325; Ed. John Gregory; Pub. David Mannis; adv.; photos; pub. size: tabloid; circ. 22,500(free).

US
LA JOLLA VILLAGE NEWS/GOLDEN TRIANGE NEWS. Thu. free. 4645 Cass, San Diego, CA 92109. TEL 619-270-3103; FAX 619-270-9325. **Owner(s):** San Diego Community Newspaper Group, 4645 Cass, San Diego, CA 92109. TEL 619-270-3103; FAX 619-270-9325; Ed. John Gregory; Pub. David Mannis; adv.; pub. size: tabloid; circ. 20,000(free).

US
LOS ANGELES LOG. bi-w. $24.95/yr. 1025 Rosecrans St., San Diego, CA 92106. TEL 619-226-1608; FAX 619-226-0573. **Owner(s):** Log Newspapers, Inc., 1025 Rosecrans St., San Diego, CA 92106. TEL 619-226-1608; FAX 619-226-0573; Ed. Susan Colby. pub. size: standard; circ. 25,000(paid).

US
MIRA MESA/SCRIPPS RANCH SENTINEL. 1928. Thu. free; $35/yr. 6312 Riverdale St., San Diego, CA 92120. TEL 619-280-2985. **Owner(s):** Sarah E. Hagerty, Western States Weeklies, Inc., 6312 Riverdale St., San Diego, CA 92160. TEL 619-280-2985; Ed. Carol Burke; Pub. Sarah E. Hagerty; adv. contact: Sarah E. Hagerty. photos; bk.rev.; pub. size: tabloid; circ. 15,000(free & paid).

US
ORANGE COUNTY LOG. bi-w. $24.95/yr. 2924 Emerson St., Ste. 200, San Diego, CA 92106. TEL 619-226-1608; FAX 619-226-0573. **Owner(s):** West Coast Community Newspapers, Inc., 2841 Loker Ave. E., Carlsbad, CA 92008. TEL 619-431-4850; Ed. Susan Colby; Pub. Dan Teckenoff; pub. size: standard; circ. 15,000(paid).

US
PENINSULA BEACON, THE. 1981. Thu. free. 4645 Cass, San Diego, CA 92109. TEL 619-270-3103; FAX 619-270-9325. **Owner(s):** San Diego Community Newspaper Group, 4645 Cass, San Diego, CA 92109. TEL 619-270-3103; FAX 619-270-9325; Ed. John Gregory; Pub. David & Julie Mannis; adv.; photos; pub. size: tabloid; circ. 21,500(free).

US
RANCHO BERNARDO NEWS JOURNAL. 1970. Thu. $.50 newsstand; $24/yr. in cy. 11650 Iberia Pl., Ste. 215, San Diego, CA 92128. TEL 619-487-5757; FAX 619-487-1264. **Owner(s):** Pomerado Publishing Co., Inc., 13247 Poway Rd., Poway, CA 92064. TEL 714-748-2311; Ed. Donna Hartings; Pub. David Calvert; adv. contact: Trudy Armstrong. pub. size: broadsheet; circ. 20,000(controlled & paid).

US
SAN DIEGO LOG. bi-w. $24.95/yr. 2924 Emerson St., Ste 200, San Diego, CA 92106. TEL 619-226-1608; FAX 619-226-0573. **Owner(s):** West Coast Community Newspapers, Inc., 2841 Loker Ave. E., Carlsbad, CA 92008. TEL 619-431-4850; Ed. Susan Colby; Pub. Dan Teckenoff; pub. size: standard; circ. 20,000(paid).

US
SAN DIEGO READER. 1972. Thu. free; $165/yr. out of cy. P.O. Box 85803, San Diego, CA 92186-0583. TEL 619-235-3000; FAX 619-231-0489. **Owner(s):** San Diego Reader, P.O. Box 85803, San Diego, CA 92186. TEL 619-235-3000; FAX 619-231-0489; Pub. James E. Holman; adv.; bk.rev.; pub. size: tabloid; circ. 160,000(free).

US
SAN DIEGO REVIEW. 1989. m. free newsstand; $25/yr. 5932 Trojan Ave., San Diego, CA 92115. TEL 619-229-8899; FAX 619-286-4026. **Owner(s):** San Diego Review, Inc., 5932 Trojan Ave., San Diego, CA 92115. TEL 619-229-8899; FAX 619-286-4026; Ed. Paul Maskut. adv.; photos; bk.rev.; pub. size: tabloid; circ. 5,000(free & paid).

US ISSN 0898-4581
UPTOWN SAN DIEGO EXAMINER. 1937. 3/wk.: Mon., Wed., Fri. free newsstand; $25/yr. 3605 30th St., San Diego, CA 92104. TEL 619-295-5432. **Owner(s):** Examiner Group, Inc., P.O. Box 4368, San Diego, CA 92164-4368. TEL 619-295-5432; Ed. J. Specht; Pub. Arthur M. Specht; photos; pub. size: standard; circ. 250(free & paid).

WEEKLY NEWSPAPERS

SAN FERNANDO

US

RECORD LEDGER. 1921. Wed. free newsstand; $20/yr. in state; $45/yr. out of state. 1024 N. Maclay Ave., Ste. 9, San Fernando, CA 91340. TEL 818-365-3111. **Owner(s):** Valley Sun Newspapers, Inc., 1024 N. Maclay Ave., Ste. 9, San Fernando, CA 91340. TEL 818-365-3111; Ed. Thelma Barrios; Pub. Thelma Barrios; adv.; pub. size: tabloid; circ. 15,000(paid).

US

SAN FERNANDO VALLEY SUN. 1904. Wed. free newsstand; $20/yr. mailed in state. 1024 N. Maclay Ave., San Fernando, CA 91340. TEL 818-365-3111. **Owner(s):** Valley Sun Newspapers, Inc., 1024 N. Maclay Ave., San Fernando, CA 91340. TEL 818-365-3111; Ed. Thelma Barrios; Pub. Thelma Barrios; adv.; pub. size: tabloid; circ. 12,000(paid).

SAN FRANCISCO

US

NORTH/SOUTH BEACH NOW. 1987. m. $24/yr. 350 Bay, Ste. 100-1066, San Francisco, CA 94133. TEL 415-391-1043; FAX 415-398-2258; E-mail: thenow@aol.com. **Owner(s):** North Beach Now, 350 Bay, Ste. 100-106, San Francisco, CA 94133. TEL 415-391-1043; FAX 415-391-1213; Ed. Joan Dahlgren. adv.; photos; bk.rev.; pub. size: tabloid; circ. 3,500(free & paid).
Formerly: North Beach Now.

US ISSN 0036-4096

SAN FRANCISCO BAY GUARDIAN. 1966. Wed. free newsstand; $20/6 mos.; $32/yr. 520 Hampshire St., San Francisco, CA 94110-1417. TEL 415-255-3100; FAX 415-255-8955. **Owner(s):** Bruce B. Brugmann & Jean Dibble, 520 Hampshire St., San Francisco, CA 94110-1417. TEL 415-255-3100; Ed. Tim Redmond; Pub. Bruce B. Brugmann; adv.; photos; bk.rev.; pub. size: tabloid; circ. 135,000(free & paid).

US

SAN FRANCISCO INDEPENDENT. 1958. 3/wk.: Tue., Thu., Sat. free. 1201 Evans Ave., San Francisco, CA 94124. TEL 415-826-1100; FAX 415-826-5371. **Owner(s):** Pan-Asian Venture Capital Corp., 1201 Evans St., San Francisco, CA 94124. TEL 415-862-5371; Ed. Vorah Basich; Pub. Ted Fang; adv.; pub. size: broadsheet; circ. 537,000(free).

US

SAN FRANCISCO METRO REPORTER. Wed. free. 270 Francisco St., San Francisco, CA 94133. TEL 415-391-2030; FAX 415-391-2525. **Owner(s):** Garry M. Goodlett, 1366 Turk St., San Francisco, CA 94115. TEL 415-931-5778; photos; bk.rev.; pub. size: tabloid.

US

SAN FRANCISCO SENTINEL. 1974. Wed. free. 285 Shipley St., San Francisco, CA 94107. TEL 415-281-3745; FAX 415-281-3714. **Owner(s):** Ray Chalker, 285 Shipley St., San Francisco, CA 94107. TEL 415-281-3745; Ed. Ray Chalker; Pub. Ray Chalker; adv. contact: Russell Rottkamp. bk.rev.; pub. size: tabloid; circ. 35,000(free). **Wire Service(s):** AP.

US

SF WEEKLY. 1981. Wed. free newsstand; $40/yr. 3rd class mailed; $80/yr. 1st class mailed. 425 Brannan St., San Francisco, CA 94107. TEL 415-541-0700; FAX 415-777-1839. **Owner(s):** New Times, Inc., 425 Brannan St., San Francisco, CA 94107. TEL 415-541-0700; Ed. Phyllis Orrick; Pub. Jim Rizzi; adv.; pub. size: broadsheet; circ. 90,000(free & paid). **Wire Service(s):** Alternet, Bay City News Service.

US

SUN REPORTER. 1944. Wed. $15/yr. 1366 Turk St., San Francisco, CA 94115. TEL 415-931-5778. **Owner(s):** Gary M. Goodlett, 1366 Turk St., San Francisco, CA 94115. TEL 415-931-5778; Ed. Amelia Ashley-Ward; Pub. Gary M. Goodlett, M.D.; adv. contact: Jessica Castle. photos; bk.rev.; pub. size: tabloid; circ. 160,000(free & paid).

US

WESTERN EDITION. 1994. m. free newsstand; $15/yr.out of cy. P.O. Box 15102, San Francisco, CA 94115-0102. TEL 415-831-6397; FAX 415-431-2021; E-mail: westednews@aol.com. **Owner(s):** Western Edition Publishing, P.O. Box 15102, San Francisco, CA 94115-0102. TEL 415-863-6397; FAX 415-431-2021; Pub. Michael Martin; adv.: 01,02,03,04,05,06,07,08,09,10,11,12,15,16, 17,18,19, 20, 21, 32, 33. pub. size: tabloid; circ. 35,000(free & paid).

SANGER

US

PARLIER POST. 1984. Wed. free; $10/yr. mailed in cy.; $13/yr. mailed out of cy. 740 N St., Sanger, CA 93657. TEL 209-875-2511; FAX 209-752-2521. **Owner(s):** Mid-Valley Publications, Inc., P.O. Box 432, Reedley, CA 93654. TEL 209-638-2244; Ed. Dorren Oken. adv.; bk.rev.; pub. size: standard; circ. 6,000(free & paid).

US

SANGER HERALD. 1888. Thu. $.50 newsstand; $17.50/yr. 740 N St., Sanger, CA 93657. TEL 209-875-2511; FAX 209-875-2521. **Owner(s):** Mid Valley Publishing Co., 740 N St., Sanger, CA 93657; Ed. William Coleman; Pub. Fred Hall; pub. size: standard; circ. 2,900(paid).

SAN JACINTO

US

SAN JACINTO VALLEY REGISTER. 1884. Wed. free. 474 W. Esplande, San Jacinto, CA 92583-8003. TEL 909-487-2200. **Owner(s):** Stephens Group, Inc., 111 Center St., Little Rock, AR 72201. TEL 501-377-2000; Ed. Dana Straheley; Pub. Jim Fredericks; adv. contact: Manny Padilla. pub. size: tabloid; circ. 4,000(controlled).
Formerly: San Jacinto Valley.

SAN JOSE

US ISSN 0882-4290

METRO. 1985. Thu. free. 550 S. First St., San Jose, CA 95113. TEL 408-298-8000. **Owner(s):** Metro Publishing Co., 550 S. First St., San Jose, CA 95113. TEL 408-298-8000; Ed. Corrine Asturias; Pub. David Cohen; adv. contact: Scott Levander. bk.rev.; pub. size: tabloid; circ. 90,000(free).

SAN LUIS OBISPO

US

NEW TIMES. 1986. Thu. free newsstand; $37/yr. 197 Santa Rosa St., San Luis Obispo, CA 93405. TEL 805-546-8208; FAX 805-546-8641. **Owner(s):** Bev Johnson & Steve Moss, 197 Santa Rosa St., San Luis Obispo, CA 93405. TEL 805-546-8208; FAX 805-546-8641; Ed. Steve Moss; Pub. Steve Moss; adv. contact: Bev Johnson. photos; bk.rev.; pub. size: tabloid; circ. 40,000(free & paid); morning 42,000. **Wire Service(s):** Alternet.

SAN MARCOS

US

SAN MARCOS NEWS REPORTER. 1970. Thu. free newsstand; $100/yr. mailed. 815 Grand Ave., Ste. 103, San Marcos, CA 92069. TEL 619-471-8701; FAX 619-471-2630. **Owner(s):** News Reporter, Inc., 815 W. San Marcos Blvd., San Marcos, CA 92069. TEL 619-471-8701; Ed. William Willoughby; Pub. William Willoughby; adv. contact: Jacqueline Ferris. pub. size: tabloid; circ. 10,000(free & paid).

SAN MARINO

US

SAN MARINO TRIBUNE. 1935. Thu. $.65 newsstand; $36/yr. 2260 Huntington Dr., San Marino, CA 91108. TEL 818-282-5707; FAX 818-457-6436. **Owner(s):** Clifton Smith, 2260 Huntington Dr., San Marino, CA 91108. TEL 818-792-3343; Pub. Clifton Smith; adv.; pub. size: broadsheet; circ. 4,000(paid).

SAN MATEO

US

COASTSIDE CHRONICLE. 1959. Sat. free. 1080 S. Amphlett Blvd., San Mateo, CA 94402. TEL 415-348-4324. **Owner(s):** Alameda Publishing Corp., 116 W. Winston Ave., Hayward, CA 94544. TEL 510-783-6111; Ed. Terry Winkler; Pub. Peter Bernhard; adv.; pub. size: standard; circ. 8,000(controlled).

US

DALY CITY RECORD. 1962. Sat. free. 1080 S. Amphlett Blvd., San Mateo, CA 94402. TEL 415-348-4321; FAX 415-348-4446. **Owner(s):** Alameda Publishing Corp., 116 W. Winton Ave., Hayward, CA 94544. TEL 510-783-6111; Ed. Terry Greenberg; Pub. John Clinton, Jr.; pub. size: standard; circ. 24,600(controlled).
Formerly: Brisbane Bee.

US

MILBRAE RECORDER-PROGRESS. Sat. free. 1080 S. Amplett Blvd., San Mateo, CA 94402. TEL 415-348-4321; FAX 415-348-4446. **Owner(s):** Alameda Publishing Corp., 116 W. Winton Ave., Hayward, CA 94544. TEL 510-783-6111; Ed. Al Bro; Pub. Peter Bernard; adv.; pub. size: broadsheet; circ. 1,320(controlled).

US

SAN BRUNO HERALD. 1895. Sun. free. 1080 S. Amplett Blvd., San Mateo, CA 94402. TEL 415-348-4321; FAX 415-348-4446. **Owner(s):** Alameda Publishing Corp., 116 W. Winton Ave., Hayward, CA 94544. TEL 510-783-6111; Ed. Terry Winkcler; Pub. Roger Grossman; adv.; pub. size: broadsheet; circ. 13,000(free).

10544 SAN MATEO, CA

SAN MATEO

US
SOUTH SAN FRANCISCO ENTERPRISE-JOURNAL. 1895. Sat. $30/yr. 1080 Amplett Blvd., San Mateo, CA 94402. TEL 415-348-4321; FAX 415-348-4446. **Owner(s):** Alameda Publishing Corp., 116 W. Winton Ave., Hayward, CA 94544. TEL 510-783-6111; Ed. Terry Greenberg; Pub. John H. Clinton, Jr.; pub. size: broadsheet; circ. 16,150(controlled).

SAN PEDRO

US ISSN 0891-6627
RANDOM LENGTHS NEWS. 1979. w. $20/yr. 1117 S. Pacific Ave., San Pedro, CA 90731. TEL 310-519-1016. E-mail: 71632.201@compuserve.com. **Owner(s):** Random Lengths News, Inc., 1117 S. Pacific Ave., San Pedro, CA 90731. TEL 310-519-1016; Ed. J. Elendorf; Pub. J.P. Allen; adv. contact: Tom Davidon. bk.rev.; pub. size: tabloid.

SAN RAFAEL

US
CLASSIFIED GAZETTE. 1968. s-w.: Wed. & Fri. free. 716 Fourth St., San Rafael, CA 94901. TEL 415-457-4151; FAX 415-454-9849. **Owner(s):** Joseph Walsh, 716 Fourth St., San Rafael, CA 94901; FAX 415-454-9849; Riley Hurd, 716 Fourth St., San Rafael, CA 94901; FAX 415-454-9849; Pub. Riley Hurd; adv.; pub. size: tabloid; circ. 52,000(free).

SANTA ANA

US ISSN 0892-6441
TUSTIN NEWS. 1922. Thu. free in surrounding cys.; $16/yr. elsewhere. 625 N. Grand Ave., Santa Ana, CA 92701. TEL 714-953-7725; FAX 714-544-9247. **Owner(s):** Freedom Communications, Inc., 17666 Fitch, Irvine, CA 92614. TEL 714-553-9292; Ed. William A. Moses, II; Pub. Jane Lee Watson; adv. contact: Judy Duncan. pub. size: broadsheet; circ. 30,000(free).

SANTA BARBARA

US
SANTA BARBARA INDEPENDENT. 1986. Thu. free. 1221 State St., 2nd Fl., Santa Barbara, CA 93101. TEL 805-965-5205; FAX 805-965-5518. **Owner(s):** Santa Barbara Independent, The, 1221 State St., 2nd Fl., Santa Barbara, CA 93101. TEL 805-965-5205; FAX 805-965-5518; Ed. Marianne Partridge; Pub. George Thurlow; adv.; pub. size: tabloid; circ. 40,000(free & paid).

SANTA CRUZ

US ISSN 0164-4033
GOOD TIMES. 1975. Thu. free newsstand; $85/yr. mailed. 1205 Pacific Ave., Ste. 301, Santa Cruz, CA 95060. TEL 408-458-1100; FAX 408-458-1296. **Owner(s):** West Coast Community Newspapers, Inc., P.O. Box 1885, Santa Cruz, CA 95061. TEL 408-458-1100; Ed. Stacy Vreeken; Pub. Carole Atkinson; adv.; bk.rev.; pub. size: tabloid; circ. 45,000(controlled).

SANTA MONICA

US
BEVERLY HILLS INDEPENDENT. 1966. Thu. free. 1920 Colorado Ave., Santa Monica, CA 90404. TEL 310-829-6811; FAX 310-453-3085. **Owner(s):** Copley Press, Inc., 7776 Ivanhoe Ave., LaJolla, CA 92037. TEL 310-829-6811; Ed. Bea Nyburg. adv.; pub. size: broadsheet; circ. 18,400(free).

US
BRENTWOOD WESTWOOD PRESS. 1928. Thu. free. 1920 Colorado Ave., Santa Monica, CA 90404. TEL 310-829-6811; FAX 310-453-3085. **Owner(s):** Copley Press, Inc., 7776 Ivanhoe Ave., LaJolla, CA 92037. TEL 310-829-6811; Ed. Bea Nyburg. adv.; pub. size: broadsheet; circ. 20,300(free).

US
CULVER CITY-LADERA INDEPENDENT. 1961. Thu. free. 1920 Colorado Ave., Santa Monica, CA 90404. TEL 310-829-6811; FAX 310-453-3085. **Owner(s):** Copley Press, Inc., 7776 Ivanhoe Ave., LaJolla, CA 92037. TEL 619-454-0411; Ed. Bea Nyburg. adv.; pub. size: broadsheet; circ. 30,100(free).
Formerly: Culver City-Ladera Independent & Star News.

US
OUTLOOK MAIL. 1982. Wed. free mailed; $.25 newsstand. 1920 Colorado Ave., Santa Monica, CA 90404. TEL 310-829-6811; FAX 310-453-3085. **Owner(s):** Copley Press, Inc., 7776 Ivanhoe Ave., La Jolla, CA 92037. TEL 310-829-6811; Ed. Lou Brancaccio. adv. contact: Tom Pullano. pub. size: broadsheet; circ. 38,000(free). **Wire Service(s):** AP.

US
VENICE-MARINA NEWS. 1961. Thu. free. 1920 Colorado Ave., Santa Monica, CA 90404. TEL 310-829-6811; FAX 310-453-3085. **Owner(s):** Copley Press, Inc., 7776 Ivanhoe Ave., La Jolla, CA 92037. TEL 310-829-6811; Ed. Bea Nyburg. adv.; pub. size: broadsheet; circ. 15,600(free).

US
WESTCHESTER OBSERVER. 1971. Thu. free. 1920 Colorado Ave., Santa Monica, CA 90404. TEL 310-829-6811; FAX 310-453-3085. **Owner(s):** Copley Press, Inc., 7776 Ivanhoe Ave., La Jolla, CA 92037. TEL 310-829-6811; Ed. Bea Nyburg. adv.; pub. size: broadsheet; circ. 13,500(free).

US
WEST LOS ANGELES INDEPENDENT. 1928. Thu. free. 1920 Colorado Ave., Santa Monica, CA 90404. TEL 310-829-6811; FAX 310-453-3085. **Owner(s):** Copley Press, Inc., 7776 Ivanhoe Ave., La Jolla, CA 92037. TEL 310-829-6811; Ed. Bea Nyburg. adv.; pub. size: broadsheet; circ. 29,300(free).

SANTA PAULA

US
SANTA PAULA TIMES. 1993. s-w.: Wed. & Fri. $.50 newsstand; $8.85/mo. mailed. 944 E. Main St., Santa Paula, CA 93060. TEL 805-525-1890; FAX 805-525-7375. **Owner(s):** Donald & Deborah Johnson, 944 E. Main St., Santa Paula, CA 93060. TEL 805-525-1890; Ed. Donald Johnson; Pub. Donald Johnson; adv.; photos; bk.rev.; pub. size: broadsheet; circ. 9,000(free & paid).

SANTA ROSA

US
SONOMA COUNTY INDEPENDENT. 1979. Thu. free newsstand; $65/yr. in cy.; $80/yr. out of cy. 540 Mendocino Ave., Santa Rosa, CA 95401. TEL 707-527-1200; FAX 707-527-1288. **Owner(s):** Metrosa, Inc., 540 Mendocino Ave., Santa Rosa, CA 95401. TEL 707-527-1200; FAX 707-527-1288; Ed. Greg Cahill; Pub. Bob Rucker; adv.; photos; bk.rev.; pub. size: tabloid; circ. 30,000(free & paid). **Wire Service(s):** Alternet.
Formerly: Paper, The.

SARATOGA

US ISSN 0745-6255
SARATOGA NEWS. 1955. Wed. $.50 newsstand; $26/yr. local; $52/yr. out of area. 14375 Saratoga, Ste. E 2, Saratoga, CA 95070. TEL 408-867-6397; FAX 408-867-1010. **Owner(s):** Metro Newspapers, Inc., 550 S. First St., San Jose, CA 95113. TEL 408-298-8000; Ed. Carolyn Leal. adv.; pub. size: tabloid; circ. 10,000(paid).

SAUSALITO

US
EBBTIDE. Fri. $.50 newsstand; $20/yr. 1050 Bridgeway, Sausalito, CA 94966-1689. TEL 415-332-3778; FAX 415-332-8714. **Owner(s):** Marin Scope Community Newspapers, Inc., P.O. Box 1689, Sausalito, CA 94966-1689. TEL 415-332-3778; FAX 415-332-8714; Ed. Billie Anderson; Pub. Paul A. Anderson; adv.; photos; pub. size: standard; circ. 4,500(paid).

US
MARIN SCOPE. 1971. Tue. $.50 newsstand; $20/yr. mailed. 1050 Bridgeway, Sausalito, CA 94966-1689. TEL 415-332-3778; FAX 415-332-8714. **Owner(s):** Marin Scope Community Newspapers, Inc., 1050 Bridgeway, Sausalito, CA 94966-1689. TEL 415-332-3778; FAX 415-332-8714; Ed. Billie Anderson; Pub. Paul Anderson; adv.; pub. size: standard; circ. 2,000(paid).

US
MILL VALLEY HERALD. Mon. $.50 newsstand; $20/yr. 1050 Bridgeway, Sausalito, CA 94965. **Owner(s):** Marin Scope Community Newspapers, Inc., 1050 Bridgeway, Sausalito, CA 94966. TEL 510-332-3778; Ed. Jordan Grant; Pub. Paul Anderson; adv.; pub. size: standard.

US
NEWS POINTER. Wed. $.50 newsstand; $20/yr. 1050 Bridgeway, Sausalito, CA 94965. TEL 415-289-4040; FAX 415-332-8714. **Owner(s):** Marin Scope Community Newspapers, 1050 Bridgeway, Sausalito, CA 94965. TEL 415-289-4040; FAX 415-332-3778; Ed. Billie Anderson; Pub. Paul Anderson; photos; pub. size: standard; circ. 11,000(free).

US
ROSS VALLEY REPORTER. 1964. Wed. $.50 newsstand; $20/yr. 1050 Bridgeway, Sausalito, CA 94966-1689. TEL 415-289-4040; FAX 415-332-8716. **Owner(s):** Marin Scope Community Newspapers, Inc., 1050 Bridgeway, Sausalito, CA 94965. TEL 415-332-3778; Ed. Billie Anderson; Pub. Paul Anderson; adv.; pub. size: broadsheet; circ. 11,050(free & paid).

WEEKLY NEWSPAPERS

SAN RAFAEL
US
SAN RAFAEL NEWS POINTER. 1968. Wed. $.50 newsstand; $20/yr. 1050 Bridgeway, Sausalito, CA 94966. TEL 415-289-4040; FAX 415-332-8714. **Owner(s):** Marin Scope Community Newspapers, Inc., 1050 Bridgeway, Sausalito, CA 94966. TEL 415-332-3778; Ed. Billie Anderson; Pub. Paul Anderson; adv.; pub. size: standard; circ. 11,000(free).
Formerly: San Rafael/Terrra Linda News.

SEAL BEACH
US
HUNTINGTON HARBOUR SUN. 1967. Thu. free home deliv.; $.25 newsstand; $45/yr. 216 Main St., Seal Beach, CA 90740. TEL 562-430-7555; FAX 562-430-3469. **Owner(s):** West Coast Community Newspapers, Inc., 2841 Loker Ave., E., Carlsbad, CA 92008. TEL 619-431-4850; Ed. John Murray; Pub. Dar Brown; adv.: $17.15/SAU. pub. size: tabloid; circ. 37,000(controlled).
Formerly: Huntington Harbour Journal.

US
LEISURE WORLD GOLDEN RAIN NEWS. 1963. Thu. $25/yr. P.O. Box 2338, Seal Beach, CA 90740. TEL 562-430-0534; FAX 562-598-1617. **Owner(s):** Golden Rain Foundation, P.O. Box 2069, Seal Beach, CA 90740. TEL 562-598-2009; Ed. David Saunders. adv.; photos; pub. size: tabloid; circ. 8,900(free & paid).

US
SUN NEWSPAPER, THE. 1967. Thu. $.25 newsstand; $75/yr. 1st class mailed; $25/yr. 3rd class mailed. 216 Main St., Seal Beach, CA 90740. TEL 310-430-7555; FAX 310-430-3469. **Owner(s):** West Coast Community Newspapers, Inc., 216 Main St., Seal Beach, CA 90740. TEL 310-430-7555; Ed. John Murray; Pub. Dar Brown; adv.; pub. size: tabloid; circ. 37,000(controlled & paid).
Formerly: Seal Beach Journal; Seal Beach Sun.

SEBASTOPAL
US
SONOMA WEST TIMES & NEWS. 1889. Wed. $.50 newsstand; $25/yr. in cy.; $37.50/yr. out of cy.; $18/yr. senior citizens. 130 S. Main St., Ste. 114, Sebastopal, CA 95472. TEL 707-823-7845; FAX 707-823-7508. **Owner(s):** Sonoma West Publishers, Inc., 130 S. Main St., Ste. 114, Sebastapol, CA 95472; Ed. Barry Dugan. pub. size: standard; circ. 6,600(paid).
Formerly: Sebastopol Times & News; Sonoma West.

SELMA
US
SELMA ENTERPRISE. 1886. Wed. $.50 newsstand; $20/yr. in cy.; $24/yr. out of cy.; $25/yr. out of state. 2045 Grant St., Selma, CA 93662. TEL 209-896-1976; FAX 209-896-9160. **Owner(s):** Community Newspapers, Inc., P.O. Box 100, Selma, CA 93662. TEL 209-896-1976; FAX 209-896-9160; Ed. Tim Sheehan; Pub. Jim Brock; adv. contact: Gerald Latham. pub. size: broadsheet; circ. 4,000(paid).

SHAFTER
US
SHAFTER PRESS. Wed. $.35 newsstand; $19/yr. in cy.; $21/yr. out of cy.; $24/yr. out of state. 107 E. Lerdo Hwy., Shafter, CA 93263. TEL 805-746-4942; FAX 805-746-5571. **Owner(s):** Reed Print, Inc., 5409 Aldrin Ct., Bakersfield, CA 93313; Ed. Frank W. Reed; Pub. Frank W. Reed; adv. contact: Donna Rowe. pub. size: broadsheet; circ. 2,300(paid).

SIERRA MADRE
US
SIERRA MADRE NEWS. 1906. Thu. $.50 newsstand; $25/yr. 49 S. Baldwin Ave., Sierra Madre, CA 91024. TEL 818-355-3324; FAX 818-355-2341. **Owner(s):** Michael DeWeese, 49 S. Baldwin, Sierra Madre, CA 91024. TEL 818-355-3324; Ed. Michael DeWeese; Pub. Michael DeWeese; adv. contact: Myrna Aquitania. pub. size: broadsheet; circ. 4,000(paid).

SOLEDAD
US
GONZALES TRIBUNE. Wed. $.50 newsstand; $25.50/yr. in cy.; $31.50/yr. out of cy. 635 Front St., Soledad, CA 93960. TEL 408-678-2660; FAX 408-385-4790. **Owner(s):** News Media Corp., 211 Hwy. 38, E., Rochelle, IL 61068; Ed. Judith Spitzer; Pub. Daniel Wright; adv.; pub. size: broadsheet; circ. 840(paid).

US
SOLEDAD BEE. Wed. $.50 newsstand; $25.50/yr. in cy.; $31.50/yr. out of cy. 635 Front St., Soledad, CA 93960. TEL 408-678-2660; FAX 408-678-3676. **Owner(s):** News Media Corp., 211 Hwy. 38, E., Rochelle, IL 61068. TEL 815-562-2061; FAX 815-562-2060; Ed. Judith Spitzer; Pub. Daniel Wright; adv. contact: Suzi Taylor. pub. size: broadsheet; circ. 1,262(paid).

SOLVANG
US
SOLVANG SANTA YNEZ VALLEY NEWS. 1925. s-w.: Tue. & Thu. $.35 newsstand; $18.50/yr. 423 Second St., Solvang, CA 93463. TEL 805-688-5522; FAX 805-688-7685. **Owner(s):** Peg L. Johnson, P.O. Box 647, Solvang, CA 93464. TEL 805-688-5522; FAX 805-688-7685; Ed. Bart Ortberg. adv.; photos; pub. size: broadsheet; circ. 7,500(paid).

SONOMA
US   ISSN 8755-9498
SONOMA INDEX TRIBUNE. 1879. s-w.: Tue. & Fri. $.50 newsstand; $45.15/yr. in Sonoma. 117 W. Napa St., Sonoma, CA 95476. TEL 707-938-2111; FAX 707-938-1600. **Owner(s):** Robert M. & Jean H. Lynch, P.O. Box C, Sonoma, CA 95476. TEL 707-938-2111; William E. Lynch, P.O. Box C, Sonoma, CA 95476. TEL 707-938-2111; James R. Lynch, P.O. Box C, Sonoma, CA 95476. TEL 707-938-2111; Ed. William E. Lynch; Pub. Robert M. Lynch; adv. contact: Pamela Austin. pub. size: broadsheet; circ. 11,500(paid).

SOUTH PASADENA
US
SOUTH PASADENA REVIEW. 1888. Wed. $.25 newsstand; $25/yr. mailed 2nd class. 1024 Mission St., South Pasadena, CA 91030. TEL 818-799-1161. **Owner(s):** South Pasadena Publishing Co., 1024 Mission St., South Pasadena, CA 91030. TEL 818-799-1161; Pub. William Ericson; adv. contact: Linda McCann. pub. size: standard; circ. 5,055(paid).

ST. HELENA
US
ST. HELENA STAR. 1874. Thu. $17.50/yr. in cy.; $23.50/yr. out of cy. 1328 Main St., St. Helena, CA 94574. TEL 707-963-2731; FAX 707-963-8957. **Owner(s):** Star Publishing Co., 25 Inverness Dr., Napa, CA 94558; Ed. Jeremy Hay; Pub. Bill Brenner; pub. size: broadsheet; circ. 4,500(paid).

SUN CITY
US
MENIFEE VALLEY NEWS. 1988. Fri. $.35 newsstand; $12/yr. mailed in cy.; $32/yr. out of cy. 27070 Sun City Blvd., Sun City, CA 92586. TEL 909-679-1195; FAX 909-679-2450. **Owner(s):** Press-Enterprise Co., P.O. Box 792, Riverside, CA 92502. TEL 714-684-1200; Ed. Dennis Brosterhous; Pub. Tom Paradis; adv.; photos; bk.rev.; pub. size: standard; circ. 7,000(free & paid).

US
SUN CITY NEWS. 1962. Fri. $.35 newsstand; $12/yr. mailed in cy.; $20/yr. out of cy. 27070 Sun City Blvd., Sun City, CA 92586. TEL 909-679-1191; FAX 909-679-2450. **Owner(s):** Press-Enterprise Co., P.O. Box 792, Riverside, CA 92502. TEL 714-684-1200; Ed. Dennis Brosterhous; Pub. Tom Paradis; pub. size: standard; circ. 5,400(paid).

TAHOE CITY
US
TAHOE WORLD. 1963. Thu. $.50 newsstand; $24/yr. in area; $39/yr.; outside of area. 241 N. Lake Blvd., Tahoe City, CA 96145. TEL 916-583-3488; FAX 916-583-7109; E-mail: world@tahoe.com; URL: http://www.tahoe.com. **Owner(s):** Mt. Rose Publishing, P.O. Box 138, Tahoe City, CA 96145. TEL 916-583-3488; Pub. Bill Kunerth; adv. contact: Bill Kunerth. photos; pub. size: broadsheet; circ. 6,500(paid).

TEHACHAPI
US
TEHACHAPI NEWS. 1900. Wed. $.50 newsstand; $24/yr. in cy.; $29/yr. out of cy.; $30/yr. out of state. 411 N. Mill St., Tehachapi, CA 93561. TEL 805-822-6828; FAX 805-822-4053. **Owner(s):** William J. Mead, P.O. Box 230, Tehachapi, CA 93581. TEL 805-822-6828; Ed. Chris Rombouts; Pub. William J. Mead; adv.; photos; pub. size: broadsheet; circ. 8,000(paid).

TRUCKEE

US

SIERRA SUN. 1869. Thu. $.50 newsstand; $22/yr. in area; $34/yr. out of area. 11429 Donner Pass Rd., Truckee, CA 96160. TEL 916-587-6061; FAX 916-587-3763; E-mail: sun@tahoe.com; URL: http://www.tahoe.com. **Owner(s):** Mt. Rose Publishing, P.O. Box 138, Tahoe City, CA 96145. TEL 916-583-3488; Ed. Peter Kostes; Pub. Bill Kunerth; pub. size: broadsheet; circ. 6,300(paid).

VALLEY CENTER

US

VALLEY ROADRUNNER. 1974. w. $.50 newsstand; $18/yr. 28904 Valley Center Rd., Valley Center, CA 92082. TEL 619-749-1112; FAX 619-749-1688. **Owner(s):** Dale & Shirley Good, 14761 Cool Valley Ranch, Valley Center, CA 92082; Ed. David Ross; Pub. Dale Good; adv. contact: Andrea Mills. photos; bk.rev.; pub. size: broadsheet; circ. 3,291(free & paid).

VENTURA

US

VENTURA COUNTY & COAST REPORTER. 1978. Thu. free; $50/yr. out of state. 1567 Spinnaker Dr., Ste. 202, Ventura, CA 93001. TEL 805-658-2244; FAX 805-658-7803. **Owner(s):** Ventura County & Coast Reporter, 1583 Spinnaker Dr., Ste. 213, Ventura, CA 93001. TEL 805-658-2244; Pub. Nancy Cloutier; pub. size: tabloid; circ. 20,000(free & paid).

WALNUT CREEK

US

ROSSMOOR NEWS. 1964. Wed. $35/yr. mailed. 1006 Stanley Dollar Dr., Walnut Creek, CA 94595. TEL 510-988-7800; FAX 510-935-8348. **Owner(s):** Golden Rain Foundation, P.O. Box 2190, Walnut Creek, CA 94595. TEL 510-939-1211; Ed. Maureen O'Rourke. adv.: $13/SAU. pub. size: tabloid; circ. 8,700(paid).

WASCO

US

WASCO TRIBUNE. Tue. free; $.35 newsstand. 911 Seventh St., Wasco, CA 93280. TEL 805-758-3063; FAX 805-758-3064. **Owner(s):** Reed Print, Inc., 5409 Aldrin Ct., Bakersfield, CA 93313; Ed. Frank W. Reed; Pub. Frank W. Reed; adv. contact: Donna Rowe. pub. size: broadsheet; circ. 5,600(free).

WEAVERVILLE

US

TRINITY JOURNAL. 1856. Wed. $.50 newsstand; $20/yr. in cy.; $29/yr. out of cy. 218 Main St., Weaverville, CA 96093-0340. TEL 916-623-2055; FAX 916-623-2065. **Owner(s):** Mike & Sarah Wenninger, 218 Main St., Weaverville, CA 96093. TEL 916-623-2055; FAX 916-623-2065; Ed. Mike Wenninger; Pub. Sarah Wenninger; photos; pub. size: broadsheet; circ. 4,650(paid).
Formerly: Weaverville Weekly Trinity Journal.

WEED

US

WEED PRESS. 1925. Wed. $17/6 mos. in cy.; $19/6 mos. out of cy. 924 N. Mt. Shasta Blvd., Weed, CA 96067. TEL 916-926-5214; FAX 916-926-4166. **Owner(s):** American Publishing Co., 606 N. Van Buren, Marion, IL 62959. TEL 618-993-1711; Ed. Steve Derace. pub. size: standard; circ. 1,825(paid).

WEST COVINA

US

AZUSA HERALD. Thu. free; $57/yr. mailed. 1210 N. Azusa Canyon Rd., West Covina, CA 91790-1003. TEL 818-854-8700; FAX 818-338-9157. **Owner(s):** Media News Inc., 1560 Broadway, Ste. 1485, Denver, CO 80202. TEL 303-820-1952; Ed. John Bender; Pub. Ike Massey; adv. contact: Monica Holbrook. pub. size: tabloid; circ. 15,000(free & paid).

US

GLENDORA PRESS. 1890. Thu. $.25 newsstand; $10/yr. home deliv. 1210 N. Azusa Canyon Rd., West Covina, CA 91790. TEL 818-854-8700; FAX 818-854-8719. **Owner(s):** Media News Group, 1560 Broadway, Ste. 1485, Denver, CO 80202. TEL 303-820-1952; FAX 303-820-1929; Ed. John Bender. adv.; pub. size: tabloid; circ. 15,140(free).

US

HIGHLANDER. 1962. Thu. free. 1210 N. Azusa Canyon Rd., West Covina, CA 91790-1003. TEL 818-854-8700; FAX 818-854-8719. **Owner(s):** Garden State Newspaper Grp., 1210 N. Azusa Canyon Rd., West Covina, CA 91790. TEL 818-854-8700; Ed. John Bender; Pub. Ike Maffey; adv. contact: Monica Holbrook. photos; pub. size: tabloid; circ. 160,000(free).

WEST SACRAMENTO

US

NEWS-LEDGER, THE. 1964. Wed. $15/yr. in cy.; $20/yr. out of cy. 816 W. Acres Rd., West Sacramento, CA 95691. TEL 916-371-8030. **Owner(s):** Michael P. Garten, P.O. Box 463, West Sacramento, CA 95691. TEL 916-371-8030; Ed. Steve Marschke. adv.; pub. size: broadsheet; circ. 3,500(paid).

US

WEST SACRAMENTO NEWS-LEDGER. 1964. Wed. $.50 newsstand; $15/yr. in cy.; $20/yr. elsewhere. 816 West Acres Rd., West Sacramento, CA 95691. TEL 916-371-8030; FAX 916-371-8030. **Owner(s):** Michael P. Garten, 816 West Acres Rd., West Sacramento, CA 95691. TEL 916-371-8030; Ed. Steven K. Marschke; Pub. Michael P. Garten; pub. size: broadsheet; circ. 3,600(paid).

WILLOWS

US

WILLOWS JOURNAL. 1877. 3/wk.: Mon., Wed., Fri. $.50 newsstand; $36/yr. carrier; $38/yr. mailed in cy.; $63/yr. mailed out of cy.; $40/yr. senior citizens. 1030 W. Wood St., Willows, CA 95988. TEL 916-934-6800; FAX 916-934-6815. **Owner(s):** Morris Communications, P.O. Box 936, Augusta, GA 30903; Ed. David Newton; Pub. Darell Phillips; adv. contact: John Taylor. pub. size: broadsheet; circ. 6,000(paid).

WINTON

US

ATWATER TIMES. Thu. $.25 newsstand; $19/yr. in cy. mailed; $23/yr. out of cy. mailed. 6950 Gerard, Winton, CA 95388. TEL 209-358-5311; FAX 209-358-7108. **Owner(s):** Mid-Valley Publications, Inc., 6950 Gerard, Winton, CA 95388. TEL 209-358-5311; FAX 209-358-7108; Ed. Charles Watson; Pub. John Derby; pub. size: tabloid; circ. 4,000(paid).
Formerly: Atwater New Times.

US

DELHI EXPRESS. Thu. $.25 newsstand; $19/yr. in cy. mailed; $23/yr. out of cy. mailed. 6950 Gerard, Winton, CA 95388. TEL 209-358-5311; FAX 209-358-7108. **Owner(s):** Mid-Valley Publications, Inc., 6950 Gerard, Winton, CA 95388. TEL 209-358-5311; Ed. John Derby; Pub. John Derby; pub. size: broadsheet; circ. 3,300(paid).

US

DENAIR DISPATCH. Wed. $.25 newsstand; $19/yr. in cy. mailed; $23/yr. out of cy. mailed. 6950 Gerard, Winton, CA 95388. TEL 209-358-5311; FAX 209-358-7108. **Owner(s):** Mid-Valley Publications, Inc., 6950 Gerard, Winton, CA 95388. TEL 209-358-5311; Ed. Mae Branagh; Pub. John Derby; pub. size: broadsheet; circ. 3,300(paid).

US

HUGHSON CHRONICLE. Tue. $.25 newsstand; $19/yr. in cy. mailed; $23/yr. out of cy. mailed. 6950 Gerard, Winton, CA 95388. TEL 209-358-5311; FAX 209-358-7108. **Owner(s):** Mid-Valley Publications, Inc., 6950 Gerard, Winton, CA 95388. TEL 209-358-5311; Ed. Miriam White; Pub. John Derby; pub. size: broadsheet; circ. 4,200(paid).

US

MERCED COUNTY TIMES. Thu. $.25 newsstand; $19/yr. in cy. mailed; $23/yr. out of cy. mailed. 6950 Gerard, Winton, CA 95388. TEL 209-358-5311; FAX 209-358-7108. **Owner(s):** Mid-Valley Publications, Inc., 6950 Gerard, Winton, CA 95388. TEL 209-358-5311; Ed. Topper Smith; Pub. John Derby; pub. size: tabloid; circ. 6,000(free & paid).

US

WATERFORD NEWS. Tue. $.25 newsstand; $19/yr. in cy. mailed; $23/yr. out of cy. mailed. 6950 Gerard, Winton, CA 95388. TEL 209-358-5311; FAX 209-358-7108. **Owner(s):** Mid-Valley Publications, Inc., 6950 Gerard, Winton, CA 95388. TEL 209-358-5311; Ed. Thais McGrath; Pub. John Derby; pub. size: broadsheet; circ. 5,200(paid).

US

WINTON TIMES. Thu. $.25 newsstand; $19/yr. in cy. mailed; $23/yr. out of cy. mailed. 6950 Gerard, Winton, CA 95388. TEL 209-358-5311; FAX 209-358-7108. **Owner(s):** Mid-Valley Publications, Inc., 6950 Gerard, Winton, CA 95388. TEL 209-358-5311; Ed. Bob Anderson; Pub. John Derby; pub. size: tabloid; circ. 3,000(paid).

WEEKLY NEWSPAPERS

WOODLAND HILLS

US ISSN 0193-9904
LAS VIRGENES ENTERPRISE. 1980. s-m.: 1st & 15th of mo. free newsstand; $30/yr. mailed. 6324 Variel Ave., Ste. 309, Woodland Hills, CA 91367-2517. TEL 818-716-4194; FAX 818-716-6577. **Owner(s):** Center News Publishing, 6324 Variel Ave., Ste. 309, Woodland Hills, CA 91367. TEL 818-716-4194; FAX 818-716-6577; Ed. Rodger Sterling; Pub. Kathleen Sterling; adv. contact: Ruth Patin. photos; pub. size: tabloid; circ. 5,000(free).

US
SOUTH OF THE BOULEVARD. 1994. s-m.: 1st & 15th of mo. free. 6324 Variel Ave., Ste. 309, Woodland Hills, CA 91367-2517. TEL 818-716-4194; FAX 818-716-6577. **Owner(s):** Center News Publishing, 6324 Variel Ave., Ste. 309, Woodland Hills, CA 91367. TEL 818-716-4194; FAX 818-716-6577; Ed. Rodger Sterling. adv.; photos; pub. size: tabloid.

US
VALLEY VANTAGE. 1949. Thu. free newsstand; $40/yr. mailed. 6324 Variel Ave., Ste. 309, Woodland Hills, CA 91367. TEL 818-906-2393; FAX 818-906-2129. **Owner(s):** Rodger & Kathleen Sterling, 6324 Variel Ave., Ste. 309, Woodland Hills, CA 91367. TEL 818-881-9460; Ed. Rodger Sterling; Pub. Rodger Sterling; adv.; pub. size: tabloid; circ. 20,000(free & paid).

US
WARNER CENTER NEWS. 1980. s-m.: 1st & 15th. free newsstand; $30/yr. mailed. 6324 Variel Ave., Ste. 309, Woodland Hills, CA 91367-2517. TEL 818-716-4161; FAX 818-716-6577. **Owner(s):** Center News Publishing, 6324 Variel Ave., Ste. 309, Woodland Hills, CA 91367-2517. TEL 818-716-4161; FAX 818-716-6577; Ed. Rodger Sterling; Pub. Kathleen Sterling; adv. contact: Ruth Patin. photos; pub. size: tabloid; circ. 10,000(paid).

YUCAIPA

US
YUCAIPA & CALIMESA NEWS-MIRROR. 1915. Thu. $.50 newsstand; $21/yr. 35154 Yucaipa Blvd., Yucaipa, CA 92399. TEL 909-797-9101; FAX 909-797-0502. **Owner(s):** Brehm Communications, Inc., 17065 Via del Campo, San Diego, CA 92127. TEL 619-451-6200; Ed. Bobbe Monk; Pub. Steve Arthur; pub. size: standard; circ. 15,000(paid).

YUCCA VALLEY

US
MORONGO BASIN ADVERTISER. 1955. Tue. free. 56-185 29 Palms Hwy., Yucca Valley, CA 92284. TEL 619-346-1729; FAX 619-346-7350. **Owner(s):** Associated Desert Shoppers, Inc., 73400 Hwy. 111, Palm Desert, CA 92260. TEL 619-345-1729; Pub. Hal Paradis; pub. size: tabloid; circ. 10,000(free).

US ISSN 0746-2301
YUCCA VALLEY HI-DESERT STAR. 1957. s-w.: Wed. & Sat. $.50 newsstand; $27/yr. 56445 29 Palms Hwy., Yucca Valley, CA 92284. TEL 619-365-3315; FAX 619-365-2650. **Owner(s):** Hi Desert Publishing Co., 56445 29 Palms Hwy., Yucca Valley, CA 92284. TEL 619-365-3315; FAX 619-365-2650; Ed. Susan Thanney; Pub. Russell Cannon; adv.; pub. size: standard; circ. 11,000(paid). **Wire Service(s):** AP.

COLORADO

AKRON

US
AKRON NEWS REPORTER. 1910. Thu. $.50 newsstand; $20/yr. in state, $23/yr. out of state. 69 Main, Akron, CO 80720-1439. TEL 970-345-2296; FAX 970-345-6638. **Owner(s):** Media News Group, 309 S. Broad St., Woodbury, NJ 08096. TEL 609-845-3300; Ed. Karen Ashley. adv.; photos; pub. size: broadsheet; circ. 2,174(paid).

AURORA

US
AURORA SENTINEL. 1910. Wed. $.50 newsstand; $26/yr. 1730 S. Abilene, Ste. 203, Aurora, CO 80012. TEL 303-750-7555; FAX 303-750-7699. **Owner(s):** Karen Sowell-Johnson, 1730 S. Abilene, Ste. 203, Aurora, CO 80012. TEL 303-750-7555; Harrison Cochran, 1730 S. Abilene, Ste. 203, Aurora, CO 80012. TEL 303-750-7555; Ed. Dave Perry; Pub. Karen Sowell-Johnson; pub. size: tabloid; circ. 25,000(paid).

BAYFIELD

US
PINE RIVER TIMES. 1985. Thu. $.50 newsstand; $20/yr. in cy.; $26/yr. out of cy. 15 W. Mill St., Bayfield, CO 81122-0830. TEL 970-884-2331; FAX 970-884-4385; E-mail: prtimes@dbbs.com. **Owner(s):** Ann McCoy, P.O. Box 830, Bayfield, CO 81122-0830. TEL 970-884-2331; FAX 970-884-4385; Pub. Ann McCoy; adv.; photos; pub. size: tabloid; circ. 1,300(paid).

BRIGHTON

US
BRIGHTON STANDARD BLADE. 1975. s-w.: Wed. & Sat. $.50 newsstand; $29/yr. 139 N. Main St., Brighton, CO 80601. TEL 303-659-1141; FAX 303-659-2901. **Owner(s):** Terry Gogerty & Anette Riesel, 139 N. Main St., Brighton, CO 80601; Pub. Terry Gogerty; adv. contact: Lisa Arkulari. pub. size: broadsheet; circ. 10,200(paid).
Formerly: Brighton/Blade Market Place.

BROOMFIELD

US
BROOMFIELD ENTERPRISE. 1975. Thu. $.50 newsstand; $52/yr. local; $52/yr. mailed. 1006 Depot Hill Rd., Ste. G, Broomfield, CO 80020. TEL 303-466-3636; FAX 303-466-8168. **Owner(s):** Boulder Publishing, Inc., Boulder, CO 80303; Ed. Shawn Stark. adv. contact: Beth Sabo. photos; pub. size: tabloid; circ. 15,000(controlled & paid).

COLORADO SPRINGS, CO 10547

BRUSH

US
BRUSH NEWS-TRIBUNE. 1894. Wed. $.50 newsstand; $22/yr. in state; $24/yr. out of state. 109 Clayton, Brush, CO 80723-0008. TEL 970-842-5516; FAX 970-842-5519. **Owner(s):** Media News Group, 309 S. Broad St., Woodbury, NJ 08096. TEL 609-845-3300; Ed. Darlene Doane; Pub. Darlene Doane; adv.; pub. size: tabloid; circ. 2,400(paid).

CARBONDALE

US
VALLEY JOURNAL. 1974. Thu. $.25 newsstand; $20/yr. in valley; $24/yr. out of valley; $10/yr. senior citizens. 36 N. Fourth, Carbondale, CO 81623. TEL 970-963-3211; FAX 970-963-3259. **Owner(s):** Roaring Fork Valley Journal, 36 N. Fourth, Carbondale, CO 81623. TEL 303-963-3211; FAX 303-963-3259; Ed. Karl Terry; Pub. Karl Terry; adv.; photos; bk.rev.; pub. size: tabloid; circ. 5,200(paid).

CASTLE ROCK

US
DOUGLAS COUNTY NEWS PRESS. 1892. Wed. $.50 newsstand; $26/yr. 319 Perry St., Castle Rock, CO 80104-2420. TEL 303-688-3128; FAX 303-660-0240. **Owner(s):** Westward Communications, Inc., 5005 LBJ Fwy., Ste. 1040, Dallas, TX 75244. TEL 214-450-1717; Ed. Richard Bangs; Pub. J. Tom Graham; adv. contact: Malcolm Smith. pub. size: broadsheet; circ. 3,800(paid).
Formerly: Daily News Press.

US
ELBERT COUNTY NEWS. Thu. $.50 newsstand. 319 Perry St., Castle Rock, CO 80104. TEL 303-688-3128; FAX 303-660-0240. **Owner(s):** Westward Communications, Inc., 5005 LBJ Frwy., Ste. 1040, Dallas, TX 75244; Pub. J. Tom Graham; pub. size: standard; circ. 2,900(paid).

COLORADO CITY

US
GREENHORN VALLEY NEWS. 1973. Thu. $.50 newsstand; $14/yr. in cy.; $17/yr. out of cy. P.O. Box 19041, Colorado City, CO 81019. TEL 719-676-3304; FAX 719-676-3304. **Owner(s):** Annie Heidrich, P.O. Box 19041, Colorado City, CO 81019. TEL 719-676-3304; FAX 719-676-3304; Ed. Annie Heidrich; Pub. Annie Heidrich; adv.; photos; pub. size: tabloid; circ. 4,000(paid).

COLORADO SPRINGS

US
BLACK FOREST NEWS. 1960. Thu. $.25 newsstand; $10/yr. 2724 Airport Rd., Colorado Springs, CO 80910. TEL 719-473-4370. E-mail: mattsonco@aol.com. **Owner(s):** Chickadee Enterprises, 2724 Airport Rd., Colorado Springs, CO 80910. TEL 719-473-4370; Ed. Charles L.R. Mattson; Pub. Charles L.R. Mattson; adv.; photos; pub. size: tabloid; circ. 1,000(paid).

ULRICH'S INTERNATIONAL PERIODICALS DIRECTORY 1998

CORTEZ

US

CORTEZ MONTEZUMA VALLEY JOURNAL. 1888. 3/wk.: Tue., Thu., Sat. $.25 newsstand; $37/yr. in area; $62/yr. out of area. 37 E. Main St., Cortez, CO 81321. TEL 970-565-8527; FAX 970-565-8532. **Owner(s):** Russell D. Brown, 37 E. Main St., Cortez, CO 81321. TEL 303-565-8527; Ed. Suzy Meyer; Pub. Russell D. Brown; pub. size: standard; circ. 6,328(paid).

US

CORTEZ SENTINEL. 1936. 3/wk.: Tue., Thu., Sat. $.25 newsstand; $37/yr. in area; $62/yr. out of area. 37 E. Main St., Cortez, CO 81321. TEL 970-565-8574; FAX 970-565-8532. **Owner(s):** Russell D. Brown, 37 E. Main St., Cortez, CO 81321. TEL 970-565-8527; Ed. Suzy Meyer; Pub. Russell D. Brown; adv. contact: Jeanne Scrivner. pub. size: standard; circ. 6,800(paid).

CRAIG

US

HAYDEN VALLEY PRESS. Thu. $.25 newsstand; $14/yr. in cy.; $17/yr. out of cy. 466 Yampa Ave., Craig, CO 81625. TEL 970-824-7031; FAX 970-824-6810. **Owner(s):** WorldWest Limited Liability Co., 609 New Hampshire, P.O. Box 688, Lawrence, KS 66044. TEL 913-843-1000; Ed. Jim Files; Pub. Bill Muldoon; adv. contact: Bill Muldoon. pub. size: tabloid; circ. 700(paid).

US

SATURDAY NORTHWEST. Sat. free. 466 Yampa Ave., Craig, CO 81625. TEL 970-824-7031; FAX 970-824-6810. **Owner(s):** WorldWest Limited Liability Co., 609 New Hampshire, Lawrence, KS 66044. TEL 913-843-1000; Ed. Jim Files; Pub. Bill Muldoon; adv. contact: Bill Muldoon. pub. size: standard; circ. 13,000(free).

DELTA

US ISSN 0891-9704

DELTA COUNTY INDEPENDENT. 1883. Wed. $.40 newsstand; $20/yr. in state; $24/yr. out of state. 401 Meeker St., Delta, CO 81416. TEL 970-874-4421; FAX 970-874-4424; E-mail: randydci@dci-press.com; URL: http://www.dci-press.com/. **Owner(s):** Leader Publishing Co., Inc., 401 Meeker St., Delta, CO 81416. TEL 970-874-4421; FAX 970-874-4424; Ed. Pat Sunderland; Pub. Norman Sunderland; adv.; photos; pub. size: broadsheet; circ. 7,714(paid).

DENVER

US

COLORADO STATESMAN. 1898. Fri. $1 newsstand; $44/yr. 1535 Grant St., Ste. 280, Denver, CO 80203. TEL 303-837-8600; FAX 303-837-9015. **Owner(s):** Colorado Statesman, P.O. Box 18129, Denver, CO 80218. TEL 303-837-8600; FAX 303-837-9015; Pub. Jody Strogoff; adv.; pub. size: tabloid; circ. 6,000(controlled & paid).

US ISSN 0898-1701

DENVER HERALD-DISPATCH. 1926. Thu. $.35 newsstand; $25/yr. 47 S. Federal Blvd., Denver, CO 80219. TEL 303-935-2453; FAX 303-936-0994. **Owner(s):** J. Ivanhoe Rosenberg, 47 S. Federal Blvd., Denver, CO 80219. TEL 303-935-2453; Ed. J. Ivanhoe Rosenburg; Pub. J. Ivanhoe Rosenberg; adv.; pub. size: tabloid; circ. 7,000(paid). **Wire Service(s):** AP.

US

WESTWORD. w. free. P.O. Box 5970, Denver, CO 80217. TEL 303-296-7744; FAX 303-296-5416; E-mail: editorial@westword.com; URL: http://www.westword.com. **Owner(s):** New Times Corp., 1201 E. Jefferson, Phoenix, AZ 85034; Ed. Patricia Calhoun. adv.; pub. size: tabloid; circ. 105,000(free).

DOVE CREEK

US

DOVE CREEK PRESS. 1940. Thu. $.25 newsstand; $11/yr. in cy.; $15/yr. out of cy. 321 N. Main St., Dove Creek, CO 81324. TEL 970-677-2214. **Owner(s):** Doug & Linda Funk, P.O. Box 598, Dove Creek, CO 81324; Ed. Linda Funk. adv.; pub. size: tabloid; circ. 1,100(paid).

EADS

US

KIOWA COUNTY PRESS. 1887. Fri. $.40 newsstand; $19.50/yr. in state; $22/yr. out of state. 1208 Maine St., Eads, CO 81036. TEL 719-438-5800; FAX 719-438-5352; E-mail: kepnews@iguana.ruralnet.net. **Owner(s):** Christopher Sorensen, P.O. Box 248, Eads, CO 81036-0248. TEL 719-438-5800; FAX 719-458-5352; Ed. Christopher Sorensen; Pub. Christopher Sorensen; adv.: $5.30/SAU. photos; bk.rev.; pub. size: standard; circ. 660(paid). **Wire Service(s):** AP.

EAGLE

US

EAGLE VALLEY ENTERPRISE. 0898. Thu. $.35 newsstand; $14/yr. in cy.; $20/yr. out of cy.; $24/yr. out of state. 11 Eagle Park Dr., E., Eagle, CO 81631. TEL 303-328-6656; FAX 303-328-6393; E-mail: getnews@vail.net; URL: http://www.adone.com/enterprise. **Owner(s):** Gojan & Leslie Nikolich, P.O. Box 1000, Eagle, CO 80030. TEL 303-428-9529; Ed. Gojan Nikolich; Pub. Gojan Nikolich; adv. contact: Kim Reed. photos; bk.rev.; pub. size: tabloid; circ. 14,000(free & paid).

EAGLE-VAIL

US ISSN 1061-1770

VAIL TRAIL. 1965. Fri. $10/3 mos.; $18/6 mos.; $25/yr. 41184 Hwy. 6 & 24, Eagle-Vail, CO 81620. TEL 970-949-4004; FAX 970-949-0199. **Owner(s):** Knox Publishing Co., P.O. Drawer 6200, Vail, CO 81658. TEL 303-949-4004; FAX 303-949-0199; Ed. Damon Arhos; Pub. Allen Knox; adv. contact: Carolyn Knox. bk.rev.; pub. size: tabloid; circ. 14,000(controlled & paid).

ESTES PARK

US

ESTES PARK TRAIL-GAZETTE. 1915. s-w.: Wed. & Fri. $.50 newsstand; $28/yr. in cy.; $38/yr. in state; $45/yr. out of state. 251 Moraine Ave., Estes Park, CO 80517. TEL 970-586-3356; FAX 970-586-9532. **Owner(s):** Estes Park Newspapers, Inc., P.O. Box 1707, Estes Park, CO 80517. TEL 303-586-3356; Ed. Timothy Asbury; Pub. Terence K. Licence; adv. contact: Elizabeth Rogers. pub. size: broadsheet; circ. 5,800(paid).

EVERGREEN

US ISSN 0192-0197

CANYON COURIER. 1954. Wed. $.50 newsstand; $20/yr. in cy.; $24/yr. out of cy. 4009 Hwy. 74, Evergreen, CO 80439. TEL 303-674-5534; FAX 303-674-4104. **Owner(s):** Dennis Rooker, P.O. Box 430, Evergreen, CO; Ed. Tony Messenger; Pub. Kamal Eways; adv. contact: John Ellis. pub. size: tabloid; circ. 9,300(paid).

FLORENCE

US

FLORENCE CITIZEN. Thu. $.35 newsstand; $16/yr. local; $18/yr. out of area. 200 S. Pikes Peak Ave., Florence, CO 81226. TEL 719-784-6383. **Owner(s):** Robert & Sue Wood, 200 S. Pikes Peak Ave., Florence, CO 81226. TEL 719-784-6383; Ed. Robert M. Wood; Pub. Robert M. Wood; adv.; pub. size: tabloid; circ. 1,500(paid).

FORT LUPTON

US ISSN 1056-2419

FORT LUPTON PRESS. 1906. s-w.: Wed. & Sat. $.50 newsstand; $29/yr. 430 Denver Ave., Ste. B, Fort Lupton, CO 80621. TEL 303-857-4440; FAX 303-857-6801. **Owner(s):** Metro West Publishing Co., 139 N. Main, Brighton, CO 80601. TEL 303-659-2522; Ed. Brad Worrell; Pub. Terry Gogerty; adv. contact: Lisa Arkulari. pub. size: tabloid; circ. 5,300(paid).

FOUNTAIN

US

FOUNTAIN VALLEY NEWS & EL PASO COUNTY NEWS. 1958. w. $.75 newsstand; $20/yr.; $17/yr. senior citizens. 120 E. Ohio, Fountain, CO 80817. TEL 719-382-5611; FAX 719-382-5614. **Owner(s):** Kathryn A. Wiese, Shopper Press, Inc., P.O. Box 400, Fountain, CO 80817. TEL 719-382-5613; FAX 719-382-5611; Pub. Kathryn A. Wiese; adv. contact: Geof Clark. photos; pub. size: tabloid; circ. 6,500(free & paid).

FOWLER

US

FOWLER TRIBUNE, THE. 1897. Thu. $.25 newsstand; $15/yr. in cy.; $18/yr. out of cy. 112 E. Cranston St., Fowler, CO 81039. TEL 719-263-5311. **Owner(s):** Karen Turner, 112 E. Cranston St., Fowler, CO 81039. TEL 719-263-5311; Ed. Dorothy Salle; Pub. Dorothy Salle; adv.; photos; pub. size: tabloid; circ. 1,520(controlled & free).

WEEKLY NEWSPAPERS

FREDERICK
US

FARMER & MINER. 1930. Wed. $19/yr. in state; $26/yr. out of state. 204 Oak St., Frederick, CO 80530. TEL 303-833-2331; FAX 303-659-2901. **Owner(s):** Terry Gogerty, 139 N. Main, Brighton, CO 80601. TEL 303-659-2522; FAX 303-659-2901; Annette Riesel, 139 N. Main, Brighton, CO 80061. TEL 303-659-2522; FAX 303-659-2901; Ed. Michael Neilson; Pub. Terry Gogerty; adv.; photos; bk.rev.; pub. size: tabloid; circ. 1,100(paid).

FRISCO
US

SUMMIT COUNTY JOURNAL. 1880. Thu. $18/yr. in cy.; $27/yr. out of cy. 40 W. Main St., Frisco, CO 80443. TEL 970-668-0750; FAX 970-668-3859. **Owner(s):** Eagle-Summit Publishing Co., P.O. Box 709, Frisco, CO 80443. TEL 970-668-0750; Ed. James Stabbins; Pub. Robert L. Brown; adv.; pub. size: tabloid; circ. 6,000(free & paid).
Formerly: Breckenridge Journal.

FRUITA
US

FRUITA TIMES, THE. 1892. Fri. $.50 newsstand; $20/yr. in cy.; $30/yr. out of cy. 217 E. Aspen Ave., Fruita, CO 81521-2285. TEL 303-858-3924; FAX 303-858-7658; E-mail: times@jgj.net. **Owner(s):** Eugene Thomas, 221 E. Aspen Ave., Apt. 2, Fruita, CO 81521-2285. TEL 970-858-3924; FAX 970-858-7658; Ed. Eugene Thomas; Pub. Eugene Thomas; adv.: $7.06/SAU. photos; bk.rev.; pub. size: tabloid; circ. 1,700(paid).

US

MESA COUNTY MAIL. Tue. free. 217 E. Aspen Ave., Fruita, CO 81521. TEL 970-858-4927; FAX 970-858-7658. **Owner(s):** Eugene Thomas, 221 E. Aspen Ave., Apt. 2, Fruita, CO 81521. TEL 970-858-3924; FAX 970-858-7658; Ed. Eugene Thomas; Pub. Eugene Thomas; adv.: $7.06/SAU. pub. size: tabloid.

GOLDEN
US ISSN 0746-6382

GOLDEN TRANSCRIPT. 1866. Fri. $.50 newsstand; $36/yr. in cy.; $50/yr. out of cy. 1000 Tenth St., Golden, CO 80401. TEL 303-279-5541; FAX 303-279-7157. **Owner(s):** Golden Media, Inc., 1000 Tenth St., Golden, CO 80401. TEL 303-279-5541; FAX 303-279-7157; Ed. Jacque Scott; Pub. Vince Bodiford; adv.: $18./SAU. photos; bk.rev.; pub. size: broadsheet; circ. 21,800(paid).

US

JEFFERSON COUNTY TRANSCRIPT. 1984. Fri. $.50 newsstand; $26/yr. 1000 Tenth St., Golden, CO 80401. TEL 303-279-5541; FAX 303-279-7157; E-mail: treditor@tesser.com; URL: http://www.tesser.com/transcript. **Owner(s): Golden Media,Inc., 1000 Tenth St., Golden, CO** 80401; Ed. Jacque Scott; Pub. Vince Bodiford; adv. contact: John Tracy. photos; pub. size: standard; circ. 5,900(controlled & free).

HAXTUN
US

HAXTUN-FLEMING HERALD, THE. 1975. Wed. $20/yr. local; $22/yr. out of area. 217 S. Colorado Ave., Haxtun, CO 80731. TEL 303-774-6118. E-mail: cjc@henge.com; URL: http://www.hfherald.com. **Owner(s):** Fletcher Street, Inc., P.O. Box 128, Haxtun, CO 80731. TEL 303-774-6221; Ed. Jean Gray; Pub. Jean Gray; adv. contact: Carol Scheel. photos; pub. size: tabloid; circ. 1,300(paid).

HUGO
US

EASTERN COLORADO PLAINSMAN. 1912. Thu. $.50 newsstand; $16/yr. in state; $20/yr. out of state. 329 Fourth St., Hugo, CO 80821. TEL 719-743-2371; FAX 719-743-2106. **Owner(s):** Becky Osterwald, P.O. Box 98, Hugo, CO 80821. TEL 719-743-2519; Ed. Becky Osterwald; Pub. Becky Osterwald; adv. contact: Becky Osterwald. pub. size: tabloid; circ. 1,350(paid).

IDAHO SPRINGS
US

CLEAR CREEK COURANT. 1973. Wed. $.50 newsstand; $23/yr. in cy.; $28/yr. out of cy.; $20/yr. senior citizens. 1634 Miner St., Idaho Springs, CO 80452-2020. TEL 303-567-4491; FAX 303-567-4492; E-mail: cccourant@aol.com. **Owner(s):** Cary Stiff & Carol Wilcox, P.O. Box 276, Idaho Springs, CO 80452. TEL 303-567-4491; FAX 303-567-4492; adv.; photos; pub. size: tabloid; circ. 2,200(paid).

JULESBURG
US

JULESBURG ADVOCATE. 1899. Thu. $.50 newsstand; $19.50/yr. in cy.; $21.75/yr. out of cy. 108 Cedar, Julesburg, CO 80737. TEL 970-474-3388; FAX 970-474-3389. **Owner(s):** Media News Group, 309 S. Broad St., Woodbury, NJ 08096. TEL 609-845-3300; Pub. Amy Lechman; adv. contact: Amy Lechman. photos; pub. size: broadsheet; circ. 1,833(paid).

LA JUNTA
US ISSN 0004-1890

AG JOURNAL. 1949. Thu. $.50 newsstand; $28/yr. in state; $30/yr. out of state. 7 W. Fifth St., La Junta, CO 81050-0500. TEL 719-384-8121; FAX 719-384-2867. **Owner(s):** Arkansas Valley Publishing Co., P.O. Box 500, La Junta, CO 81050-0500. TEL 719-384-8121; FAX 719-384-2867; Ed. Karen L. Stewart; Pub. Pat Ptoleny; adv. contact: Mary Cary. pub. size: tabloid; circ. 6,597(free & paid). **Wire Service(s):** AP.
Formerly: Arkansas Valley Journal.

LAKEWOOD
US ISSN 0899-2452

ARVADA JEFFERSON SENTINEL. 1967. Thu. $.75 newsstand; $39/yr. 1224 Wadsworth Blvd., Lakewood, CO 80215. TEL 303-239-9890; FAX 303-239-9808. **Owner(s):** Jefferson Sentinel Newspapers, 1224 Wadsworth Blvd., Lakewood, CO 80215. TEL 303-239-9890; FAX 303-239-9808; Ed. Jeff White; Pub. Robert Cox; adv. contact: Barbara Stoute. pub. size: tabloid; circ. 24,347(paid).
Formerly: Arvada Sentinel.

LITTLETON, CO 10549

US ISSN 1060-5215

JEFFERSON SENTINEL. Thu. $.75 newsstand; $39/yr. 1224 Wadsworth Blvd., Lakewood, CO 80215. TEL 303-239-9890; FAX 303-239-9808. **Owner(s):** Jefferson Sentinel Newspapers, 1224 Wadsworth Blvd., Lakewood, CO 80215. TEL 303-239-9890; FAX 303-239-9808; Pub. Robert Cox; pub. size: tabloid; circ. 22,401(controlled & paid).
Formerly: Lakewood Jefferson Sentinel.

LEADVILLE
US

HERALD-DEMOCRAT. 1878. Thu. $.50 newsstand; $19/yr. in cy.; $27/yr. out of cy. 717 Harrison Ave., Leadville, CO 80461. TEL 719-486-0641; FAX 719-486-0611. **Owner(s):** Arkansas Valley Publishing Co., Salida, CO. TEL 719-539-6691; FAX 719-539-6630; Ed. Grant Dunham. adv. contact: Judy Douglas. pub. size: tabloid; circ. 2,900(paid). **Wire Service(s):** AP.
Formerly: Leadville Herald-Democrat.

LITTLETON
US ISSN 0745-9610

ENGLEWOOD HERALD. 1911. Thu. $.75 newsstand; $19.95/yr. 2329 W. Main St., Littleton, CO 80120. TEL 303-794-7877; FAX 303-794-1909. **Owner(s):** Macari-Healey Publishing Co., 2329 W. Main St., Littleton, CO 80120. TEL 303-794-1909; Ed. Patty Burnett; Pub. Gerard Healey; adv. contact: Gates Scott. pub. size: tabloid; circ. 3,500(paid).
Formerly: Englewood Sentinel.

US

HIGHLANDS RANCH HERALD. Fri. $.50 newsstand; $14.95/yr. 2329 W. Main St., Ste. 103, Littleton, CO 80120. TEL 303-794-7877; FAX 303-794-1909. **Owner(s):** Macari-Healey Publishing Co., 2329 W. Main St., Ste. 103, Littleton, CO 80120. TEL 303-794-7877; FAX 303-794-1909; Ed. Patty Burnett; Pub. Gerard Healey; adv.: $13.25/SAU. photos; bk.rev.; pub. size: tabloid; circ. 11,000(paid).

US ISSN 0899-6318

LIFE AT KEN-CARYL. 1979. bi-w.; Wed. free local; $30/yr. outside of area. 7676 S. Continental Divide Rd., Littleton, CO 80127. TEL 303-979-1876. **Owner(s):** Ken-Caryl Ranch Master Assn., 7676 S. Continental Divide Rd., Littleton, CO 80127. TEL 303-979-1876; FAX 303-972-1272; Ed. Eleen Laubenheim. adv.; photos; pub. size: tabloid; circ. 3,700(free & paid).

US

LITTLETON INDEPENDENT. 1888. Thu. $.75 newsstand; $24.95/yr. 2329 W. Main St., Ste. 103, Littleton, CO 80120. TEL 303-794-7877; FAX 303-794-1909. **Owner(s):** Macari-Healey Publishing Co., 2329 W. Main St., Littleton, CO 80120. TEL 303-794-1909; Ed. Patty Burnett; Pub. Gerard Healey; adv. contact: Gates Scott. pub. size: tabloid; circ. 9,000(paid).
Formerly: Littleton/Sentinel Independent.

Weeklies

LYONS

US

OLD LYONS RECORDER, THE. 1910. Thu. $.50 newsstand; $35/yr. carrier. 430 Main St., Lyons, CO 80540-1729. TEL 303-823-6625; FAX 303-823-6633. **Owner(s):** Old Recorder Newspapers, P.O. Box 1729, Lyons, CO 80540-1729. TEL 303-823-6625; FAX 303-823-6633; Ed. Walter J. Kinderman; Pub. Walter J. Kinderman; adv.; photos; bk.rev.; pub. size: tabloid; circ. 2,400(paid).

MANCOS

US

MANCOS TIMES-TRIBUNE. 1892. Wed. $11/yr. in cy.; $16/yr. elsewhere. 135 Grand Ave., Mancos, CO 81328. TEL 970-533-7766; FAX 970-565-8532. **Owner(s):** Cortez Newspapers, Inc., P.O. Drawer O, Cortez, CO 81321. TEL 970-565-8527; FAX 970-565-8532; Ed. Julie Powell; Pub. R.D. Brown; adv. contact: Jeanne Shrivner. photos; bk.rev.; pub. size: tabloid; circ. 850(paid).

MANITOU SPRINGS

US

CHEYENNE MOUNTAIN JOURNAL. m: 2nd Fri. of mo. free mailed. 22 Ruxton Ave., Manitou Springs, CO 80829. TEL 719-685-9201; FAX 719-685-4424. **Owner(s):** Pikes Peak Journal, Inc., 22 Ruxton Ave., Manitou Springs, CO 80829. TEL 719-685-9201; Ed. Phil Carson; Pub. John G. Graham; adv. contact: John G. Graham. photos; pub. size: tabloid; circ. 6,400(free).

US

GARDEN OF THE GODS JOURNAL. 1990. m: 4th Fri. of mo. free mailed. 22 Ruxton Ave., Manitou Springs, CO 80829. TEL 719-685-9201; FAX 719-685-4424. **Owner(s):** Pikes Peak Journal, Inc., 22 Ruxton Ave., Manitou Springs, CO 80829. TEL 719-685-9201; FAX 719-685-4424; Ed. Phil Carson; Pub. John G. Graham; adv. contact: John G. Graham. adv.: $8/SAU. photos; pub. size: tabloid; circ. 3,700(free).

US

PIKES PEAK JOURNAL. 1882. Fri. $.50 newsstand; $15/yr. in state; $22/yr. out of state. 22 Ruxton Ave., Manitou Springs, CO 80829. TEL 719-685-9201; FAX 719-685-4424. **Owner(s):** Pikes Peak Journal, Inc., 22 Ruxton Ave., Manitou Springs, CO 80829. TEL 719-685-9201; adv. contact: John G. Graham. photos; pub. size: tabloid; circ. 4,800(free & paid).
Formerly: Manitou Springs Pikes Peak Journal.

US

ROCKRIMMON JOURNAL. 1990. s-m: 1st & 3rd Fri. free mailed. 22 Ruxton Ave., Manitou Springs, CO 80829. TEL 719-685-9201. **Owner(s):** Pikes Peak Journal, Inc., 22 Ruxton Ave., Manitou Springs, CO 80829. TEL 719-685-9201; FAX 719-685-4424; Ed. Phil Carson; Pub. John G. Graham; adv.: $8/SAU. photos; bk.rev.; pub. size: tabloid; circ. 7,500(free).

MEEKER

US

MEEKER HERALD, THE. 1885. Thu. $.50 newsstand; $16/6 mos.; $25/yr. in cy.; $23/yr. senior citizens. 178 Main St., Meeker, CO 81641-0720. TEL 970-878-4017; FAX 970-878-4017; E-mail: mkrher@rmi.net. **Owner(s):** Glenn R. & Donna L. Troester, P.O. Box 720, Meeker, CO 81641-0720. TEL 970-878-4017; FAX 970-878-4016; Ed. Glenn R. Troester; Pub. Glenn R. Troester; adv.: $5/col. in. photos; pub. size: broadsheet; circ. 2,100(paid).

MONTE VISTA

US

CENTER POST DISPATCH. Wed. $.50 newsstand; $23.75/yr. in cy.; $29.75/yr. out of cy.; $34.50/yr. out of state. 229 Adams St., Monte Vista, CO 81144. TEL 719-852-3531; FAX 719-852-3387. **Owner(s):** News Media Corp., 211 Hwy. 38, E., P.O. Box 46, Rochelle, IL 61068; Ed. Toni Vecky-Dillon; Pub. Keith Bray; pub. size: tabloid; circ. 830(paid).

US

CONEJOS COUNTY CITIZEN, THE. 1892. Wed. $.50 newsstand; $19.75/yr. in cy.; $29.75/yr. out of cy.; $34.50/yr. out of state. 229 Adams St., Monte Vista, CO 81144. TEL 719-852-3531; FAX 719-852-3387. **Owner(s):** News Media Corp., 211 Hwy. 38, E., P.O. Box 46, Rochelle, IL 61068; Ed. Toni Vecky-Dillon; Pub. Keith Bray; pub. size: tabloid; circ. 1,000(paid).

US

DEL NORTE PROSPECTOR. Wed. $.50 newsstand; $21/yr. in cy.; $28/yr. out of cy.; $31/yr. out of state. 229 Adams St., Monte Vista, CO 81144. TEL 719-852-3531; FAX 719-852-3387. **Owner(s):** News Media Corp., 211 Hwy. 38, E., P.O. Box 46, Rochelle, IL 61068; Ed. Toni Vecky-Dillon; Pub. Keith Bray; adv.; pub. size: tabloid; circ. 800(paid).

US

MINERAL COUNTY MINER. Thu. $.50 newsstand; $23.75/yr. in cy.; $29.75/yr. out of cy.; $34.50/yr. out of state. 229 Adams St., Monte Vista, CO 81144. TEL 719-852-3531; FAX 719-852-3387. **Owner(s):** News Media Corp., 211 Hwy. 38, E., P.O. Box 46, Rochelle, IL 61068; Ed. Toni Vecky-Dillon; Pub. Keith Bray; pub. size: tabloid; circ. 776(paid).

US

MONTE VISTA JOURNAL. 1888. Wed. $.50 newsstand; $23.75/yr. in cy.; $29.75/yr. out of cy.; $34.50/yr. out of state. 229 Adams St., Monte Vista, CO 81144. TEL 719-852-3531; FAX 719-852-3387. **Owner(s):** News Media Corp., 211 Hwy. 38, E., P.O. Box 46, Rochelle, IL 61068. TEL 815-562-2061; Ed. Toni Vecky-Dillon; Pub. Keith Bray; adv.; pub. size: tabloid; circ. 2,500(paid).

US

SATURDAY ADVANTAGE, THE. Sat. free. 229 Adams St., Monte Vista, CO 81144. TEL 719-852-3531; FAX 719-852-3387. **Owner(s):** News Media Corp., 211 Hwy. 38, E., P.O. Box 46, Rochelle, IL 61068; Ed. Toni Vecky-Dillon; Pub. Keith Bray; pub. size: tabloid; circ. 15,000(free).

US

SOUTH FORK TIMES. Wed. $.50 newsstand; $23.75/yr. in cy.; $29.75/yr. out of cy.; $34.50/yr. out of state. 229 Adams St., Monte Vista, CO 81144. TEL 719-852-3531; FAX 719-852-3387. **Owner(s):** News Media Corp., 211 Hwy. 38, E., P.O. Box 46, Rochelle, IL 61068; Ed. Toni Vecky-Dillon; Pub. Keith Bray; adv.; pub. size: tabloid; circ. 610(paid).

MONUMENT

US

TRIBUNE, THE. 1965. Thu. $.50 newsstand; $17/yr. in state; $23.50/yr. out of state. 283 Washington, Monument, CO 80132. TEL 719-481-3423; FAX 719-481-9005. **Owner(s):** Bill Kezzizah, P.O. Box 488, Monument, CO 80132. TEL 719-481-3423; FAX 719-481-4172; Ed. Bill Kezziah; Pub. Pat Standard; adv. contact: Pat Standard. pub. size: tabloid; circ. 3,800(paid).

OURAY

US

OURAY COUNTY PLAINDEALER. 1877. Thu. $.50 newsstand; $23/yr. in cy.; $29/yr. out of cy. 333 Sixth Ave., Ouray, CO 81427-0607. TEL 970-325-4412; FAX 970-325-4413; E-mail: ouraypd@mdependence.net. **Owner(s):** David Mullings, P.O. Box 607, Ouray, CO 81427. TEL 970-325-4412; Ed. David Mullings. adv.; pub. size: tabloid; circ. 1,900(paid).

PALISADE

US

PALISADE TRIBUNE. 1903. Thu. $.50 newsstand; $24/yr in cy.; $29/yr. out of cy.; $34/yr. out of state. 124 W. Third, Palisade, CO 81526. TEL 303-464-5614. **Owner(s):** Bob Sweeney, P.O. Box 8, Palisade, CO 81526. TEL 303-464-5614; adv.; bk.rev.; pub. size: tabloid; circ. 3,100(free & paid).

PINE

US

HIGH TIMBER TIMES. 1977. Thu. $.50 newsstand; $17/yr. local; $21/yr. elsewhere. 43 Mt. Evans Blvd., Pine, CO 80470. TEL 303-838-4884; FAX 303-838-6007. **Owner(s):** Evergreen Newspapers, Inc., 175 S. Pantops Dr., Charlottesville, VA 22901. TEL 804-977-7424; Ed. Charla Bond; Pub. Kamal P. Eways; adv. contact: John Ellis. pub. size: tabloid; circ. 3,000(paid).

RIDGWAY

US

RIDGWAY SUN. 1918. Thu. $.50 newsstand; $23/yr. in cy.; $29/yr. out of cy. 133 Lena, Ridgway, CO 81432-0529. TEL 970-626-5100; FAX 970-325-4413; E-mail: ridgsun@independence.net. **Owner(s):** David Mullings, P.O. Box 607, Ouray, CO 81427; Ed. David Mullings. adv.: $7/SAU. pub. size: tabloid; circ. 930(paid).

WEEKLY NEWSPAPERS

RIFLE
US

CITIZEN TELEGRAM, THE. 1903. Wed. $.35 newsstand; $20/yr. in cy.; $24/yr. out of cy.; $10/yr. senior citizens. 132 E. Third St., Rifle, CO 81650. TEL 970-625-3245; FAX 970-625-3628. **Owner(s):** Community Newspapers of Colorado, Inc., 132 E. Third St., Rifle, CO 81650. TEL 970-625-3245; Ed. Sandy Hanson. adv. contact: Barb Donily. photos; pub. size: tabloid; circ. 3,500(controlled & paid).

SILVERTON
US

SILVERTON STANDARD & THE MINER. 1875. Thu. $.50 newsstand; $29/yr. 1257 Greene St., Silverton, CO 81433-0008. TEL 303-387-5477. **Owner(s):** Silverton Standard & The Miner, Inc., P.O. Box 8, Silverton, CO 81433. TEL 303-387-5477; Pub. Jon Denious; adv.; photos; pub. size: tabloid; circ. 1,400(paid).

STEAMBOAT SPRINGS
US

STEAMBOAT PILOT. 1885. Wed. free newsstand; $24/yr. in cy.; $32/yr. elsewhere. 1041 Lincoln Ave., Steamboat Springs, CO 80477-4872. TEL 970-879-1502; FAX 970-879-2888. **Owner(s):** WorldWest Limited Liability Co., 609 New Hampshire, P.O. box 688, Lawrence, KS 66044. TEL 913-843-1000; Ed. Tom Ross; Pub. Suzanne Antinoro; adv. contact: Sandy Lettunich. bk.rev.; pub. size: broadsheet; circ. 7,324(free & paid). **Wire Service(s):** AP.

STRASBURG
US

EASTERN COLORADO NEWS. 1916. Thu. $18/yr. in state; $20/yr. out of state. P.O. Box 555, Strasburg, CO 80136. TEL 303-622-4417; FAX 303-622-9217. **Owner(s):** Mike Galarneau, P.O. Box 555, Strasburg, CO 80136. TEL 303-622-4417; FAX 303-622-4417; Ed. Mike Galarneau; Pub. Mike Galarneau; adv.; pub. size: broadsheet; circ. 2,000(paid).

TELLURIDE
US   ISSN 1085-1704

TELLURIDE TIMES-JOURNAL. 1962. Thu. $.25 newsstand; $24/yr. mailed. 123 S. Spruce St., Telluride, CO 81435. TEL 970-728-4488; FAX 970-728-6090; E-mail: timesj@rmii.com; URL: http://www.adone.com/telluride/. **Owner(s):** Wick Communications, Inc., 333 W. Wilcox Dr., Ste. 302, Sierra Vista, AZ 85635. TEL 970-728-4488; FAX 970-728-6090; Ed. Russell Smyth; Pub. Tom Bonfietti; adv.; $7.50/SAU. photos; bk.rev.; pub. size: tabloid; circ. 4,879(free & paid).

WALDEN
US

JACKSON COUNTY STAR. 1913. Thu. $.35 newsstand; $12/yr. in cy.; $15/yr. outside cy. 417 Fifth St., Walden, CO 80480-0397. TEL 970-723-4404; FAX 970-723-4404. **Owner(s):** Chard & Dusty Smith, 7633 State Hwy. 125, Rand, CO 80473. TEL 970-723-4404; Ed. Dusty Smith; Pub. Dusty Smith; adv. contact: Marion Trick. photos; bk.rev.; pub. size: tabloid; circ. 1,400(paid).

WESTCLIFFE
US

WET MOUNTAIN TRIBUNE. 1883. Wed. $.50 newsstand; $23/yr. 404 Main St., Westcliffe, CO 81252. TEL 719-783-2361; FAX 719-783-2879. **Owner(s):** Jim Little, 404 Main St., Westcliffe, CO 81252. TEL 719-783-2361; FAX 719-783-2879; Ed. Jim Little; Pub. Jim Little; adv. contact: Jackie Stoppe. photos; pub. size: tabloid; circ. 2,555(free & paid).

WESTMINSTER
US   ISSN 1044-4254

NORTHGLENN-THORNTON SENTINEL. 1968. Thu. $.50 newsstand; $24/yr. in cy. 7380 Lowell Blvd., Westminster, CO 80030. TEL 303-426-6000; FAX 303-430-1676. **Owner(s):** Wilbur E. Flachman, P.O. Box 215, Westminster, CO 80030. TEL 303-426-6000; FAX 303-430-1676; Ed. Mikkel Kelly. adv. contact: Scott Bumgardner. adv.: $14/SAU. photos; pub. size: tabloid; circ. 5,500(paid).

US   ISSN 1072-7576

WESTMINSTER WINDOW. 1947. Thu. $.50 newsstand; $24/yr. in cy. 7380 Lowell Blvd., Westminster, CO 80030. TEL 303-426-6000; FAX 303-430-1676. **Owner(s):** Wibur E. Flachman, P.O. Box 215, Westminster, CO 80030. TEL 303-426-6000; FAX 303-430-1676; Ed. Mikkel Kelly. adv. contact: Scott Bumgardner. adv.: $14/SAU. photos; pub. size: tabloid; circ. 5,200(paid).

WIGGINS
US

WIGGINS COURIER, THE. 1987. Thu. $.50 newsstand; $17/yr. in cy.; $18/yr. out of cy.; $20/yr. out of state. 213 Dickson, Wiggins, CO 80654. TEL 970-483-7460; FAX 970-483-7464. **Owner(s):** Verna Segelke, 213 Dickson, Wiggins, CO 80654. TEL 303-483-7460; FAX 303-483-7313; Darlene Ruyle, 213 Dickson, Wiggins, CO 80654. TEL 303-483-7460; FAX 303-483-7313; Ed. Darlene Ruyle; Pub. Verna Segelke; adv. contact: Verna Segelke. photos; pub. size: broadsheet; circ. 700(controlled & free).

WINTER PARK
US

WINTER PARK MANIFEST. 1977. Wed. $.50 newsstand; $16/yr. in cy.; $22/yr. out of cy. 78622 Winter Park Dr., Winter Park, CO 80482. TEL 970-726-5721; FAX 970-726-8789. **Owner(s):** William Potter Johnson, 445 W. Rapa Pl., Tucson, AZ 85737. TEL 520-726-5721; Ed. Harry Williamson; Pub. Patrick Brower; adv.; pub. size: tabloid; circ. 4,300(controlled).

WRAY
US

WRAY GAZETTE. 1903. Wed. $.50 newsstand; $20/yr. in area; $23/yr. out of area. 411 Main St., Wray, CO 80758. TEL 970-332-4846; FAX 970-332-4065. **Owner(s):** Wray Gazette, 411 Main St., Wray, CO 80758. TEL 303-332-4846; Ed. Michele Abbott; Pub. Ron Rieb; pub. size: oversize; circ. 3,235(paid).

YUMA
US

YUMA PIONEER. 1886. Thu. $20/yr. 207 S. Main St., Yuma, CO 80759. TEL 970-848-2174; FAX 970-848-2895. **Owner(s):** Roger Chance, 207 S. Main St., Yuma, CO 80759. TEL 303-848-2174; Ed. Roger Chance; Pub. Roger Chance; adv.; pub. size: standard; circ. 3,100(paid).

CONNECTICUT

BETHEL
US

▼**BETHEL BEACON.** 1996. Thu. $.75 newsstand; $30/yr. 214 Greenwood Ave., Bethel, CT 06801. TEL 203-798-7450; FAX 203-354-2645. **Owner(s):** Housatonic Valley Publishing, 132 Darbury Rd., P.O. Box 139, New Milford, CT 06776. TEL 203-438-6544; Ed. Susan Wolf; Pub. Tripp Rothschild; adv.; bk.rev.; pub. size: broadsheet; circ. 2,200(paid).
Formerly: Bethel Home News.

BRANFORD
US   ISSN 0888-1901

BRANFORD REVIEW. 1928. s-w.: Wed. & Sat. $.50 newsstand; $33/yr. 230 E. Main St., Branford, CT 06405. TEL 203-488-2535; FAX 203-481-4125. **Owner(s):** Journal Register Co., 50 W. State St., 12th Fl., Trenton, NJ 08608. TEL 609-396-2200; Ed. Silvio Albino. adv. contact: Jim Gibbons. photos; pub. size: tabloid; circ. 6,000(paid).

BRISTOL
US   ISSN 0746-9632

BLOOMFIELD JOURNAL. 1976. Fri. $.75 newsstand; $32/yr; $20/yr. senior citizens. 99 Main St., Bristol, CT 06010. TEL 860-236-3571; FAX 860-236-0490. **Owner(s):** Journal Register Co., 50 W. State St., 12th Fl., Trenton, NJ 08608. TEL 609-396-2200; Ed. Laurie Slye; Pub. Michael Vanacore; adv. contact: Frank G Chilinski. photos; bk.rev.; pub. size: tabloid; circ. 1,750(paid).

US   ISSN 0745-0796

NEWINGTON TOWN CRIER. 1959. Fri. $.75 newsstand; $17/6 mos.; $32/yr.; $20/yr. senior citizens. 99 Main St., Bristol, CT 06010. TEL 860-236-3571; FAX 860-236-0490. **Owner(s):** Journal Register Co., 50 W. State St., 12th Fl., Trenton, NJ 08608. TEL 609-396-2200; Ed. Bruce Beckert; Pub. Michael Vanacore; adv. contact: Julianne Scott. photos; bk.rev.; pub. size: tabloid; circ. 2,800(paid).

US

WEST HARTFORD NEWS. 1931. Thu. $.75 newsstand; $15/6 mos.; $32/yr. 99 Main St., Bristol, CT 06010. TEL 860-236-3571; FAX 860-236-0490. **Owner(s):** Journal Register Co., 50 W. State St., 12th Fl., Trenton, NJ 08608. TEL 609-396-2200; Ed. Doreen Madden; Pub. Michael Vanacore; adv. contact: Richard Rizzi. photos; pub. size: tabloid; circ. 11,000(paid).

WEEKLY NEWSPAPERS

BRISTOL, CT

US
WETHERSFIELD POST. 1959. Fri. $.75 newsstand; $32/yr.; $20/yr. senior citizens. 99 Main St., Bristol, CT 06010. TEL 860-236-3571; FAX 860-236-0490. **Owner(s):** Journal Register Co., 50 W. State St., 12th Fl., Trenton, NJ 08608. TEL 609-396-2200; Ed. Doreen Madden; Pub. Mike Vanacore; adv. contact: Richard Rizzi. photos; bk.rev.; pub. size: tabloid; circ. 3,700(paid).

US
WINDSOR JOURNAL. 1973. Fri. $.75 newsstand; $32/yr.; $20/yr. senior citizens. 99 Main St., Bristol, CT 06010. TEL 860-236-3571; FAX 860-233-2080. **Owner(s):** Journal Register Co., 50 W. State St., 12th Fl., Trenton, NJ 08608. TEL 609-396-2200; Ed. Doreen Madden; Pub. Michael Vanacore; adv. contact: Penny Carrol. photos; bk.rev.; pub. size: tabloid; circ. 2,263(paid).

US
WINDSOR LOCKS JOURNAL. 1880. Fri. $.75 newsstand; $25/yr. 99 Main St., Bristol, CT 06010. TEL 860-236-3571; FAX 860-236-0490. **Owner(s):** Imprint, Inc., 99 Main St., Bristol, CT 06010. TEL 860-236-3571; FAX 860-236-0490; Ed. Doreen Madden; Pub. Michael Vanacore; adv. contact: Rich Rizzi. photos; bk.rev.; pub. size: tabloid; circ. 1,052(paid).

BROOKFIELD

US
BROOKFIELD JOURNAL. 1957. Fri. $.75 newsstand; $29.95/yr. in cy.; $39.95/yr. out of cy.; $36.95/yr. out of state; $22/yr. senior citizens. P.O. Box 268, Brookfield, CT 06804. TEL 203-775-2533; FAX 203-354-2645; E-mail: housvalpub@aol.com. **Owner(s):** Housatonic Valley Publishing Co., P.O. Box 1139, New Milford, CT 06776. TEL 860-354-2261; FAX 860-354-2645; Ed. Jan Howard; Pub. Walter Rothschild, III; adv. contact: Tom Spano. photos; pub. size: broadsheet; circ. 2,687(paid).

CHESHIRE

US
CHESHIRE HERALD. 1953. Thu. $.45 newsstand; $18/yr. in cy.; $26/yr. out of cy. 125 Commerce Ct., Unit 11, Cheshire, CT 06410. TEL 203-272-5316; FAX 203-250-7145; E-mail: cheshireherald@snet.com. **Owner(s):** Joseph & Maureen Jakubisyn, 125 Grandview Ave., Wallingford, CT 06492; Ed. Elisa Hutcoe; Pub. Joseph Jakubisyn; adv. contact: Joseph Jakubisyn. adv.: $7.15/SAU. pub. size: tabloid; circ. 6,800(paid).

CLINTON

US ISSN 0886-6112
CLINTON RECORDER. 1900. s-w.: Tue. & Sat. $.50 newsstand; $30/yr. in cy.; $55/yr. out of cy. 16D W. Main St., Clinton, CT 06413. TEL 860-669-5727; FAX 860-664-4531. **Owner(s):** Journal Register Co., 50 W. State St., 12th Fl., Trenton, NJ 08608. TEL 609-396-2200; Ed. Michael Lemski; Pub. William Rush; pub. size: tabloid; circ. 5,000(paid).

CROMWELL

US
CROMWELL CHRONICLE. 1986. Fri. $20/yr.; $35/2 yrs. 615 Main St., Cromwell, CT 06416. TEL 860-635-1819; FAX 860-632-7203. **Owner(s):** Chronicle Communications, 615 Main St., Cromwell, CT 06416. TEL 860-635-1819; FAX 860-632-7203; Ed. Ron Nolan. photos; bk.rev.; pub. size: tabloid; circ. 2,000(free & paid).

DARIEN

US ISSN 0744-3862
DARIEN NEWS REVIEW. 1973. Thu. $.50 newsstand; $15/yr. in cy. 6 Squab Ln., Darien, CT 06820. TEL 203-655-7476; FAX 203-655-1442. **Owner(s):** Brooks Community Newspapers, Inc., 542 Westport Ave., Norwalk, CT 06880. TEL 203-849-1600; Ed. Timothy Mahin; Pub. B.V. Brooks; pub. size: tabloid; circ. 8,000(paid).

EAST HARTFORD

US ISSN 8750-9156
EAST HARTFORD GAZETTE, THE. 1885. Thu. free in town; $.35 newsstand; $20/yr. out of town. 1171 Main St., East Hartford, CT 06108. TEL 203-289-6468; FAX 203-289-6469. **Owner(s):** Journal Register Co., One Herald Sq., New Britain, CT 06040. TEL 203-225-4601; FAX 203-289-6469; Ed. William A. Doak; Pub. Gerald Garcia; adv. contact: Mike Moses. adv.: $15.58/SAU. photos; bk.rev.; pub. size: tabloid; circ. 19,981(controlled & free).

ENFIELD

US
ENFIELD PRESS. 1880. Thu. $.50 newsstand; $20/yr. in state; $28/yr. out of state. P.O. Box 1141, Enfield, CT 06083. TEL 860-745-3348; FAX 860-745-8622. **Owner(s):** Westfield Evening News, P.O. Box 1141, Enfield, CT 06083. TEL 203-745-3348; Ed. Frank Poirot; Pub. Carol Mazza; adv.; pub. size: tabloid; circ. 2,000(paid).

FAIRFIELD

US ISSN 0191-5134
FAIRFIELD CITIZEN NEWS. 1973. s-w.: Wed. & Fri. $.50 newsstand; $25/yr. in state; $35/yr. out of state. 220 Carter Henry Dr., Fairfield, CT 06430. TEL 203-255-4561; FAX 203-255-0456. **Owner(s):** B.V. Brooks, 542 Westport Ave., Norwalk, CT 06851. TEL 203-849-1600; Ed. Laura A. Nailen; Pub. B.V. Brooks; adv.; pub. size: tabloid; circ. 14,200(paid).

GEORETOWN

US
WESTON FORUM, THE. 1970. Wed. $.50 newsstand; $20-$25/yr. out of town. 3 Main St., Georetown, CT 06883. TEL 203-544-9990; FAX 203-544-9153. **Owner(s):** Acorn Press, Inc., 16 Bailey Ave., Ridgefield, CT 06877. TEL 203-438-6544; Ed. Sybil Blau; Pub. Thomas B. Nash; adv. contact: Tom Nash. photos; pub. size: broadsheet; circ. 3,500(controlled & paid). **Wire Service(s):** AP.

GEORGETOWN

US
REDDING PILOT, THE. 1966. Thu. $.75 newsstand; $30/yr. in cy.; $35/yr. out of cy.; $18/yr. military; $20/yr. students. 3 Main St., Georgetown, CT 06829. TEL 203-544-9519; FAX 203-544-9153. **Owner(s):** Acorn Press, Inc., 16 Bailey Ave., Ridgefield, CT 06877. TEL 203-438-6544; FAX 203-438-6014; Ed. Susan Wolf; Pub. Thomas Nash; adv.; photos; pub. size: broadsheet; circ. 2,233(free & paid). **Wire Service(s):** AP.

GLASTONBURY

US
GLASTONBURY CITIZEN. 1950. Thu. $.75 newsstand; $20/yr. in cy.; $24/yr. out of cy. 87 Nutmeg Ln., Glastonbury, CT 06033. TEL 860-633-4691; FAX 860-657-3258. **Owner(s):** Hallas Family, 1510 Main St., Glastonbury, CT 06033. TEL 860-633-4691; Ed. Kathleen Stack; Pub. James Hallas; adv. contact: Carole Saucier. pub. size: tabloid; circ. 8,900(paid).

US
RIVER EAST NEWS BULLETIN. 1984. Fri. free. 87 Nutmeg Ln., Glastonbury, CT 06033. TEL 203-633-4691; FAX 203-657-3258. **Owner(s):** Hallas Family, 1510 Main St., Glastonbury, CT 06033. TEL 203-633-4691; Ed. James Hallas; Pub. James Hallas; adv. contact: Carole Saucier. photos; pub. size: tabloid; circ. 26,000(free).

GREENWICH

US
▼**GREENWICH POST.** 1996. w. free. 22 W. Putnam Ave., Greenwich, CT 06830. TEL 203-861-9191; FAX 203-861-9442. **Owner(s):** Hagedorn Communications, 662 Main St., New Rochelle, NY 10801. TEL 914-636-7400; FAX 914-636-2957; Ed. Christopher Hagedorn; Pub. Christopher Hagedorn; adv. contact: Victoria Holland. adv.: $15.50/SAU. photos; bk.rev.; pub. size: tabloid.

HARTFORD

US ISSN 0192-8503
HARTFORD ADVOCATE. 1973. Thu. free newsstand; $60/yr. mailed in US. 100 Constitution Plz., Hartford, CT 06103. TEL 860-548-9300; FAX 860-548-9335. **Owner(s):** New Mass Media, Inc., 87 School St., Hatfield, MA 01038. TEL 413-247-9301; Ed. Russ Hoyle; Pub. Francis Zankowski; adv. contact: Rosemary Olson. pub. size: tabloid; circ. 60,000(paid).

KENT

US
KENT GOOD TIMES DISPATCH. 1988. Fri. $.75 newsstand; $19.95/yr. in cy.; $29.95/yr. out of state. 14 Main St., Kent, CT 06757. TEL 860-927-4621; FAX 860-927-4622. **Owner(s):** Housatonic Valley Publishing Co., P.O. Box 1139, New Milford, CT 06776. TEL 860-354-2261; Ed. Lesly Ferris; Pub. Walter Rothschild; adv.; photos; pub. size: broadsheet; circ. 1,467(free & paid).

WEEKLY NEWSPAPERS

LAKEVILLE

US
LAKEVILLE JOURNAL, THE. 1897. Thu. $.75 newsstand; $27.50/yr. local. 33 Bissell St., Lakeville, CT 06039. TEL 860-435-9873; FAX 860-435-0146; E-mail: ljournal@aol. **Owner(s):** Lakeville Journal Co., LLC, 33 Bissell St., Lakeville, CT 06039. TEL 860-435-9873; adv. contact: Anna Mae Kupferer. photos; pub. size: broadsheet; circ. 10,000(paid).

LITCHFIELD

US
LITCHFIELD ENQUIRER. 1825. Fri. $.75 newsstand; $29.95/yr. in cy.; $39.95/yr. in state; $41.95/yr. out of state. 43 West St., Litchfield, CT 06759. TEL 860-567-8766; FAX 860-567-0005; E-mail: housvalpub@aol.com. **Owner(s):** Housatonic Valley Publishing Co., P.O. Box 1139, New Milford, CT 06776. TEL 860-354-2261; FAX 860-354-2645; Ed. John McKenna; Pub. Walter Rothchild; adv.; photos; pub. size: broadsheet; circ. 7,730(free & paid).

MILFORD

US
EAST HAVEN ADVERTISER. Sat. $18/yr. 349 New Haven Ave., Milford, CT 06460. TEL 203-876-6800; FAX 203-876-6800. **Owner(s):** Journal Register Co., 50 W. State St., 12th Fl., Trenton, NJ 08608. TEL 609-396-2200; Ed. Jon Root; Pub. William Rush; circ. 3,300(free & paid).

US
HAMDEN CHRONICLE, THE. Thu. $16/yr. in cy.; $55/yr. out of cy. 349 New Haven Ave., Milford, CT 06516. TEL 203-876-6800; FAX 203-877-4772. **Owner(s):** Journal Register Co., 50 W. State St., 12th Fl., Trenton, NJ 08608. TEL 609-396-2200; Ed. Cindy Boynton; Pub. William R. Rush; adv. contact: Ann Barnhart. circ. 8,000(free & paid).
Formerly: Chronicle, The.

US
NORTH HAVEN POST, THE. Thu. free; $16/yr. 349 New Haven Ave, Milford, CT 06460. TEL 203-876-6800; FAX 203-876-6800. **Owner(s):** Journal Register Co., 50 W. State St., 12th Fl., Trenton, NJ 08608. TEL 609-396-2200; Ed. Brian Overton; Pub. William Rush; adv. contact: Ann Barnhart. circ. evening 3,700(free & paid).
Formerly: North Haven Wollingotn Post, Inc.

US
ORANGE BULLETIN. Thu. free; $10/yr. 349 New Haven Ave., Milford, CT 06460. TEL 203-876-6800; FAX 203-876-6800. **Owner(s):** Journal Register Co., 50 W. State St., 12th Fl., Trenton, NJ 08608. TEL 609-396-2200; Pub. William Rush; adv. contact: Ann Barnhart. circ. evening 10,106(free & paid).

US ISSN 1077-0844
STRATFORD BARD. 1970. Thu. $18/yr. in state; $50/yr. out of state. 349 New Haven Ave., Milford, CT 06460. TEL 203-876-6800; FAX 203-877-4772. **Owner(s):** New Haven Register, 40 Sargent Dr., New Haven, CT 06511. TEL 203-789-5200; Ed. Andrew Martin. pub. size: tabloid; circ. 17,000(free).

US
WEST HAVEN NEWS. 1931. Sat. $.35 newsstand & carrier. 349 New Haven Ave., Milford, CT 06460. TEL 203-876-6800; FAX 203-877-4772. **Owner(s):** Journal Register Co., 50 W. State St., 12th Fl., Trenton, NJ 08608. TEL 609-396-2200; pub. size: tabloid; circ. 9,000(paid).

MONROE

US
MONROE COURIER. 1965. Wed. $12/yr.; $20/2 yrs.; $30/yr. out of cy. P.O. Box 332, Monroe, CT 06468-0332. TEL 203-926-2080; FAX 203-926-2091. **Owner(s):** Hometown Publications, Inc., P.O. Box 216, Monroe, CT 06468. TEL 203-268-6234; Pub. Regina Burkhart; pub. size: broadsheet; circ. 4,800(paid). Wire Service(s): AP.

US
TRUMBULL TIMES. 1958. Thu. $.50 newsstand; $12/yr. in town; $30/yr. out of town. P.O. Box 332, Monroe, CT 06468. TEL 203-926-2080; FAX 203-926-2091. **Owner(s):** Hometown Publications Co., Milwaukee, WI; Pub. Regina Burkhart; adv.; pub. size: broadsheet; circ. 7,525(paid).

NEW CANAAN

US
NEW CANAAN ADVERTISER. 1908. Thu. $.70 newsstand; $28/yr. in state. 42 Vitti St., New Canaan, CT 06840. TEL 203-966-9541; FAX 203-966-8006; E-mail: ncadvertiser@newcanaan.com. **Owner(s):** Hersam Publishing Co., P.O. Box 605, New Canaan, CT 06840. TEL 203-966-9541; Ed. Colin McEvoy; Pub. V. Donald Hersam; adv.; pub. size: standard; circ. 7,430(paid).

NEW HAVEN

US ISSN 0192-8511
NEW HAVEN ADVOCATE. 1975. Thu. $80/yr. One Long Wharf Dr., New Haven, CT 06511-5991. TEL 203-789-0010; FAX 203-787-1418; E-mail: newhadvo@pcnet.com. **Owner(s):** New Mass Media, Inc., 87 School St., Hatfield, MA 01038. TEL 413-247-9301; FAX 413-247-5439; Ed. Joshua Mamis; Pub. Gail Thompson; adv.; bk.rev.; pub. size: tabloid; circ. 55,000(free & paid).

NEW MILFORD

US
HOUSATONIC WEEKEND. 1948. Fri. free carrier. 132 Danbury Rd., New Milford, CT 06776. TEL 860-354-2261; FAX 860-354-2645. **Owner(s):** Housatonic Valley Publishing Co., P.O. Box 1139, New Milford, CT 06776. TEL 860-354-2261; Ed. Leigh Glaizer; Pub. Walter Rothchild; adv.; pub. size: tabloid; circ. 20,000(free).
Formerly: Advertiser, The.

US ISSN 0028-6338
NEW MILFORD TIMES. 1914. Fri. $.75 newsstand; $34.95/yr. in cy.; $44.95/yr. out of cy. 132 Danbury Rd., New Milford, CT 06776. TEL 860-354-2261; FAX 860-354-2645. **Owner(s):** Housatonic Valley Publishing Co., P.O. Box 1139, New Milford, CT 06776. TEL 860-354-2261; FAX 860-354-2645; Pub. Walter Rothchild; adv.; photos; pub. size: broadsheet; circ. 8,607(free & paid).

NEWTOWN

US
NEWTOWN BEE, THE. 1877. Fri. $.50 newsstand; $24/yr. 5 Church Hill Rd., Newtown, CT 06470. TEL 203-426-3141; FAX 203-426-5169. **Owner(s):** R. Scudder Smith, 5 Church Hill Rd., P.O. Box 5503, Newtown, CT 06470. TEL 203-426-3141; FAX 203-426-1394; Ed. Curtis Clark; Pub. R. Scudder Smith; pub. size: broadsheet; circ. 9,000(paid).

OLD SAYBROOK

US
PICTORIAL GAZETTE. s-w.: Tue. & Sat. $.50 newsstand; $32/yr. in cy.; $55/yr. out of cy. 162 Main St., Old Saybrook, CT 06475. TEL 860-388-3441; FAX 860-388-5613. **Owner(s):** Journal Register Co., 50 W. State St., 12th Fl., Trenton, NJ 08608. TEL 609-396-2200; Ed. Silvio Albino; Pub. William Rush; adv. contact: Gail Rubin. pub. size: standard; circ. 10,000(paid).

RIDGEFIELD

US
LEWISBORO LEDGER, THE. 1976. Thu. $30/yr. in cy.; $35/yr. out of cy. 16 Bailey Ave., Ridgefield, CT 06877. TEL 203-438-6545. **Owner(s):** Acorn Press, Inc., 16 Bailey Ave., Ridgefield, CT 06877. TEL 203-763-8281; Pub. Thomas B. Nash; adv. contact: John Brosz. photos; bk.rev.; pub. size: broadsheet; circ. 2,077(paid). **Wire Service(s):** AP.

US
RIDGEFIELD PRESS, THE. 1875. Thu. $.75 newsstand; $30/yr. 16 Bailey Ave., Ridgefield, CT 06877. TEL 203-438-6544. E-mail: acorn@compuserve.com; URL: http://www.acorn-online.com. **Owner(s):** Acorn Press, Inc., 16 Bailey Ave., Ridgefield, CT 06877. TEL 203-438-6544; Ed. Macklin Reid; Pub. Thomas B. Nash; adv. contact: John Brosz. pub. size: broadsheet; circ. 7,010(paid). **Wire Service(s):** AP.

SHELTON

US
VALLEY GAZETTE. 1992. Wed. free mailed in area; $.50 newsstand. 1000 Bridgeport Ave., Shelton, CT 06484. TEL 203-926-2080; FAX 203-926-2091. **Owner(s):** Hometown Publications, Inc., 1000 Bridgeport Ave., Shelton, CT 06484. TEL 203-926-2080; FAX 203-926-2091; Ed. Lorraine Bukowski; Pub. Regina Burkhart; adv. contact: Robin Glowa. photos; pub. size: broadsheet; circ. 15,100(free & paid).

SOUTHBURY

US ISSN 0193-1474
VOICES. 1968. Wed. $.75 newsstand. P.O. Box 383, Southbury, CT 06488. TEL 203-263-2116; FAX 203-266-0199. **Owner(s):** Rudy Mazurosky, P. O. Box 383, Southbury, CT 06488. TEL 203-263-2116; Ed. Patty Wesley; Pub. Rudy Mazurosky; pub. size: tabloid; circ. 27,000(paid).
Formerly: Southbury Voices.

10554 SOUTHINGTON, CT   WEEKLY NEWSPAPERS

SOUTHINGTON
US

SOUTHINGTON OBSERVER. 1975. Thu. $.75 newsstand; $18/yr. local. 213 Spring St., Southington, CT 06489. TEL 860-621-6751; FAX 860-621-1841. **Owner(s):** Anthony L. Urillo, 213 Spring St., Southington, CT 06489. TEL 203-628-9645; FAX 203-621-1841; Ed. Art Secondo; Pub. Anthony L. Urillo; adv.: $7.50/SAU. photos; bk.rev.; pub. size: broadsheet; circ. 5,666(paid).

STAMFORD
US

FAIRFIELD COUNTY WEEKLY. 1979. Thu. free newsstand; $60/yr. mailed. One Dock St., Ste. 5L, Stamford, CT 06902-5838. TEL 203-406-2406; FAX 203-406-1099. **Owner(s):** New Mass Media, Inc., 50 Prospect St., Hatfield, MA 01038. TEL 413-247-9301; Ed. Lorraine Gengo; Pub. Rob Lipman; adv.; photos; pub. size: tabloid; circ. 70,000(free & paid).
Formerly: Fairfield County Advocate.

VERNON
US

REMINDER, THE. 1949. Tue. free carrier. 130 Old Town Rd., Vernon, CT 06066-2156. TEL 860-875-3366; FAX 860-875-2089. **Owner(s):** Kenneth Hovland, Sr., P.O. Box 210, Vernon Rockville, CT 06066. TEL 203-872-8515; Ed. Kenneth Hovland, Jr.; Pub. Kenneth Hovland, Jr.; adv. contact: Doug Sabian. pub. size: tabloid; circ. 130,000(free).

WESTPORT
US

WESTPORT NEWS. 1964. s-w.: Wed. & Fri. $.50 newsstand; $29/yr.; $20/yr. senior citizens. 15 Myrtle Ave., Westport, CT 06880. TEL 203-226-6311; FAX 203-454-2765; E-mail: bcnnews3@netaxis.com; URL: http://www.townline.com/brooks/westport/news/latenews.htm. **Owner(s):** Brooks Community Newspapers, Inc., 542 W. Port Ave., Norwalk, CT 06851. TEL 203-849-1600; Ed. Gary Larkin; Pub. B.V. Brooks; adv. contact: Cindy Withers. photos; bk.rev.; pub. size: tabloid; circ. 15,000(paid).

WILTON
US

WILTON BULLETIN. 1937. Wed. $.75 newsstand; $30/yr. in cy.; $35/yr. out of cy. 47 Old Richfield Rd., Wilton, CT 06897. TEL 203-762-5857; FAX 203-762-3120. **Owner(s):** Acorn Press, Inc., 16 Bailey Ave., Ridgefield, CT 06877. TEL 203-438-6544; Ed. Greg Bartlett; Pub. Thomas B. Nash; adv. contact: Jim DeFillipo. pub. size: broadsheet; circ. 4,500(paid). **Wire Service(s):** AP.

WINSTED
US

WINSTED JOURNAL. Fri. $.75 newsstand; $27.50/yr. local. 452 Main St., Winsted, CT 06098. TEL 860-738-4418. **Owner(s):** Lakeville Journal Co. LLC, 33 Bissell St., Lakeville, CT 06039. TEL 860-738-4418; Ed. Dave Parker. pub. size: broadsheet.

DELAWARE

BETHANY BEACH
US

DELAWARE WAVE. 1936. Wed. free; $35/yr. mailed 3rd class. Rte. 1, Lem Hickman Plz., Bethany Beach, DE 19930. TEL 302-537-1881; FAX 302-537-9705; E-mail: wave@dmv.com; URL: http://www.dmv.com/wave. **Owner(s):** Thomson Newspapers, Inc., Metro Centre, One Station Pl., 6th Fl., Stamford, CT 06902. TEL 203-425-2500; Ed. Steve Hoenigham; Pub. Chris Eddings; adv. contact: Susan Lyons. photos; pub. size: tabloid; circ. 12,500(free).

GEORGETOWN
US

SUSSEX COUNTIAN. 1886. Wed. $.35 newsstand; $18/yr. in state; $22/yr. out of state. 115 N. Race St., Georgetown, DE 19947. TEL 302-856-0026; FAX 302-856-0925. **Owner(s):** Robert H. Robinson Family, P.O. Box 40, Georgetown, DE 19947. TEL 302-856-0026; Pub. Dover Post; adv.: $9.60/SAU. photos; pub. size: tabloid; circ. 4,500(free & paid).
Formerly: Georgetown Sussex Countian.

HARRINGTON
US

HARRINGTON JOURNAL, THE. 1913. Wed. $.35 newsstand; $15/yr. in state; $17/yr. out of state. 110 Center St., Harrington, DE 19952. TEL 302-398-3206; FAX 302-398-3824. **Owner(s):** Independent Newspapers, Inc., P.O. Box 7001, Dover, DE 19903. TEL 302-674-4750; Ed. Carol Ann Porter. adv. contact: Helen Downing. pub. size: broadsheet; circ. 3,000(paid).

MILFORD
US

CHRONICLE, THE. 1878. Wed. $.50 newsstand; $18/yr. in cy.; $27/yr. elsewhere; $16/yr. senior citizens. 37A N. Walnut St., Milford, DE 19963. TEL 302-422-1200. **Owner(s):** Independent Newspapers, Inc., P.O. Box 7001, Dover, DE 19903. TEL 800-282-8586; Ed. Cathy Milhoan; Pub. Cathy Milhoan; adv.; pub. size: broadsheet; circ. 8,500(paid).

NEWARK
US   ISSN 1056-7658

NEWARK POST. 1910. Fri. $.50 newsstand; $15.95/yr. 153 E. Chestnut Hill Rd., Newark, DE 19713. TEL 302-737-0724; FAX 302-737-9109. **Owner(s):** Chesapeake Publishing Corp., One Airpark Dr., Easton, MD 21601. TEL 410-810-6505; Ed. James Streit; Pub. James Streit; adv. contact: Tina Winmill. photos; bk.rev.; pub. size: tabloid; circ. 12,000(paid).
Formerly: Newark Weekly Post.

REHOBOTH
US

SUSSEX POST, THE. 1972. Wed. free newsstand; $13/yr. in cy.; $16/yr. elsewhere. Midway Shopping Ctr., Rehoboth, DE 19971. TEL 302-934-9261; FAX 302-934-8590. **Owner(s):** Independent Newspapers, Inc., P.O. Box 7001, Dover, DE 19903. TEL 800-282-8586; Ed. Gwen Guerke; Pub. Tamra Brittingham; adv.; photos; pub. size: broadsheet; circ. 18,500(free & paid).

REHOBOTH BEACH
US

DELAWARE BEACHCOMBER. 1968. Fri. free. 3719 Hwy. 1, Rehoboth Beach, DE 19971. TEL 302-227-9466; FAX 302-227-9469; E-mail: dcp@dmv.com. **Owner(s):** Thomson Newspapers, Inc., Metro Centre, One Station Pl., 6th Fl., Stamford, CT 06902. TEL 203-425-2500; Ed. Terry Plowman; Pub. Sallie Harper; adv. contact: Sallie Harper. photos; bk.rev.; pub. size: tabloid; circ. 12,000(free).

US   ISSN 0740-2023
DELAWARE COAST PRESS. 1899. Wed. free newsstand; $35/yr. in cy. 3719 Hwy. 1, Rehoboth Beach, DE 19971. TEL 302-227-9466; FAX 302-227-9469; E-mail: dcp@dmv.com; URL: http://www.dmv.com/dep. **Owner(s):** Thomson Newspapers, Inc., Metro Centre, One Station Pl., 6th Fl., Stamford, CT 06902. TEL 203-425-2500; Ed. Terry Plowman. adv.; photos; pub. size: tabloid; circ. 12,500(free).

SEAFORD
US

LEADER-STATE REGISTER, THE. 1890. s-w.: Wed. & Fri. $.50 newsstand; $23.50/yr. in cy. $35/yr. elsewhere; $21/9 mos. students. 302 W. Stein Hwy., Seaford, DE 19973. TEL 302-629-5505; FAX 302-629-6700. **Owner(s):** Independent Newspapers, Inc., P.O. Box 7001, Dover, DE 19903. TEL 800-282-8586; Ed. John Sinnerty; Pub. Joe Smyth; pub. size: broadsheet; circ. 10,000(paid).
Formerly: Seaford Leader-State Register.

WILMINGTON
US

WILMINGTON DEFENDER. 1962. Wed. $25/yr. 1702 Locust St., Wilmington, DE 19802. TEL 302-656-3252; FAX 302-471-1130. **Owner(s):** Wilmington Defender, 1702 Locust St., Wilmington, DE 19802; FAX 302-471-1130; Ed. A.G. Hibbert. photos; bk.rev.; pub. size: tabloid; circ. 8,000(free & paid).

DISTRICT OF COLUMBIA

WASHINGTON
US

GEORGETOWN CURRENT, THE. 1967. Wed. $42/yr. 5125 McArthur Blvd., N.W., Washington, DC 20016. TEL 202-244-7223; FAX 202-244-7223. **Owner(s):** Current Newspapers, Inc., 5125 McArthur Blvd., N.W., Washington, DC 20016. TEL 202-244-7223; Ed. Chris Kain; Pub. Davis Kennedy; adv.; photos; pub. size: tabloid; circ. 35,000(controlled & free).

WEEKLY NEWSPAPERS

US

ISSN 0730-9082

GEORGETOWNER, THE. 1954. bi-w.: Fri. free. 1410 Wisconsin Ave., N.W., Washington, DC 20007. TEL 202-338-4833; FAX 202-342-0751. **Owner(s):** David Roffman, 1410 Wisconsin Ave., N.W., Washington, DC 20007. TEL 202-338-4833; FAX 202-342-0751; Ed. Gary Tishler; Pub. David Roffman; adv. contact: Sonya Bernhardt. photos; bk.rev.; pub. size: tabloid; circ. 15,000(controlled & free).

US

NORTHWEST CURRENT, THE. 1967. Wed. $42/yr. 5125 McArthur Blvd., N.W., Washington, DC 20016. TEL 202-244-7223; FAX 202-244-7223. **Owner(s):** Current Newspapers, Inc., 5125 McArthur Blvd., N.W., Washington, DC 20016. TEL 202-244-7223; Ed. Chris Kain; Pub. Davis Kennedy; adv.; photos; pub. size: tabloid; circ. 35,000(controlled).

US

ROCK CREEK CURRENT, THE. 1967. Wed. $42/yr. 5125 McArthur Blvd., N.W., Washington, DC 20016. TEL 202-244-7223; FAX 202-244-7223. **Owner(s):** Current Newspapers, Inc., 5125 McArthur Blvd., N.W., Washington, DC 20016. TEL 202-244-7223; Ed. Chris Kain; Pub. Davis Kennedy; adv.; photos; pub. size: tabloid; circ. 35,000(controlled).

US

SPOTLIGHT, THE. 1955. Fri. $1.50 newsstand; $59/yr. mailed. 300 Independence Ave., S.E., Washington, DC 20003. TEL 202-544-1794. **Owner(s):** Liberty Lobby, 300 Independence Ave., S.E., Washington, DC 20003. TEL 202-544-1794; Ed. Paul Croke. adv. contact: James Wolfington. pub. size: tabloid; circ. 100,000(paid).

US

WASHINGTON CITY PAPER. 1981. w. free newsstand; $35/yr. 2390 Camplain St, N.W., Washington, DC 20009. TEL 202-332-2100; FAX 202-462-8323. **Owner(s):** Tom Yoder, 11 E. Illinois St., Chicago, IL 60611. TEL 312-828-0350; Robert Roth, 11 E. Illinois St., Chicago, IL 60611. TEL 312-828-0350; Robert McCamant, 11 E. Illinois St., Chicago, IL 60611. TEL 312-828-0350; Ed. David Carr. adv. contact: Amy Austin. photos; bk.rev.; pub. size: tabloid.

FEDERATED STATES OF MICRONESIA

EASTERN CAROLINE ISLANDS

US

NATIONAL UNION. 1980. m. $8/yr. newsstand local; $12/yr. elsewhere. P.O. Box PS34, Palikir, Pohnpei, Eastern Caroline Islands, FM 96941. TEL 691-320-2548; FAX 691-320-4356. **Owner(s):** FSM Information, P.O. Box PS34, Palikir, Pohnpei, Eastern Caroline Islands, FM 96941. TEL 691-320-2548; FAX 691-320-4356; pub. size: tabloid; circ. 5,000(controlled & free).

FLORIDA

ARCADIA

US

ARCADIAN, THE. 1926. Wed. $.50 newsstand; $14.45/yr. mailed. 207 W. Oak St., Arcadia, FL 34266. TEL 941-494-2434; FAX 941-494-3533. **Owner(s):** Derrick Dunn-Rankin, 207 W. Oak St., Arcadia, FL 33821. TEL 941-492-2434; FAX 941-494-3533; Ed. Marsha Osteen. adv. contact: Margaret Turner. pub. size: broadsheet; circ. 9,600(controlled).

AUBURNDALE

US   ISSN 0745-8363

CANADA NEWS. 1982. w.: Fri; Nov.-Apr. $1.25 newsstand; $32.50/26 wks. P.O. Box 1729, Auburndale, FL 33823. TEL 941-967-6450; FAX 941-967-1954. **Owner(s):** Canada News, P.O. Box 1729, Auburndale, FL. TEL 813-967-6450; FAX 813-967-1954; Ed. Joe Braddy; Pub. Dave Perks; adv. contact: Andy Steinbergs. pub. size: tabloid; circ. 17,213(controlled & paid).

BARTOW

US

POLK COUNTY DEMOCRAT, THE. 1931. s-w.: Mon. & Thu. $.25 newsstand; $20/yr. in cy.; $30/yr. out of cy.; $35/yr. out of state. 190 S. Florida Ave., Bartow, FL 33830-4701. TEL 941-533-4183; FAX 941-533-0402; E-mail: fpcslfiv@aol.com. **Owner(s):** Frisbie Publishing Co., Inc., P.O. Box 120, Bartow, FL 33831-0120. TEL 813-533-4183; FAX 813-533-0402; Ed. Michal Holder; Pub. S.L. Frisbie, IV; adv. contact: Linda Holcom. adv.: $7.65/SAU. pub. size: broadsheet; circ. 4,483(free & paid).

BELLEVIEW

US

BELLEVIEW VOICE OF SOUTH MARION. 1969. Thu. $10/yr. in cy.; $18/yr. out of cy. 11412 S.E. US 301, Belleview, FL 34421. TEL 352-245-3161. **Owner(s):** Jim Waldron, P.O. Box 700, Belleview, FL 34421. TEL 352-245-3161; Ed. Sandy Waldron; Pub. Jim Waldron; pub. size: tabloid; circ. 2,200(paid).

BOKEELIA

US

PINE ISLAND EAGLE. 1976. Wed. free home deliv.; $30/yr. out of state mailed. 10700 Stringfellow Rd., Ste. 60, Bokeelia, FL 33922. TEL 941-283-2022; FAX 941-283-0232. **Owner(s):** Breeze Corp., 10700 Stringfellow Rd., Ste. 60, Bokeelia, FL 33922. TEL 941-283-2022; Ed. Dave Holmes. adv.; pub. size: tabloid; circ. 8,500(free & paid).

BONIFAY

US

HOLMES COUNTY ADVERTISER. 1892. Wed. $.50 newsstand; $20/yr. 112 E. Virginia Ave., Bonifay, FL 32425. TEL 904-547-2270; FAX 904-547-9200. **Owner(s):** Larry Woodham, 112 W. Virginia Ave., Bonifay, FL 32425. TEL 904-547-2770; Ed. Kathy Foster; Pub. Larry Woodham; pub. size: broadsheet; circ. 4,200(paid).

BONITA SPRINGS

US   ISSN 0191-5479

BONITA BANNER. 1959. s-w.: Wed. & Sat. $.25 newsstand; $26/6 mos.; $41.60/yr. 9102 Bonita Beach Rd., Bonita Springs, FL 34135. TEL 941-992-2110; FAX 941-992-7819. **Owner(s):** Scripps Howard, Inc., 312 Walnut St. 28th Fl., Cincinnati, OH 45202. TEL 513-977-3000; Ed. Cathy Cottrill. adv.; pub. size: broadsheet; circ. 30,000(paid). **Wire Service(s):** SHNA.

BRANDON

US

BRANDON NEWS, THE. 1957. Wed. free. 1401 Oakfield Dr., Brandon, FL 33511-2800. TEL 813-689-7764; FAX 813-689-9545. **Owner(s):** Media General, Inc., 333 E. Grace St., Richmond, VA 23219. TEL 804-649-6000; FAX 804-649-6898; Ed. D'Ann White. adv. contact: Susie Howell. photos; pub. size: tabloid; circ. 44,500(free).

US

SOUTH TAMPA NEWS. 1994. Wed. free. 1401 Oakfield Dr., Brandon, FL 33511-4854. TEL 813-664-0264. **Owner(s):** Media General, Inc., 333 E. Grace St., Richmond, VA 23219. TEL 804-649-6000; FAX 804-649-6898; Ed. Joe Rice. adv. contact: Dom Cassano. pub. size: tabloid; circ. 32,000(free).

US

TEMPLE TERRACE NEWS. 1988. Wed. free. 1401 Oakfield Dr., Brandon, FL 33511-4854. TEL 813-689-7764; FAX 813-689-9545. **Owner(s):** Media General, Inc., 333 E. Grace St., Richmond, VA 23219. TEL 804-649-6000; FAX 804-649-6898; Ed. David Loverude. adv. contact: Susie Howell. pub. size: tabloid; circ. 24,000(free).

BUSHNELL

US
SUMTER COUNTY TIMES. 1881. Thu. $.35 newsstand; $15.50/yr. 204 E. McCollum Ave., Bushnell, FL 33513. TEL 352-793-2161; FAX 352-793-1486. **Owner(s):** Landmark Community Newspapers, Inc., P.O. Box 549, Shelbyville, KY 40066. TEL 502-633-4334; FAX 502-633-0852; Ed. Bob Reichman. adv.; photos; pub. size: broadsheet; circ. 4,500(paid).

CALLAHAN

US
NASSAU COUNTY RECORD. Thu. $.50 newsstand; $16.95/yr. in cy.; $23.54/yr. out of cy. 213 W. Brandies Ave., Callahan, FL 32011. TEL 904-879-2727; FAX 904-879-5155. **Owner(s):** Tom Wood, Publ., Nassau County Record, 213 Brandies Ave., Callahan, FL 32011. TEL 904-879-2727; Ed. Jim Sparks; Pub. Tom Wood; adv. contact: Candy Wingo. photos; bk.rev.; pub. size: standard; circ. 4,600(paid).

CEDAR

US
CEDAR KEY BEACON. 1984. Thu. $.50 newsstand; $25/yr. in state; $25/yr. out of state. 6050 D St., Cedar, FL 32625-0998. TEL 904-543-5701; FAX 904-543-5928. **Owner(s):** Advertising Design, Inc., P.O. Box 532, Cedar Key, FL 32625. TEL 904-543-5701; FAX 904-543-5928; Ed. Connie Raftis; Pub. Michael J. Raftis; adv.; photos; bk.rev.; pub. size: tabloid; circ. 1,500(paid).

CHATTAHOOCHEE

US ISSN 0889-2245
TWIN CITY NEWS, THE. 1964. Thu. $.30 newsstand; $15.50/yr. in cy.; $18.85/yr. elsewhere. 314 Washington St., Chattahoochee, FL 32324. TEL 904-663-2255; FAX 904-663-8102. **Owner(s):** Stanley J. Ramsey, 620 Morgan Ave., Chattahoochee, FL 32324. TEL 904-663-2525; FAX 904-663-2255; Ed. Stanley J. Ramsey; Pub. Stanley J. Ramsey; adv.; photos; pub. size: broadsheet; circ. 2,000(paid).

CLEWISTON

US
CLEWISTON NEWS. 1928. Wed. $16.05/yr. in cy.; $19.26/yr. out of cy. 626 W. Sugarland Hwy., Clewiston, FL 33440. TEL 941-983-9148; FAX 941-983-7537. **Owner(s):** Joe Smyth, 4308 E. Lakeside Ln., Scottsdale, AZ 85253. TEL 602-991-5333; Ed. Tracy Whirls; Pub. Richard Hitt; adv. contact: Kerri Faunce. pub. size: broadsheet; circ. 3,500(paid).

US
GLADES COUNTY DEMOCRAT. 1923. Thu. $19.08/yr. 620 W. Sugarland Hwy., Clewiston, FL 33440. TEL 941-946-0511; FAX 941-983-7537. **Owner(s):** Independent Newspapers, Inc., P.O. Box 1236, Clewiston, FL 33440. TEL 813-983-9148; Ed. Tracy Worils; Pub. Richard Hitt; adv.; pub. size: tabloid; circ. 1,500(paid).

CORAL SPRINGS

US ISSN 1065-1462
BROWARD TIMES, THE. 1990. Fri. $.50 newsstand; $35/yr. 11905 W. Sample Rd., Coral Springs, FL 33065. TEL 954-345-1822; FAX 954-346-6377. **Owner(s):** Broward Times, Inc., 1001 W. Cypress Creek Rd., Ste. 111, Fort Lauderdale, FL 33309. TEL 954-351-9070; FAX 954-351-3099; Pub. Keith A. Clayborne; adv.; photos; bk.rev.; pub. size: broadsheet; circ. 25,000(controlled & paid). **Wire Service(s):** AP.

US
SUNRISE TIMES. Fri. free. 9660 W. Sample Rd., Ste. 203, Coral Springs, FL 33065. TEL 954-752-7474; FAX 954-752-7855. **Owner(s):** South Florida Newspaper Network, Inc., 601 Fairway Dr., Deerfield Beach, FL 33441. TEL 954-698-6397; FAX 954-698-4297; Ed. Van A. Gosselin; Pub. Christine Beach; adv. contact: Christine Beach. pub. size: tabloid; circ. 25,000(free).

US
TAMARAC FORUM. Fri. free. 9660 W. Sample Rd., Ste. 203, Coral Springs, FL 33065. TEL 954-752-7474; FAX 954-752-7855. **Owner(s):** South Florida Newspaper Network, Inc., 601 Fairway Dr., Deerfield Beach, FL 33441. TEL 954-698-6397; FAX 954-429-1207; Ed. Van A. Gosselin; Pub. Christine Beach; circ. 25,000(free).

CRAWFORDVILLE

US
WAKULLA NEWS. 1895. Thu. $.50 newsstand; $22/yr. in cy.; $25/yr. out of cy. P.O. Box 307, Crawfordville, FL 32326. TEL 904-926-7102; FAX 904-926-3815. **Owner(s):** Wakulla Publishing Co., P.O. Box 307, Crawfordville, FL 32326. TEL 904-926-7102; Ed. Shannon P. Turnbull; Pub. Lynda Kinsey; adv. contact: Lynda Kinsey. pub. size: broadsheet; circ. 5,000(paid).

CRESTVIEW

US
BULLETIN, THE. 1975. Wed. free local; $52/yr. mailed. 301 N. Main, Crestview, FL 32536. TEL 904-682-6524; FAX 904-682-2246. **Owner(s):** Jim Knudsen, 301 N. Main St., Crestview, FL 32536. TEL 904-682-2246; Ed. Jim Watley; Pub. Jim Knudsen; adv.; pub. size: broadsheet; circ. 14,500(free & paid).

DADE CITY

US
PASCO NEWS. 1904. Thu. $14.84/yr. in cy.; $20.14/yr. out of cy. 13032 US 301, Dade City, FL 33525. TEL 352-567-5639; FAX 352-567-5640. **Owner(s):** Sunpress Publications, Inc., P.O. Box 187, Dade City, FL 33526. TEL 352-567-5639; FAX 352-567-5640; Ed. Carlene Ellberg; Pub. J.W. Owens; adv. contact: Donna Covert. photos; bk.rev.; pub. size: broadsheet; circ. 6,000(paid).

DEERFIELD BEACH

US
BOCA MONDAY. Thu. free newsstand; $22/3 mos.; $38/6 mos.; $69/yr. 601 Fairway Dr., Deerfield Beach, FL 33441. TEL 954-698-6397; FAX 954-429-1207. **Owner(s):** South Florida Newspaper Network, Inc., 601 Fairway Dr., Deerfield Beach, FL 33441. TEL 305-698-6397; FAX 305-698-6719; Ed. Ron Buckley; Pub. Bruce Warshal; adv. contact: Jeannie Mark. photos; bk.rev.; pub. size: tabloid; circ. 35,000(controlled & free). **Wire Service(s):** CNS.

US
BOYNTON BEACH TIMES. 1979. Wed. free newsstand; $75/yr. 601 Fairway Dr., Deerfield Beach, FL 33441. TEL 954-698-6397; FAX 954-429-1207. **Owner(s):** Bruce Warshal & Scott Patterson, 601 Fairway Dr., Deerfield Beach, FL 33441; Ed. Rosemarie Donovan. pub. size: tabloid; circ. 30,000(paid).

US
DEERFIELD BEACH OBSERVER. 1972. Thu. free residents; $60/yr. out of town. 43 N.E. Second St., Deerfield Beach, FL 33441. TEL 954-428-9045; FAX 954-428-9096. **Owner(s):** Deerfield Publishing, Inc., 43 N.E. Second St., Deerfield Beach, FL 33441. TEL 305-428-9045; Ed. Judith V. Wilson; Pub. David Eller; adv.; photos; bk.rev.; pub. size: tabloid; circ. 30,000(free & paid).

US
DEERFIELD BEACH THURSDAY TIMES. Thu. free newsstand; $22/3 mos. mailed. 601 Fairway Dr., Deerfield Beach, FL 33441. TEL 954-698-6397; FAX 954-698-6719. **Owner(s):** South Florida Newspaper Network, Inc., 601 Fairway Dr., Deerfield Beach, FL 33441. TEL 954-698-6397; FAX 954-698-6719; Pub. Bruce Warshal; adv.; photos; bk.rev.; pub. size: tabloid; circ. 16,000(controlled & free).

US
DELRAY TIMES. 1980. Thu. free. 601 Fairway Dr., Deerfield Beach, FL 33441. TEL 954-698-6397; FAX 954-429-1207. **Owner(s):** South Florida Newspaper Network, Inc., 601 Fairway Dr., Deerfield Beach, FL 33487. TEL 954-698-6397; FAX 954-421-9003; Ed. Ron Buckley; Pub. Bruce Warshal; adv. contact: Jeanne Mauck. photos; bk.rev.; pub. size: tabloid; circ. 29,000(free). **Wire Service(s):** CNS.
Formerly: Delray Monday Times.

US ISSN 0191-7153
HI-RISER. 1967. Thu. free. 601 Fairway Dr., Deerfield Beach, FL 33441. TEL 954-698-6397; FAX 954-429-1207. **Owner(s):** South Florida Newspaper Network, 601 Fairway Dr., Deerfield Beach, FL 33441. TEL 954-698-6397; FAX 954-429-1207; Ed. Robert Sims; Pub. Scott Patterson; adv. contact: Suzanne Pemper. bk.rev.; pub. size: tabloid; circ. 35,000(free).

US
WEST BOCA TIMES. Wed. free. 601 Fairway Dr., Deerfield Beach, FL 33441. TEL 954-698-6397; FAX 954-698-6719. **Owner(s):** South Florida Newspaper Network, 601 Fairway Dr., Deerfield Beach, FL 33441. TEL 954-698-6397; FAX 954-698-6719; Ed. Ron Buckley; Pub. Bruce Warshal; adv.; photos; bk.rev.; pub. size: tabloid; circ. 20,000(free). **Wire Service(s):** CNS.

WEEKLY NEWSPAPERS   JASPER, FL   10557

DELAND

US

DELAND BEACON, THE. 1992. Wed. $.50 newsstand; $24/yr. 141 E. Indiana Ave., DeLand, FL 32724-0753. TEL 904-734-4622; FAX 904-734-4641; E-mail: delbeacon@aol.com. Owner(s): Barbara Shepherd, 520 N. Delaware, DeLand, FL 32720. TEL 904-736-0667; FAX 904-734-4641; Eileen Everett, 539 N. Delaware, DeLand, FL 32720. TEL 904-736-3057; FAX 904-734-4641; Joann Kramer, 141 E. Indiana, DeLand, FL 32724. TEL 904-736-5711; FAX 904-734-4641; Ed. Barbara Button. adv. contact: Eileen Everett. photos; pub. size: broadsheet; circ. 4,000(paid).

DESTIN

US

DESTIN LOG. 1974. s-w.: Wed. & Sat. $.50 newsstand; $34.98/yr. in state; $44.45/yr. out of state. 1225 Airport Rd., Destin, FL 32541. TEL 904-837-2828; FAX 904-654-5982. Owner(s): Scripps Howard, Inc., 312 Walnut St., 28th Fl., Cincinnati, OH 45202. TEL 513-977-3000; Ed. Kenneth Books; Pub. Michael A. Levi; adv. contact: Susan Sanders. pub. size: broadsheet; circ. 8,500(paid).

FERNANDINA

US

NEWS LEADER. 1858. Wed. $.50 newsstand; $19.29/yr. in cy.; $38.58/yr. out of cy. mailed; $36.40/yr. out of state. 511 Ash St., Fernandina, FL 32034. TEL 904-261-3696; FAX 904-261-3698. Owner(s): New York Times Co., The, 229 W. 43rd St., New York, NY 10036. TEL 212-556-1234; Ed. Mary Hurst; Pub. Foy Maloy; adv. contact: Mike Hankins. pub. size: broadsheet; circ. 11,200(paid).
  Formerly: Fernandina Beach News Leader.

FORT MEADE

US

FORT MEADE LEADER, THE. 1971. s-w.: Tue. & Fri. $.25 newsstand; $20/yr. in cy.; $30/yr. out of cy.; $35/yr. out of state. 25 W. Broadway, Fort Meade, FL 33841. TEL 813-285-8625; FAX 813-285-7634; E-mail: fpcslfiv@aol.com. Owner(s): Frisbie Publishing Co., Inc., P.O. Box 120, Bartow, FL 33831-0120. TEL 813-533-4183; FAX 813-533-0402; Ed. S.L. Frisbie, IV; Pub. S.L. Frisbie, IV; adv.; $6.25/SAU. photos; pub. size: broadsheet; circ. 1,285(free & paid).
  Formerly: Democrat & Leader.

FORT MYERS BEACH

US

BEACH BULLETIN. 1951. Fri. free newsstand in cy.; $30/yr. out of cy. 19260 San Carlos Blvd., Fort Myers Beach, FL 33931. TEL 941-463-4421; FAX 941-463-1402. Owner(s): Breeze Corp., 2510 Del Prado Blvd., Cape Coral, FL 33904. TEL 941-574-1110; Ed. Dee McLelland. adv.; photos; bk.rev.; pub. size: tabloid, 4 color photos/art; circ. 14,000(free & paid).

US

FORT MYERS BEACH OBSERVER. 1985. Wed. free newsstand; $25/yr. 17274 San Carlos Blvd., Fort Myers Beach, FL 33931. TEL 941-482-7111; FAX 941-482-6365. Owner(s): Ogden Newspapers, Inc., 1500 Main St., Wheeling, WV 26003. TEL 304-233-0100; Ed. Dawn Grodsky. adv.; photos; pub. size: tabloid; circ. 45,000(paid).

FROSTPROOF

US

FROSTPROOF NEWS. 1914. Thu. $.50 newsstand; $13.78/yr. in cy.; $15.90/yr. out of cy. 19 S. Scenic Hwy., Frostproof, FL 33843. TEL 941-635-2171; FAX 941-635-4265. Owner(s): Independent Newspapers, Inc., P.O. Box 7001, Dover, DE 19903. TEL 302-674-4750; Ed. Amy Polk; Pub. Richard Hitt; adv.; pub. size: broadsheet; circ. 2,000(paid).

FRUITLAND PARK

US

LAKE NEWS. Wed. free. 2891 Hwy. 441-27, Fruitland Park, FL 34731-2438. TEL 352-787-6277; FAX 352-787-8479. Owner(s): Mid-Florida Publications, 4645 Hwy. 19 A, P.O. Box 318, Mount Dora, FL 32757; Pub. Michael E. Tabor; pub. size: tabloid; circ. 21,500(free).

GAINESVILLE

US

RECORD, THE. 1963. Thu. $20/yr. in state; $24/yr. out of state. 620 N. Main St., Gainesville, FL 32601-0806. TEL 352-377-2444; FAX 352-338-1986. Owner(s): Constance & J. Ben Rowe, P.O. Box 806, Gainesville, FL 32602. TEL 352-377-2444; FAX 352-338-1986; Ed. Richard Canaday; Pub. J. Ben Rowe; adv. contact: Constance Rowe. photos; bk.rev.; pub. size: tabloid; circ. 5,000(paid).
  Formerly: Record Farm & Ranch.

GRACEVILLE

US

GRACEVILLE NEWS. 1905. Thu. $14/yr.; $12/yr. senior citizens. 1004 Tenth Ave., Graceville, FL 32440. TEL 904-263-6015. Owner(s): Ferrin-Cox, P.O. Box 187, Graceville, FL 32440. TEL 904-263-6015; FAX 904-263-1042; Ed. Sharon Taylor. pub. size: standard; circ. 1,700(paid).

GULF BREEZE

US

ISLANDER, THE. 1979. Wed. $.50 newsstand; $20/yr. in cy.; $25/yr. out of cy. 1101 Gulf Breeze Pk.; Ste. 104, Gulf Breeze, FL 32561. TEL 904-934-3417; FAX 904-932-7230. Owner(s): Island Publ. of Pensacola Beach, Inc., P.O. Box 292, Gulf Breeze, FL 32562-0292. TEL 904-934-3417; Ed. Lisa La Paglia; Pub. Barbara Bryant; adv. contact: Karen Bryant. photos; pub. size: broadsheet; circ. 3,500(paid).

US

SENTINEL, THE. 1960. Thu. $.50 newsstand; $19.26/yr. 1200 Gulf Breeze Pkwy., Gulf Breeze, FL 32561. TEL 904-932-0385; FAX 904-932-8765. Owner(s): Gannett Company, Inc., 1100 Wilson Blvd., Arlington, VA 22340. TEL 703-284-6000; Ed. Marlin Osborn; Pub. Marlin Osborn; adv.; pub. size: broadsheet; circ. 6,000(paid).

HALLANDALE

US

DIGEST, THE. 1963. Thu. free carrier in area; $3/wk. mailed. 224 S. Dixie Hwy., Hallandale, FL 33009. TEL 954-457-8029; FAX 954-457-1284. Owner(s): Dan Bluesten, 224 S. Dixie Hwy., Hollywood, FL 33009. TEL 954-457-8029; Ed. Larry Bluestein; Pub. Dan Bluesten; pub. size: broadsheet; circ. 45,000(free & paid).
  Formerly: Hallandale Digest.

HIGH SPRINGS

US   ISSN 0746-1046

HIGH SPRINGS HERALD, THE. 1951. Thu. $.25 newsstand; $12/yr. in cy.; $15/yr. out of cy.; $17/yr. out of state. 5 N.W. First St., High Springs, FL 32655. TEL 904-454-1297; FAX 904-454-4559. Owner(s): Herald Publishing Co., Inc., P.O. Box 14375, Gainesville, FL 32604-3275. TEL 904-376-4446; FAX 904-376-4556; Ed. Jim Hunter; Pub. Ed Barber; adv. contact: Carol Chidlow. photos; bk.rev.; pub. size: standard; circ. 3,600(free & paid). Wire Service(s): AP.

HOMESTEAD

US

SOUTH DADE NEWS LEADER. 1912. 3/wk.: Mon., Wed., Fri. $.50 newsstand; $19.17/13 wks.; $58.58/yr. 15 N.E. First Rd., Homestead, FL 33030. TEL 305-245-2311; FAX 305-248-0596. Owner(s): Homestead Newspapers, Inc., 15 N.E. First Rd., Homestead, FL 33090. TEL 305-245-2311; Ed. Yolanda Ulrich; Pub. Glen Martin; adv. contact: Tracy Lovitt. pub. size: broadsheet; circ. 12,514(paid). Wire Service(s): UPI.

JACKSONVILLE

US

JACKSONVILLE SHOPPING GUIDE. 1971. Wed. free. 3801 University Blvd., W., Jacksonville, FL 32217. TEL 904-737-7320; FAX 904-737-2274. Owner(s): Add, Inc., 600 Industrial Dr., P.O. Box 609, Waupoca, WI 54981. TEL 715-258-8450; Ed. Debbie Weinelt. pub. size: tabloid; circ. 150,000(free).
  Formerly: Shopping Guide.

JACKSONVILLE BEACH

US

BEACHES LEADER. 1963. s-w.: Wed. & Fri. $.50 newsstand; $20/yr. mailed. 1114 Beach Blvd., Jacksonville Beach, FL 32250. TEL 904-249-9033. Owner(s): Thomas H. Wood, P.O. Box 50129, Jacksonville, FL 32250; Ed. Kathleen Feindt Bailey; Pub. Thomas H. Wood; pub. size: broadsheet; circ. 22,500(paid).

JASPER

US

JASPER NEWS. 1869. Thu. $.50 newsstand; $12/yr. in cy.; $19/yr. out of cy. P.O. Drawer D, Jasper, FL 32052. TEL 904-792-2487; FAX 904-792-3009. Owner(s): Ricketsons & Associates, Lake City, FL; Ed. Gail Newsome; Pub. Michael Coulter; adv. contact: Chris White. photos; pub. size: standard; circ. 2,077(free & paid).

Weeklies

JUPITER

US   ISSN 0896-0283
JUPITER COURIER. 1958. s-w.: Wed. & Sun. $.50 newsstand; $54.06/yr. home deliv., $79.50/yr. mailed. 800 W. Indiantown Rd., Jupiter, FL 33458. TEL 407-746-5111; FAX 407-743-0673. **Owner(s):** Scripps-Howard, 312 Walnut St., 28th Fl., Cincinnati, OH 45202. TEL 513-977-3000; Ed. Kevin Hemstock. adv.; photos; bk.rev.; pub. size: broadsheet; circ. 11,000(paid).
    Formerly: Courier Journal.

KISSIMMEE

US   ISSN 1060-1244
OSCEOLA NEWS-GAZETTE. 1895. s-w.: Thu. & Sat. $.25 newsstand; $48.15/yr. 108 Church St., Kissimmee, FL 34741. TEL 407-846-7600; FAX 407-846-8516. **Owner(s):** Florida Sun Publishing, P.O. Box 811, Bradenton, FL 34206. TEL 800-282-3953; Ed. Bill Orben. adv.; photos; pub. size: broadsheet; circ. 29,000(controlled & paid).
    Formerly: News-Gazette.

LA BELLE

US
CALOOSA BELLE. 1922. Wed. free newsstand; $20/yr. 22 Fort Thompson Ave., La Belle, FL 33935. TEL 941-675-2541; FAX 941-675-1449. **Owner(s):** Independent Newspapers, Inc., P.O. Box 7001, Dover, DE 19903. TEL 813-983-9148; Ed. Patty Brant. adv. contact: Martha Briede. pub. size: broadsheet; circ. 7,500(paid).

LAKE PLACID

US
LAKE PLACID JOURNAL. 1957. Thu. $24.61/yr. 232 N. Main St., Lake Placid, FL 33852. TEL 941-465-2423; FAX 941-699-0331. **Owner(s):** Constance Delaney, P.O. Box 785, Lake Placid, FL 33852. TEL 813-465-4122; Pub. Mat Delaney; pub. size: broadsheet; circ. 4,990(paid).

LAKE WALES

US
LAKE WALES NEWS. 1926. Thu. $.25 newsstand; $14.84/yr. 140 E. Stuart Ave., Lake Wales, FL 33853. TEL 813-676-3467. **Owner(s):** Brice Printing-Sole Properties, 140 Stuart Ave., Lake Wales, FL 33853. TEL 813-676-3467; Pub. Owen B. Brice; adv.; pub. size: broadsheet; circ. 3,500(paid).

LAKE WORTH

US
LAKE WORTH HERALD COASTAL OBSERVER. 1912. Thu. $.50 newsstand; $12/6 mos.; $25/yr. 130 S. H St., Lake Worth, FL 33460. TEL 407-585-9387; FAX 407-585-5434. **Owner(s):** Karl Easton, 130 S. H St., Lake Worth, FL 33460. TEL 407-585-9387; Ed. Jay Kravetz; Pub. Karl J. Easton; adv.; photos; bk.rev.; pub. size: tabloid; circ. 40,000(free & paid). **Wire Service(s):** IPN.

LAND O' LAKES

US
LAKE AREA NEWS. Thu. free. P.O. Box 1669, Land O' Lakes, FL 34639. TEL 813-249-5603; FAX 813-249-5316. **Owner(s):** Media General, Inc., 333 E. Grace St., Richmond, VA 23219. TEL 804-649-6000; Ed. Robert W. Klein. adv. contact: Dom Cassano. pub. size: tabloid; circ. 25,000(free).

LEHIGH ACRES

US
NEWS-STAR. 1962. Wed. free in cy.; $13.25/yr. out of cy.; $28/yr. out of state. 1250 Business Way, Lehigh Acres, FL 33936-0908. TEL 941-369-2191; FAX 941-369-1396. **Owner(s):** News-Star Publications, Inc., 1250 Business Way, Lehigh Acres, FL 33936. TEL 941-369-2191; FAX 941-369-1396; Ed. J. Tom Wason. adv.; photos; bk.rev.; pub. size: tabloid; circ. 13,500(controlled & free).
    Formerly: Lehigh News; Lehigh Acres News-Star.

MACCLENNY

US
BAKER COUNTY PRESS, THE. 1929. Thu. $.50 newsstand; $16/yr. in cy.; $20/yr. out of cy. 104 S. Fifth St., MacClenny, FL 32063. TEL 904-259-2400. **Owner(s):** Baker County Press, Inc., 104 S. Fifth St., P.O. Box 598, MacClenny, FL 32063. TEL 904-259-2400; FAX 904-259-6502; Ed. James C. McGauley; Pub. James C. McGauley; adv. contact: Jeanie Shadd. pub. size: broadsheet; circ. 5,300(paid).

MADISON

US
MADISON COUNTY CARRIER. 1964. Wed. $.50 newsstand; $35/yr. in cy.; $36/yr. out of cy. & state. 53 South, Madison, FL 32340. TEL 904-973-4141; FAX 904-973-4121. **Owner(s):** Tommy & Mary Ellen Greene, P.O. Drawer 772, Madison, FL 32340; Ed. Jacob Bembry; Pub. Tommy Greene; adv.; pub. size: broadsheet; circ. 4,500(paid).

US
MADISON ENTERPRISE RECORDER. 1864. Fri. $.50 newsstand; $34.24/yr in cy. 111 S. Shelby St., Madison, FL 32341. TEL 904-973-4141; FAX 904-973-4121. **Owner(s):** Tommy & Mary Ellen Greene, P.O. Drawer 772, Madison, FL. TEL 904-973-4141; Ed. Harvey Greene; Pub. Tommy Greene; adv.; photos; bk.rev.; pub. size: broadsheet; circ. 3,500(paid).

MARATHON

US
FLORIDA KEYS KEYNOTER. 1953. s-w.: Wed. & Sat. $.25 newsstand; $30/yr. in cy.; $40/yr. elsewhere. 3015 Overseas Hwy., Marathon, FL 33050. TEL 305-743-5551; FAX 305-743-9586; E-mail: keynoter@aol.com; URL: http://florida-keys.fl.us/keynoter.htm. **Owner(s):** Knight-Ridder, Inc., One Herald Plz., Miami, FL 33132. TEL 305-376-3800; FAX 305-376-3875; Ed. Tom Tuell; Pub. Tom Schumaker; adv. contact: Charlotte Sikora. photos; pub. size: tabloid; circ. 15,000(free & paid). **Wire Service(s):** AP Newsfinder.
    Formerly: Keynoter.

MARCO ISLAND

US
MARCO ISLAND EAGLE, THE. 1968. Wed. $.50 newsstand; $24.50/yr. in state; $44/yr. out of state. P.O. Box 579, Marco Island, FL 34146. TEL 941-394-7592; FAX 941-394-8552. **Owner(s):** New York Times Co., The, 229 W. 43rd St., New York, NY 10036. TEL 212-556-1234; Pub. Cheryl Ferrara; pub. size: tabloid; circ. 10,000(paid).

MARGATE

US
BROWARD NEWS. 1977. Thu. free newsstand; $60/yr. 767 S. State Rd. 7, Ste. 1, Margate, FL 33068-4822. TEL 305-977-7770; FAX 305-977-7779. **Owner(s):** Harvey Lustig, 767 S. State Rd. 7, Ste. 1, Margate, FL 33068. TEL 305-977-7770; FAX 305-977-7779; Ed. Mort Luxnor; Pub. Harvey Lustig; adv. contact: Shelly Lazarus. photos; pub. size: tabloid.

MARIANNA

US
FLORIDIAN, THE. Wed. free newsstand & deliv. 4403 Constitution Ln., Marianna, FL 32448. TEL 904-526-3614; FAX 904-482-4478. **Owner(s):** Thomson Newspapers, Inc., Metro Centre, One Station Pl., 6th Fl., Stamford, CT 06902. TEL 203-425-2500; FAX 203-425-2516; Ed. Judy Green; Pub. Jane Benton; pub. size: broadsheet; circ. 10,000(free).
    Formerly: Marketplace, The.

MELBOURNE

US
BAY BULLETIN. Wed. free. One Gannett Plz., Melbourne, FL 32940. TEL 407-242-3500; FAX 407-242-0760. **Owner(s):** Gannett Company, Inc., 1100 Wilson Blvd., Arlington, VA 22340. TEL 703-284-6000; Ed. Harry McNamara; Pub. Michael Coleman; circ. 30,000(free).

US
LITTLE PAPER, THE. Thu. free newsstand. 835 E. New Haven Ave., Melbourne, FL 32901. TEL 407-723-5337; FAX 407-729-4210. **Owner(s):** Richard Sheffeld, 835 E. New Haven Ave., Melbourne, FL 32901. TEL 407-723-5337; Pub. Richard Sheffeld; adv.; pub. size: tabloid; circ. 50,000(free).

US
TIMES, THE. 1894. Wed. free. One Gannett Plz., Melbourne, FL 32940. TEL 407-242-3500; FAX 407-242-0760. **Owner(s):** Gannett Company, Inc., 1100 Wilson Blvd., Arlington, VA 22340. TEL 703-284-6000; Ed. Harry MacNamara; Pub. Michael Coleman; adv. contact: Norm Chigar. pub. size: broadsheet; circ. 51,493(free).

US
TRIBUNE, THE. 1917. Wed. free. One Gannett Plz., Melbourne, FL 32940. TEL 407-242-3500; FAX 407-242-0760. **Owner(s):** Gannett Company, Inc., 1100 Wilson Blvd., Arlington, VA 22340. TEL 703-284-6000; Ed. Harry MacNamara; Pub. Michael Coleman; pub. size: broadsheet; circ. 39,000(free).

WEEKLY NEWSPAPERS

MERRITT ISLAND

US

BREVARD REPORTER, THE. 1981. Thu. $26/yr. 142 S. Courtenay Pkwy., Merritt Island, FL 32952-4509. TEL 407-454-6300; FAX 407-454-6301; E-mail: suncoast@palmnet.net. **Owner(s):** John Barnesy, 142 S. Courtenay Pkwy., Merritt Island, FL 32952-1928. TEL 407-454-6300; FAX 407-454-6301; adv.; pub. size: tabloid; circ. 6,000(paid).

MIAMI

US

CAROL CITY/OPA-LOCKA NEWS. 1958. s-w.: Mon. & Thu. free. 6796 S.W. 62nd Ave., Miami, FL 33143. TEL 305-667-7481; FAX 305-661-0954. **Owner(s):** Community Newspapers, Inc., 6796 S.W. 62nd Ave., Miami, FL 33143. TEL 305-667-7481; Ed. Michael Miller; Pub. Grant Miller; adv. contact: Grant Miller. pub. size: tabloid; circ. 3,000(controlled & paid). **Wire Service(s):** UPI.

CORAL GABLES NEWS. 1958. s-w.: Mon. & Thu. free. 6796 S.W. 62nd Ave., Miami, FL 33143. TEL 305-667-7481; FAX 305-661-0954. **Owner(s):** Community Newspapers, Inc., 6796 S.W. 62nd Ave., Miami, FL 33143. TEL 305-667-7481; Ed. Michael Miller; Pub. Grant Miller; adv. contact: Grant Miller. pub. size: tabloid; circ. 8,000(controlled & paid). **Wire Service(s):** UPI.

US

HIALEAH/OPA-LACKA NEWS. 1958. s-w.: Mon. & Thu. $.25 newsstand; $40/yr. mailed. 6796 S.W. 62nd Ave., Miami, FL 33143. TEL 305-667-7481; FAX 305-661-0954. **Owner(s):** Community Newspapers, Inc., 6796 S.W. 62nd Ave., Miami, FL 33143. TEL 305-667-7481; Ed. Michael Miller; Pub. Grant Miller; adv. contact: Grant Miller. pub. size: tabloid; circ. 9,000(controlled & paid). **Wire Service(s):** UPI.
Formerly: Hialeah-Miami Springs News.

US

KENDALL NEWS-GAZETTE. 0958. s-w.: Mon. & Thu. free. 6796 S.W. 62nd Ave., Miami, FL 33143. TEL 305-667-7481; FAX 305-661-0954. **Owner(s):** Community Newspapers, Inc., 6796 S.W. 62nd Ave., Miami, FL 33143. TEL 305-667-7481; Ed. Michael Miller; Pub. Grant Miller; adv. contact: Grant Miller. pub. size: tabloid; circ. 25,000(free). **Wire Service(s):** UPI.
Formerly: Kendall-South Miami News.

US

MIAMI TODAY. 1983. w. $1/newsstand; $60/yr. US; $140/yr. South America, $190/yr. Europe. 710 Brickell Ave., Miami, FL 33131. TEL 305-358-1008. **Owner(s):** Today Enterprises, Inc., P.O. Box 1368, Miami, FL 33101. TEL 305-358-1008; Ed. Michael Lewis; Pub. Michael Lewis; adv.; photos; bk.rev.; pub. size: tabloid; circ. 31,602(controlled & paid). **Wire Service(s):** AP.

US

NORTH MIAMI NEWS. 1958. s-w.: Mon. & Thu. free. 6796 S.W. 62nd Ave., Miami, FL 33143. TEL 305-667-7481; FAX 305-661-0954. **Owner(s):** Community Newspapers, Inc., 6796 S.W. 62nd Ave., Miami, FL 33143. TEL 305-667-7481; Ed. Michael Miller; Pub. Grant Miller; adv. contact: Grant Miller. pub. size: tabloid; circ. morning 9,000(paid). **Wire Service(s):** UPI.

US

SOUTH MIAMI NEWS. 1958. s-w.: Mon. & Thu. free newsstand; $29.92/yr. local mailed. 6796 S.W. 62nd Ave., Miami, FL 33143. TEL 305-667-7481; FAX 305-661-0954. **Owner(s):** Community Newspapers, Inc., 6796 S.W. 62nd Ave., Miami, FL 33143. TEL 305-661-0954; Ed. Michael Miller; Pub. Grant Miller; adv.; pub. size: broadsheet; circ. 6,500(free & paid).
Formerly: South Miami Shore News.

US

SUN POST, THE. Thu. free newsstand; $35/yr. 3rd class; $80/yr. 1st class. 1688 Meridian Ave., Ste. 702, Miami, FL 33119. TEL 305-538-9700; FAX 305-538-9700. **Owner(s):** Caxton Publishing Co., 1688 Meridian Ave., Ste. 702, Miami, FL 33119. TEL 305-538-9700; Ed. Michael Sasser; Pub. Andrew Stark; adv. contact: Mark Kulwin. photos; pub. size: tabloid; circ. 35,000(controlled).

MIAMI LAKES

US

MIAMI LAKER. 1975. m. free. 6843 Main St., Ste. 310, Miami Lakes, FL 33014. TEL 305-817-4007; FAX 305-817-4197. **Owner(s):** Graham Companies, The, 6843 Main St., Miami Lakes, FL 33014. TEL 305-821-1130; Ed. Roger Reece. adv.; pub. size: tabloid; circ. 26,500(controlled).

MILTON

US

SANTA ROSA FREE PRESS. 1975. s-w.: Mon. & Thu. $.50 newsstand. 531 W. Elva St., Milton, FL 32570. TEL 904-623-3616; FAX 904-623-2007. **Owner(s):** Jim Hill, 531 W. Elva St., Milton, FL 32570. TEL 904-623-3616; Ed. Jim Fletcher; Pub. Jim Hill; adv. contact: Jim Martin. pub. size: broadsheet; circ. 8,000(free).

US ISSN 0273-5857

SANTA ROSA PRESS GAZETTE. 1907. s-w.: Mon. & Thu. $.50 newsstand; $24/yr. in cy.; $30/yr. out of cy. 531 W. Elva St., Milton, FL 32570. TEL 904-623-3131. **Owner(s):** Santa Rosa Press Gazette, 531 W. Elva St., Milton, FL 32572. TEL 904-623-2120; FAX 904-623-2007; Ed. Jim Fletcher. adv.; pub. size: broadsheet; circ. 7,500(paid).

MONTICELLO

US ISSN 0746-5297

MONTICELLO NEWS. 1869. s-w.: Wed. & Fri. $.25 newsstand; $29.26/yr. 100 W. Dogwood St., Monticello, FL 32344. TEL 904-997-3568; FAX 904-997-3774. **Owner(s):** Monticello Publishing Co., Inc., 100 W. Dogwood St., Monticello, FL 32344. TEL 904-997-3568; FAX 904-997-3774; Ed. Lazaro Almon; Pub. Ron Cichon; adv. contact: Shirley Rudd. photos; pub. size: broadsheet; circ. 3,000(paid).

MT. DORA

US

EUSTIS LAKE REGION NEWS. Thu. $.25 newsstand; $8.56/yr. in cy.; $10.17/yr. out of cy. 4645 N. Hwy. 19A, Mt. Dora, FL 32757-2039. TEL 352-357-3199; FAX 352-357-3202. **Owner(s):** William Matthew, 4645 N. Hwy. 19A, Mount Dora, FL 32757-2039; Ed. C.J. Woodring; Pub. Michael Tabor; pub. size: broadsheet; circ. 1,500(paid).

US

TAVARES CITIZEN. 1882. Thu. $8.56/yr. in cy.; $10.17/yr. out of cy. 4645 N. Hwy. 19A, Mt. Dora, FL 32757-2039. TEL 352-357-3199; FAX 352-357-3202. **Owner(s):** Mid-Florida Publications, 4645 Hwy. 19A, Mt. Dora, FL 32757. TEL 352-357-3199; Ed. C.J. Woodring; Pub. Mike Tabor; adv.; pub. size: broadsheet; circ. 400(paid).

MULBERRY

US

MULBERRY PRESS. 1909. Thu. $.50 newsstand; $24/yr. in cy. 1020 N. Church Ave., Hwy. 37-N, Mulberry, FL 33860-2040. TEL 813-425-3411. **Owner(s):** Histed Media Group, 1020 N. Church Ave., Hwy. 37-N, Mulberry, FL 33860. TEL 813-425-3411; Ed. William M. Histed. adv. contact: Barbara Wagoner. photos; bk.rev.; pub. size: broadsheet; circ. 6,000(paid).

US

POLK CITY PRESS. 1984. Thu. $.35 newsstand; $24/yr. 1020 N. Church Ave., Hwy. 37-N, Mulberry, FL 33860-2040. TEL 813-425-3411. **Owner(s):** Histed Media Group, 1020 N. Church Ave., Hwy. 37-N, Mulberry, FL 33860. TEL 813-425-3411; Ed. Martha Connell; Pub. Robert Histed; adv. contact: Barbara Wagoner. photos; bk.rev.; pub. size: broadsheet; circ. 3,050(paid).

NEW PORT RICHEY

US

SUN COAST NEWS. s-w.: Wed. & Sat. free in area; $5.30/mo. mailed; $60/yr. mailed. 6214 U.S. Hwy. 19, New Port Richey, FL 34652. TEL 813-849-7500; FAX 813-847-2902. **Owner(s):** Sunbelt Newspapers, Inc., 6214 U.S. Hwy., New Port Richey, FL 34652; Ed. Gwen Stevenson; Pub. Rich Litowchak; adv. contact: Bob Fransen. pub. size: tabloid; circ. 145,000(free & paid).
Formerly: Tarpon Springs Leader.

NICEVILLE

US

BAY BEACON, THE. 1992. Wed. $38.50/yr. 203 W. John Sims Pkwy., Ste. 2, Niceville, FL 32578. TEL 904-678-1080; FAX 904-729-3225. **Owner(s):** Stephen W. Kent, 203 W. John Sims Pkwy., Niceville, FL 32578. TEL 904-678-1080; FAX 904-729-3225; Ed. Stephen Kent; Pub. Stephen Kent; adv. contact: Sara Kent. adv.: $6.95/SAU; ads. photos; pub. size: broadsheet; circ. 12,356(free & paid).

ORANGE PARK

US

CLAY TODAY. 1974. s-w.: Wed. & Fri. $.25 newsstand; $48/yr. in cy. mailed. 1564 Kingsley Ave., Orange Park, FL 32073. TEL 904-264-3200; FAX 904-269-6958. **Owner(s):** Add, Inc., 600 Industrial Rd., P.O. Box 609, Waupaca, WI 54981. TEL 715-258-8450; Ed. Mike Mann; Pub. Joyce Lydon; pub. size: tabloid; circ. evening 15,000(free & paid).

US

GAINESVILLE BUYERS GUIDE. Wed. free newsstand & home deliv. 1564 Kingsley Ave., Orange Park, FL 32073-4594. TEL 904-264-3200; FAX 904-269-6958. **Owner(s):** Add, Inc., P.O. Box 609, Waupaca, WI 54981. TEL 715-258-8450; Ed. Mike Mann; Pub. Joyce Lydon; adv. contact: Tim Kult. pub. size: broadsheet; circ. 40,000(free).

10560 ORANGE PARK, FL **WEEKLY NEWSPAPERS**

US
TODAY. 1993. s-w.: Wed. & Fri. free newsstand. 1564 Kingsley Ave., Orange Park, FL 32073. TEL 904-264-3200; FAX 904-269-6958; E-mail: jlclay@jax-inter.net. **Owner(s):** Add, Inc., P.O. Box 609, Waupaca, WI 54981. TEL 715-258-8450; Ed. Mike Mann; Pub. Joyce Lydon; adv. contact: Tim Kult. pub. size: broadsheet; circ. 80,000(free).

ORMOND BEACH
US
DAYTONA PENNYSAVER. 1976. Wed. free. 454 S. Yonge St., Ormond Beach, FL 32174. TEL 904-677-4262; FAX 904-672-7453. **Owner(s):** News-Journal Corp., 901 Sixth St., Daytona Beach, FL 32117-8099. TEL 904-677-4262; Ed. Leonard Marsh; Pub. Leonard Marsh; adv. contact: Nancy Echard. pub. size: tabloid; circ. 75,000(free).

OVIEDO
US
OVIEDO VOICE, THE. 1992. Thu. $.35 newsstand; $17.12/yr. 169 W. Broadway, Oviedo, FL 32765. TEL 407-366-9181; FAX 407-366-7580. **Owner(s):** Oviedo Voice, The, 169 W. Broadway, Oviedo, FL 32765; Ed. Donna Mullins; Pub. James R. Noles; adv.; photos; pub. size: tabloid; circ. 2,600(paid).

PENSACOLA
US
ESCAMBIA SUN PRESS. 1948. Thu. $.25 newsstand; $16/yr. in cy.; $21.40/yr. out of cy. 3610 Barrancas Ave., Pensacola, FL 32507. TEL 904-456-3121; FAX 904-456-0103. **Owner(s):** Michael Driver, P.O. Box 4625, Pensacola, FL 32507. TEL 904-456-3121; Ed. Michael Driver; Pub. Michael Driver; adv.; pub. size: broadsheet; circ. 3,500(paid).

US
PENSACOLA VOICE. 1865. Thu. $.50 newsstand; $20/yr. 213 E. Yonge St., Pensacola, FL 32503. TEL 904-434-6963; FAX 904-469-8745. **Owner(s):** Les Humphrey, 213 E. Yonge St., Pensacola, FL 32503. TEL 904-434-6963; Ed. Hubert Jones; Pub. Les Humphrey; adv. contact: Mark Anghony. pub. size: standard; circ. 36,000(paid).

US
PERDIDO PELICAN. 1985. bi-w.: Mon. free. P.O. Box 34257, Pensacola, FL 32507. TEL 904-492-5221; FAX 904-492-7109. **Owner(s):** Gulf Breeze Publishing Co., P.O. Box 34257, Pensacola, FL 32507; Ed. Fran Thompson; Pub. Fran Thompson; adv.; photos; bk.rev.; pub. size: tabloid; circ. 10,000(free).

US
SHOPPER, THE. 1975. s-w.: Tue. & Fri. $.65 newsstand; $7/mo. 3041 E. Olive Rd., Pensacola, FL 32514. TEL 904-478-3805; FAX 904-478-2222. **Owner(s):** Susan Thibodeaux, 3041 E. Olive Rd., Pensacola, FL 32514; Ed. Susan Thibodeaux. adv.; photos; pub. size: tabloid; circ. 45,000(paid).

PERRY
US ISSN 0747-0967
PERRY NEWS-HERALD. 1887. s-w.: Wed. & Fri. $.50 newsstand; $20/yr. in cy.; $32/yr. out of cy. 123 S. Jefferson, Perry, FL 32347. TEL 904-584-5513; FAX 904-838-1566. **Owner(s):** Perry Newspapers, Inc., P.O. Box 32348, Perry, FL 32347. TEL 904-584-5513; Ed. Aaron Portwood; Pub. Don Lincoln; adv. contact: Beth Mann. pub. size: broadsheet; circ. 5,100(paid).

US ISSN 0747-2358
PERRY TACO TIMES. 1962. s-w.: Wed. & Fri. $.50 newsstand; $20/yr. in cy.; $32/yr. out of cy. 123 S. Jefferson, Perry, FL 32347. TEL 904-584-5513; FAX 904-838-1566. **Owner(s):** Perry Newspapers, Inc., P.O. Box 888, Perry, FL 32347. TEL 904-584-5513; Ed. Aaron Portwood; Pub. Don Lincoln; adv. contact: Beth Mann. pub. size: standard; circ. 5,100(paid).

PLANT CITY
US
COURIER, THE. Thu. $.25 newsstand; $18.11/yr. 102 S. Evers St., Plant City, FL 33566. TEL 813-752-3113. **Owner(s):** Media General, Inc., 333 E. Grace St., Richmond, VA 23219. TEL 804-649-6000; Ed. Bob McClure. adv. contact: Sherry Wheeler. pub. size: tabloid; circ. 4,700(paid).

US
PLANT CITY SHOPPER. Wed. free. 102 S. Evers St., Plant City, FL 33566. TEL 813-752-3113. **Owner(s):** Media General, Inc., 333 E. Grace St., Richmond, VA 23219. TEL 804-649-6000; FAX 804-649-6898; adv. contact: Sherry Wheeler. pub. size: tabloid; circ. 26,000(free).

POMPANO BEACH
US
POMPANO LEDGER, THE. 1980. Thu. $.25 newsstand; $13.78/yr. 2500 S.E. Fifth Ct., Pompano Beach, FL 33062. TEL 305-946-7277. E-mail: 72747.502@compuserve.com. **Owner(s):** Karen M. Foley, 2500 S.E. Fifth Ct., Pompano Beach, FL 33062. TEL 305-946-7277; Ed. Edward J. Foley; Pub. Karen M. Foley; adv. contact: Karen M. Foley. photos; pub. size: broadsheet; circ. 20,000(free & paid). **Wire Service(s):** AP.

QUINCY
US
GADSDEN COUNTY TIMES. 1901. Thu. $.50 newsstand; $22/yr. in cy.; $33/yr. out of cy.; $30/yr. out of state. 15 S. Madison, Quincy, FL 32351. TEL 904-627-7649; FAX 904-627-7191. **Owner(s):** Sun Press, P.O. Box 187, Tampa, FL 33526; Ed. Alice Dupont; Pub. Michael O'Holloran; adv. contact: Beverly Kirk. photos; pub. size: broadsheet; circ. 6,000(paid).
Formerly: Quincy Gadsden County Times.

ROYAL PALM BEACH
US
OBSERVER, THE. 1992. Wed. free. 240 Royal Palm Beach Blvd., Royal Palm Beach, FL 33411. TEL 561-791-9687; FAX 561-791-9690. **Owner(s):** Bruce H. & Mark J. Easton, 240 Royal Palm Beach Blvd., Royal Palm Beach, FL 33411. TEL 561-791-9687; FAX 561-791-9690; Ed. Mark Esterly; Pub. Bruce H. Easton; adv. contact: Bruce H. Easton. photos; bk.rev.; pub. size: tabloid; circ. 20,000(free).

RUSKIN
US
SHOPPER OBSERVER NEWS. 1958. Wed. free local carrier; $35/yr. 100 Shell Point Rd., E., Ruskin, FL 33570. TEL 813-645-3111; FAX 813-645-4118. **Owner(s):** M & M Printing Co., Inc., P.O. Box 5, Ruskin, FL 33570; Ed. Brenda Knowles; Pub. Brenda Knowles; adv.; photos; pub. size: tabloid; circ. 22,000(free & paid).
Formerly: Ruskin Shopper & Observer News.

SANIBEL
US
ISLAND REPORTER. 1973. Fri. $.50 newsstand; $22/yr. in cy.; $28/yr. out of cy. 2340 Periwinkle Way, Sanibel, FL 33957. TEL 941-472-1587; FAX 941-472-8398. **Owner(s):** Ogden Newspapers, Inc., 1500 Main St., Wheeling, WV 26003. TEL 304-233-0100; FAX 304-233-0327; Ed. Michelle Moran; Pub. Harry Pappas; adv. contact: Kim Crouthomel. photos; bk.rev.; pub. size: tabloid; circ. 6,500(paid).

US
SANIBEL-CAPTIVA ISLANDER. 1961. Fri. $.50 newsstand; $28/yr. 695 Tarpon Bay Rd., Sanibel, FL 33957. TEL 941-472-5185; FAX 941-472-5302. **Owner(s):** Ogden Newspapers, Inc., 1500 Main St., Wheeling, WV 26003; Ed. Scott Martell. adv. contact: Tracy Markwalter. pub. size: tabloid; circ. 7,000(paid).

SARASOTA
US
PELICAN PRESS. 1971. Thu. free newsstand; $36/yr. 230 Avenida Madera, Sarasota, FL 34242. TEL 941-349-4949; FAX 941-346-7118. **Owner(s):** John B. Davidson, 230 Avenida Madera, Sarasota, FL 34242. TEL 941-349-4949; FAX 941-346-7118; Ed. Anne Johnson; Pub. John B. Davidson; adv.; photos; bk.rev.; pub. size: tabloid; circ. 22,000(free & paid).

SEBRING
US ISSN 0163-3988
NEWS SUN, THE. 1927. 3/wk.: Wed., Fri., Sun. $.50/issue; $.75/Sun.; $36/yr. carrier; $78/yr. mailed in state; $78/yr. mailed out of state. 2227 US 27, S., Sebring, FL 33870. TEL 813-385-6155; FAX 813-385-1954; E-mail: news1@digital.net. **Owner(s):** New York Times Co., The, 229 W. 43rd St., New York, NY 10036. TEL 212-556-1234; Pub. Tim Thompson; adv. contact: Jim Hyatt. photos; bk.rev.; pub. size: broadsheet; circ. 17,000(paid); Sun. 18,000(paid). **Wire Service(s):** NYT.

WEEKLY NEWSPAPERS

SOUTH MIAMI

US
AVENTURA NEWS. 1958. s-w.: Mon. & Wed. free; $27.50/yr. in cy. 6796 S.W. 62nd Ave., South Miami, FL 33143. TEL 305-665-8214; FAX 305-661-0954. **Owner(s):** Community Newspapers, Inc., 6796 S.W. 62nd Ave., South Miami, FL 33143. TEL 305-665-8214; Ed. David Berkowitz; Pub. Grant Miller; pub. size: tabloid; circ. 20,000(free). **Wire Service(s):** AP.

US
DOWNTOWN NEWS. 1958. s-w.: Mon. & Thu. free; $27.50/yr. in cy. mailed. 6796 S.W. 62nd Ave., South Miami, FL 33143. TEL 305-665-8214; FAX 305-661-0954. **Owner(s):** Community Newspapers, Inc., 6796 S.W. 62nd Ave., South Miami, FL 33143. TEL 305-665-8214; Ed. David Berkowitz; Pub. Grant Miller; pub. size: tabloid; circ. 4,500(free). **Wire Service(s):** AP.

US
MIAMI BEACH NEWS. 1958. s-w.: Mon. & Thu. free; $27.50/yr. in cy. mailed. 6796 S.W. 62nd Ave., South Miami, FL 33143. TEL 305-665-8214; FAX 305-661-0954. **Owner(s):** Community Newspapers, Inc., 6796 S.W. 62nd Ave., South Miami, FL 33143. TEL 305-665-8214; Ed. David Berkowitz; Pub. Grant Miller; pub. size: tabloid; circ. 4,000(controlled). **Wire Service(s):** AP.

US
NORTH BAY VILLAGE NEWS. 1958. s-w.: Mon. & Thu. free newsstand; $27.50/yr. mailed in cy. 6796 S.W. 62nd Ave., South Miami, FL 33143. TEL 305-665-8214; FAX 305-661-0954. **Owner(s):** Community Newspapers, Inc., 6796 S.W. 62nd Ave., South Miami, FL 33143; Ed. David Berkowitz; Pub. Grant Miller; adv.; pub. size: broadsheet; circ. 5,800(free). **Wire Service(s):** AP.

US
NORTH MIAMI BEACH NEWS. 1965. s-w.: Mon & Thu. free. 6796 S.W. 62nd Ave., South Miami, FL 33143. TEL 305-667-7481; FAX 305-661-0954. **Owner(s):** Community Newspapers, Inc., 6796 S.W. 62nd Ave., Miami, FL 33143. TEL 305-667-7481; Ed. Michael Miller; Pub. Grant Miller; adv.; pub. size: tabloid; circ. 9,000(free). **Wire Service(s):** UPI.

US ISSN 1048-5406
SOUTH DADE NEWS. 1958. s-w.: Mon & Thu. free. 6796 S.W. 62nd Ave., South Miami, FL 33143. TEL 305-667-7481; FAX 305-661-0954. **Owner(s):** Community Newspapers, Inc., 6796 S.W. 62nd Ave., Miami, FL 33143. TEL 305-667-7481; FAX 305-661-0954; Ed. Michael Miller; Pub. Grant Miller; adv. contact: Grant Miller. pub. size: tabloid; circ. 10,500(paid). Wire Service(s): UPI.

STARKE

US
BRADFORD COUNTY TELEGRAPH. 1879. Thu. $.50 newsstand; $20/yr. in cy.; $22/yr. out of cy. 135 W. Call St., Starke, FL 32091. TEL 904-964-6305; FAX 904-964-8628; E-mail: starknet@access.net; URL: http://www.daccess.net/starknet/telegraph.htm. **Owner(s):** John M. Miller, P.O. Drawer A, Starke, FL 32091. TEL 904-964-6305; Ed. Marcia Goodge; Pub. John M. Miller; adv. contact: John M. Miller. photos; pub. size: broadsheet; circ. 10,400(paid).

ST. PETERSBURG

US
WEEKLY CHALLENGER. 1967. Thu. $.25 newsstand; $30/yr. 2500 Ninth St., S., St. Petersburg, FL 33705. TEL 813-896-2922. **Owner(s):** Cleveland Johnson, 2500 Ninth St., S., St. Petersburg, FL 33705. TEL 813-896-2922; Pub. Cleveland Johnson; adv.; photos; pub. size: standard; circ. 37,000(paid).

SUN CITY CENTER

US
EAST BAY BREEZE. Wed. free. 1507 Sun City Ctr. Plz., Sun City Center, FL 33570. TEL 813-634-9258. **Owner(s):** Media General, Inc., 333 E. Grace St., Richmond, VA 23219. TEL 804-649-6000; FAX 804-649-6898; Ed. Penny Fletcher. adv. contact: Andrea Murray. pub. size: tabloid; circ. 15,300(free).

US
SUN, THE. Wed. free. 1507 Sun City Ctr. Plz., Sun City Center, FL 33570. TEL 813-634-9258; FAX 813-634-8420. **Owner(s):** Media General, Inc., 333 E. Grace St., Richmond, VA 23219. TEL 804-649-6000; FAX 804-649-6898; Ed. Penny Fletcher. adv. contact: Andrea Murray. pub. size: tabloid; circ. 11,500(free).

TALLAHASSEE

US ISSN 1062-0885
TALLAHASSEAN. 1991. Fri. $.25 newsstand; $24.95/yr. 1230 N. Adams St., Tallahassee, FL 32303-6137. TEL 904-224-3805; FAX 904-561-6651. **Owner(s):** Sylvia Jordan, 1230 N. Adams St., Tallahassee, FL 32303-6137. TEL 904-224-3805; FAX 904-561-6651; Ed. Cathie Pedersen; Pub. Sylvia Jordan; adv.; photos; pub. size: standard; circ. 15,000(paid).

TAMPA

US
CARROLLWOOD NEWS. 1980. Wed. free. 5501 W. Waters Ave., Thompson Center #404, Tampa, FL 33634. TEL 813-249-5603; FAX 813-249-5316. **Owner(s):** Media General, Inc., 333 E. Grace St., Richmond, VA 23219. TEL 804-649-6000; FAX 804-649-6898; Ed. Sherri Vande Sande. adv. contact: David Levine. pub. size: tabloid; circ. 30,400(free).

US
FREE PRESS, THE. 1911. Sat. $12/yr. 1010 W. Cass St., Tampa, FL 33606. TEL 813-254-5888; FAX 813-251-0511. **Owner(s):** Free Press Publishing Co., 1010 W. Cass St., Tampa, FL 33606. TEL 813-254-5888; FAX 813-251-0511; Ed. Janet Harrison; Pub. John N. Harrison, IV; adv.; photos; bk.rev.; pub. size: standard; circ. 700(paid).

US
LUTZ COMMUNITY NEWS. 1961. Wed. $5.95/yr. in state; $12/yr. out of state. 15431 N. Florida Ave., Tampa, FL 33613. TEL 813-963-1918. E-mail: werbeacon@aol.com. **Owner(s):** Beacon Publishing, Inc., 119 Bullard Pkwy., Tampa, FL 33617. TEL 813-988-9175; Ed. Charlie Reese; Pub. Anne McKenna; adv.; photos; pub. size: tabloid; circ. 8,000(paid).
Formerly: Lutz Party Line.

US
TEMPLE TERRACE BEACON. Thu. $5.95/yr. in state; $12/yr. out of state. 15431 N. Florida Ave., Tampa, FL 33613. TEL 813-963-1918; FAX 813-963-3910. **Owner(s):** Beacon Publishing, Inc., 15431 N. Florida Ave., Tampa, FL 33613. TEL 813-963-1918; FAX 813-963-3910; Ed. Anne Mckenna; Pub. Anne McKenna; adv.; photos; bk.rev.; pub. size: tabloid; circ. 15,000(paid).

US
TOWN 'N COUNTRY NEWS. Wed. free. Thompson Ctr., Ste. 404, 5501 W. Water Ave., Tampa, FL 33634. TEL 813-249-5603; FAX 813-249-5316. **Owner(s):** Media General, Inc., 333 E. Grace St., Richmond, VA 23219. TEL 804-648-6000; FAX 804-649-6898; Ed. Sherri Vande Sande. adv. contact: Leigh Humes. pub. size: tabloid; circ. 20,520(free).

US
WEEKLY PLANET. 1988. Thu. free. 402 N. Reo St., Ste. 218, Tampa, FL 33609-1027. TEL 813-286-1600; FAX 813-289-8010. **Owner(s):** Ben Eason & Terry Garett, 402 N Reo St., Ste 218, Tampa, FL 33609. TEL 813-286-1600; FAX 813-289-8010; Ed. Ben Eason. adv. contact: Sharry Smith. photos; bk.rev.; pub. size: tabloid; circ. 84,000(controlled & free).

TITUSVILLE

US
STAR-ADVOCATE. 1880. Wed. free. 1100 S. Hopkins Ave., Titusville, FL 32780. TEL 407-267-4711; FAX 407-264-2228. **Owner(s):** Gannett Compnay, Inc., 1100 Wilson Blvd., Arlington, VA 22234. TEL 703-284-6000; Ed. Harry McMamara; Pub. Michael Coleman; adv. contact: Keith Johnson. pub. size: broadsheet; circ. 29,000(free).

VENICE

US
VENICE GONDOLIER. s-w.: Wed. & Sat. $.50 newsstand; $29.95/yr. in state; $44.95/yr. out of state mailed. 200 E. Venice Ave., Venice, FL 34285. TEL 941-484-2611; FAX 941-485-3036. **Owner(s):** Sun Coast Media Group, 23170 Harbor View Rd., Charlotte Harbor, FL 33980. TEL 941-629-2855; FAX 941-629-2085; Pub. Bob Vedder; adv.; pub. size: broadsheet; circ. 2,500(paid).

VERO BEACH

US
SEBASTIAN SUN. 1978. Fri. free; $18/yr. P.O. Box 1268, Vero Beach, FL 32961. TEL 561-562-2315. **Owner(s):** Scripps-Howard, 312 Walnut St., 28th Fl., Cincinnati, OH 45202. TEL 513-977-3000; Ed. Larry Reismann. pub. size: tabloid; circ. 3,500(paid).

WAUCHULA

US
HERALD-ADVOCATE. 1901. Thu. $.46 newsstand; $25./yr.in cy; $33./yr.in state; $40./yr.out of state. 115 S. Seventh Ave., Wauchula, FL 33873-0338. TEL 941-773-3255; FAX 941-773-0657. **Owner(s):** Mildred Kelly, Lynchburg, VA 24506; James R. Kelly, P.O. Box 338, Wauchula, FL 33873. TEL 813-773-3255; Jean C. Kelly, P.O. Box 338, Wauchula, FL 33873. TEL 813-773-3255; Ed. Cynthia Krahl; Pub. James R. Kelly; adv.; photos; pub. size: standard; circ. 5,380(paid).

WELLINGTON
US
WELLINGTON ROYAL PALM BEACH FORUM. Wed. free. 11320 Fortune Cir., Ste. G32, Wellington, FL 33414. TEL 954-752-7474; FAX 954-752-7855. **Owner(s):** South Florida Newspaper Network, Inc., 601 Fairway Dr., Deerfield Beach, FL 33441. TEL 954-698-6397; FAX 954-429-1207; Ed. Van A. Gosselin; Pub. Christine Beach; circ. 25,000(free).

WEST PALM BEACH
US
HOME TIMES. 1980. m. $12/yr. local. 3676 Collin Dr., Ste. 12, West Palm Beach, FL 33406-4727. TEL 561-439-3509. E-mail: 74159.363@compuserve.com. **Owner(s):** Neighbor News, Inc., P.O. Box 16096, West Palm Beach, FL 33416. TEL 561-439-3509; Ed. Dennis Lombard; Pub. Dennis Lombard; adv.; photos; bk.rev.; pub. size: tabloid; circ. 5,000(free & paid).
Formerly: Home Times Family Newspaper.

US
TOWN-CRIER. 1980. Thu. free. 12794 W. Forest Hill Blvd., Ste. 21, West Palm Beach, FL 33414-4757. TEL 561-793-7606; FAX 561-793-6090; E-mail: thecrier@magg.net; URL: http://www.thecrier.com. **Owner(s):** Robert C. Markey, Jr., 12794 W. Forest Hill Blvd., Ste. 21, West Palm Beach, FL 33414. TEL 561-793-3576; Ed. Robert Markey, II; Pub. Robert Markey, II; adv. contact: Jeff Gold. pub. size: tabloid; circ. 8,000(free).
Formerly: Wellington Town-Crier.

WINTER GARDEN
US
WEST ORANGE TIMES. 1913. Thu. $.50 newsstand; $17.50/yr. in cy.; $25/yr. out of cy. 720 S. Dillard St., Winter Garden, FL 34787. TEL 407-656-2121; FAX 407-656-6075. **Owner(s):** George Bailey, 720 S. Dillard, Winter Garden, FL 34787. TEL 407-656-2121; Ed. Maryanne Swickerath; Pub. Andrew Bailey; adv.; photos; bk.rev.; pub. size: standard; circ. 8,000(paid).

WINTER PARK
US
ORLANDO WEEKLY, THE. 1990. Thu. $32.50/6 mos. 3rd class. 807 S. Orlando Ave., Ste. R, Winter Park, FL 32789. TEL 407-645-5888; FAX 407-645-2547. **Owner(s):** Alternative Media, Detroit, MI; Ed. Jeff Truesdell; Pub. Alisa Cromer; adv.; photos; pub. size: tabloid; circ. 50,000(controlled & free).
Formerly: Weekly, The.

US ISSN 1064-3613
WINTER PARK-MAITLAND OBSERVER. 1989. w. $.35 newsstand; $24/yr. 609 Executive Dr., Winter Park, FL 32789. TEL 407-628-8500. **Owner(s):** Gerhard J.W. Munster, 609 Executive Dr., Winter Park, FL 32789. TEL 407-628-8500; Ed. Gerhard J.W. Munster; Pub. Gerhard J.W. Munster; adv.; photos; bk.rev.; pub. size: tabloid; circ. 10,000(paid).
Formerly: Winter Park Observer.

ZEPHYRHILLS
US
ZEPHYRHILLS NEWS. 1911. Thu. $.35 newsstand; $12.95.60/yr. local. 38333 Fifth Ave., Zephyrhills, FL 33540. TEL 813-782-1558; FAX 813-788-7987. **Owner(s):** Republic Newspapers, Inc., P.O. Box 769, Kings Mountain, NC 28086; Ed. Dave Walters; Pub. Janet Gillis; adv.; bk.rev.; pub. size: broadsheet; circ. 5,500.

GEORGIA

ADAIRSVILLE
US
NORTH BARTOW NEWS. Tue. $.25 newsstand; $20/yr. 321-B N. Main St., Adairsville, GA 30103. TEL 770-773-3754; FAX 770-773-3754. **Owner(s):** Walls Newspapers, Inc., P.O. Box 70, Cartersville, GA 30120. TEL 404-382-4545; Ed. Sheila Mullinax; Pub. Charles Hurley; adv. contact: Bonnie Dunbar. pub. size: broadsheet; circ. 6,000(controlled & paid).

ADEL
US
ADEL NEWS-TRIBUNE. 1888. Wed. $.50 newsstand; $19.08/yr. in cy.; $17.01/yr. senior citizens. 131 S. Hutchinson Ave., Adel, GA 31620. TEL 912-896-2233; FAX 912-896-7237. **Owner(s):** Cook Publishing Co., Inc., 131 S. Hutchinson, Adel, GA 31620. TEL 912-896-2233; Pub. Ladonna Stripling; adv. contact: Ladonna Stripling. pub. size: broadsheet; circ. 3,500(paid).

ALBANY
US
ALBANY JOURNAL. 1950. Fri. $.50 newsstand; $24.13/yr. local. 118 Roosevelt Ave., Albany, GA 31703. TEL 912-435-6222; FAX 912-435-0557. **Owner(s):** William O. Davis, P.O. Box 1628, 118 Roosevelt Ave., Albany, GA 31703. TEL 912-435-6222; Ed. William O. Davis; Pub. William O. Davis; pub. size: standard; circ. 7,958(paid).

ALPHARETTA
US
ALPHARETTA REVUE. 1981. Fri. $.25 newsstand; $35/yr. 319 N. Main St., Alpharetta, GA 30201. TEL 770-442-3278; FAX 770-475-1216; E-mail: tcb@mindspring.com; URL: http://www.appnews.com. **Owner(s):** Appen Newspapers, Inc., 319 N. Main St., Alpharetta, GA 30201. TEL 770-442-3278; Ed. Hatcher Hurd. pub. size: tabloid; circ. 22,500(free).

US
BUSINESS POST, THE. m. $.25 newsstand; $35/yr. 319 N. Main St., Alpharetta, GA 30201. TEL 770-442-3278; FAX 770-475-1216; E-mail: legacybks@aol.com. **Owner(s):** Appen Newspapers, Inc., 319 N. Main St., Alpharetta, GA 30201. TEL 404-442-3278; FAX 404-475-1216; Ed. Hatcher Hurd. pub. size: standard; circ. 8,500(paid).

ATHENS
US
ATHENS OBSERVER, THE. 1974. Thu. $.50 newsstand; $7/13 wks.; $13/26 wks.; $25/yr. in state; $40/yr. out of state. 445 N. Milledge Ave., Athens, GA 30601. TEL 706-353-9300; FAX 706-353-1008. **Owner(s):** Athens 100 Club LLC, 445 N. Milledge Ave., Athens, GA 30603. TEL 706-353-9300; FAX 706-353-1008; Ed. Mel Epps. adv. contact: Johnnie Ellis. photos; bk.rev.; pub. size: broadsheet; circ. 5,000(free & paid).

ATLANTA
US
ATLANTA BULLETIN. 1974. Sat. free; $30/yr. mailed. 1655 Peachtree St. Ste. 1003, Atlanta, GA 30309. TEL 404-874-1968; FAX 404-874-1950. **Owner(s):** David Smith, 1655 Peachtree Rd., Ste. 1003, Atlanta, GA 30309. TEL 404-874-1968; Ed. David Smith. adv.: $28.95/SAU. pub. size: tabloid; circ. 50,000(free).

US
ATLANTA DAILY WORLD. 1928. s-w.: Thu. & Sun. $.35 newsstand; $51.40/yr. mailed. 145 Auburn Ave., N.E., Atlanta, GA 30335-1201. TEL 404-659-1110. **Owner(s):** Atlanta Daily World, Inc., 145 Auburn Ave., N.E., Atlanta, GA 30303. TEL 404-659-1110; Ed. William Fowlkes; Pub. C.A. Scott; adv. contact: J.R. Simmons. pub. size: broadsheet; circ. 16,000(paid); Sun. 18,000(paid). **Wire Service(s):** UPI.

US
CHAMBLEE-DEKALB NEIGHBOR. 1969. Wed. free; $28/3 mos.; $56/6 mos.; $112/yr. mailed. 3060 Mercer University Dr., Ste. 210, Atlanta, GA 30341. TEL 770-454-9388; FAX 770-422-9533. **Owner(s):** Marietta Daily Journal & Neighbor Newspapers, Inc., P.O. Box 449, Marietta, GA 30061. TEL 770-428-9411; FAX 770-422-9533; Ed. Toby Truog; Pub. Otis Brumby; adv. contact: Julie Dollar. pub. size: broadsheet; circ. 5,100(controlled & free).

US
DORAVILLE-DEKALB NEIGHBOR. 1969. Wed. free; $28/3 mos.; $56/6 mos.; $112/yr. 3060 Mercer University Dr., Ste. 210, Atlanta, GA 30341. TEL 770-454-9388; FAX 770-422-9533. **Owner(s):** Marietta Daily Journal & Neighbor Newspapers, Inc., 580 Fairground St., Marietta, GA 30060. TEL 770-428-9411; FAX 770-422-9533; Pub. Otis A. Brumby, Jr.; adv. contact: Julie Dollar. pub. size: broadsheet; circ. 7,000(controlled).

US
DUNWOODY-DEKALB NEIGHBOR, THE. 1969. Wed. free; $28/3 mos.; $56/6 mos.; $112/yr. 3060 Mercer University Dr., Ste 210, Atlanta, GA 30341. TEL 770-428-9411; FAX 770-422-9533. **Owner(s):** Marietta Daily Journal & Neighbor Newspapers, Inc., P.O. Box 449, Marietta, GA 30061. TEL 770-428-9411; Pub. Otis Brumby, Jr.; adv. contact: Julie Dollar. pub. size: broadsheet; circ. 10,000(controlled).

US
DUNWOODY CRIER. 1975. Wed. $55/yr. 16 Perimeter Pk., Ste. 101, Atlanta, GA 30341. TEL 770-394-4147; FAX 770-394-0019. **Owner(s):** Crier Newspapers, LLC; Ed. Dick Williams. adv.; pub. size: tabloid; circ. 22,000(controlled & free).

WEEKLY NEWSPAPERS

US
NORTHSIDE NEIGHBOR, THE. 1968. Wed. free; $112/yr. mailed. 5290 Roswell Rd., N.W., Ste. M, Atlanta, GA 30342. TEL 404-256-3100; FAX 404-256-3292. **Owner(s):** Marietta Daily Journal & Neighbor Newspapers, Inc., 580 Fairground St., P.O. Box 449, Marietta, GA 30060. TEL 770-428-9411; FAX 770-422-9533; Ed. Faye Edmundson; Pub. Otis Brumby, Jr.; adv. contact: Leo Dwyer. adv.: $27.25/SAU. photos; pub. size: broadsheet; circ. 29,000(controlled).

US
ROSWELL/ALPHARETTA CRIER. 1986. s-m.: 1st & 15th. free. 16 Perimeter Pk. Dr., Ste. 101, Atlanta, GA 30341. TEL 770-451-4147; FAX 770-394-0019. **Owner(s):** Dick Williams, 16 Perimeter Pk. Dr., Ste 101, Atlanta, GA 30341; Ed. Dick Williams; Pub. Dick Williams; adv. contact: James Hart. pub. size: tabloid; circ. 15,000(controlled & free).

US
SANDY SPRINGS NEIGHBOR, THE. Wed. free. 5290 Roswell Rd., N.W., Ste. M, Atlanta, GA 30342. TEL 404-256-3100; FAX 404-256-3292. **Owner(s):** Times Journal, Inc., 580 Fairground St., Marietta, GA 30060. TEL 404-428-9411; FAX 404-422-9533; Ed. Fay Edmundson; Pub. Otis Brumby, Jr.; adv.; pub. size: broadsheet; circ. 30,000(free).

US
SOUTH DEKALB NEIGHBOR, THE. Wed. free; $28/3 mos.; $56/6 mos.; $112/yr. mailed. 3060 Mercer University Dr., Ste. 210, Atlanta, GA 30341. TEL 770-454-9388; FAX 770-454-9131. **Owner(s):** Marietta Daily Journal & Neighbor Newspapers, Inc., 580 Fairground St., Marietta, GA 30060. TEL 770-428-9411; Ed. Toby Truog; Pub. Otis Brumby, Jr.; adv. contact: Julie Dollar. pub. size: broadsheet; circ. 30,500(free & paid).

US
TUCKER-DEKALB NEIGHBOR, THE. 1969. s-w.: Wed. & Thu. free; $112/yr. mailed. 3060 Mercer University Dr., Ste. 210, Atlanta, GA 30341. TEL 770-454-9388; FAX 770-454-9131. **Owner(s):** Marietta Daily Journal & Neighbors, 580 Fairground St., Marietta, GA 30060. TEL 770-428-9411; FAX 770-422-9533; Ed. Toby Truog; Pub. Otis Brumby, Jr.; adv.; pub. size: broadsheet; circ. 5,900(controlled).

BAINBRIDGE

US
BAINBRIDGE POST-SEARCHLIGHT. 1907. s-w.: Wed. & Sat. $.50 newsstand; $29/yr. local; $44/yr. out of area. 301 N. Crawford St., Bainbridge, GA 31717. TEL 912-246-2827; FAX 912-246-7665; E-mail: postscarch@surfsouth.com. **Owner(s):** Sam M. Griffin, Bainbridge Post-Searchlight, 301 N. Crawford St., Bainbridge, GA 31717. TEL 912-246-2827; Ed. Rex Sanders; Pub. Sam M. Griffin, Jr.; pub. size: broadsheet; circ. evening 6,400(paid).

BARNESVILLE

US
HERALD-GAZETTE, THE. Tue. $.50 newsstand; $15.90/yr. 509 Greenwood St., Barnesville, GA 30204. TEL 770-358-0754; FAX 770-358-0756; E-mail: walterg@internetmci.com; URL: http://www.barnesville.com. **Owner(s):** Walter Geiger, 509 Greenwood St., Barnesville, GA 30204. TEL 770-358-0754; FAX 770-358-0756; Ed. Laura Geiger; Pub. Walter Geiger; adv. contact: Laura Geiger. adv.: $5.50/SAU. pub. size: broadsheet; circ. 5,500(paid).

BAXLEY

US
BAXLEY NEWS-BANNER. 1884. Wed. $.50 newsstand; $21.20/yr. 300 Parker St., Baxley, GA 31513. TEL 912-367-2468; FAX 912-367-0277; E-mail: baxbnr@altamaha.net. **Owner(s):** Baxley News-Banner, Inc., P.O. Box 409, Baxley, GA 31513. TEL 912-367-0277; Ed. Max Gardner; Pub. Max Gardner; adv.: $4.80/SAU. pub. size: broadsheet; circ. 4,300(paid).

BLAIRSVILLE

US
NORTH GEORGIA NEWS. 1912. Wed. $.50 newsstand; $30/yr. P.O. Box 2029, Blairsville, GA 30514. TEL 706-745-6343; FAX 706-745-1830. **Owner(s):** Wanda R. West, P.O. Box 2029, Blairsville, GA 30514. TEL 706-745-6343; FAX 706-745-1830; Ed. Norman Cooper; Pub. Wanda R. West; adv. contact: Norman Nai Pavel. pub. size: broadsheet; circ. 8,700(paid).
Formerly: Blairsville North Georgia News.

BREMEN

US
HARALSON GATEWAY-BEACON, THE. 1895. Thu. $.50 newsstand; $15-$20/yr. in area. 222 Tallapoosa St., Bremen, GA 30110. TEL 770-537-2434; FAX 770-537-0826. **Owner(s):** Paxton Media Group, Inc., P.O. Box 2300, Paducah, KY 42002. TEL 502-443-1771; Ed. Bruce Browning; Pub. Dawn Weatherby; adv. contact: Lynn Mosely. photos; pub. size: broadsheet; circ. 6,300(paid).

BRUNSWICK

US
GLYNCO OBSERVER. 1984. bi-w.: Thu. free. 3395 Cypress Mill Rd., Ste. E, Brunswick, GA 31525. TEL 912-267-7878; FAX 912-264-3357. **Owner(s):** Troy Fore, 3395 Cypress Mill Rd., Ste. E, Brunswick, GA 31525. TEL 912-267-7878; Ed. Troy Fore. pub. size: tabloid; circ. 3,500(free).

US
HARBOR SOUND. 1984. Tue. $3/mo. 1326 Newcastle St., Brunswick, GA 31520-0606. TEL 912-264-4521; FAX 912-264-4531. **Owner(s):** Jim Dryden, 1326 Newcastle St., Brunswick, GA 31520. TEL 912-264-4521; FAX 912-264-4531; Ed. Jim Dryden. adv.; photos; pub. size: tabloid; circ. 31,000(free).

US
JEKYLL'S GOLDEN ISLANDER. 1972. bi-m.: Thu. $27.50/yr. in US; $15/yr. 3rd class; $32.50/yr. Canada. 3395 Cypress Mill Rd., Ste. E, Brunswick, GA 31525. TEL 912-267-7878; FAX 912-264-3357. **Owner(s):** Glynn Press, Inc., 5000 Altana Ave., Creola, AL 36525. TEL 912-267-7878; Ed. Troy Fore; Pub. Troy Fore; pub. size: tabloid; circ. 6,000(paid).

CAIRO

US
CAIRO MESSENGER. 1904. Wed. $.35 newsstand; $13.50/yr. local; $18.50/yr. in state; $20.50/yr. out of state. 31-35 First Ave., N.E., Cairo, GA 31728. TEL 912-377-2032; FAX 912-377-4640. **Owner(s):** Messenger Publishing Co., Inc., 31-35 First Ave., N.E., Cairo, GA 31728. TEL 912-377-2032; Ed. Robert H. Wind; Pub. Robert H. Wind; adv. contact: Randolph H. Wind. pub. size: broadsheet; circ. 6,200(paid).

CALHOUN

US
CALHOUN TIMES. 1870. s-w.: Wed. & Sat. $.50 newsstand; $24/yr. in cy.; $34/yr. out of cy. 215 W. Line St., Calhoun, GA 30701. TEL 706-629-2230; FAX 706-625-0899. **Owner(s):** News Publishing Co., 305 E. Sixth Ave., Rome, GA 30162. TEL 706-291-6297; Ed. Mitch Talley; Pub. Burgitt Mooney; pub. size: broadsheet; circ. 9,250(paid).

CAMILLA

US
CAMILLA ENTERPRISE. 1903. s-w.: Wed. & Fri. $.50 newsstand; $26.50/yr. in cy.; $42.50/yr. out of cy. 13 S. Scott St., Camilla, GA 31730. TEL 912-336-5265; FAX 912-336-8476. **Owner(s):** Robert Tribble, P.O. Box 426, Manchester, GA; Pub. Roger Ann Davis; pub. size: broadsheet; circ. 3,400(paid).

CANTON

US
CHEROKEE TRIBUNE, THE. 1973. 3/wk.: Wed., Fri., Sun. $.50/day newsstand; $.75/Sun.; $38/yr. in cy. 521 E. Main St., Canton, GA 30114. TEL 770-479-1441; FAX 770-479-3505. **Owner(s):** Times Journal, Inc., 580 Fairground St., Marietta, GA 30060. TEL 770-428-9411; FAX 770-428-7945; Ed. Rebecca Johnston; Pub. Otis Brumby, Jr.; adv. contact: Rebecca Hayes. bk.rev.; pub. size: broadsheet; circ. 32,000(free & paid); Sun. 32,000(free & paid).

CARTERSVILLE

US
BARTOW NEIGHBOR, THE. Wed. free. 16 Wall St., Cartersville, GA 30120. TEL 770-386-0872; FAX 770-386-0879. **Owner(s):** Times Journal, Inc., 580 Fairground St., Marietta, GA 30060. TEL 770-428-9411; FAX 770-422-9533; Ed. Masie Underwood; Pub. Otis Brumby, Jr.; adv.; pub. size: broadsheet; circ. 15,000(free).

CARTERSVILLE, GA

US
HERALD-TRIBUNE, THE. 1926. Tue. free; $12/6 mos. in cy.; $16/yr. elsewhere; $24/yr. in state; $30/yr. out of state. 251 S. Tennessee St., Cartersville, GA 30120. TEL 770-382-4545; FAX 770-382-2711. **Owner(s):** Cleveland Newspapers, Inc., P.O. Box 3600, Cleveland, TN 37320. TEL 423-472-5041; Ed. Jim Jaquish; Pub. Charles Hurley; adv. contact: Charles Hurley. photos; pub. size: broadsheet; circ. 9,500(controlled & paid).

CEDARTOWN

US
CEDARTOWN STANDARD. 1869. s-w.: Tue. & Thu. $.50 newsstand; $24/yr. local; $34/yr. out of area. 213 Main St., Cedartown, GA 30125. TEL 770-748-1520; FAX 770-748-1524. **Owner(s):** News Publishing Co., 305 E. Sixth Ave., Rome, GA 30161. TEL 404-291-6397; Ed. James M. Penney; Pub. B.H. Mooney, III; adv. contact: Tina Carter. pub. size: broadsheet; circ. 3,500(paid).

CHATSWORTH

US
CHATSWORTH TIMES, THE. 1885. Wed. $.50 newsstand; $15.75/yr. local; $28/yr. out of city. 224 N. Third Ave., Chatsworth, GA 30705. TEL 706-695-4646; FAX 706-695-7181. **Owner(s):** Walls Newspapers, Inc., P.O. Box 70, Cartersville, GA 30120. TEL 404-382-4545; Ed. David L. Shelton; Pub. David L. Shelton; adv.; photos; pub. size: standard; circ. 5,600(paid).

CLAYTON

US
CLAYTON TRIBUNE, THE. 1898. Thu. $.50 newsstand; $18/yr. in cy.; $22/yr. out of cy. Main & Oak Crescent Dr., Clayton, GA 30525. TEL 706-782-3312; FAX 706-782-4230. **Owner(s):** Community Newspapers, Inc., P.O. Box 792, Athens, GA 30603. TEL 800-226-0692; FAX 706-548-0808; Ed. Tom Law; Pub. Russell Majors; adv.; pub. size: broadsheet; circ. 6,525(controlled & paid).

COLQUITT

US
MILLER COUNTY LIBERAL. 1897. Thu. $.50 newsstand; $14.70/yr. local; $23.10/yr. elsewhere. 157 E. Main St., Colquitt, GA 31737-0037. TEL 912-758-5549; FAX 912-758-5540. **Owner(s):** Terry Toole, 157 E. Main St., P.O. Box 37, Colquitt, GA 31737. TEL 912-758-5549; FAX 912-758-5540; Ed. Debra Jones; Pub. Terry Toole; adv. contact: Betty Jo Toole. photos; bk.rev.; pub. size: broadsheet; circ. 2,900(controlled & paid). **Wire Service(s):** AP.

COLUMBUS

US
BENNING LEADER, THE. 1991. Fri. free. 17 W. 12th St., Columbus, GA 31901. TEL 706-324-5526; FAX 706-576-6234. **Owner(s):** Knight-Ridder, Inc., One Herald Plz., Miami, FL 33132. TEL 305-376-3800; FAX 305-376-3875; Ed. Tony Adams; Pub. John Greenman; adv. contact: David Fletcher. pub. size: tabloid; circ. 25,000(controlled).
Formerly: Benning Patriot.

COMMERCE

US
COMMERCE NEWS. 1875. Wed. $.50 newsstand; $16.50/yr. in cy. 1672 S. Broad St., Commerce, GA 30529. TEL 706-335-2927; FAX 706-335-4531. **Owner(s):** Jackson Herald Publishing Co., P.O. Box 908, Jefferson, GA 30549. TEL 404-367-5233; Ed. Mark Beardsley; Pub. Herman Buffington; adv. contact: Scott Buffington. photos; pub. size: broadsheet; circ. 4,500(paid).

CONYERS

US
ROCKDALE NEIGHBOR, THE. 1969. Thu. free. 1706-D Hwy. 138, Conyers, GA 30208. TEL 770-922-8300; FAX 770-922-0899. **Owner(s):** Marietta Daily Journal & Neighbors, 580 Fairground St., Marietta, GA 30060. TEL 770-428-9411; FAX 770-422-9533; Pub. Otis Brumby; adv.; pub. size: broadsheet; circ. 16,000(free).

CORNELIA

US
NORTHEAST GEORGIAN, THE. 1892. Wed. $.50 newsstand; $17/yr. in cy.; $25/yr. out of cy. 236 Level Grove Rd., Cornelia, GA 30531. TEL 706-778-4215; FAX 706-778-4114. **Owner(s):** Community Newspapers, Inc., P.O. Box 792, Athens, GA 30603. TEL 800-226-0692; FAX 706-548-0808; Ed. Terri Blackwell; Pub. John D. Solesbee; adv. contact: Dalton Sirmans. pub. size: broadsheet; circ. 9,500(paid).
Formerly: Cornelia Northeast Georgian.

COVINGTON

US
COVINGTON NEWS. 1865. 3/wk.: Tue., Thu., Sat. $.50 newsstand; $41.34/yr. in cy.; $46.64/yr. out of cy. 1166 Usher St., N.W., Covington, GA 30210. TEL 770-787-6397; FAX 770-786-6451. **Owner(s):** Morris Communications, P.O. Box 936, Augusta, GA 30903. TEL 706-724-0851; FAX 706-722-7125; Pub. Ron Stokes; adv. contact: Kim Davis. pub. size: broadsheet; circ. 7,100(controlled & paid).
Formerly: Covington News/Multi-County Star.

STAR EXPRESS. s-w.: Tue. & Sat. free. 1166 Usher St., Covington, GA 30210. TEL 770-787-6397; FAX 770-786-6451. **Owner(s):** Morris Communications, P.O. Box 936, Augusta, GA 30903. TEL 706-724-0851; Ed. Jane Grillo; Pub. Ron Stokes; adv. contact: Kim Davis. pub. size: broadsheet; circ. 18,000(controlled).

CUMMING

US
FORSYTH COUNTY NEWS. 1908. 3/wk.: Wed., Fri., Sun. $30/yr. in cy.; $55/yr. out of cy. 121 Dahlonega St., Cumming, GA 30130. TEL 404-887-3126; FAX 404-889-6017. **Owner(s):** Swartz-Morris Media, Inc., P.O. Box 210, Cumming, GA 30128. TEL 770-887-3126; FAX 770-889-6017; Ed. Karlene Chalker; Pub. Dennis Stockton; adv. contact: Barbara Scohler. photos; bk.rev.; pub. size: broadsheet; circ. 13,800(paid); Sun. 14,500(paid). **Wire Service(s):** NYT.

DALLAS

US
DALLAS NEW ERA. 1882. Thu. $.25 newsstand; $8/yr.; $14/2 yrs. 121 W. Spring St., Dallas, GA 30132. TEL 770-445-3379. **Owner(s):** T.E. & J.T. Parker, 121 W. Spring St., Dallas, GA 30132. TEL 404-495-3379; Ed. T.E. Parker; Pub. T.E. Parker; adv. contact: Annette Manning. photos; pub. size: broadsheet; circ. 7,500(paid).

DARIEN

US
DARIEN NEWS. 1951. Wed. $.35 newsstand; $15.90/yr. in cy.; $21.20/yr. out of cy.; $25/yr. out of state. 101 Broad St., Darien, GA 31305. TEL 912-437-4251; FAX 912-437-2299. **Owner(s):** Charles M. Williamson, Jr., P.O. Box 496, Darien, GA 31305. TEL 912-437-4251; FAX 912-437-2299; Ed. Kathleen W. Russell; Pub. Charles M. Williamson, Jr.; adv.; photos; pub. size: broadsheet; circ. 2,900(paid).

DAWSON

US
DAWSON NEWS, THE. 1866. Thu. $.35 newsstand; $18/yr. in area; $21/yr. in state; $27/yr. out of state. 139 W. Lee St., Dawson, GA 31742-0350. TEL 912-995-2175; FAX 912-995-3713. **Owner(s):** Tommy Rountree, 139 W. Lee St., Dawson, GA 31742-0350. TEL 912-995-2175; FAX 912-995-3713; Ed. Tommy Rountree. adv.; photos; pub. size: broadsheet; circ. 8,200(free & paid).

DECATUR

US
DECATUR-DEKALB NEWS/ERA. 1949. Thu. $.25 newsstand; $15.75/yr. 613 Church St., Decatur, GA 30030. TEL 404-373-4488. **Owner(s):** Southern Crescent Newspapers, 138 Church St., Jonesboro, GA 30236. TEL 770-478-5753; Ed. John Sell; Pub. John Sell; adv.; pub. size: broadsheet; circ. 9,600(paid).
Formerly: DeKalb News/Sun.

DONALSONVILLE

US
DONALSONVILLE NEWS. 1916. Wed. $15.90/yr. local; $21.20/yr. elsewhere. 120 W. Second St., Donalsonville, GA 31745. TEL 912-524-2343; FAX 912-524-2343. **Owner(s):** Donalsonville News, Inc., Bo McLeod, Donalsonville, GA 31745. TEL 912-524-2343; Ed. Bo McLeod; Pub. Bo McLeod; pub. size: broadsheet; circ. 3,600(paid).

DOUGLAS

US
DOUGLAS ENTERPRISE. 1888. s-w.: Wed. & Sun. $.50 newsstand; $24.50/yr. in area; $55/yr. elsewhere. 1823 S. Peterson Ave., Douglas, GA 31533. TEL 912-384-2323; FAX 912-383-0218. **Owner(s):** Lovan B. & Patricia W. Thomas, 1823 S. Peterson Ave., Douglas, GA 31533. TEL 912-384-2323; Ed. Thomas Frier, Jr.; Pub. Jim Merritt; adv. contact: Mary Onley. photos; pub. size: standard; circ. 8,100(paid); Sun. 8,100(paid).

WEEKLY NEWSPAPERS

EASTMAN
US

DODGE COUNTY NEWS, THE. 1989. Wed. $.50 newsstand; $19/yr. in cy.; $26/yr. out of cy.; $30/yr. out of state. 218 Main St., S.E., Eastman, GA 31023-1650. TEL 912-374-0360; FAX 912-374-0361; E-mail: ceckles@mail.dodge.public.lib.ga.us. **Owner(s):** Chuck Eckles & Cindy Eckles, 218 Main St., S.E., Eastman, GA 31023. TEL 912-374-0360; FAX 912-374-0361; Ed. Cindy Eckles; Pub. Chuck Eckles; adv. contact: Cindy Eckles. adv.: $4.80/SAU. photos; pub. size: broadsheet; circ. 5,515(free & paid).

US

TIMES JOURNAL-SPOTLIGHT. 1871. Wed. $.35 newsstand; $15/yr. in cy.; $20/yr. out of cy.; $24/yr. out of state. 227 College St., Eastman, GA 31023. TEL 912-374-5562; FAX 912-374-3464. **Owner(s):** Investments & Counseling Services, Inc., P.O. Drawer 4189, Eastman, GA 31023. TEL 912-374-3464; Ed. Julia J. Roberts; Pub. Julia J. Roberts; adv.; photos; pub. size: broadsheet; circ. 5,050(paid).
Formerly: Eastman Times Journal-Spotlight.

ELBERTON
US   **ISSN 8750-6734**

ELBERTON STAR. 1887. Wed. $.50 newsstand; $16/yr. in cy.; $20/yr. in state; $28/yr. out of state; $14/yr. senior citizens. 14 N. Oliver St., Elberton, GA 30635-0280. TEL 706-283-3100; FAX 706-283-7841. **Owner(s):** Southern Crescent Publishing Co., Atlanta, GA; Ed. Carolyn E. Cann; Pub. Paula Pennell; adv. contact: Janice Crotty. photos; pub. size: broadsheet; circ. 4,900(paid).

ELLIJAY
US   **ISSN 0630-0280**

TIMES-COURIER. 1875. Wed. $.35 newsstand; $15/yr. in cy.; $18/yr. out of cy. 13 River St., Ellijay, GA 30540. TEL 706-635-4313; FAX 706-635-7006; E-mail: courier@ellijay.com. **Owner(s):** George Bunch, P.O. Box 1076, Ellijay, GA 30540. TEL 706-635-4313; FAX 706-635-7006; Ed. George N. Bunch; Pub. George N. Bunch; adv. contact: George Bunch, III. photos; pub. size: broadsheet; circ. 6,550(paid).

FAYETTEVILLE
US

FAYETTE COUNTY NEWS. 1886. 3/wk: Tue., Thu., Sat. $.50 newsstand; $26.25/yr. in cy. 180 Church St., Fayetteville, GA 30214. TEL 770-461-6317; FAX 770-460-8172. **Owner(s):** Trib Publications, Inc., P.O. Box 426, Manchester, GA 31816. TEL 706-846-3188; FAX 706-846-2206; Ed. Pat Cooper; Pub. Robert Tribble; adv.; photos; pub. size: broadsheet; circ. 9,500(paid).

US

FAYETTE NEIGHBOR, THE. 1977. Thu. free. 635 N. Glynn St., Fayetteville, GA 30214. TEL 770-461-1136; FAX 770-461-1385. **Owner(s):** Times Journal, Inc., 580 Fairground St., Marietta, GA 30060. TEL 770-428-9411; FAX 770-422-9533; Ed. Joy Denton; Pub. Otis A. Brumby, Jr.; adv.; photos; pub. size: broadsheet; circ. 16,800(free).

FITZGERALD
US

HERALD-LEADER, THE. 1895. Wed. $.50 newsstand; $35/yr. 202-204 E. Central Ave., Fitzgerald, GA 31750. TEL 912-423-9331; FAX 912-423-6533. **Owner(s):** Pryor Publications, Inc., 202-204 E. Central Ave., Fitzgerald, GA 31750. TEL 912-423-9331; FAX 912-423-6533; Ed. Barbara Ashe; Pub. Tim Anderson; adv. contact: Peggy Ross. photos; pub. size: standard; circ. 5,700(paid).

FOLKSTON
US

CHARLTON COUNTY HERALD. 1898. Wed. $.30 newsstand; $14.84/yr. in cy.; $18.02/yr. out of cy. 102 W. Love St., Folkston, GA 31537. TEL 912-496-3585; FAX 912-496-4585. **Owner(s):** David Thompson, P.O. Box 398, Falkston, GA 31537. TEL 912-496-3585; Ed. David Thompson. pub. size: broadsheet; circ. 3,000(paid).

FOREST PARK
US

CLAYTON NEIGHBOR. 1976. Wed. free; $112/yr. mailed. 5300 Frontage Rd., Ste. B, Forest Park, GA 30050. TEL 404-363-8484; FAX 404-363-0212. **Owner(s):** Times Journal, Inc., 580 Fairground St., Marietta, GA 30060. TEL 770-428-9411; FAX 770-422-9533; Ed. John Marsh; Pub. Otis Brumby, Jr.; adv. contact: Johanna Stein. pub. size: broadsheet; circ. 38,250(controlled).

US   **ISSN 0192-0693**

SOUTH FULTON NEIGHBOR, THE. 1968. Wed. free. 5300 Frontes, Ste. B, Forest Park, GA 30050. TEL 404-363-8484; FAX 404-363-0212. **Owner(s):** Times Journal, Inc., 580 Fairground St., Marietta, GA 30060. TEL 770-428-9411; FAX 770-422-9533; Ed. Martha Barksdale; Pub. Otis A. Brumby, Jr.; adv. contact: Kaye Sessions. pub. size: broadsheet; circ. 22,000(free).

FORT VALLEY
US

LEADER-TRIBUNE, THE. 1888. Wed. $.50 newsstand; $18.90/yr. in cy.; $26.50/yr. in state; $45/yr. out of state. 109 Anderson Ave., Fort Valley, GA 31030. TEL 912-825-2432; FAX 912-825-4130. **Owner(s):** Peach Publishing Co., Inc., 109 Anderson Ave., Fort Valley, GA 31030. TEL 912-825-2432; FAX 912-825-4130; Ed. Cindy Morley; Pub. Robert E. Tribble; adv.; pub. size: broadsheet; circ. 14,110(free & paid).
Formerly: Fort Valley Leader-Tribune.

GLENNVILLE
US

GLENNVILLE SENTINEL. 1925. Thu. $.50 newsstand; $16.96/yr. in state; $21.20/yr. elsewhere. 105 W. Bernard St., Glennville, GA 30427. TEL 912-654-2515; FAX 912-654-2527; E-mail: sentinel@pineland.net. **Owner(s):** Pam & Russell Terry Waters, P.O. Box 218, Glennville, GA 30427. TEL 912-654-2515; FAX 912-654-2527; Ed. Pam Waters; Pub. Pam Waters; adv.; photos; pub. size: broadsheet; circ. 3,700(free & paid).

GREENVILLE
US

MERIWETHER FREE PRESS. 1989. Wed. $.35 newsstand; $15.75/yr. in cy.; $21/yr. in state; $25/yr. out of state. 400 LaGrange St., Greenville, GA 30222. TEL 706-672-1753; FAX 706-672-1977. **Owner(s):** Kara Barnes Hamlott, Woodbury, GA. TEL 706-553-5601; Ed. Lee N. Howell; Pub. Lee N. Howell; adv. contact: Bryan Jeter. photos; bk.rev.; pub. size: broadsheet; circ. 2,200(free & paid).

HARTWELL
US

HARTWELL SUN, THE. 1877. Wed. $.50 newsstand; $22/yr. in cy.; $24/yr. out of cy. 138 N. Forest Ave., Hartwell, GA 30643. TEL 706-376-8025; FAX 706-376-3016. **Owner(s):** Southern Crescent Newspapers, L.P., 138 Church St., Jonesboro, GA 30236; Ed. Wassie Vickery; Pub. Peggy K. Vickery; adv. contact: Rita Chapman. pub. size: broadsheet; circ. 6,300(free & paid).

HAZLEHURST
US

JEFF DAVIS LEDGER. 1940. Wed. $.50 newsstand; $15/yr. in area. 104 Lattimer St., Hazlehurst, GA 31539. TEL 912-375-4225; FAX 912-375-3704. **Owner(s):** Hazlehurst Publishing Co., P.O. Box 338, Hazlehurst, GA 31539. TEL 912-375-4225; FAX 912-375-3704; Ed. Thomas H. Purser; Pub. Kay Purser; adv. contact: Kay Purser. photos; pub. size: broadsheet; circ. 3,900(paid).

HINESVILLE
US   **ISSN 1047-6636**

COASTAL COURIER. 1871. 3/wk.: Wed., Fri., Sun. $39/yr. in cy.; $41/yr. out of cy.; $46/yr. out of state. 125 S. Main St., Hinesville, GA 31313. TEL 912-876-0156; FAX 912-368-6329; E-mail: pwatkins@infoave.net. **Owner(s):** Charles Morris, P.O. Box 8167, Savannah, GA 31412. TEL 912-233-1281; Ed. Pat Watkins; Pub. Mark Griffin; adv. contact: Matt Newton. photos; bk.rev.; pub. size: standard; circ. 5,600(paid).

HOMERVILLE
US

CLINCH COUNTY NEWS. 1894. Wed. $.47 newsstand; $15/yr. in cy.; $22/yr. out of cy. 210 E. Dame Ave., Homerville, GA 31634. TEL 912-487-5337; FAX 912-487-3227; E-mail: clinnews@sowega.net. **Owner(s):** Robert & Cheryl Williams, 210 E. Dame Ave., Homerville, GA 31634. TEL 912-487-5337; FAX 912-487-3227; Ed. Len Robbins; Pub. Robert Williams; adv.; photos; pub. size: broadsheet; circ. 2,200(free & paid).

JACKSON
US

JACKSON PROGRESS-ARGUS. 1873. Wed. $.50 newsstand; $18/yr. local; $34/yr. out of area. 129 Mulberry St., Jackson, GA 30233. TEL 404-775-3107; FAX 404-775-3855. **Owner(s):** Southern Publishing Co., 138 Church St., P.O. Box 368, Jonesboro, GA 30237. TEL 770-478-5753; Ed. Larry Stanford; Pub. Herman Cawthon; pub. size: standard; circ. 4,200(paid).

JEFFERSON

US

JACKSON HERALD. 1875. Wed. $.50 newsstand; $16.50/yr. in cy.; $22/yr. out of cy.; $35.35/yr. out of state. 33 Lee St., Jefferson, GA 30549. TEL 706-367-5233; FAX 706-367-8056. **Owner(s):** Herman Buffington, 162 Jett Roberts Rd., Jefferson, GA 30549. TEL 706-367-5233; Helen Buffington, 162 Jett Roberts Rd., Jefferson, GA 30549. TEL 706-367-5233; Scott Buffington, P.O. Box 908, Jefferson, GA 30549. TEL 706-367-5233; Mike Buffington, P.O. Box 908, Jefferson, GA 30549. TEL 706-367-5233; Ed. Mike Buffington; Pub. Herman Buffington; adv. contact: Scott Buffington. pub. size: broadsheet; circ. 8,450(paid).

JESUP

US

PRESS-SENTINEL, THE. s-w.: Wed. & Sun. $.50 newsstand; $25/yr. mailed in cy.; $30/yr. out of state. 252 W. Walnut St., Jesup, GA 31545. TEL 912-427-3757; FAX 912-427-4092. **Owner(s):** Press-Sentinel Newspapers, Inc., P.O. Box 607, Jesup, GA 31598. TEL 912-427-3757; Ed. Drew Davis; Pub. Eric Denty; adv.: $6.82/SAU. photos; pub. size: broadsheet; circ. 7,200(paid).

LA FAYETTE

US

WALKER COUNTY MESSENGER. 1877. s-w.: Wed. & Fri. $.50 newsstand; $24/yr. in cy.; $34/yr. out of area. 120 E. Patton St., La Fayette, GA 30728. TEL 706-638-1859; FAX 706-638-7045. **Owner(s):** News Publishing Co., P.O. Box 1633, Rome, GA 30162. TEL 404-291-6397; Ed. Don Stilwell; Pub. Burgett Mooney; adv. contact: Nancy De Bord. pub. size: broadsheet; circ. 3,900(paid).

LAVONIA

US

FRANKLIN COUNTY CITIZEN. 1971. Thu. $17/yr. in cy.; $22/yr. out of cy.; $25/yr. out of state. 12150 Augusta Rd., Lavonia, GA 30553. TEL 706-356-8557; FAX 706-356-2008. **Owner(s):** Community Newspapers, Inc., P.O. Box 792, Athens, GA 30603. TEL 800-226-0692; Ed. Greg T. Pitts; Pub. Greg T. Pitts; adv.: $4.95/SAU. photos; pub. size: broadsheet; circ. 5,418(paid).

LUDOWICI

US

LUDOWICI NEWS. 1921. Wed. $.40 newsstand; $15/yr. in cy.; $18/yr. elsewhere. 8 McDonald St., Ludowici, GA 31316. TEL 912-545-2103; FAX 912-545-2103. **Owner(s):** Ken Buchanan, 8 McDonald St., Lusowici, GA 31316. TEL 912-545-2103; Ed. Joe Parker; Pub. Ken Buchanan; adv.; pub. size: tabloid; circ. 1,000(paid).

MADISON

US

MADISONIAN, THE. 1842. Thu. $.50 newsstand; $21.20/yr. in cy.; $24.38/yr. in state; $29/yr. out of state. 131 E. Jefferson St., Madison, GA 30650-0191. TEL 706-342-2424; FAX 706-342-1300. **Owner(s):** Robert B. Booth, P.O. Box 191, Madison, GA 30650. TEL 706-342-2424; Pub. Robert B. Booth; adv. contact: Denni Cardell. photos; bk.rev.; pub. size: broadsheet; circ. 4,800(paid).

US

OCONEE BREEZE. 1985. Sat. $.50 newsstand; $12.72/yr. mailed locally. 131 E. Jefferson St., Madison, GA 30650-0191. TEL 706-342-2424; FAX 706-342-1300. **Owner(s):** Robert B. Booth, P.O. Box 191, Madison, GA 30650-0191. TEL 706-342-2424; Pub. Robert B. Booth; adv.; pub. size: broadsheet; circ. 6,000(free & paid).
Formerly: Lake Oconee Free Press.

MANCHESTER

US

MANCHESTER STAR-MERCURY. 1911. Wed. $.50 newsstand; $19.08/yr. in cy.; $26.50/yr. out of cy.; $30/yr. out of state. 3051 Roosevelt Hwy., Manchester, GA 31816. TEL 706-846-3188; FAX 706-846-2206. **Owner(s):** Trib Publications, Inc., P.O. Box 426, Manchester, GA 31816. TEL 706-846-3188; Ed. Micky D'Avy; Pub. Robert Tribble; adv. contact: Mike Hale. photos; pub. size: broadsheet; circ. 3,650(free & paid).

US

MERIWETHER VINDICATOR. 1876. Fri. $.35 newsstand; $15.90/yr. in cy.; $23.63/yr. in state; $30/yr. out of state. 3051 Roosevelt Hwy., Manchester, GA 31816. TEL 706-846-3188; FAX 706-846-2206. **Owner(s):** Trib Publications, Inc., P.O. Box 426, Manchester, GA 31816. TEL 706-846-3188; FAX 706-846-2206; Ed. Micky D'Avy; Pub. Robert Tribble; adv. contact: Mike Hale. photos; pub. size: broadsheet; circ. 1,700(free & paid).

MARIETTA

US

ACWORTH NEIGHBOR. 1815. s-w.: Wed. & Thu. free local deliv.; $112/yr. mailed. 580 Fairground St., Marietta, GA 30060. TEL 770-795-3000; FAX 770-422-9533. **Owner(s):** Marietta Daily Journal & Neighbor Newspapers, Inc., 580 Fairground St., Marietta, GA 30060. TEL 770-428-9411; FAX 770-422-9533; Ed. Steve Allen; Pub. Otis A. Brumby, Jr.; adv.; pub. size: broadsheet; circ. 6,609(free).

US

AUSTELL NEIGHBOR. s-w.: Wed. & Thu. free local deliv.; $112/yr. mailed. 580 Fairground St., Marietta, GA 30060. TEL 770-795-3000; FAX 770-422-9533. **Owner(s):** Marietta Daily Journal & Neighbor Newspapers, Inc., 580 Fairground St., Marietta, GA 30060. TEL 770-428-9411; FAX 770-422-9533; Ed. Steve Allen; Pub. Otis A. Brumby, Jr.; adv.; pub. size: broadsheet; circ. 6,550(free).

US

DOUGLAS NEIGHBOR, THE. Thu. free. 580 Fairground St., Marietta, GA 30060. TEL 770-428-9411; FAX 770-422-9533. **Owner(s):** Times Journal, Inc., 580 Fairground St., Marietta, GA 30060. TEL 770-428-9411; FAX 770-422-9533; Ed. Joe Baggett; Pub. Otis Brumby, Jr.; adv.; pub. size: broadsheet; circ. 10,000(free).

US

KENNESAW NEIGHBOR, THE. s-w.: Wed. & Thu. free local deliv.; $112/yr. mailed. 580 Fairground St., Marietta, GA 30061. TEL 770-795-3000; FAX 404-422-9533. **Owner(s):** Marietta Daily Journal & Neighbor Newspapers, Inc., 580 Fairground St., Marietta, GA 30060. TEL 770-428-9411; FAX 770-422-9533; Ed. Steve Allen; Pub. Otis A. Brumby, Jr.; adv.; pub. size: broadsheet; circ. 8,942(free).

US

MABLETON NEIGHBOR, THE. 1973. s-w.: Wed. & Thu. free local deliv.; $112/yr. mailed. 580 Fairground St., Marietta, GA 30060. TEL 770-795-3000; FAX 770-422-9533. **Owner(s):** Marietta Daily Journal & Neighbor Newspapers, Inc., 580 Fairground St., Marietta, GA 30060. TEL 770-428-9411; FAX 770-422-9533; Ed. Rodney Shumake; Pub. Otiis A. Brumby, Jr.; adv.; pub. size: broadsheet; circ. 6,591(free).

US

PAULDING NEIGHBOR, THE. Thu. free newsstand; $52/yr. mailed. 580 Fairground St., Marietta, GA 30060. TEL 770-428-9411; FAX 770-422-9533. **Owner(s):** Times Journal, Inc., 580 Fairground St., Marietta, GA 30060. TEL 770-428-9411; FAX 770-422-9533; Ed. Stan Hardegree; Pub. Otis A. Brumby, Jr.; adv. contact: Judy Laney. pub. size: broadsheet; circ. 14,750(free & paid). **Wire Service(s):** AP.

US

POWDER SPRINGS NEIGHBOR, THE. s-w.: Wed. & Thu. free local deliv.; $112/yr. mailed. 580 Fairground St., Marietta, GA 30060. TEL 770-795-3000; FAX 770-422-9533. **Owner(s):** Marietta Daily Journal & Neighbor Newspapers, Inc., 580 Fairground St., Marietta, GA 30060. TEL 770-428-9411; FAX 770-422-9533; Ed. Steve Allen; Pub. Otis A. Brumby, Jr.; adv.; pub. size: broadsheet; circ. 7,864(free).

MARTINEZ

US

COLUMBIA NEWS TIMES, THE. 1928. s-w.: Wed. & Sun. $.50 newsstand; $33/yr. 3919 Roberts Rd., Martinez, GA 30907. TEL 706-863-6165; FAX 706-863-9080. **Owner(s):** Kim Shelnut, 3919 Roberts Rd., Martinez, GA 30907. TEL 706-863-6165; FAX 706-863-9080; Ed. Karl Haywood; Pub. Kim Shelnut; adv.; photos; pub. size: broadsheet; circ. 14,500(paid).
Formerly: Columbia News & Martinez-Evans Times.

MCDONOUGH

US

HENRY HERALD, THE. 1874. 3/wk.: Wed., Fri., Sun. $.50 newsstand; $42/yr. in cy.; $60/yr. out of cy. 32 Macon St., McDonough, GA 30253. TEL 770-957-9161; FAX 770-954-0282. **Owner(s):** Southern Crescent Newspapers LP, 138 Church St., Jonesboro, GA 30236. TEL 404-478-5753; Ed. Joe Hiett; Pub. Joe Hiett; pub. size: broadsheet; circ. 7,200(paid); Sun. 14,800(paid).

MCRAE

US

TELFAIR ENTERPRISE. 1887. Wed. $.50 newsstand; $15.90/yr. in cy; $16.96/yr. in state; $20.14/yr. out of state. 237 W. Oak, McRae, GA 31055. TEL 912-868-6015; FAX 912-868-5486. **Owner(s):** B & B Publications, Inc., P.O. Box 269, McRae, GA 31055. TEL 912-868-6015; FAX 912-868-5486; Ed. Ed Bowen, Jr. adv. contact: Ed Bowen, Jr. pub. size: standard; circ. morning 3,450.

WEEKLY NEWSPAPERS

US

THREE RIVERS GAZETTE. 1984. Tue. free. 237 W. Oak St., McRae, GA 31055. TEL 912-868-6015; FAX 912-868-5486. **Owner(s):** Corbeau Publications, Inc., P.O. Box 459, Helena, GA 31037. TEL 912-868-5776; Ed. Ed Bowen, Jr. adv.; pub. size: tabloid; circ. 8,000(free).

MONROE
US

WALTON TRIBUNE. 1900. s-w.: Wed. & Sun. $.75 newsstand; $40/yr. 124 N. Broad St., Monroe, GA 30655. TEL 770-267-8371; FAX 770-267-7780. **Owner(s):** Southern Newspapers, Inc., 1050 Wilcrest Dr., Houston, TX; Ed. Wes Swietek; Pub. Robert Hale; adv.; photos; pub. size: broadsheet; circ. 5,500(paid).

NAHUNTA
US

BRANTLEY ENTERPRISE. 1920. Wed. $.35 newsstand; $15/yr. in cy.; $20/yr. out of cy. 109 Main St., Nahunta, GA 31553. TEL 912-462-6776; FAX 912-462-6776. **Owner(s):** Ken L. Buchanan, 118C N. Main St., Nahunta, GA 31553. TEL 912-462-6776; FAX 912-462-6776; Ed. Ken Buchanan; Pub. Ken Buchanan; adv.; photos; pub. size: broadsheet; circ. 2,200(paid).

NASHVILLE
US

BERRIEN PRESS. 1959. Wed. $15/yr. in cy.; $23/yr. out of cy.; $30/yr. out of state. 200 E. McPherson Ave., Nashville, GA 31639. TEL 912-686-3523; FAX 912-686-7771. **Owner(s):** Clarice Hamilton, 200 E. McPherson Ave., Nashville, GA 31639; Ed. Donald F. Boyd; Pub. Donald F. Boyd; adv.; photos; pub. size: broadsheet; circ. 4,200(paid).

NEWNAN
US

NEWNAN TIMES-HERALD. 1865. s-w.: Wed. & Sat. $.50 newsstand; $26.50/yr. local; $30.17/yr. in state; $52/yr. out of state. 16 Jefferson St., Newnan, GA 30263. TEL 770-253-1576; FAX 770-253-2538; E-mail: webmaster@newnan.com; URL: http://newnan.com. **Owner(s):** W.W. Thomasson, P.O. Box 1052, Newnan, GA 30264. TEL 770-253-1576; Ed. Marianne Thomasson. adv. contact: Lamar Truitt. pub. size: broadsheet; circ. 13,500(paid). **Wire Service(s):** AP.

PEACHTREE CITY
US

THIS WEEK IN PEACHTREE CITY. 1974. 3/wk.: Tue., Thu., Sat. $26.25/yr. 111 Petrol Pt., Peachtree City, GA 30269. TEL 770-487-7729; FAX 770-460-8172. **Owner(s):** Robert Tribble, Fayette Newspapers, Inc., P.O. Box 2468, Peachtree City, GA 30269. TEL 770-487-7729; Ed. Pat Cooper; Pub. Robert Tribble; adv.; pub. size: broadsheet; circ. 4,300(paid).

PELHAM
US

PELHAM JOURNAL. 1902. Wed. $19/yr. cy; $26.50/yr. in state; $30/yr. out of state. 310 W. Railroad St., S., Pelham, GA 31779. TEL 912-294-3661; FAX 912-336-8426. **Owner(s):** Trib Publications, P.O. Box 426, Manchester, GA 31816. TEL 706-846-3188; Ed. Joanne Hand; Pub. Roger Anne Jones; adv.; pub. size: standard; circ. 2,500(paid).

PEMBROKE
US

BRYAN COUNTY TIMES. 1982. Wed. $.35 newsstand; $16/yr. local; $24/yr. out of state. 29 E. Bacon St., Pembroke, GA 31321. TEL 912-653-4570; FAX 912-653-4571. **Owner(s):** JAB, Inc., PO Box 798, Pembroke, GA 31321. TEL 912-653-4570; FAX 912-653-4571; Ed. Anne Butler; Pub. John Butler; adv.; photos; pub. size: broadsheet; circ. 2,400(controlled & paid).

PERRY
US

HOUSTON TIMES-JOURNAL. 1870. Wed. $.50 newsstand; $21/yr. 807 Carroll St., Perry, GA 31069. TEL 912-987-1823; FAX 912-988-1181; E-mail: timesjrnl@aol.com. **Owner(s):** Trib Publications, Inc., P.O. Box 426, Manchester, GA 31816. TEL 706-846-3188; adv. contact: John Smalley. pub. size: broadsheet; circ. 3,700(paid).
Formerly: Houston Home Journal & Perry Times.

RINCON
US

HERALD, THE. 1908. Wed. $20/yr. in cy.; $22/yr. out of cy.; $28/yr. out of state. Drawer 799, Rincon, GA 31326. TEL 912-826-5012; FAX 912-826-0318. **Owner(s):** Morris Communications, P.O. Box 936, Augusta, GA. TEL 706-724-0851; Ed. Don Lowery; Pub. Ginny Anderson; adv.; pub. size: broadsheet; circ. 4,500(paid).

RINGGOLD
US

CATOOSA COUNTY NEWS. 1949. Wed. $.50 newsstand; $14/yr. in cy.; $22/yr. out of cy. 7513 Nashville St., Ringgold, GA 30736. TEL 706-935-2621; FAX 706-965-5349. **Owner(s):** B.H. Mooney, III, P.O. Box 1633, Rome, GA 30162. TEL 706-290-5290; Ed. Richard Ball; Pub. B.H. Mooney, III; adv. contact: Amy Bagby. photos; pub. size: broadsheet; circ. 4,000(paid).

ROCKMART
US

ROCKMART JOURNAL. 1873. Wed. $.50 newsstand; $14/yr. in cy.; $22/yr. in cy. 240 S. Piedmont Ave., Rockmart, GA 30153. TEL 770-684-7811; FAX 770-684-8468. **Owner(s):** B.H. Mooney, III, P.O. Box 1633, Rome, GA 30162. TEL 706-290-5290; Ed. Orbie Thaxton; Pub. B.H. Mooney, III; adv.; pub. size: broadsheet; circ. 11,000(free & paid).

ROSWELL
US ISSN 0192-2637

ROSWELL-ALPHARETTA NEIGHBOR. 1980. Wed. $.25 newsstand; free local deliv.; $112/yr. mailed. 10479 Alpharetta St., Roswell, GA 30075. TEL 770-993-7400; FAX 770-518-6062. **Owner(s):** Times Journal, Inc., 580 Fairground St., Marietta, GA 30060. TEL 770-944-9400; FAX 770-422-9533; Ed. Rodney Shumacke; Pub. Otis Brumby, Jr.; adv. contact: Kathleen Gray. pub. size: broadsheet; circ. 37,000(controlled & paid).
Formerly: Neighborhood Newspaper Roswell-Alpharetta.

ROYSTON
US

NEWS LEADER, THE. 1978. Wed. $.25 newsstand; $13/yr. in cy. 44 Franklin Springs St., Royston, GA 30662. TEL 706-245-7351; FAX 706-245-5991. **Owner(s):** Southern Crescent Newspapers, LP, Atlanta, GA; Ed. Joe Edwards; Pub. Peggy Vickery; adv.; pub. size: broadsheet; circ. 4,000(paid).

SANDERSVILLE
US

SANDERSVILLE PROGRESS. 1887. Wed. $.50 newsstand; $21.20/yr. in cy.; $26.50/yr. out of cy.; $30/yr. out of state. 118 E. Haynes St., Sandersville, GA 31082. TEL 912-552-3161; FAX 912-552-5177. **Owner(s):** Robert Tribble, P.O. Box 431, Sandersville, GA 31082. TEL 912-552-3161; Ed. Robert Garrett; Pub. Robert Tribble; adv. contact: Melissa Brown. pub. size: broadsheet; circ. 5,300(paid).

SPARTA
US

SPARTA ISHMAELITE. 1878. Wed. $.35 newsstand; $18/yr. in cy.; $22/yr. in state; $26/yr. out of state. 109 Broad St., Sparta, GA 31087. TEL 706-444-5330; FAX 706-444-5330. **Owner(s):** R. Allen Haywood, 109 Broad St., Sparta, GA 31087. TEL 706-444-5330; FAX 706-444-5330; Ed. R. Allen Haywood; Pub. R. Allen Haywood; adv.; photos; pub. size: broadsheet; circ. 2,200(paid).

ST. MARYS
US

CAMDEN COUNTY TRIBUNE. 1950. s-w.: Wed. & Fri. $.50 newsstand; $20/yr. in cy.; $30/yr. out of cy. 707 Osborne St., St. Marys, GA 31558. TEL 912-882-4927; FAX 912-882-6519. **Owner(s):** Community Newspapers, Inc., P.O. Box 792, Athens, GA 30603. TEL 800-226-0692; FAX 706-548-0808; Pub. Linn Hudson; adv.; photos; pub. size: broadsheet; circ. 7,800(paid).

ST. SIMONS ISLAND
US

GEORGIS'S COASTAL ILLUSTRATED. 1968. Wed. free newsstand. 1626 Frederica Rd., St. Simons Island, GA 31522. TEL 912-638-3793; FAX 912-634-0623. **Owner(s):** Harry Kaufmann, P.O. Box 928, Sea Island, GA 31561. TEL 912-638-3793; Pub. Harry Kaufmann; adv.; photos; bk.rev.; pub. size: tabloid; circ. 10,000(free).
Formerly: Coastal Illustrated.

10568   ST. SIMONS ISLAND, GA

ST. SIMONS ISLAND

US

ISLANDER, THE. 1972. Mon. $.25 newsstand; $14.50/yr. in cy.; $16.50/yr. out of cy. 520 Wesley Oaks Cir., St. Simons Island, GA 31522. TEL 912-265-9654; FAX 912-638-2764. **Owner(s):** Islander, The, P.O. Box 20539, St. Simons Island, GA 31522. TEL 912-265-9654; Ed. M.J. Permar; Pub. M.J. Permar; adv.; photos; bk.rev.; pub. size: tabloid; circ. 1,000(paid).

SUMMERVILLE

US

CHATTOOGA PRESS. 1982. Wed. free. P.O. Box 485, Summerville, GA 30747. TEL 706-857-5433; FAX 706-234-6478. **Owner(s):** News Publishing Co., P.O. Box 1633, Rome, GA 30162. TEL 706-290-5330; Ed. Pamella Purcell; Pub. Bergen May; adv. contact: Gail Touchstone. pub. size: broadsheet; circ. 11,500(free).

US

SUMMERVILLE NEWS. 1886. Thu. $.25 newsstand; $10.60/yr. in cy. Rome Hwy., Summerville, GA 30747. TEL 706-857-2494; FAX 706-857-2393. **Owner(s):** David Espy, P.O. Box 310, Summerville, GA 30747. TEL 706-857-2494; FAX 706-857-2393; Winston E. Espy, P.O. Box 310, Summerville, GA 30747. TEL 706-857-2494; FAX 706-857-2393; Greg Espy, P.O. Box 310, Summerville, GA 30747. TEL 706-857-2494; FAX 706-857-2393; Ed. Gene Espy; Pub. Winston E. Espy; adv. contact: Bill Hudsputh. photos; pub. size: broadsheet; circ. 7,800(paid).

SWAINSBORO

US

BLADE, THE. 1859. s-w.: Mon. & Wed. $.50 newsstand; $24/yr. 350 W. Moring St., Swainsboro, GA 30401. TEL 912-237-9971; FAX 912-237-9451. **Owner(s):** William C. Rogers, Sr., P.O. Box 938, Swainsboro, GA 30401. TEL 912-237-9971; William C. Rogers, Jr., P.O. Box 938, Swainsboro, GA 30401. TEL 912-237-9971; Ed. Ruby Fagler; Pub. William C. Rogers, Jr.; pub. size: broadsheet; circ. 14,645(free & paid).

SYLVESTER

US

SYLVESTER LOCAL NEWS. 1884. Wed. $15/yr. in cy.; $19/yr. out of cy.; $27/yr. elsewhere. 103 E. Kelly, Sylvester, GA 31791. TEL 912-776-3991; FAX 912-776-4607. **Owner(s):** Marian A. Sumner, P.O. Box 387, Sylvester, GA 31791. TEL 912-776-7713; Ed. Marian A. Sumner; Pub. Marian A. Sumner; adv. contact: John F. Porter. pub. size: standard; circ. 3,800(paid).

THOMASTON

US

THOMASTON TIMES. 1869. 3/wk.: Mon., Wed., Fri. $.75 newsstand; $34/yr. local; $45/yr. in state; $55/yr. elsewhere. P.O. Box 430, Thomaston, GA 30286. TEL 706-647-5414; FAX 706-647-2833. **Owner(s):** Thomaston Publishing Co., Inc., P.O. Box 430, Thomaston, GA. TEL 706-647-5414; FAX 706-647-2833; Ed. Chris Smith; Pub. Chris Smith; adv.; photos; pub. size: broadsheet; circ. 6,500(free & paid).

THOMSON

US

MCDUFFIE PROGRESS, THE. 1900. s-w.: Wed. & Sun. $.50/day newsstand; $.75/Sun.; $30/yr. in cy.; $55/yr. out of cy. 101 Church St., S.W., Thomson, GA 30824-1090. TEL 706-595-1601; FAX 706-597-8974. **Owner(s):** McDuffie County Newspapers, Inc., P.O. Box 1090, Thomson, GA 30824. TEL 404-595-1601; Ed. Wesley King; Pub. Todd Rainwater; adv.; photos; pub. size: broadsheet; circ. 4,300(paid); Sun. 4,300(paid).
Formerly: Thomson McDuffie Progress.

TOCCOA

US

CHIEFTAIN & TOCCOA RECORD. Thu. $.25 newsstand; $14.84/yr. in cy.; $19.08/yr. out of cy. 151 W. Doyle St., Toccoa, GA 30577. TEL 770-886-9476; FAX 770-886-2161. **Owner(s):** Century Newspapers, Inc., P.O. Drawer 1069, Toccoa, GA 30577; Ed. Tom Law. pub. size: standard; circ. 5,000(paid).
Formerly: Chieftain, The & Toccoa Record, The.

VILLA RICA

US   ISSN 0895-7312

VILLA RICAN, THE. 1935. Thu. $12/yr. in cy.; $15/yr. out of cy.; $10/yr. senior citizens. 215 W. Wilson St., Villa Rica, GA 30180. TEL 770-459-5166; FAX 770-459-4804. **Owner(s):** Paxton Media Group, Inc., P.O. Box 2300, Paducah, KY 42002. TEL 502-443-1771; FAX 502-442-8188; Pub. Dawn Weatherby; adv.; photos; pub. size: broadsheet; circ. 2,170(paid).

WASHINGTON

US

WASHINGTON NEWS-REPORTER. 1919. Thu. $20.14/yr. in cy.; $26.50/yr. out of cy. 116 W. Robert Toombs Ave., Washington, GA 30673. TEL 706-678-2636; FAX 706-678-3857. **Owner(s):** Wilkes Publishing Co., 116 W. Robert Toombs Ave., Washington, GA 30673. TEL 706-678-2636; Ed. P. Smythe Newsome; Pub. P. Smythe Newsome; pub. size: standard; circ. 5,000(paid).

WAYNESBORO

US

TRUE CITIZEN, THE. 1882. Wed. $18/yr. in cy.; $23/yr. in state; $29/yr. elsewhere. 610 Academy Ave., Waynesboro, GA 30830. TEL 706-554-2111; FAX 706-554-2437; E-mail: chalker@csranet.com. **Owner(s):** Chalker Publishing Co., 601 E. Sixth St., Waynesboro, GA 30830. TEL 706-554-7888; Ed. Jimmy Ezzell. adv.; photos; pub. size: broadsheet; circ. 4,700(paid).

WINDER

US

WINDER NEWS. 1893. s-w.: Wed. & Sun. $.50 newsstand; $20/yr. in cy.; $30/yr. out of cy. 189 W. Athens St., Winder, GA 30680. TEL 770-867-7557; FAX 770-867-1034. **Owner(s):** Swartz-Morris Media, Inc., Cumming, GA; Ed. Leanne T. Bell; Pub. Debbie Burgamy; adv.; photos; pub. size: broadsheet; circ. 8,000(paid). **Wire Service(s):** NYT.

WOODSTOCK

US

▼**LAKESIDE LEDGER, THE.** 1995. w.: Fri. free; $15/yr. outside of area. 8364 Main St., Woodstock, GA 30188. TEL 770-928-0706; FAX 770-928-3152; E-mail: lakeledge@aol.com; URL: http://www.northga.com. **Owner(s):** P.C. Boyle, P.O. Box 928, Oil City, PA 16301. TEL 814-676-7444; Ed. Stan Handegree; Pub. Dave Caughman; adv.; photos; pub. size: tabloid; circ. 32,500(free & paid).

WRIGHTSVILLE

US   ISSN 0747-3737

WRIGHTSVILLE HEADLIGHT, THE. 1880. Thu. $.35 newsstand; $18.02/yr. local; $23.85/yr. in state; $30/yr. out of state. 102 W. Elm St., Wrightsville, GA 31096. TEL 912-864-3528; FAX 912-864-2166. **Owner(s):** Trib Publications, Inc., P.O. Box 426, Manchester, GA 31816. TEL 706-846-3188; Ed. Lori Brown. adv. contact: Lori Brown. photos; pub. size: broadsheet; circ. 2,200(free & paid).

HAWAII

KANEOHE

US

MIDWEEK. Wed. free. 45-525 Luluku Rd., Kaneohe, HI 96744. TEL 808-235-5881; FAX 808-247-7246. **Owner(s):** Ken Berry, 45-525 Luluku Rd., Kaneohe, HI 96744. TEL 808-235-5881; Ed. William Mossman; Pub. Ken Berry; adv. contact: Jay Higa. pub. size: broadsheet; circ. 280,000(free).

US

SUN PRESS. 1961. Thu. free; $1.30/mo. voluntary. 45-525 Luluku Rd., Kaneohe, HI 96744. TEL 808-235-5881; FAX 808-247-7246. **Owner(s):** Sam Newhouse, 45-525 Luluku Rd., Kaneohe, HI 96744. TEL 808-235-5881; Ed. Bill Mossman; Pub. Ken Berry; adv. contact: Chris McMahon. pub. size: broadsheet; circ. 28,000(free & paid).
Formerly: Hawaii Sun Press.

LIHUE

US

GARDEN ISLAND EXTRA. Sat. free. 3137 Kuhio Hwy., Lihue, HI 96766. TEL 808-245-3681; FAX 808-245-5286. **Owner(s):** Pulitzer Publishing Company, 900 N. Tucker Blvd., St. Louis, MO 63116. TEL 313-340-8000; Ed. Sue Dixon; Pub. Roy Callaway; circ. 10,000(paid).

IDAHO

ABERDEEN

US

ABERDEEN TIMES. 1911. Wed. $.75 newsstand; $22/yr. in state; $25/yr. out of state; $21/yr. senior citizens in state. P.O. Box X, Aberdeen, ID 83210. TEL 208-397-4440; FAX 208-226-5295. **Owner(s):** Erma Crompton, P.O. Box X, Aberdeen, ID 83210. TEL 208-397-4440; Ed. Julia Raben; Pub. Erma Crompton; adv.; pub. size: standard; circ. 1,350(paid).

WEEKLY NEWSPAPERS

AMERICAN FALLS
US

POWER COUNTY PRESS. 1898. Wed. $.75 newsstand; $22/yr. P.O. Box 547, American Falls, ID 83211. TEL 208-226-5294. **Owner(s):** Erma & Brett Crompton, P.O. Box 547, American Falls, ID 83211. TEL 208-226-5294; Ed. Brett Crompton; Pub. Erma Crompton; adv.: $6.40/SAU. photos; pub. size: broadsheet; circ. 2,100(paid).

ARCO
US ISSN 0890-1511

ARCO ADVERTISER. 1909. Thu. $.50 newsstand; $17/yr. local; $20/yr. outside area. 146 S. Front St., Arco, ID 83213-0803. TEL 208-527-3038; FAX 208-527-8210. **Owner(s):** Arco Advertiser, Inc., The, P.O. Box 803, Arco, ID 83213-0803. TEL 208-527-3038; FAX 208-527-8210; Ed. Charles L. Cammack; Pub. Don Cammack; adv.; pub. size: broadsheet; circ. 1,955(paid).

BONNERS FERRY
US

BONNERS FERRY HERALD. 1891. Wed. $.50 newsstand; $28.50/yr. in state; $29.50/yr. out of state. 7183 Main St., Bonners Ferry, ID 83805. TEL 208-267-5521; FAX 208-267-5523. **Owner(s):** Pena'Orielle Printers, Inc., Sandpoint, ID; Ed. David Keyes; Pub. David Keyes; adv.; photos; pub. size: broadsheet; circ. 3,000(paid).

BUHL
US

BUHL HERALD. 1909. Wed. $.30 newsstand; $17.85/yr. in cy. 124 S. Broadway, Buhl, ID 83316. TEL 208-543-4335; FAX 208-543-6834. **Owner(s):** Robert M. Bailey, P.O. Box 312, Buhl, ID 83316. TEL 208-543-4335; Ed. Robert M. Bailey; Pub. Robert M. Bailey; pub. size: broadsheet; circ. 3,000(paid).

CAMBRIDGE
US

UPPER COUNTRY NEWS-REPORTER. 1889. Thu. $.50 newsstand; $18/yr. 155 Superior St., Cambridge, ID 83610. TEL 208-257-3515. **Owner(s):** R. Stuart Dopf, P.O. Box 9, Cambridge, ID 83610. TEL 208-257-3515; Ed. R. Stuart Dopf; Pub. R. Stuart Dopf; pub. size: broadsheet; circ. 1,100(paid).

CASCADE
US

LONG VALLEY ADVOCATE, THE. 1985. Wed. $.50 newsstand; $19/yr. in area; $24/yr. elsewhere. 112 N. Main St., Cascade, ID 83611. TEL 208-382-3233; FAX 208-382-6728. **Owner(s):** Michael Stewart, P.O. Box 1079, Cascade, ID 83611. TEL 208-382-4707; Fred & Elzo O'Brien, P.O. Box 548, Cascade, ID 83611; Michael G. Higgins, P.O. Box 957, Cascade, ID 83611; Robin M. Simpson, P.O. Box 1079, Cascade, ID 83611; Ed. Michael Stewart; Pub. Michael Stewart; adv. contact: Robin Simpson. photos; pub. size: tabloid; circ. 5,000(free & paid).

CHALLIS
US

CHALLIS MESSENGER. 1881. Thu. $.50 newsstand; $18.90/yr. in cy.; $25.20/yr. out of cy. 310 N. Main St., Challis, ID 83226. TEL 208-879-4445. E-mail: cuspub@cyberhighwgy.net. **Owner(s):** Custer Publishing, Inc., P.O. Box 405, Challis, ID 83226. TEL 208-879-4445; Ed. Peggy Parks; Pub. Peggy Parks; adv.: $4.50/SAU. photos. pub. size: tabloid; circ. 1,970(free & paid).

COTTONWOOD
US

COTTONWOOD CHRONICLE. 1892. Thu. $18/yr. in state; $21/yr. out of state. 503 King St., Cottonwood, ID 83522-0157. TEL 208-962-3851; FAX 208-962-7131. **Owner(s):** Wherry Publishing, Inc., P.O. Box 157, Cottonwood, ID 83522-0157. TEL 208-962-3851; FAX 208-962-7131; Ed. Greg Wherry; Pub. Patricia Wherry; adv.; pub. size: tabloid; circ. 1,000(paid).

COUNCIL
US

RECORD, THE. 1977. Thu. $.47 newsstand; $18/yr. in state mailed; $18/yr. out of state. 211 Illinois Ave., Council, ID 83612. TEL 208-253-6961; FAX 208-253-6801; E-mail: record@cyberhighway.net. **Owner(s):** Tim Blevins, P.O. Box R, Council, ID 83612. TEL 208-253-6961; Ed. Tim Hohs; Pub. Tim Blevins; adv.: $3.63/SAU. photos; pub. size: broadsheet; circ. 13,000(paid).
Formerly: Council Record.

DRIGGS
US

TETON VALLEY NEWS. 1909. Thu. $20/yr. in cy.; $25/yr. out of cy. 80 E. Little Ave., Driggs, ID 83422-0049. TEL 208-354-8101; FAX 208-354-8621. **Owner(s):** Fred McCabe, P.O. Box 49, Driggs, ID 83422. TEL 208-354-8101; FAX 208-354-8257; Ed. Jeanne Anderson; Pub. Fred McCabe; adv.; bk.rev.; pub. size: tabloid; circ. 2,475(paid).

EMMETT
US

MESSENGER INDEX. 1896. Wed. $21/yr. in cy.; $34.50/yr. out of cy. 120 N. Washington, Emmett, ID 83617. TEL 208-365-6066; FAX 208-365-6068. **Owner(s):** Idaho Press-Tribune, P.O. Box 577, Emmett, ID 83617. TEL 208-467-9251; Ed. Jim Nau. adv.; photos; bk.rev.; pub. size: broadsheet; circ. 7,000(free & paid).

GOODING
US

GOODING COUNTY LEADER. 1908. Wed. $.50 newsstand; $21/yr. in cy.; $26/yr. out of cy.; $16/yr. in cy. senior citizens. 200 Main St., Gooding, ID 83330-1186. TEL 208-934-4449; FAX 208-934-4440. **Owner(s):** Magic Valley Publishing, Inc., 200 Main St., Gooding, ID 83330. TEL 208-934-4449; FAX 208-934-8815; Ed. Mary Ann Hagen; Pub. Patty Nance; adv.; photos; pub. size: tabloid; circ. 1,200(paid).

GRANGEVILLE
US

IDAHO COUNTY FREE PRESS. 1885. Wed. $.50 newsstand; $24/yr. in cy.; $32/yr. out of cy. 318 E. Main, Grangeville, ID 83530. TEL 208-983-1070; FAX 208-983-1336. **Owner(s):** Eagle Newspapers, Inc., P.O. Box 12008, Salem, OR 97309. TEL 503-393-1774; Ed. Vance Tong; Pub. Andy McNab; adv.; photos; pub. size: broadsheet; circ. 10,100(controlled & free).

HAILEY
US

WOOD RIVER JOURNAL. 1881. Wed. $16/yr. in cy.; $26/yr. out of cy. 15 E. Bullion, Hailey, ID 83333-0988. TEL 208-788-3444; FAX 208-788-0083; E-mail: wrjidaho@micron.net; URL: http://www.sunvalleyid.com/wrj. **Owner(s):** South Idaho Press, P.O. Box 988, Hailey, ID 83333-0988; Ed. Dan Gorham; Pub. Dan Gorham; adv.; photos; bk.rev.; pub. size: tabloid; circ. 12,000(free & paid). **Wire Service(s):** AP.

HOMEDALE
US

OWYHEE AVALANCHE. 1865. Wed. $25/yr. in cy.; $30/yr. out of cy. P.O. Box 97, Homedale, ID 83628. TEL 208-337-4681. **Owner(s):** Joe Aman, Homedale, ID 83628; Ed. Joe Aman; Pub. Joe Aman; pub. size: tabloid.

IDAHO FALLS
US

CABLE SCENE. 1971. Wed. $.50 newsstand; $15.75/yr. in cy. mailed. 587 Fourth St., Idaho Falls, ID 83401. TEL 208-523-7777; FAX 208-745-8703. **Owner(s):** Pioneer Publications, Inc., P.O. Box P, Shelley, ID 83274. TEL 208-357-7661; Pub. Terry Carr; adv. contact: Earlene Poole. pub. size: tabloid; circ. 7,000(paid).

JEROME
US

NORTH SIDE NEWS. 1907. Wed. $.50 newsstand; $21/yr. in cy.; $26/yr. out of state. 133 E. Main St., Jerome, ID 83338. TEL 208-324-3391; FAX 208-324-3391. **Owner(s):** Magic Valley Publishing, Inc., P.O. Box 468, Jerome, ID 83338; Ed. P. Marcantonio; Pub. P. Nance; adv.; bk.rev.; pub. size: tabloid; circ. 1,800(paid).

KENDRICK
US

KENDRICK-GAZETTE. 1890. Thu. $10.50/yr. P.O. Box 177, Kendrick, ID 83537. TEL 208-289-5731. **Owner(s):** William A. Roth, P.O. Box 177, Kendrick, ID 83537. TEL 208-289-5731; Ed. William A. Roth; Pub. William A. Roth; pub. size: broadsheet; circ. 950(paid).

10570   KETCHUM, ID   WEEKLY NEWSPAPERS

KETCHUM
US   ISSN 0279-8964
IDAHO MOUNTAIN EXPRESS. 1974. Wed. $36/yr. 591 First Ave., N., Ketchum, ID 83340. TEL 208-726-8060; FAX 208-726-2329; E-mail: express@micron.net; URL: http://www.mtexpress.com/. **Owner(s):** Express Publishing Co., Inc., P.O. Box 1013, Ketchum, ID 83340. TEL 208-726-5060; Ed. Barbara Perkins; Pub. Pam Morris; adv. contact: Mary Gibson. photos; pub. size: tabloid; circ. 13,500(paid). **Wire Service(s):** AP.

KUNA
US
KUNA-MELBA NEWS. 1983. Wed. $.30 newsstand; $18/yr. in cy.; $14/yr. senior citizens. 462 W. Third St., Kuna, ID 83634. TEL 208-466-3557; FAX 208-466-8054. **Owner(s):** Wild Horse Publishing Co., 13729 Lake Ave., Nampa, ID 83651. TEL 208-466-3557; FAX 208-466-8054. Ed. Earl L. Maggard. adv.; photos; bk.rev.; pub. size: tabloid; circ. 950(controlled & paid).

MALAD CITY
US
IDAHO ENTERPRISE. 1887. Thu. $16/yr. in cy.; $21/yr. out of cy. 100 E. 90th S., Malad City, ID 83252. TEL 208-766-4773; FAX 208-766-4774. **Owner(s):** Kris Jones Smith, P.O. Box 205, Malad City, ID 83252; Ed. Kris Jones Smith; Pub. Kris Jones Smith; pub. size: broadsheet; circ. 1,500(paid).

MCCALL
US
STAR-NEWS, THE. 1966. Thu. $.75 newsstand; $24/yr. in area. 1000 First St., McCall, ID 83638. TEL 208-634-2123; FAX 208-634-4950. **Owner(s):** Central Idaho Publishing, Inc., P.O. Box 985, McCall, ID 83638. TEL 208-634-2123; Ed. Tom Grote; Pub. A.L. "Butch" Alford, Jr.; adv. contact: Tom Grote. pub. size: broadsheet; circ. 4,200(free & paid).

MERIDIAN
US
VALLEY NEWS. 1903. s-w.: Tue. & Fri. $35/yr. 815 E. First St., Meridian, ID 83642. TEL 208-888-1941; FAX 208-888-1097. **Owner(s):** Wick Communications, Inc., 333 W. Wilcox Dr., Ste. 302, Sierra Vista, AZ 85635. TEL 520-458-0200; FAX 520-458-6166; Ed. Scot Crosby; Pub. Fran McLean; adv.; pub. size: tabloid; circ. 1,800(paid).

MIDDLETON
US
MIDDLETON GAZETTE. m. free newsstand; $8.44/yr. 418 N. Dewey, Middleton, ID 83644-5616. TEL 208-585-3472; FAX 208-585-2582. **Owner(s):** Cheri Hess & Becky O'Meara, 8522 Hwy. 44, Middleton, ID 83644. TEL 208-585-3472; Ed. Cheri Hess; Pub. Cheri Hess; adv.; photos; pub. size: tabloid; circ. 5,580(free & paid).

MONTPELIER
US
NEWS-EXAMINER. 1895. Wed. $.50 newsstand; $15/yr. local; $21.50/yr. out of area. 847 Washington, Montpelier, ID 83254. TEL 208-847-0552; FAX 208-847-0553. **Owner(s):** J. Walter Ross & Wayne D. Bell, 77 S. State, Preston, ID 83263. TEL 208-852-0155; FAX 208-852-0158; Ed. Rosa Moosman. adv.: $4.19/SAU. photos; pub. size: standard; circ. 2,500(paid).

MOUNTAIN HOME
US
MOUNTAIN HOME NEWS. 1882. Wed. $.50 newsstand; $23/yr. in cy.; $28/yr. out cy.; $33/yr. out of state. 195 S. Third E., Mountain Home, ID 83647. TEL 208-587-3331; FAX 208-587-9205. **Owner(s):** U.S. Media Group, P.O. Box 227, Crystal City, MO 63019; Pub. Coleen W. Swenson; adv. contact: Debra Shoemaker. pub. size: broadsheet; circ. 4,000(paid).

NEZPERCE
US
LEWIS COUNTY HERALD. 1897. Thu. $18/yr. in state. 517 Oak St., Nezperce, ID 83543-0159. TEL 208-937-2671; FAX 208-962-7131. **Owner(s):** Wherry Publishing, Inc., 517 Oak St., Nezperce, ID 83543. TEL 208-937-2671; Ed. Steve Wherry; Pub. Patricia Wherry; pub. size: tabloid; circ. 1,200(paid).

OROFINO
US
CLEARWATER TRIBUNE. 1912. Thu. $19.50/yr. in area; $23.50/yr. out of area. 161 Main St., Orofino, ID 83544. TEL 208-476-4571; FAX 208-476-0765. **Owner(s):** Clearwater Publishing Co., Inc., 161 Main St., Orofino, ID 83544. TEL 208-476-4571; Ed. Marcie Stanton; Pub. Cloann Wilkins-McNall; adv.; pub. size: broadsheet; circ. 3,720(free & paid).
Formerly: Orofino Clearwater.

PAYETTE
US
INDEPENDENT ENTERPRISE. 1891. Wed. $26/yr. local; $33/yr. out of area. 21 S. Main St., Payette, ID 83661-0520. TEL 208-642-3357; FAX 208-642-3560. **Owner(s):** Wick Communications, Inc., 333 W. Wilcox Dr., Ste. 302, Sierra Vista, AZ 85635. Ed. Kathleen Beckham; Pub. Eugene Rhinehart; adv.; photos; pub. size: standard; circ. 2,400(paid).

POST FALLS
US
POST FALLS TRIBUNE. 1896. Thu. $.50 newsstand; $20/yr. in cy.; $22/yr. out of cy. 318 Spokane St., Post Falls, ID 83854. TEL 208-773-7502; FAX 208-773-7002. **Owner(s):** Hagadone Corp., P.O. Box 6200, Coeur d'Alene, ID 83814. TEL 208-667-3431; Ed. Lila Horvath; Pub. Lila Horvath; adv. contact: Chandra Palm. photos; pub. size: broadsheet; circ. 2,630(paid).

PRESTON
US
PRESTON CITIZEN. 1890. Wed. $.50 newsstand; $17.50/yr. in area; $24/yr. out of area. 77 S. State St., Preston, ID 83263. TEL 208-852-0155; FAX 208-852-0158. **Owner(s):** J. Walter Ross, 77 S. State St., Preston, ID 83263. TEL 208-852-0155; FAX 208-852-0158; Ed. Necia Seamons; Pub. J. Walter Ross; adv. contact: J. Walter Ross. adv.: $6.82/SAU; $8.25/SAU classified. photos; pub. size: broadsheet; circ. 5,800(free & paid).

PRIEST RIVER
US   ISSN 0740-3348
PRIEST RIVER TIMES. 1914. Wed. $18/yr. local; $26/yr. elsewhere. 221 Cottonwood Vlge., Albeny Hwy., Priest River, ID 83856. TEL 208-448-2431; FAX 208-448-2938. **Owner(s):** Hagadone Corp., P.O. Box 6200, Coeur d'Alene, ID 83814; Pub. Linda Jordan; adv.; pub. size: broadsheet; circ. 8,400(free & paid).

REXBURG
US
STANDARD JOURNAL. 1909. s-w.: Tue. & Thu. $.50 newsstand; $39.95/yr.; $66.80/yr. in state; $70.14/yr. out of state. 23 S. 100 E., Rexburg, ID 83440. TEL 208-356-5441; FAX 208-356-8312. **Owner(s):** Porter Publications, Inc., P.O. Box 10, Rexburg, ID 83440. TEL 208-356-5411; Ed. Roger Porter; Pub. Roger Porter; pub. size: broadsheet; circ. 4,500(paid).
Formerly: The Rexburg.

RIGBY
US
JEFFERSON STAR, THE. 1903. Wed. $.50 newsstand; $19.95/yr. 134 W. Main St., Rigby, ID 83442. TEL 208-745-8701; FAX 208-745-8703. **Owner(s):** Pioneer Publications, Inc., P.O. Box P, Shelley, ID 83274. TEL 208-745-8701; FAX 208-745-8703; Ed. Terry Carr; Pub. Terry Carr; adv.; photos; pub. size: broadsheet; circ. 2,300(paid).

RUPERT
US
MINIDOKA COUNTY NEWS. 1906. Wed. $.50 newsstand; $18/yr. 518 Sixth St., Rupert, ID 83350. TEL 208-436-4201; FAX 208-436-4556. **Owner(s):** Community Newspaper Holdings, Inc., 269 W. Main St., Lexington, KY 40507. TEL 606-388-2644; FAX 606-225-8115; Ed. Judy Albertson. adv. contact: Rose Bryan. photos; bk.rev.; pub. size: broadsheet; circ. 1,414(paid).

SALMON
US
RECORDER-HERALD. 1886. Thu. $.50 newsstand; $18/yr. in state; $22/yr. out of state. 519 Van Dreff St., Salmon, ID 83467. TEL 208-756-2221; FAX 208-756-2222. **Owner(s):** Ricky G. Hodges, P.O. Box 310, Salmon, ID 83467. TEL 208-756-2221; FAX 208-756-2222; Pub. Ricky G. Hodges; adv.; pub. size: broadsheet; circ. 3,401(paid).

ULRICH'S INTERNATIONAL PERIODICALS DIRECTORY 1998

WEEKLY NEWSPAPERS

SHELLEY
US

SHELLEY PIONEER. 1905. Thu. $17.75/yr. in cy.; $27/yr. out of state. 154 E. Center, Shelley, ID 83274. TEL 208-357-7661. **Owner(s):** Pioneer Publications, Inc., P.O. Box P, Shelley, ID 83274. TEL 208-357-7661; Ed. Ken Carr; Pub. Ken Carr; adv.; pub. size: tabloid; circ. 1,700(paid).

SHOSHONE
US

LINCOLN COUNTY JOURNAL. 1884. Wed. $.50 newsstand; $21/yr. in cy.; $26/yr. out of cy.; $16/yr. senior citizens. P.O. Box 704, Shoshone, ID 83352. TEL 208-886-2740. **Owner(s):** Lincoln County Journal, P.O. Box 704, Shoshone, ID 83352. TEL 208-886-2740; Pub. P. Nance; adv.; photos; pub. size: tabloid; circ. 1,000(paid).

SODA SPRINGS
US

CARIBOU COUNTY SUN. 1930. Thu. $.50 newsstand; $16/yr. in cy.; $20/yr. out of cy. 169 S. First W., Soda Springs, ID 83276. TEL 208-547-3260. **Owner(s):** Mark Steele, P.O. Box 815, Soda Springs, ID 83276. TEL 208-547-3260; Ed. Mark Steele; Pub. Mark Steele; adv.; pub. size: tabloid; circ. 2,900(paid).

ST. ANTHONY
US

FREMONT COUNTY HERALD-CHRONICLE. 1891. s-w.: Tue. & Thu. $.50 newsstand; $39.90/yr. local; $70.14/yr. out of area. 44 N. Bridge, St. Anthony, ID 83445. TEL 208-624-4455; FAX 208-356-8312. **Owner(s):** Porter Publications, Inc., 23 S. 100 E., Rexburg, ID 83440. TEL 208-356-5441; Pub. Roger O. Porter; adv.; pub. size: broadsheet; circ. 2,300(paid).

ST. MARIES
US

ST. MARIES GAZETTE RECORD. 1906. Wed. $.75 newsstand; $24.95/yr. in cy.; $35.95/yr. out of state. 127 S. Seventh, St. Maries, ID 83861. TEL 208-245-4538; FAX 208-245-4011. **Owner(s):** St. Maries Gazette Record Corp., 127 S. Seventh, St. Maries, ID 83861. TEL 208-245-4538; Ed. Daniel Hammes; Pub. Daniel Hammes; adv. contact: Gaye Van Winkle. pub. size: broadsheet; circ. 3,504(paid).

WEISER
US

WEISER SIGNAL AMERICAN. 1882. s-w.: Mon. & Wed. $.50 newsstand; $27/yr. in state mailed; $39/yr. out of state. 18 E. Idaho St., Weiser, ID 83672-0709. TEL 208-549-1717; FAX 208-549-1718. **Owner(s):** Signal-American Printers, Inc., P.O. Box 709, Weiser, ID 83672-0709. TEL 208-549-1717; Ed. Rob Ruth; Pub. James R. Simpson; adv. contact: Eydie Huston. adv.: $7.30/SAU. photos; pub. size: broadsheet; circ. 3,150(free & paid).

ILLINOIS

ABINGDON
US

ABINGDON ARGUS. 0957. Wed. $.40 newsstand; $17/yr. in cy.; $19/yr. out of cy.; $22/yr. out of state. 405 Western Ave., Ste. 6, Abingdon, IL 61410. TEL 309-462-3189; FAX 309-462-3221. **Owner(s):** Acklin Newspaper Group, P.O. Box 32, Abingdon, IL 61410. TEL 309-462-5758; Ed. Joyce Cannon; Pub. JoAnn Muir; adv. contact: Marilyn Aden. pub. size: tabloid; circ. 2,500(free & paid).

US

AVON SENTINEL. 1879. Wed. $.40 newsstand; $17/yr. in cy.; $19/yr. in state; $22/yr. out of state. 405 Western Ave., Ste. 6, Abingdon, IL 61410-0032. TEL 309-462-5758; FAX 309-462-3221. **Owner(s):** Acklin Newspaper Group, P.O. Box 32, Abingdon, IL 61410. TEL 309-462-5758; FAX 309-462-3221; Ed. Joyce Cannon; Pub. JoAnn Muir; adv. contact: Marilyn Aden. photos; pub. size: tabloid; circ. 850(free & paid).

US

BLANDINSVILLE STAR GAZETTE. Thu. $.40 newsstand; $17/yr. in cy.; $19/yr. out of cy.; $22/yr. out of state. 405 Western Ave., Ste. 6, Abingdon, IL 61410. TEL 309-652-3328; FAX 309-462-3221. **Owner(s):** Acklin Newspaper Group, P.O. Box 32, Abingdon, IL 61410. TEL 309-462-5758; Ed. Joyce Cannon; Pub. Jo Anne Muir; pub. size: tabloid; circ. 850(paid).

ALEDO
US

TIMES RECORD. 1856. Wed. $.95 newsstand; $40/yr. local; $45/yr. elsewhere. 113 S. College Ave., Aledo, IL 61231. TEL 309-582-5112; FAX 309-582-5319. **Owner(s):** Trans-Continental Media, Inc., P.O. Box 546, St. Mary, OH 45885. TEL 419-394-1717; adv. contact: Teresa Larson. photos; bk.rev.; pub. size: broadsheet; circ. 12,000(free & paid).
Formerly: Aledo Times Record.

ALTAMONT
US

ALTAMONT NEWS, THE. 1881. Tue. $.50 newsstand; $17.50/yr. in state; $20.50/yr. out of state. 118 N. Main, Altamont, IL 62411. TEL 618-483-6176; FAX 618-483-5177. **Owner(s):** Greg Hoskins, 118 N. Main, Altamont, IL 62411. TEL 618-483-6176; Pub. Joe Baker; adv.; pub. size: standard; circ. 2,200(paid).

AMBOY
US

AMBOY NEWS, THE. 1854. Thu. $.50 newsstand; $18/yr. local; $23/yr. elsewhere. 219 E. Main St., Amboy, IL 61310-0162. TEL 815-857-2311; FAX 815-857-2517. **Owner(s):** John & Mary Koski, P.O. Box 162, Amboy, IL 61310-0162. TEL 815-857-2311; FAX 815-857-2517; Pub. John Koski; adv.: $4.80/SAU. photos; pub. size: tabloid; circ. 2,500(paid).

ANNA
US

GAZETTE-DEMOCRAT. 1849. Thu. $.50 newsstand; $19/yr. 112 Lafayette St., Anna, IL 62906. TEL 618-833-2158; FAX 618-833-5813. **Owner(s):** Jerry Reppert, P.O. Box 529, Anna, IL 62906; Ed. Geof Skinner; Pub. Jerry L. Reppert; adv.; pub. size: broadsheet; circ. 6,400(paid).

ARCOLA
US

ARCOLA RECORD HERALD. 1866. Thu. $.50 newsstand; $17/yr. local; $20/yr. out of state. 118 E. Main St., Arcola, IL 61910. TEL 217-268-4959; FAX 217-268-4815. **Owner(s):** Don Rankin, 118 E. Main St., Arcola, IL 61910. TEL 217-268-4959; Ed. Don Rankin; Pub. Don Rankin; adv.; pub. size: broadsheet; circ. 2,500(paid).

ARLINGTON HEIGHTS
US

BUFFALO GROVE COUNTRYSIDE. 1977. Thu. $.75 newsstand; $18.95/yr. 291 N. Dunton Ave., Arlington Heights, IL 60004. TEL 847-797-5100; FAX 847-797-5150. **Owner(s):** Pioneer Press, Inc., 3701 W. Lake Ave., Glenview, IL 60025. TEL 847-486-9200; Ed. David Kirkpatrick; Pub. Thomas Neri; adv. contact: Anne Kelly. pub. size: tabloid; circ. 5,580(paid).

US

PALATINE COUNTRYSIDE. 1972. Thu. $.75 newsstand; $18.95/yr. 291 N. Dunton Ave., Arlington Heights, IL 60004. TEL 847-797-5100; FAX 847-797-5150. **Owner(s):** Pioneer Press, Inc., 3701 W. Lake Ave., Glenview, IL 60025. TEL 847-486-9200; Ed. Tom Scott; Pub. Thomas Neri; adv. contact: Anne Kelly. pub. size: tabloid; circ. 6,776(paid).

ARTHUR
US

ARTHUR GRAPHIC CLARION. 1887. Thu. $.50 newsstand; $19/yr. in cy.; $22/yr. out of cy. 113 E. Illinois St., Arthur, IL 61911. TEL 217-543-2151; FAX 217-543-2152. **Owner(s):** Arthur Graphic Clarion, Inc., 113 E. Illinois St., Arthur, IL 61911. TEL 217-543-2151; Ed. Roger Bonham; Pub. Lowell Cutsinger; adv. contact: Don Newberry. photos; bk.rev.; pub. size: broadsheet; circ. 3,100(paid).

ASHTON

US

ASHTON GAZETTE. 1895. Thu. $.40 newsstand; $14/yr. in cy.; $18/yr. out of cy. 813 Main St., Ashton, IL 61006-0287. TEL 815-453-2551. **Owner(s):** David W. Townsend, 813 Main St., Ashton, IL 61006. TEL 815-453-2551; Pub. David W. Townsend; adv. contact: David W. Townsend. photos; pub. size: tabloid; circ. 1,000(paid).

ASSUMPTION

US

GOLDEN PRAIRIE NEWS. 1880. Thu. $.35 newsstand; $15/yr. 301 S. Chestnut, Assumption, IL 62510. TEL 217-226-3721; FAX 217-226-3579. **Owner(s):** Willard Raymond, 301 S. Chestnut, Assumption, IL 62510. TEL 217-226-3721; Pub. Willard Raymond; adv.; pub. size: standard; circ. 2,200(paid).

ASTORIA

US

ASTORIA SOUTH FULTON ARGUS. 1959. Wed. $14.95/yr. in cy.; $19.95/yr. out of cy. 100 N. Pearl, Astoria, IL 61501-0590. TEL 309-329-2151; FAX 309-329-2344. **Owner(s):** K.K. Stevens Publishing Co., P.O. Box 590, Astoria, IL 61501-0590. TEL 309-329-2151; Ed. Merrie Jean Perry; Pub. Thomas B. Stevens; adv. contact: Bonnie White. adv.: $3.80/SAU. photos; circ. 2,111(free & paid).

ATWOOD

US

ATWOOD HERALD. 1892. Wed. $.45 newsstand; $17.50/yr. 107 N. Main, Atwood, IL 61913. TEL 217-578-3213; FAX 217-578-2833. **Owner(s):** Mt. Zion Publications Inc., 107 N. Main, Atwood, IL 61913. TEL 217-578-3213; Ed. Mike Brothers; Pub. Mike Brothers; adv.; pub. size: tabloid; circ. 1,000(paid).

AUBURN

US

AUBURN CITIZEN. 1874. Thu. $.50 newsstand; $18/yr. 110 N. Fifth St., Auburn, IL 62615. TEL 217-438-6155; FAX 217-438-6156. **Owner(s):** South County Publications, 110 N. Fifth St., Auburn, IL 62615. TEL 217-438-6155; Ed. Joe Michelich; Pub. Joe Michelich; adv. contact: Connie McAuliff. photos; pub. size: broadsheet; circ. 1,500(paid).

US

CHATHAM CLARION. 1962. Thu. $.50 newsstand; $18/yr. 110 N. Fifth St., Auburn, IL 62615. TEL 217-438-6155; FAX 217-438-6156. **Owner(s):** South County Publications, 110 N. Fifth St., Auburn, IL 62615. TEL 217-438-6155; Ed. Joe Michelich; Pub. Joe Michelich; adv. contact: Connie McAuliff. pub. size: broadsheet; circ. 1,900(paid).

US

DIVERNON NEWS. 1897. Thu. $.50 newsstand; $18/yr. 110 N. Fifth St., Auburn, IL 62615. TEL 217-438-6155; FAX 217-438-6156. **Owner(s):** South County Publications, 110 N. Fifth St., Auburn, IL 62615. TEL 217-438-6155; Ed. Joe Michelich; Pub. Joe Michelich; adv. contact: Connie McAuliff. pub. size: broadsheet; circ. 400(paid).

US

PAWNEE POST. 1965. Thu. $.50 newsstand; $18/yr. 110 N. Fifth St., Auburn, IL 62615. TEL 217-438-6155; FAX 217-438-6156. **Owner(s):** Joe Michelich, 110 N. Fifth St., Auburn, IL 62615. TEL 217-438-6155; Ed. Joe Michelich; Pub. Joe Michelich; adv.; pub. size: broadsheet; circ. 600(paid).

US

ROCHESTER TIMES. Thu. $.50 newsstand; $18/yr. 110 N. Fifth St., Auburn, IL 62615. TEL 217-438-6155; FAX 217-438-6156. **Owner(s):** Joe Michelich, 110 N. Fifth St., Auburn, IL 62615; Ed. Joe Michelich; Pub. Joe Michelich; adv. contact: Connie McAuliff. pub. size: broadsheet; circ. 1,000(paid).

US

SOUTH COUNTY EXPRESS. 1986. Mon. free. 110 N. Fifth St., Auburn, IL 62615. TEL 217-438-6155; FAX 217-438-6156. **Owner(s):** South County Publications, 110 N. Fifth St., Auburn, IL 62615. TEL 021-743-8615; Ed. Joe Michelich; Pub. Joe Michelich; adv. contact: Connie McAuliff. pub. size: tabloid; circ. 8,800(free).

BANNOCKBURN

US

DEERFIELD REVIEW. Thu. $1 newsstand; $36.95/yr. 2201 Waukegan Rd., Ste., E175, Bannockburn, IL 60015. TEL 847-317-0500; FAX 847-317-1022. **Owner(s):** Pioneer Press, Inc., 3701 W. Lake Ave., Glenview, IL 60025. TEL 847-486-9200; Ed. Arnold Grahl; Pub. Thomas Neri; adv. contact: Susan Karol. pub. size: tabloid; circ. 6,000(paid).

US

HIGHLAND PARK NEWS. 1924. Thu. $1 newsstand; $36.95/yr. 2201 Waukegan Rd., Ste. E175, Bannockburn, IL 60015. TEL 847-317-0500; FAX 847-317-1022. **Owner(s):** Pioneer Press, Inc., 3701 W. Lake Ave., Glenview, IL 60025. TEL 847-486-9200; Ed. Kyle Leonard; Pub. Thomas Neri; adv. contact: Peggy Cunniff. pub. size: tabloid; circ. 7,635(paid).

US ISSN 0744-7973

LAKE FORESTER. 1896. Thu. $1 newsstand; $24/yr. local. 2201 Waukegan Rd., Ste. E175, Bannockburn, IL 60025. TEL 847-486-9200; FAX 847-317-1022; E-mail: leonard@pioneerlocal.com. **Owner(s):** American Publishing Co., 606 N. Van Buren, Marion, IL 62959. TEL 618-993-1711; Ed. Kyle Leonard; Pub. Tom Neri; adv. contact: Lynn Schmidt. pub. size: tabloid; circ. 6,317(paid).

US

LIBERTYVILLE REVIEW. 1974. Thu. $.75 newsstand; $18.95/yr. in cy, $41.95/yr. out of cy. 2201 Waukegan Rd., Ste. E175, Bannockburn, IL 60015. TEL 847-317-0500; FAX 847-317-1022. **Owner(s):** Pioneer Press, Inc., 3701 W. Lake Ave., Glenview, IL 60025. TEL 847-486-9200; Ed. Sheila Richard; Pub. Thomas Neri; adv. contact: Peggy Cunniss. pub. size: tabloid; circ. 2,702(paid).

US

MUNDELEIN REVIEW. 1974. Thu. $.75 newsstand; $18.50/yr. 2201 Waukegan Rd., Ste. E175, Bannockburn, IL 60015. TEL 847-317-0500; FAX 847-317-1022. **Owner(s):** Pioneer Press, Inc., 3701 W. Lake Ave., Glenview, IL 60025. TEL 847-486-9200; Ed. Sheila Richard; Pub. Thomas Neri; adv. contact: Peggy Cunniss. pub. size: tabloid; circ. 2,500(paid).

US

VERNON HILLS REVIEW. 1974. Thu. $1 newsstand; $36.95/yr. 2201 Waukegan Rd., Ste. E-175, Bannockburn, IL 60015. TEL 847-317-0500; FAX 847-317-1022. **Owner(s):** Pioneer Press, Inc., 3701 W. Lake Ave., Glenview, IL 60025. TEL 847-486-9200; Ed. Sheila Richard; Pub. Thomas Neri; adv. contact: Susan Karol. pub. size: tabloid; circ. 2,000(paid).

BARRINGTON

US

ALGONQUIN COUNTRYSIDE. 1972. Thu. $.75 newsstand; $18.95/yr. 200 James St., Barrington, IL 60010. TEL 847-381-9200; FAX 847-381-5840. **Owner(s):** Pioneer Press, Inc., 3701 W. Lake Ave., Glenview, IL 60025. TEL 847-486-9200; Ed. Terri McHugh; Pub. Thomas Neri; adv. contact: Anne Kelly. pub. size: tabloid; circ. 2,313(paid).

US

BARRINGTON COURIER REVIEW. 1981. Thu. $.75 newsstand; $24.95/yr. 200 James St., Barrington, IL 60010. TEL 847-381-9200; FAX 847-381-5840. **Owner(s):** Pioneer Press, Inc., 3701 W. Lake Ave., Glenview, IL 60025. TEL 847-486-9200; Ed. Andis Robezneks; Pub. Thomas Neri; adv. contact: Anne Kelly. pub. size: tabloid; circ. 7,313(paid).
Formerly: Courier, The.

US

CARY-GROVE COUNTRYSIDE. 1976. Thu. $.75 newsstand; $18.95/yr. in cy. $41.95/yr. out of cy. 200 James St., Barrington, IL 60010. TEL 847-381-9200; FAX 847-381-5840. **Owner(s):** Pioneer Press, Inc., 3701 W. Lake Ave., Glenview, IL 60025. TEL 847-486-9200; Pub. Thomas Neri; adv. contact: Ann Kelley. photos; pub. size: tabloid; circ. 3,049(paid).

BARRY

US

PAPER, THE. 1962. Wed. $.30 newsstand; $12/yr. in cy.; $18/yr. out of cy. 725 Bainbridge St., Barry, IL 62312. TEL 217-335-2112; FAX 217-335-2112. **Owner(s):** Debbie Harshman, 725 Bainbridge St., Barry, IL 62312. TEL 217-335-2112; Pub. Debbie Harshman; adv.; photos; pub. size: tabloid; circ. 2,200(paid).

BARTONVILLE

US

LIMESTONE INDEPENDENT NEWS. 1967. Wed. $.50 newsstand; $20/yr. 114 Roosevelt, Bartonville, IL 61607. TEL 309-697-1859; FAX 309-697-1851. **Owner(s):** Barbara Widener, 114 Roosevelt, Bartonville, IL 61607. TEL 309-697-1859; FAX 309-697-1851; Pub. Barbara Widener; adv.; photos; pub. size: tabloid; circ. 2,500(paid).

BEARDSTOWN

US

BEARDSTOWN ILLINOIAN-STAR. 1888. Thu. $.75 newsstand; $24/yr. 1210 Wall St., Beardstown, IL 62618. TEL 217-323-1010; FAX 217-323-5402. **Owner(s):** Beardstown Newspapers, Inc., 1210 Wall St., Beardstown, IL 62618. TEL 217-323-1010; FAX 217-323-5402; Ed. Salle Lael; Pub. William Mitchell; adv.; bk.rev.; pub. size: broadsheet; circ. 2,025(paid).

WEEKLY NEWSPAPERS

US
VIRGINIA GAZETTE. 1872. Thu. $.75 newsstand; $24/yr. 1210 Wall St., Beardstown, IL 62618. TEL 217-323-1010; FAX 217-323-5402. **Owner(s):** Beardstown Newspapers, Inc., 1210 Wall St., Beardstown, IL 61618. TEL 217-323-1010; FAX 217-323-5402; Ed. Nikki Kaul; Pub. William Mitchell; adv. contact: William Mitchell. bk.rev.; pub. size: broadsheet.

BEECHER CITY

US   ISSN 1066-7970
BEECHER CITY JOURNAL. 1915. Wed. $.50 newsstand; $17/yr. in cy.; $20/yr. out of cy.; $22/yr. elsewhere. 104 S. Charles, Beecher City, IL 62414-0038. TEL 618-487-5634. **Owner(s):** P.J. Ryan & Cherie Ryan, 101 S. Charles, Beecher City, IL 62414. TEL 618-487-5634; Ed. P.J. Ryan; Pub. P.J. Ryan; adv.: $3.50/SAU. photos; pub. size: tabloid.

BELLEVILLE

US
BELLEVILLE JOURNAL. s-w.: Wed. & Sun. free in cy.; $35/yr. out of cy. 219 N. Illinois, Belleville, IL 62220. TEL 618-277-7000; FAX 618-277-7018. **Owner(s):** Suburban Journals, 1714 Deer Tracks Trail, St. Louis, MO 63131; Ed. Marty Ricther; Pub. Dan Braun; adv. contact: Guy Ranney. photos; pub. size: broadsheet; circ. 35,000(free & paid).

US
COUNTY JOURNAL. Wed. free in area; $35/yr. 219 N. Illinois, Belleville, IL 62220. TEL 618-277-7000; FAX 618-277-7018. **Owner(s):** Suburban Journals, 1714 Deer Tracks Trail, St. Louis, MO 63131; Ed. Martin Richter; Pub. Tom Rice; adv. contact: Guy Ranney. photos; pub. size: broadsheet; circ. 4,500(controlled & free).

US
FAIRVIEW HEIGHTS JOURNAL. s-w.: Wed. & Sun. free in area; $35/yr. 219 N. Illinois, Belleville, IL 62220. TEL 618-277-7000; FAX 618-277-7018. **Owner(s):** Suburban Journals, 1714 Deer Tracks Trail, St. Louis, MO 63131; Ed. Marty Richter; Pub. Tom Rice; adv. contact: Guy Ranney. pub. size: broadsheet; circ. 1,500(controlled & free).

BERWYN

US
BERWYN/CICERO LIFE. 1926. 3/wk.: Wed., Fri., Sun. $.75 newsstand; $29/yr. 2601 S. Harlem Ave., Berwyn, IL 60402. TEL 708-484-1234; FAX 708-484-7778. **Owner(s):** Life Printing & Publishing Co., Inc., 2601 S. Harlem Ave., Berwyn, MA 60402; Ed. Robert Lifka; Pub. Jack R. Kubik; adv. contact: Dave Kuehl. pub. size: broadsheet; circ. 33,000(paid); Sun. 33,000(paid).
Formerly: Berwyn Life.

BLOOMINGDALE

US
BLOOMINGDALE PRESS. 1922. Thu. $.50 newsstand; $12.95/yr. in area; $28.95/yr. out of area. 134 N. Bloomingdale Rd., Bloomingdale, IL 60108. TEL 630-307-1101; FAX 630-307-1190. **Owner(s):** Press Publications, Inc., 112 S. York St., Elmhurst, IL 60126. TEL 708-834-0900; FAX 708-834-0910; Ed. Bruce A. Douglas; Pub. Jack Cruger; adv.; photos; bk.rev.; pub. size: tabloid; circ. 28,000(paid). **Wire Service(s):** CNS.

US
CAROL STREAM PRESS. 1900. Thu. $.50 newsstand; $15.95/yr. in area; $28.95/yr. out of area. 134 N. Bloomingdale Rd., Bloomingdale, IL 60108. TEL 630-307-1101; FAX 630-307-1190. **Owner(s):** Press Publications, Inc., 112 S. York St., Elmhurst, IL 60126. TEL 630-834-0900; Ed. Bruce A. Douglas; Pub. Jack Cruger; adv. contact: Lynn Hill. photos; bk.rev.; pub. size: tabloid; circ. 6,923(paid).

US
GLEN ELLYN PRESS. Thu. $.50 newsstand; $10.95/yr. in area; $12.95/yr. out of state mailed. 134 N. Bloomingdale, Bloomingdale, IL 60108. TEL 708-307-1101; FAX 708-307-1190. **Owner(s):** Press Publications, Inc., 112 S. York St., Elmhurst, IL 60126. TEL 708-834-0900; Ed. Bruce A. Douglas; Pub. Jack Cruger; adv. contact: Lynn Hill. photos; bk.rev.; pub. size: tabloid; circ. 1,000(paid).

US
WHEATON PRESS. 1922. Thu. $.50 newsstand; $12.95/yr. in city.; $28.95/yr. elsewhere. 134 N. Bloomingdale, Bloomingdale, IL 60108. TEL 630-307-1101; FAX 630-307-1190. **Owner(s):** Press Publications, Inc., 112 S. York St., Elmhurst, IL 60126. TEL 630-834-0900; Ed. Bruce A. Douglas; Pub. Jack Cruger; adv. contact: Lynn Hill. photos; bk.rev.; pub. size: tabloid; circ. 28,000(controlled & paid).

BLUE MOUND

US
BLUE MOUND LEADER. 1886. Wed. $.40 newsstand; $10/yr. in cy.; $11.50/yr. out of cy.; $13.50/yr. elsewhere. Rte. 48, Blue Mound, IL 62513-0318. TEL 217-692-2323. **Owner(s):** Cindy Stuart, P.O. Box 318, Blue Mound, IL 62513. TEL 217-692-2323; Pub. Cindy Stuart; adv. contact: Cindy Stuart. photos; pub. size: tabloid; circ. 850(free & paid).

BOLINGBROOK

US   ISSN 0885-6389
BOLINGBROOK SUN. 1963. s-w.: Wed. & Fri. $.35 newsstand; $22/yr. 339 N. Schmidt Rd., Bolingbrook, IL 60440. TEL 630-759-9169; FAX 630-759-1726. **Owner(s):** Copley Press, Inc., 7776 Ivanhoe Ave., La Jolla, CA 60540. TEL 614-454-0411; adv.; pub. size: tabloid; circ. 7,300(paid). **Wire Service(s):** CNS.

US   ISSN 0885-6397
ROMEOVILLE SUN. 1963. s-w.: Wed. & Fri. $.35 newsstand; $22.50/yr. 339 N. Schmidt Rd., Bolingbrook, IL 60440. TEL 630-759-9169; FAX 630-759-0169. **Owner(s):** Copley Press, Inc., 7776 Ivanhoe Ave., La Jolla, CA 92037; adv. contact: Rick Taden. pub. size: tabloid; circ. 2,600(paid). **Wire Service(s):** CNS.

BOURBONNAIS

US
HERALD/COUNTRY MARKET, THE. 1975. Tue. $.60 newsstand; $22/yr. in state; $25/yr. out of state. 500 Brown Blvd., Bourbonnais, IL 60914-2328. TEL 815-933-1131; FAX 815-933-3785. **Owner(s):** B & B Publishing, Inc., 500 Brown Blvd., Bourbonnais, IL 60914. TEL 815-933-1131; FAX 815-933-3785; Pub. Toby Olszewski; adv. contact: Sharon Robinson. pub. size: tabloid; circ. 32,000(free & paid).
Formerly: Country Market.

BRAIDWOOD

US
BRAIDWOOD JOURNAL, THE. 1958. Wed. $.50 newsstand; $19.50 in cy.; $22.50/yr. out of cy.; $25.50/yr. out of state. 192 E. Main, Braidwood, IL 60408. TEL 815-458-6246; FAX 815-634-5809. **Owner(s):** Bailey Printing & Publishing, 273 S. Broadway, Coal City, IL 60416. TEL 815-634-2102; Ed. Sheridan Bailey; Pub. Sheridan Bailey; adv. contact: Katie Easton. photos; pub. size: broadsheet; circ. 1,065(paid).

BREESE

US
BREESE JOURNAL. 1921. Thu. $.35 newsstand; $17.50/yr. in cy.; $21/yr. out of cy. 623-625 N. Second St., Breese, IL 62230. TEL 618-526-7211; FAX 618-526-2590. **Owner(s):** Breese Publishing Co., 623-625 N. Second St., Breese, IL 62230. TEL 618-526-7211; FAX 618-526-2590; Ed. Debbie Rehg; Pub. Dave Mahlandt; adv. contact: Vicky Albers. photos; pub. size: broadsheet; circ. 5,923(free & paid).

BRIDGEPORT

US
BRIDGEPORT LEADER. 1907. Thu. $.35 newsstand; $19.50/yr. local. 131 E. Olive, Bridgeport, IL 62417-1935. TEL 618-945-2111; FAX 618-945-2131. **Owner(s):** Louis Valbert, 131 E. Olive, Bridgeport, IL 62417. TEL 618-945-2111; Ed. Louis Valbert; Pub. Louis Valbert; adv.; pub. size: broadsheet; circ. 23,200(paid).

BRIGHTON

US
SOUTHWESTERN JOURNAL NEWS. 1972. Thu. $.30 newsstand; $10.50/yr. in cy.; $12.50/yr. out of cy.; $14.50/yr. out of state. 117 N. Main St., Brighton, IL 62012. TEL 618-372-8451; FAX 618-372-8451. **Owner(s):** Bunker Hill Publishing Co., 150 N. Washington St., Bunker Hill, IL 62014. TEL 618-585-4411; Ed. Vera Eckhardt; Pub. John M. Galer; adv. contact: Eve Pickerill. photos; pub. size: tabloid; circ. 1,550(paid).

BUNKER HILL

US
BUNKER HILL GAZETTE NEWS. 1892. Thu. $.25 newsstand; $9.50/yr. in cy.; $11.50 out of cy.; $13.50 out of state. 150 N. Washington St., Bunker Hill, IL 62014. TEL 618-585-4411; FAX 618-585-3354. **Owner(s):** John M. Galer, 150 N. Washington St., Bunker Hill, IL 62014. TEL 618-585-4411; Ed. Vera Eckhardt; Pub. John M. Galer; adv. contact: Eve Pickerill. photos; pub. size: tabloid; circ. 1,500(paid).

BUSHNELL

US
MCDONOUGH-DEMOCRAT. 9884. Mon. $17/yr. in state; $21/yr. out of state. 358 E. Main St., Bushnell, IL 61422. TEL 309-772-2129; FAX 309-772-3994. **Owner(s):** William Lorton, 358 E. Main St., Bushnell, IL 61422. TEL 309-772-2129; Pub. William Lorton; adv. pub. size: standard; circ. 2,250(paid).

BYRON
US
NORTHERN OGLE COUNTY TEMPO. Tue. $.75 newsstand; $23/yr. 110 N. Union, Byron, IL 61010. TEL 815-234-4821; FAX 815-654-4857. **Owner(s):** Rock Valley Community Press, P.O. Box 15340, Rockford, IL 61024. TEL 815-877-4044; Ed. Ellen Smith; Pub. Craig McMullin; adv. contact: Chuck Carter. photos; pub. size: tabloid; circ. 6,000(free & paid).

CAHOKIA
US
HERALD, THE. Wed. free; $50/yr. 713 Range Ln., Cahokia, IL 62206. TEL 618-337-7300. **Owner(s):** Walt Disney Co., 500 S. Buena Vista St., Burbank, CA 91521. TEL 818-560-5300; Ed. Cris Orlet; Pub. Mike Schmershal; adv.; bk.rev.; pub. size: broadsheet; circ. 12,500(free & paid).

CAIRO
US
CAIRO CITIZEN. 1887. Thu. $.50 newsstand; $26/yr. 711 Washington, Cairo, IL 62914. TEL 618-734-4242; FAX 618-734-4244. **Owner(s):** North Scott Publishing, Inc., P.O. Box 529, Anna, IL 62906. TEL 618-833-2158; Ed. James West; Pub. Jerry L. Reppert; adv. contact: Nancy Wright. photos; pub. size: broadsheet; circ. 3,500(paid).

CAMBRIDGE
US
CAMBRIDGE CHRONICLE. 1893. Thu. $.75 newsstand; $31/yr. in state; $33/yr. out of state. 119 W. Exchange, Cambridge, IL 61238. TEL 309-937-3303; FAX 309-937-3303. **Owner(s):** Terry Newspapers, Inc., 119 W. Exchange, Cambridge, IL 61238. TEL 309-937-3303; Ed. Ty Bernier; Pub. Thomas Terry; adv. contact: Linda Venable. pub. size: broadsheet; circ. 1,600(paid).

CARLINVILLE
US
CARLINVILLE DEMOCRAT. 1856. Thu. $.50 newsstand; $17/yr. in cy.; $19/yr. out of cy. 118 N. West St., Carlinville, IL 62626. TEL 217-854-2561; FAX 217-854-3366. **Owner(s):** Thomas Hatalla, P.O. Box 470, Carlinville, IL 62626. TEL 217-854-2561; FAX 217-854-3366; Edward Albracht, P.O. Box 470, Carlinville, IL 62626. TEL 217-854-2561; FAX 217-854-3366; Ed. Edward J. Albracht. adv.; photos; pub. size: standard; circ. 3,000(free & paid).

US
MACOUPIN COUNTY ENQUIRER. 1852. Thu. $.50 newsstand; $17/yr. in cy.; $19/yr. out of cy. 125 E. Main St., Carlinville, IL 62626. TEL 217-854-2534; FAX 217-854-2535. **Owner(s):** Chris Schmitt, 125 E. Main St., Carlinville, IL 62626-0200. TEL 217-854-2534; FAX 217-854-2535. Ed. Chris Schmitt; Pub. Chris Schmitt; adv.; photos; pub. size: broadsheet; circ. 4,900(paid).

CARLYLE
US
CARLYLE UNION BANNER. 1863. Wed. $.35 newsstand; $17.50/yr. in cy.; $27.50/yr. out of cy. 671 Tenth St., Carlyle, IL 62231. TEL 618-594-3131; FAX 618-594-3115. **Owner(s):** Dempsey Publishing Co., 671 Tenth St., Carlyle, IL 62231. TEL 618-594-3131; Ed. Warren Dempsey; Pub. Warren Dempsey; adv. contact: Mike Langham. pub. size: broadsheet; circ. 4,800(paid).

CARROLLTON
US
CARROLLTON GAZETTE PATRIOT. 1846. Thu. $.50 newsstand; $20/yr. in cy.; $25/yr. out of cy. 428 N. Main St., Carrollton, IL 62016-0231. TEL 217-942-3626; FAX 217-942-3699. **Owner(s):** Albert W. Scott, III, 428 N. Main St., Carrollton, IL 62016. TEL 217-942-3626; FAX 217-942-3699; Pub. Albert Scott, III; adv.; photos; pub. size: broadsheet; circ. 1,697(paid).

CARTHAGE
US
HANCOCK COUNTY JOURNAL-PILOT. 1887. Wed. $.50 newsstand; $22/yr. in cy.; $37.50/yr. out of cy. 31 N. Washington, Carthage, IL 62321. TEL 217-357-2149; FAX 217-357-2177. **Owner(s):** Brehm Communications, Inc., 17065 Via del Campo, Ste. 200, San Diego, CA 92127. TEL 619-451-3814; Ed. Joy Swearingen; Pub. Bill Ferguson; adv.; photos; pub. size: broadsheet; circ. 4,200(free & paid).
Formerly: Carthage Hancock Journal-Pilot.

CASEY
US
REPORTER, THE. 1938. s-w.: Mon. & Thu. $.50 newsstand; $38/yr. in cy.; $47/yr. out of cy.; $55/yr. out of state. 216 S. Central, Casey, IL 62420. TEL 217-932-5211; FAX 217-932-5214. **Owner(s):** Lincoln Trail Publishing Co., 216 S. Central, Casey, IL 62420. TEL 217-932-5211; Ed. Karen O'Rourke; Pub. Mary Leck; adv. contact: Don Cook. pub. size: broadsheet; circ. 3,500(paid).

CERRO GORDO
US
NEWS-RECORD, THE. 1889. Wed. $17/yr. 221 E. South St., Cerro Gordo, IL 61818-0049. TEL 217-763-3541; FAX 217-578-2833. **Owner(s):** Cleon Birkemeyer & Greg Hoskins, Mt. Zion Publications, Inc., P.O. Box 79, Mt. Zion, IL 62549-0079; Pub. Mike Brothers; adv. contact: Janice Pruitt. adv.: $3.75/SAU. pub. size: broadsheet; circ. 1,400(paid).

CHAMPAIGN
US
THRIFTY NICKEL. 1985. Thu. free. 61 E. University Ave., Champaign, IL 61820-4109. TEL 217-356-4804; FAX 217-356-4970. **Owner(s):** Randy Cooper, 306 W. Springfield, Champaign, IL 61820; adv.; pub. size: tabloid; circ. 50,000(free).

CHESTER
US
RANDOLPH COUNTY HERALD TRIBUNE. 1926. Thu. $.50 newsstand; $19.25/yr. in cy.; $22/yr. out of cy. 624 State St., Chester, IL 62233. TEL 618-826-2385; FAX 618-826-5181. **Owner(s):** American Publishing Co., 606 N. Van Buren, Marion, IL 62959. TEL 618-993-1711; Pub. Duane Bean; adv.; pub. size: broadsheet; circ. 4,500(paid).
Formerly: Chester Randolph County Herald.

CHICAGO
US
BACK OF THE YARDS JOURNAL. 1932. Wed. $.20 newsstand; $55/yr. The Yards Plz., 4642 S. Damen Ave., Chicago, IL 60609. TEL 773-927-7204. **Owner(s):** Back of the Yards Journal, The Yards Plz., 4642 S. Damen Ave., Chicago, IL 60609. TEL 773-927-7204; Pub. Patrick J. Salmon; adv.; photos; bk.rev.; pub. size: tabloid; circ. 48,000(free & paid).

US ISSN 0006-0410
BEVERLY REVIEW. 1905. Wed. $.50 newsstand; $18/yr. 10546 S. Western Ave., Chicago, IL 60643. TEL 773-238-3366; FAX 773-238-1492. **Owner(s):** TR Communications, 10546 S. Western Ave., Chicago, IL 60643. TEL 773-238-3366; Ed. Jerry Moore. adv.; pub. size: tabloid; circ. 6,000(paid).

US
BRIDGEPORT NEWS. 1943. Wed. $.20 newsstand. 3252 S. Halsted, Chicago, IL 60608. TEL 312-842-5883; FAX 312-842-5097. **Owner(s):** Chicago Bridgeport News, Inc., 3252 S. Halsted, Chicago, IL 60608. TEL 312-842-5883; FAX 312-842-5097; Ed. Janice Racinowski; Pub. Joseph L. Feldman; adv. contact: Janice Racinowski. pub. size: broadsheet; circ. 25,300(paid).
Formerly: Chicago Bridgeport News.

US
BRIGHTON PARK-MCKINLEY PARK LIFE. 1933. Thu. $.15 newsstand; $60/yr. 1st class mail. 2949 W. 43rd St., Chicago, IL 60632. TEL 773-523-3663; FAX 773-523-3983. **Owner(s):** Albert H. Silinski, 2949 W. 43rd St., Chicago, IL 60632. TEL 312-523-3663; FAX 312-523-3983; Ed. Albert H. Silinski; Pub. Albert H. Silinski; adv.: $13/SAU. photos; bk.rev.; pub. size: broadsheet; circ. 30,000(controlled & paid).
Formerly: Chicago Brighton Park-McKinley.

US
CHICAGO-LAWNDALE NEWS. 1937. s-w.: Thu. & Sun. free newsstand; $50/yr. mailed. 2300 S. Kedvale, Chicago, IL 60623. TEL 773-762-2266; FAX 773-762-5076. **Owner(s):** Chicago West Town Publications, 2300 S. Kedvale, Chicago, IL 60623. TEL 773-762-2266; Ed. Veronica Alanis; Pub. Linda Nardini; adv. contact: Gary Miller. pub. size: tabloid; circ. 50,000(paid); Sun. 150,000(paid).

US
CHICAGO'S N.W. SIDE PRESS. 1940. Wed. $.35 newsstand; $85/yr. 4937 N. Milwaukee, Chicago, IL 60630-2191. TEL 773-286-6100. **Owner(s):** Nadig Newspapers, Inc., 4937 N. Milwaukee, Chicago, IL 60640-2191. TEL 773-286-6100; Pub. Glenn Nadig; pub. size: broadsheet; circ. 40,000(free).

WEEKLY NEWSPAPERS

CHICAGO, IL 10575

US ISSN 0028-1778
CHICAGO NEAR NORTH NEWS. 1956. Sat. $.50 newsstand; $25/yr. in cy. 222 W. Ontario St., Ste. 502, Chicago, IL 60610-3695. TEL 312-787-2677; FAX 312-787-2680; E-mail: nnnews@ibm.net. **Owner(s):** Near North News, Inc., 222 W. Ontario St., Ste. 502, Chicago, IL 60610-3695. TEL 312-787-2677; FAX 312-787-2680; Ed. Arnie Matanky; Pub. Arnie Matanky; adv.: $12.60/SAU. photos; pub. size: tabloid; circ. 7,750(free & paid).

US ISSN 1068-8213
CHICAGO NEAR WEST GAZETTE. 1983. Wed. free newsstand; $18/yr. 1335 W. Harrison St., Chicago, IL 60607-3318. TEL 773-243-4288; FAX 773-243-4270; E-mail: anbcomm@interaccess.com. **Owner(s):** Mark J. Valentino, 1335 W. Morrison, Chicago, IL 60607. TEL 773-273-4288; FAX 773-243-4270; Ed. Mark J. Valentino; Pub. Mark J. Valentino; adv. contact: Laura Sorce. photos; pub. size: tabloid; circ. 15,000(controlled & free).

US
CHICAGO POST. 1984. bi-w. $12/6 mos.; $20/yr. 3647 N. Kedzie, Chicago, IL 60618. TEL 773-463-5100. **Owner(s):** Jim Boratyn, P.O. Box 18444, Chicago, IL 60618. TEL 312-463-5100; Ed. Jim Boratyn; Pub. Pat Suckow; adv.; pub. size: tabloid; circ. 35,000(paid).

US
CHICAGO READER. 1971. Thu. free; $50/yr. 11 E. Illinois, Chicago, IL 60611. TEL 312-828-0350; FAX 312-828-9926. **Owner(s):** Chicago Reader, Inc., 11 E. Illinois, Chicago, IL 60611. TEL 312-828-0350; Ed. Alison True; Pub. Jane Levine; adv. contact: Don Humbertson. bk.rev.; pub. size: tabloid; circ. 133,400(controlled).

US
CHICAGO WEST SIDE TIMES. 1940. s-w.: Thu. & Sun. free newsstand; $50/yr. mailed. 2300 S. Kedvale, Chicago, IL 60623. TEL 773-762-2266; FAX 773-762-5076. **Owner(s):** Chicago West Town Publications, 2300 S. Kedvale, Chicago, IL 60623. TEL 773-762-2266; Ed. Veronica Alanis; Pub. Linda Nardini; adv. contact: Gary Miller. pub. size: tabloid; circ. 50,000(paid); Sun. 150,000(paid).

US
CLEAR-RIDGE REPORTER. 1961. Wed. $.50 newsstand; $75/yr. mailed. 6225 S. Kedzie Ave., Chicago, IL 60629. TEL 773-476-4800; FAX 773-476-7811. **Owner(s):** Vondrak Publishing Co., 6225 S. Kedzie Ave., Chicago, IL 60629. TEL 312-476-4800; Ed. Joseph Boyle; Pub. James C. Vondrak; adv. contact: James C. Vondrak. pub. size: tabloid; circ. 24,600(free & paid).
Formerly: Chicago-Clear-Ridge Reporter.

US
HYDE PARK HERALD. 1881. Wed. $.50 newsstand; $15/yr. 5240 S. Harper Ave., Chicago, IL 60615. TEL 713-643-8533; FAX 713-643-8542; E-mail: hpherald@aol.com. **Owner(s):** Hyde Park Herald Newspapers, Inc., 5240 S. Harper Ave., Chicago, IL 60615. TEL 312-643-8533; Ed. Kevin Knapp; Pub. Bruce Sagan; adv.; pub. size: tabloid; circ. 26,000(paid).

US
INSIDE. 1968. Wed. free. 4710 N. Lincoln, Chicago, IL 60625-2010. TEL 773-878-7334; FAX 773-878-0959; E-mail: inside@suba.com. **Owner(s):** Ronald Roenigk, 4710 N. Lincoln, Chicago, IL 60625. TEL 773-878-7334; Ed. Nancy Amdur. adv. contact: Ron Roenigk. adv.: $26/SAU. photos; pub. size: tabloid; circ. 65,075(free).
Formerly: Inside Gold Coast.

US
JOURNAL, THE. Sat. $.35 newsstand; $85/yr. 4937 N. Milwaukee, Chicago, IL 60630-2191. TEL 773-286-6100. **Owner(s):** Nadig Newspapers, Inc., 4937 N. Milwaukee, Chicago, IL 60630-2191. TEL 773-286-6100; Ed. Randy Erickson; Pub. Glenn H. Nadig; adv.; pub. size: tabloid; circ. 1,000(controlled & free).

US
NEW CITY. 1986. Thu. free newsstand; $30/yr. mailed 3rd class; $75/yr. mailed 1st class. 770 N. Halsted, Ste. 208, Chicago, IL 60622. TEL 312-243-8786; FAX 312-243-8802; E-mail: letters@newcitynet.com; URL: http://www.newcitynet.com. **Owner(s):** New City Communications, Inc., 770 N. Halsted, Ste. 208, Chicago, IL 60622. TEL 312-243-8786; FAX 312-243-8802; Ed. Frank Sennett; Pub. Jan Hieggelke; adv.; photos; bk.rev.; pub. size: tabloid; circ. 70,000(controlled & free).

US ISSN 0029-2877
NORTH LOOP NEWS. 1930. Thu. free newsstand; $40.55/yr. 2nd class; $55/yr. 1st class. 1332 N. Halsted, Ste. 204, Chicago, IL 60622. TEL 312-787-5396; FAX 312-787-1616. **Owner(s):** North Loop News Corp., 1332 N. Halsted, Ste. 204, Chicago, IL 60622. TEL 312-787-5396; Ed. Deborah Madden; Pub. Michelle C. Albanese; adv. contact: Michelle C. Albanese. pub. size: tabloid; circ. 24,700(free & paid).

US
NORTHWEST LEADER. 1953. s-w.: Wed. & Sun. $.50 newsstand; $40/yr. 6010 W. Belmont Ave., Chicago, IL 60634. TEL 773-283-7900; FAX 773-283-7761. **Owner(s):** Arthur & Ramona Diaz, 6010 W. Belmont Ave., Chicago, IL 60634. TEL 773-283-7900; FAX 312-283-7761; Ed. Jackie Pledger-Skwerski. adv.; pub. size: broadsheet; circ. 25,000(paid); Sun. 6,500(paid).

US
NORTHWEST SIDE PRESS. 1940. Wed. $.35 newsstand; $85/yr. 4937 N. Milwaukee Ave., Chicago, IL 60630-2191. TEL 773-286-6100. **Owner(s):** Nadig Newspapers, Inc., 4937 N. Milwaukee Ave., Chicago, IL 60630-2191. TEL 773-286-6100; Ed. Randy Erickson; Pub. Glenn H. Nadig; adv.; photos; bk.rev.; pub. size: broadsheet; circ. 40,500(controlled & free).

US
REPORTER, THE. 1964. Sat. $.35 newsstand; $85/yr. 4937 N. Milwaukee Ave., Chicago, IL 60630-2191. TEL 773-286-6100. **Owner(s):** Nadig Newspapers, Inc., 4937 N. Milwaukee, Chicago, IL 60630; Ed. Randy Erickson; Pub. Glenn H. Nadig; pub. size: tabloid; circ. 13,000(free).

US
RIVER NORTH NEWS. 1987. bi-w. free newsstand; $36/yr. 109 W. North Ave., 2nd Fl., Chicago, IL 60610. TEL 312-944-3300; FAX 312-944-7883. **Owner(s):** William S. Petacque, 109 W. North Ave., 2nd Fl., Chicago, IL 60610. TEL 312-944-3300; Ed. David Oberhelman. adv.; photos; pub. size: tabloid; circ. 12,500(free & paid).

US
SOUTHWEST BEACON. 1982. Tue. free home deliv.; $.15 newsstand. 6225 S. Kedzie Ave., Chicago, IL 60629. TEL 773-476-4800; FAX 773-476-4800. **Owner(s):** Vondrak Publishing Co., 6225 S. Kedzie, Chicago, IL 60629. TEL 312-476-4800; Ed. Joe Boyle; Pub. James C. Vondrak; adv.; pub. size: tabloid; circ. 25,685(paid).

US
SOUTHWEST COURIER. 1986. Thu. free home deliv.; $.15 newsstand. 6225 S. Kedzie Ave., Chicago, IL 60629. TEL 773-476-4800; FAX 773-476-4800. **Owner(s):** Vondrak Publishing Co., 6225 S. Kedzie Ave., Chicago, IL 60629. TEL 312-476-4800; Ed. Timothy C. Hadac; Pub. James C. Vondrak; adv.; photos; pub. size: tabloid; circ. 13,456(paid).

US ISSN 0038-4704
SOUTHWEST NEWS-HERALD. 1924. Thu. $18.60/6 mos. home deliv.; $21/yr. mailed. 6225 S. Kedzie Ave., Chicago, IL 60629. TEL 773-476-4800; FAX 773-476-7811. **Owner(s):** Vondrak Publishing Co., 6225 S. Kedzie Ave., Chicago, IL 60629. TEL 312-476-4800; Ed. Joe Boyle; Pub. James C. Vondrak; adv.; pub. size: broadsheet; circ. 24,542(paid).

US
SOUTHWEST SHOPPER. 1960. Tue. $.15 newsstand; free home deliv. 6225 S. Kedzie Ave., Chicago, IL 60629. TEL 773-476-4800; FAX 773-476-4800. **Owner(s):** Vondrak Publishing Co., 6225 S. Kedzie Ave., Chicago, IL 60629. TEL 312-476-4800; Ed. Joe Boyle; Pub. James C. Vondrak; adv.; pub. size: broadsheet; circ. 37,000(free).

US
SUBURBAN LEADER. Sun. $.50 newsstand; $40/yr. in cy. 6008 W. Belmont Ave., Chicago, IL 60634. TEL 773-283-7900; FAX 773-283-7761. **Owner(s):** Leader/Post Newspapers, Inc., 6008 W. Belmont Ave., Chicago, IL 60634. TEL 312-283-7761; Ed. Jacki Pledger. adv.; pub. size: broadsheet; circ. 11,000(paid).

US
WEST SUBURBAN POST. 1964. Fri. $.50 newsstand; $40/yr. mailed. 6008 W. Belmont Ave., Chicago, IL 60634. TEL 773-283-7900; FAX 773-283-7761. **Owner(s):** Leader/Post Newspapers, Inc., 6008 W. Belmont Ave., Chicago, IL 60634. TEL 773-283-7900; Ed. Jackie Pledger-Swerski; Pub. Arthur Diaz; adv. contact: Patricia Cioch. photos; pub. size: tabloid; circ. 13,000(controlled).

CHILLICOTHE

US

CHILLICOTHE BULLETIN. 1883. Wed. $.50 newsstand; $18.20/yr. in cy.; $20.80/yr. out of cy. 1008 N. Fourth St., Chillicothe, IL 61523-1504. TEL 309-274-2185; FAX 309-274-2741. **Owner(s):** Fleming Publishing Co., 100 Detroit Ave., Morton, IL 61550. TEL 309-263-2211; Ed. Beth Gehrt; Pub. Ted Fleming; adv. contact: Heidi Whitman. photos; pub. size: broadsheet; circ. 2,770(paid).

CHRISMAN

US

CHRISMAN LEADER. 1972. Thu. $.35 newsstand; $18/yr. in IL & IN; $24/yr. elsewhere. 134 N. Illinois, Chrisman, IL 61924. TEL 217-269-2811; FAX 217-269-2811. **Owner(s):** Hometown Publications, 131 E. Olive St., Bridgeport, IL 62417. TEL 800-841-0888; Ed. Kevin Jenison; Pub. Louis Valvert; adv.; pub. size: tabloid; circ. 2,000(paid).

CISSNA PARK

US   ISSN 0009-7543

CISSNA PARK NEWS. 1891. Thu. $.40 newsstand; $18/yr. in cy.; $20/yr. out of cy. 119 W. Garfield, Cissna Park, IL 60924-0008. TEL 815-457-2245. **Owner(s):** Baier Publishing Co., 119 W. Garfield, Cissna Park, IL 60924-0008. TEL 815-457-2245; Ed. Rick A. Baier; Pub. Rick A. Baier; adv.: $3.50/SAU. photos; pub. size: tabloid; circ. 1,400(paid).

US

RANKIN INDEPENDENT. 1897. Thu. $.40 newsstand; $18/yr. in cy.; $20/yr. out of cy. 119 W. Garfield, Cissna Park, IL 60924. TEL 815-457-2245. **Owner(s):** Baier Publishing Co., 119 W. Garfield, Cissna Park, IL 60924. TEL 815-457-2245; Ed. Mary Ann Scott; Pub. Rick A. Baier; pub. size: tabloid; circ. 1,750(paid).

CLIFTON

US

ADVOCATE, THE. 1883. Thu. $.40 newsstand; $14.95/yr. in state; $16.95/yr. out of state. 330 N. Fourth St., Clifton, IL 60927. TEL 815-694-2122; FAX 815-694-3770. **Owner(s):** Therese Simoneau, 330 N. Fourth St., Clifton, IL 60927. TEL 815-694-2122; Ed. Therese Simoneau; Pub. Therese Simoneau; adv.; pub. size: tabloid; circ. 2,100(controlled & paid).

COAL CITY

US

COAL CITY COURANT. 1903. Wed. $.50 newsstand; $19.50/yr. in Grundy & Will cys.; $22.50/yr. in state; $25.50/yr. out of state. 273 S. Broadway, Coal City, IL 60416. TEL 815-634-2102; FAX 815-634-2815. **Owner(s):** Bailey Printing & Publishing, 273 S. Broadway, Coal City, IL 60416. TEL 815-634-2102; Ed. Sheridan Bailey; Pub. Sheridan Bailey; adv. contact: Katie Easton. photos; pub. size: broadsheet; circ. 2,360(paid).

US

GOOD NEWS SHOPPER. 1982. Mon. free. 273 S. Broadway, Coal City, IL 60416. TEL 815-634-2102; FAX 815-634-2815. **Owner(s):** Bailey Printing & Publishing, 273 S. Broadway, Coal City, IL 60416. TEL 815-634-2102; Ed. Sheridan Bailey; Pub. Sheridan Bailey; adv. contact: Katie Easton. pub. size: broadsheet; circ. 12,000(free).

COLCHESTER

US

COLCHESTER CHRONICLE. 1951. Thu. $.35 newsstand; $13.50/yr. in cy.; $16/yr. out of cy. 118 E. Market St., Colchester, IL 62326. TEL 309-776-3700. E-mail: coelho@wins.int.net. **Owner(s):** Stacey Nicholas & Joe Coelho, P.O. Box 356, Colchester, IL 62326. TEL 309-776-3700; Ed. Stacey Nicholas; Pub. Stacey Nicholas; adv.; photos; bk.rev.; pub. size: tabloid; circ. 603(paid).

COLLINSVILLE

US   ISSN 0883-6574

COLLINSVILLE HERALD. 1974. Thu. $.50 newsstand; $135/yr. local (includes Collinsville Journal). 113 E. Clay St., Collinsville, IL 62234. TEL 618-344-0264; FAX 618-344-3611. **Owner(s):** Suburban Journals, 1714 Deer Tracks Trail, St. Louis, MO 63131. TEL 314-821-1110; Ed. Dan Braun; Pub. Marty Ricther; adv. contact: Guy Ranney. pub. size: broadsheet; circ. 19,712(controlled & paid).

US

COLLINSVILLE JOURNAL. 1974. s-w.: Wed. & Sun. free distribution in cy.; $.50 newsstand; $135/yr. mailed. 113 E. Clay St., Collinsville, IL 62234. TEL 618-344-0264; FAX 618-344-3611. **Owner(s):** Suburban Journals, 1714 Deer Tracks Trail, St. Louis, MO 63131. TEL 314-821-1110; Ed. Dan Braun; Pub. Marty Richther; adv. contact: Guy Rainey. pub. size: broadsheet; circ. 19,712(free & paid).

COLUMBIA

US

CAHOKIA JOURNAL. 1969. s-w.: Wed. & Sun. free in area; $50/yr. Sun.; $58/yr. Wed. 212 W. Locust St., Columbia, IL 62236-1732. TEL 618-281-7691; FAX 618-281-7693. **Owner(s):** Suburban Journals, 1714 Deer Tracks Trail, St. Louis, MO 63131. TEL 314-821-1110; Ed. Marty Richter; Pub. Dan Braun; adv. contact: Mike Goodsell. pub. size: broadsheet; circ. 13,000(free & paid).

US

CLARION JOURNAL, THE. s-w.: Wed. & Sun. free in area; $50/yr. Sun.; $58/yr. Wed. 212 W. Locust St., Columbia, IL 62236. TEL 618-281-7691; FAX 618-281-7693. **Owner(s):** Suburban Journals, 1714 Deer Tracks Trail, St. Louis, MO 63131. TEL 314-821-1110; Ed. Marty Ricther; Pub. Dan Braun; adv. contact: Dan Braun. pub. size: broadsheet; circ. 1,500(controlled & paid); Sun. 8,500(controlled & paid).
Formerly: Columbia Star, The.

US

EAST ST. LOUIS NEWS JOURNAL. 1954. Wed. free newsstand & home deliv. 212 W. Locust St., Columbia, IL 62236. TEL 618-281-7691; FAX 618-281-7693. **Owner(s):** Suburban Journals, 1714 Deer Tracks Trail, St. Louis, MO 63131. TEL 618-332-6000; Ed. Martin Richter; Pub. Tom Rice; adv. contact: Douglas Garbs. pub. size: broadsheet; circ. 20,100(free).

US

MILLSTADT ENTERPRISE. Wed. free; $58/yr. in cy. 212 W. Locust St., Columbia, IL 62236. TEL 618-281-7691; FAX 618-281-7693. **Owner(s):** Suburban Journals, 1714 Deer Tracks Trail, St. Louis, MO 63131. TEL 314-821-1110; Ed. Martin Richter. adv. contact: Michael Goodsell. pub. size: broadsheet; circ. 4,000(free & paid).

US

MONROE COUNTY CLARION. 1939. s-w.: Wed. & Sun. $.50 newsstand; $50/yr. Sun.; $58/yr. Wed. 212 W. Locust St., Columbia, IL 62236. TEL 618-281-7691; FAX 618-281-7693. **Owner(s):** Suburban Journals, 1714 Deer Tracks Trail, St. Louis, MO 63131. TEL 314-821-1110; Ed. Martin Richter; Pub. Dan Braun; adv.; pub. size: broadsheet; circ. 14,500(paid); Sun. 8,000(paid).

DALLAS CITY

US

DALLAS CITY ENTERPRISE. 1887. Wed. $.35 newsstand; $14/yr. in cy.; $15/yr. out of cy. 395 Oak St., Dallas City, IL 62330. TEL 217-852-3511; FAX 217-852-3528. **Owner(s):** Steven & Susan Kempher, P.O. Box 455, Dallas City, IL 62330. TEL 217-852-3511; Pub. Deana Kenney; adv. contact: Deana Kenney. pub. size: standard; circ. 1,500(paid).

DECATUR

US

DECATUR TRIBUNE. 1969. Wed. $.50 newsstand; $25/yr. 240 N. Park St., Decatur, IL 62523. TEL 217-422-9702; FAX 217-422-7320. **Owner(s):** Paul V. Osbourne, 240 N. Park St., Decatur, IL 62523. TEL 217-422-9702; Pub. Paul V. Osbourne; adv. contact: Rita Gray. photos; pub. size: broadsheet; circ. 8,000(paid).

DEKALB

US

MIDWEEK, THE. 1967. Wed. free newsstand; $78/yr. out of area. P.O. Box 546, DeKalb, IL 60115. TEL 815-758-0696. **Owner(s):** Charles & Kathy Siebrasse, P.O. Box 546, DeKalb, IL 60115. TEL 815-758-0696; Ed. Sharon Emanuelson; Pub. Charles Siebrasse; adv. contact: Penny Bunnell. photos; bk.rev.; pub. size: tabloid; circ. 30,000(free & paid).

DELAVAN

US

DELAVAN TIMES, THE. 1874. Wed. $.35 newsstand; $16/yr. in state; $18/yr. out of state. 314 Locust, Delavan, IL 61734. TEL 309-244-7111. **Owner(s):** Delavan Times, Inc., 314 Locust, P.O. Box 199, Delavan, IL 61734. TEL 309-244-7111; Ed. Ruth Larimore. adv.; photos; pub. size: tabloid; circ. 1,440(paid).

DES PLAINES

US

ARLINGTON HEIGHTS JOURNAL & TOPICS. Thu. $.50 newsstand; $25/yr. in cy.; $32/yr. out of cy. 622 Graceland Ave., Des Plaines, IL 60016. TEL 847-299-5511; FAX 847-298-8549. **Owner(s):** Des Plaines Journal, Inc., 622 Graceland Ave., Des Plaines, IL 60016. TEL 847-299-5511; Ed. Todd Wessell; Pub. Richard C. Wessell, Sr.; pub. size: tabloid; circ. 12,512(paid).

US

BUFFALO GROVE JOURNAL & TOPICS. Thu. $.50 newsstand; $25/yr. in cy.; $32/yr. out of cy. 622 Graceland Ave., Des Plaines, IL 60016. TEL 847-299-5511; FAX 847-298-8549. **Owner(s):** Des Plaines Journal, Inc., 622 Graceland Ave., Des Plaines, IL 60016. TEL 847-299-5511; Ed. Todd Wessell; Pub. Richard C. Wessell, Sr.; adv.; pub. size: tabloid; circ. 3,000(paid).

WEEKLY NEWSPAPERS

GOLFMILL JOURNAL. s-w.: Wed. & Fri. $.50 newsstand; $25/yr. in cy.; $30/yr. out of cy. 622 Graceland Ave., Des Plaines, IL 60016. TEL 847-299-5511; FAX 847-298-8549. **Owner(s):** Des Plaines Journal, Inc., 622 Graceland Ave., Des Plaines, IL 60016. TEL 847-299-5511; Ed. Todd Wessell; Pub. Richard C. Wessell, Sr.; adv.; pub. size: tabloid; circ. 5,000(paid).
Formerly: Golfmill-Park Ridge Journal.

MOUNT PROSPECT JOURNAL. s-w.: Wed. & Fri. $.50 newsstand; $25/yr. in cy.; $30/yr. out of cy. 622 Graceland Ave., Des Plaines, IL 60016. TEL 847-299-5511; FAX 847-298-8549. **Owner(s):** Des Plaines Journal, Inc., 622 Graceland Ave., Des Plaines, IL 60016. TEL 847-299-5511; Ed. Todd Wessell; Pub. Richard C. Wessell, Sr.; adv.; pub. size: tabloid; circ. 6,350(paid).

NILES JOURNAL. Wed. $.50 newsstand; $22/yr. in cy.; $30/yr. out of cy. 622 Graceland Ave., Des Plaines, IL 60016. TEL 847-299-5511; FAX 847-298-8549. **Owner(s):** Des Plaines Journal, Inc., 622 Graceland Ave., Des Plaines, IL 60016. TEL 847-299-5511; Ed. Todd Wessell; Pub. Richard C. Wessell, Sr.; adv.; pub. size: tabloid; circ. 6,000(paid).

NORTHWEST JOURNAL & TOPICS. Thu. $.50 newsstand; $25/yr. in cy.; $32/yr. out of cy. 622 Graceland Ave., Des Plaines, IL 60016. TEL 847-299-5511; FAX 847-298-8549. **Owner(s):** Des Plaines Journal, Inc., 622 Graceland Ave., Des Plaines, IL 60016. TEL 847-299-5511; Ed. Todd Wessell; Pub. Richard C. Wessell, Sr.; adv.; photos; pub. size: tabloid; circ. 6,900(paid).
Formerly: Journal & Topics.

PALATINE JOURNAL & TOPICS. Thu. $.50 newsstand; $25/yr. in cy.; $32/yr. out of cy. 622 Graceland Ave., Des Plaines, IL 60016. TEL 847-299-5511; FAX 847-598-8549. **Owner(s):** Des Plaines Journal, Inc., 622 Graceland Ave., Des Plaines, IL 60016. TEL 847-299-5511; Ed. Todd Wessell; Pub. Richard C. Wessell, Sr.; adv.; pub. size: tabloid; circ. 3,850(paid).

PARK RIDGE JOURNAL. Wed. $.50 newsstand; $25/yr. in cy.; $30/yr. out of cy. mailed. 622 Graceland Ave., Des Plaines, IL 60016. TEL 847-299-5511; FAX 847-298-8549. **Owner(s):** Des Plaines Journal, Inc., 622 Graceland Ave., Des Plaines, IL 60016. TEL 847-299-5511; FAX 847-298-8549; Ed. Todd Wessell; Pub. Richard C. Wessell, Sr.; adv.; pub. size: tabloid; circ. 5,000(paid).

PROSPECT HEIGHTS JOURNAL. s-w.: Wed. & Fri. $.50 newsstand; $25/yr. in cy.; $30/yr. out of cy. 622 Graceland Ave., Des Plaines, IL 60016. TEL 847-299-5511; FAX 708-298-8549. **Owner(s):** Des Plaines Journal, Inc., 622 Graceland Ave., Des Plaines, IL 60016. TEL 847-299-5511; Ed. Todd Wessell; Pub. Richard C. Wessell, Sr.; adv.; pub. size: tabloid; circ. 1,700(paid).

ROLLING MEADOWS JOURNAL & TOPICS. Thu. $.50 newsstand; $25/yr. in cy.; $32/yr. out of cy. 622 Graceland Ave., Des Plaines, IL 60016. TEL 847-299-5511; FAX 847-298-8549. **Owner(s):** Des Plaines Journal, Inc., 622 Graceland Ave., Des Plaines, IL 60016. TEL 847-299-5511; Ed. Todd Wessell; Pub. Richard C. Wessell, Sr.; adv.; pub. size: tabloid; circ. 5,000(paid).

ROSEMONT JOURNAL. s-w.: Wed. & Fri. $.50 newsstand; $25/yr. in cy.; $30/yr. out of cy. 622 Graceland Ave., Des Plaines, IL 60016. TEL 847-299-5511; FAX 847-298-8549. **Owner(s):** Des Plaines Journal, Inc., 622 Graceland Ave., Des Plaines, IL 60016. TEL 847-299-5511; Ed. Todd Wessell; Pub. Richard C. Wessell, Sr.; adv.; pub. size: tabloid; circ. 3,500(paid).

SUBURBAN JOURNAL. Sat. $.50 newsstand; $25/yr. in cy.; $30/yr. out of cy. 622 Graceland Ave., Des Plaines, IL 60016. TEL 847-299-5511; FAX 847-298-8549. **Owner(s):** Des Plaines Journal, Inc., 622 Graceland Ave., Des Plaines, IL 60016. TEL 847-299-5511; Ed. Todd Wessell; Pub. Richard C. Wessell, Sr.; adv.; pub. size: tabloid; circ. 6,800(paid).
Formerly: Journal & Topics.

DOWNERS GROVE

CLARENDON HILLS PROGRESS. 1959. Thu. $.50 newsstand; $19/yr. carrier. 922 Warren Ave., Downers Grove, IL 60515. TEL 630-969-0188. **Owner(s):** C.J. Winter, Jr., 922 Warren Ave., Downers Grove, IL 60515. TEL 630-969-0188; P.K. Winter, 922 Warren Ave., Downers Grove, IL 60515. TEL 630-969-0188; Craig Winter, 922 Warren Ave., Downers Grove, IL 60515; Chris Winter, 922 Warren Ave., Downer Grove, IL 60515; Ed. Stuart Sudak; Pub. P.K. Winter; adv. contact: Ed Rooney. photos; bk.rev.; pub. size: tabloid; circ. 6,087(free & paid).

DARIEN PROGRESS. 1959. Thu. $.50 newsstand; $19/yr. carrier. 922 Warren Ave., Downers Grove, IL 60515. TEL 630-969-0188. **Owner(s): C.J. Winter, Jr., 922 Warren Ave., Downers Grove,** IL 60515. TEL 630-969-0188; P.K. Winter, 922 Warren Ave., Downers Grove, IL 60515. TEL 630-969-0188; Craig Winter, 922 Warren Ave., Downers Grove, IL 60505. TEL 630-969-0188; Christopher J. Winter, 922 Warren Ave., Downers Grove, IL 60515. TEL 630-969-0188; Ed. Stuart Sudak; Pub. C.J. Winter, Jr.; adv.; photos; bk.rev.; pub. size: tabloid; circ. 10,440(free & paid).

DOWNERS GROVE REPORTER. 1883. s-w.: Wed. & Fri. $.50 newsstand; $19/yr. local carrier & mailed. 922 Warren Ave., Downers Grove, IL 60515. TEL 630-969-0188; FAX 630-969-0228. **Owner(s):** C.J. Winter, Jr., 922 Warren Ave., Downers Grove, IL 60515. TEL 630-969-0188; Christopher J. Winter, 922 Warren Ave., Downers Grove, IL 60515. TEL 630-969-0188; P.K. Winter, 922 Warren Ave., Downers Grove, IL 60515. TEL 630-969-0188; Craig R. Winter, 922 Warren Ave., Downers Grove, IL 60515. TEL 630-969-0188; Ed. Jennifer Parello; Pub. P.K. Winter; adv. contact: Ed Rooney. photos; bk.rev.; pub. size: tabloid; circ. 31,464(free & paid).

LISLE SUN. Wed. $.50 newsstand; $19/yr. local carrier or mailed. 922 Warren Ave., Downers Grove, IL 60515. TEL 630-969-0188; FAX 630-969-0228. **Owner(s):** C.J. Winter, Jr., 922 Warren Ave., Downers Grove, IL 60515. TEL 630-969-0188; Christopher J. Winter, 922 Warren Ave., Downers Grove, IL 60515. TEL 630-969-0188; P.K. Winter, 922 Warren Ave., Downers Grove, IL 60515. TEL 630-969-0188; Craig R. Winter, 922 Warren Ave., Downers Grove, IL 60515. TEL 630-969-0188; Ed. Jennifer Parello; Pub. P.K. Winter; adv. contact: Ed Rooney. photos; bk.rev.; pub. size: tabloid; circ. 30,000(paid).

WESTMONT PROGRESS. 1959. Thu. $.50 newsstand; $19/yr. carrier. 922 Warren Ave., Downers Grove, IL 60515. TEL 630-969-0188; FAX 630-969-0228. **Owner(s):** C.J. Winter, Jr., 922 Warren Ave., Downers Grove, IL 60515. TEL 630-969-0188; Christopher J. Winter, 922 Warren Ave., Downers Grove, IL 60515. TEL 630-969-0188; P.K. Winter, 922 Warren Ave., Downers Grove, IL 60515. TEL 630-969-0188; Craig R. Winter, 922 Warren Ave., Downers Grove, IL 60515. TEL 630-969-0188; Ed. Stuart Sudak; Pub. C.J. Winter, Jr.; adv. contact: Ed Rooney. photos; bk.rev.; pub. size: tabloid; circ. 7,454(paid).

WILLOWBROOK PROGRESS. Thu. $.50 newsstand; $19/yr. carrier. 922 Warren Ave., Downers Grove, IL 60515. TEL 630-969-0188. **Owner(s): C.J. Winter, Jr., 922 Warren Ave., Downers Grove,** IL 60515. TEL 630-969-0188; Christopher J. Winter, 922 Warren Ave., Downers Grove, IL 60515. TEL 630-969-0188; P.K. Winter, 922 Warren Ave., Downers Grove, IL 60515. TEL 630-969-0188; Craig R. Winter, 922 Warren Ave., Downers Grove, IL 60515. TEL 630-969-0188; Ed. C.J. Winter, Jr.; Pub. P.K. Winter; adv. contact: Ed Rooney. photos; bk.rev.; pub. size: tabloid; circ. 30,000(paid).

WOODRIDGE PROGRESS. 1969. Thu. $.50 copy; $19/yr. carrier. 922 Warren Ave., Downers Grove, IL 60515. TEL 630-969-0188; FAX 630-969-0228. **Owner(s):** C.J. Winter, Jr., 922 Warren Ave., Downers Grove, IL 60515. TEL 630-969-0188; P.K. Winter, 922 Warren Ave., Downers Grove, IL 60515. TEL 630-969-0188; Christopher J. Winter, 922 Warren Ave., Downers Grove, IL 60515. TEL 630-969-0188; Craig R. Winter, 922 Warren Ave., Downers Grove, IL 60515. TEL 630-969-0188; Ed. Stuart Sudak; Pub. C.J. Winter, Jr.; adv. contact: Ed Rooney. photos; bk.rev.; pub. size: tabloid; circ. 9,133(paid).

DURAND

DURAND-DAKOTA VOLUNTEER. 1990. Thu. $.50 newsstand; $21/yr. in cy.; $35/yr. elsewhere. 109 E. Oak St., Durand, IL 61024. TEL 815-248-4407; FAX 815-248-9176. **Owner(s):** Volunteer, Inc., The, 109 E. Oak St., Durand, IL 61024. TEL 815-248-4407; FAX 815-248-9176; Pub. Curt Stalheim; adv. contact: C.J. Gregg. bk.rev.; pub. size: tabloid; circ. 10,000(free & paid).

EARLVILLE

US
EARLVILLE LEADER. 1868. Wed. $.35 newsstand; $17/yr. in cy. P.O. Box 606, Earlville, IL 60518. TEL 815-246-6911; FAX 815-246-6911. **Owner(s):** Jean Albert, P.O. Box 606, Earlville, IL 60518. TEL 815-246-6911; FAX 815-246-6911; Pub. Jean Albert; adv.; pub. size: tabloid; circ. 1,158(paid).

EAST MOLINE

US
THRIFTY NICKEL WANT ADS. 1982. Thu. free. 500 42nd Ave., East Moline, IL 61244. TEL 309-792-4747; FAX 309-792-4797. **Owner(s):** Lee Enterprises, Inc., 215 N. Main St., Davenport, IA 52801-2100. TEL 319-383-2100; adv.; pub. size: tabloid; circ. 20,000(free).

EAST ST. LOUIS

US
EAST ST. LOUIS MONITOR. 1963. Thu. $.50 newsstand; $50/yr. mailed. 1501 State St., East St. Louis, IL 62205. TEL 618-271-0468. **Owner(s):** Anne E. Jordan, 1501 State St., East St. Louis, IL 62205. TEL 618-271-0468; Ed. Frazier Garner; Pub. Anne E. Jordan; adv. contact: George Laktzian. photos; bk.rev.; pub. size: broadsheet; circ. 12,500(paid).

EDINBURG

US
HERALD-STAR, THE. 1882. Wed. $.35 newsstand; $14/yr. in state; $17/yr. out of state. 103 S. Eaton, Edinburg, IL 62531-0050. TEL 217-623-5523; FAX 217-623-4216. **Owner(s):** Glenn W. Luttrell, 103 S. Eaton, Edinburg, IL 62531. TEL 217-623-5523; Pub. Glenn W. Luttrell; adv. contact: Glenn W. Luttrell. pub. size: tabloid; circ. 750(paid).

EDWARDSVILLE

US
EDWARDSVILLE JOURNAL. 1965. Wed. free. 220 St. Louis St., Edwardsville, IL 62025. TEL 618-656-8000; FAX 618-656-5093. **Owner(s):** Madison County Publications, 1990 Troy Rd., Edwardsville, IL 62025. TEL 618-656-8000; Ed. Nicole Vaughn. adv. contact: Bob Millering. pub. size: broadsheet; circ. 12,758(free).

ELBURN

US
ELBURN HERALD. 1908. Thu. $.50 newsstand; $18/yr. in cy.; $23/yr. out of cy.; $28/yr. out of state. 123 N. Main St., Elburn, IL 60119-8023. TEL 630-365-6446; FAX 630-365-2251. **Owner(s):** Kaneland Publications, Inc., P.O. Box L, Elburn, IL 60119. TEL 630-365-6446; Ed. Kim Boyd; Pub. Richard L. Cooper; adv.; pub. size: tabloid; circ. 2,800(paid).

ELIZABETHTOWN

US
HARDIN COUNTY INDEPENDENT. 1871. Thu. $.50 newsstand; $22.50/yr. 25-27 W. First St., Elizabethtown, IL 62931. TEL 618-287-2361. **Owner(s):** Noel E. Hurford, P.O. Box 328, Elizabethtown, IL 62931. TEL 618-287-2361; Ed. Noel E. Hurford; Pub. Noel E. Hurford; adv.: $3.80/SAU. photos; pub. size: standard; circ. 3,000(paid).
Formerly: Elizabeth Hardin County Independent.

ELMHURST

US
ADDISON PRESS. 1953. s-w.: Wed. & Fri. $.50 newsstand; $24.95/yr. in city mailed; $45.95/yr. out of city mailed. 112 S. York St., Elmhurst, IL 60126. TEL 630-834-0900; FAX 630-834-0910. **Owner(s):** Press Publications, Inc., 112 S. York St., Elmhurst, IL 60126. TEL 630-834-0900; Ed. Maria Kantzavelos; Pub. John M. Cruger; adv. contact: Lynn Hill. pub. size: broadsheet; circ. 3,800(controlled).

US
BENSENVILLE PRESS. 1987. s-w.: Wed. & Fri. $.50 newsstand; $24.95/yr. in town; $45.95/yr. out of town. 112 S. York Rd., Elmhurst, IL 60126. TEL 630-834-0900; FAX 630-834-0910. **Owner(s):** Press Publications, Inc., 112 S. York St., Elmhurst, IL 60126. TEL 630-834-0900; Ed. Steve Brosinski; Pub. John M. Cruger; adv. contact: Lynn Hill. pub. size: broadsheet; circ. 865(paid).

US ISSN 1043-3236
ELMHURST PRESS. 1889. s-w.: Wed. & Fri. $.50 newsstand; $24.95/yr. in cy.; $45.95/yr. out of cy. 112 S. York St., Elmhurst, IL 60126. TEL 630-834-0900; FAX 630-834-0910. **Owner(s):** Press Publications, Inc., 112 S. York St., Elmhurst, IL 60126. TEL 630-834-0900; Ed. Rick Nagel; Pub. John M. Cruger; adv. contact: Lynn Hill. pub. size: broadsheet; circ. 9,000(paid).

US
GLENDALE HEIGHTS PRESS. Thu. $.50 newsstand; $12.95/yr. in cy.; $28.95/yr. out of cy. mailed. 112 S. York St., Elmhurst, IL 60126. TEL 630-834-0900; FAX 630-834-0910. **Owner(s):** Press Publications, Inc., 112 S. York St., Elmhurst, IL 60126. TEL 630-834-0900; Ed. Rick Nagel; Pub. John M. Cruger; adv. contact: Lynn Hill. pub. size: tabloid; circ. 2,850(paid).

US
LOMBARD SPECTATOR. s-w.: Wed. & Fri. $.50 newsstand; $39.95/yr. mailed. 112 S. York St., Elmhurst, IL 60126. TEL 630-834-0900; FAX 630-834-0910. **Owner(s):** Press Publications, Inc., 112 S. York St., Elmhurst, IL 60126. TEL 630-834-0900; Ed. Rick Nagel; Pub. John M. Cruger; adv. contact: Lynn Hill. photos; pub. size: broadsheet; circ. 10,000(paid).

US
OAK BROOK PRESS. 1895. s-w.: Wed. & Fri. $.50 newsstand; $24.95/yr. in city; $45.95/yr. out of city. 112 S. York St., Elmhurst, IL 60126. TEL 630-834-0900; FAX 630-834-0910. **Owner(s):** Press Publications, Inc., 112 S. York St., Elmhurst, IL 60126. TEL 630-834-0900; Ed. Judith Coakis; Pub. John M. Cruger; adv. contact: Lynn Hill. pub. size: broadsheet; circ. 500(paid).

US
VILLA PARK ARGUS. 1895. s-w.: Wed. & Fri. $.50 newsstand; $24.95/yr. in city mailed; $45.95/yr. out of city mailed. 112 S. York St., Elmhurst, IL 60126. TEL 630-834-0900; FAX 630-834-0910. **Owner(s):** Press Publications, Inc., 112 S. York St., Elmhurst, IL 60126. TEL 630-834-0900; Ed. Rick Nagel; Pub. John M. Cruger; adv. contact: Lynn Hill. pub. size: broadsheet; circ. 3,300(controlled & paid).

US ISSN 1050-2327
WEST COOK COUNTY PRESS. 1953. Thu. $.50 newsstand; $12.95/yr. in city; $28.95/yr. out of city. 112 S. York St., Elmhurst, IL 60126. TEL 630-834-0900; FAX 630-834-0910. **Owner(s):** Press Publications, Inc., 112 S. York St., Elmhurst, IL 60126. TEL 630-834-0900; Ed. Rick Nagel; Pub. John M. Cruger; adv. contact: Lynn Hill. pub. size: broadsheet; circ. 1,200(paid).

US
WOOD DALE PRESS. 1988. s-w.: Wed. & Fri. $.50 newsstand; $24.95/yr. in town; $45.95/yr. out of town. 112 S. York Rd., Elmhurst, IL 60126. TEL 630-834-0900; FAX 630-834-0910. **Owner(s):** Press Publications, Inc., 112 S. York St., Elmhurst, IL 60126. TEL 630-834-0900; Ed. Steve Brosinski; Pub. John M. Cruger; adv. contact: Lynn Hill. pub. size: broadsheet; circ. 1,250(paid).

ELMWOOD

US
TRI-COUNTY NEWS. 1875. Thu. $16/yr. in cy.; $18/yr. out of cy. 116 S. Magnolia, Elmwood, IL 61529. TEL 309-742-2521; FAX 309-742-2511. **Owner(s):** Tri-County News, 116 S. Magnolia, Elmwood, IL 61529. TEL 309-742-2521; FAX 309-742-2511; Ed. Sue Swindler; Pub. DeEllda Swindler; adv. contact: DeEllda Swindler. pub. size: tabloid.

EL PASO

US
EL PASO JOURNAL. 1991. w. $.50 newsstand; $24/yr. in cy. 53 W. Front, El Paso, IL 61738. TEL 309-527-8595; FAX 309-527-8850. **Owner(s):** Tazewell Publishing, 100 Detroit Ave., Morton, IL 61550. TEL 309-263-2211; Pub. Ted J. Fleming; adv.; pub. size: broadsheet; circ. 1,400(paid).

ERIE

US
REVIEW, THE. 1857. Wed. $.50 newsstand; $22/yr. cy.; $28/yr. out of cy. 910 Albany St., Erie, IL 61250. TEL 309-659-2761; FAX 309-659-2761. **Owner(s):** W.N.S. Publication, 100 E. Main St., Morrison, IL 61270. TEL 815-772-7244; Ed. Judy James; Pub. Tony Komlanc; adv. contact: Gail Possley. pub. size: broadsheet; circ. 2,300(paid).
Formerly: Erie Review.

EUREKA

US
WOODFORD COUNTY JOURNAL. 1867. Thu. $.75 newsstand; $25/yr. in cy.; $29/yr. out of cy.; $33/yr. out of state. Lakeview Shopping Ctr., Eureka, IL 61530. TEL 309-467-3314; FAX 309-467-4563. **Owner(s):** San Francisco Chronicle, 901 Mission St., San Francisco, CA 94103; Ed. Arlene Franks; Pub. Mark Barra; adv.; photos; pub. size: broadsheet; circ. 1,804(free & paid).

WEEKLY NEWSPAPERS

EVANSTON

US ISSN 1044-7733

EVANSTON REVIEW. 1953. Thu. $1 newsstand; $27.95/yr. 1600 Orrington, Ste. 500, Evanston, IL 60201. TEL 847-866-6500; FAX 847-866-0965. **Owner(s):** Pioneer Press, Inc., 3701 W. Lake Ave., Glenview, IL 60025. TEL 847-486-9200; Ed. Gary Taylor; Pub. Thomas Neri; adv. contact: Susan Karol. pub. size: tabloid; circ. 13,996(paid).

US

LINCOLNWOOD REVIEW. Thu. $.50 newsstand; $17.95/yr. 1601 Sherman Ave., Evanston, IL 60201. TEL 847-866-5250; FAX 847-866-0965. **Owner(s):** Pioneer Press, Inc., 3701 W. Lake Ave., Glenview, IL 60025. TEL 847-486-9200; Ed. Dan Obermaier; Pub. Thomas Neri; adv. contact: Jack Whisler. pub. size: tabloid; circ. 1,374(paid).

US ISSN 0193-7251

MORTON GROVE CHAMPION. 1958. Thu. $1 newsstand; $18.95/yr. 1601 Sherman Ave., Evanston, IL 60201. TEL 847-866-5250; FAX 847-866-0965. **Owner(s):** Pioneer Press, Inc., 3701 W. Lake Ave., Glenview, IL 60025. TEL 847-486-9200; Ed. Dan Obermaier; Pub. Thomas Neri; adv.; pub. size: tabloid; circ. 3,800(paid).

US ISSN 0192-2742

SKOKIE REVIEW. 1946. Thu. $1 newsstand; $18.95/yr. 1601 Sherman Ave., Evanston, IL 60201. TEL 847-866-5250; FAX 847-866-0965. **Owner(s):** Pioneer Press, Inc., 3701 W. Lake Ave., Glenview, IL 60025. TEL 847-486-9200; Ed. Dan Obermaier; Pub. Thomas Neri; adv. contact: Jack Whisler. pub. size: tabloid; circ. 7,647(paid).

FAIRFIELD

US

FAIRFIELD WAYNE COUNTY PRESS. 1866. s-w.: Mon. & Thu. $.50 newsstand; $31/yr. in cy. 213 E. Main St., Fairfield, IL 62837. TEL 618-842-2662; FAX 618-842-7912. **Owner(s):** Wayne County Press, Inc., 213 E. Main St., Fairfield, IL 62837. TEL 618-842-2662; FAX 618-842-7912; Ed. Tom Mathews, Jr.; Pub. Tom Mathews, Jr.; adv. contact: Tom Mathews, Jr. photos; pub. size: broadsheet; circ. 8,625(paid).

FARINA

US

FARINA NEWS, THE. 1882. Thu. $15/yr. in cy.; $18/yr. out of cy. $20/yr. out of state. 109 N. Walnut, Farina, IL 62838. TEL 618-245-6216; FAX 618-245-6216. **Owner(s):** Shirley Ann Quick, 109 N. Walnut, Farina, IL 62838. TEL 618-245-6216; Ed. Shirley Ann Quick; Pub. Shirley Ann Quick; pub. size: standard; circ. 1,300(paid).

FARMER CITY

US

FARMER CITY JOURNAL. 1872. Wed. $24/yr. 221 S. Main, Farmer City, IL 61842-0080. TEL 309-928-2193; FAX 309-928-2194. **Owner(s):** Illinois Valley Press, P.O. Box 80, Farmer City, IL 61842. TEL 309-928-2193; FAX 309-928-2194; Ed. Steve Hoffman. adv.; photos; pub. size: tabloid; circ. 3,100(paid).

FISHER

US

FISHER REPORTER. 1880. Wed. $12/yr. 118 S. Third St., Fisher, IL 61843. TEL 217-897-1525. **Owner(s):** Edward Pyne, 309 Beaufort St., Normal, IL 61761. TEL 309-454-5476; Ed. Susan Helle; Pub. Susan Helle; adv.; pub. size: broadsheet; circ. 1,100(paid).

FORRESTON

US

FORRESTON JOURNAL. 1865. Thu. $21/yr. in state; $26/yr. out of state. 313 E. Main St., Forreston, IL 61030. TEL 815-938-3320; FAX 815-732-4238. **Owner(s):** B.F. Shaw Printing Co., 444 Pine Hill Dr., P.O. Box 409, Dixon, IL 61021. TEL 815-284-2222; Pub. Earleen Hinton; pub. size: broadsheet; circ. 1,000(paid).

FREEPORT

US

FREEPORT ADVERTISER SHOPPING NEWS. 1970. Wed. free local; $20/yr. out of area. 1342 S. Harlem Ave., Freeport, IL 61032. TEL 815-235-4106; FAX 815-235-7077. **Owner(s):** Woodward Communications, Inc., Eighth & Bluff, Dubuque, IA 52001. TEL 319-588-5724; adv.; pub. size: tabloid; circ. 23,000(free).

FULTON

US

FULTON JOURNAL. 1854. Wed. $.50 newsstand; $14/yr. in cy.; $18/yr. out of cy. 408 Tenth Ave., Fulton, IL 61252. TEL 815-589-2424. **Owner(s):** Fulton Press, Inc., 408 Tenth Ave., Fulton, IL 61252. TEL 815-589-2424; Ed. Henry Kramer; Pub. Henry Kramer; pub. size: standard; circ. 2,200(paid).

US

WHITESIDE SHOPPER. 1940. Tue. free. 408 Tenth Ave., Fulton, IL 61252. TEL 815-589-2424. **Owner(s):** Fulton Press, Inc., 408 Tenth Ave., Fulton, IL 61252. TEL 815-589-2424; Ed. Henry Kramer; Pub. Henry Kramer; pub. size: standard; circ. 3,300(free).

GALENA

US

GALENA GAZETTE. 1834. Wed. $1 newsstand; $25/yr. local mailed; $30/yr. tri-state; $40/yr. elsewhere. 716 S. Bench St., Galena, IL 61036. TEL 815-777-0019; FAX 815-777-3809. **Owner(s):** Robert & Frances Melvold, Maquoketa Sentinel, Maquoketa, IA 52060; P. Carter & Sarah Newton, 301 Park Ave., Galena, IL 61036. TEL 815-777-1765; Ed. Theresa Riniker; Pub. P. Carter Newton; adv. contact: Robin Buss. pub. size: tabloid; circ. 6,000(paid).

GALESBURG

US

GALESBURG POST, THE. 1928. Thu. $.35 newsstand; $11.95/yr. in cy.; $21.95/yr. out of cy.; $24.95/yr. out of state. 80 S. Cherry St., Galesburg, IL 61401-4598. TEL 309-343-5617; FAX 309-343-2518. **Owner(s):** Hickory Hills Publishing, 80 S. Cherry St., Galesburg, IL 61401. TEL 309-343-2552; FAX 309-342-1986; Ed. John P. Creighton. adv.; bk.rev.; pub. size: tabloid; circ. 2,075(paid).

US

KNOXVILLE JOURNAL, THE. 1856. Thu. $.25 newsstand; $10/yr. in cy.; $18/yr. out of cy.; $20/yr. out of state. 80 S. Cherry St., Galesburg, IL 61401-4598. TEL 309-343-5617; FAX 309-343-2518. **Owner(s):** Hickory Hills Publishing, 80 S. Cherry St., Galesburg, IL 61401. TEL 309-353-3527; FAX 309-342-1986; Ed. John P. Creighton; Pub. John P. Creighton; adv.; pub. size: tabloid; circ. 3,200(paid).

GALVA

US

GALVA NEWS. 1879. Wed. $.50 newsstand; $18/yr. in state; $22/yr. out of state. 214 S. Exchange St., Galva, IL 61434. TEL 309-932-2103; FAX 309-932-3282. **Owner(s):** Copley Press, Inc., 7776 Ivanhoe Ave., La Jolla, CA 92037. TEL 619-454-0411; Ed. Rob Clark; Pub. Donald Cooper; adv. contact: Stacey Swanson. pub. size: broadsheet; circ. 2,400(paid).

GENESEO

US

GENESEO REPUBLIC. 1856. Fri. $.75 newsstand; $31/yr. in state; $33/yr. out of state. 108 W. First St., Geneseo, IL 61254. TEL 309-944-2119; FAX 309-944-6161. **Owner(s):** Terry Newspapers, Inc., 108 W. First St., Geneseo, IL 61254. TEL 309-944-2119; FAX 309-944-6161; Ed. Lisa Hammer; Pub. Thomas Terry; adv. contact: Linda Venable. pub. size: broadsheet; circ. 4,000(free & paid).

US

GENESEO SHOPPER. Wed. free. 108 W. First St., Geneseo, IL 61254. TEL 309-944-2119; FAX 309-944-6161. **Owner(s):** Terry Newspapers, Inc., 108 W. First St., Geneseo, IL 61254. TEL 309-944-2119; FAX 309-944-6161; Ed. Lisa Hammer. adv. contact: Linda Venable. circ. 14,500(free).

GENEVA

US

GENEVA REPUBLICAN. 1847. Thu. $.75 newsstand; $25/yr. 6 James St., Geneva, IL 60134. TEL 630-232-2324; FAX 630-232-9974. **Owner(s):** Wayne G. Woltman, 6 James St., Geneva, IL 60134. TEL 630-232-7400; Ed. Tim Unzicker; Pub. Wayne G. Woltman; adv. contact: Robert Langness. pub. size: tabloid; circ. 4,200(paid).

GEORGETOWN

US

INDEPENDENT NEWS. 1976. Wed. free local; $20/yr. out of area. 302 Mill St., Georgetown, IL 61846. TEL 217-662-2556; FAX 217-662-2484. **Owner(s):** Louis Valberg, 302 Mill St., Georgetown, IL 61846. TEL 217-662-2556; Ed. Vicky Delhaye; Pub. Louis Valberg; adv.; pub. size: tabloid; circ. 16,653(paid).
Formerly: Georgetown Independent News.

WEEKLY NEWSPAPERS

GIBSON CITY

US

GIBSON CITY COURIER. 1873. Wed. $.45 newsstand; $19.20/yr. in cy.; $20.30/yr. out of cy. 310 N. Sangamon Ave., Gibson City, IL 60936-0549. TEL 217-784-4244; FAX 217-784-4246. **Owner(s):** East Central Communications, Inc., P.O. Box 909, Rantoul, IL 61866. TEL 217-892-9615; Ed. Doris Benter; Pub. Dennis C. Kaster; adv.; photos; pub. size: broadsheet; circ. 2,800(paid).

GILLESPIE

US

GILLESPIE AREA NEWS. 1905. Thu. $.35 newsstand; $15/yr. in cy.; $17/yr. out of cy. 112 W. Chestnut St., Gillespie, IL 62033. TEL 217-839-2130; FAX 217-839-2139. **Owner(s):** David & Patty Ambrose, 112 W. Chestnut St., Gillespie, IL 62033. TEL 217-839-2130; Ed. David Ambrose; Pub. David Ambrose; adv.: $3.25/col. in. pub. size: broadsheet; circ. 3,000(paid).
Formerly: Area News, The.

GILMAN

US

GILMAN STAR. 1869. Thu. $.45 newsstand; $17/yr. in cy.; $20/yr. out of cy. 203 N. Central St., Gilman, IL 60938. TEL 815-265-7332; FAX 815-265-7880. **Owner(s):** John T. Elliot, 203 N. Central St., Gilman, IL 60938. TEL 815-265-7332; Ed. John T. Elliot; Pub. John T. Elliot; adv.; pub. size: broadsheet; circ. 2,900(paid).

GLASFORD

US

GLASFORD GAZETTE, THE. 1899. Thu. $.50 newsstand; $20.50/yr. in state; $23/yr. out of state. 401 Main St., Glasford, IL 61533-0260. TEL 309-389-2811. **Owner(s):** Gazette Printing Co., 401 Main St., Glasford, IL 61533-0260. TEL 309-389-2811; Ed. William Watkins; Pub. William Watkins; pub. size: tabloid; circ. 1,200(paid).

GLEN ELLYN

US   ISSN 1059-8146

GLEN ELLYN NEWS. 1922. s-w.: Wed. & Fri. $.50 newsstand; $34/yr. in cy.; $35/yr. out of cy.; $36/yr. out of state. 460 Pennsylvania Ave., Glen Ellyn, IL 60137. TEL 630-469-0100; FAX 630-469-4472. **Owner(s):** Glen News Printing Co., 460 Pennsylvania Ave., Glen Ellyn, IL 60137. TEL 630-469-0100; FAX 630-469-4472; Ed. Julia Worthen; Pub. Stuart Stone; adv. contact: Jane Rio. pub. size: tabloid; circ. 8,000(paid).

US

WHEATON LEADER. 1954. Wed. $24/yr. in cy.; $27/yr. in state; $30/yr. out of state. 460 Pennsylvania Ave., Glen Ellyn, IL 60137. TEL 630-668-7957; FAX 630-469-4472. **Owner(s):** Glen News Printing Co., 460 Pennsylvania Ave., Glen Ellyn, IL 60137. TEL 630-469-0100; Ed. Darlene Ostrowski; Pub. Stuart Stone; adv. contact: Jane Rio. pub. size: tabloid; circ. 12,000(paid).

US

WINFIELD ESTATE. 1986. Wed. $.50 newsstand; $15/yr. 460 Pennsylvania Ave., Glen Ellyn, IL 60137. TEL 630-668-7957; FAX 630-469-4472. **Owner(s):** Glen News Printing Co., 460 Pennsylvania Ave., Glen Ellyn, IL 60137. TEL 630-469-0100; Ed. Julie Worthen; Pub. Stuart Stone; pub. size: tabloid; circ. 3,000(free).

GLENVIEW

US   ISSN 0841-1646

GLENCOE NEWS. Thu. $36.95/yr. 3701 W. Lake Ave., Glenview, IL 60025. TEL 708-486-9200; FAX 708-486-7451. **Owner(s):** Pioneer Press, Inc., 3701 W. Lake Ave., Glenview, IL 60025. TEL 847-486-9200; Ed. Elaine Fandell; Pub. Tom Neri; adv.; pub. size: tabloid; circ. 2,300(paid).

US

GLENVIEW ANNOUNCEMENTS. Thu. $1 newsstand; $32.95/yr. 3701 W. Lake Ave., Glenview, IL 60025. TEL 847-486-9200; FAX 847-486-7451. **Owner(s):** Pioneer Press, Inc., 3701 W. Lake Ave., Glenview, IL 60025. TEL 847-486-9200; Pub. Thomas Neri; adv. contact: Susan Karol. pub. size: tabloid; circ. 7,728(paid).

US   ISSN 0744-9550

NORTHBROOK STAR. 1935. Thu. $1 newsstand; $36.95/yr. in cy. 3701 W. Lake Ave., Glenview, IL 60025. TEL 847-486-9200; FAX 847-486-7451. **Owner(s):** Pioneer Press, Inc., 3701 W. Lake Ave., Glenview, IL 60025. TEL 847-486-9200; pub. size: tabloid; circ. 7,500(paid).

US   ISSN 0745-0044

WILMETTE LIFE. Thu. $1 newsstand; $36.95/yr. 3701 W. Lake Ave., Glenview, IL 60025. TEL 847-486-9200; FAX 847-486-7451. **Owner(s):** Pioneer Press, Inc., 3701 W. Lake Ave., Glenview, IL 60025. TEL 847-486-9200; Ed. Elaine Fandell; Pub. Thomas Neri; adv.; photos; pub. size: tabloid; circ. 7,770(paid).

US

WINNETKA TALK. 1901. Thu. $1 newsstand; $36.95/yr. 3701 W. Lake Ave., Glenview, IL 60025. TEL 847-486-9200; FAX 847-486-7451. **Owner(s):** Pioneer Press, Inc., 3701 W. Lake Ave., Glenview, IL 60025. TEL 847-486-9200; Ed. Elaine Fandell; Pub. Thomas Neri; adv.; pub. size: tabloid; circ. 6,000(paid).

GOLCONDA

US

HERALD ENTERPRISE. 1858. Wed. $.50 newsstand; $16/yr. in cy. & adjoining area; $18/yr. out of area. Jefferson & Monroe Sts., Golconda, IL 62938-0400. TEL 618-683-3531; FAX 618-683-3531. **Owner(s):** Virginia Brenner, P.O. Box 400, Golconda, IL 62938. TEL 618-683-3531; FAX 618-683-3831; Pub. Virginia Brenner; adv. contact: Debra Carmen. adv.: $4.20/SAU. pub. size: broadsheet; circ. 2,000(paid).

GRANITE CITY

US

GRANITE CITY PRESS JOURNAL. Thu. $.50 newsstand; $18/yr. 1815 Delmar Ave., Granite City, IL 62040. TEL 618-876-2000; FAX 618-876-4240. **Owner(s):** Suburban Journals, 1714 Deer Tracks Trail, St. Louis, MO 63131. TEL 314-821-1110; Ed. Dan Barger. adv. contact: Douglas Garbs. pub. size: broadsheet; circ. 8,000(paid).

GRANVILLE

US

PUTNAM COUNTY RECORD. Wed. $.25 newsstand; $18/yr. 318 S. McCoy St., Granville, IL 61326-0048. TEL 815-339-2321; FAX 815-339-6727. **Owner(s):** Elin Arnold, 318 S. McCoy St., Granville, IL 61326. TEL 815-339-2321; FAX 815-339-6727; Ed. Elin Arnold; Pub. Elin Arnold; adv.; pub. size: tabloid; circ. 3,431(controlled & paid).

GRAYSLAKE

US

ANTIOCH NEWS-REPORTER. 1886. Thu. $.50 newsstand; $24.50/yr. mailed. 30 S. Whitney St., Grayslake, IL 60030. TEL 847-223-8161; FAX 847-223-8810. **Owner(s):** Lakeland Publishers, Inc., 30 S. Whitney St., Grayslake, IL 60030. TEL 847-223-8161; FAX 847-223-8810; Pub. William H. Schroder, Sr.; adv. contact: Esther Hebbard. pub. size: tabloid; circ. 4,427(paid).

US

FOX LAKE PRESS. 1934. Thu. $.50 newsstand; $24.50/yr. mailed. 30 S. Whitney St., Grayslake, IL 60030. TEL 847-223-8161; FAX 847-223-8810. **Owner(s):** Lakeland Publishers, Inc., 30 S. Whitney St., Grayslake, IL 60030. TEL 847-223-8161; FAX 847-223-8810; Ed. Rhonda Burke; Pub. William H. Schroder, Sr.; adv. contact: Esther Hebbard. pub. size: tabloid; circ. 4,982(paid).

US

GRAYSLAKE TIMES. 1900. Thu. $.50 newsstand; $24.50/yr. mailed. 30 S. Whitney St., Grayslake, IL 60030. TEL 847-223-8161; FAX 847-223-8810. **Owner(s):** Lakeland Publishers, Inc., 30 S. Whitney St., Grayslake, IL 60030. TEL 847-223-8161; FAX 847-223-8810; Ed. Rhonda Burke; Pub. William H. Schroeder, Sr.; adv. contact: Esther Hebbard. pub. size: tabloid; circ. 3,720(paid).

US

GURNEE PRESS. 1973. Thu. $.50 newsstand; $24.50/yr. mailed. 30 S. Whitney St., Grayslake, IL 60030. TEL 847-223-8161; FAX 847-223-8810. **Owner(s):** Lakeland Publishers, Inc., 30 S. Whitney St., Grayslake, IL 60030. TEL 847-223-8161; FAX 847-223-8810; Ed. Rhonda Burke; Pub. William H. Schroeder, Sr.; adv. contact: Esther Hebbard. pub. size: tabloid; circ. 3,347(paid).

US

LAKELAND PRESS. 1956. Thu. $.50 newsstand; $24.50/yr. 30 S. Whitney St., Grayslake, IL 60030. TEL 847-223-8161; FAX 847-223-8810. **Owner(s):** Lakeland Publishers, Inc., 30 S. Whitney St., Grayslake, IL 60030. TEL 847-223-8161; FAX 847-223-8810; Ed. Rhonda Burke; Pub. William H. Schroeder, Sr.; adv. contact: Esther Hebbard. pub. size: tabloid; circ. 38,724(paid).

US

LAKE VILLA RECORD. 1955. Thu. $.50 newsstand; $24.50/yr. mailed. 30 S. Whitney St., Grayslake, IL 60030. TEL 847-223-8161; FAX 847-223-8810. **Owner(s):** Lakeland Publishers, Inc., 30 S. Whitney St., Grayslake, IL 60030. TEL 847-223-8161; FAX 847-223-8810; Ed. Rhonda Burke; Pub. William H. Schroeder, Sr.; adv. contact: Esther Hebbard. pub. size: tabloid; circ. 2,404(paid).

WEEKLY NEWSPAPERS

HIGHLAND, IL   10581

US   ISSN 0895-8572
LAKE ZURICH ENTERPRISE. 1957. Thu. $.50 newsstand; $24.50/yr. mailed. 30 S. Whitney St., Grayslake, IL 60030. TEL 847-223-8161; FAX 847-223-8810. **Owner(s):** Lakeland Publishers, Inc., P.O. Box 268, Grayslake, IL 60030. TEL 847-223-8161; FAX 847-223-8810; Ed. Rhonda Burke; Pub. William H. Schroeder, Sr.; adv. contact: Esther Hebbard. pub. size: tabloid; circ. 4,043(paid).

US
LIBERTYVILLE NEWS. 1989. Thu. $.50 newsstand; $24.50/yr.; $22.50/yr. senior citizens. 30 S. Whitney St., Grayslake, IL 60030. TEL 847-223-8161; FAX 847-223-8810. **Owner(s):** Lakeland Publishers, Inc., 30 S. Whitney St., Grayslake, IL 60030. TEL 847-223-8161; FAX 847-223-8810; Ed. Rhonda Hetrick-Burke; Pub. William H. Schroeder, Sr.; adv. contact: Esther Hebbard. pub. size: tabloid; circ. 3,061(paid).

US
LINDENHURST NEWS. 1988. Thu. $.50 newsstand; $24.50/yr.; $22.50/yr. senior citizens. 30 S. Whitney St., Grayslake, IL 60030. TEL 847-223-8161; FAX 847-223-8810. **Owner(s):** Lakeland Publishers, Inc., 30 S. Whitney St., Grayslake, IL 60030. TEL 847-223-8161; FAX 847-223-8810; Pub. William H. Schroeder, Sr.; adv. contact: Esther Hebbard. pub. size: tabloid; circ. 2,800(paid).

US   ISSN 0746-8938
MUNDELEIN NEWS. 1942. Thu. $.50 newsstand; $24.50/yr. mailed. 30 S. Whitney St., Grayslake, IL 60030. TEL 847-223-8161; FAX 847-223-8810. **Owner(s):** Lakeland Publishers, Inc., 30 S. Whitney St., Grayslake, IL 60030. TEL 847-223-8161; FAX 847-223-8810; Ed. Rhonda Burke; Pub. William H. Schroeder, Sr.; adv. contact: Esther Hebbard. pub. size: tabloid; circ. 2,963(paid).

US
ROUND LAKE NEWS. 1938. Thu. $.50 newsstand; $24.50/yr. mailed. 30 S. Whitney St., Grayslake, IL 60030. TEL 847-223-8161; FAX 847-223-8810. **Owner(s):** Lakeland Publishers, Inc., 30 S. Whitney St., Grayslake, IL 60030. TEL 847-223-8161; FAX 847-223-8810; Ed. Rhonda Burke; Pub. William H. Schroeder, Sr.; adv. contact: Esther Hebbard. pub. size: tabloid; circ. 4,465(paid).

US
VERNON HILLS NEWS. 1958. Thu. $.50 newsstand; $24.50/yr.; $22.50/yr. senior citizens. 30 S. Whitney St., Grayslake, IL 60030. TEL 847-223-8161; FAX 847-223-8810. **Owner(s):** Lakeland Publishers, Inc., 30 S. Whitney St., Grayslake, IL 60030. TEL 847-223-8161; FAX 847-223-8110; Ed. Rhonda Hetrick-Burke; Pub. William H. Schroeder, Sr.; adv. contact: Esther Hebbard. pub. size: tabloid; circ. 2,810(paid).
Formerly: Vernon Crier.

US   ISSN 0745-8118
WARREN-NEWPORT PRESS. 1960. Thu. $.50 newsstand; $24.50/yr. mailed. 30 S. Whitney St., Grayslake, IL 60030. TEL 847-223-8161; FAX 847-223-8810. **Owner(s):** Lakeland Publishers, Inc., 30 S. Whitney St., Grayslake, IL 60030. TEL 847-223-8161; FAX 847-223-8810; Ed. Rhonda Burke; Pub. William H. Schroeder, Sr.; adv. contact: Esther Hebbard. pub. size: tabloid; circ. 2,162(paid).

US
WAUCONDA LEADER. 1888. Thu. $.50 newsstand; $24.50/yr. mailed. 30 S. Whitney St., Grayslake, IL 60030. TEL 847-223-8161; FAX 847-223-8810. **Owner(s):** Lakeland Publishers, Inc., 30 S. Whitney St., Grayslake, IL 60030. TEL 847-223-8161; FAX 847-223-8810; Ed. Rhonda Burke; Pub. William H. Schroeder, Sr.; adv. contact: Esther Hebbard. pub. size: tabloid; circ. 3,961(paid).

GREENUP

US
GREENUP PRESS. 1889. Thu. $18/yr. in state; $23/yr. out of state. 104 E. Cumberland St., Greenup, IL 62428-0127. TEL 217-923-3704; FAX 217-923-3704. **Owner(s):** William J. McMorris, P.O. Box 127, Greenup, IL 62428. TEL 217-923-3704; FAX 217-923-3704; Pub. William D. McMorris; adv. contact: Tony McMorris. photos; pub. size: standard; circ. 1,750(paid).

GREENVIEW

US
MENARD COUNTY REVIEW. 1883. Fri. $.40 newsstand; $15/yr. in state; $17/yr. out of state. 500 W. Adams, Greenview, IL 62642. TEL 217-968-5511; FAX 217-632-2237. **Owner(s):** Petersburg Observer, P.O. Box 350, Petersburg, IL 62675. TEL 217-632-2236; Ed. Carolyn Miller; Pub. Jane Cutright; adv. contact: Carolyn Miller. pub. size: tabloid; circ. 1,650(paid).

GREENVILLE

US
GREENVILLE ADVOCATE, THE. 1858. s-w.: Tue. & Thu. $.50 newsstand; $32/yr. mailed. 305 S. Secon St., Greenville, IL 62246. TEL 618-664-3144. **Owner(s):** Duane L. Reeves, P. O. Box 9, Greenville, IL 62246. TEL 618-664-3144; Ed. Duane L. Reeves; Pub. Duane L. Reeves; adv.; photos; bk.rev.; pub. size: broadsheet; circ. 5,100(paid).

HARDIN

US
CALHOUN NEWS. 1915. Wed. $16/yr. in state; $24/yr. out of state. 310 S. County Rd., Hardin, IL 62047. TEL 618-576-2244; FAX 618-576-2245. **Owner(s):** Bruce Campbell, 310 S. County Rd., Hardin, IL 62047. TEL 618-576-2244; Pub. Bruce Campbell; adv. contact: Bruce Campbell. pub. size: standard; circ. 2,500(paid).
Formerly: Hardin Calhoun News.

US
HARDIN CALHOUN HERALD. 1872. Wed. $.25 newsstand; $12/yr. One Main St., Hardin, IL 62047. TEL 618-576-2716; FAX 618-576-2716. **Owner(s):** Charles Burch, P.O. Box 389, Hardin, IL 62047. TEL 618-576-2716; FAX 618-576-2716; Ed. Charles Burch; Pub. Charles Burch; adv.; photos; pub. size: standard; circ. 1,600(paid).

HAVANA

US   ISSN 1060-2437
HAVANA MASON COUNTY DEMOCRAT. 1849. Wed. $.75 newsstand; $28/yr. 217 W. Market St., Havana, IL 62644. TEL 309-543-3311; FAX 309-543-6844. **Owner(s):** Martin Publishing Co., Inc., 219 W. Market, Havana, IL 62644. TEL 309-543-3311; Ed. Wendy Jo Martin; Pub. Robert Martin; adv.; pub. size: broadsheet; circ. 6,300(free & paid).

HENRY

US
HENRY NEWS REPUBLICAN. 1852. Wed. $.40 newsstand; $20/yr. in Marshall & Putnam cys. 709 Third St., Henry, IL 61537. TEL 309-364-3250; FAX 309-364-3858. **Owner(s):** Douglas Ziegler, P.O. Box 190, Henry, IL 61537. TEL 309-364-3250; FAX 309-364-3858; Ed. Douglas Ziegler. adv.: $4.25/SAU. photos; pub. size: broadsheet; circ. 2,850(paid).

US
WENONA INDEX. Wed. $.30 newsstand; $14/yr. in state; $16/yr. out of state. 709 Third St., Henry, IL 61537. TEL 309-364-3250; FAX 309-364-3858. **Owner(s):** George Ziegler, P.O. Box 190, Henry, IL 61537. TEL 309-364-3250; Pub. Doug Ziegler; photos; pub. size: standard; circ. 900(paid).

HERRIN

US
HERRIN SPOKESMAN. 1942. s-w.: Thu. & Sun. $.50 newsstand; $21.95/yr. in cy.; $29.95/yr. out of cy.; $32.95/yr. out of state. 216 N. Park Ave., Herrin, IL 62948. TEL 618-942-5000; FAX 618-942-4630. **Owner(s):** American Publishing Co., 606 N. Van Buren, Marion, IL 62959. TEL 618-993-1711; Ed. John Homan; Pub. G. David Green; adv. contact: Nancy Sims. pub. size: broadsheet; circ. 2,100(paid); Sun. 8,200(paid).

HERSCHER

US
HERSCHER PILOT. 1976. Thu. $.30 newsstand; $12.50/yr. in area; $15/yr. out of area; $18/yr. out of state. 100 S. Main St., Herscher, IL 60941. TEL 815-426-2132. **Owner(s):** Robert A. Mau, P.O. Box 709, Herscher, IL 60941. TEL 815-426-2132; Ed. Robert A. Mau; Pub. Robert A. Mau; adv. contact: Robert A. Mau. pub. size: tabloid; circ. 2,500(paid).

HIGHLAND

US   ISSN 8750-0007
HIGHLAND NEWS LEADER. 1861. s-w.: Mon. & Thu. $.50 newsstand; $28/yr. local. One Woodcrest Professional Park, Highland, IL 62249. TEL 618-654-2366. **Owner(s):** Walt Disney Co., 500 S. Buena Vista St., Burbank, CA 91521. TEL 818-560-5300; Pub. Kay Maue; adv.; photos; pub. size: broadsheet; circ. 15,800(free & paid).

HILLSBORO

US
HILLSBORO JOURNAL. 1853. s-w.: Mon. & Thu. $.30 newsstand; $18/yr. in cy.; $36/yr. out of cy. 431 S. Main St., Hillsboro, IL 62049. TEL 217-532-3933; FAX 217-532-3632. **Owner(s):** Phil & Nancy Galer, 431 S. Main St., Hillsboro, IL 62049. TEL 217-532-3933; John & Susie Galer, 431 S. Main St., Hillsboro, IL 62049. TEL 217-532-3933; Ed. Susie Galer; Pub. Phil Galer; pub. size: broadsheet; circ. 6,700(paid).

US
M & M JOURNAL. 1968. Mon. free. 431 S. Main St., Hillsboro, IL 62049. TEL 217-532-3933; FAX 217-532-3632. **Owner(s):** Hillsboro Journal, 431 S. Main St., Hillsboro, IL 62049. TEL 217-532-3933; Pub. Philip C. Galer; adv.; pub. size: broadsheet; circ. 21,945(free).

US
MACOUPIN & MONTGOMERY COUNTY JOURNAL. Mon. free; $10/yr. out of area. 431 S. Main St., Hillsboro, IL 62049. TEL 217-532-3933; FAX 217-532-3632. **Owner(s):** Hillsboro Journal, 431 S. Main St., Hillsboro, IL 62049. TEL 217-532-3933; Ed. Philip C. Galer; Pub. Philip C. Galer; adv. contact: John Galer. pub. size: broadsheet; circ. 1,300(paid).

US
MACOUPIN COUNTY SHOPPER. 1968. Mon. free. 431 S. Main St., Hillsboro, IL 62049. TEL 217-532-3933; FAX 217-532-3632. **Owner(s):** Hillsboro Journal, 431 S. Main St., Hillsboro, IL 62049. TEL 217-532-3933; Ed. Phillip C. Galer; Pub. Phillip C. Galer; adv.; pub. size: broadsheet; circ. 13,500(free).

US
MONTGOMERY COUNTY NEWS, THE. 1869. 3/wk.: Tue., Thu., Sat. $.35 newsstand; $25/yr. 106 W. Seward, Hillsboro, IL 62049. TEL 217-532-3929; FAX 217-532-3522; E-mail: slepicka@cnmnet.com. **Owner(s):** Hillsboro & Montgomery County News, Inc., P.O. Box 250, Hillsboro, IL 62049. TEL 217-532-3929; Ed. Richard L. Slepicka; Pub. Nancy B. Slepicka; adv. contact: Nancy B. Slepicka. pub. size: broadsheet; circ. 4,000(paid).

US
SORENTO NEWS. 1927. Thu. $.20 newsstand; $7/yr. in cy.; $14/yr. out of cy. 431 S. Main St., Hillsboro, IL 62049. TEL 217-532-3933; FAX 217-532-3632. **Owner(s):** Hillsboro Journal, 431 S. Main St., Hillsboro, IL 62049. TEL 217-532-3933; Ed. Philip C. Galer; Pub. Philip C. Galer; adv. contact: John Galer. pub. size: broadsheet; circ. 600(paid).

HINSDALE

US
BURR RIDGE DOINGS. s-w.: Wed. & Fri. $.75 newsstand; $45.50/yr. mailed. 118 W. First St., Hinsdale, IL 60521. TEL 708-887-0600; FAX 708-887-9646; E-mail: doingsnews@aol.com. **Owner(s):** Doings Newspapers, Inc., 118 W. First St., Hinsdale, IL 60521. TEL 630-887-0600; FAX 630-887-9646; Ed. Pat Lannom; Pub. J. Peter Teschner; adv. contact: Jim Slonoff. photos; pub. size: tabloid; circ. 11,000(paid).

US
CLARENDON HILLS DOINGS, THE. 1895. s-w.: Wed. & Fri. $.75 newsstand; $45.50/yr. mailed. 118 W. First St., Hinsdale, IL 60521. TEL 630-887-0600; FAX 630-887-9646; E-mail: doingsnews@aol.com; URL: http:www.//the doings.com. **Owner(s):** Doings Newspapers, Inc., 118 W. First St., Hinsdale, IL 60521. TEL 630-887-0600; FAX 630-887-9646; Ed. Pam Lannom; Pub. J. Peter Teschner; adv. contact: Jim Slonoff. photos; pub. size: tabloid; circ. 11,000(paid).

US
DARIEN DOINGS. 1895. s-w.: Wed. & Fri. $.75 newsstand; $45.50/yr. mailed. 118 W. First St., Hinsdale, IL 60521. TEL 630-887-0600; FAX 630-887-9646; E-mail: doingsnews@aol.com; URL: http://www.thedoings.com. **Owner(s):** Doings Newspapers, Inc., 118 W. First St., Hinsdale, IL 60521. TEL 630-887-0600; FAX 630-887-9646; Ed. Pam Lannom; Pub. J. Peter Teschner; adv. contact: Jim Slonoff. photos; pub. size: tabloid; circ. 11,000(paid).

US
HINSDALE DOINGS. 1895. s-w.: Wed. & Fri. $.75 newsstand; $45.50/yr. mailed. 118 W. First St., Hinsdale, IL 60521. TEL 630-887-0600; FAX 630-877-9646; E-mail: doingsnews@aol.com; URL: http://www.thedoings.com. **Owner(s):** Doings Newspapers, Inc., 118 W. First St., Hinsdale, IL 60521. TEL 630-887-0600; FAX 630-887-9646; Ed. Pam Lannom; Pub. J. Peter Teschner; adv. contact: Jim Slonoff. photos; pub. size: tabloid; circ. 11,000(paid).

US
INDIAN HEAD PARK. 1895. s-w.: Wed. & Fri. $.75 newsstand; $45.50/yr. mailed. 118 W. First St., Hinsdale, IL 60521. TEL 630-887-0600; FAX 630-877-9646; E-mail: doingsnews@aol.com; URL: http://www.thedoings.com. **Owner(s):** Doings Newspapers, Inc., 118 W. First St., Hinsdale, IL 60521. TEL 630-887-0600; FAX 630-887-9646; Ed. Pam Lannom; Pub. J. Peter Teschner; adv. contact: Jim Slonoff. photos; pub. size: tabloid; circ. 11,000(paid).

US
OAK BROOK DOINGS. 1895. s-w.: Wed. & Fri. $.75 newsstand; $45.50/yr. mailed. 118 W. First St., Hinsdale, IL 60521. TEL 630-887-0600; FAX 630-887-9646; E-mail: doingsnews@aol.com; URL: http://www.thedoings.com. **Owner(s):** Doings Newspapers, Inc., 118 W. First St., Hinsdale, IL 60521. TEL 630-887-0600; FAX 630-887-9646; Ed. Pam Lannom; Pub. J. Peter Teschner; adv.; photos; pub. size: tabloid; circ. 11,000(paid).

US
OAK BROOK TERRACE DOINGS. s-w.: Wed. & Fri. $.75 newsstand; $45.50/yr. mailed. 118 W. First St., Hinsdale, IL 60521. TEL 630-887-0600; FAX 630-887-9646; E-mail: doingsnews@aol.com; URL: http://www.thedoings.com. **Owner(s):** Doings Newspapers, Inc., 118 W. First St., Hinsdale, IL 60521. TEL 630-887-0600; FAX 630-887-9646; Ed. Pam Lannom; Pub. J. Peter Teschner; adv. contact: Jim Slonoff. photos; pub. size: 4 color photos/art; circ. 12,000(paid).

US
WESTERN SPRINGS DOINGS. s-w.: Wed. & Fri. $.75 newsstand; $45.50/yr. mailed. 118 W. First St., Hinsdale, IL 60521. TEL 630-887-0600; FAX 630-887-9646; E-mail: doingsnews@aol.com; URL: http://www.thedoings.com. **Owner(s):** Doings Newspapers, Inc., 118 W. First St., Hinsdale, IL 60521. TEL 630-887-0600; FAX 630-887-9646; Ed. Pam Lannom; Pub. J. Peter Teschner; adv. contact: James Slonoff. photos; pub. size: 4 color photos/art; circ. 11,000(paid).

US
WILLOWBROOK DOINGS. 1895. s-w.: Wed. & Fri. $.75 newsstand; $45.50/yr. mailed. 118 W. First St., Hinsdale, IL 60521. TEL 630-887-0600; FAX 630-887-9646; E-mail: doingsnews@aol.com; URL: http://www.thedoings.com. **Owner(s):** Doings Newspapers, Inc., 118 W. First St., Hinsdale, IL 60521. TEL 630-887-0600; FAX 630-887-9646; Ed. Pam Lannom; Pub. J. Peter Teschner; adv. contact: James Slonoff. photos; pub. size: tabloid; circ. 11,000(paid).

HOOPESTON

US ISSN 1076-4186
HOOPESTON CHRONICLE. 1872. s-w.: Tue. & Fri. $35/yr. in cy.; $50/yr. elsewhere. 308 E. Main St., Hoopeston, IL 60942. TEL 217-283-5111; FAX 217-283-5846. **Owner(s):** Twin States Publishing Co., Inc., 308 E. Main St., Hoopeston, IL 60942. TEL 217-283-5111; Nixon Newspapers, Inc., 33 W. Third St., P.O. Box 1149, Peru, IN. TEL 317-473-3091; Ed. Joann Gocking; Pub. Bette D. Schmid; adv. contact: Joy Neukomnn. pub. size: tabloid; circ. 2,200(paid).

HUNTLEY

US
HUNTLEY FARMSIDE, THE. 1960. Thu. $.25 newsstand; $8/yr. 11801 Main, Huntley, IL 60142. TEL 847-669-5621; FAX 847-669-5623. **Owner(s):** Suzanne L. Brown, 11801 Main, Huntley, IL 60142. TEL 847-669-5621; FAX 847-669-5623; Pub. Suzanne L. Brown; adv.: $6.50/SAU. photos; pub. size: tabloid; circ. 1,650(free & paid).

ILLIOPOLIS

US
ILLIOPOLIS SENTINEL. 1924. Thu. $.25 newsstand $15/yr.; $17.50 out of cy. P.O. Box 477, Illiopolis, IL 62539. TEL 217-486-7321. **Owner(s):** Frank Bell, P.O. Box 477, Illiopolis, IL 62539. TEL 217-486-7321; Pub. Frank Bell; adv. contact: Frank Bell. pub. size: tabloid; circ. 1,100(paid).

US
NIANTIC-HARRISTOWN COUNTY LINE OBSERVER. 1924. Fri. $.25 newsstand; $9.50/yr. in cy.; $10.50/out of cy. P.O. Box 477, Illiopolis, IL 62539. TEL 217-486-7321. **Owner(s):** Frank Bell, P.O. Box 477, Illiopolis, IL 62539. TEL 217-486-7321; Pub. Frank Bell; adv. contact: Frank Bell. pub. size: tabloid; circ. 400(paid).
Formerly: Illinois County Line Observer.

WEEKLY NEWSPAPERS

JERSEYVILLE

US

QUAD COUNTY EDITION, THE. 1989. s-w.: Tue. & Fri. $.50 newsstand; $13/4 wks. 201 N. State St., Jerseyville, IL 62052. TEL 618-498-5551; FAX 618-498-3964. **Owner(s):** Journal Register Co., 50 W. State St., 12th Fl., Trenton, NJ 08608; Pub. Tom Rice; adv. contact: Rick Jarvis. photos; pub. size: standard; circ. 10,000(paid).
Formerly: Tri-County Edition, News Journal.

US

TELEGRAPH-COUNTY EDITION. 1919. s-w.: Tue. & Fri. $.50 newsstand; $13/4 wks. subscription includes The Telegraph. 201 N. State St., Jerseyville, IL 62052. TEL 618-498-5551; FAX 618-498-3964. **Owner(s):** Telegraph, 111 E. Broadway, P.O. Box 278, Alton, IL 62002. TEL 618-463-2500; FAX 618-463-9829; Ed. Tom Wrausmann; Pub. Tom Rice; adv. contact: Doug Cooper. photos; pub. size: standard; circ. 9,660(paid).
Formerly: Tri-County Edition, News Journal.

JOLIET

US

FARMER'S WEEKLY REVIEW. 1921. Thu. $15/yr. 100 Manhattan Rd., Joliet, IL 60433. TEL 815-727-4811; FAX 815-727-5570. **Owner(s):** Patrick J. Cleary, 100 Manhattan Rd., Joliet, IL 60433. TEL 815-727-4811; Ed. Patrick J. Cleary; Pub. Patrick J. Cleary; adv. contact: Debbie Werner. bk.rev.; pub. size: tabloid; circ. 11,000(paid).

KINMUNDY

US

KINMUNDY EXPRESS. 1883. Wed. $.25; $12/yr. in state; $15/yr. elsewhere. 210 S. Madison, Kinmundy, IL 62854. TEL 618-547-3111. **Owner(s):** Rudolph Slane, 210 S. Madison, Kinmundy, IL 62854. TEL 618-547-3111; Pub. Rudolph Slane; adv. contact: Rudolph Slane. pub. size: broadsheet; circ. 990(paid).

LACON

US

LACON HOME JOURNAL. 1837. Thu. $.45 newsstand; $23/yr. 204 S. Washington St., Lacon, IL 61540. TEL 309-246-2865; FAX 309-246-3214. **Owner(s):** Marshall County Publishing Co., 204 S. Washington St., Lacon, IL 61540. TEL 309-246-2865; FAX 309-246-3214; Ed. William H. Sondag. adv.; pub. size: tabloid; circ. 2,400(paid).

LA FAYETTE

US

PRAIRIE SHOPPER, THE. 1981. Wed. $.50 newsstand; $24/yr. 101 Jefferson St., La Fayette, IL 61449. TEL 309-995-3877; FAX 309-995-3975. **Owner(s):** Lowell McKirgan, 101 Jefferson St., La Fayette, IL 61449. TEL 309-995-3877; Pub. Lowell McKirgan; adv.; pub. size: tabloid; circ. 5,840(free & paid).

US

PRAIRIE TIMES, THE. 1984. Wed. $18/yr. in state; $22/yr. out of state. 101 Jefferson St., La Fayette, IL 61449. TEL 309-995-3877; FAX 309-995-3975. **Owner(s):** Lowell McKirgan, 101 Jefferson St., La Fayette, IL 61449. TEL 309-995-3877; Pub. Lowell McKirgan; adv.; pub. size: tabloid; circ. 1,000(paid).

LA HARPE

US

HANCOCK COUNTY QUILL. 1926. Wed. $.50 newsstand; $17/yr. 103 E. Main St., La Harpe, IL 61450. TEL 217-659-3316; FAX 217-924-1212. **Owner(s):** Dessa Rodeffer, 702 Harmony St., Stronghurst, IL 61480. TEL 309-924-1558; FAX 309-924-1124; Belva Bell, 402 N. Broadway, Stronghurst, IL 61480. TEL 309-924-1263; FAX 309-924-1124; Ed. Belva Bell; Pub. Dessa Rodeffer; adv. contact: Shirley Linder. photos; bk.rev.; pub. size: tabloid; circ. 1,550(paid).

LAWRENCEVILLE

US

LAWRENCE COUNTY NEWS. 1842. Wed. $18/yr. 1209 State St., Lawrenceville, IL 62439. TEL 618-943-2331; FAX 618-943-3976. **Owner(s):** Larry L. Lewis, P.O. Box 559, Lawrenceville, IL 62439. TEL 618-943-2331; Pub. Larry L. Lewis; adv.; pub. size: standard; circ. 1,100(paid).

LEMONT

US

BOLINGBROOK METROPOLITAN. 1973. Thu. $.35 newsstand; $9.95/yr. in cy.; $15.95/yr. elsewhere. 223 Main St., Lemont, IL 60439. TEL 630-257-5300; FAX 630-257-5640. **Owner(s):** Press Publications, Inc., 112 S. York St., Elmhurst, IL 60126. TEL 708-834-0900; Ed. Karen Govera; Pub. Jack Crugar; pub. size: tabloid; circ. 17,550(paid).

US

DARIEN METROPOLITAN. 1974. Thu. $.35 newsstand; $9.95/yr. in cy.; $15.95/yr. elsewhere. 223 Main St., Lemont, IL 60439. TEL 630-257-5300; FAX 630-257-5640. **Owner(s):** Press Publications, Inc., 112 S. York St., Elmhurst, IL 60126. TEL 630-834-0900; Ed. Michael Helenthal; Pub. Jack Crugar; adv.; photos; pub. size: tabloid; circ. 17,550(paid).

US

LEMONT METROPOLITAN. 1975. Thu. $.35 newsstand; $9.95/yr. in cy.; $15.95/yr. elsewhere. 223 Main St., Lemont, IL 60439. TEL 630-257-5300; FAX 630-257-5640. **Owner(s):** Press Publications, Inc., 112 S. York St., Elmhurst, IL 60126. TEL 630-834-0900; Ed. Karen Govera; Pub. Jack Crugar; pub. size: tabloid; circ. 17,550(paid).

US

LEMONT REPORTER. 1990. Wed. $.50 newsstand; $1.50/mo. carrier. 111 Illinois St., Lemont, IL 60439. TEL 630-257-1090; FAX 630-257-1093. **Owner(s):** Reporter/Progress Newspapers, 922 Warren Ave., Downers Grove, IL 60515. TEL 708-969-0188; Ed. Stuart Sudak; Pub. P.K. Winter; adv. contact: Ed Rooney. photos; bk.rev.; pub. size: tabloid; circ. 7,875(free & paid).

US

NAPERVILLE METROPOLITAN. Thu. $.35 newsstand; $9.95/yr. in cy.; $15.95/yr. elsewhere. 223 Main St., Lemont, IL 60439. TEL 630-834-0900; FAX 708-257-5640. **Owner(s):** Press Publications, Inc., 112 S. York St., Elmhurst, IL 60126. TEL 708-834-0900; Ed. Bruce Douglas; Pub. Jack Crugar; adv. contact: Lynn Hill. pub. size: tabloid; circ. 20,000(paid).

US

ORLAND METROPOLITAN. Thu. $.35 newsstand; $9.95/yr. in cy.; $15.95 elsewhere. 223 Main St., Lemont, IL 60439. TEL 630-257-5300; FAX 630-257-5640. **Owner(s):** Press Publications, Inc., 112 S. York St., Elmhurst, IL 60126. TEL 708-834-0900; Ed. Karen Goveia; Pub. Jack Crugar; adv. contact: Vince Saputo. pub. size: tabloid; circ. 17,550(paid).

US

ROMEOVILLE METROPOLITAN. 1974. Thu. $.35 newsstand; $9.95/yr. in cy.; $15.95/yr. elsewhere. 223 Main St., Lemont, IL 60439. TEL 630-257-5300; FAX 630-257-5640. **Owner(s):** Press Publications, Inc., 112 S. York St., Elmhurst, IL 60126. TEL 708-834-0900; Ed. Karen Govera; Pub. Jack Crugar; pub. size: tabloid; circ. 17,550(paid).

LENA

US

NORTHWESTERN ILLINOIS FARMER. 1867. Wed. $18/yr. 119 W. Railroad, Lena, IL 61048-0536. TEL 815-369-2811; FAX 815-369-2816. **Owner(s):** Belvidere Daily Republican, Belvidere, IL; Stephenson Carroll Publishers, P.O. Box 536, Lena, IL 61048-0536. TEL 815-369-2811; Ed. Norman C. Templin; Pub. Norman C. Templin; adv.: $8/SAU. pub. size: tabloid; circ. 11,000(paid).

LEWISTOWN

US ISSN 1058-9619

FULTON DEMOCRAT. 1855. Wed. $.75 newsstand; $25/yr. in cy.; $36/yr. out of cy. 165 W. Lincoln, Lewistown, IL 61542. TEL 309-547-3055; FAX 309-543-6844. **Owner(s):** Martin Publishing Co., Inc., 219 W. Market St., Havana, IL 62644. TEL 309-543-3311; Ed. Ruth Lynn; Pub. Bob Martin; adv.; pub. size: broadsheet; circ. 3,200(paid).
Formerly: Lewistown-Fulton Democrat.

LINCOLNWOOD

US

ELMWOOD PARK-RIVER GROVE TIMES. 1946. Thu. $.50 newsstand; $11.95/yr. 7331 N. Lincoln Ave., Lincolnwood, IL 60646. TEL 847-329-2000; FAX 847-329-2060. **Owner(s):** Lerner Communications, Inc., 7331 N. Lincoln Ave., Lincolnwood, IL 60646. TEL 847-329-2000; FAX 847-329-2060; Ed. Brian Steele. adv.; pub. size: broadsheet; circ. 2,503(free & paid).

US

HARLEM-FOSTER-NORWOOD PARK-EDISON PARK TIMES. 1928. Wed. $.50 newsstand; $11.95/yr. 7331 N. Lincoln Ave., Lincolnwood, IL 60646. TEL 847-329-2000; FAX 847-320-2060. **Owner(s):** Lerner Communications, Inc., 7331 N. Lincoln Ave, Lincolnwood, IL 60646. TEL 847-329-2000; Ed. Leigh Hanlon. adv.; pub. size: broadsheet; circ. 4,143(free & paid).

US

HARLEM-IRVING TIMES. Wed. $.50 newsstand; $11.95/yr. 7331 N. Lincoln Ave., Lincolnwood, IL 60646. TEL 847-329-2000; FAX 847-329-2060. **Owner(s):** Lerner Communications, Inc., 7331 N. Lincoln Ave., Lincolnwood, IL 60646. TEL 847-329-2000; FAX 847-329-2060; Ed. Brian Steele. adv.; pub. size: broadsheet; circ. 4,457(free & paid).

10584 LINCOLNWOOD, IL

WEEKLY NEWSPAPERS

US
JEFFERSON PARK/PORTAGE PARK/BEL CRAGIN TIMES. Thu. $.50 newsstand; $11.95/yr. 7331 N. Lincoln Ave., Lincolnwood, IL 60646. TEL 847-329-2000; FAX 847-329-2060. **Owner(s):** Lerner Communications, Inc., 7331 Lincoln Ave., Lincolnwood, IL 60646. TEL 847-329-2000; FAX 847-329-2060; Ed. Brian Steele. adv.; pub. size: broadsheet; circ. 5,926(free & paid).
Formerly: Jefferson Portage Belmont Cragin.

US
LINCOLNWOOD LIFE. 1971. Thu. $.50 newsstand; $16.50/yr. 7331 N. Lincoln Ave., Lincolnwood, IL 60646. TEL 847-329-2000; FAX 847-329-2060. **Owner(s):** Lerner Communications, Inc., 7331 N. Lincoln Ave., Lincolnwood, IL 60646. TEL 847-329-2000; FAX 847-329-2060; Ed. Sarah Downey. adv.; pub. size: broadsheet; circ. 1,825(free & paid).

US ISSN 0194-9381
MORTON GROVE-NILES LIFE. Thu. $.50 newsstand; $16.50/yr. 7331 N. Lincoln Ave., Lincolnwood, IL 60646. TEL 847-329-2000; FAX 847-329-2060. **Owner(s):** Lerner Communications, Inc., 7331 N. Lincoln Ave., Lincolnwood, IL 60646. TEL 847-329-2000; FAX 847-329-2060; Ed. Sarah Downey. adv.; pub. size: broadsheet; circ. 2,106(free & paid).
Formerly: Morton Grove Life.

US
NEWS STAR. 1902. Wed. $.50 newsstand; $16.50/yr. 7331 N. Lincoln Ave., Lincolnwood, IL 60646. TEL 847-329-2000; FAX 847-329-2060. **Owner(s):** Lerner Communications, Inc., 7331 N. Lincoln Ave., Lincolnwood, IL 60646. TEL 847-329-2000; FAX 847-329-2060; Ed. Jack Bess. adv.; pub. size: broadsheet; circ. 13,711(free & paid).
Formerly: North Town News Star.

US
NILES LIFE. Thu. $.50 newsstand; $16.50/yr. 7331 N. Lincoln Ave., Lincolnwood, IL 60646. TEL 847-329-2000; FAX 847-329-2060. **Owner(s):** Lerner Communications, Inc., 7331 N. Lincoln Ave., Lincolnwood, IL 60646. TEL 847-329-2000; FAX 847-329-2061; Ed. Sara Downey; Pub. Lee Mortinson; adv. contact: Chuck Gekas. pub. size: broadsheet; circ. 907(paid).

US
NORRIDGE-HARWOOD HEIGHTS TIMES. Wed. $.50 newsstand; $11.95/yr. 7331 N. Lincoln Ave., Lincolnwood, IL 60646. TEL 847-329-2000; FAX 847-329-2060. **Owner(s):** Lerner Communications, Inc., 7331 N. Lincoln Ave., Lincolnwood, IL 60646. TEL 847-329-2000; FAX 847-329-2060; Ed. Brian Steele. adv.; pub. size: broadsheet; circ. 4,922(free & paid).
Formerly: Norridge-Harwood Heights-Norwood Park Times.

US
NORTH CENTER-LINCOLN BELMONT-LAKE VIEW BOOSTER. Wed. $.50 newsstand; $16.50/yr. 7331 N. Lincoln Ave., Lincolnwood, IL 60646. TEL 847-329-2000; FAX 847-329-2205. **Owner(s):** Lerner Communications, Inc., 7331 N. Lincoln Ave., Lincolnwood, IL 60053. TEL 847-329-2000; FAX 847-329-2075; Ed. Jack Bess. adv.; photos; bk.rev.; pub. size: broadsheet; circ. 7,664(free & paid).
Formerly: Booster, The.

US
ROGERS PARK/EDGEWATER NEWS/UPTOWN NEWS STAR. 1903. s-w.: Wed. & Thu. $.50 newsstand; $16.50/yr. 7331 N. Lincoln Ave., Lincolnwood, IL 60646. TEL 847-329-2000; FAX 847-329-2060. **Owner(s):** Lerner Communications, Inc., 7331 N. Lincoln Ave., Lincolnwood, IL 60646. TEL 847-329-2000; FAX 847-329-2060; Ed. Peter Strozz. adv. contact: Chuck Gekas. photos; bk.rev.; pub. size: broadsheet; circ. 5,888(paid); morning 16,073.

US ISSN 1060-0217
SKOKIE LIFE. Thu. $.50 newsstand; $16.50/yr. 7331 N. Lincoln Ave., Lincolnwood, IL 60646. TEL 847-329-2000; FAX 847-329-2060. **Owner(s):** Lerner Communications, Inc., 7331 N. Lincoln Ave., Lincolnwood, IL 60646. TEL 847-329-2000; FAX 847-329-2060; Ed. Sarah Downey. adv.; pub. size: broadsheet; circ. 6,297(free & paid).

US
SKYLINE. Thu. $24.50/yr. out of area. 7331 N. Lincoln Ave., Lincolnwood, IL 60646. TEL 847-329-2000; FAX 847-329-2060. **Owner(s):** Lerner Communications, Inc., 7331 N. Lincoln Ave., Lincolnwood, IL 60646. TEL 847-329-2000; FAX 847-329-2060; Ed. Peter L. Strazz. adv.; pub. size: broadsheet; circ. 28,503(free & paid).

LOMBARD

US
LOMBARDIAN, THE. 1957. Wed. $.45 newsstand. 613 S. Main St., Lombard, IL 60148. TEL 630-627-7010; FAX 630-627-7027; E-mail: lombardian@aol.com; URL: http://www.tccafe.com/lombardian. **Owner(s):** Scott MacKay, 613 S. Main St., Lombard, IL 60148. TEL 708-627-7010; Ed. Bonnie MacKay; Pub. Scott MacKay; adv. contact: Scott MacKay. photos; pub. size: tabloid; circ. 14,500(paid).
Formerly: Lombard Lombardian.

US
LOMBARDIAN VILLA PARK REVIEW. 1958. Wed. $.45 newsstand. 613 S. Main St., Lombard, IL 60148. TEL 630-627-7010; FAX 630-627-7027. **Owner(s):** Scott MacKay, 613 S. Main St., Lombard, IL 60148. TEL 708-627-7010; Ed. Bonnie MacKay; Pub. Scott MacKay; adv.; photos; pub. size: tabloid; circ. 11,500(paid).

LOVE PARK

US
DURAND GAZETTE. 1953. Wed. $.50 newsstand; $23/yr. home deliv. 2124 Harlem Rd., Ste. A, Love Park, IL 61111. TEL 815-624-6211; FAX 815-654-4857. **Owner(s):** Rock Valley Community Press, P.O. Box 15340, Rockford, IL 61132. TEL 815-248-2121; FAX 815-654-4857; Ed. Janine Nunes; Pub. Craig McMullin; adv. contact: Randy Johnson. photos; pub. size: tabloid; circ. 5,672(paid).

US
NEWS GAZETTE, THE. 1880. Wed. $.50 newsstand; $20/yr. carrier. 2124 Harlem Rd., Ste. A, Love Park, IL 61111. TEL 815-648-6211; FAX 815-654-4857. **Owner(s):** Rock Valley Community Press, P.O. Box 15340, Rockford, IL 61132. TEL 815-648-6211; Ed. Janine Nunes; Pub. Melanie Marshal; adv. contact: Randy Johnson. pub. size: tabloid; circ. 6,000(paid).

US
NORTH SUBURBAN HERALD. 1865. Wed. $23/yr. 2124 Harlem Rd., Ste. A, Love Park, IL 61111. TEL 815-624-6211; FAX 815-654-4857. **Owner(s):** Rock Valley Community Press, P.O. Box 15340, Rockford, IL 61132. TEL 815-877-4044; FAX 815-654-4857; Ed. Ann Tadstadt. adv. contact: Maxine Bayer. photos; bk.rev.; pub. size: tabloid; circ. 9,700(free & paid).

MARION

US
REVIEW, THE. 1990. Mon. free. P.O. Box 1111, Marion, IL 62959. TEL 618-997-2222; FAX 618-983-6227. **Owner(s):** Harry Olson, P.O. Box 1111, Marion, IL 62959. TEL 618-997-2222; Ed. Clayton Olsar; Pub. Harry Olson; adv. contact: Deborah Menley. adv.: $5/SAU. photos; pub. size: tabloid; circ. 9,000(free).
Formerly: Daily Review, The.

MASCOUTAH

US
CLINTON COUNTY NEWS. 1937. Thu. $.50 newsstand; $17.50/yr. in cy.; $20.50/yr. out of cy. 314 E. Church St., Mascoutah, IL 62258. TEL 618-588-7720; FAX 618-566-8283. **Owner(s):** Herald Publications, P.O. Drawer C, Mascoutah, IL 62258. TEL 618-566-8282; Ed. Gene Isbell; Pub. Greg Hoskins; adv.; pub. size: broadsheet;
Formerly: Clinton County Post.

US
FAIRVIEW HEIGHTS TRIBUNE. 1972. s-w.: Wed. & Thu. $.50 newsstand; $17.50/yr. in cy.; $20.50/yr. out of cy. 314 E. Church St., Mascoutah, IL 62258. TEL 618-398-8996; FAX 618-566-8283. **Owner(s):** Herald Publications, P.O. Drawer C, Mascoutah, IL 62258. TEL 618-566-8282; Ed. Gene Isbell; Pub. Greg Hoskins; adv.; pub. size: broadsheet; circ. 1,250(paid).

US
▼**LEBANON HERALD.** 1995. Thu. $.50 newsstand; $17.50 in cy.; $20.50 out of cy. 314 E. Church St., Mascoutah, IL 62258. TEL 618-588-7720; FAX 614-566-8283. **Owner(s):** Herald Publications, P.O. Drawer C, Mascoutah, IL 62258. TEL 618-566-8282; Pub. Greg Hoskins; adv.; pub. size: broadsheet; circ. 1,000(paid).

US
MASCOUTAH HERALD. 1885. Thu. $.50 newsstand; $17.50/yr. in cy.; $20.50/yr. out of cy. 314 E. Church St., Mascoutah, IL 62258. TEL 618-566-8282; FAX 618-566-8283. **Owner(s):** Herald Publications, P.O. Drawer C, Mascoutah, IL 62258. TEL 618-566-8282; Ed. Gene Isbell; Pub. Greg Hoskins; adv.; photos; bk.rev.; pub. size: broadsheet; circ. 2,400(paid).

MCLEANSBORO

US
MCLEANSBORO TIMES-LEADER. 1855. Wed. $.50 newsstand; $22/yr. in cy. 123 S. Jackson, McLeansboro, IL 62859. TEL 618-643-2387. **Owner(s):** Thomson Newspapers, Inc., One Thorn Run Ctr., Ste. 500, 1187 Thorn Run Rd. Ext., Coraopolis, PA 15108. TEL 412-262-7870; Ed. Spencer Cramer; Pub. Charles Deitz; adv. contact: Kathy Metcalf. pub. size: broadsheet; circ. 3,600(paid).

ULRICH'S INTERNATIONAL PERIODICALS DIRECTORY 1998

WEEKLY NEWSPAPERS

MIDLOTHIAN, IL 10585

MELROSE PARK

US
FRANKLIN PARK STAR-SENTINEL. 1924. Wed. $.45 newsstand; $16/yr. mailed. 1440 W. North Ave., Ste. 206, Melrose Park, IL 60160. TEL 708-345-1750; FAX 708-345-1795. **Owner(s):** Shannon Publications, Inc., P.O. Box 125, Fairbury, IL 61739. TEL 815-692-2366; Ed. David Roberts; Pub. David Roberts; pub. size: tabloid; circ. 17,000(controlled & paid).

US
MELROSE PARK STAR-SENTINEL. 1924. Wed. $.45 newsstand; $16/yr. mailed. 1440 W. North Ave., Ste. 206, Melrose Park, IL 60160. TEL 708-345-1750; FAX 708-345-1795. **Owner(s):** Shannon Publications, Inc., P.O. Box 125, Fairbury, IL 61739. TEL 815-692-2366; Ed. David Roberts; Pub. David Roberts; adv. contact: George Bellini. pub. size: tabloid; circ. 39,000(paid).

US
NORTHLAKE STAR-SENTINEL. 1924. Wed. $.45 newsstand; $16/yr. mailed. 1440 W. North Ave., Ste. 206, Melrose Park, IL 60160. TEL 708-345-1750; FAX 708-345-1795. **Owner(s):** Shannon Publications, Inc., P.O. Box 125, Fairbury, IL 61739. TEL 815-692-2366; Ed. David Roberts; Pub. David Roberts; pub. size: tabloid; circ. 17,000(controlled & paid).

US
PROVISO STAR-SENTINEL. 1924. Wed. $.45 newsstand; $16/yr. mailed. 1440 W. North Ave., Ste. 206, Melrose Park, IL 60160. TEL 708-345-1750; FAX 708-345-1795. **Owner(s):** Shannon Publications, Inc., P.O. Box 125, Fairbury, IL 61739. TEL 815-692-2366; Ed. David Roberts; Pub. David Roberts; pub. size: tabloid; circ. 17,000(controlled & paid).

MELVIN

US
FORD COUNTY PRESS. 1918. Thu. $14/yr. local; $15 yr. out of state. 115 W. Main St., Melvin, IL 60952. TEL 217-388-7721. **Owner(s):** Fred Thackeray, 115 W. Main St., Melvin, IL 60952; adv.; photos; pub. size: standard; circ. 1,050(controlled & paid).

MENDOTA

US
MENDOTA REPORTER. 1878. Wed. $.50 newsstand; $26/yr. mailed; $39.95/yr. out of state. 703 Illinois Ave., Mendota, IL 61342. TEL 815-539-9396; FAX 815-539-7862; E-mail: mendotareporter@softfarm.com; URL: http://www.softfarm.com/mendotareporter. **Owner(s):** Mendota Publishing Corp., P.O. Box 300, Mendota, IL 61342. TEL 815-539-9396; Pub. Tom Cross; adv. contact: Jeff Ohlendorf. adv.: $7.95/SAU. photos; pub. size: broadsheet; circ. 5,000(paid).

METAMORA

US
WASHBURN LEADER. 1892. Thu. $.50 newsstand; $15/yr. 214 E. Partridge, Metamora, IL 61548. TEL 309-367-2335; FAX 309-367-2616. **Owner(s):** Scott Hubbel, 214 E. Partridge, Metamora, IL 61548; Ed. Larry Schultz; Pub. Scott Hubbel; adv.; pub. size: broadsheet; circ. 925(paid).

METROPOLIS

US
METROPOLIS PLANET. 1865. Wed. $.50 newsstand; $20/yr. mailed local; $27/yr. elsewhere. 111 E. Fifth St., Metropolis, IL 62960-0820. TEL 618-524-2141; FAX 618-524-4727. **Owner(s):** Laura Harris, Richmond, KY; Ed. Clyde Wills. adv. contact: Angie Shelton. pub. size: broadsheet; circ. 5,900(paid).

MIDLOTHIAN

US
ALSIP EXPRESS. 1945. Thu. $.35 newsstand; $15/yr. in cy.; $18/yr. out of cy.; $24/yr. out of state. 3840 W. 147th St., Midlothian, IL 60445. TEL 708-388-2425; FAX 708-385-7811. **Owner(s):** Southwest Messenger Press, Inc., 3840 W. 147th St., Midlothian, IL 60445. TEL 708-388-2425; FAX 708-385-7811; Ed. Gerald Gibbons; Pub. W.H. Lysen; adv. contact: Don Talac. adv.: $712.72/pg. pub. size: tabloid; circ. 4,970(paid).

US
BEVERLY NEWS. 1948. Thu. $.35 newsstand; $15/yr. in cy.; $18/yr. out of cy. 3840 W. 147th St., Midlothian, IL 60445. TEL 708-388-2425; FAX 708-385-7811. **Owner(s):** Southwest Messenger Press, Inc., 3840 W. 147th St., Midlothian, IL 60445. TEL 708-388-2425; Ed. Gerald Gibbons; Pub. W.H. Lysen; adv. contact: Don Talac. adv.: $712.32/pg. pub. size: tabloid; circ. 4,190(paid).
Formerly: Chicago Beverly News.

US
BRIDGEVIEW INDEPENDENT. 1962. Wed. $.35 newsstand; $45/yr. 3840 W. 147th St., Midlothian, IL 60445. TEL 708-388-2425; FAX 708-385-7811. **Owner(s):** Southwest Messenger Press, Inc., 3840 W. 147th St., Midlothian, IL 60445. TEL 708-388-2425; Ed. Gerald Gibbons; Pub. W.H. Lysen; adv. contact: Don Talac. adv.: $712.32/pg. pub. size: tabloid; circ. 2,730(paid).

US
BURBANK-STICKNEY INDEPENDENT. 1962. Thu. $.35 newsstand; $15/yr. in cy.; $18/yr. out of cy.; $24/yr. out of state. 3840 W. 147th St., Midlothian, IL 60445. TEL 708-388-2425; FAX 708-385-7811. **Owner(s):** Southwest Messenger Press, Inc., 3840 W. 147th St., Midlothian, IL 60445. TEL 708-388-2425; Ed. Gerald Gibbons; Pub. W.H. Lysen; adv. contact: Don Talac. adv.: $712.32/pg. pub. size: tabloid; circ. 6,310(paid).

US
CHICAGO RIDGE CITIZEN. 1962. Thu. $.35 newsstand; $15/yr. in cy.; $18/yr. out of cy.; $24/yr. out of state. 3840 W. 147th St., Midlothian, IL 60445. TEL 708-388-2425; FAX 708-385-7811. **Owner(s):** Southwest Messenger Press, Inc., 3840 W. 147th St., Midlothian, IL 60445. TEL 708-388-2425; Ed. Gerald Gibbons; Pub. W.H. Lysen; adv. contact: Don Talac. adv.: $712.32/pg. pub. size: tabloid; circ. 2,910(paid).

US
EVERGREEN PARK COURIER. 1930. Thu. $.35 newsstand; $15/yr. in cy.; $18/yr. out of cy.; $24/yr. out of state. 3840 W. 147th St., Midlothian, IL 60445. TEL 708-388-2425; FAX 708-385-7811. **Owner(s):** Southwest Messenger Press, Inc., 3840 W. 147th St., Midlothian, IL 60445. TEL 708-388-2425; Ed. Gerald Gibbons; Pub. W.H. Lysen; adv. contact: Don Talac. adv.: $712.32/pg. pub. size: tabloid; circ. 4,370(paid).

US
HICKORY HILLS CITIZEN. 1958. Thu. $.35 newsstand; $15/yr. in cy.; $18/yr. out of cy.; $24/yr. out of state. 3840 W. 147th St., Midlothian, IL 60445. TEL 708-388-2425; FAX 708-385-7811. **Owner(s):** Southwest Messenger Press, Inc., 3840 W. 147th St., Midlothian, IL 60445. TEL 708-388-2425; Ed. Gerald Gibbons; Pub. W.H. Lysen; adv. contact: Don Talac. adv.: $712.32/pg. pub. size: tabloid; circ. 3,430(paid).

US
MIDLOTHIAN-BREMEN MESSENGER. 1930. Thu. $.35 newsstand; $15/yr. in cy.; $18/yr. out of cy.; $24/yr. out of state. 3840 W. 147th St., Midlothian, IL 60445. TEL 708-388-2425; FAX 708-385-7811. **Owner(s):** Southwest Messenger Press, Inc., 3840 W. 147th St., Midlothian, IL 60445. TEL 708-388-2425; Ed. Gerald Gibbons; Pub. W.H. Lysen; adv. contact: Don Talac. pub. size: tabloid; circ. 10,740(paid).

US
MOUNT GREENWOOD EXPRESS. 1945. Thu. $.35 newsstand; $15/yr. in cy.; $18/yr. out of cy.; $24/yr. out of state. 3840 W. 147th St., Midlothian, IL 60445. TEL 708-388-2425; FAX 708-385-7811. **Owner(s):** Southwest Messenger Press, Inc., 3840 W. 147th St., Midlothian, IL 60445. TEL 708-388-2425; Ed. Gerald Gibbons; Pub. W.H. Lysen; adv. contact: Don Talac. adv.: $712.32/pg. pub. size: tabloid; circ. 7,320(paid).

US
OAK LAWN INDEPENDENT. 1930. Thu. $.35 newsstand; $15/yr. in cy.; $18/yr. out of cy.; $24/yr. out of state. 3840 W. 147th St., Midlothian, IL 60445. TEL 708-388-2425; FAX 708-385-7811. **Owner(s):** Southwest Messenger Press, Inc., 3840 W. 147th St., Midlothian, IL 60445. TEL 708-388-2425; Ed. Gerald Gibbons; Pub. W.H. Lysen; adv. contact: Don Talac. adv.: $712.13/pg. pub. size: tabloid; circ. 11,930(paid).

US
ORLAND TOWNSHIP MESSENGER. 1980. Thu. $.35 newsstand; $15/yr. in cy.; $18/yr. out of cy.; $24/yr. out of state. 3840 W. 147th St., Midlothian, IL 60445. TEL 708-388-2425; FAX 708-385-7811. **Owner(s):** Southwest Messenger Press, Inc., 3840 W. 147th St., Midlothian, IL 60445. TEL 708-388-2425; Ed. Gerald Gibbons; Pub. W.H. Lysen; adv. contact: Don Talac. adv.: $712.32/pg. pub. size: tabloid; circ. 3,660(paid).

US
PALOS CITIZEN. 1958. Thu. $.35 newsstand; $15/yr. in cy.; $18/yr. out of cy.; $24/yr. out of state. 3840 W. 147th St., Midlothian, IL 60445. TEL 708-388-2425; FAX 708-385-7811. **Owner(s):** Southwest Messenger Press, Inc., 3840 W. 147th St., Midlothian, IL 06045. TEL 708-388-2425; Ed. Gerald Gibbons; Pub. W.H. Lysen; adv. contact: Don Talac. adv.: $712.32/pg. pub. size: tabloid; circ. 4,720(paid).

Weeklies

MIDLOTHIAN, IL

US
SCOTTSDALE-ASHBURN INDEPENDENT. 1962. Thu. $.35 newsstand; $15/yr. in cy.; $18/yr. out of cy.; $24 out of state. 3840 W. 147th St., Midlothian, IL 60445. TEL 708-388-2425. **Owner(s):** Southwest Messenger Press, Inc., 3840 W. 147th St., Midlothian, IL 60445. TEL 708-388-2425; Ed. Gerald Gibbons; Pub. W.H. Lysen; adv. contact: Don Talac. adv.: $712.32/pg. pub. size: tabloid; circ. 5,960(paid).

US
WORTH CITIZEN. 1930. Thu. $.35 newsstand; $15/yr. in cy.; $18/yr. out of cy.; $24/yr. out of state. 3840 W. 147th St., Midlothian, IL 60445. TEL 708-388-2425; FAX 708-385-7811. **Owner(s):** Southwest Messenger Press, Inc., 3840 W. 147th St., Midlothian, IL 60445. TEL 708-385-2425; Ed. Gerald Gibbons; Pub. W.H. Lysen; adv. contact: Don Talac. adv.: $712.32/pg. pub. size: tabloid; circ. 2,810(paid).

MINIER

US
OLYMPIA REVIEW. 1967. Tue. $.35 newsstand; $22/yr. 102 S. Main, Minier, IL 61759. TEL 309-392-2414; FAX 309-392-2169. **Owner(s):** Rickard Publishing Co., P.O. Box 586, Manito, IL 61546. TEL 309-968-6705; Ed. Joe Rickard. adv.; pub. size: broadsheet; circ. 6,950(paid).

MINONK

US
MINONK NEWS DISPATCH. Thu. $.75 newsstand; $25/yr. local; $33/yr. out of state. 224 E. Fifth, Minonk, IL 61760. TEL 309-432-2505; FAX 309-432-2506. **Owner(s):** Illinois Valley Press, 301 W. Washington, Normal, IL 61761. TEL 309-829-9411; Ed. Philip Wright. adv.; pub. size: broadsheet; circ. 825(free & paid).

MONTICELLO

US
PIATT COUNTY JOURNAL-REPUBLICAN. 1856. Wed. $.45 newsstand; $19.60/yr. in cy.; $20.70/yr. out of cy. 118 E. Washington St., Monticello, IL 61856. TEL 217-762-2511; FAX 217-352-1722. **Owner(s):** East Central Communications, Inc., 1332 Harmon Dr., Rantoul, IL 61866. TEL 217-892-9613; Pub. Dennis Kaster; pub. size: broadsheet; circ. 3,850(paid).
Formerly: Monticello Piatt County Journal-Republican.

MORTON

US
EAST PEORIA COURIER. 1927. Wed. free deliv.; $.50 newsstand. 100 Detroit Ave., Morton, IL 61550. TEL 309-676-2511; FAX 309-266-7385. **Owner(s):** Fleming Publishing Co., 100 Detroit Ave., P.O. Box 250, Morton, IL 61550. TEL 309-263-2211; Ed. Jill Peterson; Pub. Ted J. Fleming; pub. size: broadsheet; circ. 10,500(free & paid).

US
TAZEWELL NEWS. 1888. Wed. $.50 newsstand; $39.90/yr. carrier. 100 Detroit Ave., Morton, IL 61550. TEL 309-263-2211; FAX 309-266-7385. **Owner(s):** Fleming Publishing Co., 100 Detroit Ave., P.O. Box 250, Morton, IL 61550. TEL 309-263-2211; Ed. Sheryl Prumley. adv.; photos; pub. size: broadsheet; circ. 9,055(paid).
Formerly: Morton-Tazewell News.

US
WASHINGTON REPORTER. 1840. Wed. free; $.50 newsstand. 100 Detroit Ave., Morton, IL 61550. TEL 309-676-2511; FAX 309-266-7385. **Owner(s):** Fleming Publishing Co., 100 Detroit Ave., Morton, IL 61550. TEL 309-444-2513; FAX 309-266-7385; Ed. Jason King; Pub. Ted J. Fleming; adv.; photos; pub. size: standard; circ. evening 6,000(controlled & free). **Wire Service(s):** CNS.

MOUNDS

US
PULASKI ENTERPRISE. 1861. Wed. $.35 newsstand; $13/yr. in cy.; $20.80/yr. out of cy.; $18.20/yr. out of state. 315 First St., Mounds, IL 62964-0459. TEL 618-745-6267. **Owner(s):** Edward A. Taylor, Jr., P.O. Box 459, Mounds, IL 62964. TEL 618-745-6267; Ed. Lottie M. Taylor; Pub. Edward A. Taylor, Jr.; adv.: $14.40/SAU. photos; pub. size: broadsheet; circ. 4,260(paid).

MT. OLIVE

US
MT. OLIVE HERALD, THE. 1880. Thu. $.35 newsstand; $14/yr. local; $15/yr. in cy.; $18/yr. out of state. 102 E. Main, Mt. Olive, IL 62069. TEL 217-999-3941; FAX 217-999-5105. **Owner(s):** John M. Galer, 10 Wildwood, Hillsboro, IL 62049. TEL 217-532-3933; Ed. Linda Hasquin; Pub. John M. Galer; adv.; photos; pub. size: tabloid; circ. 1,650(paid).

MT. STERLING

US
DEMOCRAT-MESSAGE. 1848. Tue. $.50 newsstand; $17/yr. in cy.; $26/yr. elsewhere. 123 W. Main St., Mt. Sterling, IL 62353. TEL 217-773-3371; FAX 217-773-3369. **Owner(s):** Coulson Publications, 123 W. Main St., Mt. Sterling, IL 62353. TEL 217-773-3371; Ed. Warren Coulson. adv. contact: Pat Webel. pub. size: tabloid; circ. 10,000(paid).

NAPERVILLE

US
LISLE SUN. 1938. s-w.: Wed. & Fri. $.35 newsstand; $22/yr. mailed. 9 W. Jackson, Naperville, IL 60540. TEL 630-968-8200; FAX 630-355-2432. **Owner(s):** Copley Press, Inc., 7776 Ivanhoe Ave., La Jolla, CA 92037. TEL 619-454-0411; adv. contact: Rick Taden. pub. size: tabloid; circ. 5,500(paid). **Wire Service(s):** AP, CNS.

US
NAPERVILLE SUN. 1935. 3/wk.: Sun., Wed., Fri. $.50 newsstand; $36/yr. local. 9 W. Jackson, Naperville, IL 60540. TEL 630-355-0063; FAX 630-416-5163. **Owner(s):** Copley Press, Inc., 7776 Ivanhoe Ave., LaJolla, CA 92037. TEL 619-454-0411; adv. contact: Rick Taden. pub. size: tabloid; circ. 45,000(paid). **Wire Service(s):** AP, CNS.

US
WHEATON SUN. 1910. s-w.: Wed. & Fri. $.35 newsstand; $30/yr. 9 W. Jackson St., Naperville, IL 60566-0269. TEL 630-355-8012; FAX 630-355-6703. **Owner(s):** Copley Press, Inc., 7776 Ivanhoe La, Jolla, CA 92037. TEL 619-454-0411; adv. contact: Rick Taden. pub. size: tabloid; circ. 4,300(paid). **Wire Service(s):** AP, CNS.
Formerly: Wheaton Journal.

WEEKLY NEWSPAPERS

NASHVILLE

US
NASHVILLE NEWS, THE. 1934. Wed. $.40 newsstand; $17.50/yr. Washington, Perry, & Jefferson cys.; $21/yr. elsewhere. 211 W. St. Louis St., Nashville, IL 62263-0047. TEL 618-327-3411; FAX 618-327-3299. **Owner(s):** Richard & Constance Tomaszewski, 211 W. St. Louis St., Nashville, IL 62263-0047. TEL 618-327-3411; FAX 618-327-3299; Ed. Richard Tomaszewski. adv.; pub. size: broadsheet; circ. 5,500(paid).

NEWTON

US
NEWTON PRESS-MENTOR. 1862. s-w.: Mon. & Thu. $.30 newsstand; $25/yr. in cy. & adjoining cy.; $33.50/yr. in state; $34/yr. out of state. 101 S. Jackson St., Newton, IL 62448-9998. TEL 618-783-2324; FAX 618-783-2325. **Owner(s):** Jasper County Publishing, Co., 101 S. Jackson St., Newton, IL 62448-9998. TEL 618-783-2324; FAX 618-783-2325; Ed. Don Hecke; Pub. Don Hecke; adv. contact: Richard Bayler. pub. size: broadsheet; circ. 4,000(paid).

NILES

US
BUGLE, THE. 1957. s-w.: Thu. & Sat. $.50 newsstand; $26/yr. 8746 N. Shermer Rd., Niles, IL 60714. TEL 847-966-3900; FAX 847-966-0198. **Owner(s):** Besser Publications, 8746 N. Shermer Rd., Niles, IL 60714. TEL 847-966-3900; Ed. Marti Kaz; Pub. Robert Besser; adv.; pub. size: tabloid; circ. 42,000(controlled & paid). **Wire Service(s):** AP.
Formerly: Niles Bugle.

NOKOMIS

US
NOKOMIS FREE PRESS-PROGRESS. 1877. Wed. $.35 newsstand; $16.50/yr. cy. 112 W. State St., Nokomis, IL 62075. TEL 217-563-2115; FAX 217-563-7464. **Owner(s):** Free Press, Inc., 112 W. State St., Nokomis, IL 62075. TEL 217-563-2115; FAX 217-563-7464; Ed. Fred Christner; Pub. Thomas J. Phillips, Jr.; adv. contact: Cynthia Hayes. pub. size: broadsheet; circ. 2,700(paid).

O'FALLON

US
O'FALLON PROGRESS. 1895. Thu. $.50 newsstand; $20/yr. 612 E. State St., O'Fallon, IL 62269-0970. TEL 618-632-3643; FAX 618-632-6438. **Owner(s):** Walt Disney Co., 500 S. Buena Vista St., Burbank, CA 91521. TEL 818-560-5300; Ed. Jennifer Gammage; Pub. Cecil Ross; adv. contact: Caya Aufiero. adv.: $9.50/SAU. photos; pub. size: broadsheet; circ. 4,000(free & paid).

OAK BROOK

US
INDIAN HEAD PARK CITIZEN. 1947. s-w.: Wed. & Sat. $29/yr. 709 Enterprise Dr., Oak Brook, IL 60521-8814. TEL 630-368-1100; FAX 630-368-1188. **Owner(s):** Life Printing & Publishing Co., Inc., 2601 S. Harlem Ave., Berwyn, IL 60402. TEL 708-484-1234; Pub. Jack Kubik; adv. contact: Peter Manning. pub. size: broadsheet; circ. 32,500(free & paid).

US

WEEKLY NEWSPAPERS

SUBURBAN LIFE CITIZEN. 1949. s-w.: Wed. & Sat. $.75 newsstand; $29/yr. carrier. 709 Enterprise, Oak Brook, IL 60521. TEL 630-368-8847; FAX 630-368-1188. **Owner(s):** Life Printing & Publishing Co., Inc., 2601 S. Harlem Ave., Berwyn, IL 60402. TEL 630-484-1234; Ed. Bill Conkis; Pub. Jack R. Kubik; adv.; pub. size: broadsheet; circ. 29,295(paid).
   Formerly: La Grange Countryside Citizen.

US

SUBURBAN LIFE GRAPHIC. 1949. s-w.: Wed. & Sat. $.75 newsstand; $29/yr. carrier; $38/yr. mailed. 709 Enterprise, Oak Brook, IL 60521. TEL 630-368-1100; FAX 630-368-1199. **Owner(s):** Lake Printing & Publishing Co., Inc., 2601 S. Harlem Ave., Berwyn, IL 60402. TEL 630-484-1234; Ed. Joseph DeRosier; Pub. Jack R. Kubik; pub. size: broadsheet; circ. 34,000(paid).

OAK PARK

US

AUSTIN WEEKLY NEWS. 1987. Thu. free newsstand; $37.50/yr. 141 S. Oak Park Ave., Oak Park, IL 60302-2972. TEL 773-626-6332; FAX 773-237-9351. **Owner(s):** Wednesday Journal, Inc., 141 S. Oak Park Ave., Oak Park, IL 60302. TEL 708-524-8300; FAX 708-524-0447; Ed. Alonda Mccree; Pub. Don Haley; adv. contact: Deborah Sawyer. photos; bk.rev.; pub. size: tabloid; circ. 18,000(free).

US

ELM LEAVES. 1952. Wed. $1 newsstand; $18.95/yr. 1148 Westgate, Oak Park, IL 60301. TEL 708-383-3200; FAX 708-383-3678. **Owner(s):** Pioneer Press, Inc., 3701 W. Lake Ave., Glenview, IL 60025. TEL 847-486-9200; Ed. Rick Behren; Pub. Thomas Neri; adv. contact: Susan Karol. pub. size: tabloid; circ. 4,000(paid).

US

FOREST LEAVES. 1906. Wed. $1 newsstand.; $18.95/yr. in cy.; $41.95/yr. out of cy. 1148 Westgate, Oak Park, IL 60301. TEL 708-383-3200; FAX 708-383-3628. **Owner(s):** Pioneer Press, Inc., 3701 W. Lake Ave., Glenview, IL 60025. TEL 847-486-9200; Ed. Randy Blaser; Pub. Thomas Neri; adv. contact: Tom Conradi. pub. size: tabloid; circ. 2,600(paid).

US

FRANKLIN PARK HERALD-JOURNAL, THE. 1971. Wed. $1 newsstand; $18.95/yr. 1148 Westgate, Oak Park, IL 60301. TEL 708-383-3200; FAX 708-383-3678. **Owner(s):** Pioneer Press, Inc., 3701 W. Lake Ave., Glenview, IL 60025. TEL 847-486-9200; Ed. Rick Behren; Pub. Tom Neri; pub. size: tabloid; circ. 4,127(paid).

US

MAYWOOD HERALD. Wed. $1 newsstand; $18.95/yr. 1148 Westgate, Oak Park, IL 60301. TEL 708-848-9710; FAX 708-383-3678. **Owner(s):** Pioneer Press, Inc., 3701 W. Lake Ave., Glenview, IL 60025. TEL 847-486-9200; Ed. Tom Ganz; Pub. Thomas Neri; adv. contact: Susan Karol. pub. size: tabloid; circ. 3,200(paid).

US

MELROSE PARK HERALD. 1902. Wed. $1 newsstand; $18.95/yr. in cy.; $41.95/yr. out of cy. 1148 Westgate, Oak Park, IL 60301. TEL 708-383-3200; FAX 708-383-3678. **Owner(s):** Pioneer Press, Inc., 3701 W. Lake Ave., Glenview, IL 60025. TEL 847-486-9200; Ed. Greg Canfield; Pub. Thomas Neri; adv. contact: Tom Conradi. pub. size: broadsheet; circ. 2,264(paid).

US

OAK LEAVES, THE. 1878. Wed. $1 newsstand; $18.95/yr. in cy.; $41.95/yr. out of cy. 1148 Westgate, Oak Park, IL 60301. TEL 708-383-3200; FAX 708-383-3678. **Owner(s):** Pioneer Press, Inc., 3701 W. Lake Ave., Glenview, IL 60025. TEL 847-486-9200; Ed. Randy Blaser; Pub. Thomas Neri; adv. contact: Tom Conradi. pub. size: tabloid; circ. 11,941(paid).
   Formerly: Forest Park News.

US

WEDNESDAY JOURNAL OF OAK PARK & RIVER FOREST. 1980. Wed. $.50 newsstand; $20/yr. 141 S. Oak Park Ave., Oak Park, IL 60302. TEL 708-524-8300; FAX 708-524-0447; E-mail: wjinc@aol.com; URL: http://www.wjinc.com. **Owner(s):** Wednesday Journal, Inc., 141 S. Oak Park Ave., Oak Park, IL 60302. TEL 708-524-8300; Ed. Dan Haley. adv.; photos; pub. size: tabloid; circ. 11,500(paid).

US

WESTCHESTER HERALD. 1986. Wed. $1 newsstand; $18.95/yr. in cy.; $41.95/yr. out of cy. 1148 Westgate, Oak Park, IL 60301. TEL 708-383-3200; FAX 708-383-3678. **Owner(s):** Pioneer Press, Inc., 3701 W. Lake Ave., Glenview, IL 60025. TEL 847-486-9200; Ed. Greg Canfield; Pub. Thomas Neri; adv. contact: Tom Conradi. pub. size: broadsheet; circ. 2,500(paid).

US

WEST PROVISO HERALD. Wed. $1 newsstand; $17.95/yr. 1148 Westgate, Oak Park, IL 60301. TEL 708-383-3200; FAX 708-383-3678. **Owner(s):** Pioneer Press, Inc., 3701 W. Lake Ave., Glenview, IL 60025. TEL 847-486-9200; Ed. Tom Ganz; Pub. Thomas Neri; adv. contact: Susan Karol. pub. size: tabloid; circ. 2,700(paid).

OREGON

US

OGLE COUNTY LIFE. 1968. Mon. free. 200 N. Third St., Ste. B, Oregon, IL 61061. TEL 815-732-2156; FAX 815-732-6154. **Owner(s):** News Media, Corp., 211 E State, Rte. 38, Rochelle, IL 61068. TEL 815-562-4171; Ed. Doug Oleson; Pub. Tom Cross; adv.; pub. size: tabloid; circ. 13,000(free).

ORION

US

ORION GAZETTE. 1992. Thu. $.75 newsstand; $31/yr. 250 Tenth Ave., Orion, IL 61273. TEL 309-526-8085. **Owner(s):** Terry Newspapers, Inc., 108 W. First St., Geneseo, IL 61254. TEL 309-944-2119; Ed. Mindy Carls; Pub. Thomas Terry; adv. contact: Linda Venable. pub. size: broadsheet; circ. 1,671(paid).

OTTAWA

US

THRIF-T-NIKEL COMMUNITY SHOPPING GUIDE. 1973. Wed. free local; $52/yr. elsewhere mailed. 801 Canal St., Ottawa, IL 61350. TEL 815-433-5595; FAX 815-433-5596. **Owner(s):** Steve Gray & Associates, Ltd., P.O. Box 279, Ottawa, IL 61350. TEL 815-433-5595; Ed. Lillian Fricke; Pub. Stephen F. Gray; adv.; pub. size: tabloid; circ. 19,000(controlled & paid).
   Formerly: Thrif-T-Nikel Weekly Newspaper.

US

TOWN & COUNTRY WEEKLY. 1979. Wed. $.25 newsstand; $50/yr. 801 Canal St., Ottawa, IL 61350. TEL 815-433-5595; FAX 815-433-5596. **Owner(s):** Steve Gray & Associates Ltd., P.O. Box 279, Ottawa, IL 61350. TEL 815-433-5595; Ed. Linda Walter. adv.; photos; pub. size: tabloid; circ. 19,000(controlled & paid).

PALOS HEIGHTS

US

PALOS HILLS-HICKORY HILLS. 1960. Thu. $.50 newsstand; $25/yr. 12247 S. Harlem Ave., Palos Heights, IL 60463. TEL 708-448-6161; FAX 708-448-4012. **Owner(s):** Regional Publishing Corp., 12243 S. Harlem Ave., Palos Heights, IL 60463. TEL 708-448-4000; Ed. Jack Murray. adv. contact: Carol McLaughlin. bk.rev.; pub. size: broadsheet; circ. 18,545(free & paid).

US

REGIONAL NEWS. 1941. Thu. $.75 newsstand; $30/yr. 12243 S. Harlem Ave., Palos Heights, IL 60463-0932. TEL 708-448-6161. **Owner(s):** Regional Publishing Corp., 12243 S. Harlem Ave., Palos Heights, IL 60463. TEL 708-448-4000; Ed. Rich Parmeter. adv. contact: Marilyn Shaw. pub. size: broadsheet; circ. 18,858(paid).

US

REPORTER NEWSPAPER, THE. 1960. Wed. $.50 newsstand; $25/yr. 12247 S. Harlem Ave., Palos Heights, IL 60463-1431. TEL 708-448-6161. **Owner(s):** Regional Publishing Co., 12243 S. Harlem Ave., Palos Heights, IL 60463. TEL 708-448-4000; Ed. Jack Murray; Pub. Charles Richards; adv. contact: Carol McLaughlin. pub. size: broadsheet; circ. 18,402(paid).

PANA

US

PANA NEWS-PALLADIUM. 1869. s-w.: Mon. & Thu. $.50 newsstand; $28/yr. in cy.; $33/yr. in state; $35/yr. out of state. 205 S. Locust St., Pana, IL 62557. TEL 217-562-2113; FAX 217-562-3729. **Owner(s):** Pana News, Inc., 205 S. Locust, Pana, IL 62557. TEL 217-562-2113; FAX 217-562-3729; Ed. Tom Latonis. adv. contact: Patricia Spracklen. photos; pub. size: broadsheet; circ. 4,700(paid).

PARK RIDGE

US   ISSN 0745-8681

DES PLAINES TIMES. 1885. Thu. $.50 newssatnd; $18.95/yr. 130 S. Prospect Ave., Park Ridge, IL 60068. TEL 847-696-3133; FAX 847-696-3229. **Owner(s):** Pioneer Press, Inc., 3701 W. Lake Ave., Glenview, IL 60025. TEL 847-486-9200; Ed. Carroll Salman; Pub. Thomas Neri; adv. contact: John Wisler. pub. size: broadsheet; circ. 12,000(paid).

US   ISSN 0895-0105

EDGEBROOK TIMES REVIEW. 1985. Thu. $.50 newsstand; $18.95/yr. in cy. 130 S. Prospect Ave., Park Ridge, IL 60068. TEL 847-696-3133. **Owner(s):** Pioneer Press, Inc., 3701 W. Lake Ave., Glenview, IL 60025. TEL 847-846-9200; Ed. Anne Lunde; Pub. Thomas Neri; adv.; pub. size: broadsheet; circ. 2,194(paid).

PARK RIDGE, IL

US
EDISON-NORWOOD TIMES REVIEW. 1937. Thu. $.50 newsstand; $18.95/yr. in cy. 130 S. Prospect Ave., Park Ridge, IL 60068. TEL 847-696-3133; FAX 847-696-3229. **Owner(s):** Pioneer Press, Inc., 3701 W. Lake Ave., Glen View, IL 60025. TEL 847-486-9200; Ed. Tom Ganz; Pub. Thomas Neri; adv.; photos; pub. size: broadsheet; circ. 9,300(controlled & paid).

US   ISSN 0747-2595
MOUNT PROSPECT TIMES. 1980. Thu. $.50 newsstand; $33.15/yr. 130 S. Prospect Ave., Park Ridge, IL 60068. TEL 847-696-3133; FAX 847-696-3229. **Owner(s):** Pioneer Press, Inc., 3701 W. Lake Ave., Glenview, IL 60025. TEL 847-846-9200; Ed. Carroll Salman; Pub. Thomas Neri; adv. contact: John Wisler. pub. size: broadsheet; circ. 5,338(paid).

US   ISSN 0895-0121
NILES HERALD SPECTATOR. 1986. Wed. $1 newsstand; $18.95/yr. in cy. 130 S. Prospect Ave., Park Ridge, IL 60068. TEL 847-696-3133; FAX 847-696-3229. **Owner(s):** Pioneer Press, Inc., 3701 W. Lake Ave., Glen View, IL 60025. TEL 847-486-9200; Ed. Tom Ganz; Pub. Thomas Neri; adv. contact: John Wisler. pub. size: broadsheet; circ. 5,158(paid).

US   ISSN 0885-7814
NORRIDGE-HARWOOD HEIGHTS NEWS. 1985. Thu. $1 newsstand; $15.95/yr. in cy. 130 S. Prospect Ave., Park Ridge, IL 60068. TEL 847-696-3133; FAX 847-696-3229. **Owner(s):** Sun Times, Inc., 401 N. Wabash Ave., Chicago, IL 60611. TEL 312-321-3000; Ed. Kevin Beese; Pub. Thomas Neri; adv. contact: Tom Conradi. pub. size: tabloid; circ. 2,900(paid).

US   ISSN 0744-5385
PARK RIDGE HERALD ADVOCATE. 1933. Thu. $1 newsstand; $24.95/yr. 130 S. Prospect Ave., Park Ridge, IL 60068. TEL 847-696-3133; FAX 847-696-3229. **Owner(s):** Pioneer Press, Inc., 3701 W. Lake Ave., Glenview, IL 60025. TEL 847-486-9200; Ed. Tom Ganz; Pub. Thomas Neri; adv.; pub. size: tabloid; circ. 7,000(paid).

US   ISSN 0895-0113
ROSEMONT TIMES. 1981. Wed. $.50 newsstand; $18.95/yr. in cy. 130 S. Prospect Ave., Park Ridge, IL 60068. TEL 847-696-3133; FAX 847-696-3229. **Owner(s):** Pioneer Press, Inc., 3701 W. Lake Ave., Glen View, IL 60025. TEL 847-486-9200; Ed. Tom Ganz; Pub. Thomas Neri; adv.; pub. size: broadsheet; circ. 1,506(paid).

PAXTON

US
LODA TIMES. 1888. Wed. $.35 newsstand; $20/yr. in cy.; $25/yr. out of cy. 218 N. Market St., Paxton, IL 60957. TEL 217-379-4313; FAX 217-379-3104. **Owner(s):** Paxton Printing Co., 218 N. Market St., Paxton, IL 60957. TEL 217-379-4313; Ed. Bob Maney; Pub. Paul E. Anderson; adv. contact: Toni Swan. pub. size: broadsheet; circ. 400(paid).

US
RECORD TIMES, THE. 1865. Wed. $.35 newsstand; $20/yr. in cy.; $25/yr. out of cy. 218 N. Market St., Paxton, IL 60957. TEL 217-379-2356; FAX 217-379-3104. **Owner(s):** Paxton Printing Co., 218 N. Market St., Paxton, IL 60957. TEL 217-379-4313; Ed. Bob Maney; Pub. Paul E. Anderson; adv. contact: Toni Swan. pub. size: broadsheet; circ. 2,100(paid).

PEORIA

US
PEORIA OBSERVER. 1962. Wed. free local; $20.80/yr. mailed. 1616 W. Pioneer Pkwy., Peoria, IL 61615. TEL 309-692-4910; FAX 309-692-6447. **Owner(s):** Fleming Publishing Co., 100 Detroit Ave., Morton, IL 61550. TEL 309-263-2211; Ed. Kerri Skrudland. adv.; photos; pub. size: tabloid; circ. 26,300(free & paid).

PERCY

US
COUNTY JOURNAL. 1980. Thu. $.50 newsstand; $17/yr. 1101 E. Pine, Percy, IL 62272. TEL 618-497-8272; FAX 618-497-2607. **Owner(s):** Gerald Willis, 1101 E. Pine, Percy, IL 62272. TEL 618-497-8272; FAX 618-497-2607; Larry Willis, 1101 E. Pine, Percy, IL 62272. TEL 618-497-8272; FAX 618-497-2607; Pub. Larry Willis; adv. contact: Judy Willis. photos; pub. size: broadsheet; circ. 6,800(controlled & free).

PETERSBURG

US
PETERSBURG OBSERVER. 1874. Thu. $.50 newsstand; $18/yr. in state. 235 E. Sangamon, Petersburg, IL 62675-0350. TEL 217-632-2236; FAX 217-632-2237. **Owner(s):** Harriett C. Shaw, P.O. Box 350, Petersburg, IL 62675. TEL 217-632-2236; Ed. Jane Shaw Cutright. adv.; pub. size: broadsheet; circ. 3,250(paid).

PLAINFIELD

US
ENTERPRISE, THE. 1887. Wed. $.40 newsstand; $15/yr. in cy.; $22/yr. out of cy.; $30/yr. out of state. 519 W. Lockport St., Plainfield, IL 60544. TEL 815-436-2431; FAX 815-436-2592. **Owner(s):** Enterprise Printing, 519 W. Lockport St., Plainfield, IL 60544. TEL 815-436-2431; FAX 815-436-2592; Ed. Deborah Danielski; Pub. Wayne Perry; adv.; photos; pub. size: tabloid; circ. 14,000(free & paid).

US
FOX VALLEY VILLAGES. 1984. Thu. free mailed in area; $.75 newsstand. 3101 Rte. 30, Plainfield, IL 60544. TEL 815-439-5300. **Owner(s):** Copley Press, Inc., 7776 Ivanhoe Ave., La Jolla, CA 92037. TEL 619-454-0411; Ed. Sue Schmitt. adv. contact: Mike LaCombe. pub. size: tabloid; circ. 12,700(controlled & free).
Formerly: Fox Valley Sun.

US
▼**PLAINFIELD SUN.** 1997. Wed. free/mailed in school district. 3101 Rte. 30, Plainfield, IL 60544. TEL 815-439-5300. **Owner(s):** Copley Press, Inc., 7776 Ivanhoe Ave., La Jolla, CA 92037. TEL 619-454-0411; Ed. Sue Schmitt. adv. contact: Ron Matuszewski. pub. size: tabloid; circ. 13,000.

PONTIAC

US
FLANAGAN HOME TIMES. 1885. Wed. $22.50/yr. home deliv.; $25/yr. in state mailed; $27.50/yr. out of state. 318 N. Main St., Pontiac, IL 61764. TEL 815-842-1153; FAX 815-842-4388. **Owner(s):** American Publishing Co., 606 N. Van Buren, Marion, IL 62959. TEL 618-993-1711; Ed. Eric Murphy; Pub. Richard Westerfield; adv. contact: Beth Murphy. pub. size: standard; circ. 1,200(paid).

PRINCETON

US   ISSN 0894-1181
BUREAU COUNTY REPUBLICAN. 1847. 3/wk.: Tue., Thu., Sat. $.50 newsstand; $54.85/yr. local; $64.75/yr. elsewhere. P.O. Box 340, Princeton, IL 61356-0340. TEL 815-875-4461; FAX 815-872-1326. **Owner(s):** Shaw Newspaper Co., 444 Pine Hill Dr., Dixon, IL 61021. TEL 815-284-4000; Ed. Kevin Hladik; Pub. Sam Fisher; pub. size: broadsheet; circ. 7,000(paid).
Formerly: Spring Valley's Bureau County Republican.

RANTOUL

US
RANTOUL PRESS. 1874. Wed. $.45 newsstand; $25.50/yr. 1332 E. Harmon Dr., Rantoul, IL 61866-0909. TEL 217-892-9615; FAX 217-892-9451; E-mail: eastcent@aol.com. **Owner(s):** East Central Communications, Inc., 1332 E. Harmon Dr., Rantoul, IL 61866. TEL 217-892-9615; Ed. Chris Slack; Pub. Dennis C. Kaster; adv.; photos; pub. size: broadsheet; circ. 11,935(free & paid).

RED BUD

US
NORTH COUNTY NEWS. 1959. Thu. $.50 newsstand; $16/yr. in 3 cys.; $19/yr. out of cys. 122-124 S. Main St., Red Bud, IL 62278. TEL 618-282-3803; FAX 618-282-6134. **Owner(s):** Victor L. Mohr, P.O. Box 68, Red Bud, IL 62278; Ed. Victor L. Mohr; Pub. Victor L. Mohr; adv. contact: Toni Diewald. pub. size: broadsheet; circ. 4,000(paid).
Formerly: Red Bud North County News.

RIVERTON

US
RIVERTON REGISTER. 1948. Wed. $.25 newsstand; $12/yr. in cy.; $14/yr. out of cy. 100 N. Sixth St., Riverton, IL 62561-0200. TEL 217-629-9247. **Owner(s):** Rhodes Publications, 100 N. Sixth St., Riverton, IL 62561-0200. TEL 217-629-9247; Ed. Barbara Rhodes; Pub. Barbara Rhodes; adv.; photos; pub. size: tabloid; circ. 2,000(paid).

US
TRI CITY REGISTER. 1948. Wed. $.25 newsstand; $12/yr. in cy.; $14/yr. out of cy. 100 N. Sixth St., Riverton, IL 62561-0200. TEL 217-629-9247. **Owner(s):** Rhodes Publications, 100 N. Sixth St., Riverton, IL 62561-0200. TEL 217-629-9247; Ed. Barbara Rhodes; Pub. Barbara Rhodes; adv.; photos; pub. size: tabloid; circ. 2,000(paid).

WEEKLY NEWSPAPERS

WILLIAMSVILLE

US

WILLIAMSVILLE SUN. 1948. Wed. $.20 newsstand; $10/yr. in cy.; $12/yr. out of cy. 100 N. Sixth St., Riverton, IL 62561-0200. TEL 217-629-9247. **Owner(s):** Rhodes Publications, 100 N. Sixth St., Riverton, IL 62561-0200. TEL 217-629-9247; Ed. Barbara Rhodes; Pub. Barbara Rhodes; adv.; photos; pub. size: tabloid; circ. 2,000(paid).

ROANOKE

US

ROANOKE REVIEW. 1913. Thu. $.75 newsstand; $25/yr. local; $29/yr. in cy.; $33/yr. out of state. 105 E. Broad, Roanoke, IL 61561. TEL 309-923-5841; FAX 309-923-5841. **Owner(s):** San Francisco Chronicle, 901 Mission St., San Francisco, CA 94103; Ed. Cheryl Wolfe; Pub. Mark Barra; adv.; photos; pub. size: broadsheet; circ. 1,051(free & paid).

ROCHELLE

US

ROCHELLE NEWS LEADER. 1921. 3/wk.: Tue., Thu., Sun. $.50 newsstand; $68.25/yr. 211 Hwy. 38, E., Rochelle, IL 61068. TEL 815-562-4171; FAX 815-567-7048. **Owner(s):** Rochelle Newspapers, Inc., P.O. Box 46, Rochelle, IL 61068. TEL 815-562-4171; Ed. Jeff Robertson; Pub. Tom Cross; adv. contact: Pat Duffy. pub. size: broadsheet; circ. 5,500(paid).

ROSEVILLE

US

ROSEVILLE INDEPENDENT. Wed. $.40 newsstand; $17/yr. in cy.; $19/yr. out of cy.; $22/yr. out of state. 140 N. Main, Roseville, IL 61473. TEL 309-426-2255; FAX 309-462-3321. **Owner(s):** Acklin Newspaper Group, P.O. Box 32, Abington, IL 61410. TEL 309-462-5758; FAX 309-462-3221; Ed. Phil Gerding; Pub. JoAnn Muir; pub. size: tabloid; circ. 850(paid).

RUSHVILLE

US

RUSHVILLE TIMES, THE. 1848. Wed. $.40 newsstand; $15/yr. in state; $24/yr. out of state. 110 E. Lafayette, Rushville, IL 62681. TEL 217-322-3321; FAX 217-322-2138. **Owner(s):** Wayne Perry, P.O. Box 226, Rushville, IL 62681. TEL 217-322-3321; Ed. Allan Icenogle; Pub. Wayne Perry; adv. contact: Pat Grate. pub. size: standard; circ. 3,375(paid).

SALEM

US

SALEM TIMES-COMMONER. 1860. 3/wk.: Mon., Wed., Fri. $.35 newsstand; $37.62/yr. carrier. 120 S. Broadway, Salem, IL 62881-0548. TEL 618-548-3330; FAX 618-548-3593. **Owner(s):** Salem Times-Commoner, 120 S. Broadway, Salem, IL 62881-0548. TEL 618-548-3330; Ed. Lela Colclasure; Pub. Francis Rees; adv.; pub. size: broadsheet; circ. 5,000(paid).

SAVANNA

US

NORTHWESTERN ILLINOIS DISPATCH. 1960. Thu. free. 121 Main St., Savanna, IL 61074. TEL 815-273-2277; FAX 815-273-2715. **Owner(s):** Robert W. Watson, 121 Main St., Savanna, IL 61074. TEL 815-273-2277; Ed. Robert W. Watson; Pub. Robert W. Watson; adv. contact: Pat Shepherd. pub. size: tabloid; circ. 11,500(free).

US

SAVANNA TIMES JOURNAL. 1875. Thu. $.50 newsstand; $20/yr. in cy.; $26/yr. out of cy. 121 Main St., Savanna, IL 61074. TEL 815-273-2277; FAX 815-273-2751. **Owner(s):** Robert W. Watson, 121 Main St., Savanna, IL 61074. TEL 815-273-2277; Ed. Robert W. Watson; Pub. Robert W. Watson; adv. contact: Pat Shepherd. pub. size: tabloid; circ. 2,250(paid).

SOUTH HOLLAND

US

SHOPPER, THE. 1957. Wed. free. 924 E. 162nd St., South Holland, IL 60473. TEL 708-333-5901; FAX 708-333-9630. **Owner(s):** Shopper, The, 924 E. 162nd St., South Holland, IL 60473. TEL 708-333-5901; pub. size: tabloid; circ. 53,000(free).

SPARTA

US

SPARTA NEWS PLAINDEALER. 1863. Wed. $.50 newsstand; $20/yr. in cy.; $25/yr. out of cy.; $30/yr. out of state. 116 W. Main St., Sparta, IL 62286. TEL 618-443-2145; FAX 618-443-2780. **Owner(s):** Knight-Ridder, Inc., One Herald Plz., Miami, FL 33132. TEL 305-376-3800; Ed. Mike Springston; Pub. J. Bart McDowell; adv. contact: Carol Mulholland. pub. size: broadsheet; circ. 5,000(paid).

SPRINGFIELD

US

ILLINOIS TIMES. 1975. Thu. free; $38/yr. 610 S. Seventh, Springfield, IL 62703. TEL 217-753-2226; FAX 217-753-2281. **Owner(s):** Illinois Times, Inc., P.O. Box 3524, Springfield, IL 62708. TEL 217-753-2226; Ed. Fletcher Farrar, Jr.; Pub. Fletcher Farrar, Jr.; pub. size: broadsheet; circ. 33,000(free & paid). **Wire Service(s):** Alternative News Service.

US

SPRINGFIELD SHOPPER. 1975. Thu. free; $20/yr. mailed. 2001 W. Monroe, Springfield, IL 62704. TEL 217-546-3295; FAX 217-546-3133. **Owner(s):** Don Hecke, P.O. Box 142, Springfield, IL 62705. TEL 217-546-3295; pub. size: tabloid; circ. evening 29,500(free & paid).

STAUNTON

US

STAUNTON STAR-TIMES. 1878. Thu. $.35 newsstand; $15/yr. in cy.; $19/yr. out of cy. 108 W. Main St., Staunton, IL 62088. TEL 618-635-2000; FAX 618-635-5281. **Owner(s):** Star Times Publishing Co., Inc., 108 W. Main St., Staunton, IL 62088. TEL 618-635-2000; FAX 618-635-5281; Ed. Walter F. Haase. adv.; photos; bk.rev.; pub. size: broadsheet; circ. 3,900(paid).

ST. ELMO

US

SAINT ELMO BANNER. Tue. $.50 newsstand; $17.50/yr. in cy.; $20.50/yr. elsewhere. P.O. Box 10, St. Elmo, IL 62458. TEL 618-829-3246; FAX 618-483-5177. **Owner(s):** Joe Baker & Greg Hoskins, P.O. Box 10, St. Elmo, IL 62458. TEL 618-829-3246; FAX 618-829-3246; Ed. Joe Baker; Pub. Barbara Barr; adv. contact: Barbara Barr. photos; pub. size: tabloid; circ. 1,200(paid).

STOCKTON

US

STOCKTON/WARREN GAZETTE. 1834. Wed. $1 newsstand; $25/yr. local. 119 S. Main St., Stockton, IL 61085. TEL 815-947-2311; FAX 815-777-3809. **Owner(s):** P. Carter & Sarah Newton, P.O. Box 319, Galena, IL 61036. TEL 815-777-0019; Pub. P. Carter Newton; adv. contact: Robin Buss. pub. size: standard; circ. 6,000(paid).

Formerly: Gazette, The.

STRONGHURST

US

HENDERSON COUNTY QUILL. 1926. Wed. $.50 newsstand; $19/yr. in state; $20/yr. out of state. 102 N. Broadway, Stronghurst, IL 61480. TEL 309-924-1871; FAX 309-924-1212. **Owner(s):** Dessa Rodeffer, 702 Harmony St., Stronghurst, IL 61480. TEL 309-924-1871; FAX 309-924-1124; Belva Bell, 402 N. Broadway, Stronghurst, IL 61480. TEL 309-924-1263; FAX 309-924-1124; Ed. Belva Bell; Pub. Dessa Rodeffer; adv. contact: Shirley Linder. photos; bk.rev.; pub. size: tabloid; circ. 2,000(paid).

SULLIVAN

US

NEWS-PROGRESS. 1961. Wed. $.50 newsstand; $20/yr. in cy.; $25/yr. out of cy. 100 W. Monroe St., Sullivan, IL 61951. TEL 217-728-7381; FAX 217-728-2020; E-mail: newspro@cu-online.com. **Owner(s):** Marion E. Best, 1017 E. Jackson, Sullivan, IL 61951. TEL 217-728-4474; Ed. Marion E. Best; Pub. Marion E. Best; adv.; photos; pub. size: broadsheet; **Wire Service(s):** AP.

SUMNER

US

SUMNER PRESS. 1876. Wed. $.35 newsstand; $17/yr. P.O. Box 126, Sumner, IL 62466. TEL 618-936-2212; FAX 618-936-2858. **Owner(s):** Rosco & Mary Ellen Cummingham, P.O. Box 126, Sumner, IL 62466. TEL 618-936-2212; FAX 618-936-2858; Ed. Jo Ann Dowty; Pub. Rosco Cummingham; adv.; photos; pub. size: standard; circ. 2,100(free & paid).

SYCAMORE

US   ISSN 1071-9784

GENOA-KINGSTON-KIRKLAND NEWS. 1972. Wed. $.50 newsstand; $25.50/yr. in cy. mailed; $36/yr. out of cy. mailed. 322 W. State St., Sycamore, IL 60178. TEL 815-784-5138; FAX 815-899-4329. **Owner(s):** B.F. Shaw Printing Co., 444 Pine Hill Dr., P.O. Box 409, Dixon, IL 61021. TEL 815-284-2222; FAX 815-254-9290; Ed. Kim Kubiak; Pub. Roger Coleman; adv. contact: Bernice Bieber. photos; pub. size: broadsheet; circ. 2,805(paid).

SYCAMORE, IL

HAMPSHIRE REGISTER NEWS. 1894. Wed. $.50 newsstand; $23.50/yr. in cy. mailed; $33/yr. out of cy. mailed. 322 W. State St., Sycamore, IL 60178. TEL 815-899-6397; FAX 815-899-4329. **Owner(s):** B.F. Shaw Printing Co., 444 Pine Hill Dr., P.O. Box 409, Dixon, IL 61021. TEL 815-284-2222; Ed. Gary Koehler; Pub. Roger Coleman; adv. contact: Bernice Bieber. photos; pub. size: broadsheet; circ. 1,700(paid).

US   ISSN 0747-3524
SYCAMORE NEWS. 1857. Wed. $.50 newsstand; $23.50/yr. in cy. mailed; $33/yr. out of cy. mailed. 322 W. State St., Sycamore, IL 60178. TEL 815-899-6397; FAX 815-899-4329. **Owner(s):** B.F. Shaw Printing Co., 444 Pine Hill Dr., P.O. Box 409, Dixon, IL 61021. TEL 815-284-2222; Ed. Gary Koehler; Pub. Roger Coleman; adv. contact: Bernice Bieber. photos; pub. size: broadsheet; circ. 10,000(free & paid).
Formerly: Kishwaukee Independent.

THOMSON

CARROLL COUNTY REVIEW. 1863. Wed. $.50 newsstand; $18/yr. in cy. 809 Main St., Thomson, IL 61285. TEL 815-259-2131; FAX 815-259-3226. **Owner(s):** Jonathan K. Whitney, P.O. Box 369, Thomson, IL 61285. TEL 815-259-2131; Ed. Bill Gengenbach; Pub. Jonathan K. Whitney; adv. contact: Nancy G. Whitney. pub. size: tabloid; circ. 2,900(paid).

TINLEY PARK

NEWSMARKETER, THE. 1985. Wed. free. 6901 West 159th St., Tinley Park, IL 60477. TEL 708-586-8800; FAX 703-633-4859. **Owner(s):** American Publishing Co., 606 N. Van Buren, Marion, IL 62959. TEL 618-993-1711; Ed. Peter Neill; Pub. Norm Rosinski; adv. contact: Julie Ross. pub. size: broadsheet; circ. 359,994(free).

US
PENNY SAVER. 1965. Tue. free. 8231 W. 185th St., Tinley Park, IL 60477. TEL 708-429-6400; FAX 708-429-7940. **Owner(s):** Shoppers Enterprise, Inc., 125 Main St., Blue Earth, MN 56013. TEL 507-526-7326; Doug Dance, 17746 S. Oak Park Ave., Tinley Park, IL 60477. TEL 708-429-6400; Ed. Anna Staten; Pub. Doug Dance; adv.; pub. size: tabloid; circ. 300,000(free).

US
STAR, THE. 1901. s-w.: Thu. & Sun. $.50 newsstand; $43.20/yr. 6901 W. 159th St., Tinley Park, IL 60477. TEL 708-755-6161; FAX 708-802-8088. **Owner(s):** Hollinger International, Inc., 401 N. Wabash, Chicago, IL 60611. TEL 312-321-3000; Pub. Norman Rosinski; adv. contact: Mark Lacey. photos; pub. size: broadsheet; circ. 62,758(paid); Sun. 65,995(paid).
Formerly: Chicago Heights Star.

TRENTON

TRENTON SUN, THE. 1880. Wed. $.35 newsstand; $15/yr. 15 W. Broadway, Trenton, IL 62293-0118. TEL 618-224-9422; FAX 618-224-9422. **Owner(s):** Sybil & Michael Conley, 15 W. Broadway, Trenton, IL 62293-0118. TEL 618-224-9422; Ed. Michael L. Conley; Pub. Michael L. Conley; adv.; pub. size: broadsheet; circ. 1,400(paid).

TUSCOLA

TUSCOLA REVIEW. 1875. Tue. $.50 newsstand; $20/yr. in cy.; $25/yr. out of cy. 115 W. Sale St., Tuscola, IL 61953. TEL 217-253-2358; FAX 217-253-3265. **Owner(s):** Beverly Hastings, 115 W. Sale St., Tuscola, IL 61953; Randy H. Hastings, 115 W. Sale St., Tuscola, IL 61953; Greg Hastings, 115 W. Sale St., Tuscola, IL 61953; Ed. Randy H. Hastings; Pub. Randy H. Hastings; adv.; pub. size: broadsheet; circ. 3,600(paid).

VANDALIA

VANDALIA LEADER-UNION. 1865. s-w.: Wed. & Fri. $.50 newsstand; $29.50/yr. 229 S. Fifth St., Vandalia, IL 62471. TEL 618-283-3374; FAX 618-283-0977. **Owner(s):** Landmark Community Newspapers, Inc., P.O. Box 549, Shelbyville, KY 40066. TEL 502-633-4334; Ed. Rich Bauer; Pub. David R. Bell; adv.; pub. size: broadsheet; circ. 5,800(paid).

VIENNA

VIENNA TIMES, THE. 1882. Thu. $.40 newsstand; $23/yr. 305 W. Main, Vienna, IL 62995-0457. TEL 618-658-4321. **Owner(s):** Donald L. Sanders, 305 W. Main, Vienna, IL 62995. TEL 618-658-4321; Ed. Donald L. Sanders; Pub. Donald L. Sanders; pub. size: broadsheet; circ. 2,800(paid).

WARSAW

MISSISSIPPI EAGLE NEWS, THE. 1991. Mon. $.50 newsstand; $20/yr. in cy.; $25/yr. out of cy. 521 Main St., Warsaw, IL 62379. TEL 217-256-3543; FAX 217-256-3295. **Owner(s):** Crystal City Publishing Co., 602 Clay St., Warsaw, IL 62379. TEL 217-256-3543; Pub. Melinda A. Beeler; adv.; photos; bk.rev.; pub. size: tabloid; circ. 1,000(paid).

WASHINGTON

WASHINGTON COURIER. 1958. Wed. $22/yr. 100 Ford Ln., Washington, IL 61571. TEL 309-444-3139; FAX 309-444-8505. **Owner(s):** Hagel Publications, Inc., P.O. Box 349, Washington, IL 61571. TEL 309-444-3139; FAX 309-444-8505; Ed. Joi DeArmond; Pub. Roger Hagel; adv.: $12.50/SAU. photos; pub. size: tabloid; circ. 22,000(paid).

WATERLOO

WATERLOO REPUBLIC-TIMES. 1890. Wed. $.50 newsstand; $20/yr. in cy.; $25/yr. out of cy.; $30/yr. out of state. 222 S. Main St., Waterloo, IL 62298. TEL 618-939-3814. **Owner(s):** Walt Disney Co., 500 S. Buena Vista St., Burbank, CA 91521. TEL 818-560-5300; Ed. Marvin Cortner; Pub. Mark Schmershal; adv. contact: Karen Domyan. adv.: $23.66/SAU. photos; bk.rev.; pub. size: broadsheet; circ. 28,000(free & paid).

WAVERLY

WAVERLY JOURNAL. 1872. Fri. $.50 newsstand; $20/yr. 130 S. Pearl St., Waverly, IL 62692. TEL 217-435-9221; FAX 217-435-4511. **Owner(s):** Nancy Springer, 130 S. Pearl St., Waverly, IL 62692. TEL 217-435-9221; FAX 217-435-4511; Ed. Julie A. Springer; Pub. Nancy Springer; adv. contact: Julie A. Springer. photos; bk.rev.; pub. size: tabloid; circ. 1,577(paid).

WEST CHICAGO

WARRENVILLE FREE PRESS. 1986. Thu. $.50 newsstand; $25/yr. 100 Arbor Ave., West Chicago, IL 60185. TEL 630-231-0500; FAX 630-231-6813. **Owner(s):** Wayne G. Woltman, 100 Arbor Ave., West Chicago, IL 60185. TEL 630-231-0500; Ed. Marc Alberts; Pub. Wayne G. Woltman; adv. contact: Robert Langness. pub. size: tabloid; circ. 3,000(paid).

US
WEST CHICAGO PRESS. 1907. Thu. $.50 newsstand, $25/yr. 100 Arbor Ave., West Chicago, IL 60185. TEL 708-231-0500; FAX 708-231-6813. **Owner(s):** Wayne G. Woltman, 100 Arbor Ave., West Chicago, IL 60185. TEL 630-231-0500; Ed. Marc Alberts; Pub. Wayne G. Woltman; adv. contact: Robert Langness. pub. size: tabloid; circ. 5,000(paid).

US   ISSN 0273-6993
WINFIELD PRESS. 1980. Thu. $.50 newsstand; $25/yr. 100 Arbor Ave., West Chicago, IL 60185. TEL 630-231-0500; FAX 630-231-6813. **Owner(s):** Wayne G. Woltman, 100 Arbor Ave., West Chicago, IL 60185. TEL 708-231-0500; Ed. Marc Alberts; Pub. Wayne G. Woltman; adv. contact: Dustin Hawkins. pub. size: tabloid; circ. 600(paid).

WHITE HALL

GREENE PRAIRIE PRESS. Thu. $.50 newsstand; $23/yr. in cy.; $28/yr. out of cy. 112 E. Sherman, White Hall, IL 62092. TEL 217-374-2871; FAX 217-742-3596. **Owner(s):** Elmer Fedder, 112 E. Sherman, White Hall, IL 62092. TEL 217-374-2871; FAX 217-742-3596; Ed. Merrilyn Fedder; Pub. Elmer Fedder; adv.; pub. size: tabloid; circ. 3,000(paid).

WILMINGTON

BRACEVILLE EXPRESS. 1978. Wed. free. 111 S. Water St., Wilmington, IL 60481. TEL 815-476-7966; FAX 815-476-7002. **Owner(s):** George Fisher, 111 S. Water St., Wilmington, IL 60481. TEL 815-476-7966; Ed. Eric Fisher; Pub. George Fisher; adv. contact: George Fisher. pub. size: broadsheet; circ. 570(free).

WEEKLY NEWSPAPERS

US
BRAIDWOOD INDEX. 1978. Wed. free. 111 S. Water St., Wilmington, IL 60481. TEL 815-476-7966; FAX 815-476-7002. **Owner(s):** George Fisher, 111 S. Water St., Wilmington, IL 60481. TEL 815-476-7966; Ed. Eric Fisher; Pub. George Fisher; adv. contact: George Fisher. pub. size: broadsheet; circ. 2,500(free).

US
COAL CITY EXPRESS. 1978. Wed. free. 111 S. Water St., Wilmington, IL 60481. TEL 815-476-7966; FAX 815-476-7002. **Owner(s):** George Fisher, 111 S. Water Street, Wilmington, IL 60481. TEL 815-476-7966; Ed. Eric Fisher; Pub. George Fisher; adv. contact: George Fisher. pub. size: broadsheet; circ. 2,500(free).

US
ELWOOD EXPRESS. 1978. Wed. free. 111 S. Water St., Wilmington, IL 60481. TEL 815-476-7966; FAX 815-476-7002. **Owner(s):** George Fisher, 111 S. Water St., Wilmington, IL 60481. TEL 815-476-7966; Pub. George Fisher; adv. contact: George Fisher. pub. size: broadsheet; circ. 2,500(free).

US
GARDNER SOUTH WILMINGTON POST. 1978. Wed. free. 111 S. Water St., Wilmington, IL 60481. TEL 815-476-7966; FAX 815-476-7002. **Owner(s):** George Fisher, 111 S. Water St., Wilmington, IL 60481. TEL 815-476-7966; Ed. Eric Fisher; Pub. George Fisher; adv. contact: George Fisher. pub. size: broadsheet; circ. 2,500(free).

US
WILMINGTON ADVOCATE, THE. 1853. Wed. $.50 newsstand; $19.50/yr. in cy.; $22.50/yr. out of cy.; $25.50/yr. out of state. 384 W. Baltimore, Wilmington, IL 60481. TEL 815-476-7511; FAX 815-476-7544. **Owner(s):** Bailey Printing & Publishing, 273 S. Broadway, Coal City, IL 60416. TEL 815-634-2102; Ed. Sheridan Bailey; Pub. Sheridan Bailey; adv.; photos; pub. size: broadsheet; circ. 835(paid).

US
WILMINGTON EXPRESS. Wed. free. 111 S. Water St., Wilmington, IL 60481. TEL 815-476-7966; FAX 815-476-7002. **Owner(s):** George Fisher, 111 S. Water St., Wilmington, IL 60481. TEL 815-476-7966; Ed. Eric Fisher; Pub. George Fisher; adv. contact: George Fisher. pub. size: broadsheet.

US
WILMINGTON FREE PRESS. 1978. Wed. $.50 newsstand; $20/yr. in cy.; $26/yr. out of cy.; $30/yr. out of state. 111 S. Water St., Wilmington, IL 60481. TEL 815-476-7966; FAX 815-476-7002. **Owner(s):** George Fisher, 111 S. Water St., Wilmington, IL 60481. TEL 815-476-7966; Ed. Eric Fisher; Pub. George Fisher; adv. contact: George Fisher. pub. size: broadsheet; circ. 1,775(paid).
Formerly: Wilmington Express.

WOODSTOCK

US
WOODSTOCK INDEPENDENT, THE. 1987. Wed. $.75 newsstand; $26/yr. local. 671 E. Calhoun St., Woodstock, IL 60098-4262. TEL 815-338-8040; FAX 815-338-8177; E-mail: inde@il-ccom.net. **Owner(s):** Cheryl B. Wormley, 671 E. Calhoun St., Woodstock, IL 60098. TEL 815-338-8040; FAX 815-338-8177; Denise Graff Ponstein, 671 E. Calhoun St., Woodstock, IL 60098. TEL 815-338-8040; FAX 815-338-8177; Pub. Cheryl B. Wormley; adv. contact: Brent Maring. photos; pub. size: tabloid; circ. 2,500(paid).

WORDEN

US
ADVERTISER, THE. Mon. free. 125 E. Wall St., Worden, IL 62097-0490. TEL 618-459-3655; FAX 618-459-3655. **Owner(s):** Bunker Hill Publications Co., 150 N. Washington, Bunker Hill, IL 62014. TEL 618-585-4411; Pub. John M. Galer; adv. contact: Eve Pickerill. pub. size: broadsheet; circ. 7,187(free).

US
MADISON COUNTY CHRONICLE. 1978. Thu. $.25 newsstand; $10.50/yr. in cy.; $12.50/yr. out of cy.; $14.50/yr. out of state. 125 E. Wall St., Worden, IL 62097-0490. TEL 618-459-3655; FAX 618-459-3655. **Owner(s):** Bunker Hill Publications, Inc., 150 N. Washington, Bunker Hill, IL 62014. TEL 618-585-4411; Ed. Vera Eckhardt; Pub. John M. Galer; adv. contact: Eve Pickerill. photos; pub. size: tabloid; circ. 1,200(paid).

YORKVILLE

US
FOX VALLEY SHOPPING NEWS, THE. 1873. Thu. free local; $42/yr. elsewhere. P.O. Box 609, Yorkville, IL 60560. TEL 630-553-7431; FAX 630-553-0310. **Owner(s):** Copley Press, Inc., 7776 Ivanhoe Ave., La Jolla, CA 92037. TEL 619-454-0411; Ed. Dick Whitfield; Pub. Dick Whitfield; adv.; pub. size: tabloid; circ. 26,300(paid).
Formerly: Sandwich Tri-County Today.

US
KENDALL COUNTY RECORD. 1864. Thu. $.50 newsstand; $21/yr. 222 S. Bridge St., Yorkville, IL 60560. TEL 630-553-7034; FAX 630-553-7085. **Owner(s):** Jeff & Kathy Farren, 222 S. Bridge St., Yorkville, IL 60560. TEL 708-553-7034; Ed. Kathy Farren; Pub. Jeff Farren; adv.; pub. size: tabloid; circ. 4,250(paid).
Formerly: Yorkville Kendall County Record.

WOODSTOCK

US
WOODSTOCK INDEPENDENT, THE. (see above)

ZION

US
ZION-BENTON NEWS. 1929. Thu. $.50 newsstand; $17.95/yr. in cy.; $19.95/yr. out of cy. 2719 Elisha Ave., Zion, IL 60099. TEL 847-746-9000; FAX 847-746-9150. **Owner(s):** United Communications Corp., 715 58th St., Kenosha, WI 53141. TEL 414-657-1000; Ed. Mona Shannon; Pub. Frank Misureli; adv.; pub. size: tabloid; circ. 4,000(paid).

INDIANA

ALEXANDRIA

US
ALEXANDRIA TIMES-TRIBUNE. 1885. Wed. $.50 newsstand; $22/yr. in cy.; $29/yr. out of cy. One Harrison Sq., Alexandria, IN 46001. TEL 317-724-4469. **Owner(s):** Jack L. Barnes, 317 S. Anderson, Elwood, IN 46036. TEL 317-552-3355; Ed. Linda Ferris; Pub. Robert L. Nash; adv. contact: Cindy Tyner. bk.rev.; pub. size: broadsheet; circ. 3,600(paid). **Wire Service(s):** AP.

ANGOLA

US
HERALD-REPUBLICAN. 1857. s-w.: Wed. & Fri. $.50 newsstand; $39.75/yr. in cy.; $44.75/yr. out of cy. 45 S. Public Sq., Angola, IN 46703. TEL 219-665-3117; FAX 219-665-2322. **Owner(s):** Home News Enterprises, 333 Second St., Columbus, IN 47201. TEL 812-372-7811; Ed. Rick Martinez; Pub. Bill Parsons; adv. contact: David Damerow. photos; pub. size: standard; circ. 7,000(free). **Wire Service(s):** CNS.

ATTICA

US   ISSN 1060-5495
FOUNTAIN COUNTY NEIGHBOR. 1851. s-w.: Tue. & Fri. $.50/newsstand; $40/yr. in cy.; $51/yr. out of cy. & state. State Rd. 28, E., Attica, IN 47918. TEL 317-762-2411; FAX 317-762-2163. **Owner(s):** Nixon Newspapers, Inc., 35 W. Third St., Peru, IN 46970. TEL 765-473-3091; Ed. Tina McGrady; Pub. Bette D. Schmid; adv. contact: Angi Turner. pub. size: broadsheet; circ. 22,255(paid).

US
MESSENGER, THE. Tue. free. 1322 E. Main St., Attica, IN 47918. TEL 317-762-2411; FAX 317-762-2163. **Owner(s):** Nixon Newspapers, Inc., 35 W. Third St., Peru, IN 46970. TEL 765-473-3092; Ed. Tina McGrady; Pub. Bette D. Schmid; adv. contact: Angi Turner. pub. size: broadsheet; circ. 11,000(free).
Formerly: Fountain/Warren Messenger.

AUBURN

US
EVENING STAR PLUS, THE. 1958. Tue. free. 118 W. Ninth St., Auburn, IN 46706. TEL 219-925-2611; FAX 219-925-2625. **Owner(s):** Kendallville Publishing Co., P.O. Box 39, Kendallville, IN 46755. TEL 219-347-0400; adv. contact: Martin Alexander. pub. size: broadsheet; circ. 18,700(free).
Formerly: DeKalb County Advertiser.

BATESVILLE

US
HERALD-TRIBUNE. 1890. s-w.: Wed. & Sat. $.50 newsstand; $42/yr. 4 W. Pearl St., Batesville, IN 47006. TEL 812-934-4343; FAX 812-934-6406. **Owner(s):** Thomson Newspapers, Inc., Metro Centre, One Station Pl., 6th Fl., Stamford, CT 06902. TEL 203-425-2500; FAX 203-425-2516; Ed. Joel Erickson. adv. contact: Melanie Dreyer. photos; pub. size: broadsheet; circ. 7,500(paid).
Formerly: Batesville Herald-Tribune.

BEECH GROVE

US
PERRY TOWNSHIP WEEKLY. 1928. w. free. 301 Main St., Beech Grove, IN 46107. TEL 317-787-3291; FAX 317-787-3325. **Owner(s):** Reporter-Times, Inc., 60 S. Jefferson, Martinsville, IN 46151. TEL 317-342-3311; Ed. Amy Uhls; Pub. Roger Huntzinger; adv.; pub. size: broadsheet; circ. 25,000(free).
Formerly: Beech Grove Perry Township Weekly.

BERNE

US
BERNE TRI-WEEKLY NEWS. 1896. 3/wk.: Mon., Wed., Fri. $.50 newsstand; $44.95/yr. 153 S. Jefferson St., Berne, IN 46711. TEL 219-589-2101; FAX 219-589-8614. **Owner(s):** EP Graphics, 153 S. Jefferson St., Berne, IN 46711. TEL 219-589-2101; Pub. Carl H. Muselman; adv. contact: Jeremy Liechty. photos; bk.rev.; pub. size: broadsheet; circ. 3,000(paid).

BICKNELL

US   ISSN 1060-6173
NORTH KNOX NEWS. 1864. 3/wk.: Tue., Thu., Sat. $.50 newsstand; $4/mo. in town; $90/yr. in cy.; $105/yr. out of cy. 301 W. 11th St., Bicknell, IN 47512. TEL 812-735-2230; FAX 812-735-2244. **Owner(s):** Central Newspapers, Inc., 135 N. Pennsylvania Ave., Indianapolis, IN 46204. TEL 317-231-9200; Ed. Carol Gwinnup; Pub. Michael Quayle; adv.; photos; pub. size: broadsheet; circ. morning 1,400(paid). **Wire Service(s):** AP.
Formerly: Knox County Daily News.

BOONVILLE

US
BOONVILLE STANDARD. 1875. Wed. $.50 newsstand; $26/yr. 204 W. Locust St., Boonville, IN 47601. TEL 812-897-2330; FAX 812-897-3703. **Owner(s):** Warrick Publishing Co., 204 W. Locust St., Boonville, IN 47601. TEL 812-897-2330; Ed. Jan Garrett; Pub. Myra Teal; adv.; pub. size: broadsheet; circ. 4,327(paid).

BROOKVILLE

US
BROOKVILLE AMERICAN-DEMOCRAT. 1832. Wed. $.40 newsstand; $16/yr. 533 Main St., Brookville, IN 47012. TEL 317-647-4221; FAX 317-647-4811. **Owner(s):** Whitewater Publications, P.O. Box 38, Brookville, IN 47012. TEL 317-647-4221; Ed. John L. Estridge. adv. contact: Becky Trammell. photos; pub. size: broadsheet; circ. 5,600(paid).

BROWNSTOWN

US
JACKSON COUNTY BANNER. 1869. s-w.: Tue. & Thu. $.35 newsstand; $28/yr. 116 E. Cross St., Brownstown, IN 47220. TEL 812-358-2111; FAX 812-358-5606. **Owner(s):** Jackson County Banner Inc., The, 116 E. Cross St., Brownstown, IN 47220. TEL 812-358-2111; Pub. Joseph Persinger; adv. contact: Margaret Tormoehlen. photos; pub. size: broadsheet; circ. 4,052(paid). **Wire Service(s):** AP, Newsfinder.

CAMBRIDGE CITY

US
WESTERN WAYNE NEWS. 1991. Wed. $.35 newsstand; $14/yr. in cy.; $18/yr. out of cy.; $22/yr. out of state. 119 W. Main, Cambridge City, IN 47327. TEL 317-478-5448; FAX 317-478-5155. **Owner(s):** Ed Buhl, 36 W. Main, Cambridge City, IN 47327. TEL 317-478-5448; FAX 317-479-5155; Janis Buhl, 36 W. Main, Cambridge City, IN 47327. TEL 317-478-5448; FAX 317-478-5155; Pub. Janis Buhl; adv. contact: Janis Buhl. adv.: $2.75/SAU. photos; pub. size: tabloid; circ. 2,400(paid).

CENTERVILLE

US
CENTERVILLE CRUSADER. 1966. Wed. $.25 newsstand; $13/yr. in cy.; $15/yr. out of cy. P.O. Box 26, Centerville, IN 47330. TEL 756-855-5262. **Owner(s):** Nancy D. Kinder, P.O. Box 26, Centerville, IN 47330. TEL 317-825-2728; Peggy Patterson, P.O. Box 26, Centerville, IN 47330. TEL 317-855-5262; Ed. Nancy D. Kinder; Pub. Peggy Patterson; adv.; photos; pub. size: tabloid; circ. 1,360(free & paid).

CHARLESTOWN

US
LEADER, THE. 1919. Wed. $15/yr. 382 Main Cross, Charlestown, IN 47111. TEL 812-256-3377; FAX 812-967-3194. **Owner(s):** Green Banner Publications, P.O. Box 38, Charleston, IN 47111. TEL 812-256-3377; Ed. Mark Grigsby; Pub. Joe Green; adv. contact: John Roberts. pub. size: tabloid; circ. 10,439(free).

CHESTERTON

US
CHESTERTON TOWN CRIER. 1932. Mon. free. 515 Broadway, Chesterton, IN 46304-8723. TEL 219-926-7685; FAX 219-926-7685. **Owner(s):** Towndan Enterprises, Inc., 2700 Monroe, La Porte, IN 46350. TEL 219-926-7685; Ed. Gregory L. Jones; Pub. Brett Alcorn; pub. size: tabloid; circ. 10,404(free).

CLAY CITY

US
NEWS, THE. 1912. Wed. $.35 newsstand; $16/yr. 717 Main St., Clay City, IN 47841. TEL 812-939-2163; FAX 812-939-2286. **Owner(s):** News, The, 717 Main St., Clay City, IN 47841. TEL 812-939-2163; FAX 812-939-2286; adv.; photos; pub. size: standard; circ. 2,000(paid).

CORYDON

US
CLARION NEWS. 1939. Wed. free local area; $.45 newsstand; $18/yr. out of area. 301 N. Capitol Ave., Corydon, IN 47112. TEL 812-738-4552; FAX 812-738-1909. **Owner(s):** O'Bannon Publishing Co., Inc., 301 N. Capitol Ave., Corydon, IN 47112. TEL 812-738-4552; Ed. Sara Combs; Pub. Dennis L. Huber; adv. contact: Mark Young. photos; pub. size: standard; circ. 15,000(free).
Formerly: Clarion, The.

US
CORYDON DEMOCRAT. Wed. $.75 newsstand; $25/yr. in area; $24/yr. senior citizens. 301 N. Capitol Ave., Corydon, IN 47112. TEL 812-738-2211; FAX 812-738-1909. **Owner(s):** O'Bannon Publishing Co., Inc., 301 N. Capital Ave., Corydon, IN 47112. TEL 812-738-2211; Ed. Randy West; Pub. Dennis L. Huber; adv. contact: Mark Young. pub. size: broadsheet; circ. 8,500(paid).

CROTHERSVILLE

US
CROTHERSVILLE TIMES. 1980. Wed. $.25 newsstand; $10/yr. 510 Moore St., Crothersville, IN 47229. TEL 812-793-2188; FAX 812-793-2188; E-mail: ctimes@hsonline.net. **Owner(s):** Curt Kovener, P.O. Box 141, Crothersville, IN 47229. TEL 812-793-2188; FAX 812-793-2188; Mary A. Kovener, P.O. Box 141, Crothersville, IN 47229. TEL 812-723-2188; FAX 812-723-2188; Ed. Curt Kovener; Pub. Curt Kovener; adv.; photos; bk.rev.; pub. size: tabloid; circ. 1,200(paid).

CROWN POINT

US
LAKE COUNTY STAR. 1857. s-w.: Tue. & Thu. $.50 newsstand; $37/yr. 15 N. Court St., Crown Point, IN 46307. TEL 219-663-4212; FAX 219-663-0137. **Owner(s):** American Publishing Co., 606 N. Van Buren, P.O. Box 520, Marion, IL 62959. TEL 618-993-1711; Ed. Andrew Steele. adv.; photos; pub. size: broadsheet; circ. 27,000(free & paid).
Formerly: Crownpoint Lake County Star.

CULVER

US
CULVER CITIZEN. 1894. Wed. $.50/issue; $18/yr. in state; $21/yr. out of state. 107 S. Main St., Culver, IN 46511. TEL 219-842-3229; FAX 219-935-0083. **Owner(s):** Citizen Publications, Inc., 107 S. Main St., Culver, IN 46511. TEL 219-842-3229; FAX 219-935-0083; Ed. Judith L. Karst; Pub. Frederick A. Karst; adv.; photos; pub. size: broadsheet; circ. 1,600(controlled & paid).

DANVILLE

US
REPUBLICAN, THE. 1847. Thu. $.30 newsstand; $14/yr. 6 E. Main, Danville, IN 46122. TEL 317-745-2777; FAX 317-745-2777. **Owner(s):** Betty J. Weesner, 6 E. Main St., Danville, IN 46122. TEL 317-745-2777; FAX 317-745-2777; adv.; pub. size: standard; circ. 1,300(paid).

WEEKLY NEWSPAPERS

EDINBURGH

US

TRI-COUNTY NEWS. 1986. Wed. free; $40/yr. 121 E. Main Cross, Edinburgh, IN 46124. TEL 812-526-6372; FAX 812-526-6379. **Owner(s):** Gary Storie, 121 E. Main Cross, Edinburgh, IN 46124. TEL 812-526-6372; Pub. Ron Isbell; adv.; pub. size: broadsheet; circ. 8,300(paid).
  Formerly: Tri County Newspaper.

ELKHART

US

PAPER, THE. 1976. Mon. free. 229 W. Marion St., Elkhart, IN 46516. TEL 219-522-4111; FAX 219-522-7448. **Owner(s):** Papers, Inc., The, P.O. Box 188, Milford, IN 46542. TEL 219-658-4815; FAX 219-658-4701; Ed. Jeri Seely; Pub. Della Baumgartner; adv. contact: Kip Schumm. photos; pub. size: tabloid; circ. 27,360(controlled & free).

ELLETTSVILLE

US

JOURNAL, THE. 1939. Wed. $.30 newsstand; $16/yr. 211 N. Sale St., Ellettsville, IN 47429. TEL 812-876-2254; FAX 812-876-2853. **Owner(s):** John T. Gillaspy, 211 N. Sale St., Ellettsville, IN 47429. TEL 812-876-2254; FAX 812-876-2853; Ed. Tom Douglas; Pub. John T. Gillaspy; adv. contact: Jane Fiscus. photos; pub. size: standard.

FAIRMOUNT

US

NEWS-SUN. 1872. Wed. $.25 newsstand; $54/yr. 3rd class. 122 S. Main St., Fairmount, IN 46928. TEL 317-948-4165. **Owner(s):** Allen Terhune & Assn., 122 S. Main St., Fairmount, IN 46928. TEL 317-948-4165; Ed. Allen Terhune; Pub. Jim Terhune; adv.; photos; bk.rev.; pub. size: tabloid; circ. 4,400(paid).

FERDINAND

US

FERDINAND NEWS, THE. 1906. Wed. $.50 newsstand; $17/yr. local; $19/yr. in state; $23/yr. out of state. 113 W. Sixth St., Ferdinand, IN 47532. TEL 812-367-2041; FAX 812-367-2371. **Owner(s):** Dubois-Spencer County Publishing, Inc., P.O. Box 38, Ferdinand, IN 47532. TEL 812-367-2041; Ed. Richard Tretter. adv.; photos; pub. size: broadsheet; circ. 3,100(paid).

US

SPENCER COUNTY LEADER/DALE NEWS. 1960. Fri. $.50 newsstand; $20/yr. local; $25/yr. in state; $30/yr. out of state. 113 W. Sixth St., Ferdinand, IN 47532. TEL 812-367-2041; FAX 812-367-2371. **Owner(s):** Dubois-Spencer County Publishing, Inc., P.O. Box 38, Ferdinand, IN 47532. TEL 812-367-2041; Ed. Richard Tretter. adv.; photos; pub. size: broadsheet; circ. 1,700(paid).
  Formerly: The Dale News.

FISHERS

US

CARMEL NEWS TRIBUNE. 1969. Wed. free; voluntary pay subscriptions. 13095 Publishers Dr., Fishers, IN 46038. TEL 317-598-6397; FAX 317-598-6360. **Owner(s):** Central Newspapers, Inc., 135 N. Pennsylvania Ave., Ste. 1200, Indianapolis, IN 46204-2400. TEL 317-231-9200; Ed. Tom Jekel; Pub. David Lewis; adv. contact: Scott Gause. photos; pub. size: broadsheet; circ. 17,750(free & paid).

US

CASTLETON BANNER. 1966. Wed. free; voluntary pay subscriptions. 13095 Publishers Dr., Fishers, IN 46038. TEL 317-598-6397; FAX 317-593-6360. **Owner(s):** Central Newspapers, Inc., 135 N. Pennsylvania Ave., Ste 1200, Indianapolis, IN 46204-2400. TEL 317-231-9200; FAX 317-231-9208; Ed. Renee Depew; Pub. David Lewis; adv. contact: Scott Gause. photos; pub. size: broadsheet; circ. 11,700(free & paid).

US

FISHERS SUN-HERALD. 1980. Wed. free; voluntary pay subscriptions. 13095 Publishers Dr., Fishers, IN 46038. TEL 317-598-6397; FAX 317-598-6360. **Owner(s):** Central Newspapers, Inc., 135 N. Pennsylvania Ave., Ste. 1200, Indianapolis, IN 46204-2400. TEL 317-231-9201; Pub. David Lewis; adv. contact: Scott Gause. photos; pub. size: broadsheet; circ. 12,800(free & paid). **Wire Service(s):** AP.

US

GEIST GAZETTE. 1961. Wed. free; voluntary pay subscriptions. 13095 Publishers Dr., Fishers, IN 46038. TEL 317-598-6397; FAX 317-598-6360. **Owner(s):** Central Newspapers, Inc., 135 N. Pennsylvania Ave., Ste. 1200, Indianapolis, IN 46204-2400. TEL 317-231-9201; Ed. Rene Depew; Pub. David Lewis; adv. contact: Scott Gause. photos; pub. size: broadsheet; circ. 2,000(free & paid).

US

GREENWOOD GAZETTE, THE. 1986. Thu. free; voluntary pay subscriptions. 13095 Publishers Dr., Fishers, IN 46038. TEL 317-598-6397; FAX 317-598-6360. **Owner(s):** Central Newspapers, Inc., 135 N. Pennsylvania St., Ste. 1200, Indianpolis, IN 46204-2400. TEL 317-231-9200; Ed. Rebecca Collier; Pub. David Lewis; adv. contact: Scott Gause. photos; bk.rev.; pub. size: broadsheet; circ. 14,000(free & paid).

US

HEIGHTS HERALD. 1981. Thu. free; voluntary pay subscriptions. 13095 Publishers Dr., Fishers, IN 46038. TEL 317-598-6397; FAX 317-598-6360. **Owner(s):** Central Newspapers, Inc., 135 N. Pennsylvania Ave., Ste. 1200, Indianapolis, IN 46204. TEL 317-231-9200; Ed. Rebecca Colier; Pub. David Lewis; adv. contact: Scott Gause. photos; pub. size: broadsheet; circ. 3,570(free & paid).
  Formerly: Northern Heights Herald.

US

LAWRENCE TIMES. 1970. Wed. free; voluntary pay subscriptions. 13095 Publishers Dr, Fishers, IN 46038. TEL 317-598-6397; FAX 317-598-6360. **Owner(s):** Central Newspapers, Inc., 135 N. Pennsylvania Ave., Ste 1200, Indianapolis, IN 46280. TEL 317-231-9200; Ed. Tom Jekel; Pub. David Lewis; adv. contact: Scott Gause. photos; pub. size: broadsheet; circ. 10,000(free & paid).

US

NORTH MERIDIAN OBSERVER. 1972. Wed. free; voluntary pay subscriptions. 13095 Publishers Dr., Fishers, IN 46038. TEL 317-598-6397; FAX 317-598-6360. **Owner(s):** Central Newspapers, Inc., 135 N. Pennsylvania Ave., Ste. 1200, Indianapolis, IN 46204-2400. TEL 317-231-9201; Ed. Renee Depew; Pub. David Lewis; adv. contact: Scott Gause. photos; pub. size: broadsheet; circ. 3,000(free & paid).

US

NORTH SIDE TOPICS. 1961. Wed. free; voluntary pay subscriptions. 13095 Publishers Dr., Fishers, IN 46038. TEL 317-598-6397; FAX 317-598-6360. **Owner(s):** Central Newspapers, Inc., 135 N. Pennsylvania Ave., Ste. 1200, Indianapolis, IN 46204-2400. TEL 317-231-9200; Ed. Tom Jekel; Pub. David Lewis; adv. contact: Scott Gause. photos; pub. size: broadsheet; circ. 4,000(free & paid). **Wire Service(s):** UPI.

US

PIKE REGISTER. 1972. Wed. free; voluntary pay subscriptions. 13095 Publishers Dr., Fishers, IN 46038. TEL 317-598-6397; FAX 317-598-6360. **Owner(s):** Central Newspapers, Inc., 135 N. Pennsylvania Ave., Ste. 1200, Indianapolis, IN 46204-2400. TEL 317-231-9201; Ed. Renee Depew; Pub. David Lewis; adv. contact: Scott Gause. photos; pub. size: broadsheet; circ. 8,000(free & paid). **Wire Service(s):** UPI.

US

SHERIDAN NEWS. 1882. Thu. free; voluntary pay subscriptions. 13095 Publishers Dr., Fishers, IN 46038. TEL 317-598-6397; FAX 317-598-6360. **Owner(s):** Central Newspapers, Inc., 135 N. Pennsylvania Ave., Ste. 1200, Indianapolis, IN 46204-2400. TEL 317-231-9201; Ed. Laura Musall; Pub. David Lewis; adv. contact: Scott Gause. photos; bk.rev.; pub. size: broadsheet; circ. 1,675(free & paid). **Wire Service(s):** AP.

US

WESTFIELD ENTERPRISE. 1978. Wed. free; voluntary pay subscriptions. 13095 Publishers Dr., Fishers, IN 46038. TEL 317-773-1210; FAX 317-773-3872. **Owner(s):** Central Newspapers, Inc., 135 N. Pennsylvania Ave., Ste. 1200, Indianapolis, IN 46204-2400. TEL 317-231-9201; Ed. Laura Musall; Pub. David Lewis; adv. contact: Scott Gause. photos; pub. size: broadsheet; circ. 4,300(free & paid). **Wire Service(s):** AP.

US

▼**WHITE RIVER GAZETTE.** 1996. Wed. free; voluntary pay subscriptions. 13095 Publishers Dr., Fishers, IN 46038. TEL 317-598-6397; FAX 317-598-6360. **Owner(s):** Central Newspapers, Inc., 135 N. Pennsylvania Ave., Ste. 1200, Indianapolis, IN 46204-2400. TEL 317-231-9201; Ed. Rebecca Collier; Pub. David Lewis; adv. contact: Scott Gause. photos; pub. size: broadsheet.

FISHERSPOLIS

US

NORA NEWS DISPATCH. 1961. Wed. free; voluntary pay subscriptions. 13095 Publishers Dr., Fisherspolis, IN 46038. TEL 317-598-6397; FAX 317-598-6360. **Owner(s):** Central Newspapers, Inc., 135 N. Pennsylvania Ave., Ste. 1200, Indianapolis, IN 46209-2400. TEL 317-231-9200; Ed. Rene Depew; Pub. David Lewis; adv. contact: Scott Gause. photos; pub. size: broadsheet; circ. 8,130(free & paid).

10594 FLORA, IN

WEEKLY NEWSPAPERS

FLORA
US
CARROLL COUNTY COMET. 1974. Wed. $.75 newsstand; $23/yr. local. 14 E. Main St., Flora, IN 46929. TEL 219-967-4135; FAX 219-967-4657. **Owner(s):** Carroll Papers, Inc., P.O. Box 26, Flora, IN 46929. TEL 219-967-4135; FAX 219-967-4657. Ed. Susan Scholl; Pub. Joseph L. Moss; adv. contact: Joseph L. Moss. pub. size: broadsheet; circ. 5,032(paid).

FOWLER
US
BENTON REVIEW, THE. 1875. Wed. $.50 newsstand; $17.50/yr. in cy.; $21/yr. out of cy. 102 E. Fifth St., Fowler, IN 47944. TEL 765-884-1902; FAX 765-884-8110. **Owner(s):** Benton Review Newspaper, 102 E. Fifth St., Fowler, IN 47944-0527. TEL 765-884-1902; FAX 765-884-8110; Ed. Karen Moyars; Pub. Karen Moyars; adv.: $2.50/SAU. photos; bk.rev.; pub. size: broadsheet; circ. 2,040(paid).
Formerly: Fowler Benton Review.

FRENCH LICK
US
SPRINGS VALLEY HERALD. 1903. Wed. $.40 newsstand; $16.95/yr. 211 College St., French Lick, IN 47432. TEL 812-936-9630; FAX 812-936-9559. **Owner(s):** Robert Denbo, P.O. Box 311, French Lick, IN 47432. TEL 812-936-9835; FAX 812-936-9559; Ed. Ruth Marshall; Pub. Robert Denbo; adv.: $2.80/SAU. photos; bk.rev.; pub. size: broadsheet; circ. 3,000(free & paid).

GARY
US
GARY CRUSADER. Thu. $.25 newsstand; $15/yr.; $26/2 yrs. 1549 Broadway, Gary, IN 46407. TEL 219-885-4357; FAX 219-883-3317. **Owner(s):** Dorothy R. Leavell, 1549 Broadway, Gary, IN 46407. TEL 219-885-4357; Ed. David Denson; Pub. Dorothy R. Leavell; adv. contact: John Smith. photos; pub. size: tabloid; circ. 32,000(paid).

US
GARY INFO. 1963. Thu. $.25 newsstand; $12/yr. local. 1953 Broadway, Gary, IN 46407. TEL 219-882-6711; FAX 219-886-1090. **Owner(s):** Info Printing & Publishing, Inc., 1953 Broadway, Gary, IN 46401. TEL 219-882-6711; Ed. Imogene Harris; Pub. Imogene Harris; adv. contact: Huston Pugh. adv.: $14.91/SAU. photos; bk.rev.; pub. size: tabloid; circ. 40,000(paid).

GOSHEN
US
PAPER, THE. 1973. Tue. free. 134 S. Main St., Goshen, IN 46526. TEL 219-534-2591; FAX 219-533-4820. **Owner(s):** Papers, Inc., The, P.O. Box 188, Milford, IN 46542. TEL 219-658-4815; FAX 219-658-4701; Ed. Jeri Seely; Pub. Della Baumgartner; adv. contact: Kip Schumm. photos; pub. size: tabloid; circ. 30,068(free).

GREENFIELD
US
AD-NEWS. 1979. Wed. free; $52/yr. P.O. Box 602, Greenfield, IN 46140-0602. TEL 317-462-7368; FAX 317-462-7779; E-mail: t3@surf-ici.com. **Owner(s):** Jim Thomas, P.O. Box 4, Greenfield, IN 46140-0004. TEL 317-462-7368; FAX 317-462-7779; Ed. Jim Thomas; Pub. Jim Thomas; adv.; photos; bk.rev.; pub. size: tabloid; circ. 17,000(free).

US
INDIANAPOLIS WESTSIDE ENTERPRISE. 1918. Wed. free; $65/yr. P.O. Box 602, Greenfield, IN 46170-0602. TEL 317-462-7368; FAX 317-462-7779; E-mail: tt3@spitfire.net. **Owner(s):** Jim Thomas, P.O. Box 4, Greenfield, IN 46140-0602. TEL 317-462-7368; FAX 317-462-7779; Ed. Jim Thomas; Pub. Jim Thomas; adv.; photos; bk.rev.; pub. size: tabloid; circ. 10,000(free).

US
INDY SUBURBAN NEWSPAPERS. 1975. Wed. free; $52/yr. P.O. Box 602, Greenfield, IN 46140-0602. TEL 317-462-7368; FAX 317-462-7779; E-mail: t3@surf.ici.com. **Owner(s):** Jim Thomas, P.O. Box 4, Greenfield, IN 46140. TEL 317-462-7368; FAX 317-462-7779; Ed. Jim Thomas; Pub. Jim Thomas; adv. contact: Ty Thomas. photos; bk.rev.; pub. size: tabloid; circ. 47,000(free & paid).

US
WESTSIDE ENTERPRISE. 1918. Wed. free; $52/yr. P.O. Box 602, Greenfield, IN 46140. TEL 317-462-7368; FAX 317-462-7779; E-mail: t3@surf-ici.com. **Owner(s):** Jim Thomas, P.O. Box 4, Greenfield, IN 46140. TEL 317-462-7368; FAX 317-462-7779; Ed. Jim Thomas; Pub. Jim Thomas; adv. contact: Ty Thomas. photos; bk.rev.; pub. size: tabloid; circ. 10,000(free & paid).

GREENWOOD
US   ISSN 8750-7390
FRANKLIN CHALLENGER. 1984. Wed. $.25 newsstand; $12/yr. 310 W. Main, Greenwood, IN 46142. TEL 317-888-3376; FAX 317-888-3377. **Owner(s):** Guerrettaz Industries, Inc., P.O. Box 708, Greenwood, IN 46142. TEL 317-888-3376; FAX 317-888-3377; Ed. Don Guerrettaz; Pub. Don Guerrettaz; adv.; photos; bk.rev.; pub. size: tabloid; circ. 600(paid).

US
GREENWOOD & SOUTHSIDE CHALLENGER. 1972. w. $.50 newsstand; $15/yr. 310 W. Main, Greenwood, IN 46142. TEL 317-888-3376; FAX 317-888-3377. **Owner(s):** Guerrettaz Industries, Inc., 310 W. Main, Greenwood, IN 46142. TEL 317-888-3376; Ed. Don Guerrettaz; Pub. Don Guerrettaz; adv.; photos; bk.rev.; pub. size: tabloid; circ. 1,200(paid).
Formerly: Southside Challenger.

HAGERSTOWN
US
HAGERSTOWN EXPONENT, THE. 1875. Wed. $.50 newsstand; $25.50/yr. 99 S. Perry St., Hagerstown, IN 47346-1521. TEL 317-489-4035. **Owner(s):** Hagerstown Newspapers, Inc., 99 S. Perrry St., Hagerstown, IN 47346-1521. TEL 317-489-4035; Ed. Robert A. Hansen; Pub. Patricia J. Hansen; adv.: $4.75/SAU. pub. size: broadsheet; circ. 2,250(paid).

HIGHLAND
US   ISSN 1075-6981
CALUMET PRESS, THE. 1957. Wed. free; $18/yr. mailed. 8411 Kennedy Ave., Highland, IN 46322. TEL 219-838-0717; FAX 219-838-1338. **Owner(s):** Wayne & Helen Kletzing, 8411 Kennedy Ave., Highland, IN 46322. TEL 219-838-0717; H.D. Van Kooten, 747 Raymond St., Griffith, IN 46319; Ed. Jeanne Larsen; Pub. Helen D. Kletzing; adv. contact: Laura Mech. photos; pub. size: tabloid; circ. 41,193(free).

HOPE
US
STAR JOURNAL. 1912. Thu. $.50 newsstand; $16/yr. in cy.; $20/yr. out of cy. 611 Harrison St., Hope, IN 47246. TEL 812-546-6113; FAX 812-546-6114. **Owner(s):** Dion Stenneski, 611 Harrison St., Hope, IN 47246. TEL 812-546-6113; Ed. Charles Biggs; Pub. Dion Stenneski; adv.; pub. size: broadsheet; circ. 1,500(paid).

INDIANAPOLIS
US
EAST SIDE HERALD. 1968. Thu. free newsstand; $45/yr. 4309 E. Michigan St., Indianapolis, IN 46201. TEL 317-356-2487; FAX 317-356-2486. **Owner(s):** East Side Communications Corp., 4309 E. Michigan St., Indianapolis, IN 46201. TEL 317-356-2487; Ed. Helen Thoele; Pub. William K. Thoele; pub. size: tabloid; circ. 38,500(controlled).

US
INDIANAPOLIS RECORDER. 1895. Thu. $.75 newsstand; $39/yr.; $33/yr. senior citizens. 2901 N. Tacoma Ave., Indianapolis, IN 46218. TEL 317-924-5143; FAX 317-924-5148. **Owner(s):** William Mayes, 2901 N. Tacoma Ave., Indianapolis, IN 46218. TEL 317-924-5143; Ed. Connie Gaines-Hayes. adv.; photos; pub. size: broadsheet; circ. 20,000(paid). **Wire Service(s):** AP.

US
NORTHEAST REPORTER. 1935. Thu. free newsstand; $45/yr. 4309 E. Michigan St., Indianapolis, IN 46201. TEL 317-356-2487. **Owner(s):** East Side Communications Corp., 4309 E. Michigan St., Indianapolis, IN 46201. TEL 317-356-2487; Ed. Helen Thoele; Pub. William K. Thoele; pub. size: broadsheet; circ. 16,000(controlled).

US
NUVO NEWSWEEKLY. 1990. Thu. free newsstand; $8/mo.; $95/yr. 811 E. Westfield Blvd., Indianapolis, IN 46220. TEL 317-254-2400; FAX 317-254-2405. **Owner(s):** Kevin McKinney, 811 E. Westfield Blvd., Indianapolis, IN 46220. TEL 317-254-2400; FAX 317-254-2405; Ed. Harrison J. Ullmann; Pub. Kevin K. McKinney; adv. contact: Bill Platt. photos; bk.rev.; pub. size: tabloid; circ. 40,000(free).

US
SPOTLIGHT, THE. 1939. Wed. free newsstand; $45/yr. mailed. 4217 S. Meridian, Indianapolis, IN 46217. TEL 317-788-4554. **Owner(s):** Jerry Cosby, 4217 S. Meridian St., Indianapolis, IN 46217. TEL 317-788-4554; Ed. Jerry Cosby. adv.: $8/SAU. photos; pub. size: broadsheet; circ. 25,000(free & paid).

WEEKLY NEWSPAPERS

MARYVILLE, IN

US
WESTSIDE FLYER. 1993. Mon. $.50 newsstand; $21/yr. local. 7207 W. Tenth St., Indianapolis, IN 46214. TEL 317-487-1422; FAX 317-487-1158; E-mail: flyergrp@iquest.net; URL: http://www.flyergroup.com. **Owner(s):** McCarthy Media, Inc., 202 N. Mill St., Plainfield, IN 46168. TEL 317-839-5129; FAX 317-839-6546; Ed. Marc Sirkin; Pub. W. Jack McCarthy; adv. contact: Michael Schaefer. bk.rev.; pub. size: broadsheet; circ. 10,500(free & paid).

KNIGHTSTOWN

US   ISSN 0164-8640
FARMWEEK. 1955. Wed. $19.95/yr. local states. 27 N. Jefferson St., Knightstown, IN 46148. TEL 317-345-5133; FAX 800-813-1055; E-mail: farmwk@aol.com. **Owner(s):** Mayhill Publications, Inc., 27 N. Jefferson St., Knightstown, IN 46148. TEL 317-345-5133; Ed. Nancy Searfoss; Pub. R. Thomas Mayhill; adv. contact: Freda Dudley. photos; pub. size: tabloid; circ. 28,295(paid).

US
TRI-COUNTY BANNER. 1962. Wed. $.75 newsstand; $24/yr. local; $48/yr. outside area. 16 N. Washington St., Knightstown, IN 46148. TEL 317-345-2111; FAX 317-345-2186. **Owner(s):** Ty Swinsher Publishing Co., P.O. Box 116, Knightstown, IN 46148. TEL 317-345-2111; Pub. Ty Swinsher; adv. contact: Jenny Rose. pub. size: tabloid; circ. 3,500(paid).

LA CROSSE

US
REGIONAL NEWS, THE. 1915. Thu. $.40 newsstand; $20/yr. in cy.; $24/yr. out of cy. P.O. Box 358, La Crosse, IN 46348. TEL 219-785-2234. **Owner(s):** Richard N. Slater, 9852 W. State Rd., Ste. 2, LaPorte, IN 46350. TEL 219-785-2234; Ed. Richard N. Slater; Pub. Richard N. Slater; adv.; photos; bk.rev.; pub. size: broadsheet; circ. 8,100(paid).

LAFAYETTE

US
LAFAYETTE LEADER. 1883. Thu. $1 newsstand; $40/yr. 22 N. Second St., Lafayette, IN 47902-1100. TEL 317-423-2624; FAX 317-742-5156. **Owner(s):** Dennis Dunn, 22 N. Second St., Lafayette, IN 47901. TEL 317-423-2624; Ed. Lynn Holland; Pub. Dennis Dunn; adv.; pub. size: tabloid; circ. 5,000(paid).

LA GRANGE

US
LA GRANGE STANDARD NEWS. 1856. Wed. $.50 newsstand; $25/yr. local. State Rd. 9, S., La Grange, IN 46761. TEL 219-463-2166; FAX 219-463-2734. **Owner(s):** La Grange Publishing Co., Inc., P.O. Box 148, LaGrange, IN 46761. TEL 219-463-2166; Ed. William F. Connelly; Pub. William F. Connelly; adv. contact: Norm Heign. pub. size: broadsheet; circ. 7,200(paid).

LA PORTE

US
TOWN CRIER, THE. 1933. Mon. Free; $1/wk. mailed out of area. 2700 Monroe St., La Porte, IN 46350. TEL 219-362-8519; FAX 219-325-0677. **Owner(s):** Towndan Enterprises, Inc., 2700 Monroe St., La Porte, IN 46350. TEL 219-362-8519; adv.; pub. size: tabloid; circ. 75,000(free).
Formerly: Northwest Town Crier.

LAWRENCE

US
CUMBERLAND COURIER. 1983. Tue. free. 7962 Pendleton Pike, Lawrence, IN 46226. TEL 317-542-8149; FAX 317-542-1137. **Owner(s):** Joseph E. Zainey Enterprises, Inc., 7962 Pendleton Pike, Lawrence, IN 46226. TEL 317-542-8149; FAX 317-542-1137; Ed. Shelly Zainey; Pub. Joseph E. Zainey; adv. contact: Shelly Zainey. photos; bk.rev.; pub. size: tabloid; circ. 12,500(free).
Formerly: Indianapolis Ad-Courier.

US
LAWRENCE TOWNSHIP JOURNAL. 1944. Wed. $.50 newsstand; $20/yr. 7962 Pendleton Pike, Lawrence, IN 46226. TEL 317-542-8149; FAX 317-542-1137. **Owner(s):** Joseph E. Zainey Enterprises, Inc., 7962 Pendleton Ave., Lawrence, IN 46226. TEL 317-542-8149; FAX 317-542-1137; Ed. Shelly Zainey; Pub. Joseph E. Zainey; adv. contact: Shelly Zainey. photos; pub. size: tabloid; circ. 10,000(free & paid).

LAWRENCEBURG

US
DEARBORN COUNTY REGISTER. 1825. Thu. $.75 newsstand; $33/yr. in IN, combined w/Journal Press; $72/yr. elsewhere. 126 W. High St., Lawrenceburg, IN 47025. TEL 812-537-0063; FAX 812-537-5576. **Owner(s):** Delphos Newspapers, 405 N. Main St., Delphos, OH 45833. TEL 419-645-0015; Ed. Joe Awad; Pub. John Reiniger; adv. contact: Janet Essert. adv.: $6.75/SAU. pub. size: broadsheet; circ. 8,805(paid).

US
JOURNAL PRESS. 1858. Tue. $.75 newsstand; $33/yr. IN. combined with Dearborn County Register; $72/yr. elsewhere. 126 W. High St., Lawrenceburg, IN 47025. TEL 812-537-0063; FAX 812-537-5576. **Owner(s):** Delphos Newspapers, 405 N. Main St., Delphos, OH 45833. TEL 419-645-0015; Ed. Joe Awad; Pub. John Reiniger; adv. contact: Janet Essert. adv.: $6.25/SAU. pub. size: broadsheet; circ. 6,893(paid).

LIGONIER

US
ADVERTISER, THE. Mon. free. 121 S. Cavin, Ligonier, IN 46767. TEL 219-894-3102; FAX 219-894-3104. **Owner(s):** Kendallville Publishing Co., 112 N. Main St., Kendallville, IN 46755. TEL 219-347-0400; Ed. Bob Buttgen; Pub. Jim Kroemer; adv. contact: Carol Arnold. pub. size: standard; circ. 14,000(free).

US
LIGONIER ADVANCE-LEADER. 1880. Thu. $.75 newsstand; $34/yr. 121 S. Cavin, Ligonier, IN 46767. TEL 219-894-3102; FAX 219-894-3104. **Owner(s):** Kendallville Publishing Co., 112 N. Main St., Kendallville, IN 46755. TEL 219-347-0400; Ed. Bob Buttgen; Pub. Jim Kroemer; adv.; pub. size: broadsheet; circ. 3,000(paid).

LOWELL

US
CEDAR LAKE JOURNAL. 1967. Wed. free mailed. 116 Clark St., Lowell, IN 46356. TEL 219-696-7711; FAX 219-696-7713. **Owner(s):** Pilcher Publishing Co., Inc., 116 Clark St., Lowell, IN 46356; FAX 219-696-7711; Ed. L.H. Pilcher; Pub. L.H. Pilcher; adv.: $5.95/SAU. pub. size: broadsheet; circ. 5,000(free).

US
LOWELL TRIBUNE. 1885. Wed. $.25 newsstand; $12/yr. 116 Clark St., Lowell, IN 46356. TEL 219-696-7711; FAX 219-696-7713. **Owner(s):** Pilcher Publishing Co., Inc., 116 Clark St., P.O. Box 248, Lowell, IN 46356. TEL 219-696-7711; FAX 219-696-7713; Ed. L.H. Pilcher; Pub. L.H. Pilcher; adv.: $10.05/SAU. photos; pub. size: broadsheet; circ. 5,000(paid).

US
SOUTH LAKE ADVERTISER. 1885. Tue. free. 116 Clark St., Lowell, IN 46356. TEL 219-696-7711; FAX 219-696-7713. **Owner(s):** Pilcher Publishing Co., Inc., 116 Clark St., P.O. Box 248, Lowell, IN 46356. TEL 219-698-7711; Ed. L.H. Pilcher. adv.: $5.95/SAU. pub. size: broadsheet; circ. 5,000(free).
Formerly: South Lake County Advertiser.

MARYVILLE

US
CHESTERTON GUIDE. 1988. Wed. free. 3161 E. 84th Pl., Maryville, IN 46410. TEL 219-762-9564; FAX 219-942-0820. **Owner(s):** Citizen Publishing Co., 805 Park Ave., Beaver Dam, WI 53916. TEL 414-887-0321; Ed. Rory Holscher; Pub. Rory Holscher; adv. contact: Diane Kemp. pub. size: tabloid; circ. 6,100(free).
Formerly: Chesterton News.

US
GRIFFITH GUIDE. Wed. free. 3161 E. 84th St., Maryville, IN 46410-1615. TEL 219-838-5999; FAX 219-838-7999. **Owner(s):** Citizen Publishing Co., 805 Park Ave., Beaver Dam, WI 53916. TEL 414-887-0321; Ed. Greg Lenburg. adv. contact: Diane Kemp. pub. size: tabloid; circ. 12,000(free).
Formerly: Griffith News.

US
HIGHLAND GUIDE. Wed. free. 3161 E. 84th St., Maryville, IN 46410. TEL 219-838-5999; FAX 219-838-7999. **Owner(s):** Citizen Publishing Co., 805 Park Ave., Beaver Dam, WI 53916. TEL 414-887-0321; FAX 414-887-2779; Ed. Greg Lenburg. adv. contact: Diane Kemp. pub. size: tabloid; circ. 9,335(free).
Formerly: Highland News.

US
MUNSTER GUIDE. Wed. free. 3161 E. 84th Pl., Maryville, IN 46410. TEL 219-838-5999; FAX 219-838-7999. **Owner(s):** Citizen Publishing Co., 805 Park Ave., Beaver Dam, WI 53916. TEL 414-887-0321; FAX 414-887-2779; Ed. Greg Lenburg. adv. contact: Diane Kemp. pub. size: tabloid; circ. 8,450(free).
Formerly: Munster News.

10596 MARYVILLE, IN

WEEKLY NEWSPAPERS

Weeklies

US
SCHERERVILLE GUIDE. Wed. free. 3161 E. 84th Pl., Maryville, IN 46410-1615. TEL 219-924-5631; FAX 219-924-5671. **Owner(s):** Citizen Publishing Co., 805 Park Ave., Beaver Dam, WI 53916. TEL 414-887-0321; FAX 414-924-5671; Ed. Greg Lenburg. adv. contact: Diane Kemp. photos; pub. size: tabloid; circ. 18,889(free).
Formerly: Schererville News.

US
VALPARAISO GUIDE. 1985. Wed. free. 3161 E. 84th St., Maryville, IN 46410. TEL 219-762-9564; FAX 219-763-1602. **Owner(s):** Citizen Publishing Co., 805 Park Ave., Beaver Dam, WI 53916. TEL 414-887-0321; FAX 414-887-2779; Ed. Greg Lenburg. adv. contact: Diane Kemp. pub. size: tabloid; circ. 17,002(free).
Formerly: Valparaiso News.

MERRILLVILLE

US ISSN 1044-2839
HOLBERT LAKE STATION COMMUNITY SHOPPING GUIDE. 1946. Thu. free. 3161 E. 84th Pl., Merrillville, IN 46410. TEL 219-942-8914; FAX 219-942-3925. **Owner(s):** Citizen Publishing Co., 805 Park Ave., Beaver Dam, WI 53916. TEL 414-887-0321; Ed. Steve Euvino. adv. contact: Diane Kemp. pub. size: tabloid; circ. 1,500(free).
Formerly: Lake Station Herald.

US ISSN 1043-9587
MERRILLVILLE HERALD COMMUNITY SHOPPING GUIDE. 1944. Wed. free. 3161 E. 84th Pl., Merrillville, IN 46410. TEL 219-942-0521; FAX 219-942-0820. **Owner(s):** Citizen Publishing Co., 805 Park Ave., Beaver Dam, WI 53916. TEL 414-887-0321; adv. contact: Diane Kemp. pub. size: tabloid; circ. 11,375(free).
Formerly: Merrillville Herald.

MERRILVILLE

US
PORTAGE COMMUNITY SHOPPING GUIDE. 1970. Wed. free. 3161 E. 84th Pl., Merrillville, IN 46410. TEL 219-762-9564; FAX 219-763-1602. **Owner(s):** Citizen Publishing Co., 805 Park Ave., Beaver Dam, WI 53916. TEL 414-887-0321; adv. contact: Diane Kemp. pub. size: tabloid; circ. 14,868(free).
Formerly: Portage Journal-Press.

MERRIVILLE

US
HOBART GAZETTE. 1887. Wed. $20/yr. in cy.; $26/yr. out of cy. 3161 E. 84th Pl., Merriville, IN 46410. TEL 219-942-6575;
FAX 219-942-0820. **Owner(s):** Citizen Publishing Co., 805 Park Ave., Beaver Dam, WI 53916. TEL 414-692-5476; Ed. Rory Holscher. adv. contact: Diane Kemp. pub. size: tabloid; circ. 4,550(paid).

MIDDLETOWN

US
MIDDLETOWN NEWS, THE. 1885. Thu. $.50 newsstand. 469 Locust St., Middletown, IN 47356-0096. TEL 765-354-2221. **Owner(s):** Jack N. White, 469 Locust St., P.O Box 96, Middletown, IN 47356-0096. TEL 765-354-2221; FAX 765-354-2221; Ed. Cheryl Hines; Pub. Jack N. White; adv.; bk.rev.; pub. size: tabloid; circ. 1,777(paid).

MILFORD

US
MAIL-JOURNAL, THE. 1888. Wed. $.50 newsstand; $23.50/yr. 206 S. Main, Milford, IN 46542. TEL 219-658-4111; FAX 219-658-4701. **Owner(s):** Papers, Inc., The, P.O. Box 188, Milford, IN 46542. TEL 219-658-4111; FAX 219-658-4701; Ed. Jeri Seely; Pub. Della Baumgartner; adv. contact: Kip Schumn. photos; pub. size: broadsheet; circ. 3,100(paid).

MISHAWAKA

US
MISHAWAKA ENTERPRISE. Thu. $.40 newsstand; $12.50/yr. in cy. 1115 S. Spring St., Mishawaka, IN 46546. TEL 219-255-4789; FAX 219-255-4789. **Owner(s):** Ecom Corp., IN; Ed. William Nich. adv.; pub. size: tabloid; circ. 1,500(paid).

MOORESVILLE

US
MOORESVILLE TIMES, THE. 1871. Wed. $.50 newsstand; $20/yr. 23 E. Main St., Mooresville, IN 46158-0308. TEL 317-831-0280; FAX 317-831-7068. **Owner(s):** Reporter-Times, Inc., 60 S. Jefferson St., Martinsville, IN 46151. TEL 317-342-3311; FAX 317-342-1446; Ed. Steve Heath; Pub. Sharon Clipp; adv. contact: Sharon Clipp. pub. size: broadsheet; circ. 6,793(paid).

MT. VERNON

US
MOUNT VERNON DEMOCRAT. 1867. Wed. $.50 newsstand; $22/yr. 425 Main St., Mt. Vernon, IN 47620. TEL 812-838-4811; FAX 812-838-3696. **Owner(s):** Landmark Community Newspapers, Inc., P.O. Box 549, Shelbyville, KY 40066; Ed. David Pearce. adv. contact: Brenda Higgins. adv.: $6.53/SAU. pub. size: broadsheet; circ. 3,500(paid).

NASHVILLE

US
BROWN COUNTY DEMOCRAT. 1870. Wed. $.50 newsstand; $24/yr. in cy.; $34/yr. out of cy. 136 N. Van Buren St., Nashville, IN 47448-0277. TEL 812-988-2221; FAX 812-988-1570; E-mail: mlewis7664@aol.com. **Owner(s):** Greg Temple, P.O. Box 277, Nashville, IN 47448. TEL 812-988-2221; FAX 812-988-1570; Ed. Mike Lewis; Pub. Greg Temple; adv. contact: Keith Fleener. pub. size: broadsheet; circ. 4,495(paid).
Formerly: Nashville Brown County Democrat.

NEWBURGH

US
NEWBURGH-CHANDLER REGISTER. 1886. Wed. $26/yr. 501 State St., Newburgh, IN 47630. TEL 812-853-3366; FAX 812-853-8685. **Owner(s):** Brehm Communications, Inc., 17065 Via del Campo, Ste. 200, San Diego, CA 92127. TEL 619-451-6200; Ed. Robert Dewig; Pub. Myra Teal; adv. contact: Joe Stoll. pub. size: standard; circ. 3,002(paid).
Formerly: Newburgh Register.

NEW CARLISLE

US
NEW PRAIRIE TOWN CRIER. Mon. free. 115 E. Michigan St., New Carlisle, IN 46552. TEL 219-654-7468; FAX 219-654-7468. **Owner(s):** Towndan Enterprises, Inc., 2700 Monore St., La Porte, IN 46350. TEL 219-362-8519; Pub. Georgory L. Jones; circ. 4,464(free).

NEW HAVEN

US
ALLEN COUNTY TIMES. 1991. Wed. $.25 newsstand; $17.50/yr. 405 Broadway, New Haven, IN 46774-1105. TEL 219-493-2464. **Owner(s):** Ronald K. Oetting, 517 Broadway, New Haven, IN 46774. TEL 219-493-2464; Ed. Robert E. Nylund; Pub. Ronald K. Oetting; adv.; photos; pub. size: tabloid; circ. 5,000(controlled).
Formerly: New Allen News, New Haven Mews.

NORTH MANCHESTER

US
NEWS-JOURNAL. 1873. Wed. $.50 newsstand; $39/yr. 112 W. Main St., North Manchester, IN 46962-0324. TEL 219-982-6383; FAX 219-982-8233; E-mail: whweller@ctlnet.com. **Owner(s):** Susan E. Weller, 207 S. Maple St., North Manchester, IN 46962. TEL 219-982-6383; Worth Weller, 207 S. Maple St., North Manchester, IN 46962. TEL 219-982-6383; Ed. Rick Rogers; Pub. Worth Weller; adv. contact: Cheryl Wilson. pub. size: tabloid; circ. 2,500(paid).

NORTH VERNON

US
NORTH VERNON PLAIN DEALER. 1864. Thu. $.50 newsstand; $26/yr. local; $30.50/yr. in state & surrounding states; $35/yr. elsewhere. 528 E. O & M Ave., North Vernon, IN 47265. TEL 812-346-3973; FAX 812-346-8368. **Owner(s):** Barbara King, P.O. Box 410, North Vernon, IN 47265. TEL 812-346-3973; Madelan & Susan King, P.O. Box 410, North Vernon, IN 47265. TEL 812-346-3973; Ed. Barbara King; Pub. Barbara King; adv.; photos; pub. size: standard; circ. 6,800(paid).

US
NORTH VERNON SUN. 1876. Tue. $.50 newsstand; $26/yr. local; $30.50 in state & surrounding states; $35/yr. elsewhere. 528 E. O & M Ave., North Vernon, IN 47265. TEL 812-346-3973; FAX 812-346-8368. **Owner(s):** Barbara King, P.O. Box 410, North Vernon, IN 47265. TEL 812-346-3973; Viola King, P.O. Box 410, North Vernon, IN 47265. TEL 812-346-3973; Ed. Barbara King; Pub. Barbara King; adv.; photos; pub. size: standard; circ. 5,800(paid).

OSSIAN

US
OSSIAN JOURNAL. 1912. Thu. $.35 newsstand; $15.50/yr. local; $17/yr. out of area. 105 N. Jefferson St., Ossian, IN 46777. TEL 219-622-4108; FAX 219-622-4108. **Owner(s):** James C. Barbieri, 125 N. Johnson, P.O. Box 436, Bluffton, IN 46714. TEL 219-824-0224; FAX 219-824-0700; George Witwer, 125 N. Johnson St., P.O. Box 436, Bluffton, IN 46714. TEL 219-824-0224; FAX 219-824-0700; Ed. George Witwer; Pub. James C. Barbieri; adv. contact: Nila Dafforn. photos; pub. size: broadsheet; circ. 725(paid). **Wire Service(s):** AP.

ULRICH'S INTERNATIONAL PERIODICALS DIRECTORY 1998

WEEKLY NEWSPAPERS

US
SUNRISER NEWS. 1978. Tue. free. 105 N. Jefferson St., Ossian, IN 46777. TEL 219-622-4108; FAX 219-622-4108. **Owner(s):** James C. Barbieri, 125 N. Johnson, P.O. Box 436, Bluffton, IN 46714. TEL 219-824-0224; George Witwer, 125 N. Johnson St., P.O. Box 436, Bluffton, IN 46714. TEL 219-824-0224; Ed. George Witwer; Pub. James C. Barbieri; adv. contact: Nila Dafforn. photos; pub. size: tabloid; circ. 600(free).

PAOLI

US
ORANGE COUNTIAN. 1984. Wed. free. 131 N.W. Court St., Paoli, IN 47454. TEL 812-723-2572; FAX 812-723-2592. **Owner(s):** Orange County Publishing Co., Inc., P.O. Box 190, Paoli, IN 47454. TEL 812-723-2572; Ed. Brenda Cornwell; Pub. Helen M. Gooch; adv.; pub. size: standard; circ. 9,150(free).

US
PAOLI NEWS. 1872. Thu. $21/yr. local; $21/yr. area cys.; $30/yr. elsewhere. 131 N.W. Court St., Paoli, IN 47454. TEL 812-723-2572; FAX 812-723-2592. **Owner(s):** Orange County Publishing Co., Inc., P.O. Box 190, Paoli, IN 47454. TEL 812-723-2572; Ed. Brenda Cornwell; Pub. F. Wendell Gooch; adv.; pub. size: broadsheet; circ. 3,100(paid).

US
PAOLI REPUBLICAN. 1872. Tue. $21/yr. local & surrounding cys.; $30/yr. elsewhere. 131 N.W. Court St., Paoli, IN 47454. TEL 812-723-2572; FAX 812-723-2592. **Owner(s):** Orange County Publishing Co., Inc., P.O. Box 190, Paoli, IN 47454. TEL 812-723-2572; FAX 812-723-2592; Ed. Brenda Cornwell; Pub. Arthur Hampton; adv.; pub. size: broadsheet; circ. 3,200(paid).

PEKIN

US ISSN 1053-2218
AUCTIONER, THE. 1989. Wed. $.25 newsstand; $25/yr. 490 E. Hwy. 60, Pekin, IN 47165. TEL 812-967-3176; FAX 812-967-3194. **Owner(s):** Green Banner Publications, P.O. Box 38, Pekin, IN 47165. TEL 812-967-3176; Pub. Joe Green; adv. contact: John Roberts. pub. size: tabloid; circ. 500(paid).

US ISSN 0194-3545
BANNER-GAZETTE. 1919. Wed. $.25 newsstand; $18.50/yr. 490 E. Hwy. 60, Pekin, IN 47165. TEL 812-967-3176; FAX 812-967-3194. **Owner(s):** Green Banner Publications, P.O. Box 38, Pekin, IN 47165; Ed. Mark Grigsby; Pub. Joe Green; adv. contact: John Roberts. pub. size: tabloid; circ. 16,500(free & paid).

PETERSBURG

US
PRESS-DISPATCH. 1885. Thu. $.75 newsstand; $15/yr. 820 Poplar St., Petersburg, IN 47567. TEL 812-354-8500; FAX 812-354-2014. **Owner(s):** Press Dispatch, The, P.O. Box 68, Petersburg, IN 47567. TEL 812-354-8500; FAX 812-354-2014; Ed. Andy Heuring. adv. contact: John Heuring. pub. size: broadsheet; circ. 5,800(paid).

PLAINFIELD

US ISSN 0193-4910
HENDRICKS COUNTY FLYER. 1965. Mon. $.50 newsstand; $60/yr. in state; $70/yr. out of state. 202 N. Mill St., Plainfield, IN 46168. TEL 317-839-5129; FAX 317-839-6546. **Owner(s):** McCarthy Media, Inc., 202 N. Mill St., Plainfield, IN 46168. TEL 317-839-5129; FAX 317-839-6546; Ed. Tim Evans; Pub. W. Jack McCarthy; adv. contact: Michael Schaefer. photos; bk.rev.; pub. size: broadsheet; circ. 32,000(free & paid).

US
WEEKEND FLYER, THE. 1907. Thu. $.50 newsstand; $21/yr. 202 N. Mill, Plainfield, IN 46168. TEL 317-839-5129; FAX 317-839-6546; E-mail: flyergrp@iquest.net; URL: http://www.flyergroup.com. **Owner(s):** McCarthy Media, Inc., 202 N. Mill, P.O. Box 6, Plainfield, IN 46168. TEL 317-839-5129; FAX 317-839-6546; Ed. Tim Evans; Pub. W. Jack McCarthy; adv.; pub. size: broadsheet; circ. 6,000(paid).
Formerly: Plainfield Messenger.

RENSSELAER

US ISSN 1060-5231
COURIER, THE. Wed. $.50 newsstand; $25/yr. in cy.; $27/yr. out of cy.; $32/yr. out of state. 117 N. Van Rensselaer St., Rensselaer, IN 47978. TEL 219-866-5111; FAX 219-866-3775. **Owner(s):** KanKakee Valley Publishing Co., 117 N. Van Rensselaer St., Rensselaer, IL 47978; Ed. William F. Kaye. adv.; photos; bk.rev.; pub. size: standard; circ. 1,000(paid).

US
REMINGTON PRESS. 1873. Wed. $.50 newsstand; $25/yr. in cy.; $27/yr. in IN.; $32/yr. out of state. 117 N. Van Rensselaer St., Rensselaer, IN 47978. TEL 219-866-5111; FAX 219-866-3775. **Owner(s):** Kankakee Valley Publishing Co., 117 N. Van Rensselaer St., Rensselaer, IN 47978; Ed. William F. Kaye. adv. contact: Frank Copley. photos; bk.rev.; pub. size: standard; circ. 1,000(paid).

RISING SUN

US
OHIO COUNTY NEWS. 1833. Thu. $.60 newsstand; $16/yr. 235 Main St., Rising Sun, IN 47040. TEL 812-438-2011; FAX 812-537-5576. **Owner(s):** Register Publications, 126 W. High St., Lawrenceburg, IN 47025. TEL 812-537-0063; Ed. Tim Hillman; Pub. John Reiniger; pub. size: broadsheet; circ. 711(free & paid).

US
RISING SUN RECORDER. 1834. Thu. $.60 newsstand; $16/yr. 235 Main St., Rising Sun, IN 47040. TEL 812-438-2011; FAX 812-537-5576. **Owner(s):** Register Publications, 126 W. High St., Lawrenceburg, IN 47025. TEL 812-537-0063; Ed. Tim Hillman; Pub. John Reiniger; pub. size: broadsheet; circ. 1,560(paid).

ROCKPORT

US
SPENCER COUNTY JOURNAL DEMOCRAT. 1850. Thu. $.50 newsstand; $22/yr. in cy. 541 Main St., Rockport, IN 47635. TEL 812-649-4440; FAX 812-649-9197. **Owner(s):** Landmark Community Newspapers, Inc., P.O. Box 549, Shelbyville, KY 40066. TEL 502-633-4334; Ed. Stilla Janosa McMahon. adv. contact: Kim Litkenhus. photos; pub. size: broadsheet; circ. 6,100(paid).
Formerly: Journal Democrat.

ROCKVILLE

US ISSN 1044-7822
ROCKVILLE PARKE COUNTY SENTINEL. 1833. Wed. $.40 newsstand; $23/yr. in state; $25/yr. out of state. 125 W. High St., Rockville, IN 47872. TEL 765-569-2033; FAX 765-569-1424. **Owner(s):** Torch Newspapers, Inc., P.O. Box 187, Rockville, IN 47872. TEL 765-569-2033; Ed. Larry Bemis; Pub. Richard E. Harney; adv.; pub. size: broadsheet; circ. 4,400(paid).

SALEM

US
SALEM DEMOCRAT, THE. 1827. Thu. $.50 newsstand; $24/yr. local; $33/yr. in state; $39/yr. out of state. 117 E. Walnut St., Salem, IN 47167. TEL 812-883-3282; FAX 812-883-4446. **Owner(s):** Leader Publishing Co., Inc., P.O. Box 509, Salem, IN 47167. TEL 812-883-3282; FAX 812-883-4446; Ed. Cecil J. Smith; Pub. Rodger J. Grossman; adv. contact: Patricia Robertson. photos; pub. size: broadsheet; circ. 6,500(paid).

US
SALEM LEADER. 1878. Tue. $.50 newsstand; $24/yr. local; $33/yr. in state; $39/yr. out of state. 117 E. Walnut St., Salem, IN 47167-0509. TEL 812-883-3281; FAX 812-883-4446. **Owner(s):** Leader Publishing Co., Inc., P.O. Box 509, Salem, IN 47167. TEL 812-883-3281; FAX 812-883-4446; Ed. Cecil J. Smith; Pub. Rodger J. Grossman; adv. contact: Patricia Robertson. pub. size: broadsheet; circ. 6,500(paid).

US
WASHINGTON COUNTY EDITION. 1982. w. $15/yr. 105 E. Walnut St., Salem, IN 47167. TEL 812-883-5555; FAX 812-883-3658. **Owner(s):** Green Banner Publications, 105 E. Walnut St., Salem, IN 47167. TEL 812-883-5555; Ed. Mark Grigsby; Pub. Joe Green; adv. contact: John Roberts. pub. size: tabloid; circ. 10,063(free & paid).

SCOTTSBURG

US
GIVEAWAY, THE. 1937. Wed. free; $15/yr. 183 E. McLain, Scottsburg, IN 47170. TEL 812-967-3176; FAX 812-752-6468. **Owner(s):** Green Banner Publications, P.O. Box 38, Pekin, IN 47165. TEL 812-967-3176; Pub. Joe Green; adv. contact: John Roberts. pub. size: tabloid; circ. 16,277(free & paid).

US
JOURNAL & AUSTIN CHRONICLE. 1882. w.: Sat. $.25 newsstand; $8.75/yr. local. 183 E. McClain, Scottsburg, IN 47170. TEL 812-752-3171; FAX 812-752-6486. **Owner(s):** Green Banner Publications, P.O. Box 38, Pekin, IN 47165. TEL 812-967-3176; Ed. Mark Grigsby; Pub. Joe Green; adv. contact: John Roberts. pub. size: broadsheet; circ. 5,000(paid).

SOUTH BEND

US
TRI-COUNTY NEWS. 1923. Fri. $10/yr. in cy.; $17.50/2 yrs.; $14.50/yr. out of cy.; $25.50/2 yrs. P.O. Box 6666, South Bend, IN 46660-6666. TEL 219-287-0285; FAX 219-282-1716. **Owner(s):** Cherie Jolly, 918 E. Jefferson, South Bend, IN 46617. TEL 219-287-0285; FAX 219-282-1716; Ed. Cherie Jolly; Pub. Cherie Jolly; adv.; pub. size: tabloid; circ. 1,000(paid).
Formerly: South Bend Tri-County News.

SPEEDWAY

US
NORTHWEST PRESS. 1956. Wed. free. 1564 Main St., Speedway, IN 46224-6527. TEL 317-241-4345. **Owner(s):** Speedway Northwest Press, Inc., 1564 Main St., Speedway, IN 46224. TEL 317-241-4345; Ed. Elizabeth Sullivan; Pub. Elizabeth Sullivan; adv. contact: Bob Shive. photos; bk.rev.; pub. size: tabloid; circ. 700(free).
Formerly: Speedway Northwest Press.

US
SPEEDWAY TOWN PRESS. 1956. w. free. 1564 Main St., Speedway, IN 46224-6527. TEL 317-241-4345. **Owner(s):** Speedway Northwest Press, Inc., 1564 Main St., Speedway, IN 46224. TEL 317-241-4345; Ed. Elizabeth Sullivan; Pub. Elizabeth Sullivan; adv. contact: Bob Shive. photos; bk.rev.; pub. size: tabloid; circ. 7,000(free).
Formerly: Speedway Northwest Press.

US
WESTSIDE MESSENGER. 1915. Wed. free. 1564 Main St., Speedway, IN 46224-6527. TEL 317-241-4345. **Owner(s):** Speedway Northwest Press, Inc., 1564 Main St., Speedway, IN 46224. TEL 317-852-5049; Ed. Elizabeth Sullivan; Pub. Elizabeth Sullivan; adv. contact: Bob Shive. photos; bk.rev.; pub. size: tabloid; circ. 7,000(free).

TELL CITY

US
PERRY COUNTY NEWS, THE. 1891. s-w.: Mon. & Thu. $.50 newsstand; $34/yr. in cy.; $47.50/yr. out of cy.; $55/yr. out of state. 537 Main St., Tell City, IN 47586. TEL 812-547-3424; FAX 812-547-2847. **Owner(s):** Landmark Community Newspapers, Inc., P.O. Box 549, Shelbyville, KY 40066. TEL 502-633-4334; Ed. Tina Lakae; Pub. Ron Filkins; adv.; pub. size: broadsheet; circ. 7,400(paid).
Formerly: News, The.

VERSAILLES

US
OSGOOD JOURNAL. 1865. Tue. $.50 newsstand; $32/yr. in cy.; $32/yr. out of cy.; $38/yr. out of state. 115 S. Washington St., Versailles, IN 47042. TEL 812-689-6364; FAX 812-689-6508. **Owner(s):** Gene Demaree, 6709 Mad River Rd., Centerville, OH 45459. TEL 812-434-6946; Ed. Michael Baugh; Pub. Linda Chandler; adv. contact: Linda Chandler. photos; bk.rev.; pub. size: broadsheet; circ. 5,200(paid).

US
VERSAILLES REPUBLICAN. 1856. Thu. $.50 newsstand; $32/yr. 115 Washington St., Versailles, IN 47042. TEL 812-689-6364; FAX 812-689-6508. **Owner(s):** Gene Demaree, 6709 Mad River Rd., Centerville, OH 45459. TEL 812-689-6364; Ed. Michael Baugh; Pub. Linda Chandler; adv.; photos; bk.rev.; pub. size: broadsheet; circ. 5,200(paid).
Formerly: Osgood Journal & Versailles Republican.

VEVAY

US
SWITZERLAND DEMOCRAT. Thu. $.50 newsstand; $23/yr. in cy. 111 W. Market St., Vevay, IN 47043. TEL 812-427-2311. **Owner(s):** Vevay Newspapers, Inc., 111 W. Market St., Vevay, IN 47043. TEL 812-427-2311; Ed. Patrick Lanman; Pub. Don R. Wallis, Jr.; adv. contact: Dan Honeyman. pub. size: broadsheet; circ. 2,000(paid).

US
VEVAY REVEILLE-ENTERPRISE. 1816. Thu. $.50 newsstand; $23/yr. in cy.; $26/yr. in tri-states IN, KY, OH. 111 W. Market St., Vevay, IN 47043. TEL 812-427-2311. **Owner(s):** Vevay Newspapers, Inc., 111 W. Market St., Vevay, IN 47043. TEL 812-427-2311; Ed. Patrick Lanman; Pub. Don R. Wallis, Jr.; adv. contact: Dan Honeyman. pub. size: broadsheet; circ. 3,600(paid).
Formerly: Vevay Reveille-Enterprise & Switzerland Democrat.

WABASH

US
PAPER OF WABASH COUNTY, THE. 1977. Wed. free; $25/yr. mailed. Jct. 13 & 24, Wabash, IN 46992. TEL 219-563-8326; FAX 219-563-2863. **Owner(s):** Wayne & Michael Rees, Julie Frieden, P.O. Box 603, Wabash, IN 46992. TEL 219-563-8326; FAX 219-563-2863; Pub. Wayne Rees; adv. contact: Julie Frieden. photos; pub. size: tabloid; circ. 16,225(controlled & free).

WARSAW

US
PAPER, THE. 1971. Wed. free. 114 W. Market St., Warsaw, IN 46580. TEL 219-269-2932; FAX 219-269-5850. **Owner(s):** Papers, Inc., The, P.O. Box 188, Milford, IN 46542. TEL 219-658-4815; FAX 219-658-4701; Ed. Jeri Seely; Pub. Della Baumgartner; adv. contact: Kip Schumm. photos; pub. size: tabloid; circ. 23,566(free).

WASHINGTON

US
HOOSIER EXPRESS. Wed. free. Memorial at N.E. 14th St., Washington, IN 47501. TEL 812-254-7322; FAX 812-254-7837. **Owner(s):** Daco Printers, Inc., Memorial at N.E. 14th St., Washington, IN 47501. TEL 812-254-7322; Ed. Michael Crosley; Pub. Michael Crosley; adv.; photos; bk.rev.; pub. size: broadsheet; circ. 15,500(free).

WESTVILLE

US
WESTVILLE INDICATOR. 1882. Thu. $.30 newsstand; $17/yr. in cy.; $20/yr. out of cy. 9852 E. State Rd., #2, Westville, IN 46391. TEL 219-785-2234; FAX 219-785-2442. **Owner(s):** Dean H. Henrickson, 9852 E. State Rd., #2, Westville, IN 46391; Ed. Dean H. Henrickson; Pub. Dean H. Henrickson; adv.; photos; bk.rev.; pub. size: broadsheet; circ. 5,200(controlled & paid).

WINAMAC

US
INDEPENDENT, THE. 1962. Mon. free. 114 W. Main St., Winamac, IN 46996. TEL 219-946-6629. **Owner(s):** Winamac Press, Inc., 114 W. Main St., Winamac, IN 46996. TEL 219-946-6629; Ed. Terry Turner; Pub. Al Bundy; adv.; photos; pub. size: tabloid; circ. 7,600(free).

US
PULASKI COUNTY JOURNAL. 1872. Wed. $.75 newsstand; $20/yr. in cy. 114 W. Main St., Winamac, IN 46996. TEL 219-946-6628. **Owner(s):** Winamac Press, Inc., P.O. Box 19, Winamac, IN 46996. TEL 219-946-6628; Ed. Terry Turner; Pub. Douglas Haley; adv. contact: Michelle Boyce. photos; bk.rev.; pub. size: tabloid; circ. 3,800(paid).

WORTHINGTON

US
WORTHINGTON TIMES, THE. 1853. Wed. $.50 newsstand; $20/yr. in cy.; $25/yr. out of cy. 12 S. Lessie St., Worthington, IN 47471-0045. TEL 812-875-2141; FAX 812-875-2641. **Owner(s):** Worthington Times, P.O. Box 45, Worthington, IN 47471-0045. TEL 812-875-2141; Ed. Anna Rochelle; Pub. Anna Rochelle; adv.; photos; bk.rev.; pub. size: standard; circ. 1,000(free & paid).

ZIONSVILLE

US ISSN 0886-4330
ZIONSVILLE TIMES SENTINEL. 1860. Wed. $.50 newsstand; $23/yr. 250 S. Elm St., Zionsville, IN 46077. TEL 317-873-6397. **Owner(s):** Jay W. & Paula J. Endress, P.O. Box 838, Zionsville, IN 46077; Ed. Paula J. Endress; Pub. Jay W. Endress; adv. contact: Jay W. Endress. pub. size: broadsheet; circ. 4,000(paid).

IOWA

AFTON

US
AFTON STAR-ENTERPRISE. 1880. Thu. $.50 newsstand; $19/yr. in state; $24/yr. out of state. 274 N. Douglas, Afton, IA 50830. TEL 515-347-8721. **Owner(s):** Afton Star-Enterprise, P.O. Box 128, Afton, IA 50830; adv.: $3/SAU. pub. size: tabloid; circ. 1,220(paid).

WEEKLY NEWSPAPERS

ALBIA

US

ALBIA UNION-REPUBLICAN. 1862. Thu. $.50 newsstand; $30/yr. in state; $40/yr. out of state. 109-111 Benton Ave., E., Albia, IA 52531. TEL 515-932-7121; FAX 515-932-2822. **Owner(s):** Lancaster Management, P.O. Box 609, Gadsden, AL 35902. TEL 205-543-3417; Ed. David A. Paxton; Pub. David A. Paxton; adv. contact: Carol Beronisch-Jones. photos; pub. size: broadsheet; circ. 3,500(paid).

US

MONROE NEWS. 1890. Tue. $.50 newsstand; $30/yr. in state; $40/yr. out of state. 109-111 Benton Ave., E., Albia, IA 52531. TEL 515-932-7121; FAX 515-932-2822. **Owner(s):** Lancaster Management, P.O. Box 609, Gadsden, AL 35902. TEL 205-543-3417; Ed. David A. Paxton; Pub. David A. Paxton; adv. contact: Carol Beronisch-Jones. photos; pub. size: broadsheet; circ. 3,400(paid).
Formerly: Monroe County News.

ALGONA

US

ALGONA UPPER DES MOINES. 1866. Thu. $1 newsstand; $37/yr. 14 E. Nebraska St., Algona, IA 50511. TEL 515-295-3535; FAX 515-295-7217. **Owner(s):** Algona Publishing Co., P.O. Box 400, Algona, IA 50511. TEL 515-295-3535; Pub. Richard Plum; adv. contact: Nancy Steburg. pub. size: broadsheet; circ. 5,300(paid).

ALTOONA

US

ALTOONA HERALD, THE. 1888. Thu. $.50 newsstand; $21/yr. in state. 809 Eighth St., S.W., Altoona, IA 50009. TEL 515-967-4224; FAX 515-967-0553. **Owner(s):** Gannett Company, Inc., 1100 Wilson Blvd., Arlington, VA 22340; Ed. Amy Duncan. adv. contact: Beth Meyer. photos; pub. size: broadsheet; circ. 10,000(controlled & paid).

ANAMOSA

US

ANAMOSA JOURNAL-EUREKA. 1854. Thu. $.50 newsstand; $21/yr. in cy.; $27/yr. in state. 208 W. Main St., Anamosa, IA 52205-0108. TEL 319-462-3511; FAX 319-462-4540. **Owner(s):** News Publishing Co., Black Earth, WI; Ed. Jennifer Hughes; Pub. Larry K. Woellert; adv.; pub. size: broadsheet; circ. 2,600(paid).

US

JONES COUNTY TOWN CRIER. Tue. free. 208 W. Main St., Anamosa, IA 52205. TEL 319-462-3511; FAX 319-462-4540. **Owner(s):** News Publishing Co., Black Earth, WI; Pub. Larry K. Woellert; adv.; pub. size: tabloid; circ. 6,657(free).

ANKENY

US

ANKENY PRESS CITIZEN. 1955. Tue. free. 520 S.W. Third, Ankeny, IA 50021. TEL 515-964-0639; FAX 515-964-7019. **Owner(s):** Ogden Newspapers, 1500 Main St., Wheeling, WV 26003. TEL 304-233-0100; FAX 304-233-0327; Ed. Dave DeValois; Pub. Roger Smed; adv. contact: Don Gimberline. photos; pub. size: tabloid; circ. 15,470(free). **Wire Service(s):** Iowa Link.

ATLANTIC

US

FARM MONTHLY. m.: 2nd Fri. free deliv. rural rtes. 410 Walnut St., Atlantic, IA 50022. TEL 712-243-2624; FAX 712-243-4988. **Owner(s):** Community Media Group, West Frankfort, IL. TEL 618-937-3246; adv.; pub. size: broadsheet; circ. 10,000(controlled & free).

AUDUBON

US

NISHNA VALLEY TRIBUNE. Tue. free. 301 Broadway, Audubon, IA 50025. TEL 712-563-2661; FAX 712-563-3118. **Owner(s):** Audubon Media Corp., 312 Broadway, Audubon, IA 50025. TEL 712-563-2661; Ed. Jeff Oakley; Pub. Keith McGlade; adv.; pub. size: broadsheet; circ. 7,000(free).

BETTENDORF

US

BETTENDORF NEWS. 1927. Thu. $.50 newsstand; $22/yr. in cy. 1704 State St., Bettendorf, IA 52722. TEL 319-355-2644; FAX 319-355-0956. **Owner(s):** Lee Enterprises, 215 E. Main St., Davenport, IA 52801. TEL 319-383-2100; Ed. Carly Ott. adv. contact: Nancy Dorr. adv.: $8.32/SAU. photos; pub. size: tabloid; circ. 5,000(paid).

BRITT

US

BRITT NEWS-TRIBUNE. 1881. Wed. $.75 newsstand; $22/yr. in cy.; $27/yr. out of cy. 42 W. Center St., Britt, IA 50423. TEL 515-843-3851; FAX 515-843-3307. **Owner(s):** Martin Bunge, 42 W. Center St., Britt, IA 50423. TEL 515-843-3851; Ed. Joe Murphy; Pub. Martin Bunge; adv.; pub. size: broadsheet; circ. 2,000(paid).

BURLINGTON

US

SHOPPER SPREE. 1969. Wed. free. 3208 Division St., Burlington, IA 52601. TEL 319-752-4555; FAX 319-752-6410. **Owner(s):** Brehm Communications, Inc., 17065 Via Del Campo, San Diego, CA 92198. TEL 619-451-6200; Pub. John Lowman; adv.; pub. size: tabloid; circ. 22,000(controlled & free).

CHARITON

US

CHARITON HERALD-PATRIOT. 1857. Thu. $.50 newsstand; $30/yr. 817 Braden Ave., Chariton, IA 50049. TEL 515-774-2137. **Owner(s):** Chariton Publishing Co., 817 Braden Ave., Chariton, IA 50049; Ed. Karen Wilker; Pub. Don Groves; adv. contact: Don Groves. adv.: $5.40/SAU. photos; pub. size: broadsheet; circ. 11,000(free & paid).

US

CHARITON LEADER. 1867. Tue. $.50 newsstand; $30/yr. 817 Braden Ave., Chariton, IA 50049. TEL 515-774-2137; FAX 515-774-2139. **Owner(s):** Leader Publishing Co., Inc., 817 Braden Ave., Chariton, IA 50049; Ed. Karen Wilker; Pub. Don Groves; adv. contact: Don Groves. adv.: $5.40/SAU. photos; pub. size: broadsheet; circ. 11,000(free & paid).

CLARINDA

US

HERALD JOURNAL. 1858. Wed. $.75 newsstand; $25/yr. in state; $43/yr. out of state. 205 E. Main St., Clarinda, IA 51632. TEL 712-542-2181; FAX 712-542-5424. **Owner(s):** Smith Newspapers, Inc., P.O. Box 278, Clarinda, IA 51632. TEL 712-542-2181; Ed. Suzie Ensz; Pub. Cleve Dowell; adv. contact: Anne King. photos; pub. size: broadsheet; circ. 12,000(paid).
Formerly: Clarinda Herald Journal.

CLINTON

US

GATEWAY EXPRESS, THE. 1939. Sat. free. 240 Sixth Ave, S., Clinton, IA 52732. TEL 319-243-1526; FAX 319-243-5035. **Owner(s):** Lee Enterprises, Inc., 130 E. Second St., Davenport, IA 52801. TEL 319-383-2202; adv.; pub. size: tabloid; circ. 22,000(free).
Formerly: Gateway Shopper, The.

CORYDON

US

CORYDON TIMES-REPUBLICAN. Tue. $.50 newsstand; $19/yr. in cy.; $22/yr. in state; $26/yr. out of state. 205 W. Jackson, Corydon, IA 50060. TEL 515-872-1234; FAX 515-872-1965. **Owner(s):** Lancaster Management, P.O. Box 609, Gadsden, AL 35902; Ed. Tammy Courter; Pub. Rhonda Bennett; adv.; pub. size: broadsheet; circ. 3,000(paid).

CRESCO

US   ISSN 1089-8271

CRESCO TIMES-PLAIN DEALER. 1866. Wed. $.75 newsstand; $27/yr. in cy; $49/yr. out of state. 214 N. Elm St., Cresco, IA 52136. TEL 319-547-3601; FAX 319-547-4602. **Owner(s):** John Hall Publishing, Inc., P.O. Box 350, Cresco, IA 52136. TEL 319-547-3601; Ed. John Hall; Pub. John Hall; adv. contact: John Hall. photos; pub. size: broadsheet; circ. 4,231(paid).

DAVENPORT

US

LEADER, THE. 1986. Wed. free in area; $26/yr. out of area. 423 E. 32nd St., Ste. 1, Davenport, IA 52803. TEL 319-326-5848; FAX 319-326-0356. **Owner(s):** Small Newspaper Group, 1720 Fifth Ave., Moline, IL 61265. TEL 309-764-4344; FAX 309-797-0311; Ed. Michael Romkey. adv.; photos; pub. size: broadsheet; circ. 51,000(free & paid).

DECORAH

US

DECORAH PUBLIC OPINION & JOURNAL. 1864. s-w.: Tue.: Public Opinion; Thu.: Journal. $.50 newsstand; $30-42/yr. 107 E. Water St., Decorah, IA 52101. TEL 319-382-4221; FAX 319-382-5949. **Owner(s):** Decorah News Co., P.O. Box 350, Decorah, IA 52101. TEL 319-382-4221; Ed. Richard Fromm; Pub. John Anundsen; adv.; photos; pub. size: broadsheet; circ. 6,400(free & paid).
Formerly: Decorah Journal.

DENISON

US

DENISON BULLETIN & REVIEW. 1873. s-w.: Tue. & Fri. $.75 newsstand; $48/yr. local; $55/yr. elsewhere. 1410 Broadway, Denison, IA 51442-0550. TEL 712-263-2122; FAX 712-263-2125. **Owner(s):** Denison Newspapers, Inc., 1410 Broadway, Denison, IA 51442. TEL 712-263-2122; FAX 712-263-2125; Ed. Chuck Signs; Pub. Richard R.G. Knowles; adv.; photos; pub. size: broadsheet; circ. 5,500(paid).

DES MOINES

US

CENTRAL SHOPPER. Wed. free. 2221 E. Ovid St., Des Moines, IA 50313. TEL 515-262-1724; FAX 515-262-1825. **Owner(s):** Ogden Newspapers, Inc., 1500 Main St., Wheeling, WV 26033. TEL 304-233-0100; Ed. Dave DiValois; Pub. Roger Smed; adv. contact: Don Gimberline. pub. size: tabloid; circ. 16,878(free).

US

COMMUNITY SHOPPER. Wed. free. 2221 E. Ovid St., Des Moines, IA 50313. TEL 515-262-1724; FAX 515-262-1825. **Owner(s):** Ogden Newspapers, Inc., 1500 Main St., Wheeling, WV 26033. TEL 304-233-0100; Ed. Dave Di Valois; Pub. Roger Smed; adv. contact: Don Gimberlina. pub. size: tabloid; circ. 15,304(free).

US

LEE TOWN SHOPPER. 1958. Wed. free. 2221 E. Ovid St., Des Moines, IA 50313. TEL 515-262-1724; FAX 515-262-1825. **Owner(s):** Ogden Newspapers, Inc., 1500 Main St., Wheeling, WV 26033. TEL 304-233-0100; Ed. Dave DiValois; Pub. Roger Smed; adv. contact: Don Gimberline. pub. size: tabloid; circ. 15,100(free).
Formerly: Des Moines Lee Town News.

US

NORTHCENTRAL SHOPPER. Wed. free. 2221 E. Ovid St., Des Moines, IA 50313. TEL 515-262-1724; FAX 515-262-1825. **Owner(s):** Ogden Newspapers, Inc., 1500 Main St., Wheeling, WV 26033. TEL 304-233-0100; Ed. Dave DiValois; Pub. Roger Smed; adv. contact: Don Gimberlin. pub. size: tabloid; circ. 16,925(free).

US

NORTHEAST SHOPPER. Wed. free. 2221 E. Ovid St., Des Moines, IA 50313. TEL 515-262-1724; FAX 515-262-1825. **Owner(s):** Ogden Newspapers, Inc., 1500 Main St., Wheeling, WV 26033. TEL 304-233-0100; Ed. Dave DiValois; Pub. Roger Smed; adv. contact: Don Gimberline. pub. size: tabloid; circ. 14,698(free).

US

NORTHWEST SHOPPER. Wed. free. 2221 E. Ovid St., Des Moines, IA 50313. TEL 515-262-1724; FAX 515-262-1825. **Owner(s):** Ogden Newspapers, Inc., 1500 Main St., Wheeling, WV 26033. TEL 304-233-0100; Ed. Dave DiValois; Pub. Roger Smed; adv. contact: Don Gimberline. pub. size: tabloid; circ. 20,019(free).

US

SOUTHSIDE SHOPPER. Wed. free. 2221 E. Ovid St., Des Moines, IA 50313. TEL 515-262-1724; FAX 515-262-1825. **Owner(s):** Ogden Newspapers, Inc., 1500 Main St., Wheeling, WV 26033. TEL 304-233-0100; Pub. Roger Smed; adv. contact: Don Gimberlin. pub. size: tabloid; circ. 16,556(free).

US

WESTERN EXPRESS. Fri. $.25 newsstand; $15/yr. in cy. 2221 E. Ovid St., Des Moines, IA 50313. TEL 515-262-1724; FAX 515-262-1825. **Owner(s):** Ogden Newspapers, Inc., 1500 Main St., Wheeling, WV 26033. TEL 304-233-0100; Ed. Dave DiValois; Pub. Roger Smed; adv. contact: Don Gimberline. pub. size: tabloid; circ. 2,000(paid).

DEWITT

US ISSN 0886-8808

OBSERVER, THE. 1864. s-w.: Wed. & Sat. $.75 newsstand; $34/yr. local. 512 Seventh St., DeWitt, IA 52742. TEL 319-659-3121; FAX 319-659-3778. **Owner(s):** Bob Melvold, 108 W. Quarry St., Maquoketa, IA 52060. TEL 319-652-2441; Frances Melvold, 108 W. Quarry St., Maquoketa, IA 52060. TEL 319-652-2441; Ed. Mary Rueter. adv. contact: Jean Bormann. photos; pub. size: tabloid; circ. 7,000(paid).
Formerly: The DeWitt Observer.

DOON

US

DOON PRESS. 1872. Thu. $.40 newsstand; $15.70/yr. in cy.; $21/yr. out of cy. 104 First Ave., Doon, IA 51235. TEL 712-726-3313; FAX 712-726-3313. **Owner(s):** Robert Sneller, 104 First Ave., Doon, IA 51235. TEL 712-726-3313; Ed. Harold Aardema; Pub. Robert Sneller; pub. size: tabloid; circ. 3,200(paid).

DYERSVILLE

US

DYERSVILLE COMMERCIAL. 1873. Wed. $.75 newsstand; $24/yr. local; $38/yr. out of area. 137 First Ave., E., Dyersville, IA 52040-0128. TEL 319-875-7131; FAX 319-875-2279. **Owner(s):** Northeast Iowa Publishers, Inc., 137 First Ave., E., P.O. Box 128, Dyersville, IA 52040. TEL 319-875-7131; FAX 319-875-2279; Ed. Robert H. LeMay; Pub. Robert H. LeMay; adv. contact: Joyce Massey. pub. size: standard; circ. 4,200(paid).

EAGLE GROVE

US

EAGLE GROVE EAGLE. 1896. Wed. $.75 newsstand; $35/yr. 314 W. Broadway, Eagle Grove, IA 50533. TEL 515-448-4745; FAX 515-448-3182. **Owner(s):** Mid-America Publishing Corp., 314 W. Broadway, Eagle Grove, IA 50533. TEL 515-448-4745; FAX 515-448-3182; Pub. Gary L. Milks; adv. contact: Leigh Banwell. adv.: $4.70/SAU. photos; pub. size: broadsheet; circ. 2,700(paid).

EDDYVILLE

US

EDDYVILLE TRIBUNE. 1873. Thu. $.50 newsstand; $21/yr. in cy.; $24/yr. in state; $30/yr. elsewhere. P.O. Box 228, Eddyville, IA 52553. TEL 515-969-4846; FAX 515-933-4342. **Owner(s):** Mother Wit Publishing Co., P.O. Box 228, Eddyville, IA 52553. TEL 515-969-4846; Ed. Beverly Lehman; Pub. Jack Arnold; adv.; pub. size: broadsheet; circ. 450(paid).

EDGEWOOD

US

EDGEWOOD REMINDER. Tue. $.56 newsstand; $18/yr. in state; $21/yr. state. 108 E. Union, Edgewood, IA 52042. TEL 319-928-6876. **Owner(s):** Roger & Donna Skattum, 105 N. Washington, Edgewood, IA 52042. TEL 319-928-6876; adv.; photos; pub. size: tabloid; circ. 1,500(free & paid).

ELDON

US

BEACON-FORUM. 1873. Thu. $21/yr. 500 Church St., Eldon, IA 52554. TEL 515-652-7612. **Owner(s):** Jack Arnold, Mother Wit Publishing Co., P.O. Box 9, Fremont, IA 52561. TEL 515-933-4241; Ed. Virginia Hindsley; Pub. Jack Arnold; pub. size: tabloid; circ. 1,000(paid).

ELDORA

US

ELDORA HERALD-LEADER. 1880. Tue. $.50 newsstand; $29/yr. W. Edgington Ave., Eldora, IA 50627. TEL 515-858-5051; FAX 515-858-5541. **Owner(s):** Eldora Herald-Index Publishing Co., W. Edgington Ave., Eldora, IA 50627. TEL 515-858-5051; Ed. Allyn J. Schafer; Pub. Allyn J. Schafer; pub. size: broadsheet; circ. 2,850(paid).

US

HARDIN COUNTY INDEX. 1940. Fri. $.50 newsstand; $29/yr. W. Edgington Ave., Eldora, IA 50627. TEL 515-858-5051; FAX 515-858-5541. **Owner(s):** Eldora Herald-Index Publishing Co., W. Edgington Ave., Eldora, IA 50627. TEL 515-858-5051; Ed. Allyn J. Schafer. pub. size: broadsheet; circ. 2,850(paid).

ELDRIDGE

US

NORTH SCOTT PRESS, THE. 1968. Wed. $.75 newsstand; $26/yr. in cy. 214 N. Second St., Eldridge, IA 52748. TEL 319-285-8111; FAX 319-285-8114; E-mail: nspress@netins.net. **Owner(s):** North Scott Press, Inc., 214 N. Second St., Eldridge, IA 52748. TEL 319-285-8111; Ed. Charles Scott Campbell; Pub. William F. "Bill" Tubbs; adv.; pub. size: tabloid; circ. 5,500(paid).

ELKADER

US

CLAYTON COUNTY REGISTER. 1878. Wed. $1 newsstand; $24/yr. local. 106 Cedar, N.W., Elkader, IA 52043. TEL 319-245-1311. **Owner(s):** Griffith Press, Inc., 106 Cedar, N.W., Elkader, IA 52043. TEL 319-245-1311; FAX 319-245-1512; Ed. Robert Andersen; Pub. Robert P. Griffith; adv. contact: Robert P. Griffith. photos; pub. size: tabloid; circ. 3,000(paid).

EMMETSBURG

US

EMMETSBURG DEMOCRAT. 1877. Thu. $.40 newsstand; $22.50/yr. 1901 Main St., Emmetsburg, IA 50536. TEL 712-852-2323; FAX 712-852-3184. **Owner(s):** Ogden Newspapers, Inc., 1500 Main St., Wheeling, WV 26003; Ed. Jane Whitmore. adv. contact: Dan McCain. pub. size: broadsheet; circ. evening 2,300(paid).

WEEKLY NEWSPAPERS

INDEPENDENCE, IA 10601

US
EMMETSBURG REPORTER. 1877. Tue. $.40 newsstand; $22.50/yr. in cy. 1901 Main St., Emmetsburg, IA 50536. TEL 712-852-2323; FAX 712-852-3184. **Owner(s):** Ogden Newspapers, Inc., 1500 Main St., Wheeling, WV 26003; Ed. Jane Whitmore; Pub. John Schmidt; adv. contact: Dan McCain. pub. size: broadsheet; circ. 2,300(paid).

ESSEX
US
ESSEX INDEPENDENT, THE. 1895. Thu. $.50 newsstand; $16/yr. in cy.; $21/yr. out of cy. P.O. Box 59, Essex, IA 51638-0059. TEL 712-379-3313; FAX 712-246-3099. **Owner(s):** Gleason-Knowles Communications, Inc., 702 W. Sheriden Ave., Shenandoah, IA 51601. TEL 712-246-3097; FAX 712-246-3099; Ed. Robert D. Jackson; Pub. Gregg K. Knowles; adv.; pub. size: broadsheet; circ. 600(free & paid).

FOREST CITY
US
FOREST CITY SUMMIT. 1867. Tue. $.75 newsstand; $26/yr. local; $37/yr. out of state. 105 S. Clark St., Forest City, IA 50436. TEL 515-582-2112; FAX 515-582-4442. **Owner(s):** Martin Bunge, 105 S. Clark St., Forest City, IA 50436. TEL 515-582-2112; Ed. Kristie Saatmann; Pub. Martin Bunge; adv. contact: Ellen Olson. pub. size: broadsheet; circ. 10,500(paid).

FREMONT
US
FREEMONT GAZETTE. 1991. Thu. $.50 newsstand; $21/yr. P.O. Box 9, Fremont, IA 52561. TEL 515-933-4241; FAX 515-933-4341. **Owner(s):** Mother Wit Publishing Co., P.O. Box 228, Eddyville, IA 52553. TEL 515-969-4846; Ed. Chris Arnold; Pub. Jack Arnold; adv.; pub. size: tabloid; circ. 1,000(paid).

GLENWOOD
US ISSN 0746-4398
GLENWOOD OPINION-TRIBUNE. 1864. Wed. $.75 newsstand; $23.50/yr. in cy.; $31/yr. out of cy. 116 S. Walnut, Glenwood, IA 51534-0191. TEL 712-527-3191; FAX 712-587-3193. **Owner(s):** Landmark Community Newspapers, Inc., P.O. Box 549, Shelbyville, KY 40066. TEL 502-633-4334; Ed. Joe Foreman; Pub. Lois Helms; adv. contact: Lois Helms. photos; bk.rev.; pub. size: broadsheet; circ. 3,700(paid).

GREENE
US
GREENE RECORDER, THE. 1883. Wed. $.50 newsstand; $18/yr. local; $22/yr. elsewhere. 219 N. Second St., Greene, IA 50636. TEL 515-823-4525; FAX 515-823-4525. **Owner(s):** Fred J. Hawker, P.O. Box 370, Greene, IA 50636. TEL 515-823-4525; Sylvia J. Hawker, P.O. Box 370, Greene, IA 50636. TEL 515-823-4525; Ed. Syliva J. Hawker; Pub. Fred J. Hawker; adv.; photos; pub. size: broadsheet; circ. 1,300.

GREENFIELD
US ISSN 1072-7523
ADAIR COUNTY FREE PRESS. 1889. Wed. $.75/newsstand; $21/yr. 108 E. Iowa St., Greenfield, IA 50849. TEL 515-743-6121; FAX 515-743-6122. **Owner(s):** Kenneth H. Sidey, 108 E. Iowa St., Greenfield, IA 50849. TEL 515-743-6121; Ed. Kenneth H. Sidey; Pub. Edwin J. Sidey; adv.; photos; pub. size: broadsheet; circ. 3,000(paid).

GRINNELL
US
GRINNELL HERALD-REGISTER. 1868. s-w.: Mon. & Thu. $.50 newsstand; $36.50/yr. local, $42/yr. out of area. 813 Fifth Ave., Grinnell, IA 50112-0360. TEL 515-236-3113; FAX 515-236-5135. **Owner(s):** Mr. & Mrs. A.J. Pinder, 813 Fifth Ave., Grinnell, IA 50112. TEL 515-236-3113; FAX 515-236-5135; Pub. A. J. Pinder; adv. contact: Jeanne Pinder. photos; bk.rev.; pub. size: broadsheet; circ. 3,550(free & paid).

GRUNDY CENTER
US
GRUNDY REGISTER. 1868. Wed. $.75 newsstand; $26/yr. 601 G Ave., Grundy Center, IA 50638. TEL 319-824-6958. **Owner(s):** Register Printing Co., 601 G Ave., Grundy Center, IA 50638. TEL 319-824-6958; Ed. Deb Workman; Pub. Ralph Kotenbeutel; adv. contact: Ralph Kotenbeutel. pub. size: broadsheet; circ. 3,000(paid).

GUTHRIE CENTER
US
TIMES GUTHRIAN. 1856. Wed. $.50 newsstand; $18/yr. in cy. 205 State, Guthrie Center, IA 50115. TEL 515-747-3511; FAX 515-747-2208. **Owner(s):** Scott Gonzales, 100 S. 12th St., Guthrie Center, IA 50115. TEL 515-747-3044; Ed. Scott Gonzales; Pub. Charles P. Gonzales; adv. contact: Lorence Huggins. pub. size: broadsheet; circ. 4,361(paid).

GUTTENBERG
US
GUTTENBERG PRESS. Wed. $.75 newsstand; $22/yr. local. 10 Schiller St., Guttenberg, IA 52052. TEL 319-252-2421; FAX 319-252-1275. **Owner(s):** Howe Printing Co., P.O. Box 149, Prairie du Chien, WI 53821; adv. contact: Carl Neiers. pub. size: tabloid; circ. 2,758(free & paid).

HAMPTON
US
HAMPTON CHRONICLE & TIMES. 1876. s-w.: Tue. & Thu. $.75 newsstand; $30/yr. in cy.; $35/yr. out of cy. 9 Second St., N.W., Hampton, IA 50441. TEL 515-456-2585. **Owner(s):** Hampton Publishing Co., P.O. Box 29, Hampton, IA. TEL 515-456-2585; Ed. Joseph P. Roth; Pub. Joseph P. Roth; adv.; pub. size: broadsheet; circ. 4,000(paid).

HARLAN
US
HARLAN NEWS ADVERTISER. 1870. Fri. $.75 newsstand; $32/yr. 1114 Seventh St., Harlan, IA 51537-0721. TEL 712-755-3111; FAX 712-755-3324. **Owner(s):** Alan & Steve Mores, 1114 Seventh St., Harlan, IA 51537. TEL 712-755-3111; FAX 712-755-3324; Ed. Bob Bjoin; Pub. Alan Mores; adv. contact: Mike Kolbe. pub. size: broadsheet; circ. 5,390(paid).

US
HARLAN TRIBUNE. 1879. Tue. $.75 newsstand; $26/yr. Press Bldg., 1114 Seventh St., Harlan, IA 51537-0721. TEL 712-755-3111; FAX 712-755-3324; E-mail: tribnews@netins.net. **Owner(s):** Alan & Steve Mores, 1114 Seventh St., Harlan, IA 51537-0721. TEL 712-755-3111; FAX 712-755-3324; Ed. Bob Bjoin; Pub. Steve Mores; adv. contact: Alan Mores. photos; pub. size: broadsheet; circ. 5,000(paid).

HUDSON
US
HUDSON HERALD, THE. 1911. Thu. $.50 newsstand; $20/yr. 411 Jefferson St., Hudson, IA 50643-0210. TEL 319-988-3855; FAX 319-988-3855. **Owner(s):** Clifford Murray, 411 Jefferson St., Hudson, IA 50643-0210. TEL 319-988-3855; Ed. Clifford Murray. adv.: $3.50/SAU. photos; pub. size: broadsheet; circ. 1,500(paid).

HUMBOLDT
US
HUMBOLDT INDEPENDENT. 1889. Thu. $.60 newsstand; $28/yr. in state; $38/yr. out of state. 512 Sumner Ave., Humboldt, IA 50548. TEL 515-332-2514. E-mail: independent@trvnet.net; URL: http://www.trvnet.net/independent. **Owner(s):** Gargano Communications, Inc., 512 Sumner Ave., Humboldt, IA 50548. TEL 515-332-2514; Ed. Jeffrey Gargano; Pub. James Gargano; adv. contact: James Gargano. pub. size: broadsheet; circ. 4,200(paid).

HUMESTON
US
HUMESTON NEW ERA. 1880. Tue. $.50 newsstand; $15.16/yr. in area; $17/yr. elsewhere. RR 2, Humeston, IA 50123. TEL 515-877-3811; FAX 515-872-1965. **Owner(s):** James Lancaster, P.O. Box 609, Gadsden, AL 35901; Ed. Virginia Sponsler; Pub. Rhonda Bennett; adv.; pub. size: tabloid.

INDEPENDENCE
US
INDEPENDENCE BULLETIN-JOURNAL. 1860. s-w.: Wed. & Sat. $.75/Wed. newsstand; $1/Sat.; $36/yr. 116 Fifth Ave., N.E., Independence, IA 50644. TEL 319-334-2557; FAX 319-334-6752. **Owner(s):** Oelwein Publishing Co., Oelwein, IA 50662; Ed. Jim Morrison; Pub. Martin Van Ee; adv.; pub. size: broadsheet; circ. 4,500(paid).

INDIANOLA

RECORD-HERALD & INDIANOLA TRIBUNE. 1857. ISSN 0895-3287. Wed. $.75 newsstand; $27.50/yr. in cy.; $35/yr. elsewhere. 203 W. Salem Ave., Indianola, IA 50125. TEL 515-961-2511; FAX 515-961-4833. **Owner(s):** Des Moines Register & Tribune, P.O. Box 957, Des Moines, IA 50304. TEL 515-284-8000; Ed. Deb Belt; Pub. David Dear; adv.; photos; pub. size: broadsheet; circ. 20,200(free & paid). **Wire Service(s):** Media Link, AP Newsfinder.

IOWA FALLS

TIMES CITIZEN. 1881. s-w.: Wed. & Sat. $.50 newsstand; $28/yr. local; $40/yr. out of state. 406 Stevens, Iowa Falls, IA 50126. TEL 515-648-2521; FAX 515-648-4765. **Owner(s):** Times Citizen, P.O. Box 640, Iowa Falls, IA 50126. TEL 515-648-2521; Ed. Elaine Loring; Pub. Mark Hamilton; adv.; pub. size: broadsheet; circ. 3,800(paid). **Formerly:** Iowa Falls Citizen.

JEFFERSON

JEFFERSON BEE. 1866. Tue. free. 214 N. Wilson Ave., Jefferson, IA 50129. TEL 515-386-4161; FAX 515-386-4162. **Owner(s):** Jefferson Bee & Herald Publishing Co., Inc., 214 N. Wilson Ave., Jefferson, IA 50129. TEL 515-386-4161; FAX 515-386-4162; Ed. Frederick G. Morain; Pub. Frederick G. Morain; adv.; pub. size: broadsheet; circ. 8,600(free).

JEFFERSON HERALD. 1891. Thu. $24/yr. 214 N. Wilson Ave., Jefferson, IA 50129. TEL 515-386-4161; FAX 515-386-4162. **Owner(s):** Jefferson Bee & Herald Publishing Co., Inc., 214 N. Wilson Ave., Jefferson, IA 50129. TEL 515-386-4161; FAX 515-386-4162; Ed. Frederick G. Morain. adv.; pub. size: broadsheet; circ. 3,000(paid).

KALONA

KALONA NEWS, THE. 1891. Thu. $.50 newsstand; $24/yr. in cy.; $26/yr. in state; $30/yr. out of state. 419 B Ave., Kalona, IA 52247-0430. TEL 319-656-2273; FAX 319-656-2299; E-mail: knews@kctc.net; URL: http://www.kctc.net/knews. **Owner(s):** Ronald C. Slechta, 816 Tenth St., P.O. Box 430, Kalona, IA 52247-0430. TEL 319-656-2104; FAX 319-656-2299; Helen M. Slechta, 816 Tenth St., P.O. Box 430, Kalona, IA 52247-0430. TEL 319-656-2104; FAX 319-656-2299; Ed. Ronald C. Slechta; Pub. Ronald C. Slechta; adv. contact: Ronald C. Slechta. photos; pub. size: broadsheet; circ. 3,150(paid).

KNOXVILLE

JOURNAL/EXPRESS. 1855. Fri. $.75 newsstand; $27/yr.; $32/yr. out of cy. 122 E. Robinson, Knoxville, IA 50138. TEL 515-842-2155; FAX 515-842-2929. **Owner(s):** Journal-Express, 122 E. Robinson, P.O. Box 458, Knoxville, IA 50138. TEL 515-842-2155; FAX 515-842-2929; Ed. Abby St. John; Pub. Jack Crook; adv. contact: Jack Crook. photos; bk.rev.; pub. size: broadsheet; circ. 3,600(paid).

LAURENS

LAURENS SUN, THE. 1885. Thu. $.50 newsstand; $20/yr. 119 S. Third St., Laurens, IA 50554-0125. TEL 712-845-4541; FAX 712-845-4542. **Owner(s):** William H. & Darlene A. Chaffee, P.O. Box 125, Laurens, IA 50554-0125. TEL 712-845-4541; Ed. Darlene A. Chaffee; Pub. William H. Chaffee; adv.; pub. size: broadsheet; circ. 1,550(paid).

LEON

LEON JOURNAL-REPORTER. 1861. Wed. $18/yr. in area; $22/yr. out of area. 110 N. Main St., Leon, IA 50144. TEL 515-446-4151. **Owner(s):** W.R. Lindsey, 110 N. Main St., Leon, IA 50144. TEL 515-446-4940; Gary D. Lindsey, 802 N.W. White, Leon, IA 50144. TEL 515-446-6645; Ed. Margaret Lindsey. adv. contact: W.R. Lindsey. pub. size: standard; circ. 2,700(paid).

LIME SPRINGS

LIME SPRINGS HERALD. 1888. Thu. $.75 newsstand; $22.50/yr. in area; $25/yr. out of area. 111 1/2 W. Main St., Lime Springs, IA 52155. TEL 319-566-2687. **Owner(s):** Barry & Sara Casebolt, P.O. Box 187, Lime Springs, IA 52155. TEL 319-566-2687; Ed. Barry Casebolt; Pub. Barry Casebolt; adv.; photos; pub. size: broadsheet; circ. 750(paid).

LOGAN

LOGAN HERALD OBSERVER. 1886. Wed. $.50 newsstand; $18.50/yr. in cy.; $23/yr. in state; $24.50/yr. elsewhere. 112 S. Fourth Ave., Logan, IA 51546-0148. TEL 712-644-2705; FAX 712-644-2788. **Owner(s):** Bloom Publishing Co., 112 S. Fourth Ave., Logan, IA 51546. TEL 712-644-2705; FAX 712-644-2788; Ed. Karen J. Bloom; Pub. Karen J. Bloom; adv.; photos; pub. size: broadsheet; circ. 2,175(paid).

LONE TREE

LONE TREE REPORTER, THE. 1893. Tue. $.50 newsstand; $18/yr. 117 LaVoe, Lone Tree, IA 52755-0235. TEL 319-629-5207; FAX 319-629-5229. **Owner(s):** Slechta Communications, Inc., P.O. Box 430, Kalena, IA 52247. TEL 319-656-2273; FAX 319-656-2299; Ed. Cate Spears; Pub. Ronald C. Slechta; adv.; pub. size: tabloid; circ. 5,600(free & paid).

MALVERN

MALVERN LEADER, THE. 1874. Thu. $.50 newsstand; $18/yr. in cy.; $24/yr. out of cy.; $26/yr. out of state. 301 Main St., Malvern, IA 51551. TEL 712-624-8512. **Owner(s):** Mark A. Siekman, P.O. Box 129, Malvern, IA 51551. TEL 712-624-8512; Ed. Mark A. Siekman; Pub. Mark A. Siekman; adv.; photos; pub. size: broadsheet; circ. 1,300(controlled & paid).

MANCHESTER

MANCHESTER PRESS. 1871. Tue. $35/yr. 109 E. Delaware St., Manchester, IA 52057. TEL 319-927-2020; FAX 319-927-4945. **Owner(s):** Manchester Publishing Co., 109 E. Delaware St., Manchester, IA 52057. TEL 319-927-2020; Pub. Larry K. Woellert; adv. contact: Kathy Hutchinson. pub. size: broadsheet; circ. 5,000(paid).

MAQUOKETA

MAQUOKETA SENTINEL-PRESS. 1854. s-w.: Wed. & Sat. $.75 newsstand; $30/yr. in cy.; $42/yr. elsewhere. 108 W. Quarry St., Maquoketa, IA 52060. TEL 319-652-2441; FAX 319-652-6094. **Owner(s):** Maquoketa Newspapers, Inc., 108 W. Quarry St., Maquoketa, IA 52060. TEL 319-652-2441; Ed. Doug Melvold; Pub. Douglas Melvold; adv.; pub. size: broadsheet; circ. 5,000(paid).

MARENGO

PIONEER REPUBLICAN, THE. 1853. Thu. $.75 newsstand; $24/yr. in state; $29/yr. out of state. 100 W. Main St., Marengo, IA 52301. TEL 319-642-5506; FAX 319-642-5509. **Owner(s):** Marengo Publishing Corp., 100 W. Main St., Marengo, IA 52301-0208. TEL 319-642-5506; FAX 319-642-5509; Ed. Alan Sieve; Pub. Dan DeBettignies; adv. contact: Dan De Bettignies. photos; pub. size: broadsheet; circ. 5,500(paid).

MISSOURI VALLEY

MISSOURI VALLEY TIMES-NEWS. 1885. s-w.: Wed. & Fri. $.50 newsstand; $38/yr. 501 E. Erie, Missouri Valley, IA 51555. TEL 712-642-2791; FAX 712-642-2595. **Owner(s):** Mark Rhoades, 138 N. 16th, Blair, NE 68008. TEL 402-426-9860; Ed. Peter Graham. adv. contact: Charles Hickman. pub. size: broadsheet; circ. 3,000(paid).

MONTEZUMA

MONTEZUMA REPUBLICAN, THE. 1856. Wed. $.75 newsstand; $18-$23/yr. 406 E. Main St., Montezuma, IA 50171. TEL 515-623-5116; FAX 515-623-5580. **Owner(s):** Marengo Publishing Corp., 100 W. Main St., Marengo, IA 52301-0208. TEL 319-642-5506; FAX 319-642-5509; Ed. Susan Green; Pub. Dan DeBettignies; adv. contact: Roger Allen. photos; pub. size: broadsheet; circ. 5,400(free & paid).

MONTICELLO

MONTICELLO EXPRESS. 1865. Wed. $.75 newsstand; $24/yr. 111 E. Grand, Monticello, IA 52310. TEL 319-465-3555; FAX 319-465-4611. **Owner(s):** Monticello Express, Inc., 111 E. Grand, Monticello, IA 52310. TEL 319-465-3555; Ed. Craig Neises; Pub. Robert Goodyear; adv. contact: Mark Spensley. pub. size: tabloid; circ. 3,400(paid).

MT. AYR

US

MOUNT AYR RECORD-NEWS. 1864. Thu. $.50 newsstand; $19/yr. in cy. 122 W. Madison, Mt. Ayr, IA 50854. TEL 515-464-2440; FAX 515-464-2229; E-mail: renews@mtayr.heartland.net. **Owner(s):** H. Alan Smith, P.O. Box 346, Mt. Ayr, IA 50854. TEL 515-464-2440; FAX 515-464-2949; Ed. H. Alan Smith; Pub. H. Alan Smith; adv. contact: Helen Terry. pub. size: broadsheet; circ. 3,875(paid).

MT. VERNON

US

SUN, THE. 1869. Wed. $.60 newsstand; $21/yr. P.O. Box 129, Mt. Vernon, IA 52314. TEL 319-895-6216. **Owner(s):** Wedel Publishing, LC, P.O. Box 129, Mt. Vernon, IA 52314. TEL 319-895-6216; FAX 319-895-6217; adv. contact: Leann Pisarik. photos; bk.rev.; pub. size: broadsheet; circ. 2,300(paid). **Wire Service(s):** Iowa Medialink.

NASHUA

US

NASHUA REPORTER. 1878. Wed. $.50 newsstand; $19/yr. in cy.; $21/yr. in state. 216 Main St., Nashua, IA 50658. TEL 515-435-4151. **Owner(s):** Carmen Conklin, P.O. Box 67, Nashua, IA 50658. TEL 515-435-2036; Wanda Orric, P.O. Box 67, Nashua, IA 50658. TEL 515-435-2036; Ed. Conklin Orric; Pub. Carmen Conklin; adv. contact: Carmen Conklin. photos; pub. size: broadsheet; circ. 1,300(paid).

NEVADA

US

NEVADA JOURNAL. 1895. Thu. $.75 newsstand; $25/yr. 1133 Sixth St., Nevada, IA 50201. TEL 515-382-2161; FAX 515-382-4299. **Owner(s):** Partnership Press, Inc., 317 Fifth St., Ames, IA 50010. TEL 515-232-2160; adv. contact: Brian McClueary. photos; bk.rev.; pub. size: broadsheet; circ. 3,000(paid). **Wire Service(s):** AP.

NEW HAMPTON

US

NEW HAMPTON TRIBUNE. 1874. Thu. $.75 newsstand; $38/yr. 10 N. Chestnut Ave., New Hampton, IA 50659-0380. TEL 515-394-2111; FAX 515-394-2113. **Owner(s):** New Hampton Publishing Co., Inc., P.O. Box 380, New Hampton, IA 50659. TEL 515-394-2111; Ed. Beverly Kolthoff; Pub. Dan Feuling; pub. size: broadsheet; circ. 10,000(free & paid).

NEW SHARON

US

NEW SHARON STAR. 1873. Thu. $.50 newsstand; $21/yr. in cy.; $30/yr. elsewhere. 113 S. Main St., New Sharon, IA 50207. TEL 515-637-2632; FAX 515-933-4341. **Owner(s):** Mother Wit Publishing Co., P.O. Box 9, Fremont, IA 50207. TEL 515-933-4241; Ed. Tina Reed; Pub. Jack Arnold; pub. size: tabloid; circ. 750(paid).

ONAWA

US ISSN 0899-6520

ONAWA DEMOCRAT. 1890. Thu. $.50 newsstand; $15/yr. local; $20/yr. elsewhere. 720 Iowa Ave., Onawa, IA 51040-1628. TEL 712-423-2411; FAX 712-423-2411. **Owner(s):** Wonder & Son Publishing, 720 Iowa Ave., Onawa, IA 51040. TEL 712-423-2411; adv.; photos; pub. size: standard; circ. 3,000(paid).

US

ONAWA SENTINEL. 1885. Thu. $.50 newsstand; $14/yr. local; $17/yr. in state; $20/yr. out of state. 1014 Ninth St., Onawa, IA 51040. TEL 712-423-2021; FAX 712-423-3038. **Owner(s):** Onawa Sentinel-Verlee Sawyer, 1014 Ninth St., Onawa, IA 51040. TEL 712-423-2021; Ed. Verlee Sawyer; Pub. Verlee Sawyer; adv. contact: Larry Sawyer. pub. size: broadsheet; circ. 1,800(paid). **Wire Service(s):** Media Link.

OSAGE

US

MITCHELL COUNTY PRESS-NEWS. 1865. Wed. $26/yr. 112 N. Sixth St., Osage, IA 50461. TEL 515-732-3721; FAX 515-732-5689. **Owner(s):** Paul Bunge, 820 Main St., Osage, IA 50461. TEL 515-732-4716; Ed. Larry Kershner; Pub. Dave Stanley; adv.; pub. size: broadsheet; circ. 3,800(paid).
Formerly: Osage Mitchell County Press-News.

OSCEOLA

US ISSN 0745-6247

OSCEOLA SENTINEL-TRIBUNE. 1860. Thu. $.50 newsstand; $18.50/yr. local; $22/yr. elsewhere. 115 E. Washington St., Osceola, IA 50213. TEL 515-342-2131; FAX 515-342-2060. **Owner(s):** Sally & Frank Morlan, 115 E. Washington, Osceola, IA 50213. TEL 515-342-2131; Ed. Frank E. Morlan. adv.; photos; bk.rev.; pub. size: broadsheet; circ. 4,200(paid). **Wire Service(s):** Iowa Media Link.

OSSIAN

US

OSSIAN BEE, THE. 1889. Wed. $.50 newsstand; $13/yr. in cy; $15/yr. out of cy. 107 W. Main St., Ossian, IA 52161-0096. TEL 319-532-9113; FAX 319-532-9081. **Owner(s):** Dirk Amundsen, 107 W. Main St., Ossian, IA 52161. TEL 319-532-9113; FAX 319-532-9081; Ed. Marlys Amundsen; Pub. Dirk Amundsen; adv.; photos; pub. size: broadsheet; circ. 1,242(paid).

PAULLINA

US

PAULLINA TIMES. 1883. Tue. $.50 newsstand; $18/yr. 144 E. Broadway, Paullina, IA 51046-0677. TEL 712-448-3622; FAX 712-448-3622. **Owner(s):** O'Shillal Enterprises, Inc., P.O. Box 637, Paullina, IA 51046-0637. TEL 712-448-3622; FAX 712-448-3622; adv.; photos; pub. size: broadsheet; circ. 1,470(free & paid). **Wire Service(s):** Iowa Media Link.

PELLA

US

PELLA CHRONICLE. 1865. Thu. $.75 newsstand; $24/yr. in area; $27/yr. out of area. 739 Franklin St., Pella, IA 50219. TEL 515-628-3882; FAX 515-628-3905. **Owner(s):** Edwards Publications, 125 Eagle's Nest Dr., P.O. Box 1193, Seneca, SC 29679. TEL 864-882-3272; FAX 864-882-3718; Ed. Barry Johnson; Pub. Jack Crook; adv. contact: Don Abens. photos; bk.rev.; pub. size: broadsheet; circ. 3,600(paid).

PERRY

US ISSN 0746-7222

PERRY CHIEF. 1874. Wed. $.55 newsstand; $25-$28/yr. 1323 Second St., Perry, IA 50220. TEL 515-465-4666; FAX 515-465-3087. **Owner(s):** Stephen R. Whitehead, P.O. Box 98, Perry, IA 50220. TEL 515-465-4666; Ed. Denise Pierce. adv. contact: Linda Schumacher. pub. size: broadsheet; circ. 3,250(paid).

POCAHONTAS

US

POCAHONTAS RECORD-DEMOCRAT. 1884. Tue. $.75 newsstand; $22/yr. in cy.; $26.50/yr. out of cy.; $28.50/yr. out of state. 218 N. Main St., Pocahontas, IA 50574. TEL 712-335-3553; FAX 712-335-3856. **Owner(s):** Chris Godfredsen, 218 N. Main St., Pocahontas, IA 50574. TEL 712-335-3553; FAX 712-335-3856; Jerry Wiseman, 218 N. Main St., Pocahontas, IA 50574. TEL 712-335-3553; FAX 712-335-3856; Ed. Chris Godfredsen; Pub. Chris Godfredsen; adv. contact: Chris Godfredsen. pub. size: broadsheet; circ. 5,000(paid).

PRAIRIE CITY

US

PRAIRIE CITY NEWS. 1874. Thu. $.40 newsstand; $16/yr. in state; $19/yr. out of state. 108 E. Jefferson, Prairie City, IA 50228-0249. TEL 515-994-2349; FAX 515-994-3169. **Owner(s):** Orian Woods, 108 E. Jefferson, Prairie City, IA 50228. TEL 515-994-2349; FAX 515-994-3169; Ed. Orian Woods; Pub. Orian Woods; adv. contact: Christy Zerley. photos; pub. size: tabloid; circ. 1,100(paid).

RED OAK

US ISSN 0747-3281

RED OAK EXPRESS. 1867. Tue. $.75 newsstand; $23.50/yr. 2012 Commerce Dr., Red Oak, IA 51566. TEL 712-623-2566; FAX 712-623-2568. **Owner(s):** Landmark Community Newspapers, Inc., P.O. Box 549, Shelbyville, KY 40066. TEL 502-633-4334; Ed. Jan Castle Renander. adv. contact: Linda Blackburn. pub. size: broadsheet; circ. 4,800(paid).

ROCK RAPIDS

US

LYON-SIOUX PRESS. 1888. Wed. $.50 newsstand; $26/yr. in cy. & adj. cys.; $40/yr. elsewhere. 310 First Ave., Rock Rapids, IA 51246. TEL 712-472-2525; FAX 712-472-3414. **Owner(s):** New Century Press, Inc., P.O. Box 28, 310 First Ave., Rock Rapids, IA 51246. TEL 712-472-2525; Ed. Jodie Hoogendoorn; Pub. Jim Houck; pub. size: broadsheet; circ. 2,847(paid).
Formerly: Rock Rapids County Reporter.

SCHALLER
US
SCHALLER HERALD. 1881. Wed. $.50 newsstand; $20/yr. out of state. 203 S. Main St., Schaller, IA 51053. TEL 712-275-4229. **Owner(s):** Betty Bailey, P.O. Box 129, Schaller, IA 51053. TEL 712-275-4229; Ed. Betty Bailey; Pub. Betty Bailey; adv.; bk.rev.; pub. size: broadsheet; circ. 850(paid).

SHELDON
US
N'WEST IOWA REVIEW. 1972. Sat. $.95 newsstand; $24/yr. in cy.; $36/yr. out of cy. P.O. Box 160, Sheldon, IA 51201. TEL 712-324-2514; FAX 712-324-2345. **Owner(s):** Iowa Information, Inc., P.O. Box 160, Sheldon, IA 51201. TEL 712-324-2514; Pub. Peter W. Wagner; adv.: $6.93/SAU. photos; bk.rev.; pub. size: broadsheet; circ. 5,500(paid).

US
SHELDON MAIL-SUN. 1873. Wed. $.75 newsstand; $22/yr. in cy.; $30/yr. out of cy. P.O. Box 160, Sheldon, IA 51201. TEL 712-324-2514; FAX 712-324-2345. **Owner(s):** Iowa Information, Inc., P.O. Box 160, Sheldon, IA 51201. TEL 712-324-2514; Pub. Peter W. Wagner; adv.: $6.93/SAU. pub. size: broadsheet; circ. 3,000(paid).

SIBLEY
US
OSCEOLA COUNTY GAZETTE-TRIBUNE. 1872. Wed. $.50 newsstand; $19.50/yr. in cy.; $25/yr. out of cy. 201 Ninth St., Sibley, IA 51249. TEL 712-754-2551; FAX 712-754-2552. **Owner(s):** Sibley Printing & Publishing, 201 Ninth St, Sibley, IA 51249. TEL 712-754-2551; Ed. Jay L. Mohr; Pub. Jerry Wiseman; adv. contact: Jay L. Mohr. pub. size: broadsheet; circ. 1,700(paid).

SIGOURNEY
US
SIGOURNEY NEWS-REVIEW. 1870. Wed. $.75 newsstand; $24/yr. in state; $27/yr. out of state. 114 E. Washington St., Sigourney, IA 52591-0285. TEL 515-622-3110; FAX 515-622-2766; E-mail: sign@se-iowa.net. **Owner(s):** Kenneth D. Chaney, 114 E. Washington St., Sigourney, IA 52591-0285. TEL 515-622-3110; FAX 515-622-2766; Pub. Kenneth D. Chaney; adv. contact: Kim Strong. adv.: $4.15/SAU. pub. size: broadsheet; circ. 2,649(paid). **Wire Service(s):** Iowa Media Link.

SLATER
US   ISSN 0749-7040
TRI-COUNTY TIMES, THE. 1890. Wed. $.50 newsstand; $16/yr. in state; $20/yr. out of cy.; $22/yr. out of state. 312 Main St., Box 237, Slater, IA 50244-0237. TEL 515-685-3412; FAX 515-685-3668. **Owner(s):** Edwin W. Rood, 312 Main St., Box 237, Slater, IA 50244. TEL 515-685-3412; Ed. Edwin W. Rood. adv.: $5.30/SAU. photos; bk.rev.; pub. size: standard; circ. 4,800(paid).
Formerly: Slater Tri-County Times.

SOLON
US
LEADER, THE. 1950. Wed. $.50 newsstand; $18/yr. P.O. Box 249, Solon, IA 52333. TEL 319-644-2233; FAX 319-644-1356. **Owner(s):** Brian Fleck, Hybrid Publications, P.O. Box 249, Solon, IA 52333. TEL 319-644-2233; Ed. Jim Wolf; Pub. Brian Fleck; pub. size: broadsheet; circ. 900(paid).

SPENCER
US
NORTHWEST IOWA SHOPPER. s-w.: Wed. & Sat. free. 416 First Ave., W., Spencer, IA 51301. TEL 712-262-6610; FAX 712-262-3044. **Owner(s):** Edward Publications, P.O. Box 1193, Seneca, SC 29679; Pub. Joni Weerheim; adv. contact: Chris Swanson. pub. size: standard; circ. 25,000(controlled & free).

SPIRIT LAKE
US
SPIRIT LAKE BEACON. 1870. Thu. $.75 newsstand; $26/yr. 1706 Ithaca St., Spirit Lake, IA 51360. TEL 712-336-1211; FAX 712-336-1219. **Owner(s):** Edwards Publications, P.O. Box 1193, Seneca, SC 29679. TEL 803-882-3272; Ed. Frank Jaquith; Pub. Michael Kuehn; pub. size: broadsheet; circ. 3,700(paid).

STATE CENTER
US
STATE CENTER ENTERPRISE-RECORD. 1871. w. $.75 newsstand; $22/yr. local; $26/yr. elsewhere. 130 W. Main St., State Center, IA 50247-0634. TEL 515-483-2120; FAX 515-483-2938. **Owner(s):** John & Diane Strawn, 408 Second St., S.W., State Center, IA 50247-0634. TEL 515-483-2507; Ed. John C. Strawn, II; Pub. John C. Strawn, II; adv.; photos; pub. size: broadsheet; circ. 1,250.

STORM LAKE
US
STORM LAKE TIMES. 1990. s-w.: Wed. & Sat. $.75 newsstand; $39.95/yr. in cy. 220 W. Railroad St., Storm Lake, IA 50588. TEL 712-732-4991; FAX 712-732-4331. **Owner(s):** Storm Lake Times Co., Inc., Storm Lake, IA 50588; Ed. Art Cullen; Pub. John Cullen; adv. contact: Marty Gallagher. photos; bk.rev.; pub. size: tabloid; circ. 3,000(paid).

STORY CITY
US
STORY CITY HERALD. 1881. Wed. $.50 newsstand; $22/yr. in state; $26/yr. out of state. 423 Broad St., Story City, IA 50248. TEL 515-733-4318; FAX 515-733-4319. **Owner(s):** Eloise Thorson, 423 Broad St., Story City, IA 50248. TEL 515-733-4318; FAX 515-733-4319; Ed. Todd Thorson; Pub. Todd Thorson; adv. contact: Patricia Sawyer. photos; bk.rev.; pub. size: broadsheet; circ. 2,300(free & paid).

SULLY
US
DIAMOND TRAIL NEWS. 1975. Wed. $18/yr.; $23/yr. out of state; $35/yr. foreign. 303 Seventh Ave., Sully, IA 50251. TEL 515-594-4488; FAX 515-594-4498. **Owner(s):** Diamond Trail News, 303 Seventh Ave., Sully, IA 50251. TEL 515-594-4488; FAX 515-594-4498; Ed. Mark Davitt; Pub. Mark Davitt; pub. size: tabloid; circ. 18,000(paid).

SUMNER
US
SUMNER GAZETTE. 1800. Thu. $.50 newsstand; $21/yr. carrier; $19.50/yr. in cy.; $22.50/yr outside cy.; $27.50/yr. out of state. 106 E. First St., Sumner, IA 50674. TEL 319-578-3351; FAX 319-578-5784. **Owner(s):** Ken & Rosalie Schmith, 106 E. First St., Sumner, IA 50674. TEL 319-578-3351; FAX 319-578-5784; Pub. Cal Milnes; adv. contact: Katy Milnes. pub. size: broadsheet; circ. 3,000(paid).

TAMA
US
TAMA NEWS-HERALD. 1925. Thu. $32/yr. in cy. 220-224 W. Third St., Tama, IA 52339. TEL 515-484-2841; FAX 515-484-5705. **Owner(s):** Ogden Newspapers, Inc., 1500 Main St., Wheeling, WV 26033. TEL 304-233-0100; Ed. Nancy Dostal; Pub. Mike Schlesinger; adv.; photos; bk.rev.; pub. size: broadsheet; circ. 3,100(paid).

THOMPSON
US
THOMPSON-RAKE COURIER. Thu. $.40 newsstand. 160 Jackson St., Thompson, IA 50478. TEL 515-584-2770; FAX 515-584-2353. **Owner(s):** Martin Bunge, 42 W. Center St., Britt, IA 50423. TEL 515-843-3851; Ed. Kim Norftrud; Pub. Martin Bunge; adv.; pub. size: broadsheet; circ. 1,000(paid).

THORNTON
US
SOUTHERN COUNTY NEWS. Wed. $.40 newsstand; $20/yr. in state; $25/yr. out of state. 300 Main St., Thornton, IA 50479-0096. TEL 515-998-2712; FAX 515-998-2712. **Owner(s):** Southern County News, 300 Main St., Thornton, IA 50479-0096; Ed. William Schrader; Pub. William Schrader; adv.; photos; pub. size: broadsheet; circ. 1,000(free & paid).

TIPTON
US
TIPTON CONSERVATIVE & ADVERTISER. 1846. Wed. $.75 newsstand; $24/yr. W. Fifth St., Tipton, IA 52772. TEL 319-886-2131; FAX 319-886-6466. **Owner(s):** Ruth Clark, P.O. Box 271, Tipton, IA 52772. TEL 319-886-2131; Stuart & Sharon Clark, P.O. Box 271, Tipton, IA 52772. TEL 319-886-2131; FAX 319-886-6466; Ed. Stuart Clark; Pub. Stuart Clark; adv. contact: Mark Kuehnle. bk.rev.; pub. size: broadsheet; circ. 4,900(paid).

WEEKLY NEWSPAPERS

TRAER
US

TRAER STAR-CLIPPER. 1873. Thu. $.50 newsstand; $25/yr. in state. 625 Second St., Traer, IA 50675. TEL 319-478-2323. **Owner(s):** Marshalltown Newspaper, Inc., 135 W. Main, Marshalltown, IA 50158. TEL 800-542-7893; Ed. Ellen Young. adv.; photos; pub. size: broadsheet; circ. 3,200(paid).

WAUKON
US

WAUKON STANDARD. 1870. Wed. $.75 newsstand; $23/yr. local; $37/yr. out of area. 15 First St, N.W., Waukon, IA 52172. TEL 319-568-3431; FAX 319-568-4242. **Owner(s):** News Publishing Co., 1126 Mills St., Black Earth, WI 53515. TEL 319-568-3431; Ed. Dick Schilling; Pub. Tom Johnson; adv. contact: Gail Johnson. pub. size: broadsheet; circ. 4,200(paid).

WAVERLY
US

BREMER COUNTY INDEPENDENT. 1856. Tue. $.75 newsstand; $34/yr. 311 W. Bremer, Waverly, IA 50677. TEL 319-352-3335; FAX 319-352-5135. **Owner(s):** Community Media Group, 805 S. Logan, West Frankfurt, IL 62896; Ed. Ray Locke; Pub. Jayne Hall; adv. contact: Jayne Hall. pub. size: standard; circ. 6,390(paid).
Formerly: Waverly Bremer County Independent.

US

WAVERLY DEMOCRAT. 1876. Thu. $34/yr.; in state; $54/yr. out of state. 311 W. Bremer, Waverly, IA 50677. TEL 319-352-3335. **Owner(s):** Community Media Group, 805 S. Logan, West Frankfurt, IL 62896; Ed. Ray Locke; Pub. Jayne Hall; adv. contact: Jayne Hall. pub. size: standard; circ. 6,390(paid).

WEST BURLINGTON
US

DES MOINES COUNTY NEWS, THE. 1956. Fri. $16/yr. in cy.; $19/yr. in state; $23/yr. out of state. P.O. Box 177, West Burlington, IA 52655-0177. TEL 319-752-8328; FAX 319-523-8167. **Owner(s):** Louisa Publishing, Box 306, Wapello, IA 52653. TEL 319-523-4631; Pub. Mike Hodges; adv. contact: Randy Bardy. photos; pub. size: tabloid; circ. 1,900(paid).

WEST LIBERTY
US

WEST LIBERTY INDEX. 1868. Thu. $.50 newsstand; $20/yr. in cy.; $22/yr. in state; $24/yr. elsewhere. 104 E. Third St., West Liberty, IA 52776. TEL 319-627-2814; FAX 319-627-2110. **Owner(s):** Wally Johnson, P.O. Box 96, West Liberty, IA 52776-0096. TEL 319-627-2814; FAX 319-627-2110; Ed. Diane Beranek; Pub. Wally Johnson; adv.: $4.67/SAU. pub. size: tabloid; circ. 3,000(paid).

WEST UNION
US

FAYETTE COUNTY UNION. 1866. Wed. $1/ newsstand; $32/yr. in cy.; $44/yr. out of state. 119 S. Vine, West Union, IA 52175-0153. TEL 319-422-3888; FAX 319-422-3488. **Owner(s):** Union, The, 119 S. Vine, West Union, IA 52175. TEL 319-422-3888; FAX 319-422-3488; Ed. Gerald H. Blue; Pub. Gerald H. Blue; adv.; photos; pub. size: broadsheet; circ. 7,200(free & paid).
Formerly: West Union Union.

WHAT CHEER
US

WHAT CHEER PAPER. 1878. Wed. $.25 newsstand; $12/yr. 102 N. Barnes St., What Cheer, IA 50268. TEL 515-634-2092; FAX 515-522-9288. **Owner(s):** Brooklyn Publishing Co., 102 N. Barnes St., What Cheer, IA 50268; Ed. C.V. Dunham; Pub. C.V. Dunham; adv. contact: C.V. Dunham. pub. size: broadsheet; circ. 1,450(paid).
Formerly: What Cheer Patriot Chronicle.

WILLIAMSBURG
US

JOURNAL TRIBUNE. Thu. $.75 newsstand; $22/yr. in cy.; $24/yr. out of cy.; $29/yr. out of state. 208 W. State St., Williamsburg, IA 52361. TEL 319-668-1240; FAX 391-668-9112. **Owner(s):** Marengo Publishing Corp., 100 W. Main St., Marengo, IA 52301-0208. TEL 319-642-5506; FAX 319-642-5509; Ed. Todd Kimm; Pub. Dan DeBettignies; adv. contact: Michael Simmons. photos; pub. size: broadsheet; circ. 2,000(paid).

WINTERSET
US

WINTERSET MADISONIAN. 1856. Wed. $.75 newsstand; $29.50/yr. in cy.; $34.50/elsewhere. 112 W. Court Ave., Winterset, IA 50273. TEL 515-462-2101; FAX 515-462-2102. **Owner(s):** Ted Gorman, Winterset Madisonian, 112 W. Court Ave., Winterset, IA 50273. TEL 515-462-2102; Ed. Chris Dorsey; Pub. Ted Gorman; adv.; photos; pub. size: broadsheet; circ. 3,400(paid). **Wire Service(s):** Iowa Media Link.

KANSAS

ANTHONY
US

ANTHONY REPUBLICAN, THE. 1878. Wed. $.50 newsstand; $20/yr. in surrounding cys.; $25/yr. in state. 121 E. Main St., Anthony, KS 67003. TEL 316-842-5129. **Owner(s):** James W. & Vera L. Dunn, 121 E. Main St., Anthony, KS 67003. TEL 316-842-5129; Pub. James W. Dunn; adv.; contact: Larry Dunn. pub. size: broadsheet; circ. 3,100(paid).

BAXTER SPRINGS
US

BAXTER SPRINGS CITIZEN. 1872. s-w.: Tue. & Fri. $.50 newsstand; $30/yr. in cy.; $37/yr. out of cy. 1010 Military Ave., Baxter Springs, KS 66713-1547. TEL 316-856-2115; FAX 316-856-3162; E-mail: kansasnews@aol.com; URL: http://www.baxtercitizen.com. **Owner(s):** Nichols Communications, Inc., 1010 Military Ave., Baxter Springs, KS 66713. TEL 316-856-2115; FAX 316-856-3162; Ed. Brent Fisher; Pub. Jeff Nichols; adv. contact: Greg Beavers. photos; bk.rev.; pub. size: broadsheet; circ. 2,231(paid).

BELLE PLAINE
US

BELLE PLAINE NEWS, THE. 1879. Thu. $.50 newsstand; $21.50/yr. in cy.; $34/yr. out of state. 431 Merchant, Belle Plaine, KS 67013. TEL 316-488-2234; FAX 316-488-3241. **Owner(s):** William S. Clester, 431 Merchant, Belle Plaine, KS 67013. TEL 316-488-2234; FAX 316-488-3241; Ed. Brett Bohannon; Pub. William S. Clester; adv. contact: Marian Phipps. photos; bk.rev.; pub. size: tabloid; circ. 1,000(paid).

US

OXFORD REGISTER, THE. 1879. Thu. $.50 newsstand; $20/yr. 431 Merchant, Belle Plaine, KS 67013. TEL 316-455-3535; FAX 316-488-3241. **Owner(s):** William Sam Clester, P.O. Box 128, Belle Plaine, KS 67013. TEL 316-488-2234; FAX 316-488-3241; Ed. Brett Bohannon; Pub. William Sam Clester; adv.; photos; bk.rev.; pub. size: tabloid; circ. 500(free & paid).

BELLEVILLE
US   ISSN 0740-0985

BELLEVILLE TELESCOPE. 1870. Thu. $.50 newsstand; $24/yr. in cy. 1817 E. U.S. 81 Frontage Rd., Belleville, KS 66935-0349. TEL 913-527-2244; FAX 913-527-2225. **Owner(s):** Telescope, Inc., 1817 E. U.S. 81 Frontage Rd., Belleville, KS 66935. TEL 913-527-2244; Ed. Mark L. Miller; Pub. Merle M. Miller; pub. size: broadsheet; circ. 5,100(paid).

BIRD CITY
US

BIRD CITY TIMES. Thu. $.65 newsstand; $22/yr. P.O. Box 167, Bird City, KS 67731-0167. TEL 913-734-2621; FAX 913-332-3001. **Owner(s):** NorWest Newspapers, Inc., 170 S. Penn, Oberlin, KS 67749. TEL 913-475-2206; FAX 913-475-2800; Ed. Steve Haynes; Pub. Cynthia Haynes; adv. contact: Nell Frohlich. pub. size: broadsheet; circ. 688(free & paid).

BONNER SPRINGS
US

BONNER SPRINGS-EDWARDSVILLE CHIEFTAIN. 1896. Thu. $.35 newsstand; $12.75/yr. in cy.; $16/yr. out of cy. P.O. Box 256, Bonner Springs, KS 66012. TEL 913-422-4048; FAX 913-422-4233. **Owner(s):** Clausie W. & Jean Smith, P.O. Box 256, Bonner Springs, KS 66012. TEL 913-422-4048; Ed. Jean Smith; Pub. Jean Smith; adv.; photos; bk.rev.; pub. size: broadsheet; circ. 13,000(controlled & free).

BURLINGAME

US ISSN 1040-6077
OSAGE COUNTY CHRONICLE. 1863. Thu. $.60 newsstand; $21/yr. in cy.; $24/yr. out of cy. 107 E. Santa Fe, Burlingame, KS 66413-0065. TEL 913-654-3621; FAX 913-654-3438. **Owner(s):** Incunabula, Inc., 107 E. Santa Fe, Burlingame, KS 66413. TEL 913-654-3621; FAX 913-654-3438. Ed. K. Kurt Kessinger; Pub. K. Kurt Kessinger; adv. contact: Kathy Kessinger. photos; pub. size: broadsheet; circ. 5,200(paid).

BURLINGTON

US
COFFEY COUNTY TODAY. 1856. 3/wk.: Mon., Wed., Fri. $.50 newsstand; $40/yr. carrier; $46/yr. mailed in state; $50/yr. out of state. 324 Hudson St., Burlington, KS 66839. TEL 316-364-5325; FAX 316-364-2607. **Owner(s):** Glenn R. German, P.O. Drawer A, Burlington, KS 66839. TEL 316-364-8610; Ed. Mark Petterson; Pub. Glenn R. German; adv. contact: B.J. Petterson. pub. size: broadsheet; circ. 2,600(paid). **Wire Service(s):** AP.

CHENEY

US
TIMES-SENTINEL, THE. 1894. Thu. $.50 newsstand; $24/yr. 101 N. Main, Cheney, KS 67025. TEL 316-542-3111; FAX 316-542-3283. **Owner(s):** Paul Rhodes & Amy Crouch, 211 N. Garfield, Cheney, KS. TEL 316-542-0179; Ed. Paul Rhodes. adv. contact: Amy Crouch. photos; bk.rev.; pub. size: tabloid; circ. 3,550(paid).

COTTONWOOD FALLS

US ISSN 1079-8188
CHASE COUNTY LEADER-NEWS. 1871. Thu. $.75 newsstand; $24/yr. in cy.; $27/yr. out of cy. 306 Broadway, Cottonwood Falls, KS 66845-0436. TEL 316-273-6391; FAX 316-273-6864. **Owner(s):** Chase County Publishing Co., Inc., 306 Broadway, Cottonwood Falls, KS 66845-0046. TEL 316-273-6391; FAX 316-273-8674; Ed. Jerry Schwilling. adv.; photos; pub. size: standard; circ. 1,700(paid).

COURTLAND

US ISSN 0746-5750
COURTLAND JOURNAL-EMPIRE. 1891. Thu. $.35 newsstand; $12.71/yr. in state; $17/yr. out of state. 420 Main St., Courtland, KS 66939-0318. TEL 913-374-4428. **Owner(s):** Robert & Colleen Mainquist, 420 Main St., Courtland, KS 66939-0318. TEL 913-374-4428. Ed. Coleen Mainquist; Pub. Robert Mainquist; adv.; pub. size: standard; circ. 650(paid).

DODGE CITY

US ISSN 0018-1471
HIGH PLAINS JOURNAL. 1882. Mon. $56/yr. 1500 E. Wyatt Earp Blvd., Dodge City, KS 67801-0760. TEL 316-227-7171; FAX 316-227-7173. **Owner(s):** High Plains Publishers, Inc., P.O. Box 760, Dodge City, KS 67801-0760. TEL 316-227-7171; Ed. Galen Hubbs; Pub. Duane Ross; adv. contact: Tom Taylor. pub. size: negotiable; circ. 58,000(paid). **Wire Service(s):** AP, KR.

ELLSWORTH

US
ELLSWORTH REPORTER, THE. 1871. Thu. $.75 newsstand; $23.01/yr. local; $26/yr. out of state. P.O. Box 7, Ellsworth, KS 67439. TEL 913-472-3103; FAX 913-472-3268. **Owner(s):** Karl Gaston, P.O. Box 7, Ellsworth, KS 67439. TEL 913-472-3103; FAX 913-472-3268; Ed. Karl Gaston; Pub. Karl Gaston; adv.; pub. size: broadsheet; circ. 3,000(paid).

EUREKA

US
EUREKA HERALD. 1868. Thu. $.50 newsstand; $25.95/yr. in area; $36/yr. out of area. 106 W. Second, Eureka, KS 67045. TEL 316-583-5721. **Owner(s):** Greenwood County Publishing, Inc., P.O. Box 590, Eureka, KS 67045. TEL 316-583-5721; Ed. Richard W. Clasen; Pub. Richard W. Clasen; adv.; pub. size: broadsheet; circ. 3,300(paid).

FREDONIA

US
WILSON COUNTY CITIZEN. 1870. s-w.: Mon. & Thu. $.50 newsstand; $22.67/yr. in state; $27.30/yr. out of state. 406 N. Seventh, Fredonia, KS 66736. TEL 316-378-4415; FAX 316-378-4688. **Owner(s):** Joe & Rita Relph, 706 Madison, Fredonia, KS 66736. TEL 316-378-4415; Ed. Mina DeBarry; Pub. Joe Relph; adv.; bk.rev.; pub. size: broadsheet; circ. 3,995(paid).
Formerly: Fredonia Wilson County Citizen.

GIRARD

US
GIRARD PRESS. 1869. Tue. $.35 newsstand; $19.25/yr. in cy.; $24.75/yr. out of cy. 102 S. Ozark, Girard, KS 66743. TEL 316-724-4426; FAX 316-724-4493. **Owner(s):** Ed & Kris McKechnie, P.O. Box 126, Girard, KS 66743. TEL 316-724-4426; Ed. Janet Beene; Pub. Ed McKechnie; adv. contact: Jim Perona. bk.rev.; pub. size: broadsheet; circ. 2,850(free & paid).

GOODLAND

US
SHERMAN COUNTY STAR, THE. 1994. Wed. $.50 newsstand; $24/yr. local; $28/yr. elsewhere. 1015 Main Ave., Goodland, KS 67735-0599. TEL 913-899-5500; FAX 913-899-6260. **Owner(s):** Top Star, Inc., P.O. Box 599, Goodland, KS 67735; Ed. Roxanne Yonkey; Pub. Eric L. Yonkey; adv. contact: Eric L. Yonkey. bk.rev.; pub. size: broadsheet; circ. 78,611(free & paid).

HILL CITY

US
HILL CITY TIMES, THE. 1886. Wed. $.35 newsstand; $16/yr. local; $17/yr. in state; $20/yr. elsewhere. 110 N. Pomeroy Ave., Hill City, KS 67642-0308. TEL 913-421-5700. **Owner(s):** Robert A. Boyd, 805 Ash, Hill City, KS 67642. TEL 913-421-2147; James E. Logback, 77 Tenth Ave., Hill City, KS 67642. TEL 913-421-2775; Ed. Jim Logback; Pub. Robert A. Boyd; adv.; photos; pub. size: broadsheet; circ. 2,600(paid).

HILLSBORO

US
HILLSBORO STAR-JOURNAL. 1933. Wed. $.75 newsstand; $33/yr. in state; $39/yr. out of state; $50/yr. foreign. 104 S. Main, Hillsboro, KS 67063. TEL 316-947-3975; FAX 316-947-3883. **Owner(s):** Stacy Stenseng, P.O. Box A, Hillsboro, KS 67063. TEL 316-947-3975; Ed. Stacy Stenseng; Pub. Stacy Stenseng; adv. contact: Tammy Nichol. pub. size: broadsheet; circ. 3,100(paid).

HOISINGTON

US
HOISINGTON DISPATCH. 1889. Thu. $.50 newsstand; $16.94/yr. local; $19.06/yr. in state; $22.77/yr. elsewhere. 104 N. Main, Hoisington, KS 67544. TEL 316-653-4154; FAX 316-653-4720. **Owner(s):** Brown Family Publishing, Inc., P.O. Box 330, Hoisington, KS 67544. TEL 316-653-4154; Ed. Luke Brown; Pub. Luke Brown; pub. size: broadsheet; circ. 2,200(paid).

HOLTON

US
HOLTON RECORDER. 1875. s-w.: Mon. & Thu. $.50 newsstand; $24/yr. in cy.; $25/yr. out of cy.; $27/yr. out of state. 109 W. Fourth St., Holton, KS 66436. TEL 913-364-3141; FAX 913-364-3422. **Owner(s):** Bryan McDaniel, 109 W. Fourth St., Holton, KS 66436. TEL 913-564-3141; Ed. Leslie McDaniel; Pub. Bryan McDaniel; adv. contact: Terri Torrey. pub. size: broadsheet; circ. 4,800(paid).

INDEPENDENCE

US ISSN 1067-5906
INDEPENDENCE NEWS, THE. 1948. Thu. $25/yr. 210 W. Main St., Independence, KS 67301. TEL 316-331-4950; FAX 316-251-1905. **Owner(s):** John F. Vermillion, 1424 W. Eighth, Independence, KS 67301. TEL 316-331-3073; Ed. John F. Vermillion; Pub. John F. Vermillion; adv.; pub. size: broadsheet.

JETMORE

US
JETMORE REPUBLICAN. 1887. Thu. $.50 newsstand; $18.88/yr. in state; $20/yr. out of state. P.O. Box 337, Jetmore, KS 67854-0337. TEL 316-357-8316; FAX 316-357-8464. **Owner(s):** Jerry Anderson, P.O. Box 536, Cimarron, KS 67835. TEL 316-855-3902; Ed. Jerry Buxton; Pub. Jerry Anderson; pub. size: broadsheet.

JOHNSON

US
JOHNSON PIONEER. 1890. Thu. $.50 newsstand; $16.94/yr. in cy.; $19.06/yr. out of cy. 103 N. Main St., Johnson, KS 67855-0010. TEL 316-492-6244. **Owner(s):** Ronda Ford, P.O. Box 10, Johnson, KS 67855-0010. TEL 316-492-6244; Pub. Ronda Ford; adv.; bk.rev.; pub. size: broadsheet; circ. 1,100(paid).

WEEKLY NEWSPAPERS

JUNCTION CITY
US
FORT RILEY POST. 1958. Fri. $18/yr. 222 W. Sixth St., Junction City, KS 66441. TEL 913-762-5000; FAX 913-762-4584. **Owner(s):** Montgomery Communications, Inc., P.O. Box 129, Junction City, KS 66441. TEL 913-762-5000; FAX 913-762-4584; Ed. John G. Montgomery; Pub. John G. Montgomery; adv.: $12.85/SAU. pub. size: broadsheet; circ. 7,900(free).

KANSAS CITY
US
RECORD, THE. 1887. Thu. $.25 newsstand; $13.75/yr. in cy. 3414 Strong Ave., Kansas City, KS 66106. TEL 913-362-1988; FAX 913-362-1989. **Owner(s):** Jon A. Males, 3414 Strong Ave., Kansas City, KS 66106. TEL 913-362-1988; Ed. Jon A. Males; Pub. Jon A. Males; adv.; pub. size: tabloid; circ. 7,500(free & paid).

US
WYANDOTTE WEST. 1968. Thu. $.50 newsstand; $18.99/yr. 7735 Washington Ave., Kansas City, KS 66112-3312. TEL 913-788-5565; FAX 913-788-9812. **Owner(s):** Murrel W. Bland, P.O. Box 12003, Kansas City, KS 66112. TEL 913-788-5565; FAX 913-788-5565; Ed. Murrel W. Bland; Pub. Murrel W. Bland; adv. contact: Carol A. Bland. adv.: $10.36/SAU. photos; bk.rev.; pub. size: tabloid; circ. 2,548(free & paid).

KINGMAN
US
KINGMAN JOURNAL. 1880. Tue. $.50 newsstand; $30/yr. local; $33/yr. out of state; subscription includes Leader Courier. P.O. Box 353, Kingman, KS 67068. TEL 316-532-3151; FAX 316-532-3152. **Owner(s):** Robert McQuin, P.O. Box 353, Kingman, KS 67068. TEL 316-532-3151; Ed. Robert McQuin; Pub. Robert McQuin; adv.; pub. size: broadsheet; circ. 3,400(paid).
Formerly: Kingman Journal/Leader Courier.

US
LEADER-COURIER. 1885. Fri. $.50 newsstand; $30/yr. local; $33/yr. out of state; subscription includes Kingman Journal. P.O. Box 353, Kingman, KS 67068. TEL 913-532-3151; FAX 316-532-3152. **Owner(s):** Robert McQuin, P.O. Box 353, Kingman, KS 67068. TEL 316-532-3151; Ed. Robert McQuin; Pub. Robert McQuin; adv.; pub. size: broadsheet; circ. 3,400(paid).

LA CROSSE
US
RUSH COUNTY NEWS. 1940. Thu. $.50 newsstand; $21.50/yr. in state; $24.50/yr. out of state. 112 W. Eighth St., La Crosse, KS 67548. TEL 913-222-2555; FAX 913-222-2557. **Owner(s):** Rush County News, 112 W. Eighth St., La Crosse, KS 67548. TEL 913-222-2555; FAX 913-222-2557; Ed. Mary Engel; Pub. Duane Engel; adv. contact: Time Engel. adv.: $3.95/SAU. photos; pub. size: broadsheet.

LAWRENCE
US
BALDWIN CITY LEDGER. 1883. Fri. $.54 newsstand; $18.70/6 mos.; $26.73/yr.; $74.31/3 yrs. 2951 Four Wheel Dr., Lawrence, KS 66047. TEL 913-749-0006; FAX 913-749-0065. **Owner(s):** TeleGraphics, Inc., 2951 Four Wheel Dr., Lawrence, KS 66047. TEL 913-749-0006; FAX 913-749-0065; Ed. Chad Lawhorn; Pub. Doris Miller; adv.; photos; bk.rev.; pub. size: broadsheet; circ. 7,000(paid).
Formerly: Telegraphics.

LEBANON
US
LEBANON TIMES, THE. 1887. Wed. $.35 newsstand; $11.01/yr. in cy.; $12.06/yr. in state; $12.50/yr. US. 409 Walnut, Lebanon, KS 66952. TEL 913-389-6631. **Owner(s):** Darrel & Ruth Miller, P.O. Box 157, Downs, KS 67437. TEL 913-454-3514; Ed. Phyllis Bell; Pub. Darrel E. Miller; adv.; pub. size: standard; circ. 650(free & paid).

MADISON
US
MADISON NEWS INC., THE. 1879. Thu. $.40 newsstand; $25.88/yr. local. 118 S. Third St., Madison, KS 66860. TEL 316-437-2433; FAX 316-437-2433. **Owner(s):** Earl & Patsy Murphy, 242 Rd. H, Madison, KS 66860. TEL 316-475-3453; Calvin & Chris Murphy, 244 Rd. H, Madison, KS 66860. TEL 316-475-3921; Evan & Jola Casey, 121 North Adams, Council Grove, KS. TEL 316-767-6592; Ed. Jola Casey. adv.; photos; pub. size: standard; circ. 750(free & paid).

MARION
US
MARION COUNTY RECORD. 1869. Wed. $33/yr. in state; $45/yr. out of state. 117 S. Third, Marion, KS 66861-0278. TEL 316-382-2165; FAX 316-382-2262; E-mail: marcorec@southwind.net; URL: http://www.marionrecord.com. **Owner(s):** Hoch Publishing Co., Inc., P.O. Box 278, Marion, KS 66861-0278. TEL 316-382-2165; Ed. Bill Meyer; Pub. Bill Meyer; pub. size: broadsheet; circ. 3,315(paid).

MARYSVILLE
US
MARYSVILLE ADVOCATE, THE. 1885. Thu. $.79 newsstand; $26.23/yr. in area; $36/yr. elsewhere. 107 S. Ninth, Marysville, KS 66508-0271. TEL 913-562-2317; FAX 913-562-5589. **Owner(s):** Howard & Sharon Kissinger, 107 S. Ninth, Marysville, KS 66508. TEL 913-562-2317; FAX 913-562-5589; Ed. Howard D. Kessinger. adv. contact: Randy Meerian. bk.rev.; pub. size: broadsheet; circ. 6,028(paid).

MILTONVALE
US
MILTONVALE RECORD. 1899. Thu. $.30 newsstand; $16/yr. 12 Spruce St., Miltonvale, KS 67466. TEL 913-427-2680; FAX 913-427-2680. **Owner(s):** Richard Phelps, 412 Ash, Miltonvale, KS 67466. TEL 913-427-3203; Deanna Phelps, 412 Ash, Miltonvale, KS 67466. TEL 913-427-3203; Ed. Richard Phelps. adv. contact: Barbara Mikels. adv.: $2/SAU. photos; pub. size: broadsheet; circ. 750(paid).

MOUNDRIDGE
US
LEDGER, THE. 1887. Thu. $21.75/yr. in state; $28.75/yr. out of state. 135 S. Christian, Moundridge, KS 67107. TEL 316-345-2117; FAX 316-345-2170. **Owner(s):** Davies Communications, Inc., 135 S. Christian, Moundridge, KS 67107. TEL 316-345-2117; Ed. Mary Ann Musselulite. adv.; photos; pub. size: tabloid; circ. 2,000(paid).

NEODESHA
US
NEODESHA DERRICK. 1883. Thu. $.75 newsstand; $25/yr. in state; $30/yr. out of state. 501 Main St., Neodesha, KS 66757-0356. TEL 316-325-3000; FAX 316-325-2880. **Owner(s):** JoAnne Hartley Harper, P.O. Box 356, Neodesha, KS 66757. TEL 316-325-3000; Ed. JoAnne Hartley Harper; Pub. JoAnne Hartley Harper; adv. contact: Debbie Dixon. pub. size: broadsheet; circ. 1,900(paid).

NESS CITY
US
NESS COUNTY NEWS, THE. 1884. Thu. $.40 newsstand; $19.41/yr. local; $22.50/yr. out of state. 110 S. Kansas, Ness City, KS 67560. TEL 913-798-2213; FAX 913-798-2214. **Owner(s):** John Clarke, 110 S. Kansas, Ness City, KS 67560. TEL 913-798-2213; FAX 913-798-2214; Ed. Jerry Clarke; Pub. John Clarke; adv. contact: John Clarke. photos; pub. size: broadsheet; circ. 2,525(paid).

OAKLEY
US
OAKLEY GRAPHIC. 1887. Wed. $20.65/yr. local; $21.71/yr. out of area. 118 Center, Oakley, KS 67748. TEL 913-672-3228; FAX 913-672-3229. **Owner(s):** J & M Enterprises, Box 528, Cimarron, KS 67835; Ed. Barbara Glover. adv. contact: Gloria Nichols. pub. size: standard; circ. 4,400(controlled & free).

OBERLIN
US
OBERLIN HERALD, THE. 1879. Wed. $.75 newsstand; $28/yr. 170 S. Penn Ave., Oberlin, KS 67749-2243. TEL 913-475-2206; FAX 913-475-2800; E-mail: obherald@nwkansas.com. **Owner(s):** Steve & Cynthia Haynes, 170 S. Penn Ave., Oberlin, KS 67745-2243. TEL 913-475-2206; FAX 913-475-2800; Ed. Steve Haynes; Pub. Steve Haynes; adv. contact: Jennifer Lee. photos; bk.rev.; pub. size: broadsheet; circ. 2,906(paid).

OSAWATOMIE

OSAWATOMIE GRAPHIC. 1887. Thu. $.50 newsstand; $25/yr. in cy.; $35/yr. out of state; $32/yr. elswhere in KS. 635 Main St., Osawatomie, KS 66064. TEL 913-755-4151; FAX 913-755-6544. **Owner(s):** Osawatomie Publishing Co., Inc., 635 Main St., Osawatomie, KS 66064. TEL 913-755-4151; Pub. Webster Hawkins; adv. contact: Paul L. Branson. pub. size: broadsheet; circ. 7,000(paid).

OSBORNE

US   ISSN 1040-9033
OSBORNE COUNTY FARMER. 1872. Thu. $.50 newsstand; $29.94/yr. local. 210 W. Main St., Osborne, KS 67473-0130. TEL 913-346-5424; FAX 913-346-5400. **Owner(s):** Dale R. Worley, 203 N. Fourth, Osborne, KS 67473. TEL 913-346-5891; Ed. Dale R. Worley; Pub. Dale R. Worley; adv. contact: Dale R. Worley. photos; bk.rev.; pub. size: broadsheet; circ. 2,800(paid).

OSKALOOSA

US
OSKALOOSA INDEPENDENT. 1869. Thu. $.50 newsstand; $19.24/yr. in cy.; $20.31/yr. in state; $25/yr. out of state. 607 Delaware, Oskaloosa, KS 66066. TEL 913-863-2520; FAX 913-863-2730. **Owner(s):** Clarke Davis-Wilson Davis Publications, Inc., P.O. Box 187, Valley Falls, KS 66088. TEL 913-945-3257; Pub. Clarke Davis; adv. contact: Vickie Burk. pub. size: broadsheet; circ. 2,200(paid).

OTTAWA

US
OTTAWA TIMES. 1932. Thu. $.50 newsstand; $25.50/yr. in area. 401 S. Main St., Ste. 1, Ottawa, KS 66067-0246. TEL 913-242-9200; FAX 913-242-9595. **Owner(s):** Harris Publications, The Ottawa Herald, 104 S. Cedar, Ottawa, KS 66067. TEL 913-242-4700; Ed. Bill Gray; Pub. John Montgomery; adv. contact: Bonnie Ramsey. photos; bk.rev.; pub. size: tabloid; circ. 1,300(paid).

US
OTTAWA TIMES SHOPPER. 1974. Tue. free in area. 401 S. Main St., Ste. 1, Ottawa, KS 66067-0246. TEL 913-242-9200; FAX 913-242-9595. **Owner(s):** Harris Publications, The Ottawa Herald, 104 S. Cedar, Ottawa, KS 66067. TEL 913-242-4700; Ed. Bill Gray; Pub. John Montgomery; adv. contact: Bonnie Ramsey. pub. size: tabloid; circ. 13,800(free).

OVERLAND

US
SQUIRES, THE. 1994. m. free; $18/yr. mailed. 4500 College Blvd., Overland, KS 66211. TEL 913-498-2625; FAX 913-498-1561. **Owner(s):** Leathers Publishing Co., 3840 W. 75th St., Prairie Village, KS 66208. TEL 913-384-2625; FAX 913-384-5068; Ed. Barbara Thomson; Pub. Tom Leathers; adv.; bk.rev.; pub. size: standard; circ. 9,000(free & paid).
Formerly: Other Side, The.

OVERLAND PARK

US
OLATHE SUN. 1950. s-w.: Wed. & Fri. free; voluntary pay. 7373 W. 107th St., Overland Park, KS 66212. TEL 913-381-1010; FAX 913-381-9889. **Owner(s):** Sun Publications, Inc., 7373 W. 107th St., Overland Park, KS 66212. TEL 913-381-1010; Pub. Steve Rose; adv. contact: Jo Stapleton. photos; pub. size: broadsheet; circ. 112,441(free).

PAOLA

US
MIAMI COUNTY REPUBLIC. 1866. s-w.: Mon. & Wed. $.50 newsstand; $34.50/yr. in cy.; $36.30/yr. out of cy. 121 S. Pearl St., Paola, KS 66071. TEL 913-294-2311; FAX 913-294-5318. **Owner(s):** Miami County Publishing Co., Inc., 121 S. Pearl St., Paola, KS 66071. TEL 913-294-2311; Ed. Phil McLaughlin; Pub. Phil McLaughlin; adv. contact: Lorie Zahn. pub. size: broadsheet; circ. 6,000(paid).

PARSONS

US
PARSONS NEWS. Thu. $16.95/yr. 1930 Clark St., Parsons, KS 67357-0937. TEL 316-421-2990; FAX 316-421-2990; E-mail: parsonews@aol.com. Owner(s): Toni Tippet, P.O. Box 937, Parsons, KS 67357. TEL 316-421-2990; Ed. Sherri Shire; Pub. Toni Tippet; adv. contact: Jan S. Trail. photos; pub. size: tabloid; circ. 2,500(paid).

PHILLIPSBURG

US
PHILLIPS COUNTY REVIEW. 1905. Thu. $20/yr. in area; $22.50/yr. out of area. 257 F St., Phillipsburg, KS 67661. TEL 913-543-5242; FAX 913-543-5243. **Owner(s):** LST Publishing, Inc.; Ed. Perry Hanson; Pub. Ron Lower; adv. contact: Ron Lower. pub. size: broadsheet; circ. 3,500(paid).

RUSSELL

US
RUSSELL RECORD. 1872. s-w.: Mon. & Thu. $30.75/yr. 802 N. Maple St., Russell, KS 67665. TEL 913-483-2111; FAX 913-483-4012. **Owner(s):** Russell Publishing, Inc., 802 N. Maple St., Russell, KS 67665. TEL 913-483-2111; Ed. Allen D. Evans; Pub. Allen D. Evans; adv. contact: Allen D. Evans. pub. size: broadsheet; circ. 3,075(paid).

SHAWNEE

US
JOURNAL HERALD, THE. 1924. Thu. $.50 newsstand; $22.50/yr. in cy.; $27.50/yr. out of cy.; $32.50/yr. out of state. 11004 Johnson Dr., Shawnee, KS 66203. TEL 913-631-2550; FAX 913-631-6552. **Owner(s):** Kansan Publishing Co., 11004 Johnson Dr., Shawnee, KS 66203. TEL 913-631-2550; FAX 913-631-6552; Ed. Chuck Robinson. adv.; photos; pub. size: standard; circ. 19,500(paid).

SHAWNEE MISSION

US
JOHNSON COUNTY SUN. s-w.: Wed. & Fri. free; voluntary pay subscription; $78.64/yr. in cy.; $85.40/yr. elsewhere. 7373 W. 107th St., Shawnee Mission, KS 66212. TEL 913-381-1010; FAX 913-381-9889. **Owner(s):** Sun Publications, Inc., 7373 W. 107th St., Shawnee Mission, KS 66212. TEL 913-381-1010; Ed. Jack Lovelace; Pub. Steve Rose; adv. contact: Joe Mickelson. pub. size: broadsheet; circ. 11,000(paid).

US
LEAWOOD SUN. 1928. s-w.: Wed. & Fri. free; voluntary pay subscription. 7373 W. 107th St., Shawnee Mission, KS 66212. TEL 913-381-1010; FAX 913-381-9889. **Owner(s):** Sun Publications, Inc., 7373 W. 107th St., Shawnee Mission, KS 66212. TEL 913-381-1010; Ed. Jack Lovelace; Pub. Steve Rose; adv. contact: Joe Mickelson. pub. size: broadsheet; circ. 3,200(free).

US
LENEXA SUN. 1921. s-w.: Wed. & Fri. free; voluntary pay subscription; $78.46/yr. in cy. 7373 W. 107th St., Shawnee Mission, KS 66212. TEL 913-381-1010; FAX 913-381-9889. **Owner(s):** Sun Publications, Inc., 7373 W. 107th St., Shawnee Mission, KS 66212. TEL 913-381-1010; Ed. Jack Lovelace; Pub. Steve Rose; adv. contact: Joe Mickelson. pub. size: broadsheet; circ. 9,900(free).

US
NORTHEAST JOHNSON COUNTY. s-w.: Wed. & Fri. free; voluntary pay subscription; $78.46/yr. in cy. mailed. 7373 W. 107th St., Shawnee Mission, KS 66212. TEL 913-381-1010; FAX 913-381-9889. **Owner(s):** Sun Publications, Inc., 7373 W. 107th, Overland Park, KS 66212. TEL 913-381-1010; Ed. Jack Lovelace; Pub. Steve Rose; adv. contact: Joe Mickelson. pub. size: broadsheet; circ. 800(free).

US
OVERLAND PARK SUN. s-w.: Wed. & Fri. free; voluntary pay subscription; $78.46/yr. in cy. mailed. 7373 W. 107th St., Shawnee Mission, KS 66212. TEL 913-381-1010; FAX 913-381-9889. **Owner(s):** Sun Publications, Inc., 7373 W. 107th St, Shawnee Mission, KS 66212. TEL 913-381-1010; Ed. Jack Lovelace; Pub. Steve Rose; adv. contact: Joe Michelson. pub. size: broadsheet; circ. 22,841(free).

US
PRAIRIE VILLAGE SUN. s-w.: Wed. & Fri. free; voluntary pay subscription; $78.46/yr. in cy. mailed. 7373 W. 107th St., Shawnee Mission, KS 66212. TEL 913-381-1010; FAX 913-381-9889. **Owner(s):** Sun Publications, Inc., 7373 W. 107th St., Shawnee Mission, KS 66212. TEL 913-381-1010; Ed. Jack Lovelace; Pub. Steve Rose; adv. contact: Joe Mickelson. pub. size: broadsheet; circ. 7,700(free).

US
SHAWNEE/MERRIAM SUN. 1911. s-w.: Wed. & Fri. free; voluntary pay subscription; $78.46/yr. in cy. mailed. 7373 W. 107th St., Shawnee Mission, KS 66212. TEL 913-381-1010; FAX 913-381-9889. **Owner(s):** Sun Publications, Inc., 7373 W. 107th, Shawnee Mission, KS 66212. TEL 913-381-1070; Ed. Jack Lovelace; Pub. Steve Rose; adv. contact: Joe Mickelson. pub. size: broadsheet; circ. 13,100(free).
Formerly: Merriam Sun.

WEEKLY NEWSPAPERS

SMITH CENTER
US
SMITH COUNTY PIONEER. 1871. Thu. $19/yr. in cy.; $20.98/yr. out of cy.; $22/yr. out of state. 201 S. Main, Smith Center, KS 66967. TEL 913-282-3371; FAX 913-282-6383. **Owner(s):** Darrel & Ruth Miller, 201 S. Main St., Smith Center, KS 66967. TEL 913-282-3371; Ed. Darrel Miller; Pub. Darrel Miller; adv.; pub. size: standard; circ. 3,883(paid).
Formerly: Smith Center Smith County Pioneer.

ST. FRANCIS
US
ST. FRANCIS HERALD, THE. 1885. Thu. $.75 newsstand; $31/yr. P.O. Box 1050, St. Francis, KS 67756-1050. TEL 913-332-3162; FAX 913-332-3001; E-mail: stherald@nwkansas.com. **Owner(s):** NorWest Newspapers, Inc., 170 S. Penn, Oberlin, KS 67749. TEL 913-475-2206; FAX 913-475-2800; Ed. Karen Krien. adv. contact: Nell Frohlich. pub. size: broadsheet; circ. 1,813(free & paid).

ST. JOHN
US
ST. JOHN NEWS. 1880. Wed. $22/yr. in cy.; $32/yr. out of cy. 318 N. Main St., St. John, KS 67576. TEL 316-549-3201. **Owner(s):** Murphy-McGinnis Media Inc., 130 W. Superior St., Duluth, MN 55802. TEL 218-723-8000; Ed. Lisa Stevens John. pub. size: standard; circ. 1,500(paid).

ST. MARYS
US
ST. MARYS STAR. 1884. Tue. $.50 newsstand; $28.59/yr. in state; $31/yr. out of state. 517 W. Bertrand, St. Marys, KS 66536-0190. TEL 913-437-2935; FAX 913-437-2095. **Owner(s):** Anita H. Janssen, P.O. Box 190, St. Marys, KS 66536-0190. TEL 913-437-2935; FAX 913-437-2095; Ed. Anita H. Janssen; Pub. Anita H. Janssen; adv.; photos; pub. size: tabloid; circ. 2,005(paid).

ULYSSES
US
ULYSSES NEWS. 1892. Thu. $.75 newsstand; $25/yr. in cy.; $28.50/yr. out of cy. 218 N. Main, Ulysses, KS 67880. TEL 316-356-1201; FAX 316-356-4610. **Owner(s):** Karla Wood, P.O. Box 706, Ulysses, KS 67880. TEL 316-356-1201; FAX 316-356-4610; Ed. Kevin Krier. adv.; photos; pub. size: broadsheet; circ. 10,400(free & paid).

VALLEY FALLS
US
VALLEY FALLS VINDICATOR. 1864. Thu. $.50 newsstand; $18/yr. 416 Broadway, Valley Falls, KS 66088-0187. TEL 913-945-3257; FAX 913-945-3444. **Owner(s):** Wilson-Davis Publications, Inc., P.O. Box 187, Valley Falls, KS 66088-0187. TEL 913-945-3257; FAX 913-945-3444; Ed. Clarke Davis. adv.; photos; bk.rev.; pub. size: broadsheet; circ. 2,480(paid).

WASHINGTON
US
WASHINGTON COUNTY NEWS. Thu. $20/yr. in cy.; $23/yr. out of cy.; $25/yr. out of state. 211 C St., Washington, KS 66968. TEL 913-325-2219; FAX 913-325-3255; E-mail: bhays@kspress.com; URL: http://www.kspress.com/WCN/Washindex.html. **Owner(s):** Washington County News, P.O. Box 316, Washington, KS 66968. TEL 913-325-2219; Ed. William Hays. adv.; photos; pub. size: broadsheet; circ. 3,190(paid).

KENTUCKY

ALBANY
US
CLINTON COUNTY NEWS. 1949. Thu. $.30 newsstand; $14/yr. in area; $17/yr. in state; $21/yr. out of state. 116 Washington St., Albany, KY 42602. TEL 606-387-5144; FAX 606-387-7949. **Owner(s):** Gibson Printing Co., Inc., 116 Washington St., Albany, KY 42602. TEL 606-387-5144; FAX 606-387-7949; Ed. Alan B. Gibson. adv. contact: Janie U. Gibson. photos; pub. size: standard; circ. 3,750(paid).

BARBOURVILLE
US
BARBOURVILLE MOUNTAIN ADVOCATE. 1937. Thu. $.50 newsstand; $12/yr. in cy.; $26/yr. out of state. 214 Knox St., Barbourville, KY 40906. TEL 606-546-9225; FAX 606-546-3175. **Owner(s):** Robert K. Wilson, 214 Knox St., Barbourville, KY 40906. TEL 606-546-9225; FAX 606-546-3175; Ed. Robert K. Wilson; Pub. Cecil H. Wilson; adv. contact: Carolyn Kennedy. pub. size: broadsheet; circ. 6,800(paid).

BARDSTOWN
US   ISSN 8750-0760
KENTUCKY STANDARD. 1900. 3/wk.: Mon., Wed., Fri. $.50 newsstand; $44.52/yr. in cy.; $58.85/yr. in state; $79.50/yr. out of state. 110 W. Stephen Foster Ave., Bardstown, KY 40004. TEL 502-348-9003; FAX 502-348-1971. **Owner(s):** Landmark Community Newspapers, Inc., P.O. Box 549, Shelbyville, KY 40065; Ed. Teresa Rice; Pub. Steve Lowery; adv. contact: Joan Hardin. photos; pub. size: broadsheet; circ. 8,500(paid). **Wire Service(s):** AP.

US
SHOPPER'S GUIDE. 3/wk: Mon., Wed., Fri. free. 110 W. Stephen Foster Ave., Bardstown, KY 40004. TEL 502-348-9003; FAX 502-348-1971. **Owner(s):** Landmark Community Newspapers, Inc., P.O. Box 549, Shelbyville, KY 40065; Ed. Teresa Rice; Pub. Steve Lowery; adv. contact: Joan Hardin. pub. size: broadsheet; circ. 10,000(free).

BEAVER DAM
US
BEAVER DAM OHIO COUNTY MESSENGER. 1930. Wed. $8/yr. in cy.; $12/yr. out of cy.; $15/yr. out of state. 501 N. School St., Beaver Dam, KY 42320. TEL 502-274-4949. **Owner(s):** Mrs. Andy Anderson, P.O. Box 187, Beaver Dam, KY 42320; Ed. Dave McBride; Pub. Mrs. Andy Anderson; adv. contact: Tressie Brown. pub. size: standard; circ. 2,100(paid).

BENTON
US
TRIBUNE COURIER. 1888. Wed. $.50 newsstand; $24/yr. in cy.; $30/yr. out of cy.; $32/yr. out of state. 308 E. 12th St., Benton, KY 42025. TEL 502-527-3162; FAX 502-527-4567; E-mail: tribune@ldd.net. **Owner(s):** Gleaner & Journal Publishing Co., P.O. Box 4, Henderson, KY 42420. TEL 502-827-2000; Ed. Greg Travis. adv. contact: Terri Noles. photos; pub. size: broadsheet; circ. 8,000(paid). **Wire Service(s):** AP.

BRANDENBURG
US
MEADE COUNTY MESSENGER. 1892. Wed. $16.90/yr. 235 Main St., Brandenburg, KY 40108. TEL 502-422-2155; FAX 502-422-2110. **Owner(s):** Mead County Messenger Corp., 235 Main St., Brandenburg, KY 40108. TEL 502-422-2155; FAX 502-422-2110; Pub. Kay McGehee; pub. size: broadsheet; circ. 7,000(paid).

BURKESVILLE
US
CUMBERLAND COUNTY NEWS. 1920. Wed. $.35 newsstand; $14.50/yr. local. 412 Courthouse Sq., Burkesville, KY 42717. TEL 502-864-3891; FAX 502-864-3497. **Owner(s):** Patsy Judd, 412 Courthouse Sq., Burkesville, KY 42717. TEL 502-286-3891; Ed. Cyndi Pritchett; Pub. Patsy Judd; adv.; photos; pub. size: broadsheet; circ. 3,000(paid).

CADIZ
US
CADIZ RECORD, THE. 1881. Wed. $.50 newsstand; $22/yr. in cy.; $25/yr. out of cy.; $32/yr. out of state. 50 Nunn Blvd., Cadiz, KY 42211. TEL 502-522-6605; FAX 502-522-3001. **Owner(s):** Kentucky Waterland Press, Inc., P.O. Box 311, Cadiz, KY 42211. TEL 502-522-6605; FAX 502-522-3001; Ed. Robin C. Stevens; Pub. Walt Dear; adv. contact: Jan C. Witty. photos; pub. size: broadsheet; circ. 4,600(paid).

CAMPBELLSVILLE
US
CENTRAL KENTUCKY NEWS-JOURNAL. 1910. s-w.: Mon. & Thu. $.50 newsstand; $34.56/yr. in area; $47.70/yr. elsewhere. 428 Woodlawn Ave., Campbellsville, KY 42718. TEL 502-465-8111; FAX 502-465-2500. **Owner(s):** Landmark Community Newspapers, Inc., P.O. Box 549, Shelbyville, KY 40066. TEL 502-633-4334; Pub. Richard Robards; adv. contact: Cheryl Caulk. photos; pub. size: broadsheet; circ. 7,500(paid).

CAMPBELLSVILLE, KY

NEWS-JOURNAL SHOPPER. Wed. free. 428 Woodlawn Ave., Campbellsville, KY 42718. TEL 502-465-8111; FAX 502-465-2500. **Owner(s):** Landmark Community Newspapers, Inc., P.O. Box 549, Shelbyville, KY 40066; Pub. Richard Robards; adv. contact: Cheryl Caulk. pub. size: broadsheet; circ. 8,500(free).

CARLISLE

CARLISLE MERCURY, THE. 1867. Thu. $.50 newsstand; $16.96/yr. in cy.; $20.14/yr. out of cy.; $26/yr. out of state. 234 Locust St., Carlisle, KY 40311. TEL 606-289-2464; FAX 606-289-7900. **Owner(s):** Media General, Inc., 333 E. Grace St., Richmond, VA 23219. TEL 804-649-6000; FAX 804-649-6898; Ed. Leigh Stone. adv. contact: Laura Fryman. pub. size: broadsheet; circ. 3,300(paid).

CARROLLTON

NEWS-DEMOCRAT, THE. 1867. Wed. $.50 newsstand; $22.26/yr. in cy.; $36.95/yr. out of state. 422 Main St., Carrollton, KY 41008. TEL 502-732-4261; FAX 502-732-0453. **Owner(s):** Landmark Community Newspapers, Inc., P.O. Box 549, Shelbyville, KY 40066. TEL 502-633-4334; Ed. Steve Smith. adv.; photos; pub. size: broadsheet; circ. 3,891(paid).

CAVE CITY

PROGRESS, THE. 1935. Thu. $.25 newsstand; ISSN 1055-9531 $6.95/yr. in cy. & adjacent cys.; $16/yr. in state; $20/yr. out of state. 604 E. Broadway, Cave City, KY 42127. TEL 502-773-3401; FAX 502-773-8950. **Owner(s):** Aubrey C. Wilson, Sr., Barren County Progress, 604 E. Broadway, Cave City, KY 42127. TEL 502-773-3401; Ed. Nedra Morrison. pub. size: standard; circ. 8,400(paid).

CENTRAL CITY

CENTRAL CITY TIMES-ARGUS. 1906. Wed. $.25 newsstand; $9.40/yr. in cy. 202 W. Broad St., Central City, KY 42330. TEL 502-754-2331; FAX 502-754-1805. **Owner(s):** Central City Publishing Corp., 202 W. Broad St., Central City, KY 42330. TEL 502-754-2331; FAX 502-754-1805; Ed. Richard Deavers. adv.; pub. size: broadsheet; circ. 3,850(paid).

LEADER-NEWS. 1912. Tue. $.30 newsstand; $15.60/yr. in cy.; $17/yr. out of cy.; $20/yr. out of state. 1730 W. Everly Bros. Blvd., Central City, KY 42330. TEL 502-754-3000; FAX 502-754-9484. **Owner(s):** Vickie Anderson, P.O. Box 138, Greenville, KY 42345. TEL 502-754-3000; Ed. Carolyn Hillard; Pub. Vickie Anderson; adv. contact: Wayne Thompson. pub. size: broadsheet; circ. 9,000(paid).
Formerly: Greenville Leader-News.

COLUMBIA

ADAIR PROGRESS, THE. 1988. Thu. $.35 newsstand; $11/yr. 98 Grant Ln., Columbia, KY 42728. TEL 502-384-6471; FAX 502-384-6474. **Owner(s):** Adair Progress, Inc., P.O. Box 595, Columbia, KY 41278. TEL 502-384-6471; FAX 502-384-6474; Ed. Paul Hayes; Pub. Donna Crowe; adv.: $5.41/SAU. photos; bk.rev.; pub. size: broadsheet; circ. 4,900(paid).

ADAIR RUSSELL SHOPPER, THE. 1988. Mon. free. 98 Grant Ln., Columbia, KY 42728. TEL 502-384-6471; FAX 502-384-6474. **Owner(s):** Adair Progress, Inc., P.O. Box 595, Columbia, KY 42728. TEL 502-384-6471; FAX 502-384-6474; Ed. Paul Hayes; Pub. Donna Crowe; adv.: $5.85/SAU. photos; bk.rev.; pub. size: tabloid; circ. 14,244(free).

CASEY COUNTY SHOPPER, THE. 1988. Tue. free. 98 Grant Ln., Columbia, KY 42728. TEL 502-384-6471; FAX 502-384-6474. **Owner(s):** Adair Progress, Inc., P.O. Box 595, Columbia, KY 42728. TEL 502-384-6471; FAX 502-384-6474; Ed. Paul Hayes; Pub. Donna Crowe; adv.: $4.70/SAU. photos; bk.rev.; pub. size: tabloid; circ. 5,626(paid).

COLUMBIA NEWS, THE. 1988. Tue. $.35 newsstand; ISSN 1050-4311 $11/yr. 98 Grant Ln., Columbia, KY 42728. TEL 502-384-6471; FAX 502-384-6474. **Owner(s):** Adair Progress, Inc., P.O. Box 595, Columbia, KY 42728. TEL 501-384-6471; FAX 502-384-6474; Ed. Paul Hayes; Pub. Donna Crowe; adv.: $5.41/SAU. photos; bk.rev.; pub. size: broadsheet; circ. 4,200(paid).

CROMONA

LETCHER COUNTY COMMUNITY NEWS-PRESS. 1959. ISSN 0899-1820 Wed. $.50 newsstand. Rte. 805, Cromona, KY 41810. TEL 606-855-4541; FAX 606-855-9290. **Owner(s):** Superior Printing & Publishing Co., Inc., P.O. Box 156, Cromona, KY 41810. TEL 606-855-4541; Ed. Mike Whitaker; Pub. Charles Whitaker; adv.; photos; bk.rev.; pub. size: broadsheet; circ. 4,000(controlled & paid).

CUMBERLAND

TRI-CITY NEWS. 1929. Wed. $.50 newsstand; $15/yr. local; $20/yr. out of state. 805 E. Main St., Cumberland, KY 40823. TEL 606-589-2588; FAX 606-589-2589. **Owner(s):** Jeff Wilder, 850 E. Main St., Cumberland, KY 40823. TEL 606-589-2588; Ed. Jeff Wilder. adv. contact: Sandy Hodges. pub. size: broadsheet; circ. 3,600(paid).

CYNTHIANA

CYNTHIANA DEMOCRAT. 1868. Thu. $.50 newsstand; $23.32/yr. local; $22.32/yr. senior citizens. 412 Webster Ave., Cynthiana, KY 41031. TEL 606-234-1035; FAX 606-234-8096. **Owner(s):** Landmark Community Newspapers, Inc., P.O. Box 549, Shelbyville, KY 40066. TEL 502-633-4334; Ed. Becky Barnes; Pub. George Jacobs; adv. contact: William McCarty. pub. size: broadsheet; circ. 5,450(paid).

DAWSON SPRINGS

DAWSON SPRINGS PROGRESS. 1919. Thu. $.25 newsstand; $8/yr. in cy.; $15/yr. out of cy.; $20/yr. out of state. 131 S. Main St., Dawson Springs, KY 42408. TEL 502-797-3271; FAX 502-797-3271. **Owner(s):** Progress Publishing Co., Inc., 131 S. Main St., P.O. Box 460, Dawson Spring, KY 42408. TEL 502-797-3271; Ed. Jed Dillingham; Pub. Jed Dillingham; adv. contact: Scott Dillingham. photos; pub. size: standard; circ. 3,200(paid).

EDDYVILLE

HERALD LEDGER. 1905. Wed. $.50 newsstand; $17.49/yr. in cy.; $19.61/yr. out of cy.; $20.50/yr. elsewere. 214 Commerce St., Eddyville, KY 42038. TEL 502-388-2269; FAX 502-388-5540. **Owner(s):** Herald Ledger, Box 577, Eddyville, KY 42038. TEL 502-388-2269; FAX 502-388-5540; adv.; photos; pub. size: broadsheet; circ. 2,500(paid).

ELKTON

TODD COUNTY STANDARD. 1892. Wed. $.50 newsstand; $16/yr. P.O. Box 308, Elkton, KY 42220. TEL 502-265-2439. **Owner(s):** Mike Finch, P. O. Box 308, Elkton, KY 42220. TEL 502-265-2439; FAX 502-265-2571; Ed. Mike Finch; Pub. Mike Finch; adv. contact: Jo Tribble. photos; pub. size: broadsheet; circ. 2,110(paid).

FLORENCE

BOONE COUNTY RECORDER. 1875. Thu. $.50 newsstand; $18.02/yr. in cy.; $23.32/yr. in state; $27.56/yr. out of state. Colonial Sq. Plz., 7736 US Hwy. 42, Ste. D-4, Florence, KY 41042. TEL 606-283-0404; FAX 606-283-7285. **Owner(s):** Press Community Newspapers, 4910 Para Dr., Cincinnati, OH 45237. TEL 513-242-4300; Ed. Amy Charley; Pub. Gene A. Clabes; adv. contact: Jim Vieth. photos; pub. size: broadsheet; circ. 10,000(paid).

DIXIE NEWS. 1962. Thu. $.25 newsstand. 6603 Dixie Hwy., Florence, KY 41042. TEL 606-371-6177; FAX 606-371-6306. **Owner(s):** Lee Thomas, 6603 Dixie Hwy., Florence, KY 41042. TEL 606-371-6177; Ed. Lee Thomas; Pub. Lee Thomas; pub. size: tabloid; circ. 22,600(controlled & paid).

KENTON COUNTY RECORDER. 1978. Thu. $.50 newsstand; $18.02/yr. in cy.; $23.32/yr. out of cy.; $27.56/yr. in state. 7736 U.S. 42, Ste. D-4, Florence, KY 41042. TEL 606-283-0404; FAX 606-283-7285. **Owner(s):** Suburban Communications Corp., 36251 Schoolcraft Rd., Livonia, MI 48150. TEL 313-591-2300; Ed. Steve Olding; Pub. Gene Clabes; adv. contact: Jim Vieth. photos; pub. size: broadsheet; circ. 22,000(paid).

WEEKLY NEWSPAPERS

FORT THOMAS
US
CAMPBELL COUNTY RECORDER. 1978. Thu. $.50 newsstand; $18.02/yr. in cy.; $14.42/yr. senior citizens. 654 Highland Ave., Ste. 27, Fort Thomas, KY 41075. TEL 606-781-4421; FAX 606-781-2703. **Owner(s):** Press Community Newspapers, 4910 Fara Dr., Cincinatti, OH 45237. TEL 513-242-4300; Ed. Steve Olding; Pub. Gene Clabes; adv. contact: Jim Vieth. pub. size: broadsheet; circ. 10,000(paid).

FRANKLIN
US
FRANKLIN FAVORITE. 1857. Thu. $.50 newsstand; $20.50/yr. 103 N. High St., Franklin, KY 42135-0309. TEL 502-586-4481; FAX 502-586-6031. **Owner(s):** A.H. Belo Corp., 400 S. Record, Dallas, TX 75202. TEL 214-977-6606; Ed. Charles Portmann; Pub. Henry D. Stone; adv. contact: Betty Gentry. photos; pub. size: broadsheet; circ. 5,800(controlled & paid).

FULTON
US
FULTON LEADER. 1898. Thu. $.50 newsstand; $17/yr. 304 E. State Line St., Fulton, KY 42041-1200. TEL 502-472-1121; FAX 502-472-1129. **Owner(s):** Fulton Publishing Co., P.O. Box 1200, Fulton, KY 42041-1200. TEL 502-472-1121; Ed. Rita Mitchell; Pub. William Mitchell; adv. contact: Leigh Ann Moore. pub. size: broadsheet; circ. 3,000(paid).

US
FULTON SHOPPER. Wed. free. 304 E. State Line St., Fulton, KY 42041. TEL 502-472-1121; FAX 502-472-1129. **Owner(s):** Fulton Publishing Co., P.O. Box 1200, Fulton, KY 42041. TEL 502-472-1121; Ed. William Mitchell; Pub. William Mitchell; adv. contact: Leigh Ann Moore. pub. size: standard; circ. 14,500(free).

GEORGETOWN
US   ISSN 1072-9305
GEORGETOWN NEWS GRAPHIC. 1867. 3/wk.: Wed., Fri., Sun. $.50 newsstand; $45/yr. in cy.; $60/yr. out of cy.; $60/yr. out of state. 1481 Cherry Blossom Way, Georgetown, KY 40324. TEL 502-863-1111; FAX 502-863-6296. **Owner(s):** Lancaster Management, P.O. Box 609, Gadsten, AL 35902; Ed. Byron Brewer; Pub. Mike Scogin; adv.; photos; pub. size: broadsheet; circ. 5,300(paid).
  Formerly: Georgetown News & Times.

GLASGOW
US
GLASGOW REPUBLICAN. Wed. $11/yr. in state; $19/yr. out of state. 100 Commerce Dr., Glasgow, KY 42141. TEL 502-678-5171; FAX 502-678-5052. **Owner(s):** Stephens Group, Inc., P.O. Box 17017, Fort Smith, AR 72917; Ed. Frances Bastien; Pub. Bill Tinsley; pub. size: standard; circ. 2,000(paid).

GRAYSON
US
GRAYSON JOURNAL-ENQUIRER. 1968. Wed. $.50 newsstand; $15.90/yr. in cy.; $31.80/yr. out of cy.; $35/yr. out of state. 113 S. Hord St., Grayson, KY 41143. TEL 606-474-5101; FAX 606-474-0013. **Owner(s):** Media General, Inc., 333 E. Grace St., Richmond, VA 23219. TEL 804-649-6000; FAX 804-649-6898; Ed. Larry Boblitt; Pub. David Thornberry; adv. contact: Bonnie Pence. photos; pub. size: broadsheet; circ. 3,000(paid).

GREENUP
US
GREENUP COUNTY NEWS-TIMES. 1867. Thu. $.50 newsstand; $15.37/yr. in cy.; $23.32/yr. out of cy.; $24/yr. out of state. 203 Harrison St., Greenup, KY 41144. TEL 606-473-9851; FAX 606-473-7591. **Owner(s):** Media General, Inc., 333 E. Grace St., Richmond, VA 23219. TEL 804-649-6000; FAX 804-649-6898; Ed. Mason Branham. adv. contact: Betty Blevin. pub. size: broadsheet; circ. 5,700(paid).
  Formerly: Greenup News.

HARDINSBURG
US
BRECKINRIDGE COUNTY HERALD-NEWS. 1874. Wed. $.50 newsstand; $16.96/yr. in cy.; $23.32/yr. in state; $28/yr. out of state. U.S. Hwy. 60, E., Hardinsburg, KY 40143. TEL 502-756-2109; FAX 502-756-1003. **Owner(s):** Brucie Beard, P.O. Box 6, Hardinsburg, KY 40143. TEL 502-756-2109; Ed. Nancy Beard; Pub. Brucie Beard; adv. contact: B. Masterson. pub. size: broadsheet; circ. 6,400(paid).

HARRODSBURG
US
HARRODSBURG HERALD. 1884. Thu. $.50 newsstand; $21/yr. local home deliv. 101 W. Broadway, Harrodsburg, KY 40330. TEL 606-734-2726; FAX 606-734-0737. **Owner(s):** Bill Randolph, 101 W. Broadway, Harrodsburg, KY 40330. TEL 606-734-2726; Hutton Pyles Trust, 101 W. Broadway, Harrodsburg, KY 40330. TEL 606-734-2726; Ed. Bill Randolph. adv. contact: Cathy Lewis. photos; pub. size: broadsheet; circ. 6,150(paid).

HARTFORD
US
OHIO COUNTY TIMES NEWS. 1965. Thu. $.25 newsstand; $10/yr. local; $12/yr. adjoining cys.; $20/yr. out of state. 108 W. Center St., Hartford, KY 42347. TEL 502-298-7100; FAX 502-298-7592. **Owner(s):** Andy Anderson Corp., P.O. Box 226, Hartford, KY 42347. TEL 502-298-7100; Ed. Dave McBride; Pub. Gina Gibbons; adv. contact: Gina Gibbons. adv.: $4.02/SAU. pub. size: broadsheet; circ. 6,800(paid).

HAWESVILLE
US
HANCOCK CLARION. 1893. Thu. $.50 newsstand; $16/yr. in cy.; $20/yr. out of cy. Main St., Hawesville, KY 42348. TEL 502-927-6945; FAX 502-927-6947. **Owner(s):** Donn K. Wimmer, P.O. Box 39, Hawesville, KY 42348. TEL 502-927-6945; FAX 502-927-6947; Ed. Donn K. Wimmer; Pub. Donn K. Wimmer; adv. contact: Lynn Roberts. pub. size: broadsheet; circ. 4,000(paid).

HAZARD
US
HAZARD HERALD-VOICE. 1911. Thu. $.50 newsstand; $17/yr. in cy.; $23/yr. elsewhere. 380 Main St., Hazard, KY 41701. TEL 606-436-5771; FAX 606-436-3140. **Owner(s):** Pulitzer Publishing Co., 900 N. Tucker Blvd., St. Louis, MO 63101. TEL 313-340-8000; Pub. Jack G. Thomas; adv.; photos; pub. size: broadsheet; circ. 5,057(paid).

HODGENVILLE
US
LARUE COUNTY HERALD-NEWS. 1885. Wed. $.50 newsstand; $19.08/yr. in cy.; $25.44/yr. in state; $31/yr. out of state. 40 Shawnee Dr., Hodgenville, KY 42748. TEL 502-358-3118; FAX 502-358-4852; E-mail: lcherald@ne.infi.net. **Owner(s):** Landmark Community Newspapers, Inc., P.O. Box 549, Shelbyville, KY 40066. TEL 502-633-4335; Ed. Debbie Polly; Pub. Tammy Harding; adv. contact: Tammy Harding. adv.: $4.49/SAU. pub. size: broadsheet; circ. 3,975(paid).

HYDEN
US
LESLIE COUNTY NEWS. 1968. Thu. $.50 newsstand; $18.55/yr. in cy.; $26/yr. out of cy. 100 Main St., Hyden, KY 41749. TEL 606-672-2841; FAX 606-672-7409. **Owner(s):** Reba & Vernon Baker, P.O. Box 967, Hyden, KY 41749. TEL 606-672-2841; Ed. Vernon Baker; Pub. Vernon Baker; adv. contact: Bernetta York. photos; pub. size: broadsheet; circ. 5,000(paid).

US
THOUSANDSTICKS. Tue. $.50 newsstand; $18.55/yr. in cy.; $26/yr. out of cy. P.O. Box 917, Hyden, KY 41749. TEL 606-672-2841; FAX 606-672-7409. **Owner(s):** Vernon & Reba Baker, P.O. Box 967, Hyden, KY 41749. TEL 606-672-2841; Pub. Reba Baker; adv. contact: Ron Williams. pub. size: standard; circ. 4,200(paid).

INEZ
US
MOUNTAIN CITIZEN, THE. 1975. Wed. $.50 newsstand; $15/yr. in cy. Main St., Cain Bldg., Inez, KY 41224. TEL 606-298-7570; FAX 606-298-3711. **Owner(s):** New Wave Community Papers, Inc., P.O. Box 1029, Inez, KY 41224. TEL 606-298-7570; Ed. Lisa Stayton; Pub. Lisa Stayton; adv. contact: Susie Skyles. pub. size: broadsheet; circ. 5,800(paid).
  Formerly: Martin Countian & Mercury.

Weeklies

IRVINE
US

CITIZEN VOICE & TIMES. 1973. s-w.: Sun. & Thu. $.50 newsstand; $15.95/yr. in cy.; $23.95/yr. out of cy.; $32/yr. out of state. 108 Court St., Irvine, KY 40336-1093. TEL 606-723-5161; FAX 606-723-5509; E-mail: cvt@aol.com. **Owner(s):** Guy Hatfield, 108 Court St., Irvine, KY 40336-1093. TEL 606-723-5161; FAX 606-723-5509; Ed. Beth Curlin; Pub. Guy Hatfield; adv. contact: Traci Cahal. pub. size: broadsheet; circ. 4,700(paid); Sun. 9,700(paid). **Wire Service(s):** AP.

US

ESTILL COUNTY TRIBUNE, THE. 1982. Wed. $.25 newsstand; $9/yr. local; $15/yr. elsewhere. 6135 Winchester Rd., Irvine, KY 40336. TEL 606-723-5012. **Owner(s):** Tracy R. Patrick, 7665 Winchester Rd., Irvine, KY 40336. TEL 606-723-7155; Ed. Delores L. Patrick; Pub. Tracy R. Patrick; pub. size: standard; circ. 2,200(paid).

LACENTER
US

ADVANCE-YEOMAN. 1882. Wed. $.50 newsstand; $22/yr. in cy.; $27/yr. out of cy. 347 Broadway, Lacenter, KY 42056-0417. TEL 502-665-9492; FAX 502-665-9463. **Owner(s):** Chris McGhee, Louisville, KY; Ed. Teresa Leneave; Pub. Chris McGhee; adv.; pub. size: standard; circ. 3,500(paid).
Formerly: Wickliffe Advance-Yeoman.

LA GRANGE
US

OLDHAM ERA, THE. 1876. Thu. $.50 newsstand; $23.32/yr. in cy.; $31.27/yr. in state; $42/yr. out of state. 204 S. First St., La Grange, KY 40031-0005. TEL 502-222-7183; FAX 502-222-7194. **Owner(s):** Landmark Community Newspapers, Inc., P.O. Box 549, Shelbyville, KY 40066. TEL 502-633-4334; Ed. Kit Millay; Pub. Dorothy Abernathy; adv. contact: Doris Armstrong. photos; pub. size: broadsheet; circ. 7,000(paid).

LAWRENCEBURG
US

ANDERSON NEWS, THE. 1903. Wed. $.75 newsstand; $23.32/yr. in cy.; $31.27/yr. out of cy. 133 Main St., Lawrenceburg, KY 40342. TEL 502-839-6906; FAX 502-839-3118. **Owner(s):** Landmark Community Newspapers, Inc., P.O. Box 549, Shelbyville, KY 40065. TEL 502-633-4334; Ed. Don White; Pub. Don White; adv. contact: Bud Garrison. pub. size: broadsheet; circ. 6,000(paid).

LEBANON
US

LEBANON ENTERPRISE. 1985. Wed. $.75 newsstand; $22.26/yr. in cy.; $29.68/yr. out of cy.; $38/yr. out of state. 119 S. Proctor Knott Ave., Lebanon, KY 40033. TEL 502-692-6026; FAX 502-692-2118. **Owner(s):** Landmark Community Newspapers, Inc., P.O. Box 549, Shelbyville, KY 40065. TEL 502-633-4334; Ed. Tim Ballard; Pub. Tim Ballard; adv. contact: Mary Anne Blair. pub. size: broadsheet; circ. 6,400(paid).

LEITCHFIELD
US

GRAYSON ADVERTISER. s-w: Mon. & Thu. free. 208 S. Main St., Leitchfield, KY 42754. TEL 502-259-9622; FAX 502-259-5537. **Owner(s):** Media General, Inc., 333 E. Grace St., Richmond, VA 23219. TEL 804-649-6000; FAX 804-649-6898; Ed. Carol Bond; Pub. Carol Bond; adv. contact: Nancy Farmer. pub. size: broadsheet; circ. 5,000(free).

US

GRAYSON COUNTY NEWS-GAZETTE. 1881. s-w.: Mon. & Thu. $.50 newsstand; $20/yr. in cy.; $25/yr. out of cy. 208 S. Main St., Leitchfield, KY 42754. TEL 502-259-9622; FAX 502-259-5537. **Owner(s):** Media General, Inc., 333 E. Grace St., Richmond, VA 23219. TEL 804-649-6000; FAX 804-649-6898; Ed. Carol Bond; Pub. Carol Bond; adv. contact: Nancy Farmer. pub. size: broadsheet; circ. 6,000(paid).

LIBERTY
US

CASEY COUNTY NEWS. 1904. Wed. $.50 newsstand; $23.32/yr. in cy.; $31.27. out of cy.; $38.95/yr. out of state. 704 Campbellsville St., Liberty, KY 42539. TEL 606-787-7171; FAX 606-787-8306. **Owner(s):** Landmark Community Newspapers, Inc., P.O. Box 549, Shelbyville, KY 40066. TEL 502-633-4334; Ed. Maleena Streeval; Pub. Randall Vaught; adv.; photos; bk.rev.; pub. size: broadsheet; circ. 6,200(paid).
Formerly: Liberty Casey County News.

LONDON
US

SENTINEL-ECHO. 1893. 3/wk.: Mon., Wed., Fri. $.50 newsstand; $41.34/yr. in cy. 123 W. Fifth St., London, KY 40741. TEL 606-878-7400; FAX 606-878-7404. **Owner(s):** Media General, Inc., 333 E. Grace St., Richmond, VA 23219. TEL 804-649-6000; FAX 804-649-6898; Ed. Ken Shmidheiser. adv. contact: Michael Bryant. pub. size: broadsheet; circ. 15,100(controlled & paid).
Formerly: London Sentinel-Echo.

LOUISA
US

ADVERTISER, THE. 1982. Thu. free. 106 Pocahantas St., Louisa, KY 41230. TEL 606-638-9957; FAX 606-638-1293. **Owner(s):** C.D. Watts, P.O. Box 129, Louisa, KY 41230. TEL 606-638-9957; FAX 606-638-9957; Ed. C.D. Watts; Pub. C.D. Watts; adv.; pub. size: tabloid; circ. 21,000(free).

US

BIG SANDY NEWS, THE. 1885. Wed. $.50 newsstand; $20/yr. in cy.; $24/yr. out of state. 101 Ricky Skaggs Blvd., Louisa, KY 41230. TEL 606-638-4581; FAX 606-638-9949; E-mail: bsnews@eastky.com. **Owner(s):** Sandy Valley Press, Inc., 101 Ricky Skaggs Blvd., Louisa, KY 41230. TEL 606-638-4541; FAX 606-638-9949; Ed. Jerry Pennington; Pub. Allan S. Perry; adv. contact: Marjie Hale. photos; pub. size: standard; circ. 4,300(paid).

LOUISVILLE
US

SOUTHWEST NEWSWEEK, THE. 1954. Fri. $.25 newsstand; $18/2 yrs. 4500 Dixie Hwy., Louisville, KY 40216-0128. TEL 502-448-4581; FAX 502-447-3999. **Owner(s):** Southwest Jefferson Media, Inc., 4500 Dixie Hwy., Louisville, KY 40216. TEL 502-448-4581; Ed. Diane Vanderford; Pub. Diane Vanderford; adv.; photos; pub. size: tabloid; circ. 2,000(paid).
Formerly: Newsweek, The.

US

VOICE-TRIBUNE, THE. Wed. $.50 newsstand; $14.95/yr. in cy.; $16.95/yr. out of cy. 3818 Shelbyville Rd., Louisville, KY 40207. TEL 502-897-8900; FAX 502-897-8915. **Owner(s):** Southern Publishing Inc., 3818 Shelbyville Rd., Louisville, KY 40207. TEL 502-897-8900; Ed. Steve Rush; Pub. John Harralson; adv. contact: Don Wood. pub. size: broadsheet; circ. 15,000(paid).
Formerly: New Voice.

MANCHESTER
US

MANCHESTER ENTERPRISE. 1890. Thu. $.75 newsstand; $22/yr. in cy.; $27/yr. elsewhere. 103 Third St., Manchester, KY 40962. TEL 606-598-2319; FAX 606-598-2330. **Owner(s):** Manchester Enterprise, P.O. Box 449, Manchester, KY 40962. TEL 606-598-2319; Ed. Mark Hoskins; Pub. Melissa Walker; adv.; photos; bk.rev.; pub. size: broadsheet; circ. 8,200(paid).

MARION
US

CRITTENDEN PRESS. 1876. Thu. $.50 newsstand; $18/yr. in cy.; $21/yr. in state; $23/yr. elsewhere. 125 E. Bellville St., Marion, KY 42064. TEL 502-965-3191; FAX 502-965-2516. **Owner(s):** Nancy Mick, 125 E. Bellville St., Marion, KY 42064. TEL 502-965-3191; FAX 502-965-2516; Ed. Chris Evans; Pub. Nancy Mick; adv. contact: Marty Kares. photos; pub. size: broadsheet; circ. 4,500(paid).

MIDDLESBORO
US

CUMBERLAND TRADING POST, THE. 1978. Thu. free; $60/yr. mailed. 110 N. 11th St., Middlesboro, KY 40965. TEL 606-248-2274; FAX 606-248-8386. **Owner(s):** American Publishing Co., 606 N. Van Buren, Marion, IL 62959. TEL 618-993-1711; Ed. J.T. Hurst. adv. contact: Steve Bernard. pub. size: tabloid; circ. 20,000(free).

MONTICELLO
US

WAYNE COUNTY OUTLOOK. 1904. Wed. $.50 newsstand; $21/yr. local; $29/yr. elsewhere. 109 E. Columbia Ave., Monticello, KY 42633. TEL 606-348-3338; FAX 606-348-8848. **Owner(s):** Larry Traylor, 109 E. Columbia Ave., Monticello, KY 42633. TEL 606-348-3338; FAX 606-348-8848; Pub. Melinda Jones; adv.; photos; pub. size: broadsheet; circ. 6,000(paid).

WEEKLY NEWSPAPERS

MOREHEAD

US

MINIFEE COUNTY NEWS. Wed. $.50 newsstand; $12.72/yr. in cy. 722 First St., Morehead, KY 40351. TEL 606-784-4116; FAX 606-784-7337. **Owner(s):** Park Communications, Inc., Vine Ctr. Office Tower, 333 W. Vine St., 17th Fl., Lexington, KY 40507. TEL 606-252-7275; Ed. Shirley Smith. adv. contact: Brett Janke. circ. 822(paid).

US

MOREHEAD NEWS. 1883. s-w.: Tue. & Fri. $.50 newsstand; $26.50/yr. in cy. 722 W. First St., Morehead, KY 40351. TEL 606-784-4116; FAX 606-784-7337. **Owner(s):** Media General, Inc., 333 E. Church St., Richmond, VA 23219. TEL 804-649-6000; FAX 804-649-6898; Ed. Shirley Smith. adv. contact: Brent Janke. pub. size: broadsheet; circ. 6,500(paid).

US

OLIVEVILLE TIMES. Wed. $.50 newsstand; $12.72/yr. in cy. 722 W. First St., Morehead, KY 40351. TEL 606-784-4116; FAX 606-784-7337. **Owner(s):** Park Communications, Inc., Vine Ctr. Office Tower, 333 W. Vine St., 17th Fl., Lexington, KY 40507. TEL 606-252-7275; Ed. Mary Bobbitt. adv. contact: Brett Janke. circ. 822(paid).

MORGANFIELD

US

UNION COUNTY ADVOCATE. 1924. Wed. $.50 newsstand; $18/yr. in cy.; $25/yr. out of cy.; $30/yr. out of state. 214 W. Main, Morganfield, KY 42437. TEL 502-389-1833; FAX 502-389-3926. **Owner(s):** A.H. Belo Corp., 400 S. Record, Dallas, TX 75202. TEL 214-977-6606; Ed. Mike Banks. adv.; photos; bk.rev.; pub. size: broadsheet; circ. 5,500(paid).

MORGANTOWN

US   ISSN 0745-7006

BUTLER COUNTY & GREEN RIVER REPUBLICAN BANNER, THE. 1982. w. $.35 newsstand; $10/yr. in cy. 119 N. Main, Morgantown, KY 42261. TEL 502-526-4151; FAX 502-526-3111. **Owner(s):** Butler County Banner, Inc., 119 N. Main, Morgantown, KY 42261. TEL 502-526-4151; FAX 502-526-3111; Pub. Roger G. Givens; adv.; photos; pub. size: broadsheet; circ. 5,300(paid).

MOUNT STERLING

US

ADVERTISER, THE. 1978. Mon. free. 40 S. Bank St., Mount Sterling, KY 40353. TEL 606-498-2222; FAX 606-498-2228. **Owner(s):** Hasco Newspapers, Martinsville, VA; Ed. Glen Greene; Pub. Douglas S. Taylor; adv.; pub. size: broadsheet; circ. 17,369(free).

US

MOUNT STERLING ADVOCATE. Wed. $.50 newsstand; $19.61/yr. in cy. 40 S. Bank St., Mount Sterling, KY 40353. TEL 606-498-2222; FAX 606-498-2228. **Owner(s):** Hasco Newspapers, 40 S. Bank St., Mount Sterling, KY 40353. TEL 606-498-2222; Ed. Glen Greene. adv.; pub. size: broadsheet; circ. 6,350(paid).

MUNFORDVILLE

US   ISSN 1075-4628

HART COUNTY NEWS-HERALD. 1878. Tue. $.25 newsstand; $6.95/yr. in cy. 113 E. South St., Munfordville, KY 42765. TEL 502-524-2481; FAX 502-524-2482. **Owner(s):** Aubrey C. Wilson, Sr., 604 E. Broadway, Cave City, KY 42127. TEL 502-773-3401; Ed. Aubrey C. Wilson, Jr. adv.; pub. size: standard; circ. 8,600(paid).

NEW CASTLE

US

HENRY COUNTY LOCAL. 1876. Wed. $.50 newsstand; $22.25/yr. in cy. Hwy. 421 & 55, New Castle, KY 40050. TEL 502-845-2858; FAX 502-845-2921. **Owner(s):** Landmark Community Newspapers, Inc., P.O. Box 549, Shelbyville, KY 40065. TEL 502-633-4334; adv.; photos; pub. size: standard; circ. 4,500(paid).

NICHOLASVILLE

US

JESSAMINE JOURNAL. 1873. Thu. $.50 newsstand; $19.50/yr. in cy.; $25/yr. out of cy.; $30/yr. out of state. 507 N. Main St., Nicholasville, KY 40356. TEL 606-885-5381; FAX 606-887-2966. **Owner(s):** Republic Newspapers, Inc., P.O. Box 8, Nicholasville, KY 40340. TEL 606-885-5381; Ed. Randy Patrick; Pub. Tony Cox; adv. contact: Tony Cox. photos; pub. size: broadsheet; circ. 6,011(paid).

OLIVE HILL

US

OLIVE HILL TIMES. Wed. $.50 newsstand; $15.90/yr. in cy.; $31.80/yr. out of cy.; $35/yr. out of state. Post Office Bldg., Olive Hill, KY 41164. TEL 606-286-4201. **Owner(s):** Media General, Inc., 333 E. Grace St., Richmond, VA 23219. TEL 804-649-6000; FAX 804-649-6898; Ed. Larry Boblitt; Pub. David Thornberry; adv.; photos; pub. size: broadsheet; circ. 2,350(paid).

OWINGSVILLE

US

BATH COUNTY NEWS-OUTLOOK. 1878. Thu. $.50 newsstand; $14/yr. in cy.; $18/yr. in state; $24/yr. out of state. 18 Water St., Owingsville, KY 40360. TEL 606-674-2181; FAX 606-674-2181. **Owner(s):** Russell L. & Margaret C. Metz, P.O. Box 577, Owingsville, KY 40360. TEL 606-674-2181; Ken E. & Gloria Metz, P.O. Box 577, Owingsville, KY 40360. TEL 606-674-2181; Pub. Kenneth E. Metz; adv. contact: Margaret C. Metz. pub. size: broadsheet; circ. 3,600(paid).

PADUCAH

US

WEST KENTUCKY NEWS. 1967. Wed. $.25 newsstand; $20/yr. in cy. mailed; $27/yr. out of state mailed. 701 Jefferson St., Paducah, KY 42001-1135. TEL 502-442-7380; FAX 502-442-5220. **Owner(s):** Chris McGhee, P.O. Box 1135, Paducah, KY 42002. TEL 502-442-7380; Pub. Chris McGhee; adv. contact: Brian Wyatt. pub. size: broadsheet; circ. 20,000(paid).
Formerly: Kentucky News.

PAINTSVILLE

US

EASTERN KENTUCKY SHOPPER. Mon. free. 604 W. Third St., Paintsville, KY 42140. TEL 606-789-5315; FAX 606-789-9717. **Owner(s):** P.T.S., Inc., P.O. Box 22, Tuscaloosa, AL 30967; Ed. Ralph Davis; Pub. Ron Ditz; adv. contact: Justin Newton. pub. size: broadsheet; circ. 20,500(free & paid).

US

PAINTSVILLE HERALD, THE. 1901. Wed. $.75 newsstand; $25/yr. in cy. 604 W. Third St., Paintsville, KY 41240. TEL 606-789-5315; FAX 606-789-9717. **Owner(s):** P.T.S., Inc., P.O. Box 22, Tuscaloosa, AL 30967; Ed. Ralph Davis; Pub. Ron Dietz; adv. contact: Chris Long. photos; pub. size: broadsheet; circ. 6,500(paid).

PARIS

US

ADVERTISER, THE. 1807. Mon. free; $23/yr. mailed. 123 W. Eighth St., Paris, KY 40361. TEL 606-987-1870; FAX 606-987-3729. **Owner(s):** Brannon Family, 123 W. Eighth St., Paris, KY 40361. TEL 606-987-1870; Ed. Jim Brannon; Pub. Genevieve Brannon; adv.; photos; pub. size: standard; circ. 12,800(free).
Formerly: Citizen Advertiser.

US

BOURBON COUNTY CITIZEN. Wed. $.50 newsstand; $16/yr.; $18/yr. out of state. 123 W. Eighth St., Paris, KY 40361. TEL 606-987-1870; FAX 606-987-3729. **Owner(s):** Brannon Family, 123 Eighth St., Paris, KY 40361. TEL 606-987-1870; Ed. Jim Brannon; Pub. Genevieve Brannon; pub. size: standard; circ. 3,400(paid).

PIKEVILLE

US

APPALACHIAN NEWS-EXPRESS. 1913. 3/wk.: Wed., Fri., Sun. $.50 newsstand; $52/yr. home deliv.; $85/yr. out of area. 201 Caroline Ave., Pikeville, KY 41501. TEL 606-432-0148; FAX 606-437-4246. **Owner(s):** Appalachian Newspapers, Inc., P.O. Box 802, Pikeville, KY 41502. TEL 606-437-4054; Ed. Larry Martin; Pub. Marty Backus; adv. contact: Paula Whitt. photos; pub. size: broadsheet; circ. 11,300(paid).

PINEVILLE

US

PINEVILLE SUN-CUMBERLAND COURIER. 1907. Thu. $.50 newsstand; $12.50/yr. in cy.; $23.50/yr. elsewhere. 210 Virginia Ave., Pineville, KY 40977. TEL 606-337-2333. **Owner(s):** Pineville Sun-Cumberland Courier, P.O. Box 250, Pineville, KY 40977. TEL 606-337-2333; Pub. Lin Hobbes; adv. contact: Lin Hobbes. pub. size: broadsheet; circ. 3,250(paid).

PRESTONSBURG

US

FLOYD COUNTY TIMES. 1928. s-w.: Wed. & Fri. $.75 newsstand; $28/yr. in cy. carrier. 112 S. Central, Prestonsburg, KY 41653. TEL 606-886-8506; FAX 606-886-3603. **Owner(s):** Smith Newspapers, Inc., P.O. Box 27, Fort Payne, AL 35967. TEL 205-845-5510; Ed. Janice Sheppard; Pub. Scott Perry; adv. contact: Shawn Hamilton. pub. size: broadsheet; circ. 17,006(paid).

PRINCETON

TIMES LEADER, THE. 1871. s-w.: Wed. & Sat. $.50 newsstand; $33/yr. in cy.; $39/yr. in state; $48/yr. out of state. 607 W. Washington St., Princeton, KY 42445. TEL 502-365-5588; FAX 502-365-7299; E-mail: timesleader@ziggycom.net; URL: http://www.wkynet.com/princetonnet/timesleader/. Owner(s): Times Leader, Inc., 607 W. Washington St., Princeton, KY 42445. TEL 502-365-5588; FAX 502-365-7299; Ed. Anita Baker; Pub. John Hutcheson, III; adv. contact: Ellen Franklin. photos; pub. size: broadsheet; circ. 5,800(free & paid).
Wire Service(s): AP.
Formerly: Caldwell County Times; Princeton Leader, The.

PROVIDENCE

JOURNAL-ENTERPRISE. 1899. Thu. $.35 newsstand; $15/yr. 100 Walnut St., Providence, KY 42450. TEL 502-667-2068; FAX 502-667-9160. Owner(s): Providence Journal-Enterprise, Inc., P.O. Box 190, Providence, KY 42450; FAX 502-667-9160; Ed. Charles Hust; Pub. Edd Hust; pub. size: standard; circ. 4,500(paid).
Formerly: Providence Journal-Enterprise.

RADCLIFF

SENTINEL, THE. 1961. Thu. $.25 newsstand; $7.95/yr. 1558 Hill St., Radcliff, KY 40160. TEL 502-351-4407; FAX 502-351-4407. Owner(s): Sentinel, The, 1558 Hill St., Radcliff, KY 40160. TEL 502-351-4407; Ed. O.J. Royalty; Pub. O.J. Royalty; adv.; pub. size: standard; circ. 3,500(paid).

RUSSELL SPRINGS

ISSN 8750-1651
RUSSELL COUNTY NEWS, THE. 1913. Sun. free newsstand; $40/yr. 120 Wilson St., Russell Springs, KY 42642-0190. TEL 502-866-3191; FAX 502-866-3198. Owner(s): Russell County Newspapers, Inc., 120 Wilson St., Russell Springs, KY 42642-0190. TEL 502-866-3191; FAX 502-866-3198; Ed. Jay Albrecht; Pub. Jay Albrecht; adv.; photos; pub. size: broadsheet; circ. Sun. 9,000(free & paid).

TIMES JOURNAL, THE. 1949. Thu. $.50 newsstand; $17.57/yr. in cy.; $27.11/yr. out of cy.; $26/yr. out of state; $80/yr. elsewhere. 120 Wilson St., Russell Springs, KY 42642-0190. TEL 502-866-3191; FAX 502-866-3198. Owner(s): Russell County Newspapers, Inc., P.O. Box 190, Russell Springs, KY 42642. TEL 502-866-3191; FAX 502-866-3198; Pub. Jay Albrecht; adv. contact: Jay Albrecht. photos; bk.rev.; pub. size: broadsheet; circ. 4,200(paid).
Formerly: Russell Springs Times Journal.

RUSSELLVILLE

NEWS DEMOCRAT & LEADER. 1904. s-w.: Tue. & Fri. $.50 newsstand; $25/yr. in cy.; $35/yr. out of cy. 120 Public Sq., Russellville, KY 42276. TEL 502-726-8394; FAX 502-726-8398. Owner(s): Park Communications, Inc., Vine Ctr. Office Tower, 333 W. Vine St., 17th Fl., Lexington, KY 40507. TEL 606-252-7275; adv.; pub. size: standard; circ. 6,800(free & paid).

SALYERSVILLE

SALYERSVILLE INDEPENDENT. 1921. Thu. $.50 newsstand; $18.02/yr. in cy.; $24.14/yr. out of cy; $22/yr. out of state. 7 W. Maple St., Salyersville, KY 41465. TEL 606-349-2915. Owner(s): Tim & Carol Bostic, P.O. Box 29, Salyersville, KY 44165. TEL 606-349-2915; Ed. Tim Bostic; Pub. Tim Bostic; adv.: $3.40/SAU; classified, $.20 per word. photos; bk.rev.; pub. size: standard; circ. 4,200(paid).

SCOTTSVILLE

SCOTTSVILLE CITIZEN-TIMES. 1890. Thu. $.40 newsstand; $12/yr. in cy.; $15/yr. out of cy. 611 E. Main, Scottsville, KY 42164. TEL 502-237-3441; FAX 502-237-4943; E-mail: citzntimes@aol.com. Owner(s): Billie Hatcher & Robert B. Pitchford, III, P.O. Box 310, Scottsville, KY 42164. TEL 502-237-3441; FAX 502-237-4840; Ed. Robert B. Pitchford, III; Pub. Billie Hatcher; adv.: $4.50/SAU. pub. size: standard; circ. 5,000(paid).

SHELBYVILLE

SHELBYVILLE SENTINEL-NEWS. 1840. s-w.: Wed. & Fri. $.50 newsstand; $32.50/yr. 703 Taylorsville Rd., Shelbyville, KY 40065. TEL 502-633-2526; FAX 502-633-2618. Owner(s): Landmark Community Newspapers, Inc., P.O. Box 549, Shelbyville, KY 40065. TEL 502-633-4334; Ed. DuAnne Puckett; Pub. James L. Edelen; adv.; photos; bk.rev.; pub. size: broadsheet; circ. 7,700(paid).

SHOPPER/PLUS. 1983. Mon. free. 703 Taylorsville Rd., Shelbyville, KY 40065. TEL 502-633-2526; FAX 502-633-2618. Owner(s): Landmark Community Newspapers, Inc., P.O. Box 549, Shelbyville, KY 40065. TEL 502-633-4334; Ed. DuAnne Puckett; Pub. James L. Edelen; adv. contact: Angela Crosson. pub. size: broadsheet; circ. 15,600(free).

SHEPHERDSVILLE

PIONEER-NEWS. 1882. s-w.: Mon. & Wed. $.50 newsstand; $25.95/yr. 455 N. Buckman St., Shepherdsville, KY 40165. TEL 502-543-2288; FAX 502-955-9704. Owner(s): Landmark Community Newspapers, Inc., P.O. Box 549, Shelbyville, KY 40066. TEL 502-633-4334; Ed. Thomas Barr; Pub. Thomas Barr; adv. contact: Thomas Barr. pub. size: broadsheet; circ. 22,500(free & paid).

SPRINGFIELD

SPRINGFIELD SUN. 1904. Wed. $.75 newsstand; $23.32/yr. in cy.; $31.27/yr. out of cy.; $40/yr. out of state. 117 Cross Main, Springfield, KY 40069. TEL 606-336-3716; FAX 606-336-7718. Owner(s): Landmark Community Newspapers, Inc., P.O. Box 549, Shelbyville, KY 40066; Ed. Tim Ballard; Pub. Tim Ballard; pub. size: broadsheet; circ. 4,100(paid).

STANFORD

INTERIOR JOURNAL. 1860. Thu. $.35 newsstand; $15.50/yr. in state; $29.75/yr. out of state. 111 E. Main St., Stanford, KY 40484. TEL 606-365-2104; FAX 606-365-2105. Owner(s): Thomas J. Moore, 111 E. Main St., Stanford, KY 40484. TEL 606-365-2104; Sharman P. Moore, 111 E. Main St., Stanford, KY 40484. TEL 606-365-2104; Ed. Thomas J. Moore. adv.: $3.85/SAU. pub. size: broadsheet; circ. 4,339(paid).

STANTON

CLAY CITY TIMES, THE. 1896. Thu. $.50 newsstand; $15/yr. local; $20/yr. in state; $25/yr. out of state. 209 N. Main St., Stanton, KY 40380. TEL 606-663-5540; FAX 606-663-6397. Owner(s): Hatfield Newspapers, Inc., P.O. Box 547, Stanton, KY 40380. TEL 606-663-5540; FAX 606-663-6397; Ed. Matt McCarty; Pub. Guy Hatfield; adv.; photos; pub. size: broadsheet; circ. 4,100(paid).

STURGIS

STURGIS NEWS. 1885. Wed. $.35 newsstand; $9.54/yr. 617 N. Adams, Sturgis, KY 42459-0218. TEL 502-333-5545; FAX 502-333-9943. Owner(s): Betty P. Catlett, P.O. Box 36, Sebree, KY 42455. TEL 502-835-7521; FAX 502-825-9521; Ed. Paul J. Monsour; Pub. Betty P. Catlett; adv.; photos; pub. size: standard; circ. 3,200(paid).

TAYLORSVILLE

SPENCER MAGNET. Wed. $.50 newsstand. 51 W. Main St., Taylorsville, KY 40071. TEL 502-477-2239; FAX 502-477-2110. Owner(s): Landmark Community Newspapers, Inc., P.O. Box 549, Shelbyville, KY 40065. TEL 502-633-4334; Ed. Kimberly Rich. adv.; photos; pub. size: broadsheet; circ. 2,700(paid).

TOMPKINSVILLE

T-VILLE NEWS TRADER. Mon. free. 105 N. Main, Tompkinsville, KY 42167. TEL 502-487-5576; FAX 502-487-8839. Owner(s): Monroe County Press, Inc., 105 N. Main St., Tompkinsville, KY 42167. TEL 502-487-5576; FAX 502-487-8839; Ed. Gina Kinslow; Pub. Blanche B. Trimble; adv. contact: Sharon Fister. pub. size: tabloid; circ. 7,800(free).

TOMPKINSVILLE NEWS. 1903. Thu. $.25 newsstand; $12/yr. in cy.; $16/yr. out of cy.; $21/yr. out of state. 105 N. Main, Tompkinsville, KY 42167. TEL 502-487-5576; FAX 502-487-8839. Owner(s): Monroe County Press, Inc., 105 N. Main, Tompkinsville, KY 42167. TEL 502-487-5624; FAX 502-487-8839; Ed. Gina Kinslow; Pub. Blanche B. Trimble; adv. contact: Gina Kinslow. photos; pub. size: standard; circ. 4,800(paid).

WEEKLY NEWSPAPERS

VERSAILLES

US

WOODFORD SUN. 1869. Thu. $.50 newsstand; $17/yr. in cy.; $28/yr. out of state. 184 S. Main St., Versailles, KY 40383. TEL 606-873-4131; FAX 606-873-0300. **Owner(s):** Woodford Sun Co., Inc., P.O. Box 29, Versailles, KY 40383. TEL 606-873-4131; FAX 606-873-0300; Ed. H. Moss Vance; Pub. A.B. Chandler, Jr.; adv.; pub. size: broadsheet; circ. 6,000(paid).

WEST LIBERTY

US

LICKING VALLEY COURIER. 1910. Thu. $.50 newsstand; $13.50/yr. in cy.; $16/yr. out of cy.; $18/yr. out of state. 142 Prestonsburg St., West Liberty, KY 41472. TEL 606-743-3551; FAX 606-743-3565. **Owner(s):** Earl W. Kinner, P.O. Box 187, West Liberty, KY 41472. TEL 606-743-3551; Ed. Earl W. Kinner; Pub. Earl W. Kinner; adv. contact: Sue H. Kinner. pub. size: broadsheet; circ. 4,200(paid).
Formerly: West Liberty Licking Valley Courier.

WHITESBURG

US

MOUNTAIN EAGLE, THE. 1907. Wed. $.75 newsstand; $24.50/yr. in cy.; $31.50/yr. out of cy. 367B Hazard Rd., Whitesburg, KY 41858. TEL 606-633-2252; FAX 606-633-2843. **Owner(s):** Tom Gish, P.O. Box 808, Whitesburg, KY 41858. TEL 606-633-2252; Ed. Ben Gish; Pub. Tom Gish; adv. contact: Freddy Oakes. pub. size: broadsheet; circ. 7,800(paid).
Formerly: Whitesburg Mountain Eagle.

WHITLEY CITY

US

MCCREARY COUNTY RECORD. 1919. Tue. $.50 newsstand; $14.65/yr. in cy.; $28/yr. in state; $30/yr. out of state. Courthouse Sq., Whitley City, KY 42653-0009. TEL 606-376-5356; FAX 606-376-5357. **Owner(s):** Media General, Inc., 333 E. Grace St., Richmond, VA 23219. TEL 804-649-6000; FAX 804-649-6898; Ed. Ken Shmidheiser; Pub. James T. Stratton; adv. contact: Janie West. pub. size: broadsheet; circ. 5,400(paid).

WILLIAMSBURG

US

WHITLEY REPUBLICAN NEWS JOURNAL. 1908. Wed. $.50 newsstand; $20/yr. in cy.; $22/yr. out of cy. 105 S. Second St., Williamsburg, KY 40769. TEL 606-549-0643; FAX 606-528-9779. **Owner(s):** Terry Forcht, N. Barton & Don Estep, 105 S. Second St., Williamsburg, KY 40769. TEL 606-549-0643; Ed. Mark White; Pub. Don Estep; adv. contact: Don Estep. adv.: $6.90/SAU. photos; pub. size: broadsheet; circ. 7,600(paid).

WILLIAMSTOWN

US

GRANT COUNTY NEWS. 1906. Thu. $.50 newsstand; $17/yr. locally; $26/yr. in state; $35/yr. out of state. 151 N. Main St., Williamstown, KY 41097-0247. TEL 606-824-3344; FAX 606-824-5888; E-mail: grantnews@kih.net. **Owner(s):** Landmark Community Newspapers, Inc., P.O. Box 549, Shelbyville, KY 40066. TEL 502-633-4334; Ed. Jamie Baker-Nantz; Pub. Ken Stone; adv. contact: John Hurston. photos; pub. size: broadsheet; circ. 5,200(free & paid).

LOUISIANA

ALEXANDRIA

US

ALEXANDRIA NEWS WEEKLY. 1963. Thu. $.25 newsstand; $39/yr. in state. 1746 Mason St., Alexandria, LA 71301. TEL 318-443-7664. **Owner(s):** Leon Coleman, Sr., P.O. Box 608, Alexandria, LA 71309. TEL 318-443-7664; Alice G. Coleman, 1746 Mason St., Alexandria, LA 71301. TEL 318-443-7664; Ed. Alice G. Coleman; Pub. Alice G. Coleman; pub. size: broadsheet; circ. 13,800(paid).

AMITE

US

AMITE TANGI DIGEST. 1928. Wed. $.50 newsstand; $22.50/yr. in state; $32.50/yr. out of state. 120 N.E. Central Ave., Amite, LA 70422. TEL 504-748-6343; FAX 504-748-7104. **Owner(s):** Louisiana State Newspapers, Lafayette, LA; Ed. Trish Adams; Pub. Carol Brooke; adv.; pub. size: broadsheet; circ. 4,100(paid).
Formerly: Tangi Talk/News Digest.

ARABI

US

ST. BERNARD VOICE, THE. 1890. Fri. $.30 newsstand; $12/yr. in state; $14/yr. out of state. 234 Mehle Ave., Arabi, LA 70032-0088. TEL 504-279-7488; FAX 504-277-2231. **Owner(s):** St. Bernard Voice, Inc., The, 234 Mehle Ave., Arabi, LA 70032. TEL 504-279-7488; FAX 504-277-2231; Ed. Edwin M. Roy, Jr.; Pub. Edwin M. Roy, Jr.; adv.; photos; bk.rev.; pub. size: broadsheet; circ. 3,000(paid).

ARCADIA

US

BIENVILLE DEMOCRAT & RINGGOLD RECORD. 1909. Thu. $.50 newsstand; $30/yr. in state; $25/yr. trade area. Railroad St., Arcadia, LA 71001. TEL 318-263-2922; FAX 318-263-8897. **Owner(s):** Natchitoches Times, Inc., P.O. Box 448, Natchitoches, LA 71458. TEL 318-352-3618; Ed. Wayne Dring. adv.; pub. size: broadsheet; circ. 3,500(paid).

BAKER

US

BAKER OBSERVER. 1957. Thu. $.50 newsstand; $20/yr. in cy.; $42/yr. out of state. 5240 Groom Rd., Baker, LA 70714-3126. TEL 504-775-2315; FAX 504-774-9212. **Owner(s):** Louisiana Suburban Press, P.O. Box 539, Baker, LA 70704. TEL 504-775-2315; Ed. Mark C. Smith; Pub. Mitchell D. Lynch; adv. contact: Sherri Romero. photos; pub. size: broadsheet; circ. 2,100(paid).

BATON ROUGE

US

BATON ROUGE SHOPPER. Wed. $1.50 newsstand; $32/6 mos.; $60/yr. 8252 W. El Cajon Dr., Baton Rouge, LA 70815. TEL 504-926-8882; FAX 504-927-2742. **Owner(s):** H.M. Mike Cannon, 8252 W. El Cajon Dr., Baton Rouge, LA 70815. TEL 504-926-8882; Ed. Veronica Spegell. adv. contact: Lisa S. Cannon. photos; pub. size: tabloid; circ. 35,000(paid).

US

CONSUMERS' EDGE. Wed. free. 8252 W. El Cajon Dr., Baton Rouge, LA 70815. TEL 504-926-8882; FAX 504-927-2742. **Owner(s):** H.M. Mike Cannon, 8252 W. El Cajon Dr., Baton Rouge, LA 70815. TEL 504-926-8882; Ed. Veronica Spegell. adv. contact: Lisa S. Cannon. pub. size: tabloid; circ. 30,000(free).

US

GREATER BATON ROUGE BUSINESS REPORT. 1982. bi-w: Tue. $1.50 newsstand; $39/yr. in state; $47/yr. out of state. 5757 Corporate Blvd., Ste. 402, Baton Rouge, LA 70808. TEL 504-928-1700; FAX 504-923-3448. **Owner(s):** Rolfe McCollister, 5757 Corporate Blvd., Ste. 402, Baton Rouge, LA 70808. TEL 504-928-1700; FAX 504-923-3448; Ed. Paulette Senior. adv. contact: Sara Wilensky. pub. size: tabloid; circ. 14,000(paid).

US

WEEKLY PRESS. 1981. Thu. $.50 newsstand; $25/yr. 1384 Swan Ave., Baton Rouge, LA 70807. TEL 504-775-2002; FAX 054-775-4216. **Owner(s):** Ivory Payne, 1384 Swan Ave., Baton Rouge, LA 70807; Ed. Cassie Payne; Pub. Ivory Payne; adv.; pub. size: broadsheet; circ. 7,500(paid).

BELLE CHASSE

US

PLAQUEMINES GAZETTE. 1926. Fri. $.35 newsstand; $25/yr. 7952 Hwy. 23, Belle Chasse, LA 70037. TEL 504-392-1619; FAX 504-393-9327. **Owner(s):** Plaquemines Newspaper Publishing, Inc., 7952 Hwy. 23, Belle Chasse, LA 70037. TEL 504-392-1619; Ed. Dale Benoit. adv. contact: Norris J. Babin, Jr. pub. size: broadsheet; circ. 2,950(paid).

US

PLAQUEMINES WATCHMAN. 1981. Wed. $25/yr. in parish; $30/yr. out of parish; $35/yr. out of state. 7952 Hwy. 23, Belle Chasse, LA 70037. TEL 504-392-1619; FAX 504-393-9327. **Owner(s):** Plaquemines Newspaper Publishings, Inc., 7952 Hwy. 23, Belle Chasse, LA 70037. TEL 504-392-1619; adv.; photos; pub. size: broadsheet; circ. 2,950(paid).

BOSSIER CITY

BOSSIER BANNER-PROGRESS
US
BOSSIER BANNER-PROGRESS. 1859. s-w.: Wed. & Sun. $39/yr. in parish; $50/yr. out of parish. 409 Barksdale Blvd., Bossier City, LA 71171. TEL 318-965-0101; FAX 318-747-5298. **Owner(s):** Robert Barton, P.O Box 6267, Bossier City, LA 71171. TEL 318-965-0101; FAX 318-747-5298; Ed. Pat Culverhouse; Pub. Robert Barton; adv. contact: Kathy Spivey. pub. size: broadsheet; circ. 500(paid).

US   ISSN 0747-4733
BOSSIER PRESS-TRIBUNE. 1928. s-w.: Wed. & Sun. $.50 newsstand; $50/yr. 409 Barksdale Blvd., Bossier City, LA 71111. TEL 318-747-7900; FAX 318-747-5298. **Owner(s):** Bossier Newspapers Publishing Co., Inc., 409 Barksdale Blvd., Bossier City, LA 71111. TEL 318-747-4010; Ed. Pat Culverhouse; Pub. Bob Barton; adv. contact: Kathy Spivey. pub. size: broadsheet; circ. 7,000(controlled).

CHURCH POINT

US
CHURCH POINT NEWS. 1933. Wed. $.75 newsstand; $21/yr. in parish; $25/yr. in state; $32/yr. out of state. 315 N. Main, Church Point, LA 70525. TEL 318-684-5711; FAX 318-684-5793. **Owner(s):** Louisiana State Newspapers, P.O. Box 5010, Lafayette, LA 70507. TEL 318-334-3186; Ed. Diane Daigle; Pub. Willie Petre; adv. contact: Liz Horecky. pub. size: broadsheet; circ. 1,600(paid).

CLINTON

US
EAST FELICIANA WATCHMAN. 1878. Thu. $.50 newsstand; $20/yr. in state. 12311 St. Helena St., Clinton, LA 70722. TEL 504-683-5195; FAX 504-683-4276. **Owner(s):** Louisiana State Newspapers, P.O. Box 5010, Lafayette, LA 70502. TEL 504-266-2100; Ed. Jack Roberts. adv. contact: Mitchell Lynch. photos; pub. size: standard; circ. 20,000(controlled).
Formerly: Clinton Watchman.

COUSHATTA

US
COUSHATTA CITIZEN. 1871. Thu. $.50 newsstand; $17/yr. 1703 Ringgold Ave., Coushatta, LA 71019-1365. TEL 318-932-4201; FAX 318-932-4285. **Owner(s):** Lovan Thomas, 1703 Ringgold Ave., Coushatta, LA 71019-1365. TEL 318-932-4201; FAX 318-932-4285; Pub. Marsha Loftin; adv.; photos; pub. size: broadsheet; circ. 6,200(free & paid).

COVINGTON

US
COVINGTON ST. TAMMANY FARMER. 1874. Thu. $.35 newsstand; $15/yr. 321 N. New Hampshire St., Covington, LA 70433. TEL 504-892-2323; FAX 504-892-2325. **Owner(s):** St. Tammany Farmer, Inc., P.O. Box 269, Covington, LA 70434-0269. TEL 504-892-2323; FAX 504-892-2232; Ed. Ron Barthet. adv.; photos; pub. size: broadsheet; circ. 4,000(paid).

US
NEWS-BANNER, THE. 1963. 3/wk.: Wed., Fri., Sun. $.75 newsstand; $72/yr. in parish mailed; $50.96/yr. home deliv.; $72/yr. elsewhere mailed. 19290 19th Ave., Covington, LA 70433. TEL 504-892-7980; FAX 504-892-8242; E-mail: banner@neosofti.com. **Owner(s):** Wick Communications, Inc., 333 W. Wilcox, Ste. 302, Sierra Vista, AZ 85632. TEL 602-458-0200; Ed. Don Redman; Pub. Floyd Burckel; photos; bk.rev.; pub. size: broadsheet; circ. 26,500(paid); Sun. 21,000(paid).

DENHAM SPRINGS

US
DENHAM SPRINGS-LIVINGSTON PARISH NEWS. 1898. s-w.: Thu. & Sun. $.50 newsstand; $36.16/yr. in parish; $50.96 out of state. 688 Hatchell Ln., Denham Springs, LA 70726. TEL 504-665-5176; FAX 504-667-0167. **Owner(s):** Denham Springs Publishing Co., P.O. Box 1529, Denham Springs, LA 70727. TEL 504-665-5342; Ed. Mike Dowty; Pub. Jeff M. David; adv. contact: Debbie Johnson. pub. size: broadsheet; circ. 10,544(paid).

US
LIVINGSTON LEADER. Thu. free. 688 Hatchell Ln., Denham Springs, LA 70726. TEL 504-665-5176; FAX 504-667-0167. **Owner(s):** Denham Springs Publishing Co., 688 Hatchell Ln., Denham Springs, LA 70727. TEL 504-665-5176; FAX 504-667-0167; Ed. Mike Dowty; Pub. Jeff M. David; adv. contact: Rhonda Morris. pub. size: broadsheet; circ. 5,000(free).

DE QUINCY

US
DE QUINCY NEWS. 1926. Wed. $15.45/yr. 203 E. Harrison, De Quincy, LA 70633. TEL 318-786-8004; FAX 318-786-8131. **Owner(s):** De Quincy News, 203 E. Harrison, De Quincy, LA 70633. TEL 318-786-8004; FAX 318-786-8131; Ed. Jerry Wise; Pub. Jerry Wise; adv.; bk.rev.; pub. size: standard; circ. 3,800(paid).

DONALDSONVILLE

US
DONALDSONVILLE CHIEF. 1871. Thu. $20/yr. 402 Railroad Ave., Donaldsonville, LA 70346. TEL 504-473-3101; FAX 504-473-4060. **Owner(s):** Donaldsonville Newspapers, Inc., P.O. Box 309, Donaldsonville, LA 70346. TEL 504-473-3101; FAX 504-473-4060; Ed. Juanita Wagvespack; Pub. Ella Metrejean; adv. contact: Monica Dubois. pub. size: standard; circ. 3,100(paid).

EUNICE

US
EUNICE NEWS. 1904. s-w.: Thu. & Sun. $.75 newsstand; $30/yr. in parish; $40/yr. out of parish; $50/yr. elsewhere. 251 N. Second St., Eunice, LA 70535. TEL 318-457-3061; FAX 318-457-3122. **Owner(s):** Louisiana State Newspapers, P.O. Box 4033-C, Lafayette, LA 70502. TEL 318-233-7000; Ed. Jerry Hoffpauir; Pub. Willie Pitre; adv. contact: Chad Fontonot. pub. size: broadsheet; circ. 6,000(paid); Sun. 6,500(paid).

FERRIDAY

US
CONCORDIA SENTINEL. 1876. Wed. $.50 newsstand; $20/yr. in parish; $25/yr. in state; $30/yr. out of state. 1308 N. First St., Ferriday, LA 71334. TEL 318-757-3646; FAX 318-757-3001. **Owner(s):** Hanna Publishing Co., P.O. Box 312, Ferriday, LA 71334. TEL 318-757-3646; FAX 318-757-3001; Ed. Samuel A. Hanna; Pub. Samuel A. Hanna; adv. contact: Barbara Jackson. pub. size: broadsheet; circ. 5,500(paid).

GONZALES

US
COMMUNITY MIRROR. Tue. free. 205 W. Worthey, Gonzales, LA 70737. TEL 504-647-4569; FAX 504-644-8238. **Owner(s):** Gonzales Weekly, Inc., 205 W. Worthey, Gonzales, LA 70737. Ed. Arlene E. Bishop; Pub. Crawford A. Bishop; adv. contact: Arlene E. Bishop. pub. size: broadsheet; circ. 22,000(free).

US
GONZALES WEEKLY. 1920. Fri. $.50 newsstand; $20/yr. in state; $25/yr. out of state. 205 W. Worthey, Gonzales, LA 70737. TEL 504-647-4569; FAX 504-644-8238. **Owner(s):** Gonzales Weekly, Inc., 205 W. Worthey, Gonzales, LA 70737. TEL 504-647-4569; Ed. Arlene E. Bishop; Pub. Crawford A. Bishop; adv.; photos; pub. size: broadsheet; circ. 8,000(paid).

JEANERETTE

US
JEANERETTE ENTERPRISE. 1942. Wed. $.25 newsstand; $30/yr. 808 E. Main St., Jeanerette, LA 70544. TEL 318-276-5171; FAX 318-367-9640. **Owner(s):** Wick Communications, Inc., 333 Wilcox Dr., Ste. 302, Sierra Vista, AZ 85635. TEL 520-728-4488; FAX 520-728-6090; Ed. Karma Champaigne; Pub. Will Chapman; adv. contact: Jane Collier. pub. size: broadsheet; circ. 4,200(paid).

JENA

US
JENA TIMES OLLA-TULLOS SIGNAL. 1905. Wed. $.50 newsstand; $32/yr. P.O. Drawer 1384, Jena, LA 71342. TEL 318-992-4121; FAX 318-992-2287. **Owner(s):** Sammy J. Franklin, P.O. Box 1384, Jena, LA 71342. TEL 318-992-4121; FAX 318-992-2287; Ed. Sammy J. Franklin; Pub. Sammy J. Franklin; adv. contact: Karla Fitzgerald. adv.: $4.80/SAU. pub. size: broadsheet; circ. 4,600(paid).

JONESBORO

US
JACKSON INDEPENDENT, THE. 1892. Thu. $.50 newsstand; $16.70/yr. in parish; $27.14/yr. out of parish; $32/yr. out of state. 624 Hudson Ave., Jonesboro, LA 71251. TEL 318-259-2551. **Owner(s):** T.L. Colvin, Jr., 624 Hudson Ave., Jonesboro, LA 71251; Ed. T.L. Colvin, III; Pub. T.L. Colvin, Jr.; photos; pub. size: broadsheet; circ. 3,500(free & paid).
Formerly: Jonesboro Jackson Independent.

WEEKLY NEWSPAPERS

KENTWOOD
US

KENTWOOD NEWS-LEDGER. 1965. Wed. $.50 newsstand; $20/yr. in parish; $30/yr. out of parish. 212 Ave. F, Kentwood, LA 70444. TEL 504-229-8607; FAX 504-229-8698. **Owner(s):** Louisiana State Newspapers, P.O. Box AD, Kentwood, LA 70444. TEL 504-229-8607; FAX 504-748-7104; Ed. Steve Byrd. adv.; photos; pub. size: broadsheet; circ. 14,646(free & paid).

LA PLACE
US

L'OBSERVATEUR. 1913. s-w.: Wed. & Sat. $.50 newsstand; $23.70/yr. 116 Newspaper Dr., La Place, LA 70068. TEL 504-652-9545; FAX 504-652-3885. **Owner(s):** Wick Communications, Inc., 333 Wilcox Dr., Ste. 302, Sierra Vista, AZ 85635. TEL 520-728-4488; FAX 520-728-6090; Ed. Debbie Mustian; Pub. Joy Kennon; adv. contact: Robyn Zeringue. photos; pub. size: broadsheet; circ. 5,000(paid).
Formerly: La Place L'Observateur.

LUTCHER
US

NEWS EXAMINER, THE. Thu. $.50 newsstand; $15.45/yr. mailed. 2290 Texas St., Lutcher, LA 70071. TEL 504-869-5784; FAX 504-869-4386. **Owner(s):** Ruhr Valley Publishing, 2290 Texas St., Lutcher, LA 70071. TEL 504-869-5784; FAX 504-869-4386; Ed. Huey Stein; Pub. Wilbur Raynaud; adv. contact: Cynthia Rouyea. photos; pub. size: broadsheet; circ. 4,000(paid).

MAMOU
US

MAMOU ACADIAN PRESS. 1956. Thu. free; $18/yr. mailed. P.O. Drawer 360, Mamou, LA 70554. TEL 318-363-3939; FAX 318-363-2841. **Owner(s):** Louisiana State Newspapers, P.O. Drawer 260, Lafayette, LA 70501. TEL 318-363-3939; Ed. Florence Washam. adv.; photos; bk.rev.; pub. size: broadsheet; circ. 3,000(free).

MANSFIELD
US

MANSFIELD ENTERPRISE. 1904. Thu. $.50 newsstand; $20/yr. in parish; $35/yr. out of parish. 202 Adams St., Mansfield, LA 71052. TEL 318-872-4120; FAX 318-872-6038. **Owner(s):** Natchitoches Times, Inc., P.O. Box 448, Natchitoches, LA 71458. TEL 318-352-5501; Ed. Vickie Welborn; Pub. Keenan C. Gingles; adv. contact: Bennie Hall. pub. size: broadsheet; circ. 5,000(paid).

MANY
US

SABINE BANNER. Tue. free. 850 San Antonio Ave., Many, LA 71449. TEL 318-256-3495; FAX 318-256-9151. **Owner(s):** Robert Gentry, P.O. Box 850, Many, LA 71449. TEL 318-256-3495; Ed. Shannon Clements; Pub. Robert Gentry; adv.; pub. size: tabloid; circ. 15,000(free).

US

SABINE INDEX. 1879. Wed. free; $.75 newsstand; $24/yr. in parish; $36/yr. out of parish. 850 San Antonio Ave., Many, LA 71449. TEL 318-256-3495; FAX 318-256-9151. **Owner(s):** Robert Gentry, P.O. Box 850, Many, LA 71449. TEL 318-256-3495; Ed. Shannon Clements; Pub. Robert Gentry; adv. contact: Melinda Crosier. photos; bk.rev.; pub. size: tabloid; circ. 6,200(controlled & paid).

MARKSVILLE
US

AVOYELLES JOURNAL. 1978. s-w.: Sun. & Wed. free. 100 Main St., Marksville, LA 71351. TEL 318-253-5413; FAX 318-253-7223. **Owner(s):** Avoyelles Publishing Co., P.O. Box 523, Marksville, LA 71351. TEL 318-253-5413; Ed. Randy DeCuir; Pub. Randy DeCuir; adv. contact: Kathie Lipe. photos; pub. size: broadsheet; circ. 16,500(free).

US

WEEKLY NEWS. Thu. $13.50/yr. in parish; $24/yr. out of parish; $28/yr. out of state. 100 N. Main St., Marksville, LA 71351. TEL 318-253-9247; FAX 318-253-7223. **Owner(s):** Avoyelles Publishing Co., P.O. Box 253, Marksville, LA 71351. TEL 318-253-9247; Ed. Randy DeCuir; Pub. Randy DeCuir; pub. size: broadsheet; circ. 4,000(paid).

MORGAN CITY
US

ST. MARY JOURNAL. 1960. s-w.: Sun. & Wed. free. 1014 Front St., Morgan City, LA 70380. TEL 504-384-1350; FAX 504-384-4255. **Owner(s):** Morgan City Newspapers, Inc., P.O. Box 948, Morgan City, LA 70381. TEL 504-384-8370; Ed. Steve Shirley; Pub. Doyle E. Shirley; adv. contact: Andy Shirley. photos; pub. size: broadsheet; circ. 10,500(free).

NEW ROADS
US

POINTE COUPEE BANNER. 1880. Thu. $.50 newsstand; $20.80/yr. in state; $30/yr. out of state; $30/yr. out of cy. 123 St. Mary St., New Roads, LA 70760. TEL 504-638-7155; FAX 504-638-8442. **Owner(s):** Pointe Coupee Printing & Publishing, Inc., 123 St. Mary St., New Roads, LA 70760. TEL 504-638-7155; Pub. Mary Catherine Roy LaCour; adv. contact: Amy Braud. pub. size: broadsheet; circ. 5,400(paid).

OAKDALE
US ISSN 0746-5920

OAKDALE JOURNAL. 1913. Thu. $.75 newsstand; $22/yr. in parish; $26/yr. out of parish; $32.50/yr. out of state. 122 E. Sixth Ave., Oakdale, LA 71463. TEL 318-335-0635; FAX 318-335-0431. **Owner(s):** Louisiana State Newspapers, 122 E. Sixth Ave., Oakdale, LA 71463. TEL 318-335-0635; FAX 318-335-0431; Ed. Barbara Doyle. adv.; photos; pub. size: broadsheet; circ. 14,000(paid).

OAK GROVE
US

WEST CARROLL GAZETTE. 1910. Wed. $.50 newsstand; $15/yr. in parish; $18/yr. out of parish; $27.50/yr. out of state. 512 S. Constitution Ave., Oak Grove, LA 71263. TEL 318-428-3207; FAX 318-428-2747. **Owner(s):** Moody Co., P.O. Box 4033C, Lafayette, LA 70502; Pub. David Clevenger; adv. contact: Bill Vaughn. photos; pub. size: standard; circ. 3,348(paid).

PLAQUEMINE
US ISSN 1053-5691

POST SOUTH. 1957. Thu. $.50 newsstand; $20.80/yr. local. 58640 Belleview Rd., Plaquemine, LA 70764. TEL 504-687-3288; FAX 504-687-1814. **Owner(s):** Joyce S. Hebert, P.O. Box 589, Plaquemine, LA 70765-0589. TEL 504-687-3288; FAX 504-687-1814; Ed. Ellie Hebert; Pub. Joyce S. Hebert; adv.: $5.60/SAU. photos; pub. size: standard; circ. 5,900(paid).
Formerly: Plaquemine Post/Iberville South.

PONCHATOULA
US ISSN 0889-0684

ENTERPRISE, THE. 1921. Wed. $.25 newsstand; $12/yr. 240 E. Pine St., Ponchatoula, LA 70454. TEL 504-386-6537. **Owner(s):** Don Ellzey, P.O. Box 218, Ponchatoula, LA 70454. TEL 504-386-6537; Pub. Don Ellzey; adv.; pub. size: broadsheet; circ. 2,300(paid).

US

PONCHATOULA TIMES, THE. 1981. Thu. $.50 newsstand; $11/yr. in parish; $13/yr. elsewhere. 145 W. Pine St., Ste. A, Ponchatoula, LA 70454. TEL 504-386-2877; FAX 504-386-0458. **Owner(s):** Bryan T. McMahon, 145 W. Pine St., Ste. A, Ponchatoula, LA 70454. TEL 504-386-2877; FAX 504-386-0458; adv.; photos; bk.rev.; pub. size: broadsheet; circ. 5,000(controlled & paid).

PORT ALLEN
US

WEST SIDE JOURNAL. 1938. Thu. $.35 newsstand; $10/yr. in parish; $12/yr. out of parish. 668 N. Jefferson, Port Allen, LA 70767. TEL 504-343-2540; FAX 504-344-0923. **Owner(s):** Lora Mae Young, 668 N. Jefferson, Port Allen, LA 70767. TEL 504-343-2540; Pub. Loretta Decuir; adv.; photos; pub. size: broadsheet; circ. 4,000(paid).

RAYNE
US ISSN 1069-2398

RAYNE ACADIAN-TRIBUNE. 1893. Thu. $.25 newsstand; $13/yr. in parish. 108 N. Adams, Rayne, LA 70578. TEL 318-334-3186; FAX 318-334-8474. **Owner(s):** Louisiana State Newspapers, 318 N. Main, P.O. Box 400, Abbeville, LA 70510. TEL 318-893-4223; Ed. Paul Kedinger; Pub. Milo Nickel; adv. contact: Frances Bihm. pub. size: broadsheet; circ. 4,700(paid).

US

RAYNE INDEPENDENT. 1967. Thu. $.25 newsstand; $14/yr. in parish; $17/yr. out of parish. 201 E.S. First St., Rayne, LA 70578. TEL 318-334-2128. **Owner(s):** Independent Publishing Corp., 201 E.S. First St., Rayne, LA 70578. TEL 318-334-2128; Ed. Jo Cart. adv. contact: Walter T. Cart. photos; pub. size: broadsheet; circ. 4,610(paid).

WEEKLY NEWSPAPERS

RAYVILLE
US
RICHLAND BEACON-NEWS. 1846. Thu. $.50 newsstand; $15/yr. local; $20/yr. in state; $25/yr. out of state. 603 N. Louisa, Rayville, LA 71269. TEL 318-728-2250; FAX 318-728-5991. **Owner(s):** Louisiana State Newspapers, P.O. Box 5010, Lafayette, LA 70507. TEL 318-334-3186; Ed. Bill Hardin; Pub. Terry Stockton; adv.; photos; pub. size: broadsheet; circ. 5,500(paid).

SPRINGHILL
US
SPRINGHILL PRESS. Thu. $21/yr. local; $31/yr. out of parish. 127 Main St., Springhill, LA 71075. TEL 318-539-3511; FAX 318-539-3512. **Owner(s):** Lovan B. & Patricia W. Thomas, 127 Main St., Springhill, LA 71075. TEL 318-539-3511; Ed. Steve Colwell; Pub. Steve Colwell; adv. contact: Vicky Dorst. pub. size: broadsheet; circ. 4,000(paid).
Formerly: Springhill Press & News Journal.

ST. MARTINVILLE
US
ST. MARTINVILLE TECHE NEWS. 1886. Wed. $.75 newsstand; $18.72/yr. in parish; $24.96/yr. out of parish; $30/yr. out of state. 214 N. Main St., St. Martinville, LA 70582. TEL 318-394-6232; FAX 318-394-7511. **Owner(s):** Louisiana Suburban Press, 214 N. Main St., P.O. Box 69, St. Martinville, LA 70582. TEL 318-394-6232; FAX 318-394-7511; Ed. Henri C. Bienvenu; Pub. Henri C. Bienvenu; adv. contact: Mary Johnson. photos; bk.rev.; pub. size: broadsheet; circ. 6,200(paid).

TALLULAH
US
MADISON JOURNAL. 1869. Wed. $.35 newsstand; $20/yr. in parish; $23/yr. out of parish. 300 S. Chestnut St., Tallulah, LA 71282. TEL 318-574-1404; FAX 318-574-4219. **Owner(s):** L.P. Cashman, III, 300 S. Chestnut St., Tallulah, LA 71282. TEL 318-574-1404; Pub. Pete Sanders; adv.; pub. size: broadsheet; circ. 3,400(paid).

VILLE PLATTE
US
VILLE PLATTE GAZETTE. 1914. s-w.: Thu. & Sun. $.75 newsstand; $28.50/yr. local; $32/yr. out of area. 145 Court St., Ville Platte, LA 70586. TEL 318-363-4416; FAX 318-363-2841. **Owner(s):** Louisiana State Newspapers, 122 E. Sixth Ave., Oakdale, LA 71463. TEL 318-335-0635; Ed. Danielle Wood. adv.; photos; pub. size: broadsheet; circ. 4,000(paid).

VIVIAN
US
CADDO CITIZEN. 1912. Thu. $24.96/yr. in parish; $29.12/yr. in state;. 109 W. Louisiana Ave., Vivian, LA 71082. TEL 318-375-3294; FAX 318-375-4578. **Owner(s):** Westward Communications, Inc., 5005 LBJ Fwy., Dallas, TX 75244. TEL 214-450-1717; FAX 214-450-1770; Ed. Barbara Dendy; Pub. Jill Boswell; pub. size: broadsheet; circ. 2,400(paid).

WEST MONROE
US
OUACHITA CITIZEN. 1924. Thu. $.50 newsstand; $22/yr. in parish; $31/yr. out of parish. 810 Natchitoches, West Monroe, LA 71291. TEL 318-322-3161; FAX 318-325-2285. **Owner(s):** SJH Publishing, P.O. Box 758, West Monroe, LA 71294. TEL 318-322-3161; FAX 318-325-2285; Ed. Sam Hanna, Jr. adv.; bk.rev.; pub. size: broadsheet; circ. 8,000(paid).

WINNFIELD
US
WINN PARISH ENTERPRISE. 1925. Wed. $.50 newsstand; $20/yr. local. Lafayette & Long, Winnfield, LA 71483. TEL 318-628-2712; FAX 318-628-6196. **Owner(s):** Lovan B. & Patricia W. Thomas, P.O. Box 448, Natchitoches, LA 71458; Pub. Bob Holeman; adv. contact: Linda Bumbalough. photos; pub. size: broadsheet; circ. 4,500(paid).
Formerly: Winnfield Winn Parish Enterprise.

WINNSBORO
US
FRANKLIN SUN, THE. 1856. Wed. $.50 newsstand; $18.50/yr. in parish; $27.50/yr. out of parish; $33.50/yr. out of state. 514 Prairie, Winnsboro, LA 71295. TEL 318-435-4521; FAX 318-435-9220. **Owner(s):** Hanna Publishing Co., 514 Prairie, Winnsboro, LA 71295. TEL 318-435-4521; Ed. Leslie Young; Pub. Sam Hanna; adv. contact: Monica Huff. photos; pub. size: broadsheet; circ. 6,100(paid).

ZACHARY
US
ZACHARY PLAINSMAN-NEWS. 1953. Thu. $.50 newsstand; $20/yr. in parish; $25/yr. out of parish. 5145 Main St., Ste. C, Zachary, LA 70791. TEL 504-654-6841; FAX 504-654-8271. **Owner(s):** Louisiana State Newspapers, 5240 Groom Rd., Baker, LA 70714. TEL 504-654-6841; FAX 504-654-8271; Ed. Katherine Gilbert. adv. contact: Sherry Romero. pub. size: broadsheet; circ. 2,000(paid).

MAINE

AUGUSTA
US
▼**CAPITAL WEEKLY.** 1995. Thu. $.35 newsstand; $14/yr.in state;$28/yr. out of st.atetate. 173 State St., Augusta, ME 04332-2788. TEL 207-621-6000. **Owner(s):** Courier Publications, One Park Dr., Rockland, ME 04841. TEL 207-594-4401; Ed. Tom Farkas; Pub. David Morse; adv. contact: Ron Belyea. photos; pub. size: broadsheet; circ. 7,500(paid).

BAR HARBOR
US
BAR HARBOR TIMES. 1914. Thu. $.75 newsstand; $28/yr. in state; $45/yr. out of state. 76 Cottage St., Bar Harbor, ME 04609. TEL 207-288-3311; FAX 207-288-5814; E-mail: bhtmail@courierpub.com. **Owner(s):** Courier Publications, One Park Dr., Rockland, ME 04841. TEL 207-594-4401; Ed. Earl Brechlin; Pub. David Morse; adv. contact: Shannon Polchies. bk.rev.; pub. size: broadsheet; circ. 8,500(paid).

BELFAST
US   ISSN 0034-5075
REPUBLICAN JOURNAL. 1829. Thu. $.50 newsstand; $20/yr. in cy.; $28/yr. in state; $30/yr. out of state. 71 High St., Belfast, ME 04915. TEL 207-338-3333; FAX 207-338-5498. **Owner(s):** Courier Publications, One Park Dr., Rockford, ME 04841. TEL 207-594-4401; Ed. Tom Groening; Pub. David Morse; adv. contact: Greg Whitcomb. photos; pub. size: broadsheet; circ. 7,000(paid).

BIDDEFORD
US
BIDDEFORD-SACO-OOB COURIER. 1989. Thu. $.35 newsstand; $45/yr. 5 Washington St., Biddeford, ME 04005. TEL 207-282-4337; FAX 207-282-4339. **Owner(s):** David & Carolyn Flood, 5 Washington St., Biddeford, ME 04005. TEL 207-282-4337; FAX 207-282-4339; Pub. David Flood; adv.; photos; pub. size: tabloid; circ. 22,000(controlled & free). **Wire Service(s):** AP.

BLUE HILL
US
WEEKLY PACKET. 1961. Thu. $.60 newsstand; $24.95/yr. in state; $33.95/yr. out of state. Main St., Blue Hill, ME 04614. TEL 207-374-2341; FAX 207-374-2343. **Owner(s):** Penobscot Bay Press, P.O. Box 36, Stonington, ME 04681. TEL 207-367-2200; FAX 207-374-2439; Ed. Nathaniel W. Barrows; Pub. Nathaniel W. Barrows; adv.; photos; pub. size: tabloid; circ. 2,200(paid).

BOOTHBAY HARBOR
US
BOOTHBAY REGISTER. 1876. Thu. $.50 newsstand; $22/yr. in cy.; $30/yr. out of cy. 95 Townsend Ave., Boothbay Harbor, ME 04538. TEL 207-633-4620; FAX 207-633-7123. **Owner(s):** Maine-OK Enterprises, Inc., P.O. Box 357, Boothbay Harbor, ME 04538-0357. TEL 207-633-4620; Ed. Mary Brewer; Pub. Marylouise Cowan; adv.; photos; pub. size: broadsheet; circ. 5,640(paid).

BRIDGTON
US
BRIDGTON NEWS. 1870. Thu. $.50 newsstand; $20/yr. in state; $24/yr. out of state. 42 Main St., Bridgton, ME 04009. TEL 207-647-2851. **Owner(s):** Bridgton News Corp., P.O. Box 244, Bridgton, ME. TEL 207-647-2851; Ed. Wayne E. Rivet; Pub. Henry A. Shorey; adv. contact: Gail Stretton. photos; pub. size: broadsheet; circ. 6,600(free & paid).

CALAIS
US
CALAIS ADVERTISER. 1836. Wed. $27/yr. in state; $31/yr. out of state. 19 Church St., Calais, ME 04619-0660. TEL 207-454-3561; FAX 207-454-3458. **Owner(s):** Calais Advertiser, The, P.O. Box 660, Calais, ME 04619. TEL 207-454-3561; FAX 207-454-3458; Ed. Ferguson Calder. adv. contact: Maxine Geroux. photos; pub. size: tabloid; circ. 4,350(paid).

WEEKLY NEWSPAPERS

CARIBOU

US

AROOSTOOK REPUBLICAN & NEWS. 1880. Wed. $.75 newsstand; $28.60/yr. in cy.; $37/yr. out of cy.; $39.50/yr. out of state. 159 Bennett Dr., Caribou, ME 04736. TEL 207-496-3251; FAX 207-492-4351; E-mail: aroosrep@bangornews.infi.net. **Owner(s):** Northeast Publishing Co., P.O. Box 510, Presque Isle, ME 04769. TEL 207-768-4471; pub. size: broadsheet; circ. 4,800(paid).
  Formerly: Caribou Aroostook Republican & News.

DEXTER

US

EASTERN GAZETTE, THE. 1853. Mon. free; $30/yr. 380 Main St., Dexter, ME 04930-0306. TEL 207-924-7402. **Owner(s):** Robert & Janice Shank, P.O. Box 306, Dexter, ME 04930. TEL 207-924-7402; Ed. Robert Shank; Pub. Robert Shank; adv. contact: Robert Shank. photos; pub. size: tabloid; circ. 15,000(free & paid).

DOVER-FOXCROFT

US

COUNTY WIDE. 1977. Mon. free; $28/yr. 78 River St., Dover-Foxcroft, ME 04426. TEL 207-564-7548; FAX 207-564-7051. **Owner(s):** County Wide Communications, Inc., P.O. Box 497, Machias, ME 04654. TEL 207-564-7548; FAX 207-564-7051; Pub. Bob Berta; adv. contact: Joyce Hartford. photos; bk.rev.; pub. size: tabloid; circ. 4,400(free & paid).

US

GUILFORD AMERICAN. 1989. Wed. $28/yr. 78 River St., Dover-Foxcroft, ME 04654. TEL 207-564-7548; FAX 207-564-7051. **Owner(s):** County Wide Communications, Inc., 78 River St., Dover-Foxcroft, ME 04426-1321. TEL 207-564-7548; Ed. Bob Berta. adv. contact: Joyce Hartford. photos; bk.rev.; pub. size: tabloid; circ. 3,200(paid).
  Formerly: Guilford Journal.

US

PISCATAQUIS OBSERVER, THE. 1838. Wed. $.60 newsstand; $23.50/yr. in cy.; $33/yr. out of state. 126 Union Sq., Dover-Foxcroft, ME 04426. TEL 207-564-8355; FAX 207-564-7056. **Owner(s):** Northeast Publishing Co., P.O. Box 510, Presque Isle, ME 04769. TEL 207-764-4471; Ed. Martha Lostron; Pub. Richard Warren; adv.; photos; pub. size: standard; circ. 4,400(paid).

EASTPORT

US

QUODDY TIDES. 1968. bi-w.: 2nd & 4th Fri. $.75 newsstand; $22/yr. in cy.; $25/yr. elsewhere. 123 Water St., Eastport, ME 04631. TEL 207-853-4806; FAX 207-853-4095. **Owner(s):** Edward B. French, P.O. Box 213, Water St., Eastport, ME 04631. TEL 207-853-4806; Robert French, 36915 Harper Ave., Apt. 7, Mt. Clemens, MI 48035; Hugh French, 295 Brackett St., Portland, ME 04102; Ann Townsend, P.O. Box 29, Bradford, ME 04410; Ed. Edward French; Pub. Edward French; adv.; pub. size: tabloid; circ. 5,634(paid).

ELLSWORTH

US

ELLSWORTH AMERICAN, THE. 1851. Thu. $.75 newsstand; $27/yr. local; $33/yr. out of area; $44/yr. out of state. 63 Main St., Ellsworth, ME 04605-0509. TEL 207-667-2576; FAX 207-667-7656. **Owner(s):** Ellsworth American, Inc., P.O. Box 509, Ellsworth, ME 04605-0509. TEL 207-667-2576; FAX 207-667-7656; Ed. Stephen Fay; Pub. Alan Baker; adv. contact: Terry L. Young. adv.: $10.50/SAU. photos; bk.rev.; pub. size: broadsheet; circ. 10,803(paid). **Wire Service(s):** API Newsfinder.

FARMINGDALE

US

COMMUNITY ADVERTISER. 1936. Mon. free newsstand; $15/yr. 324-A Maine Ave., Farmingdale, ME 04344. TEL 207-582-8486; FAX 207-582-4530. **Owner(s):** Keith Peters, 324-A Maine Ave., Farmingdale, ME 04344. TEL 207-582-8486; FAX 207-582-4530; Ed. Keith Peters. adv.; bk.rev.; pub. size: tabloid; circ. 21,000(free & paid).

FARMINGTON

US

FRANKLIN JOURNAL & FARMINGTON CHRONICLE. 1840. s-w.: Tue. & Fri. $.50 newsstand; $25/yr. in state; $35/yr. out of state. Wilton Rd., Farmington, ME 04938-0750. TEL 207-778-2075; FAX 207-778-6970. **Owner(s):** Mt. Blue Publishing Co., Inc., P.O. Box 750, Farmington, ME 04938. TEL 207-778-2075; FAX 207-778-6970; Ed. Greg Davis; Pub. Janet K. Warner; adv. contact: Laura McFarlane. adv.: $7.13/SAU. photos; pub. size: broadsheet; circ. 9,900(paid).

FORT FAIRFIELD

US

FORT FAIRFIELD REVIEW. 1893. Wed. $.45 newsstand; $20.50/yr. in area. 128 Main St., Fort Fairfield, ME 04742. TEL 207-472-3111; FAX 207-473-7977; E-mail: ffreview@ainop.com. **Owner(s):** Eastern Publishing Ltd., P.O. Box 304, Houlton, ME 04730. TEL 207-328-8863; FAX 207-328-3208; Ed. Marcia Reed. adv.; photos; pub. size: broadsheet; circ. 2,300(paid).

HOULTON

US

HOULTON PIONEER TIMES. Wed. $28.60/yr. in cy.; $37/yr. out of cy.; $39.50/yr. out of state; $60/yr. foreign. 23 Court St., Houlton, ME 04730. TEL 207-532-2281; FAX 207-532-2403. **Owner(s):** Northeast Publishing Co., Skyway Industrial Pk., Presque Isle, ME 04769. TEL 207-764-4471; adv.; pub. size: standard; circ. 5,650(paid).

ISLESBORO

US ISSN 1071-1473

ISLESBORO ISLAND NEWS. 1985. 11/yr. $2.50 newsstand; $24/yr. HC 60, Box 227, Islesboro, ME 04848. TEL 207-734-6745; FAX 207-734-6519. **Owner(s):** Agatha Cabaniss, HC 60, Box 227, Islesboro, ME 04848. TEL 207-754-6745; FAX 207-734-6519; Ed. Agatha Cabaniss. adv.; photos; pub. size: tabloid; circ. 600(free & paid).

KENNEBUNK

US

YORK COUNTY COAST STAR. 1878. Wed. $.75 newsstand; $25/yr. in cy. deliv.; $45/yr. out of cy.; $80/yr. foreign. Rte. 1 S., Kennebunk, ME 04043. TEL 207-985-2961; FAX 207-985-9050. **Owner(s):** Journal Transcript Newspapers, 327 Broadway, Revere, MA 02151. TEL 617-284-2400; Ed. John Martins; Pub. Lou McGrew; adv.; photos; pub. size: broadsheet; circ. 11,000(paid).

LINCOLN

US

LINCOLN NEWS. 1959. Thu. $.50 newsstand; $23/yr. in state; $25/yr. out of state. P.O. Box 35, Lincoln, ME 04457. TEL 207-794-6532; FAX 207-794-2004. **Owner(s):** M. Sheila Tenggren, P. O. Box 35, Lincoln, ME 04457. TEL 207-794-6532; FAX 207-794-2004; Ed. M. Sheila Tenggren; Pub. M. Sheila Tenggren; adv. contact: M. Sheila Tenggren. photos; pub. size: tabloid; circ. 5,696(paid).

LIVERMORE FALLS

US

LIVERMORE FALLS ADVERTISER. 1892. Thu. $.40 newsstand; $17/yr. in state; $24/yr. out of state. 59 Main St., Livermore Falls, ME 04254-0701. TEL 207-897-4321; FAX 207-897-4322. **Owner(s):** Mt. Blue Publishing Co., Inc., P.O. Box 750, Farmington, ME 04938. TEL 207-778-2075; Ed. Mitchell C. Thomas; Pub. Janet K. Warner; adv. contact: Carol A. Lanier. adv.: $7.13/SAU. photos; pub. size: broadsheet; circ. 3,200(paid).

MACHIAS

US

MACHIAS VALLEY NEWS OBSERVER. 1853. Wed. $.75 newsstand; $25/yr. in cy.; $26/yr. out of cy. 31 Broadway, Machias, ME 04654-0357. TEL 207-255-6561; FAX 207-255-4058. **Owner(s):** Jay B. Hinson, Robbinston, ME 04671; Eugene M. Townsend, Calais, ME 04619; Ed. Jay B. Hinson. adv.: $4.90/SAU. pub. size: tabloid; circ. 3,400(paid).

MADAWASKA

US

ST. JOHN VALLEY TIMES. 1957. Wed. $.75 newsstand; $30/yr. 696 W. Main St., Madawaska, ME 04756. TEL 207-728-3336; FAX 207-728-3825. **Owner(s):** Walls Newspapers, Inc., P.O. Box 7346-A, Birmingham, AL 35253. TEL 205-870-1684; Ed. Julia Bayly; Pub. Don Levesque; adv. contact: Carole Michaud. photos; pub. size: tabloid; circ. 6,550(controlled & paid).

MILLINOCKET

US ISSN 1064-0657

KATAHDIN TIMES. 1976. Tue. $.50 newsstand; $24./yr. in cy.; $31/yr. in state; $38/yr. out of state. 202 Penobscot Ave., Millinocket, ME 04462. TEL 207-723-8118; FAX 207-723-4434; E-mail: ktimes@agate.net. **Owner(s):** David S. & Marlene Henley, P.O. Box 304, Houlton, ME 04730. TEL 207-328-8863; Ed. Barbara M. Waters; Pub. David S. Henley; adv. contact: Kathy Beaumont. photos; pub. size: broadsheet; circ. 4,200(free & paid).

NEWCASTLE

US

LINCOLN COUNTY NEWS. 1875. Thu. $.30 newsstand; $15/yr. in cy.; $18/yr. out of cy. Mills Rd., Newcastle, ME 04553. TEL 207-563-3171; FAX 207-563-3127. **Owner(s):** Lincoln County Publishing Co., Inc., P.O. Box 36, Damariscotta, ME 04543. TEL 207-563-3171; FAX 207-563-3127; Ed. Judi Finn; Pub. Christopher A. Roberts; adv.; pub. size: broadsheet; circ. 8,000(paid).

NORWAY

US

NORWAY ADVERTISER-DEMOCRAT. 1826. Thu. $.50 newsstand; $17.50/6 mos. in cy. 2 Bridge St., Norway, ME 04268. TEL 207-743-7011; FAX 207-743-2256. **Owner(s):** Howard James, P.O. Box 269, Norway, ME 04268; Ed. Susan Reana; Pub. Howard James; adv.; photos; pub. size: standard; circ. 7,100(paid).

OLD TOWN

US

PENOBSCOT TIMES. 1891. Thu. $.60 newsstand; $20/yr. in cy.; $30/yr. out of cy. 400 N. Main St., Old Town, ME 04468. TEL 207-827-4451; FAX 207-827-2280. **Owner(s):** David Woldstadt, Penobscot Times, Inc., 400 N. Main St., Old Town, ME 04468. TEL 207-827-4451; FAX 207-827-2280; Ed. Robert Diebold; Pub. David Wollstadt; adv. contact: Beverly King. photos; pub. size: tabloid; circ. 3,900(paid).
Formerly: Old Town-Orono Times.

PORTLAND

US   ISSN 0025-0783

MAINE TIMES. 1968. Wed. $.95 newsstand; $1.95/seasonal guide; $25/yr. 561 Congress St., Portland, ME 04101. TEL 207-828-5432; FAX 207-828-5438. **Owner(s):** Maine Publishing Corp.; Ed. Doug Rooks; Pub. Seth Sprague; adv.; pub. size: tabloid; circ. 15,000(paid).

PRESQUE ISLE

US

STAR-HERALD, THE. 1871. Wed. $.75 newsstand; $28.60/yr. in cy.; $37/yr. in state; $39.50/yr. out of state. 40 North St., Ste. B, Presque Isle, ME 04769. TEL 207-768-5431; FAX 207-764-7585; E-mail: starhrld@bangornews.infi.net. **Owner(s):** Northeast Publishing Co., P.O. Box 510, Presque Isle, ME 04769. TEL 207-764-4471; adv.; pub. size: broadsheet; circ. 8,000(paid).
Formerly: Presque Isle Star-Herald.

ROCKLAND

US

COURIER-GAZETTE. 1846. 3/wk.: Tue., Thu., Sat. $.75 newsstand; $75/yr. in state; $95/yr. out of state. One Park Dr., Rockland, ME 04841. TEL 207-594-4401; FAX 207-596-6981; E-mail: cgmail@courierpub.com. **Owner(s):** Courier Publications, One Park Dr., Rockland, ME 04841. TEL 207-594-4401; Ed. Steve Betts; Pub. David E. Morse; adv.; photos; bk.rev.; pub. size: broadsheet; circ. 9,000(paid).

RUMFORD

US

RUMFORD FALLS TIMES. Wed. $.50 newsstand; $30/yr in cy.; $36/yr. northern New England; $44/yr. western New England. 71 Canal St., Rumford, ME 04276. TEL 207-364-7893; FAX 207-369-0170. **Owner(s):** James Newspapers, Bridge St., Norway, ME 04268. TEL 207-743-8996; FAX 207-743-2256; Ed. Greg Davis. adv.; photos; bk.rev.; pub. size: broadsheet; circ. 5,000(paid).

SANFORD

US   ISSN 1090-8293

SANFORD NEWS. 1980. Tue. $.50 newsstand; $19.99/yr. 6 School St., Sanford, ME 04073. TEL 207-324-5986; FAX 207-490-1431. **Owner(s):** Buzz & Dusty Dietterle, 6 School St., Sanford, ME 03906. TEL 207-324-5986; FAX 207-490-1431; Pub. Buzz Dietterle; adv. contact: Donna Bourque. photos; pub. size: broadsheet; circ. evening 7,000(paid).

STONINGTON

US

ISLAND AD-VANTAGES. 1934. Thu. $.60 newsstand; $24.95/yr. in state; $33.95/yr. out of state. Main St., Stonington, ME 04681-0036. TEL 207-367-2200; FAX 207-374-2439. **Owner(s):** Penobscot Bay Press, P.O. Box 36, Stonington, ME 04681. TEL 207-367-2200; FAX 207-374-2439; Ed. R. Nathaniel W. Barrows. adv.; photos; pub. size: tabloid; circ. 2,600(paid).

WESTBROOK

US   ISSN 0092-0119

AMERICAN JOURNAL. 1950. Wed. $.50 newsstand; $25/yr.; $44/2 yrs. 4 Dana St., Westbrook, ME 04092. TEL 207-854-2577; FAX 207-854-0018. **Owner(s):** Durgin-Snow Publishing Co., Inc., 4 Dana St., Westbrook, ME 04092. TEL 207-854-2577; FAX 207-854-0018; Ed. Raymond M. Foote; Pub. Harry T. Foote; adv.; pub. size: tabloid; circ. 7,500(free & paid).

WINDHAM

US

SUBURBAN NEWS, THE. 1992. Tue. free newsstand; $50/yr. 733 Roosevelt Trail, Windham, ME 04062. TEL 207-892-1166; FAX 207-892-1171. **Owner(s):** Ray Roux, Gary Cooper & Bill Diamond, 690 Roosevelt Trail, Windham, ME 04062. TEL 207-892-1166; FAX 207-892-1171; Ed. Kay Soldier. adv. contact: Bill Foss. adv.; $8/SAU. photos; pub. size: tabloid; circ. 10,000(free).

MARYLAND

BALTIMORE

US   ISSN 0748-5271

ARBUTUS TIMES. 1961. Wed. $.50 newsstand; $16/yr. 835 Frederick Rd., Baltimore, MD 21228. TEL 410-788-4500; FAX 410-788-4103. **Owner(s):** Patuxent Publishing Co., 10750 Little Patuxent Pkwy., Columbia, MD 21044. TEL 301-730-3620; Ed. Jim Joyner; Pub. Zeke Orlinsky; pub. size: tabloid; circ. 3,800(paid).

US

AVENUE NEWS. 1974. s-w.: Wed. & Thu. $.10 newsstand. 442 Eastern Blvd., Baltimore, MD 21221. TEL 410-687-7775; FAX 410-687-7881. **Owner(s):** Avenue, Inc., 442 Eastern Blvd., Baltimore, MD 21221. TEL 410-687-7775; FAX 410-687-7881; Ed. Jay Livingston; Pub. Kenneth C. Coldwell; adv.; bk.rev.; pub. size: tabloid; circ. 80,000(free & paid).

US

BALTIMORE CHRONICLE. 1973. m.: 1st Wed. $10/yr. mailed 1st class. 30 W. 25th St., Baltimore, MD 21218. TEL 410-243-4141. **Owner(s):** Laurence N. Krause, 30 W. 25th St., Baltimore, MD 21218. TEL 410-243-4141; Alice C. Cherbonnier, 30 W. 25th St., Baltimore, MD 21218. TEL 410-243-4141; Ed. Alice Cherbonnier. adv.; photos; pub. size: tabloid.

US   ISSN 1041-0872

BALTIMORE MESSENGER. Thu. free; $.50 newsstand. 409 Washington Ave., Baltimore, MD 21204. TEL 410-337-2400; FAX 410-337-2490. **Owner(s):** Patuxent Publishing Co., 409 Washington Ave., Baltimore, MD 21204. TEL 410-337-2400; Ed. Paul Milton; Pub. Zeke Orlinsky; adv. contact: Karleen Pate. photos; bk.rev.; pub. size: tabloid; circ. 15,000(free).

US   ISSN 0748-5256

CATONSVILLE TIMES. 1881. Wed. $.50 newsstand; $19.95/yr. 835 Frederick Rd., Baltimore, MD 21228. TEL 410-788-4500; FAX 410-788-4103. **Owner(s):** Patuxent Publishing Co., 10750 Little Patuxent Pkwy., Columbia, MD 21044; Ed. Jim Joyner; Pub. Zeke Orlinsky; pub. size: tabloid; circ. 12,000(paid).

US

CITY PAPER. 1977. Wed. free; $50/yr. mailed. 812 Park Ave., Baltimore, MD 21201. TEL 410-523-2300; FAX 410-523-2222; E-mail: amarkowitz@citypaper.com; URL: http://www.citypaper.com. **Owner(s):** Times/Shamrock Communications, 812 Park Ave., Baltimore, MD 21201. TEL 410-539-5200; Ed. Andy Markowitz; Pub. Don Farley; adv. contact: Matt Stegman. pub. size: tabloid; circ. 91,500(free & paid).

US

DUNDALK EAGLE, THE. 1969. Thu. $.27 newsstand; $10.50/yr. local; $20/yr. out of state. 4 N. Center Pl., Baltimore, MD 21222. TEL 410-288-6060; FAX 410-288-2712. **Owner(s):** Dundalk Eagle, The, 4 N. Center Pl., Baltimore, MD 21222. TEL 410-288-6060; Ed. Deborah Cornely; Pub. Kimbel E. Oelke; adv.; photos; pub. size: tabloid; circ. 26,000(paid).

US

EAST BALTIMORE GUIDE. 1927. Thu. $15/yr. 526 S. Conkling St., Baltimore, MD 21224. TEL 410-732-6600; FAX 410-732-6336. **Owner(s):** R & B Publishing Co., 526 S. Conkling St., Baltimore, MD 21224. TEL 410-732-6600; FAX 410-732-6336; Ed. Jacqueline Watts; Pub. Richard W. Sandza; adv. contact: Fran Schuyler. photos; bk.rev.; pub. size: tabloid; circ. 40,000(controlled & free). **Wire Service(s):** AP.

WEEKLY NEWSPAPERS

US
ENTERPRISE & INNER HARBOR NEWS. 1934. Thu. free; $22/yr. mailed. 1316 Light St., Baltimore, MD 21230-4308. TEL 410-752-0711; FAX 410-752-0712. **Owner(s):** Bryan R. Moorhouse, 1316 Light St., Baltimore, MD 21230. TEL 410-752-0711; FAX 410-752-0712; R. Charles Avera, 1316 Light St., Baltimore, MD 21230. TEL 410-752-0711; FAX 410-752-0712; Ed. Bryan R. Moorhouse; Pub. Bryan R. Moorhouse; adv. contact: Darla Young. photos; pub. size: tabloid; circ. 30,000(free & paid).

US
JEFFERSONIAN, THE. Thu. $.50 newsstand; $15.65/yr. in state. 409 Washington Ave., Baltimore, MD 21204. TEL 410-337-2400; FAX 410-337-2490. **Owner(s):** Patuxent Publishing Co., 409 Washington Ave., Baltimore, MD 21204. TEL 410-337-2640; Ed. Cynthia Prairie; Pub. Zeke Orlinsky; adv.; pub. size: broadsheet; circ. 5,601(paid).

US
LABOR HERALD. 1936. bi-w. $.50 newsstand; $10/yr. 4005 Seven Mile Ln., Baltimore, MD 21208-6116. TEL 410-484-3832. **Owner(s):** Labor Herald Press, The, 4005 Seven Mile Ln., Baltimore, MD 21208-6116. TEL 410-484-3832; Ed. Daniel Bernstein; Pub. Daniel Bernstein; adv.; bk.rev.; pub. size: tabloid; circ. 36,000(paid).

US
OWINGS MILLS TIMES. 1986. Thu. free; $.50 newsstand. 409 Washington Ave., Baltimore, MD 21204. TEL 410-337-2400; FAX 410-337-2490. **Owner(s):** Patuxent Publishing Co., 10750 Little Patuxent Pkwy., Columbia, MD 21044. TEL 410-730-3620; Ed. Elizabeth Eck; Pub. Zeke Orlinsky; adv.; photos; pub. size: tabloid; circ. 35,000(free & paid).

BEL AIR
US
AEGIS, THE. 1856. Wed. $32/yr. 10 Hays St., Bel Air, MD 21014. TEL 410-838-4400; FAX 410-838-7867. **Owner(s):** Baltimore Sun, The, 501 N. Calvert St., Baltimore, MD 21278. TEL 410-332-6265; Ed. Allan Vought. adv. contact: Kay Kline. pub. size: broadsheet; circ. 34,500(paid).

BOWIE
US
BOWIE BLADE-NEWS. 1958. Thu. $.35 newsstand; $19.50/yr. 6000 Laurel-Bowie Rd., Ste. 101, Bowie, MD 20715. TEL 301-262-3700; FAX 301-464-7027. **Owner(s):** Capital-Gazette Newspapers, 2000 Capital Dr., Annapolis, MD 21401. TEL 301-262-3700; Ed. Susan Gross. pub. size: standard; circ. 14,500(paid). **Wire Service(s):** AP.

US
CROFTON NEWS-CRIER. 1972. Thu. $.25 newsstand; free in cy. 6000 Laurel-Bowie Rd., Ste. 101, Bowie, MD 20715. TEL 301-262-3700; FAX 301-464-7027. **Owner(s):** Capital-Gazette Newspapers, 6800 Laurel-Bowie Rd., Bowie, MD 20715. TEL 301-261-2200; FAX 301-464-7027; Ed. Susan Gross; Pub. Philip Merrill; adv.; photos; bk.rev.; pub. size: standard; circ. 8,500(controlled & paid).

BRUNSWICK
US
BRUNSWICK CITIZEN. 1974. Wed. $.35 newsstand; $12.60/yr. in cy. 2 S. Maryland Ave., Brunswick, MD 21716. TEL 301-834-7722. **Owner(s):** Citizen Communications, 2 S. Maryland Ave., Brunswick, MD 21716. TEL 301-834-7722; Ed. Julia Maynard. pub. size: tabloid; circ. 3,500(paid).

US ISSN 1056-7674
MIDDLETOWN VALLEY CITIZEN. 1974. w. $.25 newsstand; $12.60/yr. 2 S. Maryland Ave., Brunswick, MD 21716. TEL 301-834-7722. **Owner(s):** Citizen Newspapers, 2 S. Maryland Ave., Brunswick, MD 21716; pub. size: tabloid; circ. 1,100(paid).

CAMBRIDGE
US
DORCHESTER STAR. 1867. Fri. free. 300 Academy St., Cambridge, MD 21613. TEL 410-228-0222; FAX 410-228-0685. **Owner(s):** Chesapeake Publishing Corp., P.O. Box 600, Easton, MD 21601. TEL 410-822-1500; Ed. Gail Dean; Pub. Larry Effingham; adv. contact: Beverly Travers. pub. size: broadsheet; circ. 11,500(free).

CENTREVILLE
US
QUEEN ANNE'S RECORD-OBSERVER. Fri. $16.80/yr. in cy. 114 Broadway, Centreville, MD 21617. TEL 410-758-1400; FAX 410-758-1701. **Owner(s):** Chesapeake Publishing Corp., One Airpark Dr., Easton, MD 21601. TEL 410-822-1500; Ed. William Kirby; Pub. Larry Effingham; adv. contact: Barbara Mulligan. pub. size: broadsheet; circ. 5,500(paid).

CHESTERTOWN
US
KENT COUNTY NEWS. 1793. w. $30/yr. 217 High St., Chestertown, MD 21620. TEL 410-778-2011; FAX 410-778-6522. **Owner(s):** Chesapeake Publishing Corp., One Airpark Dr., Easton, MD 21601. TEL 301-820-7070; Ed. Trish McGee; Pub. Mary Burton; adv.; pub. size: broadsheet; circ. 7,991(paid).

COLUMBIA
US
COLUMBIA FLIER. 1969. Thu. free in area; $156/yr. plus tax outside of area. 10750 Little Patuxent Pkwy., Columbia, MD 21044. TEL 410-730-3620; FAX 410-730-7053. **Owner(s):** Patuxent Publishing Co., 10750 Little Patuxent Pkwy., Columbia, MD 21044. TEL 301-730-3620; Ed. Tom Graham; Pub. S. Zeke Orlinsky; adv.; photos; bk.rev.; pub. size: tabloid; circ. 35,000(free).

US ISSN 0748-5298
HOWARD COUNTY TIMES. 1979. Thu. $19/yr. in cy.; $21/yr. out of cy.; $25yr. out of state. 10750 Little Patuxent Pkwy., Columbia, MD 21044. TEL 410-730-3620; FAX 410-730-7053. **Owner(s):** Patuxent Publishing Co., 10750 Little Patuxent Pkwy., Columbia, MD 21044. TEL 410-730-3620; Ed. Tom Graham; Pub. Zeke Orlinsky; adv.; photos; pub. size: tabloid; circ. 20,000(paid).

DENTON
US ISSN 0746-1658
TIMES-RECORD, THE. 1922. Wed. $.50 newsstand; $16.80/yr. in cy.; $22.05 out of cy. 219 Market St., Denton, MD 21629. TEL 410-479-1800; FAX 410-479-3174. **Owner(s):** Chesapeake Publishing Corp., P.O. Box 600, Easton, MD 21601. TEL 410-822-1500; FAX 410-820-6519; Ed. Peter Howell; Pub. Larry Effingham; adv. contact: Julia Millionie. photos; pub. size: broadsheet; circ. 4,500(paid).

GAITHERSBURG
US
GAITHERSBURG GAZETTE. 1959. Wed. $12.50/mo.; $75/6 mos.; $150/yr. 1200 Quince Orchard Blvd., Gaithersburg, MD 20878. TEL 301-948-3120; FAX 301-670-7183. **Owner(s):** Washington Post Co., 1150 15th St., N.W., Washington, DC 20071. TEL 202-334-6000; Ed. Georgia MacDonald; Pub. Bill Schlossenberg; adv.; pub. size: tabloid; circ. 42,000(free & paid).

US
MONTGOMERY COUNTY SENTINEL. 1855. s-w.: Wed. & Thu. $.25 newsstand; $22.05/yr. 615 S. Fredrick Ave., Ste. 303, Gaithersburg, MD 20877. TEL 301-417-1200; FAX 301-417-1210. **Owner(s):** Bernard Kapiloff, P.O. Box 1272, Rockville, MD 20849-1272. TEL 301-417-1200; Lynn G. Kapiloff, P.O. Box 1272, Rockville, MD 20849-1272. TEL 301-417-1200; Pub. Lynn Kapiloff; adv.; pub. size: tabloid; circ. 8,700(paid).

US
SILVER SPRING GAZETTE. 1943. Wed. free home deliv.; $.25 newsstand. 1200 Quince Orchard Blvd., Gaithersburg, MD 20878. TEL 301-948-3120; FAX 301-670-7170. **Owner(s):** Gazette Newspapers, 18705 N. Fredrick Ave., Gaithersburg, MD 20884. TEL 301-670-7100; Ed. Judy Hruz; Pub. Bill Schlossenburg; adv.; bk.rev.; pub. size: tabloid; circ. 30,000(free). **Formerly:** Silver Spring Record.

GATORSBURG
US
DAMASCUS GAZETTE. 1964. Wed. $35.50/3 mos.; $150/yr. local. 1200 Quince Orchard Blvd., Gatorsburg, MD 20878. TEL 301-253-6161; FAX 301-670-7183. **Owner(s):** Washington Post Co., 1150 15th St., N.W., Washington, DC 20071. TEL 202-334-6000; Ed. Tom Grant; Pub. Bill Schlossenberg; adv. contact: Bill Schlossenberg. pub. size: tabloid; circ. 7,000(controlled). **Formerly:** Damascus Courier-Gazette.

GLEN BURNIE
US
MARYLAND GAZETTE. 1727. s-w.: Wed. & Sat. $39/yr. home deliv. 306 Crain Highway, S.W., Glen Burnie, MD 21061. TEL 410-766-3700; FAX 410-766-7031. **Owner(s):** Capital-Gazette Newspapers, 2000 Capital Dr., Annapolis, MD 21401. TEL 301-268-5000; Ed. Robert Mosier; Pub. Philip Merrill; adv. contact: Tom Bazzell. photos; pub. size: standard; circ. 38,000(paid).

10622 GREENBELT, MD — **WEEKLY NEWSPAPERS**

GREENBELT
US
GREENBELT NEWS REVIEW. 1937. Thu. free; $32/yr. mailed. 15 Crescent Rd., Ste. 100, Greenbelt, MD 20770-0068. TEL 301-474-4131; FAX 301-474-5880. **Owner(s):** Greenbelt Cooperative Publishing Association, Inc., 15 Crescent Rd., Ste. 100, Greenbelt, MD 20768. TEL 301-474-4131; Ed. Mary Lou Williamson. adv.; photos; pub. size: tabloid; circ. 10,500(paid).

HANCOCK
US
HANCOCK NEWS. 1914. Wed. $.48 newsstand; $16.80/yr. in state; $18/yr. out of state. 263 Pennsylvania Ave., Hancock, MD 21750. TEL 301-678-6255; FAX 301-678-5520. **Owner(s):** Berkeley Springs Morgan Messenger, Mercer St., Berkeley Springs, WV 25411. TEL 304-258-1800; FAX 304-258-8441; Ed. J. Warren Buzzerd. adv.; bk.rev.; pub. size: standard; circ. 2,900(paid).

HAVRE DE GRACE
US
RECORD, THE. Fri. $.50 newsstand; $16.80/yr. in cy.; $21/yr. out of cy. 316 Saint John St., Havre De Grace, MD 21078. TEL 410-939-4040; FAX 410-939-2390. **Owner(s):** Homestead Publishing Co., Havre de Grace, MD 21078; Ed. Erika Compton. pub. size: broadsheet; circ. 5,500(paid).

LAUREL
US
LAUREL LEADER. 1897. Thu. free. 615 Main St., Laurel, MD 20707. TEL 301-725-2000; FAX 301-317-8736. **Owner(s):** Patuxent Publishing Co., 10750 Little Patuxent Pkwy., Columbia, MD 21044. TEL 301-730-3620; Ed. Joe Murchison; Pub. Zeke Orlinsky; adv. contact: David Tomasini. bk.rev.; pub. size: tabloid; circ. 28,158(controlled & free).

LEXINGTON PARK
US
ENTERPRISE, THE. 1883. s-w.: Wed. & Fri. $.75 newsstand; $37.80/yr. P.O. Box 700, Lexington Park, MD 20653. TEL 301-862-2111; FAX 301-737-2896. **Owner(s):** Chesapeake Publishing Corp., 29088 Airpark Dr., P.O. Box 600, Easton, MD 21601. TEL 410-822-1500; Ed. Donnie Morgan; Pub. Ralph Martin; adv. contact: Mickey Carlock. photos; pub. size: broadsheet; circ. 16,500(free & paid).

MONTGOMERY VILLAGE
US
VILLAGE NEWS. 1968. bi-w.: Fri. free newsstand; $25/yr. out of cy. 10120 Apple Ridge Rd., Montgomery Village, MD 20879. TEL 301-948-0110; FAX 301-990-7071. **Owner(s):** Montgomery Village Foundation, 10120 Apple Ridge Rd., Gaithersburg, MD 20879. TEL 301-948-0110; Ed. Dagmar Kane. adv.; pub. size: tabloid; circ. 12,000(controlled & paid).
 Formerly: Montgomery Village Foundation News.

OAKLAND
US
REPUBLICAN, THE. 1877. Thu. $.35 newsstand; $16.28/yr. local. 108 S. Second St., Oakland, MD 21550. TEL 301-334-3963; FAX 301-334-5904. **Owner(s):** Sincell Publishing Co., 108 S. Second St., Oakland, MD 21550. TEL 301-334-3963; FAX 301-334-5904; Ed. Donald W. Sincell; Pub. Robert B. Sincell; adv. contact: Lisa Rook. pub. size: broadsheet; circ. 11,500(controlled & paid).

OCEAN CITY
US
MARYLAND TIMES-PRESS. 1923. Wed. $.25 newsstand; $10.45/yr. local; $18/yr. out of area. 214 16th St., Ocean City, MD 21842. TEL 410-289-6834; FAX 410-289-6838; E-mail: atlantic@shore.intercom.net; URL: http://www.atbeach.com/mdtimes.html. **Owner(s):** Thomson Newspapers, Inc., Metro Ctr., One Station Pl., Stamford, CT 06902. TEL 203-425-2500; Ed. Joe Harris; Pub. Chris Eddings; adv. contact: Connie Taylor. pub. size: tabloid; circ. 5,500(paid).

POCOMOKE CITY
US
WORCESTER COUNTY MESSENGER. 1869. Wed. $.50 newsstand; $18/yr. in cy.; $30/yr. out of cy. 129 Market St., Pocomoke City, MD 21851. TEL 410-957-1700; FAX 410-957-4314. **Owner(s):** Thomson Newspapers, Inc., Metro Ctr., One Station Pl., Stamford, CT 06902. TEL 203-425-2500; Ed. Bill Kerbin. adv. contact: Donna Bloxom. photos; pub. size: broadsheet; circ. 3,250(paid).

POTOMAC
US
BETHESDA/CHEVY CHASE ALMANAC. Wed. free newsstand & home deliv.; $61.71/yr. mailed. 10220 River Rd., Potomac, MD 20854. TEL 301-983-3350; FAX 301-983-3923. **Owner(s):** DCI Publishing, Inc., 7670 Old Spring House Rd., McClean, VA 22101; Ed. Susan Pardys; Pub. Mary Kimm Dixon; adv. contact: Dan Laibstain. pub. size: tabloid; circ. 4,673(free & paid).

US
POTOMAC ALMANAC. 1957. Wed. free newsstand & home deliv.; $61.71/yr. mailed. 10220 River Rd., Ste. 303, Potomac, MD 20854. TEL 301-983-2600; FAX 301-983-3923. **Owner(s):** DCI Publishing, Inc., 7670 Old Spring House Rd., Mc Lean, VA 22102; Ed. James Currie; Pub. Mary Kimm Dixon; adv. contact: Dan Laibstain. photos; bk.rev.; pub. size: tabloid; circ. 20,522(free & paid).

PRINCE FREDERICK
US
RECORDER, THE. 1971. s-w.: Wed. & Fri. $.50 newsstand; $22.10/yr. in cy. 440 Main St., Prince Frederick, MD 20678. TEL 410-535-1214; FAX 410-535-5883. **Owner(s):** Chesapeake Publishing Corp., Airpark Dr., Easton, MD 21601. TEL 410-820-7070; Ed. Kevin Conron; Pub. Ralph Martin; adv. contact: Jeannie Green. pub. size: broadsheet; circ. 8,500(paid).

PRINCE FREDRICK
US
CALVERT INDEPENDENT. 1940. Wed. $.50 newsstand; $15.75/yr. in cy.; $21/yr. out of cy. 424 Soloman's Island Rd., Prince Fredrick, MD 20678. TEL 410-535-1575; FAX 410-855-9070. **Owner(s):** News World Communications, Inc., 401 Fifth Ave., New York, NY 10016. TEL 212-532-8300; adv. contact: Sandy Worsham. photos; pub. size: broadsheet; circ. 10,000(paid).

PRINCESS ANNE
US   ISSN 8756-6397
SOMERSET HERALD. 1826. Wed. $.50 newsstand; $18.90/yr.; $31.50/yr. elsewhere. 11763 Somerset Herald, Princess Anne, MD 21853. TEL 410-651-1600; FAX 410-651-3785. **Owner(s):** Thomson Newspapers, Inc., Metro Ctr., One Station Pl., Stamford, CT 06902. TEL 203-425-2500; Ed. R. Crumbacker; Pub. C. Eddings; adv. contact: D. Westbrook. photos; pub. size: broadsheet; circ. 5,800(free & paid).

SALISBURY
US
SALISBURY NEWS & ADVERTISER, THE. 1867. Wed. free newsstand; $15/yr. 307 E. Market St., Salisbury, MD 21801. TEL 410-749-0272; FAX 410-749-5073; E-mail: snapaper@aol.com. **Owner(s):** Independent Newspapers, Inc., P.O. Box 7001, Dover, DE 19903. TEL 302-674-4750; FAX 302-674-5910; Ed. Robin Adamopoulos; Pub. Anthony W. Bertino, Jr.; adv.; pub. size: broadsheet; circ. morning 13,511(free & paid).

SEABROOK
US
PRINCE GEORGES SENTINEL. 1932. Wed. $.25 newsstand; $15/yr. 9458 Lanham-Severn Rd., Ste. 203, Seabrook, MD 20706. TEL 301-306-9500; FAX 301-306-9596. **Owner(s):** Berlyn, Inc., P.O. Box 1247, Lanham, MD 20703. TEL 301-306-9500; FAX 301-306-9596; Ed. Lea Alexander Greve; Pub. Lynn Kapiloff; adv.; pub. size: tabloid; circ. 104,000(free & paid).

STEVENSVILLE
US
BAY TIMES. 1963. Wed. $.50 newsstand; $16.80/yr. in cy.; $21/yr. out of cy. 102 E. Main St., Ste. 101, Stevensville, MD 21666. TEL 410-643-7770; FAX 410-643-8374. **Owner(s):** Chesapeake Publishing Corp., Airpark Dr., Easton, MD 21601. TEL 410-820-7070; Ed. Angela Price; Pub. Larry Effingham; adv. contact: Franny Lynch. pub. size: tabloid; circ. 5,200(paid).

TIMONIUM
US
TIMES-HERALD. 1963. bi-w.: Thu. free; $15/yr. 2300 York Rd., Ste. 216, Timonium, MD 21093. TEL 410-453-0092; FAX 410-453-0065. **Owner(s):** JRM Incorp., 2300 York Rd., Ste. 216, Timonium, MD 21093. TEL 410-453-0092; Ed. Marina Brockman; Pub. Marina Brockman; adv. contact: Barbara Gray. photos; pub. size: tabloid; circ. 32,000(paid).

WEEKLY NEWSPAPERS

TOWSON

US
NORTHEAST REPORTER. 1949. Wed. free. 409 Washington Ave., Towson, MD 21204. TEL 410-337-2400; FAX 410-337-2490. **Owner(s):** Patuxent Publishing Co., 10750 Little Patuxent Pkwy., Columbia, MD 21044-3184. TEL 410-337-2400; FAX 410-337-2490; Ed. Angela Bornemann. adv. contact: Karleen Pate. pub. size: tabloid; circ. 18,000(controlled & free).

US ISSN 1041-0899
TOWSON TIMES. 1968. Wed. $.50 newsstand; free in cy.; $104/yr. mailed. 409 Washington Ave., Towson, MD 21204. TEL 410-337-2400; FAX 410-337-2490. **Owner(s):** Patuxent Publishing Co., 409 Washington Ave., Baltimore, MD 21204. TEL 410-337-2640; Ed. Len Lazarick; Pub. Zeke Orlinsky; adv. contact: Amy Newton. photos; pub. size: tabloid; circ. 39,000(free & paid).

UPPER MARLBORO

US
ENQUIRER-GAZETTE. Thu. $.25 newsstand; $10.50/yr. in cy.; $15.75/yr. out of cy. 14760 Main St., Upper Marlboro, MD 20773. TEL 301-627-2833; FAX 301-627-2835. **Owner(s):** Chesapeake Publishing Corp., P.O. Box 429, Elkton, MD 21922. TEL 410-398-3311; Ed. Joseph Norris; Pub. Ralph Martin; adv. contact: Joey Crossen. circ. 6,000(paid).

WALDORF

US
MARYLAND INDEPENDENT. 1872. s-w.: Wed. & Fri. $29.90/yr. 7 Industrial Park Dr., Waldorf, MD 20602. TEL 301-645-9480; FAX 301-645-2175. **Owner(s):** Chesapeake Publishing Corp., P.O Box 429, Elkton, MD 21922. TEL 410-398-3311; Ed. Angela Breck; Pub. Ralph Martin; adv. contact: Joey Crossen. pub. size: broadsheet; circ. 22,000(paid).

WESTMINSTER

US
COMMUNITY TIMES. 1928. Wed. $24.15/yr. 201 Railroad Ave., Westminster, MD 21157. TEL 410-876-4670; FAX 410-876-7084. **Owner(s):** Landmark Community Newspapers of Maryland, Inc., 201 Railroad Ave., Westminster, MD 21157. TEL 410-848-4400; FAX 410-876-7084; Ed. Brian Ditto; Pub. Robin Saul; adv. contact: Ron Thomas. photos; pub. size: broadsheet; circ. 13,580(free & paid).

MASSACHUSETTS

AMESBURY

US
AMESBURY NEWS. 1888. Fri. $.75 newsstand; $18/yr. 16 Millyard, Amesbury, MA 01913. TEL 508-388-2406; FAX 508-834-3151. **Owner(s):** Community Newspaper Co., 254 Second Ave., Meedham, MA 02194. TEL 617-433-6700; Ed. Jim Malone; Pub. Asa Cole; adv. contact: Mary Beth Gerard. pub. size: tabloid; circ. 3,557(paid).

US
MERRIMACK VALLEY SUNDAY. Sun. free. 16 Millyard, Amesbury, MA 01913. TEL 508-388-2406; FAX 508-834-3151. **Owner(s):** Community Newspaper Co., 254 Second Ave., Needham, MA 02194. TEL 508-433-6700; Ed. Jim Malone. adv. contact: Mary Beth Gerard. pub. size: standard.

ANDOVER

US
ANDOVER TOWNSMAN. 1887. Thu. $.75 newsstand; $37.50/yr. local; $42.50/yr. out of state. 33 Chestnut, Andover, MA 01810. TEL 508-475-1943; FAX 508-475-5731; E-mail: townsman2@aol.com; townsman@aol.com. **Owner(s):** Irving E. Rogers, Jr., 100 Turnpike St., North Andover, MA 01845. TEL 508-685-1000; Pub. Irving E. Rogers, III; adv.; bk.rev.; pub. size: tabloid; circ. 7,216(paid).

ARLINGTON

US
ARLINGTON ADVOCATE. 1872. Thu. $.75 newsstand; $31.75/yr. in cy.; $18.75/yr. senior citizens in cy. 5 Water St., Arlington, MA 02174. TEL 617-643-7900; FAX 617-641-5567. **Owner(s):** Community Newspaper Co., 245 Second Ave., Needham, MA 02194. TEL 617-433-6700; Ed. Tom Rose; Pub. Kirk Davis; pub. size: broadsheet; circ. 10,582(free & paid).

US
BELMONT CITIZEN-HERALD. 1919. Thu. $.75 newsstand; $31.75/yr. 5 Water St., Arlington, MA 02194. TEL 617-641-5560; FAX 617-641-5567. **Owner(s):** Community Newspaper Co., 254 Second Ave., Needham, MA 02194. TEL 617-433-6700; Ed. Chris Begley; Pub. Kirk Davis; adv. contact: Sue Wallace. pub. size: broadsheet; circ. 5,700(paid).

AUBURN

US
AUBURN NEWS. 1949. Wed. $.50 newsstand; $18/yr. local; $25/yr. out of town. One St. Mark St., Auburn, MA 01501. TEL 508-832-2222; FAX 508-832-2431. **Owner(s):** Stonebridge Press, Inc., 25 Elm St., Southbridge, MA 01550. TEL 508-764-4325; Ed. Ron McGilvray; Pub. David Cutler; adv. contact: Fran Boutilier. pub. size: tabloid; circ. 3,000(paid).

AYER

US
GROTON LANDMARK. Wed. $.75 newsstand; $39/yr. in state; $45/yr. out of state. 69 Fitchburg Rd., Ayer, MA 01432. TEL 508-772-0777; FAX 508-772-4012. **Owner(s):** Nashoba Publications, Inc., 69 Fitchburg Rd., Ayer, MA 01432. TEL 508-772-0777; Ed. Frank J. Hartnett, Jr.; Pub. Frank J. Hartnett, Sr.; pub. size: broadsheet; circ. 17,000.

US
HARVARD SPIRIT. Thu. $.75 newsstand; $39/yr. in state; $45/yr. out of state. 69 Fitchburg Rd., Ayer, MA 01432. TEL 508-772-0777; FAX 508-772-4012. **Owner(s):** Nashoba Publications, Inc., 60 Fitchburg Rd., Ayer, MA 01432. TEL 508-772-0777; Ed. Frank J. Hartnett, Jr.; Pub. Frank J. Hartnett, Sr.; pub. size: broadsheet; circ. 17,000.

US
PEPPERELL FREE PRESS. Wed. $.75 newsstand; $25/yr. in state; $45/yr. out of state. 69 Fitchburg Rd., Ayer, MA 01432. TEL 508-772-0777; FAX 508-772-4012. **Owner(s):** Nashoba Publications, Inc., 69 Fitchburg Rd., Ayer, MA 01432. TEL 508-772-0777; Ed. Frank Hartnett, Jr.; Pub. Frank J. Hartnett, Sr.; photos; bk.rev.; pub. size: broadsheet; circ. 17,000(free & paid).

US
PUBLIC SPIRIT. Wed. $.75 newsstand; $30/yr. in state; $45/yr. out of state. 69 Fitchburg Rd., Ayer, MA 01432. TEL 508-772-0777; FAX 508-772-4012. **Owner(s):** Nashoba Publications, Inc., 69 Fitchburg Rd., ayer, MA 01432. TEL 508-772-0777; Ed. Frank Hartnett, Jr.; Pub. Frank J. Hartnett, Sr.; adv. contact: C.Walmsley. pub. size: broadsheet; circ. 17,000.

US
TOWNSEND TIMES. 1869. Wed. $.75 newsstand; $25/yr. in state; $45/yr. out of state. 69 Fitchburg Rd., Ayer, MA 01432. TEL 508-772-0777; FAX 508-772-4012. **Owner(s):** Nashoba Publications, Inc., 69 Fitchburg Rd., Ayer, MA 01432. TEL 508-772-0777; FAX 508-772-4012; Ed. Frank Hartnett, Jr.; Pub. Frank J. Hartnett, Sr.; adv. contact: C.Walmsley. photos; bk.rev.; pub. size: broadsheet; circ. 17,000(free & paid).
Formerly: Times Free Press.

BELCHERTOWN

US
BELCHERTOWN SENTINEL. 1915. Thu. free local; $15/yr. out of town. 10 S. Main St., Belchertown, MA 01007. TEL 413-323-7040; FAX 413-323-9424. **Owner(s):** Turley Publications, 24 Water St., Palmer, MA 01069; Ed. Dave Anderson; Pub. Thomas A. Turley; pub. size: tabloid; circ. 8,500(paid).

BOLTON

US
BOLTON COMMON. 1988. Fri. $.75/newsstand; $28/yr. P.O. Box 8, Bolton, MA 01740. TEL 508-779-5113. **Owner(s):** Harvard Post Newspapers, Inc., 53 Bolton Rd., P.O. Box 308, Harvard, MA 01451. TEL 508-456-8122; Ed. Bill Latimer; Pub. Kathleen Cushman; adv. contact: Jodie Guerard. photos; bk.rev.; pub. size: tabloid; circ. 3,100(paid).

BOSTON

US
BAY STATE BANNER. 1965. Thu. $.50 newsstand; $20/yr.; $33/2 yrs. 68 Fargo St., Ste. 811, Boston, MA 02210-2122. TEL 617-357-4900; FAX 617-542-7119. **Owner(s):** Banner Publications, Inc., 68 Fargo St., Ste. 1811, Boston, MA 02210. TEL 617-357-4900; FAX 617-542-7119; Ed. Yawu Miller; Pub. Melvin B. Miller; adv. contact: Sandra Casagrand. pub. size: tabloid; circ. 10,500(paid).

US ISSN 0163-3015
BOSTON PHOENIX. 1966. Thu. $1.50 newsstand; $40/6 mos.; $75/yr. 126 Brookline Ave., Boston, MA 02215. TEL 617-859-3200; FAX 617-536-1313; E-mail: smindich@phx.com. **Owner(s):** Stephen M. Mindich, 126 Brookline Ave., Boston, MA 02215. TEL 617-859-3200; Ed. Cliff Garboden; Pub. Stephen M. Mindich; adv.; photos; bk.rev.; pub. size: tabloid; circ. 118,000(free & paid). **Wire Service(s):** AP.

BOSTON, MA

US
IMPROPER BOSTONIAN, THE. 1991. bi-w. $40/yr. 45 Newbury St., Ste. 509, Boston, MA 02116-3106. TEL 617-859-1400; FAX 617-859-1446; E-mail: improperb@aol.com. Owner(s): Improper Publications, Inc., 45 Newbury St., Ste. 509, Boston, MA 02116. TEL 617-859-1400; FAX 617-859-1446; Ed. Danielle Dubin. adv.; photos; bk.rev.; pub. size: tabloid; circ. 80,000(paid).

US
SOUTH BOSTON TRIBUNE. 1938. Thu. $23/yr. 395 W. Broadway, Boston, MA 02127. TEL 617-268-3440; FAX 617-268-6420. Owner(s): Daniel J. Horgan, P.O. Box 6, Boston, MA 02127. TEL 617-268-3440; Pub. Daniel J. Horgan; pub. size: broadsheet; circ. 8,500(paid). Wire Service(s): AP.

BRAINTREE

US
WEYMOUTH NEWS & GAZETTE. 1867. Wed. $.75 newsstand; $22/yr. 720 Union St., Braintree, MA 02185. TEL 617-337-1944; FAX 617-849-3319. Owner(s): Community Newspapers, Inc., 254 Second Ave., Needham, MA 02194. TEL 517-433-6700; Ed. Patsy Murray; Pub. Asa Cole; adv. contact: Tom Booth. pub. size: tabloid; circ. 5,400(paid).

CANTON

US
CANTON JOURNAL. 1876. Thu. $.75 newsstand; $24/yr. in cy.; $28/yr. out of cy. 12 Revere St., Canton, MA 02021. TEL 617-828-0006; FAX 617-828-9039. Owner(s): Community Newspaper Co., 254 Second Ave., Needham, MA 02194. TEL 617-433-6700; Ed. Marilyn Jackson; Pub. Asa Cole; adv.; pub. size: tabloid; circ. 4,500(paid).

CHELMSFORD

US
CHELMSFORD INDEPENDENT. 1952. Thu. $.75 newsstand; $28/yr. in cy.; $46/yr. out of cy. 15 Fletcher St., Chelmsford, MA 01824. TEL 508-256-7196; FAX 508-256-6111. Owner(s): Community Newspapers Co., 165 Enterprise Dr., Marshfield, MA 01742-6170. TEL 617-837-3500; Ed. Richard Lodge; Pub. Mark O'Neil; adv. contact: Jamie Tomasic. pub. size: tabloid; circ. 6,500(paid). Wire Service(s): AP.
Formerly: Chelmsford Newsweekly.

US
WESTFORD EAGLE. 1970. Thu. $.75 newsstand; $28/yr. in cy.; $46/yr. out of cy. 15 Fletcher St., Chelmsford, MA 01824. TEL 508-256-7196; FAX 508-256-6111. Owner(s): Community Newspaper Co., 150 Baker Ave. Extension, Ste. 305, Concord, MA 01742; Ed. Richard Lodge; Pub. Mark O'Neil; adv. contact: Jamie Tomasic. pub. size: broadsheet; circ. 3,700(paid).

CHICOPEE

US
CHICOPEE HERALD WEEKLY, THE. 1991. Thu. free. 143 E. Main St., Chicopee, MA 01020. TEL 413-592-1400; FAX 413-592-5286. Owner(s): John Maslar, P.O. Box 950, Chicopee, MA 01014. TEL 413-592-1400; FAX 413-592-5286; Ed. Joanne Despard; Pub. John Maslar; adv.: $10/SAU. photos; pub. size: tabloid; circ. 30,000(free).
Formerly: Herald-American.

CLINTON

US
ITEM. 1893. Fri. $.50 newsstand; $26/yr. 156 Church St., Clinton, MA 01510. TEL 508-368-0176; FAX 508-368-1151. Owner(s): Chronicle Publishing Co., 156 Church St., Clinton, MA 01510. TEL 508-368-0176; FAX 508-368-1157; Ed. Lisa Drueke; Pub. Frank R. Hewitt; adv. contact: Ron Chapdelaine. pub. size: broadsheet; circ. evening 6,000(paid). Wire Service(s): AP.
Formerly: Daily Item.

CONCORD

US ISSN 0744-7930
BEACON, THE. 1950. Thu. $.75 newsstand; $29/yr. in cy.; $45/yr. out of cy. 150 Baker Ave., Concord, MA 01722-9191. TEL 508-369-2800; FAX 508-371-9058. Owner(s): Community Newspaper Co., 82 Devonshire St., Boston, MA 02109. TEL 508-728-6553; Ed. Richard K. Lodge; Pub. Mark O'Neil; adv. contact: Jamie Tomasic. pub. size: broadsheet; circ. 5,344(paid).

US
BEDFORD MINUTEMAN. 1958. Thu. $.75 newsstand; $29/yr. in cy.; $46/yr. out of cy. 150 Baker Ave. Ext., Concord, MA 01742. TEL 617-861-9110; FAX 617-863-8662. Owner(s): Community Newspaper Co., 254 Second Ave., Needham, MA 02194. TEL 617-837-3500; FAX 617-872-2131; Ed. Richard Lodge; Pub. Mark O'Neil; adv. contact: Jamie Tomasic. pub. size: broadsheet; circ. 3,500(paid).

US
CONCORD JOURNAL. Thu. $.75 newsstand; $29/yr. in cy.; $45/yr. out of cy. 150 Baker Ave., Ste. 305, Concord, MA 01720. TEL 508-369-2800; FAX 508-371-9058. Owner(s): Community Newspaper Co., 82 Devonshire St., Boston, MA 02109. TEL 617-728-6553; Ed. Lucile Daniels; Pub. Mark O'Neil; adv. contact: Allan Mushliz. pub. size: broadsheet; circ. 5,575(paid).

US
LITTLETON INDEPENDENT. 1950. Thu. $.75 newsstand; $28/yr. in cy.; $46/yr. out of cy. 150 Baker Ave. Ext., Concord, MA 01742. TEL 508-369-2800; FAX 508-371-9058. Owner(s): Community Newspaper Co., 82 Devonshire St., Boston, MA 02109. TEL 617-728-6553; Ed. Richard Lodge; Pub. Mark O'Neil; adv. contact: Jamie Tomasic. photos; pub. size: broadsheet; circ. 1,760(paid).

US
MAYNARD BEACON. 1950. Thu. $.75 newsstand; $25/yr. in cy.; $45/2 yrs. 150 Baker Ave., Ste. 305, Concord, MA 01742. TEL 508-369-2800; FAX 508-264-9396. Owner(s): Community Newspaper Co., 82 Devonshire St., Boston, MA 02109. TEL 617-728-6553; Ed. June Morgon; Pub. Mark O'Neil; adv. contact: Allan Mushliz. pub. size: broadsheet; circ. 2,743(paid).

DANVERS

US
DANVERS HERALD. 1863. Thu. $.75 newsstand; $18/yr. 152 Sylvan St., Danvers, MA 01923. TEL 508-774-0505; FAX 508-774-6365. Owner(s): Community Newspaper Co., 254 Second Ave., Needham, MA 02194. TEL 617-837-3500; FAX 617-872-2131; Ed. Howard Iverson; Pub. Asa Cole; adv. contact: Mary Beth Gerard. pub. size: tabloid; circ. 5,500(paid).

WEEKLY NEWSPAPERS

US
NORTH SHORE SUNDAY. 1977. Sun. free newsstand; $31/yr. mailed. 152 Sylvan St., Danvers, MA 01923-0293. TEL 508-774-0505; FAX 508-774-6365. Owner(s): Community Newspaper Co., 254 Second Ave., Needham, MA 02194-0293. TEL 617-837-3500; FAX 617-872-2131; Ed. Jim Malone; Pub. Charles F. Goodrich; adv. contact: Mary Beth Gerard. photos; pub. size: tabloid; circ. 111,000(free & paid). Wire Service(s): AP Newsfinder.
Formerly: North Shore.

US
TRI-TOWN TRANSCRIPT. 1959. Thu. $.75 newsstand; $24/yr. 152 Sylvan St., Danvers, MA 01923. TEL 508-739-1300; FAX 508-762-9767. Owner(s): Community Newspaper Co., 254 Second Ave., Needham, MA 02194. TEL 617-837-3500; FAX 617-872-2131; Ed. Faye Raynard; Pub. Charles F. Goodrich; adv.; pub. size: tabloid; circ. 4,244(paid).

DEDHAM

US
PARKWAY TRANSCRIPT. 1929. Wed. $.75 newsstand; $20/yr. mailed in cy.; $25/yr. mailed out of cy. 367 Washington St., Dedham, MA 02026. TEL 617-327-2608; FAX 617-326-9675. Owner(s): Community Newspaper Co., 254 Second Ave., Needham, MA 02194. TEL 617-433-6700; Ed. James Harder; Pub. Asa Cole; adv.; pub. size: broadsheet; circ. 4,500(paid).

US
WEST ROXBURY TRANSCRIPT. 1941. Wed. $.50 newsstand; $20/yr. mailed in cy.; $25/yr. mailed out of cy. 367 Washington St., Dedham, MA 02026. TEL 617-327-2608; FAX 617-326-9675. Owner(s): Community Newspaper Co., 254 Second Ave., Needham, MA 02194. TEL 617-433-6700; Ed. James Harder; Pub. Asa Cole; adv.; pub. size: broadsheet; circ. 9,000(paid).

DRACUT

US ISSN 8750-1341
DRACUT DISPATCH, THE. 1973. Thu. $.35 newsstand; $14/yr. 434 Textile Ave., Dracut, MA 01826. TEL 508-957-0007; FAX 508-457-1051. Owner(s): William J. Themelis, 434 Textile Ave., Dracut, MA 01826; Geraldine Themelis, 434 Textile Ave., Dracut, MA 01826; Ed. Geraldine Katin; Pub. Geraldine Themelis; adv. contact: Geraldine Katin. photos; bk.rev.; pub. size: tabloid; circ. 6,600(paid).

EAST BRIDGEWATER

US
EAST BRIDGEWATER STAR. 1812. Thu. $.50 newsstand; $17.50/yr. in cy.; $14.50/yr. senior citizens. 232 Broad St., East Bridgewater, MA 02324. TEL 508-697-2881; FAX 508-947-1763. Owner(s): Independent Newspapers, Inc., 25 Center St., Middleboro, MA 02346. TEL 508-947-0031; Ed. Terence Egan; Pub. John Anderson; adv.; bk.rev.; pub. size: tabloid; circ. 600(paid).

WEEKLY NEWSPAPERS

EDGARTOWN
US

VINEYARD GAZETTE. 1846. s-w.: Tue. & Fri. summer; Fri. winter. $.50 newsstand; $37/yr. in cy. 34 S. Summer St., Edgartown, MA 02539. TEL 508-627-4311; FAX 508-627-7444; E-mail: gazette@vineyard.net; URL: http://www.vineyard.net/biz/gazette. **Owner(s):** Richard & Mary Jo Reston, S. Summer St., Edgartown, MA 02539. TEL 508-627-4311; Ed. Richard Reston; Pub. Eileen Holley; adv. contact: Eileen Holley. adv.: $1,735/pg. photos; bk.rev.; pub. size: broadsheet; circ. 13,500(paid).

FALMOUTH
US ISSN 0744-2114

ENTERPRISE, THE. 1895. s-w.: Tue. & Fri. $.50 newsstand; $42.50/yr. in cy.; $45/yr. out of cy. 50 Depot Ave., Falmouth, MA 02541. TEL 508-548-4700; FAX 508-540-8407. **Owner(s):** Falmouth Publishing, 50 Depot Ave., Falmouth, MA 01541. TEL 508-540-4700; Ed. Janice Walford; Pub. Margaret H. Russell; adv. contact: Christopher Megan. pub. size: broadsheet; circ. 10,500(paid).

FOXBORO
US

FOXBORO REPORTER, THE. 1884. Thu. $.50 newsstand; $22/yr.; $32/yr. foreign; $18/yr. senior citizens; $29/yr. senior citizens foreign. 36 Mechanic St., Foxboro, MA 02035. TEL 508-543-4851; FAX 508-543-4888. **Owner(s):** Sun Chronicle, S. Main St., Attleboro, MA 02703; Ed. Jeffrey Peterson; Pub. Paul Rixon; adv. contact: Edward Wilson. pub. size: broadsheet; circ. 5,000(paid).

GREAT BARRINGTON
US

BERKSHIRE RECORD. 1989. Thu. $.50 newsstand; $20/yr. in cy.; $24/yr. outside cy. 21 Elm St., Great Barrington, MA 01230. TEL 413-528-5380; FAX 413-528-9449. **Owner(s):** Anthony & Donna Prisendorf, 21 Elm St., Great Barrington, MA 01230. TEL 413-528-5380; FAX 413-528-9449; Ed. Donna Prisendorf; Pub. Anthony Prisendorf; adv. contact: Jim Hurley. photos; bk.rev.; pub. size: broadsheet; circ. 4,500(paid).

HATFIELD
US

VALLEY ADVOCATE. 1973. Thu. free; $80/yr. mailed. 87 School St., Hatfield, MA 01038. TEL 413-247-9301. **Owner(s):** New Mass Media, Inc., 87 School St., Hatfield, MA 01038. TEL 413-247-9301; Ed. Dan Caccavaro; Pub. Geofrey Robinson; adv.; pub. size: standard; circ. 65,000(free & paid).

HYANNIS
US ISSN 0744-7221

BARNSTABLE PATRIOT, THE. 1830. Thu. $.75 newsstand; $21/yr. 326 Main St., Hyannis, MA 02601. TEL 508-771-1427; FAX 508-790-3997; E-mail: barnpat@cape.com. **Owner(s):** Robert F. & Anne G. Sennott, 326 Main St., P.O. Box 1208, Hyannis, MA 02601. TEL 508-771-1427; Ed. David Still, II; Pub. Anne G. Sennott; adv. contact: Lucinda Harrison. adv.: $8.75/SAU. photos; pub. size: broadsheet; circ. 3,000(paid).

IPSWICH
US

GEORGETOWN RECORD. 1982. Wed. $.75 newsstand; $20/yr. local; $33/yr. out of area. 2 Washington St., Ipswich, MA 01938. TEL 508-352-7288; FAX 508-412-1564. **Owner(s):** Community Newspaper Co., 82 Devonshire St., Boston, MA 02109. TEL 508-728-6553; Ed. Ted Wadsworth; Pub. Charles Goodrich; adv.; pub. size: broadsheet; circ. 2,000(paid).

US

HAMILTON-WENHAM CHRONICLE. 1949. Wed. $.75 newsstand; $28/yr. in cy.; $35/yr. out of cy. 2 Washington St., Ipswich, MA 01938. TEL 617-837-3500; FAX 617-872-2131. **Owner(s):** Community Newspaper Co., 254 Second Ave., Needham, MA 02194. TEL 617-837-3500; FAX 617-872-2131; Ed. Sasha Paulsen; Pub. Charles Goodrich; adv. contact: John Vistorino. pub. size: tabloid; circ. 2,706(paid).

US

IPSWICH CHRONICLE. 1872. Thu. $.75 newsstand; $28/yr. in cy.; $35/yr. out of cy. 2 Washington St., Ipswich, MA 01938. TEL 508-356-5141; FAX 508-412-1564. **Owner(s):** Community Newspaper Co., 254 Second Ave., Needham, MA 02194. TEL 617-837-3500; FAX 617-872-2131; Ed. Janet McKay Smith; Pub. Charles F. Goodrich; adv.; pub. size: tabloid; circ. 4,644(paid).

LEE
US

BERKSHIRE PENNY SAVER. 1963. Tue. free. 14 Park Pl., Lee, MA 01238-0300. TEL 413-243-2341; FAX 413-243-4662. **Owner(s):** J.W. McWhirk Publishers, Inc., 14 Park Pl., P.O. Box 300, Lee, MA 01238-0300. TEL 413-243-2341; FAX 413-243-4662; adv.: $5.75/SAU. photos; pub. size: tabloid; circ. 16,000(controlled & free).

LYNN
US

SUNDAY POST. 1960. Sun. $.75 newsstand; $45/yr. 617-619 Chestnut St., Lynn, MA 01904. TEL 617-592-4600; FAX 617-592-1811. **Owner(s):** Community Newspaper Co., 254 Second Ave., Needham, MA 02194. TEL 617-837-3500; FAX 617-872-2131; Pub. Charles Goodrich; pub. size: broadsheet; circ. 5,000(paid); Sun. 7,500(paid).

MANSFIELD
US

MANSFIELD NEWS. 1873. Fri. $.35 newsstand; $23/yr. local; $28/yr. out of area. 154 Copeland Dr., Mansfield, MA 02048. TEL 508-339-8977; FAX 508-339-0340. **Owner(s):** Community Newspaper Co., 254 Second Ave., P.O. Box9112, Needham, MA 02048. TEL 617-433-8200; Ed. Garreth Charter; Pub. Kirk Davis; adv. contact: Sean Burke. pub. size: tabloid; circ. 3,600(paid).

MARBLEHEAD
US

MARBLEHEAD REPORTER. 1871. Thu. free home deliv.; $33/yr. mailed. 40 South St., Ste. 100, Marblehead, MA 01945. TEL 617-631-7700; FAX 617-639-4801. **Owner(s):** Community Newspaper Co., 2 Washington St., P.O. Box 192, Ipswich, MA 01938. TEL 617-356-5141; FAX 617-872-2131; Ed. Bruce Brock; Pub. Charles F. Goodrich; adv. contact: Barbara Silva. photos; pub. size: tabloid; circ. 10,442(free & paid).

US

SWAMPSCOTT REPORTER. 1871. Thu. $.75 newsstand; $24/yr. 40 South St., Ste. 100, Marblehead, MA 01945. TEL 617-631-7700; FAX 617-639-4801. **Owner(s):** Community Newspaper Co., 254 Second Ave., Needham, MA 02194. TEL 617-837-3500; FAX 617-872-2131; Ed. Jim Malone; Pub. Charles F. Goodrich; adv. contact: Robert Tisi. pub. size: tabloid; circ. 4,000(paid).

MARION
US

SENTINEL, THE. 1963. Thu. $.50 newsstand; $18/yr. in cy.; $30/yr. out of cy. 312 Wareham Rd., Marion, MA 02738. TEL 508-748-1123; FAX 508-748-1128; E-mail: mpgnews@aol.com; URL: http://www.mpgnews.com/plymouth. **Owner(s):** G.W. Prescott Publishing Co., 400 Crown Colony Dr., Quincy, MA 02169. TEL 617-786-7000; Pub. Phyllis J. Hughes; adv.: $7.95/SAU. photos; bk.rev.; pub. size: tabloid; circ. 2,558(paid).

US

WAREHAM COURIER. 1894. Thu. $.75 newsstand; $21/yr. in cy.; $32/yr. out of cy. 312 Wareham Rd., Marion, MA 02738-0959. TEL 508-748-1123; FAX 508-748-1128; E-mail: mpgnews@aol.com; URL: http://www.mpgnews.com/plymouth. **Owner(s):** G.W. Prescott Publishing Co., 400 Crown Colony Dr., Quincy, MA 02169. TEL 617-786-7000; Pub. Phyllis J. Hughes; adv.: $9.95/SAU. photos; bk.rev.; pub. size: tabloid; circ. 5,109(paid).

MARSHFIELD
US

BRAINTREE FORUM. 1877. Wed. $.75 newsstand; $20/yr. 165 Enterprise Dr., Marshfield, MA 02050. TEL 617-837-3500; FAX 617-837-9619. **Owner(s):** Community Newspaper Co., 165 Enterprise Dr., Marshfield, MA 02050. TEL 617-466-1800; Ed. Cathy Conley; Pub. Asa Cole; adv. contact: Amy Dwyer. pub. size: tabloid; circ. 3,500(paid).

US

COHASSET MARINER. 1978. Wed. $.75 newsstand; $26/yr. 165 Enterprise Dr., Marshfield, MA 02050. TEL 617-837-3500; FAX 617-837-4541. **Owner(s):** Fidelity Investments, 82 Devonshire St., Boston, MA 02109. TEL 617-563-7000; Ed. Mary Ford; Pub. Asa Cole; adv. contact: Amy Dwyer. pub. size: tabloid; circ. 1,772(controlled & paid).

US ISSN 0745-7960

HANOVER MARINER. 1981. Wed. $.75 newsstand; $26/yr. 165 Enterprise Dr., Marshfield, MA 02050. TEL 617-837-3500; FAX 617-837-4540. **Owner(s):** Fidelity Investments, 82 Devonshire St., Boston, MA 02109. TEL 617-563-7000; Ed. Judy Enright; Pub. Asa Cole; adv. contact: Amy Dwyer. pub. size: tabloid; circ. 2,314(paid).

MARSHFIELD, MA

US ISSN 0745-6301
HINGHAM JOURNAL & MARINER. 1867. Thu. $.75 newsstand; $26/yr. 165 Enterprise Dr., Marshfield, MA 02050. TEL 617-749-0031; FAX 617-837-4541. **Owner(s):** Fidelity Investments, 82 Devonshire St., Boston, MA 02109. TEL 617-563-7000; Ed. Mary Ford; Pub. Asa Cole; adv. contact: Amy Dwyer. pub. size: broadsheet; circ. 4,443(controlled & paid).
Formerly: Hingham Journal.

US
HOLBROOK SUN. 1958. Wed. $.75 newsstand; $21/yr. 165 Enterprise Dr., Marshfield, MA 02050. TEL 617-837-3500; FAX 617-837-4541. **Owner(s):** Fidelity Investments, 82 Devonshire St., Boston, MA 02109. TEL 617-563-7000; Ed. Cathy Conley; Pub. Asa Cole; adv. contact: Amy Dwyer. pub. size: tabloid; circ. 1,882(paid).

US
KINGSTON INDEPENDENT. 1976. Wed. free. 165 Enterprise Dr., Marshfield, MA 02050. TEL 617-837-3500; FAX 617-837-4541. **Owner(s):** Fidelity Investments, 82 Devonshire St., Boston, MA 02109. TEL 617-563-7000; Ed. Cathy Conley. adv. contact: Amy Dwyer. pub. size: tabloid; circ. 3,000(controlled & paid).
Formerly: Marina & Independent Voice.

US
MARSHFIELD MARINER. 1972. Wed. $.75 newsstand; $26/yr. 165 Enterprise Dr., Marshfield, MA 02050. TEL 617-837-3500; FAX 617-837-4541. **Owner(s):** Fidelity Investments, 82 Devonshire St., Boston, MA 02109. TEL 617-563-7000; Ed. Bob Rodgers; Pub. Asa Cole; adv. contact: Amy Dwyer. pub. size: tabloid; circ. 4,339(controlled & paid).

US
NORWELL MARINER. 1974. Wed. $.75 newsstand; $26/yr. in town; $30/yr. out of town; $24/yr. senior citizens. 165 Enterprise Dr., Marshfield, MA 02050. TEL 617-837-3500; FAX 617-837-4541. **Owner(s):** Community Newspaper Co., 254 Second Ave., Needham, MA 02194. TEL 617-837-3500; FAX 617-872-2131; Ed. Judy Enright; Pub. Asa Cole; adv. contact: Paul Farrell. pub. size: tabloid; circ. 2,100(paid).

US
PEMBROKE MARINER. 1983. Wed. $.75 newsstand; $21/yr. 165 Enterprise Dr., Marshfield, MA 02050. TEL 617-837-3500; FAX 617-837-4541. **Owner(s):** Fidelity Investments, 82 Devonshire St., Boston, MA 02109. TEL 617-563-7000; Ed. Paula Woodhull; Pub. Asa Cole; adv. contact: Amy Dwyer. pub. size: tabloid; circ. 1,229(paid).

US
WEYMOUTH NEWS. 1867. Thu. $.75 newsstand; $20/yr. in cy; $25/yr. in state. 165 Enterprise Dr., Marshfield, MA 02050. TEL 617-837-3500; FAX 617-837-9619. **Owner(s):** Community Newspaper Co., 165 Enterprise Dr., Marshfield, MA 02050. TEL 617-466-1800; Ed. Patsy Murray; Pub. Asa Cole; adv. contact: Amy Dwyer. pub. size: tabloid; circ. 4,365(paid).

MELROSE

US
MELROSE FREE PRESS. 1901. Thu. $.50 newsstand; $26/yr. in area; $35/yr. out of area. 40 W. Foster St., Melrose, MA 02176. TEL 617-665-4000; FAX 617-979-5671. **Owner(s):** Community Newspaper Co., 254 Second Ave., Needham, MA 02194. TEL 617-837-3500; FAX 617-872-2131; Ed. Marie Lingblom; Pub. Chuck Goodrich; pub. size: broadsheet; circ. 6,500(paid).

US
SAUGUS ADVERTISER. 1881. Thu. $.50 newsstand; $23/yr. in area; $35/yr. out of area. 40 W. Foster St., Melrose, MA 02176. TEL 617-665-4000; FAX 617-979-5671. **Owner(s):** Community Newspaper Co., 254 Second Ave., Needham, MA 02194. TEL 617-837-3500; FAX 617-872-2131; Ed. Sue Ellen Woodcock; Pub. Chuck Goodridge; pub. size: broadsheet; circ. 5,000(paid).

MIDDLEBORO

US ISSN 1050-0936
BRIDGEWATER INDEPENDENT. 1856. Thu. $.50 newsstand; $17.50/yr.; $14.50/yr. senior citizens. 25 Center St., Middleboro, MA 02346. TEL 508-697-2881; FAX 508-947-1763. **Owner(s):** Independent Newspapers, Inc., 25 Center St., Middleboro, MA 02346. TEL 508-947-0031; Ed. Terence Egan; Pub. John Anderson; adv.; photos; pub. size: standard; circ. 2,500(paid).

US
CAPEWAY NEWS. 1955. Tue. free deliv. 25 Center St., Middleboro, MA 02346. TEL 508-947-1111; FAX 508-947-1763. **Owner(s):** Franklin Publishing Co., 65 Grove St., Middleboro, MA 02346. TEL 508-947-1763; Ed. Terrance Egan; Pub. John Anderson; adv.; photos; bk.rev.; pub. size: tabloid; circ. 22,000(free).

US
LAKEVILLE INDEPENDENT. 1985. Thu. $.50 newsstand; $17.50/yr.; $14.50/yr. senior citizens. 25 Center St., Middleboro, MA 02346. TEL 508-947-0031; FAX 508-947-1763. **Owner(s):** Independent Newspapers, Inc., 25 Center St., Middleboro, MA 02346. TEL 508-947-0031; FAX 508-947-1763; Ed. Terrence Egan; Pub. John Anderson; adv.; pub. size: tabloid; circ. 1,400(paid).

US
MIDDLEBORO GAZETTE. 1852. Thu. $.50 newsstand; $20/yr. in cy. 148 W. Grove St., Middleboro, MA 02346. TEL 508-947-1760. **Owner(s):** Hathaway Publishing Corp., 780 County St., Somerset, MA 02726. TEL 617-674-4656; Ed. Jane Lopes; Pub. Warren Hathaway; adv. contact: Jay Vogel. photos; pub. size: broadsheet; circ. 6,073(paid).

US
TAUNTON INDEPENDENT. Thu. $.50 newsstand; $17.50/yr.; $14.50/yr. senior citizens. 25 Center St., Middleboro, MA 02346. TEL 508-947-0031; FAX 508-947-1763. **Owner(s):** Independent Newspapers, Inc., 25 Center St., Middleboro, MA 02346. TEL 508-947-0031; Ed. Terrence Egan; Pub. John Anderson; adv.; pub. size: tabloid; circ. 1,400(paid).

US
WEST BRIDGEWATER STAR. 1812. Thu. $.50 newsstand; $17.50/yr. in cy.; $14.50/yr. senior citizens. 25 Center St., Middleboro, MA 02346. TEL 508-697-2881; FAX 508-947-1763. **Owner(s):** Independent Newspapers, Inc., 25 Center St., Middleboro, MA 02346. TEL 508-947-0031; Ed. Terrence Egan; Pub. John Anderson; adv.; photos; pub. size: tabloid; circ. 350(paid).

MILLBURY

US
MILLBURY/SUTTON CHRONICLE. 1986. Thu. $.35 newsstand; $9/yr. 117 Elm St., Millbury, MA 01527. TEL 508-865-1645. **Owner(s):** Andree Belisle, 117 Elm St., Millbury, MA 01527. TEL 508-865-1645; Ed. Andree Belisle; Pub. A.G. Belisle; adv. contact: A.G. Belisle. photos; bk.rev.; pub. size: tabloid; circ. 2,000(paid).

MILTON VILLAGE

US
MILTON RECORD TRANSCRIPT. 1900. Fri. $.50 newsstand; $20/yr. in cy.; $22/yr. out of cy. 26 High St., Milton Village, MA 02186. TEL 617-361-6500; FAX 617-361-8909. **Owner(s):** Tribune Publications, 1261 Hyde Park Ave., Hyde Park, MA 02136. TEL 617-361-6500; Ed. Daniel J. Horgan Jr.; Pub. Daniel J. Horgan Jr.; adv. contact: Karen Willette. photos; pub. size: broadsheet; circ. 5,900(paid).

NANTUCKET

US
INQUIRER & MIRROR, THE. 1821. Thu. $.75 newsstand; $34/yr. on Isl.; $42/yr. out of area; $95/yr. foreign; $26/yr. students (Sept.-June). One Old South Rd., Nantucket, MA 02554. TEL 508-228-0001; FAX 508-325-5089; E-mail: mstanton@nantucket.net; URL: http://www.nantucket.net/InkyM/. **Owner(s):** Ottaway Newspapers, Inc., P.O. Box 401, Campbell Hall, NY 10916. TEL 914-294-8181; Ed. Marianne Giffin Stanton; Pub. Marianne Giffin Stanton; adv. contact: Denese Allen. pub. size: broadsheet; circ. 8,900(paid).

US ISSN 1046-6304
NANTUCKET BEACON. 1989. Wed. $.75 newsstand; $35/yr. 64 Old South Rd., Nantucket, MA 02554. TEL 508-228-8455; FAX 508-228-8994; E-mail: staff@nantucketbeacon.com; URL: http://www.nantucketbeacon.com. **Owner(s):** Ottaway Newspapers Inc., P.O. Box 401, Campbell Hall, NY 10916. TEL 914-294-8181; Ed. Don Costanzo; Pub. Scott Himstead; adv. contact: Keith Connolly. photos; bk.rev.; pub. size: broadsheet; circ. 6,000(paid).

NEEDHAM

US
DOVER-SHERBORN SUBURBAN PRESS. 1958. Thu. $30/yr. 992 Great Plain Ave., Needham, MA 02192. TEL 617-444-1706; FAX 617-444-1795; E-mail: dover@suburbanworld.com. **Owner(s):** Suburban World, Inc., 992 Great Plain Ave., Needham, MA 02192. TEL 617-444-1706; Ed. Elizabeth Banks; Pub. William Barrett; adv. contact: R. Shomphe, Jr. pub. size: tabloid; circ. 6,000(paid).

WEEKLY NEWSPAPERS

US
MEDFIELD SUBURBAN PRESS. 1932. Thu. $.75 newsstand; $32/yr. local; $39/yr. out of area. 992 Great Plain Ave., Needham, MA 02192. TEL 617-359-4278; FAX 617-359-4223. **Owner(s):** Suburban World, Inc., 992 Great Plain Ave., Needham, MA 02192. TEL 617-444-1706; Ed. Susan O'Keefe; Pub. William Barrett; adv. contact: Bob Shomphe. pub. size: tabloid; circ. 7,100(controlled & paid).

US
NATICK BULLETIN. 1865. Thu. $.75 newsstand; $32/yr. in town; $39/yr. out of town. 992 Great Plain Ave., Needham, MA 02192. TEL 617-653-4460; FAX 617-444-1795. **Owner(s):** Suburban World, Inc., 992 Great Plain Ave., Needham, MA 02192. TEL 617-444-1706; Ed. Joyce Bain; Pub. William Barrett; adv. contact: Bob Shomphe. pub. size: tabloid; circ. 4,500(paid).

US
SUDBURY TOWN CRIER. 1951. Thu. $.75 newsstand; $29/yr. local; $31.25 out of area; $34.50/yr. out of state. 254 Second Ave., Needham, MA 02194. TEL 617-443-8948; FAX 617-433-7835. **Owner(s):** Community Newspaper Co., 254 Second Ave., Needham, MA 02194. TEL 508-443-8948; Ed. Andrea Haynes. adv.; pub. size: tabloid; circ. 3,637(paid).

US
TAB, THE. 1979. Tue. free. 254 Second Ave, Needham, MA 02192. TEL 617-969-0340; FAX 617-433-8202. **Owner(s):** Community Newspaper Co., 254 Second Ave., Needham, MA 02194. TEL 617-433-6700; Ed. George Donnolly; Pub. Kirk Davis; adv. contact: Cris Warren. pub. size: tabloid; circ. 146,000(free).

US
WAYLAND-WESTON TOWN CRIER. 1951. Thu. $29/yr.; $34.50/yr. mailed; $26.50/yr. senior citizens. 254 Second Ave., Needham, MA 02194. TEL 617-443-8948; FAX 617-433-7835. **Owner(s):** Fidelity Investments, P.O. Box 109, Mansfield, MA 02048. TEL 508-339-8977; Ed. Andrea Haynes; Pub. Kirk Davis; pub. size: tabloid; circ. 6,500(paid).

NORTH BILLERICA

US
BILLERICA MINUTEMAN. 1971. Thu. $.50 newsstand; $24/yr. in cy. 2 Survey Cir., North Billerica, MA 01862. TEL 508-369-2800; FAX 508-262-9947. **Owner(s):** Community Newspaper Co., 254 Second Ave., Needham, MA 02194. TEL 617-837-3500; FAX 617-872-2131; Ed. Daniel Fellini; Pub. Mark O'Neil; adv. contact: Donna Rice. pub. size: broadsheet; circ. 5,403(paid).

NORTH DARTMOUTH

US
CHRONICLE, THE. 1969. Wed. $.50 newsstand; $19/yr. in cy.; $32/yr. out of cy. 45 Slocum Rd., North Dartmouth, MA 02747-0268. TEL 508-992-1522; FAX 508-992-1689. **Owner(s):** Hathaway Publishing Corp., P.O. Box 80268, South Dartmouth, MA 02748-0268. TEL 617-992-1522; Ed. Susan Gonsalves; Pub. Warren Hathaway; adv.; pub. size: broadsheet; circ. 6,500(paid).
Formerly: Dartmouth Chronicle.

ORLEANS

US
CAPE CODDER. 1946. s-w.: Tue. & Fri. $.75 newsstand; $32/yr. on the Cape; $47/yr. off the Cape. 5 Namskaket Rd., Orleans, MA 02653. TEL 508-255-2121; FAX 508-240-0333. **Owner(s):** Community Newspaper Co., 254 Second Ave., Needham, MA 02194. TEL 617-837-3500; FAX 617-872-2131; Ed. Victoria Ogden; Pub. Victoria Ogden; pub. size: tabloid; circ. 13,500(paid).

US
HARWICH ORACLE. 1986. Thu. $.50 newsstand; $19.95/yr. on the Cape; $26.95/yr. off the Cape. 5 Namskaket Rd., Orleans, MA 02653. TEL 508-255-1212; FAX 508-240-0333. **Owner(s):** Community Newspaper Co., 254 Second Ave., Needham, MA 02194. TEL 617-433-6700; Ed. Victoria Ogden; Pub. Victoria Ogden; adv.; pub. size: tabloid; circ. 4,000(controlled & paid).

US
SANDWICH BROADSIDER. 1974. Thu. $.50 newsstand $19.95/yr. in town; $26.95/yr. out of town. 5 Namskaket Rd., Orleans, MA 02653. TEL 508-255-2121; FAX 508-240-0333. **Owner(s):** Community Newspaper Co., 254 Second Ave., Needham, MA 02194. TEL 617-433-6700; Ed. Victoria Ogden; Pub. Victoria Ogden; adv. contact: George Martin. pub. size: tabloid; circ. 3,907(paid).

PALMER

US
JOURNAL REGISTER. 1850. Thu. $.50 newsstand; $28/yr. in state; $32/yr. out of state. 24 Water St., Palmer, MA 01069. TEL 413-283-8393; FAX 413-289-1977. **Owner(s):** Turley Publications, Inc., 24 Water St., Palmer, MA 01069. TEL 413-283-8393; Ed. Tina McNaughton. pub. size: broadsheet; circ. 5,000(paid).

US
LUDLOW REGISTER. 1946. Wed. free newsstand; $25/yr. in state; $28/yr. out of state. 24 Water St., Palmer, MA 01069. TEL 413-583-3095; FAX 413-289-1977. **Owner(s):** Turley Publications, Inc., 24 Water St., Palmer, MA 01069. TEL 413-283-8393; Ed. Tina McNaughton. pub. size: tabloid; circ. 11,800(free).

US
STATE LINE SHOPPING GUIDE. 1962. Tue. free. 24 Water St., Palmer, MA 01069. TEL 413-283-8393; FAX 413-289-1977. **Owner(s):** Turley Publications, Inc., 24 Water St., Palmer, MA 01069. TEL 413-283-1977; Ed. Tina McNaughton; Pub. Patrick H. Turley; pub. size: tabloid; circ. 14,300(free).

PITTSFIELD

US
PITTSFIELD GAZETTE, THE. 1991. Thu. $20/yr. in cy.; $30/yr. out of cy.; $20 in city. 38 West St., Pittsfield, MA 01201. TEL 413-443-2010; FAX 413-443-2445. **Owner(s):** Pittsfield Gazette, Inc., 38 West St., Pittsfield, MA 01201. TEL 413-443-2010; FAX 413-443-2445; Ed. Jonathan Levine; Pub. Jonathan Levine; adv.; photos; pub. size: tabloid; circ. 8,000(free & paid).

PLYMOUTH, MA 10627

PLYMOUTH

US
CARVER REPORTER. 1988. Thu. $.75 newsstand; $15/yr. in cy.; $32/yr. out of cy. 9 Long Pond Rd., Plymouth, MA 02360-0959. TEL 508-746-5555; FAX 508-747-2148; E-mail: mpgnews@aol.com; URL: http://www.mpgnews.com/plymouth. **Owner(s):** G.W. Prescott Publishing Co., 400 Crown Colony Dr., Quincy, MA 02169. TEL 617-786-7000; Pub. Phyllis J. Hughes; adv.: $7.25/SAU. photos; bk.rev.; pub. size: tabloid; circ. 2,708(paid).

US   ISSN 0899-6229
DUXBURY REPORTER. 1987. Wed. free newsstand; $32/yr. out of cy. 9 Long Pond Rd., Plymouth, MA 02360-0959. TEL 508-746-5555; FAX 508-747-2148; E-mail: mpgnews@aol.com; URL: http://www.mpgnews.com/plymouth. **Owner(s):** G.W. Prescott Publishing Co., 400 Crown Colony Dr., Quincy, MA 02169. TEL 617-786-7000; Pub. Phyllis J. Hughes; adv.: $7.45/SAU. photos; bk.rev.; pub. size: tabloid; circ. 4,938(free).

US
HALIFAX REPORTER. 1984. Thu. $.75 newsstand; $20/yr. in cy.; $32/yr. out of cy. 9 Long Pond Rd., Plymouth, MA 02360-0959. TEL 508-746-5555; FAX 508-747-2148; E-mail: mpgnews@aol.com; URL: http://www.mpgnews.com/plymouth. **Owner(s):** G.W. Prescott Publishing Co., 400 Crown Colony Dr., Quincy, MA 02169. TEL 617-786-7000; Pub. Phyllis J. Hughes; adv.: $6.85/SAU. photos; bk.rev.; pub. size: tabloid; circ. 1,456(free & paid).
Formerly: Halifax-Plympton Reporter.

US
KINGSTON REPORTER. 1984. Thu. mailed free to residents; $.75 newsstand; $32/yr.out of cy. 9 Long Pond Rd., Plymouth, MA 02360-0959. TEL 508-746-5555; FAX 508-747-2148; E-mail: mpgnews@aol.com; URL: http://mpgnews.com/plymouth. **Owner(s):** G.W. Prescott Publishing Co., 400 Crown Colony Dr., Quincy, MA 02169. TEL 617-786-7000; Pub. Phyliss J. Hughes; adv.: $7.45/SAU. photos; bk.rev.; pub. size: tabloid; circ. 3,768(free).

US
MARSHFIELD REPORTER. 1984. Thu. free newsstand; mailed free to town residents; $32/yr. out of cy. 9 Long Pond Rd., Plymouth, MA 02362-0959. TEL 508-746-5555; FAX 508-747-2148; E-mail: mpgnews@aol.com; URL: http://www.mpgnews.com/plymouth. **Owner(s):** G.W. Prescott Publishing Co., 400 Crown Colony Dr., Quincy, MA 02169. TEL 617-786-7000; Pub. Phyllis J. Hughes; adv.: $7.45/SAU. photos; bk.rev.; pub. size: tabloid; circ. 6,364(free).

US
OLD COLONY MEMORIAL. 1822. Thu. $1 newsstand; $29/yr. in cy.; $42/yr. out of cy. 9 Long Pond Rd., Plymouth, MA 02360-0959. TEL 508-746-5555; FAX 508-747-2148; E-mail: mpgnews@aol.com; URL: http://www.mpgnews.com/plymouth. **Owner(s):** G.W. Prescott Publishing Co., 400 Crown Colony Dr., Quincy, MA 02169. TEL 617-786-7000; Pub. Phyllis J. Hughes; adv.: $17.95/SAU. photos; bk.rev.; pub. size: broadsheet; circ. 12,388(paid).

10628   PLYMOUTH, MA   **WEEKLY NEWSPAPERS**

US
PEMBROKE REPORTER. 1983. Thu. $.75 newsstand; $20/yr. in cy.; $32/yr. out of cy. 9 Long Pond Rd., Plymouth, MA 02360-0959. TEL 508-746-5555; FAX 508-747-2148; E-mail: mpgnews@aol.com; URL: http://www.mpgnews.com/plymouth. **Owner(s):** G.W. Prescott Publishing Co., 400 Crown Colony Dr., Quincy, MA 02169. TEL 617-786-7000; Pub. Phyllis J. Hughes; adv.: $6.85/SAU. photos; bk.rev.; pub. size: tabloid; circ. 1,606(paid).

PROVINCETOWN
US
PROVINCETOWN ADVOCATE. 1869. Thu. $1 newsstand; $28.50/yr. 100 Bradford St., Provincetown, MA 02657. TEL 508-487-1170; FAX 508-487-3878. **Owner(s):** Hometown Newspapers, 323 E. Grand River, Howell, MI 48843. TEL 517-548-2003; Ed. Duane A. Steele; Pub. Duane A. Steele; pub. size: tabloid; circ. 12,000(paid).

QUINCY
US
QUINCY SUN. 1968. Thu. $.35 newsstand; $14/yr. in town; $16/yr. out of town; $19/yr. out of state. 1372 Hancock St., Quincy, MA 02169. TEL 617-471-3100; FAX 617-472-3963. **Owner(s):** Henry W. Bosworth, 1372 Hancock St., Quincy, MA 02169. TEL 617-471-3100; Ed. Robert Bosworth; Pub. Henry W. Bosworth; adv. contact: Mark Crosby. pub. size: tabloid; circ. 7,000(paid).

REVERE
US   ISSN 1054-6529
CHELSEA RECORD. 1890. s-w.: Wed. & Fri. $.35 newsstand; $29/yr. in town; $55/yr. out of town. 327 Broadway, Revere, MA 02151. TEL 617-284-2400; FAX 617-289-5352. **Owner(s):** Journal Transcript Newspapers, 327 Broadway, Revere, MA 02151. TEL 617-284-2400; Ed. Ed Coletta; Pub. Lincoln McKie; adv. contact: Charles Anderson. pub. size: broadsheet; circ. 5,000(paid).

US
REVERE JOURNAL. 1881. Wed. $.50 newsstand; $19/yr. local; $29/yr. elsewhere. 327 Broadway, Revere, MA 02151. TEL 617-284-2400; FAX 617-289-5352. **Owner(s):** Journal Transcript Newspapers, 327 Broadway, Revere, MA 02151. TEL 617-284-2400; Ed. Dave Procopio; Pub. Linc McKie; adv. contact: Charlie Anderson. pub. size: standard; circ. 9,000(paid).

ROCKLAND
US
SOUTH SHORE NEWS. 1965. Mon. free. 65 Grove St., Rockland, MA 02370. TEL 617-878-5100; FAX 617-878-1318. **Owner(s):** Franklin Publishing Co., Mayflower Dr., Hanover, MA 02339. TEL 617-878-3444; FAX 617-878-1318; Ed. Michael Lenny; Pub. John Anderson; adv.; photos; bk.rev.; pub. size: tabloid; circ. 70,729(controlled & paid).

SHARON
US
SHARON ADVOCATE. 1873. Fri. $.50 newsstand; $23/yr. in town; $28/yr. out of town; $17/yr. senior citizens. 28-A S. Main St., Sharon, MA 02067. TEL 617-784-2131; FAX 617-784-6724. **Owner(s):** Community Newspapers, 254 Second Ave., Needham, MA 02194. TEL 617-784-2131; Ed. Gareth Charter; Pub. Kirk Davis; adv. contact: Sean Burke. pub. size: broadsheet; circ. 4,326(paid).

SOMERSET
US
SPECTATOR, THE. 1932. Wed. $.50 newsstand; $22/yr. 780 County St., Somerset, MA 02726. TEL 508-674-4656; FAX 508-677-1210. **Owner(s):** Hathaway Publishing Corp., 780 County St., Somerset, MA 02726. TEL 508-674-4656; Ed. George Austin; Pub. Warren G. Hathaway; adv.; bk.rev.; pub. size: broadsheet; circ. 8,000(free & paid).

SOMERVILLE
US
CAMBRIDGE CHRONICLE. 1846. Thu. $.75 newsstand; $26/yr. in cy.; $35/yr. out of cy.; $17/yr. senior citizens. 240 A. Elm St., Ste. 20, Somerville, MA 02144. TEL 617-629-3380; FAX 617-629-3381. **Owner(s):** Fidelity Investments, 82 Devonshire St., Boston, MA 02019. TEL 617-728-6488; Ed. John Breneman; Pub. Kirk Davis; pub. size: broadsheet; circ. 9,500(paid).

US
WATERTOWN TAB & PRESS. 1955. Thu. $.75 newsstand; $26/yr. in cy.; $35/yr. out of cy.; $17/yr. senior citizens. 240A Elm St., Ste. 20, Somerville, MA 02144. TEL 617-629-3380; FAX 617-629-3381. **Owner(s):** Fidelity Investments, 82 Devonshire St., Rm. 25 C, Boston, MA 02109; pub. size: broadsheet; circ. 4,500(paid).
Formerly: Watertown Press.

SPENCER
US
NEW LEADER. 1977. Wed. $24/yr. in state; $36/yr. out of state; $20/yr. senior citizens. 369 Main St., Spencer, MA 01562. TEL 508-885-5041; FAX 508-885-4213. **Owner(s):** Stonebridge Press, Inc., 475 Washington St., Auburn, MA 01501. TEL 617-832-5876; Ed. Laurie Griggs. adv.; pub. size: tabloid; circ. 3,500(paid).

US
WICK-QUA-BOAG WEEKLY. 1955. Fri. free. 369 Main St., Spencer, MA 01562. TEL 508-885-9402; FAX 508-885-4213. **Owner(s):** Stonebridge Press, Inc., 25 Elm St. , Southbridge, MA 01550. TEL 508-764-4325; Ed. Laurie Griggs; Pub. John Coots; adv. contact: Fran Leppanen. pub. size: tabloid; circ. 15,800(free).

SPRINGFIELD
US
SPRINGFIELD ADVOCATE. 1975. Thu. free newsstand; $80/yr. mailed. 1127 Main St., Springfield, MA 01103. TEL 413-781-1900; FAX 413-781-1906. **Owner(s):** New Mass Media, Inc., 87 School St., Hatfield, MA 01038. TEL 413-247-9301; Ed. Dan Caccavaro; Pub. Kathy Nylic; adv. contact: Kathy Nylic. pub. size: tabloid; circ. 38,750(free & paid).

STOUGHTON
US
ASSOCIATED NEWSPAPER. Wed. $.25 newsstand; $19.50/yr. 7 Cabot Pl., Stoughton, MA 02072. TEL 617-341-1111; FAX 617-341-9475. **Owner(s):** Franklin Publishing Co., 66 W. Grove St., Middleboro, MA 02346. TEL 508-697-2881; Ed. Michael Lenney; Pub. Richard Dailey; adv. contact: Chris MacDonald. photos; bk.rev.; pub. size: tabloid; circ. 20,000(paid).

US
EASTON BULLETIN. 1929. Wed. $.25 newsstand; $19.50/yr.; $35.50/2 yrs. 1044 Central St., Stoughton, MA 02072. TEL 617-341-1111; FAX 617-341-9475. **Owner(s):** Richard R. Dailey, 1044 Central St., Stoughton, MA 02072. TEL 617-341-1111; FAX 617-341-9475; Ed. Michael Lenney; Pub. Richard R. Dailey; adv. contact: Richard R. Dailey. bk.rev.; pub. size: tabloid; circ. 1,916(paid).

US
HOLBROOK TIMES. 1929. Wed. $.25 newsstand; $19.50/yr.; $35.50/2 yrs. 1044 Central St., Stoughton, MA 02072. TEL 617-341-1111; FAX 617-341-9475. **Owner(s):** Associated Newspapers, 1044 Central St., Stoughton, MA 02072. TEL 617-341-1111; FAX 617-341-9475; Ed. Michael Lenny; Pub. Richard R. Dailey; adv. contact: Richard R. Dailey. bk.rev.; pub. size: tabloid; circ. 700(paid).

US
NORTON COURIER. 1986. Wed. $.25 newsstand; $19.50/yr.; $35.50/2 yrs. 1044 Central St., Stoughton, MA 02072. TEL 617-341-1111; FAX 617-341-9475. **Owner(s):** Associated Newspapers, 1044 Central St., Stoughton, MA 02072. TEL 617-341-1111; FAX 617-341-9475; Ed. Michael Lenney; Pub. Richard R. Dailey; adv. contact: Richard R. Dailey. bk.rev.; pub. size: tabloid; circ. 1,270(paid).

US
RAYNHAM JOURNAL. 1982. Wed. $.25 newsstand; $19.50/yr.; $35.50/2 yrs. 1044 Central St., Stoughton, MA 02072. TEL 617-341-1111; FAX 617-341-9475. **Owner(s):** Associated Newspapers, 7 Cabot Pl., Stoughton, MA 02072; Ed. Michael Lenney; Pub. Richard R. Dailey; adv.; bk.rev.; pub. size: tabloid; circ. 505(paid).

US
STOUGHTON CHRONICLE. 1861. Wed. $.25 newsstand; $19.50/yr.; $35.50/2 yrs. 1044 Central St., Stoughton, MA 02072-0441. TEL 617-341-1111; FAX 617-341-9475. **Owner(s):** Associated Newspapers, 1044 Central St., Stoughton, MA 02072. TEL 617-341-1111; FAX 617-341-1194; Ed. Michael Lenney. adv. contact: C. MacDonald. bk.rev.; pub. size: tabloid; circ. 4,469(paid).

US
WHITMAN TIMES. 1873. Wed. $19.50/yr.; $35/2 yrs. 7 Cabot Pl., Stoughton, MA 02072. TEL 617-341-1111; FAX 617-341-1194. **Owner(s):** Associated Newspapers, 7 Cabot Pl., Stoughton, MA 02072. TEL 617-341-1111; Ed. Michael Lenney. adv. contact: C. MacDonald. bk.rev.; pub. size: tabloid; circ. 552(paid).

WEEKLY NEWSPAPERS

TOWNSEND

US

MAIN STREET TRILOGY. 1991. Wed. $.50 newsstand; $.50/wk. deliv.; $17.50/50 wks. 8 Jefts St., Townsend, MA 01469-0571. TEL 508-597-5465; FAX 508-597-5365. **Owner(s):** Mary-Flora & Robert E. Hale, P.O. Box 571, Townsend, MA 01469. TEL 508-597-5465; FAX 508-597-5365; Ed. David Henshaw. adv.: $6.50/SAU. photos; bk.rev.; pub. size: tabloid; circ. 12,500(free & paid).

WALPOLE

US

WALPOLE TIMES, THE. 1915. Thu. $.50 newsstand; $25/yr. in cy. mailed; $30/yr. out of cy. 7 West St., Walpole, MA 02081. TEL 508-668-0243; FAX 508-668-5174. **Owner(s):** Harris D. Lang, 257 Elm St., Walpole, MA 02081. TEL 617-668-0243; Ed. Bill Bilodeau; Pub. Jack Authelet; adv. contact: Albie Nudel. pub. size: broadsheet; circ. 6,100(paid).

WALTHAM

US   ISSN 0739-3849

NEWTON GRAPHIC. 1872. Wed. $.50 newsstand; $22/yr. in cy.; $24/yr. out of cy. 99 Moody St., Waltham, MA 02154. TEL 617-398-8000; FAX 617-398-8010. **Owner(s):** Community Newspaper Co., 254 Second Ave., Needham, MA 02194. TEL 617-433-6700; Ed. Ellen Ishkanian; Pub. Asa Cole; adv. contact: Robert Cardosa. photos; pub. size: tabloid; circ. 28,000(free & paid). **Wire Service(s):** AP.

WARE

US

WARE RIVER NEWS. 1888. Thu. $.50 newsstand; $21/yr. 4 Church St., Ware, MA 01082. TEL 413-967-3505. **Owner(s):** Ware River News, Inc., 4 Church St., Ware, MA 01082. TEL 413-967-3505; Ed. Glenn H. Ickler; Pub. Patrick H. Turley; adv. contact: Margaret Stacy. photos; pub. size: broadsheet; circ. 4,000(paid).

WEBSTER

US

SOUTH COUNTY WEEKENDER. 1962. Sat. free. 8-10 Mechanic St., Webster, MA 01570. TEL 508-943-4800; FAX 508-943-5524. **Owner(s):** Stonebridge Press, Inc., 25 Elm St., Southbridge, MA 01550. TEL 508-764-4325; Ed. Heather Sill; Pub. John Coots; adv. contact: Sandra Warner. pub. size: tabloid; circ. 17,000(free).
Formerly: South County Advertiser.

US

WEBSTER TIMES, THE. 1859. Wed. $.50 newsstand; $24/yr. in cy.; $36/yr. out of cy.; $20/yr. senior citizens. 8-10 Mechanic St., Webster, MA 01570. TEL 508-943-4800; FAX 508-943-5524. **Owner(s):** Stonebridge Press, Inc., 25 Elm St., Southbridge, MA 01550. TEL 508-764-4325; Ed. Heather Sill; Pub. John Coots; adv. contact: Sandra Warner. pub. size: broadsheet; circ. 5,400(paid).
Formerly: Times, The.

WELLESLEY

US

WELLESLEY TOWNSMAN. 1906. Thu. $.75 newsstand; $29.75 local mailed. One Crest Rd., Wellesley, MA 02181. TEL 617-431-2000; FAX 617-431-2001. **Owner(s):** Community Newspapers, Inc., 254 Second Ave., Needham, MA 02194. TEL 617-433-6700; Ed. Cathy Brauner; Pub. Kirk Davis; adv.; pub. size: standard; circ. 9,000.

WESTFIELD

US

LONGMEADOW NEWS. Thu. $.40 newsstand; $14/6 mos.; $20/yr.; $17/yr. senior citizens. 62-64 School St., Westfield, MA 01086. TEL 413-562-4181; FAX 413-562-4185. **Owner(s):** Westfield News Publishing Co., 62-64 School St., Westfield, MA 01085. TEL 413-562-4181; Ed. Maria Trombley; Pub. Carol Mazza; pub. size: standard; circ. 2,700(paid).

WEST SOMERVILLE

US

SOMERVILLE JOURNAL. 1870. Thu. $.75 newsstand; $26/yr. in cy; $35/yr. out of cy.;$17/yr. senior citizens. 240 A. Elm St., Ste. 20, West Somerville, MA 02144. TEL 617-629-3380; FAX 617-629-3381. **Owner(s):** Fidelity Investments, 82 Devonshire St., Boston, MA 02109. TEL 617-728-6488; pub. size: broadsheet; circ. 8,000(paid).

WEST SPRINGFIELD

US

WEST SPRINGFIELD RECORD. 1953. Thu. $11/yr. in cy.; $24/yr. out of cy. 516 Main St., West Springfield, MA 01089. TEL 413-736-1587. **Owner(s):** Marie A. Coburn, 516 Main St., W. Springfield, MA 01089. TEL 413-736-1587; FAX 413-739-2477; Ed. Thomas Coburn. adv.; pub. size: tabloid; circ. 5,500(paid).

WHITINSVILLE

US   ISSN 0745-8673

BLACKSTONE VALLEY TRIBUNE. 1976. s-w.: Wed. & Fri. $.50 Wed. newsstand; free Fri. newsstand; $24/yr.; $20/yr. senior citizens. 110 Church St., Whitinsville, MA 01588. TEL 508-234-2107; FAX 508-234-7506. **Owner(s):** Stonebridge Press, Inc., 475 Washington St., Auburn, MA 01501. TEL 617-832-5876; Ed. Deborah Gauthier; Pub. David Cutler; adv.; photos; pub. size: tabloid; circ. 5,500 (free & paid).

US

WEEKENDER, THE. Fri. free home deliv. 60 Church St., Whitinsville, MA 01588. TEL 508-234-5686; FAX 508-234-7506. **Owner(s):** Stonebridge Press, Inc., 25 Elm St., Southbridge, MA 01550. TEL 508-764-4325; Ed. Debbie Gauthier; Pub. David Cutler; adv. contact: Cindy Crozier. photos; pub. size: tabloid; circ. 13,000(free).

WILLIAMSTOWN

US

ADVOCATE/SOUTH ADVOCATE, THE. 1982. Wed. $100/yr. P.O. Box 95, Williamstown, MA 01267. TEL 413-458-9000; FAX 413-458-5715. **Owner(s):** Ellen J. Bernstein, P.O. Box 95, Wiliamstown, MA 01267. TEL 413-458-9000; FAX 413-458-5715; Ed. Mark Rondeau; Pub. Ellen J. Bernstein; adv. contact: Gail King. photos; pub. size: tabloid; circ. 21,750(free & paid).

WILMINGTON

US

WILMINGTON-TEWKSBURY TOWN CRIER. 1955. Wed. $.50 newsstand; $20/yr. local. 104 Lowell St., Wilmington, MA 01887. TEL 508-658-2346; FAX 508-658-2266. **Owner(s):** Woburn Daily Times, Inc., 104 Lowell St., Wilmington, MA 01887. TEL 508-658-2346; Ed. C. Stuart Neilson; Pub. Peter Haggerty; adv. contact: John O'Neil. pub. size: broadsheet; circ. 7,081(controlled & paid).

WINCHENDON

US

WINCHENDON CHRONICLE. 1800. Wed. $.50 newsstand; $24/yr. in cy.; $36/yr. out of cy. 110 Front St., Winchendon, MA 01475. TEL 508-297-0050; FAX 508-297-2177. **Owner(s):** Stonebridge Press, Inc., 25 Elm St., Southbridge, MA 01550. TEL 508-987-0754; Ed. Kris Spofford; Pub. David Cutler; adv. contact: Mary Delaney. pub. size: tabloid; circ. 3,000(paid).
Formerly: Jaffrey-Rindge Chronicle.

US

WINCHENDON COURIER. 1800. Wed. $.50 newsstand; $24/yr. in cy.; $36/yr. out of cy.; $20/yr. senior citizens. 20 Front St., Winchendon, MA 01475. TEL 508-297-0050; FAX 508-297-2177. **Owner(s):** Stonebridge Press, Inc., 25 Elm St., Southbridge, MA 01550. TEL 508-764-4325; Ed. Kristen Spofford; Pub. David Cutler; adv. contact: Fran Boutileir. pub. size: broadsheet; circ. 2,500(paid).

WOBURN

US

BURLINGTON UNION. 1956. Thu. $.50 newsstand; $24/yr. in cy.; $42/yr. out of cy. 186 Cambridge Rd., Woburn, MA 01801. TEL 617-229-0918; FAX 617-863-8662. **Owner(s):** Community Newspaper Co., 254 Second Ave., Needham, MA 02194-5080. TEL 617-433-6700; Ed. Richard Lodge; Pub. Mark O'Neil; adv. contact: Jamie Tomasic. pub. size: broadsheet; circ. 4,000(paid).
Formerly: Burlington News.

US

LEXINGTON MINUTEMAN. 1871. Thu. $.75 newsstand; $24/yr. in cy.; $42/yr. out of cy. 186 Cambridge Rd., Woburn, MA 01801. TEL 617-229-0918; FAX 617-863-8662. **Owner(s):** Community Newspaper Co., 254 Second Ave., Needham, MA 02194. TEL 617-837-3500; FAX 617-872-2131; Ed. Richard K. Lodge; Pub. Mark O'Neil; adv. contact: Jamie Tomasic. pub. size: broadsheet; circ. 8,200(paid).

US

WINCHESTER STAR. 1880. Thu. $.75 newsstand; $24/yr. mailed; $18/yr. senior citizens. 186 Cambridge Rd., Woburn, MA 01801. TEL 617-729-6100; FAX 617-939-3441. **Owner(s):** Fidelity Investments, 82 Devonshire St., Boston, MA 02019; Ed. Nancy Schwalbert; Pub. Paul Farrell; adv. contact: Paul Farrell. pub. size: broadsheet; circ. 6,000(paid).

US   ISSN 1071-9806

WOBURN ADVOCATE. 1991. Thu. $.50 newsstand; $39/yr. 186 Cambridge Rd., Woburn, MA 01801. TEL 617-937-8000; FAX 617-939-3441. **Owner(s):** Community Newspaper Co., 254 Second Ave., Needham, MA 02194. TEL 617-433-6700; Ed. Larry Walsh; Pub. Mark O'Neil; adv.; photos; pub. size: tabloid; circ. 17,250(paid).

WORCESTER

US   ISSN 0191-4960
WORCESTER MAGAZINE. 1976. Wed. free newsstand; $26/yr. 3rd class. 172 Shrewsbury St., Worcester, MA 01604. TEL 508-755-8004; FAX 508-755-8860. **Owner(s):** Allen Fletcher, 172 Shrewsbury St., Worcester, MA 01604. TEL 508-755-8004; FAX 508-755-8860; Paul Giorgio, 172 Shrewsbury St., Worcester, MA 01604. TEL 508-755-8004; FAX 508-755-8860; Peter Stanton, 172 Shrewsbury St., Worcester, MA 01604. TEL 508-755-8004; FAX 508-755-8860; Ed. Walter Crockett; Pub. Peter Stanton; adv. contact: Mark Murray. photos; bk.rev.; pub. size: tabloid; circ. 40,000(free & paid).

YARMOUTH

US
MASHPEE MESSENGER. 1985. Thu. free. 923 G, Rte. 6A, Yarmouth, MA 02675. TEL 508-362-2111; FAX 508-240-0333. **Owner(s):** Community Newspaper Co., 254 Second Ave., Needham, MA 02194. TEL 617-433-6700; Ed. Victoria Ogden; Pub. Victoria Ogden; adv.; pub. size: tabloid; circ. 4,600(free).

YARMOUTHPORT

US
BOURNE COURIER. 1976. Thu. $.50 newsstand; $19.95/yr. in cy.; $26.95/yr. out of cy. 923 G, Rte. 6A, Yarmouthport, MA 02675. TEL 508-362-2111; FAX 508-240-0333. **Owner(s):** Community Newspaper Co., 254 Second Ave., Needham, MA 02194. TEL 617-433-6700; Pub. Victoria Ogden; adv. contact: George Martin. pub. size: tabloid; circ. 7,000(paid).

US
PENNYSAVER, THE. 1964. Wed. free. 923 G Main St., Sun Flower Market Pl., Yarmouthport, MA 02675-0716. TEL 508-833-2930; FAX 508-375-4901. **Owner(s):** Fidelity Investments, 82 Devonshire St., Boston, MA 02109. TEL 617-563-7000; Pub. Asa Cole; pub. size: tabloid; circ. 209,000(free & paid).

US
REGISTER, THE. 1836. Thu. $.50 newsstand; $18.95/yr. mailed on Cape Cod. 923 G, Rte. 6A, Yarmouthport, MA 02675. TEL 508-362-2111; FAX 508-675-4901. **Owner(s):** Community Newspaper Co., 923 G, Rte 6A, Yarmouthport, MA 02675. TEL 508-362-1111; Ed. Asa Cole; Pub. Victoria Ogden; adv. contact: Jim Horvath. pub. size: tabloid; circ. 12,048(paid).
Formerly: Yarmouth Register Sun.

MICHIGAN

ALLEGAN

US
ALLEGAN COUNTY NEWS. 1882. Thu. $.50 newsstand; $18/yr. in cy.; $23/yr. out of cy.; $27/yr. out of state. 231 Trowbridge St., Allegan, MI 49010. TEL 616-673-5534; FAX 616-673-5535. **Owner(s):** Kaechele Publications, Inc., P.O. Box 189, Allegan, MI 49010. TEL 616-673-5534; Ed. Dave Trinka. adv.; pub. size: broadsheet; circ. 6,500.
Formerly: Allegan County News & Gazette.

ALPENA

US
ALPENA STAR. 1972. Sun. free. 431 Ripley Blvd., Alpena, MI 49707. TEL 517-356-2121. **Owner(s):** Star Publications, P.O. Box 620, Gaylord, MI 49735. TEL 517-732-5125; Pub. James R. Glasser; adv. contact: Mike Adams. adv.: $6.23/SAU. pub. size: tabloid; circ. 18,921(free).
Formerly: Alpena Advertiser.

BATTLE CREEK

US
BATTLE CREEK SHOPPER. 1947. Thu. free in area. 1361 E. Columbia, Battle Creek, MI 49014. TEL 616-965-3955; FAX 616-968-8586. **Owner(s):** J-Ad Graphics, Inc., 1952 N. Broadway, Hastings, MI 49058. TEL 616-965-3955; FAX 616-945-5192; Ed. Joyce Ryan; Pub. Fred Jacobs; adv.; photos; bk.rev.; pub. size: tabloid; circ. 50,855(controlled & paid).

BAY CITY

US
VALLEY FARMER, THE. 1929. Thu. $.50 newsstand; $18/yr. 905 S. Henry, Bay City, MI 48706. TEL 517-893-6507. **Owner(s):** David Hebert, 905 S. Henry, Bay City, MI 48706. TEL 517-893-6507; Ed. Mark Schanhals; Pub. David Hebert; adv.; photos; pub. size: tabloid; circ. 2,100(paid).

BEULAH

US
AD-VISOR. 1966. Sun. free home deliv.; $20/yr. out of area mailed. 254 S. Benzie Blvd., Beulah, MI 49617. TEL 616-882-9613; FAX 616-882-9615. **Owner(s):** Noverr Publications Inc., P.O. Box 797, Beulah, MI 49617. TEL 616-882-9613; Ed. Joe Noverr; Pub. Frank Noverr; pub. size: tabloid; circ. 8,600(free & paid).

BIG RAPIDS

US
LAKE COUNTY STAR. Thu. $.50 newsstand; $18/yr. in cy.; $28/yr. out of cy. 502 N. State St., Big Rapids, MI 49307. TEL 616-796-4831; FAX 616-796-1152. **Owner(s):** Pioneer Group, 502 N. State St., Big Rapids, MI 49307. TEL 616-796-4831; FAX 616-796-1152; Ed. Jim Bruskotter. adv. contact: D. Clasen. photos; pub. size: tabloid; circ. 2,850(paid). **Wire Service(s):** AP.

US
LAKEVIEW ENTERPRISE. Wed. $.50 newsstand; $18/yr. in cy. 502 N. State St., Big Rapids, MI 49307. TEL 616-796-4831; FAX 616-796-1152. **Owner(s):** Pioneer Group, 502 N. State St., Big Rapids, MI 49307. TEL 616-796-4831; FAX 616-796-1152; Ed. Jim Bruskotter. adv. contact: Sharon Fredricks. photos; pub. size: broadsheet; circ. 1,300(paid).

BIRMINGHAM

US
BIRMINGHAM ECCENTRIC, THE. 1970. s-w.: Mon. & Thu. $.75 newsstand; $42/yr. 805 E. Maple, Birmingham, MI 48009. TEL 810-644-1100; FAX 810-644-1314. **Owner(s):** Suburban Communications Corp., 36251 Schoolcraft Rd., Livonia, MI 48150. TEL 313-591-2300; Ed. Bob Sklar. adv. contact: Kathy Hirschfield. pub. size: broadsheet; circ. 18,000(paid).

US
BLOOMFIELD ECCENTRIC, THE. s-w.: Thu. & Sun. $.75 newsstand; $42/yr. in cy. 805 E. Maple, Birmingham, MI 48009. TEL 810-644-1100; FAX 810-644-1314. **Owner(s):** Suburban Communications Corp., 36251 Schoolcraft Rd., Livonia, MI 48150. TEL 313-591-2300; Ed. Bob Sklar. adv. contact: Kathy Hirschfield. pub. size: broadsheet; circ. 85,000(paid).
Formerly: West Bloomfield Eccentric.

US
SOUTHFIELD ECCENTRIC. 1949. s-w.: Mon. & Thu. $.75 newsstand; $42/yr. in cy. 805 E. Maple, Birmingham, MI 48009. TEL 810-644-1100; FAX 810-591-9202. **Owner(s):** Suburban Communications Corp., 36251 Schoolcraft Rd., Livonia, MI 48150. TEL 313-591-2300; Ed. Bob Sklar. adv. contact: Kathy Hirschfield. pub. size: broadsheet; circ. 13,000(paid).

US
ST. CLAIR SHORES HERALD. 1973. Thu. $6/yr.; $10/2 yrs.; $14/3 yrs. 2648 Dorchester Rd., Birmingham, MI 48009-5989. TEL 810-649-0749. **Owner(s):** Detroit Northeast Detroiter, 2648 Dorchester Rd., Birmingham, MI 48009. TEL 810-649-0749; Ed. Lloyd Saulter; Pub. Lloyd Saulter; adv. contact: Kevin Saulter. pub. size: broadsheet; circ. 8,900(paid).

BLISSFIELD

US
BLISSFIELD ADVANCE. 1874. Wed. $.50 newsstand; $20/yr. local; $30/yr. out of state. 121 Newspaper St., Blissfield, MI 49228. TEL 517-486-2400. **Owner(s):** Marcia Loader, 121 Newspaper St., Blissfield, MI 49228. TEL 517-486-2400; Ed. Doug Goodnough; Pub. Marcia Loader; adv.; photos; bk.rev.; pub. size: tabloid; circ. 2,800(paid).

BOYNE CITY

US
CITIZEN, THE. 1879. Wed. $.50 newsstand; $22/yr. in cy.; $32/yr. out of cy. 112 S. Park, Boyne City, MI 49712. TEL 616-582-6761; FAX 616-582-6762. **Owner(s):** Husan Publishing Co., P.O. Box A, Boyne City, MI 49712. TEL 616-582-6761; FAX 616-582-6762; Pub. Hugh Conklin; adv.; photos; bk.rev.; pub. size: broadsheet; circ. 3,000(free & paid).
Formerly: Charlevoix County Press.

BRIGHTON

US
BRIGHTON ARGUS. Wed. $.50 newsstand; $26/yr. in cy. mailed. 113 E. Grand River, Brighton, MI 48116. TEL 810-227-0171; FAX 810-227-0175. **Owner(s):** Hometown Newspapers, 323 E. Grand River, Howell, MI 48843. TEL 517-548-2000; Ed. Buddy Morehouse. adv. contact: John Utter. pub. size: broadsheet; circ. 13,000(paid).

BROOKLYN

US
EXPONENT, THE. 1881. Tue. $.50 newsstand; $25/yr. 160 S. Main St., Brooklyn, MI 49230. TEL 517-592-2122; FAX 517-592-3241. **Owner(s):** Schepeler Corp., 160 S. Main, Brooklyn, MI 49230. TEL 517-592-2122; Ed. Joyce Brown; Pub. Matt Schepeler; adv. contact: Sharon Coffman. pub. size: tabloid; circ. 5,000(paid).

WEEKLY NEWSPAPERS

BUCHANAN
US
BERRIEN COUNTY RECORD. 1867. Wed. $.75 newsstand; $25/yr. in cy.; $32/yr. out of cy. 109 Days Ave., Buchanan, MI 49107-1612. TEL 616-695-3878; FAX 616-695-3880. **Owner(s):** Donald W. Holmes, 408 W. Roe St., Buchanan, MI 49107. TEL 616-695-1133; Ed. Mark Anderson; Pub. Donald W. Holmes; adv.; photos; pub. size: broadsheet; circ. 2,600(free & paid).

CADILLAC
US ISSN 0194-3014
NORTHERN MICHIGAN NEWS. 1972. Mon. free. 130 N. Mitchell, Cadillac, MI 49601-0640. TEL 616-775-6565. **Owner(s):** Thomas C. Huckle, 130 N. Mitchell, Cadillac, MI 49601-0640. TEL 616-775-6565; Ed. Matt Seward; Pub. Thomas C. Huckle; pub. size: broadsheet; circ. 17,690(controlled).

CAMDEN
US
FARMERS' ADVANCE. 1898. Wed. $1 newsstand; $28/yr. mailed. 331 E. Bell, Camden, MI 49232. TEL 517-368-0365; FAX 517-368-5131. **Owner(s):** Suburban Communications Corp., 36251 Schoolcraft Rd., Livonia, MI 48150. TEL 313-591-2300; pub. size: tabloid; circ. 25,000(paid).

CARO
US
TUSCOLA COUNTY ADVERTISER. 1868. Wed. $.75 newsstand; $24/yr. 344 N. State St., Caro, MI 48723. TEL 517-673-3181; FAX 517-673-5662. **Owner(s):** Edwards Publications, 125 Eagles Nest, Seneca, SC 29679. TEL 803-882-3272; Ed. Dean Bohn; Pub. Brett McLaughlin; adv. contact: Jamie McCoy. photos; pub. size: broadsheet; circ. 9,950(paid).

CASS CITY
US
CASS CITY CHRONICLE. 1917. Wed. $.50 newsstand; $15/yr. local; $18/yr. in state; $20/yr. elsewhere. 6550 Main St., Cass City, MI 48726. TEL 517-872-2010; FAX 517-872-2010. **Owner(s):** John Haire, 6550 Main St., Cass City, MI 48726. TEL 517-872-2010; FAX 517-872-2010; Ed. Tom Montgomery; Pub. John Haire; adv.; photos; pub. size: broadsheet; circ. 3,875(paid).

CHARLEVOIX
US
CHARLEVOIX COURIER. 1883. Wed. $47/yr. 112 Mason St., Charlevoix, MI 49720-0117. TEL 616-547-6558; FAX 616-547-4992. **Owner(s):** Charlevoix Courier, 319 State St., Petoskey, MI 49770. TEL 616-347-2544; FAX 616-347-6833; Ed. Janenne Irene Harrington. adv. contact: Kim Taylor. pub. size: tabloid; circ. 2,026(paid).

US
NORTH WOODS CALL. 1953. bi-w.: Wed. $1 newsstand; $25/yr. mailed; $16/6 mos.; $44/2 yr. Rte. 1, 00509 Turkey Run, Charlevoix, MI 49720. TEL 616-547-9797; FAX 616-547-0367. **Owner(s):** North Woods Call, Inc., Rte. 1, 00509 Turkey Run, Charlevoix, MI 49720. TEL 616-547-9797; FAX 616-547-0367; Ed. Glen Sheppard. adv.; bk.rev.; pub. size: tabloid; circ. 16,500(paid).

CHARLOTTE
US
CHARLOTTE SHOPPING GUIDE. 1948. Sun. free newsstand; $104/yr. 1st class mailed. 239 S. Cochran Ave., Charlotte, MI 48813. TEL 517-543-9913; FAX 517-543-0665. **Owner(s):** Suburban Communications Corp., 36251 Schoolcraft Rd., Livonia, MI 48150. TEL 313-591-2300; Ed. Tim Strickland; Pub. Pete Cantine; adv.; pub. size: tabloid; circ. 18,000(controlled).

US
EATON COUNTY NEWS. 1854. Sun. free home deliv.; $.35 newsstand; $32.50/yr. 239 S. Cochran, Charlotte, MI 48813. TEL 517-543-9913; FAX 517-543-3677. **Owner(s):** Suburban Communications Corp., 36251 Schoolcraft Rd., Livonia, MI 48150. TEL 313-591-2300; Ed. Tim Strickland; Pub. Tricia Johnson; adv. contact: Kathy Fountain. pub. size: tabloid; circ. 17,000(free & paid).

CHATHAM
US
PORCUPINE PRESS. 1989. Wed. $.75 newsstand; $24/yr. E. 3724 Autrain St., Chatham, MI 49816-0200. TEL 906-439-5111; FAX 906-439-5337. E-mail: porkypress@aol.com. **Owner(s):** Porcupine Press, Inc., P.O. Box 200, Chatham, MI 49816. TEL 906-439-5111; FAX 906-439-5337; Ed. M.J. VanDenBranden; Pub. M.J. VanDenBranden; adv.; photos; pub. size: tabloid; circ. 4,665(paid). **Wire Service(s):** AP.

CHEBOYGAN
US
STRAITS AREA STAR. 1986. Sun. free. 111 N. Main, Cheboygan, MI 49721. TEL 616-627-3151. **Owner(s):** Star Publications, P.O. Box 620, Gaylord, MI 49735. TEL 517-732-5125; Pub. James R. Glasser; adv. contact: Sue Duffiney. pub. size: tabloid; circ. 15,154(free).
Formerly: Community Shopper.

CHELSEA
US
CHELSEA STANDARD, THE. 1871. Thu. $.50 newsstand; $20/yr. 101 N. Main, Chelsea, MI 48118. TEL 313-475-1371; FAX 313-475-1371. **Owner(s):** Heritage Newspapers, Inc., 101 N. Main St., Chelsea, MI 48118. TEL 313-475-1371; FAX 313-475-1413; Ed. Brian Hamilton. adv. contact: K. Crimmins. adv.: $6.50/SAU. photos; pub. size: broadsheet; circ. 5,800(paid).

CHESANING
US
TRI-COUNTY CITIZEN. 1983. Sun. free; $3/mo. out of area. 9996 E. M-57, Chesaning, MI 48616. TEL 517-845-7403; FAX 517-845-4397. **Owner(s):** Daniel Lea, 9996 E. M-57, Chesaning, MI 48616. TEL 517-845-7403; FAX 517-845-4397; Ed. Carol Coty; Pub. Daniel Lea; adv.; photos; pub. size: tabloid; circ. 18,200(free).

CLARE
US
CLARE SENTINEL. 1897. Tue. $.50 newsstand; $19.50/yr. 112 W. Fourth St., Clare, MI 48617. TEL 517-386-9937; FAX 517-386-9938. **Owner(s):** Clare Sentinel, 112 W. Fourth St., Clare, MI 48617. TEL 517-386-9937; Ed. Alfred R. Bransdorfer; Pub. Alfred R. Bransdorfer; adv.; pub. size: broadsheet; circ. 3,500(paid).

CLARKSTON
US
CLARKSTON NEWS. 1930. Wed. $.50 newsstand; $16/yr. mailed. 5 S. Main St., Clarkston, MI 48346. TEL 810-625-3370; FAX 810-625-0706. **Owner(s):** Sherman Publications, Inc., 666 S. Lapeer, Oxford, MI 48371. TEL 810-628-4801; FAX 810-628-9750; Ed. Annette Kingsbury; Pub. James A. Sherman, Jr.; adv. contact: Eric Lewis. photos; pub. size: tabloid; circ. 4,465(free & paid).

CROSWELL
US
JEFFERSONIAN, THE. 1858. Mon. $16.95/yr. in cy. mailed. 14 Wells St., Croswell, MI 48422. TEL 810-679-4500; FAX 810-679-4504. **Owner(s):** John D. Johnson, 465 N. Sandusky Rd., Sandusky, MI 48471. TEL 810-648-4000; Ed. John D. Johnson. adv. contact: Carlene Soroka. pub. size: tabloid; circ. 7,700(paid).
Formerly: Croswell Sanilac Jeffersonian.

DAVISON
US
DAVISON INDEX, THE. 0889. Wed. $.50 newsstand; $15/yr. in area. 220 N. Main St., Davison, MI 48423. TEL 810-653-3511. **Owner(s):** Jim Sherman, P.O. Box 100, Davison, MI 48423-0100. TEL 810-653-3511; Ed. Don Schelske. adv.; photos; pub. size: tabloid; circ. 9,000(free & paid).

DEARBORN
US
DEARBORN PRESS & GUIDE. 1918. Thu. $.75 newsstand; $36/yr. 15340 Michigan Ave., Dearborn, MI 48126. TEL 313-943-4250; FAX 313-846-5531. **Owner(s):** Heritage Newspapers, Inc., 15340 Michigan Ave., Dearborn, MI 48126. TEL 313-943-4250; Pub. Robert Riddell; adv. contact: Darrell Futo. photos; bk.rev.; circ. 48,000(controlled & paid).

DEARBORN, MI

US ISSN 0193-0230
DEARBORN TIMES-HERALD. 1963. s-w.: Wed. & Sun. $.50 newsstand; $24.95/yr. 13730 Michigan Ave., Dearborn, MI 48126-3520. TEL 313-584-4000; FAX 313-584-1357. **Owner(s):** Dearborn Management Co., 13730 Michigan Avenue, Dearborn, MI 48126-3520. TEL 313-584-4000; Ed. Tom Edwards; Pub. Frank N. Bewick; adv. contact: Louise Parker. photos; bk.rev.; pub. size: broadsheet; circ. 28,000(paid); Sun. 34,000(paid). **Wire Service(s):** Newsfinder.

US
HEIGHTS TIMES-HERALD. 1963. s-w.: Wed. & Sun. $.50 newsstand; $24.95/yr. 13730 Michigan, Dearborn, MI 48126-3520. TEL 313-584-4000; FAX 313-584-1357. **Owner(s):** Laurie Bewick, 13730 Michigan, Dearborn, MI 48126-3520. TEL 313-584-4000; FAX 313-584-1357; Scott Bewick, 13730 Michigan, Dearborn, MI 48126-3520. TEL 313-584-4000; FAX 313-584-1357; Ed. Tom Edwards; Pub. Frank H. Bewick; adv. contact: Louise Parker. photos; bk.rev.; pub. size: broadsheet; circ. 27,000(free & paid); Sun. 37,000(free & paid). **Wire Service(s):** ARI, United Media.

DETROIT

US
METRO TIMES. Wed. free; $30/6 mos. 3rd class mailed; $65/6 mos. 1st class mailed. 733 St. Antoine St., Detroit, MI 48226. TEL 313-961-4060; FAX 313-961-6598. **Owner(s):** Ron Williams, Detroit Metro Times, 733 Saint Antoine St., Detroit, MI 48226. TEL 313-961-4060; FAX 313-961-6598; Pub. Jim McCarter; adv. contact: Jim Cohen. pub. size: tabloid; circ. 107,000(paid). **Wire Service(s):** Alternet.

US
MICHIGAN CHRONICLE. 1936. Wed. $.50 newsstand; $25/yr. 479 Ledyard St., Detroit, MI 48201. TEL 313-963-5522; FAX 313-963-8788. **Owner(s):** John S. Sengstacke, 2400 S. Michigan Ave., Chicago, IL 60616. TEL 312-225-2400; Ed. Carol Archer; Pub. Sam Logan; adv.; photos; bk.rev.; pub. size: broadsheet; circ. 30,000(paid). **Wire Service(s):** AP, API, GNS, N, UPI.

DURAND

US
DURAND EXPRESS, THE. 1888. Thu. $.35 newsstand; $20/yr. 219 N. Saginaw St., Durand, MI 48429-0168. TEL 517-288-3164; FAX 517-288-4666. **Owner(s):** Owen & Arlene Rood, 505 N. Saginaw St., Durand, MI 48429-0415. TEL 517-288-3164; FAX 517-288-4666; Ed. Bryan Myrkle; Pub. Owen Rood; adv.: $6.15/SAU. photos; pub. size: broadsheet; circ. 3,000(paid).

EAST LANSING

US
TOWNE COURIER. 1972. Sat. $.50 newsstand; $26/yr. in cy. mailed; $30/yr. out of cy.; $40/yr. out of state. 210 Abbott, Ste. 28, East Lansing, MI 48823. TEL 517-333-7272; FAX 517-333-7275. **Owner(s):** Ingham Newspapers, P.O. Box 160, Mason, MI 48854; Ed. Dirk Milliman; Pub. Dirk Milliman; pub. size: tabloid; circ. 40,000(paid).

EAST TAWAS

US
IOSCO COUNTY NEWS HERALD. Wed. $.50 newsstand; $22/yr. local mailed; $26/yr. in state; $32/yr. out of state. 110 W. State St., East Tawas, MI 48730. TEL 517-362-3456; FAX 517-362-6601. **Owner(s):** J. Berkeley Smith, News Press Publishing Co., P.O. Box 72, East Tawas, MI 48730. TEL 517-362-3456; Neal Miller, New Press Publishing Co., P.O Box 72, East Tawas, MI 48730. TEL 517-362-3456; Ed. Neal Miller; Pub. Neal Miller; pub. size: tabloid; circ. 7,500(paid).
Formerly: Tawas City Tawas Herald.

EVART

US ISSN 0192-8678
EVART REVIEW, THE. Wed. $.50 newsstand, $18/yr. 125 N. Main St., Evart, MI 49631. TEL 616-734-5587; FAX 616-796-1152. **Owner(s):** Pioneer Group, 125 N. Main St., Evart, MI 49631. TEL 616-734-5587; FAX 616-796-1152; Ed. Jim Bruskotter. adv. contact: Denise Clasen. photos; pub. size: broadsheet; circ. 2,450(paid). **Wire Service(s):** Pioneer News Network, AP.

FARMINGTON

US
FARMINGTON OBSERVER. s-w.: Thu. & Sun. $.75 newsstand; $42/yr. in cy. 33411 Grand River Ave., Farmington, MI 48335-3521. TEL 313-591-2300; FAX 313-591-7279. **Owner(s):** Suburban Communications Corp., 36251 Schoolcraft Rd., Livonia, MI 48150. TEL 313-591-2300; Ed. Bob Sklar; Pub. Tom Bird; adv. contact: Rich Ficorelli. pub. size: broadsheet; circ. 140,000(paid); Sun. 152,000.

FLINT

US
CLIO MESSENGER, THE. s-w.: Thu. & Sun. free deliv.; $.25 newsstand. G-5085 Miller Rd., Flint, MI 48507. TEL 810-733-2239; FAX 810-733-2688. **Owner(s):** Flint Advance Newspapers, G-5085 Miller Rd., Flint, MI 48507. TEL 810-733-2239; FAX 810-733-2688; Ed. Dennis Setter; Pub. John J. Badoud, Jr.; adv. contact: Tom Reynolds. pub. size: broadsheet; circ. 8,889(free & paid).

US
FLUSHING OBSERVER. s-w.: Thu. & Sun. free deliv.; $.25 newsstand. G-5085 Miller Rd., Flint, MI 48507. TEL 810-733-2239; FAX 810-733-2688. **Owner(s):** Flint Advance Newspapers, G-5085 Miller Rd., Flint, MI 48507. TEL 810-733-2239; FAX 810-733-2688; Ed. Dennis Setter; Pub. John J. Badoud, Jr.; adv. contact: Tom Reynolds. pub. size: broadsheet; circ. 9,371(free & paid).

US
GRAND BLANC NEWS, THE. s-w.: Thu. & Sun. free deliv.; $.25 newsstand. G-5085 Miller Rd., Flint, MI 48507. TEL 810-733-2239; FAX 810-733-2688. **Owner(s):** Flint Advance Newspapers, G-5085 Miller Rd., Flint, MI 48507. TEL 810-733-2239; FAX 810-733-2688; Ed. Dennis Setter; Pub. John J. Badoud, Jr.; adv. contact: Tom Reynolds. pub. size: broadsheet; circ. 14,000(free & paid).

WEEKLY NEWSPAPERS

US
INDEPENDENT, THE. 1868. s-w.: Thu. & Sun. free deliv.; $.25 newsstand. G-5085 Miller Rd., Flint, MI 48507. TEL 810-733-2239; FAX 810-733-2688. **Owner(s):** Flint Advance Newspapers, G-5085 Miller Rd., Flint, MI 48507. TEL 810-733-2239; Ed. Dennis Setter; Pub. John J. Badoud, Jr.; adv. contact: Tom Reynolds. pub. size: broadsheet; circ. 15,360(free & paid).

US
SUBURBAN NEWS, THE. s-w.: Thu. & Sun. free deliv.; $.25 newsstand. G-5085 Miller Rd., Flint, MI 48507. TEL 810-733-2239; FAX 810-733-2688. **Owner(s):** Flint Advance Newspapers, G-5085 Miller Rd., Flint, MI 48507. TEL 810-733-2239; FAX 810-733-2688; Ed. Dennis Setter; Pub. John J. Badoud, Jr.; adv. contact: Tom Reynolds. pub. size: broadsheet; circ. 13,804(free & paid).

US
WEST VALLEY NEWS/SUNDAY ADVANCE. s-w.: Thu. & Sun. free deliv.; $.25 newsstand. G-5085 Miller Rd., Flint, MI 48507. TEL 810-733-2239; FAX 810-733-2688. **Owner(s):** Flint Advance Newspapers, G-5085 Miller Rd., Flint, MI 48507. TEL 810-733-2239; Ed. Dennis Setter; Pub. John J. Badoud, Jr.; adv. contact: Tom Reynolds. pub. size: broadsheet; circ. 13,000(free & paid).

FRANKENMUTH

US
FRANKENMUTH NEWS. 1906. Wed. $.50 newsstand; $22.50/yr. in cy.; $22.50/yr. in state; $23/yr. out of state. 231 Hubinger St., Frankenmuth, MI 48734. TEL 517-652-3246; FAX 517-652-3247. **Owner(s):** Frankenmuth News, 410 E. Tuscola, Frankenmuth, MI 48734. TEL 517-652-6773; FAX 517-652-3247; Ed. Scott A. Wenzel; Pub. Steve Grainger; adv. contact: Robert Wilkinson. photos; pub. size: broadsheet; circ. 5,000(paid).

FREMONT

US
TIMES-INDICATOR. 1878. Wed. $.60 newsstand; $23/yr. in cy.; $32/yr. out of cy.; $43/yr out of state. 44 W. Main St., Fremont, MI 49412. TEL 616-924-4400; FAX 616-924-4066. **Owner(s):** T.I. Publication, P.O. Box 387, Morrison, IL 61270. TEL 815-772-4123; Ed. Richard Wheater; Pub. Richard Wheater; adv. contact: Debbie Reinhold. photos; bk.rev.; pub. size: broadsheet; circ. 7,500(paid).

GAYLORD

US
CHARLEVOIX COUNTY STAR. 1970. Sun. free. 1966 Old 27, S., Gaylord, MI 49735. TEL 517-732-5125; FAX 517-732-9323. **Owner(s):** Star Publications, P.O. Box 620, Gaylord, MI 49735. TEL 517-732-5125; FAX 517-732-9323; Pub. James R. Glasser; adv. contact: David G. Baragrey. pub. size: tabloid; circ. 16,000(free).

US
GAYLORD HERALD TIMES. 1875. Thu. $.75 newsstand; $32.50/yr. local; $45/yr. out of area. 2066 Old 27, S., Gaylord, MI 49735-0598. TEL 517-732-1111; FAX 517-732-3490. **Owner(s):** Otsego County Herald Times, Inc., P.O. Box 598, Gaylord, MI 49735. TEL 517-732-1111; Ed. Chris Jenkins; Pub. James L. Grisso; adv. contact: Angie Love. photos; pub. size: broadsheet; circ. 24,500(free & paid). **Wire Service(s):** AP, Newsfinder.

WEEKLY NEWSPAPERS

US
NORTHERN STAR. 1960. Sun. free. 1966 Old 27, S., Gaylord, MI 49735. TEL 517-732-5125; FAX 517-732-9323. **Owner(s):** Star Publications, P.O. Box 620, Gaylord, MI 49735. TEL 517-732-5125; FAX 517-732-9323; Pub. James R. Glasser; adv. contact: David G. Baragrey. pub. size: tabloid; circ. 17,654(free).
Formerly: Gaylord Northern Star.

US
PETOSKY STAR AD-VERTISER. 1956. Sun. free. 1966 Old 27, S., Gaylord, MI 49735. TEL 517-732-5125; FAX 517-732-9323. **Owner(s):** Star Publications, P.O. Box 620, Gaylord, MI 40735. TEL 517-732-5125; FAX 517-732-9323; Pub. James R. Glasser; adv. contact: Dan McDonald. pub. size: tabloid; circ. 12,807(free).
Formerly: Emmet Ad-Vertiser.

US
PRESQUE ISLE STAR. 1975. Sun. free. 1966 Old 27, S., Gaylord, MI 49735. TEL 517-732-5125; FAX 517-732-9323. **Owner(s):** Star Publications, P.O. Box 620, Gaylord, MI 49735. TEL 517-732-5125; Ed. Mike Adams; Pub. James R. Glasser; adv. contact: Mike Adams. pub. size: tabloid; circ. 7,318(free).
Formerly: Huron Shores Buyers Guide.

GLADWIN

US
GLADWIN COUNTY RECORD & BEAVERTON CLARION. 1877. Wed. $.50 newsstand; $24.95/yr. 700 E. Cedar Ave., Gladwin, MI 48624-0425. TEL 517-426-9411; FAX 517-426-2023. **Owner(s):** Gladwin County Newspapers, Inc, Fort Payne, AL; Pub. Charles Johnson; adv.; photos; pub. size: broadsheet; circ. 8,000(free & paid).

GOBLES

US
VAN BUREN COUNTY ADVERTISER. 1946. Wed. free. 205 S. State St., Gobles, MI 49055. TEL 616-628-5122; FAX 616-628-5198. **Owner(s):** Michigan Printing Co., P.O. Box 340, Gobles, MI 49055; Ed. Pam Harris. pub. size: tabloid; circ. 7,000(controlled & free).

GRAND LEDGE

US
DELTA WAVERLY COMMUNITY NEWS. 1984. Mon. free home deliv.; $.35 newsstand; $104/yr. 1st class mailed. 219 S. Bridge St., Grand Ledge, MI 48837. TEL 517-627-6085; FAX 517-627-3497. **Owner(s):** Suburban Communications Corp., 36251 Schoolcraft Rd,, Livonia, MI 48150. TEL 313-591-2300; FAX 313-591-9424; Ed. Nancy Zeimen; Pub. Terry Fitzwater; adv. contact: Kathy Fountain. photos; pub. size: tabloid; circ. 9,000(free & paid).
Formerly: Delta Waverly News Herald, The.

US
GRAND LEDGE INDEPENDENT, THE. 1869. Tue. free home deliv.; $.35 newsstand; $104/yr. 1st class mailed. 219 S. Bridge St., Grand Ledge, MI 48837. TEL 517-627-6085; FAX 517-627-3497. **Owner(s):** Community Newspapers, 239 S. Cochran, Charlotte, MI 48813. TEL 517-543-9913; Ed. Michelle Munson; Pub. Terry Fitzwater; adv.; photos; bk.rev.; pub. size: broadsheet; circ. 12,175(free & paid).

US
PORTLAND REVIEW & OBSERVER. 1867. Mon. free home deliv.; $.35 newsstand; $104/yr. 1st class mailed. 219 S. Bridge St., Grand Ledge, MI 48837. TEL 517-627-6085; FAX 517-627-3497. **Owner(s):** Suburban Communications Corp., 36251 Schoolcraft Rd., Livonia, MI 48150. TEL 313-591-2300; FAX 313-591-9424; Ed. Nan Simons; Pub. Terry Fitzwater; adv. contact: Kathy Fountain. pub. size: tabloid; circ. 6,000(free & paid).

GRAND MARAIS

US
GREAT LAKES PILOT, THE. m. free. 123 Lake Ave., Grand Marais, MI 49839. TEL 906-494-2391; FAX 906-494-2527. **Owner(s):** Rick & Marge Capogrossa, P.O. Box 339, Grand Marais, MI 49839. TEL 906-494-2391; Ed. Rick Capogrossa; Pub. Mary Capogrossa; adv. contact: Mary Capogrossa. pub. size: tabloid; circ. 35,000(free).

GROSSE ILE

US
ILE CAMERA, THE. 1945. Fri. $.50 newsstand; $26/yr. 8801 Macomb, Grosse Ile, MI 48138. TEL 313-676-0515; FAX 313-676-0638. **Owner(s):** Heritage Newspapers, Inc., One Heritage Pl., Southgate, MI 48195. TEL 313-246-7800; FAX 313-284-2028; Ed. Michael Raveane; Pub. Fred Manuel; adv. contact: Lee Atkinson. adv.: $6.60/SAU. photos; pub. size: tabloid.

GROSSE POINT

US
CONNECTION, THE. 1991. Thu. free. 96 Kercheval Rd., Grosse Point, MI 48236. TEL 313-882-3500; FAX 313-882-1585. **Owner(s):** Robert G. Edgar, 96 Kercheval Rd., Grosse Point, MI 48236. TEL 313-882-3500; Pub. Robert G. Edgar; adv. contact: Roger Hages. pub. size: broadsheet; circ. 35,000(controlled & free).

GROSSE POINTE FARMS

US
GROSSE POINTE NEWS. 1940. Thu. $.75 newsstand; $29/yr. in state; $35/yr. out of state. 96 Kercheval Ave., Grosse Pointe Farms, MI 48236. TEL 313-882-6900; FAX 313-882-1585. **Owner(s):** Anteebo Publishers, 96 Kercheval, Grosse Pointe, MI 48236. TEL 313-882-6900; Ed. John Minnis; Pub. Robert G. Edgar; adv. contact: Roger Hages. photos; bk.rev.; pub. size: broadsheet; circ. 18,556(paid).

HAMTRAMCK

US   ISSN 1042-6906
CITIZEN, THE. 1934. Thu. $.50 newsstand; $18/yr. in cy.; $21/yr. out of cy. 11901 Joseph Campau, Hamtramck, MI 48212-3099. TEL 313-365-9500. **Owner(s):** Hamtramck Citizen, Inc., 11901 Joseph Campau, Hamtramck, MI 48212-3099. TEL 313-365-9500; Ed. Karen Kargol Spang; Pub. Karen Kargol Spang; adv.; photos; pub. size: broadsheet; circ. 9,765(controlled & paid).
Formerly: Hamtramck Citizen.

HARBOR BEACH

US
HARBOR BEACH TIMES. 1834. Thu. $.50 newsstand; $18/yr. 123 N. First St., Harbor Beach, MI 48441. TEL 517-479-3605; FAX 517-479-9697. **Owner(s):** Michael & Kathy Murphy, 123 N. First St., Harbor Beach, MI 48441. TEL 517-479-3605; Ed. Michael Murphy; Pub. Michael Murphy; adv.; pub. size: broadsheet; circ. 3,200(paid).

HART

US
OCEANA'S HERALD-JOURNAL. 1981. Thu. $.50 newsstand; $18/yr. in cy.; $21/yr. out of cy.; $26/yr. out of state. 123 State St., Hart, MI 49420. TEL 616-873-5602; FAX 616-873-4775. **Owner(s):** Maxine Huggard, 86 Fourth St., Shelby, MI 49455. TEL 616-861-2946; Richard Lound, 3335 W. Johnson, Shelby, MI 49455. TEL 616-861-4235; Ed. Mary Sanford; Pub. Maxine Huggard; adv. contact: James O. Young. photos; pub. size: broadsheet; circ. 7,400(paid).

HASTINGS

US
HASTINGS BANNER. 1856. Thu. $.50 newsstand; $25/yr. in cy. mailed; $27/yr. out of cy. mailed. 1952 N. Broadway, Hastings, MI 49058. TEL 616-948-8051; FAX 616-945-5192. **Owner(s):** J-Ad Graphics, Inc., 1952 N. Broadway, Hastings, MI 49058. TEL 616-945-9554; Ed. David T. Young; Pub. Fred Jacobs; adv. contact: Scott Ommen. pub. size: broadsheet; circ. 7,000(paid). **Wire Service(s):** AP.

US
HASTINGS REMINDER. Tue. free; $28/yr. 1952 N. Broadway, Hastings, MI 49058. TEL 616-945-9554; FAX 616-945-5192. **Owner(s):** John Jacobs, 1952 N. Broadway, Hastings, MI 49058. TEL 616-945-9554; FAX 616-945-5192; Fredric Jacobs, 1952 N. Broadway, Hastings, MI 49058. TEL 616-945-9554; FAX 616-945-5192; Joyce Ryan, 1952 N. Broadway, Hastings, MI 49508. TEL 616-945-9554; FAX 616-945-5192; Stephan Jacobs, 1952 N. Broadway, Hastings, MI 49058. TEL 616-945-9554; FAX 616-645-5192; Ed. David Youngs. adv.; photos; bk.rev.; pub. size: tabloid; circ. 28,450(free & paid).

US
MAPLE VALLEY NEWS. 1975. Tue. free newsstand; $20/yr. mailed. 1952 N. Broadway, Hastings, MI 49058. TEL 616-945-9554; FAX 616-945-5192. **Owner(s):** J-Ad Graphics, Inc., 1952 N. Broadway, Hastings, MI 49058. TEL 616-945-9554; Ed. David Young. adv. contact: Jerry Johnson. pub. size: tabloid; circ. 3,200(free).

US
SUN & NEWS, THE. 1871. Tue. free newsstand; $20/yr. 1952 N. Broadway, Hastings, MI 49058. TEL 616-795-3345; FAX 616-945-5192. **Owner(s):** John Jacobs, 1952 N. Broadway, Hastings, MI 49058. TEL 616-945-9554; FAX 616-945-5192; Ed. David Young; Pub. John Jacobs; adv.; photos; bk.rev.; pub. size: tabloid; circ. 8,000(free).

HOLT

US

HOLT COMMUNITY NEWS. Sun. free home deliv.; $.35 newsstand. 2068 Cedar St., Holt, MI 48842. TEL 517-694-8484; FAX 517-694-3497. **Owner(s):** Lansing Suburban Newspaper Network, Inc., 239 S. Cochran, Charlotte, MI 48113. TEL 517-627-6085; Pub. Peter Cantine; adv.: $8/SAU. photos; pub. size: broadsheet; circ. 10,600(free & paid).

HOUGHTON LAKE

US

HOUGHTON LAKE RESORTER. 1939. Thu. $.50 newsstand; $18/yr. in cy.; $22/yr. out of cy. 4049 W. Houghton Lake Dr., Houghton Lake, MI 48629. TEL 517-366-5341; FAX 517-366-4472. **Owner(s):** Thomas W. Hamp, 4049 W. Houghton Lake Dr., Houghton Lake, MI 48629; Ed. Thomas W. Hamp. adv.; photos; pub. size: broadsheet; circ. 8,000(paid). **Wire Service(s):** AP.

HOWELL

US

FOWLERVILLE REVIEW SHOPPING GUIDE. 1874. Wed. free. 323 E. Grand River, Howell, MI 48843. TEL 517-548-2000; FAX 517-548-3005. **Owner(s):** Hometown Newspapers, 323 E. Grand River, Howell, MI 48843. TEL 517-548-2000; adv. contact: Michael Preville. pub. size: tabloid; circ. 9,000(free).

US

HARTLAND HERALD SHOPPING GUIDE. 1980. Wed. free. 323 E. Grand River, Howell, MI 48843. TEL 517-548-2000; FAX 517-548-3005. **Owner(s):** Hometown Newspapers, 323 E. Grand River, Howell, MI 48843. TEL 517-548-2000; adv. contact: Michael Preville. pub. size: tabloid; circ. 7,500(free).

IMLAY CITY

US

TRI-CITY TIMES. 1977. Wed. $.50 newsstand; $13/yr. in cy. mailed; $15/yr. out of cy.; $24/yr. out of state. 594 N. Almont Ave., Imlay City, MI 48444. TEL 810-724-6191; FAX 810-724-8552. **Owner(s):** Delores Heim, P.O. Box 278, Imlay City, MI 48444; Ed. Cathy Barringer-Rourke; Pub. Delores Heim; adv. contact: Kim Jorgensen. pub. size: broadsheet; circ. 8,760(paid).

IRON MOUNTAIN

US

ADVERTISER, THE. 1975. Tue. free. 333 S. Stephenson Ave., Iron Mountain, MI 49801. TEL 906-774-3708; FAX 906-774-1088. **Owner(s):** John & Marilyn Lutz, 1026 Prospect, Iron Mountain, MI 49801. TEL 906-774-9641; Pub. John Lutz; adv.; photos; pub. size: tabloid; circ. 20,600(free).

IRON RIVER

US

IRON RIVER REPORTER. 1885. Wed. $.75 newsstand; $36/yr. out of cy. 801 W. Adams St., Iron River, MI 49935. TEL 906-265-9927; FAX 906-265-5755; E-mail: biged@up.net. **Owner(s):** Northland Publishers, Inc., P.O. Box 311, Iron River, MI 49935. TEL 906-265-9927; FAX 906-265-5755; Ed. Edward J. Erickson, III. adv.; photos; pub. size: broadsheet; circ. 5,000(paid).

IRONWOOD

US

NORTH COUNTRY SUN. 1977. Mon. free in area; $25/yr. mailed. 216 E. Aurora St., Ironwood, MI 49938. TEL 906-932-3530; FAX 906-932-3074. **Owner(s):** La Pean Publications, 417 Ninth Ave., W., Ashland, WI 54806. TEL 715-682-8131; FAX 715-682-6400; Ed. Gary La Pean; Pub. Gary La Pean; adv.; pub. size: tabloid; circ. 16,739(free & paid).

ITHACA

US

GRATIOT COUNTY HERALD. 1887. Thu. $.50 newsstand; $21/yr. in cy.; $23/yr. out of cy.; $26/yr. out of state. 123 N. Main St., Ithaca, MI 48847. TEL 517-875-4151; FAX 517-875-3159. **Owner(s):** Patricia R. MacDonald, 123 N. Main St., Ithaca, MI 48847. TEL 517-875-4151; Thomas P. MacDonald, 123 N. Main St., Ithaca, NY 48847. TEL 517-875-4151; Ed. Randy Williams; Pub. Thomas P. MacDonald; adv.; photos; pub. size: tabloid; circ. 7,000(paid).

JACKSON

US

BLAZER NEWS. 1963. Wed. $15/yr. 404 McNeal St., Jackson, MI 49203. TEL 517-788-4600; FAX 517-788-5300. **Owner(s):** New City Resources, 404 McNeal St., Jackson, MI 49203. TEL 517-788-4600; FAX 517-788-5300; Ed. Ron Davis. adv. contact: Ron Davis. adv.: $12.50/SAU. photos; bk.rev.; pub. size: tabloid; circ. 5,000(free).

JENISON

US

ADA/CASCADE/FOREST HILLS ADVANCE. Tue. $.35 newsstand. 2141 Port Sheldon Rd., Jenison, MI 49428. TEL 616-669-2700; FAX 616-669-1162. **Owner(s):** Valley Media, Inc., 2141 Port Sheldon Rd., Jenison, MI 49428. TEL 616-669-2700; FAX 616-669-1162; Ed. Tim Gortsema; Pub. Joel Holland; pub. size: tabloid; circ. 12,450(free & paid).

US

CALEDONIA/GAINES ADVANCE. Tue. free. 2141 Port Sheldon Rd., Jenison, MI 49428. TEL 616-669-2700; FAX 616-669-1162. **Owner(s):** John Badoud, 2141 Port Sheldon Rd., Jenison, MI 49428. TEL 616-669-2700; FAX 616-669-1162; Ed. Mike Wyngarden; Pub. Joel Holland; adv.; pub. size: broadsheet; circ. 6,300(free).

US

EAST GRAND RAPIDS CADENCE. Tue. free. 2141 Port Sheldon Rd., Jenison, MI 49428. TEL 616-669-2700; FAX 616-669-1162. **Owner(s):** Valley Media, Inc., 2141 Port Sheldon Rd., Jenison, MI 49428. TEL 616-669-2700; FAX 616-669-1162; Ed. Mike Wyngarden; Pub. Joel Holland; pub. size: tabloid; circ. 5,250(free).

US

GRAND RAPIDS ADVANCE. Tue. $.35 newsstand; 30/yr. mailed. 2141 Port Sheldon Rd., Jenison, MI 49428. TEL 616-669-2700; FAX 616-669-1162. **Owner(s):** Valley Media, Inc., 2141 Port Sheldon Rd., Jenison, MI 49428. TEL 616-669-2700; FAX 616-669-1162; Ed. Mike Wyndgarden; Pub. Joel Holland; pub. size: tabloid; circ. 13,000(paid).

US

GRAND VALLEY ADVANCE. 1966. Tue. free. 2141 Port Sheldon Rd., Jenison, MI 49428. TEL 616-669-2700; FAX 616-669-1162. **Owner(s):** Valley Media, Inc., 2141 Port Sheldon Rd., Jenison, MI 49428. TEL 616-669-2700; FAX 616-669-1162; Ed. Mike Wyngarden; Pub. Joel Holland; pub. size: tabloid; circ. 24,885(free).

US

KENTWOOD ADVANCE. 1982. Tue. free. 2141 Port Sheldon Rd., Jenison, MI 49428. TEL 616-669-2700; FAX 616-669-1162. **Owner(s):** Valley Media, Inc., 2141 Port Sheldon Rd., Jenison, MI 49428. TEL 616-669-2700; FAX 616-669-1162; Ed. Mike Wyngarden; Pub. Joel Holland; pub. size: tabloid; circ. 151,570(free).

US

NORTHFIELD ADVANCE. 1982. s-w.: Tue & Wed. free. 2141 Port Sheldon Rd., Jenison, MI 49428. TEL 616-669-2700; FAX 616-669-1162. **Owner(s):** Valley Media, Inc., 2141 Port Sheldon Rd., Jenison, MI 49428. TEL 616-669-2700; FAX 616-669-1162; Ed. Mike Wyngarden; Pub. Joel Holland; pub. size: tabloid; circ. 19,650(free).

US

OTTAWA ADVANCE. 1968. Tue. free. 2141 Port Sheldon Rd., Jenison, MI 49428. TEL 616-669-2700; FAX 616-669-1162. **Owner(s):** Valley Media, Inc., 2141 Port Sheldon Rd., Jenison, MI 49428. TEL 616-669-2700; FAX 616-669-1162; Ed. Mike Wyngarden; Pub. Joel Holland; pub. size: tabloid; circ. 9,000(free).

US

ROCKFORD/CEDAR SPRINGS ADVANCE. 1989. Tue. free. 2141 Port Sheldon Rd., Jenison, MI 49428. TEL 616-669-2700; FAX 616-669-1162. **Owner(s):** Valley Media, Inc., 2141 Port Sheldon Rd., Jenison, MI 49428. TEL 616-669-2700; FAX 616-669-1162; Ed. Mike Wyngarden; Pub. Joel Holland; pub. size: tabloid; circ. 14,700(free).

US

WALKER-WESTSIDE ADVANCE. 1968. Tue. free. 2141 Port Sheldon Rd., Jenison, MI 49428. TEL 616-669-2700; FAX 616-669-1162. **Owner(s):** Valley Media, Inc., 2141 Port Sheldon Rd., Jenison, MI 49428. TEL 616-669-2700; FAX 616-669-1162; Ed. Mike Wyngarden; Pub. Joel Holland; pub. size: tabloid; circ. 23,425(free).

US

WYOMING ADVANCE. 1982. Tue. free. 2141 Port Sheldon Rd., Jenison, MI 49428. TEL 616-669-2700; FAX 616-669-3930. **Owner(s):** Valley Media, Inc., 2141 Port Sheldon Rd., Jenison, MI 49428. TEL 616-669-2700; FAX 616-669-1162; Ed. Mike Wyngarden; Pub. Joel Holland; pub. size: tabloid; circ. 22,425(free).

WEEKLY NEWSPAPERS

KALKASKA

US

STAR ADVERTISER. 1970. Sun. free. 134 S. Cedar, Kalkaska, MI 49646. TEL 616-258-3226; FAX 616-732-9323. **Owner(s):** Star Publications, P.O. Box 620, Gaylord, MI 49735. TEL 517-732-5125; Pub. James R. Glasser; adv. contact: Susan Kelly. pub. size: tabloid; circ. 12,844(free).

L'ANSE

US

L'ANSE SENTINEL. 1880. Wed. $28/yr. local; $31/yr. in state; $34/yr. out of state. 202 N. Main, L'Anse, MI 49946. TEL 906-524-6194; FAX 906-524-6197. **Owner(s):** LDJ Publishers, Inc., 636 Broad St., L'Anse, MI 49946. TEL 906-524-7132; Ed. Barry Drue; Pub. Ed Danner; adv. contact: Pauline Kahkonen. photos; pub. size: broadsheet; circ. 3,800(paid).

LANSING

US

AD-VISOR. 1963. m. free. 1521 S. Pennsylvania, Lansing, MI 48910. TEL 517-372-8433. **Owner(s):** Jeanne & Manuel Castro, 1521 S. Pennsylvania, Lansing, MI. TEL 517-372-8433; Ed. Manuel Castro; Pub. Manuel Castro; adv. contact: Jeanne Castro. bk.rev.; pub. size: tabloid; circ. 15,000(free).

LAPEER

US ISSN 8750-4561

COUNTY PRESS, THE. 1839. s-w.: Wed. & Sun. $.75 newsstand; $34.50/yr. in cy.; $36.50/yr. out of cy. 1521 Imlay City Rd., Lapeer, MI 48446. TEL 810-664-0811; FAX 810-664-5852. **Owner(s):** Walt Disney Co., 500 S. Buena Vista St., Burbank, CA 91521. TEL 818-560-5300; Ed. Mark Haney; Pub. Ernest Slade; adv.; pub. size: broadsheet; circ. 19,000(paid); Sun. 33,000.

Formerly: Lapeer County Press.

LELAND

US

LEELANAU ENTERPRISE. 1877. Thu. $.50 newsstand; $17/yr. in cy.; $33/yr. out of cy. 112 Chandler St., Leland, MI 49654-0527. TEL 616-256-9827. **Owner(s):** Leelanau Publishing Co., Inc., P.O. Box 527, Leland, MI 49654. TEL 616-256-9827; Ed. Dick Kerr; Pub. R.C. Kerr; adv.: $7/SAU. pub. size: tabloid; circ. 7,637(paid).

LESLIE

US

LESLIE LOCAL INDEPENDENT. 1869. Tue. $.25 newsstand; $12/yr. in state; $14/yr. out of state. 109 Carney, Leslie, MI 49251. TEL 517-589-8228; FAX 517-589-8526. **Owner(s):** S.G. Publications, 140 E. Ash St., Mason, MI 48854. TEL 517-676-5100; FAX 517-676-6753; Ed. Larry Hook; Pub. George Raymond; adv. contact: Tami Stanfield. bk.rev.; pub. size: tabloid; circ. 7,415(free & paid).

LIVONIA

US

GARDEN CITY OBSERVER. s-w.: Mon. & Thu. $.75 newsstand; $42/yr. in cy. 36251 Schoolcraft Rd., Livonia, MI 48150. TEL 313-591-2300; FAX 313-591-7279. **Owner(s):** Suburban Communications Corp., 36251 Schoolcraft Rd., Livonia, MI 48150. TEL 313-591-2300; Ed. Sue Rosiek; Pub. Banks Dishman; adv. contact: Peg Knoespel. pub. size: broadsheet; circ. 8,500(paid).

US

LIVONIA OBSERVER. s-w.: Mon. & Thu. $.75 newsstand; $42/yr. in cy. 36251 Schoolcraft Rd., Livonia, MI 48150. TEL 313-591-2300; FAX 313-951-7279. **Owner(s):** Suburban Communications Corp., 36251 Schoolcraft Rd., Livonia, MI 48150. TEL 313-591-2300; Ed. Sue Rosiek; Pub. Banks Dishman; adv. contact: Peg Knoespel. pub. size: broadsheet; circ. 29,500(paid).

US

REDFORD OBSERVER. s-w.: Mon. & Thu. $.75 newsstand; $42/yr. in cy. 36251 Schoolcraft Rd., Livonia, MI 48150. TEL 313-591-2300; FAX 313-591-7279. **Owner(s):** Suburban Communications Corp., 36251 Schoolcraft Rd., Livonia, MI 48150. TEL 313-591-2300; Ed. Emory Daniels. adv. contact: Bob Kampf. pub. size: broadsheet; circ. 12,600(paid).

US

WESTLAND OBSERVER. 1965. s-w.: Mon. & Thu. $.75 newsstand; $43.20/yr. in cy. 36251 Schoolcraft Rd., Livonia, MI 48150. TEL 313-591-2300; FAX 313-591-7279. **Owner(s):** Suburban Communications Corp., 36251 Schoolcraft Rd., Livonia, MI 48150. TEL 313-591-2300; Ed. Bob Sklar. adv. contact: Kathy Hirshfield. pub. size: broadsheet; circ. 12,000(paid).

LOWELL

US

LOWELL LEDGER. 1956. Wed. $.35 newsstand; $12.50/yr. mailed. 105 N. Broadway, Lowell, MI 49331. TEL 616-897-9261; FAX 616-897-4809. **Owner(s):** Roger K. Brown, 105 N. Broadway, Lowell, MI 49331. TEL 616-897-9261; Ed. Roger K. Brown; Pub. Roger K. Brown; adv.; pub. size: broadsheet; circ. 3,000(paid).

MANISTEE

US

MANISTEE OBSERVER. Sun. free local; $18/yr. voluntary pay. 75 Maple St., Manistee, MI 49660. TEL 616-723-3593; FAX 616-723-4733. **Owner(s):** J.B. Publishing Co., 75 Maple St., Manistee, MI 49660. TEL 616-723-3593; FAX 616-723-4733; Ed. Phil Watson; Pub. Jack Batdorff; adv. contact: Marilyn Barker. photos; pub. size: tabloid; circ. Sun. 18,000(paid).

MANISTIQUE

US

MANISTIQUE PIONEER-TRIBUNE. 1876. Wed. $17.50/yr. in cy.; $22.50/yr. out of cy. 212 Walnut St., Manistique, MI 49854. TEL 906-341-5200. **Owner(s):** Leanne Trebilcock, 212 Walnut, Manistique, MI 49854. TEL 906-341-5200; Pub. Leanne Trebilcock; adv. contact: Leanne Trebilcock. pub. size: broadsheet; circ. 3,800(paid).

MARSHALL

US

COMMUNITY ADVISOR. 1969. Wed. free newsstand; $26/yr. mailed. 215 W. Michigan Ave., Marshall, MI 49068. TEL 616-781-5444; FAX 616-781-7766. **Owner(s):** J-Ad Graphics, Inc., 1952 N. Broadway, Hastings, MI 49058; Ed. Tom Isham; Pub. John Jacobs; adv.; pub. size: tabloid; circ. 19,500(free & paid).

MASON

US

ENTERPRISE, THE. Wed. $.50 newsstand; $20/yr. 624 S. Cedar, Mason, MI 48854. TEL 517-676-9393; FAX 517-676-9402. **Owner(s):** Milliman Communications, Inc., P.O. Box 160, Mason, MI 48854. TEL 517-676-9393; Ed. George Pinkerton; Pub. Dirk Milliman; adv.; pub. size: tabloid; circ. 2,500(paid).

US

INGHAM COUNTY NEWS. 1858. Wed. $.50 newsstand; $20/yr. 624 S. Cedar St., Mason, MI 48854. TEL 517-676-9393; FAX 517-676-9402. **Owner(s):** Milliman Communications, Inc., P.O. Box 160, Mason, MI 48854. TEL 517-676-9393; Ed. George Pinkerton; Pub. Dirk Milliman; adv.; pub. size: tabloid; circ. 8,500(paid).

MAYVILLE

US

MAYVILLE MONITOR. 1884. Thu. $.35 newsstand; $13/yr. in cy.; $15/yr. elsewhere in state; $18/yr. out of state. 6071 Fulton St., Mayville, MI 48744-0299. TEL 517-843-6441; FAX 517-843-0054. **Owner(s):** Gale & Debra Langford, 6071 Fulton St., Mayville, MI 08744-0299. TEL 517-843-6441; FAX 517-843-0054; Ed. Gale Langford; Pub. Gale Langford; adv.; photos; bk.rev.; pub. size: tabloid; circ. 1,200(paid).

MILAN

US

MILAN AREA LEADER. 1881. Wed. $.30 newsstand; $14/yr. Washtenau & Monroe cys; $16/yr. out of cys. 37 E. Main St., Milan, MI 48160-0017. TEL 313-439-8150; FAX 313-439-2278. **Owner(s):** Milan Area Leader, 37 E. Main, Milan, MI 48160. TEL 313-439-8118; FAX 313-439-2278; Pub. G.R. Jones; adv. contact: Timothy Troin. photos; bk.rev.; pub. size: tabloid; circ. 3,725(paid).

MILFORD

US

MILFORD TIMES. 1871. Thu. $.50 newsstand; $26/yr. local mailed. 405 N. Main St., Milford, MI 48381. TEL 810-685-1509; FAX 810-437-9460. **Owner(s):** Hometown Newspapers, 323 E. Grand River Ave., Howell, MI 48843. TEL 517-548-2000; Ed. Maggie Wolfgang. adv. contact: Michael Preville. pub. size: broadsheet; circ. 6,568(paid).

MORENCI
US
MORENCI OBSERVER. 1872. Wed. $.50 newsstand; $18/yr. in area; $22/yr. out of area. 120 North St., Morenci, MI 49256. TEL 517-458-6811; FAX 517-458-6811. **Owner(s):** David Green, 120 North St., Morenci, MI 49256. TEL 517-458-6811; Ed. David Green; Pub. David Green; adv.: $4.20/SAU. pub. size: tabloid; circ. 2,377(paid).

MUNISING
US ISSN 1074-0201
MUNISING NEWS. 1896. Wed. $20/yr. in cy.; $25/yr. out of cy. P.O. Box 38, Munising, MI 49862-0038. TEL 906-387-3282. **Owner(s):** Esley M. Mattson, Munising, MI; John Williams, Munising, MI; Ed. Dan Wilson; Pub. Esley M. Mattson; pub. size: broadsheet; circ. 3,450(paid).

MUSKEGON
US
LAKE MICHIGAN EXAMINER, THE. 1968. Wed. $.50 newsstand; $24/yr. 3494 Peninsula Dr., Muskegon, MI 49444. TEL 616-739-6397; FAX 616-737-1520; E-mail: examiner95@aol.com. **Owner(s):** SCS Publishing, Inc., 3494 Peninsula Dr., Muskegon, MI 49444. TEL 616-739-6397; FAX 616-737-1520; Ed. Susan Carrington. adv.; photos; bk.rev.; pub. size: tabloid; circ. 5,000(controlled & paid). **Wire Service(s):** AP.
  Formerly: Examiner, The.

NEW BALTIMORE
US ISSN 8750-7188
BAY VOICE. 1983. Wed. $21/yr. 31950 23 Mile Rd., New Baltimore, MI 48047. TEL 810-949-7900; FAX 810-949-2217. **Owner(s):** Tom & Beth Stanton, P.O. Box 760, New Baltimore, MI 48047. TEL 810-949-7900; FAX 810-949-2217; Dorothy & Joe Stabile, P.O. Box 760, New Baltimore, MI 48047; Ed. Tom Stanton. adv.; photos; pub. size: tabloid; circ. 22,000(paid).

US
BLUE WATER VOICE. 1985. Wed. $21/yr. 31950 23 Mile Rd., New Baltimore, MI 48047. TEL 810-765-4059; FAX 810-949-2217. **Owner(s):** Tom & Beth Stanton, 31950 23 Mile Rd., New Baltimore, MI 48047. TEL 810-765-4059; Joe & Dorothy Stabile, 31950 23 Mile Rd., New Baltimore, MI 48047; Ed. Tom Stanton. photos; pub. size: tabloid; circ. 11,000(paid).

US
DOWNRIVER VOICE. 1985. Wed. $21/yr. 31950 23 Mile Rd., Box 760, New Baltimore, MI 48047. TEL 810-765-4059. **Owner(s):** Tom & Beth Stanton, 31950 23 Mile Rd., Box 760, New Baltimore, MI 48047; Joe & Dorothy Stabile, 31950 23 Mile Rd., New Baltimore, MI 48047; Ed. Donna Remer. adv. contact: Debbie Loggins. photos; pub. size: tabloid; circ. 11,000(paid).

US
MACOMB VOICE, THE. 1985. Wed. free in area; $21/yr. out of area. P.O. Box 760, New Baltimore, MI 48047. TEL 810-949-7900; FAX 810-949-2217. **Owner(s):** Tom & Beth Stanton, 31950 23 Mile Rd., New Baltimore, MI 48047. TEL 810-949-7900; Joe & Dorothy Stabile, 31950 23 Mile Rd., New Baltimore, MI 48047; Ed. Donna Remer. adv. contact: Debbie Loggins. photos; pub. size: tabloid; circ. 56,909(controlled & paid).

US
NORTH MACOMB VOICE. 1985. Wed. $25/yr. 31950 23 Mile Rd., New Baltimore, MI 48047. TEL 313-765-4059. **Owner(s):** Tom & Beth Stanton, 31950 23 Mile Rd., New Baltimore, MI 48047; Joe & Dorothy Stabile, 31950 23 Mile Rd., New Baltimore, MI 48047; Ed. Donna Remer. adv.; photos; pub. size: tabloid; circ. 9,000(paid).

NEW BUFFALO
US
NEW BUFFALO TIMES. 1943. Wed. $.50 newsstand; $26/yr. 102 S. Whittaker St., New Buffalo, MI 49117. TEL 616-469-1100; FAX 616-469-4812. **Owner(s):** M.B. Moriarty, P.O. Box 369, New Buffalo, MI 49117. TEL 616-469-1100; Ed. M.B. Moriarty; Pub. M.B. Moriarty; pub. size: tabloid; circ. 3,500(paid).

NORTHVILLE
US ISSN 1050-2467
NORTHVILLE RECORD. 1869. Thu. $.50 newsstand; $26/yr. mailed. 104 W. Main St., Northville, MI 48167. TEL 810-349-1700; FAX 810-349-1050. **Owner(s):** Hometown Newspapers, 323 E. Grand River, Howell, MI 48843. TEL 517-548-2003; Pub. Rich Perlberg; adv. contact: Michael Preville. pub. size: broadsheet; circ. 5,781(paid).

US
NOVI NEWS. 1977. Thu. $.50 newstand; $26/yr. 104 W. Main St., Northville, MI 48167. TEL 810-349-1700; FAX 810-349-1050; E-mail: mikem@oeonline.com. **Owner(s):** Hometown Newspapers, 323 E. Grand River Ave., Howell, MI 48843. TEL 517-548-2000; FAX 517-548-3005; Ed. Mike Malott. adv. contact: Michael Preville. pub. size: broadsheet; circ. 6,500(paid).

NORWAY
US ISSN 1071-2607
NORWAY CURRENT. 1885. Wed. $.50 newsstand; $23/yr. 821 Main St., Norway, MI 49870. TEL 906-563-5212; FAX 906-563-5904. **Owner(s):** Larry & Vicki Underhill, 723 Main St., Norway, MI 49870. TEL 906-563-5212; FAX 906-563-5904; Ed. Vicki Underhill; Pub. L.A. Underhill; adv. contact: L.A. Underhill. photos; bk.rev.; pub. size: tabloid; circ. 1,500(controlled & paid).

ONAWAY
US
ONAWAY OUTLOOK. 1974. Fri. $.35 newsstand; $21/yr. local mailed. 319 Washington Ave., Onaway, MI 49765. TEL 517-733-6543. **Owner(s):** Milliman Communications, Inc., P.O. Box 160, Mason, MI 48854. TEL 517-676-1260; Ed. Bill Breed; Pub. Richard Lamb; adv.; pub. size: tabloid; circ. 2,400(paid).

ONTONAGON
US
ONTONAGON HERALD. 1881. Wed. $.60 newsstand; $26.50/yr. in cy.; $30.50/yr. out of cy. 326 River St., Ontonagon, MI 49953-0098. TEL 906-884-2826; FAX 906-884-2939. **Owner(s):** Maureen Guzek, P.O. Box 98, Ontonagon, MI 49953-0098. TEL 906-884-2826; FAX 906-884-2939; Ed. Maureen Guzek; Pub. Maureen Guzek; adv.; photos; bk.rev.; pub. size: broadsheet; circ. 3,700(paid).

ORTONVILLE
US
COUNTY LINE REMINDER. 1953. Sun. free. 48 South St., Ortonville, MI 48462. TEL 810-627-2843; FAX 810-627-3473. **Owner(s):** Walt Disney Co., 500 S. Buena Vista St., Burbank, CA 91521. TEL 818-560-5300; Ed. Kathleen Steffen; Pub. Ernest Slade; adv.; photos; pub. size: broadsheet; circ. 11,000(free).

OSCODA
US
OSCODA PRESS. 1800. Wed. $.50 newsstand; $22/yr. in cy.; $26/yr. out of cy.; $32/yr. out of state. 311 S. State, Oscoda, MI 48750. TEL 517-739-2055; FAX 517-739-3201. **Owner(s):** News Press Publishers, P.O. Box 663, Oscoda, MI 48750. TEL 517-739-3201; Neal Miller, P.O. Box 663, Oscoda, MI 48750, TEL 517-739-3201; Pub. J. Berkeley Smith; pub. size: tabloid; circ. 6,700(paid).

OWOSSO
US
SUNDAY INDEPENDENT, THE. 1968. Sun. $20/6 mos.; $30/yr. 1907 W M-21, Owosso, MI 48867-9317. TEL 517-723-1118; FAX 517-725-1834; E-mail: sundayindy@aol.com. **Owner(s):** Michael Flores, 1907 W M-21, Owosso, MI 48867. TEL 517-723-1118; FAX 517-725-7925; Leonard Krawczyk, 1106 S. Washington, Owosso, MI 48867. TEL 517-725-5322; Ed. Bill Constine; Pub. Michael Flores; adv.: $25/SAU. pub. size: tabloid; circ. 40,577(free).

PARMA
US
COUNTY PRESS. 1868. Wed. $.50 newsstand; $20/yr. 123 W. Main St., Parma, MI 49269. TEL 517-531-4542; FAX 517-531-3576. **Owner(s):** Schepeler Corp., 123 W. Main St., Parma, MI 49269. TEL 517-531-4542; FAX 517-531-3576; Ed. Jeanine Kohler-Schepeler. adv. contact: LuAnn Faling. photos; pub. size: tabloid; circ. 1,500(free & paid).
  Formerly: Parma News, West County Press.

PAW PAW
US
PAW PAW COURIER-LEADER. 1844. Fri. $.50 newsstand; $14/yr. local; $16/yr. elsewhere. 32280 Red Arrow, Paw Paw, MI 49079-0129. TEL 616-657-3072; FAX 616-657-5723. **Owner(s):** Vineyard Press, Inc., P.O. Box 129, Paw Paw, MI 49079-0129. TEL 616-657-3072; FAX 616-657-5723; Ed. Felix A. Racette. adv.; photos; pub. size: broadsheet; circ. 4,100(paid).

WEEKLY NEWSPAPERS

PERRY
US
SHIAWASSEE COUNTY JOURNAL. 1893. Wed. $.35 newsstand; $20/yr. mailed; $18/yr. senior citizens. 130 N. Main St., Perry, MI 48872. TEL 517-625-3181; FAX 517-288-4666. **Owner(s):** Owen & Arlene Rood, 219 N. Saginaw, Durand, MI 48429. TEL 517-288-3164; Ed. Bryan Myrkle; Pub. Owen Rood; adv. contact: Dan Dolihanti. pub. size: tabloid; circ. 6,035(paid).

PINCKNEY
US
PINCKNEY POST SHOPPING GUIDE. 1980. Wed. free. 107 E. Main St., Pinckney, MI 48169. TEL 313-878-3107; FAX 313-878-9247. **Owner(s):** Hometown Newspapers, 323 E. Grand River, Howell, MI 48843. TEL 517-548-2000; FAX 517-548-3005; Pub. Richard Perlberg; adv. contact: Michael Preville. pub. size: tabloid; circ. 10,400(free).

PLAINWELL
US
UNION ENTERPRISE. 1869. Thu. $.35 newsstand; $15/yr. in cy.; $18/yr. out of cy.; $22/yr. out of state. 352 12th St., Plainwell, MI 49080. TEL 616-685-9571. **Owner(s):** Cherly Kaechele, P.O. Box 417, Plainwell, MI 49080. TEL 616-685-9571; Ed. Dave Trinka; Pub. Cheryl Kaechele; adv.; pub. size: tabloid; circ. 5,625(free & paid).

PLYMOUTH
US
CANTON OBSERVER. s-w.: Mon & Thu. $.75 newsstand; $42/yr. in cy. 794 S. Main, Plymouth, MI 48170. TEL 313-459-2700; FAX 313-459-4224. **Owner(s):** Suburban Communications Corp., 36251 Schoolcraft Rd., Livonia, MI 48150. TEL 313-591-2300; Ed. Sue Rosiek; Pub. Banks Dishman; adv. contact: Peg Knoepsel. pub. size: broadsheet; circ. 6,000(paid).

US
PLYMOUTH OBSERVER. 1967. s-w.: Mon. & Thu. $.75 newsstand; $42/yr. in cy. 744 Wing St., Plymouth, MI 48170. TEL 313-459-2700; FAX 313-459-4224. **Owner(s):** Suburban Communications Corp., 36251 Schoolcraft Rd., Livonia, MI 48150. TEL 313-591-2300; Ed. Sue Rosiek; Pub. Banks Dishman; adv. contact: Peg Knoepsel. pub. size: broadsheet; circ. 10,000(paid).

PONTIAC
US
IN YOUR COMMUNITY/OAKLAND PRESS. Thu. $.35 newsstand; $79/yr. mailed. 48 W. Huron St., Pontiac, MI 48342. TEL 810-745-4626; FAX 810-332-8885. **Owner(s):** Walt Disney Co., 500 S. Buena Vista St., Burbank, CA 91521. TEL 818-560-5300; Ed. Al Adler. pub. size: broadsheet; circ. 142,000(free).
Formerly: Reminder, The.

REED CITY
US
HERALD NEWS, THE. Thu. $.50 newsstand; $18/yr. in cy.; $28/yr. out of cy.; $38/yr. out of state. 101 W. Slosson St., Reed City, MI 49677. TEL 616-832-5566; FAX 616-832-5558. **Owner(s):** Pioneer Group, 502 N. State St., Big Rapids, MI 49307. TEL 616-796-4831; Ed. Molly Van Black; Pub. Jack Batdorff; adv.; photos; pub. size: broadsheet; circ. 3,000(paid).
Formerly: Reed City Osceola County Herald.

RICHMOND
US
RICHMOND REVIEW, THE. 1876. Mon. $.50 newsstand; $19.95/yr. local mailed. 68834 S. Main St., Richmond, MI 48062. TEL 810-727-3745; FAX 810-727-3929. **Owner(s):** Sanilac Publishing Inc., 4325 S. Sandusky Rd., Sandusky, MI 48471. TEL 810-648-4000; Ed. Jim Hopper; Pub. Bruce David; adv. contact: Helga Wissell. pub. size: tabloid; circ. 8,500(free & paid).

ROCHESTER
US
ROCHESTER CLARION. 1898. Thu. $.50 newsstand; $19/yr. in cy.; $24/yr. out of cy. 429 Walnut St., Rochester, MI 48308. TEL 810-651-4321; FAX 810-651-8243. **Owner(s):** Justin W. Wilcox, P.O. Box 9, Rochester, MI 48307. TEL 313-651-4321; Ed. Tony Manolatos. pub. size: broadsheet; circ. 10,000(paid).

ROCHESTER HILLS
US
ROCHESTER ECCENTRIC. 1972. s-w.: Mon. & Thu. $.75 newsstand; $42/yr. in cy. 1814 S. Rochester Rd., Rochester Hills, MI 48307. TEL 810-651-7575; FAX 810-651-9080. **Owner(s):** Suburban Communications Corp., 36251 Schoolcraft Rd., Livonia, MI 48150. TEL 313-591-2300; Ed. Bob Sklar. adv. contact: Bob Kampf. pub. size: broadsheet; circ. 10,000(paid).

US
TROY ECCENTRIC. 1972. s-w.: Mon. & Thu. $.50 newsstand; $36.40/yr. in cy. 1814 S. Rochester Rd., Rochester Hills, MI 48307. TEL 810-651-7575; FAX 810-651-9080. **Owner(s):** Suburban Communications Corp., 36251 Schoolcraft Rd., Livonia, MI 48150. TEL 313-591-2300; Ed. Bob Sklar. adv. contact: Tom Byrd. photos; bk.rev.; pub. size: broadsheet; circ. 10,500(paid).

ROCKFORD
US
ROCKFORD SQUIRE. 1983. Thu. free local; $20/yr. mailed. 51 E. Bridge St., Rockford, MI 49341. TEL 616-866-4465; FAX 616-866-3810; E-mail: shoewich@aol.com. **Owner(s):** Rockford Publishing Co., 51 E. Bridge St., Rockford, MI 48341. TEL 616-866-3810; Pub. Roger Allen; adv. contact: Alan Richard. bk.rev.; pub. size: tabloid; circ. 8,700(free & paid).

ROGERS CITY
US
PRESQUE ISLE ADVANCE. 1878. Thu. $.50 newsstand; $23/yr. in cy.; $24/yr. in state; $25/yr. out of state. 104 S. Third St., Rogers City, MI 49779. TEL 517-734-2105. **Owner(s):** Presque Isle Newspapers, Inc., 104 S. Third St., Rogers City, MI 49779. TEL 517-734-2105; Ed. Richard Lamb; Pub. Richard Lamb; pub. size: broadsheet; circ. 4,300(paid).

ROMEO
US
ROMEO OBSERVER. 1866. Wed. $.50 newsstand; $10/yr. 124 W. St. Clair, Romeo, MI 48065-0096. TEL 810-752-3524. **Owner(s):** Romeo Observer Inc., 124 W. St. Clair, Romeo, MI 48065-0096. TEL 313-752-3524; Ed. Melvin E. Bleich; Pub. Melvin E. Bleich; pub. size: standard; circ. 19,000(free & paid).

ROSCOMMON
US
ROSCOMMON COUNTY HERALD-NEWS. 1875. Sun. $.50 newsstand; $25/yr. in state mailed; $30/yr. out of state. 905 Lake St., Roscommon, MI 48653. TEL 517-275-5100. **Owner(s):** Robert Perlberg, P.O. Box 247, West Branch, MI 48661; Ed. Phil Bendely; Pub. Robert Perlberg; adv.; pub. size: broadsheet; circ. 15,000(paid).

ROYAL OAK
US
TRIBUNE PLUS. Sun. free; voluntary contribution. 210 E. Third St., Royal Oak, MI 48067. TEL 810-541-3000; FAX 810-541-7903. **Owner(s):** Independent Newspapers, Inc., 100 Macomb Daily Dr., Mount Clemens, MI 48043. TEL 810-469-4510; Ed. Joe Ballor; Pub. R.D. Isham; adv. contact: Matt Fasing. photos; bk.rev.; pub. size: tabloid; circ. 101,000(free).

SAGINAW
US
SAGINAW PRESS, THE. 1912. Fri. $.30 newsstand; $12/yr. 410 Hancock St., Saginaw, MI 48602-4279. TEL 517-793-8070; FAX 517-793-7225. **Owner(s):** Saginaw Publishing Co., 410 Hancock St., Saginaw, MI 48602. TEL 517-793-8070; Ed. George W. Baxter, III. adv.: $4.76/SAU. pub. size: standard; circ. 700(controlled & paid).

US
TOWNSHIP TIMES. 1964. Wed. $.50 newsstand; $24/yr. 2089 Wieneke Rd., Saginaw, MI 48603-3338. TEL 517-799-3200; FAX 517-799-7085. **Owner(s):** Saginaw Community News, 2089 Wienke Rd., Saginaw, MI 48603. TEL 517-799-3200; Pub. Edward Belles; adv. contact: Bob Grnak. photos; pub. size: tabloid; circ. 6,000(paid).

SALINE
US
SALINE REPORTER. 1948. Wed. $.50 newsstand; $20/yr. in city; $20/yr. out of city. 106 W. Michigan Ave., Saline, MI 48176. TEL 313-429-7380; FAX 313-429-3621. **Owner(s):** Heritage Newspapers, Inc., One Heritage Pl., Ste. 100, Southgate, MI 48195. TEL 313-246-0800; Ed. Tom Kirvan. adv.; pub. size: broadsheet; circ. 4,800(paid).

SANDUSKY
US
SANILAC COUNTY NEWS. 1971. Wed. $.75 newsstand; $17.75/yr. in cy. mailed; $32.50/yr. out of cy.; $16.50/yr. senior citizens. 432 S. Sandusky Rd., Sandusky, MI 48471. TEL 810-648-4000; FAX 810-648-4002. **Owner(s):** Sanilac Publishing, Inc., 432 S. Sandusky Rd., Sandusky, MI 48471. TEL 810-648-4000; Ed. Eric Levine; Pub. John D. Johnson; adv. contact: Carlene Soroka. photos; pub. size: tabloid; circ. 32,500(free & paid).
Formerly: Sandusky Sanilac County News.

SAUGATUCK
US
COMMERCIAL RECORD. 1882. Thu. $.50 newsstand; $15/yr. in cy. P.O. Box 246, Saugatuck, MI 49453. TEL 616-857-2570; FAX 616-857-4637. **Owner(s):** Kaechele Publications, Inc., P.O. Box 189, Allegan, MI 49010. TEL 616-673-5534; Ed. Donita Hunt; Pub. Cheryl Kaechele; adv.; photos; pub. size: broadsheet; circ. 5,000(paid).

SEBEWAING
US
NEWSWEEKLY, THE. 1890. Tue. $.50 newsstand; $21/yr. mailed locally; $31/yr. elsewhere. 236 N. Center St., Sebewaing, MI 48759. TEL 517-883-3100; FAX 517-883-9211. **Owner(s):** Walt Disney Co., 500 S. Buena Vista St., Burbank, CA 91521. TEL 818-560-5300; Ed. Mark Rummel. adv. contact: Lorrine Kuhl. pub. size: tabloid; circ. 7,200(paid).
Formerly: Blade & Progress Newsweekly.

SOUTHGATE
US
NEWS-HERALD, THE. s-w.: Wed. & Sun. $.75 newsstand; $48/yr. home deliv.; $78/yr. mailed. One Heritage Pl., Ste. 100, Southgate, MI 48195. TEL 313-246-0800; FAX 313-284-2028. **Owner(s):** Heritage Newspapers, Inc., One Heritage Pl., Ste. 100, Southgate, MI 48195. TEL 313-246-0800; Ed. Karl Ziomek; Pub. Fredrick Manuel; adv. contact: Darrell Futo. photos; pub. size: broadsheet; circ. 84,902(controlled & paid); Sun. 90,000(controlled & paid).
Formerly: Lincoln Park News-Herald, The.

SOUTH LYON
US
SOUTH LYON HERALD. 1880. Thu. $.50 newsstand; $26/yr. in cy.; $32/yr. out of cy. 101 N. Lafayette, South Lyon, MI 48178. TEL 810-437-2011; FAX 810-437-9460. **Owner(s):** Hometown Newspapers, 323 E. Grand River, Howell, MI 48843. TEL 517-548-2000; Ed. Rick Byrne; Pub. Rich Perlberg; adv. contact: Lisa M. Dranginis. pub. size: broadsheet; circ. 6,000(paid).

SPARTA
US
SPARTA/KENT CITY ADVANCE. 1989. Tue. free in area; $20/6 mos. out of area; $30/yr. out of area. 151 E. Division, Sparta, MI 49345. TEL 616-887-8400; FAX 616-887-7230. **Owner(s):** Valley Media, Inc., 2141 Port Sheldon Rd., Jenison, MI 49428. TEL 616-669-2700; FAX 616-669-1162; Ed. Mike Wyngarden; Pub. Joel Holland; pub. size: tabloid; circ. 12,075(free & paid).

STANDISH
US
ARENAC COUNTY INDEPENDENT. 1883. Wed. $.50 newsstand; $18/yr. in cy. mailed; $25/yr. out of cy.; $30/yr. out of state. 203 E. Cedar, Standish, MI 48658. TEL 517-846-4531; FAX 517-846-9868. **Owner(s):** R.E. Perlberg, P.O. Box 699, Standish, MI 48658. TEL 517-846-4531; Ed. Ben Welmers; Pub. Robert Perlberg; adv. contact: Kip Pomranky. pub. size: broadsheet; circ. 6,000(paid).
Formerly: Standish Arenac County Independent.

ST. IGNACE
US
ST. IGNACE NEWS, THE. 1878. Thu. $.50 newsstand; $24/yr. 359 Reagon St., St. Ignace, MI 49781-0277. TEL 906-643-9150; FAX 906-643-9122. **Owner(s):** St. Ignace News, 359 Reagon St., St. Ignace, MI 49781-0277. TEL 906-643-9150; Ed. Wesley H. Maurer, Jr.; Pub. Wesley H. Maurer; adv. contact: Richard Hayden. photos; bk.rev.; pub. size: broadsheet; circ. 6,700(paid).

ST. JOHNS
US
CLINTON COUNTY NEWS. 1930. Sun. free newsstand & local deliv.; $104/yr. mailed 1st class. 215 N. Clinton Ave., St. Johns, MI 48879. TEL 517-224-2361; FAX 517-224-4452. **Owner(s):** Community Newspapers, Inc., 239 S. Cochran St., Charlotte, MI 48813; Ed. Jennifer Vincent; Pub. Preston Odette; photos; pub. size: tabloid; circ. 13,767(free & paid).

DEWITT BATH REVIEW. 1979. Sun. free home deliv.; $.35 newsstand. 215 N. Clinton, St. Johns, MI 48879. TEL 517-224-2361; FAX 517-224-4452. **Owner(s):** Suburban Communications Corp., 36251 Schoolcraft Rd., Livonia, MI 48150. TEL 313-591-2300; FAX 313-591-9424; Ed. Jennifer Vincent; Pub. Preston O'Dette; adv.; pub. size: tabloid; circ. 8,050(free & paid).

ST. JOHNS REMINDER. 1949. Sat. free; $32/yr. 109 W. Higham, St. Johns, MI 48879. TEL 517-224-8356; FAX 517-224-9458. **Owner(s):** Central Michigan Newspapers, P.O. Box 766, Mt. Pleasant, MI 48804-0766; Pub. Rhonda Westfall; adv.; pub. size: tabloid; circ. 16,200(paid).

STOCKBRIDGE
US
TOWN CRIER. 1967. Tue. $.35 newsstand; $15/yr. in state; $29/yr. out of state. 510 Water St., Stockbridge, MI 49285-0548. TEL 517-851-7833; FAX 517-851-4641. **Owner(s):** Charlotte Camp, P.O. Box 548, Stockbridge, MI 49285. TEL 517-851-7833; Ed. Ruth Camp Wellman; Pub. Ruth Camp Wellman; adv. contact: Brian White. pub. size: tabloid; circ. 10,000(paid).

SWARTZ CREEK
US
DAVISON FLAGSTAFF. s-w.: Thu. & Sun. free deliv.; $.25 newsstand. P.O. Box 497, Swartz Creek, MI 48473. TEL 810-733-2239; FAX 810-733-2688. **Owner(s):** Flint Advance Newspapers, G 5085 Miller Rd., Flint, MI 48507. TEL 810-238-5070; Ed. Dennis Setter; Pub. John J. Badoud, Jr.; adv. contact: Tom Reynolds. pub. size: broadsheet; circ. 8,808(free).

TECUMSEH
US
TECUMSEH HERALD. 1850. Thu. $.50 newsstand; $22/yr. in cy.; $24/yr. out of cy. 110 E. Logan St., Tecumseh, MI 49286. TEL 517-423-2174; FAX 517-423-6258. **Owner(s):** James C., Dorothy L., & James L. Lincoln, 499 Seminole Dr., Tecumseh, MI 49286. TEL 517-423-7096; Ed. James L. Lincoln; Pub. James C. Lincoln; adv.; photos; pub. size: broadsheet; circ. 5,500(paid).

THREE RIVERS
US
PENNY SAVER. 1985. Sun. free. 124 N. Main St., Three Rivers, MI 49093. TEL 616-279-7488; FAX 616-279-6007. **Owner(s):** Richard L. Milliman, 124 N. Main St., Three Rivers, MI 49093. TEL 616-279-7488; Ed. Joe Albertson; Pub. Lori Bogda; adv. contact: Lori Bogda. pub. size: tabloid; circ. 16,400(free). **Wire Service(s):** AP, NEA, CNS.

TROY
US
TROY-SOMERSET GAZETTE. 1980. Mon. free newsstand; $.75/wk. mailed. 1903 E. Wattles, Troy, MI 48098. TEL 810-524-4868; FAX 810-524-9140. **Owner(s):** Claire M. Springer, 6506 Tanglewood, Troy, MI 48098. TEL 810-828-8523; Ed. Cynthia Kmett; Pub. Claire M. Springer; adv. contact: Kathy Troshyski. photos; pub. size: tabloid; circ. 25,000(free). **Wire Service(s):** PR.

UTICA
US
ADVISOR/SOURCE. 1972. s-w.: Sun. & Thu. $1 newsstand; $65/yr. local mailed. 48075 Van Dyke Ave., Utica, MI 48317. TEL 810-731-1000; FAX 810-781-8172. **Owner(s):** Independent Newspapers, Inc., 48075 Van Dyke Ave., Utica, MI 48317. TEL 313-731-1000; Ed. Gary Winkleman. adv. contact: Phil Marien. photos; pub. size: broadsheet; circ. 113,500(paid); Sun. 115,000(paid).

VANDERBILT
US
OUR HOME TOWN. 1956. Thu. $.35 newsstand; $14/yr. local. 540 E. Main St., Vanderbilt, MI 49795. TEL 517-732-7167; FAX 517-732-7167. **Owner(s):** Tom Serino, P.O. Box 101, Vanderbilt, MI 49795-0101. TEL 517-983-4132; FAX 517-732-7167; Ed. Tom Serino; Pub. Tom Serino; adv.; photos; bk.rev.; pub. size: tabloid; circ. 1,100(paid).

WEEKLY NEWSPAPERS

VASSAR
US
VASSAR PIONEER TIMES. 1857. Wed. $12/yr. 113 S. Main St., Vassar, MI 48768. TEL 517-823-8579; FAX 517-823-8778. **Owner(s):** Hearst Corp., 959 Eighth Ave., New York, NY 10019. TEL 216-642-5516; Ed. Sandy Walker. adv.: $5.50/SAU. photos; bk.rev.; pub. size: tabloid; circ. 1,813(paid).

VICKSBURG
US
COMMERCIAL-EXPRESS. 1879. Wed. $.50 newsstand; $18/yr. 109 S. Main, Vicksburg, MI 49097. TEL 616-649-2333; FAX 616-649-2335. **Owner(s):** McGraw Publishing Inc., 109 S. Main, Vicksburg, MI 49097. TEL 616-649-2333; Ed. Scott McGraw; Pub. Scott McGraw; pub. size: tabloid; circ. 2,200(paid).

WATERFORD
US
SPINAL COLUMN NEWSWEEKLY. 1960. Wed. $.50 newsstand; $26/yr. in area. 7196 Cooley Lake Rd., Waterford, MI 48327. TEL 810-360-6397. **Owner(s):** Union Lake Spinal Column, 7196 Cooley Lake Rd., Union Lake, MI 48327. TEL 313-360-6397; Ed. Tim Dmoch; Pub. James W. Fancy; adv.; pub. size: tabloid; circ. 50,000(controlled).

WATERVLIET
US
TRI-CITY RECORD, THE. 1882. Wed. $.50 newsstand; $22/yr. in cy.; $26/yr. out of cy.; $30/yr. out of state. 138 N. Main St., Watervliet, MI 49098. TEL 616-463-6397; FAX 616-463-8329. **Owner(s):** Anne & Karl Bayer, 138 N. Main St., Watervliet, MI 49098; Ed. Karl Bayer; Pub. Anne Bayer; adv.; pub. size: broadsheet; circ. 2,700(paid).

WAYNE
US
BELLEVILLE ENTERPRISE. 1886. s-w.: Thu. & Sun. $.50 newsstand; $26/yr. in area; $28/yr. out of area. 35540 Michigan Ave., W., Wayne, MI 48184. TEL 313-729-4000; FAX 313-729-6088. **Owner(s):** Mike Wilcox, P.O. Box 578, Wayne, MI 48184. TEL 313-729-4000; Ed. Joan Byer-Zinner; Pub. Mike Wilcox; adv. contact: Ron Spielman. pub. size: broadsheet; circ. 5,241(paid).

US
CANTON EAGLE. 1945. s-w.: Thu. & Sun. $.50 newsstand; $26/yr. in area; $28/yr. out of area. 35540 Michigan Ave., Wayne, MI 48184. TEL 313-729-4000; FAX 313-729-6088. **Owner(s):** Mike Wilcox, P.O. Box 578, Wayne, MI 48184; Ed. Joan Dyer-Zinner; Pub. Mike Wilcox; adv. contact: Ron Spielman. pub. size: broadsheet; circ. 10,148(controlled).

US
INKSTER LEDGER-STAR. 1945. s-w.: Thu. & Sun. $.50 newsstand; $26/yr. in area; $28/yr. out of area. 35540 Michigan Ave., W., Wayne, MI 48184. TEL 313-729-4000; FAX 313-729-6088. **Owner(s):** Mike Wilcox, P.O. Box 578, Wayne, MI 48184. TEL 313-729-4000; FAX 313-729-6088; Ed. Joan Dyer-Zinner; Pub. Mike Wilcox; adv. contact: Ron Spielman. photos; pub. size: broadsheet; circ. 4,500(paid).

US
ROMULUS ROMAN. 1885. s-w.: Thu. & Sun. $.50 newsstand; $26/yr. in area; $28/yr. out of area. 35540 Michigan Ave., W., Wayne, MI 48184. TEL 313-729-4000; FAX 313-729-6088. **Owner(s):** Mike Wilcox, P.O. Box 578, Wayne, MI 48184. TEL 313-729-4000; Ed. Joan Byer-Zinner; Pub. Mike Wilcox; adv. contact: Ron Spielman. photos; pub. size: broadsheet; circ. 5,039(paid).

US
WAYNE EAGLE. 1945. s-w.: Thu. & Sun. $.50 newsstand; $26/yr. in area; $28/yr. out of area. 35540 Michigan Ave., W., Wayne, MI 48184. TEL 313-729-4000; FAX 313-729-6088. **Owner(s):** Mike Wilcox, P.O. Box 578, Wayne, MI 48184. TEL 313-729-4000; Ed. Joan Dyer-Zinner; Pub. Mike Wilcox; adv. contact: Ron Spielman. pub. size: broadsheet; circ. 6,069(paid).

US
WESTLAND EAGLE. 1945. s-w.: Thu. & Sun. $.50 newsstand; $26/yr. in area; $28/yr. out of area. 35540 Michigan Ave., W., Wayne, MI 48184. TEL 313-729-4000; FAX 313-729-6088. **Owner(s):** Mike Wilcox, P.O. Box 578, Wayne, MI 48184. TEL 313-729-4000; Ed. Joan Zinner; Pub. Mike Wilcox; adv. contact: Ron Spielman. photos; pub. size: broadsheet; circ. 17,459(paid).

WEST BRANCH
US
OGEMAW COUNTY HERALD. 1880. Thu. $18/yr. in cy.; $25/yr. out of cy.; $30/yr. out of state. 215 W. Houghton Ave., West Branch, MI 48661. TEL 517-345-0044. **Owner(s):** Robert Perlberg, 215 W. Houghton Ave., West Branch, MI 48661. TEL 517-345-0044; Ed. Bruce Buschoff; Pub. Robert Pearlberg; adv. contact: Kipp Pomranky. pub. size: broadsheet; circ. 10,000(paid).

US
STAR BUYERS GUIDE. 1972. Sun. free. 420 W. Houghton Ave., West Branch, MI 48661. TEL 517-345-0510; FAX 517-732-5125. **Owner(s):** Star Publications, P.O. Box 620, Gaylord, MI 49735. TEL 517-732-5125; FAX 517-732-9322; Pub. James R. Glasser; adv. contact: Susan Kelly. pub. size: tabloid; circ. 25,858(free).

WHITEHALL
US
WHITE LAKE BEACON. 1983. Mon. free home deliv.; $.50 newsstand. 432 Spring St., Whitehall, MI 49461. TEL 616-894-5356; FAX 616-894-2174. **Owner(s):** White Lake Beacon, Inc., 432 Spring St., Whitehall, MI 49461. TEL 616-894-5356; FAX 616-894-2174; Ed. Gregory N. Means. adv. contact: James Young. photos; pub. size: tabloid; circ. 11,700(free).

MINNESOTA

ADA
US
ADA NORMAN COUNTY INDEX. 1880. Tue. $.75 newsstand; $22/yr. in cy.; $26/yr. in state; $30/yr. out of state. 307 W. Main St., Ada, MN 56510-0148. TEL 218-784-2541; FAX 218-784-2551; E-mail: nci@ada.polaristel.net. **Owner(s):** Index Printing, Inc., 307 W. Main St., Ada, MN 56510. TEL 218-784-2541; FAX 218-784-2551; Ed. Ross D. Pfund; Pub. John R. Pfund; adv.; photos; pub. size: standard; circ. 2,450(free & paid).

AITKIN
US
AITKIN INDEPENDENT AGE. 1883. Wed. $25/yr. local; $30/yr. out of cy.; $35/yr. out of state. 213 Minnesota Ave., N., Aitkin, MN 56431-0259. TEL 218-927-3761; FAX 218-927-3763. **Owner(s):** Dick Norlander, P. O. Box 259, Aitkin, MN 56431. TEL 218-927-3761; Ed. Ann Schwartz. adv. contact: Eric Heglund. pub. size: broadsheet; circ. 5,860(paid).

ALEXANDRIA
US
ECHO PRESS, THE. 1875. s-w.: Wed. & Fri. $.75 newsstand; $41/yr. in state mailed; $54/yr. out of state. 225 Seventh Ave., E., Alexandria, MN 56308. TEL 612-763-3133; FAX 612-763-3258; E-mail: echo@rea-alp.com; URL: http://www.echopress.com. **Owner(s):** Forum Communications Co., 101 Fifth St., N., Fargo, ND 58102; Ed. Al Edenloff; Pub. Jon O. Haaven; adv. contact: Jody Hansen. photos; bk.rev.; pub. size: broadsheet; circ. 10,000(paid).
Formerly: Echo, The.

BAGLEY
US   ISSN 0889-3470
FARMERS INDEPENDENT. 1918. Wed. $.75 newsstand; $17.50/yr. in cy.; $21.50/yr. out of cy.; $22.50/yr. out of state. 102 N. Main, Bagley, MN 56621. TEL 218-694-6265; FAX 218-694-6015. **Owner(s):** Farmers Independent, 102 N. Main, Bagley, MN 56621. TEL 218-694-6265; Ed. Tom Burford; Pub. Tom Burford; adv.; photos; pub. size: broadsheet; circ. 2,650(free & paid).

BAUDETTE

US

BAUDETTE REGION, THE. 1902. Wed. $.50 newsstand; $20/yr. local; $26/yr. out of area. P.O. Drawer C, Baudette, MN 56623-0240. TEL 218-634-1722; FAX 218-634-1224. **Owner(s):** North Star Publishing Co., P.O. Box 951, International Falls, MN 56649. TEL 218-285-7411; Ed. John C. Oren; Pub. John C. Oren; adv.: $4.10/SAU. photos; pub. size: broadsheet; circ. 2,250(free & paid).

BELGRADE

US

OBSERVER, THE. 1969. Wed. $.35 newsstand; $12/yr. in cy.; $14/yr. elsewhere. 303 Washburn Ave., Belgrade, MN 56312. TEL 320-254-8250; FAX 320-254-3215. **Owner(s):** Jim Lemmer, 303 Washburn Ave., Belgrade, MN 56326-0720. TEL 320-254-8250; Ed. Jim Lemmer; Pub. Jim Lemmer; adv. contact: Grace Scheel. photos; pub. size: tabloid; circ. 1,200(controlled & paid).

BEMIDJI

US

ADVERTISER, THE. s-w.: Wed. & Sun. free. 1320 Neilson Ave., S.E., Bemidji, MN 56601. TEL 218-751-3740; FAX 218-751-6914. **Owner(s):** Fargo Forum, 101 Fifth St., Fargo, ND 58102; adv. contact: Jeff Halversen. pub. size: standard; circ. 20,000(free).

BENSON

US

SWIFT COUNTY MONITOR-NEWS. 1887. Wed. $27/yr. local; $31/yr. in state; $35/yr. out of state. 101 12th St., S., Benson, MN 56215. TEL 320-843-4111; FAX 320-843-3246. **Owner(s):** Reed Anfinson, 101 12th St., S., Benson, MN 56215. TEL 320-843-4111; Rob Anfinson, 101 12th St., S., Benson, MN 56215. TEL 320-843-4111; Ed. Reed Anfinson; Pub. Reed Anfinson; adv. contact: Rob Anfinson. pub. size: broadsheet; circ. 3,104(paid).
Formerly: Benson Swift County Monitor-News.

BIRD ISLAND

US

BIRD ISLAND UNION. 1881. Wed. $.65 newsstand; $24/yr. in cy.; $27/yr. out of cy.; $32/yr. out of state. 750 Ash Ave., Bird Island, MN 55310. TEL 320-365-3266; FAX 320-365-3266. **Owner(s):** Hubin Publishing, 201 Main St., Hector, MN. TEL 320-848-2248; FAX 320-848-2249; Ed. Bren McDowell; Pub. John Hubin; adv.; photos; pub. size: broadsheet; circ. 1,000(paid).

BLAINE

US

BLAINE BANNER. 1985. m.: 1st Wed. free newsstand; $22/yr. 12570 Raddison Rd., N.E., Blaine, MN 55449. **Owner(s):** Blaine Banner, 12570 Raddison Rd., N.E., Blaine, MN 55449; adv.; photos; pub. size: tabloid; circ. 10,000(free & paid).

BLOOMINGTON

US

BLOOMINGTON SUN-CURRENT. 1954. Wed. $.75 newsstand; voluntary subscription; $40/yr. mailed. 7831 E. Bush Lake Rd., Bloomington, MN 55439. TEL 612-896-4700; FAX 612-896-4728. **Owner(s):** Minnesota Sun Publications LLC, 7831 E. Bush Lake Rd., Minneapolis, MN 55439. TEL 612-896-4700; Ed. Yvonne Klinnert; Pub. Denis Mindak; adv.: $1,424/B&W pg. pub. size: tabloid; circ. 29,510(free & paid).

US

EDEN PRAIRIE SUN-CURRENT. 1932. Wed. $.75 newsstand; voluntary subscription; $40/yr. mailed. 7831 E. Bushlake Rd., Bloomington, MN 55439. TEL 612-896-4700; FAX 612-896-4728. **Owner(s):** Minnesota Sun Publications LLC, 7831 E. Bush Lake Rd., Bloomington, MN 55439. TEL 612-896-4700; Ed. Yvonne Klinnert; Pub. Denis Mindak; adv.: $730/B&W pg. pub. size: tabloid; circ. 12,840(free & paid).

US

RICHFIELD SUN-CURRENT. Wed. free deliv.; $.75 newsstand; voluntary subscription; $25/yr. mailed. 7831 E. Bush Lake Rd., Bloomington, MN 55439. TEL 612-896-4700; FAX 612-896-4728. **Owner(s):** Minnesota Sun Publications LLC, 7831 E. Bush Lake Rd., Minneapolis, MN 55439. TEL 612-896-4700; Ed. Yvonne Klinnert; Pub. Denis Mindak; adv.: $762/B&W pg. photos; pub. size: tabloid; circ. 9,400(free & paid).

BLUE EARTH

US

FARIBAULT COUNTY REGISTER. 1869. Mon. $.75 newsstand; $24.50/yr. in cy.; $29.50/yr. out of cy. 125 N. Main St., Blue Earth, MN 56013. TEL 507-526-7324; FAX 507-526-4080. **Owner(s):** Ogden Newspapers, Inc., 1500 Main St., Wheeling, WV 26003. TEL 304-233-0100; FAX 304-233-0327; Ed. Kyle MacArthur. adv.; photos; bk.rev.; pub. size: tabloid; circ. 3,500(paid).

BUFFALO

US

WRIGHT COUNTY JOURNAL-PRESS. 1887. Thu. $25/yr. in state; $32/yr. out of state. 108 Central Ave., Buffalo, MN 55313. TEL 612-682-1221; FAX 612-682-5458. **Owner(s):** James P. McDonnell, Jr., 108 Central Ave., Buffalo, MN 55313. TEL 612-545-8000; Ed. James P. McDonnell; Pub. James P. McDonnell; pub. size: broadsheet; circ. 6,500(paid).

BURNSVILLE

US

APPLE VALLEY/ROSEMONT SUN-CURRENT. 1975. Wed. free deliv.; $.75 newsstand; voluntary subscription; $40/yr. mailed. 1209 E. Cliff Rd., Burnsville, MN 55337. TEL 612-890-4456; FAX 612-890-4970. **Owner(s):** Minnesota Sun Publications LLC, 7831 E. Bush Lake Rd., Bloomington, MN 55439. TEL 612-896-4700; Ed. Yvonne Klinnert; Pub. Denis Mindak; adv.: $1,288/B&W pg. pub. size: tabloid; circ. 15,043(free & paid).

US

BURNSVILLE/SAVAGE SUN-CURRENT. 1976. Wed. free deliv.; $.75 newsstand; voluntary subscription; $40/yr. mailed. 1209 E. Cliff Rd., Burnsville, MN 55337. TEL 612-890-4456; FAX 612-890-4970. **Owner(s):** Minnesota Sun Publications LLC, 7831 E. Bush Lake Rd., Minneapolis, MN 55439. TEL 612-896-4700; Ed. Yvonne Klinnert; Pub. Denis Mindak; adv. contact: Mike Maslow. adv.: $1,288/B&W pg. pub. size: tabloid; circ. 19,920(free & paid).

US ISSN 8750-2895

DAKOTA COUNTY TRIBUNE. 1884. Thu. $.50 newsstand; $24/yr. 1525 E. Hwy. 13, Burnsville, MN 55337. TEL 612-894-1111; FAX 612-894-1859. **Owner(s):** Joseph R. Clay, 1525 E. Hwy. 13, Burnsville, MN 55337. TEL 612-894-1111; Daniel H. Clay, 1525 E. Hwy. 13, Burnsville, MN 55337. TEL 612-894-1111; Ed. B. Haugen. adv. contact: Cindy Warweg. pub. size: tabloid; circ. 2,000(paid).

US

EAGAN SUN-CURRENT. Wed. free; $.75 newsstand; voluntary subscription; $40/yr. mailed. 1209 E. Cliff Rd., Burnsville, MN 55337. TEL 612-890-4456; FAX 612-890-4970. **Owner(s):** Minnesota Sun Publications LLC, 7831 E. Bush Lake Rd., Minneapolis, MN 55439. TEL 612-896-4700; Ed. Yvonne Klinnert; Pub. Denis Mindak; adv. contact: Mike Maslow. adv.: $1,288/B&W pg. pub. size: tabloid; circ. 17,855(free & paid).
Formerly: Eagan Chronicle.

US

LAKEVILLE SUN-CURRENT. 1975. Wed. free; $.75 newsstand; voluntary subscription; $40/yr. in state. 1209 E. Cliff Rd., Burnsville, MN 55337. TEL 612-890-4456; FAX 612-890-4970. **Owner(s):** Minnesota Sun Publications LLC, 7831 E. Bush Lake Rd., Bloomington, MN 55439. TEL 612-896-4700; Ed. Yvonne Klinnert; Pub. Denis Mindak; adv. contact: Mike Maslow. adv.: $1,288/B&W pg. pub. size: tabloid; circ. 276,000(free & paid).

US

SOUTH ST. PAUL/INVER GROVE HEIGHTS SUN-CURRENT. 1950. Wed. free deliv.; $.75 newsstand; voluntary subscription; $40/yr. mailed. 1209 E. Cliff Rd., Burnsville, MN 55337. TEL 612-890-4465; FAX 612-890-4970. **Owner(s):** Minnesota Sun Publications LLC, 7831 E. Bush Lake Rd., Edina, MN 55439. TEL 612-896-4700; Ed. Yvonne Klinnert; Pub. Denis Mindak; adv.: $1,109/B&W pg. photos; pub. size: tabloid; circ. 14,500(free & paid).

US

WEST ST. PAUL/MENDOTA HEIGHTS SUN-CURRENT. Wed. free deliv.; $.75 newsstand; voluntary subscription; $40/yr. mailed. 1209 E. Cliff Rd., Burnsville, MN 55337. TEL 612-890-4456; FAX 612-890-4970. **Owner(s):** Minnesota Sun Publications LLC, 7831 E. Bush Lake Rd., Minneapolis, MN 55439. TEL 612-896-4700; Ed. Yvonne Klinnert; Pub. Denis Mindak; adv.: $1,109/B&W pg. photos; pub. size: tabloid; circ. 10,200(free & paid).

CANBY

US

CANBY NEWS. 1878. Wed. $22/yr. in cy.; $25/yr. out of cy. 123 First St., E., Canby, MN 56220. TEL 507-223-5303; FAX 507-223-5404. **Owner(s):** Don & Ellie Beman, P.O. Box 129, Canby, MN 56220. TEL 507-223-5303; Ed. Don Beman; Pub. Don Beman; pub. size: broadsheet; circ. 3,947(paid).

WEEKLY NEWSPAPERS

CHANHASSEN
US

CHANHASSEN VILLAGER. 1987. Thu. free; $23/yr. in cy. mailed; $35/yr. out of cy. 80 W. 78th St., Chanhassen, MN 55317. TEL 612-445-3333; FAX 612-934-7960. **Owner(s):** Southwest Suburban Publishing Co., P.O. Box 8, 327 Marschall Rd., Shakopee, MN 55379; Ed. Dean Trippler; Pub. Mark Weber; adv. contact: Gary Klatt. adv.: $828/B&W pg. photos; pub. size: broadsheet; circ. 5,000(free & paid).

CHASKA
US

CHASKA HERALD. 1862. Thu. $24/yr. in cy.; $35/yr. out of cy. P.O. Box 113, Chaska, MN 55318. TEL 612-448-2650; FAX 612-448-3146. **Owner(s):** Southwest Suburban Publishing, P.O. Box 8, Shakopee, MN 55379; Ed. LaVonne Barac; Pub. Stan Rolfsrud; adv.; pub. size: broadsheet; circ. 4,700(paid).

CHISHOLM
US

CHISHOLM TRIBUNE PRESS. 1947. s-w.: Tue. & Thu. $.50 newsstand; $20/yr. in cy.; $24/yr. out of cy. 216 W. Lake St., Chisholm, MN 55719. TEL 218-254-4432; FAX 218-254-7141. **Owner(s):** County Journal, Inc., 216 W. Lake St., Chisholm, MN 55719; Ed. Brian Anderson; Pub. Eric Erickson; adv.; photos; pub. size: tabloid; circ. 3,250(paid).
Formerly: Chisholm Free Press & Tribune Press.

CLARISSA
US   ISSN 1065-0628

INDEPENDENT NEWS HERALD. 1891. Wed. $.50 newsstand; $20/yr. 310 W. Main St., Clarissa, MN 56440. TEL 218-756-2131; FAX 218-756-2126; E-mail: inhnews@eaglebend.polaristel.net. **Owner(s):** Ernest & Diane Silbernagel, 310 W. Main St., Clarissa, MN 56440. TEL 218-756-2131; FAX 218-756-2126; Pub. Ernest J. Silbernagel; adv.; photos; bk.rev.; pub. size: broadsheet; circ. 2,557(paid).
Formerly: News Herald.

CLINTON
US

NORTHERN STAR, THE. 1965. Thu. $.50 newsstand; $20/yr. in cy.; $23/yr. elsewhere. Main St., Clinton, MN 56225-0368. TEL 320-325-5152; FAX 320-325-5280. **Owner(s):** Kaercher Publications, Inc., Ortonville, MN 56278. TEL 612-839-6163; Ed. Lois Torgerson; Pub. James D. Kaercher; adv. contact: Denese Gustafson. pub. size: broadsheet; circ. 2,000(paid).

CLOQUET
US

CLOQUET BILLBOARD SHOPPER. 1962. s-w.: Wed. & Sat. free. 1418 S. Hwy. 33, Cloquet, MN 55720. TEL 218-879-6761; FAX 218-879-6696. **Owner(s):** Cloquet Newspapers, Inc., 1418 S. Hwy. 33, Cloquet, MN 55720. TEL 218-879-6761; Ed. Pat Faherty; Pub. Scott L. Elwood; adv. contact: Scott L. Elwood. pub. size: broadsheet; circ. 21,000(free).

US

CLOQUET PINE KNOT. 1884. s-w.: Wed. & Sat. $.50 newsstand; $23/yr. in cy. mailed; $29/yr. out of cy. 1418 S. Hwy. 33, Cloquet, MN 55720. TEL 218-879-6761. **Owner(s):** Cloquet Newspapers, Inc., 1418 S. Hwy. 33, Cloquet, MN 55720. TEL 218-879-6761; Ed. Scott L. Elwood; Pub. Scott L. Elwood; adv. contact: Karen Bakke. pub. size: broadsheet; circ. 4,100(paid).

COON RAPIDS
US   ISSN 1059-9525

ANOKA COUNTY UNION. 1865. Fri. $.60 newsstand; $21/yr. 4101 Coon Rapids Blvd., Coon Rapids, MN 55433. TEL 612-421-4444; FAX 612-421-4315. **Owner(s):** ECM Publishers, Inc., 4101 Coon Rapids Blvd., Coon Rapids, MN 55433. TEL 612-421-4444; FAX 612-421-4315; Ed. Peter Bodley; Pub. Elmer L. Andersen; adv. contact: Phil Frebault. photos; pub. size: broadsheet; circ. 5,800(paid).

US   ISSN 1059-9533

BLAINE-SPRING LAKE PARK LIFE. 1961. Fri. $.60 newsstand; $21/yr. 4101 Coon Rapids Blvd., Coon Rapids, MN 55433. TEL 612-421-4444; FAX 612-421-4315. **Owner(s):** ECM Publishers, Inc., 4101 Coon Rapids Blvd., Coon Rapids, MN 55433. TEL 612-421-4444; FAX 612-421-4315; Ed. Peter Bodley; Pub. Elmer L. Andersen; adv. contact: Phil Fribault. photos; pub. size: broadsheet; circ. 2,100(paid).

US   ISSN 1059-9541

COON RAPIDS HERALD. 1875. Fri. $.60 newsstand; $21/yr. 4101 Coon Rapids Blvd., Coon Rapids, MN 55433. TEL 612-421-4444; FAX 612-421-4315. **Owner(s):** ECM Publishers, Inc., 4101 Coon Rapids Blvd., Coon Rapids, MN 55433. TEL 612-421-4444; FAX 612-421-4315; Ed. Peter G. Bailey; Pub. Elmer L. Andersen; adv. contact: Phil Frebault. photos; pub. size: broadsheet; circ. 4,000(paid).

DETROIT LAKES
US

BECKER COUNTY RECORD. 1871. Wed. free local carrier; $.75 newsstand. 511 Washington Ave., Detroit Lakes, MN 56501. TEL 218-847-3151; FAX 218-847-9409. **Owner(s):** Forum Communications Co., 101 Fifth St., N., P.O. Box 2020, Fargo, ND 58102. TEL 701-235-7311; Ed. Jamie Marks; Pub. Dennis Winskowski; adv. contact: Dave Aune. photos; pub. size: broadsheet; circ. 13,500(free & paid).

US

DETROIT LAKES TRIBUNE. 1907. Sun. $.75 newsstand; $29.50/yr. mailed & motor rte. in cy.; $35/yr. out of cy.; $42/yr. in state; $45/yr. out of state. 511 Washington St., Detroit Lakes, MN 56501. TEL 218-847-3151; FAX 218-847-9409. **Owner(s):** Forum Communications Co., 101 Fifth St., N., P.O. Box 2020, Fargo, ND 58102. TEL 701-235-7311; Ed. Stephanie Corneliussen; Pub. Dennis Winskowski; adv. contact: Dave Aune. pub. size: broadsheet; circ. 7,000(paid).

DULUTH
US

BUDGETEER PRESS. 1931. Sun. free; $26/yr. out of area mailed. 5807 Grand Ave., Duluth, MN 55807-2459. TEL 218-624-3665; FAX 218-624-7927. **Owner(s):** McGinnis Media, 625 First Bank Pl., 130 W. Superior St., Duluth, MN 55802. TEL 218-723-8000; Ed. Paul Lungdren. adv. contact: John Hyduke. pub. size: broadsheet; circ. 60,000(free & paid).

US

SKYWORLD DULUTH NEWS. Sun. free; $26/yr. out of area mailed. 5807 Grand Ave., Duluth, MN 55807. TEL 218-624-3665; FAX 218-624-7927. **Owner(s):** McGinnis Media, 625 First Bank Pl., 130 W. Superior St., Duluth, MN 55802. TEL 218-723-8000; Ed. Paul Lungdren. adv. contact: John Hyduke. pub. size: broadsheet.

EDGERTON
US

EDGERTON ENTERPRISE, THE. 1883. Wed. $.50 newsstand; $21/yr. in 561 zip code; $26.50/yr. elsewhere. 831 Main St., Edgerton, MN 56128. TEL 507-442-6161; FAX 507-442-6161. **Owner(s):** Melvin DeBoer, 831 Main St., Edgerton, MN 56128-0397. TEL 507-442-6161; FAX 507-442-6161; Ed. Melvin DeBoer; Pub. Melvin DeBoer; adv. contact: Melvin DeBoer. adv.: $3.40/SAU. photos; pub. size: broadsheet; circ. 2,000(paid).

ELY
US   ISSN 0746-7087

ELY ECHO. 1972. Mon. $.75 newsstand; $20/yr. in cy.; $30/yr. out of cy.; $40/yr. out of state. 2 E. Sheridan St., Ely, MN 55731-1257. TEL 218-365-3141; FAX 218-365-3142. **Owner(s):** Milestones, Inc., 2 E. Sheridan St., Ely, MN 55731. TEL 218-365-3141; FAX 218-365-3142; Ed. Tom Coombe; Pub. Anne Wognum; adv. contact: Anne Wognum. pub. size: broadsheet; circ. 4,403(paid).

ERSKINE
US

ERSKINE ECHO, THE. 1902. w. $.50 newsstand; $18/yr. 309 First St., Erskine, MN 56535-0016. TEL 218-687-3775. **Owner(s):** Robert M. Hole, 309 First St., Erskine, MN 56535. TEL 218-687-3775; Pub. Robert M. Hole; adv.: $3.75/SAU. photos; pub. size: standard; circ. 1,200(paid).

FAIRMONT
US

FAIRMONT PHOTO PRESS. 1963. Wed. free carrier & motor rte.; $26.20/yr. mailed 3rd class; $41.65/yr. mailed 1st class. 112 E. First St., Fairmont, MN 56031. TEL 507-238-9456; FAX 507-238-9457. **Owner(s):** Wayne L. Schroeder, 112 E. First St., Fairmont, MN 56031. TEL 507-235-3855; Sherman L. Kumba, 238 Amber Lake Dr., Fairmont, MN 56031. TEL 507-238-1192; Ed. Sherman L. Kumba; Pub. Wayne L. Schroeder; adv.; pub. size: tabloid; circ. 11,750(free & paid).

FOREST LAKE

US   ISSN 0892-1784
ST. CROIX VALLEY PEACH. 1954. Sun. free in area; $1 newsstand out of area; $85/yr. out of area. 880 S.W. 15th St., Forest Lake, MN 55025-1381. TEL 612-464-4601; FAX 612-464-4605; E-mail: peach.fl@ecm-inc.com; URL: http://www.ecm-inc.com. **Owner(s):** ECM Publishers, Inc., Princeton, MN; adv. contact: Roxie Muehlberg. adv.: $13.28/SAU. pub. size: tabloid; circ. 33,684(paid).

US
TIMES, THE. 1903. Thu. free deliv.; $1 newsstand; $31/yr. in state; $36/yr. out of state. 880 S.W. 15th St., Forest Lake, MN 55025. TEL 612-464-4601; FAX 612-464-4605; E-mail: eitor.times@inc.com; URL: http://www.ecm-inc.com/news/fltimes. **Owner(s):** ECM Publishers, Inc., 4101 Coon Rapids Blvd., Coon Rapids, MN 55433. TEL 612-421-4444; Pub. Carol Deitner; adv. contact: Carol Deitner. adv.: $9.95/SAU. pub. size: tabloid; circ. 3,903(paid).

FOSSTON

US
FOSSTON THIRTEEN TOWNS. 1884. Mon. $.50 newsstand; $16/yr. in cy.; $20/yr. out of cy. 116 Second St., N.W., Fosston, MN 56542. TEL 218-435-1313; FAX 218-435-1309. **Owner(s):** C & K Publishing, Inc., 606 Second St., N.W., Fosston, MN 56542. TEL 218-435-1313; FAX 218-435-1309; Ed. David S. Carr. adv.; pub. size: broadsheet; circ. 3,250(paid).

GLENCOE

US
GLENCOE ENTERPRISE. 1873. Thu. $22/yr. in cy.; $25/yr. out of cy. 831 11th St., Glencoe, MN 55336. TEL 612-864-4715; FAX 612-864-6472. **Owner(s):** Annamarie Tudhope, P.O. Box 97, Glencoe, MN 55336. TEL 612-864-4715; Ed. Annamarie Tudhope; Pub. Annamarie Tudhope; adv.; photos; bk.rev.; pub. size: standard; circ. 4,200(paid).

GLENWOOD

US
POPE COUNTY TRIBUNE. 1920. Mon. $.75 newsstand; $23/yr. 108 S. Franklin, Glenwood, MN 56334. TEL 612-634-4571; FAX 612-634-5522. **Owner(s):** John R. Stone, P.O. Box 157, Glenwood, MN 56334. TEL 612-634-4571; Pub. John R. Stone; adv. contact: Stacy Gerdes. photos; pub. size: broadsheet; circ. 4,000(paid).
Formerly: Glenwood Pope County Tribune.

GONVICK

US
LEADER-RECORD. w. $.75 newsstand; $18/yr. in cy.; $23/yr. out of cy. P.O. Box 159, Gonvick, MN 56644. TEL 218-776-3665; FAX 218-487-5251; E-mail: richards@gonvick.means.net. **Owner(s):** Richards Publishing Co., Inc., P.O. Box 159, Gonvick, MN 56644. TEL 218-487-5225; Ed. C.J. Richards; Pub. Dick Richards; adv.; photos; bk.rev.; pub. size: tabloid; circ. 2,252(paid).

GRAND RAPIDS

US
GRAND RAPIDS/HERALD-REVIEW. 1894. s-w.: Sun. & Wed. $.75 newsstand; $38/yr. carrier; $40/yr. motor rte.; $45/yr. mailed. 301 First Ave., N.W., Grand Rapids, MN 55744. TEL 218-326-6623; FAX 218-326-6627. **Owner(s):** Murphy-McGinnis Media, 625 First Bank Pl., 130 W. Superior St., Duluth, MN 55802. TEL 218-723-8000; Ed. Wanda Moeller. adv. contact: Steve Lynch. photos; pub. size: tabloid; circ. 21,000(paid).

GRANITE FALLS

US
GRANITE FALLS/CLERKFIELD ADVOCATE TRIBUNE. 1883. w. $32/yr. 138 Eighth Ave., Granite Falls, MN 56241. TEL 320-564-2126; FAX 320-564-4293. **Owner(s):** Mainstream Publications, P.O. Box 58, Northfield, MN 55057; Ed. Linda Larson; Pub. Tim Douglass; pub. size: broadsheet; circ. 3,400(paid).
Formerly: Granite Falls Tribune.

GREENBUSH

US
EXPONENT, THE. 1902. Tue. $22/yr. in cy.; $28/yr. out of cy. P.O. Box F, Greenbush, MN 56726. TEL 218-782-2275; FAX 218-782-2277; E-mail: tribune@grandforks.polaristel.net. **Owner(s):** Page 1 Publications, P.O. Box F, Greenbush, MN 56726. TEL 218-782-2275; FAX 218-782-2277; adv.; pub. size: broadsheet; circ. 2,100(paid).

US   ISSN 0747-4407
NEW RIVER RECORD. 1902. Tue. $19/yr. in cy.; $25/yr. out of cy. P.O. Box F, Greenbush, MN 56726. TEL 218-782-2275; FAX 218-782-2277; E-mail: tribune@grandforks.polaristel.net. **Owner(s):** Page 1 Publications, P.O. Box F, Greenbush, MN 56726. TEL 218-782-2275; FAX 218-782-2277; adv.; pub. size: broadsheet; circ. 1,275(paid).

US
NORTHERN LIGHT, THE. 1902. Tue. $19/yr. in cy; $25/yr. out of cy. P.O. Box F, Greenbush, MN 56726. TEL 218-782-2275; FAX 218-782-2277; E-mail: tribune@grandforks.polaristel.net. **Owner(s):** Page 1 Publications, P.O. Box F, Greenbush, MN 56726. TEL 218-782-2275; FAX 218-782-2277; adv.; pub. size: broadsheet; circ. 1,200(paid).

US
NORTH STAR NEWS. 1902. Wed. $22/yr. in cy; $28/yr. out of cy. P.O. Box F, Greenbush, MN 56726. TEL 218-782-2275; FAX 218-782-2277; E-mail: tribune@grandforks.polaristel.net. **Owner(s):** Page 1 Publications, P.O. Box F, Greenbush, MN 56726. TEL 218-782-2275; FAX 218-782-2277; adv.; pub. size: broadsheet; circ. 2,300(paid).

US
TRIBUNE, THE. 1902. Wed. $22/yr,. in cy.; $28/yr. out of cy. P.O.Box F, Greenbush, MN 56726. TEL 218-782-2275; FAX 218-782-2277; E-mail: tribune@grandforks.polaristel.net. **Owner(s):** Page 1 Publications, P.O. Box F, Greenbush, MN 56726. TEL 218-782-2275; FAX 218-782-2277; adv.; pub. size: broadsheet; circ. 1,800(paid).

US
WARROAD PIONEER. 1902. Wed. $22/yr. in cy; $28/yr. out of cy. P.O. Box F, Greenbush, MN 56726. TEL 218-782-2275; FAX 218-782-2277; E-mail: tribune@grandforks.polaristel.net. **Owner(s):** Page 1 Publications, P.O. Box F, Greenbush, MN 56726. TEL 218-782-2275; FAX 218-782-2277; adv.; pub. size: broadsheet; circ. 2,100(paid).

GRYGLA

US
GRYGLA EAGLE. 1973. Thu. $.75 newsstand; $18/yr. in trade area; $23/yr. outside of area. 127 N. Main St., Grygla, MN 56727. TEL 218-294-6220; FAX 218-294-6220. **Owner(s):** Richards Publishing Co., Inc., P.O. Box 159, Gonvick, MN 56644. TEL 218-487-5225; Ed. Joy Nordby; Pub. Dick Richards; adv.; pub. size: tabloid; circ. 1,000(paid).

HASTINGS

US
HASTINGS STAR GAZETTE. 1857. Thu. $1 newsstand; $33/yr. local area; $50/yr. out of area. 741 Spiral Blvd., Hastings, MN 55033. TEL 612-437-6153; FAX 612-437-5911. **Owner(s):** Arlin Albright, P.O. Box 25, 2760 N. Service Dr., Red Wing, MN 55066; Ed. Doug Schult; Pub. Steve Messick; adv. contact: Ross Ulrich. pub. size: broadsheet; circ. 6,500(paid).

HAWLEY

US
HAWLEY HERALD. 1890. Mon. $.65 newsstand; $20/yr. in cy.; $22.50/yr. out of cy. 608 Main St., Hawley, MN 56549. TEL 218-483-3306; FAX 218-483-4457. **Owner(s):** Eugene Prim, P.O. Box 709, Hawley, MN 56549. TEL 218-483-3306; Ed. Marc C. Ness. adv.: $6.30/SAU. photos; bk.rev.; pub. size: broadsheet; circ. 1,700(paid).

HUTCHINSON

US
HUTCHINSON LEADER. 1882. s-w.: Tue. & Thu. $42.50/yr. local. 36 Washington Ave., W., Hutchinson, MN 55350-2240. TEL 612-587-5000; FAX 612-587-6104; E-mail: hulead@hutchel.net. **Owner(s):** Red Wing Publishing Co., P.O. Box 82, Red Wing, MN 55066. TEL 612-388-8235; FAX 612-388-8912; Ten Part, 36 Washington Ave., W., Hutchinson, MN 55350. TEL 612-587-5000; Ed. Richard Crawford. adv. contact: Tina Berglund. photos; bk.rev.; pub. size: broadsheet; circ. 6,011(paid).

JACKSON

US
JACKSON COUNTY LIVEWIRE. 1929. Mon. free in area; $14/yr. out of area. 310 Second St., Jackson, MN 56143-0208. TEL 507-847-3771; FAX 507-847-5822; E-mail: editor@rconnect.com. **Owner(s):** Jim Keul, P.O. Box 208, Jackson, MN 56143-0208. TEL 507-847-3771; FAX 507-847-5822; Ed. Tim Gallagher; Pub. Jim Keul; adv. contact: Dallas Luhmann. adv.: $6.25/SAU. pub. size: tabloid; circ. 9,200(free & paid).

WEEKLY NEWSPAPERS

JASPER
US ISSN 0744-3110
JASPER JOURNAL. 1888. Mon. $.50 newsstand; $17/yr. local; $21.50/yr. elsewhere. P.O. Box 188, Jasper, MN 56144. TEL 507-348-4176; FAX 507-825-2168. **Owner(s):** Pipestone Publishing Co., P.O. Box 277, Pipestone, MN 56164. TEL 507-825-3333; Ed. Chuck Draper; Pub. Chuck Draper; adv. contact: Deloris Quissell. pub. size: tabloid; circ. 933(paid).

KENYON
US
KENYON LEADER. 1885. Wed. $.50 newsstand; $19/yr. in cy.; $21/yr. in state; $25/yr. out of state. 638 Second St., Kenyon, MN 55946. TEL 507-789-6161; FAX 507-789-6161. **Owner(s):** Noah Publishing, Inc., 638 Second St., Kenyon, MN 55946. TEL 507-789-6161; FAX 507-789-6161; Ed. Douglas A. Noah; Pub. Robert Noah; adv.: $3.60/SAU. photos; pub. size: broadsheet; circ. 1,996(paid).

LAKEFIELD
US
LAKEFIELD STANDARD. 1884. s-w: Wed. & Thu. $.75 newsstand; $23/yr. in cy.; $26.50/yr. out of cy. 403 Main St., Lakefield, MN 56150. TEL 507-662-5555; FAX 507-662-6770. **Owner(s):** Lakefield Publishing Co., P.O. Box 249, Lakefield, MN 56150. TEL 507-662-5555; FAX 507-662-6770; Ed. Mark O. Erickson; Pub. Jim Keul; pub. size: broadsheet; circ. 1,750(paid).

LAKEVILLE
US
LAKEVILLE LIFE & TIMES. 1979. Sat. free; $1.50/wk. mailed. 20777 Holyoke Ave., W., Lakeville, MN 55044. TEL 612-469-2181; FAX 612-469-2184; E-mail: lkvlpub@aol.com. **Owner(s):** Richard M. Sherman, 14135 Guthrie Ave., Apple Valley, MN 55124-6720; Barbara W. Sherman, 14135 Guthrie Ave., Apple Valley, MN 55124-6720; Ed. Richard M. Sherman; Pub. Richard M. Sherman; adv.; photos; pub. size: tabloid; circ. 19,000(free & paid).

LAMBERTON
US
LAMBERTON NEWS. 1923. Wed. $.50 newsstand; $17.50/yr. local; $20/yr. in state; $22.50/yr. out of state. 218 Main St., Lamberton, MN 56152-0308. TEL 507-752-7181; FAX 507-752-7181. **Owner(s):** Joseph G. Dietl, 218 Main St., Lamberton, MN 56152. TEL 507-752-7181; FAX 507-752-7181; Pub. Joseph G. Dietl; adv.; photos; pub. size: standard; circ. 1,750(paid).

LE CENTER
US
LE CENTER LEADER. 1895. Wed. $1 newsstand; $29/yr. in state; $40/yr. out of state. 62 E. Minnesota Ave., Le Center, MN 56057. TEL 507-357-2233; FAX 507-357-6656. **Owner(s):** Bob Bradford, 62 E. Minnesota St., Le Center, MN 56057. TEL 507-357-2233; Pub. Terri McMillen; adv. contact: Terri McMillen. pub. size: broadsheet; circ. 2,000(paid).

LEWISTON
US
LEWISTON JOURNAL. 1929. Tue. $.50 newsstand; $20/yr. in cy.; $27/yr. out of cy. 220 E. Main, Lewiston, MN 55952. TEL 507-523-2119; FAX 507-523-2891. **Owner(s):** Mack Publishing, 924 Whitewater Ave., St. Charles, MN 55972. TEL 507-932-3663; Ed. Jan Mack; Pub. Tim Mack; adv. contact: Tim Mack. pub. size: broadsheet; circ. 1,700(paid).

LINDSTROM
US
CHICAGO COUNTY PRESS. 1898. Thu. $.75 newsstand; $32/yr. in cy.; $37.50/yr. out of cy. 12615 Lake Blvd., Lindstrom, MN 55045-0748. TEL 612-257-5115; FAX 612-257-5500. **Owner(s):** John A. Silver, 12615 Lake Blvd., P.O. Box 748, Lindstrom, MN 55045. TEL 612-257-5115; FAX 612-257-5500; Ed. Denise Martin; Pub. John A. Silver; adv. contact: Ellen Glenna. photos; bk.rev.; pub. size: broadsheet; circ. 4,333(free & paid).

LITCHFIELD
US
LITCHFIELD INDEPENDENT REVIEW. 1876. Thu. $.60 newsstand; $20/yr. in cy. $26/yr. out of cy. $28/yr. out of state. P.O. Box 921, Litchfield, MN 55355. TEL 320-693-3266; FAX 320-693-9177. **Owner(s):** Vernon Madson, P.O. Box 921, Litchfield, MN 55355. TEL 320-693-3266; FAX 320-693-9177; Stanley Roeser, P.O. Box 921, Litchfield, MN 55355. TEL 320-693-3266; FAX 320-693-9177; adv.; pub. size: broadsheet; circ. 4,000(paid).

LONG PRAIRIE
US
LONG PRAIRIE LEADER. 1887. Wed. $.75 newsstand; $25/yr. in cy.; $30/yr. out of cy. 21 Third St., S., Long Prairie, MN 56347. TEL 320-732-2151; FAX 320-732-2152. **Owner(s):** Gary & Sharon Brown, P.O. Box 479, Long Prairie, MN 56387. TEL 612-732-2151; Ed. Sue Farmer; Pub. Gary Brown; adv.; pub. size: broadsheet; circ. 3,500(paid).

LUVERNE
US
ROCK COUNTY STAR HERALD. 1873. Thu. $.75 newsstand; $28/yr. in cy.; $36/yr. out of cy. 117 W. Main, Luverne, MN 56156. TEL 507-283-2333; FAX 507-283-2335. **Owner(s):** Tollefson Publishing, P.O. Box 837, Luverne, MN 56156. TEL 507-283-2333; Pub. Roger S. Tollefson; adv.; photos; pub. size: broadsheet; circ. 3,200(paid).

MADISON
US
MADISON WESTERN GUARD, THE. 1892. Wed. $.75 newsstand; $25/yr. in state; $27/yr. out of state. 216 Sixth Ave., Madison, MN 56256. TEL 320-598-7521; FAX 320-598-7523. **Owner(s):** RBM Publications, Main St., Wheaton, MN 56296; Ed. Richard Gail; Pub. Richard Gail; adv. contact: Missy Schmidt. photos; pub. size: broadsheet; circ. 2,700(paid).

MAHNOMEN
US
MAHNOMEN PIONEER, THE. 1905. w. $.50 newsstand; $17/yr. in cy; $22/yr. in state; $24/yr. out of state. P.O. Box 219, Mahnomen, MN 56557. TEL 218-935-5296. **Owner(s):** Patrick D. Kelly, P.O. Box 219, Mahnomen, MN 56557. TEL 218-935-5296; Ed. Debra Harmon. adv. contact: Patrick Kelly. photos; pub. size: broadsheet.

MCINTOSH
US
MCINTOSH TIMES. 1888. Wed. $18/yr. local; $23/yr. out of cy. 115 Broadway, N.W., McIntosh, MN 55556. TEL 218-563-3585; FAX 218-487-5251. **Owner(s):** Richards Publishing Co., Inc., P.O. Box 159, Gonvick, MN 56644. TEL 218-487-5225; Ed. Mary Horacek. adv.; photos; pub. size: tabloid; circ. 1,350(paid).

MELROSE
US
MELROSE BEACON. 1890. Mon. $.60 newsstand; $19/yr. in area; $25/yr. in state; $30/yr. out of state. 408 E. Main St., Melrose, MN 56352. TEL 320-256-3240; FAX 320-256-3363. **Owner(s):** Stearns County Publishing, Inc., P.O. Box 186, Melrose, MN 56352. TEL 320-256-3240; Ed. Mike Kosik; Pub. Don Larson; adv. contact: Richard Raeker. photos; pub. size: broadsheet; circ. 4,500(paid).

MILACA
US
MILLE LACS COUNTY TIMES. 1892. Wed. $.60 newsstand; $21/yr. local & surrounding cys.; $25/yr. in state; $30/yr. out of state. 225 S.W. Second St., Milaca, MN 56353. TEL 320-983-6111; FAX 320-983-6112. **Owner(s):** Elmer L. Andersen, 800 Rosedale Towers, St. Paul, MN 55113; Ed. Gary Larson. adv.; pub. size: broadsheet; circ. 3,500(paid).

MINNEAPOLIS
US
BROOKLYN CENTER SUN POST. 1956. Wed. free deliv.; $.75 newsstand; voluntary subscription; $40/yr. mailed. 4080 W. Broadway, Ste. 113, Minneapolis, MN 55428. TEL 612-896-4700; FAX 612-536-7519. **Owner(s):** Minnesota Sun Publications LLC, 7831 E. Bush Lake Rd., Bloomington, MN 55439. TEL 612-896-4700; Ed. Yvonne Klinnert; Pub. Denis Mindak; adv.: $1,250/B&W pg. pub. size: tabloid; circ. 9,551(controlled & free).

US
BROOKLYN PARK SUN POST. 1965. Wed. free deliv.; $.75 newsstand; voluntary subscription; $40/yr. mailed. 4080 W. Broadway, Ste. 113, Minneapolis, MN 55422. TEL 612-896-4700; FAX 612-536-7519. **Owner(s):** Minnesota Sun Publications LLC, 7831 E. Bush Lake Rd., Bloomington, MN 55439. TEL 612-896-4700; Ed. Yvonne Klinnert; Pub. Denis Mindak; adv.: $1,250/B&W pg. pub. size: tabloid; circ. 16,357(controlled & free). Formerly: Brooklyn Park Post.

WEEKLY NEWSPAPERS

MINNEAPOLIS, MN

US
EDINA SUN-CURRENT. 1932. Wed. free deliv.; $.75 newsstand; voluntary subscription; $40/yr. mailed. 4080 W. Broadway, Ste. 113, Minneapolis, MN 55422. TEL 612-896-4700; FAX 612-536-7519. **Owner(s):** Minnesota Sun Publications LLC, 7831 E. Bush Lake Rd., Bloomington, MN 55439. TEL 617-896-4700; Ed. Yvonne Klinnert; Pub. Denis Mindak; adv.: $925/B&W pg. pub. size: tabloid; circ. 12,375(free & paid).

US
NEW HOPE-GOLDEN VALLEY SUN POST. 1974. Wed. free; $.75 newsstand; voluntary subscription; $40/yr. mailed. 4080 W. Broadway, Ste. 113, Minneapolis, MN 55422. TEL 612-536-7500; FAX 612-536-7519. **Owner(s):** Minnesota Sun Publications LLC, 7831 E. Bush Lake Rd., Bloomington, MN 55439. TEL 612-896-4700; Ed. Yvonne Klinnert; Pub. Denis Mindak; adv.: $1,250/B&W pg. pub. size: tabloid; circ. 13,400(free & paid).

US
NORTH MINNEAPOLIS SUN POST. Wed. free deliv.; $.75 newsstand; voluntary subscription; $40/yr. mailed. 4080 W. Broadway Ave., Ste. 113, Minneapolis, MN 55422-5605. TEL 612-896-4700; FAX 612-536-7519. **Owner(s):** Minnesota Sun Publications LLC, 7831 E. Bush Lake Rd., Bloomington, MN 55439. TEL 612-896-4700; Ed. Yvonne Klinnert; Pub. Denis Mindak; adv.: $518/B&W pg. pub. size: tabloid; circ. 9,334(controlled & paid).

US   ISSN 0193-2802
TWIN CITIES READER. 1977. Wed. $30/yr. 10 S. Fifth St., Ste. 200, Minneapolis, MN 55402-1012. TEL 612-321-7300; FAX 612-321-7333. **Owner(s):** American City Business Journals, 128 S. Tryon St., Ste. 2200, Charlotte, NC 28202. TEL 704-375-8129; FAX 704-371-3299; Ed. Claude Peck; Pub. Donna Schnieder; adv. contact: Chrissy Harrison. photos; bk.rev.; pub. size: tabloid; circ. 95,000(free).

MINNEPOLIS

US
CITY PAGES. Wed. free; $39/yr. 401 N. Third St., Ste. 550, Minneapolis, MN 55401. TEL 612-375-1015; FAX 612-372-6737; E-mail: citypages.com. **Owner(s):** Stern Publishing, 401 N. Third St., Ste. 550, Minneapolis, MN 55401. TEL 612-375-1015; FAX 612-372-6737; Ed. Steve Perry; Pub. Kristin Henning; circ. 117,000(paid).

MINNETONKA

US
EXCELSIOR/SHOREWOOD/CHANHASSEN SUN-SAILOR. Wed. free; $.75 newsstand; voluntary subscription; $40/yr. mailed. W. Wind Plz., 4785 Hwy. 101., S., Minnetonka, MN 55345. TEL 612-896-4700; FAX 612-935-1452. **Owner(s):** Minnesota Sun Publications, LLC, 7831 E. Bush Lake Rd., Bloomington, MN 55439. TEL 612-896-4700; Ed. Yvonne Klinnert; Pub. Denis Mindak; adv.: $828/B&W pg. pub. size: tabloid; circ. 6,132(free & paid).

US
HOPKINS SUN-SAILOR. Wed. free; $.75 newsstand; voluntary subscription; $40/yr. mailed. W. Wind Plz., 4785 Hwy. 101, S., Minnetonka, MN 55435. TEL 612-932-6660; FAX 612-935-1452. **Owner(s):** Minnesota Sun Publications LLC, 7831 E. Bush Lake Rd., Bloomington, MN 55439. TEL 612-896-4700; FAX 612-536-7519; Ed. Yvonne Klinnert; Pub. Denis Mindak; adv.: $1,319/B&W pg. pub. size: tabloid; circ. 4,158(free).
Formerly: Westonka Sailor.

US
MINNETONKA/DEEPHAVEN SUN-SAILOR. Wed. free; $.75 newsstand; voluntary subscription; $40/yr. W. Wind Plz., 4785 Hwy. 101, S., Minnetonka, MN 55345. TEL 612-896-4700; FAX 612-896-4728. **Owner(s):** Minnesota Sun Publications LLC, 7831 E. Bush Lake Rd., Bloomington, MN 55439. TEL 612-896-4700; Ed. Yvonne Klinnert; Pub. Denis Mindak; adv.: $850/B&W pg. pub. size: tabloid; circ. 16,170(free).

US
PLYMOUTH SUN-SAILOR. Wed. free; $.75 newsstand; voluntary subscription; $40/yr. mailed. W. Wind Plz., 4785 Hwy. 101, S., Minnetonka, MN 55345. TEL 612-932-6660; FAX 612-935-1452. **Owner(s):** Minnesota Sun Publications LLC, 7831 E. Bush Lake Rd., Bloomington, MN 55439. TEL 612-895-4700; FAX 612-896-4728; Ed. Yvonne Klinnert; Pub. Denis Mindak; adv.; pub. size: tabloid; circ. 17,500(free).

US
ST. LOUIS PARK SUN-SAILOR. 1984. Wed. free; $.75 newsstand; voluntary subscription; $40/yr. mailed in state; $60/yr. mailed out of state. W. Wind Plz., 4785 Hwy. 10l, S., Minnetonka, MN 55345. TEL 612-932-6660; FAX 612-935-1452. **Owner(s):** Minnesota Sun Publications LLC, 7831 E. Bush Lake Rd., Minneapolis, MN 55439. TEL 612-896-4700; Ed. Yvonne Klinnert; Pub. Denis Mindak; adv. contact: Mike Maslow. adv.: $1,319/B&W pg. pub. size: tabloid; circ. 11,772(free).

US
WAYZATA/ORONO/LONG LAKE SUN-SAILOR. Wed. free; $.75 newsstand; voluntary subscription; $40/yr. mailed. W. Wind Plz., 4785 Hwy. 101, S., Minnetonka, MN 55345. TEL 612-932-6660; FAX 612-935-1452. **Owner(s):** Minnesota Sun Publications LLC, 7831 E. Bush Lake Rd., Bloomington, MN 55439. TEL 612-896-4700; Ed. Yvonne Klinnert; Pub. Denis Mindak; adv. contact: Mike Maslow. adv.: $1,231/B&W pg. pub. size: tabloid; circ. 5,000(free).

MONTEVIDEO

US
MONTEVIDEO AMERICAN-NEWS. 1911. Thu. $1 newsstand; $34/yr. local. 223 S. First St., Montevideo, MN 56265. TEL 320-269-2156; FAX 320-269-2159. **Owner(s):** Montevideo Publishing Co., Inc., P.O. Box 736, Montevideo, MN 56265. TEL 320-269-2156; Pub. Louis Seesz; adv. contact: Kurt Dahl. photos; pub. size: broadsheet; circ. 5,025(paid).

MOOSE LAKE

US   ISSN 0746-2980
MOOSE LAKE STAR-GAZETTE. 1895. w. $.50 newsstand; $20/yr. local. 308 Elm Ave., Moose Lake, MN 55767. TEL 218-485-4406; FAX 218-485-0237. **Owner(s):** Jerry DeRungs, 3122 Twlight Ln., Moose Lake, MN 55767. TEL 218-485-8304; Ed. Jerry DeRungs; Pub. Jerry DeRungs; adv.; photos; pub. size: broadsheet; circ. 2,800(controlled & paid).

MORA

US
KANABEC COUNTY TIMES. 1884. Thu. $.75 newsstand; $23/yr. in cy; $29.50/yr. out of cy. 106 N.W. Railroad Ave., Mora, MN 55051. TEL 320-679-2661; FAX 320-679-2663. **Owner(s):** Eugene Johnson, P.O. Box 239, Mora, MN 55051. TEL 320-679-2661; Ed. Lee Ostrom; Pub. Wade Weber; adv. contact: Annette Krist. pub. size: broadsheet; circ. 3,000(paid).

MORRIS

US
MORRIS SUN. Tue. $.50 newsstand; $29/yr. in area w. Morris Tribune; $36/yr. out of area. 108 E. Sixth St., Morris, MN 56267-0470. TEL 320-589-2525; FAX 320-589-4357. **Owner(s):** Morris Tribune, Inc., P.O. Box 470, Morris, MN 56267. TEL 320-589-2525; FAX 320-589-4357; Ed. Nick Ripperger. adv. contact: Anne Erickson. pub. size: broadsheet; circ. 4,000(paid).

US
MORRIS TRIBUNE. Thu. $.50 newsstand; $29/yr. in area w. Morris Sun; $36/yr. out of area. 108 E. Sixth St., Morris, MN 56267-0470. TEL 320-589-2525; FAX 320-589-4357. **Owner(s):** Morris Tribune, Inc., P.O. Box 470, Morris, MN 56267. TEL 320-589-2525; FAX 320-589-4357; Ed. Nick Ripperger. adv. contact: Anne Erickson. pub. size: broadsheet; circ. 4,000(paid).

NEW PRAGUE

US
NEW PRAGUE TIMES. 1889. Thu. $.75 newsstand; $20/yr. in cy.; $25/yr. in state; $30/yr. out of state. 200 E. Main St., New Prague, MN 56071. TEL 612-758-4435; FAX 612-758-4135. **Owner(s):** Suel Printing Co., P.O. Box 25, New Prague, MN 56071. TEL 612-758-4435; Ed. Lois Suel Wann; Pub. E. Charles Wann; adv. contact: Mark Slavik. pub. size: broadsheet; circ. 4,500(paid).

NORTH BRANCH

US   ISSN 0891-0731
ECM POST-REVIEW. 1875. Wed. $.65 newsstand; $24/yr. 612 Main St., North Branch, MN 55056-0366. TEL 612-674-7025; FAX 612-674-7026. **Owner(s):** ECM Publishers, Inc., 1201 15th Ave., S., Princeton, MN 55373-2306. TEL 612-333-2980; Ed. Twyla Ring; Pub. Elmer L. Andersen; adv. contact: Mary Eslinger. pub. size: tabloid; circ. 2,500(paid).

WEEKLY NEWSPAPERS

NORTHFIELD
US
NORTHFIELD NEWS. 1876. s-w.: Wed. & Fri. $1 newsstand; $42/yr. in state; $52.50/yr. out of state. 115 W. Fifth St., Northfield, MN 55057. TEL 507-645-5615. **Owner(s):** Bradford Family, 1118 Lia Ct., Northfield, MN 55057. TEL 507-645-5615; Ed. Evelyn Hoover; Pub. Robert Bradford; adv. contact: Doug Fitzgerald. photos; bk.rev.; pub. size: broadsheet; circ. 6,200(paid).

NORTHOME
US
NORTHOME RECORD & MIZPAH MESSAGE. 1901. Tue. $.35 newsstand; $16.50/yr. in cy.; $20/yr. in state; $22.50/yr. out of state. Main St., Northome, MN 56661-0025. TEL 218-897-5278. **Owner(s):** Bernard & Kathryn E. Elhard, Northome, MN 56601; Pub. Kathryn E. Elhard; adv.; pub. size: tabloid; circ. 1,000(paid).

NORTH ST. PAUL
US
EAST SIDE REVIEW. 1938. Mon. free. 2515 E. Seventh Ave., North St. Paul, MN 55109-3098. TEL 612-777-8800; FAX 612-777-8288. **Owner(s):** Lillie Suburban Newspapers, Inc., 2515 E. Seventh Ave., St. Paul, MN 55109. TEL 612-777-8800; FAX 612-777-8200; Ed. Mary Lee Hagert; Pub. N. Ted Lillie; adv. contact: Mark Beckstrom. pub. size: broadsheet; circ. 19,822(free).

US
ST. ANTHONY BULLETIN. 1938. Wed. free home deliv./ $.50 newsstand; $23.95/yr. out of area. 2515 E. Seventh Ave., North St. Paul, MN 55109. TEL 612-777-8800; FAX 612-777-8200. **Owner(s):** Lillie Suburban Newspapers, Inc., 2515 E. Seventh Ave., St. Paul, MN 55109-3098. TEL 612-777-8800; FAX 612-777-8288; Ed. Mary Lee Hagert; Pub. N. Ted Lillie; adv. contact: Mark Beckstrom. pub. size: broadsheet; circ. 3,000(free & paid).

OAKDALE
US
OAKDALE CLARION. 1992. Fri. $19/yr. in state mailed; $21/yr. out of state. 1979 Geneva Ave. N., Oakdale, MN 55128. TEL 612-730-9116; FAX 612-730-0340. **Owner(s):** Oakdale Clarion, P.O. Box 28303, Oakdale, MN 55128. TEL 612-730-9116; FAX 612-730-0340; Pub. Lisa Heikkila; adv.: $6.50/SAU. pub. size: standard; circ. 2,123(paid).

OKLEE
US
OKLEE HERALD. 1917. Wed. $.75 newsstand; $18/yr. in cy.; $23/yr. out of cy. Main St., Oklee, MN 56742. TEL 218-796-5181; FAX 218-487-5251. **Owner(s):** Richards Publishing Co., Inc., P.O. Box 159, Gonvick, MN 56644. TEL 218-487-5225; Ed. Marilyn Whyte; Pub. Dick Richards; adv.; photos; pub. size: tabloid; circ. 1,200(paid).

OLIVIA
US
OLIVIA TIMES JOURNAL. Mon. $.75 newsstand; $24/yr. in cy. 816 E. Lincoln Ave., Olivia, MN 56277. TEL 320-523-2032; FAX 320-523-2033. **Owner(s):** Olivia Publishing, Inc., 816 E. Lincoln, Olivia, MN. TEL 612-523-2032; Ed. Rick Herman. adv.; photos; pub. size: broadsheet; circ. 1,750(controlled & paid).

US
RENVILLE COUNTY SHOPPER. 1967. Mon. free. 816 E. Lincoln, Olivia, MN 56277. TEL 320-523-2032; FAX 320-523-2033. **Owner(s):** Olivia Publishing, Inc., 816 E. Lincoln, Olivia, MN 56277; Pub. Rose Hettig; adv.; pub. size: broadsheet; circ. 5,100(free).

ORTONVILLE
US
ORTONVILLE INDEPENDENT. 1920. Tue. $.75 newsstand; $25/yr. in cy.; $29/yr. out of cy.; $33/yr. out of state. 29 N.W. Second St., Ortonville, MN 56278. TEL 320-839-6163; FAX 320-839-6173. **Owner(s):** James D., Jeannette Kaercher, Sue Kaercher-Blake, P.O. Box 336, Ortonville, MN 56278. TEL 320-839-6163; Ed. James D. Kaercher; Pub. Jeanette Kaercher; adv.; pub. size: broadsheet; circ. 3,700(controlled & paid).

OSAKIS
US ISSN 1040-6069
OSAKIS REVIEW, THE. 1890. Tue. $.75 newsstand; $20/yr. in cy.; $23/yr. in state; $26/yr. out of state. 28 E. Main St., Osakis, MN 56360-0220. TEL 320-859-2143; FAX 320-859-2054. **Owner(s):** John & Roberta Olson, 28 E. Main St., Osakis, MN 56360. TEL 320-859-2143; FAX 320-859-2054; Pub. John Olson; adv. contact: John Olson. pub. size: tabloid; circ. 1,350(controlled & free).

OWATONNA
US
OWATONNA WEEKLY SHOPPER. Sat. free. 135 W. Pearl St., Owatonna, MN 55060. TEL 507-451-2840; FAX 507-451-6020. **Owner(s):** Huckle Publishing, Inc., P.O. Box 346, Owatonna, MN 55060; Pub. Ken Lynam; adv. contact: Holly Westercamp. pub. size: standard; circ. Sun. 18,000(free).

PARK RAPIDS
US
PARK RAPIDS ENTERPRISE. 1882. s-w.: Wed. & Sat. $30/yr. in cy.; $40/yr. out of cy.; $42/yr. out of state. 203 N. Henrietta Ave., Park Rapids, MN 56470. TEL 218-732-3364; FAX 218-732-8757; E-mail: entrpris@parkrapids.polavistel.net. **Owner(s):** Forum Communications Co., P.O. Box 2020, Fargo, ND 58107. TEL 701-241-5400; Ed. LuAnn Hurd-Lof. adv.; photos; pub. size: broadsheet; circ. 6,000(paid).

PAYNESVILLE
US
PAYNESVILLE PRESS, THE. 1887. Wed. $.75 newsstand; $23/yr. 211 Washburne, Paynesville, MN 56362. TEL 320-243-3772; FAX 320-243-4492; E-mail: paypress@lkdllink.net; URL: http://www.edtechweb.com/paynesvillearea. **Owner(s):** Paynesville Press, The, P.O. Box 54, Paynesville, MN 56362. TEL 320-243-3772; FAX 320-243-3772; Pub. Peter J. Jacobsa; adv.; pub. size: broadsheet; circ. 2,970(paid).

PELICAN RAPIDS
US
PELICAN RAPIDS PRESS. 1897. Wed. $.50 newsstand; $22/yr. 29 W. Mill, Pelican Rapids, MN 56572-0632. TEL 218-863-1421; FAX 218-863-1423. **Owner(s):** Gary E. & Richard E. Peterson, P.O. Box L, Pelican Rapids, MN 56572. TEL 218-863-1421; FAX 218-863-1423; Ed. Gary E. Peterson; Pub. Richard E. Peterson; adv.; pub. size: standard; circ. 3,452(paid).

PERHAM
US
PERHAM ENTERPRISE-BULLETIN. 1882. Thu. $.75 newsstand; $22/yr. in cy.; $24/yr. out of cy.; $26/yr. out of state. 135 E. Main St., Perham, MN 56573. TEL 218-346-5900; FAX 218-346-5901. **Owner(s):** Mike Parta, Parta Printers, 135 E. Main St., New York Mills, MN 56567. TEL 218-385-2275; Ed. Charles Johnson; Pub. Mike Parta; adv. contact: Cleone Stewart. photos; pub. size: broadsheet; circ. 3,200(paid).

PIPESTONE
US
PIPESTONE COUNTY STAR. 1879. Wed. $.75 newsstand; $26/yr. in cy.; $32/yr. out of cy. 101 Second St., N.E., Pipestone, MN 56164. TEL 507-825-3333; FAX 507-825-2168. **Owner(s):** Pipestone Publishing Co., P.O. Box 277, Pipestone, MN 56164-0277. TEL 507-825-3333; Ed. Mark Fode; Pub. Chuck Draper; adv. contact: Ray Fuder. pub. size: broadsheet; circ. 4,040(paid).

PLAINVIEW
US
PLAINVIEW NEWS. Tue. $.50 newsstand; $20/yr. in surrounding cys.; $27/yr. elsewhere. 409 W. Broadway, Plainview, MN 55964. TEL 507-534-3121; FAX 507-534-3920. **Owner(s):** Timothy Mack, P.O. Box 457, Plainview, MN 55964; Ed. Janet Mack; Pub. Timothy Mack; adv. contact: Julie Stoning. pub. size: broadsheet; circ. 2,500(paid).

PRINCETON
US
PRINCETON UNION-EAGLE. 1876. Thu. $.60 newsstand; $21/yr. in cy.; $16/yr. senior citizens. 208 N. LaGrande, Princeton, MN 55371. TEL 612-389-1222; FAX 612-389-1728. **Owner(s):** ECM Publishers, Inc., 4101 Coon Rapids Blvd., Coon Rapids, MN 55433; Ed. Luther Dorr; Pub. Elmer L. Andersen; adv.; photos; pub. size: broadsheet; circ. 3,600(paid).

PROCTOR

US

PROCTOR JOURNAL. 1906. Thu. $.75 newsstand; $25/yr. in cy.; $26/yr. out of cy.; $27/yr in state. 215 Fifth St., Proctor, MN 55810-1686. TEL 218-624-3344; FAX 218-624-7037. **Owner(s):** Jake Benson, 215 Fifth St., Proctor, MN 55810-1686. TEL 218-624-3344; FAX 218-624-7037; Pub. Jake Benson; adv. contact: Diane Giuliani. photos; pub. size: tabloid; circ. 2,000(paid).

RED WING

US

HIAWATHA VALLEY SHOPPER. 1955. Sun. free. P.O. Box 324, Red Wing, MN 55066. TEL 715-792-2880; FAX 715-273-4769; E-mail: helmprint@aol.com. **Owner(s):** Helmer Printing Co., Inc., P.O. Box 40, Beldenville, WI 54003; Ed. Milton Helmer; Pub. W.M.A. Helmer; adv.; photos; pub. size: tabloid; circ. 43,000(free).

REDWOOD FALLS

US

REDWOOD GAZETTE, THE. 1869. s-w.: Mon. & Thu. $1 newsstand; $44.50/yr. in surrounding cys.; $54.50/yr. out of area. 140 E. Second St., Redwood Falls, MN 56283. TEL 507-637-2929; FAX 507-637-3175. **Owner(s):** Bob Bradford, P.O. Box 299, Redwood Falls, MN 36283. TEL 507-637-2929; Ed. Rick Peterson; Pub. Rick Peterson; adv. contact: Shelly Doering. pub. size: broadsheet; circ. 5,500(paid).

ROSEAU

US

ROSEAU TIMES-REGION. 1889. Mon. $21/yr. in cy.; $28/yr. out of cy. 106 W. Center St., Roseau, MN 56751. TEL 218-463-1521; FAX 218-463-1530. **Owner(s):** Warren Sheaf Publishing Co., P.O. Box 45, Warren, MN 56762. TEL 218-745-5174; Ed. Jeri Thompson. adv. contact: Jodi Wiskow. pub. size: broadsheet; circ. 4,450(paid).

ROSEVILLE

US

FOCUS NEWS. 1985. Thu. free newsstand; $80/yr. mailed. 2819 N. Hamline Ave., Ste. 101, Roseville, MN 55113-7118. TEL 612-633-3434; FAX 612-633-9550. **Owner(s):** Focus Newspapers, 2819 N. Hamline, Ste. 101, Roseville, MN 55113; Ed. Rick Rotzien; Pub. Richard Roberts; adv. contact: Collette Roberts. pub. size: tabloid; circ. 50,000(free).

Formerly: Roseville-Falcon Heights-Arden Hill Focus.

US

FRIDLEY FOCUS. Thu. free newsstand; $80/yr. 2819 N. Hamline Ave., Ste. 101, Roseville, MN 55113-7118. TEL 612-633-3434; FAX 612-571-1026. **Owner(s):** Focus Newspapers, 2819 N. Hamline Ave., Ste. 101, Roseville, MN 55113-7118. TEL 612-633-3434; Ed. Rick Rotzein; Pub. Richard Roberts; adv. contact: Collette Roberts. pub. size: tabloid; circ. 10,168(free).

Formerly: Fridley/Columbia Heights Focus.

US

MOUNDS VIEW-NEW BRIGHTON-ST. ANTHONY FOCUS. 1985. Thu. free newsstand; $75/yr. mailed. 2819 N. Hamline Ave., Ste. 101, Roseville, MN 55113-7118. TEL 612-633-3434; FAX 612-633-9550. **Owner(s):** Focus Newspapers, 2819 N. Hamline Ave., Ste. 101, Roseville, MN 55113-7118; Ed. Collette Roberts; Pub. Richard Roberts; adv. contact: Collette Roberts. pub. size: tabloid; circ. 52,000(free).

Formerly: Shoreview/Moundsview/Arden Hills Focus.

RUSHFORD

US

TRI-COUNTY RECORD. 1915. Thu. $.60 newsstand; $21/yr.; $25/yr. out of cy. 300 S. Mill St., Rushford, MN 55971. TEL 507-864-7700. **Owner(s):** Tri-County Publishing, Inc., 300 S. Mill St., Rushford, MN 55971; Ed. Myron J. Schober; Pub. Darlene J. Schober; adv.; photos; pub. size: broadsheet; circ. 1,750(paid).

RUTHTON

US

BUFFALO RIDGE GAZETTE, THE. 1974. Wed. $.50 newsstand; $17/yr. 320 Aetna, Ruthton, MN 56170. TEL 507-658-3919; FAX 507-247-5502. **Owner(s):** Hunt & Hunt Newspapers, 151 N. Tyler St., Tyler, MN 56178. TEL 507-247-5502; FAX 507-247-5502; Ed. Lorry Sanderson; Pub. Charles Hunt; adv.; photos; pub. size: broadsheet; circ. 500(paid).

SAUK CENTRE

US

SAUK CENTRE HERALD. 1867. Tue. $.75 newsstand; $22.50/yr. in area; $26.50/yr. out of area; $27.50/yr. out of state. 522 Sinclair Lewis Ave., Sauk Centre, MN 56378. TEL 320-352-6577; FAX 320-352-5647. **Owner(s):** Dave Simpkins, 522 Sinclair Lewis Ave., Sauk Centre, MN 56378. TEL 612-352-2345; Pub. Dave Simpkins; adv. contact: Glenn Domine. pub. size: broadsheet; circ. 3,550(paid).

SEBEKA

US

SEBEKA/MENAHGA REVIEW MESSENGER. 1898. Wed. $.75 newsstand; $22/yr. in trade area; $26/yr. in state; $30/yr. out of state. 112 Minnesota Ave., W., Sebeka, MN 56477-0309. TEL 218-837-5558; FAX 218-837-5560. **Owner(s):** Marjon Printers, Inc., P.O. Box 309, Sebeka, MN 56477. TEL 218-837-5558; FAX 218-837-5560; Ed. T.M. Bloomquist. adv.: $5.70/SAU. photos; pub. size: broadsheet; circ. 3,545(free & paid).

SHAKOPEE

US

SHAKOPEE VALLEY NEWS. 1900. Thu. $.75 newsstand; $22/yr. in cy.; $33/yr. out of cy. 327 Marschall Rd., Shakopee, MN 55379. TEL 612-445-3333. **Owner(s):** Southwest Suburban Publishing, P.O. Box 8, Shakopee, MN 55379. TEL 612-445-3333; Ed. Pat Minelli; Pub. Stan Rolffrug; pub. size: broadsheet; circ. 4,009(paid).

SHERBURN

US ISSN 1056-8999

WEST MARTIN WEEKLY NEWS. 1888. Wed. $.75 newsstand; $21/yr. in cy. 10 N. Main St., Sherburn, MN 56171. TEL 507-764-6681; FAX 507-764-2756. **Owner(s):** Harwood & Polly Schaffer, P.O. Box 820, Sherburn, MN 56171. TEL 507-764-6681; FAX 507-764-2756; adv.; photos; pub. size: broadsheet; circ. 1,000(paid).

SLAYTON

US

MURRAY COUNTY WHEEL HERALD. Mon. $.50 newsstand; $24/yr. in cy. 2734 Broadway Ave., Slayton, MN 56172. TEL 507-836-8726; FAX 507-836-8726. **Owner(s):** Will Beers, P.O. Box 263, Slayton, MN 36172. TEL 507-386-8726; Ed. Sherri Halbur; Pub. Will Beers; adv. contact: Randy Beers. pub. size: broadsheet; circ. 7,100(paid).

SPRINGFIELD

US

SPRINGFIELD ADVANCE-PRESS. 1896. Wed. $.75 newsstand; $23.50/yr. 13 S. Marshall Ave., Springfield, MN 56087. TEL 507-723-4225; FAX 507-723-4400. **Owner(s):** Don R. Peterson, 135 Interlaken Rd., Fairmont, MN 56031; D.J. Hedstrom, 518 N. Marshall Ave., Springfield, MN 56087. TEL 507-723-5078; FAX 507-723-6534; Ed. Peter Hedstrom; Pub. Peter Hedstrom; adv. contact: Peter Hedstrom. adv.: $3.75/SAU. photos; pub. size: broadsheet; circ. 232,906(paid).

SPRING VALLEY

US

RIVER VALLEY SHOPPER. Mon. free. 141 S. Broadway, Spring Valley, MN 55975-0112. TEL 507-346-7365; FAX 507-346-7366. **Owner(s):** Phillips Publishing, Inc., P.O. Box 112, Spring Valley, MN 55975. TEL 507-346-7365; Pub. David Phillips; adv.; pub. size: standard; circ. 13,785(free).

US

SPRING VALLEY TRIBUNE. 1880. Wed. $.60 newsstand; $18/yr. locally. 141 S. Broadway, Spring Valley, MN 55975-0112. TEL 507-346-7365; FAX 507-346-7366. **Owner(s):** Phillips Publishing, Inc., P.O. Box 112, Spring Valley, MN 55975. TEL 507-346-7365; FAX 507-346-7366; Pub. David Phillips; photos; pub. size: broadsheet; circ. 2,000(paid).

STAPLES

US

STAPLES WORLD. 1890. Thu. $.75 newsstand; $22/yr. in surrounding cys.; $26/yr. out of area; $30/yr. out of state. 224 Fourth St., N., Staples, MN 56479. TEL 218-894-1112; FAX 218-894-3570; E-mail: staworld@brainerd.net. **Owner(s):** Devlin Newspapers, Inc., 224 Fourth St., N., Staples, MN 56479-0100. TEL 218-894-1112; FAX 218-894-3570; Ed. Tom Crawford; Pub. Russ Devlin; adv. contact: Gary Mueller. adv.: $5.50/SAU. photos; pub. size: broadsheet; circ. 2,728(free & paid).

ST. CHARLES

US

ST. CHARLES PRESS. 1877. Tue. $.50 newsstand; $20/yr. in cy.; $27/yr. out of cy. 924 Whitewater Ave., St. Charles, MN 55972. TEL 507-932-3663; FAX 507-932-5537. **Owner(s):** Mack Publishing, 924 Whitewater Ave., St. Charles, MN 55972. TEL 507-932-3663; Ed. Sue Benedett; Pub. Tim Mack; adv.; pub. size: broadsheet; circ. 2,700(paid).

ST. JAMES

US

ST. JAMES PLAINDEALER. 1891. Thu. $1 newsstand; $27/yr. in cy. 604 First Ave., S., St. James, MN 56081. TEL 507-375-3161; FAX 507-375-3221. **Owner(s):** Robert Bradford, Northfield, MN 55057; FAX 507-375-3221; Ed. Pat Beck; Pub. R. Joseph Flanagan; adv.; pub. size: broadsheet; circ. 3,000(paid).

ST. PAUL

US

FOREST LAKE PRESS. Fri. $.50 newsstand; $25/yr. in cy. 4779 Bloom Ave., St. Paul, MN 55110. TEL 612-407-1200; FAX 612-429-1242. **Owner(s):** Press Publications, Inc., 4779 Bloom Ave., St. Paul, MN 55110. TEL 612-429-7781; Ed. Paul Wahl; Pub. Eugene D. Johnson; adv. contact: Michelle Larson. pub. size: broadsheet; circ. 14,020(paid).

US

GRAND GAZETTE. 1972. m.: 4th Sat. free newsstand; $15/yr. out of area mailed. 757 S. Snelling Ave., St. Paul, MN 55116-2250. TEL 612-699-1462; FAX 612-699-6501. **Owner(s):** Michael Mischke, 757 S. Snelling Ave., St. Paul, MN 55116-2250. TEL 612-699-1462; FAX 612-699-6501; Ed. Dale Mischke; Pub. Michael Mischke; adv.; photos; bk.rev.; pub. size: tabloid; circ. 22,000(free & paid).

US

LILLIE SUBURBAN SHOPPING REVIEW. 1938. Mon. free. 2515 E. Seventh Ave., St. Paul, MN 55109-3098. TEL 612-777-8800; FAX 612-777-8288. **Owner(s):** Lillie Suburban Newspapers, Inc., 2515 E. Seventh Ave., St. Paul, MN 55109-3098. TEL 612-777-8800; FAX 612-777-8288; Ed. Mary Lee Hagert; Pub. Jeff Enright; adv. contact: Mark Beckstrom. pub. size: broadsheet; circ. 20,000(free).

US

MAPLEWOOD REVIEW. 1938. Wed. $.50 newsstand; $19.95/yr. in area; $23.95/yr. out of area. 2515 E. Seventh Ave., St. Paul, MN 55109-3098. TEL 612-777-8800; FAX 612-777-8288. **Owner(s):** Lillie Suburban Newspapers, Inc., 2515 E. Seventh Ave., St. Paul, MN 55109. TEL 612-777-8800; FAX 612-777-8288; Ed. Mary Lee Hagert; Pub. N. Ted Lillie; adv. contact: Mark Beckstrom. pub. size: broadsheet; circ. 1,100(free & paid).

US

NEW BRIGHTON-MOUNDS VIEW BULLETIN. 1938. Wed. free home deliv.; $.50 newsstand; $23.95/yr. out of area. 2515 E. Seventh Ave., St. Paul, MN 55109. TEL 612-777-8800; FAX 612-777-8200. **Owner(s):** Lillie Suburban Newspapers, Inc., 2515 E. Seventh Ave., St. Paul, MN 55109-3098. TEL 612-777-8800; FAX 612-777-8288; Ed. Mary Lee Hagert; Pub. N. Ted Lillie; adv. contact: Mark Beckstrom. pub. size: broadsheet; circ. 10,000(free & paid).

US

OAKDALE-LAKE ELMO REVIEW. 1938. Wed. $.50 newsstand; $19.95/yr. in area; $23.95/yr. out of area. 2515 E. Seventh Ave., St. Paul, MN 55109. TEL 612-777-8800; FAX 612-777-8288. **Owner(s):** Lillie Suburban Newspapers, Inc., 2515 E. Seventh Ave., St. Paul, MN 55109. TEL 612-777-8800; Ed. Mary Lee Hagert; Pub. N. Ted Lillie; adv. contact: Mark Beckstrom. pub. size: broadsheet; circ. 780(free & paid).

US

RAMSEY COUNTY REVIEW. 1938. Wed. $.50 newsstand; $16/yr. in area; $20/yr. out of area. 2515 E. Seventh Ave., St. Paul, MN 55109-3098. TEL 612-777-8800; FAX 612-777-8288. **Owner(s):** Lillie Suburban Newspapers, Inc., 2515 E. Seventh Ave., St. Paul, MN 55109. TEL 612-777-8800; FAX 612-777-8288; Ed. Mary Lee Hagert; Pub. N. Ted Lillie; adv. contact: Mark Beckstrom. pub. size: broadsheet; circ. 1,500(free & paid).

US

ROOSEVELT REVIEW. 1938. Tue. free home deliv.; $.40 newsstand; $19.95/yr. in cy.; $23.95/yr. out of cy. 2515 E. Seventh Ave., St. Paul, MN 55109. TEL 612-777-8800; FAX 612-777-8288. **Owner(s):** Lillie Suburban Newspapers, Inc., 2515 E. Seventh Ave., St. Paul, MN 55109. TEL 612-777-8800; FAX 612-777-8200; Ed. Mary Lee Hagert; Pub. N. Ted Lillie; adv. contact: Mark Beckstrom. photos; pub. size: broadsheet; circ. 16,000(paid).

US

ROSEVILLE REVIEW. 1938. Tue. free in area; $1/wk. out of area mailed. 2515 E. Seventh Ave., St. Paul, MN 55109-3098. TEL 612-777-8800; FAX 612-777-8288. **Owner(s):** Lillie Suburban Newspapers, Inc., 2515 E. Seventh Ave., St. Paul, MN 55109-3098. TEL 612-777-8800; FAX 612-777-8288; Ed. Mary Lee Hagert; Pub. N. Ted Lillie; adv. contact: Mark Beckstrom. photos; pub. size: broadsheet; circ. 16,684(free).

US

SHOREVIEW-ARDEN HILLS BULLETIN. 1938. Wed. free home deliv.; $.50 newsstand; $23.95/yr. out of area. 2515 E. Seventh Ave., St. Paul, MN 55109-3098. TEL 612-777-8800; FAX 612-777-8288. **Owner(s):** Lillie Suburban Newspapers, Inc., 2515 E. Seventh Ave., St. Paul, MN 55109-3098. TEL 612-777-8800; FAX 612-777-8288; Ed. Mary Lee Hagert; Pub. N. Ted Lillie; adv. contact: Mark Beckstrom. pub. size: broadsheet; circ. 16,214(free & paid).

US

SHOREVIEW PRESS. Tue. $.50 newsstand; $25/yr. in cy. 4779 Bloom Ave., St. Paul, MN 55110. TEL 612-407-1200; FAX 612-429-1242. **Owner(s):** Press Publications, Inc., 4779 Bloom Ave., St. Paul, MN 55110. TEL 612-429-7781; Ed. Paul Wahl; Pub. Eugene D. Johnson; adv. contact: Michelle Larson. pub. size: broadsheet; circ. 8,700.

US

SOUTH-WEST REVIEW. 1938. Sun. free. 2515 E. Seventh Ave., St. Paul, MN 55109-3098. TEL 612-777-8800; FAX 612-777-8288. **Owner(s):** Lillie Suburban Newspapers, Inc., 2515 E. Seventh Ave., St. Paul, MN 55109-3098. TEL 612-777-8800; FAX 612-777-8288; Ed. Mary Lee Hagert; Pub. N. Ted Lillie; adv. contact: Mark Beckstrom. pub. size: broadsheet; circ. 22,509(free).

US

ST. CROIX VALLEY PRESS. 1978. Wed. $.50 newsstand; $25/yr. in area. 4779 Bloom Ave., St. Paul, MN 55100. TEL 612-429-7781; FAX 612-429-1242. **Owner(s):** Press Publications, Inc., 4779 Bloom Ave., St. Paul, MN 55110. TEL 612-429-7781; Ed. Paul Wahl; Pub. Eugene D. Johnson; adv. contact: Michelle Larson. pub. size: broadsheet; circ. 12,899(paid).

US

VADNAIS HEIGHTS PRESS. Wed. $.50 newsstand; $25/yr. in cy. 4779 Bloom Ave., St. Paul, MN 55110. TEL 612-407-1200; FAX 612-429-1242. **Owner(s):** Press Publications, Inc., 4779 Bloom Ave., St. Paul, MN 55110. TEL 612-429-7781; Ed. Paul Wahl; Pub. Eugene D. Johnson; adv. contact: Michelle Larson. pub. size: broadsheet; circ. 4,000.

US

VILLAGER. s-m.: Wed. free; $25/yr out of area mailed. 757 S. Snelling Ave., St. Paul, MN 55116. TEL 612-699-1462; FAX 612-699-6501. **Owner(s):** Michael Mischke, 757 S. Snelling Ave., St. Paul, MN 55116. TEL 612-699-1462; Ed. Dale Mischke; Pub. Michael Mischke; adv.; photos; bk.rev./ circ. 44,500(controlled & free).

US

WHITE BEAR PRESS. Tue. $.50 newsstand; $25/yr. in cy. White Bear Press, 4779 Bloom Ave., St. Paul, MN 55110. TEL 612-407-1200; FAX 612-429-1242. **Owner(s):** Press Publications, Inc., 4779 Bloom Ave., St. Paul, MN 55110. TEL 612-429-7781; Ed. Paul Wahl; Pub. Eugene D. Johnson; adv. contact: Michelle Larson. pub. size: broadsheet; circ. 18,800(paid).

US

WOODBURY-SOUTH MAPLEWOOD REVIEW. 1938. Mon. $.50 newsstand; free in area. 2515 E. Seventh Ave., St. Paul, MN 55109-3098. TEL 612-777-8800; FAX 612-777-8288. **Owner(s):** Lillie Suburban Newspapers, Inc., 2515 E. Seventh Ave., St. Paul, MN 55109-3098. TEL 612-777-8800; FAX 612-777-8288; Ed. Mary Lee Hagert; Pub. N. Ted Lillie; adv. contact: Mark Beckstrom. photos; pub. size: broadsheet; circ. 9,510(free).

ST. PETER

US

ST. PETER HERALD. 1884. Thu. $1 newsstand; $22.50/yr in cy; $38/yr. out of cy.; $43/yr. out of state. 311 S. Minnesota Ave., St. Peter, MN 56082. TEL 507-931-4520; FAX 507-931-4522. **Owner(s):** St. Peter Publishing Co., 311 S. Minnesota Ave., St. Peter, MN 56082. TEL 507-931-4520; Ed. Peggy Palmer; Pub. Peggy Palmer; adv.; photos; pub. size: broadsheet; circ. 2,900(paid).

THIEF RIVER FALLS

US

NORTHERN WATCH. 1991. Sat. free in trade area; $.75/copy outside of trade area. 324 Main Ave., N., Thief River Falls, MN 56701. TEL 218-681-4450; FAX 218-681-4455. **Owner(s):** Thief River Falls Times, Inc., 324 Main Ave., N., Thief River Falls, MN 56701. TEL 218-681-4450; FAX 218-681-4455; Ed. Marvin Lundin; Pub. John Mattson; adv. contact: Denise Laymon. adv.: $8/SAU. pub. size: broadsheet; circ. 22,500(free).

10648 THIEF RIVER FALLS, MN

US   ISSN 8750-3883
THIEF RIVER FALLS TIMES. 1910. Wed. $.75 newsstand; $24/yr. in area; $29/yr. out of area. 324 Main Ave., N., Thief River Falls, MN 56701. TEL 218-681-4450; FAX 218-681-4455. **Owner(s):** Thief River Falls Times, Inc., 324 Main Ave., N., Thief River Falls, MN 56701-0100. TEL 218-681-4450; FAX 218-681-4455; Ed. Marvin Lundin; Pub. John P. Mattson; adv. contact: Denise Laymon. adv.: $5.50/SAU. pub. size: broadsheet; circ. 5,800(paid).
Formerly: Times, The.

TRACY
US
TRACY HEADLIGHT-HERALD. 1879. Wed. $.75 newsstand; $26/yr. in cy.; $35/yr. out of cy. 207 Fourth St., Tracy, MN 56175. TEL 507-629-4300; FAX 507-629-4301. **Owner(s):** James Keul, 207 Fourth St., Tracy, MN 56175. TEL 507-629-4300; Seth Schmidt, 207 Fourth St., Tracy, MN 56175. TEL 507-629-4300; Ed. Seth Schmidt; Pub. Seth Schmidt; adv. contact: Lisa Sell. pub. size: broadsheet; circ. 2,300(paid).

TWO HARBORS
US
LAKE COUNTY NEWS-CHRONICLE. 1895. Thu. $.75 newsstand; $25.31/yr. in cy.; $34/yr. out of cy.; $34/yr. out of state. 109 Waterfront Dr., Two Harbors, MN 55616. TEL 218-834-2141. **Owner(s):** Mary E. Williams, 109 Waterfront Dr., Two Harbors, MN 55616. TEL 218-834-2141; George Williams, Jr., 109 Waterfront Dr., Two Harbors, MN 55616. TEL 218-834-2141; Ed. Forrest Johnson; Pub. George Williams; adv. contact: Donna Carlson. pub. size: broadsheet; circ. 3,200(paid).

TYLER
US
TYLER TRIBUTE. 1972. Thu. $.50 newsstand; $19/yr. in cy.; $23/yr. in state. 151 N. Tyler St., Tyler, MN 56178-0466. TEL 507-247-5502; FAX 507-247-5502; E-mail: tribute@compuserve.com; URL: http://onsworld.compuserve.com/homepages/tribute. Owner(s): Hunt & Hunt Newspapers, 151 N. Tyler St., Tyler, MN 56178. TEL 507-247-5502; FAX 507-247-5502; Ed. Charles R. Hunt; Pub. Charles R. Hunt; adv.: $3.99/SAU. photos; pub. size: broadsheet; circ. 1,680(paid).

WACONIA
US
WACONIA PATRIOT, THE. 1895. Thu. $.75 newsstand; $25.60/yr. carrier in state; $32.90/yr. out of state. 8 Elm St., S., Waconia, MN 55387. TEL 612-442-4414; FAX 612-442-4428. **Owner(s):** Carver County News, Inc., Watertown, MN 55388. TEL 612-955-1111; Ed. Keith Anderson; Pub. James Berreth; adv. contact: Karen Miller. pub. size: broadsheet; circ. 4,200(paid).

WADENA
US
WADENA PIONEER JOURNAL. 1878. Thu. $.75 newsstand; $23/yr. in area; $27/yr. in state; $32/yr. out state. 314 S. Jefferson, Wadena, MN 56482. TEL 218-631-2561; FAX 218-631-1621. **Owner(s):** Fargo Forum Communications, 101 Fifth St., N., P.O. Box 2020, Fargo, ND 58102. TEL 701-241-5404; Ed. Dee George; Pub. Jackie Schmitz; adv. contact: Jackie Schmitz. photos; pub. size: broadsheet; circ. 4,000(paid).

WARREN
US
WARREN SHEAF. 6880. Wed. $.50 newsstand; $21/yr. local; $25/yr. out of cy. 127 W. Johnson Ave., Warren, MN 56762. TEL 218-745-5174; FAX 218-745-5175. **Owner(s):** Warren Sheaf Publishing Co., P.O. Box 45, Warren, MN 56762. TEL 218-745-5174; FAX 218-745-5174; Ed. Eric Mattson; Pub. Eric Mattson; pub. size: broadsheet; circ. 3,150(paid).

WASECA
US   ISSN 0745-8177
WASECA COUNTY NEWS. 1981. s-w.: Tue. & Thu. $1 newsstand; $37/yr. in area; $48/yr. out of area. 213 Second St. N.W., Waseca, MN 56093-0465. TEL 507-835-3380; FAX 507-835-3435. **Owner(s):** Waseca Publishing Co., Inc., 108 Second Ave. NW, Waseca, MN 56093. TEL 507-835-3380; FAX 507-835-3435; Ed. Tom West; Pub. Tom West; adv. contact: Cheryl Neid. photos; bk.rev.; pub. size: broadsheet; circ. 7,236(paid). **Wire Service(s):** AP, Datafinder.

WAYZATA
US
LAKESHORE WEEKLY NEWS. 1982. Thu. free newsstand; $16/6 mos.; $28/yr. 18178 Minnetonka Blvd., Wayzata, MN 55391. TEL 612-473-0890; FAX 612-473-0895; E-mail: billb@weeklynews.com; URL: http://www.weeklynews.com. **Owner(s):** Peter H. May, 18178 Minnetonka Blvd., Wayzata, MN 55391. TEL 612-473-0890; FAX 612-473-0895; Pub. Peter H. May; adv. contact: Mark Gardner. adv.: $19/SAU. pub. size: tabloid; circ. 25,000(free & paid); morning 25,000(free & paid).
Formerly: Weekly News.

WELLS
US
WELLS MIRROR, THE. 1913. Thu. $.60 newsstand; $24/yr. in cy. 40 W. Franklin, Wells, MN 56097. TEL 507-553-3131; FAX 507-553-3132. **Owner(s):** Wells Mirror Co., 40 W. Franklin, Wells, MN 56097. TEL 507-553-3131; FAX 507-553-3132; Ed. Tracy Madden; Pub. Mike Johnson; adv. contact: Tammy Madsen. photos; pub. size: standard; circ. 2,000(paid).

WHITE BEAR LAKE
US
QUAD COMMUNITY PRESS. 1983. Tue. $.50 newsstand; $25/yr. 4779 Bloom Ave., White Bear Lake, MN 55110. TEL 612-429-7781; FAX 612-429-1242. **Owner(s):** Press Publications, Inc., 4779 Bloom Ave., St. Paul, MN 55110. TEL 612-429-7781; Pub. Eugene D. Johnson; adv. contact: Michelle Larson. pub. size: broadsheet; circ. 7,000(paid).

WINDOM
US
WINDOM COTTONWOOD COUNTY CITIZEN. Wed. $.75 newsstand; $29.95/yr. in area; $41.95/yr. out of area. 260 Tenth St., Windom, MN 56101. TEL 507-831-3455; FAX 507-831-3740. **Owner(s):** Kim Anderson, 260 Tenth St., Windom, MN 56101; Ed. Rahn Larson. adv.; pub. size: broadsheet; circ. 4,000(paid).

MISSISSIPPI

ABERDEEN
US
ABERDEEN EXAMINER. 1866. Wed. $.50 newsstand; $18/yr. in cy.; $25/yr. out of cy.; $32/yr. out of state. 209 E. Commerce St., Aberdeen, MS 39730. TEL 601-369-4507; FAX 601-369-4508. **Owner(s):** Northeast Mississippi Community Newspapers, Inc., P.O. Box 909, Tupelo, MS 38802. TEL 601-842-2611; Ed. Barry Burleson; Pub. Barry Burleson; adv. contact: Jimmy Willis. pub. size: broadsheet; circ. 5,000(paid).

AMORY
US   ISSN 0899-0085
AMORY ADVERTISER, THE. 1917. Wed. $.50 newsstand; $25/yr. out of cy.; $32/yr. out of state. 113 S. Main St., Amory, MS 38821. TEL 601-256-5647; FAX 601-256-5701. **Owner(s):** Northeast Mississippi Community Newspapers, Inc., P.O. Box 519, Amory, MS 38821. TEL 601-256-5647; Ed. Chris Wilson; Pub. Barry Burleson; adv. contact: Bonnie Parham. photos; bk.rev.; pub. size: broadsheet; circ. 5,800(paid).

BATESVILLE
US
▼**PANOLIAN ADVANTAGE, THE.** 1996. Wed. $.75 newsstand; $39.95/yr. 174 Hwy. 51, N., Batesville, MS 38606. TEL 601-563-4591; FAX 601-563-5610. **Owner(s):** John H. Howell, 174 Hwy. 51, N., P.O. Box 393, Batesville, MS 38606. TEL 601-563-4591; Rupert K. Howell, 174 Hwy. 51, N., P.O. Box 393, Batesville, MS 38606. TEL 601-563-4591; Ed. Tawanda Tinkersley; Pub. Tawanda Tinkersley; adv. contact: Sandy Richardson. circ. 10,700(paid).

US
PANOLIAN, THE. 1882. bi-w.: Tue. & Fri. $.75 newsstand; $20/yr. in state; $30.50/yr. out of state. 363 Hwy. 51, N., Batesville, MS 38606. TEL 601-563-4591; FAX 601-563-5610. **Owner(s):** John H. Howell, 174 Hwy. 51, N., P.O. Box 393, Batesville, MS 38606. TEL 601-563-4591; Rupert K. Howell, 174 Hwy. 51, N., P.O. Box 393, Batesville, MS 38606. TEL 601-563-4591; Ed. Tawanda Tinkersley; Pub. Tawanda Tinkersley; adv. contact: Sandy Richardson. pub. size: standard; circ. 10,000(paid).

WEEKLY NEWSPAPERS

BAY SPRINGS
US
JASPER COUNTY NEWS, THE. 1920. Wed. $15/yr. in cy.; $20/yr. out of cy.; $23/yr. out of state. Hwy. 15 N., Industrial Park, Bay Springs, MS 39422. TEL 601-764-3104; FAX 601-764-3106. **Owner(s):** Ronnie L. Buckley, P.O. Box 449, Bay Springs, MS 39422. TEL 601-764-2388; Ed. Kevin Williams; Pub. Ronnie L. Buckley; pub. size: standard; circ. 4,200(paid).
Formerly: Bay Springs Jasper County News.

BAY ST. LOUIS
US
BAY ST. LOUIS SEA COAST ECHO. 1892. s-w.: Thu. & Sun. $.50 newsstand; $29/yr. in cy.; $43.50/yr. out of cy.; $49.50/yr. out of state. 124 Court St., Bay St. Louis, MS 39520-2009. TEL 601-467-5474; FAX 601-467-0333. **Owner(s):** Bay St. Louis Newspapers, Inc., P.O. Box 2009, Bay St. Louis, MS 39521. TEL 601-467-5474; Ed. Richard Meek; Pub. Ellis C. Cuevas; pub. size: standard; circ. 7,800(paid).

BOONEVILLE
US
BOONEVILLE BANNER-INDEPENDENT. 1898. Thu. $.50 newsstand; $20/yr. local; $30/yr. elsewhere. 208 Main St., Booneville, MS 38829. TEL 601-728-6214; FAX 601-728-1636. **Owner(s):** Paxton Media Group, Inc., 408 Kentucky Ave., Paducah, KY 42002. TEL 502-575-8600; Ed. Kenny Goode; Pub. Don Swartz; adv. contact: Jim Burnett. pub. size: broadsheet; circ. 5,600(paid).

BRANDON
US
RANKIN COUNTY NEWS, THE. 1848. Wed. $.50 newsstand; $15/yr. in cy.; $20/yr. out of state. Town Sq., 207 Government St., Brandon, MS 39042. TEL 601-825-8333; FAX 601-825-8334. **Owner(s):** RCN Corp., P.O. Box 107, Brandon, MS 39043. TEL 601-825-8333; Ed. Marcus Bowers, Jr.; Pub. Marcus Bowers, Jr.; adv. contact: Marcus Bowers, Jr. pub. size: broadsheet; circ. 6,000(paid).

BRUCE
US
BRUCE CALHOUN COUNTY JOURNAL. 1953. Thu. $.50 newsstand; $17/yr.; $22/yr. out of town. 207 N. Newberger St., Bruce, MS 38915. TEL 601-983-2570; FAX 601-983-7667. **Owner(s):** S. Gale Denley, P.O. Box 278, Bruce, MS 38915; Ed. Celia Denley-Hillhouse; Pub. S. Gale Denley; pub. size: broadsheet; circ. 3,500(paid).

CANTON
US
MADISON COUNTY HERALD. 1906. Thu. $.25 newsstand; $12/yr. in cy.; $15/yr. out of cy. 159 E. Center St., Canton, MS 39046. TEL 601-859-1221; FAX 601-859-9409. **Owner(s):** Mississippi Publishers Corp., P.O. Box 40, Jackson, MS 39205. TEL 601-961-7022; Ed. Bill Zimmerman; Pub. Joe Dove; pub. size: broadsheet; circ. 4,500(paid).

CARROLLTON
US
CONSERVATIVE, THE. 1864. Thu. $.25 newsstand; $14/yr. in cy.; $20/yr. out of cy. Lexington Ave., Carrollton, MS 38917. TEL 601-283-1131. **Owner(s):** Montgomery Publishing Co., P.O. Box 345, Carrollton, MS 38917. TEL 601-283-1131; Ed. Tim James; Pub. Tim James; adv. contact: Ken Strahan. pub. size: broadsheet; circ. 1,000(paid).

CARTHAGE
US
CARTHAGINIAN, THE. 1872. Thu. $.50 newsstand; $21/yr. in cy.; $23/yr. out of cy; $27/yr. out of state. 122 W. Franklin St., Carthage, MS 39051. TEL 601-267-4501; FAX 601-267-5290. **Owner(s):** John H. Keith, The Carthaginian, 122 Franklin St., Carthage, MS 39051. TEL 601-267-4501; Ed. Wade Prather; Pub. John H. Keith; adv.; pub. size: broadsheet; circ. 5,400(paid).

COLUMBIA
US
COLUMBIAN-PROGRESS. 1882. s-w.: Thu. & Sat. $.50 newsstand; $30/yr. in cy.; $35/yr. in state; $40/yr. out of state. 318 Second St., Columbia, MS 39429. TEL 601-736-2611; FAX 601-736-4507. **Owner(s):** Emmerich Newspapers, Inc., P.O. Box 16709, Jackson, MS 39236. TEL 601-957-1122; Ed. Ken Prillhart; Pub. Ken Prillhart; adv. contact: Bonnie Hudson. pub. size: standard; circ. 12,900(paid).

COLUMBUS
US
GOLDEN TRIANGLE SHOPPER. Tue. free. 516 Main St., Columbus, MS 39701. TEL 601-328-2424; FAX 601-329-8937; E-mail: letters@cdispatch.com. **Owner(s):** Commercial Dispatch, Inc., 516 Main St., Columbus, MS 39701. TEL 601-328-2424; FAX 601-329-8937; adv. contact: Dianne Medley. bk.rev.; pub. size: standard; circ. 15,000(free). **Wire Service(s):** AP.

D'IBERVILLE
US
BILOXI-D'IBERVILLE PRESS. 1973. Wed. $.25 newsstand; $14/yr. mailed in Harrison & Jackson cys.; $12/yr. senior citizens; $25/yr. elsewhere. 9450 Central Ave., D'Iberville, MS 39532. TEL 601-392-3307; FAX 601-392-7043. **Owner(s):** S & F Publishing Co., Inc., P.O. Box 194, Biloxi, MS 39533. TEL 601-392-3307; Ed. Walter Fountain; Pub. Charles R. Stein, Sr.; adv.; pub. size: broadsheet; circ. 6,000(paid).

DEKALB
US
KEMPER COUNTY MESSENGER. 1940. Thu. $.50 newsstand; $12/yr. in cy.; $15/yr. out of cy.; $18/yr. out of state. Main St., DeKalb, MS 39328. TEL 601-743-5760; FAX 601-743-2760. **Owner(s):** Jeff & Jayne Jowers, P.O. Box 546, DeKalb, MS 39328. TEL 601-743-5760; James & Bettye Sledge, 107 Lavern, Crystal Springs, MS 39059. TEL 601-892-5510; Ed. Jeff Jowers; Pub. James L. Sledge, Jr.; adv. contact: Patty Jowers. bk.rev.; pub. size: broadsheet; circ. 2,200(free & paid).

EUPORA
US
WEBSTER PROGRESS-TIMES. 1879. Wed. $.50 newsstand; $16/yr. in state; $20/yr. out of state. 122 Dunn St., Eupora, MS 39744. TEL 601-258-7532; FAX 601-258-6474. **Owner(s):** Robert Anderson, P.O. Box Drawer D, Eupora, MS 39744. TEL 601-258-7532; FAX 601-258-6474; Ed. Betsy Mordecai; Pub. Robert Anderson; adv. contact: Timothy R. James. photos; pub. size: broadsheet; circ. 2,638(paid).

FOREST
US
SCOTT COUNTY TIMES. 1939. Wed. $.50 newsstand; $21/yr. in cy.; $24/yr. in state; $27/yr. out of state. 311 Smith St., Forest, MS 39074. TEL 601-469-2561; FAX 601-469-2004. **Owner(s):** Scott Publishing, Inc., P.O. Box 89, Forest, MS 39074. TEL 601-469-2561; FAX 601-469-2004; Ed. S.L. Salter; Pub. S.L. Salter; adv. contact: Nicole Nichols. pub. size: broadsheet; circ. 5,500(paid).

FULTON
US
ITAWAMBA COUNTY TIMES, THE. 1945. Wed. $.50 newsstand; $18/yr. in cy.; $25/yr. in state; $32/yr. out of state. 106 W. Main St., Fulton, MS 38843-5149. TEL 601-862-3141; FAX 601-862-7804. **Owner(s):** Journal Publishing Co., P.O. Box 909, Tupelo, MS 38801. TEL 601-862-2611; FAX 601-862-7804; Ed. Susan Harp; Pub. Rubye Del Harden; adv.; pub. size: broadsheet; circ. 6,600(paid).

HAZLEHURST
US
COPIAH COUNTY COURIER. 1884. Wed. $.50 newsstand; $14/yr. in cy.; $16/yr. out of cy.; $20/yr. out of state. 103 S. Ragsdale Ave., Hazlehurst, MS 39083-0135. TEL 601-894-3141; FAX 601-894-3144. **Owner(s):** James & Wilma S. Lambert, 103 S. Ragsdale Ave., Hazlehurst, MS 39083; Ed. James Lambert; Pub. James Lambert; adv.; photos; pub. size: standard; circ. 6,036(free & paid).

HOLLY SPRINGS
US
SOUTH REPORTER, THE. 1865. Thu. $.50 newsstand; $17/yr. in cy.; $22/yr. out of cy. 157 S. Center St., Holly Springs, MS 38635. TEL 601-252-4261; FAX 601-252-3388. **Owner(s):** Walter W. Webb, 157 S. Center St., Holly Springs, MS 38635. TEL 601-252-4261; FAX 601-252-3388; Ed. Walter W. Webb; Pub. Walter W. Webb; pub. size: broadsheet; circ. 6,500(paid).

HOUSTON
US
TIMES POST, THE. 1906. Wed. $.50 newsstand; $24/yr. in cy.; $30/yr. in state; $40/yr. out of state. 225 E. Madison, Houston, MS 38851. TEL 601-456-3771; FAX 601-456-5202. **Owner(s):** Houston Newspapers, Inc., 225 E. Madison, Houston, MS 38851. TEL 601-456-3771; Ed. Kenny Hoblitzell; Pub. Kenny Hoblitzell; adv. contact: Laura Bray. pub. size: broadsheet; circ. 15,000(paid).

10650 IUKA, MS

WEEKLY NEWSPAPERS

IUKA
US
IUKA TISHOMINGO COUNTY NEWS. 1885. Thu. $.35 newsstand; $15/yr. in state; $25/yr. out of state. 120 W. Front St., Iuka, MS 38852. TEL 601-423-2211; FAX 601-423-3667. **Owner(s):** John H. Biggs, 120 W. Front St., Iuka, MS 38852. TEL 601-423-3666; Caroline Morris, Sheffield, AL; Ed. John H. Biggs; Pub. John H. Biggs; pub. size: standard; circ. 6,000(paid).

JACKSON
US
NORTHSIDE SUN, THE. 1967. Thu. $.50 newsstand; $16/yr. in cy. 246 Briarwood, Jackson, MS 39206. TEL 601-957-1122; FAX 601-957-1533. **Owner(s):** Sunland Publishing Co., Inc., P.O. Box 16709, Jackson, MS 39236. TEL 601-957-1122; FAX 601-957-1533; Ed. Jimmye Sweat. adv. contact: Jonni Webb. photos; bk.rev.; pub. size: broadsheet; circ. 9,500(paid).
   Formerly: Sunland.

KOSCIUSKO
US
STAR-HERALD, THE. 1866. Thu. $.50 newsstand; $28/yr. local in state; $35/yr. out of state. 317 N. Madison, Kosciusko, MS 39090. TEL 601-289-2251; FAX 601-289-2254. **Owner(s):** American Publishing Co., 606 N. Van Buren, P.O. Box 520, Marion, IL 62959. TEL 618-993-1711; Ed. Rayne Bruce; Pub. Neal H. Turnage; adv. contact: Donna Peeples. pub. size: broadsheet; circ. 8,500(paid).
   Formerly: Kosciusko Star-Herald.

LAUREL
US
IMPACT OF LAUREL. 1976. s-w.: Wed. & Sun. free. 1010 N. 16th Ave., Laurel, MS 39440. TEL 601-649-1129; FAX 601-649-0424. **Owner(s):** Buckley Newspapers, Inc., Box 449, Bay Springs, MS 39422. TEL 601-764-3104; Ed. Ronnie L. Buckley. adv. contact: Suzanne Smith. pub. size: tabloid; circ. 60,000(free).

LIBERTY
US   ISSN 0893-3790
SOUTHERN HERALD, THE. 1825. Thu. $.50 newsstand; $17/yr. in cy.; $20/yr. out of cy. & state. 258 Main St., Liberty, MS 39645. TEL 601-657-4818; FAX 601-657-4818. **Owner(s):** Richard H. Stratton, P.O. Box 674, Liberty, MS 39645. TEL 601-657-4818; Ed. Richard H. Stratton; Pub. Richard H. Stratton; adv.; photos; pub. size: standard; circ. 1,100(free & paid).
   Formerly: Liberty Southern Herald.

LOUISVILLE
US
LOUISVILLE WINSTON COUNTY JOURNAL. 1892. Wed. $.75 newsstand; $24/yr. in cy.; $40/yr. out of cy. 119 N. Court Ave., Louisville, MS 39339. TEL 601-773-6241; FAX 601-773-6242. **Owner(s):** Louisville Newspapers, Inc., P.O. Box 469, Louisville, MS 39339. TEL 601-773-6241; Ed. Sarah Stevens; Pub. Jerry Shiverdecker; pub. size: broadsheet; circ. 5,300(paid).

US
SHOPPER'S GUIDE, THE. 1892. Wed. free. 119 N. Court Ave., Louisville, MS 39339. TEL 601-773-6241; FAX 601-773-6242. **Owner(s):** Louisville Newspapers, Inc., P.O. Box 469, Louisville, MS 39339; Ed. Sarah Stevenson; Pub. Jerry Shiverdecker; circ. 9,600(free & paid).

LUCEDALE
US
GEORGE COUNTY TIMES. Thu. $.25 newsstand; $11/yr. in cy.; $15/yr. in state; $18/yr. out of state. P.O. Box 238, Lucedale, MS 39452. TEL 601-947-2967; FAX 601-947-6828. **Owner(s):** O.G. Sellers, P.O. Box 238, Lucedale, MS 39452. TEL 601-947-7967; Ed. O.G. Sellers; Pub. O.G. Sellers; pub. size: standard; circ. 5,000(paid).
   Formerly: Lucedale George County Times.

MACON
US
MACON BEACON, THE. 1849. Thu. $.50 newsstand; $17/yr. in state; $20/yr. out of state. 403 S. Jefferson, Macon, MS 39341. TEL 601-726-4747; FAX 601-726-4742. **Owner(s):** R. Scott Boyd, P.O. Box 32, Macon, MS 39341. TEL 601-726-4747; FAX 601-726-4742; Ed. R. Scott Boyd; Pub. R. Scott Boyd; pub. size: broadsheet; circ. 2,900(paid).

MAGEE
US
MAGEE COURIER. 1899. Thu. $.50 newsstand; $18/yr. in cy. 206 N. Main St., Magee, MS 39111. TEL 601-849-3434; FAX 601-849-6828. **Owner(s):** Simpson Publishing Co., Inc., P.O. Box 338, Magee, MS 39111. TEL 601-849-3434; FAX 601-849-6828; Ed. Pat Brown; Pub. Pat Brown; adv.; photos; pub. size: broadsheet; circ. 3,500(paid).

MAGNOLIA
US
MAGNOLIA GAZETTE, THE. 1874. Wed. $.50 newsstand; $10/yr. in cy.; $20/yr. out of state. 279 E. Bay, Magnolia, MS 39652. TEL 601-783-2441; FAX 504-748-7104. **Owner(s):** Louisiana State Newspapers, P.O. Box 4033C, Lafayette, LA 70502. TEL 318-266-2154; Ed. Cathy Haroin. adv. contact: Cathy Haroin. photos; pub. size: broadsheet; circ. 1,200(paid).

NEW ALBANY
US
NEW ALBANY GAZETTE. 1887. s-w.: Wed. & Fri. $.50 newsstand; $32.50/yr. local. 713 Carter Ave., New Albany, MS 38652. TEL 601-534-6321; FAX 601-534-6355; E-mail: janlynn@dixie-net.com. **Owner(s):** Landmark Community Newspapers, Inc., Hwy. 55, S., Shelbyville, KY 40065. TEL 502-633-4334; FAX 502-633-0852; Ed. Betty Jo Stewart. adv.; pub. size: broadsheet; circ. 16,000(paid).

NEWTON
US
NEWTON RECORD. 1901. Wed. $.50 newsstand; $22/yr. in cy.; $27/yr. out of cy.; $32/yr. out of state. 120 S. Main St., Newton, MS 39345. TEL 601-683-2001; FAX 601-683-2360. **Owner(s):** American Publishing Co., 606 N. Van Buren, P.O. Box 520, Marion, IL 62959. TEL 618-993-1711; Ed. J.E. Strange; Pub. J.E. Strange; adv.; photos; pub. size: broadsheet; circ. 2,674(paid).

US
SHOPPING NEWS, THE. 1980. Wed. free. 120 S. Main St., Newton, MS 39345. TEL 601-683-2001; FAX 601-683-2360. **Owner(s):** American Publishing Co., 606 N. Van Buren, P.O. Box 520, Marion, IL 62959. TEL 618-993-1711; Ed. J.E. Strange; Pub. J.E. Strange; adv.; pub. size: broadsheet; circ. 8,600(free).

OCEAN SPRINGS
US
OCEAN SPRINGS RECORD. 1965. Thu. $.50 newsstand; $19.75/yr. in cy.; $27.75/yr. out of cy.; $12.50/yr. senior citizen in cy.; $26.50/yr. senior citizen out of cy. 715 Cox Ave., Ocean Springs, MS 39564. TEL 601-875-2791; FAX 601-875-9569. **Owner(s):** Gannett Company, Inc., 1100 Wilson Blvd., Arlington, VA 22234. TEL 703-284-6000; Pub. James Ricketts; adv. contact: Peter D. Logan. photos; pub. size: standard; circ. 3,600(paid).

PHILADELPHIA
US
NESHOBA DEMOCRAT, THE. 1881. Wed. $.50 newsstand; $21/yr. in cy.; $27/yr. out of state. 439 Beacon St., Philadelphia, MS 39350. TEL 601-656-4000; FAX 601-656-6379. **Owner(s):** Neshoba Democrat Publishing Co., P.O. Box 30, Philadelphia, MS 39350. TEL 601-656-4000; Ed. Stanley Dearman; Pub. Stanley Dearman; adv.; photos; bk.rev.; pub. size: standard; circ. 7,500(paid).

PONTOTOC
US
PONTOTOC PROGRESS. 1929. Wed. $.50 newsstand; $23/yr. in cy.; $28/yr. elsewhere. 19 S. Liberty, Pontotoc, MS 38863. TEL 601-489-3511; FAX 601-489-6714. **Owner(s):** Daily Journal Newspapers, Green St., Tupelo, MS 38801. TEL 601-937-6411; Ed. Brenda Owens; Pub. David Helms; pub. size: broadsheet; circ. 6,800(paid).

PORT GIBSON
US
PORT GIBSON REVEILLE. 1851. Thu. $.35 newsstand; $14/yr. in state; $19.50/yr. out of state. 708 Main St., Port Gibson, MS 39150. TEL 601-437-5103; FAX 601-437-4410. **Owner(s):** Edgar T. Crisler, Jr., P.O. Box 1002, Port Gibson, MS 39150. TEL 601-437-5103; FAX 601-437-4410; Ed. Edgar T. Crisler, Jr.; Pub. Edgar T. Crisler, Jr.; adv. contact: Janice Bufkin. photos; bk.rev.; pub. size: standard; circ. 2,247(free & paid).

WEEKLY NEWSPAPERS

QUITMAN
US

CLARKE COUNTY TRIBUNE. 1908. Wed. $18/yr. in cy.; $20/yr. out of cy.; $22/yr. out of state. 101 Main St., Quitman, MS 39355. TEL 601-776-3726; FAX 601-776-5793. **Owner(s):** James T. Speed, 101 Main St., Quitman, MS 39355. TEL 601-776-3726; Ed. Steve Swogetinsky; Pub. James T. Speed; adv. contact: Rhonda Kelley. pub. size: standard; circ. 4,000(paid).

RALEIGH
US

SMITH COUNTY REFORMER. 1889. Wed. $.50 newsstand; $15/yr. in cy.; $20/yr. out of cy.; $23/yr. out of state. Main St., Raleigh, MS 39153. TEL 601-782-4358; FAX 601-764-3106. **Owner(s):** Ronnie L. Buckley, Buckley Newspapers, P.O. Box 449, Bay Springs, MS 39422. TEL 601-764-3104; Ed. Blenda Singleton. adv. contact: Brenda Ingram. bk.rev.; pub. size: standard; circ. 3,800(paid).

RICHTON
US

RICHTON DISPATCH, THE. 1905. Thu. $.30 newsstand; $13/yr. in cy.; $16/yr. out of cy. 110 Walnut St., Richton, MS 39476-1521. TEL 601-788-6031; FAX 601-788-6031; E-mail: richtonl@aol.com. **Owner(s):** Richton Dispatch, P.O. Drawer X, Richton, KS 39476-1521. TEL 601-788-6031; FAX 601-788-6031; Ed. Larry A. Wilson. adv.; photos; pub. size: standard; circ. 1,600(paid).

RIPLEY
US

RIPLEY SOUTHERN SENTINEL. 1879. s-w.: Wed. & Sat. $.50 newsstand; $38.50/yr. in cy.; $45.50/yr. out of cy.; $56/yr. elsewhere. 1701 City Ave. N., Ripley, MS 38663. TEL 601-837-8111; FAX 601-837-4504. **Owner(s):** Sentinel, Inc., P.O. Box 558, Ripley, MS 38663. TEL 601-837-8111; adv. contact: Jane Matthews. pub. size: broadsheet; circ. 7,200(paid).

SENATOBIA
US

DEMOCRAT, THE. 1881. Tue. $.50 newsstand; $18/yr. local; $23/yr. in state; $28/yr. out of state. 219 E. Main St., Senatobia, MS 38668-0369. TEL 601-562-4414; FAX 601-562-8866; E-mail: sarah-bondurant@mspress.tfnet.org. **Owner(s):** North Mississippi Newspapers, Inc., 219 E. Main St., Senatobia, MS 38668-0369. TEL 601-562-4414; FAX 601-562-8866; Ed. Sarah Bondurant; Pub. Joe Lee, III; adv. contact: Sarah Bondurant. adv.: $6.25/SAU. photos; bk.rev.; pub. size: broadsheet; circ. 5,000(free & paid).
Formerly: Tate County Democrat.

SOUTHAVEN
US

DE SOTO TIMES. 1939. Wed. $23/yr. in cy.; $36/yr. out of cy. 1283 Stateline Rd., Southaven, MS 38671. TEL 601-393-6397; FAX 601-393-6463. **Owner(s):** Bailey Publications, Inc., 1283 Stateline Rd., Southaven, MS 38671. TEL 601-393-6397; Ed. William Bailey. adv.; photos; pub. size: standard; circ. 6,559(paid).

TYLERTOWN
US

TYLERTOWN TIMES. 1907. Thu. $15/yr. 727 Beulah Ave., Tylertown, MS 39667. TEL 601-876-5111; FAX 601-876-5280. **Owner(s):** Tylertown Times, 727 Beulah Ave., Tylertown, MS 39667; Ed. Carolyn Dillon. pub. size: broadsheet; circ. 3,950(paid).

WAYNESBORO
US

WAYNE COUNTY NEWS. 1891. Thu. $.50 newsstand; $18.75/yr. local. 608 Station St., Waynesboro, MS 39367. TEL 601-735-4341; FAX 601-735-1111. **Owner(s):** American Publishing Co., 606 N. Van Buren, Marion, IL 62959. TEL 618-993-1711; Ed. Gene O'Gordon. adv.; pub. size: broadsheet; circ. 5,000(paid).

WIGGINS
US

STONE COUNTY ENTERPRISE. 1906. Wed. $.50 newsstand; $15/yr. in cy.; $25/yr. out of cy.; $30/yr. out of state. 143 First St., Wiggins, MS 39577. TEL 601-928-4802; FAX 601-928-2191. **Owner(s):** Stone County Enterprise, P.O. Box 157, Wiggins, MS 39577. TEL 601-928-4802; Ed. Kirk Boyer; Pub. Don Groves; adv. contact: Heather Freret. pub. size: broadsheet; circ. 3,100(paid).

WINONA
US

WINONA TIMES. Thu. $.50 newsstand; $20/yr. in cy.; $25/yr. out of cy. 401 Summit St., Winona, MS 38967. TEL 601-283-1131; FAX 601-283-5374. **Owner(s):** Montgomery Publishing Co., P.O. Box 151, Winona, MS 38967. TEL 601-283-1131; Ed. Tim James; Pub. Tim James; adv. contact: Ken Strahan. photos; pub. size: broadsheet; circ. 3,600(paid).

YAZOO CITY
US

YAZOO HERALD. 1872. s-w.: Wed. & Sat. $.50 newsstand; $26/yr. in state; $38/yr. out of state. 1035 Grand Ave., Yazoo City, MS 39194. TEL 601-746-4911; FAX 601-746-4915; E-mail: herald@capital2.com. **Owner(s):** Yazoo Newspaper Co., Inc., P.O. Box 720, Yazoo City, MS 39194. TEL 601-746-4911; Ed. Steve Stewart; Pub. Steve Stewart; adv. contact: Steve Stewart. adv.: $5.48/SAU. pub. size: broadsheet; circ. 4,200(paid).

MISSOURI

ALBANY
US

ALBANY LEDGER, THE. 1868. Wed. $.50 newsstand; $20/yr. in cy.; $24/yr. in state; $28/yr. out of state. P.O. Box 247, Albany, MO 64402. TEL 816-726-3997; FAX 816-726-3997. **Owner(s):** Terry & Nancy Holub, Smith & Clay Sts., P.O. Box 247, Albany, MO 64402. TEL 816-726-3997; Ed. Terry Holub; Pub. Terry Holub; adv.; pub. size: broadsheet; circ. 1,600(paid).
Formerly: Ledger-Highlight, The.

ARNOLD
US

JEFFERSON COUNTY JOURNAL. s-w.: Sun. & Wed. free. 27 Fox Valley Ctr., Arnold, MO 63010. TEL 314-296-2800; FAX 314-296-2800. **Owner(s):** Suburban Journals, P.O. Box 309, Festus, MO 63028. TEL 314-296-1800; Ed. Jennifer Florian. pub. size: broadsheet; circ. 19,000(free).

ASHLAND
US

BOONE COUNTY JOURNAL. 1969. Wed. $16/yr. in state; $20/yr. out of state. 104 W. Broadway, Ashland, MO 65010. TEL 573-657-2334; FAX 573-657-2002. **Owner(s):** Richard Flink, 104 W. Broadway, Ashland, MO 65010. TEL 573-657-2334; Ed. Jane Flink; Pub. Richard Flink; adv.; pub. size: broadsheet; circ. 1,700(paid).

AURORA
US ISSN 1041-1275

AURORA ADVERTISER. 1886. 3/wk.: Mon., Wed., Fri. $.35 newsstand; $16/yr. in cy. 226 W. Church St., Aurora, MO 65605-0509. TEL 417-678-2115. E-mail: advert@dialnet.net. **Owner(s):** Lawrence County Newspapers, Inc., 226 W. Church St., P.O. Box 509, Aurora, MO 65605. TEL 417-678-2115; Ed. Paul E. Donley; Pub. Paul E. Donley; adv. contact: Jowell Bagby. photos; bk.rev.; pub. size: standard; circ. 3,500(paid).

AVA
US

DOUGLAS COUNTY HERALD. 1887. Thu. $.35 newsstand; $14/yr. in cy.; $19/yr. out of cy. 304 E. Washington Ave., Ava, MO 65608-0577. TEL 417-683-4181. **Owner(s):** James E. Curry, 304 E. Washington Ave., Ava, MO 65608. TEL 417-683-4181; D. Keith Moore, 304 E. Washington Ave., Ava, MO 65608. TEL 417-683-4181; Ed. D. Keith Moore; Pub. James E. Curry; adv. contact: Jody Porter. pub. size: broadsheet; circ. 5,000(paid).

BELLE
US

BELLE BANNER. 1907. Wed. $.40 newsstand; $17.61/yr. local; $20.28/yr. in state; $20/yr. out of state. 307 S. Alvarado Ave., Belle, MO 65013-0711. TEL 573-859-3328; FAX 573-859-6274. **Owner(s):** Tri-County Newspapers, 307 Alvarado, P.O. Box 711, Belle, MO 65013-0711. TEL 573-859-3328; FAX 573-859-6274; Ed. Ron Lewis; Pub. Ron Lewis; adv.; photos; pub. size: broadsheet; circ. 2,750(paid).

US

BLAND COURIER. 1901. Wed. $.40 newsstand; $17.61/yr. local; $20.28/yr. in state; $20/yr. out of state. 307 Alvarado, Belle, MO 65014. TEL 314-646-3312; FAX 314-859-6274. **Owner(s):** Tri-County Newspapers, 307 Alvarado, P.O. Box 711, Belle, MO 65013-0711. TEL 314-859-3328; FAX 314-859-6274; Ed. Ron Lewis; Pub. Ron Lewis; adv.; photos; pub. size: broadsheet; circ. 900(paid).

BELTON
US

10652 BELTON, MO

STAR-HERALD. 1892. Thu. $.50 newsstand; $19/yr. in cy.; $26/yr. out of cy.; $26/yr. in state; $31/yr. out of state. 419 Main St., Belton, MO 64012. TEL 816-331-5353; FAX 816-322-2943. **Owner(s):** Belton Publishing Co., Inc., 419 Main St., Belton, MO 64012. TEL 816-331-5353; Ed. Mark E. Cox; Pub. Mark E. Cox; adv. contact: Vicki Daniel. pub. size: broadsheet; circ. 5,348(paid).

BETHANY
US
BETHANY REPUBLICAN-CLIPPER. 1873. Wed. $.50 newsstand; $25/yr. 214 N. 16th St., Bethany, MO 64424. TEL 816-425-6325; FAX 816-425-3441. **Owner(s):** Bethany Printing Co., P.O. Box 351, Bethany, MO 64424. TEL 816-425-6325; FAX 816-425-3441; Ed. Philip Conger; Pub. Philip Conger; adv. contact: Kathy Conger. photos; pub. size: broadsheet; circ. 20,900(free & paid).

US
HARRISON COUNTY ADVISOR. 1967. Tue. free in cy.; $35/yr. mailed 1st class; $13/yr. mailed 3rd class. 303 N. 25th, Bethany, MO 64424. TEL 816-425-3433; FAX 816-425-6984. **Owner(s):** Harrison County Advisor, Inc., P.O. Box 106, Bethany, MO 64424. TEL 816-425-3433; adv.; pub. size: tabloid; circ. 7,000(free).

BOLIVAR
US
BOLIVAR HERALD-FREE PRESS. 1868. Wed. $.50 newsstand; $25/yr. in cy. 335 S. Springfield, Bolivar, MO 65613-0330. TEL 417-326-7636; FAX 417-326-8701. **Owner(s):** Sterling Media, Ltd., P.O. Box 330, Bolivar, MO 65613-0330. TEL 417-326-7636; Ed. Judy Kallenbach. adv. contact: Linda Simmon. pub. size: broadsheet; circ. 7,400(paid).

BOONVILLE
US
RECORD, THE. Tue. $.50 newsstand; $32.09/yr. 412 High St., Boonville, MO 65233. TEL 816-882-5335; FAX 816-882-2256. **Owner(s):** American Publishing Co., 606 N. Van Buren, Marion, IL 62959. TEL 816-993-1711; Ed. Steve Thomas; Pub. Scott Jackson; adv. contact: Kim Alberts. photos; pub. size: broadsheet; circ. 10,000(paid).

BOWLING GREEN
US
BOWLING GREEN TIMES. 1874. Wed. $.50 newsstand; $21/yr. in cy.; $31/yr. out of cy. 106 W. Main, Bowling Green, MO 63334. TEL 573-324-2222; FAX 573-324-3991. **Owner(s):** Pike/Lincoln Publishing Co., P.O. Box 3204, Tuscalusca, AL 35401; Pub. Candace Velvin; pub. size: broadsheet; circ. 3,000(paid).

BUFFALO
US
BUFFALO REFLEX. 1869. Wed. $.70 newsstand; $25/yr. local; $40/yr. out of state. 114 E. Lincoln, Buffalo, MO 65622. TEL 417-345-2224; FAX 417-345-2235. **Owner(s):** James Sterling, P.O. Box 330, Bolivar, MO 65622. TEL 417-325-7636; FAX 417-326-8701; Ed. Dave Abner; Pub. James Hamilton; adv. contact: Steve Johnson. bk.rev.; pub. size: broadsheet; circ. 4,700(paid).

BUTLER
US
NEWS-X PRESS. 1984. Fri. $.53 newsstand; $18.50/yr. in cy.; $22.73/yr. out of cy.; $25.90/yr. out of state. 5 N. Main, Butler, MO 64730-0210. TEL 816-679-6126; FAX 816-679-4905. **Owner(s):** Jim & Carol Peters, 5 N. Main St., Butler, MO 64730. TEL 816-679-6126; FAX 816-679-4905; Ed. C.A. Moore. adv.; pub. size: standard; circ. 3,800(paid).

CALIFORNIA
US
CALIFORNIA DEMOCRAT. 1858. Wed. $.50 newsstand; $22.75/yr. in cy.; $25/yr. in state; $27.50/yr. out of state. 319 S. High St., California, MO 65018. TEL 573-796-2135; FAX 573-796-4220. **Owner(s):** Freedom Communications, Inc., 17666 Fitch, Irvine, CA 92714. TEL 714-553-9292; FAX 714-474-7675; Ed. Connie Bestgen; Pub. Ray Grimes; pub. size: broadsheet; circ. 4,000(paid).

CAMERON
US
CAMERON CITIZEN OBSERVER. Thu. $.75 newsstand; $26/yr. in cy.; $28/yr. out of cy.; $36/yr. out of state. P.O. Box 70, Cameron, MO 64429. TEL 816-632-7281; FAX 816-632-4508. **Owner(s):** Smith Publishing Co., P.O. Box 70, Cameron, MO 64429. TEL 816-632-7281; Ed. Craig Watkins; Pub. Craig Watkins; pub. size: broadsheet; circ. 2,500(paid).

CANTON
US
PRESS-NEWS JOURNAL. 1863. Thu. $.50 newsstand; $20-$23/yr. 130 N. Fourth St., Canton, MO 63435. TEL 573-288-5668. **Owner(s):** Americanton Enterprises Inc., 130 N. Fourth St., Canton, MO 63435. TEL 573-288-5668; FAX 573-288-0000; Ed. Daniel W. Steinbeck; Pub. Daniel W. Steinbeck; adv.: $3.25/SAU. photos; pub. size: broadsheet; circ. 3,500(paid).
Formerly: Canton Press-News Journal.

CARROLLTON
US
CARROLLTON DEMOCRAT. 1881. s-w.: Tue. & Fri. $.50 newsstand; $31.34/yr. carrier; $43.43/yr. out of cy.; $39/yr. out of state. Hwy. 65 & 24 S., Carrollton, MO 64633. TEL 816-542-0881; FAX 816-542-2580. **Owner(s):** Standard Herald, Inc., 132 W. Pine, Lawrence, KS; Ed. Mike Johnson; Pub. Frank Mescer; adv. contact: Judy Stroud. pub. size: broadsheet; circ. evening 2,800(paid).
Formerly: Carrollton Daily Democrat.

CARUTHERSVILLE
US
DEMOCRAT-ARGUS, THE. 1868. s-w.: Wed. & Fri. $.50 newsstand; $30/yr. 111 E. Fifth St., Caruthersville, MO 63830. TEL 573-333-4336; FAX 573-333-2307. **Owner(s):** Rust Communications, P.O. Box 699, Cape Girardeau, MO 63702-0699. TEL 800-879-1210; Ed. Jennifer Dodson. adv. contact: Sheila Roufe. pub. size: broadsheet; circ. 13,000(free & paid).

WEEKLY NEWSPAPERS

CASSVILLE
US   ISSN 0194-1542
BARRY COUNTY ADVERTISER. 1966. Wed. $.25 newsstand; $32.02/yr. 904 West St., Cassville, MO 65625. TEL 417-847-3155; FAX 417-847-4523. **Owner(s):** Barry County Advertiser, 904 West St., P.O. Box 488, Cassville, MO 65625. TEL 417-847-4475; FAX 417-847-4523; Ed. Jennie Herrin; Pub. Jean Melton; adv. contact: Johnie Edie. photos; pub. size: tabloid; circ. 11,500(paid).

US
CASSVILLE DEMOCRAT. 1872. Wed. $.30 newsstand; $25/yr. 600 Main St., Cassville, MO 65625. TEL 417-847-2610; FAX 417-847-3092. **Owner(s):** Mike & Lisa Schlichtman, P.O. Box 486, Cassville, MO 65625. TEL 417-847-2610; FAX 417-847-3092; Ed. Mike Schlichtman. adv.; photos; pub. size: broadsheet; circ. 3,500(paid).

CENTRALIA
US
CENTRALIA FIRESIDE GUARD. 1868. Wed. $25.50/yr. local; $25.50/yr. in state; $29/yr. out of state. 118 W. Sneed, Centralia, MO 65240. TEL 573-682-2133; FAX 573-682-3361. **Owner(s):** Charles & Janann Hedberg, 118 W. Sneed, Centralia, MO 65240; Ed. Janann Hedberg; Pub. Charles Hedberg; pub. size: broadsheet; circ. 4,300(paid).

CHARLESTON
US
CHARLESTON ENTERPRISE-COURIER. 1874. Thu. $.30 newsstand; $18.70/yr. in state; $20/yr. out of state. 206 S. Main St., Charleston, MO 63834. TEL 573-683-3351; FAX 573-683-2217. **Owner(s):** Enterprise-Courier, Inc., P.O. Box 69, Charleston, MO 63834; Ed. Jim Anderson; Pub. Mildred Wallhausen; adv. contact: Beth Ohmes. pub. size: broadsheet; circ. 3,500(paid).

CLINTON
US
CLINTON EYE, THE. Thu. $.30 newsstand. 212 S. Washington St., Clinton, MO 64735-0586. TEL 816-885-2281; FAX 816-885-2265. **Owner(s):** Democrat Publishing Co., 212 S. Washington St., Clinton, MO 64735-0586. TEL 816-885-2281; FAX 816-885-2265; Ed. Kathleen Miles; Pub. Kathleen Miles; pub. size: broadsheet; circ. 665(paid).

US
KAYO, THE. Wed. free. 212 S. Washington St., Clinton, MO 64735-0586. TEL 816-885-2281; FAX 816-885-2265. **Owner(s):** Democrat Publishing Co., 212 S. Washington St., Clinton, MO 64735-0586. TEL 816-885-2281; FAX 816-885-2265; Ed. Kathleen Miles; Pub. Kathleen Miles; adv. contact: Kathleen Miles. pub. size: broadsheet; circ. 15,000(free).

COLUMBIA
US   ISSN 0026-6671
MISSOURI PRESS NEWS. 1938. m. $7.50/yr. 802 Locust, Columbia, MO 65201. TEL 573-449-4167; FAX 573-874-5894; E-mail: kford@digmo.org. **Owner(s):** Missouri Press Association, 802 Locust, Columbia, MO 65201. TEL 573-449-4167; Ed. Kent M. Ford; Pub. Doug Crews; adv.; photos; pub. size: standard; circ. 900.

WEEKLY NEWSPAPERS

US
WHEELS 'N DEALS. bi-m. free. 1203 Wilks Blvd., Columbia, MO 65201. TEL 573-443-6014; FAX 573-874-9594. **Owner(s):** Tom Ridge, P.O. Box 256, Columbia, MO 65201. TEL 314-443-6014; Ed. Tom Ridge; Pub. Tom Ridge; pub. size: broadsheet; circ. 17,000(free).

CUBA
US
CUBA FREE PRESS. 1960. Thu. $.50 newsstand; $18.16/yr. 110 S. Buchanan, Cuba, MO 65453. TEL 573-885-7460; FAX 573-885-3803. **Owner(s):** Cuba Free Press, Inc., 110 S. Buchanan, Cuba, MO 65453. TEL 573-885-7460; Ed. Percy Pascoe; Pub. Percy Pascoe; adv. contact: Sherry Wycoff. pub. size: broadsheet; circ. 3,657(free & paid).

DIXON
US
DIXON PILOT. 1910. Thu. $.35 newsstand; $21.35/yr. in cy. 302 Locust St., Dixon, MO 65459. TEL 573-759-2127; FAX 573-759-6226. **Owner(s):** Rick Blackburn, 302 Locust St., P.O. Drawer V, Dixon, MA 65459. TEL 573-759-2127; Ed. Ralph Nelson; Pub. Rick Blackburn; adv. contact: Connie Blackburn. pub. size: broadsheet; circ. 2,500(paid).

DONIPHAN
US
PROSPECT-NEWS, THE. 1874. Wed. $.50 newsstand; $20/yr. local; $30/yr. elsewhere. 110 Washington, Doniphan, MO 63935. TEL 573-996-2103; FAX 573-996-2217. **Owner(s):** Rust Communications, P.O. Box 600, Cape Girardeau, MO 63702. TEL 314-335-6611; Ed. Barbara Horton; Pub. Don Schrieber; adv.; pub. size: broadsheet; circ. 5,300(paid).

US
PROSPECTOR, THE. Wed. $20/yr. in area; $30/yr. outside area. 110 Washington St., Doniphan, MO 63935. TEL 573-996-2103; FAX 573-996-2217. **Owner(s):** Butler County Publishing, 208 Poplar St., Poplar Bluff, MO 63901. TEL 573-785-1414; Ed. Barbara Horton; Pub. Don Schrieber; adv.; pub. size: broadsheet; circ. 6,800(free).

ELDON
US
ELDON ADVERTISER. 1894. Wed. $.50 newsstand; $28.50/yr. in cy.; $34/yr. out of cy.; $42/yr. out of state. 409-15 S. Maple St., Eldon, MO 65026-0315. TEL 314-392-5658; FAX 314-392-7755. **Owner(s):** Vernon Publishing, Inc., 409-15 S. Maple St., Eldon, MO 65026. TEL 573-392-5659; Ed. Ginny Duffield; Pub. Jeffrey D. Vernon; adv.; photos; pub. size: broadsheet; circ. 5,400(paid).

ELLINGTON
US
REYNOLDS COUNTY COURIER. 1876. Thu. $.50 newsstand; $20.50/yr. in surrounding cys.; $30/yr. elsewhere. 318 Main St., Ellington, MO 63638. TEL 573-663-2243; FAX 573-663-2763. **Owner(s):** Ellinghouse Publishing Co., Inc., 101 W. Elm, Piedmont, MO 63957. TEL 314-223-7122; FAX 314-223-7871; Pub. Mary Beth Stivers; adv. contact: Carol Whitehead. photos; pub. size: broadsheet; circ. 2,850(paid). **Wire Service(s):** AP.

FAYETTE
US ISSN 0746-9934
DEMOCRAT-LEADER. 1874. Sat. $.30 newsstand; $12/yr. in cy.; $29/yr. in state; $34/yr. out of state. 202 E. Morrison St., Fayette, MO 65248-0032. TEL 816-248-2235; FAX 816-298-1200. **Owner(s):** Wood Creek Corp., 202 E. Morrison St., Fayette, MO 65248. TEL 816-248-5223; FAX 816-298-1200; Ed. H. Denny Davis; Pub. H. Denny Davis; adv.; pub. size: standard; circ. 2,512(free & paid).

US ISSN 0746-9942
FAYETTE ADVERTISER, THE. 1840. Wed. $.30 newsstand; $12/yr. in cy.; $18/yr. 202 E. Morrison St., Fayette, MO 65248-0032. TEL 816-248-2235; FAX 816-248-1200. **Owner(s):** Wood Creek Corp., 202 E. Morrison St., Fayette, MO 65248. TEL 816-248-5223; FAX 816-248-1200; Ed. H. Denny Davis; Pub. H. Denny Davis; adv.; pub. size: standard; circ. 4,912(paid).

FESTUS
US
NEWS DEMOCRAT JOURNAL. 1865. s-w.: Sun. & Wed. $.50 newsstand; free home deliv. 988 E. Gannon Dr., Festus, MO 63028-0309. TEL 314-937-9811; FAX 314-931-2638. **Owner(s):** Suburban Journals, 1714 Deer Tracks Trail, St. Louis, MO 63131. TEL 314-821-1110; Ed. Lois Kendal; Pub. Thomas Rice; adv. contact: Janice Feltner. pub. size: broadsheet; circ. 23,800(paid).

FLORISSANT
US
FLORISSANT VALLEY REPORTER. 1950. Tue. $.50 newsstand; $12.95/yr. in cy.; $17.95/yr. out of cy. 525 Rue St. Francois, Florissant, MO 63031. TEL 314-839-1111; FAX 314-839-1111. **Owner(s):** Reynolds Publishing Co., Inc, P.O. Box 69, Florissant, MO 63032. TEL 314-839-1111; Ed. David L. Reynolds; Pub. David L. Reynolds; adv.; photos; bk.rev.; pub. size: tabloid; circ. 9,000(paid).

FORSYTH
US
▼**TANEY COUNTY TIMES.** 1995. w. $.35 newsstand; $15/yr. in cy.; $25/yr. out of cy. 253 Main St., Forsyth, MO 65653. TEL 417-546-3305; FAX 417-546-2326. **Owner(s):** Pat & Wendy Fitzgerald, P.O. Box 220, Forsyth, MO 65653. TEL 417-546-3305; FAX 417-546-2326; Ed. Patrick D. Fitzgerald; Pub. Patrick D. Fitzgerald; adv. contact: W. A. Fitzgerald. photos; pub. size: broadsheet; circ. 2,400(free & paid).

FREDERICKTOWN
US
DEMOCRAT-NEWS. 1870. Wed. $.50 newsstand; $25/yr. in state; $31/yr. out of state. 131 S. Main, Fredericktown, MO 63645. TEL 573-783-3366; FAX 573-783-6890. **Owner(s):** American Publishing Co., 606 N. Van Buren, Marion, IL 62959. TEL 618-993-1711; Ed. Alan Kopitsky; Pub. Mary Cissell; adv.; photos; bk.rev.; pub. size: broadsheet; circ. 3,400(paid). **Formerly:** Fredericktown Democrat-News.

GAINESVILLE
US
OZARK COUNTY TIMES. 1883. Wed. $.50 newsstand. P.O. Box 188, Gainesville, MO 65655. TEL 417-679-4641; FAX 417-679-3423; E-mail: walt@ozcool.com. **Owner(s):** Dalton Wright, P.O. Box 188, Gainesville, MO. TEL 417-679-4641; FAX 417-679-3423; Ed. Walt Sanders; Pub. Walt Sanders; adv. contact: Annette Lane. photos; bk.rev.; pub. size: broadsheet; circ. 3,800(paid).

GALLATIN
US
NORTH MISSOURIAN. 1864. Wed. $.50 newsstand; $18-$24/yr. 203 N. Main, Gallatin, MO 64640. TEL 816-663-2154; FAX 816-663-2054; E-mail: gpc@ponyexpress.net. **Owner(s):** Gallatin Publishing Co., 203 N. Main, P.O. Box 37, Gallatin, MO 64640. TEL 816-663-2154; FAX 816-663-2498; Ed. Darryl Wilkinson. adv.; photos; bk.rev.; pub. size: tabloid; circ. 2,600(paid).

HARRISONVILLE
US
HARRISONVILLE CASS COUNTY DEMOCRAT MISSOURIAN. 1881. Fri. $.50 newsstand; $24.50/yr. 310 S. Lexington, Harrisonville, MO 64701. TEL 816-380-3228; FAX 816-380-2095. **Owner(s):** Clark O. Murray, P.O. Box 15999, Shawnee Mission, KS 66285. TEL 913-492-9050; Ed. William E. James. adv. contact: Gavin Fenwick. photos; pub. size: broadsheet; circ. 6,181(paid).

HERMANN
US
HERMANN ADVERTISER-COURIER. 1854. Wed. $.50 newsstand; $25/yr. in cy.; $30/yr. out of cy.; $40/yr. out of state. 136 E. Fourth St., Hermann, MO 65041-0350. TEL 573-486-5418; FAX 573-486-5524. **Owner(s):** Spirit Newspapers of Missouri, Inc., 136 E. Fourth St., Hermann, MO 65041. TEL 573-486-5418; Ed. Don Kruse. adv. contact: Katy Van Kamp. pub. size: broadsheet; circ. 4,000(paid).

HERMITAGE
US
HERMITAGE INDEX. 1885. Thu. $.50 newsstand; $18.50/yr. in cy.; $24/yr. out of cy.; $30/yr. out of state. 108 Polk St., Hermitage, MO 65668. TEL 417-745-6404; FAX 417-745-2222. **Owner(s):** Earl Jenkins, P.O. Box 127, Hermitage, MO 65668. TEL 417-745-6404; FAX 417-745-2222; Ed. Don Ginnings; Pub. Earl Jenkins; adv. contact: Don Ginnings. pub. size: broadsheet; circ. 4,400(paid).

HOLDEN

US

HOLDEN IMAGE-PROGRESS, THE. 1904. Wed. $.50 newsstand; $18/yr. local; $29/yr. out of state. 117 E. 2nd St., Holden, MO 64040. TEL 816-732-5552; FAX 816-732-4696. **Owner(s):** Rusty Hartwell, 117 E. 2nd St., Holden, MO 64040. TEL 816-732-5552; FAX 816-732-4696; Pub. Rusty Hartwell; adv. contact: Cindy Reynolds. pub. size: standard; circ. 7,700(free & paid).
  Formerly: Holden Progress, The.

HOLTS SUMMIT

US

CALLAWAY COURIER. 1994. Wed. $.35 newsstand; $15/yr. in cy.; $20/yr. out of cy. P.O. Box 635, Holts Summit, MO 65043. TEL 573-896-9311; FAX 573-896-8725. **Owner(s):** Callaway Courier, Inc., P.O. Box 635, Holts Summit, MO 65043. TEL 573-896-9311; Ed. Dwight Warren. adv.; photos; pub. size: broadsheet; circ. 3,000(paid).

HOPKINS

US

HOPKINS JOURNAL, THE. 1874. Wed. $.35 newsstand; $12.57/yr. 411 E. Barnard St., Hopkins, MO 64461-0170. TEL 816-778-3464; FAX 816-778-3345. **Owner(s):** Paul E. Thompson, P.O. Box 170, Hopkins, MO 64461-0170. TEL 816-778-3464; FAX 816-778-3345; Ed. Darla Thompson; Pub. Paul E. Thompson; adv. contact: Paul E. Thompson. photos; pub. size: standard.

HOUSTON

US

HOUSTON HERALD & REPUBLICAN. 1878. Thu. $.50 newsstand; $18.65/yr. in cy.; $29/yr. out of cy.; $27.55/yr. elsewhere in MO. 113 N. Grand, Houston, MO 65483. TEL 417-967-2000; FAX 417-967-2096; E-mail: hstherald@aol.com. **Owner(s):** Houston Newspapers, Inc., P.O. Box 70, Houston, MO 65483. TEL 417-967-2000; FAX 417-967-2096; Ed. Bradley G. Gentry. adv.; pub. size: broadsheet; circ. 9,800(free & paid).

IRONTON

US

MOUNTAIN ECHO. 1937. Wed. $.50 newsstand; $21/yr. local; $33/yr. out of area; $33/yr. out of state. 110 N. Main St., Ironton, MO 63650-0025. TEL 573-546-3917; FAX 573-546-3919. **Owner(s):** Smith Newspapers, Inc., 110 N. Main St., Ironton, MO 63650-0025. TEL 573-546-3917; FAX 573-546-3919; Ed. Mark Cheaney; Pub. Judy Schaaf; adv.; photos; pub. size: broadsheet; circ. 6,700(free & paid).

JACKSON

US

CASH-BOOK JOURNAL. 1870. Wed. $.50 newsstand; $17/yr. in surrounding cys.; $19/yr. out of cy.; $23/yr. in state; $32/yr. out of state. 210 W. Main St., Jackson, MO 63755. TEL 573-243-3515; FAX 573-243-3517. **Owner(s):** Gerald Jones, Sr., P.O. Box 369, Jackson, MO 63755. TEL 573-243-3515; Ed. David Bloom; Pub. Gerald Jones, II; adv. contact: Pam Jones. photos; pub. size: broadsheet; circ. 8,500(free & paid).
  Formerly: Jackson Cash-Book Journal.

KANSAS CITY

US

CLAY DISPATCH-TRIBUNE. 1964. Wed. $.50 newsstand; $18/yr. 7007 N.E. Parvin Rd., Kansas City, MO 64117. TEL 816-454-9660; FAX 816-454-7523. **Owner(s):** Townsend Communications, Inc., 7007 N.E. Parvin Road, Kansas City, MO 64117. TEL 816-454-9660; Ed. Linn Brown; Pub. Harold G. Townsend, Jr.; adv. contact: Dorothy Baum. pub. size: broadsheet; circ. 63,500(paid).

US

LIBERTY TRIBUNE. Wed. $.50 newsstand; $18/yr. 7007 N.E. Parvin Rd., Kansas City, MO 64117. TEL 816-454-9660; FAX 816-454-7523. **Owner(s):** Townsend Communications, Inc., 7007 N.E. Parvin Rd., Kansas City, MO 64117. TEL 816-454-9660; Ed. Linn Brown; Pub. Harold G. Townsend, Jr.; adv.; pub. size: broadsheet; circ. 10,200(paid).

US

NEW TIMES, THE. 1991. Thu. free newsstand; $40/yr. mailed. 207 Westport Rd., Ste. 201, Kansas City, MO 64111. TEL 816-753-7880; FAX 816-753-4207. **Owner(s):** J. Patrick O'Connor, 207 Westport Rd., Ste. 201, Kansas City, MO 64111. TEL 816-753-7880; FAX 816-561-6252; Pub. Chuck Saults; adv.; photos; bk.rev.; pub. size: tabloid; circ. evening 40,000.

US

PITCH WEEKLY. 1980. Thu. free newsstand; $35/yr. 3535 Broadway, Ste. 400, Kansas City, MO 64111. TEL 816-561-6061; FAX 816-756-0502; E-mail: pitch@pitch.com; URL: http://www.pitch.com. **Owner(s):** Hal Brody, 3535 Broadway, Ste. 400, Kansas City, MO 64111. TEL 816-561-6061; FAX 816-756-0502; Ed. Jeffrey Drake; Pub. Hal Brody; adv. contact: Julie Brecht. photos; bk.rev.; pub. size: tabloid; circ. 85,000(controlled & free).

US

PLATTE DISPATCH TRIBUNE. 1914. Wed. $.50 newsstand; $15/yr. in cy. 7007 N.E. Parvin Rd., Kansas City, MO 64117. TEL 816-454-9660; FAX 816-452-5889. **Owner(s):** Townsend Communications, Inc., 7007 N.E. Parvin Road, Kansas City, MO 64117. TEL 816-454-9660; FAX 816-452-5889; Ed. Linn Brown; Pub. Harold G. Townsend, Jr.; adv. contact: Dorothy Baum. pub. size: broadsheet; circ. 13,400(paid).

US

PRESS DISPATCH. 1914. Wed. $.50 newsstand; $17/yr. in cy.; $20/yr. out of cy. 7007 N.E. Parvin Rd., Kansas City, MO 64117. TEL 816-454-9660; FAX 816-452-5889. **Owner(s):** Townsend Communications, Inc., 7007 N.E. Parvin Road, Kansas City, MO 64117. TEL 816-454-9660; FAX 816-452-9660; Ed. Linn Brown; Pub. Harold G. Townsend, Jr.; adv. contact: Dorothy Baum. pub. size: broadsheet; circ. 1,770(paid).

US

WEDNESDAY MAGAZINE. 1937. Wed. free newsstand; $20/yr. in cy.; $35/2 yrs. 20 E. Gregory Blvd., Kansas City, MO 64114. TEL 816-361-0616; FAX 816-822-1856. **Owner(s):** Townsend Communications, Inc., 7007 N.E. Parvin Road, Kansas City, MO 64116. TEL 816-454-9660; Ed. David Knofs; Pub. Harold G. Townsend, Jr.; adv. contact: Jim Seitnater. pub. size: tabloid; circ. 34,000(paid).

KIMBERLING CITY

US   ISSN 0894-0568

TABLE ROCK GAZETTE. 1961. Thu. $.50 newsstand; $20.86/yr. in cy.; $30.94/yr. out of cy.; $33.94/yr. out of state. Kimberling City Shopping Center, Hwy. 13, Kimberling City, MO 65686. TEL 417-739-4694; FAX 417-739-4695. **Owner(s):** Donald Sumner, P.O. Box 432, Kimberling City, MO 65686. TEL 417-739-4694; FAX 417-739-4695; Ed. Pam Soetaert; Pub. Donald Sumner; adv.; pub. size: broadsheet; circ. 2,000(paid).
  Formerly: Kimberling City Table Rock Gazette.

LAMAR

US

LAMAR DEMOCRAT. 1870. s-w.: Wed. & Sat. $.50 newsstand; $39.50/yr. 900 N. Gulf St., Lamar, MO 64759. TEL 417-682-5529; FAX 417-682-5595. **Owner(s):** Lamar Democrat, Inc., 900 N. Gulf, Lamar, MO 64759. TEL 417-682-5529; Pub. Douglas D. Davis; adv. contact: Douglas D. Davis. photos; bk.rev.; pub. size: broadsheet; circ. 3,800(paid).

LEE'S SUMMIT

US

LEE'S SUMMIT JOURNAL. 1881. 3/wk.: Mon., Wed., Fri. $.50 newsstand; $36/yr. in cy.; $47/yr. out of cy. 415 S. Douglas St., Lee's Summit, MO 64063. TEL 816-524-2345; FAX 816-524-5136. **Owner(s):** Inland Industries, Inc., 105th & Santa Fe, Shawnee, KS 66215. TEL 913-492-9050; Ed. Roy Harryman; Pub. W. Ferrell Shuck; adv. contact: Jane Drummond. pub. size: broadsheet; circ. 7,650(paid). **Wire Service(s):** AP.

LEXINGTON

US

LEXINGTON NEWS. 1800. s-w.: Wed. & Fri. $.50 newsstand; $25.73/yr. local; $40/yr. out of state. 925 Main St., Lexington, MO 64067. TEL 816-259-2266; FAX 816-259-4870. **Owner(s):** Jack Krier, P.O. Box 69, Carrollton, MO 64633. TEL 816-542-0881; Ed. Eric Cramer; Pub. Frank Mercer; adv. contact: Amy Eckhoff. photos; bk.rev.; pub. size: standard; circ. 2,200(paid).

LINN

US

LINN UNTERRIFIED DEMOCRAT. 1866. Wed. $.50 newsstand; $23/yr. in cy.; $29/yr. out of cy.; $33/yr. out of state. 300 E. Main St., Linn, MO 65051. TEL 573-897-3150; FAX 573-897-0076. **Owner(s):** Jerrilynn Voss, 300 E. Main St., Linn, MO 65051; Ed. Paul Slater; Pub. Jerrilynn Voss; adv.; pub. size: broadsheet; circ. 4,750(paid).

LOUISIANA

US

LOUISIANA PRESS-JOURNAL. 1855. Wed. $.50 newsstand; $21/yr. local. 3406 Georgia St., Louisiana, MO 63353. TEL 573-754-5566; FAX 573-754-4749. **Owner(s):** Press-Journal Publishing Co., Inc., 3406 Georgia St., Louisiana, MO 63353. TEL 573-754-5566; Ed. Walt Gilbert; Pub. Walt Gilbert; adv. contact: Walt Gilbert. photos; pub. size: broadsheet; circ. 3,500(paid).

WEEKLY NEWSPAPERS

MARBLE HILL
US

BOLLINGER COUNTY BANNER-PRESS. 1881. Thu. $.50 newsstand; $17/yr. local. 103 Walnut St., Marble Hill, MO 63764. TEL 573-238-2821; FAX 573-238-0020. **Owner(s):** Concord Publishing, 301 Broadway, Cape Girardeau, MO 63701. TEL 573-335-6611; Ed. Julie A. Kridelbaugh; Pub. Wally Lage; adv.: $4.25/SAU. photos; bk.rev.; pub. size: broadsheet; circ. 4,500(paid).
Formerly: Marble Hill Bollinger County Banner-Press.

MARCELINE
US

MARCELINE PRESS. 1966. Thu. $.50 newsstand; $35/yr. 123 S. Kansas, Marceline, MO 64658. TEL 816-376-3508; FAX 816-376-2757; E-mail: bllevans@aol.com. **Owner(s):** American Publishing Co., 606 N. Van Buren, P.O. Box 520, Marion, IL 62959. TEL 618-993-1711; Ed. Jason Baldwin. adv.; pub. size: broadsheet; circ. 16,650(free & paid).

MARSHFIELD
US

MARSHFIELD MAIL. 1892. Wed. $.50 newsstand; $21/yr. local; $30/yr. elsewhere. 225 N. Clay St., Marshfield, MO 65706-1652. TEL 417-468-2013; FAX 417-859-7930. **Owner(s):** Gordon E. Nordquist, 9164 Riverview Dr., Rogersville, MO 65742. TEL 417-753-7083; Beverly Hickey, 853 Queen St., Maize, KS 67101; Robert Bolitho Design Benefit Trust No. 1, P.O. Box 3008, Palm Beach, FL 33480; Ed. Gordon E. Nordquist. adv.; photos; pub. size: standard; circ. 5,500(free & paid).

MARTHASVILLE
US

MARTHASVILLE RECORD, THE. 1896. Thu. $.35 newsstand; $18.50/yr. local; $20.65/yr. in state; $20.50/yr. out of state. 203 W. South St., Marthasville, MO 63357-0077. TEL 314-433-2223. **Owner(s):** Rueben Eichmeyer, P.O. Box 77, Marthasville, MO 63357-0077. TEL 314-433-2223; Mabel Eichmeyer, P.O. Box 77, Marthasville, MO 63357-0077. TEL 314-433-2223; adv.: $5.04/SAU. pub. size: broadsheet; circ. 784(paid).

MILAN
US

MILAN STANDARD, THE. 1872. Thu. $.40 newsstand; $16.84/yr. in cy.; $17.88/yr. out of cy.; $23/yr. out of state. 105 S. Market St., Milan, MO 63556. TEL 816-265-4244; FAX 816-265-3180. **Owner(s):** Bertha B. Wilson, 431 E. Second St., Milan, MO 63556. TEL 816-265-3122; Robert W. Wilson, 431 E. Second St., Milan, MO 63556. TEL 816-265-4323; Mary Ann Cowgill, 402 S. Water, Milan, MO 63556. TEL 816-265-4524; Ed. Robert W. Wilson; Pub. Robert W. Wilson; adv. contact: David T. Wilson. photos; pub. size: broadsheet; circ. 3,993(paid).

MONTGOMERY CITY
US

MONTGOMERY STANDARD. 1868. Wed. $.25 newsstand; $12/yr. in cy.; $16/yr. out of cy. 115 W. Second St., Montgomery City, MO 63361. TEL 573-564-2339; FAX 573-564-2313. **Owner(s):** Montgomery Standard, Inc., 115 W. Second St., Montgomery City, MO 63361. TEL 573-564-2339; Ed. John Fisher. adv.; pub. size: broadsheet; circ. 3,500(paid).

MOUND CITY
US

MOUND CITY NEWS. 1879. Thu. $.50 newsstand; $18/yr. in cy.; $20/yr. in state; $22/yr. elsewhere. 511 State St., Mound City, MO 64470-0175. TEL 816-442-5423; FAX 816-442-5423. **Owner(s):** Mound City News, Inc., 511 State St., Mound City, MO 64470-0175. TEL 816-442-5423; FAX 816-442-5423; Pub. Linda Boultinghouse; adv.; photos; pub. size: broadsheet; circ. 2,409(paid).
Formerly: Mound City News Independent.

MOUNTAIN GROVE
US

MOUNTAIN GROVE NEWS-JOURNAL. 1890. Wed. $.45 newsstand; $15.50/yr. local; $18.50/yr. out of area; $22/yr. out of state. 150 E. First St., Mountain Grove, MO 65711. TEL 417-926-5148; FAX 417-926-6648. **Owner(s):** Dean DeVries, 150 E. First St., Mountain Grove, MO 65711. TEL 417-926-5148; FAX 417-926-6648; Ed. Doug Berger; Pub. Dean DeVries; adv. contact: Sandy Anderson. photos; bk.rev.; pub. size: broadsheet; circ. 12,200(free & paid).

MT. VERNON
US

LAWRENCE COUNTY RECORD. 1875. Wed. $.50 newsstand; $16.50/yr. local; $24/yr. out of state. 312 S. Hickory, Mt. Vernon, MO 65712. TEL 417-466-2185; FAX 417-466-2187. **Owner(s):** Stephen C. & Kathy S. Fairchild, P.O. Box 348, Mt. Vernon, MO 65712. TEL 417-466-2185; FAX 417-466-2187; Ed. Kathy S. Fairchild; Pub. Stephen C. Fairchild; adv. contact: Rosemary Hailey. pub. size: broadsheet; circ. 3,500(paid).

O'FALLON
US

O'FALLON JOURNAL. 1963. 3/wk.: Wed., Fri., Sun. free local; $56.25/yr. elsewhere. 216 E. Elm St., O'Fallon, MO 63366. TEL 314-240-4949; FAX 314-272-7913. **Owner(s):** Suburban Journals, 1714 Deer Tracks Trail, St. Louis, MO 63131. TEL 314-821-1110; Ed. Jim O'Neal; Pub. Tom Rice; adv. contact: Heather Masters. photos; bk.rev.; pub. size: broadsheet; circ. 13,000(free).
Formerly: O'Fallon Tribune Journal.

OWENSVILLE
US

GASCONADE COUNTY REPUBLICAN. 1904. Wed. $.50 newsstand; $25.25/yr. 106 E. Washington Ave., Owensville, MO 65066. TEL 573-437-2323; FAX 573-437-3033. **Owner(s):** Warden Publishing Co., Inc., P.O. Box 540, Owensville, MO 65066. TEL 573-437-2323; FAX 573-437-3033; Ed. Thomas C. Warden; Pub. Thomas C. Warden; adv. contact: Don Warden. pub. size: standard; circ. 7,700(free & paid).
Formerly: Owensville Gasconade County Republican.

OZARK
US

CHRISTIAN COUNTY HEADLINER NEWS. 1967. s-w.: Wed. & Sat. $.50 newsstand; $34/yr. mailed. 427 E. South St., Ozark, MO 65721. TEL 417-581-3541; FAX 417-581-3577. **Owner(s):** Lancaster Management, P.O. Box 609, Gadsen, AL 35209. TEL 205-543-3417; Ed. Clayton Berry; Pub. Roger Frieze; pub. size: broadsheet; circ. 4,500(paid).
Formerly: Ozark Headliner.

PACIFIC
US   ISSN 0746-1712

TRI-COUNTY JOURNAL. 1962. Wed. $.50 newsstand; $30/3 mos.; $39/6 mos.; $90/yr. 111 W. St. Louis St., Pacific, MO 63069. TEL 314-227-1286; FAX 314-227-1272. **Owner(s):** Suburban Journals, 1714 Deer Tracks Trail, St. Louis, MO 63131. TEL 314-821-1110; Ed. Danette Thompson; Pub. Jeff Littlejohn; adv.; photos; pub. size: broadsheet; circ. 11,000(free).

PALMYRA
US

PALMYRA SPECTATOR. 1839. Wed. $24/yr. 304 S. Main, Palmyra, MO 63461. TEL 573-769-3111; FAX 573-769-3554. **Owner(s):** Mark & Patricia Cheffey, P.O. Box 391, Palmyra, MO 63461. TEL 573-769-3111; Ed. Mark Cheffey; Pub. Mark Cheffey; pub. size: broadsheet; circ. 3,300(paid).

PARIS
US

MONROE COUNTY APPEAL. 1865. Thu. $.50 newsstand; $21/yr. in area; $23/yr. in state; $24/yr. out of state. 230 N. Main St., Paris, MO 65275. TEL 816-327-4192; FAX 816-327-4847. **Owner(s):** Richard Fredrick, P.O. Box 207, Paris, MO 65275. TEL 816-327-4192; FAX 816-327-4847; Pub. Richard Fredrick; adv.; photos; pub. size: broadsheet; circ. 2,300(paid).

PARKVILLE
US   ISSN 0899-5737

PLATTE COUNTY GAZETTE. 1885. Wed. $.35 newsstand; $15/yr. 6201 N.W. Hwy. 9, Parkville, MO 64512. TEL 816-741-9530; FAX 816-741-9593. **Owner(s):** Dan O'Dell, 6201 N.W. Hwy. 9, Parkville, MO 64512. TEL 816-781-1044; FAX 816-781-1755; Ed. Jason Offutt; Pub. Randall Battagler; adv. contact: Carol Allen. photos; bk.rev.; pub. size: standard; circ. 15,588(free & paid).

PERRYVILLE

US
PERRY COUNTY REPUBLIC-MONITOR, THE. 1889. s-w.: Tue. & Thu. $.75 newsstand; $35.22/yr. in cy.; $58.70/yr. out of cy.; $58.70/yr. out of state. 10 W. St. Maries, Perryville, MO 63775. TEL 573-547-4567; FAX 573-547-1643. **Owner(s):** P.T.S., Inc., P.O. Box 32040, Tuscaloosa, AL 30967. TEL 205-752-7500; FAX 205-752-5600; Ed. Randall J. Pribble; Pub. Randall J. Pribble; adv. contact: Randall J. Pribble. photos; pub. size: broadsheet; circ. 11,457(free & paid).

US
SUN TIMES. 1989. Wed. $.50 newsstand; $19.12/yr. 10 Perry Plz., Perryville, MO 63775. TEL 573-883-2980; FAX 573-547-8085. **Owner(s):** Elmo Donze, 10 Perry Plz., Perryville, MO 63775. TEL 573-883-2980; FAX 573-547-8085; Ed. John Meacham; Pub. Elmo Donze; adv. contact: Bob Scott. photos; pub. size: broadsheet; circ. 3,000(controlled & paid).

PIEDMONT

US
WAYNE COUNTY JOURNAL-BANNER. 1876. Thu. $.50 newsstand; $21/yr. local; $32/yr. elsewhere. 101 W. Elm St., Piedmont, MO 63957. TEL 573-223-7122; FAX 573-223-7871. **Owner(s):** Harold Ellinghouse, 101 W. Elm St., Piedmont, MO 63957. TEL 573-223-7122; FAX 573-223-7871; Mary Beth Stivers, 101 W. Elm St., Piedmont, MO 63957. TEL 573-223-7122; FAX 573-223-7871; Ed. Harold T. Ellinghouse; Pub. Harold T. Ellinghouse; adv.; photos; pub. size: broadsheet; circ. 5,300(paid). **Wire Service(s):** AP.

PIERCE CITY

US
PIERCE CITY LEADER-JOURNAL. 1905. Thu. $.50 newsstand; $17.50/yr. local; $20/yr. elsewhere. 105 W. Commercial St., Pierce City, MO 65723. TEL 417-476-2232; FAX 417-476-2230. **Owner(s):** Linda Eck Elderton, R.R. 2, Box 345A, Sarcoxie, MO 64862. TEL 417-548-3311; FAX 417-548-3312; adv. contact: Marlene Gisn. bk.rev.; pub. size: tabloid; circ. 1,000(paid).

POTOSI

US
INDEPENDENT-JOURNAL, THE. 1872. Thu. $.50 newsstand; $24/yr. 119 E. High St., Potosi, MO 63664-0340. TEL 573-438-5141; FAX 573-438-4472. **Owner(s):** Independent-Journal, Inc., P.O. Box 340, 119 E. High St., Potosi, MO 63664. TEL 573-438-5141; FAX 573-438-4472; Ed. Neil Richards. adv.; photos; bk.rev.; pub. size: broadsheet; circ. 5,479(free & paid).

RAYTOWN

US
RAYTOWN DISPATCH TRIBUNE. 1926. Wed. $.50 newsstand; $17/yr. in state; $20/yr. out of state. 10227 E. 61st St., Raytown, MO 64133. TEL 816-358-6398; FAX 816-358-5141. **Owner(s):** Townsend Communications, Inc., 7007 N.E. Parvin Rd., Kansas City, MO 64117. TEL 816-454-9660; Ed. Gene Gentrup; Pub. Harold G. Townsend, Jr.; adv. contact: Lori Richmond. pub. size: broadsheet; circ. 25,300(paid).

ROCK PORT

US
ATCHISON COUNTY MAIL, THE. 1848. Thu. $.50 newsstand; $21/yr. in cy.; $26.50/yr. elsewhere. 300 S. Main St., Rock Port, MO 64482. TEL 816-744-6245; FAX 816-744-2645. **Owner(s):** William W. & Marilyn S. Farmer, 300 S. Main St., Rock Port, MO 64482. TEL 816-744-6245; FAX 816-744-2645; Ed. William C. Farmer; Pub. William W. Farmer; adv. contact: Michael P. Farmer. adv.: $3.75/SAU. photos; bk.rev.; pub. size: broadsheet; circ. 2,550(paid). **Wire Service(s):** MO Line.

SALEM

US
SALEM NEWS. 1923. s-w.: Tue. & Thu. $.53 newsstand; $32.77/yr. 500 N. Washington St., Salem, MO 65560-0798. TEL 573-729-4126; FAX 573-729-4920. **Owner(s):** Salem Publishing Co., P.O. Box 798, Salem, MO 65560. TEL 573-729-4126; Ed. Donald Dodd; Pub. W. Ray Vickery; adv. contact: Karen Barred. adv.: $5.25, local, non-commisionable rate. pub. size: broadsheet; circ. 12,250(free & paid).

SARCOXIE

US
SARCOXIE RECORD, THE. 1901. Thu. $.50 newsstand; $17.50/yr. in cy.; $20/yr. out of cy. 101 N. Sixth St., Sarcoxie, MO 64862. TEL 417-548-3311; FAX 417-548-3312. **Owner(s):** Linda Eck Elderton, R.R. 2, Box 345A, Sarcoxie, MO 64862. TEL 417-548-3311; FAX 417-548-3312; adv. contact: Marlene Gish. photos; pub. size: tabloid; circ. 1,400(paid).

SAVANNAH

US
SAVANNAH REPORTER & ANDREW COUNTY DEMOCRAT. 1876. Thu. $.50 newsstand; $18/yr. local; $21/yr. in state; $23/yr. out of state. 115 S. Fourth St., Savannah, MO 64485. TEL 816-324-3149; FAX 816-324-3632. **Owner(s):** Ray Communications, Inc., Savannah Reporter, 115 S. Fourth, Savannah, MO 64485. TEL 816-324-3149; Ed. Amy Brant; Pub. Gary Ray; adv.; photos; pub. size: standard; circ. 4,050(paid).

SEDALIA

US
CENTRAL MISSOURI NEWS. 1985. Wed. $22/yr. in cy.; $26/yr. out of cy.; $30/yr. out of state. 406 S. Ohio, Sedalia, MO 65301. TEL 816-827-2425; FAX 816-827-2427. **Owner(s):** Melton Publishing Co., 406 S. Ohio St., Sedalia, MO 65301. TEL 816-827-2425; FAX 816-827-2427; Ed. Pete Daniels; Pub. Greg Melton; adv.; photos; bk.rev.; pub. size: broadsheet; circ. 6,000(paid).

US
PLAINSMAN WEEKLY NEWS. 1980. Wed. free; $65/yr. mailed 1st class. 700 S. Massachusetts, Sedalia, MO 65301-1566. TEL 816-826-1000; FAX 816-826-3913. **Owner(s):** Freedom Communications of Missouri, 700 S. Massachusetts, Sedalia, MO 65301. TEL 816-826-1000; FAX 816-826-3913; adv. contact: Denise L. McMillen. photos; pub. size: tabloid; circ. 61,784(free).

SEYMOUR

US
WEBSTER COUNTY CITIZEN. 1907. Wed. $.50 newsstand; $12-$25/yr. 221 S. Commercial, Seymour, MO 65746-0190. TEL 417-935-2257. **Owner(s):** Gary & Helen Sosniecki, 221 S. Commercial, Seymour, MO 65746-0190. TEL 417-935-2257; Pub. Helen Sosniecki; adv.: $3.25/SAU. pub. size: broadsheet; circ. 4,913(free & paid). **Wire Service(s):** AP.

SHELBYVILLE

US
SHELBY COUNTY HERALD. 1870. Wed. $.50 newsstand; $20/yr. local; $25/yr. elsewhere. 106 E. Main St., Shelbyville, MO 63469-0225. TEL 573-633-2261; FAX 573-633-2133. **Owner(s):** W. Rogers Hewitt, 207 S. Cleveland, Shelbyville, MO 63469. TEL 573-633-2261; FAX 573-633-2133; Ed. W. Rogers Hewitt; Pub. W. Rogers Hewitt; adv. contact: Betty Thrasher. adv.: $3.60/SAU. photos; pub. size: broadsheet; circ. 2,500(paid).

SHERIDAN

US   ISSN 0747-0444
QUAD RIVER NEWS. 1983. Wed. $.35 newsstand; $12/yr. R.R. 1, Box 16, Sheridan, MO 64486. TEL 816-799-3735; FAX 816-564-3707. **Owner(s):** Joe & Elise Stark, R.R. 1, Box 16, Sheridan, MO 64486. TEL 816-799-3735; FAX 816-564-3707; Ed. Joe Stark; Pub. Joe Stark; adv.: $2/SAU. pub. size: broadsheet; circ. 750(paid).

SMITHVILLE

US
SMITHVILLE LAKE HERALD, THE. 1888. Wed. $.50 newsstand; $18/yr. in cy.; $28/yr. out of cy.; $25/yr. out of state. 110 N. Bridge St., Smithville, MO 64089-0269. TEL 816-532-4444; FAX 816-532-4918. **Owner(s):** David T. Peery, P.O. Box 269, Smithville, MO 64089-0269. TEL 816-532-4444; FAX 816-532-4918; Ed. David T. Peery; Pub. David T. Peery; adv. contact: Becky Black. adv.: $4/SAU. photos; pub. size: broadsheet; circ. 2,380(paid).
Formerly: Smithville Lake Democrat-Herald.

ST. CHARLES

US
ST. CHARLES JOURNAL. 1957. 3/wk.: Sun., Wed., Fri. free. 1529 Old Hwy. 94 S., Ste. 108, St. Charles, MO 63303-3707. TEL 314-724-1111; FAX 314-946-5955. **Owner(s):** Suburban Journals, 1417 Deer Tracks Trail, St. Louis, MO 63113. TEL 314-821-1110; Ed. Jim O'Neal. adv. contact: Tom McCullen. pub. size: broadsheet; circ. 78,000(controlled).

ST. CLAIR

US
ST. CLAIR MISSOURIAN. 1924. s-w.: Wed. & Sat. $.75/Wed. newsstand; $.50/Sat. newsstand; $31.21/yr. in cy.; $34.24/yr. out of cy.; $55/yr. out of state. 515 S. Main, St. Clair, MO 63077. TEL 314-629-1027; FAX 314-629-2810. **Owner(s):** Missourian Publishing Co., 14 W. Main St., Washington, MO 63090. TEL 314-239-7701; Ed. Ed Pruneau. adv. contact: Laurie Pinnell. pub. size: broadsheet; circ. 26,945(paid). **Wire Service(s):** AP.

WEEKLY NEWSPAPERS

ST. LOUIS, MO

STEEL

US
STEELE ENTERPRISE. 1921. Thu. $.35 newsstand; $12.50/yr. in cy.; $30/yr. out of cy. 227 W. Main, Steel, MO 63877. TEL 573-695-3415; FAX 573-695-2114. **Owner(s):** David Tennyson, 677 N. Hwy. 181, Blythville, AR 72315. TEL 314-695-3415; FAX 314-695-2114; Karen Tennyson, Rte. 1, Box 160, Steele, MO 63877; Ed. Karen Tennyson. adv.; photos; bk.rev.; pub. size: standard; circ. 2,450(paid).

STEELVILLE

US
STEELVILLE STAR/CRAWFORD MIRROR. 1872. Wed. $.50 newsstand; $12.76/yr. in cy. 106 S. First St., Steelville, MO 65565. TEL 573-775-5454; FAX 573-775-2668. **Owner(s):** Percy Pascoe, P.O. Box BG, Steelville, MO 65565. TEL 573-775-5454; FAX 573-775-2668; Ed. Ava Viehman; Pub. Percy Pascoe; adv. contact: Lori Viehman. pub. size: tabloid; circ. 2,900(paid).

STE. GENEVIEVE

US
STE. GENEVIEVE HERALD. 1881. Wed. $.50 newsstand; $19/yr. in cy.; $27/yr. out of area. 330 Market St., Ste. Genevieve, MO 63670-1638. TEL 573-883-2222; FAX 573-883-2833. **Owner(s):** Ste. Genevieve Newspapers, Inc., 330 Market St., Ste. Genevieve, MO 63670-1638. TEL 573-883-2222; FAX 573-883-2833; Ed. Jean Rissover; Pub. Bob Burr; adv.: $5/SAU. pub. size: standard; circ. 5,000(paid). **Wire Service(s):** Mo. Medialink.

ST. JAMES

US
ST. JAMES LEADER JOURNAL. 1896. Wed. $.50 newsstand; $18.75/yr. in cy.; $22.25/yr. out of cy.; $22.50/yr. out of state. 125 W. Springfield, St. James, MO 65559. TEL 573-265-3321; FAX 573-265-3197. **Owner(s):** American Publishing Co., 606 N. Van Buren, Marion, IL 62959. TEL 618-993-1711; Ed. Angela Gwillim; Pub. Joe Arnold; adv.; photos; bk.rev.; pub. size: broadsheet; circ. 2,000(paid). **Wire Service(s):** AP.

ST. JOSEPH

US
ST. JOSEPH TELEGRAPH, THE. 1989. Thu. $1 newsstand; $28/yr. 620 Frances St., Rm. 318, St. Joseph, MO 64501. TEL 816-364-1323; FAX 816-364-3083. **Owner(s):** Leo S. Johnson, P.O. Box 1087, St. Joseph, MO 64052-1087. TEL 816-364-1323; FAX 816-364-3083; Pub. Scott Johnson; adv.: $6/SAU. photos; bk.rev.; pub. size: tabloid; circ. 1,700(free & paid).

ST. LOUIS

US
CENTRAL WEST END JOURNAL. 1984. s-w.: Wed. & Sun. free. 1714 Deer Tracks Trail, St. Louis, MO 63131. TEL 314-821-2462; FAX 314-821-0843. **Owner(s):** Suburban Journals, 1714 Deer Tracks Trail, St. Louis, MO 63131. TEL 314-821-1110; Ed. Dan Barger. adv. contact: Dave Wittman. pub. size: broadsheet; circ. 7,500(free).

US
CHESTERFIELD JOURNAL. 1990. s-w.: Wed. & Sun. free. 1714 Deer Tracks Trail, St. Louis, MO 63131-1825. TEL 314-821-2462; FAX 314-821-0843. **Owner(s):** Suburban Journals, 1714 Deer Tracks Trail, St. Louis, MO 63131-1825. TEL 314-821-1110; Ed. Mary Shapiro. adv. contact: Dave Wittman. pub. size: broadsheet; circ. 15,220(free).

US
CITIZEN JOURNAL. 1968. s-w.: Sun. & Wed. free. 1714 Deer Tracks Trail, St. Louis, MO 63131. TEL 314-821-2462; FAX 314-821-0843. **Owner(s):** Suburban Journals, 1714 Deer Tracks Trail, Saint Louis, MO 63131. TEL 314-821-1110; Ed. Dan Barger. adv.; pub. size: broadsheet; circ. 20,994(free); Sun. 20,566(free).

US
COMMUNITY NEWS. 1921. Wed. $104/yr. 5748 Helen Ave., St. Louis, MO 63136. TEL 314-261-5555; FAX 314-261-2776. **Owner(s):** Huneke Publications, Inc., 5748 Helen Ave., St. Louis, MO 63136. TEL 314-261-5555; FAX 314-261-2776; Ed. C.R. Bockskopf; Pub. Robert Huneke, Jr.; adv.: $20/SAU. photos; pub. size: tabloid; circ. 30,000(free).

US
COUNTY STAR JOURNAL EAST. 1993. s-w.: Sun. & Wed. free; $26/3 mos. mailed. 4305 Woodson Rd., St. Louis, MO 63134. TEL 314-426-2222; FAX 314-426-4883. **Owner(s):** Suburban Journals, 1714 Deer Tracks Trail, St. Louis, MO 63131. TEL 314-821-1110; Ed. Dan Barger. adv. contact: Mark Gehrs. adv.: $14.43/SAU. photos; pub. size: broadsheet; circ. 27,300(free & paid).

US
COUNTY STAR JOURNAL WEST. 1993. s-w.: Sun. & Wed. free; $26/3 mos. mailed. 4305 Woodson Rd., St. Louis, MO 63134. TEL 314-426-2222; FAX 314-426-4883. **Owner(s):** Suburban Journals, 1714 Deer Tracks Trail, St. Louis, MO 63131. TEL 314-821-1110; Ed. Dan Barger. adv. contact: Mark Gehrs. adv.: $10.70/SAU. photos; pub. size: broadsheet; circ. 12,251(free & paid). **Formerly:** Maryland Heights Bridgeton Journal.

US
MID-COUNTY JOURNAL. s-w.: Sun. & Wed. free. 1714 Deer Tracks Trail, St. Louis, MO 63131. TEL 314-821-2462; FAX 314-821-0843. **Owner(s):** Suburban Journals, 1714 Deer Tracks Trail, St. Louis, MO 63131. TEL 314-821-1110; Ed. Dan Barger. adv. contact: Mairian King. pub. size: broadsheet; circ. 13,400.

US
NORTH COUNTY JOURNAL EAST. 1960. s-w.: Sun. & Wed. free; $26/3 mos. mailed. 4305 Woodson Rd., St. Louis, MO 63134. TEL 314-426-2222; FAX 314-426-4883. **Owner(s):** Suburban Journals, 1714 Deer Tracks Trail, St. Louis, MO 63131. TEL 314-821-1110; Ed. Dan Barger. adv. contact: Mark Gehrs. adv.: $16.39/SAU; $3.22/SAU classified. photos; pub. size: broadsheet; circ. 43,683(free & paid). **Formerly:** North County Journal.

US
NORTH COUNTY JOURNAL WEST. 1993. s-w.: Sun. & Wed. free; $26/3 mos. mailed. 4305 Woodson Rd., St. Louis, MO 63134. TEL 314-426-2222; FAX 314-426-4883. **Owner(s):** Suburban Journals, 1714 Deer Tracks Trail, St. Louis, MO 63131. TEL 314-821-1110; Ed. Dan Barger. adv. contact: Mark Gehrs. adv.: $20.06/SAU. photos; pub. size: broadsheet; circ. 49,484(free & paid).

US
NORTHSIDE JOURNAL. 1993. s-w.: Sun. & Wed. free; $26/3 mos. mailed. 4305 Woodson Rd., St. Louis, MO 63134. TEL 314-426-2222; FAX 314-426-2222. **Owner(s):** Suburban Journals, 1714 Deer Tracks Trail, St. Louis, MO 63131. TEL 314-821-1110; Ed. Dan Barger. adv. contact: Mark Gehrs. adv.: $17.60/SAU. photos; pub. size: broadsheet; circ. 36,000(free & paid).

US
OAKVILLE-MEHVILLE JOURNAL. s-w.: Sun. & Wed. free. 4210 Chippewa, St. Louis, MO 63116. TEL 314-664-2700; FAX 314-664-8533. **Owner(s):** Suburban Journals, 1714 Deer Tracks Trail, St. Louis, MO 63131. TEL 314-821-1110; Ed. Lois Kendall. pub. size: broadsheet; circ. 19,975(free).

US
PRESS JOURNAL. s-w.: Sun. & Wed. free. 1714 Deer Tracks Trail, St. Louis, MO 63131. TEL 314-821-2462; FAX 314-821-0843. **Owner(s):** Suburban Journals, 1714 Deer Tracks Trail, St. Louis, MO 63131. TEL 314-821-1110; Ed. Dan Barger. adv. contact: Mairian King. pub. size: broadsheet; circ. 35,200.

US
SOUTH CITY JOURNAL. Wed. free. 4210 Chippewa, St. Louis, MO 63116. TEL 314-664-2700; FAX 314-664-8533. **Owner(s):** Suburban Journals, 1714 Deer Tracks Trail, St. Louis, MO 63131. TEL 314-821-1110; Ed. Linda Fischer. pub. size: broadsheet; circ. 23,200(free).

US
SOUTH COUNTY JOURNAL. 1965. s-w.: Sun. & Wed. free. 4210 Chippewa, St. Louis, MO 63116. TEL 314-664-2700; FAX 314-664-8533. **Owner(s):** Suburban Journals, 1714 Deer Tracks Trail, St. Louis, MO 63131. TEL 314-821-1110; Ed. Linda Fischer. pub. size: broadsheet; circ. 67,850(free).

US
SOUTHSIDE JOURNAL. s-w.: Sun. & Wed. free. 4210 Chippewa, St. Louis, MO 63131. TEL 314-664-2700; FAX 314-664-8533. **Owner(s):** Suburban Journals, 1714 Deer Tracks Trail, St. Louis, MO 63131. TEL 314-821-1110; Ed. Linda Fischer. pub. size: broadsheet; circ. 38,500(free).

US
SOUTHWEST CITY JOURNAL. 1921. s-w.: Sun. & Wed. free. 4210 Chippewa, St. Louis, MO 63119. TEL 314-664-2700; FAX 314-664-9777. **Owner(s):** Suburban Journals, 1714 Deer Tracks Trail, St. Louis, MO 63131. TEL 314-821-1110; Ed. Linda Fischer. pub. size: broadsheet; circ. 26,125(free).

10658 ST. LOUIS, MO

WEEKLY NEWSPAPERS

Weeklies

US
SOUTHWEST COUNTY JOURNAL. 1990. s-w.: Sun. & Wed. free. 4210 Chippewa, St. Louis, MO 63116. TEL 314-644-2700; FAX 314-644-4777. **Owner(s):** Suburban Journals, 1714 Deer Tracks Trail, St. Louis, MO 63131. TEL 314-821-1110; Ed. Linda Fischer. pub. size: broadsheet; circ. 29,907(free).

US
ST. LOUIS AMERICAN NEWSPAPER. 1928. Thu. $35/yr. in cy. 4144 Lindell Blvd., Ste. B-5, St. Louis, MO 63108. TEL 314-533-8000; FAX 314-533-0038. **Owner(s):** Dr. Donald M. Suggs, 4144 Lindell Blvd., Ste. B-5, St. Louis, MO 63108. TEL 314-533-8000; FAX 314-533-0038; Ed. Eric Clark; Pub. Dr. Donald M. Suggs; adv. contact: Kevin Jones. pub. size: broadsheet; circ. 65,500(paid). **Wire Service(s):** AP.

US
WEST COUNTY JOURNAL. s-w.: Sun. & Wed. free. 1714 Deer Tracks Trail, St. Louis, MO 63131. TEL 314-821-1110; FAX 314-821-0843. **Owner(s):** Suburban Journals, 1714 Deer Tracks Trail, St. Louis, MO 63131. TEL 314-821-1110; Ed. Dan Barger. pub. size: broadsheet; circ. 30,000(free).

STOCKTON

US
CEDAR COUNTY REPUBLICAN. 1888. Wed. $.50 newsstand; $17/yr. in cy.; $32/yr. out of cy.; $39/yr. out of state. 108 S.E. Arcad St., Stockton, MO 65785. TEL 417-276-4211; FAX 417-276-5760. **Owner(s):** Sterling Media, Ltd., Rt. 3, Box 559, Bolivar, MO 65613. TEL 417-326-7636; Ed. Sandra Woodard; Pub. Dave Berry; adv. contact: Marilyn Picard. pub. size: broadsheet; circ. 2,800(paid).

SULLIVAN

US
SULLIVAN INDEPENDENT NEWS. 1962. Wed. $.50 newsstand; $20.50/yr. in cy.; $26/yr. out of cy.; $30/yr. out of state. Scottsdale & Springfield Rd., Sullivan, MO 63080. TEL 314-468-6511; FAX 314-468-4046. **Owner(s):** Kathleen Manion, Scottsdale & Springfield Rd., Sullivan, MO 63080. TEL 314-468-6511; Ed. Jim Bartle; Pub. Kathleen Manion; adv. contact: Jim Bartle. photos; bk.rev.; pub. size: tabloid; circ. 7,000(paid).

TARKIO

US
TARKIO AVALANCHE. 1884. Thu. $.50 newsstand; $21/yr. surrounding cys; $26.50/yr. elsewhere. 107 N. Third, Tarkio, MO 64491-0278. TEL 816-736-4111; FAX 816-736-5700. **Owner(s):** Will Johnson, 107 N. Third, Tarkio, MO 64491. TEL 816-736-4111; FAX 816-736-5700; Ed. Will Johnson. adv. contact: Will Johnson. photos; pub. size: broadsheet; circ. evening 1,760(controlled & paid). **Wire Service(s):** AP.

THAYER

US
SOUTH MISSOURIAN NEWS. 1991. Thu. $.50 newsstand; $18-$23/yr. 101 Chestnut St., Thayer, MO 65791. TEL 417-264-3085; FAX 417-264-3814. **Owner(s):** Paducah Newspapers, Inc., 408 Kentucky Ave., Paducah, KY 42002. TEL 502-443-1771; FAX 502-442-8188; Ed. Max Cates; Pub. Janie Flynn; adv. contact: Carolyn Clarke. photos; pub. size: broadsheet; circ. 1,532(paid).

TRENTON

US
GREEN HILLS WEEKLY. 1972. Wed. free. 122 E. Eighth St., Trenton, MO 64683. TEL 816-359-2212; FAX 816-359-4414. **Owner(s):** Wendell J. Lenhart, P.O. Box 548, Trenton, MO 64683. TEL 816-359-2212; Ed. Diane Raines; Pub. Wendell Lenhart; adv. contact: DeLane Hein. pub. size: broadsheet; circ. 13,000(free).

TROY

US
TROY FREE PRESS & SILEX INDEX. Wed. $.50 newsstand; $23/yr. in cy.; $35/yr. out of cy.; $18/yr. in cy. senior citizens; $30/yr. out of cy. senior citizens. 615 E. Cherry St., Troy, MO 63379. TEL 314-462-4720; FAX 314-528-6694. **Owner(s):** Smith Publishing Co., 615 E. Cherry St., Troy, MO 63379. TEL 314-426-4720; FAX 314-528-6694; Ed. Bob Simons; Pub. Pat Whiteside; pub. size: broadsheet; circ. 3,000(paid).

UNIONVILLE

US
UNIONVILLE REPUBLICAN, THE. 1865. Wed. $15/yr. in cy; $18/yr. out of cy. 111 S. 16th St., Unionville, MO 63565-0365. TEL 816-947-2222; FAX 816-947-2223. **Owner(s):** Ron & Theresa Kinzler, 111 S. 16th St., Unionville, MO 63565. TEL 816-947-2222; Ed. Theresa Kinzler; Pub. Ron Kinzler; pub. size: standard; circ. 3,800(paid).

VERSAILLES

US
VERSAILLES LEADER-STATESMAN. 1887. Thu. $.50 newsstand; $39/yr. 104 W. Jasper, Versailles, MO 65084. TEL 573-378-5441; FAX 573-378-4292. **Owner(s):** Dane Vernon, P.O. Box 348, Versailles, MO 65084-0348. TEL 573-378-5441; Ed. Duane Johnson; Pub. Dane Vernon; adv.; photos; pub. size: broadsheet; circ. 3,900(paid).

VIENNA

US
MARIES COUNTY GAZETTE. 1876. Wed. $.40 newsstand; $17.61/yr. local; $20.28/yr. in state; $20 /yr. out of state. Courthouse Sq., Vienna, MO 65582-0202. TEL 573-422-3441; FAX 573-859-6274. **Owner(s):** Tri-County Newspapers, 307 Alvarado, Belle, MO 65013. TEL 573-859-3328; FAX 573-859-6274; Pub. Ron Lewis; adv.; photos; pub. size: broadsheet; circ. 2,300(paid).

WARRENTON

US
WARRENTON JOURNAL. 1973. Wed. free. 111 W. Main, Warrenton, MO 63383. TEL 314-456-3481; FAX 314-456-3020. **Owner(s):** Suburban Journals, 1714 Deer Tracks Trail, St. Louis, MO 63131. TEL 314-821-1110; Ed. Marie Hollenbeck; Pub. Tom Rice; pub. size: broadsheet; circ. 12,272(free).
Formerly: Warrenton News-Journal.

WARSAW

US
WARSAW BENTON COUNTY ENTERPRISE. 1879. Thu. $19.95/yr. in cy; $25/yr. out of cy.; $25/yr. out of state. 107 Main St., Warsaw, MO 65355. TEL 816-438-6312; FAX 816-438-3464. **Owner(s):** M.K. White, 107 Main St., Warsaw, MO 65355. TEL 816-438-5933; Ed. M.K. White; Pub. M.K. White; adv. contact: M.K. White. pub. size: standard; circ. 5,200(paid).

WASHINGTON

US
WASHINGTON MISSOURIAN. 1860. s-w.: Wed. & Sat. $.75/Wed. newsstand; $.50/Sat. newsstand; $31.21/yr. in cy.; $34.24/yr. out of cy.; $55/yr. out of state. 14 W. Main, Washington, MO 63090. TEL 314-239-7701; FAX 314-239-0915. **Owner(s):** Missourian Publishing Co., 14 W. Main, Washington, MO 63090. TEL 314-239-7701; Ed. William L. Miller; Pub. William L. Miller; adv. contact: Nancy Schafer. pub. size: broadsheet; circ. morning 26,024(paid). **Wire Service(s):** AP.

WENTZVILLE

US ISSN 0192-6896
WENTZVILLE JOURNAL. 1966. 3/wk.: Wed., Fri., Sun. $450/yr. 501 E. Pearce Blvd., Wentzville, MO 63385. TEL 314-327-6463; FAX 314-327-6411. **Owner(s):** Suburban Journals, 1714 Deer Tracks Trail, St. Louis, MO 63131. TEL 314-821-1110; Pub. Tom Rice; adv. contact: Heather Masters. pub. size: broadsheet; circ. 10,000(free & paid).
Formerly: Wentzville Messenger.

WINDSOR

US
WINDSOR REVIEW. 1870. Thu. $.50 newsstand; $17.95/yr. in cy.; $24.95/yr. out of cy. 205 S. Main, Windsor, MO 65360. TEL 816-647-2121; FAX 816-647-2122. **Owner(s):** Dave Tapp, 205 S. Main, Windsor, MO 65360. TEL 816-647-2121; Pub. Dave Tapp; adv.; photos; bk.rev.; pub. size: broadsheet; circ. 1,850(paid).

MONTANA

ANACONDA

US
ANACONDA LEADER. 1969. s-w.: Wed. & Fri. $25.50/yr. 121 Main St., Anaconda, MT 59711. TEL 406-563-5283; FAX 406-563-5284. **Owner(s):** Leader Printing & Supply, Inc., 121 Main St., Anaconda, MT 59711. TEL 406-563-5283; Ed. Dick Crockford; Pub. Dean A. Neitz; adv. contact: Micky Gee. photos; pub. size: broadsheet; circ. 4,000(free & paid).

WEEKLY NEWSPAPERS

BIGFORK
US

BIGFORK EAGLE. 1979. Wed. $.50 newsstand; $20/yr. in cy.; $24/yr. out of cy.; $35/yr. out of state. P.O. Box 406, Bigfork, MT 59911. TEL 406-837-5131; FAX 406-837-1132; E-mail: marcus@netrix.net; URL: http://www.townnews.com/mt/mteagle. **Owner(s):** Lee Enterprises, Inc., 215 N. Main St., Ste. 400, Davenport, IA 52801. TEL 319-383-2100; Ed. Don Schwennesen; Pub. Don Schwennesen; pub. size: broadsheet; circ. 3,500(paid).

BIG SANDY
US

MOUNTAINEER, THE. 1911. Wed. $.50 newsstand; $22/yr. in cy.; $24/yr. in state; $26/yr. out of state. 123 Main St., Big Sandy, MT 59520. TEL 406-378-2176; FAX 406-378-2176. **Owner(s):** Rettig Publishing, Inc., P.O. Box 529, Big Sandy, MT 59520. TEL 406-378-2176; FAX 406-378-2176; Ed. James L Rettig; Pub. James L. Rettig; pub. size: broadsheet; circ. 1,200(paid). Formerly: Big Sandy Mountaineer.

COLUMBIA FALLS
US

HUNGRY HORSE NEWS. 1946. Thu. $.75 newsstand; $23/yr. local; $30/yr. out of area; $35/yr. out of state. 926 Nucleus Ave., Columbia Falls, MT 59912-0189. TEL 406-892-2151; FAX 406-892-5600. **Owner(s):** Brian & Carol Kennedy, 926 Nucleus Ave., Coumbia Falls, MT 59912. TEL 406-892-2151; Ed. Brian M. Kennedy. adv. contact: Noreen Hanson. pub. size: broadsheet; circ. 7,200(paid).

CUT BANK
US

WESTERN BREEZE. 1942. s-w.: Tue. & Fri. $.50 newsstand; $25/yr. in cy.; $27.50/yr. out of cy.; $30/yr. out of state. 32 S. Central Ave., Cut Bank, MT 59427-1253. TEL 406-873-4128; FAX 406-873-4129. **Owner(s):** James M. O'Day, P.O. Box 1253, Cut Bank, MT 59427-1253. TEL 406-873-4128; FAX 406-873-4129; Ed. James M. O'Day; Pub. James M. O'Day; adv. contact: Penne Swenson. photos; pub. size: tabloid; circ. 1,950(paid).

FORT BENTON
US

RIVER PRESS, THE. 1880. Wed. $.50 newsstand; $18/yr. in cy.; $22/yr. out of cy. 1114 Front St., Fort Benton, MT 59442-0069. TEL 406-622-3311; FAX 406-622-5446. **Owner(s):** Stanley E. & Esther C. Tichenor, P.O. Box 69, Fort Benton, MT 59442. TEL 406-622-3311; FAX 406-622-5446; Ed. Esther C. Tichenor; Pub. Esther C. Tichenor; adv.; photos; bk.rev.; pub. size: standard; circ. 2,100(paid).

GLASGOW
US

GLASGOW COURIER, THE. 1913. Thu. $.75 newsstand; $33/yr. in cy.; $37/yr. out of cy.; $47/yr. out of state. 341 Third Ave., S., Glasgow, MT 59230. TEL 406-228-9301; FAX 406-228-2665. **Owner(s):** Bruce Wright, MT; John Stanislaw, MT; Ed. Mike Brant; Pub. John Stanislaw; pub. size: standard; circ. 4,200(paid).

GLENDIVE
US

GLENDIVE RANGER-REVIEW. 1881. s-w.: Sun. & Thu. $.75 newsstand; $36/yr. carrier; $46/yr. mailed; $49.30/yr. out of state. 119 W. Bell St., Glendive, MT 59330. TEL 406-365-3303; FAX 406-365-5435. **Owner(s):** Yellowstone Newspapers, P.O. Box 665, Livingston, MT 59047. TEL 406-222-2000; Ed. Mervin Mecklenberg; Pub. G.R. Zander; adv.; photos; pub. size: broadsheet; circ. 3,357(paid).

HARLOWTON
US   ISSN 0889-5627

TIMES-CLARION, THE. 1917. Thu. $.50 newsstand; $20/yr. in cy.; $23/yr. in state. 111 S. Central St., Harlowton, MT 59036-0307. TEL 406-632-5633; FAX 406-632-5644. **Owner(s):** Gerald H. & Audrey J. Miller, 14 W. Division, Harlowton, MT 59036-0307. TEL 406-632-5566; FAX 406-632-5644; Ed. Gerald H. Miller; Pub. Gerald H. Miller; adv.; photos; pub. size: standard; circ. 1,675(paid). **Wire Service(s):** AP.

LEWISTOWN
US

LEWISTOWN NEWS-ARGUS. 1883. s-w.: Wed. & Sun. $.50 newsstand; $39.01/yr. local. 521 W. Main St., Lewistown, MT 59457-0900. TEL 406-538-3401; FAX 406-538-3405. **Owner(s):** Central Montana Publishing, P.O. Box 900, Lewistown, MT 59457; Ed. Jane McFarlane; Pub. Ken Byerly; adv. contact: Mitch Kottas. pub. size: standard; circ. 5,000(paid).

LIBBY
US

WESTERN NEWS. 1902. s-w.: Wed. & Fri. $.50 newsstand; $35/yr. in cy.; $45/yr. out of cy. 311 California Ave., Libby, MT 59923. TEL 406-293-4124; FAX 406-293-7187. **Owner(s):** Cabinet Publishing Co., P.O. Box 1377, Libby, MT 59923; Ed. Roger Morris; Pub. Mark McMahon; adv. contact: Lee Bothman. pub. size: broadsheet; circ. 4,600(paid).

PHILIPSBURG
US

PHILIPSBURG MAIL, THE. 1886. Wed. $.50 newsstand; $20/yr. 123 Broadway, Philipsburg, MT 59858-0160. TEL 406-859-3223; FAX 406-859-3690. **Owner(s):** James J. & Lee Tracy, 123 Broadway, Philipsburg, MT 59858-0160. TEL 406-859-3223; FAX 406-858-3640; Pub. Lee Tracy; adv.; photos; pub. size: broadsheet; circ. 1,500(paid).

RONAN
US

LAKE COUNTY LEADER. 1910. Thu. $.50 newsstand; $20.95/yr. in cy.; $24.95/yr. out of cy.; $26.95/yr. out of state. 229 Main St., S.W., Ronan, MT 59864. TEL 406-676-3800; FAX 406-676-3801. **Owner(s):** Todd Mowbray, Courier/Pioneer/Advertiser, P.O. Box 1090, Polson, MT 59860. TEL 406-883-4343; Pub. John Schnase; pub. size: broadsheet; circ. 5,900(paid).

SIDNEY
US

SIDNEY HERALD-LEADER. 1908. s-w.: Sun. & Wed. $.50 newsstand; $35/yr. in cy. 310 Second Ave., N.E., Sidney, MT 59270. TEL 406-482-2706; FAX 406-482-7802. **Owner(s):** Wick Communications, Inc., 333 Wilcox Dr., Ste. 302, Sierra Vista, AZ 85635. TEL 520-458-0200; FAX 520-458-6166; Ed. Steve Merritt; Pub. Rick Schneider; adv. contact: Dianne Swanson. pub. size: broadsheet; circ. 4,500(paid).

WHITEFISH
US

WHITEFISH PILOT. 1902. Thu. $.75 newsstand; $23/yr. in cy.; $35/yr. out of cy. P.O. Box 488, Whitefish, MT 59937. TEL 406-862-3505; FAX 406-862-3636. **Owner(s):** Betty Kennedy, P.O. Box 189, Columbia Falls, MT; Ed. Brian Kennedy; Pub. Brian Kennedy; adv. contact: Darrin Tyree. pub. size: broadsheet; circ. 4,400(paid).

WOLF POINT
US

HERALD-NEWS. 1913. Thu. $.75 newsstand; $25/yr. local; $31/yr. in state; $35/yr. out of state; $46.80/yr. foreign. 408 Main St., Wolf Point, MT 59201. TEL 406-653-2222; FAX 406-653-2221. **Owner(s):** Herald-News, Inc., Box 639, Wolf Point, MT 59201. TEL 406-405-2222; FAX 406-653-2221; Ed. Greg Little. adv.; photos; pub. size: broadsheet; circ. 3,500(paid).

NEBRASKA

ALBION
US

ALBION NEWS. 1879. Wed. $.50 newsstand; $17/yr. local; $20/yr. out of state. 328 W. Church St., Albion, NE 68620. TEL 402-395-2115; FAX 402-395-2772. **Owner(s):** Albion News, P.O. Box 431, Albion, NE 68620. TEL 402-395-2115; FAX 402-395-2772; Ed. Jean Kaup. adv.; photos; bk.rev.; pub. size: broadsheet; circ. 3,200(paid).

ALMA
US

HARLAN COUNTY JOURNAL. 1896. Thu. $.50 newsstand; $20/yr. local; $22/yr. elsewhere. 713 W. Main St., Alma, NE 68920. TEL 308-928-2143. **Owner(s):** Wayne & Marilyn Lingg, 900 Brown, Alma, NE 68920. TEL 308-928-2710; Ed. Marilyn Lingg; Pub. Marilyn Lingg; adv.; photos; pub. size: broadsheet; circ. 2,230(paid).

ARAPAHOE
US

ARAPAHOE PUBLIC MIRROR. 1880. Wed. $.50 newsstand; $18-$22/yr. 420 Nebraska Ave., Arapahoe, NE 68922-0660. TEL 308-962-7261; FAX 308-962-7861. **Owner(s):** Arapahoe Public Mirror, 420 Nebraska Ave., Arapahoe, NE 68922-0660. TEL 308-962-7261; FAX 308-962-7262; Ed. Gayle Gill Schutz; Pub. T.M. Gill; adv.; pub. size: broadsheet; circ. evening 13,500.

ARTHUR
US
ARTHUR ENTERPRISE, THE. 1911. w. $.25 newsstand; $12/yr. in cy.; $12/yr. in state; $13.50/yr. out of state. P.O. Box 165, Arthur, NE 69121-0165. TEL 308-764-2402. E-mail: artent@neb-sandhills.net. **Owner(s):** Robert J. Crouse, Arthur, NE 69121. TEL 308-764-2402; Ed. Robert J. Crouse; Pub. Robert J. Crouse; adv. contact: Karen A. Sizer. photos; pub. size: tabloid; circ. 480(free & paid).

ATKINSON
US
ATKINSON GRAPHIC, THE. 1882. Wed. $.50 newsstand; $14.50/yr. in state; $20/yr. out of state. 207 E. State St., Atkinson, NE 68713. TEL 402-925-5411. **Owner(s):** Gerald Z. & Roxanne Hollingsworth, 306 W. First St., Atkinson, NE 68713. TEL 402-925-5411; Ed. Gerald Z. Hollingsworth; Pub. Gerald Z. Hollingsworth; pub. size: broadsheet; circ. 2,300(paid).

AUBURN
US
AUBURN PRESS TRIBUNE. 1882. Tue. $22/yr. in cy.; $28/yr. out of cy. 830 Central Ave., Auburn, NE 68305. TEL 402-274-3185; FAX 402-274-3273. **Owner(s):** Auburn Newspapers, 830 Central Ave., Auburn, NE 68305. TEL 402-274-3185; FAX 402-274-3185; Ed. Darrell Wellman; Pub. Mark A. Cramer; pub. size: broadsheet; circ. 3,650(paid).

US
NEMAHA COUNTY HERALD. 1888. Tue. $.35 newsstand; $22/yr. local; $28/yr. out of area. 830 Central Ave., Auburn, NE 68305. TEL 402-274-3185; FAX 402-274-3273. **Owner(s):** Mark A. Cramer, P.O. Box 250, Auburn, NE 68305. TEL 402-274-3185; FAX 402-274-3273; Ed. Darrell Wellman; Pub. Mark A. Cramer; adv. contact: Paula Winkelman. pub. size: broadsheet; circ. 3,700(paid).

AURORA
US
AURORA NEWS-REGISTER. 1870. Wed. $20/yr. in cy.; $24/yr. out of cy.; $27/yr. out of state. 1320 K. St., Aurora, NE 68818. TEL 402-694-2131; FAX 402-694-2133; E-mail: NewsRegister@hamilton.net; URL: http://www.hamilton.net/aurora/newsreg/anewsreg.htm. Owner(s): Aurora Publishing Co., 1320 K St., Aurora, NE 68818. TEL 402-694-2131; Ed. Hap Fruits; Pub. Ron Furse; pub. size: standard; circ. 4,000(paid).

BELLEVUE
US   ISSN 0193-0389
BELLEVUE LEADER. 1973. Wed. $.50 newsstand; $28/yr. in cy. 604 Fort Crook Rd., N., Bellevue, NE 68005. TEL 402-733-7300; FAX 402-733-9116. **Owner(s):** Bellevue Leader Co., 604 Fort Crook Rd., N., Bellevue, NE 68005. TEL 402-733-7300; FAX 402-733-9116; Ed. Ron Petak; Pub. Dixie Cavner; adv.; photos; pub. size: broadsheet; circ. 25,629(free & paid).

BLAIR
US
ARLINGTON CITIZEN. 1954. Wed. $.25 newsstand; $13/yr. 138 N. 16th St., Blair, NE 68008. TEL 402-426-2121; FAX 402-426-2227. **Owner(s):** Blair Enterprise Co., Inc., 138 N. 16th, Blair, NE 68008. TEL 402-426-2121; Ed. Carrie Larkins. adv. contact: Lynette Hansen. photos; pub. size: broadsheet; circ. 746(paid).

US
BLAIR ENTERPRISE. 1892. Thu. $.50 newsstand; $25/yr. in cy.; $36/yr. out of cy.; $38/yr. out of state. 138 N. 16th, Blair, NE 68008. TEL 402-426-2121; FAX 402-426-2227. **Owner(s):** Blair Enterprise Co., Inc., 138 N. 16th, Blair, NE 68008. TEL 402-426-2121; Ed. Carrie Larkins. adv. contact: Lynette Hansen. photos; pub. size: broadsheet; circ. 4,200(controlled & paid).

US
BLAIR PILOT-TRIBUNE. 1905. s-w.: Tue. & Thu. $.50 newsstand; $25/yr. in cy.; $36/yr. out of cy.; $38/yr. out of state. 16th & Front St., Blair, NE 68008. TEL 402-426-2121; FAX 402-426-2227. **Owner(s):** Blair Enterprise Co., Inc., 138 N. 16th, Blair, NE 68008. TEL 402-426-3144; Ed. Mark Rhoades; Pub. Mark Rhoades; adv. contact: Lynette Hansen. photos; pub. size: broadsheet; circ. 14,000(controlled & paid).

BROKEN BOW
US
CUSTER COUNTY CHIEF. 1892. s-w.: Mon. & Thu. $.75 newsstand; $28/yr. in area; $38/yr. out of area. 305 S. 10th, Broken Bow, NE 68822. TEL 308-872-2471; FAX 308-872-2415. **Owner(s):** Smith Newspapers, Inc., P.O. Box 27, Fort Payne, AL 35967. TEL 205-845-5510; Ed. Jeff Billser; Pub. Charley Najacht; adv. contact: Mary Coffman. pub. size: broadsheet; circ. morning 3,300(paid).

BURWELL
US
BURWELL TRIBUNE, THE. 1892. Wed. $.75 newsstand; $23/yr. local; $25/yr. in state; $27/out of state. 757 H St., Burwell, NE 68823. TEL 308-346-4504; FAX 308-346-4018. **Owner(s):** Kendall Neiman, P.O. Box 547, Burwell, NE 68823. TEL 308-346-4504; Ed. Kendall Neiman; Pub. Kendall Neiman; pub. size: broadsheet; circ. 2,400(paid).

US
SARGENT LEADER. Wed. $.75 newsstand; $23/yr. in cy.; $25/yr. our of cy.; $27/yr. out of state. 757 H. St., Burwell, NE 68823. TEL 308-346-4504; FAX 308-346-4018. **Owner(s):** Kendall Neiman, P.O. Box 547, Burwell, NE 68823. TEL 308-346-4504; FAX 308-346-4018; Steve DeLashmutt, P.O. Box 547, Burwell, NE 68823. TEL 308-346-4504; FAX 308-346-4018; Ed. Kendall Neiman; Pub. Steve DeLashmutt; pub. size: broadsheet; circ. 2,900(paid).

CENTRAL CITY
US
CENTRAL CITY REPUBLICAN NONPAREIL. 1893. Thu. $17.50/yr. local; 19.50/yr. in state; $23/yr. out of state. 802 C. Ave., Central City, NE 68826. TEL 308-946-3081; FAX 308-946-3082. **Owner(s):** Robert M. Jensen, 802 C Ave., Central City, NE 68826. TEL 308-946-3081; Ed. Robert M. Jensen; Pub. Robert M. Jensen; adv. contact: Ronna Kutlas. adv.: $4.95/SAU. photos; bk.rev.; pub. size: tabloid; circ. 2,000(paid).

COZAD
US
TRI-CITY TRIB. 1965. Thu. $.50 newsstand; $21.50/yr. 320 W. Eighth St., Cozad, NE 69130. TEL 308-784-3644; FAX 308-784-3647. **Owner(s):** Tri-City Trib, 320 W. Eighth St., Cozad, NE 69130. TEL 308-784-3644; FAX 308-784-3647; Ed. Dean Dorsey. adv.; photos; pub. size: tabloid; circ. 3,000(paid).

CRETE
US
CRETE NEWS, THE. 1871. Wed. $24.75/yr. in cy.; $35/yr. out of cy. 1201 Linden, Crete, NE 68333. TEL 402-826-2147; FAX 402-826-5072. **Owner(s):** Crete News, Inc., P.O. Box 40, Crete, NE 68333. TEL 402-826-2147; Pub. Lloyd Reeves; pub. size: broadsheet; circ. 4,400(paid).

DAVID CITY
US
DAVID CITY BANNER-PRESS, THE. 1873. Thu. $24/yr. local; $28/yr. in state; $33/yr. out of state. 331 E St., David City, NE 68632. TEL 402-367-3054; FAX 402-367-3055. **Owner(s):** Banner Press Publishing Co., Inc., Box 407, David City, NE 68632. TEL 402-367-3054; Ed. Zean Carney; Pub. Zean Carney; pub. size: broadsheet; circ. 4,300(paid).

DESHLER
US
DESHLER RUSTLER, THE. 1986. Wed. $.45 newsstand; $17.50/yr. in state; $20/yr. out of state. 706 Fourth St., Deshler, NE 68340. TEL 402-365-7221; FAX 402-365-7243. **Owner(s):** Harold W. Struve, 307 Alice St., Deshler, NE 68340. TEL 402-365-7575; FAX 402-365-7228; Ed. Harold W. Struve; Pub. Harold W. Struve; adv.; photos; pub. size: standard; circ. 1,600(paid).

ELKHORN
US   ISSN 0746-1437
DOUGLAS COUNTY POST GAZETTE. 1895. Tue. $.50 newsstand; $18.75/yr. in cy.; $24/yr. out of cy.; $28.50/yr. out of state. 113 Hillrise, Elkhorn, NE 68022. TEL 402-289-2329; FAX 402-289-0861; E-mail: postgazette@top.net. Owner(s): Penny Overmann, 113 Hillrise, Elkhorn, NE 68022. TEL 402-289-2329; FAX 402-289-0861; Ed. Mark Thiessen. adv. contact: Penny Overmann. adv.: $7.25/SAU. photos; bk.rev.; pub. size: broadsheet; circ. 8,200(free & paid).

WEEKLY NEWSPAPERS   SEWARD, NE 10661

FAIRBURY
US
FAIRBURY JOURNAL-NEWS, THE. 1892. s-w.: Tue. & Fri. $.50 newsstand; $29/yr. 516 Fifth St., Fairbury, NE 68352. TEL 402-729-6141; FAX 402-729-3892. **Owner(s):** McBattas Co., 516 Fifth St., Fairbury, NE 68352. TEL 402-729-6141; Pub. Fred A. Arnold, Jr.; adv. contact: Darrel Junker. photos; pub. size: standard; circ. 4,808(paid).

FALLS CITY
US
FALLS CITY JOURNAL. 1857. s-w.: Tue. & Fri. $.50 newsstand; $30/yr. 1810 Harlan St., Falls City, NE 68355. TEL 402-245-2431; FAX 402-245-4404. **Owner(s):** Journal Publishing Co., 1810 Harlan St., P.O. Box 128, Falls City, NE 68355. TEL 402-245-2431; Ed. Bill Schock. adv. contact: Linda Thout. pub. size: broadsheet; circ. 4,100(paid).

GENEVA
US
NEBRASKA SIGNAL. 1874. Wed. $.75 newsstand; $23/yr. local; $27/yr. out of area. 131 N. Ninth, Geneva, NE 68361. TEL 402-759-3117; FAX 402-759-4214. **Owner(s):** John Edgecombe, Jr., 131 N. Ninth, Geneva, NE 68361. TEL 402-759-3117; FAX 402-759-4214; Ed. Claudia Bohn; Pub. John F. Edgecombe, Jr.; adv.; photos; pub. size: broadsheet; circ. 3,707(paid).

GERING
US
GERING COURIER. 1887. Thu. $.50 newsstand; $21.75/yr. in cy.; $27.75/yr. out of cy. 1428 Tenth St., Gering, NE 69341. TEL 308-436-2222; FAX 308-436-7127. **Owner(s):** Jack & Carol Ann Lewis, 1428 Tenth St., Gering, NE 69341; Ed. Jack Lewis; Pub. Carol Ann Lewis; pub. size: broadsheet; circ. 2,361(paid).

LEXINGTON
US
CLIPPER-HERALD. 1891. s-w.: Wed. & Sat. $.50 newsstand; $29/yr. in cy.; $39/yr. out of cy. 114 W. Fifth St., Lexington, NE 68850-0599. TEL 308-324-5511; FAX 308-324-5240. **Owner(s):** Western Publishing Co., P.O. Box 1228, North Platte, NE 69103-1228; Pub. Peter J. Cook; adv.; bk.rev.; pub. size: broadsheet; circ. 4,100(paid).

LYONS
US
LYONS MIRROR-SUN. 1883. Thu. $.60 newsstand; $25-30/yr. P.O. Box 59, Lyons, NE 68038. TEL 402-687-2616. **Owner(s):** Bobbie & Dewaine Gahan, 215 N. Engdahl Ave., Oakland, NE 68045. TEL 402-685-6229; Ed. Anne O'Mara; Pub. Dewaine Gahan; adv.; pub. size: broadsheet; circ. 1,500(paid).

MINDEN
US
MINDEN COURIER, THE. 1890. w. $.50 newsstand; $20/yr. 317 N. Minden Ave., Minden, NE 68959-0379. TEL 308-832-2220; FAX 308-832-2221; E-mail: mc70720@itec.net. **Owner(s):** John & JoAnn Edgecombe, 317 N. Minden Ave., Minden, NE 68959. TEL 308-832-2220; FAX 308-832-2221; Ed. Julinne Gasseling; Pub. John Edgecombe, Jr.; adv. contact: JoAnn Edgecombe. photos; pub. size: broadsheet; circ. 2,800(paid).

O'NEILL
US
FRONTIER & HOLT COUNTY INDEPENDENT. Thu. $22.50/yr. in cy.; $27.50/yr. out of cy.; $35/yr. out of state. 114 N. Fourth St., O'Neill, NE 68763. TEL 402-336-1220; FAX 402-336-1222. **Owner(s):** G.A. Miles, P.O. Box 360, O'Neill, NE 68763. TEL 402-336-1220; Ed. Burnes McCulloch; Pub. G.A. Miles; adv. contact: George T. Miles. pub. size: broadsheet; circ. 4,870(paid).

OAKLAND
US
OAKLAND INDEPENDENT. 1880. Thu. $.75 newsstand; $28-$36/yr. 217 N. Oakland Ave., Oakland, NE 68045-0085. TEL 402-685-5624; FAX 402-685-5625. **Owner(s):** Bobbie & Dewaine Gahan, 215 N. Engdahl Ave., Oakland, NE 68045. TEL 402-685-6229; Pub. Dewaine Gahan; adv.; pub. size: standard; circ. 1,913(paid).

OGALLALA
US
KEITH COUNTY NEWS. 1885. s-w.: Mon. & Wed. $29/yr. 116 W. A St., Ogallala, NE 69153. TEL 308-284-4046; FAX 308-284-4048. **Owner(s):** Jack Pollock, 116 W. A St., Ogallala, NE 69153. TEL 308-284-4046; FAX 308-284-4048; Ed. Tom Huddleson; Pub. Jack Pollock; adv. contact: Marilee Perlinger. pub. size: broadsheet; circ. 4,500(paid).
Formerly: Ogallala Keith County News.

OMAHA
US
OMAHA STAR. 1938. Thu. $.35 newsstand; $24/yr. local; $26/yr. out of area. 2216 N. 24th St., Omaha, NE 68110. TEL 402-346-4041. **Owner(s):** Marquerita Washington, 2216 N. 24th St., Omaha, NE 68110. TEL 402-346-4041; adv.; bk.rev.; pub. size: standard; circ. 30,000(paid).

ORD
US
ORD QUIZ. 1882. Thu. $.75 newsstand; $27.50/yr. in state; $30/yr. out of state. 305 S. 16th St., Ord, NE 68862-0197. TEL 308-728-3262; FAX 308-728-5715. **Owner(s):** Quiz Graphic Arts, Inc., 305 S. 16th St., Ord, NE 68862. TEL 308-728-3262; FAX 308-728-5715; Ed. Doug Barber; Pub. Kerry E. Leggett; adv. contact: Lynn Griffith. adv.: $4.70/SAU. photos; pub. size: broadsheet; circ. 2,904(paid).

OVERTON
US
BEACON OBSERVER, THE. 1898. Wed. $.50 newsstand; $29/yr. P.O. Box 330, Overton, NE 68863. TEL 308-987-2451; FAX 308-987-2452. **Owner(s):** Norman & Polly Taylor, P.O. Box 330, Overton, NE 68863. TEL 308-907-2451; FAX 308-987-2452; adv.; photos; pub. size: broadsheet; circ. 1,518(controlled & paid).

PAPILLION
US
PAPILLION TIMES. 1874. Wed. $.50 newsstand; $23.40/yr. in cy.; $31.20/yr. elsewhere. 138 N. Washington, Papillion, NE 68046. TEL 402-339-3331; FAX 402-339-8562. **Owner(s):** Papillion Times Printing Co., 138 N. Washington St., Papillion, NE 68046. TEL 402-339-3331; Ed. Mark Martin; Pub. Shon Barenklau; adv. contact: Carolyn Hatting. pub. size: broadsheet; circ. 4,200(paid).

PLAINVIEW
US
PLAINVIEW NEWS. 1892. Wed. $.50 newsstand; $21/yr. 508 W. Locust, Plainview, NE 68769. TEL 402-582-4921; FAX 402-582-4922. **Owner(s):** Lee Warneke, P.O. Box 9, Plainview, NE 68769-0009. TEL 402-582-4921; FAX 402-582-4922; Pub. Lee Warneke; adv.; photos; pub. size: broadsheet; circ. 1,814(paid).

PLATTSMOUTH
US
PLATTSMOUTH JOURNAL. 1882. s-w.: Mon. & Thu. $.50 newsstand; $27/yr. in cy.; $34/yr. elsewhere. 410 Main St., Plattsmouth, NE 68048. TEL 402-296-2141; FAX 402-296-3401. **Owner(s):** Lee Corp., E. Moline, IL; Pub. Lou Prohaska; adv. contact: Kathy Herndon. pub. size: standard; circ. evening 5,400.

SCHUYLER
US
SCHUYLER SUN. 1871. Thu. $.50 newsstand; $25/yr. in cy.; $27/yr. out of state. 1112 C St., Schuyler, NE 68661. TEL 402-352-2424; FAX 402-352-3332. **Owner(s):** Francis Svoboda, P.O. Box 506, Schuyler, NE 68661. TEL 402-352-2424; FAX 402-352-3332; Ed. Michael Rea; Pub. Francis Svoboda; adv. contact: Curt Mentzer. pub. size: broadsheet; circ. 3,800(paid).

SEWARD
US
SEWARD COUNTY INDEPENDENT. 1897. Wed. $.75 newsstand; $23/yr. in cy.; $25/yr. out of cy.; $36/yr. out of state. 129 S. Sixth St., Seward, NE 68434. TEL 402-643-3676; FAX 402-643-6774. **Owner(s):** Rhoades Publishing, Blair, NE 68008. TEL 402-426-2121; Ed. Lori Shriner; Pub. Mark Rhoades; adv. contact: Lynn Dance. photos; pub. size: broadsheet; circ. 3,683(paid).

Weeklies

ULRICH'S INTERNATIONAL PERIODICALS DIRECTORY 1998

SIDNEY
US

SIDNEY TELEGRAPH. 1873. 3/wk.: Tue., Thu., Sat. $61/yr.; $56/yr. senior citizens. 809 Illinois St., Sidney, NE 69162. TEL 308-254-5555; FAX 308-254-5607. **Owner(s):** Western Publishing Co., P.O. Box 1228, N. Platter, NE 69103. TEL 800-951-6700; Ed. Gordon Tustin; Pub. Don Evans; adv. contact: Sue Kilgore. photos; bk.rev.; pub. size: broadsheet; circ. 2,650(paid). **Wire Service(s):** AP.

SOUTH SIOUX CITY
US

SOUTH SIOUX CITY STAR. 1909. Thu. $.75 newsstand; $22.50/yr. in state; $30/yr. out of state. 2520 Dakota Ave., South Sioux City, NE 68776-0157. TEL 402-494-4264; FAX 402-494-2414. **Owner(s):** Star Printing & Publishing, 2520 Dakota Ave., South Sioux City, NE 68776. TEL 402-494-4264; FAX 402-494-2414; Ed. Peggy Williams. adv.; photos; pub. size: broadsheet; circ. 3,800(paid).

SPRINGVIEW
US

SPRINGVIEW HERALD. 1886. Thu. $.35 newsstand; $16/yr. local; $18/yr. in state; $20/yr. out of state. W. L St., Springview, NE 68778-0369. TEL 402-497-3651; FAX 402-497-2651. **Owner(s):** Springview Herald, P.O. Box 369, Springview, NE 68778-0369. TEL 402-497-3651; FAX 402-497-2651; Ed. Karen Kurzenberger; Pub. Karen Kurzenberger; adv.: $2.67/SAU. photos; pub. size: tabloid; circ. 900(free & paid).

SUPERIOR
US   ISSN 0740-0969

SUPERIOR EXPRESS, THE. 1900. Thu. $.50 newsstand; $16/yr. local; $23/yr. elsewhere. 148 E. Third St., Superior, NE 68978. TEL 402-879-3291; FAX 402-879-3293; E-mail: bblauvelt@aol.com. **Owner(s):** Superior Publishing Co., P.O. Box 408, Superior, NE 68978. TEL 402-879-3291; Pub. Bill Blauvelt; adv. contact: Sherri Nun. photos; pub. size: broadsheet; circ. 4,239(paid).

SUTHERLAND
US

COURIER-TIMES. 1895. Thu. $.25 newsstand; $13/yr. in state; $18/yr. out of state. 824 First, Sutherland, NE 69165. TEL 308-386-4617; FAX 308-386-2437. **Owner(s):** Courier-Times, 824 First, Sutherland, NE 69165. TEL 308-386-4617; FAX 308-386-2426; Pub. Trenda Seifer; adv.; pub. size: tabloid; circ. 1,000(paid).

SYRACUSE
US

SYRACUSE JOURNAL-DEMOCRAT. 1878. Thu. $.50 newsstand; $18/yr. 123 W. 17th St., Syracuse, NE 68446. TEL 402-269-2135; FAX 402-269-2392. **Owner(s):** Midwest Newspapers, Inc., P.O. Box 380, Ames, IA 50010. TEL 515-232-2160; Ed. David Swanson; Pub. W.R. Welsh; adv. contact: Bill Holland. pub. size: tabloid; circ. 3,415(paid).

WAHOO
US

WAHOO NEWSPAPER. 1885. Thu. $.75 newsstand; $28/yr. 564 N. Broadway, Wahoo, NE 68066. TEL 402-443-4162; FAX 402-443-4459. **Owner(s):** Saunders County Publishing, Inc., 564 N. Broadway, P.O. Box 147, Wahoo, NE 68066. TEL 402-443-4162; Ed. Zean Carney; Pub. Zean Carney; adv.; pub. size: broadsheet; circ. 4,500(paid).

WAYNE
US

WAYNE HERALD. 1876. Thu. $.75 newsstand; $28/yr. in area; $35/yr. in state; $45/yr. out of state. 114 Main St., Wayne, NE 68787-0070. TEL 402-375-2600; FAX 402-375-1888. **Owner(s):** Smith Newspaper, Inc., P.O. Box 27, Fort Payne, AL 35967. TEL 205-845-5510; FAX 205-845-5509; Ed. Kevin Peterson; Pub. Jim Shanks; pub. size: standard; circ. morning 2,600(paid). **Wire Service(s):** AP, Newsfinder.

WEST POINT
US

WEST POINT NEWS. 1870. Wed. $29.50/yr. 134 E. Grove St., West Point, NE 68788. TEL 402-372-2461; FAX 402-372-3530. **Owner(s):** Tom Kelly, P.O. Box 40, West Point, NE 68788. TEL 402-372-2461; Ed. Willis Mahannah; Pub. Tom Kelly; adv.; pub. size: broadsheet; circ. 3,900(paid).

NEVADA

BOULDER CITY
US

BOULDER CITY NEWS. 1937. Thu. $.25 newsstand; $20/yr. home deliv.; $25/yr. mailed. 1227 Arizona St., Boulder City, NV 89005. TEL 702-293-2302; FAX 702-294-0977. **Owner(s):** HBC Publications, Two Commerce Center, Henderson, NV 89014. TEL 702-564-1881; Ed. Paul Szydelko; Pub. Mike O'Callaghan; adv. contact: Anne Picking. pub. size: broadsheet; circ. 5,500(paid).

CARSON CITY
US

CHRONICLE, THE. 1927. Wed. free. 200 Bath St., Carson City, NV 89702. TEL 702-882-2111; FAX 702-887-2420; E-mail: appeal@tahoe.com. **Owner(s):** Western Nevada Communications, P.O. Box 2288, Carson City, NV 89702-3209. TEL 702-883-8282; Ed. Barry Smith; Pub. Jeff Ackerman; adv. contact: Steve Reynolds. pub. size: broadsheet; circ. 34,000(free). **Wire Service(s):** AP.

HAWTHORNE
US

MINERAL COUNTY INDEPENDENT-NEWS. 1928. Wed. $.35 newsstand; $25/yr. mailed. 501 D St., Hawthorne, NV 89415. TEL 702-945-2414; FAX 702-945-1270. **Owner(s):** Mineral County Independent, 501 D St., Hawthorne, NV 89415. TEL 702-945-2414; Ed. Ted Hughes. adv.; photos; pub. size: broadsheet; circ. 2,900(free).

INCLINE VILLAGE
US

NORTH LAKE TAHOE BONANZA. 1964. s-w.: Wed. & Fri. $.50 newsstand; $36/yr. 917 Tahoe Blvd., Ste. 100, Incline Village, NV 89452. TEL 702-831-4666; FAX 916-546-2507; E-mail: bonanza@tahoe.com; URL: http://www.tahoe.com. **Owner(s):** North Lake Tahoe Bonanza, P.O. Box 7820, Incline Village, NV 89452. TEL 702-831-4666; Ed. Irwin Goldberg. adv.: negotiable. photos; pub. size: standard; circ. 7,900(free & paid). **Wire Service(s):** Swift News Service.

LAS VEGAS
US

LAS VEGAS TODAY. 1975. Thu. free newsstand; $75/yr. 4440 S. Arville, Ste. 12, Las Vegas, NV 89103. TEL 702-221-5000; FAX 702-221-5099. **Owner(s):** Desert Media Group, 4440 S. Arville, Ste. 12, Las Vegas, NV 89103. TEL 702-221-5000; Ed. Tom W. Westmoreland. adv.; pub. size: broadsheet; circ. 50,000(controlled).

LOVELOCK
US

LOVELOCK REVIEW-MINER. 1903. Thu. $.35 newsstand; $18/yr. in state; $25/yr. out of state. 230 Main St., Lovelock, NV 89419. TEL 702-273-7245. **Owner(s):** Gwendolyn Bogh Carter, 230 Main St., Lovelock, NV 89419. TEL 702-273-7245; FAX 702-273-0500; Ed. Gwendolyn Bogh Carter; Pub. Gwendolyn Bogh Carter; adv.; pub. size: broadsheet; circ. 1,500(paid).

TONOPAH
US

EUREKA SENTINEL. 1870. Thu. $.35 newsstand; $21/yr. 150 Main St., Tonopah, NV 89049. TEL 702-482-3365; FAX 702-482-5042. **Owner(s):** Central Nevada Newspapers, Inc., P.O. Box 193, Tonopah, NV 89049. TEL 702-482-3365; Ed. William G. Roberts; Pub. William G. Roberts; adv.; pub. size: tabloid; circ. 550(paid).

US

TONOPAH TIMES-BONANZA & GOLDFIELD NEWS. 1900. Thu. $.25 newsstand; $21/yr. in cy.; $22/yr. out of cy. 150 Main St., Tonopah, NV 89049. TEL 702-482-3365; FAX 702-482-5042. **Owner(s):** Central Nevada Newspapers, Inc., P.O. Box 193, Tonopah, NV 89049. TEL 702-482-3365; Ed. William G. Roberts; Pub. William G. Roberts; adv.; pub. size: tabloid; circ. 2,800(paid).

YERINGTON
US

FERNLEY LEADER-DAYTON COURIER. 1983. Wed. $.50 newsstand; $18.95/yr. 41 N. Main St., Yerington, NV 89447. TEL 702-463-4242; FAX 702-463-5547. **Owner(s):** Mason Valley News, Inc., 41 N. Main St., Yerington, NV 89447. TEL 702-463-4242; Ed. Laura Tennant; Pub. Bob Sanford; adv.: $4.90/SAU. photos; pub. size: broadsheet; circ. 2,600(controlled & paid).

WEEKLY NEWSPAPERS

US

MASON VALLEY NEWS. 1917. Fri. $.50 newsstand; $22.50/yr. 41 N. Main St., Yerington, NV 89447. TEL 702-463-4242; FAX 702-463-5547. **Owner(s):** Mason Valley News, Inc., 41 N. Main St., Yerington, NV 89447. TEL 702-463-4242; FAX 702-463-5547; Ed. David Sanford; Pub. Bob Sanford; adv.: $5.70/SAU. photos; pub. size: broadsheet; circ. 4,000(controlled & paid).
Formerly: Yerington Mason Valley News.

NEW HAMPSHIRE

CENTER OSSIPEE

US

CARROLL COUNTY INDEPENDENT. 1881. Wed. $20/yr. in cy.; $28/yr. out of cy. Moultonville Rd., Center Ossipee, NH 03814. TEL 603-539-4111; FAX 603-539-5564. **Owner(s):** Jacob J. & Ann Burghardt, 324 Wentworth Hill Rd., Sandwich, NH 03270. TEL 603-284-7001; Ed. Jeanne Tempest; Pub. Jacob J. Burghardt; adv. contact: Robin DeMello. photos; pub. size: broadsheet; circ. 5,500(paid).

COLEBROOK

US

NEWS & SENTINEL, THE. 1870. Wed. $.60 newsstand; $28/yr. One Bridge St., Colebrook, NH 03576. TEL 603-237-5501; FAX 603-237-5060; E-mail: sentinel@colbsent.com; URL: http://www.colbsent.com. **Owner(s):** John D. Harrigan, P.O. Box 39, Colebrook, NH 03576. TEL 603-237-5001; FAX 603-237-5060; Ed. Dennis Joos; Pub. John D. Harrigan; adv.; photos; pub. size: tabloid; circ. 4,454(free & paid).

CONWAY

US

MT. WASHINGTON VALLEY MOUNTAIN EAR. 1976. Thu. free newsstand; $30/yr. out of area. Mt. River Village, Rte. 16, Conway, NH 03818. TEL 603-447-6336; FAX 603-447-5474. **Owner(s):** R. Stephen Eastman, Mt. River Village, Rte. 16, Conway, NH 03818. TEL 603-447-6336; FAX 603-447-5474; Sarah W. Eastman, Mt. River Village, Rte. 16, Conway, NH 03818. TEL 603-447-6336; FAX 603-447-5474; Ed. R. Stephen Eastman. adv. contact: Paula Tetreault. photos; pub. size: tabloid; circ. 12,000(free).

DERRY

US

DERRY NEWS. 1880. s-w.: Wed. & Fri. $.50 newsstand; $32/yr. 46 W. Broadway, Derry, NH 03038. TEL 603-437-7000; FAX 603-432-4510; E-mail: info@derrynews.com. **Owner(s):** Eagle Tribune, The, 100 Tpke. St., N. Andover, MA 01847. TEL 603-432-3363; Ed. Daniel Griffin; Pub. Tom Kirk; adv. contact: Tom Kirk. pub. size: broadsheet; circ. 10,700(paid).

DOVER

US

TRI-TOWN TRANSCRIPT, THE. 1975. Thu. $.35 newsstand; $18.50/yr. 563 Central Ave., Dover, NH 03820. TEL 603-742-3735; FAX 603-742-6442. **Owner(s):** Tri-Town Publishers, Inc., 563 Central Ave., Dover, NH 03820. TEL 603-742-3735; FAX 603-742-6442; adv.: $11.07/SAU. photos; pub. size: broadsheet; circ. 6,700(paid).
Formerly: The Transcript.

HILLSBOROUGH

US

NEW HAMPSHIRE WEEK IN REVIEW. 1868. Mon. free. 202 W. Main St., Hillsborough, NH 03244-1190. TEL 603-464-5588; FAX 603-464-4106. **Owner(s):** Granite Quill Publishers, P.O. Box 917, Hillsborough, NH 03244. TEL 603-464-5588; Ed. Joyce Bosse; Pub. Leigh Bosse; adv.; pub. size: tabloid; circ. 18,000(free & paid).

HUDSON

US

HUDSON-LITCHFIELD NEWS. 1990. Fri. free. 222 Central St., Ste. 5, Hudson, NH 03051. TEL 603-883-1432. **Owner(s):** PBR Enterprises, Inc., 222 Central St., Ste. 5, Hudson, NH 03051. TEL 603-880-1516; Ed. Diane Thoms. adv. contact: Ed Koenig. photos; pub. size: tabloid; circ. 9,800(free).

LANCASTER

US

COOS COUNTY DEMOCRAT. 1838. Wed. $.60 newsstand; $25/yr. in NH & VT; $28/yr. elsewhere. 79 Main St., Lancaster, NH 03584. TEL 603-788-4939; FAX 603-788-3022. **Owner(s):** North Country Publishing Inc., P.O. Box 28, Lancaster, NH 03584. TEL 603-788-4939; Ed. Eugene Ehlert; Pub. John D. Harrigan; adv.; photos; pub. size: broadsheet; circ. 6,500(paid).

LITTLETON

US

COURIER, THE. 1889. Wed. $.50 newsstand; $21/yr. in cy.; $26/yr. out of cy. 365 Union St., Littleton, NH 03561. TEL 603-444-3927; FAX 603-444-3920. **Owner(s):** White Mountain Publishing Partnership, P.O. Box 230, Littleton, NH 03561. TEL 603-444-3927; Ed. Tim McCarthy; Pub. Thomas C. Hepner; adv. contact: Georgia Golden. photos; bk.rev.; pub. size: broadsheet; circ. 7,000(paid).

MILFORD

US   ISSN 1071-9206

MILFORD CABINET & WILTON JOURNAL. 1802. Wed. $.75 newsstand; $26/yr. in state; $38/yr. out of state. 54 School St., Milford, NH 03055-0180. TEL 603-673-3100; FAX 603-673-8250; E-mail: cabinet@cabinet.com; URL: http://www.cabinet.com. **Owner(s):** Frank & Martha Manley, P.O. Box 180, Milford, NH 03055. TEL 603-673-3100; FAX 603-673-8250; Ed. Michael Cleveland; Pub. Frank Manley; adv.; pub. size: broadsheet; circ. 9,000(paid).

NASHUA

US   ISSN 0192-8597

1590 BROADCASTER. 1964. Wed. free. 502 W. Hollis St., Nashua, NH 03062-0548. TEL 603-889-1590; FAX 603-883-4344. **Owner(s):** 1590 Broadcasting Corp., 502 W. Hollis St., Nashua, NH 03062. TEL 603-889-1590; Ed. Maurice R. Parent; Pub. Maurice R. Parent; adv. contact: Maurice R. Parent. photos; pub. size: tabloid; circ. 64,000(free).

NEWPORT

US

ARGUS-CHAMPION, THE. 1825. Wed. $.50 newsstand; $19.95/yr. in state; $24.95/yr. out of state. 86 Sunapee St., Newport, NH 03773. TEL 603-863-1776; FAX 603-863-0066. **Owner(s):** Dirk Ippen, 86 Sunapee St., Newport, NH 03773. TEL 603-863-1776; Ed. Mark DiPietro. adv. contact: Roger Carroll. pub. size: broadsheet; circ. 5,100(paid).

PETERBOROUGH

US

MONADNOCK LEDGER. 1956. Thu. $.50 newsstand; $24/yr. in state; $30/yr. out of state. 20 Grove St., Peterborough, NH 03458. TEL 603-924-7172; FAX 603-924-3681. **Owner(s):** Newspapers of New England, Inc., 3 N. State St., Concord, NH 03301. TEL 603-224-5301; Pub. Heather McKernan; adv.; pub. size: broadsheet; circ. 7,000(paid).

US

PETERBOROUGH TRANSCRIPT. 1849. Thu. $.50 newsstand; $20/yr. in state; $24/yr. out of state. 43 Grove St., Peterborough, NH 03458. TEL 603-924-3333; FAX 603-924-7946. **Owner(s):** Joseph D. Cummings, 220 Sand Hill Rd., Peterborough, NH 03458. TEL 603-924-6486; Paul C. Cummings, Jr., 220 Sand Hill Rd., Peterborough, NH 03458. TEL 603-924-6486; Ed. Bob McElroy; Pub. Joseph D. Cummings; adv. contact: Heidi Bourgeois. pub. size: broadsheet; circ. 5,900(paid).

PLYMOUTH

US

RECORD ENTERPRISE, THE. Wed. $.50 newsstand; $21/yr. in cy.; $26/yr. out of cy. Brimstone House, Rte. 3, Fairgrounds Rd., Plymouth, NH 03264. TEL 603-536-1311; FAX 603-536-8940. **Owner(s):** White Mountain Publishing Partnership, P.O. Box 230, Littleton, NH 03561. TEL 603-444-3927; Ed. William York; Pub. Thomas Hepner; adv. contact: Georgia Golden. photos; bk.rev.; pub. size: tabloid; circ. 6,500(paid).

ROCHESTER

US

ROCHESTER TIMES, THE. 1993. Thu. 77 N. Main St., Rochester, NH 03867. TEL 603-332-2300; FAX 603-330-0718. **Owner(s):** Lou McGrew, 77 N. Main St., Rochester, NH 03870. TEL 603-332-2300; FAX 603-330-0718; Ed. John Nolan; Pub. Brad Lipe; adv. contact: Brad Lipe. photos; pub. size: tabloid.

SALEM

SALEM OBSERVER. 1966. Thu. $.50 newsstand; $18/yr. in state; $21/yr. out of state. 380 Main St., Salem, NH 03079. TEL 603-893-4356; FAX 603-898-0249. **Owner(s):** Observer, Inc., The, P.O. Box 720, Salem, NH 03079. TEL 603-893-4356; FAX 603-898-0249; Ed. Carol Moore; Pub. Arthur Mueller, Jr.; adv. contact: Armand Beliveau. photos; bk.rev.; pub. size: broadsheet; circ. 6,000(paid).

STRATHAM

EXETER NEWS-LETTER. 1831. s-w.: Tue. & Fri. $.75 newsstand; $36.40/yr. in cy. 7 Portsmouth Ave., Stratham, NH 03885. TEL 603-772-6000; FAX 603-772-3830. **Owner(s):** Ottaway Newspapers, Inc., P.O. Box 401, Campbell Hall, NY 10916. TEL 914-294-8181; Ed. Howard Altschiller; Pub. John Tabor; adv. contact: Michael Rabideau. pub. size: broadsheet; circ. morning 7,125(paid). **Wire Service(s):** AP, Newsfinder.

HAMPTON UNION. 1901. s-w.: Tue. & Fri. $.75 newsstand; $41.60/yr. Fern Crossing Mall, 7 Portsmouth Ave., Stratham, NH 03885. TEL 603-926-4511; FAX 603-772-3830. **Owner(s):** Ottaway Newspapers, Inc., P.O. Box 401, Campbell Hall, NY 10916. TEL 914-294-8181; Ed. Howard Altschiller; Pub. John Tabor; pub. size: broadsheet; circ. 7,200(paid).

WOLFEBORO

GRANITE STATE NEWS. 1859. Wed. $.50 newsstand; $20/yr. in cy.; $28/yr. out of cy. 10 Endicott Street, Wolfeboro, NH 03894. TEL 603-569-3126; FAX 603-569-4743; E-mail: gsn@conket.com; URL: http://www.granitestatenews.com. **Owner(s):** Jacob J. & Ann Burghardt, 324 Wentworth Hill Rd., Sandwich, NH 03270. TEL 603-284-7001; Ed. Jeanne Tempest; Pub. Jacob J. Burghardt; adv. contact: Jeffry Morris. photos; pub. size: broadsheet; circ. 5,500(paid). ISSN 1060-0590

NEW JERSEY

BAYONNE

BAYONNE COMMUNITY NEWS. 1978. Wed. $60/yr. 13 E. 21st St., Bayonne, NJ 07002. TEL 201-437-2460; FAX 201-437-7127. **Owner(s):** Edward M. Kukowski, Bayonne, NJ; Victor J. Ruggiero, Bayonne, NJ; Pub. Edward M. Kukowski; adv. contact: Renee Pavlick. photos; pub. size: tabloid; circ. 28,525(controlled & free).

BELVIDERE

NEWS, THE. 1962. Wed. $.35 newsstand; $21/yr. P.O. Box 265, Belvidere, NJ 07823. TEL 908-475-1848; FAX 908-362-9223. **Owner(s):** North Jersey Newspapers Co., 988 Main St., Passaic, NJ 07005. TEL 201-365-3000; FAX 201-365-5887; Ed. Enid Scharf; Pub. Rosemarie Maio; adv. contact: Rosemarie Maio. photos; pub. size: broadsheet; circ. 1,300(paid).

BERNARDSVILLE

BERNARDSVILLE NEWS. 1896. Wed. $.75 newsstand; $29/yr. in cy. 17-19 Morristown Rd., Bernardsville, NJ 07924. TEL 908-766-3900; FAX 908-766-6365. **Owner(s):** Recorder Publishing Co., 17-19 Morristown Rd., Bernardsville, NJ 07924. TEL 908-766-3900; Ed. Charles Zavalick; Pub. Cortlandt Parker; adv. contact: Allison Spinella. photos; bk.rev.; pub. size: broadsheet; circ. 8,619(paid).

RANDOLPH REPORTER. Thu. $.50 newsstand; $15/yr. in cy.; $25/yr. out of cy. 17-19 Morristown Rd., Bernardsville, NJ 07924. TEL 908-766-3900; FAX 201-691-2396. **Owner(s):** Recorder Publishing Co., 17-19 Morristown Rd., Bernardsville, NJ 07924. TEL 201-766-3900; Ed. Claire Seedburg; Pub. Cortland Parker; pub. size: standard; circ. 4,043(paid).

BLACKWOOD

NEWS REPORT. 1960. Thu. $.50 newsstand; $14/yr. Black Horse Pike, Blackwood, NJ 08012. TEL 609-228-7300; FAX 609-227-1207. **Owner(s):** Intercounty Newspaper Group, P.O. Box 67, Blackwood, NJ 08012. TEL 609-228-7300; Ed. John Worthington; Pub. Art Thompson; adv.; photos; bk.rev.; pub. size: tabloid; circ. 3,500(paid).

PLAIN DEALER. 1926. Thu. $17/yr. Black Horse Pike, Blackwood, NJ 08012. TEL 609-228-7300; FAX 609-227-1207. **Owner(s):** Intercounty Newspaper Group, P.O. Box 67, Blackwood, NJ 08012. TEL 609-228-7300; Ed. John Worthington; Pub. Art Thompson; adv. contact: James Pearce. photos; bk.rev.; pub. size: tabloid; circ. 6,200(paid).

RECORD-BREEZE. 1919. Thu. $17/yr. in cy.; $20/yr. out of cy. Black Horse Pike, Blackwood, NJ 08012. TEL 609-228-7300; FAX 609-227-1207; E-mail: ingrews@aol.com. **Owner(s):** Intercounty Newspaper Group, P.O. Box 67, Blackwood, NJ 08012; Ed. John Worthington; Pub. Art Thompson; adv. contact: James Pearce. photos; bk.rev.; pub. size: tabloid; circ. 3,500(paid).

BLAIRSTOWN

BLAIRSTOWN PRESS. 1877. Wed. $.50 newsstand; $21/yr. in cy. 122 Rte. 94, Blairstown, NJ 07825. TEL 908-362-6161; FAX 908-362-9223. **Owner(s):** North Jersey Newspapers Co., 988 Main Ave., Passaic, NJ 07005. TEL 201-365-3000; FAX 201-365-5887; Ed. Enid Scharf; Pub. Rosemarie Maio; pub. size: broadsheet; circ. 4,000(paid).

BLOOMFIELD

BELLEVILLE POST. 1982. Thu. $22/yr. in cy. 266 Liberty St., Bloomfield, NJ 07003. TEL 973-743-4040; FAX 973-680-8848. **Owner(s):** Worrall Community Newspapers, Inc., P.O. Box 3109, Union, NJ 07083. TEL 908-686-7700; Pub. David Worrall; adv. contact: Peter Worrall. pub. size: broadsheet; circ. 12,000(paid).

GLEN RIDGE PAPER, THE. 1935. Thu. $22/yr. in cy. 266 Liberty St., Bloomfield, NJ 07003. TEL 973-743-4040; FAX 973-680-8848. **Owner(s):** Worrall Community Newspapers, Inc., P.O. Box 3109, Union, NJ 07083. TEL 908-686-7700; Ed. Anthony Buccino; Pub. David Worrall; adv. contact: Peter Worrall. pub. size: broadsheet; circ. 1,512(paid).

INDEPENDENT PRESS OF BLOOMFIELD, THE. 1883. Thu. $22/yr. in cy. 266 Liberty St., Bloomfield, NJ 07003. TEL 973-743-4040; FAX 973-680-8848. **Owner(s):** Worrall Community Newspapers, Inc., P.O. Box 3109, Union, NJ 07083. TEL 908-686-7700; Ed. Russell Roemmele; Pub. David Worrall; adv. contact: Peter Worrall. pub. size: broadsheet; circ. 3,976(paid).

NUTLEY JOURNAL. 1982. Thu. $22/yr. in cy. 266 Liberty St., Bloomfield, NJ 07003. TEL 973-743-4040; FAX 973-680-8848. **Owner(s):** Worrall Community Newspapers, Inc., P.O. Box 3109, Union, NJ 07083. TEL 908-686-7700; Pub. David Worrall; adv. contact: Peter Worrall. pub. size: broadsheet; circ. 10,400(paid).

BORDENTOWN

REGISTER-NEWS. 1845. Thu. $.25 newsstand; $13/yr. in state; $16.50/yr. out of state; $11/yr. senior citizens. 137 Farnsworth Ave., Bordentown, NJ 08505. TEL 609-298-7111; FAX 609-298-7107. **Owner(s):** Lorraine Publishing, Inc., 137 Farnsworth Ave., P.O. Box 189, Bordentown, NJ 08505. TEL 609-298-7111; FAX 609-298-7107; Ed. Jennifer L. Collins; Pub. Hershel M. Brown; adv. contact: Michael Atkins. photos; pub. size: tabloid; circ. 7,800(paid).

BRICK

BRICK TOWNSHIP TOWN NEWS. 1980. Thu. $.35 newsstand; $9/yr. in town; $14/yr. out of town. 526 Jackson Ave., Brick, NJ 08723. TEL 908-477-9110; FAX 908-477-8305. **Owner(s):** Edward C. Mueller, 526 Jackson Ave., Brick, NJ 08723. TEL 908-477-9110; FAX 908-477-8305; Pub. Edward C. Mueller; adv.; photos; bk.rev.; pub. size: tabloid; circ. 5,000(free & paid).

BUDD LAKE

MT. OLIVE CHRONICLE. Thu. $.50 newsstand; $18/yr. mailed in cy.; $25/yr. out of cy. 336 Rte. 46, Budd Lake, NJ 07828. TEL 201-691-8181; FAX 201-691-2396. **Owner(s):** Recorder Publishing Co., 17-19 Morristown Rd., Bernardsville, NJ 07924. TEL 908-766-3900; Ed. Phillip J. Nardone; Pub. Cortlandt Parker; adv.; pub. size: standard; circ. 5,000(paid).

WEEKLY NEWSPAPERS

BUTLER

US
LAKELAND TODAY. 1961. s-w.: Wed. & Sun. free. 10 Park Pl., Butler, NJ 07405. TEL 201-283-5507; FAX 201-838-1495. **Owner(s):** North Jersey Newspapers Co., 988 Main Ave., Passaic, NJ 07055; Pub. Richard Vezza; adv.; pub. size: standard; circ. 23,000(free & paid).

US
PASSAIC VALLEY TODAY. s-w.: Wed. & Sun. free home deliv.; $.25 newsstand. 10 Park Pl., Butler, NJ 07405. TEL 201-283-5507; FAX 201-838-1495. **Owner(s):** North Jersey Newspapers Co., 988 Main Ave., Passaic, NJ 07055. TEL 201-365-3000; Ed. Nancy Rubenstein; Pub. Richard Vezza; adv. contact: Tony Roselli. pub. size: broadsheet; circ. 10,926(paid).

US
SUBURBAN LIFE. 1961. Wed. $31/yr. 10 Park Pl., Butler, NJ 07405. TEL 201-283-5511; FAX 201-838-1495. **Owner(s):** North Jersey Newspapers Co., 988 Main Ave., Passaic, NJ 07055. TEL 201-365-3000; Ed. Robert Errera; Pub. Richard Vezza; adv. contact: Tony Viggiano. photos; pub. size: broadsheet; circ. 32,579(paid). **Wire Service(s):** AP.
   Formerly: Suburban Life Today.

US
SUBURBAN TRENDS. 1955. s-w.: Sun. & Wed. $54.60/yr. 10 Park Pl., Butler, NJ 07405-1377. TEL 201-838-9000; FAX 201-838-1495. **Owner(s):** North Jersey Newspapers Co., 998 Main Ave., Passaic, NJ 07055. TEL 201-492-3500; Ed. Jack Carle. adv. contact: Joseph Onegri. photos; bk.rev.; pub. size: broadsheet; circ. 12,160(paid); Sun. 14,287(paid).

US
WAYNE TODAY. 1962. s-w.: Sun. & Wed. $31.20/yr. 10 Park Pl., Butler, NJ 07405. TEL 201-283-5507; FAX 201-492-3548. **Owner(s):** North Jersey Newspapers Co., 988 Main Ave., Passaic, NJ 07055. TEL 201-365-3000; Ed. Nancy Rubenstein; Pub. Richard Vezza; adv.; photos; pub. size: broadsheet; circ. 48,000(controlled & paid).

BYRAM

US
SUSSEX COUNTY CHRONICLE. 1993. Wed. $.35 newsstand; $21/yr. 23 Rte. 206, Byram, NJ 07874. TEL 201-691-9530; FAX 201-691-1183. **Owner(s):** North Jersey Newspapers Co., 988 Main Ave., Passaic, NJ 07055. TEL 201-492-3000; Pub. Rosemarie Maio; adv.; photos; pub. size: broadsheet; circ. 2,400(paid).

CALDWELL

US
PROGRESS, THE. 1911. Thu. $18/yr. in cy. 6 Brookside Ave., Caldwell, NJ 07006-0072. TEL 201-226-8900; FAX 201-226-0553; E-mail: jean.conlon@njnetpath.net. **Owner(s):** John A. Sullivan, III & Jean E. Conlon, 6 Brookside Ave., Caldwell, NJ 07006. TEL 201-226-8900; Ed. Jean E. Conlon. adv. contact: Roger White. photos; pub. size: broadsheet; circ. 9,300(paid).

CAMDEN

US
CAMDEN COUNTY RECORD. 1939. Thu. $.15 newsstand; $18/yr. 519 Federal St., Ste. 207, Camden, NJ 08103. TEL 609-757-9200; FAX 609-541-4036. **Owner(s):** Tymes Publications, P.O. Box 389, Camden, NJ 08011. TEL 609-757-9200; FAX 609-541-4036; Ed. Veronica Miles; Pub. Jeffrey Gunning; adv.; pub. size: tabloid; circ. 12,000(paid).

CAPE MAY

US
CAPE MAY STAR & WAVE. 1854. Thu. $.50 newsstand; $22/yr. in cy.; $25/yr. out of cy. 513 Washington Mall, Cape May, NJ 08204. TEL 609-884-3466; FAX 609-884-2893; E-mail: rcooper@acy.digex.net; URL: http://www.acy.digex.net/'mwave. **Owner(s):** American Publishing Co., 606 N. Van Buren, P.O. Box 520, Marion, IL 62959. TEL 618-993-1711; Ed. Mary Keely; Pub. Ralph Cooper; adv. contact: R. Merrick-Borgo. pub. size: standard; circ. 7,800(paid).

CHERRY HILL

US
THIS WEEK. 1991. Thu. free. 301 S. Cuthbert Blvd., Cherry Hill, NJ 08002. TEL 609-663-4200; FAX 609-663-7664. **Owner(s):** Gannett Company, Inc., 1100 Wilson Blvd., Arlington, VA 22234. TEL 703-284-6000; Ed. Tom Engleman; Pub. Robert Collins; adv. contact: Michael Fanelli. pub. size: broadsheet; circ. 4,800(free).
   Formerly: Suburban, The.

CHESTER

US
OBSERVER-TRIBUNE. 1936. Thu. $.75 newsstand; $29/yr. in cy.; $32/yr. out of cy.; $38/yr. out of state. 530 E. Main St., Chester, NJ 07930. TEL 908-879-4100; FAX 908-879-6141. **Owner(s):** Recorder Publishing Co., 17-19 Morristown Rd., Bernardsville, NJ 07924. TEL 201-766-3900; Ed. Philip Nardone; Pub. Cortlandt Parker; adv. contact: Alison Spinella. pub. size: broadsheet; circ. 6,970(paid).

CLIFTON

US   ISSN 0745-8908
NORTH JERSEY PROSPECTOR. 1933. Thu. $.35 newsstand; $30/yr. 85 Crooks Ave., Clifton, NJ 07011. TEL 201-773-8300. **Owner(s):** North Jersey Prospector, Inc., 85 Crooks Ave., Clifton, NJ 07011. TEL 201-773-8300; Ed. Marsha Razumov; Pub. Blanche Kubat; adv. contact: Rich Grudzinski. photos; bk.rev.; pub. size: tabloid; circ. 109,023(controlled & paid).

CLOSTER

US
SUBURBANITE, THE. 1958. Wed. free home deliv. 231 Herbert Ave., Closter, NJ 07624. TEL 201-784-0903; FAX 201-784-2592. **Owner(s):** North Jersey Newspapers Co., 998 Main Ave., Passaic, NJ 07055. TEL 201-492-3000; Ed. Beverly O'Shea; Pub. Sherwood Spitz; pub. size: tabloid; circ. 49,000(free).
   Formerly: Northern N.J. Suburbanite.

COLLINGSWOOD

US
RETROSPECT, THE. 1902. Fri. $.35 newsstand; $13/yr. 732 Haddon Ave., Collingswood, NJ 08108-0296. TEL 609-854-1400. **Owner(s):** Retrospect, Inc., 732 Haddon Ave., Camden, NJ 08108. TEL 609-854-1400; Ed. Kenneth W. Roberts. adv.; pub. size: tabloid; circ. 4,300(paid).

COLOGNE

US
SOUTH JERSEY ADVISOR. 1970. Thu. free; $35/yr. 644 W. White Horse Pike, Cologne, NJ 08213. TEL 609-646-5843; FAX 609-965-2814. **Owner(s):** Ronald G. Moissinac, 509 S. Fourth Ave., Absecon, NJ 08201. TEL 609-646-5843; FAX 609-965-2814; Ed. Kenneth Platt; Pub. Ronald G. Moissinac; adv. contact: Helen Miranda. photos; pub. size: tabloid; circ. 22,481(free & paid).

CRANFORD

US
CRANFORD CHRONICLE. 1893. Wed. $.50 newsstand; $25/yr. in cy. 102 Walnut Ave., Cranford, NJ 07016. TEL 908-276-6000; FAX 908-276-6220. **Owner(s):** North Jersey Newspaper, Co., 988 Main St., Passaic, NJ 07055. TEL 201-492-3500; Ed. Andrew Simpson; Pub. Louis Barsony; pub. size: broadsheet; circ. 7,331(paid).

DAYTON

US
CENTRAL POST. 1958. Thu. $.60 newsstand; $29/yr. 397 Ridge Rd., Ste. 4, Dayton, NJ 08810. TEL 908-329-9214; FAX 908-329-9286. **Owner(s):** Princeton Packet, Inc., 300 Witherspoon St., Princeton, NJ 08540. TEL 609-924-5412; Ed. Helene Ragovin; Pub. James Kilgore; adv. contact: Martin Hillson. pub. size: broadsheet; circ. 3,500(paid).

US
CRANBURY PRESS. Fri. $.60 newsstand; $29/yr. 397 Ridge Rd., Ste. 4, Dayton, NJ 08810. TEL 908-329-9216; FAX 908-329-9286. **Owner(s):** Princeton Packet, Inc., 300 Witherspoon St., Princeton, NJ 08540. TEL 609-924-5412; Ed. Helene Ragovin; Pub. James Kilgore; adv. contact: Martin Hillson. pub. size: broadsheet; circ. 5,000(paid).

US
NORTH BRUNSWICK POST. Fri. $.50 newsstand; $61/yr. 397 Ridge Rd., Ste. 4, Dayton, NJ 08810. TEL 908-329-9216; FAX 908-329-9286. **Owner(s):** Princeton Packet, Inc., 300 Witherspoon St., Princeton, NJ 08540. TEL 609-924-5412; Ed. Helen Ragovin; Pub. James Kilgore; adv. contact: Martin Hillson. pub. size: broadsheet; circ. 8,000(paid).

DENVILLE

US
CITIZEN OF MORRIS COUNTY, THE. Wed. $15/yr. in cy.; $25/yr. out of cy. 124 E. Main St., Denville, NJ 07834. TEL 201-627-0400; FAX 201-627-0403. **Owner(s):** Andis, Inc., 125 E. Main St., Denville, NJ 07834. TEL 201-627-0400; Ed. Audrey Davie. adv. contact: Diane Goldthwait. pub. size: broadsheet; circ. 7,000(paid).

FAIR LAWN

NEWS BEACON. 1959. Thu. $.25 newsstand; $9/yr. 12-38 River Rd., Fair Lawn, NJ 07410. TEL 201-791-8400; FAX 201-794-3259. **Owner(s):** North Jersey Newspapers Co., 988 Main Ave., Passaic, NJ 07055. TEL 201-492-3500; Pub. Woody Spitz; adv. contact: Joe Brenan. photos; pub. size: tabloid; circ. 36,400(controlled).

FLEMINGTON

HUNTERDON COUNTY DEMOCRAT. Thu. $.75 newsstand; $29/yr. P.O. Box 32, Flemington, NJ 08822-0032. TEL 908-782-4747; FAX 908-782-6572. **Owner(s):** Hunterdon County Democrat, P.O. Box 32, Flemington, NJ 08822-0032. TEL 908-782-4747; Ed. Sally Graziano; Pub. Catherine Langley; adv.; photos; pub. size: standard; circ. 25,000(paid).

FRANKLIN LAKES

GLEN ROCK GAZETTE. Fri. $.50 newsstand; $18/yr. 799 Franklin Ave., Franklin Lakes, NJ 07417. TEL 201-847-0400; FAX 201-847-1144. **Owner(s):** Bergen County Newspapers, Inc., 799 Franklin Ave., Franklin Lakes, NJ 07417. TEL 201-847-0400; FAX 201-847-1144; Pub. Stephen E. Clark; adv.; photos; pub. size: tabloid.

REPORTER, THE. Fri. $.50 newsstand; $18/yr. 799 Franklin Ave., Franklin Lakes, NJ 07417. TEL 201-847-0400; FAX 201-847-1144. **Owner(s):** Bergen County Newspapers, Inc., 799 Franklin Ave., Franklin Lakes, NJ 07417. TEL 201-847-0400; FAX 201-847-1144; Pub. Stephen E. Clark; adv.; photos; pub. size: tabloid; circ. 10,000(paid).

VILLAGE GAZETTE OF RIDGEWOOD. Fri. $.50 newsstand; $18/yr. 799 Franklin Ave., Franklin Lakes, NJ 07417. TEL 201-847-0400; FAX 201-847-1144. **Owner(s):** Bergen County Newspapers, Inc., 799 Franklin Ave., Franklin Lakes, NJ 07417. TEL 201-847-0400; FAX 201-847-1144; Pub. Stephen E. Clark; adv.; photos; pub. size: tabloid.

WYCKOFF GAZETTE. Fri. $.50 newsstand; $18/yr. 799 Franklin Ave., Franklin Lakes, NJ 07417. TEL 201-847-0400; FAX 201-847-1144. **Owner(s):** Bergen County Newspapers, Inc., 799 Franklin Ave., Franklin Lakes, NJ 07417. TEL 201-847-0400; FAX 201-847-1144; Pub. Stephen E. Clark; adv.; photos; pub. size: tabloid.

FRANKLINVILLE

ISSN 0016-0040
FRANKLIN TOWNSHIP SENTINEL. 1942. Thu. $.35 newsstand; $15/yr. P.O. Box 367, Franklinville, NJ 08322. TEL 609-694-1600; FAX 609-694-0469. **Owner(s):** James R. Kinkade, RD 2, P. O. Box 670, Elmer, NJ 08318; Ed. James R. Kinkade; Pub. James R. Kinkade; adv. contact: Monica Billings. pub. size: broadsheet; circ. 4,700(paid).
Formerly: Franklinville Sentinel.

FRENCHTOWN

DELAWARE VALLEY NEWS. 1879. Thu. $.40 newsstand; $18/yr. 207 Harrison St., Frenchtown, NJ 08825-0244. TEL 908-996-4047; FAX 908-996-2238. **Owner(s):** Hunterdon County Democrat, P.O. Box 32, Flemington, NJ 08822. TEL 908-782-4747; Ed. Nick DiGiovanni; Pub. Catherine Langley; adv. contact: Jane Leuthauser. pub. size: broadsheet; circ. 4,800(paid).

GARFIELD

MESSENGER, THE. 1940. Thu. $10/yr. mailed only. 48 Harrison Ave., Garfield, NJ 07026. TEL 201-473-1927; FAX 201-546-4233. **Owner(s):** James & Nancy Huffman, 629 Victoria Ave., Paramus, NJ 07652. TEL 201-652-6155; FAX 201-652-7126; Ed. James A. Huffman. adv.; pub. size: tabloid; circ. 1,500(paid).

GLOUCESTER CITY

GLOUCESTER CITY NEWS. 1927. Thu. $.50 newsstand; $14/yr. 34 S. Broadway, Gloucester City, NJ 08030. TEL 609-456-1199; FAX 609-456-1330. **Owner(s):** William E. Cleary, P.O. Box 151, Gloucester City, NJ 08030. TEL 609-456-1199; FAX 609-456-1330; Ed. William E. Cleary; Pub. William E. Cleary; photos; bk.rev.; pub. size: tabloid; circ. 5,000(free & paid).

HACKETTSTOWN

COMMUNITY FORUM. 1972. Fri. free. 106 E. Moore St., Hackettstown, NJ 07840. TEL 908-852-1212; FAX 908-852-9320. **Owner(s):** North Jersey Newspapers Co., 988 Main Ave., Passaic, NJ 07055. TEL 201-492-3000; Ed. Dan Hirshberg. adv.; photos; pub. size: broadsheet; circ. 53,511(free & paid).
Formerly: Forum, The.

STAR GAZETTE. Thu. $.50 newsstand; $24/yr. in cy.; $27/yr. out of cy. 106 E. Moore St., Hackettstown, NJ 07840. TEL 908-852-1212; FAX 908-852-9320. **Owner(s):** North Jersey Newspapers Co., 988 Main Ave., Passaic, NJ 07005. TEL 201-365-3000; Ed. Enid Scharf. adv.; photos; pub. size: broadsheet; circ. 4,300(paid).

HAMMONTON

ATLANTIC COUNTY RECORD. Thu. $.50 newsstand; $21/yr. 12th St. & West End Ave., Hammonton, NJ 08037. TEL 609-641-3100; FAX 609-646-0516. **Owner(s):** Gannett Company, Inc., 1100 Wilson Blvd., Arlington, VA 22340. TEL 703-284-6000; adv.; pub. size: broadsheet; circ. 3,500(paid).

ISSN 0746-7036
EGG HARBOR NEWS. 1911. Thu. $.50/newsstand; $21/yr. 12th St. & West End Ave., Hammonton, NJ 08037. TEL 609-561-2300; FAX 609-567-2249. **Owner(s):** Gannett Company, Inc., 1100 Wilson Blvd., Arlington, VA 22340. TEL 703-284-6000; adv.; pub. size: broadsheet; circ. 2,000(paid).

HAMMONTON NEWS. 1858. Thu. $.50 newsstand; $21/yr. 12th St. & West End Ave., Hammonton, NJ 08037. TEL 609-561-2300; FAX 609-646-0561. **Owner(s):** Gannett Company, Inc., 1100 Wilson Blvd., Arlington, VA 22340. TEL 703-284-6000; Pub. Ron Jacovini; adv.; photos; pub. size: broadsheet; circ. 6,500(paid).

MAINLAND JOURNAL. 1894. Thu. $21/yr. 12th St. & West End Ave., Hammonton, NJ 08037. TEL 609-641-3100; FAX 609-646-0561. **Owner(s):** Gannett Company, Inc., 1100 Wilson Blvd., Arlington, VA 22340. TEL 703-284-6000; Pub. Ron Jacovini; adv. contact: Lee Goeke. pub. size: broadsheet; circ. 5,000(paid).
Formerly: Pleasantville Mainland Journal.

HAWTHORNE

HAWTHORNE PRESS. 1924. Thu. $.25 newsstand; $15/yr. local; $18/yr. in state; $22/yr. out of state. 463 Lafayette Ave., Hawthorne, NJ 07507-0001. TEL 201-427-3330. **Owner(s):** William R. Missonellie, P.O. Box 1, Hawthorne, NJ 07507-0001. TEL 201-427-3330; Ed. Linda Missonellie; Pub. William R. Missonellie; adv.; photos; bk.rev.; pub. size: tabloid; circ. 5,600(paid).

HIGHTSTOWN

MESSENGER-PRESS. 1903. Thu. $.60 newsstand; $16/6 mos. in cy.; $20/yr. in cy. 510 Rte. 130, S., Hightstown, NJ 08520. TEL 609-448-2100; FAX 609-448-8044. **Owner(s):** Princeton Packet, Inc., 300 Witherspoon St., Princeton, NJ 08540; Ed. Frank Herrick; Pub. James Kilgore; adv. contact: Debra Richford. pub. size: broadsheet; circ. 5,000(paid).

HOBOKEN

HOBOKEN REPORTER. 1983. Sun. free newsstand; $50/yr. 1400 Washington St., Hoboken, NJ 07030. TEL 201-798-7800; FAX 201-798-0018. **Owner(s):** Joseph Barry, P.O. Box 3069, Hoboken, NJ 07030. TEL 201-798-7800; Ed. Michael Richardson; Pub. Joseph Barry; adv. contact: David Unger. bk.rev.; pub. size: tabloid; circ. 6,600(controlled).

HUDSON CURRENT. Thu. free; $25/6 mos.; $50/yr. 1400 Washington St., Hoboken, NJ 07030. TEL 201-798-7800; FAX 201-798-0018. **Owner(s):** Joseph Barry, 1400 Washington St., Hoboken, NJ 07030. TEL 201-798-7800; Ed. Michael Richardson; Pub. Joseph Barry; adv. contact: David S. Unger. photos; bk.rev.; pub. size: tabloid; circ. 6,500(free & paid).

JERSEY CITY REPORTER. Sat. free; $50/yr. 1400 Washington St., Hoboken, NJ 07030. TEL 201-798-7800; FAX 201-798-0018. **Owner(s):** Joseph Barry, 1400 Washington St., Hoboken, NJ 07030. TEL 201-798-7800; Ed. Michael Richardson; Pub. Joseph Barry; adv. contact: David Unger. photos; pub. size: tabloid.

WEEKLY NEWSPAPERS

US
NORTH BERGEN REPORTER. 1985. Fri. free; $15/3 mos.; $25/6 mos; $50/yr. 1400 Washington St., Hoboken, NJ 07030. TEL 201-798-7800; FAX 201-798-0018. **Owner(s):** Joseph Barry, 1400 Washington St., Hoboken, NJ 07030. TEL 201-798-7800; Ed. Michael Richardson; Pub. Joseph Barry; adv. contact: David Unger. pub. size: tabloid; circ. 120,000(controlled).

US
SECAUCUS REPORTER. 1983. Fri. free; $25/6 mos.; $50/yr. 1400 Washington St., Hoboken, NJ 07030. TEL 201-798-7800; FAX 201-798-0018. **Owner(s):** Joseph Barry, 1400 Washington St., Hoboken, NJ 07030. TEL 201-798-7800; Ed. Michael Richardson; Pub. Joseph Barry; adv. contact: David S. Unger. pub. size: tabloid.

US
UNION CITY REPORTER. Fri. free; $50/yr. 1400 Washington St., Hoboken, NJ 07030. TEL 201-798-7800; FAX 201-798-0018. **Owner(s):** Joseph Barry, 1400 Washington St., Hoboken, NJ 07030. TEL 201-798-7800; Ed. Michael Richardson; Pub. Joseph Barry; adv. contact: David Unger. photos; pub. size: tabloid.

US
WEEHAWKEN REPORTER. 1986. Sat. free newsstand; $50/yr. 1400 Washington St., Hoboken, NJ 07030. TEL 201-798-7800; FAX 201-798-0018. **Owner(s):** Joseph Barry, 1321 Washington St., Hoboken, NJ 07030. TEL 201-798-7800; Ed. Michael Richardson; Pub. Joseph Barry; adv. contact: David Unger. pub. size: tabloid; circ. 6,600(free & paid).

US
WEST NEW YORK REPORTER. Fri. free; $50/yr. 1400 Washington Ave., Hoboken, NJ 07030. TEL 201-798-7800; FAX 201-798-0018. **Owner(s):** Joseph Barry, 1400 Washington St., Hoboken, NJ 07030. TEL 201-798-7800; Ed. Michael Richardson; Pub. Joseph Barry; adv. contact: David Unger. photos; pub. size: tabloid.

HOPEWELL
US
BEACON, THE. 1845. Thu. $.60 newsstand; $26/yr. in state; $49/yr. out of state; $21/yr. senior citizens. P.O. Box 8, Hopewell, NJ 08525. TEL 609-466-1190; FAX 609-466-2123. **Owner(s):** Princeton Packet, Inc., 300 Witherspoon St., Princeton, NJ 08540; Ed. Mae Rhine; Pub. James Kilgore; adv. contact: Debra Richford. pub. size: broadsheet; circ. 3,500(paid).
Formerly: The Beacon-Record.

KEARNY
US
OBSERVER, THE. 1887. Wed. free; $30/yr. 531 Kearny Ave., Kearny, NJ 07032. TEL 201-991-1600; FAX 201-991-8941. **Owner(s):** Observer, The, 531 Kearny Ave., Kearny, NJ 07032. TEL 201-991-1600; FAX 201-991-8941; Pub. Mary Tortoreti; adv. contact: Antoinette Zuest. photos; pub. size: broadsheet; circ. 25,000(free & paid).
Formerly: Kearny Observer.

LAKEHURST
US
ADVANCE NEWS. 1968. Wed. $.15 newsstand; $7.50/yr.; $15/2 yrs.; $22.50/3 yrs. 2048 Rte. 37, Lakehurst, NJ 08733. TEL 908-657-8936; FAX 908-657-2970. **Owner(s):** Advance Nickel Dime News, 2048 Rte. 37, Lakehurst, NJ 08733. TEL 908-657-8936; Pub. Jerri T. Varelli; adv. contact: Rose Mauder. photos; bk.rev.; pub. size: tabloid; circ. 25,000(paid).

LEBANON
US
HUNTERDON REVIEW. 1868. Wed. $.50 newsstand; $20/yr. local. 1128 Rte. 31 N., Lebanon, NJ 08833. TEL 908-735-4081; FAX 908-735-2945. **Owner(s):** Recorder Publishing Co., 17-19 Morristown Rd., Bernardsville, NJ 07924. TEL 201-766-3900; Ed. Richard Hartten; Pub. Cortlandt Parker; adv. contact: Joyce Flynn. pub. size: broadsheet; circ. 4,900(paid).

LEDGEWOOD
US
WEST MORRIS STAR-JOURNAL. 1962. Wed. $.35 newsstand; $21/yr. in cy.; $24/yr. out of cy.; $28/yr. out of state. 50 Main St., Ledgewood, NJ 07852. TEL 201-584-7176; FAX 201-584-7403. **Owner(s):** North Jersey Newspapers Co., 988 Main Ave., Passaic, NJ 07005. TEL 201-362-3000; FAX 201-365-5887; Ed. Enid Sharf; Pub. Rosemarie Maio; adv.; pub. size: broadsheet; circ. 6,000(paid).

LIVINGSTON
US
WEST ESSEX TRIBUNE. 1929. Thu. $.40 newsstand; $18/yr. in cy.; $22/yr. out of cy.; $24/yr. out of state. 495 S. Livingston Ave., Livingston, NJ 07039-0065. TEL 201-992-1771; FAX 201-992-7015. **Owner(s):** E. Christopher Cone, 18 Midway Dr., Livingston, NJ 07039. TEL 201-992-1771; FAX 201-992-7015; Ed. Nancy B. Dinar; Pub. E. Christopher Cone; adv. contact: Donna Cota. adv.: $9.75/SAU. pub. size: broadsheet; circ. 8,000(paid).

MADISON
US
CHATHAM COURIER. 1930. Thu. $.50 newsstand; $22/yr. in cy.; $25/yr. out of cy.; $30/yr. out of state; $20/college yr. 155 Main St., Madison, NJ 07940. TEL 201-377-2000; FAX 201-377-7721. **Owner(s):** Parker Publishing Co., 17-19 Morristown Rd., Bernardsville, NJ 07924. TEL 908-766-3900; Ed. Gene Robbins; Pub. Cortlandt Parker; adv. contact: Carmel Clancy. photos; pub. size: standard; circ. 3,400(paid).

US
FLORHAM PARK EAGLE. 1882. Thu. $.50 newsstand; $22/yr. in cy.; $30/yr. out of cy.; $20/college yr. students. 155 Main St., Madison, NJ 07940. TEL 201-377-2000; FAX 201-377-7721. **Owner(s):** Recorder Publishing Co., 17-19 Morristown Rd., Bernardsville, NJ 07924. TEL 908-766-3900; Ed. Gene Robbins; Pub. Cortlandt Parker; adv. contact: Carmel Clancy. photos; pub. size: broadsheet; circ. 1,892(paid).
Formerly: Florham Park Eagle & Community News.

US
HANOVER EAGLE & REGIONAL NEWS. 1956. Thu. $.50 newsstand; $18/yr. in cy.; $25/yr. out of cy.; $30/yr. out of state. 155 Main St., Madison, NJ 07940. TEL 201-377-2000; FAX 201-377-7721. **Owner(s):** Recorder Publishing Co., 17-19 Morristown Rd., Bernardsville, NJ 07924. TEL 908-766-3900; Ed. Gene Robbins; Pub. Cortlandt Parker; adv. contact: Carmel Clancy. pub. size: tabloid; circ. 4,500(paid).

US
MADISON EAGLE. 1880. Thu. $.50 newsstand; $22/yr. in cy.; $25/yr. out of cy.; $30/yr. out of state; $20/college yr. 155 Main St., Madison, NJ 07940. TEL 201-377-2000; FAX 201-377-7721. **Owner(s):** Recorder Publishing Co., 17-19 Morristown Rd., Bernardsville, NJ 07924. TEL 908-766-3900; Ed. Gene Robbins; Pub. Cortlandt Parker; adv. contact: Carmel Clancy. photos; pub. size: broadsheet; circ. 3,315(paid).

US
MORRIS NEWS BEE. 1946. Thu. $.50 newsstand; $18/yr. in cy.; $25/yr. out of cy.; $30/yr. out of state. 155 Main St., Madison, NJ 07940. TEL 201-377-2000; FAX 201-377-7721. **Owner(s):** Recorder Publishing Co., 17-19 Morristown Rd., Bernardsville, NJ 07924. TEL 908-766-3900; Ed. Gene Robbins; Pub. Cortlandt Parker; adv. contact: Carmel Clancy. pub. size: broadsheet; circ. 4,500(paid).

MANAHAWKIN
US
BEACH HAVEN TIMES. 1923. Wed. $24/yr. in cy.; $28/yr. out of cy. 345 E. Bay Ave., Manahawkin, NJ 08050. TEL 609-597-3211; FAX 609-597-8169. **Owner(s):** Goodson Newspaper Group, 1009 Lenox Dr., Lawrenceville, NJ 08648. TEL 609-895-2600; Ed. Jan Zollinger; Pub. J. Peter Lindquist; adv. contact: Tim Wallace. pub. size: broadsheet; circ. 7,819(paid).

US
BEACON, THE. 1889. Thu. $24/yr. in cy.; $28/yr. out of cy. 345 E. Bay Ave., Manahawkin, NJ 08050. TEL 609-597-3211; FAX 609-597-8169. **Owner(s):** Goodson Newspaper Group, 1009 Lenox Dr., Lawrenceville, NJ 08648. TEL 609-895-2600; Ed. Jan Zollinger; Pub. J. Peter Lindquist; adv. contact: Tim Wallace. photos; pub. size: broadsheet; circ. 13,000(controlled).

MAPLE SHADE
US
MAPLE SHADE PROGRESS. 1918. Thu. $.35 newsstand; $15/yr. 306 E. Main St., Maple Shade, NJ 08052. TEL 609-779-7788. **Owner(s):** Frank E. Gerkens, 306 E. Main St., Maple Shade, NJ 08502. TEL 609-779-7788; Ed. Frank E. Gerkens; Pub. Frank E. Gerkens; pub. size: broadsheet; circ. 10,000(free & paid).

US
MT. LAUREL PROGRESS PRESS. Thu. $.35 newsstand; $12/yr. 306 E. Main St., Maple Shade, NJ 08052. TEL 609-779-7788. **Owner(s):** Frank E. Gerkens, 306 E. Main St., Maple Shade, NJ 08502. TEL 609-779-7788; Ed. Frank E. Gerkens; Pub. Frank E. Gerkens; pub. size: broadsheet; circ. 5,000(free & paid).

MAPLEWOOD

NEWS-RECORD OF MAPLEWOOD & SOUTH ORANGE. 1886. Thu. $22/yr. in cy.; $32/yr. out of cy.; $17/yr. senior citizens. 463 Valley St., Maplewood, NJ 07040. TEL 973-763-0700; FAX 973-763-2557. **Owner(s):** Worrall Community Newspapers, Inc., 1291 Stuyvesant Ave., Union, NJ 07083. TEL 908-686-7700; Ed. Tom Caravan; Pub. David Worrall; adv. contact: Peter Worrall. pub. size: broadsheet; circ. 6,745(paid).

VAILSBURG LEADER. 1950. Thu. $.50 newsstand; $22/yr. 463 Valley St., Maplewood, NJ 07040. TEL 908-686-7700; FAX 908-763-2557. **Owner(s):** Worrall Community Newspapers, Inc., 1291 Stuyvesant Ave., Union, NJ 07083. TEL 908-686-7700; Ed. Yolanda McBride; Pub. David Worrall; adv. contact: Peter Worrall. pub. size: standard; circ. 500(paid).

MAYWOOD

OUR TOWN. ISSN 0048-2404. 1948. Thu. $.35 newsstand; $12/yr.; $22/2 yrs. 58 W. Pleasant Ave., Maywood, NJ 07607. TEL 201-843-5700. **Owner(s):** Jim & Kathy Panos, 680 Jersey Ave., Maywood, NJ 07607; Ed. Katherine J. Panos. adv.; pub. size: tabloid; circ. 3,500(free & paid).

MIDDLETOWN

MIDDLETOWN COURIER. 1955. Thu. $.40 newsstand; $13/yr. in state; $16/yr. out of state. 320 Kings Hwy., E., Middletown, NJ 07748. TEL 908-957-0070; FAX 908-957-0143. **Owner(s):** Bayshore Press, Inc., 320 Kings Hwy., E., Middletown, NJ 07748. TEL 201-957-0070; Ed. Alfred F. Muzer, Jr.; Pub. John Famulary; adv.; photos; bk.rev.; pub. size: tabloid; circ. 11,000(paid).

MILLBURN

MILLBURN & SHORT HILLS ITEM. 1888. Thu. $.50 newsstand; $18/yr. 100 Millburn Ave., Millburn, NJ 07041. TEL 201-376-1200; FAX 201-376-8556. **Owner(s):** BAL Communications, Inc., 100 Millburn Ave., Millburn, NJ 07041. TEL 201-376-1200; FAX 201-376-8550; Ed. Carter J. Bennett; Pub. Barbara A. Lewis; adv. contact: Tracy DuPuis. adv.: $10.88/SAU. pub. size: broadsheet; circ. 5,000(paid).

MONTCLAIR

MONTCLAIR TIMES, THE. 1877. Thu. $.50 newsstand; $18/yr. 114 Valley Rd., Montclair, NJ 07042. TEL 201-746-1100; FAX 201-746-0995. **Owner(s):** Montgrove Publications, 114 Valley Rd., Montclair, NJ 07042. TEL 201-746-1100; FAX 201-746-8131; Ed. Lucinda Smith; Pub. Barbara A. Lewis; adv. contact: Sara Singleton. photos; pub. size: broadsheet; circ. 12,003(paid).

MORGANVILLE

INDEPENDENT, THE. 1970. Wed. free deliv. 25 Kilmer Dr., Ste. 109, Morganville, NJ 07751-1561. TEL 908-254-7000; FAX 908-972-6746. **Owner(s):** Greater Media, Inc., 2 Kennedy Blvd., East Brunswick, NJ 08816. TEL 908-247-6161; Ed. Marilyn Duff; Pub. Kevin Wittman; adv.; pub. size: tabloid; circ. 34,000(free). **Wire Service(s):** AP, Newsfinder.

NEWS TRANSCRIPT. 1888. Wed. $.40 newsstand; $32/yr. 25 Kilmer Dr., Ste. 109, Morganville, NJ 07751. TEL 908-972-6740; FAX 908-972-6746. **Owner(s):** Greater Media, Inc., 2 Kennedy Blvd., East Brunswick, NJ 07728. TEL 908-247-6161; Ed. Mark Rosman; Pub. Kevin Wittman; adv. contact: Elaine Clisham. photos; pub. size: tabloid; circ. 40,000.

MT. HOLLY

GAZETTE, THE. 1986. Thu. $.35 newsstand; $15/yr. 69 High St., Mt. Holly, NJ 08060. TEL 609-261-7341; FAX 609-261-7392. **Owner(s):** Robert Reichenbach, 69 High St., Mt. Holly, NJ 08060. TEL 609-261-7341; FAX 609-261-7392; Ed. Paul Fowler; Pub. Robert Reichenbach; adv. contact: Elda Goss. adv.: $7/SAU. photos; pub. size: tabloid; circ. 3,000(paid).

MT. LAUREL

NEWS WEEKLY. 1966. Thu. $.50 newsstand; $14/yr. in cy.; $20/yr. out of cy. 155 Gaither Dr., Mt. Laurel, NJ 08054. TEL 609-231-7600; FAX 609-231-4333. **Owner(s):** Intercounty Newspaper Group, 6220 Ridge Ave., Philadelphia, PA 19128. TEL 215-483-7300; Ed. Sandra McGuire; Pub. Fred W. Donaldson; adv. contact: John Brookover. photos; bk.rev.; pub. size: tabloid; circ. 8,600(paid).

NETCONG

NETCONG NEWS-LEADER. Wed. $.35 newsstand; $21/yr. P.O. Box 637, Netcong, NJ 07857. TEL 201-347-0300; FAX 201-691-1183. **Owner(s):** North Jersey Newspapers Co., 988 Main Ave., Passaic, NJ 07005. TEL 201-365-3000; FAX 201-365-5887; Ed. Lynn Apolinaro; Pub. Rosemarie Maio; pub. size: broadsheet; circ. 3,000(paid).

NEW PROVIDENCE

DISPATCH, THE. 1950. Sat. $.50 newsstand; $20/yr. 80 South St., New Providence, NJ 07974. TEL 908-464-1025; FAX 908-464-9085. **Owner(s):** North Jersey Newspapers Co., 988 Main Ave., Passaic, NJ 07055. TEL 201-365-3000; FAX 201-365-5887; Ed. Christopher Moore; Pub. Michael Kelly; pub. size: broadsheet; circ. 3,000(paid).

INDEPENDENT PRESS. 1965. Wed. free home deliv.; $.50 newsstand; $60/yr. mailed. 80 South St., New Providence, NJ 07974. TEL 908-464-1025; FAX 908-464-9085. **Owner(s):** North Jersey Newspapers Co., 988 Main Ave., Passaic, NJ 07005. TEL 201-365-3000; FAX 201-365-5887; Ed. Christopher Moore; Pub. Michael J. Kelly; adv. contact: Brad Tomilson. adv.: $19.50/SAU. photos; bk.rev.; pub. size: broadsheet; circ. 35,200(free & paid).

NUTLEY

BELLEVILLE TIMES NEWS. 1909. Thu. $.50 newsstand; $16/yr. in state; $18/yr. out of state. 800 Bloomfield Ave., Nutley, NJ 07110. TEL 201-759-3200; FAX 201-667-3904. **Owner(s):** Orechio Publications, 155A Washington Ave., Belleville, NJ 07109. TEL 201-759-3200; Ed. Howard Klausner; Pub. Frank Orechio; pub. size: standard; circ. 7,500(paid).

BLOOMFIELD LIFE. 1980. Thu. $.50 newsstand; $16/yr.; $8/yr. senior citizens. 800 Bloomfield Ave., Nutley, NJ 07110. TEL 201-759-3200; FAX 201-667-3904. **Owner(s):** Orechio Publications, 800 Bloomfield Ave., Nutley, NJ 07110. TEL 201-759-3200; Ed. Steve Galvacky; Pub. Frank A. Orechio; adv. contact: Maria Paladino. pub. size: broadsheet; circ. 5,000(paid).

NUTLEY SUN, THE. 1895. Thu. $.50 newsstand; $16/yr. in state mailed; $18/yr. out of state; $8/yr. in state senior citizens. 800 Bloomfield Ave., Nutley, NJ 07110. TEL 201-759-3200; FAX 201-667-3904. **Owner(s):** Orechio Publications, 800 Bloomfield Ave., Nutley, NJ 07110. TEL 201-759-3200; Ed. James Zocolli; Pub. Frank A. Orechio; adv. contact: Celeste Federico. pub. size: broadsheet; circ. 8,000(paid).

OCEAN CITY

SENTINEL-LEDGER, THE. 1881. Thu. $.50 newsstand; $25/yr. in cy.; $29/yr. out of cy.; $29/yr. out of state. 112 E. Eighth St., Ocean City, NJ 08226-0238. TEL 609-399-5411; FAX 609-399-0416; E-mail: rcooper@acy.digex.net; URL: http://www.acy.digex.net. **Owner(s):** American Publishing Co., 606 N. Van Buren, Marion, IL 62959. TEL 618-993-1711; Ed. John H. Andrus, II; Pub. Ralph J. Cooper; adv. contact: Barbara Bradley. photos; bk.rev.; pub. size: broadsheet; circ. 10,000(paid).

ORANGE

EAST ORANGE RECORD. 1899. Thu. $22/yr. in cy.; $32/yr. out of cy.; $17/yr. senior citizens. 170 Scotland Rd., Orange, NJ 07050. TEL 973-674-8000; FAX 973-674-2038. **Owner(s):** Worrall Community Newspapers, Inc., 1291 Stuyvesant Ave., Union, NJ 07083. TEL 908-686-7700; Ed. Anthony Puglisi; Pub. David Worrall; adv. contact: Peter Worrall. pub. size: broadsheet; circ. 2,531(paid).

WEEKLY NEWSPAPERS

ORANGE

US

ORANGE TRANSCRIPT. 1898. Thu. $22/yr. in cy.; $22/yr. out of cy.; $17/yr. senior citizens. 170 Scotland Rd., Orange, NJ 07050. TEL 903-674-8000; FAX 903-674-2038. **Owner(s):** Worrall Community Newspapers, Inc., P.O. Box 3109, Union, NJ 07083. TEL 908-686-7700; Ed. Anthony Puglisi; Pub. David Worrall; adv. contact: Peter Worrall. pub. size: broadsheet; circ. 2,500(paid).

US

WEST ORANGE CHRONICLE. 1931. Thu. $22/yr. in cy.; $22/yr. out of cy.; $17/yr. senior citizens. 170 Scotland Rd., Orange, NJ 07050. TEL 201-674-8000; FAX 201-674-2038. **Owner(s):** Worrall Community Newspapers, Inc., P.O. Box 3109, Union, NJ 07083. TEL 908-686-7700; Ed. Tom Caravan; Pub. David Worrall; adv. contact: Peter Worrall. pub. size: broadsheet; circ. 6,000(paid).

PALISADES PARK

US

BERGEN NEWS, THE. 1950. Wed. $.50 newsstand; $32/yr. in state; $42/yr. out of state. 111 Grand Ave., Palisades Park, NJ 07650. TEL 201-947-5000; FAX 201-947-6968. **Owner(s):** News Publishing Group, 111 Grand Ave., Palisades Park, NJ 07650. TEL 201-947-5000; FAX 201-947-6968; Ed. Eleanor Marra; Pub. William Cohen; adv.; photos; pub. size: tabloid; circ. 38,962(controlled).
Formerly: Bergen News-Palisades, South & Valley Editions.

US

PRESS JOURNAL, THE. 1874. Thu. $.50 newsstand; $32/yr. in cy.; $42/yr. out of cy. 111 Grand Ave., Palisades Park, NJ 07650. TEL 201-871-6900; FAX 201-947-6968. **Owner(s):** News Publishing Group, 111 Grand Ave., Palisades Park, NJ 07650. TEL 201-947-5000; FAX 201-947-0968; Ed. Eleanor Marra; Pub. Phylis Cohen; adv.; photos; pub. size: broadsheet; circ. 10,987(controlled & paid).
Formerly: Press Journal-North & South Editions.

US

RAMSEY-MAHWAH REPORTER. 1976. Fri. $.50 newsstand; $30/yr. in town; $42/yr. out of town. 111 Grand Ave., Palisades Park, NJ 07650. TEL 800-640-1896; FAX 201-947-5055. **Owner(s):** News Publishing Group, 111 Grand Ave., Palisades Park, NJ 07650. TEL 201-947-5000; Ed. Eleanor Marra; Pub. Phyllis Cohen; adv. contact: Jill Cohen. photos; pub. size: tabloid; circ. 4,468(paid).

US

SUN-BULLETIN, THE. 1893. Fri. $.50 newsstand; $32/yr. in state; $42/yr. out of state. 111 Grand Ave., Palisades Park, NJ 07650. TEL 201-947-5000; FAX 201-947-6968. **Owner(s):** News Publishing Group, 111 Grand Ave., Palisades Park, NJ 07650. TEL 201-947-5000; FAX 201-947-6968; Ed. Eleanor Marra; Pub. Phyllis Cohen; adv. contact: Lesley Ann Cohen. photos; pub. size: tabloid; circ. 18,454(paid).
Formerly: Sun-Bulletin-East & Central Editions.

PARAMUS

US

POST REVIEW, THE. s-w.: Sun. & Thu. $.50 newsstand; $39/yr. in cy. includes The Review. 50 Eisenhower Dr., Paramus, NJ 07652. TEL 201-843-0500; FAX 201-368-0706. **Owner(s):** North Jersey Newspapers Co., 988 Main Ave., Passaic, NJ 07055. TEL 201-365-3000; FAX 201-365-5887; Ed. Ellen Walsh. adv. contact: Sharon Puser. pub. size: broadsheet; circ. Sun. 10,000(paid).
Formerly: Sunday Post.

US

REVIEW, THE. 1920. Thu. $.35 newsstand; $15.60/yr.; $39/yr. includes Sunday Post. 50 Eisenhower Dr., Paramus, NJ 07652. TEL 201-843-0500; FAX 201-843-2388. **Owner(s):** North Jersey Newspapers Co., 988 Main Ave., Passaic, NJ 07055. TEL 201-365-3000; Ed. Christina Rossi; Pub. Sherwood L. Spitz; adv. contact: Brian Winterberg. pub. size: tabloid; circ. 10,000(paid).

US

RIDGEWOOD NEWS. 1889. s-w.: Sun. & Thu. $.35/Thu.; $.50/Sun.; $15.60/yr. Thu. only; $23.40/yr. Sun. only; $39/yr. both editions. 50 Eisenhower Dr., Paramus, NJ 07652. TEL 201-843-0500; FAX 201-368-0706. **Owner(s):** North Jersey Newspapers Co., 988 Main Ave., Passaic, NJ 07055. TEL 201-365-3000; Ed. Christina Rossi; Pub. Sherwood L. Spitz; adv. contact: Brian Winterberg. pub. size: broadsheet; circ. 8,900(paid); Sun. 12,000(paid).
Formerly: Sunday News.

US

SUBURBAN TOWN NEWS. 1952. Wed. free. 50 Eisenhower Dr., Paramus, NJ 07652. TEL 201-368-0100; FAX 201-368-0706. **Owner(s):** North Jersey Newspapers Co., 988 Main Ave., Passaic, NJ 07055. TEL 201-365-3000; FAX 201-365-5887; Ed. Paul Rabin; Pub. S. Spitz; adv.; pub. size: tabloid; circ. 114,000(free). **Wire Service(s):** SNS.

PENNINGTON

US ISSN 0746-1771

LAWRENCE LEDGER. 1969. Thu. $.60 newsstand; $33/yr. 53 Pennington-Hopewell Rd., Pennington, NJ 08534. TEL 609-466-8650; FAX 609-466-2123. **Owner(s):** Princeton Packet, Inc., 300 Witherspoon, P.O. Box 350, Princeton, NJ 08540. TEL 609-924-3244; Ed. Tom Ledder. pub. size: standard; circ. 3,100(paid).

PHILLIPSBURG

US

PHILLIPSBURG FREE PRESS. 1961. Thu. $.40 newsstand; $18/yr. in NJ & PA; $23/yr. elsewhere. 198 Chamber St., Phillipsburg, NJ 08865. TEL 908-859-4444; FAX 908-859-3084. **Owner(s):** Montclair Newspapers, Inc., Montclair, NJ; Ed. Michael C. O'Connor; Pub. Rosemary Maio; adv.; pub. size: tabloid; circ. 3,100(paid).

POINT PLEASANT BEACH

US

LEADER, THE. 1916. Thu. $.50 newsstand; $17.50/yr. 707 Arnold Ave., Point Pleasant Beach, NJ 08742. TEL 908-899-1000; FAX 908-899-2135. **Owner(s):** Rockfleet Media, Inc., P.O. Box 1771, Point Pleasant Beach, NJ 08742. TEL 908-899-1000; FAX 908-899-2135; Ed. Jeannie Tomaselli. pub. size: broadsheet; circ. 8,500(paid).

US ISSN 1053-4555

REVIEW, THE. Thu. $.50 newsstand; $17.50/yr. 707 Arnold Ave., Point Pleasant Beach, NJ 08742. TEL 908-899-1000; FAX 908-899-2135. **Owner(s):** Rockfleet Media, Inc., P.O. Box 1771, Point Pleasant Beach, NJ 08742. TEL 908-899-1000; FAX 908-899-2135; Ed. James Purcell; Pub. Sheila O'Malley; adv.; pub. size: broadsheet; circ. 8,000(paid).

PRINCETON

US

FRANKLIN NEWS-RECORD. Fri. free; $27/yr. out of area. 300 Witherspoon St., Princeton, NJ 08542. TEL 609-924-3244; FAX 609-924-3842. **Owner(s):** Princeton Packet, Inc., 300 Witherspoon St., Princeton, NJ 08540. TEL 609-924-3244; adv. contact: Allison Spinella. pub. size: standard; circ. 4,900(free & paid).

US

PRINCETON PACKET, THE. 1786. s-w.: Tue. & Fri. $.60 newsstand; $47/yr. 300 Witherspoon St., Princeton, NJ 08542. TEL 609-924-3244; FAX 609-921-2714. **Owner(s):** Princeton Packet, Inc., 300 Witherspoon St., P.O. Box 350, Princeton, NJ 08542. TEL 609-924-3244; Ed. Randy Bergmann. adv.; photos; bk.rev.; pub. size: broadsheet; circ. 14,420(paid).

US ISSN 0191-7056

TOWN TOPICS. 1946. Wed. $.50 newsstand; $20/yr. local; $25/yr. elsewhere. 4 Mercer St., Princeton, NJ 08540. TEL 609-924-2200. **Owner(s):** Donald C. Stuart, III, 4 Mercer St., Princeton, NJ 08540; Ed. Donald C. Stuart, III. adv. contact: Linda Sproehnle. pub. size: tabloid; circ. 14,435(free & paid).

RAHWAY

US

CLARK PATRIOT. 1965. Thu. $.25 newsstand; $15/yr.; in cy.; $20/yr. out of cy. 1544 Irving St., Ste. 201, Rahway, NJ 07065. TEL 908-574-1200; FAX 908-388-4143. **Owner(s):** Shore News, P.O. Box 1061, Rahway, NJ 07065. TEL 908-574-1200; Ed. Patty Rinsky; Pub. Ellen Vigilante; adv.; photos; pub. size: broadsheet; circ. 1,300(free & paid).

US

RAHWAY NEWS-RECORD. 1822. Thu. $.25 newsstand; $15/yr.; in cy.; $20/yr. out of cy. 1544 Irving St., Ste. 201, Rahway, NJ 07065. TEL 908-574-1200; FAX 908-388-4143. **Owner(s):** Shore News, P.O. Box 1061, Rahway, NJ 07065. TEL 908-574-1200; Ed. Patty Rinsky; Pub. Ellen Vigilante; adv.; photos; pub. size: broadsheet; circ. 1,300(paid).

RAMSEY
US
HOME & STORE NEWS. 1960. Wed. free. 6A E. Main St., Ramsey, NJ 07446-0329. TEL 201-327-1212; FAX 201-327-3684. **Owner(s):** Arthur Aldrich, P.O. Box 329, Ramsey, NJ 07446-0329. TEL 201-327-1212; FAX 201-327-3684; Ed. Arthur Aldrich; Pub. Arthur Aldrich; adv. contact: Jo Bosakowski. photos; pub. size: tabloid; circ. 30,000(free).

RIO GRANDE
US
CAPE MAY HERALD DISPATCH. 1984. Wed. $20/yr. 1508 Rte. 47, S., Rio Grande, NJ 08242. TEL 609-886-8600; FAX 609-886-1879. **Owner(s):** Seawave Corp., P.O. Box 400, Rio Grande, NJ 08242. TEL 609-886-8600; FAX 609-886-1879; Ed. Joseph R. Zelnik; Pub. Arthur R. Hall; adv. contact: Beth Huber. photos; bk.rev.; pub. size: tabloid; circ. 29,626(free & paid).

US
LOWER TOWNSHIP LANTERN. 1979. Wed. free newsstand; $20/yr. 1508 Rte. 47, S., Rio Grande, NJ 08242. TEL 609-886-8600; FAX 609-886-1879. **Owner(s):** Seawave Corp., P.O. Box 400, Rio Grande, NJ 08242. TEL 609-886-8600; Ed. Joseph R. Zelnik; Pub. Arthur R. Hall; adv. contact: Beth Huber. photos; bk.rev.; pub. size: tabloid; circ. 29,600(free & paid).

RUTHERFORD
US
SOUTH BERGENITE. 1970. Wed. free. 71 Union Ave., Rutherford, NJ 07070. TEL 201-933-1166; FAX 201-933-5496. **Owner(s):** North Jersey Newspapers Co., 988 Main Ave., Passaic, NJ 07005. TEL 201-365-3000; FAX 201-365-5887; Ed. Edward Kensik; Pub. Sherwood Spitz; adv. contact: Sharon Puser. pub. size: tabloid; circ. 36,178(free).

SALEM
US
SALEM COUNTY RECORD. 1819. Fri. free. 93 Fifth St., Salem, NJ 08079. TEL 609-935-1500; FAX 609-845-3139. **Owner(s):** Media News Group, 4888 Loop Central Dr., Ste. 525, Houston, TX 77081. TEL 713-295-3800; Ed. Matt Gray; Pub. Wayne Studer; adv. contact: Ceil Smith. pub. size: broadsheet; circ. 7,000(free).

SECAUCUS
US
SECAUCUS HOME NEWS. 1910. Thu. $.35 newsstand; $13/yr. in cy.; $15/yr. in state; $16/yr. out of state. 766 Irving Pl., Secaucus, NJ 07094. TEL 201-867-2071; FAX 201-865-3806. **Owner(s):** Gretchen Henkel, 766 Irving Pl., Secaucus, NJ 07094. TEL 201-867-2071; Ed. Gretchen Henkel; Pub. Gretchen Henkel; adv. contact: Debbie Zapoluch. pub. size: tabloid; circ. 5,500(paid).

SOMERSET
US
SOMERSET SPECTATOR. 1969. Thu. $.35 newsstand; $16.95/yr. 102 Walnut Ave., Somerset, NJ 08873-5717. TEL 908-247-8700; FAX 908-247-3707. **Owner(s):** Somerset Spectator, Inc., P.O. Box 5717, Somerset, NJ 08875. TEL 908-247-8700; FAX 908-247-3707; Pub. Ed Briencke; adv. contact: Ed Briencke. pub. size: standard; circ. 6,300(paid).

SOMERVILLE
US
BOUND BROOK CHRONICLE. 1866. Thu. $.50 newsstand; $25/yr. in cy.; $28/yr. out of cy. 44 Veterans Memorial Dr., E., Somerville, NJ 08876. TEL 908-722-3000; FAX 908-231-1385. **Owner(s):** Forbes Newspapers, Inc., P.O. Box 95, Bedminster, NJ 07921; Ed. Michael Deaks; Pub. Louis Barsony; adv. contact: Rick Kestenbaum. pub. size: broadsheet; circ. 2,700(paid).

US
HILLSBOROUGH BEACON. 1956. Thu. $32/yr. 307 Omni Dr., Somerville, NJ 08876. TEL 908-359-0850; FAX 908-359-3930. **Owner(s):** Princeton Packet, Inc., 300 Witherspoon, Princeton, NJ 08540. TEL 609-924-3244; Ed. John Patten. adv.; bk.rev.; pub. size: broadsheet; circ. 4,000(paid).

US ISSN 1058-6857
MANVILLE NEWS. 1945. Thu. $.60 newsstand; $34/yr. 307 Omni Dr., Somerville, NJ 08876. TEL 908-359-3930; FAX 908-359-3936. **Owner(s):** Princeton Packet, Inc., 300 Witherspoon St., Princeton, NJ 08540. TEL 609-924-3244; FAX 609-921-2714; Ed. John Patten. adv.; pub. size: broadsheet; circ. 1,400(paid).

US
MIDDLESEX-DUNELLEN CHRONICLE. 1956. Thu. $.50 newsstand; $25/yr. 44 Veterans Memorial Dr., E., Somerville, NJ 08876. TEL 908-722-3000; FAX 908-526-2509. **Owner(s):** North Jersey Newspapers, P.O. Box 699, Somerville, NJ 08876; Pub. Louis Barsony; adv. contact: Lena Moore. pub. size: broadsheet; circ. 3,268(paid).
 Formerly: Chronicle, The.

US
SOMERSET MESSENGER GAZETTE. 1823. Thu. $.60 newsstand; $16/yr. 44 Veterans Memorial Dr., E., Somerville, NJ 08876. TEL 908-722-3000; FAX 908-526-2509. **Owner(s):** Forbes Newspapers, Inc., P.O. Box 95, Bedminster, NJ 07921. TEL 908-722-3000; Ed. Andrew Simpson; Pub. Louis Barsony; adv. contact: Rick Kestenbaum. photos; pub. size: broadsheet; circ. 20,000(paid).

SPARTA
US
SPARTA INDEPENDENT. 1985. Thu. free. 270 Sparta Ave., Ste. 101, Sparta, NJ 07871. TEL 201-729-7620; FAX 201-729-0513. **Owner(s):** Straus Media of New Jersey, Inc., 328-C Sparta Ave., Sparta, NJ 07871. TEL 201-729-7620; FAX 201-729-0513; Ed. David Slavin; Pub. David Slavin; adv.; photos; pub. size: tabloid; circ. 8,600(free).

STIRLING
US
ECHOES-SENTINEL. 1954. Wed. $.50 newsstand; $22/yr. in cy.; $40/yr. out of cy. 256 Mercer St., Stirling, NJ 07980. TEL 908-647-1134; FAX 908-647-7679. **Owner(s):** Recorder Publishing Co., 17-19 Morristown Road, Bernardsville, NJ 07924. TEL 908-766-3900; Ed. Christy Kass; Pub. Cortlandt Parker; adv. contact: Allison Spinello. pub. size: broadsheet; circ. 6,500(paid).

SURF CITY
US ISSN 0194-6307
BEACHCOMBER, THE. 1950. Fri. (May-Sep.). free. 1816 Long Beach Blvd., Surf City, NJ 08008. TEL 609-494-5900; FAX 609-494-1437. **Owner(s):** Jersey Shore News Magazines, Inc., 1816 Long Beach Blvd., Surf City, NJ 08008. TEL 609-494-5900; FAX 609-494-1437; Ed. Margaret Buchholz; Pub. Margaret Buchholz; adv. contact: Norman Scull. bk.rev.; pub. size: tabloid; circ. 25,000(free).

TOMS RIVER
US
OCEAN COUNTY REPORTER. 1956. s-w.: Thu. & Sat. free. 8 Robbins St., Toms River, NJ 08753. TEL 908-349-1501; FAX 908-240-0545. **Owner(s):** Goodson Newspaper Group, 1009 Lenox Dr., Lawrenceville, NJ 08648. TEL 609-895-2600; Pub. Robert Juzwiak; adv. contact: Paul Haney. photos; pub. size: tabloid; circ. 100,107(free). **Wire Service(s):** CNS.

UNION
US
CLARK EAGLE. 1990. Thu. $.25 newsstand; $15/yr. 1291 Stuyvesant Ave., Union, NJ 07083. TEL 908-686-6700; FAX 908-686-4169. **Owner(s):** Worrall Community Newspapers, Inc., 1291 Stuyvesant Ave., Union, NJ 07083. TEL 908-686-6700; Ed. Tom Canavan; Pub. David Worrall; adv. contact: Peter Worrall. photos; bk.rev.; pub. size: broadsheet; circ. 1,500(free & paid).

US
ELIZABETH GAZETTE. Thu. $.50 newsstand; $22/yr. 1291 Stuyesant Ave., Union, NJ 07083. TEL 908-686-6700; FAX 908-686-4169. **Owner(s):** Worrall Community Newspapers, 1291 Stuyvesant Ave., Union, NJ 07083. TEL 908-686-6700; Ed. Tom Canavan; Pub. David Worrall; adv. contact: Peter Worrall. photos; bk.rev.; pub. size: broadsheet.

US
HILLSIDE LEADER. 1990. Thu. $.50 newsstand; $22/yr. 1291 Stuyvesant Ave., Union, NJ 07083. TEL 908-686-4169. **Owner(s):** Worrall Community Newspapers, Inc., 1291 Stuyvesant Ave., Union, NJ 07083. TEL 908-686-6700; Ed. Tom Canavan; Pub. David Worrall; adv. contact: Peter Worrall. photos; bk.rev.; pub. size: broadsheet; circ. 1,500(paid).

US ISSN 8750-8664
KENILWORTH LEADER. 1945. Thu. $.50 newsstand; $22/yr. 1291 Stuyvesant Ave., Union, NJ 07083. TEL 908-686-6700; FAX 908-686-4169. **Owner(s):** Worrall Community Newspapers, 1291 Stuyvesant Ave., Union, NJ 07083. TEL 908-686-6700; Ed. Thomas Canavan. adv. contact: Peter Worrall. photos; bk.rev.; pub. size: broadsheet; circ. 1,000(paid).

WEEKLY NEWSPAPERS

US

LINDEN LEADER. Thu. $.50 newsstand; $22/yr. 1291 Stuyvesant Ave., Union, NJ 07083. TEL 908-686-7700; FAX 908-686-4169. **Owner(s):** Worrall Community Newspapers, Inc., 1291 Stuyvesant Ave., Union, NJ 07083. TEL 908-686-7700; Ed. Thomas Canavan. adv. contact: Nancy Seyboth. photos; bk.rev.; pub. size: broadsheet; circ. 2,650(paid).

US

MOUNTAINSIDE ECHO. Thu. $.50 newsstand; $22/yr. 1291 Stuyvesant Ave., Union, NJ 07083. TEL 908-686-7700; FAX 908-686-4169. **Owner(s):** Worrall Community Newspapers, Inc., 1291 Stuyvesant Ave., Union, NJ 07083. TEL 908-686-7700; Ed. Thomas Canavan; Pub. David Worrall; adv. contact: Peter Worrall. photos; pub. size: broadsheet; circ. 850(paid).

US

RAHWAY PROGRESS. 1990. Thu. $.25 newsstand; 15/yr. 1291 Stuyvesant Ave., Union, NJ 07083. TEL 908-686-7700; FAX 908-686-4169. **Owner(s):** Worrall Community Newspapers, Inc., 1291 Stuyvesant Ave., Union, NJ 07083. TEL 908-686-7700; Ed. Thomas Canavan; Pub. David Worrall; adv. contact: Peter Worrall. photos; bk.rev.; pub. size: broadsheet; circ. 1,500(paid).

US

ROSELLE PARK LEADER. 1990. Thu. $.50 newsstand; $22/yr. 1291 Stuyvesant Ave., Union, NJ 07083. TEL 908-686-7700; FAX 908-686-4169. **Owner(s):** Worrall Community Newspapers, Inc., 1291 Stuyvesant Ave., Union, NJ 07083. TEL 908-686-7700; Ed. Thomas Canavan; Pub. David Worrall; adv. contact: Peter Worrall. photos; bk.rev.; pub. size: broadsheet; circ. 1,000(paid).

US

ROSELLE SPECTATOR. 1917. Thu. $.50 newsstand; $22/yr. 1291 Stuyvesant Ave., Union, NJ 07083. TEL 908-686-7700; FAX 908-686-4169. **Owner(s):** Worrall Community Newspapers, Inc., 1291 Stuyvesant Ave., Union, NJ 07083. TEL 908-686-7700; Ed. Thomas Canavan; Pub. David Worrall; adv. contact: Peter Worrall. photos; pub. size: broadsheet; circ. 1,050(paid).

US

SPRINGFIELD LEADER. 1945. Thu. $.50 newsstand; $22/yr. 1291 Stuyvesant Ave., Union, NJ 07083. TEL 908-686-7700; FAX 908-686-4169. **Owner(s):** Worrall Community Newspapers, Inc., 1291 Stuyvesant Ave., Union, NJ 07083. TEL 908-686-7700; Ed. Thomas Canavan. adv. contact: Peter Worrall. photos; bk.rev.; pub. size: broadsheet; circ. 2,250(paid).

US

SUMMIT OBSERVER. Thu. $.50 newsstand; $20/yr. mailed in cy.; $35/2 yrs. mailed in cy. 1291 Stuyvesant Ave., Union, NJ 07083. TEL 908-686-7700; FAX 908-686-4169; E-mail: wcn22@aol.com. **Owner(s):** Worrall Community Newspapers, 1291 Stuyvesant Ave., Union, NJ 07083. TEL 908-686-7700; Ed. Thomas Canavan; Pub. David Worrall; adv. contact: Peter Worrall. bk.rev.; pub. size: broadsheet; circ. 1,000(paid).

US

UNION LEADER. 1928. Thu. $.50 newsstand; $22/yr. 1291 Stuyvesant Ave., Union, NJ 07083. TEL 908-686-7700; FAX 908-686-4169. **Owner(s):** Worrall Community Newspapers, Inc., 1291 Stuyvesant Ave., Union, NJ 07083. TEL 908-686-7700; Ed. Tom Canavan; Pub. David Worrall; adv. contact: Peter Worrall. photos; bk.rev.; pub. size: broadsheet; circ. 7,100(paid).

VERONA

US

VERONA-CEDAR GROVE TIMES. 1948. Thu. $.50 newsstand; $18/yr.; $10/yr. senior citizens. 685 Bloomfield Ave., Verona, NJ 07044. TEL 201-239-0900; FAX 201-239-7739. **Owner(s):** Montgrove Publications, 114 Valley Rd., Montclair, NJ 07042. TEL 201-746-1100; Ed. Ward Miele; Pub. Barbara A. Lewis; adv. contact: Sally Morris. photos; pub. size: broadsheet; circ. 6,000(paid).

VOORHEES

US

JOURNAL, THE. 1973. Fri. $.30 newsstand; $15/yr.; $12/yr. senior citizens. 157 S. Rte. 73, Voorhees, NJ 08043. TEL 609-767-1640; FAX 609-768-4320. **Owner(s):** Consumer & Community News, Inc., P.O. Box 399, Berlin, NJ 08009-0399. TEL 609-767-1640; FAX 609-768-4320; Ed. Louis A. Chimenti; Pub. Ed McCartney; adv.; photos; pub. size: tabloid; circ. evening 15,000(free & paid).

WEST CALDWELL

US

FAIRFIELD CHRONICLE, THE. Wed. $.20 newsstand; $6/yr. in cy.; $12/yr. in state; $24/yr. out of state. P.O. Box 6123, West Caldwell, NJ 07007-6123. TEL 201-227-4433; FAX 201-882-8553. **Owner(s):** Reboli Publishing Co., P.O. Box 6123, West Caldwell, NJ 07007. TEL 201-227-4433; FAX 201-882-8553; Ed. Kelly J. Kilborn; Pub. John A. Reboli; adv. contact: Joan C. Beechey. photos; bk.rev.; pub. size: tabloid.

US

MORRISTOWN NEWS, THE. Wed. $.20 newsstand; $6/yr. in area; $12/yr. in state; $24/yr. out of state. P.O. Box 6123, West Caldwell, NJ 07007-6123. TEL 201-227-4433; FAX 201-882-8553. **Owner(s):** Reboli Publishing Co., P.O. Box 6123, West Caldwell, NJ 07007-6123. TEL 201-227-4433; FAX 201-882-8553; Ed. Kelly J. Kilborn; Pub. John A. Reboli; adv. contact: Joan C. Beechey. photos; bk.rev.; pub. size: tabloid; **Wire Service(s):** Parsippany News Service, NJ Wire Service.

US

PARSIPPANY NEWS, THE. Thu. $.20 newsstand. P.O. Box 6123, West Caldwell, NJ 07007-6123. TEL 201-227-4433; FAX 201-882-8553. **Owner(s):** Reboli Publishing Co., P.O. Box 6123, West Caldwell, NJ 07007. TEL 201-227-4433; FAX 201-882-8553; Ed. Kelly J. Kilborn; Pub. John A. Reboli; adv. contact: Joan C. Beechey. photos; bk.rev.; pub. size: tabloid; **Wire Service(s):** Parsippany News Service, NJ Wire Service.

WESTFIELD

US

TIMES OF SCOTCH PLAINS & FANWOOD, THE. 1958. Thu. $.50 newsstand; $20/yr. in cy.; $24/yr. out of cy. 50 Elm St., Westfield, NJ 07090. TEL 908-232-4407; FAX 908-232-0473; E-mail: goleader@aol.com; URL: http://www.quintillon.com/leader. **Owner(s):** Horace R. & Gail S. Corbin, 50 Elm St., Westfield, NJ 07090. TEL 908-232-4407; FAX 908-232-0473; Ed. Paul J. Peyton; Pub. Horace R. Corbin; adv.; pub. size: standard; circ. 1,600(paid).
Formerly: Times, The.

US

WESTFIELD LEADER. 1890. Thu. $20/yr. in cy.; $24/yr. out of cy. 50 Elm St., Westfield, NJ 07090. TEL 908-232-4407; FAX 908-232-0473; E-mail: goleader@aol.com URL: http: www.quintillon.com/leader. **Owner(s):** Horace R. & Gail S. Corbin, 50 Elm St., Westfield, NJ 07090. TEL 908-232-4407; FAX 908-232-0473; Ed. Paul J. Peyton; Pub. Horace R. Corbin; adv. contact: Kathleen L. Norman. pub. size: standard; circ. 5,700(paid).

WESTWOOD

US

PASCACK VALLEY COMMUNITY LIFE. 1928. Wed. free; $45/yr. out of town. 345 Kinderkamack Rd., Westwood, NJ 07675. TEL 201-664-2501; FAX 201-664-1332. **Owner(s):** North Jersey Newspapers Co., 988 Main Ave., Passaic, NJ 07005. TEL 201-365-3000; FAX 201-365-5887; Ed. Barbara J. Stewart; Pub. Sherwood Spitz; adv. contact: Doug McBride. photos; pub. size: tabloid; circ. 24,350(paid).
Formerly: Pascack Valley News.

WILDWOOD

US

CAPE MAY COUNTY GAZETTE LEADER. 1976. Wed. $.50 newsstand; $18/yr. in cy.; $22/yr. out of cy. 1212 Atlantic Ave., Wildwood, NJ 08260. TEL 609-522-3423; FAX 609-522-7451. **Owner(s):** Catamarin Media LLC, 1816 Long Beach Blvd., Ship Bottom, NJ 08008. TEL 609-494-5900; FAX 609-494-1437; Ed. Rob Seitzinger; Pub. Rick Travers; adv. contact: Marylou Trottnow. photos; pub. size: broadsheet; circ. 7,000(paid).
Formerly: Gazette Leader.

US

FREE TIME. Wed. free. 1212 Atlantic Ave., Wildwood, NJ 08260. TEL 609-522-3423; FAX 609-522-7451. **Owner(s):** Catamorran Media, 1816 Long Beach Blvd., Ship Bottom, NJ 08008. TEL 609-494-5900; FAX 609-494-1437; Ed. Rob Seitzinger; Pub. Rick Travers; pub. size: standard; circ. 25,000(free).

WILDWOOD, NJ

US
WILDWOOD LEADER. Wed. $.50 newsstand; $22/yr. 1212 Atlantic Ave., Wildwood, NJ 08260. TEL 609-522-3423; FAX 609-522-7451. **Owner(s):** Travers Brothers, P.O. Box 469, Wildwood, NJ 08620. TEL 609-522-3423; FAX 609-522-7451; Ed. Rob Seitzinger; Pub. Rick Travers; pub. size: standard; circ. 8,000(paid).

NEW MEXICO

ALBUQUERQUE

US
ALBUQUERQUE STREET NEWS. 1990. s-m.: 1st & 16th. $.75 newsstand. 1019 Second St., S.W., Albuquerque, NM 87102. TEL 505-842-8314. **Owner(s):** Albuquerque Help for the Homeless, P.O. Box 26896, Albuquerque, NM 87125. TEL 505-842-8314; Pub. Karen Krueger; adv.; photos; bk.rev.; pub. size: tabloid; circ. 6,000(free).

BELEN

US
VALENCIA COUNTY NEWS-BULLETIN. 1911. s-w.: Wed. & Sat. $.50 newsstand; $36/yr. in cy.; $42/yr. elsewhere. 1837 Sosimo Padilla Blvd., Belen, NM 87002. TEL 505-864-4472; FAX 505-864-3549; E-mail: cristop555@aol.com. **Owner(s):** WorldWest Limited Liability Co., 609 New Hampshire, P.O. Box 688, Lawrence, KS 66044. TEL 913-843-1000; FAX 913-832-7207; Ed. Sandy Battin; Pub. Chris Baker; adv.; photos; bk.rev.; pub. size: broadsheet; circ. 6,000(paid). **Wire Service(s):** AP.

ESPANOLA

US
RIO GRANDE SUN. 1956. Thu. $.40 newsstand; $15/yr. 123 N. Railroad, Espanola, NM 87532. TEL 505-753-2126. **Owner(s):** Sun Co., Inc., P.O. Box 790, Espanola, NM 87532. TEL 505-753-2126; Ed. Robert E. Trapp; Pub. Robert E. Trapp; adv. contact: Robert B. Trapp. pub. size: broadsheet; circ. 10,800(paid).

ESTANCIA

US
ESTANCIA VALLEY CITIZEN. 1958. Fri. $.50 newsstand; $16/yr. in state; $22/yr. elsewhere. 400 S. Fifth St., Estancia, NM 87016-0288. TEL 505-384-2744. E-mail: giraf@aol.comm. **Owner(s):** Carolyn Appelman, P.O. Box 288, Estancia, NM 87016-0288. TEL 505-384-2744; Ed. Morrow Hall; Pub. Carolyn Appelman; adv.; photos; bk.rev.; pub. size: broadsheet; circ. 2,800(free & paid).
Formerly: Torrance County Citizen.

GRANTS

US
CIBOLA COUNTY BEACON. 1941. s-w.: Wed. & Fri. $.50 newsstand; $48/yr. 300 N. Second St., Grants, NM 87020. TEL 505-287-4411; FAX 505-287-7822. **Owner(s):** Wick Communications, 333 W. Wilcox Dr., Ste. 302, Sierra Vista, AZ 85635; Ed. J.D. Meisner; Pub. Jamie Honeycutt; adv.; photos; pub. size: broadsheet; circ. 3,500(paid).

HOBBS

US
HOBBS FLARE. 1948. Thu. $.50 newsstand; $18/yr. in cy.; $24/yr. out of cy.; $30/yr. out of state. 114 E. Dunnam, Hobbs, NM 88240. TEL 505-393-5141; FAX 505-393-1831. **Owner(s):** Sun Publishing, Inc., Lake Charles, LA; Ed. Steve Snyder; Pub. Ralph Colinenda; adv. contact: Ralph Colinenda. pub. size: standard; circ. 2,800(paid).

RATON

US ISSN 0896-1093
RATON RANGE, THE. 1881. s-w.: Tue. & Fri. $.75 newsstand; $40/yr. in cy.; $45/yr. out of cy. 208 S. Third St., Raton, NM 87740. TEL 505-445-2721; FAX 505-445-2723. **Owner(s):** Raton Newspaper Inc., 208 S. Third St., Raton, NM 87740. TEL 505-445-2721; FAX 505-445-2723; Ed. Todd Wildermuth; Pub. Paula Pachorek; adv. contact: Laura Oliver. photos; pub. size: broadsheet; circ. 3,000(paid).

RIO RANCHO

US ISSN 1049-7374
OBSERVER, THE. 1973. s-w.: Wed. & Fri. $.50 newsstand; $22/yr. 1594 Sara Rd., Rio Rancho, NM 87124. TEL 505-892-8080; FAX 505-892-5719; E-mail: theobserve@aol.com. **Owner(s):** Wick Communications, Inc., 333 Wilcox Dr., Ste. 302, Sierra Vista, AZ 85635-1756. TEL 520-458-0200; FAX 520-458-6166; Pub. Michael J. Ryan; adv. contact: Marisa Gilles. photos; bk.rev.; pub. size: broadsheet; circ. 8,000(controlled & paid).

RUIDOSO

US
RUIDOSO NEWS, THE. 1946. s-w.: Wed. & Fri. $.50 newsstand; $34/yr. mailed; $68/yr. home deliv. 104 Park Ave., Ruidoso, NM 88355. TEL 505-257-4001; FAX 505-257-7053; E-mail: rvidosonws@aol.com. **Owner(s):** WorldWest Limited Liability Co., 609 New Hampshire, P.O. Box 688, Lawrence, KS 66044. TEL 913-843-1000; Ed. Joanna Dodder; Pub. Barbara Triemble; adv. contact: Chris Volquardsen. photos; pub. size: broadsheet; circ. evening 5,800(paid).

SANTA FE

US
SANTA FE REPORTER, THE. 1974. Wed. free newsstand; $50/yr. mailed in US. 132 E. Marcy St., Santa Fe, NM 87501. TEL 505-988-5541; FAX 505-988-5348. **Owner(s):** Santa Fe Reporter, Inc., The, P.O. Box 2306, Santa Fe, NM 87504; Ed. Hope Aldrich; Pub. Hope Aldrich; adv.; pub. size: tabloid; circ. 25,000. **Wire Service(s):** Alternet.

SOCORRO

US ISSN 0011-7633
DEFENSOR CHIEFTAIN. 1865. s-w.: Wed. & Sun. $.35 newsstand; $28/yr. in cy.; $38/yr. elsewhere. 200 Winkler, S.W., Socorro, NM 87801. TEL 505-835-0520; FAX 505-835-1837; E-mail: defensocor@aol.com. **Owner(s):** WorldWest Limited Liability Co., 609 New Hampshire, P.O. Box 688, Lawrence, KS 66044. TEL 913-843-1000; Ed. Gwen Roath; Pub. Gwen Roath; adv. contact: Daniel Gaines. pub. size: broadsheet; circ. 2,800(paid).

TAOS

US
TAOS NEWS. 1893. Thu. $.75 newsstand; $26/yr. in cy.; $30/yr. out of cy.; $35/yr. out of state. 120 Camino de la Placita, Taos, NM 87571. TEL 505-758-2241; FAX 505-758-9647. **Owner(s):** Robin McKinney Martin, P.O. Box U, Taos, NM 87571. TEL 505-758-2241; Ed. Deborah Ensor; Pub. George Fellows; adv. contact: Joanne Crass. pub. size: broadsheet; circ. 10,500(paid).

TRUTH OR CONSEQUENCES

US
HERALD, THE. 1916. Wed. $.50 newsstand; $20/yr. in cy.; $30/yr. out of cy. 1204 N. Date St., Truth or Consequences, NM 87901-0752. TEL 505-894-2143; FAX 505-894-7824. **Owner(s):** Herald Publishing Co., Inc., 1204 N. Date St., Truth or Consequences, NM 87901-0752. TEL 505-894-2143; FAX 505-894-7824; Pub. Bob Tooley; adv. contact: Maureen Tooley. photos; pub. size: broadsheet; circ. 4,500(paid).

US
SIERRA COUNTY SENTINEL. 1967. Wed. $.50 newsstand; $25/yr. in cy.; $30/yr. out of cy. 1747 E. Third, Truth or Consequences, NM 87901. TEL 505-894-3088; FAX 505-894-3998. **Owner(s):** Myrna Baird-Kohs, P.O. Box 351, Truth or Consequences, NM 87901. TEL 505-894-3088; Ed. Myrna Baird-Kohs; Pub. Myrna Baird-Kohs; pub. size: standard; circ. 4,300(paid).

TUCUMCARI

US
QUAY COUNTY SUN. 1975. s-w.: Wed. & Sat. $.50 newsstand; $36/yr. 902 S. First St., Tucumcari, NM 88401-1408. TEL 505-461-1952; FAX 505-461-1965. **Owner(s):** Freedom Newspapers of NM, 521 Pile St., Clovis, NM 88102; Ed. Ruth Friedberg; Pub. Ron V. Wilmot; adv.; photos; pub. size: broadsheet; circ. 3,600(paid).

NEW YORK

ADAMS

US
JEFFERSON COUNTY JOURNAL. 1844. Wed. $.35 newsstand; $18/yr. in cy.; $22/yr. out of cy.; $24/yr. out of state. 7 Main St., Adams, NY 13605-0068. TEL 315-232-2141; FAX 315-232-4586. **Owner(s):** Journal Publishing Co., 7 Main St., Adams, NY 13605. TEL 315-232-2141; FAX 315-232-4586; Ed. Karl Fowler; Pub. Karl Fowler; adv. contact: Rick Sidman. photos; pub. size: broadsheet; circ. 3,000(controlled).

WEEKLY NEWSPAPERS

ALBION
US

ALBION ADVERTISER. 1824. Wed. $.50 newsstand; $27/yr. 116 N. Main St., Albion, NY 14411. TEL 716-589-4455; FAX 716-589-4488. **Owner(s):** Community Newspaper Holdings, Inc., 269 N. Main St., 6th Fl., Lexington, KY 40507. TEL 606-388-2644; FAX 606-225-8115; Ed. Owen P. Toale. adv. contact: Gregory Kerth. adv.: $5.79/SAU. pub. size: broadsheet; circ. 2,000(paid).

ALDEN
US

WEISBECK, THE. 1914. Thu. $.50 newsstand; $18/yr. 13200 Broadway, Alden, NY 14004. TEL 716-937-9226. **Owner(s):** Weisbeck Publishing & Printing, Inc., 13200 Broadway, Alden, NY 14004. TEL 716-937-9226; Ed. Leonard A. Weisbeck, Sr.; Pub. Leonard A. Weisbeck, Jr.; adv.; pub. size: tabloid; circ. 3,588(paid).

ALEXANDRIA BAY
US

THOUSAND ISLANDS SUN. 1901. Wed. $.50 newsstand; $22/yr. in cy.; $26/yr. out of cy; $32/yr. Canada. P.O. Box 277, Alexandria Bay, NY 13607-0277. TEL 315-482-2581; FAX 315-482-6315. **Owner(s):** Thousand Islands Printing Co., Inc., P.O. Box 277, Alexandria Bay, NY 13607. TEL 315-482-2581; FAX 315-482-6315; Ed. Jeanne Snow; Pub. Jeanne Snow; adv. contact: Craig Snow. photos; pub. size: standard; circ. 6,422(paid).

ALTAMONT
US   ISSN 0890-6025

ALTAMONT ENTERPRISE, THE. 1884. Thu. $.50 newsstand; $24/yr. in cy.; $26/yr. out of cy. 123 Maple Ave., Altamont, NY 12009. TEL 518-861-6641; FAX 518-861-5105. **Owner(s):** James E. Gardner, 123 Maple Ave., Altamont, NY 12009. TEL 518-861-6641; FAX 518-861-5105; Ed. Melissa Hale-Spencer; Pub. James E. Gardner; adv.; bk.rev.; pub. size: tabloid; circ. 7,200(paid).

AMENIA
US

HARLEM VALLEY TIMES. 1852. Thu. $.60 newsstand; $29.50/yr. E. Main St., Amenia, NY 12501. TEL 914-373-8084; FAX 914-373-8908. **Owner(s):** Taconic Media, Inc., P.O. Box 316, Millbrook, NY 12545. TEL 914-677-8241; Ed. Bob Lomicky; Pub. Hamilton Meserve; adv.; pub. size: broadsheet; circ. 3,800(paid).

AMITYVILLE
US

AMITYVILLE RECORD. 1904. Wed. $.50 newsstand; $14/yr. 85 Broadway, Amityville, NY 11701. TEL 516-264-0077; FAX 516-264-5310. **Owner(s):** ACJ Communications, Inc., 85 Broadway, Amityville, NY 11701. TEL 516-264-0077; Ed. Jim Custer; Pub. Alfred James; adv.; photos; pub. size: tabloid; circ. 8,000(paid).

BABYLON
US

BEACON NEWSPAPER. 1966. Thu. $.50 newsstand; $17/yr.; $29/2 yrs.; $42/3 yrs. 65 Deerpark Ave., Babylon, NY 11702. TEL 516-587-5612; FAX 516-587-0198. **Owner(s):** Beacon Newspapers, Inc., 65 Deerpark Ave., Babylon, NY 11702. TEL 516-587-5612; Ed. Terry Bouquet; Pub. John Mangano; adv.; photos; pub. size: tabloid; circ. 52,000(free & paid).
Formerly: Babylon Beacon.

BALLSTON SPA
US

BALLSTON JOURNAL. 1798. Wed. $.50 newsstand; $16/yr. in cy.; $18/yr. out of cy.; $20/yr. out of state. 72 W. High St., Ballston Spa, NY 12020. TEL 518-885-4341; FAX 518-885-4344. **Owner(s):** Journal Newspapers, Inc., 72 W. High St., Ballston Spa, NY 12020. TEL 518-885-4341; Ed. Charles Hogan; Pub. Charles Hogan; adv. contact: Nancy Rochford. pub. size: broadsheet; circ. 2,200(paid).

US

MALTA MESSENGER. Mon. free. 72 W. High St., Ballston Spa, NY 12020. TEL 518-885-4341; FAX 518-885-4344. **Owner(s):** Journal Newspapers, Inc., 72 W. High St., Ballston Spa, NY 12020. TEL 518-885-4341; Ed. Charles Hogan; Pub. Charles Hogan; adv.; pub. size: standard; circ. 6,000(free).

US

MONEYSAVER, THE. 1969. Tue. free. 72 W. High St., Ballston Spa, NY 12020-1927. TEL 518-885-4341; FAX 518-885-4344. **Owner(s):** Journal Newspapers, Inc., 72 W. High St., Ballston Spa, NY 12020-1927. TEL 518-885-4341; Ed. Charles Hogan; Pub. Charles Hogan; adv.; pub. size: tabloid; circ. 15,000(free).

BATH
US

STEUBEN COURIER-ADVOCATE. 1843. Sun. free in cy.; $2/wk. mailed. 10 W. Steuben St., Bath, NY 14810. TEL 607-776-2121; FAX 607-776-3967. **Owner(s):** American Publishing Co., 606 N. Van Buren, Marion, IL 62959. TEL 618-993-1711; Ed. Mark Raven; Pub. Colleen Neeley; adv. contact: Colleen Neeley. pub. size: broadsheet; circ. Sun. 11,313(free).

BAYSIDE
US

BAYSIDE TIMES, THE. 1934. Thu. $.50 newsstand; $19/yr. local; $35/2 yrs. in cy.; $29/yr. elsewhere. 41-02 Bell Blvd., 2nd Fl., Bayside, NY 11361. TEL 718-229-0300; FAX 718-225-7117. **Owner(s):** Queens Publishing Corp., 41-02 Bell Blvd., 2nd Fl., Bayside, NY 11361. TEL 718-229-0300; FAX 718-225-7117; Ed. Roz Liston; Pub. Steve Blank; adv.; photos; pub. size: tabloid; circ. 11,044(paid).

US

FLUSHING TIMES, THE. 1992. Thu. $.50 newsstand; $19/yr.; $35/2 yrs. in cy. 41-02 Bell Blvd., 2nd Fl., Bayside, NY 11361. TEL 718-229-0300; FAX 718-225-7117. **Owner(s):** Queens Publishing Corp., 41-02 Bell Blvd., 2nd Fl., Bayside, NY 11361. TEL 718-229-0300; FAX 718-225-7117; Ed. Roz Liston; Pub. Steve Blank; adv. contact: Joseph Tiegal. photos; pub. size: tabloid; circ. 5,400(paid).

US

GLEN OAKS LEDGER, THE. 1993. Thu. $.50 newsstand; $19/yr.; $35/2 yr. in cy. 41-02 Bell Blvd., 2nd Fl., Bayside, NY 11361. TEL 718-229-0300; FAX 718-225-7117. **Owner(s):** Queens Publishing Corp., 214-11 41st Ave., Flushing, NY 11361. TEL 718-229-0300; FAX 718-225-7171; Ed. Roz Liston; Pub. Steven Blank; adv.; photos; pub. size: tabloid; circ. 2,424(paid).

US

WHITESTONE TIMES, THE. 1991. Thu. $.50 newsstand; $19/yr. in cy.; $35/2 yrs. in cy. 41-02 Bell Blvd., 2nd Fl., Bayside, NY 11361. TEL 718-229-0300; FAX 718-225-7117. **Owner(s):** Queens Publishing Corp., 41-02 Bell Blvd., 2nd Fl., Bayside, NY 11361. TEL 718-229-0300; FAX 718-225-7117; Ed. Roz Liston; Pub. Steven Blank; adv.; photos; pub. size: tabloid; circ. 3,603(paid).

BELLMORE
US

BELLMORE-MERRICK OBSERVER. 1949. Thu. $7/yr. P.O. Box 407, Bellmore, NY 11710. TEL 516-679-9888; FAX 516-731-0338. **Owner(s):** Observer Newspapers, Inc., 2262 Centre Ave., Bellmore, NY; Ed. Jackson B. Pokress; Pub. Wilma J. Pokress; adv.; photos; bk.rev.; pub. size: tabloid; circ. 5,000(paid).

US

BELLMORE LIFE. 1964. Wed. $.35 newsstand; $14.50/yr. in cy.; $19.50/yr. out of cy. 2818 Merrick Rd., Bellmore, NY 11710. TEL 516-826-0333; FAX 516-826-0814. **Owner(s):** L & M Publications, Inc., 1840 Merrick Ave., Merrick, NY 11566. TEL 516-378-5320; Ed. Paul Laursen; Pub. Linda Toscano; adv. contact: Mike Diller. pub. size: tabloid; circ. 5,127(free & paid).

US

WANTAGH-SEAFORD CITIZEN. 1953. Thu. $.30 newsstand; $11.50/yr. 2818 Merrick Rd., Bellmore, NY 11710. TEL 516-826-0812; FAX 516-826-0814. **Owner(s):** L & M Publications, Inc., 1840 Merrick Ave., Merrick, NY 11566. TEL 516-378-5320; Ed. Paul Laursen; Pub. Linda Laursen Toscano; adv. contact: Carole Friedman. photos; pub. size: tabloid; circ. 4,137(free & paid).

BOONVILLE
US

BOONVILLE HERALD & ADIRONDACK TOURIST. 1852. Wed. $.40 newsstand; $16/yr. surrounding cys.; $18/yr. elsewhere. E. Schuyler St., Boonville, NY 13309. TEL 315-942-4449. **Owner(s):** Kathy Lansing, Jackson Hill Rd., Boonville, NY 13309. TEL 315-942-4844; Ed. Kathy Lansing; Pub. Kathy Lansing; adv. contact: John Isley. photos; pub. size: broadsheet; circ. 3,400(free & paid).
Formerly: Boonville Herald.

BRIDGEHAMPTON
US

DAN'S PAPERS. 1960. Thu. free; $26/yr. 2221 Montauk Hwy., Bridgehampton, NY 11932. TEL 516-537-0500; FAX 516-537-3330. **Owner(s):** News Communications, Inc., 174-15 Harding Expy., Queens, NY 11365. TEL 718-357-7400; Ed. Dan Rattiner; Pub. Dan Rattiner; adv. contact: Leslie Halligan. photos; bk.rev.; pub. size: tabloid; circ. 71,000(free).

10674 BRIDGEHAMPTON, NY

WEEKLY NEWSPAPERS

Weeklies

US
MONTAUK PIONEER. Thu. free; $26/yr. 2221 Montauk Hwy., Bridgehampton, NY 11932. TEL 516-537-0500; FAX 516-537-3330. **Owner(s):** News Communications, Inc., 174-15 Harding Expy., Queens, NY 11365. TEL 718-357-7400; Ed. Dan Rattiner; Pub. Dan Rattiner; pub. size: broadsheet; circ. 13,000(free & paid).

BROCKPORT

US
BROCKPORT POST, THE. 1968. Thu. $21/yr. 2 S. Main St., Brockport, NY 14420. TEL 716-381-3300; FAX 716-637-5637. **Owner(s):** Canandaigua Messenger, Inc., 73 Buffalo St., Canandaigua, NY 14424. TEL 716-394-0770; Ed. Mark Syverud; Pub. George Ewing, Jr.; pub. size: broadsheet; circ. 1,600(paid).

US
TRI-COUNTY ADVERTISER. 1957. Mon. free. 15 Main St., Brockport, NY 14420. TEL 716-637-5100; FAX 716-637-0111. **Owner(s):** Sally A. Becht, 15 Main St., Brockport, NY 14420. TEL 716-637-5100; Ed. Sally A. Becht. adv. contact: David G. Abrams. pub. size: tabloid; circ. 16,000(free).

BRONX

US
BRONX NEWS. 1982. Thu. $10/yr. 135 Dreiser Loop, Bronx, NY 10475. TEL 718-671-1234. **Owner(s):** C.G. Hagedorn, 135 Dreiser Loop, Bronx, NY 10475. TEL 718-671-1234; Pub. C.G. Hagedorn; adv.; pub. size: tabloid; circ. 8,000(paid).

US
BRONX PRESS-REVIEW. 1940. Thu. $.35 newsstand; $9/yr. in town; $25/yr. out of town. 170 W. 233rd St., Bronx, NY 10463. TEL 718-543-5200; FAX 718-543-4206. **Owner(s):** Parkchester Publishing, Inc., 170 W. 233rd St., Bronx, NY 10463. TEL 718-543-5200; Ed. Melody Zivancev; Pub. Andrew Wolf; adv.; bk.rev.; pub. size: tabloid; circ. 15,000(paid).

US
CITY NEWS. 1969. Sat. free. 135 Dreiser Loop, Bronx, NY 10475. TEL 718-671-1234. **Owner(s):** C.G. Hagedorn, 135 Dreiser Loop, Bronx, NY 10475. TEL 718-671-1234; Ed. C.G. Hagedorn; Pub. C.G. Hagedorn; adv.; pub. size: tabloid; circ. 15,500(free).

US
PARKCHESTER NEWS. 1974. Fri. free. 135 Dreiser Loop, Bronx, NY 10475. TEL 718-671-1234. **Owner(s):** C.G. Hagedorn, 135 Dreiser Loop, Bronx, NY 10475. TEL 718-671-1234; Ed. C.G. Hagedorn; Pub. C.G. Hagedorn; adv.; pub. size: tabloid; circ. 12,500(free).

US
RIVERDALE PRESS. 1950. Thu. $.75 newsstand; $19/yr.; $33/2 yrs. 6155 Broadway, Bronx, NY 10471. TEL 718-543-6065; FAX 718-548-4038. **Owner(s):** Dale Press, Inc., 6155 Broadway, Bronx, NY 10471. TEL 718-543-6065; Ed. Bernard L. Stein; Pub. Bernard L. Stein; adv. contact: Phyllis Steele. photos; pub. size: broadsheet; circ. 14,500(paid).

BROOKLYN

US
BAY NEWS. 1945. Mon. $.50 newsstand; $20/yr. 1733 Sheepshead Bay Rd., Brooklyn, NY 11235. TEL 718-769-4400; FAX 718-769-5048. **Owner(s):** Courier-Life, Inc., 1733 Sheepshead Bay Rd., Brooklyn, NY 11235; Ed. Ken Brown; Pub. Edward E. Luster; adv. contact: Clifford Luster. photos; bk.rev.; pub. size: tabloid; circ. 76,000(controlled & paid).

US
BAY RIDGE COURIER. 1978. Thu. $.50 newsstand; $20/yr. mailed. 1733 Sheepshead Bay Rd., Brooklyn, NY 11235. TEL 718-769-4400; FAX 718-769-5048. **Owner(s):** Courier-Life Publications, 1733 Sheepshead Bay Rd., Brooklyn, NY 11235. TEL 718-769-4400; Ed. Kenneth Brown; Pub. Edward Luster; adv. contact: Clifford Luster. photos; bk.rev.; pub. size: tabloid; circ. 79,000(controlled & paid).

US
BROOKLYN GRAPHIC. 1953. Mon. $.50 newsstand; $20/yr. 1733 Sheepshead Bay Rd., Brooklyn, NY 11235. TEL 718-769-4400; FAX 718-769-5048. **Owner(s):** Courier-Life, Inc., 1733 Sheepshead Bay Rd., Brooklyn, NY 11235. TEL 718-769-4400; Ed. Kenneth Brown; Pub. Edward Luster; adv. contact: Clifford Luster. pub. size: tabloid; circ. 13,500(paid).

US
BROOKLYN HEIGHTS COURIER. 1990. bi-w.: Mon. free. 1733 Sheepshead Bay Rd., Brooklyn, NY 11235. TEL 718-769-4400; FAX 718-769-5048. **Owner(s):** Courier-Life, Inc., 1733 Sheepshead Bay Rd., Brooklyn, NY 11235. TEL 718-769-4400; Ed. Kenneth Brown; Pub. Edward Luster; adv. contact: Clifford Luster. photos; bk.rev.; pub. size: tabloid; circ. 72,000(free).

US
BROOKLYN HEIGHTS PRESS. 1937. Thu. $.50 newsstand; $25/yr. 125 Montague St., 2nd Fl., Brooklyn, NY 11201. TEL 718-624-0536; FAX 718-624-2716. **Owner(s):** Brooklyn Journal Publications, 125 Montague St., Lower Level, Brooklyn, NY 11201. TEL 718-624-0536; Ed. Henrik Krogius; Pub. Dozier Hasty; adv. contact: Patricia Higgins. pub. size: tabloid; circ. 19,500(paid).

US
BROOKLYN HOME REPORTER & SUNSET NEWS. 1953. Fri. $.50 newsstand; $35/yr. 8723 Third Ave., Brooklyn, NY 11209. TEL 718-238-6600; FAX 718-238-6630. **Owner(s):** Modern Media, Inc., 8723 Third Ave., Brooklyn, NY 11209; Ed. Sara Otey; Pub. J. Frank Griffin; adv.; pub. size: tabloid; circ. 18,000(paid).

US ISSN 0740-2643
BROOKLYN RECORD. 1938. Fri. $.25 newsstand; $25/yr. 125 Montague St, 2nd Fl., Brooklyn, NY 11201. TEL 718-624-6033; FAX 718-624-2716. **Owner(s):** Fredrick Halla, 125 Montague St., Brooklyn, NY 11201; Ed. Fredrick Halla; Pub. Fredrick Halla; adv.; bk.rev.; pub. size: tabloid; circ. 4,500(paid).

US
BROOKLYN SPECTATOR. 1933. Fri. $.50 newsstand; $35/yr. 8723 Third Ave., Brooklyn, NY 11209. TEL 718-238-6603; FAX 718-238-6630. **Owner(s):** Modern Media, Inc., 8723 Third Ave., Brooklyn, NY 11209; Ed. Sara Otey; Pub. J. Frank Griffin; pub. size: tabloid; circ. 18,000(paid).

US
CANARSIE COURIER. 1921. Thu. $.25 newsstand; $11.50/yr. local; $17/yr. out of town. 1142 E. 92nd St., Brooklyn, NY 11236. TEL 718-257-0600; FAX 718-272-0870. **Owner(s):** Mary Samitz, 1142 E. 92 St., Brooklyn, NY 11236. TEL 212-257-0600; Ed. Charles Rogers; Pub. Mary Samitz; adv.; photos; pub. size: tabloid; circ. 15,000(paid).

US
CANARSIE DIGEST. 1959. Mon. $.50 newsstand; $20/yr. 1733 Sheepshead Bay Rd., Brooklyn, NY 11235. TEL 718-769-4400; FAX 718-769-5408. **Owner(s):** Courier-Life, Inc., 1733 Sheepshead Bay Rd., Brooklyn, NY 11235. TEL 718-769-4400; Ed. Ken Brown; Pub. Edward Luster; adv. contact: Clifford Luster. photos; bk.rev.; pub. size: tabloid; circ. 10,900(paid).

US
CARROLL GARDENS/COBBLE HILL COURIER. 1990. bi-w.: Mon. free. 1733 Sheepshead Bay Rd., Brooklyn, NY 11235. TEL 718-769-4400; FAX 718-769-5048. **Owner(s):** Courier-Life, Inc., 1733 Sheepshead Bay Rd., Brooklyn, NY 11235. TEL 718-769-4400; Ed. Kenneth Brown; Pub. Edward Luster; adv. contact: Clifford Luster. photos; bk.rev.; pub. size: tabloid; circ. 81,000(free).

US
FLATBUSH LIFE. 1956. Mon. $.50 newsstand; $20/yr. 1733 Sheepshead Bay Rd., Brooklyn, NY 11235. TEL 718-769-4400; FAX 718-769-5048. **Owner(s):** Courier-Life, Inc., 1733 Sheepshead Bay Rd., Brooklyn, NY 11235. TEL 718-769-4400; Ed. Kenneth Brown; Pub. Edward Luster; adv. contact: Clifford Luster. photos; bk.rev.; pub. size: tabloid; circ. 13,600(paid).

US
GREENPOINT GAZETTE/ADVERTISER. 1973. Wed. $.25 newsstand; $20/yr. in Brooklyn; $25/yr. out of Brooklyn. 597 Manhattan Ave., Brooklyn, NY 11222-3919. TEL 718-389-6067; FAX 718-349-3471. **Owner(s):** Community Gazette, Inc., 597 Manhattan Ave., Brooklyn, NY 11222-3919. TEL 718-389-6067; FAX 718-349-3471; Ed. Virginia Bednarek. adv.; photos; bk.rev.; pub. size: tabloid; circ. 5,010(free & paid). **Wire Service(s):** CNS.

US
HARBORWATCH. 1989. Thu. free to military; $15/yr. mailed. 1733 Sheepshead Bay Rd., Brooklyn, NY 11235. TEL 718-769-4400; FAX 718-769-5048. **Owner(s):** Courier-Life, Inc., 1733 Sheepshead Bay Road, Brooklyn, NY 11235. TEL 718-769-4400; Ed. Kenneth Brown; Pub. Edward Luster; adv. contact: Clifford Luster. photos; bk.rev.; pub. size: tabloid; circ. 12,000(controlled & paid).

US
KINGS COUNTY NEWS. 1976. Mon. $.50 newsstand; $26/yr. 2446 E. 65th St., Brooklyn, NY 11234. TEL 718-763-7034; FAX 718-763-7035. **Owner(s):** EWA Publications, 275 Bay 37th St., Brooklyn, NY 11214. TEL 718-996-5406; FAX 718-373-1352; Ed. Kevin Browne. adv.; photos; bk.rev.; pub. size: tabloid; circ. 71,000(controlled & paid).

WEEKLY NEWSPAPERS

KINGS COURIER. 1951. Mon. $.50 newsstand; $20/yr. 1733 Sheepshead Bay Rd., Brooklyn, NY 11235. TEL 718-769-4400; FAX 718-769-5408. **Owner(s):** Courier-Life, Inc., 1733 Sheepshead Bay Rd., Brooklyn, NY 11235; Ed. Ken Brown; Pub. Edward Luster; adv. contact: Clifford Luster. photos; bk.rev.; pub. size: tabloid; circ. 10,700(controlled & paid).

US

METROPOLITAN NEWS. 1970. Fri. $.50 newsstand; $26/yr. 2446 E. 65th St., Brooklyn, NY 11234. TEL 718-763-7034; FAX 718-763-7035. **Owner(s):** EWA Publications, 2446 E. 65th St., Brooklyn, NY 11234. TEL 718-763-7034; FAX 718-763-7035; photos; bk.rev.; pub. size: tabloid; circ. 132,000(controlled & paid).

US

NEW YORK METROPOLITAN NEWS. 1962. Mon. $.50 newsstand; $26/yr. 2446 E. 65th St., Brooklyn, NY 11234. TEL 718-763-7034; FAX 718-763-7035. **Owner(s):** EWA Publications, 2446 E. 65th St., Brooklyn, NY 11234. TEL 718-763-7034; FAX 718-763-7035; Ed. Kevin Browne. photos; bk.rev.; pub. size: tabloid; circ. 216,000(controlled & paid).

US

PARK SLOPE COURIER. 1990. bi-w.: Mon. free. 1733 Sheepshead Bay Rd., Brooklyn, NY 11235. TEL 718-769-4400; FAX 718-769-5048. **Owner(s):** Courier-Life, Inc., 1733 Sheepshead Bay Rd., Brooklyn, NY 11235. TEL 718-769-4400; Ed. Kenneth Brown; Pub. Edward Luster; adv. contact: Clifford Luster. photos; bk.rev.; pub. size: tabloid; circ. 101,000(free).

US

PHOENIX NEWSPAPER, THE. 1972. Mon. $.50 newsstand; $18/yr. 125 Montague St., Brooklyn, NY 11201. TEL 718-625-7500; FAX 718-624-2716. **Owner(s):** J.D. Hasty, 125 Montague St., Brooklyn, NY 11201. TEL 718-643-1400; FAX 718-643-1033; Frederick Halla, 125 Montague St., Brooklyn, NY 11202. TEL 718-643-1400; FAX 718-643-1033; Ed. Dennis Holt; Pub. J.D. Hasty; adv. contact: Patricia Higgins. photos; pub. size: tabloid; circ. 13,000(paid).

BUFFALO

US

BUFFALO ROCKET. 1969. Wed. $30/yr. 2503 Delaware, Buffalo, NY 14216. TEL 716-873-2594; FAX 716-873-0809. **Owner(s):** David Gallagher, 2503 Delaware, Buffalo, NY 14216. TEL 716-873-2594; Ed. Craig W. Turner; Pub. David H. Gallagher; adv.; pub. size: tabloid; circ. 15,000(paid).

US

RIVERSIDE REVIEW. 1923. Wed. free newsstand; $39.50/yr. mailed. 215 Military Rd., Buffalo, NY 14207. TEL 716-877-8400; FAX 716-877-8742. **Owner(s):** Worrall Community Newspapers, Inc., 1291 Stuyvesant Ave., Union, NJ 07083. TEL 908-686-7700; Ed. Richard Mack; Pub. Richard Mack; adv. contact: James Smith. pub. size: tabloid; circ. 14,300(free & paid).

US

WEST SIDE TIMES. 1893. Tue. $30/yr. 2503 Delaware, Buffalo, NY 14216. TEL 716-873-2594; FAX 716-873-0809. **Owner(s):** David H. Gallagher, 2503 Delaware Ave., Buffalo, NY 14216. TEL 716-873-2594; FAX 716-873-0809; Ed. Dennis Gallagher; Pub. David H. Gallagher; adv.; photos; pub. size: tabloid; circ. 13,000(free).

CAMBRIDGE

US ISSN 0745-9831

EAGLE, THE. 1981. Wed. $28/yr. in state; $30/yr. out of state. P.O. Box 36, Cambridge, NY 12816. TEL 518-677-5158; FAX 518-677-8323. **Owner(s):** Eagle, The, P.O. Box 36, Cambridge, NY 12816. TEL 518-677-5158; FAX 518-677-8323; Ed. Richard F. Farrell; Pub. Richard F. Farrell; adv.; photos; bk.rev.; pub. size: tabloid; circ. 4,220(free & paid).

CANASTOTA

US

CANASTOTA BEE-JOURNAL. Wed. $.75 newsstand; $25/yr.; $13/yr. student; $21/yr. senior citizens. 114 Canal St., Canastota, NY 13032. TEL 315-697-7142; FAX 315-434-8883. **Owner(s):** Eagle Newspapers, Inc., P.O. Box 65, Fayetteville, NY 13066, free & paid. TEL 315-637-3121; Ed. Rich Petrillo; Pub. Stewart Hancock; pub. size: broadsheet; circ. 2,200(paid).

CANTON

US

ST. LAWRENCE PLAINDEALER. Tue. $18.90/yr. in cy.; $19.95/yr. out of cy. 75 Main St., Canton, NY 13617. TEL 315-386-8521; FAX 315-386-8887. **Owner(s):** Johnson Acquisitions Corp., 260 Washington St., Watertown, NY 13601. TEL 315-782-1000; Ed. Paul Mitchell. pub. size: broadsheet; circ. 3,500(paid).

CARMEL

US ISSN 0890-1147

PUTNAM COURIER-TRADER, THE. 1841. Thu. $.50 newsstand; $24.95/yr. in cy.; $34.95/yr. out of cy.; $16/yr. senior citizens. 73 Gleneida, Carmel, NY 10512. TEL 914-225-3633; FAX 914-225-1914; E-mail: housvalpub@aol.com. **Owner(s):** Housatonic Valley Publishing Co., P.O. Box 1139, New Milford, CT 06776. TEL 860-354-2261; FAX 860-354-2645; Ed. Barbara Gallo Farrell; Pub. John Norton; adv. contact: Joan Byrnes. photos; pub. size: broadsheet; circ. 6,200(paid).

CARTHAGE

US

CARTHAGE REPUBLICAN TRIBUNE. 1860. Wed. $.75 newsstand; $29/yr. local; $35/yr. elsewhere. 3 Front St., Carthage, NY 13619. TEL 315-493-1270; FAX 315-493-1271. **Owner(s):** Johnson Newspaper Corp., 260 Washington St., Watertown, NY 13601. TEL 315-782-1000; adv. contact: Charles Howlett. photos; bk.rev.; pub. size: broadsheet; circ. 3,000(paid).

CAZENOVIA

US

CAZENOVIA REPUBLICAN. 1794. Wed. $.75 newsstand; $25/yr. in cy.; $21/yr. senior citizens; $13/yr. students; $30/yr. out of state. 72 Albany St., Cazenovia, NY 13035. TEL 315-655-3415; FAX 315-655-3813. **Owner(s):** Eagle Newspapers, Inc., P.O. Box 65, Fayetteville, NY 13066. TEL 315-637-3121; Ed. Peter Anderson; Pub. Stewart Hancock; adv. contact: Pam Kennedy. pub. size: broadsheet; circ. 3,871(paid).

CHATHAM

US ISSN 1064-4644

CHATHAM COURIER. 1825. Thu. $.50 newsstand; $32/yr. 24 Park Row, Chatham, NY 12037. TEL 518-392-4141; FAX 518-392-7322. **Owner(s):** Johnson Newspaper Corp., 260 Washington St., Watertown, NY 13601. TEL 315-782-1000; Ed. Barbara Hauley; Pub. Tony Panetta; adv.; photos; pub. size: tabloid; circ. 3,500(paid). **Wire Service(s):** AP. **Formerly:** Courier-Roughnotes.

CHEEKTOWAGA

US

CHEEKTOWAGA TIMES. 1946. Thu. $.75 newsstand; $25/yr. 343 Maryvale Dr., Cheektowaga, NY 14225. TEL 716-892-5323; FAX 716-892-4925. **Owner(s):** Eve J. Allis, 403 Walton Dr., Cheektowaga, NY 14225. TEL 716-892-5323; adv.; photos; pub. size: tabloid; circ. 5,600(paid).

CLIFTON PARK

US

COMMUNITY NEWS. 1969. Fri. free. Clifton Corporate Park, Bldg. 400, Ste. 482, Clifton Park, NY 12065. TEL 518-371-7108; FAX 518-371-0933. **Owner(s):** Gannett Company, Inc., 1100 Wilson Blvd., Arlington, VA 22234. TEL 703-284-6000; Ed. Cindy Chin; Pub. Monte Trammer; adv. contact: Kim Rich. photos; pub. size: broadsheet; circ. 26,000(controlled & free). **Wire Service(s):** AP, GNS.

CLINTON

US

CLINTON COURIER. 1846. Wed. $.75 newsstand; $25/yr. in cy.; $30/yr. out of cy.; $19.75/yr. student. 4 Meadow St., Clinton, NY 13323-0294. TEL 315-853-3490; FAX 315-853-3522; E-mail: courier@delphi.com. **Owner(s):** Charles & Cynthia Kershner, 4 Meadow St., P.O. Box 294, Clinton, NY 13323-0294. TEL 315-853-3490; FAX 315-853-3522; Ed. Charles J. Kershner; Pub. Cynthia Kershner; adv.: $10.32/SAU. bk.rev.; pub. size: tabloid; circ. 2,170(paid).

COBLESKILL

US

TIMES JOURNAL. 1876. Wed. $.60 newsstand; $25/yr. in cy.; $40/yr. out of cy. 19 Division St., Cobleskill, NY 12043. TEL 518-234-2515; FAX 518-234-7898. **Owner(s):** Jim Poole, P.O. Box 339, Cobleskill, NY 12043. TEL 518-234-2515; Ed. Patsy Nicosia; Pub. Jim Poole; adv. contact: Marilyn Swartout. photos; pub. size: broadsheet; circ. 6,000(paid). **Formerly:** Cobleskill Times Journal.

CONKLIN

US ISSN 1065-5891
COUNTRY COURIER, THE. 1976. Wed. $.45 newsstand; $19/yr. mailed in cy. 1035 Conklin Rd., Conklin, NY 13748. TEL 607-775-0472; FAX 607-775-5863. **Owner(s):** Masthead Publications, Inc., 1035 Conklin Rd., Conklin, NY 13748. TEL 607-775-0472; FAX 607-775-5863; Ed. Elizabeth Einstein; Pub. Don Einstein; adv.; photos; pub. size: tabloid; circ. 1,600(paid).

US ISSN 1051-3574
VESTAL TOWN CRIER. 1989. Wed. $.45 newsstand; $19/yr. mailed in cy.; $20/yr. out of cy. 1035 Conklin Rd., Conklin, NY 13748. TEL 607-775-0472; FAX 607-775-5863. **Owner(s):** Masthead Publications, Inc., P.O. Box 208, Conklin, NY 13748. TEL 607-775-0472; FAX 607-775-5863; Ed. Elizabeth Einstein; Pub. Don Einstein; adv.; photos; pub. size: tabloid; circ. 1,400(paid).

US ISSN 1059-5449
WINDSOR STANDARD. 1879. Wed. $.45 newsstand; $19/yr. in cy.; $21/yr. out of cy. 1035 Conklin Rd., Conklin, NY 13748. TEL 607-775-0472; FAX 607-775-5863. **Owner(s):** Masthead Publications, Inc., P.O. Box 208, Conklin, NY 13748. TEL 607-775-0472; FAX 607-775-5863; Ed. Elizabeth Einstein; Pub. Don Einstein; adv.; photos; pub. size: tabloid; circ. 1,500(paid).

CORAM

US
YANKEE TRADER. 1966. Wed. free. One Glenmere Ln., Coram, NY 11727. TEL 516-331-3300; FAX 516-331-3481. **Owner(s):** Newport Media, 250 Miller Pl., Hicksville, NY 11801; Pub. John W. Sutter; adv.; pub. size: tabloid; circ. 252,399(free).

CROSS RIVER

US ISSN 0746-1836
PATENT TRADER. 1956. Thu. $.75 newsstand; $45/yr. Cross River Shopping Plz., Corner of Rte. 121 & 35, Cross River, NY 10518. TEL 914-763-3200; FAX 914-763-3911. **Owner(s):** Tucker Communications, Inc., Cross River Shopping Plz., P.O. Box 1000, Cross River, NY 10518. TEL 914-763-3200; Ed. Susan Pronovost; Pub. Carll Tucker; adv.; pub. size: broadsheet; circ. 16,000(paid). **Wire Service(s):** AP.

CUBA

US
PATRIOT & FREE PRESS. 1862. Wed. $.50 newsstand; $21/yr. in cy.; $23/yr. out of cy. 34 Water St., Cuba, NY 14727-1490. TEL 716-968-2580; FAX 716-968-2622; E-mail: 71342.3575@compuserve.com. **Owner(s):** Empire Phoenix Corp., 97 Pennsylvania Ave., Friendship, NY 14739. TEL 716-973-2025; Ed. John Arden-Hopkins; Pub. Christina Arden-Hopkins; adv.; photos; pub. size: broadsheet; circ. 4,300(paid).
Formerly: Cuba Patriot & Free Press; New Patriot; Free Press.

DANSVILLE

US
DANSVILLE GENESEE COUNTRY EXPRESS. 1851. Thu. $.75 newsstand; $28/yr. in cy. 113 Main St., Dansville, NY 14437. TEL 716-335-2272; FAX 716-335-6957. **Owner(s):** American Publishing Co., 606 N. Van Buren, Marion, IL 61959. TEL 618-993-1711; Ed. Brian Langen; Pub. Frederick W. Kurtz; adv. contact: Barbara Nagle. pub. size: broadsheet; circ. 14,842(free & paid).

DELHI

US ISSN 0745-0206
DELAWARE COUNTY TIMES. 1978. Fri. $.35 newsstand; $15/yr. in cy.; $17.50/yr. out of cy. 56 Main St., Delhi, NY 13753. TEL 607-746-2176; FAX 607-746-3135; E-mail: kaatslife@digital-marketplace.net. **Owner(s):** Donald F. Bishop, II, Hobart, NY 13788. TEL 607-746-2176; FAX 607-746-3135; Pub. Donald F. Bishop; adv. contact: Richard Craft. adv.: $3.50/SAU. photos; bk.rev.; pub. size: broadsheet; circ. 1,500(paid).

DELMAR

US
COLONIE SPOTLIGHT. Tue. $.50 newsstand; $24/yr. in cy. 125 Adams St., Delmar, NY 12054. TEL 518-439-4949; FAX 518-439-0609. **Owner(s):** Spotlight Newspapers, Inc., 125 Adams St., Delmar, NY 12054. TEL 518-439-4949; Ed. Martin Kelly; Pub. Richard A. Ahlstrom; adv. contact: Louise Havens. pub. size: tabloid; circ. 4,000(paid).

US
LOUDENVILLE WEEKLY. Wed. $.50 newsstand; free in area; $24/yr. in cy. 125 Adams St., Delmar, NY 12054. TEL 518-439-4949; FAX 518-439-0609. **Owner(s):** Spotlight Newspapers, Inc., 125 Adams St., Delmar, NY 12054. TEL 518-439-4949; Ed. Martin Kelly; Pub. Richard A. Ahlstrom; adv. contact: Louise Havens. pub. size: tabloid; circ. 5,000(free & paid).

US
SPOTLIGHT, THE. 1955. Wed. $.50 newsstand; $24/yr. in cy.; $32/yr. out of cy. 125 Adams St., Delmar, NY 12054. TEL 518-439-4949; FAX 518-439-0609. **Owner(s):** Spotlight Newspapers, Inc., 125 Adams St., Delmar, NY 12054. TEL 518-439-4949; Ed. Susan Graves; Pub. Richard A. Ahlstrom; adv.; pub. size: tabloid; circ. 7,000(paid).

DEPOSIT

US
DEPOSIT COURIER. 1848. w. $.50 newsstand; $16/yr. in cy.; $19/yr. out of cy. 138 Front St., Deposit, NY 13754. TEL 607-467-3600; FAX 607-467-5330. **Owner(s):** Hilton A. Evans, 138 Front St., Deposit, NY 13754. TEL 607-467-3600; Ed. Hilton A. Evans. pub. size: broadsheet; circ. 2,200(paid).

DUNDEE

US
DUNDEE OBSERVER. 1878. Wed. $.60 newsstand; $23/yr. in state; $27/yr. out of state. 45 Water St., Dundee, NY 14837. TEL 607-243-8351; FAX 607-243-5833. **Owner(s):** Mary Geo Tomion, 45 Water St., Dundee, NY 14837. TEL 607-243-7600; FAX 607-243-5833; Ed. Mary Geo Tomion; Pub. Mary Geo Tomion; adv. contact: Lori Knapp. adv.: $4.25/SAU. photos; pub. size: tabloid; circ. 3,200(free & paid).

EAST AURORA

US
EAST AURORA ADVERTISER. 1872. Tue. $.50 newsstand; $23/yr. in cy.; $29/yr. out of cy. 710 Main St., East Aurora, NY 14052. TEL 716-652-0320. **Owner(s):** Grant M. Hamilton, 710 Main St., East Aurora, NY 14052. TEL 716-652-0320; Ed. Grant M. Hamilton; Pub. Grant M. Hamilton; adv.; pub. size: broadsheet; circ. 4,400(paid).

US
ELMA REVIEW. 1972. Wed. $.25 newsstand; $13/yr. in cy.; $15/yr. out of cy. 710 Main St., East Aurora, NY 14052. TEL 716-652-0327. **Owner(s):** Grant M. Hamilton, P.O. Box 118, Elma, NY 14052. TEL 716-652-0327; Ed. Grant M. Hamilton; Pub. Grant M. Hamilton; adv. contact: Sharon Nieman. pub. size: tabloid; circ. 1,200(paid).

EAST HAMPTON

US
EAST HAMPTON STAR. 1885. Thu. $1 newsstand; $30/yr. in cy.; $40/yr. out of cy.; $45/yr. Manhattan deliv. 153 Main St., East Hampton, NY 11937. TEL 516-324-0002; FAX 516-324-7943; E-mail: editore@easthamptonstar.com; URL: http://www.easthamptonstar.com. **Owner(s):** Helen S. Rattray, P.O. Box 5002, East Hampton, NY 11937. TEL 516-324-0002; FAX 516-324-7943; Arthur L. Carter, 54 E. 64th St., New York, NY 10021. TEL 212-755-2400; Ed. Helen S. Rattray; Pub. Arthur L. Carter; adv. contact: Gregg Robinson. photos; bk.rev.; pub. size: broadsheet; circ. 14,223(paid).

EAST SETAUKET

US
THREE VILLAGE HERALD. 1954. Wed. $.50 newsstand; $18/yr. in cy.; $24/yr. out of cy. 60 Rt. 25A, East Setauket, NY 11733. TEL 516-751-1550; FAX 516-751-8592. **Owner(s):** North Suffolk Publishing Co., P.O. Box BH, Stony Brook, NY 11790; Ed. Sue Bridson; Pub. Gardner Cowles, III; adv. contact: Pearl Knight. photos; pub. size: tabloid; circ. 30,000(paid).

ELIZABETHTOWN

US
NORTH COUNTRYMAN, THE. 1928. Sat. $25/yr. in cy.; $30/yr. out of cy. P.O. Box 338, Elizabethtown, NY 12932. TEL 518-873-6368; FAX 518-873-6360. **Owner(s):** Elizabethtown Denton Publications, Inc., P.O. Box 338, Elizabethtown, NY 12932. TEL 518-873-6368; Ed. John Gereau; Pub. Dan Alexander. pub. size: tabloid; circ. 3,000(paid).
Formerly: Rouses Point North Countryman.

WEEKLY NEWSPAPERS

US
VALLEY NEWS. 1839. Wed. $.50 newsstand; $25/yr. in cy.; $30/yr. out of cy. P.O. Box 338, Elizabethtown, NY 12932. TEL 518-873-6368; FAX 518-873-6360. **Owner(s):** Elizabethtown Denton Publications, Inc., P.O. Box 338, Elizabethtown, NY 12932. TEL 518-873-6368; Ed. John Gereau; Pub. Dan Alexander; pub. size: tabloid; circ. 4,800(paid).

US
WARRENSBURG-LAKE GEORGE NEWS. 1868. Wed. $25/yr. in cy.; $30/yr. out of cy. P.O. Box 338, Elizabethtown, NY 12932. TEL 518-623-3411; FAX 518-623-9264. **Owner(s):** Elizabethtown Denton Publications, Inc., P.O. Box 338, Elizabethtown, NY 12932. TEL 518-873-6368; Ed. John Gereau; Pub. Dan Alexander; adv. contact: John Macglire. pub. size: tabloid; circ. 3,000(paid).

ELLENVILLE

US   ISSN 1077-6133
ELLENVILLE PRESS. 1873. Wed. $.35 newsstand; $16.50/yr. 7 Cape Ave., Ellenville, NY 12428. TEL 914-647-7222. **Owner(s):** Rondout Valley Publishing Co., Inc., P.O. Box 31, Ellenville, NY 12428. TEL 914-647-7222; Ed. Minnie L. Wainer; Pub. Minnie L. Wainer; adv.; photos; bk.rev.; pub. size: tabloid; circ. 1,970(paid).

ELMONT

US
ELMONT HERALD. 1978. Fri. $.35 newsstand; $14/yr. in cy.; $16/yr. out of cy. 591 Bauer Ct., Elmont, NY 11003-4312. TEL 516-354-3379; FAX 516-328-8586. **Owner(s):** Rita Mezzapelle, 591 Bauer Ct., Elmont, NY 11003. TEL 516-354-3379; FAX 516-328-8586; Ed. Roy J. Mezzapelle; Pub. Roy J. Mezzapelle; adv. contact: Roy J. Mezzapelle. photos; pub. size: tabloid; circ. 5,000(paid).

ELMSFORD

US
PENNYSAVER. 1985. Sat. free. 101 Executive Blvd., Elmsford, NY 10523. TEL 914-592-5222; FAX 914-592-4816. **Owner(s):** Pennysaver Group, Inc., 101 Executive Blvd., P.O. Box 481, Elmsford, NY 10523. TEL 914-592-5222; Ed. Herb Solomon. adv.; pub. size: standard; circ. 388,210(controlled & free).
Formerly: Pennysaver/Westchester Life.

ENDWELL

US
VALLEY NEWS, THE. 1989. Wed. $.75 newsstand; $32/yr. 3128 Watson Blvd., Endwell, NY 13760-3532. TEL 607-757-0753; FAX 607-757-0784. **Owner(s):** Brad Manchester, 3128 Watson Blvd., Endwell, NY 13760. TEL 607-757-0753; FAX 607-757-0784; Keith Manchester, 3128 Watson Blvd., Endwell, NY 13760. TEL 607-757-0753; FAX 607-757-0784; Ed. Tom Melville; Pub. Brad Manchester; adv. contact: Brad Manchester. photos; bk.rev.; pub. size: broadsheet; circ. 1,500(paid).

FISHERS

US
BRIGHTON-PITTSFORD POST, THE. 1932. Wed. $.75 newsstand; $28/yr. P.O. Box C, Fishers, NY 14453. TEL 716-381-3300; FAX 716-924-7734. **Owner(s):** Canandaigua Messenger, Inc., 73 Buffalo St., Canandaigua, NY 14424. TEL 716-394-0770; Ed. Mark Syverud; Pub. George W. Ewing, Jr.; pub. size: broadsheet; circ. 11,100(paid).

US
GREECE POST, THE. 1960. Thu. $.50 newsstand; $21/yr. P.O. Box C, Fishers, NY 14453. TEL 716-381-3300; FAX 716-924-7734. **Owner(s):** Canandaigua Messenger, Inc., 73 Buffalo St., Canandaigua, NY 14424. TEL 716-394-0770; Ed. Andrew D. Wolfe; Pub. Jillian St. Jaques; pub. size: broadsheet; circ. 8,500(paid).

US
HENRIETTA POST. 1964. Wed. $.50 newsstand; $21/yr. mailed. P.O. Box C, Fishers, NY 14453. TEL 716-381-3300; FAX 716-924-7734. **Owner(s):** Canandaigua Messenger, Inc., 73 Buffalo St., Canandaigua, NY 14424. TEL 716-394-0770; Ed. Mark Syverud; Pub. George Ewing, Jr.; pub. size: broadsheet; circ. 2,500(paid).

US
PENFIELD POST-REPUBLICAN, THE. 1950. Thu. $.50 newsstand; $21/yr. P.O. Box C, Fishers, NY 14453. TEL 716-381-3300; FAX 716-924-7734. **Owner(s):** Canandaigua Messenger, Inc., 73 Buffalo St., Canandaigua, NY 14424. TEL 716-394-0770; Ed. Mark Syverud; Pub. Mark Syverud; adv.; pub. size: broadsheet; circ. 3,800(paid).

FLORAL PARK

US
FLORAL PARK BULLETIN. 1941. w. $.35 newsstand; $15/yr. P.O. Box 227, Floral Park, NY 11001. **Owner(s):** Carla Cohen, P.O. Box 227, Floral Park, NY 11001; Ed. Carla Cohen; Pub. Carla Cohen; adv. contact: Janis Murphy. pub. size: tabloid.

US
FRANKLIN SQUARE BULLETIN. 1938. Thu. $.35 newsstand; $15/yr. 139 Tulip Ave., Floral Park, NY 11001. TEL 516-775-7700. **Owner(s):** Nassau Border Papers, Inc., P.O. Box 155, Franklin Square, NY 11010. TEL 516-775-7700; Ed. Carla Cohen; Pub. Carla Cohen; adv. contact: Janis Murphy. photos; pub. size: tabloid; circ. 8,700(paid).

US
GATEWAY, THE. 1926. Wed. $15/yr. P.O. Box 227, Floral Park, NY 11002. TEL 516-775-2700. **Owner(s):** Carla Cohen, P.O. Box 227, Floral Park, NY 11002. TEL 516-775-2700; Ed. Carla Cohen. adv.; photos; pub. size: tabloid; circ. 12,000(paid).

FLUSHING

US
FRESH MEADOWS TIMES, THE. 1993. Thu. $.50 newsstand; $19/yr.; $35/2 yrs. in cy. 41-02 Bell Blvd., 2nd Fl., Flushing, NY 11361. TEL 718-229-0300; FAX 718-225-7117. **Owner(s):** Queens Publishing Corp., 41-02 Bell Blvd., 2nd Fl., Flushing, NY 11361. TEL 718-229-0300; Ed. Roz Liston; Pub. Steve Blank; adv.; photos; pub. size: tabloid; circ. 1,552(paid).

US
▼**JAMAICA TIMES, THE.** 1995. Thu. $.50 newsstand; $19/yr.; $35/2 yrs. in cy. 41-02 Bell Blvd., 2nd Fl., Flushing, NY 11361. TEL 718-229-0300; FAX 718-225-7117. **Owner(s):** Queens Publishing Corp., 214-11 41st Ave., Flushing, NY 11361. TEL 718-229-0300; Ed. Roz Liston; Pub. Steve Blank; adv.; photos; pub. size: tabloid; circ. 1,019.

US
LITTLE NECK LEDGER, THE. 1919. Thu. $.50 newsstand; $19/yr.; $35/2 yrs. 41-02 Bell Blvd., 2nd Fl., Flushing, NY 11361. TEL 718-229-0300; FAX 718-225-7117. **Owner(s):** Queens Publishing Corp., 214-11 41st Ave., Flushing, NY 11361. TEL 718-229-0300; Ed. Roz Liston; Pub. Steven Blank; adv.; photos; pub. size: tabloid; circ. 3,723(paid).

US
QUEENS VILLAGE TIMES, THE. 1994. Thu. $.50 newsstand; $19/yr.; $35/2 yrs. in cy. 41-02 Bell Blvd., 2nd Fl., Flushing, NY 11361. TEL 718-229-0300; FAX 718-225-7117. **Owner(s):** Queens Publishing Corp., 41-02 Bell Blvd., 2nd Fl., Flushing, NY 11361. TEL 718-229-0300; Ed. Roz Liston; Pub. Steve Blank; adv.; photos; pub. size: tabloid; circ. 2,039(paid).

FORT PLAIN

US
COURIER-STANDARD-ENTERPRISE. 1876. Wed. $.50 newsstand; $18/yr. in cy. 41 Main St., Fort Plain, NY 13339. TEL 518-993-2321; FAX 518-993-4919. **Owner(s):** Tri-Village Publishers, Inc., One Venner Rd., Amsterdam, NY 12010. TEL 518-843-1100; Ed. Robert P. Lindsay; Pub. Richard A. Barker; adv. contact: John Larkin. photos; pub. size: broadsheet; circ. 4,700(paid).

FREEPORT

US
FREEPORT BALDWIN LEADER, THE. 1935. Thu. $.30 newsstand; $11.50/yr. 30 S. Ocean Ave., Ste. 204, Freeport, NY 11520. TEL 516-378-3133; FAX 516-378-3139. **Owner(s):** L & M Publications, Inc., 1840 Merrick Ave., Merrick, NY 11566. TEL 516-378-5320; FAX 516-378-0287; Ed. Laura Shofer; Pub. Linda L. Toscano; adv. contact: Mark Treske. pub. size: tabloid; circ. 2,700(paid).

US
LEADER, THE. 1935. Thu. $11.50/yr. 30 S. Ocean Ave., Ste. 204, Freeport, NY 11520. TEL 516-378-3133. **Owner(s):** L & M Publications, Inc., 1840 Merrick Ave., Merrick, NY 11566. TEL 516-378-5320; FAX 516-378-0287; Ed. Paul Laursen; Pub. Linda Toscano. pub. size: tabloid; circ. 3,000(paid).

US
VALLEY STREAM COURIER. 1966. Thu. $20/yr. 244 Whaley St., Freeport, NY 11520. TEL 516-378-5002. **Owner(s):** Rosemary McCarthy, Freeport, NY. TEL 516-378-5002; Ed. Rosemary A. McCarthy; Pub. Rosemary A. McCarthy; pub. size: tabloid; circ. 1,400(paid).

FRESH MEADOWS

US

QUEENS TRIBUNE. 1970. Thu. $12/yr.; $21/2 yrs.; $29/3 yrs. 174-15 Horace Harding Expy., Fresh Meadows, NY 11365. TEL 718-357-7400; FAX 718-357-9417. **Owner(s):** News Communications, Inc., Fresh Meadows, NY; Ed. David Oats; Pub. Steven Goldstein; adv. contact: Steven Goldstein. pub. size: tabloid; circ. 146,000(free & paid).

FULTON

US

FULTON PATRIOT. 1823. Mon. free newsstand; $7/yr. in cy.; $14/yr. out of cy. P.O. Box 299, Fulton, NY 13069. TEL 315-592-2459. **Owner(s):** Fulton Newspapers, Inc., P.O. Box 805, Fulton, NY 13069. TEL 315-598-6397; Ed. Roy N. Hodge; Pub. Roy N. Hodge; pub. size: standard; circ. 6,235(paid).

US ISSN 1067-7755
VALLEY NEWS. 1947. s-w.: Mon. & Thu. $.35 newsstand; $17/yr. in cy. 117 Oneida St., Fulton, NY 13069. TEL 315-598-6397. **Owner(s):** Fulton Newspapers, Inc., P.O. Box 805, Fulton, NY 13069. TEL 315-598-6397; Ed. Ronald L. Caravan; Pub. Isabelle Caravan; adv. contact: Allison McManus. pub. size: tabloid; circ. 10,000(paid).

GLENS FALLS

US

CHRONICLE, THE. 1980. Thu. free; $35/yr. P.O. Box 153, Glens Falls, NY 12801-0153. TEL 518-792-1126. **Owner(s):** Chronicle, The, P.O. Box 153, Glens Falls, NY 12801. TEL 518-792-1126. Ed. Mark Frost; Pub. Patricia Maddock; adv.; photos; bk.rev.; pub. size: tabloid; circ. 25,000(free & paid).

GOSHEN

US

INDEPENDENT REPUBLICAN. 1812. Wed. $.50 newsstand; $24/yr. in cy.; $26/yr. out of cy. 132 W. Main, Goshen, NY 10924-0628. TEL 914-294-6111; FAX 914-294-0532. **Owner(s):** Betty J. Wright, 132 W. Main, Goshen, NY 10924-0628. TEL 914-294-6111; FAX 914-294-0532; Ed. Betty Jane Wright. adv.; photos; pub. size: tabloid; circ. 3,800(paid).

GOUVERNEUR

US

GOUVERNEUR TRIBUNE PRESS. 1886. Wed. $.50 newsstand; $18/yr. in state; $25/yr. out of state. 74 Trinity Ave., Gouverneur, NY 13642. TEL 315-287-2100. **Owner(s):** Gouverneur Tribune Press, Inc., 74 Trinity Ave., Gouverneur, NY 13642. TEL 315-287-2100; Pub. M. Dan McClennan; adv. contact: Colin Graves. bk.rev.; pub. size: standard; circ. 5,000(paid).

GOWANDA

US

GOWANDA PENNYSAVER NEWS. 1939. Mon. free. 62 W. Main St., Gowanda, NY 14070. TEL 716-532-2288; FAX 716-532-3056. **Owner(s):** H & K Publications, Inc., 50 Buffalo St., Hamburg, NY 14075. TEL 716-649-4413; FAX 716-649-6374; Ed. Maureen Spockdale; Pub. H & K Publication; pub. size: tabloid; circ. 11,800(free).

GRAND ISLAND

US

GRAND ISLAND PENNYSAVER. 1949. Tue. free. 1854C Whitehaven Rd., Grand Island, NY 14072-0130. TEL 716-773-7676; FAX 716-773-7190. **Owner(s):** Niagara Frontier Publications, Inc., 1854C Whitehaven Rd., Grand Island, NY 14072. TEL 716-773-7676; FAX 716-773-7190; Ed. Deanne Bartha; Pub. Arthur J. Mazenauer; adv.; photos; pub. size: tabloid; circ. 7,000(free).

US

ISLAND DISPATCH. 1944. Fri. $.65 newsstand; $20.95/yr. in cy.; $25.95/yr. out of cy. 1854C Whitehaven Rd., Grand Island, NY 14072-0130. TEL 716-773-7676; FAX 716-773-7190. **Owner(s):** Niagara Frontier Publications, Inc., 1845C Whitehaven Rd., P.O. Box 130, Grand Island, NY 14072-0130. TEL 716-773-7676; FAX 716-773-7190; Ed. Deanne Bartha; Pub. Arthur J. Mazenauer; photos; bk.rev.; pub. size: tabloid; circ. 3,602(free & paid). **Wire Service(s):** NY Press Assn.

US

LEWISTON-PORTER SENTINEL. 1987. Sat. free. 1854C Whitehaven Rd., Grand Island, NY 14072. TEL 716-773-7676; FAX 716-773-7190. **Owner(s):** Niagara Frontier Publications, Inc., 1854C Whitehaven Rd., Grand Island, NY 14072. TEL 716-773-7676; FAX 716-773-7190; Ed. Deanne Bartha; Pub. Arthur J. Mazenauer; adv.; photos; pub. size: tabloid; circ. 15,000(free). **Wire Service(s):** NY Press Assn.

US

NIAGARA/WHEATFIELD TRIBUNE. Thu. free. 1854C Whitehaven Rd., Grand Island, NY 14072-0130. TEL 716-773-7676; FAX 716-773-7190. **Owner(s):** Niagara Frontier Publications, Inc., 1854C Whitehaven Rd., Grand Island, NY 14072. TEL 716-773-7676; FAX 716-773-7190; Ed. Deanne Bartha; Pub. Arthur J. Mazenauer; adv.; photos; pub. size: tabloid; circ. 15,000(free). **Wire Service(s):** NY Press Assn.

GRANVILLE

US

GRANVILLE SENTINEL. 1875. Wed. $.60 newsstand; $20/yr. in cy.; $26/yr. in N.Y.-New England; $.36/yr. elsewhere. 14 E. Main St., Granville, NY 12832. TEL 518-642-1234; FAX 518-642-1344. **Owner(s):** Manchester Newspapers, Inc., 6 North St., Granville, NY 12832; Ed. John N. Manchester; Pub. John N. Manchester; adv. contact: Jennifer Barrett. pub. size: broadsheet; circ. 3,300(paid).

US

LAKES REGION FREE PRESS, THE. Sat. free. 14 E. Main St., Granville, NY 12832. TEL 518-642-1234; FAX 518-642-1344. **Owner(s):** Manchester Newspapers, Inc., 6 North St., Granville, NY 12832; Ed. Alex Hyatt; Pub. John Manchester; adv. contact: John Manchester. pub. size: tabloid; circ. 7,680(free).

US

NORTH COUNTRY FREE PRESS. 1985. Sat. free. 14 E. Main St., Granville, NY 12832. TEL 518-642-1234; FAX 518-642-1344. **Owner(s):** Manchester Newspapers, Inc., 6 North St., Granville, NY 12832; Ed. Alex Hyatt; Pub. John Manchester; adv. contact: John Manchester. pub. size: tabloid; circ. 22,000(paid). **Formerly:** Free Press.

US

NORTHSHIRE FREE PRESS, THE. Sat. free. 14 E. Main St., Granville, NY 12832. TEL 518-642-1234; FAX 518-642-1344. **Owner(s):** Manchester Newspapers, Inc., 6 North St., Granville, NY 12832; Ed. Alex Hyatt; Pub. John Manchester; adv. contact: John Manchester. pub. size: tabloid; circ. 6,417(free).

GREAT NECK

US

GREAT NECK NEWS. 1925. Fri. $.35 newsstand; $9.50/yr. 643 Middle Neck Rd., Great Neck, NY 11023. TEL 516-487-1100; FAX 516-487-1100. **Owner(s):** Litmore Publications, Inc., P.O. Box 398, Great Neck, NY 11022. TEL 516-931-0012; Ed. Karen Rubin; Pub. Margaret Morgan; pub. size: tabloid; circ. 6,700(paid).

GREENE

US

CHENANGO AMERICAN. 1855. Tue. $14/yr. in city; $16/yr. in cy.; $20/yr. out of cy. 12 S. Chenango St., Greene, NY 13778. TEL 607-656-4511; FAX 607-656-8544. **Owner(s):** Kenneth S. Paden & Paul Hamilton, Sr., 5 Winkler Rd., Sidney, NY 13838. TEL 607-563-3526; Ed. Pete Mansheffer; Pub. Kenneth S. Paden; adv.; pub. size: broadsheet; circ. 3,500(paid).

US

OXFORD REVIEW-TIMES. 1960. Tue. $16/yr. in area; $20/yr. out of area. 12 S. Chenango St., Greene, NY 13778. TEL 607-656-4511; FAX 607-656-8544. **Owner(s):** Kenneth S. Paden & Paul Hamilton, Sr., 12 S. Chenango St., Greene, NY 13778. TEL 607-563-3526; Ed. Pete Mansheffer; Pub. Ken Paden; adv.; photos; pub. size: broadsheet; circ. 3,500(paid).

US

WHITNEY POINT REPORTER. 1850. Tue. $16/yr. local; $20/yr. out of area. 12 S. Chenango St., Greene, NY 13778. TEL 607-656-4511; FAX 607-656-8544. **Owner(s):** Kenneth S. Paden & Paul Hamilton, Sr., 12 S. Chenango St., Greene, NY 13778; Ed. Peter Mansheffer; Pub. Kenneth Paden; adv.; pub. size: broadsheet; circ. 3,500(paid).

GREENWICH

US

GREENWICH JOURNAL & SALEM PRESS. 1842. Thu. $.60 newsstand; $23/yr. in cy.; $26/yr. elsewhere. 35 Salem St., Greenwich, NY 12834. TEL 518-692-2266. **Owner(s):** Sally B. Tefft, 35 Salem St., P.O. Box 185, Greenwich, NY 12834. TEL 518-692-2266; Pub. Sally B. Tefft; adv.; pub. size: broadsheet; circ. 3,816(paid).

GREENWOOD LAKE

US

GREENWOOD LAKE & WEST MILFORD NEWS. 1964. Wed. $26/yr. in cy.; $29.50/yr. out of cy. Windermere Ave., Greenwood Lake, NY 10925. TEL 914-477-2575; FAX 914-477-2577. **Owner(s):** Greenwood Lake News, Inc., P.O. Box 1117, Greenwood Lake, NY 10925. TEL 914-477-2575; Pub. Ann Chaimowitz; adv. contact: Ann Chaimowitz. pub. size: tabloid; circ. 4,000(paid).

WEEKLY NEWSPAPERS

HAMBURG

US
SUN & ERIE COUNTY INDEPENDENT, THE. 1875. Thu. $.75 newsstand; $17.50/yr. 46 Buffalo St., Hamburg, NY 14075. TEL 716-649-4040; FAX 716-649-6374. **Owner(s):** H & K Publications, Inc., P.O. Box 590, Hamburg, NY 14075. TEL 716-649-4040; Ed. Eileen Hotho. adv.; photos; bk.rev.; pub. size: tabloid; circ. 10,000(paid). **Wire Service(s):** Empire News Service.

HAMILTON

US
HAMILTON MID-YORK WEEKLY. 1828. Thu. free newsstand; $19/yr. outside area. 55 Utica St., Hamilton, NY 13346. TEL 315-824-2150; FAX 315-824-4220. **Owner(s):** Oneida Madison Pennysaver, The, P.O. Box 203, Clinton, NY 13323. TEL 315-853-6103; Ed. Carolyn Godfrey; Pub. Wayne Cleary; adv. contact: Bonny Bean. pub. size: broadsheet; circ. 9,000(free & paid).

US
▼**HAMILTON TRIBUNE.** 1995. Wed. $.50 newsstand; $25/yr.; $21/yr. senior citizens; $13/yr. students. 18 Broad, Hamilton, NY 13346. TEL 315-824-3147; FAX 315-655-3813. **Owner(s):** Eagle Newspapers, Inc., P.O. Box 65, Fayetteville, NY 13066. TEL 315-637-3121; Pub. Stewart Hancock; adv.; photos; bk.rev.; pub. size: broadsheet.

HASTINGS-ON-HUDSON

US   ISSN 0745-3477
ENTERPRISE, THE. Fri. $24/yr. in cy.; $30/yr. out of cy. 5 Boulanger Plz., Hastings-on-Hudson, NY 10706. TEL 914-478-2787; FAX 914-478-2863. **Owner(s):** Deborah White, P.O. Box 278, Hastings-on-Hudson, NY 10706. TEL 914-478-2787; Ed. Terri Salvatore; Pub. Deborah White; pub. size: standard; circ. 4,900(paid).
Formerly: Hastings Enterprise.

HAVERSTRAW

US
ROCKLAND COUNTY TIMES. 1889. Thu. $.50 newsstand; $21/yr. in cy.; $27/yr. out of cy. 11 New Main St., Haverstraw, NY 10927. TEL 914-429-2000; FAX 914-429-8990. **Owner(s):** RCT Publishing Co., Inc., 11 New Main St., Haverstraw, NY 10927. TEL 914-429-2000; FAX 914-429-8990; Ed. David Gordon; Pub. Randy Davis; adv. contact: Arlene Adler. adv.: $10.65/SAU. photos; bk.rev.; pub. size: broadsheet; circ. 8,000(paid).

HICKSVILLE

US
EAST MEADOW BEACON. 1950. Thu. $9.50/yr. One Jonathan Ave., Hicksville, NY 11801-5201. TEL 516-931-1400. **Owner(s):** Nassau County Publications, Inc., One Jonathan Ave., Hicksville, NY 11801; Ed. Peter Hoegl; Pub. Peter Hoegl; adv.; photos; bk.rev.; pub. size: tabloid; circ. 5,800(paid).

US
HEMPSTEAD BEACON. 1951. Fri. $9.50/yr. One Jonathan Ave., Hicksville, NY 11801-5201. TEL 516-931-1400. **Owner(s):** Nassau County Publications, Inc., One Jonathan Ave., Hicksville, NY 11801. TEL 516-931-1400; Pub. Pete Hoegl; adv.; photos; bk.rev.; pub. size: tabloid; circ. 5,100(paid).

US
MERRICK BEACON. 1950. Fri. $9.50/yr. One Jonathan Ave., Hicksville, NY 11801-5201. TEL 516-931-1400. **Owner(s):** Nassau County Publications, Inc., One Jonathan Ave., Hicksville, NY 11801; Ed. Peter Hoegl; Pub. Peter Hoegl; adv.; photos; bk.rev.; pub. size: tabloid; circ. 4,000(paid).

US   ISSN 0747-4741
MID-ISLAND TIMES. Fri. $.35/newsstand; $10.50/yr. mailed. 81 E. Barclay St., Hicksville, NY 11801. TEL 516-931-0012. **Owner(s):** Litmore Publications, Inc., 81 E. Barclay St., Hicksville, NY 11801. TEL 516-931-0012; Ed. Meg Norris; Pub. Meg Norris; adv.; pub. size: tabloid; circ. 5,685(paid).

US
UNIONDALE BEACON. 1951. Fri. $9.50/yr. One Jonathan Ave., Hicksville, NY 11801-5201. TEL 516-931-1400. **Owner(s):** Nassau County Publications, Inc., One Jonathan Ave., Hicksville, NY 11801-5201. TEL 516-931-1400; Pub. Peter Hoegl; adv.; photos; bk.rev.; pub. size: tabloid; circ. 5,300(paid).

US
WEST HEMPSTEAD BEACON. 1951. Fri. $.35 newsstand; $9.50/yr. local; $12/yr. elsewhere. One Jonathan Ave., Hicksville, NY 11801-5201. TEL 516-931-1400. **Owner(s):** Nassau County Publications, Inc., One Jonathan Ave., Hicksville, NY 11801. TEL 516-931-1400; Ed. Peter Hoegl; Pub. Peter Hoegl; adv.; photos; bk.rev.; pub. size: tabloid; circ. 5,200(paid).

HIGHLAND FALLS

US
NEWS OF THE HIGHLANDS. 1891. Wed. $.50 newsstand; $21/yr. Webb Ln., Highland Falls, NY 10928. TEL 914-446-4519. **Owner(s):** News of the Highlands, Inc., P.O. Box 278, Highland Falls, NY 10928. TEL 914-446-4519; FAX 914-446-0532; Ed. Frederick Brennan. pub. size: broadsheet; circ. 3,000(paid).
Formerly: Highland Falls News of the Highlands.

HORNELL

US
SUNDAY SPECTATOR. 1851. Sun. $1.50 newsstand. 85 Canisteo St., Hornell, NY 14843. TEL 607-324-1425; FAX 607-324-1753. **Owner(s):** American Publishing Co., 606 N. Van Buren, Marion, IL 62959. TEL 618-993-1711; Ed. Andy Tompson; Pub. Kelly Luvison; adv. contact: John Frungillo. pub. size: broadsheet; circ. Sun. 17,000(paid). **Wire Service(s):** AP.

HORSEHEADS

US   ISSN 1064-4091
CHEMUNG VALLEY REPORTER. 1856. Thu. $.50 newsstand; $20/yr. in cy.; $22/yr. out of cy. 207 S. Main St., Horseheads, NY 14845. TEL 607-739-3001; FAX 607-739-2935. **Owner(s):** Roots & Wings, Inc., P.O. Box 474, Horseheads, NY 14845. TEL 607-739-3001; FAX 607-739-2935; Ed. Randy Denierio; Pub. Chris Denierio; adv. contact: Chris Denierio. photos; bk.rev.; pub. size: tabloid; circ. 1,500(free & paid).

HUNTINGTON

US
RECORD, THE. 1932. Thu. $15/yr. 322 Main St., Huntington, NY 11743. TEL 516-427-7000; FAX 516-427-5820; E-mail: longisler@aol.com. **Owner(s):** James Koutsis, 322 Main St., Huntington, NY 11743. TEL 516-427-7000; Ed. Peter Sloggatt; Pub. James Koutsis; adv.; photos; bk.rev.; pub. size: tabloid; circ. 60,000(paid).
Formerly: Huntington Record, The.

HYDE PARK

US
HYDE PARK TOWNSMAN. 1959. Thu. $.75 newsstand; $29/yr. 639 Albany Post Rd., Hyde Park, NY 12538. TEL 914-229-7126; FAX 914-229-6283. **Owner(s):** Taconic Media, Inc., P.O. Box 316, Millbrook, NY 12545. TEL 914-677-8241; Ed. Dan Barton; Pub. Hamilton W. Meserve; pub. size: broadsheet; circ. 2,000(paid).

IRVINGTON

US
IRVINGTON VIEWPOINT, THE. 1990. m. free; $15/yr. out of town. 37 Barney Park, Irvington, NY 10533. TEL 914-591-3700; FAX 914-591-9226. **Owner(s):** Berger Communications, Inc., 37 Barney Park, Irvington, NY 10533. TEL 914-591-3700; FAX 914-591-9226; Ed. George Berger; Pub. George Berger; adv.; pub. size: tabloid; circ. 6,500(controlled & free).

ITHACA

US
ITHACA TIMES. 1972. Thu. free; $22.95/yr. 109 N. Cayuga St., Ithaca, NY 14850-0027. TEL 607-277-7000; FAX 607-277-1012. **Owner(s):** Finger Lakes Community Newspapers, Inc., P.O. Box 6475, Ithaca, NY 14851. TEL 607-277-7000; Ed. Jay Wrolstad; Pub. James Bilinski; adv.; pub. size: tabloid; circ. 24,500(controlled).

JOHNSON CITY

US
BROOME PENNYSAVER. Thu. free. 353 Harry L. Dr., Johnson City, NY 13790. TEL 607-770-4991. **Owner(s):** Owego Pennysaver Press, P.O. Box 149, Owego, NY 13827. TEL 607-687-2434; Ed. Kim Depew. adv.; pub. size: standard; circ. 56,000(free).

LACKAWANNA

US

FRONT PAGE. 1959. Wed. $14/yr. in cy.; $22/yr. out of cy. 2703 S. Park Ave., Lackawanna, NY 14218. TEL 716-823-8222; FAX 716-821-0550. **Owner(s):** Front Page Group, Inc., 2703 S. Park Ave., Lackawanna, NY 14218. TEL 716-823-8222; FAX 716-821-0550; Pub. William Delmont; photos; pub. size: tabloid; circ. 14,500(paid).

US

SOUTH BUFFALO NEWS. 1919. Wed. $14/yr. in cy; $22/yr. out of cy. 2703 S. Park Ave., Lackawanna, NY 14218-1591. TEL 716-823-8222; FAX 716-821-0550. **Owner(s):** Front Page Group, Inc., 2703 S. Park Ave., Lackawanna, NY 14218. TEL 716-823-8222; Pub. William Delmont; adv.: $8.78/SAU. photos; pub. size: tabloid; circ. 5,500(paid).

LAKE PLACID

US

LAKE PLACID NEWS. 1905. Fri. $.75 newsstand; $30/yr. in zip 129; $39/yr. outside zip 129. 412 S. Main St., Lake Placid, NY 12946. TEL 518-523-4401; FAX 518-523-1351. **Owner(s):** Ogden Newspapers, Inc., 1500 Main St., Wheeling, WV 26033. TEL 304-233-0100; Ed. Shir Filler. adv. contact: Sandra Johnston. photos; pub. size: broadsheet; circ. 3,500(paid).

LAWRENCE

US

BALDWIN HERALD. 1943. Wed. $.75 newsstand; $22/yr. in cy.; $30/yr. out of cy. 379 Central Ave., Lawrence, NY 11559. TEL 516-569-4000; FAX 516-569-4942. **Owner(s):** Richner Communications, Inc., 379 Central Ave., Lawrence, NY 11559. TEL 516-569-4000; FAX 516-569-4942; Ed. Fran Evans; Pub. Cifford Richner; adv. contact: Barbara Klein. photos; bk.rev.; pub. size: broadsheet; circ. 4,400(free & paid).
Formerly: South Shore Reporter-Baldwin.

US

LONG ISLAND GRAPHIC-ROOSEVELT PRESS. Wed. $.25 newsstand; $12/yr. 379 Central Ave., Lawrence, NY 11559. TEL 516-569-4000; FAX 516-569-4942. **Owner(s):** Richner Communications, Inc., 379 Central Ave., Lawrence, NY 11559. TEL 516-569-4000; FAX 516-569-4942; Ed. Jean Graham; Pub. Stuart Richner; adv. contact: Barbara Kline. photos; bk.rev.; pub. size: tabloid; circ. 1,200(paid).

US

MEADOWBROOK TIMES. 1964. Wed. $.25 newsstand; $12/yr. in cy.; $20/yr. out of cy. 379 Central Ave., Lawrence, NY 11559. TEL 516-569-4000; FAX 516-569-4942. **Owner(s):** Richner Communications, Inc., 379 Central Ave., Lawrence, NY 11559. TEL 516-569-4000; FAX 516-569-4942; Ed. Fran Evans; Pub. Clifford Richner; adv. contact: Barbara Klein. pub. size: tabloid; circ. 3,000(paid).

US

NASSAU HERALD. 1924. Wed. $22/yr. in cy.; $30/yr. out of cy. 379 Central Ave., Lawrence, NY 11559. TEL 516-569-4000; FAX 516-569-4942. **Owner(s):** Richner Communications, Inc., 379 Central Ave., Lawrence, NY 11559. TEL 516-569-4000; FAX 516-569-4942; Ed. Randi Kreiss; Pub. Clifford Richner; pub. size: tabloid; circ. 10,500(paid).
Formerly: Nassau Herald-Lawrence.

US

PRIMETIME. 1987. Fri. free. 379 Central Ave., Lawrence, NY 11559. TEL 516-569-4444; FAX 516-569-4942. **Owner(s):** Richner Communications, Inc., 379 Central Ave., Lawrence, NY 11559. TEL 516-569-4444; FAX 516-569-4942; Ed. Clifford Richner; Pub. Stuart Richner; pub. size: tabloid; circ. 110,000(free).

US

ROCKAWAY JOURNAL. 1883. Wed. $.25 newsstand; $12/yr. in cy.; $20/yr. out of cy. 379 Central Ave., Lawrence, NY 11559. TEL 516-569-4000; FAX 516-569-4942. **Owner(s):** Richner Communications, Inc., 379 Central Ave., Lawrence, NY 11559. TEL 516-569-4000; FAX 516-569-4942; Ed. Fran Evans; Pub. Cliff Richner; pub. size: tabloid; circ. 1,917(paid).

US

ROCKVILLE CENTRE HERALD. 1991. Thu. $.75 newsstand; $22/yr. in town; $26/yr. elsewhere. 379 Central Ave., Lawrence, NY 11559. TEL 516-569-4000; FAX 516-569-4942. **Owner(s):** Richner Communications, Inc., 379 Central Ave., Lawrence, NY 11559. TEL 516-569-4000; FAX 516-569-4942; Ed. Jeff Kleuwer; Pub. Clifford Richner; adv. contact: Barbara Klein. pub. size: tabloid; circ. 5,400(paid).

US

VALLEY STREAM HERALD. 1990. Thu. $.75 newsstand; $22/yr.; $36/2 yrs.; $44/3 yrs.; $30/yr. out of cy. 379 Central Ave., Lawrence, NY 11559. TEL 516-569-4000; FAX 516-569-4942. **Owner(s):** Richner Communications, Inc., 379 Central Ave., Lawrence, NY 11559. TEL 516-569-4000; FAX 516-569-4942; Ed. Fran Evans; Pub. Clifford Richner; adv. contact: Barbara Klien. pub. size: tabloid; circ. 9,121(paid).

US

VILLAGE HERALD. 1964. Wed. $.75 newsstand; $22/yr. in cy.; $30/yr. out of cy. 379 Central Ave., Lawrence, NY 11559. TEL 516-569-4000; FAX 516-569-4942. **Owner(s):** Richner Communications, Inc., 379 Central Ave., Lawrence, NY 11559. TEL 516-569-4000; FAX 516-569-4942; Ed. Bob Clark; Pub. Clifford Richner; adv. contact: Barbara Klein. pub. size: tabloid; circ. 5,500(paid).
Formerly: Lynbrook Herald.

LINDENHURST

US

SOUTH BAY'S NEWSPAPER. 1953. Wed. free. 150 W. Hoffman Ave., Lindenhurst, NY 11757-4043. TEL 516-226-2636. **Owner(s):** Excel Promotions Corp., 150 W. Hoffman Ave., Lindenhurst, NY 11757-4043. TEL 516-226-2636; FAX 516-226-2680; Ed. J.M. Freedman. adv.; photos; bk.rev.; pub. size: tabloid; circ. 96,129(free).

LOCKPORT

US

TRI-COUNTY NEWS. Sat. free. 459-491 S. Transit St., Lockport, NY 14094. TEL 716-439-9222; FAX 716-439-9249. **Owner(s):** Newspaper Holdings, Inc., 269 W. Main St., 6th Fl., Lexington, KY 40507. TEL 606-388-2644; Ed. Dan Kane. pub. size: broadsheet; circ. 8,000(free).
Formerly: Lockport Tri-County News.

LOCUST VALLEY

US

LOCUST VALLEY LEADER. 1946. Thu. $.40 newsstand; $18/yr. 160 Birch Hill Rd., Locust Valley, NY 11560. TEL 516-676-1434; FAX 516-671-7442. **Owner(s):** Edith Hay Wyckoff, 160 Birch Hill Rd., Locust Valley, NY 11560. TEL 516-671-7442; Ed. Edith Hay Wyckoff; Pub. Edith Hay Wyckoff; adv. contact: Claudia De Vecchi. pub. size: tabloid; circ. 3,800(paid).

LONG BEACH

US

LONG BEACH HERALD. 1990. Thu. $.75 newsstand; $22/yr. in town; $30/yr. elsewhere. 143 E. Park Ave., Long Beach, NY 11561. TEL 516-431-3400; FAX 516-889-4419. **Owner(s):** Richner Publications, Inc., 379 Central Ave., Lawrence, NY 11559. TEL 516-569-4000; FAX 516-569-4942; Ed. Mike Harrison; Pub. Clifford Richner; adv. contact: Barbara Klein. photos; bk.rev.; pub. size: tabloid; circ. 6,228(paid).

US

OCEANSIDE/ISLAND PARK HERALD. 1966. Wed. $.75 newsstand; $18/yr. 143 E. Park Ave., Long Beach, NY 11561. TEL 516-431-3400; FAX 516-889-4419. **Owner(s):** Richner Publications, Inc., 379 Central Ave., Lawrence, NY 11559. TEL 516-569-4000; FAX 516-569-4942; Ed. Mark Poleo; Pub. Clifford Richner; adv.; photos; bk.rev.; pub. size: broadsheet; circ. 5,500(paid).

LOWVILLE

US

JOURNAL & REPUBLICAN. 1830. Wed. $.75 newsstand; $29/yr. in state; $35/yr. out of state. 7556 State St., Lowville, NY 13367. TEL 315-376-3525; FAX 315-376-4136. **Owner(s):** Lowville Newspapers Corp./Johnson Newspaper Corp., 7556 State St., Lowville, NY 13367. TEL 315-376-3525; FAX 315-376-4136; Ed. Gordon H. Allen; Pub. Pamala J. Spry; adv. contact: Bonnie Franklin. pub. size: broadsheet; circ. 6,273(paid).

LYONS

US   ISSN 1064-7619

WAYNE COUNTY STAR. 1821. s-w.: Wed. & Sat. $.50 newsstand; $27/yr. in cy.; $38/yr. out of cy. 36 B Canal St., Lyons, NY 14489-0430. TEL 315-946-9701; FAX 315-946-4382. **Owner(s):** Wayuga Community Newspapers, Inc., Main St., Red Creek, NY 13143-0031. TEL 315-754-6229; FAX 315-754-6431; Ed. Mary K. Henderberg; Pub. Christopher M. Palermo; adv.; photos; pub. size: tabloid; circ. 4,700(free & paid). **Wire Service(s):** Newsfinder.
Formerly: Lyons Wayne County Star.

MAHOPAC

US

BEACON LIGHT. Wed. $.20 newsstand; $10/yr. in cy.; $20/yr. out of cy. 83 E. Lake Blvd., Mahopac, NY 10541. TEL 914-628-8400; FAX 914-628-8400. **Owner(s):** Gateway Papers, Inc., P.O. Drawer H, Mahopac, NY 10541. TEL 914-628-8400; Ed. Karen Placek; Pub. Don Hall; adv. contact: Don Hall. pub. size: tabloid; circ. 2,700(paid).

WEEKLY NEWSPAPERS

US
BREWSTER TIMES. Wed. $.20 newsstand; $10/yr. in cy.; $20/yr. out of cy. 83 E. Lake Blvd., Mahopac, NY 10541. TEL 914-628-8400; FAX 914-628-8400. **Owner(s):** Gateway Papers, Inc., P.O. Drawer H, Mahopac, NY 10541. TEL 914-628-8400; Ed. Karen Placek; Pub. Don Hall; adv. contact: Don Hall. pub. size: tabloid; circ. 8,200(paid).

US
CARMEL TIMES. Wed. $.20 newsstand; $10/yr. in cy.; $20/yr. out of cy. 83 E. Lake Blvd., Mahopac, NY 10541. TEL 914-628-8400; FAX 914-628-8400. **Owner(s):** Gateway Papers, Inc., P.O. Box 608, Mahopac, NY 10541. TEL 914-628-8400; Ed. Donald Hall; Pub. Donald Hall; adv.; pub. size: tabloid; circ. 11,800(paid).

US
EAST FISHKILL RECORD. 1858. Wed. $.20 newsstand; $10/yr. in cy.; $20/yr. out of cy. 83 E. Lake Blvd., Mahopac, NY 10541. TEL 914-628-8400; FAX 914-628-8400. **Owner(s):** Gateway Papers, Inc., P.O. Drawer H, Mahopac, NY 10541. TEL 914-628-8400; Ed. Karen Placek; Pub. Don Hall; adv. contact: Don Hall. pub. size: tabloid; circ. 3,100(paid).

US
FISHKILL STANDARD. Wed. $.20 newsstand; $10/yr. in cy.; $20/yr. out of cy. 83 E. Lake Blvd., Mahopac, NY 10541. TEL 914-628-8400; FAX 914-628-8400. **Owner(s):** Gateway Papers, Inc., P.O. Drawer H, Mahopac, NY 10541. TEL 914-628-8400; Ed. Karen Placek; Pub. Don Hall; adv. contact: Don Hall. pub. size: tabloid; circ. 6,200(paid).

US
LA GRANGE INDEPENDENT. Wed. $.10 newsstand; $5/yr. in cy.; $20/yr. out of cy. 83 E. Lake Blvd., Mahopac, NY 10541. TEL 914-628-8400; FAX 914-628-8400. **Owner(s):** Gateway Papers, Inc., P.O. Drawer H, Mahopac, NY 10541. TEL 914-628-8400; Ed. Karen Placek; Pub. Don Hall; adv. contact: Don Hall. pub. size: tabloid; circ. 2,600(paid).

US
MAHOPAC PRESS. Wed. $.20 newsstand; $10/yr. in cy.; $20/yr. out of cy. 83 E. Lake Blvd., Mahopac, NY 10541. TEL 914-628-8400; FAX 914-628-8400. **Owner(s):** Gateway Papers, Inc., P.O. Box 608, Mahopac, NY 10541. TEL 914-628-8400; Ed. Donald Hall; Pub. Donald Hall; adv.; pub. size: tabloid; circ. 3,200(paid).

MARATHON

US
CORTLAND DEMOCRAT. 1864. Sun. $.50 newsstand; $20/yr. in state; $21/yr. out of state. P.O. Box 878, Marathon, NY 13803-0878. TEL 607-849-4555; FAX 607-849-4654. **Owner(s):** Lakeside Printing, Inc., P.O. Box 150, 819 W. Genesee St., Skaneateles, NY 13152. TEL 315-685-8904; Ed. Sharon Fox. adv. contact: Mike Rifamberg. pub. size: tabloid; circ. 1,250(paid).

MASPETH

US
▼**FOREST HILLS/REGO PARK TIMES.** 1995. Thu. $.35 newsstand; $12/yr. 5551 69th St., Maspeth, NY 11378. TEL 718-639-7000; FAX 718-429-1234. **Owner(s):** Walter H. Sanchez, II, 5551 69th St., Maspeth, NY 11378. TEL 718-639-7000; FAX 718-429-1234; Ed. Alice Wenz; Pub. Walter H. Sanchez, II; adv.: $15/SAU. photos; bk.rev.; pub. size: tabloid; circ. 8,000(paid).

US
GLENDALE REGISTER. 1935. Thu. $12/yr. in area; $16/yr. out of area. 5551 69th St., Maspeth, NY 11378. TEL 718-639-7000; FAX 718-429-1234. **Owner(s):** Walter H. Sanchez, II, 5551 69th St., Maspeth, NY 11378. TEL 718-639-7000; FAX 718-429-1234; Ed. Alice Wenz; Pub. Walter H. Sanchez, II; adv.: $15/SAU. photos; bk.rev.; pub. size: tabloid; circ. 10,000(paid).

US
▼**HOWARD BEACH RESIDENT.** 1996. Thu. $.35 newsstand; $12/yr. 5551 69th St., Maspeth, NY 11378. TEL 718-639-7000; FAX 718-429-1234. **Owner(s):** Walter H. Sanchez, II, 5551 69th St., Maspeth, NY 11378. TEL 718-639-7000; FAX 718-429-1234; Ed. Alice Wenz; Pub. Walter H. Sanchez, II; adv.: $15/SAU. photos; bk.rev.; pub. size: tabloid.

US
JACKSON HEIGHTS NEWS. 1986. Thu. $.35 newsstand; $12/yr. 5551 69th St., Maspeth, NY 11378. TEL 718-639-7000; FAX 718-429-1234. **Owner(s):** Walter H. Sanchez, II, 5551 69th St., Maspeth, NY 11378. TEL 718-639-7000; FAX 718-429-1234; Ed. Alice Wenz; Pub. Walter H. Sanchez, II; adv.: $15/SAU. photos; bk.rev.; pub. size: tabloid; circ. 25,000(paid).

US
LEADER OBSERVER. 1909. Thu. $.35 newsstand; $12/yr. in cy. 5551 69th St., Maspeth, NY 11378. TEL 718-639-7000; FAX 718-429-1234. **Owner(s):** Walter H. Sanchez, II, 5551 69th St., Maspeth, NY 11378. TEL 718-639-7000; FAX 718-429-1234; Ed. Alice Wenz; Pub. Walter H. Sanchez, II; adv.: $15/SAU. photos; bk.rev.; pub. size: tabloid; circ. 7,000(paid).

US
LONG ISLAND CITY/ASTORIA JOURNAL. 1986. Thu. $.35 newsstand; $12/yr. in cy.; $16/yr. out of cy. 5551 69th St., Maspeth, NY 11378. TEL 718-639-7000; FAX 718-429-1234. **Owner(s):** Walter H. Sanchez, II, 5551 69th St., Maspeth, NY 11378. TEL 718-639-7000; FAX 718-429-1234; Ed. Alice Wenz; Pub. Walter H. Sanchez, II; adv.: $15/SAU. photos; bk.rev.; pub. size: tabloid; circ. 32,000(paid).
Formerly: Long Island City Journal.

US
QUEENS LEDGER. 1873. Thu. $.35 newsstand; $12/yr.; $16/yr. out of cy. 5551 69th St., Maspeth, NY 11378. TEL 718-639-7000; FAX 718-429-1234. **Owner(s):** Walter H. Sanchez, II, 5551 69th St., Maspeth, NY 11378. TEL 718-639-7000; FAX 718-429-1234; Ed. Alice Wenz; Pub. Walter H. Sanchez, II; adv.: $15/SAU. pub. size: tabloid; circ. 10,000(paid).

MASSAPEQUA PARK

US
MASSAPEQUA POST. 1954. Wed. $.50 newsstand; $15/yr. 1045B Park Blvd., Massapequa Park, NY 11762. TEL 516-798-5100; FAX 516-798-5296; E-mail: recpost@aol.com. **Owner(s):** ACJ Communications, Inc., 197 Broadway, Amityville, NY 11701. TEL 516-264-0077; FAX 516-264-5310; Ed. Carolyn James; Pub. Carolyn James; adv.; photos; pub. size: tabloid; circ. 8,000(paid).

MASSENA

US
FREE TRADER. 1981. Thu. free. W. Hatfield St., Massena, NY 13662. TEL 315-769-3770; FAX 315-764-7440. **Owner(s):** Bob Noreault, W. Hatfield St., Massena, NY 13662. TEL 315-769-7149; Ed. Bob Noreault; Pub. Bob Noreault; adv.; pub. size: tabloid; circ. 14,000(controlled).

MATTITUCK

US
NEWS-REVIEW, THE. 1950. Thu. $1 newsstand; $35/yr. in cy.; $44/yr. out of cy. 7785 Main Rd., Mattituck, NY 11952. TEL 516-298-3200; FAX 516-298-3287. **Owner(s):** Times/Review Newspapers, P.O. Box 1500, Mattituck, NY 11952. TEL 516-298-3200; Ed. Ruth Jernick; Pub. Joan Gustavson; pub. size: tabloid; circ. 5,000(paid).

US
SUFFOLK TIMES. 1857. Thu. $1 newsstand; $35/yr. in cy.; $44/yr. out of cy. 7785 Main Rd., Mattituck, NY 11952. TEL 516-298-3200; FAX 516-298-3287; E-mail: stnrnews@aol.com. **Owner(s):** Times/Review Newspapers, P.O. Box 1500, Mattituck, NY 11952. TEL 516-298-3200; Pub. Troy Gustavson; adv.; photos; bk.rev.; pub. size: tabloid; circ. 10,450(free & paid).

MERRICK

US
MERRICK LIFE. 1938. Thu. $.40 newsstand; $17/yr. 1840 Merrick Ave., Merrick, NY 11566. TEL 516-378-5320; FAX 516-378-0287. **Owner(s):** L & M Publications, Inc., 1840 Merrick Ave., Merrick, NY 11566. TEL 516-378-5320; Ed. Paul Laursen; Pub. Linda Toscano; adv. contact: Lois Roos. pub. size: tabloid; circ. 6,444(free & paid).

MEXICO

US
CITIZEN OUTLET. Wed. $.50 newsstand; $10/yr. 80 N. Jefferson St., Mexico, NY 13114. TEL 315-963-7813; FAX 315-963-4087. **Owner(s):** Mark Backus, P.O. Box 129, Mexico, NY 13114. TEL 315-963-7813; Ed. Roseann Parsons; Pub. Mark Backus; adv. contact: Charles Seaman. pub. size: tabloid; circ. 16,000(paid).

US
INDEPENDENT MIRROR. 1861. Wed. $.50 newsstand; 10/yr. P.O. Box 129, Mexico, NY 13114. TEL 315-963-7813; FAX 310-963-4087. **Owner(s):** Mark Backus, P.O. Box 129, Mexico, NY 13114. TEL 315-963-7813; FAX 315-963-4087; Ed. Rose Ann Parsons. pub. size: tabloid; circ. 3,100(paid).

MILLBROOK

US

MILLBROOK ROUND TABLE. 1888. Thu. $.75 newsstand; $29/yr.; $49/2 yrs.; $59/3 yrs. Front St. & Merritt Ave., Millbrook, NY 12545. TEL 914-677-8241; FAX 914-677-6337. **Owner(s):** Taconic Media, Inc., P.O. Box 316, Millbrook, NY 12545. TEL 914-677-8241; Ed. Marty Sweeney; Pub. Helen Meserve; adv. contact: Marty Sweeney. pub. size: broadsheet; circ. 2,500(paid).

US

VOICE LEDGER, THE. 1969. Thu. $.75 newsstand; $29/yr. Front St. & Merritt Ave., Millbrook, NY 12545. TEL 914-677-8241; FAX 914-677-6337. **Owner(s):** Taconic Media, Inc., P.O. Box 316, Millbrook, NY 12545. TEL 914-677-8241; Ed. Matt Bechard; Pub. Hamilton Meserve; adv. contact: Marty Sweeney. photos; bk.rev.; pub. size: broadsheet; circ. 2,500(paid).
Formerly: Pleasant Valley Voice.

MILLERTON

US

MILLERTON NEWS, THE. 1934. Thu. $.75 newsstand; $29.95/yr. in cy.; $38/yr. out of cy. Main St., Millerton, NY 12546. TEL 518-789-4401; FAX 518-789-9247; E-mail: mnews@aol.com. **Owner(s):** Lakeville Journal Co., LLC, 33 Bissell St., P.O. Box 353, Lakeville, CT 06039. TEL 860-435-9873; Ed. Kathryn Boughton; Pub. A. Whitney Ellsworth; adv. contact: Anna Mae Kupferer. photos; bk.rev.; pub. size: broadsheet; circ. 12,000(paid).

MINEOLA

US

BALDWIN CITIZEN. 1925. Thu. $.35 newsstand; $15/yr.; $23/2 yrs. 216 E. Second St., Mineola, NY 11501. TEL 516-739-6400; FAX 516-739-5404. **Owner(s):** Nassau Community Newspaper Group, Inc., 216 E. Second St., Mineola, NY 11501. TEL 516-739-6400; FAX 516-739-5404; Ed. Pat Horwell; Pub. Barry Manning; pub. size: tabloid; circ. 5,500(paid).

US ISSN 0746-2093

EAST ROCKAWAY OBSERVER. 1967. Thu. $.40 newsstand; $15/yr. 216 E. Second St., Mineola, NY 11501. TEL 516-739-6400; FAX 516-739-5404. **Owner(s):** Nassau Community Newspaper Group, Inc., 216 E. Second St., Mineola, NY 11501. TEL 516-739-6400; Ed. Patricia Horwell; Pub. Barry Manning; adv. contact: Rhonda Glickman. pub. size: tabloid; circ. 4,500(paid).
Formerly: East Rockaway/Lynbrook Observer.

US

FARMINGDALE OBSERVER. 1962. Thu. $.75 newsstand; $18/yr. in state; $31/2 yrs. in state; $42/3 yrs. in state; $28/yr. out of state. 132 E. Second St., Mineola, NY 11501. TEL 516-747-8282; FAX 516-742-5867. **Owner(s):** Anton Publications, 132 E. Second St., Mineola, NY 11501. TEL 516-747-8287; Ed. Christine Leonard; Pub. Karl V. Anton, Jr.; adv. contact: Harriett Heffernan. photos; bk.rev.; pub. size: tabloid; circ. 3,471(paid).

US

GLEN COVE RECORD PILOT. 1875. Thu. $.75 newsstand; $21/yr. in area; $31/yr. out of state. 132 E. Second St., Mineola, NY 11501. TEL 516-747-8282; FAX 516-742-5867. **Owner(s):** Anton Publications, 132 E. Second St., Mineola, NY 11501. TEL 516-747-8282; FAX 516-742-5867; Ed. Zesy Christapoulas; Pub. Karl V. Anton, Jr.; adv. contact: Harriet Heffernan. pub. size: tabloid; circ. 7,735(paid).

US

GREAT NECK RECORD. Thu. $.75 newsstand; $21/yr. in area; $31/yr. out of state. 132 E. Second St., Mineola, NY 11501. TEL 516-747-8282; FAX 516-742-5867. **Owner(s):** Anton Publications, 132 E. Second St., Mineola, NY 11501. TEL 516-747-8282; Ed. Wendy Kreitzman; Pub. Karl V. Anton, Jr.; adv. contact: Harriet Heffernan. pub. size: tabloid; circ. 6,734(paid).

US

HICKSVILLE ILLUSTRATED NEWS. Thu. $.75 newsstand; $21/yr. in area; $28/yr. out of state. 132 E. Second St., Mineola, NY 11501. TEL 516-747-8282. **Owner(s):** Anton Publications, 132 E. Second St., Mineola, NY 11501. TEL 516-747-8282; FAX 516-742-5867; Ed. Chris Grillo; Pub. Karl V. Anton, Jr.; adv. contact: Harriet Heffernan. pub. size: tabloid; circ. 5,500(paid).
Formerly: Hicksville Mid-Island Herald.

US

LEVITTOWN TRIBUNE. 1947. Fri. $.75 newsstand; $18/yr. in state; $31/2 yrs.; $42/3 yrs. in state; $28/yr. out of state. 132 E. Second St., Mineola, NY 11501. TEL 516-747-8282. **Owner(s):** Anton Publications, 132 E. Second St., Mineola, NY 11501. TEL 516-747-8282; FAX 516-742-5867; Ed. Neil McKenna; Pub. Karl V. Anton; adv. contact: Harriet Heffernan. bk.rev.; pub. size: tabloid; circ. 4,275(paid).

US

LONG BEACH INDEPENDENT VOICE. 1932. Thu. $.35 newsstand; $11/yr.; $19/2 yrs. 216 E. Second St., Mineola, NY 11501. TEL 516-739-6400; FAX 516-739-5404. **Owner(s):** Nassau Community Newspapers, 216 E. Second St., Mineola, NY 11501. TEL 516-739-6400; FAX 516-739-5404; Pub. Barry Manning; pub. size: tabloid; circ. 5,000(paid).

US

▼**LONG ISLAND VOICE.** 1997. Thu. free. 393 Jericho Tpke., Mineola, NY 11501-1205. TEL 516-877-7373; FAX 516-877-0987. **Owner(s):** Stern Publishing, Inc., 393 Jericho Tpke., Mineola, NY 11501-1205. TEL 516-877-7373; Ed. John Mancini; Pub. Andrea Stern; adv.; pub. size: tabloid; circ. 60,000(free).

US

LYNBROOK USA. Wed. $.35 newsstand; $15/yr.; $23/2 yrs. 216 E. Second St., Mineola, NY 11501. TEL 516-739-6400; FAX 516-739-5404. **Owner(s):** Nassau Community Newspapers, 216 E. Second St., Mineola, NY 11501. TEL 516-739-6400; Ed. Pat Horwell; Pub. Barry Manning; adv. contact: Rhonda Glickman. pub. size: tabloid; circ. 10,000(paid).

US

MALVERNE COMMUNITY TIMES. Wed. $.35 newsstand; $15/yr.; $23/2 yrs. 216 E. Second St., Mineola, NY 11501. TEL 516-739-6400; FAX 516-739-5404. **Owner(s):** Nassau Community Newspapers, 216 E. Second St., Mineola, NY 11501. TEL 516-739-6400; Ed. Pat Horwell; Pub. Barry Manning; adv. contact: Rhonda Glickman. pub. size: tabloid; circ. 10,000(paid).
Formerly: Malverne Times.

US

MANHASSET PRESS. 1958. Thu. $.75 newsstand; $21/yr. in area; $31/yr. out of state. 132 E. Second St., Mineola, NY 11501. TEL 516-747-8282; FAX 516-742-5867. **Owner(s):** Anton Publications, 132 E. Second St., Mineola, NY 11501. TEL 516-747-8282; Ed. Eileen Brennan; Pub. Karl V. Anton, Jr.; adv. contact: Harriet Heffernan. pub. size: tabloid; circ. 4,700(paid).

US

MASSAPEQUAN OBSERVER. 1957. Thu. $.75 newsstand; $12/yr. in area; $22/yr. out of state. 132 E. Second St., Mineola, NY 11501. TEL 516-747-8282; FAX 516-742-5867. **Owner(s):** Anton Publications, 132 E. Second St., Mineola, NY 11501. TEL 516-747-8282; Ed. Christine Leonard; Pub. Karl V. Anton; adv. contact: Harriet Heffernan. pub. size: tabloid; circ. 2,475(paid).

US

MINEOLA AMERICAN. 1952. Wed. $.75 newsstand; $12/yr. local; $22/yr. out of area. 132 E. Second St., Mineola, NY 11501. TEL 516-747-8282; FAX 516-742-5867. **Owner(s):** Anton Publications, 132 E. Second St., Mineola, NY 11501. TEL 516-747-8282; Ed. James Kennedy; Pub. Karl V. Anton, Jr.; adv. contact: Harriet Heffernan. pub. size: tabloid; circ. 3,975(paid).

US

OCEANSIDE CENTRE BEACON. 1935. Thu. $.35 newsstand; $15/yr. 216 E. Second St., Mineola, NY 11501. TEL 516-739-6400; FAX 516-739-5404. **Owner(s):** Nassau Community Newspaper Group., Inc., 100 E. Second St., Mineola, NY 11501. TEL 516-739-6400; Ed. Pat Horwell; Pub. Barry Manning; adv. contact: Rhonda Glickman. photos; pub. size: tabloid; circ. 6,500(paid).
Formerly: Oceanside-Rockville Centre Beacon.

US

OYSTER BAY ENTERPRISE PILOT. 1885. Thu. $.75 newsstand; $21/yr. in area. 132 E. Second St., Mineola, NY 11501. TEL 516-747-8282; FAX 516-742-5867. **Owner(s):** Anton Publications, 132 E. Second St., Mineola, NY 11501. TEL 516-747-8282; Ed. Dagmar Fors Karppi; Pub. Karl V. Anton, Jr.; adv. contact: Harriet Heffernan. pub. size: tabloid; circ. 2,200(paid).

US

ROCKVILLE CENTRE NEWS & OWL. 1908. Wed. $.15 216 E. Second St., Mineola, NY 11501. TEL 516-739-6400; FAX 516-739-5404. **Owner(s):** Nassau Community Newspapers, 216 E. Second St., Mineola, NY 11501. TEL 516-739-6400; Ed. Pat Horwell; Pub. Barry Manning; adv. contact: Rhoda Glickmann. pub. size: tabloid; circ. 3,900(paid).
Formerly: Rockville Centre Long Island News & Owl.

WEEKLY NEWSPAPERS

US
SYOSSET JERICHO TRIBUNE. Fri. $.75 newsstand; $18/yr. in area; $18/15 mos. senior citizens. 132 E. Second St., Mineola, NY 11501. TEL 516-747-8282; FAX 516-742-5867. **Owner(s):** Anton Publications, 132 E. Second St., Mineola, NY 11501. TEL 516-747-8282; FAX 516-742-5867; Ed. Kathy Gerber; Pub. Karl V. Anton, Jr.; adv. contact: Harriet Heffernan. pub. size: tabloid; circ. 5,800(paid).
Formerly: Syosset Tribune.

US
THREE VILLAGE TIMES. 1948. Fri. $.75 newsstand; $18/yr. in cy.; $28/yr. out of cy. 132 E. Second St., Mineola, NY 11501. TEL 516-747-8282; FAX 516-742-5867. **Owner(s):** Anton Publications, 132 E. Second St., Mineola, NY 11501. TEL 516-747-8282; Ed. Danny McCue; Pub. Karl V. Anton, Jr.; adv. contact: Harriet Heffernan. pub. size: tabloid; circ. 1,563(paid).

US
VALLEY STREAM MAILEADER. 1923. Wed. $.35 newsstand; $15/yr. 216 E. Second St., Mineola, NY 11501. TEL 516-739-6400; FAX 516-739-5404. **Owner(s):** Nassau Community Newspapers, P.O. Box 159, Valley Stream, NY 11582. TEL 516-825-0155; Ed. Patricia Horwell; Pub. Barry Manning; adv. contact: Rhonda Glickman. photos; pub. size: tabloid; circ. 8,800(paid).

US
WESTBURY TIMES. 1964. Thu. $.75 newsstand; $18/yr. in state; $23/yr. out of state. 132 E. Second St., Mineola, NY 11501. TEL 516-747-8282; FAX 516-742-5287. **Owner(s):** Anton Publications, 132 E. Second St., Mineola, NY 11501. TEL 516-747-8282; Ed. Danny McCue; Pub. Karl V. Anton, Jr.; adv. contact: Harriet Heffernan. pub. size: tabloid; circ. 3,575(paid).

MONROE

US
PHOTO NEWS. 1967. Wed. $.50 newsstand; $21/yr. in cy.; $25/yr. out of cy. 45 Gilbert St., Monroe, NY 10950. TEL 914-782-4000; FAX 914-782-1711. **Owner(s):** Straus Communications, P.O. Box 190, Warwick, NY 10990. TEL 914-986-2061; Ed. Stan Martin; Pub. Stan Martin; pub. size: tabloid; circ. 4,900(paid).
Formerly: Monroe-Woodbury Photo News.

MORAVIA

US
MORAVIA REPUBLICAN REGISTER. 1863. Wed. $.50 newsstand; $18.50/yr. in cy.; $22/yr. out of cy. 6 Central St., Moravia, NY 13118. TEL 315-497-1551. **Owner(s):** Community Newspapers, 6 Central St., Moravia, NY 13118. TEL 315-497-1551; Ed. Bernard McGuerty, III. adv.; photos; pub. size: tabloid; circ. 2,500(paid).

US
SOUTHERN CAYUGA TRIBUNE. Wed. $.50 newsstand; $18.50/yr. in cy.; $22/yr. out of cy. 6 Central St., Moravia, NY 13118. TEL 315-497-1551; FAX 315-497-1551. **Owner(s):** Community Newspapers, 6 Central St., P.O. Box 591, Moravia, NY 13118. TEL 315-497-1551; Ed. Bernard McGuerty, III; Pub. Bernard McGuerty, III; photos; pub. size: tabloid; circ. 2,500(paid).

NAPLES

US
NAPLES RECORD, THE. 1870. Wed. $.50 newsstand; $24/yr. in state; $30/yr. out of state. 23 Mill St., Naples, NY 14512. TEL 716-374-5260; FAX 716-374-8590. **Owner(s):** Naples Record, P.O. Box 370, Naples, NY 14512. TEL 716-374-5260; Ed. Mike Fowler; Pub. Mike Fowler; adv.; photos; bk.rev.; pub. size: tabloid; circ. 1,350(paid).

NARROWSBURG

US
RIVER REPORTER, THE. 1975. Thu. $.60 newsstand; $22/yr. 8 Main St., Narrowsburg, NY 12764. TEL 914-252-7414; FAX 914-252-3298; E-mail: riverrep@zelacom.com. **Owner(s):** Suart Communications, Inc., P.O. Box 20, Narrowsburg, NY 12764. TEL 914-252-7414; FAX 914-252-3298; Ed. Pam Chergotis. adv.; photos; bk.rev.; pub. size: tabloid; circ. 3,700(paid).

NEWARK

US
COURIER GAZETTE. 1846. Fri. $.50 newsstand; $19/yr. in cy.; $26/yr. out of cy. 613 S. Main St., Newark, NY 14513. TEL 315-331-1000; FAX 315-331-1053; E-mail: adgroup@epix.net; URL: http://www.our-hometown.com/ny/wayne/newark/news.html. **Owner(s):** Ad Group, Inc., 613 S. Main St., Newark, NY 14513. TEL 315-331-6956; FAX 315-331-1053; Ed. Sandra Marcano; Pub. John H. VanDusen; pub. size: broadsheet; circ. 4,000(paid).

NEW ROCHELLE

US
TOMORROW. 1983. m. $10/yr. 459 Main St., Ste. 204, New Rochelle, NY 10801. TEL 914-636-4646. **Owner(s):** Marketing Tomorrow, Inc., 459 Main St., New Rochelle, NY 10801. TEL 914-636-4646; Ed. Glenda Palmer; Pub. Philip Wanderman; pub. size: broadsheet; circ. 47,000(paid).

NEW YORK

US
CHELSEA CLINTON NEWS. 1939. Thu. $.50 newsstand; $24/yr. 242 W. 30th St., 5th Fl., New York, NY 10001. TEL 212-268-3087; FAX 212-268-2935. **Owner(s):** News Communications, Inc., 242 W. 30th St., 5th Fl., New York, NY 10001. TEL 212-268-3087; FAX 212-268-2935; Ed. Doug Fricke. pub. size: tabloid; circ. 12,000(paid).

US
DOWNTOWN EXPRESS. 1986. bi-w. Tue. free. 80 Eighth Ave., 2nd Fl., New York, NY 10011. TEL 212-242-6162. **Owner(s):** Clean Slate Corp., 80 Eighth Ave., 2nd Fl., New York, NY 10011. TEL 212-242-6162; Ed. Thomas Butson. adv. contact: Loren Granville. photos; pub. size: tabloid; circ. 15,000(free).

US
NEW YORK OBSERVER. 1987. Wed. $1 newsstand; $22/yr. mailed. 54 E. 64th St., New York, NY 10021. TEL 212-755-2400; FAX 212-688-4889; E-mail: editorial@observer.con. **Owner(s):** Arthur Carter, 54 E. 64th St., New York, NY 10021. TEL 212-755-2400; FAX 212-688-4889; Ed. Peter Kaplan; Pub. Arthur Carter; pub. size: broadsheet; circ. 51,000(paid).

US
NEW YORK PRESS. 1988. Wed. free; $25/yr. mailed. 295 Lafayette St., 9th Fl., New York, NY 10012-3920. TEL 212-941-1130; FAX 212-941-7824. **Owner(s):** New York Press, Inc., 295 Lafayette St., 9th Fl., New York, NY 10012-3920. TEL 212-941-1130; FAX 212-941-7824; Ed. Russ Smith; Pub. Ron Mann; adv. contact: Jill Muller. pub. size: tabloid; circ. 100,000(controlled & free).

US ISSN 0473-5900
OUR TOWN. 1970. Wed. free newsstand; $69/yr. mailed. 242 W. 30th St., 5th Fl., New York, NY 10001. TEL 212-268-8600; FAX 212-268-0614. **Owner(s):** News Communications, Inc., 242 W. 30th St., 5th Fl., New York, NY 10001. TEL 212-268-0454; FAX 212-268-0614; Ed. Mark Boal. adv.; photos; pub. size: tabloid; circ. 118,000(free).

US ISSN 1076-0091
PEOPLE'S WEEKLY WORLD. 1967. Thu. $.50 newsstand; $20/yr. 235 W. 23rd St., New York, NY 10011. TEL 212-924-2523; FAX 212-645-5436. **Owner(s):** Long View Publishing Co. Inc., 239 W. 23rd St., New York, NY 10011. TEL 212-924-2523; Ed. Carolyn Rummel. adv.; pub. size: tabloid; circ. 60,000(paid). **Wire Service(s):** UPI, TASS.
Formerly: People's Daily World.

US ISSN 0042-6202
VILLAGER, THE. 1933. Wed. $.50 newsstand; $21/yr. 80 Eighth Ave., Ste. 200, New York, NY 10011. TEL 212-229-1890; FAX 212-229-2790. **Owner(s):** Clean Slate Corp., 80 Eighth Ave., New York, NY 10011. TEL 212-229-1890; Ed. Thomas Butson; Pub. Elizabeth Butson; adv.; photos; pub. size: tabloid; circ. 20,000(paid).

US ISSN 0042-6180
VILLAGE VOICE, THE. 1955. Wed. free in Manhattan; $1.25 newsstand; $47.95/yr. 36 Cooper Sq., New York, NY 10003. TEL 212-475-3300; FAX 212-475-8944. **Owner(s):** Stern Publishing, Inc., 393 Jericho Tpke., Minneola, NY 11501-1205. TEL 516-877-7373; Ed. Donald Forst. adv.; photos; bk.rev.; pub. size: tabloid; circ. 235,206(paid). **Wire Service(s):** AP.

US
WESTSIDER, THE. 1973. Thu. $22/yr. 242 W. 30th St., 5th Fl., New York, NY 10001. TEL 212-268-3087; FAX 212-268-2935. **Owner(s):** News Communications, Inc., 242 W. 30th St., 5th Fl., New York, NY 10001. TEL 212-268-3087; Ed. Doug Fricke. pub. size: tabloid; circ. 15,000(paid).

NORTHPORT

US
OBSERVER, THE. 1922. Thu. $.75 newsstand; $20/yr. 188 Main St., Northport, NY 11768. TEL 516-261-6124; FAX 516-265-6237. **Owner(s):** North Shore News Group, P.O. Box 805, Smithtown, NY 11787. TEL 516-265-2100; Ed. David Ambro; Pub. Bernard Paley; adv. contact: Jennifer Paley. pub. size: tabloid; circ. 10,000(paid).

NORTH SYRACUSE
US
STAR-NEWS, THE. 1924. Wed. $.75 newsstand; $25/yr. 428 S. Main St., North Syracuse, NY 13212. TEL 315-434-8889; FAX 315-434-8883. **Owner(s):** Eagle Newspapers, Inc., P.O. Box 270, Baldwinsville, NY 13027. TEL 315-635-3921; FAX 315-635-3914; Ed. Maria Forastiero. adv. contact: John Mott. photos; pub. size: broadsheet; circ. 7,200(paid).

NORTH TONAWANDA
US
RECORD-ADVERTISER. 1914. Wed. free. 435 River Rd., North Tonawanda, NY 14120. TEL 716-693-1000; FAX 716-693-8573. **Owner(s):** Tonawanda News, 435 River Rd., North Tonawanda, NY. TEL 716-693-1000; Ed. Terry Shaw; Pub. Joseph P. Armenia; adv.: $12.70/SAU. pub. size: broadsheet; circ. 33,000(free). **Wire Service(s):** AP.

OGDENSBURG
US
ADVANCE, THE. 1830. Sun. $1/issue. 308 Isabella, Ogdensburg, NY 13669. TEL 315-393-1000; FAX 315-393-5108. **Owner(s):** Johnson Newspaper Corp., 260 Washington St., Watertown, NY 13601. TEL 315-782-1000; Ed. James Reagen. adv. contact: Mary McGee. pub. size: broadsheet; circ. Sun. 12,000(paid). **Wire Service(s):** AP.

ORCHARD PARK
US
SOUTHTOWNS CITIZEN. 1932. Sat. $.70 newsstand; $25/yr. 6519 E. Quaker St., Orchard Park, NY 14127. TEL 716-662-0001; FAX 716-667-3002. **Owner(s):** Coleman Communications Corp., 6519 E. Quaker St., Orchard Park, NY 14127. TEL 716-662-0001; Ed. Christopher Coleman; Pub. Christopher Coleman; adv. contact: Gail Ford. pub. size: tabloid; circ. 5,000(paid).

OWEGO
US
OWEGO PENNYSAVER. Sun. free. 181-183 Front St., Owego, NY 13827. TEL 607-687-2434; FAX 607-687-2931. **Owner(s):** Owego Pennysaver Press, P.O. Box 149, Owego, NY 13827. TEL 607-687-2434; Ed. Kim Depew. adv.; pub. size: standard; circ. 24,000(free).

OYSTER BAY
US
OYSTER BAY-SYOSSET GUARDIAN. 1899. Fri. $.50 newsstand; $20/yr. local; $24/yr. out of state; $16/yr. senior citizen. 32 E. Main St., Oyster Bay, NY 11771. TEL 516-922-4215; FAX 516-922-4227. **Owner(s):** Helen Dolan, P.O. Box 28, Oyster Bay, NY 11771. TEL 516-922-4215; Ed. David Criblez. adv. contact: Eileen Reilly. pub. size: broadsheet; circ. 30,000(paid).

OZONE PARK
US
FORUM OF QUEENS. 1977. Fri. free; $65/yr. 137-05 Cross Bay Blvd., Ozone Park, NY 11417. TEL 718-845-3221; FAX 718-738-7645. **Owner(s):** Queens Herald Corp., 137-05 Cross Bay Blvd., Ozone Park, NY 11417. TEL 718-845-3221; FAX 718-738-7645; Ed. Alex Lutz; Pub. Thomas J. LaVecchia; adv.; photos; bk.rev.; pub. size: tabloid; circ. 25,000(free & paid).
Formerly: Forum of South Queens.

PALMYRA
US
COURIER-JOURNAL. 1838. Wed. $.35 newsstand; $14.50/yr. 612 E. Main St., Palmyra, NY 14522. TEL 315-597-6655; FAX 315-597-6947. **Owner(s):** Suburban Circle Publications, Inc., 2808 Dewey Ave., Rochester, NY 14616. TEL 716-663-0068; Ed. Stephen Buchiere; Pub. Lawrence Lucieer; adv.; pub. size: tabloid; circ. 2,700(paid).

PATCHOGUE
US
LONG ISLAND ADVANCE. 1871. Thu. $24/yr. 20 Medford Ave., Patchogue, NY 11772. TEL 516-475-1000; FAX 516-475-1565; E-mail: advletters@aol.com. **Owner(s):** John T. Tuthill, III, P.O. Box 780, Patchogue, NY 11772. TEL 516-475-1000; Ed. Jeff Sievers; Pub. John T. Tuthill, III; adv. contact: Terry Tuthill. pub. size: tabloid; circ. 10,500(paid).

PAWLING
US ISSN 0747-2188
PAWLING NEWS CHRONICLE. 1870. Thu. $.60 newsstand; $18.65/yr. in cy. 3 Memorial Ave., Pawling, NY 12564. TEL 914-855-1100; FAX 914-855-1106. **Owner(s):** Taconic Media, Inc., P.O. Box 316, Millbrook, NY 12545; Pub. Hamilton Meserve; adv.; photos; pub. size: tabloid; circ. 2,357(paid).

PEARL RIVER
US
CLARKSTOWN COURIER, THE. 1992. Wed. $.50 newsstand; $100/yr. 25 W. Central Ave., Pearl River, NY 10965. TEL 914-732-8200; FAX 914-732-9214. **Owner(s):** Aldrich Family Trust, 25 W. Central Ave., Pearl River, NY 10965. TEL 914-732-8200; FAX 914-732-9214; Sluys Family Trust, 25 W. Central Ave., Pearl River, NY 10965. TEL 914-732-8200; FAX 914-732-9214; Ed. Arthur R. Aldrich; Pub. Arthur R. Aldrich; adv. contact: Judith C. Haber. bk.rev.; pub. size: tabloid; circ. 12,000(free).

US
OUR TOWN. 1973. Wed. free. 25 W. Central Ave., Pearl River, NY 10965. TEL 914-732-8200; FAX 914-732-9214. **Owner(s):** Community Media, Inc., 25 W. Central Ave., Pearl River, NY 10965. TEL 914-732-8200; FAX 914-732-9214; Ed. Arthur R. Aldrich; Pub. Arthur R. Aldrich; adv. contact: Judith C. Haber. bk.rev.; pub. size: tabloid; circ. 22,000(free).

US
ROCKLAND INDEPENDENT, THE. 1992. Wed. $.25 newsstand. 25 W. Central Ave., Pearl River, NY 10965. TEL 914-732-8200; FAX 914-732-9214. **Owner(s):** Aldrich Family Trust, 25 W. Central Ave., Pearl River, NY 10965. TEL 914-732-8200; FAX 914-732-9214; Sluys Family Trust, 25 W. Central Ave., Pearl River, NY 10965. TEL 914-732-8200; FAX 914-732-9214; Ed. Arthur R. Aldrich; Pub. Arthur R. Aldrich; adv. contact: Judith C. Haber. bk.rev.; pub. size: tabloid; circ. 14,000(free).

PEEKSKILL
US
PEEKSKILL HERALD. 1986. Thu. $30/yr. local; $40/yr. out of area. 927 South St., Peekskill, NY 10566. TEL 914-737-7747. **Owner(s):** Highland Publications, Inc., P.O. Box 2250, Peekskill, NY 10566; Ed. Kathy Daley. pub. size: tabloid; circ. 5,000(paid).

PENN YAN
US
CHRONICLE-EXPRESS. 1824. Wed. $.75 newsstand; $28/yr. 138 Main St., Penn Yan, NY 14527. TEL 315-536-4422; FAX 315-536-0682. **Owner(s):** American Publishing Co. of NY, 85 Canisteo St., Hornell, NY 14843. TEL 607-324-1425; Ed. Gwen Chamberlin; Pub. George M. Barnes; adv. contact: George M. Barnes. pub. size: broadsheet; circ. 4,550(paid).

PHOENIX
US
PHOENIX REGISTER. 1912. Wed. $.50 newsstand; $10/yr. 71 State St., Phoenix, NY 13135. TEL 315-695-4771; FAX 315-695-4771. **Owner(s):** Oswego County Weeklies, P.O. Box 129, Mexico, NY 13114. TEL 315-963-7813; FAX 315-963-4087; Ed. Andrew Freeman. adv. contact: Charles Seaman. pub. size: tabloid; circ. 3,400(paid).

PINE PLAINS
US
PINE PLAINS REGISTER-HERALD. 1859. Thu. $29/yr. 24 Popler Ave., Pine Plains, NY 12567. TEL 518-398-1737; FAX 914-677-6337. **Owner(s):** Taconic Media, Inc., P.O. Box 316, Millbrook, NY 12545. TEL 914-677-8241; Ed. Bob Lonicky; Pub. Hamilton W. Meserve; pub. size: broadsheet; circ. 2,300(paid).

PITTSFORD
US
PERINTON-FAIRPORT POST, THE. 1932. Wed. $.75 newsstand; $25/yr. mailed. 4 S. Main St., Pittsford, NY 14534. TEL 716-924-4040; FAX 716-924-7734; E-mail: wolfepub@frontiernet.com. **Owner(s):** Canandaigua Messenger, Inc., 73 Buffalo St., Canandaigua, NY 14424. TEL 716-394-0770; Pub. Andrew D. Wolfe; adv.; $7.70/SAU. photos; pub. size: broadsheet; circ. 4,500(paid).

WEEKLY NEWSPAPERS

PORT CHESTER
US ISSN 0680-0660
WESTMORE NEWS. 1964. Thu. $.50 newsstand; $18/yr. 38 Broad St., Port Chester, NY 10573-4197. TEL 914-939-6864. **Owner(s):** Westmore News, Inc., 38 Broad St., Port Chester, NY 10573. TEL 914-939-6864; Ed. Jananne Abel; Pub. Richard Abel; adv.; photos; pub. size: tabloid; circ. 3,000(paid).

PORT JERVIS
US
GAZETTE, THE. 1850. Thu. $.50 newsstand; $18.50/yr. deliv. & mailed. 84-88 Fowler St., Port Jervis, NY 12771. TEL 914-856-5383; FAX 914-858-8484. **Owner(s):** Ottaway Newspapers, Inc., P.O. Box 401, Campbell Hall, NY 10916. TEL 914-294-8181; Ed. Janis Osborne. adv.; photos; pub. size: tabloid; circ. 9,500(free & paid).
Formerly: Tri-State Gazette.

PORT WASHINGTON
US
PORT WASHINGTON NEWS. 1903. Thu. $.75 newsstand; $21/yr. 270 Main St., Port Washington, NY 11050. TEL 516-767-0035; FAX 516-944-7743. **Owner(s):** Anton Publications, 132 E. Second St., Mineola, NY 11501. TEL 516-747-8282; FAX 516-742-5867; Ed. Jackie Pierangelo; Pub. Karl V. Anton; adv. contact: Richard Gaudet. pub. size: tabloid; circ. 6,969(paid).

POTSDAM
US
CLARKSON INTEGRATOR. 1920. Mon. $10/yr. Clarkson Ave., Potsdam, NY 13699. TEL 315-265-9050; FAX 315-268-7661. **Owner(s):** Clarkson Integrator, P.O. Box 8710, Potsdam, NY 13699-8710. TEL 315-265-9050; FAX 315-268-7661; Ed. David King. adv. contact: Pat Murphy. photos; bk.rev. pub. size: tabloid; circ. 6,000(controlled & paid). **Wire Service(s):** AP.

POUND RIDGE
US
COUNTRY SHOPPER. m. free. 40 Westchester Ave., Pound Ridge, NY 10576. TEL 914-764-4678; FAX 914-764-4662. **Owner(s):** Country Shopper, P.O. Box 190, Pound Ridge, NY 10576. TEL 914-764-4678; Ed. Lillian Petruccione. pub. size: tabloid; circ. 31,000(free).

PULASKI
US
SALMON RIVER NEWS. 1973. Wed. $.50 newsstand; $10/yr. 7549 Broad St., Pulaski, NY 13142. TEL 315-963-7813; FAX 315-963-7813. **Owner(s):** Oswego County Weeklies, P.O. Box 129, Mexico, NY 13114. TEL 315-963-7813; FAX 315-963-4087; Ed. Rose Ann Parsons; Pub. Mark Backus; adv. contact: Charles Seaman. pub. size: tabloid; circ. 8,000(paid).

RAVENA
US
GREENVILLE LOCAL. 1932. Thu. $20/yr. local; $24/yr. out of cy. 164 Main St., Ravena, NY 12143-0370. TEL 518-756-2030; FAX 518-756-8555. **Owner(s):** Bleezarde Publishing, Inc., 164 Main Street, Ravena, NY 12143-0370. TEL 518-756-2030; Pub. Richard G. Bleezarde; pub. size: tabloid; circ. 1,350(paid).

US
RAVENA NEWS HERALD. Thu. $20/yr. Albany & Greene cys.; $24/yr.elsewhere. 164 Main St., Ravena, NY 12143-0370. TEL 518-756-2030; FAX 518-756-8555. **Owner(s):** Bleezarde Publishing, Inc., 164 Main St., Ravena, NY 12143-0307. TEL 518-756-2030; FAX 518-756-8555; Ed. Gene Levy; Pub. Richard G. Bleezarde; adv.; photos; pub. size: tabloid; circ. 4,650(paid).

RED CREEK
US
POST-HERALD. 1894. Thu. $.45 newsstand; $20/yr. local; $30/yr. out of state. Main St., Red Creek, NY 13143-0199. TEL 315-754-6229; FAX 315-754-6431. **Owner(s):** Angelo G. Palermo, Main St., Red Creek, NY 13143. TEL 315-754-6229; Ed. Dana McIntyre; Pub. Christopher Palermo; adv. contact: Donna Malcott. pub. size: tabloid; circ. 1,200(paid). **Wire Service(s):** Empire Information System.
Formerly: Red Creek Herald, Fair Haven Register, Cato Citizen.

REGO PARK
US
QUEENS CHRONICLE. 1979. Thu. $75/yr. 62-33 Woodhaven Blvd., Rego Park, NY 11374. TEL 718-205-8000; FAX 718-205-0150. **Owner(s):** Susan Merzon, 151-15 84th St., Howard Beach, NY 11414. TEL 718-738-1704; Ed. Liz Rhoades; Pub. Susan Merzon; adv. contact: Mark Weidler. photos; bk.rev.; pub. size: tabloid; circ. 5,500(controlled & free). **Wire Service(s):** CNS.

RHINEBECK
US
GAZETTE-ADVERTISER. 1846. Thu. $.75 newsstand; $29/yr. in state; $35/yr. out of state. 7 Livingston St., Rhinebeck, NY 12572. TEL 914-876-3033; FAX 914-876-2361. **Owner(s):** Taconic Media, Inc., Front St. & Merritt Ave., Millbrook, NY 12545; Ed. Gabe Wasserman; Pub. Hamilton W. Meserve; adv. contact: Marty Sweeney. pub. size: broadsheet; circ. 5,500(paid).

RIDGEWOOD
US
TIMES NEWSWEEKLY. 1908. Thu. $.40 newsstand; $14/yr. local; $16/yr. out of area. 6658 Fresh Pond Rd., Ridgewood, NY 11385-3245. TEL 718-821-7500; FAX 718-456-0120. **Owner(s):** Ridgewood Times Printing & Publishing Co., P.O. Box C-299, Flushing, NY 11385; Ed. James P. Devlin; Pub. Maureen E. Walthers; adv.; pub. size: tabloid; circ. 23,000(paid).
Formerly: Ridgewood Times.

ROCHESTER
US
FAIRFIELD-PENFIELD COMMUNITY NEWS. 1948. Tue. free in area; $15/yr. out of area. 2808 Dewey Ave., Rochester, NY 14616. TEL 716-663-0068; FAX 716-663-0146. **Owner(s):** Suburban Circle Publications, 2808 Dewey Ave., Rochester, NY 14612. TEL 716-663-0068; FAX 716-663-0146; Ed. Molly Stone. pub. size: tabloid; circ. 16,000(free & paid).
Formerly: Shopping News.

US
GATES-CHILI NEWS. 1958. Wed. $.45 newsstand; $16/yr.; $31/2 yrs. 2361 Chili Ave., Rochester, NY 14624-3319. TEL 716-247-9200; FAX 716-247-9210. **Owner(s):** Patricia M. Smith, 2361 Chili Ave., Rochester, NY 14624. TEL 716-247-9200; Ed. Christine C. Fien; Pub. Patricia M. Smith; adv.; photos; pub. size: tabloid; circ. 9,800(controlled & paid).

US
GOLDEN TIMES. 1976. s-m.: 1st & 3rd Wed. $15/yr.; $25/2 yrs. 80 Rockwood Pl., Rochester, NY 14610. TEL 716-242-2930; FAX 716-256-2765. **Owner(s):** Carmen J. Viglucci, 80 Rockwood Pl., Rochester, NY 14610. Ed. Carmen J. Viglucci. adv. contact: Ralph Hyman. photos; bk.rev.; pub. size: tabloid; circ. 20,000(free & paid).

US
IRONDEQUOIT PRESS. 1932. Thu. $.50 newsstand; $21/yr.; $18/yr. senior citizens. 657 Titus Ave., Rochester, NY 14617. TEL 716-342-9450; FAX 716-342-6146. **Owner(s):** Canandaigua Messenger, Inc., 73 Buffalo St., Canandaigua, NY 14424. TEL 716-394-0770; Ed. Mark Syverud; Pub. George Ewing, Jr.; adv.; photos; pub. size: broadsheet; circ. 7,700(paid).

SAUGERTIES
US
SAUGERTIES POST STAR. 1877. Thu. $30/yr. in cy.; $35/yr. out of cy. 141 Ulster Ave., Saugerties, NY 12477. TEL 914-246-4985; FAX 914-246-5108. **Owner(s):** American Publishing Co., 606 N. Van Buren, Marion, IL 62959. TEL 618-993-1711; Ed. Scott Hallum. pub. size: tabloid; circ. 2,400(paid).
Formerly: Sunday Old Dutch Post-Star.

SAYVILLE
US
FIRE ISLAND TIDE. 1976. bi-w.: May-Sep. $1 newsstand; $10/yr. 49 Main St., Sayville, NY 11782. TEL 516-567-7470. **Owner(s):** Fire Island Tide, Inc., P.O. Box 8, Patchogue, NY 11772. TEL 516-567-7470; Pub. Warren C. McDowell; adv.; photos; bk.rev.; pub. size: tabloid; circ. 15,000(paid).

US
ISLIP BULLETIN. 1946. Thu. $.50 newsstand; $20/yr. in cy.; $27/yr. out of cy. P.O. Box 367, Sayville, NY 11782. TEL 516-589-6200; FAX 516-475-1565. **Owner(s):** John-Lor Publications, P.O. Box 780, Patchogue, NY 11772. TEL 516-475-1000; Ed. John Lee; Pub. John T. Tuthill, III; pub. size: tabloid; circ. 10,000(paid).

10686 SAYVILLE, NY

WEEKLY NEWSPAPERS

US
SUFFOLK COUNTY NEWS. 1884. Thu. $.75 newsstand; $24/yr. 23 Candee Ave., Sayville, NY 11782. TEL 516-589-6200; FAX 516-589-3246. **Owner(s):** John-Lor Publications, P.O. Box 780, Patchogue, NY 11772. TEL 516-475-1000; Ed. John Lee; Pub. John Tuthill; adv. contact: John Tuthill. pub. size: tabloid; circ. 10,000(paid).

SCARSDALE

US
SCARSDALE INQUIRER, THE. 1901. Fri. $.75 newsstand; $33/yr. The Harwood Bldg., Ste. 510, Scarsdale, NY 10583. TEL 914-725-2500; FAX 914-725-1552. **Owner(s):** S.I. Communications, Inc., P.O. Box 418, Scarsdale, NY 10583. TEL 914-725-2500; FAX 914-725-1552; Ed. Linda Leavitt; Pub. Deborah White; adv.; photos; pub. size: broadsheet; circ. 7,000(free & paid).

SENECA FALLS

US
REVEILLE/BETWEEN THE LAKES. 1855. Thu. $.50 newsstand; $26.95/yr. out of cy. 2024 Rte. 5 & 20, Seneca Falls, NY 13148-0557. TEL 315-568-6400; FAX 315-568-4200; E-mail: lakes@lynnet.com. **Owner(s):** Reveille Publishing Co., Inc., 2024 Rte. 5 & 20, Seneca Falls, NY 13148. TEL 315-568-6400; FAX 315-568-4200; Pub. Joe Siccardi; adv.; photos; bk.rev.; pub. size: tabloid; circ. 1,845(paid).
Formerly: Seneca Falls-Waterloo Reveille.

SETAUKET

US
PORT TIMES-RECORD, THE. 1989. Thu. $.75 newsstand; $23/yr. in cy.; $31/yr. out of cy. 185 Rte. 25A, Setauket, NY 11733. TEL 516-751-7744. **Owner(s):** Leah S. Dunaief, P.O. Box 707, Setauket, NY 11733. TEL 516-751-7744; FAX 516-751-4165; Ed. Marie Murtagh; Pub. Leah S. Dunaief; adv.; photos; bk.rev.; pub. size: tabloid; circ. 7,680(paid).
Formerly: Port Times.

US
TIMES OF NESCONSET, THE. 1993. Thu. $.75 newsstand; $23/yr. 185 Rte. 25A, Setauket, NY 11733. TEL 516-751-7744; FAX 516-751-4165. **Owner(s):** Leah S. Dunaief, P.O. Box 707, Setauket, NY 11733. TEL 516-751-7744; FAX 516-751-4165; Ed. Jane O'Sullivan; Pub. Leah S. Dunaief; adv.; photos; bk.rev.; pub. size: tabloid; circ. 4,000(paid).

US
TIMES OF SMITHTOWN. 1993. Thu. $.75 newsstand; $23/yr. in cy.; $31/yr. out of cy. 185 Rte. 25A, Setauket, NY 11733. TEL 516-751-7744; FAX 516-751-4165. **Owner(s):** Leah S. Dunaief, P.O. Box 707, Setauket, NY 11733. TEL 516-751-7744; FAX 516-751-4165; Ed. Jane O'Sullivan; Pub. Leah S. Dunaief; adv.; photos; bk.rev.; pub. size: tabloid; circ. 23,000(paid).

US
TIMES OF ST. JAMES. 1989. Thu. $.75 newsstand; $23/yr. in cy.; $31/yr. out of cy. 185 Rte. 25A, Setauket, NY 11733. TEL 516-751-7744; FAX 516-751-4165. **Owner(s):** Leah S. Dunaief, P.O. Box 707, Setauket, NY 11733. TEL 516-751-7744; FAX 516-751-4165; Ed. Jane O'Sullivan; Pub. Leah S. Dunaief; adv.; photos; bk.rev.; pub. size: tabloid; circ. 32,000(paid).

US
VILLAGE BEACON-RECORD, THE. 1986. Thu. $.75 newsstand; $23/yr. in cy.; $31/yr. out of cy. 185 Rte. 25A, Setauket, NY 11733. TEL 516-331-1154; FAX 516-751-4165. **Owner(s):** Leah S. Dunaief, P.O. Box 707, Setauket, NY 11733. TEL 516-751-7744; FAX 516-751-4165; Ed. Leah S. Dunaief; Pub. Leah S. Dunaief; adv.; photos; bk.rev.; pub. size: tabloid; circ. 35,000(paid).

US   ISSN 0889-8677
VILLAGE TIMES, THE. 1976. Thu. $.75 newsstand; $27/yr. in cy.; $35/yr. out of cy. 185 Rte. 25A, Setauket, NY 11733. TEL 516-751-7744; FAX 516-751-4165. **Owner(s):** Leah S. Dunaief, P.O. Box 707, Setauket, NY 11733. TEL 516-751-7744; Ed. Leah S. Dunaief; Pub. Leah S. Dunaief; adv.; photos; bk.rev.; pub. size: tabloid; circ. 10,000(paid).

SHELTER ISLAND HEIGHTS

US   ISSN 0746-0668
SHELTER ISLAND REPORTER. 1959. Thu. $.75 newsstand; $20/yr. in cy.; $25/yr. out of cy. 9 Grand Ave., Shelter Island Heights, NY 11965. TEL 516-749-1000; FAX 516-749-0144. **Owner(s):** Gardner Cowles, III, P.O. Box 3020, Shelter Island Heights, NY 11965. TEL 516-749-1000; Ed. Elizabeth A. Bonora; Pub. Gardner Cowles, III; adv.; bk.rev.; pub. size: tabloid; circ. 2,800(paid).

SIDNEY

US
TRI-TOWN NEWS. Wed. $.50 newsstand; $19/yr. local; $22/yr. out of area. 5 Winkler Rd., Sidney, NY 13838. TEL 607-563-3526; FAX 607-563-7118. **Owner(s):** Paul Hamilton, Sr. & Ken Paden, P.O. Box 388, Sidney, NY 13838. TEL 607-563-3526; Ed. Nancy Burns. adv. contact: Anna Ritchey. photos; pub. size: standard; circ. 6,000(paid).

SKANEATELES

US   ISSN 1066-1352
MARCELLUS OBSERVER. 1879. Wed. $.75 newsstand; $25/yr. 2 Fennel St., Skaneateles, NY 13152. TEL 315-685-8338; FAX 315-685-8338. **Owner(s):** Eagle Newspapers, Inc., P.O. Box 65, Fayetteville, NY 13066. TEL 315-637-3121; Ed. Guy Hulberg; Pub. Stewart Hancock; adv. contact: Laurie Whiting. pub. size: broadsheet; circ. 1,418(paid).

US
SKANEATELES PRESS. 1939. Wed. $.75 newsstand; $21/yr. 2 Fennel St., Skaneateles, NY 13152. TEL 315-685-8338; FAX 315-685-8338. **Owner(s):** Eagle Newspapers, Inc., 5910 Firestone Dr., Syracuse, NY 13206; Ed. Guy Hulbert; Pub. Stewart Hancock; adv. contact: Laurie Smart. pub. size: broadsheet; circ. 4,000(paid).

SMITHTOWN

US
BROOKHAVEN REVIEW. 1888. Thu. $.50 newsstand; $15.50/yr. in cy.; $21/yr. out of cy. 127 E. Main St., Smithtown, NY 11787. TEL 516-265-3500; FAX 516-265-3504. **Owner(s):** ESP Publications, P.O. Box 925, Smithtown, NY 11787; Ed. Terry Gilberti; Pub. Phil Sciarillo; adv. contact: Phil Sciarillo. pub. size: tabloid; circ. 3,000(paid).

US
COMMACK NEWS. 1964. Thu. $.75 newsstand; $20/yr. One Brooksite Dr., Smithtown, NY 11787. TEL 516-265-2100; FAX 516-265-6237. **Owner(s):** North Shore News Group, P.O. Box 805, Smithtown, NY 11787. TEL 516-265-2100; Pub. Bernard Paley; adv.; photos; pub. size: tabloid; circ. 4,500(paid).

US
ISLIP NEWS. 1950. Thu. $.75 newsstand; $20/yr. One Brooksite Dr., Smithtown, NY 11787. TEL 516-265-2100; FAX 516-265-6237. **Owner(s):** Northshore News Group, P.O. Box 805, Smithtown, NY 11787. TEL 516-265-2100; Ed. Jennifer Paley. adv.; pub. size: tabloid; circ. 3,100(paid).

US
RONKONKOMA REVIEW. 1959. Thu. $.50 newsstand; $15.50/yr. in cy.; $21/yr. out of cy. 127 E. Main St., Smithtown, NY 11787. TEL 516-567-8730. **Owner(s):** ESP Publishing, P.O. Box 925, Smithtown, NY 11787. TEL 516-265-3500; Ed. Terry Gilberti; Pub. Sal DiPeri; adv. contact: Phil Sciarillo. pub. size: tabloid; circ. 2,500(paid).

US
SMITHTOWN MESSENGER. 1887. Thu. $.50 newsstand; $15.50/yr. in cy. 127 E. Main St., Smithtown, NY 11787. TEL 516-265-3500; FAX 516-265-3504. **Owner(s):** Sal Diperi, 127 E. Main St., Smithtown, NY 11787. TEL 516-265-3500; Ed. Terry Gilberti. adv. contact: Phil Sciarillo. photos; pub. size: tabloid; circ. 9,820(paid).

US
SMITHTOWN NEWS, THE. 1945. Thu. $.75 newsstand; $20/yr. One Brooksite Dr., Smithtown, NY 11787. TEL 516-265-2100; FAX 516-265-6237. **Owner(s):** North Shore News Group, One Brooksite Dr., Smithtown, NY 11787. TEL 516-265-2100; Ed. David Ambro. adv.; photos; bk.rev.; pub. size: tabloid; circ. 9,650(paid).

SOUTHAMPTON

US   ISSN 0745-6484
SOUTHAMPTON PRESS. 1897. Thu. $.75 newsstand; $28/yr. in cy.; $36/yr. out of cy. 135 Windmill Ln., Southampton, NY 11968. TEL 516-283-4100; FAX 516-283-4927; E-mail: mailbag@shpress.com. **Owner(s):** Southampton Press Publishing Co., Inc., 135 Windmill Ln., Southampton, NY 11968. TEL 516-283-4100; FAX 516-283-4927; Ed. Peter B. Boody. adv.; photos; bk.rev.; pub. size: broadsheet; circ. 12,000(controlled & paid).

SOUTHOLD

US
TRAVELER/WATCHMAN. 1824. Thu. $1 newsstand; $30/yr. in cy.; $38/yr. out of cy. Traveler St., Southold, NY 11971. TEL 516-765-3425; FAX 516-765-1756. **Owner(s):** Emanuel Konto Kosta, Traveler St., Southold, NY 11971. TEL 516-765-3425; FAX 516-756-1756; Ed. Glen Jochem; Pub. Emanuel Konto Kosta; adv. contact: Pat Lollot. pub. size: tabloid; circ. 10,000(paid).

WEEKLY NEWSPAPERS　　　　　　　　　　　　　　　　　　　　　　　　　　　　　　**SYRACUSE, NY　10687**

SPECULATOR

US
HAMILTON COUNTY NEWS. 1947. Tue. $.50 newsstand; $20/yr. in cy.; $22/yr. out of cy.; $25/yr. out of state. Rte. 8 & 30, Speculator, NY 12164. TEL 518-548-6898; FAX 518-548-5305; E-mail: hcn@superior.net; URL: http://www.mohawkvalley.com/mvpapers/hamco. **Owner(s):** Willim J. Kline & Sons, Inc., Rte. 8 & 30, Speculator, NY 12164. TEL 518-548-6898; FAX 518-548-5305; Ed. Cristine Meixner; Pub. Richard Barker; adv. contact: Arthur Simmons. adv.: $6.90/SAU. photos; pub. size: tabloid; circ. 3,600(paid).

SPENCERPORT

US
BROCKPORT/HOLLEY SUBURBAN NEWS. 1989. Mon. free; $35/yr. 1835 N. Union St., Spencerport, NY 14559-0106. TEL 716-352-3411; FAX 716-352-4811. **Owner(s):** Keith A. Ryan, 1835 N. Union St., Spencerport, NY 14559. TEL 716-352-3411; FAX 716-352-4811; Pub. Keith A. Ryan; adv.; photos; pub. size: tabloid; circ. 7,355(free & paid).

US
HAMLIN-CLARKSON HERALD. 1988. Mon. free local; $35/yr. elsewhere. 1835 N. Union St., Spencerport, NY 14559-0106. TEL 716-352-3411; FAX 716-352-4811. **Owner(s):** Keith Ryan, 1835 N. Union St., Spencerport, NY 14559-0106. TEL 716-352-3411; FAX 716-352-4611; Pub. Keith Ryan; adv.; photos; pub. size: tabloid; circ. 5,994(free & paid).

US
SUBURBAN NEWS. 1953. Mon. free; $35/yr. 1835 N. Union St., Spencerport, NY 14559. TEL 716-352-3411; FAX 716-352-4811. **Owner(s):** Keith A. Ryan, P.O. Box 106, Spencerport, NY 14559-0106. TEL 716-352-3411; Ed. Evelyn Dow; Pub. Keith A. Ryan; adv.; photos; pub. size: tabloid; circ. 32,000(free & paid).
Formerly: Spencerport Suburban News.

SPRINGVILLE

US
SPRINGVILLE JOURNAL. 1867. Thu. $.75 newsstand; $17.50/yr. in state; $14/yr. senior citizens & military. 33 E. Main St., Springville, NY 14141-0099. TEL 716-592-4550; FAX 716-592-4663. **Owner(s):** H & K Publications, Inc., 50 Buffalo St., Hamburg, NY 14075. TEL 716-649-4413; Ed. David Pierce; Pub. Steve Klukhohn; adv.; photos; bk.rev.; pub. size: tabloid; circ. 4,368(free & paid).

STATEN ISLAND

US
STATEN ISLAND REGISTER. 1966. Tue. $.50 newsstand; $20/yr. local. 2100 Clove Rd., Staten Island, NY 10305. TEL 718-447-4700; FAX 718-816-7719. **Owner(s):** Joseph Sclafani & Diane Sclafani, 2100 Clove Rd., Staten Island, NY 10305. TEL 718-447-4700; FAX 718-816-7719; Ed. Diane Sclafani; Pub. Joanne Lent; adv.: $36/SAU. photos; pub. size: tabloid; circ. 20,000(paid). **Wire Service(s):** SHNA.

SUNNYSIDE

US
WOODSIDE HERALD. 1935. Fri. $.25 newsstand; $15/yr. 43-11 Greenpoint Ave., Sunnyside, NY 11104. TEL 718-729-3444; FAX 718-718-7294. **Owner(s):** Joseph Sabba, 43-11 Greenpoint Ave., Sunnyside, NY 11104. TEL 718-729-3444; Ed. Douglas Kennedy; Pub. Joseph Sabba; adv. contact: Joseph Sabba. pub. size: tabloid; circ. 14,212(paid).

SYRACUSE

US
BALDWINSVILLE MESSENGER. 1846. Wed. $.75 newsstand; $21/yr.; $13/yr. students; $21/yr. senior citizens. 5910 Firestone Dr., Syracuse, NY 13206. TEL 315-434-8889; FAX 315-434-8883. **Owner(s):** Eagle Newspapers, Inc., 5910 Firestone Dr., Syracuse, NY 13206. TEL 315-434-8889; FAX 315-434-8883; Ed. Rebecca Sernett; Pub. Stewart F. Hancock, III; adv.; photos; pub. size: broadsheet; circ. 7,500(paid).

US
CAMILLUS ADVOCATE. 1926. Wed. $.75 newsstand; $24/yr.; $13/yr. students; $21/yr. senior citizens. 5910 Firestone Dr., Syracuse, NY 13206. TEL 315-434-8889; FAX 315-434-8883. **Owner(s):** Eagle Newspapers, Inc., 5910 Firestone Dr., Syracuse, NY 13206. TEL 315-434-8889; FAX 315-434-8883; Ed. Richard Palmer; Pub. Stewart Hancock; adv. contact: Tammy Grashof. photos; pub. size: broadsheet; circ. 3,475(paid).

US
CHITTENANGO-BRIDGEPORT TIMES. 1910. Wed. $.75 newsstand; $25/yr.; $13/yr. students; $21/yr. senior citizens. 5910 Firestone Dr., Syracuse, NY 13206. TEL 315-434-8889; FAX 315-434-8883. **Owner(s):** Eagle Newspapers, Inc., 5910 Firestone Dr., Syracuse, NY 13206. TEL 315-434-8889; Ed. Todd Fielding; Pub. Stewart Hancock; adv. contact: Becky Cooper. pub. size: broadsheet; circ. 2,206(paid).

US
DEWITT TIMES. 1970. Wed. $.75 newsstand; $25/yr.; $13/yr. students; $21/yr. senior citizens. 5910 Firestone Dr., Syracuse, NY 13206. TEL 315-434-8889; FAX 315-434-8883. **Owner(s):** Eagle Newspapers, Inc., 5910 Firestone Dr., Syracuse, NY 13206. TEL 315-635-9321; Ed. David Tyler; Pub. Stewart Hancock; adv. contact: Hunter Hillers. pub. size: tabloid; circ. 1,703(paid).
Formerly: De Witt Suburban Times.

US
EAGLE BULLETIN. 1850. Wed. $.75 newsstand; $21/yr. in cy.; $13/yr. students. 5910 Firestone Dr., Syracuse, NY 13206. TEL 315-434-8889; FAX 315-434-8883. **Owner(s):** Eagle Newspapers, Inc., 7 E. Genesee St., P.O. Box 270, Baldwinsville, NY 13027. TEL 315-635-9321; Ed. Chris Donlon; Pub. Stewart Hancock; adv. contact: John Mott. pub. size: tabloid; circ. 7,032(paid).

US
LIVERPOOL REVIEW. 1926. Wed. $.75 newsstand; $25/yr.; $13/yr. students; $21/yr. senior citizens. 5910 Firestone Dr., Syracuse, NY 13206. TEL 315-434-8889; FAX 315-434-8883. **Owner(s):** Eagle Newspapers, Inc., 5910 Firestone Dr., Syracuse, NY 13206. TEL 315-434-8889; Ed. Ali Holtzapple; Pub. Stewart Hancock; adv. contact: Jack Mott. photos; pub. size: broadsheet; circ. 14,916(paid).
Formerly: Review, The.

US
NORTH SYRACUSE STAR-NEWS. 1924. Wed. $.75 newsstand; $21/yr. in cy.; $13/yr. students. 5910 Firestone Dr., Syracuse, NY 13206. TEL 315-434-8889; FAX 315-434-8883. **Owner(s):** Eagle Newspapers, Inc., 5910 Firestone Dr., Syracuse, NY 13206. TEL 315-434-8889; Ed. Kathy Fanella; Pub. Stewart Hancock; adv. contact: Jack Mott. photos; pub. size: broadsheet; circ. 6,275(paid).
Formerly: Star News.

US
ONONDAGA VALLEY NEWS. 1956. Mon. free; $.25 newsstand; $15/yr. mailed. 250 Bear St., W., Syracuse, NY 13204. TEL 315-472-7825; FAX 315-478-1434. **Owner(s):** John Badoud, 250 Bear St., W., Syracuse, NY 13221. TEL 315-472-7825; Ed. Marylou Singer; Pub. A. Loren Colburn; adv. contact: Greg Borowski. adv.: $6.18/SAU. photos; bk.rev.; pub. size: tabloid; circ. 24,000(controlled & free).

US
SCOTSMAN PRESS, THE. 1954. Mon. free; $.30 newsstand; $15/yr. mailed. 250 Bear St., W., Syracuse, NY 13204. TEL 315-472-7825; FAX 315-478-1434. **Owner(s):** John Badoud, 250 Bear St., W., Syracuse, NY 13204. TEL 315-472-7825; FAX 315-478-1434; Ed. Marylou Singer; Pub. A. Loren Colburn; adv.: $5.09/SAU. photos; bk.rev.; pub. size: tabloid; circ. 206,534(controlled & free).

US
SYRACUSE NEW TIMES. 1969. Wed. free; $24.95/yr. 1415 W. Genesee St., Syracuse, NY 13204-2156. TEL 315-422-7011; FAX 315-422-1721; E-mail: newtimes@ras.com; URL: http://www.rway.com/newtimes/. **Owner(s):** Art Zimmer, Ltd., 1415 W. Genesee St., Syracuse, NY 13204-2156. TEL 315-422-7011; FAX 315-422-1721; Ed. Mike Greenstein; Pub. Art Zimmer; adv. contact: Karen Belgrader. photos; bk.rev.; pub. size: tabloid; circ. 45,000(controlled & free). **Wire Service(s):** Alternet.

US
VILLAGER, THE. Mon. free; $.30 newsstand; $15/yr. local mailed. 250 Bear St., W., Syracuse, NY 13221. TEL 315-472-7825; FAX 315-478-1434; E-mail: scotsmanpr@aol.com. **Owner(s):** John Badoud, 250 Bear St., W., Syracuse, NY 13221. TEL 315-472-7825; FAX 315-478-1434; Ed. Marylou Singer; Pub. A. Loren Colburn; adv.: $5.09/SAU. photos; bk.rev.; pub. size: tabloid; circ. 11,841(controlled & free).

TANNERSVILLE

US

MOUNTAIN EAGLE. 1982. Thu. $.75 newsstand; $35/yr. in state; $45/yr. out of state. Railroad Ave., Tannersville, NY 12485. TEL 518-589-7007; FAX 518-589-7028. **Owner(s):** Eagle Newspapers, Inc., P.O. Box 65, Fayetteville, NY 13066. TEL 315-637-3121; Ed. Paul Smart; Pub. Carol Ricken; adv.; pub. size: broadsheet; circ. 6,000(paid).

TICONDEROGA

US

TIMES OF TI. 1974. s-w.: Wed. & Sat. $.50 newsstand; $25/yr. in cy.; $30/yr. out of cy. 146 Montcalm St., Ticonderoga, NY 12883. TEL 518-585-6204; FAX 518-873-6360. **Owner(s):** Denton Publications, Inc., P.O. Box 338, Elizabethtown, NY 12932. TEL 518-873-6368; Ed. John Gereau; Pub. Dan Alexander; adv. contact: Scarlet Keller. pub. size: tabloid; circ. 9,400(paid).
  Formerly: Ticonderoga Times of Ti.

TRUMANSBURG

US

CANDOR CHRONICLE. Wed. $.50 newsstand; $20/yr. in cy.; $24/yr. out of cy.; $19/yr. senior citizens. 51 N. Main St., Trumansburg, NY 14886. TEL 607-387-3181; FAX 607-387-9421. **Owner(s):** Finger Lakes Community Newspapers, Inc., P.O. Box 6475, Ithaca, NY 14851. TEL 607-277-7000; Ed. Cliff Creech; Pub. James Bilinski; adv. contact: Jim Graney. photos; pub. size: tabloid; circ. 10,000(paid).

US

INTERLAKEN REVIEW. Wed. $.50 newsstand; $20/yr. in cy.; $25/yr. out of cy.; $19/yr. senior citizens. 51 N. Main St., Trumansburg, NY 14886. TEL 607-387-3181; FAX 607-387-9421. **Owner(s):** Finger Lakes Community Newspapers, Inc., P.O. Box 6475, Ithaca, NY 14851. TEL 607-277-7000; Ed. Cliff Creech; Pub. James Bilinski; adv. contact: Jim Graney. photos; pub. size: tabloid; circ. 6,000(paid).

US

NEWFIELD NEWS. Wed. $.50 newsstand; $20/yr. in cy.; $24/yr. out of cy.; $19/yr. senior citizens. 51 N. Main St., Trumansburg, NY 14886. TEL 607-387-3181; FAX 607-387-9421. **Owner(s):** Finger Lakes Community Newspapers, Inc., P.O. Box 27, Ithaca, NY 14850. TEL 607-277-7000; Ed. Cliff Creech; Pub. James Bilinski; adv. contact: Jim Graney. pub. size: tabloid; circ. 5,000(paid).

US

OVID GAZETTE. Wed. $.50 newsstand; $20/yr. in cy.; $25/yr. out of cy.; $19/yr. senior citizens. 51 N. Main St., Trumansburg, NY 14886. TEL 607-387-3181; FAX 607-387-9421. **Owner(s):** Finger Lakes Community Newspapers, Inc., P.O. Box 6475, Ithaca, NY 14851. TEL 607-277-7000; Ed. Cliff Creech; Pub. James Bilinski; adv. contact: Jim Graney. photos; pub. size: tabloid; circ. 7,000(paid).

US

SPENCER RANDOM HARVEST WEEKLY. Wed. $.50 newsstand; $20/yr. in cy.; $24/yr. out of cy.; $19/yr. senior citizens. 51 N. Main St., Trumansburg, NY 14886. TEL 607-387-3181; FAX 607-387-9421. **Owner(s):** Finger Lakes Community Newspapers, Inc., P.O. Box 6475, Ithaca, NY 14851. TEL 607-277-7000; Ed. Cliff Creech; Pub. James Bilinski; adv. contact: Jim Graney. photos; pub. size: tabloid; circ. 7,000(paid).

US

TRUMANSBURG FREE PRESS. Wed. $.50 newsstand; $20/yr. in cy.; $25/yr. out of cy.; $19/yr. senior citizens. 51 N. Main St., Trumansburg, NY 14886. TEL 607-387-3181; FAX 607-387-9421. **Owner(s):** Finger Lakes Community Newspapers, Inc., P.O. Box 6475, Ithaca, NY 14851. TEL 607-277-7000; Ed. Cliff Creech; Pub. James Bilinski; adv. contact: Jim Graney. pub. size: tabloid; circ. 10,000(paid).

TUPPER LAKE

US

TUPPER LAKE FREE PRESS & HERALD. 1895. Wed. $.50 newsstand; $25/yr. in cy.; $26/yr. out of cy. 136 Park St., Tupper Lake, NY 12986. TEL 518-359-2166. **Owner(s):** M. Dan McClelland, P.O. Box 1210, Tupper Lake, NY 12986. TEL 518-359-2166; Ed. Sue Mitchell. adv. contact: Chantel Skiff. pub. size: broadsheet; circ. 3,700(free & paid).

VICTOR

US

EAST ROCHESTER POST-HERALD. 1989. Thu. $.50 newsstand; $21/yr. mailed; $18/yr. senior citizens. 666 Phillips Rd., Victor, NY 14564. TEL 716-924-4040; FAX 716-924-7734. **Owner(s):** Canandaigua Messenger, Inc., 73 Buffalo St., Canandaigua, NY 14424. TEL 716-395-0770; Ed. Mark Syverud; Pub. George Ewing; pub. size: broadsheet; circ. 1,100(paid).

WADING RIVER

US

COMMUNITY JOURNAL. 1978. Wed. $.10 newsstand. Rte. 25A & Dogwood Dr., Wading River, NY 11792. TEL 516-929-8882. **Owner(s):** Bernadette Smith Budd, Rte. 25A & Dogwood Dr., Wading River, NY 11792. TEL 516-929-8882; Ed. Bernadette Smith Budd; Pub. Bernadette Smith Budd; photos; pub. size: tabloid.

WALDEN

US

MID HUDSON TIMES. Wed. $.75 newsstand; $24/yr. 23 E. Main St., Walden, NY 12586. TEL 914-778-2181; FAX 914-778-1196. **Owner(s):** Wallkill Valley Publications, Inc., P.O. Box 10234, Newburgh, NY 12552-0234. TEL 914-561-0170; Ed. Carl J. Aiello; Pub. Carl J. Aiello; adv. contact: Daniel Stewart. adv.: $8.30/SAU. photos; bk.rev.; pub. size: tabloid; circ. 3,500(paid).

US

WALLKILL VALLEY TIMES, THE. 1983. Wed. $.75 newsstand; $24/yr. 23 E. Main St., Walden, NY 12586. TEL 914-778-2181; FAX 914-778-1196. **Owner(s):** Wallkill Valley Publications, Inc., P.O. Box 446, Walden, NY 12586. TEL 434-778-2181; Ed. Carl J. Aiello; Pub. Carl J. Aiello; adv. contact: Dan Stewart. photos; bk.rev.; pub. size: tabloid; circ. 5,000(paid).

WALTON

US

WALTON REPORTER, THE. 1881. Wed. $.75 newsstand; $26/yr. in cy.; $30/yr. out of cy. 181 Delaware St., Walton, NY 13856. TEL 607-865-4131; FAX 607-865-8983. **Owner(s):** Leonard & Amy Govern, 181 Delaware St., Walton, NY 13856. TEL 607-865-4131; Ed. Glenn S. Graves. adv. contact: David MacDonald. photos; pub. size: tabloid; circ. 7,491(paid).
  Formerly: Reporter, The.

WAPPINGERS FALLS

US

BEACON FREE PRESS. 1962. Wed. $25/yr. 84 E. Main St., Wappingers Falls, NY 12590-2599. TEL 914-297-3723; FAX 914-297-6810; E-mail: newsplace@aol.com. **Owner(s):** Wappingers Falls Shopper, Inc., 84 E. Main St., Wappingers Falls, NY 12590-2599. TEL 914-297-3723; FAX 914-297-6810; Ed. Albert Osten; Pub. Albert Osten; adv.: $6.25/SAU. pub. size: broadsheet; circ. 8,300(paid).

US   ISSN 0192-9631

SOUTHERN DUTCHESS NEWS. 1958. Wed. $.50/wk; $23/yr. 84 E. Main St., Wappingers Falls, NY 12590-2599. TEL 914-297-3723; FAX 914-297-6810; E-mail: newsplace@aol.com. **Owner(s):** Wappingers Falls Shopper, Inc., 84 E. Main St., Wappingers Falls, NY 12590-2599. TEL 914-297-3723; FAX 914-297-6810; Pub. Albert Osten; adv.: $11.75/SAU. pub. size: broadsheet; circ. 20,000(controlled & paid).

US

SPACKENKILL SENTINEL. 1972. Wed. $25/yr. 84 E. Main St., Wappingers Falls, NY 12590-2599. TEL 914-297-3723; FAX 914-297-6810; E-mail: newsplace@aol.com. **Owner(s):** Wappingers Falls Shopper, Inc., 84 E. Main St., Wappingers Falls, NY 12590-2599. TEL 914-297-3723; FAX 914-297-6810; Ed. Albert Osten; Pub. Albert Osten; adv.: display, $5. net. pub. size: broadsheet; circ. 4,000(free).

WARWICK

US

WARWICK ADVERTISER, THE. 1866. Wed. $.50 newsstand; $21/yr. 10 Oakland Ave., Warwick, NY 10990. TEL 914-986-2061; FAX 914-986-2063. **Owner(s):** Straus Communications, P.O. Box 190, Warwick, NY 10990. TEL 914-986-2061; Ed. Stan Martin; Pub. Stan Martin; pub. size: tabloid; circ. 4,800(paid).

US

WARWICK VALLEY DISPATCH. 1885. Wed. $.50 newsstand; $20/yr. in cy.; $22/yr. out of cy. 2 Oakland Ave., Warwick, NY 10990. TEL 914-986-2216. **Owner(s):** Betty Jane Wright, 2 Oakland Ave., Warwick, NY 10990. 914-986-2216; FAX 914-987-1180; Ed. Betty Jane Wright; Pub. Betty Jane Wright; pub. size: tabloid; circ. 3,000(paid).

WEEKLY NEWSPAPERS

WATKINS GLEN

US   ISSN 1041-6250
WATKINS REVIEW & EXPRESS. 1854. Wed. $.50 newsstand; $20/yr. in cy.; $22/yr. in state; $22/yr. out of state. 210 N. Franklin, Watkins Glen, NY 14891. TEL 607-535-2711; FAX 607-535-2500. **Owner(s):** Gary R. Herzig, 210 N. Franklin St., Watkins Glen, NY 14891. TEL 607-535-2711; Lynn B. Herzig, 210 N. Franklin St., Watkins Glen, NY 14891. TEL 607-535-2711; Ed. Glenda Gephart. adv.; photos; bk.rev.; pub. size: tabloid; circ. 3,000(paid).

WEBSTER

US   ISSN 0745-7685
WAYNE COUNTY MAIL. 1887. Thu. $.35 newsstand; $14/yr. 2010 Empire Blvd., Webster, NY 14580. TEL 716-671-1533; FAX 716-671-7067. **Owner(s):** Richard Calus & W. David Young, 2010 Empire Blvd., Webster, NY 14580. TEL 716-671-1533; Ed. James J. Gertner. adv.; photos; pub. size: tabloid; circ. 2,500(paid).

US   ISSN 0745-1377
WEBSTER HERALD. 1899. Wed. $.40 newsstand; $18/yr. 2010 Empire Blvd., Webster, NY 14580. TEL 716-671-1533; FAX 716-671-7067. **Owner(s):** Empire State Weeklies, 2010 Empire Blvd., Webster, NY 14580. TEL 716-671-1533; FAX 716-671-7061; Ed. James J. Gertner; Pub. James J. Gertner; adv. contact: Jan Glende. adv.: $8.33/SAU. photos; pub. size: tabloid; circ. 4,897(paid).

US
WEBSTER POST, THE. 1992. Wed. $.50 newsstand; $21/yr. mailed. 40 North Ave., Webster, NY 14580. TEL 716-872-2221; FAX 716-872-0494. **Owner(s):** Canandaigua Messenger, Inc., 73 Buffalo St., Canandaigua, NY 14424. TEL 716-394-0770; Pub. George M. Ewing, Jr.; adv.; pub. size: broadsheet; circ. 2,700(paid).

WESTFIELD

US
MAYVILLE SENTINEL/CHAUTAUQUA NEWS. 1834. Thu. $.35 newsstand; $19/yr. in cy.; $20/yr. out of cy. 41 E. Main St., Westfield, NY 14787. TEL 716-326-3163; FAX 716-326-3165. **Owner(s):** Ogden Newspapers, Inc., 1500 Main St., Wheeling, WV 26003. TEL 304-233-0100; Ed. Wendy Link; Pub. Donald L. Meyer; adv. contact: David Rigas. photos; bk.rev.; pub. size: broadsheet; circ. 1,100(paid).

US   ISSN 1071-1074
WESTFIELD REPUBLICAN. 1855. Thu. $.40 newsstand; $21.50/yr. in cy.; $24/yr. out of cy. 41 E. Main St., Westfield, NY 14787. TEL 716-326-3163; FAX 716-326-3165. **Owner(s):** Ogden Newspapers, Inc., 1500 Main St., Wheeling, WV 26003. TEL 304-233-0100; Ed. Wendy Link; Pub. Donald L. Meyer; adv. contact: David Rigas. photos; bk.rev.; pub. size: broadsheet; circ. 2,000(paid).

WESTHAMPTON BEACH

US
SOUTHHAMPTON PRESS, THE/WESTERN EDITION. 1907. Thu. $.90 newsstand; $28/yr. in cy.; $36/yr. out of cy. 12 Mitchell Rd., Westhampton Beach, NY 11978. TEL 516-288-1100; FAX 516-288-4965. **Owner(s):** Donald H. Louchheim, P.O. Box 1071, Westhampton Beach, NY 11978; Ed. W. Michael Pitcher; Pub. Donald H. Louchheim; adv. contact: Carol Mantell. photos; pub. size: broadsheet; circ. 8,000(paid).
Formerly: Hampton Chronicle-News.

WHITEHALL

US
WHITEHALL TIMES. 1815. Thu. $.60 newsstand; $20/yr. 126 Main St., Whitehall, NY 12887. TEL 518-499-1500; FAX 518-499-1500. **Owner(s):** Manchester Newspapers, Inc., P.O. Box 330, Grandville, NY 12832. TEL 518-642-1234; FAX 518-642-1344; Ed. Alex Hyatt; Pub. John Manchester; adv.; photos; pub. size: tabloid; circ. 2,300(paid).

WHITE PLAINS

US
SUBURBAN STREET NEWS. 1976. m. $25/yr. 199 Main St., White Plains, NY 10601. TEL 914-428-0930; FAX 914-428-9077. **Owner(s):** Suburban Street News, Inc., 199 Main St., White Plains, NY 10601. TEL 914-428-0930; Ed. James Benerofe; Pub. James Benerofe; pub. size: tabloid; circ. 25,000(paid).

WILLIAMSVILLE

US
AMHERST BEE. 1879. Wed. $.75 newsstand; $36/yr. in cy. 5564 Main St., Williamsville, NY 14221. TEL 716-632-4700; FAX 716-633-8601. **Owner(s):** Bee Publications, Inc., P.O. Box 150, Williamsville, NY 14221. TEL 716-632-4700; FAX 716-633-8601; Ed. David Sherman; Pub. Trey Measer; adv.; pub. size: tabloid; circ. 10,000(paid).

US
CHEEKTOWAGA BEE. 1977. Thu. $.75 newsstand; $32/yr. 5564 Main St., Williamsville, NY 14221. TEL 716-632-4700; FAX 716-633-8601. **Owner(s):** Bee Publications, Inc., P.O. Box 150, Williamsville, NY 14221-0150. TEL 716-632-4700; FAX 716-633-8601; Ed. David Sherman; Pub. Trey Measer; adv.; pub. size: tabloid; circ. 1,900(paid).

US
CLARENCE BEE. 1937. Wed. $.75 newsstand; $32/yr. in cy.; $40/yr. out of cy. 5564 Main St., Williamsville, NY 14221. TEL 716-632-4700; FAX 716-633-8601. **Owner(s):** Bee Publications, Inc., P.O. Box 150, Buffalo, NY 14221. TEL 716-632-4700; Ed. David Sherman; Pub. Trey Measer; adv.; pub. size: tabloid; circ. 4,700(paid).

US
DEPEW BEE. 1893. Thu. $.75 newsstand; $36/yr. in cy. 5564 Main St., Williamsville, NY 14221. TEL 716-632-4700; FAX 716-633-8601. **Owner(s):** Bee Publications, Inc., P.O. Box 150, Williamsville, NY 14221. TEL 716-632-4700; Ed. David Sherman; Pub. Trey Measer; adv.; pub. size: tabloid; circ. 2,000(paid).

US
EAST AURORA BEE. 1987. Thu. $.75 newsstand; $32/yr. in cy. 5564 Main St., Williamsville, NY 14221. TEL 716-632-4700; FAX 716-633-8601. **Owner(s):** Bee Publications, Inc., P.O. Box 150, Buffalo, NY 14231-0150. TEL 716-632-4700; Ed. Kathy Mason; Pub. Trey Measer; adv.; pub. size: tabloid; circ. 1,900(free).

US
KEN-TON BEE. 1892. Wed. $.75 newsstand; $32/yr. in cy. 5564 Main St., Williamsville, NY 14221. TEL 716-632-4700; FAX 716-633-8601. **Owner(s):** Bee Publications, Inc., P.O. Box 150, Buffalo, NY 14221-0150. TEL 716-632-4700; Ed. David Sherman; Pub. Trey Measer; adv.; photos; pub. size: tabloid; circ. 1,800(paid).

US
LANCASTER BEE. 1877. Thu. $.75 newsstand; $32/yr. in cy. 5564 Main St., Williamsville, NY 14221. TEL 716-632-4700; FAX 716-633-8601. **Owner(s):** Bee Publications, Inc., P.O. Box 150, Buffalo, NY 14231. TEL 716-632-4700; Ed. David Sherman; Pub. Trey Measer; adv.; pub. size: tabloid; circ. 3,712(paid).

US
ORCHARD PARK BEE. 1986. Thu. $.75 newsstand; $32/yr. in cy. 5564 Main St., Williamsville, NY 14221. TEL 716-632-4700; FAX 716-633-8601. **Owner(s):** Bee Publications, Inc., P.O. Box 150, Buffalo, NY 14221. TEL 716-632-4700; Ed. Joe Iannarelli; Pub. Trey Measer; adv. contact: Dean Hutter. pub. size: tabloid; circ. 11,000(free).

US
WEST SENECA BEE. 1980. Thu. $.75 newsstand; $32/yr. 5564 Main St., Williamsville, NY 14221. TEL 716-632-4700; FAX 716-633-8601. **Owner(s):** Bee Publications, Inc., P.O. Box 150, Bufflo, NY 14231. TEL 716-632-4700; Ed. David Sherman; Pub. Trey Measer; adv.; pub. size: tabloid; circ. 4,100(paid).

WINDHAM

US
WINDHAM JOURNAL. 1857. Thu. $.75 newsstand; $29.20/yr. in cy.; $35/yr. out of cy. Main St., Windham, NY 12496. TEL 518-734-4400; FAX 518-734-5179. **Owner(s):** Catskill Daily Mail, 30 Church St., Catskill, NY 12414; Ed. Laurie Anander; Pub. A. Panetta; adv.; pub. size: broadsheet; circ. 1,950(paid).

WOODMERE

US
SOUTH SHORE RECORD. 1953. Thu. $.50 newsstand; $20/yr. 990 Railroad Ave., Woodmere, NY 11598. TEL 516-374-9200; FAX 516-374-9209. **Owner(s):** Florence B. Schwartzberg, 990 Railroad Ave., Woodmere, NY 11598. TEL 516-374-9200; Ed. Florence B. Schwartzberg. adv.; pub. size: tabloid; circ. 22,000(free & paid).

WOODSTOCK

US
ULSTER COUNTY TOWNSMAN. 1953. Thu. $.40 newsstand; $24/yr. in cy.; $28/yr. out of cy. 18 Rock City Rd., Woodstock, NY 12498-0308. TEL 914-679-2145; FAX 914-589-7028. **Owner(s):** J. Blake Killin, P.O. Box 308, Woodstock, NY 12498-0308. TEL 914-679-2145; Ed. J. Blake Killin; Pub. J. Blake Killin; adv.; pub. size: broadsheet; circ. 2,500(paid).

YONKERS

US
EASTCHESTER RECORD. Thu. $.75 newsstand; $25/yr. 40 Larkin Plz., Yonkers, NY 10701. TEL 914-965-4000; FAX 914-965-2892. **Owner(s):** Martinelli Publications, 40 Larkin Plz., Yonkers, NY 10701. TEL 914-965-4000; Ed. Louise Montclare; Pub. Ralph R. Martinelli; adv. contact: John Alfieri. pub. size: broadsheet; circ. 4,058(paid).

US
HARRISON INDEPENDENT. 1962. Thu. $.75 newsstand; $25/yr. 40 Larkin Plz., Yonkers, NY 10701. TEL 914-965-4000; FAX 914-965-2892. **Owner(s):** Martinelli Publications, 40 Larkin Plz., Yonkers, NY 10701. TEL 914-965-4000; Ed. Louise Montclare; Pub. Ralph R. Martinelli; adv. contact: John Alfieri. pub. size: broadsheet; circ. 4,300(paid).

US
MOUNT VERNON INDEPENDENT. Thu. $.75 newsstand; $25/yr. 40 Larkin Plz., Yonkers, NY 10701. TEL 914-965-4000; FAX 914-965-2892. **Owner(s):** Martinelli Publications, 40 Larkin Plz., Yonkers, NY 10701. TEL 914-965-4000; Ed. Louise Montclare; Pub. Ralph R. Martinelli; adv. contact: John Alfieri. pub. size: broadsheet; circ. 6,000(paid).

US
NORTH CASTLE NEWS. 1963. Thu. $.75 newsstand; $25/yr. 40 Larkin Plz., Yonkers, NY 10701. TEL 914-965-4000; FAX 914-965-2892. **Owner(s):** Martinelli Publications, 40 Larkin Plz., Yonkers, NY 10701. TEL 914-965-4000; Ed. Louise Montclare; Pub. Ralph R. Martinelli; adv. contact: John Alfieri. pub. size: broadsheet; circ. 3,300(paid).

US
PELHAM SUN. 1910. Thu. $.75 newsstand; $25/yr. 40 Larkin Plz., Yonkers, NY 10701. TEL 914-965-4000; FAX 914-965-2892. **Owner(s):** Martinelli Publications, 40 Larkin Plz., Yonkers, NY 10701. TEL 914-965-4000; Ed. Louise Montclaire; Pub. Ralph R. Martinelli; adv. contact: Pete Roth. pub. size: broadsheet; circ. 3,606(paid).

US
REVIEW PRESS REPORTER. 1902. Thu. $.35 newsstand; $26/yr. One Odell Plz., Yonkers, NY 10701. TEL 914-694-9300; FAX 914-696-8208. **Owner(s):** Gannett Company, Inc., 1100 Wilson Blvd., Arlington, VA 22340; Ed. Meryl Harris; Pub. Gary Shurlock; adv.; photos; pub. size: broadsheet; circ. 2,200(paid).

US
RYE CHRONICLE. 1905. Thu. $.75 newsstand; $25/yr. 40 Larkin Plz., Yonkers, NY 10701. TEL 914-965-4000; FAX 914-965-2892. **Owner(s):** Martinelli Publications, 40 Larkin Plz., Yonkers, NY 10701. TEL 914-965-4000; Ed. Louise Montclare; Pub. Ralph R. Martinelli; adv. contact: John Alfieri. pub. size: broadsheet; circ. 3,966(paid).

US
SOUND VIEW NEWS. Thu. $.75 newsstand; $25/yr. 40 Larkin Plz., Yonkers, NY 10701. TEL 914-965-4000; FAX 914-965-2892. **Owner(s):** Martinelli Publications, 40 Larkin Plz., Yonkers, NY 10701. TEL 914-965-4000; Ed. Louise Montclare; Pub. Ralph R. Martinelli; adv. contact: John Alfieri. pub. size: broadsheet; circ. 6,000(paid).

US
YONKERS HOME NEWS & TIMES. Fri. $.75 newsstand; $25/yr. carrier. 40 Larkin Plz., Yonkers, NY 10701. TEL 914-965-4000; FAX 914-965-2892. **Owner(s):** Martinelli Publications, 40 Larkin Plz., Yonkers, NY 10701. TEL 914-965-4000; Ed. Louise Montclare; Pub. Ralph R. Martinelli; adv. contact: John Alfieri. photos; pub. size: broadsheet; circ. 20,100(paid).
Formerly: Home News & Times.

YORKTOWN HEIGHTS

US
NORTH COUNTY NEWS. 1966. Wed. $.75 newsstand; $35/yr. local; $40/yr. elsewhere. 1520 Front St., Yorktown Heights, NY 10598. TEL 914-962-4748; FAX 914-962-6763. **Owner(s):** Northern Tier Publishing Corp., 1520 Front St., Yorktown Heights, NY 10598. TEL 914-962-4748; Ed. Rick Pezzulo; Pub. Cynthia Smith; adv. contact: Bill Hitt. pub. size: tabloid; circ. 10,000(paid).

US
PENNYSAVER. 1958. Wed. free. 1520 Front St., Yorktown Heights, NY 10598. TEL 914-962-3871; FAX 914-962-5123. **Owner(s):** Yorktown Printing & Pennysaver Corp., 1520 Front St., Yorktown Heights, NY 10598. TEL 914-962-3871; Pub. John W. Chase; adv.; pub. size: tabloid; circ. 320,550(free).

NORTH CAROLINA

AHOSKIE

US
ROANOKE-CHOWAN NEWS-HERALD, THE. 1909. 3/wk.: Tue., Thu., Sat. $.50 newsstand; $53.42/yr. surrounding cys.; $59.36/yr. out of area; $62.40/yr. out of state. 801 Parker Ave., Ahoskie, NC 27910. TEL 919-332-2123; FAX 919-332-3940. **Owner(s):** Media General, Inc., 333 E. Grace St., Richmondn, VA 23219. TEL 804-649-6000; FAX 804-649-6898; Ed. Jay Jenkins; Pub. Joe Vaughn; adv. contact: Phyllis Frymyer. pub. size: broadsheet; circ. 7,810(paid).

ALBEMARLE

US
STANLY NEWS & PRESS. 1880. 3/wk.: Tue., Thu., Sun. $.75 newsstand; $44.40/yr. local; $54.50/yr. in state; $67/yr. out of state. 237 W. North St., Albemarle, NC 28001. TEL 704-982-2121; FAX 704-983-7999. **Owner(s):** Stanly County Newspapers, Inc., 237 W. North St., Albemarle, NC 28001. TEL 704-982-2121; Ed. David Deese; Pub. J.L. Waggoner; adv. contact: Jane Harned. photos; pub. size: broadsheet; circ. 12,000(paid).

ANGIER

US
ANGIER INDEPENDENT. 1972. Tue. $20/yr. in state; $30/yr. out of state. P.O.Box 878, Angier, NC 27501. TEL 919-639-4913; FAX 919-639-0289. **Owner(s):** Angier Independent, Inc., P.O. Box 878, Angier, NC 27501. TEL 919-639-4913; Ed. Terri Brooks; Pub. Bart Adams; adv.; photos; pub. size: broadsheet; circ. 5,000(paid).

APEX

US
APEX HERALD, THE. 1956. Wed. $.50 newsstand; $17/yr. in cy.; $25/yr. out of cy. 616 W. Chatham St., Apex, NC 27502-1539. TEL 919-362-8356; FAX 919-362-1369. **Owner(s):** Kirkland Newspapers, Inc., 1577 Haermitage Ct., Durham, NC 27707; Ed. Robbie Robertson; Pub. Ann Kirkland; adv.; pub. size: broadsheet; circ. 4,000(paid).
Formerly: Western Wake Herald.

ASHEBORO

US
RANDOLPH GUIDE, THE. 1954. Wed. $.50 newsstand; $19.50/yr. in cy.; $27/yr. elsewhere. 431 S. Fayetteville St., Asheboro, NC 27203. TEL 910-625-5576; FAX 910-675-5577. **Owner(s):** Robert M. Derr, Jr., P.O. Box 1044, Asheboro, NC 27204-1044. TEL 910-625-5576; Ed. Kathie Keyes; Pub. Robert M. Derr, Jr.; adv. contact: Brenda West. photos; bk.rev.; pub. size: broadsheet; circ. 3,200(free & paid).

ASHEVILLE

US
▼**MOUNTAIN XPRESS.** 1995. Wed. free newsstand. 2 Wall St., Asheville, NC 28802. TEL 704-251-1333; FAX 704-251-1311; E-mail: xpress@circle.net. **Owner(s):** Green Lined Media, Inc., P.O. Box 144, Asheville, NC 28802. TEL 704-251-1333; FAX 704-251-1311; Ed. Jeff Fobes; Pub. Jeff Forbes; adv. contact: Wanda Edney. photos; bk.rev.; pub. size: tabloid; circ. 18,100(controlled & paid).
Formerly: Green Line.

BELMONT

US
BELMONT BANNER. 1929. Wed. $.50 newsstand; $18.02/yr. in cy.; $20.14/yr. out of cy.; $23.32/yr. out of state. 812 Woodlawn St., Belmont, NC 28012. TEL 704-827-7526; FAX 704-739-0611. **Owner(s):** Republic Newspapers, Inc., P.O. Box 769, Kings Mountain, NC 28086; Ed. Dwight Frady; Pub. Dean Ridings; adv.; photos; pub. size: broadsheet; circ. 5,000(controlled).

WEEKLY NEWSPAPERS

MOUNT HOLLY NEWS. 1929. Wed. $.50 newsstand; $18.02/yr. in cy.; $20.14/yr out of cy.; $22.32/yr. out of state. 812 Woodlawn St., Belmont, NC 28012. TEL 704-827-7526; FAX 704-827-1037. **Owner(s):** Republic Newspapers, Inc., P.O. Box 769, Kings Mountain, NC 28086; Ed. Dwight Frady; Pub. Dean Ridings; adv.: $7.50/SAU. photos; pub. size: broadsheet; circ. 2,300(paid).

BENSON
US

FOUR OAKS-BENSON NEWS IN REVIEW. 1910. Wed. $.50 newsstand; $11.50/yr. in cy.; $13.50/yr. out of cy. 113 S. Market St., Benson, NC 27504. TEL 919-894-3331; FAX 919-894-1069. **Owner(s):** Ralph E. Delano, P.O. Box 9, Benson, NC 27504. TEL 919-894-3331; Ed. Mike Dart; Pub. Norman Delano; adv. contact: Phil Burgess. pub. size: broadsheet; circ. 4,500(paid).
Formerly: Benson Review, The.

BLACK MOUNTAIN
US

BLACK MOUNTAIN NEWS. 1945. Thu. $.35 newsstand; $15/yr. in cy.; $22/yr. out of cy.; $25/yr. out of state. 118 Cherry St., Ste. 201, Black Mountain, NC 28711. TEL 704-669-8727; FAX 704-669-8619. **Owner(s):** Gannett Company, Inc., 1100 Wilson Blvd., Arlington, VA 22340. TEL 703-284-6000; Ed. Roger Watson; Pub. Anna Day; adv. contact: Anna Day. photos; pub. size: broadsheet; circ. 4,000(free & paid).

BLOWING ROCK
US   ISSN 1071-0574

BLOWING ROCKET, THE. 1932. Thu. $.50 newsstand; $20/yr. in state; $25/yr. out of state. 452 Sunset Dr., Blowing Rock, NC 28605. TEL 704-295-7522; FAX 704-295-7507. **Owner(s):** Watauga Newspaper, Inc., P.O. Box 3050, Boone, NC 28607. TEL 704-264-3612; Ed. Jerry W. Burns. adv.; photos; bk.rev.; pub. size: broadsheet; circ. 4,500(paid).

BOONE
US

BOONE WATAUGA DEMOCRAT. 1888. 3/wk.: Mon., Wed., Fri. $.50 newsstand; $41/yr. home deliv.; $76/yr. out of state mailed. 474 Industrial Park Dr., Boone, NC 28607. TEL 704-264-3612; FAX 704-262-0282. **Owner(s):** Watauga Newspapers, Inc., P.O. Box 3050, Boone, NC 28607; Ed. Sandra Shook; Pub. William S. Cummings, III; adv. contact: Lana Brantz. photos; pub. size: broadsheet; circ. 9,255(paid). **Wire Service(s):** AP.

BREVARD
US

TRANSYLVANIA TIMES, THE. 1900. s-w.: Mon. & Thu. $.35 newsstand; $23/yr. in cy.; $26/yr. out of cy. 100 N. Broad St., Brevard, NC 28712. TEL 704-883-8156; FAX 704-883-8158. **Owner(s):** Stella A. Trapp, 100 N. Broad St., Brevard, LA 28712. TEL 704-833-8156; FAX 704-883-8158; Ed. Stella A. Trapp; Pub. Stella A. Trapp; adv.; photos; pub. size: broadsheet; circ. 8,300(paid).

BURGAW
US

PENDER CHRONICLE. 1896. Wed. $.25 newsstand; $15/yr. in cy.; $22/yr. out of cy.; $26/yr. out of state. 110 Courthouse Ave., Burgaw, NC 28425. TEL 910-259-2351; FAX 910-285-3179. **Owner(s):** H.L. Oswald Enterprises, Inc., P.O. Box 699, Wallace, NC 28466. TEL 919-285-2178; Pub. H.L. Oswald; adv. contact: Nancy Bradshaw. photos; pub. size: broadsheet; circ. 6,300(paid).

PENDER POST. 1971. Wed. $.25 newsstand; $18/yr. in cy.; $24/yr. out of cy. 210 Fremont St., Burgaw, NC 28425. TEL 910-259-9111; FAX 910-259-9112. **Owner(s):** Post Newspapers, Inc., P.O. Box 955, Burgaw, NC 28425; Ed. Patrick Thomas; Pub. Patrick Thomas; adv.; photos; pub. size: broadsheet; circ. 5,000(paid).

BURNSVILLE
US

YANCEY COMMON TIMES JOURNAL. 1920. Wed. $.50 newsstand; $18.50/yr. in cy.; $26.50/yr. in state; $33/yr. out of state. 5 Town Sq., Burnsville, NC 28714. TEL 704-682-2120; FAX 704-682-3701. **Owner(s):** Trib Publications, Inc., P.O. Box 426, Manchester, GA 31816. TEL 404-846-3188; Ed. Jody Higgins; Pub. Jody Higgins; adv. contact: Pat Randolph. bk.rev.; pub. size: broadsheet; circ. 7,000(paid).
Formerly: Yancey Journal, The.

CANTON
US

ENTERPRISE MOUNTAINEER, THE. 1903. 3/wk.: Mon., Wed., Fri. $.50 newsstand; $45/yr. in cy.; $68.95/yr. in state. 119 Main St., Canton, NC 28716. TEL 704-253-7416. **Owner(s):** Mountaineer Publishing Co., Inc., 413 N. Main St., P.O. Box 129, Waynesville, NC 28786. TEL 704-452-0661; FAX 704-452-0665; Ed. Scott McLeod. adv.; photos; bk.rev.; pub. size: broadsheet; circ. 1,912(paid).
Formerly: Mountaineer, The.

CARY
US

CARY NEWS. 1963. s-w.: Wed. & Sat. $.50 newsstand; $27/yr. 212 E. Chatham St., Cary, NC 27511. TEL 919-460-2600; FAX 919-460-6034. **Owner(s):** McClatchy Newspapers, P.O. Box 15774, Sacramento, CA 95816. TEL 916-321-1000; Ed. Jane Paige; Pub. Jack Andrews; adv.; pub. size: standard; circ. 12,250(paid).

CHAPEL HILL
US   ISSN 1070-2741

CHAPEL HILL NEWS. 1923. 3/wk: Wed., Fri., Sun. free. 505 W. Franklin St., Chapel Hill, NC 27516. TEL 919-967-7045; FAX 919-968-4953. **Owner(s):** McClatchy Newspapers, P.O. Box 15774, Sacramento, CA 95816. TEL 916-321-1000; Ed. Richard Hart; Pub. Ted Vaden; adv. contact: Peter Tompkins. photos; pub. size: broadsheet; circ. 35,000(paid); Sun. 35,000(paid). **Wire Service(s):** NYT, AP.
Formerly: Chapel Hill Newspaper.

US

VILLAGE ADVOCATE. 1969. s-w.: Wed. & Sun. free newsstand; $20/mo. 88 McClamroch Cir., Chapel Hill, NC 27514. TEL 919-968-4801; FAX 919-942-2826. **Owner(s):** Village Companies, 88 McClamroch Cir., Chapel Hill, NC 27514. TEL 919-968-4801; Pub. Doug Rogers; adv.; photos; pub. size: tabloid; circ. 35,000(free & paid).

CHERRYVILLE
US

CHERRYVILLE EAGLE. 1906. Wed. $.50 newsstand; $18.02/yr. in Gaston & Cleveland cys.; $20.14/yr. out of area; $23.32/yr. out of state. P.O. Box 699, Cherryville, NC 28021. TEL 704-435-6752; FAX 704-435-8293. **Owner(s):** Republic Newspapers, Inc., P.O. Box 769, Kings Mountain, NC 28086. TEL 704-739-7496; Ed. Christin Stone. adv. contact: Bill Fulton. photos; pub. size: broadsheet; circ. 3,000(paid).

CLAYTON
US

CLAYTON NEWS-STAR. 1911. Tue. $.50 newsstand; $12.75/yr. in cy.; $26.50/yr. out of cy.; $38/yr. out of state. 222 W. Main St., Clayton, NC 27520. TEL 919-553-7234; FAX 919-553-5858. **Owner(s):** Stew McLeod, P.O. Box 9, Benson, NC 27504. TEL 919-894-3331; Pub. Stew McLeod; adv. contact: Shirley Johnson. photos; pub. size: broadsheet; circ. 10,000(paid).
Formerly: Clayton News.

CLEMMONS
US

CLEMMONS COURIER. 1960. Thu. $.50 newsstand; $15/yr. in state; $20/yr. out of state. 3600 Clemmons Rd., Clemmons, NC 27012. TEL 910-766-4126; FAX 910-766-7350. **Owner(s):** Dwight Spark, 3600 Clemmons Rd., Clemmons, NC 27012. TEL 919-766-4126; Ed. Dwight Sparks; Pub. Dwight Sparks; pub. size: standard; circ. 3,200(paid).

CREEDMOOR
US

BUTNER-CREEDMOOR NEWS, THE. 1965. Thu. $.50 newsstand; $22.26/yr. in state; $25/yr. out of state. 418 N. Main, Creedmoor, NC 27522. TEL 919-528-2393; FAX 919-528-0288. **Owner(s):** Harry R. Coleman, P.O. Box 726, Creedmoor, NC 27522. TEL 919-528-2393; FAX 919-528-0288; Ed. Harry R. Coleman; Pub. Harry R. Coleman; adv. contact: Tracy Byrd. photos; pub. size: standard; circ. 4,400(paid).

DAVIDSON
US

MECKLENBURG GAZETTE. 1948. Wed. $.50 newsstand; $18.50/yr. 108 S. Main St., Davidson, NC 28036. TEL 704-892-8809; FAX 704-664-3614. **Owner(s):** Media General, Inc., 333 E. Grace St., Richmond, VA 23219. TEL 804-649-6000; FAX 804-649-6898; Ed. Amy Ledbetter. adv. contact: Kristin Powell. photos; bk.rev.; pub. size: broadsheet; circ. 12,546(paid).

DURHAM

US

CAROLINA TIMES, THE. 1926. Thu. $.30 newsstand; $19.08/yr. in cy.; $22.32/yr. out of cy.; $22/yr. out of state. 923 Old Fayetteville St., Durham, NC 27701. TEL 919-682-2913; FAX 919-682-2913; E-mail: 76061.3630@compuserve.com. **Owner(s):** United Publishers, Inc., P.O. Box 3825, Durham, NC 27702. TEL 919-682-2913; FAX 919-682-2913; Ed. V.A. Edmonds; Pub. V.A. Edmonds; adv. contact: Kenneth Edmonds. photos; bk.rev.; pub. size: broadsheet; circ. 5,800(paid). **Wire Service(s):** AP.

US

INDEPENDENT, THE. 1983. Wed. free newsstand; $29/yr. mailed. 2810 Hillsborough Rd., Durham, NC 27705. TEL 919-286-1972; FAX 919-286-4274. **Owner(s):** Carolina Independent Publications, P.O. Box 2690, Durham, NC 27715. TEL 919-286-1972; Ed. Bob Moser; Pub. Steve Schewel; adv. contact: Susan Watson. pub. size: tabloid; circ. 50,000(free & paid).

ELKIN

US

TRIBUNE, THE. 1911. 3/wk.: Mon., Wed., Fri. $.50 newsstand; $44.52/yr. home deliv. 214 E. Main St., Elkin, NC 28621. TEL 910-835-1513; FAX 910-835-8742. **Owner(s):** Mid-South Management Co., Inc., P.O. Box 1634, Spartanburg, SC 29304. TEL 803-583-2907; Ed. Bill Watson; Pub. R. Fletcher Good, IV; adv. contact: Sarah Byrd. photos; pub. size: broadsheet; circ. 11,000(paid).

FOREST CITY

US

COUNTY NEWS ENTERPRISE. 1926. Wed. free. 601 Oak St., Forest City, NC 28043. TEL 704-287-3327; FAX 704-248-2490. **Owner(s):** Forest City Publishing, 601 Oak St., Forest City, NC 28043; Ed. Jean Gordon; Pub. Doug Flowe; adv. contact: Doug Flowe. photos; pub. size: broadsheet; circ. 12,000(free).
Formerly: Enterprise; Rutherford County News Enterprise.

FRANKLIN

US

FRANKLIN PRESS. 1886. s-w.: Wed. & Fri. $.50 newsstand; $22.50/yr. in cy.; $36/yr. out of cy. 40 Depot St., Franklin, NC 28734. TEL 704-524-2010; FAX 704-524-8821. **Owner(s):** Community Newspapers, Inc., P.O. Box 792, Athens, GA 30603. TEL 706-548-0010; FAX 706-548-0808; Ed. Scott McRae; Pub. Kenneth Hudgins; adv. contact: Tom Brown. photos; pub. size: broadsheet; circ. 8,300(paid).

FREMONT

US

WAYNE WILSON NEWS LEADER. Wed. $.50 newsstand; $12/yr. local; $16.50/yr. out of area. 113 N. Wilson St., Fremont, NC 27830. TEL 919-242-6301; FAX 919-936-2065. **Owner(s):** Barry Merrill, P.O. Box 158, Fremont, NC 27830. TEL 919-242-6301; FAX 919-936-2065; Ed. Barry Merrill; Pub. Barry Merrill; adv.; pub. size: standard; circ. 1,500(paid).

GARNER

US

GARNER NEWS. 1962. Wed. $.50 newsstand; $17/yr. in cy.; $26/yr. out of cy. 503-L U.S. Hwy. 70, Garner, NC 27529. TEL 919-772-1166; FAX 919-779-7824. **Owner(s):** William Kirkland, 503-L U.S. Hwy. 70, Garner, NC 27529; Ed. Amy Griggs; Pub. William Kirkland; adv. contact: Chris Minshew. pub. size: broadsheet; circ. 6,000(paid).

GATESVILLE

US

GATES COUNTY INDEX. 1932. Wed. $.50 newsstand; $19.08/yr. in cy.; $25.18/yr. out of cy. W. Maple St., Gatesville, NC 27938. TEL 919-357-0960; FAX 919-332-3940. **Owner(s):** Media General, Inc., 333 E. Grace St., Richmond, VA 23219. TEL 804-649-6000; FAX 804-649-6898; Ed. Helene Knight. adv. contact: Tammy Perry. pub. size: broadsheet; circ. 2,800(paid).

GOLDSBORO

US

EASTERN CAROLINA TIMES-INQUIRER. 1975. Wed. free newsstand. 1201 C. Wayne Memorial Dr., Goldsboro, NC 27533. TEL 919-734-5444; FAX 919-734-0290. **Owner(s):** Joe C. Dougherty, P.O. Box 1659, Goldsboro, NC 27533. TEL 919-734-5444; FAX 919-734-0290; Ed. Ken Plummer. adv.; photos; bk.rev.; pub. size: tabloid; circ. 35,000(free).
Formerly: Goldsboro Times Newspaper.

GRAHAM

US

ALAMANCE NEWS. 1875. Thu. $.50 newsstand; $20/yr. in cy.; $29/yr. out of cy. 114 W. Elm St., Graham, NC 27253-0431. TEL 910-228-7851; FAX 910-229-9602. **Owner(s):** Boney Publishers, Inc., P.O. Box 431, Graham, NC 27253-0431. TEL 919-228-7851; Ed. Tom Boney, Jr.; Pub. Tom Boney, Jr.; adv.; pub. size: standard; circ. 7,429(paid).

HERTFORD

US

PERQUIMANS WEEKLY. 1932. Thu. $.35 newsstand; $24.20/yr. in state; $26.40/yr. out of state. 119 W. Grubb St., Hertford, NC 27944. TEL 919-426-5728; FAX 919-426-4625. **Owner(s):** Cox Enterprises, Inc., P.O. Box 105357, Atlanta, GA 30348. TEL 404-843-5000; Ed. Susan Harris; Pub. Belinda Gaudet; adv. contact: Anzie Ziemba. pub. size: standard; circ. 2,000(paid).

HICKORY

US

HICKORY NEWS/EXTRA, THE. 1970. Thu. $.50 newsstand; $20/yr. in area; $25/yr. out of state. 270 Union Sq. Common, Hickory, NC 28601. TEL 704-328-6164; FAX 704-322-6398. **Owner(s):** Charles H. Deal, P.O. Box 2650, Hickory, NC 28603. TEL 704-328-6164; Valerie M. Deal, P.O. Box 2650, Hickory, NC 28603. TEL 704-328-6164; Ed. Charles H. Deal; Pub. Charles H. Deal; adv. contact: Mickey L. Price. photos; bk.rev.; pub. size: broadsheet; circ. 16,000(free & paid).

HILLSBOROUGH

US   ISSN 1071-1716

NEWS OF ORANGE COUNTY, THE. 1893. Wed. $.50 newsstand; $18.93/yr. Churton St., Hillsborough, NC 27278. TEL 919-732-2171; FAX 919-732-4852. **Owner(s):** Womack Publishing Co., Inc., P.O. Box 111, Chatham, VA 24531. TEL 804-432-1654; Ed. Jonathan Butler; Pub. Charles A. Womack, Jr.; adv.: $6.25/SAU. pub. size: broadsheet; circ. 4,600(free & paid).

KENLY

US

KENLY NEWS. 1973. Wed. $.50 newsstand; $15/yr. 201 W. Second St., Kenly, NC 27542. TEL 919-284-2295. E-mail: stewnews@aol.com. **Owner(s):** Richard D. Stewart, P.O. Box 39, Kenly, NC 27542. TEL 919-284-2295; Pub. Richard D. Stewart; adv. contact: Karen B. Stewart. photos; bk.rev.; pub. size: broadsheet; circ. 3,200(paid).

KERNERSVILLE

US

KERNERSVILLE NEWS. 1938. 3/wk.: Tue., Thu., Sat. $.50 newsstand; $28.95/yr. local. 300 E. Mountain St., Kernersville, NC 27284. TEL 910-993-2161; FAX 910-993-0931. **Owner(s):** Carter Publishing Co., 300 E. Mountain St., Kernersville, NC 27284. TEL 919-993-2161; Ed. John Staples; Pub. John Owensby; adv. contact: J.C. Grose. pub. size: standard; circ. 19,900(free & paid).

KING

US

KING TIMES NEWS. 1961. Thu. $.50 newsstand; $17.50/yr. in cy.; $21.50/yr. out of cy.; $25.50/yr. out of state; $15.50/yr. senior citizens. 141 Pineview Dr., King, NC 27021. TEL 910-983-3109; FAX 910-983-8203. **Owner(s):** CM Publishing Co., 141 Pineview Dr., King, NC 27021. TEL 919-983-3109; Ed. Karen McConkey; Pub. T.J. "Turk" Tergliafera; adv.; pub. size: broadsheet; circ. 6,800(paid).

KINGS MOUNTAIN

US

BESSEMER CITY RECORD. 1956. Wed. $.50 newsstand; $16/yr. in cy.; $18/yr. out of cy.; $21/yr. out of state. E. King St. & Canterbury Rd., Kings Mountain, NC 28086. TEL 704-629-2376; FAX 704-739-0611. **Owner(s):** Republic Newspapers, Inc., P.O. Box 769, Kings Mountain, NC 28086; Ed. Jim Hefner; Pub. Bob Rop; adv. contact: Darrell Austin. photos; pub. size: broadsheet; circ. 1,200(paid).

US

KINGS MOUNTAIN HERALD. 1888. Thu. $.50 newsstand; $17/yr. in cy.; $19/yr. out of cy.; $22/yr. out of state. E. King St. & Canterbury Rd., Kings Mountain, NC 28086. TEL 704-739-7496; FAX 704-739-0611. **Owner(s):** Republic Newspapers, Inc., P.O. Box 769, Kings Mountain, NC 28086; Ed. Gary & Lib Stewart; Pub. Bob Rop; adv.; photos; pub. size: broadsheet; circ. 6,500(paid).

WEEKLY NEWSPAPERS

LINCOLNTON
US
LINCOLN TIMES-NEWS. 1903. 3/wk.: Mon., Wed., Fri. $.35 newsstand; $31.20/yr. 119 W. Water St., Lincolnton, NC 28092. TEL 704-735-3031; FAX 704-735-3037. **Owner(s):** Western Carolina Publishing Co., P.O. Box 40, Lincolnton, NC 28093-0040. TEL 704-735-3031; FAX 704-735-3037; Ed. Kathryn Yarboro; Pub. Jerry G. Leedy; adv. contact: Trudy Ingel. photos; bk.rev.; pub. size: standard; circ. 10,600(paid). **Wire Service(s):** AP.

LITTLETON
US
LITTLETON OBSERVER. 1955. Thu. $.50 newsstand; $18/yr. in cy.; $20/yr. out of cy.; $22/yr. out of state. 101 E.S. Main St., Littleton, NC 27850-0417. TEL 919-586-6397. E-mail: lgastan@3rddr.com. **Owner(s):** Jack Sharpe, P.O. Box 417, Littleton, NC 27850-0417. TEL 919-586-6397; Pub. Hal Sharpe; adv. contact: Jane Boney. photos; bk.rev.; pub. size: broadsheet; circ. 2,500(paid).

LOUISBURG
US
FRANKLIN TIMES. 1870. s-w.: Wed. & Sat. $.50 newsstand; $25/yr. 109 S. Bickett Blvd., Louisburg, NC 27549. TEL 919-496-6503; FAX 919-496-1689. **Owner(s):** Gary Cunard, P.O. Box 119, Louisburg, NC 27549. TEL 919-496-6503; Ed. Anna Meadows; Pub. Gary Cunard; adv.; pub. size: broadsheet; circ. 8,700(paid).

MADISON
US ISSN 0892-1814
MADISON MESSENGER, THE. 1915. s-w.: Wed. & Fri. $.50 newsstand; $40/yr. in state; $52/yr. out of state. 208 W. Murphy St., Madison, NC 27025. TEL 910-548-6047; FAX 910-548-2853. **Owner(s):** Media General, Inc., 333 E. Grace St., Richmond, VA 23219. TEL 804-649-6000; FAX 804-775-8090; Ed. Bruce A. Webb; Pub. Bruce A. Webb; adv. contact: Wendy Hayden. photos; bk.rev.; pub. size: broadsheet; circ. 6,000(paid).

MANTEO
US
COASTLAND TIMES. 1935. 3/wk.: Tue., Thu., Sun. $.50 newsstand; $25.66/yr. in cy. 501 Budleigh St., Manteo, NC 27954. TEL 919-473-2105; FAX 919-473-1515. **Owner(s):** Times Printing Co., 501 Budleigh St., Manteo, NC 27454. TEL 919-473-2105; Ed. F.W. Meekins; Pub. F.W. Meekins; pub. size: broadsheet; circ. 12,000(paid). **Wire Service(s):** AP.

MARSHVILLE
US
HOME NEWS, THE. 1892. Thu. $.50 newsstand; $14/yr. in Union & Anson cys.; $22/yr. elsewhere. 123 E. Union St., Marshville, NC 28103. TEL 704-624-5068. **Owner(s):** Beaver Dam Press, Inc., P.O. Box 100, Marshville, NC 28103. TEL 704-624-5068; Ed. Rosemary Osborn. adv. contact: William Osborn. photos; pub. size: broadsheet; circ. 2,950(paid).

MEBANE
US
MEBANE ENTERPRISE. 1908. Wed. $.50 newsstand; $18.43/yr. 106 N. Fourth St., Mebane, NC 27302. TEL 919-563-3555; FAX 919-563-9242. **Owner(s):** Womack Publishing Co., Inc., P.O. Box 111, Chatham, VA 24531. TEL 804-432-1654; Ed. Kitty Brandon. adv.; photos; pub. size: standard; circ. 6,100(free & paid).

MOCKSVILLE
US
DAVIE COUNTY ENTERPRISE-RECORD. 1916. Thu. $.50 newsstand; $20/yr. in state; $25/yr. out of state. S. Main St., Mocksville, NC 27028. TEL 704-634-2129; FAX 704-634-9760. **Owner(s):** Davie County Publishing Co., Inc., P.O. Box 525, Mocksville, NC 27028. TEL 704-634-2129; Ed. Mike Barnhardt; Pub. Dwight Sparks; adv. contact: Becky Snyder. photos; pub. size: broadsheet; circ. 8,000(paid).
Formerly: Mocksville Davie County Enterprise.

MOORESVILLE
US
MOORESVILLE TRIBUNE. Wed. $.50 newsstand; $18.37/yr. local; $21/yr. out of state. 147 E. Center Ave., Mooresville, NC 28115. TEL 704-664-5554; FAX 704-664-3614. **Owner(s):** Park Communications, Inc., Vine Ctr. Office Tower, 333 W. Vine St., 17th Fl., Lexington, KY 40507. TEL 606-242-7252; Ed. Annette Privette. adv. contact: Kristin Powell. photos; bk.rev.; pub. size: broadsheet; circ. 10,304(paid).

MOREHEAD CITY
US
CARTERET COUNTY NEWS-TIMES. 1912. 3/wk.: Sun., Wed., Fri. $.50 newsstand; $52/yr. in cy. 4034 Arendell St., Morehead City, NC 28557. TEL 919-726-7081; FAX 919-726-6016. **Owner(s):** Carteret Publishing, Inc., 4034 Arendell St., Morehead City, NC 28557. TEL 919-726-7081; Ed. Walter D. Phillips. adv.; photos; bk.rev.; pub. size: broadsheet; circ. 12,800(paid); Sun. 13,700(paid). **Wire Service(s):** AP.
Formerly: Morehead City Carteret County News-Times.

MORGANTON
US
BURKE COUNTY OBSERVER. Wed. free. 301 Collett St., Morganton, NC 28655. TEL 704-437-2161; FAX 704-437-5372; E-mail: ann@tsl.dana.edu. **Owner(s):** Media General, Inc., 333 E. Grace St., Richmond, VA 23219. TEL 804-649-6000; FAX 804-649-6898; Ed. Bill Poteat. adv. contact: Randy Hart. pub. size: broadsheet; circ. 8,000(free).

US
VALDESE NEWS. 1935. Wed. $.20 newsstand; $12/yr. 301 Collett St., Morganton, NC 28655. TEL 704-437-2161; FAX 704-437-5372; E-mail: ann@tsl.dana.edu. **Owner(s):** Media General, Inc., 333 E. Grace St., Richmond, VA 23219. TEL 804-649-6000; FAX 804-649-6898; Ed. Bill Poteat. adv. contact: Randy Hart. pub. size: broadsheet; circ. 4,000(paid).

MOUNT AIRY
US
SURRY SCENE, THE. 1881. Tue. free. 319 Renfro St., Mount Airy, NC 27030. TEL 910-786-4141; FAX 910-789-2816. **Owner(s):** Mount Airy Newspapers, Inc., P.O. Box 808, Mount Airy, NC 27030. TEL 919-786-4141; Ed. R.J. Berrier; Pub. George W. Summerlin; adv. contact: Bernard Flippin. pub. size: tabloid; circ. 20,000(free).

MT. OLIVE
US
MOUNT OLIVE TRIBUNE. 1904. s-w.: Tue. & Fri. $.50 newsstand; $21.20/yr. in cy.; $31.09/yr. out of cy. 301 Hwy. 55, W., Mt. Olive, NC 28365. TEL 919-658-9456; FAX 919-658-9559. **Owner(s):** McClatchy Newspapers, P.O. Box 15779, Sacramento, CA 95816. TEL 916-321-1000; Ed. Steve Herring; Pub. S.B. Pierce, Jr.; adv. contact: Gary Scott. pub. size: broadsheet; circ. 5,000(paid).

MURPHY
US ISSN 0746-3987
CHEROKEE SCOUT. 1891. Tue. $.50 newsstand; $14/yr. in cy.; $22/yr. out of cy. One Church St., Murphy, NC 28906. TEL 704-837-5122; FAX 704-837-5832. **Owner(s):** Community Newspapers, Inc., 255 E. Hancock Ave., P.O. Box 792, Athens, GA 30603. TEL 706-548-0010; FAX 706-548-0808; Ed. Patty Little; Pub. Weaver Carrington; adv. contact: Donna Kook. photos; bk.rev.; pub. size: broadsheet; circ. 8,000(paid).
Formerly: Cherokee Scout.

NASHVILLE
US
NASHVILLE GRAPHIC. 1895. Thu. $.50 newsstand; $18.70/yr. in cy. 106 N. Boddie St., Nashville, NC 27856. TEL 919-459-7101; FAX 919-459-3052. **Owner(s):** Nash County Newspapers, Inc.; Pub. Gary Cunard; adv. contact: Sam Taylor. photos; bk.rev.; pub. size: broadsheet; circ. 4,500(controlled & paid).

NORTH WILKESBORO
US
JOURNAL-PATRIOT. 1906. s-w.: Wed. & Fri. $.35 newsstand; $33.92/yr. in cy.; $35/yr. out of cy. 711 Main St., North Wilkesboro, NC 28659. TEL 910-838-4117; FAX 910-838-9864. **Owner(s):** Carter-Hubbard Publishing Co., Inc., 711 Main St., North Wilkesboro, NC 28659. TEL 919-838-4117; Ed. Charles Williams; Pub. John Hubbard; adv. contact: Carolyn Barker. photos; pub. size: broadsheet; circ. 17,600(paid).

OLD FORT
US
NEWS BULLETIN OF MCDOWELL COUNTY, THE. 1973. Wed. $.25 newsstand; $15/yr. in cy.; $20/yr. out of cy. P.O. Box 638, Old Fort, NC 28762-0638. TEL 704-668-4783; FAX 704-668-4722. **Owner(s):** McDowell Publishing Associates, Inc., P.O. Box 305, Marion, NC 28752-0305. TEL 704-668-4783; adv.; photos; pub. size: standard; circ. 2,000(controlled & paid).
Formerly: Old Fort Bulletin; News Bulletin. The.

OXFORD

US

OXFORD PUBLIC LEDGER. 1881. s-w.: Mon. & Thu. $.50 newsstand; $21.20/yr. in cy.; $24.38/yr. in state; $26.50/yr. out of state. 200 W. Spring St., Oxford, NC 27565. TEL 919-693-2646; FAX 919-693-3704. **Owner(s):** Royster Critcher, 200 W. Spring St., Oxford, NC 27565. TEL 919-693-2646; FAX 919-693-3704; Ed. Johnny Whitfield. adv. contact: Ronald N. Critcher. pub. size: broadsheet; circ. 8,200(paid).

PLYMOUTH

US

ROANOKE BEACON. 1889. Wed. $.50 newsstand; $21.73/yr. 210-212 W. Water St., Plymouth, NC 27962. TEL 919-793-2123; FAX 919-793-5365. **Owner(s):** Hote Jones, P.O. Box 726, Plymouth, NC 27962. TEL 919-793-2123; Ed. Doward N. Jones, Jr. adv.; pub. size: broadsheet; circ. 4,700(paid).

PRINCETON

US

PRINCETON NEWS LEADER. Wed. $.50 newsstand; $12/yr. local; $16.50/yr. out of area. 109 S. Center St., Princeton, NC 27569. TEL 919-936-9891; FAX 919-936-2065. **Owner(s):** Barry Merrill, P.O. Box 597, Princeton, NC 27590. TEL 919-936-9891; FAX 919-936-2065; Ed. Barry Merrill; Pub. Barry Merrill; circ. 1,500(paid).

RAEFORD

US

RAEFORD NEWS-JOURNAL, THE. 1905. Wed. $.50 newsstand; $14/yr. in cy.; $17/yr. in state; $20/yr. out of state. 119 W. Elwood Ave., Raeford, NC 28376. TEL 910-875-2121; FAX 910-875-7256; E-mail: njournal@coastalnet.com; URL: http://www4.dicksonpress.com. **Owner(s):** Dickson Press, Inc., P.O. Box 550, Raeford, NC 28376. TEL 910-875-2121; FAX 910-875-7256; Ed. Wendy Brown; Pub. Robert A. Dickson; adv. contact: Susan Stauffer. photos; pub. size: broadsheet; circ. 4,700(paid).

RALEIGH

US   ISSN 0045-5873

CAROLINIAN, THE. 1940. s-w.: Mon. & Thu. $.50 newsstand; $30/yr. locally. 610 Maywood Ave., Raleigh, NC 27603. TEL 919-834-5558; FAX 919-832-3243. **Owner(s):** Paul & Evelyn H. Jervey, 610 Maywood Ave., Raleigh, NC 27603. TEL 919-834-5558; FAX 919-832-3243; Ed. Paul Jervey; Pub. Paul Jervey; pub. size: broadsheet; circ. 21,000(paid).

US   ISSN 0896-3363

SPECTATOR MAGAZINE. 1978. Thu. free newsstand; $30/yr. mailed. 1318 Dale St., Raleigh, NC 27605. TEL 919-828-7393; FAX 919-831-9217. **Owner(s):** Spectator Publications, Inc., 1318 Dale St., Raleigh, NC 27605. TEL 919-828-7393; Ed. Art Taylor; Pub. R.B. Reeves; adv.; photos; bk.rev.; pub. size: tabloid; circ. 55,000(free).

RANDLEMAN

US   ISSN 1074-5157

RANDLEMAN REPORTER. 1982. Wed. $.35 newsstand; $18/yr. 125 W. Academy St., Randleman, NC 27317. TEL 910-498-4151; FAX 910-498-4152. **Owner(s):** Randolph Publishing Co., 125 Academy St., Randleman, NC 27317. TEL 910-498-4151; FAX 910-498-4152; Ed. Robert M. Derr, Jr.; Pub. Robert M. Deer, Jr.; adv.; photos; pub. size: broadsheet; circ. 2,150(controlled & paid).

RICHLANDS

US

RICHLANDS-BEULAVILLE ADVERTISER-NEWS. 1975. Wed. $.25 newsstand; $15/yr. in cy.; $22/yr. out of cy.; $26/yr. out of state. 105 W. Frank St., Richlands, NC 28574. TEL 910-324-5062; FAX 910-324-6267. **Owner(s):** H.L. Oswald Enterprises, Inc., 107 N. College St., Wallace, NC 28466. TEL 910-285-2178; FAX 910-285-3179; Ed. Sammie Carter; Pub. H.L. Oswald, III; adv. contact: Mary Hart Oswald. photos; pub. size: broadsheet; circ. 4,200(paid).

ROXBORO

US

COURIER-TIMES, THE. 1881. s-w.: Wed. & Sat. $.50 newsstand; $34.95/yr. in state; $38.22/yr. out of state. 109 Clayton Ave., Roxboro, NC 27573. TEL 910-599-0162; FAX 910-597-2773; E-mail: tpbrinn@interpath.com. **Owner(s):** Jerry M. Clayton, P.O. Box 311, Roxboro, NC 27573. TEL 910-599-0162; FAX 910-597-2773; Ed. Neal F. Rattican; Pub. Jerry M. Clayton; adv.: $6.40/SAU. photos; bk.rev.; pub. size: broadsheet; circ. 7,900(paid). **Wire Service(s):** AP.
Formerly: Roxboro Courier-Times.

SCOTLAND NECK

US

COMMONWEALTH PROGRESS. Wed. $.50 newsstand; $19.08/yr. in area; $17.17/yr. senior citizens. +107 Main St., Scotland Neck, NC 27874. TEL 919-826-2111; FAX 919-826-2111. **Owner(s):** Media General, Inc., 333 E. Grace St., Richmond, VA 23219. TEL 804-649-6000; FAX 804-649-6898; Ed. Yolanda Wiggins; Pub. Marie Harrison; adv. contact: Marie Harrison. pub. size: broadsheet; circ. 1,050(paid).
Formerly: Enfield Progress.

SELMA

US

SMITHFIELD-SELMA SUN. 1887. Thu. $.50 newsstand; $18/yr. local; $21/yr. out of area; $24/yr. out of state. 101 N. Webb St., Selma, NC 27576. TEL 919-965-2033; FAX 919-965-5903. **Owner(s):** Hometown Heritage Publishing Co., Inc., P.O. Box 278, Selma, NC 27576. TEL 919-965-2033; Ed. Wingate Lassiter; Pub. Wingate Lassiter; pub. size: broadsheet; circ. 4,500(paid).
Formerly: Johnstonian Sun.

SHALLOTTE

US

BRUNSWICK BEACON, THE. 1962. Thu. $.50 newsstand; $12.25/yr. in cy.; $18.30/yr. out of cy.; $20.90/yr. out of state. 106 Cheers St., Shallotte, NC 28459. TEL 910-754-6890; FAX 910-754-5407; E-mail: beacon@infoave.net; URL: http://www.weblync.com/beacon. **Owner(s):** Brunswick Beacon, Inc., The, 106 Cheers St., P.O. Box 2558, Shallotte, NC 28459. TEL 910-754-6890; FAX 910-754-5407; Ed. Lynn S. Carlson. adv.; pub. size: broadsheet; circ. 15,000(paid).

SHELBY

US

CLEVELAND TIMES. 1941. Thu. $.25 newsstand; $12.72/yr. 824-1 E. King at Canterbury Rd., Shelby, NC 28151. TEL 704-481-8202; FAX 704-481-1031. **Owner(s):** Republic Newspapers, Inc., 824-1 E. King at Canterbury Rd., Shelby, NC 28151. TEL 704-481-8202; FAX 704-481-1031; Ed. Michelle Hill; Pub. Dean Ridings; adv. contact: Aron Goss. photos; pub. size: broadsheet; circ. 2,500(free & paid).

SILER CITY

US

CHATHAM NEWS, THE. Thu. $.50 newsstand; $17/yr. in cy.; $20/yr. out of cy. 303 W. Raleigh, Siler City, NC 27344. TEL 919-663-3232; FAX 919-663-4042. **Owner(s):** Chatham News Publishing Co., 303 W. Raleigh, Siler City, NC 27344. TEL 919-663-3232; FAX 919-663-4042; Ed. Alan D. Resch; Pub. Alan D. Resch; adv. contact: Georgia Trogdon. photos; pub. size: broadsheet; circ. 9,100(paid).
Formerly: Siler City Chatham News.

SMITHFIELD

US

SMITHFIELD HERALD. 1882. s-w.: Tue. & Fri. $.50 newsstand; $48/yr. out of state mailed. 125 S. Fourth St., Smithfield, NC 27577. TEL 919-934-2176; FAX 919-989-7093. **Owner(s):** McClatchy Newspapers, P.O. Box 15774, Sacramento, CA 95816. TEL 916-321-1000; Ed. Scott Bolejack; Pub. S.E. Thorndyke, Sr.; adv. contact: Robert Dixon. pub. size: broadsheet; circ. 14,697(paid).

SOUTHERN PINES

US

SOUTHERN PINES PILOT. 1920. s-w.: Mon. & Thu. $.50 newsstand; $30/yr. in cy.; $35/yr. out of cy. 145 W. Pennsylvania Ave., Southern Pines, NC 28387. TEL 910-692-7271; FAX 910-692-9382. **Owner(s):** Sam & Marjorie Ragan, P.O. Box 58, Southern Pines, NC 28387. TEL 910-692-7271; Ed. Florence Gilkeson; Pub. David Wororoff; adv. contact: John Hubbard. photos; bk.rev.; pub. size: broadsheet; circ. 16,500(paid).

WEEKLY NEWSPAPERS

SOUTHPORT
US

STATE PORT PILOT, THE. 1928. Wed. $.50 newsstand; $10.87/yr. in cy.; $16.47/yr. out of cy.; $19/yr. out of state. 105 S. Howe St., Southport, NC 28461-0548. TEL 910-457-4568; FAX 910-457-9427; E-mail: stateport@aol.com; URL: http://www.southport.net. **Owner(s):** Margaret Harper, P.O. Box 10548, Southport, NC 28461. TEL 910-457-4568; FAX 910-457-9427; Ed. Ed Harper. adv. contact: Kim Adams. pub. size: broadsheet; circ. 7,400(free & paid).

SPRING HOPE
US

SPRING HOPE ENTERPRISE. 1947. Thu. $18/yr. in cy.; $30/yr. out of cy. 113 Ash St., Spring Hope, NC 27882. TEL 919-478-3651; FAX 919-478-3075. **Owner(s):** Spring Hope Enterprise, P.O. Box 399, Spring Hope, NC 27882. TEL 919-478-3651; FAX 919-478-3075; Ed. Ken Ripley; Pub. Ken Ripley; adv. contact: Raymond Renfrow. photos; pub. size: standard; circ. 3,000(free & paid).

SPRUCE PINE
US

MITCHELL NEWS JOURNAL. 1927. Wed. $.50 newsstand; $17/yr. in cy.; $25/yr. out of cy.; $30/yr. out of state. 401 Locust St., Spruce Pine, NC 28777. TEL 704-765-2071; FAX 704-765-1616. **Owner(s):** CNI Newspapers, Inc., P.O. Box 1492, Spartanburg, SC 29304; Ed. Rachel Hoskins; Pub. Rick Bacon; adv.; pub. size: broadsheet; circ. 6,500(paid).

SYLVA
US ISSN 0531-0300

SYLVA HERALD & RURALITE. 1926. Thu. $.50 newsstand; $18/yr. in cy. 539 W. Main St., Sylva, NC 28779. TEL 704-586-2611; FAX 704-586-2637. **Owner(s):** Sylva Herald Publishing Co., Inc., P.O. Box 307, Sylva, NC 28779-0307. TEL 704-586-2611; FAX 704-586-2637; Ed. J.A. Gray. adv. contact: Margo Gray. photos; pub. size: broadsheet; circ. 7,000(paid).

TABOR CITY
US

TRIBUNE, THE. 1946. Wed. $.25 newsstand; $14.95/yr. in town; $18.95/yr. out of town. 1108 E. Fifth St., Tabor City, NC 28463. TEL 910-653-3153; FAX 910-653-9440. **Owner(s):** W. Horace Carter, P.O. Box 67, Tabor City, NC 28463. TEL 919-653-3153; Ed. Deuce Niven; Pub. Deuce Niven; adv. contact: Linda Carter. pub. size: broadsheet; circ. 3,800(paid).
Formerly: Tabor City Tribune.

TAYLORSVILLE
US

TAYLORSVILLE TIMES, THE. 1886. Wed. $.50 newsstand; $18.50/yr. in cy.; $27.50/yr. out of cy. 106 E. Main St., Taylorsville, NC 28681. TEL 704-632-2532; FAX 704-632-8233. **Owner(s):** Walter L. Sharpe, 106 E. Main St., Taylorsville, NC 28681. TEL 704-632-2532; FAX 704-632-8233; Ed. David Icenhour; Pub. Walter L. Sharpe; adv. contact: Linda Jones. pub. size: broadsheet; circ. 7,000(paid).

THOMASVILLE
US

THOMASVILLE TIMES. 1890. 3/wk.: Tue., Thu., Sat. $.50 newsstand; $3.50/mo. carrier. 512 Turner St., Thomasville, NC 27360. TEL 910-472-9500; FAX 910-476-7272. **Owner(s):** High Point Enterprises, Inc., 210 Church St., High Point, NC 27262. TEL 910-888-3500; Ed. Gary Evans; Pub. Robert Schoolfield; adv.; pub. size: broadsheet; circ. 7,000(paid). **Wire Service(s):** AP.

TROY
US

MONTGOMERY HERALD. 1884. Wed. $.50 newsstand; $19.08/yr. in cy.; $27.56/yr. out of cy. 139 Bruton St., Troy, NC 27371. TEL 910-576-6051; FAX 910-576-1050. **Owner(s):** Womack Publications Co., Inc., P.O. Box 466, Troy, NC 27371. TEL 909-576-6051; Ed. Tammy Dunn; Pub. Charles A. Womack, III; adv. contact: Jenefer Kimery. pub. size: broadsheet; circ. 7,075(paid).

WADESBORO
US

ANSON RECORD, THE. 1881. Wed. $.50 newsstand; $18/yr. in cy.; $22/yr. in zones 1 & 2; $25/yr. in zones 3-10. 210 E. Morgan, Wadesboro, NC 28170. TEL 704-694-2161; FAX 704-694-7060. **Owner(s):** Community Newspapers, Inc., P.O. Box 792, Athens, GA 30603. TEL 800-226-0692; FAX 706-548-0808; Ed. Sandy Bruney; Pub. Ellen W. Hanson; adv.; pub. size: broadsheet; circ. 7,500(paid).

WAKE FOREST
US

WAKE WEEKLY, THE. 1947. Thu. $.50 newsstand; $21.20/yr. in Wake, Franklin & Durham cys.; $29.04/yr. out of area.; $30/yr. out of state. 229 E. Owen, Wake Forest, NC 27587. TEL 919-556-3182; FAX 919-556-2233. **Owner(s):** Robert W. Allen, 229 E. Owen, Wake Forest, NC 27587. TEL 919-556-3182; Ed. Margret Allen; Pub. Robert W. Allen; adv.; pub. size: broadsheet; circ. 7,500(paid).

WALLACE
US

WALLACE ENTERPRISE. 1923. s-w.: Mon. & Thu. $.25 newsstand; $25/yr. local; $40/yr. out of cy.; $50/yr. out of state. 107 N. College St., Wallace, NC 28466. TEL 910-285-2178; FAX 910-285-3179. **Owner(s):** H.L. Oswald Enterprises, Inc., 107 N. College St., Wallace, NC 28466. TEL 919-285-2178; Ed. Sammie Carter; Pub. H.L. Oswald, III; adv. contact: Mary Hart Oswald. photos; pub. size: broadsheet; circ. 7,500(paid).

US

WARSAW-FAISON NEWS. 1955. Thu. $.25 newsstand; $15/yr. in cy.; $22/yr. out of cy.; $26/yr. out of state. 107 N. College St., Wallace, NC 28466. TEL 910-285-2178; FAX 910-285-3179. **Owner(s):** H.L. Oswald Enterprises, Inc., 107 N. College St., Wallace, NC 28466. TEL 910-285-2178; FAX 910-285-3179; Ed. Sammie Carter; Pub. H.L. Oswald, III; adv. contact: Mary Hart Oswald. photos; pub. size: broadsheet; circ. 4,000(paid).

WALNUT COVE
US

DANBURY REPORTER. 1872. Thu. $.50 newsstand; $17.50/yr. in cy.; $21.50/yr. out of cy.; $15.50/yr. senior citizens. Main St., Walnut Cove, NC 27052. TEL 910-591-8191; FAX 910-591-4379. **Owner(s):** C.M. Publishing, P.O. Box 545, King, NC 27021. TEL 910-983-3109; FAX 910-983-8203; Ed. Denise Petree; Pub. T.J. Tergliafera; adv.; pub. size: broadsheet; circ. 6,500(paid).

WARRENTON
US

WARREN RECORD, THE. 1896. Wed. $.50 newsstand; $20/yr. in cy.; $26/yr. out of cy. 123 S. Main St., Warrenton, NC 27589. TEL 919-257-3341; FAX 919-257-1413. **Owner(s):** Record Publishing Co., Inc., P.O. Box 70, Warrenton, NC 27589. TEL 919-257-3341; Ed. Howard Jones; Pub. Howard Jones; adv. contact: Jean Reid. photos; pub. size: broadsheet; circ. 5,700(paid).

WENDELL
US

GOLD LEAF FARMER, THE. 1924. Thu. $.50 newsstand; $14.84/yr. in cy.; $21/yr. out of state. 10 S. Main St., Wendell, NC 27591. TEL 919-365-6262; FAX 919-269-8383. **Owner(s):** McClatchy Newspapers, P.O. Box 15779, Sacramento, CA 95816. TEL 916-321-1000; Ed. Marty Coward; Pub. D. Mark Wilson; adv.; photos; pub. size: broadsheet; circ. 4,700(paid).

WEST JEFFERSON
US

JEFFERSON POST. 1929. s-w.: Tue. & Thu. $.50 newsstand; $22/yr. in cy.; $39.85/yr. out of cy. 203 S. Second Ave., West Jefferson, NC 28694. TEL 910-246-4121; FAX 910-246-7165. **Owner(s):** Mid-South Management Co., Inc., P.O. Box 334, Spartanburg, SC 29304. TEL 919-583-2907; Ed. Joe Morgan. adv. contact: Sherry Rinehart. photos; pub. size: broadsheet; circ. 11,700(free & paid).
Formerly: Skyland Post.

WHITEVILLE
US

NEWS REPORTER, THE. 1896. s-w.: Mon. & Thu. $.50 newsstand; $22.50/yr. in cy.; $35/yr. out of cy.; $42/yr. out of state. 127 W. Columbus St., Whiteville, NC 28472-0707. TEL 910-642-4104; FAX 910-642-1856. **Owner(s):** News Reporter, Inc., P.O. Box 707, Whiteville, NC 28472-0707. TEL 910-642-4104; FAX 910-642-1856; Ed. Jim High. adv. contact: Max N. Greer, Jr. photos; pub. size: broadsheet; circ. 10,100(free & paid). **Wire Service(s):** AP.
Formerly: Whiteville News Reporter.

WILLIAMSTON

US

ENTERPRISE, THE. 1899. s-w.: Tue. & Thu. $.50 newsstand; $29.95/yr. 108 W. Main St., Williamston, NC 27892. TEL 919-792-1181; FAX 919-792-1921. **Owner(s):** Cox North Carolina Publications, Inc., P.O. Box 105357, Atlanta, GA 30348. TEL 404-843-5000; Ed. Bobby Burns; Pub. Dallas F. Coltrain; adv. contact: Dallas F. Coltrain. adv.: $4.40/SAU. photos; pub. size: broadsheet; circ. 4,500(paid).

US

ROBERSONVILLE WEEKLY HERALD. 1914. Wed. $.35 newsstand; $11-$15/yr. 108 W. Main St., Williamston, NC 27892. TEL 919-792-1181; FAX 919-792-1921. **Owner(s):** Cox North Carolina Publications, Inc., P.O. Box 105357, Atlanta, GA 30348. TEL 404-843-5000; Ed. Bobby Burns; Pub. Dallas F. Coltrain; adv. contact: Dallas F. Coltrain. photos; pub. size: standard; circ. 600(paid).

US

WILLIAMSTON ENTERPRISE. 1899. s-w.: Tue. & Thu. $.50 newsstand; $29.95/yr. in cy.; $39.95/yr. out of cy. 108 W. Main St., Williamston, NC 27892. TEL 919-792-1181; FAX 919-792-1921. **Owner(s):** Cox North Carolina Publications, Inc., 106-108 Main St., Williamston, NC 27892. TEL 404-843-5000; Ed. Bobby Burns; Pub. Dallas F. Coltrain; adv. contact: Dallas F. Coltrain. photos; pub. size: standard; circ. 5,600(paid).

WILMINGTON

US

WILMINGTON JOURNAL. 1927. Thu. $.50 newsstand; $22/yr. mailed in US. 412 S. Seventh St., Wilmington, NC 28401. TEL 910-762-5502; FAX 910-343-1334. **Owner(s):** Jerzay Family, P.O. Box 1618, Wilmington, NC 28402. TEL 910-762-5502; Ed. Mary Chatch; Pub. Willy E. Jerzay; adv.; photos; pub. size: standard; circ. 6,100(paid).

WINDSOR

US

BERTIE LEDGER-ADVANCE. 1928. Thu. $.50 newsstand; $15.90/yr. in cy.; $23.32/yr. in state; $25/yr. out of state. 124 S. King, Windsor, NC 27983-0069. TEL 919-794-3185; FAX 919-794-2835. **Owner(s):** Cox Enterprises, Inc., P.O. Box 105357, Atlanta, GA 30348. TEL 404-843-5000; Ed. Laura Harrell; Pub. Laura Harrell; adv. contact: Sue Brett. pub. size: standard; circ. 4,450(paid).

YADKINVILLE

US

YADKIN RIPPLE, THE. 1892. Thu. $.50 newsstand; $15/yr. in cy.; $15/yr. out of cy.; $21/yr. out of state. P.O. Box 7, Yadkinville, NC 27055. TEL 910-679-2341; FAX 910-679-2340. **Owner(s):** Craig Rutledge, Jr., P.O. Box 7, Yadkinville, NC 27055. TEL 910-679-2341; FAX 910-679-2340; Ed. Charles Mathis; Pub. Craig Rutledge; adv. contact: Carol Rutledge. adv.: $5/SAU. pub. size: standard; circ. 6,250(paid).

YANCEYVILLE

US

CASWELL MESSENGER. 1926. Wed. $.50 newsstand; $19.79/yr. in cy. 137 Main St., Yanceyville, NC 27379. TEL 910-694-4145; FAX 910-694-5637. **Owner(s):** Womack Publishing Co., Inc., P.O. Box 111, Chatham, VA 24531. TEL 804-432-1654; Ed. Gordon Bendall; Pub. Charles A. Womack, Jr.; adv. contact: Pam Durham. pub. size: broadsheet; circ. 4,800(paid).
Formerly: Yanceyville Caswell Messenger.

ZEBULON

US

ZEBULON RECORD, THE. 1925. Thu. $.50 newsstand; $14.84/yr. local; $18.55/yr. in state; $21/yr. out of state. 110 N. Ardendell Ave., Zebulon, NC 27597. TEL 919-269-6101; FAX 919-269-8383; E-mail: zrecord@mindspring.com. **Owner(s):** McClatchy Newspapers, P.O. Box 15774, Sacramento, CA 95816. TFl 916-321-1000; Ed. Marty Coward; Pub. D. Mark Wilson; adv.; photos; pub. size: broadsheet; circ. 3,450(paid).

NORTH DAKOTA

BEULAH

US

BEULAH BEACON. 1970. Thu. $.50 newsstand; $23/yr. in state; $30/yr. out of state. 324 Second Ave., N.E., Beulah, ND 58523-0609. TEL 701-873-4381. **Owner(s):** BHG, Inc., P.O. Box 309, Garrison, ND 58540; Pub. Mike Gackle; adv. contact: Ken Beauchamp. photos; bk.rev.; pub. size: broadsheet; circ. 2,500(paid).

BOTTINEAU

US

COURANT, THE. 1885. Tue. $22/yr. in state; $30/yr. out of state. 419 Main St., Bottineau, ND 58318. TEL 701-228-2605; FAX 701-228-5864. **Owner(s):** Hills & Plains Free Press, Inc., P.O. Box 29, Bottineau, ND 58318. TEL 701-228-2605; Pub. Mike Getzloff; adv. contact: Jackie Bullinger. pub. size: standard; circ. 3,500(paid).

BOWMAN

US

BOWMAN FINDER. 1962. Wed. free in surrounding cys.; $20/yr. out of area. 18 S. Main St., Bowman, ND 58623. TEL 701-523-5623; FAX 701-523-3441. **Owner(s):** Dickson Media, Inc., P.O. Box F, Bowman, ND 58623. TEL 701-523-5623; Ed. Jeff Schumacher; Pub. Jeff Schumacher; adv.; pub. size: standard; circ. 11,500(free & paid).

CASSELTON

US ISSN 1074-1801

CASS COUNTY REPORTER. 1881. Wed. $.50 newsstand; $22/yr. local; $29.50/yr. elsewhere. 122 Sixth Ave., N., Casselton, ND 58012-0190. TEL 701-347-4493; FAX 701-347-4495. **Owner(s):** Sean & Cheryl Kelly, 122 Sixth Ave., N., Casselton, ND 58012. TEL 701-347-4493; FAX 701-347-4495; Ed. Michael Utt; Pub. Sean Kelly; adv. contact: David Overland. pub. size: broadsheet; circ. 3,400(controlled & paid).

CROSBY

US

JOURNAL, THE. 1902. Wed. $.50 newsstand; $24/yr. in area; $34/yr. out of area. 217 N. Main, Crosby, ND 58730. TEL 701-965-6088; FAX 701-965-6089. **Owner(s):** Journal, The, P.O. Box E, Crosby, ND 58730. TEL 701-965-6088; Ed. Steve Andrist; Pub. Steve Andrist; pub. size: broadsheet; circ. 3,000(paid).

ELGIN

US

CARSON PRESS. 1905. Wed. $20/yr. in cy.; $23/yr. in state; $26/yr. out of state. 119 Main St., Elgin, ND 58533. TEL 701-584-2900. **Owner(s):** Duane & Gail Schatz, P.O. Box 100, Elgin, ND 58533. TEL 701-584-2900; Ed. Duane Schatz; Pub. Gail Schatz; pub. size: broadsheet; circ. 1,200(paid).

US

GRANT COUNTY NEWS. 1910. Wed. $.75 newsstand; $17/yr. in cy.; $20/yr. in state; $23/yr. out of state. 119 Main St., Elgin, ND 58533. TEL 701-584-2900; FAX 701-584-2900. **Owner(s):** Duane & Gail Schatz, 119 Main St., Elgin, ND 58533. TEL 701-584-2900; FAX 701-584-2900; Ed. Duane Schatz; Pub. Duane Schatz; adv.; pub. size: broadsheet; circ. 2,312(free & paid).

ENDERLIN

US

ENDERLIN INDEPENDENT. 1882. Wed. $.50 newsstand; $22/yr. in state; $26/yr. out of state. 209 Fourth Ave., Enderlin, ND 58027. TEL 701-437-3131; FAX 701-437-3131. **Owner(s):** Ruth E. McCleerey, 209 Fourth Ave., Enderlin, ND 58027. TEL 701-437-3131; FAX 701-437-3131; Gerald P. Harris, P.O. Box 196, La Moure, ND 58458. TEL 701-884-5393; Ed. Ruth E. McCleerey; Pub. Ruth E. McCleerey; adv. contact: Ruth E. McCleerey. photos; bk.rev.; pub. size: broadsheet; circ. 1,000(paid).

GARRISON

US

MCLEAN COUNTY INDEPENDENT. 1905. Thu. $23/yr. in area; $35/yr. out of state. 71 N. Main St., Garrison, ND 58540. TEL 701-463-2201; FAX 701-463-7487. **Owner(s):** BHG, Inc., P.O. Box 309, Garrison, ND 58540. TEL 701-463-2201; Ed. Alan Reed; Pub. Don Gackle; adv. contact: Jude Iverson. pub. size: tabloid; circ. 3,875(paid).

GRAFTON

US ISSN 1067-5922

WALSH COUNTY RECORD, THE. 1889. Tue. $.75 newsstand; $29/yr. in area. 402 Hill Ave., Grafton, ND 58237. TEL 701-352-0640; FAX 701-352-1502; E-mail: mpi@polar.polarcamm.com. **Owner(s):** Morgan Publishing Co., 420 Hill Ave., Grafton, ND 58237. TEL 701-352-0640; Ed. Jason Flaig; Pub. Jackie Thompson; adv.; pub. size: broadsheet; circ. 3,600(paid).
Formerly: Grafton Record.

WEEKLY NEWSPAPERS

HARVEY
US

HERALD-PRESS. 1897. Sat. $.75 newsstand; $24/yr. in cy.; $26/yr. in state; $34/yr. out of state. 1015 Lincoln Ave., Harvey, ND 58341. TEL 701-324-4646. **Owner(s):** Charles & Marion Eldredge, 1015 Lincoln Ave., Harvey, ND 58341. TEL 701-324-4646; Pub. Charles Eldredge; adv.; pub. size: broadsheet; circ. 3,728(paid).

HAZEN
US

HAZEN STAR. 1914. Thu. $.50 newsstand; $23/yr. in state; $30/yr. out of state. 26 E. Main St., Hazen, ND 58545. TEL 701-748-2255; FAX 701-748-5768. **Owner(s):** BHG, Inc., P.O. Box 309, Garrison, ND 58540; Ed. Lauren Donovan. adv. contact: Doreen Ost. photos; bk.rev.; pub. size: broadsheet; circ. 2,300(paid).

JAMESTOWN
US

PRAIRIE POST. 1972. Tue. free. 217 First Ave., N., Jamestown, ND 58402-1268. TEL 701-252-2796; FAX 701-252-5751. **Owner(s):** American Publishing Co., 606 N. Van Buren, P.O. Box 520, Marion, IL 62959. TEL 618-993-1711; Pub. Bruce Henke; adv. contact: Zenithe Mayer. pub. size: tabloid; circ. 19,000(free).

LANGDON
US

CAVALIER COUNTY REPUBLICAN. 1888. Mon. $.75 newsstand; $25/yr. in city; $35/yr. out of city. 710 Third St., Langdon, ND 58249. TEL 701-256-5311; FAX 701-256-5841. **Owner(s):** Dickson Media, 710 Third St., Langdon, ND 58249. TEL 701-256-5311; FAX 701-256-5841; Ed. Marvin Baker; Pub. Marvin Baker; adv. contact: Diane Wenzel. bk.rev.; pub. size: broadsheet; circ. 2,700(paid).

LINTON
US

LINTON EMMONS COUNTY RECORD. 1884. Tue. $.75 newsstand; $24/yr. in area; $33/yr. out of state. 201 N. Broadway, Linton, ND 58552-0038. TEL 701-254-4537; FAX 701-254-4909. **Owner(s):** Allan C. Burke, P.O. Box 38, Linton, ND 58552-0038; Leah Burke, P.O. Box 38, Linton, ND 58552-0038; Ed. Allan C. Burke; Pub. Allan C. Burke; adv.: $4.10/SAU. photos. pub. size: broadsheet; circ. 2,980(paid).

LISBON
US

LISBON RANSOM COUNTY GAZETTE & ENTERPRISE. 1882. Mon. $.50 newsstand; $26/yr. in state; $30/yr. out of state. 310 Main St., Lisbon, ND 58054. TEL 701-683-4128; FAX 701-683-4129. **Owner(s):** Sean W. Kelly, 310 Main St., Lisbon, ND 58054. TEL 701-683-4128; Ed. Sean W. Kelly; Pub. Sean W. Kelly; adv. contact: Cheryl A. Kelly. pub. size: broadsheet; circ. 3,600(paid).

MANDAN
US

FINDER, THE. Wed. free in town; $.25/copy. 303 First St., N.E., Mandan, ND 58554. TEL 701-663-6823; FAX 701-663-6823. **Owner(s):** Lee Enterprises, Inc., 130 E. Second St., Davenport, IA 52801; pub. size: tabloid; circ. 39,000(controlled & free).

US

MANDAN NEWS. 1975. Thu. $.50 newsstand; $25/yr. 303 First St., N.E., Mandan, ND 58554. TEL 701-663-6823; FAX 701-663-2442. **Owner(s):** Lee Enterprises, Inc., 130 E. Second St., Davenport, IA 52801; pub. size: tabloid; circ. 1,800(paid).

MINNEWAUKAN
US

BENSON COUNTY FARMERS PRESS. 1884. Wed. $.60 newsstand; $30/yr. in state; $36/yr. out of state; $42/yr. foreign. 120 B Ave., N., Minnewaukan, ND 58351-0098. TEL 701-473-5436; FAX 701-473-5736; E-mail: farmerspress@stellarnet.com. **Owner(s):** Benson County Farmers Press, Inc., 120 B Ave., N., Minnewaukan, ND 58351. TEL 701-473-5436; FAX 701-473-5736; Consolidated Newspapers, Inc., 120 B Ave., N., Minnewaukan, ND 58351. TEL 701-473-5436; FAX 701-473-5736; Ed. Richard M. Peterson; Pub. Richard M. Peterson; adv.; photos; bk.rev.; pub. size: broadsheet; circ. 2,936(free & paid).

NORTHWOOD
US

LARIMORE PIONEER. Mon. $.60 newsstand; $21.75/yr. in state; $29.50/yr. out of state. 22 N. Main St., Northwood, ND 58267. TEL 701-587-6126; FAX 701-587-5219. **Owner(s):** David & Leslie Pfeifle, 22 N. Main St., Northwood, ND 58267. TEL 701-587-6126; FAX 701-587-5219; Pub. David Pfeifle; pub. size: broadsheet; circ. 1,000(paid).

US

LEADER, THE. Fri. $.50 newsstand; $21.75/yr. 22 N. Main St., Northwood, ND 58367. TEL 701-587-6126; FAX 701-587-5219. **Owner(s):** David & Leslie Pfeifle, 22 N. Main St., Northwood, ND 58267. TEL 701-587-6126; FAX 701-587-5219; Pub. David Pfeifle; pub. size: broadsheet; circ. 5,800(paid).

US

NORTHWOOD GLEANER. 1890. Mon. $.60 newsstand; $21.75/yr. in state; $29.50/yr. out of state. 22 N. Main St., Northwood, ND 58267. TEL 701-587-6126; FAX 701-587-5219. **Owner(s):** David & Leslie Pfeifle, 22 N. Main St., Northwood, ND 58267. TEL 701-587-5697; FAX 701-587-5134; Pub. David Pfeifle; adv. contact: Chris Ostlie. pub. size: broadsheet; circ. 1,650(paid).

PARK RIVER
US

WALSH COUNTY PRESS. 1881. Sat. $.90 newsstand; $36/yr. in cy.; $56/yr. in state; $56/yr. out of state. 404 Briggs Ave., S., Park River, ND 58270. TEL 701-284-6333; FAX 701-284-6091. **Owner(s):** Walsh County Press, Inc., 404 Briggs Ave., S., Park River, SD 58270. TEL 701-284-6333; FAX 701-284-6091; Ed. Holly Anderson; Pub. Henry W. Kelly; adv. contact: Joan Schumacher. pub. size: broadsheet; circ. 3,800(paid).

ROLLA
US

TURTLE MOUNTAIN STAR, THE. 1888. Mon. $.50 newsstand; $24/yr. in cy.; $26/yr. out of cy.; $34/yr. out of state. 11 First Ave., N.E., Rolla, ND 58367. TEL 701-477-6495; FAX 701-477-3182. **Owner(s):** Roger Bailey, P.O. Box 849, Rolla, ND 58367. TEL 701-477-6495; FAX 701-477-3182; Ed. Roger Bailey; Pub. Roger Bailey; pub. size: broadsheet; circ. 4,000(paid). **Formerly:** Rolla Turtle Mountain Star.

RUGBY
US

PIERCE COUNTY TRIBUNE. 1887. Sat. $.50 newsstand; $25/yr. in state; $30/yr. out of state. 219 S. Main Ave., Rugby, ND 58368. TEL 701-776-5252; FAX 701-776-2159. **Owner(s):** Ogden Newspapers, Inc., 1500 Main St., Wheeling, WV 26003. TEL 304-233-0100; Ed. Matt Mullalley. adv. contact: Kim Brown. pub. size: broadsheet; circ. 31,000(paid).

TURTLE LAKE
US

MCLEAN COUNTY JOURNAL. 1902. w. $.50 newsstand; $19.50/yr. in state; $27.50/yr. out of state. 210 Main St., Turtle Lake, ND 58575-0220. TEL 701-448-2649; FAX 701-448-2649. **Owner(s):** Gerald W. Anderson, 210 Main St., Turtle Lake, ND 58575-0220. TEL 701-448-2649; FAX 701-448-2649; Pub. Gerald W. Anderson; adv.; photos; pub. size: tabloid; circ. 925(controlled & free).

UNDERWOOD
US

UNDERWOOD NEWS. Thu. $.50 newsstand; $25/yr. in state; $30/yr. out of state. P.O. Box 179, Underwood, ND 58576. TEL 701-442-5535. **Owner(s):** BHG, Inc., Garrison, ND 58540. TEL 701-463-2201; Ed. Linda Hermanson; Pub. Mike Gackle; pub. size: broadsheet; circ. 1,000(paid).

WASHBURN
US

CENTER REPUBLICAN. 1906. Thu. $.50 newsstand; $25/yr. in cy.; $35/yr. out of cy. P.O. Box 340, Washburn, ND 58577. TEL 701-462-8126. **Owner(s):** BHG, Inc., P.O. Box 309, Garrison, ND 58540. TEL 701-463-2201; Ed. Lucille Gullickson; Pub. Mike Gackle; adv.; photos; bk.rev.; pub. size: standard; circ. 700(paid).

US   ISSN 0888-0220

LEADER-NEWS. Thu. $25/yr. in town; $29/yr. out of town; $35/yr. out of state. Box 340, Washburn, ND 58577. TEL 701-462-8126. **Owner(s):** BHG, Inc., P.O. 309, Garrison, ND 58540. TEL 701-463-2201; Ed. Joe Froleich; Pub. Mike Gackle; adv.; photos; bk.rev.; pub. size: tabloid; circ. 2,500(paid).

WEST FARGO
US
MIDWEEK EAGLE. 1970. Mon. free in cy.; $75/yr. outside cy. 322 Sheyenne St., West Fargo, ND 58078. TEL 701-282-2443; FAX 701-282-9248. **Owner(s):** Donovan C. Witham, 322 Sheyenne St., West Fargo, ND 58078. TEL 701-282-2443; Ed. Donovan C. Witham; Pub. Donovan C. Witham; adv. contact: Dave Braton. pub. size: tabloid; circ. 63,000(free & paid).

US
MIDWEEK PLUS. 1970. Thu. free in cy.; $50/yr. elsewhere. 322 Sheyenne St., West Fargo, ND 58078. TEL 701-282-2443; FAX 701-282-9248. **Owner(s):** Donovan C. Witham, 322 Sheyenne St., West Fargo, ND 58078. TEL 701-282-2443; Ed. Donovan C. Witham; Pub. Donovan C. Witham; adv. contact: Dave Braton. pub. size: tabloid; circ. 45,900(free & paid).

US
WEST FARGO PIONEER. 1967. Wed. $.50 newsstand; $18/yr. in cy.; $21/yr. out of cy. 322 Sheyenne St., West Fargo, ND 58078. TEL 701-282-2443; FAX 701-282-9248. **Owner(s):** Pioneer Press, Inc., P.O. Box 457, West Fargo, ND 58078; Ed. Thomas Jensen; Pub. Donovan C. Witham; adv.; photos; pub. size: tabloid; circ. 3,300(paid).

WILLISTON
US
WILLISTON PLAINS REPORTER. Wed. free. 14 W. Fourth St., Williston, ND 58801. TEL 701-572-6311; FAX 701-572-1965. **Owner(s):** Wick Communications, Inc., 333 W. Wilcox Dr., Ste. 302, Sierra Vista, AZ 85635; Ed. Donald J. Mrachek; Pub. Donald J. Mrachek; adv.; photos; pub. size: broadsheet; circ. 3,900(free).

OHIO

AKRON
US
SUBURBANITE, THE. 1968. Mon. $.25 newsstand; $20/yr. local; $25/yr. out of state. 3830 S. Main St., Akron, OH 44319. TEL 330-644-2249; FAX 330-644-6037. **Owner(s):** Thomson Newspapers, Inc., One Thorn Run Ctr., Ste. 500, 1187 Thorn Run Rd. Ext., Coraopolis, PA 15108. TEL 412-262-7870; Ed. Paul R. Harbaugh; Pub. Ron Thrash; pub. size: tabloid; circ. 26,000(paid).

AMHERST
US
NEWS TIMES. 1874. Wed. $.50 newsstand; $20/yr. 155 N. Leavitt, Amherst, OH 44001. TEL 216-988-2801; FAX 216-988-2802. **Owner(s):** Gazette Publishing Co., 607 N. Sandusky St., Bellevue, OH 44811. TEL 419-483-4190; Ed. Kathleen Koshar; Pub. Tom Smith; adv. contact: Dorri Sturges. pub. size: standard; circ. 2,500(paid).

ANDOVER
US
PYMATUNING AREA NEWS. 1970. Wed. $.50 newsstand; $20/yr. in cy.; $30/yr. out of cy. 37 Public Sq., Andover, OH 44003. TEL 216-293-6097; FAX 216-293-7374. **Owner(s):** Gazette Newspapers, P.O. Box 166, Jefferson, OH 44047. TEL 216-576-9115; Ed. Stephen Siff; Pub. John Lampson; adv. contact: Robert Halstead. pub. size: tabloid; circ. 2,100(paid).

ARCHBOLD
US
ARCHBOLD BUCKEYE. 1905. Wed. $.75 newsstand; $29/yr. in state; $34/yr. out of state. 207 N. Defiance St., Archbold, OH 43502-1187. TEL 419-445-4466; FAX 419-445-4177. **Owner(s):** Archbold Buckeye, Inc., 207 N. Defiance St., Archbold, OH 43502. TEL 419-445-4466; FAX 419-445-4177; Pub. Ross W. Taylor; adv. contact: Mary Huber. adv.: $7/SAU. photos; pub. size: broadsheet; circ. 3,250(paid).

US ISSN 0093-5832
FARMLAND NEWS. 1959. Tue. $.60 newsstand; $21/yr. local. 104 Depot St., Archbold, OH 43502-0240. TEL 419-445-9456; FAX 419-445-4444. **Owner(s):** O. Roger Taylor, 309 Murbach St., Archbold, OH 43502. TEL 419-445-5411; Ed. Jeremy J. Rohrs; Pub. O. Roger Taylor; adv. contact: Doug Nutter. photos; pub. size: tabloid; circ. 14,572(controlled & paid).

ATHENS
US
ATHENS NEWS. 1977. s-w.: Mon. & Thu. free. 14 N. Court St., Athens, OH 45701. TEL 614-594-8219; FAX 614-592-5695. **Owner(s):** Athens News Inc., The, 14 N. Court St., Athens, OH 45701. TEL 614-594-8219; FAX 614-592-5695; Ed. Terry Smith; Pub. Bruce Mitchell; pub. size: tabloid; circ. 17,500(free).

ATTICA
US
ATTICA HUB. 1896. Thu. $.50 newsstand; $18.50/yr. 26 N. Main St., Attica, OH 44807-0516. TEL 419-426-3491; FAX 419-426-3491. **Owner(s):** Jeffrey Cook, 9606 SR 269 N., Bellevue, OH 44811; Ed. Dawn Martin; Pub. Jeffrey Cook; adv.; pub. size: broadsheet; circ. 2,800(paid).

US
BLOOMVILLE GAZETTE. 1901. Thu. $.50 newsstand; $18.50/yr. 26 N. Main St., Attica, OH 44807-0516. TEL 419-426-3491; FAX 419-426-3491. **Owner(s):** Seneca Publishing, Inc., 9606 SR 269 N., Bellevue, OH 44811; Ed. Dawn Martin; Pub. Jeffrey Cook; adv.; pub. size: broadsheet; circ. 500(paid).

AVON LAKE
US
PRESS, THE. Wed. $.60 newsstand; $2/mos. carrier; $25/yr. in area mailed; $30/yr. out of area mailed. 158 Lear Rd., Avon Lake, OH 44012. TEL 216-933-5100; FAX 216-933-7904. **Owner(s):** Richard Hemmer, Jr., 158 Lear Rd., Avon Lake, OH 44012. TEL 216-935-5100; Ed. Richard Hemmer, Jr.; Pub. Richard Hemmer, Jr.; adv. contact: Linda Hemmer. pub. size: tabloid; circ. 13,000(paid).
Formerly: Avon Lake Press.

BARBERTON
US
BARBERTON HERALD. 1927. Thu. $.50 newsstand; $15/yr. in 4 cys. area mailed; $24/yr. out of area mailed. 70 Fourth St., N.W., Barberton, OH 44203. TEL 330-753-1068; FAX 330-753-1021. **Owner(s):** Richardson Publishing Co., 70 Fourth St., N.W., Barberton, OH 44203. TEL 330-753-1068; Ed. D.A. Richardson; Pub. D.A. Richardson; adv. contact: Rosalie Marquette. pub. size: broadsheet; circ. 7,500(paid).

BARNESVILLE
US
BARNESVILLE ENTERPRISE. 1866. Wed. $.60 newsstand; $19.50/yr. in state; $23/yr. out of state. 166 E. Main St., Barnesville, OH 43713. TEL 614-425-1912; FAX 614-425-2545. **Owner(s):** Dix News Media, P.O. Box 30, Barnesville, OH 43713. TEL 614-425-1912; FAX 614-425-2545; Ed. Pamela McCort; Pub. Robert C. Dix; adv. contact: Connie Burkhart. pub. size: standard; circ. 5,000(paid).

BATAVIA
US
CLERMONT SUN. 1828. Thu. $.45 newsstand; $15/yr. 465 E. Main St., Batavia, OH 45103. TEL 513-732-2511; FAX 513-732-6344. **Owner(s):** Clermont Sun Publishing Co., P.O. Box 366, Batavia, OH 45103. TEL 513-732-2511; FAX 513-732-6344; Ed. Jean Kowalski; Pub. William Latham; adv. contact: Carla Marasek. bk.rev.; pub. size: broadsheet; circ. 5,000(paid).

BEACHWOOD
US
BEDFORD SUN BANNER. 1970. Thu. $.60 newsstand; $32.50/yr. 3355 Richmond Rd., Ste. 171, Beachwood, OH 44122. TEL 216-464-6397; FAX 216-524-7792. **Owner(s):** Sun Media, Inc., 5510 Cloverleaf Pkwy., Cleveland, OH 44125-4887. TEL 216-524-0830; FAX 216-642-5547; Ed. Mark Morilak. adv.: $10.20/SAU. photos; pub. size: broadsheet; circ. 5,491(paid).

US
CHAGRIN HERALD SUN. 1948. Thu. $.60 newsstand; $32.50/yr. 3355 Richmond Rd., Ste. 171, Beachwood, OH 44122. TEL 216-464-6397; FAX 216-524-7792. **Owner(s):** Sun Media, Inc., 5510 Cloverleaf Pkwy., Cleveland, OH 44125-4887. TEL 216-524-0830; FAX 216-642-5547; Ed. Mary Jane Skala. adv.: $21.20/SAU. photos; bk.rev. pub. size: broadsheet; circ. 18,127(paid).
Formerly: Chagrin Valley Herald Sun.

US
EUCLID SUN JOURNAL. 1945. Thu. $.60 newsstand; $32.50/yr. 3355 Richmond Rd., Ste. 171, Beachwood, OH 44122. TEL 216-464-6397; FAX 216-524-7792. **Owner(s):** Sun Media, Inc., 5510 Cloverleaf Pkwy., Cleveland, OH 44125-4887. TEL 216-524-0830; FAX 216-642-5547; Ed. Mark Morilak. adv.: $19.90/SAU. photos; bk.rev.; pub. size: broadsheet; circ. 12,176(paid).

WEEKLY NEWSPAPERS

US
SOLON HERALD SUN. 1948. Thu. $.60 newsstand; $32.50/yr. 3355 Richmond Rd., Ste. 171, Beachwood, OH 44122. TEL 216-464-6397; FAX 216-464-8816. **Owner(s):** Sun Media, Inc., 510 Cloverleaf Pkwy., Cleveland, OH 44125. TEL 216-524-0830; FAX 216-464-5547; Ed. Mary Jane Skala. adv. contact: John Zeigler. adv.: $21.20/SAU. photos; pub. size: broadsheet; circ. 5,889(paid).

US
SUN MESSENGER, THE. 1952. Thu. $.60 newsstand; $32.50/yr. 3355 Richmond Rd., Ste. 171, Beachwood, OH 44122. TEL 216-464-6397. **Owner(s):** Sun Media, Inc., 5510 Cloverleaf Pkwy., Cleveland, OH 44125-4887. TEL 216-524-0830; FAX 216-642-5547; Ed. Mark Morilak. adv.: $23.95/SAU. pub. size: broadsheet; circ. 14,613(paid).

US
SUN PRESS, THE. 1946. Thu. $.60 newsstand; $32.50/yr. 3355 Richmond Rd., Ste. 171, Beachwood, OH 44122. TEL 216-464-6397; FAX 216-524-7792. **Owner(s):** Sun Media, Inc., 5510 Cloverleaf Pkwy., Cleveland, OH 44125-4887. TEL 216-524-0830; FAX 216-642-5547; Ed. Mary Jane Skala. adv.: $27.95/SAU. photos; bk.rev.; pub. size: broadsheet; circ. 20,478(paid).

US
SUN SCOOP JOURNAL. 1919. Thu. $.60 newsstand; $32.50/yr. 3355 Richmond Rd., Ste. 171, Beachwood, OH 44122. TEL 216-464-6397; FAX 216-524-7792. **Owner(s):** Sun Media, Inc., 5510 Cloverleaf Pkwy., Cleveland, OH 44125-4887. TEL 216-524-0830; FAX 216-642-5547; Ed. Mark Morilak. adv.: $10.40/SAU. photos; bk.rev.; pub. size: broadsheet; circ. 4,700(paid).

US
WEST GEAUGA SUN. 1994. Thu. $.60 newsstand; $32.50/yr. 3355 Richmond Rd., Ste. 171, Beachwood, OH 44122. TEL 216-464-6397; FAX 216-524-7792. **Owner(s):** Sun Media, Inc., 5510 Cloverleaf Pkwy., Cleveland, OH 44125-4887. TEL 216-524-0830; FAX 216-642-5547; Ed. Mary Jane Skala. adv.: $21.20/SAU. photos; pub. size: broadsheet; circ. 11,986(paid).

BEDFORD

US
BEDFORD TIME REGISTER. Thu. $.50 newsstand; $16/yr. mailed. 711 Broadway, Bedford, OH 44146-0059. TEL 216-232-4055; FAX 216-232-8861; E-mail: ald119@ald.net; URL: http://www.recordpub.com. **Owner(s):** Record Publishing Co., LLC, 1619 Commerce Dr., Cuyahoga Falls, OH 44224; Ed. Mindi Gabarik. photos; pub. size: tabloid; circ. 3,400(paid).

US
BULLETIN, THE. Thu. $.50 newsstand; $16/yr. 711 Broadway, Bedford, OH 44146. TEL 216-232-4055; FAX 216-232-8861; E-mail: ald119@ald.net; URL: http://www.recordpub.com. **Owner(s):** Record Publishing Co., LLC, 126 N. Chestnut St., Ravenna, OH 44266. TEL 330-296-9657; FAX 330-296-2698; adv. contact: Diana Kelly. pub. size: tabloid; circ. 7,000(paid).

US
MAPLE HEIGHTS PRESS. 1948. Thu. $.50 newsstand; $16/yr. 711 Broadway, Bedford, OH 44146-0059. TEL 216-232-4055; FAX 216-232-8861; E-mail: ald119@ald.net; URL: http://www.recordcom. **Owner(s):** Record Publishing Co., LLC, 1619 Commerce Dr., Stow, OH 44224. TEL 216-688-0088; Ed. Mindi Gabarik; Pub. David Dix; adv.; photos; pub. size: tabloid; circ. 5,500(paid).

BELLEVUE

US
RFD NEWS, THE. 1958. s-m.: 2nd & 4th Mon. $12/yr. 131 E. Main St., Bellevue, OH 44811. TEL 419-483-7410; FAX 419-483-3617. **Owner(s):** Gazette Publishing Co., 127 N. Sandusky Ave., Bellevue, OH 44811. TEL 419-483-3737; Ed. Thomas L. Ackerman. adv.; bk.rev.; pub. size: tabloid; circ. 75,331(controlled & paid).

BEREA

US
PARMA SUN POST. 1918. Thu. $.60 newsstand; $32.50/yr. 32 Park Dr., Berea, OH 44017. TEL 216-243-3725; FAX 216-524-7792. **Owner(s):** Sun Media, Inc., 5510 Cloverleaf Pkwy., Cleveland, OH 44125-4887. TEL 216-524-0830; FAX 216-642-5547; Ed. Linda Kinsey. adv.: $29.95/SAU. photos; pub. size: broadsheet; circ. 26,401(paid).

US
SUN STAR, THE. 1918. Thu. $.60 newsstand; $32.50/yr. 32 Park Dr., Berea, OH 44017. TEL 216-243-3725; FAX 216-524-7792. **Owner(s):** Sun Media, Inc., 5510 Cloverleaf Pkwy., Cleveland, OH 44125-4887. TEL 216-524-0830; FAX 216-642-5547; Ed. Linda Kinsey. adv.: $16.75/SAU. photos; bk.rev.; pub. size: broadsheet; circ. 11,712(paid).

BLUFFTON

US
BLUFFTON NEWS, THE. 1875. Thu. $30/yr. in state; $35/yr. out of state. 101 N. Main St., Bluffton, OH 45817. TEL 419-358-8010; FAX 419-358-5027. **Owner(s):** Bluffton News Printing & Publishing Co., 101 N. Main St., Bluffton, OH 45817. TEL 419-358-8010; Ed. Fred Steiner; Pub. Tom Edwards; adv.; bk.rev.; pub. size: standard; circ. 2,800(paid).

BOARDMAN

US
BOARDMAN NEWS. 1947. Thu. $.25 newsstand; $15/yr. renewal; $20/yr. 6221 Market St., Boardman, OH 44512. TEL 330-758-2658; FAX 330-758-2658. **Owner(s):** John A. Darnell, Sr. & John A. Darnell, Jr., 6221 Market St., Youngstown, OH 44512. TEL 330-758-2658; Ed. John Darnell, Jr.; Pub. John Darnell, Sr.; adv. contact: Richard Bingham. photos; bk.rev.; pub. size: broadsheet; circ. 9,000(paid).

BRYAN

US
COUNTYLINE, THE. 1967. Sun. free; $7.90/yr. mailed. 127 S. Walnut St., Bryan, OH 43506. TEL 419-636-1111. **Owner(s):** Bryan Publishing Co., The, 127 S. Walnut St., Bryan, OH 43506. TEL 419-636-1111; adv.; pub. size: tabloid; circ. Sun. 23,871(free & paid).

CADIZ

US
HARRISON NEWS-HERALD, THE. 1968. Mon. $.50 newsstand; $16.50/yr. local; $36.50/yr. out of cy.; $47/yr. out of state. P.O. Box 127, Cadiz, OH 43907. TEL 614-942-2118; FAX 614-942-4667. **Owner(s):** Patricia O'Grady, P.O. Box 127, Cadiz, OH 43907. TEL 614-942-2796; Ed. Kay Keyser Sedgmer; Pub. Patricia O'Grady; adv.; pub. size: broadsheet; circ. 8,000(paid).
Formerly: Cadiz Harrison News-Herald.

CALDWELL

US
JOURNAL-LEADER. 1859. Mon. $.50 newsstand; $22/yr. in cy.; $24/yr. out of cy. 309 Main St., Caldwell, OH 43724. TEL 614-732-2341; FAX 614-732-7288. **Owner(s):** Southeast Publications, Inc., 309 Main St., Caldwell, OH 43724. TEL 614-732-2341; FAX 614-732-7288; Pub. David Evans; adv.; photos; pub. size: broadsheet; circ. 5,000(controlled & paid).

CANTON

US
FREE PRESS, THE. Sun. free in cy. 808 Monument Rd., N.W., Canton, OH 44703. TEL 330-456-0040; FAX 330-456-1153. **Owner(s):** Youngstown Vindicator, P.O. Box 780, Youngstown, OH 44503. TEL 330-747-1471; adv. contact: Robert Wagner. pub. size: broadsheet; circ. 110,000(free).

CARDINGTON

US
MORROW COUNTY INDEPENDENT. 1848. Wed. $.35 newsstand; $23/yr. in cy.; $25/yr. out of cy.; $27/yr. out of state. 123 E. Main St., Cardington, OH 43315. TEL 419-864-6046; FAX 419-947-7241. **Owner(s):** Hirt Publishing, P.O. Box 303, Bellevue, OH 44811. TEL 419-483-7000; Ed. Susie Dye. adv.; photos; pub. size: broadsheet; circ. 1,100(free & paid).

CAREY

US
PROGRESSOR-TIMES, THE. 1873. Wed. $.50 newsstand; $25/yr. in state; $30/yr. out of state. 1198 E. Findlay St., Carey, OH 43316-0037. TEL 419-396-7567; FAX 419-396-7527. **Owner(s):** Stephen C. Zender, 1198 E. Findlay St., P.O. Box 37, Carey, OH 43316-0037. TEL 419-396-7567; FAX 419-396-7527; Ed. Stephen C. Zender; Pub. Stephen C. Zender; adv. contact: Amy Zender. pub. size: standard; circ. 4,200(paid).

CARROLL

US
LANCASTER FAIRFIELD ADVERTISER. 1974. Wed. free. 3675 Dolson Ct., Carroll, OH 43112. TEL 614-654-6856; FAX 614-654-5617. **Owner(s):** Add, Inc., 600 Industrial Dr., Waupaca, WI 54981. TEL 715-258-8450; pub. size: tabloid; circ. 38,450(free).

CARROLLTON

US
FREE PRESS STANDARD. 1831. Thu. $.50 newsstand; $17.50/yr. local; $35/yr. out of area; $45/yr. out of state. 43 E. Main St., Carrollton, OH 44615-9983. TEL 330-627-5591; FAX 330-627-3195. **Owner(s):** Maynard A. Buck, Jr., 135 Poplar Ln., Cadiz, OH 43907. TEL 614-942-2796; Ed. Carol McIntire; Pub. Maynard A. Buck, Jr.; adv. contact: Judith Ray. photos; pub. size: broadsheet; circ. 7,800(free & paid).
Formerly: Carrollton Free Press Standard.

CHAGRIN FALLS

US ISSN 0194-3685
CHAGRIN VALLEY TIMES. 1971. Thu. $.50 newsstand; $24.75/yr. 525 E. Washington St., Chagrin Falls, OH 44022. TEL 216-247-5335; FAX 216-247-5615. **Owner(s):** Chagrin Valley Publishing Co., 525 E. Washington St., Chagrin Falls, OH 44022. TEL 216-247-5335; FAX 216-247-5615; Ed. David C. Lange. adv.; photos; pub. size: tabloid; circ. 18,000(paid).

US ISSN 0194-3677
SOLON TIMES, THE. 1977. Thu. $.50 newsstand; $24.75/yr. 525 E. Washington St., Chagrin Falls, OH 44022. TEL 216-247-5335. **Owner(s):** Chagrin Valley Publishing Co., 525 W. Washington St., Chagrin Falls, OH 44022. TEL 216-247-5335; Ed. David C. Lange. adv.; photos; pub. size: tabloid; circ. 3,544(paid).

CHESTERLAND

US
CHESTERLAND NEWS. 1967. Wed. free in area; $15/yr. out of area. 8525 Herrick Dr., Chesterland, OH 44026-2619. TEL 216-729-7667. **Owner(s):** Pamela Gable, 8525 Herrick Dr., Chesterland, OH 44026. TEL 216-729-7667; Pub. Pamela Gable; adv.; photos; pub. size: tabloid; circ. 6,000(free).

CHILLICOTHE

US
ADVERTISER, THE. 1913. Sun. free. 147 W. Water St., Chillicothe, OH 45601. TEL 614-773-5010; FAX 614-773-5021. **Owner(s):** Add, Inc., 600 Industrial Dr., Waupaca, WI 54981. TEL 715-258-8450; Pub. Mark Karavakis; adv. contact: H.F. Scharfetter. pub. size: tabloid; circ. 30,000(free).

CINCINNATI

US
DELHI PRESS. 1924. Wed. free deliv.; $.50 newsstand; $2/4 wks. voluntary pay; $104/yr. mailed. 5552 Cheviot Rd., Cincinnati, OH 45247. TEL 513-923-3111; FAX 513-923-1806. **Owner(s):** Community Newspapers, 4910 Para Dr., Cincinnati, OH 45237. TEL 513-242-4300; Pub. Tony Schad; adv. contact: Gary Hughes. photos; pub. size: broadsheet; circ. 11,000(free & paid).

US
EVERYBODY'S NEWS. Fri. free. 1310 Pendleton St., Ste. 700, Cincinnati, OH 45210. TEL 513-381-2606; FAX 513-287-8643. **Owner(s):** Goodwin Communications, 1310 Pendleton St., Ste., 700, Cincinnati, OH 45210. TEL 513-381-2606; FAX 513-287-8643; Ed. Pat Morris; Pub. Donna Goodwin; pub. size: broadsheet; circ. 42,000(paid).

US
HILLTOP NEWS-PRESS. 1918. Wed. free deliv.; $.50 newsstand; $2/4 wks. voluntary pay; $104/yr. mailed. 5552 Cheviot Rd., Cincinnati, OH 45247. TEL 513-923-3111; FAX 513-923-1806. **Owner(s):** Community Newspapers, 4910 Para Dr., Cincinnati, OH 45237; Pub. Tony Schad; adv. contact: Gary Hughes. pub. size: broadsheet; circ. 20,000(controlled & paid).

US
NORTHWEST PRESS. 1918. Wed. free deliv.; $.50 newsstand; $2/4 wks. voluntary pay; $104./yr. mailed. 5552 Cheviot Rd., Cincinnati, OH 45247. TEL 513-923-3111; FAX 513-923-1806. **Owner(s):** Community Newspapers, 4910 Para Dr., Cincinnati, OH 45237. TEL 513-242-4300; Pub. Tony Schad; adv. contact: Gary Hughes. pub. size: broadsheet; circ. 18,000(paid).

US
PRICE HILL PRESS. 1924. Wed. free deliv.; $.50 newsstand; $2/4 wks. voluntary pay; $104/yr. mailed. 5552 Cheviot Rd., Cincinnati, OH 45247. TEL 513-923-3111; FAX 513-923-1806. **Owner(s):** Community Newspapers, 4910 Para Dr., Cincinnati, OH 45237. TEL 513-242-4300; Pub. Tony Schad; adv. contact: Gary Hughes. pub. size: broadsheet; circ. 9,000(paid).

US
TRI-COUNTY PRESS. Wed. free deliv.; $.50 newsstand; $2/4 wks. voluntary pay; $104/yr. mailed. 5552 Cheviot Rd., Cincinnati, OH 45247. TEL 513-923-3111; FAX 513-923-1806. **Owner(s):** Community Newspapers, 4910 Para Dr., Cincinnati, OH 45237. TEL 513-242-4300; Pub. Tony Schad; adv. contact: Gary Hughes. pub. size: broadsheet; circ. 9,200(paid).

US
WESTERN HILLS PRESS. 1924. Wed. free deliv.; $.50 newsstand; $2/4 wks. voluntary pay; $104/yr. 5552 Cheviot Rd., Cincinnati, OH 45247. TEL 513-923-3111; FAX 513-923-1806. **Owner(s):** Community Newspapers, 4910 Para Dr., Cincinnati, OH 45237. TEL 513-242-4300; Pub. Tony Schad; adv. contact: Gary Hughes. pub. size: broadsheet; circ. 18,000(paid).

CLEVELAND

US
BRECKSVILLE GAZETTE. 1975. bi-w.: Wed. $.35 newsstand; $7/yr.; $12/2 yrs. 7014 Mill Rd., Cleveland, OH 44141. TEL 216-526-7977; FAX 216-526-7114. **Owner(s):** Gazette Newspapers, 7014 Mill Rd., Cleveland, OH 44141. TEL 216-526-7977; pub. size: tabloid; circ. 8,000(paid).

US
BROOKLYN SUN JOURNAL. 1918. Thu. $.60 newsstand; $32.50/yr. 5510 Cloverleaf Pkwy., Cleveland, OH 44125-4887. TEL 216-524-0830; FAX 216-524-7792. **Owner(s):** Sun Media, Inc., 5510 Cloverleaf Pkwy., Cleveland, OH 44125-4887. TEL 216-524-0830; FAX 216-642-5547; Ed. Carol Kovach. adv.: $15.30/SAU. photos; bk.rev.; pub. size: broadsheet; circ. 9,169(paid).

US
FREE TIMES, THE. Wed. free. 1846 Coventry Rd., Ste. 100, Cleveland, OH 44118-1682. TEL 216-321-2300; FAX 216-321-4456. **Owner(s):** Free Times, The, 1846 Coventry Rd., Ste. 100, Cleveland, OH 44118-1682. TEL 216-321-2300; Ed. Eric Broder; Pub. Randy Siegel; pub. size: tabloid; circ. 50,000(controlled & free).

US
GARFIELD MAPLE-SUN. 1918. Thu. $.60 newsstand; $32.50/yr. 5510 Cloverleaf Pkwy., Cleveland, OH 44125-4887. TEL 216-524-0830; FAX 216-524-7792. **Owner(s):** Sun Media, Inc., 5510 Cloverleaf Pkwy., Cleveland, OH 44125-4887. TEL 216-524-0830; FAX 216-642-5547; Ed. Carol Kovach. adv.: $19.85/SA. photos; pub. size: broadsheet; circ. 10,431(paid).
Formerly: Garfield Sun-Banner.

US
GAZETTE SHOPPER. 1975. m.: 1st. Wed. free. 7014 Mill Rd., Cleveland, OH 44141. TEL 216-526-7977; FAX 216-526-7114. **Owner(s):** Brecksville-Broadview Hts. & Independence Gazette, 7014 Mill Rd., Cleveland, OH 44141. TEL 216-526-7977; Ed. Joyce McFadden. circ. 12,500.

US
LEADER, THE. 1946. Thu. $18/yr. 4818 Turney Rd., Cleveland, OH 44125. TEL 216-883-0300; FAX 216-271-7133. **Owner(s):** William Kleinschmidt, 4818 Turney Rd., Cleveland, OH 44125. TEL 216-883-0300; FAX 216-271-7447; Ed. William Kleinschmidt. adv. contact: H. Kleinschmidt. pub. size: broadsheet; circ. 6,000(paid).

US
NEWS SUN, THE. 1924. Thu. $.60 newsstand; $32.50/yr. 5510 Cloverleaf Pkwy., Cleveland, OH 44125-4887. TEL 216-524-0830; FAX 216-524-7792. **Owner(s):** Sun Media, Inc., 5510 Cloverleaf Pkwy., Cleveland, OH 44125-4887. TEL 216-524-0830; FAX 216-642-5547; Ed. Linda Kinsey. adv.: $21.20/SAU. photos; bk.rev.; pub. size: broadsheet; circ. 16,404(paid).

US
NORDONIA HILLS SUN. 1994. Thu. $.60 newsstand. 5510 Cloverleaf Pkwy., Cleveland, OH 44125-4887. TEL 216-524-0830; FAX 216-524-7792. **Owner(s):** Sun Media, Inc., 5510 Cloverleaf Pkwy., Cleveland, OH 44125-4887. TEL 216-524-0830; FAX 216-642-5547; Ed. Carol Kovach. adv.: $11.70/SAU. photos; pub. size: broadsheet; circ. 3,327(paid).

US
SUN COURIER, THE. 1969. Thu. $.60 newsstand; $32.50/yr. 5510 Cloverleaf Pkwy., Cleveland, OH 44125-4887. TEL 216-524-0830; FAX 216-524-7792. **Owner(s):** Sun Media, Inc., 5510 Cloverleaf Pkwy., Cleveland, OH 44125-4887. TEL 216-524-0830; FAX 216-642-5547; Ed. Carol Kovach. adv.: $15.25/SAU. photos; bk.rev.; pub. size: broadsheet; circ. 8,570(paid).

US
TWINSBURG SUN, THE. 1994. Thu. $.60 newsstand; $32.50/yr. 5510 Cloverleaf Pkwy., Cleveland, OH 44125-4887. TEL 216-524-0830; FAX 216-524-7792. **Owner(s):** Sun Media, Inc., 5510 Cloverleaf Pkwy., Cleveland, OH 44125-4887. TEL 216-524-0830; FAX 216-642-5547; Ed. Carol Kovach. adv.: $11.70/SAU. photos; bk.rev.; pub. size: broadsheet; circ. 2,375(paid).

WEEKLY NEWSPAPERS

COLUMBUS, OH 10701

CLYDE

US

CLYDE ENTERPRISE. 1878. Wed. $.65 newsstand; $28/yr. out of state; $21.50/yr. senior citizens in state; $25/yr. senior citizens out of state. 107 S. Main St., Clyde, OH 43410. TEL 419-547-9194. **Owner(s):** Gazette Publishing Co., 107 N. Sandusky St., Bellevue, OH. TEL 419-483-4190; Ed. John W. Brewer; Pub. Thomas Smith; adv.; photos; pub. size: broadsheet; circ. 2,200(paid).

COLDWATER

US

MERCER COUNTY CHRONICLE. 1902. Wed. $.75 newsstand; $24/yr. in cy.; $27/yr. out of cy; $32/yr. out of state. 116 W. Main St., Coldwater, OH 45828-0105. TEL 419-678-2324; FAX 419-678-4659. **Owner(s):** Delphos Newspapers, 405 N. Main St., Delphos, OH 45833. TEL 419-695-0015; FAX 419-692-7704; Ed. Bonnie J. VanDeMark; Pub. Bonnie J. VanDeMark; adv.; photos; pub. size: broadsheet; circ. 2,300(paid).

COLUMBIA STATION

US

RURAL-URBAN RECORD. 1955. Mon. free local; $20/yr. out of area. 24487 Squires Rd., Columbia Station, OH 44028. TEL 216-236-8982. **Owner(s):** Rural-Urban-Record, Inc., P.O. Box 966, Columbia Station, OH 44028. TEL 216-238-8982; Ed. Leonard Boise; Pub. Leonard Boise; adv.: $6.50/SAU. pub. size: tabloid; circ. 16,221(free & paid).

COLUMBUS

US

BEXLEY NEWS. 1964. Wed. $.25 newsstand; $20/yr. in cy.; $25/yr. out of cy. 5257 Sinclair Rd., Columbus, OH 43229. TEL 614-785-1212; FAX 614-842-4760. **Owner(s):** Suburban News Publications, 5257 Sinclair Rd., Columbus, OH 43229. TEL 614-785-1212; Ed. Joe Meyer; Pub. James Toms; adv. contact: Carol Zimmer. pub. size: broadsheet; circ. 6,000(paid).

US

BIG WALNUT/SUNBURY. Thu. free; $75/yr. P.O. Box 341890, Columbus, OH 43234-1890. TEL 614-841-0444; FAX 614-438-8159. **Owner(s):** John Wolf, P.O. Box 341890, Columbus, OH 43240-1890. TEL 614-438-8100; FAX 614-438-8110; Ed. Craig McDonald. adv. contact: Jerry O'Connell. adv.: $5.35/SAU. photos; pub. size: broadsheet; circ. 11,532(free & paid).

US

BOOSTER, THE. 1933. Wed. $.40 newsstand; $20/yr. in cy.; $25/yr. elsewhere. 5257 Sinclair Rd., Columbus, OH 43229. TEL 614-785-1212; FAX 614-842-4760. **Owner(s):** Suburban News Publications, 5257 Sinclair Rd., Columbus, OH 43229. TEL 614-785-1212; Ed. Martin Rozenman; Pub. James Toms; adv.; pub. size: tabloid; circ. 18,500(paid).

US

COLUMBUS ALIVE. 1984. Wed. free newsstand; $35/yr. mailed. 17 Brickel St., Columbus, OH 43215-0309. TEL 614-221-2449; FAX 614-221-2456. **Owner(s):** Columbus Alive, Inc., P.O. Box 15309, Columbus, OH 43215-0309. TEL 614-221-2449; FAX 614-221-2456; Ed. Sally Crane MacPhail; Pub. Sally Crane MacPhail; adv.; photos; bk.rev.; pub. size: tabloid; circ. 33,000(free & paid).

US

COLUMBUS MESSENGER. 1974. Mon. $52/yr. mailed. 3378 Sullivant Ave., Columbus, OH 43204. TEL 614-272-5422; FAX 614-272-0684. **Owner(s):** Columbus Messenger, 3378 Sullivant Ave., Columbus, OH 43204. TEL 614-272-5422; Pub. Phil Daubel; adv. contact: Douglas Henry. pub. size: tabloid; circ. 151,000(controlled & free).

US

DUBLIN SUBURBIA NEWS. 1978. Wed. $.40 newsstand; $20/yr. in cy. $25/yr. out of cy. 5257 Sinclair Rd., Columbus, OH 43229. TEL 614-785-1212; FAX 614-842-4760. **Owner(s):** Suburban News Publications, 5257 Sinclair Rd., Columbus, OH 43229. TEL 614-785-1212; FAX 614-842-4760; Ed. Joe Meyer; Pub. James Toms; adv.; photos; pub. size: tabloid; circ. 18,133(paid).

US

GROVE CITY RECORD. 1927. w.: Wed. $.50 newsstand; $21/yr. mailed. P.O. Box 341890, Columbus, OH 43234-1890. TEL 614-438-8100; FAX 614-438-8110; E-mail: thisweek@infinet.com; URL: http://www.this weeknews.com. **Owner(s):** John Wolf, P.O. Box 341890, Columbus, OH 43234-1890. TEL 614-438-8100; FAX 614-438-8110; Ed. Craig McDonald. adv. contact: Jerry O'Connell. adv.: $9.50/SAU. photos; pub. size: broadsheet; circ. 2,484(free).

US

JOHNSTOWN INDEPENDENT. 1884. w.: Wed. $.50 newsstand; $21/yr. mailed. P.O. Box 341890, Columbus, OH 43234-1890. TEL 614-438-8100; FAX 614-438-8110; E-mail: thisweek@infinet.com; URL: http://thisweeknews.com. **Owner(s):** John Wolf, P.O. Box 341890, Columbus, OH 43232-1890. TEL 614-438-8100; FAX 614-438-8110; Ed. Craig McDonald. adv. contact: Jerry O'Connell. adv.: $7.50/SAU. photos; pub. size: broadsheet; circ. 1,116(paid).

US

NORTHLAND NEWS. Wed. $.40 newsstand; $25/yr. in cy.; $30/yr. out of cy. 5257 Sinclair Rd., Columbus, OH 43229. TEL 614-785-1212. **Owner(s):** Suburban News Publications, 5257 Sinclair Rd., Columbus, OH 43229. TEL 614-785-1212; Ed. Joe Meyer; Pub. James Toms; adv. contact: Carol Zimmer. pub. size: broadsheet; circ. 21,400(paid).

US

NORTHWEST COLUMBUS NEWS. 1980. Wed. $.40 newsstand; $20/yr. in cy.; $25/yr. out of cy. 5257 Sinclair Rd., Columbus, OH 43229. TEL 614-785-1212; FAX 614-842-4760. **Owner(s):** Suburban News Publications, 5257 Sinclair Rd., Columbus, OH 43229. TEL 614-785-1214; FAX 614-842-4760; Ed. Joe Meyer; Pub. James Toms; adv.; photos; pub. size: tabloid; circ. 19,500(paid).

US

OTHER PAPER, THE. Thu. free. P.O. Box 29913, Columbus, OH 43229. TEL 614-847-3800; FAX 614-848-3838. **Owner(s):** Max S. Brown, P.O. Box 29913, Columbus, OH 43229. TEL 614-847-3800; FAX 614-848-3838; Ed. Danny Russell; Pub. Max S. Brown; pub. size: broadsheet; circ. 50,000(paid).

US

PICKERINGTON TIMES-SUN. Wed. $.40 newsstand; $15/yr. mailed. 5257 Sinclair Rd., Columbus, OH 43229. TEL 614-237-2500; FAX 614-837-3441. **Owner(s):** CM Media, 5257 Sinclair Rd., Columbus, OH 43229. TEL 614-785-1212; Ed. Martin Rozenman; Pub. James Toms; adv. contact: Carol Zimmer. pub. size: tabloid; circ. 8,700(paid).

US

ROCKY FORK ENTERPRISE. 1994. Thu. free. P.O. Box 341890, Columbus, OH 43234-1890. TEL 614-438-8100; FAX 614-438-8110; E-mail: thisweek@infinet.com; URL: http://www.thisweeknews.com. **Owner(s):** John Wolf, P.O. Box 341890, Columbus, OH 43234-1890. TEL 614-438-8100; FAX 614-438-8110; Ed. Craig McDonald. adv. contact: Jerry O'Connell. adv.: $8.30/SAU. photos; pub. size: broadsheet; circ. 11,532(free).

US

THIS WEEK IN BEXLEY. 1990. Mon. free newsstand; $75/yr. mailed. P.O. Box 341890, Columbus, OH 43234-1890. TEL 614-438-8100; FAX 614-438-8110; E-mail: thisweek@infinet.com; URL: http://www.thisweeknews.com. **Owner(s):** John Wolf, P.O. Box 341890, Columbus, OH 43234-1890. TEL 614-438-8100; FAX 614-438-8110; Ed. Craig McDonald. adv. contact: Jerry O'Connell. adv.: $7.20/SAU. photos; pub. size: tabloid; circ. 9,681(free).

US

THIS WEEK IN CLINTONVILLE. 1990. Mon. free newsstand; $75/yr. mailed. P.O. Box 341890, Columbus, OH 43234-1890. TEL 614-438-8100; FAX 614-438-8110; E-mail: thisweek@infinet.com; URL: http://www.thisweeknews.com. **Owner(s):** John Wolf, P.O. Box 341890, Columbus, OH 43234-1890. TEL 614-438-8100; FAX 614-438-8110; Ed. Craig McDonald. adv. contact: Jerry O'Connell. adv.: $8.65/SAU. photos; pub. size: tabloid; circ. 14,959(free).

US

THIS WEEK IN DELAWARE. 1990. Mon. free newsstand; $75/yr. mailed. P.O. Box 341890, Columbus, OH 43234-1890. TEL 614-438-8100; FAX 614-438-8110; E-mail: thisweek@infinet.com; URL: http://www.thisweeknews.com. **Owner(s):** John Wolf, P.O. Box 341890, Columbus, OH 43234-1890. TEL 614-438-8100; FAX 614-438-8110; Ed. Craig McDonald. adv. contact: Jerry O'Connell. adv.: $8.65/SAU. photos; pub. size: tabloid; circ. 13,309(free).

US

THIS WEEK IN EASTSIDE. 1990. Mon. free newsstand; $75/yr. mailed. P.O. Box 341890, Columbus, OH 43234-1890. TEL 614-438-8100; FAX 614-438-8110; E-mail: thisweek@infinet.com; URL: http://www.thisweeknews.com. **Owner(s):** John Wolf, P.O. Box 341890, Columbus, OH 43234-1890. TEL 614-438-8100; FAX 614-438-8110; Ed. Craig McDonald. adv. contact: Jerry O'Connell. adv.: $8.65/SAU. photos; pub. size: tabloid; circ. 14,526(free).

Weeklies

COLUMBUS, OH

WEEKLY NEWSPAPERS

US
THIS WEEK IN GRANDVIEW. 1990. Mon. free newsstand; $75/yr. mailed. P.O. Box 341890, Columbus, OH 43230-1890. TEL 614-438-8100; FAX 614-438-8110; E-mail: thisweek@infinet.com; URL: http://www.thisweeknews.com. **Owner(s):** John Wolf, P.O. Box 341890, Columbus, OH 43234-1890. TEL 614-438-8100; FAX 614-438-8110; Ed. Craig McDonald. adv. contact: Jerry O'Connell. photos; pub. size: tabloid; circ. 6,008(free).

US
THIS WEEK IN HILLIARD. 1990. Mon. free newsstand; $75/yr. mailed. P.O. Box 341890, Columbus, OH 43234-1890. TEL 614-438-8100; FAX 614-438-8110; E-mail: thisweek@infinet.com; URL: http://www.thisweeknews.com. **Owner(s):** John Wolf, P.O. Box 341890, Columbus, OH 43234-1890. TEL 614-438-8100; FAX 614-438-8110; Ed. Craig McDonald. adv. contact: Jerry O'Connell. adv.: $8.05/SAU. photos; pub. size: tabloid; circ. 21,357(free).

US
THIS WEEK IN NEW ALBANY. 1993. Mon. free newsstand; $75/yr. mailed. P.O. Box 341890, Columbus, OH 43234-1890. TEL 614-438-8100; FAX 614-438-8110; E-mail: thisweek@infinet.com; URL: http://www.thisweeknews.com. **Owner(s):** John Wolf, P.O. Box 341890, Columbus, OH 43234-1890. TEL 614-438-8100; FAX 614-438-8110; Ed. Craig McDonald. adv. contact: Jerry O'Connell. adv.: $5.75/SAU. photos; pub. size: tabloid; circ. 3,263(free).

US
THIS WEEK IN NORTHLAND. 1990. Mon. free newsstand; $75/yr. mailed. P.O. Box 341890, Columbus, OH 43234-1890. TEL 614-438-8100; FAX 614-438-8110; E-mail: thisweek@infinet.com; URL: http://www.thisweeknews.com. **Owner(s):** John Wolf, P.O. Box 341890, Columbus, OH 43234-1890. TEL 614-438-8100; FAX 614-438-8110; Ed. Craig McDonald. adv. contact: Jerry O'Connell. adv.: $9.70/SAU. photos; pub. size: tabloid; circ. 25,861(free).

US
THIS WEEK IN PICKERINGTON. 1990. Mon. free newsstand; $75/yr. mailed. P.O. Box 341890, Columbus, OH 43234-1890. TEL 614-438-8100; FAX 614-438-8110; E-mail: thisweek@infinet.com; URL: http://www.thisweeknews.com. **Owner(s):** John Wolf, P.O. Box 341890, Columbus, OH 43234-1890. TEL 614-438-8100; FAX 614-438-8110; Ed. Craig McDonald. adv. contact: Jerry O'Connell. adv.: $7.65/SAU. photos; pub. size: tabloid; circ. 13,034(free).

US
THIS WEEK IN POWELL. 1990. Mon. free newsstand; $75/yr mailed. P.O. Box 341890, Columbus, OH 43234-1890. TEL 614-438-8100; FAX 614-438-8110; E-mail: thisweek@infinet.com; URL: http://www.thisweeknews.com. **Owner(s):** John Wolf, P.O. Box 341890, Columbus, OH 43234-1890. TEL 614-438-8100; FAX 614-438-8110; Ed. Jerry O'Connell. adv. contact: Jerry O'Connell. adv.: $6.50/SAU. photos; pub. size: tabloid; circ. 8,158(free).

US
THIS WEEK IN REYNOLDSBURG. 1990. Mon. free newsstand; $75/yr. mailed. P.O. Box 341890, Columbus, OH 43234-1890. TEL 614-438-8100; FAX 614-438-8110; E-mail: thisweek@infinet.com; URL: http://www.thisweeknews.com. **Owner(s):** John Wolf, P.O. Box 341890, Columbus, OH 43234-1890. TEL 614-438-8100; FAX 614-438-8110; Ed. Craig McDonald. adv. contact: Jerry O'Connell. adv.: $7.65/SAU. photos; pub. size: tabloid; circ. 14,029(free).

US
THIS WEEK IN SOUTHSIDE. 1990. Mon. free newsstand; $75/yr. mailed. P.O. Box 341890, Columbus, OH 43234-1890. TEL 614-438-8100; FAX 614-438-8110; E-mail: thisweek@infinet.com; URL: http://www.thisweeknews.com. **Owner(s):** John Wolf, P.O. Box 341890, Columbus, OH 43234-1890. TEL 614-438-8100; FAX 614-438-8110; Ed. Craig McDonald. adv. contact: Jerry O'Connell. adv.: $9.25/SAU. photos; pub. size: tabloid; circ. 20,079(free).

US
THIS WEEK IN UNION COUNTY. 1990. Sun. free newsstand; $75/yr. mailed. P.O. Box 341890, Columbus, OH 43234-1890. TEL 614-438-8100; FAX 614-438-8110; E-mail: thisweek@infinet.com; URL: http://www.thisweeknews.com. **Owner(s):** John Wolf, P.O. Box 3471890, Columbus, OH 43234-1890. TEL 614-438-8100; FAX 614-438-8110; Ed. Craig McDonald. adv. contact: Jerry O'Connell. adv.: $7.65/SAU. photos; pub. size: tabloid; circ. 6,749(free); evening 7,200.

US
THIS WEEK IN WESTERVILLE. 1990. Mon. free newsstand; $75/yr. mailed. P.O. Box 341890, Columbus, OH 43234-1890. TEL 614-438-8100; FAX 614-438-8110; E-mail: thisweek@infinet.com; URL: http://www.thisweeknews.com. **Owner(s):** John Wolf, P.O. Box 34189, Columbus, OH 43234-1890. TEL 614-438-8100; FAX 614-438-8110; Ed. Craig McDonald. adv. contact: Jerry O'Connell. adv.: $9/SAU. photos; pub. size: tabloid; circ. 24,567(free).

US
THIS WEEK IN WESTSIDE. 1990. Mon. free newsstand; $75/yr. mailed. P.O. Box 341890, Columbus, OH 43234-1890. TEL 614-438-8100; FAX 614-438-8110; E-mail: thisweek@infinet.com; URL: http://www.thisweeknews.com. **Owner(s):** John Wolf, P.O. Box 341890, Columbus, OH 43234-1890. TEL 614-438-8100; FAX 614-438-8110; Ed. Craig McDonnel. adv.: $9.25/SAU. photos; pub. size: tabloid; circ. 26,028.

US
THIS WEEK IN WORTHINGTON. 1990. Mon. free newsstand; $75/yr. mailed. P.O. Box 341890, Columbus, OH 43234-1890. TEL 614-438-8100; FAX 614-438-8110; E-mail: thisweek@infinet.com; URL: http://www.thisweeknews.com. **Owner(s):** John Wolf, P.O. Box 341890, Columbus, OH 43234-1890. TEL 614-438-8100; FAX 614-438-8110; Ed. Craig McDonald. adv. contact: Jerry O'Connell. adv.: $9.25/SAU. photos; pub. size: tabloid; circ. 24,697(free).

US
TIMES, THE. 1871. Wed. $.40 newsstand; $12/yr. in cy.; $15/yr. out of cy. 5257 Sinclair Rd., Columbus, OH 43229. TEL 614-237-2500; FAX 614-237-1888. **Owner(s):** CM Media, 5257 Sinclair Rd., Columbus, OH 43229. TEL 614-785-1212; Ed. Martin Rozenman; Pub. James Toms; adv.; pub. size: broadsheet; circ. 2,500(paid).
Formerly: Canal Winchester Times.

US
TRI-VILLAGE NEWS. 1931. Wed. $.25 newsstand; $20/yr. in cy.; $25/yr. out of cy. 5257 Sinclair Rd., Columbus, OH 43229. TEL 614-785-1212; FAX 614-842-4760. **Owner(s):** Suburban News Publications, 5257 Sinclair Rd., Columbus, OH 43229. TEL 614-785-1212; FAX 614-842-4760; Ed. Martin Rozenman; Pub. James Toms; adv.; pub. size: tabloid; circ. 4,100(paid).

US
UA THIS WEEK. 1990. Mon. free newsstand; $75/yr. mailed. P.O. Box 341890, Columbus, OH 43234-1890. TEL 614-438-8100; FAX 614-438-8110; E-mail: thisweek@infinet.com; URL: http://www.thisweeknews.com. **Owner(s):** John Wolf, P.O. Box 341890, Columbus, OH 43234-1890. TEL 614-438-8100; FAX 614-438-8110; Ed. Craig McDonald. adv. contact: Jerry O'Connell. adv.: $9.70/SAU. photos; pub. size: tabloid; circ. 21,495(free).

US
UPPER ARLINGTON NEWS. 1933. Wed. $.25 newsstand; $20/yr. in cy.; $25/yr. out of cy. 5257 Sinclair Rd., Columbus, OH 43229. TEL 614-785-1212; FAX 614-842-4760. **Owner(s):** Suburban News Publications, 5257 Sinclair Rd., Columbus, OH 43229. TEL 614-785-1212; Ed. Joe Meyer; Pub. James Toms; adv. contact: Carol Zimmer. pub. size: tabloid; circ. 17,000(paid).

US
WHITEHALL NEWS. 1986. Wed. $.25 newsstand; $20/yr. in cy.; $25/yr. out of cy. 5257 Sinclair Rd., Columbus, OH 43229. TEL 614-785-1212; FAX 614-842-4760. **Owner(s):** Suburban News Publications, 5257 Sinclair Rd., Columbus, OH 43229. TEL 614-785-1212; FAX 614-842-4760; Ed. Joe Meyer; Pub. James Toms; adv. contact: Carol Zimmer. photos; pub. size: tabloid; circ. 10,237(free).

US
WORTHINGTON SUBURBIA NEWS. 1926. Wed. $.40 newsstand; $20/yr. in cy.; $25/yr. out of cy. 5257 Sinclair Rd., Columbus, OH 43229. TEL 614-785-1212; FAX 614-842-4760. **Owner(s):** Suburban News Publications, 5257 Sinclair Rd., Columbus, OH 43229. TEL 614-785-1212; FAX 614-842-4760; Ed. Joe Meyer; Pub. James Toms; adv. contact: Ron Boyd. photos; pub. size: tabloid; circ. 18,425(paid).

COLUMBUS GROVE

US
PUTNAM COUNTY VIDETTE. 1873. Wed. $.50 newsstand; $23/yr. in cy.; $25/ yr. in state; $27/yr. elsewhere. 111 E. Sycamore St., Columbus Grove, OH 45830-0127. TEL 419-659-2173; FAX 419-659-2760. **Owner(s):** Hirt Publishing, P.O. Box 352, Bellevue, OH 44811. TEL 419-483-7000; Ed. John R. Marshall. adv. contact: Tatia R. Farthing. photos; pub. size: broadsheet; circ. 2,000(paid).

WEEKLY NEWSPAPERS

CONNEAUT
US

COURIER, THE. 1992. Wed. $.50 newsstand; $20/yr.; $30/yr. out of town. 218 Washington St., Conneaut, OH 44030. TEL 216-593-6030; FAX 216-593-6061. **Owner(s):** Gazette Printing Co., Inc., P.O. Box 166, Jefferson, OH 44047. TEL 216-576-9115; FAX 216-576-2735; Ed. Patrick Williams; Pub. John Lampson; adv. contact: Bill Creed. pub. size: tabloid; circ. 1,650(paid).

COVINGTON
US

PENNY SAVER. Mon. $.25 newsstand; $14/yr. mailed. 395 S. High St., Covington, OH 45318. TEL 513-473-2028; FAX 513-473-3299. **Owner(s):** Covington Arens Corp., P.O. Box 69, Covington, OH 45318; Ed. Carol Wood; Pub. Gary L. Godfrey; pub. size: tabloid; circ. 10,700(paid).

US

STILLWATER VALLEY ADVERTISER. 1954. Wed. $.25 newsstand; $13/yr. mailed. 395 S. High St., Covington, OH 45318. TEL 513-473-2028; FAX 513-473-3299. **Owner(s):** Covington Arens Corp., P.O. Box 69, Covington, OH 45318. TEL 513-473-2028; Ed. Jean Devlin; Pub. Gary L. Godfrey; adv.; pub. size: tabloid; circ. 10,500(paid).

CRESTLINE
US

CRESTLINE ADVOCATE. 1869. Wed. $.50 newsstand; $25/yr. 312 N. Seltzer St., Crestline, OH 44827-0226. TEL 419-683-3355. **Owner(s):** Brouwer-Marken, Inc., 312 N. Seltzer St., Crestline, OH 44827-0226. TEL 419-683-3355; Ed. Joseph J. Petti. adv.; photos; pub. size: standard; circ. 2,300(paid).

DALTON
US

DALTON GAZETTE & KIDRON NEWS. 1875. w. $.35 newsstand; $14.50/yr. in cy.; $15/yr. in state; $15.50/yr. out of state. P.O. Box 495, Dalton, OH 44618-0495. TEL 330-828-8401. **Owner(s):** Francis Woodruff, P.O. Box 495, Dalton, OH 44618-0495. TEL 330-828-8401; Pub. Francis Woodruff; adv.; photos; pub. size: tabloid; circ. 1,300(paid).

DAYTON
US

HUBER HEIGHTS COURIER. 1960. Wed. $.50/newsstand; $24/yr. local; $26/yr. in cy. mailed; $31/yr. out of cy. mailed. 7089 Taylorsville Rd., Dayton, OH 45424. TEL 937-236-4990; FAX 937-236-4176. **Owner(s):** Bowling-Mooreman Publications, Inc., 1455 W. Main St., Tipp City, OH 45371. TEL 513-667-2214; Ed. Chuck Vosskuehler; Pub. Vernon T. Bowling; adv.; photos; pub. size: broadsheet; circ. 12,000(controlled & free).

DELTA
US

DELTA ATLAS. 1882. Tue. $.40 newsstand; $14/yr.; $13/yr. senior citizens. 212 Main St., Delta, OH 43515. TEL 419-822-3231. **Owner(s):** Thomas W. Mack, 212 Main St., Delta, OH 43515. TEL 419-822-3231; Ed. Thomas W. Mack. adv. contact: Larry Favorite. pub. size: broadsheet; circ. 2,000(paid).

EATON
US

REGISTER-HERALD. 1820. Wed. $.50 newsstand; $26/yr. in cy.; $33/yr. out of cy.; $37/yr. out of state. 542 N. Barron, Eaton, OH 45320. TEL 513-456-5553; FAX 513-456-3558. **Owner(s):** Brown Publishing Co., P.O. Box 555, Urbana, OH 43078. TEL 513-652-2100; Ed. Deron Newman; Pub. James R. Hardin; adv. contact: Nona J. Wigger. pub. size: broadsheet; circ. 6,800(paid).

FAIRFIELD
US

FAIRFIELD ECHO. 1956. Wed. free. 5120 Dixie Hwy., Fairfield, OH 45014. TEL 513-829-7900; FAX 513-829-7950. **Owner(s):** Thomson Newspapers, Inc., One Thorn Run Ctr., Ste. 500, 1187 Thorn Run Rd. Ext., Coraopolis, PA 15108. TEL 412-262-7870; Ed. Emily York; Pub. Bob Murphy; photos; bk.rev.; pub. size: broadsheet; circ. 19,000(free).
Formerly: Fairfield Echo/Journal-News.

FAYETTE
US ISSN 1065-0083

FAYETTE REVIEW, THE. 1901. w. $17.50-$19.50/yr. P.O. Box 219, Fayette, OH 43521-0219. TEL 419-237-2591. **Owner(s):** Cynthia L. Potter, P.O. Box 219, Fayette, OH 43521-0219. TEL 419-237-2591; Ed. Cynthia L. Potter; Pub. Yvonne Potter; adv.; circ. 1,300(paid).

FRANKLIN
US

FRANKLIN CHRONICLE. 1875. Tue. $.35 newsstand; $15.60/yr. in cy.; $17.60/yr. out of cy. 42 E. Fourth St., Franklin, OH 45005. TEL 513-746-3691; FAX 513-746-6013. **Owner(s):** Thomson Newspapers, Inc., One Thorn Run Ctr., Ste. 500, 1187 Thorn Run Rd. Ext., Coraopolis, PA 15108. TEL 412-262-7870; Ed. Dan Darragh. adv. contact: Barb Stapies. pub. size: standard; circ. 13,500(free & paid).

GAHANNA
US

ROCKY FORK ENTERPRISE. 1931. Thu. free home deliv.; $.50 newsstand; $75/yr. mailed. 110 N. High St., Gahanna, OH 43230. TEL 614-471-1600; FAX 614-471-1764. **Owner(s):** This Week Newspapers, 670 Lakeview Plz. Blvd., Ste. F, Worthington, OH 43085; Ed. Gaylon Vickers. pub. size: broadsheet; circ. 12,908(paid).
Formerly: Gahanna Village Post.

GRANVILLE
US

COMMUNITY BOOSTER, THE. 1949. Mon. free newsstand; $23/yr. in cy.; $25/yr. out of cy. 110 E. Elm St., Granville, OH 43023. TEL 614-587-3397; FAX 614-587-3398. **Owner(s):** Thomson Newspapers, 65 Queen St., Toronto, ON M5H 2M2, Canada; Ed. Chuck Peterson. adv.; photos; bk.rev.; pub. size: tabloid; circ. 10,000(controlled & free).
Formerly: Granville Booster, The.

US

GRANVILLE SENTINEL, THE. 1970. Thu. $.50 newsstand; $23/yr. in cy.; $28 out of cy. 110 E. Elm St., Granville, OH 43023. TEL 614-587-3397; FAX 614-587-3398. **Owner(s):** Thomson Newspapers, One Thorn Run Ctr., Ste. 500, 1187 Thorn Run Rd. Ext., Coraopolis, PA 15108. TEL 412-262-7870; Ed. Chuck Peterson. adv.; photos; bk.rev.; pub. size: tabloid; circ. 2,000(paid).

GREENVILLE
US

DARKE COUNTY EARLY BIRD, THE. 1968. Sun. free; $.50 newsstand. 5312 Sebring-Warner Rd., Greenville, OH 45331. TEL 937-548-3330; FAX 937-548-3376; E-mail: clball@bright.net. **Owner(s):** John F. & Carol L. Ball, 5312 Sebring-Warner Rd., Greenville, OH 45331. TEL 937-548-3330; FAX 937-548-3376; Ed. Norma Jenkins; Pub. Carol L. Ball; adv.: $14/SAU. photos; pub. size: broadsheet; circ. 26,677(free).

HARTVILLE
US

HARTVILLE NEWS. 1930. Wed. $.50 newsstand; $22/yr. in area; $24/yr. elsewhere. 316 E. Maple St., Hartville, OH 44632-0428. TEL 330-877-9345; FAX 330-877-1364. **Owner(s):** Knowles Press, Inc., The, 316 E. Maple St., Hartville, OH 44632-0428. TEL 330-877-9345; FAX 330-877-1364; Ed. Rosalee Haines. adv.; pub. size: tabloid; circ. 3,000(paid).

HEATH
US

ACE NEWS, THE. 1963. Thu. $.30 newsstand; $14/yr. in cy.; $20/yr. out of cy. 619 Industrial Pkwy., Heath, OH 43056. TEL 614-522-8566. **Owner(s):** Boeckman Communications, 409 S. 22nd St., Heath, OH 43056. TEL 614-522-8566; Ed. Elaine Landis; Pub. Ron Boeckman; pub. size: tabloid; circ. 5,000(paid).

HILLIARD
US

HILLIARD NORTHWEST NEWS. Wed. $.40 newsstand; $1/mo. out of area. 5314 Center St., Hilliard, OH 43026. TEL 614-785-1212; FAX 614-785-1881. **Owner(s):** Suburban News Publications, 5257 Sinclair Rd., Columbus, OH 43229. TEL 614-451-1212; Ed. Martin Rozenman; Pub. Jim Toms; adv. contact: Carol Zimmer. pub. size: tabloid; circ. 15,800(free & paid).

JACKSON
US

JACKSON-VINTON JOURNAL-HERALD. 1847. 3/wk.: Wed., Fri., Sun. $.50 newsstand; $51.75/yr. home deliv.; $67.38/yr. mailed; $49.16/yr. senior citizens. 295 Broadway St., Jackson, OH 45640. TEL 614-286-2187; FAX 614-286-5854. **Owner(s):** Mid-South Management Co., Inc., 314 Pine St., P.O. Box 1634, Spartanburg, SC 29304. TEL 614-286-2187; Ed. Bob Farley; Pub. P. Dale Gardner, Jr.; adv. contact: Jeanne Gillum. adv.: $8.50/SAU display; $5.19/SAU classified. pub. size: broadsheet; circ. 7,100(paid); Sun. 16,000(paid).
Formerly: Jackson Journal Herald; Vinton County Courier & Wellston Sentry.

JEFFERSON, OH

WEEKLY NEWSPAPERS

JEFFERSON

US
GAZETTE, THE. 1876. Wed. $.50 newsstand; $20/yr. local; $30/yr. out of state. 46 W. Jefferson St., Jefferson, OH 44047-0166. TEL 216-576-9115; FAX 216-576-2735. **Owner(s):** Gazette Printing Co., Inc., P.O. Box 166, Jefferson, OH 44047-0166. TEL 216-576-9115; FAX 216-576-2735; Ed. Lucille Donley; Pub. John Lampson; pub. size: broadsheet; circ. 3,058(paid).

US
SENTINEL, THE. 1968. Fri. $.25 newsstand; $15/yr. mailed. 46 W. Jefferson St., Jefferson, OH 44047-0166. TEL 216-576-9115; FAX 216-576-2735. **Owner(s):** Gazette Printing Co., Inc., 46 W. Jefferson St., P.O. Box 166, Jefferson, OH 44047-0166. TEL 216-576-9115; FAX 216-576-2735; Ed. Chuck Altonen; Pub. John Lampson; adv.; pub. size: broadsheet; circ. 2,500(free & paid).

US
VALLEY NEWS, THE. 1895. Wed. $.50 newsstand; $20/yr. P.O. Box 166, Jefferson, OH 44047. TEL 800-860-2775; FAX 216-437-6532. **Owner(s):** Gazette Printing Co., Inc., P.O. Box 166, Jefferson, OH 44047-0166. TEL 216-576-9115; FAX 216-576-2734; Ed. Sean Linhart; Pub. John Lampson; pub. size: tabloid; circ. 1,227(free & paid).

KETTERING

US ISSN 1049-8117
CENTERVILLE-BELLBROOK TIMES. 1984. s-w.: Wed. & Sat. free Wed. newsstand; $.50/Sat.; $26/yr. 3085 Woodman Dr., Ste. 170, Kettering, OH 45420. TEL 513-294-7000; FAX 513-294-2981. **Owner(s):** Amos Press, Inc., 3085 Woodman Dr., Kettering, OH 45420. TEL 513-294-7000; FAX 513-294-6981; Ed. Mark Kellam; Pub. Mark Raymond; adv. contact: John Carnahan. pub. size: broadsheet; circ. 20,000(free & paid).

US ISSN 8750-8141
KETTERING-OAKWOOD TIMES. 1956. s-w.: Wed. & Sat. $.50 newsstand; $32/yr. 3085 Woodman Dr., Ste. 170, Kettering, OH 45420. TEL 513-294-7000; FAX 513-294-2981. **Owner(s):** Amos Press, Inc., 3085 Woodman Dr., Ste. 170, Kettering, OH 45420. TEL 513-294-7000; Ed. Nick Blizzard; Pub. Mark Raymond; adv. contact: John Carnahan. pub. size: broadsheet; circ. 6,000(paid).

LEBANON

US
WESTERN STAR. 1807. Wed. $.75 newsstand; $39/yr. local carrier; $46/yr. in state mailed; $58/yr. out of state mailed. 200 Harmon Ave., Lebanon, OH 45036. TEL 513-932-3010; FAX 513-932-6056. **Owner(s):** Brown Publishing Co., P.O. Box 555, Urbana, OH 43078. TEL 513-652-2100; Ed. Fred Gibson; Pub. Fred Gibson; adv.; photos; bk.rev.; pub. size: broadsheet; circ. 8,926(paid).

LIBERTY CENTER

US
LIBERTY PRESS, THE. 1882. w.: Thu. $.40 newsstand; $17/yr. 107-1 East St., Liberty Center, OH 43532-0006. TEL 419-533-2401. **Owner(s):** Donald & Susan Mickens, 107-1 East St., Liberty Corner, OH 43532-0006. TEL 419-533-2401; Pub. Donald Mickens; adv.; pub. size: broadsheet; circ. 1,300(paid).

LOGAN

US
HOCKING VALLEY ADVERTISER. 1984. Sun. free. 53 W. Main St., Logan, OH 43138. TEL 614-385-1969; FAX 614-385-8758; E-mail: hva@hockinghills.net. **Owner(s):** Add, Inc., 600 Industrial Dr., P.O. Box 609, Waupaca, WI 54981. TEL 715-258-8450; adv.; photos; pub. size: tabloid; circ. 9,800(free).

LONDON

US
PRESS REVIEW. Mon. free to non-subscribers. 30 S. Oak St., London, OH 43140. TEL 614-852-1616; FAX 614-852-1620. **Owner(s):** Central Ohio Printing Corp., P.O. Box 390, London, OH 43140. TEL 614-852-1616; Ed. Bill MCullick; Pub. Donald L. Hartley; adv.; pub. size: standard; circ. 10,000.

LOUDONVILLE

US
LOUDONVILLE TIMES, THE. 1873. Tue. $.50 newsstand; $20/yr. in cy.; $21/yr. in state; $25/yr. out of state. 225 W. Main St., Loudonville, OH 44842. TEL 419-994-5049; FAX 419-994-5826. **Owner(s):** Ashland Publishing Co., 225 W. Main St., Loudonville, OH 44842. TEL 419-994-5049; FAX 419-994-5826; Ed. Jim Brewer. adv.; photos; bk.rev.; pub. size: broadsheet; circ. 2,300(paid).

LOUISVILLE

US
LOUISVILLE HERALD, THE. 1887. Thu. $.50 newsstand; $20/yr. in cy. 308 S. Mill St., Louisville, OH 44641-0170. TEL 330-875-5610; FAX 330-875-4475. **Owner(s):** Paul M. & Shirley J. Clapper, P.O. Box 170, Louisville, OH 44641-0170. TEL 330-875-5610; FAX 330-875-4475; Ed. Frank H. Clapper; Pub. Paul M. Clapper; adv. contact: Shirley J. Clapper. adv.: $4.13/SAU. photos; pub. size: broadsheet; circ. 3,201(paid).

LOVELAND

US ISSN 1066-7458
BETHEL JOURNAL, THE. 1899. Thu. $.30 newsstand; $15/yr. mailed. 394 Wards Corner Rd., Ste. 170, Loveland, OH 45140-8300. TEL 513-734-4017; FAX 513-753-1117. **Owner(s):** Press Community Newspapers, 4910 Para Dr., Cincinnati, OH 45237. TEL 513-242-4300; adv.; photos; pub. size: broadsheet; circ. 1,750(free & paid).
Formerly: Bethel Journal-Press, The.

US
COMMUNITY JOURNAL, SOUTH. 1970. Wed. $.50 newsstand; $2/4 wks.; $105/yr. mailed. 394 Wards Corner Rd, Ste. 170, Loveland, OH 45140-6300. TEL 513-248-8600; FAX 513-248-1938. **Owner(s):** Community Press, 4910 Para Dr., Cincinnati, OH 45237. TEL 513-242-4300; Ed. Gary L. Presley. adv. contact: Steve Means. photos; pub. size: broadsheet; circ. 26,141(free & paid).
Formerly: Community Journal-Press.

US
COMMUNITY PRESS, MASON. 1988. Wed. $.50 newsstand; $2/4 wks.; $105/yr. mailed. 394 Wards Corner Rd., Loveland, OH 45140-8300. TEL 513-248-8600; FAX 513-248-1938. **Owner(s):** Community Press, 4910 Para Dr., Cincinnati, OH 45237. TEL 513-242-4300; Ed. Gary L. Presley. adv. contact: Steve Means. photos; pub. size: broadsheet; circ. 8,000(free).
Formerly: Community Press.

US
EASTERN HILLS JOURNAL. 1935. Wed. $.50 newsstand; $2/4 wks.; $105/yr. mailed. 394 Wards Corner Rd., Loveland, OH 45140-8300. TEL 513-248-8600; FAX 513-248-1938. **Owner(s):** Community Press, 4910 Para Dr., Cincinnati, OH 45237. TEL 513-242-4300; Ed. Gary L. Presley. adv. contact: Steve Means. photos; pub. size: broadsheet; circ. 14,400(paid).

US
FOREST HILLS JOURNAL. 1961. Wed. $2/4 wks.; $104/yr. mailed. 394 Wards Corner Rd., Ste. 170, Loveland, OH 45140-8300. TEL 513-248-8600; FAX 513-248-1938; E-mail: localmail@aol.com. **Owner(s):** Press Community Newspapers, 4910 Para Dr., Cincinnati, OH 45237. TEL 513-242-4300; Ed. Gary Presley; Pub. Thomas E. Niehaus; adv.; pub. size: broadsheet; circ. 16,600(paid).
Formerly: Forest Hills Journal-Press.

US ISSN 0745-2756
LOVELAND HERALD PRESS. 1916. Wed. $.50 newsstand; $2/4 wks. voluntary pay; $105/yr. mailed. 394 Wards Corner Rd., Ste. 170, Loveland, OH 45140-8300. TEL 513-248-8600; FAX 513-248-1938. **Owner(s):** Suburban Communications Corp., 36251 Schoolcraft Rd., Livonia, MI 48150. TEL 313-591-2300; Ed. Gary Presley; Pub. Thomas E. Niehaus; pub. size: broadsheet; circ. 4,942.
Formerly: Loveland Herald.

US ISSN 0745-2764
MILFORD ADVERTISER. 1951. Wed. $.50 newsstand; $2/4 wks.; $105/yr. mailed. 394 Wards Corner Rd., Ste. 170, Loveland, OH 45140-6300. TEL 513-753-1111; FAX 513-753-1117. **Owner(s):** Suburban Communications Corp., 36251 Schoolcraft Rd., Livonia, MI 48150. TEL 313-591-2300; Pub. Thomas E. Niehaus; adv.; pub. size: broadsheet; circ. 8,900(paid).
Formerly: Milford Advertiser-Press.

US
NORTH CLERMONT COMMUNITY JOURNAL. 1970. Wed. $2/4 wks.; $104/yr. mailed. 394 Wards Corner Rd., Ste. 170, Loveland, OH 45140-8300. TEL 513-753-1111; FAX 513-753-1117. **Owner(s):** Press Community Newspapers, 4910 Para Dr., Cincinnati, OH 45237. TEL 513-242-4300; Ed. Gary Presley; Pub. Thomas E. Niehaus; adv.; pub. size: broadsheet; circ. 6,800(paid).
Formerly: Community Journal Press, North.

WEEKLY NEWSPAPERS

NEWARK, OH 10705

US
NORTHEAST SUBURBAN LIFE PRESS. 1963. Wed. $.50 newsstand; $2/4 wks.; $105/yr. mailed. 394 Wards Corner Rd., Ste. 170, Loveland, OH 45140. TEL 513-248-8600; FAX 513-248-1938. **Owner(s):** Community Press, 4910 Para Dr., Cincinnati, OH 45237. TEL 513-242-4300; Ed. Gary L. Presley. adv. contact: Steve Means. photos; pub. size: broadsheet; circ. 8,900(paid).

US
SUBURBAN LIFE. 1961. Wed. $.50 newsstand; $2/4 wks. voluntary pay; $105/yr. mailed. 394 Wards Corner Rd., Loveland, OH 45140-8300. TEL 513-248-8600; FAX 513-248-1938. **Owner(s):** Community Press, 4910 Para Dr., Cincinnati, OH 45237. TEL 313-242-4300; Ed. Gary L. Presley. adv. contact: Steve Means. photos; pub. size: broadsheet; circ. 11,200(free & paid).

MANCHESTER

US
MANCHESTER SIGNAL. 1883. Thu. $.35 newsstand; $11/yr. in cy.; $14/yr. out of cy. 414 E. Seventh St., Manchester, OH 45144-1402. TEL 937-549-2800; FAX 937-549-3611. **Owner(s):** Wm. G. Woolard, Jr., 414 E. Seventh St., Manchester, OH 45144. TEL 513-549-2800; Ed. William G. Woolard, Jr.; Pub. William G. Woolard, Jr.; adv. contact: Nicolle Politt. photos; bk.rev.; pub. size: broadsheet; circ. 5,100(paid).

MASON

US
PULSE-JOURNAL. 1976. Wed. free home deliv.; $.50 newsstand; voluntary pay. 1074 Reading Rd., Mason, OH 45040. TEL 513-398-8856; FAX 513-459-7965. **Owner(s):** Thomson Newspapers, Inc., Metro Centre, One Station Pl., 6th Fl., Stamford, CT 06902. TEL 203-425-2500; FAX 203-425-2516; Ed. Mary Hitt; Pub. Rhonda L. Ford; adv.; photos; pub. size: broadsheet; circ. 25,000(free & paid).

MCCONNELSVILLE

US
MORGAN COUNTY HERALD. 1844. Wed. $.75 newsstand; $30/yr. 89 W. Main St., McConnelsville, OH 43756-0268. TEL 614-962-3377; FAX 614-962-6861. **Owner(s):** Morgan County Publishing Co., 89 W. Main St., P.O. Box 268, McConnellsville, OH 43756. TEL 614-962-3377; FAX 614-962-6861; Ed. Don Keller. pub. size: broadsheet; circ. 5,100(free & paid).

MEDINA

US ISSN 0894-1645
BRUNSWICK SUN TIMES. 1972. Thu. $.60 newsstand; $32.50/yr. 2795 Medina Rd., Medina, OH 44256-4887. TEL 216-524-0830; FAX 216-524-7792. **Owner(s):** Sun Media, Inc., 5510 Cloverleaf Pkwy., Cleveland, OH 44125-4887. TEL 216-524-0830; FAX 216-642-5547; Ed. Glenn Wojciak. adv.: $12.70/SAU. photos; bk.rev.; pub. size: broadsheet; circ. 5,990(paid).

US
▼**MEDINA SUN, THE.** 1995. Thu. $.60 newsstand; $32.50/yr. 2795 Medina Rd., Medina, OH 44256-4887. TEL 216-524-0830; FAX 216-524-7792. **Owner(s):** Sun Media, Inc., 5510 Cloverleaf Pkwy., Cleveland, OH 44125. TEL 216-524-0830; Ed. Glenn Wojciak. adv.: $10.10/SAU. photos; bk.rev.; pub. size: broadsheet; circ. 12,025(paid).

US
SUN BANNER PRIDE. 1865. Thu. $.60 newsstand; $32.50/yr. 2795 Medina Rd., Medina, OH 44256-4887. TEL 216-524-0830; FAX 216-524-7792. **Owner(s):** Sun Media, Inc., 5510 Cloverleaf Pkwy., Cleveland, OH 44125-4887. TEL 216-524-0830; FAX 216-642-5547; Ed. Charles Aukerman. adv.: $11.65/SAU. photos; bk.rev.; pub. size: broadsheet; circ. 4,463(paid).

MIAMISBURG

US
MIAMISBURG NEWS. 1880. Wed. $.50 newsstand; $26/yr. in cy. 230 S. Second St., Miamisburg, OH 45342. TEL 937-866-3331; FAX 937-652-2448. **Owner(s):** Brown Publishing Co., P.O. Box 555, Urbana, OH 43078. TEL 513-652-2100; Ed. Jim Pickering; Pub. Kimm Mote; adv. contact: Ruemel Lambke. photos; pub. size: broadsheet; circ. 7,000(paid). **Wire Service(s):** CNS.

MILLBURY

US
METRO PRESS. 1971. Mon. $.50 newsstand; $20/yr. 1550 Woodville Rd., Millbury, OH 43447. TEL 419-836-2221; FAX 419-836-1319. **Owner(s):** Photojournal, Inc., 620 Warren, Sandusky, OH 44870. TEL 419-625-5825; Ed. John Szozda. pub. size: tabloid; circ. 19,676(paid).

US
PRESS, THE. 1971. Mon. free in area; $.50 newsstand; $24/yr. out of state. 1550 Woodville Rd., Millbury, OH 43447. TEL 419-836-2221; FAX 419-836-1319. **Owner(s):** Douthit Communications, Inc., 620 Warren, Sandusky, OH 44870. TEL 419-625-5825; Ed. John Szozda. pub. size: tabloid; circ. 36,313(free).

MILLERSBURG

US
HOLMES COUNTY HUB. 1825. Thu. $.75 newsstand; $28/yr. in area; $33/yr. out of area. 25 N. Clay St., Millersburg, OH 44654. TEL 216-674-5676; FAX 216-674-3780. **Owner(s):** Wooster Republican Printing Co., 212 E. Liberty St., Wooster, OH 44691. TEL 216-264-1811; Ed. Jeanine Kendle; Pub. R. Victor Dix; adv. contact: Jeff Massaro. photos; pub. size: broadsheet; circ. 4,800(paid).

MINERVA

US
MALVERN COMMUNITY NEWS. 1920. Thu. $.50 newsstand; $21/yr. in state; $33/yr. out of state. 177 Curry St., Minerva, OH 44657-0527. TEL 330-868-3408; FAX 330-868-3273. **Owner(s):** Alliance Publishing Co., P.O. Box 2180, Alliance, OH 44601. TEL 330-821-1200; FAX 330-821-8258; Ed. Sarah Reed. adv. contact: Lynn Brumbaugh. pub. size: broadsheet; circ. 1,100(paid).

US ISSN 1078-0858
MINERVA LEADER. 1937. Thu. $.50 newsstand; $21/yr. in state; $33/yr. out of state. 177 Curry St., Minerva, OH 44657-0030. TEL 330-868-5164; FAX 330-868-5164. **Owner(s):** Dix Communications Group, 210 E. Liberty St., Wooster, OH 44691; Ed. Sarah Reed; Pub. G. Charles Dix, II; adv. contact: Lynn Brumbaugh. pub. size: broadsheet; circ. 4,000(paid).

US
PRESS-NEWS, THE. 1897. Thu. $.50 newsstand; $21/yr. in state; $33/yr. out of state. 177 Curry St., Minerva, OH 44657-0777. TEL 330-868-5164; FAX 330-868-3273. **Owner(s):** Alliance Publishing Co., P.O.Box 2180, Alliance, OH 44601. TEL 330-821-1200; FAX 330-821-8258; Ed. Karen Mundy; Pub. Chuck Dix; adv. contact: Linda Stark. pub. size: standard; circ. 3,000(paid).

MONTPELIER

US
LEADER ENTERPRISE. 1880. Wed. $.50 newsstand; $17.50/yr. in cy.; $20.50/yr. out of cy. 319 W. Main, Montpelier, OH 43543. TEL 419-485-3113; FAX 419-485-3114. **Owner(s):** Bryan Publishing Co., The, Walnut St., Bryan, OH 43506. TEL 419-636-1111; Ed. David Belden. adv.; photos; pub. size: standard; circ. 2,000(paid).

MT. GILEAD

US
MORROW COUNTY ADVERTISER. s-w.: Wed. & Sun. free newsstand & home deliv. 255 Neal Ave., Mt. Gilead, OH 43338. TEL 419-946-3010; FAX 419-947-7241. **Owner(s):** Hirt Publishing, P.O. Box 352, Bellevue, OH 44811. TEL 419-483-7000; Ed. Al Gress; Pub. William Kreeger; adv. contact: Nancy Daehnke. pub. size: tabloid; circ. 17,831(free).

US
MORROW COUNTY SENTINEL. 1848. Wed. $1 newsstand; $32/yr. in cy.; $34/yr. out of cy.; $36/yr. out of state. 255 Neal Ave., Mt. Gilead, OH 43338. TEL 419-946-3010; FAX 419-947-7241. **Owner(s):** Hirt Publishing, P.O. Box 352, Bellevue, OH 44811. TEL 419-483-7000; Pub. William Kreeger; adv. contact: Nancy Daehnke. photos; pub. size: broadsheet; circ. 4,100(paid).

MT. ORAB

US
BROWN COUNTY PRESS. 1973. Mon. $.25 newsstand; free. 106 N. High St., Mt. Orab, OH 45154. TEL 513-444-3441; FAX 513-444-2652. **Owner(s):** Batavia Buying Guide, The, 465 E. Main St., Batavia, OH 45103. TEL 513-444-3441; FAX 513-444-2652; Ed. Eunice Ott. adv.; photos; pub. size: broadsheet; circ. 14,350(free & paid).

NEWARK

US
NEWARK/LICKING ADVERTISER. 1978. Sat. free. 195 Union St., Newark, OH 43055. TEL 614-522-2502; FAX 614-522-2498. **Owner(s):** Add, Inc., 600 Industrial Dr., Waupaca, WI 54981. TEL 715-258-8450; Ed. Roman Dymerski. adv.; pub. size: tabloid; circ. 279,147(free).

NEW CARLISLE

US

NEW CARLISLE SUN. 1882. Wed. $.50 newsstand; $26/yr. in cy.; $31/yr. out of cy. 225 S. Main St., New Carlisle, OH 45344. TEL 513-845-3861; FAX 513-845-3577. **Owner(s):** Bowling-Mooreman Publications, Inc., 1455 W. Main St., Tipp City, OH 45371. TEL 513-667-8512; Ed. Elaine Bouret; Pub. David Copen; pub. size: broadsheet; circ. 4,800(free & paid).

NEWCOMERSTOWN

US

NEWCOMERSTOWN NEWS. 1898. Wed. $.50 newsstand; $20/yr. in state; $30/yr. out of state. 140 Main St., Newcomerstown, OH 43832-0030. TEL 614-498-7117; FAX 614-498-5624. **Owner(s):** Wooster Republican Printing Co., Wooster, OH 44691; Ed. R.H. Booth. adv.; photos; bk.rev.; pub. size: broadsheet; circ. 3,700(paid).

NEW LEXINGTON

US

PERRY COUNTY TRIBUNE. 1940. Wed. $1 newsstand; $31/yr. in area; $35/yr. out of area. 399 Lincoln Park Dr., New Lexington, OH 43764. TEL 614-342-4121; FAX 614-342-4131. **Owner(s):** Hirt Publishing, P.O. Box 352, Bellevue, OH 44811. TEL 419-483-7000; Ed. Deb Hutmire. adv. contact: David Schubert. pub. size: broadsheet; circ. 4,150(paid).

US

TRIBUNE SHOPPING NEWS. Sun. free. 399 Lincoln Pk. Dr., Ste. A, New Lexington, OH 43764. TEL 614-342-4121; FAX 614-342-4131. **Owner(s):** Hirt Publishing, P.O. Box 352, Bellevue, OH 44811. TEL 419-483-7000; Ed. Deb Hutmire; Pub. Gary Hirt; adv. contact: David Schubert. circ. 4,000(free).

NORTH CANTON

US

SUN JOURNAL, THE. 1922. Wed. $.50 newsstand; $15.99/yr. 7215 Whipple Ave., N.W., North Canton, OH 44720. TEL 330-966-1121; FAX 330-966-1202. **Owner(s):** Suarez Corp., 7215 Whipple Ave., N.W., North Canton, OH 44720. TEL 216-966-1121; FAX 216-966-1202; Ed. Robert Cillela; Pub. Mike McNulty; adv.; pub. size: broadsheet; circ. 10,000(paid).
Formerly: The Sun.

NORTH OLMSTED

US

LAKEWOOD SUN POST. 1918. Thu. $.60 newsstand; $32.50/yr. 28895 Lorain Rd., North Olmsted, OH 44070. TEL 216-777-3800; FAX 216-524-7792. **Owner(s):** Sun Media, Inc., 5510 Cloverleaf Pkwy., Cleveland, OH 44125-4887. TEL 216-524-0830; FAX 216-642-5547; Ed. Kevin Burns. adv.: $22/SAU. photos; bk.rev.; pub. size: broadsheet; circ. 11,314(paid).

US

SUN HERALD, THE. 1965. Thu. $.60 newsstand; $32.50/yr. 28895 Lorain Rd., North Olmsted, OH 44070. TEL 216-777-3800. FAX 216-524-7792. **Owner(s):** Sun Media, Inc., 5510 Cloverleaf Pkwy., Cleveland, OH 44125-4887. TEL 216-524-0830; FAX 216-642-5547; Ed. Kevin Burns. adv.: $26.15/SAU. photos; pub. size: broadsheet; circ. 16,575(paid).

US

SUN, THE. 1990. Thu. $.60 newsstand; $32.50/yr. 28895 Lorain Rd., North Olmsted, OH 44070-4887. TEL 216-777-3800; FAX 216-524-7792. **Owner(s):** Sun Media, Inc., 5510 Cloverleaf Pkwy., Cleveland, OH 44125-4887. TEL 216-524-0830; FAX 216-642-5547; adv.: $10.35/SAU. photos; bk.rev.; pub. size: broadsheet; circ. 6,824(paid).

US

WEST SIDE SUN NEWS. 1918. Thu. $.60 newsstand; $32.50/yr. 28895 Lorain Rd., North Olmsted, OH 44122. TEL 216-777-3800; FAX 216-524-7792. **Owner(s):** Sun Media, Inc., 5510 Cloverleaf Pkwy., Cleveland, OH 44125-4887. TEL 216-524-0830; FAX 216-642-5547; adv.: $20.80/SAU. photos; pub. size: broadsheet; circ. 17,339(paid).

OAK HARBOR

US   ISSN 1059-9045

OTTAWA COUNTY EXPONENT, THE. 1871. Wed. $15/yr. in town; $22/yr. in state; $25/yr. out of state. 264 W. Water St., Oak Harbor, OH 43449. TEL 419-898-5361; FAX 419-898-0501; E-mail: wwayned@aol.com. **Owner(s):** Catherine M. Freed, P.O. Box 70, Oak Harbor, OH 43449. TEL 419-898-5361; FAX 419-848-0501; Ed. Wayne Dreier; Pub. Catherine M. Freed; adv.; photos; bk.rev.; pub. size: broadsheet; circ. 2,700(paid).
Formerly: Exponent, The.

ONTARIO

US

TRIBUNE-COURIER. 1961. Thu. $.35 newsstand; $12/yr. local; $20/yr. elsewhere. 347 Allen Dr., Ontario, OH 44862-0127. TEL 419-529-2847. E-mail: huminbrd96@aol.com. **Owner(s):** Frank & Betty Stumbo, 347 Allen Dr., Ontario, OH 44862-0127. TEL 419-529-2847; Ed. John J. Kirschenheiter; Pub. Frank A. Stumbo; adv. contact: Betty Stumbo. photos; bk.rev.; pub. size: broadsheet; circ. 2,600(paid).

OTTAWA

US

PUTNAM COUNTY SENTINEL. 1855. Wed. $1 newsstand; $35/yr. mailed. 232 E. Main St., Ottawa, OH 45875. TEL 419-523-5709; FAX 419-523-3512. **Owner(s):** Hirt Publishing, P.O. Box 352, Bellevue, OH 44811. TEL 419-483-7000; Ed. Amy Sealts. adv.; pub. size: broadsheet; circ. 7,600(paid).

OXFORD

US

OXFORD PRESS. 1932. Thu. $.50 newsstand; $20/yr. local. 15 S. Beech St., Oxford, OH 45056. TEL 513-523-4139; FAX 513-523-1935; E-mail: pub@oxfordpress.com. **Owner(s):** Thomson Newspapers, Inc., Metro Centre, One Station Pl., 6th Fl., Stamford, CT 06902. TEL 203-425-2500; FAX 203-425-2516; Ed. Robert A. Ratterman; Pub. William Cusack; adv.: $6.81/SAU. photos; pub. size: broadsheet; circ. 4,000(paid).

PATASKALA

US

PATASKALA STANDARD. 1886. Wed. $.50 newsstand; $18/yr. in state; $20/yr. out of state. 350 S. Main St., Pataskala, OH 43062-0007. TEL 614-927-2991; FAX 614-927-2930. **Owner(s):** Thomson Newspapers, Inc., Metro Centre, One Station Pl., 6th Fl., Stamford, CT 06902. TEL 203-425-2500; Ed. Sheila Reiser; Pub. Mark Richmond; adv.; photos; pub. size: standard; circ. 4,800(paid).

PAULDING

US

PAULDING PROGRESS. 1945. Wed. $.70 newsstand; $21/yr. in cy.; $26/yr. out of cy. 113 S. Williams St., Paulding, OH 45879. TEL 419-399-4015; FAX 419-399-4030. **Owner(s):** Delphos Newspapers, 405 N. Main St., Delphos, OH 45833. TEL 419-695-0015; Ed. Anna Brewster; Pub. Anna Brewster; pub. size: broadsheet; circ. 4,200(paid).

US

WEEKLY REMINDER. Tue. free. 113 S. Williams St., Paulding, OH 45879. TEL 419-399-4015; FAX 419-399-4030. **Owner(s):** Delphos Newspapers, 405 N. Main St., Delphos, OH 45833. TEL 419-695-0015; Ed. Anna Brewster; Pub. Anna Brewster; adv. contact: Terri Daniels. pub. size: broadsheet; circ. 9,000(free).

PERRYSBURG

US   ISSN 1064-2021

PERRYSBURG MESSENGER-JOURNAL. 1853. Wed. $.50 newsstand; $18/yr. in cy. 117 E. Second St., Perrysburg, OH 43551. TEL 419-874-2528. E-mail: welch@perrysburg.com; URL: http://www.perrysburg.com. **Owner(s):** Welch Publishing Co., P.O. Box 267, Perrysburg, OH 42552. TEL 419-874-2528; Ed. Robert C. Welch; Pub. Robert C. Welch; adv. contact: Matt Welch. photos; bk.rev.; pub. size: broadsheet; circ. 13,000(free & paid).

US

ROSSFORD RECORD-JOURNAL. 1939. Thu. $.50 newsstand; $12/yr. in cy.; $15/yr. out of cy. 117 E. 2nd. St., Perrysburg, OH 43551. TEL 419-874-4491. **Owner(s):** Welch Publishing Co., P.O. Box 267, Perrysburg, OH 43552. TEL 419-874-2528; Ed. Robert C. Welch; Pub. Robert C. Welch; adv.; pub. size: broadsheet; circ. 1,600(paid).

WEEKLY NEWSPAPERS

PORT CLINTON
US

BEACON, THE. 1983. Thu. free in cy.; $28/yr. mailed out of cy. 106 W. Perry St., Port Clinton, OH 43452. TEL 419-732-2154; FAX 419-734-5382. **Owner(s):** John R. Schaffner, P.O. Box 87, Clinton, OH 43452; Pub. John R. Schaffner; pub. size: tabloid; circ. 17,000(free & paid).

ROCKY RIVER
US

LORAIN COUNTY TIMES, THE. 1968. Thu. $.35 newsstand; $29.50/yr. 21010 Center Ridge Rd., Ste. G8, Rocky River, OH 44116. TEL 216-356-0920; FAX 216-356-0515. **Owner(s):** Gottschalk Publishing Co., Inc., 21010 Center Ridge Rd., Ste. G8, Rocky River, OH 44116. TEL 216-356-0920; FAX 216-356-0515; Ed. Aharon Bucholtz; Pub. Eleanor J. Gottschalk; adv. contact: Fred L. Klein. photos; bk.rev.; pub. size: broadsheet; circ. 3,000(free & paid).

US

WESTLAKER TIMES, THE. 1983. Thu. $.35 newsstand; $29.50/yr. 21010 Center Ridge Rd., Ste. G8, Rocky River, OH 44116. TEL 216-356-0920; FAX 216-356-0515. **Owner(s):** Gottschalk Publishing Co., Inc., 21010 Center Ridge Rd., Suite G8, Rocky River, OH 44116. TEL 216-356-0920; FAX 216-356-0515; Ed. Aharon Bucholtz; Pub. Eleanor J. Gottschalk; adv. contact: Fred L. Klein. adv.: $15.44/SAU. photos; bk.rev.; pub. size: broadsheet; circ. 7,000(free & paid). **Wire Service(s):** CNS.
Formerly: Bay Times.

SABINA
US

SABINA ADVERTISER. 1948. Fri. free. 58 N. Howard, Sabina, OH 45169. TEL 513-584-2122; FAX 513-584-2122. **Owner(s):** Gaskins Printing, 58 N. Howard, Sabina, OH 45169. TEL 513-584-2122; FAX 513-584-2122; Ed. Brenda Gaskins May. adv.; photos; pub. size: tabloid; circ. 4,300(free).

SEBRING
US

SEBRING TIMES. Thu. $.35 newsstand. 185 W. Ohio, Sebring, OH 44672. TEL 330-938-2060; FAX 330-821-8218. **Owner(s):** Dix Communications Group, 210 E. Liberty St., Wooster, OH 44691; Ed. K.C. Held, Jr.; Pub. G. Charles Dix, II; adv.; pub. size: broadsheet; circ. 750(paid).

SPENCERVILLE
US

JOURNAL NEWS. Thu. $.35 newsstand; $15/yr. in cy.; $18/yr. out of cy.; $21/yr. out of state. 126 N. Broadway, Spencerville, OH 45887. TEL 419-647-4981. **Owner(s):** Journal News, The, 126 N. Broadway, Spencerville, OH 45887. TEL 419-647-4981; Pub. Doris Beebe; adv.; pub. size: standard.

SPRINGBORO
US

STAR PRESS. 1976. s-w.: Tue. & Sun. $.50 newsstand; $20/yr. local; $30/yr. in state. 25 E. Central, Springboro, OH 45066. TEL 513-748-2550; FAX 513-748-1165. **Owner(s):** Brown Publishing Co., P.O. Box 555, Urbana, OH 43078. TEL 513-652-2100; Ed. Terry Baver; Pub. Fred Gibson; adv. contact: Barbara Parks. pub. size: broadsheet; circ. 14,000(paid).

ST. MARYS
US

EXTRA MERCHANDISER. 1982. Wed. free. 102 E. Spring St., St. Marys, OH 45885. TEL 419-394-7414; FAX 419-394-7202. **Owner(s):** American Publishing Co., 606 N. Van Buren, Marion, IL 62959. TEL 618-993-1711; Ed. Jose Nogueran; Pub. David Creech; adv. contact: David Creech. pub. size: broadsheet; circ. 10,500(free).
Formerly: West Auglaize Merchandiser.

STOW
US

AURORA ADVOCATE. 1972. Wed. $.50 newsstand; $18/yr. in cy. carrier; $40/yr. mailed. 1619 Commerce Dr., Stow, OH 44224. TEL 330-688-0088; FAX 330-688-1588. **Owner(s):** Record Publishing Co., LLC, 126 N. Chestnut St., Ravenna, OH 44266. TEL 216-296-9657; Ed. Ken Lahmers; Pub. David Dix; adv. contact: Diana Kelly. pub. size: tabloid; circ. 5,700(free & paid).

US

CUYAHOGA FALLS NEWS-PRESS. 1929. Sun. $.35 newsstand; $14/yr. carrier; $20/yr. mailed. 1619 Commerce Dr., Stow, OH 44224. TEL 330-688-0088; FAX 330-688-1588. **Owner(s):** Record Publishing Co., LLC, 126 N. Chestnut St., Ravenna, OH 44266. TEL 330-296-9657; Ed. Ellin Walsh; Pub. David Dix; adv.; pub. size: tabloid; circ. 24,400(paid).
Formerly: Falls News-Press.

US

HUDSON HUB-TIMES. s-w.: Wed. & Sun. $.50 newsstand; $36/yr. carrier; $46/yr. mailed. 1619 Commerce Dr., Stow, OH 44224. TEL 216-688-0088; FAX 216-688-1588. **Owner(s):** Record Publishing Co. LLC, 126 N. Chestnut St., Ravenna, OH 44266. TEL 330-296-9657; Ed. Debbie DiMafcio; Pub. David Dix; adv. contact: Larry Kinney. pub. size: tabloid; circ. 6,600(free & paid).

US

NEWS LEADER. Wed. $.50 newsstand; $14/yr. carrier; $20/yr. mailed. 1619 Commerce Dr., Stow, OH 44224. TEL 330-688-0088; FAX 330-688-1588; E-mail: ald119@ald.net; URL: http://www.recordpub.com. **Owner(s):** Record Publishing Co. LLC, 126 N. Chesnut St., Ravenna, OH 44266. TEL 216-296-9657; Ed. Linda Hoy; Pub. David Dix; adv.; pub. size: tabloid; circ. 11,106(free & paid).

US   ISSN 0192-9410

STOW SENTRY. 1969. Sun. $.50 newsstand; $20/yr. 1619 Commerce Dr., Stow, OH 44224. TEL 330-688-0088; FAX 330-688-1588. **Owner(s):** Record Publishing Co. LLC, 125 N. Chestnut St., Ravenna, OH 44266. TEL 330-296-9657; Ed. Beverly Ocasek; Pub. David Dix; adv.; photos; pub. size: tabloid; circ. Sun. 13,416(paid).

US

TALLMADGE EXPRESS. Sun. $.50 newsstand; $18/yr. carrier; $40/yr. mailed. 1619 Commerce Dr., Stow, OH 44224. TEL 330-688-0088; FAX 330-688-1588. **Owner(s):** Record Publishing Co. LLC, 126 N. Chestnut St., Ravenna, OH 44266. TEL 216-296-9657; Pub. David Dix; adv.; pub. size: tabloid; circ. 6,416(free & paid).

STREETSBORO
US

GATEWAY NEWS, THE. 1918. Wed. free in area; $.50 newsstand; $12/yr. carrier. 1675 State Rte. 303, Streetsboro, OH 44241. TEL 330-626-5558; FAX 330-626-5550. **Owner(s):** Record Publishing Co. LLC, 126 N. Chestnut St., Ravenna, OH 44266. TEL 216-296-9657; Ed. Laura White; Pub. David Dix; adv.; pub. size: tabloid; circ. 5,000(free & paid).
Formerly: Record-News.

STRUTHERS
US

JOURNAL, THE. Thu. $16.50/yr. 23 Lowellville Rd., Struthers, OH 44471. TEL 216-755-2155. **Owner(s):** Journal Publishing Co., 23 Lowellville Rd., Struthers, OH 44471. TEL 216-755-2155; Ed. Karen Spaite; Pub. Ralph Baker; adv. contact: Karen Spaite. pub. size: standard.

SUNBURY
US

SUNBURY NEWS. 1873. Thu. $.50 newsstand; $18/yr. 40 S. Vernon St., Sunbury, OH 43074. TEL 614-965-3891; FAX 614-965-3992. **Owner(s):** Delaware Gazette, 18 E. William St., Delaware, OH; Ed. Susan Wright; Pub. W.D. Thompson; adv. contact: Don Cardwell. pub. size: broadsheet; circ. 3,200(paid).

SWANTON
US

SWANTON ENTERPRISE. 1886. Tue. $28/yr. 97 N. Main St., Swanton, OH 43558. TEL 419-826-3580; FAX 419-826-3590. **Owner(s):** Gazette Publishing Co., 107 N. Sandusky St., Bellevue, OH 44811. TEL 419-483-4190; Ed. Brian Liskai. pub. size: broadsheet; circ. 2,000(paid).

TIPP CITY
US

TIPP CITY HERALD. 1859. Tue. $.50 newsstand; $26/yr. in cy.; $31/yr. out of cy. 1455 W. Main St., Tipp City, OH 45371. TEL 513-667-2214; FAX 513-667-8987. **Owner(s):** Vernon T. Bowling, P.O. Box 430, Tipp City, OH 45371; Ed. Tom Barnett; Pub. Vernon T. Bowling; pub. size: broadsheet; circ. 7,100(paid).

TOLEDO
US

POINT & SHORELAND JOURNAL. 1978. Tue. free in area; $.50 newsstand; $15/yr. mailed. 5198 N. Summit St., Toledo, OH 43611. TEL 419-729-2855; FAX 419-874-7311. **Owner(s):** Welch Publishing Co., P.O. Box 267, Perrysburg, OH 43552. TEL 419-874-2528; Ed. James Welch; Pub. Robert C. Welch; adv.; photos; bk.rev.; pub. size: broadsheet; circ. 7,800(free & paid).

10708 TOLEDO, OH   **WEEKLY NEWSPAPERS**

US
SYLVANIA HERALD. 1910. Wed. $.25 newsstand; $12/yr. 4444 W. Alexis St., Toledo, OH 43623. TEL 419-475-6000; FAX 419-472-7774. **Owner(s):** Herald Newspapers, 4444 W. Alexis Rd., Toledo, OH 43623. TEL 419-475-1501; Ed. Paula Gibson; Pub. Allen C. Foster; adv.; photos; bk.rev.; pub. size: standard; circ. 2,500(paid).

US
WEST TOLEDO HERALD. 1970. Wed. $.25 newsstand; $15/yr. mailed. 4444 W. Alexis Rd., Toledo, OH 43623. TEL 419-475-6000; FAX 419-472-7774. **Owner(s):** Herald Newspapers, 4444 Alexis Rd., Toledo, OH 43623; Ed. Paula Gibson; Pub. Allen C. Foster; adv., photos; pub. size: broadsheet; circ. 37,000(paid).
Formerly: Toledo Edition.

UTICA
US
UTICA HERALD. 1878. Wed. $.25 newsstand; $12/yr. in cy.; $14/yr. out of cy.; $16/yr. out of state. 120 S. Main St., Utica, OH 43080. TEL 614-892-2771. **Owner(s):** Nelson A. Smith, 120 S. Main St., P.O. Box 515, Utica, OH 43080-0515. TEL 614-892-2771; adv.: $4/SAU. photos; pub. size: broadsheet; circ. 2,100(paid).

VERMILION
US
VERMILION PHOTOJOURNAL. 1959. Thu. $.50 newsstand; $24/yr. 630 N. Main St., Vermilion, OH 44089. TEL 216-967-5268; FAX 216-967-2535. **Owner(s):** Photojournal, Inc., 520 Warren St., Sandusky, OH 44870. TEL 419-625-5825; Ed. Karen Cornelius. adv.; photos; pub. size: tabloid; circ. 3,500(free & paid).

VERSAILLES
US
VERSAILLES POLICY, THE. 1875. Wed. $.50 newsstand; $21/yr. in state; $25/yr. out of state. P.O. Box 74, Versailles, OH 45380. TEL 513-526-9131; FAX 513-526-9131. **Owner(s):** Scott Langston, 1080 Aubert Dr., Versailles, OH 45380; Ed. Scott Langston; Pub. Scott Langston; adv.; photos; bk.rev.; pub. size: standard; circ. 2,450(paid).

WAPAKONETA
US
SHELBY REVIEW. 1978. Tue. $20/yr. 8 Willipie St., Wapakoneta, OH 45895. TEL 419-738-2128; FAX 419-738-5352. **Owner(s):** American Publishing Co., 606 N. Van Buren, Marion, IL 62959. TEL 618-993-1711; Ed. Dianna Epperly. adv. contact: Karen Brown. photos; bk.rev.; pub. size: tabloid; circ. 4,550.

WAUSEON
US
FULTON COUNTY EXPOSITOR. 1854. s-w.: Tue. & Thu. $.75 newsstand; $39/yr. in cy. mailed; $52/yr. out of cy.; $56/yr. out of state. 201 N. Fulton, Wauseon, OH 43567. TEL 419-335-2010; FAX 419-335-2030. **Owner(s):** Gazette Publishing Co., 107 N. Sandsky St., Bellview, OH 44811; Ed. Brian Liskai; Pub. Robert Krumm; adv. contact: Sherry Garrison. photos; pub. size: broadsheet; circ. 7,500(paid).

WAVERLY
US
NEWS WATCHMAN, THE. 1975. s-w.: Wed. & Sun. $.50 newsstand; $40.25/yr.; $49/yr. out of cy. 101 W. Second St., Waverly, OH 45690. TEL 614-947-2149; FAX 614-947-1344. **Owner(s):** Mid-South Management Co., Inc., 314 Pine St., Spartanburg, SC 29302. TEL 803-573-7640; FAX 803-573-7640; Ed. Betty McAdow; Pub. Dale Gardner; adv. contact: Jeanne Gillum. photos; bk.rev.; pub. size: broadsheet; circ. 3,800(paid).

US
PIKE COUNTY NEWS WATCHMAN. s-w.: Wed. & Sun. $.50 newsstand; $40.25/yr.; $49/yr. mailed; $38.24/yr. senior citizens. 101 W. Second St., Waverly, OH 45690. TEL 614-947-2149; FAX 614-286-5854. **Owner(s):** Jackson Publishing Co., Inc., 295 E. Broadway, Jackson, OH 45640. TEL 614-286-2187; Ed. Betty McAdow; Pub. P. Dale Gardener; pub. size: standard; circ. 4,500(paid).

WELLSTON
US
WELLSTON TELEGRAM, THE. 1896. Thu. free newsstand; $25/yr. 12 S. Ohio Ave., Wellston, OH 45692. TEL 614-384-6102; FAX 614-384-3063. **Owner(s):** Steven P. Keller, 12. S. Ohio Ave., Wellston, OH 45692. TEL 614-384-6102; FAX 614-384-3063; Ed. Steven P. Keller; Pub. Steven P. Keller; adv. contact: Steven P. Keller. pub. size: broadsheet; circ. 5,400(free & paid).

WESTERVILLE
US
WESTERVILLE NEWS & PUBLIC OPINION. 1867. Wed. $.40 newsstand; $25/yr. in cy.; $30/yr. out of state. 130 Graphic Way, Westerville, OH 43081. TEL 614-882-2244; FAX 614-842-7460. **Owner(s):** Suburban News Publications, 5257 Sinclair Rd., Columbus, OH 43229. TEL 614-464-4567; Ed. Martin Rozeman; Pub. James A. Toms; pub. size: broadsheet; circ. 20,515(free & paid).
Formerly: Westerville Public Opinion & News.

WEST LAKE
US
PRESS & LIGHT. 1983. Wed. $.50 newsstand; $24/yr. local; $25.50/yr. elsewhere. 27006 Center Ridge Rd., West Lake, OH 44145. TEL 216-871-5797; FAX 216-871-5797. **Owner(s):** Douthit Communications, Inc., P.O. Box 760, Sandusky, OH 44871. TEL 419-625-5825; Ed. Carol Klear. adv. contact: Toni Musgrove. pub. size: tabloid; circ. 7,200(paid).

US
WEST LIFE. 1958. Wed. $.60 newsstand; $27.50/yr. in cy.; $30.50/yr. out of cy. 27006 Center Ridge Rd., West Lake, OH 44145. TEL 216-871-5797; FAX 216-871-3824. **Owner(s):** PICT Partnership, P.O. Box 760, Sandusky, OH 44870. TEL 419-625-5825; Ed. Mary Slama; Pub. Kenneth Douthit III; adv.; pub. size: tabloid; circ. 15,000(paid).

WEST MILTON
US
WEST MILTON RECORD. Wed. $.50 newsstand; $18.20/yr. local; $26/yr. in cy.; $31/yr. out of cy. 2 S. Miami St., West Milton, OH 45383. TEL 937-698-4451; FAX 937-667-8987. **Owner(s):** Vernon Bowling, 1455 W. Main, Tipp City, OH 45371. TEL 513-698-8512; Ed. Erik Shrewsberry; Pub. David Copen; adv. contact: Roger Leibold. pub. size: broadsheet; circ. 3,000(paid).

WEST UNION
US
PEOPLE'S DEFENDER, THE. 1866. Wed. $.50 newsstand; $14.50/yr. in cy.; $16/yr. out of cy. 229 N. Cross St., West Union, OH 45693. TEL 513-544-2391; FAX 513-544-2298. **Owner(s):** Brown Publishing Co., P.O. Box 555, Urbana, OH 43078. TEL 513-652-2100; FAX 513-652-2448; Ed. Herbert H. Lax; Pub. Herbert H. Lax; adv. contact: Garry Messer. pub. size: broadsheet; circ. 9,200(paid).

WHEELERSBURG
US
SCIOTO VOICE. 1973. Thu. $.50 newsstand; $15/yr. in cy.; $22/yr. out of cy. 8019 Hayport Rd., Wheelersburg, OH 45694-0400. TEL 614-574-8494; FAX 614-574-2329. **Owner(s):** Voice Newspapers, Inc., P.O. Box 400, Wheerlersburg, OH 45694; Ed. James G. Kegley; Pub. James G. Kegley; adv.; pub. size: broadsheet; circ. 4,000(paid).

WILLARD
US
WILLARD TIMES-JUNCTION. 1883. s-w.: Mon. & Thu. $.35 newsstand; $30/yr. in cy.; $37.50/yr. out of cy. 211 Myrtle Ave., Willard, OH 44890. TEL 419-935-0184; FAX 419-933-2031. **Owner(s):** Shelby Daily Globe, Inc., 37 W. Main, Shelby, OH 44875. TEL 419-342-4276; Pub. Ken Gove; pub. size: broadsheet; circ. 4,200(paid).

WILLSHIRE
US
PHOTO STAR. 1895. Wed. free; $25/yr. mailed. 307 State St., Willshire, OH 45898. TEL 419-495-2696; FAX 419-495-2143. **Owner(s):** Judith Bunner, 307 State St., Willshire, OH 45898. TEL 419-495-2696; Ed. Judith Bunner; Pub. Judith Bunner; adv.; photos; pub. size: tabloid; circ. 11,600(paid).

WILMINGTON
US
CLINTON COUNTY SHOPPERS GUIDE. 1986. Wed. free. 47 S. South St., Wilmington, OH 45177-2213. TEL 513-382-6761; FAX 513-382-4392. **Owner(s):** Brown Publishing Co., P.O. Box 555, Urbana, OH 43078. TEL 513-652-2100; Ed. Jay Carey; Pub. Clarence Graham; adv. contact: Rick Irvin. bk.rev.; pub. size: tabloid; circ. 16,500(free).

WEEKLY NEWSPAPERS

US

STAR REPUBLICAN. 1870. Mon. $18.75/yr. 47 S. South St., Wilmington, OH 45177. TEL 513-382-7796; FAX 513-382-4392. **Owner(s):** Brown Publishing Co., P.O. Box 555, Urbanna, OH 43078. TEL 513-652-2100; Ed. Rose Cooper; Pub. Clarence Graham; adv. contact: Rick Irvin. photos; pub. size: broadsheet; circ. 22,000(free & paid).

WOODSFIELD

US

MONROE COUNTY BEACON. 1937. Thu. $.75 newsstand; $22/yr. in school district; $39/yr. elsewhere; $19/yr. senior citizens. P.O. Box 70, Woodsfield, OH 43793-0070. TEL 614-472-0734; FAX 614-472-0735. **Owner(s):** Delphos Newspapers, 405 N. Main St., Delphos, OH 45833. TEL 419-695-0015; Ed. Arlene Selvey; Pub. Kristina L. Vineyard; adv.; photos; pub. size: broadsheet; circ. 5,650(paid).

WORTHINGTON

US

DUBLIN VILLAGER. Mon. free newsstand; $75/yr. mailed. 70 Lakeview Plz. Blvd., Ste. F, Worthington, OH 43085. TEL 614-841-1781; FAX 614-841-0436; E-mail: thisweek@infinet.com; URL: http://www.thisweeknews.com. **Owner(s):** Dispatch Newspapers, Inc., 34 S. Third St., Columbus, OH 43229. TEL 614-461-5000; Ed. Craig McDonald. adv. contact: Jerry O'Connell. adv.: $8.90/SAU. photos; pub. size: tabloid; circ. 21,479(free).

YOUNGSTOWN

US

BUCKEYE REVIEW, THE. 1937. Wed. $.50 newsstand; $20/yr. 1555 Belmont Ave., Youngstown, OH 44501-0287. TEL 216-743-2250; FAX 216-746-2340. **Owner(s):** The Buckeye Review Publishing Co., LLC, 1555 Belmont Ave., Youngstown, OH 44501-0287. TEL 216-743-2250; FAX 216-746-2340; Ed. M. Mike McNair; Pub. M. Mike McNair; adv. contact: M. Mike McNair. photos; bk.rev.; pub. size: tabloid; circ. 20,100(free & paid).
Formerly: Youngstown Buckeye Review.

ZANESVILLE

US

ZANESVILLE MUSKINGUM ADVERTISER. 1976. Sat. free. 760 Linden Ave., Zanesville, OH 43701. TEL 614-453-0615; FAX 614-453-9504. **Owner(s):** Add, Inc., 600 Industrial Dr., Waupaca, WI 54981. TEL 715-258-8450; Ed. Ernie Bruns. adv.; pub. size: tabloid; circ. 36,055(free).

OKLAHOMA

ATOKA

US

ATOKA COUNTY TIMES. Wed. $.50 newsstand; $20/yr. in cy. mailed; $27.50/yr. out of cy.; $35/yr. out of state. 1004 W. 13th, Atoka, OK 74525. TEL 405-889-3319; FAX 405-889-2300. **Owner(s):** Foster & Louise Cain, 1004 W. 13th, Atoka, OK 74525. TEL 405-889-3319; FAX 405-889-2300; Ed. Kenneth Hamilton; Pub. Louise Cain; adv. contact: Ron Linscott. adv.: $4.60/SAU. photos; pub. size: broadsheet; circ. 4,190(paid).

BETHANY

US

TRIBUNE, THE. 1923. Thu. $.35 newsstand; $16.50/yr. in cy.; $19.50/yr. out of cy.; $24.50/yr. out of state; $14/yr. senior citizens. 3813 N. College St., Bethany, OK 73008. TEL 405-789-1962; FAX 405-789-4253. **Owner(s):** K. Brett Wesner, P.O. Box 40, Bethany, OK 73008. TEL 405-789-1962; FAX 405-789-4253; Ed. Shannon Williams; Pub. K. Brett Wesner; adv. contact: Jerry Rakosky. bk.rev.; pub. size: broadsheet; circ. 3,300(paid).

BOISE CITY

US

BOISE CITY NEWS, THE. 1898. Wed. $.50 newsstand; $21.50/yr. 105 W. Main St., Boise City, OK 73933. TEL 405-544-2222; FAX 405-544-3281. **Owner(s):** Jim Rosebery, 105 W. Main St., Boise City, OK 73933. TEL 405-544-2222; FAX 405-544-3281; Ed. Jim Rosebery; Pub. Jim Rosebery; adv. contact: Deb Crabtree. photos; circ. 1,700(paid).

BRISTOW

US

BRISTOW NEWS. 1948. Wed. $.50 newsstand; $18/yr. in cy.; $24/yr. out of cy.; $31/yr. out of state. 112 W. Sixth Ave., Bristow, OK 74010. TEL 918-367-2282; FAX 918-367-2724. **Owner(s):** East Central Oklahoma Publishers, Inc., P.O. Box 840, Bristow, OK 74010. TEL 918-367-2282; adv.; pub. size: broadstreet; circ. 3,225(free & paid).

US

RECORD-CITIZEN, THE. 1898. Fri. $18/yr. in cy.; $24/yr. out of cy.; $31/yr. out of state. 112 W. Sixth Ave., Bristow, OK 74010. TEL 918-367-2282. **Owner(s):** East Central Oklahoma Publishers, Inc., P.O. Box 840, Bristow, OK 74010. TEL 918-367-2282; adv.; pub. size: broadsheet; circ. 3,150(free & paid).

BROKEN ARROW

US

BROKEN ARROW LEDGER. 1903. 3/wk.: Tue., Thu., Sun. $.50 newsstand; $45/yr. home deliv. 110 W. Kenosh, Broken Arrow, OK 74012. TEL 918-258-7171; FAX 918-258-9908. **Owner(s):** Retherford Publications, Inc., 8584 E. 41st St., Tulsa, OK 74145. TEL 918-663-1414; FAX 918-664-8161; Ed. Wayne Bishop; Pub. Bill Retherford; pub. size: broadsheet; circ. 4,500(paid); Sun. 17,000.
Formerly: Broken Arrow Ledger & Scout.

CATOOSA

US

CATOOSA TIMES HERALD. 1965. Wed. $15/yr. local. 650 S. Cherokee, Catoosa, OK 74015. TEL 918-266-3664; FAX 918-266-3666. **Owner(s):** NEOK Publishing, P.O. Box 40, Catoosa, OK 74015; Ed. John Kester; Pub. Eula Kester; adv.; pub. size: standard; circ. 1,400(paid).

CHANDLER

US

LINCOLN COUNTY NEWS. 1891. Thu. $.50 newsstand; $17/yr. in cy.; $19/yr. out of cy.; $23/yr. out of state. 718 Manvel Ave., Chandler, OK 74834. TEL 405-258-1818; FAX 405-258-1824. **Owner(s):** Stephen E. Mathis, P.O. Box 248, Chandler, OK 74834. TEL 405-258-1818; FAX 405-258-1824; Ed. Stephen E. Mathis; Pub. Stephen E. Mathis; adv. contact: P. Dawn Mathis. photos; bk.rev.; pub. size: standard; circ. 4,100(paid).
Formerly: Chandler Lincoln County News.

CHEROKEE

US

CHEROKEE MESSENGER & REPUBLICAN. 1900. Thu. $.50 newsstand; $16/yr. in cy.; $25/yr. out of cy.; $30/yr. out of state. 216 S. Grand, Cherokee, OK 73728. TEL 405-596-3344. **Owner(s):** Larry Hammer, P.O. Box 245, Cherokee, OK 73728. TEL 405-596-3344; Ed. Carol Angle; Pub. Larry Hammer; adv.; bk.rev.; pub. size: broadsheet; circ. 2,500(paid).
Formerly: Cherokee Messenger.

CORDELL

US

CORDELL BEACON, THE. Wed. $.50 newsstand; $19.75/yr. in cy.; $26/yr. out of cy.; $30/yr. out of state. 115 E. Main St., Cordell, OK 73632. TEL 405-832-3333. **Owner(s):** Wesner Publications, 115 E. Main St., Cordell, OK 73632. TEL 405-832-3333; Ed. Ray Wallace; Pub. Brett Wesner; adv. contact: Kay Igo. pub. size: standard; circ. 3,700(paid).

COVINGTON

US ISSN 0746-6633

COVINGTON RECORD. 1905. Thu. $.35 newsstand; $15.50/yr. 310 Main St., Covington, OK 73730-0535. TEL 405-864-7612; FAX 405-864-7612. **Owner(s):** Covington Publishing Corp., 310 Main St., Covington, OK 73730. TEL 405-864-7612; Ed. Janet Smith; Pub. John W. Smith; adv. contact: John W. Smith. photos; bk.rev.; pub. size: broadsheet; circ. 900(paid).

10710 COWETA, OK

COWETA

US

COWETA AMERICAN. Wed. $.50 newsstand; $16.50/yr. 107 S. Broadway, Coweta, OK 74429. TEL 918-486-4444; FAX 918-486-3827. **Owner(s):** Retherford Publishing, 8545 E. 41st St., Tulsa, OK 74145. TEL 918-663-1414; Ed. Christy Wheeland; Pub. Betty Woodward; adv. contact: Sherry Yocham. pub. size: broadsheet; circ. 3,000(paid).

DURANT

US

BRYAN COUNTY STAR. Thu. $.35 newsstand; $12/yr. 301 W. Arkansas, Durant, OK 74702. TEL 405-924-6499; FAX 405-924-6664; E-mail: bcstar@redriverok.com. **Owner(s):** Cecil Plyler, P.O. Box 1427, Durant, OK 74702. TEL 405-924-6499; FAX 405-924-6664; Ed. Cecil Plyler. adv.; pub. size: standard; circ. 5,000(paid).

US

SHOPPER ZONE I. 1976. Wed. free. 120 N. 12th St., Durant, OK 74701. TEL 405-924-1770; FAX 405-924-1792. **Owner(s):** Cox Publishing Co., 4905 Hwy. 75, S., Denison, TX 75020. TEL 903-465-1400; Pub. H. Wayne Cox; pub. size: tabloid; circ. 17,000(free).

US   ISSN 0747-2633

SOUTHERN OKLAHOMA LEADER. 1905. Tue. free. P.O. Box 1427, Durant, OK 74702. TEL 405-924-6499; FAX 405-924-6664. **Owner(s):** Cecil Plyler, P.O. Box 1427, Durant, OK 74702. TEL 405-924-6499; FAX 405-924-6664; Ed. Cecil Plyler. adv.; pub. size: standard; circ. 14,000(controlled & paid).

EAKLY

US   ISSN 0746-4789

COUNTRY CONNECTION NEWS. 1982. Wed. $.50 newsstand; $23/yr. in state; $26/yr. out of state. 315 Main St., Eakly, OK 73033. TEL 405-797-3648; FAX 405-797-3663; E-mail: bblock@prodigy.com. **Owner(s):** Joyce Carney, 315 Main St., Eakly, OK 73033. TEL 405-797-3648; FAX 405-797-3663; Ed. Joyce Carney; Pub. Joyce Carney; adv. contact: Pat Thiessen. photos; pub. size: broadsheet; circ. 2,000(paid).

EL RENO

US

EL RENO TRIBUNE. 1934. s-w.: Wed. & Sun. $.50 newsstand; $3/mo. home deliv.; $8.75/4 mos. home deliv. 201 N. Rock Island, El Reno, OK 73036. TEL 405-262-5180; FAX 405-262-3541. **Owner(s):** Tribune Corp., P.O. Box 9, El Reno, OK 73036. TEL 405-262-5180; FAX 405-262-3541; Ed. Ray Dyer; Pub. Sean Dyer; adv. contact: Erin Dyer. pub. size: broadsheet; circ. 4,500(paid); Sun. 5,200(paid).

FAIRVIEW

US

FAIRVIEW REPUBLICAN. 1900. Thu. $.50 newsstand; $19/yr. in cy.; $27/yr. out of cy.; $32/yr. out of state. 112 N. Main St., Fairview, OK 73737. TEL 405-227-4439; FAX 405-227-4430. **Owner(s):** Larry Hammer, P.O. Box 245, Cherokee, OK 73728. TEL 405-596-3344; Ed. Dave Altman; Pub. Larry Hammer; adv.; pub. size: broadsheet; circ. 3,500(controlled & paid).

FREDERICK

US

FREDERICK LEADER. 1904. s-w.: Wed & Sun. $.50 newsstand; $30/yr. carrier; $30/yr. mailed in cy. 304 W. Grand Ave., Frederick, OK 73542. TEL 405-335-2188; FAX 405-335-2047. **Owner(s):** DonRey Media Group, P.O. Box 17017, Fort Smith, AR 72901. TEL 501-785-7810; Ed. Terri Erickson. adv. contact: Roxie Heil. pub. size: broadsheet; circ. evening 2,300(paid); Sun. 2,300(paid).

Formerly: Frederick Daily Leader.

GROVE

US

GROVE SUN. 1898. 3/wk.: Tue., Thu., Fri. $.50 newsstand; $35/yr. in cy.; $45/yr. out of cy.; $90/yr. out of state. 14 W. Third St., Grove, OK 74344. TEL 918-786-2228; FAX 918-786-2156. **Owner(s):** Grove Sun Newspaper Co., 14 W. Third St., Grove, OK 74344. TEL 918-786-2228; Ed. Randy Webb; Pub. M. Gerald Stone; adv.; pub. size: broadsheet; circ. 6,000(paid).

HARRAH

US

HARRAH NEWS, THE. 1959. Thu. $.50 newsstand; $12.50/yr. in state; $19/yr out of state. 2041 Church St., Harrah, OK 73045. TEL 405-454-2451; FAX 405-454-3567. **Owner(s):** Harrah News, Inc., P.O. Box 448, Harrah, OK 73045. TEL 405-454-2451; FAX 405-454-3567; Pub. Hank Foster; adv.; photos; bk.rev.; pub. size: tabloid; circ. 1,969(paid).

HOBART

US

HOBART DEMOCRAT-CHIEF. 1901. Thu. $.50 newsstand; $18/yr. in cy.; $28/yr. in state. 407 S. Main St., Hobart, OK 73651. TEL 405-726-3333; FAX 405-726-3431. **Owner(s):** Democrat-Chief Publishing Co., 407 S. Main St., Hobart, OK 73651. TEL 405-726-3333; Pub. Joe Hancock; adv.; photos; pub. size: broadsheet; circ. 3,200(paid).

HOMINY

US

HOMINY NEWS-PROGRESS. 1973. Wed. $.50 newsstand; $15/yr. 115 W. Main St., Hominy, OK 74035. TEL 918-885-2101. **Owner(s):** Ferguson & Ferguson, S. Broadway, Cleveland, OK 74020; Ed. Ramona Brown; Pub. Romona Brown; pub. size: standard; circ. 1,800(paid).

KINGFISHER

US

KINGFISHER TIMES & FREE PRESS. 1889. s-w.: Wed. & Sun. $.50 newsstand; $26/yr. 323 N. Main St., Kingfisher, OK 73750. TEL 405-375-3220; FAX 405-375-3222. **Owner(s):** Kingfisher Newspapers Inc., 323 N. Main St., Kingfisher, OK 73750. TEL 405-375-3220; FAX 405-375-3222; Ed. Gary Reid; Pub. Gary Reid; adv.; photos; pub. size: broadsheet; circ. 4,200(paid).

Formerly: Kingfisher Times.

KONAWA

US

KONAWA LEADER. 1893. Thu. $.45 newsstand; $18/yr. 102 N. Broadway, Konawa, OK 74849. TEL 405-925-3187; FAX 405-925-3187. **Owner(s):** Ed Gallagher, P.O. Box 157, Konawa, OK 74849. TEL 405-925-3187; FAX 405-925-3729; Ed. Ed Gallagher; Pub. Ed Gallagher; pub. size: broadsheet; circ. 2,000(paid).

US

STRATFORD STAR. Thu. $.35 newsstand; $15/yr. 102 N. Broadway, Konawa, OK 74849. TEL 405-925-3187; FAX 405-925-3729. **Owner(s):** Ed Gallagher, P.O. Box 157, Konawa, OK. TEL 405-925-3187; FAX 405-925-3729; Ed. Ed Gallagher; Pub. Ed Gallagher; adv.; pub. size: standard; circ. 1,500(paid).

MADILL

US

MADILL RECORD. 1895. Thu. $20/yr. in cy.; $27/yr. in OK & TX; $32/yr. elsewhere. 211 Plaza, Madill, OK 73446. TEL 405-795-3355; FAX 405-795-3530. **Owner(s):** John D. Montgomery, P.O. Box 529, Madill, OK 73446. TEL 405-795-3355; FAX 405-795-3530; G. Montgomery, S. Codner, M. Codner, P.O. Box 529, Madill, OK 73446; Ed. Mark Codner; Pub. Mark Codner; adv.; photos; pub. size: broadsheet; circ. 4,450(paid).

MOORE

US   ISSN 0747-1947

MOORE AMERICAN. 1935. Fri. $.50 newsstand; $19.95/yr. 623 N. Broadway, Moore, OK 73160. TEL 405-794-5555; FAX 405-799-8046. **Owner(s):** Redden, Inc., 325 W. I-35 Service Rd., S., Moore, OK 73160. TEL 405-794-5555; FAX 405-799-8046; Ed. Oran C. Redden; Pub. Oran C. Redden; adv.; photos; pub. size: broadsheet; circ. 9,500(free & paid). **Wire Service(s):** AP.

US

SOUTH OKLAHOMA CITY LEADER. Wed. $.50 newsstand; $19.95/yr. 623 N. Broadway, Moore, OK 73160. TEL 405-794-5555; FAX 405-799-8046. **Owner(s):** Redden, Inc., 325 W. I-35 Service Rd., S., Moore, OK 73160. TEL 405-794-5555; Ed. Oran C. Redden; Pub. Oran C. Redden; pub. size: broadsheet; circ. 9,500(paid).

NEWCASTLE

US

NEWCASTLE PACER, THE. 1978. Thu. $.35 newsstand; $12/yr. local; $13.50/yr. elsewhere. 120 N.E. Second St., Ste. 102, Newcastle, OK 73065. TEL 405-387-5277. **Owner(s):** Newcastle Pacer, Inc., P.O. Box 429, Newcastle, OK 73065. TEL 405-387-5277; Ed. Marvin Leyerle; Pub. Marvin Leyerle; adv. contact: Jocile Leyerle. pub. size: broadsheet; circ. 1,500(controlled & paid).

NOWATA

US

NOWATA STAR. 1904. Wed. $.50 newsstand; $18/yr. 213 N. Maple St., Nowata, OK 74048. TEL 918-273-2446. **Owner(s):** Nowata Newspapers, Inc., P.O. Box 429, Nowata, OK 74048. TEL 918-273-2446; Ed. Janet Reeder; Pub. David Reid; adv. contact: Pat Morrison. pub. size: broadsheet; circ. 2,700(free & paid).

WEEKLY NEWSPAPERS

OKLAHOMA CITY

US

CAPITOL HILL BEACON. 1905. Thu. $.25 newsstand; $25/yr. mailed. 124 W. Commerce, Oklahoma City, OK 73109. TEL 405-232-4151; FAX 405-235-0818. **Owner(s):** Beacon Publishing Co., 124 W. Commerce, Oklahoma City, OK 73109; Ed. David Sellers; Pub. David Sellers; adv. contact: David Sellers. pub. size: standard; circ. 1,200(paid).

US

OKLAHOMA CITY FRIDAY. 1974. Fri. $1 newsstand; $20/yr. in cy. 10801 N. Quail Plaza Dr., Oklahoma City, OK 73120. TEL 405-755-3311. **Owner(s):** Nichols Hills Publishing Co., 1605 W. Wilshire, Oklahoma City, OK 73116; Ed. Gordon Walker; Pub. J. Leland Gourley; adv. contact: Cindy Shea. bk.rev.; pub. size: broadsheet; circ. 8,119(paid).

US

OKLAHOMA GAZETTE. Thu. $21/6 mos.; $38/yr. 801 N.W. 36th St., Oklahoma City, OK 73154. TEL 405-528-6000; FAX 405-528-4600. **Owner(s):** Bill Bleakley, 801 N.W. 36th St., Oklahoma City, OK 73154. TEL 405-528-6000; Ed. Mike Easterling; Pub. Bill Bleakley; pub. size: broadsheet; circ. 50,000(paid).

OOLOGAH

US   ISSN 0688-0470

OOLOGAH LAKE LEADER. 1982. Thu. $.50 newsstand; $17/yr. in cy.; $20/yr. in state; $30/yr. out of state. 109 S. Maple, Oologah, OK 74053. TEL 918-443-2428. E-mail: oologah-leader@okpress.com. **Owner(s):** John M. Wylie, II, 109 S. Maple, Oologah, OK 74053. TEL 918-443-2428; Ed. John M. Wylie, II; Pub. John M. Wylie, II; adv. contact: Harriet Estep. photos; bk.rev.; pub. size: broadsheet; circ. 3,560(free & paid).

OWASSO

US

OWASSO REPORTER. 1970. Thu. $.50 newsstand; $17.50/yr. 202 E. Second Ave., Owasso, OK 74055. TEL 918-272-1155. **Owner(s):** Retherford Publications, Inc., 8545 E. 41st St., Tulsa, OK 74145. TEL 918-663-1414; Ed. Ralph Schaefer; Pub. Bill R. Retherford; adv. contact: Charles Cagle. photos; pub. size: broadsheet; circ. 5,000(paid).

PAWHUSKA

US

PAWHUSKA JOURNAL-CAPITAL. 1904. s-w.: Wed. & Sat. $.50 newsstand; $42/yr. in cy.; $60/yr. out of cy. 700 Kihekaa, Pawhuska, OK 74056. TEL 918-287-1590; FAX 918-287-1804. **Owner(s):** Don Rey Media Grp., 3600 Wheeler Ave., P.O. Box 17017, Fort Smith, AR 72917. TEL 502-785-7810; adv. contact: Terry Collins. pub. size: broadsheet; circ. 2,400(paid).

PRYOR

US

ORYOR JEFFERSONIAN. 1907. Thu. free. 105 S. Adair St., Pryor, OK 74362. TEL 918-825-3292; FAX 918-825-1965. **Owner(s):** Pryor Publishing Co., Inc., 105 S. Adair St., P.O. Box 308, Pryor, OK 74361. TEL 918-825-3292; Ed. Henry Goodman; Pub. Henry Goodman; pub. size: broadsheet; circ. 6,000(free).

PURCELL

US

PURCELL REGISTER. 1887. Thu. $.50 newsstand; $18/yr. 225 W. Main St., Purcell, OK 73080. TEL 405-527-2126; FAX 405-527-3299. **Owner(s):** McClain County Publishing Co., Inc., P.O. Box 191, Purcell, OK 73080. TEL 405-527-2126; FAX 405-527-3299; Ed. Bill Moakley. adv. contact: Vickie Foraker. photos; pub. size: broadsheet; circ. 6,200(paid).

SALLISAW

US

SEQUOYAH COUNTY TIMES. 1932. s-w.: Thu. & Sun. $.35 newsstand; $17/yr. in OK. & adjoining states; $44/yr. elsewhere. 111 N. Oak St., Sallisaw, OK 74955-4637. TEL 918-775-4433; FAX 918-775-3023. **Owner(s):** Cookson Hills Publishers, Inc., 11 N. Oak St., Sallisaw, OK 74955. TEL 918-775-4433; FAX 918-775-3023; Ed. Jim Mayo; Pub. Jim Mayo; adv. contact: Delanna Nutter. pub. size: broadsheet; circ. 6,948(free & paid).

SAND SPRINGS

US

SAND SPRINGS LEADER. 1912. s-w.: Wed. & Sun. $.50 newsstand; $25/yr. local. 303 N. McKinley Ave., Sand Springs, OK 74063. TEL 918-245-6634; FAX 918-241-3610. **Owner(s):** Retherford Publications, Inc., 8545 E. 41st St., Tulsa, OK 74145. TEL 918-663-1414; Pub. Bill Retherford; adv. contact: Dan Rodgers. photos; pub. size: broadsheet; circ. 5,228(paid).

SAYRE

US

SAYRE JOURNAL. 1891. Thu. $.35 newsstand; $19.26/yr. in area; $24.50/yr. elsewhere. 110 N. Fourth St., Sayre, OK 73662-0340. TEL 405-928-3372. **Owner(s):** To-Mo-Ca Comm., Inc., P.O. Box 340, Sayre, OK 73662-0340. TEL 405-928-3372; Ed. Sonya Blackshear; Pub. Tom Higley; adv.: $3/SAU. pub. size: broadsheet; circ. 2,125(paid).

SKIATOOK

US

SKIATOOK JOURNAL. 1985. Wed. $.50 newsstand; $13.75/yr. local. 501 W. Rogers, Skiatook, OK 74070. TEL 918-396-1616. **Owner(s):** Retherford Publications, Inc., 8545 E. 41st St., Tulsa, OK 74145. TEL 918-663-1414; Ed. Ralph Schaefer; Pub. Bill R. Retherford; adv.: $6.85/SAU. pub. size: broadsheet; circ. 2,321(paid).

STIGLER

US

COUNTRY STAR. Thu. free. 204 S. Broadway, Stigler, OK 74462. TEL 918-967-4655; FAX 918-967-4289. **Owner(s):** Linus G. Williams, 204 S. Broadway, Stigler, OK 74462. TEL 918-967-4655; Ed. Sharon Johnson; Pub. Linus G. Williams; adv. contact: Mike Higley. pub. size: broadsheet; circ. 4,000(free).
Formerly: County Star.

US

STIGLER NEWS-SENTINEL. 1930. Thu. $.50 newsstand; $20/yr. 204 S. Broadway, Stigler, OK 74462. TEL 918-967-4655; FAX 918-967-4289. **Owner(s):** Linus G. Williams, 204 S. Broadway, Stigler, OK 74462. TEL 918-967-4655; Ed. Sharon Johnson; Pub. Linus G. Williams; adv. contact: Mike Higley. pub. size: broadsheet; circ. 4,100(paid).

STILWELL

US

STILWELL DEMOCRAT-JOURNAL. 1897. Thu. $.50 newsstand; $16.50/yr. out of state. 118 N. Second St., Stilwell, OK 74960. TEL 918-696-2228; FAX 918-696-7066. **Owner(s):** Indian Nations Communications, Inc., P.O. Box 508, Stilwell, OK 74960. TEL 918-696-2228; adv. contact: Pam Muskrat. pub. size: standard; circ. 6,300(paid).

TISHOMINGO

US

JOHNSTON COUNTY CAPITAL-DEMOCRAT. 1900. Thu. $.50 newsstand; $20/yr. in cy.; $28/yr. out of cy.; $32/yr. out of state. 103 N. Neshoba, Tishomingo, OK 73460. TEL 405-371-2356. **Owner(s):** Ray Lokey, P.O. Box 400, Tishomingo, OK 73460. TEL 405-371-2356; Ed. Ray Lokey; Pub. Ray Lokey; adv.; pub. size: broadsheet; circ. 3,150(paid).

TONKAWA

US

TONKAWA NEWS, THE. 1894. Thu. $.50 newsstand; 19.50/yr. 108 N. Seventh St., Tonkawa, OK 74653-0250. TEL 405-628-2532; FAX 405-628-4044. **Owner(s):** H. Lyle Becker, 108 N. Seventh St., Tonkawa, OK 74653-0250. TEL 405-628-2532; FAX 405-628-4044; Ed. H. Lyle Becker; Pub. H. Lyle Becker; adv.; photos; bk.rev.; pub. size: broadsheet; circ. 1,800(paid).

TULSA

US

BIXBY BULLETIN. 1905. Thu. $15.50/yr. in cy.; $29/yr. out of cy.; $36/yr. out of state. 8545 41st St., Tulsa, OK 74145. TEL 918-663-1414; FAX 918-664-8161. **Owner(s):** Retherford Publications, 8545 E. 41st St., Tulsa, OK 74145. TEL 918-663-1414; Ed. Ralph Schaefer; Pub. Bill R. Retherford; adv.: $6.25/SAU. pub. size: standard; circ. 1,463(paid).

US   ISSN 0890-9040

COLLINSVILLE NEWS. 1899. Wed. $.50 newsstand; $16.50/yr. in cy.; $24/yr. out of cy. 9545 E. 41st St., Tulsa, OK 74145. TEL 918-663-1414. **Owner(s):** Retherford Publications, Inc., 8545 E. 41st St., Tulsa, OK 74145. TEL 918-663-1414; Ed. Ralph Schaefer; Pub. Bill R. Retherford; adv.: $6.85/SAU. pub. size: broadsheet; circ. 2,000(paid).

US

JENKS JOURNAL. 1957. w. $.50 newsstand; $15.50/yr. 8545 E. 41st St., Tulsa, OK 74145. TEL 918-663-1414; FAX 918-664-8161. **Owner(s):** Retherford Publications, Inc., 8545 E. 41st St., Tulsa, OK 74145. TEL 918-663-1414; FAX 918-664-8161; Pub. Bill R. Retherford; adv. contact: Rick Collins. photos; pub. size: broadsheet; circ. 1,300(paid).

TULSA, OK

US
OKLAHOMA EAGLE. 1921. Thu. $.50 newsstand; $23/yr. 624 E. Archer St., Tulsa, OK 74120. TEL 918-582-7124; FAX 918-582-8905. **Owner(s):** James O. Goodwin, 624 E. Archer, Tulsa, OK 74120. TEL 918-582-7124; Edward L. Goodwin, Jr., 624 E. Archer St., Tulsa, OK 74120. TEL 918-582-7124; Ed. Carolyn Chappele; Pub. James G. Goodwin; adv.; photos; pub. size: standard; circ. 12,800(paid).

US
SOUTHWEST TULSA NEWS. Thu. $.50 newsstand; $13.75/yr. 8545 E. 41st St., Tulsa, OK 74145. TEL 918-663-1414. **Owner(s):** Retherford Publications, Inc., 8545 E. 41st St., Tulsa, OK 74145. TEL 918-663-1414; Ed. Ralph Schaefer. adv.: $6.25/SAU. pub. size: tabloid; circ. 3,800(paid).
Formerly: Tulsa County News.

WAGONER
US
WAGONER TRIBUNE, THE. 1894. Thu. $17.50/yr. 221 E. Cherokee, Wagoner, OK 74467. TEL 918-485-5505; FAX 918-485-8442. **Owner(s):** Retherford Publications, Inc., 8545 E. 41st St., Tulsa, OK 74145. TEL 918-663-1414; Ed. Ralph Schaefer. adv.; pub. size: broadsheet; circ. 3,700(paid).

WATONGA
US
WATONGA REPUBLICAN, THE. 1892. Wed. $.50 newsstand; $26/yr. in state; $30/yr. out of state. 104 E. Main, Watonga, OK 73772-0030. TEL 405-623-4922; FAX 405-623-4925. **Owner(s):** Mr. & Mrs. Tim Curtin, 802 N. Prouty, Watonga, OK 73772. TEL 405-623-4922; Pub. Tim Curtin; adv. contact: Tim Curtin. adv.: $4.20/SAU. pub. size: broadsheet; circ. 3,552(paid).

WETUMKA
US
HUGHES COUNTY TIMES. 1930. Thu. $.25 newsstand; $17.50/yr. in cy.; $22.50/yr. out of cy.; $27.50 out of state. 120 S. Main, Wetumka, OK 74883. TEL 405-452-3294; FAX 405-452-3329. **Owner(s):** William C. Morgan, 120 S. Main, Wetumka, OK 74883. TEL 405-452-3294; Ed. William C. Morgan; Pub. William C. Morgan; adv. contact: Donna Ramsey. pub. size: broadsheet; circ. 2,500(paid).

WEWOKA
US
WEWOKA TIMES. 1926. Wed. $.50 newsstand; $24/yr. mailed. 210 S. Wewoka St., Wewoka, OK 74884. TEL 405-257-3342; FAX 405-257-3313. **Owner(s):** Bill & Dana Robinson, 210 S. Wewoka St., Wewoka, AR 74884; Ed. Bill Robinson; Pub. Bill Robinson; adv. contact: Cindy Davis. photos; pub. size: tabloid; circ. evening 1,200(paid).

YALE
US
YALE NEWS, THE. 1902. Wed. $.35 newsstand; $15.50/yr. 103 N. Main St., Yale, OK 74085. TEL 918-387-2125. E-mail: yale-news@okpress.tfnet.org. **Owner(s):** Beth & Homer Ray, 103 N. Main St., P.O. Box 307, Yale, OK 74085. TEL 918-387-2125; adv.; photos; bk.rev.; pub. size: standard; circ. 1,500(paid).

YUKON
US
CANADIAN COUNTY CHRONICLE. q.; 1st weekend. free. 110 S. Fifth, Yukon, OK 73099. TEL 405-354-5264; FAX 405-350-3044. **Owner(s):** Randel & Karen Grigsby, 110 S. Fifth, Yukon, OK 73099. TEL 405-354-5264; Ed. Conrad Dudderar; Pub. Randel Gribsby; adv.; pub. size: broadsheet; circ. 30,000(free).

US
YUKON REVIEW. 1963. s-w.: Wed. & Sat. $.50 newsstand; $26/yr. 110 S. Fifth, Yukon, OK 73099. TEL 405-354-5264; FAX 405-350-3044. **Owner(s):** Randel & Karen Grigsby, 110 S. Fifth, Yukon, OK 73099. TEL 405-354-5264; Ed. Conrad Dudderar; Pub. Randel Grigsby; adv.; photos; pub. size: broadsheet; circ. 7,100(paid).

OREGON

BAKER CITY
US
BAKER RECORD-COURIER. 1901. Thu. $15/yr. local; $18/yr. out of area. 1718-1720 Main, Baker City, OR 97814-0070. TEL 541-523-5353. **Owner(s):** Byron Brinton, 2517 Valley, Baker City, OR 97814. TEL 503-523-4395; Ed. Ron Brinton; Pub. Byron Brinton; adv. contact: Doyle Perry. pub. size: broadsheet; circ. 5,040(paid).

BANDON
US
WESTERN WORLD. 1912. Wed. $.50 newsstand; $18/yr. cy.; $22/yr. out of cy.; $30/yr.out of state. 1185 Baltimore St., Bandon, OR 97411. TEL 541-347-2423; FAX 541-347-2424. **Owner(s):** Greg & Mary McNair, P.O. Box 248, Bandon, OR 97411-0248. TEL 541-347-2423; FAX 541-347-2424; Ed. Greg McNair. adv. contact: Lori Osborne. photos; pub. size: broadsheet; circ. 2,800(paid).

BROOKINGS
US
CURRY COASTAL PILOT. 1946. s-w.: Wed. & Sat. $.50 newsstand; $34/yr. local; $44/yr. elsewhere. 507 Chetco Ave., Brookings, OR 97415. TEL 541-469-3123; FAX 541-469-4679. **Owner(s):** Western Communications, Inc., 1526 N.W. Hill St., Bend, OR 97701. TEL 541-382-1811; Ed. Jerry Teague; Pub. Charles Kocher; adv. contact: Craig Michaelson. pub. size: broadsheet; circ. 7,055(free & paid).

BURNS
US
BURNS TIMES-HERALD. 1887. Wed. $.50 newsstand; $25/yr. in cy.; $30/yr. out of cy. 355 N. Broadway, Burns, OR 97720. TEL 541-573-2022; FAX 541-573-3915. **Owner(s):** Western Communications, Inc., 1526 N.W. Hill St., Bend, OR 97701. TEL 541-382-1811; Ed. Pauline Braymen; Pub. Donna Clark; adv.; photos; pub. size: broadsheet; circ. 3,200(paid).

CANBY
US
CANBY HERALD. 1906. Wed. $.50 newsstand; $22/yr. in cy.; $30/yr. out of cy. 241 N. Grant St., Canby, OR 97013. TEL 503-266-6831. **Owner(s):** Eagle Newspapers, Inc., 4901 Indian School Rd., N.E., Salem, OR 97305. TEL 503-393-1774; Ed. Cam Sivesind; Pub. William D. Cassel; adv. contact: William D. Cassel. pub. size: standard; circ. 10,200(paid).

CONDON
US
TIMES-JOURNAL, THE. 1886. Thu. $.35 newsstand; $19/yr. 319 S. Main St., Condon, OR 97823-0746. TEL 541-384-2421; FAX 541-384-2411. **Owner(s):** McLaren & Janet Stinchfield, 319 S. Main St., Condon, OR 97823-0746. TEL 541-384-2421; FAX 541-384-2411; Ed. McLaren Stinchfield; Pub. McLaren Stinchfield; adv.; photos; bk.rev.; pub. size: standard; circ. 1,677(paid).

COQUILLE
US
COQUILLE VALLEY SENTINEL. 1882. Wed. $.50 newsstand; $16/yr. in cy. One Barton's Alley, Coquille, OR 97423. TEL 503-396-3191; FAX 503-396-3624. **Owner(s):** Coquille Valley Publishing, P.O. Box 400, Coquille, OR 97423. TEL 541-396-3191; FAX 541-396-3624; Ed. Frederick Taylor; Pub. Frederick Taylor; adv.; pub. size: standard; circ. 1,900(paid).

COTTAGE GROVE
US
COTTAGE GROVE SENTINEL. 1889. Wed. $20.50/yr. in area; $26/yr. out of area. 116 N. Sixth St., Cottage Grove, OR 97424. TEL 503-942-3325; FAX 503-942-3328. **Owner(s):** Walt Disney Co., 500 S. Buena Vista St., Burbank, CA 91521. TEL 818-560-5300; Ed. Mark Bowder; Pub. Jody Rolnick; adv. contact: Brad Chambers. pub. size: standard; circ. 5,000(paid).

CRESWELL
US   ISSN 0739-9758
CHRONICLE, THE. 1966. Wed. $.75 newsstand; $18/yr. in cy.; $21/yr. out of cy. 244 W. Oregon Ave., Creswell, OR 97426. TEL 541-895-2197. **Owner(s):** Gerri O'Rourke, P.O. Box 428, Creswell, OR 97426. TEL 541-895-2197; Ed. Gerri O'Rourke; Pub. Gerri O'Rourke; adv. contact: Gerri O'Rourke. pub. size: tabloid; circ. 3,600(free & paid).
Formerly: Creswell Chronicle.

DALLAS
US
DALLAS POLK COUNTY ITEMIZER-OBSERVER. 1875. Wed. $.50 newsstand; $18/yr. in cy.; $24/yr. out of cy.; $30/yr. out of state. 147 S.E. Court St., Dallas, OR 97338. TEL 503-623-2373; FAX 503-623-2395. **Owner(s):** Eagle Newspapers, Inc., 4901 Indian School Rd., N.E., Salem, OR 97305. TEL 503-393-1774; Ed. Virginia Henderson; Pub. Nancy J. Adams; adv. contact: Korri Miller. photos; pub. size: tabloid; circ. 13,700(free & paid).

WEEKLY NEWSPAPERS

DAYTON
US

DAYTON TRIBUNE. 1912. Thu. $.10 newsstand; $6/yr. in cy. 408 Fourth St., Dayton, OR 97114-0069. TEL 503-864-2310; FAX 503-864-2310. **Owner(s):** George & Edwina Meitzen, P.O. Box 69, Dayton, OR 97114-0069. TEL 503-864-2310; FAX 503-864-2310; Ed. George Meitzen. adv.; pub. size: tabloid; circ. 428(paid).

DRAIN
US

DRAIN ENTERPRISE. 1950. Wed. $.30 newsstand; $11/yr. in cy. 309 First St., Drain, OR 97435-0026. TEL 503-836-2241. **Owner(s):** Betty Anderson, P.O. Box 26, Drain, OR 97435; Ed. Sue Anderson. adv.; pub. size: tabloid; circ. 1,200(paid).

EAGLE POINT
US

UPPER ROGUE INDEPENDENT. 1976. Tue. $.25 newsstand; $11.50/yr. in area; $23/yr. out of area; $8.65/yr. senior citizens. 11136 Hwy. 62, Eagle Point, OR 97524. TEL 503-826-7700; FAX 503-826-1340. **Owner(s):** Nancy Leonard, 11136 Hwy. 62, Eagle Point, OR 97524. TEL 503-826-7700; FAX 503-826-1340; Ed. Nancy Leonard; Pub. Nancy Leonard; adv.; photos; pub. size: tabloid; circ. 10,000(free & paid).

EUGENE
US

EUGENE WEEKLY. Thu. free; $60/yr. 1251 Lincoln St., Eugene, OR 97401. TEL 541-484-0519; FAX 541-484-4044. **Owner(s):** Sonja Snyder, 1251 Lincoln St., Eugene, OR 97401. TEL 541-484-0519; Ed. Debra Gwartney; Pub. Sonja Snyder; pub. size: tabloid; circ. 27,000(paid).

FLORENCE
US

SIUSLAW NEWS, THE. 1890. Wed. $.50 newsstand; $20/yr. in cy.; $30/yr. out of cy.; $55/yr. out of state. 148 Maple St., Florence, OR 97439. TEL 541-997-3441; FAX 541-997-7979. **Owner(s):** Mr. & Mrs. Paul R. Holman, 1490 Myrtle Loop, Florence, OR 97439. TEL 541-997-6615; Ed. Bob Serra; Pub. Paul R. Holman; adv. contact: Pam Girard. pub. size: broadsheet; circ. 7,000(paid).

FOREST GROVE
US   ISSN 1042-8518

NEWS TIMES. 1887. Wed. $24/yr. in cy.; $37/yr. out of cy. 2038 Pacific Ave., Forest Grove, OR 97116-0408. TEL 503-357-3181; FAX 503-359-8456. **Owner(s):** Community Newspapers, Inc., 2038 Pacific Ave., Forest Grove, OR 97116. TEL 503-357-3181; Ed. Jim Hart. adv.; photos; pub. size: standard; circ. 9,100(free & paid).

GOLD BEACH
US

GOLD BEACH CURRY COUNTY REPORTER. 1914. Wed. $.50 newsstand; $17/yr. in cy.; $24/yr. out of cy. 29835 Ellensburg, Gold Beach, OR 97444. TEL 541-247-6643; FAX 541-247-6644. **Owner(s):** Curry County Reporter, Inc., P.O. Box 766, Gold Beach, OR 97444. TEL 541-247-6643; Ed. Molly Walker. adv.; pub. size: broadsheet; circ. 3,241(paid).

GRANTS PASS
US

CENTRAL VALLEY TIMES. Wed. $15/yr. home deliv. P.O. Box 1468, Grants Pass, OR 97526. TEL 541-664-5665; FAX 541-664-7000. **Owner(s):** Courier Publishing Co., P.O. Box 1468, Grants Pass, OR 97526. TEL 503-474-3700; FAX 503-474-3723; Ed. Steve Baily; Pub. Dennis Mack; adv. contact: Michele Thomas. pub. size: broadsheet; circ. 15,000(paid).

US

COUNTRY WEEKLY. Wed. free. 409 S.E. Seventh St., Grants Pass, OR 97526. TEL 541-474-3700; FAX 541-474-3824. **Owner(s):** Courier Publishing Co., P.O. Box 1468, Grants Pass, OR 97526. TEL 503-474-3700; FAX 503-474-3723; Ed. Barbara Hahn; Pub. Dennis Mack; adv. contact: Michele Thomas. pub. size: broadsheet; circ. 21,750(free).

GRESHAM
US

GRESHAM OUTLOOK. 1911. s-w.: Wed. & Sat. $.50 newsstand; $30/yr. carrier; $34/yr. in cy. mailed; $38/yr. out of cy. 1190 N.E. Division St., Gresham, OR 97030. TEL 503-665-2181; FAX 503-665-2187. **Owner(s):** Walt Disney Co., 500 S. Buena Vista St., Burbank, CA 91521. TEL 818-560-5300; Ed. Dave Magnuson; Pub. William R. Hunter; adv. contact: Bruce Tarbet. pub. size: standard; circ. 12,500(paid).

HERMISTON
US

HERMISTON HERALD. 1906. Tue. $.75 newsstand; $18.50/yr. local; $16.50/yr. senior citizens. 193 E. Main St., Hermiston, OR 97838. TEL 541-567-6457; FAX 541-567-4125. **Owner(s):** Western Communications, Inc., 1526 N.W. Hill St., Bend, OR 97701. TEL 541-382-1811; Ed. Michael Kane. adv.; photos; pub. size: broadsheet; circ. 13,500(free & paid). **Wire Service(s):** AP.

HILLSBORO
US

ALOHA BREEZE. 1974. Wed. free. 150 S.E. Third Ave., Hillsboro, OR 97123. TEL 503-648-1131; FAX 503-648-9191. **Owner(s):** Hillsboro Argus, 150 S.E. Third Ave., P.O. Box 588, Hillsboro, OR 97123. TEL 503-648-1131; Ed. Val Hess; Pub. Walter V. McKinney; adv. contact: Dick Bixler. pub. size: standard; circ. 5,450(free).

US   ISSN 8750-5479

HILLSBORO ARGUS. 1873. s-w.: Tue. & Thu. $.50 newsstand; $30/yr. 150 S.E. Third Ave., Hillsboro, OR 97123. TEL 503-648-1131; FAX 503-648-9191. **Owner(s):** McKinney Publishing Co., 150 S.E. Third Ave., Hillsboro, OR 97123-0588. TEL 503-648-1131; FAX 503-648-9191; Ed. Val Hess. adv. contact: Dick Bixler. photos; bk.rev.; pub. size: broadsheet; circ. 15,271(free & paid).

US

WEST VALLEY COURIER. 1965. Wed. free. 150 S.E. Third Ave., Hillsboro, OR 97123. TEL 503-648-1131. **Owner(s):** McKinney Publishing Co., 150 S.E. Third Ave., Hillsboro, OR 97123. TEL 503-648-1131; FAX 503-648-9191; Ed. Val Hess. adv. contact: Dick Bixler. pub. size: broadsheet; circ. 28,310(free).

HOOD RIVER
US

HOOD RIVER NEWS. 1905. s-w.: Wed. & Sat. $.50 newsstand; $38/yr. local; $61/yr. elsewhere; $31/yr. senior citizens local. 419 State Ave., Hood River, OR 97031. TEL 541-386-1234; FAX 541-386-6796. **Owner(s):** Eagle Newspapers, Inc., P.O. Box 12008, Salem, OR 97309. TEL 541-393-1774; Pub. James Kelly; adv.; photos; pub. size: broadsheet; circ. 5,973(paid).

LAKE OSWEGO
US   ISSN 0889-2369

LAKE OSWEGO REVIEW. Thu. $.75 newsstand; $24/yr. tri-cy. area; $37/yr. out of state. 111 A Ave., Lake Oswego, OR 97034. TEL 503-635-8811; FAX 503-635-8817. **Owner(s):** Steve & Randalyn Clark, P.O. Box 370, Beaverton, OR 97075. TEL 503-684-0360; Ed. Dana Haynes; Pub. Bob Bigelow; pub. size: standard; circ. 9,400(paid).

US

WEST LINN TIDINGS. 1981. Thu. $.50 newsstand; $24/yr. 111 A Ave., Lake Oswego, OR 97034. TEL 503-635-8811; FAX 503-635-8817. **Owner(s):** Community News, Inc., P.O. Box 370, Beaverton, OR 97075. TEL 503-684-0360; FAX 503-620-3433; Ed. Julie Vertrees; Pub. Bob Bigelow; adv.; pub. size: standard; circ. 6,925(paid).

LAKEVIEW
US   ISSN 1062-5313

LAKE COUNTY EXAMINER. Thu. $.45 newsstand; $20/yr. in cy.; $24/yr. out of cy. 305 N. F St., Lakeview, OR 97630. TEL 541-947-3378; FAX 541-947-4359. **Owner(s):** Clamath Publishing Co., P.O. Box 271, Lakeview, OR 97630. TEL 541-947-3378; FAX 541-947-4359; Ed. Eric Hogstrom; Pub. Tillie Flynn; adv.; pub. size: broadsheet; circ. 3,100(paid).

LEBANON
US

LEBANON EXPRESS. 1887. Wed. $.35 newsstand; $18.50/yr. local. 90 E. Grant St., Lebanon, OR 97355. TEL 541-258-3151; FAX 541-259-3569. **Owner(s):** Walt Disney Co., 500 S. Buena Vista St., Burbank, CA 91521. TEL 818-560-5300; Ed. Theresa Rice; Pub. John Buckner; adv.; photos; pub. size: broadsheet; circ. 4,500(paid).

LINCOLN CITY
US

NEWS GUARD, THE. 1927. Wed. $.50 newsstand; $24/yr. in cy.; $36/yr. out of cy. 930 S.E. Hwy. 101, Lincoln City, OR 97367. TEL 541-994-2178; FAX 541-994-7613; E-mail: newsguard@orcoastnews.com; URL: http://www.orcoastnews.com/newsguard. **Owner(s):** Pacific Coast Newspapers, Inc., P.O. Box 848, Lincoln City, OR 97367. TEL 503-842-7535; Ed. Niki Price; Pub. David Price; adv. contact: Heather Hatton. photos; pub. size: broadsheet; circ. 6,500(paid).

MADRAS

US

MADRAS PIONEER, THE. 1904. Wed. $.50 newsstand; $18/yr. in cy.; $24/yr. out of cy. 241 S.E. Sixth St., Madras, OR 97741-1635. TEL 503-475-2275; FAX 503-475-3710. **Owner(s):** Eagle Newspapers, Inc., P.O. Box 12008, Salem, OR 97309. TEL 503-393-1774; Ed. Susan Matheny; Pub. Tony Ahern; adv. contact: Teena Hubbard. pub. size: standard; circ. 3,400(paid).

MCMINNVILLE

US

NEWS-REGISTER. 1866. 3/wk.: Tue., Thu., Sat. $.50 newsstand; $13.50/3 mos. 611 E. Third, McMinnville, OR 97128. TEL 503-472-5114; FAX 503-472-9151. **Owner(s):** Bladine Family, 611 E. Third, McMinnville, OR 97128. TEL 503-472-5114; Ed. Jeb Bladine; Pub. Jeb Bladine; adv. contact: Rick McDonald. pub. size: broadsheet; circ. 10,400(paid).

MERRILL

US

BUTTE VALLEY STAR. 1927. Tue. $.30 newsstand; $13.50/yr. 365 Front St., Merrill, OR 97633. TEL 541-798-5668; FAX 541-798-5668. **Owner(s):** Star Syndicate, 111 W. Third, Dorris, CA 96023. TEL 916-397-2601; Ed. Beth Sikes; Pub. Carol McKay; adv. contact: Ron Edwards. pub. size: broadsheet; circ. 3,000(free & paid).

US

LOST RIVER STAR. 1927. Wed. $.30 newsstand; $13.50/yr. 365 Front St., Merrill, OR 97633. TEL 541-798-5668; FAX 541-798-5668. **Owner(s):** Star Syndicate, 111 W. Third, Dorris, CA 96023. TEL 916-397-2601; Ed. Beth Sikes; Pub. Carol McKay; adv. contact: Ron Edwards. pub. size: broadsheet; circ. 3,500(free & paid).

MILWAUKEE

US

CLACKAMAS REVIEW. 1922. Fri. free in area; $22/yr. out of area; $30/yr. out of state; $18/yr. senior citizens. 4287 S.E. International Way, Ste. F, Milwaukee, OR 97222-8825. TEL 503-786-1996; FAX 503-786-6977; E-mail: 76440.1042@compuserve.com. **Owner(s):** Columbia River Newspapers, Inc., 4287 S.E. International Way, Ste. F, Milwaukee, OR 97222-8825. TEL 503-786-1996; FAX 503-786-6977; Ed. Robert Wederquist; Pub. William Swindells; pub. size: broadsheet; circ. 25,000(paid).
Formerly: Clackamas County Review.

MYRTLE CREEK

US   ISSN 0745-7588

UMPQUA FREE PRESS. 1902. Thu. $.35 newsstand; $16/yr. in cy.; $20/yr. out of cy. 119 S. Main St., Myrtle Creek, OR 97457. TEL 541-863-5233; FAX 541-863-5234. **Owner(s):** Umpqua Free Press, Inc., P.O. Box 729, Myrtle Creek, OR 97457. TEL 541-863-5234; Pub. Robert F. Scherer; pub. size: tabloid; circ. 2,900(paid).

NEWBERG

US

NEWBERG GRAPHIC. 1888. s-w.: Wed. & Sat. $.50 newsstand; $30/yr. in cy. 109 N. School St., Newberg, OR 97132. TEL 503-538-2181; FAX 503-538-1632. **Owner(s):** Eagle Newspapers, Inc., 4091 Indian School Rd., N.E., Salem, OR 97305. TEL 503-393-1774; FAX 503-463-9898; Ed. David Thouvenel; Pub. David Thouvenel; adv.; photos; bk.rev.; pub. size: broadsheet; circ. 10,400(free & paid).

NEWPORT

US

NEWS-TIMES. 1892. s-w.: Wed. & Fri. $.50 newsstand; $52/yr. in cy.; $104/yr. out of cy. 831 N.E. Avery, Newport, OR 97365. TEL 541-265-8571; FAX 541-265-3103. **Owner(s):** Walt Disney Co., 500 S. Buena Vista St., Burbank, CA 91521. TEL 818-560-5300; Ed. Leslie O'Donnell; Pub. Mary Jo Parker; adv. contact: Mary Jo Parker. photos; pub. size: broadsheet; circ. 10,500(controlled & paid).
Formerly: Newport News Times.

PENDLETON

US

PENDLETON RECORD, THE. 1911. Thu. $20/yr. 809 S.E. Court, Pendleton, OR 97801-9998. TEL 541-276-2853. **Owner(s):** Pendleton Record, The, 809 S.E. Court, Pendleton, OR 97801. TEL 541-276-2853; Ed. R.E. Maznaritz; Pub. Margaret Maznaritz; adv.; pub. size: standard; circ. 1,000(paid).

PHILOMATH

US

BENTON BULLETIN. 1976. Thu. $.50 newsstand; $21/yr.; $35/yr. out of state. 1324 Main St., Philomath, OR 97370-0340. TEL 541-929-3043; FAX 541-929-7250. **Owner(s):** Edward Hawley, 25027 Dunham, P.O. Box 188, Veneta, OR 97487. TEL 541-929-3043; FAX 541-929-3043; Ed. Judy Hunt; Pub. Edward Hawley; adv. contact: Patricia Hunt. photos; bk.rev.; pub. size: tabloid; circ. 1,100(paid).

PORTLAND

US

BEE, THE. 1906. m.: 3rd Thu. free newsstand; $12/yr. mailed. P.O. Box 82127, Portland, OR 97282-0127. TEL 503-692-8527; FAX 503-692-8527; E-mail: jdillin@class.orednet.org. **Owner(s):** Three Rivers Communications, Inc., 17605 S.W. 108th Pl., Tualatin, OR 97062. TEL 503-692-8527; FAX 503-692-8527; Ed. John F. Dillin, Jr.; Pub. John F. Dillin, Jr.; adv. contact: John F. Dillin, Jr. photos; bk.rev.; pub. size: tabloid; circ. 14,000(free & paid).

US

ISLAND CONNECTION. m. free. 700 N. Haden Island Dr., Ste. 210, Portland, OR 97217. TEL 503-283-5086; FAX 503-735-1446. **Owner(s):** Gayla Whitman, 700 N. Haden Island Dr., Ste. 210, Portland, OR 97217. TEL 503-283-5086; FAX 503-735-1446; Ed. Gayla Whitman; Pub. Gayla Whitman; adv.; pub. size: tabloid.

US

ST. JOHNS REVIEW. 1904. bi-w.: Fri $12/yr. 700 N. Haden Island Dr., Ste. 210, Portland, OR 97217. TEL 503-283-5086; FAX 503-735-1446. **Owner(s):** Gayla Whitman, 700 N. Haden Island Dr., Ste. 210, Portland, OR 97217. TEL 503-283-5865; FAX 503-735-1446; Ed. Ty Walker; Pub. Gayla Whitman; pub. size: tabloid; circ. 3,500(paid).

US

WILLAMETTE WEEK. 1974. Wed. free newsstand; $90/yr. mailed in OR & WA. 822 S.W. Tenth Ave., Portland, OR 97205-2519. TEL 503-243-2122; FAX 503-243-1115; E-mail: rmeeker@wweek.com. **Owner(s):** City of Roses Newspaper Co., 822 S.W. Tenth Ave., Portland, OR 97205. TEL 503-243-2122; Ed. Mark L. Zusman; Pub. Richard H. Meeker; adv. contact: Russ Martineau. photos; bk.rev.; pub. size: tabloid; circ. 75,000(free & paid). **Wire Service(s):** AlterNet.

PRINEVILLE

US

CENTRAL OREGONIAN, THE. 1881. s-w.: Tue. & Thu. $.50 newsstand; $24/yr. 558 N. Main St., Prineville, OR 97754. TEL 503-447-6205; FAX 503-447-1754. **Owner(s):** Eagle Newspapers, Inc., P.O. Box 12008, Salem, OR 97309. TEL 503-393-7980; Ed. James O. Smith; Pub. James O. Smith; adv.; $7.50/SAU. pub. size: broadsheet; circ. 6,300(free & paid).
Formerly: Prineville Central Oregonian.

REDMOND

US

REDMOND SPOKESMAN. 1910. Wed. $.35 newsstand; $18/yr. in state; $25/yr. out of state. 226 N. Sixth St., Redmond, OR 97756. TEL 541-548-2184; FAX 541-548-3203. **Owner(s):** Western Communications, Inc., 1526 N.W. Hill St., Bend, OR 97701. TEL 541-382-1811; Ed. Scott Maben; Pub. Carl Vertrees; adv. contact: Lane Jorgenson. photos; bk.rev.; pub. size: broadsheet; circ. 4,700(paid).

REEDSPORT

US

COURIER, THE. Thu. $.50 newsstand; $19/yr. in cy.; $24/yr. out of cy. 174 N. 16th St., Reedsport, OR 97467. TEL 541-271-3633; FAX 541-271-3138. **Owner(s):** Dan Olson, 174 N. 16th St., Reedsport, OR 97467. TEL 541-271-3633; FAX 541-271-3138; Ed. Dan Olson; Pub. Dan Olson; adv.; photos; pub. size: broadsheet; circ. 2,900(paid).

ROGUE RIVER

US

ROGUE RIVER PRESS. 1962. Wed. $.50 newsstand; $18/yr. in cy.; $28/yr. out of cy. 105 Gardiner St., Rogue River, OR 97537. TEL 541-582-1707; FAX 541-582-0201; E-mail: rrpress@echoweb.net. **Owner(s):** River Press Publishers, Inc., 105 Gardiner St., Rogue River, OR 97537. TEL 541-582-1707; Ed. Dave Ehrhardt; Pub. Heidi Ehrhardt; adv.; photos; bk.rev.; pub. size: tabloid; circ. 2,000(free & paid).
Formerly: River Press.

SANDY

US

SANDY POST. Wed. $.35 newsstand; $15/yr. in cy. mailed; $18/yr. out of cy.; $23/yr. out of state. 17270 S.E. Bluff Rd., Sandy, OR 97055. TEL 503-668-5548; FAX 503-665-2187. **Owner(s):** Walt Disney Co., 500 S. Buena Vista St., Burbank, CA 91521. TEL 818-560-5300; Ed. Dave Magnuson; Pub. William R. Hunter; adv. contact: Bruce Tarbet. pub. size: standard; circ. 3,000(paid).

SEASIDE

US

SEASIDE SIGNAL. 1905. Thu. $.50 newsstand; $24/yr. in cy.; $36/yr. out of cy. 113 N. Holladay, Seaside, OR 97138. TEL 503-738-5561; FAX 503-738-5672. **Owner(s):** Pacific Coast Newspapers, Inc., 1902 Second, Tillamook, OR 97141. TEL 503-842-7535; Ed. Cat Mauldin; Pub. Tom Mauldin; adv.; photos; bk.rev.; pub. size: broadsheet; circ. 3,600(paid).

SILVERTON

US

SILVERTON APPEAL-TRIBUNE/MT. ANGEL NEWS. 1881. Wed. $.50 newsstand; $24/yr. mailed. 399 S. Water St., Silverton, OR 97381. TEL 503-873-8385; FAX 503-873-8064. **Owner(s):** East Valley Newspapers, P.O. Box 35, Silverton, OR 97381. TEL 503-873-8385; Ed. Joe Petshow; Pub. Paula Marbey; adv. contact: Jim Kinghorn. photos; pub. size: standard; circ. 7,800(free & paid).

SPRINGFIELD

US

SPRINGFIELD NEWS, THE. 1903. s-w.: Wed. & Sat. $.35 newsstand; $4/mo. in cy; $4.50/mo. out of cy.; $29/yr. carrier; $48/yr. out of cy. 1887 Laura St., Springfield, OR 97477. TEL 541-746-1671; FAX 541-746-0633; E-mail: thenews@axessnw.com; URL: http://www.axessnw.com/~henews. **Owner(s):** Walt Disney Co., 500 S. Buena Vista, Burbank, CA 91521. TEL 818-560-5300; Pub. David Holgate; adv. contact: Janet Rumsey. pub. size: broadsheet; circ. 10,500(paid). **Wire Service(s):** UPI.

STAYTON

US

STAYTON MAIL. 1892. Tue. $.50 newsstand; $15/yr. P.O. Box 400, Stayton, OR 97383. TEL 503-769-6338; FAX 503-769-6207. **Owner(s):** Gannett Company, Inc., 1100 Wilson Blvd., Arlington, VA 22234. TEL 703-284-6000; Pub. Paula Mabry; adv.; photos; pub. size: broadsheet; circ. 2,700(paid).

ST. HELENS

US

ST. HELENS CHRONICLE. 1881. s-w.: Wed. & Sat. $.35 newsstand; $22/yr. in cy. 195 S. 15th St., St. Helens, OR 97051. TEL 503-397-0116; FAX 503-397-4093. **Owner(s):** Parsons Associates, Inc., P.O. Box 1153, St. Helens, OR 97051. TEL 503-397-0116; FAX 503-397-4093; Ed. Greg Cohen; Pub. Pamela Petersen; adv.; pub. size: standard; circ. 17,900(free & paid).

SWEET HOME

US

NEW ERA, THE. 1929. Wed. $.50 newsstand; $24/yr. in cy.; $29/yr. out of cy. 313 Main, Sweet Home, OR 97386. TEL 541-367-2135; FAX 541-367-2137. **Owner(s):** Alex & Debra Paul, P.O. Box 39, Sweet Home, OR 97386. TEL 503-367-8426; Ed. Alex Paul; Pub. Alex Paul; adv. contact: Debra Paul. pub. size: broadsheet; circ. 8,000(paid).

Formerly: Sweet Home New Era.

TIGARD

US

BEAVERTON VALLEY TIMES. 1920. Thu. $.50 newsstand; $24/yr. 6975 S.W. Sandburg Rd., Tigard, OR 97223. TEL 503-684-0360; FAX 503-620-3433. **Owner(s):** Steve & Randalyn Clark, P.O. Box 370, Beaverton, OR 97075; Ed. Mikel Kelly; Pub. Steve Clark; adv. contact: Steve Clark. pub. size: broadsheet; circ. 5,972(paid).

US

TIGARD TIMES. 1956. Thu. $.50 newsstand; $24/yr. 6975 S.W. Sandburg Rd., Tigard, OR 97223. TEL 503-684-0360; FAX 503-620-3433. **Owner(s):** Steve & Randalyn Clark, P.O. Box 370, Beaverton, OR 97075; Ed. Mikel Kelly; Pub. Steve Clark; adv. contact: Fred Board. photos; pub. size: broadsheet; circ. 9,603(paid).

TILLAMOOK

US

HEADLIGHT-HERALD. 1888. Wed. $.50 newsstand; $24/yr. in cy.; $36/yr. out of cy. 1908 Second St., Tillamook, OR 97141. TEL 503-842-7535; FAX 503-842-8842; E-mail: shaffer@orcoastnews.com. **Owner(s):** Pacific Coast Newspapers, Inc., P.O. Box 444, Tillamook, OR 97141. TEL 503-842-7535; FAX 503-842-8842; Ed. Scott Frank; Pub. Linda Shaffer; adv. contact: Mary K. Hanthorn. photos; pub. size: broadsheet; circ. 8,052(paid).

VALE

US

MALHEUR ENTERPRISE. 1909. Wed. $.50 newsstand; $20/yr. in cy.; $30/yr. out of cy.; $15/yr. senior citizens; $15/yr. students. P.O. Box 310, Vale, OR 97918. TEL 541-473-3377; FAX 541-473-3268. **Owner(s):** Barbara Schaffeld, P.O. Box 310, Vale, OR 97918. TEL 503-473-3377; FAX 503-473-3268; Ed. Rachel Haueter. adv. contact: Matt Kunzman. pub. size: broadsheet; circ. 2,350(paid).

PALAU

KOROR

US

PALAU GAZETTE. 1980. m. free. Palau Government, Koror, PW 96940. TEL 680-488-3257; FAX 680-488-1662. **Owner(s):** Palau Government/Office of the President, P.O. Box 100, Koror, PW 96940, paid. TEL 680-488-3257; FAX 680-488-1662; Ed. Sally Soalabai; Pub. Kunkod Nakamura; photos; pub. size: standard; circ. 2,000(free).

PENNSYLVANIA

ALBION

US

ALBION NEWS, THE. 1921. Wed. $.45 newsstand; $16/yr. 16 Market St., Albion, PA 16401. TEL 814-756-4133; FAX 814-756-5643. **Owner(s):** Penn-Ohio Graphics, Inc., P.O. Box 245, Jefferson, OH 44047. TEL 216-576-9115; FAX 216-576-2735; Ed. Vickie Canfield Peters; Pub. John Lampson; adv. contact: Bill Creed. photos; bk.rev.; pub. size: tabloid; circ. 3,550(paid).

ALIQUIPPA

US

NEWS, THE. 1961. Thu. free. 1181 Airport Rd., Aliquippa, PA 15001-0629. TEL 412-375-6611. E-mail: thenews@tristate.pgh.net; URL: http://www.tristate.pgh.net/news. **Owner(s):** R.A. Palket Co., Inc., P.O. Box 629, Aliquippa, PA 15001-0629; Pub. R.A. Palket; adv.; pub. size: tabloid; circ. 66,656(free).

ALLENTOWN

US

EAST PENN PRESS. 1959. Wed. $.50 newsstand; $23.40/yr. 1633 N. 26th St., Allentown, PA 18104. TEL 610-740-0944; FAX 610-740-0947. **Owner(s):** Pencor Services, Inc., P.O. Box 215, Palmerton, PA 18071. TEL 215-826-2551; Ed. Julia Foster Nazimov; Pub. Fred Masenheimer; adv. contact: Peg Stocking. pub. size: broadsheet; circ. 7,000(free & paid).

ARDMORE

US
MAIN LINE LIFE. 1988. Thu. $.50 newsstand; $19.95/yr. local. 110 Ardmore Ave., Ardmore, PA 19003. TEL 610-896-9555; FAX 610-896-9560. **Owner(s):** Montgomery Publishing Co., Fort Washington, PA; Ed. Warren Patton; Pub. Art Howe; adv. contact: Julian Rosado. pub. size: broadsheet; circ. 18,000(paid). **Formerly:** Mainliner, The.

US
MAIN LINE TIMES. 1930. Thu. $.50 newsstand; $31.20/yr. carrier; mail rate by zone. 311 E. Lancaster Ave., Ardmore, PA 19003. TEL 610-642-4300; FAX 610-649-9318. **Owner(s):** Acme Newspapers, Inc., 311 E. Lancaster Ave., Ardmore, PA 19003. TEL 215-642-4300; Ed. Daniel A. Eisenhuth; Pub. Deborah Shaw; adv. contact: Joyce Sullivan. photos; pub. size: broadsheet; circ. 16,300(controlled & paid). **Formerly:** Main Line Times/Main Line Sunday.

BANGOR

US
SLATEBELT HOMETOWN NEWS, THE. 1893. Thu. $.25 newsstand; $15/yr. in Slatebelt area; $17/yr. out of area. 13-15 Main St., Bangor, PA 18013. TEL 610-588-2196; FAX 610-759-4003. **Owner(s):** Janson Publishing Co., Inc., 13-15 S. Main St., Bangor, PA 18013. TEL 610-588-2196; Ed. Kathleen J. McFall; Pub. Kathleen J. McFall; adv. contact: Candi Martin. pub. size: tabloid; circ. 1,700(paid).

BARNESBORO

US
BARNESBORO STAR, THE. 1902. Wed. $.45 newsstand; $19.75/yr. in cy.; $23/yr. out of cy.; $26/yr. out of state. 520 Philadelphia Ave., Barnesboro, PA 15714. TEL 814-948-6210; FAX 814-948-7563. **Owner(s):** Sedloff Publications, Inc., P.O. Box 395, Portage, PA 15946. TEL 814-736-9666; Ed. Connie Miller. adv.; pub. size: broadsheet; circ. 5,404(paid).

BOYERTOWN

US
BOYERTOWN AREA TIMES. 1857. Thu. $.50 newsstand; $24/yr. 124 N. Chestnut St., Boyertown, PA 19512. TEL 610-367-6041; FAX 610-369-0233. **Owner(s):** Berks-Mont Newspapers, Inc., 124 N. Chestnut St., Boyertown, PA 19512. TEL 610-367-6041; Ed. Jeff Bell; Pub. James C. Webb; adv.; photos; pub. size: broadsheet; circ. 6,500(free & paid).

US
NEWS OF SOUTHERN BERKS, THE. 1885. Wed. $.50 newsstand; $20/yr. 124 N. Chestnut St., Boyertown, PA 19512. TEL 610-367-6041; FAX 610-369-0233. **Owner(s):** Berks-Mont Newspapers, Inc., 124 N. Chestnut St., Boyertown, PA 19512. TEL 610-367-6041; FAX 610-369-0233; Ed. Jolynn Weiler. adv.; photos; pub. size: broadsheet; circ. 2,500(paid).

BRADDOCK

US
FREE PRESS, THE. 1913. Thu. free newsstand; $27/yr. 522 Braddock Ave., Braddock, PA 15104-1807. TEL 412-271-0622; FAX 412-351-1593; E-mail: woodpub@aol.com. **Owner(s):** Woodland Publishing Co., 522 Braddock Ave., Braddock, PA 15104-1807. TEL 412-271-0622; Ed. Anthony Munson. adv.: $9/SAU. photos; pub. size: tabloid; circ. 19,700(free & paid).

BRADFORD

US
BRADFORD JOURNAL/MINER. 1832. Thu. $.45 newsstand; $23/yr. local; $33/yr. out of cy. 265 South Ave., Bradford, PA 16701. TEL 814-362-6563; FAX 814-368-8202. **Owner(s):** Grant & Debra Nichols, P.O. Box 17, Bradford, PA 16701. TEL 814-362-6563; Michelle Sherrick, P.O. Box 17, Bradford, PA 16701. TEL 814-362-6563; Adam & Steve Nichols, P.O. Box 17, Bradford, PA 16701. TEL 814-362-6563; Ed. Grant Nichols. adv. contact: Grant Nichols. photos; bk.rev.; pub. size: tabloid; circ. 5,500(paid). **Formerly:** McKean County Miner.

BRISTOL

US
BRISTOL PILOT. 1986. Thu. $.35 newsstand; $18/yr. 2100 Frost Rd., Bristol, PA 19007. TEL 215-788-1682; FAX 215-788-6328. **Owner(s):** Intercounty Newspaper Group, 6220 Ridge Ave., Philadelphia, PA 19128. TEL 215-483-7300; Ed. Kathleen Fratti; Pub. R. Arthur Thompson; adv. contact: Linda Tecce. pub. size: tabloid; circ. 4,200(paid).

BROOKVILLE

US
JEFFERSONIAN DEMOCRAT. 1839. Thu. $.50 newsstand; $26/yr. mailed. 301 Main St., Brookville, PA 15825. TEL 814-849-5339; FAX 814-849-4333. **Owner(s):** Independent Publications, Inc., 175 Main St., Brookville, PA 15825. TEL 814-949-5339; Ed. Randy Bartley; Pub. Dock Lias; adv. contact: Linda Smith. pub. size: broadsheet; circ. 4,500(paid).

CANTON

US
CANTON INDEPENDENT-SENTINEL. 1842. Thu. $.40 newsstand; $22-$25/yr. 41 Lycoming St., Canton, PA 17724-0127. TEL 717-673-5151; FAX 717-673-5152. **Owner(s):** John Shaffer, 70 Union St., Canton, PA 17724. TEL 717-673-4296; Ed. John Shaffer; Pub. John Shaffer; adv. contact: Lynda Juinn. photos; pub. size: broadsheet; circ. 2,000(free & paid).

CARBONDALE

US ISSN 0746-3510
CARBONDALE NEWS. 1872. Wed. $17/yr. local; $25/yr. out of state. 41 N. Church St., Carbondale, PA 18407. TEL 717-282-3300; FAX 717-282-3950. **Owner(s):** Hometown Publications, Inc., 41 N. Church St., Carbondale, PA 18407. TEL 717-282-3300; FAX 717-282-3950; Ed. Tom Fontana; Pub. Philip T. Heth; adv.: $4.98/SAU. pub. size: broadsheet; circ. 6,500(paid).

CLARION

US
CLARION NEWS. 1840. s-w.: Tue. & Thu. $.50 newsstand; $34.32/yr. home deliv. 645 Main St., Clarion, PA 16214. TEL 814-226-7000; FAX 814-226-7518. **Owner(s):** Western Penn Newspapers, 645 Main St., Clarion, PA 16214. TEL 814-226-7000; Ed. Paul Hambke; Pub. Patrick C. Boyle; adv. contact: Mary Logue. pub. size: broadsheet; circ. 7,000(paid).

CLARKS SUMMIT

US ISSN 1058-6865
ABINGTON JOURNAL. 1929. Wed. $.50 newsstand; $18/yr. 211 S. State St., Clarks Summit, PA 18411. TEL 717-587-1148; FAX 717-586-3980. **Owner(s):** Bartsen Media, Inc., P.O. Box 366, Dallas, PA 18612. TEL 717-675-5211; Ed. John Wharton, Jr.; Pub. Ronald Bartizek; adv. contact: David Gribbins. photos; bk.rev.; pub. size: broadsheet; circ. 3,800(paid).

CLAYSVILLE

US
WEEKLY RECORDER, THE. 1888. Fri. $.50 newsstand; $22/yr. in state; $24/yr. elsewhere. 256 Main St., Claysville, PA 15323-0506. TEL 412-663-7742. **Owner(s):** Weekly Recorder, P.O. Box F, Claysville, PA 15323-0506. TEL 412-663-7742; Ed. Douglas R. Teagarden; Pub. Douglas R. Teagarden; adv. contact: Susan Burd. pub. size: tabloid; circ. 3,500(paid).

COLLEGEVILLE

US
INDEPENDENT, THE. 1875. Tue. $.35 newsstand; $18/yr. in cy.; $20/yr. out of cy.; $24/yr. out of state. 350 Walnut St., Collegeville, PA 19426-0039. TEL 610-489-3001; FAX 610-489-8633. **Owner(s):** Montgomery Transcript Publishing Co., P.O. Box 39, Collegeville, PA 19426. TEL 610-489-3001; Ed. James T. Stewart; Pub. John Stewart; adv.: $6/SAU. photos; bk.rev.; pub. size: broadsheet; circ. 6,300(paid). **Formerly:** Independent News, The.

CONNEAUTVILLE

US
AREA SHOPPER. 1953. Mon. $18/yr. home deliv. 1022 Water St., Conneautville, PA 16406. TEL 814-587-2425; FAX 814-587-3302. **Owner(s):** Miller Printing & Publishing Co., 1022 Water St., Conneautville, PA 16406; Ed. Brian Miller; Pub. Brian Miller; pub. size: standard; circ. 90,000(paid).

US
CONNEAUTVILLE COURIER. Fri. $18/yr. Main St., Conneautville, PA 16406. TEL 814-587-2425; FAX 814-587-3302. **Owner(s):** Miller Printing & Publishing Co., Inc., 1022 Water St., Conneautville, PA 16406; Ed. Rhonda Curlowicz. pub. size: tabloid; circ. 1,000(free & paid).

WEEKLY NEWSPAPERS

CONSHOHOCKEN
US
RECORDER, THE. 1869. Thu. $.50 newsstand; $13/yr. in cy.; $18/yr. out of cy. Seventh & Fayette, Conshohocken, PA 19428. TEL 610-828-4600. **Owner(s):** Intercounty Newspaper Group, 6220 Ridge Ave., Philadelphia, PA 19128. TEL 215-483-7300; Ed. Nancy O'Brien; Pub. Fred W. Donaldson; adv. contact: Mike Cooper. photos; pub. size: tabloid; circ. 3,500(paid).

CORAOPOLIS
US   ISSN 1047-0689
RECORD, THE. 1903. Wed. $.50 newsstand; $.40/wk. home deliv.; $25.00/yr. 705 Fifth Ave., Coraopolis, PA 15108. TEL 412-264-4140; FAX 412-264-8269; E-mail: gateway@ghplus.infi.net; URL: http://www.ghplus.com. **Owner(s):** Trinity Holdings, Inc., 610 Beatty Rd., Monroeville, PA 15146. TEL 412-856-7400; FAX 412-856-7954; Ed. Harry Funk; Pub. Kevin Aylmer; adv.; pub. size: tabloid; circ. 4,862(paid).

COUDERSPORT
US
POTTER LEADER-ENTERPRISE. 1874. Wed. $.75 newsstand; $25/yr. in cy.; $28/yr. in state; $30/yr. out of state. 6 W. Second St., Coudersport, PA 16915. TEL 814-274-8044; FAX 814-274-8120. **Owner(s):** Leader Publishing Co., Inc., P.O. Box 29, Coudersport, PA 16915. TEL 814-274-8141; Ed. Teri L. McDowell; Pub. Joseph Majot; adv.; photos; pub. size: broadsheet; circ. 12,000(paid).

CRESSON
US   ISSN 0745-7499
CRESSON-GALLITZIN MAINLINER, THE. Wed. $.45 newsstand; $19.75/yr. in cy.; $23/yr. in state; $26/yr. out of state. 719 Front St., Cresson, PA 16630. TEL 814-886-2117. **Owner(s):** Sedloff Publications, Inc., P.O. Box 395, Portage, PA 15946. TEL 814-736-9666; Ed. Connie Miller; Pub. Colleen Krug; adv. contact: Colleen Krug. pub. size: broadsheet; circ. 3,642(paid).

DALLAS
US
DALLAS POST. 1889. Wed. $.50 newsstand; $20/yr. in state. 607 Main Rd., Dallas, PA 18612. TEL 717-675-5211. **Owner(s):** Bartsen Media, Inc., P.O. Box 366, Dallas, PA 18612. TEL 717-675-5211; Ed. Ronald Bartizek. adv.: $8.50/SAU. pub. size: broadsheet; circ. 3,000(paid).

DREXEL HILL
US
MARCUS HOOK PRESS. 1916. Thu. $7/yr. 3245 Garrett Rd., Drexel Hill, PA 19026. TEL 610-259-4141. **Owner(s):** Press Publishing Co., 3245 Garrett Rd., Drexel Hill, PA 19026. TEL 610-259-4141; Ed. M.M. Girard. adv.; photos; pub. size: tabloid; circ. 3,500(paid).

US
RIDLEY PRESS. 1963. Thu. $7/yr. 3245 Garrett Rd., Drexel Hill, PA 19026. TEL 610-259-4141. **Owner(s):** Press Publishing Co., 3245 Garrett Rd., Drexel Hill, PA 19026. TEL 610-259-4141; Ed. P.A. Girard; Pub. P.A. Girard; adv.; photos; pub. size: tabloid; circ. 7,000(paid).

US
UPPER DARBY PRESS. 1926. Thu. $7/yr. 3245 Garrett Rd., Drexel Hill, PA 19026. TEL 610-259-4141. **Owner(s):** Press Publishing Co., 3245 Garrett Rd., Drexel Hill, PA 19026. TEL 610-259-4141; Ed. P.A. Girard. adv.; photos; pub. size: tabloid; circ. 4,000(paid).

DUSHORE
US
SULLIVAN REVIEW. 1878. Thu. $.50 newsstand; $22/yr. in cy.; $27/yr. out of cy.; $32/yr. out of state. Main & Water Sts., Dushore, PA 18614. TEL 717-928-8403; FAX 717-928-8006. **Owner(s):** John A. Shoemaker, P.O. Box 305, Dushore, PA 18614. TEL 717-928-8403; Christine S. Shoemaker, P.O. Box 305, Dushore, PA 18614; Ed. T.W. Shoemaker; Pub. T.W. Shoemaker; adv. contact: Carmela Walosin. pub. size: broadsheet; circ. 7,000(paid).

EAST STROUDSBURG
US
POCONO SHOPPER. 1975. Wed. free. 96 S. Courtland St., East Stroudsburg, PA 18301. TEL 717-421-4800; FAX 717-421-4255. **Owner(s):** Scranton Times, Penn Ave., Scranton, PA; Ed. Toni Cusumano. adv. contact: Danny Brown. bk.rev.; pub. size: tabloid; circ. 38,000(controlled & free).

EBENSBURG
US
EBENSBURG NEWS LEADER, THE. Wed. $.45 newsstand; $19.75/yr. in cy.; $23/yr. out of cy.; $26/yr. out of state. 975 Rowena Dr., Ebensburg, PA 15931. TEL 814-472-4110. **Owner(s):** Sedloff Publications, Inc., Mainline Newspapers, P.O. Box 395, Portage, PA 15946. TEL 814-472-4110; Ed. Connie Miller. adv. contact: Barbara Cordoro. pub. size: broadsheet; circ. 2,225(paid).

US
MOUNTAINEER-HERALD, THE. 1853. Wed. $.45 newsstand; $23.40/yr. in cy.; $26/yr. out of cy. 113 S. Center St., Ebensburg, PA 15931. TEL 814-472-8240; FAX 814-472-8660. **Owner(s):** David E. Thompson, P.O. Box 359, Ebensburg, PA 15931. TEL 814-472-8240; Ed. Kathleen P. Nikolishen; Pub. David E. Thompson; adv.; photos; bk.rev.; pub. size: broadsheet; circ. 3,200(paid).

ELIZABETHTOWN
US   ISSN 0745-9122
ELIZABETHTOWN CHRONICLE. 1869. Thu. $.50 newsstand; $18/yr. in state; $25/yr. out of state. 25 Center Sq., Elizabethtown, PA 17022-2014. TEL 717-367-7152; FAX 717-367-3655. **Owner(s):** Reid Newspapers, Inc., 513 Chocolate Ave., Hershey, PA 17033. TEL 717-533-2900; FAX 717-531-2561; Ed. Jim Hazen; Pub. Wanda S. Reid; adv. contact: Barbara Smith. pub. size: broadsheet; circ. 3,520(free & paid).
Formerly: Chronicle, The.

EMPORIUM
US
CAMERON COUNTY ECHO. 1963. Wed. $.75 newsstand; $28/yr. 300 S. Broad St., Emporium, PA 15834. TEL 814-486-3711; FAX 814-486-0990. **Owner(s):** Cameron County Echo, P.O. Box 308, Emporium, PA 15834. TEL 814-486-3711; Ed. David A. Brown. adv. contact: Nancy A. Brown. photos; bk.rev.; pub. size: broadsheet; circ. 4,000(paid).

EPHRATA
US
EPHRATA REVIEW. Wed. $.30 newsstand; $15.50/yr. in cy.; $18/yr. out of cy.; $21/yr. out of state. One E. Main St., Ephrata, PA 17522. TEL 717-733-6397; FAX 717-733-6058. **Owner(s):** Lancaster Newspapers, Inc., 8 W. King St., Lancaster, PA 17603. TEL 717-733-6397; Ed. Andy Fasnacht. adv. contact: Doug Dussinger. pub. size: standard; circ. 13,000(paid).

ERIE
US
MILLCREEK SUN. Sun. $.60 newsstand; $20/yr.; $18/yr. senior citizens. 2126 Filmore Ave., Erie, PA 16506-2941. TEL 814-438-7666; FAX 814-838-9802. **Owner(s):** Brown-Thompson Newspapers, W. High St. Ext., Union City, PA 16438. TEL 814-438-7666; Ed. Claudia Mosso. adv.; photos; pub. size: standard; circ. 52,000(paid).

FORT WASHINGTON
US
AMBLER GAZETTE. 1882. Wed. $.75 newsstand; $31.20/yr. mailed. 290 Commerce Dr., Fort Washington, PA 19034. TEL 215-542-0200; FAX 215-643-9475. **Owner(s):** Montgomery Publishing Co., 290 Commerce Dr., Fort Washington, PA 19034. TEL 215-542-0200; Ed. Gillian H. Gordon; Pub. Arthur W. Howe, IV; adv. contact: Susan Gleaser. adv.: $23.24/SAU. pub. size: broadsheet; circ. 10,050(paid).

US
COLONIAL, THE. 1961. Thu. $.50 newsstand; $14/yr. home deliv. 290 Commerce Dr., Fort Washington, PA 19034. TEL 215-542-0200; FAX 215-643-9475. **Owner(s):** Montgomery Publishing Co., 290 Commerce Dr., Fort Washington, PA 19034. TEL 215-542-0200; Ed. Gillian Gordon; Pub. Arthur W. Howe, IV; adv. contact: Sue Greaser. pub. size: tabloid; circ. 6,000(paid).

US
MONTGOMERYVILLE SPIRIT. 1974. Wed. $.50 newsstand; $26/yr. carrier; $31.20/yr. mailed. 290 Commerce Dr., Fort Washington, PA 19034. TEL 215-542-0200; FAX 215-643-9457. **Owner(s):** Montgomery Publishing Co., 290 Commerce Dr., Fort Washington, PA 19034. TEL 215-542-0200; Ed. Elaine Abse; Pub. Arthur W. Howe, IV; adv. contact: Sue Greaser. adv.: $10.92/SAU. pub. size: broadsheet; circ. 11,414(paid).

FORT WASHINGTON, PA

US
SPRINGFIELD SUN. 1946. Thu. $.75 newsstand; $26/yr. carrier; $31.50/yr. mailed. 290 Commerce Dr., Fort Washington, PA 19034. TEL 215-542-0200; FAX 215-643-9475. **Owner(s):** Montgomery Publishing Co., 290 Commerce Dr., Fort Washington, PA 19034. TEL 215-646-5100; Ed. Gillian H. Gordon; Pub. Arthur W. Howe, IV; adv. contact: Susan Greaser. adv.: $23.24/SAU. pub. size: broadsheet; circ. 2,723(paid).

US
WILLOW GROVE GUIDE. 1925. Wed. $.75 newsstand; $31.20/yr. carrier; $36/yr. mailed. 290 Commerce Dr., Fort Washington, PA 19034. TEL 215-542-0200; FAX 215-643-9475. **Owner(s):** Montgomery Publishing Co., 290 Commerce Drive, Fort Washington, PA 19034. TEL 215-646-5100; Ed. Christina Hecker; Pub. Arthur W. Howe, IV; adv. contact: Susan Greaser. photos; pub. size: broadsheet; circ. 10,000(paid).

GIRARD

US
COSMOPOLITE-HERALD. 1866. Sun. $.60 newsstand; $20/yr.; $18/yr. senior citizens. P.O. Box 403, Girard, PA 16437. TEL 814-774-9648; FAX 814-774-0328. **Owner(s):** Brown-Thompson Newspapers, W. High St. Ext., Union City, PA 16438. TEL 814-438-7666; FAX 814-438-2898; Ed. Peggy J. Machinski. adv.; photos; pub. size: broadsheet; circ. 3,770(paid).
Formerly: Girard Cosmopolite-Herald.

GROVE CITY

US
ALLIED NEWS. 1879. Wed. $.50 newsstand; $15/yr. carrier & motor rte.; $16/yr. mailed in area; $19/yr. mailed out of area; $14/yr. senior citizens. 201A Erie St., Grove City, PA 16127. TEL 412-458-5010; FAX 412-458-1609. **Owner(s):** Ottaway Newspapers, Inc., P.O. Box 401, Campbell Hall, NY 10916. TEL 914-294-8181; Ed. Brian David; Pub. John Lima; adv.; pub. size: broadsheet; circ. 15,000(paid).

HAMBURG

US
HAMBURG ITEM. 1875. Wed. $18/yr. local; $22/yr. out of cy. P.O. Box 31, Hamburg, PA 19526. TEL 610-562-7515; FAX 610-562-7516. **Owner(s):** Avery D. Piersons, P.O. Box 31, Hamburg, PA 19526. TEL 610-562-7515; Ed. Avery D. Piersons; Pub. Avery D. Piersons; adv. contact: William Colunio. pub. size: standard; circ. 4,200(paid).

HAVERTOWN

US
NEWS OF DELAWARE COUNTY. 1930. Wed. $26/yr. home deliv.; $31.20/yr. in cy. mailed. Manoa Shopping Ctr., West Chester Pike, Havertown, PA 19083. TEL 610-446-8700; FAX 610-449-0419. **Owner(s):** Acme Newspapers, Inc., 311 E. Lancaster Ave., Ardmore, PA 19003. TEL 610-642-4300; Ed. Joan C. Toenniessen; Pub. Deb Shaw; adv. contact: John Coverdall. photos; bk.rev.; pub. size: broadsheet; circ. 46,000(free & paid).

HAWLEY

US
NEWS EAGLE. 1957. 3/wk.: Tue., Thu., Sat. $45/yr. Wayne & Pike cys.; $71/yr. out of area. 522 Spring St., Hawley, PA 18428. TEL 717-226-4547; FAX 717-226-4548. **Owner(s):** News Eagle, Inc., P.O. Box E, Hawley, PA 18428. TEL 717-226-4547; Pub. John C. Dyson, Jr.; adv. contact: Glenn Khoury. photos; pub. size: broadsheet; circ. 7,400(paid). **Wire Service(s):** AP.

HERSHEY

US ISSN 8750-8753
HERSHEY CHRONICLE, THE. 1984. Thu. $.50 newsstand; $18/yr. in state; $30/yr. out of state. 513 W. Chocolate Ave., Hershey, PA 17033. TEL 717-533-2900; FAX 717-531-2561. **Owner(s):** Reid Newspapers, Inc., 513 W. Chocolate Ave., Hershey, PA 17033. TEL 717-533-2900; FAX 717-531-2561; Ed. Susan Erb; Pub. Wanda S. Reid; adv.: $5.80/SAU. photos; pub. size: broadsheet; circ. 4,300(paid).

HOLMES

US
DELAWARE COUNTY JOURNAL. Wed. free newsstand. 1914 Parker Ave., Holmes, PA 19043. TEL 610-583-4432; FAX 610-583-0503. **Owner(s):** Wing Publications, 1300 MacDade Blvd., Folsom, PA 19033; Ed. Phil Anderson; Pub. Lewis Lax; adv. contact: Marian Asel. pub. size: tabloid; circ. 15,000(free).

US
TOWN TALK. 1963. Wed. free newsstand & carrier. 1914 Parker Ave., Holmes, PA 19043. TEL 610-583-4432; FAX 610-583-0503. **Owner(s):** Wing Publications, 1300 MacDade Blvd., Folsom, PA 19033. TEL 610-583-4432; Ed. Phil Anderson; Pub. Lewis Lax; adv. contact: Marian Asel. pub. size: tabloid; circ. 50,000(free).

HONESDALE

US ISSN 1063-2794
WEEKLY ALMANAC, THE. 1990. Wed. $.45 newsstand; $24/yr. mailed. 709 Church St., Honesdale, PA 18431-1831. TEL 717-253-9270; FAX 717-253-8937. **Owner(s):** James A. Kalbaugh, 709 Church St., Honesdale, PA 18431-1831. TEL 717-253-9270; FAX 717-253-8937; Judie G. Kalbaugh, 709 Church St., Honesdale, PA 18431-1831. TEL 717-253-9270; FAX 717-253-8937; Ed. James A. Kalbaugh; Pub. James A. Kalbaugh; adv. contact: Judie G. Kalbaugh. photos; bk.rev.; pub. size: tabloid; circ. 4,500(paid).

HORSHAM

US
BUCKS COUNTY TRIBUNE. 1961. Wed. free newsstand & carrier; $59/yr. mailed out of area. 390 Easton Rd., Horsham, PA 19044-2592. TEL 215-675-6600; FAX 215-675-8251. **Owner(s):** Progress Newspapers, Inc., 390 Easton Rd., Horsham, PA 19044. TEL 215-368-8600; Ed. Sandra L. Petersohn; Pub. Matthew Petersohn; adv. contact: Matthew Petersohn. adv.: $21.88/SAU. pub. size: tabloid; circ. 17,000(controlled & paid).

US
MONTGOMERY COUNTY PROGRESS. 1953. Wed. free newsstand & carrier; $59/yr. mailed. 390 Easton Rd., Horsham, PA 19044. TEL 215-675-8250; FAX 215-675-8251. **Owner(s):** Progress Newspapers, Inc., 390 Easton Rd., Horsham, PA 19044. TEL 215-368-8600; Ed. Sandra L. Petersohn; Pub. Matthew Petersohn; adv.: $21.88/SAU. pub. size: tabloid; circ. 17,200(free & paid).

US
SUNDAY BUCKS COUNTY TELEGRAPH. 1982. Sun. free newsstand & carrier; $59/yr. mailed. 390 Easton Rd., Horsham, PA 19044. TEL 215-675-8250. **Owner(s):** Progress Newspapers, Inc., 390 Easton Rd., Horsham, PA 19044. TEL 215-368-8600; Ed. Sandra L. Petersohn; Pub. Matthew Petersohn; adv.: $34/SAU. pub. size: tabloid; circ. Sun. 8,100(free & paid).
Formerly: Bucks County Telegraph.

HUMMELSTOWN

US
SUN, THE. 1871. Wed. $.45 newsstand; $15/yr. in state; $18/yr. out of state. 115-117 S. Water St., Hummelstown, PA 17036. TEL 717-566-3251; FAX 717-566-6196. **Owner(s):** William S. & Rosemary K. Jackson, 1406 Bradley Ave., Hummelstown, PA 17036. TEL 717-566-8958; Ed. William S. Jackson; Pub. Rosemary Jackson; adv.; photos; bk.rev.; pub. size: broadsheet; circ. 6,800(free & paid).

JEANNETTE

US ISSN 0746-5971
JEANNETTE SPIRIT. 1983. Wed. $.40 newsstand; $20.60/yr. in cy.; $28.60/yr. out of cy.; $30.60/yr. out of state. 107 S. Second St., Jeannette, PA 15644. TEL 412-527-2868; FAX 412-887-5115. **Owner(s):** Laurel Group Press, 229 Pittsburgh St., Scottdale, PA 15683. TEL 412-887-7400; Ed. Gregory L. Stock; Pub. Ralph Heanrley; adv. contact: Art Meyers. photos; pub. size: standard; circ. 2,300(paid).

JENKINTOWN

US
GLENSIDE NEWS. 1923. Wed. $.75 newsstand; $31.20/yr. 101 Greenwood Ave., Ste. 130, Jenkintown, PA 19046. TEL 215-885-1345; FAX 215-884-9112. **Owner(s):** Montgomery Publishing Co., 290 Commerce Dr., Fort Washington, PA 19034. TEL 215-542-0200; Pub. Arthur W. Howe, IV; adv. contact: Susan Greser. pub. size: broadsheet; circ. 3,200(paid).

US
GLOBE, THE. 1927. Thu. $.75 newsstand; $31.20/yr. mailed. 101 Greenwood Ave., Ste. 130, Jenkintown, PA 19046. TEL 215-885-1345; FAX 215-884-9112. **Owner(s):** Montgomery Publishing Co., 290 Commerce Dr., Fort Washington, PA 19034. TEL 215-646-5100; Pub. Arthur W. Howe, IV; adv. contact: Susan Greaser. pub. size: broadsheet; circ. 4,000(paid).

WEEKLY NEWSPAPERS

US

TIMES CHRONICLE. 1894. Wed. $.75 newsstand; $26/yr. carrier; $31.20/yr. mailed. 101 Greenwood Ave., Ste. 130, Jenkintown, PA 19046. TEL 215-885-1345; FAX 215-884-9112. **Owner(s):** Montgomery Publishing Co., 290 Commerce Dr., Fort Washington, PA 19034. TEL 215-646-8170; Ed. Regis D'Angiolini; Pub. Arthur W. Howe, IV; adv. contact: Leslie Hamada. pub. size: broadsheet; circ. 10,000(paid).

JOHNSONBURG

US

JOHNSONBURG PRESS, INC., THE. 1900. Wed. $.60 newsstand; $22.50-$26/yr. 517 Market St., Johnsonburg, PA 15845. TEL 814-965-2503; FAX 814-965-2504. **Owner(s):** Johnsonburg Press, Inc., The, 517 Market St., Johnsonburg, PA 15845. TEL 814-965-2503; FAX 814-965-2504; Ed. Frances Fowler. adv.; photos; pub. size: standard; circ. 2,500(paid).

KING OF PRUSSIA

US

KING OF PRUSSIA COURIER. 1964. Wed. free delivery. 707 W. Dekalb Pike, King of Prussia, PA 19406. TEL 610-265-0775; FAX 610-265-0776; E-mail: swtimes@aol.com. **Owner(s):** Suburban Publications, 134 N. Wayne Ave., Wayne, PA 19087. TEL 610-688-3000; FAX 610-254-8522; Ed. James Lewis. adv.; photos; pub. size: broadsheet; circ. 7,000(free).

KUTZTOWN

US ISSN 1041-4029

PATRIOT, THE. 1874. Thu. $.50 newsstand; $18,50/yr. 15076 Kutztown Rd., Kutztown, PA 19530. TEL 610-683-7343; FAX 610-683-5136. **Owner(s):** Kutztown Publishing Co., P.O. Box 346, Kutztown, PA 19530. TEL 610-683-7343; FAX 610-683-5136; Pub. Jacob R. Esser; adv. contact: Lois Esser. photos; pub. size: standard; circ. 5,700(paid).

LANCASTER

US

SUNDAY NEWS. Sun. $1.50 newsstand. 8 King St., Lancaster, PA 17608. TEL 717-291-8811; FAX 717-399-6506. **Owner(s):** Lancaster Newspapers, Inc., 8 King St., Lancaster, PA 17608. TEL 717-291-8811; Ed. Dave Hennigen. adv.; pub. size: broadsheet; circ. morning 105,000(paid). **Wire Service(s):** AP, NYT, KR.

LANSFORD

US ISSN 1056-4853

VALLEY GAZETTE. 1972. m. $.75 newsstand; $16/yr. mailed. 102 W. Water St., Lansford, PA 18232-1920. TEL 717-645-4692. **Owner(s):** Gazette Publications, 102 W. Water St., Lansford, PA 18232. TEL 717-645-4692; Ed. Edward Gildea. adv.; photos; bk.rev.; pub. size: tabloid; circ. 1,500(paid).

LEWISBURG

US ISSN 0888-0999

VALLEY TRADER. 1980. w. $25/yr. 637 Market St., Lewisburg, PA 17837-1451. TEL 800-800-4047; FAX 717-529-4048; E-mail: oberpub@theway2sell.com; URL: http://www.theway2sell.com. **Owner(s):** Oberdorf Publishing Co., 637 Market St., Lewisburg, PA 17837-1451. TEL 717-524-9850; Ed. Max Oberdorf. adv.; photos; bk.rev.; pub. size: tabloid; circ. 16,000(controlled & free).

LIBRARY

US

PARK NEWS. 1981. m. $6/yr. 2550 Brownsville, Library, PA 15129. TEL 412-831-2588; FAX 412-831-2588; E-mail: parknews@nb.net. **Owner(s):** Wayne Perry, 3104 Trapper Dr., Library, PA 15129. TEL 412-348-6773; FAX 412-831-2588; Constance Perry, 3104 Trapper Dr., Library, PA 15129. TEL 412-348-6773; FAX 412-831-2588; Ed. Wayne Perry. adv.; photos; pub. size: tabloid; circ. 7,500(controlled & free).

LIGONIER

US

LIGONIER ECHO. 1888. Wed. $.45 newsstand; $23.60/yr. in cy.; $35.60/yr. out of cy.; $37.60/yr. out of state. 112 W. Main St., Ligonier, PA 15658. TEL 412-238-2111; FAX 412-887-5115. **Owner(s):** Laurel Group Press, 229 Pittsburgh St., Scottdale, PA 15683-0222. TEL 412-887-7400; Ed. Richard P. Schwab. pub. size: broadsheet; circ. 4,734(paid).

US

LIGONIER FREE GAZETTE, THE. 1990. q. free/distributed & mailed. P.O. Box G, Ligonier, PA 15658-1607. TEL 412-238-5749; FAX 412-238-5190; E-mail: ekmyers@westol.com. **Owner(s):** E. Kay Myers Advertising/PR, P.O. Box G, Ligonier, PA 15658-1607. TEL 412-238-5749; FAX 412-238-5190; Pub. E. Kay Myers; adv.; photos; pub. size: tabloid; circ. 15,000(controlled & free).

LITITZ

US

LITITZ RECORD EXPRESS, THE. 1877. Thu. $.30 newsstand; $9.50/yr. 22 E. Main St., Lititz, PA 17543. TEL 717-626-2191; FAX 717-733-6058. **Owner(s):** Lancaster Newspapers, Inc., 8 W. King St., Lancaster, PA 17603. TEL 717-291-8811; FAX 717-399-6518; adv. contact: Donald Campbell. adv.: $7.50/SAU. photos; pub. size: broadsheet; circ. 7,200(free & paid).

MARTINSBURG

US

MORRISONS COVE HERALD. 1885. Thu. $.50 newsstand; $20/yr. in state; $23/yr. out of state. 113 N. Market St., Martinsburg, PA 16662-0277. TEL 814-793-2144; FAX 814-793-4882. **Owner(s):** Morrisons Cove Herald, Inc., P.O. Box 277, Martinsburg, PA 16662. TEL 814-793-2144; FAX 814-793-4882; Pub. David Snyder; adv. contact: William Keagle. photos; pub. size: standard; circ. 6,200(paid).

MCCONNELLSBURG

US

MCCONNELLSBURG FULTON COUNTY NEWS. 1899. Thu. $18/yr. in cy.; $19/yr. out of cy.; $23/yr. out of state. E. Market & Fifth, McConnellsburg, PA 17233. TEL 717-485-3811; FAX 717-485-5187; E-mail: fcnews@cvn.net. **Owner(s):** Jamie S. Greathead, 321 S. Second, McConnellsburg, PA 17233. TEL 717-485-4513; FAX 717-485-5187; Ed. Bob Saul. adv. contact: Tina Gress. pub. size: standard; circ. 6,300(paid). **Wire Service(s):** AP.

MCDONALD

US

RECORD-ENTERPRISE. 1886. Wed. $30/yr. mailed; $26/yr. by carrier. 116 E. Lincoln Ave., McDonald, PA 15057. TEL 412-926-2111; FAX 412-926-2123. **Owner(s):** Observer Publishing Co., S. Main St., Washington, PA 15301. TEL 412-222-2200; Ed. Eliza A. Northrop. adv.; photos; pub. size: broadsheet; circ. 5,700(paid).
Formerly: Record-Outlook & Enterprise.

MCKEES ROCKS

US

SUBURBAN GAZETTE. 1892. Wed. $20/yr. in cy.; $32/yr. out of cy. 421 Locust St., McKees Rocks, PA 15136-3599. TEL 412-331-2645. **Owner(s):** Virginia A. Schramm, 421 Locust St., McKees Rocks, PA 15136. TEL 412-331-2645; Ed. James C. DiNardo. adv.; pub. size: tabloid; circ. 8,700(paid).

MCMURRAY

US

ADVERTISER, THE. 1965. Thu. free; $22.50/yr. out of area. 3801 Washington Rd., McMurray, PA 15317. TEL 412-941-7725; FAX 412-941-8685. **Owner(s):** Observer-Reporter, 122 S. Main St., Washington, PA 15301. TEL 412-222-2200; Ed. Debbie Popp. adv. contact: Alice Bonnim. pub. size: broadsheet; circ. 34,641(free & paid).

US

ALMANAC, THE. 1968. Wed. free local; $22.50/yr. elsewhere. 3801 Washington Rd., McMurray, PA 15317. TEL 412-561-0700; FAX 412-941-8685. **Owner(s):** Observer-Reporter, 122 S. Main St., Washington, PA 15301. TEL 412-222-2200; Ed. Debbie Popp. adv. contact: Alice Bonnim. pub. size: broadsheet; circ. 33,279(free & paid).

MEDIA

US

TOWN TALK. 1963. Wed. free newsstand & carrier. 39 Old State Rd., Media, PA 19063. TEL 215-566-6755; FAX 215-566-1261. **Owner(s):** Town Talk Newspapers, P.O. Box 110, Media, PA 19063. TEL 215-566-6755; FAX 215-566-1261; Ed. Chris Parker; Pub. Edward Berman; adv.; photos; bk.rev.; pub. size: tabloid; circ. 85,000(free).

MIDDLEBURG

US
POST, THE. 1856. Wed. $17/yr. in cy.; $22.75/yr. out of cy.; $31.85/yr. out of state. 11 S. Main St., Middleburg, PA 17842. TEL 717-837-6065; FAX 717-837-0776. **Owner(s):** Sun County Times, P.O. Box 356, Middleburg, PA 17842; Ed. Kevin Kelley; Pub. Sue Weaver; adv.; pub. size: broadsheet; circ. 2,500(paid).

MIDDLETOWN

US
PRESS & JOURNAL, THE. 1854. Wed. $.50 newsstand; $22/yr. in state; $34/yr. out of state. 20 S. Union St., Middletown, PA 17057. TEL 717-944-4628; FAX 717-944-2083. **Owner(s):** Joseph G. Sukle, P.O. Box 310, Middletown, PA 17057. TEL 717-944-4628; David Graybill, P.O. Box 310, Middletown, PA 17057. TEL 717-944-4628; Mike Graybill, P.O. Box 310, Middletown, PA 17057. TEL 717-944-4628; Louise Sukle, P.O. Box 310, Middletown, PA 17057. TEL 717-944-4628; Ed. Joseph G. Sukle; Pub. Joseph G. Sukle; adv. contact: Maxine J. Etter. photos; pub. size: broadsheet; circ. 11,400(controlled & paid).
Formerly: Middletown Press & Journal.

MIFFLINBURG

US
MIFFLINBURG TELEGRAPH, THE. 1862. Thu. $.25 newsstand; $8/yr. in cy; $9/yr. out of cy. 358 Walnut St., Mifflinburg, PA 17844. TEL 717-966-2255; FAX 717-966-9706. **Owner(s):** John Stamm, 358 Walnut St., Mifflinburg, PA 17844. TEL 717-966-2255; FAX 717-966-9706; Pub. John Stamm; adv.; photos; pub. size: tabloid; circ. 756(paid).

MIFFLINTOWN

US
JUNIATA SENTINEL. 1846. Wed. $.50 newsstand; $15/yr. in cy.; $20/yr. out of cy. Old Rte. 22, R.D. 1, Mifflintown, PA 17059. TEL 717-436-8206; FAX 717-436-5174. **Owner(s):** Swank-Fowler Publications, Inc., P.O. Box 127, Mifflintown, PA 17059. TEL 717-436-8206; FAX 717-436-5174; Ed. Polly Digen. adv.; pub. size: standard; circ. 8,000(paid).

MILFORD

US ISSN 1059-2377
PIKE COUNTY DISPATCH. 1856. Thu. $24/yr. in state; $27/yr. out of state. 105 W. Catharine St., Milford, PA 18337. TEL 717-296-6641; FAX 717-296-2610. **Owner(s):** Sue Doty-Lloyd, P.O. Box 186, Milford, PA 18337. TEL 717-296-6641; Ed. Christopher Jones; Pub. Sue Doty-Lloyd; adv.; photos; pub. size: broadsheet; circ. 5,500(paid).

MILLERSBURG

US
UPPER DAUPHIN SENTINEL. 1972. Tue. $.50 newsstand; $21/yr. in state. 510 Union St., Millersburg, PA 17061. TEL 717-692-4737; FAX 717-692-2420; E-mail: uds@epix.net. **Owner(s):** Kocher Enterprises, Inc., P.O. Box 169, Millersburg, PA 17061. TEL 717-692-4737; FAX 717-692-2420; Ed. Duane Good; Pub. Ben L. Kocher; adv. contact: Dale Hoy. photos; pub. size: broadsheet; circ. 9,500(paid).

MONROEVILLE

US
ADVANCE LEADER. 1901. Wed. $.50 newsstand; $25/yr. 610 Beatty Rd., Monroeville, PA 15146. TEL 412-856-7400; FAX 412-856-7954; E-mail: gateway@ghplus.com. URL: http:www.ghplus.com. **Owner(s):** Trinity Holdings, Inc., 610 Beatty Rd., Monroeville, PA 15146. TEL 412-856-7400; FAX 412-856-7954; Pub. Kevin Aylmer; adv. contact: Rick Vaccarelli. photos; pub. size: broadsheet; circ. 5,879(paid).

US ISSN 1047-0670
BRIDGEVILLE AREA NEWS. 1926. Wed. $.50 newsstand; $25/yr. 610 Beatty Rd., Monroeville, PA 15146. TEL 412-221-6397. E-mail: newsitem@ghplus.infi.net; URL: http://www.ghplus.com/hometown/bridgeville. **Owner(s):** Trinity Holdings, Inc., 600 Beatty Rd., Monroeville, PA 15146. TEL 412-856-7400; FAX 412-856-7954; Ed. Donna Selling; Pub. Kevin Aylmer; adv.; pub. size: tabloid; circ. 2,519(paid).

US
MURRYSVILLE AREA STAR. 1972. Wed. $.50 newsstand; $25/yr. 610 Beatty Rd., Monroeville, PA 15146. TEL 412-856-7400; FAX 412-856-7954; E-mail: gateway@ghplus.infl.net; URL: http:llwww.ghplus.com. **Owner(s):** Trinity Holdings, Inc., 610 Beatty Rd., Monroeville, PA 15146. TEL 412-856-7400; FAX 412-856-7954; Pub. Kevin Aylmer; adv. contact: Rick Vaccarelli. pub. size: broadsheet; circ. 5,721(free & paid).

US
PROGRESS, THE. 1948. Wed. $.50 newsstand; $25/yr. 610 Beatty Rd., Monroeville, PA 15146. TEL 412-856-7400; FAX 412-856-7954; E-mail: gateway@ghplus.infl.net; URL: http://www.ghplus.com. **Owner(s):** Trinity Holdings, Inc., 610 Beatty Rd., Monroeville, PA 15146. TEL 412-856-7400; FAX 412-856-7954; Pub. Kevin Aylmer; adv. contact: Rick Vaccarelli. photos; pub. size: broadsheet; circ. 7,004(paid).

US ISSN 1047-0697
SEWICKLEY HERALD. 1903. Wed. $.50 newsstand; $25/yr. 610 Beatty Rd., Monroeville, PA 15146. TEL 412-856-7400; FAX 412-856-7954; E-mail: sherald@ghplus.infi.net; URL: http://www.ghplus.com. **Owner(s):** Trinity Holdings, Inc., 610 Beatty Rd., Monroeville, PA 15146. TEL 412-856-7400; FAX 412-856-7954; Pub. Kevin Aylmer; adv. contact: Rick Vaccarelli. pub. size: tabloid; circ. 4,160(paid).

US ISSN 1047-0662
SIGNAL-ITEM. 1873. Wed. $.50 newsstand; $25/yr. 610 Beatty Rd., Monroeville, PA 15146. TEL 412-856-7400; FAX 412-856-7954; E-mail: newsitem@ghplus.infi.net; URL: http://www.ghplus.com/hometown/signal. **Owner(s):** Trinity Holdings, Inc., 610 Beatty Rd., Monroeville, PA 15146. TEL 412-856-7400; FAX 412-856-7954; Ed. Donna Selling; Pub. Kevin Aylmer; adv. contact: Rick Vaccarelli. pub. size: tabloid; circ. 4,537(paid).

US
TIMES-EXPRESS. 1893. Wed. $.50 newsstand; $25/yr. home deliv. 610 Beatty Rd., Monroeville, PA 15146. TEL 412-856-7400; FAX 412-856-7954; E-mail: gateway@ghplus.:infi.net; URL: http://www.ghplus.com. **Owner(s):** Trinity Holdings, Inc., 610 Beatty Rd., Monroeville, PA 15146. TEL 412-856-7400; FAX 412-856-7954; Pub. Kevin Aylmer; adv. contact: Rick Vaccarelli. photos; pub. size: broadsheet; circ. 5,847(paid).

MONTROSE

US
INDEPENDENT, THE. Wed. $.55 newsstand; $21/yr.; $25 out of cy. 24 S. Main St., Montrose, PA 18801. TEL 717-278-6397; FAX 717-278-6397. **Owner(s):** County Publishers Corp., 24 S. Main St., Montrose, PA 18801. TEL 717-278-6397; Ed. Teri Olcott; Pub. Elizabeth Taylor; adv. contact: Debbie Oaks. photos; pub. size: tabloid; circ. 1,500(paid).

US
SUSQUEHANNA COUNTY INDEPENDENT. 1816. Wed. $.55 newsstand; $21/yr. in cy.; $25/yr. out of cy. 24 S. Main St., Montrose, PA 18801. TEL 717-278-6397; FAX 717-278-4305. **Owner(s):** Earl Wootton, County Publishers Corp., 24 S. Main St., Montrose, PA 18801. TEL 717-278-6397; Robert Wootton, County Publishers Corp., 24 S. Main St., Montrose, PA 18801. TEL 717-278-6397; Ed. Elizabeth Taylor; Pub. Elizabeth Taylor; adv.; pub. size: tabloid; circ. 5,000(paid).

US
WEEKEND NEWS. 1990. Sat. free. 24 S. Main St., Montrose, PA 18801. TEL 717-278-6397; FAX 717-278-6397. **Owner(s):** County Publishers Corp., 24 S. Main St., Montrose, PA 18801. TEL 717-278-6397; Ed. Teri Olcott; Pub. Elizabeth Taylor; adv. contact: Debbie Oaks. pub. size: tabloid; circ. 16,500(free).

MOSCOW

US
VILLAGER, THE. 1961. Wed. $17/yr. in state; $21/yr. out of state. R.D. 2, Box 2186B, Moscow, PA 18444. TEL 717-842-8789; FAX 717-842-9841. **Owner(s):** Hometown Publications, Inc., 41 N. Church St., Carbondale, PA 18407. TEL 717-282-3300; Ed. Philip Heth; Pub. Philip Heth; adv.: $4.78/SAU. pub. size: broadsheet; circ. 4,300(paid).
Formerly: Moscow Hamlin Villager.

MOUNTAIN TOP

US
MOUNTAINTOP EAGLE. 1969. Wed. $.50 newsstand; $18/yr. 85 S. Main Rd., Mountain Top, PA 18707. TEL 717-474-6397; FAX 717-474-9272. **Owner(s):** Stephanie Grubert, 13 Wilderness Dr., Mountain Top, PA 18707. TEL 717-868-3617; Ed. Kathy Flower; Pub. Stephanie Grubert; adv. contact: Stephanie Grubert. pub. size: broadsheet; circ. 3,000(paid).

WEEKLY NEWSPAPERS

MT. JOY

US

ELIZABETHTOWN MOUNT JOY MERCHANDISER.
1975. Wed. $36/yr. 3rd class mailed; $70/yr.
1st class mailed. 1425 W. Main St., Mt. Joy, PA
17552. TEL 717-653-1835;
FAX 717-653-5606. **Owner(s):** Charles &
Pauline Engle, P.O. Box 500, Mt. Joy, PA 17552.
TEL 717-653-1833; Ed. Joanna Smith; Pub.
Charles Engle; adv.; pub. size: tabloid; circ.
17,665(free).
  Formerly: Mount Joy Merchandiser.

MT. PLEASANT

US

ADVISOR, THE. 1978. Wed. $.35 newsstand;
$18.60/yr. 23-33 S. Church St., Mt. Pleasant,
PA 15666. TEL 412-547-5722;
FAX 412-887-5115. **Owner(s):** Laurel Group
Press, 229 Pittsburgh St., Scottdale, PA
15683-0222. TEL 412-887-7400; Ed. Jonna L.
Stairs. pub. size: broadsheet; circ. 3,418(paid).

US

MOUNT PLEASANT JOURNAL. 1873. Wed. $.45
newsstand; $23.60/yr. 23 S. Church St., Mt.
Pleasant, PA 15666. TEL 412-547-5722;
FAX 412-887-5115. **Owner(s):** Laurel Group
Press, 229 Pittsburgh St., Scottdale, PA 15683.
TEL 412-887-7400; Ed. Marsha L. Forys; Pub.
Joseph F. Soforic; adv. contact: Charles D. Hixson.
pub. size: broadsheet; circ. 5,935(paid).

NANTY GLO

US   ISSN 0746-4037

NANTY GLO JOURNAL, THE. Wed. $.45 newsstand;
$19.75/yr. in cy.; $23/yr. in state; $26/yr. out
of state. 975 Roberts St., Nanty Glo, PA 15943.
TEL 814-749-8631. **Owner(s):** Sedloff
Publications, Inc., P.O. Box 395, Portage, PA
15946; Ed. Connie Miller; Pub. Barbara Cordoro;
adv. contact: Barbara Cordoro. pub. size:
broadsheet; circ. 3,088(paid).

NEW BETHLEHEM

US

LEADER-VINDICATOR, THE. 1885. Wed. $.40
newsstand; $20/yr. in state; $40/yr. out of state.
435 Broad St., New Bethlehem, PA 16242.
TEL 814-275-3131; FAX 814-275-3531.
Owner(s): Southern Clarion County Newspapers,
Inc., 435 Broad St., New Bethlehem, PA 16242.
TEL 814-275-3131; FAX 814-275-3531; Pub.
James R. Shaffer; adv. contact: James R. Shaffer.
adv.: $5.40/SAU. photos; pub. size: standard;
circ. 5,200(paid).

NEW BLOOMFIELD

US

DUNCANNON RECORD. 1886. Thu. $17/yr. in cy.;
$25/yr. out of cy. 51 N. Church St., New
Bloomfield, PA 17068. TEL 717-582-4305.
Owner(s): Swank-Fowler Publications, Inc., P.O.
Box 130, New Bloomfield, PA 17068; Ed. Gary
Thomas; Pub. Rick White; circ. evening
3,609(paid).

US   ISSN 0889-3810

NEWS-SUN, THE. 1868. Wed. $17/yr. in state. 51
N. Church St., New Bloomfield, PA 17068.
TEL 717-582-4305; FAX 717-582-7933.
Owner(s): Swank-Fowler Publications, Inc., 51 N.
Church St., New Bloomfield, PA 17068. TEL
717-582-4305; Ed. Gary Thomas; Pub. Rick
White; adv.; bk.rev.; pub. size: standard; circ.
3,239(paid).

US

PERRY COUNTY TIMES. 1886. Thu. $17/yr. in cy.
51 N. Church St., New Bloomfield, PA 17068.
TEL 717-582-4305; FAX 715-582-7933.
Owner(s): Swank-Fowler Publications, Inc., P.O.
Box 130, New Bloomfield, PA 17068. TEL
717-582-4305; Ed. Gary Thomas; Pub. Rick
White; adv.; bk.rev.; pub. size: broadsheet; circ.
5,770(paid).

NEW HOPE

US

NEW HOPE GAZETTE. 1948. Thu. $18.50/yr.;
$23/yr. out of cy.; $32/2 yrs. 170 Old York Rd.,
New Hope, PA 18938-0180.
TEL 215-862-9435; FAX 215-862-2160.
Owner(s): Intercounty Newspaper Group, 6220
Ridge Ave., Philadelphia, PA 19128. TEL
215-483-7300; Ed. Bridget Wingert; Pub. R.A.
Thompson; adv. contact: Victoria Burke. pub. size:
tabloid; circ. 4,000(paid).

NEWTOWN

US

ADVANCE OF BUCKS COUNTY. 1877. Thu. $.50
newsstand; $22/yr. 9 W. Centre Ave., Newtown,
PA 18940. TEL 215-968-2244;
FAX 215-968-2244. **Owner(s):** Intercounty
Newspaper Group, 6220 Ridge Ave., Philadelphia,
PA 19128. TEL 215-483-7300; Ed. Nancy
Pickering; Pub. Art Thompson; adv. contact: Kay
Williams. photos; pub. size: tabloid; circ.
6,000(paid).

NEWTOWN SQUARE

US

COUNTY PRESS. 1931. Wed. $18/yr.; $30/2 yrs.;
$42/3 yrs. 3732 West Chester Pike, Newtown
Square, PA 19073-0249. TEL 610-356-6664;
FAX 610-353-5321. **Owner(s):** Richard Crowe,
3732 West Chester Pike, Newtown Square, PA
19073. TEL 610-356-6664; William Lawrence,
3732 West Chester Pike, Newtown Square, PA
19073. TEL 610-356-6664; Ed. William
Lawrence; Pub. Richard Crowe; adv.: $8.40/SAU.
pub. size: tabloid; circ. 8,250(free & paid).

US

DREXEL HILL PRESS. 1990. Wed. free deliv.; $.35
newsstand; $15/yr. 3732 West Chester Pike,
Newtown Square, PA 19073.
TEL 610-356-6664; FAX 610-353-5321.
Owner(s): Richard Crowe, 3732 West Chester
Pike, Newton Square, PA 19073; William
Lawrence, 3732 West Chester Pike, Newtown
Square, PA 19073; Ed. William Lawrence; Pub.
Richard Crowe; adv.: $7.80/SAU. pub. size:
tabloid; circ. 2,600(free & paid).

US

HAVERFORD PRESS. 1985. Wed. $.50 newsstand;
$18/yr. 3732 West Chester Pike, Newtown
Square, PA 19073-0249. TEL 610-356-3820;
FAX 610-353-5321. **Owner(s):** Richard Crowe,
3732 West Chester Pike, Newton Square, PA
19073. TEL 610-356-6664; William Lawrence,
3732 West Chester Pike, Newton Square, PA
19073. TEL 610-356-6664; Reese Crowe, 3732
West Chester Pike, Newton Square, PA 19073;
Ed. William Lawrence; Pub. Richard Crowe; adv.:
$7.80/SAU. pub. size: tabloid; circ. 2,900(free &
paid).

NEWVILLE

US

VALLEY TIMES-STAR. 1858. Wed. $.40 newsstand;
$18.20/yr. 23 W. Big Spring Ave., Newville, PA
17241. TEL 717-776-3197;
FAX 717-776-9290. **Owner(s):** Shippensburg
News-Chronicle Co., Inc., P.O. Box 100,
Shippensburg, PA 17257. TEL 717-532-4101;
FAX 717-532-3020; Ed. Barbara Thompson; Pub.
Kenneth W. Wolfrom; adv. contact: Steve Helm.
photos; pub. size: broadsheet; circ. 3,500(paid).

NORRISTOWN

US

MONTGOMERY POST, THE. 1961. Thu. $.50
newsstand; $12/yr. 416 Egypt Rd., Norristown,
PA 19403. TEL 610-630-6200;
FAX 610-630-9765. **Owner(s):** Montgomery
Publishing Co., 290 Commerce Dr., Fort
Washington, PA 19034. TEL 215-542-0200; Ed.
Maggie Lockwood; Pub. Arthur Howe, IV; adv.;
pub. size: broadsheet; circ. 15,000(paid).
  Formerly: Post, The.

NORTH EAST

US

NORTH EAST BREEZE. 1868. Fri. $.60 newsstand;
$20/yr. 35-39 S. Lake St., North East, PA
16428. TEL 814-725-4557. **Owner(s):**
Brown-Thompson Newspapers, W. High St.
Extension, Union City, PA 16438. TEL
814-438-7666; Ed. Peggy Machinski. adv.; pub.
size: broadsheet; circ. 3,368(paid).

ORBISONIA

US

VALLEY LOG, THE. 1980. Wed. $.50 newsstand;
$18/yr. 111 S. Ridgley St., Orbisonia, PA
17243-0219. TEL 814-447-5506;
FAX 814-447-3050. **Owner(s):** C. Arnold
McClure, RD1, Shirleysburg, PA 17260. TEL
814-542-2588; FAX 814-447-3050; Ed. Lloyd
M. Dell; Pub. C. Arnold McClure; adv.; photos;
pub. size: broadsheet; circ. 3,300(paid).

OXFORD

US

BRANDYWINE CHRONICLE. 1982. Thu. free. 309
Limestone Rd., Oxford, PA 19363-0520.
TEL 610-932-2444; FAX 610-932-2246.
Owner(s): Andrew & Randall Lieberman, P.O. Box
520, Oxford, PA 19363-0520. TEL
215-932-2444; adv.; pub. size: tabloid; circ.
20,000(free). **Wire Service(s):** AP.
  Formerly: Chronicle News Magazine.

US

CHESTER COUNTY PRESS. 1866. Wed. $.60
newsstand; $20/yr. in cy.; $35/yr. out of cy.
5000 Limestone Rd., Oxford, PA 19363-0520.
TEL 610-932-2444; FAX 610-932-2246; E-mail:
mfmm182@prodigy.com. **Owner(s):** AdPro, Inc.,
P.O. Box 520, Oxford, PA 19363. TEL
610-932-2444; Ed. JoAnn Silva; Pub. Andrew H.
Lieberman; adv. contact: Alan E. Tuens. photos;
bk.rev.; pub. size: broadsheet; circ. 15,200(paid).
Wire Service(s): AP.
  Formerly: The Chronicle.

PATTON

US
UNION PRESS-COURIER. 1906. Thu. $.40 newsstand; $19/yr. in cy.; $22/yr. in state; $23/yr. out of state. 452 Magee Ave., Patton, PA 16668. TEL 814-674-3666; FAX 814-674-3628. **Owner(s):** Frank J. Cammarata, P.O. Box 116, Patton, PA 16668. TEL 814-674-3666; FAX 814-674-3628; Ed. Gretchen Smith; Pub. Frank J. Cammarata; adv.; photos; pub. size: standard; circ. 4,300(paid).

PENNSBURG

US
TOWN & COUNTRY. 1899. Thu. $.50 newsstand; $26/yr. in state; $31.20/yr. out of state. Rte. 663 & Dotts St., Pennsburg, PA 18073. TEL 215-679-9561; FAX 215-679-9563. **Owner(s):** Gannett Satellite Information Network, Inc., 1100 Wilson Blvd., Arlington, VA 22234. TEL 703-284-6000; Ed. Michael Tittinger; Pub. Suzanne Bush; adv.; photos; pub. size: broadsheet; circ. 5,000(paid). **Wire Service(s):** GNS.

PERKASIE

US
PERKASIE NEWS-HERALD. 1881. Wed. $.50 newsstand; $24/yr. in state; $30/yr. out of state. 320 S. Seventh St., Perkasie, PA 18944. TEL 215-257-6839; FAX 215-257-8701. **Owner(s):** Baum Publishing Co., 320 S. Seventh St., Perkasie, PA 18944. TEL 215-257-6839; FAX 215-257-8701; Ed. John A. Gerner. adv. contact: Eric L. Brunner. pub. size: broadsheet; circ. 7,000(free & paid).

PHILADELPHIA

US ISSN 0009-3394
CHESTNUT HILL LOCAL. 1958. Thu. $.50 newsstand; $20/yr. mailed. 8434 Germantown Ave., Philadelphia, PA 19118. TEL 215-248-8800; FAX 215-248-8814. **Owner(s):** Chestnut Hill Community Association, 8434 Germantown Ave., Philadelphia, PA 19118. TEL 215-248-8800; Ed. Marie Reinhart Jones. adv. contact: Jason Scarpello. photos; pub. size: tabloid; circ. 8,400(paid).

US
FISHTOWN STAR. 1975. Wed. free; $85/yr. mailed. 250 W. Girard Ave., Philadelphia, PA 19123. TEL 215-925-7827; FAX 215-925-2339. **Owner(s):** News Star, Inc., 250 W. Girard Ave., Philadelphia, PA 19123. TEL 215-925-7827; Ed. Debbie Szumowski; Pub. Jonathan Stern; adv. contact: Pat Buzine. photos; bk.rev.; pub. size: tabloid; circ. 12,000(controlled & paid).

US
GERMANTOWN COURIER. 1936. Wed. $.35 newsstand; $20/yr. 6622 Germantown Ave., Philadelphia, PA 19119-0971. TEL 215-848-4300; FAX 215-848-9160. **Owner(s):** Acme Newspapers, Inc., 311 E. Lancaster Ave., Ardmore, PA 19003. TEL 215-642-4300; Ed. Sharon Bender; Pub. V. Clark McNeight; adv. contact: Allan Ash. photos; bk.rev.; pub. size: tabloid; circ. 21,000(controlled & paid).

US
GERMANTOWN PAPER. 1980. Wed. $78/yr. 2385 W. Cheltenham, Philadelphia, PA 19150. TEL 215-885-4111. **Owner(s):** Intercounty Newspaper Group, 6220 Ridge Ave., Philadelphia, PA 19128. TEL 215-483-7300; Ed. Marshall Rothman; Pub. Fred W. Donaldson; adv. contact: Leslie Sharpless. photos; pub. size: tabloid; circ. 8,000(controlled).

US
GIRARD HOME NEWS. 1937. Thu. free; $85/yr. mailed. 250 W. Girard Ave., Philadelphia, PA 19123. TEL 215-925-7827; FAX 215-925-2339. **Owner(s):** News Star, Inc., 250 W. Girard Ave., Philadelphia, PA 19123. TEL 215-925-7827; Ed. Debbie Szumowski; Pub. Jonathan Stern; adv. contact: Pat Buzine. photos; pub. size: tabloid; circ. 13,500(free).
Formerly: Philadelphia Girard Home News.

US
JUNIATA NEWS. 1934. Tue. $.25 newsstand; $49/yr. 2241 N. Fifth St., Philadelphia, PA 19133-2599. TEL 215-739-8197; FAX 215-739-9290. **Owner(s):** Gerard R. Lineman, Juniata News, 2241 N. Fifth St., Philadelphia, PA 19133. TEL 215-739-8197; FAX 215-739-9290; Ed. Gerard R. Lineman; Pub. Gerard R. Lineman; adv.; photos; pub. size: tabloid; circ. 10,000(free & paid).

US
LEADER, THE. 1963. Wed. $.50 newsstand; $48/yr. 2385 W. Cheltenham Ave., Ste. 182, Philadelphia, PA 19150-1506. TEL 215-885-4111; FAX 215-885-0226. **Owner(s):** Intercounty Newspaper Group, 6220 Ridge Ave., Philadelphia, PA 19128. TEL 215-483-7300; Ed. Marshall Rothman; Pub. Fred W. Donaldson; adv. contact: Leslie Sharpless. photos; pub. size: tabloid; circ. 29,000(controlled & paid).
Formerly: West Oak Lane Leader.

US
MT. AIRY TIMES. 1991. Wed. free in area; $.35 newsstand; $20/yr. 6622 Germantown Ave., Philadelphia, PA 19119. TEL 215-848-4300; FAX 215-848-9160. **Owner(s):** Acme Newspapers, Inc., 311 E. Lancaster Ave., Ardmore, PA 19003. TEL 215-642-4300; Ed. Sharon Bender; Pub. Deborah Shaw; adv. contact: Allan Ash. photos; bk.rev.; pub. size: tabloid; circ. 14,000(free & paid).
Formerly: Mt. Airy Times Express.

US
NEWS GLEANER PUBLICATIONS. 1882. Wed. free; $.25 newsstand; $90/yr. mailed. 1612 Margaret St., Philadelphia, PA 19124. TEL 215-535-4275; FAX 215-533-0566. **Owner(s):** Coulston S. Henry, 1612 Margaret St., Philadelphia, PA 19124. TEL 215-535-4275; Pub. Coulston S. Henry; adv. contact: John Steinruck. pub. size: broadsheet; circ. 109,262(free & paid). **Wire Service(s):** AP.

US
NORTHEAST TIMES. 1934. s-w.: Wed. & Thu. $25/yr. 8001 Roosevelt Blvd., Ste. 401, Philadelphia, PA 19152. TEL 215-332-3300. **Owner(s):** Times Newspapers, Inc., 8001 Roosevelt Blvd., Ste. 401, Philadelphia, PA 19152. TEL 215-332-3300; Ed. John J. Scanlon; Pub. Robert T. Smylie; adv. contact: Timothy Smylie. photos; pub. size: tabloid; circ. 116,000(free & paid).

US
NORTH STAR. 1975. Wed. free; $85/yr. mailed. 250 W. Girard Ave., Philadelphia, PA 19123. TEL 215-925-7827; FAX 215-925-2339. **Owner(s):** News Star, Inc., 250 W. Girard Ave., Philadelphia, PA 19123. TEL 215-925-7827; FAX 215-925-2339; Ed. Debbie Szumowski; Pub. Jonathan Stern; adv. contact: Pat Buzine. photos; bk.rev.; pub. size: tabloid; circ. 6,000(controlled & free).

US
OLNEY TIMES. 1909. Thu. free deliv.; $60/yr. mailed. 5703 N. Fifth St., Philadelphia, PA 19120. TEL 215-424-0700; FAX 215-424-4082. **Owner(s):** Olney Times, 5703 N. Fifth St., Philadelphia, PA 19120. TEL 215-424-0700; Pub. David Henry; adv.; bk.rev.; pub. size: broadsheet; circ. 25,000(free).

US ISSN 0733-6349
PHILADELPHIA CITY PAPER. 1981. Wed. $52/yr. 206 S. 13th St., Philadelphia, PA 19146. TEL 215-735-8444; FAX 215-732-9033. **Owner(s):** City Communications, Inc., 206 S. 13th St., Philadelphia, PA 19146; Ed. David Warner; Pub. Paul Curci; adv.; bk.rev.; pub. size: tabloid; circ. 109,000.

US
PHILADELPHIA GUIDE NEWSPAPER. 1939. s-w.: Thu. & Fri. $50/yr. 2022 E. Allegheny Ave., Philadelphia, PA 19134. TEL 215-423-1000; FAX 215-426-4438. **Owner(s):** H. Robert Jacobs, Jr., 47 Bank St., Medford, NJ 08055. TEL 609-654-0726; H. Robert Jacobs, Sr., 5550 Gulfstream Way Indian River, Stuart, FL 34996. TEL 609-654-9644; Graphic News, Inc., AKA Guide Newspapers, 2022 E. Allegheny Ave., Philadelphia, PA 19134. TEL 215-423-1000; Ed. H.R. Jacobs, Jr.; Pub. Michelle O'Connell; adv. contact: Michelle O'Connell. pub. size: tabloid; circ. morning 51,000(free & paid).

US
PHILADELPHIA WEEKLY. 1971. Wed. $30/6 mos.; $55/yr. 1701 Walnut St., Philadelphia, PA 19103-5220. TEL 215-563-7400; FAX 215-563-6799. **Owner(s):** Review Publishing, Ltd., 1701 Walnut St., 3rd Fl., Philadelphia, PA 19103-5220. TEL 215-563-7400; FAX 215-563-6799; Ed. Sara Kelly; Pub. Joseph Trachtman; adv. contact: Nicholas Riggio. adv.: $29/SAU. photos; bk.rev.; pub. size: tabloid; circ. 112,000(controlled).
Formerly: Philadelphia Welcomat.

US
PORT RICHMOND STAR. Wed. free; $85/yr. mailed. 250 W. Girard Ave., Philadelphia, PA 19123. TEL 215-925-7827; FAX 215-925-2339. **Owner(s):** News Star, Inc., 250 W. Girard Ave., Philadelphia, PA 19123. TEL 215-925-7827; FAX 215-925-2339; Ed. Debbie Szumowski; Pub. Jonathan Stern; adv. contact: Pat Buzine. photos; bk.rev.; pub. size: tabloid; circ. 12,000(controlled & free).

US
ROXBOROUGH REVIEW. 1902. Wed. $.50 newsstand; $85/yr. 6220 Ridge Ave., Philadelphia, PA 19128. TEL 215-483-7300; FAX 215-483-2073. **Owner(s):** Intercounty Newspaper Group, 6220 Ridge Ave., Philadelphia, PA 19128. TEL 215-483-7300; Ed. George Beetham; Pub. Fred Donaldson; adv. contact: Peter Damato. photos; pub. size: broadsheet; circ. 23,500(paid).

WEEKLY NEWSPAPERS

US
SOUTH PHILADELPHIA CHRONICLE. 1947. Thu. free newsstand; $60/yr. 12th & Porter Sts., N.W. Corner, Philadelphia, PA 19148. TEL 215-336-2500; FAX 215-336-1112. **Owner(s):** Review Publishing, Ltd., 12th & Porter, P.O. Box 2427, Philadelphia, PA 19148. TEL 215-336-2500; Ed. Dave Kramer; Pub. Michael Cohen; adv. contact: John Gallo. pub. size: tabloid; circ. 74,050(free & paid).

US
SOUTH PHILADELPHIA REVIEW. 1947. Thu. free newsstand; $60/yr. 12th & Porter Sts., Philadelphia, PA 19148. TEL 215-336-2500; FAX 215-336-1112. **Owner(s):** Review Publishing, Ltd., 12th & Porter Sts., P.O. Box 2027, Philadelphia, PA 19148. TEL 215-336-2500; Ed. Sandra Philips; Pub. Michael Cohen; adv. contact: John Gallo. pub. size: tabloid; circ. 72,000(paid).

US
SOUTHWEST GLOBE TIMES. 1945. Wed. free newsstand; $50/yr. deliv. 6330 Paschall Ave., Philadelphia, PA 19142. TEL 215-727-7777; FAX 215-727-5116. **Owner(s):** Southwest Globe Times, 6330 Paschall Ave., Philadelphia, PA 19142. TEL 215-727-7777; Ed. Lenora Iannuzzelli; Pub. Joseph Bartash; adv. contact: Theresa Nichols. photos; pub. size: tabloid; circ. 18,500(free & paid).

US
THREE STAR EDITION. 1975. Wed. free; $85/yr. mailed. 250 W. Girard Ave., Philadelphia, PA 19123. TEL 215-925-7827; FAX 215-925-2339. **Owner(s):** News Star, Inc., 250 W. Girard Ave., Philadelphia, PA 19123. TEL 215-925-7827; FAX 215-925-2339; Ed. Debbie Szumowski; Pub. Jonathan Stern; adv.; photos; bk.rev.; pub. size: tabloid; circ. 6,000(controlled & paid).

PHOENIXVILLE
US
VOICE, THE. Thu. free. 225 Bridge St., Phoenixville, PA 19460. TEL 610-933-8926; FAX 610-933-1187. **Owner(s):** Journal Register Co., 50 W. State St., 12th Fl., Trenton, NJ. TEL 609-396-2200; Ed. Lynn Vanderburg. pub. size: broadsheet; circ. 30,000(free).

PINE GROVE
US
PRESS HERALD. 1877. Thu. $.50 newsstand; $24/yr. in cy.; $30/yr. out of cy.; $35/yr. out of state. 181 S. Tulpehocken, Pine Grove, PA 17963. TEL 717-345-4455; FAX 717-345-8467. **Owner(s):** Fred Knecht, Call Newspapers, Inc., 960 E. Main St., Schuylkill Haven, PA 17972; Ed. Paula Schaeffer. pub. size: standard; circ. 3,157(paid).

PITTBURGH
US
IN PITTSBURGH NEWSWEEKLY. 1984. Thu. $35/6 mos.; $60/yr. 2000 E. Carson St., Pittsburgh, PA 15203. TEL 412-488-1212; FAX 412-488-1217. **Owner(s):** Review Publications, Pittsburgh, PA; Ed. Sara Kelly; Pub. John Burnstein; adv.; pub. size: standard; circ. 55,000(paid).

PITTSBURGH
US
HERALD, THE. Wed. $.50 newsstand; $30/yr. in cy.; $35/yr. out of cy. 101 Emerson Ave., Pittsburgh, PA 15215. TEL 412-782-2121; FAX 412-782-1195. **Owner(s):** Gannett Company, Inc., One Gannett Dr., White Plains, NY 10604. TEL 914-694-9300; Ed. Matthew Clark; Pub. Scott Brown; adv.; pub. size: broadsheet; circ. 5,000(paid).

US   ISSN 1066-0062
PITTSBURGH CITY PAPER. 1991. Wed. free newsstand; $50/yr. 911 Penn Ave., 6th Fl., Pittsburgh, PA 15222. TEL 412-560-2489; FAX 412-281-1962; E-mail: info@pghcitypaper.com; URL: http://www.pghcitypaper.com. **Owner(s):** Brad Witherell, 1582 S. Parker Rd., Ste. 212, Denver, CO 80231. TEL 303-750-3865; FAX 303-696-4271; Andy March, 1582 S. Parker Rd., Ste. 212, Denver, CO 80231. TEL 303-750-3865; FAX 303-696-2471; Ed. John Hayes; Pub. Brad Witherell; adv. contact: Greg Brozovich. photos; bk.rev.; pub. size: tabloid; circ. 50,000(free & paid).

US
PITTSBURGH RENAISSANCE NEWS. 1965. Wed. $25/yr. 1516 Fifth Ave., Pittsburgh, PA 15219. TEL 412-391-8208; FAX 412-391-8006. **Owner(s):** Connie Portis, 1516 Fifth Ave., Pittsburgh, PA 15219. TEL 412-391-8208; FAX 412-391-8006; Ed. Connie Portis; Pub. Connie Portis; adv.; photos; bk.rev.; pub. size: tabloid; circ. 30,000(free & paid).

US
SOUTH HILLS RECORD. 1903. Thu. $.50 newsstand; $20.80/yr. carrier; $25/yr. mailed in cy.; $40/yr. out of cy. 3623 Brownsville, Pittsburgh, PA 15227. TEL 412-884-3111; FAX 412-884-3106; E-mail: shillsl@ghplusinfi.net; URL: http://www.ghplus.com. **Owner(s):** Trinity Holdings, Inc., 610 Beatty Rd., Monroeville, PA 15146. TEL 412-856-7400; FAX 412-856-7954; Ed. Jeff Jones; Pub. Kevin Aylmer; adv. contact: Rick Vaccarelli. pub. size: tabloid; circ. 6,119(paid).

US
SOUTH PITTSBURGH REPORTER. 1939. Tue. $36/yr. 1301 E. Carson St., Pittsburgh, PA 15203-0285. TEL 412-481-0266; FAX 412-488-8011. **Owner(s):** South Pittsburgh Reporter, P.O. Box 4285, Pittsburgh, PA 15203-0285. TEL 412-481-0266; Ed. Roberta F. Smith; Pub. Roberta F. Smith; adv.; $5.10/SAU. photos; pub. size: tabloid; circ. 12,000(controlled & free).

PITTSTON
US
SUNDAY DISPATCH. 1948. Sun. $1 newsstand; $52/yr. 109 New St., Pittston, PA 18640. TEL 717-655-1418; FAX 717-883-1266. **Owner(s):** Knight Ridder, Inc., One Herald Plz., Miami, FL 33132. TEL 305-376-3800; Ed. Kim Capatino; Pub. John Watson; adv. contact: Laurie Nocito. pub. size: tabloid; circ. Sun. 13,000(paid). **Formerly:** Pittston Sunday Dispatch.

PORTAGE
US
PORTAGE DISPATCH, THE. 1904. Wed. $.45 newsstand; $19.75/yr. in cy.; $23/yr. in state; $26/yr. out of state. 722 Dulancey Dr., Portage, PA 15946. TEL 814-736-9666. **Owner(s):** Sedloff Publications, Inc., P.O. Box 395, Portage, PA 15946. TEL 814-472-4110; Ed. Connie Miller. adv.; pub. size: broadsheet; circ. 5,303(paid).

PORT ROYAL
US
TIMES, THE. 1876. Wed. $.35 newsstand; $12/yr. in cy.; $18/yr. out of cy. 111 W. Fourth St., Port Royal, PA 17082. TEL 717-527-2213; FAX 717-527-2787. **Owner(s):** Donna K. Swartz, 111 W. Fourth St., Port Royal, PA 17082. TEL 717-527-2213; Ed. Donna K. Swartz; Pub. Donna K. Swartz; adv. contact: Donna K. Swartz. pub. size: standard; circ. 2,500(paid). **Formerly:** Port Royal Times.

PUNXSUTAWNEY
US
COUNTY NEIGHBORS. 1991. Wed. $19/yr. in cy.; $29/yr. out of cy. 510 Pine St., Punxsutawney, PA 15767. TEL 814-938-8740; FAX 814-938-3794. **Owner(s):** American Publishing Co., 606 N. Van Buren, P.O. Box 520, Marion, IL 62959. TEL 618-993-1711; Ed. Wick Divelbiss; Pub. William Anderson; adv. contact: Valerie Pasternak. photos; pub. size: standard; circ. 5,500(free & paid). **Wire Service(s):** AP.

QUAKERTOWN
US
QUAKERTOWN FREE PRESS. 1881. Wed. $.40 newsstand; $18/yr. 312 W. Broad St., Quakertown, PA 18951. TEL 215-536-6820; FAX 215-536-7201. **Owner(s):** Morning Call, The, P.O. Box 1260, Allentown, PA 18105. TEL 610-820-6695; pub. size: tabloid; circ. 5,000(paid). **Formerly:** Free Press.

ROCKLEDGE
US
BREEZE, THE. 1927. Thu. $.35 newsstand; $40/yr. 54 Park Ave., Rockledge, PA 19046. TEL 215-379-5500. **Owner(s):** Intercounty Newspaper Group, 6220 Ridge Ave., Philadelphia, PA 19128. TEL 215-483-7300; Ed. Robert Kent; Pub. Fred W. Donaldson; adv.; photos; pub. size: tabloid; circ. 2,200(paid).

ROYERSFORD
US
REPORTER OF THE SPRING-FORD AREA. 1872. Thu. $.50 newsstand; $18/yr. carrier local; $20/yr. mailed local; $24/yr. mail elsewhere. Park Towne Plz., Royersford, PA 19468. TEL 610-948-4850; FAX 610-948-5914. **Owner(s):** Montgomery Publishing Co., 290 Commerce Dr., Fort Washington, PA 19034. TEL 610-542-0200; Ed. Alethea Lynch; Pub. Arthur Howe; adv.; photos; pub. size: broadsheet; circ. 5,008(free & paid).

SAXTON

US

BROAD TOP BULLETIN. 1947. Wed. $.50 newsstand; $20/yr. 900 Sixth St., Saxton, PA 16678-0188. TEL 814-635-2851. **Owner(s):** Jon Baughman, P.O. Box 215, Dudley, PA 16634. TEL 814-635-2851; Judy Baughman, P.O. Box 215, Dudley, PA 16634. TEL 814-635-2851; Ed. Jon Baughman; Pub. Jon Baughman; adv. contact: Peggy Whited. adv.: $3.50/SAU. photos; pub. size: broadsheet; circ. 3,250(paid).

SCHUYLKILL HAVEN

US

CALL, THE. 1891. Thu. $.50 newsstand; $24/yr. in cy.; $30/yr. out of cy.; $35/yr. out of state. 960 E. Main St., Schuylkill Haven, PA 17972. TEL 717-385-3120; FAX 717-385-0725. **Owner(s):** Call Newspapers, Inc., P.O. Box 178, Schuylkill Haven, PA 17972. TEL 717-385-3120; FAX 717-385-0725; Ed. LaJeune Steidle. adv.: $8.25/SAU. pub. size: standard; circ. 5,100(paid).
Formerly: Schuylkill Haven Call.

SCOTTDALE

US

INDEPENDENT OBSERVER, THE. 1879. Wed. $.45 newsstand; $23.60/yr. in cy.; $35.60/yr. out of cy.; $37.60/yr. out of state. 229 Pittsburgh St., Scottdale, PA 15683-0222. TEL 412-887-6101; FAX 412-887-5115. **Owner(s):** Laurel Group Press, 229 Pittsburgh St., Scottdale, PA 15683. TEL 412-887-7400; Ed. Dirk W. Kaufman; Pub. Joseph F. Soforic; pub. size: broadsheet; circ. 3,473(paid).

US

SOUTHWESTERN PENNSYLVANIA SCENE. 1971. bi-m. $1.50 newsstand; $9/yr. 229 Pittsburgh St., Scottdale, PA 15683. TEL 412-887-7400. E-mail: scene@laurelgrouppress.com. **Owner(s):** Laurel Group Press, 229 Pittsburgh St., Scottdale, PA 15683. TEL 412-887-7400; Ed. Dirk W. Kaufman; Pub. Joseph F. Soforic; adv.; pub. size: standard; circ. 8,000(free & paid).
Formerly: Laurel Highlands Scene.

SHIPPENSBURG

US

SHIPPENSBURG NEWS-CHRONICLE. 1875. s-w.: Mon. & Thu. $.40 newsstand; $36.40/yr. in cy.; $47.80/yr. zones 1-5; $52/yr. zones 6-8. 1011 Ritner Hwy., Shippensburg, PA 17257-0100. TEL 717-532-4101; FAX 717-532-3020. **Owner(s):** News Chronicle Co., Inc., P.O. Box 100, Shippensburg, PA 17257. TEL 717-532-4101; Ed. James Curtis. adv. contact: Steve Helm. photos; bk.rev.; pub. size: broadsheet; circ. 6,100(free & paid). **Wire Service(s):** CNS, AP.

SOUDERTON

US

SOUDERTON INDEPENDENT. 1878. Wed. $.50 newsstand; $20/yr. 673 E. Broad St., Souderton, PA 18964. TEL 215-723-4801; FAX 215-723-8779. **Owner(s):** Montgomery Publishing Co., 290 Commerce Dr., Fort Washington, PA 19034. TEL 215-542-0200; Ed. Barbara McClennen; Pub. Art Howe; adv. contact: John Derr. photos; pub. size: broadsheet; circ. 5,400(paid).

SPRINGFIELD

US

SPRINGFIELD PRESS. 1931. Wed. $.50 newsstand; $18/yr. 204 Ballymore Rd., Springfield, PA 19064. TEL 610-544-6660; FAX 610-544-4530. **Owner(s):** Crowe Printers & Publishers, P.O. Box 291, Springfield, PA 19064. TEL 610-544-6660; Ed. Dorothy B. Koetzle; Pub. Reese Crowe, Jr.; adv. contact: Reese Crowe, Jr. pub. size: tabloid; circ. 7,000(paid).

SUSQUEHANNA

US

COUNTY TRANSCRIPT. 1886. Thu. $.55 newsstand; $20/yr. Exchange St., Susquehanna, PA 18847. TEL 717-853-3134; FAX 717-853-4707. **Owner(s):** Charles W. Ficarro, R.D. 2, Box 152 A1, Susquehanna, PA 18847. TEL 717-853-3284; FAX 717-853-4707; Pub. Charles W. Ficarro; adv.; photos; pub. size: tabloid; circ. 3,500(paid).
Formerly: Susquehanna Transcript.

TIONESTA

US

FOREST PRESS. 1867. Wed. $.50 newsstand; $19/yr. in cy. $22/yr. out of cy. 165 Elm St., Tionesta, PA 16353-0366. TEL 814-755-4900; FAX 814-755-4429. **Owner(s):** Edwin R. Patrick, P.O. Box 366, Tionesta, PA 16353. TEL 814-755-4900; Ed. Virginia Patrick; Pub. Edwin R. Patrick; adv. contact: Leslie Holt. photos; pub. size: tabloid; circ. 4,500(paid).

TOWER CITY

US

WEST SCHUYLKILL HERALD. 1898. Thu. $.50 newsstand; $28/yr. in cy.; $31/yr. in state; $35/yr. out of state. 613 E. Grand Ave., Tower City, PA 17980. TEL 717-647-2191; FAX 717-647-2420. **Owner(s):** Call Newspapers, Inc., P.O. Box 17980, Schuylkill, PA 17972. TEL 717-385-3120; Ed. June Reibsane. adv.: $5.75/SAU. pub. size: standard; circ. 2,250(paid).

TUNKHANNOCK

US

TUNKHANNOCK NEW AGE-EXAMINER. 1870. s-w.: Tue. & Fri. $.60 newsstand; $37/yr. in cy.; $38/yr. out of cy. 16 E. Tioga St., Tunkhannock, PA 18657. TEL 717-836-2123; FAX 717-836-3378. **Owner(s):** Scranton Times, 149 Penn Ave., Scranton, PA 18503. TEL 717-348-9101; Ed. Mary Baldwin; Pub. James E. Towner; adv. contact: Nancy Kaufmann. pub. size: standard; circ. 5,600(paid).

UNION CITY

US

TIMES-LEADER. 1872. Sun. $.60 newsstand; $20/yr. 8230 W. High St. Extension, Union City, PA 16438-0151. TEL 814-438-7666; FAX 814-438-2898. **Owner(s):** Erie Times, Erie, PA; Ed. Mary Holt; Pub. Mark Laskowski; adv.: $8.34/SAU display retail; $17.95/SAU classified. photos; pub. size: standard; circ. 9,699(free & paid).

VALLEY VIEW

US

CITIZEN-STANDARD, THE. 1932. s-m. $.50 newsstand; $25/yr. in cy.; $26/yr. out of cy. 100 W. Main St., Valley View, PA 17983. TEL 717-682-9081; FAX 717-682-8734; E-mail: gzyla@prolog.net. **Owner(s):** Scranton Times, 149 Penn Ave., Scranton, PA 18503. TEL 717-348-9101; Pub. Gregory J. Zyla; adv. contact: Linda Schlaskye. bk.rev.; pub. size: broadsheet; circ. 4,570(free & paid). **Wire Service(s):** Thomson News Service.

VANDERGRIFT

US

VANDERGRIFT NEWS. 1905. s-w.: Wed. & Sat. $.50 newsstand; $33.40/yr. mailed in area; $37/yr. mailed out of area; $31.20/yr. senior citizens. 143 Washington Ave., Vandergrift, PA 15690. TEL 412-567-5656; FAX 412-568-3818. **Owner(s):** Buttermilk Falls, 143 Washington Ave., Vandergrift, PA 15690. TEL 412-567-5656; FAX 412-568-3818; Ed. JoJo Bodnar; Pub. Donald Cole; adv. contact: Kurt Amendola. pub. size: broadsheet; circ. 3,000(paid).

WAYNE

US

SUBURBAN & WAYNE TIMES. 1885. Thu. $.50 newsstand; $35.95/yr. carrier in state; $41.95 mailed in state. 134 N. Wayne Ave., Wayne, PA 19087. TEL 610-688-3000; FAX 610-254-8522. **Owner(s):** Journal Register Co., 50 W. State St., 12th Fl., Trenton, NJ 08608. TEL 609-396-2200; Ed. Jim Lewis. adv. contact: Shelly Meenan. pub. size: broadsheet; circ. 12,000(paid).

US

SUBURBAN ADVERTISER. 1961. Thu. free. 134 N. Wayne Ave., Wayne, PA 19087. TEL 610-688-3000. **Owner(s):** Journal Register Co., 134 N. Wayne Ave., Wayne, PA 19087. TEL 610-688-3000; Ed. Jim Lewis. adv. contact: Shelly Meenan. pub. size: broadsheet; circ. 18,000(free).

WEEDVILLE

US

BENNETTS VALLEY NEWS. 1953. Thu. $17/yr. in state; $20/yr. out of state. P.O. Box 158, Weedville, PA 15868. TEL 814-787-4454. **Owner(s):** Jim Leonard, P.O. Box 158, Weedville, PA 15868. TEL 814-787-4454; adv.; pub. size: tabloid; circ. 1,000(paid).

WELLSBORO

US

WELLSBORO GAZETTE. 1874. Wed. $.75 newsstand; $39/yr. in cy.; $44/yr. out of cy. 25 East Ave., Wellsboro, PA 16901. TEL 717-724-2287; FAX 717-724-2278. **Owner(s):** Community Media Group, 805 S. Logan, West Frankfort, IL 62896. TEL 618-937-3246; Ed. Jeffrey A. Fetzer; Pub. Jeffrey Fetzer; adv. contact: Robert Miller. pub. size: broadsheet; circ. 7,200(paid).

WEEKLY NEWSPAPERS

WESTFIELD
US
FREE PRESS-COURIER. 1878. Wed. $.60 newsstand; $24/yr. in state; $24/yr. out of state. 199 Main St., Westfield, PA 16950-0515. TEL 814-367-2230; FAX 814-367-5092. **Owner(s):** Tioga Publishing Corp., 25 East Ave., Wellsboro, PA 16901. TEL 717-724-2287; FAX 717-724-2278. Ed. Marie Pepero. adv.; photos; pub. size: standard; circ. 4,000(paid).
Formerly: Westfield Free Press-Courier.

WEST NEWTON
US
TIMES-SUN, THE. 1878. Wed. $.45 newsstand; $23.60/yr. in cy.; $35.60/yr. out of cy.; $37.60/yr. out of state. 205 E. Main St., West Newton, PA 15089-1153. TEL 412-872-6800; FAX 412-887-5115. **Owner(s):** Laurel Group Press, 229 Pittsburgh St., Scottsdale, PA 15683-0222. TEL 412-887-7400; FAX 412-887-5115; Ed. Colleen A. Pollock; Pub. H. Ralph Hernley; adv. contact: Rich Zahrobsky. photos; pub. size: broadsheet; circ. 3,200(paid).

WHITE HAVEN
US
JOURNAL-HERALD, THE. 1879. Thu. $.40 newsstand; $20/yr. in cy.; $25/yr. out of cy. 211 Main St., White Haven, PA 18661. TEL 717-443-9131. **Owner(s):** Clara Holder, 211 Main St., White Haven, PA 18661. TEL 717-443-9131; Seth & Ruth Isenberg, 403 Second St., Weatherly, PA 18255. TEL 717-427-4433; Pub. Clara Holder; adv. contact: Seth Isenberg. adv.: $3/SAU. photos; pub. size: broadsheet; circ. 1,780(paid).

US
JOURNAL/VALLEY VIEWS. 1994. m. free; $6/yr. out of town. 211 Main St., White Haven, PA 18661. TEL 717-443-9131. **Owner(s):** Jay & Clara Holder, 211 Main St., White Haven, PA 18661. TEL 717-443-9131; Seth & Ruth Isenberg, 211 Main St., White Haven, PA 18661. TEL 717-443-9131; Ed. Ruth Isenberg. adv.: $7/SAU. photos; pub. size: standard; circ. 5,500(controlled & free).

YARDLEY
US
YARDLEY NEWS. 1946. Thu. $.50 newsstand; $18.50/yr. 10 Penn Valley Dr., Unit B, Yardley, PA 19067. TEL 215-493-2794. **Owner(s):** Intercounty Newspaper Group, 6220 Ridge Ave., Philadelphia, PA 19128. TEL 215-483-7300; Ed. Jeffrey Werner; Pub. Art Thompson; adv. contact: Resa Hall. photos; pub. size: tabloid; circ. 6,000(controlled & paid).

YEAGERTOWN
US
COUNTY OBSERVER. 1975. Wed. $.50 newsstand; $18/yr. in cy.; $25/yr. out of cy. 310 S. Main St., Yeagertown Plz., Ste. A-1, Yeagertown, PA 17099. TEL 717-248-9366; FAX 717-248-9377. **Owner(s):** Ogden Newspapers, Inc., 1500 Main St., Wheeling, WV 26003. TEL 304-233-0100; Ed. Susan Rupe. adv.; pub. size: broadsheet; circ. 6,200(paid).

RHODE ISLAND

BRISTOL
US
BRISTOL PHOENIX. 1837. Thu. $.60 newsstand; $24/yr. in cy.; $35/yr. out of cy.; $40/yr. elsewhere. One Bradford St., Bristol, RI 02809. TEL 401-253-6000; FAX 401-253-6055. **Owner(s):** Roswell Bosworth, Jr., P.O. Box 90, Bristol, RI 02809-0090. TEL 401-253-6000; Ed. Scott Pickering; Pub. Matthew Hayes; adv. contact: Jane McHenry. photos; pub. size: tabloid; circ. 6,100(paid).

CRANSTON
US
CRANSTON HERALD. 1921. Thu. $.50 newsstand; $23/yr. 798 Park Ave., Cranston, RI 02910. TEL 401-781-4240; FAX 401-781-4241. **Owner(s):** Beacon Communications Corp., 1944 Warwick Ave., Warwick, RI 02889. TEL 401-732-3100; Ed. Joe Kernan; Pub. John Howell; pub. size: standard; circ. 5,200(paid).

EAST GREENWICH
US
EAST GREENWICH PENDULUM. 1854. Thu. $.75 newsstand; $30/yr. 580 Main St., East Greenwich, RI 02818. TEL 401-884-4662; FAX 401-884-9819. **Owner(s):** Southern Rhode Island Newspaper, 187 Main St., Wakefield, RI 02880. TEL 401-789-9744; Ed. Jennifer L. Sano; Pub. Michael F. O'Sullivan; adv.; photos; pub. size: broadsheet; circ. 4,000(paid).

EAST PROVIDENCE
US
EAST PROVIDENCE POST. 1906. Thu. $.35 newsstand; $12/yr. 1000A Waterman Ave., East Providence, RI 02914. TEL 401-434-7210; FAX 401-434-9469. **Owner(s):** Herald Press, 99 Webster St., Pautucket, RI 72644; Ed. David Howard. adv. contact: Mary Whelan. bk.rev.; pub. size: tabloid; circ. 12,000(paid).

US
SEEKONK STAR. Thu. $.35 newsstand; $12/yr. 1000 A. Waterman Ave., East Providence, RI 02914. TEL 401-434-7210; FAX 401-434-9469. **Owner(s):** Herald Press, 99 Webster St., Pawtucket, RI 02861. TEL 401-434-7110; Ed. David Howard; Pub. Mary Whelon; adv. contact: Mary Whelon. photos; bk.rev.; pub. size: tabloid; circ. 4,000(paid).

GREENVILLE
US
OBSERVER, THE. 1956. Thu. $.50 newsstand; $22/yr. One Whipple Ln., Greenville, RI 02828. TEL 401-949-2700; FAX 401-949-2420. **Owner(s):** Observer Publishing Co., One Whipple Ln., Greenville, RI 02828. TEL 401-949-2700; FAX 401-949-2420; Ed. Laurence Sasso, Jr. photos; bk.rev.; pub. size: tabloid; circ. 10,500(paid).

JAMESTOWN
US
JAMESTOWN PRESS, THE. 1989. Thu. free; $30/yr. voluntary. 42 Narragansett Ave., Jamestown, RI 02835. TEL 401-423-3200; FAX 401-423-1661; E-mail: jtownpress@aol.com. **Owner(s):** Jeff McDonough, 42 Narragansett Ave., Jamestown, RI 02835. TEL 401-423-3200; FAX 401-423-1661; Ed. Jeff McDonough; Pub. Jeff McDonough; adv. contact: Jeff McDonough. photos; bk.rev.; pub. size: tabloid; circ. 5,600(controlled & free).

NEWPORT
US   ISSN 1052-6935
NEWPORT MERCURY. 1758. Fri. $.50 newsstand; $45/yr. 101 Malbone Rd., Newport, RI 02840. TEL 401-849-3300. **Owner(s):** E.A. Sherman Publishing Co., 101 Malbone Rd., Newport, RI 02840. TEL 401-849-3300; FAX 401-849-3300; Ed. David B. Offer; Pub. Albert K. Sherman, Jr.; pub. size: broadsheet; circ. 1,273(paid).

US
NEWPORT THIS WEEK. 1973. Thu. free newsstand; $20/yr. 3rd class; $50/yr. 1st class. 38 Bellevue Ave., Newport, RI 02840. TEL 401-847-7766; FAX 401-846-4974. **Owner(s):** Community Communications Co., P.O. Box 159, Newport, RI 02840. TEL 401-847-7766; adv.; photos; bk.rev.; pub. size: tabloid; circ. 12,000(free & paid).

NORTH KINGSTOWN
US
STANDARD-TIMES. 1888. Thu. $.75 newsstand; $34/yr. in cy.; $55/yr. out of cy. 13 W. Main St., North Kingstown, RI 02852. TEL 401-294-4576; FAX 401-294-9736. **Owner(s):** Journal Register Co., 50 W. State St.,12th Fl., Trenton, NJ 08608. TEL 609-396-2200; Ed. Rudi Hempe; Pub. Marc Romanow; adv. contact: Laurie Ramaker. bk.rev.; pub. size: broadsheet; circ. 6,500(paid).

PORTSMOUTH
US
SAKONNET TIMES. 1966. Thu. $.60 newsstand; $24/yr. in cy.; $35/yr. out of cy.; $40/yr. elsewhere. 2829 East Main Rd., Portsmouth, RI 02871. TEL 401-683-1000; FAX 401-683-6688. **Owner(s):** Phoenix-Times Publishing Co., One Bradford St., Bristol, RI 02809. TEL 401-253-6000; Ed. Matthew Hayes; Pub. Matthew Hayes; adv. contact: Jane McHenry. pub. size: tabloid; circ. 6,378(paid).

PROVIDENCE

US

EASTSIDE MONTHLY. 1976. m. free; $18/yr. mailed. One Park Row, Providence, RI 02903. TEL 401-453-3937; FAX 401-331-0237. **Owner(s):** Barry Fain, 48 Congdon St., Providence, RI 02906. TEL 401-453-3937; John Howell, 3288 Post Rd., Warwick, RI 02886. TEL 401-331-0237; Ed. Barry Fain. adv. contact: Alice Stanelun. photos; bk.rev.; pub. size: tabloid; circ. 17,000(controlled & free).

US

PROVIDENCE PHOENIX. Thu. free; $45/yr. 150 Chestnut St., Providence, RI 02903. TEL 401-273-6397; FAX 401-273-0920. **Owner(s):** Stephen M. Mindich, 150 Chestnut St., Prividence, RI 02903. TEL 401-273-6397; FAX 401-273-0920; Ed. Lou Papineau; Pub. Stephen M. Mindich; pub. size: tabloid; circ. 60,000(free & paid).

WAKEFIELD

US   ISSN 1040-1938

NARRAGANSETT TIMES, THE. 1855. s-w.: Wed. & Fri. $.75 newsstand; $48/yr. in state; $84/yr. out of state. 187 Main St., Wakefield, RI 02879. TEL 401-789-1081; FAX 401-783-5610. **Owner(s):** Journal Register Co., 50 W. State St., 12th Fl., Trenton, NJ 08608. TEL 609-396-2200; Ed. Michael Pare; Pub. Michael O'Sullivan; adv. contact: Bob Semple. photos; pub. size: broadsheet; circ. 19,000(paid).

WARREN

US

BARRINGTON TIMES. 1958. Wed. $.60 newsstand; $24/yr. in cy.; $35/yr. in New England; $40/yr. elsewhere. 139 Main St., Warren, RI 02885. TEL 401-245-6000; FAX 401-245-3640. **Owner(s):** Phoenix-Times Publishing Co., One Bradford St., Bristol, RI 02809. TEL 401-253-6000; Ed. Monica Allen; Pub. Matthew Hayes; pub. size: tabloid; circ. 5,300(paid).

US

WARREN TIMES GAZETTE. 1866. Wed. $.60 newsstand; $24/yr. in cy.; $35/yr. out of state; $40/yr. elsewhere. 139 Main St., Warren, RI 02885. TEL 401-245-6002. **Owner(s):** East Bay Newspapers, P.O. Box 90, Bristol, RI 02809. TEL 401-253-6000; Ed. Scott Pickering. pub. size: tabloid; circ. 3,094(paid).

WARWICK

US

WARWICK BEACON. 1952. s-w.: Tue. & Thu. $.50 newsstand; $36/yr. 1944 Warwick Ave., Warwick, RI 02889. TEL 401-732-3100; FAX 401-732-3110; E-mail: feedback@warwickonline.com; URL: http://www.warwickonline.com. **Owner(s):** Beacon Communications Corp., 1944 Warwick Ave., Warwick, RI 02889. TEL 401-732-3100; Ed. John I. Howell; Pub. John I. Howell. adv. contact: Alice Stanelun. adv.: $11/SAU. bk.rev.; pub. size: broadsheet; circ. 12,500(paid).

SOUTH CAROLINA

BAMBERG

US

BAMBERG ADVERTIZER-HERALD, THE. 1967. Wed. $.50 newsstand; $22/yr. in cy.; $25/yr. out of cy.; $30/yr. out of state. 102 McGee St., Bamberg, SC 29003. TEL 803-245-5204; FAX 803-245-3900. **Owner(s):** UpState Newspapers Inc., Manchester, GA; Pub. Bob Tribble; adv. contact: Joyce Searson. pub. size: broadsheet; circ. 4,350(paid).

BARNWELL

US

PEOPLE-SENTINEL. 1877. Wed. $.50 newsstand; $20/yr. in cy.; $26/yr. out of cy. 1411 Dunbarton Blvd., Barnwell, SC 29812. TEL 803-259-3501; FAX 803-259-2703. **Owner(s):** Community Newspapers, Inc., P.O. Box 1777, Spartanburg, SC 29304. TEL 803-585-3678; Ed. Sharon Taylor; Pub. Rick Bacon; pub. size: broadsheet; circ. 6,000(paid). **Formerly:** Barnwell People-Sentinel.

BATESBURG-LEESVILLE

US

TWIN-CITY NEWS, THE. 1925. Wed. $.50 newsstand; $15/yr. local; $25/yr. out of state. 114 E. Columbia Ave., Batesburg-Leesville, SC 29006. TEL 803-532-6203; FAX 803-532-6204. **Owner(s):** Bruner Press, P.O. Box 311, Batesburg, SC 29006. TEL 803-532-6203; Pub. Sara F. Bruner; adv.; photos; pub. size: standard; circ. 5,500(paid).

BEAUFORT

US

BEAUFORT SHOPPER. 1972. Wed. free. 3052-C Boundary St., Beaufort, SC 29903. TEL 803-524-3494. **Owner(s):** Beaufort Gazette, P.O. Box 4549, Beaufort, SC 29903. TEL 803-524-3183; adv.; pub. size: tabloid; circ. 17,300(free).

BENNETTSVILLE

US

MARLBORO HERALD-ADVOCATE. 1874. s-w.: Mon. & Thu. $.50 newsstand; $30/yr. local; $35/yr. out of cy. 100 Fayetteville Ave., Bennettsville, SC 29512. TEL 803-479-3815; FAX 803-479-7671. **Owner(s):** Marlboro Publishing Co., Inc., 100 Fayetteville Ave., Bennettsville, SC 29512. TEL 803-479-3815; Ed. William L. Kinney, Jr.; Pub. William L. Kinney, Jr.; adv. contact: Linda Wilson. photos; bk.rev.; pub. size: broadsheet; circ. 6,800(paid).

US

MARLBORO SHOPPER. 1984. Wed. free. 100 Fayetteville Ave., Bennettsville, SC 29512. TEL 803-479-3815; FAX 803-479-7671. **Owner(s):** Marlboro Publishing Co., Inc., P.O. Box 656, Bennettsville, SC 29512. TEL 803-479-3815; FAX 803-479-7671; Ed. William L. Kinney, Jr. adv.; pub. size: standard; circ. 13,000(free).

BISHOPVILLE

US

LEE COUNTY OBSERVER. 1977. Wed. $.50 newsstand; $14/yr. in cy.; $16/yr. out of cy.; $20/yr. out of state. 218 N. Main St., Bishopville, SC 29010. TEL 803-484-9431; FAX 803-484-5055. **Owner(s):** Womack Publishing Co., Inc., P.O. Box 111, Chatham, VA. TEL 803-432-1654; Ed. Todd Hudak; Pub. Charles Womack, III; adv. contact: Millie Watson. pub. size: broadsheet; circ. 4,000(paid)

CAMDEN

US

CHRONICLE-INDEPENDENT. 1888. 3/wk.: Mon., Wed., Fri. $.35 newsstand; $48/yr. mailed. 909 W. Dekalb St., Camden, SC 29020. TEL 803-432-6157; FAX 803-432-7609. **Owner(s):** Morris Communications, P.O. Box 9367, Augusta, GA. TEL 706-724-0851; Ed. Martha Bruce; Pub. Glenn Tucker; pub. size: broadsheet; circ. 8,000(paid).

CHARLESTON

US

COASTAL TIMES. 1983. Wed. $.35 newsstand; $18/yr. local; $20/yr. out of area. 2106 Mt. Pleasant St., Ste. 3, Charleston, SC 29403. TEL 803-723-5318; FAX 803-723-5326. **Owner(s):** Mignon Clyburn, 2106 Mt. Pleasant St., Ste. 1, Charleston, SC 29403. TEL 803-723-5318; Pub. Mignon Clyburn; bk.rev.; pub. size: broadsheet; circ. 5,000(controlled & free).

CHERAW

US   ISSN 0889-0617

CHERAW CHRONICLE, THE. 1885. Thu. $.50 newsstand; $18/yr. 114 Front St., Cheraw, SC 29520. TEL 803-537-5261; FAX 803-537-4518. **Owner(s):** C.N.I., P.O. Box 792, Athens, GA 30603; Ed. Ross Norton; Pub. Ross Norton; adv.; photos; bk.rev.; pub. size: standard; circ. 6,500(free & paid).

CHESTER

US

CHESTER NEWS & REPORTER. 1869. s-w.: Wed. & Fri. $.50 newsstand; $27.50/yr. in cy.; $40/yr. in state; $48.50/yr. out of state. 104 York St., Chester, SC 29706. TEL 803-385-3177; FAX 803-581-2518. **Owner(s):** Landmark Community Newspapers, Inc., P.O. Box 549, Shelbyville, KY 40066. TEL 502-633-4334; Ed. L.D. McKeown. adv. contact: Fran T. Dodds. photos; pub. size: broadsheet; circ. 7,500(paid).

WEEKLY NEWSPAPERS

CLEMSON
US
MESSENGER, THE. 1954. s-w.: Wed. & Sat. $.50 newsstand; $35/yr.; $42/yr. out of state. By Pass 123 Tiger Blvd., Clemson, SC 29631. TEL 864-654-2451; FAX 864-882-2381. **Owner(s):** Edwards Publications, P.O. Box 547, Seneca, SC 29679. TEL 864-882-2375; Pub. Steve Edwards; adv.; pub. size: standard; circ. 4,000(free & paid).

CLINTON
US
CLINTON CHRONICLE, THE. 1900. Wed. $.50 newsstand; $24/yr. 513 N. Broad St., Clinton, SC 29325. TEL 803-833-1900; FAX 803-833-1902. **Owner(s):** Laurens County Newspapers, Inc., P.O. Box 180, Clinton, SC 29325. TEL 803-833-1900; Ed. Rick Hendricks; Pub. Larry B. Franklin; adv.; pub. size: broadsheet; circ. 5,000(controlled & paid).

CLOVER
US
CLOVER HERALD. 1928. Thu. $.25 newsstand; $14/yr. in cy.; $18/yr. out of cy. P.O. Box 38, Clover, SC 29710. TEL 803-684-9903; FAX 803-628-0300. **Owner(s):** McClatchy Newspapers, P.O. Box 15774, Sacramento, CA 95852. TEL 916-321-1006; Ed. Mike Faulkenberry. adv.; bk.rev.; pub. size: broadsheet; circ. 2,900(paid).

CONWAY
US
HORRY INDEPENDENT. 1980. Thu. $22/yr. 2510 Main St., Conway, SC 29526. TEL 803-248-6882. **Owner(s):** Waccamaw Publishers, P.O. Box 740, Conway, SC 29526. TEL 803-248-6671; Ed. Kathy Ropp; Pub. Steve Robertson; adv.; photos; pub. size: broadsheet; circ. 6,000(free & paid).

DARLINGTON
US
NEWS & PRESS, THE. 1874. Thu. $14/yr. in cy.; $16/yr. in state; $20/yr. out of state. 141 S. Main St., Darlington, SC 29532. TEL 803-393-3811; FAX 803-393-6811. **Owner(s):** Morrell L. Thomas, Jr., P. O. Box 513, Darlington, SC 29532. TEL 803-393-3811; FAX 803-393-6811; Ed. Jim Faile; Pub. Morrell L. Thomas, Jr.; adv. contact: Crystal Eisson. pub. size: standard; circ. 6,000(paid).
Formerly: Darlington News & Press.

DILLON
US
DILLON HERALD, THE. 1894. s-w.: Tue. & Thu. $.50 newsstand; $24/yr. local; $32.75/yr. elsewhere. 505 Hwy. 301, N., Dillon, SC 29536. TEL 803-774-3311; FAX 803-841-1930. **Owner(s):** Herald Publishing Co., Inc., P.O. Box 1288, Dillon, SC 29536-1288. TEL 803-774-3311; FAX 803-841-1930; Ed. Paul Jones. adv. contact: Johnnie Daniels. photos; pub. size: broadsheet; circ. 6,034(free & paid). **Wire Service(s):** AP.

EASLEY
US
EASLEY PROGRESS. 1902. Wed. $.50 newsstand; $12.50/yr.in cy. 205 Russell St., Easley, SC 29640. TEL 864-855-0355; FAX 864-855-6825; E-mail: easleyprogress@worldnet.att.net. **Owner(s):** Crescent Communications, Inc., P.O. Box 709, Easley, SC 29641. TEL 864-855-0355; FAX 864-855-6825; Pub. Jerry D. Vickery; adv. contact: Jane Jones. photos; bk.rev.; pub. size: broadsheet; circ. 9,000(controlled & paid).

FORT MILL
US
FORT MILL TIMES. 1892. Wed. $18/yr. 116 Main St., Fort Mill, SC 29715. TEL 864-547-2353; FAX 864-547-2321. **Owner(s):** Mantle Publications, Inc., P.O. Box 250, Fort Mill, SC 29716. TEL 864-547-2353; Ed. Jerry McGuire; Pub. John E. Mantle; adv. contact: Carol Mantle. pub. size: broadsheet; circ. 7,000(paid).

FOUNTAIN INN
US   ISSN 0747-1165
TRIBUNE-TIMES. 1911. Wed. $.50 newsstand; $18/yr. in cy. 1314 N. Main St., Fountain Inn, SC 29644. TEL 864-967-9580; FAX 864-967-9585. **Owner(s):** Multimedia, Inc., 305 S. Main St., Greenville, SC 29601. TEL 864-298-4000; Ed. Ernie Kastner; Pub. Melody Bishop; adv. contact: Melody Bishop. photos; bk.rev.; pub. size: broadsheet; circ. 7,300(paid).

GAFFNEY
US
GAFFNEY LEDGER, THE. 1894. 3/wk.: Mon., Wed., Fri. $.50 newsstand; $33/yr. in cy.; $55/yr. out of cy. 1604 Baker Blvd., Gaffney, SC 29342. TEL 864-489-1131; FAX 864-487-7667. **Owner(s):** Louis Sossamon, Gaffney Ledger, Inc., The, P.O. Box 670, Gaffney, SC 29342. TEL 864-489-1131; FAX 864-487-7667; Cody Sossamon, Gaffney Ledger, Inc., The, P.O. Box 670, Gaffney, SC 29342. TEL 864-489-1131; FAX 864-487-7667; Ed. Klonie Jordan; Pub. Louis Sossamon; adv. contact: Robert Martin. photos; bk.rev.; pub. size: standard; circ. morning 9,589(paid). **Wire Service(s):** AP.

GEORGETOWN
US
GEORGETOWN TIMES, THE. 1797. 3/wk.: Tue., Thu., Sat. $.25 newsstand; $24/yr. in cy. 615 Front St., Georgetown, SC 29440. TEL 803-546-4148; FAX 803-546-2395. **Owner(s):** Georgetown Communications, Inc., 615 Front St., Georgetown, SC 29440. TEL 803-546-4148; Ed. Jesse Tullos; Pub. John Burbage; adv.; photos; pub. size: broadsheet; circ. 7,000(paid). **Wire Service(s):** AP.

GREER
US
GREER CITIZEN, THE. 1918. Wed. $.50 newsstand; $15-$28/yr. 105 Victoria, Greer, SC 29651. TEL 864-877-2076; FAX 864-877-3563. **Owner(s):** Walter M. Burch, 105 Victoria, Greer, SC 29651. TEL 864-877-2076; Leland E. Burch, 105 Victoria, Greer, SC 29651. TEL 864-877-2076; Ed. Leland E. Burch; Pub. Walter M. Burch; adv.; photos; bk.rev.; pub. size: standard; circ. 11,350(paid).

HARTSVILLE
US
DARCO NEWS & BUYERS GUIDE. Wed. free. 416 W. Carolina Ave., Hartsville, SC 29550-4524. TEL 803-667-9656. **Owner(s):** News-Journal, Inc., 146 W. Evans St., Florence, SC 29501. TEL 803-667-9656; Pub. Jim Harris; adv. contact: Carl Campbell. pub. size: broadsheet; circ. 17,333(controlled & free).

US
HARTSVILLE MESSENGER, THE. 1893. s-w.: Mon. & Wed. $.25 newsstand; $20/yr. in cy.; $30/yr. out of cy. 207 E. Carolina Ave., Hartsville, SC 29550. TEL 803-332-6545; FAX 803-332-1341. **Owner(s):** H.D. Osteen, Jr., 207 E. Carolina St., Hartsville, SC 29550; Ed. Dennie Truesdale; Pub. H.D. Osteen, Jr.; adv. contact: Myrtleen Tyner. pub. size: broadsheet; circ. 5,000(paid).

HEMINGWAY
US
WEEKLY OBSERVER, THE. 1973. Thu. $12/yr.; $20/yr. out of cy; $10/yr. senior citizens. 108 N. Main St., Hemingway, SC 29554. TEL 803-558-3323; FAX 803-558-9601. **Owner(s):** Community Newspapers, Inc., P.O. Box 792, Athens, GA 30601. TEL 706-548-0010; FAX 706-548-0808; Ed. Russ Pace; Pub. Robert Ryder; adv.: $4/SAU. photos; pub. size: broadsheet; circ. 2,485(free & paid).

HOLLY HILL
US
HOLLY HILL OBSERVER, THE. 1972. Wed. $.50 newsstand; $15/yr. in Orangeburg cy.; $17 out of cy.; $25 out of state. 605 Gardner Blvd., Holly Hill, SC 29059-0715. TEL 803-496-3242; FAX 803-496-3051. **Owner(s):** Bob Tribble, St. George, SC 29477. TEL 803-563-3121; FAX 803-496-3051; adv.; photos; pub. size: broadsheet; circ. 3,000(paid).
Formerly: Observer, The.

KINGSTREE
US
NEWS, THE. 1972. Wed. $.50 newsstand; $15/yr. in cy.; $18/yr. out of cy.; $24/yr. out of state. 107 E. Mill St., Kingstree, SC 29556-0574. TEL 803-354-7454; FAX 803-354-6530; E-mail: thenews@net.alley.com; URL: http://www.net.alley.com/thenews. **Owner(s):** Evening Post Publishing Co., 134 Columbus St., Charleston, SC 29403. TEL 803-577-7111; Pub. Vickey Boyd; adv.: $4.52/SAU. pub. size: standard; circ. 5,200(paid).
Formerly: Kingstree News.

LADSON
US
GOOSE CREEK GAZETTE. 1978. Wed. $.25 newsstand; $12/yr. mailed in US. 101 Spring Hall Dr., Ste. A, Ladson, SC 29456. TEL 803-572-0511; FAX 803-572-0312. **Owner(s):** William C. Collins, P.O. Box 715, Summerville, SC 29484. TEL 803-572-0511; Ed. Judy S. Watts; Pub. William C. Collins; adv. contact: William C. Collins. photos; pub. size: broadsheet; circ. 3,500(controlled & paid).

10728 LANCASTER, SC **WEEKLY NEWSPAPERS**

LANCASTER
US ISSN 0745-7421
LANCASTER NEWS. 1852. 3/wk.: Wed., Fri., Sun. $.50 newsstand; $45/yr. 701 N. White St., Lancaster, SC 29720. TEL 803-283-1133. **Owner(s):** Landmark Communications, Inc., 701 N. White St., Lancaster, SC 29720. TEL 803-283-1133; Ed. Barbara Howell; Pub. David L. Ernest; adv. contact: Susan Rowell. pub. size: standard; circ. 13,000(paid). **Wire Service(s):** AP.

LANDRUM
US
NEWS LEADER, THE. 1955. Wed. $.35 newsstand; $15/yr. local. 146 Trade Ave., Landrum, SC 29356. TEL 864-457-3337; FAX 864-472-6900. **Owner(s):** Trib Publications, Inc., P.O. Box 426, Manchester, GA 31816; Ed. John F. Lawrence; Pub. John F. Lawrence; adv.; pub. size: broadsheet; circ. 4,800(paid).

LAURENS
US
LAURENS COUNTY ADVERTISER. 1885. 3/wk.: Wed., Fri., Sun. $.50 newsstand; $29/yr. in cy.; $45/yr. in state; $55/yr. out of state. 218 W. Laurens, Laurens, SC 29360. TEL 864-984-2586; FAX 864-984-4039. **Owner(s):** W.J. Brown, P.O. Box 490, Laurens, SC 29360. TEL 864-984-2586; FAX 864-984-4039; Ed. Rich Browne; Pub. W.J. Brown; adv. contact: James D. Brown. pub. size: broadsheet; circ. 18,465(paid).

LEXINGTON
US
DISPATCH-NEWS, THE. 1870. Wed. $.50 newsstand; $20/yr. in state; $26/yr. out of state. 115 E. Main St., Lexington, SC 29072. TEL 803-359-3195; FAX 803-359-1378. **Owner(s):** Community Newspapers, Inc., P.O. Box 792, Athens, GA 30603. TEL 800-226-0692; FAX 706-548-0808; Ed. Tim Chamberlin; Pub. Rick Bacon; adv. contact: Linda Melton. photos; pub. size: broadsheet; circ. 7,300(paid).

US
LAKE EDITION, THE. 1993. Fri. $.50 newsstand; $14/yr. P.O. Box 502, Lexington, SC 29071. TEL 803-730-8383; FAX 803-892-5757; E-mail: 76066.104@compuserve.com. **Owner(s):** Jackie Black, P.O. Box 1015, Irmo, SC 29063. TEL 803-781-1210; FAX 803-892-5757; Sam Bruce, P.O. Box 502, Lexington, SC 29071. TEL 803-730-8363; FAX 803-892-5757; Ed. Jackie Black; Pub. Jackie Black; adv. contact: R.K. King. photos; bk.rev.; pub. size: standard; circ. 7,350(free & paid).
Formerly: Irmo Independent News.

LORIS
US
LORIS TIMES. 1991. Thu. $.25 newsstand; $11/yr. in cy.; $15/yr. out of cy.; $23/yr. out of state. 4111 Walnut St., Loris, SC 29569. TEL 803-756-7224; FAX 803-756-7812. **Owner(s):** Pauline L. Lowman, P.O. Box 725, North Myrtle Beach, SC 29597. TEL 803-249-3525; FAX 803-249-7012; Ed. Pauline L. Lowman; Pub. Pauline L. Lowman; adv.; photos; bk.rev.; pub. size: broadsheet; circ. 4,500(paid).

MARION
US
MARION STAR & MULLINS ENTERPRISE. Wed. $18/yr. in cy.; $28/yr. out of cy. 211 Railroad Ave., Marion, SC 29571. TEL 803-423-2050; FAX 803-423-2542. **Owner(s):** Community Newspapers, Inc., P.O. Box 792, Athens, SC 30603. TEL 800-226-0692; FAX 706-548-0808; Ed. Tim Chamberlin; Pub. Robert Rider; pub. size: broadsheet; circ. 12,000(paid).
Formerly: Marion Star.

MONCKS CORNER
US
BERKELEY INDEPENDENT. 1987. Wed. $.50 newsstand; $18/yr. 320 E. Main St., Moncks Corner, SC 29461. TEL 803-761-6397; FAX 803-899-6996; E-mail: berkeleyind@infoave.net; URL: http://www.hometeleo.com/home. **Owner(s):** Manuel Cohen, P.O. Box 427, Moncks Corner, SC 29461. TEL 803-761-6397; FAX 803-899-6996; Allen & Tony Morris, P.O. Box 427, Moncks Corner, SC 29461. TEL 803-761-6397; FAX 803-899-6996; Pub. H. Allen Morris; adv. contact: Micah Ponce. photos; bk.rev.; pub. size: broadsheet; circ. 11,200(paid).

MT. PLEASANT
US
JOURNAL, THE. 1968. bi-w.: Thu. $.25 newsstand; $7/yr. in cy. 1558 Ben Sawyer Blvd., Ste. B, Mt. Pleasant, SC 29464-4538. TEL 803-849-1778; FAX 803-849-0214. **Owner(s):** Community Press, Inc., 1558 Ben Sawyer Blvd., Ste. B, Mt. Pleasant, SC 29464-4538. TEL 803-849-1778; FAX 803-849-0214; Ed. Charles P. Diggle; Pub. Charles P. Diggle; adv.; bk.rev.; pub. size: broadsheet; circ. 4,000(free & paid).

US
MOULTRIE NEWS, THE. 1964. Wed. free deliv., $25/yr. mailed. 1558 Ben Sawyer Blvd., Ste. B, Mt. Pleasant, SC 29464-4538. TEL 803-849-1779; FAX 803-849-0214. **Owner(s):** Community Press, Inc., 1558 Ben Sawyer Blvd., Ste. B, Mt. Pleasant, SC 29464-4538. TEL 803-849-1778; FAX 803-849-0214; Ed. Chuck Diggle; Pub. Charles P. Diggle; adv.: $8/SAU. bk.rev.; pub. size: broadsheet; circ. 16,000(free & paid).

MYRTLE BEACH
US
ALTERNATIVES NEWS MAGAZINE. 1984. fortn. $21.95/yr. 1111 N. Tenth Ave., Myrtle Beach, SC 29577. TEL 803-444-5556; FAX 803-444-5558; E-mail: altnews@ns.sccoast.net; URL: http://www.myrtlebeachlive.com.newsalternatives. **Owner(s):** Alternative Publications, Ltd., Drawer 2485, Myrtle Beach, SC 29578. TEL 803-444-5556; FAX 803-444-5558; Ed. Ray Bartlett; Pub. William E. Darry; adv.; photos; bk.rev.; pub. size: tabloid; circ. 20,000(paid).

NEWBERRY
US
NEWBERRY OBSERVER, THE. 1865. 3/wk.: Mon., Wed., Fri. $.35 newsstand; $38/yr. mailed. 1716 Main St., Newberry, SC 29108. TEL 803-276-0625; FAX 803-276-1517. **Owner(s):** Knight-Ridder, Inc., One Herald Plz., Miami, FL 33132. TEL 305-376-3800; FAX 305-376-3875; Pub. Fred Mott; adv. contact: Debbie Waldrop. photos; pub. size: standard; circ. 6,543(paid).

NORTH CHARLESTON
US
HANAHAN NEWS. 1959. Wed. $.25 newsstand; $12/yr. mailed in US. 1924 E. Montaque Ave., North Charleston, SC 29406. TEL 803-747-5773; FAX 803-744-5505. **Owner(s):** Carl Meynardie, P.O. Box 60580, Charleston, SC 29419. TEL 803-747-5773; Ed. Carl Meynardie; Pub. Carl Meynardie; adv. contact: Paul Meynardie. pub. size: tabloid; circ. 20,500(paid).

NORTH MYRTLE BEACH
US
NORTH MYRTLE BEACH TIMES. 1971. Thu. $.50 newsstand; $25/yr. local; $30/yr. out of cy.; $40/yr. out of state. 203 N. Kings Hwy., North Myrtle Beach, SC 29582. TEL 803-249-3525; FAX 803-249-7012. **Owner(s):** Pauline L. Lowman, P.O. Box 725, N. Myrtle Beach, SC 29597. TEL 803-249-3525; FAX 803-249-7012; Ed. Pauline L. Lowman; Pub. Pauline L. Lowman; adv.; bk.rev.; pub. size: standard; circ. 20,000(paid).

PAGELAND
US ISSN 1063-8415
PAGELAND PROGRESSIVE-JOURNAL, THE. 1910. Tue. $.30 newsstand; $12/yr. in cy.; $17/yr. out of cy. Hwy. 9 E., Pageland, SC 29728. TEL 803-672-2358; FAX 803-672-5593. **Owner(s):** Brian & Jane Hough, 937 E. Maynard St., Pageland, SC 29728. TEL 803-672-2367; FAX 803-672-5593; Ed. Brian Hough; Pub. Brian Hough; adv. contact: Jane Hough. photos; pub. size: broadsheet; circ. 4,300(paid).

PICKENS
US
PICKENS SENTINEL. 1872. Wed. $.50 newsstand; $12/yr. in cy.; $20/yr. out of cy. 109 Garvin St., Pickens, SC 29671. TEL 803-878-2453; FAX 803-878-2454. **Owner(s):** Pickens County Publishing, Inc., P.O. Box 95, Pickens, SC 29671. TEL 803-878-2453; FAX 803-878-2454; Pub. Jerry Alexander; adv.; photos; pub. size: broadsheet; circ. 7,000(paid).

RIDGELAND
US ISSN 1072-3986
JASPER COUNTY SUN. 1993. Wed. $.35 newsstand; $16.50/yr. in cy.; $25/yr. out of cy. 104 S. Railroad St., Ridgeland, SC 29936. TEL 803-726-6161; FAX 803-726-8661. **Owner(s):** Larry & Renee Miller, P.O. Box 788, Ridgeland, SC 29936. TEL 803-726-6161; FAX 803-726-8661; Ed. Larry Miller. adv. contact: Renee Miller. photos; bk.rev.; pub. size: broadsheet; circ. 3,000(paid).

WEEKLY NEWSPAPERS

ROEBUCK
US

YOUR PAPER. 1994. bi-w.: Tue. free newsstand. 100 Peak Rd. Ste. B, Roebuck, SC 29376. TEL 864-574-2777. **Owner(s):** Your Paper, Inc., P.O. Box 2524, Spartanburg, SC 29302. TEL 803-573-8505; Ed. Jeff Hayes; Pub. Jeff Hayes; adv.; photos; pub. size: tabloid; circ. 10,000(free).

SALUDA
US

SALUDA STANDARD SENTINEL. 1946. Thu. $.25 newsstand; $10/yr. in cy.; $13/yr. out of cy. P.O. Box 676, Saluda, SC 29138. TEL 864-445-2527; FAX 864-445-8679. **Owner(s):** Ralph Shealy, P.O. Box 676, Saluda, SC 29138. TEL 864-445-2527; FAX 864-445-8679; Ed. Ralph Shealy; Pub. Ralph Shealy; adv.; photos; bk.rev.; pub. size: standard; circ. 4,300(paid).

SENECA
US

JOURNAL TRIBUNE. s-w.: Wed. & Sat. $.50 newsstand; $34.95/yr. in cy.; $42/yr. out of cy. 210 W. North First St., Seneca, SC 29678. TEL 864-882-2375; FAX 864-882-2381. **Owner(s):** Edwards Publications, 210 W. North First St., Seneca, SC 29678. TEL 864-882-3272; FAX 864-882-0903; Ed. Dan Brannan; Pub. Steve Edwards; pub. size: broadsheet; circ. 13,000(paid).
Formerly: Seneca Journal & Tribune.

ST. GEORGE
US

DORCHESTER EAGLE RECORD. 1899. Thu. $.35 newsstand; $14/yr. in cy.; $16/yr. out of cy. 5549 Memorial Blvd., St. George, SC 29477. TEL 803-563-3121; FAX 803-563-5355. **Owner(s):** William M. Owens, 5549 Memorial Blvd., St. George, SC 29477. TEL 803-563-3121; Ed. William M. Owens; Pub. William M. Owens; adv.; photos; pub. size: broadsheet; circ. 3,100(paid).

SUMMERVILLE
US

SUMMERVILLE JOURNAL SCENE. 1972. s-w.: Wed. & Fri. $.50 newsstand; $25/yr. in state; $40/yr. out of state. 104 E. Doty Ave., Summerville, SC 29483. TEL 803-873-9424. **Owner(s):** Journal Co., P.O. Box 715, Summerville, SC 29484. TEL 803-873-9424; Ed. William C. Collins; Pub. William C. Collins; adv. contact: Jane Barrineau. photos; pub. size: broadsheet; circ. 9,000(paid).

WALTERBORO
US

PRESS & STANDARD, THE. 1877. s-w.: Tue. & Fri. $.50 newsstand; $32/yr. in cy.; $44/yr. out of cy. 113 E. Washington St., Walterboro, SC 29488-3915. TEL 803-549-2586; FAX 803-549-2446. **Owner(s):** Smith Newspapers, Inc., P.O. Box 27, Fort Payne, AL 35967. TEL 205-845-5510; Ed. Taylor M. Smith; Pub. Taylor M. Smith; adv. contact: Anne Padget. adv.: $6/SAU. pub. size: broadsheet; circ. 6,000(paid).

WILLIAMSTON
US

JOURNAL, THE. 1955. Wed. $.50 newsstand; $18/yr. in cy.; $20.50/yr. out of cy.; $25/yr. out of state. 106 W. Main St., Williamston, SC 29697. TEL 864-847-7361; FAX 864-847-9879. **Owner(s):** William C. Meade, P.O. Box 369, Williamston, SC 29697. TEL 864-847-7361; Ed. Sharon Crout; Pub. David Meade; adv. contact: David Meade. photos; pub. size: broadsheet; circ. 5,600(paid).

WINNSBORO
US

HERALD-INDEPENDENT, THE. 1844. Thu. $.50 newsstand; $15/yr. in cy.; $25/yr. out of state. 127 N. Congress St., Winnsboro, SC 29180. TEL 803-635-4016; FAX 803-635-2948. **Owner(s):** Community Newspapers, Inc., P.O. Box 792, Athens, GA 30603. TEL 800-226-0692; FAX 706-548-0808; Pub. Patricia Smith; adv. contact: Mary Douglas. photos; bk.rev.; pub. size: broadsheet; circ. 5,000(free & paid). **Wire Service(s):** AP.

YORK
US

YORKVILLE ENQUIRER. 1855. Thu. $.25 newsstand; $14/yr. in cy.; $18/yr. out of cy. 20 W. Liberty St., York, SC 29745. TEL 803-684-9903; FAX 803-628-0300. **Owner(s):** McClatchy Newspapers, 2100 Q St., Sacramento, CA 95816. TEL 916-321-1000; Ed. Gene Graham. adv.; bk.rev.; pub. size: standard; circ. 3,200(paid).

SOUTH DAKOTA

BELLE FOURCHE
US

BELLE FOURCHE POST. 1902. s-w.: Wed. & Sat. $.50 newsstand; $33.92/yr. local; $38. 48/yr. mailed. 1004 Fifth Ave., Belle Fourche, SD 57717. TEL 605-892-2528; FAX 605-892-2529. **Owner(s):** Dickson Media, Inc., Charlottesville, VA; Ed. Tim Velder; Pub. Tim Velder; adv. contact: Chrisann Mateer. pub. size: broadsheet; circ. 2,500(paid).

BUFFALO
US

NATION'S CENTER NEWS. 1979. Wed. $.55 newsstand; $26/yr. in state; $25/yr. out of state. 507 W. Fifth St., Buffalo, SD 57720. TEL 605-375-3228; FAX 605-375-3318. **Owner(s):** Linda & Walter Stephens, 507 W. Fifth St., Buffalo, SD 57720. TEL 605-375-3228; Ed. Walter Stephens; Pub. Linda Stephens; adv.; pub. size: broadsheet; circ. 3,200(controlled & paid).

CANISTOTA
US

CANISTOTA CLIPPER. 1902. Thu. $21.20/yr. in cy. P.O. Box 128, Canistota, SD 57012. TEL 605-296-3181; FAX 605-296-3289. **Owner(s):** Matt Anderson, P.O. Box 128, Canistota, SD 57012. TEL 605-296-3181; Ed. Matt Anderson; Pub. Matt Anderson; pub. size: broadsheet; circ. 752(paid).

CANOVA HERALD
US

CANOVA HERALD. Thu. $12/yr. Main St., Canistota, SD 57012. TEL 605-296-3181; FAX 605-296-3289. **Owner(s):** Matt Anderson, P.O. Box 128, Canistota, SD 57012. TEL 605-296-3181; FAX 605-296-3289; Ed. Matt Anderson; Pub. Matt Anderson; adv.; photos; pub. size: broadsheet; circ. 450(paid).

HARTFORD AREA NEWS
US

HARTFORD AREA NEWS. 1902. Thu. $16.96/yr. in cy. P.O. Box 128, Canistota, SD 57012. TEL 605-296-3181; FAX 605-296-3289. **Owner(s):** Matt Anderson, P.O. Box 128, Canistota, SD 57012. TEL 605-296-3181; Ed. Matt Anderson; Pub. Matt Anderson; adv.; pub. size: broadsheet; circ. 640(paid).

HUMBOLT JOURNAL
US

HUMBOLT JOURNAL. 1902. Thu. $16/yr. in cy. Main St., Canistota, SD 57012. TEL 605-296-3181; FAX 605-296-3289. **Owner(s):** Matt Anderson, P.O. Box 128, Canistota, SD 57012. TEL 605-396-3181; Ed. Matt Anderson; Pub. Matt Anderson; adv.; photos; pub. size: broadsheet; circ. 600(paid).

MONTROSE HERALD
US

MONTROSE HERALD. Thu. $16/yr. in cy. P.O. Box 128, Canistota, SD 57012. TEL 605-296-3181; FAX 605-296-3289. **Owner(s):** Wendell Anderson, P.O. Box 128, Cansistota, SD 57012. TEL 605-296-3181; Ed. Matt Anderson; Pub. Matt Anderson; adv.; pub. size: broadsheet; circ. 500(paid).

DEADWOOD
US

LAWRENCE COUNTY CENTENNIAL. 1973. s-w.: Wed. & Sat. $.50 newsstand; $32/yr. 68 Sherman St., Deadwood, SD 57732. TEL 605-578-3305; FAX 605-578-2023. **Owner(s):** Dickson Media, Inc., 2568 Ivy Rd., Ste. D., Charlottesville, VA 22903. TEL 804-971-8350; Ed. George Lodbetter; Pub. Gary Greene; adv. contact: Barb Shepardson. adv.: $4.50/SAU. photos; pub. size: broadsheet; circ. 2,675(paid). **Wire Service(s):** UPI.

DELL RAPIDS
US

BALTIC BEACON. 1889. Wed. $.50 newsstand; $18/yr. local; $23/yr. elsewhere. 414 Fourth St., Dell Rapids, SD 57022. TEL 605-428-5441; FAX 605-428-5992. **Owner(s):** Prairie Publishing, Inc., P.O. Box 99, Dell Rapids, SD 57022. TEL 605-428-5441; Ed. Bruce Benham. adv. contact: James Wilber. pub. size: tabloid; circ. 320(paid).

US

BRANDON VALLEY CHALLENGER. 1985. Wed. $.50 newsstand; $24/yr. in cy.; $29/yr. out of cy. 414 Fourth St., Dell Rapids, SD 57022. TEL 605-428-5441; FAX 605-428-5992. **Owner(s):** James Wilber, 414 Fourth St., Dell Rapids, SD 57022. TEL 605-428-5441; Ed. Bruce Benham; Pub. Jim Wilber; adv.; photos; pub. size: tabloid; circ. 1,000(paid).

US

DELL RAPIDS TRIBUNE. 1985. Wed. $.50 newsstand; $24/yr. in cy.; $29/yr. out of cy. mailed. 414 Fourth St., Dell Rapids, SD 57022. TEL 605-428-5441; FAX 605-428-5992. **Owner(s):** James Wilber, 414 Fourth St., Dell Rapids, SD 57022. TEL 605-428-5441; Ed. Bruce Benham; Pub. James Wilber; adv.; photos; pub. size: tabloid; circ. 3,119(free & paid).

WEEKLY NEWSPAPERS

EUREKA
US

NORTHWEST BLADE, THE. 1884. Wed. $.50 newsstand; $21/yr. local; $25/yr. elsewhere. P.O. Box 797, Eureka, SD 57437-0797. TEL 605-284-2631; FAX 605-284-2501. **Owner(s):** Arlo & Bonnie Mehlhaff, P.O. Box 797, Eureka, SD 57437. TEL 605-284-2631; Ed. Bonnie Mehlhaff; Pub. Arlo Mehlhaff; adv. contact: Arlo Mehlhaff. pub. size: broadsheet; circ. 1,750(paid).

FLANDREAU
US

MOODY COUNTY ENTERPRISE. 1885. Wed. $.50 newsstand; $21/yr. in area; $27/yr. elsewhere. 107 Second St., Flandreau, SD 57028. TEL 605-997-3725; FAX 605-997-3194. **Owner(s):** Chuck Cecil, 1209 Second St., Brookings, SD 57006. TEL 605-692-2329, Ed. C.F. Cecil; Pub. C.F. Cecil; adv. contact: Roger Janssen. photos; bk.rev.; pub. size: broadsheet; circ. 3,600(paid).

HILL CITY
US

PENNINGTON COUNTY PREVAILER-NEWS. 1972. Wed. $.40 newsstand; $18/yr. in state; $24/yr. out of state. 114 Main St., Ste. 1, Hill City, SD 57745-0266. TEL 605-574-2538. **Owner(s):** Custer Chronicle, P.O. Box 551, Custer, SD 57730; Ed. Don Gerken. adv.; photos; pub. size: standard; circ. 1,600(free & paid).

IPSWICH
US

IPSWICH TRIBUNE. Wed. $20/yr. in cy.; $23/yr. in state; $25/yr. out of state. 103 Main St., Ipswich, SD 57451-0007. TEL 605-426-6471; FAX 605-426-6471. **Owner(s):** Gibson Publishing Co., 103 Main St., Ipswich, SD 57451-0007. TEL 605-426-6471; Ed. Tena Gibson; Pub. Dwain Gibson; adv.; pub. size: broadsheet; circ. 1,105(paid).

US

ROSCOE HOSMER INDEPENDENT. Wed. $20/yr. in cy.; $23/yr. in state; $25/yr. out of state. 103 Main St., Ipswich, SD 57451-0007. TEL 605-426-6471; FAX 605-426-6471. **Owner(s):** Gibson Publishing Co., 103 Main St., Ipswich, SD 57451-0007. TEL 605-426-6471; Ed. Tena Gibson; Pub. Dwain Gibson; adv.; pub. size: broadsheet; circ. 700(paid).

MENNO
US

HUTCHINSON HERALD, THE. 1882. Wed. $.40 newsstand; $20/yr. in state; $22/yr. out of state. 154 E. Poplar St., Menno, SD 57045-0537. TEL 605-387-5158; FAX 605-387-5148. **Owner(s):** William J. Headley, P.O. Box 537, Menno, SD 57045. TEL 605-387-5270; Ed. William J. Headley; Pub. William J. Headley; adv.; photos; bk.rev.; pub. size: standard; circ. 1,145(free & paid).

MILBANK
US

GRANT COUNTY REVIEW. 1880. Wed. $.50 newsstand; $23/yr. in cy.; $28/out of cy. 225 S. Main St., Milbank, SD 57252-0390. TEL 605-432-4516. **Owner(s):** Phyllis Justice, P.O. Box 390, Milbank, SD 57252. TEL 605-432-4516; Ed. Phyllis Justice; Pub. Phyllis Justice; adv. contact: Phyllis Justice. pub. size: broadsheet; circ. 4,450(paid).
Formerly: Milbank Grant County Review.

NEWELL
US

BUTTE COUNTY VALLEY IRRIGATOR. 1900. Wed. $22/yr. in cy.; $26/yr. out of cy.; $30/yr. out of state. 119 Third St., Newell, SD 57760. TEL 605-456-2585; FAX 605-456-2585. **Owner(s):** Dickson Media, Inc., 2568 Ivy Rd., Ste. D, Charlottesville, VA 22903. TEL 804-971-8350; Ed. Tim Veldor; Pub. Tim Veldor; adv. contact: Austin Post. pub. size: broadsheet; circ. 1,400(free). **Wire Service(s):** UP.

PIERRE
US

PIERRE TIMES, THE. 1875. Thu. $22/yr. 333 W. Dakota, Pierre, SD 57501. TEL 605-224-7301; FAX 605-224-9210. **Owner(s):** Hipple Printing Co., Inc., P.O. Box 878, Pierre, SD 57501. TEL 605-224-7301; FAX 605-225-9210; Ed. Dana Hess; Pub. Terry Hipple; adv.; photos; pub. size: broadsheet; circ. 1,600(paid). **Wire Service(s):** AP.

REDFIELD
US

REDFIELD PRESS. 1898. Wed. $30/yr. in trade area; $40/yr. out of area. 16 E. Seventh Ave., Redfield, SD 57469. TEL 605-472-0822; FAX 605-472-3634. **Owner(s):** Walter Mundstock, Redfield Press, P.O. Box 440, Redfield, SD 57469. TEL 605-692-6826; Ed. Sonyna Suetter; Pub. Walter Mundstock; adv. contact: Walter Mundstock. bk.rev.; pub. size: broadsheet; circ. 3,662(paid).

SELBY
US

SELBY RECORD. 1888. Wed. $.75 newsstand; $29/yr. local; $32/yr. elsewhere. P.O. Box 421, Selby, SD 57472-0421. TEL 605-649-7866; FAX 605-649-7054. **Owner(s):** Leona Wager, P.O. Box 421, Selby, SD 57472; Ed. Leona Wager; Pub. Leona Wager; adv.; pub. size: tabloid; circ. 1,100(free & paid).

SISSETON
US

SISSETON COURIER. 1892. Wed. $27-$32/yr. 117 E. Oak, Sisseton, SD 57262. TEL 605-698-7642; FAX 605-698-3641. **Owner(s):** Harley Deutsch, P.O. Box 169, 117 E. Oak, Sisseton, SD 57262. TEL 605-698-7642; FAX 605-698-3641; Ed. Harley Deutsch; Pub. Harley Deutsch; pub. size: broadsheet; circ. 3,941(paid).

STURGIS
US

BLACK HILLS PRESS. 1900. Sat. $.50 newsstand; $32/yr. 1238 Main, Sturgis, SD 57785. TEL 605-347-2503; FAX 605-347-2321. **Owner(s):** Dickson Media, Inc., Charlottesville, VA; Ed. Jerry Steinley. pub. size: broadsheet; circ. 4,500(paid).

US

MEADE COUNTY TIMES-TRIBUNE. 1930. s-w.: Wed. & Sat. $.50 newsstand; $32/yr. in cy.; $37/yr. out of cy.; $44/yr. out of state. 1238 Main St., Sturgis, SD 57785. TEL 605-347-2503; FAX 605-347-2321. **Owner(s):** Dickson Media, Inc., 2568 Ivy Rd., Ste. D, Charlottesville, VA 22903. TEL 804-971-8350; Ed. Jerry Steinley; Pub. Gary Greene; adv.; pub. size: broadsheet, circ. 3,800(free & paid).

VERMILLION
US ISSN 1054-3449

PRATT TRIBUNE. 1884. Thu. $.75 newsstand; $24.38/yr. 201 W. Cherry St., Vermillion, SD 57069. TEL 605-624-2695; FAX 605-624-2696. **Owner(s):** Morris Communications, P.O. Box 936, P.O. Box 256, Augusta, GA. TEL 706-724-0856; Ed. David Lias. adv. contact: Jim Frye. bk.rev.; pub. size: standard; circ. 1,600(paid).

WEBSTER
US

WEBSTER REPORTER & FARMER. 1881. Mon. $.75 newsstand; $24.50/yr. in area; $30/yr. in state; $31/yr. out of state. 624 Main St., Webster, SD 57274-0030. TEL 605-345-3356; FAX 605-345-3739; E-mail: ripsnort@itchel.com. Owner(s): Larry & Janet Ingalls, 450 W. Eighth Ave., P.O. Box 30, Webster, SD. TEL 605-345-3356; FAX 605-345-3739; John & Le Ann Suhr, 619 E. 12th Ave., Webster, SD 57274. TEL 605-345-3356; FAX 605-345-3739; Ed. Larry Ingalls. adv. contact: John Suhr. photos; pub. size: broadsheet; circ. 3,837(paid).

WESSINGTON SPRINGS
US

TRUE DAKOTAN, THE. 1975. Tue. $25/yr. in state; $35/yr. out of state. 113 E. Main, Wessington Springs, SD 57382. TEL 605-539-1281; FAX 605-539-9315. **Owner(s):** J. Craig Wenzel, P.O. Box 305, Wessington Springs, SD 57382. TEL 605-539-1281; FAX 605-539-9315; Dennis P. Wenzel, P.O. Box T, Wessington Springs, SD 57382. TEL 605-539-1281; FAX 605-539-9315; Ed. J. Craig Wenzel. adv.; photos; pub. size: broadsheet; circ. 1,800(paid).
Formerly: Dakotan, The.

WEEKLY NEWSPAPERS

WINNER
US

WINNER ADVOCATE. 1910. Wed. $31.75/yr. local; $40.23/yr. elsewhere. 125 W. Third St., Winner, SD 57580-0071. TEL 605-842-1481; FAX 605-842-1979. **Owner(s):** Bill Sniffin, 28 Boulder Loop, Lander, WY 82520; Ed. Dan Bechtold; Pub. Mylan Schroeder; adv. contact: Mylan Schroeder. adv.: $6.61/SAU. pub. size: broadsheet; circ. 4,000(paid).
Formerly: Advocate.

TENNESSEE

ALAMO
US

CROCKETT TIMES, THE. 1873. Wed. $20/yr. in cy.; $30/yr. out of cy. 128 W. Main, Alamo, TN 38001. TEL 901-696-4558; FAX 901-696-4550. **Owner(s):** Robert B. and Patricia Sims, 128 W. Main, Alamo, TX 38001; Ed. Patricia Sims. pub. size: broadsheet; circ. 4,200(paid).

BLOUNTVILLE
US

SULLIVAN COUNTY NEWS. 1944. Thu. $.50 newsstand; $17/yr. 3200 Hwy. 126, Blountville, TN 37617. TEL 423-323-5700; FAX 423-323-1681. **Owner(s):** T.E. Worrell, Sr., c/o Bristol Newspapers, Bristol, VA 24201. TEL 703-669-2181; Ed. David McGee. adv.; photos; bk.rev.; pub. size: broadsheet; circ. 4,800(paid).

BOLIVAR
US

BOLIVAR BULLETIN-TIMES. 1865. Wed. $.75 newsstand; $26/yr. in cy.; $33/yr. in state; $50/yr. out of state. 410 W. Market, Bolivar, TN 38008. TEL 901-658-3691; FAX 901-658-7222. **Owner(s):** Delphos Newspapers, 405 N. Main, Delphos, OH 45833. TEL 419-692-5050; Ed. Anne Ingle; Pub. Richard Fry; adv. contact: Rita Blackard. pub. size: broadsheet; circ. 6,200(paid).

BRENTWOOD
US

BRENTWOOD JOURNAL. 1813. Thu. $.50 newsstand; $18/yr. carrier; $25/yr. mailed. 750 Old Hickory Blvd., Bldg. 2, Ste. 150, Brentwood, TN 37027. TEL 615-373-0445; FAX 615-377-3130. **Owner(s):** Morris Communications, P.O. Box 8167, Savannah, GA 31412; Ed. Lauren Lexa; Pub. Betty Brooks; adv. contact: Betty Brooks. photos; pub. size: broadsheet; circ. 11,000(free & paid). **Wire Service(s):** AP.
Formerly: Review Appeal.

BROWNSVILLE
US   ISSN 0893-3839

BROWNSVILLE STATES-GRAPHIC. 1867. Thu. $.50 newsstand; $18/yr. in cy.; $22/yr. in state; $30/yr. out of state. 42 S. Washington, Brownsville, TN 38012. TEL 901-772-1172. **Owner(s):** Wireless Group, Inc., 42 S. Washington, P.O. Box 198, Brownsville, TN 38012. TEL 901-772-1172; Ed. Christy Smith. adv.; photos; bk.rev.; pub. size: standard; circ. 5,400(paid).

BYRDSTOWN
US

PICKETT COUNTY PRESS. 1974. Thu. $.50 newsstand; $15/yr. 23 Courthouse Sq., Byrdstown, TN 38549. TEL 615-864-3675. **Owner(s):** James E. Hill, Main St., P.O. Box 268, Byrdstown, TN 38549. TEL 615-864-3675; Pub. James E. Hill; adv.; pub. size: broadsheet.

CAMDEN
US

CAMDEN CHRONICLE, THE. 1889. Wed. $.50 newsstand; $17/yr. in cy.; $16.50/yr. in state; $20/yr. out of state; $12/yr. senior citizens. 144 W. Main St., Camden, TN 38320. TEL 901-584-7200; FAX 901-584-4943; E-mail: johatiswt.com. **Owner(s):** Dennis & Lisa Richardson, 144 W. Main St., Camden, TN 38320. TEL 901-584-7200; Elton C. & Joan T. Hatley, 144 W. Main St., Camden, TN 38320. TEL 901-584-7200; Ed. Joan Hatley; Pub. Lisa Richardson; adv. contact: Vanessa Bell. pub. size: broadsheet; circ. 5,000(paid).

MAGIC VALLEY SHOPPER'S NEWS. 1979. Wed. $.35 newsstand; free mailed. 144 Main St., Camden, TN 38320. TEL 901-584-8700; FAX 901-584-7200. **Owner(s):** Magic Valley Publishing, P.O. Box 899, Camden, TN 38320. TEL 901-584-7200; Ed. Dennis Richardson; Pub. Dennis Richardson; adv. contact: Vanessa Bells. pub. size: broadsheet; circ. 8,700.
Formerly: Majic Valley Shopper's News.

CARTHAGE
US

CARTHAGE COURIER. 1807. Thu. $.35 newsstand; $12/yr. in cy.; $14/yr. out of cy.; $17/yr. out of state. 509 Main, Carthage, TN 37030-0239. TEL 615-735-1110; FAX 615-735-0635. **Owner(s):** Hershel Lake, P.O. Box 239, Carthage, TN 37030. TEL 615-735-1110; Ed. Eddie West; Pub. Scott Winfree; adv. contact: Scott Winfree. pub. size: broadsheet; circ. 5,152(paid).

CLINTON
US

COURIER-NEWS. 1887. s-w.: Wed. & Sun. $.50 newsstand; $32/yr. in cy.; $34/yr. in surrounding cys.; $45/yr. out of area. 233 N. Hicks St., Clinton, TN 37716. TEL 423-457-2515; FAX 423-457-1586. **Owner(s):** Courier Publications, P.O. Box 1630, Greeneville, TN 37744. TEL 615-638-4181; Ed. Doug Morris; Pub. Doug Morris; adv.; photos; pub. size: standard; circ. 17,112(controlled & paid).

COLLIERVILLE
US   ISSN 0746-5939

COLLIERVILLE HERALD, THE. 1870. Thu. $.50 newsstand; $15/yr. in cy.; $18/yr. out of cy. 139 N. Main St., Collierville, TN 38017. TEL 901-853-2241; FAX 901-853-8507. **Owner(s):** Van Pritchartt, P.O. Box 427, Collierville, TN 38027. TEL 901-853-2241; Thomas Hart, P.O. Box 427, Collierville, TN 38027; Frayser Humphreys, P.O. Box 427, Collierville, TN 38027; Ed. Van Pritchartt; Pub. Van Pritchartt; adv.; photos; bk.rev.; pub. size: broadsheet; circ. 5,500(paid).

US

INDEPENDENT. 1982. Wed. $.50 newsstand; $15/yr. 151 N. Main St., Collierville, TN 38017-2617. TEL 901-853-7060. **Owner(s):** Shoppers Press of Memphis, 622 S. Highland St., Memphis, TN 38111. TEL 901-458-8030; Ed. Stephen Craven. adv.; pub. size: broadsheet; circ. 12,400(free & paid).

COVINGTON
US

COVINGTON LEADER. 1886. Wed. $.50 newsstand; $18/yr. in cy.; $24/yr. out of cy.; $30/yr. out of state. 2001 Hwy. 51 S., Covington, TN 38019. TEL 901-476-7116; FAX 901-476-0373. **Owner(s):** Press Holding Corp., P.O. Box 529, Covington, TN 38019-0529. TEL 901-476-7116; FAX 901-476-0373; Ed. George T. Whitley; Pub. George T. Whitley; adv. contact: Larry Whitley. photos; bk.rev.; pub. size: broadsheet; circ. 9,200(paid).

CROSSVILLE
US

CROSSVILLE CHRONICLE. 1886. 3/wk.: Tue., Wed., Fri. $.50 newsstand; $43/yr. in state; $50/yr. out of state; $35/yr. senior citizens. 120 S. Main, Ste. 102, Crossville, TN 38555. TEL 615-484-5145; FAX 615-456-7683; E-mail: chronicle@midtenn.net. **Owner(s):** American Publishing Co., 606 N. Van Buren, Marion, IL 62959. TEL 618-993-1711; Ed. Mike Moser; Pub. Pauline Sherrer; photos; bk.rev.; pub. size: broadsheet; circ. 89,000(paid).

DAYTON
US

HERALD-NEWS. 1898. s-w.: Sun. & Wed. $.50 newsstand; $32/yr. in cy.; $42/yr. in state; $45/yr. out of state. 3687 Rhea County Hwy., Dayton, TN 37321. TEL 423-775-6111; FAX 423-775-8218. **Owner(s):** Media Services Group, Inc., P.O. Box 1630, Greeneville, TN 37744. TEL 615-638-4181; Ed. John Carpenter; Pub. Ed Emens; adv. contact: Jim Kinser. pub. size: broadsheet; circ. Sun. 13,500(paid).

DICKSON
US

DICKSON HERALD, THE. 1907. s-w.: Wed. & Fri. $.50 newsstand; $20/yr. in cy. 104 Church St., Dickson, TN 37055. TEL 615-446-2811; FAX 615-446-5560. **Owner(s):** Leaf Chronicle Co., 200 Commerce St., Clarksville, TN 37040. TEL 615-552-1808; FAX 615-648-8001; Ed. Chris Norman. adv.; photos; pub. size: broadsheet; circ. 19,500(free & paid).

DRESDEN
US   ISSN 0016-1040

DRESDEN ENTERPRISE. 1883. Wed. $14/yr. in cy.; $16/yr. out of cy.; $24/yr. out of state. 113 Wilson, Dresden, TN 38225-0139. TEL 901-364-2234; FAX 901-364-5774. **Owner(s):** Ramona Washburn, P.O. Box 100, McKenzie, TN 38201. TEL 901-352-3323; Jeff Washburn, P.O. Box 139, Dresden, TN 38225. TEL 901-364-2234; Joel Washburn, P.O. Box 100, McKenzie, TN 38201. TEL 901-352-3323; Ed. Jeff Washburn; Pub. Ramona Washburn; adv.; photos; pub. size: broadsheet; circ. 6,200(paid).

DYER

US
TRI-CITY REPORTER. 1892. Wed. $.50 newsstand; $17.95/yr. in cy.; $22.50/yr. in state; $27.50/yr. elsewhere. 101 N. Main St., Dyer, TN 38330. TEL 901-692-3506; FAX 901-692-4844. **Owner(s):** Warmath Communications, P.O. Box 408, Humboldt, TN 38343. TEL 901-784-5000; Ed. April Jackson; Pub. Frank Warmath; adv.; photos; pub. size: broadsheet; circ. 3,500(paid).

ERWIN

US
ERWIN RECORD. 1927. Wed. $.35 newsstand; $14/yr. in cy.; $22/yr. out of cy. 218 Gay St., Erwin, TN 37650. TEL 423-743-4112; FAX 423-743-6125. **Owner(s):** Press Holding Corp., 218 Gay St., Erwin, TN 37650. TEL 423-743-4112; FAX 423-743-6125; Ed. Tom Harris; Pub. Tom Harris. adv.: $4.17/SAU. photos; pub. size: standard; circ. 4,500(paid).

FAYETTEVILLE

US
ELK VALLEY TIMES. 1965. Wed. $.50 newsstand; $17/yr. local; $23/yr. elswhere. 418 N. Elk Ave., Fayetteville, TN 37334. TEL 615-433-6151; FAX 615-433-6151. **Owner(s):** Lakeway Publishers, Inc., P.O. Box 625, Morristown, TN 37815. TEL 615-581-5630; Ed. Lucy A. Carter; Pub. Lucy A. Carter; pub. size: broadsheet; circ. 8,100(paid).

FRANKLIN

US
WILLIAMSON LEADER, THE. 1973. Thu. $.25 newsstand; $15/yr. in state; $25/yr. out of state. 128 Holiday Ct. Ste. 121, Franklin, TN 37067. TEL 615-794-4564; FAX 615-794-9581. **Owner(s):** Williamson Leader, Inc., P.O. Box 729, Franklin, TN 37065-0729. TEL 615-794-4564; FAX 615-794-9581; Ed. Bailey Leopard; Pub. Bailey Leopard; adv.; photos; pub. size: broadsheet; circ. 6,100(paid).

GALLATIN

US
NEWS-EXAMINER. 1840. 3/wk.: Mon., Wed., Fri. $.50 newsstand; $36/yr. One Examiner Ct., Gallatin, TN 37066. TEL 615-452-2561; FAX 615-452-9110. **Owner(s):** Gannett Company, Inc., 1100 Wilson Blvd., Arlington, VA 22234. TEL 703-284-6000; Ed. Steve Rogers; Pub. Bob Atkins; adv.; photos; bk.rev.; pub. size: broadsheet; circ. 10,800(paid). **Wire Service(s):** AP.

GERMANTOWN

US
GERMANTOWN NEWS, THE. 1974. Thu. $.50 newsstand; $25/yr. 7545 North St., Germantown, TN 38138. TEL 901-754-0337; FAX 901-754-2961. **Owner(s):** Ricketson Publishing, 7545 North St., Memphis, TN 38138. TEL 901-754-0337; FAX 901-754-2961; adv.; photos; pub. size: broadsheet; circ. 8,000(paid).

US
SHELBY SUN TIMES. 1987. Thu. $.25 newsstand; $20/yr. mailed. 7508 Capital Dr., Ste. 2, Germantown, TN 38138-0801. TEL 901-755-7386; FAX 901-755-0827. **Owner(s):** Lynn H. Sanders, 7508 Capital Dr., Germantown, TN 38138. TEL 901-755-7386; FAX 901-755-0827; Ed. Patricia Pair. adv.; photos; pub. size: tabloid; circ. 22,400(free).

HARTSVILLE

US
HARTSVILLE VIDETTE, THE. 1862. Thu. $.25 newsstand; $7/yr. in cy.; $15/yr. out of cy. 111 Marlene St., Hartsville, TN 37074. TEL 615-374-3556. **Owner(s):** Lebanon Democrat, Lebanon, TN 37087. TEL 615-444-3952; Pub. Angelene Anderson; adv. contact: Tina Kay Davis. photos; pub. size: standard; circ. 2,300(paid).

HENDERSONVILLE

US   ISSN 0193-5143
HENDERSONVILLE STAR NEWS. 1951. s-w.: Wed. & Fri. $.50 newsstand; $36/yr. mailed; $41/yr. out of state. 110 Sanders Ferry, Hendersonville, TN 37077. TEL 615-824-8480; FAX 615-824-3126. **Owner(s):** Gannett Company, Inc., 1100 Wilson Blvd., Arlington, VA 22340. TEL 615-824-8480; Ed. Mike McClanahan. adv.; photos; pub. size: broadsheet; circ. 13,300(paid). **Wire Service(s):** AP.

HUMBOLDT

US
CHRONICLE, THE. 1887. Wed. $18.50/yr. in cy.; $25/yr. in state; $30/yr. out of state. 2606 E. End Dr., Humboldt, TN 38343. TEL 901-784-2531; FAX 901-784-2533. **Owner(s):** Chronicle, Inc., 2606 E. End Dr., Humboldt, TN 38343. TEL 901-784-2531; FAX 901-784-2533; Ed. Martha Dodson; Pub. Frank Warmath; adv.; photos; pub. size: broadsheet; circ. 4,000(paid).
Formerly: Courier Chronicle, The.

HUNTINGDON

US
CARROLL COUNTY NEWS-LEADER. 1887. Wed. $.50 newsstand; $19/yr. in cy.; $24/yr. out of cy.; $29/yr. out of state. 163 Court Sq., Huntingdon, TN 38344. TEL 901-986-2253; FAX 901-986-3585. **Owner(s):** Magic Valley Publishing Co., P.O. Box 389, Huntington, TN 38344. TEL 901-986-2253; Elton C. & Joan T. Hatley, P.O. Box 389, Huntington, TN 38344. TEL 901-986-2253; Ed. Shirley Nanney. pub. size: broadsheet; circ. 6,700(paid).
Formerly: Huntington Carroll News.

JASPER

US
JASPER JOURNAL. 1938. Tue. $.75 newsstand; $25/yr. in cy.; $32/yr. out of cy. 6615 Hwy. 41, Jasper, TN 37347. TEL 423-942-2433; FAX 423-942-8835. **Owner(s):** Marin County Newspapers, 6615 Hwy. 41, Jasper, TN 37347. TEL 615-942-2348; Ed. Linda Rector; Pub. Allen Kirk; adv. contact: Allen Kirk. pub. size: standard; circ. 3,600(paid).

JEFFERSON

US
STANDARD BANNER. 1927. s-w.: Tue. & Thu. $.50 newsstand; $25/yr. in cy.; $40/yr. out of cy. 122 W. Andrew Johnson Hwy., Jefferson, TN 37760-0310. TEL 423-475-2081; FAX 423-475-8539. **Owner(s):** Jefferson County Standard Publishing Co., Inc., P.O. Box 310, Jefferson, TN 37760-0310. TEL 423-475-2081; FAX 423-475-8539; Ed. Dale Gentry; Pub. Tom Gentry; adv. contact: Shane Cook. pub. size: broadsheet; circ. 6,400(paid).

JONESBOROUGH

US
HERALD & TRIBUNE. 1869. Wed. $.25 newsstand; $10/yr. mailed. 702 W. Jackson Blvd., Jonesborough, TN 37659. TEL 615-753-3136; FAX 615-753-6528. **Owner(s):** Johnson City Press, P.O. Box 277, Johnson City, TN; Ed. Kelly Arnold. adv. contact: Lois Hicks. pub. size: broadsheet; circ. 4,500(paid).

KINGSTON

US
HARRIMAN RECORD. 1865. Tue. $.35 newsstand; $7.95/yr. 204 Franklin St., Kingston, TN 37763. TEL 423-376-3481; FAX 423-376-1945. **Owner(s):** Landmark Community Newspapers, Inc., P.O. Box 549, Shelbyville, KY 40066. TEL 502-633-4334; Ed. Darrell Richardson. adv. contact: Glenda Danflyke. pub. size: broadsheet; circ. 850(paid).

US
ROANE COUNTY NEWS, THE. 1957. 3/wk.: Mon., Wed., Fri. $.50 newsstand; $34.95/yr. in cy.; $53/yr. out of cy.; $74/yr. out of state. 204 Franklin St., Kingston, TN 37763. TEL 423-376-3481; FAX 423-376-1945. **Owner(s):** Landmark Community Newspapers, Inc., P.O. Box 549, Shelbyville, KY 40066. TEL 502-633-4334; Ed. Darrell Richardson. adv. contact: Glenda Vanslyke. pub. size: broadsheet; circ. 8,937(paid).

US
ROCKWOOD TIMES. Tue. $.35 newsstand; $9.95/yr. P.O. Box 610, Kingston, TN 37763. TEL 423-376-3481; FAX 423-376-1945. **Owner(s):** Landmark Community Newspapers, Inc., P.O. Box 549, Shelbyville, KY 40066. TEL 502-633-4334; Ed. Darrell Richardson. adv. contact: Glenda Vanslyke. photos; bk.rev.; pub. size: broadsheet; circ. morning 681(controlled & paid).

KNOXVILLE

US
TRI-COUNTY NEWS. 1955. Tue. $.30 newsstand; $15/yr. local; $20/yr. out of area. 9010 Chapman Hwy., Knoxville, TN 37920. TEL 423-577-5935; FAX 423-577-9896. **Owner(s):** Gladys E. Hamilton, P.O. Box 130, Seymour, TN 37865. TEL 615-577-5935; FAX 615-577-9896; Ed. Gladys E. Hamilton; Pub. Gladys E. Hamilton; pub. size: tabloid; circ. 2,500(free & paid).

WEEKLY NEWSPAPERS

LAFAYETTE

US   ISSN 0745-5976
MACON COUNTY TIMES. 1919. Thu. $.50 newsstand; $15/yr. 200 Times Ave., Lafayette, TN 37083. TEL 615-666-2440; FAX 615-666-4909. **Owner(s):** Macon County Newspapers, Inc., P.O. Box 69, Lafayette, TN 37083. TEL 615-666-2440; Ed. Truett Langston; Pub. Truett Langston; adv.; pub. size: broadsheet; circ. 6,400(paid).

LA FOLLETTE

US
JELLICO ADVANCE SENTINEL. 1880. Wed. $.25 newsstand; $8.50/yr. in cy.; $10.50/yr. elsewhere. P.O. Box 1261, La Follette, TN 37766. TEL 423-562-8468; FAX 423-566-7060. **Owner(s):** La Follette Press, Inc., P.O. Box 1261, La Follette, TN 37766. TEL 615-562-8468; Ed. Rex Hickey; Pub. Larry K. Smith; pub. size: broadsheet; circ. 850(paid).

US
LA FOLLETTE PRESS. 1910. Thu. $.50 newsstand; $15.25/yr. local; $27.50/yr. out of state. 220 N. First St., La Follette, TN 37766. TEL 615-562-8468; FAX 615-566-7060. **Owner(s):** La Follette Press, Inc., P.O. Box 1261, La Follette, TN 37766. TEL 615-562-8468; Ed. Charles Winfrey; Pub. Larry Smith; adv. contact: Larry Dilbeck. pub. size: tabloid; circ. 8,300(paid).

US
LAKE CITY TOWN CRIER. 1910. Tue. $.15 newsstand; $7/yr. in cy.; $9/yr. out of cy. 220 N. First St., La Follette, TN 37766. TEL 423-562-8468; FAX 423-566-7060. **Owner(s):** La Follette Press, Inc., P.O. Box 1261, La Follette, TN 37766. TEL 423-562-8468; Ed. Rex Hickey; Pub. Larry Smith; pub. size: tabloid; circ. 1,500(paid).

LAWRENCEBURG

US
DEMOCRAT-UNION. 1884. s-w.: Tue. & Fri. $.25 newsstand; $18/yr. 238 Hughes St., Lawrenceburg, TN 38464. TEL 615-762-2222; FAX 615-762-4191. **Owner(s):** Jim Crawford, Jr., P.O. Box 685, Goodspring, TN 38460. TEL 615-762-2222; Ed. Charlie Crawford; Pub. Jim Crawford, Jr.; adv. contact: Charlie Crawford. pub. size: broadsheet; circ. 10,000(paid).

LEBANON

US
WILSON WORLD, THE. 1978. Thu. $.25 newsstand; $5/yr. local. 115-A East Main St., Lebanon, TN 37087. TEL 615-444-6008; FAX 615-444-6018. **Owner(s):** Tommy A. Bryan, 115-A East Main St., Lebanon, TN 37087. TEL 615-444-6008; FAX 615-444-6018; John B. Bryan, 115-A East Main St., Lebanon, TN 37087. TEL 615-444-6008; FAX 615-444-6018; W. Troy Putman, 115-A East Main St., Lebanon, TN 37087. TEL 615-444-6008; FAX 615-444-6018; Ed. Tommy A. Bryan; Pub. Tommy A. Bryan; adv. contact: John B. Bryan. photos; pub. size: tabloid; circ. 5,400(paid).

LENOIR CITY

US
NEWS HERALD. 1885. s-w.: Mon. & Thu. $.50 newsstand; $40/yr. 508 E. Broadway, Lenoir City, TN 37771. TEL 423-986-6581; FAX 423-988-3261. **Owner(s):** Loudon Publishing Co., 508 E. Broadway, Lenoir City, TN 37771. TEL 423-988-3261; Ed. Linda Brewer. adv. contact: Phylis Burnette. photos; bk.rev.; pub. size: broadsheet; circ. 14,892(free & paid).

LEWISBURG

US
LEWISBURG TRIBUNE. s-w.: Tue. & Thu. $.35 newsstand; $22/yr. in cy.; $28/yr. out of cy. 121 First Ave., S., Lewisburg, TN 37091. TEL 615-359-1188; FAX 615-359-1847. **Owner(s):** Lewisburg Tribune, Inc., 121 First Ave., S., Lewisburg, TN 37091. TEL 615-359-1188; Ed. Betty Orr; Pub. Tommy Hawkins, III; adv. contact: Bonnie Phillips. pub. size: standard; circ. 7,800(paid).

US
MARSHALL GAZETTE. Tue. $.35 newsstand; $22/yr. in cy.; $29/yr. out of cy. 121 First Ave. S., Lewisburg, TN 37091. TEL 615-359-1188. **Owner(s):** Lewisburg Tribune, Inc., 121 First Ave., S., Lewisburg, TN 37091. TEL 615-359-1188; Ed. Betty Orr; Pub. Tommy Hawkins, III; adv. contact: Bonnie Phillips. pub. size: broadsheet; circ. 7,800(paid).

LEXINGTON

US
LEXINGTON PROGRESS. Wed. $.50 newsstand; $13/yr. in cy.; $18/yr. in state; $22/yr. out of state. 60 S. Broad St., Lexington, TN 38351. TEL 901-968-6397; FAX 901-968-9560. **Owner(s):** Lexington Progress Inc., 60 S. Broad St., Lexington, TN 38351; Ed. Mike Reed; Pub. Tom Franklin; pub. size: broadsheet; circ. 8,300(paid).

LINDEN

US
BUFFALO RIVER REVIEW. 1976. Wed. $.35 newsstand; $13/yr. 115 S. Mill St., Linden, TN 37096. TEL 615-589-2169; FAX 615-589-3858. **Owner(s):** Buffalo Review, P.O. Box 914, Linden, TN 37096. TEL 615-589-2169; FAX 615-589-3858; Ed. Randy Mackin; Pub. Sam Kennedy; adv.; pub. size: broadsheet; circ. 3,000(paid).

LIVINGSTON

US
LIVINGSTON ENTERPRISE. 1892. Wed. $.50 newsstand; $15/yr. in area; $30/yr. out of area. 203 S. Church St., Livingston, TN 38570. TEL 615-823-1274; FAX 615-268-9125. **Owner(s):** Richard F. Knight, 203 S. Church St., P.O. Box 129, Livingston, TN 38570; Ed. Richard F. Knight; Pub. Richard F. Knight; adv. contact: Mickey Ledbetter. photos; pub. size: standard; circ. 5,300(paid).

MADISON

US
MESSENGER, THE. 1982. Wed. free. 322 E. Old Hickory Blvd., Madison, TN 37115. TEL 615-868-0475; FAX 615-868-6888. **Owner(s):** Messenger Newspapers, Inc., P.O. Box 711, Mt. Juliet, TN 37122. TEL 615-754-6111; Ed. Susan Rotkiewcz; Pub. Bill C. Robinson; adv.: $7.99/SAU; $8.49/SAU classified. photos; pub. size: broadsheet; circ. 8,000(free).

MADISONVILLE

US
ADVOCATE DEMOCRAT. 1870. 3/wk.: Wed., Fri., Sun. $.50 newsstand; $39/yr. in cy.; $66/yr. out of area. 509 Cook St., Madisonville, TN 37354. TEL 423-442-4575; FAX 423-442-1416. **Owner(s):** Advocate Democrat, 509 Cook St., Madisonville, TN 37354. TEL 423-337-7101; Ed. Ann Wallace; Pub. Thomas G. Wilson, III; adv. contact: Ann Roberts. pub. size: broadsheet; circ. 5,000(paid); Sun. 15,000(paid).
  Formerly: Democrat/Laker.

MANCHESTER

US
MANCHESTER TIMES. 1881. Wed. $.50 newsstand; $18/yr. local; $32/yr. out of area. 300 N. Spring St., Manchester, TN 37355. TEL 615-728-7577; FAX 615-728-7614. **Owner(s):** Lakeway Publishers, Inc., Morristown, TN; Ed. Robert Long; Pub. Chuck Cunningham; adv. contact: Susie Gilliam. pub. size: broadsheet; circ. 6,500(paid).

MARTIN

US
WEAKLEY COUNTY PRESS. 1885. s-w.: Tue. & Thu. $.50 newsstand; $18/yr. 235 Lindell, Martin, TN 38237. TEL 901-587-3144; FAX 901-587-3147. **Owner(s):** David Critchlow, P.O. Box 410, Martin, TN 38237; Ed. Joe Lofaro; Pub. David Critchlow; adv. contact: Donna Wright. pub. size: standard; circ. 5,700(paid).
  Formerly: Martin Weakley County Press.

MCKENZIE

US
MCKENZIE BANNER. 1870. Wed. $.50 newsstand; $15/yr. surrounding cys.; $19/yr. in state; $25/yr. elsewhere. 3 Banner Row, McKenzie, TN 38201-0100. TEL 901-352-3323. **Owner(s):** Jeff Washburn, P.O. Box 139, Dresden, TN 38225. TEL 901-364-2234; Joel Washburn, P.O. Box 125, McKenzie, TN 38201. TEL 901-352-3323; Ramona Washburn, P.O. Box 28, McKenzie, TN 38201. TEL 901-352-3323; FAX 901-352-3322; Ed. Joel Washburn; Pub. Ramona Washburn; adv.; photos; pub. size: broadsheet; circ. 5,500(paid). **Wire Service(s):** AP.

MCMINNVILLE

US
SOUTHERN STANDARD. 1879. 3/wk.: Sun., Wed., Fri. $.50 newsstand; $51/yr. deliv. 105 College St., McMinnville, TN 37110. TEL 615-473-2191; FAX 615-473-6823. **Owner(s):** Morris Newspaper Corp., P.O. Box 8167, Savannah, GA 31412. TEL 912-233-1281; Ed. Susan Newby; Pub. William R. Fryar; adv. contact: Sharon Patrick. photos; bk.rev.; pub. size: broadsheet; circ. 8,400(paid).

MEMPHIS, TN

MEMPHIS
US
MEMPHIS FLYER. Thu. free; $50/yr. 460 Tennesse St., Memphis, TN 38103. TEL 901-521-9000; FAX 901-521-0129. **Owner(s):** Contemporary Media, 460 Tennesse St., Memphis, TN 38103. TEL 901-521-9000; Ed. Cheryl Bader; Pub. Kenneth Neill; pub. size: tabloid; circ. 245,000(free & paid).

MILAN
US
MIRROR-EXCHANGE. 1964. Tue. $.50 newsstand; $15/yr. in cy.; $20/yr. out of cy.; $25/yr. out of state. 1104 S. Main, Milan, TN 38358. TEL 901-686-8114; FAX 901-686-9005. **Owner(s):** Mirror-Exchange, Inc., P.O. Box 549, Milan; TN 38358. TEL 901-686-1632; Ed. Bob Parkins; Pub. Bob Parkins; adv. contact: Melanie Day. photos; pub. size: broadsheet; circ. 5,500(paid).
Formerly: Milan Mirror-Exchange.

MILLINGTON
US
MILLINGTON STAR, THE. 1952. Wed. $.50 newsstand; $18/yr. in cy.; $21/yr. out of cy. 5107 Easley, Millington, TN 38053-0305. TEL 901-872-2286; FAX 901-872-2965. **Owner(s):** J.T.S. Inc., P.O. Box 305, Millington, TN 38083-0305. TEL 901-872-2965; FAX 901-872-2965; Ed. Patricia Stumb; Pub. Jeff Stumb; adv. contact: Kay Black. photos; pub. size: broadsheet; circ. 2,178(paid).

MOUNTAIN CITY
US
TOMAHAWK, THE. 1874. Wed. $.35 newsstand; $25/yr. in cy.; $35/yr. out of cy.; $18/yr. senior citizens. 118 S. Church St., Mountain City, TN 37683. TEL 423-727-6121; FAX 423-727-4833. **Owner(s):** Press, Inc., P.O. Box 1717, Johnson City, TN 37605. TEL 615-929-3111; Ed. Deidra Smith. adv. contact: Rita Cornett. bk.rev.; pub. size: standard; circ. 5,700(paid).
Formerly: Mountain City Tomahawk.

MURFREESBORO
US
COVER STORY, THE. 1975. Wed. free. 224 N. Walnut St., Murfreesboro, TN 37130. TEL 615-893-5860; FAX 615-896-8702. **Owner(s):** Morris Communications, P.O. Box 8167, Savannah, GA 31412. TEL 912-233-1281; Ed. Mike Pirtle. pub. size: tabloid; circ. 24,000(free).
Formerly: Merchant's Advocate.

NASHVILLE
US
NASHVILLE SCENE, THE. Thu. free; $50/yr. 209 Tenth Ave., S., Ste.222, Nashville, TN 37203. TEL 615-244-7989; FAX 615-244-8578. **Owner(s):** Albie Del Favero, Nashville, TN 37203. TEL 615-244-7989; Ed. Bruce Dobie; Pub. Albie Del Favero; circ. 50,000(free & paid).

NEWBERN
US
DYER COUNTY TENNESSEAN. 1888. Fri. $14/yr. in cy.; $16.50/yr. in state; $19/yr. out of state. 113 Jefferson, Newbern, TN 38059. TEL 901-627-3247; FAX 901-287-1551; E-mail: jkrvst@aol.com. **Owner(s):** Rust Communications, P.O. Box 699, Cape Girardeau, MO 63702-0699. TEL 314-335-6611; Ed. Chris Rimal; Pub. John Rust; adv.; pub. size: broadsheet; circ. 4,100(paid).

NEWPORT
US
NEWPORT PLAINTALK. 1900. 3/wk.: Mon., Wed., Fri. $.50 newsstand; $43/yr. in cy.; $66/yr. out of cy. 145 E. Broadway, Newport, TN 37821. TEL 423-623-6171; FAX 423-625-1995. **Owner(s):** Newport Publishing Co., 145 E. Broadway, Newport, RI 37821. TEL 615-623-6171; FAX 615-625-1995; Pub. John M. Jones; adv.; bk.rev.; pub. size: broadsheet; circ. 9,200(paid).
Formerly: Plain Talk.

ONEIDA
US   ISSN 8750-5940
SCOTT COUNTY NEWS. 1916. Thu. $13/yr. in cy.; $15/yr. in state; $18/yr. out of cy. 224 Alberta Ave., Oneida, TN 37841. TEL 423-569-8351; FAX 423-569-4500. **Owner(s):** Bell Press, Inc., P.O. Box 4399, Oneida, TN 37841. TEL 615-569-8351; FAX 615-569-4500; Ed. Richard Magyar, Jr.; Pub. Shelia K. Erwin; adv. contact: Gary Hollis. pub. size: standard; circ. 7,000(controlled & paid).
Formerly: Oneida Scott County News.

PARSONS
US
NEWS LEADER, THE. 1926. Wed. $10/yr. in cy.; $16/yr. out of cy.; $20/yr. out of state. 113 S. Tennessee Ave., Parsons, TN 38363-0340. TEL 901-847-6354; FAX 901-847-9120. **Owner(s):** Sam Kennedy, P.O. Box 340, Parsons, TN 38363. TEL 901-847-6354; FAX 901-847-9120; Ed. Mary Alexander. adv.; pub. size: broadsheet; circ. 4,833(paid).

PULASKI
US
CITIZEN/PRESS PLUS. 1982. Tue. free. 308 W. College, Pulaski, TN 38478. TEL 615-363-3544; FAX 615-363-4319. **Owner(s):** S. Hershel Lake, 308 W. College St., Pulaski, TN 38478. TEL 615-363-3544; FAX 615-363-4319; Ed. Joe Collins; Pub. S. Hershel Lake; adv.; photos; pub. size: broadsheet; circ. 5,400(free).

US
PULASKI CITIZEN. 1854. Tue. $.50 newsstand; $24/yr. 308 W. College, Pulaski, TN 38478. TEL 615-363-4548; FAX 615-363-4319. **Owner(s):** S. Hershel Lake, P.O. Box E, Pulaski, TN 38478. TEL 615-363-3544; Pub. S. Hershel Lake; adv. contact: Juanita Hoover. adv.: $6.30/SAU. pub. size: broadsheet; circ. 8,200(paid).

US
PULASKI GILES FREE PRESS. 1961. Thu. $.50 newsstand; $24/yr. in cy. 308 W. College, Pulaski, TN 38478. TEL 615-363-4548; FAX 615-363-4319. **Owner(s):** S. Hershel Lake, P.O. Box E, Pulaski, TN 38478. TEL 615-363-4548; FAX 615-363-4319; Ed. Dana Keeton; Pub. S. Hershel Lake; adv. contact: Juanita Hoover. adv.: $6.30/SAU. pub. size: broadsheet; circ. 8,400(paid).

RIPLEY
US
HALLS GRAPHIC. 1894. Thu. $10/yr. in cy.; $12/yr. elsewhere. 145 E. Jackson, Ripley, TN 38063. TEL 901-635-1771; FAX 901-635-2111. **Owner(s):** William A. Klutts, 145 E. Jackson, Ripley, TN 38063. TEL 901-635-1771; Ed. William A. Klutts; Pub. William A. Klutts; pub. size: broadsheet; circ. 1,231(paid).

US
LAUDERDALE COUNTY ENTERPRISE. 1885. Thu. $.35 newsstand; $15/yr. in cy.; $18/yr. out of cy.; $24/yr. out of state. 145 E. Jackson Ave., Ripley, TN 38063. TEL 901-635-1771; FAX 901-635-2111. **Owner(s):** William A. Klutts, P.O. Box 289, Ripley, TN 38063. TEL 901-635-1771; Ed. William A. Klutts; Pub. William A. Klutts; pub. size: standard; circ. 4,800(paid).

ROGERSVILLE
US
ROGERSVILLE REVIEW. 1885. s-w.: Wed. & Sat. $.50 newsstand; $26/yr. in cy.; $28/yr. out of cy.; $34/yr. elsewhere. 207 Washington St., Rogersville, TN 37857. TEL 423-272-7422; FAX 423-272-7889. **Owner(s):** Hawkins County Publishers, Inc., P.O. Box 100, Rogersville, TN 37857. TEL 615-272-7422; Pub. Duane Uls; adv. contact: Ben Addison. pub. size: standard; circ. 7,012(paid).

RUTLEDGE
US
GRAINGER COUNTY NEWS. 1928. Wed. $.35 newsstand; $10/yr. in cy. Cherry St., Rutledge, TN 37861. TEL 423-828-5254. **Owner(s):** Linda Witt, P.O. Box 218, Rutledge, TN 37861. TEL 615-828-5254; Ed. Linda Witt; Pub. Linda Witt; adv. contact: Kim Carpenter. adv.: $3.75/SAU. pub. size: broadsheet; circ. 3,900(paid).

SAVANNAH
US
COURIER, THE. 1884. Thu. $.50 newsstand; $16/yr. local; $21/yr. out of area; $28/yr. out of state. 801 Main St., Savannah, TN 38372. TEL 901-925-6397; FAX 901-925-6310. **Owner(s):** Savannah Publishing Co., Inc., P.O. Box 340, Savannah, TN 38372. TEL 901-925-6397; Ed. Jim Thompson; Pub. Kathryn Craddock; adv. contact: Beth Jerrolds. pub. size: broadsheet; circ. 9,200(paid).
Formerly: Savannah Courier.

WEEKLY NEWSPAPERS

SELMER
US
INDEPENDENT APPEAL. 1902. Thu. $.50 newsstand; $12/yr. in cy.; $18/yr. out of cy.; $25/yr. out of state. 111 N. Second St., Selmer, TN 38375. TEL 901-645-5346; FAX 901-645-3591. **Owner(s):** William Rail, 111 N. Second St., Selmer, TN 38375. TEL 901-645-5346; Pub. Bill Rail; adv. contact: Janet Rail. pub. size: broadsheet; circ. 7,500(paid).
Formerly: Selmer Independent Appeal.

SMITHVILLE
US
SMITHVILLE REVIEW. 1892. Wed. $.50 newsstand; $20/yr. in cy.; $28/yr. elsewhere. 106 S. First St., Smithville, TN 37166. TEL 615-597-5485; FAX 615-597-5489. **Owner(s):** Morris Communications, P.O. Box 8167, Savannah, GA 31412. TEL 912-233-1281; Ed. Dennis Stanley; Pub. William R. Fryar; pub. size: broadsheet; circ. 4,400(paid).

SMYRNA
US
RUTHERFORD COURIER, THE. 1931. Thu. $.50 newsstand; $18/yr. in state; $22/yr. out of state. 103 Front St., Smyrna, TN 37167. TEL 615-459-3868; FAX 615-459-3878. **Owner(s):** Charles H. Morris, P.O. Box 8167, Savannah, GA 31412. TEL 912-233-1281; Ed. Ric Gross. pub. size: broadsheet; circ. 3,300(paid).

SOMERVILLE
US
EAST SHELBY REVIEW. 1989. Wed. $.35 newsstand; mailed free in area. 16814 Hwy. 64, Somerville, TN 38068. TEL 901-867-2306; FAX 901-465-5493. **Owner(s):** Don Dowdle, P.O. Box 423, Somerville, TN 38068. TEL 901-465-4042; FAX 901-465-5493; Ed. Bob Koenig; Pub. Don Dowdle; adv.; photos; bk.rev.; pub. size: broadsheet; circ. 5,400(free).

US
FAYETTE COUNTY REVIEW. Wed. $.35 newsstand; free/mailed in area. 16814 Hwy. 64, Somerville, TN 38068. TEL 901-465-4042; FAX 901-465-5493. **Owner(s):** Don Dowdle, 16814 Hwy. 64, P.O. Box 280, Somerville, TN 38068. TEL 901-465-4042; FAX 901-465-5493; Ed. Don Dowdle. pub. size: broadsheet; circ. 8,214.

US
FAYETTE FALCON, THE. 1837. Wed. $.25 newsstand; $10/yr. in cy.; $17/yr. out of state. 101 W. Court Sq., Somerville, TN 38068. TEL 901-465-3567; FAX 901-465-3568. **Owner(s):** Carl A. Jones, P.O. Box 1717, Johnson City, TN 37605; Ed. Butch Rhea. adv. contact: Debby Smith. photos; pub. size: standard; circ. 4,000(free & paid). **Wire Service(s):** AP.

US
MID-SOUTH HORSE REVIEW. m. free; $36/yr. 1st class; $18/yr. 2nd class. 16814 Hwy. 64, Somerville, TN 38068. TEL 901-465-4042; FAX 901-465-5493; E-mail: fcreview@bellsouth.net. **Owner(s):** Don Dowdle, 16814 Hwy. 64, P.O. Box 519, Somerville, TN 38068. TEL 901-465-4042; FAX 901-465-5493; Ed. Sharon Keith; Pub. Don Dowdle; pub. size: tabloid; circ. 13,500(free).

SOUTH PITTSBURG
US
HUSTLER, THE. 1899. Thu. $.75 newsstand; $25/yr. in cy.; $32/yr. out of cy. 307 1/2 Elm Ave., South Pittsburg, TN 37380. TEL 423-837-6312; FAX 423-837-8715. **Owner(s):** Marion County Newspapers, Inc., 307 1/2 Elm St., South Pittsburg, TN 37380. TEL 615-837-6312; Ed. Penny Hyatt; Pub. Bill Hoch; adv. contact: Allan Kirk. circ. 3,800(paid).
Formerly: South Pittsburg Hustler.

SPARTA
US   ISSN 0745-6026
SPARTA EXPOSITOR. 1876. s-w.: Mon. & Thu. $.50 newsstand; $29/yr. local; $35/yr. out of area; $40/yr. out of state; $26/yr. senior citizens. 34 W. Bockman Way, Sparta, TN 38583. TEL 615-836-3284. **Owner(s):** Smith Newspapers, Inc., P.O. Box 27, Fort Payne, AL 35967. TEL 205-845-5510; Ed. Suzanne Dickerson; Pub. Suzanne Dickerson; adv.; photos; pub. size: broadsheet; circ. 11,900(free & paid).

SPRINGFIELD
US
ROBERTSON COUNTY TIMES. 1922. Wed. $.50 newsstand; $16/yr. in cy.; $30/yr. out of cy.; $30/yr. out of state. West Court Sq., Springfield, TN 37172. TEL 615-384-3567; FAX 615-384-1221. **Owner(s):** Gannett Company, Inc., P.O. Box 637, Springfield, TN 37172. TEL 615-384-3567; FAX 615-384-1221; Ed. Tom Beesley; Pub. Hugh Braddock; adv. contact: Hugh Braddock. pub. size: broadsheet; circ. 10,000(paid).

SWEETWATER
US
ADVOCATE PENNY SAVER. 1927. Sun. free in cy. P.O. Box 389, Sweetwater, TN 37874. TEL 423-337-7101; FAX 423-442-1416. **Owner(s):** County Publishers, Inc., P.O. Box 389, Sweetwater, TN 37874. TEL 423-337-7101; Ed. Ann Wallace; Pub. Thomas G. Wilson, III; adv. contact: Ann Roberts. pub. size: broadsheet; circ. Sun. 20,000(free).

TAZEWELL
US
CLAIBORNE PROGRESS. 1887. Wed. $.50 newsstand; $17/yr. in cy.; $19.25/yr. out of cy.; $21/yr. out of state. 302 Court St., Tazewell, TN 37879. TEL 423-626-3222; FAX 423-626-6868. **Owner(s):** American Publishing Co., 606 N. Van Buren, P.O. Box 520, Marion, IL 62959. TEL 618-993-1711; Ed. Ron Morgan; Pub. J.T. Hurst; adv. contact: Judy Buchanan. photos; pub. size: broadsheet; circ. 6,850(paid).

TRACY CITY
US
GRUNDY COUNTY HERALD. 1932. Thu. $.50 newsstand; $17/yr. in cy.; $24/yr. out of cy. 1234 Oak St., Tracy City, TN 37387. TEL 615-592-2781; FAX 615-598-5812. **Owner(s):** Grundy County Herald, Oak St., P.O. Box 189, Tracy City, TN 37387. TEL 615-592-2781; FAX 615-598-5812; Ed. Dawn J. Brothers; Pub. Dawn J. Brothers; adv. contact: Carrie Jones. pub. size: broadsheet; circ. 4,800(paid).

TRENTON
US
HERALD GAZETTE, THE. 1968. Wed. $.50 newsstand; $20/yr. in cy.; $25/yr. in state; $30/yr. out of state. 111 E. First St., Trenton, TN 38382. TEL 901-855-1711; FAX 901-855-9587. **Owner(s):** Herald Gazette, Inc., The, P.O. Box 7, Trenton, TN 38382. TEL 901-855-1711; Ed. Danny Jones; Pub. Danny Jones; adv. contact: Danny Jones. pub. size: broadsheet; circ. 5,000(paid).

TULLAHOMA
US
TULLAHOMA NEWS. 1946. 3/wk.: Sun., Wed., Fri. $.50/day newsstand; $.75/Sun.; $38/yr. local; $48/yr. elsewhere. 505 Lakeway Pl., Tullahoma, TN 37388. TEL 615-455-4545; FAX 615-455-9229. **Owner(s):** Lakeway Publishers, Inc., Morristown, TN; Ed. Bob Kyer; Pub. Terry Craig; adv. contact: Harry Hill. photos; bk.rev.; pub. size: standard; circ. 8,500(paid); Sun. 10,000(paid).

WARTBURG
US
MORGAN COUNTY NEWS. Thu. $.50 newsstand; $16.95/yr. 224 Maiden, Wartburg, TN 37887. TEL 423-346-6225; FAX 423-346-5788. **Owner(s):** Landmark Community Newspapers, Inc., P.O. Box 549, Shelbyville, KY 40066. TEL 502-633-4334; Ed. Judy Underwood; Pub. Dave Commons; adv. contact: Betty Crabtree. pub. size: broadsheet; circ. 4,350(paid).

WAYNESBORO
US
WAYNE COUNTY NEWS. 1857. Wed. $.25 newsstand; $10/yr.; $12/yr. out of cy. 119 E. Hollis St., Waynesboro, TN 38485. TEL 615-722-5429; FAX 615-722-5429. **Owner(s):** Nelle B. Cole, P.O. Box 156, Waynesboro, TN 38485. TEL 615-722-5429; Ed. Kathy Brison. adv. contact: Kathy Brison. pub. size: broadsheet; circ. 7,000(paid).

WINCHESTER
US
HERALD-CHRONICLE, THE. 1845. s-w.: Mon. & Thu. $.50 newsstand; $24/yr. in cy.; $32/yr. out of cy. 906 Dinah Shore Blvd., Winchester, TN 37398. TEL 615-967-2272; FAX 615-967-2299. **Owner(s):** Franklin County Publishing Co., Inc., 906 Dinah Shore Ave., Winchester, TN 37398. TEL 615-967-2272; Ed. Dick Wolff; Pub. Charles Sons; adv.; pub. size: broadsheet; circ. 10,000(paid).
Formerly: Winchester Herald-Chronicle.

TEXAS

ABERNATHY
US   ISSN 0895-4291
ABERNATHY WEEKLY REVIEW. 1921. Fri. $.50 newsstand; $17/yr. in cy.; $24/yr. out of cy. 916 Ave. D, Abernathy, TX 79311. TEL 806-298-2033. **Owner(s):** Scott & Judy Luce, 411 13th St., Abernathy, TX 79311. TEL 806-298-2909; Ed. Scott Luce; Pub. Scott Luce; adv. contact: Judy Luce. photos; pub. size: broadsheet; circ. 1,032(paid).

ALPINE

US
ALPINE AVALANCHE. 1890. Thu. $20/yr. in cy.; $24/yr. out of cy.; $28/yr., in state. 112 N. Fifth, Alpine, TX 79830. TEL 915-837-3334; FAX 915-837-7181. **Owner(s):** Granite Publications, 304 Gate Way Loop, Marble Falls, TX 78654. TEL 210-693-3334; Ed. Burnis Lawrence; Pub. Burnis Lawrence; adv.: $5.18/SAU. pub. size: broadsheet; circ. 4,050(paid).

ALVARADO

US
ALVARADO POST. Thu. $.50 newsstand; $16.50/yr. mailed; $18/yr. in cy.; $21/yr. out of cy. 206 N. Parkway, Alvarado, TX 76009. TEL 817-790-8717; FAX 817-783-7606. **Owner(s):** Alvarado Newspapers, Inc., 206 N. Parkway, Alvarado, TX 76009. TEL 817-790-8717; Pub. Wade J. Parker; adv.: $4/SAU. pub. size: broadsheet; circ. 2,600(paid).

ALVIN

US
ALVIN ADVERTISER. 1890. s-w.: Wed. & Sun. free. 201 E. House St., Alvin, TX 77511. TEL 281-331-4421; FAX 281-331-4424. **Owner(s):** Henderson Newspapers, Inc., 201 E. House St., Alvin, TX. TEL 281-331-4421; FAX 331-331-4424; Ed. Wade Wootton; Pub. Jim Schwind; adv. contact: Debbie Griffin. adv.: $7.15/SAU. pub. size: broadsheet; circ. 17,000(free).

US
ALVIN SUN. 1890. Mon. $.50 newsstand; $18/yr. 201 E. House St., Alvin, TX 77511. TEL 281-331-4421; FAX 281-331-4424. **Owner(s):** Henderson Newspapers, Inc., 201 E. House, Alvin, TX 77511. TEL 281-331-4421; FAX 281-331-4424; Ed. Wade Wootton; Pub. Jim Schwind; adv. contact: Debbie Griffin. adv.: $5.57/SAU. photos; pub. size: broadsheet; circ. 2,000(free & paid).

ANAHUAC

US
PROGRESS, THE. 1908. Wed. $.50 newsstand; $17.50/yr. in cy. 209 Willcox St., Anahuac, TX 77514. TEL 409-267-6131; FAX 409-336-3345. **Owner(s):** Hartman Newspapers, Inc., P.O. Box 1390, Rosenberg, TX 77471. TEL 713-342-4474; FAX 713-342-3219; Pub. E.E. Zieschang; adv. contact: Sue Hawthorne. pub. size: broadsheet; circ. 2,200(paid).

ANDREWS

US
ANDREWS COUNTY NEWS. 1934. s-w.: Wed. & Sun. $.50 newsstand; $18.90/yr. in cy.; $36.90/yr. surrounding cys.; $36.90/yr. out of area. 210 E. Broadway, Andrews, TX 79714. TEL 915-523-2085; FAX 915-523-9492. **Owner(s):** James Roberts, 210 E. Broadway, Andrews, TX 79714; Ed. James Roberts; Pub. James Roberts; adv. contact: James Egan. bk.rev.; pub. size: standard; circ. 3,500(controlled & free).

ANGLETON

US
ANGLETON TIMES. 1893. s-w.: Wed. & Sat. $.50 newsstand; $42/yr. carrier. 700 Western Ave., Angleton, TX 77515. TEL 409-849-8581; FAX 409-849-0230. **Owner(s):** Southern Newspapers, Inc., 1050 Wilcrest St., Houston, TX 77042; Pub. Mike Reddell; adv. contact: Tommy Crow. photos; pub. size: broadsheet; circ. 4,000(paid). **Wire Service(s):** UPI.

ARLINGTON

US   ISSN 1044-0097
GRAND PRAIRIE NEWS. 1906. s-w.: Thu. & Sun. $.50 newsstand; $28/yr. 1000 Ave. H, E., Arlington, TX 76011. TEL 817-695-0500; FAX 817-695-0555. **Owner(s):** DFW Suburban Newspapers, Inc., 1000 Ave. H, E., Arlington, TX 76011. TEL 817-695-0500; Ed. Pat Wascovich. adv. contact: Kyle Gibson. photos; pub. size: broadsheet; circ. 7,000(paid); Sun. 7,500(paid). **Wire Service(s):** Southwest Business Wire.

US   ISSN 8750-7870
IRVING NEWS. 1956. s-w.: Thu. & Sun. $.50 newsstand; $7/mo. mailed; $13.50/3 mos. carrier. 1000 Ave. H., East, Arlington, TX 76011. TEL 817-695-0483; FAX 817-695-0555. **Owner(s):** DFW Suburban Newspapers, Inc., 1000 Ave. H, E., Arlington, TX 76011. TEL 817-633-0500; Ed. Donny Jackson. adv. contact: Richard Conley. pub. size: broadsheet; circ. 10,425(paid); Sun. 9,472(paid).

ATLANTA

US
ATLANTA CITIZENS JOURNAL. 1879. s-w.: Sun. & Wed. $.50 newsstand; $42/yr. local; $47/yr. elsewhere. 306 W. Main St., Atlanta, TX 75551. TEL 903-796-7133; FAX 903-796-3294. **Owner(s):** Westward Communications, Inc., 5005 LBJ Freeway, Ste. 1040, Dallas, TX 75244. TEL 214-450-1717; Ed. Annette Calaway; Pub. Debbie Milton; adv. contact: Debbie Milton. pub. size: broadsheet; circ. 3,700(paid).

AUSTIN

US   ISSN 1074-0740
AUSTIN CHRONICLE. 1981. Thu. free local; $60/yr. bulk mail; $135/yr. 1st class mail. 4000 N. IH-35 N., Austin, TX 78751. TEL 512-454-5766; FAX 512-458-6910. **Owner(s):** Austin Chronicle Corp., 4000 N. IH-35 N., Austin, TX 78751. TEL 512-454-5766; Ed. Louis Black; Pub. Nick Barbaro; adv.; photos; bk.rev.; pub. size: tabloid; circ. 80,000(controlled & free).

US   ISSN 0040-4519
TEXAS OBSERVER. 1954. bi-w.: Fri. $2.25 newsstand; $32/yr. 307 W. Seventh St., Austin, TX 78701. TEL 512-477-0746; FAX 512-475-1175. **Owner(s):** Texas Democracy Foundation, 307 W. Seventh St., Austin, TX 78701. TEL 512-477-0746; Ed. Louis Dubose; Pub. Geoffrey Rips; adv. contact: Amanda Toerning. photos; bk.rev.; pub. size: broadsheet; circ. 8,300(paid).

US
VILLAGER NEWSPAPER. 1973. Fri. free; $20/yr. 1223-A Rosewood Ave., Austin, TX 78702. TEL 512-476-0082; FAX 512-476-0179. **Owner(s):** T.L. Wyatt, 1223-A Rosewood Ave., Austin, TX 78702. TEL 512-476-0082; Ed. T.L. Wyatt; Pub. T.L. Wyatt; pub. size: broadsheet; circ. 6,000(free & paid).

US
WESTLAKE PICAYUNE. 1977. Thu. $.50 newsstand; $32/yr. in cy.; $37/yr. outside of cy. 3103 Bee Cave Rd., Ste. 102, Austin, TX 78746. TEL 512-327-2990; FAX 512-328-6470. **Owner(s):** Westward Communications, Inc., 5005 LBJ Fwy., #1040, Dallas, TX 75244. TEL 214-450-1717; Pub. Jason Jared; adv. contact: Betty Wilson. pub. size: tabloid; circ. 3,500(paid).

AZLE

US   ISSN 0546-0920
AZLE NEWS. 1953. Thu. $.50 newsstand; $21/yr. in cy.; $27.50/yr. out of cy.; $18.50/yr. senior citizen. 1121 S.E. Parkway, Azle, TX 76020. TEL 817-237-1184; FAX 817-238-9617. **Owner(s):** Azle Tri-County Advertiser, Inc., 1121 S.E. Parkway, Azle, TX 76020. TEL 817-237-1184; FAX 817-238-9617; Ed. Bob Buckel; Pub. Bob Buckel; adv.; pub. size: broadsheet; circ. 5,500(free & paid).

BAIRD

US
CALLAHAN COUNTY STAR. 1887. Thu. $15/yr. in cy.; $16/yr. out of cy.; $18/yr. in state. 211 Market St., Baird, TX 79504. TEL 915-854-1008. **Owner(s):** H.V. O'Brien, 215 S. Seaman, Eastland, TX 76448. TEL 817-629-1707; Ed. Lupe Garcia. pub. size: broadsheet; circ. 1,400(paid).

BALCH SPRINGS

US
SUBURBAN TRIBUNE. 1951. Wed. $.50 newsstand; $16/yr. in cy.; $20/yr. out of cy. 11401 Elam Rd., Ste. 106, Balch Springs, TX 75180. TEL 214-286-8850; FAX 214-286-8862. **Owner(s):** Mary Freeman, 11401 Elam Rd., Ste. 106, Balch Springs, TX 75180. TEL 214-286-8550; Ed. Mary Freeman; Pub. Mary Freeman; adv.; pub. size: tabloid; circ. 4,500(paid).

BEEVILLE

US   ISSN 0889-8618
BEEVILLE BEE-PICAYUNE. 1886. s-w.: Wed. & Sat. $.50 newsstand; $44.25/yr. in cy.; $57.20/yr. out of cy.; $59.28/yr. elsewhere. 111 N. Washington St., Beeville, TX 78102. TEL 512-358-2550; FAX 512-358-5323. **Owner(s):** F.C. Latcham III, P.O. Box 10, Beeville, TX 78102. TEL 512-358-9478; FAX 512-358-5323; Fred C. Latcham, Jr., P.O. Box 10, Beeville, TX 78102. TEL 512-358-2232; FAX 512-358-5323; G.G. (Jeff) Latcham, P.O. Box 10, Beeville, TX 78102. TEL 512-358-2232; FAX 512-358-5323; Joyce Latcham, P.O. Box 10, Beeville, TX 78102. TEL 512-358-2232; FAX 512-358-5323; Ed. F.C. (Chip) Latcham, III; Pub. Fred C. Latcham, Jr.; adv. contact: Richard Carter. photos; pub. size: broadsheet; circ. 5,403(free & paid).

BELLVILLE

US
BELLVILLE TIMES. 1879. Thu. $.50 newsstand; $20.50/yr. in cy.; $25/yr. out of cy.; $30/yr. out of state. 106 E. Palm St., Bellville, TX 77418. TEL 409-865-3131; FAX 409-865-3132. **Owner(s):** Austin County Publishing Co., Inc., 106 E. Palm St., Bellville, TX 77418. TEL 409-865-3131; Ed. Bruce White; Pub. Bruce White; adv.; pub. size: broadsheet; circ. 4,200(paid).

WEEKLY NEWSPAPERS

BLANCO
US   ISSN 1049-2216
BLANCO COUNTY NEWS. 1932. Wed. $.50 newsstand; $19/yr. P.O. Box 429, Blanco, TX 78606. TEL 210-833-4812; FAX 210-833-4246. **Owner(s):** Roy McNett, P.O. Box 429, Blanco, TX 78606. TEL 210-833-4812; FAX 210-833-4246; Pub. Roy McNett; adv. contact: Ava Ninett. photos; bk.rev.; pub. size: broadsheet; circ. 2,900(controlled & paid). **Wire Service(s):** AP.

BOOKER
US
BOOKER NEWS, THE. 1921. Wed, $.40 newsstand; $14/yr. in cy.; $16/yr. elsewhere. 204 S. Main, Booker, TX 79005. TEL 806-658-4732; FAX 806-658-4424. **Owner(s):** Kayla & Jerry Parvin, 204 S. Main, Booker, TX 79005. TEL 806-658-4732; Ed. Kayla Parvin; Pub. Kayla Parvin; adv.; photos; pub. size: standard; circ. 1,300(free & paid).

BOWIE
US
BOWIE NEWS. 1920. s-w.: Sun. & Thu. $.50 newsstand; $20/yr. in cy.; $25/yr. out of cy.; $30/yr. out of state. 218 W. Tarrant, Bowie, TX 76230. TEL 817-872-2247; FAX 817-872-4812. **Owner(s):** James H. Winter, P.O. Box 831, Bowie, TX 76230. TEL 817-872-2247; Ed. Barbara Beckwith; Pub. James H. Winter; adv.; pub. size: broadsheet; circ. morning 4,500(paid).

US
MONTAGUE COUNTY SHOPPER, THE. 1980. w. free in cy.; $10/yr. mailed outside of cy. 114 Mason St., Bowie, TX 76230. TEL 817-872-6186; FAX 817-872-3559. **Owner(s):** Montague County Shopper, 114 N. Mason St., Bowie, TX 76230. TEL 817-872-6186; Ed. Sharon McKinley; Pub. Lynn Morgan; adv. contact: Cindy Croxton. pub. size: tabloid; circ. 11,900(free & paid).

BRACKETTVILLE
US
BRACKETT NEWS THE. 1989. Thu. $.50 newsstand; $20/yr. in state; $27.50yr. out of state. P.O. Box 1039, Brackettville, TX 78832-1039. TEL 210-563-2852; FAX 210-563-9538. **Owner(s):** Jewel F. Robinson, P.O. Box 1039, Brackettville, TX 78832. TEL 210-563-2852; FAX 210-563-9538; Ed. J.J. Guidry; Pub. Jewel F. Robinson; adv.; photos; pub. size: standard; circ. 1,100(free & paid).

BRADY
US
BRADY STANDARD. 1909. s-w.: Tue. & Fri. $.50 newsstand; $22/yr. in cy.; $26/yr. in state; $32/yr. out of state. 201 S. Bridge, Brady, TX 76825. TEL 915-597-2959; FAX 915-597-1434. **Owner(s):** Brady Standard-Herald Publishing Inc., 201 S. Bridge St., Brady, TX 76825. TEL 915-597-2959; Ed. Larry Smith; Pub. Larry Smith; adv.; pub. size: broadsheet; circ. 3,500(paid).

BRIDGEPORT
US
BRIDGEPORT INDEX. 1898. Thu. $20/yr. in cy.; $25/yr. out of cy. 916 Halsell, Bridgeport, TX 76426. TEL 940-683-4021; FAX 940-683-3841. **Owner(s):** Bridwell Publishing Co., 916 Halsell, Bridgeport, TX 76426. TEL 817-683-4021; Ed. Harlan Bridwell; Pub. Harlan Bridwell; adv.; pub. size: broadsheet; circ. 3,400(paid).

BROWNFIELD
US
BROWNFIELD NEWS. 1904. s-w.: Wed. & Sun. $.50 newsstand; $23.80/yr. in cy.; $28.75/yr. in state; $34.10/yr. out of state. 409 W. Hill St., Brownfield, TX 79316. TEL 806-637-4535; FAX 806-637-3795; E-mail: bnews@hub.ofthe.net. **Owner(s):** Lynn Brisendine, 409 W. Hill St., Brownfield, TX 79316. TEL 806-637-4535; FAX 806-637-3795; Ed. Lynn Brisendine. adv.; photos; bk.rev.; pub. size: broadsheet; circ. 3,100(paid).

BRYAN
US
BRYAN COLLEGE STATION PRESS. 1966. Thu. free. 725 E. Villa Maria, Bryan, TX 77802. TEL 409-823-0088; FAX 409-822-3649. **Owner(s):** A.H. Belo Corp., 400 S. Record, Dallas, TX 75202. TEL 214-977-6606; Ed. Greg Huchingson; Pub. Greg Huchingson; adv. contact: W.F. Moore, Jr. photos; pub. size: broadsheet; circ. 34,000(free).

BURLESON
US
BURLESON STAR. 1965. s-w.: Sun. & Wed. $.50 newsstand; $29.95/yr. 319 N. Burleson Blvd., Burleson, TX 76028. TEL 817-295-0486; FAX 817-295-5278; E-mail: burlstar@onramp.net. **Owner(s):** Susan Hutson, P.O. Drawer 909, Burleson, TX 76028. TEL 817-295-0486; James Moody, P.O. Drawer 909, Burleson, TX 76028. TEL 817-295-0486; Ed. Sally Ellertson; Pub. James Moody; adv. contact: Cathy Smith. pub. size: broadsheet; circ. 7,400(paid).

US   ISSN 1041-3081
CROWLEY REVIEW. 1970. Thu. $.50 newsstand; $13.50/yr. 319 N. Burleson Blvd., Burleson, TX 76028. TEL 817-295-0486; FAX 817-295-5278; E-mail: burlstar@onramp.net. **Owner(s):** James Moody, P.O. Box 300, Crowley, TX 76036. TEL 817-295-0486; Susan Hutson, P.O. Box 300, Crowley, TX 76036. TEL 817-295-0486; Ed. Nancy Huckaby; Pub. James Moody; adv. contact: Cathy Smith. pub. size: broadsheet; circ. 3,000(paid).

BURNET
US
BURNET BULLETIN. 1873. Wed. $.50 newsstand; $21/yr. in cy.; $30/yr. out of cy. 101 E. Jackson, Burnet, TX 78611. TEL 512-756-6136; FAX 512-756-8911. **Owner(s):** Granite Publications, 304 Gate Way Loop, Marble Falls, TX 78654. TEL 210-693-3334; Ed. Brenda Sommer; Pub. Tim Prince; adv. contact: Tim Prince. pub. size: broadsheet; circ. 4,400(paid).

CALDWELL
US
BURLESON COUNTY CITIZEN TRIBUNE. 1898. Thu. $.60 newsstand; $21.50/yr. in cy.; $26.50/yr. in state; $35/yr. out of state. 205 W. Buck, Caldwell, TX 77836. TEL 409-567-3286. **Owner(s):** Burleson County Publishing Co., 205 W. Buck, Caldwell, TX 77836. TEL 409-567-3286; Ed. Sam Preuss. adv.; pub. size: broadsheet; circ. 4,000(paid).

CAMERON
US
CAMERON HERALD. 1860. Thu. $.50 newsstand; $18/yr in cy.; $21/yr. out of cy. 108 E. First St., Cameron, TX 76520. TEL 817-697-6671; FAX 817-697-4902. **Owner(s):** Granite Publications, 304 Gate Way Loop, Marble Falls, TX 78654. TEL 210-693-3334; Pub. Wayne E. Green; adv. contact: Jacquie Green. pub. size: broadsheet; circ. 4,077(paid).

CANYON
US
CANYON NEWS. 1896. s-w.: Thu. & Sun. $.50 newsstand; $26/yr. local; $35/yr. elsewhere. 1500 Fifth Ave., Canyon, TX 79015. TEL 806-655-7121; FAX 806-655-0823; E-mail: canyonnews@amaonline.com; URL: http://www.canyonnews.com. **Owner(s):** Randall County Publishing Co., 1500 Fifth Ave., Canyon, TX 79015. TEL 806-655-7121; FAX 806-655-0823; Ed. Brad Tooley. adv. contact: Brad Tooley. photos; bk.rev.; pub. size: broadsheet; circ. 4,300(free & paid); Sun. 4,300(free & paid).

CARTHAGE
US
PANOLA WATCHMAN. 1873. s-w.: Wed. & Sun. $.50 newsstand; $35/yr. in cy. 109 W. Panola St., Carthage, TX 75633. TEL 903-693-7888; FAX 903-693-5857. **Owner(s):** Westward Communications, Inc., P.O. Box 518, Dallas, TX 75633; Ed. Ted Leach; Pub. Bill Holder; adv. contact: Bill Holder. photos; bk.rev.; pub. size: standard; circ. 5,000(paid); Sun. 5,000(paid). **Formerly:** Carthage Panola Watchman.

CENTER
US
LIGHT & CHAMPION. 1877. s-w.: Tue. & Fri. $.75 newsstand; $30/yr. in cy.; $55/yr. elsewhere. 137 San Augustine St., Center, TX 75935. TEL 409-598-3377; FAX 409-598-6394. **Owner(s):** PTS, Inc., 600 Lurleen Blvd., Ste.600, Tuscaloosa, AL 35967. TEL 205-752-7500; Ed. Matthew Postins; Pub. Michael A. Pace; adv.; photos; pub. size: broadsheet; circ. 5,300(paid).

CHILDRESS
US
CHILDRESS INDEX. 1888. 3/wk.: Sun., Tue., Thu. $.50 newsstand; $36/yr. carrier; $38/yr. mailed. 226 Main St., Childress, TX 79201. TEL 817-937-2525; FAX 817-937-2239. **Owner(s):** Childress Index, Inc., 226 Main St., Childress, TX 79201. TEL 817-937-2525; Ed. Christopher Blackburn. pub. size: standard; circ. evening 3,300(paid); Sun. 3,300(paid). **Wire Service(s):** AP.

CISCO
US
CISCO PRESS. 1870. s-w.: Sun. & Thu. $.50 newsstand; $22/yr. in cy.; $28/yr. in state; $40/yr. out of state. 700 Conrad Hilton Ave., Cisco, TX 76437. TEL 817-442-2244; FAX 817-629-2092. **Owner(s):** H.V. O'Brien, 215 S. Seman, Eastland, TX 76448. TEL 817-629-1707; Ed. Richard Kurklin; Pub. H.V. O'Brien; pub. size: broadsheet; circ. 1,800(paid).

CLARKSVILLE
US ISSN 1040-2489
CLARKSVILLE TIMES, THE. 1875. Thu. $.25 newsstand; $15/yr. in cy.; $24/yr. out of cy. 106 E. Main St., Clarksville, TX 75426. TEL 903-427-5616; FAX 903-427-5617. **Owner(s):** Red River Media, Mt. Pleasant, TX; Ed. Ben Black. adv. contact: Barbara Mitchell. photos; bk.rev.; pub. size: broadsheet; circ. 3,500(paid).

CLEVELAND
US
CLEVELAND ADVOCATE. 1917. Wed. $.50 newsstand; $22/yr. 106 W. Hanson St., Cleveland, TX 77327. TEL 281-592-2626; FAX 281-592-2629. **Owner(s):** Westward Communications, Inc., P.O. Box 609, Conroe, TX 77305. TEL 409-756-6671; Ed. Jerry Vincent; Pub. Diana Lobner; adv. contact: Diana Lobner. photos; pub. size: broadsheet; circ. morning 3,900(paid).

COLEMAN
US
COLEMAN CHRONICLE & DEMOCRAT VOICE. 1933. s-w.: Tue. & Thu. $.35 newsstand; $25.95/yr. in cy.; $36.95/yr. out of cy. 208-212 W. Pecan, Coleman, TX 76834. TEL 915-625-4128; FAX 915-625-4129. **Owner(s):** Brett Autry, P.O. Box 840, Coleman, TX 76834. TEL 915-625-4128; FAX 915-625-4129; Stan Brudney, P.O. Box 840, Coleman, TX 76834. TEL 915-625-4357; FAX 915-625-4129; Ed. Brett Autry; Pub. Brett Autry; adv. contact: Stan Brudney. pub. size: broadsheet; circ. 3,350(paid).
Formerly: Coleman County Chronicle.

COLUMBUS
US ISSN 0891-1118
BANNER PRESS NEWSPAPER, THE. 1985. Thu. $.50 newsstand; $23/yr. in cy.; $28/yr. in state; $33/yr. out of state. 1038 Milam, Columbus, TX 78934. TEL 409-732-6243; FAX 409-732-6245. **Owner(s):** Regional Newspapers, Inc., 1038 Milam, P.O. Box 490, Columbus, OH 78934. TEL 409-732-6243; Ed. Chad Ferguson. adv.; photos; bk.rev.; pub. size: broadsheet; circ. 4,700.
Formerly: Banner Newspaper, The.

COMANCHE
US
COMANCHE CHIEF. 1873. Thu. $.50 newsstand; $17/yr. in cy.; $18.50/yr. out of cy.; $20/yr. out of state. 203 W. Grand St., Comanche, TX 76442. TEL 915-356-2636; FAX 915-356-5380. **Owner(s):** James C. & Mary Wilkerson, 205 W. Grand St., Comanche, TX 76442; Ed. James C. Wilkerson; Pub. James C. Wilkerson; adv.; pub. size: broadsheet; circ. 4,300(paid).

COMMERCE
US
COMMERCE JOURNAL. 1889. s-w.: Sun. & Wed. $.50 newsstand; $284/yr. 1219 Washington St., Commerce, TX 75428. TEL 903-886-3196; FAX 903-886-3198. **Owner(s):** American Publishing Co., 606 N. Van Buren, P.O. Box 520, Marion, IL 62959. TEL 618-993-1711; Ed. Matt Shrum; Pub. Paul Harris; adv. contact: Paul Harris. bk.rev.; pub. size: broadsheet; circ. Sun. 2,817(paid).

COPPELL
US
CITIZENS' ADVOCATE NEWSPAPER. 1984. Fri. $.35 newsstand; $15/yr. 408 Bethel Rd., Coppell, TX 75019. TEL 972-462-8192. **Owner(s):** Dan Mara Corp., 408 Bethel Rd., Coppell, TX 75019. TEL 972-462-8192; Ed. Jean Murph; Pub. Jean Murph; pub. size: standard; circ. 5,500(paid).

COPPERAS COVE
US
COPPERAS COVE LEADER PRESS. 1895. Thu. $.35 newsstand; $15/yr. local. 115 W. Ave D, Copperas Cove, TX 76522. TEL 817-547-4207; FAX 817-542-3299. **Owner(s):** Roberts Publishing Co., Andrews, TX; Ed. Connie Landmann; Pub. David Landmann; adv. contact: Katie Baty. adv.: $5.20/SAU. pub. size: broadsheet; circ. 3,100(free & paid).

CORRIGAN
US
CORRIGAN TIMES, THE. 1954. Thu. $.50 newsstand; $13/yr. in cy.; $16/yr. in state; $19/yr. out of state. 202 E. Front St., Corrigan, TX 75939. TEL 409-398-2535; FAX 409-327-7156. **Owner(s):** Polk County Publishing Co., P.O. Box 1276, Livingston, TX 77351. TEL 409-327-4357; FAX 409-327-7156; Ed. Gregory L. Peak; Pub. Alvin Holley; adv.; pub. size: broadsheet; circ. 1,450(paid).

CRANE
US
CRANE NEWS. 1947. Thu. $.50 newsstand; $18/yr. in cy.; $21/yr. in state; $24/yr. outside of state. 401 S. Gaston, Crane, TX 79731. TEL 915-558-3541; FAX 915-558-2676. **Owner(s):** Wood Publication LLC, 401 S. Gaston, Crane, TX 79731. TEL 915-558-3541; FAX 915-558-2676; Ed. Scott Wood; Pub. Scott Wood; adv. contact: Barbara Leach. photos; bk.rev.; pub. size: broadsheet; circ. 1,758(paid).

CROCKETT
US
HOUSTON COUNTY COURIER. 1890. s-w.: Sun. & Thu. $.50 newsstand; $16.95/yr. local; $18.95/yr. in state; $20.95/yr. out of state. 102 S. Seventh St., Crockett, TX 75835. TEL 409-544-2238; FAX 409-544-4088. **Owner(s):** Polk County Publishing Co., P.O. Box 1276, Livingston, TX 77351; Ed. LaDeanne Smith; Pub. Bassett Keller; adv. contact: Billy Clark. pub. size: broadsheet; circ. 5,600(paid).

CUERO
US
CUERO RECORD. 1894. Wed. $.50 newsstand; $19/yr. in cy.; $24/yr. out of cy. 119 E. Main St., Cuero, TX 77954. TEL 512-275-3464; FAX 512-275-3131. **Owner(s):** Hartman Newspapers, Inc., 1904 Fourth St., Roseberg, TX 77471. TEL 713-342-4474; Ed. Glenn Rea; Pub. Glenn Rea; adv. contact: Connie Young. pub. size: broadsheet; circ. 3,600(paid).

DALLAS
US
DALLAS PARK CITIES NEWS. 1943. Thu. $.25 newsstand; $25/yr. in state; $40/yr. out of state. 8115 Preston Rd., Ste. 120, LB10, Dallas, TX 75225. TEL 214-369-7570; FAX 214-369-7736. **Owner(s):** Marjorie B. Waters, 8115 Preston Rd., Ste. 120, LB10, Dallas, TX 75225; Thomas R. Waters, 8115 Preston Rd., Ste. 120, LB10, Dallas, TX 75225. TEL 214-369-7570; Ed. Pete Waters. pub. size: broadsheet; circ. 8,000(paid).

US ISSN 1049-3387
DALLAS WHITE ROCKER NEWS. 1945. Thu. $.35 newsstand; $17/yr.; $30/2 yrs. mailed; $45/3 yrs. mailed. P.O. Box 180698, 10809 Garland Rd., Dallas, TX 75218-0698. TEL 214-327-9335. **Owner(s):** Retta Hanie, 10809 Garland Rd., Dallas, TX 75218-0698. TEL 214-327-9335; Ed. Retta Hanie; Pub. Retta Hanie; adv. contact: Frances Gunter. bk.rev.; pub. size: broadsheet; circ. 4,008(paid).

US
OAK CLIFF TRIBUNE. 1903. bi-w.: Thu. $.50 newsstand; $20/yr. 400 S. Zang, Ste. C101, Dallas, TX 75208. TEL 214-943-7755; FAX 214-943-7775. **Owner(s):** Oak Cliff Tribune, Inc., 400 S. Zang, Ste. C101, Dallas, TX 75200; Ed. Kathy Magers; Pub. Joseph D. Whitney; adv. contact: Cheryl Rice. pub. size: tabloid; circ. 4,100(paid).

DECATUR
US ISSN 0746-8679
WISE COUNTY MESSENGER. 1880. s-w.: Thu. & Sun. $.50 newsstand; $30/yr. in cy.; $35/yr. out of cy.; $40/yr. out of state. 115 S. Trinity, Decatur, TX 76234-0149. TEL 940-627-5987; FAX 940-627-1004. **Owner(s):** Wise County Messenger, Inc., P.O. Box 149, Decatur, TX 76234. TEL 817-627-5987; FAX 817-627-1004; Ed. Jimmy Rainey; Pub. Roy Eaton; adv. contact: Lisa Davis. photos; pub. size: broadsheet; circ. 23,500(free & paid); Sun. 5,500(paid).

DEER PARK
US
DEER PARK BROADCASTER, THE. 1957. Wed. free. 102 W. Pasadena Blvd., Deer Park, TX 77536-0369. TEL 281-479-2760; FAX 281-479-3415. **Owner(s):** Larry & B.J. Power, Broadcaster Publications, Inc., P.O. Box 369, Deer Park, TX 77536. TEL 281-479-2760; FAX 281-479-3415; Ed. Mary Ellen Wilson; Pub. Larry Power; adv. contact: Randy Wilson. photos; bk.rev.; pub. size: broadsheet; circ. 11,000(free & paid).

WEEKLY NEWSPAPERS

EVERMAN, TX 10739

US
DEER PARK PROGRESS, THE. Sat. $.50 newsstand; $18/yr. in cy.; $30/yr. out of cy. 102 W. Pasadena Blvd., Deer Park, TX 77536. TEL 281-479-2760; FAX 281-479-3415. **Owner(s):** Larry & B.J. Power, Broadcaster Publications, Inc., P.O. Box 369, Deer Park, TX 77536. TEL 281-479-2760; FAX 281-479-3415; Ed. Mary Ellen Wilson; Pub. Larry Power; adv. contact: Randy Wilson. circ. 4,000(paid).

DENISON

US
GRAYSON COUNTY SHOPPER. 1970. Wed. free. 4101 Texoma Pkwy., Denison, TX 75020. TEL 903-465-1400; FAX 903-465-1453. **Owner(s):** Cox Publishing Co., P.O. Box 1249, Denison, TX 75021. TEL 903-465-1403; Ed. H. Wayne Cox; Pub. H. Wayne Cox; pub. size: tabloid; circ. 47,000(free).

US
SHOPPER ZONE II. 1986. Wed. free. 4101 Texoma Pky., Denison, TX 75020. TEL 903-465-1400. **Owner(s):** H. Wayne Cox, P.O. Box 1249, Denison, TX 75021. TEL 903-465-1400; Pub. H. Wayne Cox; pub. size: tabloid; circ. 9,191(free).

DESOTO

US
CEDAR HILL TODAY. 1965. Thu. $.50 newsstand; $23.50/yr. in city; $32.50/yr. out of city. 1701 N. Hampton, Ste. A, DeSoto, TX 75115. TEL 214-298-4211; FAX 214-298-6369. **Owner(s):** Richard Collins, P.O. Box 381029, Duncanville, TX 75138. TEL 214-298-4211; Ed. Mark Victry; Pub. Richard Collins; adv. contact: Linda Nasche. photos; pub. size: standard; circ. 5,400(free & paid).
Formerly: Cedar Hill Chronicle.

US ISSN 0704-0428
DESOTO TODAY. 1977. Thu. $.50 newsstand; $20.50/yr. in cy.; $32.50/yr. out of cy. 1701 N. Hampton, Ste. A, DeSoto, TX 75115. TEL 214-298-4211; FAX 214-298-6369. **Owner(s):** Richard Collins, 1701 N. Hampton, Ste. A, Duncanville, TX 75115. TEL 214-298-4211; Ed. Mark Victory; Pub. Richard Collins; adv. contact: Linda Nasche. pub. size: standard; circ. 8,900(free & paid).
Formerly: DeSoto News Advertiser.

US ISSN 0888-1960
DUNCANVILLE TODAY. 1960. Thu. $.50 newsstand; $23.50/yr. in city; $32.50/yr. out of city. 1701 N. Hampton, Ste. A, DeSoto, TX 75115. TEL 214-298-4211; FAX 214-298-6369. **Owner(s):** Richard Collins, 1701 N. Hampton, Ste. A, Dallas, TX 75115. TEL 214-298-4211; Ed. Mark Victry; Pub. Richard Collins; adv. contact: Leslie Nasche. pub. size: broadsheet; circ. 10,500(paid).
Formerly: Duncanville Suburban.

US ISSN 1065-0644
LANCASTER TODAY. 1975. Thu. $.50 newsstand; $20.50/yr. in city; $32.50/yr. out of city. 1701 N. Hampton, Ste. A, DeSoto, TX 75115. TEL 214-298-4211; FAX 214-298-6369. **Owner(s):** Richard Collins, 1701 N. Hampton, Ste. A, Duncanville, TX 75115. TEL 214-298-4211; Ed. Mark Victry; Pub. Richard Collins; adv. contact: Leslie Nasche. pub. size: standard; circ. 4,500(free & paid).
Formerly: Lancaster News.

US
MIDLOTHIAN TODAY. 1968. Thu. $.50 newsstand; $19/yr. in city; $32.50/yr. out of city. 1701 N. Hampton, Ste. A., DeSoto, TX 75115. TEL 214-775-2371; FAX 214-298-6369. **Owner(s):** Richard Collins, P.O. Box 381029, Duncanville, TX 75138. TEL 214-298-4211; FAX 214-298-6369; Ed. Mark Victry; Pub. Richard Collins; adv. contact: Leslie Nasche. photos; bk.rev.; pub. size: standard; circ. 1,725(paid).
Formerly: Midlothian Reporter.

DIBOLL

US
ANGELINA FREE PRESS. 1953. Thu. $.50 newsstand; $16/yr. in cy.; $20/yr. out of cy. 201 N. Temple Dr., Diboll, TX 75941. TEL 409-829-1801; FAX 409-829-1811. **Owner(s):** Temple-Inland, Inc., 30 S. Temple Dr., Diboll, TX 75941. TEL 800-262-5512; Ed. Gary Willmon; Pub. Gary Willmon; adv. contact: Betty Jo Jared. pub. size: broadsheet; circ. 3,561(free).

DRIPPING SPRINGS

US
DRIPPING SPRINGS DISPATCH. 1982. Thu. $.50 newsstand; $18/yr. Promenade Ctr., Ste. 4, Dripping Springs, TX 78620. TEL 512-858-7893; FAX 512-858-4828. **Owner(s):** Dale Roberson, P.O. Box 550, Dripping Springs, TX 78620. TEL 512-858-7893; FAX 512-858-4828; Ed. Dale Roberson; Pub. Dale Roberson; adv. contact: Joyce Kovacs. photos; pub. size: tabloid; circ. 2,000(paid).

DUMAS

US
MOORE COUNTY NEWS-PRESS. 1927. s-w.: Thu. & Sun. $.50 newsstand; $37/yr. in cy.; $52/yr. out of cy. Seventh & Meredith Sts., Dumas, TX 79029. TEL 806-935-4111. **Owner(s):** Southern Newspapers, Inc., Houston, TX; Ed. Todd Hepler; Pub. Mike Coggins; adv. contact: Mike Coggins. photos; pub. size: broadsheet; circ. 4,654(free & paid).

EAGLE LAKE

US
EAGLE LAKE HEADLIGHT. 1903. Thu. $.35 newsstand; $12/yr. in cy.; $15/yr. out of cy. 220 E. Main St., Eagle Lake, TX 77434. TEL 409-234-5521. **Owner(s):** Jeannine Fearing, P.O. Box 67, Eagle Lake, TX 77434. TEL 713-234-5521; Ed. Jeannine Fearing; Pub. Jeannine Fearing; adv.; photos; pub. size: broadsheet; circ. 2,200(paid).

EAGLE PASS

US
EAGLE PASS NEWS GUIDE/BRIEF. 1886. Guide: Thu. & Sun.; Brief: Wed. $.50/day newsstand; $19.50/yr. mailed local; $34.50/yr. mailed in state; $38.50/yr. out of state. 1342 Main St., Eagle Pass, TX 78852. TEL 210-773-2309; FAX 217-773-3398. **Owner(s):** Guide Publishing Co., 1342 Main St., P.O. Box 764, Eagle Pass, TX 78852. TEL 512-773-2309; Ed. Maggie McBeath; Pub. Rex McBeath; adv.; pub. size: standard; circ. morning 2,500(free); Sun. 5,000(free).

EASTLAND

US
EASTLAND TELEGRAM. 1968. s-w.: Thu. & Sun. $.50 newsstand; $22/yr. in cy. 215 S. Seaman St., Eastland, TX 76448-0029. TEL 817-629-1707; FAX 817-629-2092. **Owner(s):** Eastland County Newspapers, Inc., P.O. Box 29, Eastland, TX 76448. TEL 817-629-1707; Ed. H.V. O'Brien; Pub. H.V. O'Brien; adv.; bk.rev.; pub. size: broadsheet; circ. 2,200(paid); Sun. 2,500(paid).

EDGEWOOD

US
EDGEWOOD ENTERPRISE. Thu. $.25 newsstand; $16.50/yr. in cy.; $22/yr. out of cy. 109 Front St., Edgewood, TX 75117. TEL 903-896-4401; FAX 903-962-3660. **Owner(s):** Westward Communications, Inc., 5005 LBJ Fwy., Ste. 1040, Dallas, TX 25244. TEL 214-450-1717; Ed. Glenda Lee. adv.; pub. size: broadsheet; circ. 1,500(paid).

EDNA

US
JACKSON COUNTY HERALD/TRIBUNE. 1906. Thu. $.50 newsstand; $21.50/yr. in cy.; $31.50/yr. out of cy.; $35.50/yr. out of state. 306 N. Wells St., Edna, TX 77957. TEL 512-782-3547; FAX 512-782-6002. **Owner(s):** Dennis Simons, 201 1/2 N. Wells, Edna, TX 77957. TEL 512-782-3504; Joe Hermes, 606 N. Wells, Edna, TX 77957; Harrison Stafford, II, 508 Gilbert, Edna, TX 77957; Mark Rose, 105 E. Main, Edna, TX 77957. TEL 512-782-5274; David Rose, 105 E. Main, Edna, TX 77957. TEL 512-782-5274; Willard Ulbricht, 114 W. Main, Edna, TX 77957. TEL 512-782-5655; Ed. Bert West; Pub. Bert West; adv. contact: Pam Harvey. pub. size: standard; circ. 4,300(paid).

EL CAMPO

US
EL CAMPO LEADER-NEWS. 1885. s-w.: Wed. & Sat. $.50 newsstand; $32/yr. in cy.; $42/yr. out of cy. 203 E. Jackson, El Campo, TX 77437-1180. TEL 409-543-3363; FAX 409-543-0097. **Owner(s):** El Campo Newspapers, Inc., P.O. Box 1180, El Campo, TX 77437. TEL 409-543-3363; FAX 409-543-0097; Ed. Chris F. Barbee; Pub. Fred V. Barbee, Jr.; adv. contact: Rena Dlukas. photos; pub. size: broadsheet; circ. 6,350(paid).

EULESS

US
D/FW PEOPLE. 1983. Thu. free to airport employees; $75/yr. mailed. 400 Fuller-Wiser, Ste. 125, Euless, TX 76039. TEL 817-540-4666; FAX 817-685-7562. **Owner(s):** Wood Publications, Atlanta, GA 30301; Ed. Bill Leader; Pub. Jim Wood; adv. contact: Janie Ross. pub. size: tabloid; circ. 13,000(free & paid).

EVERMAN

US
EVERMAN TIMES. 1962. Thu. $.35 newsstand; $12/yr. in cy.; $17/yr. out of cy. 833 E. Enon, Everman, TX 76140. TEL 817-478-4661. **Owner(s):** B & B Publishing, Inc., P.O. Box 40230, Fort Worth, TX 76140. TEL 817-478-4661; Ed. Gene S. Blessing; Pub. Gene S. Blessing; adv.: $4.40/SAU. photos; bk.rev.; pub. size: broadsheet; circ. 494(paid).

Weeklies

10740 EVERMAN, TX

FOREST HILL NEWS
US
FOREST HILL NEWS. 1945. Thu. free newsstand; $45/yr. mailed. 833 E. Enon, Everman, TX 76140. TEL 817-478-4661. **Owner(s):** B & B Publishing, Inc., P.O. Box 40230, Everman, TX 76140. TEL 817-478-4661; Ed. Gene S. Blessing; Pub. Gene S. Blessing; adv.: $6.20/SAU. photos; bk.rev.; pub. size: broadsheet; circ. 7,000(free & paid).

US
KENNEDALE NEWS. 1965. Thu. $.35 newsstand; $12/yr. in cy.; $17/yr. out of cy. 833 E. Enon, Everman, TX 76140-3523. TEL 817-478-4661. **Owner(s):** B & B Publishing, Inc., P.O. Box 40230, Fort Worth, TX 76140. TEL 817-478-4661; Ed. Gene S. Blessing; Pub. Gene S. Blessing; adv.; photos; bk.rev.; pub. size: broadsheet; circ. 350(paid).

FALFURRIAS
US
FALFURRIAS FACTS. 1906. Thu. $.50 newsstand; $20/yr. local; $22/yr. out of area. 219 E. Rice St., Falfurrias, TX 78355. TEL 512-325-2200. **Owner(s):** Falfurrias Publishing Co., Inc., 219 E. Rice St., P.O. Box 619, Falfurrias, TX 78355. TEL 512-325-2200; FAX 512-325-2200; Ed. Marcelo Silva; Pub. Marcelo Silva; adv. contact: SanJuanita Olivarez. adv.: $3.50/SAU. pub. size: broadsheet; circ. 2,247(paid).

FLORESVILLE
US
FLORESVILLE CHRONICLE-JOURNAL. 1877. Wed. $.40 newsstand; $20/yr. 1433 Third, Floresville, TX 78114-0820. TEL 210-393-2111; FAX 210-393-9012. **Owner(s):** Joe H. & Marjorie Fietsam, 1401 Hospital Blvd., Floresville, TX 78114. TEL 210-393-2111; FAX 210-393-9012; Ed. Marjorie Fietsam. adv. contact: James Fietsam. pub. size: broadsheet; circ. 4,320(controlled & paid).

FLOYDADA
US
FLOYD COUNTY HESPERIAN-BEACON. 1896. Thu. $.50 newsstand; $16/yr. in cy.; $18/yr. out of cy.; $19/yr. out of state. 111 E. Missouri, Floydada, TX 79235. TEL 806-983-3737. **Owner(s):** Caprock-Sentinel Corp., 706 Barton Blvd., Austin, TX 78704. TEL 512-443-7918; Ed. Alice Towery Gilroy; Pub. Alice Towery Gilroy; pub. size: broadsheet; circ. 2,430(controlled & paid).

FORT STOCKTON
US
FORT STOCKTON PIONEER. 1908. Thu. $.50 newsstand; $21/yr. in cy.; $28/yr. out of cy.; $33/yr. out of state. 210 N. Nelson St., Fort Stockton, TX 79735. TEL 915-336-2281; FAX 915-336-6432. **Owner(s):** Big Bend Communications, Inc., P.O. Box 1528, Ft. Stockton, TX 79735. TEL 915-336-2281; Ed. Jeffrey McDonald; Pub. John Cordsen; adv. contact: Colin Wilson. pub. size: broadsheet; circ. 3,700(paid).

FORT WORTH
US
BENBROOK NEWS. 1939. Thu. free in cy.; $40/yr. out of cy. mailed. 7820 Wyatt Dr., Fort Worth, TX 76108-2533. TEL 817-246-2473; FAX 817-246-2474. **Owner(s):** Suburban Newspapers, Inc., 7820 Wyatt Dr., Fort Worth, TX 76108. TEL 817-246-2473; Ed. Janice Underwood; Pub. Janice Underwood; adv.: $624/B&W pg. photos; pub. size: tabloid; circ. 6,000(free & paid).

US
RIVER OAKS NEWS. 1940. Thu. free in cy.; $40/yr. out of cy. mailed. 7820 Wyatt Dr., Fort Worth, TX 76108-2533. TEL 817-246-2473; FAX 817-246-2474. **Owner(s):** Suburban Newspapers, Inc., 7820 Wyatt Dr., Fort Worth, TX 76108. TEL 817-247-2474; Ed. Janice Underwood; Pub. Janice Underwood; adv.: $624/B&W pg. photos; pub. size: tabloid; circ. 7,000(free).

US
SOUTH COUNTY NEWS & ADVERTISER. 1975. Thu. free; $45/yr. mailed. 833 E. Enon, Fort Worth, TX 76140. TEL 817-478-4661. **Owner(s):** B & B Publishing, Inc., P.O. Box 40230, Fort Worth, TX 76140. TEL 817-478-4661; Ed. Gene S. Blessing; Pub. Gene S. Blessing; adv.: $6.20/SAU. pub. size: broadsheet; circ. 7,000(free).

US
WHITE SETTLEMENT NEWS. 1941. Thu. free in cy.; $40/yr. out of cy. mailed. 7820 Wyatt Dr., Fort Worth, TX 76108-2533. TEL 817-246-2473; FAX 817-246-2474. **Owner(s):** Suburban Newspapers, Inc., 7820 Wyatt Dr., Fort Worth, TX 76108. TEL 817-246-2473; Ed. Janice Underwood; Pub. Janice Underwood; adv.: $624/B&W pg. photos; pub. size: tabloid; circ. 6,000(free & paid).

FREDERICKSBURG
US   ISSN 0747-0061
FREDERICKSBURG STANDARD/RADIO POST. 1888. Wed. $.50 newsstand; $19/yr.; $23/yr. elsewhere. 108 E. Main, Fredericksburg, TX 78624-0473. TEL 210-997-2155; FAX 210-990-0036. **Owner(s):** Fredericksburg Publishing Co, Inc., P.O. Box 473, Fredericksbrg, TX 78624. TEL 210-997-2155; FAX 210-990-0036; Ed. Terrill D. Collier; Pub. Arthur H. Kowert; adv. contact: Elaine Kanz. photos; bk.rev.; pub. size: broadsheet; circ. 9,787(paid).

GAIL
US
BORDEN STAR. 1972. Wed. $.25 newsstand; $12/yr. 100 Kincaid Ave., Gail, TX 79738. TEL 806-756-4402; FAX 806-756-4310. **Owner(s):** Borden Star, The, P.O. Box 137, 100 Kincaid Ave., Gail, TX 79738. TEL 806-756-4402; Ed. Verna Adcock; Pub. Cookie Dyess; adv. contact: Clara Jane Dyess. photos; bk.rev.; pub. size: broadsheet; circ. 450(free & paid).

GARLAND
US   ISSN 1045-3997
GARLAND NEWS. 1887. s-w.: Thu. & Sun. $.50 newsstand; $3/mo.; $36/yr. 613 State St., Garland, TX 75040. TEL 214-272-6591; FAX 214-487-0655. **Owner(s):** DFW Suburban Newspapers, Inc., 1000 Ave. H, E., Arlington, TX 76011. TEL 817-633-0500; Ed. Ray Leszczynski. adv. contact: Neil Tait. photos; pub. size: standard; circ. 10,750(paid). **Wire Service(s):** Southwest News.
Formerly: Garland Daily News.

GATESVILLE
US   ISSN 0894-4954
GATESVILLE MESSENGER. 1881. Wed. & Thu. $.50 newsstand; $22.75/yr. in cy.; $31.95/out of cy. 116 S. Sixth St., Gatesville, TX 76528. TEL 817-865-5212; FAX 817-865-2361. **Owner(s):** Roberts Publishing Co., Andrews, TX; Ed. Larry Kennedy; Pub. Marshall Day; adv. contact: Debbie Day. photos; bk.rev.; pub. size: broadsheet; circ. 5,500(paid).

GEORGETOWN
US
SUNDAY SUN. 1975. Sat. $.50 newsstand; $14/yr. in cy.; $21.50/yr. out of cy. 707 Main St., Georgetown, TX 78626. TEL 512-930-4824. **Owner(s):** Linda Scarbrough, P.O. Box 39, Georgetown, TX 78627-0039. TEL 512-930-4824; Ed. Linda Scarbrough; Pub. Clark Thurmond; adv. contact: Melissa Gentry. photos; pub. size: broadsheet; circ. 8,690(paid).

US
WILLIAMSON COUNTY SUN. 1877. w. $.50 newsstand; $28/yr. 709 Main St., Georgetown, TX 78626-0039. TEL 512-930-4824. **Owner(s):** Williamson County Sun, Inc., P.O. Box 39, Georgetown, TX 78627. TEL 512-930-4824; Ed. Clark Thurmond. adv.; photos; pub. size: broadsheet; circ. 8,690(paid).

GIDDINGS
US
GIDDINGS TIMES & NEWS. 1888. Thu. $22.50/yr. in cy.; $25/yr. out of cy.; $35/yr. out of state. 170 N. Knox Ave., Giddings, TX 78942. TEL 409-542-2222. **Owner(s):** Preuss Printing Co., 170 N. Knox Ave., Giddings, TX 78942; Ed. David True; Pub. L. M. Preuss; pub. size: broadsheet; circ. 6,200(paid).

GILMER
US   ISSN 8750-0884
GILMER MIRROR. 1877. s-w.: Wed. & Sat. $.50 newsstand; $27/yr. in cy.; $31/yr. out of cy; $35/yr. out of state. 214 E. Marshall St., Gilmer, TX 75644. TEL 903-843-2503; FAX 903-843-5123. **Owner(s):** Greeneway Enterprises, P.O. Box 250, Gilmer, TX 75644. TEL 903-843-2503; Pub. Sarah Greene; adv. contact: Susan Patterson. photos; bk.rev.; pub. size: broadsheet; circ. 5,000(paid).

WEEKLY NEWSPAPERS

HOUSTON, TX 10741

GLADEWATER
US

GLADEWATER MIRROR. 1949. Wed. $.50 newsstand; $26/yr. in cy.; $28/yr. out of cy.; $36.50/yr. out of state. 201 S. Dean St., Gladewater, TX 75647. TEL 903-845-2235; FAX 903-845-2237. **Owner(s):** Westward Communications, Inc., 5005 LBJ Freeway #1040, Dallas, TX 75244. TEL 214-450-1717; FAX 214-450-1770; Ed. Garth Maier; Pub. Floydell Borchardt; adv. contact: Tonya Hunt. pub. size: broadsheet; circ. 1,850(paid).

GLEN ROSE
US

GLEN ROSE REPORTER. 1887. Thu. $.35 newsstand; $13.50/yr in cy; $18/yr. out of cy.: $28/yr. out of state. 100 S.W. Vernon St., Glen Rose, TX 76043. TEL 817-897-2282; FAX 817-897-9423. **Owner(s):** Glen Rose Publishing Co., P.O. Box 2009, Glen Rose, TX 76043. TEL 817-897-2282; FAX 817-897-9423; Ed. Dan McCarty; Pub. Dan McCarty; adv. contact: Linda Nix. photos; pub. size: broadsheet; circ. 2,900(paid).

GONZALES
US

GONZALES INQUIRER. 1853. s-w.: Tue. & Fri. $.50 newsstand; $28/yr. in cy.; $33/yr. out of cy. 622 St. Paul St., Gonzales, TX 78629. TEL 210-672-2861; FAX 210-672-7029. **Owner(s):** Granite Publications, 304 Gate Way Loop, Marble Falls, TX 78654. TEL 210-693-3334; Ed. Charles Wood; Pub. Jim Cunningham; adv. contact: Judy Stewart. pub. size: broadsheet; circ. 4,000(paid).

GORMAN
US

GORMAN PROGRESS, THE. 1900. Wed. $.30 newsstand; $11/yr. in cy.; $15.50/yr. in state; $17.50/yr. out of state. 106 S. Kent, Gorman, TX 76454-0068. TEL 817-734-2410; FAX 817-734-2799. **Owner(s):** Joe Bennett, 106 S. Kent St., P.O. Box 68, Gorman, TX 76454-0068. TEL 817-734-2410; FAX 817-734-2799; Ed. Elania Lingle; Pub. Joe Bennett; adv.; pub. size: broadsheet; circ. 1,000(paid).

GRANBURY
US

HOOD COUNTY NEWS. 1886. s-w.: Wed. & Sat. $.50 newsstand; $30/yr. in cy.; $45/yr. out of cy.; $60/yr. out of state. 1501 S. Morgan St., Granbury, TX 76048. TEL 817-573-7066; FAX 817-279-8371. **Owner(s):** Jerry Tidwell, 1501 S. Morgan St., Granbury, TX 76048; Ed. Jerry Tidwell; Pub. Jerry Tidwell; adv. contact: Cherri Medcalf. pub. size: broadsheet; circ. 10,034(paid).

GRAND SALINE
US

GRAND SALINE SUN. 1894. Thu. $.50 newsstand; $19.50/yr. in cy.; $28.50/yr. out of cy.; $32.50/yr. out of state. 116 N. Main St., Grand Saline, TX 75140. TEL 903-962-4275; FAX 903-962-3660. **Owner(s):** Westward Communications, Inc., 5005 LBJ Freeway, Ste. 1040, Dallas, TX 75244. TEL 214-450-1717; Ed. Jan Adamson; Pub. Jan Adamson; adv. contact: Donna Limberger. adv. $4.25/SAU. pub. size: broadsheet; circ. 2,500(paid).

GREENVILLE
US

HUNT COUNTY SHOPPER. 1965. w. free newsstand; $8.50/yr. out of area. 3617 Wesley, Greenville, TX 75401. TEL 903-455-5254; FAX 903-455-3297. **Owner(s):** Hunt County Shopper, 3617 Wesley, Greenville, TX 75401. TEL 903-455-5254; FAX 903-455-3297; Ed. Warren Hope; Pub. Warren Hope; adv.: $4.85/SAU. pub. size: tabloid; circ. 24,161(free & paid).

GROESBECK
US

GROESBECK JOURNAL. 1892. Thu. $.40 newsstand; $12/yr. in cy.; $15/yr. in state; $17/yr. out of state; $19/yr. foreign. 115-117 N. Ellis, Groesbeck, TX 76642. TEL 817-729-5103; FAX 817-729-5555. **Owner(s):** Groesbeck Journal, Inc., P.O. Box 440, Groesbeck, TX 76642. TEL 817-729-5103; Ed. Thomas E. Hawkins; Pub. Thomas E. Hawkins; pub. size: broadsheet; circ. 4,600(paid).

GUN BARREL CITY
US ISSN 1046-8633

CEDAR CREEK PILOT. 1970. s-w.: Thu. & Sun. $.50 newsstand; $22/yr. 828 W. Main St., Gun Barrel City, TX 75147. TEL 903-432-3132. **Owner(s):** Stephens Group, Inc., P.O. Box 1359, Fort Smith, AR 72901-7017. TEL 501-785-7810; Pub. Dan Dwelle; adv. contact: Kathi Nailling. photos; pub. size: broadsheet; circ. 5,300(paid); Sun. 6,150(paid).

HALLETTSVILLE
US

HALLETTSVILLE TRIBUNE-HERALD. 1931. Wed. $.60 newsstand; $19.50/yr. in cy.; $28.50/yr. out of cy.; $30/yr. out of state. 108 S. Texana, Hallettsville, TX 77964. TEL 512-798-2481; FAX 512-798-9902. **Owner(s):** L.M. Preuss, 170 N. Knox, Giddings, TX 78942. TEL 409-542-2222; Pub. Larry Rothbauer; adv. contact: Anne Kubicek. pub. size: standard; circ. 4,000(paid).

HAMILTON
US

HAMILTON HERALD-NEWS. 1875. Thu. $.40 newsstand; $20/yr. in cy.; $25/yr. out of cy. 112 E. Main, Hamilton, TX 76531. TEL 817-386-3145; FAX 817-386-3001. **Owner(s):** Hamilton Publishing Co., Inc., 112 E. Main, Hamilton, TX 76531. TEL 817-386-3145; Ed. Roger P. Miller; Pub. Kenneth Miller; pub. size: broadsheet; circ. 3,700(paid).

HASKELL
US

HASKELL FREE PRESS. 1886. Thu. $.50 newsstand; $20/yr. in cy.; $28/yr. elsewhere. 401 S. First St., Haskell, TX 79521. TEL 817-864-2686; FAX 817-864-2686. **Owner(s):** John McDougal, 401 S. First St., Haskell, TX 79521. TEL 817-864-2686; Pub. John McDougal; adv. contact: John McDougal. pub. size: broadsheet; circ. 2,550(paid).

HEMPHILL
US

SABINE COUNTY REPORTER-RAMBLER. 1883. Wed. $.75 newsstand; $22/yr. in cy.; $33/yr. out of cy. 211 Worth St., Hemphill, TX 75948. TEL 409-787-2643; FAX 409-787-4300. **Owner(s):** Smith Newspapers, Inc., P.O. Box 27, Fort Payne, AL 35967. TEL 205-845-5510; Ed. Stephanie Corley; Pub. Stephanie Corley; pub. size: standard; circ. 4,000(paid).
Formerly: San Augustine Rambler.

HEMPSTEAD
US ISSN 0164-4203

WALLER COUNTY NEWS-CITIZEN. 1890. Wed. $.50 newsstand; $22/yr. in cy.; $26/yr. out of cy. 705 12th St., Hempstead, TX 77445. TEL 409-826-3361; FAX 409-826-3360. **Owner(s):** Westward Communications, 705 12th St., Hempstead, TX 77445. TEL 409-826-3360; FAX 409-826-3361; Ed. Jim Belew; Pub. Jim Belew; adv.; photos; pub. size: broadsheet; circ. 2,500(paid).

HONDO
US

HONDO ANVIL HERALD. 1886. Thu. $.50 newsstand; $15/yr. local; $25/yr. out of area. 1601 Ave. K, Hondo, TX 78861. TEL 210-426-3346; FAX 210-426-3348. **Owner(s):** Associated Texas Newspapers, Inc., 1801 Exposition, Austin, TX 78703. TEL 512-476-3950; FAX 512-476-6356; Pub. William E. Berger; adv.; bk.rev.; pub. size: broadsheet; circ. 3,917(paid); morning 8,300.

SABINAL SAMPLER. 1950. Wed. free in area. 1601 Ave. K, Hondo, TX 78861. TEL 210-426-3346; FAX 210-426-3348. **Owner(s):** W.E. Berger, P.O. Box 400, Hondo, TX 78861. TEL 210-426-3346; FAX 210-426-3348; Ed. Frances Guinn. adv.: $2/SAU. pub. size: broadsheet; circ. 1,483(free).

HOUSTON
US

CITIZEN, THE. 1960. Wed. $.50 newsstand; $18/yr. in area mailed. 17511 El Camino Real, Houston, TX 77058. TEL 281-488-1108; FAX 281-286-0750. **Owner(s):** Gulf Coast Newspapers, 17511 El Camino Real, Houston, TX 77058. TEL 713-488-1108; FAX 713-286-0750; Ed. Lori Williams; Pub. Lonnie Clement; adv.; pub. size: broadsheet; circ. 25,000(controlled & paid).

10742 HOUSTON, TX

US
EXCHANGE, THE. Wed. $.50 newsstand; $18/yr. in area mailed. 17511 El Camino Real, Houston, TX 77058. TEL 281-488-1108; FAX 281-286-0750. **Owner(s):** Gulf Coast Newspapers, 17511 El Camino Real, Houston, TX. TEL 281-488-1108; FAX 281-286-0750; Ed. Lori Williams; Pub. Lonnie Clement; adv.; pub. size: broadsheet; circ. 21,000(paid).

US
HOUSTON FORWARD TIMES. 1960. Wed. $.50 newsstand; $13.50/6 mos. in cy.; $25/yr. in cy.; $25/yr. out of cy. 4411 Almeda, Houston, TX 77004. TEL 713-526-4727; FAX 713-526-3170. **Owner(s):** Lenora Carter, 411 Almeda, Houston, TX 77004; Ed. Lenora Carter; Pub. Lenora Carter; adv. contact: Henrietta Smith. pub. size: broadsheet; circ. 63,000(paid).

US
HOUSTON INFORMER. 1893. Tue. $1 newsstand; $32/yr. in cy. 4209 Dowling, Houston, TX 77004. TEL 713-527-8261; FAX 713-524-7028. **Owner(s):** Lorenza P. Butler, Jr., 3906 Daphne St., Houston, TX 77021. TEL 713-527-8261; Ed. George McElroy; Pub. Lorenza P. Butler, Jr.; adv. contact: William Handout. pub. size: broadsheet; circ. 23,000(paid).

HOWE

US
HOWE ENTERPRISE. 1963. Thu. $.50 newsstand; $17/yr. in cy.; $222/yr. out of cy. 106 E. Haning St., Howe, TX 75459-0488. TEL 903-532-6012. E-mail: howeenterprise@texoma.com; URL: http://www.texoma.com/newspapers/howe-enterprise. Owner(s): Dale Rideout, 106 E. Haning St., Howe, TX 75459-0488. TEL 903-532-6012; Ed. Lana Rideout; Pub. Dale Rideout; adv. contact: Dale Rideout. photos; bk.rev.; pub. size: standard; circ. 736(free & paid).

HUMBLE

US
HUMBLE SUN. Wed. free. 9810 FM 1960 W. By pass, Ste. 115, Humble, TX 77338. TEL 281-446-3733; FAX 281-446-0201. **Owner(s):** Houston Community Newspapers, Inc., P.O. Box 280, Channelview, TX 77530. TEL 281-452-0530; Ed. Norm Rowland; Pub. Tony Burt, Jr.; adv.; photos; pub. size: broadsheet; circ. 17,998(controlled & free).
Formerly: Humble Echo.

US
KINGWOOD SUN. 1942. Wed. free. 9810 FM 1960 W. By Pass Ste., 115, Humble, TX 77338. TEL 281-446-3733; FAX 281-446-0201. **Owner(s):** Houston Community Newspapers, Inc., P.O. Box 280, Channelview, TX 77530. TEL 713-452-0530; Ed. Barbara Newman; Pub. Tony Burt, Jr.; adv.; photos; pub. size: broadsheet; circ. 16,000(controlled & free).
Formerly: Kingwood Echo/New Caney Echo.

US
PORTER/NEW CANEY SUN. 1942. Wed. free. 1960 W. By Pass, Ste. 115, Humble, TX 77338. TEL 281-446-3733; FAX 281-446-0201. **Owner(s):** Houston Community Newspapers, Inc., P.O. Box 280, Channelview, TX 77530. TEL 713-452-0530; Ed. Norm Rowland; Pub. Tony Burt, Jr.; adv.; photos; pub. size: broadsheet; circ. 12,000(controlled & free).
Formerly: Porter/New Caney Echo.

IDALOU

US
IDALOU BEACON. 1957. w. $.50 newsstand; $15/yr. local; $17/yr. out of cy. & state. 818 Frontage Rd., Idalou, TX 79329. TEL 806-892-2233. **Owner(s):** Scott & Judy Luce, 1108 Ave. J, Abernathy, TX 79311. TEL 806-298-2909; Ed. Scott Luce; Pub. Scott Luce; adv.; photos; pub. size: broadsheet; circ. 675(free & paid).

IOWA PARK

US
IOWA PARK LEADER. 1969. Thu. $.50 newsstand; $15/yr. in cy.; $17/yr. out of cy. $20/yr out of state. P.O. Box 430, Iowa Park, TX 76367. TEL 817-592-4431. **Owner(s):** Bob & Dolores Hamilton, P.O. Box 430, Iowa Park, TX 76367. TEL 817-592-4431; adv.: $2.88/SAU. photos; pub. size: standard; circ. 2,560(paid).

JASPER

US
JASPER NEWSBOY. 1865. s-w.: Wed. & Sun. $.50 newsstand; $12/yr. in cy.; $15/yr. out of cy.; $18/yr. elsewhere. 302 N. Wheeler, Jasper, TX 75951. TEL 409-384-3441; FAX 409-384-8803. **Owner(s):** Hearst Corp., 959 Eighth Ave., New York, NY 10019; Pub. Willis Webb; pub. size: broadsheet; circ. 6,390(paid).

US
JASPER NEWSBOY SHOPPER. s-w: Wed. & Sun. $.50/newsstand; $12/yr. in cy.; $15/yr. out of cy. 302 N. Wheeler, Jasper, TX 75951. TEL 409-384-3441; FAX 409-384-8803. **Owner(s):** Enterprise Co., P.O. Box 3071, Beaumont, TX 77704. TEL 409-833-3311; Ed. Willis Webb; Pub. Willis Webb; pub. size: broadsheet; circ. 17,700(free).

JEFFERSON

US   ISSN 1060-3476
JEFFERSON JIMPLECUTE. 1848. Thu. $.50 newsstand; $20/yr. in cy.; $23/yr. in state; $26/yr. out of state. 205 W. Austin, Jefferson, TX 75657. TEL 903-665-2462; FAX 903-665-3802. **Owner(s):** Cox Enterprises, Inc., 1400 Lake Hearn Dr., N.E., P.O. Box 105720, Atlanta, GA 30319; Ed. Lou Anne Suber; Pub. Joe Wayne Dennis; adv.; pub. size: broadsheet; circ. 2,500(paid).

JUNCTION

US
JUNCTION EAGLE, THE. 1882. Wed. $.50 newsstand; $17/yr. in cy.; $19/yr. out of cy.; $20/yr. out of state. 215 N. Sixth St., Junction, TX 76849. TEL 915-446-2610; FAX 915-446-4025. **Owner(s):** Debbie W. Cooper, 215 N. Sixth St., Junction, TX 76849. TEL 915-446-2610; FAX 915-446-4025; Ed. Debbie Cooper; Pub. Debbie Cooper; adv. contact: Roy Cooper. photos; bk.rev.; pub. size: standard.

KARNES CITY

US
KARNES CITATION. 1895. Wed. $.50 newsstand; $20/yr. in cy.; $26/yr. out of cy. 110 S. Market St., Karnes City, TX 78118. TEL 210-780-3924. Owner(s): Karnes Multimedia, Inc., 110 S. Market St., Karnes City, TX 78118. TEL 210-780-3924; Ed. Bill DeFries; Pub. Bill DeFries; adv. contact: Sharon Menn. pub. size: standard; circ. 2,550(paid).

US
KENNEDY ADVANCED TIMES. Wed. $.50 newsstand; $20/yr. in cy.; $26/yr. out of cy. 110 S. Market St., Karnes City, TX 78118. TEL 210-780-3924. Owner(s): Karnes Multimedia, Inc., 110 S. Market St., Karnes City, TX 78118. TEL 210-780-3924; Ed. Bill DeFries; Pub. Bill DeFries; adv. contact: Sharon Menn. pub. size: standard; circ. 1,900(paid).

KAUFMAN

US
KAUFMAN HERALD, THE. 1886. Thu. $.50 newsstand; $18/yr. in cy.; $21/yr. out of cy. 300 N. Washington, Kaufman, TX 75142. TEL 972-932-2171; FAX 972-932-2172. **Owner(s):** Hartman Newspapers, Inc., P.O. Box 1390, Rosenberg, TX 77471. TEL 713-342-8691; Ed. Pam High; Pub. Les Linebarger; adv.; pub. size: broadsheet; circ. 4,200(paid).

KELLER

US
KELLER CITIZEN, THE. 1980. Tue. $.25 newsstand; $30/yr. 538 E. Price St., Keller, TX 76248. TEL 817-431-2231; FAX 817-431-5534; E-mail: kcitizen@aol.com. **Owner(s):** William C. Lewis, P.O. Box 615, Keller, TX 76244. TEL 817-431-2231; FAX 817-431-2231; Pub. William C. Lewis; adv. contact: Sandra S. Lewis. adv.: $7/SAU. photos; pub. size: broadsheet; circ. 14,700(free & paid).

KERMIT

US
WINKLER COUNTY NEWS. 1936. Thu. $.50 newsstand; $16/yr. in cy. deliv.; $27/yr. out of cy. mailed. 109 S. Poplar, Kermit, TX 79745. TEL 915-586-2561; FAX 915-586-2562. **Owner(s):** Golden West Free Press Co., 109 S. Poplar, Kermit, TX 79745. TEL 915-586-2561; Ed. Bert Brewer; Pub. Richard E. McLaughlin; adv. contact: Beth Murray. pub. size: standard; circ. 3,700(paid).

KERRVILLE

US
MOUNTAIN SUN, THE. 1881. Wed. $.50 newsstand; $20/yr. in cy.; $22.50/yr. out of cy.; $25/yr. out of state. 516 Quinlan, Kerrville, TX 78028. TEL 210-257-3300; FAX 210-257-3329. **Owner(s):** Las Trampas, P.O. Box 790, Espanola, NM 87532. TEL 505-753-2126; Pub. Robert Trapp, Jr.; adv.; photos; pub. size: broadsheet; circ. 4,500(paid).

WEEKLY NEWSPAPERS

LIVINGSTON, TX 10743

KINGSVILLE

US

KINGSVILLE RECORD, THE. 1906. s-w.: Sun. & Wed. $33.50/yr. home deliv.; $36.50/yr. mailed. 105 S. Fifth St., Kingsville, TX 78363. TEL 512-592-4304; FAX 512-592-1015. **Owner(s):** Kingsville Publishing Co., P.O. Box 951, Kingsville, TX 78364. TEL 512-592-4304; Ed. Bob Odom; Pub. Bob Odom; pub. size: broadsheet; circ. 6,800(paid).

LA FERIA

US ISSN 1084-2578

LA FERIA NEWS. 1923. Wed. $.50 newsstand; $22/yr. in cy.; $27/yr. in state. 116 W. Oleander St., La Feria, TX 78559-0308. TEL 210-797-1813; FAX 210-797-9217. **Owner(s):** Golden Media, Inc., P.O. Box 308, La Feria, TX 78559. TEL 210-797-1813; FAX 210-797-9217; Ed. Vincent W. Bodiford; Pub. Vincent W. Bodiford; adv.; photos; bk.rev.; pub. size: broadsheet; circ. 3,450(free & paid).

LA GRANGE

US

FAYETTE COUNTY RECORD, THE. 1922. s-w.: Tue. & Fri. $.50 newsstand; $17.50/yr. 127 S. Washington, La Grange, TX 78945. TEL 409-968-3155; FAX 409-968-6767. **Owner(s):** Richard L. Barton, Jr., P.O. Box 400, La Grange, TX 78945. TEL 409-968-3155; FAX 409-968-6767; Ed. Richard L. Barton, Jr.; Pub. Richard L. Barton, Jr.; adv.; photos; pub. size: broadsheet; circ. 6,161(paid).

LAKE DALLAS

US

ARGYLE SUN, THE. 1986. Thu. free. 275 Market St., Lake Dallas, TX 75065. TEL 817-497-4141. **Owner(s):** Sun Newspapers, 275 Market St., P.O. Box 879, Lake Dallas, TX 75065. TEL 817-497-4141; Pub. Terry Lantrip; adv. contact: Terry Lantrip. photos; pub. size: broadsheet; circ. 1,600(free).

US

DENTON COUNTY EXPRESS. 1992. Wed. free/incl. with Lake City Sun & The Argyle Sun. 275 Market St., Lake Dallas, TX 75065. TEL 817-497-4141. **Owner(s):** Sun Newspapers, 275 Market St., Lake Dallas, TX 75065. TEL 817-497-4141; Pub. Terry Lantrip; adv. contact: Terry Lantrip. photos; pub. size: broadsheet; circ. 3,000(free).

US

LAKE CITIES SUN, THE. 1974. Wed. $.50 newsstand; $18/yr. in cy.; $26/yr. in state. 275 Market St., Lake Dallas, TX 75065. TEL 817-497-4141. **Owner(s):** Sun Newspapers, 275 Market St., P.O. Box 879, Lake Dallas, TX 75065. TEL 817-497-4141; Pub. Terry Lantrip; adv. contact: Terry Lantrip. photos; pub. size: broadsheet; circ. 1,700(paid).

LA MARQUE

US

LA MARQUE TIMES. 1946. Wed. $.25 newsstand; $16/yr. in cy.; $21/yr. elsewhere. 1118 Bayou Rd., La Marque, TX 77568. TEL 409-935-2431; FAX 409-925-1399. **Owner(s):** Santa Fe Newspapers, Inc., P.O. Box 158, La Marque, TX 77568. TEL 409-935-2511; Ed. Harry Monych; Pub. Harry Monych; adv. contact: Harry Monych. pub. size: broadsheet; circ. 3,100(paid).

LAMESA

US

LAMESA PRESS-REPORTER. 1905. s-w.: Wed. & Sun. $.50 newsstand; $25.25/yr. 523 N. First St., Lamesa, TX 79331. TEL 806-872-2177; FAX 806-872-2623. **Owner(s):** Roberts Publishing Co., 210 E. Broadway, Andrews, TX 79714. TEL 915-523-3232; Walter Buckel, 523 N. First St., Lamesa, TX 79331. TEL 806-872-2177; Russell Skiles, 523 N. First St., Lamesa, TX 79331. TEL 806-872-2177; B. McCormick, 523 N. First St., Lamesa, TX 79331. TEL 806-872-2177; B. Buckel, 523 N. First St., Lamesa, TX 79331. TEL 806-872-2177; Barbara Buckel, 523 N. First St., Lamesa, TX 79331. TEL 806-872-2177; Venita Loftin, 523 N. First St., Lamesa, TX 79331. TEL 806-872-2177; FAX 806-872-2623; Ed. Russel Skiles; Pub. Russel Skiles; adv.: $4/SAU. pub. size: broadsheet; circ. 4,027(free & paid).

LA PORTE

US

BAYSHORE SUN. 1947. s-w.: Wed. & Sun. $.25 newsstand; $26.50/yr. in cy.; $30/yr. out of cy. 1200 Hwy. 146 S., Ste. 150, La Porte, TX 77571. TEL 281-471-1234; FAX 281-471-5763. **Owner(s):** Hartman Newspapers, Inc., P.O. Box 1390, Rosenberg, TX 77471; Ed. John Black; Pub. John Black; pub. size: broadsheet; circ. 13,000(paid); Sun. 5,300(paid).

LEAKEY

US

REAL AMERICAN. 1951. w. $.50 newsstand; $15/yr. in cy.; $20/yr. out of cy. Main St., Leakey, TX 78873. TEL 210-232-5204; FAX 210-232-5630. **Owner(s):** Vice Stadter, Main St., P.O. Box 1140, Leakey, TX 78873. TEL 210-232-5204; FAX 210-232-5630; Ed. Pat Thurmond; Pub. Vic Stadter; adv. contact: Pat Thurmond. photos; pub. size: standard; circ. 1,250(controlled & paid).

LEVELLAND

US

LEVELLAND HOCKLEY COUNTY NEWS-PRESS. 1925. s-w.: Wed. & Sun. $.50 newsstand; $24/yr. 711 Austin St., Levelland, TX 79336. TEL 806-894-3121; FAX 806-894-7957. **Owner(s):** Stephen & Pat Enterprises, Drawer 1628, Levelland, TX 79336. TEL 806-894-3121; FAX 806-894-7957; Ed. Stephen A. Henry; Pub. Stephen Henry; adv.; photos; pub. size: standard; circ. 4,761(free & paid); Sun. 5,045(free & paid).

LEWISVILLE

US

COPPELL GAZETTE. Thu. $.50 newsstand; $36/yr. mailed. 1165 S. Stemmons, Ste. 100, Lewisville, TX 75067. TEL 972-436-3566; FAX 972-219-0719. **Owner(s):** Harte-Hanks Communications, Inc., P.O. Box 269, San Antonio, TX 78291. TEL 512-344-8000; Ed. Tim Waterson; Pub. Beth Roddy; adv. contact: Debbie Rauen. pub. size: broadsheet; circ. 8,500(paid).

US ISSN 0745-6174

LEWISVILLE LEADER. 1895. s-w.: Wed. & Sat. free. 1165 S. Stemmons, Ste. 100, Lewisville, TX 75057. TEL 214-436-3566; FAX 214-436-7432. **Owner(s):** Harte-Hanks Communications, Inc., P.O. Box 269, San Antonio, TX 78291; Ed. Kristine Hughes; Pub. Beth Roddy; adv. contact: Debbie Raven. pub. size: broadsheet; circ. 29,500(free). **Wire Service(s):** UPI.
Formerly: Lewisville Daily Leader.

LIBERTY

US

LIBERTY GAZETTE. 1960. Wed. free. 314 Main St., Liberty, TX 77575. TEL 409-336-6416; FAX 409-336-9400. **Owner(s):** Lawrence & Cynthia Kuslich, 314 Main St., Liberty, TX 77575. TEL 409-336-6416; FAX 409-336-9400; Ed. Edith Smith; Pub. Lawrence Kuslich; adv.; pub. size: broadsheet; circ. 8,800(free).

US

PONY EXPRESS MAIL. 1981. Tue. free. 314 Main St., Liberty, TX 77575. TEL 409-336-6416; FAX 409-336-9400. **Owner(s):** Lawrence & Cynthia Kuslich, 314 Main St., Liberty, TX 77575. TEL 409-336-6416; FAX 409-336-9400; Ed. Edith Smith; Pub. Lawrence Kuslich; adv.; pub. size: broadsheet; circ. 8,012(free).

US ISSN 0746-6838

VINDICATOR, THE. 1887. s-w.: Wed. & Sun. $.50 newsstand; $30/yr. in cy. 301 Vera Ln., Liberty, TX 77575. TEL 409-336-3611; FAX 409-336-3345. **Owner(s):** Hartman Newspapers, Inc., P.O. Box 1390, Rosenberg, TX 77471. TEL 713-342-8691; Ed. Ernie E. Zieschang; Pub. Ernie E. Zieschang; adv. contact: Jeff Meadows. photos; pub. size: broadsheet; circ. 4,745(free & paid).
Formerly: Vindicator Advertiser, The.

LITTLEFIELD

US

LAMB COUNTY LEADER-NEWS. 1923. s-w.: Wed. & Sun. $.50 newsstand; $22/yr. in cy.; $28/yr. out of cy.; $32/yr out of state. 313 W. Fourth St., Littlefield, TX 79339. TEL 806-385-4481; FAX 806-385-4640. **Owner(s):** Stephen & Pat Enterprises, P.O. Drawer 1628, Levelland, TX 79336. TEL 806-385-4481; Ed. Joella Lovvorn; Pub. Stephen A. Henry; adv.; photos; pub. size: standard; circ. 2,465(free & paid); Sun. 2,755(free & paid).

LIVINGSTON

US

POLK COUNTY ENTERPRISE. 1882. s-w.: Thu. & Sun. $.50 newsstand; $20/yr. in cy.; $22/yr. out of cy.; $24/yr. out of state. 100 Calhoun, Livingston, TX 77351. TEL 409-327-4357; FAX 409-327-7156. **Owner(s):** Polk County Publishing Co., P.O. Box 1276, Livingston, TX 77351. TEL 409-327-4357; Ed. Barbara White; Pub. Alvin Holly; adv.; pub. size: broadsheet; circ. 8,300(paid).
Formerly: Livingston Polk County Enterprise.

Weeklies

LLANO

US

LLANO NEWS. 1889. Thu. $.50 newsstand; $19/yr. in cy.; $26/yr. out of cy.; $40/yr. out of state. 813 Berry St., Llano, TX 78643. TEL 915-247-4433; FAX 915-247-4433. **Owner(s):** Walter L. Buckner, P.O. Box 187, Llano, TX 78643. TEL 915-247-4433; FAX 915-247-4433; Pub. Walter L. Buckner; adv. contact: Walter L. Buckner. pub. size: standard; circ. 3,300(paid).

LOCKHART

US

LOCKHART POST REGISTER. 1872. Thu. $.50 newsstand; $35/yr. 111 S. Church St., Lockhart, TX 78644. TEL 512-398-4886; FAX 512-398-4888. **Owner(s):** Dana Garrett, 111 S. Church St., Lockhart, TX 78644. TEL 512-398-4886; Pub. Dana Garrett; adv. contact: Wayne Bock. pub. size: broadsheet; circ. 3,980(paid).

LORENZO

US

LORENZO EXAMINER. 1986. Fri. $.50 newsstand; $12/yr. in cy.; $15/yr. in state; $20/yr. out of state. 513 Harrison, Lorenzo, TX 79343. TEL 806-634-5390; FAX 806-634-5390. **Owner(s):** Bill & Charlotte Gibbs, 1106 Fifth, P.O. Box 331, Lorenzo, TX 79343. TEL 806-634-5390; FAX 806-634-5390; Ed. Bill Gibbs; Pub. Bill Gibbs; adv. contact: Charlotte Gibbs. adv.: $2.55/SAU. photos; pub. size: standard; circ. 650(paid).

LULING

US

LULING NEWSBOY & SIGNAL. 1940. Thu. $.50 newsstand; $20.50/yr. in cy.; $22.50/yr. out of cy.; $25/yr. out of state. 415 E. Davis, Luling, TX 78648. TEL 210-875-2116; FAX 210-875-2124. **Owner(s):** Luling Publishing Co., Inc., 415 E. Davis, Luling, TX 78648. TEL 210-875-2116; FAX 210-875-2124; Ed. Karen G. McCrary. adv.; photos; bk.rev.; pub. size: broadsheet; circ. 2,500(paid).

MABANK

US ISSN 1049-3409

MONITOR, THE. Wed. $.25 newsstand; $15/yr. 1316 S. Third St., Mabank, TX 75147-7680. TEL 903-887-4511; FAX 903-887-4510. **Owner(s):** Charlotte Whitaker, P.O. Box 1144, Mabank, TX 75147. TEL 903-887-4511; FAX 903-887-4510; Ed. Jim McKee; Pub. Charlotte Whitaker; adv. contact: Jim McKee. photos; pub. size: broadsheet; circ. 21,000(free & paid).

MANSFIELD

US ISSN 0746-3847

MANSFIELD NEWS-MIRROR. 1883. s-w.: Mon. & Thu. $.50 newsstand; $32.95/yr. in cy. 119 N. Main, Mansfield, TX 76063. TEL 817-473-4451; FAX 817-473-0730. **Owner(s):** Jerry T. Ebensberger, P.O. Box 337, Mansfield, TX 76063. TEL 817-473-4451; Ed. Jerry T. Ebensberger; Pub. Jerry T. Ebensberger; adv.; pub. size: broadsheet; circ. 4,000(paid).

MARBLE FALLS

US

MARBLE FALLS HIGHLANDER. 1956. s-w.: Tue. & Fri. $.50 newsstand; $35/yr. 208 Main, Marble Falls, TX 78654. TEL 210-693-4367; FAX 210-693-3650. **Owner(s):** Granite Publishers, 304 Gate Way Loop, Marble Falls, TX 78654. TEL 210-693-3334; Ed. Richard Stone; Pub. Jim Chionsini; adv.; photos; bk.rev.; pub. size: broadsheet; circ. 6,500(paid).

MASON

US

MASON COUNTY NEWS. 1877. Wed. $.50 newsstand; $16/yr. in cy.; $18/yr. out of cy.; $20/yr. elsewhere. 110 Live Oak, Mason, TX 76856. TEL 915-347-5757; FAX 915-347-5668. **Owner(s):** G.W. Lyon, 110 Live Oak, Mason, TX 76856. TEL 915-347-5157; FAX 915-347-5668; Ed. G.W. Lyon; Pub. G.W. Lyon; adv.; pub. size: broadsheet; circ. 2,750(paid).

MATADOR

US ISSN 0897-4322

MOTLEY COUNTY TRIBUNE. 1892. w. $.50 newsstand. Hwy. 70, E., Matador, TX 79244-0490. TEL 806-347-2400. **Owner(s):** Carla M. Meador, 724 Dundee, Matador, TX 79244. TEL 806-347-2400; Ed. Carla M. Meador. adv.; photos; pub. size: standard; circ. 1,200(paid).

MATHIS

US

MATHIS NEWS. 1914. Thu. $23.50/yr. 620 E. San Patricio Ave., Mathis, TX 78368. TEL 512-547-3274; FAX 512-547-3275. **Owner(s):** San Patricio Publishing Co., Inc., P.O. Drawer B, Sinton, TX 78387. TEL 512-364-1270; Ed. Charles Sullivan; Pub. John Tracy; adv. contact: Charles Sullivan. photos; pub. size: broadsheet; circ. 2,550(paid).

MCALLEN

US

VALLEY TOWN CRIER. 1964. Wed. free. 1811 N. 23rd St., McAllen, TX 78501. TEL 956-682-2423; FAX 956-630-6371. **Owner(s):** Valley Media, Inc., 1811 N. 23rd St., McAllen, TX 78501. TEL 956-682-2423; Pub. Mike McKinney; adv. contact: Jack Wilson. pub. size: broadsheet; circ. 90,000(free).

MENARD

US

MENARD NEWS & MESSENGER, THE. 1893. Thu. $.50 newsstand; $18/yr. in cy.; $22/yr. in state; $25/yr. out of state. 220 Gay St., Menard, TX 76859. TEL 915-396-2243. **Owner(s):** Dan Feather, Jr., 220 Gay St., Menard, TX 76859. TEL 915-396-2243; Ed. Dorothy Kerns; Pub. Dan Feather, Jr.; adv.; $4/SAU. photos; pub. size: standard; circ. 1,272(paid).

MERIDIAN

US

BOSQUE COUNTY NEWS. 1990. Wed. $.50 newsstand; $20/yr. in cy.; $24/yr. out of cy. 114 N. Main St., Meridian, TX 76665. TEL 817-435-6333; FAX 817-435-6335. **Owner(s):** Robby James, 114 N. Main St., Meridian, TX 76665. TEL 817-435-6333; FAX 817-435-6335; Ed. Robby James; Pub. Robby James; adv. contact: Carolyn Frerking. bk.rev.; pub. size: standard; circ. 1,500(controlled & paid). **Wire Service(s):** TPA.
Formerly: Meridian Tribune.

MESQUITE

US ISSN 0746-4126

MESQUITE NEWS. 1882. Thu. $.50 newsstand. 303 N. Galloway, Mesquite, TX 75149. TEL 972-285-6301; FAX 972-288-9383. **Owner(s):** Harte-Hanks Communications, Inc., P.O. Box 269, San Antonio, TX 78291. TEL 210-829-9000; FAX 210-829-9403; Ed. Tim Watterson; Pub. Beth Roddy; adv. contact: Scott Moon. photos; bk.rev.; pub. size: broadsheet; circ. 31,000(free & paid).

MEXIA

US ISSN 1067-7305

HUBBARD CITY NEWS. 1881. Thu. $.50 newsstand; $14/yr. in cy.; $16/yr. out of cy.; $18/yr. out of state. 214 N. Railroad, Mexia, TX 76667. TEL 817-562-2868; FAX 817-562-3121. **Owner(s):** American Publishing Co., 606 N. Van Buren, Marion, IL 62959. TEL 618-993-1711; Ed. Barbara Minze; Pub. Lynette Copley; adv.; bk.rev.; pub. size: broadsheet; circ. 1,450(paid).

MIAMI

US ISSN 0746-0082

MIAMI CHIEF, THE. 1899. Thu. $.50 newsstand; $18/yr. local; $24/yr. elsewhere. 401 E. Commercial St., Miami, TX 79059-0396. TEL 806-868-2521; FAX 806-868-5381. **Owner(s):** Valda G. Traughber, P.O. Box 396, Miami, TX 79059-0396. TEL 806-868-2521; FAX 806-868-5381; Clarence L. Traughber, P.O. Box 396, Miami, TX 79059-0396. TEL 806-868-2521; FAX 806-868-5381; Ed. Valda G. Traughber; Pub. C.L. Traughber; adv. contact: C.L. Traughber. bk.rev.; pub. size: tabloid; circ. 550(paid).

MIDLOTHIAN

US

MIDLOTHIAN MIRROR. 1882. Thu. $.25 newsstand; $12/yr. in cy.; $14/yr. in state; $17/yr. out of state. 214 W. Ave. F, Midlothian, TX 76065. TEL 214-775-3322. **Owner(s):** Midlothian Mirror, 214 W. Ave. F, Midlothian, TX 76065. TEL 214-775-3322; Pub. Debbie Garvin; adv.; pub. size: standard.

MONAHANS

US

MONAHANS NEWS. 1931. Thu. $25/yr. in cy.; $36/yr. in surrounding cys.; $58/yr. out of area. 107 W. Second, Monahans, TX 79756. TEL 915-943-4313; FAX 915-943-4314. **Owner(s):** Ward Newspapers, Inc., 107 W. Second, Monahans, TX 79756; Pub. Steve Paterson; adv.; photos; pub. size: broadsheet; circ. 3,400(paid).

MOODY
US
MOODY COURIER, THE. 1890. Thu. $.35 newsstand; $14/yr. in cy.; $17/yr. out of cy.; $17/yr. out of state. 827 S. Hwy. 317, Moody, TX 76557. TEL 817-853-2801; FAX 817-754-3541. **Owner(s):** Bill Foster, P.O. Box 3280, Waco, TX 76707. TEL 817-754-3511; FAX 817-754-3541; Ed. Bill Foster; Pub. Bill Foster; adv.: $3.50/SAU. photos; bk.rev.; pub. size: broadsheet; circ. 900(paid).

MUNDAY
US ISSN 8750-6750
MUNDAY COURIER, THE. 1971. Wed. $.50 newsstand; $15/yr. in cy.; $20/yr. out of cy. 111 E. B St., Munday, TX 76371-0130. TEL 817-422-4314; FAX 817-422-4314. **Owner(s):** Munday Courier, The, 111 E. B St., Munday, TX 76371. TEL 817-422-4314; FAX 817-422-4314; Ed. Michael L. Waggoner; Pub. Michael L. Waggoner; adv.; photos; pub. size: broadsheet; circ. 1,340(free & paid).

NAVASOTA
US
NAVASOTA EXAMINER REVIEW. 1894. Thu. $.50 newsstand; $20/yr. in cy.; $23/yr. in state; $27/yr. out of state. 115 Railroad St., Navasota, TX 77868. TEL 409-825-6484; FAX 409-825-2230. **Owner(s):** Whitten & Son, Inc., P.O. Box 751, Navasota, TX 77868. TEL 409-825-6484; FAX 409-825-2230; Ed. Clark Whitten; Pub. Daphne Kopycinski; adv. contact: Daphne Kopycinski. photos; pub. size: broadsheet; circ. 5,602(free & paid).

NEDERLAND
US
MIDCOUNTY CHRONICLE. 1931. Wed. free; $26/yr. mailed. 2112 Nederland Ave., Nederland, TX 77627. TEL 409-722-0479; FAX 409-729-7626. **Owner(s):** Hearst Corp., 959 Eighth Ave., New York, NY 10019. TEL 212-262-5700; Ed. Regina Throop; Pub. John Butters; adv.: $8.70/SAU. pub. size: standard; circ. 25,000(controlled & free).

NEW ULM
US
NEW ULM ENTERPRISE. 1910. Thu. $.50 newsstand; $16/yr. 200 Hwy. 109, S., New Ulm, TX 78950-0128. TEL 409-992-3351. **Owner(s):** Raymond L. Dungen, Jr., P.O. Box 128, New Ulm, TX 78950-0128. TEL 409-992-3351; Ed. Raymond L. Dungen, Jr. adv.; pub. size: standard; circ. 1,475(paid).

OLNEY
US
OLNEY ENTERPRISE, THE. 1910. Thu. $.25 newsstand; $11/yr. 213 E. Main St., Olney, TX 76374. **Owner(s):** David H. Penn, 213 E. Main St., Olney, TX 76374. TEL 817-564-5558; Pub. David H. Penn; adv.; photos; pub. size: broadsheet; circ. 2,518(paid).

PALACIOS
US
PALACIOS BEACON. 1906. Wed. $.50 newsstand; $18/yr. in cy.; $24/yr. out of cy. 453 Commerce St., Palacios, TX 77465. TEL 512-972-3009; FAX 512-972-2610; E-mail: nickwest@sat.net. **Owner(s):** Toney Publishing, 113 E. Bernard, West Columbia, TX 77486. TEL 409-345-3128; Ed. Nick West; Pub. Nick West; adv. contact: Lucy White. photos; bk.rev.; pub. size: standard; circ. 1,700(paid).

PEARLAND
US
FRIENDSWOOD & PEARLAND REPORTER NEWS. 1970. Wed. $.50 newsstand; $25/yr. 2404 S. Park, Pearland, TX 77581. TEL 713-485-7501; FAX 713-485-6397. **Owner(s):** Randy & Laura Emmons, 2404 S. Park, Pearland, TX 77581. TEL 713-485-7501; FAX 713-485-6397; Ed. Laura Emmons; Pub. Laura Emmons; adv. contact: Pam Walston. photos; pub. size: broadsheet; circ. 12,500(free & paid).
Formerly: Friendswood Reporter News.

PITTSBURG
US
PITTSBURG GAZETTE. 1884. Thu. $.50 newsstand; $26/yr. in cy.; $32/yr. out of cy.; $40/yr. out of state. 112 Quitman St., Pittsburg, TX 75686. TEL 903-856-6629; FAX 903-856-0510. **Owner(s):** Westward Communications, Inc., 5005 LBJ Fwy., Ste. 1048, Dallas, TX 75244; Ed. Susan Taft; Pub. Debbie Knox; adv. contact: Debbie Malone. photos; bk.rev.; pub. size: standard; circ. 3,150(paid).

PLEASANTON
US
PLEASANTON EXPRESS. 1909. Wed. $.50 newsstand; $23/yr. in cy.; $28/yr. out of cy; $33/yr. out of state; $20/yr. senior citizens. 114 Goodwin, Pleasanton, TX 78064. TEL 210-281-2341; FAX 210-569-6100. **Owner(s):** Wilkerson Publishing Co., 89 Pulliam, Pleasanton, TX 78064; Ed. David B. Wilkerson. adv. contact: Mary Gallegos. pub. size: broadsheet; circ. 7,800(paid).

PORT ISABEL
US
PORT ISABEL-SOUTH PADRE ITEM PRESS. 1950. s-w.: Mon. & Thu. $.50 newsstand; $22.50/yr. in cy.; $36/yr. out of cy. 101 Maxan, Port Isabel, TX 78578. TEL 210-943-5545; FAX 210-943-4782. **Owner(s):** New Horizon Publishers, Inc., P.O. Box 1791, San Benito, TX 78586. TEL 210-399-2436; FAX 210-233-9604; Ed. Elizabeth Sweeten; Pub. Ben Brooks; adv.; pub. size: broadsheet; circ. 4,500(free & paid).
Formerly: Port Isabel-South Padre Press.

PORTLAND
US
PORTLAND NEWS. Thu. $.50 newsstand; $23.50/yr. in cy.; $29.60/yr. out of cy.; $30.60/yr. out of state. 101 Cedar Pl., Ste. G, Portland, TX 78374. TEL 512-643-1566; FAX 512-643-1567. **Owner(s):** San Patricio Publishing Co., Inc., P.O. Drawer B, Sinton, TX 78387. TEL 512-364-1270; Ed. Cindi Wright; Pub. John Tracy; adv.; pub. size: broadsheet; circ. 2,500(paid).

PORT LAVACA
US
PORT LAVACA WAVE. 1890. s-w.: Wed. & Sat. $.50 newsstand; $30/yr. in cy.; $60/yr. out of cy. 107 E. Austin, Port Lavaca, TX 77979-0088. TEL 512-552-9788; FAX 512-552-3108. **Owner(s):** Port Lavaca Wave, Inc., P.O. Box 88, Port Lavaca, TX 77979-0088. TEL 512-552-9788; FAX 512-552-3108; Ed. Steve Bales; Pub. Steve Bales; adv. contact: Cathy Buehring. adv.: $6.50/SAU. photos; bk.rev.; pub. size: broadsheet; circ. 8,000(free & paid).

POTTSBORO
US
POTTSBORO PRESS. 1984. Thu. $15/yr. in cy.; $20/yr. in state; $25/yr. out of state. P.O. Box 837, Pottsboro, TX 75076-0837. TEL 903-786-4051; FAX 903-786-9336. **Owner(s):** Pottsboro Press, P.O. Box 837, Pottsboro, TX 75076-0837. TEL 903-786-4051; Ed. Lori Conary; Pub. Lori Conary; bk.rev.; pub. size: standard; circ. 1,355(paid).

QUITMAN
US
WOOD COUNTY DEMOCRAT. 1893. Wed. $.50 newsstand; $24.50/yr. in cy.; $34/yr. in state; $39/yr. out of state. 111 W. Lipscomb, Quitman, TX 75783. TEL 903-763-4522; FAX 903-763-2313. **Owner(s):** Westward Communications, Inc., 5005 LBJ Fwy., Ste. 1040, Dallas, TX 25244. TEL 214-450-1717; Ed. Larry Tucker; Pub. Nell French; adv. contact: Monte Coleman. pub. size: broadsheet; circ. 3,200(paid).

RANGER
US
RANGER TIMES. 1919. s-w.: Sun. & Thu. $.50 newsstand; $22/yr. in cy.; $28/yr. out of cy.; $40/yr. out of state. 211 Elm St., Ranger, TX 76470. TEL 817-647-1101; FAX 817-629-2092. **Owner(s):** H.V. O'Brien, 1201 S. Seaman, Eastland, TX 76448. TEL 817-629-2413; Ed. Sheila McCoy; Pub. H.V. O'Brien; adv. contact: Sheila McCoy. photos; bk.rev.; pub. size: broadsheet; circ. 1,200(paid); Sun. 1,200(paid).

RICHARDSON
US ISSN 1045-4004
RICHARDSON NEWS. 1958. s-w.: Thu. & Sun. $.50 newsstand; $36/yr. carrier. 409 Belle Grove, Richardson, TX 75080. TEL 214-234-3198; FAX 214-234-6906. **Owner(s):** Dallas-Fort Worth Suburban Newspapers, Inc, 1000 Ave. H, E., Arlington, TX 76011. TEL 817-695-0500; Ed. Lois Wetzel Brown; Pub. Randy Chandler; adv. contact: Mary Bell. pub. size: broadsheet; circ. 10,000(paid); Sun. 10,000(paid).
Formerly: Richardson Daily News.

RISING STAR
US
RISING STAR, THE. 1892. Thu. $.50 newsstand; $1.25/mo.; $7.50/6 mos.; $15/yr. local; $18/yr. Texas cy.; $21/yr. out of state. 105 N. Main St., Rising Star, TX 76471. TEL 817-643-4141; FAX 817-629-2029. **Owner(s):** Eastland County Newspapers, Inc., P.O. Box 29, Eastland, TX 76448. TEL 817-629-1707; Ed. Elaine Coleman; Pub. H.V. O'Brien; adv.; photos; bk.rev.; pub. size: standard; circ. 747(free & paid).

ROBSTOWN

NUECES COUNTY RECORD STAR. 1919. Thu. $25.50/yr. 104 N. Fifth St., Robstown, TX 78380. TEL 512-387-4511. **Owner(s):** Keach & Co., Inc., P.O. Box 1192, Robstown, TX 78380. TEL 512-387-4511; FAX 512-767-8827; Ed. Sam Keach; Pub. Sam Keach; adv. contact: Darrell Keach. photos; bk.rev.; pub. size: broadsheet; circ. 7,000(paid).

ROCKDALE

ROCKDALE REPORTER. 1873. Thu. $.50 newsstand; $22/yr. local; $26/yr. in state; $32/yr. out of state. 221-225 E. Cameron, Rockdale, TX 76567. TEL 512-446-5838; FAX 512-446-5317. **Owner(s):** J.W. Cooke, P.O. Box 552, Rockdale, TX 76567-0552. TEL 512-446-5838; FAX 512-446-5317; Ed. J.W. Cooke; Pub. J.W. Cooke; adv. contact: Judy Shelander. adv.: $5/SAU. pub. size: broadsheet; circ. 4,564(paid).

ROSENBERG

FORT BEND MIRROR. 1956. Thu. $.25 newsstand; $15/yr. 1902 Fourth St., Rosenberg, TX 77471. TEL 281-242-9104; FAX 281-342-3219. **Owner(s):** Hartman Newspapers, Inc., P.O. Box 1088, Rosenberg, TX 77471. TEL 281-342-8691; Ed. Robert Haenel; Pub. Clyde King; pub. size: broadsheet; circ. 3,000(paid).

ROUND ROCK

US   ISSN 0164-9124
ROUND ROCK LEADER. 1876. s-w.: Mon. & Thu. $.50 newsstand; $11.50/3 mos.; $29.50/yr. 105 S. Blair, Round Rock, TX 78664. TEL 512-255-5827; FAX 512-255-3733; E-mail: rrtxleader@aol.com. **Owner(s):** Todd Publications, Inc., 2304 Hancock Dr., Austin, TX 78756. TEL 512-451-3900; FAX 512-450-1506; Ed. Will Hampton; Pub. Ken Long; adv. contact: Bobby Seiferman. photos; pub. size: broadsheet; circ. 5,719(paid).

SAN ANTONIO

FORT SAN ANTONIO NEWS LEADER. Thu. free. 7137 Military Dr., W., San Antonio, TX 78227. TEL 210-675-4500; FAX 210-675-4597. **Owner(s):** Prime Time, Inc., 7137 Military Dr., W., San Antonio, TX 78227. TEL 210-675-4500; FAX 210-675-4577; Ed. Gary Gossett; Pub. Gregg Rosenfield; adv.; photos; pub. size: tabloid; circ. 10,000(free).

US
KELLY OBSERVER. Thu. free. 7137 Military Dr., W., San Antonio, TX 78227. TEL 210-675-4500; FAX 210-675-4577. **Owner(s):** Prime Time, Inc., 7137 Military Dr., W., San Antonio, TX 78227. TEL 210-675-4500; FAX 210-675-4577; Ed. Ross Day; Pub. Gregg Rosenfield; adv.; photos; pub. size: tabloid; circ. 18,000(free).

US
LACKLAND TALE SPINNER. Fri. free. 7137 Military Dr., W., San Antonio, TX 00007. TEL 210-675-4500; FAX 210-675-4577. **Owner(s):** Prime Time, Inc., 7137 Military Dr., W., San Antonio, TX 78227. TEL 210-675-4500; Ed. Wayne Bryant; Pub. Gregg Rosenfield; adv.; photos; bk.rev.; pub. size: tabloid; circ. 20,000(free).

US
METROCOM HERALD, THE. Thu. free. 7137 Military Dr., W., San Antonio, TX 78227. TEL 210-675-4500; FAX 210-675-4577. **Owner(s):** Prime Time, Inc., 7137 Military Dr., W., San Antonio, TX 78227. TEL 210-675-4500; FAX 210-675-4577; Ed. Gary Gossett; Pub. Kim Sipper; adv.; photos; pub. size: tabloid; circ. 33,600(free).

US
NORTH SAN ANTONIO TIMES. Thu. free; $.50 newsstand. 8603 Botts Ln., San Antonio, TX 78217. TEL 210-828-3321; FAX 210-828-3787; E-mail: shenry@onr.com; URL: http://www.onr.com/usatimes. **Owner(s):** Prime Time, Inc., 8603 Botts Ln., San Antonio, TX 78217. TEL 210-828-3321; Ed. Steve Henry; Pub. Robert Jones; adv. contact: Linda Hardin. photos; bk.rev.; pub. size: broadsheet; circ. 10,000.

US
NORTHSIDE RECORDER TIMES, THE. 1971. Thu. free; $.50 newsstand. 8603 Botts Ln., San Antonio, TX 78217. TEL 210-828-3321; FAX 210-828-3787; E-mail: shenry@onr.com; URL: http://www.onr.com/usatimes. **Owner(s):** Prime Time, Inc., 8603 Botts Ln., San Antonio, TX 78217. TEL 512-828-3321; Ed. Steve Henry; Pub. Robert Jones; adv. contact: Linda Hardin. photos; bk.rev.; pub. size: broadsheet; circ. 10,000(free & paid).
Formerly: Recorder Times, The.

US
SOUTHSIDE REPORTER. Thu. free; $.50 newsstand. 2203 S. Hackberry, San Antonio, TX 78210. TEL 210-534-8848; FAX 210-532-9329. **Owner(s):** Prime Time, Inc., 6222 IH-10 N.W., Ste. 101, San Antonio, TX 78201. TEL 210-736-4450; Ed. Theresa Rabe; Pub. Paul Davis; adv.; photos; pub. size: tabloid; circ. 50,000(free & paid).

SAN AUGUSTINE

SAN AUGUSTINE TRIBUNE. 1909. Thu. $.25 newsstand; $6/yr. in cy.; $9/yr. out of cy. 315 W. Columbia St., San Augustine, TX 75972. TEL 409-275-2181. **Owner(s):** Arlan Hays, P.O. Box M, San Augustine, TX 75972. TEL 409-275-2181; Ed. Arlan Hays; Pub. Arlan Hays; adv.: $5/SAU. photos; bk.rev.; pub. size: standard; circ. 5,300(paid).

SAN BENITO

SAN BENITO NEWS. 1946. s-w.: Wed. & Sun. $.50 newsstand; $32/yr. in cy. mailed; $38/yr. out of cy. mailed; $30/yr. carrier. 356 N. Sam Houston, San Benito, TX 78586. TEL 210-399-2436; FAX 210-233-9604. **Owner(s):** New Horizon Publishers, Inc., P.O. Box 1791, San Benito, TX 78586. TEL 512-399-2436; Ed. Martha McClain; Pub. Jim Elam; adv.: $5/SAU. photos; bk.rev.; pub. size: broadsheet; circ. 5,100(paid).

SANTA FE

BULLETIN, THE. 1969. Wed. free in area; $80/yr. mailed elsewhere. 13201 Hwy. 6, Santa Fe, TX 77510. TEL 409-925-2517; FAX 409-925-1399. **Owner(s):** Santa Fe Newspapers, Inc., Drawer 730, Santa Fe, TX 77510. TEL 409-925-2517; FAX 409-925-1399; Ed. Harry Monych; Pub. Harry Monych; adv.; photos; pub. size: broadsheet; circ. 9,100(free & paid).

SEALY

SEALY NEWS. 1887. s-w.: Tue. & Fri. $.50 newsstand; $28/yr. local; $35/yr. in state; $60/yr. out of state. 208 Schmidt Rd., Sealy, TX 77474-2390. TEL 409-885-3562; FAX 409-885-3564; E-mail: sealynew@phoenix.net. **Owner(s):** Sealy Publications, Inc., P.O. Box 480, Sealy, TX 77474. TEL 409-885-3562; Ed. Wilma Petrusek; Pub. Michelle Novicke; adv. contact: Joanie Griffin. pub. size: broadsheet; circ. 5,500(paid).

SEYMOUR

BAYLOR COUNTY BANNER. 1895. Thu. $.50 newsstand; $15/yr. in cy.; $18/yr. out of cy.; $20/yr. out of state. 109 E. Morris St., Seymour, TX 76380-0912. TEL 817-888-2616; FAX 817-888-3610. **Owner(s):** Earl Gwinn, 109 E. Morris, P.O. Box 912, Seymour, TX 76380-0912. TEL 817-888-2616; FAX 817-888-3610; Ed. Earl Gwinn; Pub. Earl Gwinn; adv. contact: Lita Slaggle. adv.: $3.30/SAU. photos; bk.rev.; pub. size: standard; circ. 2,700(paid).

SILSBEE

SILSBEE BEE. 1919. Thu. $.35 newsstand; $12/yr. local; $17.50/yr. elsewhere. 410 Hwy. 96, S., Silsbee, TX 77656. TEL 409-385-5278; FAX 409-385-5270. **Owner(s):** Danny Reneau, P.O. Box 547, Silsbee, TX 77656. TEL 409-385-2151; Ed. Sherri Watson; Pub. Danny Reneau; adv. contact: Jan Reneau. pub. size: broadsheet; circ. 6,500(paid).

SINTON

ODEM-EDROY TIMES. 1948. Thu. $.40 newsstand; $23.50/yr. 117 S. Rachal St., Sinton, TX 78387. TEL 512-364-1270; FAX 512-364-3833. **Owner(s):** San Patricio Publishing Co., Inc., P.O. Drawer B, Sinton, TX 78387. TEL 512-364-1270; Ed. Jim McElhaney; Pub. Helen S. Tracy; adv. contact: Johnnie Sue Littleton. pub. size: broadsheet; circ. 650(paid).

US
SAN PATRICIO COUNTY NEWS. 1908. Wed. $.50 newsstand; $23.50/yr. 117 S. Rachal St., Sinton, TX 78387. TEL 512-364-1270; FAX 512-364-3833. **Owner(s):** San Patricio Publishing Co., Inc., P.O. Drawer B, Sinton, TX 78387. TEL 512-364-1270; Ed. James F. Tracy, Jr. adv.; pub. size: broadsheet; circ. 2,500(paid).

WEEKLY NEWSPAPERS

WEST COLUMBIA, TX 10747

SOUTH PADRE ISLAND

US

COASTAL CURRENT, THE. 1990. Fri. free. 1004 Padre Blvd., South Padre Island, TX 78597. TEL 210-761-9341; FAX 210-761-1436. **Owner(s):** Jim Goller, 116 W. Esperanza, South Padre Island, TX 78597. TEL 210-761-2421; FAX 210-761-9436; Jonathan Deeley, 203 Huisache, South Padre Island, TX. TEL 210-761-9417; FAX 210-761-1436; Ed. Lori Todd; Pub. Jonathan Deeley; adv. contact: Stan Hulse. photos; bk.rev.; pub. size: tabloid; circ. 10,000(controlled & free).

SPEARMAN

US

HANSFORD COUNTY REPORTER-STATESMAN. 1907. Thu. $.50 newsstand; $20/yr. in cy.; $25/yr. out of cy. 213 Main St., Spearman, TX 79081. TEL 806-659-3434; FAX 806-659-3368. **Owner(s):** Gary Smith, 213 Main St., Sperrman, TX 79081. TEL 806-659-3434; Ed. Catherine Smith; Pub. Gary Smith; adv. contact: Debra McNeely. pub. size: standard; circ. 1,500(paid).

SPRINGTOWN

US

SPRINGTOWN EPIGRAPH, THE. Thu. $.50 newsstand. 109 N. First St., Springtown, TX 76082. TEL 817-220-7217; FAX 817-238-9617. **Owner(s):** Azle News, 1121 S.E. Parkway, Azle, TX 76020. TEL 817-237-1184; Ed. Bob Buckel; Pub. Bob Buckel; adv.; photos; pub. size: broadsheet; circ. 1,884(free & paid).

STAMFORD

US

STAMFORD AMERICAN. 1922. Thu. $.50 newsstand; $15/yr. in cy.; $17/yr. out of cy.; $20/yr. out of state. 112 E. Hamilton, Stamford, TX 79553. TEL 915-773-3621; FAX 915-773-3622. **Owner(s):** Becky Alambar, P.O. Box 1207, Stamford, TX 79553. TEL 915-773-3621; FAX 915-773-3622; Ed. Michelle Sanchez. adv. contact: Timmy Sanchez. pub. size: standard; circ. 2,500(paid).

SUGAR LAND

US

FORT BEND SUN. 1967. Thu. $.35 newsstand; free home deliv.; $10/mo. local mailed. 13735 Southwest Fwy., Sugar Land, TX 77478. TEL 713-242-1812; FAX 713-242-1891. **Owner(s):** Houston Community Newspapers, Inc., 1136 Sheldon Rd., Channelview, TX 77530; Ed. Trinth T. Le; Pub. Chris Colihan; adv.; pub. size: broadsheet; circ. 4,200(free & paid).

US

SOUTHWEST SUN. 1967. Thu. free newsstand; $10/mo. carrier. 13735 Southwest Fwy., Sugar Land, TX 77478. TEL 713-242-1812; FAX 713-242-1891. **Owner(s):** Houston Community Newspapers, Inc., 1136 Sheldon Rd., Channelview, TX 72530. TEL 713-452-0530; Ed. Trinh Le. adv.; pub. size: broadsheet; circ. 29,000(free & paid).
Formerly: Southwest Advocate.

TAFT

US

TAFT TRIBUNE. 1922. Wed. $.50 newsstand; $23.50/yr. in cy.; $29.60/out of cy.; $30.60/yr. out of state. 325 Green Ave., Taft, TX 78390. TEL 512-528-2515; FAX 512-364-3833. **Owner(s):** San Patricio Publishing Co., Inc., P.O. Drawer B, Sinton, TX 78387. TEL 512-364-1270; Ed. Belinda Tracy; Pub. John Henry Tracy; adv. contact: Belinda Tracy. pub. size: broadsheet; circ. 1,200(paid).

TRENTON

US

TRENTON TRIBUNE. 1909. Thu. $.25 newsstand; $18-$23/yr. 115 Hamilton, Trenton, TX 75490-0043. TEL 903-989-2325. **Owner(s):** Tom M. Holmes, 115 Hamilton, Trenton, TX 75490-0043. TEL 903-989-2325; Pub. Tom M. Holmes; adv.; pub. size: standard; circ. 1,100(paid).

UVALDE

US

UVALDE LEADER-NEWS. 1879. s-w.: Thu. & Sun. $30/yr. in cy.; $32.50/yr. out of cy.; $49/yr. out of state. 110 N. East St., Uvalde, TX 78801. TEL 210-278-3335; FAX 210-278-9191. **Owner(s):** Craig K. Garnett, P.O. Box 740, Uvalde, TX 78802. TEL 210-278-3335; Ed. Bill Cockerill; Pub. Craig K. Garnett; adv. contact: Steve Balke. pub. size: broadsheet; circ. 6,000(paid); Sun. 6,500(paid).

VAN HORN

US

VAN HORN ADVOCATE. 1910. Thu. $.50 newsstand; $22/yr. 701 W. Broadway, Van Horn, TX 79855-0008. TEL 915-283-2003; FAX 915-283-7334. **Owner(s):** Larry Simpson, P.O. Box 8, Van Horn, TX 79855. TEL 915-283-2003; FAX 915-283-7334; Pub. Larry Simpson; adv.; pub. size: standard.

VEGA

US

VEGA ENTERPRISE, THE. Thu. $.25 newsstand; $15/yr. 116 S. Main St., Vega, TX 79092. TEL 806-267-2230; FAX 806-267-2889. **Owner(s):** Quincy Taylor, 116 S. Main St., Vega, TX 79092; Pub. Quincy Taylor; adv.; photos; pub. size: standard.

VIDOR

US

VIDORIAN, THE. 1959. s-w.: Wed. & Fri. $.25 newsstand; $12.50/yr. 450 W. Bolivar, Vidor, TX 77662. TEL 409-769-5428; FAX 409-769-2600. **Owner(s):** A. Randall Luker, 450 W. Bolivar, Vidor, TX 77662. TEL 409-769-5428; FAX 409-769-2600; Ed. A. Randall Luker; Pub. A. Merle Luker; adv. contact: Adair Luker. bk.rev.; pub. size: broadsheet; circ. 12,700(free & paid).

WACO

US

WACO CITIZEN, THE. 1946. s-w.: Wed. & Sun. $.25 newsstand; $26/yr. in cy.; $36/yr. out of cy. 1020 N. 25th St., Waco, TX 76707. TEL 817-754-3511; FAX 817-754-3541. **Owner(s):** Citizen Newspapers, Inc., 1020 N. 25th St., Waco, TX 76700. TEL 817-754-3511; FAX 817-754-3541; Pub. Bill C. Foster; adv. contact: Bill C. Foster. photos; bk.rev.; pub. size: broadsheet; circ. 3,700(paid).

WALLIS

US

WALLIS NEWS-REVIEW. Thu. $.50 newsstand; $14/yr.; $16/yr. out of state. 6109 Commerce, Wallis, TX 77485. TEL 409-478-6412; FAX 406-478-6412. **Owner(s):** Raymond L. Dungen, Jr., P.O. Box 128, New Ulm, TX 78950-0128. TEL 409-992-3351; Ed. Lucille Jemela. pub. size: broadsheet; circ. 1,250(paid).

WEIMAR

US ISSN 1071-0329

WEIMAR MERCURY. 1888. Thu. $.50 newsstand; $18/yr. in cy.; $19/yr. out of cy.; $20/yr. out of state. 200 W. Main, Weimar, TX 78962. TEL 409-725-9595; FAX 409-725-9051. **Owner(s):** Weimer Mercury, 200 W. Main, Weimer, TX 78962. TEL 409-725-9595; Ed. Bruce Beal; Pub. Bruce Beal; pub. size: standard; circ. 3,500(paid).

WESLACO

US

MID VALLEY TOWN CRIER. 1967. s-w.: Wed. & Sat. free newsstand & home deliv. 401 S. Iowa, Weslaco, TX 78596. TEL 210-969-2543; FAX 210-968-0855. **Owner(s):** P.T.S., Inc., Tuscaloosa, AL 35401; Ed. Charles Robinson; Pub. James Beaver; adv.; pub. size: broadsheet; circ. 23,500(free).

WEST

US

WEST NEWS. 1890. Thu. $.35 newsstand; $21/yr. 214 W. Oak, West, TX 76691. TEL 817-826-3718. **Owner(s):** Cechoslovak Publishing Co., P.O. Box 38, West, TX 76691. TEL 817-826-3718; Ed. Larry Knapek; Pub. Linn Pescaia; adv. contact: Sue Pescaia. adv.: $4/SAU. bk.rev.; pub. size: broadsheet; circ. 3,100(paid).

WEST COLUMBIA

US

GULF COAST TRIBUNE, THE. 1962. w. $.35 newsstand; $25/yr. 113 E. Bemord St., West Columbia, TX 77486. TEL 409-345-3127. **Owner(s):** David Toney, P.O. Box 488, West Columbia, TX 77486. TEL 409-345-3127; Ed. Richard Kotrla; Pub. David Toney; adv. contact: Jeri Mager. pub. size: broadsheet; circ. 1,400(paid).

US

WEST COLUMBIA BRAZORIA COUNTY NEWS. 1962. Thu. $.35 newsstand; $40/yr. 113 E. Bernard St., West Columbia, TX 77486. TEL 713-345-3127. **Owner(s):** David Toney, P.O. Box 488, West Columbia, TX 77486; Ed. David Toney. adv.; photos; pub. size: broadsheet; circ. 10,300(free & paid).

WHARTON

WHARTON JOURNAL-SPECTATOR. 1888. s-w.: Wed. & Sat. $.50 newsstand; $30/yr. in cy.; $40/yr. in state; $45/yr. out of state. 115 W. Burleson St., Wharton, TX 77488. TEL 409-532-8840; FAX 409-532-8845. **Owner(s):** River Publishers, Inc., P.O. Box 111, Wharton, TX 77488. TEL 713-532-8840; FAX 713-532-8845; Ed. Ron Sanders. adv. contact: Missy Justice. pub. size: broadsheet; circ. 5,000(paid).

WHITE OAK

US   ISSN 1053-1513
WHITE OAK INDEPENDENT. 1990. Thu. $.50 newsstand; $20/yr. 201-B Hwy. 80, E., White Oak, TX 75693. TEL 903-759-4410; FAX 903-759-8100; E-mail: newman@rapidramp.com. **Owner(s):** Jeff & Winnie Newman, 201-B Hwy. 80, E., White Oak, TX 75693. TEL 903-759-4410; FAX 903-759-8100; Ed. Jeff Newman; Pub. Jeff Newman; adv.; photos; pub. size: broadsheet; circ. 1,200(paid).

WHITEWRIGHT

US   ISSN 0886-4322
WHITEWRIGHT SUN, THE. 1884. Thu. $.50 newsstand; $15/yr. in cy.; $18/yr. out of cy.; $22/yr. out of state. 121 Grand Ave., Whitewright, TX 75491. TEL 903-364-2276; FAX 903-364-2276. **Owner(s):** Dennis & Clara Combs, 121 Grand Ave., Whitewright, TX 75491. TEL 903-364-2276; Ed. Clara Combs; Pub. Clara Combs; adv.; photos; pub. size: standard; circ. 1,000(paid).

WIMBERLEY

US
WIMBERLEY VALLEY-NEWS. 1985. Thu. free; $20/yr. out of area. P.O. Box 989, Wimberley, TX 78676. TEL 512-858-7893; FAX 512-858-4828. **Owner(s):** Dale Roberson, P.O. Box 989, Wimberley, TX 78676. TEL 512-858-7893; FAX 512-858-4828; Ed. Dale Roberson; Pub. Dale Roberson; adv. contact: Joyce Kovacs. photos; pub. size: tabloid; circ. 1,900(controlled & paid).

WINNSBORO

US
WINNSBORO NEWS. 1907. Thu. $18/yr. in cy.; $25/yr. elsewhere. 105 E. Locust, Winnsboro, TX 75494. TEL 903-342-5247. **Owner(s):** Pen-Wheel Press, P.O. Box 87, Winnsboro, TX 75494. TEL 903-342-5247; Ed. Karen W. Pendergast; Pub. Thomas F. Pendergast; adv. contact: Linda Henry. photos; pub. size: standard; circ. 4,150(paid).

WOODVILLE

US   ISSN 1043-0350
TYLER COUNTY BOOSTER. 1930. Wed. $.50 newsstand; $13.75/yr. local. 205 W. Bluff St., Woodville, TX 75979. TEL 409-283-2516; FAX 409-283-2560. **Owner(s):** Polk County Publishing Co., P.O. Box 1276, Livingston, TX 77351. TEL 409-327-4357; FAX 409-327-7156; Ed. Gregory Peak; Pub. Alvin Holley; adv. contact: John Morrison. photos; pub. size: broadsheet; circ. 4,550(free & paid).
Formerly: Woodville Tyler County Booster.

WYLIE

US
WYLIE NEWS, THE. 1947. Wed. $.50 newsstand; $15/yr. local; $17/yr. out of cy. 113 W. Oak, Wylie, TX 75098. TEL 972-442-5515; FAX 972-442-4318. **Owner(s):** C & S Media, Inc., P.O. Box 369, Wylie, TX 75098. TEL 214-442-5515; Ed. Margaret Cook; Pub. Chad B. Engbrock; adv. contact: Chad B. Engbrock. photos; bk.rev.; pub. size: broadsheet; circ. 3,950(paid).

YOAKUM

US
YOAKUM HERALD-TIMES. 1892. Wed. $.50 newsstand; 18.50/yr. in cy.; $25/yr. out of cy.; $30/yr. elsewhere. 312 Lott St., Yoakum, TX 77995. TEL 512-293-2335; FAX 512-293-5267. **Owner(s):** L.M. Preuss, III, P.O. Box 798, Yoakum, TX 77995. TEL 512-293-2335; Ed. James Johnson; Pub. L.M. Preuss, III; adv. contact: Anne Kubicek. photos; pub. size: broadsheet; circ. 3,000(paid).
Formerly: Yoakum Herald-Times & Four Star Reporter.

UTAH

AMERICAN FORK

US
CITIZEN. 1903. Wed. $.50 newsstand; $24/yr. in cy.; $30/yr. out of cy. 59 W. Main St., American Fork, UT 84003-0007. TEL 801-756-7669; FAX 801-756-5274; E-mail: newtah@aol.com. **Owner(s):** Newtah News Group, P.O. Box 7, American Fork, UT 84003. TEL 801-756-7669; FAX 801-756-5274; Ed. Marc Haddock; Pub. Brett Bezzant; adv. contact: Tom Hollingsworth. pub. size: broadsheet; circ. 4,600(paid).
Formerly: American Fork Citizen.

US
LEHI FREE PRESS. 1903. Wed. $.50 newsstand; $24/yr. in cy.; $30/yr. out of cy. 59 W. Main St., American Fork, UT 84003. TEL 801-756-7669; FAX 801-756-5274. **Owner(s):** Newtah News Group, P.O. Box 7, American Fork, UT 84003. TEL 801-756-7669; FAX 801-756-5274; Ed. Marc Haddock; Pub. Brett Bezzant; adv. contact: Tom Hollingsworth. adv.: $11/SAU. pub. size: broadsheet; circ. 2,800(paid).

US
NORTH UTAH COUNTY SHOPPER. Wed. free. 59 W. Main St., American Fork, UT 84003. TEL 801-756-7669; FAX 801-756-5274. **Owner(s):** Newtah News Group, P.O. Box 7, American Fork, UT 84003. TEL 801-756-7669; FAX 801-756-5274; Ed. Mark Haddock; Pub. Brett Bezzant; adv. contact: Tom Hollingsworth. adv.: $11/SAU. pub. size: broadsheet; circ. 11,400(free).

US
PLEASANT GROVE REVIEW. 1905. Wed. $.50 newsstand; $24/yr. in cy.; $30/yr. out of cy. 59 W. Main St., American Fork, UT 84003. TEL 801-756-7669; FAX 801-756-5274. **Owner(s):** Newtah News Group, P.O. Box 7, American Fork, UT 84003. TEL 801-756-7669; FAX 801-756-5274; Ed. Marc Haddock; Pub. Brett Bezzant; adv. contact: Tom Hollingsworth. adv.: $11/SAU. pub. size: broadsheet; circ. 3,200(paid).

BOUNTIFUL

US   ISSN 1061-1223
DAVIS COUNTY CLIPPER. 1891. s-w.: Tue. & Fri. $.50 newsstand; $25/yr. in cy.; $35/yr. out of cy. 1370 S. 500 W., Bountiful, UT 84010. TEL 801-295-2251; FAX 801-295-3044. **Owner(s):** Gail Stahle, 125 W. First St., Bountiful, UT 84010. TEL 801-295-2001; Ed. Judy Jensen; Pub. Gail Stahle; adv.; photos; bk.rev.; pub. size: standard; circ. 30,000(free & paid).

US
EAGLE NEWS. 1891. s-w.: Tue. & Fri. $.50 newsstand; $25/yr. in cy.; $35/yr. out of cy. 1370 S. 500 W., Bountiful, UT 84010. TEL 801-295-2251; FAX 801-295-3044. **Owner(s):** Gail Stahle, 125 W. First St., Bountiful, UT 84010. TEL 801-295-2001; Ed. Darren Tucker; Pub. Gail Stahle; adv.; photos; bk.rev.; pub. size: standard; circ. 30,000(free & paid).

US
TODAY'S NEWS. 1891. s-w.: Tue. & Fri. $.50 newsstand; $25/yr. in cy.; $35/yr. out of cy. 1370 S. 500 W., Bountiful, UT 84010. TEL 801-295-2251; FAX 801-295-3044. **Owner(s):** Gail Stahle, 125 W. First St., Bountiful, UT 84010. TEL 801-295-2001; Ed. Judy Jensen; Pub. Gail Stahle; adv.; photos; bk.rev.; pub. size: standard; circ. 30,000(free & paid).

US
WEST VALLEY EAGLE. 1927. Thu. free newsstand; $1/mo. voluntary; $15/yr. mailed. 1370 S. Fifth W., Bountiful, UT 84010. TEL 801-292-1088; FAX 801-295-3044. **Owner(s):** Spectrum Press, Inc., 1370 S. Fifth W., Bountiful, UT 84010; Ed. Darren Tucker; Pub. Gail Stahle; pub. size: broadsheet; circ. 32,000(free & paid).
Formerly: West Valley View.

BRIGHAM CITY

US
BOX ELDER NEWS JOURNAL. 1896. Wed. $.50 newsstand; $25/yr. in cy.; $35/yr. out of cy. 55 S. 100 W., Brigham City, UT 84302. TEL 801-723-3471; FAX 801-723-5247. **Owner(s):** Box Elder News & Journal, Inc., P.O. Box 370, Brigham City, UT 84302. TEL 801-723-3471; FAX 801-723-5247; Ed. Sarah Yates; Pub. Charles C. Claybaugh; adv.; photos; pub. size: broadsheet; circ. 10,000(free & paid).

CASTLE DALE

US
EMERY COUNTY PROGRESS. Tue. $.50 newsstand; $21/yr. in cy.; $25/yr. out of cy. 190 E. Main St., Castle Dale, UT 84513. TEL 801-381-2431; FAX 801-381-5431; E-mail: progress@etv.net. **Owner(s):** Brehm Communications, Inc., P.O. Box 28429, San Diego, CA 92128. TEL 619-451-6200; Ed. Scott Niendorf; Pub. Kevin Ashby; adv.; photos; bk.rev.; pub. size: broadsheet; circ. 2,500(controlled).

DELTA

US
MILLARD COUNTY GAZETTE. 1978. Tue. $.25 newsstand; free in cy.; $1 out of cy. 175 N. 100 E., Delta, UT 84624. TEL 801-743-6983; FAX 801-864-4050. **Owner(s):** Dale Whipple, 250 W. 2855 S., Salt Lake City, UT 84115. TEL 801-486-8999; FAX 801-466-8806; pub. size: tabloid; circ. 5,000(free & paid).

WEEKLY NEWSPAPERS

MAGNA
US
MAGNA TIMES. Thu. $.50 newsstand; $15/yr. 8980 W. 2700 S., Magna, UT 84044. TEL 801-250-5656; FAX 801-250-5685. **Owner(s):** Howard Stahle, 8980 W. 2700 S., Magna, UT 84044. TEL 801-250-5656; Ed. Gary R. Blodgett; Pub. J. Howard Stahle; adv. contact: Bonnie Stahle. pub. size: tabloid; circ. 2,500(paid).

US
WEST VALLEY NEWS. Thu. free newsstand; $18/yr. 8980 W. 2700 S., Magna, UT 84044. TEL 801-250-5656. **Owner(s):** Howard H. Stahle, 8980 W. 2700 S., Magna, UT 84044. TEL 801-250-5656; Ed. Gary R. Blodgett; Pub. J. Howard Stahle; adv. contact: Bonnie Stahle. pub. size: tabloid; circ. 2,500(paid).

MT. PLEASANT
US
PYRAMID, THE. 1892. Wed. $.50 newsstand; $20/yr. in cy.; $23/yr. out of cy. 49 W. Main St., Mt. Pleasant, UT 84647. TEL 801-462-2134; FAX 801-462-2459. **Owner(s):** Pyramid Publishing, Inc., 49 W. Main St., Mt. Pleasant, UT 84647. TEL 801-462-2134; FAX 801-462-2459; Ed. Penny Hamilton; Pub. Martin Conover; adv.: $8.50/SAU. pub. size: broadsheet; circ. 2,500(paid).

OREM
US
OREM-GENEVA TIMES. 1937. Wed. $.50 newsstand; $16/yr.; $26/2 yrs. 546 S. State St., Orem, UT 84058. TEL 801-225-1340; FAX 801-225-1341. **Owner(s):** Brent Sumner, P.O. Box 65, Orem, UT 84059. TEL 801-225-1340; Ed. Brent Sumner; Pub. Brent Sumner; adv.; pub. size: standard; circ. 5,400(controlled & paid).

PARK CITY
US ISSN 0745-9483
PARK RECORD, THE. 1880. s-w. Wed. & Sat. $.50 newsstand; $32/yr. local; $60/yr. elsewhere. 1670 Bonanza Dr., Park City, UT 84060-3688. TEL 801-649-9014; FAX 801-649-4942. **Owner(s):** Peter Bernharad, 1670 Bonanza Dr., Park City, UT 84060-3688. TEL 801-649-9014; FAX 801-649-4942; Ed. Nan Chalat-Noaker; Pub. Andy Bernhard; adv. contact: Tracy Harden. pub. size: broadsheet; circ. 8,500(controlled & paid).

PRICE
US
SUN ADVOCATE. 1891. s-w.: Tue. & Thu. $35/yr. in cy.; $38/yr. out of cy.; $42/yr. out of state. 76 W. Main St., Price, UT 84501. TEL 801-637-0732; FAX 801-637-2716; E-mail: kashbysisna.com. **Owner(s):** Brehm Communications, Inc., P.O. Box 28429, San Diego, CA 92128. TEL 619-451-6200; Ed. Lynnda Johnson; Pub. Kevin Ashby; adv.; photos; pub. size: broadsheet; circ. 5,400(free & paid).

RICHFIELD
US
RICHFIELD REAPER. 1964. Wed. $.75 newsstand; $24/yr. in cy.; $34/yr. out of cy. 65 W. Center, Richfield, UT 84701. TEL 801-896-5476; FAX 801-896-8123. **Owner(s):** Gull Communications, Inc., 65 W. Center, Richfield, UT 84701. TEL 801-896-5476; Ed. Hal Edwards; Pub. Mark Fuellenbach; adv. contact: Charles Hawley. pub. size: broadsheet; circ. 6,600(free).
Formerly: Reaper Extra.

ROOSEVELT
US
UINTAH BASIN STANDARD. 1913. Tue. $.50 newsstand; $20/yr. in area; $32/yr. out of area. 268 S. 200 E., Roosevelt, UT 84066. TEL 801-722-5131; FAX 801-722-4140. **Owner(s):** Craig Ashby, 268 S. 200 E., Roosevelt, UT 84066. TEL 801-722-5131; Ed. Lezlee Whiting; Pub. Craig Ashby; pub. size: broadsheet; circ. 4,200(paid).

SALT LAKE CITY
US
PRIVATE EYE WEEKLY. 1984. Thu. free newsstand; $30/yr. 60 W. 400 S., Salt Lake City, UT 84101. TEL 801-575-7003; FAX 801-575-6106. **Owner(s):** John Saltas, 68 W. 400 S., Salt Lake City, UT 84101. TEL 801-575-7003; FAX 801-575-6106; Ed. Christopher Smart. adv.; photos; bk.rev.; pub. size: tabloid; circ. 50,000(controlled & free).

TOOELE
US
TOOELE TRANSCRIPT-BULLETIN. 1894. s-w.: Tue. & Thu. $.50 newsstand; $30/yr. carrier; $35/yr. in cy. mailed; $38/yr. out of cy. mailed. 58 N. Main, Tooele, UT 84074. TEL 801-882-0050; FAX 801-882-6123. **Owner(s):** Joel Dunn, P.O. Box 390, Tooele, UT 84074. TEL 801-882-0050; Scott Dunn, P.O. Box 390, Tooele, UT 84074. TEL 801-882-0050; Perry Dunn, P.O. Box 390, Tooele, UT 84074. TEL 801-882-0050; Clayton Dunn, P.O. Box 390, Tooele, UT 84074. TEL 801-882-0050; Curtis Dunn, P.O. Box 390, Tooele, UT 84074. TEL 801-882-0050; Bruce Dunn, P.O. Box 390, Tooele, UT 84074. TEL 801-882-0050; Ed. David Bern; Pub. Scott C. Dunn; adv. contact: Clayton Dunn. adv.: $5.50/SAU. photos; bk.rev.; pub. size: broadsheet; circ. 7,200(paid).

TREMONTON
US ISSN 0747-1416
LEADER, THE. 1914. Wed. $.50 newsstand; $18.50/yr. in cy.; $24.50/yr. out of cy. 119 E. Main St., Tremonton, UT 84337. TEL 801-257-5182; FAX 801-257-6175. **Owner(s):** J. Walter Ross & Wayne D. Bell, 77 S. State, Preston, ID 83263. TEL 208-852-0155; Ed. Diana Myers; Pub. Greg Madson; adv. contact: Lisa Carter. pub. size: standard; circ. 5,500(free & paid).

VERNAL
US ISSN 0892-1091
VERNAL EXPRESS. 1891. Wed. $.50 newsstand; $19/yr. local; $30/yr. out of area; $33/yr. out of state. 54 N. Vernal Ave., Vernal, UT 84078. TEL 801-789-3511; FAX 801-789-8690. **Owner(s):** Vernal Express Publishing Co., P.O. Box 1000, Vernal, UT 84078. TEL 801-789-3511; FAX 801-789-8690; Ed. Steven R. Wallis. adv. contact: Janet D. Wallis. pub. size: broadsheet; circ. 4,000(paid).

VERMONT

BELLOWS FALLS
US
BELLOWS FALLS TOWN CRIER. 1984. Fri. free newsstand; $12.50/3 mos. mailed; $20/6 mos. mailed. 55 Square, Bellows Falls, VT 05101-0459. TEL 802-463-9591; FAX 802-463-9818. **Owner(s):** Roger Miller, Putney Rd., Brattleboro, VT 05301. TEL 802-257-7771; FAX 802-257-2211; Ed. Steve Crimmin; Pub. Bill Bedard; adv.; photos; pub. size: tabloid; circ. 13,600(controlled & free).

BENNINGTON
US
PENNYSAVER PRESS. 1958. Fri. free. 109 South St., Bennington, VT 05201. TEL 802-447-3381; FAX 802-447-3270. **Owner(s):** Add, Inc., 600 Industrial Dr., Waupaca, WI 54981. TEL 715-258-8450; Ed. Kelly Nesbitt; Pub. Dan McKay; pub. size: tabloid; circ. 37,000(free).

BRADFORD
US ISSN 0746-1674
JOURNAL OPINION. 1866. Wed. $.50 newsstand; $15/yr. Main St., Bradford, VT 05033. TEL 802-222-5281; FAX 802-222-5438. **Owner(s):** Robert F. Huminski, P.O. Box 378, Bradford, VT 05033. TEL 802-222-5281; FAX 802-222-5438; Ed. Robert F. Huminski; Pub. Robert F. Huminski; adv. contact: Jim Jung. photos; bk.rev.; pub. size: broadsheet; circ. 4,500(paid).

CHESTER
US
MESSAGE FOR THE WEEK. 1972. Wed. free. Elm St., Chester, VT 05143. TEL 802-875-4790; FAX 802-875-4792. **Owner(s):** Wes & Teresa Johnson, P.O. Box 759, Chester, VT 05147. TEL 802-875-4790; FAX 802-875-4792; Ed. Wes Johnson; Pub. Wes Johnson; adv. contact: Teresa Johnson. pub. size: tabloid; circ. 22,000(controlled & free).

ENOSBURG FALLS
US
COUNTY COURIER. 4895. Thu. $.75 newsstand; $20/yr. in cy.; $25/yr. out of cy. 209 Main St., Enosburg Falls, VT 05450-0398. TEL 802-933-4375; FAX 802-933-4907. **Owner(s):** Franklin Press, 209 Main St., Enosburg Falls, VT 05450-0398. TEL 802-933-4375; FAX 802-933-4907; Ed. Steve Cusick. adv.: $4.95/SAU. bk.rev.; pub. size: tabloid; circ. 4,300(free & paid).
Formerly: Franklin County Courier.

HARDWICK

US   ISSN 0744-5512
HARDWICK GAZETTE. 1889. Wed. $.50 newsstand; $22/yr. in state; $26/yr. out of state. Main St., Hardwick, VT 05843. TEL 802-472-6521. **Owner(s):** Hardwick Publishing Co., Inc., P.O. Box 367, Hardwick, VT 05843. TEL 802-472-6521; Ed. Ross Connelly; Pub. Ross Connelly; adv. contact: Susan Jarzyna. photos; bk.rev.; pub. size: broadsheet; circ. 3,000(paid).

KILLINGTON

US
MOUNTAIN TIMES. 1971. Thu. free; $65/yr. mailed. P.O. Box 183, Killington, VT 05751. TEL 802-422-2399; FAX 802-422-2395; E-mail: rbarn64850Aad.com; URL: http://www.mtntimes-killington.com. **Owner(s):** BRD Corp., P.O. Box 183, Killington, VT 05751. TEL 802-422-2399; FAX 802-422-2395; Ed. Royal Barnard; Pub. Royal Barnard; adv. contact: Zip Barnard. adv.: $8/SAU. photos; pub. size: tabloid; circ. 13,000(free & paid).

MANCHESTER CENTER

US   ISSN 1062-5070
MANCHESTER JOURNAL. 1861. Wed. $.50 newsstand; $36/yr. P.O. Box 569, Manchester Center, VT 05255-0569. TEL 802-362-2222; FAX 802-362-5327. **Owner(s):** New England Newspapers, Inc., 23 Exchange St., Pittsfield, MA 02860; Ed. Cathy Palumbo; Pub. Jeff Shippe; adv.; photos; bk.rev.; pub. size: broadsheet; circ. 5,000(paid),

MANCHESTER VILLAGE

US
VERMONT NEWS GUIDE. 1960. Wed. free; $35/yr. out of state mailed. Rte. 7A, Manchester Village, VT 05254. TEL 802-362-3535; FAX 802-362-5368. **Owner(s):** Add, Inc., 600 Industrial Dr., Waupaca, WI 54981. TEL 715-258-8450; Ed. David Lewis; Pub. Holly McCaughey; adv. contact: Holly McCaughey. pub. size: half-tabloid; circ. 16,000(free & paid).

MIDDLEBURY

US
ADDISON COUNTY INDEPENDENT. 1946. s-w.: Mon. & Thu. $.50 newsstand; $27.50/yr. in state; $38/yr. out of state. 4 Maple St., Middlebury, VT 05753. TEL 802-388-4944. **Owner(s):** Addison Press, Inc., P.O. Box 31, Middlebury, VT 05753. TEL 802-388-4944; Pub. Angelo S. Lynn; adv. contact: Jane Spencer. pub. size: tabloid; circ. 16,000(controlled & paid). **Wire Service(s):** AP.

MORRISVILLE

US
TRANSCRIPT, THE. 1973. Mon. free. Brooklyn St., Morrisville, VT 05661. TEL 802-888-2212; FAX 802-888-2173. **Owner(s):** Bradley Limoge Publishers, Inc., Brooklyn St., Morrisville, VT 05661. TEL 802-888-2212; Ed. Paulette Wallace; Pub. Bradley A. Limoge; adv. contact: Ramona Audet. pub. size: tabloid; circ. 12,135(free).
   Formerly: Morrisville Transcript.

RANDOLPH

US
HERALD OF RANDOLPH. 1874. Thu. $.65 newsstand; $22/yr. local; $25/yr. out of VT & NH. 30 Pleasant St., Randolph, VT 05060. TEL 802-728-3232; FAX 802-728-9275. **Owner(s):** M.D. Drysdale, RFD 2, Randolph, VT 05060; Ed. M.D. Drysdale; Pub. M.D. Drysdale; pub. size: broadsheet; circ. 6,000(paid).

RUTLAND

US
RUTLAND TRIBUNE, THE. 1966. Thu. free; $17/yr. 98 Allen St., Rutland, VT 05701. TEL 802-775-4221; FAX 802-775-9535; E-mail: ruttrib@vermontel.com; URL: http://www.rutlandvt.com. **Owner(s):** Robert Maguire, 98 Allen St., Rutland, VT 05701. TEL 802-775-4221; FAX 802-775-9535; Pub. Robert Maguire; adv. contact: R. O'Connor. photos; pub. size: tabloid; circ. 16,287(free).

SHELBURNE

US
VERMONT TIMES. 1990. Wed. free newsstand; $90/yr. 1st class; $35/yr. 3rd class. One Pine Haven Shore Rd., Shelburne, VT 05482. TEL 802-985-2400; FAX 802-985-2490; E-mail: vttimes@ad.com; URL: http://www.vt-times.com. **Owner(s):** New Market Press, P.O. Box 940, Shelburne, VT 05482-0940. TEL 802-985-2400; FAX 802-985-2490; Ed. Shay Totten; Pub. Ed Coats; adv. contact: Ed Coats. photos; bk.rev.; pub. size: tabloid; circ. 23,000(free).

SOUTH HERO

US
ISLANDER, THE. 1975. Tue. free; $1.25/wk. out of area. Sunset View Rd., South Hero, VT 05486. TEL 802-372-5600; FAX 802-372-3025; E-mail: ilander@together.net. **Owner(s):** Northern Champlain Islander, Inc., P.O. Box 212, South Hero, VT 05486. TEL 802-372-5600; FAX 802-372-5600; Ed. George D. Fowler. adv.; photos; bk.rev.; pub. size: tabloid; circ. 7,000(free & paid).

SPRINGFIELD

US
SPRINGFIELD REPORTER, THE. 1976. Wed. $.50 newsstand; $28/yr. 151 Summer St., Springfield, VT 05156-3503. TEL 802-885-2246; FAX 802-885-9821; E-mail: reporter@vermontel.com. **Owner(s):** Rodney W. Arnold, 151 Sumner St., Springfield, VT 05156-3507. TEL 802-885-2246; FAX 802-885-9821; Ed. Rodney W. Arnold; Pub. Rodney W. Arnold; adv. contact: S. Cofrancesco. photos; bk.rev.; pub. size: tabloid; circ. 2,400(free & paid).

STOWE

US
STOWE REPORTER. 1958. Thu. $.50 newsstand; $17/yr. in state; $25/yr. out of state; $32/yr. Canada. School St., Stowe, VT 05672. TEL 802-253-2101; FAX 802-253-8332. **Owner(s):** Reporter Press, Inc., P.O. Box 489, Stowe, VT 05672-0489. TEL 802-253-2101; FAX 802-253-8332; Ed. Gregory Popa; Pub. D. Trowbridge Elliman; adv. contact: Janka Heath. adv.: $6.16/SAU. photos; bk.rev.; pub. size: tabloid; circ. 5,600(paid). **Wire Service(s):** AP.

WAITSFIELD

US
VALLEY REPORTER, THE. 1971. Thu. $.50 newsstand; $14.50/yr. in state; $24/yr. out of state. P.O. Box 119, Waitsfield, VT 05673-0119. TEL 802-496-3928; FAX 802-496-4703. **Owner(s):** Valley Reporter, Inc., P.O. Box 119, Mad River Valley, Waitsfield, VT 05673-0119. TEL 802-496-3928; FAX 802-496-4703; Ed. Al Benjamin; Pub. Al Benjamin; adv.; photos; pub. size: tabloid; circ. 3,500(free & paid).

WOODSTOCK

US
VERMONT STANDARD. Thu. $.50 newsstand; $8/13 wks.; $15/6 mos.; $30/yr.; $56/2 yrs.; $27/yr. senior citizens. Rte. 4, Woodstock, VT 05091. TEL 802-457-1313; FAX 802-457-3639; E-mail: vstand@souer.net. **Owner(s):** Vermont Standard, Route 4, P.O. Box 88, Woodstock, VT 05091. TEL 808-457-1313; FAX 802-457-3639; Ed. Kevin Forrest; Pub. Phillip C. Camp; adv. contact: Jonathan Estey. adv.: $7/SAU. pub. size: standard; circ. 12,000.

VIRGIN ISLANDS

ST. JOHN

US   ISSN 0895-0970
TRADEWINDS. 1977. bi-w. $.50 newsstand; $30/yr. P.O. Box 1500, Cruz Bay, St. John, VI 00831. TEL 809-776-6496; FAX 809-693-8885. **Owner(s):** St. John Tradewinds, Inc., P.O. Box 1500, Cruz Bay, St. John, VI 00830; Ed. Tom Oat. circ. 3,000(paid).

VIRGINIA

ABINGDON

US
ABINGDON VIRGINIAN. 1841. Wed. $20/yr. in cy.; $25/yr. out of cy. 170 E. Main St., Abingdon, VA 24210. TEL 540-628-2962. **Owner(s):** Martha M. Weisfeld, 170 E. Main St., Abingdon, VA 24210. TEL 703-628-2962; Ed. Martha M. Weisfeld; Pub. Martha M. Weisfeld; adv.; photos; pub. size: standard; circ. 4,500(paid).

US
WASHINGTON COUNTY NEWS. 1948. Wed. $.50 newsstand; $21/yr. 143 W. Main St., Abingdon, VA 24210. TEL 540-628-7101; FAX 540-628-9396. **Owner(s):** Abingdon Newspapers, Inc., 143 W. Main St., Abingdon, VA 24210. TEL 703-628-7101; Ed. Pennie Anderson; Pub. Donna Moore; adv. contact: Bill Thomas. photos; bk.rev.; pub. size: standard; circ. 5,000(paid).

ALEXANDRIA

US
ALEXANDRIA GAZETTE PACKET. 1784. Thu. $.25 newsstand; $25/yr. carrier. 1610 King St., Alexandria, VA 22314. TEL 703-549-7185; FAX 703-548-2228. **Owner(s):** Peter Labovitz, 1610 King St., Alexandria, VA 22314. TEL 703-549-0004; Ed. Mary Anne Weber; Pub. Jerry Vernon; pub. size: tabloid; circ. 20,000(controlled & paid).

WEEKLY NEWSPAPERS

MOUNT VERNON
US
MOUNT VERNON GAZETTE. Thu. $.25 newsstand; $25/yr. carrier. 1610 King St., Alexandria, VA 22314. TEL 817-695-0500. **Owner(s):** Peter Labovitz, 1610 King St., Alexandria, VA 22314. TEL 817-695-0500; Ed. Mary Anne Weber. pub. size: tabloid; circ. 15,000(paid).

ALTAVISTA
US
ALTAVISTA JOURNAL. 1909. Wed. $.50 newsstand; $20/yr. in cy.; $24/yr. out of cy. 600 Main St., Altavista, VA 24517. TEL 804-369-6688; FAX 804-369-6689. **Owner(s):** Womack Publishing Co., Inc., P.O. Box 111, Chatham, VA 24531. TEL 804-432-1654; Ed. Betty Gilliam. adv. contact: Terri Haynes. pub. size: broadsheet; circ. 6,600(paid).

AMELIA COURT HOUSE
US ISSN 0746-1798
AMELIA BULLETIN MONITOR, THE. 1973. Thu. $.25 newsstand; $16/yr. in state; $22/yr. out of state. 16301 Goodesbridge Rd., Amelia Court House, VA 23002. TEL 804-561-3655; FAX 804-561-2065. **Owner(s):** Ann B. Salster, P.O. Box 123, Amelia Court House, VA 23002-0123. TEL 804-561-3655; Ed. Michael D. Salster; Pub. Ann B. Salster; adv. contact: B. Thompson. photos; bk.rev.; pub. size: tabloid; circ. 8,300(free & paid).

AMHERST
US
AMHERST NEW ERA-PROGRESS. 1881. Thu. $.50 newsstand; $14/yr. in cy.; $20/yr. out of cy. 134 Second St., Amherst, VA 24521. TEL 804-946-7195; FAX 804-946-2684. **Owner(s):** Thomas T. Byrd, 2 N. Kent St., Winchester, VA 22601. TEL 703-667-3200; Ed. Nancy Cruthfield; Pub. Thomas T. Byrd; adv.; photos; pub. size: broadsheet; circ. 5,000(paid).

US
NELSON COUNTY TIMES. Thu. $.50 newsstand; $14/yr. in cy.; $20/yr. out of cy. 134 Second St., Amherst, VA 24521. TEL 804-946-7195; FAX 804-946-2684. **Owner(s):** Thomas T. Byrd, 2 N. Kent St., Winchester, VA 22601. TEL 703-667-3200; Ed. Jim Manner; Pub. Thomas Byrd; adv.; photos; pub. size: tabloid; circ. 4,700(paid).

APPOMATTOX
US
APPOMATTOX TIMES-VIRGINIAN. 1892. Wed. $.50 newsstand; $20/yr. local; $24/yr. out of state. 507 Court St., Appomattox, VA 24522. TEL 804-352-8215; FAX 804-352-2216. **Owner(s):** Womack Publishing Co., Inc., P.O. Box 111, Chatham, VA 24531. TEL 804-432-1654; Ed. Louis Wood; Pub. Charles Womack; adv. contact: Peggy Kidd. photos; pub. size: broadsheet; circ. 3,800(paid).

ARLINGTON
US
ARLINGTON COURIER, THE. 1988. Thu. $.25 newsstand; $17/yr. local; $24/yr. elsewhere. 3030 Clarendon Blvd., #219, Arlington, VA 22201. TEL 703-522-9898; FAX 703-522-8788; E-mail: arlcourier.com. **Owner(s):** Emily Schlesinger, P.O. Box 10089, Arlington, VA 22210. TEL 703-522-9898; FAX 703-522-8788; Ed. Emily Schlesinger; Pub. Emily Schlesinger; adv.; photos; bk.rev.; pub. size: tabloid; circ. 20,000(controlled & paid).

ASHLAND
US
HERALD-PROGRESS. 1881. s-w.: Mon. & Thu. $.50 newsstand; $20/yr. in cy.; $26/yr. out of cy. 11293 Air Park Rd., Ashland, VA 23005-3203. TEL 804-798-9031; FAX 804-798-9036. **Owner(s):** Herald-Progress, Inc., 11293 Air Park Rd., Ashland, VA 23005. TEL 804-798-9031; FAX 804-798-9036; Pub. J.M. Pace, III; adv. contact: Janice Henicheck. pub. size: broadsheet; circ. 8,400(free & paid). **Wire Service(s):** AP.
Formerly: Hanover Herald-Progress.

BEDFORD
US
BEDFORD BULLETIN. 1857. Wed. $.75 newsstand; $23/yr. in cy.; $31/yr. out of cy.; $36/yr. out of state. 402 E. Main St., Bedford, VA 24523. TEL 540-586-8612; FAX 540-586-0834. **Owner(s):** Landmark Community Newspapers, Inc., P.O. Box 549, Shelbyville, KY 40065; Ed. Rebecca Jackson-Clause; Pub. Jay Bondurant; adv. contact: Lynn Hurst. photos; pub. size: broadsheet; circ. 8,500(paid).

BERRYVILLE
US
CLARK COURIER. Thu. $.50 newsstand; $16/yr. in cy.; $20/yr. out of cy. 16 W. Main St., Berryville, VA 22611. TEL 540-955-1111; FAX 540-955-1334. **Owner(s):** Arcom Publications Co., Inc., 1760 Reston Blvd., Ste. 411, Reston, VA 22090. TEL 703-437-5400; FAX 703-437-6019; Ed. Janet Rems; Pub. Arthur W. Arundel; adv. contact: pub. size: broadsheet; circ. 2,600(paid).

BIG STONE GAP
US
POST, THE. 1890. Wed. $.40 newsstand; $20/yr. in cy.; $40/yr. elsewhere. 215 Wood Ave., Big Stone Gap, VA 24219. TEL 703-523-1141; FAX 703-523-1175; E-mail: thepost@mounet.com. **Owner(s):** Wise Printing Co., P.O. Box 250, Big Stone Gap, VA 24219. TEL 703-523-1141; Ed. Jeff Moore; Pub. Robbie G. Tate; adv.; pub. size: broadsheet; circ. 4,921(free & paid).

BLACKSTONE
US
BLACKSTONE COURIER-RECORD. 1898. Wed. $.50 newsstand; $15/yr. 207 S. Main St., Blackstone, VA 23824. TEL 804-292-3019; FAX 804-292-5966. **Owner(s):** Nottoway Publishing Co., Inc., 207 S. Main St., P.O. Box 450, Blackstone, VA 23824. TEL 804-292-3019; FAX 804-292-5966; Ed. William D. Coleburn. adv.; photos; pub. size: broadsheet; circ. 7,100(free & paid).

BOWLING GREEN
US
CAROLINE PROGRESS, THE. 1919. Wed. $.40 newsstand; $19/yr. in cy.; $34/yr. out of cy. 115 N. Main St., Bowling Green, VA 22427. TEL 804-633-5005; FAX 804-633-6740. **Owner(s):** Chesapeake Publishing Corp., 216 Ironbound, Williamsburg, VA 23188. TEL 804-220-1736; Ed. Greg Belcher. adv. contact: Karen Oyler. pub. size: broadsheet; circ. 9,000(paid).

BROOKNEAL
US
UNION STAR. Wed. $.50 newsstand; $20/yr. in cy.; $24/yr. out of cy. 241 Main St., Brookneal, VA 24528. TEL 804-376-2795; FAX 804-376-2676. **Owner(s):** Charles A. Womack, Jr., P.O. Box 180, Brookneal, VA 24528. TEL 804-376-1795; FAX 804-376-2676; Ed. Paula Bryant; Pub. Charles A. Womack, Jr.; adv.: $5.30/SAU. photos; pub. size: broadsheet; circ. 3,200(paid).

CHARLOTTESVILLE
US
CHARLOTTESVILLE-ALBEMARLE TRIBUNE. 1954. Thu. $.50 newsstand; $25/yr. 250 W. Main St., Ste. 402, Charlottesville, VA 22902. TEL 804-979-0373; FAX 804-971-5821. **Owner(s):** Agnes White, 250 W. Main St., Ste. 402, Charlottesville, VA 22902. TEL 804-979-0373; FAX 804-971-5821; Ed. Agnes White; Pub. David White; adv.; photos; bk.rev.; pub. size: tabloid; circ. 8,000(free & paid).

US
RURAL VIRGINIAN. Wed. free. 685 W. Rio Rd., Charlottesville, VA 22906. TEL 804-978-7200; FAX 804-978-7223. **Owner(s):** Media General, Inc., 411 E. Franklin St., Richmond, VA 23219; Ed. Robert Knapp; Pub. Lawrence McConnell; adv. contact: Wanda Birckhead. pub. size: tabloid; circ. 10,700(paid).

CHASE CITY
US
NEWS-PROGRESS, THE. 1888. s-w.: Mon. & Wed. $.25 newsstand; $16/yr. in cy.; $30/yr. out of cy. 850 E. Second St., Chase City, VA 23924. TEL 804-372-5156; FAX 804-372-3911. **Owner(s):** Mecklenburg News, Inc., P.O. Box 337, Chase City, VA 23924. TEL 804-374-0103; Ed. Cathy Cochelin; Pub. Keith A. Shelton; adv.; photos; pub. size: broadsheet; circ. 7,675(paid).
Formerly: Clarksville Mecklenberg News.

CHATHAM
US ISSN 1074-5114
STAR-TRIBUNE. 1869. Wed. $.50 newsstand; $20/yr. in cy.; $24/yr. out of cy. 30 N. Main St., Chatham, VA 24531. TEL 804-432-2791; FAX 804-432-4033. **Owner(s):** Womack Publishing Co., Inc., P.O. Box 111, Chatham, VA 24531. TEL 804-432-1654; Ed. Tim Davis; Pub. Charles Womack, Jr.; adv. contact: Margie Dawson. photos; pub. size: broadsheet; circ. 8,900(paid).

CHESAPEAKE

US
CHESAPEAKE POST. 1962. Fri. $.35 newsstand; $15.95/yr. in cy. 1024 N. Battlefield Blvd., Chesapeake, VA 23320. TEL 804-547-4571; FAX 804-548-0390. **Owner(s):** Byerly Publications, Inc., 1000 Armory Dr., Franklin, VA 23851. TEL 804-562-3187; Ed. Victoria Hecht; Pub. Hanes Byerly; adv. contact: Sandra Snelley. photos; pub. size: broadsheet; circ. 8,425(paid).

US
PORTSMOUTH TIMES. Fri. $.35 newsstand; $15.95/yr. in cy. 1024 N. Battlefield Blvd., Chesapeake, VA 23320. TEL 804-397-7606; FAX 804-548-0390. **Owner(s):** Byerly Publications, Inc., 1000 Armory Dr., Franklin, VA 23851. TEL 804-562-3187; Ed. Victoria Hecht; Pub. Hanes Byerly; adv. contact: Sandra Snelley. photos; pub. size: broadsheet; circ. 7,000(paid).

US
VIRGINIA BEACH SUN. 1925. Fri. $.35 newsstand; $15.95/yr. in cy.; $18.95/yr. out of cy. 138 S. Rosemont Rd., Chesapeake, VA 23452. TEL 757-486-3430; FAX 757-548-0390. **Owner(s):** Byerly Publications, Inc., 1000 Armory Dr., Franklin, VA 23851. TEL 804-562-3187; Ed. Victoria Hecht; Pub. Hanes Byerly; adv. contact: Sandra Snelley. photos; pub. size: broadsheet; circ. 7,500(paid).

CHRISTIANSBURG

US
BLACKSBURG SENTINEL. s-w.: Wed. & Sat. $.50 newsstand. 3325 N. Franklin St., Christiansburg, VA 24073. TEL 540-382-6171; FAX 540-382-3009. **Owner(s):** New River Newspapers, LLC, 3325 N. Franklin St., Christiansburg, VA 24073. TEL 540-382-6171; FAX 540-382-3009; Ed. Gene Morrell; Pub. John Reynolds; adv.; photos; pub. size: broadsheet; circ. 10,000(controlled & paid).

US
NEWS MESSENGER, THE. 1884. s-w.: Wed. & Sat. $.50 newsstand. 3325 N. Franklin St., Christiansburg, VA 24073. TEL 540-382-6171; FAX 540-382-3009. **Owner(s):** New River Newspapers, LLC, 3325 N. Franklin St., Christiansburg, VA 24073. TEL 540-382-6171; FAX 540-382-3009; Ed. Gene Morrell; Pub. John Reynolds; adv. contact: Shellby Roope. photos; pub. size: broadsheet; circ. 10,000(controlled & paid); Sun. 13,200(paid).

US
RADFORD NEWS JOURNAL. s-w.: Wed. & Sat. $.50 newsstand. 3325 N. Franklin St., Christiansburg, VA 24073. TEL 540-382-6171; FAX 540-382-3009. **Owner(s):** New River Newspapers, LLC, 3325 N. Franklin St., Christiansburg, VA 24073. TEL 540-382-6171; FAX 540-382-3009; Ed. Gene Morrell; Pub. John Reynolds; adv.; photos; pub. size: broadsheet; circ. 10,000(controlled & paid).

CLARKSVILLE

US
MECKLENBURG SUN. 1976. Wed. $.25 newsstand; $7/yr. in cy. 602 Virginia Ave., Clarksville, VA 23927. TEL 804-374-8152; FAX 804-374-8153. **Owner(s):** Tucker W. Mclaughlin, Sr., P.O. Drawer 100, South Boston, VA 24592. TEL 804-572-2928; Hugh M. Moore, P.O. Drawer 100, South Boston, VA 24592. TEL 804-572-2928; Ed. Tom McLaughlin, Jr.; Pub. Hugh M. Moore; adv.; photos; pub. size: broadsheet; circ. 5,200(paid).

CLINTWOOD

US
DICKENSON STAR/CUMBERLAND TIMES, THE. 1966. Wed. $.35 newsstand; $20/yr. in cy.; $28/yr. out of cy. Main St., Clintwood, VA 24228-0707. TEL 540-926-8816; FAX 540-926-8827; E-mail: npimedici@compunet.net. **Owner(s):** Robbie G. Tate, 564 Oak Ave., Norton, VA 24273. TEL 703-679-1056; Michael N. & Jenay Tate, P.O. Box 380, Norton, VA 24273. TEL 703-679-1101; Ed. Ida Holyfield; Pub. Robbie G. Tate; adv. contact: Bill Endean. photos; bk.rev.; pub. size: standard; circ. 6,800(paid). **Wire Service(s):** AP.

CREWE

US   ISSN 8755-9463
CREWE-BURKEVILLE JOURNAL. 1959. Thu. $.50 newsstand; $20/yr. in state; $25/yr. out of state. 107 W. Carolina Ave., Crewe, VA 23930. TEL 804-645-7534; FAX 804-645-1848. **Owner(s):** Jim R. Eanes, Eanes & Hudgins Publishing Co., Inc., 107 W. Carolina Ave., Crewe, VA 23930; Ed. Jim R. Eanes. adv.; photos; pub. size: standard; circ. 7,000(paid).

CULPEPER

US
CULPEPER NEWS. 1975. Thu. $.50 newsstand; $24/yr. in cy.; $28/yr. out of cy. 605 S. Main St., Culpeper, VA 22701. TEL 540-825-3232; FAX 540-825-5670. **Owner(s):** Virginia Newspapers, Inc., 333 E. Grace St., Richmond, VA 23219. TEL 804-649-6000; FAX 804-775-8090; Ed. Theresa Knight. adv. contact: Sherri Lutz. photos; pub. size: broadsheet; circ. 5,000(controlled & paid).

US
NORTHERN PIEDMONT EXPRESS. Wed. free. 122 W. Spencer St., Culpeper, VA 22701. TEL 540-825-0771; FAX 540-825-0771. **Owner(s):** Media General, Inc., 411 E. Franklin St., Richmond, VA 23219. TEL 804-775-8030; Pub. Robin L. Quillum; adv. contact: Diane Holt. pub. size: standard; circ. 20,000(controlled & free).

DRAKES BRANCH

US
CHARLOTTE GAZETTE. 1873. Wed. $.50 newsstand; $14/yr. in cy.; $18/yr. out of cy.; $20/yr. out of state. Main St., Drakes Branch, VA 23937. TEL 804-568-3341; FAX 804-568-3731. **Owner(s):** Dorothy C. Tucker, P.O. Box 214, Drakes Branch, VA 23937. TEL 804-568-3341; Ed. O.O. Tucker, III; Pub. Dorothy C. Tucker; pub. size: broadsheet; circ. 3,300(paid).

ELKTON

US
VALLEY BANNER, THE. 1966. Thu. $.25 newsstand; $13/yr. local; $18/yr. elsewhere. 157 W. Spotswood Ave., Elkton, VA 22827-0126. TEL 540-298-9444; FAX 540-298-2560; E-mail: frontpg@aol.com. **Owner(s):** Rockingham Publishing Co., Inc., P.O. Box 193, Harrisonburg, VA 22801. TEL 540-298-9444; FAX 540-298-2560; Ed. R.C. Murphey, IV. adv. contact: Travis Fox. adv.: $6.25/SAU. photos; pub. size: standard; circ. 4,500(free & paid).

EMPORIA

US
INDEPENDENT-MESSENGER. 1896. s-w.: Sun. & Thu. $.35 newsstand; $24.85/yr. in cy.; $31.85/yr. in VA & NC; $40/yr. elsewhere. 441 S. Main St., Emporia, VA 23847. TEL 804-634-4153; FAX 804-634-0783. **Owner(s):** Byerly Publications, Inc., 1000 Armory Dr., Franklin, VA 23851. TEL 804-562-3187; Ed. Dawn Dondibley; Pub. Hanes Byerly; adv. contact: Bill Edwards. photos; pub. size: broadsheet; circ. 6,800(paid).

FAIRFAX

US   ISSN 1065-1632
NORTHERN VIRGINIA SUN, THE. 1937. s-w.: Tue. & Fri. $.25 newsstand; $24/yr. 2710 C Prosperity Ave., Fairfax, VA 22031. TEL 703-204-2800; FAX 703-204-3455. **Owner(s):** Sun Newspapers, Inc., 2710 C Prosperity Ave., Fairfax, VA 22031. TEL 703-204-2800; Ed. Scott McCaffrey; Pub. Debora Crook; adv.; pub. size: tabloid; circ. 2,000(paid). **Wire Service(s):** AP.
Formerly: Arlington Northern Virginia Sun.

FALLS CHURCH

US
FALLS CHURCH NEWS-PRESS. 1991. Wed. free newsstand; $39/yr. 929 W. Broad St., Ste. 200, Falls Church, VA 22046. TEL 703-532-3267; FAX 703-532-3396. **Owner(s):** Century News Service, Inc., 929 W. Broad St., Ste. 200, Falls Church, VA 22046. TEL 703-532-3267; FAX 703-532-3396; Ed. Nicholas Benton; Pub. Nicholas Benton; adv.; bk.rev.; pub. size: tabloid; circ. 8,000(free).

FARMVILLE

US
FARMVILLE HERALD, THE. 1890. 3/wk.: Wed., Fri., Sun. $.35 newsstand; $24/yr. in cy.; $35/yr. out of cy. 114 North St., Farmville, VA 23901. TEL 804-392-4151; FAX 804-392-3366. **Owner(s):** William B. Wall, 114 North St., Farmville, VA 23901. TEL 804-392-4151; Ed. Ken Woodley; Pub. Steven E. Wall; pub. size: broadsheet; circ. 8,200(paid).

US
FREE NEWS, THE. Mon. free. 114 North St., Farmville, VA 23901. TEL 804-392-4151; FAX 804-392-6298. **Owner(s):** William B. Wall, 114 North St., Farmville, VA 23901. TEL 804-392-4151; FAX 804-392-6298; Ed. Kim Woodley; Pub. Steven E. Wall; pub. size: broadsheet; circ. 15,000(free).

FINCASTLE

US
FINCASTLE HERALD, THE. 1866. Wed. $.50 newsstand; $20/yr. 211 Catawba St., Fincastle, VA 24090. TEL 703-473-2741; FAX 703-473-2741. **Owner(s):** Salem Publishing Co., 1633 W. Main St., Salem, VA 24153. TEL 703-389-9355; FAX 703-389-2930; Ed. Edwin Taylor; Pub. Ray Robinson; adv. contact: Steve Parker. photos; bk.rev.; pub. size: standard; circ. 5,900(paid).
Formerly: Botetourt County News.

WEEKLY NEWSPAPERS

FLOYD
US

FLOYD PRESS. 1891. Thu. $.50 newsstand; $20/yr. in cy.; $29/yr. out of cy. 710 E. Main St., Floyd, VA 24091. TEL 540-745-2127; FAX 540-745-2126. **Owner(s):** William B. & Dorothy V. Sumner, 710 E. Main St., Floyd, VA 24091. TEL 703-745-2127/ Ed. Wanda Combs; Pub. Dorothy V. Sumner; adv. contact: Carman Harman. photos; pub. size: standard; circ. 5,200(paid).

FRANKLIN
US

TIDEWATER NEWS, THE. s-w.: Thu. & Sun. $.35 newsstand; $26.85/yr. in cy. 1000 Armory Dr., Franklin, VA 23851. TEL 757-562-3187; FAX 757-562-6795. **Owner(s):** Byerly Publications, Inc., P.O. Box 497, Franklin, VA 23851; Ed. Jamie Brown; Pub. Hanes Byerly; adv.: $8.20/SAU. photos; pub. size: standard; circ. 9,000(paid).

FRONT ROYAL
US

WARREN SENTINEL, THE. Thu. $.25 newsstand; $10/yr. in cy.; $12/yr. out of cy. 429 N. Royal Ave., Front Royal, VA 22630. TEL 540-635-4174; FAX 540-635-7478. **Owner(s):** Thomas T. Byrd, P.O. Box 1297, Front Royal, VA 22630. TEL 540-635-4174; FAX 540-635-7478. Ed. Michelle Sullivan; Pub. Thomas T. Byrd; adv.; photos; pub. size: broadsheet; circ. 6,000(paid).

GALAX
US

GALAX GAZETTE, THE. 1876. 3/wk.: Mon., Wed., Fri. $.50 newsstand; $39.95/yr. in state; $53.74/yr. out of state. 108 W. Stuart Dr., Galax, VA 24333. TEL 540-236-5178; FAX 540-236-0756. **Owner(s):** Landmark Community Newspapers, Inc., P.O. Box 549, Shelbyville, KY 40066. TEL 502-633-4334; Ed. Amy Hauslohner; Pub. Chuck Burress; adv. contact: Robin Porterfield. photos; pub. size: broadsheet; circ. 8,600(paid).

GLOUCESTER
US

GLOUCESTER-MATHEWS GAZETTE JOURNAL. 1904. Thu. $.50 newsstand; $20/yr. in cy.; $24/yr. out of cy. Main St. & Lewis Ave., Gloucester, VA 23061. TEL 804-693-3101; FAX 804-693-7844. **Owner(s):** Tidewater Newspapers, Inc., P.O. Box J, Gloucester, VA 23061. TEL 804-693-3101; Ed. Elsa V. Cooke-Verbyla; Pub. John W. Cooke; adv. contact: June Byrd. photos; pub. size: broadsheet; circ. 10,500(paid). **Wire Service(s):** AP, Newsfinder.

GOOCHLAND
US

GOOCHLAND GAZETTE. 1955. Sat. $.50 newsstand; $20/yr. in cy.; $30/yr. out of cy. 3052 River Rd., W., Goochland, VA 23063. TEL 804-556-3135; FAX 804-556-4237. **Owner(s):** JGF Media, Inc., P.O. Box 5146, Charlottesville, VA 22905. TEL 804-977-2002; Ed. McGregor McCance; Pub. J. Grey Ferguson; adv. contact: Tom Haynie. photos; bk.rev.; pub. size: broadsheet; circ. 3,400(paid).

GRUNDY
US

VIRGINIA MOUNTAINEER. 1922. Thu. $.50 newsstand; $20/yr. in cy.; $30/yr. out of cy. 105 Main St., Grundy, VA 24614-2040. TEL 540-935-2123; FAX 540-935-2125. **Owner(s):** Mountaineer Publishing Co., Inc., P.O. Box 2040, Grundy, VA 24614-2040. TEL 540-935-2123; FAX 540-935-2125; Ed. Lodge Compton; Pub. Lodge Compton; adv. contact: John Whited. adv.: $6.72/SAU. photos; pub. size: broadsheet; circ. 8,600(paid).

HEATHSVILLE
US

NORTHUMBERLAND ECHO. 1902. Wed. $.35 newsstand; $17/yr. in cy.; $32/yr. out of cy. Rte. 360-Echo Bldg., Heathsville, VA 22473. TEL 804-580-3444; FAX 804-580-6826. **Owner(s):** Chesapeake Publishing Corp., Airport Industrial Park, Easton, MD 21601. TEL 301-822-1500; Ed. Priscilla Dawson; Pub. William C. O'Donovan; pub. size: broadsheet; circ. 5,000(paid).

HILLSVILLE
US

CARROLL NEWS, THE. 1920. Wed. $.50 newsstand; $20.50/yr. in cy. 1026 W. Stuart Dr., Hillsville, VA 24343. TEL 540-728-7311; FAX 540-728-4119. **Owner(s):** Wayne Brockenbrough, P. O. Box 57, Christiansberg, VA 24073; Ed. Wendy Turner; Pub. Ina Horton; adv. contact: Joyce Cromer. pub. size: broadsheet; circ. 6,700(paid).

INDEPENDENCE
US

DECLARATION, THE. 1980. Wed. $.50 newsstand; $19/yr. local; $30/yr. out of area. 304 Davis St., Independence, VA 24348-0070. TEL 540-773-2222; FAX 540-773-2287. **Owner(s):** John E. North, 304 Davis St., Independence, VA 24348-0070. TEL 703-773-2222; FAX 703-773-2287; Ed. John E. North; Pub. John E. North; adv. contact: Leslie Shifflett. photos; bk.rev.; pub. size: broadsheet; circ. 3,500(free & paid).

KILMARNOCK
US

RAPPAHANNOCK RECORD. 1916. Thu. $.50 newsstand; $18/yr. in cy.; $26/yr. out of cy. 27 Main St., Kilmarnock, VA 22482. TEL 804-435-1701; FAX 804-435-2632; E-mail: rprecord@crosslink.net. **Owner(s):** Rappahannock Record, Inc., 27 Main St., Kilmarnock, VA 22482. TEL 804-435-1701; FAX 804-435-2632; Ed. John C. Wilson; Pub. Fred A. Gaskins; adv. contact: Linda Troise. adv.: $7.50/SAU. pub. size: broadsheet; circ. 8,082(free & paid).

KING GEORGE
US

JOURNAL, THE. Wed. $.35 newsstand; $17.25/yr. in cy. 10250 Kings Hwy., King George, VA 22485. TEL 540-775-2024; FAX 540-775-4099. **Owner(s):** Ruth Herrink, P.O. Box 409, King George, VA 22485. TEL 540-775-2024; FAX 540-775-4099; Ed. Ruth Herrink; Pub. Ruth Herrink; adv. contact: Lorene Rich. photos; pub. size: broadsheet; circ. 8,000(paid).

LAWRENCEVILLE
US

BRUNSWICK TIMES-GAZETTE. 1887. Wed. $.35 newsstand; $12/yr. in cy. 213 Main St., Lawrenceville, VA 23868. TEL 804-848-2114; FAX 804-848-2115. **Owner(s):** Byerly Publications, Inc., 1000 Armory Dr., Franklin, VA 23851. TEL 804-562-3187; Ed. Jennifer Sullivan; Pub. Hanes Byerly; adv. contact: Tom Childrey. photos; pub. size: broadsheet; circ. 5,800(paid).

LEBANON
US

LEBANON NEWS. 1880. Wed. $.50 newsstand; $20/yr. in cy.; $26/yr. out of cy. 308 Main St., Lebanon, VA 24266. TEL 540-889-2112; FAX 540-889-5017. **Owner(s):** Jerry E. Lark, P.O. Box 1268, Lebanon, VA 24266. TEL 703-889-2112; A.G. Griffith, P.O. Box 1268, Lebanon, PA 24266; Bob Hillman, P.O. Box 1268, Lebanon, PA 24266; Bill McFarlane, P.O. Box 1268, Lebanon, PA 24266; Ed. Jerry E. Lark; Pub. Jerry E. Lark; adv.; photos; pub. size: broadsheet; circ. 5,600(paid).

LEESBURG
US

LEESBURG TODAY. 1988. Wed. free newsstand; $80/yr. 1st class. 112-Q South St., S.E., Leesburg, VA 22075. TEL 703-771-8800; FAX 703-771-7289. **Owner(s):** Amendment I, Inc., 112-Q South St., S.E., Leesburg, VA 22075. TEL 703-771-8800; FAX 703-771-8833; Pub. Brett Phillips; adv. contact: Jack Allen. pub. size: tabloid; circ. 29,900(controlled & free).

US

LOUDOUN TIMES-MIRROR. 1798. Wed. $.50 newsstand; $23.95/yr. in cy. carrier; $29.95/yr. in cy. mailed; $39.95/yr. out of cy. 9 E. Market St., Leesburg, VA 20175. TEL 703-777-1111; FAX 703-771-0036. **Owner(s):** Arcom Publications Co., Inc., 1760 Reston Pkwy., Ste. 411, Reston, VA 22091. TEL 703-437-5400; FAX 703-437-6019; Ed. Martin Casey; Pub. Arthur W. Arundel; adv. contact: Martie Curran. photos; pub. size: broadsheet; circ. 18,000(paid).

LEXINGTON
US

NEWS-GAZETTE. 1801. Wed. $.50 newsstand; $18/yr. in cy.; $30/yr. out of cy. 20 W. Nelson St., Lexington, VA 24450. TEL 540-463-3113; FAX 540-464-6397. **Owner(s):** News-Gazette Corp., 20 W. Nelson St., Lexington, VA 24450. TEL 540-463-3113; Ed. Darryl Woodson; Pub. M.W. Paxton, IV; adv. contact: Marsha Rexrode. pub. size: broadsheet; circ. 9,560(paid).

US   ISSN 1064-7759

ROCKBRIDGE WEEKLY. 1981. Wed. $.50 newsstand; $15/yr. in area; $30/yr. out of area. College Sq. Shopping Ctr., Lexington, VA 24450. TEL 540-464-6600; FAX 540-464-6603. **Owner(s):** Jerry Clark, P.O. Box 791, Buena Vista, VA 24416; Ed. Jerry Clark; Pub. Jerry Clark; adv.; photos; pub. size: broadsheet; circ. 5,400(paid).

US

WEEKENDER, THE. 1989. Sat. free. 20 W. Nelson St., Lexington, VA 24450. TEL 540-463-3113; FAX 540-464-6397. **Owner(s):** News-Gazette Corp., 20 W. Nelson St., Lexington, VA 00623. TEL 540-463-3113; Ed. Darryl Woodson; Pub. M.W. Paxton, IV; adv. contact: Marshal Rexrode. pub. size: broadsheet; circ. 14,000(controlled).

10754 LOUISA, VA WEEKLY NEWSPAPERS

LOUISA
US
CENTRAL VIRGINIAN, THE. 1912. Thu. $.50 newsstand; $17/yr. in cy.; $22/yr. in state; $25/yr. out of state. 101 Elm Ave., Louisa, VA 23093. TEL 540-967-0368; FAX 540-967-0457. **Owner(s):** C.V. Corporation of Virginia, P.O. Box 464, Louisa, VA 23093. TEL 540-967-0368; FAX 540-967-0457; Ed. Cathy Collins; Pub. Hilda D. Miller; adv. contact: Keli Harold. photos; pub. size: broadsheet; circ. 7,000(paid).

LURAY
US
PAGE NEWS & COURIER. 1867. Thu. $.50 newsstand; $12/yr. in cy.; $15/yr. out of cy. 17 S. Broad St., Luray, VA 22835. TEL 540-743-5123. E-mail: pagenews@shentel.net. **Owner(s):** Page-Shenandoah Newspaper Corp., 17 S. Broad St., Luray, VA 22835. TEL 703-743-5123; Ed. R. Cort Kirkwood. adv. contact: L. E. Osborne. photos; pub. size: standard; circ. 7,200(paid).
Formerly: Luray Page News & Courier.

MADISON
US
MADISON COUNTY EAGLE. 1911. Thu. $.50 newsstand; $24/yr. in cy. 200 Main St., Madison, VA 22727. TEL 540-948-5121; FAX 540-948-3045. **Owner(s):** Media General, Inc., 333 E. Grace St., Richmond, VA 23219. TEL 804-649-6000; FAX 804-775-8090; Ed. Greg K. Glassner. adv. contact: Debbie Lowe. photos; bk.rev.; pub. size: broadsheet; circ. 4,500(paid).

MARION
US
NEWS BUYERS CATALOG. 1980. Sat. free. 119 Sheffey St., Marion, VA 24354. TEL 540-783-5121; FAX 540-783-9713. **Owner(s):** D. Gregory Rooker, 460 W. Main St., Wytheville, VA 24382. TEL 703-228-6611; FAX 703-228-7260; Ed. Pam Thornton; Pub. Debbie Maxwell; adv. contact: Debbie Overbay. pub. size: tabloid; circ. 9,100(free).
Formerly: Appalachian Shopper.

US ISSN 0744-0766
SMYTH COUNTY NEWS & MESSENGER. 1884. s-w.: Wed. & Sat. $.50 newsstand; $30/yr. in cy.; $43/yr. in state; $51.20/yr. out of state. 119 Sheffey St., Marion, VA 24354. TEL 540-783-5121; FAX 540-783-9713. **Owner(s):** Family Community Newspapers, 460 W. Main St., Wytheville, VA 24382. TEL 540-228-6611; FAX 540-228-7260; adv.; photos; pub. size: broadsheet; circ. 8,100(paid).

MCLEAN
US
FAIRFAX CONNECTION. 1987. Thu. free. 7670 Old Springhouse Rd., McLean, VA 22102. TEL 703-917-6444; FAX 703-917-0991. **Owner(s):** DCI Publishing, Inc., 7670 Old Springhouse Rd., McLean, VA 22102; Ed. Kimm Dixon; Pub. Renee Britton; adv. contact: Renee Britton. photos; pub. size: standard; circ. 22,050(controlled).

MECHANICSVILLE
US
MECHANICSVILLE LOCAL. Wed. free; $18/yr. in cy.; $28/yr. out of cy. mailed. 7235 Stonewall Pkwy., Mechanicsville, VA 23111. TEL 804-746-1235; FAX 804-730-0476. **Owner(s):** JGF Media, Inc., Charlottesville, VA; Ed. Bob Rayner; Pub. J. Grey Ferguson; adv. contact: Tom Haynie. pub. size: tabloid; circ. 18,500(free & paid).

MONETA
US
SMITH MOUNTAIN EAGLE. Wed. $.50 newsstand; $20/yr. in area; $24/yr. out of area. Rte. 122, Moneta, VA 24121. TEL 540-297-1222; FAX 540-297-1944. **Owner(s):** Womack Publishing Co., Inc., P.O. Box 111, Chatham, VA 24531. TEL 804-432-1650; Ed. Rob Lyon; Pub. Charles Womack; adv.; pub. size: broadsheet; circ. 4,000(paid).

MONTEREY
US ISSN 0888-9473
RECORDER, THE. 1877. Fri. $.75 newsstand; $19/yr. in cy.; $24/yr. in state; $26/yr. out of state. 3 Water St., Monterey, VA 24465. TEL 540-468-2147; FAX 540-468-2048. **Owner(s):** Recorder Publishing of Virginia, Inc., P.O. Box 10, Monterey, VA 24465. TEL 540-468-2147; Ed. Suzanne Simmons. adv.; pub. size: tabloid; circ. 5,600(paid).

MONTROSS
US
WESTMORELAND NEWS. 1947. Thu. $.40 newsstand; $19/yr. in cy.; $34/yr. out of cy. Courthouse Ln., Montross, VA 22520. TEL 804-493-8096; FAX 804-493-8009. **Owner(s):** Chesapeake Publishing Corp., Airport Industrial Park, Easton, MD 21601. TEL 301-822-1500; Ed. Lynn Norris; Pub. William C. O'Donovan; adv. contact: Kathi Beam. pub. size: broadsheet; circ. 8,200(free & paid).

NEW CASTLE
US
NEW CASTLE RECORD. 1885. Wed. $.50 newsstand; $20/yr. local; $24/yr. out of cy.; $28/yr. out of state. P.O. Box 116, New Castle, VA 24127. TEL 540-864-5944; FAX 540-864-5944. **Owner(s):** Salem Publishing Co., 1633 W. Main St., Salem, VA 24153. TEL 703-389-9355; FAX 703-389-2930; Ed. Edwin Taylor; Pub. Ray Robinson; adv.; pub. size: broadsheet; circ. 1,750(paid).

NORFOLK
US
METRO WEEKENDERS, THE. Fri. free. 362 Campastella Rd., Norfolk, VA 23523. TEL 804-543-6531; FAX 804-543-7620. **Owner(s):** Brenda H. Andrews, 362 Campastella Rd., Norfolk, VA 23523. TEL 804-543-6531; Ed. Leonard Colvin; Pub. Brenda H. Andrews; adv. contact: M. Pritchard. pub. size: broadsheet; circ. 25,000(free).

NORTON
US ISSN 0889-3330
COALFIELD PROGRESS. 1911. s-w.: Tue. & Thu. $.50 newsstand; $40/yr. in cy. 725 Park Ave., Norton, VA 24273-0380. TEL 540-679-1101; FAX 540-679-5922; E-mail: npimedia@compunet.net. **Owner(s):** Norton Press, Inc., P.O. Box 380, Norton, VA 24273. TEL 703-679-1101; Ed. Jenay Tate; Pub. Robbie G. Tate; adv. contact: Bill Endean. photos; bk.rev.; pub. size: broadsheet; circ. 8,885(free & paid). **Wire Service(s):** AP.

ORANGE
US
ORANGE COUNTY REVIEW. 1931. Thu. $.50 newsstand; $24/yr. in cy.; $26/yr. out of cy. 110 Berry Hill Rd., Orange, VA 22960. TEL 540-672-1266; FAX 540-672-5831. **Owner(s):** Media General, Inc., 333 E. Grace St., Richmond, VA 23219. TEL 804-649-6000; FAX 804-775-8090; Ed. Jeff Poole; Pub. Peter S. Yates; adv. contact: Stacey Weakley. pub. size: broadsheet; circ. 7,450(paid).

PEARISBURG
US
VIRGINIAN-LEADER. 1857. Wed. $.50 newsstand; $25/yr. 511 Mountain Lake Ave., Pearisburg, VA 24134. TEL 540-921-3434; FAX 540-921-2563. **Owner(s):** Virginian Leader Corp., P.O. Drawer C, Pearisburg, VA 24134. TEL 703-921-3434; Ed. Amy Rakes; Pub. Kenneth Rakes; adv.; photos; pub. size: standard; circ. 6,400(paid).

PENNINGTON GAP
US
POWELL VALLEY NEWS. 1920. Wed. $.50 newsstand; $25/yr. in surrounding cys.; $30/yr. out of area. 125 E. Morgan Ave., Pennington Gap, VA 24277. TEL 540-546-1210; FAX 540-546-5468. **Owner(s):** Donald R. & Shirley A. Watson, P.O. Box 459, Pennington Gap, VA 24277. TEL 540-546-1210; Ed. Donald R. Watson; Pub. Donald R. Watson; adv. contact: Rick L. Watson. photos; pub. size: broadsheet; circ. 7,537(paid).
Formerly: Pennington Gap Powell Valley.

PURCELLVILLE
US
BLUE RIDGE LEADER, THE. 1984. Fri. $.25 newsstand; $20/yr. 769 E. Main St., Purcellville, VA 20132. TEL 703-338-6200; FAX 703-338-2647. **Owner(s):** Philip Y. Hahn, 769 E. Main St., Purcellville, VA 22132. TEL 703-338-6200; FAX 703-338-2647; Ed. Philip Y. Hahn; Pub. Philip Y. Hahn; adv. contact: Carol Riggs. photos; bk.rev.; pub. size: tabloid; circ. 20,000(controlled & paid).

RESTON
US
BURKE TIMES, THE. Thu. $.25 newsstand; $29.95/yr. in cy.; $39.95/yr. out of cy. 1760 Reston Pkwy., Ste. 411, Reston, VA 20190. TEL 703-437-5400; FAX 703-437-6019. **Owner(s):** Arcom Publications Co., Inc., 1760 Reston Pkwy., Ste. 411, Reston, VA 20190. TEL 703-437-5400; FAX 703-437-6019; Pub. Arthur W. Arundel; adv. contact: Mike Randolph. photos; pub. size: broadsheet; circ. 13,006(controlled & paid).

WEEKLY NEWSPAPERS

US
CENTREVILLE TIMES. Thu. $.25 newsstand; $29.95/yr. in cy.; $39.95/yr. out of cy. 1760 Reston Pkwy., Ste. 411, Reston, VA 22090. TEL 703-437-5400; FAX 703-437-6019. **Owner(s):** Arcom Publications Co., Inc., 1760 Reston Pkwy., Ste. 411, Reston, VA 22091. TEL 703-437-5400; FAX 703-437-6019; Ed. Janet Rems; Pub. Arthur W. Arundel; adv. contact: Mike Randolph. pub. size: broadsheet; circ. 13,948(free & paid).
Formerly: Centreville Times Mirror.

US
CHANTILLY TIMES. Thu. $.25 newsstand; $29.95/yr. in cy.; $39.95/yr. out of cy. 1760 Reston Pkwy., Ste. 411, Reston, VA 22090. TEL 703-437-5400; FAX 703-437-6019. **Owner(s):** Arcom Publications Co., Inc., 1760 Reston Pkwy., Ste. 411, Reston, VA 22091. TEL 703-437-5400; FAX 703-437-6019; Ed. Janet Rems; Pub. Arthur W. Arundel; adv. contact: Mike Randolph. photos; pub. size: broadsheet; circ. 6,980(free & paid).
Formerly: Chantilly Times Mirror.

US
FAIRFAX STATION TIMES. Thu. $.25 newsstand; $29.95/yr. in cy.; $39.95/yr. out of cy. 1760 Reston Pkwy., Reston, VA 20190. TEL 703-437-5400; FAX 703-437-6019. **Owner(s):** Arcom Publications Co., Inc., 1760 Reston Pkwy., Ste. 411, Reston, VA 20190. TEL 703-437-5400; FAX 703-437-6019; Pub. Arthur W. Arundel; adv. contact: Mike Randolph. pub. size: broadsheet; circ. 5,250(controlled & paid).

US
FAIRFAX TIMES. Thu. $.25 newsstand; $29.95/yr. in cy.; $39.95/yr. out of cy. 1760 Reston Pkwy., Ste. 411, Reston, VA 20190. TEL 703-437-5400; FAX 703-437-6019. **Owner(s):** Arcom Publications Co., Inc., 1760 Reston Pkwy., Ste. 411, Reston, VA 20190. TEL 703-437-5400; FAX 703-437-6019; Ed. Janet Rems; Pub. Arthur W. Arundel; adv. contact: Mike Ranolph. pub. size: broadsheet; circ. 19,150(controlled & paid).

US
GREAT FALLS TIMES. 1986. Wed. $13.50/yr. in cy.; $20/yr. out of cy. 1760 Reston Pkwy., Ste. 411, Reston, VA 20190-3303. TEL 703-437-5400; FAX 703-437-6019; E-mail: nvtimes@aol.com. **Owner(s):** Arcom Publications Co., Inc., 1760 Reston Pkwy., Ste. 411, Reston, VA 20190. TEL 703-437-5400; FAX 703-435-6019; Ed. Janet Rems; Pub. Arthur W. Arundel; adv. contact: Donna Hirsch. photos; pub. size: tabloid; circ. 4,000(free).
Formerly: Great Falls Current.

US
HERNDON TIMES. Wed. $.25 newsstand; $29.95/yr. in cy.; $39.95/yr. out of cy. 1760 Reston Pkwy., Ste. 411, Reston, VA 22090. TEL 703-437-5400; FAX 703-437-6019. **Owner(s):** Arcom Publications Co., Inc., 1760 Reston Pkwy., Ste. 411, Reston, VA 22090-3285. TEL 703-437-5400; FAX 703-437-6019; Ed. Janet Rems; Pub. Arthur W. Arundel; adv. contact: Donna Hirsch. pub. size: broadsheet; circ. 12,041(free & paid).
Formerly: Herndon Times Mirror.

US
MCLEAN PROVIDENCE JOURNAL. Wed. $13.50/yr. in cy.; $20/yr. out of cy. 1760 Reston Pkwy., Ste. 411, Reston, VA 20190-3303. TEL 703-437-5400; FAX 703-437-6019; E-mail: nvtimes.aol.com. **Owner(s):** Arcom Publications Co., Inc., 1760 Reston Pkwy., Ste. 411, Reston, VA 20190-3285. TEL 703-437-5400; FAX 703-437-6019; Ed. Janet Rems; Pub. Arthur W. Arundel; adv. contact: Donna Hirsch. photos; pub. size: tabloid; circ. 14,000(free).

US
RESTON TIMES. 1965. Wed. $.25 newsstand; $29.95/yr. in cy.; $39.95/yr. out of cy. 1760 Reston Pkwy., Ste. 411, Reston, VA 22090. TEL 703-437-5400; FAX 703-437-6019. **Owner(s):** Arcom Publications Co., Inc., 1760 Reston Pkwy., Ste. 411, Reston, VA 22091. TEL 703-437-5400; FAX 703-437-6019; Ed. Janet Rems; Pub. Arthur W. Arundel; adv. contact: Mike Randolph. photos; pub. size: broadsheet; circ. 16,527(free & paid).
Formerly: Reston Times Mirror.

US
SPRINGFIELD TIMES COURIER. Thu. $.25 newsstand; $29.95/yr. in cy.; $39.95/yr. out of cy. 1760 Reston Pkwy., Ste. 411, Reston, VA 20190. TEL 703-437-5400; FAX 703-437-6019. **Owner(s):** Arcom Publications Co., Inc., 1760 Reston Pkway., Ste. 411, Reston, VA 20190. TEL 703-437-5400; FAX 703-437-6019; Pub. Arthur W. Arundel; adv. contact: Mike Randolph. pub. size: broadsheet; circ. 23,500(controlled & paid).

US
VIENNA TIMES. 1985. Thu. $.25 newsstand; $29.95/yr. in cy.; $39.95/yr. out of cy. 1760 Reston Pkwy., Ste. 411, Reston, VA 22090. TEL 703-437-5400; FAX 703-437-6019. **Owner(s):** Arcom Publications Co., Inc., 1760 Reston Pkwy., Ste. 411, Reston, VA 22091-3285. TEL 703-437-5400; FAX 703-437-6019; Ed. Janet Rems; Pub. Arthur W. Arundel; adv. contact: Donna Hirsch. pub. size: broadsheet; circ. 11,339(free & paid).
Formerly: Vienna Times Mirror.

RICHLANDS

US
MOUNTAIN ADVISOR. Sat. free. 1206 Second St., Richlands, VA 24641. TEL 540-963-1081; FAX 540-963-0123. **Owner(s):** Media General, Inc., 333 E. Grace St., Richmond, VA 23126. TEL 804-649-6000; Pub. William H. Hall; adv. contact: Audira Leffel. pub. size: broadsheet; circ. 14,000(free).

US
RICHLANDS NEWS PRESS. 1933. Wed. $.50 newsstand; $26/yr. in cy. 1206 Second St., Richlands, VA 24641. TEL 540-963-1081; FAX 540-963-0123. **Owner(s):** Media General, Inc., 333 E. Grace St., Richmond, VA 23126. TEL 804-649-6000; FAX 804-775-8090; Pub. William H. Hall; adv. contact: Audria Leffel. photos; pub. size: broadsheet; circ. 7,900(paid).

US
TAZEWELL COUNTY FREE PRESS. 1976. Wed. free newsstand; $20/6 mos. 1249 Front St., Richlands, VA 24641. TEL 540-963-0127; FAX 703-963-0127; E-mail: freepres@netscope.net. **Owner(s):** Loren & Lynna Mitchell, 406 Buchanan St., Richlands, VA 24641. TEL 540-963-2308; Ed. Loren Mitchell; Pub. Loren Mitchell; adv. contact: Lynna Mitchell. photos; bk.rev.; pub. size: standard; circ. 13,000(controlled & free). **Wire Service(s):** AP.

ROCKY MOUNT

US
FRANKLIN NEWS-POST. 1905. 3/wk.: Mon., Wed., Fri. $.50 newsstand; $40/yr. in cy.; $45/yr. out of cy. 310 Main St., Rocky Mount, VA 24151. TEL 540-483-5113; FAX 540-483-8013. **Owner(s):** Franklin County Newspapers, Inc., P.O. Box 250, Rocky Mount, VA 24151. TEL 540-483-5113; Ed. R.B. Hundley; Pub. R.B. Hundley; adv. contact: Ken Bradley. photos; pub. size: broadsheet; circ. 8,600(paid).

SALEM

US
SALEM TIMES-REGISTER. 1854. Thu. $.50 newsstand; $20/yr. in town; $24/yr. out of town; $28/yr. out of state. 1633 W. Main St., Salem, VA 24153. TEL 540-389-9355; FAX 540-389-2930. **Owner(s):** Ray Robinson, 1633 W. Main St., Salem, VA 24153. TEL 540-389-9355; FAX 540-389-2930; Ed. Edwin Taylor; Pub. Ray Robinson; adv. contact: Judy Bradshaw. photos; pub. size: broadsheet; circ. 5,000(paid).

SOUTH BOSTON

US
SOUTH BOSTON GAZETTE-VIRGINIAN. 1903. 3/wk.: Mon., Wed., Fri. $.25 newsstand; $20/yr. in cy.; $36/yr. out of cy. 3201 Halifax Rd., South Boston, VA 24592. TEL 804-572-3945; FAX 804-572-1173. **Owner(s):** Keith A. Shelton, 3201 Halifax Rd., South Boston, VA 24592. TEL 804-572-3492; FAX 804-572-1173; Ed. Hugh M. Moore; Pub. Keith A. Shelton; adv. contact: Dell Satterfield. photos; bk.rev.; pub. size: broadsheet; circ. 11,500(paid).

US
SOUTH BOSTON NEWS & RECORD. 1892. s-w.: Mon. & Thu. $.25 newsstand; $12/yr. in cy.; $24/yr. out of cy. Halifax Sq. Shopping Ctr., Rte. 501, N., South Boston, VA 24592. TEL 804-572-2928; FAX 804-572-2920. **Owner(s):** Tucker McLaughlin, Sr., P.O. Drawer 100, South Boston, VA 24592. TEL 804-572-2928; Hugh M. Moore, P.O. Drawer 100, South Boston, VA 24592. TEL 804-572-2928; Ed. Sylvia McLaughlin; Pub. Tucker McLaughlin, Sr.; adv. contact: Sue Cain. pub. size: broadsheet; circ. 7,600(paid).

SOUTH HILL

US
SOUTH HILL ENTERPRISE. Wed. $.50 newsstand; $18/yr. in cy.; $25/yr. out of cy. 914 W. Danville St., South Hill, VA 23970. TEL 804-447-3178; FAX 804-447-5931. **Owner(s):** Womack Publishing Co., Inc., P.O. Box 111, Chatham, VA 24531. TEL 804-432-1654; Ed. Res Spears. pub. size: broadsheet; circ. 8,575(paid).

STANARDSVILLE

US
GREENE COUNTY RECORD. 1914. Thu. $.50 newsstand; $22/yr. Main St., Stanardsville, VA 22973. TEL 804-985-2315; FAX 804-985-8356. **Owner(s):** Media General, Inc., 333 E. Grace St., Richmond, VA 23219. TEL 804-649-6000; FAX 804-775-8090; Ed. Chris R. Brasted; Pub. Peter S. Yates; adv.; bk.rev.; pub. size: broadsheet; circ. 3,100(paid).

WEEKLY NEWSPAPERS

STUART
US

ENTERPRISE, THE. 1876. Wed. $.35 newsstand; $15/yr. local; $20/yr. elsewhere. 22 E. Main St., Stuart, VA 24171-0348. TEL 540-694-3101; FAX 540-694-3102. **Owner(s):** Gail M. Harding, 22 E. Main St., Stuart, VA 24171-0348. TEL 540-694-3101; Ed. Nancy M. Lindsey; Pub. Gail M. Harding; adv. contact: Teresa Roberson. pub. size: broadsheet; circ. 5,900(paid).

TAZEWELL
US

CLINCH VALLEY NEWS. 1845. Wed. $.50 newsstand; $26/yr. in cy. 119 Fincastle Tpke., Tazewell, VA 24651. TEL 540-988-4770; FAX 540-963-0123. **Owner(s):** Media General, Inc., 333 E. Grace St., Richmond, VA 23219. TEL 804-649-6000; FAX 804-775-8090; Pub. William H. Hall; adv. contact: Audria Leffel. photos; pub. size: broadsheet; circ. 3,900(paid).

URBANNA
US

SOUTHSIDE SENTINEL. 1896. Thu. $.50 newsstand; $17/yr. in cy.; $23/yr. out of cy. 276 Virginia St., Urbanna, VA 23175-0549. TEL 804-758-2328; FAX 804-758-5896; E-mail: sentinel@inna.net. **Owner(s):** Frederick A. & Elizabeth Lee Gaskins, P.O. Box 549, Urbanna, VA 23175. TEL 804-758-2328; Ed. John T. Hardin; Pub. Frederick A. Gaskins; adv. contact: Anita Minuth. photos; bk.rev.; pub. size: broadsheet; circ. 5,416(free & paid).
Formerly: Urbanna Southside Sentinel.

VICTORIA
US

KENBRIDGE-VICTORIA DISPATCH. 1970. Wed. $.50 newsstand; $14/yr. in cy.; $18/yr. out of cy.; $20/yr. out of state. 1404 Nottoway Blvd., Victoria, VA 23974. TEL 804-696-5550; FAX 804-696-2958. **Owner(s):** Dorothy C. Tucker, P.O. Box 40, Victoria, VA 23974. TEL 804-696-5550; Ed. Dorothy C. Tucker; Pub. Dorothy C. Tucker; adv.; pub. size: broadsheet; circ. 3,300(paid).

VINTON
US   ISSN 8750-7919

VINTON MESSENGER. 1962. Thu. $.50 newsstand; $20/yr. in city; $24/yr. out of city; $28/yr. out of state. 118 Lee Ave., Vinton, VA 24179. TEL 540-343-0720; FAX 540-343-2648. **Owner(s):** Salem Publishing Co., 1633 W. Main St., Salem, VA 24153. TEL 540-389-9355; FAX 540-389-2930; Ed. Anne Waelti; Pub. Ray Robinson; adv.; photos; pub. size: standard; circ. 3,000(paid).

WAKEFIELD
US   ISSN 0745-9467

SUSSEX-SURRY DISPATCH. 1888. Wed. $.35 newsstand; $19/yr. in cy.; $34/yr. out of state. 228 Fleetwood St., Wakefield, VA 23888. TEL 804-899-6397; FAX 804-899-7312. **Owner(s):** Chesapeake Publishing Corp., Airport Industrial Park, Easton, MD 21601. TEL 301-822-1500; Ed. Brian Rafferty. adv. contact: Lorrie Akers. photos; pub. size: broadsheet; circ. 3,300(paid).

WARRENTON
US

FAUQUIER CITIZEN. Fri. $.50 newsstand; $19/yr. in cy.; $26/yr. out of cy. 17 S. Fifth St., Warrenton, VA 20186. TEL 540-347-5522; FAX 540-347-7363. **Owner(s):** Ellen F. & Lawrence K. Emerson, P.O. Box 3430, Warrenton, VA 20186. TEL 540-347-5522; Ed. Lawrence K. Emerson; Pub. Ellen F. Emerson; adv.; photos; pub. size: broadsheet; circ. 7,700(paid).

US

FAUQUIER TIMES-DEMOCRAT. 1817. Wed. $.50 newsstand; $29.95/yr. local; $39.95/yr. out of state. 39 Culpepper St., Warrenton, VA 20186. TEL 540-347-4222; FAX 540-349-8676. **Owner(s):** Arcom Publications Co., Inc., 1760 Reston Pkwy., Ste. 411, Reston, VA 22091. TEL 703-437-5400; FAX 703-437-6019; Pub. Arthur W. Arundel; adv. contact: Kathleen Keller. pub. size: broadsheet; circ. 16,000(paid).

WASHINGTON
US

RAPPAHANNOCK NEWS. Thu. $.50 newsstand; $19/yr. in cy.; $24/yr. out of cy. 249 Main St., Washington, VA 22747. TEL 540-675-3349; FAX 540-437-6019. **Owner(s):** Arcom Publications Co., Inc., 1760 Reston Pkwy., Ste. 411, Reston, VA 22090. TEL 703-437-5400; FAX 703-437-6019; Ed. Janet Rems; Pub. Arthur W. Arundel; pub. size: broadsheet; circ. 3,000.

WEST POINT
US

TIDEWATER REVIEW. 1889. Wed. $.40 newsstand; $19/yr. in cy.; $34/yr. out of cy. 702 Main St., West Point, VA 23181. TEL 804-843-2282; FAX 804-843-4404. **Owner(s):** Chesapeake Publishing Corp., Airport Industrial Park, Easton, MD 21601. TEL 301-822-1500; Ed. Colston Newton; Pub. William C. O'Donovan; adv. contact: Rosemary Sims. photos; pub. size: broadsheet; circ. 5,000(paid).

WILLIAMSBURG
US   ISSN 0049-6480

VIRGINIA GAZETTE. 1736. s-w.: Wed. & Sat. $.50 newsstand; $31.99/yr. home deliv.; $44/yr. in state mailed; $50/yr. out of state. 216 Ironbound Rd., Williamsburg, VA 23188. TEL 757-220-1736; FAX 757-220-1665. **Owner(s):** Chesapeake Publishing Corp., Airport Industrial Park, Easton, MD 21601. TEL 410-822-1500; Ed. Rusty Carter; Pub. William C. O'Donovan; adv. contact: Michael Curry. pub. size: broadsheet; circ. 14,500(paid).

WOODSTOCK
US   ISSN 0746-6846

SHENANDOAH VALLEY-HERALD, THE. 1806. Wed. $12/yr. 207 N. Main St., Woodstock, VA 22664. TEL 540-459-4078; FAX 540-459-4077. **Owner(s):** Page-Shenandoah Newspaper Corp., P.O. Box 507, Woodstock, VA 22664. TEL 540-459-4078; FAX 540-459-4077; Ed. C.L. Earehart. adv. contact: Carol Holmes. pub. size: broadsheet; circ. 6,400(paid).

WYTHEVILLE
US

BLAND MESSENGER. 1922. Thu. $.50 newsstand; $19/yr. in cy. 460 W. Main St., Wytheville, VA 24382. TEL 800-655-1406; FAX 540-228-7260; E-mail: wneus@naxs.com; URL: http://www.blandnews.com. **Owner(s):** Family Community Newspapers, 460 W. Main St., Wytheville, VA 24382. TEL 540-228-6611; FAX 540-228-7260; Ed. Stephanie Porter-Nichols; Pub. D. Gregory Rooker; adv.; photos; pub. size: broadsheet; circ. 2,500(paid).

US

ENTERPRISE BUYER'S CATALOGUE. 1986. Fri. free. 460 W. Main St., Wytheville, VA 24382. TEL 540-228-6611; FAX 540-228-7260. **Owner(s):** Family Community Newspapers, 460 W. Main St., Wytheville, VA 14382. TEL 540-228-6611; FAX 540-228-7260; Ed. Stephanie Porter-Nichols; Pub. D. Gregory Rooker; adv. contact: Linda Crigger. pub. size: tabloid; circ. 7,350(free).
Formerly: Penny Saver.

US

NEWS BUYER'S CATALOGUE. Fri. free. 460 W. Main St., Wytheville, VA 24382. TEL 540-228-6611; FAX 540-228-7260. **Owner(s):** Family Community Newspapers, 460 W. Main St., Wytheville, VA 24382. TEL 540-228-6611; FAX 540-228-7260; Pub. D. Gregory Rooker; adv. contact: Debbie Overbay. pub. size: tabloid; circ. 9,800(free).

US

SOUTHWEST VIRGINIA ENTERPRISE. 1870. s-w.: Wed. & Sat. $.50 newsstand; $30/yr. in cy.; $43.24/yr. out of cy.; $51.20/yr. out of state. 460 W. Main St., Wytheville, VA 24382. TEL 540-228-6611; FAX 540-228-7260. **Owner(s):** Family Community Newspapers, 460 W. Main St., Wytheville, VA 24382. TEL 540-228-6611; FAX 540-228-7260; Ed. Stephanie Porter-Nichols; Pub. D. Gregory Rooker; adv.; pub. size: broadsheet; circ. 7,900(paid).

YORKTOWN
US

DENBIGH GAZETTE. 1987. Thu. $.35 newsstand; $15/yr. in state mailed; $20/yr. out of state. 4824 George Washington Hwy., Yorktown, VA 23692. TEL 757-898-7225; FAX 757-890-0119. **Owner(s):** Media General, Inc., 333 E. Grace St., Richmond, VA 23219. TEL 804-649-6000; FAX 804-649-6898; Ed. Beth Meisner; Pub. Gaither Perry; adv. contact: Peggy Brown. photos; pub. size: broadsheet; circ. 5,000(controlled & paid).

US

POQUOSON POST. Wed. $.25 newsstand; $12/yr. in state; $17/yr. out of state. 4824 George Washington Hwy., Yorktown, VA 23692. TEL 757-898-7225; FAX 757-890-0119. **Owner(s):** Media General, Inc, 333 E. Grace St., Richmond, VA 23219. TEL 804-649-6000; FAX 804-649-6898; Ed. Beth Meisner; Pub. Gaither Perry; adv. contact: Peggy Brown. pub. size: tabloid; circ. 4,000(paid).

WEEKLY NEWSPAPERS

EPHRATA, WA 10757

US
YORK TOWN CRIER. 1978. Wed. $.25/newsstand; $15/yr. in state; $20/yr. out of state. 4824 George Washington Hwy., Yorktown, VA 23692. TEL 757-898-7225; FAX 757-890-0119. **Owner(s):** Media General, Inc., 333 E. Grace St., Richmond, VA 23219. TEL 804-649-6000; FAX 804-649-6898; Ed. Beth Meisner; Pub. D. Gaither Perry; adv. contact: Peggy Brown. photos; bk.rev.; pub. size: broadsheet; circ. 5,000(free & paid).

WASHINGTON

ANACORTES
US
ANACORTES AMERICAN. 1890. Wed. $.50 newsstand; $30/yr. in cy.; $40/yr. out of cy. Sixth & Q Sts., Anacortes, WA 98221. TEL 360-293-3122; FAX 360-293-5000. **Owner(s):** Skagit Valley Publishing Co., P.O. Box 578, Mt. Vernon, WA 92873; Ed. Duncan Frazier; Pub. Duncan Frazier; adv. contact: Connie Mears. pub. size: broadsheet; circ. 4,500(paid).

ARLINGTON
US
NORTH SNOHOMISH WEEKLY. 1981. Thu. $.50 newsstand; $55/yr. 3611 168th St., N.E., Smokey Point, Arlington, WA 98223-3187. TEL 360-653-8000; FAX 360-653-9848. **Owner(s):** Skagit Valley Publishing Co., 1000 E. College Way, Mount Vernon, WA 98273. TEL 206-424-3251; FAX 206-424-5300; Ed. Kristin Kinnamon; Pub. Leighton P. Wood; adv. contact: Ken G. Larson. pub. size: broadsheet; circ. 23,000(controlled & free).

BAINBRIDGE ISLAND
US   ISSN 0745-7391
BAINBRIDGE REVIEW. 1926. s-w.: Wed. & Sat. $.75 newsstand; $32.50/yr. in cy.; $42/yr. out of cy.; $83/yr. out of state. 221 Winslow Way W., Bainbridge Island, WA 98110. TEL 206-842-6613; FAX 206-842-5867. **Owner(s):** Sound Publishing, Inc., 7689 N.E. Day Rd., Bainbridge Island, WA 98110; Ed. Jack Swanson; Pub. Christiana C. Allen; adv.; pub. size: tabloid; circ. 6,100(paid).

BATTLE GROUND
US
REFLECTOR, THE. 1909. Wed. $.35 newsstand; $20/yr. in cy. mailed; $35/yr. out of state mailed. 20 N.W. 20th Ave., Battle Ground, WA 98604-2020. TEL 360-687-5151; FAX 360-687-5162. **Owner(s):** Case Publishing Co., Inc., 20 N.W. 20th Ave., Battle Ground, WA 98604. TEL 360-687-5151; FAX 360-687-5162; Pub. Marvin F. Case; adv. contact: Darlene Carr. photos; pub. size: broadsheet; circ. 29,000(free & paid).

BOTHELL
US   ISSN 0739-9286
NORTHSHORE CITIZEN. 1903. Wed. $.50 newsstand; $24/yr. in area. 18120 Bothell Way, N.E., Bothell, WA 98011. TEL 206-486-1231; FAX 206-483-3286; E-mail: nscitizen@aol.com. **Owner(s):** Horvitz Newspapers, Inc., P.O. Box 90130, Bellevue, WA 98009-0130. TEL 206-624-2233; Ed. Craig Degginger; Pub. Howard Mullenary; adv. contact: Kathleen Maloy. photos; pub. size: broadsheet; circ. 6,800(paid).

CAMAS
US
CAMAS/WASHOUGAL POST RECORD. 1905. Tue. $.50 newsstand; $18/yr. in cy.; $35/yr. out of cy. 425 N.E. Fourth Ave., Camas, WA 98607. TEL 360-834-2141; FAX 360-834-3423. **Owner(s):** Eagle Newspapers, Inc., P.O. Box 12008, Salem, OR 97309; Ed. Craig Clohessy; Pub. Michael Gallagher; adv. contact: Don Dire. pub. size: broadsheet; circ. 8,600(paid).

CASHMERE
US
CASHMERE VALLEY RECORD. Wed. $.50 newsstand; $19/yr. in cy. mailed. P.O. Box N, Cashmere, WA 98815. TEL 509-782-3781; FAX 509-548-4789. **Owner(s):** Prairie Media, Inc., 215 14th St., Leavenworth, WA 98826. TEL 509-548-5286; Ed. Jeff Gauger. adv. contact: Cassidy Roehm. pub. size: broadsheet; circ. 1,800(paid).

CATHLAMET
US
WAHKIAKUM COUNTY EAGLE, THE. 1891. Thu. $.50 newsstand. 77 Main St., Cathlamet, WA 98612-0368. TEL 360-795-3391; FAX 360-795-3983. **Owner(s):** Eric R. Nelson, 77 Main St., Cathlamet, WA 98612. TEL 360-795-3391; FAX 360-795-3983; Ed. Eric R. Nelson. adv. contact: Eric R. Nelson. bk.rev.; pub. size: broadsheet; circ. 1,611(paid).

CHENEY
US
CHENEY FREE PRESS. 1896. Thu. $.50 newsstand; $20/yr. in cy.; $27/yr. out of cy. 1616 W. First St., Cheney, WA 99004. TEL 509-235-6184; FAX 509-235-2887. **Owner(s):** Journal News Publishing Co., 1616 W. First St., Cheney, WA 99004. TEL 509-747-7395; Ed. Kevin Hanson; Pub. William Ifft; adv. contact: Mary Mossman. pub. size: broadsheet; circ. 3,000(paid).

COLFAX
US
WHITMAN COUNTY GAZETTE. 1877. Thu. $.50 newsstand; $21/yr. in cy.; $30/yr. out of cy. 211 N. Main St., Colfax, WA 99111. TEL 509-397-4333; FAX 509-397-4527. **Owner(s):** Tribune Publishing Co., P.O. Box 957, Lewiston, ID 83501. TEL 208-743-9411; Ed. Jerry Jones; Pub. Gordon Forgey; adv. contact: Dick Bruce. pub. size: broadsheet; circ. 4,450(paid).
Formerly: Colfax Gazette.

COLVILLE
US
STATESMAN-EXAMINER. 1948. Wed. $.60 newsstand; $23/yr. in cy.; $30/yr. out of cy. 220 S. Main St., Colville, WA 99114. TEL 509-684-4567; FAX 509-684-3849. **Owner(s):** American Publishing Co., 606 N. Van Buren, Marion, IL 62959. TEL 618-993-1711; Ed. Chris Cowbrough; Pub. Don Birch; adv. contact: Marty Deubel. pub. size: broadsheet; circ. 6,535(free & paid).
Formerly: Colville Statesman-Examiner.

CONNELL
US
FRANKLIN COUNTY GRAPHIC. Thu. $.40 newsstand; $20/yr. in cy.; $25/yr. out of cy. 346 S. Columbia, Connell, WA 99326-0160. TEL 509-234-3181; FAX 509-234-3182. **Owner(s):** Duane & Dee Russer, 346 S. Columbia, Connell, WA 99326. TEL 509-234-3181; FAX 509-234-3182; Ed. Kathy Valdez; Pub. Duane Russer; pub. size: broadsheet; circ. 2,762(free & paid).

DAYTON
US
DAYTON CHRONICLE. 1877. w. $.50 newsstand; $20/yr. local; $25/yr. in OR, WA, ID; $29/yr. elsewhere. 358 E. Main St., Dayton, WA 99328. TEL 509-382-2221. **Owner(s):** Jack Williams, 358 E. Main St., Dayton, WA 99328. TEL 509-382-2221; Ed. Jackie Williams. adv.; bk.rev.; pub. size: standard; circ. 1,500(controlled & paid).

DEER PARK
US
TRIBUNE. 1906. Wed. $.50 newsstand; $23/yr. local; $33/yr. out of state. 104 N. Main St., Deer Park, WA 99006. TEL 509-276-5043; FAX 509-276-2041. **Owner(s):** American Publishing Co., 606 N. Van Buren, Marion, IL 62959. TEL 618-993-1711; Ed. Tom Costigan; Pub. Barbara Hanna; adv.: $6.45/SAU. pub. size: broadsheet; circ. 8,728(paid).

ENUMCLAW
US
ENUMCLAW COURIER-HERALD. 1901. Wed. $.50 newsstand; $22/yr. in King & Pierce cys.; $24/yr. in state; $30/yr. out of state. 1627 Cole St., Enumclaw, WA 98022. TEL 360-825-2555; FAX 360-825-1092. **Owner(s):** Courier Herald Publishing Co., Inc., P.O. Box 157, Enumclaw, WA 98022. TEL 360-825-2555; Pub. Jack Darnton; adv. contact: Bill Hinrichsen. pub. size: broadsheet; circ. 6,500(paid).

EPHRATA
US
GRANT COUNTY JOURNAL. 1907. s-w.: Mon. & Thu. $.50 newsstand; $28/yr. in cy. carrier or mailed; $38/yr. out of cy. mailed. 29 Alder, S.W., Ephrata, WA 98823. TEL 509-754-4636; FAX 509-754-5112. **Owner(s):** Jeffrey G. Fletcher, P.O. Box 998, Ephrata, WA 98823. TEL 509-754-4636; Ed. Randy Bracht; Pub. Jeffrey G. Fletcher; adv. contact: Steve Wallace. photos; pub. size: broadsheet; circ. 3,500(controlled & paid). **Wire Service(s):** AP.
Formerly: Ephrata Grant County Journal.

10758 FEDERAL WAY, WA   WEEKLY NEWSPAPERS

FEDERAL WAY
US

FEDERAL WAY NEWS. 1954. s-w.: Wed. & Sat. $.50 newsstand; $36/yr. 533 S. 336th St., Ste. C, Federal Way, WA 98003. TEL 206-529-2300; FAX 206-241-2788. **Owner(s):** Seattle Times Co., 207 S.W. 150th, Seattle, WA 98166. TEL 206-241-2700; Ed. Brad Broberg; Pub. Craig Dennis; adv. contact: Carla Royter. pub. size: broadsheet; circ. 45,962(free & paid).

FERNDALE
US

WESTSIDE RECORD-JOURNAL. 1885. Wed. $.50 newsstand; $20/yr. 2008 Main St., Ferndale, WA 98248-0038. TEL 360-384-1411; FAX 360-384-1417; E-mail: recjourn@telcomplus.com. **Owner(s):** Ferndale Record, Inc., P.O. Box 38, Ferndale, WA 98248. TEL 360-384-1411; Pub. Michael D. Lewis; adv. contact: Kim Winjum. photos; pub. size: broadsheet; circ. 8,360(free & paid).

GIG HARBOR
US

BUSINESS EXAMINER. 1985. bi-w. $25/yr. 3123 56th St., N.W., Ste. 6, Gig Harbor, WA 98335-1311. TEL 206-851-3705. **Owner(s):** Pierce County Business Examiner, 3123 56th St., N.W., Ste. 6, Gig Harbor, WA 98335-1311. TEL 206-851-3705; Pub. Jeff Rounce; adv.; photos; pub. size: tabloid; circ. 16,500(controlled & paid). Wire Service(s): AP.

US

PENINSULA GATEWAY. 1917. Wed. $.50 newsstand; $20/yr. in cy.; $40/yr. out of cy.; $17/yr. senior citizens. 3555 Erickson St., Gig Harbor, WA 98335. TEL 206-851-9921; FAX 206-851-3939. **Owner(s):** McClatchy Newspapers, 2100 Q St., Sacramento, CA 95852. TEL 916-321-1936; Ed. Tony Hazarian; Pub. Tom Taylor; adv.: $17.00/SAU. photos; pub. size: broadsheet; circ. 27,500(free & paid).

GOLDENDALE
US

GOLDENDALE SENTINEL. Thu. $25/yr. in cy.; $34/yr. out of cy. 117 W. Main, Goldendale, WA 98620-9526. TEL 509-773-3777; FAX 509-773-4737. **Owner(s):** Andrew J. McNab, 117 W. Main St., Goldendale, WA 98620. TEL 509-773-3777; Ed. Mike Federman. pub. size: standard; circ. 3,500(paid).

GRANDVIEW
US

GRANDVIEW HERALD. 1922. Wed. $.50 newsstand; $26/yr. local. 107 Division St., Grandview, WA 98930. TEL 509-882-3712; FAX 509-786-1779. **Owner(s):** Fournier Media Services, P.O. Box 750, Prosser, WA 99350. TEL 509-882-3712; Ed. Christa Lond; Pub. John Fournier Jr.; adv. contact: Diane Buxton. pub. size: standard; circ. 25,500(paid).

ISSAQUAH
US

ISSAQUAH PRESS. 1900. Wed. $.75 newsstand; $20/yr. in cy. mailed; $35/yr. out of cy. 45 Front St., S., Issaquah, WA 98027-1328. TEL 206-392-6434; FAX 206-391-1541; E-mail: ispress@accessone.com. **Owner(s):** Seattle Times Co., P.O. Box 70, Seattle, WA 98111. TEL 206-464-2111; Ed. Karl Kunkel; Pub. Deborah L. Berto; adv. contact: June Ford. photos; pub. size: broadsheet; circ. 8,600(paid).

LEAVENWORTH
US

LEAVENWORTH ECHO. 1906. Wed. $.50 newsstand; $19/yr. in cy. mailed. 215 14th St., Leavenworth, WA 98826. TEL 509-548-5286; FAX 509-548-4789. **Owner(s):** Prairie Media, Inc., 215 14th St., Leavenworth, WA 98826. TEL 509-548-5286; FAX 509-548-4789; Ed. Liz Gauger. adv. contact: Cassidy Roehm. pub. size: broadsheet; circ. 2,400.

LONG BEACH
US ISSN 0739-9200

LONG BEACH CHINOOK OBSERVER. 1900. Tue. $.50 newsstand; $20/yr. in cy.; $30/yr. out of cy. 212 S. Oregon St., Long Beach, WA 98631. TEL 360-642-8181; FAX 360-642-8105; E-mail: chinook@aone.com. **Owner(s):** East Oregonian Publishing Co., 211 S.E. Byers Ave., P.O. Box 1089, Pendleton, OR 97801. TEL 541-276-2211; Ed. Matt Winters. adv.; pub. size: broadsheet; circ. 7,200(paid).

LYNDEN
US

LYNDEN TRIBUNE. 1888. Wed. $.75 newsstand; $23/yr. in cy.; $32/yr. out of cy.; $35/yr. out of state. 113 N. Sixth St., Lynden, WA 98264. TEL 360-354-4444; FAX 360-398-1731; E-mail: lyndentrib@nas.com; URL: http://lyndentrib.com. **Owner(s):** Lewis Publishing Co., Inc., P.O. Box 153, Lynden, WA 98264. TEL 360-354-4444; FAX 360-398-1731; Ed. Dave Brumbaugh; Pub. Michael D. Lewis; adv. contact: Maggy Jones. bk.rev.; pub. size: broadsheet; circ. 14,265(free & paid).

LYNNWOOD
US

ENTERPRISE, THE. 1958. Wed. free; $25/yr. mailed. 7300 196th St., S.W., Ste. E, Lynnwood, WA 98036. TEL 206-775-7521; FAX 206-774-8622. **Owner(s):** Herald Inc., The, P.O. Box 930, Everett, WA 98206. TEL 206-339-3000; Ed. Tom Pearce; Pub. Allen Funk; adv.; photos; pub. size: broadsheet; circ. 80,000(paid).

MAPLE VALLEY
US

VOICE OF THE VALLEY. 1968. Wed. free; $20/yr. P.O. Box 307, Maple Valley, WA 98038. TEL 206-432-9696; FAX 206-432-0701. **Owner(s):** S. Hipple, P.O. Box 307, Maple Valley, WA 98038. TEL 206-432-9696; FAX 206-432-0701; Pub. S. Hipple; adv. contact: R.B. Hipple. photos; pub. size: tabloid; circ. 19,000(free & paid).

MERCER ISLAND
US

MERCER ISLAND REPORTER. 1954. Wed. $.75 newsstand; $36/yr. 7845 S.E. 30th St., Mercer Island, WA 98040. TEL 206-232-1215; FAX 206-232-1284; E-mail: mireprtr@horvitz.com. **Owner(s):** Horvitz Newspapers, Inc., P.O. Box 3110, Bellevue, WA 98004. TEL 206-455-2222; Ed. Jane Meyer; Pub. Peter A. Horvitz; adv. contact: Diana Reul. pub. size: standard; circ. 5,000(paid).

NEWPORT
US

GEM STATE MINER. 1901. Wed. $.50 newsstand; $17.50/yr. in cy.; $26.50/yr. out of cy. 317 S. Union St., Newport, WA 99156. TEL 509-447-2433; FAX 509-447-9222. **Owner(s):** Willenbrock Publishers, Inc., P.O. Box 349, Newport, WA 99156. TEL 509-447-2433; FAX 509-447-9222; Pub. Fred J. Willenbrock, II; pub. size: broadsheet; circ. 6,000(paid).

US

NEWPORT MINER. 1901. Wed. $.50 newsstand; $17.50/yr. mailed in cy.; $26.50/yr. out of cy. 317 S. Union St., Newport, WA 99156. TEL 509-447-2433; FAX 509-447-9222; E-mail: theminer@povn.com. **Owner(s):** Willenbrock Publishers, Inc., P.O. Box 349, Newport, WA 99156. TEL 509-447-2433; Ed. Mike Denuty; Pub. Fred J. Willenbrock, II; adv.; photos; pub. size: broadsheet; circ. 3,992(paid).

OAK HARBOR
US

WHIDBEY NEWS-TIMES. 1891. s-w.: Wed. & Sat. $.50 newsstand; $36/yr. carrier; $46/yr. in cy. mailed; $64/yr. out of cy. mailed. 8000 S.E. Barrington Dr., Oak Harbor, WA 98277. TEL 360-675-6611; FAX 360-675-2732; E-mail: wnt@whidbey.net. **Owner(s):** Sound Publishing, Inc., 7689 N.E. Day Rd., Bainbridge Island, WA 98110; Ed. Dave Fisher; Pub. Gregg McConnell; adv. contact: Kayla Connor. photos; pub. size: broadsheet; circ. 14,000(paid).

OMAK
US

OMAK-OKANOGAN COUNTY CHRONICLE. 1910. Wed. $.50 newsstand; $19/yr. home deliv.; $35/yr. out of state mailed. 618 Okoma Dr., Omak, WA 98841. TEL 509-826-1110; FAX 509-826-5819. **Owner(s):** Omak Chronicle, Inc., P.O. Box 553, Omak, WA 98841. TEL 509-826-1110; Pub. Judy Z. Smith; adv.; pub. size: broadsheet; circ. 16,000(paid).

OTHELLO
US ISSN 1056-8328

OUTLOOK, THE. 1951. Wed. $.75 newsstand; $25/yr. 180 E. Main St., Othello, WA 99344. TEL 509-488-3342; FAX 509-488-3345. **Owner(s):** Zaser-Longston, 1802-136th Pl., N.E., Seattle, WA 98005. TEL 206-562-7997; FAX 206-562-4785; Ed. Mark Grim; Pub. Bill Edlin; adv. contact: Richard Rex. pub. size: standard; circ. 2,700(paid).
Formerly: Othello Outlook, The.

ULRICH'S INTERNATIONAL PERIODICALS DIRECTORY 1998

WEEKLY NEWSPAPERS

SEATTLE, WA

PORT ORCHARD

US

PORT ORCHARD INDEPENDENT. 1886. s-w.: Wed. & Sat. $.50 newsstand; $26/yr. carrier. 1035 Bethel Ave., Port Orchard, WA 98366. TEL 360-876-4414; FAX 360-292-9521. **Owner(s):** Sound Publishing, Inc., 7689 N.E. Day Rd., Bainbridge Island, WA 98110; Ed. Pat Jenkins; Pub. Mike Shepard; adv.; photos; pub. size: tabloid; circ. 18,150(free & paid).

PORT TOWNSEND

US   ISSN 1050-1460

PORT TOWNSEND/JEFFERSON COUNTY LEADER. 1889. Wed. $.75 newsstand; $21/yr. in cy.; $32/yr. out of cy. 226 Adams St., Port Townsend, WA 98368. TEL 360-385-2900. E-mail: leader@olympus.net; URL: http://www.olympus.net/biz/leader. **Owner(s):** Port Townsend Publishing Co., Inc., 226 Adams St., Port Townsend, WA 98368. TEL 360-385-2900; Ed. Frank W. Garred. pub. size: broadsheet; circ. 9,247(paid).

POULSBO

US

NORTH KITSAP HERALD. 1901. b-w. $.50 newsstand; $26/yr. 19062 Hwy. 305, Ste. 203, Poulsbo, WA 98370. TEL 360-779-4464; FAX 360-779-8276. **Owner(s):** Sound Publishing, Inc., 7689 N.E. Day Rd., Bainbridge Island, WA 98110. TEL 360-842-8305; FAX 360-682-1107; Pub. Doug Weese; photos; pub. size: tabloid; circ. 10,500(free & paid).

PUYALLUP

US

PIERCE COUNTY HERALD. s-w.: Tue. & Fri. $.50 newsstand; $25/yr. in cy. 822 E. Main St., Puyallup, WA 98371. TEL 206-841-2487; FAX 206-840-8249. **Owner(s):** McClatchy Newspapers, 2100 Q St., Sacramento, CA 95852. TEL 916-321-1936; Ed. Gale Robinette; Pub. Gale Robinette; adv. contact: Kim Barkley. photos; pub. size: standard; circ. 16,000(paid).

RAYMOND

US   ISSN 1065-3805

WILLAPA HARBOR HERALD. 1906. Wed. $17/yr. in cy.; $22/yr. out of cy.; $14/yr. senior citizens. 335 Third St., Raymond, WA 98577. TEL 360-942-3466; FAX 360-942-3487. **Owner(s):** Flannery Publications, 335 Third St., Raymond, WA 98577; Ed. Doug Blossen. adv. contact: Ron Ulrich. pub. size: broadsheet; circ. 4,302(free & paid).

REDMOND

US

REDMOND SAMMAMISH VALLEY NEWS. 1946. Wed. free; $25/yr. in cy.; $35/yr. out of cy.; $20/yr. senior citizen. 14796 N.E. 95th St., Redmond, WA 98052. TEL 206-883-7187; FAX 206-881-9567. **Owner(s):** Pacific Publishing Co., 2314 Third Ave., Seattle, WA. TEL 206-461-1300; FAX 206-461-1347; Ed. Daven Rosener; Pub. Kim Nolan; adv. contact: Laurie Dugan. photos; bk.rev.; pub. size: tabloid; circ. 11,700(free & paid).

ROYAL CITY

US

ROYAL REVIEW. 1985. Wed. $.50 newsstand; $14.50/yr. in cy.; $17.50/yr. out of cy. 321 Camelia St., Royal City, WA 99357-0219. TEL 509-346-9723; FAX 509-346-9453. **Owner(s):** Andrew & Rachel Perkins, 321 Camilia St., Royal City, WA 99357. TEL 509-346-9723; FAX 509-346-9453; Ed. Rachel Perkins; Pub. Andrew Perkins; adv.; photos; circ. 1,200(controlled & paid).

SEATAC

US

HIGHLINE NEWS. 1946. s-w.: Wed. & Sat. $.50 newsstand; $36/yr. home deliv. 4800 S. 188th St., Ste. 360, Seatac, WA 98188. TEL 206-241-2700; FAX 206-241-2788. **Owner(s):** Seattle Times Co., P.O. Box 70, Seattle, WA 98111; Ed. Rob Smith; Pub. Craig Dennis; adv. contact: Paul Wood. photos; pub. size: broadsheet; circ. 47,000(free & paid).
Formerly: Highline Times.

SEATTLE

US

BEACON HILL NEWS, THE/SOUTH DISTRICT JOURNAL. 1924. Wed. $.50 newsstand; $30/yr. mailed. 2314 Third Ave., Seattle, WA 98121. TEL 206-461-1300; FAX 206-461-1340. **Owner(s):** Pacific Publishing Co., 2314 Third Ave., Seattle, WA 98121. TEL 206-461-1300; Ed. Jenny Yim; Pub. Brenda French; adv. contact: Sandy Hood. adv.: $22/SAU. photos; pub. size: tabloid; circ. 20,000(controlled & paid).

US

CAPITOL HILL TIMES. 1926. Wed. $.50 newsstand; $30/yr. 2314 Third Ave., Seattle, WA 98121. TEL 206-461-1300; FAX 206-461-1340. **Owner(s):** Pacific Publishing Co., 2314 Third Ave., Seattle, WA 98121. TEL 206-461-1300; Ed. Dennis Fitzgerald; Pub. Brenda French; adv. contact: Sandy C. Hood. adv.: $22/SAU. pub. size: tabloid; circ. 15,000(controlled & paid).

US

DES MOINES NEWS. 1959. s-w.: Wed. & Sat. $.50 newsstand; $36/yr. home deliv. 207 S.W. 150th St., Seattle, WA 98166. TEL 206-242-0100; FAX 206-241-2788. **Owner(s):** Seattle Times Co., P.O. Box 70, Seattle, WA 98166; Ed. Rob Smith; Pub. Craig Dennis; adv. contact: Craig McMurray. pub. size: broadsheet; circ. 11,883(paid).

US

MADISON PARK TIMES. 1983. bi-m. $.50 newsstand; $25/yr. 2314 Third Ave., Seattle, WA 98121. TEL 206-461-1300. **Owner(s):** Pacific Publishing Co., 2314 Third Ave., Seattle, WA 98121. TEL 206-461-1300; Ed. Dennis Fitzgerald; Pub. Brenda L. French; adv. contact: Sandy Hood. bk.rev.; pub. size: tabloid; circ. 6,000(paid).

US

NORTH CENTRAL OUTLOOK. 1917. Wed. $.50 newsstand; $30/yr. 2314 Third Ave., Seattle, WA 98121. TEL 206-461-1300. **Owner(s):** Pacific Publishing Co., 2314 Third Ave., Seattle, WA 98121. TEL 206-461-1300; Ed. Dennis Fitzgerald; Pub. Brenda L. French; adv. contact: Sandy Hood. photos; pub. size: tabloid; circ. 9,500(controlled & paid).

US

QUEEN ANNE-MAGNOLIA NEWS. 1919. Wed. $.75 newsstand; $1.50/mo. home deliv.; $35/yr. mailed. 529 Warren Ave., N., Seattle, WA 98109-4527. TEL 206-282-0900; FAX 206-285-1085; E-mail: qanews@seanet.com. **Owner(s):** Pacific Publishing Co., 2314 Third Ave., Seattle, WA 98121. TEL 206-461-1300; FAX 206-461-1340; Ed. Jack Arends; Pub. Mike Dillon; adv.; photos; pub. size: tabloid; circ. 21,800(controlled & paid).

US

SEATTLE FACTS. 1961. Wed. $60/yr. mailed. 2765 E. Cherry, Seattle, WA 98122. TEL 206-324-0552; FAX 206-324-1007. **Owner(s):** Elizabeth Beaver Fitzgerald, P.O. Box 22015, Seattle, WA 98122. TEL 206-324-0552; Ed. Elizabeth Beaver; Pub. Elizabeth Beaver; pub. size: oversize; circ. 50,000(paid).

US

SEATTLE SKANNER, THE. 1990. Wed. $35/yr. 1326 Fifth Ave., Ste. 825, Seattle, WA 98101. TEL 206-233-9888; FAX 206-233-9795; E-mail: info@theskanner; URL: http://www.theskanner.com. **Owner(s):** Bernard V. Foster, 2337 N. Williams, Portland, OR 97227-1989. TEL 503-287-3562; FAX 503-284-8200; Bobbie Dore Foster, 2337 N. Williams, Portland, OR 97227-1989. TEL 503-287-3562; FAX 503-284-8200; Ed. Bobbie Dore Foster; Pub. Bernard V. Foster; adv. contact: Ted Banks. photos; bk.rev.; pub. size: tabloid; circ. 25,000(free & paid).

US

SEATTLE WEEKLY. 1976. Wed. free. 1008 Western Ave., Ste. 300, Seattle, WA 98104. TEL 206-623-0500; FAX 206-467-4377. **Owner(s):** Quickfish Media, Inc., 1008 Western Ave., Ste. 300, Seattle, WA 98104; Ed. David Brewster; Pub. David Brewster; adv. contact: Ellen Cole. photos; bk.rev.; pub. size: tabloid; circ. 75,000(free & paid).

US

SOUTH DISTRICT JOURNAL. 1924. Wed. $.50 newsstand; $30/yr. 2314 Third Ave., Seattle, WA 98121. TEL 206-461-1300; FAX 206-461-1340. **Owner(s):** Pacific Publishing Co., 2314 Third Ave., Seattle, WA 98121. TEL 206-461-1311; Ed. Jenny Yim; Pub. Brenda French; adv.; $22/SAU. pub. size: tabloid; circ. 20,000(controlled & paid).

US

UNIVERSITY HERALD. 1925. Wed. $.35 newsstand; $24/yr. 2314 Third Ave., Seattle, WA 98121. TEL 206-461-3333; FAX 206-461-1340. **Owner(s):** Pacific Publishing Co., 2314 Third Ave., Seattle, WA 98121. TEL 206-461-1346; Ed. Jenny Yim; Pub. Brenda L. French; adv. contact: Sandy Hood. photos; pub. size: tabloid; circ. 10,000(controlled & paid).

US

WEST SEATTLE HERALD. 1923. Wed. $.50 newsstand; $24/yr. home deliv.; $40/yr. mailed. 3500 S.W. Alaska St., Seattle, WA 98126. TEL 206-932-0300; FAX 206-937-1223. **Owner(s):** West Seattle Herald, Inc., 3500 S.W. Alaska St., Seattle, WA 98126. TEL 206-932-0300; Ed. Gloria Kruzner; Pub. Jerry Robinson; pub. size: tabloid; circ. 16,000(paid).
Formerly: West Seattle Herald/White Center News.

SEQUIM

US

SEQUIM GAZETTE. 1974. Wed. $.50 newsstand; $18/yr. local; $25/yr. elsewhere. 147 W. Washington, Sequim, WA 98382. TEL 360-683-3311; FAX 360-683-6670. **Owner(s):** Olympic View Publishing Co., P.O. Box 1750, Sequim, WA 98382. TEL 206-683-3311; Ed. James Manders; Pub. Brown M. Maloney; pub. size: tabloid; circ. 11,000(paid).

SHELTON

US

SHELTON-MASON COUNTY JOURNAL. 1886. Thu. $.50 newsstand; $25/yr. in cy.; $35/yr. out of cy.; $45/yr. out of state. Third & Cota, Shelton, WA 98584. TEL 206-426-4412. **Owner(s):** Henry G. Gay, P.O. Box 430, Shelton, WA 98584. TEL 206-426-4412; Ed. Charles Gay; Pub. Henry G. Gay; adv.; photos; pub. size: broadsheet; circ. 9,977(paid).

SNOHOMISH

US

SNOHOMISH COUNTY TRIBUNE. 1891. Wed. $.50 newsstand; $20/yr. mailed in cy.; $28/yr. out of cy. 127 Ave. C, Snohomish, WA 98290. TEL 425-568-4121; FAX 425-568-1484. **Owner(s):** Mach Publishing, P.O. Box 499, Snohomish, WA 98291. TEL 360-568-4121; FAX 360-568-1484; Ed. Leslie Hynes; Pub. Dave Mach; adv. contact: Becky Reed. adv.: $22.67/SAU. pub. size: tabloid; circ. 30,000(paid).

SPOKANE

US

VALLEY NEWS HERALD. 1920. Fri. $50 newsstand; $20/yr. in cy.; $30/yr. out of cy. 8940 E. Sprague Ave., Spokane, WA 99212. TEL 509-924-2440; FAX 509-927-1154. **Owner(s):** Journal News Publishing Co., 8940 E. Sprague Ave., Spokane, WA 99212. TEL 509-924-2440; Ed. Mike Huffman; Pub. William Lfft; adv.; photos; pub. size: broadsheet; circ. 8,070(paid).
Formerly: The Valley Herald.

SPRAGUE

US

SPRAGUE ADVOCATE, THE. 1888. Thu. $.50 newsstand; $26/yr. in state; $29/yr. out of state; $25/yr. senior citizens. 113 N. C St., Sprague, WA 99032-0327. TEL 509-257-2928. **Owner(s):** Tess Canaday, P.O. Box 68, Sprague, WA 99032. TEL 509-257-2928; Pub. Tess Canaday; adv.; photos; pub. size: broadsheet; circ. 232,906(paid).

TACOMA

US

TACOMA CITY PAPER. Thu. free. 10507 Gravelly Lake Dr., S.E., Ste. 4, Tacoma, WA 98499. TEL 206-584-1212; FAX 206-581-5962; E-mail: swarnercom@aol.com. **Owner(s):** Thomas H. Swarner, Ranger Publishing Co., Inc., The, P.O. Box 98801, Tacoma, WA 98498. TEL 206-548-1212; FAX 206-581-5962; Ed. John Atkins; Pub. Thomas H. Swarner; adv. contact: Kenneth Swarner. pub. size: tabloid; circ. 38,000(controlled).

TENINO

US

ROCHESTER SUN NEWS, THE. 1922. Fri. $.50 newsstand; $18/yr. in cy.; $21/yr. out of cy.; $26/yr. out of state. 297 Suffex Ave., W., Tenino, WA 98589-4004. TEL 360-264-2500; FAX 360-264-2955. **Owner(s):** DeVaul Publishing, Inc., 459 N.E. Washington Ave., Chehalis, WA 98532. TEL 360-748-6848; Ed. Glen Dickason; Pub. Frank DeVaul; adv.; pub. size: tabloid; circ. 1,800(free).
Formerly: Sun, The.

TENINO INDEPENDENT. 1922. Fri. $.50 newsstand; $18/yr. in cy.; $21/yr. in state; $26/yr. out of state. P.O. Box 4004, Tenino, WA 98589-4004. TEL 360-264-2500; FAX 360-264-2955. **Owner(s):** DeVaul Publishing, Inc., 107 N. Tower, Ste. 5, Centralia, WA 98531. TEL 360-736-3580; FAX 360-736-3581; Ed. Glen E. Dickason; Pub. Frank DeVaul; adv.; photos; pub. size: tabloid; circ. 3,000(paid).

TOPPENISH

US

TOPPENISH REVIEW. 1905. Wed. $20/yr. in cy.; $25/yr. out of cy. 11 E. Toppenish Ave., Toppenish, WA 98948. TEL 509-865-4055; FAX 509-865-2655. **Owner(s):** James A. Flint, 11 E. Toppenish Ave., Toppenish, WA 98948; Ed. Pat Jones; Pub. James Flint; pub. size: broadsheet; circ. 6,000(paid).

VASHON

US

VASHON-MAURY ISLAND BEACHCOMBER. 1957. Wed. $.50 newsstand; $20/yr. on island; $34/yr. off island; $18/yr. senior citizens. 17500 Vashon Hwy., S.W., Vashon, WA 98070. TEL 206-463-9195; FAX 206-463-6122. **Owner(s):** Sound Publishing, Inc., 7689 N.E. Day Rd., Bainbridge Island, WA 98110; Ed. Allison Arthur; Pub. Jim Long; adv. contact: Todd Brown. photos; pub. size: tabloid; circ. 3,783(paid).

WAITSBURG

US

TIMES, THE. 1878. Thu. $.50 newsstand; $20/yr. in Walla Walla & Columbia cys.; $22/yr. in state; $25/yr. out of state. 139 Main St., Waitsburg, WA 99361-0097. TEL 509-337-6631; FAX 509-337-6045; E-mail: loyalbaker@juno.com. **Owner(s):** Loyal & Kathy Baker, 139 Main St., Waitsburg, WA 99361-0097. TEL 509-337-6631; FAX 509-337-6045; Ed. Loyal Baker. adv. contact: Loyal Baker. pub. size: standard; circ. 1,850(paid).

WAPATO

US

WAPATO INDEPENDENT. 1906. Wed. $.50 newsstand; $20/yr. in cy.; $25/yr. out of cy.; $18/yr. senior citizens. 113 S. Wapato Ave., Wapato, WA 98951-0067. TEL 509-877-3322; FAX 509-877-2577. **Owner(s):** James A. Flint, P.O. Box 511, Toppenish, WA 98948. TEL 509-865-4055; FAX 509-862-2655; Ed. Stephen McFadden; Pub. James A. Flint; adv. contact: Larry Watkins. pub. size: broadsheet; circ. 2,100(paid).

WOODLAND

US

LEWIS RIVER NEWS. 1919. Wed. $35/yr. 435 Davidson St., Woodland, WA 98674. TEL 360-225-8287; FAX 360-225-8289. **Owner(s):** Stern Wheeler Publishing Co., P. O. Box 368, Castle Rock, WA 98611. TEL 360-225-8287; FAX 360-225-8289; Pub. John Hayden; adv.; photos; pub. size: broadsheet; circ. 7,782(paid).
Formerly: Woodland River News.

YELM

US

NISQUALLY VALLEY NEWS. 1921. Thu. $.50 newsstand; $23/yr. in state; $30/yr. out of state. 207 Yelm Ave., W., Yelm, WA 98597. TEL 360-458-2681; FAX 360-458-5741. **Owner(s):** Lafromboise Newspapers, Inc., 321 N. Pearl St., Centralia, WA 98531. TEL 360-736-3311; Ed. Fiona Reeves; Pub. Dennis R. Waller; adv.; photos; bk.rev.; pub. size: standard; circ. 3,600(paid).

WEST VIRGINIA

BECKLEY

US

POST REPORT, THE. 1965. Thu. $.50 newsstand; $13/yr. in state. 801 N. Kanawha St., Beckley, WV 25801. TEL 304-255-4400; FAX 304-255-4427. **Owner(s):** Thomson Newspapers, Inc., Metro Centre, One Station Pl., 6th Fl., Stamford, CT 06902. TEL 203-425-2500; FAX 203-425-2516; Ed. Dawn Keys; Pub. Rob Hammon; adv. contact: Jack Scott. pub. size: standard; circ. 35,000(paid).

BERKELEY SPRINGS

US   ISSN 0895-1594

MORGAN MESSENGER, THE. 1893. Wed. $.50 newsstand; $18.02/yr. in town. P.O. Box 567, Berkeley Springs, WV 25411. TEL 304-258-1800; FAX 304-258-8441. **Owner(s):** Morgan Messenger, Inc., P.O. Box 567, Berkeley Springs, WV 25411. TEL 304-258-1800; FAX 304-258-8441; Ed. J. Warren Buzzerd; Pub. J. Warren Buzzerd; adv. contact: Sandy Buzzerd. photos; pub. size: standard; circ. 5,400(paid).

BUCKHANNON

US

RECORD-DELTA, THE. 1976. 3/wk.: Mon., Wed., Fri. $62.54/yr. home deliv. in cy.; $59/yr. in state; $68.90/yr. out of state. 2-B Clarksburg Rd., Buckhannon, WV 26201. TEL 304-472-2800; FAX 304-472-0537; E-mail: medemail@aol.com. **Owner(s):** Mountaineer Newspapers, 2-B Clarksburg Rd., Buckhannon, WV 26201. TEL 304-472-2800; Pub. Mark Davis; adv. contact: Mark Davis. photos; pub. size: broadsheet; circ. 5,000(paid).
Formerly: Buckhannon Record-Delta.

WEEKLY NEWSPAPERS

CHARLES TOWN

US

SPIRIT OF JEFFERSON-ADVOCATE. 1844. Thu. $.45 newsstand; $22/yr. in state; $23/yr. out of state. 210 N. George St., Charles Town, WV 25414-0966. TEL 304-725-2046. **Owner(s):** Jefferson Publishing Co., Inc., P.O. Box 966, Charles Town, WV 25414-0966. TEL 304-725-2046; Ed. Edward W. Dockeney, Jr. adv. contact: R. Meade Dorsey. adv.: $6.90/SAU. photos; pub. size: broadsheet; circ. 4,893(free & paid).

CLAY

US

CLAY COUNTY FREE PRESS. 1888. Wed. $.50 newsstand; $12/yr. in cy.; $15/yr. out of cy.; $18/yr. out of state. P.O. Box 180, Clay, WV 25043-0180. TEL 304-587-4250; FAX 304-587-7300. **Owner(s):** Clinton Nichols, P.O. Box 180, Clay, WV 02503-0180. TEL 304-587-4250; FAX 304-587-7329; Ed. Clinton Nichols; Pub. Clinton Nichols; pub. size: tabloid; circ. 3,500(paid).

CULLODEN

US

CABELL RECORD. 1898. Thu. $12/yr. in state; $20/yr. out of state. 2085 Rte. 60, Culloden, WV 25510. TEL 304-743-1222; FAX 304-562-6214. **Owner(s):** Phyllis Robinson, P.O. Box 186, Culloden, WV 25510-0186. TEL 304-743-1222; Frances Fallecker, 2235 Lincoln Ave., St. Albans, WV 25177. TEL 304-727-1757; Ed. Marie Hedrick. adv. contact: Jim Drown. adv.: $4.40/SAU. photos; pub. size: broadsheet; circ. 2,525(paid).

US

PUTNAM-CABELL POST. 1955. Sun. free in area; $26.50/yr. out of area. 2085 Rte. 60, Culloden, WV 25510. TEL 304-562-6214; FAX 304-562-6214. **Owner(s):** Phyllis C. Robinson, P.C. Publishing Co., P.O. Box 186, Culloden, WV 25510. TEL 304-562-6214; Frances Fallecker, 2235 Lincoln Ave., St. Albans, WV 25510. TEL 304-727-1757; Ed. Marie Hedrick. adv. contact: Jim Drown. adv.: $13.86/SAU. photos; pub. size: tabloid; circ. 27,022(controlled & paid).
Formerly: Putnam Post-Cabell Bulletin.

DANVILLE

US

COAL VALLEY NEWS. 1925. Wed. $.50 newsstand; $24/yr. in state mailed; $33/yr. out of state; $21/yr. senior citizens. One Smoot Ave., Danville, WV 25053. TEL 304-369-1165; FAX 304-369-1166. **Owner(s):** Smith Newspapers, Inc., P.O. Box 27, Fort Payne, AL 35967. TEL 205-845-5510; Ed. Terry Headley; Pub. Marc Glenn; adv. contact: Marc Glenn. pub. size: broadsheet; circ. 6,000(paid).
Formerly: Madison Coal Valley News.

FRANKLIN

US

FRANKLIN PENDLETON TIMES. 1913. Thu. $.35 newsstand; $15/yr. mailed anywhere. Main St., Franklin, WV 26807. TEL 304-358-2304; FAX 304-358-2304. **Owner(s):** William McCoy, Jr., P.O. Box 906, Franklin, WV 26807. TEL 304-358-2261; Ed. William McCoy, Jr.; Pub. William McCoy, Jr.; adv.; pub. size: standard; circ. 5,500(paid).

GLENVILLE

US

GLENVILLE DEMOCRAT, THE. 1906. Thu. $16.96/yr. in cy.; $21.20/yr. out of cy.; $22/yr. out of state. 206 E. Main St., Glenville, WV 26351. TEL 304-462-7309; FAX 304-462-7300. **Owner(s):** David Corcoran, P.O. Box 458, Glenville, WV 26351; Pub. David Corcoran; adv. contact: Angela McHenry. pub. size: broadsheet; circ. 1,970(paid).

US

GLENVILLE PATHFINDER. Thu. $16.96/yr. in cy.; $20/yr. in state; $22/yr. out of state. 109 E. Main St., Glenville, WV 26351. TEL 304-462-7309. **Owner(s):** Gilmer County Publishing, Inc., P.O. Box 458, Glenville, WV 26351. TEL 304-462-7309; Pub. David Corcoran; adv. contact: Angela McHenry. pub. size: broadsheet; circ. 1,530(paid).

GRAFTON

US ISSN 0745-1334

MOUNTAIN STATESMAN. 3/wk.: Mon., Wed., Fri. $.35 newsstand; $57.24/yr. in cy. home deliv. 914 W. Main St., Grafton, WV 26354. TEL 304-265-3333; FAX 304-265-3342; E-mail: medemail@aol.com. **Owner(s):** News Media Corp., Rochelle, IL 61068. TEL 815-562-2061; Ed. Marvin Gelhausen; Pub. James Clark; adv.; pub. size: broadsheet; circ. 3,300(paid).

GRANTSVILLE

US

CALHOUN CHRONICLE. 1883. Thu. $15.90/yr. in cy.; $20.67/yr. out of cy.; $23/yr. out of state. 353 Main St., Grantsville, WV 26147. TEL 304-354-6917; FAX 304-354-7142. **Owner(s):** Carl Morris, 353 Main St., Grantsville, WV 26147. TEL 304-354-6672; FAX 304-354-7142; Ed. Newton Nichols; Pub. Carl Morris; adv. contact: Maureen Wright. photos; pub. size: standard; circ. 3,300(paid).

HAMLIN

US

LINCOLN JOURNAL. 1903. Tue. $.50 newsstand; $21/yr. in cy.; $28.50/yr. out of cy.; $37.30/yr. out of state. 328 Walnut St., Hamlin, WV 25523. TEL 304-824-5101; FAX 304-824-5210. **Owner(s):** Thomas A. Robinson, 328 Walnut St., Hamlin, WV 25523. TEL 304-824-5101; FAX 304-824-5210; Ed. Charles Damron; Pub. Thomas A. Robinson; adv. contact: Barbara Cummings. photos; bk.rev.; pub. size: broadsheet; circ. 5,200(free & paid). **Wire Service(s):** WV Press Assn.

US

LINCOLN TIMES, THE. Fri. free. 328 Walnut St., Hamlin, WV 25523. TEL 304-824-5101; FAX 304-824-5210. **Owner(s):** Thomas A. Robinson, P.O. Box 308, Hamlin, WV 25523. TEL 304-824-5101; FAX 304-824-5210; Pub. Thomas A. Robinson; adv. contact: Barbara Cummings. pub. size: broadsheet; circ. 12,133(paid).

US

LINCOLN WEEKLY NEWS SENTINEL. Tue. $.50 newsstant; $21/yr. in cy.; $28.50/yr. out of cy. 328 Walnut St., Hamlin, WV 25523. TEL 304-824-5101; FAX 304-824-5210. **Owner(s):** Thomas A. Robinson, P.O. Box 308, Hamlin, WV 25523. TEL 304-824-5101; FAX 304-824-5210; Ed. Charles Damron; Pub. Thomas A. Robinson; adv. contact: Barbara Cummings. photos; pub. size: broadsheet; circ. 4,500(paid).

HARRISVILLE

US

RITCHIE GAZETTE. 1873. Thu. $15.37/yr. in cy.; $19.61/yr. in state; $22/yr. out of state. 200 E. Main St., Harrisville, WV 26362. TEL 304-643-2221; FAX 304-643-2156. **Owner(s):** Ritchie Gazette Publishing, LLC, P.O. Box 215, Harrisville, WV 26362. TEL 304-643-2221; FAX 304-643-2156; Ed. Kent R. Spellman. adv. contact: D.J. Allen. photos; bk.rev.; pub. size: standard; circ. 3,820(paid).

HINTON

US

HINTON NEWS. 1901. Tue. $.32 newsstand; $16.43/yr. in cy.; $19.50/yr. out of state. 210 Second Ave., Hinton, WV 25951. TEL 304-466-0005. **Owner(s):** Hinton Publishing Co., Inc., 210 Second Ave., Hinton, WV 25951. TEL 304-466-0005; Ed. Fred Long; Pub. Fred Long; adv. contact: Fred Long. photos; pub. size: broadsheet; circ. 4,200(paid).

HURRICANE

US

HURRICANE BREEZE. 1900. Thu. $.35 newsstand; $12.72/yr. in cy.; $16.96/yr. in state; $19.08/yr. out of state. 488 Hurricane Creek Rd., Hurricane, WV 25526. TEL 304-562-9881. **Owner(s):** Cookie Allen, 488 Hurricane Creek Rd., Hurricane, WV 25526. TEL 304-562-9881; Ed. Ron Allen; Pub. Cookie Allen; adv. contact: Ron Allen. pub. size: broadsheet; circ. 1,500(paid).

KINGWOOD

US

PRESTON COUNTY JOURNAL. Wed. $.35 newsstand; $18/yr. in cy.; $23/yr. out of cy. 110 W. Main St., Kingwood, WV 26537. TEL 304-329-0090; FAX 304-329-2450. **Owner(s):** Preston Publications, Inc., 110 W. Main St., Kingwood, WV 26537. TEL 304-329-0090; Ed. Tina Bolyard; Pub. Gary Bolyard; adv. contact: Carol Peters. photos; pub. size: broadsheet; circ. 5,700(paid).

US ISSN 1072-0057

PRESTON COUNTY NEWS. 1866. Sat. $.35 newsstand; $18/yr. in cy.; $23/yr. out of cy. 110 W. Main St., Kingwood, WV 26537. TEL 304-329-0090; FAX 304-329-2450. **Owner(s):** Preston Publications, Inc., 110 W. Main St., Kingwood, WV 26537. TEL 304-329-0090; Ed. Tina Bolyard; Pub. Gary Bolyard; adv. contact: Carol Peters. pub. size: broadsheet; circ. 5,400(paid).

LEWISBURG

GREENBRIER VALLEY RANGER. 1981. s-w.: Wed. & Sun. free. 200 S. Court St., Lewisburg, WV 24901-0471. TEL 304-645-1206; FAX 304-645-7104. **Owner(s):** Moffitt Newspapers, Inc., P.O. Box 8565, Roanoke, VA 24014. TEL 540-344-2489; Ed. Kerri Flaganan; Pub. Frank Spicer; adv. contact: Judy Dowdy. photos; pub. size: broadsheet; circ. 26,762(free).

MOUNTAIN MESSENGER. 1985. Sun. $15/yr. carrier; $19.08/yr. mailed; $24/yr. out of state. 122 N. Court St., Lewisburg, WV 24901. TEL 304-647-5724; FAX 304-647-5767. **Owner(s):** Michael Showell, 122 N. Court St., Lewisburg, WV 24901. TEL 304-647-5724; Ed. Carol Hall; Pub. Michael Showell; adv. contact: Linda Hudson. photos; bk.rev.; pub. size: broadsheet; circ. Sun. 5,000(paid). Wire Service(s): AP.

MADISON

HOMETOWN NEWS. 1986. Wed. $.50 newsstand; $21/yr. 475 Main St., Lower Level, Madison, WV 25130. TEL 304-369-5175; FAX 304-369-5176. **Owner(s):** Hometown News, P.O. Box 597, Madison, WV 25130. TEL 304-369-5175; FAX 304-369-5176; Ed. Janet Yeager; Pub. Janet Yeager; adv. contact: Arthur Bias. photos; pub. size: broadsheet; circ. 4,500(paid).

MARLINTON

POCAHONTAS TIMES. 1883. Wed. $.30 newsstand; $12.72/yr. in cy.; $21.20/yr. in state; $22/yr. out of state. 810 Second Ave., Marlinton, WV 24954. TEL 304-799-4973. **Owner(s):** Jane P. Sharp, 1118 Second Ave., Marlinton, WV 24954. TEL 304-799-4913; William P. McNeel, 1118 Second Ave., Marlinton, WV 24954; Pamela E. Pritt, 810 Second Ave., Marlinton, WV 24954; Ed. Pamela E. Pritt. adv.: $4/SAU. bk.rev.; pub. size: standard; circ. 6,500(free & paid).

MONTGOMERY

MONTGOMERY HERALD. 1940. Wed. $18/yr. in state; $19.50/yr. out of state. 406 Lee St., Montgomery, WV 25136. TEL 304-442-4156; FAX 304-442-8753. **Owner(s):** Thomson Newspapers, Inc., Metro Centre, One Station Pl., 6th Fl., Stamford, CT 06902. TEL 203-425-2500; FAX 203-425-2516; Ed. Cheryl Keenan; Pub. Robert Hammond; adv. contact: Nancy Shelton. pub. size: broadsheet; circ. 4,700(paid).

MOOREFIELD

MOOREFIELD EXAMINER. 1845. Wed. $.40 newsstand; $16.96/yr. in cy; $21/yr. out of state. 132 S. Main St., Moorefield, WV 26836-0380. TEL 304-538-2342; FAX 304-538-7294. **Owner(s):** R.E. Fisher Co., Inc., 132 S. Main St., P.O. Box 380, Moorefield, WV 26836-0380. TEL 304-538-2342; FAX 304-538-7294; Ed. Phoebe F. Heishman; Pub. Phoebe F. Heishman; adv. contact: Serena Cline. photos; bk.rev.; pub. size: broadsheet; circ. 4,400(paid).

MOUNDSVILLE

GREEN TAB. 1926. Sun. free. 518 Seventh St., Moundsville, WV 26041. TEL 304-845-4050; FAX 304-845-4312. **Owner(s):** Robert W. Munn, Jr., 518 Seventh St., Moundsville, WV 26041. TEL 304-845-4050; Ed. Robert W. Munn, Jr. adv. contact: Ralph DeRemigio. pub. size: tabloid; circ. 60,000(free).

MULLEN

MULLENS ADVOCATE. 1913. Tue. $.25 newsstand; $11/yr. in cy.; $15/yr. out of cy. 217 Moran Ave., Mullen, WV 25882. TEL 304-294-4144. **Owner(s):** Jack Moffitt, 217 Moran Ave., Mullen, WV 25882. TEL 304-294-4144; Pub. W.A. Tony Johnson; adv.; pub. size: broadsheet; circ. 3,500(paid).

NEW MARTINSVILLE

WETZEL CHRONICLE. 1888. Wed. $.47 newsstand; $25/yr. in state mailed; $28/yr. out of state. 1100 Third St., New Martinsville, WV 26155. TEL 304-455-3300; FAX 304-455-1275. **Owner(s):** Wetzel Chronicle Co., 1100 Third St., New Martinsville, WV 26155. TEL 304-455-3300; Ed. Ray Sweeney; Pub. Kenneth M. Sickle; adv. contact: Michael Galluzzo. photos; pub. size: standard; circ. 7,000(paid).

OAK HILL

FAYETTE TRIBUNE. 1897. s-w: Mon. & Thu. $.35 newsstand; $30/yr. in cy.; $35/yr. in state; $40/yr. out of state. 417 Main St., Oak Hill, WV 25901. TEL 304-469-3373; FAX 304-469-4105. **Owner(s):** Thomson Newspapers, Inc., Metro Centre, One Station Pl., 6th Fl., Stamford, CT 06902. TEL 203-425-2500; FAX 203-425-2516; Ed. Cheryl Keenan; Pub. Robert Hammond; adv. contact: Nancy Shelton. pub. size: broadsheet; circ. 6,000(paid).

PARSONS

ISSN 0747-3303
PARSONS ADVOCATE. 1896. Wed. $.50 newsstand; $20/yr. in state; $25/yr. out of state. 212 Main St., Parsons, WV 26287. TEL 304-478-3533; FAX 304-478-4658. **Owner(s):** George A. & Mariwyn Smith, 205 Main St., Parsons, WV 26287; Ed. Mariwyn M. Smith. adv.; pub. size: standard; circ. 3,900(paid).

PENNSBORO

PENNSBORO NEWS. 1892. Wed. $.50 newsstand; $7.47/yr. in cy.; $12.72/yr. out of cy. 409 Main St., Pennsboro, WV 26415. TEL 304-659-2441; FAX 304-659-2441. **Owner(s):** James McGoldrick, 409 Main St., Pennsboro, WV 26415. TEL 304-659-2441; Ed. James McGoldrick; Pub. James McGoldrick; pub. size: broadsheet; circ. 5,100(paid).

PETERSBURG

GRANT COUNTY PRESS. 1896. Tue. $15.90/yr. in cy.; $16.96/yr. in state; $19.50/yr. out of state. 47 S. Main St., Petersburg, WV 26847. TEL 304-257-1844; FAX 304-257-1691. **Owner(s):** Potomac Valley Press, Inc., 47 S. Main St., Petersburg, WV 26847; Ed. William E. Fouch. adv. contact: Jodi Fouch. pub. size: broadsheet; circ. 5,200(paid).

PHILIPPI

BARBOUR DEMOCRAT, THE. 1893. Wed. $19.08/yr. in state; $21.50/yr. out of state. 113 Church St., Philippi, WV 26416. TEL 304-457-2222; FAX 304-457-2703. **Owner(s):** Barbour Publishing Co., Inc., 113 Church St., Philippi, WV 24616; Ed. Robert A. Byrne. pub. size: standard; circ. 5,300(paid).
Formerly: Philippi Barbour Democrat.

PIEDMONT

PIEDMONT HERALD. 1879. Tue. $20/yr. in cy.; $21/yr. out of cy. 34 Railroad St., Piedmont, WV 26750. TEL 304-355-2381; FAX 304-355-2383. **Owner(s):** Herald Printing House, Piedmont, WV. TEL 304-355-2381; FAX 304-355-2383; Ed. Margaret J. Hood; Pub. William T. Hood; adv.; photos; pub. size: standard; circ. 2,000(paid).

PINEVILLE

INDEPENDENT HERALD, THE. 1914. Wed. $8.48/yr. in cy.; $12.72/yr. out of cy. Rte. 10, Pineville, WV 24874. TEL 304-732-6060; FAX 304-732-8228. **Owner(s):** Charles R. Cline, Rte. 10, Pineville, WV 24874. TEL 304-732-6060; Ed. Ron Mullens; Pub. Charles R. Cline; adv.; photos; pub. size: standard; circ. 5,000(paid).

PRINCETON

PRINCETON TIMES. 1961. Thu. $15/yr. in state; $20/yr. out of state. 109 Thorn St., Princeton, WV 24740. TEL 304-425-8191; FAX 304-487-1632. **Owner(s):** Thomson Newspapers, Inc., Metro Centre, One Station Pl., 6th Fl., Stamford, CT 06902. TEL 203-425-2500; FAX 203-425-2516; Ed. Sasrah Rosen. adv. contact: Jerry L. Morgan. pub. size: broadsheet; circ. 3,000(paid).

RAVENSWOOD

JACKSON STAR NEWS. 1955. s-w.: Wed. & Sat. $.75 newsstand; $29.15/yr. in cy. 237 Washington St., Ravenswood, WV 26164. TEL 304-273-9333; FAX 304-273-3401. **Owner(s):** Smith Newspapers, Inc., P.O. Box 27, Fort Payne, AL 35967. TEL 205-845-5510; Ed. Greg Matics; Pub. Greg Matics; pub. size: broadsheet; circ. 14,500(paid).

RICHWOOD
US

NEWS LEADER. 1946. Wed. $.50 newsstand; $21/yr. in state; $25/yr. out of state. 4 Railroad Ave., Richwood, WV 26261. TEL 304-846-2666; FAX 304-846-4972. **Owner(s):** Jim Comstock, P.O. Box 430, Richwood, WV 26261. TEL 304-846-2667; Jay Comstock, P.O. Box 430, Richmond, VA 26261. TEL 304-846-2667; Ed. Russell McCauley; Pub. Jay Comstock; adv.; pub. size: broadsheet; circ. 4,200(paid).

US

WEST VIRGINIA HILLBILLY. 1958. Wed. $30/yr. 4 Railroad Ave., Richwood, WV 26261. TEL 304-846-2667; FAX 304-846-4972. **Owner(s):** Russell McCulley, P.O. Box 430, Richwood, WV 26261. TEL 304-846-2667; Pub. Russell McCulley; adv. contact: Russell McCulley. pub. size: tabloid; circ. 5,000(paid).

RIPLEY
US

JACKSON HERALD. 1877. Wed. $.75 newsstand; $29.15/yr. in cy.; $34.98/yr. out of cy.; $47.70/yr. out of state. 117 Court St., Ripley, WV 25271. TEL 304-372-2421; FAX 304-372-8240. **Owner(s):** Ripley Newspapers Inc., P.O. Box 27, Fort Payne, AL 35967; Ed. Mike Ruben; Pub. Carol Haun; adv.; photos; pub. size: broadsheet; circ. 6,500(free & paid).

US

STAR HERALD. Sat. free home deliv.; $.75 newsstand. 117 Court St., Ripley, WV 25271. TEL 304-372-2421; FAX 304-372-8240. **Owner(s):** Ripley Newspapers, Inc., P.O. Box 27, Fort Payne, AL 35967; Ed. Mike Ruben; Pub. Carol Haun; adv.; pub. size: tabloid; circ. 14,500(free & paid).

ROMNEY
US

HAMPSHIRE REVIEW. 1829. Wed. $.50 newsstand; $25.44/yr. in cy. mailed; $26.50/yr. in state; $27.56/yr. out of state. 25 S. Grafton St., Romney, WV 26757. TEL 304-822-3871; FAX 304-822-4487. **Owner(s):** Cornwell & Ailes, Inc., 25 S. Grafton St., Romney, WV 26757. TEL 304-822-3871; Ed. Charles See. adv. contact: Lana Bean. pub. size: broadsheet; circ. 6,200(paid).

SHEPHERDSTOWN
US

SHEPHERDSTOWN CHRONICLE. 1991. Fri. $.35 newsstand; $13.50/yr. in cy.; $22.50/yr. out of cy. Duke & Washington Sts., Shepherdstown, WV 25443. TEL 304-876-3380; FAX 304-876-1957; E-mail: shepchrn@intrepid.net. **Owner(s):** Corcoran Publications, Ltd., P.O. Box 2088, Shepherdstown, WV 25443. TEL 304-876-3380; FAX 304-876-3380; Ed. Mary Corcoran; Pub. John Lehman; adv. contact: John Lehman. photos; pub. size: tabloid; circ. 2,000(paid).

SISTERSVILLE
US

TYLER STAR NEWS. 1878. Wed. $25/yr. in state; $28/yr. out of state. 727 Wells St., Sistersville, WV 26175. TEL 304-652-4141; FAX 304-652-1454. **Owner(s):** Ogden Newspapers, Inc., 1500 Main St., Wheeling, WV 26003. TEL 304-233-0100; Ed. Charles A. Mason; Pub. Kenneth Sickle; adv. contact: Michael Galluzzo. bk.rev.; pub. size: standard; circ. 4,200(paid).

SPENCER
US

ROANE COUNTY REPORTER. 1915. Thu. $.50 newsstand; $21/yr. in state; $25/yr. out of state. 210 E. Main St., Spencer, WV 25276-0647. TEL 304-927-2360; FAX 304-927-2361. **Owner(s):** Spencer Newspapers, Inc., P.O. Box 647, Spencer, WV 25276. TEL 304-927-2360; FAX 304-927-2361; Ed. Jim Cooper; Pub. David J. Hedges; adv. contact: Danny Jarvis. pub. size: broadsheet; circ. 2,000(free & paid).

US

TIMES RECORD. 1914. Thu. $.50 newsstand; $21/yr. in state; $25/yr. out of state. 210 E. Main St., Spencer, WV 25276. TEL 304-927-2360; FAX 304-927-2361. **Owner(s):** Spencer Newspapers, Inc., P.O. Box 647, Spencer, WV 25276. TEL 304-927-2360; Ed. Jim Cooper; Pub. David J. Hedges; adv. contact: Danny Jarvis. pub. size: broadsheet; circ. 3,562(free & paid).

SUMMERSVILLE
US

NICHOLAS CHRONICLE. 1880. Thu. $.50 newsstand; $25/yr. in state; $30/yr. out of state. 603 Church St., Summersville, WV 26651. TEL 304-872-2251; FAX 304-872-2254. **Owner(s):** Nicholas County Publishing Co., Inc., P.O. Box 503, Summersville, WV 26651. TEL 304-872-2251; FAX 304-872-2254; Ed. Matthew R. Yeager; Pub. Charles Yeager; adv.; photos; bk.rev.; pub. size: standard; circ. 6,510(paid). **Wire Service(s):** AP.

SUTTON
US

BRAXTON CITIZEN'S NEWS. 1976. Mon. $.16 newsstand; $10/yr. in cy.; $9/yr. senior citizens. 501 Main St., Sutton, WV 26601. TEL 304-765-5193; FAX 304-765-2754. **Owner(s):** Ed Given, 501 Main St., Sutton, WV 26601. TEL 304-765-5193; FAX 304-765-2754; Ed. Del Thayer; Pub. Ed Given; adv. contact: Jeanine Given. photos; pub. size: tabloid; circ. 6,500(paid).

US

BRAXTON DEMOCRAT-CENTRAL. 1883. Thu. $.25 newsstand; $9.50/yr. in cy.; $14/yr. out of cy.; $19.50/yr. out of state. 205 Main St., Sutton, WV 26601-1399. TEL 304-765-5555; FAX 304-765-5555. **Owner(s):** Craig A. Smith, 205 Main St., Sutton, WV 26601. TEL 304-765-5555; FAX 304-765-5555; Ed. Craig A. Smith; Pub. Craig A. Smith; adv. contact: Joan Bias. pub. size: broadsheet; circ. 4,200(paid).

UNION
US

MONROE WATCHMAN. 1872. Thu. $.50 newsstand; $18.55/yr. in state; $20/yr. out of state. Main St., Union, WV 24983. TEL 304-772-3016. **Owner(s):** Dale Mohler, P.O. Box 179, Union, WV 24983. TEL 304-772-3016; Ed. Dr. H. Craig Mohler; Pub. Dale Mohler; adv. contact: John Honaker. pub. size: broadsheet; circ. 4,000(paid).

WAYNE
US

WAYNE COUNTY NEWS. 1874. Wed. $.50 newsstand; $22.95/yr. in cy.; $25.44/yr. out of cy.; $28.80/yr. out of state. 310 Central Ave., Wayne, WV 25570. TEL 304-272-3433; FAX 304-522-3910. **Owner(s):** Thomas J. George, 310 Central Ave., Wayne, WV 25570. TEL 304-272-3433; Pub. Thomas J. George; adv.; pub. size: broadsheet; circ. 4,600(paid).

WEBSTER SPRINGS
US

WEBSTER ECHO. 1882. Wed. $.34 newsstand; $19.64/yr. in cy. mailed; $24.19/yr. out of state. 219 Back Fork St., Webster Springs, WV 26288. TEL 304-847-5828. **Owner(s):** D. Boyd Dotson, Jr., Back Fork St., Webster Springs, WV 26288. TEL 304-847-5828; Ed. Elizabeth Tracy; Pub. D. Boyd Dotson, Jr.; adv.; photos; pub. size: broadsheet; circ. 3,000(paid).

US

WEBSTER REPUBLICAN. 1882. Wed. $.48 newsstand; $22.81/yr. mailed in cy.; $28.69/yr. out of state. 219 Back Fork St., Webster Springs, WV 26288. TEL 304-847-5828; FAX 304-847-5991. **Owner(s):** D. Boyd Dotson, Jr., 219 Back Fork St., Webster Springs, WV 26288. TEL 304-847-5828; Ed. Elizabeth Tracy; Pub. D. Boyd Dotson, Jr.; pub. size: broadsheet; circ. 1,800(paid).

WELLSBURG
US

BROOKE COUNTY REVIEW. 1937. Thu. $.25 newsstand; $14/yr. mailed. 319 Charles St., Wellsburg, WV 26070. TEL 304-737-0946; FAX 304-737-0297; E-mail: jwallace@weir.net. **Owner(s):** Brooke Publishing Inc., 319 Charles St., Wellsburg, WV 26070. TEL 304-737-0946; FAX 304-737-0297; Pub. J.W. George Wallace; adv.; photos; pub. size: broadsheet; circ. 2,000(paid). **Wire Service(s):** WV Pressnet.
Formerly: Brooke News & Follansbee Review.

WESTON
US

WESTON DEMOCRAT, THE. 1867. Wed. $.33 newsstand; $14.83/yr. in state; $18/yr. out of state. 238 Main Ave., Weston, WV 26452. TEL 304-269-1600; FAX 304-269-4035. **Owner(s):** Robert Billeter, P.O. Box 968, Weston, WV 26452. TEL 304-269-1600; FAX 304-269-4035; Ed. George Whelan; Pub. Robert Billeter; adv. contact: Julia Spelsberg. photos; bk.rev.; pub. size: standard; circ. 8,000(paid).

WEST UNION

US
HERALD RECORD. Tue. $.35 newsstand; $10.60/yr. local; $11.66/yr. out of cy.; $12/yr. out of state. 202 E. Main St., West Union, WV 26456. TEL 304-873-1600. **Owner(s):** Virginia Nicholson, 202 E. Main St., West Union, WV 26456. TEL 304-873-1600; Ed. Virginia Nicholson. adv.; pub. size: standard; circ. 3,150(paid).

WISCONSIN

ABBOTSFORD

US
ABBOTSFORD TRIBUNE-PHONOGRAPH. w. $.75 newsstand, $23/yr. in state; $26/yr. In IA, IL, MI, & MN; $32/yr. elsewhere. P.O. Box 677, Abbotsford, WI 54405. TEL 715-223-2342; FAX 715-223-3505. **Owner(s):** J.A. O'Leary, P.O. Box 677, Abbotsford, WI 54405. TEL 715-223-2342; Ed. Charles Runnoe; Pub. J.A. O'Leary; pub. size: tabloid; circ. 2,450(paid).

US
RECORD-REVIEW, THE. 1964. Wed. $.75 newsstand; $20/yr. in state; $23/yr. out of state. 103 W. Spruce St., Abbotsford, WI 54405. TEL 715-223-2342; FAX 715-223-3505. **Owner(s):** J.A. & Carol O'Leary, 103 W. Spruce St., Abbotsford, WI 54405. TEL 715-223-2342; FAX 715-223-3505; Ed. Peter Weinschenk; Pub. J.A. O'Leary; adv. contact: Carol O'Leary. photos; pub. size: tabloid; circ. 1,900(paid).

ADAMS

US
ADAMS COUNTY TIMES. 1940. Wed. $28/yr. in cy.; $30/yr. out of cy.; $37/yr. out of state. 116 S. Main St., Adams, WI 53910. TEL 608-339-7844; FAX 608-339-3903. **Owner(s):** Richard A. Hannagan, P.O. Box 99, Adams, WI 53910. TEL 608-339-7844; Pub. Richard A. Hannagan; pub. size: standard; circ. 4,600(paid).

ALGOMA

US
ALGOMA RECORD HERALD. s-w. Wed. & Sun. $.50 newsstand; $20/yr. local; $25/yr. out of state. 602 Third St., Algoma, WI 54201. TEL 414-487-2222; FAX 414-487-3194. **Owner(s):** Frank Wood, P.O. Box 68, Algoma, WI 54201; Ed. Lee Lawrenz; Pub. Frank Wood; adv.; photos; pub. size: broadsheet; circ. 4,200(paid).
 Formerly: Record Herald.

AMERY

US
AMERY FREE PRESS. 1889. Tue. $.75 newsstand; $25/yr. in cy.; $30/yr. out of cy.; $35/yr. out of state. 215 S. Keller, Amery, WI 54001. TEL 715-268-8101; FAX 715-268-8125. **Owner(s):** Sondreal Enterprises, Inc., 215 S. Keller, Amery, WI 54001. TEL 715-268-8101; Ed. Palmer Sondreal; Pub. Palmer Sondreal; adv. contact: Pamela Humpal. pub. size: broadsheet; circ. 5,000(paid). **Wire Service(s):** UPI.

ANTIGO

US
ANTIGO AREA SHOPPERS GUIDE. 1954. Tue. free local. 813 Fifth Ave., Antigo, WI 54409. TEL 715-623-5024; FAX 715-623-5389; E-mail: ashoppr@newnorth.net. **Owner(s):** Antigo Area Shoppers Guide, Inc., 813 Fifth Ave., Antigo, WI 54409. TEL 715-623-5024; FAX 715-623-5389; adv.; pub. size: tabloid; circ. 12,969(free).

ARCADIA

US
ARCADIA NEWS-LEADER. 1875. Thu. $.75 newsstand; $22/yr. in cy.; $24/yr. in state; $26/yr. out of state. 625 Dettloff Dr., Arcadia, WI 54612-0220. TEL 608-323-3366; FAX 608-323-2185. **Owner(s):** Blaschko Enterprises, P.O. Box 220, Arcadia, WI 54612. TEL 608-323-3366; Pub. Chuck Blaschko; adv. contact: Lisa Wolfe. photos; pub. size: standard; circ. 2,500(paid).

ARGYLE

US
ARGYLE AGENDA. 1961. Wed., local; Thu., rural. $.50 newsstand; $22/yr. in state mailed; $35/yr. out of state mailed. 101 N. State St., Argyle, WI 53504-0426. TEL 608-543-3773; FAX 608-543-3724. **Owner(s):** Dan Witte & Mark Witte, Mt. Horeb, WI 53572. TEL 608-437-5553; Pub. Dan Witte; adv.; photos; bk.rev.; pub. size: tabloid; circ. 1,000(paid).

AUGUSTA

US ISSN 0749-7083
AUGUSTA AREA TIMES. 1900. Wed. $.50 newsstand; $18/yr. in area; $21/yr. out of area; $25/yr. out of state. 156 E. Lincoln, Augusta, WI 54722. TEL 715-286-2655; FAX 715-286-2655. **Owner(s):** Michael D. Jensen, P.O. Box 465, Augusta, WI 54722. TEL 715-286-2655; FAX 715-597-8705; Ed. Beth Ellie; Pub. Michael D. Jensen; adv. contact: Tamy Cuddy. pub. size: standard; circ. 1,500(paid).

BALDWIN

US
BALDWIN BULLETIN. 1872. Tue. $17/yr. in cy.; $22/yr. out of cy.; $25/yr. out of state. 805 Main St., Baldwin, WI 54002. TEL 715-684-2484; FAX 715-684-4937. **Owner(s):** Thomas A. Hawley, P.O. Box 66, Baldwin, WI 54002. TEL 715-684-2484; Peter C. Hawley, P.O. Box 66, Baldwin, WI 54002; Muriel Hawley, P.O. Box 66, Baldwin, WI 54002; Ed. Thomas A. Hawley; Pub. Thomas A. Hawley; pub. size: broadsheet; circ. 3,000(paid).

BALSAM LAKE

US
COUNTY LEDGER-PRESS. 1898. Thu. $19/yr. in cy.; $24/yr. out of cy. 105 Main St., Balsam Lake, WI 54810. TEL 715-485-3121. **Owner(s):** Ledger Publications, Inc., 105 Main St., Balsam Lake, WI 54810. TEL 715-485-3121; Ed. Linda Peterson; Pub. Thomas C. Miller; adv. contact: Thomas C. Miller. photos; pub. size: broadsheet; circ. 6,500(paid).

BARRON

US
BARRON NEWS SHIELD. 1876. Wed. $.75 newsstand; $21/yr. local; $22.50/yr. out of cy.; $26/yr. out of state. 219 E. La Salle, Barron, WI 54812. TEL 715-537-3117; FAX 715-537-5640. **Owner(s):** Bell Press, Inc., P.O. Box 189, Barron, WI 54812. TEL 715-532-5591; Ed. Robert Groshong; Pub. James Bell; pub. size: broadsheet; circ. 4,400(paid).
 Formerly: Barron County News Shield.

BELLEVILLE

US
BELLEVILLE RECORDER. 1866. w. $.50 newsstand; $20.50/yr. in state; $22.50/yr. out of state. 38 River St., Belleville, WI 53508. TEL 608-424-3232. **Owner(s):** Stuart M. Shapiro, P.O. Box 50, Belleville, WI 53508. TEL 608-424-3232; Pub. Stuart M. Shapiro; adv. contact: Stuart M. Shapiro. pub. size: tabloid; circ. 1,450(paid).

BERLIN

US
BERLIN BUYERS' GUIDE. 1945. Tue. free local; $52/yr. elsewhere. 124 W. Huron St., Berlin, WI 54923. TEL 414-361-2444; FAX 414-361-4959. **Owner(s):** Add, Inc., 600 Industrial Dr., P.O. Box 609, Waupaca, WI 54981. TEL 715-258-8450; FAX 715-258-4896; Ed. David Schroeder. adv.; pub. size: tabloid; circ. 22,400(free).

US ISSN 8755-4003
BERLIN JOURNAL. 1870. Thu. $.75 newsstand; $24/yr. in cy.; $42/yr. out of cy. 301 June St., Berlin, WI 54923. TEL 414-361-1515; FAX 414-361-1518. **Owner(s):** R.M. Gonyo, 135 E. Moore, Berlin, WI 54923. TEL 414-361-0377; Ed. Jim Wolff; Pub. R.M. Gonyo; adv.; pub. size: tabloid; circ. 4,100(paid).

US
BILLBOARD, THE. Tue. free. 301 June St., Berlin, WI 54923. TEL 414-361-1515; FAX 514-361-1518. **Owner(s):** R.M. Gonyo, 135 E. Moore, Berlin, WI 54923. TEL 414-361-0377; Ed. Jime Wolff; Pub. R.M. Gonyo; pub. size: tabloid; circ. 23,600.

US
GREEN LAKE COUNTY REPORTER. 1900. Thu. $.75 newsstand; $24/yr. local; $42/yr. in state; $55/yr. out of state. 301 June St., Berlin, WI 54923. TEL 414-361-1515; FAX 414-361-1518. **Owner(s):** R.M. Gonyo, 135 E. Moore, Berlin, WI 54923. TEL 414-316-0377; Ed. Jim Wolff; Pub. R.M. Gonyo; adv.; pub. size: broadsheet; circ. 1,350(paid).

BLACK RIVER FALLS

US
BANNER JOURNAL. 1856. Wed. $.75/newsstand; $28/yr. local. 409 E. Main St., Black River Falls, WI 54615. TEL 715-284-4304; FAX 715-284-4634. **Owner(s):** News Publishing Co., 1126 Mills St., Black Earth, WI 53515. TEL 608-767-3655; Ed. Jeanette Ruxton; Pub. Dan Witte; adv.; photos; pub. size: tabloid; circ. 4,400(paid).

BLAIR
US
BLAIR PRESS. 1893. Thu. $.50 newsstand; $20/yr. in cy.; $22/yr. out of cy.; $26/yr. out of state. 109 N. Gilbert St., Blair, WI 54616. TEL 608-989-2531; FAX 608-989-9615. **Owner(s):** Gerald Hjornevik, P.O. Box 187, Blair, WI 54616. TEL 608-989-2531; FAX 608-989-2531; Pub. Gerald Hjornevik; adv. contact: Liz Hjornevik. photos; pub. size: broadsheet; circ. 2,150(paid).

BLANCHARDVILLE
US
BLADE ATLAS. 1888. Thu. $.40 newsstand; $15/yr. in state mailed; $18/yr. out of state mailed. 205 S. Main St., Blanchardville, WI 53516. TEL 608-523-4284; FAX 608-523-1019. **Owner(s):** John P. Riley & Thomas M. Riley, Dodgeville, WI 53533. TEL 608-935-2331; Ed. Gary McKenzie. adv.; bk.rev.; pub. size: tabloid; circ. 1,300(paid).

BLOOMER
US
BLOOMER ADVANCE. 1888. Wed. $.50 newsstand; $17/yr. in cy. $19/yr. out of cy. 1210 15th, Bloomer, WI 54724. TEL 715-568-3100; FAX 715-568-3111. **Owner(s):** Don Bell, 1210 15th, Bloomer, WI 54724. TEL 715-568-3100; FAX 715-568-3111; Pub. Al Bauer; pub. size: standard; circ. 3,900.

BOSCOBEL
US
BOSCOBEL DIAL. 1872. Thu. $.75 newsstand; $26/yr. in state mailed; $31/yr. out of state. 805 Wisconsin Ave., Boscobel, WI 53805. TEL 608-375-4458; FAX 608-375-2369. **Owner(s):** Southwest Publishing Co., P.O. Box 128, Boscobel, WI 53805; Ed. David Krier; Pub. William S. Hale; adv. contact: Jean Roth. photos; pub. size: broadsheet; circ. 6,100(paid).

BRILLION
US ISSN 0749-7210
BRILLION NEWS. 1894. Wed. $.40 newsstand; $20/yr. 425 W. Ryan St., Brillion, WI 54110. TEL 414-756-2222; FAX 414-756-2701. **Owner(s):** Zander Press, Inc., 425 W. Ryan St., Brillion, WI 54110. TEL 414-756-2222; FAX 414-756-2701; Pub. Zane Zander; adv. contact: Zane Zander. photos; pub. size: tabloid; circ. 2,100(paid).

BRODHEAD
US
INDEPENDENT-REGISTER, THE. 1861. w. $.70 newsstand; $19/yr. in cy.; $21/yr. in state; $28/yr. out of state. 922 Exchange St., Brodhead, WI 53520. TEL 608-897-2193; FAX 608-897-4137; E-mail: paper@indreg.com; URL: http://www.indreg.com. **Owner(s):** M.D. Markham, 922 Exchange St., Brodhead, WI 53520. TEL 608-897-2193; FAX 608-897-4137; Ed. M.D. Markham; Pub. Kim Markham; adv. contact: M.D. Markham. bk.rev.; pub. size: tabloid; circ. 7,900(free & paid).

BURLINGTON
US
BURLINGTON STANDARD PRESS. 1863. s-w.: Wed. & Sun. $1 newsstand; $28/yr. in area mailed; $29.50/yr. in cy.; $47.50/yr. out of state. 140 Commerce St., Burlington, WI 53105. TEL 414-763-3511; FAX 414-763-2238. **Owner(s):** Robert Branen, 140 Commerce St., Burlington, WI 35105. TEL 414-763-3511; Pub. Robert Branen; adv. contact: Dave Wright. photos; pub. size: broadsheet; circ. 9,846(paid).

CADOTT
US ISSN 0885-0798
CADOTT SENTINEL. 1917. Thu. $.75 newsstand; $20/yr. local; $22/yr. in state; $28/yr. elsewhere. 327 Main St., Cadott, WI 54727. TEL 715-289-4978; FAX 715-239-6200. **Owner(s):** Trygg J. Hansen, P.O. Box 70, Cadott, WI 54727. TEL 715-289-4978; FAX 715-239-6200; Pub. Trygg Hansen; adv.; photos; pub. size: broadsheet; circ. 3,000(paid).

CAMBRIDGE
US ISSN 0749-7202
CAMBRIDGE NEWS. 1892. Thu. $.50 newsstand; $20/yr. in cy.; $24/yr. elsewhere. 201 W. North St., Cambridge, WI 53523-0008. TEL 608-423-3213; FAX 414-648-8187. **Owner(s):** Leader Printing Co., P.O. Box 60, Lake Mills, WI 53551. TEL 414-648-2334; FAX 414-648-8187; Pub. Dennis Hawkes; adv. contact: Karen DeWall. pub. size: tabloid; circ. 2,000(paid).

CAMPBELLSPORT
US
CAMPBELLSPORT NEWS. 1899. Thu. $.40 newsstand; $21/yr. in state; $23/yr. out of state. 101 N. Fond du Lac Ave., Campbellsport, WI 53010. TEL 414-533-8338; FAX 414-533-5579. **Owner(s):** James R. Ninneman, P.O. Box 138, Campbellsport, WI 53010. TEL 414-533-8338; Pub. James R. Ninneman; adv. contact: James R. Ninneman. pub. size: tabloid; circ. 2,300(paid).

CASHTON
US
CASHTON RECORD. 1896. Wed. $.50 newsstand; $18/yr. local; $28/yr. out of state. 713 Broadway, Cashton, WI 54619-0100. TEL 608-654-7330. **Owner(s):** Gerald Eddy, P.O. Box 100, Cashton, WI 54619. TEL 608-654-7330; Pub. Gerald Eddy; adv. contact: Rose Eddy. pub. size: tabloid; circ. 1,600(free & paid).

CEDARBURG
US ISSN 1056-9006
OZAUKEE COUNTY NEWS GRAPHIC. 1883. s-w.: Mon. & Thu. $.75 newsstand; $30.95/yr. mailed. N19 W6733 Commerce Ct., Cedarburg, WI 53012. TEL 414-375-5100; FAX 414-375-5107. **Owner(s):** Lakeshore Newspapers, Inc., Beaver Dam, WI 53916; Pub. Phil Paige; adv. contact: Jim Baumgart. pub. size: tabloid; circ. 10,000(paid).
Formerly: News Graphic Pilot.

US
OZAUKEE GUIDE. Wed. free. N19 W6733 Commerce Ct., Cedarburg, WI 53012. TEL 414-375-5100; FAX 414-375-5107. **Owner(s):** Lake Shore Newspapers, Inc., Beaver Dam, WI; Ed. Mark Jaegar; Pub. Phil Paige; adv. contact: Jim Baumgart. pub. size: tabloid; circ. 35,000(free).

CHETEK
US
CHETEK ALERT, THE. 1882. Wed. $.50 newsstand; $16/yr. in cy.; $20/yr. out of cy.; $26/yr. out of state. 312 Knapp St., Chetek, WI 54728. TEL 715-924-4118; FAX 715-924-4122. **Owner(s):** Paul H. Lange, P.O. Box 5, Chetek, WI 54728. TEL 715-924-3032; Melodee A. Eckerman, P.O. Box 5, Chetek, WI 54728. TEL 715-924-2922; Ed. Melodee A. Eckerman; Pub. Paul H. Lange; pub. size: broadsheet; circ. 3,600(paid).

CHILTON
US
CHILTON TIMES-JOURNAL. 1857. Thu. $.50 newsstand; $15.50/yr. in cy. 19 E. Main St., Chilton, WI 53014. TEL 414-849-7036; FAX 414-849-4651. **Owner(s):** Vercauteren Publishing, 19 E. Main, Chilton, WI 53014. TEL 414-849-7036; FAX 414-849-4651; Ed. Debbie Dins; Pub. Gary Vercauteren; adv.; photos; pub. size: broadsheet; circ. 3,800(paid).

CLINTON
US
CLINTON TOPPER. 1938. Thu. $.50 newsstand; $20/yr. in cy.; $25/yr. out of cy. 400-B Front St., Clinton, WI 53525. TEL 608-676-4664; FAX 608-676-4664. **Owner(s):** Independent Newspapers Corp., 400-B Front St., Clinton, WI 53525. TEL 608-676-4664; FAX 608-676-4664; Ed. Robert Gard; Pub. Henry W. Schroeder; adv. contact: Sharon Bobolz. photos; pub. size: tabloid; circ. 1,500(paid).

CLINTONVILLE
US
CLINTONVILLE TRIBUNE-GAZETTE. 1881. Thu. $.75 newsstand; $22.50/yr. in cy.; $27.50/yr. in state; $32.50/yr. out of state. 13 11th St., Clintonville, WI 54929. TEL 715-823-3151; E-mail: teegee@mail.atw.fullfeed.com; URL: http://www.clintonville-online.com. **Owner(s):** Clintonville Publishing Co., 13 11th St., Clintonville, WI 54929. TEL 718-823-3151; Ed. Scott McGraw; Pub. Scott McGraw; adv. contact: Jeff Vollendorf. adv.: $5.75/SAU. pub. size: broadsheet; circ. 3,450(paid).

COCHRANE
US
BUFFALO COUNTY JOURNAL. 1861. Thu. $.50 newsstand; $19/yr. surrounding area; $22/yr. out of cy.; $28/yr. out of state. 104 Fifth St., Cochrane, WI 54622-0046. TEL 608-248-2451; FAX 608-248-2422. **Owner(s):** Valley Publications, P.O. Box 109, Wabasha, MN 55981. TEL 612-565-3368; Ed. Ed McFarlaine; Pub. Gary Stumpf; adv.; pub. size: tabloid; circ. 875(paid).

10766 COLFAX, WI — **WEEKLY NEWSPAPERS**

COLFAX
US
COLFAX MESSENGER. 1897. Wed. $.50 newsstand; $20/yr. in cy. mailed; $24/yr. out of cy. mailed. P.O. Box 517, Colfax, WI 54730-0517. TEL 715-962-3535; FAX 715-962-3413. **Owner(s):** Carleton DeWitt, P.O. Box 517, Colfax, WI 54730-0517. TEL 715-962-3535; Ed. Marlin Raveling; Pub. Carleton DeWitt; adv.; photos; pub. size: broadsheet; circ. 1,250(paid).

COLUMBUS
US
COLUMBUS JOURNAL. 1861. Mon. $.75 newsstand; $25/yr. in state; $35/yr. out of state. 101 S. Ludington St., Columbus, WI 53925. TEL 414-623-3160; FAX 414-623-9383. **Owner(s):** Citizen Publishing Co., 805 Park Ave., Beaver Dam, WI 53916; Ed. Jason Cramer. adv. contact: Geri Schwarrtz. pub. size: tabloid; circ. 2,000(paid)
Formerly: Columbus Journal-Republican.

CORNELL
US
CORNELL & LAKE HOLCOMBE COURIER. 1915. Thu. $.75 newsstand; $20/yr. local; $22/yr. in state; $28/yr. out of state. 121 Main St., Cornell, WI 54732. TEL 715-239-6688; FAX 715-239-6200. **Owner(s):** Trygg J. Hansen, P.O. Box 546, Cornell, WI 54732-0546. TEL 715-239-6688; FAX 715-239-6200; Ed. John Rykhus; Pub. Trygg J. Hansen; adv.; pub. size: broadsheet; circ. 3,200(paid).

CRANDON
US
FOREST REPUBLICAN, THE. 1885. Wed. $.50 newsstand; $14.50/yr. in cy.; $17.50/yr. out of cy. 108-110 W. Madison St., Crandon, WI 54520. TEL 715-478-3315; FAX 715-478-5385. **Owner(s):** Russell H. Steel, P.O. Box 367, Crandon, WI 54520. TEL 715-478-3315; Ed. Russell H. Steel; Pub. Russell H. Steel; pub. size: broadsheet; circ. 3,900(paid).

CUBA CITY
US
TRI-COUNTY PRESS. 1894. Wed. $.75 newsstand; $23/yr. in state; $25/yr. in IA & IL; $36/yr. other states. 301 S. Main St., Cuba City, WI 53807. TEL 608-744-2107; FAX 608-744-2108. **Owner(s):** Tri-County Press, Inc., 301 S. Main St., Cuba City, WI 53807. TEL 608-744-2107; Ed. Jennifer Wilkinson; Pub. William S. Hale; adv. contact: Rick Goldthorpe. photos; pub. size: tabloid; circ. 3,000(paid).
Formerly: Cuba City Tri-County Press.

CUMBERLAND
US
CUMBERLAND ADVOCATE. 1881. w. $.60 newsstand; $21/yr. 1375 Second Ave., Cumberland, WI 54829. TEL 715-822-4469. **Owner(s):** Jackson County Publications, Inc., P.O. Box 637, Cumberland, WI 54829. TEL 715-234-2121; Ed. Sharon Bucher; Pub. Craig Bucher; adv.; $4.90/SAU. photos; pub. size: broadsheet; circ. 3,000(paid).

DARLINGTON
US
REPUBLICAN-JOURNAL. 1862. Thu. $.75 newsstand; $28/yr. in area; $34/yr. out of area. 316 Main St., Darlington, WI 53530. TEL 608-776-4425; FAX 608-776-4301. **Owner(s):** Darlington Publishing Co., Inc., 316 Main St., Darlington, WI 53530. TEL 608-776-4425; Ed. Cindy Lund; Pub. Brian A. Lund; adv. contact: Nancy Fink. pub. size: broadsheet; circ. 3,600(paid).

DEERFIELD
US
INDEPENDENT. 1885. Thu. $.60 newsstand; $20/yr. 7 S. Main St., Deerfield, WI 53531. TEL 608-764-5515; FAX 608-764-8214. **Owner(s):** Hometown News, L.P., 114 Columbus St., Sun Prairie, WI 53590. TEL 608-837-2521; FAX 608-825-4460; Ed. Mary Pohlman; Pub. Brian Knox; pub. size: broadsheet; circ. 1,500(paid).
Formerly: Deerfield Independent.

DE FOREST
US
FOREST TIMES-TRIBUNE. 1895. Thu. $.60 newsstand; $21/yr. in cy; $24.50/yr. out of state; $20/yr. senior citizens; $17.50/yr. students. 108 Market St., De Forest, WI 53115. TEL 608-846-5576; FAX 608-846-5757. **Owner(s):** Richard H. & Molly Emerson, 108 Market Street, De Forest, WI 53532. TEL 608-846-5576; FAX 608-846-5757; Ed. Richard H. Emerson; Pub. Richard H. Emerson; adv.; pub. size: broadsheet; circ. 2,300(paid).

DELAVAN
US
DELAVAN ENTERPRISE. 1878. Wed. $.75 newsstand; $23.50/yr. in cy. mailed; $26.50/yr. out of cy.; $32/yr. out of state. 1436 Mound Rd., Delavan, WI 53115. TEL 414-728-3411; FAX 414-728-5706. **Owner(s):** Bliss Communications, Inc., One S. Parker Dr., Janesville, WI 53545. TEL 414-754-3311; Ed. Tom Sheeham; Pub. Tom Sheeham; adv. contact: Dave Erickson. pub. size: tabloid; circ. 5,000(paid).

DENMARK
US
DENMARK PRESS. 1883. Tue. $.50 newsstand; $20/yr. in state; $25/yr. out of state. 138 Main St., Denmark, WI 54208. TEL 414-863-2154; FAX 414-863-6102. **Owner(s):** Frank Wood, P.O. Box 610, Denmark, WI 54208. TEL 414-863-2154; FAX 414-863-6102; Pub. Frank Wood; adv.; photos; pub. size: tabloid; circ. 2,700(paid).

DE PERE
US   ISSN 0748-6219
DE PERE JOURNAL. 1871. Thu. $.50 newsstand; $16/yr. local carrier. 126 S. Broadway, De Pere, WI 54115-0188. TEL 414-336-4221. **Owner(s):** Journal Publishing Co., Inc., 126 S. Broadway, De Pere, WI 54115. TEL 414-336-4221; Ed. Marie S. Creviere; Pub. Paul J. Creviere, Sr.; adv.; photos; pub. size: broadsheet; circ. 3,895(paid).

DODGEVILLE
US
DODGEVILLE CHRONICLE, INC. 1862. Thu. $.50 newsstand; $21/yr. mailed. 106 W. Merrimac St., Dodgeville, WI 53533-0096. TEL 608-935-2331; FAX 608-935-9531. **Owner(s):** Reilly & Reilly, Inc., P.O. Box 96, Dodgeville, WI 53533. TEL 608-935-2331; FAX 608-935-9531; Ed. J. Patrick Reilly; Pub. Pat Reilly; adv. contact: Kim Gleichauf. photos; bk.rev./ pub. size: broadsheet; circ. 5,600(paid).

DURAND
US
COURIER-WEDGE. 1861. Thu. $.50 newsstand; $21/yr. in cy. 103 W. Main St., Durand, WI 54736. TEL 715-672-4252; FAX 715-672-4254. **Owner(s):** Gary Stumpf, 200 Industrial Ct., Wabasha, MN 55981; Ed. Karl Drews; Pub. Gary Stumpf; pub. size: broadsheet; circ. 4,300(paid).
Formerly: Durand Courier-Wedge.

EAGLE RIVER
US
VILAS COUNTY NEWS-REVIEW. 1886. Wed. $1 newsstand; $32/yr. local; $36/yr. in state; $44/yr. out of state. 346 W. Division St., Eagle River, WI 54521-1929. TEL 715-479-4421; FAX 715-479-6242. **Owner(s):** Delphos Newspapers, 405 N. Main St., Delphos, OH 45833. TEL 419-692-5050; Ed. Kurt Krueger; Pub. Byron McNutt; adv.; photos; pub. size: broadsheet; circ. 10,250(paid).

EAST TROY
US   ISSN 0749-5943
EAST TROY NEWS. 1893. Thu. $1 newsstand; $24/yr.; $18/yr. senior citizens. 2100 Church St., East Troy, WI 53120. TEL 414-642-7451; FAX 414-642-5934. **Owner(s):** Southern Lakes Media, P.O. Box 47, East Troy, WI 53120. TEL 414-642-7451; Pub. Robert Branen; adv. contact: David Wright. pub. size: tabloid; circ. 2,344(paid).

EDGERTON
US
EDGERTON REPORTER. 1878. Wed. $.75 newsstand; $22/yr. in cy.; $23/yr. out of cy.; $25/yr. out of state. 21 N. Henry St., Edgerton, WI 53534. TEL 608-884-3367; FAX 608-884-8187. **Owner(s):** Reporter Co., Inc., The, 21 N. Henry St., Edgerton, WI 53534. TEL 608-884-3367; FAX 608-884-8187; Ed. Helen Everson; Pub. Helen Everson; adv.; $8.56/SAU. photos; bk.rev.; pub. size: broadsheet; circ. 3,812(paid).

ELKHORN
US   ISSN 1076-4569
ELKHORN INDEPENDENT. 1853. Wed. $.75 newsstand; $25.50/yr. in area; $27/yr. in surrounding cys.; $30/yr. in state; $19.50/yr. senior citizens. 11 W. Walworth St., Elkhorn, WI 53121. TEL 414-723-2250; FAX 414-723-7424. **Owner(s):** Southern Lakes Media, Inc., WI; Ed. Nancy Jacobson; Pub. Robert Brannen; adv. contact: Riene Wells. pub. size: broadsheet; circ. 2,750(controlled & paid).

ELLSWORTH
US
PIERCE COUNTY HERALD. 1867. Wed. $1 newsstand; $26/yr. in cy.; $41/yr. out of cy. 126 S. Chestnut St., Ellsworth, WI 54011. TEL 715-273-4334; FAX 715-273-4335. **Owner(s):** Western Wisconsin Publishing Co., 226 Locust, Hudson, WI 54016. TEL 715-386-9333; Ed. Bill Kirk; Pub. Steve Dzubay; adv. contact: Robin Kruse. photos; pub. size: standard; circ. 4,500(paid).

ELROY
US
KEYSTONE REPORTER. s-w.: Wed. & Sat. $.75 newsstand; $35/yr. in cy.; $37/yr. out of cy. 249 Main St., Elroy, WI 53929. TEL 608-462-8224; FAX 608-462-5678. **Owner(s):** South Central Wisconsin Newspapers Inc., 309 DeWitt St., Portage, WI 53901. TEL 608-742-2111; Ed. Bill Smith; Pub. David Gentry; adv. contact: Matt Gorsuch. pub. size: tabloid; circ. 2,073(paid).
Formerly: Wonewoc Reporter.

FENNIMORE
US
FENNIMORE TIMES. 1881. Thu. $21/yr. 1150 Lincoln Ave., Fennimore, WI 53809. TEL 608-822-3912; FAX 608-822-3916. **Owner(s):** William S. Hale, 1196 Lincoln Ave., Fennimore, WI 53809. TEL 608-723-2151; Ed. Matthew Johnson; Pub. William S. Hale; pub. size: broadsheet; circ. 2,000(paid).

FLORENCE
US
FLORENCE MINING NEWS. 1880. Wed. $.60 newsstand; $23/yr. in cy.; $26/yr. in surrounding cys.; $29/yr. out of cy. 140 Florence Ave., Florence, WI 54121. TEL 715-696-3400; FAX 715-528-4986. **Owner(s):** Nancy Gomez & Margie Yadro, 140 Florence Ave., Florence, WI 54121. TEL 715-528-3276; Ed. Nancy Gomez; Pub. Nancy Gomez; adv.; photos; pub. size: tabloid; circ. 2,200(paid).

FOND DU LAC
US
ACTION ADVERTISER. 1970. s-w.: Sun. & Wed. free newsstand; $59/yr. mailed. 6637 N. Rolling Meadows Dr., Fond Du Lac, WI 54935-9452. TEL 414-922-8640; FAX 414-922-0125. **Owner(s):** James Carew, 6637 N. Rolling Meadows Dr., Fond Du Lac, WI 54937. TEL 414-922-8640; FAX 414-922-0125; Ed. Scott Witchow; Pub. Robert Carew; adv. contact: Paul Krasin. pub. size: tabloid; circ. 34,000(free & paid).

FOX LAKE
US
FOX LAKE REPRESENTATIVE. 1868. Thu. $.75 newsstand; $24/yr. local; $42/yr. in state; $55/yr. out of state. P.O. Box 66, Fox Lake, WI 53933. TEL 414-928-2626; FAX 414-361-1518. **Owner(s):** R.M. Gonyo, 135 E. Moore, Berlin, WI 54923. TEL 414-361-0377; Ed. Jim Wolff; Pub. R.M. Gonyo; adv.; pub. size: tabloid; circ. 500(paid).

FREDERIC
US
INDIANHEAD ADVERTISER. Mon. free. 303 N. Wisconsin Ave., Frederic, WI 54837. TEL 715-327-4236; FAX 715-327-4870. **Owner(s):** Inter-County Cooperative Publishing Association, P.O. Box 490, Frederic, WI 54837. TEL 715-327-4236; FAX 715-327-4870; adv.; pub. size: tabloid; circ. 18,200(free).

INTER-COUNTY LEADER. 1933. Wed. $.75 newsstand; $22/yr. in cy. mailed; $25/yr. out of cy. 303 N. Wisconsin Ave., Frederic, WI 54837. TEL 715-327-4236; FAX 715-327-4870. **Owner(s):** Inter-County Cooperative Publishing Association, P.O. Box 490, Frederic, WI 54837. TEL 715-327-4236; Ed. Gary King; Pub. Doug Panek; adv. contact: Wayne Boniface. pub. size: tabloid; circ. 6,200(paid).
Formerly: Frederic Inter-County Leader.

GALESVILLE
US
GALESVILLE REPUBLICAN. 1874. Wed. $.50 newsstand; $20/yr. in cy.; $25/yr. out of cy.; $35/yr. out of state. 19852 Court Ave., Galesville, WI 54630-0695. TEL 608-582-2330; FAX 608-582-2455. **Owner(s):** John P.H. Graf, 139 S. Davis, Galesville, WI 54630. TEL 608-582-2330; Pub. John P.H. Graf; pub. size: tabloid; circ. 1,875(paid).

GAY MILLS
US
CRAWFORD COUNTY INDEPENDENT-KICKAPOO SCOUT. Thu. $.75 newsstand; $21/yr. in state; $25.50/yr. out of state. Rebecca St., Gay Mills, WI 54631. TEL 608-375-4458. **Owner(s):** Southwest Publishing Co., Boscobel, WI 53805; Ed. David Kirer. adv. contact: Bonnie Olson. pub. size: broadsheet; circ. 2,600(paid).

GLENWOOD CITY
US
TRIBUNE PRESS REPORTER. 1889. Wed. $.50 newsstand; $18/yr. 217 Oak St., Glenwood City, WI 54013-0038. TEL 715-265-4646; FAX 715-265-7496. **Owner(s):** Carlton DeWitt, 215 Oak St., Glenwood City, WI 54013. TEL 715-265-4646; FAX 715-265-7496; Pub. Carlton DeWitt; adv. contact: Shawn DeWitt. photos; pub. size: broadsheet; circ. 2,800(paid).

GLIDDEN
US
GLIDDEN ENTERPRISE. 1906. Wed. $.50 newsstand; $18/yr. in cy.; $21/yr. out of cy. P.O. Box 128, Glidden, WI 54527. TEL 715-264-3481. **Owner(s):** Glidden Enterprises, Inc., P.O. Box 128, Glidden, WI 54527. TEL 715-264-3481; Ed. Matthew Hart; Pub. Matthew Hart; adv.; pub. size: broadsheet; circ. 1,450(paid).

GRANTSBURG
US
BURNETT COUNTY SENTINEL. 1962. Wed. $1 newsstand; $25/yr. in state; $32/yr. out of state. 114 Madison Ave., Grantsburg, WI 54840-0397. TEL 715-463-2341. **Owner(s):** Mainstream Publications, 114 Madison Ave., Grantsburg, WI 54840. TEL 715-463-2341; Pub. Byron Higgin; adv. contact: Sandy Eng. pub. size: broadsheet; circ. 4,500(paid). **Wire Service(s):** AP.

HAMMOND
US
CENTRAL SAINT CROIX NEWS. 1873. Wed. $.50 newsstand; $15/yr. in cy.; $18/yr. out of cy. 815 Davis St., Hammond, WI 54015. TEL 715-796-2355. **Owner(s):** Barbara & Robert Gardner, P.O. Box 208, Hammond, WI 54015. TEL 715-796-2355; Ed. Barbara Gardner; Pub. Barbara Gardner; adv.; photos; bk.rev.; pub. size: broadsheet; circ. 1,215(paid).

HARTFORD
US
TIMES-PRESS. 1876. Thu. $.50 newsstand; $18/yr. home deliv. & mailed. 225 N. Main St., Hartford, WI 53027. TEL 414-673-3500; FAX 414-673-5260. **Owner(s):** John McLoone, 225 N. Main St., Hartford, WI 53027. TEL 414-673-3500; FAX 414-673-5260; Ed. John McLoone; Pub. John McLoone; adv. contact: Ken Ubert. pub. size: tabloid; circ. 7,100(paid).
Formerly: Hartford Times-Press.

HARTLAND
US
KETTLE MORAINE INDEX. 1942. Thu. $19.20/yr. in cy.; $23/yr. out of cy.; $26.80/yr. out of state. 440 Cardinal Ln., Hartland, WI 53029. TEL 414-367-3272; FAX 414-367-7414; E-mail: lake@mke.follfeed.com. **Owner(s):** Add, Inc., 600 Industrial Dr., Waupaca, WI 54981. TEL 715-258-8450; Ed. Scott Peterson; Pub. Gary J. Jasiek; adv.; photos; pub. size: tabloid; circ. 1,725(paid).

US
LAKE COUNTRY REPORTER. 1960. s-w.: Mon. & Thu. $.50 newsstand; $27.75/yr. in cy.; $33.60/yr. in state; $38.85/yr. out of state. 440 Cardinal Ln., Hartland, WI 53029. TEL 414-367-3272; FAX 414-367-7414. **Owner(s):** Add, Inc., 600 Industrial Dr., P.O. Box 609, Waupaca, WI 54981. TEL 715-258-8450; Ed. Scott Peterson; Pub. Gary Jasiek; adv. contact: Lori Marchek. pub. size: tabloid; circ. 8,011(paid).

US ISSN 1064-2102
SUSSEX SUN. 1963. Tue. $.50 newsstand; $19.20/yr. in cy.; $22.10/yr. out of cy.; $25.75/yr. out of state. 440 Cardinal Ln., Hartland, WI 53029. TEL 414-367-3272; FAX 414-367-7414. **Owner(s):** Add, Inc., 600 Industrial Dr., Waupaca, WI 54981. TEL 715-258-8450; Ed. Scott Peterson. pub. size: tabloid; circ. 2,800(paid).

HAYWARD
US
SAWYER COUNTY RECORD. 1893. Wed. $.75 newsstand; $29/yr. mailed local; $45/yr. out of area. 220 W. First St., Hayward, WI 54843. TEL 715-634-4881; FAX 715-634-8191. **Owner(s):** Northwest Wisconsin Media, Inc., 220 First St., Hayward, WI 54843. TEL 715-634-4881; Ed. Paul Mitchell; Pub. Gary Pennington; adv. contact: Gary Pennington. pub. size: broadsheet; circ. 7,000(paid).

HILLSBORO

HILLSBORO SENTRY-ENTERPRISE. 1885. Thu. $.60 newsstand; $20/yr. in area; $24/yr. in state; $30/yr. out of state. 839 Water Ave., Hillsboro, WI 54634. TEL 608-489-2264; FAX 608-489-2348. **Owner(s):** Jack Knowles, P.O. Box 469, Hillsboro, WI 54634. TEL 608-489-2264; FAX 608-489-2348; Ed. Jack Knowles; Pub. Jack Knowles; adv. contact: Kelli Mitchell. photos; bk.rev.; pub. size: tabloid; circ. 2,200(controlled & paid).

US
ISSN 0749-7016

US

NEIGHBORS. m. free. 839 Water Ave., Hillsboro, WI 54634. TEL 608-489-2264; FAX 608-489-2348. **Owner(s):** Jack Knowles, P.O. Box 469, Hillboro, WI 54634. TEL 608-489-2264; FAX 608-489-2348; Ed. Jack Knowles; Pub. Jack Knowles; adv. contact: Kelli Mitchell. pub. size: standard; circ. 6,000(free).

HORICON

US
ISSN 1053-9972

HORICON REPORTER. 1883. Thu. $.50 newsstand; $18/yr. in cy.; $19/yr. out of cy.; $21/yr. out of state. 319 E. Lake St., Horicon, WI 53032. TEL 414-485-2016; FAX 414-485-4820. **Owner(s):** Wisconsin Free Press, Inc., 126 Bridge St., Mayville, WI 53050; Ed. Edward J. Zagorski, III; Pub. Andrew Johnson; adv. contact: Tina Stambough. photos; bk.rev.; pub. size: broadsheet; circ. 2,100(paid).

HUDSON

US
ISSN 0749-7008

HUDSON STAR-OBSERVER. 1854. Wed. $1 newsstand; $34/yr. carrier or mailed. 226 Locust St., Hudson, WI 54016-0147. TEL 715-386-9333; FAX 715-386-9891; E-mail: starobs@rival.com; URL: http://www.rival.com. **Owner(s):** Star-Observer Publishing Co., 226 Locust St., Hudson, WI 54016-0147. TEL 715-386-9333; FAX 715-386-9891; Ed. Robert Zientara; Pub. Steve Dzubay; adv. contact: Theda Hilt. photos; pub. size: broadsheet; circ. 5,600(paid). **Wire Service(s):** AP, Newsfinder.

HURLEY

US

IRON COUNTY MINER. 1885. Thu. $.50 newsstand; $24/yr. 216 Copper, Hurley, WI 54534. TEL 715-561-3405; FAX 715-561-3799. **Owner(s):** Iron County Miner, 216 Copper, Hurley, WI 54534; Ed. H.M. Moore. adv.; photos; pub. size: broadsheet; circ. 3,000(paid).

INDEPENDENCE

US

INDEPENDENCE NEWS-WAVE. 1878. Wed. $18/yr. in cy.; $20/yr. out of cy.; $22/yr. elsewhere. 23701 Washington St., Independence, WI 54747. TEL 715-985-3815; FAX 715-985-9330. **Owner(s):** O.J. Evenson, P.O. Box 47, Independence, WI 54747. TEL 715-985-3815; Pub. O.J. Evenson; adv. contact: O.J. Evenson. pub. size: broadsheet; circ. 1,150(paid).

IOLA

US
ISSN 0886-8360

IOLA HERALD. 1891. Thu. $.75 newsstand; $20/yr. in area; $24/yr. out of area. 165 N. Main St., Iola, WI 54945-0235. TEL 715-445-3415; FAX 715-445-3988. **Owner(s):** Trey & Mary Foerster, P.O. Box 235, Iola, WI 54945. TEL 715-445-3415; FAX 715-445-3988; Pub. Trey Foerster; adv. contact: Trey Foerster. photos; pub. size: tabloid; circ. 2,000(paid).

JUNEAU

US

DODGE COUNTY INDEPENDENT-NEWS. 1893. Thu. $.50 newsstand; $17/yr. local. 122 S. Main St., Juneau, WI 53039. TEL 414-386-2421; FAX 414-386-2421. **Owner(s):** Independent Publishing Corp., 122 S. Main St., Juneau, WI 53039. TEL 414-386-2421; Ed. Bonnie Fitzgerald; Pub. James M. Clifford; adv. contact: Rhonda Boyd. photos; pub. size: broadsheet; circ. 1,200(paid).

KAUKAUNA

US

KAUKAUNA TIMES. 1880. s-w.: Tue. & Thu. $.30 newsstand; $20/yr. home deliv.; $26/yr. mailed in state; $30/yr. out of state. 1900 Crooks Ave., Kaukauna, WI 54130-0109. TEL 414-766-4651; FAX 414-766-4736. **Owner(s):** James W. Lang, 1900 Crooks Ave., Kaukauna, WI 54130. TEL 414-766-4651; FAX 414-766-4736; Glenn P. & Lyle J. Hansen, 1900 Crooks Ave., Kaukauna, WI 54130-0109. TEL 414-766-4651; FAX 414-766-4736; Ed. Joyce Schubring. adv. contact: George Kailhofer. pub. size: broadsheet; circ. 6,800(free & paid).

KENOSHA

US

BULLETIN, THE. 1981. Mon. free. 715 58th St., Lower Level, Kenosha, WI 53140. TEL 414-656-1101; FAX 414-656-1255. **Owner(s):** United Communications, Corp., 715 58th St., Kenosha, WI 53140. TEL 414-657-1000; FAX 414-656-1255; Ed. Darren Hillock. adv.; photos; pub. size: tabloid; circ. 69,500(free).

KEWASKUM

US

KEWASKUM STATESMAN. 1895. Thu. $.40 newsstand; $19/yr. in state; $22/yr. out of state. 250 Main St., Kewaskum, WI 53040-0098. TEL 414-626-2626; FAX 414-626-2626. **Owner(s):** Lana Kuehl, 250 Main St., Kewaskum, WI 53040. TEL 414-626-3312; FAX 414-626-2626; Ed. Lana Kuehl. adv.; photos; bk.rev.; pub. size: standard; circ. 3,500(paid).

KEWAUNEE

US

KEWAUNEE ENTERPRISE. 1859. Wed. $.50 newsstand; $20/yr. in cy.; $25/yr. out of cy. 206 Ellis St., Kewaunee, WI 54216. TEL 414-388-3175; FAX 414-388-0609. **Owner(s):** Brown County Publishing Co., Denmark, WI 52508; Pub. Frank Wood; adv. contact: Russ Ritchie. photos; pub. size: broadsheet; circ. 2,650(paid).

KIEL

US

KIEL TRI-COUNTY RECORD. 1893. Thu. $20/yr. in tri-county; $28/yr. out of cy.; $38/yr. out of state. 705 Seventh St., Kiel, WI 53042. TEL 414-894-2828; FAX 414-894-2161. **Owner(s):** Delta Publications Co., Inc., P.O. Box 7, Kiel, WI 53042. TEL 414-894-2828; Pub. Mike Mathes; adv. contact: Joe Mathes. pub. size: tabloid; circ. 2,063(paid).

LADYSMITH

US

LADYSMITH NEWS. 1895. Thu. $.75 newsstand; $24/yr. in surrounding cys.; $30/yr. elsewhere. 120 W. Third St., S., Ladysmith, WI 54848. TEL 715-532-5591. **Owner(s):** Donald L. Bell, P.O. Box 189, Ladysmith, WI 54848. TEL 715-532-5591; Thomas D. & James L. Bell, P.O. Box 189, Ladysmith, WI 54848. TEL 715-532-5591; Michael D. & Audrey M. Bell, P.O. Box 189, Ladysmith, WI 54848. TEL 715-532-5591; Ed. John M. Terrill; Pub. Thomas D. Bell; adv. contact: Christine Bell. pub. size: broadsheet; circ. 5,700(paid).

LAKE GENEVA

US

LAKE GENEVA REGIONAL NEWS. 1873. Thu. $.50 newsstand; $20/yr. mailed in cy.; $25/yr. in state; $35/yr. elsewhere. 315 Broad St., Lake Geneva, WI 53147. TEL 414-248-4444; FAX 414-248-4476. **Owner(s):** Donald W. Bearder, 315 Broad St., Lake Geneva, WI 53147. TEL 414-248-4444; Pub. Donald W. Bearder; adv. contact: Donald W. Bearder. pub. size: standard; circ. 7,000(paid).

LAKE MILLS

US

LAKE MILLS LEADER. 1878. Thu. $.50 newsstand; $20/yr. 320 N. Main St., Lake Mills, WI 53551-0060. TEL 414-648-2334; FAX 414-648-8187. **Owner(s):** Dennis Hawkes, 322 N. Main, Lake Mills, WI 53551. TEL 414-648-2334; FAX 414-648-8187; Pub. Dennis Hawkes; adv. contact: Arlys Hawkes. photos; pub. size: broadsheet; circ. 3,200(paid).

LANCASTER

US

GRANT COUNTY HERALD INDEPENDENT. 1843. Thu. $.75 newsstand; $27/yr. in cy.; $30/yr. out of cy.; $40/yr. out of state. 208 W. Cherry St., Lancaster, WI 53813-0310. TEL 608-723-2151; FAX 608-723-7272. **Owner(s):** Lancaster Newspapers, P.O. Box 310, Lancaster, WI 53813. TEL 608-723-2151; FAX 608-723-7272; Ed. John D. Ingebritsen; Pub. William S. Hale; adv. contact: Kevin Kelly. pub. size: broadsheet; circ. 4,450(paid).

LODI

US

LODI ENTERPRISE. 1894. Thu. $.75 newsstand; $27/yr. in area; $33/yr. out of area. 146 S. Main St., Lodi, WI 53555. TEL 608-592-3261; FAX 608-592-3866. **Owner(s):** Bill Haupt, P.O. Box 16, Lodi, WI 53555. TEL 608-592-3261; Ed. Peg Zaeminch; Pub. Bill Haupt; adv. contact: Eric Simons. pub. size: broadsheet; circ. 2,500(paid).

WEEKLY NEWSPAPERS

LOYAL
US

LOYAL TRIBUNE-RECORD-GLEANER. 1894. Wed. $.75 newsstand; $24/yr. in state. 318 N. Main St., Loyal, WI 54446-0187. TEL 715-255-8531; FAX 715-255-8357. **Owner(s):** TRG, Inc., 318 N. Main St., Loyal, WI 54446-0187. TEL 715-255-8357; Ed. Dean Lesar. adv.; pub. size: broadsheet; circ. 3,612(paid).

LUXEMBURG
US

LUXEMBURG NEWS. 1909. Wed. $.50 newsstand; $20/yr. in state; $25/yr. out of state. 406 Elm St., P.O. Box 130, Luxemburg, WI 54217-0130. TEL 414-845-2525; FAX 414-845-2525. **Owner(s):** Brown County Publishing Co., 138 Main St., Denmark, WI 54208; Ed. Lee Lawrenz. adv. contact: Larry Wilken. photos; pub. size: broadsheet; circ. 1,100(paid).

MADISON
US ISSN 1081-4043

ISTHMUS. 1976. w. $25/yr. 101 King St., Madison, WI 53703. TEL 608-251-5627; FAX 608-251-2165. **Owner(s):** Vincent O'Hern, 101 King St., Madison, WI 53703. TEL 608-251-5627; Ed. Marc Eisen; Pub. Vincent O'Hern; adv. contact: Linda Baldwin O'Hern. photos; bk.rev.; pub. size: tabloid; circ. 62,000(free & paid).

MANITOWOC
US

LAKESHORE CHRONICLE. 1972. s-w.: Wed. & Sun. free home deliv.; $10 voluntary subscription. 909 S. 29th St., Manitowoc, WI 54220. TEL 414-682-5231; FAX 414-682-1804. **Owner(s):** Thomson Newspapers, Inc., Metro Ctr., One Station Pl., 6th Fl., Stamford, CT 06902. TEL 203-425-2500; FAX 203-425-2516; Ed. Debra Horn; Pub. John Clark; adv.; photos; pub. size: broadsheet; circ. 32,500(free). **Wire Service(s):** AP.

MARION
US

MARION ADVERTISER. 1895. Thu. $.50 newsstand; $17/yr. in surrounding cys.; $20/yr. in state; $22/yr. elsewhere. 109 N. Main, Marion, WI 54950. TEL 715-754-5444. **Owner(s):** Daniel S. Brandenburg, 109 N. Main, Marion, WI 54950. TEL 715-754-5444; Ed. Patsy Brandenburg; Pub. Daniel S. Brandenburg; adv.; pub. size: broadsheet; circ. 2,850(paid).

MARKESAN
US

NEIGHBORS. 1881. Sat. $1 newsstand; $31.20/yr. in state; $31.20/yr. out of state. 51 E. John St., Markesan, WI 53946. TEL 414-398-2334; FAX 414-398-3835. **Owner(s):** Citizen Publishing Co., 51 E. John St., Markesan, WI 53946. TEL 414-398-2334; FAX 414-398-2334; Pub. James Conley; adv. contact: Mark Stormberg. pub. size: tabloid; circ. 1,831(free & paid).
Formerly: Herald, The.

MAUSTON
US

BUYER'S GUIDE CENT SAVER. Sat. free. 500 La Crosse St., Mauston, WI 53948. TEL 608-847-6224; FAX 608-847-5457. **Owner(s):** South Central Wisconsin Newspapers, Inc., P.O. Box 470, Portage, WI 53901. TEL 608-742-2111; Pub. David Gentry; adv. contact: Timothy Benson. pub. size: tabloid; circ. 15,155(free).

JUNEAU COUNTY STAR-TIMES. s-w.: Wed. & Sat. $.75 newsstand; $37/yr. in cy.; $39/yr. out of cy.; $50/yr. out of state. 500 La Crosse St., Mauston, WI 53948. TEL 608-847-6224; FAX 608-847-5457. **Owner(s):** South Central Wisconsin Newspapers, Inc., P.O. Box 470, Portage, WI 53901. TEL 608-742-2111; Ed. Georga Bray; Pub. David Gentry; adv. contact: Timothy Benson. pub. size: tabloid; circ. 3,800(paid).

MAYVILLE
US

MAYVILLE NEWS, THE. 1892. Thu. $.50 newsstand; $18/yr. 126 Bridge St., Mayville, WI 53050. TEL 414-387-2211; FAX 414-387-5515. **Owner(s):** Andrew Johnson, P.O. Box 271, Mayville, WI 53050. TEL 414-387-5515; Ed. Michael Harvey; Pub. Andrew Johnson; pub. size: broadsheet; circ. 4,333(paid).

MEDFORD
US

STAR NEWS, THE. 1875. Wed. $1 newsstand; $27.50/yr. in cy.; $31/yr. in state; $40/yr. out of state. 116 S. Wisconsin Ave., Medford, WI 54451-0180. TEL 715-748-2626; FAX 715-748-2299; E-mail: starnews@tpsnet.com. **Owner(s):** J.A. O'Leary, P.O. Box 180, Medford, WI 54451. TEL 715-748-2626; FAX 715-748-2699; Ed. Don Woerpel; Pub. J.A. O'Leary; adv.; pub. size: tabloid; circ. 6,900(paid).
Formerly: Medford Star News.

MELROSE
US

MELROSE CHRONICLE. 1895. Wed. $.75 newsstand; $26/yr. in state; $35/yr. out of state. P.O. Box 8, Melrose, WI 54642. TEL 608-488-3201; FAX 608-488-7851. **Owner(s):** Tom Besl, P.O. Box 8, Melrose, WI 54642. TEL 608-488-3201; Pub. Tom Besl; adv.; pub. size: tabloid; circ. 4,200(paid).

MENOMONIE
US

DUNN COUNTY NEWS. 1860. s-w.: Wed. & Sun. $.75 newsstand; $48/yr. in cy.; $56/yr. in state; $63/yr. out of state. 710 Main St., Menomonie, WI 54751. TEL 715-235-3411; FAX 715-235-0936. **Owner(s):** Independent Media Group, 321 Frenette, Chippewa Falls, WI 54729. TEL 715-723-5515; Ed. Margo Hecker; Pub. Steve Jahn; adv. contact: Denny Boduh. photos; bk.review; pub. size: broadsheet; circ. 5,000(paid); Sun. 5,000(paid).

MERRILL
US ISSN 0191-8958

FOTO NEWS. 1953. Wed. free newsstand; $.25/office; $30/yr. mailed in US. 805 E. Main St., Merrill, WI 54452. TEL 715-536-7121. **Owner(s):** James O'Day, 805 E. Main St., Merrill, WI 54452. TEL 715-536-7121; Ed. Lauree O'Day; Pub. James O'Day; adv.; photos; pub. size: tabloid; circ. 17,360(controlled & paid).

MERRIMAC
US

SHOPPER STOPPER. 1970. Tue. free. 327 Palisade St., Merrimac, WI 53561. TEL 608-493-2291; FAX 608-493-2074. **Owner(s):** Shopper Stopper, Inc., 327 Palisade St., Merrimac, WI 53561. TEL 608-493-2291; FAX 608-493-2074; adv.: $6.82/SAU. pub. size: tabloid; circ. 127,000(free).

MIDDLETON
US

MIDDLETON TIMES-TRIBUNE. 1893. Thu. $.75 newsstand; $29/yr. in state mailed; $44/yr. out of state mailed. 7507 Hubbard Ave., Ste. 100, Middleton, WI 53562. TEL 608-836-1601; FAX 608-836-3759. **Owner(s):** News Publishing Co., 1126 Mill St., Black Earth, WI 53515. TEL 608-767-3655; Ed. Susan Brook. adv. contact: Candy Tracy. pub. size: broadsheet; circ. 2,700(paid).

MILTON
US

MILTON COURIER. 1879. Wed. $.50 newsstand; $20/yr. in state; $23/yr. out of state. 513 Vernal, Milton, WI 53563. TEL 608-868-2442; FAX 608-869-4664. **Owner(s):** Hometown News, L.P., 28 W. Milwaukee Ave., Fort Atkinson, WI 53538. TEL 414-563-5551; Ed. Doug Welch; Pub. Brian Knox; adv. contact: Susan Angell. pub. size: tabloid; circ. 3,000(paid).

MILWAUKEE
US

BARGAIN EXPRESS NEWSPAPER. 1980. Tue. free/home deliv. 10001 W. Lisbon Ave., Milwaukee, WI 53222. TEL 414-466-3933. **Owner(s):** Ads Ex-Press Publications, Inc., 10001 W. Lisbon Ave., Milwaukee, WI 53222. TEL 414-466-3933; pub. size: tabloid; circ. 162,000(free).

US

MILWAUKEE STAR. 1960. Thu. free; $12.50/yr. 3815 N. Teutonia Ave., Milwaukee, WI 53206. TEL 414-449-4870; FAX 414-449-4872. **Owner(s):** Jerrel Jones, P.O. Box 06279 St., Milwaukee, WI 53206. TEL 414-449-4870; Ed. Walter Jones; Pub. Carole Geary; adv. contact: Faithe Colas. pub. size: tabloid; circ. 5,000(free).

MINERAL POINT
US

DEMOCRAT TRIBUNE, THE. 1892. Thu. $15/yr. in state; $18/yr. out of state. 334 High St., Mineral Point, WI 53565. TEL 608-987-2141. **Owner(s):** T. Michael Reilly & J. Patrick Reilly, 334 High St., Mineral Point, WI 53565. TEL 608-987-2141; Ed. Jeanie Lewis; Pub. T. Michael Reilly; adv. contact: T. Michael Reilly. bk.rev.; pub. size: tabloid; circ. 1,196(paid).

MINOCQUA

LAKELAND TIMES. 1891. s-w.: Tue. & Fri. $.75 newsstand; $31/yr. in cy.; $40/yr. out of cy. Chippewa & Milwaukee Sts., Minocqua, WI 54548. TEL 715-356-5236; FAX 715-358-2121. **Owner(s):** Lakeland Printing Co., P.O. Box 790, Minocqua, WI 54548. TEL 715-356-5236; Pub. Don Walker; adv.; photos; pub. size: tabloid; circ. 10,500(paid).

ISSN 0746-4274

MONDOVI

MONDOVI HERALD NEWS. 1900. Thu. $18/yr. in cy.; $21/yr. out of cy.; $25/yr. out of state. 123 W. Main St., Mondovi, WI 54755. TEL 715-926-4970; FAX 715-926-4928. **Owner(s):** Perry Nyseth, P.O. Box 67, Mondovi, WI 54755. TEL 715-926-4970; Pub. Perry Nyseth; adv. contact: Perry Nyseth. pub. size: standard; circ. 3,500(paid).

MONONA

ISSN 0745-6646

COMMUNITY HERALD. 1968. Thu. $.75 newsstand; $28/yr. 6041 Monona Dr., Monona, WI 53716. TEL 608-221-1544; FAX 608-221-0463. **Owner(s):** Community Herald Newspapers Corp., 6041 Monona Dr., Monona, WI 53716. TEL 608-221-1544; Ed. Kathleen Osten; Pub. Henry W. Schroeder; pub. size: tabloid; circ. 1,710(paid).

GOOD NEWS. 1968. Mon. free. 6041 Monona Dr., Monona, WI 53716. TEL 608-221-1544. **Owner(s):** Community Herald Newspapers Corp., 6041 Monona Dr., Monona, WI 53716. TEL 608-221-1544; Pub. Henry W. Schroeder; adv. contact: Kim Moore. pub. size: tabloid; circ. 15,500(free).

ISSN 0883-6566

MCFARLAND COMMUNITY LIFE. 1966. Thu. $.75 newsstand; $28/yr. 6041 Monona Dr., Monona, WI 53716. TEL 608-221-1544; FAX 608-221-0463. **Owner(s):** Community Herald Newspapers Corp., 6041 Monona Dr., Monona, WI 53716. TEL 608-221-1544; Ed. Kathleen Osten; Pub. Henry W. Schroeder; pub. size: tabloid; circ. 1,629(paid).

MONTELLO

MARQUETTE COUNTY TRIBUNE. 1859. Thu. $.50 newsstand; $19/yr. in state; $23/yr. out of state. 120 Underwood Ave., Montello, WI 53949. TEL 608-297-2424; FAX 608-297-9293. **Owner(s):** News Publishing Co., 1126 Mills St., Black Earth, WI 53515. TEL 608-767-3655; FAX 608-767-2222; Ed. Mary Faltz; Pub. Mark Witte; adv.; photos; pub. size: tabloid; circ. 4,500(free & paid).

MOSINEE

ISSN 0748-8297

MOSINEE TIMES, THE. 1895. Thu. $.35 newsstand; $14/yr. in cy.; $19/yr. in state; $21/yr. out of state. 407 Third St., Mosinee, WI 54455-1495. TEL 715-693-2300; FAX 715-693-1574. **Owner(s):** Mosinee Publishing Inc., 407 Third St., Mosinee, WI 54455-1495. TEL 715-693-2300; FAX 715-693-1574; Pub. John Durst; adv. contact: Jim Kress. adv.: $5.25/SAU. photos; pub. size: broadsheet; circ. 2,520(free & paid).

MUKWONAGO

MUKWONAGO CHIEF. 1889. Wed. $.50 newsstand; $22/yr. in cy. 555 Bay View Rd., Mukwonago, WI 53149-0204. TEL 414-363-4045; FAX 414-363-8573; E-mail: mukpubs@all-inc.com. **Owner(s):** Add, Inc., 600 Industrial Dr., Waupaca, WI 54891. TEL 715-258-8450; Ed. Jim Flaherty; Pub. Terri Blazek; adv. contact: Terri Blazek. pub. size: tabloid; circ. 4,500(controlled & paid).

NEILLSVILLE

CLARK COUNTY PRESS. 1989. Wed. $.75 newsstand; $26/yr. in cy.; 30/yr. out of cy.; $39/yr. elsewhere. 614 Hewitt, Neillsville, WI 54456. TEL 715-743-2600; FAX 715-743-5460. **Owner(s):** News Publishing Co., 1126 Mills St., Black Earth, WI 53515. TEL 715-743-2600; Pub. Dan Witte; adv. contact: Kathy Potter. photos; pub. size: tabloid; circ. 3,200(paid).

NEW BERLIN

ISSN 0895-2817

BAY VIEWER. 1976. Thu. $.50 newsstand; $24/yr. local; $51/yr. out of area; $75.70/yr. elsewhere. 15770 W. Cleveland, New Berlin, WI 53151. TEL 414-938-5000; FAX 414-938-5001. **Owner(s):** Community Newspapers, Inc., P.O. Box 510210, New Berlin, WI 53151. TEL 414-938-5000; Ed. Ellen Hickok-Wall; Pub. Thomas H. Krekel; adv. contact: Howard J. Hoerl. photos; pub. size: tabloid; circ. 1,527(paid).

BROOKFIELD NEWS. Thu. $.50 newsstand; $24/yr. local; $51/yr. out of area; $75.70/yr. elsewhere. 15770 W. Cleveland Ave., New Berlin, WI 53151. TEL 414-938-5000; FAX 414-938-5001. **Owner(s):** Community Newspapers, Inc., P.O. Box 510210, New Berlin, WI 53151-0210. TEL 414-938-5000; Ed. Mary Lou Stover; Pub. Thomas H. Krekel; adv.; photos; bk.rev.; pub. size: tabloid; circ. 6,807(paid).

BROWN DEER HERALD. Thu. $.50 newsstand; $24/yr. local; $51/yr. out of area; $75.70/yr. elsewhere. 15770 W. Cleveland, New Berlin, WI 53151. TEL 414-938-5000; FAX 414-938-5012. **Owner(s):** Community Newspapers, Inc., P.O. Box 510210, New Berlin, WI 53151-0210. TEL 414-938-5000; Ed. Ellen Hickok-Wall; Pub. Thomas H. Krekel; pub. size: tabloid; circ. 1,500(paid).

CUDAHY REMINDER-ENTERPRISE. Thu. $.50 newsstand; $24/yr. local; $51/yr. out of area; $75.70/yr. elsewhere. 15770 W. Cleveland, New Berlin, WI 53151. TEL 414-938-5000; FAX 414-938-5001. **Owner(s):** Community Newspapers, Inc., P.O. Box 510210, New Berlin, WI 53151. TEL 414-938-5000; Ed. Ellen Hickok-Wall; Pub. Thomas H. Krekel; adv.; photos; pub. size: tabloid; circ. 5,175(paid).

ELM GROVE ELM LEAVES. Thu. $.50 newsstand; $24/yr. local; $51/yr. out of area; $75.70/yr. elsewhere. 15770 W. Cleveland, New Berlin, WI 53151. TEL 414-938-5000; FAX 414-938-5001. **Owner(s):** Community Newspapers, Inc., P.O. Box 510210, New Berlin, OH 53151-0210. TEL 216-642-5516; Ed. Mary Lou Stover; Pub. Thomas H. Krekel; adv.; photos; bk.rev.; pub. size: tabloid; circ. 1,581(paid).

FOX POINT, BAYSIDE, RIVER HILLS HERALD. Thu. $.50 newsstand; $24/yr. local; $51/yr. out of area; $75.70/yr. elsewhere. 15770 W. Cleveland, New Berlin, WI 53151. TEL 414-938-5000; FAX 414-938-5012. **Owner(s):** Community Newspapers, Inc., P.O. Box 510210, New Berlin, WI 51020. TEL 414-938-5000; Ed. Ellen Hickok-Wall; Pub. Thomas H. Krekel; adv. contact: Howard J. Hoerl. photos; bk.rev.; pub. size: tabloid; circ. 2,053(paid).

FRANKLIN-HALES CORNER HUB. Thu. $.50 newsstand; $24/yr. local; $51/yr. out of area; $75.70/yr. elsewhere. 15770 W. Cleveland, New Berlin, WI 53152. TEL 414-938-5000; FAX 414-938-5001. **Owner(s):** Community Newspapers, Inc., P.O. Box 510210, New Berlin, WI 53151-0210. TEL 414-938-5000; FAX 414-938-5001; Ed. Mary Lou Stover; Pub. Thomas H. Krekel; adv. contact: Howard J. Hoerl. photos; bk.rev.; pub. size: tabloid; circ. 4,491(paid).

GERMANTOWN BANNER-PRESS. 1975. Thu. $.50 newsstand; $24/yr. local; $51/yr. out of area; $75.70/yr. elsewhere. 15770 W. Cleveland Ave., New Berlin, WI 53151. TEL 414-938-5000; FAX 414-938-5001. **Owner(s):** Community Newspapers, Inc., P.O. Box 510210, New Berlin, WI 53151-0210. TEL 414-938-5000; Ed. Mary Lou Stover; Pub. Thomas H. Kreckel; adv. contact: Howard Hoerl. photos; bk.rev.; pub. size: tabloid; circ. 2,238(paid).

GLENDALE HERALD. Thu. $.50 newsstand; $24/yr. local; $51/yr. out of area; $75.70/yr. elsewhere. 15770 W. Cleveland, New Berlin, WI 53151. TEL 414-938-5000; FAX 414-938-5001. **Owner(s):** Community Newspapers, Inc., P.O. Box 510210, New Berlin, WI 53151. TEL 414-938-5000; Ed. Ellen Hickok-Wall; Pub. Thomas H. Krekel; adv.; photos; pub. size: tabloid; circ. 1,714(paid).

GREENDALE VILLAGE LIFE. Thu. $.50 newsstand; $24/yr. local; $51/yr. out of area; $75.70/yr. elsewhere. 15770 W. Cleveland, New Berlin, WI 53151. TEL 414-938-5000; FAX 414-938-5001. **Owner(s):** Community Newspapers, Inc., P.O. Box 510210, New Berlin, WI 53151. TEL 414-938-5000; Ed. Ellen Hickok-Wall; Pub. Thomas H. Krekel; adv. contact: Howard J. Hoerl. photos; pub. size: tabloid; circ. 2,768(paid).

GREENFIELD OBSERVER. Thu. $.50 newsstand; $24/yr. local; $51/yr. out of area; $75.70/yr. elsewhere. 15770 W. Cleveland, New Berlin, WI 53151. TEL 414-938-5000; FAX 414-938-5001. **Owner(s):** Community Newspapers, Inc., P.O. Box 510210, New Berlin, WI 53151. TEL 414-938-5000; Ed. Ellen Hickok-Wall; Pub. Thomas H. Krekel; adv. contact: Howard J. Hoerl. photos; pub. size: tabloid; circ. 3,326(paid).

WEEKLY NEWSPAPERS

US

MENOMONEE FALLS NEWS. 1894. Thu. $.50 newsstand; $24/yr. local; $51/yr. out of area; $75.70/yr. elsewhere. 15770 W. Cleveland, New Berlin, WI 53151. TEL 414-768-5832; FAX 414-938-5001. **Owner(s):** Community Newspapers, Inc., P.O. Box 510210, New Berlin, WI 53151-0210. TEL 414-938-5000; Ed. Ellen Hickok-Wall; Pub. Thomas Kreckel; adv. contact: Howard Hoerl. pub. size: tabloid; circ. 5,024(paid).

US

MEQUON-THIENSVILLE COURANT. Thu. $.50 newsstand; $24/yr. local; $51/yr. out of area; $75.70/yr. elsewhere. 15770 W. Cleveland, New Berlin, WI 53151. TEL 414-938-5000; FAX 414-938-5001. **Owner(s):** Community Newspapers, Inc., P.O. Box 510210, New Berlin, WI 53151. TEL 414-938-5000; Ed. Mary Lou Stover; Pub. Thomas H. Krekel; adv.; photos; bk.rev.; pub. size: tabloid; circ. 3,000(paid).

US

MUSKEGO SUN. Thu. $.50 newsstand; $24/yr. local; $51/yr. out of area; $75.70/yr. elsewhere. 15770 W. Cleveland, New Berlin, WI 53151. TEL 414-938-5000; FAX 414-938-5001. **Owner(s):** Community Newspapers,Inc., P.O. Box 510210, New Berlin, WI 53151. TEL 414-938-5000; Ed. Ellen Hickok-Wall; Pub. Thomas H. Krekel; adv. contact: Howard J. Hoerl. photos; bk.rev.; pub. size: tabloid; circ. 3,309(paid).

US

NEW BERLIN CITIZEN. Thu. $.50 newsstand; $24/yr. local; $51/yr. out of area; $75.70/yr. elsewhere. 15770 W. Cleveland, New Berlin, WI 53151. TEL 414-938-5000; FAX 414-938-5001. **Owner(s):** Community Newspapers, Inc., P.O. Box 510210, New Berlin, WI 53151. TEL 414-938-5000; Ed. Mary Lou Stover; Pub. Thomas H. Krekel; adv. contact: Howard J. Hoerl. photos; bk.rev.; pub. size: tabloid; circ. 4,491(paid).

US

OAK CREEK PICTORIAL. Thu. $.50 newsstand; $24/yr. local; $51/yr. out of area; $75.70/yr. elsewhere. 15770 W. Cleveland, New Berlin, WI 53151. TEL 414-938-5000; FAX 414-938-5001. **Owner(s):** Community Newspapers, Inc., P.O. Box 510210, New Berlin, WI 53151. TEL 414-938-5000; Ed. Ellen Hickok-Wall; Pub. Thomas H. Krekel; adv.; photos; bk.rev.; pub. size: tabloid; circ. 4,536(paid).

US

SHOREWOOD HERALD. Thu. $.50 newsstand; $24/yr. local; $51/yr. out of area; $75.70/yr. elsewhere. 15770 W. Cleveland, New Berlin, WI 53151. TEL 414-938-5000; FAX 414-938-5001. **Owner(s):** Community Newspapers, Inc., P.O. Box 510210, New Berlin, WI 53151. TEL 414-938-5000; Ed. Ellen Hickok-Wall; Pub. Thomas H. Krekel; adv. contact: Howard J. Hoerl. photos; pub. size: tabloid; circ. 1,700(paid).

US

SOUTH MILWAUKEE VOICE GRAPHIC. Thu. $.50 newsstand; $19.50/yr. local; $43.50/yr. out of area; $64.50/yr. elsewhere. 15770 W. Cleveland, New Berlin, WI 53151. TEL 414-938-5000; FAX 414-938-5001. **Owner(s):** Community Newspapers, Inc., P.O. Box 510210, New Berlin, WI 53151. TEL 414-938-5000; Ed. Mary Lou Stover; Pub. Thomas H. Krekel; adv.; photos; bk.rev.; pub. size: tabloid; circ. 4,140(paid).

US

ST. FRANCIS REMINDER-ENTERPRISE. Thu. $.50 newsstand; $24/yr. local; $51/yr. out of area; $75.70/yr. elsewhere. 15770 W. Cleveland, New Berlin, WI 53151. TEL 414-938-5000; FAX 414-938-5001. **Owner(s):** Community Newspapers, Inc., P.O. Box 15770, New Berlin, WI 53151. TEL 414-938-5000; Ed. Mary Lou Stover; Pub. Thomas H. Kreckel; photos; pub. size: tabloid; circ. 5,120(paid).
Formerly: St. Francis Free Press Reminder.

US

SUSSEX-LANNON-LISBON NEWS. Thu. $.50 newsstand; $24/yr. local; $51/yr. out of area; $75.70/yr. elsewhere. 15770 W. Cleveland, New Berlin, WI 53151. TEL 414-938-5000; FAX 414-938-5001. **Owner(s):** Community Newspapers, Inc., P.O. Box 510210, New Berlin, WI 53151. TEL 414-938-5000; Ed. Mary Lou Stover; Pub. Thomas H. Krekel; adv.; photos; bk.rev.; pub. size: tabloid; circ. 500(paid).

US

WEST ALLIS STAR. Thu. $.50 newsstand; $24/yr. local; $51/yr. out of area; $75.70/yr. elsewhere. 15770 W. Cleveland, New Berlin, WI 53151. TEL 414-938-5000; FAX 414-938-5001. **Owner(s):** Community Newspapers, Inc., P.O. Box 510210, West Berlin, WI 53151. TEL 414-938-5000; Ed. Mary Lou Stover; Pub. Thomas H. Krekel; adv. contact: Howard J. Hoerl. pub. size: tabloid; circ. 4,143(paid).

US

WHITEFISH BAY HERALD. Thu. $.50 newsstand; $24/yr. local; $51/yr. out of area; $75.70/yr. elsewhere. 15770 W. Cleveland, New Berlin, WI 53151. TEL 414-938-5000; FAX 414-938-5001. **Owner(s):** Community Newspapers, Inc., P.O. Box 510210, New Berlin, WI 53151. TEL 414-938-5000; Ed. Ellen Hickok-Wall; Pub. Thomas H. Krekel; adv.; photos; bk.rev.; pub. size: tabloid; circ. 2,900(paid).

NEW HOLSTEIN

US

NEW HOLSTEIN REPORTER. 1905. Thu. $.75 newsstand; $20/yr. local cys.; $28/yr. in state; $38/yr. out of state. 2118 Wisconsin Ave., New Holstein, WI 53061. TEL 414-898-4276; FAX 414-894-2161. **Owner(s):** Mark Sherry, Mike Mathes & Joe Mathes, 1803 Park Ave., New Holstein, WI 53061. TEL 414-898-4276; Pub. Mark Sherry; adv. contact: Greg Fictum. pub. size: tabloid; circ. 2,200(paid).

NEW LONDON

US

PRESS-STAR. 1891. Fri. $.75 newsstand; $20/yr. in cy.; $26/yr. in state; $32/yr. out of state. 416 N. Water St., New London, WI 54961-0283. TEL 414-982-4321; FAX 414-982-7672. **Owner(s):** Add, Inc., 600 Industrial Dr., Waupaca, WI 54981. TEL 715-258-8450; Ed. Nancy Wieneke; Pub. William Melendes; adv. contact: William Melendes. photos; bk.rev.; pub. size: tabloid; circ. 2,630(free & paid).
Formerly: New London Press-Star.

NEW RICHMOND

US

NEW RICHMOND NEWS. 1869. Thu. $1 newsstand; $32/yr. mailed in state; $39/yr. out of state. 127 S. Knowles Ave., New Richmond, WI 54017. TEL 715-246-6881; FAX 715-246-7117. **Owner(s):** Robert Bradford, 127 S. Knowles Ave., New Richmond, WI 54017. TEL 715-246-6881; Ed. Larry Hubner; Pub. Michael Burke; adv. contact: Rene Findlay. pub. size: broadsheet; circ. 5,000(paid).

NEWVERLAND

US

WAUWATOSA NEWS-TIMES. Thu. $.50 newsstand; $24/yr. local; $51/yr. out of area; $75.70/yr. elsewhere. 15770 W. Cleveland Ave., Newverland, WI 53151. TEL 414-938-5000; FAX 414-938-5001. **Owner(s):** Community Newspapers, Inc., P.O. Box 510210, New Berlin, WI 53151-0210. TEL 414-938-5000; Ed. Mary Lou Stover; Pub. Thomas H. Krekle; adv.; photos; pub. size: tabloid; circ. 6,760(paid).

OCONOMOWOC

US

OCONOMOWOC ENTERPRISE. 1888. Wed. $.50 newsstand; $20.80/yr. in city; $28.60/yr. mailed out of city; $36.40/yr. out of state. 212 E. Wisconsin Ave., Oconomowoc, WI 53066. TEL 414-567-5511; FAX 414-567-4422. **Owner(s):** Thomson Newspapers, Inc., Metro Centre, One Station Pl., 6th Fl., Stamford, CT 06902. TEL 203-425-2500; FAX 203-425-2516; Ed. Pat Walker. adv. contact: Jan Gust. photos; pub. size: broadsheet; circ. 8,000(paid).

OCONTO FALLS

US

OCONTO COUNTY TIMES-HERALD. 1890. Wed. $.50 newsstand; $20/yr. 107 S. Main St., Oconto Falls, WI 54154-0128. TEL 414-846-3427; FAX 414-846-3430. **Owner(s):** Roger F. Shellman, 107 S. Main St., Oconto Falls, WI 54154-0128. TEL 414-846-3427; FAX 414-846-3430; Ed. Roger F. Shellman; Pub. Roger F. Shellman; adv. contact: Gayle Smoot. photos; pub. size: broadsheet; circ. 5,500(controlled & paid).

OMRO

US

OMRO HERALD. 1895. Thu. $.75 newsstand; $24/yr. local; $42/yr. in state; $55/yr. out of state. 127 W. Main St., Omro, WI 54963. TEL 414-685-2707; FAX 414-361-1518. **Owner(s):** R.M. Gonyo, 135 E. Moore, Berlin, WI 54923. TEL 414-316-0377; Berlin Journal Co., P.O. Box 502, Omro, WI 54963; Ed. Jim Wolff. adv.; pub. size: tabloid; circ. 1,125(paid).

OREGON

US

OREGON OBSERVER. 1844. Wed. $.75 newsstand; $28/yr. 845 Market St., Oregon, WI 53575. TEL 608-251-3252; FAX 608-251-0582. **Owner(s):** Henry W. Schroeder, 120 W. Verona Ave., P.O. Box 6, Verona, WI 53575. TEL 608-251-3252; FAX 608-251-0582; Pub. Henry Schroeder; adv.; pub. size: tabloid; circ. 3,050(paid).

ORFORDVILLE

US

ORFORDVILLE JOURNAL & FOOTVILLE NEWS. 1909. Wed. $.35 newsstand; $12/yr. 124 E. Spring St., Orfordville, WI 53576-0248. TEL 608-879-2211; FAX 608-879-2211. **Owner(s):** George E. Stewart, 124 E. Spring St., Orfordville, WI 53576-0248. TEL 608-879-2211; FAX 608-879-2211; Pub. George E. Stewart; adv. contact: B.L. Stewart. pub. size: tabloid; circ. morning 1,250(paid).

OSCEOLA

US

OSCEOLA SUN. 1897. Wed. $.50 newsstand; $15/yr. 108 Cascade St., Osceola, WI 54020-0248. TEL 715-294-2314; FAX 715-755-3314. **Owner(s):** Jeff & Julie Holmquist, 524 Eric Dr., Osceola, WI 54020-0248. TEL 715-294-4580; Ed. Jeff Holmquist; Pub. Julie Holmquist; adv.; pub. size: broadsheet; circ. 2,000(paid).

OSHKOSH

US

OSHKOSH BUYERS GUIDE. 1937. Wed. free newsstand. 314 N. Koeller St., Oshkosh, WI 54901. TEL 414-235-1790; FAX 414-235-1833. **Owner(s):** Add, Inc., 600 Industrial Dr., Waupaca, WI 54981. TEL 715-258-8450; Ed. Ed Lowe; Pub. Jeff Thorkildsen; adv.; photos; pub. size: tabloid; circ. 23,200(free).

OSSEO

US

TRI-COUNTY NEWS. 1900. Wed. 51119 Omaha St., Osseo, WI 54758-0460. TEL 715-597-3313; FAX 715-597-2705. **Owner(s):** Michael D. Jensen, P.O. Box 460, Osseo, WI 54758. TEL 715-597-3313; Pub. Michael D. Jensen; pub. size: standard; circ. 3,500(paid).
Formerly: Osseo Tri-County News.

PARK FALLS

US

PARK FALLS HERALD. 1900. Thu. $.75 newsstand; $25/yr. in cy.; $30/yr. out of cy.; $35/yr. out of state. 259 Second Ave., N., Park Falls, WI 54552. TEL 715-762-4940; FAX 715-762-2757. **Owner(s):** Bee Hive Press, Inc., P.O. Box 170, Phillips, WI 54555. TEL 715-339-3036; Ed. Kenneth Dischler; Pub. Kenneth Dischler; adv. contact: Wilma Thier. pub. size: tabloid; circ. 3,437(paid).

PESHTIGO

US

PESHTIGO TIMES. Wed. $.50 newsstand; $18/yr. in cy.; $28/yr. in state; $30/yr. out of state. 851 Maple Ave., Peshtigo, WI 54157. TEL 715-582-4541; FAX 715-582-4662. **Owner(s):** Pesch Publishing Co., Inc., P.O. Box 187, Peshtigo, WI 54157. TEL 715-582-4541; Ed. Leo Pesch; Pub. Mary Ann Gardon; adv. contact: Chuck Gardon. photos. pub. size: broadsheet; circ. 12,000(paid).

PHILLIPS

US

BEE, THE. 1884. Thu. $.75 newsstand; $25-$35/yr. 115 N. Lake, Phillips, WI 54555-0170. TEL 715-339-3036; FAX 715-339-4300. **Owner(s):** Bee Hive Press, Inc., P.O. Box 170, Phillips, WI 54555-0170. TEL 715-339-3036; Pub. T.L. Kempkes; adv. contact: Jennifer Zillman. photos; pub. size: tabloid; circ. 4,700(paid).

PLATTEVILLE

US

PLATTEVILLE JOURNAL. 1899. s-w.: Tue. & Thu. $.75 newsstand; $22/yr. in cy.; $29/yr. out of cy. 1190 U.S. Hwy. 151, Platteville, WI 53818. TEL 608-348-3006; FAX 608-348-7979. **Owner(s):** Richard Brockman, 855 N. Elm, Platteville, WI 53818. TEL 608-348-3006; FAX 608-348-7979; Ed. Richard Brockman; Pub. Richard Brokman; adv.; pub. size: broadsheet; circ. 7,000(paid).

US

SHOPPING NEWS. 1950. Tue. free; $35/yr. out of area. 11 Means Dr., Platteville, WI 53818-0500. TEL 608-348-2374; FAX 608-348-3388. **Owner(s):** Woodward Communications, Inc., P.O. Box 688, Dubuque, IA 52004. TEL 319-588-5611; Ed. George Louthain; Pub. George Louthain; adv. contact: Kathy Neumeister. pub. size: tabloid; circ. 37,877(free).

PLYMOUTH

US

REVIEW, THE. s-w.: Tue & Thu. $.75 newsstand; $28/yr. in cy.; $45/yr. out of cy. & state. 113 E. Mill St., Plymouth, WI 53073-1776. TEL 414-893-6411; FAX 414-893-5505. **Owner(s):** Wisconsin News Press, Inc., 113 E. Mill St., Plymouth, WI 53073-1776. TEL 414-893-6411; FAX 414-893-5505; Ed. Emmett Feldner; Pub. Barry S. Johanson; adv. contact: Nancy Juskey. pub. size: broadsheet.

PORT WASHINGTON

US ISSN 0749-7164

OZAUKEE PRESS. 1939. Thu. $1 newsstand; $26/yr. 125 E. Main St., Port Washington, WI 53074. TEL 414-284-3494; FAX 414-284-0067. **Owner(s):** Port Publications, 125 E. Main St., Port Washington, WI 53074. TEL 414-284-3494; FAX 414-284-0067; Ed. William Schanen, III; Pub. William Schanen, III; adv. contact: Ray Haverkamps. pub. size: tabloid; circ. 15,000(paid).

POYNETTE

US

POYNETTE PRESS. w. . $.50 newsstand; $16/yr. 125 N. Main St., Poynette, WI 53955-0037. TEL 608-635-2565; FAX 608-846-9664. **Owner(s):** Deforest Times Tribune, 108 Market, Deforest, WI 53932; Ed. Molly Emerson; Pub. Richard Emerson; adv. contact: Richard Emerson. pub. size: tabloid; circ. 1,300.

PRAIRIE DU CHIEN

US

COURIER PRESS. 1845. s-w.: Mon. & Wed. $37.50/yr. in area; $47.50/yr out of area. 132 S. Beaumont Rd., Prairie du Chien, WI 53821. TEL 608-326-2441; FAX 608-326-2443. **Owner(s):** Howe Printing Co., P.O. Box 149, Prairie du Chien, WI; Ed. William Howe; Pub. E.B. Howe; adv. contact: Gary J. Howe. photos; bk.rev.; pub. size: tabloid; circ. 13,500(controlled).

PRESCOTT

US

PRESCOTT JOURNAL. 1855. Thu. $24/yr. in cy.; $36/yr. elsewhere. 311 Dakota St., Prescott, WI 54021. TEL 715-262-5454; FAX 715-262-5474; E-mail: pres,our@pressenter.com. **Owner(s):** Gary B. Rawn, 255 Lawrence St., Prescott, WI 54021. TEL 715-262-5454; Ed. Gary B. Rawn; Pub. Gary B. Rawn; adv. contact: Rita Kemp. adv.: $6.06/SAU. photos; bk.rev.; pub. size: standard; circ. 6,500(paid).

PRESQUE ISLE

US

NORTH STAR JOURNAL. 1976. Thu. $.65 newsstand; $27.50/yr. in state. 8378 Lake St., Presque Isle, WI 54557. TEL 715-686-2525; FAX 715-686-2080. **Owner(s):** Thomas Forster, 8378 Lake St., Presque Isle, WI 54557. TEL 715-686-2938; Ed. Thomas Forster; Pub. Thomas Forster; adv.; pub. size: tabloid; circ. 2,800(paid).

PRINCETON

US

PRINCETON TIMES-REPUBLIC. Thu. $.75 newsstand; $24/yr. local; $42/yr. in state; $55/yr. out of state. 439 W. Water, Princeton, WI 54968. TEL 414-295-6261; FAX 414-295-0110. **Owner(s):** R.M. Gonyo, 135 E. Moore, Berlin, WI 54923. TEL 414-361-0377; Ed. Jim Wolff; Pub. R.M. Gonyo; pub. size: broadsheet; circ. 1,475(paid).

RANDOM LAKE

US

SOUNDER, THE. 1918. Thu. $.50 newsstand; $14/yr. in state; $19/yr. out of state. 405 Second St., Random Lake, WI 53075-0346. TEL 414-994-9244; FAX 414-994-4817. **Owner(s):** Times Printing Co., Inc., 100 Industrial Dr., Random Lake, WI 53075-1636. TEL 414-994-4396; FAX 414-994-2088; Ed. Gary J. Feider. adv. contact: Gary J. Feider. adv.: $3.20/SAU. photos; pub. size: tabloid; circ. 2,768(paid).

REEDSBURG

US

REEDSBURG TIMES-PRESS. 1860. s-w.: Wed. & Sat. $.60 newsstand; $22/yr. in cy.; $24/yr. out of cy. 117 S. Walnut St., Reedsburg, WI 53959. TEL 608-524-4336; FAX 608-524-4337. **Owner(s):** South Central Wisconsin Newspapers, Inc., P.O. Box 470, Portage, WI 53901. TEL 608-742-2111; Ed. Pete Margolis; Pub. David Gentry; adv. contact: Larry Crawford. pub. size: tabloid; circ. 4,400(paid).

WEEKLY NEWSPAPERS

RICE LAKE
US

RICE LAKE CHRONOTYPE. 1874. Wed. $.75 newsstand; $30/yr. 28 S. Main St., Rice Lake, WI 54868. TEL 715-234-2121; FAX 715-234-5232. **Owner(s):** Chronotype Publishing, Inc., 28 S. Main St., Rice Lake, WI 54868. TEL 715-234-2121; Ed. Sam Finazzo; Pub. Warren Dorrance; pub. size: broadsheet; circ. 9,013(paid). **Wire Service(s):** AP Newsfinder.

RICHLAND CENTER
US

RICHLAND OBSERVER. 1854. Thu. $.75 newsstand; $17/yr. in state; $28/yr. out of state. 172 E. Court St., Richland Center, WI 53581. TEL 608-647-6141; FAX 608-647-6143. **Owner(s):** Erik R. Olson, 172 E. Court St., P.O. Box 31, Richland Center, WI 53581. TEL 608-647-6141; Ed. Erik R. Olson; Pub. Erik R. Olson; adv. contact: Michael Lee. pub. size: tabloid; circ. 5,000(paid).
Formerly: Richland Center Observer.

RIPON
US

FIVE COUNTY/BUYER'S GUIDE. Tue. free newsstand & home deliv.; $1/copy mailed out of area. 321 Watson St., Ripon, WI 54971. TEL 414-748-2848; FAX 414-748-2750. **Owner(s):** Schroeder Media LLC, P.O. Box 301, Ripon, WI 54971; Ed. David R. Schroeder; Pub. David R. Schroeder; pub. size: standard; circ. 21,500(free).
Formerly: Five County Shopping News.

US ISSN 0748-6863

RIPON COMMONWEALTH PRESS. 1864. Thu. $27/yr. in cy.; $33/yr. out of cy.; $40/yr. out of state. 646 Douglas St., Ripon, WI 54971. TEL 414-748-3017; FAX 414-748-3028. **Owner(s):** Ripon Community Publications, 646 Douglas St., P.O. Box 344, Ripon, WI 54971. TEL 414-748-3017; Ed. Pam Evans; Pub. Tim Lyke; adv.; pub. size: broadsheet; circ. 3,600(paid).

RIVER FALLS
US

RIVER FALLS JOURNAL. 1854. Thu. $1 newsstand; $31/yr. in cy.; $52/yr. out of cy. 112 E. Walnut St., River Falls, WI 54022-0025. TEL 715-425-1561; FAX 715-425-5666. **Owner(s):** Arlin Albrecht, 112 E. Walnut St., River Falls, WI 54022-0025. TEL 715-425-1561; Ed. Phil Pfuehler; Pub. Steve Dzubay; adv. contact: Gina Boury. pub. size: standard; circ. 4,362(paid). Wire Service(s): AP Newsfinder, WNA.

SAUK CITY
US

SAUK-PRAIRIE STAR. 1844. Thu. $.75 newsstand; $29/yr. in state; $44/yr. out of state. 801 Water St., Sauk City, WI 53583. TEL 608-643-3444; FAX 608-643-4988. **Owner(s):** News Publishing Co., 1126 Mill St., Black Earth, WI 53515; Ed. Dan Satran, Jr.; Pub. Dan Witte; adv. contact: D. Baumgartner. pub. size: tabloid; circ. 3,000(paid).

SEYMOUR
US

TIMES-PRESS. 1886. Thu. $.50 newsstand; $20/yr. 205 N. Main St., Seymour, WI 54165-0128. TEL 414-833-2517; FAX 414-833-2454. **Owner(s):** Journal-Sentinel, P.O. Box 661, Milwaukee, WI 53201. TEL 414-224-2115; Ed. Teresa Hilgenberg. adv.; photos; bk.rev.; pub. size: tabloid; circ. 2,400(paid).

SHARON
US

SHARON REPORTER, THE. 1878. Wed. $.50 newsstand; $20/yr. in cy.; $24/yr. in state; $28/yr. in IL; $32/yr. elsewhere. 213 Baldwin, Sharon, WI 53585-0508. TEL 414-736-4380; FAX 414-275-5259. **Owner(s):** Walworth Papers, 630 Kenosha St., Walworth, WI 53184. TEL 414-275-2166; FAX 414-275-5259; Ed. Mabel Jackson. adv.; pub. size: broadsheet; circ. 850(paid).

SHEBOYGAN
US

SHORELINE CHRONICLE. 1976. Tue. free. 614 N. Sixth St., Sheboygan, WI 53081. TEL 414-459-8820; FAX 414-459-7449. **Owner(s):** Thomson Newspapers, Inc., Metro Centre, One Station Pl., 6th fl., Stamford, CT 06902. TEL 203-425-2500; FAX 203-425-2516; Pub. Dennis Brooks; adv. contact: L. Tuzinekewich. pub. size: tabloid; circ. 40,200(free).

SHEBOYGAN FALLS
US ISSN 0897-4543

SHEBOYGAN FALLS NEWS. 1980. Wed. $.50 newsstand; $22/yr. in cy.; $35/yr. out cy. P.O. Box 183, Sheboygan Falls, WI 53085. TEL 414-467-6591; FAX 414-893-5505. **Owner(s):** Wisconsin News Press, Inc., 113 E. Mill St., Plymouth, WI 53073; Ed. Sandra Kimball; Pub. Sandra Kimball; adv. contact: Nancy Jusky. pub. size: broadsheet; circ. 2,200(paid).

SHELL LAKE
US ISSN 8755-0520

WASHBURN COUNTY REGISTER. 1889. Thu. $.60 newsstand; $19/yr. in cy.; $29.75/yr. out of cy. 21 W. Fifth Ave., Shell Lake, WI 54871. TEL 715-468-2314; FAX 715-468-2314. **Owner(s):** Marc & Connie Parentau, P.O. Box 455, Shell Lake, WI 54871. TEL 715-468-2314; FAX 715-468-2314; Ed. Marc Parentau; Pub. Marc Parentau; adv. contact: Connie Parentau. photos; pub. size: tabloid; circ. 1,800(paid).

SPARTA
US

FOXXY SHOPPER. 1975. Tue. free newsstand; $55/yr. P.O. Box 526, Sparta, WI 54656. TEL 608-269-5054; FAX 608-269-1488. **Owner(s):** Lee Enterprises, Inc., 400 Putnam Bldg., 215 N. Main St., Davenport, IA 52801. TEL 312-383-2100; pub. size: tabloid; circ. 74,000(paid).

US

MONROE COUNTY DEMOCRAT. 1859. Thu. $27/yr. in cy.; $30/yr. out of cy.; $37/yr. out of state. 132 River Rd., Sparta, WI 54656. TEL 608-269-3186; FAX 608-269-6876. **Owner(s):** Sparta Monroe County Publishers, Inc., P.O. Box 252, Sparta, WI 54656. TEL 608-269-3186; Ed. William Gleiss; Pub. William Gleiss; adv. contact: Jill Bisinger. photos; bk.rev.; pub. size: broadsheet; circ. 5,600(paid).

US

SPARTA HERALD. 1858. Mon. $.75 newsstand; $27/yr. locally mailed; $30/yr. in state; $37/yr. out of state. 1302 River Rd., Sparta, WI 54656-0252. TEL 608-269-3186; FAX 608-269-6876. **Owner(s):** Sparta Monroe County Publishers, Inc., P.O. Box 252, Sparta, WI 54656. TEL 608-269-3186; Ed. Theodore C. Radde; Pub. Theodore C. Radde; adv.; pub. size: broadsheet; circ. 5,050(paid).

SPOONER
US

EVERGREEN SHOPPING GUIDE. Thu. free. 509 Front St., Spooner, WI 54801. TEL 715-635-2181; FAX 715-635-2186. **Owner(s):** Northwest Wisconsin Media, Inc., P.O. Box 338, Spooner, WI 54801. TEL 715-635-2181; FAX 715-635-2186; Ed. Bill Thornley; Pub. Janet Krokson; pub. size: broadsheet; circ. 16,800(free & paid).

US ISSN 8755-6995

SPOONER ADVOCATE. 1901. Thu. $.75 newsstand; $29/yr. in area; $44/yr. out of area. 509 Front St., Spooner, WI 54801. TEL 715-635-2181; FAX 715-635-2186. **Owner(s):** Northwest Wisconsin Media, Inc., P.O. Box 338, Spooner, WI 54801. TEL 715-635-2181; FAX 715-635-2186; Ed. William Thornley; Pub. Janet Krokson; adv. contact: Michelle Carlson. photos; pub. size: broadsheet; circ. 5,000(paid).

SPRING VALLEY
US

SPRING VALLEY SUN. 1921. Wed. $.25 newsstand; $11/yr. in cy.; $15/yr. out of cy. 216 S. McKay Ave., Spring Valley, WI 54767. TEL 715-778-4395. **Owner(s):** Duane Kelley, 216 S. McKay Ave., Spring Valley, WI 54767. TEL 715-778-4395; Ed. Duane Kelley; Pub. Duane Kelley; adv.; photos; pub. size: tabloid; circ. 700(paid).

US

VALLEY VALUE SHOPPER. Tue. free. 216 S. McKay Ave., Spring Valley, WI 54767. TEL 715-778-4395. **Owner(s):** Duane Kelley, 216 S. McKay Ave., Spring Valley, WI 54767. TEL 715-778-4395; Ed. Duane Kelley; Pub. Duane Kelley; adv.: $4.50/SAU. photos; pub. size: tabloid; circ. 2,000(controlled).

STANLEY
US

STANLEY REPUBLICAN. 1896. Thu. $18/yr. in area; $20/yr. in state; $27/yr. out of state. 131 E. First Ave., Stanley, WI 54768-0185. TEL 715-644-3319; FAX 715-644-5452. **Owner(s):** B.J. Fazendin, 131 E. First Ave., P.O. Box 185, Stanley, WI 54768-0185. TEL 715-644-3319; FAX 715-644-5452; Ed. B.J. Fazendin. adv.; photos; pub. size: standard; circ. 2,500(paid).

10774 STOUGHTON, WI — **WEEKLY NEWSPAPERS**

STOUGHTON
US ISSN 1049-0655

COURIER HUB. 1867. Thu. $.75 newsstand; $26.50/yr. in cy.; $35/yr. out of cy. 301 W. Main St., Stoughton, WI 53589-0577. TEL 608-873-6671; FAX 608-873-3473. **Owner(s):** Woodward Communications, Inc., P.O. Box 688, Dubuque, IA 52004-0688. TEL 319-588-5687; FAX 319-588-5739; Ed. Eric Neuwirth; Pub. Tom Courbari; adv. contact: Tom Courbari. bk.rev.; pub. size: tabloid; circ. 4,374(paid).

STRATFORD
US

STRATFORD JOURNAL. 1914. Wed. $15/yr. local; $22.50/yr. in state; $30/yr. out of state. P.O. Box 5, Stratford, WI 54484. TEL 715-687-4112. Owner(s): Paul Hale, P.O. Box 5, Stratford, WI 54484. TEL 715-687-4112; Pub. Paul Hale; adv. contact: Paul Hale. adv.: $7.16/SAU. photos; pub. size: tabloid; circ. 750(paid).

STURGEON BAY
US ISSN 0749-7180

DOOR COUNTY ADVOCATE. 1862. s-w.: Tue. & Fri. $.50 newsstand; $36/yr. home deliv.; $41/yr. mailed in state; $47/yr. out of state. 233 N. Third Ave., Sturgeon Bay, WI 54235-0130. TEL 414-743-3321; FAX 414-743-5817. **Owner(s):** Brown County Publishing Co., P.O. Box 278, Denmark, WI 54208. TEL 414-863-2154; Ed. Thomas Brooker; Pub. Frank A. Wood; adv.; photos; pub. size: broadsheet; circ. 15,384(free & paid).
Formerly: Sturgeon Bay Door County Advocate.

SUN PRAIRIE
US

COURIER, THE. 1870. Thu. $.60 newsstand; $20/yr. in cy.; $28/yr. out of cy. 114 Columbus St., Sun Prairie, WI 53590-0645. TEL 608-478-2188; FAX 608-478-3618. **Owner(s):** Hometown News, L.P., P.O. Box 645, Sun Prairie, WI 53590-0645. TEL 608-837-2521; FAX 608-825-4460; Ed. Pam Chickoring. adv.; photos; pub. size: broadsheet; circ. 2,500(paid).

US

STAR, THE. 1877. Thu. $.60 newsstand; $22.50/yr. in cy.; $30.50/yr. out of cy. 114 Columbus St., Sun Prairie, WI 53590-0645. TEL 608-837-2521; FAX 608-825-4460. **Owner(s):** Hometown News, L.P., P.O. Box 645, Sun Prairie, WI 53590-0645. TEL 608-837-2521; FAX 698-825-4460; Ed. Chris Mertes. adv.; photos; pub. size: broadsheet; circ. 5,200(paid).

THORP
US ISSN 0885-2375

THORP COURIER. 1883. Thu. $.50 newsstand; $16/yr. in cy.; $21/yr. out of cy.; $24/yr. out of state. 403 N. Washington, Thorp, WI 54771-0487. TEL 715-669-5525; FAX 715-669-5596. **Owner(s):** Thorp Courier Printing Publications, Inc., P.O. Box 487, Thorp, WI 54771-0487. TEL 715-669-5525; Ed. Mark J. LaGasse; Pub. Mark J. LaGasse; adv.; pub. size: broadsheet; circ. 3,100(free & paid).

TOMAH
US

JOURNAL & MONITOR HERALD. 1867. s-w.: Mon. & Thu. $.75 newsstand; $28/yr. in cy.; $33/yr. in state; $42/yr. out of state. 1108 Superior Ave., Tomah, WI 54660-0190. TEL 608-372-4123; FAX 608-372-2791. **Owner(s):** John R. Kenny, 1108 Superior Ave., Tomah, WI 54660. TEL 608-372-4123; FAX 608-372-2791; Ed. John Froelich; Pub. ohn R. Kenny; adv. contact: Patrick Adler. pub. size: broadsheet; circ. 5,600(paid).

US

TOMAH JOURNAL. 1867. Thu. $.75 newsstand; $28/yr. in cy. mailed subscription incl. Tomah Monitor-Herald. 1108 Superior Ave., Tomah, WI 54660. TEL 608-372-4123; FAX 608-372-2791. **Owner(s):** Tomah Journal Printing Co., Inc., 1108 Superior Ave., Tomah, WI 54660. TEL 608-372-4729; Ed. John R. Kenny; Pub. John R. Kenny; adv. contact: P.J. Adler. pub. size: broadsheet; circ. 5,500(paid). **Wire Service(s):** AP.

US

TOMAH MONITOR-HERALD. 1881. Mon. $.75 newsstand; $28/yr. in cy. mailed subscription incl. Tomah Journal. 1108 Superior Ave., Tomah, WI 54660. TEL 608-372-4123; FAX 608-372-2791. **Owner(s):** Tomah Journal Printing Co., Inc., 1108 Superior Ave., Tomah, WI 54660. TEL 608-372-4729; Ed. John R. Kenny; Pub. John R. Kenny; adv. contact: P.J. Adler. pub. size: broadsheet; circ. 5,500(paid). **Wire Service(s):** AP.

TOMAHAWK
US

TOMAHAWK LEADER. 1886. Tue. $.75 newsstand; $22/yr. in area; $34/yr. in state; $41/yr. out of state. 315 W. Wisconsin Ave., Tomahawk, WI 54487. TEL 715-453-2151. **Owner(s):** Larry & Kathy Tobin, P.O. Box 345, Tomahawk, WI 54487. TEL 715-453-2151; Ed. Kathy Tobin; Pub. Kathy Tobin; adv. contact: Larry Tobin. adv.: $6.85/SAU. pub. size: broadsheet; circ. 8,050(free & paid).

TURTLE LAKE
US

TURTLE LAKE TIMES, THE. 1900. Thu. $.40 newsstand; $12/yr. in surrounding cys.; $15/yr. elsewhere. 419 S. Maple, Turtle Lake, WI 54889. TEL 715-986-4675. **Owner(s):** James P. Slack, P.O. Box 88, Turtle Lake, WI 54889. TEL 715-986-4675; Ed. Anne Slack; Pub. James P. Slack; adv. contact: Denise Slack. pub. size: standard; circ. 1,250(paid).

TWIN LAKES
US

WESTOSHA REPORT. 1956. Mon. $.75 newsstand; $16.50/yr. mailed in state; $38/yr. mailed out of state. 316 N. Lake Ave., Twin Lakes, WI 53181. TEL 414-877-2813; FAX 414-877-3619. **Owner(s):** Southern Lakes Media, Inc., P.O. Box 437, Burlington, WI 53105. TEL 414-763-3511; FAX 414-763-2238; Ed. Diane Jahnke; Pub. Robert Branen; adv. contact: Dave Wright. photos; pub. size: broadsheet; circ. 12,000(paid).

UNION GROVE
US ISSN 0749-6990

WESTINE REPORT. 1869. Wed. $.75 newsstand; $14.85/yr. in cy.; $28.05/yr. in state; $42.35/yr. out of state. 1113 Main St., Union Grove, WI 53182. TEL 414-878-1300; FAX 414-763-2238. **Owner(s):** Zimmermann & Sons, Inc., 140 Commerce St., Burlington, WI 53105. TEL 414-763-3511; Ed. Rosalyn Calek; Pub. Robert Branen; adv. contact: David Wright. pub. size: tabloid; circ. 2,200(paid).

VALDERS
US

VALDERS JOURNAL. 1940. Thu. $15/yr. in cy.; $22/yr. out of cy. 204 N. Liberty St., Valders, WI 54245-0400. TEL 414-775-4431. **Owner(s):** Marion F. Brockman, 332 N. Jackson St., Valders, WI 54245-0400. TEL 414-775-4316; Brian Thomsen, 204B N. Liberty St., Valders, WI 54245-0400. TEL 414-775-9268; Ed. Brian Thomsen; Pub. Marion F. Brockman; adv. contact: Brian Thomsen. adv.: $5.08/SAU. pub. size: tabloid; circ. 2,225(paid). **Wire Service(s):** AP.

VERONA
US

FITCHBURG STAR. 1974. Thu. $.50 newsstand; $24/yr. 120 W. Verona Ave., Verona, WI 53593. TEL 608-273-3576; FAX 608-845-9500. **Owner(s):** Henry W. Schroeder, 2752 Cross Country Cir., Verona, WI 53593. TEL 608-845-9559; Pub. Henry W. Schroeder; adv. contact: Deb Harville. pub. size: tabloid; circ. 500(paid).

US

VERONA PRESS. 1965. Thu. $.75 newsstand; $28/yr. in cy.; $30/yr. out of cy.; $38/yr. out of state. 120 W. Verona Ave., Verona, WI 53593-0006. TEL 608-845-9559; FAX 608-845-9550. **Owner(s):** Henry W. Schroeder, 120 W. Verona Ave., Verona, WI 53593-0006. TEL 608-845-9559; FAX 608-845-9550; Pub. Henry W. Schroeder; adv. contact: Terry Leonard. pub. size: tabloid; circ. 6,274(free & paid).

VIROQUA
US

VERNON COUNTY BROADCASTER. 1856. Thu. $.75 newsstand; $25/yr. local; $30/yr. out of cy.; $35/yr. out of state. 122 W. Jefferson St., Viroqua, WI 54665. TEL 608-637-3137; FAX 608-637-8557. **Owner(s):** Peter L. Hollister, P.O. Box 472, Viroqua, WI 54665. TEL 608-637-3137; Mary M. Hollister, P.O. Box 472, Viroqua, WI 54665. TEL 608-637-3137; Ed. Mary Hollister; Pub. Peter Hollister; adv. contact: Peter Hollister. adv.: $6.10/SAU. pub. size: broadsheet; circ. 6,180(paid).

WALWORTH
US

WALWORTH TIMES, THE. 1904. Wed. $.75 newsstand; $20/yr. in cy. 325 Kenosha St., Walworth, WI 53184-0129. TEL 414-275-2166; FAX 414-275-5259. **Owner(s):** Robert Branen, P.O. Box 129, Walworth, WI 53184. TEL 414-275-2166; FAX 414-275-5219; Ed. Kent Johnson. adv.; photos; pub. size: broadsheet; circ. 4,000(paid).

WEEKLY NEWSPAPERS

WASHBURN
US   ISSN 1041-9942

COUNTY JOURNAL, THE. 1984. Wed. $.50 newsstand; $23/yr. in area; $28/yr. out of area. P.O. Box 637, Washburn, WI 54891-0637. TEL 715-373-5500; FAX 715-373-5546. **Owner(s):** Country Journal, Inc., P.O. Box 637, Washburn, WI 54891. TEL 715-373-5500; FAX 715-373-5546; Ed. Darrell Pendergrass. adv.; photos; pub. size: broadsheet; circ. 4,547(free & paid).

    Formerly: Bayfield County Journal.

WATERFORD
US

WATERFORD POST. 1877. Sun. $1 newsstand; $21.50/yr. 224A N. Milwaukee St., Waterford, WI 53185. TEL 414-534-4668; FAX 414-534-3616. **Owner(s):** Southern Lakes Media, inc., 140 Commerce St., Burlington, WI 53105; FAX 414-534-3616; Ed. Pete Wicklund; Pub. Robert Branen; adv. contact: David Wright. pub. size: tabloid; circ. 1,500(paid).

WAUNAKEE
US

WAUNAKEE TRIBUNE. 1920. Thu. $.60 newsstand; $27.50/ in state; $34/yr. out of state. 105 South St., Waunakee, WI 53597. TEL 608-849-5227; FAX 608-849-4225. **Owner(s):** Arthur M. Drake, 105 South St., Waunakee, WI 53597. TEL 608-849-5227; Ed. Arthur M. Drake; Pub. Arthur M. Drake; adv. contact: Arthur M. Drake. pub. size: broadsheet; circ. 3,500(paid).

WAUPACA
US

PICTURE POST. Fri. free. 717 Tenth St., Waupaca, WI 54981. TEL 715-258-5546; FAX 715-258-8162. **Owner(s):** Waupaca Publishing Co., P.O. Box 152, Waupaca, WI 54981. TEL 715-258-5546; Ed. Scott Turner. adv.; pub. size: broadsheet.

US

WISCONSIN STATE FARMER. 1956. Fri. $.50 newsstand; $18/yr. mailed. 717 Tenth St., Waupaca, WI 54981. TEL 715-258-5546; FAX 715-258-8162. **Owner(s):** Waupaca Publishing Co., P.O. Box 152, Waupaca, WI 54981. TEL 715-258-5546; FAX 715-258-8162; Ed. Carla Gunst; Pub. Scott B. Turner; adv. contact: Tom Barton. adv.: $13/SAU. pub. size: broadsheet; circ. 30,100(free & paid). **Wire Service(s):** AP.

WAUPUN
US

▼**NEIGHBORS.** 1996. Sat. $1 newsstand; $31.20/yr. 520 E. Main St., Waupun, WI 53963. TEL 414-324-5555; FAX 414-324-8582. **Owner(s):** Citizen Publishing Co., 805 Park Ave., Beaver Dam, WI 53956. TEL 414-887-0321; Ed. Kevin Passon. adv.; pub. size: tabloid; circ. 8,500(free & paid).

    Formerly: Waupun Leader News.

WAUTOMA
US

WAUSHARA ARGUS. 1859. Wed. $.70 newsstand; $23/yr. mailed local. Hwy. 21 & 73 E., Wautoma, WI 54982. TEL 414-787-3334; FAX 414-787-2883. **Owner(s):** Delphos Newspapers, Delphos, OH 45833. TEL 419-695-0015; Ed. Mary Kunasch; Pub. Mary Kunasch; adv.; photos; pub. size: broadsheet; circ. 6,800(paid).

    Formerly: Wautoma Waushara Argus.

WESTBY
US

TIMES, THE. 1895. Wed. $22/yr. local; $26/yr. in state; $32/yr. out of state. 005 E. First St., Westby, WI 54667. TEL 608-634-4317; FAX 608-637-8557. **Owner(s):** Peter L. Hollister, 105 E. First St., Westby, WI 54667. TEL 608-634-4317; Mary Bormann Hollister, 105 E. First St., Westby, WI 54667. TEL 608-634-4317; Pub. Peter Hollister; adv. contact: Peter Hollister. pub. size: broadsheet; circ. 2,500(paid).

WEST SALEM
US

LA CROSSE COUNTY COUNTRYMAN. 1879. Thu. $.75 newsstand; $25/yr. in cy.; $27/yr. out of cy.; $40/yr. out of state. 153 S. Leonard St., West Salem, WI 54669. TEL 608-786-1950; FAX 608-786-1670. **Owner(s):** South Central Wisconsin Newspapers, Inc., P.O. Box 470, Portage, WI 53901. TEL 608-742-2111; Ed. Ron Marose; Pub. Dave Gentry; adv. contact: Ben Baker. photos; pub. size: tabloid; circ. 2,250(paid).

WHITEHALL
US

WHITEHALL TIMES. 1861. Thu. $.75 newsstand; $22/yr. in cy.; $29/yr. out of state. 36435 Main St., Whitehall, WI 54773-0095. FAX 715-538-4540. **Owner(s):** Charles Gauger, P.O. Box 95, Whitehall, WI 54773. TEL 715-538-4765; Ed. Scott Thomson; Pub. Robert Gauger; adv. contact: Charles Gauger. pub. size: standard; circ. 2,450(paid).

WINNECONNE
US

WINNECONNE NEWS. 1930. Wed. $15/yr. in cy.; $20/yr. out of state. 908 E. Main St., Winneconne, WI 54986-0370. TEL 414-582-4541; FAX 414-582-4417. **Owner(s):** John Rogers, 908 E. Main St., Winneconne, WI 54986-0370. TEL 414-582-4541; Ed. Margaret Rogers; Pub. John Rogers; pub. size: tabloid; circ. 1,750(paid).

WINTER
US

SAWYER COUNTY GAZETTE. 1908. Wed. $.35 newsstand; $15/yr. in cy.; $17.50/yr. out of cy. P.O. Box 99, Winter, WI 54896-0099. TEL 715-266-2511; FAX 715-266-2511. **Owner(s):** Meredith Rickert, P.O. Box 99, Winter, WI 54896-0099. TEL 715-266-2511; Pub. Meredith Rickert; adv. contact: Meredith Rickert. photos; pub. size: standard; circ. 2,250(free & paid).

WISCONSIN DELLS
US

WISCONSIN DELLS EVENTS. 1905. s-w. Wed. & Sat. $.75 newsstand; $37/yr. in cy.; $39/yr. out of cy.; $50/yr. out of state. 716 Elm St., Wisconsin Dells, WI 53965. TEL 608-254-8327; FAX 608-254-8328. **Owner(s):** South Central Wisconsin Newspapers, Inc., P.O. Box 470, Portage, WI 53901. TEL 608-742-2111; Ed. Kay J. James; Pub. David Gentry; adv. contact: Jay Anderle. photos; pub. size: broadsheet; circ. 3,000(paid).

WITHEE
US   ISSN 1047-8361

O-W ENTERPRISE. 1910. Wed. $.75 newsstand; $25/yr. in cy.; $30/yr. in state; $35/yr. elsewhere. 1006 Division St., Withee, WI 54498. TEL 715-229-2103; FAX 715-229-2104. **Owner(s):** Larry Shimono, 1006 Division St., Withee, WI 54498; Ed. Larry Shimono; Pub. Larry Shimono; adv.; pub. size: tabloid; circ. 1,100(paid).

    Formerly: Owen Enterprise.

WITTENBERG
US

WITTENBERG ENTERPRISE NEWS. 1893. w. $.35 newsstand; $16.25/yr. in state; $17.75/yr. out of state. 110 W. Vinal St., Wittenberg, WI 54499-0190. TEL 715-253-2737; FAX 715-253-2700. **Owner(s):** Gordon C. & Sally Boldig, P.O. Box 190, Wittenberg, WI 54499. TEL 715-253-2737; Steve & Darlene Block, P.O. Box 190, Wittenberg, WI 54499. TEL 715-253-2737; Pub. Gordon C. Boldig; adv. contact: Darlene Block. photos; pub. size: standard; circ. 2,000(paid).

WYOMING

BUFFALO
US

BUFFALO BULLETIN. 1891. Thu. $.50 newsstand; $18/yr. in state; $26/yr. out of state. 58 N. Lobban, Buffalo, WY 82834. TEL 307-684-2223. **Owner(s):** Buffalo Bulletin, P.O. Box 730, Buffalo, WY 82834. TEL 307-684-2223; Ed. Robert Waggener; Pub. Robert H. Hicks; adv. contact: Robert H. Hicks. photos; bk.rev.; pub. size: standard; circ. 4,150(paid).

CHEYENNE
US

SENTINEL. Fri. free newsstand; $48/yr. 1810 Westland Rd., Cheyenne, WY 82001. TEL 307-632-5666; FAX 307-632-1554. **Owner(s):** News Media Corp., P.O. Box 46, Rochelle, IL 61068. TEL 307-532-7097; Pub. Jim Wood; adv.; pub. size: tabloid; circ. 5,200(free & paid).

CODY

US ISSN 0747-2498
CODY ENTERPRISE. 1899. s-w.: Mon. & Wed. $.50 newsstand; $26/yr. 1549 Sheridan, Cody, WY 82414. TEL 307-587-2231; FAX 307-587-5208. **Owner(s):** Sage Publishing Co., Inc., P.O. Box 1090, Cody, WY 82414. TEL 307-587-2231; Ed. Bruce McCormack; Pub. Bruce McCormack; adv. contact: John Malmberg. pub. size: broadsheet; circ. 5,999(controlled & paid).

EVANSTON

US
UINTA COUNTY HERALD. 1938. s-w.: Tue. & Fri. $.50 newsstand; $46.75/yr. mailed in state; $49.75/yr. out of state. 1565 S. Hwy. 150, Ste. D, Evanston, WY 82930-0210. TEL 307-789-6560; FAX 307-789-2700. **Owner(s):** Wyoming Newspapers, Inc., 1565 S. Hwy. 150, Ste. D, Evanston, WY 82930. TEL 307-789-6560; FAX 307-789-6560; Ed. Shawn Hubbell; Pub. Mike Jensen; adv.: $7.78/SAU. photos; pub. size: standard; circ. 7,700(free & paid). **Wire Service(s):** AP.
Formerly: Evanston Uinta County Herald.

GUERNSEY

US ISSN 1061-1789
GUERNSEY GAZETTE/LINGLE GUIDE. 1902. Tue. $.50 newsstand; $20.25/yr. in cy.; $24.55/yr. out of cy. 40 S. Wyoming, Guernsey, WY 82214. TEL 307-836-2021; FAX 307-837-2255. **Owner(s):** Wyoming Newspapers, Inc., 2025 Main St., Torrington, WY 82240. TEL 307-532-2184; FAX 307-532-2283; Ed. Sandra Hansen; Pub. Bill Hanson; adv.; photos; pub. size: tabloid; circ. 800(paid).

JACKSON

US
JACKSON HOLE GUIDE. 1952. Wed. $.75 newsstand; $26/yr. in cy.; $32/yr. out of cy. 185 N. Glenwood, Jackson, WY 83001. TEL 307-733-2430; FAX 307-733-7841. **Owner(s):** Grand Teton Printing & Publishing Co., 185 N. Glenwood, Jackson, WY 83001. TEL 307-733-2430; Ed. Curtis Hubbard; Pub. Curtis Hubbard; adv. contact: Monty Nethercott. photos; bk.rev.; pub. size: tabloid; circ. 8,000(paid). **Wire Service(s):** AP.

US
JACKSON HOLE NEWS. 1970. Wed. $.50 newsstand; $26/yr. in cy. mailed; $33/yr. out of cy. 1225 Maple Way, Jackson, WY 83001. TEL 307-733-2047; FAX 307-733-2138. **Owner(s):** Jackson Hole News, Inc., P.O. Box 7445, Jackson, WY 83001. TEL 307-733-2047; FAX 307-733-2138; Ed. Angus M. Thuemer, Jr.; Pub. Michael Sellett; adv. contact: Michael Sellett. pub. size: tabloid; circ. 9,000(paid). **Wire Service(s):** AP.

KEMMERER

US
KEMMERER GAZETTE. 1901. Thu. $.35 newsstand; $22.50/yr. 708 J.C. Penny Dr., Kemmerer, WY 83101-0030. TEL 307-877-3347; FAX 307-877-3736. **Owner(s):** Mark Steele, P.O. Box 815, Soda Springs, ID 83276. TEL 208-547-3260; Ed. Tracy Thompson; Pub. Mark Steele; adv. contact: Kathleen Rosa. photos; pub. size: standard; circ. morning 2,000(free & paid).

LANDER

US
LANDER WYOMING STATE JOURNAL. 1886. s-w.: Mon. & Wed. $.50 newsstand; $34.95/yr. in cy. mailed; $42.95/yr. out of cy. 453 Main St., Lander, WY 82520. TEL 307-332-2323; FAX 307-332-9332. **Owner(s):** WCS Corp., P.O. Box 900, Lander, WY 82520. TEL 307-332-2323; FAX 307-332-9332; Ed. William Sniffin; Pub. William Sniffin; adv.; photos; pub. size: broadsheet; circ. 4,750(paid).

US
WIND RIVER NEWS. 1978. Thu. $.50 newsstand; $18.75/yr. in cy.; $21.75/yr. out of cy. 453 Main St., Lander, WY 82520. TEL 307-332-2323; FAX 307-332-9332. **Owner(s):** William Sniffin, P.O. Box 900, Lander, WY 82520. TEL 307-332-2323; Ed. Todd Simchuk; Pub. William Sniffin; pub. size: broadsheet; circ. 3,000(paid).
Formerly: Lander-Wind River News.

US
WYOMING STATE JOURNAL. 1978. s-w.: Mon. & Wed. $34.95/yr. in cy.; $42.95/yr. out of cy. 453 Main St., Lander, WY 82520. TEL 307-332-2323; FAX 307-332-9332. **Owner(s):** W.C.S. Corporation, P.O. Box 900, Lander, WY 82520. TEL 307-332-2323; Ed. Todd Simchuk. circ. morning 5,000(paid); evening 4,400(paid).

LOVELL

US
LOVELL CHRONICLE, THE. 1906. Thu. $.50 newsstand; $14/yr. in cy.; $22/yr. in state; $25/yr. out of state. 234 E. Main St., Lovell, WY 82431. TEL 307-548-2217. **Owner(s):** David & Susan Peck, P.O. Box 787, Lovell, WY 82431. TEL 307-548-2217; Margaret Peck, 1002 W. Park Ave., Riverton, WY 82501; Pub. David H. Peck; adv. contact: David H. Peck. pub. size: broadsheet; circ. 2,184(free & paid).

LUSK

US
LUSK HERALD. 1886. Wed. $.50 newsstand; $33.25/yr. in cy.; $35.25/yr. out of cy. 227 S. Main St., Lusk, WY 82225. TEL 307-334-2867; FAX 307-334-2514. **Owner(s):** Wyoming Newspapers, Inc., P.O. Box 1058, Torrington, WY 82240. TEL 307-532-7097; Pub. Bill Hanson; pub. size: tabloid; circ. 1,300(paid).

LYMAN

US
BRIDGER VALLEY PIONEER. 1976. Fri. $.50 newsstand; $19.75/yr. in cy.; $21.50/yr. out of cy. 1718 Center St., Lyman, WY 82937. TEL 307-787-3229; FAX 307-787-6795. **Owner(s):** Wyoming Newspapers, Inc., P.O. Box 46, Rochelle, IL 61068. TEL 815-562-2061; Ed. Wade Williams; Pub. Debbie Smith; adv. contact: Debbie Smith. pub. size: broadsheet; circ. 4,100(controlled & paid).
Formerly: Uinta County Pioneer.

MOORCROFT

US
MOORCROFT LEADER. 1912. Thu. $.50 newsstand; $15.40/yr. in cy.; $16.50/yr. out of cy. 304 Riley, Moorcroft, WY 82721-0067. TEL 307-756-3371; FAX 307-756-9827. **Owner(s):** Margaret Larson, P.O. Box 221 Rd., Moorcroft, WY 82721-0221. TEL 307-756-9812; Theron & Mary Hepker, P.O. Box 315, Deadwood, SD. TEL 605-578-3419; Ed. Margaret Larson; Pub. Margaret Larson; adv. contact: Margaret Larson. adv.: $5.15/SAU. photos; bk.rev.; pub. size: tabloid; circ. 1,100.

NEWCASTLE

US
NEWS LETTER JOURNAL. 1889. Wed. $.75 newsstand; $22/yr. local; $26/yr. elsewhere. 14 W. Main St., Newcastle, WY 82701. TEL 307-746-2777; FAX 307-746-2660. **Owner(s):** Robb Hicks, P.O. Box 40, Newcastle, WY 82701. TEL 307-746-2777; FAX 307-746-2660; Pub. Tom Mullen; adv.: $6/SAU. photos; pub. size: standard; circ. 2,700(paid).

SARATOGA

US
SARATOGA SUN. 1888. Wed. $.50 newsstand; $20/yr. in cy.; $28/yr. out of state. 116 E. Bridge St., Saratoga, WY 82331. TEL 307-326-8311. **Owner(s):** Saratoga Sun, Inc., 116 E. Bridge St., Saratoga, WY 82331. TEL 307-326-8311; Ed. Toby F. Marlett; Pub. Gary Stevenson; adv.; pub. size: tabloid; circ. 1,900(paid).

TORRINGTON

US
TORRINGTON TELEGRAM. 1907. s-w.: Wed. & Fri. $.50 newsstand; $52.95/yr. in cy.; $59.85/yr. out of cy. 2025 Main St., Torrington, WY 82240. TEL 307-532-2184; FAX 307-532-2283. **Owner(s):** Wyoming Newspapers, Inc., P.O. Box 1058, Torrington, WY 82240. TEL 307-532-7097; Ed. Sandra Hanson; Pub. Bill Hanson; adv. contact: Bill Hanson. pub. size: broadsheet; circ. 3,400(paid). **Wire Service(s):** AP.

WHEATLAND

US
PLATTE COUNTY RECORD-TIMES. 1900. Wed. $.50 newsstand; $29.95/yr. in cy.; $36/yr. out of cy. 1007 Eighth St., Wheatland, WY 82201. TEL 307-322-2627; FAX 307-322-9612. **Owner(s):** Wyoming Newspapers, Inc., P.O. Box 1054, Torrington, WY 82240. TEL 307-532-7097; Ed. Susie Geringer; Pub. Jim Woods; adv. contact: Ken Barnes. photos; bk.rev.; pub. size: broadsheet; circ. 2,800(paid).

Title Index

A

Abbeville Herald (Abbeville, AL) **10517**
Abbeville Meridional (Abbeville, LA) **10453**
Abbotsford Tribune-Phonograph (Abbotsford, WI) **10764**
Aberdeen American News (Aberdeen, SD) **10499**
Aberdeen Examiner (Aberdeen, MS) **10648**
Aberdeen Times (Aberdeen, ID) **10568**
Abernathy Weekly Review (Abernathy, TX) **10735**
Abilene Reflector-Chronicle (Abilene, KS) **10449**
Abilene Reporter-News (Abilene, TX) **10502**
Abingdon Argus (Abingdon, IL) **10571**
Abingdon Virginian (Abingdon, VA) **10750**
Abington Journal (Clarks Summit, PA) **10716**
Ace News, The (Heath, OH) **10703**
Acorn, The (Agoura Hills, CA) **10530**
Action Advertiser (Fond Du Lac, WI) **10767**
Acworth Neighbor (Marietta, GA) **10566**
Ad-News (Greenfield, IN) **10594**
Ad-Visor (Beulah, MI) **10630**
Ad-Visor (Lansing, MI) **10635**
Ada/Cascade/Forest Hills Advance (Jenison, MI) **10634**
Ada Evening News (Ada, OK) **10488**
Adair County Free Press (Greenfield, IA) **10601**
Adair Progress, The (Columbia, KY) **10610**
Adair Russell Shopper, The (Columbia, KY) **10610**
† Adams County Leader (Council, ID)
Adams County Times (Adams, WI) **10764**
Ada Norman County Index (Ada, MN) **10639**
Addison County Independent (Middlebury, VT) **10750**
Addison Press (Elmhurst, IL) **10578**
† Adelanto Bulletin, The (Adelanto, CA)
Adel News-Tribune (Adel, GA) **10562**
Ad Express & Daily Iowegian (Centerville, IA) **10447**
Adirondack Daily Enterprise (Saranac Lake, NY) **10477**
Advance-Monticellonian (Monticello, AR) **10528**
Advance-Yeoman (Lacenter, KY) **10612**
Advance Leader (Monroeville, PA) **10720**
Advance News (Lakehurst, NJ) **10667**
Advance of Bucks County (Newtown, PA) **10721**
Advance, The (Ogdensburg, NY) **10684**
Advertiser-Gleam (Guntersville, AL) **10520**
Advertiser-Tribune (Tiffin, OH) **10487**
Advertiser, The (Van Buren, AR) **10529**
Advertiser, The (Worden, IL) **10591**
Advertiser, The (Ligonier, IN) **10595**
Advertiser, The (Louisa, KY) **10612**
Advertiser, The (Mount Sterling, KY) **10613**
Advertiser, The (Paris, KY) **10613**

ULRICH'S INTERNATIONAL PERIODICALS DIRECTORY 1998

Advertiser, The (Iron Mountain, MI) **10634**
Advertiser, The (Bemidji, MN) **10640**
Advertiser, The (Chillicothe, OH) **10700**
Advertiser, The (McMurray, PA) **10719**
Advisor/Source (Utica, MI) **10638**
Advisor, The (Mt. Pleasant, PA) **10721**
Advocate-Messenger (Danville, KY) **10452**
Advocate/South Advocate, The (Williamstown, MA) **10629**
Advocate Democrat (Madisonville, TN) **10733**
Advocate Penny Saver (Sweetwater, TN) **10735**
Advocate, The (Stamford, CT) **10430**
Advocate, The (Clifton, IL) **10576**
Advocate, The (Baton Rouge, LA) **10454**
Advocate, The (Newark, OH) **10486**
Aegis, The (Bel Air, MD) **10621**
Afton Star-Enterprise (Afton, IA) **10598**
AG Journal (La Junta, CO) **10549**
Aiken Standard (Aiken, SC) **10498**
Aitkin Independent Age (Aitkin, MN) **10639**
Ajo Copper News (Ajo, AZ) **10524**
Akron Beacon Journal (Akron, OH) **10482**
Akron News Reporter (Akron, CO) **10547**
† Alabama Journal (Montgomery, AL)
Alabama Messenger (Birmingham, AL) **10518**
Alamance News (Graham, NC) **10692**
Alameda Times Star (Oakland, CA) **10423**
Alamogordo Daily News (Alamogordo, NM) **10473**
Alaska Star (Eagle River, AK) **10523**
Albany Democrat-Herald (Albany, OR) **10491**
Albany Herald, The (Albany, GA) **10434**
Albany Journal (Albany, GA) **10562**
Albany Ledger, The (Albany, MO) **10651**
Albert Lea Tribune (Albert Lea, MN) **10462**
Albia Union-Republican (Albia, IA) **10599**
Albion Advertiser (Albion, NY) **10673**
Albion News (Albion, NE) **10659**
Albion News, The (Albion, PA) **10715**
Albion Recorder (Albion, MI) **10459**
Albuquerque Journal (Albuquerque, NM) **10473**
Albuquerque Street News (Albuquerque, NM) **10672**
Albuquerque Tribune, The (Albuquerque, NM) **10473**
Alexander City Outlook (Alexander City, AL) **10415**
Alexandria Daily Town Talk (Alexandria, LA) **10453**
Alexandria Gazette Packet (Alexandria, VA) **10750**
Alexandria Journal (Fairfax, VA) **10509**
Alexandria News Weekly (Alexandria, LA) **10615**

Alexandria Times-Tribune (Alexandria, IN) **10591**
Algoma Record Herald (Algoma, WI) **10764**
† Algonac Courier Journal (Marine City, MI)
Algona Upper Des Moines (Algona, IA) **10599**
Algonquin Countryside (Barrington, IL) **10572**
Alhambra Post Advocate (Los Angeles, CA) **10537**
Alice Echo-News (Alice, TX) **10502**
Aliso Viejo News (Lake Forest, CA) **10536**
Allegan County News (Allegan, MI) **10630**
Allegheny Times (Moon Township, PA) **10495**
Allen County Times (New Haven, IN) **10596**
Alliance Review (Alliance, OH) **10482**
Alliance Times-Herald (Alliance, NE) **10469**
Allied News (Grove City, PA) **10718**
Almanac, The (McMurray, PA) **10719**
Aloha Breeze (Hillsboro, OR) **10713**
† Alpena Journal (Wessington Springs, SD)
Alpena News (Alpena, MI) **10459**
Alpena Star (Alpena, MI) **10630**
Alpharetta Revue (Alpharetta, GA) **10562**
Alpine Avalanche (Alpine, TX) **10736**
Alsip Express (Midlothian, IL) **10585**
Altamont Enterprise, The (Altamont, NY) **10673**
Altamont News, The (Altamont, IL) **10571**
Altavista Journal (Altavista, VA) **10751**
Alternatives News Magazine (Myrtle Beach, SC) **10728**
Altoona Herald, The (Altoona, IA) **10599**
Altoona Mirror (Altoona, PA) **10492**
Altus Times (Altus, OK) **10488**
Alvarado Post (Alvarado, TX) **10736**
Alva Review-Courier (Alva, OK) **10488**
Alvin Advertiser (Alvin, TX) **10736**
Alvin Sun (Alvin, TX) **10736**
† Alvin Tiller (Lamont, CA)
Amador/Calavaras Ledger Dispatch (Jackson, CA) **10535**
Amarillo Daily News/Sunday News Globe (Amarillo, TX) **10502**
Amarillo Globe Times (Amarillo, TX) **10502**
Ambler Gazette (Fort Washington, PA) **10717**
Amboy News, The (Amboy, IL) **10571**
Amelia Bulletin Monitor, The (Amelia Court House, VA) **10751**
American Journal (Westbrook, ME) **10620**
Americus Times-Recorder (Americus, GA) **10434**
Amery Free Press (Amery, WI) **10764**
Amesbury News (Amesbury, MA) **10623**
Amherst Bee (Williamsville, NY) **10689**
Amherst New Era-Progress (Amherst, VA) **10751**
Amite Tangi Digest (Amite, LA) **10615**

Amityville Record (Amityville, NY) **10673**
Amory Advertiser, The (Amory, MS) **10648**
† Amsterdam Star, The (Albany, NY)
Anaconda Leader (Anaconda, MT) **10658**
Anacortes American (Anacortes, WA) **10757**
Anadarko Daily News (Anadarko, OK) **10488**
Anaheim Bulletin (Anaheim, CA) **10530**
Anaheim Hills News (Anaheim, CA) **10530**
Anamosa Journal-Eureka (Anamosa, IA) **10599**
Anchorage Daily News (Anchorage, AK) **10417**
† Anchor Bay Beacon (New Baltimore, MI)
Andalusia Star News (Andalusia, AL) **10415**
† Anderson Countian (Garnett, KS)
Anderson Independent-Mail (Anderson, SC) **10498**
Anderson News, The (Lawrenceburg, KY) **10612**
Andover Townsman (Andover, MA) **10623**
Andrews County News (Andrews, TX) **10736**
Angelina Free Press (Diboll, TX) **10739**
Angier Independent (Angier, NC) **10690**
Angleton Times (Angleton, TX) **10736**
Ankeny Press Citizen (Ankeny, IA) **10599**
Ann Arbor News (Ann Arbor, MI) **10459**
Anniston Star (Anniston, AL) **10415**
Anoka County Union (Coon Rapids, MN) **10641**
Anson Record, The (Wadesboro, NC) **10695**
Antelope Valley Press (Palmdale, CA) **10423**
Anthony Republican, The (Anthony, KS) **10605**
Antigo Area Shoppers Guide (Antigo, WI) **10764**
Antigo Daily Journal (Antigo, WI) **10513**
Antioch News-Reporter (Grayslake, IL) **10580**
Apache Junction Independent (Apache Junction, AZ) **10524**
Apex Herald, The (Apex, NC) **10690**
Appalachian News-Express (Pikeville, KY) **10613**
Appeal-Democrat (Marysville, CA) **10423**
Apple Valley/Rosemont Sun-Current (Burnsville, MN) **10640**
Apple Valley News (Apple Valley, CA) **10530**
† Applewood/Wheat Ridge Transcript (Golden, CO)
Appomattox Times-Virginian (Appomattox, VA) **10751**
Arab Tribune (Arab, AL) **10517**
Arapahoe Public Mirror (Arapahoe, NE) **10659**
Arbutus Times (Baltimore, MD) **10620**
Arcadia News-Leader (Arcadia, WI) **10764**
Arcadian, The (Arcadia, FL) **10555**
† Arcadia Tribune (Arcadia, CA)
Archbold Buckeye (Archbold, OH) **10698**
Arco Advertiser (Arco, ID) **10569**
Arcola Record Herald (Arcola, IL) **10571**

Arctic Sounder, The (Barrow, AK) **10522**
Area Shopper (Conneautville, PA) **10716**
Arenac County Independent (Standish, MI) **10638**
Argonaut, The (Los Angeles, CA) **10537**
Argus-Champion, The (Newport, NH) **10663**
Argus-Press, The (Owosso, MI) **10461**
Argus Leader (Sioux Falls, SD) **10500**
Argus Observer (Ontario, OR) **10492**
Argus, The (Fremont, CA) **10422**
Argyle Agenda (Argyle, WI) **10764**
Argyle Sun, The (Lake Dallas, TX) **10743**
Arizona City Independent (Arizona City, AZ) **10524**
Arizona Daily Star (Tucson, AZ) **10418**
Arizona Daily Sun (Flagstaff, AZ) **10418**
Arizona Republic (Phoenix, AZ) **10418**
Arizona Silver Belt (Globe, AZ) **10525**
Arkadelphia Daily Siftings Herald (Arkadelphia, AR) **10419**
Arkansas City Traveler (Arkansas City, KS) **10449**
Arkansas Democrat-Gazette (Little Rock, AR) **10420**
Ark, The (Bel Tiburon, CA) **10531**
Arlington Advocate (Arlington, MA) **10623**
Arlington Citizen (Blair, NE) **10660**
Arlington Courier, The (Arlington, VA) **10751**
Arlington Heights Journal & Topics (Des Plaines, IL) **10576**
Arlington Journal (Fairfax, VA) **10509**
▼Arlington Morning News (Arlington, TX) **10502**
Arlington Star Telegram (Arlington, TX) **10502**
Aroostook Republican & News (Caribou, ME) **10619**
▼Arrowhead Ranch Independent (Sun City, AZ) **10526**
Arrow, The (Glendale, AZ) **10525**
Artesia Daily Press (Artesia, NM) **10473**
Arthur Enterprise, The (Arthur, NE) **10660**
Arthur Graphic Clarion (Arthur, IL) **10571**
Arvada Jefferson Sentinel (Lakewood, CO) **10549**
Asbury Park Press (Neptune, NJ) **10472**
Asheboro Courier-Tribune (Asheboro, NC) **10478**
Asheville Citizen-Times (Asheville, NC) **10478**
Ashland Daily Tidings (Ashland, OR) **10491**
Ashland Times-Gazette (Ashland, OH) **10482**
Ashley County Shoppers Guide (Crossett, AR) **10527**
Ashley News Observer (Crossett, AR) **10527**
Ashtabula Star-Beacon (Ashtabula, OH) **10482**
Ashton Gazette (Ashton, IL) **10572**
Aspen Daily News (Aspen, CO) **10427**

Aspen Times, The (Aspen, CO) **10427**
Associated Newspaper (Stoughton, MA) **10628**
Astoria South Fulton Argus (Astoria, IL) **10572**
Atascadero News (Atascadero, CA) **10530**
Atchison County Mail, The (Rock Port, MO) **10656**
Atchison Daily Globe (Atchison, KS) **10449**
Athens Banner Herald (Athens, GA) **10434**
Athens Daily News (Athens, GA) **10434**
Athens Daily Post (Athens, TN) **10500**
Athens Daily Review (Athens, TX) **10502**
Athens Messenger, The (Athens, OH) **10482**
Athens News (Athens, OH) **10698**
Athens Observer, The (Athens, GA) **10562**
Athol Daily News (Athol, MA) **10457**
Atkins Chronicle, The (Atkins, AR) **10526**
Atkinson Graphic, The (Atkinson, NE) **10660**
Atlanta Bulletin (Atlanta, GA) **10562**
Atlanta Citizens Journal (Atlanta, TX) **10736**
Atlanta Daily World (Atlanta, GA) **10562**
Atlanta Journal-Constitution (Atlanta, GA) **10434**
Atlantic County Record (Hammonton, NJ) **10666**
Atlantic News-Telegraph (Atlantic, IA) **10446**
Atmore Advance (Atmore, AL) **10517**
Atoka County Times (Atoka, OK) **10709**
Attica Hub (Attica, OH) **10698**
Atwater Times (Winton, CA) **10546**
Atwood Herald (Atwood, IL) **10572**
Auburn Citizen (Auburn, IL) **10572**
Auburn Journal (Auburn, CA) **10421**
Auburn News (Auburn, MA) **10623**
Auburn Press Tribune (Auburn, NE) **10660**
Auctioner, The (Pekin, IN) **10597**
Augusta Area Times (Augusta, WI) **10764**
Augusta Chronicle, The (Augusta, GA) **10434**
Augusta Daily Gazette (Augusta, KS) **10449**
† Augusta Herald (Augusta, GA)
Aurora Advertiser (Aurora, MO) **10651**
Aurora Advocate (Stow, OH) **10707**
Aurora News-Register (Aurora, NE) **10660**
Aurora Sentinel (Aurora, CO) **10547**
† Ausable Forks Adirondack Record Post (Elizabethtown, NY)
Austell Neighbor (Marietta, GA) **10566**
Austin American-Statesman (Austin, TX) **10502**
Austin Chronicle (Austin, TX) **10736**
Austin Daily Herald (Austin, MN) **10462**
† Austintown Leader (Niles, OH)
Austin Weekly News (Oak Park, IL) **10587**
Avalon Bay News, The (Avalon, CA) **10530**
Avenal Progress (Avenal, CA) **10531**
Aventura News (South Miami, FL) **10561**
Avenue News (Baltimore, MD) **10620**

Avon Sentinel (Abingdon, IL) **10571**
Avoyelles Journal (Marksville, LA) **10617**
† Azalea City News & Review (Bayou Labatre, AL)
Azle News (Azle, TX) **10736**
Azusa Herald (West Covina, CA) **10546**

B

Back of the Yards Journal (Chicago, IL) **10574**
Bainbridge Post-Searchlight (Bainbridge, GA) **10563**
Bainbridge Review (Bainbridge Island, WA) **10757**
Baker City Herald (Baker City, OR) **10491**
Baker County Press, The (MacClenny, FL) **10558**
Baker Observer (Baker, LA) **10615**
Baker Record-Courier (Baker City, OR) **10712**
Bakersfield Californian (Bakersfield, CA) **10421**
Baldwin Bulletin (Baldwin, WI) **10764**
Baldwin Citizen (Mineola, NY) **10682**
Baldwin City Ledger (Lawrence, KS) **10607**
Baldwin Herald (Lawrence, NY) **10680**
Baldwinsville Messenger (Syracuse, NY) **10687**
Baldwin Times (Bay Minette, AL) **10517**
† Bal Harbor/Bay Harbour News (South Miami, FL)
Ballston Journal (Ballston Spa, NY) **10673**
Baltic Beacon (Dell Rapids, SD) **10729**
Baltimore Chronicle (Baltimore, MD) **10620**
Baltimore Messenger (Baltimore, MD) **10620**
Baltimore Sun (Baltimore, MD) **10456**
Bamberg Advertizer-Herald, The (Bamberg, SC) **10726**
Bangor Daily News (Bangor, ME) **10455**
Banner-Gazette (Pekin, IN) **10597**
Banner-Graphic (Greencastle, IN) **10443**
Banner-News (Magnolia, AR) **10420**
Banner Journal (Black River Falls, WI) **10764**
Banner Press Newspaper, The (Columbus, TX) **10738**
Banning Record Gazette (Banning, CA) **10421**
Baraboo News-Republic (Baraboo, WI) **10514**
Barberton Herald (Barberton, OH) **10698**
Barbour Democrat, The (Philippi, WV) **10762**
Barbourville Mountain Advocate (Barbourville, KY) **10609**
Bargain Express Newspaper (Milwaukee, WI) **10769**
Bar Harbor Times (Bar Harbor, ME) **10618**
Barnesboro Star, The (Barnesboro, PA) **10716**
Barnesville Enterprise (Barnesville, OH) **10698**
Barnstable Patriot, The (Hyannis, MA) **10625**

Barrington Courier Review (Barrington, IL) **10572**
Barrington Times (Warren, RI) **10726**
Barron News Shield (Barron, WI) **10764**
Barry County Advertiser (Cassville, MO) **10652**
Bartlesville Examiner-Enterprise (Bartlesville, OK) **10488**
Bartow Neighbor, The (Cartersville, GA) **10563**
Bastrop Daily Enterprise (Bastrop, LA) **10453**
Batavia Daily News (Batavia, NY) **10474**
Batesville Guard (Batesville, AR) **10419**
Bath County News-Outlook (Owingsville, KY) **10613**
Baton Rouge Shopper (Baton Rouge, LA) **10615**
Battle Creek Enquirer (Battle Creek, MI) **10459**
Battle Creek Shopper (Battle Creek, MI) **10630**
Baudette Region, The (Baudette, MN) **10640**
Baxley News-Banner (Baxley, GA) **10563**
Baxter Bulletin (Mountain Home, AR) **10420**
Baxter Springs Citizen (Baxter Springs, KS) **10605**
Bay Area Press (Oakland, CA) **10540**
Bay Beacon, The (Niceville, FL) **10559**
Bay Bulletin (Melbourne, FL) **10558**
Bay City Times (Bay City, MI) **10459**
Baylor County Banner (Seymour, TX) **10746**
Bay News (Brooklyn, NY) **10674**
Bayonne Community News (Bayonne, NJ) **10664**
Bay Ridge Courier (Brooklyn, NY) **10674**
Bayshore Sun (La Porte, TX) **10743**
Bayside Times, The (Bayside, NY) **10673**
Bay State Banner (Boston, MA) **10623**
Bay St. Louis Sea Coast Echo (Bay St. Louis, MS) **10649**
Bay Times (Stevensville, MD) **10622**
Baytown Sun (Baytown, TX) **10502**
Bay Viewer (New Berlin, WI) **10770**
Bay Voice (New Baltimore, MI) **10636**
Beach & Bay Press (San Diego, CA) **10542**
Beach Bulletin (Fort Myers Beach, FL) **10557**
Beachcomber, The (Surf City, NJ) **10670**
Beaches Leader (Jacksonville Beach, FL) **10557**
Beach Haven Times (Manahawkin, NJ) **10667**
Beach Reporter, The (Manhattan Beach, CA) **10539**
Beacon-Forum (Eldon, IA) **10600**
Beacon Free Press (Wappingers Falls, NY) **10688**
Beacon Hill News, The/South District Journal (Seattle, WA) **10759**
Beacon Light (Mahopac, NY) **10680**
Beacon News (Aurora, IL) **10438**
Beacon Newspaper (Babylon, NY) **10673**
Beacon Observer, The (Overton, NE) **10661**
Beacon, The (Concord, MA) **10624**
Beacon, The (Hopewell, NJ) **10667**
Beacon, The (Manahawkin, NJ) **10667**
Beacon, The (Port Clinton, OH) **10707**
Beardstown Illinoian-Star (Beardstown, IL) **10572**
Beatrice Daily Sun (Beatrice, NE) **10469**
Beaufort Gazette (Beaufort, SC) **10498**
Beaufort Shopper (Beaufort, SC) **10726**
Beaumont Enterprise (Beaumont, TX) **10502**
Beauregard Daily News (De Ridder, LA) **10454**
Beaver County Times (Beaver, PA) **10492**
Beavercreek News-Current (Dayton, OH) **10484**
Beaver Dam Daily Citizen (Beaver Dam, WI) **10514**
Beaver Dam Ohio County Messenger (Beaver Dam, KY) **10609**
Beaverton Valley Times (Tigard, OR) **10715**
Becker County Record (Detroit Lakes, MN) **10641**
Bedford Bulletin (Bedford, VA) **10751**
Bedford Gazette/Gazette Sunday (Bedford, PA) **10492**
Bedford Minuteman (Concord, MA) **10624**
Bedford Sun Banner (Beachwood, OH) **10698**
Bedford Time Register (Bedford, OH) **10699**
Beebe News (Beebe, AR) **10526**
Beecher City Journal (Beecher City, IL) **10573**
Bee, The (Portland, OR) **10714**
Bee, The (Phillips, WI) **10772**
Beeville Bee-Picayune (Beeville, TX) **10736**
Belchertown Sentinel (Belchertown, MA) **10623**
Belevedere Citizen (Los Angeles, CA) **10537**
Belle Banner (Belle, MO) **10651**
Bellefontaine Examiner (Bellefontaine, OH) **10482**
Belle Fourche Post (Belle Fourche, SD) **10729**
Belle Plaine News, The (Belle Plaine, KS) **10605**
Belleview Voice of South Marion (Belleview, FL) **10555**
Belleville Enterprise (Wayne, MI) **10639**
Belleville Journal (Belleville, IL) **10573**
Belleville News-Democrat (Belleville, IL) **10438**
Belleville Post (Bloomfield, NJ) **10664**
Belleville Recorder (Belleville, WI) **10764**
Belleville Telescope (Belleville, KS) **10605**
Belleville Times News (Nutley, NJ) **10668**
Bellevue Gazette (Bellevue, OH) **10483**
Bellevue Leader (Bellevue, NE) **10660**
Bell Gardens Review (Los Angeles, CA) **10537**

Bellingham Herald (Bellingham, WA) **10510**
Bell Maywood Cudahy Industrial Post (Los Angeles, CA) **10537**
Bellmore-Merrick Observer (Bellmore, NY) **10673**
Bellmore Life (Bellmore, NY) **10673**
Bellows Falls Town Crier (Bellows Falls, VT) **10749**
Bellville Times (Bellville, TX) **10736**
Belmont Banner (Belmont, NC) **10690**
Belmont Citizen-Herald (Arlington, MA) **10623**
Beloit Daily Call (Beloit, KS) **10449**
Beloit Daily News (Beloit, WI) **10514**
Belvidere Daily Republican (Belvidere, IL) **10438**
Benbrook News (Fort Worth, TX) **10740**
Benicia Herald (Benicia, CA) **10421**
Bennetts Valley News (Weedville, PA) **10724**
Benning Leader, The (Columbus, GA) **10564**
Bennington Banner (Bennington, VT) **10508**
Bensenville Press (Elmhurst, IL) **10578**
Benson County Farmers Press (Minnewaukan, ND) **10697**
Benton Bulletin (Philomath, OR) **10714**
Benton County Daily Record (Bentonville, AR) **10419**
Benton Courier (Benton, AR) **10419**
Benton Review, The (Fowler, IN) **10594**
Bergen News, The (Palisades Park, NJ) **10669**
Bering Strait Record (None, AK) **10523**
Berkeley Independent (Moncks Corner, SC) **10728**
† Berkshire Courier (Great Barrington, MA)
Berkshire Eagle (Pittsfield, MA) **10458**
Berkshire Penny Saver (Lee, MA) **10625**
Berkshire Record (Great Barrington, MA) **10625**
Berlin Buyers' Guide (Berlin, WI) **10764**
Berlin Daily Sun (Berlin, NH) **10471**
Berlin Journal (Berlin, WI) **10764**
Berlin Reporter, The (Berlin, NH) **10471**
Bernardsville News (Bernardsville, NJ) **10664**
Berne Tri-Weekly News (Berne, IN) **10592**
Berrien County Record (Buchanan, MI) **10631**
Berrien Press (Nashville, GA) **10567**
Berryessa Sun (Milpitas, CA) **10539**
Bertie Ledger-Advance (Windsor, NC) **10696**
Berwyn/Cicero Life (Berwyn, IL) **10573**
Bessemer City Record (Kings Mountain, NC) **10692**
Bethany Republican-Clipper (Bethany, MO) **10652**
▼Bethel Beacon (Bethel, CT) **10551**
Bethel Journal, The (Loveland, OH) **10704**
Bethesda/Chevy Chase Almanac (Potomac, MD) **10622**

Bettendorf News (Bettendorf, IA) **10599**
Beulah Beacon (Beulah, ND) **10696**
Beverly Hills Courier (Beverly Hills, CA) **10531**
Beverly Hills Independent (Santa Monica, CA) **10544**
Beverly News (Midlothian, IL) **10585**
Beverly Review (Chicago, IL) **10574**
Bexley News (Columbus, OH) **10701**
Biddeford-Saco-OOB Courier (Biddeford, ME) **10618**
Bienville Democrat & Ringgold Record (Arcadia, LA) **10615**
Big Bear Life (Big Bear Lake, CA) **10531**
Bigfork Eagle (Bigfork, MT) **10659**
Big Rapids Pioneer (Big Rapids, MI) **10459**
Big Sandy News, The (Louisa, KY) **10612**
Big Spring Herald (Big Spring, TX) **10502**
Big Walnut/Sunbury (Columbus, OH) **10701**
Billboard, The (Berlin, WI) **10764**
Billerica Minuteman (North Billerica, MA) **10627**
Billings Gazette (Billings, MT) **10468**
Biloxi-D'Iberville Press (D'Iberville, MS) **10649**
Bird City Times (Bird City, KS) **10605**
Bird Island Union (Bird Island, MN) **10640**
Birmingham Eccentric, The (Birmingham, MI) **10630**
† Birmingham Free Press (Birmingham, AL)
Birmingham News (Birmingham, AL) **10415**
Birmingham Post-Herald (Birmingham, AL) **10415**
Birmingham World (Birmingham, AL) **10518**
Bisbee Daily Review (Bisbee, AZ) **10417**
▼Bisbee News, The (Bisbee, AZ) **10524**
Bisbee Observer, The (Bisbee, AZ) **10524**
Bismarck Tribune (Bismarck, ND) **10481**
Bixby Bulletin (Tulsa, OK) **10711**
† Biz (Oxford, PA)
Blackfoot Morning News (Blackfoot, ID) **10437**
Black Forest News (Colorado Springs, CO) **10547**
Black Hills Pioneer (Spearfish, SD) **10500**
Black Hills Press (Sturgis, SD) **10730**
Black Mountain News (Black Mountain, NC) **10691**
Blacksburg Sentinel (Christiansburg, VA) **10752**
Blackstone Courier-Record (Blackstone, VA) **10751**
Blackstone Valley Tribune (Whitinsville, MA) **10629**
Blackwell Journal-Tribune (Blackwell, OK) **10488**
Blade Atlas (Blanchardville, WI) **10765**
Bladen Journal (Elizabethtown, NC) **10479**
Blade, The (Swainsboro, GA) **10568**

Blaine-Spring Lake Park Life (Coon Rapids, MN) **10641**
Blaine Banner (Blaine, MN) **10640**
Blair Enterprise (Blair, NE) **10660**
Blair Pilot-Tribune (Blair, NE) **10660**
Blair Press (Blair, WI) **10765**
Blairstown Press (Blairstown, NJ) **10664**
Blanco County News (Blanco, TX) **10737**
Bland Courier (Belle, MO) **10651**
Blandinsville Star Gazette (Abingdon, IL) **10571**
Bland Messenger (Wytheville, VA) **10756**
Blazer News (Jackson, MI) **10634**
Blissfield Advance (Blissfield, MI) **10630**
Bloomer Advance (Bloomer, WI) **10765**
Bloomfield Eccentric, The (Birmingham, MI) **10630**
Bloomfield Journal (Bristol, CT) **10551**
Bloomfield Life (Nutley, NJ) **10668**
Bloomingdale Press (Bloomingdale, IL) **10573**
Bloomington Sun-Current (Bloomington, MN) **10640**
Bloomville Gazette (Attica, OH) **10698**
Blount Countian, The (Oneonta, AL) **10521**
Blowing Rocket, The (Blowing Rock, NC) **10691**
Bluefield Daily Telegraph (Bluefield, WV) **10512**
Blue Mound Leader (Blue Mound, IL) **10573**
Blue Ridge Leader, The (Purcellville, VA) **10754**
Blue Springs Examiner (Blue Springs, MO) **10465**
Blue Water Voice (New Baltimore, MI) **10636**
Bluffton News-Banner (Bluffton, IN) **10442**
Bluffton News, The (Bluffton, OH) **10699**
Blythe Advertiser (Palm Desert, CA) **10540**
Boardman News (Boardman, OH) **10699**
Boca Monday (Deerfield Beach, FL) **10556**
Boca Raton News (Boca Raton, FL) **10431**
Bogalusa Daily News & Sunday News (Bogalusa, LA) **10454**
Boise City News, The (Boise City, OK) **10709**
Bolingbrook Metropolitan (Lemont, IL) **10583**
Bolingbrook Sun (Bolingbrook, IL) **10573**
Bolivar Bulletin-Times (Bolivar, TN) **10731**
Bolivar Herald-Free Press (Bolivar, MO) **10652**
Bollinger County Banner-Press (Marble Hill, MO) **10655**
Bolton Common (Bolton, MA) **10623**
Bonham Daily Favorite (Bonham, TX) **10502**
Bonita Banner (Bonita Springs, FL) **10555**
Bonner County Daily Bee (Sandpoint, ID) **10437**
Bonners Ferry Herald (Bonners Ferry, ID) **10569**
Bonner Springs-Edwardsville Chieftain (Bonner Springs, KS) **10605**
Booker News, The (Booker, TX) **10737**
Boone County Journal (Ashland, MO) **10651**
Boone County Recorder (Florence, KY) **10610**
Boone News-Republican (Boone, IA) **10447**
Booneville Banner-Independent (Booneville, MS) **10649**
Boone Watauga Democrat (Boone, NC) **10691**
Boonville Daily News (Boonville, MO) **10465**
Boonville Herald & Adirondack Tourist (Boonville, NY) **10673**
Boonville Standard (Boonville, IN) **10592**
Booster, The (Columbus, OH) **10701**
Boothbay Register (Boothbay Harbor, ME) **10618**
Borden Star (Gail, TX) **10740**
Borger News-Herald (Borger, TX) **10502**
Boscobel Dial (Boscobel, WI) **10765**
Bosque County News (Meridian, TX) **10744**
Bossier Banner-Progress (Bossier City, LA) **10616**
Bossier Press-Tribune (Bossier City, LA) **10616**
Boston Globe (Boston, MA) **10457**
Boston Herald (Boston, MA) **10457**
Boston Phoenix (Boston, MA) **10623**
Boulder City News (Boulder City, NV) **10662**
Bound Brook Chronicle (Somerville, NJ) **10670**
Bourbon County Citizen (Paris, KY) **10613**
Bourne Courier (Yarmouthport, MA) **10630**
Boutique & Villager (Burlingame, CA) **10531**
Bowie Blade-News (Bowie, MD) **10621**
Bowie News (Bowie, TX) **10737**
Bowling Green Times (Bowling Green, MO) **10652**
Bowman Finder (Bowman, ND) **10696**
Box Elder News Journal (Brigham City, UT) **10748**
Boyertown Area Times (Boyertown, PA) **10716**
Boynton Beach Times (Deerfield Beach, FL) **10556**
Bozeman Daily Chronicle (Bozeman, MT) **10468**
Braceville Express (Wilmington, IL) **10590**
Brackett News The (Brackettville, TX) **10737**
Bradenton Herald, The (Bradenton, FL) **10431**
Bradford County Telegraph (Starke, FL) **10561**
Bradford Era, The (Bradford, PA) **10492**
Bradford Journal/Miner (Bradford, PA) **10716**
Brady Standard (Brady, TX) **10737**
Braidwood Index (Wilmington, IL) **10591**
Braidwood Journal, The (Braidwood, IL) **10573**
Brainerd Daily Dispatch (Brainerd, MN) **10462**
Braintree Forum (Marshfield, MA) **10625**
Brandon News, The (Brandon, FL) **10555**

Brandon Valley Challenger (Dell Rapids, SD) **10729**
Brandywine Chronicle (Oxford, PA) **10721**
Branford Review (Branford, CT) **10551**
Branson Daily News (Hollister, MO) **10466**
Brantley Enterprise (Nahunta, GA) **10567**
Brattleboro Reformer (Brattleboro, VT) **10508**
Brawley Advertiser (El Centro, CA) **10533**
Braxton Citizen's News (Sutton, WV) **10763**
Braxton Democrat-Central (Sutton, WV) **10763**
Brazil Times (Brazil, IN) **10442**
Brazosport Facts, The (Clute, TX) **10503**
Brea Progress (Anaheim, CA) **10530**
Breckinridge County Herald-News (Hardinsburg, KY) **10611**
Brecksville Gazette (Cleveland, OH) **10700**
Breese Journal (Breese, IL) **10573**
† Breeze Herald (Conneut Lake Park, PA)
Breeze, The (Rockledge, PA) **10723**
Bremer County Independent (Waverly, IA) **10605**
Brenham Banner-Press (Brenham, TX) **10503**
Brentwood Journal (Brentwood, TN) **10731**
Brentwood Westwood Press (Santa Monica, CA) **10544**
Brevard Reporter, The (Merritt Island, FL) **10559**
† Brewery Gulch Gazette (Bisbee, AZ)
Brewster Times (Mahopac, NY) **10681**
Brewton Standard, The (Brewton, AL) **10518**
Brick Township Town News (Brick, NJ) **10664**
Bridgeport Index (Bridgeport, TX) **10737**
Bridgeport Leader (Bridgeport, IL) **10573**
Bridgeport News (Chicago, IL) **10574**
Bridger Valley Pioneer (Lyman, WY) **10776**
Bridgeton Evening News (Bridgeton, NJ) **10471**
Bridgeview Independent (Midlothian, IL) **10585**
Bridgeville Area News (Monroeville, PA) **10720**
Bridgewater Independent (Middleboro, MA) **10626**
† Bridgewater Townsman (Bridgewater, MA)
Bridgton News (Bridgton, ME) **10618**
Brighton-Pittsford Post, The (Fishers, NY) **10677**
Brighton Argus (Brighton, MI) **10630**
Brighton Park-McKinley Park Life (Chicago, IL) **10574**
Brighton Standard Blade (Brighton, CO) **10547**
Brillion News (Brillion, WI) **10765**
Brinkley Argus (Brinkley, AR) **10527**
Bristol Bay Times, The (Dillingham, AK) **10523**
Bristol Herald-Courier, The (Bristol, VA) **10509**
Bristol Phoenix (Bristol, RI) **10725**
Bristol Pilot (Bristol, PA) **10716**
Bristol Press, The (Bristol, CT) **10429**

Bristow News (Bristow, OK) **10709**
Britt News-Tribune (Britt, IA) **10599**
Broad Top Bulletin (Saxton, PA) **10724**
Brockport/Holley Suburban News (Spencerport, NY) **10687**
Brockport Post, The (Brockport, NY) **10674**
Broken Arrow Ledger (Broken Arrow, OK) **10709**
† Broken Arrow Scout (Broken Arrow, OK)
Bronx News (Bronx, NY) **10674**
Bronx Press-Review (Bronx, NY) **10674**
Brooke County Review (Wellsburg, WV) **10763**
Brookfield Journal (Brookfield, CT) **10552**
Brookfield News (New Berlin, WI) **10770**
Brookhaven Daily Leader (Brookhaven, MS) **10464**
Brookhaven Review (Smithtown, NY) **10686**
Brookings Register (Brookings, SD) **10499**
Brooklyn Center Sun Post (Minneapolis, MN) **10643**
Brooklyn Daily Eagle & Daily Bulletin (Brooklyn, NY) **10474**
Brooklyn Graphic (Brooklyn, NY) **10674**
Brooklyn Heights Courier (Brooklyn, NY) **10674**
Brooklyn Heights Press (Brooklyn, NY) **10674**
Brooklyn Home Reporter & Sunset News (Brooklyn, NY) **10674**
Brooklyn Park Sun Post (Minneapolis, MN) **10643**
Brooklyn Record (Brooklyn, NY) **10674**
Brooklyn Spectator (Brooklyn, NY) **10674**
Brooklyn Sun Journal (Cleveland, OH) **10700**
† Brooklyn Times (Brooklyn, NY)
† Brooksville Sun Journal (Brooksville, FL)
† Brookville American (Brookville, PA)
Brookville American-Democrat (Brookville, IN) **10592**
Broome Pennysaver (Johnson City, NY) **10679**
Broomfield Enterprise (Broomfield, CO) **10547**
Broward News (Margate, FL) **10558**
Broward Times, The (Coral Springs, FL) **10556**
Brown County Democrat (Nashville, IN) **10596**
Brown County Press (Mt. Orab, OH) **10705**
Brown Deer Herald (New Berlin, WI) **10770**
Brownfield News (Brownfield, TX) **10737**
Brownsville Herald (Brownsville, TX) **10503**
Brownsville States-Graphic (Brownsville, TN) **10731**
Brownwood Bulletin (Brownwood, TX) **10503**
Bruce Calhoun County Journal (Bruce, MS) **10649**
Brunswick Beacon, The (Shallotte, NC) **10694**
Brunswick Citizen (Brunswick, MD) **10621**
Brunswick News, The (Brunswick, GA) **10434**
Brunswick Sun Times (Medina, OH) **10705**

Brunswick Times-Gazette
(Lawrenceville, VA) **10753**
Brush News-Tribune (Brush, CO) **10547**
Bryan College Station Eagle (Bryan, TX) **10503**
Bryan College Station Press (Bryan, TX) **10737**
Bryan County Star (Durant, OK) **10710**
Bryan County Times (Pembroke, GA) **10567**
Bryan Times (Bryan, OH) **10483**
Buckeye Review, The (Youngstown, OH) **10709**
Buckeye Valley News (Buckeye, AZ) **10524**
Bucks County Courier Times
(Levittown, PA) **10495**
Bucks County Tribune (Horsham, PA) **10718**
Bucyrus Telegraph-Forum
(Bucyrus, OH) **10483**
Budgeteer Press (Duluth, MN) **10641**
Buffalo Bulletin (Buffalo, WY) **10775**
Buffalo County Journal (Cochrane, WI) **10765**
Buffalo Grove Countryside (Arlington
Heights, IL) **10571**
Buffalo Grove Journal & Topics (Des
Plaines, IL) **10576**
Buffalo News, The (Buffalo, NY) **10474**
Buffalo Reflex (Buffalo, MO) **10652**
Buffalo Ridge Gazette, The
(Ruthton, MN) **10646**
Buffalo River Review (Linden, TN) **10733**
Buffalo Rocket (Buffalo, NY) **10675**
Bugle, The (Niles, IL) **10586**
Buhl Herald (Buhl, ID) **10569**
Bulletin, The (Crestview, FL) **10556**
Bulletin, The (Bedford, OH) **10699**
Bulletin, The (Bend, OR) **10491**
Bulletin, The (Santa Fe, TX) **10746**
Bulletin, The (Kenosha, WI) **10768**
Bunker Hill Gazette News (Bunker
Hill, IL) **10573**
Burbank-Stickney Independent
(Midlothian, IL) **10585**
Bureau County Republican
(Princeton, IL) **10588**
Burke County Observer
(Morganton, NC) **10693**
Burke Times, The (Reston, VA) **10754**
Burleson County Citizen Tribune
(Caldwell, TX) **10737**
Burleson Star (Burleson, TX) **10737**
Burlington County Times
(Willingboro, NJ) **10473**
Burlington Free Press (Burlington, VT) **10508**
Burlington Standard Press
(Burlington, WI) **10765**
Burlington Union (Woburn, MA) **10629**
Burnet Bulletin (Burnet, TX) **10737**
Burnett County Sentinel
(Grantsburg, WI) **10767**

Burns Times-Herald (Burns, OR) **10712**
Burnsville/Savage Sun-Current
(Burnsville, MN) **10640**
Burr Ridge Doings (Hinsdale, IL) **10582**
Burwell Tribune, The (Burwell, NE) **10660**
Business Examiner (Gig Harbor, WA) **10758**
Business Post, The (Alpharetta, GA) **10562**
Butler County & Green River Republican Banner,
The (Morgantown, KY) **10613**
Butler County News (Georgiana, AL) **10519**
Butler Eagle (Butler, PA) **10493**
Butner-Creedmoor News, The
(Creedmoor, NC) **10691**
Butte County Valley Irrigator
(Newell, SD) **10730**
Butte Valley Star (Merrill, OR) **10714**
† Buyer's Guide (Napa, CA)
Buyer's Guide Cent Saver
(Mauston, WI) **10769**
† Byron Center/Dorr Advance (Jenison, MI)

C

Cabell Record (Culloden, WV) **10761**
Cable Scene (Idaho Falls, ID) **10569**
Caddo Citizen (Vivian, LA) **10618**
Cadillac Evening News (Cadillac, MI) **10459**
Cadiz Record, The (Cadiz, KY) **10609**
Cadott Sentinel (Cadott, WI) **10765**
Cahokia Journal (Columbia, IL) **10576**
Cairo Citizen (Cairo, IL) **10574**
Cairo Messenger (Cairo, GA) **10563**
Calais Advertiser (Calais, ME) **10618**
Caledonia/Gaines Advance
(Jenison, MI) **10634**
Caledonian-Record, The (St.
Johnsbury, VT) **10508**
Calexico Advertiser (El Centro, CA) **10533**
Calhoun Chronicle (Grantsville, WV) **10761**
Calhoun News (Hardin, IL) **10581**
Calhoun Times (Calhoun, GA) **10563**
California Advocate, The (Fresno, CA) **10534**
California Courier (Glendale, CA) **10534**
California Democrat (California, MO) **10652**
Californian, The (Salinas, CA) **10425**
Californian, The (Temecula, CA) **10426**
Call-Leader (Elwood, IN) **10443**
Callahan County Star (Baird, TX) **10736**
Callaway Courier (Holts Summit, MO) **10654**
Call, The (Schuylkill Haven, PA) **10724**
Call, The (Woonsocket, RI) **10498**
Caloosa Belle (La Belle, FL) **10558**
Calumet Press, The (Highland, IN) **10594**
Calvert Independent (Prince
Fredrick, MD) **10622**
Camarillo Star (Camarillo, CA) **10421**

Camas/Washougal Post Record
(Camas, WA) **10757**
Cambridge Chronicle (Cambridge, IL) **10574**
Cambridge Chronicle (Somerville, MA) **10628**
Cambridge News (Cambridge, WI) **10765**
Camden Chronicle, The (Camden, TN) **10731**
Camden County Record (Camden, NJ) **10665**
Camden County Tribune (St. Marys, GA) **10567**
Camden News (Camden, AR) **10419**
Cameron Citizen Observer (Cameron, MO) **10652**
Cameron County Echo (Emporium, PA) **10717**
Cameron Herald (Cameron, TX) **10737**
Camilla Enterprise (Camilla, GA) **10563**
Camillus Advocate (Syracuse, NY) **10687**
Campbell County Recorder (Fort Thomas, KY) **10611**
Campbellsport News (Campbellsport, WI) **10765**
Canada News (Auburndale, FL) **10555**
Canadian County Chronicle (Yukon, OK) **10712**
Canandaigua Daily Messenger (Canandaigua, NY) **10474**
Canarsie Courier (Brooklyn, NY) **10674**
Canarsie Digest (Brooklyn, NY) **10674**
Canastota Bee-Journal (Canastota, NY) **10675**
Canby Herald (Canby, OR) **10712**
Canby News (Canby, MN) **10640**
Candor Chronicle (Trumansburg, NY) **10688**
Canistota Clipper (Canistota, SD) **10729**
Canova Herald (Canistota, SD) **10729**
Canton Eagle (Wayne, MI) **10639**
Canton Independent-Sentinel (Canton, PA) **10716**
Canton Journal (Canton, MA) **10624**
Canton Observer (Plymouth, MI) **10637**
Canyon Courier (Evergreen, CO) **10548**
Canyon News (Canyon, TX) **10737**
Cape Codder (Orleans, MA) **10627**
† Cape Cod News (Yarmouth Port, MA)
Cape Cod Times (Hyannis, MA) **10457**
Cape Coral Daily Breeze, The (Cape Coral, FL) **10431**
Cape May County Gazette Leader (Wildwood, NJ) **10671**
Cape May Herald Dispatch (Rio Grande, NJ) **10670**
Cape May Star & Wave (Cape May, NJ) **10665**
Capeway News (Middleboro, MA) **10626**
Capistrano Valley News (Lake Forest, CA) **10536**
Capital-Journal (Topeka, KS) **10452**
Capital City Weekly (Juneau, AK) **10523**
Capital Journal (Pierre, SD) **10499**
Capital, The (Annapolis, MD) **10456**
Capital Times, The (Madison, WI) **10514**
▼Capital Weekly (Augusta, ME) **10618**
Capitol Hill Beacon (Oklahoma City, OK) **10711**
Capitol Hill Times (Seattle, WA) **10759**
Carbondale News (Carbondale, PA) **10716**
Caribou County Sun (Soda Springs, ID) **10571**
Carlinville Democrat (Carlinville, IL) **10574**
Carlisle Mercury, The (Carlisle, KY) **10610**
Carlisle Sentinel (Carlisle, PA) **10493**
Carlsbad Current-Argus (Carlsbad, NM) **10473**
Carlsbad Sun (Carlsbad, CA) **10532**
Carlyle Union Banner (Carlyle, IL) **10574**
Carmel News Tribune (Fishers, IN) **10593**
Carmel Pine Cone (Carmel, CA) **10532**
Carmel Times (Mahopac, NY) **10681**
Carmichael Times (Carmichael, CA) **10532**
Carmi Times (Carmi, IL) **10438**
Carol City/Opa-Locka News (Miami, FL) **10559**
Carolina Times, The (Durham, NC) **10692**
Caroline Progress, The (Bowling Green, VA) **10751**
Carolinian, The (Raleigh, NC) **10694**
Carol Stream Press (Bloomingdale, IL) **10573**
† Carpinteria Herald (Goleta, CA)
Carroll County Comet (Flora, IN) **10594**
Carroll County Independent (Center Ossipee, NH) **10663**
Carroll County News-Leader (Huntingdon, TN) **10732**
Carroll County Review (Thomson, IL) **10590**
Carroll County Sun (Westminster, MD) **10456**
Carroll County Times (Westminster, MD) **10457**
Carroll Gardens/Cobble Hill Courier (Brooklyn, NY) **10674**
Carroll News, The (Hillsville, VA) **10753**
† Carrollton Chronicle (Carrollton, TX)
Carrollton Democrat (Carrollton, MO) **10652**
Carrollton Gazette Patriot (Carrollton, IL) **10574**
Carrollwood News (Tampa, FL) **10561**
Carson Bulletin (Compton, CA) **10532**
Carson Press (Elgin, ND) **10696**
Carson Wave (Los Angeles, CA) **10537**
Carteret County News-Times (Morehead City, NC) **10693**
Cartersville Daily Tribune News (Cartersville, GA) **10434**
Carthage Courier (Carthage, TN) **10731**
Carthage Press (Carthage, MO) **10466**
Carthage Republican Tribune (Carthage, NY) **10675**
Carthaginian, The (Carthage, MS) **10649**
Carver Reporter (Plymouth, MA) **10627**

Cary-Grove Countryside (Barrington, IL) **10572**
Cary News (Cary, NC) **10691**
Casa Grande Dispatch (Casa Grande, AZ) **10417**
Casey County News (Liberty, KY) **10612**
Casey County Shopper, The (Columbia, KY) **10610**
Cash-Book Journal (Jackson, MO) **10654**
Cashmere Valley Record (Cashmere, WA) **10757**
Cashton Record (Cashton, WI) **10765**
Casper Star Tribune (Casper, WY) **10516**
Cass City Chronicle (Cass City, MI) **10631**
Cass County Reporter (Casselton, ND) **10696**
Cassville Democrat (Cassville, MO) **10652**
Castleton Banner (Fishers, IN) **10593**
Caswell Messenger (Yanceyville, NC) **10696**
Catalina Islander, The (Avalon, CA) **10530**
† Cato Citizen (Red Creek, NY)
Catonsville Times (Baltimore, MD) **10620**
Catoosa County News (Ringgold, GA) **10567**
Catoosa Times Herald (Catoosa, OK) **10709**
Cavalier County Republican (Langdon, ND) **10697**
Cazenovia Republican (Cazenovia, NY) **10675**
Cecil Whig (Elkton, MD) **10456**
Cedar County Republican (Stockton, MO) **10658**
Cedar Creek Pilot (Gun Barrel City, TX) **10741**
Cedar Hill Today (DeSoto, TX) **10739**
Cedar Key Beacon (Cedar, FL) **10556**
Cedar Lake Journal (Lowell, IN) **10595**
Cedar Rapids Gazette (Cedar Rapids, IA) **10447**
Cedartown Standard (Cedartown, GA) **10564**
Cedar Valley Daily Times (Vinton, IA) **10449**
Center Post Dispatch (Monte Vista, CO) **10550**
Center Republican (Washburn, ND) **10697**
Centerville-Bellbrook Times (Kettering, OH) **10704**
Centerville Crusader (Centerville, IN) **10592**
Central City Republican Nonpareil (Central City, NE) **10660**
Central City Times-Argus (Central City, KY) **10610**
Central Coast Sun-Bulletin (Morro Bay, CA) **10539**
† Central Coast Times (Paso Robles, CA)
Centralia Fireside Guard (Centralia, MO) **10652**
Centralia Sentinel (Centralia, IL) **10438**
Central Kentucky News-Journal (Campbellsville, KY) **10609**
Central Maine Morning Sentinel (Waterville, ME) **10456**
Central Missouri News (Sedalia, MO) **10656**

Central Oregonian, The (Prineville, OR) **10714**
Central Post (Dayton, NJ) **10665**
Central Saint Croix News (Hammond, WI) **10767**
Central Shopper (Des Moines, IA) **10600**
Central Valley Times (Grants Pass, OR) **10713**
Central Virginian, The (Louisa, VA) **10754**
Central West End Journal (St. Louis, MO) **10657**
Centre Daily Times (State College, PA) **10496**
Centreville Press (Centreville, AL) **10518**
Centreville Times (Reston, VA) **10755**
Ceres Courier (Ceres, CA) **10532**
Chagrin Herald Sun (Beachwood, OH) **10698**
Chagrin Valley Times (Chagrin Falls, OH) **10700**
Challis Messenger (Challis, ID) **10569**
Chamblee-DeKalb Neighbor (Atlanta, GA) **10562**
Champaign News Gazette (Champaign, IL) **10438**
Chandler Arizonan Tribune (Chandler, AZ) **10418**
Chandler Independent (Chandler, AZ) **10524**
† Chandler Post (Boonville, IN)
Chanhassen Villager (Chanhassen, MN) **10641**
Chantilly Times (Reston, VA) **10755**
Chanute Tribune (Chanute, KS) **10449**
Chapel Hill Herald (Chapel Hill, NC) **10478**
Chapel Hill News (Chapel Hill, NC) **10691**
Chariton Herald-Patriot (Chariton, IA) **10599**
Chariton Leader (Chariton, IA) **10599**
Charles City Press (Charles City, IA) **10447**
Charleston Daily Mail (Charleston, WV) **10512**
Charleston Enterprise-Courier (Charleston, MO) **10652**
Charleston Gazette, The (Charleston, WV) **10512**
Charleston Post & Courier (Charleston, SC) **10498**
Charleston Times-Courier (Charleston, IL) **10438**
† Charlestown Citizen (Brookline, MA)
Charlevoix County Star (Gaylord, MI) **10632**
Charlevoix Courier (Charlevoix, MI) **10631**
Charlotte Gazette (Drakes Branch, VA) **10752**
Charlotte Observer (Charlotte, NC) **10478**
Charlotte Shopping Guide (Charlotte, MI) **10631**
Charlotte Sun Herald (Charlotte Harbor, FL) **10431**
Charlottesville-Albemarle Tribune (Charlottesville, VA) **10751**
Charlton County Herald (Folkston, GA) **10565**
Chase County Leader-News (Cottonwood Falls, KS) **10606**

Chaska Herald (Chaska, MN) **10641**
† Chateaugay Record (Chateaugay, NY)
Chatham Clarion (Auburn, IL) **10572**
Chatham Courier (Madison, NJ) **10667**
Chatham Courier (Chatham, NY) **10675**
Chatham News, The (Siler City, NC) **10694**
Chatsworth Times, The (Chatsworth, GA) **10564**
Chattanooga Free Press (Chattanooga, TN) **10500**
Chattanooga Times (Chattanooga, TN) **10500**
Chattooga Press (Summerville, GA) **10568**
Cheboygan Daily Tribune (Cheboygan, MI) **10459**
Cheektowaga Bee (Williamsville, NY) **10689**
Cheektowaga Times (Cheektowaga, NY) **10675**
Chelmsford Independent (Chelmsford, MA) **10624**
Chelsea Clinton News (New York, NY) **10683**
Chelsea Record (Revere, MA) **10628**
Chelsea Standard, The (Chelsea, MI) **10631**
Chemung Valley Reporter (Horseheads, NY) **10679**
Chenango American (Greene, NY) **10678**
Cheney Free Press (Cheney, WA) **10757**
Cheraw Chronicle, The (Cheraw, SC) **10726**
Cherokee County Herald (Centre, AL) **10518**
Cherokee Daily Times (Cherokee, IA) **10447**
Cherokee Messenger & Republican (Cherokee, OK) **10709**
Cherokee Scout (Murphy, NC) **10693**
Cherokee Tribune, The (Canton, GA) **10563**
† Cherry Hill News (Cherry Hill, NJ)
Cherryville Eagle (Cherryville, NC) **10691**
Chesapeake Post (Chesapeake, VA) **10752**
Cheshire Herald (Cheshire, CT) **10552**
Chester County Press (Oxford, PA) **10721**
Chesterfield Journal (St. Louis, MO) **10657**
Chesterland News (Chesterland, OH) **10700**
Chester News & Reporter (Chester, SC) **10726**
Chesterton Guide (Maryville, IN) **10595**
Chesterton Town Crier (Chesterton, IN) **10592**
Chesterton Tribune (Chesterton, IN) **10442**
Chestnut Hill Local (Philadelphia, PA) **10722**
Chetek Alert, The (Chetek, WI) **10765**
Cheyenne Mountain Journal (Manitou Springs, CO) **10550**
Chicago-Lawndale News (Chicago, IL) **10574**
Chicago's N.W. Side Press (Chicago, IL) **10574**
Chicago County Press (Lindstrom, MN) **10643**
Chicago Defender (Chicago, IL) **10438**
Chicago Near North News (Chicago, IL) **10575**
Chicago Near West Gazette (Chicago, IL) **10575**
Chicago Post (Chicago, IL) **10575**
Chicago Reader (Chicago, IL) **10575**
Chicago Ridge Citizen (Midlothian, IL) **10585**
Chicago Sun Times (Chicago, IL) **10438**
Chicago Tribune (Chicago, IL) **10438**
Chicago West Side Times (Chicago, IL) **10575**
Chickasha Daily Express (Chickasha, OK) **10488**
Chico Enterprise-Record (Chico, CA) **10421**
Chicopee Herald Weekly, The (Chicopee, MA) **10624**
Chieftain & Toccoa Record (Toccoa, GA) **10568**
Childress Index (Childress, TX) **10737**
Chilkat Valley News (Haines, AK) **10523**
Chillicothe Bulletin (Chillicothe, IL) **10576**
Chillicothe Constitution-Tribune (Chillicothe, MO) **10466**
Chillicothe Gazette (Chillicothe, OH) **10483**
Chilton Times-Journal (Chilton, WI) **10765**
Chino Valley Review (Chino Valley, AZ) **10524**
Chippewa Herald-Telegram (Chippewa Falls, WI) **10514**
Chisholm Tribune Press (Chisholm, MN) **10641**
Chittenango-Bridgeport Times (Syracuse, NY) **10687**
Choctaw Advocate (Butler, AL) **10518**
Chrisman Leader (Chrisman, IL) **10576**
Christian County Headliner News (Ozark, MO) **10655**
Chronicle-Express (Penn Yan, NY) **10684**
Chronicle-Independent (Camden, SC) **10726**
Chronicle-Tribune (Marion, IN) **10444**
Chronicle News, The (Trinidad, CO) **10429**
Chronicle, The (Atwater, CA) **10530**
Chronicle, The (Willimantic, CT) **10431**
Chronicle, The (Milford, DE) **10554**
Chronicle, The (North Dartmouth, MA) **10627**
Chronicle, The (Carson City, NV) **10662**
Chronicle, The (Glens Falls, NY) **10678**
Chronicle, The (Creswell, OR) **10712**
Chronicle, The (Humboldt, TN) **10732**
Chronicle, The (Centralia, WA) **10511**
Church Point News (Church Point, LA) **10616**
Cibola County Beacon (Grants, NM) **10672**
Cincinnati Enquirer, The (Cincinnati, OH) **10483**
Cincinnati Post (Cincinnati, OH) **10483**
Circleville Herald (Circleville, OH) **10483**
Cisco Press (Cisco, TX) **10738**
Cissna Park News (Cissna Park, IL) **10576**
Citizen (American Fork, UT) **10748**
Citizen-Standard, The (Valley View, PA) **10724**
Citizen/Press Plus (Pulaski, TN) **10734**
Citizen Journal (St. Louis, MO) **10657**
Citizen of Morris County, The (Denville, NJ) **10665**

Citizen Outlet (Mexico, NY) **10681**
Citizen Register (Yorktown Heights, NY) **10478**
Citizens' Advocate Newspaper (Coppell, TX) **10738**
Citizen Telegram, The (Rifle, CO) **10551**
Citizen, The (Mansfield, AR) **10528**
Citizen, The (Boyne City, MI) **10630**
Citizen, The (Hamtramck, MI) **10633**
Citizen, The (Laconia, NH) **10471**
Citizen, The (Auburn, NY) **10474**
Citizen, The (Houston, TX) **10741**
Citizen Tribune (Morristown, TN) **10501**
Citizen Voice & Times (Irvine, KY) **10612**
Citrus County Chronicle (Crystal River, FL) **10431**
City News (Bronx, NY) **10674**
City Pages (Minneapolis, MN) **10644**
City Paper (Baltimore, MD) **10620**
City Terrace Comet (City of Commerce, CA) **10532**
Civic Center NEWSource (Los Angeles, CA) **10537**
Clackamas Review (Milwaukee, OR) **10714**
Claiborne Progress (Tazewell, TN) **10735**
Clanton Advertiser (Clanton, AL) **10518**
Claremont Courier (Claremont, CA) **10532**
Claremore Progress (Claremore, OK) **10488**
Clarence Bee (Williamsville, NY) **10689**
Clarendon Hills Doings, The (Hinsdale, IL) **10582**
Clarendon Hills Progress (Downers Grove, IL) **10577**
Clare Sentinel (Clare, MI) **10631**
Clarion-Ledger, The (Jackson, MS) **10464**
Clarion Journal, The (Columbia, IL) **10576**
Clarion News (Corydon, IN) **10592**
Clarion News (Clarion, PA) **10716**
Clark County Press (Neillsville, WI) **10770**
Clark Courier (Berryville, VA) **10751**
Clark Eagle (Union, NJ) **10670**
Clarke County Democrat (Grove Hill, AL) **10519**
Clarke County Tribune (Quitman, MS) **10651**
Clark Patriot (Rahway, NJ) **10669**
Clarksburg Exponent (Clarksburg, WV) **10512**
Clarksburg Telegram (Clarksburg, WV) **10512**
Clarksdale Press Register (Clarksdale, MS) **10464**
Clarkson Integrator (Potsdam, NY) **10685**
Clarkston News (Clarkston, MI) **10631**
Clarkstown Courier, The (Pearl River, NY) **10684**
Clarksville Times, The (Clarksville, TX) **10738**
Classified Gazette (San Rafael, CA) **10544**
Clay Center Dispatch (Clay Center, KS) **10449**
Clay City Times, The (Stanton, KY) **10614**

† Clay Countian (Orange Park, FL)
† Clay County Crescent (Orange Park, FL)
Clay County Free Press (Clay, WV) **10761**
Clay Dispatch-Tribune (Kansas City, MO) **10654**
Clay Times Journal (Lineville, AL) **10520**
Clay Today (Orange Park, FL) **10559**
Clayton County Register (Elkader, IA) **10600**
Clayton Neighbor (Forest Park, GA) **10565**
Clayton News-Star (Clayton, NC) **10691**
Clayton News Daily (Jonesboro, GA) **10435**
Clayton Record (Clayton, AL) **10518**
† Clayton Sun (Atlanta, GA)
Clayton Tribune, The (Clayton, GA) **10564**
Clear-Ridge Reporter (Chicago, IL) **10575**
Clear Creek Courant (Idaho Springs, CO) **10549**
Clear Lake Observer-American (Clearlake, CA) **10532**
Clearwater Tribune (Orofino, ID) **10570**
Cleburne News (Heflin, AL) **10520**
Clemmons Courier (Clemmons, NC) **10691**
† Clermont County Review (Cincinnati, OH)
† Clermont Courier (Cincinnati, OH)
Clermont Sun (Batavia, OH) **10698**
Cleveland Advocate (Cleveland, TX) **10738**
Cleveland Bolivar Commercial (Cleveland, MS) **10464**
Cleveland Daily Banner (Cleveland, TN) **10500**
Cleveland Plain Dealer (Cleveland, OH) **10483**
Cleveland Times (Shelby, NC) **10694**
Clewiston News (Clewiston, FL) **10556**
Clinch County News (Homerville, GA) **10565**
Clinch Valley News (Tazewell, VA) **10756**
Clinton Chronicle, The (Clinton, SC) **10727**
Clinton County News (Mascoutah, IL) **10584**
Clinton County News (Albany, KY) **10609**
Clinton County News (St. Johns, MI) **10638**
Clinton County Shoppers Guide (Wilmington, OH) **10708**
Clinton Courier (Clinton, NY) **10675**
Clinton Daily Democrat (Clinton, MO) **10466**
Clinton Daily Journal (Clinton, IL) **10438**
Clinton Daily News (Clinton, OK) **10489**
Clinton Eye, The (Clinton, MO) **10652**
Clinton Herald (Clinton, IA) **10447**
Clinton Recorder (Clinton, CT) **10552**
Clinton Topper (Clinton, WI) **10765**
Clinton Van Buren County Democrat (Clinton, AR) **10527**
Clintonville Tribune-Gazette (Clintonville, WI) **10765**
Clio Messenger, The (Flint, MI) **10632**
Clipper-Herald (Lexington, NE) **10661**
Cloquet Billboard Shopper (Cloquet, MN) **10641**

Cloquet Pine Knot (Cloquet, MN) **10641**
Cloverdale Reveille (Cloverdale, CA) **10532**
Clover Herald (Clover, SC) **10727**
Clovis Independent (Clovis, CA) **10532**
Clovis News Journal (Clovis, NM) **10473**
Clyde Enterprise (Clyde, OH) **10701**
Coal City Courant (Coal City, IL) **10576**
Coal City Express (Wilmington, IL) **10591**
Coalfield Progress (Norton, VA) **10754**
Coalinga Record (Coalinga, CA) **10532**
Coal Valley News (Danville, WV) **10761**
Coastal Courier (Hinesville, GA) **10565**
Coastal Current, The (South Padre Island, TX) **10747**
Coastal Post (Bolinas, CA) **10531**
Coastal Times (Charleston, SC) **10726**
Coastland Times (Manteo, NC) **10693**
Coastside Chronicle (San Mateo, CA) **10543**
Cody Enterprise (Cody, WY) **10776**
Coeur d'Alene Press (Coeur d'Alene, ID) **10437**
Coffey County Today (Burlington, KS) **10606**
Coffeyville Journal, The (Coffeyville, KS) **10449**
Cohasset Mariner (Marshfield, MA) **10625**
Colbert County Reporter (Tuscumbia, AL) **10522**
Colby Free Press (Colby, KS) **10449**
Colchester Chronicle (Colchester, IL) **10576**
Coleman Chronicle & Democrat Voice (Coleman, TX) **10738**
Colfax Messenger (Colfax, WI) **10766**
Collierville Herald, The (Collierville, TN) **10731**
Collinsville Herald (Collinsville, IL) **10576**
Collinsville Journal (Collinsville, IL) **10576**
Collinsville News (Tulsa, OK) **10711**
Colonial, The (Fort Washington, PA) **10717**
Colonie Spotlight (Delmar, NY) **10676**
Colorado Statesman (Denver, CO) **10548**
Columbia Basin Herald (Moses Lake, WA) **10511**
Columbia Daily Tribune (Columbia, MO) **10466**
Columbia Flier (Columbia, MD) **10621**
Columbia Missourian (Columbia, MO) **10466**
Columbian-Progress (Columbia, MS) **10649**
Columbia News, The (Columbia, KY) **10610**
Columbia News Times, The (Martinez, GA) **10566**
Columbian, The (Vancouver, WA) **10512**
Columbus Alive (Columbus, OH) **10701**
Columbus Daily Advocate (Columbus, KS) **10449**
Columbus Dispatch (Columbus, OH) **10483**
Columbus Journal (Columbus, WI) **10766**
Columbus Ledger-Enquirer (Columbus, GA) **10435**
Columbus Messenger (Columbus, OH) **10701**

Columbus Telegram (Columbus, NE) **10469**
Colusa County Sun-Herald (Colusa, CA) **10532**
Comanche Chief (Comanche, TX) **10738**
Commack News (Smithtown, NY) **10686**
Commerce Journal (Commerce, TX) **10738**
Commerce News (Commerce, GA) **10564**
Commercial-Express (Vicksburg, MI) **10639**
Commercial-News (Danville, IL) **10439**
Commercial Appeal, The (Memphis, TN) **10501**
Commercial Dispatch, The (Columbus, MS) **10464**
Commercial Record (Saugatuck, MI) **10638**
Commonwealth Journal (Somerset, KY) **10453**
Commonwealth Progress (Scotland Neck, NC) **10694**
† Communicator Community News (Reno, NV)
Community Advertiser (Farmingdale, ME) **10619**
Community Adviser (Beaumont, CA) **10531**
Community Advisor (Marshall, MI) **10635**
Community Booster, The (Granville, OH) **10703**
Community Forum (Hackettstown, NJ) **10666**
Community Herald (Monona, WI) **10770**
Community Journal (Wading River, NY) **10688**
Community Journal, South (Loveland, OH) **10704**
Community Mirror (Gonzales, LA) **10616**
Community News (St. Louis, MO) **10657**
Community News (Clifton Park, NY) **10675**
Community News, The (Dora, AL) **10518**
Community Press, Mason (Loveland, OH) **10704**
Community Press, The (Millbrook, AL) **10520**
† Community Press, West Chester (Loveland, OH)
Community Shopper (Birmingham, AL) **10518**
Community Shopper (Des Moines, IA) **10600**
Community Times (Westminster, MD) **10623**
Compton Bulletin (Compton, CA) **10533**
Compton Wave (Los Angeles, CA) **10537**
Concordia Blade-Empire (Concordia, KS) **10449**
Concordia Sentinel (Ferriday, LA) **10616**
Concord Journal (Concord, MA) **10624**
Concord Monitor (Concord, NH) **10471**
Conejos County Citizen, The (Monte Vista, CO) **10550**
† Conneaut News-Herald (Conneaut, OH)
Conneautville Courier (Conneautville, PA) **10716**
Connecticut Post (Bridgeport, CT) **10429**
Connection, The (Grosse Point, MI) **10633**
Connersville News-Examiner (Connersville, IN) **10442**

Conroe Courier, The (Conroe, TX) **10503**
Conservative, The (Carrollton, MS) **10649**
Consumers' Edge (Baton Rouge, LA) **10615**
Contra Costa Sun (Lafayette, CA) **10535**
Contra Costa Times (Walnut Creek, CA) **10427**
Conway County Petit Jean Country Headlight (Morrilton, AR) **10528**
Conway Daily Sun, The (North Conway, NH) **10471**
† Conway Field & Herald (Conway, SC)
Coolidge Examiner (Coolidge, AZ) **10524**
Coon Rapids Herald (Coon Rapids, MN) **10641**
Coos County Democrat (Lancaster, NH) **10663**
Copiah County Courier (Hazlehurst, MS) **10649**
Coppell Gazette (Lewisville, TX) **10743**
Copperas Cove Leader Press (Copperas Cove, TX) **10738**
Copper Country News (Globe, AZ) **10525**
Copper Era (Clifton, AZ) **10524**
Coquille Valley Sentinel (Coquille, OR) **10712**
Coral Gables News (Miami, FL) **10559**
Corbin Times-Tribune (Corbin, KY) **10452**
Cordele Dispatch (Cordele, GA) **10435**
Cordell Beacon, The (Cordell, OK) **10709**
Cordova Times (Cordova, AK) **10523**
Cornell & Lake Holcombe Courier (Cornell, WI) **10766**
Corning Observer (Corning, CA) **10533**
Corona-Norco Independent (Corona, CA) **10533**
Coronado Journal (Coronado, CA) **10533**
Corpus Christi Caller-Times (Corpus Christi, TX) **10503**
Corridor News (Poway, CA) **10541**
Corrigan Times, The (Corrigan, TX) **10738**
Corry Journal (Corry, PA) **10493**
Corsicana Daily Sun (Corsicana, TX) **10503**
Cortez Montezuma Valley Journal (Cortez, CO) **10548**
Cortez Sentinel (Cortez, CO) **10548**
Cortland Democrat (Marathon, NY) **10681**
Cortland Standard (Cortland, NY) **10475**
Corvallis Gazette-Times (Corvallis, OR) **10491**
Corydon Democrat (Corydon, IN) **10592**
Corydon Times-Republican (Corydon, IA) **10599**
Coshocton Tribune (Coshocton, OH) **10483**
Cosmopolite-Herald (Girard, PA) **10718**
Cottage Grove Sentinel (Cottage Grove, OR) **10712**
Cottonwood Chronicle (Cottonwood, ID) **10569**
Cottonwood Journal Extra (Cottonwood, AZ) **10524**
Council Grove Republican (Council Grove, KS) **10449**

Country Almanac (Menlo Park, CA) **10539**
Country Connection News (Eakly, OK) **10710**
Country Courier, The (Conklin, NY) **10676**
Country News-Press (Paso Robles, CA) **10424**
Country Shopper (Pound Ridge, NY) **10685**
Country Star (Stigler, OK) **10711**
Country Weekly (Grants Pass, OR) **10713**
County Courier (Enosburg Falls, VT) **10749**
County Journal (Belleville, IL) **10573**
County Journal (Percy, IL) **10588**
County Journal, The (Washburn, WI) **10775**
County Ledger-Press (Balsam Lake, WI) **10764**
County Line Reminder (Ortonville, MI) **10636**
Countyline, The (Bryan, OH) **10699**
County Neighbors (Punxsutawney, PA) **10723**
County News Enterprise (Forest City, NC) **10692**
County Observer (Yeagertown, PA) **10725**
County Press (Parma, MI) **10636**
County Press (Newtown Square, PA) **10721**
County Press, The (Lapeer, MI) **10635**
County Reporter, The (Andalusia, AL) **10517**
County Star Journal East (St. Louis, MO) **10657**
County Star Journal West (St. Louis, MO) **10657**
County Transcript (Susquehanna, PA) **10724**
County Wide (Dover-Foxcroft, ME) **10619**
† Countywide News (Westminster, MD)
Courant, The (Bottineau, ND) **10696**
Courier-Express (Du Bois, PA) **10493**
Courier-Gazette (Rockland, ME) **10620**
Courier-Journal (Palmyra, NY) **10684**
Courier-Journal, The (Louisville, KY) **10453**
Courier-News (Clinton, TN) **10731**
Courier-News, The (Elgin, IL) **10439**
Courier-News, The (Bridgewater, NJ) **10472**
Courier-Post, The (St. Charles, MO) **10468**
Courier-Post, The (Cherry Hill, NJ) **10472**
Courier-Standard-Enterprise (Fort Plain, NY) **10677**
Courier-Times (Sutherland, NE) **10662**
Courier-Times, The (Roxboro, NC) **10694**
Courier-Wedge (Durand, WI) **10766**
Courier Gazette (Newark, NY) **10683**
Courier Herald, The (Dublin, GA) **10435**
Courier Hub (Stoughton, WI) **10774**
Courier Journal (Florence, AL) **10519**
Courier News (Blytheville, AR) **10419**
Courier Press (Prairie du Chien, WI) **10772**
Courier, The (Russellville, AR) **10420**
Courier, The (Plant City, FL) **10560**
† Courier, The (Thomasville, GA)
Courier, The (Rensselaer, IN) **10597**
Courier, The (Houma, LA) **10454**
Courier, The (Littleton, NH) **10663**

Courier, The (Conneaut, OH) **10703**
Courier, The (Findlay, OH) **10484**
Courier, The (Reedsport, OR) **10714**
Courier, The (Savannah, TN) **10734**
Courier, The (Sun Prairie, WI) **10774**
Courtland Journal-Empire
 (Courtland, KS) **10606**
Coushatta Citizen (Coushatta, LA) **10616**
Cover Story, The (Murfreesboro, TN) **10734**
Covington Leader (Covington, TN) **10731**
Covington News (Covington, GA) **10564**
Covington Record (Covington, OK) **10709**
Covington St. Tammany Farmer
 (Covington, LA) **10616**
Coweta American (Coweta, OK) **10710**
Cranbury Press (Dayton, NJ) **10665**
Crane News (Crane, TX) **10738**
Cranford Chronicle (Cranford, NJ) **10665**
Cranston Herald (Cranston, RI) **10725**
Crawford County Independent-Kickapoo Scout
 (Gay Mills, WI) **10767**
Crawfordsville Journal Review
 (Crawfordsville, IN) **10443**
Crescent-News (Defiance, OH) **10484**
Cresco Times-Plain Dealer (Cresco, IA) **10599**
Cresson-Gallitzin Mainliner, The
 (Cresson, PA) **10717**
Crestline Advocate (Crestline, OH) **10703**
Crestline Courier-News (Crestline, CA) **10533**
Creston News Advertiser (Creston, IA) **10447**
† Crestview Okaloosa-News Journal
 (Crestview, FL)
Crete News, The (Crete, NE) **10660**
Crewe-Burkeville Journal (Crewe, VA) **10752**
Crittenden Press (Marion, KY) **10612**
Crockett Times, The (Alamo, TN) **10731**
Crofton News-Crier (Bowie, MD) **10621**
Cromwell Chronicle (Cromwell, CT) **10552**
Crookston Daily Times (Crookston, MN) **10462**
Crossville Chronicle (Crossville, TN) **10731**
Crothersville Times (Crothersville, IN) **10592**
Crowley Post-Signal (Crowley, LA) **10454**
Crowley Review (Burleson, TX) **10737**
Cuba Free Press (Cuba, MO) **10653**
† Cuba Journal (Cuba, IL)
Cudahy Reminder-Enterprise (New
 Berlin, WI) **10770**
Cuero Record (Cuero, TX) **10738**
Cullman Times (Cullman, AL) **10415**
Cullman Tribune (Cullman, AL) **10518**
Culpeper News (Culpeper, VA) **10752**
Culpeper Star Exponent (Culpeper, VA) **10509**
Culver Citizen (Culver, IN) **10592**
Culver City-Ladera Independent (Santa
 Monica, CA) **10544**
Culver City Star (Los Angeles, CA) **10537**

Cumberland Advocate
 (Cumberland, WI) **10766**
Cumberland County News
 (Burkesville, KY) **10609**
Cumberland Courier (Lawrence, IN) **10595**
† Cumberland Times (Crossville, TN)
Cumberland Times-News
 (Cumberland, MD) **10456**
Cumberland Trading Post, The
 (Middlesboro, KY) **10612**
Cupertino Courier (Cupertino, CA) **10533**
† Current (Potsdam, NY)
Curry Coastal Pilot (Brookings, OR) **10712**
Cushing Daily Citizen (Cushing, OK) **10489**
Custer County Chief (Broken Bow, NE) **10660**
Cuyahoga Falls News-Press (Stow, OH) **10707**
Cynthiana Democrat (Cynthiana, KY) **10610**

D

D/FW People (Euless, TX) **10739**
Dadeville Record (Alexander City, AL) **10517**
Daily & Sunday Freeman (Kingston, NY) **10475**
Daily & Sunday Sentinel (Rome, NY) **10477**
Daily Advance (Elizabeth City, NC) **10479**
Daily Advocate (Greenville, OH) **10484**
Daily American (West Frankfort, IL) **10442**
Daily American (Somerset, PA) **10496**
Daily American Republic (Poplar
 Bluff, MO) **10467**
Daily Ardmoreite (Ardmore, OK) **10488**
Daily Astorian (Astoria, OR) **10491**
Daily Banner (Cambridge, MD) **10456**
Daily Breeze (Torrance, CA) **10426**
Daily Californian, The (El Cajon, CA) **10421**
Daily Camera (Boulder, CO) **10428**
Daily Chronicle (De Kalb, IL) **10439**
Daily Citizen (Searcy, AR) **10420**
Daily Citizen News (Dalton, GA) **10435**
Daily Clay County Advocate-Press
 (Flora, IL) **10439**
Daily Clintonian (Clinton, IN) **10442**
Daily Comet (Thibodaux, LA) **10455**
Daily Commercial (Leesburg, FL) **10432**
Daily Corinthian (Corinth, MS) **10464**
Daily Courier (Forest City, NC) **10479**
Daily Courier Observer, The
 (Massena, NY) **10476**
Daily Courier, The (Prescott, AZ) **10418**
Daily Courier, The (Connellsville, PA) **10493**
Daily Democrat (Woodland, CA) **10427**
Daily Dispatch (Douglas, AZ) **10418**
Daily Dispatch, The (Henderson, NC) **10479**
Daily Dunklin Democrat (Kennett, MO) **10467**
Daily Evening Item (Lynn, MA) **10458**

Daily Freeman Journal (Webster City, IA) **10449**
Daily Gazette (Sterling, IL) **10441**
Daily Gazette (Schenectady, NY) **10477**
Daily Guide (St. Robert, MO) **10468**
Daily Hampshire Gazette (Northampton, MA) **10458**
Daily Herald (Arlington Heights, IL) **10437**
Daily Herald (Delphos, OH) **10484**
Daily Herald (Columbia, TN) **10500**
Daily Herald, The (Tyrone, PA) **10497**
Daily Herald, The (Provo, UT) **10508**
Daily Home (Talladega, AL) **10416**
Daily Iberian (New Iberia, LA) **10455**
Daily Independent, The (Ridgecrest, CA) **10424**
Daily Independent, The (Ashland, KY) **10452**
Daily Inter Lake, The (Kalispell, MT) **10469**
Daily Item, The (New Rochelle, NY) **10476**
Daily Item, The (Sunbury, PA) **10497**
Daily Jefferson County Union (Fort Atkinson, WI) **10514**
Daily Jeffersonian, The (Cambridge, OH) **10483**
Daily Journal (Kankakee, IL) **10440**
Daily Journal (Franklin, IN) **10443**
Daily Journal (Park Hills, MO) **10467**
† Daily Journal (Elizabeth, NJ)
Daily Journal (Vineland, NJ) **10473**
Daily Journal, The (Fergus Falls, MN) **10463**
Daily Journal, The (International Falls, MN) **10463**
Daily Ledger (Canton, IL) **10438**
Daily Ledger (Fisher, IN) **10443**
Daily Local News (West Chester, PA) **10497**
Daily Mail (Catskill, NY) **10474**
Daily Mail & Sunday Herald (Nevada, MO) **10467**
Daily Mail, The (Hagerstown, MD) **10456**
Daily Midway Driller (Taft, CA) **10426**
† Daily Milford Citizen (Milford, CT)
Daily Mining Gazette (Houghton, MI) **10460**
Daily News (Mountain Home, AR) **10420**
Daily News (Woodland Hills, CA) **10427**
Daily News (Palatka, FL) **10433**
Daily News (Bowling Green, KY) **10452**
Daily News (Greenville, MI) **10460**
Daily News (Iron Mountain, MI) **10460**
Daily News (Richmond, MO) **10467**
Daily News (Jacksonville, NC) **10479**
Daily News (Wahpeton, ND) **10482**
Daily News (Wapakoneta, OH) **10487**
Daily News (Huntingdon, PA) **10494**
Daily News (Longview, WA) **10511**
Daily News (West Bend, WI) **10516**

Daily News-Bulletin, The (Brookfield, MO) **10465**
Daily News-Record (Harrisonburg, VA) **10509**
Daily News-Sun (Sun City, AZ) **10418**
Daily News Leader, The (Staunton, VA) **10510**
Daily News of Newburyport, The (Newburyport, MA) **10458**
Daily News, The (Eden, NC) **10479**
Daily Nonpareil (Council Bluffs, IA) **10447**
Daily Okeechobee News, The (Okeechobee, FL) **10433**
Daily Oklahoman (Oklahoma City, OK) **10490**
Daily Pilot, The (Costa Mesa, CA) **10421**
Daily Press (Victorville, CA) **10427**
Daily Press, The (Escanaba, MI) **10460**
Daily Press, The (St. Marys, PA) **10496**
Daily Press, The (Newport News, VA) **10510**
Daily Press, The (Ashland, WI) **10513**
Daily Progress (Charlottesville, VA) **10509**
Daily Record (Canon City, CO) **10428**
Daily Record (Parsippany, NJ) **10472**
Daily Record (Ellensburg, WA) **10511**
† Daily Record, The (Westchester, PA)
Daily Register, The (Portage, WI) **10515**
Daily Reporter (Greenfield, IN) **10443**
Daily Reporter (Columbus, OH) **10483**
Daily Reporter, The (Derby, KS) **10449**
Daily Reporter, The (Coldwater, MI) **10459**
Daily Republic (Fairfield, CA) **10422**
Daily Republic (Mitchell, SD) **10499**
Daily Review (Hayward, CA) **10422**
Daily Review & Sunday Review (Towanda, PA) **10497**
Daily Review Atlas (Monmouth, IL) **10440**
Daily Review, The (Morgan City, LA) **10454**
Daily Sentinel-Star, The (Grenada, MS) **10464**
Daily Sentinel, The (Scottsboro, AL) **10416**
Daily Sentinel, The (Grand Junction, CO) **10428**
Daily Sentinel, The (Pomeroy, OH) **10486**
Daily Sentinel, The (Nacogdoches, TX) **10505**
Daily Sitka Sentinel (Sitka, AK) **10417**
Daily Southerner, The (Tarboro, NC) **10481**
Daily Southtown (Tinley Park, IL) **10441**
Daily Sparks Tribune, The (Sparks, NV) **10471**
Daily Standard (Excelsior Springs, MO) **10466**
Daily Standard (Celina, OH) **10483**
Daily Star-Journal, The (Warrensburg, MO) **10468**
Daily Star, The (Oneonta, NY) **10476**
Daily Statesman (Dexter, MO) **10466**
Daily Sun-News (Sunnyside, WA) **10512**
Daily Sun, The (Warner Robins, GA) **10436**
Daily Telegraph (Adrian, MI) **10459**
Daily Times (Ottawa, IL) **10441**
Daily Times (Salisbury, MD) **10456**

Daily Times (Farmington, NM) **10473**
Daily Times (Maryville, TN) **10501**
Daily Times (Weirton, WV) **10513**
Daily Times & Chronicle (Reading, MA) **10458**
Daily Times-Call (Longmont, CO) **10429**
Daily Times Chronicle (Woburn, MA) **10459**
Daily Times Herald (Carroll, IA) **10447**
Daily Times Leader (West Point, MS) **10465**
Daily Times, The (New Rochelle, NY) **10476**
Daily Times, The (Rawlins, WY) **10516**
Daily Transcript (Dedham, MA) **10457**
Daily Tribune News (Cartersville, GA) **10435**
Daily Tribune. The (Ames, IA) **10446**
Daily Tribune, The (Royal Oak, MI) **10462**
Daily Tribune, The (Bay City, TX) **10502**
Daily Tribune, The (Wisconsin Rapids, WI) **10516**
Daily Whale, The (Rehoboth Beach, DE) **10431**
Daily World (Opelousas, LA) **10455**
Daily World, The (Aberdeen, WA) **10510**
Dakota County Tribune (Burnsville, MN) **10640**
Dalhart Daily Texan (Dalhart, TX) **10503**
Dallas City Enterprise (Dallas City, IL) **10576**
Dallas Morning News, The (Dallas, TX) **10503**
Dallas New Era (Dallas, GA) **10564**
Dallas Park Cities News (Dallas, TX) **10738**
Dallas Polk County Itemizer-Observer (Dallas, OR) **10712**
Dallas Post (Dallas, PA) **10717**
Dallas White Rocker News (Dallas, TX) **10738**
Dalton Gazette & Kidron News (Dalton, OH) **10703**
Daly City Record (San Mateo, CA) **10543**
Damascus Gazette (Gatorsburg, MD) **10621**
Dan's Papers (Bridgehampton, NY) **10673**
Dana Point News (Lake Forest, CA) **10536**
Danbury Reporter (Walnut Cove, NC) **10695**
Dansville Genesee Country Express (Dansville, NY) **10676**
Danvers Herald (Danvers, MA) **10624**
Danville News (Danville, PA) **10493**
Danville Register & Bee (Danville, VA) **10509**
Darco News & Buyers Guide (Hartsville, SC) **10727**
Darien Doings (Hinsdale, IL) **10582**
Darien Metropolitan (Lemont, IL) **10583**
Darien News (Darien, GA) **10564**
Darien News Review (Darien, CT) **10552**
Darien Progress (Downers Grove, IL) **10577**
Darke County Early Bird, The (Greenville, OH) **10703**
David City Banner-Press, The (David City, NE) **10660**
Davie County Enterprise-Record (Mocksville, NC) **10693**
Davis County Clipper (Bountiful, UT) **10748**
Davis Enterprise (Davis, CA) **10421**
Davison Flagstaff (Swartz Creek, MI) **10638**
Davison Index, The (Davison, MI) **10631**
Dawson News, The (Dawson, GA) **10564**
Dawson Springs Progress (Dawson Springs, KY) **10610**
Day, The (New London, CT) **10430**
Daytona Pennysaver (Ormond Beach, FL) **10560**
Dayton Chronicle (Dayton, WA) **10757**
Dayton Daily News (Dayton, OH) **10484**
Dayton Tribune (Dayton, OR) **10713**
Dearborn County Register (Lawrenceburg, IN) **10595**
Dearborn Press & Guide (Dearborn, MI) **10631**
Dearborn Times-Herald (Dearborn, MI) **10632**
Decatur-DeKalb News/Era (Decatur, GA) **10564**
Decatur Daily (Decatur, AL) **10416**
Decatur Daily Democrat (Decatur, IN) **10443**
Decatur Herald (Gentry, AR) **10527**
Decatur Tribune (Decatur, IL) **10576**
Declaration, The (Independence, VA) **10753**
Decorah Public Opinion & Journal (Decorah, IA) **10599**
Deerfield Beach Observer (Deerfield Beach, FL) **10556**
Deerfield Beach Thursday Times (Deerfield Beach, FL) **10556**
Deerfield Review (Bannockburn, IL) **10572**
Deer Park Broadcaster, The (Deer Park, TX) **10738**
Deer Park Progress, The (Deer Park, TX) **10739**
Defensor Chieftain (Socorro, NM) **10672**
† DeKalb News/Sun (Decatur, GA)
DeLand Beacon, The (DeLand, FL) **10557**
Delano Record (Delano, CA) **10533**
Delavan Enterprise (Delavan, WI) **10766**
Delavan Times, The (Delavan, IL) **10576**
Delaware Beachcomber (Rehoboth Beach, DE) **10554**
Delaware Coast Press (Rehoboth Beach, DE) **10554**
Delaware County Daily-Sunday Times (Clifton Heights, PA) **10493**
Delaware County Journal (Holmes, PA) **10718**
Delaware County Times (Delhi, NY) **10676**
Delaware Gazette (Delaware, OH) **10484**
Delaware State News (Dover, DE) **10431**
Delaware Valley News (Frenchtown, NJ) **10666**
Delaware Wave (Bethany Beach, DE) **10554**
Delhi Express (Winton, CA) **10546**
Delhi Press (Cincinnati, OH) **10700**
Dell Rapids Tribune (Dell Rapids, SD) **10729**

Del Mar, Solana Beach, Carmel Valley, Rancho Santa Fe Sun (Carlsbad, CA) **10532**
Del Norte Prospector (Monte Vista, CO) **10550**
Del Norte Triplicate (Crescent City, CA) **10421**
Delray Times (Deerfield Beach, FL) **10556**
Del Rio News-Herald (Del Rio, TX) **10503**
Delta Atlas (Delta, OH) **10703**
Delta County Independent (Delta, CO) **10548**
Delta Democrat-Times (Greenville, MS) **10464**
† Delta Paper (Delta Jct, AK)
Delta Waverly Community News (Grand Ledge, MI) **10633**
Delta Wind, The (Delta Junction, AK) **10523**
Deming Headlight (Deming, NM) **10473**
Democrat-Argus, The (Caruthersville, MO) **10652**
Democrat-Leader (Fayette, MO) **10653**
Democrat-Message (Mt. Sterling, IL) **10586**
Democrat-News (Fredericktown, MO) **10653**
Democrat-Reporter, The (Linden, AL) **10520**
Democrat-Union (Lawrenceburg, TN) **10733**
Democrat, The (Senatobia, MS) **10651**
Democrat Tribune, The (Mineral Point, WI) **10769**
Demopolis Times (Demopolis, AL) **10518**
Denair Dispatch (Winton, CA) **10546**
Denbigh Gazette (Yorktown, VA) **10756**
Denham Springs-Livingston Parish News (Denham Springs, LA) **10616**
Denison Bulletin & Review (Denison, IA) **10600**
Denmark Press (Denmark, WI) **10766**
† Dennis Bulletin (South Yarmouth, MA)
Denton County Express (Lake Dallas, TX) **10743**
Denton Record-Chronicle (Denton, TX) **10503**
Denver Herald-Dispatch (Denver, CO) **10548**
Denver Post (Denver, CO) **10428**
De Pere Journal (De Pere, WI) **10766**
Depew Bee (Williamsville, NY) **10689**
Deposit Courier (Deposit, NY) **10676**
De Queen Bee (De Queen, AR) **10527**
De Queen Daily Citizen (De Queen, AR) **10419**
De Quincy News (De Quincy, LA) **10616**
Derrick, The (Oil City, PA) **10495**
Derry News (Derry, NH) **10663**
Desert Dispatch (Barstow, CA) **10421**
Desert Mailer News (Lancaster, CA) **10536**
Desert Mobile Home News (Palm Desert, CA) **10540**
† Desert Mountain Express (Hesperia, CA)
Desert Sentinel, The (Desert Hot Springs, CA) **10533**
Desert Sun, The (Palm Springs, CA) **10424**
Desert Winds, The (Cave Creek, AZ) **10524**
Deshler Rustler, The (Deshler, NE) **10660**

Des Moines County News, The (West Burlington, IA) **10605**
Des Moines News (Seattle, WA) **10759**
Des Moines Register (Des Moines, IA) **10447**
De Soto Times (Southaven, MS) **10651**
DeSoto Today (DeSoto, TX) **10739**
Des Plaines Journal (Des Plaines, IL) **10439**
Des Plaines Times (Park Ridge, IL) **10587**
Destin Log (Destin, FL) **10557**
Detroit Free Press (Detroit, MI) **10460**
Detroit Lakes Tribune (Detroit Lakes, MN) **10641**
Detroit News (Detroit, MI) **10460**
Devil's Lake Daily Journal (Devil's Lake, ND) **10481**
DeWitt Bath Review (St. Johns, MI) **10638**
DeWitt Times (Syracuse, NY) **10687**
Dexter Daily Statesman (Dexter, MO) **10466**
† Diamond Drill, The (Crystal Falls, MI)
Diamond Trail News (Sully, IA) **10604**
Dickenson Star/Cumberland Times, The (Clintwood, VA) **10752**
Dickinson Press, The (Dickinson, ND) **10481**
Dickson Herald, The (Dickson, TN) **10731**
Digest, The (Hallandale, FL) **10557**
Digger Shopper & News, The (Oroville, CA) **10540**
Dillon Herald, The (Dillon, SC) **10727**
Dispatch-News, The (Lexington, SC) **10728**
Dispatch, The (Gilroy, CA) **10422**
Dispatch, The (Lexington, NC) **10480**
Dispatch, The (New Providence, NJ) **10668**
† Dispatch, The (Cookeville, TN)
Divernon News (Auburn, IL) **10572**
Dixie News (Florence, KY) **10610**
Dixon Pilot (Dixon, MO) **10653**
Dodge City Daily Globe (Dodge City, KS) **10450**
Dodge County Independent-News (Juneau, WI) **10768**
Dodge County News, The (Eastman, GA) **10565**
Dodgeville Chronicle, Inc. (Dodgeville, WI) **10766**
Dominion Post, The (Morgantown, WV) **10513**
Donaldsonville Chief (Donaldsonville, LA) **10616**
Donalsonville News (Donalsonville, GA) **10564**
Doon Press (Doon, IA) **10600**
Door County Advocate (Sturgeon Bay, WI) **10774**
Doraville-DeKalb Neighbor (Atlanta, GA) **10562**
Dorchester Eagle Record (St. George, SC) **10729**
Dorchester Star (Cambridge, MD) **10621**
Dothan Eagle (Dothan, AL) **10416**

Douglas County Herald (Ava, MO) **10651**
Douglas County News Press (Castle Rock, CO) **10547**
Douglas County Post Gazette (Elkhorn, NE) **10660**
Douglas County Sentinel (Douglasville, GA) **10435**
Douglas Enterprise (Douglas, GA) **10564**
Douglas Neighbor, The (Marietta, GA) **10566**
Dove Creek Press (Dove Creek, CO) **10548**
Dover-Sherborn Suburban Press (Needham, MA) **10626**
Dowagiac Daily News (Dowagiac, MI) **10460**
Downers Grove Reporter (Downers Grove, IL) **10577**
Downey Herald American (Los Angeles, CA) **10537**
Downriver Voice (New Baltimore, MI) **10636**
Downtown Express (New York, NY) **10683**
Downtown Gazette (Long Beach, CA) **10537**
Downtown News (South Miami, FL) **10561**
Dracut Dispatch, The (Dracut, MA) **10624**
Drain Enterprise (Drain, OR) **10713**
Dresden Enterprise (Dresden, TN) **10731**
Drexel Hill Press (Newtown Square, PA) **10721**
Dripping Springs Dispatch (Dripping Springs, TX) **10739**
Dublin Suburbia News (Columbus, OH) **10701**
Dublin Villager (Worthington, OH) **10709**
Duluth News-Tribune (Duluth, MN) **10462**
Dumas Clarion (Dumas, AR) **10527**
Duncan Banner (Duncan, OK) **10489**
Duncannon Record (New Bloomfield, PA) **10721**
Duncanville Today (DeSoto, TX) **10739**
Dundalk Eagle, The (Baltimore, MD) **10620**
Dundee Observer (Dundee, NY) **10676**
Dunn County News (Menomonie, WI) **10769**
Dunn Daily Record (Dunn, NC) **10478**
Dunwoody-DeKalb Neighbor, The (Atlanta, GA) **10562**
Dunwoody Crier (Atlanta, GA) **10562**
† DuPage Press Service (Wheaton, IL)
Du Quoin Evening Call (Du Quoin, IL) **10439**
Durand-Dakota Volunteer (Durand, IL) **10577**
Durand Express, The (Durand, MI) **10632**
Durand Gazette (Love Park, IL) **10584**
Durango Herald (Durango, CO) **10428**
Durant Daily Democrat (Durant, OK) **10489**
Dutch Harbor Fisherman, The (Dutch Harbor, AK) **10523**
Duxbury Reporter (Plymouth, MA) **10627**
Dyer County Tennessean (Newbern, TN) **10734**
Dyersville Commercial (Dyersville, IA) **10600**

E

Eagan Sun-Current (Burnsville, MN) **10640**
Eagle-Herald (Marinette, WI) **10515**
Eagle-Times (Claremont, NH) **10471**
Eagle Bulletin (Syracuse, NY) **10687**
Eagle Grove Eagle (Eagle Grove, IA) **10600**
Eagle Lake Headlight (Eagle Lake, TX) **10739**
Eagle News (Bountiful, UT) **10748**
Eagle Pass News Guide/Brief (Eagle Pass, TX) **10739**
Eagle Rock Sentinel (Los Angeles, CA) **10537**
Eagle, The (Cambridge, NY) **10675**
Eagle Tribune, The (North Andover, MA) **10458**
Eagle Valley Enterprise (Eagle, CO) **10548**
Earlville Leader (Earlville, IL) **10578**
Easley Progress (Easley, SC) **10727**
East Aurora Advertiser (East Aurora, NY) **10676**
East Aurora Bee (Williamsville, NY) **10689**
East Baltimore Guide (Baltimore, MD) **10620**
East Bay Breeze (Sun City Center, FL) **10561**
East Bay Express (Berkeley, CA) **10531**
East Bridgewater Star (East Bridgewater, MA) **10624**
Eastchester Record (Yonkers, NY) **10690**
† East County Chronicle (Kimberly, ID)
Eastern Arizona Courier (Safford, AZ) **10526**
Eastern Carolina Times-Inquirer (Goldsboro, NC) **10692**
Eastern Colorado News (Strasburg, CO) **10551**
Eastern Colorado Plainsman (Hugo, CO) **10549**
Eastern Gazette, The (Dexter, ME) **10619**
Eastern Hills Journal (Loveland, OH) **10704**
Eastern Kentucky Shopper (Paintsville, KY) **10613**
East Feliciana Watchman (Clinton, LA) **10616**
East Fishkill Record (Mahopac, NY) **10681**
East Grand Rapids Cadence (Jenison, MI) **10634**
East Greenwich Pendulum (East Greenwich, RI) **10725**
East Hampton Star (East Hampton, NY) **10676**
East Hartford Gazette, The (East Hartford, CT) **10552**
East Haven Advertiser (Milford, CT) **10553**
East L.A./Commerce Tribune (Los Angeles, CA) **10537**
Eastland Telegram (Eastland, TX) **10739**
East Lauderdale News (Rogersville, AL) **10521**
† East Los Angeles Gazette (South Gate, CA)
† East Los Angeles Tribune (South Gate, CA)
East Meadow Beacon (Hicksville, NY) **10679**
East Mesa Independent (Apache Junction, AZ) **10524**

Easton Bulletin (Stoughton, MA) **10628**
East Orange Record (Orange, NJ) **10668**
East Oregonian, The (Pendleton, OR) **10492**
† East Palestine Heritage, The (Columbiana, OH)
East Penn Press (Allentown, PA) **10715**
East Peoria Courier (Morton, IL) **10586**
East Providence Post (East Providence, RI) **10725**
East Riverside Advertiser (Palm Desert, CA) **10540**
East Rochester Post-Herald (Victor, NY) **10688**
East Rockaway Observer (Mineola, NY) **10682**
East Shelby Review (Somerville, TN) **10735**
East Side Herald (Indianapolis, IN) **10594**
Eastside Journal (Los Angeles, CA) **10537**
Eastside Journal (Bellevue, WA) **10510**
Eastside Monthly (Providence, RI) **10726**
East Side Review (North St. Paul, MN) **10645**
Eastside Sun (City of Commerce, CA) **10532**
† Eastside Times (Tulsa, OK)
East St. Louis Monitor (East St. Louis, IL) **10578**
East St. Louis News Journal (Columbia, IL) **10576**
East Troy News (East Troy, WI) **10766**
Easy Reader (Hermosa Beach, CA) **10535**
Eaton County News (Charlotte, MI) **10631**
Ebbtide (Sausalito, CA) **10544**
Ebensburg News Leader, The (Ebensburg, PA) **10717**
Echoes-Sentinel (Stirling, NJ) **10670**
Echo Press, The (Alexandria, MN) **10639**
† Echo, The (Berlin, NY)
ECM Post-Review (North Branch, MN) **10644**
Eddyville Tribune (Eddyville, IA) **10600**
Eden Prairie Sun-Current (Bloomington, MN) **10640**
Edgebrook Times Review (Park Ridge, IL) **10587**
Edgerton Enterprise, The (Edgerton, MN) **10641**
Edgerton Reporter (Edgerton, WI) **10766**
Edgewood Enterprise (Edgewood, TX) **10739**
Edgewood Reminder (Edgewood, IA) **10600**
Edina Sun-Current (Minneapolis, MN) **10644**
Edinburg Daily Review (Edinburg, TX) **10503**
Edison-Norwood Times Review (Park Ridge, IL) **10588**
Edmond Evening Sun (Edmond, OK) **10489**
Edwardsville Intelligencer (Edwardsville, IL) **10439**
Edwardsville Journal (Edwardsville, IL) **10578**
Effingham Daily News (Effingham, IL) **10439**
Egg Harbor News (Hammonton, NJ) **10666**
Elba Clipper, The (Elba, AL) **10519**
Elbert County News (Castle Rock, CO) **10547**

Elberton Star (Elberton, GA) **10565**
Elburn Herald (Elburn, IL) **10578**
El Campo Leader-News (El Campo, TX) **10739**
El Centro Advertiser (El Centro, CA) **10533**
Eldon Advertiser (Eldon, MO) **10653**
Eldorado Daily Journal (Eldorado, IL) **10439**
El Dorado News-Times (El Dorado, AR) **10419**
El Dorado Times (El Dorado, KS) **10450**
Eldora Herald-Leader (Eldora, IA) **10600**
Elizabeth Gazette (Union, NJ) **10670**
Elizabethton Star (Elizabethton, TN) **10500**
Elizabethtown Chronicle (Elizabethtown, PA) **10717**
Elizabethtown Mount Joy Merchandiser (Mt. Joy, PA) **10721**
Elk City Daily News (Elk City, OK) **10489**
Elk Grove Citizen (Elk Grove, CA) **10533**
Elkhart Truth, The (Elkhart, IN) **10443**
Elkhorn Independent (Elkhorn, WI) **10766**
Elko Daily Free Press (Elko, NV) **10470**
Elk Valley Times (Fayetteville, TN) **10732**
Ellenville Press (Ellenville, NY) **10677**
Ellsworth American, The (Ellsworth, ME) **10619**
Ellsworth Reporter, The (Ellsworth, KS) **10606**
Ellwood City Ledger (Ellwood City, PA) **10493**
Elma Review (East Aurora, NY) **10676**
Elm Grove Elm Leaves (New Berlin, WI) **10770**
Elmhurst Press (Elmhurst, IL) **10578**
Elm Leaves (Oak Park, IL) **10587**
Elmont Herald (Elmont, NY) **10677**
Elmwood Park-River Grove Times (Lincolnwood, IL) **10583**
Eloy Enterprise (Eloy, AZ) **10525**
El Paso Herald-Post (El Paso, TX) **10504**
El Paso Journal (El Paso, IL) **10578**
El Paso Times (El Paso, TX) **10504**
El Reno Tribune (El Reno, OK) **10710**
El Segundo Herald (El Segundo, CA) **10534**
El Sereno Star (Los Angeles, CA) **10537**
Elwood Express (Wilmington, IL) **10591**
Ely Daily Times (Ely, NV) **10470**
Ely Echo (Ely, MN) **10641**
Elyria Chronicle-Telegram (Elyria, OH) **10484**
Emery County Progress (Castle Dale, UT) **10748**
Emmetsburg Democrat (Emmetsburg, IA) **10600**
Emmetsburg Reporter (Emmetsburg, IA) **10601**
Emporia Gazette (Emporia, KS) **10450**
Encinitas Sun (Encinitas, CA) **10534**
Enderlin Independent (Enderlin, ND) **10696**
Enfield Press (Enfield, CT) **10552**
England Democrat (England, AR) **10527**
Englewood Herald (Littleton, CO) **10549**

Englewood Sun Herald (Englewood, FL) **10432**
Enid News & Eagle (Enid, OK) **10489**
Ennis Daily News (Ennis, TX) **10504**
Enquirer-Gazette (Upper Marlboro, MD) **10623**
Enquirer-Journal, The (Monroe, NC) **10480**
Enquirer Bulletin (Burlingame, CA) **10531**
Enterprise & Inner Harbor News (Baltimore, MD) **10621**
Enterprise Buyer's Catalogue (Wytheville, VA) **10756**
Enterprise Ledger (Enterprise, AL) **10416**
Enterprise Mountaineer, The (Canton, NC) **10691**
† Enterprise News (Pixley, CA)
† Enterprise Sun (Marlborough, MA)
Enterprise, The (Fallbrook, CA) **10534**
Enterprise, The (Plainfield, IL) **10588**
Enterprise, The (Ponchatoula, LA) **10617**
Enterprise, The (Brockton, MA) **10457**
Enterprise, The (Falmouth, MA) **10625**
Enterprise, The (Lexington Park, MD) **10622**
Enterprise, The (Mason, MI) **10635**
Enterprise, The (Williamston, NC) **10696**
Enterprise, The (Hastings-on-Hudson, NY) **10679**
Enterprise, The (Stuart, VA) **10756**
Enterprise, The (Lynnwood, WA) **10758**
Enumclaw Courier-Herald (Enumclaw, WA) **10757**
Ephrata Review (Ephrata, PA) **10717**
† Erie County Reporter (Huron, OH)
Erie Daily Times/Sunday Times News (Erie, PA) **10493**
Erie Morning News (Erie, PA) **10493**
Erskine Echo, The (Erskine, MN) **10641**
Erwin Record (Erwin, TN) **10732**
Escambia Sun Press (Pensacola, FL) **10560**
Escondido News-Reporter (Escondido, CA) **10534**
Essex Independent, The (Essex, IA) **10601**
Estancia Valley Citizen (Estancia, NM) **10672**
Estes Park Trail-Gazette (Estes Park, CO) **10548**
Estherville Daily News (Estherville, IA) **10447**
Estill County Tribune, The (Irvine, KY) **10612**
Euclid Sun Journal (Beachwood, OH) **10698**
Eufaula Tribune (Eufaula, AL) **10519**
Eugene Weekly (Eugene, OR) **10713**
Eunice News (Eunice, LA) **10616**
Eureka Herald (Eureka, KS) **10606**
Eureka Sentinel (Tonopah, NV) **10662**
Eureka Springs Times-Echo (Berryville, AR) **10527**
Eustis Lake Region News (Mt. Dora, FL) **10559**
Evanston Review (Evanston, IL) **10579**
Evansville Courier (Evansville, IN) **10443**

Evansville Press (Evansville, IN) **10443**
Evart Review, The (Evart, MI) **10632**
Evening-Observer (Dunkirk, NY) **10475**
† Evening Express (Portland, ME)
Evening Leader, The (St. Marys, OH) **10487**
Evening News (Benton, IL) **10438**
† Evening Sentinel (Ansonia, CT)
Evening Star (Auburn, IN) **10442**
Evening Star Plus, The (Auburn, IN) **10591**
Evening Sun (Hanover, PA) **10494**
Evening Sun, The (Norwich, NY) **10476**
Evening Telegram (Herkimer, NY) **10475**
Evening Times (West Memphis, AR) **10421**
Evening Times (Sayre, PA) **10496**
Evening Times, The (Little Falls, NY) **10475**
Evening World (Bloomfield, IN) **10442**
Evergreen Courant, The (Evergreen, AL) **10519**
Evergreen Park Courier (Midlothian, IL) **10585**
Evergreen Shopping Guide (Spooner, WI) **10773**
Everman Times (Everman, TX) **10739**
Everybody's News (Cincinnati, OH) **10700**
Excelsior/Shorewood/Chanhassen Sun-Sailor (Minnetonka, MN) **10644**
Exchange, The (Houston, TX) **10742**
Exeter News-Letter (Stratham, NH) **10664**
Exeter Sun, The (Exeter, CA) **10534**
Exponent, The (Brooklyn, MI) **10630**
Exponent, The (Greenbush, MN) **10642**
Express (Lock Haven, PA) **10495**
Express-Times, The (Easton, PA) **10493**
Extra Merchandiser (St. Marys, OH) **10707**

F

Fairbanks Daily News-Miner (Fairbanks, AK) **10417**
Fairborn Daily Herald (Fairborn, OH) **10484**
Fairbury Journal-News, The (Fairbury, NE) **10661**
† Fairchild Strikehawk (Spokane, WA)
Fairfax Connection (McLean, VA) **10754**
Fairfax Journal (Fairfax, VA) **10509**
Fairfax Station Times (Reston, VA) **10755**
Fairfax Times (Reston, VA) **10755**
Fairfield-Penfield Community News (Rochester, NY) **10685**
Fairfield Chronicle, The (West Caldwell, NJ) **10671**
Fairfield Citizen News (Fairfield, CT) **10552**
Fairfield County Weekly (Stamford, CT) **10554**
Fairfield Daily Ledger (Fairfield, IA) **10447**
Fairfield Echo (Fairfield, OH) **10703**
Fairfield Wayne County Press (Fairfield, IL) **10579**

† Fair Haven Register (Red Creek, NY)
Fairhope Courier, The (Fairhope, AL) **10519**
Fairmont Photo Press (Fairmont, MN) **10641**
Fairmont Sentinel (Fairmont, MN) **10463**
† Fairport-Perinton Herald-Mail (Webster, NY)
Fairview Heights Journal (Belleville, IL) **10573**
Fairview Heights Tribune (Mascoutah, IL) **10584**
Fairview Republican (Fairview, OK) **10710**
Falfurrias Facts (Falfurrias, TX) **10740**
† Fallon Eagle Standard (Fallon, NV)
Falls Church News-Press (Falls Church, VA) **10752**
Falls City Journal (Falls City, NE) **10661**
Faribault County Register (Blue Earth, MN) **10640**
Faribault Daily News (Faribault, MN) **10463**
Farina News, The (Farina, IL) **10579**
Farmer & Miner (Frederick, CO) **10549**
Farmer's Weekly Review (Joliet, IL) **10583**
Farmer City Journal (Farmer City, IL) **10579**
Farmers' Advance (Camden, MI) **10631**
† Farmers Branch Times (Carrollton, TX)
Farmers Independent (Bagley, MN) **10639**
Farmingdale Observer (Mineola, NY) **10682**
Farmington Observer (Farmington, MI) **10632**
† Farmington Valley Herald (Simsbury, CT)
Farmland News (Archbold, OH) **10698**
Farm Monthly (Atlantic, IA) **10599**
Farmville Herald, The (Farmville, VA) **10752**
Farmweek (Knightstown, IN) **10595**
Fauquier Citizen (Warrenton, VA) **10756**
Fauquier Times-Democrat (Warrenton, VA) **10756**
Fayette Advertiser, The (Fayette, MO) **10653**
Fayette County News (Fayetteville, GA) **10565**
Fayette County Record, The (La Grange, TX) **10743**
Fayette County Review (Somerville, TN) **10735**
Fayette County Union (West Union, IA) **10605**
Fayette Falcon, The (Somerville, TN) **10735**
Fayette Neighbor, The (Fayetteville, GA) **10565**
Fayette Review, The (Fayette, OH) **10703**
† Fayette Sun (Fayetteville, GA)
Fayette Tribune (Oak Hill, WV) **10762**
Fayetteville Observer-Times (Fayetteville, NC) **10479**
Federal Way News (Federal Way, WA) **10758**
Fennimore Times (Fennimore, WI) **10767**
Ferdinand News, The (Ferdinand, IN) **10593**
Fernley Leader-Dayton Courier (Yerington, NV) **10662**
Fillmore Herald (Fillmore, CA) **10534**
Fincastle Herald, The (Fincastle, VA) **10752**
Finder, The (Mandan, ND) **10697**
Finger Lakes Times, The (Geneva, NY) **10475**
Firebaugh/Mendota Journal (Kerman, CA) **10535**
Fire Island Tide (Sayville, NY) **10685**
Fisher Reporter (Fisher, IL) **10579**
Fishers Sun-Herald (Fishers, IN) **10593**
Fishkill Standard (Mahopac, NY) **10681**
Fishtown Star (Philadelphia, PA) **10722**
Fitchburg Star (Verona, WI) **10774**
Five Cities Times-Press-Recorder (Arroyo Grande, CA) **10530**
Five County/Buyer's Guide (Ripon, WI) **10773**
Flanagan Home Times (Pontiac, IL) **10588**
Flatbush Life (Brooklyn, NY) **10674**
† Flat River Lead Belt News (Flat River, MO)
Flint Journal (Flint, MI) **10460**
Florala News, The (Florala, AL) **10519**
Floral Park Bulletin (Floral Park, NY) **10677**
Florence Citizen (Florence, CO) **10548**
Florence Mining News (Florence, WI) **10767**
Florence Morning News (Florence, SC) **10498**
Florence Reminder & Blade-Tribune (Florence, AZ) **10525**
Floresville Chronicle-Journal (Floresville, TX) **10740**
Florham Park Eagle (Madison, NJ) **10667**
Florida Keys Keynoter (Marathon, FL) **10558**
Florida Times-Union (Jacksonville, FL) **10432**
Florida Today (Melbourne, FL) **10432**
Floridian, The (Marianna, FL) **10558**
Florissant Valley Reporter (Florissant, MO) **10653**
Floyd County Hesperian-Beacon (Floydada, TX) **10740**
Floyd County Times (Prestonsburg, KY) **10613**
Floyd Press (Floyd, VA) **10753**
Flushing Observer (Flint, MI) **10632**
Flushing Times, The (Bayside, NY) **10673**
Focus News (Roseville, MN) **10646**
Folsom Telegraph (Folsom, CA) **10534**
Fontana Herald News (Fontana, CA) **10534**
Foothills Sentinel (Cave Creek, AZ) **10524**
Ford County Press (Melvin, IL) **10585**
Forest City Summit (Forest City, IA) **10601**
Forest Hill News (Everman, TX) **10740**
▼Forest Hills/Rego Park Times (Maspeth, NY) **10681**
Forest Hills Journal (Loveland, OH) **10704**
Forest Lake Press (St. Paul, MN) **10647**
Forest Leaves (Oak Park, IL) **10587**
Forest Press (Tionesta, PA) **10724**
Forest Republican, The (Crandon, WI) **10766**
Forest Times-Tribune (De Forest, WI) **10766**
Forrest City Times-Herald (Forrest City, AR) **10419**
Forreston Journal (Forreston, IL) **10579**
Forsyth County News (Cumming, GA) **10564**

Fort Bend Mirror (Rosenberg, TX) **10746**
Fort Bend Sun (Sugar Land, TX) **10747**
Fort Bragg Advocate-News (Fort Bragg, CA) **10534**
Fort Collins Coloradoan (Fort Collins, CO) **10428**
Fort Dodge Messenger (Fort Dodge, IA) **10447**
Fort Fairfield Review (Fort Fairfield, ME) **10619**
Fort Lupton Press (Fort Lupton, CO) **10548**
Fort Madison Daily Democrat (Fort Madison, IA) **10448**
Fort Meade Leader, The (Fort Meade, FL) **10557**
Fort Mill Times (Fort Mill, SC) **10727**
Fort Morgan Times, The (Fort Morgan, CO) **10428**
Fort Myers Beach Observer (Fort Myers Beach, FL) **10557**
† Fort Myers Observer (Fort Myers, FL)
Fort Riley Post (Junction City, KS) **10607**
Fort San Antonio News Leader (San Antonio, TX) **10746**
Fort Scott Tribune, The (Fort Scott, KS) **10450**
Fort Stockton Pioneer (Fort Stockton, TX) **10740**
Fort Wayne News-Sentinel (Fort Wayne, IN) **10443**
Fort Worth Star-Telegram (Fort Worth, TX) **10504**
Forum of Queens (Ozone Park, NY) **10684**
Forum, The (Fargo, ND) **10482**
Fosston Thirteen Towns (Fosston, MN) **10642**
Foster's Daily Democrat (Dover, NH) **10471**
Foster City Progress (Burlingame, CA) **10531**
Foto News (Merrill, WI) **10769**
Fountain County Neighbor (Attica, IN) **10591**
Fountain Valley News & El Paso County News (Fountain, CO) **10548**
Four Oaks-Benson News in Review (Benson, NC) **10691**
Fowler Tribune, The (Fowler, CO) **10548**
Fowlerville Review Shopping Guide (Howell, MI) **10634**
Foxboro Reporter, The (Foxboro, MA) **10625**
Fox Lake Press (Grayslake, IL) **10580**
Fox Lake Representative (Fox Lake, WI) **10767**
Fox Point, Bayside, River Hills Herald (New Berlin, WI) **10770**
Fox Valley Shopping News, The (Yorkville, IL) **10591**
Fox Valley Villages (Plainfield, IL) **10588**
Foxxy Shopper (Sparta, WI) **10773**
Frankenmuth News (Frankenmuth, MI) **10632**
Frankfort Times (Frankfort, IN) **10443**

Franklin-Hales Corner Hub (New Berlin, WI) **10770**
Franklin Banner-Tribune (Franklin, LA) **10454**
Franklin Challenger (Greenwood, IN) **10594**
Franklin Chronicle (Franklin, OH) **10703**
Franklin County Citizen (Lavonia, GA) **10566**
Franklin County Graphic (Connell, WA) **10757**
Franklin County Plus (Russellville, AL) **10522**
Franklin County Times (Russellville, AL) **10522**
Franklin Favorite (Franklin, KY) **10611**
Franklin Journal & Farmington Chronicle (Farmington, ME) **10619**
Franklin News-Post (Rocky Mount, VA) **10755**
Franklin News-Record (Princeton, NJ) **10669**
Franklin Park Herald-Journal, The (Oak Park, IL) **10587**
Franklin Park Star-Sentinel (Melrose Park, IL) **10585**
Franklin Pendleton Times (Franklin, WV) **10761**
Franklin Press (Franklin, NC) **10692**
Franklin Square Bulletin (Floral Park, NY) **10677**
Franklin Sun, The (Winnsboro, LA) **10618**
Franklin Times (Louisburg, NC) **10693**
Franklin Township Sentinel (Franklinville, NJ) **10666**
Frederick Leader (Frederick, OK) **10710**
Frederick Post, The (Frederick, MD) **10456**
Fredericksburg Free Lance-Star (Fredericksburg, VA) **10509**
Fredericksburg Standard/Radio Post (Fredericksburg, TX) **10740**
† Freeborn County Register (Albert Lea, MN)
Free Lance (Hollister, CA) **10422**
Freeman, The (Waukesha, WI) **10515**
Freemont Gazette (Fremont, IA) **10601**
Free News, The (Farmville, VA) **10752**
Freeport Advertiser Shopping News (Freeport, IL) **10579**
Freeport Baldwin Leader, The (Freeport, NY) **10677**
Freeport Journal-Standard (Freeport, IL) **10439**
Free Press (Mankato, MN) **10463**
Free Press-Courier (Westfield, PA) **10725**
Free Press Standard (Carrollton, OH) **10700**
Free Press, The (Tampa, FL) **10561**
Free Press, The (Canton, OH) **10699**
Free Press, The (Braddock, PA) **10716**
Free Time (Wildwood, NJ) **10671**
Free Times, The (Cleveland, OH) **10700**
Free Trader (Massena, NY) **10681**
Fremont County Herald-Chronicle (St. Anthony, ID) **10571**
Fremont Tribune (Fremont, NE) **10469**

Fresh Meadows Times, The
 (Flushing, NY) **10677**
Fresno Bee, The (Fresno, CA) **10422**
Fridley Focus (Roseville, MN) **10646**
Friendswood & Pearland Reporter News
 (Pearland, TX) **10745**
Frontier & Holt County Independent
 (O'Neill, NE) **10661**
Frontiersman, The (Wasilla, AK) **10523**
Front Page (Lackawanna, NY) **10680**
Frostproof News (Frostproof, FL) **10557**
Fruita Times, The (Fruita, CO) **10549**
Fulton County Expositor (Wauseon, OH) **10708**
Fulton Democrat (Lewistown, IL) **10583**
Fulton Journal (Fulton, IL) **10579**
Fulton Leader (Fulton, KY) **10611**
Fulton Patriot (Fulton, NY) **10678**
Fulton Shopper (Fulton, KY) **10611**
Fulton Sun Gazette, The (Fulton, MO) **10466**

G

Gadsden County Times (Quincy, FL) **10560**
Gadsden Times (Gadsden, AL) **10416**
Gaffney Ledger, The (Gaffney, SC) **10727**
Gainesville Buyers Guide (Orange
 Park, FL) **10559**
Gainesville Daily Register
 (Gainesville, TX) **10504**
Gainesville Sun, The (Gainesville, FL) **10432**
Gaithersburg Gazette
 (Gaithersburg, MD) **10621**
Galax Gazette, The (Galax, VA) **10753**
Galena Gazette (Galena, IL) **10579**
Galesburg Post, The (Galesburg, IL) **10579**
Galesville Republican (Galesville, WI) **10767**
Galion Inquirer (Galion, OH) **10484**
Gallipolis Daily Tribune (Gallipolis, OH) **10484**
Galt Herald (Galt, CA) **10534**
Galva News (Galva, IL) **10579**
Galveston County Daily News, The
 (Galveston, TX) **10504**
Gardena Valley News (Gardena, CA) **10534**
Garden City Observer (Livonia, MI) **10635**
Garden City Telegram (Garden
 City, KS) **10450**
Garden Island Extra (Lihue, HI) **10568**
Garden of the Gods Journal (Manitou
 Springs, CO) **10550**
Gardner News (Gardner, MA) **10457**
Gardner South Wilmington Post
 (Wilmington, IL) **10591**
Garfield Maple-Sun (Cleveland, OH) **10700**
Garland News (Garland, TX) **10740**
Garner News (Garner, NC) **10692**
† Garnett Review (Garnett, KS)

Gary Crusader (Gary, IN) **10594**
Gary Info (Gary, IN) **10594**
Gasconade County Republican
 (Owensville, MO) **10655**
Gaston Gazette (Gastonia, NC) **10479**
Gates-Chili News (Rochester, NY) **10685**
Gates County Index (Gatesville, NC) **10692**
Gatesville Messenger (Gatesville, TX) **10740**
Gateway Express, The (Clinton, IA) **10599**
Gateway News, The (Streetsboro, OH) **10707**
Gateway, The (Floral Park, NY) **10677**
Gaylord Herald Times (Gaylord, MI) **10632**
Gazette-Advertiser (Rhinebeck, NY) **10685**
Gazette-Democrat (Anna, IL) **10571**
Gazette Shopper (Cleveland, OH) **10700**
Gazette, The (Colorado Springs, CO) **10428**
Gazette, The (Mt. Holly, NJ) **10668**
Gazette, The (Port Jervis, NY) **10685**
Gazette, The (Jefferson, OH) **10704**
† Geauga Times-Leader (Chardon, OH)
Geist Gazette (Fishers, IN) **10593**
Gem State Miner (Newport, WA) **10758**
Geneseo Republic (Geneseo, IL) **10579**
Geneseo Shopper (Geneseo, IL) **10579**
Geneva County Reaper (Geneva, AL) **10519**
Geneva Republican (Geneva, IL) **10579**
Genoa-Kingston-Kirkland News
 (Sycamore, IL) **10589**
Gentry Courier-Journal (Gentry, AR) **10527**
George County Times (Lucedale, MS) **10650**
Georgetown Current, The
 (Washington, DC) **10554**
Georgetowner, The (Washington, DC) **10555**
Georgetown News Graphic
 (Georgetown, KY) **10611**
Georgetown Record (Ipswich, MA) **10625**
Georgetown Times, The
 (Georgetown, SC) **10727**
Georgia Times-Union (Brunswick, GA) **10434**
Georgis's Coastal Illustrated (St. Simons
 Island, GA) **10567**
Gering Courier (Gering, NE) **10661**
Germantown Banner-Press (New
 Berlin, WI) **10770**
Germantown Courier (Philadelphia, PA) **10722**
Germantown News, The
 (Germantown, TN) **10732**
Germantown Paper (Philadelphia, PA) **10722**
Gettysburg Times (Gettysburg, PA) **10493**
Gibson City Courier (Gibson City, IL) **10580**
Giddings Times & News (Giddings, TX) **10740**
Gilbert Independent (Scottsdale, AZ) **10526**
Gilbert Tribune (Chandler, AZ) **10418**
Gillespie Area News (Gillespie, IL) **10580**
Gilman Star (Gilman, IL) **10580**
Gilmer Mirror (Gilmer, TX) **10740**

Girard Home News (Philadelphia, PA) **10722**
† Girard News (Niles, OH)
Girard Press (Girard, KS) **10606**
Giveaway, The (Scottsburg, IN) **10597**
Glades County Democrat
  (Clewiston, FL) **10556**
Gladewater Mirror (Gladewater, TX) **10741**
† Gladstone Delta Reporter (Escanaba, MI)
Gladwin County Record & Beaverton Clarion
  (Gladwin, MI) **10633**
Glasford Gazette, The (Glasford, IL) **10580**
Glasgow Courier, The (Glasgow, MT) **10659**
Glasgow Daily Times (Glasgow, KY) **10452**
Glasgow Republican (Glasgow, KY) **10611**
Glastonbury Citizen (Glastonbury, CT) **10552**
Glencoe Enterprise (Glencoe, MN) **10642**
Glencoe News (Glenview, IL) **10580**
Glen Cove Record Pilot (Mineola, NY) **10682**
Glendale Heights Press (Elmhurst, IL) **10578**
Glendale Herald (New Berlin, WI) **10770**
Glendale News-Press (Glendale, CA) **10422**
Glendale Register (Maspeth, NY) **10681**
Glendale Star, The (Glendale, AZ) **10525**
Glendive Ranger-Review (Glendive, MT) **10659**
Glendora Press (West Covina, CA) **10546**
Glen Ellyn News (Glen Ellyn, IL) **10580**
Glen Ellyn Press (Bloomingdale, IL) **10573**
Glennville Sentinel (Glennville, GA) **10565**
Glen Oaks Ledger, The (Bayside, NY) **10673**
Glen Ridge Paper, The (Bloomfield, NJ) **10664**
Glen Rock Gazette (Franklin Lakes, NJ) **10666**
Glen Rose Reporter (Glen Rose, TX) **10741**
Glenside News (Jenkintown, PA) **10718**
Glenview Announcements (Glenview, IL) **10580**
Glenville Democrat, The (Glenville, WV) **10761**
Glenville Pathfinder (Glenville, WV) **10761**
Glenwood Herald (Glenwood, AR) **10527**
Glenwood Opinion-Tribune
  (Glenwood, IA) **10601**
Glenwood Post (Glenwood Springs, CO) **10428**
Glidden Enterprise (Glidden, WI) **10767**
Globe-Gazette (Mason City, IA) **10448**
Globe, The (Jenkintown, PA) **10718**
Gloucester-Mathews Gazette Journal
  (Gloucester, VA) **10753**
Gloucester City News (Gloucester
  City, NJ) **10666**
Gloucester County Times
  (Woodbury, NJ) **10473**
Gloucester Daily Times
  (Gloucester, MA) **10457**
Glynco Observer (Brunswick, GA) **10563**
Gold Beach Curry County Reporter (Gold
  Beach, OR) **10713**
Goldendale Sentinel (Goldendale, WA) **10758**
Golden Prairie News (Assumption, IL) **10572**
Golden Times (Rochester, NY) **10685**
Golden Transcript (Golden, CO) **10549**
Golden Triangle Shopper
  (Columbus, MS) **10649**
Gold Leaf Farmer, The (Wendell, NC) **10695**
Gold River News (Sacramento, CA) **10542**
Goldsboro News-Argus (Goldsboro, NC) **10479**
† Goleta Review (Goleta, CA)
† Goleta Sun (Santa Barbara, CA)
Golfmill Journal (Des Plaines, IL) **10577**
Gonzales Inquirer (Gonzales, TX) **10741**
Gonzales Tribune (Soledad, CA) **10545**
Gonzales Weekly (Gonzales, LA) **10616**
Goochland Gazette (Goochland, VA) **10753**
Gooding County Leader (Gooding, ID) **10569**
Goodland Daily News (Goodland, KS) **10450**
Good News (Monona, WI) **10770**
Good News Shopper (Coal City, IL) **10576**
Good Times (Santa Cruz, CA) **10544**
† Good Times News (Fayette, MO)
Goose Creek Gazette (Ladson, SC) **10727**
Gorman Progress, The (Gorman, TX) **10741**
Goshen News, The (Goshen, IN) **10443**
Gouverneur Tribune Press
  (Gouverneur, NY) **10678**
Gowanda Pennysaver News
  (Gowanda, NY) **10678**
† Grace Citizen (Preston, ID)
Graceville News (Graceville, FL) **10557**
Grainger County News (Rutledge, TN) **10734**
Grand Blanc News, The (Flint, MI) **10632**
Grand Forks Herald (Grand Forks, ND) **10482**
Grand Gazette (St. Paul, MN) **10647**
Grand Haven Tribune (Grand
  Haven, MI) **10460**
Grand Island Independent (Grand
  Island, NE) **10469**
Grand Island Pennysaver (Grand
  Island, NY) **10678**
Grand Ledge Independent, The (Grand
  Ledge, MI) **10633**
Grand Prairie News (Arlington, TX) **10736**
Grand Rapids/Herald-Review (Grand
  Rapids, MN) **10642**
Grand Rapids Advance (Jenison, MI) **10634**
Grand Rapids Press, The (Grand
  Rapids, MI) **10460**
Grand Saline Sun (Grand Saline, TX) **10741**
Grand Valley Advance (Jenison, MI) **10634**
Grandview Herald (Grandview, WA) **10758**
Granite City Press Journal (Granite
  City, IL) **10580**
Granite Falls/Clerkfield Advocate Tribune
  (Granite Falls, MN) **10642**
Granite State News (Wolfeboro, NH) **10664**

Grant County Herald Independent (Lancaster, WI) **10768**
Grant County Journal (Ephrata, WA) **10757**
Grant County News (Williamstown, KY) **10615**
Grant County News (Elgin, ND) **10696**
Grant County Press (Petersburg, WV) **10762**
Grant County Review (Milbank, SD) **10730**
Grants Pass Daily Courier (Grants Pass, OR) **10491**
Granville Sentinel (Granville, NY) **10678**
Granville Sentinel, The (Granville, OH) **10703**
Gratiot County Herald (Ithaca, MI) **10634**
Gravette News Herald (Gravette, AR) **10527**
Grayslake Times (Grayslake, IL) **10580**
Grayson Advertiser (Leitchfield, KY) **10612**
Grayson County News-Gazette (Leitchfield, KY) **10612**
Grayson County Shopper (Denison, TX) **10739**
Grayson Journal-Enquirer (Grayson, KY) **10611**
Great Bend Tribune (Great Bend, KS) **10450**
Greater Baton Rouge Business Report (Baton Rouge, LA) **10615**
Great Falls Times (Reston, VA) **10755**
Great Falls Tribune (Great Falls, MT) **10468**
Great Lakes Pilot, The (Grand Marais, MI) **10633**
Great Lander Bush Mailer (Anchorage, AK) **10522**
Great Neck News (Great Neck, NY) **10678**
Great Neck Record (Mineola, NY) **10682**
Greece Post, The (Fishers, NY) **10677**
Greeley Tribune (Greeley, CO) **10428**
Green Bay News-Chronicle (Green Bay, WI) **10514**
Green Bay Press-Gazette (Green Bay, WI) **10514**
Greenbelt News Review (Greenbelt, MD) **10622**
Greenbrier Valley Ranger (Lewisburg, WV) **10762**
Greendale Village Life (New Berlin, WI) **10770**
Greene County Independent (Eutaw, AL) **10519**
Greene County Record (Stanardsville, VA) **10755**
Greene Prairie Press (White Hall, IL) **10590**
Greene Recorder, The (Greene, IA) **10601**
Greeneville Sun (Greeneville, TN) **10500**
Greenfield News (Greenfield, CA) **10534**
Greenfield Observer (New Berlin, WI) **10770**
Green Forest Tribune (Berryville, AR) **10527**
Green Hills Weekly (Trenton, MO) **10658**
Greenhorn Valley News (Colorado City, CO) **10547**

Green Lake County Reporter (Berlin, WI) **10764**
Greenpoint Gazette/Advertiser (Brooklyn, NY) **10674**
† Green River Republican (Morgantown, KY)
Greensboro Watchman, The (Greensboro, AL) **10519**
Greensburg Daily News (Greensburg, IN) **10443**
Green Sheet, The (San Bernardino, CA) **10542**
Green Tab (Moundsville, WV) **10762**
Greenup County News-Times (Greenup, KY) **10611**
Greenup Press (Greenup, IL) **10581**
Green Valley News & Sun (Green Valley, AZ) **10525**
Greenville Advocate, The (Greenville, AL) **10519**
Greenville Advocate, The (Greenville, IL) **10581**
Greenville Daily Advocate (Greenville, OH) **10484**
Greenville Daily Reflector (Greenville, NC) **10479**
Greenville Herald Banner (Greenville, TX) **10504**
Greenville Local (Ravena, NY) **10685**
Greenville News (Greenville, SC) **10499**
† Greenville Piedmont (Greenville, SC)
Greenville Record-Argus (Greenville, PA) **10494**
Greenwich Journal & Salem Press (Greenwich, NY) **10678**
† Greenwich News (Greenwich, CT)
▼Greenwich Post (Greenwich, CT) **10552**
Greenwich Time (Greenwich, CT) **10430**
Greenwood & Southside Challenger (Greenwood, IN) **10594**
Greenwood Commonwealth (Greenwood, MS) **10464**
Greenwood Democrat (Greenwood, AR) **10527**
Greenwood Gazette, The (Fishers, IN) **10593**
Greenwood Lake & West Milford News (Greenwood Lake, NY) **10678**
Greer Citizen, The (Greer, SC) **10727**
Gresham Outlook (Gresham, OR) **10713**
Gridley Herald, The (Gridley, CA) **10534**
Griffin Daily News (Griffin, GA) **10435**
Griffith Guide (Maryville, IN) **10595**
Grinnell Herald-Register (Grinnell, IA) **10601**
Grizzly, The (Big Bear Lake, CA) **10531**
Groesbeck Journal (Groesbeck, TX) **10741**
Grosse Pointe News (Grosse Pointe Farms, MI) **10633**
Groton Landmark (Ayer, MA) **10623**
Grove City Record (Columbus, OH) **10701**

▼Grove Daily News (Grove, OK) **10489**
Grove Sun (Grove, OK) **10710**
Grundy County Herald (Tracy City, TN) **10735**
Grundy Register (Grundy Center, IA) **10601**
Grunion Gazette (Long Beach, CA) **10537**
Grygla Eagle (Grygla, MN) **10642**
Guernsey Gazette/Lingle Guide (Guernsey, WY) **10776**
Guilford American (Dover-Foxcroft, ME) **10619**
Gulf Coast Tribune, The (West Columbia, TX) **10747**
Gunnison Country Times (Gunnison, CO) **10428**
Gurnee Press (Grayslake, IL) **10580**
Guthrie News Leader (Guthrie, OK) **10489**
Guttenberg Press (Guttenberg, IA) **10601**
Guymon Daily Herald (Guymon, OK) **10489**
† Gwinnett Daily News (Lawrenceville, GA)
Gwinnett Daily Post (Lawrenceville, GA) **10435**

H

† Haddon Gazette (Cherry Hill, NJ)
Hagerstown Exponent, The (Hagerstown, IN) **10594**
† Haines City Herald (Haines City, FL)
Half Moon Bay Review (Half Moon Bay, CA) **10534**
Halifax Reporter (Plymouth, MA) **10627**
Hallettsville Tribune-Herald (Hallettsville, TX) **10741**
Halls Graphic (Ripley, TN) **10734**
Hamburg Item (Hamburg, PA) **10718**
Hamden Chronicle, The (Milford, CT) **10553**
Hamilton-Wenham Chronicle (Ipswich, MA) **10625**
† Hamilton County News (Elizabethtown, NY)
Hamilton County News (Speculator, NY) **10687**
Hamilton Herald-News (Hamilton, TX) **10741**
Hamilton Mid-York Weekly (Hamilton, NY) **10679**
▼Hamilton Tribune (Hamilton, NY) **10679**
Hamlin-Clarkson Herald (Spencerport, NY) **10687**
Hammond Daily Star (Hammond, LA) **10454**
Hammonton News (Hammonton, NJ) **10666**
Hampshire Register News (Sycamore, IL) **10590**
Hampshire Review (Romney, WV) **10763**
Hampton Chronicle & Times (Hampton, IA) **10601**
Hampton Union (Stratham, NH) **10664**
Hanahan News (North Charleston, SC) **10728**
Hanceville Herald (Hanceville, AL) **10520**
Hancock Clarion (Hawesville, KY) **10611**

Hancock County Journal-Pilot (Carthage, IL) **10574**
Hancock County Quill (La Harpe, IL) **10583**
Hancock News (Hancock, MD) **10622**
Hanford Sentinel, The (Hanford, CA) **10422**
Hannibal Courier-Post (Hannibal, MO) **10466**
Hanover Eagle & Regional News (Madison, NJ) **10667**
Hanover Mariner (Marshfield, MA) **10625**
† Hanover Park Township Times (Carol Stream, IL)
Hansford County Reporter-Statesman (Spearman, TX) **10747**
Haralson Gateway-Beacon, The (Bremen, GA) **10563**
Harbor Beach Times (Harbor Beach, MI) **10633**
Harbor Sound (Brunswick, GA) **10563**
Harborwatch (Brooklyn, NY) **10674**
Hardin Calhoun Herald (Hardin, IL) **10581**
Hardin County Independent (Elizabethtown, IL) **10578**
Hardin County Index (Eldora, IA) **10600**
Hardwick Gazette (Hardwick, VT) **10750**
Harlan County Journal (Alma, NE) **10659**
Harlan Daily Enterprise (Harlan, KY) **10452**
Harlan News Advertiser (Harlan, IA) **10601**
Harlan Tribune (Harlan, IA) **10601**
Harlem-Foster-Norwood Park-Edison Park Times (Lincolnwood, IL) **10583**
Harlem-Irving Times (Lincolnwood, IL) **10583**
Harlem Valley Times (Amenia, NY) **10673**
† Harper Woods Herald (Birmingham, MI)
Harrah News, The (Harrah, OK) **10710**
Harriman Record (Kingston, TN) **10732**
Harrington Journal, The (Harrington, DE) **10554**
Harrisburg Daily Register (Harrisburg, IL) **10439**
Harrison County Advisor (Bethany, MO) **10652**
Harrison Daily Times (Harrison, AR) **10419**
Harrison Independent (Yonkers, NY) **10690**
Harrison News-Herald, The (Cadiz, OH) **10699**
Harrisonville Cass County Democrat Missourian (Harrisonville, MO) **10653**
Harrodsburg Herald (Harrodsburg, KY) **10611**
Hart County News-Herald (Munfordville, KY) **10613**
Harte-Hanks Pennysaver (Brea, CA) **10531**
Hartford Advocate (Hartford, CT) **10552**
Hartford Area News (Canistota, SD) **10729**
Hartford Courant (Hartford, CT) **10430**
Hartland Herald Shopping Guide (Howell, MI) **10634**
Hartselle Enquirer (Hartselle, AL) **10520**

Hartsville Messenger, The (Hartsville, SC) **10727**
Hartsville Vidette, The (Hartsville, TN) **10732**
Hartville News (Hartville, OH) **10703**
Hartwell Sun, The (Hartwell, GA) **10565**
Harvard Spirit (Ayer, MA) **10623**
Harwich Oracle (Orleans, MA) **10627**
† Harwood Heights News (Park Ridge, IL)
Haskell Free Press (Haskell, TX) **10741**
Hastings Banner (Hastings, MI) **10633**
Hastings Daily Tribune (Hastings, NE) **10469**
Hastings Reminder (Hastings, MI) **10633**
Hastings Star Gazette (Hastings, MN) **10642**
Hattiesburg American (Hattiesburg, MS) **10464**
Havana Mason County Democrat (Havana, IL) **10581**
Haverford Press (Newtown Square, PA) **10721**
Haverhill Gazette (Haverhill, MA) **10457**
Havre Daily News (Havre, MT) **10469**
Hawaii Tribune-Herald (Hilo, HI) **10436**
Hawk Eye, The (Burlington, IA) **10447**
Hawley Herald (Hawley, MN) **10642**
Hawthorne Press (Hawthorne, NJ) **10666**
Haxtun-Fleming Herald, The (Haxtun, CO) **10549**
Hayden Valley Press (Craig, CO) **10548**
Hays Daily News (Hays, KS) **10450**
Hazard Herald-Voice (Hazard, KY) **10611**
Hazen Star (Hazen, ND) **10697**
Hazleton Standard Speaker (Hazleton, PA) **10494**
Headland Observer (Headland, AL) **10520**
Headlight-Herald (Tillamook, OR) **10715**
Healdsburg Tribune (Healdsburg, CA) **10535**
Heights Herald (Fishers, IN) **10593**
Heights Times-Herald (Dearborn, MI) **10632**
Helena West Helena Daily World (Helena, AR) **10420**
Hemet News, The (San Jacinto, CA) **10425**
Hempstead Beacon (Hicksville, NY) **10679**
Henderson County Quill (Stronghurst, IL) **10589**
Henderson Daily News (Henderson, TX) **10504**
Henderson Gleaner (Henderson, KY) **10452**
† Hendersonville Free Press (Hendersonville, TN)
Hendersonville Star News (Hendersonville, TN) **10732**
Hendersonville Times-News (Hendersonville, NC) **10479**
Hendricks County Flyer (Plainfield, IN) **10597**
† Hendricks County Guide Gazette (Plainfield, IN)
† Henrico Gazette (Richmond, VA)
Henrietta Post (Fishers, NY) **10677**

Henry County Local (New Castle, KY) **10613**
Henryetta Daily Free-Lance (Henryetta, OK) **10489**
Henry Herald, The (McDonough, GA) **10566**
Henry News Republican (Henry, IL) **10581**
Herald & News (Klamath Falls, OR) **10492**
Herald & Review (Decatur, IL) **10439**
Herald & Tribune (Jonesborough, TN) **10732**
Herald-Advocate (Wauchula, FL) **10561**
Herald-Chronicle, The (Winchester, TN) **10735**
Herald-Citizen (Cookeville, TN) **10500**
Herald-Democrat (Leadville, CO) **10549**
Herald-Democrat (Denison, TX) **10503**
Herald-Gazette, The (Barnesville, GA) **10563**
Herald-Independent, The (Winnsboro, SC) **10729**
Herald-Journal (Syracuse, NY) **10477**
Herald-Journal (Spartanburg, SC) **10499**
Herald-Journal, The (Monticello, IN) **10445**
Herald-Leader (Siloam Springs, AR) **10529**
Herald-Leader, The (Fitzgerald, GA) **10565**
Herald-Mail, The (Hagerstown, MD) **10456**
Herald-News (Wolf Point, MT) **10659**
Herald-News (Dayton, TN) **10731**
Herald-News, The (Joliet, IL) **10440**
Herald-Palladium (St. Joseph, MI) **10462**
Herald-Press (Huntington, IN) **10444**
Herald-Press (Harvey, ND) **10697**
Herald-Progress (Ashland, VA) **10751**
Herald-Republican (Angola, IN) **10591**
Herald-Star (Steubenville, OH) **10487**
Herald-Star, The (Edinburg, IL) **10578**
Herald-Sun, The (Durham, NC) **10478**
Herald-Times (Bloomington, IN) **10442**
Herald-Times Reporter (Manitowoc, WI) **10514**
Herald-Tribune (Batesville, IN) **10592**
Herald-Tribune, The (Cartersville, GA) **10564**
Herald/Country Market, The (Bourbonnais, IL) **10573**
Herald Bulletin (Anderson, IN) **10442**
Herald Coaster (Rosenberg, TX) **10506**
Herald Enterprise (Golconda, IL) **10580**
Herald Gazette, The (Trenton, TN) **10735**
Herald Journal (Clarinda, IA) **10599**
Herald Journal, The (Logan, UT) **10507**
Herald Ledger (Eddyville, KY) **10610**
Herald News, The (Fall River, MA) **10457**
Herald News, The (Reed City, MI) **10637**
Herald of Randolph (Randolph, VT) **10750**
Herald Record (West Union, WV) **10764**
Herald Standard (Uniontown, PA) **10497**
Herald Statesman (Yonkers, NY) **10478**
Herald, The (New Britain, CT) **10430**
† Herald, The (Tarpon Springs, FL)
Herald, The (Rincon, GA) **10567**
Herald, The (Cahokia, IL) **10574**

Herald, The (Jasper, IN) **10444**
Herald, The (Truth or Consequences, NM) **10672**
Herald, The (Pittsburgh, PA) **10723**
Herald, The (Sharon, PA) **10496**
Herald, The (Rock Hill, SC) **10499**
Herald, The (Everett, WA) **10511**
Hereford Brand (Hereford, TX) **10504**
Hermann Advertiser-Courier (Hermann, MO) **10653**
Hermiston Herald (Hermiston, OR) **10713**
Hermitage Index (Hermitage, MO) **10653**
Hernando Today (Brooksville, FL) **10431**
Herndon Times (Reston, VA) **10755**
Herrin Spokesman (Herrin, IL) **10581**
Herscher Pilot (Herscher, IL) **10581**
Hershey Chronicle, The (Hershey, PA) **10718**
Hesperia Resorter (Hesperia, CA) **10535**
Hi-Riser (Deerfield Beach, FL) **10556**
Hialeah/Opa-Lacka News (Miami, FL) **10559**
Hiawatha Daily World (Hiawatha, KS) **10450**
Hiawatha Valley Shopper (Red Wing, MN) **10646**
Hibbing Daily Tribune (Hibbing, MN) **10463**
Hickory Daily Record (Hickory, NC) **10479**
Hickory Hills Citizen (Midlothian, IL) **10585**
Hickory News/Extra, The (Hickory, NC) **10692**
Hicksville Illustrated News (Mineola, NY) **10682**
Highlander (West Covina, CA) **10546**
Highland Guide (Maryville, IN) **10595**
Highland News Leader (Highland, IL) **10581**
Highland Park News (Bannockburn, IL) **10572**
Highland Park News/Herald/Journal (Los Angeles, CA) **10537**
† Highlands Press (Mulberry, FL)
Highlands Ranch Herald (Littleton, CO) **10549**
Highline News (Seatac, WA) **10759**
High Plains Journal (Dodge City, KS) **10606**
High Point Enterprise (High Point, NC) **10479**
High Springs Herald, The (High Springs, FL) **10557**
High Timber Times (Pine, CO) **10550**
Hill City Times, The (Hill City, KS) **10606**
Hilliard Northwest News (Hilliard, OH) **10703**
Hillsboro Argus (Hillsboro, OR) **10713**
Hillsboro Journal (Hillsboro, IL) **10582**
Hillsboro Sentry-Enterprise (Hillsboro, WI) **10768**
Hillsboro Star-Journal (Hillsboro, KS) **10606**
Hillsborough Beacon (Somerville, NJ) **10670**
Hillsdale Daily News (Hillsdale, MI) **10460**
Hillside Leader (Union, NJ) **10670**
Hilltop News-Press (Cincinnati, OH) **10700**
Hilmar Times (Hilmar, CA) **10535**

Hilton Head Island Packet (Hilton Head, SC) **10499**
Hingham Journal & Mariner (Marshfield, MA) **10626**
Hinsdale Doings (Hinsdale, IL) **10582**
Hinton News (Hinton, WV) **10761**
Hobart Democrat-Chief (Hobart, OK) **10710**
Hobart Gazette (Merriville, IN) **10596**
Hobbs Daily News-Sun (Hobbs, NM) **10473**
Hobbs Flare (Hobbs, NM) **10672**
Hoboken Reporter (Hoboken, NJ) **10666**
Hocking Valley Advertiser (Logan, OH) **10704**
† Hodgkins Citizen (La Grange, IL)
Hoisington Dispatch (Hoisington, KS) **10606**
Holbert Lake Station Community Shopping Guide (Merrillville, IN) **10596**
Holbrook Sun (Marshfield, MA) **10626**
Holbrook Times (Stoughton, MA) **10628**
Holbrook Tribune News & Snowflake Herald (Holbrook, AZ) **10525**
Holden Image-Progress, The (Holden, MO) **10654**
Holdenville Daily News (Holdenville, OK) **10489**
Holdrege Daily Citizen (Holdrege, NE) **10469**
Holland Sentinel (Holland, MI) **10460**
Holly Hill Observer, The (Holly Hill, SC) **10727**
† Hollywood Citizen News (Los Angeles, CA)
† Hollywood Sun (Hollywood, FL)
Holmes County Advertiser (Bonifay, FL) **10555**
Holmes County Hub (Millersburg, OH) **10705**
Holt Community News (Holt, MI) **10634**
Holton Recorder (Holton, KS) **10606**
Holtville Tribune (Holtville, CA) **10535**
Home & Store News (Ramsey, NJ) **10670**
Home News & Tribune, The (East Brunswick, NJ) **10472**
Home News, The (Marshville, NC) **10693**
Homer News (Homer, AK) **10523**
† Homestead/Florida City News (Miami, FL)
Home Times (West Palm Beach, FL) **10562**
Hometown News (Madison, WV) **10762**
Hominy News-Progress (Hominy, OK) **10710**
Hondo Anvil Herald (Hondo, TX) **10741**
Honolulu Advertiser (Honolulu, HI) **10436**
Honolulu Star-Bulletin (Honolulu, HI) **10436**
Hood County News (Granbury, TX) **10741**
Hood River News (Hood River, OR) **10713**
Hoopeston Chronicle (Hoopeston, IL) **10582**
Hoosier Express (Washington, IN) **10598**
Hope Star, The (Hope, AR) **10420**
Hopewell News (Hopewell, VA) **10509**
Hopkins Journal, The (Hopkins, MO) **10654**
Hopkins Sun-Sailor (Minnetonka, MN) **10644**
Horicon Reporter (Horicon, WI) **10768**
Hornell Evening Tribune (Hornell, NY) **10475**

Horry Independent (Conway, SC) **10727**
Houghton Lake Resorter (Houghton Lake, MI) **10634**
Houlton Pioneer Times (Houlton, ME) **10619**
Hour, The (Norwalk, CT) **10430**
Housatonic Weekend (New Milford, CT) **10553**
Houston Chronicle (Houston, TX) **10504**
Houston County Courier (Crockett, TX) **10738**
Houston Forward Times (Houston, TX) **10742**
Houston Herald & Republican (Houston, MO) **10654**
Houston Informer (Houston, TX) **10742**
† Houston Post (Houston, TX)
Houston Times-Journal (Perry, GA) **10567**
▼Howard Beach Resident (Maspeth, NY) **10681**
Howard County Times (Columbia, MD) **10621**
Howe Enterprise (Howe, TX) **10742**
Hubbard City News (Mexia, TX) **10744**
† Hubbard News (Niles, OH)
Huber Heights Courier (Dayton, OH) **10703**
Hudson-Litchfield News (Hudson, NH) **10663**
Hudson Current (Hoboken, NJ) **10666**
Hudson Herald, The (Hudson, IA) **10601**
Hudson Hub-Times (Stow, OH) **10707**
Hudson Star-Observer (Hudson, WI) **10768**
Hughes County Times (Wetumka, OK) **10712**
Hughson Chronicle (Winton, CA) **10546**
Hugo Daily News (Hugo, OK) **10489**
Humble Sun (Humble, TX) **10742**
Humboldt Beacon (Fortuna, CA) **10534**
Humboldt Independent (Humboldt, IA) **10601**
† Humboldt Republican (Humboldt, IA)
Humboldt Sun (Winnemucca, NV) **10471**
Humbolt Journal (Canistota, SD) **10729**
Humeston New Era (Humeston, IA) **10601**
Hungry Horse News (Columbia Falls, MT) **10659**
Hunt County Shopper (Greenville, TX) **10741**
Hunterdon County Democrat (Flemington, NJ) **10666**
Hunterdon Review (Lebanon, NJ) **10667**
† Huntingdon Carroll Leader (Huntingdon, TN)
Huntington Beach/Fountain Valley Independent (Huntington Beach, CA) **10535**
Huntington Harbour Sun (Seal Beach, CA) **10545**
Huntington Herald-Dispatch (Huntington, WV) **10512**
Huntley Farmside, The (Huntley, IL) **10582**
Huntsville Item (Huntsville, TX) **10504**
† Huntsville News (Huntsville, AL)
Huntsville Times, The (Huntsville, AL) **10416**
Huron Daily Tribune (Bad Axe, MI) **10459**
Hurricane Breeze (Hurricane, WV) **10761**
Hustler, The (South Pittsburg, TN) **10735**

Hutchinson Herald, The (Menno, SD) **10730**
Hutchinson Leader (Hutchinson, MN) **10642**
Hutchinson News (Hutchinson, KS) **10450**
Hyde Park Herald (Chicago, IL) **10575**
Hyde Park Townsman (Hyde Park, NY) **10679**

I

Idaho County Free Press (Grangeville, ID) **10569**
Idaho Enterprise (Malad City, ID) **10570**
Idaho Falls Post Register (Idaho Falls, ID) **10437**
Idaho Mountain Express (Ketchum, ID) **10570**
Idaho Press-Tribune (Nampa, ID) **10437**
Idaho State Journal (Pocatello, ID) **10437**
Idaho Statesman, The (Boise, ID) **10437**
Idalou Beacon (Idalou, TX) **10742**
Ile Camera, The (Grosse Ile, MI) **10633**
Illinois Times (Springfield, IL) **10589**
Illiopolis Sentinel (Illiopolis, IL) **10582**
Impact of Laurel (Laurel, MS) **10650**
Imperial Valley Press (El Centro, CA) **10422**
Improper Bostonian, The (Boston, MA) **10624**
Independence Bulletin-Journal (Independence, IA) **10601**
Independence Daily Reporter (Independence, KS) **10450**
Independence Examiner, The (Independence, MO) **10466**
Independence News-Wave (Independence, WI) **10768**
Independence News, The (Independence, KS) **10606**
Independent (Collierville, TN) **10731**
Independent (Deerfield, WI) **10766**
Independent-Journal, The (Potosi, MO) **10656**
Independent-Messenger (Emporia, VA) **10752**
Independent-Register, The (Brodhead, WI) **10765**
Independent Appeal (Selmer, TN) **10735**
Independent Enterprise (Payette, ID) **10570**
Independent Herald, The (Pineville, WV) **10762**
Independent Mirror (Mexico, NY) **10681**
Independent News (Georgetown, IL) **10579**
Independent News Herald (Clarissa, MN) **10641**
Independent Observer, The (Scottdale, PA) **10724**
† Independent Press (Marine City, MI)
Independent Press (New Providence, NJ) **10668**
Independent Press of Bloomfield, The (Bloomfield, NJ) **10664**
Independent Record (Helena, MT) **10469**
Independent Republican (Goshen, NY) **10678**

Independent, The (Robertsdale, AL) **10521**
Independent, The (Livermore, CA) **10536**
Independent, The (Winamac, IN) **10598**
Independent, The (Flint, MI) **10632**
Independent, The (Durham, NC) **10692**
Independent, The (Morganville, NJ) **10668**
Independent, The (Massillon, OH) **10486**
Independent, The (Collegeville, PA) **10716**
Independent, The (Montrose, PA) **10720**
Independent Tribune (Kannapolis, NC) **10479**
Index-Journal (Greenwood, SC) **10499**
Indiana Gazette (Indiana, PA) **10494**
Indianapolis News (Indianapolis, IN) **10444**
Indianapolis Recorder (Indianapolis, IN) **10594**
Indianapolis Star (Indianapolis, IN) **10444**
Indianapolis Westside Enterprise (Greenfield, IN) **10594**
Indianhead Advertiser (Frederic, WI) **10767**
Indian Head Park (Hinsdale, IL) **10582**
Indian Head Park Citizen (Oak Brook, IL) **10586**
Indio Advertiser (Palm Desert, CA) **10540**
Indio Post (Indio, CA) **10535**
Indy Suburban Newspapers (Greenfield, IN) **10594**
Ingham County News (Mason, MI) **10635**
Inglewood/Hawthorne Wave (Los Angeles, CA) **10537**
Inglewood Tribune (Compton, CA) **10533**
Inkster Ledger-Star (Wayne, MI) **10639**
Inland Valley Daily Bulletin (Ontario, CA) **10423**
In Pittsburgh Newsweekly (Pittsburgh, PA) **10723**
Inquirer & Mirror, The (Nantucket, MA) **10626**
Inside (Chicago, IL) **10575**
† Inside Ravenswood (Chicago, IL)
Intelligencer/Record, The (Doylestown, PA) **10493**
Intelligencer Journal (Lancaster, PA) **10494**
Intelligencer, The (Wheeling, WV) **10513**
Inter-County Leader (Frederic, WI) **10767**
Inter-Mountain, The (Elkins, WV) **10512**
† Interboro News (Prospect Park, PA)
Interior Journal (Stanford, KY) **10614**
Interlaken Review (Trumansburg, NY) **10688**
Intermountain News (Burney, CA) **10531**
Inyo Register (Bishop, CA) **10531**
In Your Community/Oakland Press (Pontiac, MI) **10637**
Iola Herald (Iola, WI) **10768**
Iola Register (Iola, KS) **10450**
Ionia Sentinel-Standard (Ionia, MI) **10460**
Iosco County News Herald (East Tawas, MI) **10632**
Iowa City Press-Citizen (Iowa City, IA) **10448**

Iowa Park Leader (Iowa Park, TX) **10742**
Ipswich Chronicle (Ipswich, MA) **10625**
Ipswich Tribune (Ipswich, SD) **10730**
Iron County Miner (Hurley, WI) **10768**
Irondequoit Press (Rochester, NY) **10685**
Iron River Reporter (Iron River, MI) **10634**
Ironton Tribune (Ironton, OH) **10485**
Ironwood Daily Globe (Ironwood, MI) **10460**
Iroquois County Times Republic (Watseka, IL) **10442**
Irvine World News (Irvine, CA) **10535**
Irving News (Arlington, TX) **10736**
Irvington Viewpoint, The (Irvington, NY) **10679**
Island Ad-Vantages (Stonington, ME) **10620**
Island Connection (Portland, OR) **10714**
Island Dispatch (Grand Island, NY) **10678**
Islander, The (Gulf Shores, AL) **10519**
Islander, The (Gulf Breeze, FL) **10557**
Islander, The (St. Simons Island, GA) **10568**
Islander, The (South Hero, VT) **10750**
Island Reporter (Sanibel, FL) **10560**
Island Times (Lihue, HI) **10436**
Islesboro Island News (Islesboro, ME) **10619**
Islip Bulletin (Sayville, NY) **10685**
Islip News (Smithtown, NY) **10686**
Issaquah Press (Issaquah, WA) **10758**
Isthmus (Madison, WI) **10769**
Itawamba County Times, The (Fulton, MS) **10649**
Item (Clinton, MA) **10624**
Item, The (Sumter, SC) **10499**
Ithaca Journal, The (Ithaca, NY) **10475**
Ithaca Times (Ithaca, NY) **10679**
Iuka Tishomingo County News (Iuka, MS) **10650**

J

Jackson-Vinton Journal-Herald (Jackson, OH) **10703**
Jackson Citizen Patriot (Jackson, MI) **10460**
Jackson County Banner (Brownstown, IN) **10592**
Jackson County Floridan (Marianna, FL) **10432**
Jackson County Herald/Tribune (Edna, TX) **10739**
Jackson County Livewire (Jackson, MN) **10642**
Jackson County Star (Walden, CO) **10551**
Jackson Heights News (Maspeth, NY) **10681**
Jackson Herald (Jefferson, GA) **10566**
Jackson Herald (Ripley, WV) **10763**
Jackson Hole Guide (Jackson, WY) **10776**
Jackson Hole News (Jackson, WY) **10776**
Jackson Independent, The (Jonesboro, LA) **10616**
Jackson Progress-Argus (Jackson, GA) **10565**

Jackson Star News (Ravenswood, WV) **10762**
Jackson Sun, The (Jackson, TN) **10500**
Jacksonville Daily Progress
 (Jacksonville, TX) **10504**
Jacksonville Journal-Courier
 (Jacksonville, IL) **10440**
Jacksonville News (Jacksonville, AL) **10520**
Jacksonville Patriot (Jacksonville, AR) **10420**
Jacksonville Shopping Guide
 (Jacksonville, FL) **10557**
▼ Jamaica Times, The (Flushing, NY) **10677**
Jamestown Press, The (Jamestown, RI) **10725**
Jamestown Sun, The (Jamestown, ND) **10482**
Janesville Gazette (Janesville, WI) **10514**
Jasper County News, The (Bay
 Springs, MS) **10649**
Jasper County Sun (Ridgeland, SC) **10728**
Jasper Daily Mountain Eagle
 (Jasper, AL) **10416**
Jasper Journal (Jasper, MN) **10643**
Jasper Journal (Jasper, TN) **10732**
Jasper News (Jasper, FL) **10557**
Jasper NewsBoy (Jasper, TX) **10742**
Jasper NewsBoy Shopper (Jasper, TX) **10742**
Jeanerette Enterprise (Jeanerette, LA) **10616**
Jeannette Spirit (Jeannette, PA) **10718**
Jeff Davis Ledger (Hazlehurst, GA) **10565**
Jefferson Bee (Jefferson, IA) **10602**
Jefferson County Journal (Arnold, MO) **10651**
Jefferson County Journal (Adams, NY) **10672**
Jefferson County Transcript
 (Golden, CO) **10549**
Jefferson Herald (Jefferson, IA) **10602**
Jeffersonian Democrat (Brookville, PA) **10716**
Jeffersonian, The (Baltimore, MD) **10621**
Jeffersonian, The (Croswell, MI) **10631**
Jefferson Jimplecute (Jefferson, TX) **10742**
Jefferson Park/Portage Park/Bel Cragin Times
 (Lincolnwood, IL) **10584**
Jefferson Post (West Jefferson, NC) **10695**
† Jefferson Republic, The (De Soto, MO)
Jefferson Sentinel (Lakewood, CO) **10549**
Jefferson Star, The (Rigby, ID) **10570**
Jeffersonville Evening News
 (Jeffersonville, IN) **10444**
Jekyll's Golden Islander
 (Brunswick, GA) **10563**
Jellico Advance Sentinel (La
 Follette, TN) **10733**
Jena Times Olla-Tullos Signal
 (Jena, LA) **10616**
Jenks Journal (Tulsa, OK) **10711**
Jennings Daily News (Jennings, LA) **10454**
Jersey City Reporter (Hoboken, NJ) **10666**
Jersey Journal, The (Jersey City, NJ) **10472**
Jessamine Journal (Nicholasville, KY) **10613**
† Jet Gazette (Austin, TX)
Jetmore Republican (Jetmore, KS) **10606**
† Jet Visitor (Cherokee, OK)
Jewish Journal of Greater Los Angeles, The (Los
 Angeles, CA) **10537**
Johnsonburg Press, Inc., The
 (Johnsonburg, PA) **10719**
Johnson City Press (Johnson City, TN) **10501**
Johnson County Graphic
 (Clarksville, AR) **10527**
Johnson County Sun (Shawnee
 Mission, KS) **10608**
Johnson Pioneer (Johnson, KS) **10606**
Johnston County Capital-Democrat
 (Tishomingo, OK) **10711**
Johnstown Independent
 (Columbus, OH) **10701**
Jonesboro Sun (Jonesboro, AR) **10420**
Jones County Town Crier
 (Anamosa, IA) **10599**
Joplin Globe, The (Joplin, MO) **10467**
Journal & Austin Chronicle
 (Scottsburg, IN) **10597**
Journal & Courier (Lafayette, IN) **10444**
Journal & Monitor Herald (Tomah, WI) **10774**
Journal & Republican (Lowville, NY) **10680**
Journal-Enterprise (Providence, KY) **10614**
Journal-Gazette, The (Fort Wayne, IN) **10443**
Journal-Herald, The (White Haven, PA) **10725**
Journal-Leader (Caldwell, OH) **10699**
Journal-Patriot (North Wilkesboro, NC) **10693**
Journal-Register (Medina, NY) **10476**
Journal-World, The (Lawrence, KS) **10451**
Journal/Express (Knoxville, IA) **10602**
Journal/Valley Views (White Haven, PA) **10725**
† Journal Courier (Moravia, NY)
Journal Herald, The (Shawnee, KS) **10608**
Journal Inquirer (Manchester, CT) **10430**
Journal Messenger (Manassas, VA) **10509**
Journal News (Hamilton, OH) **10485**
Journal News (Spencerville, OH) **10707**
Journal Opinion (Bradford, VT) **10749**
Journal Press (Lawrenceburg, IN) **10595**
Journal Record (Hamilton, AL) **10520**
Journal Register (Palmer, MA) **10627**
Journal, The (Chicago, IL) **10575**
Journal, The (Ellettsville, IN) **10593**
Journal, The (New Ulm, MN) **10463**
Journal, The (Crosby, ND) **10696**
Journal, The (Voorhees, NJ) **10671**
Journal, The (Ogdensburg, NY) **10476**
Journal, The (Struthers, OH) **10707**
Journal, The (Mt. Pleasant, SC) **10728**
Journal, The (Williamston, SC) **10729**
Journal, The (King George, VA) **10753**
Journal, The (Martinsburg, WV) **10513**

Journal Times (Racine, WI) **10515**
† Journal Transcript (Franklin, NH)
Journal Tribune (Williamsburg, IA) **10605**
Journal Tribune (Biddeford, ME) **10455**
Journal Tribune (Seneca, SC) **10729**
Julesburg Advocate (Julesburg, CO) **10549**
Junction City Daily Union (Junction City, KS) **10450**
Junction Eagle, The (Junction, TX) **10742**
Juneau County Star-Times (Mauston, WI) **10769**
Juneau Empire (Juneau, AK) **10417**
Juniata News (Philadelphia, PA) **10722**
Juniata Sentinel (Mifflintown, PA) **10720**
Jupiter Courier (Jupiter, FL) **10558**

K

Kalamazoo Gazette (Kalamazoo, MI) **10461**
Kalona News, The (Kalona, IA) **10602**
Kanabec County Times (Mora, MN) **10644**
Kane County Chronicle (Geneva, IL) **10439**
Kane Republican (Kane, PA) **10494**
† Kansas Business News (Augusta, KS)
† Kansas City Evening News (Shawnee Mission, KS)
Kansas City Kansan (Kansas City, KS) **10450**
Kansas City Star (Kansas City, MO) **10467**
Karnes Citation (Karnes City, TX) **10742**
Katahdin Times (Millinocket, ME) **10619**
Kaufman Herald, The (Kaufman, TX) **10742**
Kaukauna Times (Kaukauna, WI) **10768**
Kayo, The (Clinton, MO) **10652**
Kearney Hub (Kearney, NE) **10469**
Keene Sentinel (Keene, NH) **10471**
Keith County News (Ogallala, NE) **10661**
Keller Citizen, The (Keller, TX) **10742**
Kelly Observer (San Antonio, TX) **10746**
Kemmerer Gazette (Kemmerer, WY) **10776**
Kemper County Messenger (DeKalb, MS) **10649**
Ken-Ton Bee (Williamsville, NY) **10689**
Kenbridge-Victoria Dispatch (Victoria, VA) **10756**
Kendall County Record (Yorkville, IL) **10591**
Kendall News-Gazette (Miami, FL) **10559**
Kendallville News-Sun (Kendallville, IN) **10444**
Kendrick-Gazette (Kendrick, ID) **10569**
Kenilworth Leader (Union, NJ) **10670**
Kenly News (Kenly, NC) **10692**
Kennebec Journal (Augusta, ME) **10455**
Kennedale News (Everman, TX) **10740**
Kennedy Advanced Times (Karnes City, TX) **10742**
Kennesaw Neighbor, The (Marietta, GA) **10566**
Kenosha News (Kenosha, WI) **10514**

Kent-Ravenna Record-Courier (Ravenna, OH) **10486**
Kent County Daily Times (West Warwick, RI) **10498**
Kent County News (Chestertown, MD) **10621**
Kent Good Times Dispatch (Kent, CT) **10552**
Kenton County Recorder (Florence, KY) **10610**
Kenton Times (Kenton, OH) **10485**
Kentucky New Era (Hopkinsville, KY) **10452**
Kentucky Post, The (Covington, KY) **10452**
Kentucky Standard (Bardstown, KY) **10609**
Kentwood Advance (Jenison, MI) **10634**
Kentwood News-Ledger (Kentwood, LA) **10617**
Kenyon Leader (Kenyon, MN) **10643**
Keokuk Daily Gate City (Keokuk, IA) **10448**
Kerman News (Kerman, CA) **10535**
Kernersville News (Kernersville, NC) **10692**
Kern Valley Sun (Lake Isabella, CA) **10536**
Kerrville Daily Times (Kerrville, TX) **10504**
Ketchikan Daily News (Ketchikan, AK) **10417**
Kettering-Oakwood Times (Kettering, OH) **10704**
Kettle Moraine Index (Hartland, WI) **10767**
Kewanee Star-Courier (Kewanee, IL) **10440**
Kewaskum Statesman (Kewaskum, WI) **10768**
Kewaunee Enterprise (Kewaunee, WI) **10768**
Keystone Reporter (Elroy, WI) **10767**
Key West Citizen (Key West, FL) **10432**
Kiel Tri-County Record (Kiel, WI) **10768**
Kilgore News Herald (Kilgore, TX) **10504**
Killeen Daily Herald (Killeen, TX) **10504**
King City Rustler (King City, CA) **10535**
Kingfisher Times & Free Press (Kingfisher, OK) **10710**
Kingman Daily Miner (Kingman, AZ) **10418**
Kingman Journal (Kingman, KS) **10607**
King of Prussia Courier (King of Prussia, PA) **10719**
Kingsburg Recorder (Kingsburg, CA) **10535**
Kings County News (Brooklyn, NY) **10674**
Kings Courier (Brooklyn, NY) **10675**
Kings Mountain Herald (Kings Mountain, NC) **10692**
Kingsport Daily News (Kingsport, TN) **10501**
Kingsport Times-News (Kingsport, TN) **10501**
Kingston Independent (Marshfield, MA) **10626**
Kingston Reporter (Plymouth, MA) **10627**
Kingsville Record, The (Kingsville, TX) **10743**
King Times News (King, NC) **10692**
Kingwood Sun (Humble, TX) **10742**
Kinmundy Express (Kinmundy, IL) **10583**
Kinston Daily Free Press (Kinston, NC) **10480**
Kiowa County Press (Eads, CO) **10548**
Kirksville Daily Express (Kirksville, MO) **10467**
† Kirtland Enterprise (Willoughby, OH)
Knoxville Journal, The (Galesburg, IL) **10579**

Knoxville News-Sentinel (Knoxville, TN) **10501**
Kodiak Daily Mirror (Kodiak, AK) **10417**
Kokomo Tribune, The (Kokomo, IN) **10444**
Konawa Leader (Konawa, OK) **10710**
† Kossuth County Advance (Algona, IA)
Kuna-Melba News (Kuna, ID) **10570**

L

L'Anse Sentinel (L'Anse, MI) **10635**
L'Observateur (La Place, LA) **10617**
Labor Herald (Baltimore, MD) **10621**
La Canada Valley Sun (La Canada, CA) **10535**
Lackland Tale Spinner (San Antonio, TX) **10746**
Lacon Home Journal (Lacon, IL) **10583**
La Crosse County Countryman (West Salem, WI) **10775**
La Crosse Tribune (La Crosse, WI) **10514**
Ladysmith News (Ladysmith, WI) **10768**
Lafayette Advertiser (Lafayette, LA) **10454**
Lafayette Leader (Lafayette, IN) **10595**
Lafayette Sun, The (Lafayette, AL) **10520**
La Feria News (La Feria, TX) **10743**
La Follette Press (La Follette, TN) **10733**
La Grange Daily News (La Grange, GA) **10435**
La Grange Independent (Mahopac, NY) **10681**
La Grange Standard News (La Grange, IN) **10595**
Laguna News Post (Lake Forest, CA) **10536**
Laguna Niguel News (Lake Forest, CA) **10536**
La Habra Star (Anaheim, CA) **10530**
Lahontan Valley News (Fallon, NV) **10470**
La Jolla Light (La Jolla, CA) **10536**
La Jolla Village News/Golden Triange News (San Diego, CA) **10542**
La Junta Tribune-Democrat (La Junta, CO) **10429**
† Lake Alfred Press (Mulberry, FL)
Lake Area News (Land O' Lakes, FL) **10558**
Lake Charles American Press (Lake Charles, LA) **10454**
Lake Cities Sun, The (Lake Dallas, TX) **10743**
Lake City Reporter (Lake City, FL) **10432**
Lake City Town Crier (La Follette, TN) **10733**
† Lake Country Chronicle (Buchanan, MI)
Lake Country Reporter (Hartland, WI) **10767**
Lake County Examiner (Lakeview, OR) **10713**
Lake County Leader (Ronan, MT) **10659**
Lake County News-Chronicle (Two Harbors, MN) **10648**
Lake County Record-Bee (Lakeport, CA) **10422**
Lake County Star (Crown Point, IN) **10592**
Lake County Star (Big Rapids, MI) **10630**
Lake Edition, The (Lexington, SC) **10728**

Lake Elsinore Valley Sun-Tribune (Lake Elsinore, CA) **10536**
Lakefield Standard (Lakefield, MN) **10643**
Lake Forester (Bannockburn, IL) **10572**
Lake Geneva Regional News (Lake Geneva, WI) **10768**
Lake Havasu City Advertiser (Lake Havasu City, AZ) **10525**
Lake Havasu City Herald (Lake Havasu City, AZ) **10418**
Lakeland Press (Grayslake, IL) **10580**
Lakeland Times (Minocqua, WI) **10770**
Lakeland Today (Butler, NJ) **10665**
Lake Michigan Examiner, The (Muskegon, MI) **10636**
Lake Mills Leader (Lake Mills, WI) **10768**
Lake News (Fruitland Park, FL) **10557**
Lake Oswego Review (Lake Oswego, OR) **10713**
Lake Placid Journal (Lake Placid, FL) **10558**
Lake Placid News (Lake Placid, NY) **10680**
Lake Powell Chronicle (Page, AZ) **10525**
Lakeshore Chronicle (Manitowoc, WI) **10769**
Lakeshore Weekly News (Wayzata, MN) **10648**
▼Lakeside Ledger, The (Woodstock, GA) **10568**
Lakes Region Free Press, The (Granville, NY) **10678**
Lake Sun Leader (Camdenton, MO) **10465**
Lakeview Enterprise (Big Rapids, MI) **10630**
Lake Villa Record (Grayslake, IL) **10580**
Lakeville Independent (Middleboro, MA) **10626**
Lakeville Journal, The (Lakeville, CT) **10553**
Lakeville Life & Times (Lakeville, MN) **10643**
Lakeville Sun-Current (Burnsville, MN) **10640**
† Lake Wales Highlander (Winter Haven, FL)
Lake Wales News (Lake Wales, FL) **10558**
Lakewood Sun Post (North Olmsted, OH) **10706**
Lake Worth Herald Coastal Observer (Lake Worth, FL) **10558**
Lake Zurich Enterprise (Grayslake, IL) **10581**
Lamar Daily News (Lamar, CO) **10429**
Lamar Democrat (Vernon, AL) **10522**
Lamar Democrat (Lamar, MO) **10654**
Lamar Leader (Sulligent, AL) **10522**
La Marque Times (La Marque, TX) **10743**
Lamb County Leader-News (Littlefield, TX) **10743**
Lamberton News (Lamberton, MN) **10643**
La Mesa Forum (Lemon Grove, CA) **10536**
Lamesa Press-Reporter (Lamesa, TX) **10743**
Lamont Reporter (Lamont, CA) **10536**
Lancaster Bee (Williamsville, NY) **10689**
Lancaster Eagle-Gazette (Lancaster, OH) **10485**

Lancaster Fairfield Advertiser (Carroll, OH) **10699**
Lancaster Intelligencer Journal (Lancaster, PA) **10494**
Lancaster New Era (Lancaster, PA) **10494**
Lancaster News (Lancaster, SC) **10728**
Lancaster Today (DeSoto, TX) **10739**
Lander Wyoming State Journal (Lander, WY) **10776**
Lansing State Journal (Lansing, MI) **10461**
La Porte Herald-Argus (La Porte, IN) **10444**
Laramie Daily Boomerang (Laramie, WY) **10516**
Laredo Morning Times (Laredo, TX) **10505**
Larimore Pioneer (Northwood, ND) **10697**
LaRue County Herald-News (Hodgenville, KY) **10611**
Las Cruces Sun-News (Las Cruces, NM) **10473**
Las Vegas Daily Optic (Las Vegas, NM) **10473**
Las Vegas Review-Journal (Las Vegas, NV) **10470**
Las Vegas Sun (Las Vegas, NV) **10470**
Las Vegas Today (Las Vegas, NV) **10662**
Las Virgenes Enterprise (Woodland Hills, CA) **10547**
Latrobe Bulletin (Latrobe, PA) **10494**
Lauderdale County Enterprise (Ripley, TN) **10734**
Laurel Leader (Laurel, MD) **10622**
Laurel Leader-Call (Laurel, MS) **10465**
Laurens County Advertiser (Laurens, SC) **10728**
Laurens Sun, The (Laurens, IA) **10602**
Laurinburg Exchange (Laurinburg, NC) **10480**
LaVilla News (Hot Springs Village, AR) **10528**
L.A. Weekly (Los Angeles, CA) **10538**
Lawrence County Centennial (Deadwood, SD) **10729**
Lawrence County News (Lawrenceville, IL) **10583**
Lawrence County Record (Mt. Vernon, MO) **10655**
Lawrence Ledger (Pennington, NJ) **10669**
Lawrence Times (Fishers, IN) **10593**
Lawrence Township Journal (Lawrence, IN) **10595**
Lawrenceville Daily Record (Lawrenceville, IL) **10440**
Lawton Constitution (Lawton, OK) **10489**
† Lead Call (Lead, SD)
Leader-Courier (Kingman, KS) **10607**
Leader-Herald, The (Gloversville, NY) **10475**
Leader-News (Central City, KY) **10610**
Leader-News (Washburn, ND) **10697**
Leader-Record (Gonvick, MN) **10642**
Leader-State Register, The (Seaford, DE) **10554**
Leader-Telegram (Eau Claire, WI) **10514**
Leader-Tribune, The (Fort Valley, GA) **10565**
Leader-Vindicator, The (New Bethlehem, PA) **10721**
Leader Enterprise (Montpelier, OH) **10705**
Leader Observer (Maspeth, NY) **10681**
Leader, The (Davenport, IA) **10599**
Leader, The (Solon, IA) **10604**
Leader, The (Charlestown, IN) **10592**
† Leader, The (Lansing, KS)
Leader, The (Northwood, ND) **10697**
Leader, The (Point Pleasant Beach, NJ) **10669**
Leader, The (Corning, NY) **10474**
Leader, The (Freeport, NY) **10677**
Leader, The (Cleveland, OH) **10700**
† Leader, The (East Palestine, OH)
Leader, The (Philadelphia, PA) **10722**
Leader, The (Tremonton, UT) **10749**
Leader Times (Kittanning, PA) **10494**
Leaf-Chronicle, The (Clarksville, TN) **10500**
Leavenworth Echo (Leavenworth, WA) **10758**
Leavenworth Times (Leavenworth, KS) **10451**
Leawood Sun (Shawnee Mission, KS) **10608**
† Lebanon Connecticut Valley Reporter (Lebanon, NH)
Lebanon Daily News (Lebanon, PA) **10495**
Lebanon Daily Record (Lebanon, MO) **10467**
Lebanon Democrat, The (Lebanon, TN) **10501**
Lebanon Enterprise (Lebanon, KY) **10612**
Lebanon Express (Lebanon, OR) **10713**
▼Lebanon Herald (Mascoutah, IL) **10584**
Lebanon News (Lebanon, VA) **10753**
Lebanon Times, The (Lebanon, KS) **10607**
Le Center Leader (Le Center, MN) **10643**
Ledger-Independent (Maysville, KY) **10453**
† Ledger-Star (Norfolk, VA)
Ledger Dispatch & Sunday Times, The (Antioch, CA) **10421**
Ledger, The (Lakeland, FL) **10432**
Ledger, The (Moundridge, KS) **10607**
Ledger Tribune, The (New Albany, IN) **10445**
Lee's Summit Journal (Lee's Summit, MO) **10654**
Lee County Eagle, The (Auburn, AL) **10517**
Lee County Observer (Bishopville, SC) **10726**
Leeds News (Leeds, AL) **10520**
Leelanau Enterprise (Leland, MI) **10635**
Leesburg Today (Leesburg, VA) **10753**
Leesville Daily Leader (Leesville, LA) **10454**
Lee Town Shopper (Des Moines, IA) **10600**
Lehi Free Press (American Fork, UT) **10748**
Leisure World Golden Rain News (Seal Beach, CA) **10545**
Leisure World News (Laguna Hills, CA) **10536**

Le Mars Daily Sentinel (Le Mars, IA) **10448**
Lemon Grove Review (Lemon Grove, CA) **10536**
Lemont Metropolitan (Lemont, IL) **10583**
Lemont Reporter (Lemont, IL) **10583**
Lenexa Sun (Shawnee Mission, KS) **10608**
Lenoir News-Topic (Lenoir, NC) **10480**
Leon Journal-Reporter (Leon, IA) **10602**
Leslie County News (Hyden, KY) **10611**
Leslie Local Independent (Leslie, MI) **10635**
Letcher County Community News-Press (Cromona, KY) **10610**
Levelland Hockley County News-Press (Levelland, TX) **10743**
Levittown Tribune (Mineola, NY) **10682**
Lewisboro Ledger, The (Ridgefield, CT) **10553**
Lewisburg Daily Journal (Milton, PA) **10495**
Lewisburg Tribune (Lewisburg, TN) **10733**
Lewis County Herald (Nezperce, ID) **10570**
Lewis River News (Woodland, WA) **10760**
Lewiston-Porter Sentinel (Grand Island, NY) **10678**
Lewiston Journal (Lewiston, MN) **10643**
Lewiston Morning Tribune (Lewiston, ID) **10437**
Lewistown News-Argus (Lewistown, MT) **10659**
Lewisville Leader (Lewisville, TX) **10743**
Lexington Herald-Leader (Lexington, KY) **10453**
Lexington Minuteman (Woburn, MA) **10629**
Lexington News (Lexington, MO) **10654**
Lexington Progress (Lexington, TN) **10733**
Liberal Southwest Daily Times (Liberal, KS) **10451**
Liberty Gazette (Liberty, TX) **10743**
† Liberty News (Niles, OH)
Liberty Press, The (Liberty Center, OH) **10704**
Liberty Tribune (Kansas City, MO) **10654**
Libertyville News (Grayslake, IL) **10581**
Libertyville Review (Bannockburn, IL) **10572**
† Licking Countian (Newark, OH)
Licking Valley Courier (West Liberty, KY) **10615**
Life at Ken-Caryl (Littleton, CO) **10549**
Light & Champion (Center, TX) **10737**
Ligonier Advance-Leader (Ligonier, IN) **10595**
Ligonier Echo (Ligonier, PA) **10719**
Ligonier Free Gazette, The (Ligonier, PA) **10719**
Lillie Suburban Shopping Review (St. Paul, MN) **10647**
Lima News (Lima, OH) **10485**
Lime Springs Herald (Lime Springs, IA) **10602**
Limestone Independent News (Bartonville, IL) **10572**
† Lincoln-Belmont Booster (Chicago, IL)

Lincoln County Journal (Shoshone, ID) **10571**
Lincoln County News (Newcastle, ME) **10620**
Lincoln County News (Chandler, OK) **10709**
Lincoln Courier (Lincoln, IL) **10440**
Lincoln Heights Bulletin-News (Los Angeles, CA) **10538**
Lincoln Journal (Hamlin, WV) **10761**
Lincoln Journal Star (Lincoln, NE) **10470**
Lincoln Ledger (Star City, AR) **10529**
Lincoln News (Lincoln, ME) **10619**
Lincoln Times-News (Lincolnton, NC) **10693**
Lincoln Times, The (Hamlin, WV) **10761**
Lincoln Weekly News Sentinel (Hamlin, WV) **10761**
Lincolnwood Life (Lincolnwood, IL) **10584**
Lincolnwood Review (Evanston, IL) **10579**
Linden Herald (Linden, CA) **10536**
Lindenhurst News (Grayslake, IL) **10581**
Linden Leader (Union, NJ) **10671**
Lindsay Gazette (Lindsay, CA) **10536**
† Linesville Herald (Conneaut Lake, PA)
Linn Unterrified Democrat (Linn, MO) **10654**
Linton Daily Citizen (Linton, IN) **10444**
Linton Emmons County Record (Linton, ND) **10697**
Lisbon Ransom County Gazette & Enterprise (Lisbon, ND) **10697**
Lisle Sun (Downers Grove, IL) **10577**
Lisle Sun (Naperville, IL) **10586**
Litchfield Enquirer (Litchfield, CT) **10553**
Litchfield Independent Review (Litchfield, MN) **10643**
Litchfield News-Herald (Litchfield, IL) **10440**
Lititz Record Express, The (Lititz, PA) **10719**
† Little Falls Transcript (Little Falls, MN)
Little Neck Ledger, The (Flushing, NY) **10677**
Little Paper, The (Melbourne, FL) **10558**
Littleton Independent (Littleton, CO) **10549**
Littleton Independent (Concord, MA) **10624**
Littleton Observer (Littleton, NC) **10693**
† Littleton Times (Littleton, CO)
Livermore Falls Advertiser (Livermore Falls, ME) **10619**
Liverpool Review (Syracuse, NY) **10687**
† Livingston East Texas Eye (Livingston, TX)
Livingston Enterprise (Livingston, MT) **10469**
Livingston Enterprise (Livingston, TN) **10733**
Livingston Leader (Denham Springs, LA) **10616**
Livonia Observer (Livonia, MI) **10635**
Llano News (Llano, TX) **10744**
Lockeford-Clements News (Lockeford, CA) **10537**
Lockhart Post Register (Lockhart, TX) **10744**
Locust Valley Leader (Locust Valley, NY) **10680**

Loda Times (Paxton, IL) **10588**
Lodi Enterprise (Lodi, WI) **10768**
Lodi News-Sentinel (Lodi, CA) **10422**
Logan Banner (Logan, WV) **10513**
Logan Daily News (Logan, OH) **10485**
Logan Herald Observer (Logan, IA) **10602**
Log Cabin Democrat (Conway, AR) **10419**
Lombardian, The (Lombard, IL) **10584**
Lombardian Villa Park Review (Lombard, IL) **10584**
Lombard Spectator (Elmhurst, IL) **10578**
Lompoc Record (Lompoc, CA) **10422**
† London Mills Times (Roseville, IL)
Lone Tree Reporter, The (Lone Tree, IA) **10602**
Long Beach Chinook Observer (Long Beach, WA) **10758**
† Long Beach Community News (Long Beach, CA)
Long Beach Herald (Long Beach, NY) **10680**
Long Beach Independent Voice (Mineola, NY) **10682**
Long Island Advance (Patchogue, NY) **10684**
Long Island City/Astoria Journal (Maspeth, NY) **10681**
Long Island Graphic-Roosevelt Press (Lawrence, NY) **10680**
† Long Island Journal Newspaper Group (Long Beach, NY)
▼ Long Island Voice (Mineola, NY) **10682**
Longmeadow News (Westfield, MA) **10629**
Long Prairie Leader (Long Prairie, MN) **10643**
Long Valley Advocate, The (Cascade, ID) **10569**
Longview News Journal (Longview, TX) **10505**
Lorain County Times, The (Rocky River, OH) **10707**
Lorenzo Examiner (Lorenzo, TX) **10744**
Loris Times (Loris, SC) **10728**
Los Altos Town Crier (Los Altos, CA) **10537**
Los Angeles Bulletin (Los Angeles, CA) **10422**
Los Angeles Independent (Los Angeles, CA) **10538**
Los Angeles Log (San Diego, CA) **10542**
Los Angeles Times (Los Angeles, CA) **10423**
Los Banos Enterprise (Los Banos, CA) **10538**
Los Gatos Weekly-Times (Los Gatos, CA) **10539**
Lost River Star (Merrill, OR) **10714**
Loudenville Weekly (Delmar, NY) **10676**
Loudonville Times, The (Loudonville, OH) **10704**
Loudoun Times-Mirror (Leesburg, VA) **10753**
Louisiana Press-Journal (Louisiana, MO) **10654**
Louisville Herald, The (Louisville, OH) **10704**

Louisville Winston County Journal (Louisville, MS) **10650**
Loveland Daily Reporter-Herald (Loveland, CO) **10429**
Loveland Herald Press (Loveland, OH) **10704**
Lovell Chronicle, The (Lovell, WY) **10776**
Lovelock Review-Miner (Lovelock, NV) **10662**
Lovington Daily Leader (Lovington, NM) **10474**
Lowell Ledger (Lowell, MI) **10635**
Lowell Sun (Lowell, MA) **10458**
Lowell Tribune (Lowell, IN) **10595**
Lower Township Lantern (Rio Grande, NJ) **10670**
Loyal Tribune-Record-Gleaner (Loyal, WI) **10769**
Lubbock Avalanche-Journal (Lubbock, TX) **10505**
Ludington Daily News (Ludington, MI) **10461**
Ludlow Register (Palmer, MA) **10627**
Ludowici News (Ludowici, GA) **10566**
Lufkin Daily News (Lufkin, TX) **10505**
Luling Newsboy & Signal (Luling, TX) **10744**
Lusk Herald (Lusk, WY) **10776**
Lutz Community News (Tampa, FL) **10561**
Luverne Journal & News (Luverne, AL) **10520**
Luxemburg News (Luxemburg, WI) **10769**
Lynbrook USA (Mineola, NY) **10682**
Lynden Tribune (Lynden, WA) **10758**
Lynwood Journal (Compton, CA) **10533**
Lynwood Press (Los Angeles, CA) **10538**
Lyon-Sioux Press (Rock Rapids, IA) **10603**
Lyons Daily News (Lyons, KS) **10451**
Lyons Mirror-Sun (Lyons, NE) **10661**

M

M & M Journal (Hillsboro, IL) **10582**
Mableton Neighbor, The (Marietta, GA) **10566**
Machias Valley News Observer (Machias, ME) **10619**
Macomb Daily (Mt. Clemens, MI) **10461**
Macomb Journal (Macomb, IL) **10440**
Macomb Voice, The (New Baltimore, MI) **10636**
Macon Beacon, The (Macon, MS) **10650**
Macon Chronicle-Herald (Macon, MO) **10467**
Macon County Times (Lafayette, TN) **10733**
Macon Telegraph (Macon, GA) **10435**
Macoupin & Montgomery County Journal (Hillsboro, IL) **10582**
Macoupin County Enquirer (Carlinville, IL) **10574**
Macoupin County Shopper (Hillsboro, IL) **10582**
Madera Tribune (Madera, CA) **10423**
Madill Record (Madill, OK) **10710**

Madison County Carrier (Madison, FL) **10558**
Madison County Chronicle (Worden, IL) **10591**
Madison County Eagle (Madison, VA) **10754**
Madison County Herald (Canton, MS) **10649**
Madison County Record (Madison, AL) **10520**
Madison County Record
 (Huntsville, AR) **10528**
Madison Courier (Madison, IN) **10444**
Madison Daily Leader (Madison, SD) **10499**
Madison Eagle (Madison, NJ) **10667**
Madison Enterprise Recorder
 (Madison, FL) **10558**
Madisonian, The (Madison, GA) **10566**
Madison Journal (Tallulah, LA) **10618**
Madison Messenger, The (Madison, NC) **10693**
Madison News Inc., The (Madison, KS) **10607**
Madison Park Times (Seattle, WA) **10759**
Madison Press, The (London, OH) **10485**
† Madison Tribune (Ontario, OH)
Madison Western Guard, The
 (Madison, MN) **10643**
Madras Pioneer, The (Madras, OR) **10714**
Magee Courier (Magee, MS) **10650**
Magic Valley Shopper's News
 (Camden, TN) **10731**
Magna Times (Magna, UT) **10749**
Magnolia Gazette, The (Magnolia, MS) **10650**
Mahnomen Pioneer, The
 (Mahnomen, MN) **10643**
Mahopac Press (Mahopac, NY) **10681**
Mail-Journal, The (Milford, IN) **10596**
Mail Tribune (Medford, OR) **10492**
Maine Times (Portland, ME) **10620**
Mainland Journal (Hammonton, NJ) **10666**
† Main Line Chronicle (West Chester, PA)
Main Line Life (Ardmore, PA) **10716**
Main Line Times (Ardmore, PA) **10716**
Main Street Trilogy (Townsend, MA) **10629**
Malden Evening News (Malden, MA) **10458**
† Malden Press-Merit (Malden, MO)
Malheur Enterprise (Vale, OR) **10715**
Malibu Surfside News (Malibu, CA) **10539**
Malibu Times (Malibu, CA) **10539**
Malone Telegram (Malone, NY) **10475**
Malta Messenger (Ballston Spa, NY) **10673**
Malvern Community News
 (Minerva, OH) **10705**
Malvern Daily Record (Malvern, AR) **10420**
Malverne Community Times
 (Mineola, NY) **10682**
Malvern Leader, The (Malvern, IA) **10602**
† Mammoth Lakes Review/Mono Herald
 (Mammoth Lakes, CA)
Mammoth Times (Mammoth Lakes, CA) **10539**
Mamou Acadian Press (Mamou, LA) **10617**

Manchester Enterprise
 (Manchester, KY) **10612**
Manchester Journal (Manchester
 Center, VT) **10750**
Manchester Press (Manchester, IA) **10602**
Manchester Signal (Manchester, OH) **10705**
Manchester Star-Mercury
 (Manchester, GA) **10566**
Manchester Times (Manchester, TN) **10733**
Mancos Times-Tribune (Mancos, CO) **10550**
Mandan News (Mandan, ND) **10697**
Manhasset Press (Mineola, NY) **10682**
Manhattan Mercury (Manhattan, KS) **10451**
Manistee News-Advocate (Manistee, MI) **10461**
Manistee Observer (Manistee, MI) **10635**
Manistique Pioneer-Tribune
 (Manistique, MI) **10635**
Mansfield Enterprise (Mansfield, LA) **10617**
Mansfield News (Mansfield, MA) **10625**
Mansfield News-Mirror (Mansfield, TX) **10744**
Manteca Bulletin (Manteca, CA) **10423**
Manville News (Somerville, NJ) **10670**
Maple Heights Press (Bedford, OH) **10699**
Maple Shade Progress (Maple
 Shade, NJ) **10667**
Maple Valley News (Hastings, MI) **10633**
Maplewood Review (St. Paul, MN) **10647**
Maquoketa Sentinel-Press
 (Maquoketa, IA) **10602**
† Marathon Independent Newspaper
 (Marathon, NY)
Marble Falls Highlander (Marble
 Falls, TX) **10744**
Marblehead Reporter (Marblehead, MA) **10625**
Marceline Press (Marceline, MO) **10655**
Marcellus Observer (Skaneateles, NY) **10686**
Marco Island Eagle, The (Marco
 Island, FL) **10558**
Marcus Hook Press (Drexel Hill, PA) **10717**
Marianas Variety News & Views
 (Saipan, MP) **10482**
Marianna Courier Index (Marianna, AR) **10528**
Maries County Gazette (Vienna, MO) **10658**
Marietta Daily Journal (Marietta, GA) **10435**
Marietta Times (Marietta, OH) **10485**
† Marin County Daily Recording (San
 Rafael, CA)
Marin Independent Journal
 (Novato, CA) **10423**
Marin Scope (Sausalito, CA) **10544**
Marion Advertiser (Marion, WI) **10769**
Marion County Record (Marion, KS) **10607**
Marion Daily Republican (Marion, IL) **10440**
Marion Star (Marion, OH) **10485**
Marion Star & Mullins Enterprise
 (Marion, SC) **10728**

Marion Times-Standard (Marion, AL) **10520**
Mariposa Gazette (Mariposa, CA) **10539**
† Market Place (Vandergrift, PA)
Market Shopper, The (Delano, CA) **10533**
Marlboro Herald-Advocate
　(Bennettsville, SC) **10726**
Marlboro Shopper (Bennettsville, SC) **10726**
Marquette County Tribune
　(Montello, WI) **10770**
Marshall Chronicle (Marshall, MI) **10461**
† Marshall County Life (Culver, IN)
Marshall Democrat-News
　(Marshall, MO) **10467**
Marshall Gazette (Lewisburg, TN) **10733**
Marshall Independent (Marshall, MN) **10463**
Marshall Mountain Wave (Marshall, AR) **10528**
Marshalltown Times-Republican
　(Marshalltown, IA) **10448**
Marshfield Mail (Marshfield, MO) **10655**
Marshfield Mariner (Marshfield, MA) **10626**
Marshfield News-Herald
　(Marshfield, WI) **10515**
Marshfield Reporter (Plymouth, MA) **10627**
Marthasville Record, The
　(Marthasville, MO) **10655**
† Mart Herald (Mart, TX)
† Martin County News (Stuart, FL)
Martinez News Gazette (Martinez, CA) **10539**
Martinsville Bulletin (Martinsville, VA) **10509**
Martinsville Daily Reporter
　(Martinsville, IN) **10445**
Maryland Gazette (Glen Burnie, MD) **10621**
Maryland Independent (Waldorf, MD) **10623**
Maryland Times-Press (Ocean
　City, MD) **10622**
Marysville Advocate, The
　(Marysville, KS) **10607**
Marysville Journal-Tribune
　(Marysville, OH) **10485**
Maryville Daily Forum (Maryville, MO) **10467**
Mascoutah Herald (Mascoutah, IL) **10584**
Mashpee Messenger (Yarmouth, MA) **10630**
Mason County News (Mason, TX) **10744**
Mason Valley News (Yerington, NV) **10663**
Massapequan Observer (Mineola, NY) **10682**
Massapequa Post (Massapequa
　Park, NY) **10681**
Mathis News (Mathis, TX) **10744**
† Matthews News (Matthews, NC)
Mattoon Journal Gazette (Mattoon, IL) **10440**
Maui News (Wailuku, HI) **10437**
† Maumee Valley Herald (Toledo, OH)
Mayfield Messenger (Mayfield, KY) **10453**
Maynard Beacon (Concord, MA) **10624**
Mayville Monitor (Mayville, MI) **10635**
Mayville News, The (Mayville, WI) **10769**

Mayville Sentinel/Chautauqua News
　(Westfield, NY) **10689**
Maywood Herald (Oak Park, IL) **10587**
McAllen Monitor (McAllen, TX) **10505**
McComb Enterprise-Journal
　(McComb, MS) **10465**
McConnellsburg Fulton County News
　(McConnellsburg, PA) **10719**
McCook Daily Gazette (McCook, NE) **10470**
McCreary County Record (Whitley
　City, KY) **10615**
McCurtain Daily Gazette (Idabel, OK) **10489**
McDonough-Democrat (Bushnell, IL) **10573**
McDowell News, The (Marion, NC) **10480**
McDuffie Progress, The (Thomson, GA) **10568**
McFarland Community Life
　(Monona, WI) **10770**
† McFarland Leader (Monona, WI)
McIntosh Times (McIntosh, MN) **10643**
McKeesport Daily News
　(McKeesport, PA) **10495**
McKenzie Banner (McKenzie, TN) **10733**
McKinney Courier Gazette
　(McKinney, TX) **10505**
McLean County Independent
　(Garrison, ND) **10696**
McLean County Journal (Turtle
　Lake, ND) **10697**
McLean Providence Journal
　(Reston, VA) **10755**
McLeansboro Times-Leader
　(McLeansboro, IL) **10584**
McPherson Sentinel (McPherson, KS) **10451**
Meade County Messenger
　(Brandenburg, KY) **10609**
Meade County Times-Tribune
　(Sturgis, SD) **10730**
Meadowbrook Times (Lawrence, NY) **10680**
Meadville Tribune, The (Meadville, PA) **10495**
Mebane Enterprise (Mebane, NC) **10693**
Mechanicsville Local
　(Mechanicsville, VA) **10754**
Mecklenburg Gazette (Davidson, NC) **10691**
Mecklenburg Sun (Clarksville, VA) **10752**
Medfield Suburban Press
　(Needham, MA) **10627**
Medford Daily Mercury (Malden, MA) **10458**
Medina County Gazette (Medina, OH) **10486**
▼Medina Sun, The (Medina, OH) **10705**
Meeker Herald, The (Meeker, CO) **10550**
Melrose Beacon (Melrose, MN) **10643**
Melrose Chronicle (Melrose, WI) **10769**
Melrose Free Press (Melrose, MA) **10626**
Melrose Park Herald (Oak Park, IL) **10587**
Melrose Park Star-Sentinel (Melrose
　Park, IL) **10585**

† Melrose Shoppers News (Stoneham, MA)
Memphis Flyer (Memphis, TN) **10734**
Menard County Review (Greenview, IL) **10581**
Menard News & Messenger, The (Menard, TX) **10744**
Mena Star (Mena, AR) **10528**
Mendocino Beacon, The (Mendocino, CA) **10539**
Mendota Reporter (Mendota, IL) **10585**
Menifee Valley News (Sun City, CA) **10545**
Menomonee Falls News (New Berlin, WI) **10771**
Mequon-Thiensville Courant (New Berlin, WI) **10771**
Merced County Times (Winton, CA) **10546**
Merced Sun-Star (Merced, CA) **10423**
Mercer County Chronicle (Coldwater, OH) **10701**
Mercer Island Reporter (Mercer Island, WA) **10758**
Mercury, The (Pottstown, PA) **10496**
Meridian Star (Meridian, MS) **10465**
Meriwether Free Press (Greenville, GA) **10565**
Meriwether Vindicator (Manchester, GA) **10566**
Merrick Beacon (Hicksville, NY) **10679**
Merrick Life (Merrick, NY) **10681**
Merrillville Herald Community Shopping Guide (Merrillville, IN) **10596**
Merrimack Valley Sunday (Amesbury, MA) **10623**
Mesabi Daily News (Virginia, MN) **10464**
Mesa County Mail (Fruita, CO) **10549**
Mesa Tribune (Mesa, AZ) **10418**
Mesa Tribune Wave (Los Angeles, CA) **10538**
Mesquite News (Mesquite, TX) **10744**
Message for the Week (Chester, VT) **10749**
Messenger-Press (Hightstown, NJ) **10666**
Messenger Index (Emmett, ID) **10569**
Messenger, The (Troy, AL) **10417**
Messenger, The (Attica, IN) **10591**
Messenger, The (Madisonville, KY) **10453**
Messenger, The (Garfield, NJ) **10666**
Messenger, The (Clemson, SC) **10727**
Messenger, The (Madison, TN) **10733**
Metro (San Jose, CA) **10543**
Metrocom Herald, The (San Antonio, TX) **10746**
Metropolis Planet (Metropolis, IL) **10585**
Metropolitan News (Brooklyn, NY) **10675**
Metro Press (Millbury, OH) **10705**
Metro Times (Detroit, MI) **10632**
Metro Weekenders, The (Norfolk, VA) **10754**
Mexia Daily News (Mexia, TX) **10505**
Mexico Ledger (Mexico, MO) **10467**
Miami Beach News (South Miami, FL) **10561**

Miami Chief, The (Miami, TX) **10744**
Miami County Republic (Paola, KS) **10608**
Miami Herald (Miami, FL) **10432**
Miami Laker (Miami Lakes, FL) **10559**
Miami News-Record (Miami, OK) **10490**
Miamisburg News (Miamisburg, OH) **10705**
† Miami Shores News (Miami, FL)
Miami Today (Miami, FL) **10559**
Michigan Chronicle (Detroit, MI) **10632**
Michigan City News-Dispatch (Michigan City, IN) **10445**
† Mid-Cities News (Arlington, TX)
Mid-County Journal (St. Louis, MO) **10657**
† Mid-County Times (Pardeeville, WI)
Mid-Island Times (Hicksville, NY) **10679**
Mid-South Horse Review (Somerville, TN) **10735**
Midcounty Chronicle (Nederland, TX) **10745**
Middleboro Gazette (Middleboro, MA) **10626**
Middlesboro Daily News (Middlesboro, KY) **10453**
Middlesex-Dunellen Chronicle (Somerville, NJ) **10670**
Middlesex News (Framingham, MA) **10457**
Middleton Gazette (Middleton, ID) **10570**
Middleton Times-Tribune (Middleton, WI) **10769**
Middletown Courier (Middletown, NJ) **10668**
Middletown Journal (Middletown, OH) **10486**
Middletown News, The (Middletown, IN) **10596**
Middletown Press (Middletown, CT) **10430**
Middletown Valley Citizen (Brunswick, MD) **10621**
Mid Hudson Times (Walden, NY) **10688**
Midland Daily News (Midland, MI) **10461**
Midland Reporter-Telegram (Midland, TX) **10505**
Midlothian-Bremen Messenger (Midlothian, IL) **10585**
Midlothian Mirror (Midlothian, TX) **10744**
Midlothian Today (DeSoto, TX) **10739**
† MidMon Observer (Washington, PA)
Mid Valley News (El Monte, CA) **10533**
Mid Valley Town Crier (Weslaco, TX) **10747**
MidWeek (Kaneohe, HI) **10568**
Midweek Eagle (West Fargo, ND) **10698**
Midweek Plus (West Fargo, ND) **10698**
MidWeek, The (DeKalb, IL) **10576**
Mifflinburg Telegraph, The (Mifflinburg, PA) **10720**
Milan Area Leader (Milan, MI) **10635**
Milan Standard, The (Milan, MO) **10655**
Milbrae Recorder-Progress (San Mateo, CA) **10543**
Miles City Star (Miles City, MT) **10469**
Milford Advertiser (Loveland, OH) **10704**

Milford Cabinet & Wilton Journal (Milford, NH) **10663**
† Milford Citizen (Milford, CT)
Milford Daily News (Milford, MA) **10458**
Milford Times (Milford, MI) **10635**
Millard County Gazette (Delta, UT) **10748**
Millbrae & San Bruno Sun (Burlingame, CA) **10531**
Millbrook Round Table (Millbrook, NY) **10682**
Millburn & Short Hills Item (Millburn, NJ) **10668**
Millbury/Sutton Chronicle (Millbury, MA) **10626**
Millcreek Sun (Erie, PA) **10717**
Mille Lacs County Times (Milaca, MN) **10643**
Miller County Liberal (Colquitt, GA) **10564**
Millerton News, The (Millerton, NY) **10682**
Millington Star, The (Millington, TN) **10734**
Millstadt Enterprise (Columbia, IL) **10576**
Mill Valley Herald (Sausalito, CA) **10544**
Milpitas Post (Milpitas, CA) **10539**
Milton Courier (Milton, WI) **10769**
Milton Daily Standard (Milton, PA) **10495**
Milton Record Transcript (Milton Village, MA) **10626**
Miltonvale Record (Miltonvale, KS) **10607**
Milville News (Bridgeton, NJ) **10472**
Milwaukee Journal Sentinel (Milwaukee, WI) **10515**
Milwaukee Star (Milwaukee, WI) **10769**
Minden Courier, The (Minden, NE) **10661**
Minden Press-Herald (Minden, LA) **10454**
Mineola American (Mineola, NY) **10682**
Mineral County Independent-News (Hawthorne, NV) **10662**
Mineral County Miner (Monte Vista, CO) **10550**
Mineral Daily Tribune (Keyser, WV) **10513**
Mineral Wells Index (Mineral Wells, TX) **10505**
Minerva Leader (Minerva, OH) **10705**
Minidoka County News (Rupert, ID) **10570**
Minifee County News (Morehead, KY) **10613**
Mining Journal (Marquette, MI) **10461**
Minnetonka/Deephaven Sun-Sailor (Minnetonka, MN) **10644**
Minonk News Dispatch (Minonk, IL) **10586**
Minot Daily News (Minot, ND) **10482**
Mira Mesa/Scripps Ranch Sentinel (San Diego, CA) **10542**
Mirror-Exchange (Milan, TN) **10734**
† Mirror-Recorder (Stamford, NY)
Mishawaka Enterprise (Mishawaka, IN) **10596**
Mississippi Eagle News, The (Warsaw, IL) **10590**
Mississippi Press (Pascagoula, MS) **10465**
Missoulian, The (Missoula, MT) **10469**

Missouri Press News (Columbia, MO) **10652**
Missouri Valley Times-News (Missouri Valley, IA) **10602**
Mitchell County Press-News (Osage, IA) **10603**
Mitchell News Journal (Spruce Pine, NC) **10695**
Moberly Monitor Index (Moberly, MO) **10467**
Mobile Beacon (Mobile, AL) **10521**
† Mobile Press (Mobile, AL)
Mobile Register, The (Mobile, AL) **10416**
Modern News (Harrisburg, AR) **10527**
Modesto Bee, The (Modesto, CA) **10423**
Modoc County Record (Alturas, CA) **10530**
Mohave Valley Daily News (Bullhead City, AZ) **10417**
Mojave Desert News, The (California City, CA) **10531**
Monadnock Ledger (Peterborough, NH) **10663**
Monahans News (Monahans, TX) **10744**
Mondovi Herald News (Mondovi, WI) **10770**
Monett Times (Monett, MO) **10467**
Moneysaver, The (Ballston Spa, NY) **10673**
Monitor, The (Los Alamos, NM) **10474**
Monitor, The (Mabank, TX) **10744**
Monroe County Appeal (Paris, MO) **10655**
Monroe County Beacon (Woodsfield, OH) **10709**
Monroe County Clarion (Columbia, IL) **10576**
Monroe County Democrat (Sparta, WI) **10773**
† Monroe County Sentinel (Woodsfield, OH)
Monroe Courier (Monroe, CT) **10553**
Monroe Evening News (Monroe, MI) **10461**
Monroe Journal (Monroeville, AL) **10521**
Monroe News (Albia, IA) **10599**
Monroe Times, The (Monroe, WI) **10515**
Monroe Watchman (Union, WV) **10763**
Montague County Shopper, The (Bowie, TX) **10737**
Montana Standard (Butte, MT) **10468**
Montauk Pioneer (Bridgehampton, NY) **10674**
Montclair Times, The (Montclair, NJ) **10668**
Montclarion (Oakland, CA) **10540**
Montebello News (Los Angeles, CA) **10538**
† Montecito Life (Goleta, CA)
Monterey County Herald, The (Monterey, CA) **10423**
Monterey Park Progress (Los Angeles, CA) **10538**
Montevideo American-News (Montevideo, MN) **10644**
Monte Vista Journal (Monte Vista, CO) **10550**
Montezuma Republican, The (Montezuma, IA) **10602**
Montgomery Advertiser (Montgomery, AL) **10416**

Montgomery County News, The (Hillsboro, IL) **10582**
Montgomery County Progress (Horsham, PA) **10718**
Montgomery County Sentinel (Gaithersburg, MD) **10621**
Montgomery Herald (Troy, NC) **10695**
Montgomery Herald (Montgomery, WV) **10762**
Montgomery Independent (Montgomery, AL) **10521**
Montgomery Journal, The (Rockville, MD) **10456**
Montgomery Post, The (Norristown, PA) **10721**
Montgomery Standard (Montgomery City, MO) **10655**
Montgomeryville Spirit (Fort Washington, PA) **10717**
Monticello Express (Monticello, IA) **10602**
Monticello News (Monticello, FL) **10559**
Montrose Daily Press (Montrose, CO) **10429**
Montrose Herald (Canistota, SD) **10729**
▼Montrose Morning Sun (Montrose, CO) **10429**
Moody County Enterprise (Flandreau, SD) **10730**
Moody Courier, The (Moody, TX) **10745**
Moorcroft Leader (Moorcroft, WY) **10776**
Moore American (Moore, OK) **10710**
Moore County News-Press (Dumas, TX) **10739**
Moorefield Examiner (Moorefield, WV) **10762**
Mooresville Times, The (Mooresville, IN) **10596**
Mooresville Tribune (Mooresville, NC) **10693**
Moorpark Star (Moorpark, CA) **10423**
Moose Lake Star-Gazette (Moose Lake, MN) **10644**
Moravia Republican Register (Moravia, NY) **10683**
Morehead News (Morehead, KY) **10613**
Morenci Observer (Morenci, MI) **10636**
Morgan County Herald (McConnelsville, OH) **10705**
Morgan County News (Wartburg, TN) **10735**
Morgan Hill Times (Morgan Hill, CA) **10539**
Morgan Messenger, The (Berkeley Springs, WV) **10760**
Morning Call, The (Allentown, PA) **10492**
Morning Journal (Lisbon, OH) **10485**
Morning Journal (Lorain, OH) **10485**
Morning News of Northwest Arkansas (Springdale, AR) **10421**
Morning Sun (Mt. Pleasant, MI) **10461**
Morongo Basin (Palm Desert, CA) **10540**
Morongo Basin Advertiser (Yucca Valley, CA) **10547**

Morris Daily Herald (Morris, IL) **10440**
Morris News Bee (Madison, NJ) **10667**
Morrisons Cove Herald (Martinsburg, PA) **10719**
Morris Sun (Morris, MN) **10644**
Morristown News, The (West Caldwell, NJ) **10671**
Morris Tribune (Morris, MN) **10644**
Morrow County Advertiser (Mt. Gilead, OH) **10705**
Morrow County Independent (Cardington, OH) **10699**
Morrow County Sentinel (Mt. Gilead, OH) **10705**
Morton Grove-Niles Life (Lincolnwood, IL) **10584**
Morton Grove Champion (Evanston, IL) **10579**
Moscow/Pullman Daily News (Moscow, ID) **10437**
Mosinee Times, The (Mosinee, WI) **10770**
Motley County Tribune (Matador, TX) **10744**
Moulton Advertiser (Moulton, AL) **10521**
Moultrie News, The (Mt. Pleasant, SC) **10728**
Mound City News (Mound City, MO) **10655**
Mounds View-New Brighton-St. Anthony Focus (Roseville, MN) **10646**
Moundsville Daily Echo (Moundsville, WV) **10513**
Moundville Times (Moundville, AL) **10521**
Mountain Advisor (Richlands, VA) **10755**
Mountain Citizen, The (Inez, KY) **10611**
Mountain Democrat (Placerville, CA) **10424**
Mountain Eagle (Tannersville, NY) **10688**
Mountain Eagle, The (Whitesburg, KY) **10615**
Mountain Echo (Yellville, AR) **10530**
Mountain Echo (Ironton, MO) **10654**
Mountaineer-Herald, The (Ebensburg, PA) **10717**
Mountaineer, The (Big Sandy, MT) **10659**
† Mountaineer, The (Waynesville, NC)
Mountain Grove News-Journal (Mountain Grove, MO) **10655**
Mountain Home News (Mountain Home, ID) **10570**
Mountain Life (Mariposa, CA) **10539**
Mountain Mail (Salida, CO) **10429**
Mountain Messenger (Downieville, CA) **10533**
Mountain Messenger (Lewisburg, WV) **10762**
Mountain News, The (Lake Arrowhead, CA) **10536**
Mountain Press (Prather, CA) **10541**
Mountain Press, The (Sevierville, TN) **10501**
Mountainside Echo (Union, NJ) **10671**
Mountain Statesman (Grafton, WV) **10761**
Mountain Sun, The (Kerrville, TX) **10742**
Mountain Times (Killington, VT) **10750**

Mountaintop Eagle (Mountain Top, PA) **10720**
† Mountain Visitor (Sevierville, TN)
▼Mountain Xpress (Asheville, NC) **10690**
Mount Airy News (Mt. Airy, NC) **10480**
Mount Ayr Record-News (Mt. Ayr, IA) **10603**
Mount Carmel Daily Republican-Register (Mt. Carmel, IL) **10440**
Mount Greenwood Express (Midlothian, IL) **10585**
Mount Holly News (Belmont, NC) **10691**
Mount Olive Tribune (Mt. Olive, NC) **10693**
Mount Pleasant Daily Tribune (Mt. Pleasant, TX) **10505**
Mount Pleasant Journal (Mt. Pleasant, PA) **10721**
Mount Pleasant News (Mt. Pleasant, IA) **10448**
Mount Prospect Journal (Des Plaines, IL) **10577**
Mount Prospect Times (Park Ridge, IL) **10588**
Mount Shasta Herald (Mt. Shasta, CA) **10539**
Mount Sterling Advocate (Mount Sterling, KY) **10613**
Mount Vernon Democrat (Mt. Vernon, IN) **10596**
Mount Vernon Gazette (Alexandria, VA) **10751**
Mount Vernon Independent (Yonkers, NY) **10690**
Mount Vernon News (Mt. Vernon, OH) **10486**
Mt. Airy Times (Philadelphia, PA) **10722**
Mt. Laurel Progress Press (Maple Shade, NJ) **10667**
Mt. Olive Chronicle (Budd Lake, NJ) **10664**
Mt. Olive Herald, The (Mt. Olive, IL) **10586**
Mt. Vernon Argus (Yonkers, NY) **10478**
† Mt. Washington Press (Cincinnati, OH)
Mt. Washington Star Review (Los Angeles, CA) **10538**
Mt. Washington Valley Mountain Ear (Conway, NH) **10663**
Mukwonago Chief (Mukwonago, WI) **10770**
Mulberry Press (Mulberry, FL) **10559**
Mullens Advocate (Mullen, WV) **10762**
Munday Courier, The (Munday, TX) **10745**
Mundelein News (Grayslake, IL) **10581**
Mundelein Review (Bannockburn, IL) **10572**
Munising News (Munising, MI) **10636**
Munster Guide (Maryville, IN) **10595**
Murfreesboro Daily News Journal (Murfreesboro, TN) **10501**
Murfreesboro Diamond (Murfreesboro, AR) **10528**
Murray County Wheel Herald (Slayton, MN) **10646**
† Murray Eagle (Salt Lake City, UT)
Murray Ledger & Times (Murray, KY) **10453**
Murrysville Area Star (Monroeville, PA) **10720**

Muscatine Journal (Muscatine, IA) **10448**
Muskegon Chronicle, The (Muskegon, MI) **10461**
Muskego Sun (New Berlin, WI) **10771**
Muskogee Daily Phoenix & Times-Democrat (Muskogee, OK) **10490**

N

N'West Iowa Review (Sheldon, IA) **10604**
Nantucket Beacon (Nantucket, MA) **10626**
Nanty Glo Journal, The (Nanty Glo, PA) **10721**
Napa County Record (Napa, CA) **10540**
Napa Valley Register (Napa, CA) **10423**
Naperville Metropolitan (Lemont, IL) **10583**
Naperville Sun (Naperville, IL) **10586**
Naples Daily News (Naples, FL) **10433**
Naples Record, The (Naples, NY) **10683**
Narragansett Times, The (Wakefield, RI) **10726**
Nashua Reporter (Nashua, IA) **10603**
Nashville Banner (Nashville, TN) **10501**
Nashville Graphic (Nashville, NC) **10693**
Nashville News (Nashville, AR) **10528**
Nashville News, The (Nashville, IL) **10586**
Nashville Scene, The (Nashville, TN) **10734**
Nassau County Record (Callahan, FL) **10556**
Nassau Herald (Lawrence, NY) **10680**
Natchez Democrat (Natchez, MS) **10465**
Natchitoches Times (Natchitoches, LA) **10454**
Natick Bulletin (Needham, MA) **10627**
Nation's Center News (Buffalo, SD) **10729**
National Union (Eastern Caroline Islands, FM) **10555**
Naugatuck Daily News (Naugatuck, CT) **10430**
Navasota Examiner Review (Navasota, TX) **10745**
† Near South Herald (Chicago, IL)
Nebraska City News-Press (Nebraska City, NE) **10470**
Nebraska Signal (Geneva, NE) **10661**
Needles Desert Star (Needles, CA) **10540**
Neighbors (Hillsboro, WI) **10768**
Neighbors (Markesan, WI) **10769**
▼Neighbors (Waupun, WI) **10775**
Nelson County Times (Amherst, VA) **10751**
Nemaha County Herald (Auburn, NE) **10660**
Neodesha Derrick (Neodesha, KS) **10607**
Neosho Daily News (Neosho, MO) **10467**
Neshoba Democrat, The (Philadelphia, MS) **10650**
Ness County News, The (Ness City, KS) **10607**
Netcong News-Leader (Netcong, NJ) **10668**
Nevada Appeal (Carson City, NV) **10470**
Nevada County Picayune (Prescott, AR) **10529**
Nevada Journal (Nevada, IA) **10603**

† New Alaskan (Ketchikan, AK)
New Albany Gazette (New Albany, MS) **10650**
Newark/Licking Advertiser (Newark, OH) **10705**
Newark Post (Newark, DE) **10554**
Newberg Graphic (Newberg, OR) **10714**
New Berlin Citizen (New Berlin, WI) **10771**
Newberry Observer, The (Newberry, SC) **10728**
New Braunfels Herald & Zeitung (New Braunfels, TX) **10505**
New Brighton-Mounds View Bulletin (St. Paul, MN) **10647**
New Buffalo Times (New Buffalo, MI) **10636**
Newburgh-Chandler Register (Newburgh, IN) **10596**
† Newburgh Evening News (Newburgh, NY)
New Canaan Advertiser (New Canaan, CT) **10553**
New Carlisle Sun (New Carlisle, OH) **10706**
New Castle Courier-Times (New Castle, IN) **10445**
New Castle News (New Castle, PA) **10495**
Newcastle Pacer, The (Newcastle, OK) **10710**
New Castle Record (New Castle, VA) **10754**
New City (Chicago, IL) **10575**
Newcomerstown News (Newcomerstown, OH) **10706**
New Era, The (Sweet Home, OR) **10715**
Newfield News (Trumansburg, NY) **10688**
New Hampshire Week in Review (Hillsborough, NH) **10663**
† New Hampton Economist (New Hampton, IA)
New Hampton Tribune (New Hampton, IA) **10603**
New Haven Advocate (New Haven, CT) **10553**
New Haven Register (New Haven, CT) **10430**
New Holstein Reporter (New Holstein, WI) **10771**
New Hope-Golden Valley Sun Post (Minneapolis, MN) **10644**
New Hope Gazette (New Hope, PA) **10721**
Newington Town Crier (Bristol, CT) **10551**
New Jersey Herald (Newton, NJ) **10472**
New Leader (Spencer, MA) **10628**
† Newman News, The (Newman, CA)
New Milford Times (New Milford, CT) **10553**
Newnan Times-Herald (Newnan, GA) **10567**
Newport Daily Express (Newport, VT) **10508**
Newport Daily Independent (Newport, AR) **10420**
Newport Daily News, The (Newport, RI) **10498**
Newport Mercury (Newport, RI) **10725**
Newport Miner (Newport, WA) **10758**
Newport Plaintalk (Newport, TN) **10734**
Newport This Week (Newport, RI) **10725**

New Prague Times (New Prague, MN) **10644**
New Prairie Town Crier (New Carlisle, IN) **10596**
New Richmond News (New Richmond, WI) **10771**
New River Record (Greenbush, MN) **10642**
News & Advance (Lynchburg, VA) **10509**
News & Observer (Raleigh, NC) **10480**
News & Press, The (Darlington, SC) **10727**
News & Record, The (Greensboro, NC) **10479**
News & Sentinel, The (Colebrook, NH) **10663**
News-Banner, The (Covington, LA) **10616**
News-Capital & Democrat (McAlester, OK) **10490**
News-Courier (Athens, AL) **10415**
News-Democrat, The (Carrollton, KY) **10610**
News-Enterprise (Elizabethtown, KY) **10452**
News-Examiner (Montpelier, ID) **10570**
News-Examiner (Gallatin, TN) **10732**
News-Gazette (Lexington, VA) **10753**
News-Gazette, The (Winchester, IN) **10446**
News-Herald (Port Clinton, OH) **10486**
News-Herald (Willoughby, OH) **10487**
News-Herald (Oil City, PA) **10495**
News-Herald, The (Southgate, MI) **10638**
News-Item (Shamokin, PA) **10496**
News-Journal (North Manchester, IN) **10596**
News-Journal Shopper (Campbellsville, KY) **10610**
News-Journal, The (Daytona Beach, FL) **10432**
News-Ledger, The (West Sacramento, CA) **10546**
News-Messenger (Fremont, OH) **10484**
† News-Messenger, The (Rockingham, NC)
News-Pilot, The (San Pedro, CA) **10425**
News-Press, The (Fort Myers, FL) **10432**
News-Progress (Sullivan, IL) **10589**
News-Progress, The (Chase City, VA) **10751**
News-Record (Gillette, WY) **10516**
News-Record of Maplewood & South Orange (Maplewood, NJ) **10668**
News-Record, The (Cerro Gordo, IL) **10574**
News-Register (McMinnville, OR) **10714**
News-Review (Roseburg, OR) **10492**
News-Review, The (Mattituck, NY) **10681**
News-Star (Lehigh Acres, FL) **10558**
News-Star, The (Monroe, LA) **10454**
News-Sun (Fairmount, IN) **10593**
News-Sun, The (Waukegan, IL) **10442**
News-Sun, The (New Bloomfield, PA) **10721**
News-Times (Hartford City, IN) **10444**
News-Times (Newport, OR) **10714**
News-Times, The (Danbury, CT) **10429**
News-Tribune (La Salle, IL) **10440**
News-Tribune (Framingham, MA) **10457**
News-Virginian (Waynesboro, VA) **10510**

News-X Press (Butler, MO) **10652**
News Beacon (Fair Lawn, NJ) **10666**
News Bulletin of McDowell County, The (Old Fort, NC) **10693**
News Buyer's Catalogue (Wytheville, VA) **10756**
News Buyers Catalog (Marion, VA) **10754**
News Chief (Winter Haven, FL) **10434**
Newsday (Melville, NY) **10476**
News Democrat & Leader (Russellville, KY) **10614**
News Democrat Journal (Festus, MO) **10653**
News Eagle (Hawley, PA) **10718**
† NewsEAST (Columbus, OH)
News Enterprise, The (Los Alamitos, CA) **10537**
News Examiner, The (Lutcher, LA) **10617**
News Gazette, The (Love Park, IL) **10584**
News Gleaner Publications (Philadelphia, PA) **10722**
News Guard, The (Lincoln City, OR) **10713**
New Sharon Star (New Sharon, IA) **10603**
News Herald (Lenoir City, TN) **10733**
† News Herald, The (Mobile, AL)
News Herald, The (Panama City, FL) **10433**
News Herald, The (Morganton, NC) **10480**
News Journal (Mansfield, OH) **10485**
News Journal, The (New Castle, DE) **10431**
News Leader (Fernandina, FL) **10557**
News Leader (Stow, OH) **10707**
News Leader (Richwood, WV) **10763**
News Leader, The (Royston, GA) **10567**
News Leader, The (Landrum, SC) **10728**
News Leader, The (Parsons, TN) **10734**
News Letter Journal (Newcastle, WY) **10776**
NewsMarketer, The (Tinley Park, IL) **10590**
News Messenger (Marshall, TX) **10505**
News Messenger, The (Christiansburg, VA) **10752**
New Smyrna Beach Observer (New Smyrna, FL) **10433**
News of Delaware County (Havertown, PA) **10718**
News of Orange County, The (Hillsborough, NC) **10692**
† News of Paterson (Passaic, NJ)
News of Southern Berks, The (Boyertown, PA) **10716**
News of the Highlands (Highland Falls, NY) **10679**
† News Outlook (Aberdeen, NC)
News Pointer (Sausalito, CA) **10544**
News Press, The (Paso Robles, CA) **10424**
News Report (Blackwood, NJ) **10664**
News Reporter, The (Whiteville, NC) **10695**
News Review (Ridgecrest, CA) **10541**
News Star (Lincolnwood, IL) **10584**
News Sun, The (Sebring, FL) **10560**
News Sun, The (Cleveland, OH) **10700**
News, The (Salem, AR) **10529**
News, The (Clay City, IN) **10592**
News, The (Southbridge, MA) **10458**
News, The (Frederick, MD) **10456**
News, The (Belvidere, NJ) **10664**
News, The (Aliquippa, PA) **10715**
News, The (Kingstree, SC) **10727**
News Times (Amherst, OH) **10698**
News Times (Forest Grove, OR) **10713**
News Transcript (Morganville, NJ) **10668**
News Tribune, The (Tacoma, WA) **10512**
News Watchman, The (Waverly, OH) **10708**
News Weekly (Mt. Laurel, NJ) **10668**
Newsweekly, The (Sebewaing, MI) **10638**
New Times (Phoenix, AZ) **10525**
New Times (San Luis Obispo, CA) **10543**
New Times, The (Kansas City, MO) **10654**
Newton Daily News (Newton, IA) **10448**
Newton Graphic (Waltham, MA) **10629**
Newton Kansan (Newton, KS) **10451**
Newton Press-Mentor (Newton, IL) **10586**
Newton Record (Newton, MS) **10650**
Newtown Bee, The (Newtown, CT) **10553**
New Ulm Enterprise (New Ulm, TX) **10745**
† New York City Tribune (New York, NY)
New York Daily Challenge (Brooklyn, NY) **10474**
New York Daily News, The (New York, NY) **10476**
New York Metropolitan News (Brooklyn, NY) **10675**
† New York Newsday (New York, NY)
New York Observer (New York, NY) **10683**
New York Post (New York, NY) **10476**
New York Press (New York, NY) **10683**
New York Times, The (New York, NY) **10476**
Niagara/Wheatfield Tribune (Grand Island, NY) **10678**
Niagara Gazette (Niagara Falls, NY) **10476**
Niantic-Harristown County Line Observer (Illiopolis, IL) **10582**
† Niantic News (East Lyme, CT)
Nicholas Chronicle (Summersville, WV) **10763**
Niles Daily Star (Niles, MI) **10461**
Niles Herald Spectator (Park Ridge, IL) **10588**
Niles Journal (Des Plaines, IL) **10577**
Niles Life (Lincolnwood, IL) **10584**
Nishna Valley Tribune (Audubon, IA) **10599**
Nisqually Valley News (Yelm, WA) **10760**
Nokomis Free Press-Progress (Nokomis, IL) **10586**
Nome Nugget (Nome, AK) **10523**
Nora News Dispatch (Fisherspolis, IN) **10593**

Nordonia Hills Sun (Cleveland, OH) **10700**
Norfolk Daily News (Norfolk, NE) **10470**
Norman Transcript (Norman, OK) **10490**
Norridge-Harwood Heights News (Park Ridge, IL) **10588**
Norridge-Harwood Heights Times (Lincolnwood, IL) **10584**
North/South Beach Now (San Francisco, CA) **10543**
North Bartow News (Adairsville, GA) **10562**
North Bay Village News (South Miami, FL) **10561**
North Bergen Reporter (Hoboken, NJ) **10667**
Northbrook Star (Glenview, IL) **10580**
North Brunswick Post (Dayton, NJ) **10665**
North Castle News (Yonkers, NY) **10690**
North Center-Lincoln Belmont-Lake View Booster (Lincolnwood, IL) **10584**
North Central Outlook (Seattle, WA) **10759**
Northcentral Shopper (Des Moines, IA) **10600**
North Clermont Community Journal (Loveland, OH) **10704**
North Country Free Press (Granville, NY) **10678**
North Countryman, The (Elizabethtown, NY) **10676**
North Country Sun (Ironwood, MI) **10634**
North County Journal East (St. Louis, MO) **10657**
North County Journal West (St. Louis, MO) **10657**
North County News (Red Bud, IL) **10588**
North County News (Yorktown Heights, NY) **10690**
North County Shopping News (Atascadero, CA) **10530**
North County Times (Escondido, CA) **10422**
North East Breeze (North East, PA) **10721**
† Northeast Detroiter (Detroit, MI)
Northeast Georgian, The (Cornelia, GA) **10564**
Northeast Johnson County (Shawnee Mission, KS) **10608**
Northeast Mississippi Daily Journal (Tupelo, MS) **10465**
Northeast Reporter (Indianapolis, IN) **10594**
Northeast Reporter (Towson, MD) **10623**
Northeast Shopper (Des Moines, IA) **10600**
Northeast Suburban Life Press (Loveland, OH) **10705**
Northeast Sun (City of Commerce, CA) **10532**
Northeast Times (Philadelphia, PA) **10722**
Northern Light, The (Greenbush, MN) **10642**
Northern Michigan News (Cadillac, MI) **10631**
Northern Ogle County Tempo (Byron, IL) **10574**

Northern Piedmont Express (Culpeper, VA) **10752**
Northern Star (Gaylord, MI) **10633**
Northern Star, The (Clinton, MN) **10641**
Northern Virginia Daily (Strasburg, VA) **10510**
Northern Virginia Sun, The (Fairfax, VA) **10752**
Northern Watch (Thief River Falls, MN) **10647**
Northern Wyoming Daily News (Worland, WY) **10516**
Northfield Advance (Jenison, MI) **10634**
Northfield News (Northfield, MN) **10645**
North Georgia News (Blairsville, GA) **10563**
Northglenn-Thornton Sentinel (Westminster, CO) **10551**
North Haven Post, The (Milford, CT) **10553**
North Hills News Record (Warrendale, PA) **10497**
North Jackson Progress (Stevenson, AL) **10522**
North Jefferson News (Gardendale, AL) **10519**
North Jersey Herald & News, The (Passaic, NJ) **10472**
North Jersey Prospector (Clifton, NJ) **10665**
North Kitsap Herald (Poulsbo, WA) **10759**
North Knox News (Bicknell, IN) **10592**
Northlake Star-Sentinel (Melrose Park, IL) **10585**
North Lake Tahoe Bonanza (Incline Village, NV) **10662**
Northland News (Columbus, OH) **10701**
North Loop News (Chicago, IL) **10575**
North Macomb Voice (New Baltimore, MI) **10636**
North Meridian Observer (Fishers, IN) **10593**
North Miami Beach News (South Miami, FL) **10561**
North Miami News (Miami, FL) **10559**
North Minneapolis Sun Post (Minneapolis, MN) **10644**
North Missourian (Gallatin, MO) **10653**
North Myrtle Beach Times (North Myrtle Beach, SC) **10728**
Northome Record & Mizpah Message (Northome, MN) **10645**
North Port Sun Herald (North Port, FL) **10433**
North San Antonio Times (San Antonio, TX) **10746**
North Scott Press, The (Eldridge, IA) **10600**
† North Scottsdale Independent (Scottsdale, AZ)
Northshire Free Press, The (Granville, NY) **10678**
Northshore Citizen (Bothell, WA) **10757**
North Shore Shopper (Pacific Palisades, CA) **10540**
North Shore Sunday (Danvers, MA) **10624**

Northside Journal (St. Louis, MO) **10657**
Northside Neighbor, The (Atlanta, GA) **10563**
North Side News (Jerome, ID) **10569**
Northside Recorder Times, The (San Antonio, TX) **10746**
Northside Sun, The (Jackson, MS) **10650**
North Side Topics (Fishers, IN) **10593**
North Snohomish Weekly (Arlington, WA) **10757**
North Star (Philadelphia, PA) **10722**
North Star Journal (Presque Isle, WI) **10772**
North Star News (Greenbush, MN) **10642**
North Suburban Herald (Love Park, IL) **10584**
North Syracuse Star-News (Syracuse, NY) **10687**
North Tahoe/Truckee Week (Carnelian Bay, CA) **10532**
Northumberland Echo (Heathsville, VA) **10753**
North Utah County Shopper (American Fork, UT) **10748**
North Vernon Plain Dealer (North Vernon, IN) **10596**
North Vernon Sun (North Vernon, IN) **10596**
Northville Record (Northville, MI) **10636**
Northwest Alabamian (Haleyville, AL) **10520**
Northwest Arkansas Times (Fayetteville, AR) **10419**
Northwest Blade, The (Eureka, SD) **10730**
Northwest Colorado Daily Press (Craig, CO) **10428**
Northwest Columbus News (Columbus, OH) **10701**
Northwest Current, The (Washington, DC) **10555**
Northwestern Illinois Dispatch (Savanna, IL) **10589**
Northwestern Illinois Farmer (Lena, IL) **10583**
Northwest Florida Daily News (Fort Walton Beach, FL) **10432**
Northwest Herald (Crystal Lake, IL) **10438**
Northwest Iowa Shopper (Spencer, IA) **10604**
Northwest Journal & Topics (Des Plaines, IL) **10577**
Northwest Leader (Chicago, IL) **10575**
Northwest Press (Speedway, IN) **10598**
Northwest Press (Cincinnati, OH) **10700**
Northwest Shopper (Des Moines, IA) **10600**
Northwest Side Press (Chicago, IL) **10575**
Northwest Signal (Napoleon, OH) **10486**
Northwood Gleaner (Northwood, ND) **10697**
North Woods Call (Charlevoix, MI) **10631**
Norton Courier (Stoughton, MA) **10628**
Norton Daily Telegram (Norton, KS) **10451**
Norwalk Herald American (Los Angeles, CA) **10538**
† Norwalk News (Westport, CT)

Norwalk Reflector (Norwalk, OH) **10486**
Norway Advertiser-Democrat (Norway, ME) **10620**
Norway Current (Norway, MI) **10636**
Norwell Mariner (Marshfield, MA) **10626**
Norwich Bulletin (Norwich, CT) **10430**
Novato Advance (Novato, CA) **10540**
Novi News (Northville, MI) **10636**
Nowata Star (Nowata, OK) **10710**
Nueces County Record Star (Robstown, TX) **10746**
Nutley Journal (Bloomfield, NJ) **10664**
Nutley Sun, The (Nutley, NJ) **10668**
NUVO Newsweekly (Indianapolis, IN) **10594**

O

O-W Enterprise (Withee, WI) **10775**
O'Fallon Journal (O'Fallon, MO) **10655**
O'Fallon Progress (O'Fallon, IL) **10586**
Oak Brook Doings (Hinsdale, IL) **10582**
Oak Brook Press (Elmhurst, IL) **10578**
Oak Brook Terrace Doings (Hinsdale, IL) **10582**
Oak Cliff Tribune (Dallas, TX) **10738**
Oak Creek Pictorial (New Berlin, WI) **10771**
Oakdale-Lake Elmo Review (St. Paul, MN) **10647**
Oakdale Clarion (Oakdale, MN) **10645**
Oakdale Journal (Oakdale, LA) **10617**
Oakdale Leader (Oakdale, CA) **10540**
Oakland Independent (Oakland, NE) **10661**
Oakland Press, The (Pontiac, MI) **10461**
Oakland Tribune, The (Oakland, CA) **10423**
Oak Lawn Independent (Midlothian, IL) **10585**
Oak Leaves, The (Oak Park, IL) **10587**
Oakley Graphic (Oakley, KS) **10607**
Oak Ridger, The (Oak Ridge, TN) **10501**
Oakville-Mehville Journal (St. Louis, MO) **10657**
Oberlin Herald, The (Oberlin, KS) **10607**
Observer-Dispatch (Utica, NY) **10477**
† Observer-Patriot (Putnam, CT)
Observer-Reporter (Waynesburg, PA) **10497**
Observer-Reporter, Washington County Edition (Washington, PA) **10497**
Observer-Tribune (Chester, NJ) **10665**
Observer News (Newton, NC) **10480**
Observer, The (New Smyrna, FL) **10433**
Observer, The (Royal Palm Beach, FL) **10560**
Observer, The (Moultrie, GA) **10435**
Observer, The (DeWitt, IA) **10600**
Observer, The (Belgrade, MN) **10640**
† Observer, The (Blackwood, NJ)
Observer, The (Kearny, NJ) **10667**
Observer, The (Rio Rancho, NM) **10672**

Observer, The (Northport, NY) **10683**
Observer, The (La Grande, OR) **10492**
Observer, The (Greenville, RI) **10725**
Ocala Star Banner (Ocala, FL) **10433**
Oceana's Herald-Journal (Hart, MI) **10633**
Ocean County's Observer (Toms River, NJ) **10472**
Ocean County Reporter (Toms River, NJ) **10670**
Oceanside/Island Park Herald (Long Beach, NY) **10680**
Oceanside Centre Beacon (Mineola, NY) **10682**
Ocean Springs Record (Ocean Springs, MS) **10650**
Oconee Breeze (Madison, GA) **10566**
Oconomowoc Enterprise (Oconomowoc, WI) **10771**
Oconto County Times-Herald (Oconto Falls, WI) **10771**
▼OC Weekly (Los Angeles, CA) **10538**
Odem-Edroy Times (Sinton, TX) **10746**
Odessa American (Odessa, TX) **10505**
Oelwein Daily Register (Oelwein, IA) **10448**
Ogemaw County Herald (West Branch, MI) **10639**
Ogle County Life (Oregon, IL) **10587**
Ohio County News (Rising Sun, IN) **10597**
Ohio County Times News (Hartford, KY) **10611**
Ojai Valley News (Ojai, CA) **10540**
Oklahoma City Friday (Oklahoma City, OK) **10711**
Oklahoma Eagle (Tulsa, OK) **10712**
Oklahoma Gazette (Oklahoma City, OK) **10711**
Oklee Herald (Oklee, MN) **10645**
Okmulgee Times (Okmulgee, OK) **10490**
Olathe Daily News (Olathe, KS) **10451**
Olathe Sun (Overland Park, KS) **10608**
Old Colony Memorial (Plymouth, MA) **10627**
Oldham Era, The (La Grange, KY) **10612**
Old Lyons Recorder, The (Lyons, CO) **10550**
Olean Times Herald (Olean, NY) **10476**
Olive Hill Times (Olive Hill, KY) **10613**
Oliveville Times (Morehead, KY) **10613**
Olivia Times Journal (Olivia, MN) **10645**
Olney Daily Mail (Olney, IL) **10441**
Olney Enterprise, The (Olney, TX) **10745**
Olney Times (Philadelphia, PA) **10722**
Olympian, The (Olympia, WA) **10511**
Olympia Review (Minier, IL) **10586**
Omaha Star (Omaha, NE) **10661**
Omaha World-Herald (Omaha, NE) **10470**
Omak-Okanogan County Chronicle (Omak, WA) **10758**
Omro Herald (Omro, WI) **10771**
Onawa Democrat (Onawa, IA) **10603**
Onawa Sentinel (Onawa, IA) **10603**
Onaway Outlook (Onaway, MI) **10636**
Oneida Daily Dispatch (Oneida, NY) **10476**
Onlooker, The (Foley, AL) **10519**
Onondaga Valley News (Syracuse, NY) **10687**
Ontario Advertiser (San Bernardino, CA) **10542**
Ontonagon Herald (Ontonagon, MI) **10636**
Oologah Lake Leader (Oologah, OK) **10711**
Opelika-Auburn News (Opelika, AL) **10416**
Opp News (Opp, AL) **10521**
Orange Bulletin (Milford, CT) **10553**
Orange Countian (Paoli, IN) **10597**
Orange County Log (San Diego, CA) **10542**
Orange County News (Garden Grove, CA) **10534**
Orange County Register, The (Santa Ana, CA) **10425**
Orange County Review (Orange, VA) **10754**
Orange Cove Mountain Times (Reedley, CA) **10541**
Orange Leader (Orange, TX) **10505**
Orange Transcript (Orange, NJ) **10669**
† Orangevale News (Folsom, CA)
Orchard Park Bee (Williamsville, NY) **10689**
Ord Quiz (Ord, NE) **10661**
Oregonian, The (Portland, OR) **10492**
Oregon Observer (Oregon, WI) **10771**
Orem-Geneva Times (Orem, UT) **10749**
Orfordville Journal & Footville News (Orfordville, WI) **10772**
Orion Gazette (Orion, IL) **10587**
† Orion Times (Orion, IL)
Orland Metropolitan (Lemont, IL) **10583**
Orlando Sentinel (Orlando, FL) **10433**
Orlando Weekly, The (Winter Park, FL) **10562**
Orland Press-Register (Orland, CA) **10540**
Orland Township Messenger (Midlothian, IL) **10585**
Oroville Mercury-Register (Oroville, CA) **10423**
† Orrville Courier-Crescent (Orrville, OH)
Ortonville Independent (Ortonville, MN) **10645**
Oryor Jeffersonian (Pryor, OK) **10711**
Osage County Chronicle (Burlingame, KS) **10606**
Osakis Review, The (Osakis, MN) **10645**
Osawatomie Graphic (Osawatomie, KS) **10608**
Osborne County Farmer (Osborne, KS) **10608**
Osceola County Gazette-Tribune (Sibley, IA) **10604**
Osceola News-Gazette (Kissimmee, FL) **10558**
Osceola Sentinel-Tribune (Osceola, IA) **10603**
Osceola Sun (Osceola, WI) **10772**
Osceola Times (Osceola, AR) **10529**
Oscoda Press (Oscoda, MI) **10636**
Osgood Journal (Versailles, IN) **10598**

Oshkosh Buyers Guide (Oshkosh, WI) **10772**
Oshkosh Northwestern (Oshkosh, WI) **10515**
Oskaloosa Herald (Oskaloosa, IA) **10448**
Oskaloosa Independent (Oskaloosa, KS) **10608**
Ossian Bee, The (Ossian, IA) **10603**
Ossian Journal (Ossian, IN) **10596**
Other Paper, The (Columbus, OH) **10701**
Ottawa Advance (Jenison, MI) **10634**
Ottawa County Exponent, The (Oak Harbor, OH) **10706**
Ottawa Herald (Ottawa, KS) **10451**
Ottawa Times (Ottawa, KS) **10608**
Ottawa Times Shopper (Ottawa, KS) **10608**
Ottumwa Courier (Ottumwa, IA) **10448**
Ouachita Citizen (West Monroe, LA) **10618**
Ouray County Plaindealer (Ouray, CO) **10550**
Our Home Town (Vanderbilt, MI) **10638**
Our Town (Maywood, NJ) **10668**
Our Town (New York, NY) **10683**
Our Town (Pearl River, NY) **10684**
Outlook Mail (Santa Monica, CA) **10544**
Outlook, The (Santa Monica, CA) **10426**
Outlook, The (Othello, WA) **10758**
Overland Park Sun (Shawnee Mission, KS) **10608**
Over the Mountain Journal (Birmingham, AL) **10518**
Ovid Gazette (Trumansburg, NY) **10688**
Oviedo Voice, The (Oviedo, FL) **10560**
Owasso Reporter (Owasso, OK) **10711**
Owatonna People's Press (Owatonna, MN) **10463**
Owatonna Weekly Shopper (Owatonna, MN) **10645**
Owego Pennysaver (Owego, NY) **10684**
Owensboro Messenger-Inquirer (Owensboro, KY) **10453**
Owings Mills Times (Baltimore, MD) **10621**
Owyhee Avalanche (Homedale, ID) **10569**
Oxford Eagle (Oxford, MS) **10465**
Oxford Press (Oxford, OH) **10706**
Oxford Public Ledger (Oxford, NC) **10694**
Oxford Register, The (Belle Plaine, KS) **10605**
Oxford Review-Times (Greene, NY) **10678**
† Oxnard Press-Courier (Oxnard, CA)
Oyster Bay-Syosset Guardian (Oyster Bay, NY) **10684**
Oyster Bay Enterprise Pilot (Mineola, NY) **10682**
Ozark County Times (Gainesville, MO) **10653**
Ozark Journal (Imboden, AR) **10528**
Ozaukee County News Graphic (Cedarburg, WI) **10765**
Ozaukee Guide (Cedarburg, WI) **10765**
Ozaukee Press (Port Washington, WI) **10772**

P

Pacifica Tribune (Pacifica, CA) **10540**
Pacific Daily News (Agana, GU) **10436**
Pacific Sun (Mill Valley, CA) **10539**
Paducah Sun, The (Paducah, KY) **10453**
Pageland Progressive-Journal, The (Pageland, SC) **10728**
Page News & Courier (Luray, VA) **10754**
Paintsville Herald, The (Paintsville, KY) **10613**
Palacios Beacon (Palacios, TX) **10745**
Palatine Countryside (Arlington Heights, IL) **10571**
Palatine Journal & Topics (Des Plaines, IL) **10577**
Palau Gazette (Koror, PW) **10715**
Palestine Herald-Press (Palestine, TX) **10506**
Palisade Tribune (Palisade, CO) **10550**
Palisadian-Post (Pacific Palisades, CA) **10540**
Palladium-Times, The (Oswego, NY) **10476**
Palm Beach Daily News (Palm Beach, FL) **10433**
Palm Beach Post (West Palm Beach, FL) **10434**
Palm Desert Advertiser (Palm Desert, CA) **10540**
Palm Desert Post (Indio, CA) **10535**
Palm Spring Advertiser (Palm Desert, CA) **10540**
Palmyra Spectator (Palmyra, MO) **10655**
▼Palo Alto Daily News (Palo Alto, CA) **10424**
Palo Alto Weekly (Palo Alto, CA) **10541**
Palos Citizen (Midlothian, IL) **10585**
Palos Hills-Hickory Hills (Palos Heights, IL) **10587**
Palos Verdes Peninsula News (Palos Verdes Peninsula, CA) **10541**
Palo Verde Valley Times (Blythe, CA) **10531**
Pampa News (Pampa, TX) **10506**
Pana News-Palladium (Pana, IL) **10587**
† Panhandle Press (Chester, WV)
Panola Watchman (Carthage, TX) **10737**
▼Panolian Advantage, The (Batesville, MS) **10648**
Panolian, The (Batesville, MS) **10648**
Pantagraph, The (Bloomington, IL) **10438**
Paoli News (Paoli, IN) **10597**
Paoli Republican (Paoli, IN) **10597**
Paper of Wabash County, The (Wabash, IN) **10598**
Paper, The (Barry, IL) **10572**
Paper, The (Elkhart, IN) **10593**
Paper, The (Goshen, IN) **10594**
Paper, The (Warsaw, IN) **10598**
† Paper, The (Spartanburg, SC)
Papillion Times (Papillion, NE) **10661**
Paradise Post (Paradise, CA) **10541**

Paradise Valley Independent
  (Scottsdale, AZ) **10526**
Paragould Daily Press (Paragould, AR) **10420**
Paris Beacon News (Paris, IL) **10441**
Paris Express (Paris, AR) **10529**
Paris News, The (Paris, TX) **10506**
Paris Post-Intelligencer, The (Paris, TN) **10501**
Parkchester News (Bronx, NY) **10674**
Parker Advertiser (Parker, AZ) **10525**
Parker Pioneer (Parker, AZ) **10525**
Parkersburg Sentinel
  (Parkersburg, WV) **10513**
Park Falls Herald (Park Falls, WI) **10772**
Park LaBrea News/Beverly Press (Los
  Angeles, CA) **10538**
Park News (Library, PA) **10719**
Park Rapids Enterprise (Park
  Rapids, MN) **10645**
Park Record, The (Park City, UT) **10749**
Park Ridge Herald Advocate (Park
  Ridge, IL) **10588**
Park Ridge Journal (Des Plaines, IL) **10577**
Park Slope Courier (Brooklyn, NY) **10675**
Parkway Transcript (Dedham, MA) **10624**
Parlier Post (Sanger, CA) **10543**
Parma Sun Post (Berea, OH) **10699**
† Parsippany Focus (Morris Plains, NJ)
Parsippany News, The (West
  Caldwell, NJ) **10671**
Parsons Advocate (Parsons, WV) **10762**
Parsons News (Parsons, KS) **10608**
Parsons Sun (Parsons, KS) **10451**
Pasadena Citizen (Pasadena, TX) **10506**
Pasadena Star-News, The
  (Pasadena, CA) **10424**
Pasadena Weekly (Pasadena, CA) **10541**
Pascack Valley Community Life
  (Westwood, NJ) **10671**
Pasco News (Dade City, FL) **10556**
Passaic Valley Today (Butler, NJ) **10665**
Pataskala Standard (Pataskala, OH) **10706**
Patent Trader (Cross River, NY) **10676**
Patriot & Free Press (Cuba, NY) **10676**
Patriot-News (Harrisburg, PA) **10494**
Patriot Ledger (Quincy, MA) **10458**
Patriot, The (Kutztown, PA) **10719**
Paulding Neighbor, The (Marietta, GA) **10566**
Paulding Progress (Paulding, OH) **10706**
Paullina Times (Paullina, IA) **10603**
Pauls Valley Daily Democrat (Pauls
  Valley, OK) **10490**
Pawhuska Journal-Capital
  (Pawhuska, OK) **10711**
Pawling News Chronicle (Pawling, NY) **10684**
Pawnee Post (Auburn, IL) **10572**
Paw Paw Courier-Leader (Paw Paw, MI) **10636**

Paxton Daily Record (Paxton, IL) **10441**
Paynesville Press, The
  (Paynesville, MN) **10645**
Payson Roundup (Payson, AZ) **10525**
† Peabody Times (Peabody, MA)
Pecos Enterprise (Pecos, TX) **10506**
Peekskill Herald (Peekskill, NY) **10684**
Peekskill Star (Yorktown Heights, NY) **10478**
Pekin Daily Times (Pekin, IL) **10441**
Pelham Journal (Pelham, GA) **10567**
Pelham Sun (Yonkers, NY) **10690**
Pelican Press (Sarasota, FL) **10560**
Pelican Rapids Press (Pelican
  Rapids, MN) **10645**
Pella Chronicle (Pella, IA) **10603**
Pembroke Mariner (Marshfield, MA) **10626**
Pembroke Reporter (Plymouth, MA) **10628**
Pender Chronicle (Burgaw, NC) **10691**
Pender Post (Burgaw, NC) **10691**
Pendleton Record, The (Pendleton, OR) **10714**
Penfield Post-Republican, The
  (Fishers, NY) **10677**
Peninsula Beacon, The (San Diego, CA) **10542**
Peninsula Clarion (Kenai, AK) **10417**
Peninsula Daily News (Port
  Angeles, WA) **10511**
Peninsula Gateway (Gig Harbor, WA) **10758**
Peninsula Independent
  (Burlingame, CA) **10531**
† Peninsula Review, The (Carmel, CA)
Pennington County Prevailer-News (Hill
  City, SD) **10730**
Pennsboro News (Pennsboro, WV) **10762**
† Pennysaver (Vista, CA)
Penny Saver (Tinley Park, IL) **10590**
Penny Saver (Three Rivers, MI) **10638**
Pennysaver (Elmsford, NY) **10677**
Pennysaver (Yorktown Heights, NY) **10690**
Penny Saver (Covington, OH) **10703**
Pennysaver Press (Bennington, VT) **10749**
Pennysaver, The (Yarmouthport, MA) **10630**
Penobscot Times (Old Town, ME) **10620**
Pensacola News Journal
  (Pensacola, FL) **10433**
Pensacola Voice (Pensacola, FL) **10560**
People-Sentinel (Barnwell, SC) **10726**
People's Defender, The (West
  Union, OH) **10708**
People's Weekly World (New York, NY) **10683**
Peoria Journal Star (Peoria, IL) **10441**
Peoria Observer (Peoria, IL) **10588**
Peoria Times (Glendale, AZ) **10525**
Pepperell Free Press (Ayer, MA) **10623**
Perdido Pelican (Pensacola, FL) **10560**
Perham Enterprise-Bulletin
  (Perham, MN) **10645**

Perinton-Fairport Post, The
  (Pittsford, NY) **10684**
Perkasie News-Herald (Perkasie, PA) **10722**
Perquimans Weekly (Hertford, NC) **10692**
Perry Chief (Perry, IA) **10603**
Perry County News, The (Tell City, IN) **10598**
Perry County Petit Jean Country Headlight
  (Morrilton, AR) **10528**
Perry County Republic-Monitor, The
  (Perryville, MO) **10656**
Perry County Times (New
  Bloomfield, PA) **10721**
Perry County Tribune (New
  Lexington, OH) **10706**
Perry Daily Journal (Perry, OK) **10490**
Perry News-Herald (Perry, FL) **10560**
Perrysburg Messenger-Journal
  (Perrysburg, OH) **10706**
Perry Taco Times (Perry, FL) **10560**
Perry Township Weekly (Beech
  Grove, IN) **10592**
Peru Tribune (Peru, IN) **10445**
Peshtigo Times (Peshtigo, WI) **10772**
Petaluma Argus-Courier (Petaluma, CA) **10541**
Peterborough Transcript
  (Peterborough, NH) **10663**
Petersburg Observer (Petersburg, IL) **10588**
Petersburg Pilot (Petersburg, AK) **10523**
Petoskey News-Review (Petoskey, MI) **10461**
Petosky Star Ad-Vertiser (Gaylord, MI) **10633**
Pharos-Tribune (Logansport, IN) **10444**
Phenix-Citizen (Phenix City, AL) **10521**
Philadelphia City Paper
  (Philadelphia, PA) **10722**
Philadelphia Daily News
  (Philadelphia, PA) **10495**
Philadelphia Guide Newspaper
  (Philadelphia, PA) **10722**
Philadelphia Inquirer (Philadelphia, PA) **10495**
Philadelphia Weekly (Philadelphia, PA) **10722**
Philipsburg Mail, The (Philipsburg, MT) **10659**
Phillipsburg Free Press
  (Phillipsburg, NJ) **10669**
Phillips County Review
  (Phillipsburg, KS) **10608**
† Phoenix Gazette (Phoenix, AZ)
Phoenix Newspaper, The (Brooklyn, NY) **10675**
Phoenix Register (Phoenix, NY) **10684**
Phoenix, The (Phoenixville, PA) **10496**
Photo News (Monroe, NY) **10683**
Photo Star (Willshire, OH) **10708**
Piatt County Journal-Republican
  (Monticello, IL) **10586**
Picayune Item (Picayune, MS) **10465**
Pickens County Herald (Carrollton, AL) **10518**
Pickens Sentinel (Pickens, SC) **10728**

Pickerington Times-Sun
  (Columbus, OH) **10701**
Pickett County Press (Byrdstown, TN) **10731**
Pico Rivera News (Los Angeles, CA) **10538**
Pictorial Gazette (Old Saybrook, CT) **10553**
† Pictorial Press (Tahlequah, OK)
Picture Post (Waupaca, WI) **10775**
Piedmonter, The (Oakland, CA) **10540**
Piedmont Herald (Piedmont, WV) **10762**
Piedmont Journal-Independent
  (Piedmont, AL) **10521**
Pierce City Leader-Journal (Pierce
  City, MO) **10656**
Pierce County Herald (Puyallup, WA) **10759**
Pierce County Herald (Ellsworth, WI) **10767**
Pierce County Tribune (Rugby, ND) **10697**
Pierre Times, The (Pierre, SD) **10730**
Piggott Times, The (Piggott, AR) **10529**
Pike County Dispatch (Milford, PA) **10720**
Pike County News Watchman
  (Waverly, OH) **10708**
Pike Register (Fishers, IN) **10593**
Pikes Peak Journal (Manitou
  Springs, CO) **10550**
Pilot-News (Plymouth, IN) **10445**
Pinckney Post Shopping Guide
  (Pinckney, MI) **10637**
Pine Bluff Commercial (Pine Bluff, AR) **10420**
Pine Bluff News (Pine Bluff, AR) **10529**
Pine Island Eagle (Bokeelia, FL) **10555**
Pine Plains Register-Herald (Pine
  Plains, NY) **10684**
Pine River Times (Bayfield, CO) **10547**
Pineville Sun-Cumberland Courier
  (Pineville, KY) **10613**
Pinnacle, The (Hollister, CA) **10535**
Pioneer-News (Shepherdsville, KY) **10614**
Pioneer Republican, The (Marengo, IA) **10602**
Pioneer, The (Bemidji, MN) **10462**
Pipestone County Star (Pipestone, MN) **10645**
Piqua Daily Call (Piqua, OH) **10486**
Piscataquis Observer, The
  (Dover-Foxcroft, ME) **10619**
Pitch Weekly (Kansas City, MO) **10654**
Pittsburg Gazette (Pittsburg, TX) **10745**
Pittsburgh City Paper (Pittsburgh, PA) **10723**
Pittsburgh Post-Gazette
  (Pittsburgh, PA) **10496**
† Pittsburgh Press (Pittsburgh, PA)
Pittsburgh Renaissance News
  (Pittsburgh, PA) **10723**
Pittsburg Morning Sun (Pittsburg, KS) **10451**
Pittsfield Gazette, The (Pittsfield, MA) **10627**
Placentia News-Times (Anaheim, CA) **10530**
Placer Herald (Rocklin, CA) **10541**
Plain Dealer (Blackwood, NJ) **10664**

▼Plainfield Sun (Plainfield, IL) **10588**
Plainsman, The (Huron, SD) **10499**
Plainsman Weekly News (Sedalia, MO) **10656**
Plainview Daily Herald (Plainview, TX) **10506**
Plainview News (Plainview, MN) **10645**
Plainview News (Plainview, NE) **10661**
Plano Star Courier (Plano, TX) **10506**
Plant City Shopper (Plant City, FL) **10560**
Plaquemines Gazette (Belle Chasse, LA) **10615**
Plaquemines Watchman (Belle Chasse, LA) **10615**
Platte County Gazette (Parkville, MO) **10655**
Platte County Record-Times (Wheatland, WY) **10776**
Platte Dispatch Tribune (Kansas City, MO) **10654**
Platteville Journal (Platteville, WI) **10772**
Plattsmouth Journal (Plattsmouth, NE) **10661**
Pleasant Grove Review (American Fork, UT) **10748**
Pleasanton Express (Pleasanton, TX) **10745**
Plymouth Observer (Plymouth, MI) **10637**
Plymouth Sun-Sailor (Minnetonka, MN) **10644**
Pocahontas Record-Democrat (Pocahontas, IA) **10603**
Pocahontas Star Herald (Pocahontas, AR) **10529**
Pocahontas Times (Marlinton, WV) **10762**
Pocono Record (Stroudsburg, PA) **10497**
Pocono Shopper (East Stroudsburg, PA) **10717**
Point & Shoreland Journal (Toledo, OH) **10707**
Pointe Coupee Banner (New Roads, LA) **10617**
Point Pleasant Register (Point Pleasant, WV) **10513**
Point Reyes Light (Point Reyes Station, CA) **10541**
† Poland Leader (Niles, OH)
Polk City Press (Mulberry, FL) **10559**
Polk County Democrat, The (Bartow, FL) **10555**
Polk County Enterprise (Livingston, TX) **10743**
Pompano Ledger, The (Pompano Beach, FL) **10560**
Ponca City News (Ponca City, OK) **10490**
Ponchatoula Times, The (Ponchatoula, LA) **10617**
Pontiac Daily Leader (Pontiac, IL) **10441**
Pontotoc Progress (Pontotoc, MS) **10650**
Pony Express Mail (Liberty, TX) **10743**
Pope County Tribune (Glenwood, MN) **10642**
Poquoson Post (Yorktown, VA) **10756**
Porcupine Press (Chatham, MI) **10631**
Portage Community Shopping Guide (Merrillville, IN) **10596**
Portage Dispatch, The (Portage, PA) **10723**

Portales News-Tribune (Portales, NM) **10474**
Port Arthur News (Port Arthur, TX) **10506**
Porter/New Caney Sun (Humble, TX) **10742**
Porterville Recorder (Porterville, CA) **10424**
Port Gibson Reveille (Port Gibson, MS) **10650**
Port Isabel-South Padre Item Press (Port Isabel, TX) **10745**
Portland Commercial Review (Portland, IN) **10445**
Portland News (Portland, TX) **10745**
Portland Press Herald (Portland, ME) **10455**
Portland Review & Observer (Grand Ledge, MI) **10633**
Port Lavaca Wave (Port Lavaca, TX) **10745**
Port Orchard Independent (Port Orchard, WA) **10759**
Port Richmond Star (Philadelphia, PA) **10722**
Portsmouth Daily Times (Portsmouth, OH) **10486**
Portsmouth Herald (Portsmouth, NH) **10471**
Portsmouth Times (Chesapeake, VA) **10752**
Port Times-Record, The (Setauket, NY) **10686**
Port Townsend/Jefferson County Leader (Port Townsend, WA) **10759**
Port Washington News (Port Washington, NY) **10685**
Post & Mail, The (Columbia City, IN) **10442**
Post-Bulletin (Rochester, MN) **10463**
Post-Crescent, The (Appleton, WI) **10513**
Post-Herald (Red Creek, NY) **10685**
Post-Journal, The (Jamestown, NY) **10475**
Post-Standard (Syracuse, NY) **10477**
Post-Star (Glens Falls, NY) **10475**
Post-Tribune (Gary, IN) **10443**
Post-Tribune (Jefferson City, MO) **10466**
Post Falls Tribune (Post Falls, ID) **10570**
Post News (San Clemente, CA) **10542**
Post Report, The (Beckley, WV) **10760**
Post Review, The (Paramus, NJ) **10669**
Post South (Plaquemine, LA) **10617**
Post, The (Middleburg, PA) **10720**
Post, The (Big Stone Gap, VA) **10751**
Poteau Daily News & Sun (Poteau, OK) **10490**
Potomac Almanac (Potomac, MD) **10622**
Potomac News (Woodbridge, VA) **10510**
Potter Leader-Enterprise (Coudersport, PA) **10717**
Pottsboro Press (Pottsboro, TX) **10745**
Pottsville Republican & Evening Herald (Pottsville, PA) **10496**
Poughkeepsie Journal (Poughkeepsie, NY) **10477**
† ▼Poultney News, The (Rutland, VT)
Poway News Chieftain (Poway, CA) **10541**
Powder Springs Neighbor, The (Marietta, GA) **10566**

Powell Valley News (Pennington Gap, VA) **10754**
Power County Press (American Falls, ID) **10569**
Poynette Press (Poynette, WI) **10772**
Prairie City News (Prairie City, IA) **10603**
Prairie Post (Jamestown, ND) **10697**
Prairie Shopper, The (La Fayette, IL) **10583**
Prairie Times, The (La Fayette, IL) **10583**
Prairie Village Sun (Shawnee Mission, KS) **10608**
Pratt Tribune (Pratt, KS) **10451**
Pratt Tribune (Vermillion, SD) **10730**
Prattville Progress (Prattville, AL) **10521**
Prescott Journal (Prescott, WI) **10772**
Prescott Valley Tribune, The (Prescott Valley, AZ) **10526**
Presque Isle Advance (Rogers City, MI) **10637**
Presque Isle Star (Gaylord, MI) **10633**
Press & Journal, The (Middletown, PA) **10720**
Press & Light (West Lake, OH) **10708**
Press & Standard, The (Walterboro, SC) **10729**
Press & Sun-Bulletin (Vestal, NY) **10477**
Press-Dispatch (Petersburg, IN) **10597**
Press-Enterprise, The (Riverside, CA) **10424**
Press-Journal (Vero Beach, FL) **10434**
Press-News Journal (Canton, MO) **10652**
Press-News, The (Minerva, OH) **10705**
Press-Republican (Plattsburgh, NY) **10477**
Press-Sentinel, The (Jesup, GA) **10566**
Press-Star (New London, WI) **10771**
Press-Telegram (Long Beach, CA) **10422**
Press Argus-Courier (Van Buren, AR) **10529**
Press Dispatch (Kansas City, MO) **10654**
Press Enterprise, The (Bloomsburg, PA) **10492**
Press Herald (Pine Grove, PA) **10723**
Press Journal (St. Louis, MO) **10657**
Press Journal, The (Palisades Park, NJ) **10669**
Press Leader, The (Farmington, MO) **10466**
Press of Atlantic City, The (Pleasantville, NJ) **10472**
Press Review (London, OH) **10704**
Press, The (Los Angeles, CA) **10538**
† Press, The (Alexandria, MN)
Press, The (Avon Lake, OH) **10698**
Press, The (Millbury, OH) **10705**
Preston Citizen (Preston, ID) **10570**
Preston County Journal (Kingwood, WV) **10761**
Preston County News (Kingwood, WV) **10761**
Price Hill Press (Cincinnati, OH) **10700**
Priest River Times (Priest River, ID) **10570**
PrimeTime (Lawrence, NY) **10680**
Prince Georges Journal (Lanham, MD) **10456**

Prince Georges Sentinel (Seabrook, MD) **10622**
Princeton Daily Clarion (Princeton, IN) **10445**
Princeton News Leader (Princeton, NC) **10694**
Princeton Packet, The (Princeton, NJ) **10669**
Princeton Times (Princeton, WV) **10762**
Princeton Times-Republic (Princeton, WI) **10772**
Princeton Union-Eagle (Princeton, MN) **10645**
▼ Prince William Journal (Manassas, VA) **10509**
Private Eye Weekly (Salt Lake City, UT) **10749**
Proctor Journal (Proctor, MN) **10646**
Progress-Index (Petersburg, VA) **10510**
Progressor-Times, The (Carey, OH) **10699**
Progress, The (Cave City, KY) **10610**
Progress, The (Caldwell, NJ) **10665**
† Progress, The (Clearfield, PA)
Progress, The (Monroeville, PA) **10720**
Progress, The (Anahuac, TX) **10736**
Prospect-News, The (Doniphan, MO) **10653**
Prospect Heights Journal (Des Plaines, IL) **10577**
Prospector, The (Doniphan, MO) **10653**
Providence Journal-Bulletin (Providence, RI) **10498**
Providence Phoenix (Providence, RI) **10726**
Provincetown Advocate (Provincetown, MA) **10628**
Proviso Star-Sentinel (Melrose Park, IL) **10585**
Pryor Daily Times (Pryor, OK) **10490**
Public Opinion, The (Chambersburg, PA) **10493**
Public Spirit (Ayer, MA) **10623**
Pueblo Chieftain (Pueblo, CO) **10429**
Pulaski Citizen (Pulaski, TN) **10734**
Pulaski County Journal (Winamac, IN) **10598**
Pulaski Enterprise (Mounds, IL) **10586**
Pulaski Giles Free Press (Pulaski, TN) **10734**
Pulse-Journal (Mason, OH) **10705**
Punxsutawney Spirit (Punxsutawney, PA) **10496**
Purcell Register (Purcell, OK) **10711**
Putnam-Cabell Post (Culloden, WV) **10761**
Putnam County Record (Granville, IL) **10580**
Putnam County Sentinel (Ottawa, OH) **10706**
Putnam County Vidette (Columbus Grove, OH) **10702**
Putnam Courier-Trader, The (Carmel, NY) **10675**
Pymatuning Area News (Andover, OH) **10698**
Pyramid, The (Mt. Pleasant, UT) **10749**

Q

Quad-City Times (Davenport, IA) **10447**

Quad Community Press (White Bear Lake, MN) **10648**
Quad County Edition, The (Jerseyville, IL) **10583**
Quad River News (Sheridan, MO) **10656**
Quakertown Free Press (Quakertown, PA) **10723**
Quay County Sun (Tucumcari, NM) **10672**
Queen Anne-Magnolia News (Seattle, WA) **10759**
Queen Anne's Record-Observer (Centreville, MD) **10621**
Queens Chronicle (Rego Park, NY) **10685**
Queens Ledger (Maspeth, NY) **10681**
Queens Tribune (Fresh Meadows, NY) **10678**
Queens Village Times, The (Flushing, NY) **10677**
† Quik Quarter Want Ads (Hobbs, NM)
Quincy Herald-Whig (Quincy, IL) **10441**
Quincy Sun (Quincy, MA) **10628**
Quoddy Tides (Eastport, ME) **10619**

R

Radford News Journal (Christiansburg, VA) **10752**
Raeford News-Journal, The (Raeford, NC) **10694**
Rahway News-Record (Rahway, NJ) **10669**
Rahway Progress (Union, NJ) **10671**
Ramona Sentinel (Ramona, CA) **10541**
Ramsey-Mahwah Reporter (Palisades Park, NJ) **10669**
Ramsey County Review (St. Paul, MN) **10647**
Rancho Bernardo News Journal (San Diego, CA) **10542**
Rancho Santa Margarita News (Lake Forest, CA) **10536**
Randleman Reporter (Randleman, NC) **10694**
Randolph County Herald Tribune (Chester, IL) **10574**
† Randolph County Times-Herald (Moberly, MO)
Randolph Guide, The (Asheboro, NC) **10690**
Randolph Leader (Roanoke, AL) **10521**
† Randolph Mariner (Marshfield, MA)
Randolph Reporter (Bernardsville, NJ) **10664**
Random Lengths News (San Pedro, CA) **10544**
Ranger Times (Ranger, TX) **10745**
Rankin County News, The (Brandon, MS) **10649**
Rankin Independent (Cissna Park, IL) **10576**
† Rantoul Pacesetter (Rantoul, IL)
Rantoul Press (Rantoul, IL) **10588**
Rapid City Journal (Rapid City, SD) **10499**
Rappahannock News (Washington, VA) **10756**
Rappahannock Record (Kilmarnock, VA) **10753**
Raton Range, The (Raton, NM) **10672**
Ravalli Republic (Hamilton, MT) **10469**
Ravena News Herald (Ravena, NY) **10685**
Rayne Acadian-Tribune (Rayne, LA) **10617**
Rayne Independent (Rayne, LA) **10617**
Raynham Journal (Stoughton, MA) **10628**
Raytown Dispatch Tribune (Raytown, MO) **10656**
Reading Eagle & Reading Times (Reading, PA) **10496**
Real American (Leakey, TX) **10743**
Record-Advertiser (North Tonawanda, NY) **10684**
Record-Breeze (Blackwood, NJ) **10664**
Record-Citizen, The (Bristow, OK) **10709**
Record-Delta, The (Buckhannon, WV) **10760**
Record-Enterprise (McDonald, PA) **10719**
Record-Herald & Indianola Tribune (Indianola, IA) **10602**
Record-Journal (Meriden, CT) **10430**
Record-Review, The (Abbotsford, WI) **10764**
Record Enterprise, The (Plymouth, NH) **10663**
Recorder-Herald (Salmon, ID) **10570**
Recorder, The (Greenfield, MA) **10457**
Recorder, The (Prince Frederick, MD) **10622**
Recorder, The (Amsterdam, NY) **10474**
Recorder, The (Conshohocken, PA) **10717**
Recorder, The (Monterey, VA) **10754**
Record Herald (Washington Court House, OH) **10487**
Record Herald (Waynesboro, PA) **10497**
Record Ledger (San Fernando, CA) **10543**
Record Searchlight (Redding, CA) **10424**
Record, The (Stockton, CA) **10426**
Record, The (Gainesville, FL) **10557**
Record, The (Council, ID) **10569**
Record, The (Kansas City, KS) **10607**
Record, The (Havre De Grace, MD) **10622**
Record, The (Boonville, MO) **10652**
Record, The (Hackensack, NJ) **10472**
Record, The (Huntington, NY) **10679**
Record, The (Troy, NY) **10477**
Record, The (Coraopolis, PA) **10717**
Record, The (Horsham, PA) **10494**
Record Times, The (Paxton, IL) **10588**
Red Bay News (Red Bay, AL) **10521**
Red Bluff Daily News (Red Bluff, CA) **10424**
Redding Pilot, The (Georgetown, CT) **10552**
Redfield Press (Redfield, SD) **10730**
Redford Observer (Livonia, MI) **10635**
Redlands Advertiser (Redlands, CA) **10541**
Redlands Daily Facts (Redlands, CA) **10424**
Redmond Sammamish Valley News (Redmond, WA) **10759**

Redmond Spokesman (Redmond, OR) **10714**
Red Oak Express (Red Oak, IA) **10603**
Red Wing Republican Eagle (Red Wing, MN) **10463**
Redwood City Tribune (Redwood City, CA) **10541**
Redwood Gazette, The (Redwood Falls, MN) **10646**
Reedley Exponent (Reedley, CA) **10541**
Reedsburg Times-Press (Reedsburg, WI) **10772**
Reflector, The (Battle Ground, WA) **10757**
Regional News (Palos Heights, IL) **10587**
Regional News, The (La Crosse, IN) **10595**
Register-Guard (Eugene, OR) **10491**
Register-Herald (Eaton, OH) **10703**
Register-Mail (Galesburg, IL) **10439**
Register-News (Mt. Vernon, IL) **10440**
Register-News (Bordentown, NJ) **10664**
Register-Pajaronian (Watsonville, CA) **10427**
Register-Star (Hudson, NY) **10475**
Register/Herald (Beckley, WV) **10512**
Register Citizen (Torrington, CT) **10430**
Register Star (Rockford, IL) **10441**
Register, The (Yarmouthport, MA) **10630**
† Register, The (Shrewsbury, NJ)
Reidsville Review (Reidsville, NC) **10480**
Reminder, The (Vernon, CT) **10554**
Remington Press (Rensselaer, IN) **10597**
Reno Gazette-Journal (Reno, NV) **10470**
Rensselaer Republican (Rensselaer, IN) **10445**
Renville County Shopper (Olivia, MN) **10645**
Reporter Dispatch, The (White Plains, NY) **10478**
Reporter Newspaper, The (Palos Heights, IL) **10587**
Reporter of the Spring-Ford Area (Royersford, PA) **10723**
Reporter, The (Vacaville, CA) **10426**
† Reporter, The (Tampa, FL)
Reporter, The (Casey, IL) **10574**
Reporter, The (Chicago, IL) **10575**
Reporter, The (Lebanon, IN) **10444**
Reporter, The (Franklin Lakes, NJ) **10666**
Reporter, The (Lansdale, PA) **10494**
Reporter, The (Fond Du Lac, WI) **10514**
Repository, The (Canton, OH) **10483**
Republican-Journal (Darlington, WI) **10766**
Republican Journal (Belfast, ME) **10618**
Republican, The (Danville, IN) **10592**
Republican, The (Oakland, MD) **10622**
Republic, The (Columbus, IN) **10442**
† ▼Resident Community News (New York, NY)
Reston Times (Reston, VA) **10755**
Retrospect, The (Collingswood, NJ) **10665**

Reveille/Between the Lakes (Seneca Falls, NY) **10686**
Revere Journal (Revere, MA) **10628**
† Review-Enterprise (Blackwood, NJ)
Review Herald, The (Mammoth Lakes, CA) **10539**
Review Press Reporter (Yonkers, NY) **10690**
Review, The (Erie, IL) **10578**
Review, The (Marion, IL) **10584**
Review, The (Paramus, NJ) **10669**
Review, The (Point Pleasant Beach, NJ) **10669**
Review, The (East Liverpool, OH) **10484**
Review, The (Plymouth, WI) **10772**
Review Times (Fostoria, OH) **10484**
Reynolds County Courier (Ellington, MO) **10653**
RFD News, The (Bellevue, OH) **10699**
Rhinelander Daily News (Rhinelander, WI) **10515**
Rialto Record (San Bernardino, CA) **10542**
Rice Lake Chronotype (Rice Lake, WI) **10773**
Richardson News (Richardson, TX) **10745**
Richfield Reaper (Richfield, UT) **10749**
Richfield Sun-Current (Bloomington, MN) **10640**
Richland Beacon-News (Rayville, LA) **10618**
Richland Observer (Richland Center, WI) **10773**
Richlands-Beulaville Advertiser-News (Richlands, NC) **10694**
Richlands News Press (Richlands, VA) **10755**
Richmond County Daily Journal (Rockingham, NC) **10481**
Richmond Palladium-Item (Richmond, IN) **10445**
Richmond Register (Richmond, KY) **10453**
Richmond Review, The (Richmond, MI) **10637**
Richmond Times-Dispatch (Richmond, VA) **10510**
Richton Dispatch, The (Richton, MS) **10651**
Ridgefield Press, The (Ridgefield, CT) **10553**
Ridgewood News (Paramus, NJ) **10669**
Ridgway Record (Ridgway, PA) **10496**
Ridgway Sun (Ridgway, CO) **10550**
Ridley Press (Drexel Hill, PA) **10717**
Rio Grande Sun (Espanola, NM) **10672**
Ripley Southern Sentinel (Ripley, MS) **10651**
Ripon Commonwealth Press (Ripon, WI) **10773**
Rising Star, The (Rising Star, TX) **10745**
Rising Sun Recorder (Rising Sun, IN) **10597**
Ritchie Gazette (Harrisville, WV) **10761**
Riverdale Press (Bronx, NY) **10674**
River East News Bulletin (Glastonbury, CT) **10552**
River Falls Journal (River Falls, WI) **10773**

River North News (Chicago, IL) **10575**
River Oaks News (Fort Worth, TX) **10740**
River Press, The (Fort Benton, MT) **10659**
River Reporter, The (Narrowsburg, NY) **10683**
Riverside Advertiser (San Bernardino, CA) **10542**
Riverside Bulletin, The (Los Angeles, CA) **10538**
Riverside Review (Buffalo, NY) **10675**
Riverton Ranger (Riverton, WY) **10516**
Riverton Register (Riverton, IL) **10588**
River Valley Shopper (Spring Valley, MN) **10646**
Roane County News, The (Kingston, TN) **10732**
Roane County Reporter (Spencer, WV) **10763**
Roanoke-Chowan News-Herald, The (Ahoskie, NC) **10690**
Roanoke Beacon (Plymouth, NC) **10694**
Roanoke Rapids Daily & Sunday Herald (Roanoke Rapids, NC) **10480**
Roanoke Review (Roanoke, IL) **10589**
Roanoke Times, The (Roanoke, VA) **10510**
Robersonville Weekly Herald (Williamston, NC) **10696**
Robertson County Times (Springfield, TN) **10735**
Robesonian, The (Lumberton, NC) **10480**
Robinson Daily News (Robinson, IL) **10441**
Rochelle News Leader (Rochelle, IL) **10589**
Rochester Clarion (Rochester, MI) **10637**
† Rochester Courier (Rochester, NH)
Rochester Democrat & Chronicle (Rochester, NY) **10477**
Rochester Eccentric (Rochester Hills, MI) **10637**
Rochester Sentinel, The (Rochester, IN) **10445**
Rochester Sun News, The (Tenino, WA) **10760**
Rochester Times (Auburn, IL) **10572**
Rochester Times, The (Rochester, NH) **10663**
Rockaway Journal (Lawrence, NY) **10680**
Rockbridge Weekly (Lexington, VA) **10753**
Rock County Star Herald (Luverne, MN) **10643**
Rock Creek Current, The (Washington, DC) **10555**
Rockdale Citizen (Conyers, GA) **10435**
Rockdale Neighbor, The (Conyers, GA) **10564**
Rockdale Reporter (Rockdale, TX) **10746**
Rockford/Cedar Springs Advance (Jenison, MI) **10634**
Rockford Squire (Rockford, MI) **10637**
Rock Island Argus & The Dispatch (Moline, IL) **10440**
Rockland County Times (Haverstraw, NY) **10679**
Rockland Independent, The (Pearl River, NY) **10684**
Rockland Journal-News (West Nyack, NY) **10478**
Rockmart Journal (Rockmart, GA) **10567**
Rockrimmon Journal (Manitou Springs, CO) **10550**
Rock Springs Daily Rocket-Miner (Rock Springs, WY) **10516**
Rockville Centre Herald (Lawrence, NY) **10680**
Rockville Centre News & Owl (Mineola, NY) **10682**
Rockville Parke County Sentinel (Rockville, IN) **10597**
Rockwood Times (Kingston, TN) **10732**
Rocky Ford Daily Gazette (Rocky Ford, CO) **10429**
Rocky Fork Enterprise (Columbus, OH) **10701**
Rocky Fork Enterprise (Gahanna, OH) **10703**
Rocky Mountain News (Denver, CO) **10428**
Rocky Mount Telegram (Rocky Mount, NC) **10481**
Rogers Park/Edgewater News/Uptown News Star (Lincolnwood, IL) **10584**
Rogersville Review (Rogersville, TN) **10734**
Rogue River Press (Rogue River, OR) **10714**
† Rohnert Park Cotati Clarion (Cotati, CA)
Rolla Daily News (Rolla, MO) **10468**
Rolling Meadows Journal & Topics (Des Plaines, IL) **10577**
Rome News-Tribune (Rome, GA) **10436**
Romeo Observer (Romeo, MI) **10637**
Romeoville Metropolitan (Lemont, IL) **10583**
Romeoville Sun (Bolingbrook, IL) **10573**
Romulus Roman (Wayne, MI) **10639**
Ronkonkoma Review (Smithtown, NY) **10686**
Roosevelt Review (St. Paul, MN) **10647**
Rosamond News (Rosamond, CA) **10541**
Roscoe Hosmer Independent (Ipswich, SD) **10730**
Roscommon County Herald-News (Roscommon, MI) **10637**
Roseau Times-Region (Roseau, MN) **10646**
Roselle Park Leader (Union, NJ) **10671**
† Roselle Record (Carol Stream, IL)
Roselle Spectator (Union, NJ) **10671**
Rosemont Journal (Des Plaines, IL) **10577**
Rosemont Times (Park Ridge, IL) **10588**
Roseville Independent (Roseville, IL) **10589**
Roseville Press-Tribune (Roseville, CA) **10542**
Roseville Review (St. Paul, MN) **10647**
Rossford Record-Journal (Perrysburg, OH) **10706**
Rossmoor News (Walnut Creek, CA) **10546**
Ross Valley Reporter (Sausalito, CA) **10544**

Roswell-Alpharetta Neighbor
(Roswell, GA) **10567**
Roswell/Alpharetta Crier (Atlanta, GA) **10563**
Roswell Daily Record (Roswell, NM) **10474**
Round Lake News (Grayslake, IL) **10581**
Round Rock Leader (Round Rock, TX) **10746**
Round Valley Paper, The (Eagar, AZ) **10525**
Roxborough Review (Philadelphia, PA) **10722**
Royal Review (Royal City, WA) **10759**
Ruidoso News, The (Ruidoso, NM) **10672**
Rumford Falls Times (Rumford, ME) **10620**
Rural-Urban Record (Columbia
Station, OH) **10701**
Rural Virginian (Charlottesville, VA) **10751**
Rush County News (La Crosse, KS) **10607**
Rushville Republican (Rushville, IN) **10445**
Rushville Times, The (Rushville, IL) **10589**
Russell County News, The (Russell
Springs, KY) **10614**
Russell Daily News (Russell, KS) **10451**
Russell Record (Russell, KS) **10608**
Ruston Daily Leader (Ruston, LA) **10455**
Rutherford Courier, The (Smyrna, TN) **10735**
Rutland Herald (Rutland, VT) **10508**
Rutland Tribune, The (Rutland, VT) **10750**
Rye Chronicle (Yonkers, NY) **10690**

S

Sabina Advertiser (Sabina, OH) **10707**
Sabinal Sampler (Hondo, TX) **10741**
Sabine Banner (Many, LA) **10617**
Sabine County Reporter-Rambler
(Hemphill, TX) **10741**
Sabine Index (Many, LA) **10617**
Sacramento Bee (Sacramento, CA) **10425**
Sacramento Bulletin, The
(Sacramento, CA) **10542**
† Sacramento Union (Sacramento, CA)
Saddleback Valley News (Lake
Forest, CA) **10536**
Saginaw News (Saginaw, MI) **10462**
Saginaw Press, The (Saginaw, MI) **10637**
Saint Elmo Banner (St. Elmo, IL) **10589**
Saipan Tribune (Saipan, MP) **10482**
Sakonnet Times (Portsmouth, RI) **10725**
Salamanca Press (Salamanca, NY) **10477**
Salem County Record (Salem, NJ) **10670**
Salem Democrat, The (Salem, IN) **10597**
Salem Evening News (Beverly, MA) **10457**
Salem Leader (Salem, IN) **10597**
Salem News (Salem, MO) **10656**
Salem News (Salem, OH) **10486**
Salem Observer (Salem, NH) **10664**
Salem Times-Commoner (Salem, IL) **10589**
Salem Times-Register (Salem, VA) **10755**

Salina Journal (Salina, KS) **10451**
Saline Reporter (Saline, MI) **10637**
Salisbury News & Advertiser, The
(Salisbury, MD) **10622**
Salisbury Post (Salisbury, NC) **10481**
Salmon River News (Pulaski, NY) **10685**
Salt Lake City Deseret News (Salt Lake
City, UT) **10508**
Salt Lake Tribune (Salt Lake City, UT) **10508**
Saluda Standard Sentinel (Saluda, SC) **10729**
Salyersville Independent
(Salyersville, KY) **10614**
Samford Crimson (Birmingham, AL) **10518**
Samoa News (Pago Pago, AS) **10417**
Sampson Independent, The
(Clinton, NC) **10478**
Samson Ledger (Geneva, AL) **10519**
San Angelo Standard-Times (San
Angelo, TX) **10506**
San Antonio Express-News (San
Antonio, TX) **10506**
† San Antonio Light (San Antonio, TX)
San Augustine Tribune (San
Augustine, TX) **10746**
San Benito News (San Benito, TX) **10746**
San Bernardino Advertiser (San
Bernardino, CA) **10542**
San Bernardino Bulletin, The (Los
Angeles, CA) **10538**
San Bernardino County Sun (San
Bernardino, CA) **10425**
San Bruno Herald (San Mateo, CA) **10543**
San Carlos Apache Moccasin
(Globe, AZ) **10525**
† San Clemente News (San Clemente, CA)
Sandersville Progress
(Sandersville, GA) **10567**
† ▼Sandhills Living (Southern Pines, NC)
† San Diego Bulletin (Los Angeles, CA)
San Diego Log (San Diego, CA) **10542**
San Diego Reader (San Diego, CA) **10542**
San Diego Review (San Diego, CA) **10542**
San Diego Union-Tribune (San
Diego, CA) **10425**
Sand Mountain Reporter
(Albertville, AL) **10517**
† Sandpoint News-Bulletin (Sandpoint, ID)
Sand Springs Leader (Sand
Springs, OK) **10711**
Sandusky Register (Sandusky, OH) **10486**
Sandwich Broadsider (Orleans, MA) **10627**
Sandy Post (Sandy, OR) **10715**
Sandy Springs Neighbor, The
(Atlanta, GA) **10563**
San Fernando Valley Sun (San
Fernando, CA) **10543**

Sanford Herald (Sanford, FL) **10433**
Sanford Herald, The (Sanford, NC) **10481**
Sanford News (Sanford, ME) **10620**
San Francisco Bay Guardian (San Francisco, CA) **10543**
San Francisco Chronicle (San Francisco, CA) **10425**
San Francisco Examiner (San Francisco, CA) **10425**
San Francisco Independent (San Francisco, CA) **10543**
San Francisco Metro Reporter (San Francisco, CA) **10543**
San Francisco Sentinel (San Francisco, CA) **10543**
San Gabriel Progress (Los Angeles, CA) **10538**
San Gabriel Valley Tribune (West Covina, CA) **10427**
Sanger Herald (Sanger, CA) **10543**
Sanibel-Captiva Islander (Sanibel, FL) **10560**
Sanilac County News (Sandusky, MI) **10638**
San Jacinto Valley Register (San Jacinto, CA) **10543**
San Jose Mercury News (San Jose, CA) **10425**
San Luis Obispo County Telegram-Tribune (San Luis Obisopo, CA) **10425**
San Marcos Daily Record (San Marcos, TX) **10506**
San Marcos News Reporter (San Marcos, CA) **10543**
San Marino Tribune (San Marino, CA) **10543**
San Mateo County Times (San Mateo, CA) **10425**
San Mateo Weekly (Burlingame, CA) **10531**
San Patricio County News (Sinton, TX) **10746**
San Pedro Valley News-Sun (Benson, AZ) **10524**
San Rafael News Pointer (Sausalito, CA) **10545**
San Ramon Valley Times, The (Danville, CA) **10421**
Santa Barbara Independent (Santa Barbara, CA) **10544**
Santa Barbara News Press (Santa Barbara, CA) **10425**
Santa Cruz County Sentinel (Santa Cruz, CA) **10425**
Santa Fe New Mexican (Santa Fe, NM) **10474**
Santa Fe Reporter, The (Santa Fe, NM) **10672**
Santa Fe Springs News (Los Angeles, CA) **10538**
Santa Maria Times (Santa Maria, CA) **10425**
† Santa Monica Life (Santa Monica, CA)
Santa Paula Times (Santa Paula, CA) **10544**
Santa Rosa Free Press (Milton, FL) **10559**

Santa Rosa Press Democrat (Santa Rosa, CA) **10426**
Santa Rosa Press Gazette (Milton, FL) **10559**
Sapulpa Daily Herald (Sapulpa, OK) **10490**
Sarasota Herald Tribune (Sarasota, FL) **10433**
Saratoga News (Saratoga, CA) **10544**
Saratoga Sun (Saratoga, WY) **10776**
Saratogian, The (Saratoga Springs, NY) **10477**
Sarcoxie Record, The (Sarcoxie, MO) **10656**
Sargent Leader (Burwell, NE) **10660**
Saturday Advantage, The (Monte Vista, CO) **10550**
Saturday Northwest (Craig, CO) **10548**
† Saturday Post-Star (Saugerties, NY)
Saugerties Post Star (Saugerties, NY) **10685**
Saugus Advertiser (Melrose, MA) **10626**
Sauk-Prairie Star (Sauk City, WI) **10773**
Sauk Centre Herald (Sauk Centre, MN) **10646**
Sault Ste. Marie Evening News (Sault Ste. Marie, MI) **10462**
Savannah Morning News (Savannah, GA) **10436**
Savannah Reporter & Andrew County Democrat (Savannah, MO) **10656**
Savanna Times Journal (Savanna, IL) **10589**
Sawyer County Gazette (Winter, WI) **10775**
Sawyer County Record (Hayward, WI) **10767**
Sayre Journal (Sayre, OK) **10711**
Scarsdale Inquirer, The (Scarsdale, NY) **10686**
Schaller Herald (Schaller, IA) **10604**
Schererville Guide (Maryville, IN) **10596**
Schuyler Sun (Schuyler, NE) **10661**
Scioto Voice (Wheelersburg, OH) **10708**
Scotsman Press, The (Syracuse, NY) **10687**
Scott County Advertiser (Waldron, AR) **10529**
Scott County News (Oneida, TN) **10734**
Scott County Times (Forest, MS) **10649**
Scottsdale-Ashburn Independent (Midlothian, IL) **10586**
Scottsdale Progress Tribune (Scottsdale, AZ) **10418**
Scottsville Citizen-Times (Scottsville, KY) **10614**
Scranton Times/Sunday Times (Scranton, PA) **10496**
Sealy News (Sealy, TX) **10746**
Seaside Signal (Seaside, OR) **10715**
Seattle Daily Journal of Commerce (Seattle, WA) **10511**
Seattle Facts (Seattle, WA) **10759**
Seattle Post-Intelligencer (Seattle, WA) **10511**
Seattle Skanner, The (Seattle, WA) **10759**
Seattle Times, The (Seattle, WA) **10511**
Seattle Weekly (Seattle, WA) **10759**
Sebastian Sun (Vero Beach, FL) **10561**

Sebeka/Menahga Review Messenger
  (Sebeka, MN) **10646**
Sebring Times (Sebring, OH) **10707**
Secaucus Home News (Secaucus, NJ) **10670**
Secaucus Reporter (Hoboken, NJ) **10667**
Sedalia Democrat, The (Sedalia, MO) **10468**
Sedona Red Rock News (Sedona, AZ) **10526**
Seekonk Star (East Providence, RI) **10725**
Seguin Gazette-Enterprise (Seguin, TX) **10506**
Selby Record (Selby, SD) **10730**
Selma Enterprise (Selma, CA) **10545**
Selma Times-Journal (Selma, AL) **10416**
Seminole Daily Producer
  (Seminole, OK) **10490**
† Seminole Outlook (Oviedo, FL)
Sentinel (Cheyenne, WY) **10775**
Sentinel & Enterprise (Fitchburg, MA) **10457**
Sentinel-Echo (London, KY) **10612**
Sentinel-Ledger, The (Ocean City, NJ) **10668**
Sentinel-Record, The (Hot Springs, AR) **10420**
Sentinel-Tribune (Bowling Green, OH) **10483**
† Sentinel/Altitudes (Frisco, CO)
Sentinel, The (Auburn, CA) **10530**
Sentinel, The (Gulf Breeze, FL) **10557**
† Sentinel, The (Chicago, IL)
Sentinel, The (Radcliff, KY) **10614**
Sentinel, The (Marion, MA) **10625**
Sentinel, The (Jefferson, OH) **10704**
Sentinel, The (Lewistown, PA) **10495**
Sequim Gazette (Sequim, WA) **10760**
Sequoyah County Times (Sallisaw, OK) **10711**
Seward County Independent
  (Seward, NE) **10661**
Seward Phoenix Log (Seward, AK) **10523**
Sewickley Herald (Monroeville, PA) **10720**
SF Weekly (San Francisco, CA) **10543**
Shafter Press (Shafter, CA) **10545**
Shakopee Valley News (Shakopee, MN) **10646**
Sharon Advocate (Sharon, MA) **10628**
Sharon Reporter, The (Sharon, WI) **10773**
Shawano Leader (Shawano, WI) **10515**
† Shawnee-Cridersville Press (Wapakoneta, OH)
Shawnee/Merriam Sun (Shawnee
  Mission, KS) **10608**
Shawnee News-Star (Shawnee, OK) **10490**
Sheboygan Falls News (Sheboygan
  Falls, WI) **10773**
Sheboygan Press, The (Sheboygan, WI) **10515**
Shelby County Herald (Shelbyville, MO) **10656**
Shelby County Reporter
  (Columbiana, AL) **10518**
Shelby Globe (Shelby, OH) **10487**
Shelby Review (Wapakoneta, OH) **10708**
Shelby Star (Shelby, NC) **10481**
Shelby Sun Times (Germantown, TN) **10732**
Shelbyville Daily Union (Shelbyville, IL) **10441**
Shelbyville News (Shelbyville, IN) **10446**
Shelbyville Sentinel-News
  (Shelbyville, KY) **10614**
Shelbyville Times-Gazette
  (Shelbyville, TN) **10501**
Sheldon Mail-Sun (Sheldon, IA) **10604**
Shelley Pioneer (Shelley, ID) **10571**
Shelter Island Reporter (Shelter Island
  Heights, NY) **10686**
Shelton-Mason County Journal
  (Shelton, WA) **10760**
Shenandoah Valley-Herald, The
  (Woodstock, VA) **10756**
Shepherdstown Chronicle
  (Shepherdstown, WV) **10763**
Sheridan Headlight (Sheridan, AR) **10529**
Sheridan News (Fishers, IN) **10593**
Sheridan Press (Sheridan, WY) **10516**
Sherman County Star, The
  (Goodland, KS) **10606**
Shiawassee County Journal (Perry, MI) **10637**
Shippensburg News-Chronicle
  (Shippensburg, PA) **10724**
Shopper/PLUS (Shelbyville, KY) **10614**
Shopper's Guide (Bardstown, KY) **10609**
Shopper's Guide, The (Louisville, MS) **10650**
Shopper Observer News (Ruskin, FL) **10560**
Shopper Spree (Burlington, IA) **10599**
Shopper Stopper (Merrimac, WI) **10769**
Shopper, The (Pensacola, FL) **10560**
Shopper, The (South Holland, IL) **10589**
Shopper Zone I (Durant, OK) **10710**
Shopper Zone II (Denison, TX) **10739**
Shopping News (Platteville, WI) **10772**
Shopping News, The (Newton, MS) **10650**
Shoreline Chronicle (Sheboygan, WI) **10773**
Shoreview-Arden Hills Bulletin (St.
  Paul, MN) **10647**
Shoreview Press (St. Paul, MN) **10647**
Shorewood Herald (New Berlin, WI) **10771**
Shoshone News-Press (Kellogg, ID) **10437**
† Shreveport Journal (Shreveport, LA)
Sidney Daily News (Sidney, OH) **10487**
Sidney Herald-Leader (Sidney, MT) **10659**
Sidney Telegraph (Sidney, NE) **10662**
Sierra County Sentinel (Truth or
  Consequences, NM) **10672**
Sierra Madre News (Sierra Madre, CA) **10545**
Sierra Sun (Truckee, CA) **10546**
Sierra Vista Herald (Sierra Vista, AZ) **10418**
Signal-Item (Monroeville, PA) **10720**
Signal, The (Atwater, CA) **10530**
Signal, The (Valencia, CA) **10427**
† Signal, The (Canal Fulton, OH)
Sigourney News-Review (Sigourney, IA) **10604**

Sikeston Standard Democrat, The (Sikeston, MO) **10468**
Silsbee Bee (Silsbee, TX) **10746**
Silver City Daily Press & Independent (Silver City, NM) **10474**
Silver Spring Gazette (Gaithersburg, MD) **10621**
Silverton Appeal-Tribune/Mt. Angel News (Silverton, OR) **10715**
Silverton Standard & The Miner (Silverton, CO) **10551**
Simi Valley Star (Simi Valley, CA) **10426**
Sioux City Journal, The (Sioux City, IA) **10448**
Siskiyou Daily News (Yreka, CA) **10427**
Sisseton Courier (Sisseton, SD) **10730**
Siuslaw News, The (Florence, OR) **10713**
Skagit Valley Herald (Mt. Vernon, WA) **10511**
Skaneateles Press (Skaneateles, NY) **10686**
Skiatook Journal (Skiatook, OK) **10711**
Skokie Life (Lincolnwood, IL) **10584**
Skokie Review (Evanston, IL) **10579**
Skyline (Lincolnwood, IL) **10584**
Skyworld Duluth News (Duluth, MN) **10641**
Slatebelt Hometown News, The (Bangor, PA) **10716**
Slidell Sentry-News (Slidell, LA) **10455**
Smith County Pioneer (Smith Center, KS) **10609**
Smith County Reformer (Raleigh, MS) **10651**
Smithfield-Selma Sun (Selma, NC) **10694**
Smithfield Herald (Smithfield, NC) **10694**
Smith Mountain Eagle (Moneta, VA) **10754**
Smithtown Messenger (Smithtown, NY) **10686**
Smithtown News, The (Smithtown, NY) **10686**
Smithville Lake Herald, The (Smithville, MO) **10656**
Smithville Review (Smithville, TN) **10735**
Smyth County News & Messenger (Marion, VA) **10754**
† Snake River Press (Craig, CO)
Snohomish County Tribune (Snohomish, WA) **10760**
Snyder Daily News (Snyder, TX) **10506**
Soledad Bee (Soledad, CA) **10545**
Solon Herald Sun (Beachwood, OH) **10699**
Solon Times, The (Chagrin Falls, OH) **10700**
Solvang Santa Ynez Valley News (Solvang, CA) **10545**
Somerset Herald (Princess Anne, MD) **10622**
Somerset Messenger Gazette (Somerville, NJ) **10670**
Somerset Spectator (Somerset, NJ) **10670**
Somerville Journal (West Somerville, MA) **10629**
Sonoma County Independent (Santa Rosa, CA) **10544**
Sonoma Index Tribune (Sonoma, CA) **10545**
Sonoma West Times & News (Sebastopal, CA) **10545**
Sorento News (Hillsboro, IL) **10582**
Souderton Independent (Souderton, PA) **10724**
Sounder, The (Random Lake, WI) **10772**
Sound View News (Yonkers, NY) **10690**
South-West Review (St. Paul, MN) **10647**
South Alabamian (Jackson, AL) **10520**
Southampton Press (Southampton, NY) **10686**
South Bay's Newspaper (Lindenhurst, NY) **10680**
† South Bay's Shopper (Lindenhurst, NY)
South Bend Tribune (South Bend, IN) **10446**
South Bergenite (Rutherford, NJ) **10670**
South Boston Gazette-Virginian (South Boston, VA) **10755**
South Boston News & Record (South Boston, VA) **10755**
South Boston Tribune (Boston, MA) **10624**
South Buffalo News (Lackawanna, NY) **10680**
South City Journal (St. Louis, MO) **10657**
South Coast Shoppers/Penny Savers (Laguna Hills, CA) **10536**
South County Express (Auburn, IL) **10572**
South County Journal (St. Louis, MO) **10657**
South County Journal (Kent, WA) **10511**
South County News & Advertiser (Fort Worth, TX) **10740**
South County Weekender (Webster, MA) **10629**
South Dade News (South Miami, FL) **10561**
South Dade News Leader (Homestead, FL) **10557**
South Dekalb Neighbor, The (Atlanta, GA) **10563**
South District Journal (Seattle, WA) **10759**
† South East Metro Shopper (Cottage Grove, MN)
Southeast Missourian (Cape Girardeau, MO) **10466**
Southern Cayuga Tribune (Moravia, NY) **10683**
Southern County News (Thornton, IA) **10604**
Southern Dutchess News (Wappingers Falls, NY) **10688**
Southern Herald, The (Liberty, MS) **10650**
Southern Illinoisan (Carbondale, IL) **10438**
Southern Oklahoma Leader (Durant, OK) **10710**
Southern Pines Pilot (Southern Pines, NC) **10694**
Southern Standard (McMinnville, TN) **10733**
Southern Star (Ozark, AL) **10521**
Southfield Eccentric (Birmingham, MI) **10630**
South Fork Times (Monte Vista, CO) **10550**

South Fulton Neighbor, The (Forest Park, GA) **10565**
South Gate Press (Los Angeles, CA) **10538**
Southhampton Press, The/Western Edition (Westhampton Beach, NY) **10689**
South Haven Daily Tribune (South Haven, MI) **10462**
South Hill Enterprise (South Hill, VA) **10755**
South Hills Record (Pittsburgh, PA) **10723**
South Idaho Press (Burley, ID) **10437**
Southington Observer (Southington, CT) **10554**
South Jersey Advisor (Cologne, NJ) **10665**
South Lake Advertiser (Lowell, IN) **10595**
South Lyon Herald (South Lyon, MI) **10638**
South Miami News (Miami, FL) **10559**
South Milwaukee Voice Graphic (New Berlin, WI) **10771**
South Missourian News (Thayer, MO) **10658**
South of the Boulevard (Woodland Hills, CA) **10547**
South Oklahoma City Leader (Moore, OK) **10710**
† South Pasadena Journal (Los Angeles, CA)
South Pasadena Review (South Pasadena, CA) **10545**
South Philadelphia Chronicle (Philadelphia, PA) **10723**
South Philadelphia Review (Philadelphia, PA) **10723**
South Pittsburgh Reporter (Pittsburgh, PA) **10723**
South Reporter, The (Holly Springs, MS) **10649**
South San Francisco Enterprise-Journal (San Mateo, CA) **10544**
South San Gabriel/Rosemead Progress (Los Angeles, CA) **10538**
South Shore News (Rockland, MA) **10628**
South Shore Record (Woodmere, NY) **10689**
Southside Journal (Los Angeles, CA) **10538**
Southside Journal (St. Louis, MO) **10657**
Southside Reporter (San Antonio, TX) **10746**
Southside Sentinel (Urbanna, VA) **10756**
Southside Shopper (Des Moines, IA) **10600**
† Southside Sun (East Point, GA)
South Sioux City Star (South Sioux City, NE) **10662**
South St. Paul/Inver Grove Heights Sun-Current (Burnsville, MN) **10640**
South Tampa News (Brandon, FL) **10555**
Southtowns Citizen (Orchard Park, NY) **10684**
† South Valley Eagle (Salt Lake City, UT)
Southwest Beacon (Chicago, IL) **10575**
Southwest City Journal (St. Louis, MO) **10657**
Southwest County Journal (St. Louis, MO) **10658**
Southwest Courier (Chicago, IL) **10575**
Southwest Daily News (Sulphur, LA) **10455**
Southwestern Journal News (Brighton, IL) **10573**
Southwestern Pennsylvania Scene (Scottdale, PA) **10724**
Southwest Globe Times (Philadelphia, PA) **10723**
† Southwest News (South Miami, FL)
Southwest News-Herald (Chicago, IL) **10575**
Southwest Newsweek, The (Louisville, KY) **10612**
Southwest Shopper (Chicago, IL) **10575**
Southwest Sun (Sugar Land, TX) **10747**
Southwest Times Record (Fort Smith, AR) **10419**
Southwest Times, The (Pulaski, VA) **10510**
Southwest Tulsa News (Tulsa, OK) **10712**
Southwest Virginia Enterprise (Wytheville, VA) **10756**
Southwest Wave/News (Los Angeles, CA) **10538**
Spackenkill Sentinel (Wappingers Falls, NY) **10688**
Sparta/Kent City Advance (Sparta, MI) **10638**
Sparta Expositor (Sparta, TN) **10735**
Sparta Herald (Sparta, WI) **10773**
Sparta Independent (Sparta, NJ) **10670**
Sparta Ishmaelite (Sparta, GA) **10567**
Sparta News Plaindealer (Sparta, IL) **10589**
Spectator Magazine (Raleigh, NC) **10694**
Spectator, The (Somerset, MA) **10628**
Spectrum, The (St. George, UT) **10508**
Speedway Town Press (Speedway, IN) **10598**
Spencer County Journal Democrat (Rockport, IN) **10597**
Spencer County Leader/Dale News (Ferdinand, IN) **10593**
Spencer Daily Reporter (Spencer, IA) **10448**
Spencer Evening World (Spencer, IN) **10446**
Spencer Magnet (Taylorsville, KY) **10614**
Spencer Random Harvest Weekly (Trumansburg, NY) **10688**
Spinal Column Newsweekly (Waterford, MI) **10639**
Spirit Lake Beacon (Spirit Lake, IA) **10604**
† Spirit of Bucks County (Hatboro, PA)
Spirit of Jefferson-Advocate (Charles Town, WV) **10761**
Spokesman-Review, The (Spokane, WA) **10511**
Spooner Advocate (Spooner, WI) **10773**
Spotlight, The (Washington, DC) **10555**
Spotlight, The (Indianapolis, IN) **10594**
Spotlight, The (Delmar, NY) **10676**

Sprague Advocate, The (Sprague, WA) **10760**
Springfield Advance-Press
  (Springfield, MN) **10646**
Springfield Advocate (Springfield, MA) **10628**
Springfield Leader (Union, NJ) **10671**
Springfield News-Leader, The
  (Springfield, MO) **10468**
Springfield News-Sun (Springfield, OH) **10487**
Springfield News, The (Springfield, OR) **10715**
Springfield Press (Springfield, PA) **10724**
Springfield Reporter, The
  (Springfield, VT) **10750**
Springfield Shopper (Springfield, IL) **10589**
Springfield Sun (Springfield, KY) **10614**
Springfield Sun (Fort Washington, PA) **10718**
Springfield Times Courier (Reston, VA) **10755**
Springhill Press (Springhill, LA) **10618**
Spring Hope Enterprise (Spring
  Hope, NC) **10695**
Springs Valley Herald (French Lick, IN) **10594**
Springtown Epigraph, The
  (Springtown, TX) **10747**
Spring Valley Bulletin (Lemon
  Grove, CA) **10536**
Spring Valley Sun (Spring Valley, WI) **10773**
Spring Valley Tribune (Spring
  Valley, MN) **10646**
Springview Herald (Springview, NE) **10662**
Springville Journal (Springville, NY) **10687**
Squires, The (Overland, KS) **10608**
† Squire, The (Prairie Village, KS)
St. Albans Messenger (St. Albans, VT) **10508**
Stamford American (Stamford, TX) **10747**
Standard & Times (Tuscumbia, AL) **10522**
Standard-Examiner (Ogden, UT) **10508**
Standard-Observer (Greensburg, PA) **10493**
Standard-Star (New Rochelle, NY) **10476**
Standard-Times (North Kingstown, RI) **10725**
Standard-Times, The (New
  Bedford, MA) **10458**
Standard Banner (Jefferson, TN) **10732**
Standard Journal (Rexburg, ID) **10570**
Stanley Republican (Stanley, WI) **10773**
Stanly News & Press (Albemarle, NC) **10690**
St. Anthony Bulletin (North St.
  Paul, MN) **10645**
Staples World (Staples, MN) **10646**
Star-Advocate (Titusville, FL) **10561**
Star-Democrat, The (Easton, MD) **10456**
Star-Gazette (Elmira, NY) **10475**
Star-Herald (Belton, MO) **10651**
Star-Herald (Scottsbluff, NE) **10470**
Star-Herald, The (Presque Isle, ME) **10620**
Star-Herald, The (Kosciusko, MS) **10650**
Star-Ledger (Newark, NJ) **10472**
Star-News, The (McCall, ID) **10570**

Star-News, The (North Syracuse, NY) **10684**
Star-Progress, The (Berryville, AR) **10527**
Star-Tribune (Chatham, VA) **10751**
Star Advertiser (Kalkaska, MI) **10635**
Star Buyers Guide (West Branch, MI) **10639**
Star Express (Covington, GA) **10564**
Star Gazette (Hackettstown, NJ) **10666**
Star Herald (Ripley, WV) **10763**
Star Journal (Hope, IN) **10594**
Starkville Daily News (Starkville, MS) **10465**
Star News, The (Chula Vista, CA) **10532**
Star News, The (Medford, WI) **10769**
Star Press (Springboro, OH) **10707**
Star Press, The (Muncie, IN) **10445**
Star Republican (Wilmington, OH) **10709**
Star, The (Tinley Park, IL) **10590**
Star, The (Sun Prairie, WI) **10774**
Star Tribune (Minneapolis, MN) **10463**
State Center Enterprise-Record (State
  Center, IA) **10604**
State Gazette (Dyersburg, TN) **10500**
State Journal (Frankfort, KY) **10452**
State Journal-Register (Springfield, IL) **10441**
State Line Shopping Guide
  (Palmer, MA) **10627**
Staten Island Advance (Staten
  Island, NY) **10477**
Staten Island Register (Staten
  Island, NY) **10687**
State Port Pilot, The (Southport, NC) **10695**
Statesboro Herald (Statesboro, GA) **10436**
Statesman-Examiner (Colville, WA) **10757**
Statesman Journal (Salem, OR) **10492**
Statesville Record & Landmark
  (Statesville, NC) **10481**
State, The (Columbia, SC) **10498**
St. Augustine Record (St.
  Augustine, FL) **10433**
Staunton Star-Times (Staunton, IL) **10589**
Stayton Mail (Stayton, OR) **10715**
St. Bernard Voice, The (Arabi, LA) **10615**
St. Charles Journal (St. Charles, MO) **10656**
St. Charles Press (St. Charles, MN) **10647**
St. Clair Missourian (St. Clair, MO) **10656**
St. Clair News-Aegis (Pell City, AL) **10521**
St. Clair Shores Herald
  (Birmingham, MI) **10630**
St. Cloud Times (St. Cloud, MN) **10463**
St. Croix Avis (St. Croix, VI) **10508**
St. Croix Valley Peach (Forest
  Lake, MN) **10642**
St. Croix Valley Press (St. Paul, MN) **10647**
Steamboat Pilot (Steamboat
  Springs, CO) **10551**
Steamboat Today (Steamboat
  Springs, CO) **10429**

Steele Enterprise (Steel, MO) **10657**
Steelville Star/Crawford Mirror (Steelville, MO) **10657**
Ste. Genevieve Herald (Ste. Genevieve, MO) **10657**
Stephenville Empire-Tribune (Stephenville, TX) **10506**
Sterling Journal-Advocate (Sterling, CO) **10429**
Steuben Courier-Advocate (Bath, NY) **10673**
Stevens Point Journal (Stevens Point, WI) **10515**
St. Francis Herald, The (St. Francis, KS) **10609**
St. Francis Reminder-Enterprise (New Berlin, WI) **10771**
St. Helena Star (St. Helena, CA) **10545**
St. Helens Chronicle (St. Helens, OR) **10715**
Stigler News-Sentinel (Stigler, OK) **10711**
St. Ignace News, The (St. Ignace, MI) **10638**
Stillwater Gazette (Stillwater, MN) **10463**
Stillwater News-Press (Stillwater, OK) **10490**
Stillwater Valley Advertiser (Covington, OH) **10703**
Stilwell Democrat-Journal (Stilwell, OK) **10711**
St. James Leader Journal (St. James, MO) **10657**
St. James Plaindealer (St. James, MN) **10647**
St. John News (St. John, KS) **10609**
St. Johns Reminder (St. Johns, MI) **10638**
St. Johns Review (Portland, OR) **10714**
St. John Valley Times (Madawaska, ME) **10619**
St. Joseph News-Press (St. Joseph, MO) **10468**
St. Joseph Telegraph, The (St. Joseph, MO) **10657**
St. Lawrence Plaindealer (Canton, NY) **10675**
St. Louis American Newspaper (St. Louis, MO) **10658**
† St. Louis Naborhood Link News (St. Louis, MO)
St. Louis Park Sun-Sailor (Minnetonka, MN) **10644**
St. Louis Post-Dispatch (St. Louis, MO) **10468**
† St. Louis South St. Louis County News (St. Louis, MO)
St. Maries Gazette Record (St. Maries, ID) **10571**
St. Martinville Teche News (St. Martinville, LA) **10618**
St. Mary Journal (Morgan City, LA) **10617**
St. Marys Star (St. Marys, KS) **10609**
Stockton/Warren Gazette (Stockton, IL) **10589**
Stone County Citizen (Mountain View, AR) **10528**
Stone County Enterprise (Wiggins, MS) **10651**
Stone County Leader (Mountain View, AR) **10528**
† Stoneham Weekender News (Stoneham, MA)
Storm Lake Pilot Tribune (Storm Lake, IA) **10448**
Storm Lake Times (Storm Lake, IA) **10604**
Story City Herald (Story City, IA) **10604**
Stoughton Chronicle (Stoughton, MA) **10628**
Stowe Reporter (Stowe, VT) **10750**
Stow Sentry (Stow, OH) **10707**
St. Paul Pioneer Press (St. Paul, MN) **10463**
St. Peter Herald (St. Peter, MN) **10647**
St. Petersburg Times (St. Petersburg, FL) **10433**
Straits Area Star (Cheboygan, MI) **10631**
Stratford Bard (Milford, CT) **10553**
Stratford Journal (Stratford, WI) **10774**
Stratford Star (Konawa, OK) **10710**
Streator Times-Press (Streator, IL) **10441**
Stuart News (Stuart, FL) **10434**
Sturgis Journal (Sturgis, MI) **10462**
Sturgis News (Sturgis, KY) **10614**
Stuttgart Daily Leader (Stuttgart, AR) **10421**
Suburban & Wayne Times (Wayne, PA) **10724**
Suburban Advertiser (Wayne, PA) **10724**
Suburban Gazette (McKees Rocks, PA) **10719**
Suburbanite, The (Closter, NJ) **10665**
Suburbanite, The (Akron, OH) **10698**
Suburban Journal (Des Plaines, IL) **10577**
Suburban Leader (Chicago, IL) **10575**
Suburban Life (Butler, NJ) **10665**
Suburban Life (Loveland, OH) **10705**
Suburban Life Citizen (Oak Brook, IL) **10586**
Suburban Life Graphic (Oak Brook, IL) **10587**
† Suburban News (Reading, MA)
Suburban News (Spencerport, NY) **10687**
Suburban News, The (Windham, ME) **10620**
Suburban News, The (Flint, MI) **10632**
Suburban Street News (White Plains, NY) **10689**
Suburban Town News (Paramus, NJ) **10669**
Suburban Trends (Butler, NJ) **10665**
Suburban Tribune (Balch Springs, TX) **10736**
Sudbury Town Crier (Needham, MA) **10627**
Suffolk County News (Sayville, NY) **10686**
Suffolk News-Herald (Suffolk, VA) **10510**
Suffolk Times (Mattituck, NY) **10681**
Sullivan County News (Blountville, TN) **10731**
Sullivan Daily Times (Sullivan, IN) **10446**
Sullivan Independent News (Sullivan, MO) **10658**
Sullivan Review (Dushore, PA) **10717**
Sulphur Springs News-Telegram (Sulphur Springs, TX) **10507**
Summerville Journal Scene (Summerville, SC) **10729**

Summerville News (Summerville, GA) **10568**
Summit County Journal (Frisco, CO) **10549**
Summit Daily News (Frisco, CO) **10428**
Summit Observer (Union, NJ) **10671**
Sumner Gazette (Sumner, IA) **10604**
Sumner Press (Sumner, IL) **10589**
Sumter County Record-Journal, The (Livingston, AL) **10520**
Sumter County Times (Bushnell, FL) **10556**
Sun & Erie County Independent, The (Hamburg, NY) **10679**
Sun & News, The (Hastings, MI) **10633**
Sun-Bulletin, The (Palisades Park, NJ) **10669**
Sun-Journal (Lewiston, ME) **10455**
Sun-Journal (New Bern, NC) **10480**
Sun-Sentinel (Fort Lauderdale, FL) **10432**
Sun Advocate (Price, UT) **10749**
Sun Banner Pride (Medina, OH) **10705**
Sunbury News (Sunbury, OH) **10707**
Sun Chronicle (Attleboro, MA) **10457**
Sun Cities Independent (Sun City, AZ) **10526**
Sun City/Youngtown (Sun City, AZ) **10526**
Sun City News (Sun City, CA) **10545**
Sun City West (Sun City, AZ) **10526**
Sun Coast News (New Port Richey, FL) **10559**
Sun Courier, The (Cleveland, OH) **10700**
Sunday Bucks County Telegraph (Horsham, PA) **10718**
Sunday Dispatch (Pittston, PA) **10723**
† Sunday Glades Trend (Clewiston, FL)
Sunday Independent, The (Owosso, MI) **10636**
Sunday News (Lancaster, PA) **10719**
Sunday Post (Lynn, MA) **10625**
Sunday Spectator (Hornell, NY) **10679**
† Sunday Sun (Scranton, PA)
Sunday Sun (Georgetown, TX) **10740**
Sun Herald, The (Gulfport, MS) **10464**
Sun Herald, The (North Olmsted, OH) **10706**
Sun Journal, The (North Canton, OH) **10706**
Sun Messenger, The (Beachwood, OH) **10699**
Sun Newspaper, The (Seal Beach, CA) **10545**
Sun News, The (Myrtle Beach, SC) **10499**
Sun Post, The (Miami, FL) **10559**
Sun Press (Kaneohe, HI) **10568**
Sun Press, The (Beachwood, OH) **10699**
Sun Reporter (San Francisco, CA) **10543**
Sunriser News (Ossian, IN) **10597**
Sunrise Times (Coral Springs, FL) **10556**
Sun Scoop Journal (Beachwood, OH) **10699**
Sun Star, The (Berea, OH) **10699**
Sun, The (Sun City Center, FL) **10561**
Sun, The (Mt. Vernon, IA) **10603**
Sun, The (North Olmsted, OH) **10706**
Sun, The (Hummelstown, PA) **10718**
Sun, The (Bremerton, WA) **10511**
Sun Times (Heber Springs, AR) **10528**

Sun Times (Perryville, MO) **10656**
Superior Daily Telegram (Superior, WI) **10515**
Superior Express, The (Superior, NE) **10662**
† Surfside News (South Miami, FL)
Surry Scene, The (Mount Airy, NC) **10693**
Susquehanna County Independent (Montrose, PA) **10720**
Sussex-Lannon-Lisbon News (New Berlin, WI) **10771**
Sussex-Surry Dispatch (Wakefield, VA) **10756**
Sussex Countian (Georgetown, DE) **10554**
Sussex County Chronicle (Byram, NJ) **10665**
Sussex Post, The (Rehoboth, DE) **10554**
Sussex Sun (Hartland, WI) **10767**
Swampscott Reporter (Marblehead, MA) **10625**
Swanton Enterprise (Swanton, OH) **10707**
Swap Sheet (Ridgecrest, CA) **10541**
Sweetwater Reporter (Sweetwater, TX) **10507**
Swift County Monitor-News (Benson, MN) **10640**
Switzerland Democrat (Vevay, IN) **10598**
† Sycamore Messenger (Cincinnati, OH)
Sycamore News (Sycamore, IL) **10590**
Sylva Herald & Ruralite (Sylva, NC) **10695**
Sylvania Herald (Toledo, OH) **10708**
Sylvester Local News (Sylvester, GA) **10568**
Syosset Jericho Tribune (Mineola, NY) **10683**
Syracuse Journal-Democrat (Syracuse, NE) **10662**
Syracuse New Times (Syracuse, NY) **10687**

T

T-Ville News Trader (Tompkinsville, KY) **10614**
Table Rock Gazette (Kimberling City, MO) **10654**
Tab, The (Needham, MA) **10627**
Tacoma City Paper (Tacoma, WA) **10760**
Taft Tribune (Taft, TX) **10747**
Tahlequah Daily Press (Tahlequah, OK) **10491**
Tahoe Daily Tribune (South Lake Tahoe, CA) **10426**
Tahoe World (Tahoe City, CA) **10545**
Tallahassean (Tallahassee, FL) **10561**
Tallahassee Democrat (Tallahassee, FL) **10434**
Tallassee Tribune (Tallassee, AL) **10522**
Tallmadge Express (Stow, OH) **10707**
Tama News-Herald (Tama, IA) **10604**
Tamarac Forum (Coral Springs, FL) **10556**
Tampa Tribune, The (Tampa, FL) **10434**
▼Taney County Times (Forsyth, MO) **10653**
Taos News (Taos, NM) **10672**
Tarkio Avalanche (Tarkio, MO) **10658**
Tarrytown Daily News (White Plains, NY) **10478**

Taunton Daily Gazette (Taunton, MA) **10458**
Taunton Independent (Middleboro, MA) **10626**
Tavares Citizen (Mt. Dora, FL) **10559**
Taylor Daily Press (Taylor, TX) **10507**
Taylorsville Times, The (Taylorsville, NC) **10695**
Taylorville Breeze-Courier (Taylorville, IL) **10441**
Tazewell County Free Press (Richlands, VA) **10755**
Tazewell News (Morton, IL) **10586**
Tecumseh Herald (Tecumseh, MI) **10638**
Tehachapi News (Tehachapi, CA) **10545**
Telegram & Gazette (Worcester, MA) **10459**
Telegraph-County Edition (Jerseyville, IL) **10583**
Telegraph Herald (Dubuque, IA) **10447**
Telegraph, The (Alton, IL) **10437**
Telegraph, The (Dixon, IL) **10439**
Telegraph, The (North Platte, NE) **10470**
Telegraph, The (Hudson, NH) **10471**
Telfair Enterprise (McRae, GA) **10566**
Telluride Daily Planet (Telluride, CO) **10429**
Telluride Times-Journal (Telluride, CO) **10551**
Tempe Daily News Tribune (Tempe, AZ) **10418**
Temple Daily Telegram (Temple, TX) **10507**
Temple Terrace Beacon (Tampa, FL) **10561**
Temple Terrace News (Brandon, FL) **10555**
Tenino Independent (Tenino, WA) **10760**
Tennessean, The (Nashville, TN) **10501**
Terrell Tribune (Terrell, TX) **10507**
Teton Valley News (Driggs, ID) **10569**
Texarkana Gazette (Texarkana, TX) **10507**
Texas City Sun (Texas City, TX) **10507**
Texas Observer (Austin, TX) **10736**
The Dalles Daily Chronicle (The Dalles, OR) **10492**
Thief River Falls Times (Thief River Falls, MN) **10648**
† This Week (Aledo, IL)
This Week (Cherry Hill, NJ) **10665**
This Week In Bexley (Columbus, OH) **10701**
This Week In Clintonville (Columbus, OH) **10701**
This Week In Delaware (Columbus, OH) **10701**
This Week In Eastside (Columbus, OH) **10701**
This Week In Grandview (Columbus, OH) **10702**
This Week In Hilliard (Columbus, OH) **10702**
This Week In New Albany (Columbus, OH) **10702**
This Week In Northland (Columbus, OH) **10702**
This Week In Peachtree City (Peachtree City, GA) **10567**
This Week In Pickerington (Columbus, OH) **10702**
This Week In Powell (Columbus, OH) **10702**
This Week In Reynoldsburg (Columbus, OH) **10702**
This Week In Southside (Columbus, OH) **10702**
This Week In Union County (Columbus, OH) **10702**
This Week In Westerville (Columbus, OH) **10702**
This Week In Westside (Columbus, OH) **10702**
This Week In Worthington (Columbus, OH) **10702**
Thomaston Times (Thomaston, GA) **10568**
Thomasville Times (Thomasville, NC) **10695**
Thomasville Times-Enterprise (Thomasville, GA) **10436**
Thomasville Times, The (Thomasville, AL) **10522**
Thompson-Rake Courier (Thompson, IA) **10604**
Thorp Courier (Thorp, WI) **10774**
Thousand Islands Sun (Alexandria Bay, NY) **10673**
Thousand Oaks Star (Thousand Oaks, CA) **10426**
Thousandsticks (Hyden, KY) **10611**
Three Rivers Commercial-News (Three Rivers, MI) **10462**
Three Rivers Gazette (McRae, GA) **10567**
Three Star Edition (Philadelphia, PA) **10723**
Three Village Herald (East Setauket, NY) **10676**
Three Village Times (Mineola, NY) **10683**
Thrif-T-Nikel Community Shopping Guide (Ottawa, IL) **10587**
Thrifty Nickel (Birmingham, AL) **10518**
Thrifty Nickel (Champaign, IL) **10574**
Thrifty Nickel Want Ads (East Moline, IL) **10578**
Tidewater News, The (Franklin, VA) **10753**
Tidewater Review (West Point, VA) **10756**
Tifton Gazette (Tifton, GA) **10436**
Tigard Times (Tigard, OR) **10715**
Tiller & Toiler (Larned, KS) **10450**
Times & Democrat, The (Orangeburg, SC) **10499**
Times-Bulletin (Van Wert, OH) **10487**
Times-Clarion, The (Harlowton, MT) **10659**
Times-Courier (Ellijay, GA) **10565**
Times-Express (Monroeville, PA) **10720**
Times-Gazette (Greenfield, OH) **10484**
Times-Georgian (Carrollton, GA) **10434**
Times-Herald (Timonium, MD) **10622**
Times-Indicator (Fremont, MI) **10632**

Times-Journal, The (Fort Payne, AL) **10416**
Times-Journal, The (Condon, OR) **10712**
Times-Leader (Union City, PA) **10724**
Times-Mail (Bedford, IN) **10442**
Times-News, The (Burlington, NC) **10478**
Times-Picayune (New Orleans, LA) **10455**
Times-Press (Hartford, WI) **10767**
Times-Press (Seymour, WI) **10773**
Times-Record (Brunswick, ME) **10455**
Times-Record, The (Denton, MD) **10621**
Times-Reporter, The (New Philadelphia, OH) **10486**
Times-Review (Cleburne, TX) **10503**
Times-Sentinel, The (Cheney, KS) **10606**
Times-Standard (Eureka, CA) **10422**
Times-Sun, The (West Newton, PA) **10725**
Times-Union (Warsaw, IN) **10446**
† Times-Union (Rochester, NY)
Times Argus (Barre, VT) **10508**
Times Chronicle (Jenkintown, PA) **10719**
Times Citizen (Iowa Falls, IA) **10602**
Times Daily (Florence, AL) **10416**
Times Dispatch (Walnut Ridge, AR) **10529**
Times Gazette, The (Hillsboro, OH) **10485**
Times Guthrian (Guthrie Center, IA) **10601**
Times Herald (Port Huron, MI) **10462**
Times Herald-Record (Middletown, NY) **10476**
Times Herald, The (Norristown, PA) **10495**
Times Journal (Cobleskill, NY) **10675**
Times Journal-Spotlight (Eastman, GA) **10565**
Times Journal, The (Russell Springs, KY) **10614**
Times Leader (Martins Ferry, OH) **10485**
Times Leader, The (Princeton, KY) **10614**
Times Leader, The (Wilkes Barre, PA) **10497**
Times News (Lehighton, PA) **10495**
Times Newsweekly (Ridgewood, NY) **10685**
Times of Fountain Hills & Rio Verde (Fountain Hills, AZ) **10525**
Times of Nesconset, The (Setauket, NY) **10686**
Times of Northeast Benton County (Pea Ridge, AR) **10529**
Times of Scotch Plains & Fanwood, The (Westfield, NJ) **10671**
Times of Smithtown (Setauket, NY) **10686**
Times of St. James (Setauket, NY) **10686**
Times of Ti (Ticonderoga, NY) **10688**
Times Post, The (Houston, MS) **10649**
Times Record (Fayette, AL) **10519**
Times Record (Aledo, IL) **10571**
Times Record (Spencer, WV) **10763**
Times Recorder, The (Zanesville, OH) **10488**
Times Record News (Wichita Falls, TX) **10507**
Times, The (North Little Rock, AR) **10528**
Times, The (Melbourne, FL) **10558**

Times, The (Gainesville, GA) **10435**
Times, The (Munster, IN) **10445**
† Times, The (Augusta, KY)
Times, The (Shreveport, LA) **10455**
Times, The (Forest Lake, MN) **10642**
Times, The (Trenton, NJ) **10472**
Times, The (Columbus, OH) **10702**
Times, The (Port Royal, PA) **10723**
Times, The (Pawtucket, RI) **10498**
Times, The (Waitsburg, WA) **10760**
Times, The (Westby, WI) **10775**
† Times Tribune (Palo Alto, CA)
Times Union (Albany, NY) **10474**
Times West Virginian (Fairmont, WV) **10512**
† Tioga County Gazette & Times (Owego, NY)
Tipp City Herald (Tipp City, OH) **10707**
Tipton Conservative & Advertiser (Tipton, IA) **10604**
† Tipton News Leader (Altus, OK)
Tipton Tribune (Tipton, IN) **10446**
Titusville Herald (Titusville, PA) **10497**
Today (Orange Park, FL) **10560**
Today's News (Bountiful, UT) **10748**
Today's News-Herald (Lake Havasu City, AZ) **10418**
Today's Sunbeam (Salem, NJ) **10472**
Todd County Standard (Elkton, KY) **10610**
Toledo Blade (Toledo, OH) **10487**
Tomahawk Leader (Tomahawk, WI) **10774**
Tomahawk, The (Mountain City, TN) **10734**
Tomah Journal (Tomah, WI) **10774**
Tomah Monitor-Herald (Tomah, WI) **10774**
Tombstone Epitaph, The (Tombstone, AZ) **10526**
Tomorrow (New Rochelle, NY) **10683**
Tompkinsville News (Tompkinsville, KY) **10614**
Tonawanda News (North Tonawanda, NY) **10476**
Tonkawa News, The (Tonkawa, OK) **10711**
Tonopah Times-Bonanza & Goldfield News (Tonopah, NV) **10662**
Tooele Transcript-Bulletin (Tooele, UT) **10749**
Topics Sun Wave (Los Angeles, CA) **10538**
Toppenish Review (Toppenish, WA) **10760**
Torrington Telegram (Torrington, WY) **10776**
† Total, The (Heflin, AL)
† Town & Country (Bradford, PA)
Town & Country (Pennsburg, PA) **10722**
Town & Country Weekly (Ottawa, IL) **10587**
Town-Crier (West Palm Beach, FL) **10562**
Town 'n Country News (Tampa, FL) **10561**
Town Crier (Stockbridge, MI) **10638**
Town Crier, The (La Porte, IN) **10595**
† Towne & Country Shopper (Columbus, KS)
Towne Courier (East Lansing, MI) **10632**

Town of Paradise Valley Independent
  (Scottsdale, AZ) **10526**
Townsend Times (Ayer, MA) **10623**
Township Times (Saginaw, MI) **10637**
Town Talk (Holmes, PA) **10718**
Town Talk (Media, PA) **10719**
Town Topics (Princeton, NJ) **10669**
Towson Times (Towson, MD) **10623**
Tracy Headlight-Herald (Tracy, MN) **10648**
Tracy Press (Tracy, CA) **10426**
Tradewinds (St. John, VI) **10750**
Traer Star-Clipper (Traer, IA) **10605**
† Transcript-Telegram (Holyoke, MA)
Transcript, The (North Adams, MA) **10458**
Transcript, The (Morrisville, VT) **10750**
Transylvania Times, The (Brevard, NC) **10691**
Traveler/Watchman (Southold, NY) **10686**
Traverse City Record-Eagle (Traverse
  City, MI) **10462**
Trentonian, The (Trenton, NJ) **10473**
Trenton Republican Times
  (Trenton, MO) **10468**
Trenton Sun, The (Trenton, IL) **10590**
Trenton Tribune (Trenton, TX) **10747**
Tri-City Herald (Kennewick, WA) **10511**
† Tri-City Independent (Margate, FL)
Tri-City Ledger (Flomaton, AL) **10519**
Tri-City News (Cumberland, KY) **10610**
Tri-City Record, The (Watervliet, MI) **10639**
Tri-City Reporter (Dyer, TN) **10732**
† Tri-City Times (Geraldine, AL)
Tri-City Times (Imlay City, MI) **10634**
Tri-City Trib (Cozad, NE) **10660**
Tri-City Tribune (Marked Tree, AR) **10528**
Tri-County Advertiser (Brockport, NY) **10674**
Tri-County Banner (Knightstown, IN) **10595**
Tri-County Citizen (Chesaning, MI) **10631**
Tri-County Journal (Pacific, MO) **10655**
Tri-County News (Elmwood, IL) **10578**
Tri-County News (Edinburgh, IN) **10593**
Tri-County News (South Bend, IN) **10598**
Tri-County News (Lockport, NY) **10680**
Tri-County News (Knoxville, TN) **10732**
Tri-County News (Osseo, WI) **10772**
Tri-County Press (Cincinnati, OH) **10700**
Tri-County Press (Cuba City, WI) **10766**
Tri-County Record (Rushford, MN) **10646**
Tri-County Times, The (Slater, IA) **10604**
Tri-County Trader (Waldron, AR) **10529**
Tri-State Advertiser (Bullhead City, AZ) **10524**
Tri-Town News (Sidney, NY) **10686**
Tri-Town Transcript (Danvers, MA) **10624**
Tri-Town Transcript, The (Dover, NH) **10663**
Tri-Valley Herald (Pleasanton, CA) **10424**
Tri-Village News (Columbus, OH) **10702**
Tribune (Chandler, AZ) **10418**
Tribune (Deer Park, WA) **10757**
Tribune-Courier (Ontario, OH) **10706**
Tribune-Democrat, The
  (Johnstown, PA) **10494**
Tribune-Review (Greensburg, PA) **10493**
Tribune-Star (Terre Haute, IN) **10446**
Tribune-Times (Fountain Inn, SC) **10727**
Tribune Chronicle, The (Warren, OH) **10487**
Tribune Courier (Benton, KY) **10609**
Tribune Plus (Royal Oak, MI) **10637**
Tribune Press Reporter (Glenwood
  City, WI) **10767**
Tribune Shopping News (New
  Lexington, OH) **10706**
Tribune, The (Monument, CO) **10550**
Tribune, The (Fort Pierce, FL) **10432**
Tribune, The (Melbourne, FL) **10558**
Tribune, The (Seymour, IN) **10446**
Tribune, The (Greenbush, MN) **10642**
Tribune, The (Elkin, NC) **10692**
Tribune, The (Tabor City, NC) **10695**
Tribune, The (Bethany, OK) **10709**
Tribune, The/Sunday Times
  (Scranton, PA) **10496**
Tri City Register (Riverton, IL) **10588**
Trinity Journal (Weaverville, CA) **10546**
Troy-Somerset Gazette (Troy, MI) **10638**
Troy Daily News (Troy, OH) **10487**
Troy Eccentric (Rochester Hills, MI) **10637**
Troy Free Press & Silex Index
  (Troy, MO) **10658**
Troy Progress (Troy, AL) **10522**
True Citizen, The (Waynesboro, GA) **10568**
True Dakotan, The (Wessington
  Springs, SD) **10730**
Trumann Democrat (Trumann, AR) **10529**
Trumansburg Free Press
  (Trumansburg, NY) **10688**
Trumbull Times (Monroe, CT) **10553**
Tryon Daily Bulletin (Tryon, NC) **10481**
Tucker-DeKalb Neighbor, The
  (Atlanta, GA) **10563**
Tucson Citizen (Tucson, AZ) **10419**
Tulare Advance-Register (Tulare, CA) **10426**
Tullahoma News (Tullahoma, TN) **10735**
Tulsa World (Tulsa, OK) **10491**
Tundra Drums (Bethel, AK) **10523**
Tundra Times (Anchorage, AK) **10522**
Tunkhannock New Age-Examiner
  (Tunkhannock, PA) **10724**
Tupper Lake Free Press & Herald (Tupper
  Lake, NY) **10688**
Turlock Journal (Turlock, CA) **10426**
Turtle Lake Times, The (Turtle
  Lake, WI) **10774**
Turtle Mountain Star, The (Rolla, ND) **10697**

Tuscaloosa News, The (Tuscaloosa, AL) **10417**
Tuscola County Advertiser (Caro, MI) **10631**
Tuscola Review (Tuscola, IL) **10590**
Tuskegee News (Tuskegee, AL) **10522**
Tustin News (Santa Ana, CA) **10544**
Twin-City News, The
  (Batesburg-Leesville, SC) **10726**
Twin Cities Reader (Minneapolis, MN) **10644**
Twin Cities Times (Corte Madera, CA) **10533**
Twin City News, The
  (Chattahoochee, FL) **10556**
Twin Falls Times-News (Twin Falls, ID) **10437**
Twinsburg Sun, The (Cleveland, OH) **10700**
Tyler County Booster (Woodville, TX) **10748**
Tyler Morning Telegraph (Tyler, TX) **10507**
Tyler Star News (Sistersville, WV) **10763**
Tylertown Times (Tylertown, MS) **10651**
Tyler Tribute (Tyler, MN) **10648**

U

UA This Week (Columbus, OH) **10702**
Uinta County Herald (Evanston, WY) **10776**
Uintah Basin Standard (Roosevelt, UT) **10749**
Ukiah Daily Journal (Ukiah, CA) **10426**
Ulster County Townsman
  (Woodstock, NY) **10690**
Ulysses News (Ulysses, KS) **10609**
Umpqua Free Press (Myrtle Creek, OR) **10714**
Underwood News (Underwood, ND) **10697**
Union-News (Springfield, MA) **10458**
Union-Recorder (Milledgeville, GA) **10435**
Union-Sun & Journal (Lockport, NY) **10475**
Union City Daily Messenger (Union
  City, TN) **10502**
Union City Reporter (Hoboken, NJ) **10667**
Union County Advocate
  (Morganfield, KY) **10613**
Union Daily Times (Union, SC) **10499**
Uniondale Beacon (Hicksville, NY) **10679**
Union Democrat, The (Sonora, CA) **10426**
Union Enterprise (Plainwell, MI) **10637**
Union Leader (Union, NJ) **10671**
Union Leader/New Hampshire Sunday News
  (Manchester, NH) **10471**
Union Press-Courier (Patton, PA) **10722**
† Union Shopper, The (Arcata, CA)
Union Springs Herald (Union
  Springs, AL) **10522**
Union Star (Brookneal, VA) **10751**
† Union, The (Arcata, CA)
Union, The (Grass Valley, CA) **10422**
Unionville Republican, The
  (Unionville, MO) **10658**
University Herald (Seattle, WA) **10759**
Upper Arlington News (Columbus, OH) **10702**

Upper Country News-Reporter
  (Cambridge, ID) **10569**
Upper Darby Press (Drexel Hill, PA) **10717**
Upper Dauphin Sentinel
  (Millersburg, PA) **10720**
Upper Rogue Independent (Eagle
  Point, OR) **10713**
Upper Sandusky Daily Chief-Union (Upper
  Sandusky, OH) **10487**
Uptown San Diego Examiner (San
  Diego, CA) **10542**
Urbana Daily Citizen (Urbana, OH) **10487**
Utica Herald (Utica, OH) **10708**
Uvalde Leader-News (Uvalde, TX) **10747**

V

Vadnais Heights Press (St. Paul, MN) **10647**
Vail Daily (Avon, CO) **10428**
Vailsburg Leader (Maplewood, NJ) **10668**
Vail Trail (Eagle-Vail, CO) **10548**
Valders Journal (Valders, WI) **10774**
Valdese News (Morganton, NC) **10693**
Valdez Vanguard (Valdez, AK) **10523**
Valdosta Daily Times (Valdosta, GA) **10436**
Valencia County News-Bulletin
  (Belen, NM) **10672**
Vallejo Times-Herald (Vallejo, CA) **10427**
Valley Advocate (Hatfield, MA) **10625**
Valley Banner, The (Elkton, VA) **10752**
Valley City Times-Record (Valley
  City, ND) **10482**
Valley Courier (Alamosa, CO) **10427**
Valley Falls Vindicator (Valley Falls, KS) **10609**
Valley Farmer, The (Bay City, MI) **10630**
Valley Gazette (Shelton, CT) **10553**
Valley Gazette (Lansford, PA) **10719**
Valley Independent (Monessen, PA) **10495**
Valley Journal (Carbondale, CO) **10547**
Valley Log, The (Orbisonia, PA) **10721**
Valley Morning Star (Harlingen, TX) **10504**
Valley News (Meridian, ID) **10570**
Valley News (West Lebanon, NH) **10471**
Valley News (Elizabethtown, NY) **10677**
Valley News (Fulton, NY) **10678**
Valley News Dispatch (Tarentum, PA) **10497**
Valley News Herald (Spokane, WA) **10760**
Valley News, The (Endwell, NY) **10677**
Valley News, The (Jefferson, OH) **10704**
Valley News Today-Daily Sentinel
  (Shenandoah, IA) **10448**
Valley Post (Anderson, CA) **10530**
Valley Reporter, The (Waitsfield, VT) **10750**
Valley Roadrunner (Valley Center, CA) **10546**
Valley Stream Courier (Freeport, NY) **10677**
Valley Stream Herald (Lawrence, NY) **10680**

Valley Stream Maileader (Mineola, NY) **10683**
Valley Sun (Wasilla, AK) **10523**
Valley Sun, The (Scottsboro, AL) **10522**
Valley Times (Pleasanton, CA) **10424**
Valley Times-News (Lanett, AL) **10416**
Valley Times-Star (Newville, PA) **10721**
Valley Times, The (Moreno Valley, CA) **10539**
Valley Town Crier (McAllen, TX) **10744**
Valley Trader (Lewisburg, PA) **10719**
Valley Value Shopper (Spring Valley, WI) **10773**
Valley Vantage (Woodland Hills, CA) **10547**
Valparaiso Guide (Maryville, IN) **10596**
Valparaiso Vidette-Times (Valparaiso, IN) **10446**
Van Buren County Advertiser (Gobles, MI) **10633**
Vandalia Leader-Union (Vandalia, IL) **10590**
Vandergrift News (Vandergrift, PA) **10724**
Van Horn Advocate (Van Horn, TX) **10747**
Vashon-Maury Island Beachcomber (Vashon, WA) **10760**
Vassar Pioneer Times (Vassar, MI) **10639**
Vega Enterprise, The (Vega, TX) **10747**
Venice-Marina News (Santa Monica, CA) **10544**
Venice Gondolier (Venice, FL) **10561**
† Ventura Bulletin, The (Los Angeles, CA)
Ventura County & Coast Reporter (Ventura, CA) **10546**
Ventura County Star (Ventura, CA) **10427**
Verde Independent (Cottonwood, AZ) **10525**
Vermilion Photojournal (Vermilion, OH) **10708**
Vermont News Guide (Manchester Village, VT) **10750**
Vermont Standard (Woodstock, VT) **10750**
Vermont Times (Shelburne, VT) **10750**
Vernal Express (Vernal, UT) **10749**
Vernon County Broadcaster (Viroqua, WI) **10774**
Vernon Daily Record (Vernon, TX) **10507**
Vernon Hills News (Grayslake, IL) **10581**
Vernon Hills Review (Bannockburn, IL) **10572**
Verona-Cedar Grove Times (Verona, NJ) **10671**
Verona Press (Verona, WI) **10774**
Versailles Leader-Statesman (Versailles, MO) **10658**
Versailles Policy, The (Versailles, OH) **10708**
Versailles Republican (Versailles, IN) **10598**
Vestal Town Crier (Conklin, NY) **10676**
Vevay Reveille-Enterprise (Vevay, IN) **10598**
Vicksburg Post (Vicksburg, MS) **10465**
† Victor-Farmington Herald (Webster, NY)
Victoria Advocate (Victoria, TX) **10507**

Victor Valley Advertiser (San Bernardino, CA) **10542**
† Victor Valley Living (Hesperia, CA)
Vidorian, The (Vidor, TX) **10747**
Vienna Times (Reston, VA) **10755**
Vienna Times, The (Vienna, IL) **10590**
Vilas County News-Review (Eagle River, WI) **10766**
Village Advocate (Chapel Hill, NC) **10691**
Village Beacon-Record, The (Setauket, NY) **10686**
Village Gazette of Ridgewood (Franklin Lakes, NJ) **10666**
Village Herald (Lawrence, NY) **10680**
† Village Journal (Osterville, MA)
Village News (Montgomery Village, MD) **10622**
Villager (St. Paul, MN) **10647**
Villager Newspaper (Austin, TX) **10736**
Villager, The (New York, NY) **10683**
Villager, The (Syracuse, NY) **10687**
Villager, The (Moscow, PA) **10720**
Village Times, The (Setauket, NY) **10686**
Village Voice, The (New York, NY) **10683**
Villa Park Argus (Elmhurst, IL) **10578**
Villa Rican, The (Villa Rica, GA) **10568**
Ville Platte Gazette (Ville Platte, LA) **10618**
Vincennes Sun-Commercial (Vincennes, IN) **10446**
† Vincennes Valley Advance (Vincennes, IN)
Vindicator, The (Youngstown, OH) **10488**
Vindicator, The (Liberty, TX) **10743**
Vineyard Gazette (Edgartown, MA) **10625**
Vinita Daily Journal (Vinita, OK) **10491**
† Vinton County Courier (McArthur, OH)
Vinton Messenger (Vinton, VA) **10756**
Virginia Beach Sun (Chesapeake, VA) **10752**
Virginia Gazette (Beardstown, IL) **10573**
Virginia Gazette (Williamsburg, VA) **10756**
Virginia Mountaineer (Grundy, VA) **10753**
Virginian-Leader (Pearisburg, VA) **10754**
Virginian-Pilot, The (Norfolk, VA) **10510**
Virginian Pilot (Nags Head, NC) **10480**
Virginian Review (Covington, VA) **10509**
Virgin Islands Daily News (St. Thomas, VI) **10509**
Visalia Times-Delta (Visalia, CA) **10427**
† Vista Press (Kansas City, MO)
Vistas (King City, CA) **10535**
Voice-Tribune, The (Louisville, KY) **10612**
Voice Ledger, The (Millbrook, NY) **10682**
Voice of the Valley (Maple Valley, WA) **10758**
Voices (Southbury, CT) **10553**
Voice, The (Phoenixville, PA) **10723**

W

Wabash Plain Dealer (Wabash, IN) **10446**
Waco Citizen, The (Waco, TX) **10747**

Waconia Patriot, The (Waconia, MN) **10648**
Waco Tribune Herald (Waco, TX) **10507**
Wadena Pioneer Journal (Wadena, MN) **10648**
Wagoner Tribune, The (Wagoner, OK) **10712**
Wahkiakum County Eagle, The (Cathlamet, WA) **10757**
Wahoo Newspaper (Wahoo, NE) **10662**
Wakefield Item (Wakefield, MA) **10459**
Wake Weekly, The (Wake Forest, NC) **10695**
Wakulla News (Crawfordville, FL) **10556**
Walker-Westside Advance (Jenison, MI) **10634**
Walker County Messenger (La Fayette, GA) **10566**
Wallace Enterprise (Wallace, NC) **10695**
† Wallace Miner (Kellogg, ID)
Walla Walla Union-Bulletin (Walla Walla, WA) **10512**
Waller County News-Citizen (Hempstead, TX) **10741**
Wallis News-Review (Wallis, TX) **10747**
Wallkill Valley Times, The (Walden, NY) **10688**
Walpole Times, The (Walpole, MA) **10629**
Walsh County Press (Park River, ND) **10697**
Walsh County Record, The (Grafton, ND) **10696**
Walton Reporter, The (Walton, NY) **10688**
Walton Tribune (Monroe, GA) **10567**
Walworth Times, The (Walworth, WI) **10774**
Wampum Saver (Show Low, AZ) **10526**
Wantagh-Seaford Citizen (Bellmore, NY) **10673**
Wapato Independent (Wapato, WA) **10760**
Wareham Courier (Marion, MA) **10625**
Ware River News (Ware, MA) **10629**
Warner Center News (Woodland Hills, CA) **10547**
Warren-Newport Press (Grayslake, IL) **10581**
Warren Record, The (Warrenton, NC) **10695**
Warrensburg-Lake George News (Elizabethtown, NY) **10677**
Warren Sentinel, The (Front Royal, VA) **10753**
Warren Sheaf (Warren, MN) **10648**
Warren Times Gazette (Warren, RI) **10726**
Warren Times Observer (Warren, PA) **10497**
† Warrenton Banner (Warrenton, MO)
Warrenton Journal (Warrenton, MO) **10658**
Warrenville Free Press (West Chicago, IL) **10590**
Warroad Pioneer (Greenbush, MN) **10642**
Warsaw-Faison News (Wallace, NC) **10695**
Warsaw Benton County Enterprise (Warsaw, MO) **10658**
Warwick Advertiser, The (Warwick, NY) **10688**
Warwick Beacon (Warwick, RI) **10726**
Warwick Valley Dispatch (Warwick, NY) **10688**

Wasco Tribune (Wasco, CA) **10546**
Waseca County News (Waseca, MN) **10648**
Washburn County Register (Shell Lake, WI) **10773**
Washburn Leader (Metamora, IL) **10585**
Washington City Paper (Washington, DC) **10555**
Washington County Edition (Salem, IN) **10597**
Washington County News (Chatom, AL) **10518**
Washington County News (Washington, KS) **10609**
Washington County News (Abingdon, VA) **10750**
Washington Courier (Washington, IL) **10590**
Washington Daily News (Washington, NC) **10481**
Washington Evening Journal (Washington, IA) **10449**
Washington Missourian (Washington, MO) **10658**
Washington News-Reporter (Washington, GA) **10568**
Washington Post, The (Washington, DC) **10431**
Washington Reporter (Morton, IL) **10586**
Washington Times (Washington, DC) **10431**
Washington Times-Herald (Washington, IN) **10446**
Waterbury Republican-American (Waterbury, CT) **10430**
Waterford News (Winton, CA) **10546**
Waterford Post (Waterford, WI) **10775**
Waterloo Courier (Waterloo, IA) **10449**
Waterloo Republic-Times (Waterloo, IL) **10590**
Watertown Daily Times (Watertown, NY) **10477**
Watertown Daily Times (Watertown, WI) **10515**
Watertown Public Opinion (Watertown, SD) **10500**
Watertown Tab & Press (Somerville, MA) **10628**
Watkins Review & Express (Watkins Glen, NY) **10689**
Watonga Republican, The (Watonga, OK) **10712**
Wauconda Leader (Grayslake, IL) **10581**
Waukon Standard (Waukon, IA) **10605**
Waunakee Tribune (Waunakee, WI) **10775**
Wausau Daily Herald (Wausau, WI) **10515**
Waushara Argus (Wautoma, WI) **10775**
Wauwatosa News-Times (Newverland, WI) **10771**
Waverly Democrat (Waverly, IA) **10605**
Waverly Journal (Waverly, IL) **10590**
Waxahachie Daily Light (Waxahachie, TX) **10507**

Waycross Journal Herald
  (Waycross, GA) **10436**
Wayland-Weston Town Crier
  (Needham, MA) **10627**
Wayne County Journal-Banner
  (Piedmont, MO) **10656**
Wayne County Mail (Webster, NY) **10689**
Wayne County News (Waynesboro, MS) **10651**
Wayne County News (Waynesboro, TN) **10735**
Wayne County News (Wayne, WV) **10763**
Wayne County Outlook (Monticello, KY) **10612**
Wayne County Star (Lyons, NY) **10680**
Wayne Eagle (Wayne, MI) **10639**
Wayne Herald (Wayne, NE) **10662**
Wayne Independent, The
  (Honesdale, PA) **10494**
Wayne Today (Butler, NJ) **10665**
Wayne Wilson News Leader
  (Fremont, NC) **10692**
Wayzata/Orono/Long Lake Sun-Sailor
  (Minnetonka, MN) **10644**
Weakley County Press (Martin, TN) **10733**
Weatherford Daily News
  (Weatherford, OK) **10491**
Weatherford Democrat
  (Weatherford, TX) **10507**
Webster County Citizen (Seymour, MO) **10656**
Webster Echo (Webster Springs, WV) **10763**
Webster Herald (Webster, NY) **10689**
Webster Post, The (Webster, NY) **10689**
Webster Progress-Times (Eupora, MS) **10649**
Webster Reporter & Farmer
  (Webster, SD) **10730**
Webster Republican (Webster
  Springs, WV) **10763**
Webster Times, The (Webster, MA) **10629**
Wednesday Journal of Oak Park & River Forest
  (Oak Park, IL) **10587**
Wednesday Magazine (Kansas
  City, MO) **10654**
Weed Press (Weed, CA) **10546**
Weehawken Reporter (Hoboken, NJ) **10667**
† Weekender Enquirer (Boonville, IN)
Weekender, The (Whitinsville, MA) **10629**
† Weekender, The (Bronx, NY)
Weekender, The (Lexington, VA) **10753**
Weekend Flyer, The (Plainfield, IN) **10597**
Weekend News (Montrose, PA) **10720**
Weekly Almanac, The (Honesdale, PA) **10718**
Weekly Calistogan (Calistoga, CA) **10532**
Weekly Challenger (St. Petersburg, FL) **10561**
Weekly News (Marksville, LA) **10617**
Weekly Observer, The (Hemingway, SC) **10727**
Weekly Packet (Blue Hill, ME) **10618**
Weekly Planet (Tampa, FL) **10561**
Weekly Post (Rainsville, AL) **10521**

Weekly Press (Baton Rouge, LA) **10615**
Weekly Recorder, The (Claysville, PA) **10716**
Weekly Reminder (Paulding, OH) **10706**
† Weekly Territorial (Tucson, AZ)
Weimar Mercury (Weimar, TX) **10747**
Weisbeck, The (Alden, NY) **10673**
Weiser Signal American (Weiser, ID) **10571**
Welch Daily News (Welch, WV) **10513**
Wellesley Townsman (Wellesley, MA) **10629**
Wellington Daily News (Wellington, KS) **10452**
Wellington Royal Palm Beach Forum
  (Wellington, FL) **10562**
Wellsboro Gazette (Wellsboro, PA) **10724**
Wells Mirror, The (Wells, MN) **10648**
† Wellston Sentry (Wellston, OH)
Wellston Telegram, The (Wellston, OH) **10708**
Wellsville Daily Reporter (Wellsville, NY) **10478**
Wenatchee World (Wenatchee, WA) **10512**
Wenona Index (Henry, IL) **10581**
Wentzville Journal (Wentzville, MO) **10658**
West Alabama Gazette (Millport, AL) **10521**
West Allis Star (New Berlin, WI) **10771**
West Boca Times (Deerfield Beach, FL) **10556**
West Bridgewater Star
  (Middleboro, MA) **10626**
Westbury Times (Mineola, NY) **10683**
West Carroll Gazette (Oak Grove, LA) **10617**
West Central Tribune (Willmar, MN) **10464**
Westchester Herald (Oak Park, IL) **10587**
Westchester Observer (Santa
  Monica, CA) **10544**
Westchester Star (Los Angeles, CA) **10538**
West Chicago Press (West Chicago, IL) **10590**
West Columbia Brazoria County News (West
  Columbia, TX) **10747**
West Cook County Press (Elmhurst, IL) **10578**
West County Journal (St. Louis, MO) **10658**
West County Times (Richmond, CA) **10424**
Westerly Sun (Westerly, RI) **10498**
Western Breeze (Cut Bank, MT) **10659**
Western Edition (San Francisco, CA) **10543**
Western Express (Des Moines, IA) **10600**
Western Hills Press (Cincinnati, OH) **10700**
Western News (Libby, MT) **10659**
Western Springs Doings (Hinsdale, IL) **10582**
Western Star (Bessemer, AL) **10517**
Western Star (Lebanon, OH) **10704**
Western Wayne News (Cambridge
  City, IN) **10592**
Western World (Bandon, OR) **10712**
Westerville News & Public Opinion
  (Westerville, OH) **10708**
West Essex Tribune (Livingston, NJ) **10667**
West Fargo Pioneer (West Fargo, ND) **10698**
Westfield Enterprise (Fishers, IN) **10593**
Westfield Evening News (Westfield, MA) **10459**

Westfield Leader (Westfield, NJ) **10671**
Westfield Republican (Westfield, NY) **10689**
Westford Eagle (Chelmsford, MA) **10624**
West Geauga Sun (Beachwood, OH) **10699**
West Hartford News (Bristol, CT) **10551**
West Haven News (Milford, CT) **10553**
West Hawaii Today (Kailua Kona, HI) **10436**
West Hempstead Beacon
   (Hicksville, NY) **10679**
Westine Report (Union Grove, WI) **10774**
West Kentucky News (Paducah, KY) **10613**
Westlake Picayune (Austin, TX) **10736**
Westlaker Times, The (Rocky
   River, OH) **10707**
Westland Eagle (Wayne, MI) **10639**
Westland Observer (Livonia, MI) **10635**
West Liberty Index (West Liberty, IA) **10605**
West Life (West Lake, OH) **10708**
West Linn Tidings (Lake Oswego, OR) **10713**
West Los Angeles Independent (Santa
   Monica, CA) **10544**
West Martin Weekly News
   (Sherburn, MN) **10646**
West Milton Record (West Milton, OH) **10708**
Westminster Window
   (Westminster, CO) **10551**
Westmont Progress (Downers
   Grove, IL) **10577**
Westmoreland News (Montross, VA) **10754**
Westmore News (Port Chester, NY) **10685**
West Morris Star-Journal
   (Ledgewood, NJ) **10667**
West News (West, TX) **10747**
West New York Reporter (Hoboken, NJ) **10667**
Weston Democrat, The (Weston, WV) **10763**
Weston Forum, The (Georetown, CT) **10552**
West Orange Chronicle (Orange, NJ) **10669**
West Orange Times (Winter
   Garden, FL) **10562**
Westosha Report (Twin Lakes, WI) **10774**
West Plains Daily Quill (West
   Plains, MO) **10468**
† West Plains Tribune (Spokane, WA)
West Point News (West Point, NE) **10662**
Westport News (Westport, CT) **10554**
West Proviso Herald (Oak Park, IL) **10587**
West Roxbury Transcript
   (Dedham, MA) **10624**
West Sacramento News-Ledger (West
   Sacramento, CA) **10546**
West San Bernardino Advertiser (San
   Bernardino, CA) **10542**
West Schuylkill Herald (Tower City, PA) **10724**
West Seattle Herald (Seattle, WA) **10759**
West Seneca Bee (Williamsville, NY) **10689**
West Side Advance (Kerman, CA) **10535**

Westside Enterprise (Greenfield, IN) **10594**
Westside Flyer (Indianapolis, IN) **10595**
West Side Journal (Port Allen, LA) **10617**
Westside Messenger (Speedway, IN) **10598**
Westside Record-Journal
   (Ferndale, WA) **10758**
Westsider, The (New York, NY) **10683**
West Side Sun News (North
   Olmsted, OH) **10706**
West Side Times (Buffalo, NY) **10675**
West Springfield Record (West
   Springfield, MA) **10629**
West St. Paul/Mendota Heights Sun-Current
   (Burnsville, MN) **10640**
West Suburban Post (Chicago, IL) **10575**
West Toledo Herald (Toledo, OH) **10708**
West Valley Courier (Hillsboro, OR) **10713**
West Valley Eagle (Bountiful, UT) **10748**
West Valley News (Magna, UT) **10749**
West Valley News/Sunday Advance
   (Flint, MI) **10632**
West Valley View (Avondale, AZ) **10524**
Westville Indicator (Westville, IN) **10598**
West Virginia Daily News
   (Lewisburg, WV) **10513**
West Virginia Hillbilly (Richwood, WV) **10763**
Westword (Denver, CO) **10548**
Wethersfield Post (Bristol, CT) **10552**
Wet Mountain Tribune (Westcliffe, CO) **10551**
Wetumpka Herald (Wetumpka, AL) **10522**
Wetzel Chronicle (New
   Martinsville, WV) **10762**
Wewoka Times (Wewoka, OK) **10712**
Weymouth News (Marshfield, MA) **10626**
Weymouth News & Gazette
   (Braintree, MA) **10624**
Wharton Journal-Spectator
   (Wharton, TX) **10748**
What Cheer Paper (What Cheer, IA) **10605**
Wheaton Leader (Glen Ellyn, IL) **10580**
Wheaton Press (Bloomingdale, IL) **10573**
Wheaton Sun (Naperville, IL) **10586**
† Wheat Ridge Sentinel (Lakewood, CO)
Wheeling News-Register (Wheeling, WV) **10513**
Wheels 'N Deals (Columbia, MO) **10653**
Whidbey News-Times (Oak Harbor, WA) **10758**
White Bear Press (St. Paul, MN) **10647**
Whitefish Bay Herald (New Berlin, WI) **10771**
Whitefish Pilot (Whitefish, MT) **10659**
White Hall Journal (Pine Bluff, AR) **10529**
Whitehall News (Columbus, OH) **10702**
Whitehall Times (Whitehall, NY) **10689**
Whitehall Times (Whitehall, WI) **10775**
White Lake Beacon (Whitehall, MI) **10639**
White Mountain Independent (Show
   Low, AZ) **10526**

White Oak Independent (White Oak, TX) **10748**
White River Current (Calico Rock, AR) **10527**
▼White River Gazette (Fishers, IN) **10593**
White River Journal (Des Arc, AR) **10527**
White Settlement News (Fort Worth, TX) **10740**
Whiteside Shopper (Fulton, IL) **10579**
Whitestone Times, The (Bayside, NY) **10673**
Whitewright Sun, The (Whitewright, TX) **10748**
Whitley Republican News Journal (Williamsburg, KY) **10615**
Whitman County Gazette (Colfax, WA) **10757**
Whitman Times (Stoughton, MA) **10628**
Whitney Point Reporter (Greene, NY) **10678**
Whittier Daily News (Whittier, CA) **10427**
Wichita Eagle (Wichita, KS) **10452**
Wick-Qua-Boag Weekly (Spencer, MA) **10628**
Wickenburg Sun, The (Wickenburg, AZ) **10526**
Wiggins Courier, The (Wiggins, CO) **10551**
Wilcox Progressive Era (Camden, AL) **10518**
Wildwood Leader (Wildwood, NJ) **10672**
Wilkes-Barre Citizens' Voice (Wilkes Barre, PA) **10497**
† Wilkes-Barre Sunday Independent (Wilkes Barre, PA)
Willamette Week (Portland, OR) **10714**
Willapa Harbor Herald (Raymond, WA) **10759**
Willard Times-Junction (Willard, OH) **10708**
Williams Grand Canyon News (Williams, AZ) **10526**
Williamson County Sun (Georgetown, TX) **10740**
Williamson Daily News (Williamson, WV) **10513**
Williamson Leader, The (Franklin, TN) **10732**
Williamsport Sun-Gazette (Williamsport, PA) **10498**
Williamston Enterprise (Williamston, NC) **10696**
Williamsville Sun (Riverton, IL) **10589**
Williston Herald (Williston, ND) **10482**
Williston Plains Reporter (Williston, ND) **10698**
Willowbrook Doings (Hinsdale, IL) **10582**
Willowbrook Progress (Downers Grove, IL) **10577**
Willow Grove Guide (Fort Washington, PA) **10718**
Willows Journal (Willows, CA) **10546**
Wilmette Life (Glenview, IL) **10580**
Wilmington-Tewksbury Town Crier (Wilmington, MA) **10629**
Wilmington Advocate, The (Wilmington, IL) **10591**
Wilmington Beacon (Compton, CA) **10533**
Wilmington Defender (Wilmington, DE) **10554**
Wilmington Express (Wilmington, IL) **10591**

Wilmington Free Press (Wilmington, IL) **10591**
Wilmington Journal (Wilmington, NC) **10696**
Wilmington Morning Star (Wilmington, NC) **10481**
Wilmington News-Journal (Wilmington, OH) **10488**
Wilson County Citizen (Fredonia, KS) **10606**
Wilson Daily Times (Wilson, NC) **10481**
Wilson World, The (Lebanon, TN) **10733**
Wilton Bulletin (Wilton, CT) **10554**
Wimberley Valley-News (Wimberley, TX) **10748**
Winchendon Chronicle (Winchendon, MA) **10629**
Winchendon Courier (Winchendon, MA) **10629**
Winchester Star (Woburn, MA) **10629**
Winchester Star (Winchester, VA) **10510**
Winchester Sun (Winchester, KY) **10453**
Winder News (Winder, GA) **10568**
Windham Journal (Windham, NY) **10689**
Windom Cottonwood County Citizen (Windom, MN) **10648**
Wind River News (Lander, WY) **10776**
Windsor Journal (Bristol, CT) **10552**
Windsor Locks Journal (Bristol, CT) **10552**
Windsor Review (Windsor, MO) **10658**
Windsor Standard (Conklin, NY) **10676**
Winfield Daily Courier (Winfield, KS) **10452**
Winfield Estate (Glen Ellyn, IL) **10580**
Winfield Press (West Chicago, IL) **10590**
Winkler County News (Kermit, TX) **10742**
Winneconne News (Winneconne, WI) **10775**
Winner Advocate (Winner, SD) **10731**
Winnetka Talk (Glenview, IL) **10580**
Winn Parish Enterprise (Winnfield, LA) **10618**
Winnsboro News (Winnsboro, TX) **10748**
Winona Daily News (Winona, MN) **10464**
Winona Times (Winona, MS) **10651**
Winslow Mail (Winslow, AZ) **10526**
Winsted Journal (Winsted, CT) **10554**
Winston-Salem Journal (Winston-Salem, NC) **10481**
Winter Park-Maitland Observer (Winter Park, FL) **10562**
Winter Park Manifest (Winter Park, CO) **10551**
Winterset Madisonian (Winterset, IA) **10605**
† Winter Visitor Independent (Mesa, AZ)
Winton Times (Winton, CA) **10546**
Wisconsin Dells Events (Wisconsin Dells, WI) **10775**
Wisconsin State Farmer (Waupaca, WI) **10775**
Wisconsin State Journal (Madison, WI) **10514**
Wise County Messenger (Decatur, TX) **10738**
Wittenberg Enterprise News (Wittenberg, WI) **10775**
Woburn Advocate (Woburn, MA) **10629**

Woodbury-South Maplewood Review (St. Paul, MN) **10647**
Wood County Democrat (Quitman, TX) **10745**
Wood Dale Press (Elmhurst, IL) **10578**
Woodford County Journal (Eureka, IL) **10578**
Woodford Sun (Versailles, KY) **10615**
Woodridge Progress (Downers Grove, IL) **10577**
Wood River Journal (Hailey, ID) **10569**
Woodruff County Monitor Leader Advocate (McCrory, AR) **10528**
Woodside Herald (Sunnyside, NY) **10687**
Woodstock Independent, The (Woodstock, IL) **10591**
Woodward News (Woodward, OK) **10491**
Wooster Daily Record (Wooster, OH) **10488**
Worcester County Messenger (Pocomoke City, MD) **10622**
Worcester Magazine (Worcester, MA) **10630**
World, The (Coos Bay, OR) **10491**
Worth Citizen (Midlothian, IL) **10586**
Worthington Daily Globe (Worthington, MN) **10464**
Worthington Suburbia News (Columbus, OH) **10702**
Worthington Times, The (Worthington, IN) **10598**
Wrangell Sentinel (Wrangell, AK) **10524**
Wray Gazette (Wray, CO) **10551**
Wright County Journal-Press (Buffalo, MN) **10640**
Wrightsville Headlight, The (Wrightsville, GA) **10568**
† Wrova Reporter (Galva, IL)
Wyandotte West (Kansas City, KS) **10607**
Wyckoff Gazette (Franklin Lakes, NJ) **10666**
Wylie News, The (Wylie, TX) **10748**
Wynne Progress (Wynne, AR) **10530**
Wyoming Advance (Jenison, MI) **10634**
Wyoming State Journal (Lander, WY) **10776**
Wyoming Tribune-Eagle (Cheyenne, WY) **10516**

X

Xenia Daily Gazette (Xenia, OH) **10488**

Y

Yadkin Ripple, The (Yadkinville, NC) **10696**
Yakima Herald-Republic (Yakima, WA) **10512**
Yale News, The (Yale, OK) **10712**
Yancey Common Times Journal (Burnsville, NC) **10691**
Yankee Trader (Coram, NY) **10676**
Yankton Daily Press & Dakotan (Yankton, SD) **10500**
Yardley News (Yardley, PA) **10725**
† Yarmouth Sun (Yarmouth Port, MA)
Yazoo Herald (Yazoo City, MS) **10651**
Yoakum Herald-Times (Yoakum, TX) **10748**
Yonkers Home News & Times (Yonkers, NY) **10690**
York County Coast Star (Kennebunk, ME) **10619**
York Daily Record (York, PA) **10498**
York Dispatch/York Sunday News (York, PA) **10498**
York News-Times (York, NE) **10470**
York Town Crier (Yorktown, VA) **10757**
Yorkville Enquirer (York, SC) **10729**
Your Paper (Roebuck, SC) **10729**
Yucaipa & Calimesa News-Mirror (Yucaipa, CA) **10547**
Yucca Valley Hi-Desert Star (Yucca Valley, CA) **10547**
Yukon Review (Yukon, OK) **10712**
Yuma Daily Sun (Yuma, AZ) **10419**
Yuma Pioneer (Yuma, CO) **10551**

Z

Zachary Plainsman-News (Zachary, LA) **10618**
Zanesville Muskingum Advertiser (Zanesville, OH) **10709**
Zebulon Record, The (Zebulon, NC) **10696**
Zephyrhills News (Zephyrhills, FL) **10562**
Zion-Benton News (Zion, IL) **10591**
† Zionsville Eagle (Indianapolis, IN)
Zionsville Times Sentinel (Zionsville, IN) **10598**
1590 Broadcaster (Nashua, NH) **10663**

Daily Newspapers Index

Abbeville Meridional (Abbeville, LA) **10453**
Aberdeen American News (Aberdeen, SD) **10499**
Abilene Reflector-Chronicle (Abilene, KS) **10449**
Abilene Reporter-News (Abilene, TX) **10502**
Ada Evening News (Ada, OK) **10488**
Ad Express & Daily Iowegian (Centerville, IA) **10447**
Adirondack Daily Enterprise (Saranac Lake, NY) **10477**
Advertiser-Tribune (Tiffin, OH) **10487**
Advocate-Messenger (Danville, KY) **10452**
Advocate, The (Stamford, CT) **10430**
Advocate, The (Baton Rouge, LA) **10454**
Advocate, The (Newark, OH) **10486**
Aiken Standard (Aiken, SC) **10498**
Akron Beacon Journal (Akron, OH) **10482**
† Alabama Journal (Montgomery, AL)
Alameda Times Star (Oakland, CA) **10423**
Alamogordo Daily News (Alamogordo, NM) **10473**
Albany Democrat-Herald (Albany, OR) **10491**
Albany Herald, The (Albany, GA) **10434**
Albert Lea Tribune (Albert Lea, MN) **10462**
Albion Recorder (Albion, MI) **10459**
Albuquerque Journal (Albuquerque, NM) **10473**
Albuquerque Tribune, The (Albuquerque, NM) **10473**
Alexander City Outlook (Alexander City, AL) **10415**
Alexandria Daily Town Talk (Alexandria, LA) **10453**
Alexandria Journal (Fairfax, VA) **10509**
Alice Echo-News (Alice, TX) **10502**
Allegheny Times (Moon Township, PA) **10495**
Alliance Review (Alliance, OH) **10482**
Alliance Times-Herald (Alliance, NE) **10469**
Alpena News (Alpena, MI) **10459**
Altoona Mirror (Altoona, PA) **10492**
Altus Times (Altus, OK) **10488**
Alva Review-Courier (Alva, OK) **10488**
Amarillo Daily News/Sunday News Globe (Amarillo, TX) **10502**
Amarillo Globe Times (Amarillo, TX) **10502**
Americus Times-Recorder (Americus, GA) **10434**
† Amsterdam Star, The (Albany, NY)
Anadarko Daily News (Anadarko, OK) **10488**
Anchorage Daily News (Anchorage, AK) **10417**
Andalusia Star News (Andalusia, AL) **10415**
Anderson Independent-Mail (Anderson, SC) **10498**
Ann Arbor News (Ann Arbor, MI) **10459**
Anniston Star (Anniston, AL) **10415**
Antelope Valley Press (Palmdale, CA) **10423**
Antigo Daily Journal (Antigo, WI) **10513**
Appeal-Democrat (Marysville, CA) **10423**
Argus-Press, The (Owosso, MI) **10461**

Argus Leader (Sioux Falls, SD) **10500**
Argus Observer (Ontario, OR) **10492**
Argus, The (Fremont, CA) **10422**
Arizona Daily Star (Tucson, AZ) **10418**
Arizona Daily Sun (Flagstaff, AZ) **10418**
Arizona Republic (Phoenix, AZ) **10418**
Arkadelphia Daily Siftings Herald (Arkadelphia, AR) **10419**
Arkansas City Traveler (Arkansas City, KS) **10449**
Arkansas Democrat-Gazette (Little Rock, AR) **10420**
Arlington Journal (Fairfax, VA) **10509**
▼Arlington Morning News (Arlington, TX) **10502**
Arlington Star Telegram (Arlington, TX) **10502**
Artesia Daily Press (Artesia, NM) **10473**
Asbury Park Press (Neptune, NJ) **10472**
Asheboro Courier-Tribune (Asheboro, NC) **10478**
Asheville Citizen-Times (Asheville, NC) **10478**
Ashland Daily Tidings (Ashland, OR) **10491**
Ashland Times-Gazette (Ashland, OH) **10482**
Ashtabula Star-Beacon (Ashtabula, OH) **10482**
Aspen Daily News (Aspen, CO) **10427**
Aspen Times, The (Aspen, CO) **10427**
Atchison Daily Globe (Atchison, KS) **10449**
Athens Banner Herald (Athens, GA) **10434**
Athens Daily News (Athens, GA) **10434**
Athens Daily Post (Athens, TN) **10500**
Athens Daily Review (Athens, TX) **10502**
Athens Messenger, The (Athens, OH) **10482**
Athol Daily News (Athol, MA) **10457**
Atlanta Journal-Constitution (Atlanta, GA) **10434**
Atlantic News-Telegraph (Atlantic, IA) **10446**
Auburn Journal (Auburn, CA) **10421**
Augusta Chronicle, The (Augusta, GA) **10434**
Augusta Daily Gazette (Augusta, KS) **10449**
† Augusta Herald (Augusta, GA)
Austin American-Statesman (Austin, TX) **10502**
Austin Daily Herald (Austin, MN) **10462**
Baker City Herald (Baker City, OR) **10491**
Bakersfield Californian (Bakersfield, CA) **10421**
Baltimore Sun (Baltimore, MD) **10456**
Bangor Daily News (Bangor, ME) **10455**
Banner-Graphic (Greencastle, IN) **10443**
Banner-News (Magnolia, AR) **10420**
Banning Record Gazette (Banning, CA) **10421**
Baraboo News-Republic (Baraboo, WI) **10514**
Bartlesville Examiner-Enterprise (Bartlesville, OK) **10488**
Bastrop Daily Enterprise (Bastrop, LA) **10453**
Batavia Daily News (Batavia, NY) **10474**

Batesville Guard (Batesville, AR) **10419**
Battle Creek Enquirer (Battle Creek, MI) **10459**
Baxter Bulletin (Mountain Home, AR) **10420**
Bay City Times (Bay City, MI) **10459**
Baytown Sun (Baytown, TX) **10502**
Beacon News (Aurora, IL) **10438**
Beatrice Daily Sun (Beatrice, NE) **10469**
Beaufort Gazette (Beaufort, SC) **10498**
Beaumont Enterprise (Beaumont, TX) **10502**
Beauregard Daily News (De Ridder, LA) **10454**
Beaver County Times (Beaver, PA) **10492**
Beavercreek News-Current (Dayton, OH) **10484**
Beaver Dam Daily Citizen (Beaver Dam, WI) **10514**
Bedford Gazette/Gazette Sunday (Bedford, PA) **10492**
Bellefontaine Examiner (Bellefontaine, OH) **10482**
Belleville News-Democrat (Belleville, IL) **10438**
Bellevue Gazette (Bellevue, OH) **10483**
Bellingham Herald (Bellingham, WA) **10510**
Beloit Daily Call (Beloit, KS) **10449**
Beloit Daily News (Beloit, WI) **10514**
Belvidere Daily Republican (Belvidere, IL) **10438**
Benicia Herald (Benicia, CA) **10421**
Bennington Banner (Bennington, VT) **10508**
Benton County Daily Record (Bentonville, AR) **10419**
Benton Courier (Benton, AR) **10419**
Berkshire Eagle (Pittsfield, MA) **10458**
Berlin Daily Sun (Berlin, NH) **10471**
Berlin Reporter, The (Berlin, NH) **10471**
Big Rapids Pioneer (Big Rapids, MI) **10459**
Big Spring Herald (Big Spring, TX) **10502**
Billings Gazette (Billings, MT) **10468**
Birmingham News (Birmingham, AL) **10415**
Birmingham Post-Herald (Birmingham, AL) **10415**
Bisbee Daily Review (Bisbee, AZ) **10417**
Bismarck Tribune (Bismarck, ND) **10481**
Blackfoot Morning News (Blackfoot, ID) **10437**
Black Hills Pioneer (Spearfish, SD) **10500**
Blackwell Journal-Tribune (Blackwell, OK) **10488**
Bladen Journal (Elizabethtown, NC) **10479**
Bluefield Daily Telegraph (Bluefield, WV) **10512**
Blue Springs Examiner (Blue Springs, MO) **10465**
Bluffton News-Banner (Bluffton, IN) **10442**
Boca Raton News (Boca Raton, FL) **10431**
Bogalusa Daily News & Sunday News (Bogalusa, LA) **10454**

DAILY NEWSPAPERS

Bonham Daily Favorite (Bonham, TX) **10502**
Bonner County Daily Bee (Sandpoint, ID) **10437**
Boone News-Republican (Boone, IA) **10447**
Boonville Daily News (Boonville, MO) **10465**
Borger News-Herald (Borger, TX) **10502**
Boston Globe (Boston, MA) **10457**
Boston Herald (Boston, MA) **10457**
Bozeman Daily Chronicle (Bozeman, MT) **10468**
Bradenton Herald, The (Bradenton, FL) **10431**
Bradford Era, The (Bradford, PA) **10492**
Brainerd Daily Dispatch (Brainerd, MN) **10462**
Branson Daily News (Hollister, MO) **10466**
Brattleboro Reformer (Brattleboro, VT) **10508**
Brazil Times (Brazil, IN) **10442**
Brazosport Facts, The (Clute, TX) **10503**
Brenham Banner-Press (Brenham, TX) **10503**
Bridgeton Evening News (Bridgeton, NJ) **10471**
Bristol Herald-Courier, The (Bristol, VA) **10509**
Bristol Press, The (Bristol, CT) **10429**
Brookhaven Daily Leader (Brookhaven, MS) **10464**
Brookings Register (Brookings, SD) **10499**
Brooklyn Daily Eagle & Daily Bulletin (Brooklyn, NY) **10474**
Brownsville Herald (Brownsville, TX) **10503**
Brownwood Bulletin (Brownwood, TX) **10503**
Brunswick News, The (Brunswick, GA) **10434**
Bryan College Station Eagle (Bryan, TX) **10503**
Bryan Times (Bryan, OH) **10483**
Bucks County Courier Times (Levittown, PA) **10495**
Bucyrus Telegraph-Forum (Bucyrus, OH) **10483**
Buffalo News, The (Buffalo, NY) **10474**
Bulletin, The (Bend, OR) **10491**
Burlington County Times (Willingboro, NJ) **10473**
Burlington Free Press (Burlington, VT) **10508**
Butler Eagle (Butler, PA) **10493**
Cadillac Evening News (Cadillac, MI) **10459**
Caledonian-Record, The (St. Johnsbury, VT) **10508**
Californian, The (Salinas, CA) **10425**
Californian, The (Temecula, CA) **10426**
Call-Leader (Elwood, IN) **10443**
Call, The (Woonsocket, RI) **10498**
Camarillo Star (Camarillo, CA) **10421**
Camden News (Camden, AR) **10419**
Canandaigua Daily Messenger (Canandaigua, NY) **10474**
Cape Cod Times (Hyannis, MA) **10457**
Cape Coral Daily Breeze, The (Cape Coral, FL) **10431**
Capital-Journal (Topeka, KS) **10452**
Capital Journal (Pierre, SD) **10499**
Capital, The (Annapolis, MD) **10456**
Capital Times, The (Madison, WI) **10514**
Carlisle Sentinel (Carlisle, PA) **10493**
Carlsbad Current-Argus (Carlsbad, NM) **10473**
Carmi Times (Carmi, IL) **10438**
Carroll County Sun (Westminster, MD) **10456**
Carroll County Times (Westminster, MD) **10457**
Cartersville Daily Tribune News (Cartersville, GA) **10434**
Carthage Press (Carthage, MO) **10466**
Casa Grande Dispatch (Casa Grande, AZ) **10417**
Casper Star Tribune (Casper, WY) **10516**
Cecil Whig (Elkton, MD) **10456**
Cedar Rapids Gazette (Cedar Rapids, IA) **10447**
Cedar Valley Daily Times (Vinton, IA) **10449**
Centralia Sentinel (Centralia, IL) **10438**
Central Maine Morning Sentinel (Waterville, ME) **10456**
Centre Daily Times (State College, PA) **10496**
Champaign News Gazette (Champaign, IL) **10438**
Chandler Arizonan Tribune (Chandler, AZ) **10418**
Chanute Tribune (Chanute, KS) **10449**
Chapel Hill Herald (Chapel Hill, NC) **10478**
Charles City Press (Charles City, IA) **10447**
Charleston Daily Mail (Charleston, WV) **10512**
Charleston Gazette, The (Charleston, WV) **10512**
Charleston Post & Courier (Charleston, SC) **10498**
Charleston Times-Courier (Charleston, IL) **10438**
Charlotte Observer (Charlotte, NC) **10478**
Charlotte Sun Herald (Charlotte Harbor, FL) **10431**
Chattanooga Free Press (Chattanooga, TN) **10500**
Chattanooga Times (Chattanooga, TN) **10500**
Cheboygan Daily Tribune (Cheboygan, MI) **10459**
Cherokee Daily Times (Cherokee, IA) **10447**
Chesterton Tribune (Chesterton, IN) **10442**
Chicago Defender (Chicago, IL) **10438**
Chicago Sun Times (Chicago, IL) **10438**
Chicago Tribune (Chicago, IL) **10438**
Chickasha Daily Express (Chickasha, OK) **10488**
Chico Enterprise-Record (Chico, CA) **10421**
Chillicothe Constitution-Tribune (Chillicothe, MO) **10466**

Chillicothe Gazette (Chillicothe, OH) **10483**
Chippewa Herald-Telegram (Chippewa Falls, WI) **10514**
Chronicle-Tribune (Marion, IN) **10444**
Chronicle News, The (Trinidad, CO) **10429**
Chronicle, The (Willimantic, CT) **10431**
Chronicle, The (Centralia, WA) **10511**
Cincinnati Enquirer, The (Cincinnati, OH) **10483**
Cincinnati Post (Cincinnati, OH) **10483**
Circleville Herald (Circleville, OH) **10483**
Citizen Register (Yorktown Heights, NY) **10478**
Citizen, The (Laconia, NH) **10471**
Citizen, The (Auburn, NY) **10474**
Citizen Tribune (Morristown, TN) **10501**
Citrus County Chronicle (Crystal River, FL) **10431**
Claremore Progress (Claremore, OK) **10488**
Clarion-Ledger, The (Jackson, MS) **10464**
Clarksburg Exponent (Clarksburg, WV) **10512**
Clarksburg Telegram (Clarksburg, WV) **10512**
Clarksdale Press Register (Clarksdale, MS) **10464**
Clay Center Dispatch (Clay Center, KS) **10449**
Clayton News Daily (Jonesboro, GA) **10435**
Cleveland Bolivar Commercial (Cleveland, MS) **10464**
Cleveland Daily Banner (Cleveland, TN) **10500**
Cleveland Plain Dealer (Cleveland, OH) **10483**
Clinton Daily Democrat (Clinton, MO) **10466**
Clinton Daily Journal (Clinton, IL) **10438**
Clinton Daily News (Clinton, OK) **10489**
Clinton Herald (Clinton, IA) **10447**
Clovis News Journal (Clovis, NM) **10473**
Coeur d'Alene Press (Coeur d'Alene, ID) **10437**
Coffeyville Journal, The (Coffeyville, KS) **10449**
Colby Free Press (Colby, KS) **10449**
Columbia Basin Herald (Moses Lake, WA) **10511**
Columbia Daily Tribune (Columbia, MO) **10466**
Columbia Missourian (Columbia, MO) **10466**
Columbian, The (Vancouver, WA) **10512**
Columbus Daily Advocate (Columbus, KS) **10449**
Columbus Dispatch (Columbus, OH) **10483**
Columbus Ledger-Enquirer (Columbus, GA) **10435**
Columbus Telegram (Columbus, NE) **10469**
Commercial-News (Danville, IL) **10439**
Commercial Appeal, The (Memphis, TN) **10501**
Commercial Dispatch, The (Columbus, MS) **10464**
Commonwealth Journal (Somerset, KY) **10453**

Concordia Blade-Empire (Concordia, KS) **10449**
Concord Monitor (Concord, NH) **10471**
† Conneaut News-Herald (Conneaut, OH)
Connecticut Post (Bridgeport, CT) **10429**
Connersville News-Examiner (Connersville, IN) **10442**
Conroe Courier, The (Conroe, TX) **10503**
Contra Costa Times (Walnut Creek, CA) **10427**
Conway Daily Sun, The (North Conway, NH) **10471**
Corbin Times-Tribune (Corbin, KY) **10452**
Cordele Dispatch (Cordele, GA) **10435**
Corpus Christi Caller-Times (Corpus Christi, TX) **10503**
Corry Journal (Corry, PA) **10493**
Corsicana Daily Sun (Corsicana, TX) **10503**
Cortland Standard (Cortland, NY) **10475**
Corvallis Gazette-Times (Corvallis, OR) **10491**
Coshocton Tribune (Coshocton, OH) **10483**
Council Grove Republican (Council Grove, KS) **10449**
Country News-Press (Paso Robles, CA) **10424**
† Countywide News (Westminster, MD)
Courier-Express (Du Bois, PA) **10493**
Courier-Journal, The (Louisville, KY) **10453**
Courier-News, The (Elgin, IL) **10439**
Courier-News, The (Bridgewater, NJ) **10472**
Courier-Post, The (St. Charles, MO) **10468**
Courier-Post, The (Cherry Hill, NJ) **10472**
Courier Herald, The (Dublin, GA) **10435**
Courier News (Blytheville, AR) **10419**
Courier, The (Russellville, AR) **10420**
Courier, The (Houma, LA) **10454**
Courier, The (Findlay, OH) **10484**
Crawfordsville Journal Review (Crawfordsville, IN) **10443**
Crescent-News (Defiance, OH) **10484**
Creston News Advertiser (Creston, IA) **10447**
Crookston Daily Times (Crookston, MN) **10462**
Crowley Post-Signal (Crowley, LA) **10454**
Cullman Times (Cullman, AL) **10415**
Culpeper Star Exponent (Culpeper, VA) **10509**
Cumberland Times-News (Cumberland, MD) **10456**
Cushing Daily Citizen (Cushing, OK) **10489**
Daily & Sunday Freeman (Kingston, NY) **10475**
Daily & Sunday Sentinel (Rome, NY) **10477**
Daily Advance (Elizabeth City, NC) **10479**
Daily Advocate (Greenville, OH) **10484**
Daily American (West Frankfort, IL) **10442**
Daily American (Somerset, PA) **10496**
Daily American Republic (Poplar Bluff, MO) **10467**
Daily Ardmoreite (Ardmore, OK) **10488**
Daily Astorian (Astoria, OR) **10491**

DAILY NEWSPAPERS

Daily Banner (Cambridge, MD) **10456**
Daily Breeze (Torrance, CA) **10426**
Daily Californian, The (El Cajon, CA) **10421**
Daily Camera (Boulder, CO) **10428**
Daily Chronicle (De Kalb, IL) **10439**
Daily Citizen (Searcy, AR) **10420**
Daily Citizen News (Dalton, GA) **10435**
Daily Clay County Advocate-Press (Flora, IL) **10439**
Daily Clintonian (Clinton, IN) **10442**
Daily Comet (Thibodaux, LA) **10455**
Daily Commercial (Leesburg, FL) **10432**
Daily Corinthian (Corinth, MS) **10464**
Daily Courier (Forest City, NC) **10479**
Daily Courier Observer, The (Massena, NY) **10476**
Daily Courier, The (Prescott, AZ) **10418**
Daily Courier, The (Connellsville, PA) **10493**
Daily Democrat (Woodland, CA) **10427**
Daily Dispatch (Douglas, AZ) **10418**
Daily Dispatch, The (Henderson, NC) **10479**
Daily Dunklin Democrat (Kennett, MO) **10467**
Daily Evening Item (Lynn, MA) **10458**
Daily Freeman Journal (Webster City, IA) **10449**
Daily Gazette (Sterling, IL) **10441**
Daily Gazette (Schenectady, NY) **10477**
Daily Guide (St. Robert, MO) **10468**
Daily Hampshire Gazette (Northampton, MA) **10458**
Daily Herald (Arlington Heights, IL) **10437**
Daily Herald (Delphos, OH) **10484**
Daily Herald (Columbia, TN) **10500**
Daily Herald, The (Tyrone, PA) **10497**
Daily Herald, The (Provo, UT) **10508**
Daily Home (Talladega, AL) **10416**
Daily Iberian (New Iberia, LA) **10455**
Daily Independent, The (Ridgecrest, CA) **10424**
Daily Independent, The (Ashland, KY) **10452**
Daily Inter Lake, The (Kalispell, MT) **10469**
Daily Item, The (New Rochelle, NY) **10476**
Daily Item, The (Sunbury, PA) **10497**
Daily Jefferson County Union (Fort Atkinson, WI) **10514**
Daily Jeffersonian, The (Cambridge, OH) **10483**
Daily Journal (Kankakee, IL) **10440**
Daily Journal (Franklin, IN) **10443**
Daily Journal (Park Hills, MO) **10467**
† Daily Journal (Elizabeth, NJ)
Daily Journal (Vineland, NJ) **10473**
Daily Journal, The (Fergus Falls, MN) **10463**
Daily Journal, The (International Falls, MN) **10463**
Daily Ledger (Canton, IL) **10438**

Daily Ledger (Fisher, IN) **10443**
Daily Local News (West Chester, PA) **10497**
Daily Mail (Catskill, NY) **10474**
Daily Mail & Sunday Herald (Nevada, MO) **10467**
Daily Mail, The (Hagerstown, MD) **10456**
Daily Midway Driller (Taft, CA) **10426**
Daily Mining Gazette (Houghton, MI) **10460**
Daily News (Mountain Home, AR) **10420**
Daily News (Woodland Hills, CA) **10427**
Daily News (Palatka, FL) **10433**
Daily News (Bowling Green, KY) **10452**
Daily News (Greenville, MI) **10460**
Daily News (Iron Mountain, MI) **10460**
Daily News (Richmond, MO) **10467**
Daily News (Jacksonville, NC) **10479**
Daily News (Wahpeton, ND) **10482**
Daily News (Wapakoneta, OH) **10487**
Daily News (Huntingdon, PA) **10494**
Daily News (Longview, WA) **10511**
Daily News (West Bend, WI) **10516**
Daily News-Bulletin, The (Brookfield, MO) **10465**
Daily News-Record (Harrisonburg, VA) **10509**
Daily News-Sun (Sun City, AZ) **10418**
Daily News Leader, The (Staunton, VA) **10510**
Daily News of Newburyport, The (Newburyport, MA) **10458**
Daily News, The (Eden, NC) **10479**
Daily Nonpareil (Council Bluffs, IA) **10447**
Daily Okeechobee News, The (Okeechobee, FL) **10433**
Daily Oklahoman (Oklahoma City, OK) **10490**
Daily Pilot, The (Costa Mesa, CA) **10421**
Daily Press (Victorville, CA) **10427**
Daily Press, The (Escanaba, MI) **10460**
Daily Press, The (St. Marys, PA) **10496**
Daily Press, The (Newport News, VA) **10510**
Daily Press, The (Ashland, WI) **10513**
Daily Progress (Charlottesville, VA) **10509**
Daily Record (Canon City, CO) **10428**
Daily Record (Parsippany, NJ) **10472**
Daily Record (Ellensburg, WA) **10511**
† Daily Record, The (Westchester, PA)
Daily Register, The (Portage, WI) **10515**
Daily Reporter (Greenfield, IN) **10443**
Daily Reporter (Columbus, OH) **10483**
Daily Reporter, The (Derby, KS) **10449**
Daily Reporter, The (Coldwater, MI) **10459**
Daily Republic (Fairfield, CA) **10422**
Daily Republic (Mitchell, SD) **10499**
Daily Review (Hayward, CA) **10422**
Daily Review & Sunday Review (Towanda, PA) **10497**
Daily Review Atlas (Monmouth, IL) **10440**
Daily Review, The (Morgan City, LA) **10454**

Daily Sentinel-Star, The (Grenada, MS) **10464**
Daily Sentinel, The (Scottsboro, AL) **10416**
Daily Sentinel, The (Grand Junction, CO) **10428**
Daily Sentinel, The (Pomeroy, OH) **10486**
Daily Sentinel, The (Nacogdoches, TX) **10505**
Daily Sitka Sentinel (Sitka, AK) **10417**
Daily Southerner, The (Tarboro, NC) **10481**
Daily Southtown (Tinley Park, IL) **10441**
Daily Sparks Tribune, The (Sparks, NV) **10471**
Daily Standard (Excelsior Springs, MO) **10466**
Daily Standard (Celina, OH) **10483**
Daily Star-Journal, The (Warrensburg, MO) **10468**
Daily Star, The (Oneonta, NY) **10476**
Daily Statesman (Dexter, MO) **10466**
Daily Sun-News (Sunnyside, WA) **10512**
Daily Sun, The (Warner Robins, GA) **10436**
Daily Telegraph (Adrian, MI) **10459**
Daily Times (Ottawa, IL) **10441**
Daily Times (Salisbury, MD) **10456**
Daily Times (Farmington, NM) **10473**
Daily Times (Maryville, TN) **10501**
Daily Times (Weirton, WV) **10513**
Daily Times & Chronicle (Reading, MA) **10458**
Daily Times-Call (Longmont, CO) **10429**
Daily Times Chronicle (Woburn, MA) **10459**
Daily Times Herald (Carroll, IA) **10447**
Daily Times Leader (West Point, MS) **10465**
Daily Times, The (New Rochelle, NY) **10476**
Daily Times, The (Rawlins, WY) **10516**
Daily Transcript (Dedham, MA) **10457**
Daily Tribune News (Cartersville, GA) **10435**
Daily Tribune, The (Ames, IA) **10446**
Daily Tribune, The (Royal Oak, MI) **10462**
Daily Tribune, The (Bay City, TX) **10502**
Daily Tribune, The (Wisconsin Rapids, WI) **10516**
Daily Whale, The (Rehoboth Beach, DE) **10431**
Daily World (Opelousas, LA) **10455**
Daily World, The (Aberdeen, WA) **10510**
Dalhart Daily Texan (Dalhart, TX) **10503**
Dallas Morning News, The (Dallas, TX) **10503**
Danville News (Danville, PA) **10493**
Danville Register & Bee (Danville, VA) **10509**
Davis Enterprise (Davis, CA) **10421**
Day, The (New London, CT) **10430**
Dayton Daily News (Dayton, OH) **10484**
Decatur Daily (Decatur, AL) **10416**
Decatur Daily Democrat (Decatur, IN) **10443**
Delaware County Daily-Sunday Times (Clifton Heights, PA) **10493**
Delaware Gazette (Delaware, OH) **10484**
Delaware State News (Dover, DE) **10431**
Del Norte Triplicate (Crescent City, CA) **10421**
Del Rio News-Herald (Del Rio, TX) **10503**

Delta Democrat-Times (Greenville, MS) **10464**
Deming Headlight (Deming, NM) **10473**
Denton Record-Chronicle (Denton, TX) **10503**
Denver Post (Denver, CO) **10428**
De Queen Daily Citizen (De Queen, AR) **10419**
Derrick, The (Oil City, PA) **10495**
Desert Dispatch (Barstow, CA) **10421**
Desert Sun, The (Palm Springs, CA) **10424**
Des Moines Register (Des Moines, IA) **10447**
Des Plaines Journal (Des Plaines, IL) **10439**
Detroit Free Press (Detroit, MI) **10460**
Detroit News (Detroit, MI) **10460**
Devil's Lake Daily Journal (Devil's Lake, ND) **10481**
Dexter Daily Statesman (Dexter, MO) **10466**
Dickinson Press, The (Dickinson, ND) **10481**
Dispatch, The (Gilroy, CA) **10422**
Dispatch, The (Lexington, NC) **10480**
Dodge City Daily Globe (Dodge City, KS) **10450**
Dominion Post, The (Morgantown, WV) **10513**
Dothan Eagle (Dothan, AL) **10416**
Douglas County Sentinel (Douglasville, GA) **10435**
Dowagiac Daily News (Dowagiac, MI) **10460**
Duluth News-Tribune (Duluth, MN) **10462**
Duncan Banner (Duncan, OK) **10489**
Dunn Daily Record (Dunn, NC) **10478**
Du Quoin Evening Call (Du Quoin, IL) **10439**
Durango Herald (Durango, CO) **10428**
Durant Daily Democrat (Durant, OK) **10489**
Eagle-Herald (Marinette, WI) **10515**
Eagle-Times (Claremont, NH) **10471**
Eagle Tribune, The (North Andover, MA) **10458**
East Oregonian, The (Pendleton, OR) **10492**
Eastside Journal (Bellevue, WA) **10510**
Edinburg Daily Review (Edinburg, TX) **10503**
Edmond Evening Sun (Edmond, OK) **10489**
Edwardsville Intelligencer (Edwardsville, IL) **10439**
Effingham Daily News (Effingham, IL) **10439**
Eldorado Daily Journal (Eldorado, IL) **10439**
El Dorado News-Times (El Dorado, AR) **10419**
El Dorado Times (El Dorado, KS) **10450**
Elizabethton Star (Elizabethton, TN) **10500**
Elk City Daily News (Elk City, OK) **10489**
Elkhart Truth, The (Elkhart, IN) **10443**
Elko Daily Free Press (Elko, NV) **10470**
Ellwood City Ledger (Ellwood City, PA) **10493**
El Paso Herald-Post (El Paso, TX) **10504**
El Paso Times (El Paso, TX) **10504**
Ely Daily Times (Ely, NV) **10470**
Elyria Chronicle-Telegram (Elyria, OH) **10484**
Emporia Gazette (Emporia, KS) **10450**
Englewood Sun Herald (Englewood, FL) **10432**

Enid News & Eagle (Enid, OK) **10489**
Ennis Daily News (Ennis, TX) **10504**
Enquirer-Journal, The (Monroe, NC) **10480**
Enterprise Ledger (Enterprise, AL) **10416**
† Enterprise Sun (Marlborough, MA)
Enterprise, The (Brockton, MA) **10457**
Erie Daily Times/Sunday Times News
    (Erie, PA) **10493**
Erie Morning News (Erie, PA) **10493**
Estherville Daily News (Estherville, IA) **10447**
Evansville Courier (Evansville, IN) **10443**
Evansville Press (Evansville, IN) **10443**
Evening-Observer (Dunkirk, NY) **10475**
† Evening Express (Portland, ME)
Evening Leader, The (St. Marys, OH) **10487**
Evening News (Benton, IL) **10438**
† Evening Sentinel (Ansonia, CT)
Evening Star (Auburn, IN) **10442**
Evening Sun (Hanover, PA) **10494**
Evening Sun, The (Norwich, NY) **10476**
Evening Telegram (Herkimer, NY) **10475**
Evening Times (West Memphis, AR) **10421**
Evening Times (Sayre, PA) **10496**
Evening Times, The (Little Falls, NY) **10475**
Evening World (Bloomfield, IN) **10442**
Express (Lock Haven, PA) **10495**
Express-Times, The (Easton, PA) **10493**
Fairbanks Daily News-Miner
    (Fairbanks, AK) **10417**
Fairborn Daily Herald (Fairborn, OH) **10484**
Fairfax Journal (Fairfax, VA) **10509**
Fairfield Daily Ledger (Fairfield, IA) **10447**
Fairmont Sentinel (Fairmont, MN) **10463**
† Fallon Eagle Standard (Fallon, NV)
Faribault Daily News (Faribault, MN) **10463**
Fayetteville Observer-Times
    (Fayetteville, NC) **10479**
Finger Lakes Times, The (Geneva, NY) **10475**
Flint Journal (Flint, MI) **10460**
Florence Morning News (Florence, SC) **10498**
Florida Times-Union (Jacksonville, FL) **10432**
Florida Today (Melbourne, FL) **10432**
Forrest City Times-Herald (Forrest
    City, AR) **10419**
Fort Collins Coloradoan (Fort
    Collins, CO) **10428**
Fort Dodge Messenger (Fort Dodge, IA) **10447**
Fort Madison Daily Democrat (Fort
    Madison, IA) **10448**
Fort Morgan Times, The (Fort
    Morgan, CO) **10428**
Fort Scott Tribune, The (Fort Scott, KS) **10450**
Fort Wayne News-Sentinel (Fort
    Wayne, IN) **10443**
Fort Worth Star-Telegram (Fort
    Worth, TX) **10504**

Forum, The (Fargo, ND) **10482**
Foster's Daily Democrat (Dover, NH) **10471**
Frankfort Times (Frankfort, IN) **10443**
Franklin Banner-Tribune (Franklin, LA) **10454**
Frederick Post, The (Frederick, MD) **10456**
Fredericksburg Free Lance-Star
    (Fredericksburg, VA) **10509**
Free Lance (Hollister, CA) **10422**
Freeman, The (Waukesha, WI) **10515**
Freeport Journal-Standard
    (Freeport, IL) **10439**
Free Press (Mankato, MN) **10463**
Fremont Tribune (Fremont, NE) **10469**
Fresno Bee, The (Fresno, CA) **10422**
Fulton Sun Gazette, The (Fulton, MO) **10466**
Gadsden Times (Gadsden, AL) **10416**
Gainesville Daily Register
    (Gainesville, TX) **10504**
Gainesville Sun, The (Gainesville, FL) **10432**
Galion Inquirer (Galion, OH) **10484**
Gallipolis Daily Tribune (Gallipolis, OH) **10484**
Galveston County Daily News, The
    (Galveston, TX) **10504**
Garden City Telegram (Garden
    City, KS) **10450**
Gardner News (Gardner, MA) **10457**
Gaston Gazette (Gastonia, NC) **10479**
Gazette, The (Colorado Springs, CO) **10428**
† Geauga Times-Leader (Chardon, OH)
Georgia Times-Union (Brunswick, GA) **10434**
Gettysburg Times (Gettysburg, PA) **10493**
Gilbert Tribune (Chandler, AZ) **10418**
Glasgow Daily Times (Glasgow, KY) **10452**
Glendale News-Press (Glendale, CA) **10422**
Glenwood Post (Glenwood Springs, CO) **10428**
Globe-Gazette (Mason City, IA) **10448**
Gloucester County Times
    (Woodbury, NJ) **10473**
Gloucester Daily Times
    (Gloucester, MA) **10457**
Goldsboro News-Argus (Goldsboro, NC) **10479**
Goodland Daily News (Goodland, KS) **10450**
Goshen News, The (Goshen, IN) **10443**
Grand Forks Herald (Grand Forks, ND) **10482**
Grand Haven Tribune (Grand
    Haven, MI) **10460**
Grand Island Independent (Grand
    Island, NE) **10469**
Grand Rapids Press, The (Grand
    Rapids, MI) **10460**
Grants Pass Daily Courier (Grants
    Pass, OR) **10491**
Great Bend Tribune (Great Bend, KS) **10450**
Great Falls Tribune (Great Falls, MT) **10468**
Greeley Tribune (Greeley, CO) **10428**

Green Bay News-Chronicle (Green Bay, WI) **10514**
Green Bay Press-Gazette (Green Bay, WI) **10514**
Greeneville Sun (Greeneville, TN) **10500**
Greensburg Daily News (Greensburg, IN) **10443**
Greenville Daily Advocate (Greenville, OH) **10484**
Greenville Daily Reflector (Greenville, NC) **10479**
Greenville Herald Banner (Greenville, TX) **10504**
Greenville News (Greenville, SC) **10499**
† Greenville Piedmont (Greenville, SC)
Greenville Record-Argus (Greenville, PA) **10494**
Greenwich Time (Greenwich, CT) **10430**
Greenwood Commonwealth (Greenwood, MS) **10464**
Griffin Daily News (Griffin, GA) **10435**
▼Grove Daily News (Grove, OK) **10489**
Gunnison Country Times (Gunnison, CO) **10428**
Guthrie News Leader (Guthrie, OK) **10489**
Guymon Daily Herald (Guymon, OK) **10489**
† Gwinnett Daily News (Lawrenceville, GA)
Gwinnett Daily Post (Lawrenceville, GA) **10435**
Hammond Daily Star (Hammond, LA) **10454**
Hanford Sentinel, The (Hanford, CA) **10422**
Hannibal Courier-Post (Hannibal, MO) **10466**
Harlan Daily Enterprise (Harlan, KY) **10452**
Harrisburg Daily Register (Harrisburg, IL) **10439**
Harrison Daily Times (Harrison, AR) **10419**
Hartford Courant (Hartford, CT) **10430**
Hastings Daily Tribune (Hastings, NE) **10469**
Hattiesburg American (Hattiesburg, MS) **10464**
Haverhill Gazette (Haverhill, MA) **10457**
Havre Daily News (Havre, MT) **10469**
Hawaii Tribune-Herald (Hilo, HI) **10436**
Hawk Eye, The (Burlington, IA) **10447**
Hays Daily News (Hays, KS) **10450**
Hazleton Standard Speaker (Hazleton, PA) **10494**
Helena West Helena Daily World (Helena, AR) **10420**
Hemet News, The (San Jacinto, CA) **10425**
Henderson Daily News (Henderson, TX) **10504**
Henderson Gleaner (Henderson, KY) **10452**
Hendersonville Times-News (Hendersonville, NC) **10479**
Henryetta Daily Free-Lance (Henryetta, OK) **10489**
Herald & News (Klamath Falls, OR) **10492**

Herald & Review (Decatur, IL) **10439**
Herald-Citizen (Cookeville, TN) **10500**
Herald-Democrat (Denison, TX) **10503**
Herald-Journal (Syracuse, NY) **10477**
Herald-Journal (Spartanburg, SC) **10499**
Herald-Journal, The (Monticello, IN) **10445**
Herald-Mail, The (Hagerstown, MD) **10456**
Herald-News, The (Joliet, IL) **10440**
Herald-Palladium (St. Joseph, MI) **10462**
Herald-Press (Huntington, IN) **10444**
Herald-Star (Steubenville, OH) **10487**
Herald-Sun, The (Durham, NC) **10478**
Herald-Times (Bloomington, IN) **10442**
Herald-Times Reporter (Manitowoc, WI) **10514**
Herald Bulletin (Anderson, IN) **10442**
Herald Coaster (Rosenberg, TX) **10506**
Herald Journal, The (Logan, UT) **10507**
Herald News, The (Fall River, MA) **10457**
Herald Standard (Uniontown, PA) **10497**
Herald Statesman (Yonkers, NY) **10478**
Herald, The (New Britain, CT) **10430**
Herald, The (Jasper, IN) **10444**
Herald, The (Sharon, PA) **10496**
Herald, The (Rock Hill, SC) **10499**
Herald, The (Everett, WA) **10511**
Hereford Brand (Hereford, TX) **10504**
Hernando Today (Brooksville, FL) **10431**
Hiawatha Daily World (Hiawatha, KS) **10450**
Hibbing Daily Tribune (Hibbing, MN) **10463**
Hickory Daily Record (Hickory, NC) **10479**
High Point Enterprise (High Point, NC) **10479**
Hillsdale Daily News (Hillsdale, MI) **10460**
Hilton Head Island Packet (Hilton Head, SC) **10499**
Hobbs Daily News-Sun (Hobbs, NM) **10473**
Holdenville Daily News (Holdenville, OK) **10489**
Holdrege Daily Citizen (Holdrege, NE) **10469**
Holland Sentinel (Holland, MI) **10460**
† Hollywood Sun (Hollywood, FL)
Home News & Tribune, The (East Brunswick, NJ) **10472**
Honolulu Advertiser (Honolulu, HI) **10436**
Honolulu Star-Bulletin (Honolulu, HI) **10436**
Hope Star, The (Hope, AR) **10420**
Hopewell News (Hopewell, VA) **10509**
Hornell Evening Tribune (Hornell, NY) **10475**
Hour, The (Norwalk, CT) **10430**
Houston Chronicle (Houston, TX) **10504**
† Houston Post (Houston, TX)
Hugo Daily News (Hugo, OK) **10489**
Humboldt Sun (Winnemucca, NV) **10471**
Huntington Herald-Dispatch (Huntington, WV) **10512**
Huntsville Item (Huntsville, TX) **10504**
† Huntsville News (Huntsville, AL)

Huntsville Times, The (Huntsville, AL) **10416**
Huron Daily Tribune (Bad Axe, MI) **10459**
Hutchinson News (Hutchinson, KS) **10450**
Idaho Falls Post Register (Idaho
 Falls, ID) **10437**
Idaho Press-Tribune (Nampa, ID) **10437**
Idaho State Journal (Pocatello, ID) **10437**
Idaho Statesman, The (Boise, ID) **10437**
Imperial Valley Press (El Centro, CA) **10422**
Independence Daily Reporter
 (Independence, KS) **10450**
Independence Examiner, The
 (Independence, MO) **10466**
Independent Record (Helena, MT) **10469**
Independent, The (Massillon, OH) **10486**
Independent Tribune (Kannapolis, NC) **10479**
Index-Journal (Greenwood, SC) **10499**
Indiana Gazette (Indiana, PA) **10494**
Indianapolis News (Indianapolis, IN) **10444**
Indianapolis Star (Indianapolis, IN) **10444**
Inland Valley Daily Bulletin
 (Ontario, CA) **10423**
Intelligencer/Record, The
 (Doylestown, PA) **10493**
Intelligencer Journal (Lancaster, PA) **10494**
Intelligencer, The (Wheeling, WV) **10513**
Inter-Mountain, The (Elkins, WV) **10512**
Iola Register (Iola, KS) **10450**
Ionia Sentinel-Standard (Ionia, MI) **10460**
Iowa City Press-Citizen (Iowa City, IA) **10448**
Ironton Tribune (Ironton, OH) **10485**
Ironwood Daily Globe (Ironwood, MI) **10460**
Iroquois County Times Republic
 (Watseka, IL) **10442**
Island Times (Lihue, HI) **10436**
Item, The (Sumter, SC) **10499**
Ithaca Journal, The (Ithaca, NY) **10475**
Jackson Citizen Patriot (Jackson, MI) **10460**
Jackson County Floridan (Marianna, FL) **10432**
Jackson Sun, The (Jackson, TN) **10500**
Jacksonville Daily Progress
 (Jacksonville, TX) **10504**
Jacksonville Journal-Courier
 (Jacksonville, IL) **10440**
Jacksonville Patriot (Jacksonville, AR) **10420**
Jamestown Sun, The (Jamestown, ND) **10482**
Janesville Gazette (Janesville, WI) **10514**
Jasper Daily Mountain Eagle
 (Jasper, AL) **10416**
Jeffersonville Evening News
 (Jeffersonville, IN) **10444**
Jennings Daily News (Jennings, LA) **10454**
Jersey Journal, The (Jersey City, NJ) **10472**
Johnson City Press (Johnson City, TN) **10501**
Jonesboro Sun (Jonesboro, AR) **10420**
Joplin Globe, The (Joplin, MO) **10467**

Journal & Courier (Lafayette, IN) **10444**
Journal-Gazette, The (Fort Wayne, IN) **10443**
Journal-Register (Medina, NY) **10476**
Journal-World, The (Lawrence, KS) **10451**
Journal Inquirer (Manchester, CT) **10430**
Journal Messenger (Manassas, VA) **10509**
Journal News (Hamilton, OH) **10485**
Journal, The (New Ulm, MN) **10463**
Journal, The (Ogdensburg, NY) **10476**
Journal, The (Martinsburg, WV) **10513**
Journal Times (Racine, WI) **10515**
Journal Tribune (Biddeford, ME) **10455**
Junction City Daily Union (Junction
 City, KS) **10450**
Juneau Empire (Juneau, AK) **10417**
Kalamazoo Gazette (Kalamazoo, MI) **10461**
Kane County Chronicle (Geneva, IL) **10439**
Kane Republican (Kane, PA) **10494**
† Kansas City Evening News (Shawnee
 Mission, KS)
Kansas City Kansan (Kansas City, KS) **10450**
Kansas City Star (Kansas City, MO) **10467**
Kearney Hub (Kearney, NE) **10469**
Keene Sentinel (Keene, NH) **10471**
Kendallville News-Sun (Kendallville, IN) **10444**
Kennebec Journal (Augusta, ME) **10455**
Kenosha News (Kenosha, WI) **10514**
Kent-Ravenna Record-Courier
 (Ravenna, OH) **10486**
Kent County Daily Times (West
 Warwick, RI) **10498**
Kenton Times (Kenton, OH) **10485**
Kentucky New Era (Hopkinsville, KY) **10452**
Kentucky Post, The (Covington, KY) **10452**
Keokuk Daily Gate City (Keokuk, IA) **10448**
Kerrville Daily Times (Kerrville, TX) **10504**
Ketchikan Daily News (Ketchikan, AK) **10417**
Kewanee Star-Courier (Kewanee, IL) **10440**
Key West Citizen (Key West, FL) **10432**
Kilgore News Herald (Kilgore, TX) **10504**
Killeen Daily Herald (Killeen, TX) **10504**
Kingman Daily Miner (Kingman, AZ) **10418**
Kingsport Daily News (Kingsport, TN) **10501**
Kingsport Times-News (Kingsport, TN) **10501**
Kinston Daily Free Press (Kinston, NC) **10480**
Kirksville Daily Express (Kirksville, MO) **10467**
Knoxville News-Sentinel (Knoxville, TN) **10501**
Kodiak Daily Mirror (Kodiak, AK) **10417**
Kokomo Tribune, The (Kokomo, IN) **10444**
La Crosse Tribune (La Crosse, WI) **10514**
Lafayette Advertiser (Lafayette, LA) **10454**
La Grange Daily News (La Grange, GA) **10435**
Lahontan Valley News (Fallon, NV) **10470**
La Junta Tribune-Democrat (La
 Junta, CO) **10429**

Lake Charles American Press (Lake Charles, LA) **10454**
Lake City Reporter (Lake City, FL) **10432**
Lake County Record-Bee (Lakeport, CA) **10422**
Lake Havasu City Herald (Lake Havasu City, AZ) **10418**
Lake Sun Leader (Camdenton, MO) **10465**
Lamar Daily News (Lamar, CO) **10429**
Lancaster Eagle-Gazette (Lancaster, OH) **10485**
Lancaster Intelligencer Journal (Lancaster, PA) **10494**
Lancaster New Era (Lancaster, PA) **10494**
Lansing State Journal (Lansing, MI) **10461**
La Porte Herald-Argus (La Porte, IN) **10444**
Laramie Daily Boomerang (Laramie, WY) **10516**
Laredo Morning Times (Laredo, TX) **10505**
Las Cruces Sun-News (Las Cruces, NM) **10473**
Las Vegas Daily Optic (Las Vegas, NM) **10473**
Las Vegas Review-Journal (Las Vegas, NV) **10470**
Las Vegas Sun (Las Vegas, NV) **10470**
Latrobe Bulletin (Latrobe, PA) **10494**
Laurel Leader-Call (Laurel, MS) **10465**
Laurinburg Exchange (Laurinburg, NC) **10480**
Lawrenceville Daily Record (Lawrenceville, IL) **10440**
Lawton Constitution (Lawton, OK) **10489**
† Lead Call (Lead, SD)
Leader-Herald, The (Gloversville, NY) **10475**
Leader-Telegram (Eau Claire, WI) **10514**
Leader, The (Corning, NY) **10474**
Leader Times (Kittanning, PA) **10494**
Leaf-Chronicle, The (Clarksville, TN) **10500**
Leavenworth Times (Leavenworth, KS) **10451**
Lebanon Daily News (Lebanon, PA) **10495**
Lebanon Daily Record (Lebanon, MO) **10467**
Lebanon Democrat, The (Lebanon, TN) **10501**
Ledger-Independent (Maysville, KY) **10453**
† Ledger-Star (Norfolk, VA)
Ledger Dispatch & Sunday Times, The (Antioch, CA) **10421**
Ledger, The (Lakeland, FL) **10432**
Ledger Tribune, The (New Albany, IN) **10445**
Leesville Daily Leader (Leesville, LA) **10454**
Le Mars Daily Sentinel (Le Mars, IA) **10448**
Lenoir News-Topic (Lenoir, NC) **10480**
Lewisburg Daily Journal (Milton, PA) **10495**
Lewiston Morning Tribune (Lewiston, ID) **10437**
Lexington Herald-Leader (Lexington, KY) **10453**
Liberal Southwest Daily Times (Liberal, KS) **10451**
Lima News (Lima, OH) **10485**

Lincoln Courier (Lincoln, IL) **10440**
Lincoln Journal Star (Lincoln, NE) **10470**
Linton Daily Citizen (Linton, IN) **10444**
Litchfield News-Herald (Litchfield, IL) **10440**
† Little Falls Transcript (Little Falls, MN)
Livingston Enterprise (Livingston, MT) **10469**
Lodi News-Sentinel (Lodi, CA) **10422**
Logan Banner (Logan, WV) **10513**
Logan Daily News (Logan, OH) **10485**
Log Cabin Democrat (Conway, AR) **10419**
Lompoc Record (Lompoc, CA) **10422**
Longview News Journal (Longview, TX) **10505**
Los Angeles Bulletin (Los Angeles, CA) **10422**
Los Angeles Times (Los Angeles, CA) **10423**
Loveland Daily Reporter-Herald (Loveland, CO) **10429**
Lovington Daily Leader (Lovington, NM) **10474**
Lowell Sun (Lowell, MA) **10458**
Lubbock Avalanche-Journal (Lubbock, TX) **10505**
Ludington Daily News (Ludington, MI) **10461**
Lufkin Daily News (Lufkin, TX) **10505**
Lyons Daily News (Lyons, KS) **10451**
Macomb Daily (Mt. Clemens, MI) **10461**
Macomb Journal (Macomb, IL) **10440**
Macon Chronicle-Herald (Macon, MO) **10467**
Macon Telegraph (Macon, GA) **10435**
Madera Tribune (Madera, CA) **10423**
Madison Courier (Madison, IN) **10444**
Madison Daily Leader (Madison, SD) **10499**
Madison Press, The (London, OH) **10485**
Mail Tribune (Medford, OR) **10492**
Malden Evening News (Malden, MA) **10458**
Malone Telegram (Malone, NY) **10475**
Malvern Daily Record (Malvern, AR) **10420**
Manhattan Mercury (Manhattan, KS) **10451**
Manistee News-Advocate (Manistee, MI) **10461**
Manteca Bulletin (Manteca, CA) **10423**
Marianas Variety News & Views (Saipan, MP) **10482**
Marietta Daily Journal (Marietta, GA) **10435**
Marietta Times (Marietta, OH) **10485**
† Marin County Daily Recording (San Rafael, CA)
Marin Independent Journal (Novato, CA) **10423**
Marion Daily Republican (Marion, IL) **10440**
Marion Star (Marion, OH) **10485**
Marshall Chronicle (Marshall, MI) **10461**
Marshall Democrat-News (Marshall, MO) **10467**
Marshall Independent (Marshall, MN) **10463**
Marshalltown Times-Republican (Marshalltown, IA) **10448**
Marshfield News-Herald (Marshfield, WI) **10515**

DAILY NEWSPAPERS

Martinsville Bulletin (Martinsville, VA) **10509**
Martinsville Daily Reporter
 (Martinsville, IN) **10445**
Marysville Journal-Tribune
 (Marysville, OH) **10485**
Maryville Daily Forum (Maryville, MO) **10467**
Mattoon Journal Gazette (Mattoon, IL) **10440**
Maui News (Wailuku, HI) **10437**
Mayfield Messenger (Mayfield, KY) **10453**
McAllen Monitor (McAllen, TX) **10505**
McComb Enterprise-Journal
 (McComb, MS) **10465**
McCook Daily Gazette (McCook, NE) **10470**
McCurtain Daily Gazette (Idabel, OK) **10489**
McDowell News, The (Marion, NC) **10480**
McKeesport Daily News
 (McKeesport, PA) **10495**
McKinney Courier Gazette
 (McKinney, TX) **10505**
McPherson Sentinel (McPherson, KS) **10451**
Meadville Tribune, The (Meadville, PA) **10495**
Medford Daily Mercury (Malden, MA) **10458**
Medina County Gazette (Medina, OH) **10486**
Merced Sun-Star (Merced, CA) **10423**
Mercury, The (Pottstown, PA) **10496**
Meridian Star (Meridian, MS) **10465**
Mesabi Daily News (Virginia, MN) **10464**
Mesa Tribune (Mesa, AZ) **10418**
Messenger, The (Troy, AL) **10417**
Messenger, The (Madisonville, KY) **10453**
Mexia Daily News (Mexia, TX) **10505**
Mexico Ledger (Mexico, MO) **10467**
Miami Herald (Miami, FL) **10432**
Miami News-Record (Miami, OK) **10490**
Michigan City News-Dispatch (Michigan
 City, IN) **10445**
Middlesboro Daily News
 (Middlesboro, KY) **10453**
Middlesex News (Framingham, MA) **10457**
Middletown Journal (Middletown, OH) **10486**
Middletown Press (Middletown, CT) **10430**
Midland Daily News (Midland, MI) **10461**
Midland Reporter-Telegram
 (Midland, TX) **10505**
Miles City Star (Miles City, MT) **10469**
† Milford Citizen (Milford, CT)
Milford Daily News (Milford, MA) **10458**
Milton Daily Standard (Milton, PA) **10495**
Milville News (Bridgeton, NJ) **10472**
Milwaukee Journal Sentinel
 (Milwaukee, WI) **10515**
Minden Press-Herald (Minden, LA) **10454**
Mineral Daily Tribune (Keyser, WV) **10513**
Mineral Wells Index (Mineral Wells, TX) **10505**
Mining Journal (Marquette, MI) **10461**
Minot Daily News (Minot, ND) **10482**

Mississippi Press (Pascagoula, MS) **10465**
Missoulian, The (Missoula, MT) **10469**
Moberly Monitor Index (Moberly, MO) **10467**
† Mobile Press (Mobile, AL)
Mobile Register, The (Mobile, AL) **10416**
Modesto Bee, The (Modesto, CA) **10423**
Mohave Valley Daily News (Bullhead
 City, AZ) **10417**
Monett Times (Monett, MO) **10467**
Monitor, The (Los Alamos, NM) **10474**
Monroe Evening News (Monroe, MI) **10461**
Monroe Times, The (Monroe, WI) **10515**
Montana Standard (Butte, MT) **10468**
Monterey County Herald, The
 (Monterey, CA) **10423**
Montgomery Advertiser
 (Montgomery, AL) **10416**
Montgomery Journal, The
 (Rockville, MD) **10456**
Montrose Daily Press (Montrose, CO) **10429**
▼Montrose Morning Sun
 (Montrose, CO) **10429**
Moorpark Star (Moorpark, CA) **10423**
Morning Call, The (Allentown, PA) **10492**
Morning Journal (Lisbon, OH) **10485**
Morning Journal (Lorain, OH) **10485**
Morning News of Northwest Arkansas
 (Springdale, AR) **10421**
Morning Sun (Mt. Pleasant, MI) **10461**
Morris Daily Herald (Morris, IL) **10440**
Moscow/Pullman Daily News
 (Moscow, ID) **10437**
Moundsville Daily Echo
 (Moundsville, WV) **10513**
Mountain Democrat (Placerville, CA) **10424**
Mountain Mail (Salida, CO) **10429**
Mountain Press, The (Sevierville, TN) **10501**
Mount Airy News (Mt. Airy, NC) **10480**
Mount Carmel Daily Republican-Register (Mt.
 Carmel, IL) **10440**
Mount Pleasant Daily Tribune (Mt.
 Pleasant, TX) **10505**
Mount Pleasant News (Mt. Pleasant, IA) **10448**
Mount Vernon News (Mt. Vernon, OH) **10486**
Mt. Vernon Argus (Yonkers, NY) **10478**
Murfreesboro Daily News Journal
 (Murfreesboro, TN) **10501**
Murray Ledger & Times (Murray, KY) **10453**
Muscatine Journal (Muscatine, IA) **10448**
Muskegon Chronicle, The
 (Muskegon, MI) **10461**
Muskogee Daily Phoenix & Times-Democrat
 (Muskogee, OK) **10490**
Napa Valley Register (Napa, CA) **10423**
Naples Daily News (Naples, FL) **10433**
Nashville Banner (Nashville, TN) **10501**

Natchez Democrat (Natchez, MS) **10465**
Natchitoches Times (Natchitoches, LA) **10454**
Naugatuck Daily News (Naugatuck, CT) **10430**
Nebraska City News-Press (Nebraska City, NE) **10470**
Neosho Daily News (Neosho, MO) **10467**
Nevada Appeal (Carson City, NV) **10470**
New Braunfels Herald & Zeitung (New Braunfels, TX) **10505**
† Newburgh Evening News (Newburgh, NY)
New Castle Courier-Times (New Castle, IN) **10445**
New Castle News (New Castle, PA) **10495**
New Haven Register (New Haven, CT) **10430**
New Jersey Herald (Newton, NJ) **10472**
Newport Daily Express (Newport, VT) **10508**
Newport Daily Independent (Newport, AR) **10420**
Newport Daily News, The (Newport, RI) **10498**
News & Advance (Lynchburg, VA) **10509**
News & Observer (Raleigh, NC) **10480**
News & Record, The (Greensboro, NC) **10479**
News-Capital & Democrat (McAlester, OK) **10490**
News-Courier (Athens, AL) **10415**
News-Enterprise (Elizabethtown, KY) **10452**
News-Gazette, The (Winchester, IN) **10446**
News-Herald (Port Clinton, OH) **10486**
News-Herald (Willoughby, OH) **10487**
News-Herald (Oil City, PA) **10495**
News-Item (Shamokin, PA) **10496**
News-Journal, The (Daytona Beach, FL) **10432**
News-Messenger (Fremont, OH) **10484**
News-Pilot, The (San Pedro, CA) **10425**
News-Press, The (Fort Myers, FL) **10432**
News-Record (Gillette, WY) **10516**
News-Review (Roseburg, OR) **10492**
News-Star, The (Monroe, LA) **10454**
News-Sun, The (Waukegan, IL) **10442**
News-Times (Hartford City, IN) **10444**
News-Times, The (Danbury, CT) **10429**
News-Tribune (La Salle, IL) **10440**
News-Tribune (Framingham, MA) **10457**
News-Virginian (Waynesboro, VA) **10510**
News Chief (Winter Haven, FL) **10434**
Newsday (Melville, NY) **10476**
News Herald, The (Panama City, FL) **10433**
News Herald, The (Morganton, NC) **10480**
News Journal (Mansfield, OH) **10485**
News Journal, The (New Castle, DE) **10431**
News Messenger (Marshall, TX) **10505**
New Smyrna Beach Observer (New Smyrna, FL) **10433**
† News of Paterson (Passaic, NJ)
† News Outlook (Aberdeen, NC)
News Press, The (Paso Robles, CA) **10424**

News, The (Southbridge, MA) **10458**
News, The (Frederick, MD) **10456**
News Tribune, The (Tacoma, WA) **10512**
Newton Daily News (Newton, IA) **10448**
Newton Kansan (Newton, KS) **10451**
† New York City Tribune (New York, NY)
New York Daily Challenge (Brooklyn, NY) **10474**
New York Daily News, The (New York, NY) **10476**
† New York Newsday (New York, NY)
New York Post (New York, NY) **10476**
New York Times, The (New York, NY) **10476**
Niagara Gazette (Niagara Falls, NY) **10476**
Niles Daily Star (Niles, MI) **10461**
Norfolk Daily News (Norfolk, NE) **10470**
Norman Transcript (Norman, OK) **10490**
North County Times (Escondido, CA) **10422**
Northeast Mississippi Daily Journal (Tupelo, MS) **10465**
Northern Virginia Daily (Strasburg, VA) **10510**
Northern Wyoming Daily News (Worland, WY) **10516**
North Hills News Record (Warrendale, PA) **10497**
North Jersey Herald & News, The (Passaic, NJ) **10472**
North Port Sun Herald (North Port, FL) **10433**
Northwest Arkansas Times (Fayetteville, AR) **10419**
Northwest Colorado Daily Press (Craig, CO) **10428**
Northwest Florida Daily News (Fort Walton Beach, FL) **10432**
Northwest Herald (Crystal Lake, IL) **10438**
Northwest Signal (Napoleon, OH) **10486**
Norton Daily Telegram (Norton, KS) **10451**
Norwalk Reflector (Norwalk, OH) **10486**
Norwich Bulletin (Norwich, CT) **10430**
Oakland Press, The (Pontiac, MI) **10461**
Oakland Tribune, The (Oakland, CA) **10423**
Oak Ridger, The (Oak Ridge, TN) **10501**
Observer-Dispatch (Utica, NY) **10477**
Observer-Reporter (Waynesburg, PA) **10497**
Observer-Reporter, Washington County Edition (Washington, PA) **10497**
Observer News (Newton, NC) **10480**
Observer, The (New Smyrna, FL) **10433**
Observer, The (Moultrie, GA) **10435**
Observer, The (La Grande, OR) **10492**
Ocala Star Banner (Ocala, FL) **10433**
Ocean County's Observer (Toms River, NJ) **10472**
Odessa American (Odessa, TX) **10505**
Oelwein Daily Register (Oelwein, IA) **10448**
Okmulgee Times (Okmulgee, OK) **10490**

DAILY NEWSPAPERS

Olathe Daily News (Olathe, KS) **10451**
Olean Times Herald (Olean, NY) **10476**
Olney Daily Mail (Olney, IL) **10441**
Olympian, The (Olympia, WA) **10511**
Omaha World-Herald (Omaha, NE) **10470**
Oneida Daily Dispatch (Oneida, NY) **10476**
Opelika-Auburn News (Opelika, AL) **10416**
Orange County Register, The (Santa Ana, CA) **10425**
Orange Leader (Orange, TX) **10505**
Oregonian, The (Portland, OR) **10492**
Orlando Sentinel (Orlando, FL) **10433**
Oroville Mercury-Register (Oroville, CA) **10423**
Oshkosh Northwestern (Oshkosh, WI) **10515**
Oskaloosa Herald (Oskaloosa, IA) **10448**
Ottawa Herald (Ottawa, KS) **10451**
Ottumwa Courier (Ottumwa, IA) **10448**
Outlook, The (Santa Monica, CA) **10426**
Owatonna People's Press (Owatonna, MN) **10463**
Owensboro Messenger-Inquirer (Owensboro, KY) **10453**
Oxford Eagle (Oxford, MS) **10465**
† Oxnard Press-Courier (Oxnard, CA)
Pacific Daily News (Agana, GU) **10436**
Paducah Sun, The (Paducah, KY) **10453**
Palestine Herald-Press (Palestine, TX) **10506**
Palladium-Times, The (Oswego, NY) **10476**
Palm Beach Daily News (Palm Beach, FL) **10433**
Palm Beach Post (West Palm Beach, FL) **10434**
▼Palo Alto Daily News (Palo Alto, CA) **10424**
Pampa News (Pampa, TX) **10506**
Pantagraph, The (Bloomington, IL) **10438**
Paragould Daily Press (Paragould, AR) **10420**
Paris Beacon News (Paris, IL) **10441**
Paris News, The (Paris, TX) **10506**
Paris Post-Intelligencer, The (Paris, TN) **10501**
Parkersburg Sentinel (Parkersburg, WV) **10513**
Parsons Sun (Parsons, KS) **10451**
Pasadena Citizen (Pasadena, TX) **10506**
Pasadena Star-News, The (Pasadena, CA) **10424**
Patriot-News (Harrisburg, PA) **10494**
Patriot Ledger (Quincy, MA) **10458**
Pauls Valley Daily Democrat (Pauls Valley, OK) **10490**
Paxton Daily Record (Paxton, IL) **10441**
† Peabody Times (Peabody, MA)
Pecos Enterprise (Pecos, TX) **10506**
Peekskill Star (Yorktown Heights, NY) **10478**
Pekin Daily Times (Pekin, IL) **10441**
Peninsula Clarion (Kenai, AK) **10417**
Peninsula Daily News (Port Angeles, WA) **10511**
Pensacola News Journal (Pensacola, FL) **10433**
Peoria Journal Star (Peoria, IL) **10441**
Perry Daily Journal (Perry, OK) **10490**
Peru Tribune (Peru, IN) **10445**
Petoskey News-Review (Petoskey, MI) **10461**
Pharos-Tribune (Logansport, IN) **10444**
Philadelphia Daily News (Philadelphia, PA) **10495**
Philadelphia Inquirer (Philadelphia, PA) **10495**
† Phoenix Gazette (Phoenix, AZ)
Phoenix, The (Phoenixville, PA) **10496**
Picayune Item (Picayune, MS) **10465**
Pilot-News (Plymouth, IN) **10445**
Pine Bluff Commercial (Pine Bluff, AR) **10420**
Pioneer, The (Bemidji, MN) **10462**
Piqua Daily Call (Piqua, OH) **10486**
Pittsburgh Post-Gazette (Pittsburgh, PA) **10496**
† Pittsburgh Press (Pittsburgh, PA)
Pittsburg Morning Sun (Pittsburg, KS) **10451**
Plainsman, The (Huron, SD) **10499**
Plainview Daily Herald (Plainview, TX) **10506**
Plano Star Courier (Plano, TX) **10506**
Pocono Record (Stroudsburg, PA) **10497**
Point Pleasant Register (Point Pleasant, WV) **10513**
Ponca City News (Ponca City, OK) **10490**
Pontiac Daily Leader (Pontiac, IL) **10441**
Portales News-Tribune (Portales, NM) **10474**
Port Arthur News (Port Arthur, TX) **10506**
Porterville Recorder (Porterville, CA) **10424**
Portland Commercial Review (Portland, IN) **10445**
Portland Press Herald (Portland, ME) **10455**
Portsmouth Daily Times (Portsmouth, OH) **10486**
Portsmouth Herald (Portsmouth, NH) **10471**
Post & Mail, The (Columbia City, IN) **10442**
Post-Bulletin (Rochester, MN) **10463**
Post-Crescent, The (Appleton, WI) **10513**
Post-Journal, The (Jamestown, NY) **10475**
Post-Standard (Syracuse, NY) **10477**
Post-Star (Glens Falls, NY) **10475**
Post-Tribune (Gary, IN) **10443**
Post-Tribune (Jefferson City, MO) **10466**
Poteau Daily News & Sun (Poteau, OK) **10490**
Potomac News (Woodbridge, VA) **10510**
Pottsville Republican & Evening Herald (Pottsville, PA) **10496**
Poughkeepsie Journal (Poughkeepsie, NY) **10477**
Pratt Tribune (Pratt, KS) **10451**
Press & Sun-Bulletin (Vestal, NY) **10477**

Press-Enterprise, The (Riverside, CA) **10424**
Press-Journal (Vero Beach, FL) **10434**
Press-Republican (Plattsburgh, NY) **10477**
Press-Telegram (Long Beach, CA) **10422**
Press Enterprise, The (Bloomsburg, PA) **10492**
Press Leader, The (Farmington, MO) **10466**
Press of Atlantic City, The (Pleasantville, NJ) **10472**
Prince Georges Journal (Lanham, MD) **10456**
Princeton Daily Clarion (Princeton, IN) **10445**
▼Prince William Journal (Manassas, VA) **10509**
Progress-Index (Petersburg, VA) **10510**
† Progress, The (Clearfield, PA)
Providence Journal-Bulletin (Providence, RI) **10498**
Pryor Daily Times (Pryor, OK) **10490**
Public Opinion, The (Chambersburg, PA) **10493**
Pueblo Chieftain (Pueblo, CO) **10429**
Punxsutawney Spirit (Punxsutawney, PA) **10496**
Quad-City Times (Davenport, IA) **10447**
Quincy Herald-Whig (Quincy, IL) **10441**
Rapid City Journal (Rapid City, SD) **10499**
Ravalli Republic (Hamilton, MT) **10469**
Reading Eagle & Reading Times (Reading, PA) **10496**
Record-Journal (Meriden, CT) **10430**
Recorder, The (Greenfield, MA) **10457**
Recorder, The (Amsterdam, NY) **10474**
Record Herald (Washington Court House, OH) **10487**
Record Herald (Waynesboro, PA) **10497**
Record Searchlight (Redding, CA) **10424**
Record, The (Stockton, CA) **10426**
Record, The (Hackensack, NJ) **10472**
Record, The (Troy, NY) **10477**
Record, The (Horsham, PA) **10494**
Red Bluff Daily News (Red Bluff, CA) **10424**
Redlands Daily Facts (Redlands, CA) **10424**
Red Wing Republican Eagle (Red Wing, MN) **10463**
Register-Guard (Eugene, OR) **10491**
Register-Mail (Galesburg, IL) **10439**
Register-News (Mt. Vernon, IL) **10440**
Register-Pajaronian (Watsonville, CA) **10427**
Register-Star (Hudson, NY) **10475**
Register/Herald (Beckley, WV) **10512**
Register Citizen (Torrington, CT) **10430**
Register Star (Rockford, IL) **10441**
† Register, The (Shrewsbury, NJ)
Reidsville Review (Reidsville, NC) **10480**
Reno Gazette-Journal (Reno, NV) **10470**
Rensselaer Republican (Rensselaer, IN) **10445**

Reporter Dispatch, The (White Plains, NY) **10478**
Reporter, The (Vacaville, CA) **10426**
Reporter, The (Lebanon, IN) **10444**
Reporter, The (Lansdale, PA) **10494**
Reporter, The (Fond Du Lac, WI) **10514**
Repository, The (Canton, OH) **10483**
Republic, The (Columbus, IN) **10442**
Review, The (East Liverpool, OH) **10484**
Review Times (Fostoria, OH) **10484**
Rhinelander Daily News (Rhinelander, WI) **10515**
Richmond County Daily Journal (Rockingham, NC) **10481**
Richmond Palladium-Item (Richmond, IN) **10445**
Richmond Register (Richmond, KY) **10453**
Richmond Times-Dispatch (Richmond, VA) **10510**
Ridgway Record (Ridgway, PA) **10496**
Riverton Ranger (Riverton, WY) **10516**
Roanoke Rapids Daily & Sunday Herald (Roanoke Rapids, NC) **10480**
Roanoke Times, The (Roanoke, VA) **10510**
Robesonian, The (Lumberton, NC) **10480**
Robinson Daily News (Robinson, IL) **10441**
Rochester Democrat & Chronicle (Rochester, NY) **10477**
Rochester Sentinel, The (Rochester, IN) **10445**
Rockdale Citizen (Conyers, GA) **10435**
Rock Island Argus & The Dispatch (Moline, IL) **10440**
Rockland Journal-News (West Nyack, NY) **10478**
Rock Springs Daily Rocket-Miner (Rock Springs, WY) **10516**
Rocky Ford Daily Gazette (Rocky Ford, CO) **10429**
Rocky Mountain News (Denver, CO) **10428**
Rocky Mount Telegram (Rocky Mount, NC) **10481**
Rolla Daily News (Rolla, MO) **10468**
Rome News-Tribune (Rome, GA) **10436**
Roswell Daily Record (Roswell, NM) **10474**
Rushville Republican (Rushville, IN) **10445**
Russell Daily News (Russell, KS) **10451**
Ruston Daily Leader (Ruston, LA) **10455**
Rutland Herald (Rutland, VT) **10508**
Sacramento Bee (Sacramento, CA) **10425**
Saginaw News (Saginaw, MI) **10462**
Saipan Tribune (Saipan, MP) **10482**
Salamanca Press (Salamanca, NY) **10477**
Salem Evening News (Beverly, MA) **10457**
Salem News (Salem, OH) **10486**
Salina Journal (Salina, KS) **10451**
Salisbury Post (Salisbury, NC) **10481**

DAILY NEWSPAPERS

Salt Lake City Deseret News (Salt Lake City, UT) **10508**
Salt Lake Tribune (Salt Lake City, UT) **10508**
Samoa News (Pago Pago, AS) **10417**
Sampson Independent, The (Clinton, NC) **10478**
San Angelo Standard-Times (San Angelo, TX) **10506**
San Antonio Express-News (San Antonio, TX) **10506**
† San Antonio Light (San Antonio, TX)
San Bernardino County Sun (San Bernardino, CA) **10425**
San Diego Union-Tribune (San Diego, CA) **10425**
Sandusky Register (Sandusky, OH) **10486**
Sanford Herald (Sanford, FL) **10433**
Sanford Herald, The (Sanford, NC) **10481**
San Francisco Chronicle (San Francisco, CA) **10425**
San Francisco Examiner (San Francisco, CA) **10425**
San Gabriel Valley Tribune (West Covina, CA) **10427**
San Jose Mercury News (San Jose, CA) **10425**
San Luis Obispo County Telegram-Tribune (San Luis Obisopo, CA) **10425**
San Marcos Daily Record (San Marcos, TX) **10506**
San Mateo County Times (San Mateo, CA) **10425**
San Ramon Valley Times, The (Danville, CA) **10421**
Santa Barbara News Press (Santa Barbara, CA) **10425**
Santa Cruz County Sentinel (Santa Cruz, CA) **10425**
Santa Fe New Mexican (Santa Fe, NM) **10474**
Santa Maria Times (Santa Maria, CA) **10425**
Santa Rosa Press Democrat (Santa Rosa, CA) **10426**
Sapulpa Daily Herald (Sapulpa, OK) **10490**
Sarasota Herald Tribune (Sarasota, FL) **10433**
Saratogian, The (Saratoga Springs, NY) **10477**
Sault Ste. Marie Evening News (Sault Ste. Marie, MI) **10462**
Savannah Morning News (Savannah, GA) **10436**
Scottsdale Progress Tribune (Scottsdale, AZ) **10418**
Scranton Times/Sunday Times (Scranton, PA) **10496**
Seattle Daily Journal of Commerce (Seattle, WA) **10511**
Seattle Post-Intelligencer (Seattle, WA) **10511**
Seattle Times, The (Seattle, WA) **10511**

Sedalia Democrat, The (Sedalia, MO) **10468**
Seguin Gazette-Enterprise (Seguin, TX) **10506**
Selma Times-Journal (Selma, AL) **10416**
Seminole Daily Producer (Seminole, OK) **10490**
Sentinel & Enterprise (Fitchburg, MA) **10457**
Sentinel-Record, The (Hot Springs, AR) **10420**
Sentinel-Tribune (Bowling Green, OH) **10483**
Sentinel, The (Lewistown, PA) **10495**
Shawano Leader (Shawano, WI) **10515**
Shawnee News-Star (Shawnee, OK) **10490**
Sheboygan Press, The (Sheboygan, WI) **10515**
Shelby Globe (Shelby, OH) **10487**
Shelby Star (Shelby, NC) **10481**
Shelbyville Daily Union (Shelbyville, IL) **10441**
Shelbyville News (Shelbyville, IN) **10446**
Shelbyville Times-Gazette (Shelbyville, TN) **10501**
Sheridan Press (Sheridan, WY) **10516**
Shoshone News-Press (Kellogg, ID) **10437**
† Shreveport Journal (Shreveport, LA)
Sidney Daily News (Sidney, OH) **10487**
Sierra Vista Herald (Sierra Vista, AZ) **10418**
Signal, The (Valencia, CA) **10427**
Sikeston Standard Democrat, The (Sikeston, MO) **10468**
Silver City Daily Press & Independent (Silver City, NM) **10474**
Simi Valley Star (Simi Valley, CA) **10426**
Sioux City Journal, The (Sioux City, IA) **10448**
Siskiyou Daily News (Yreka, CA) **10427**
Skagit Valley Herald (Mt. Vernon, WA) **10511**
Slidell Sentry-News (Slidell, LA) **10455**
Snyder Daily News (Snyder, TX) **10506**
South Bend Tribune (South Bend, IN) **10446**
South County Journal (Kent, WA) **10511**
Southeast Missourian (Cape Girardeau, MO) **10466**
Southern Illinoisan (Carbondale, IL) **10438**
South Haven Daily Tribune (South Haven, MI) **10462**
South Idaho Press (Burley, ID) **10437**
Southwest Daily News (Sulphur, LA) **10455**
Southwest Times Record (Fort Smith, AR) **10419**
Southwest Times, The (Pulaski, VA) **10510**
Spectrum, The (St. George, UT) **10508**
Spencer Daily Reporter (Spencer, IA) **10448**
Spencer Evening World (Spencer, IN) **10446**
Spokesman-Review, The (Spokane, WA) **10511**
Springfield News-Leader, The (Springfield, MO) **10468**
Springfield News-Sun (Springfield, OH) **10487**
St. Albans Messenger (St. Albans, VT) **10508**
Standard-Examiner (Ogden, UT) **10508**
Standard-Observer (Greensburg, PA) **10493**

Standard-Star (New Rochelle, NY) **10476**
Standard-Times, The (New Bedford, MA) **10458**
Star-Democrat, The (Easton, MD) **10456**
Star-Gazette (Elmira, NY) **10475**
Star-Herald (Scottsbluff, NE) **10470**
Star-Ledger (Newark, NJ) **10472**
Starkville Daily News (Starkville, MS) **10465**
Star Press, The (Muncie, IN) **10445**
Star Tribune (Minneapolis, MN) **10463**
State Gazette (Dyersburg, TN) **10500**
State Journal (Frankfort, KY) **10452**
State Journal-Register (Springfield, IL) **10441**
Staten Island Advance (Staten Island, NY) **10477**
Statesboro Herald (Statesboro, GA) **10436**
Statesman Journal (Salem, OR) **10492**
Statesville Record & Landmark (Statesville, NC) **10481**
State, The (Columbia, SC) **10498**
St. Augustine Record (St. Augustine, FL) **10433**
St. Cloud Times (St. Cloud, MN) **10463**
St. Croix Avis (St. Croix, VI) **10508**
Steamboat Today (Steamboat Springs, CO) **10429**
Stephenville Empire-Tribune (Stephenville, TX) **10506**
Sterling Journal-Advocate (Sterling, CO) **10429**
Stevens Point Journal (Stevens Point, WI) **10515**
Stillwater Gazette (Stillwater, MN) **10463**
Stillwater News-Press (Stillwater, OK) **10490**
St. Joseph News-Press (St. Joseph, MO) **10468**
St. Louis Post-Dispatch (St. Louis, MO) **10468**
Storm Lake Pilot Tribune (Storm Lake, IA) **10448**
St. Paul Pioneer Press (St. Paul, MN) **10463**
St. Petersburg Times (St. Petersburg, FL) **10433**
Streator Times-Press (Streator, IL) **10441**
Stuart News (Stuart, FL) **10434**
Sturgis Journal (Sturgis, MI) **10462**
Stuttgart Daily Leader (Stuttgart, AR) **10421**
Suffolk News-Herald (Suffolk, VA) **10510**
Sullivan Daily Times (Sullivan, IN) **10446**
Sulphur Springs News-Telegram (Sulphur Springs, TX) **10507**
Summit Daily News (Frisco, CO) **10428**
Sun-Journal (Lewiston, ME) **10455**
Sun-Journal (New Bern, NC) **10480**
Sun-Sentinel (Fort Lauderdale, FL) **10432**
Sun Chronicle (Attleboro, MA) **10457**
Sun Herald, The (Gulfport, MS) **10464**
Sun News, The (Myrtle Beach, SC) **10499**

Sun, The (Bremerton, WA) **10511**
Superior Daily Telegram (Superior, WI) **10515**
Sweetwater Reporter (Sweetwater, TX) **10507**
Tahlequah Daily Press (Tahlequah, OK) **10491**
Tahoe Daily Tribune (South Lake Tahoe, CA) **10426**
Tallahassee Democrat (Tallahassee, FL) **10434**
Tampa Tribune, The (Tampa, FL) **10434**
Tarrytown Daily News (White Plains, NY) **10478**
Taunton Daily Gazette (Taunton, MA) **10458**
Taylor Daily Press (Taylor, TX) **10507**
Taylorville Breeze-Courier (Taylorville, IL) **10441**
Telegram & Gazette (Worcester, MA) **10459**
Telegraph Herald (Dubuque, IA) **10447**
Telegraph, The (Alton, IL) **10437**
Telegraph, The (Dixon, IL) **10439**
Telegraph, The (North Platte, NE) **10470**
Telegraph, The (Hudson, NH) **10471**
Telluride Daily Planet (Telluride, CO) **10429**
Tempe Daily News Tribune (Tempe, AZ) **10418**
Temple Daily Telegram (Temple, TX) **10507**
Tennessean, The (Nashville, TN) **10501**
Terrell Tribune (Terrell, TX) **10507**
Texarkana Gazette (Texarkana, TX) **10507**
Texas City Sun (Texas City, TX) **10507**
The Dalles Daily Chronicle (The Dalles, OR) **10492**
Thomasville Times-Enterprise (Thomasville, GA) **10436**
Thousand Oaks Star (Thousand Oaks, CA) **10426**
Three Rivers Commercial-News (Three Rivers, MI) **10462**
Tifton Gazette (Tifton, GA) **10436**
Tiller & Toiler (Larned, KS) **10450**
Times & Democrat, The (Orangeburg, SC) **10499**
Times-Bulletin (Van Wert, OH) **10487**
Times-Gazette (Greenfield, OH) **10484**
Times-Georgian (Carrollton, GA) **10434**
Times-Journal, The (Fort Payne, AL) **10416**
Times-Mail (Bedford, IN) **10442**
Times-News, The (Burlington, NC) **10478**
Times-Picayune (New Orleans, LA) **10455**
Times-Record (Brunswick, ME) **10455**
Times-Reporter, The (New Philadelphia, OH) **10486**
Times-Review (Cleburne, TX) **10503**
Times-Standard (Eureka, CA) **10422**
Times-Union (Warsaw, IN) **10446**
† Times-Union (Rochester, NY)
Times Argus (Barre, VT) **10508**
Times Daily (Florence, AL) **10416**

DAILY NEWSPAPERS

Times Gazette, The (Hillsboro, OH) **10485**
Times Herald (Port Huron, MI) **10462**
Times Herald-Record (Middletown, NY) **10476**
Times Herald, The (Norristown, PA) **10495**
Times Leader (Martins Ferry, OH) **10485**
Times Leader, The (Wilkes Barre, PA) **10497**
Times News (Lehighton, PA) **10495**
Times Recorder, The (Zanesville, OH) **10488**
Times Record News (Wichita Falls, TX) **10507**
Times, The (Gainesville, GA) **10435**
Times, The (Munster, IN) **10445**
Times, The (Shreveport, LA) **10455**
Times, The (Trenton, NJ) **10472**
Times, The (Pawtucket, RI) **10498**
† Times Tribune (Palo Alto, CA)
Times Union (Albany, NY) **10474**
Times West Virginian (Fairmont, WV) **10512**
Tipton Tribune (Tipton, IN) **10446**
Titusville Herald (Titusville, PA) **10497**
Today's News-Herald (Lake Havasu City, AZ) **10418**
Today's Sunbeam (Salem, NJ) **10472**
Toledo Blade (Toledo, OH) **10487**
Tonawanda News (North Tonawanda, NY) **10476**
Tracy Press (Tracy, CA) **10426**
Transcript, The (North Adams, MA) **10458**
Traverse City Record-Eagle (Traverse City, MI) **10462**
Trentonian, The (Trenton, NJ) **10473**
Trenton Republican Times (Trenton, MO) **10468**
Tri-City Herald (Kennewick, WA) **10511**
Tri-Valley Herald (Pleasanton, CA) **10424**
Tribune (Chandler, AZ) **10418**
Tribune-Democrat, The (Johnstown, PA) **10494**
Tribune-Review (Greensburg, PA) **10493**
Tribune-Star (Terre Haute, IN) **10446**
Tribune Chronicle, The (Warren, OH) **10487**
Tribune, The (Fort Pierce, FL) **10432**
Tribune, The (Seymour, IN) **10446**
Tribune, The/Sunday Times (Scranton, PA) **10496**
Troy Daily News (Troy, OH) **10487**
Tryon Daily Bulletin (Tryon, NC) **10481**
Tucson Citizen (Tucson, AZ) **10419**
Tulare Advance-Register (Tulare, CA) **10426**
Tulsa World (Tulsa, OK) **10491**
Turlock Journal (Turlock, CA) **10426**
Tuscaloosa News, The (Tuscaloosa, AL) **10417**
Twin Falls Times-News (Twin Falls, ID) **10437**
Tyler Morning Telegraph (Tyler, TX) **10507**
Ukiah Daily Journal (Ukiah, CA) **10426**
Union-News (Springfield, MA) **10458**
Union-Recorder (Milledgeville, GA) **10435**

Union-Sun & Journal (Lockport, NY) **10475**
Union City Daily Messenger (Union City, TN) **10502**
Union Daily Times (Union, SC) **10499**
Union Democrat, The (Sonora, CA) **10426**
Union Leader/New Hampshire Sunday News (Manchester, NH) **10471**
Union, The (Grass Valley, CA) **10422**
Upper Sandusky Daily Chief-Union (Upper Sandusky, OH) **10487**
Urbana Daily Citizen (Urbana, OH) **10487**
Vail Daily (Avon, CO) **10428**
Valdosta Daily Times (Valdosta, GA) **10436**
Vallejo Times-Herald (Vallejo, CA) **10427**
Valley City Times-Record (Valley City, ND) **10482**
Valley Courier (Alamosa, CO) **10427**
Valley Independent (Monessen, PA) **10495**
Valley Morning Star (Harlingen, TX) **10504**
Valley News (West Lebanon, NH) **10471**
Valley News Dispatch (Tarentum, PA) **10497**
Valley News Today-Daily Sentinel (Shenandoah, IA) **10448**
Valley Times (Pleasanton, CA) **10424**
Valley Times-News (Lanett, AL) **10416**
Valparaiso Vidette-Times (Valparaiso, IN) **10446**
Ventura County Star (Ventura, CA) **10427**
Vernon Daily Record (Vernon, TX) **10507**
Vicksburg Post (Vicksburg, MS) **10465**
Victoria Advocate (Victoria, TX) **10507**
Vincennes Sun-Commercial (Vincennes, IN) **10446**
Vindicator, The (Youngstown, OH) **10488**
Vinita Daily Journal (Vinita, OK) **10491**
Virginian-Pilot, The (Norfolk, VA) **10510**
Virginian Pilot (Nags Head, NC) **10480**
Virginian Review (Covington, VA) **10509**
Virgin Islands Daily News (St. Thomas, VI) **10509**
Visalia Times-Delta (Visalia, CA) **10427**
Wabash Plain Dealer (Wabash, IN) **10446**
Waco Tribune Herald (Waco, TX) **10507**
Wakefield Item (Wakefield, MA) **10459**
Walla Walla Union-Bulletin (Walla Walla, WA) **10512**
Warren Times Observer (Warren, PA) **10497**
Washington Daily News (Washington, NC) **10481**
Washington Evening Journal (Washington, IA) **10449**
Washington Post, The (Washington, DC) **10431**
Washington Times (Washington, DC) **10431**
Washington Times-Herald (Washington, IN) **10446**

Waterbury Republican-American (Waterbury, CT) **10430**
Waterloo Courier (Waterloo, IA) **10449**
Watertown Daily Times (Watertown, NY) **10477**
Watertown Daily Times (Watertown, WI) **10515**
Watertown Public Opinion (Watertown, SD) **10500**
Wausau Daily Herald (Wausau, WI) **10515**
Waxahachie Daily Light (Waxahachie, TX) **10507**
Waycross Journal Herald (Waycross, GA) **10436**
Wayne Independent, The (Honesdale, PA) **10494**
Weatherford Daily News (Weatherford, OK) **10491**
Weatherford Democrat (Weatherford, TX) **10507**
Welch Daily News (Welch, WV) **10513**
Wellington Daily News (Wellington, KS) **10452**
Wellsville Daily Reporter (Wellsville, NY) **10478**
Wenatchee World (Wenatchee, WA) **10512**
West Central Tribune (Willmar, MN) **10464**
West County Times (Richmond, CA) **10424**
Westerly Sun (Westerly, RI) **10498**
Westfield Evening News (Westfield, MA) **10459**
West Hawaii Today (Kailua Kona, HI) **10436**
West Plains Daily Quill (West Plains, MO) **10468**
West Virginia Daily News (Lewisburg, WV) **10513**
Wheeling News-Register (Wheeling, WV) **10513**
Whittier Daily News (Whittier, CA) **10427**
Wichita Eagle (Wichita, KS) **10452**

Wilkes-Barre Citizens' Voice (Wilkes Barre, PA) **10497**
Williamson Daily News (Williamson, WV) **10513**
Williamsport Sun-Gazette (Williamsport, PA) **10498**
Williston Herald (Williston, ND) **10482**
Wilmington Morning Star (Wilmington, NC) **10481**
Wilmington News-Journal (Wilmington, OH) **10488**
Wilson Daily Times (Wilson, NC) **10481**
Winchester Star (Winchester, VA) **10510**
Winchester Sun (Winchester, KY) **10453**
Winfield Daily Courier (Winfield, KS) **10452**
Winona Daily News (Winona, MN) **10464**
Winston-Salem Journal (Winston-Salem, NC) **10481**
Wisconsin State Journal (Madison, WI) **10514**
Woodward News (Woodward, OK) **10491**
Wooster Daily Record (Wooster, OH) **10488**
World, The (Coos Bay, OR) **10491**
Worthington Daily Globe (Worthington, MN) **10464**
Wyoming Tribune-Eagle (Cheyenne, WY) **10516**
Xenia Daily Gazette (Xenia, OH) **10488**
Yakima Herald-Republic (Yakima, WA) **10512**
Yankton Daily Press & Dakotan (Yankton, SD) **10500**
York Daily Record (York, PA) **10498**
York Dispatch/York Sunday News (York, PA) **10498**
York News-Times (York, NE) **10470**
Yuma Daily Sun (Yuma, AZ) **10419**

Weekly Newspapers Index

Abbeville Herald (Abbeville, AL) **10517**
Abbotsford Tribune-Phonograph
 (Abbotsford, WI) **10764**
Aberdeen Examiner (Aberdeen, MS) **10648**
Aberdeen Times (Aberdeen, ID) **10568**
Abernathy Weekly Review
 (Abernathy, TX) **10735**
Abingdon Argus (Abingdon, IL) **10571**
Abingdon Virginian (Abingdon, VA) **10750**
Abington Journal (Clarks Summit, PA) **10716**
Ace News, The (Heath, OH) **10703**
Acorn, The (Agoura Hills, CA) **10530**
Action Advertiser (Fond Du Lac, WI) **10767**
Acworth Neighbor (Marietta, GA) **10566**
Ad-News (Greenfield, IN) **10594**
Ad-Visor (Beulah, MI) **10630**
Ad-Visor (Lansing, MI) **10635**
Ada/Cascade/Forest Hills Advance
 (Jenison, MI) **10634**
Adair County Free Press
 (Greenfield, IA) **10601**
Adair Progress, The (Columbia, KY) **10610**
Adair Russell Shopper, The
 (Columbia, KY) **10610**
† Adams County Leader (Council, ID)
Adams County Times (Adams, WI) **10764**
Ada Norman County Index (Ada, MN) **10639**
Addison County Independent
 (Middlebury, VT) **10750**
Addison Press (Elmhurst, IL) **10578**
† Adelanto Bulletin, The (Adelanto, CA)
Adel News-Tribune (Adel, GA) **10562**
Advance-Monticellonian
 (Monticello, AR) **10528**
Advance-Yeoman (Lacenter, KY) **10612**
Advance Leader (Monroeville, PA) **10720**
Advance News (Lakehurst, NJ) **10667**
Advance of Bucks County
 (Newtown, PA) **10721**
Advance, The (Ogdensburg, NY) **10684**
Advertiser-Gleam (Guntersville, AL) **10520**
Advertiser, The (Van Buren, AR) **10529**
Advertiser, The (Worden, IL) **10591**
Advertiser, The (Ligonier, IN) **10595**
Advertiser, The (Louisa, KY) **10612**
Advertiser, The (Mount Sterling, KY) **10613**
Advertiser, The (Paris, KY) **10613**
Advertiser, The (Iron Mountain, MI) **10634**
Advertiser, The (Bemidji, MN) **10640**
Advertiser, The (Chillicothe, OH) **10700**
Advertiser, The (McMurray, PA) **10719**
Advisor/Source (Utica, MI) **10638**
Advisor, The (Mt. Pleasant, PA) **10721**
Advocate/South Advocate, The
 (Williamstown, MA) **10629**
Advocate Democrat (Madisonville, TN) **10733**
Advocate Penny Saver
 (Sweetwater, TN) **10735**
Advocate, The (Clifton, IL) **10576**
Aegis, The (Bel Air, MD) **10621**

Afton Star-Enterprise (Afton, IA) **10598**
AG Journal (La Junta, CO) **10549**
Aitkin Independent Age (Aitkin, MN) **10639**
Ajo Copper News (Ajo, AZ) **10524**
Akron News Reporter (Akron, CO) **10547**
Alabama Messenger (Birmingham, AL) **10518**
Alamance News (Graham, NC) **10692**
Alaska Star (Eagle River, AK) **10523**
Albany Journal (Albany, GA) **10562**
Albany Ledger, The (Albany, MO) **10651**
Albia Union-Republican (Albia, IA) **10599**
Albion Advertiser (Albion, NY) **10673**
Albion News (Albion, NE) **10659**
Albion News, The (Albion, PA) **10715**
Albuquerque Street News (Albuquerque, NM) **10672**
Alexandria Gazette Packet (Alexandria, VA) **10750**
Alexandria News Weekly (Alexandria, LA) **10615**
Alexandria Times-Tribune (Alexandria, IN) **10591**
Algoma Record Herald (Algoma, WI) **10764**
† Algonac Courier Journal (Marine City, MI)
Algona Upper Des Moines (Algona, IA) **10599**
Algonquin Countryside (Barrington, IL) **10572**
Alhambra Post Advocate (Los Angeles, CA) **10537**
Aliso Viejo News (Lake Forest, CA) **10536**
Allegan County News (Allegan, MI) **10630**
Allen County Times (New Haven, IN) **10596**
Allied News (Grove City, PA) **10718**
Almanac, The (McMurray, PA) **10719**
Aloha Breeze (Hillsboro, OR) **10713**
† Alpena Journal (Wessington Springs, SD)
Alpena Star (Alpena, MI) **10630**
Alpharetta Revue (Alpharetta, GA) **10562**
Alpine Avalanche (Alpine, TX) **10736**
Alsip Express (Midlothian, IL) **10585**
Altamont Enterprise, The (Altamont, NY) **10673**
Altamont News, The (Altamont, IL) **10571**
Altavista Journal (Altavista, VA) **10751**
Alternatives News Magazine (Myrtle Beach, SC) **10728**
Altoona Herald, The (Altoona, IA) **10599**
Alvarado Post (Alvarado, TX) **10736**
Alvin Advertiser (Alvin, TX) **10736**
Alvin Sun (Alvin, TX) **10736**
† Alvin Tiller (Lamont, CA)
Amador/Calavaras Ledger Dispatch (Jackson, CA) **10535**
Ambler Gazette (Fort Washington, PA) **10717**
Amboy News, The (Amboy, IL) **10571**
Amelia Bulletin Monitor, The (Amelia Court House, VA) **10751**

American Journal (Westbrook, ME) **10620**
Amery Free Press (Amery, WI) **10764**
Amesbury News (Amesbury, MA) **10623**
Amherst Bee (Williamsville, NY) **10689**
Amherst New Era-Progress (Amherst, VA) **10751**
Amite Tangi Digest (Amite, LA) **10615**
Amityville Record (Amityville, NY) **10673**
Amory Advertiser, The (Amory, MS) **10648**
Anaconda Leader (Anaconda, MT) **10658**
Anacortes American (Anacortes, WA) **10757**
Anaheim Bulletin (Anaheim, CA) **10530**
Anaheim Hills News (Anaheim, CA) **10530**
Anamosa Journal-Eureka (Anamosa, IA) **10599**
† Anchor Bay Beacon (New Baltimore, MI)
† Anderson Countian (Garnett, KS)
Anderson News, The (Lawrenceburg, KY) **10612**
Andover Townsman (Andover, MA) **10623**
Andrews County News (Andrews, TX) **10736**
Angelina Free Press (Diboll, TX) **10739**
Angier Independent (Angier, NC) **10690**
Angleton Times (Angleton, TX) **10736**
Ankeny Press Citizen (Ankeny, IA) **10599**
Anoka County Union (Coon Rapids, MN) **10641**
Anson Record, The (Wadesboro, NC) **10695**
Anthony Republican, The (Anthony, KS) **10605**
Antigo Area Shoppers Guide (Antigo, WI) **10764**
Antioch News-Reporter (Grayslake, IL) **10580**
Apache Junction Independent (Apache Junction, AZ) **10524**
Apex Herald, The (Apex, NC) **10690**
Appalachian News-Express (Pikeville, KY) **10613**
Apple Valley/Rosemont Sun-Current (Burnsville, MN) **10640**
Apple Valley News (Apple Valley, CA) **10530**
† Applewood/Wheat Ridge Transcript (Golden, CO)
Appomattox Times-Virginian (Appomattox, VA) **10751**
Arab Tribune (Arab, AL) **10517**
Arapahoe Public Mirror (Arapahoe, NE) **10659**
Arbutus Times (Baltimore, MD) **10620**
Arcadia News-Leader (Arcadia, WI) **10764**
Arcadian, The (Arcadia, FL) **10555**
† Arcadia Tribune (Arcadia, CA)
Archbold Buckeye (Archbold, OH) **10698**
Arco Advertiser (Arco, ID) **10569**
Arcola Record Herald (Arcola, IL) **10571**
Arctic Sounder, The (Barrow, AK) **10522**
Area Shopper (Conneautville, PA) **10716**
Arenac County Independent (Standish, MI) **10638**

Argonaut, The (Los Angeles, CA) **10537**
Argus-Champion, The (Newport, NH) **10663**
Argyle Agenda (Argyle, WI) **10764**
Argyle Sun, The (Lake Dallas, TX) **10743**
Arizona City Independent (Arizona City, AZ) **10524**
Arizona Silver Belt (Globe, AZ) **10525**
Ark, The (Bel Tiburon, CA) **10531**
Arlington Advocate (Arlington, MA) **10623**
Arlington Citizen (Blair, NE) **10660**
Arlington Courier, The (Arlington, VA) **10751**
Arlington Heights Journal & Topics (Des Plaines, IL) **10576**
Aroostook Republican & News (Caribou, ME) **10619**
▼Arrowhead Ranch Independent (Sun City, AZ) **10526**
Arrow, The (Glendale, AZ) **10525**
Arthur Enterprise, The (Arthur, NE) **10660**
Arthur Graphic Clarion (Arthur, IL) **10571**
Arvada Jefferson Sentinel (Lakewood, CO) **10549**
Ashley County Shoppers Guide (Crossett, AR) **10527**
Ashley News Observer (Crossett, AR) **10527**
Ashton Gazette (Ashton, IL) **10572**
Associated Newspaper (Stoughton, MA) **10628**
Astoria South Fulton Argus (Astoria, IL) **10572**
Atascadero News (Atascadero, CA) **10530**
Atchison County Mail, The (Rock Port, MO) **10656**
Athens News (Athens, OH) **10698**
Athens Observer, The (Athens, GA) **10562**
Atkins Chronicle, The (Atkins, AR) **10526**
Atkinson Graphic, The (Atkinson, NE) **10660**
Atlanta Bulletin (Atlanta, GA) **10562**
Atlanta Citizens Journal (Atlanta, TX) **10736**
Atlanta Daily World (Atlanta, GA) **10562**
Atlantic County Record (Hammonton, NJ) **10666**
Atmore Advance (Atmore, AL) **10517**
Atoka County Times (Atoka, OK) **10709**
Attica Hub (Attica, OH) **10698**
Atwater Times (Winton, CA) **10546**
Atwood Herald (Atwood, IL) **10572**
Auburn Citizen (Auburn, IL) **10572**
Auburn News (Auburn, MA) **10623**
Auburn Press Tribune (Auburn, NE) **10660**
Auctioner, The (Pekin, IN) **10597**
Augusta Area Times (Augusta, WI) **10764**
Aurora Advertiser (Aurora, MO) **10651**
Aurora Advocate (Stow, OH) **10707**
Aurora News-Register (Aurora, NE) **10660**
Aurora Sentinel (Aurora, CO) **10547**
† Ausable Forks Adirondack Record Post (Elizabethtown, NY)

Austell Neighbor (Marietta, GA) **10566**
Austin Chronicle (Austin, TX) **10736**
† Austintown Leader (Niles, OH)
Austin Weekly News (Oak Park, IL) **10587**
Avalon Bay News, The (Avalon, CA) **10530**
Avenal Progress (Avenal, CA) **10531**
Aventura News (South Miami, FL) **10561**
Avenue News (Baltimore, MD) **10620**
Avon Sentinel (Abingdon, IL) **10571**
Avoyelles Journal (Marksville, LA) **10617**
† Azalea City News & Review (Bayou Labatre, AL)
Azle News (Azle, TX) **10736**
Azusa Herald (West Covina, CA) **10546**
Back of the Yards Journal (Chicago, IL) **10574**
Bainbridge Post-Searchlight (Bainbridge, GA) **10563**
Bainbridge Review (Bainbridge Island, WA) **10757**
Baker County Press, The (MacClenny, FL) **10558**
Baker Observer (Baker, LA) **10615**
Baker Record-Courier (Baker City, OR) **10712**
Baldwin Bulletin (Baldwin, WI) **10764**
Baldwin Citizen (Mineola, NY) **10682**
Baldwin City Ledger (Lawrence, KS) **10607**
Baldwin Herald (Lawrence, NY) **10680**
Baldwinsville Messenger (Syracuse, NY) **10687**
Baldwin Times (Bay Minette, AL) **10517**
† Bal Harbor/Bay Harbour News (South Miami, FL)
Ballston Journal (Ballston Spa, NY) **10673**
Baltic Beacon (Dell Rapids, SD) **10729**
Baltimore Chronicle (Baltimore, MD) **10620**
Baltimore Messenger (Baltimore, MD) **10620**
Bamberg Advertiser-Herald, The (Bamberg, SC) **10726**
Banner-Gazette (Pekin, IN) **10597**
Banner Journal (Black River Falls, WI) **10764**
Banner Press Newspaper, The (Columbus, TX) **10738**
Barberton Herald (Barberton, OH) **10698**
Barbour Democrat, The (Philippi, WV) **10762**
Barbourville Mountain Advocate (Barbourville, KY) **10609**
Bargain Express Newspaper (Milwaukee, WI) **10769**
Bar Harbor Times (Bar Harbor, ME) **10618**
Barnesboro Star, The (Barnesboro, PA) **10716**
Barnesville Enterprise (Barnesville, OH) **10698**
Barnstable Patriot, The (Hyannis, MA) **10625**
Barrington Courier Review (Barrington, IL) **10572**
Barrington Times (Warren, RI) **10726**
Barron News Shield (Barron, WI) **10764**
Barry County Advertiser (Cassville, MO) **10652**

Bartow Neighbor, The (Cartersville, GA) **10563**
Bath County News-Outlook (Owingsville, KY) **10613**
Baton Rouge Shopper (Baton Rouge, LA) **10615**
Battle Creek Shopper (Battle Creek, MI) **10630**
Baudette Region, The (Baudette, MN) **10640**
Baxley News-Banner (Baxley, GA) **10563**
Baxter Springs Citizen (Baxter Springs, KS) **10605**
Bay Area Press (Oakland, CA) **10540**
Bay Beacon, The (Niceville, FL) **10559**
Bay Bulletin (Melbourne, FL) **10558**
Baylor County Banner (Seymour, TX) **10746**
Bay News (Brooklyn, NY) **10674**
Bayonne Community News (Bayonne, NJ) **10664**
Bay Ridge Courier (Brooklyn, NY) **10674**
Bayshore Sun (La Porte, TX) **10743**
Bayside Times, The (Bayside, NY) **10673**
Bay State Banner (Boston, MA) **10623**
Bay St. Louis Sea Coast Echo (Bay St. Louis, MS) **10649**
Bay Times (Stevensville, MD) **10622**
Bay Viewer (New Berlin, WI) **10770**
Bay Voice (New Baltimore, MI) **10636**
Beach & Bay Press (San Diego, CA) **10542**
Beach Bulletin (Fort Myers Beach, FL) **10557**
Beachcomber, The (Surf City, NJ) **10670**
Beaches Leader (Jacksonville Beach, FL) **10557**
Beach Haven Times (Manahawkin, NJ) **10667**
Beach Reporter, The (Manhattan Beach, CA) **10539**
Beacon-Forum (Eldon, IA) **10600**
Beacon Free Press (Wappingers Falls, NY) **10688**
Beacon Hill News, The/South District Journal (Seattle, WA) **10759**
Beacon Light (Mahopac, NY) **10680**
Beacon Newspaper (Babylon, NY) **10673**
Beacon Observer, The (Overton, NE) **10661**
Beacon, The (Concord, MA) **10624**
Beacon, The (Hopewell, NJ) **10667**
Beacon, The (Manahawkin, NJ) **10667**
Beacon, The (Port Clinton, OH) **10707**
Beardstown Illinoian-Star (Beardstown, IL) **10572**
Beaufort Shopper (Beaufort, SC) **10726**
Beaver Dam Ohio County Messenger (Beaver Dam, KY) **10609**
Beaverton Valley Times (Tigard, OR) **10715**
Becker County Record (Detroit Lakes, MN) **10641**
Bedford Bulletin (Bedford, VA) **10751**

Bedford Minuteman (Concord, MA) **10624**
Bedford Sun Banner (Beachwood, OH) **10698**
Bedford Time Register (Bedford, OH) **10699**
Beebe News (Beebe, AR) **10526**
Beecher City Journal (Beecher City, IL) **10573**
Bee, The (Portland, OR) **10714**
Bee, The (Phillips, WI) **10772**
Beeville Bee-Picayune (Beeville, TX) **10736**
Belchertown Sentinel (Belchertown, MA) **10623**
Belevedere Citizen (Los Angeles, CA) **10537**
Belle Banner (Belle, MO) **10651**
Belle Fourche Post (Belle Fourche, SD) **10729**
Belle Plaine News, The (Belle Plaine, KS) **10605**
Belleview Voice of South Marion (Belleview, FL) **10555**
Belleville Enterprise (Wayne, MI) **10639**
Belleville Journal (Belleville, IL) **10573**
Belleville Post (Bloomfield, NJ) **10664**
Belleville Recorder (Belleville, WI) **10764**
Belleville Telescope (Belleville, KS) **10605**
Belleville Times News (Nutley, NJ) **10668**
Bellevue Leader (Bellevue, NE) **10660**
Bell Gardens Review (Los Angeles, CA) **10537**
Bell Maywood Cudahy Industrial Post (Los Angeles, CA) **10537**
Bellmore-Merrick Observer (Bellmore, NY) **10673**
Bellmore Life (Bellmore, NY) **10673**
Bellows Falls Town Crier (Bellows Falls, VT) **10749**
Bellville Times (Bellville, TX) **10736**
Belmont Banner (Belmont, NC) **10690**
Belmont Citizen-Herald (Arlington, MA) **10623**
Benbrook News (Fort Worth, TX) **10740**
Bennetts Valley News (Weedville, PA) **10724**
Benning Leader, The (Columbus, GA) **10564**
Bensenville Press (Elmhurst, IL) **10578**
Benson County Farmers Press (Minnewaukan, ND) **10697**
Benton Bulletin (Philomath, OR) **10714**
Benton Review, The (Fowler, IN) **10594**
Bergen News, The (Palisades Park, NJ) **10669**
Bering Strait Record (None, AK) **10523**
Berkeley Independent (Moncks Corner, SC) **10728**
† Berkshire Courier (Great Barrington, MA)
Berkshire Penny Saver (Lee, MA) **10625**
Berkshire Record (Great Barrington, MA) **10625**
Berlin Buyers' Guide (Berlin, WI) **10764**
Berlin Journal (Berlin, WI) **10764**
Bernardsville News (Bernardsville, NJ) **10664**
Berne Tri-Weekly News (Berne, IN) **10592**
Berrien County Record (Buchanan, MI) **10631**

WEEKLY NEWSPAPERS

Berrien Press (Nashville, GA) **10567**
Berryessa Sun (Milpitas, CA) **10539**
Bertie Ledger-Advance (Windsor, NC) **10696**
Berwyn/Cicero Life (Berwyn, IL) **10573**
Bessemer City Record (Kings
    Mountain, NC) **10692**
Bethany Republican-Clipper
    (Bethany, MO) **10652**
▼Bethel Beacon (Bethel, CT) **10551**
Bethel Journal, The (Loveland, OH) **10704**
Bethesda/Chevy Chase Almanac
    (Potomac, MD) **10622**
Bettendorf News (Bettendorf, IA) **10599**
Beulah Beacon (Beulah, ND) **10696**
Beverly Hills Courier (Beverly Hills, CA) **10531**
Beverly Hills Independent (Santa
    Monica, CA) **10544**
Beverly News (Midlothian, IL) **10585**
Beverly Review (Chicago, IL) **10574**
Bexley News (Columbus, OH) **10701**
Biddeford-Saco-OOB Courier
    (Biddeford, ME) **10618**
Bienville Democrat & Ringgold Record
    (Arcadia, LA) **10615**
Big Bear Life (Big Bear Lake, CA) **10531**
Bigfork Eagle (Bigfork, MT) **10659**
Big Sandy News, The (Louisa, KY) **10612**
Big Walnut/Sunbury (Columbus, OH) **10701**
Billboard, The (Berlin, WI) **10764**
Billerica Minuteman (North
    Billerica, MA) **10627**
Biloxi-D'Iberville Press (D'Iberville, MS) **10649**
Bird City Times (Bird City, KS) **10605**
Bird Island Union (Bird Island, MN) **10640**
Birmingham Eccentric, The
    (Birmingham, MI) **10630**
† Birmingham Free Press (Birmingham, AL)
Birmingham World (Birmingham, AL) **10518**
▼Bisbee News, The (Bisbee, AZ) **10524**
Bisbee Observer, The (Bisbee, AZ) **10524**
Bixby Bulletin (Tulsa, OK) **10711**
† Biz (Oxford, PA)
Black Forest News (Colorado
    Springs, CO) **10547**
Black Hills Press (Sturgis, SD) **10730**
Black Mountain News (Black
    Mountain, NC) **10691**
Blacksburg Sentinel
    (Christiansburg, VA) **10752**
Blackstone Courier-Record
    (Blackstone, VA) **10751**
Blackstone Valley Tribune
    (Whitinsville, MA) **10629**
Blade Atlas (Blanchardville, WI) **10765**
Blade, The (Swainsboro, GA) **10568**

Blaine-Spring Lake Park Life (Coon
    Rapids, MN) **10641**
Blaine Banner (Blaine, MN) **10640**
Blair Enterprise (Blair, NE) **10660**
Blair Pilot-Tribune (Blair, NE) **10660**
Blair Press (Blair, WI) **10765**
Blairstown Press (Blairstown, NJ) **10664**
Blanco County News (Blanco, TX) **10737**
Bland Courier (Belle, MO) **10651**
Blandinsville Star Gazette
    (Abingdon, IL) **10571**
Bland Messenger (Wytheville, VA) **10756**
Blazer News (Jackson, MI) **10634**
Blissfield Advance (Blissfield, MI) **10630**
Bloomer Advance (Bloomer, WI) **10765**
Bloomfield Eccentric, The
    (Birmingham, MI) **10630**
Bloomfield Journal (Bristol, CT) **10551**
Bloomfield Life (Nutley, NJ) **10668**
Bloomingdale Press (Bloomingdale, IL) **10573**
Bloomington Sun-Current
    (Bloomington, MN) **10640**
Bloomville Gazette (Attica, OH) **10698**
Blount Countian, The (Oneonta, AL) **10521**
Blowing Rocket, The (Blowing
    Rock, NC) **10691**
Blue Mound Leader (Blue Mound, IL) **10573**
Blue Ridge Leader, The
    (Purcellville, VA) **10754**
Blue Water Voice (New Baltimore, MI) **10636**
Bluffton News, The (Bluffton, OH) **10699**
Blythe Advertiser (Palm Desert, CA) **10540**
Boardman News (Boardman, OH) **10699**
Boca Monday (Deerfield Beach, FL) **10556**
Boise City News, The (Boise City, OK) **10709**
Bolingbrook Metropolitan (Lemont, IL) **10583**
Bolingbrook Sun (Bolingbrook, IL) **10573**
Bolivar Bulletin-Times (Bolivar, TN) **10731**
Bolivar Herald-Free Press (Bolivar, MO) **10652**
Bollinger County Banner-Press (Marble
    Hill, MO) **10655**
Bolton Common (Bolton, MA) **10623**
Bonita Banner (Bonita Springs, FL) **10555**
Bonners Ferry Herald (Bonners
    Ferry, ID) **10569**
Bonner Springs-Edwardsville Chieftain (Bonner
    Springs, KS) **10605**
Booker News, The (Booker, TX) **10737**
Boone County Journal (Ashland, MO) **10651**
Boone County Recorder (Florence, KY) **10610**
Booneville Banner-Independent
    (Booneville, MS) **10649**
Boone Watauga Democrat (Boone, NC) **10691**
Boonville Herald & Adirondack Tourist
    (Boonville, NY) **10673**
Boonville Standard (Boonville, IN) **10592**

Booster, The (Columbus, OH) **10701**
Boothbay Register (Boothbay Harbor, ME) **10618**
Borden Star (Gail, TX) **10740**
Boscobel Dial (Boscobel, WI) **10765**
Bosque County News (Meridian, TX) **10744**
Bossier Banner-Progress (Bossier City, LA) **10616**
Bossier Press-Tribune (Bossier City, LA) **10616**
Boston Phoenix (Boston, MA) **10623**
Boulder City News (Boulder City, NV) **10662**
Bound Brook Chronicle (Somerville, NJ) **10670**
Bourbon County Citizen (Paris, KY) **10613**
Bourne Courier (Yarmouthport, MA) **10630**
Boutique & Villager (Burlingame, CA) **10531**
Bowie Blade-News (Bowie, MD) **10621**
Bowie News (Bowie, TX) **10737**
Bowling Green Times (Bowling Green, MO) **10652**
Bowman Finder (Bowman, ND) **10696**
Box Elder News Journal (Brigham City, UT) **10748**
Boyertown Area Times (Boyertown, PA) **10716**
Boynton Beach Times (Deerfield Beach, FL) **10556**
Braceville Express (Wilmington, IL) **10590**
Brackett News The (Brackettville, TX) **10737**
Bradford County Telegraph (Starke, FL) **10561**
Bradford Journal/Miner (Bradford, PA) **10716**
Brady Standard (Brady, TX) **10737**
Braidwood Index (Wilmington, IL) **10591**
Braidwood Journal, The (Braidwood, IL) **10573**
Braintree Forum (Marshfield, MA) **10625**
Brandon News, The (Brandon, FL) **10555**
Brandon Valley Challenger (Dell Rapids, SD) **10729**
Brandywine Chronicle (Oxford, PA) **10721**
Branford Review (Branford, CT) **10551**
Brantley Enterprise (Nahunta, GA) **10567**
Brawley Advertiser (El Centro, CA) **10533**
Braxton Citizen's News (Sutton, WV) **10763**
Braxton Democrat-Central (Sutton, WV) **10763**
Brea Progress (Anaheim, CA) **10530**
Breckinridge County Herald-News (Hardinsburg, KY) **10611**
Brecksville Gazette (Cleveland, OH) **10700**
Breese Journal (Breese, IL) **10573**
† Breeze Herald (Conneut Lake Park, PA)
Breeze, The (Rockledge, PA) **10723**
Bremer County Independent (Waverly, IA) **10605**
Brentwood Journal (Brentwood, TN) **10731**
Brentwood Westwood Press (Santa Monica, CA) **10544**

Brevard Reporter, The (Merritt Island, FL) **10559**
† Brewery Gulch Gazette (Bisbee, AZ)
Brewster Times (Mahopac, NY) **10681**
Brewton Standard, The (Brewton, AL) **10518**
Brick Township Town News (Brick, NJ) **10664**
Bridgeport Index (Bridgeport, TX) **10737**
Bridgeport Leader (Bridgeport, IL) **10573**
Bridgeport News (Chicago, IL) **10574**
Bridger Valley Pioneer (Lyman, WY) **10776**
Bridgeview Independent (Midlothian, IL) **10585**
Bridgeville Area News (Monroeville, PA) **10720**
Bridgewater Independent (Middleboro, MA) **10626**
† Bridgewater Townsman (Bridgewater, MA)
Bridgton News (Bridgton, ME) **10618**
Brighton-Pittsford Post, The (Fishers, NY) **10677**
Brighton Argus (Brighton, MI) **10630**
Brighton Park-McKinley Park Life (Chicago, IL) **10574**
Brighton Standard Blade (Brighton, CO) **10547**
Brillion News (Brillion, WI) **10765**
Brinkley Argus (Brinkley, AR) **10527**
Bristol Bay Times, The (Dillingham, AK) **10523**
Bristol Phoenix (Bristol, RI) **10725**
Bristol Pilot (Bristol, PA) **10716**
Bristow News (Bristow, OK) **10709**
Britt News-Tribune (Britt, IA) **10599**
Broad Top Bulletin (Saxton, PA) **10724**
Brockport/Holley Suburban News (Spencerport, NY) **10687**
Brockport Post, The (Brockport, NY) **10674**
Broken Arrow Ledger (Broken Arrow, OK) **10709**
† Broken Arrow Scout (Broken Arrow, OK)
Bronx News (Bronx, NY) **10674**
Bronx Press-Review (Bronx, NY) **10674**
Brooke County Review (Wellsburg, WV) **10763**
Brookfield Journal (Brookfield, CT) **10552**
Brookfield News (New Berlin, WI) **10770**
Brookhaven Review (Smithtown, NY) **10686**
Brooklyn Center Sun Post (Minneapolis, MN) **10643**
Brooklyn Graphic (Brooklyn, NY) **10674**
Brooklyn Heights Courier (Brooklyn, NY) **10674**
Brooklyn Heights Press (Brooklyn, NY) **10674**
Brooklyn Home Reporter & Sunset News (Brooklyn, NY) **10674**
Brooklyn Park Sun Post (Minneapolis, MN) **10643**
Brooklyn Record (Brooklyn, NY) **10674**
Brooklyn Spectator (Brooklyn, NY) **10674**
Brooklyn Sun Journal (Cleveland, OH) **10700**
† Brooklyn Times (Brooklyn, NY)

WEEKLY NEWSPAPERS

† Brooksville Sun Journal (Brooksville, FL)
† Brookville American (Brookville, PA)
Brookville American-Democrat (Brookville, IN) **10592**
Broome Pennysaver (Johnson City, NY) **10679**
Broomfield Enterprise (Broomfield, CO) **10547**
Broward News (Margate, FL) **10558**
Broward Times, The (Coral Springs, FL) **10556**
Brown County Democrat (Nashville, IN) **10596**
Brown County Press (Mt. Orab, OH) **10705**
Brown Deer Herald (New Berlin, WI) **10770**
Brownfield News (Brownfield, TX) **10737**
Brownsville States-Graphic (Brownsville, TN) **10731**
Bruce Calhoun County Journal (Bruce, MS) **10649**
Brunswick Beacon, The (Shallotte, NC) **10694**
Brunswick Citizen (Brunswick, MD) **10621**
Brunswick Sun Times (Medina, OH) **10705**
Brunswick Times-Gazette (Lawrenceville, VA) **10753**
Brush News-Tribune (Brush, CO) **10547**
Bryan College Station Press (Bryan, TX) **10737**
Bryan County Star (Durant, OK) **10710**
Bryan County Times (Pembroke, GA) **10567**
Buckeye Review, The (Youngstown, OH) **10709**
Buckeye Valley News (Buckeye, AZ) **10524**
Bucks County Tribune (Horsham, PA) **10718**
Budgeteer Press (Duluth, MN) **10641**
Buffalo Bulletin (Buffalo, WY) **10775**
Buffalo County Journal (Cochrane, WI) **10765**
Buffalo Grove Countryside (Arlington Heights, IL) **10571**
Buffalo Grove Journal & Topics (Des Plaines, IL) **10576**
Buffalo Reflex (Buffalo, MO) **10652**
Buffalo Ridge Gazette, The (Ruthton, MN) **10646**
Buffalo River Review (Linden, TN) **10733**
Buffalo Rocket (Buffalo, NY) **10675**
Bugle, The (Niles, IL) **10586**
Buhl Herald (Buhl, ID) **10569**
Bulletin, The (Crestview, FL) **10556**
Bulletin, The (Bedford, OH) **10699**
Bulletin, The (Santa Fe, TX) **10746**
Bulletin, The (Kenosha, WI) **10768**
Bunker Hill Gazette News (Bunker Hill, IL) **10573**
Burbank-Stickney Independent (Midlothian, IL) **10585**
Bureau County Republican (Princeton, IL) **10588**
Burke County Observer (Morganton, NC) **10693**
Burke Times, The (Reston, VA) **10754**

Cambridge Chronicle **10877**

Burleson County Citizen Tribune (Caldwell, TX) **10737**
Burleson Star (Burleson, TX) **10737**
Burlington Standard Press (Burlington, WI) **10765**
Burlington Union (Woburn, MA) **10629**
Burnet Bulletin (Burnet, TX) **10737**
Burnett County Sentinel (Grantsburg, WI) **10767**
Burns Times-Herald (Burns, OR) **10712**
Burnsville/Savage Sun-Current (Burnsville, MN) **10640**
Burr Ridge Doings (Hinsdale, IL) **10582**
Burwell Tribune, The (Burwell, NE) **10660**
Business Examiner (Gig Harbor, WA) **10758**
Business Post, The (Alpharetta, GA) **10562**
Butler County & Green River Republican Banner, The (Morgantown, KY) **10613**
Butler County News (Georgiana, AL) **10519**
Butner-Creedmoor News, The (Creedmoor, NC) **10691**
Butte County Valley Irrigator (Newell, SD) **10730**
Butte Valley Star (Merrill, OR) **10714**
† Buyer's Guide (Napa, CA)
Buyer's Guide Cent Saver (Mauston, WI) **10769**
† Byron Center/Dorr Advance (Jenison, MI)
Cabell Record (Culloden, WV) **10761**
Cable Scene (Idaho Falls, ID) **10569**
Caddo Citizen (Vivian, LA) **10618**
Cadiz Record, The (Cadiz, KY) **10609**
Cadott Sentinel (Cadott, WI) **10765**
Cahokia Journal (Columbia, IL) **10576**
Cairo Citizen (Cairo, IL) **10574**
Cairo Messenger (Cairo, GA) **10563**
Calais Advertiser (Calais, ME) **10618**
Caledonia/Gaines Advance (Jenison, MI) **10634**
Calexico Advertiser (El Centro, CA) **10533**
Calhoun Chronicle (Grantsville, WV) **10761**
Calhoun News (Hardin, IL) **10581**
Calhoun Times (Calhoun, GA) **10563**
California Advocate, The (Fresno, CA) **10534**
California Courier (Glendale, CA) **10534**
California Democrat (California, MO) **10652**
Callahan County Star (Baird, TX) **10736**
Callaway Courier (Holts Summit, MO) **10654**
Call, The (Schuylkill Haven, PA) **10724**
Caloosa Belle (La Belle, FL) **10558**
Calumet Press, The (Highland, IN) **10594**
Calvert Independent (Prince Fredrick, MD) **10622**
Camas/Washougal Post Record (Camas, WA) **10757**
Cambridge Chronicle (Cambridge, IL) **10574**

Weeklies Index

Cambridge Chronicle (Somerville, MA) **10628**
Cambridge News (Cambridge, WI) **10765**
Camden Chronicle, The (Camden, TN) **10731**
Camden County Record (Camden, NJ) **10665**
Camden County Tribune (St. Marys, GA) **10567**
Cameron Citizen Observer (Cameron, MO) **10652**
Cameron County Echo (Emporium, PA) **10717**
Cameron Herald (Cameron, TX) **10737**
Camilla Enterprise (Camilla, GA) **10563**
Camillus Advocate (Syracuse, NY) **10687**
Campbell County Recorder (Fort Thomas, KY) **10611**
Campbellsport News (Campbellsport, WI) **10765**
Canada News (Auburndale, FL) **10555**
Canadian County Chronicle (Yukon, OK) **10712**
Canarsie Courier (Brooklyn, NY) **10674**
Canarsie Digest (Brooklyn, NY) **10674**
Canastota Bee-Journal (Canastota, NY) **10675**
Canby Herald (Canby, OR) **10712**
Canby News (Canby, MN) **10640**
Candor Chronicle (Trumansburg, NY) **10688**
Canistota Clipper (Canistota, SD) **10729**
Canova Herald (Canistota, SD) **10729**
Canton Eagle (Wayne, MI) **10639**
Canton Independent-Sentinel (Canton, PA) **10716**
Canton Journal (Canton, MA) **10624**
Canton Observer (Plymouth, MI) **10637**
Canyon Courier (Evergreen, CO) **10548**
Canyon News (Canyon, TX) **10737**
Cape Codder (Orleans, MA) **10627**
† Cape Cod News (Yarmouth Port, MA)
Cape May County Gazette Leader (Wildwood, NJ) **10671**
Cape May Herald Dispatch (Rio Grande, NJ) **10670**
Cape May Star & Wave (Cape May, NJ) **10665**
Capeway News (Middleboro, MA) **10626**
Capistrano Valley News (Lake Forest, CA) **10536**
Capital City Weekly (Juneau, AK) **10523**
▼Capital Weekly (Augusta, ME) **10618**
Capitol Hill Beacon (Oklahoma City, OK) **10711**
Capitol Hill Times (Seattle, WA) **10759**
Carbondale News (Carbondale, PA) **10716**
Caribou County Sun (Soda Springs, ID) **10571**
Carlinville Democrat (Carlinville, IL) **10574**
Carlisle Mercury, The (Carlisle, KY) **10610**
Carlsbad Sun (Carlsbad, CA) **10532**
Carlyle Union Banner (Carlyle, IL) **10574**
Carmel News Tribune (Fishers, IN) **10593**

Carmel Pine Cone (Carmel, CA) **10532**
Carmel Times (Mahopac, NY) **10681**
Carmichael Times (Carmichael, CA) **10532**
Carol City/Opa-Locka News (Miami, FL) **10559**
Carolina Times, The (Durham, NC) **10692**
Caroline Progress, The (Bowling Green, VA) **10751**
Carolinian, The (Raleigh, NC) **10694**
Carol Stream Press (Bloomingdale, IL) **10573**
† Carpinteria Herald (Goleta, CA)
Carroll County Comet (Flora, IN) **10594**
Carroll County Independent (Center Ossipee, NH) **10663**
Carroll County News-Leader (Huntingdon, TN) **10732**
Carroll County Review (Thomson, IL) **10590**
Carroll Gardens/Cobble Hill Courier (Brooklyn, NY) **10674**
Carroll News, The (Hillsville, VA) **10753**
† Carrollton Chronicle (Carrollton, TX)
Carrollton Democrat (Carrollton, MO) **10652**
Carrollton Gazette Patriot (Carrollton, IL) **10574**
Carrollwood News (Tampa, FL) **10561**
Carson Bulletin (Compton, CA) **10532**
Carson Press (Elgin, ND) **10696**
Carson Wave (Los Angeles, CA) **10537**
Carteret County News-Times (Morehead City, NC) **10693**
Carthage Courier (Carthage, TN) **10731**
Carthage Republican Tribune (Carthage, NY) **10675**
Carthaginian, The (Carthage, MS) **10649**
Carver Reporter (Plymouth, MA) **10627**
Cary-Grove Countryside (Barrington, IL) **10572**
Cary News (Cary, NC) **10691**
Casey County News (Liberty, KY) **10612**
Casey County Shopper, The (Columbia, KY) **10610**
Cash-Book Journal (Jackson, MO) **10654**
Cashmere Valley Record (Cashmere, WA) **10757**
Cashton Record (Cashton, WI) **10765**
Cass City Chronicle (Cass City, MI) **10631**
Cass County Reporter (Casselton, ND) **10696**
Cassville Democrat (Cassville, MO) **10652**
Castleton Banner (Fishers, IN) **10593**
Caswell Messenger (Yanceyville, NC) **10696**
Catalina Islander, The (Avalon, CA) **10530**
† Cato Citizen (Red Creek, NY)
Catonsville Times (Baltimore, MD) **10620**
Catoosa County News (Ringgold, GA) **10567**
Catoosa Times Herald (Catoosa, OK) **10709**
Cavalier County Republican (Langdon, ND) **10697**
Cazenovia Republican (Cazenovia, NY) **10675**

WEEKLY NEWSPAPERS

Cedar County Republican
(Stockton, MO) **10658**
Cedar Creek Pilot (Gun Barrel City, TX) **10741**
Cedar Hill Today (DeSoto, TX) **10739**
Cedar Key Beacon (Cedar, FL) **10556**
Cedar Lake Journal (Lowell, IN) **10595**
Cedartown Standard (Cedartown, GA) **10564**
Center Post Dispatch (Monte Vista, CO) **10550**
Center Republican (Washburn, ND) **10697**
Centerville-Bellbrook Times
(Kettering, OH) **10704**
Centerville Crusader (Centerville, IN) **10592**
Central City Republican Nonpareil (Central
City, NE) **10660**
Central City Times-Argus (Central
City, KY) **10610**
Central Coast Sun-Bulletin (Morro
Bay, CA) **10539**
† Central Coast Times (Paso Robles, CA)
Centralia Fireside Guard
(Centralia, MO) **10652**
Central Kentucky News-Journal
(Campbellsville, KY) **10609**
Central Missouri News (Sedalia, MO) **10656**
Central Oregonian, The (Prineville, OR) **10714**
Central Post (Dayton, NJ) **10665**
Central Saint Croix News
(Hammond, WI) **10767**
Central Shopper (Des Moines, IA) **10600**
Central Valley Times (Grants Pass, OR) **10713**
Central Virginian, The (Louisa, VA) **10754**
Central West End Journal (St.
Louis, MO) **10657**
Centreville Press (Centreville, AL) **10518**
Centreville Times (Reston, VA) **10755**
Ceres Courier (Ceres, CA) **10532**
Chagrin Herald Sun (Beachwood, OH) **10698**
Chagrin Valley Times (Chagrin
Falls, OH) **10700**
Challis Messenger (Challis, ID) **10569**
Chamblee-DeKalb Neighbor
(Atlanta, GA) **10562**
Chandler Independent (Chandler, AZ) **10524**
† Chandler Post (Boonville, IN)
Chanhassen Villager (Chanhassen, MN) **10641**
Chantilly Times (Reston, VA) **10755**
Chapel Hill News (Chapel Hill, NC) **10691**
Chariton Herald-Patriot (Chariton, IA) **10599**
Chariton Leader (Chariton, IA) **10599**
Charleston Enterprise-Courier
(Charleston, MO) **10652**
† Charlestown Citizen (Brookline, MA)
Charlevoix County Star (Gaylord, MI) **10632**
Charlevoix Courier (Charlevoix, MI) **10631**
Charlotte Gazette (Drakes Branch, VA) **10752**

Chicago Ridge Citizen **10879**

Charlotte Shopping Guide
(Charlotte, MI) **10631**
Charlottesville-Albemarle Tribune
(Charlottesville, VA) **10751**
Charlton County Herald (Folkston, GA) **10565**
Chase County Leader-News (Cottonwood
Falls, KS) **10606**
Chaska Herald (Chaska, MN) **10641**
† Chateaugay Record (Chateaugay, NY)
Chatham Clarion (Auburn, IL) **10572**
Chatham Courier (Madison, NJ) **10667**
Chatham Courier (Chatham, NY) **10675**
Chatham News, The (Siler City, NC) **10694**
Chatsworth Times, The
(Chatsworth, GA) **10564**
Chattooga Press (Summerville, GA) **10568**
Cheektowaga Bee (Williamsville, NY) **10689**
Cheektowaga Times (Cheektowaga, NY) **10675**
Chelmsford Independent
(Chelmsford, MA) **10624**
Chelsea Clinton News (New York, NY) **10683**
Chelsea Record (Revere, MA) **10628**
Chelsea Standard, The (Chelsea, MI) **10631**
Chemung Valley Reporter
(Horseheads, NY) **10679**
Chenango American (Greene, NY) **10678**
Cheney Free Press (Cheney, WA) **10757**
Cheraw Chronicle, The (Cheraw, SC) **10726**
Cherokee County Herald (Centre, AL) **10518**
Cherokee Messenger & Republican
(Cherokee, OK) **10709**
Cherokee Scout (Murphy, NC) **10693**
Cherokee Tribune, The (Canton, GA) **10563**
† Cherry Hill News (Cherry Hill, NJ)
Cherryville Eagle (Cherryville, NC) **10691**
Chesapeake Post (Chesapeake, VA) **10752**
Cheshire Herald (Cheshire, CT) **10552**
Chester County Press (Oxford, PA) **10721**
Chesterfield Journal (St. Louis, MO) **10657**
Chesterland News (Chesterland, OH) **10700**
Chester News & Reporter (Chester, SC) **10726**
Chesterton Guide (Maryville, IN) **10595**
Chesterton Town Crier (Chesterton, IN) **10592**
Chestnut Hill Local (Philadelphia, PA) **10722**
Chetek Alert, The (Chetek, WI) **10765**
Cheyenne Mountain Journal (Manitou
Springs, CO) **10550**
Chicago-Lawndale News (Chicago, IL) **10574**
Chicago's N.W. Side Press (Chicago, IL) **10574**
Chicago County Press (Lindstrom, MN) **10643**
Chicago Near North News (Chicago, IL) **10575**
Chicago Near West Gazette
(Chicago, IL) **10575**
Chicago Post (Chicago, IL) **10575**
Chicago Reader (Chicago, IL) **10575**
Chicago Ridge Citizen (Midlothian, IL) **10585**

ULRICH'S INTERNATIONAL PERIODICALS DIRECTORY 1998

Chicago West Side Times (Chicago, IL) **10575**
Chicopee Herald Weekly, The (Chicopee, MA) **10624**
Chieftain & Toccoa Record (Toccoa, GA) **10568**
Childress Index (Childress, TX) **10737**
Chilkat Valley News (Haines, AK) **10523**
Chillicothe Bulletin (Chillicothe, IL) **10576**
Chilton Times-Journal (Chilton, WI) **10765**
Chino Valley Review (Chino Valley, AZ) **10524**
Chisholm Tribune Press (Chisholm, MN) **10641**
Chittenango-Bridgeport Times (Syracuse, NY) **10687**
Choctaw Advocate (Butler, AL) **10518**
Chrisman Leader (Chrisman, IL) **10576**
Christian County Headliner News (Ozark, MO) **10655**
Chronicle-Express (Penn Yan, NY) **10684**
Chronicle-Independent (Camden, SC) **10726**
Chronicle, The (Atwater, CA) **10530**
Chronicle, The (Milford, DE) **10554**
Chronicle, The (North Dartmouth, MA) **10627**
Chronicle, The (Carson City, NV) **10662**
Chronicle, The (Glens Falls, NY) **10678**
Chronicle, The (Creswell, OR) **10712**
Chronicle, The (Humboldt, TN) **10732**
Church Point News (Church Point, LA) **10616**
Cibola County Beacon (Grants, NM) **10672**
Cisco Press (Cisco, TX) **10738**
Cissna Park News (Cissna Park, IL) **10576**
Citizen (American Fork, UT) **10748**
Citizen-Standard, The (Valley View, PA) **10724**
Citizen/Press Plus (Pulaski, TN) **10734**
Citizen Journal (St. Louis, MO) **10657**
Citizen of Morris County, The (Denville, NJ) **10665**
Citizen Outlet (Mexico, NY) **10681**
Citizens' Advocate Newspaper (Coppell, TX) **10738**
Citizen Telegram, The (Rifle, CO) **10551**
Citizen, The (Mansfield, AR) **10528**
Citizen, The (Boyne City, MI) **10630**
Citizen, The (Hamtramck, MI) **10633**
Citizen, The (Houston, TX) **10741**
Citizen Voice & Times (Irvine, KY) **10612**
City News (Bronx, NY) **10674**
City Pages (Minneapolis, MN) **10644**
City Paper (Baltimore, MD) **10620**
City Terrace Comet (City of Commerce, CA) **10532**
Civic Center NEWSource (Los Angeles, CA) **10537**
Clackamas Review (Milwaukee, OR) **10714**
Claiborne Progress (Tazewell, TN) **10735**
Clanton Advertiser (Clanton, AL) **10518**

Claremont Courier (Claremont, CA) **10532**
Clarence Bee (Williamsville, NY) **10689**
Clarendon Hills Doings, The (Hinsdale, IL) **10582**
Clarendon Hills Progress (Downers Grove, IL) **10577**
Clare Sentinel (Clare, MI) **10631**
Clarion Journal, The (Columbia, IL) **10576**
Clarion News (Corydon, IN) **10592**
Clarion News (Clarion, PA) **10716**
Clark County Press (Neillsville, WI) **10770**
Clark Courier (Berryville, VA) **10751**
Clark Eagle (Union, NJ) **10670**
Clarke County Democrat (Grove Hill, AL) **10519**
Clarke County Tribune (Quitman, MS) **10651**
Clark Patriot (Rahway, NJ) **10669**
Clarkson Integrator (Potsdam, NY) **10685**
Clarkston News (Clarkston, MI) **10631**
Clarkstown Courier, The (Pearl River, NY) **10684**
Clarksville Times, The (Clarksville, TX) **10738**
Classified Gazette (San Rafael, CA) **10544**
Clay City Times, The (Stanton, KY) **10614**
† Clay Countian (Orange Park, FL)
† Clay County Crescent (Orange Park, FL)
Clay County Free Press (Clay, WV) **10761**
Clay Dispatch-Tribune (Kansas City, MO) **10654**
Clay Times Journal (Lineville, AL) **10520**
Clay Today (Orange Park, FL) **10559**
Clayton County Register (Elkader, IA) **10600**
Clayton Neighbor (Forest Park, GA) **10565**
Clayton News-Star (Clayton, NC) **10691**
Clayton Record (Clayton, AL) **10518**
† Clayton Sun (Atlanta, GA)
Clayton Tribune, The (Clayton, GA) **10564**
Clear-Ridge Reporter (Chicago, IL) **10575**
Clear Creek Courant (Idaho Springs, CO) **10549**
Clear Lake Observer-American (Clearlake, CA) **10532**
Clearwater Tribune (Orofino, ID) **10570**
Cleburne News (Heflin, AL) **10520**
Clemmons Courier (Clemmons, NC) **10691**
† Clermont County Review (Cincinnati, OH)
† Clermont Courier (Cincinnati, OH)
Clermont Sun (Batavia, OH) **10698**
Cleveland Advocate (Cleveland, TX) **10738**
Cleveland Times (Shelby, NC) **10694**
Clewiston News (Clewiston, FL) **10556**
Clinch County News (Homerville, GA) **10565**
Clinch Valley News (Tazewell, VA) **10756**
Clinton Chronicle, The (Clinton, SC) **10727**
Clinton County News (Mascoutah, IL) **10584**
Clinton County News (Albany, KY) **10609**

WEEKLY NEWSPAPERS

Clinton County News (St. Johns, MI) **10638**
Clinton County Shoppers Guide
 (Wilmington, OH) **10708**
Clinton Courier (Clinton, NY) **10675**
Clinton Eye, The (Clinton, MO) **10652**
Clinton Recorder (Clinton, CT) **10552**
Clinton Topper (Clinton, WI) **10765**
Clinton Van Buren County Democrat
 (Clinton, AR) **10527**
Clintonville Tribune-Gazette
 (Clintonville, WI) **10765**
Clio Messenger, The (Flint, MI) **10632**
Clipper-Herald (Lexington, NE) **10661**
Cloquet Billboard Shopper
 (Cloquet, MN) **10641**
Cloquet Pine Knot (Cloquet, MN) **10641**
Cloverdale Reveille (Cloverdale, CA) **10532**
Clover Herald (Clover, SC) **10727**
Clovis Independent (Clovis, CA) **10532**
Clyde Enterprise (Clyde, OH) **10701**
Coal City Courant (Coal City, IL) **10576**
Coal City Express (Wilmington, IL) **10591**
Coalfield Progress (Norton, VA) **10754**
Coalinga Record (Coalinga, CA) **10532**
Coal Valley News (Danville, WV) **10761**
Coastal Courier (Hinesville, GA) **10565**
Coastal Current, The (South Padre
 Island, TX) **10747**
Coastal Post (Bolinas, CA) **10531**
Coastal Times (Charleston, SC) **10726**
Coastland Times (Manteo, NC) **10693**
Coastside Chronicle (San Mateo, CA) **10543**
Cody Enterprise (Cody, WY) **10776**
Coffey County Today (Burlington, KS) **10606**
Cohasset Mariner (Marshfield, MA) **10625**
Colbert County Reporter
 (Tuscumbia, AL) **10522**
Colchester Chronicle (Colchester, IL) **10576**
Coleman Chronicle & Democrat Voice
 (Coleman, TX) **10738**
Colfax Messenger (Colfax, WI) **10766**
Collierville Herald, The (Collierville, TN) **10731**
Collinsville Herald (Collinsville, IL) **10576**
Collinsville Journal (Collinsville, IL) **10576**
Collinsville News (Tulsa, OK) **10711**
Colonial, The (Fort Washington, PA) **10717**
Colonie Spotlight (Delmar, NY) **10676**
Colorado Statesman (Denver, CO) **10548**
Columbia Flier (Columbia, MD) **10621**
Columbian-Progress (Columbia, MS) **10649**
Columbia News, The (Columbia, KY) **10610**
Columbia News Times, The
 (Martinez, GA) **10566**
Columbus Alive (Columbus, OH) **10701**
Columbus Journal (Columbus, WI) **10766**
Columbus Messenger (Columbus, OH) **10701**

Colusa County Sun-Herald (Colusa, CA) **10532**
Comanche Chief (Comanche, TX) **10738**
Commack News (Smithtown, NY) **10686**
Commerce Journal (Commerce, TX) **10738**
Commerce News (Commerce, GA) **10564**
Commercial-Express (Vicksburg, MI) **10639**
Commercial Record (Saugatuck, MI) **10638**
Commonwealth Progress (Scotland
 Neck, NC) **10694**
† Communicator Community News (Reno, NV)
Community Advertiser
 (Farmingdale, ME) **10619**
Community Adviser (Beaumont, CA) **10531**
Community Advisor (Marshall, MI) **10635**
Community Booster, The
 (Granville, OH) **10703**
Community Forum (Hackettstown, NJ) **10666**
Community Herald (Monona, WI) **10770**
Community Journal (Wading River, NY) **10688**
Community Journal, South
 (Loveland, OH) **10704**
Community Mirror (Gonzales, LA) **10616**
Community News (St. Louis, MO) **10657**
Community News (Clifton Park, NY) **10675**
Community News, The (Dora, AL) **10518**
Community Press, Mason
 (Loveland, OH) **10704**
Community Press, The (Millbrook, AL) **10520**
† Community Press, West Chester
 (Loveland, OH)
Community Shopper (Birmingham, AL) **10518**
Community Shopper (Des Moines, IA) **10600**
Community Times (Westminster, MD) **10623**
Compton Bulletin (Compton, CA) **10533**
Compton Wave (Los Angeles, CA) **10537**
Concordia Sentinel (Ferriday, LA) **10616**
Concord Journal (Concord, MA) **10624**
Conejos County Citizen, The (Monte
 Vista, CO) **10550**
Conneautville Courier
 (Conneautville, PA) **10716**
Connection, The (Grosse Point, MI) **10633**
Conservative, The (Carrollton, MS) **10649**
Consumers' Edge (Baton Rouge, LA) **10615**
Contra Costa Sun (Lafayette, CA) **10535**
Conway County Petit Jean Country Headlight
 (Morrilton, AR) **10528**
† Conway Field & Herald (Conway, SC)
Coolidge Examiner (Coolidge, AZ) **10524**
Coon Rapids Herald (Coon Rapids, MN) **10641**
Coos County Democrat (Lancaster, NH) **10663**
Copiah County Courier
 (Hazlehurst, MS) **10649**
Coppell Gazette (Lewisville, TX) **10743**
Copperas Cove Leader Press (Copperas
 Cove, TX) **10738**

Copper Country News (Globe, AZ) **10525**
Copper Era (Clifton, AZ) **10524**
Coquille Valley Sentinel (Coquille, OR) **10712**
Coral Gables News (Miami, FL) **10559**
Cordell Beacon, The (Cordell, OK) **10709**
Cordova Times (Cordova, AK) **10523**
Cornell & Lake Holcombe Courier (Cornell, WI) **10766**
Corning Observer (Corning, CA) **10533**
Corona-Norco Independent (Corona, CA) **10533**
Coronado Journal (Coronado, CA) **10533**
Corridor News (Poway, CA) **10541**
Corrigan Times, The (Corrigan, TX) **10738**
Cortez Montezuma Valley Journal (Cortez, CO) **10548**
Cortez Sentinel (Cortez, CO) **10548**
Cortland Democrat (Marathon, NY) **10681**
Corydon Democrat (Corydon, IN) **10592**
Corydon Times-Republican (Corydon, IA) **10599**
Cosmopolite-Herald (Girard, PA) **10718**
Cottage Grove Sentinel (Cottage Grove, OR) **10712**
Cottonwood Chronicle (Cottonwood, ID) **10569**
Cottonwood Journal Extra (Cottonwood, AZ) **10524**
Country Almanac (Menlo Park, CA) **10539**
Country Connection News (Eakly, OK) **10710**
Country Courier, The (Conklin, NY) **10676**
Country Shopper (Pound Ridge, NY) **10685**
Country Star (Stigler, OK) **10711**
Country Weekly (Grants Pass, OR) **10713**
County Courier (Enosburg Falls, VT) **10749**
County Journal (Belleville, IL) **10573**
County Journal (Percy, IL) **10588**
County Journal, The (Washburn, WI) **10775**
County Ledger-Press (Balsam Lake, WI) **10764**
County Line Reminder (Ortonville, MI) **10636**
Countyline, The (Bryan, OH) **10699**
County Neighbors (Punxsutawney, PA) **10723**
County News Enterprise (Forest City, NC) **10692**
County Observer (Yeagertown, PA) **10725**
County Press (Parma, MI) **10636**
County Press (Newtown Square, PA) **10721**
County Press, The (Lapeer, MI) **10635**
County Reporter, The (Andalusia, AL) **10517**
County Star Journal East (St. Louis, MO) **10657**
County Star Journal West (St. Louis, MO) **10657**
County Transcript (Susquehanna, PA) **10724**
County Wide (Dover-Foxcroft, ME) **10619**
Courant, The (Bottineau, ND) **10696**
Courier-Gazette (Rockland, ME) **10620**

Courier-Journal (Palmyra, NY) **10684**
Courier-News (Clinton, TN) **10731**
Courier-Standard-Enterprise (Fort Plain, NY) **10677**
Courier-Times (Sutherland, NE) **10662**
Courier-Times, The (Roxboro, NC) **10694**
Courier-Wedge (Durand, WI) **10766**
Courier Gazette (Newark, NY) **10683**
Courier Hub (Stoughton, WI) **10774**
Courier Journal (Florence, AL) **10519**
Courier Press (Prairie du Chien, WI) **10772**
Courier, The (Plant City, FL) **10560**
† Courier, The (Thomasville, GA)
Courier, The (Rensselaer, IN) **10597**
Courier, The (Littleton, NH) **10663**
Courier, The (Conneaut, OH) **10703**
Courier, The (Reedsport, OR) **10714**
Courier, The (Savannah, TN) **10734**
Courier, The (Sun Prairie, WI) **10774**
Courtland Journal-Empire (Courtland, KS) **10606**
Coushatta Citizen (Coushatta, LA) **10616**
Cover Story, The (Murfreesboro, TN) **10734**
Covington Leader (Covington, TN) **10731**
Covington News (Covington, GA) **10564**
Covington Record (Covington, OK) **10709**
Covington St. Tammany Farmer (Covington, LA) **10616**
Coweta American (Coweta, OK) **10710**
Cranbury Press (Dayton, NJ) **10665**
Crane News (Crane, TX) **10738**
Cranford Chronicle (Cranford, NJ) **10665**
Cranston Herald (Cranston, RI) **10725**
Crawford County Independent-Kickapoo Scout (Gay Mills, WI) **10767**
Cresco Times-Plain Dealer (Cresco, IA) **10599**
Cresson-Gallitzin Mainliner, The (Cresson, PA) **10717**
Crestline Advocate (Crestline, OH) **10703**
Crestline Courier-News (Crestline, CA) **10533**
† Crestview Okaloosa-News Journal (Crestview, FL)
Crete News, The (Crete, NE) **10660**
Crewe-Burkeville Journal (Crewe, VA) **10752**
Crittenden Press (Marion, KY) **10612**
Crockett Times, The (Alamo, TN) **10731**
Crofton News-Crier (Bowie, MD) **10621**
Cromwell Chronicle (Cromwell, CT) **10552**
Crossville Chronicle (Crossville, TN) **10731**
Crothersville Times (Crothersville, IN) **10592**
Crowley Review (Burleson, TX) **10737**
Cuba Free Press (Cuba, MO) **10653**
† Cuba Journal (Cuba, IL)
Cudahy Reminder-Enterprise (New Berlin, WI) **10770**
Cuero Record (Cuero, TX) **10738**

WEEKLY NEWSPAPERS

Cullman Tribune (Cullman, AL) **10518**
Culpeper News (Culpeper, VA) **10752**
Culver Citizen (Culver, IN) **10592**
Culver City-Ladera Independent (Santa Monica, CA) **10544**
Culver City Star (Los Angeles, CA) **10537**
Cumberland Advocate (Cumberland, WI) **10766**
Cumberland County News (Burkesville, KY) **10609**
Cumberland Courier (Lawrence, IN) **10595**
† Cumberland Times (Crossville, TN)
Cumberland Trading Post, The (Middlesboro, KY) **10612**
Cupertino Courier (Cupertino, CA) **10533**
† Current (Potsdam, NY)
Curry Coastal Pilot (Brookings, OR) **10712**
Custer County Chief (Broken Bow, NE) **10660**
Cuyahoga Falls News-Press (Stow, OH) **10707**
Cynthiana Democrat (Cynthiana, KY) **10610**
D/FW People (Euless, TX) **10739**
Dadeville Record (Alexander City, AL) **10517**
† Daily Milford Citizen (Milford, CT)
Dakota County Tribune (Burnsville, MN) **10640**
Dallas City Enterprise (Dallas City, IL) **10576**
Dallas New Era (Dallas, GA) **10564**
Dallas Park Cities News (Dallas, TX) **10738**
Dallas Polk County Itemizer-Observer (Dallas, OR) **10712**
Dallas Post (Dallas, PA) **10717**
Dallas White Rocker News (Dallas, TX) **10738**
Dalton Gazette & Kidron News (Dalton, OH) **10703**
Daly City Record (San Mateo, CA) **10543**
Damascus Gazette (Gatorsburg, MD) **10621**
Dan's Papers (Bridgehampton, NY) **10673**
Dana Point News (Lake Forest, CA) **10536**
Danbury Reporter (Walnut Cove, NC) **10695**
Dansville Genesee Country Express (Dansville, NY) **10676**
Danvers Herald (Danvers, MA) **10624**
Darco News & Buyers Guide (Hartsville, SC) **10727**
Darien Doings (Hinsdale, IL) **10582**
Darien Metropolitan (Lemont, IL) **10583**
Darien News (Darien, GA) **10564**
Darien News Review (Darien, CT) **10552**
Darien Progress (Downers Grove, IL) **10577**
Darke County Early Bird, The (Greenville, OH) **10703**
David City Banner-Press, The (David City, NE) **10660**
Davie County Enterprise-Record (Mocksville, NC) **10693**
Davis County Clipper (Bountiful, UT) **10748**
Davison Flagstaff (Swartz Creek, MI) **10638**

Davison Index, The (Davison, MI) **10631**
Dawson News, The (Dawson, GA) **10564**
Dawson Springs Progress (Dawson Springs, KY) **10610**
Daytona Pennysaver (Ormond Beach, FL) **10560**
Dayton Chronicle (Dayton, WA) **10757**
Dayton Tribune (Dayton, OR) **10713**
Dearborn County Register (Lawrenceburg, IN) **10595**
Dearborn Press & Guide (Dearborn, MI) **10631**
Dearborn Times-Herald (Dearborn, MI) **10632**
Decatur-DeKalb News/Era (Decatur, GA) **10564**
Decatur Herald (Gentry, AR) **10527**
Decatur Tribune (Decatur, IL) **10576**
Declaration, The (Independence, VA) **10753**
Decorah Public Opinion & Journal (Decorah, IA) **10599**
Deerfield Beach Observer (Deerfield Beach, FL) **10556**
Deerfield Beach Thursday Times (Deerfield Beach, FL) **10556**
Deerfield Review (Bannockburn, IL) **10572**
Deer Park Broadcaster, The (Deer Park, TX) **10738**
Deer Park Progress, The (Deer Park, TX) **10739**
Defensor Chieftain (Socorro, NM) **10672**
† DeKalb News/Sun (Decatur, GA)
DeLand Beacon, The (DeLand, FL) **10557**
Delano Record (Delano, CA) **10533**
Delavan Enterprise (Delavan, WI) **10766**
Delavan Times, The (Delavan, IL) **10576**
Delaware Beachcomber (Rehoboth Beach, DE) **10554**
Delaware Coast Press (Rehoboth Beach, DE) **10554**
Delaware County Journal (Holmes, PA) **10718**
Delaware County Times (Delhi, NY) **10676**
Delaware Valley News (Frenchtown, NJ) **10666**
Delaware Wave (Bethany Beach, DE) **10554**
Delhi Express (Winton, CA) **10546**
Delhi Press (Cincinnati, OH) **10700**
Dell Rapids Tribune (Dell Rapids, SD) **10729**
Del Mar, Solana Beach, Carmel Valley, Rancho Santa Fe Sun (Carlsbad, CA) **10532**
Del Norte Prospector (Monte Vista, CO) **10550**
Delray Times (Deerfield Beach, FL) **10556**
Delta Atlas (Delta, OH) **10703**
Delta County Independent (Delta, CO) **10548**
† Delta Paper (Delta Jct, AK)
Delta Waverly Community News (Grand Ledge, MI) **10633**
Delta Wind, The (Delta Junction, AK) **10523**

Democrat-Argus, The
 (Caruthersville, MO) **10652**
Democrat-Leader (Fayette, MO) **10653**
Democrat-Message (Mt. Sterling, IL) **10586**
Democrat-News (Fredericktown, MO) **10653**
Democrat-Reporter, The (Linden, AL) **10520**
Democrat-Union (Lawrenceburg, TN) **10733**
Democrat, The (Senatobia, MS) **10651**
Democrat Tribune, The (Mineral
 Point, WI) **10769**
Demopolis Times (Demopolis, AL) **10518**
Denair Dispatch (Winton, CA) **10546**
Denbigh Gazette (Yorktown, VA) **10756**
Denham Springs-Livingston Parish News
 (Denham Springs, LA) **10616**
Denison Bulletin & Review (Denison, IA) **10600**
Denmark Press (Denmark, WI) **10766**
† Dennis Bulletin (South Yarmouth, MA)
Denton County Express (Lake
 Dallas, TX) **10743**
Denver Herald-Dispatch (Denver, CO) **10548**
De Pere Journal (De Pere, WI) **10766**
Depew Bee (Williamsville, NY) **10689**
Deposit Courier (Deposit, NY) **10676**
De Queen Bee (De Queen, AR) **10527**
De Quincy News (De Quincy, LA) **10616**
Derry News (Derry, NH) **10663**
Desert Mailer News (Lancaster, CA) **10536**
Desert Mobile Home News (Palm
 Desert, CA) **10540**
† Desert Mountain Express (Hesperia, CA)
Desert Sentinel, The (Desert Hot
 Springs, CA) **10533**
Desert Winds, The (Cave Creek, AZ) **10524**
Deshler Rustler, The (Deshler, NE) **10660**
Des Moines County News, The (West
 Burlington, IA) **10605**
Des Moines News (Seattle, WA) **10759**
De Soto Times (Southaven, MS) **10651**
DeSoto Today (DeSoto, TX) **10739**
Des Plaines Times (Park Ridge, IL) **10587**
Destin Log (Destin, FL) **10557**
Detroit Lakes Tribune (Detroit
 Lakes, MN) **10641**
DeWitt Bath Review (St. Johns, MI) **10638**
DeWitt Times (Syracuse, NY) **10687**
† Diamond Drill, The (Crystal Falls, MI)
Diamond Trail News (Sully, IA) **10604**
Dickenson Star/Cumberland Times, The
 (Clintwood, VA) **10752**
Dickson Herald, The (Dickson, TN) **10731**
Digest, The (Hallandale, FL) **10557**
Digger Shopper & News, The
 (Oroville, CA) **10540**
Dillon Herald, The (Dillon, SC) **10727**
Dispatch-News, The (Lexington, SC) **10728**

Dispatch, The (New Providence, NJ) **10668**
† Dispatch, The (Cookeville, TN)
Divernon News (Auburn, IL) **10572**
Dixie News (Florence, KY) **10610**
Dixon Pilot (Dixon, MO) **10653**
Dodge County Independent-News
 (Juneau, WI) **10768**
Dodge County News, The
 (Eastman, GA) **10565**
Dodgeville Chronicle, Inc.
 (Dodgeville, WI) **10766**
Donaldsonville Chief
 (Donaldsonville, LA) **10616**
Donalsonville News (Donalsonville, GA) **10564**
Doon Press (Doon, IA) **10600**
Door County Advocate (Sturgeon
 Bay, WI) **10774**
Doraville-DeKalb Neighbor (Atlanta, GA) **10562**
Dorchester Eagle Record (St.
 George, SC) **10729**
Dorchester Star (Cambridge, MD) **10621**
Douglas County Herald (Ava, MO) **10651**
Douglas County News Press (Castle
 Rock, CO) **10547**
Douglas County Post Gazette
 (Elkhorn, NE) **10660**
Douglas Enterprise (Douglas, GA) **10564**
Douglas Neighbor, The (Marietta, GA) **10566**
Dove Creek Press (Dove Creek, CO) **10548**
Dover-Sherborn Suburban Press
 (Needham, MA) **10626**
Downers Grove Reporter (Downers
 Grove, IL) **10577**
Downey Herald American (Los
 Angeles, CA) **10537**
Downriver Voice (New Baltimore, MI) **10636**
Downtown Express (New York, NY) **10683**
Downtown Gazette (Long Beach, CA) **10537**
Downtown News (South Miami, FL) **10561**
Dracut Dispatch, The (Dracut, MA) **10624**
Drain Enterprise (Drain, OR) **10713**
Dresden Enterprise (Dresden, TN) **10731**
Drexel Hill Press (Newtown Square, PA) **10721**
Dripping Springs Dispatch (Dripping
 Springs, TX) **10739**
Dublin Suburbia News (Columbus, OH) **10701**
Dublin Villager (Worthington, OH) **10709**
Dumas Clarion (Dumas, AR) **10527**
Duncannon Record (New
 Bloomfield, PA) **10721**
Duncanville Today (DeSoto, TX) **10739**
Dundalk Eagle, The (Baltimore, MD) **10620**
Dundee Observer (Dundee, NY) **10676**
Dunn County News (Menomonie, WI) **10769**
Dunwoody-DeKalb Neighbor, The
 (Atlanta, GA) **10562**

WEEKLY NEWSPAPERS

Dunwoody Crier (Atlanta, GA) **10562**
† DuPage Press Service (Wheaton, IL)
Durand-Dakota Volunteer (Durand, IL) **10577**
Durand Express, The (Durand, MI) **10632**
Durand Gazette (Love Park, IL) **10584**
Dutch Harbor Fisherman, The (Dutch Harbor, AK) **10523**
Duxbury Reporter (Plymouth, MA) **10627**
Dyer County Tennessean (Newbern, TN) **10734**
Dyersville Commercial (Dyersville, IA) **10600**
Eagan Sun-Current (Burnsville, MN) **10640**
Eagle Bulletin (Syracuse, NY) **10687**
Eagle Grove Eagle (Eagle Grove, IA) **10600**
Eagle Lake Headlight (Eagle Lake, TX) **10739**
Eagle News (Bountiful, UT) **10748**
Eagle Pass News Guide/Brief (Eagle Pass, TX) **10739**
Eagle Rock Sentinel (Los Angeles, CA) **10537**
Eagle, The (Cambridge, NY) **10675**
Eagle Valley Enterprise (Eagle, CO) **10548**
Earlville Leader (Earlville, IL) **10578**
Easley Progress (Easley, SC) **10727**
East Aurora Advertiser (East Aurora, NY) **10676**
East Aurora Bee (Williamsville, NY) **10689**
East Baltimore Guide (Baltimore, MD) **10620**
East Bay Breeze (Sun City Center, FL) **10561**
East Bay Express (Berkeley, CA) **10531**
East Bridgewater Star (East Bridgewater, MA) **10624**
Eastchester Record (Yonkers, NY) **10690**
† East County Chronicle (Kimberly, ID)
Eastern Arizona Courier (Safford, AZ) **10526**
Eastern Carolina Times-Inquirer (Goldsboro, NC) **10692**
Eastern Colorado News (Strasburg, CO) **10551**
Eastern Colorado Plainsman (Hugo, CO) **10549**
Eastern Gazette, The (Dexter, ME) **10619**
Eastern Hills Journal (Loveland, OH) **10704**
Eastern Kentucky Shopper (Paintsville, KY) **10613**
East Feliciana Watchman (Clinton, LA) **10616**
East Fishkill Record (Mahopac, NY) **10681**
East Grand Rapids Cadence (Jenison, MI) **10634**
East Greenwich Pendulum (East Greenwich, RI) **10725**
East Hampton Star (East Hampton, NY) **10676**
East Hartford Gazette, The (East Hartford, CT) **10552**
East Haven Advertiser (Milford, CT) **10553**
East L.A./Commerce Tribune (Los Angeles, CA) **10537**
Eastland Telegram (Eastland, TX) **10739**

East Lauderdale News (Rogersville, AL) **10521**
† East Los Angeles Gazette (South Gate, CA)
† East Los Angeles Tribune (South Gate, CA)
East Meadow Beacon (Hicksville, NY) **10679**
East Mesa Independent (Apache Junction, AZ) **10524**
Easton Bulletin (Stoughton, MA) **10628**
East Orange Record (Orange, NJ) **10668**
† East Palestine Heritage, The (Columbiana, OH)
East Penn Press (Allentown, PA) **10715**
East Peoria Courier (Morton, IL) **10586**
East Providence Post (East Providence, RI) **10725**
East Riverside Advertiser (Palm Desert, CA) **10540**
East Rochester Post-Herald (Victor, NY) **10688**
East Rockaway Observer (Mineola, NY) **10682**
East Shelby Review (Somerville, TN) **10735**
East Side Herald (Indianapolis, IN) **10594**
Eastside Journal (Los Angeles, CA) **10537**
Eastside Monthly (Providence, RI) **10726**
East Side Review (North St. Paul, MN) **10645**
Eastside Sun (City of Commerce, CA) **10532**
† Eastside Times (Tulsa, OK)
East St. Louis Monitor (East St. Louis, IL) **10578**
East St. Louis News Journal (Columbia, IL) **10576**
East Troy News (East Troy, WI) **10766**
Easy Reader (Hermosa Beach, CA) **10535**
Eaton County News (Charlotte, MI) **10631**
Ebbtide (Sausalito, CA) **10544**
Ebensburg News Leader, The (Ebensburg, PA) **10717**
Echoes-Sentinel (Stirling, NJ) **10670**
Echo Press, The (Alexandria, MN) **10639**
† Echo, The (Berlin, NY)
ECM Post-Review (North Branch, MN) **10644**
Eddyville Tribune (Eddyville, IA) **10600**
Eden Prairie Sun-Current (Bloomington, MN) **10640**
Edgebrook Times Review (Park Ridge, IL) **10587**
Edgerton Enterprise, The (Edgerton, MN) **10641**
Edgerton Reporter (Edgerton, WI) **10766**
Edgewood Enterprise (Edgewood, TX) **10739**
Edgewood Reminder (Edgewood, IA) **10600**
Edina Sun-Current (Minneapolis, MN) **10644**
Edison-Norwood Times Review (Park Ridge, IL) **10588**
Edwardsville Journal (Edwardsville, IL) **10578**
Egg Harbor News (Hammonton, NJ) **10666**
Elba Clipper, The (Elba, AL) **10519**
Elbert County News (Castle Rock, CO) **10547**
Elberton Star (Elberton, GA) **10565**

Elburn Herald (Elburn, IL) **10578**
El Campo Leader-News (El Campo, TX) **10739**
El Centro Advertiser (El Centro, CA) **10533**
Eldon Advertiser (Eldon, MO) **10653**
Eldora Herald-Leader (Eldora, IA) **10600**
Elizabeth Gazette (Union, NJ) **10670**
Elizabethtown Chronicle
  (Elizabethtown, PA) **10717**
Elizabethtown Mount Joy Merchandiser (Mt.
  Joy, PA) **10721**
Elk Grove Citizen (Elk Grove, CA) **10533**
Elkhorn Independent (Elkhorn, WI) **10766**
Elk Valley Times (Fayetteville, TN) **10732**
Ellenville Press (Ellenville, NY) **10677**
Ellsworth American, The
  (Ellsworth, ME) **10619**
Ellsworth Reporter, The (Ellsworth, KS) **10606**
Elma Review (East Aurora, NY) **10676**
Elm Grove Elm Leaves (New Berlin, WI) **10770**
Elmhurst Press (Elmhurst, IL) **10578**
Elm Leaves (Oak Park, IL) **10587**
Elmont Herald (Elmont, NY) **10677**
Elmwood Park-River Grove Times
  (Lincolnwood, IL) **10583**
Eloy Enterprise (Eloy, AZ) **10525**
El Paso Journal (El Paso, IL) **10578**
El Reno Tribune (El Reno, OK) **10710**
El Segundo Herald (El Segundo, CA) **10534**
El Sereno Star (Los Angeles, CA) **10537**
Elwood Express (Wilmington, IL) **10591**
Ely Echo (Ely, MN) **10641**
Emery County Progress (Castle
  Dale, UT) **10748**
Emmetsburg Democrat
  (Emmetsburg, IA) **10600**
Emmetsburg Reporter
  (Emmetsburg, IA) **10601**
Encinitas Sun (Encinitas, CA) **10534**
Enderlin Independent (Enderlin, ND) **10696**
Enfield Press (Enfield, CT) **10552**
England Democrat (England, AR) **10527**
Englewood Herald (Littleton, CO) **10549**
Enquirer-Gazette (Upper Marlboro, MD) **10623**
Enquirer Bulletin (Burlingame, CA) **10531**
Enterprise & Inner Harbor News
  (Baltimore, MD) **10621**
Enterprise Buyer's Catalogue
  (Wytheville, VA) **10756**
Enterprise Mountaineer, The
  (Canton, NC) **10691**
† Enterprise News (Pixley, CA)
Enterprise, The (Fallbrook, CA) **10534**
Enterprise, The (Plainfield, IL) **10588**
Enterprise, The (Ponchatoula, LA) **10617**
Enterprise, The (Falmouth, MA) **10625**
Enterprise, The (Lexington Park, MD) **10622**

Enterprise, The (Mason, MI) **10635**
Enterprise, The (Williamston, NC) **10696**
Enterprise, The
  (Hastings-on-Hudson, NY) **10679**
Enterprise, The (Stuart, VA) **10756**
Enterprise, The (Lynnwood, WA) **10758**
Enumclaw Courier-Herald
  (Enumclaw, WA) **10757**
Ephrata Review (Ephrata, PA) **10717**
† Erie County Reporter (Huron, OH)
Erskine Echo, The (Erskine, MN) **10641**
Erwin Record (Erwin, TN) **10732**
Escambia Sun Press (Pensacola, FL) **10560**
Escondido News-Reporter
  (Escondido, CA) **10534**
Essex Independent, The (Essex, IA) **10601**
Estancia Valley Citizen (Estancia, NM) **10672**
Estes Park Trail-Gazette (Estes
  Park, CO) **10548**
Estill County Tribune, The (Irvine, KY) **10612**
Euclid Sun Journal (Beachwood, OH) **10698**
Eufaula Tribune (Eufaula, AL) **10519**
Eugene Weekly (Eugene, OR) **10713**
Eunice News (Eunice, LA) **10616**
Eureka Herald (Eureka, KS) **10606**
Eureka Sentinel (Tonopah, NV) **10662**
Eureka Springs Times-Echo
  (Berryville, AR) **10527**
Eustis Lake Region News (Mt. Dora, FL) **10559**
Evanston Review (Evanston, IL) **10579**
Evart Review, The (Evart, MI) **10632**
Evening Star Plus, The (Auburn, IN) **10591**
Evergreen Courant, The
  (Evergreen, AL) **10519**
Evergreen Park Courier (Midlothian, IL) **10585**
Evergreen Shopping Guide
  (Spooner, WI) **10773**
Everman Times (Everman, TX) **10739**
Everybody's News (Cincinnati, OH) **10700**
Excelsior/Shorewood/Chanhassen Sun-Sailor
  (Minnetonka, MN) **10644**
Exchange, The (Houston, TX) **10742**
Exeter News-Letter (Stratham, NH) **10664**
Exeter Sun, The (Exeter, CA) **10534**
Exponent, The (Brooklyn, MI) **10630**
Exponent, The (Greenbush, MN) **10642**
Extra Merchandiser (St. Marys, OH) **10707**
Fairbury Journal-News, The
  (Fairbury, NE) **10661**
† Fairchild Strikehawk (Spokane, WA)
Fairfax Connection (McLean, VA) **10754**
Fairfax Station Times (Reston, VA) **10755**
Fairfax Times (Reston, VA) **10755**
Fairfield-Penfield Community News
  (Rochester, NY) **10685**

WEEKLY NEWSPAPERS

Fairfield Chronicle, The (West Caldwell, NJ) **10671**
Fairfield Citizen News (Fairfield, CT) **10552**
Fairfield County Weekly (Stamford, CT) **10554**
Fairfield Echo (Fairfield, OH) **10703**
Fairfield Wayne County Press (Fairfield, IL) **10579**
† Fair Haven Register (Red Creek, NY)
Fairhope Courier, The (Fairhope, AL) **10519**
Fairmont Photo Press (Fairmont, MN) **10641**
† Fairport-Perinton Herald-Mail (Webster, NY)
Fairview Heights Journal (Belleville, IL) **10573**
Fairview Heights Tribune (Mascoutah, IL) **10584**
Fairview Republican (Fairview, OK) **10710**
Falfurrias Facts (Falfurrias, TX) **10740**
Falls Church News-Press (Falls Church, VA) **10752**
Falls City Journal (Falls City, NE) **10661**
Faribault County Register (Blue Earth, MN) **10640**
Farina News, The (Farina, IL) **10579**
Farmer & Miner (Frederick, CO) **10549**
Farmer's Weekly Review (Joliet, IL) **10583**
Farmer City Journal (Farmer City, IL) **10579**
Farmers' Advance (Camden, MI) **10631**
† Farmers Branch Times (Carrollton, TX)
Farmers Independent (Bagley, MN) **10639**
Farmingdale Observer (Mineola, NY) **10682**
Farmington Observer (Farmington, MI) **10632**
† Farmington Valley Herald (Simsbury, CT)
Farmland News (Archbold, OH) **10698**
Farm Monthly (Atlantic, IA) **10599**
Farmville Herald, The (Farmville, VA) **10752**
Farmweek (Knightstown, IN) **10595**
Fauquier Citizen (Warrenton, VA) **10756**
Fauquier Times-Democrat (Warrenton, VA) **10756**
Fayette Advertiser, The (Fayette, MO) **10653**
Fayette County News (Fayetteville, GA) **10565**
Fayette County Record, The (La Grange, TX) **10743**
Fayette County Review (Somerville, TN) **10735**
Fayette County Union (West Union, IA) **10605**
Fayette Falcon, The (Somerville, TN) **10735**
Fayette Neighbor, The (Fayetteville, GA) **10565**
Fayette Review, The (Fayette, OH) **10703**
† Fayette Sun (Fayetteville, GA)
Fayette Tribune (Oak Hill, WV) **10762**
Federal Way News (Federal Way, WA) **10758**
Fennimore Times (Fennimore, WI) **10767**
Ferdinand News, The (Ferdinand, IN) **10593**
Fernley Leader-Dayton Courier (Yerington, NV) **10662**
Fillmore Herald (Fillmore, CA) **10534**
Fincastle Herald, The (Fincastle, VA) **10752**

Finder, The (Mandan, ND) **10697**
Firebaugh/Mendota Journal (Kerman, CA) **10535**
Fire Island Tide (Sayville, NY) **10685**
Fisher Reporter (Fisher, IL) **10579**
Fishers Sun-Herald (Fishers, IN) **10593**
Fishkill Standard (Mahopac, NY) **10681**
Fishtown Star (Philadelphia, PA) **10722**
Fitchburg Star (Verona, WI) **10774**
Five Cities Times-Press-Recorder (Arroyo Grande, CA) **10530**
Five County/Buyer's Guide (Ripon, WI) **10773**
Flanagan Home Times (Pontiac, IL) **10588**
Flatbush Life (Brooklyn, NY) **10674**
† Flat River Lead Belt News (Flat River, MO)
Florala News, The (Florala, AL) **10519**
Floral Park Bulletin (Floral Park, NY) **10677**
Florence Citizen (Florence, CO) **10548**
Florence Mining News (Florence, WI) **10767**
Florence Reminder & Blade-Tribune (Florence, AZ) **10525**
Floresville Chronicle-Journal (Floresville, TX) **10740**
Florham Park Eagle (Madison, NJ) **10667**
Florida Keys Keynoter (Marathon, FL) **10558**
Floridian, The (Marianna, FL) **10558**
Florissant Valley Reporter (Florissant, MO) **10653**
Floyd County Hesperian-Beacon (Floydada, TX) **10740**
Floyd County Times (Prestonsburg, KY) **10613**
Floyd Press (Floyd, VA) **10753**
Flushing Observer (Flint, MI) **10632**
Flushing Times, The (Bayside, NY) **10673**
Focus News (Roseville, MN) **10646**
Folsom Telegraph (Folsom, CA) **10534**
Fontana Herald News (Fontana, CA) **10534**
Foothills Sentinel (Cave Creek, AZ) **10524**
Ford County Press (Melvin, IL) **10585**
Forest City Summit (Forest City, IA) **10601**
Forest Hill News (Everman, TX) **10740**
▼Forest Hills/Rego Park Times (Maspeth, NY) **10681**
Forest Hills Journal (Loveland, OH) **10704**
Forest Lake Press (St. Paul, MN) **10647**
Forest Leaves (Oak Park, IL) **10587**
Forest Press (Tionesta, PA) **10724**
Forest Republican, The (Crandon, WI) **10766**
Forest Times-Tribune (De Forest, WI) **10766**
Forreston Journal (Forreston, IL) **10579**
Forsyth County News (Cumming, GA) **10564**
Fort Bend Mirror (Rosenberg, TX) **10746**
Fort Bend Sun (Sugar Land, TX) **10747**
Fort Bragg Advocate-News (Fort Bragg, CA) **10534**

WEEKLY NEWSPAPERS

Fort Fairfield Review (Fort Fairfield, ME) **10619**
Fort Lupton Press (Fort Lupton, CO) **10548**
Fort Meade Leader, The (Fort Meade, FL) **10557**
Fort Mill Times (Fort Mill, SC) **10727**
Fort Myers Beach Observer (Fort Myers Beach, FL) **10557**
† Fort Myers Observer (Fort Myers, FL)
Fort Riley Post (Junction City, KS) **10607**
Fort San Antonio News Leader (San Antonio, TX) **10746**
Fort Stockton Pioneer (Fort Stockton, TX) **10740**
Forum of Queens (Ozone Park, NY) **10684**
Fosston Thirteen Towns (Fosston, MN) **10642**
Foster City Progress (Burlingame, CA) **10531**
Foto News (Merrill, WI) **10769**
Fountain County Neighbor (Attica, IN) **10591**
Fountain Valley News & El Paso County News (Fountain, CO) **10548**
Four Oaks-Benson News in Review (Benson, NC) **10691**
Fowler Tribune, The (Fowler, CO) **10548**
Fowlerville Review Shopping Guide (Howell, MI) **10634**
Foxboro Reporter, The (Foxboro, MA) **10625**
Fox Lake Press (Grayslake, IL) **10580**
Fox Lake Representative (Fox Lake, WI) **10767**
Fox Point, Bayside, River Hills Herald (New Berlin, WI) **10770**
Fox Valley Shopping News, The (Yorkville, IL) **10591**
Fox Valley Villages (Plainfield, IL) **10588**
Foxxy Shopper (Sparta, WI) **10773**
Frankenmuth News (Frankenmuth, MI) **10632**
Franklin-Hales Corner Hub (New Berlin, WI) **10770**
Franklin Challenger (Greenwood, IN) **10594**
Franklin Chronicle (Franklin, OH) **10703**
Franklin County Citizen (Lavonia, GA) **10566**
Franklin County Graphic (Connell, WA) **10757**
Franklin County Plus (Russellville, AL) **10522**
Franklin County Times (Russellville, AL) **10522**
Franklin Favorite (Franklin, KY) **10611**
Franklin Journal & Farmington Chronicle (Farmington, ME) **10619**
Franklin News-Post (Rocky Mount, VA) **10755**
Franklin News-Record (Princeton, NJ) **10669**
Franklin Park Herald-Journal, The (Oak Park, IL) **10587**
Franklin Park Star-Sentinel (Melrose Park, IL) **10585**
Franklin Pendleton Times (Franklin, WV) **10761**
Franklin Press (Franklin, NC) **10692**

Franklin Square Bulletin (Floral Park, NY) **10677**
Franklin Sun, The (Winnsboro, LA) **10618**
Franklin Times (Louisburg, NC) **10693**
Franklin Township Sentinel (Franklinville, NJ) **10666**
Frederick Leader (Frederick, OK) **10710**
Fredericksburg Standard/Radio Post (Fredericksburg, TX) **10740**
† Freeborn County Register (Albert Lea, MN)
Freemont Gazette (Fremont, IA) **10601**
Free News, The (Farmville, VA) **10752**
Freeport Advertiser Shopping News (Freeport, IL) **10579**
Freeport Baldwin Leader, The (Freeport, NY) **10677**
Free Press-Courier (Westfield, PA) **10725**
Free Press Standard (Carrollton, OH) **10700**
Free Press, The (Tampa, FL) **10561**
Free Press, The (Canton, OH) **10699**
Free Press, The (Braddock, PA) **10716**
Free Time (Wildwood, NJ) **10671**
Free Times, The (Cleveland, OH) **10700**
Free Trader (Massena, NY) **10681**
Fremont County Herald-Chronicle (St. Anthony, ID) **10571**
Fresh Meadows Times, The (Flushing, NY) **10677**
Fridley Focus (Roseville, MN) **10646**
Friendswood & Pearland Reporter News (Pearland, TX) **10745**
Frontier & Holt County Independent (O'Neill, NE) **10661**
Frontiersman, The (Wasilla, AK) **10523**
Front Page (Lackawanna, NY) **10680**
Frostproof News (Frostproof, FL) **10557**
Fruita Times, The (Fruita, CO) **10549**
Fulton County Expositor (Wauseon, OH) **1070**
Fulton Democrat (Lewistown, IL) **10583**
Fulton Journal (Fulton, IL) **10579**
Fulton Leader (Fulton, KY) **10611**
Fulton Patriot (Fulton, NY) **10678**
Fulton Shopper (Fulton, KY) **10611**
Gadsden County Times (Quincy, FL) **10560**
Gaffney Ledger, The (Gaffney, SC) **10727**
Gainesville Buyers Guide (Orange Park, FL) **10559**
Gaithersburg Gazette (Gaithersburg, MD) **10621**
Galax Gazette, The (Galax, VA) **10753**
Galena Gazette (Galena, IL) **10579**
Galesburg Post, The (Galesburg, IL) **10579**
Galesville Republican (Galesville, WI) **10767**
Galt Herald (Galt, CA) **10534**
Galva News (Galva, IL) **10579**
Gardena Valley News (Gardena, CA) **10534**

Garden City Observer (Livonia, MI) **10635**
Garden Island Extra (Lihue, HI) **10568**
Garden of the Gods Journal (Manitou Springs, CO) **10550**
Gardner South Wilmington Post (Wilmington, IL) **10591**
Garfield Maple-Sun (Cleveland, OH) **10700**
Garland News (Garland, TX) **10740**
Garner News (Garner, NC) **10692**
† Garnett Review (Garnett, KS)
Gary Crusader (Gary, IN) **10594**
Gary Info (Gary, IN) **10594**
Gasconade County Republican (Owensville, MO) **10655**
Gates-Chili News (Rochester, NY) **10685**
Gates County Index (Gatesville, NC) **10692**
Gatesville Messenger (Gatesville, TX) **10740**
Gateway Express, The (Clinton, IA) **10599**
Gateway News, The (Streetsboro, OH) **10707**
Gateway, The (Floral Park, NY) **10677**
Gaylord Herald Times (Gaylord, MI) **10632**
Gazette-Advertiser (Rhinebeck, NY) **10685**
Gazette-Democrat (Anna, IL) **10571**
Gazette Shopper (Cleveland, OH) **10700**
Gazette, The (Mt. Holly, NJ) **10668**
Gazette, The (Port Jervis, NY) **10685**
Gazette, The (Jefferson, OH) **10704**
Geist Gazette (Fishers, IN) **10593**
Gem State Miner (Newport, WA) **10758**
Geneseo Republic (Geneseo, IL) **10579**
Geneseo Shopper (Geneseo, IL) **10579**
Geneva County Reaper (Geneva, AL) **10519**
Geneva Republican (Geneva, IL) **10579**
Genoa-Kingston-Kirkland News (Sycamore, IL) **10589**
Gentry Courier-Journal (Gentry, AR) **10527**
George County Times (Lucedale, MS) **10650**
Georgetown Current, The (Washington, DC) **10554**
Georgetowner, The (Washington, DC) **10555**
Georgetown News Graphic (Georgetown, KY) **10611**
Georgetown Record (Ipswich, MA) **10625**
Georgetown Times, The (Georgetown, SC) **10727**
Georgis's Coastal Illustrated (St. Simons Island, GA) **10567**
Gering Courier (Gering, NE) **10661**
Germantown Banner-Press (New Berlin, WI) **10770**
Germantown Courier (Philadelphia, PA) **10722**
Germantown News, The (Germantown, TN) **10732**
Germantown Paper (Philadelphia, PA) **10722**
Gibson City Courier (Gibson City, IL) **10580**
Giddings Times & News (Giddings, TX) **10740**
Gilbert Independent (Scottsdale, AZ) **10526**
Gillespie Area News (Gillespie, IL) **10580**
Gilman Star (Gilman, IL) **10580**
Gilmer Mirror (Gilmer, TX) **10740**
Girard Home News (Philadelphia, PA) **10722**
† Girard News (Niles, OH)
Girard Press (Girard, KS) **10606**
Giveaway, The (Scottsburg, IN) **10597**
Glades County Democrat (Clewiston, FL) **10556**
Gladewater Mirror (Gladewater, TX) **10741**
† Gladstone Delta Reporter (Escanaba, MI)
Gladwin County Record & Beaverton Clarion (Gladwin, MI) **10633**
Glasford Gazette, The (Glasford, IL) **10580**
Glasgow Courier, The (Glasgow, MT) **10659**
Glasgow Republican (Glasgow, KY) **10611**
Glastonbury Citizen (Glastonbury, CT) **10552**
Glencoe Enterprise (Glencoe, MN) **10642**
Glencoe News (Glenview, IL) **10580**
Glen Cove Record Pilot (Mineola, NY) **10682**
Glendale Heights Press (Elmhurst, IL) **10578**
Glendale Herald (New Berlin, WI) **10770**
Glendale Register (Maspeth, NY) **10681**
Glendale Star, The (Glendale, AZ) **10525**
Glendive Ranger-Review (Glendive, MT) **10659**
Glendora Press (West Covina, CA) **10546**
Glen Ellyn News (Glen Ellyn, IL) **10580**
Glen Ellyn Press (Bloomingdale, IL) **10573**
Glennville Sentinel (Glennville, GA) **10565**
Glen Oaks Ledger, The (Bayside, NY) **10673**
Glen Ridge Paper, The (Bloomfield, NJ) **10664**
Glen Rock Gazette (Franklin Lakes, NJ) **10666**
Glen Rose Reporter (Glen Rose, TX) **10741**
Glenside News (Jenkintown, PA) **10718**
Glenview Announcements (Glenview, IL) **10580**
Glenville Democrat, The (Glenville, WV) **10761**
Glenville Pathfinder (Glenville, WV) **10761**
Glenwood Herald (Glenwood, AR) **10527**
Glenwood Opinion-Tribune (Glenwood, IA) **10601**
Glidden Enterprise (Glidden, WI) **10767**
Globe, The (Jenkintown, PA) **10718**
Gloucester-Mathews Gazette Journal (Gloucester, VA) **10753**
Gloucester City News (Gloucester City, NJ) **10666**
Glynco Observer (Brunswick, GA) **10563**
Gold Beach Curry County Reporter (Gold Beach, OR) **10713**
Goldendale Sentinel (Goldendale, WA) **10758**
Golden Prairie News (Assumption, IL) **10572**
Golden Times (Rochester, NY) **10685**
Golden Transcript (Golden, CO) **10549**
Golden Triangle Shopper (Columbus, MS) **10649**

Gold Leaf Farmer, The (Wendell, NC) **10695**
Gold River News (Sacramento, CA) **10542**
† Goleta Review (Goleta, CA)
† Goleta Sun (Santa Barbara, CA)
Golfmill Journal (Des Plaines, IL) **10577**
Gonzales Inquirer (Gonzales, TX) **10741**
Gonzales Tribune (Soledad, CA) **10545**
Gonzales Weekly (Gonzales, LA) **10616**
Goochland Gazette (Goochland, VA) **10753**
Gooding County Leader (Gooding, ID) **10569**
Good News (Monona, WI) **10770**
Good News Shopper (Coal City, IL) **10576**
Good Times (Santa Cruz, CA) **10544**
† Good Times News (Fayette, MO)
Goose Creek Gazette (Ladson, SC) **10727**
Gorman Progress, The (Gorman, TX) **10741**
Gouverneur Tribune Press (Gouverneur, NY) **10678**
Gowanda Pennysaver News (Gowanda, NY) **10678**
† Grace Citizen (Preston, ID)
Graceville News (Graceville, FL) **10557**
Grainger County News (Rutledge, TN) **10734**
Grand Blanc News, The (Flint, MI) **10632**
Grand Gazette (St. Paul, MN) **10647**
Grand Island Pennysaver (Grand Island, NY) **10678**
Grand Ledge Independent, The (Grand Ledge, MI) **10633**
Grand Prairie News (Arlington, TX) **10736**
Grand Rapids/Herald-Review (Grand Rapids, MN) **10642**
Grand Rapids Advance (Jenison, MI) **10634**
Grand Saline Sun (Grand Saline, TX) **10741**
Grand Valley Advance (Jenison, MI) **10634**
Grandview Herald (Grandview, WA) **10758**
Granite City Press Journal (Granite City, IL) **10580**
Granite Falls/Clerkfield Advocate Tribune (Granite Falls, MN) **10642**
Granite State News (Wolfeboro, NH) **10664**
Grant County Herald Independent (Lancaster, WI) **10768**
Grant County Journal (Ephrata, WA) **10757**
Grant County News (Williamstown, KY) **10615**
Grant County News (Elgin, ND) **10696**
Grant County Press (Petersburg, WV) **10762**
Grant County Review (Milbank, SD) **10730**
Granville Sentinel (Granville, NY) **10678**
Granville Sentinel, The (Granville, OH) **10703**
Gratiot County Herald (Ithaca, MI) **10634**
Gravette News Herald (Gravette, AR) **10527**
Grayslake Times (Grayslake, IL) **10580**
Grayson Advertiser (Leitchfield, KY) **10612**
Grayson County News-Gazette (Leitchfield, KY) **10612**

Grayson County Shopper (Denison, TX) **10739**
Grayson Journal-Enquirer (Grayson, KY) **10611**
Greater Baton Rouge Business Report (Baton Rouge, LA) **10615**
Great Falls Times (Reston, VA) **10755**
Great Lakes Pilot, The (Grand Marais, MI) **10633**
Great Lander Bush Mailer (Anchorage, AK) **10522**
Great Neck News (Great Neck, NY) **10678**
Great Neck Record (Mineola, NY) **10682**
Greece Post, The (Fishers, NY) **10677**
Greenbelt News Review (Greenbelt, MD) **10622**
Greenbrier Valley Ranger (Lewisburg, WV) **10762**
Greendale Village Life (New Berlin, WI) **10770**
Greene County Independent (Eutaw, AL) **10519**
Greene County Record (Stanardsville, VA) **10755**
Greene Prairie Press (White Hall, IL) **10590**
Greene Recorder, The (Greene, IA) **10601**
Greenfield News (Greenfield, CA) **10534**
Greenfield Observer (New Berlin, WI) **10770**
Green Forest Tribune (Berryville, AR) **10527**
Green Hills Weekly (Trenton, MO) **10658**
Greenhorn Valley News (Colorado City, CO) **10547**
Green Lake County Reporter (Berlin, WI) **10764**
Greenpoint Gazette/Advertiser (Brooklyn, NY) **10674**
† Green River Republican (Morgantown, KY)
Greensboro Watchman, The (Greensboro, AL) **10519**
Green Sheet, The (San Bernardino, CA) **10542**
Green Tab (Moundsville, WV) **10762**
Greenup County News-Times (Greenup, KY) **10611**
Greenup Press (Greenup, IL) **10581**
Green Valley News & Sun (Green Valley, AZ) **10525**
Greenville Advocate, The (Greenville, AL) **10519**
Greenville Advocate, The (Greenville, IL) **10581**
Greenville Local (Ravena, NY) **10685**
Greenwich Journal & Salem Press (Greenwich, NY) **10678**
† Greenwich News (Greenwich, CT)
▼Greenwich Post (Greenwich, CT) **10552**
Greenwood & Southside Challenger (Greenwood, IN) **10594**
Greenwood Democrat (Greenwood, AR) **10527**

WEEKLY NEWSPAPERS

Greenwood Gazette, The (Fishers, IN) **10593**
Greenwood Lake & West Milford News (Greenwood Lake, NY) **10678**
Greer Citizen, The (Greer, SC) **10727**
Gresham Outlook (Gresham, OR) **10713**
Gridley Herald, The (Gridley, CA) **10534**
Griffith Guide (Maryville, IN) **10595**
Grinnell Herald-Register (Grinnell, IA) **10601**
Grizzly, The (Big Bear Lake, CA) **10531**
Groesbeck Journal (Groesbeck, TX) **10741**
Grosse Pointe News (Grosse Pointe Farms, MI) **10633**
Groton Landmark (Ayer, MA) **10623**
Grove City Record (Columbus, OH) **10701**
Grove Sun (Grove, OK) **10710**
Grundy County Herald (Tracy City, TN) **10735**
Grundy Register (Grundy Center, IA) **10601**
Grunion Gazette (Long Beach, CA) **10537**
Grygla Eagle (Grygla, MN) **10642**
Guernsey Gazette/Lingle Guide (Guernsey, WY) **10776**
Guilford American (Dover-Foxcroft, ME) **10619**
Gulf Coast Tribune, The (West Columbia, TX) **10747**
Gurnee Press (Grayslake, IL) **10580**
Guttenberg Press (Guttenberg, IA) **10601**
† Haddon Gazette (Cherry Hill, NJ)
Hagerstown Exponent, The (Hagerstown, IN) **10594**
† Haines City Herald (Haines City, FL)
Half Moon Bay Review (Half Moon Bay, CA) **10534**
Halifax Reporter (Plymouth, MA) **10627**
Hallettsville Tribune-Herald (Hallettsville, TX) **10741**
Halls Graphic (Ripley, TN) **10734**
Hamburg Item (Hamburg, PA) **10718**
Hamden Chronicle, The (Milford, CT) **10553**
Hamilton-Wenham Chronicle (Ipswich, MA) **10625**
† Hamilton County News (Elizabethtown, NY)
Hamilton County News (Speculator, NY) **10687**
Hamilton Herald-News (Hamilton, TX) **10741**
Hamilton Mid-York Weekly (Hamilton, NY) **10679**
▼Hamilton Tribune (Hamilton, NY) **10679**
Hamlin-Clarkson Herald (Spencerport, NY) **10687**
Hammonton News (Hammonton, NJ) **10666**
Hampshire Register News (Sycamore, IL) **10590**
Hampshire Review (Romney, WV) **10763**
Hampton Chronicle & Times (Hampton, IA) **10601**
Hampton Union (Stratham, NH) **10664**
Hanahan News (North Charleston, SC) **10728**

Hanceville Herald (Hanceville, AL) **10520**
Hancock Clarion (Hawesville, KY) **10611**
Hancock County Journal-Pilot (Carthage, IL) **10574**
Hancock County Quill (La Harpe, IL) **10583**
Hancock News (Hancock, MD) **10622**
Hanover Eagle & Regional News (Madison, NJ) **10667**
Hanover Mariner (Marshfield, MA) **10625**
† Hanover Park Township Times (Carol Stream, IL)
Hansford County Reporter-Statesman (Spearman, TX) **10747**
Haralson Gateway-Beacon, The (Bremen, GA) **10563**
Harbor Beach Times (Harbor Beach, MI) **10633**
Harbor Sound (Brunswick, GA) **10563**
Harborwatch (Brooklyn, NY) **10674**
Hardin Calhoun Herald (Hardin, IL) **10581**
Hardin County Independent (Elizabethtown, IL) **10578**
Hardin County Index (Eldora, IA) **10600**
Hardwick Gazette (Hardwick, VT) **10750**
Harlan County Journal (Alma, NE) **10659**
Harlan News Advertiser (Harlan, IA) **10601**
Harlan Tribune (Harlan, IA) **10601**
Harlem-Foster-Norwood Park-Edison Park Times (Lincolnwood, IL) **10583**
Harlem-Irving Times (Lincolnwood, IL) **10583**
Harlem Valley Times (Amenia, NY) **10673**
† Harper Woods Herald (Birmingham, MI)
Harrah News, The (Harrah, OK) **10710**
Harriman Record (Kingston, TN) **10732**
Harrington Journal, The (Harrington, DE) **10554**
Harrison County Advisor (Bethany, MO) **10652**
Harrison Independent (Yonkers, NY) **10690**
Harrison News-Herald, The (Cadiz, OH) **10699**
Harrisonville Cass County Democrat Missourian (Harrisonville, MO) **10653**
Harrodsburg Herald (Harrodsburg, KY) **10611**
Hart County News-Herald (Munfordville, KY) **10613**
Harte-Hanks Pennysaver (Brea, CA) **10531**
Hartford Advocate (Hartford, CT) **10552**
Hartford Area News (Canistota, SD) **10729**
Hartland Herald Shopping Guide (Howell, MI) **10634**
Hartselle Enquirer (Hartselle, AL) **10520**
Hartsville Messenger, The (Hartsville, SC) **10727**
Hartsville Vidette, The (Hartsville, TN) **10732**
Hartville News (Hartville, OH) **10703**
Hartwell Sun, The (Hartwell, GA) **10565**
Harvard Spirit (Ayer, MA) **10623**

Harwich Oracle (Orleans, MA) **10627**
† Harwood Heights News (Park Ridge, IL)
Haskell Free Press (Haskell, TX) **10741**
Hastings Banner (Hastings, MI) **10633**
Hastings Reminder (Hastings, MI) **10633**
Hastings Star Gazette (Hastings, MN) **10642**
Havana Mason County Democrat (Havana, IL) **10581**
Haverford Press (Newtown Square, PA) **10721**
Hawley Herald (Hawley, MN) **10642**
Hawthorne Press (Hawthorne, NJ) **10666**
Haxtun-Fleming Herald, The (Haxtun, CO) **10549**
Hayden Valley Press (Craig, CO) **10548**
Hazard Herald-Voice (Hazard, KY) **10611**
Hazen Star (Hazen, ND) **10697**
Headland Observer (Headland, AL) **10520**
Headlight-Herald (Tillamook, OR) **10715**
Healdsburg Tribune (Healdsburg, CA) **10535**
Heights Herald (Fishers, IN) **10593**
Heights Times-Herald (Dearborn, MI) **10632**
Hempstead Beacon (Hicksville, NY) **10679**
Henderson County Quill (Stronghurst, IL) **10589**
† Hendersonville Free Press (Hendersonville, TN)
Hendersonville Star News (Hendersonville, TN) **10732**
Hendricks County Flyer (Plainfield, IN) **10597**
† Hendricks County Guide Gazette (Plainfield, IN)
† Henrico Gazette (Richmond, VA)
Henrietta Post (Fishers, NY) **10677**
Henry County Local (New Castle, KY) **10613**
Henry Herald, The (McDonough, GA) **10566**
Henry News Republican (Henry, IL) **10581**
Herald & Tribune (Jonesborough, TN) **10732**
Herald-Advocate (Wauchula, FL) **10561**
Herald-Chronicle, The (Winchester, TN) **10735**
Herald-Democrat (Leadville, CO) **10549**
Herald-Gazette, The (Barnesville, GA) **10563**
Herald-Independent, The (Winnsboro, SC) **10729**
Herald-Leader (Siloam Springs, AR) **10529**
Herald-Leader, The (Fitzgerald, GA) **10565**
Herald-News (Wolf Point, MT) **10659**
Herald-News (Dayton, TN) **10731**
Herald-Press (Harvey, ND) **10697**
Herald-Progress (Ashland, VA) **10751**
Herald-Republican (Angola, IN) **10591**
Herald-Star, The (Edinburg, IL) **10578**
Herald-Tribune (Batesville, IN) **10592**
Herald-Tribune, The (Cartersville, GA) **10564**
Herald/Country Market, The (Bourbonnais, IL) **10573**
Herald Enterprise (Golconda, IL) **10580**

Herald Gazette, The (Trenton, TN) **10735**
Herald Journal (Clarinda, IA) **10599**
Herald Ledger (Eddyville, KY) **10610**
Herald News, The (Reed City, MI) **10637**
Herald of Randolph (Randolph, VT) **10750**
Herald Record (West Union, WV) **10764**
† Herald, The (Tarpon Springs, FL)
Herald, The (Rincon, GA) **10567**
Herald, The (Cahokia, IL) **10574**
Herald, The (Truth or Consequences, NM) **10672**
Herald, The (Pittsburgh, PA) **10723**
Hermann Advertiser-Courier (Hermann, MO) **10653**
Hermiston Herald (Hermiston, OR) **10713**
Hermitage Index (Hermitage, MO) **10653**
Herndon Times (Reston, VA) **10755**
Herrin Spokesman (Herrin, IL) **10581**
Herscher Pilot (Herscher, IL) **10581**
Hershey Chronicle, The (Hershey, PA) **10718**
Hesperia Resorter (Hesperia, CA) **10535**
Hi-Riser (Deerfield Beach, FL) **10556**
Hialeah/Opa-Lacka News (Miami, FL) **10559**
Hiawatha Valley Shopper (Red Wing, MN) **10646**
Hickory Hills Citizen (Midlothian, IL) **10585**
Hickory News/Extra, The (Hickory, NC) **10692**
Hicksville Illustrated News (Mineola, NY) **10682**
Highlander (West Covina, CA) **10546**
Highland Guide (Maryville, IN) **10595**
Highland News Leader (Highland, IL) **10581**
Highland Park News (Bannockburn, IL) **10572**
Highland Park News/Herald/Journal (Los Angeles, CA) **10537**
† Highlands Press (Mulberry, FL)
Highlands Ranch Herald (Littleton, CO) **10549**
Highline News (Seatac, WA) **10759**
High Plains Journal (Dodge City, KS) **10606**
High Springs Herald, The (High Springs, FL) **10557**
High Timber Times (Pine, CO) **10550**
Hill City Times, The (Hill City, KS) **10606**
Hilliard Northwest News (Hilliard, OH) **10703**
Hillsboro Argus (Hillsboro, OR) **10713**
Hillsboro Journal (Hillsboro, IL) **10582**
Hillsboro Sentry-Enterprise (Hillsboro, WI) **10768**
Hillsboro Star-Journal (Hillsboro, KS) **10606**
Hillsborough Beacon (Somerville, NJ) **10670**
Hillside Leader (Union, NJ) **10670**
Hilltop News-Press (Cincinnati, OH) **10700**
Hilmar Times (Hilmar, CA) **10535**
Hingham Journal & Mariner (Marshfield, MA) **10626**
Hinsdale Doings (Hinsdale, IL) **10582**

WEEKLY NEWSPAPERS   Independent Herald, The   10893

Hinton News (Hinton, WV)   **10761**
Hobart Democrat-Chief (Hobart, OK)   **10710**
Hobart Gazette (Merriville, IN)   **10596**
Hobbs Flare (Hobbs, NM)   **10672**
Hoboken Reporter (Hoboken, NJ)   **10666**
Hocking Valley Advertiser (Logan, OH)   **10704**
† Hodgkins Citizen (La Grange, IL)
Hoisington Dispatch (Hoisington, KS)   **10606**
Holbert Lake Station Community Shopping
   Guide (Merrillville, IN)   **10596**
Holbrook Sun (Marshfield, MA)   **10626**
Holbrook Times (Stoughton, MA)   **10628**
Holbrook Tribune News & Snowflake Herald
   (Holbrook, AZ)   **10525**
Holden Image-Progress, The
   (Holden, MO)   **10654**
Holly Hill Observer, The (Holly Hill, SC)   **10727**
† Hollywood Citizen News (Los Angeles, CA)
Holmes County Advertiser (Bonifay, FL)   **10555**
Holmes County Hub (Millersburg, OH)   **10705**
Holt Community News (Holt, MI)   **10634**
Holton Recorder (Holton, KS)   **10606**
Holtville Tribune (Holtville, CA)   **10535**
Home & Store News (Ramsey, NJ)   **10670**
Home News, The (Marshville, NC)   **10693**
Homer News (Homer, AK)   **10523**
† Homestead/Florida City News (Miami, FL)
Home Times (West Palm Beach, FL)   **10562**
Hometown News (Madison, WV)   **10762**
Hominy News-Progress (Hominy, OK)   **10710**
Hondo Anvil Herald (Hondo, TX)   **10741**
Hood County News (Granbury, TX)   **10741**
Hood River News (Hood River, OR)   **10713**
Hoopeston Chronicle (Hoopeston, IL)   **10582**
Hoosier Express (Washington, IN)   **10598**
Hopkins Journal, The (Hopkins, MO)   **10654**
Hopkins Sun-Sailor (Minnetonka, MN)   **10644**
Horicon Reporter (Horicon, WI)   **10768**
Horry Independent (Conway, SC)   **10727**
Houghton Lake Resorter (Houghton
   Lake, MI)   **10634**
Houlton Pioneer Times (Houlton, ME)   **10619**
Housatonic Weekend (New Milford, CT)   **10553**
Houston County Courier (Crockett, TX)   **10738**
Houston Forward Times (Houston, TX)   **10742**
Houston Herald & Republican
   (Houston, MO)   **10654**
Houston Informer (Houston, TX)   **10742**
Houston Times-Journal (Perry, GA)   **10567**
▼Howard Beach Resident
   (Maspeth, NY)   **10681**
Howard County Times (Columbia, MD)   **10621**
Howe Enterprise (Howe, TX)   **10742**
Hubbard City News (Mexia, TX)   **10744**
† Hubbard News (Niles, OH)
Huber Heights Courier (Dayton, OH)   **10703**

Hudson-Litchfield News (Hudson, NH)   **10663**
Hudson Current (Hoboken, NJ)   **10666**
Hudson Herald, The (Hudson, IA)   **10601**
Hudson Hub-Times (Stow, OH)   **10707**
Hudson Star-Observer (Hudson, WI)   **10768**
Hughes County Times (Wetumka, OK)   **10712**
Hughson Chronicle (Winton, CA)   **10546**
Humble Sun (Humble, TX)   **10742**
Humboldt Beacon (Fortuna, CA)   **10534**
Humboldt Independent (Humboldt, IA)   **10601**
† Humboldt Republican (Humboldt, IA)
Humbolt Journal (Canistota, SD)   **10729**
Humeston New Era (Humeston, IA)   **10601**
Hungry Horse News (Columbia
   Falls, MT)   **10659**
Hunt County Shopper (Greenville, TX)   **10741**
Hunterdon County Democrat
   (Flemington, NJ)   **10666**
Hunterdon Review (Lebanon, NJ)   **10667**
† Huntingdon Carroll Leader (Huntingdon, TN)
Huntington Beach/Fountain Valley Independent
   (Huntington Beach, CA)   **10535**
Huntington Harbour Sun (Seal
   Beach, CA)   **10545**
Huntley Farmside, The (Huntley, IL)   **10582**
Hurricane Breeze (Hurricane, WV)   **10761**
Hustler, The (South Pittsburg, TN)   **10735**
Hutchinson Herald, The (Menno, SD)   **10730**
Hutchinson Leader (Hutchinson, MN)   **10642**
Hyde Park Herald (Chicago, IL)   **10575**
Hyde Park Townsman (Hyde Park, NY)   **10679**
Idaho County Free Press
   (Grangeville, ID)   **10569**
Idaho Enterprise (Malad City, ID)   **10570**
Idaho Mountain Express (Ketchum, ID)   **10570**
Idalou Beacon (Idalou, TX)   **10742**
Ile Camera, The (Grosse Ile, MI)   **10633**
Illinois Times (Springfield, IL)   **10589**
Illiopolis Sentinel (Illiopolis, IL)   **10582**
Impact of Laurel (Laurel, MS)   **10650**
Improper Bostonian, The (Boston, MA)   **10624**
Independence Bulletin-Journal
   (Independence, IA)   **10601**
Independence News-Wave
   (Independence, WI)   **10768**
Independence News, The
   (Independence, KS)   **10606**
Independent (Collierville, TN)   **10731**
Independent (Deerfield, WI)   **10766**
Independent-Journal, The (Potosi, MO)   **10656**
Independent-Messenger (Emporia, VA)   **10752**
Independent-Register, The
   (Brodhead, WI)   **10765**
Independent Appeal (Selmer, TN)   **10735**
Independent Enterprise (Payette, ID)   **10570**
Independent Herald, The (Pineville, WV)   **10762**

ULRICH'S INTERNATIONAL PERIODICALS DIRECTORY 1998

Independent Mirror (Mexico, NY) **10681**
Independent News (Georgetown, IL) **10579**
Independent News Herald
  (Clarissa, MN) **10641**
Independent Observer, The
  (Scottdale, PA) **10724**
† Independent Press (Marine City, MI)
Independent Press (New
  Providence, NJ) **10668**
Independent Press of Bloomfield, The
  (Bloomfield, NJ) **10664**
Independent Republican (Goshen, NY) **10678**
Independent, The (Robertsdale, AL) **10521**
Independent, The (Livermore, CA) **10536**
Independent, The (Winamac, IN) **10598**
Independent, The (Flint, MI) **10632**
Independent, The (Durham, NC) **10692**
Independent, The (Morganville, NJ) **10668**
Independent, The (Collegeville, PA) **10716**
Independent, The (Montrose, PA) **10720**
Indianapolis Recorder (Indianapolis, IN) **10594**
Indianapolis Westside Enterprise
  (Greenfield, IN) **10594**
Indianhead Advertiser (Frederic, WI) **10767**
Indian Head Park (Hinsdale, IL) **10582**
Indian Head Park Citizen (Oak
  Brook, IL) **10586**
Indio Advertiser (Palm Desert, CA) **10540**
Indio Post (Indio, CA) **10535**
Indy Suburban Newspapers
  (Greenfield, IN) **10594**
Ingham County News (Mason, MI) **10635**
Inglewood/Hawthorne Wave (Los
  Angeles, CA) **10537**
Inglewood Tribune (Compton, CA) **10533**
Inkster Ledger-Star (Wayne, MI) **10639**
In Pittsburgh Newsweekly
  (Pittsburgh, PA) **10723**
Inquirer & Mirror, The (Nantucket, MA) **10626**
Inside (Chicago, IL) **10575**
† Inside Ravenswood (Chicago, IL)
Inter-County Leader (Frederic, WI) **10767**
† Interboro News (Prospect Park, PA)
Interior Journal (Stanford, KY) **10614**
Interlaken Review (Trumansburg, NY) **10688**
Intermountain News (Burney, CA) **10531**
Inyo Register (Bishop, CA) **10531**
In Your Community/Oakland Press
  (Pontiac, MI) **10637**
Iola Herald (Iola, WI) **10768**
Iosco County News Herald (East
  Tawas, MI) **10632**
Iowa Park Leader (Iowa Park, TX) **10742**
Ipswich Chronicle (Ipswich, MA) **10625**
Ipswich Tribune (Ipswich, SD) **10730**
Iron County Miner (Hurley, WI) **10768**
Irondequoit Press (Rochester, NY) **10685**
Iron River Reporter (Iron River, MI) **10634**
Irvine World News (Irvine, CA) **10535**
Irving News (Arlington, TX) **10736**
Irvington Viewpoint, The (Irvington, NY) **10679**
Island Ad-Vantages (Stonington, ME) **10620**
Island Connection (Portland, OR) **10714**
Island Dispatch (Grand Island, NY) **10678**
Islander, The (Gulf Shores, AL) **10519**
Islander, The (Gulf Breeze, FL) **10557**
Islander, The (St. Simons Island, GA) **10568**
Islander, The (South Hero, VT) **10750**
Island Reporter (Sanibel, FL) **10560**
Islesboro Island News (Islesboro, ME) **10619**
Islip Bulletin (Sayville, NY) **10685**
Islip News (Smithtown, NY) **10686**
Issaquah Press (Issaquah, WA) **10758**
Isthmus (Madison, WI) **10769**
Itawamba County Times, The
  (Fulton, MS) **10649**
Item (Clinton, MA) **10624**
Ithaca Times (Ithaca, NY) **10679**
Iuka Tishomingo County News
  (Iuka, MS) **10650**
Jackson-Vinton Journal-Herald
  (Jackson, OH) **10703**
Jackson County Banner
  (Brownstown, IN) **10592**
Jackson County Herald/Tribune
  (Edna, TX) **10739**
Jackson County Livewire (Jackson, MN) **10642**
Jackson County Star (Walden, CO) **10551**
Jackson Heights News (Maspeth, NY) **10681**
Jackson Herald (Jefferson, GA) **10566**
Jackson Herald (Ripley, WV) **10763**
Jackson Hole Guide (Jackson, WY) **10776**
Jackson Hole News (Jackson, WY) **10776**
Jackson Independent, The
  (Jonesboro, LA) **10616**
Jackson Progress-Argus (Jackson, GA) **10565**
Jackson Star News (Ravenswood, WV) **10762**
Jacksonville News (Jacksonville, AL) **10520**
Jacksonville Shopping Guide
  (Jacksonville, FL) **10557**
▼Jamaica Times, The (Flushing, NY) **10677**
Jamestown Press, The (Jamestown, RI) **10725**
Jasper County News, The (Bay
  Springs, MS) **10649**
Jasper County Sun (Ridgeland, SC) **10728**
Jasper Journal (Jasper, MN) **10643**
Jasper Journal (Jasper, TN) **10732**
Jasper News (Jasper, FL) **10557**
Jasper NewsBoy (Jasper, TX) **10742**
Jasper NewsBoy Shopper (Jasper, TX) **10742**
Jeanerette Enterprise (Jeanerette, LA) **10616**
Jeannette Spirit (Jeannette, PA) **10718**

WEEKLY NEWSPAPERS

Jeff Davis Ledger (Hazlehurst, GA) **10565**
Jefferson Bee (Jefferson, IA) **10602**
Jefferson County Journal (Arnold, MO) **10651**
Jefferson County Journal (Adams, NY) **10672**
Jefferson County Transcript
  (Golden, CO) **10549**
Jefferson Herald (Jefferson, IA) **10602**
Jeffersonian Democrat (Brookville, PA) **10716**
Jeffersonian, The (Baltimore, MD) **10621**
Jeffersonian, The (Croswell, MI) **10631**
Jefferson Jimplecute (Jefferson, TX) **10742**
Jefferson Park/Portage Park/Bel Cragin Times
  (Lincolnwood, IL) **10584**
Jefferson Post (West Jefferson, NC) **10695**
† Jefferson Republic, The (De Soto, MO)
Jefferson Sentinel (Lakewood, CO) **10549**
Jefferson Star, The (Rigby, ID) **10570**
Jekyll's Golden Islander
  (Brunswick, GA) **10563**
Jellico Advance Sentinel (La
  Follette, TN) **10733**
Jena Times Olla-Tullos Signal
  (Jena, LA) **10616**
Jenks Journal (Tulsa, OK) **10711**
Jersey City Reporter (Hoboken, NJ) **10666**
Jessamine Journal (Nicholasville, KY) **10613**
† Jet Gazette (Austin, TX)
Jetmore Republican (Jetmore, KS) **10606**
† Jet Visitor (Cherokee, OK)
Jewish Journal of Greater Los Angeles, The (Los
  Angeles, CA) **10537**
Johnsonburg Press, Inc., The
  (Johnsonburg, PA) **10719**
Johnson County Graphic
  (Clarksville, AR) **10527**
Johnson County Sun (Shawnee
  Mission, KS) **10608**
Johnson Pioneer (Johnson, KS) **10606**
Johnston County Capital-Democrat
  (Tishomingo, OK) **10711**
Johnstown Independent
  (Columbus, OH) **10701**
Jones County Town Crier
  (Anamosa, IA) **10599**
Journal & Austin Chronicle
  (Scottsburg, IN) **10597**
Journal & Monitor Herald (Tomah, WI) **10774**
Journal & Republican (Lowville, NY) **10680**
Journal-Enterprise (Providence, KY) **10614**
Journal-Herald, The (White Haven, PA) **10725**
Journal-Leader (Caldwell, OH) **10699**
Journal-Patriot (North Wilkesboro, NC) **10693**
Journal/Express (Knoxville, IA) **10602**
Journal/Valley Views (White Haven, PA) **10725**
† Journal Courier (Moravia, NY)
Journal Herald, The (Shawnee, KS) **10608**

Journal News (Spencerville, OH) **10707**
Journal Opinion (Bradford, VT) **10749**
Journal Press (Lawrenceburg, IN) **10595**
Journal Record (Hamilton, AL) **10520**
Journal Register (Palmer, MA) **10627**
Journal, The (Chicago, IL) **10575**
Journal, The (Ellettsville, IN) **10593**
Journal, The (Crosby, ND) **10696**
Journal, The (Voorhees, NJ) **10671**
Journal, The (Struthers, OH) **10707**
Journal, The (Mt. Pleasant, SC) **10728**
Journal, The (Williamston, SC) **10729**
Journal, The (King George, VA) **10753**
† Journal Transcript (Franklin, NH)
Journal Tribune (Williamsburg, IA) **10605**
Journal Tribune (Seneca, SC) **10729**
Julesburg Advocate (Julesburg, CO) **10549**
Junction Eagle, The (Junction, TX) **10742**
Juneau County Star-Times
  (Mauston, WI) **10769**
Juniata News (Philadelphia, PA) **10722**
Juniata Sentinel (Mifflintown, PA) **10720**
Jupiter Courier (Jupiter, FL) **10558**
Kalona News, The (Kalona, IA) **10602**
Kanabec County Times (Mora, MN) **10644**
† Kansas Business News (Augusta, KS)
Karnes Citation (Karnes City, TX) **10742**
Katahdin Times (Millinocket, ME) **10619**
Kaufman Herald, The (Kaufman, TX) **10742**
Kaukauna Times (Kaukauna, WI) **10768**
Kayo, The (Clinton, MO) **10652**
Keith County News (Ogallala, NE) **10661**
Keller Citizen, The (Keller, TX) **10742**
Kelly Observer (San Antonio, TX) **10746**
Kemmerer Gazette (Kemmerer, WY) **10776**
Kemper County Messenger
  (DeKalb, MS) **10649**
Ken-Ton Bee (Williamsville, NY) **10689**
Kenbridge-Victoria Dispatch
  (Victoria, VA) **10756**
Kendall County Record (Yorkville, IL) **10591**
Kendall News-Gazette (Miami, FL) **10559**
Kendrick-Gazette (Kendrick, ID) **10569**
Kenilworth Leader (Union, NJ) **10670**
Kenly News (Kenly, NC) **10692**
Kennedale News (Everman, TX) **10740**
Kennedy Advanced Times (Karnes
  City, TX) **10742**
Kennesaw Neighbor, The (Marietta, GA) **10566**
Kent County News (Chestertown, MD) **10621**
Kent Good Times Dispatch (Kent, CT) **10552**
Kenton County Recorder (Florence, KY) **10610**
Kentucky Standard (Bardstown, KY) **10609**
Kentwood Advance (Jenison, MI) **10634**
Kentwood News-Ledger (Kentwood, LA) **10617**
Kenyon Leader (Kenyon, MN) **10643**

Kerman News (Kerman, CA) **10535**
Kernersville News (Kernersville, NC) **10692**
Kern Valley Sun (Lake Isabella, CA) **10536**
Kettering-Oakwood Times (Kettering, OH) **10704**
Kettle Moraine Index (Hartland, WI) **10767**
Kewaskum Statesman (Kewaskum, WI) **10768**
Kewaunee Enterprise (Kewaunee, WI) **10768**
Keystone Reporter (Elroy, WI) **10767**
Kiel Tri-County Record (Kiel, WI) **10768**
King City Rustler (King City, CA) **10535**
Kingfisher Times & Free Press (Kingfisher, OK) **10710**
Kingman Journal (Kingman, KS) **10607**
King of Prussia Courier (King of Prussia, PA) **10719**
Kingsburg Recorder (Kingsburg, CA) **10535**
Kings County News (Brooklyn, NY) **10674**
Kings Courier (Brooklyn, NY) **10675**
Kings Mountain Herald (Kings Mountain, NC) **10692**
Kingston Independent (Marshfield, MA) **10626**
Kingston Reporter (Plymouth, MA) **10627**
Kingsville Record, The (Kingsville, TX) **10743**
King Times News (King, NC) **10692**
Kingwood Sun (Humble, TX) **10742**
Kinmundy Express (Kinmundy, IL) **10583**
Kiowa County Press (Eads, CO) **10548**
† Kirtland Enterprise (Willoughby, OH)
Knoxville Journal, The (Galesburg, IL) **10579**
Konawa Leader (Konawa, OK) **10710**
† Kossuth County Advance (Algona, IA)
Kuna-Melba News (Kuna, ID) **10570**
L'Anse Sentinel (L'Anse, MI) **10635**
L'Observateur (La Place, LA) **10617**
Labor Herald (Baltimore, MD) **10621**
La Canada Valley Sun (La Canada, CA) **10535**
Lackland Tale Spinner (San Antonio, TX) **10746**
Lacon Home Journal (Lacon, IL) **10583**
La Crosse County Countryman (West Salem, WI) **10775**
Ladysmith News (Ladysmith, WI) **10768**
Lafayette Leader (Lafayette, IN) **10595**
Lafayette Sun, The (Lafayette, AL) **10520**
La Feria News (La Feria, TX) **10743**
La Follette Press (La Follette, TN) **10733**
La Grange Independent (Mahopac, NY) **10681**
La Grange Standard News (La Grange, IN) **10595**
Laguna News Post (Lake Forest, CA) **10536**
Laguna Niguel News (Lake Forest, CA) **10536**
La Habra Star (Anaheim, CA) **10530**
La Jolla Light (La Jolla, CA) **10536**
La Jolla Village News/Golden Triange News (San Diego, CA) **10542**

† Lake Alfred Press (Mulberry, FL)
Lake Area News (Land O' Lakes, FL) **10558**
Lake Cities Sun, The (Lake Dallas, TX) **10743**
Lake City Town Crier (La Follette, TN) **10733**
† Lake Country Chronicle (Buchanan, MI)
Lake Country Reporter (Hartland, WI) **10767**
Lake County Examiner (Lakeview, OR) **10713**
Lake County Leader (Ronan, MT) **10659**
Lake County News-Chronicle (Two Harbors, MN) **10648**
Lake County Star (Crown Point, IN) **10592**
Lake County Star (Big Rapids, MI) **10630**
Lake Edition, The (Lexington, SC) **10728**
Lake Elsinore Valley Sun-Tribune (Lake Elsinore, CA) **10536**
Lakefield Standard (Lakefield, MN) **10643**
Lake Forester (Bannockburn, IL) **10572**
Lake Geneva Regional News (Lake Geneva, WI) **10768**
Lake Havasu City Advertiser (Lake Havasu City, AZ) **10525**
Lakeland Press (Grayslake, IL) **10580**
Lakeland Times (Minocqua, WI) **10770**
Lakeland Today (Butler, NJ) **10665**
Lake Michigan Examiner, The (Muskegon, MI) **10636**
Lake Mills Leader (Lake Mills, WI) **10768**
Lake News (Fruitland Park, FL) **10557**
Lake Oswego Review (Lake Oswego, OR) **10713**
Lake Placid Journal (Lake Placid, FL) **10558**
Lake Placid News (Lake Placid, NY) **10680**
Lake Powell Chronicle (Page, AZ) **10525**
Lakeshore Chronicle (Manitowoc, WI) **10769**
Lakeshore Weekly News (Wayzata, MN) **10648**
▼Lakeside Ledger, The (Woodstock, GA) **10568**
Lakes Region Free Press, The (Granville, NY) **10678**
Lakeview Enterprise (Big Rapids, MI) **10630**
Lake Villa Record (Grayslake, IL) **10580**
Lakeville Independent (Middleboro, MA) **10626**
Lakeville Journal, The (Lakeville, CT) **10553**
Lakeville Life & Times (Lakeville, MN) **10643**
Lakeville Sun-Current (Burnsville, MN) **10640**
† Lake Wales Highlander (Winter Haven, FL)
Lake Wales News (Lake Wales, FL) **10558**
Lakewood Sun Post (North Olmsted, OH) **10706**
Lake Worth Herald Coastal Observer (Lake Worth, FL) **10558**
Lake Zurich Enterprise (Grayslake, IL) **10581**
Lamar Democrat (Vernon, AL) **10522**
Lamar Democrat (Lamar, MO) **10654**
Lamar Leader (Sulligent, AL) **10522**
La Marque Times (La Marque, TX) **10743**

Lamb County Leader-News
  (Littlefield, TX) **10743**
Lamberton News (Lamberton, MN) **10643**
La Mesa Forum (Lemon Grove, CA) **10536**
Lamesa Press-Reporter (Lamesa, TX) **10743**
Lamont Reporter (Lamont, CA) **10536**
Lancaster Bee (Williamsville, NY) **10689**
Lancaster Fairfield Advertiser
  (Carroll, OH) **10699**
Lancaster News (Lancaster, SC) **10728**
Lancaster Today (DeSoto, TX) **10739**
Lander Wyoming State Journal
  (Lander, WY) **10776**
Larimore Pioneer (Northwood, ND) **10697**
LaRue County Herald-News
  (Hodgenville, KY) **10611**
Las Vegas Today (Las Vegas, NV) **10662**
Las Virgenes Enterprise (Woodland
  Hills, CA) **10547**
Lauderdale County Enterprise
  (Ripley, TN) **10734**
Laurel Leader (Laurel, MD) **10622**
Laurens County Advertiser
  (Laurens, SC) **10728**
Laurens Sun, The (Laurens, IA) **10602**
LaVilla News (Hot Springs Village, AR) **10528**
L.A. Weekly (Los Angeles, CA) **10538**
Lawrence County Centennial
  (Deadwood, SD) **10729**
Lawrence County News
  (Lawrenceville, IL) **10583**
Lawrence County Record (Mt.
  Vernon, MO) **10655**
Lawrence Ledger (Pennington, NJ) **10669**
Lawrence Times (Fishers, IN) **10593**
Lawrence Township Journal
  (Lawrence, IN) **10595**
Leader-Courier (Kingman, KS) **10607**
Leader-News (Central City, KY) **10610**
Leader-News (Washburn, ND) **10697**
Leader-Record (Gonvick, MN) **10642**
Leader-State Register, The
  (Seaford, DE) **10554**
Leader-Tribune, The (Fort Valley, GA) **10565**
Leader-Vindicator, The (New
  Bethlehem, PA) **10721**
Leader Enterprise (Montpelier, OH) **10705**
Leader Observer (Maspeth, NY) **10681**
Leader, The (Davenport, IA) **10599**
Leader, The (Solon, IA) **10604**
Leader, The (Charlestown, IN) **10592**
† Leader, The (Lansing, KS)
Leader, The (Northwood, ND) **10697**
Leader, The (Point Pleasant Beach, NJ) **10669**
Leader, The (Freeport, NY) **10677**
Leader, The (Cleveland, OH) **10700**
† Leader, The (East Palestine, OH)
Leader, The (Philadelphia, PA) **10722**
Leader, The (Tremonton, UT) **10749**
Leavenworth Echo (Leavenworth, WA) **10758**
Leawood Sun (Shawnee Mission, KS) **10608**
† Lebanon Connecticut Valley Reporter
  (Lebanon, NH)
Lebanon Enterprise (Lebanon, KY) **10612**
Lebanon Express (Lebanon, OR) **10713**
▼Lebanon Herald (Mascoutah, IL) **10584**
Lebanon News (Lebanon, VA) **10753**
Lebanon Times, The (Lebanon, KS) **10607**
Le Center Leader (Le Center, MN) **10643**
Ledger, The (Moundridge, KS) **10607**
Lee's Summit Journal (Lee's
  Summit, MO) **10654**
Lee County Eagle, The (Auburn, AL) **10517**
Lee County Observer (Bishopville, SC) **10726**
Leeds News (Leeds, AL) **10520**
Leelanau Enterprise (Leland, MI) **10635**
Leesburg Today (Leesburg, VA) **10753**
Lee Town Shopper (Des Moines, IA) **10600**
Lehi Free Press (American Fork, UT) **10748**
Leisure World Golden Rain News (Seal
  Beach, CA) **10545**
Leisure World News (Laguna Hills, CA) **10536**
Lemon Grove Review (Lemon
  Grove, CA) **10536**
Lemont Metropolitan (Lemont, IL) **10583**
Lemont Reporter (Lemont, IL) **10583**
Lenexa Sun (Shawnee Mission, KS) **10608**
Leon Journal-Reporter (Leon, IA) **10602**
Leslie County News (Hyden, KY) **10611**
Leslie Local Independent (Leslie, MI) **10635**
Letcher County Community News-Press
  (Cromona, KY) **10610**
Levelland Hockley County News-Press
  (Levelland, TX) **10743**
Levittown Tribune (Mineola, NY) **10682**
Lewisboro Ledger, The (Ridgefield, CT) **10553**
Lewisburg Tribune (Lewisburg, TN) **10733**
Lewis County Herald (Nezperce, ID) **10570**
Lewis River News (Woodland, WA) **10760**
Lewiston-Porter Sentinel (Grand
  Island, NY) **10678**
Lewiston Journal (Lewiston, MN) **10643**
Lewistown News-Argus (Lewistown, MT) **10659**
Lewisville Leader (Lewisville, TX) **10743**
Lexington Minuteman (Woburn, MA) **10629**
Lexington News (Lexington, MO) **10654**
Lexington Progress (Lexington, TN) **10733**
Liberty Gazette (Liberty, TX) **10743**
† Liberty News (Niles, OH)
Liberty Press, The (Liberty Center, OH) **10704**
Liberty Tribune (Kansas City, MO) **10654**
Libertyville News (Grayslake, IL) **10581**

Libertyville Review (Bannockburn, IL) **10572**
† Licking Countian (Newark, OH)
Licking Valley Courier (West Liberty, KY) **10615**
Life at Ken-Caryl (Littleton, CO) **10549**
Light & Champion (Center, TX) **10737**
Ligonier Advance-Leader (Ligonier, IN) **10595**
Ligonier Echo (Ligonier, PA) **10719**
Ligonier Free Gazette, The (Ligonier, PA) **10719**
Lillie Suburban Shopping Review (St. Paul, MN) **10647**
Lime Springs Herald (Lime Springs, IA) **10602**
Limestone Independent News (Bartonville, IL) **10572**
† Lincoln-Belmont Booster (Chicago, IL)
Lincoln County Journal (Shoshone, ID) **10571**
Lincoln County News (Newcastle, ME) **10620**
Lincoln County News (Chandler, OK) **10709**
Lincoln Heights Bulletin-News (Los Angeles, CA) **10538**
Lincoln Journal (Hamlin, WV) **10761**
Lincoln Ledger (Star City, AR) **10529**
Lincoln News (Lincoln, ME) **10619**
Lincoln Times-News (Lincolnton, NC) **10693**
Lincoln Times, The (Hamlin, WV) **10761**
Lincoln Weekly News Sentinel (Hamlin, WV) **10761**
Lincolnwood Life (Lincolnwood, IL) **10584**
Lincolnwood Review (Evanston, IL) **10579**
Linden Herald (Linden, CA) **10536**
Lindenhurst News (Grayslake, IL) **10581**
Linden Leader (Union, NJ) **10671**
Lindsay Gazette (Lindsay, CA) **10536**
† Linesville Herald (Conneaut Lake, PA)
Linn Unterrified Democrat (Linn, MO) **10654**
Linton Emmons County Record (Linton, ND) **10697**
Lisbon Ransom County Gazette & Enterprise (Lisbon, ND) **10697**
Lisle Sun (Downers Grove, IL) **10577**
Lisle Sun (Naperville, IL) **10586**
Litchfield Enquirer (Litchfield, CT) **10553**
Litchfield Independent Review (Litchfield, MN) **10643**
Lititz Record Express, The (Lititz, PA) **10719**
Little Neck Ledger, The (Flushing, NY) **10677**
Little Paper, The (Melbourne, FL) **10558**
Littleton Independent (Littleton, CO) **10549**
Littleton Independent (Concord, MA) **10624**
Littleton Observer (Littleton, NC) **10693**
† Littleton Times (Littleton, CO)
Livermore Falls Advertiser (Livermore Falls, ME) **10619**
Liverpool Review (Syracuse, NY) **10687**
† Livingston East Texas Eye (Livingston, TX)

Livingston Enterprise (Livingston, TN) **10733**
Livingston Leader (Denham Springs, LA) **10616**
Livonia Observer (Livonia, MI) **10635**
Llano News (Llano, TX) **10744**
Lockeford-Clements News (Lockeford, CA) **10537**
Lockhart Post Register (Lockhart, TX) **10744**
Locust Valley Leader (Locust Valley, NY) **10680**
Loda Times (Paxton, IL) **10588**
Lodi Enterprise (Lodi, WI) **10768**
Logan Herald Observer (Logan, IA) **10602**
Lombardian, The (Lombard, IL) **10584**
Lombardian Villa Park Review (Lombard, IL) **10584**
Lombard Spectator (Elmhurst, IL) **10578**
† London Mills Times (Roseville, IL)
Lone Tree Reporter, The (Lone Tree, IA) **10602**
Long Beach Chinook Observer (Long Beach, WA) **10758**
† Long Beach Community News (Long Beach, CA)
Long Beach Herald (Long Beach, NY) **10680**
Long Beach Independent Voice (Mineola, NY) **10682**
Long Island Advance (Patchogue, NY) **10684**
Long Island City/Astoria Journal (Maspeth, NY) **10681**
Long Island Graphic-Roosevelt Press (Lawrence, NY) **10680**
† Long Island Journal Newspaper Group (Long Beach, NY)
▼Long Island Voice (Mineola, NY) **10682**
Longmeadow News (Westfield, MA) **10629**
Long Prairie Leader (Long Prairie, MN) **10643**
Long Valley Advocate, The (Cascade, ID) **10569**
Lorain County Times, The (Rocky River, OH) **10707**
Lorenzo Examiner (Lorenzo, TX) **10744**
Loris Times (Loris, SC) **10728**
Los Altos Town Crier (Los Altos, CA) **10537**
Los Angeles Independent (Los Angeles, CA) **10538**
Los Angeles Log (San Diego, CA) **10542**
Los Banos Enterprise (Los Banos, CA) **10538**
Los Gatos Weekly-Times (Los Gatos, CA) **10539**
Lost River Star (Merrill, OR) **10714**
Loudenville Weekly (Delmar, NY) **10676**
Loudonville Times, The (Loudonville, OH) **10704**
Loudoun Times-Mirror (Leesburg, VA) **10753**

WEEKLY NEWSPAPERS

Louisiana Press-Journal (Louisiana, MO) **10654**
Louisville Herald, The (Louisville, OH) **10704**
Louisville Winston County Journal (Louisville, MS) **10650**
Loveland Herald Press (Loveland, OH) **10704**
Lovell Chronicle, The (Lovell, WY) **10776**
Lovelock Review-Miner (Lovelock, NV) **10662**
Lowell Ledger (Lowell, MI) **10635**
Lowell Tribune (Lowell, IN) **10595**
Lower Township Lantern (Rio Grande, NJ) **10670**
Loyal Tribune-Record-Gleaner (Loyal, WI) **10769**
Ludlow Register (Palmer, MA) **10627**
Ludowici News (Ludowici, GA) **10566**
Luling Newsboy & Signal (Luling, TX) **10744**
Lusk Herald (Lusk, WY) **10776**
Lutz Community News (Tampa, FL) **10561**
Luverne Journal & News (Luverne, AL) **10520**
Luxemburg News (Luxemburg, WI) **10769**
Lynbrook USA (Mineola, NY) **10682**
Lynden Tribune (Lynden, WA) **10758**
Lynwood Journal (Compton, CA) **10533**
Lynwood Press (Los Angeles, CA) **10538**
Lyon-Sioux Press (Rock Rapids, IA) **10603**
Lyons Mirror-Sun (Lyons, NE) **10661**
M & M Journal (Hillsboro, IL) **10582**
Mableton Neighbor, The (Marietta, GA) **10566**
Machias Valley News Observer (Machias, ME) **10619**
Macomb Voice, The (New Baltimore, MI) **10636**
Macon Beacon, The (Macon, MS) **10650**
Macon County Times (Lafayette, TN) **10733**
Macoupin & Montgomery County Journal (Hillsboro, IL) **10582**
Macoupin County Enquirer (Carlinville, IL) **10574**
Macoupin County Shopper (Hillsboro, IL) **10582**
Madill Record (Madill, OK) **10710**
Madison County Carrier (Madison, FL) **10558**
Madison County Chronicle (Worden, IL) **10591**
Madison County Eagle (Madison, VA) **10754**
Madison County Herald (Canton, MS) **10649**
Madison County Record (Madison, AL) **10520**
Madison County Record (Huntsville, AR) **10528**
Madison Eagle (Madison, NJ) **10667**
Madison Enterprise Recorder (Madison, FL) **10558**
Madisonian, The (Madison, GA) **10566**
Madison Journal (Tallulah, LA) **10618**
Madison Messenger, The (Madison, NC) **10693**
Madison News Inc., The (Madison, KS) **10607**

Madison Park Times (Seattle, WA) **10759**
† Madison Tribune (Ontario, OH)
Madison Western Guard, The (Madison, MN) **10643**
Madras Pioneer, The (Madras, OR) **10714**
Magee Courier (Magee, MS) **10650**
Magic Valley Shopper's News (Camden, TN) **10731**
Magna Times (Magna, UT) **10749**
Magnolia Gazette, The (Magnolia, MS) **10650**
Mahnomen Pioneer, The (Mahnomen, MN) **10643**
Mahopac Press (Mahopac, NY) **10681**
Mail-Journal, The (Milford, IN) **10596**
Maine Times (Portland, ME) **10620**
Mainland Journal (Hammonton, NJ) **10666**
† Main Line Chronicle (West Chester, PA)
Main Line Life (Ardmore, PA) **10716**
Main Line Times (Ardmore, PA) **10716**
Main Street Trilogy (Townsend, MA) **10629**
† Malden Press-Merit (Malden, MO)
Malheur Enterprise (Vale, OR) **10715**
Malibu Surfside News (Malibu, CA) **10539**
Malibu Times (Malibu, CA) **10539**
Malta Messenger (Ballston Spa, NY) **10673**
Malvern Community News (Minerva, OH) **10705**
Malverne Community Times (Mineola, NY) **10682**
Malvern Leader, The (Malvern, IA) **10602**
† Mammoth Lakes Review/Mono Herald (Mammoth Lakes, CA)
Mammoth Times (Mammoth Lakes, CA) **10539**
Mamou Acadian Press (Mamou, LA) **10617**
Manchester Enterprise (Manchester, KY) **10612**
Manchester Journal (Manchester Center, VT) **10750**
Manchester Press (Manchester, IA) **10602**
Manchester Signal (Manchester, OH) **10705**
Manchester Star-Mercury (Manchester, GA) **10566**
Manchester Times (Manchester, TN) **10733**
Mancos Times-Tribune (Mancos, CO) **10550**
Mandan News (Mandan, ND) **10697**
Manhasset Press (Mineola, NY) **10682**
Manistee Observer (Manistee, MI) **10635**
Manistique Pioneer-Tribune (Manistique, MI) **10635**
Mansfield Enterprise (Mansfield, LA) **10617**
Mansfield News (Mansfield, MA) **10625**
Mansfield News-Mirror (Mansfield, TX) **10744**
Manville News (Somerville, NJ) **10670**
Maple Heights Press (Bedford, OH) **10699**
Maple Shade Progress (Maple Shade, NJ) **10667**

Maple Valley News (Hastings, MI) **10633**
Maplewood Review (St. Paul, MN) **10647**
Maquoketa Sentinel-Press (Maquoketa, IA) **10602**
† Marathon Independent Newspaper (Marathon, NY)
Marble Falls Highlander (Marble Falls, TX) **10744**
Marblehead Reporter (Marblehead, MA) **10625**
Marceline Press (Marceline, MO) **10655**
Marcellus Observer (Skaneateles, NY) **10686**
Marco Island Eagle, The (Marco Island, FL) **10558**
Marcus Hook Press (Drexel Hill, PA) **10717**
Marianna Courier Index (Marianna, AR) **10528**
Maries County Gazette (Vienna, MO) **10658**
Marin Scope (Sausalito, CA) **10544**
Marion Advertiser (Marion, WI) **10769**
Marion County Record (Marion, KS) **10607**
Marion Star & Mullins Enterprise (Marion, SC) **10728**
Marion Times-Standard (Marion, AL) **10520**
Mariposa Gazette (Mariposa, CA) **10539**
† Market Place (Vandergrift, PA)
Market Shopper, The (Delano, CA) **10533**
Marlboro Herald-Advocate (Bennettsville, SC) **10726**
Marlboro Shopper (Bennettsville, SC) **10726**
Marquette County Tribune (Montello, WI) **10770**
† Marshall County Life (Culver, IN)
Marshall Gazette (Lewisburg, TN) **10733**
Marshall Mountain Wave (Marshall, AR) **10528**
Marshfield Mail (Marshfield, MO) **10655**
Marshfield Mariner (Marshfield, MA) **10626**
Marshfield Reporter (Plymouth, MA) **10627**
Marthasville Record, The (Marthasville, MO) **10655**
† Mart Herald (Mart, TX)
† Martin County News (Stuart, FL)
Martinez News Gazette (Martinez, CA) **10539**
Maryland Gazette (Glen Burnie, MD) **10621**
Maryland Independent (Waldorf, MD) **10623**
Maryland Times-Press (Ocean City, MD) **10622**
Marysville Advocate, The (Marysville, KS) **10607**
Mascoutah Herald (Mascoutah, IL) **10584**
Mashpee Messenger (Yarmouth, MA) **10630**
Mason County News (Mason, TX) **10744**
Mason Valley News (Yerington, NV) **10663**
Massapequan Observer (Mineola, NY) **10682**
Massapequa Post (Massapequa Park, NY) **10681**
Mathis News (Mathis, TX) **10744**
† Matthews News (Matthews, NC)

† Maumee Valley Herald (Toledo, OH)
Maynard Beacon (Concord, MA) **10624**
Mayville Monitor (Mayville, MI) **10635**
Mayville News, The (Mayville, WI) **10769**
Mayville Sentinel/Chautauqua News (Westfield, NY) **10689**
Maywood Herald (Oak Park, IL) **10587**
McConnellsburg Fulton County News (McConnellsburg, PA) **10719**
McCreary County Record (Whitley City, KY) **10615**
McDonough-Democrat (Bushnell, IL) **10573**
McDuffie Progress, The (Thomson, GA) **10568**
McFarland Community Life (Monona, WI) **10770**
† McFarland Leader (Monona, WI)
McIntosh Times (McIntosh, MN) **10643**
McKenzie Banner (McKenzie, TN) **10733**
McLean County Independent (Garrison, ND) **10696**
McLean County Journal (Turtle Lake, ND) **10697**
McLean Providence Journal (Reston, VA) **10755**
McLeansboro Times-Leader (McLeansboro, IL) **10584**
Meade County Messenger (Brandenburg, KY) **10609**
Meade County Times-Tribune (Sturgis, SD) **10730**
Meadowbrook Times (Lawrence, NY) **10680**
Mebane Enterprise (Mebane, NC) **10693**
Mechanicsville Local (Mechanicsville, VA) **10754**
Mecklenburg Gazette (Davidson, NC) **10691**
Mecklenburg Sun (Clarksville, VA) **10752**
Medfield Suburban Press (Needham, MA) **10627**
▼Medina Sun, The (Medina, OH) **10705**
Meeker Herald, The (Meeker, CO) **10550**
Melrose Beacon (Melrose, MN) **10643**
Melrose Chronicle (Melrose, WI) **10769**
Melrose Free Press (Melrose, MA) **10626**
Melrose Park Herald (Oak Park, IL) **10587**
Melrose Park Star-Sentinel (Melrose Park, IL) **10585**
† Melrose Shoppers News (Stoneham, MA)
Memphis Flyer (Memphis, TN) **10734**
Menard County Review (Greenview, IL) **10581**
Menard News & Messenger, The (Menard, TX) **10744**
Mena Star (Mena, AR) **10528**
Mendocino Beacon, The (Mendocino, CA) **10539**
Mendota Reporter (Mendota, IL) **10585**
Menifee Valley News (Sun City, CA) **10545**

WEEKLY NEWSPAPERS

Menomonee Falls News (New Berlin, WI) **10771**
Mequon-Thiensville Courant (New Berlin, WI) **10771**
Merced County Times (Winton, CA) **10546**
Mercer County Chronicle (Coldwater, OH) **10701**
Mercer Island Reporter (Mercer Island, WA) **10758**
Meriwether Free Press (Greenville, GA) **10565**
Meriwether Vindicator (Manchester, GA) **10566**
Merrick Beacon (Hicksville, NY) **10679**
Merrick Life (Merrick, NY) **10681**
Merrillville Herald Community Shopping Guide (Merrillville, IN) **10596**
Merrimack Valley Sunday (Amesbury, MA) **10623**
Mesa County Mail (Fruita, CO) **10549**
Mesa Tribune Wave (Los Angeles, CA) **10538**
Mesquite News (Mesquite, TX) **10744**
Message for the Week (Chester, VT) **10749**
Messenger-Press (Hightstown, NJ) **10666**
Messenger Index (Emmett, ID) **10569**
Messenger, The (Attica, IN) **10591**
Messenger, The (Garfield, NJ) **10666**
Messenger, The (Clemson, SC) **10727**
Messenger, The (Madison, TN) **10733**
Metro (San Jose, CA) **10543**
Metrocom Herald, The (San Antonio, TX) **10746**
Metropolis Planet (Metropolis, IL) **10585**
Metropolitan News (Brooklyn, NY) **10675**
Metro Press (Millbury, OH) **10705**
Metro Times (Detroit, MI) **10632**
Metro Weekenders, The (Norfolk, VA) **10754**
Miami Beach News (South Miami, FL) **10561**
Miami Chief, The (Miami, TX) **10744**
Miami County Republic (Paola, KS) **10608**
Miami Laker (Miami Lakes, FL) **10559**
Miamisburg News (Miamisburg, OH) **10705**
† Miami Shores News (Miami, FL)
Miami Today (Miami, FL) **10559**
Michigan Chronicle (Detroit, MI) **10632**
† Mid-Cities News (Arlington, TX)
Mid-County Journal (St. Louis, MO) **10657**
† Mid-County Times (Pardeeville, WI)
Mid-Island Times (Hicksville, NY) **10679**
Mid-South Horse Review (Somerville, TN) **10735**
Midcounty Chronicle (Nederland, TX) **10745**
Middleboro Gazette (Middleboro, MA) **10626**
Middlesex-Dunellen Chronicle (Somerville, NJ) **10670**
Middleton Gazette (Middleton, ID) **10570**

Middleton Times-Tribune (Middleton, WI) **10769**
Middletown Courier (Middletown, NJ) **10668**
Middletown News, The (Middletown, IN) **10596**
Middletown Valley Citizen (Brunswick, MD) **10621**
Mid Hudson Times (Walden, NY) **10688**
Midlothian-Bremen Messenger (Midlothian, IL) **10585**
Midlothian Mirror (Midlothian, TX) **10744**
Midlothian Today (DeSoto, TX) **10739**
† MidMon Observer (Washington, PA)
Mid Valley News (El Monte, CA) **10533**
Mid Valley Town Crier (Weslaco, TX) **10747**
MidWeek (Kaneohe, HI) **10568**
Midweek Eagle (West Fargo, ND) **10698**
Midweek Plus (West Fargo, ND) **10698**
MidWeek, The (DeKalb, IL) **10576**
Mifflinburg Telegraph, The (Mifflinburg, PA) **10720**
Milan Area Leader (Milan, MI) **10635**
Milan Standard, The (Milan, MO) **10655**
Milbrae Recorder-Progress (San Mateo, CA) **10543**
Milford Advertiser (Loveland, OH) **10704**
Milford Cabinet & Wilton Journal (Milford, NH) **10663**
Milford Times (Milford, MI) **10635**
Millard County Gazette (Delta, UT) **10748**
Millbrae & San Bruno Sun (Burlingame, CA) **10531**
Millbrook Round Table (Millbrook, NY) **10682**
Millburn & Short Hills Item (Millburn, NJ) **10668**
Millbury/Sutton Chronicle (Millbury, MA) **10626**
Millcreek Sun (Erie, PA) **10717**
Mille Lacs County Times (Milaca, MN) **10643**
Miller County Liberal (Colquitt, GA) **10564**
Millerton News, The (Millerton, NY) **10682**
Millington Star, The (Millington, TN) **10734**
Millstadt Enterprise (Columbia, IL) **10576**
Mill Valley Herald (Sausalito, CA) **10544**
Milpitas Post (Milpitas, CA) **10539**
Milton Courier (Milton, WI) **10769**
Milton Record Transcript (Milton Village, MA) **10626**
Miltonvale Record (Miltonvale, KS) **10607**
Milwaukee Star (Milwaukee, WI) **10769**
Minden Courier, The (Minden, NE) **10661**
Mineola American (Mineola, NY) **10682**
Mineral County Independent-News (Hawthorne, NV) **10662**
Mineral County Miner (Monte Vista, CO) **10550**
Minerva Leader (Minerva, OH) **10705**

Minidoka County News (Rupert, ID) **10570**
Minifee County News (Morehead, KY) **10613**
Minnetonka/Deephaven Sun-Sailor
 (Minnetonka, MN) **10644**
Minonk News Dispatch (Minonk, IL) **10586**
Mira Mesa/Scripps Ranch Sentinel (San
 Diego, CA) **10542**
Mirror-Exchange (Milan, TN) **10734**
† Mirror-Recorder (Stamford, NY)
Mishawaka Enterprise (Mishawaka, IN) **10596**
Mississippi Eagle News, The
 (Warsaw, IL) **10590**
Missouri Press News (Columbia, MO) **10652**
Missouri Valley Times-News (Missouri
 Valley, IA) **10602**
Mitchell County Press-News (Osage, IA) **10603**
Mitchell News Journal (Spruce
 Pine, NC) **10695**
Mobile Beacon (Mobile, AL) **10521**
Modern News (Harrisburg, AR) **10527**
Modoc County Record (Alturas, CA) **10530**
Mojave Desert News, The (California
 City, CA) **10531**
Monadnock Ledger (Peterborough, NH) **10663**
Monahans News (Monahans, TX) **10744**
Mondovi Herald News (Mondovi, WI) **10770**
Moneysaver, The (Ballston Spa, NY) **10673**
Monitor, The (Mabank, TX) **10744**
Monroe County Appeal (Paris, MO) **10655**
Monroe County Beacon
 (Woodsfield, OH) **10709**
Monroe County Clarion (Columbia, IL) **10576**
Monroe County Democrat (Sparta, WI) **10773**
† Monroe County Sentinel (Woodsfield, OH)
Monroe Courier (Monroe, CT) **10553**
Monroe Journal (Monroeville, AL) **10521**
Monroe News (Albia, IA) **10599**
Monroe Watchman (Union, WV) **10763**
Montague County Shopper, The
 (Bowie, TX) **10737**
Montauk Pioneer (Bridgehampton, NY) **10674**
Montclair Times, The (Montclair, NJ) **10668**
Montclarion (Oakland, CA) **10540**
Montebello News (Los Angeles, CA) **10538**
† Montecito Life (Goleta, CA)
Monterey Park Progress (Los
 Angeles, CA) **10538**
Montevideo American-News
 (Montevideo, MN) **10644**
Monte Vista Journal (Monte Vista, CO) **10550**
Montezuma Republican, The
 (Montezuma, IA) **10602**
Montgomery County News, The
 (Hillsboro, IL) **10582**
Montgomery County Progress
 (Horsham, PA) **10718**

Montgomery County Sentinel
 (Gaithersburg, MD) **10621**
Montgomery Herald (Troy, NC) **10695**
Montgomery Herald (Montgomery, WV) **10762**
Montgomery Independent
 (Montgomery, AL) **10521**
Montgomery Post, The
 (Norristown, PA) **10721**
Montgomery Standard (Montgomery
 City, MO) **10655**
Montgomeryville Spirit (Fort
 Washington, PA) **10717**
Monticello Express (Monticello, IA) **10602**
Monticello News (Monticello, FL) **10559**
Montrose Herald (Canistota, SD) **10729**
Moody County Enterprise
 (Flandreau, SD) **10730**
Moody Courier, The (Moody, TX) **10745**
Moorcroft Leader (Moorcroft, WY) **10776**
Moore American (Moore, OK) **10710**
Moore County News-Press (Dumas, TX) **10739**
Moorefield Examiner (Moorefield, WV) **10762**
Mooresville Times, The
 (Mooresville, IN) **10596**
Mooresville Tribune (Mooresville, NC) **10693**
Moose Lake Star-Gazette (Moose
 Lake, MN) **10644**
Moravia Republican Register
 (Moravia, NY) **10683**
Morehead News (Morehead, KY) **10613**
Morenci Observer (Morenci, MI) **10636**
Morgan County Herald
 (McConnelsville, OH) **10705**
Morgan County News (Wartburg, TN) **10735**
Morgan Hill Times (Morgan Hill, CA) **10539**
Morgan Messenger, The (Berkeley
 Springs, WV) **10760**
Morongo Basin (Palm Desert, CA) **10540**
Morongo Basin Advertiser (Yucca
 Valley, CA) **10547**
Morris News Bee (Madison, NJ) **10667**
Morrisons Cove Herald
 (Martinsburg, PA) **10719**
Morris Sun (Morris, MN) **10644**
Morristown News, The (West
 Caldwell, NJ) **10671**
Morris Tribune (Morris, MN) **10644**
Morrow County Advertiser (Mt.
 Gilead, OH) **10705**
Morrow County Independent
 (Cardington, OH) **10699**
Morrow County Sentinel (Mt.
 Gilead, OH) **10705**
Morton Grove-Niles Life
 (Lincolnwood, IL) **10584**
Morton Grove Champion (Evanston, IL) **10579**

Mosinee Times, The (Mosinee, WI) **10770**
Motley County Tribune (Matador, TX) **10744**
Moulton Advertiser (Moulton, AL) **10521**
Moultrie News, The (Mt. Pleasant, SC) **10728**
Mound City News (Mound City, MO) **10655**
Mounds View-New Brighton-St. Anthony Focus (Roseville, MN) **10646**
Moundville Times (Moundville, AL) **10521**
Mountain Advisor (Richlands, VA) **10755**
Mountain Citizen, The (Inez, KY) **10611**
Mountain Eagle (Tannersville, NY) **10688**
Mountain Eagle, The (Whitesburg, KY) **10615**
Mountain Echo (Yellville, AR) **10530**
Mountain Echo (Ironton, MO) **10654**
Mountaineer-Herald, The (Ebensburg, PA) **10717**
Mountaineer, The (Big Sandy, MT) **10659**
† Mountaineer, The (Waynesville, NC)
Mountain Grove News-Journal (Mountain Grove, MO) **10655**
Mountain Home News (Mountain Home, ID) **10570**
Mountain Life (Mariposa, CA) **10539**
Mountain Messenger (Downieville, CA) **10533**
Mountain Messenger (Lewisburg, WV) **10762**
Mountain News, The (Lake Arrowhead, CA) **10536**
Mountain Press (Prather, CA) **10541**
Mountainside Echo (Union, NJ) **10671**
Mountain Statesman (Grafton, WV) **10761**
Mountain Sun, The (Kerrville, TX) **10742**
Mountain Times (Killington, VT) **10750**
Mountaintop Eagle (Mountain Top, PA) **10720**
† Mountain Visitor (Sevierville, TN)
▼Mountain Xpress (Asheville, NC) **10690**
Mount Ayr Record-News (Mt. Ayr, IA) **10603**
Mount Greenwood Express (Midlothian, IL) **10585**
Mount Holly News (Belmont, NC) **10691**
Mount Olive Tribune (Mt. Olive, NC) **10693**
Mount Pleasant Journal (Mt. Pleasant, PA) **10721**
Mount Prospect Journal (Des Plaines, IL) **10577**
Mount Prospect Times (Park Ridge, IL) **10588**
Mount Shasta Herald (Mt. Shasta, CA) **10539**
Mount Sterling Advocate (Mount Sterling, KY) **10613**
Mount Vernon Democrat (Mt. Vernon, IN) **10596**
Mount Vernon Gazette (Alexandria, VA) **10751**
Mount Vernon Independent (Yonkers, NY) **10690**
Mt. Airy Times (Philadelphia, PA) **10722**
Mt. Laurel Progress Press (Maple Shade, NJ) **10667**
Mt. Olive Chronicle (Budd Lake, NJ) **10664**
Mt. Olive Herald, The (Mt. Olive, IL) **10586**
† Mt. Washington Press (Cincinnati, OH)
Mt. Washington Star Review (Los Angeles, CA) **10538**
Mt. Washington Valley Mountain Ear (Conway, NH) **10663**
Mukwonago Chief (Mukwonago, WI) **10770**
Mulberry Press (Mulberry, FL) **10559**
Mullens Advocate (Mullen, WV) **10762**
Munday Courier, The (Munday, TX) **10745**
Mundelein News (Grayslake, IL) **10581**
Mundelein Review (Bannockburn, IL) **10572**
Munising News (Munising, MI) **10636**
Munster Guide (Maryville, IN) **10595**
Murfreesboro Diamond (Murfreesboro, AR) **10528**
Murray County Wheel Herald (Slayton, MN) **10646**
† Murray Eagle (Salt Lake City, UT)
Murrysville Area Star (Monroeville, PA) **10720**
Muskego Sun (New Berlin, WI) **10771**
N'West Iowa Review (Sheldon, IA) **10604**
Nantucket Beacon (Nantucket, MA) **10626**
Nanty Glo Journal, The (Nanty Glo, PA) **10721**
Napa County Record (Napa, CA) **10540**
Naperville Metropolitan (Lemont, IL) **10583**
Naperville Sun (Naperville, IL) **10586**
Naples Record, The (Naples, NY) **10683**
Narragansett Times, The (Wakefield, RI) **10726**
Nashua Reporter (Nashua, IA) **10603**
Nashville Graphic (Nashville, NC) **10693**
Nashville News (Nashville, AR) **10528**
Nashville News, The (Nashville, IL) **10586**
Nashville Scene, The (Nashville, TN) **10734**
Nassau County Record (Callahan, FL) **10556**
Nassau Herald (Lawrence, NY) **10680**
Natick Bulletin (Needham, MA) **10627**
Nation's Center News (Buffalo, SD) **10729**
National Union (Eastern Caroline Islands, FM) **10555**
Navasota Examiner Review (Navasota, TX) **10745**
† Near South Herald (Chicago, IL)
Nebraska Signal (Geneva, NE) **10661**
Needles Desert Star (Needles, CA) **10540**
Neighbors (Hillsboro, WI) **10768**
Neighbors (Markesan, WI) **10769**
▼Neighbors (Waupun, WI) **10775**
Nelson County Times (Amherst, VA) **10751**
Nemaha County Herald (Auburn, NE) **10660**
Neodesha Derrick (Neodesha, KS) **10607**
Neshoba Democrat, The (Philadelphia, MS) **10650**
Ness County News, The (Ness City, KS) **10607**

Netcong News-Leader (Netcong, NJ) **10668**
Nevada County Picayune (Prescott, AR) **10529**
Nevada Journal (Nevada, IA) **10603**
† New Alaskan (Ketchikan, AK)
New Albany Gazette (New Albany, MS) **10650**
Newark/Licking Advertiser
  (Newark, OH) **10705**
Newark Post (Newark, DE) **10554**
Newberg Graphic (Newberg, OR) **10714**
New Berlin Citizen (New Berlin, WI) **10771**
Newberry Observer, The
  (Newberry, SC) **10728**
New Brighton-Mounds View Bulletin (St.
  Paul, MN) **10647**
New Buffalo Times (New Buffalo, MI) **10636**
Newburgh-Chandler Register
  (Newburgh, IN) **10596**
New Canaan Advertiser (New
  Canaan, CT) **10553**
New Carlisle Sun (New Carlisle, OH) **10706**
Newcastle Pacer, The (Newcastle, OK) **10710**
New Castle Record (New Castle, VA) **10754**
New City (Chicago, IL) **10575**
Newcomerstown News
  (Newcomerstown, OH) **10706**
New Era, The (Sweet Home, OR) **10715**
Newfield News (Trumansburg, NY) **10688**
New Hampshire Week in Review
  (Hillsborough, NH) **10663**
† New Hampton Economist (New Hampton, IA)
New Hampton Tribune (New
  Hampton, IA) **10603**
New Haven Advocate (New Haven, CT) **10553**
New Holstein Reporter (New
  Holstein, WI) **10771**
New Hope-Golden Valley Sun Post
  (Minneapolis, MN) **10644**
New Hope Gazette (New Hope, PA) **10721**
Newington Town Crier (Bristol, CT) **10551**
New Leader (Spencer, MA) **10628**
† Newman News, The (Newman, CA)
New Milford Times (New Milford, CT) **10553**
Newnan Times-Herald (Newnan, GA) **10567**
Newport Mercury (Newport, RI) **10725**
Newport Miner (Newport, WA) **10758**
Newport Plaintalk (Newport, TN) **10734**
Newport This Week (Newport, RI) **10725**
New Prague Times (New Prague, MN) **10644**
New Prairie Town Crier (New
  Carlisle, IN) **10596**
New Richmond News (New
  Richmond, WI) **10771**
New River Record (Greenbush, MN) **10642**
News & Press, The (Darlington, SC) **10727**
News & Sentinel, The (Colebrook, NH) **10663**
News-Banner, The (Covington, LA) **10616**

News-Democrat, The (Carrollton, KY) **10610**
News-Examiner (Montpelier, ID) **10570**
News-Examiner (Gallatin, TN) **10732**
News-Gazette (Lexington, VA) **10753**
News-Herald, The (Southgate, MI) **10638**
News-Journal (North Manchester, IN) **10596**
News-Journal Shopper
  (Campbellsville, KY) **10610**
News-Ledger, The (West
  Sacramento, CA) **10546**
† News-Messenger, The (Rockingham, NC)
News-Progress (Sullivan, IL) **10589**
News-Progress, The (Chase City, VA) **10751**
News-Record of Maplewood & South Orange
  (Maplewood, NJ) **10668**
News-Record, The (Cerro Gordo, IL) **10574**
News-Register (McMinnville, OR) **10714**
News-Review, The (Mattituck, NY) **10681**
News-Star (Lehigh Acres, FL) **10558**
News-Sun (Fairmount, IN) **10593**
News-Sun, The (New Bloomfield, PA) **10721**
News-Times (Newport, OR) **10714**
News-X Press (Butler, MO) **10652**
News Beacon (Fair Lawn, NJ) **10666**
News Bulletin of McDowell County, The (Old
  Fort, NC) **10693**
News Buyer's Catalogue
  (Wytheville, VA) **10756**
News Buyers Catalog (Marion, VA) **10754**
News Democrat & Leader
  (Russellville, KY) **10614**
News Democrat Journal (Festus, MO) **10653**
News Eagle (Hawley, PA) **10718**
† NewsEAST (Columbus, OH)
News Enterprise, The (Los
  Alamitos, CA) **10537**
News Examiner, The (Lutcher, LA) **10617**
News Gazette, The (Love Park, IL) **10584**
News Gleaner Publications
  (Philadelphia, PA) **10722**
News Guard, The (Lincoln City, OR) **10713**
New Sharon Star (New Sharon, IA) **10603**
News Herald (Lenoir City, TN) **10733**
† News Herald, The (Mobile, AL)
News Leader (Fernandina, FL) **10557**
News Leader (Stow, OH) **10707**
News Leader (Richwood, WV) **10763**
News Leader, The (Royston, GA) **10567**
News Leader, The (Landrum, SC) **10728**
News Leader, The (Parsons, TN) **10734**
News Letter Journal (Newcastle, WY) **10776**
NewsMarketer, The (Tinley Park, IL) **10590**
News Messenger, The
  (Christiansburg, VA) **10752**
News of Delaware County
  (Havertown, PA) **10718**

News of Orange County, The (Hillsborough, NC) **10692**
News of Southern Berks, The (Boyertown, PA) **10716**
News of the Highlands (Highland Falls, NY) **10679**
News Pointer (Sausalito, CA) **10544**
News Report (Blackwood, NJ) **10664**
News Reporter, The (Whiteville, NC) **10695**
News Review (Ridgecrest, CA) **10541**
News Star (Lincolnwood, IL) **10584**
News Sun, The (Sebring, FL) **10560**
News Sun, The (Cleveland, OH) **10700**
News, The (Salem, AR) **10529**
News, The (Clay City, IN) **10592**
News, The (Belvidere, NJ) **10664**
News, The (Aliquippa, PA) **10715**
News, The (Kingstree, SC) **10727**
News Times (Amherst, OH) **10698**
News Times (Forest Grove, OR) **10713**
News Transcript (Morganville, NJ) **10668**
News Watchman, The (Waverly, OH) **10708**
News Weekly (Mt. Laurel, NJ) **10668**
Newsweekly, The (Sebewaing, MI) **10638**
New Times (Phoenix, AZ) **10525**
New Times (San Luis Obispo, CA) **10543**
New Times, The (Kansas City, MO) **10654**
Newton Graphic (Waltham, MA) **10629**
Newton Press-Mentor (Newton, IL) **10586**
Newton Record (Newton, MS) **10650**
Newtown Bee, The (Newtown, CT) **10553**
New Ulm Enterprise (New Ulm, TX) **10745**
New York Metropolitan News (Brooklyn, NY) **10675**
New York Observer (New York, NY) **10683**
New York Press (New York, NY) **10683**
Niagara/Wheatfield Tribune (Grand Island, NY) **10678**
Niantic-Harristown County Line Observer (Illiopolis, IL) **10582**
† Niantic News (East Lyme, CT)
Nicholas Chronicle (Summersville, WV) **10763**
Niles Herald Spectator (Park Ridge, IL) **10588**
Niles Journal (Des Plaines, IL) **10577**
Niles Life (Lincolnwood, IL) **10584**
Nishna Valley Tribune (Audubon, IA) **10599**
Nisqually Valley News (Yelm, WA) **10760**
Nokomis Free Press-Progress (Nokomis, IL) **10586**
Nome Nugget (Nome, AK) **10523**
Nora News Dispatch (Fisherspolis, IN) **10593**
Nordonia Hills Sun (Cleveland, OH) **10700**
Norridge-Harwood Heights News (Park Ridge, IL) **10588**
Norridge-Harwood Heights Times (Lincolnwood, IL) **10584**

North/South Beach Now (San Francisco, CA) **10543**
North Bartow News (Adairsville, GA) **10562**
North Bay Village News (South Miami, FL) **10561**
North Bergen Reporter (Hoboken, NJ) **10667**
Northbrook Star (Glenview, IL) **10580**
North Brunswick Post (Dayton, NJ) **10665**
North Castle News (Yonkers, NY) **10690**
North Center-Lincoln Belmont-Lake View Booster (Lincolnwood, IL) **10584**
North Central Outlook (Seattle, WA) **10759**
Northcentral Shopper (Des Moines, IA) **10600**
North Clermont Community Journal (Loveland, OH) **10704**
North Country Free Press (Granville, NY) **10678**
North Countryman, The (Elizabethtown, NY) **10676**
North Country Sun (Ironwood, MI) **10634**
North County Journal East (St. Louis, MO) **10657**
North County Journal West (St. Louis, MO) **10657**
North County News (Red Bud, IL) **10588**
North County News (Yorktown Heights, NY) **10690**
North County Shopping News (Atascadero, CA) **10530**
North East Breeze (North East, PA) **10721**
† Northeast Detroiter (Detroit, MI)
Northeast Georgian, The (Cornelia, GA) **10564**
Northeast Johnson County (Shawnee Mission, KS) **10608**
Northeast Reporter (Indianapolis, IN) **10594**
Northeast Reporter (Towson, MD) **10623**
Northeast Shopper (Des Moines, IA) **10600**
Northeast Suburban Life Press (Loveland, OH) **10705**
Northeast Sun (City of Commerce, CA) **10532**
Northeast Times (Philadelphia, PA) **10722**
Northern Light, The (Greenbush, MN) **10642**
Northern Michigan News (Cadillac, MI) **10631**
Northern Ogle County Tempo (Byron, IL) **10574**
Northern Piedmont Express (Culpeper, VA) **10752**
Northern Star (Gaylord, MI) **10633**
Northern Star, The (Clinton, MN) **10641**
Northern Virginia Sun, The (Fairfax, VA) **10752**
Northern Watch (Thief River Falls, MN) **10647**
Northfield Advance (Jenison, MI) **10634**
Northfield News (Northfield, MN) **10645**
North Georgia News (Blairsville, GA) **10563**

Northglenn-Thornton Sentinel (Westminster, CO) **10551**
North Haven Post, The (Milford, CT) **10553**
North Jackson Progress (Stevenson, AL) **10522**
North Jefferson News (Gardendale, AL) **10519**
North Jersey Prospector (Clifton, NJ) **10665**
North Kitsap Herald (Poulsbo, WA) **10759**
North Knox News (Bicknell, IN) **10592**
Northlake Star-Sentinel (Melrose Park, IL) **10585**
North Lake Tahoe Bonanza (Incline Village, NV) **10662**
Northland News (Columbus, OH) **10701**
North Loop News (Chicago, IL) **10575**
North Macomb Voice (New Baltimore, MI) **10636**
North Meridian Observer (Fishers, IN) **10593**
North Miami Beach News (South Miami, FL) **10561**
North Miami News (Miami, FL) **10559**
North Minneapolis Sun Post (Minneapolis, MN) **10644**
North Missourian (Gallatin, MO) **10653**
North Myrtle Beach Times (North Myrtle Beach, SC) **10728**
Northome Record & Mizpah Message (Northome, MN) **10645**
North San Antonio Times (San Antonio, TX) **10746**
North Scott Press, The (Eldridge, IA) **10600**
† North Scottsdale Independent (Scottsdale, AZ)
Northshire Free Press, The (Granville, NY) **10678**
Northshore Citizen (Bothell, WA) **10757**
North Shore Shopper (Pacific Palisades, CA) **10540**
North Shore Sunday (Danvers, MA) **10624**
Northside Journal (St. Louis, MO) **10657**
Northside Neighbor, The (Atlanta, GA) **10563**
North Side News (Jerome, ID) **10569**
Northside Recorder Times, The (San Antonio, TX) **10746**
Northside Sun, The (Jackson, MS) **10650**
North Side Topics (Fishers, IN) **10593**
North Snohomish Weekly (Arlington, WA) **10757**
North Star (Philadelphia, PA) **10722**
North Star Journal (Presque Isle, WI) **10772**
North Star News (Greenbush, MN) **10642**
North Suburban Herald (Love Park, IL) **10584**
North Syracuse Star-News (Syracuse, NY) **10687**
North Tahoe/Truckee Week (Carnelian Bay, CA) **10532**
Northumberland Echo (Heathsville, VA) **10753**

North Utah County Shopper (American Fork, UT) **10748**
North Vernon Plain Dealer (North Vernon, IN) **10596**
North Vernon Sun (North Vernon, IN) **10596**
Northville Record (Northville, MI) **10636**
Northwest Alabamian (Haleyville, AL) **10520**
Northwest Blade, The (Eureka, SD) **10730**
Northwest Columbus News (Columbus, OH) **10701**
Northwest Current, The (Washington, DC) **10555**
Northwestern Illinois Dispatch (Savanna, IL) **10589**
Northwestern Illinois Farmer (Lena, IL) **10583**
Northwest Iowa Shopper (Spencer, IA) **10604**
Northwest Journal & Topics (Des Plaines, IL) **10577**
Northwest Leader (Chicago, IL) **10575**
Northwest Press (Speedway, IN) **10598**
Northwest Press (Cincinnati, OH) **10700**
Northwest Shopper (Des Moines, IA) **10600**
Northwest Side Press (Chicago, IL) **10575**
Northwood Gleaner (Northwood, ND) **10697**
North Woods Call (Charlevoix, MI) **10631**
Norton Courier (Stoughton, MA) **10628**
Norwalk Herald American (Los Angeles, CA) **10538**
† Norwalk News (Westport, CT)
Norway Advertiser-Democrat (Norway, ME) **10620**
Norway Current (Norway, MI) **10636**
Norwell Mariner (Marshfield, MA) **10626**
Novato Advance (Novato, CA) **10540**
Novi News (Northville, MI) **10636**
Nowata Star (Nowata, OK) **10710**
Nueces County Record Star (Robstown, TX) **10746**
Nutley Journal (Bloomfield, NJ) **10664**
Nutley Sun, The (Nutley, NJ) **10668**
NUVO Newsweekly (Indianapolis, IN) **10594**
O-W Enterprise (Withee, WI) **10775**
O'Fallon Journal (O'Fallon, MO) **10655**
O'Fallon Progress (O'Fallon, IL) **10586**
Oak Brook Doings (Hinsdale, IL) **10582**
Oak Brook Press (Elmhurst, IL) **10578**
Oak Brook Terrace Doings (Hinsdale, IL) **10582**
Oak Cliff Tribune (Dallas, TX) **10738**
Oak Creek Pictorial (New Berlin, WI) **10771**
Oakdale-Lake Elmo Review (St. Paul, MN) **10647**
Oakdale Clarion (Oakdale, MN) **10645**
Oakdale Journal (Oakdale, LA) **10617**
Oakdale Leader (Oakdale, CA) **10540**
Oakland Independent (Oakland, NE) **10661**

WEEKLY NEWSPAPERS

Oak Lawn Independent (Midlothian, IL) **10585**
Oak Leaves, The (Oak Park, IL) **10587**
Oakley Graphic (Oakley, KS) **10607**
Oakville-Mehville Journal (St. Louis, MO) **10657**
Oberlin Herald, The (Oberlin, KS) **10607**
† Observer-Patriot (Putnam, CT)
Observer-Tribune (Chester, NJ) **10665**
Observer, The (Royal Palm Beach, FL) **10560**
Observer, The (DeWitt, IA) **10600**
Observer, The (Belgrade, MN) **10640**
† Observer, The (Blackwood, NJ)
Observer, The (Kearny, NJ) **10667**
Observer, The (Rio Rancho, NM) **10672**
Observer, The (Northport, NY) **10683**
Observer, The (Greenville, RI) **10725**
Oceana's Herald-Journal (Hart, MI) **10633**
Ocean County Reporter (Toms River, NJ) **10670**
Oceanside/Island Park Herald (Long Beach, NY) **10680**
Oceanside Centre Beacon (Mineola, NY) **10682**
Ocean Springs Record (Ocean Springs, MS) **10650**
Oconee Breeze (Madison, GA) **10566**
Oconomowoc Enterprise (Oconomowoc, WI) **10771**
Oconto County Times-Herald (Oconto Falls, WI) **10771**
▼ OC Weekly (Los Angeles, CA) **10538**
Odem-Edroy Times (Sinton, TX) **10746**
Ogemaw County Herald (West Branch, MI) **10639**
Ogle County Life (Oregon, IL) **10587**
Ohio County News (Rising Sun, IN) **10597**
Ohio County Times News (Hartford, KY) **10611**
Ojai Valley News (Ojai, CA) **10540**
Oklahoma City Friday (Oklahoma City, OK) **10711**
Oklahoma Eagle (Tulsa, OK) **10712**
Oklahoma Gazette (Oklahoma City, OK) **10711**
Oklee Herald (Oklee, MN) **10645**
Olathe Sun (Overland Park, KS) **10608**
Old Colony Memorial (Plymouth, MA) **10627**
Oldham Era, The (La Grange, KY) **10612**
Old Lyons Recorder, The (Lyons, CO) **10550**
Olive Hill Times (Olive Hill, KY) **10613**
Oliveville Times (Morehead, KY) **10613**
Olivia Times Journal (Olivia, MN) **10645**
Olney Enterprise, The (Olney, TX) **10745**
Olney Times (Philadelphia, PA) **10722**
Olympia Review (Minier, IL) **10586**
Omaha Star (Omaha, NE) **10661**
Omak-Okanogan County Chronicle (Omak, WA) **10758**

Ottawa Advance **10907**

Omro Herald (Omro, WI) **10771**
Onawa Democrat (Onawa, IA) **10603**
Onawa Sentinel (Onawa, IA) **10603**
Onaway Outlook (Onaway, MI) **10636**
Onlooker, The (Foley, AL) **10519**
Onondaga Valley News (Syracuse, NY) **10687**
Ontario Advertiser (San Bernardino, CA) **10542**
Ontonagon Herald (Ontonagon, MI) **10636**
Oologah Lake Leader (Oologah, OK) **10711**
Opp News (Opp, AL) **10521**
Orange Bulletin (Milford, CT) **10553**
Orange Countian (Paoli, IN) **10597**
Orange County Log (San Diego, CA) **10542**
Orange County News (Garden Grove, CA) **10534**
Orange County Review (Orange, VA) **10754**
Orange Cove Mountain Times (Reedley, CA) **10541**
Orange Transcript (Orange, NJ) **10669**
† Orangevale News (Folsom, CA)
Orchard Park Bee (Williamsville, NY) **10689**
Ord Quiz (Ord, NE) **10661**
Oregon Observer (Oregon, WI) **10771**
Orem-Geneva Times (Orem, UT) **10749**
Orfordville Journal & Footville News (Orfordville, WI) **10772**
Orion Gazette (Orion, IL) **10587**
† Orion Times (Orion, IL)
Orland Metropolitan (Lemont, IL) **10583**
Orlando Weekly, The (Winter Park, FL) **10562**
Orland Press-Register (Orland, CA) **10540**
Orland Township Messenger (Midlothian, IL) **10585**
† Orrville Courier-Crescent (Orrville, OH)
Ortonville Independent (Ortonville, MN) **10645**
Oryor Jeffersonian (Pryor, OK) **10711**
Osage County Chronicle (Burlingame, KS) **10606**
Osakis Review, The (Osakis, MN) **10645**
Osawatomie Graphic (Osawatomie, KS) **10608**
Osborne County Farmer (Osborne, KS) **10608**
Osceola County Gazette-Tribune (Sibley, IA) **10604**
Osceola News-Gazette (Kissimmee, FL) **10558**
Osceola Sentinel-Tribune (Osceola, IA) **10603**
Osceola Sun (Osceola, WI) **10772**
Osceola Times (Osceola, AR) **10529**
Oscoda Press (Oscoda, MI) **10636**
Osgood Journal (Versailles, IN) **10598**
Oshkosh Buyers Guide (Oshkosh, WI) **10772**
Oskaloosa Independent (Oskaloosa, KS) **10608**
Ossian Bee, The (Ossian, IA) **10603**
Ossian Journal (Ossian, IN) **10596**
Other Paper, The (Columbus, OH) **10701**
Ottawa Advance (Jenison, MI) **10634**

Weeklies Index

ULRICH'S INTERNATIONAL PERIODICALS DIRECTORY 1998

Ottawa County Exponent, The (Oak Harbor, OH) **10706**
Ottawa Times (Ottawa, KS) **10608**
Ottawa Times Shopper (Ottawa, KS) **10608**
Ouachita Citizen (West Monroe, LA) **10618**
Ouray County Plaindealer (Ouray, CO) **10550**
Our Home Town (Vanderbilt, MI) **10638**
Our Town (Maywood, NJ) **10668**
Our Town (New York, NY) **10683**
Our Town (Pearl River, NY) **10684**
Outlook Mail (Santa Monica, CA) **10544**
Outlook, The (Othello, WA) **10758**
Overland Park Sun (Shawnee Mission, KS) **10608**
Over the Mountain Journal (Birmingham, AL) **10518**
Ovid Gazette (Trumansburg, NY) **10688**
Oviedo Voice, The (Oviedo, FL) **10560**
Owasso Reporter (Owasso, OK) **10711**
Owatonna Weekly Shopper (Owatonna, MN) **10645**
Owego Pennysaver (Owego, NY) **10684**
Owings Mills Times (Baltimore, MD) **10621**
Owyhee Avalanche (Homedale, ID) **10569**
Oxford Press (Oxford, OH) **10706**
Oxford Public Ledger (Oxford, NC) **10694**
Oxford Register, The (Belle Plaine, KS) **10605**
Oxford Review-Times (Greene, NY) **10678**
Oyster Bay-Syosset Guardian (Oyster Bay, NY) **10684**
Oyster Bay Enterprise Pilot (Mineola, NY) **10682**
Ozark County Times (Gainesville, MO) **10653**
Ozark Journal (Imboden, AR) **10528**
Ozaukee County News Graphic (Cedarburg, WI) **10765**
Ozaukee Guide (Cedarburg, WI) **10765**
Ozaukee Press (Port Washington, WI) **10772**
Pacifica Tribune (Pacifica, CA) **10540**
Pacific Sun (Mill Valley, CA) **10539**
Pageland Progressive-Journal, The (Pageland, SC) **10728**
Page News & Courier (Luray, VA) **10754**
Paintsville Herald, The (Paintsville, KY) **10613**
Palacios Beacon (Palacios, TX) **10745**
Palatine Countryside (Arlington Heights, IL) **10571**
Palatine Journal & Topics (Des Plaines, IL) **10577**
Palau Gazette (Koror, PW) **10715**
Palisade Tribune (Palisade, CO) **10550**
Palisadian-Post (Pacific Palisades, CA) **10540**
Palm Desert Advertiser (Palm Desert, CA) **10540**
Palm Desert Post (Indio, CA) **10535**

Palm Spring Advertiser (Palm Desert, CA) **10540**
Palmyra Spectator (Palmyra, MO) **10655**
Palo Alto Weekly (Palo Alto, CA) **10541**
Palos Citizen (Midlothian, IL) **10585**
Palos Hills-Hickory Hills (Palos Heights, IL) **10587**
Palos Verdes Peninsula News (Palos Verdes Peninsula, CA) **10541**
Palo Verde Valley Times (Blythe, CA) **10531**
Pana News-Palladium (Pana, IL) **10587**
† Panhandle Press (Chester, WV)
Panola Watchman (Carthage, TX) **10737**
▼Panolian Advantage, The (Batesville, MS) **10648**
Panolian, The (Batesville, MS) **10648**
Paoli News (Paoli, IN) **10597**
Paoli Republican (Paoli, IN) **10597**
Paper of Wabash County, The (Wabash, IN) **10598**
Paper, The (Barry, IL) **10572**
Paper, The (Elkhart, IN) **10593**
Paper, The (Goshen, IN) **10594**
Paper, The (Warsaw, IN) **10598**
† Paper, The (Spartanburg, SC)
Papillion Times (Papillion, NE) **10661**
Paradise Post (Paradise, CA) **10541**
Paradise Valley Independent (Scottsdale, AZ) **10526**
Paris Express (Paris, AR) **10529**
Parkchester News (Bronx, NY) **10674**
Parker Advertiser (Parker, AZ) **10525**
Parker Pioneer (Parker, AZ) **10525**
Park Falls Herald (Park Falls, WI) **10772**
Park LaBrea News/Beverly Press (Los Angeles, CA) **10538**
Park News (Library, PA) **10719**
Park Rapids Enterprise (Park Rapids, MN) **10645**
Park Record, The (Park City, UT) **10749**
Park Ridge Herald Advocate (Park Ridge, IL) **10588**
Park Ridge Journal (Des Plaines, IL) **10577**
Park Slope Courier (Brooklyn, NY) **10675**
Parkway Transcript (Dedham, MA) **10624**
Parlier Post (Sanger, CA) **10543**
Parma Sun Post (Berea, OH) **10699**
† Parsippany Focus (Morris Plains, NJ)
Parsippany News, The (West Caldwell, NJ) **10671**
Parsons Advocate (Parsons, WV) **10762**
Parsons News (Parsons, KS) **10608**
Pasadena Weekly (Pasadena, CA) **10541**
Pascack Valley Community Life (Westwood, NJ) **10671**
Pasco News (Dade City, FL) **10556**

WEEKLY NEWSPAPERS

Passaic Valley Today (Butler, NJ) **10665**
Pataskala Standard (Pataskala, OH) **10706**
Patent Trader (Cross River, NY) **10676**
Patriot & Free Press (Cuba, NY) **10676**
Patriot, The (Kutztown, PA) **10719**
Paulding Neighbor, The (Marietta, GA) **10566**
Paulding Progress (Paulding, OH) **10706**
Paullina Times (Paullina, IA) **10603**
Pawhuska Journal-Capital
 (Pawhuska, OK) **10711**
Pawling News Chronicle (Pawling, NY) **10684**
Pawnee Post (Auburn, IL) **10572**
Paw Paw Courier-Leader (Paw Paw, MI) **10636**
Paynesville Press, The
 (Paynesville, MN) **10645**
Payson Roundup (Payson, AZ) **10525**
Peekskill Herald (Peekskill, NY) **10684**
Pelham Journal (Pelham, GA) **10567**
Pelham Sun (Yonkers, NY) **10690**
Pelican Press (Sarasota, FL) **10560**
Pelican Rapids Press (Pelican
 Rapids, MN) **10645**
Pella Chronicle (Pella, IA) **10603**
Pembroke Mariner (Marshfield, MA) **10626**
Pembroke Reporter (Plymouth, MA) **10628**
Pender Chronicle (Burgaw, NC) **10691**
Pender Post (Burgaw, NC) **10691**
Pendleton Record, The (Pendleton, OR) **10714**
Penfield Post-Republican, The
 (Fishers, NY) **10677**
Peninsula Beacon, The (San Diego, CA) **10542**
Peninsula Gateway (Gig Harbor, WA) **10758**
Peninsula Independent
 (Burlingame, CA) **10531**
† Peninsula Review, The (Carmel, CA)
Pennington County Prevailer-News (Hill
 City, SD) **10730**
Pennsboro News (Pennsboro, WV) **10762**
† Pennysaver (Vista, CA)
Penny Saver (Tinley Park, IL) **10590**
Penny Saver (Three Rivers, MI) **10638**
Pennysaver (Elmsford, NY) **10677**
Pennysaver (Yorktown Heights, NY) **10690**
Penny Saver (Covington, OH) **10703**
Pennysaver Press (Bennington, VT) **10749**
Pennysaver, The (Yarmouthport, MA) **10630**
Penobscot Times (Old Town, ME) **10620**
Pensacola Voice (Pensacola, FL) **10560**
People-Sentinel (Barnwell, SC) **10726**
People's Defender, The (West
 Union, OH) **10708**
People's Weekly World (New York, NY) **10683**
Peoria Observer (Peoria, IL) **10588**
Peoria Times (Glendale, AZ) **10525**
Pepperell Free Press (Ayer, MA) **10623**
Perdido Pelican (Pensacola, FL) **10560**

Perham Enterprise-Bulletin
 (Perham, MN) **10645**
Perinton-Fairport Post, The
 (Pittsford, NY) **10684**
Perkasie News-Herald (Perkasie, PA) **10722**
Perquimans Weekly (Hertford, NC) **10692**
Perry Chief (Perry, IA) **10603**
Perry County News, The (Tell City, IN) **10598**
Perry County Petit Jean Country Headlight
 (Morrilton, AR) **10528**
Perry County Republic-Monitor, The
 (Perryville, MO) **10656**
Perry County Times (New
 Bloomfield, PA) **10721**
Perry County Tribune (New
 Lexington, OH) **10706**
Perry News-Herald (Perry, FL) **10560**
Perrysburg Messenger-Journal
 (Perrysburg, OH) **10706**
Perry Taco Times (Perry, FL) **10560**
Perry Township Weekly (Beech
 Grove, IN) **10592**
Peshtigo Times (Peshtigo, WI) **10772**
Petaluma Argus-Courier (Petaluma, CA) **10541**
Peterborough Transcript
 (Peterborough, NH) **10663**
Petersburg Observer (Petersburg, IL) **10588**
Petersburg Pilot (Petersburg, AK) **10523**
Petosky Star Ad-Vertiser (Gaylord, MI) **10633**
Phenix-Citizen (Phenix City, AL) **10521**
Philadelphia City Paper
 (Philadelphia, PA) **10722**
Philadelphia Guide Newspaper
 (Philadelphia, PA) **10722**
Philadelphia Weekly (Philadelphia, PA) **10722**
Philipsburg Mail, The (Philipsburg, MT) **10659**
Phillipsburg Free Press
 (Phillipsburg, NJ) **10669**
Phillips County Review
 (Phillipsburg, KS) **10608**
Phoenix Newspaper, The (Brooklyn, NY) **10675**
Phoenix Register (Phoenix, NY) **10684**
Photo News (Monroe, NY) **10683**
Photo Star (Willshire, OH) **10708**
Piatt County Journal-Republican
 (Monticello, IL) **10586**
Pickens County Herald (Carrollton, AL) **10518**
Pickens Sentinel (Pickens, SC) **10728**
Pickerington Times-Sun
 (Columbus, OH) **10701**
Pickett County Press (Byrdstown, TN) **10731**
Pico Rivera News (Los Angeles, CA) **10538**
Pictorial Gazette (Old Saybrook, CT) **10553**
† Pictorial Press (Tahlequah, OK)
Picture Post (Waupaca, WI) **10775**
Piedmonter, The (Oakland, CA) **10540**

Piedmont Herald (Piedmont, WV) **10762**
Piedmont Journal-Independent (Piedmont, AL) **10521**
Pierce City Leader-Journal (Pierce City, MO) **10656**
Pierce County Herald (Puyallup, WA) **10759**
Pierce County Herald (Ellsworth, WI) **10767**
Pierce County Tribune (Rugby, ND) **10697**
Pierre Times, The (Pierre, SD) **10730**
Piggott Times, The (Piggott, AR) **10529**
Pike County Dispatch (Milford, PA) **10720**
Pike County News Watchman (Waverly, OH) **10708**
Pike Register (Fishers, IN) **10593**
Pikes Peak Journal (Manitou Springs, CO) **10550**
Pinckney Post Shopping Guide (Pinckney, MI) **10637**
Pine Bluff News (Pine Bluff, AR) **10529**
Pine Island Eagle (Bokeelia, FL) **10555**
Pine Plains Register-Herald (Pine Plains, NY) **10684**
Pine River Times (Bayfield, CO) **10547**
Pineville Sun-Cumberland Courier (Pineville, KY) **10613**
Pinnacle, The (Hollister, CA) **10535**
Pioneer-News (Shepherdsville, KY) **10614**
Pioneer Republican, The (Marengo, IA) **10602**
Pipestone County Star (Pipestone, MN) **10645**
Piscataquis Observer, The (Dover-Foxcroft, ME) **10619**
Pitch Weekly (Kansas City, MO) **10654**
Pittsburg Gazette (Pittsburg, TX) **10745**
Pittsburgh City Paper (Pittsburgh, PA) **10723**
Pittsburgh Renaissance News (Pittsburgh, PA) **10723**
Pittsfield Gazette, The (Pittsfield, MA) **10627**
Placentia News-Times (Anaheim, CA) **10530**
Placer Herald (Rocklin, CA) **10541**
Plain Dealer (Blackwood, NJ) **10664**
▼Plainfield Sun (Plainfield, IL) **10588**
Plainsman Weekly News (Sedalia, MO) **10656**
Plainview News (Plainview, MN) **10645**
Plainview News (Plainview, NE) **10661**
Plant City Shopper (Plant City, FL) **10560**
Plaquemines Gazette (Belle Chasse, LA) **10615**
Plaquemines Watchman (Belle Chasse, LA) **10615**
Platte County Gazette (Parkville, MO) **10655**
Platte County Record-Times (Wheatland, WY) **10776**
Platte Dispatch Tribune (Kansas City, MO) **10654**
Platteville Journal (Platteville, WI) **10772**
Plattsmouth Journal (Plattsmouth, NE) **10661**
Pleasant Grove Review (American Fork, UT) **10748**
Pleasanton Express (Pleasanton, TX) **10745**
Plymouth Observer (Plymouth, MI) **10637**
Plymouth Sun-Sailor (Minnetonka, MN) **10644**
Pocahontas Record-Democrat (Pocahontas, IA) **10603**
Pocahontas Star Herald (Pocahontas, AR) **10529**
Pocahontas Times (Marlinton, WV) **10762**
Pocono Shopper (East Stroudsburg, PA) **10717**
Point & Shoreland Journal (Toledo, OH) **10707**
Pointe Coupee Banner (New Roads, LA) **10617**
Point Reyes Light (Point Reyes Station, CA) **10541**
† Poland Leader (Niles, OH)
Polk City Press (Mulberry, FL) **10559**
Polk County Democrat, The (Bartow, FL) **10555**
Polk County Enterprise (Livingston, TX) **10743**
Pompano Ledger, The (Pompano Beach, FL) **10560**
Ponchatoula Times, The (Ponchatoula, LA) **10617**
Pontotoc Progress (Pontotoc, MS) **10650**
Pony Express Mail (Liberty, TX) **10743**
Pope County Tribune (Glenwood, MN) **10642**
Poquoson Post (Yorktown, VA) **10756**
Porcupine Press (Chatham, MI) **10631**
Portage Community Shopping Guide (Merrillville, IN) **10596**
Portage Dispatch, The (Portage, PA) **10723**
Porter/New Caney Sun (Humble, TX) **10742**
Port Gibson Reveille (Port Gibson, MS) **10650**
Port Isabel-South Padre Item Press (Port Isabel, TX) **10745**
Portland News (Portland, TX) **10745**
Portland Review & Observer (Grand Ledge, MI) **10633**
Port Lavaca Wave (Port Lavaca, TX) **10745**
Port Orchard Independent (Port Orchard, WA) **10759**
Port Richmond Star (Philadelphia, PA) **10722**
Portsmouth Times (Chesapeake, VA) **10752**
Port Times-Record, The (Setauket, NY) **10686**
Port Townsend/Jefferson County Leader (Port Townsend, WA) **10759**
Port Washington News (Port Washington, NY) **10685**
Post-Herald (Red Creek, NY) **10685**
Post Falls Tribune (Post Falls, ID) **10570**
Post News (San Clemente, CA) **10542**
Post Report, The (Beckley, WV) **10760**
Post Review, The (Paramus, NJ) **10669**
Post South (Plaquemine, LA) **10617**

WEEKLY NEWSPAPERS

Post, The (Middleburg, PA) **10720**
Post, The (Big Stone Gap, VA) **10751**
Potomac Almanac (Potomac, MD) **10622**
Potter Leader-Enterprise
   (Coudersport, PA) **10717**
Pottsboro Press (Pottsboro, TX) **10745**
† ▼Poultney News, The (Rutland, VT)
Poway News Chieftain (Poway, CA) **10541**
Powder Springs Neighbor, The
   (Marietta, GA) **10566**
Powell Valley News (Pennington
   Gap, VA) **10754**
Power County Press (American
   Falls, ID) **10569**
Poynette Press (Poynette, WI) **10772**
Prairie City News (Prairie City, IA) **10603**
Prairie Post (Jamestown, ND) **10697**
Prairie Shopper, The (La Fayette, IL) **10583**
Prairie Times, The (La Fayette, IL) **10583**
Prairie Village Sun (Shawnee
   Mission, KS) **10608**
Pratt Tribune (Vermillion, SD) **10730**
Prattville Progress (Prattville, AL) **10521**
Prescott Journal (Prescott, WI) **10772**
Prescott Valley Tribune, The (Prescott
   Valley, AZ) **10526**
Presque Isle Advance (Rogers City, MI) **10637**
Presque Isle Star (Gaylord, MI) **10633**
Press & Journal, The (Middletown, PA) **10720**
Press & Light (West Lake, OH) **10708**
Press & Standard, The
   (Walterboro, SC) **10729**
Press-Dispatch (Petersburg, IN) **10597**
Press-News Journal (Canton, MO) **10652**
Press-News, The (Minerva, OH) **10705**
Press-Sentinel, The (Jesup, GA) **10566**
Press-Star (New London, WI) **10771**
Press Argus-Courier (Van Buren, AR) **10529**
Press Dispatch (Kansas City, MO) **10654**
Press Herald (Pine Grove, PA) **10723**
Press Journal (St. Louis, MO) **10657**
Press Journal, The (Palisades Park, NJ) **10669**
Press Review (London, OH) **10704**
Press, The (Los Angeles, CA) **10538**
† Press, The (Alexandria, MN)
Press, The (Avon Lake, OH) **10698**
Press, The (Millbury, OH) **10705**
Preston Citizen (Preston, ID) **10570**
Preston County Journal
   (Kingwood, WV) **10761**
Preston County News (Kingwood, WV) **10761**
Price Hill Press (Cincinnati, OH) **10700**
Priest River Times (Priest River, ID) **10570**
PrimeTime (Lawrence, NY) **10680**
Prince Georges Sentinel
   (Seabrook, MD) **10622**
Princeton News Leader (Princeton, NC) **10694**
Princeton Packet, The (Princeton, NJ) **10669**
Princeton Times (Princeton, WV) **10762**
Princeton Times-Republic
   (Princeton, WI) **10772**
Princeton Union-Eagle (Princeton, MN) **10645**
Private Eye Weekly (Salt Lake City, UT) **10749**
Proctor Journal (Proctor, MN) **10646**
Progressor-Times, The (Carey, OH) **10699**
Progress, The (Cave City, KY) **10610**
Progress, The (Caldwell, NJ) **10665**
Progress, The (Monroeville, PA) **10720**
Progress, The (Anahuac, TX) **10736**
Prospect-News, The (Doniphan, MO) **10653**
Prospect Heights Journal (Des
   Plaines, IL) **10577**
Prospector, The (Doniphan, MO) **10653**
Providence Phoenix (Providence, RI) **10726**
Provincetown Advocate
   (Provincetown, MA) **10628**
Proviso Star-Sentinel (Melrose Park, IL) **10585**
Public Spirit (Ayer, MA) **10623**
Pulaski Citizen (Pulaski, TN) **10734**
Pulaski County Journal (Winamac, IN) **10598**
Pulaski Enterprise (Mounds, IL) **10586**
Pulaski Giles Free Press (Pulaski, TN) **10734**
Pulse-Journal (Mason, OH) **10705**
Purcell Register (Purcell, OK) **10711**
Putnam-Cabell Post (Culloden, WV) **10761**
Putnam County Record (Granville, IL) **10580**
Putnam County Sentinel (Ottawa, OH) **10706**
Putnam County Vidette (Columbus
   Grove, OH) **10702**
Putnam Courier-Trader, The
   (Carmel, NY) **10675**
Pymatuning Area News (Andover, OH) **10698**
Pyramid, The (Mt. Pleasant, UT) **10749**
Quad Community Press (White Bear
   Lake, MN) **10648**
Quad County Edition, The
   (Jerseyville, IL) **10583**
Quad River News (Sheridan, MO) **10656**
Quakertown Free Press
   (Quakertown, PA) **10723**
Quay County Sun (Tucumcari, NM) **10672**
Queen Anne-Magnolia News
   (Seattle, WA) **10759**
Queen Anne's Record-Observer
   (Centreville, MD) **10621**
Queens Chronicle (Rego Park, NY) **10685**
Queens Ledger (Maspeth, NY) **10681**
Queens Tribune (Fresh Meadows, NY) **10678**
Queens Village Times, The
   (Flushing, NY) **10677**
† Quik Quarter Want Ads (Hobbs, NM)
Quincy Sun (Quincy, MA) **10628**

Quoddy Tides (Eastport, ME) **10619**
Radford News Journal
 (Christiansburg, VA) **10752**
Raeford News-Journal, The
 (Raeford, NC) **10694**
Rahway News-Record (Rahway, NJ) **10669**
Rahway Progress (Union, NJ) **10671**
Ramona Sentinel (Ramona, CA) **10541**
Ramsey-Mahwah Reporter (Palisades
 Park, NJ) **10669**
Ramsey County Review (St. Paul, MN) **10647**
Rancho Bernardo News Journal (San
 Diego, CA) **10542**
Rancho Santa Margarita News (Lake
 Forest, CA) **10536**
Randleman Reporter (Randleman, NC) **10694**
Randolph County Herald Tribune
 (Chester, IL) **10574**
† Randolph County Times-Herald (Moberly, MO)
Randolph Guide, The (Asheboro, NC) **10690**
Randolph Leader (Roanoke, AL) **10521**
† Randolph Mariner (Marshfield, MA)
Randolph Reporter (Bernardsville, NJ) **10664**
Random Lengths News (San Pedro, CA) **10544**
Ranger Times (Ranger, TX) **10745**
Rankin County News, The
 (Brandon, MS) **10649**
Rankin Independent (Cissna Park, IL) **10576**
† Rantoul Pacesetter (Rantoul, IL)
Rantoul Press (Rantoul, IL) **10588**
Rappahannock News (Washington, VA) **10756**
Rappahannock Record
 (Kilmarnock, VA) **10753**
Raton Range, The (Raton, NM) **10672**
Ravena News Herald (Ravena, NY) **10685**
Rayne Acadian-Tribune (Rayne, LA) **10617**
Rayne Independent (Rayne, LA) **10617**
Raynham Journal (Stoughton, MA) **10628**
Raytown Dispatch Tribune
 (Raytown, MO) **10656**
Real American (Leakey, TX) **10743**
Record-Advertiser (North
 Tonawanda, NY) **10684**
Record-Breeze (Blackwood, NJ) **10664**
Record-Citizen, The (Bristow, OK) **10709**
Record-Delta, The (Buckhannon, WV) **10760**
Record-Enterprise (McDonald, PA) **10719**
Record-Herald & Indianola Tribune
 (Indianola, IA) **10602**
Record-Review, The (Abbotsford, WI) **10764**
Record Enterprise, The (Plymouth, NH) **10663**
Recorder-Herald (Salmon, ID) **10570**
Recorder, The (Prince Frederick, MD) **10622**
Recorder, The (Conshohocken, PA) **10717**
Recorder, The (Monterey, VA) **10754**
Record Ledger (San Fernando, CA) **10543**

Record, The (Gainesville, FL) **10557**
Record, The (Council, ID) **10569**
Record, The (Kansas City, KS) **10607**
Record, The (Havre De Grace, MD) **10622**
Record, The (Boonville, MO) **10652**
Record, The (Huntington, NY) **10679**
Record, The (Coraopolis, PA) **10717**
Record Times, The (Paxton, IL) **10588**
Red Bay News (Red Bay, AL) **10521**
Redding Pilot, The (Georgetown, CT) **10552**
Redfield Press (Redfield, SD) **10730**
Redford Observer (Livonia, MI) **10635**
Redlands Advertiser (Redlands, CA) **10541**
Redmond Sammamish Valley News
 (Redmond, WA) **10759**
Redmond Spokesman (Redmond, OR) **10714**
Red Oak Express (Red Oak, IA) **10603**
Redwood City Tribune (Redwood
 City, CA) **10541**
Redwood Gazette, The (Redwood
 Falls, MN) **10646**
Reedley Exponent (Reedley, CA) **10541**
Reedsburg Times-Press
 (Reedsburg, WI) **10772**
Reflector, The (Battle Ground, WA) **10757**
Regional News (Palos Heights, IL) **10587**
Regional News, The (La Crosse, IN) **10595**
Register-Herald (Eaton, OH) **10703**
Register-News (Bordentown, NJ) **10664**
Register, The (Yarmouthport, MA) **10630**
Reminder, The (Vernon, CT) **10554**
Remington Press (Rensselaer, IN) **10597**
Renville County Shopper (Olivia, MN) **10645**
Reporter Newspaper, The (Palos
 Heights, IL) **10587**
Reporter of the Spring-Ford Area
 (Royersford, PA) **10723**
† Reporter, The (Tampa, FL)
Reporter, The (Casey, IL) **10574**
Reporter, The (Chicago, IL) **10575**
Reporter, The (Franklin Lakes, NJ) **10666**
Republican-Journal (Darlington, WI) **10766**
Republican Journal (Belfast, ME) **10618**
Republican, The (Danville, IN) **10592**
Republican, The (Oakland, MD) **10622**
† ▼Resident Community News (New York, NY)
Reston Times (Reston, VA) **10755**
Retrospect, The (Collingswood, NJ) **10665**
Reveille/Between the Lakes (Seneca
 Falls, NY) **10686**
Revere Journal (Revere, MA) **10628**
† Review-Enterprise (Blackwood, NJ)
Review Herald, The (Mammoth
 Lakes, CA) **10539**
Review Press Reporter (Yonkers, NY) **10690**
Review, The (Erie, IL) **10578**

WEEKLY NEWSPAPERS

Review, The (Marion, IL) **10584**
Review, The (Paramus, NJ) **10669**
Review, The (Point Pleasant Beach, NJ) **10669**
Review, The (Plymouth, WI) **10772**
Reynolds County Courier
  (Ellington, MO) **10653**
RFD News, The (Bellevue, OH) **10699**
Rialto Record (San Bernardino, CA) **10542**
Rice Lake Chronotype (Rice Lake, WI) **10773**
Richardson News (Richardson, TX) **10745**
Richfield Reaper (Richfield, UT) **10749**
Richfield Sun-Current
  (Bloomington, MN) **10640**
Richland Beacon-News (Rayville, LA) **10618**
Richland Observer (Richland
  Center, WI) **10773**
Richlands-Beulaville Advertiser-News
  (Richlands, NC) **10694**
Richlands News Press (Richlands, VA) **10755**
Richmond Review, The (Richmond, MI) **10637**
Richton Dispatch, The (Richton, MS) **10651**
Ridgefield Press, The (Ridgefield, CT) **10553**
Ridgewood News (Paramus, NJ) **10669**
Ridgway Sun (Ridgway, CO) **10550**
Ridley Press (Drexel Hill, PA) **10717**
Rio Grande Sun (Espanola, NM) **10672**
Ripley Southern Sentinel (Ripley, MS) **10651**
Ripon Commonwealth Press
  (Ripon, WI) **10773**
Rising Star, The (Rising Star, TX) **10745**
Rising Sun Recorder (Rising Sun, IN) **10597**
Ritchie Gazette (Harrisville, WV) **10761**
Riverdale Press (Bronx, NY) **10674**
River East News Bulletin
  (Glastonbury, CT) **10552**
River Falls Journal (River Falls, WI) **10773**
River North News (Chicago, IL) **10575**
River Oaks News (Fort Worth, TX) **10740**
River Press, The (Fort Benton, MT) **10659**
River Reporter, The (Narrowsburg, NY) **10683**
Riverside Advertiser (San
  Bernardino, CA) **10542**
Riverside Bulletin, The (Los
  Angeles, CA) **10538**
Riverside Review (Buffalo, NY) **10675**
Riverton Register (Riverton, IL) **10588**
River Valley Shopper (Spring
  Valley, MN) **10646**
Roane County News, The
  (Kingston, TN) **10732**
Roane County Reporter (Spencer, WV) **10763**
Roanoke-Chowan News-Herald, The
  (Ahoskie, NC) **10690**
Roanoke Beacon (Plymouth, NC) **10694**
Roanoke Review (Roanoke, IL) **10589**

Robersonville Weekly Herald
  (Williamston, NC) **10696**
Robertson County Times
  (Springfield, TN) **10735**
Rochelle News Leader (Rochelle, IL) **10589**
Rochester Clarion (Rochester, MI) **10637**
† Rochester Courier (Rochester, NH)
Rochester Eccentric (Rochester
  Hills, MI) **10637**
Rochester Sun News, The (Tenino, WA) **10760**
Rochester Times (Auburn, IL) **10572**
Rochester Times, The (Rochester, NH) **10663**
Rockaway Journal (Lawrence, NY) **10680**
Rockbridge Weekly (Lexington, VA) **10753**
Rock County Star Herald (Luverne, MN) **10643**
Rock Creek Current, The
  (Washington, DC) **10555**
Rockdale Neighbor, The (Conyers, GA) **10564**
Rockdale Reporter (Rockdale, TX) **10746**
Rockford/Cedar Springs Advance
  (Jenison, MI) **10634**
Rockford Squire (Rockford, MI) **10637**
Rockland County Times
  (Haverstraw, NY) **10679**
Rockland Independent, The (Pearl
  River, NY) **10684**
Rockmart Journal (Rockmart, GA) **10567**
Rockrimmon Journal (Manitou
  Springs, CO) **10550**
Rockville Centre Herald (Lawrence, NY) **10680**
Rockville Centre News & Owl
  (Mineola, NY) **10682**
Rockville Parke County Sentinel
  (Rockville, IN) **10597**
Rockwood Times (Kingston, TN) **10732**
Rocky Fork Enterprise (Columbus, OH) **10701**
Rocky Fork Enterprise (Gahanna, OH) **10703**
Rogers Park/Edgewater News/Uptown News
  Star (Lincolnwood, IL) **10584**
Rogersville Review (Rogersville, TN) **10734**
Rogue River Press (Rogue River, OR) **10714**
† Rohnert Park Cotati Clarion (Cotati, CA)
Rolling Meadows Journal & Topics (Des
  Plaines, IL) **10577**
Romeo Observer (Romeo, MI) **10637**
Romeoville Metropolitan (Lemont, IL) **10583**
Romeoville Sun (Bolingbrook, IL) **10573**
Romulus Roman (Wayne, MI) **10639**
Ronkonkoma Review (Smithtown, NY) **10686**
Roosevelt Review (St. Paul, MN) **10647**
Rosamond News (Rosamond, CA) **10541**
Roscoe Hosmer Independent
  (Ipswich, SD) **10730**
Roscommon County Herald-News
  (Roscommon, MI) **10637**
Roseau Times-Region (Roseau, MN) **10646**

Roselle Park Leader (Union, NJ) **10671**
† Roselle Record (Carol Stream, IL)
Roselle Spectator (Union, NJ) **10671**
Rosemont Journal (Des Plaines, IL) **10577**
Rosemont Times (Park Ridge, IL) **10588**
Roseville Independent (Roseville, IL) **10589**
Roseville Press-Tribune (Roseville, CA) **10542**
Roseville Review (St. Paul, MN) **10647**
Rossford Record-Journal (Perrysburg, OH) **10706**
Rossmoor News (Walnut Creek, CA) **10546**
Ross Valley Reporter (Sausalito, CA) **10544**
Roswell-Alpharetta Neighbor (Roswell, GA) **10567**
Roswell/Alpharetta Crier (Atlanta, GA) **10563**
Round Lake News (Grayslake, IL) **10581**
Round Rock Leader (Round Rock, TX) **10746**
Round Valley Paper, The (Eagar, AZ) **10525**
Roxborough Review (Philadelphia, PA) **10722**
Royal Review (Royal City, WA) **10759**
Ruidoso News, The (Ruidoso, NM) **10672**
Rumford Falls Times (Rumford, ME) **10620**
Rural-Urban Record (Columbia Station, OH) **10701**
Rural Virginian (Charlottesville, VA) **10751**
Rush County News (La Crosse, KS) **10607**
Rushville Times, The (Rushville, IL) **10589**
Russell County News, The (Russell Springs, KY) **10614**
Russell Record (Russell, KS) **10608**
Rutherford Courier, The (Smyrna, TN) **10735**
Rutland Tribune, The (Rutland, VT) **10750**
Rye Chronicle (Yonkers, NY) **10690**
Sabina Advertiser (Sabina, OH) **10707**
Sabinal Sampler (Hondo, TX) **10741**
Sabine Banner (Many, LA) **10617**
Sabine County Reporter-Rambler (Hemphill, TX) **10741**
Sabine Index (Many, LA) **10617**
Sacramento Bulletin, The (Sacramento, CA) **10542**
† Sacramento Union (Sacramento, CA)
Saddleback Valley News (Lake Forest, CA) **10536**
Saginaw Press, The (Saginaw, MI) **10637**
Saint Elmo Banner (St. Elmo, IL) **10589**
Sakonnet Times (Portsmouth, RI) **10725**
Salem County Record (Salem, NJ) **10670**
Salem Democrat, The (Salem, IN) **10597**
Salem Leader (Salem, IN) **10597**
Salem News (Salem, MO) **10656**
Salem Observer (Salem, NH) **10664**
Salem Times-Commoner (Salem, IL) **10589**
Salem Times-Register (Salem, VA) **10755**
Saline Reporter (Saline, MI) **10637**

Salisbury News & Advertiser, The (Salisbury, MD) **10622**
Salmon River News (Pulaski, NY) **10685**
Saluda Standard Sentinel (Saluda, SC) **10729**
Salyersville Independent (Salyersville, KY) **10614**
Samford Crimson (Birmingham, AL) **10518**
Samson Ledger (Geneva, AL) **10519**
San Augustine Tribune (San Augustine, TX) **10746**
San Benito News (San Benito, TX) **10746**
San Bernardino Advertiser (San Bernardino, CA) **10542**
San Bernardino Bulletin, The (Los Angeles, CA) **10538**
San Bruno Herald (San Mateo, CA) **10543**
San Carlos Apache Moccasin (Globe, AZ) **10525**
† San Clemente News (San Clemente, CA)
Sandersville Progress (Sandersville, GA) **10567**
† ▼Sandhills Living (Southern Pines, NC)
† San Diego Bulletin (Los Angeles, CA)
San Diego Log (San Diego, CA) **10542**
San Diego Reader (San Diego, CA) **10542**
San Diego Review (San Diego, CA) **10542**
Sand Mountain Reporter (Albertville, AL) **10517**
† Sandpoint News-Bulletin (Sandpoint, ID)
Sand Springs Leader (Sand Springs, OK) **10711**
Sandwich Broadsider (Orleans, MA) **10627**
Sandy Post (Sandy, OR) **10715**
Sandy Springs Neighbor, The (Atlanta, GA) **10563**
San Fernando Valley Sun (San Fernando, CA) **10543**
Sanford News (Sanford, ME) **10620**
San Francisco Bay Guardian (San Francisco, CA) **10543**
San Francisco Independent (San Francisco, CA) **10543**
San Francisco Metro Reporter (San Francisco, CA) **10543**
San Francisco Sentinel (San Francisco, CA) **10543**
San Gabriel Progress (Los Angeles, CA) **10538**
Sanger Herald (Sanger, CA) **10543**
Sanibel-Captiva Islander (Sanibel, FL) **10560**
Sanilac County News (Sandusky, MI) **10638**
San Jacinto Valley Register (San Jacinto, CA) **10543**
San Marcos News Reporter (San Marcos, CA) **10543**
San Marino Tribune (San Marino, CA) **10543**
San Mateo Weekly (Burlingame, CA) **10531**

WEEKLY NEWSPAPERS

San Patricio County News (Sinton, TX) **10746**
San Pedro Valley News-Sun (Benson, AZ) **10524**
San Rafael News Pointer (Sausalito, CA) **10545**
Santa Barbara Independent (Santa Barbara, CA) **10544**
Santa Fe Reporter, The (Santa Fe, NM) **10672**
Santa Fe Springs News (Los Angeles, CA) **10538**
† Santa Monica Life (Santa Monica, CA)
Santa Paula Times (Santa Paula, CA) **10544**
Santa Rosa Free Press (Milton, FL) **10559**
Santa Rosa Press Gazette (Milton, FL) **10559**
Saratoga News (Saratoga, CA) **10544**
Saratoga Sun (Saratoga, WY) **10776**
Sarcoxie Record, The (Sarcoxie, MO) **10656**
Sargent Leader (Burwell, NE) **10660**
Saturday Advantage, The (Monte Vista, CO) **10550**
Saturday Northwest (Craig, CO) **10548**
† Saturday Post-Star (Saugerties, NY)
Saugerties Post Star (Saugerties, NY) **10685**
Saugus Advertiser (Melrose, MA) **10626**
Sauk-Prairie Star (Sauk City, WI) **10773**
Sauk Centre Herald (Sauk Centre, MN) **10646**
Savannah Reporter & Andrew County Democrat (Savannah, MO) **10656**
Savanna Times Journal (Savanna, IL) **10589**
Sawyer County Gazette (Winter, WI) **10775**
Sawyer County Record (Hayward, WI) **10767**
Sayre Journal (Sayre, OK) **10711**
Scarsdale Inquirer, The (Scarsdale, NY) **10686**
Schaller Herald (Schaller, IA) **10604**
Schererville Guide (Maryville, IN) **10596**
Schuyler Sun (Schuyler, NE) **10661**
Scioto Voice (Wheelersburg, OH) **10708**
Scotsman Press, The (Syracuse, NY) **10687**
Scott County Advertiser (Waldron, AR) **10529**
Scott County News (Oneida, TN) **10734**
Scott County Times (Forest, MS) **10649**
Scottsdale-Ashburn Independent (Midlothian, IL) **10586**
Scottsville Citizen-Times (Scottsville, KY) **10614**
Sealy News (Sealy, TX) **10746**
Seaside Signal (Seaside, OR) **10715**
Seattle Facts (Seattle, WA) **10759**
Seattle Skanner, The (Seattle, WA) **10759**
Seattle Weekly (Seattle, WA) **10759**
Sebastian Sun (Vero Beach, FL) **10561**
Sebeka/Menahga Review Messenger (Sebeka, MN) **10646**
Sebring Times (Sebring, OH) **10707**
Secaucus Home News (Secaucus, NJ) **10670**
Secaucus Reporter (Hoboken, NJ) **10667**

Sedona Red Rock News (Sedona, AZ) **10526**
Seekonk Star (East Providence, RI) **10725**
Selby Record (Selby, SD) **10730**
Selma Enterprise (Selma, CA) **10545**
† Seminole Outlook (Oviedo, FL)
Sentinel (Cheyenne, WY) **10775**
Sentinel-Echo (London, KY) **10612**
Sentinel-Ledger, The (Ocean City, NJ) **10668**
† Sentinel/Altitudes (Frisco, CO)
Sentinel, The (Auburn, CA) **10530**
Sentinel, The (Gulf Breeze, FL) **10557**
† Sentinel, The (Chicago, IL)
Sentinel, The (Radcliff, KY) **10614**
Sentinel, The (Marion, MA) **10625**
Sentinel, The (Jefferson, OH) **10704**
Sequim Gazette (Sequim, WA) **10760**
Sequoyah County Times (Sallisaw, OK) **10711**
Seward County Independent (Seward, NE) **10661**
Seward Phoenix Log (Seward, AK) **10523**
Sewickley Herald (Monroeville, PA) **10720**
SF Weekly (San Francisco, CA) **10543**
Shafter Press (Shafter, CA) **10545**
Shakopee Valley News (Shakopee, MN) **10646**
Sharon Advocate (Sharon, MA) **10628**
Sharon Reporter, The (Sharon, WI) **10773**
† Shawnee-Cridersville Press (Wapakoneta, OH)
Shawnee/Merriam Sun (Shawnee Mission, KS) **10608**
Sheboygan Falls News (Sheboygan Falls, WI) **10773**
Shelby County Herald (Shelbyville, MO) **10656**
Shelby County Reporter (Columbiana, AL) **10518**
Shelby Review (Wapakoneta, OH) **10708**
Shelby Sun Times (Germantown, TN) **10732**
Shelbyville Sentinel-News (Shelbyville, KY) **10614**
Sheldon Mail-Sun (Sheldon, IA) **10604**
Shelley Pioneer (Shelley, ID) **10571**
Shelter Island Reporter (Shelter Island Heights, NY) **10686**
Shelton-Mason County Journal (Shelton, WA) **10760**
Shenandoah Valley-Herald, The (Woodstock, VA) **10756**
Shepherdstown Chronicle (Shepherdstown, WV) **10763**
Sheridan Headlight (Sheridan, AR) **10529**
Sheridan News (Fishers, IN) **10593**
Sherman County Star, The (Goodland, KS) **10606**
Shiawassee County Journal (Perry, MI) **10637**
Shippensburg News-Chronicle (Shippensburg, PA) **10724**
Shopper/PLUS (Shelbyville, KY) **10614**

Shopper's Guide (Bardstown, KY) **10609**
Shopper's Guide, The (Louisville, MS) **10650**
Shopper Observer News (Ruskin, FL) **10560**
Shopper Spree (Burlington, IA) **10599**
Shopper Stopper (Merrimac, WI) **10769**
Shopper, The (Pensacola, FL) **10560**
Shopper, The (South Holland, IL) **10589**
Shopper Zone I (Durant, OK) **10710**
Shopper Zone II (Denison, TX) **10739**
Shopping News (Platteville, WI) **10772**
Shopping News, The (Newton, MS) **10650**
Shoreline Chronicle (Sheboygan, WI) **10773**
Shoreview-Arden Hills Bulletin (St. Paul, MN) **10647**
Shoreview Press (St. Paul, MN) **10647**
Shorewood Herald (New Berlin, WI) **10771**
Sidney Herald-Leader (Sidney, MT) **10659**
Sidney Telegraph (Sidney, NE) **10662**
Sierra County Sentinel (Truth or Consequences, NM) **10672**
Sierra Madre News (Sierra Madre, CA) **10545**
Sierra Sun (Truckee, CA) **10546**
Signal-Item (Monroeville, PA) **10720**
Signal, The (Atwater, CA) **10530**
† Signal, The (Canal Fulton, OH)
Sigourney News-Review (Sigourney, IA) **10604**
Silsbee Bee (Silsbee, TX) **10746**
Silver Spring Gazette (Gaithersburg, MD) **10621**
Silverton Appeal-Tribune/Mt. Angel News (Silverton, OR) **10715**
Silverton Standard & The Miner (Silverton, CO) **10551**
Sisseton Courier (Sisseton, SD) **10730**
Siuslaw News, The (Florence, OR) **10713**
Skaneateles Press (Skaneateles, NY) **10686**
Skiatook Journal (Skiatook, OK) **10711**
Skokie Life (Lincolnwood, IL) **10584**
Skokie Review (Evanston, IL) **10579**
Skyline (Lincolnwood, IL) **10584**
Skyworld Duluth News (Duluth, MN) **10641**
Slatebelt Hometown News, The (Bangor, PA) **10716**
Smith County Pioneer (Smith Center, KS) **10609**
Smith County Reformer (Raleigh, MS) **10651**
Smithfield-Selma Sun (Selma, NC) **10694**
Smithfield Herald (Smithfield, NC) **10694**
Smith Mountain Eagle (Moneta, VA) **10754**
Smithtown Messenger (Smithtown, NY) **10686**
Smithtown News, The (Smithtown, NY) **10686**
Smithville Lake Herald, The (Smithville, MO) **10656**
Smithville Review (Smithville, TN) **10735**
Smyth County News & Messenger (Marion, VA) **10754**

† Snake River Press (Craig, CO)
Snohomish County Tribune (Snohomish, WA) **10760**
Soledad Bee (Soledad, CA) **10545**
Solon Herald Sun (Beachwood, OH) **10699**
Solon Times, The (Chagrin Falls, OH) **10700**
Solvang Santa Ynez Valley News (Solvang, CA) **10545**
Somerset Herald (Princess Anne, MD) **10622**
Somerset Messenger Gazette (Somerville, NJ) **10670**
Somerset Spectator (Somerset, NJ) **10670**
Somerville Journal (West Somerville, MA) **10629**
Sonoma County Independent (Santa Rosa, CA) **10544**
Sonoma Index Tribune (Sonoma, CA) **10545**
Sonoma West Times & News (Sebastopal, CA) **10545**
Sorento News (Hillsboro, IL) **10582**
Souderton Independent (Souderton, PA) **10724**
Sounder, The (Random Lake, WI) **10772**
Sound View News (Yonkers, NY) **10690**
South-West Review (St. Paul, MN) **10647**
South Alabamian (Jackson, AL) **10520**
Southampton Press (Southampton, NY) **10686**
South Bay's Newspaper (Lindenhurst, NY) **10680**
† South Bay's Shopper (Lindenhurst, NY)
South Bergenite (Rutherford, NJ) **10670**
South Boston Gazette-Virginian (South Boston, VA) **10755**
South Boston News & Record (South Boston, VA) **10755**
South Boston Tribune (Boston, MA) **10624**
South Buffalo News (Lackawanna, NY) **10680**
South City Journal (St. Louis, MO) **10657**
South Coast Shoppers/Penny Savers (Laguna Hills, CA) **10536**
South County Express (Auburn, IL) **10572**
South County Journal (St. Louis, MO) **10657**
South County News & Advertiser (Fort Worth, TX) **10740**
South County Weekender (Webster, MA) **10629**
South Dade News (South Miami, FL) **10561**
South Dade News Leader (Homestead, FL) **10557**
South Dekalb Neighbor, The (Atlanta, GA) **10563**
South District Journal (Seattle, WA) **10759**
† South East Metro Shopper (Cottage Grove, MN)
Southern Cayuga Tribune (Moravia, NY) **10683**
Southern County News (Thornton, IA) **10604**

WEEKLY NEWSPAPERS

Southern Dutchess News (Wappingers Falls, NY) **10688**
Southern Herald, The (Liberty, MS) **10650**
Southern Oklahoma Leader (Durant, OK) **10710**
Southern Pines Pilot (Southern Pines, NC) **10694**
Southern Standard (McMinnville, TN) **10733**
Southern Star (Ozark, AL) **10521**
Southfield Eccentric (Birmingham, MI) **10630**
South Fork Times (Monte Vista, CO) **10550**
South Fulton Neighbor, The (Forest Park, GA) **10565**
South Gate Press (Los Angeles, CA) **10538**
Southhampton Press, The/Western Edition (Westhampton Beach, NY) **10689**
South Hill Enterprise (South Hill, VA) **10755**
South Hills Record (Pittsburgh, PA) **10723**
Southington Observer (Southington, CT) **10554**
South Jersey Advisor (Cologne, NJ) **10665**
South Lake Advertiser (Lowell, IN) **10595**
South Lyon Herald (South Lyon, MI) **10638**
South Miami News (Miami, FL) **10559**
South Milwaukee Voice Graphic (New Berlin, WI) **10771**
South Missourian News (Thayer, MO) **10658**
South of the Boulevard (Woodland Hills, CA) **10547**
South Oklahoma City Leader (Moore, OK) **10710**
† South Pasadena Journal (Los Angeles, CA)
South Pasadena Review (South Pasadena, CA) **10545**
South Philadelphia Chronicle (Philadelphia, PA) **10723**
South Philadelphia Review (Philadelphia, PA) **10723**
South Pittsburgh Reporter (Pittsburgh, PA) **10723**
South Reporter, The (Holly Springs, MS) **10649**
South San Francisco Enterprise-Journal (San Mateo, CA) **10544**
South San Gabriel/Rosemead Progress (Los Angeles, CA) **10538**
South Shore News (Rockland, MA) **10628**
South Shore Record (Woodmere, NY) **10689**
Southside Journal (Los Angeles, CA) **10538**
Southside Journal (St. Louis, MO) **10657**
Southside Reporter (San Antonio, TX) **10746**
Southside Sentinel (Urbanna, VA) **10756**
Southside Shopper (Des Moines, IA) **10600**
† Southside Sun (East Point, GA)
South Sioux City Star (South Sioux City, NE) **10662**

South St. Paul/Inver Grove Heights Sun-Current (Burnsville, MN) **10640**
South Tampa News (Brandon, FL) **10555**
Southtowns Citizen (Orchard Park, NY) **10684**
† South Valley Eagle (Salt Lake City, UT)
Southwest Beacon (Chicago, IL) **10575**
Southwest City Journal (St. Louis, MO) **10657**
Southwest County Journal (St. Louis, MO) **10658**
Southwest Courier (Chicago, IL) **10575**
Southwestern Journal News (Brighton, IL) **10573**
Southwestern Pennsylvania Scene (Scottdale, PA) **10724**
Southwest Globe Times (Philadelphia, PA) **10723**
† Southwest News (South Miami, FL)
Southwest News-Herald (Chicago, IL) **10575**
Southwest Newsweek, The (Louisville, KY) **10612**
Southwest Shopper (Chicago, IL) **10575**
Southwest Sun (Sugar Land, TX) **10747**
Southwest Tulsa News (Tulsa, OK) **10712**
Southwest Virginia Enterprise (Wytheville, VA) **10756**
Southwest Wave/News (Los Angeles, CA) **10538**
Spackenkill Sentinel (Wappingers Falls, NY) **10688**
Sparta/Kent City Advance (Sparta, MI) **10638**
Sparta Expositor (Sparta, TN) **10735**
Sparta Herald (Sparta, WI) **10773**
Sparta Independent (Sparta, NJ) **10670**
Sparta Ishmaelite (Sparta, GA) **10567**
Sparta News Plaindealer (Sparta, IL) **10589**
Spectator Magazine (Raleigh, NC) **10694**
Spectator, The (Somerset, MA) **10628**
Speedway Town Press (Speedway, IN) **10598**
Spencer County Journal Democrat (Rockport, IN) **10597**
Spencer County Leader/Dale News (Ferdinand, IN) **10593**
Spencer Magnet (Taylorsville, KY) **10614**
Spencer Random Harvest Weekly (Trumansburg, NY) **10688**
Spinal Column Newsweekly (Waterford, MI) **10639**
Spirit Lake Beacon (Spirit Lake, IA) **10604**
† Spirit of Bucks County (Hatboro, PA)
Spirit of Jefferson-Advocate (Charles Town, WV) **10761**
Spooner Advocate (Spooner, WI) **10773**
Spotlight, The (Washington, DC) **10555**
Spotlight, The (Indianapolis, IN) **10594**
Spotlight, The (Delmar, NY) **10676**
Sprague Advocate, The (Sprague, WA) **10760**

ULRICH'S INTERNATIONAL PERIODICALS DIRECTORY 1998

Springfield Advance-Press
 (Springfield, MN) **10646**
Springfield Advocate (Springfield, MA) **10628**
Springfield Leader (Union, NJ) **10671**
Springfield News, The (Springfield, OR) **10715**
Springfield Press (Springfield, PA) **10724**
Springfield Reporter, The
 (Springfield, VT) **10750**
Springfield Shopper (Springfield, IL) **10589**
Springfield Sun (Springfield, KY) **10614**
Springfield Sun (Fort Washington, PA) **10718**
Springfield Times Courier (Reston, VA) **10755**
Springhill Press (Springhill, LA) **10618**
Spring Hope Enterprise (Spring
 Hope, NC) **10695**
Springs Valley Herald (French Lick, IN) **10594**
Springtown Epigraph, The
 (Springtown, TX) **10747**
Spring Valley Bulletin (Lemon
 Grove, CA) **10536**
Spring Valley Sun (Spring Valley, WI) **10773**
Spring Valley Tribune (Spring
 Valley, MN) **10646**
Springview Herald (Springview, NE) **10662**
Springville Journal (Springville, NY) **10687**
Squires, The (Overland, KS) **10608**
† Squire, The (Prairie Village, KS)
Stamford American (Stamford, TX) **10747**
Standard & Times (Tuscumbia, AL) **10522**
Standard-Times (North Kingstown, RI) **10725**
Standard Banner (Jefferson, TN) **10732**
Standard Journal (Rexburg, ID) **10570**
Stanley Republican (Stanley, WI) **10773**
Stanly News & Press (Albemarle, NC) **10690**
St. Anthony Bulletin (North St.
 Paul, MN) **10645**
Staples World (Staples, MN) **10646**
Star-Advocate (Titusville, FL) **10561**
Star-Herald (Belton, MO) **10651**
Star-Herald, The (Presque Isle, ME) **10620**
Star-Herald, The (Kosciusko, MS) **10650**
Star-News, The (McCall, ID) **10570**
Star-News, The (North Syracuse, NY) **10684**
Star-Progress, The (Berryville, AR) **10527**
Star-Tribune (Chatham, VA) **10751**
Star Advertiser (Kalkaska, MI) **10635**
Star Buyers Guide (West Branch, MI) **10639**
Star Express (Covington, GA) **10564**
Star Gazette (Hackettstown, NJ) **10666**
Star Herald (Ripley, WV) **10763**
Star Journal (Hope, IN) **10594**
Star News, The (Chula Vista, CA) **10532**
Star News, The (Medford, WI) **10769**
Star Press (Springboro, OH) **10707**
Star Republican (Wilmington, OH) **10709**
Star, The (Tinley Park, IL) **10590**
Star, The (Sun Prairie, WI) **10774**
State Center Enterprise-Record (State
 Center, IA) **10604**
State Line Shopping Guide
 (Palmer, MA) **10627**
Staten Island Register (Staten
 Island, NY) **10687**
State Port Pilot, The (Southport, NC) **10695**
Statesman-Examiner (Colville, WA) **10757**
Staunton Star-Times (Staunton, IL) **10589**
Stayton Mail (Stayton, OR) **10715**
St. Bernard Voice, The (Arabi, LA) **10615**
St. Charles Journal (St. Charles, MO) **10656**
St. Charles Press (St. Charles, MN) **10647**
St. Clair Missourian (St. Clair, MO) **10656**
St. Clair News-Aegis (Pell City, AL) **10521**
St. Clair Shores Herald
 (Birmingham, MI) **10630**
St. Croix Valley Peach (Forest
 Lake, MN) **10642**
St. Croix Valley Press (St. Paul, MN) **10647**
Steamboat Pilot (Steamboat
 Springs, CO) **10551**
Steele Enterprise (Steel, MO) **10657**
Steelville Star/Crawford Mirror
 (Steelville, MO) **10657**
Ste. Genevieve Herald (Ste.
 Genevieve, MO) **10657**
Steuben Courier-Advocate (Bath, NY) **10673**
St. Francis Herald, The (St.
 Francis, KS) **10609**
St. Francis Reminder-Enterprise (New
 Berlin, WI) **10771**
St. Helena Star (St. Helena, CA) **10545**
St. Helens Chronicle (St. Helens, OR) **10715**
Stigler News-Sentinel (Stigler, OK) **10711**
St. Ignace News, The (St. Ignace, MI) **10638**
Stillwater Valley Advertiser
 (Covington, OH) **10703**
Stilwell Democrat-Journal (Stilwell, OK) **10711**
St. James Leader Journal (St.
 James, MO) **10657**
St. James Plaindealer (St. James, MN) **10647**
St. John News (St. John, KS) **10609**
St. Johns Reminder (St. Johns, MI) **10638**
St. Johns Review (Portland, OR) **10714**
St. John Valley Times (Madawaska, ME) **10619**
St. Joseph Telegraph, The (St.
 Joseph, MO) **10657**
St. Lawrence Plaindealer (Canton, NY) **10675**
St. Louis American Newspaper (St.
 Louis, MO) **10658**
† St. Louis Naborhood Link News (St.
 Louis, MO)
St. Louis Park Sun-Sailor
 (Minnetonka, MN) **10644**

WEEKLY NEWSPAPERS

† St. Louis South St. Louis County News (St. Louis, MO)
St. Maries Gazette Record (St. Maries, ID) **10571**
St. Martinville Teche News (St. Martinville, LA) **10618**
St. Mary Journal (Morgan City, LA) **10617**
St. Marys Star (St. Marys, KS) **10609**
Stockton/Warren Gazette (Stockton, IL) **10589**
Stone County Citizen (Mountain View, AR) **10528**
Stone County Enterprise (Wiggins, MS) **10651**
Stone County Leader (Mountain View, AR) **10528**
† Stoneham Weekender News (Stoneham, MA)
Storm Lake Times (Storm Lake, IA) **10604**
Story City Herald (Story City, IA) **10604**
Stoughton Chronicle (Stoughton, MA) **10628**
Stowe Reporter (Stowe, VT) **10750**
Stow Sentry (Stow, OH) **10707**
St. Peter Herald (St. Peter, MN) **10647**
Straits Area Star (Cheboygan, MI) **10631**
Stratford Bard (Milford, CT) **10553**
Stratford Journal (Stratford, WI) **10774**
Stratford Star (Konawa, OK) **10710**
Sturgis News (Sturgis, KY) **10614**
Suburban & Wayne Times (Wayne, PA) **10724**
Suburban Advertiser (Wayne, PA) **10724**
Suburban Gazette (McKees Rocks, PA) **10719**
Suburbanite, The (Closter, NJ) **10665**
Suburbanite, The (Akron, OH) **10698**
Suburban Journal (Des Plaines, IL) **10577**
Suburban Leader (Chicago, IL) **10575**
Suburban Life (Butler, NJ) **10665**
Suburban Life (Loveland, OH) **10705**
Suburban Life Citizen (Oak Brook, IL) **10586**
Suburban Life Graphic (Oak Brook, IL) **10587**
† Suburban News (Reading, MA)
Suburban News (Spencerport, NY) **10687**
Suburban News, The (Windham, ME) **10620**
Suburban News, The (Flint, MI) **10632**
Suburban Street News (White Plains, NY) **10689**
Suburban Town News (Paramus, NJ) **10669**
Suburban Trends (Butler, NJ) **10665**
Suburban Tribune (Balch Springs, TX) **10736**
Sudbury Town Crier (Needham, MA) **10627**
Suffolk County News (Sayville, NY) **10686**
Suffolk Times (Mattituck, NY) **10681**
Sullivan County News (Blountville, TN) **10731**
Sullivan Independent News (Sullivan, MO) **10658**
Sullivan Review (Dushore, PA) **10717**
Summerville Journal Scene (Summerville, SC) **10729**
Summerville News (Summerville, GA) **10568**
Summit County Journal (Frisco, CO) **10549**
Summit Observer (Union, NJ) **10671**
Sumner Gazette (Sumner, IA) **10604**
Sumner Press (Sumner, IL) **10589**
Sumter County Record-Journal, The (Livingston, AL) **10520**
Sumter County Times (Bushnell, FL) **10556**
Sun & Erie County Independent, The (Hamburg, NY) **10679**
Sun & News, The (Hastings, MI) **10633**
Sun-Bulletin, The (Palisades Park, NJ) **10669**
Sun Advocate (Price, UT) **10749**
Sun Banner Pride (Medina, OH) **10705**
Sunbury News (Sunbury, OH) **10707**
Sun Cities Independent (Sun City, AZ) **10526**
Sun City/Youngtown (Sun City, AZ) **10526**
Sun City News (Sun City, CA) **10545**
Sun City West (Sun City, AZ) **10526**
Sun Coast News (New Port Richey, FL) **10559**
Sun Courier, The (Cleveland, OH) **10700**
Sunday Bucks County Telegraph (Horsham, PA) **10718**
Sunday Dispatch (Pittston, PA) **10723**
† Sunday Glades Trend (Clewiston, FL)
Sunday Independent, The (Owosso, MI) **10636**
Sunday News (Lancaster, PA) **10719**
Sunday Post (Lynn, MA) **10625**
Sunday Spectator (Hornell, NY) **10679**
† Sunday Sun (Scranton, PA)
Sunday Sun (Georgetown, TX) **10740**
Sun Herald, The (North Olmsted, OH) **10706**
Sun Journal, The (North Canton, OH) **10706**
Sun Messenger, The (Beachwood, OH) **10699**
Sun Newspaper, The (Seal Beach, CA) **10545**
Sun Post, The (Miami, FL) **10559**
Sun Press (Kaneohe, HI) **10568**
Sun Press, The (Beachwood, OH) **10699**
Sun Reporter (San Francisco, CA) **10543**
Sunriser News (Ossian, IN) **10597**
Sunrise Times (Coral Springs, FL) **10556**
Sun Scoop Journal (Beachwood, OH) **10699**
Sun Star, The (Berea, OH) **10699**
Sun, The (Sun City Center, FL) **10561**
Sun, The (Mt. Vernon, IA) **10603**
Sun, The (North Olmsted, OH) **10706**
Sun, The (Hummelstown, PA) **10718**
Sun Times (Heber Springs, AR) **10528**
Sun Times (Perryville, MO) **10656**
Superior Express, The (Superior, NE) **10662**
† Surfside News (South Miami, FL)
Surry Scene, The (Mount Airy, NC) **10693**
Susquehanna County Independent (Montrose, PA) **10720**
Sussex-Lannon-Lisbon News (New Berlin, WI) **10771**
Sussex-Surry Dispatch (Wakefield, VA) **10756**

Sussex Countian (Georgetown, DE) **10554**
Sussex County Chronicle (Byram, NJ) **10665**
Sussex Post, The (Rehoboth, DE) **10554**
Sussex Sun (Hartland, WI) **10767**
Swampscott Reporter
 (Marblehead, MA) **10625**
Swanton Enterprise (Swanton, OH) **10707**
Swap Sheet (Ridgecrest, CA) **10541**
Swift County Monitor-News
 (Benson, MN) **10640**
Switzerland Democrat (Vevay, IN) **10598**
† Sycamore Messenger (Cincinnati, OH)
Sycamore News (Sycamore, IL) **10590**
Sylva Herald & Ruralite (Sylva, NC) **10695**
Sylvania Herald (Toledo, OH) **10708**
Sylvester Local News (Sylvester, GA) **10568**
Syosset Jericho Tribune (Mineola, NY) **10683**
Syracuse Journal-Democrat
 (Syracuse, NE) **10662**
Syracuse New Times (Syracuse, NY) **10687**
T-Ville News Trader (Tompkinsville, KY) **10614**
Table Rock Gazette (Kimberling
 City, MO) **10654**
Tab, The (Needham, MA) **10627**
Tacoma City Paper (Tacoma, WA) **10760**
Taft Tribune (Taft, TX) **10747**
Tahoe World (Tahoe City, CA) **10545**
Tallahassean (Tallahassee, FL) **10561**
Tallassee Tribune (Tallassee, AL) **10522**
Tallmadge Express (Stow, OH) **10707**
Tama News-Herald (Tama, IA) **10604**
Tamarac Forum (Coral Springs, FL) **10556**
▼Taney County Times (Forsyth, MO) **10653**
Taos News (Taos, NM) **10672**
Tarkio Avalanche (Tarkio, MO) **10658**
Taunton Independent (Middleboro, MA) **10626**
Tavares Citizen (Mt. Dora, FL) **10559**
Taylorsville Times, The
 (Taylorsville, NC) **10695**
Tazewell County Free Press
 (Richlands, VA) **10755**
Tazewell News (Morton, IL) **10586**
Tecumseh Herald (Tecumseh, MI) **10638**
Tehachapi News (Tehachapi, CA) **10545**
Telegraph-County Edition
 (Jerseyville, IL) **10583**
Telfair Enterprise (McRae, GA) **10566**
Telluride Times-Journal (Telluride, CO) **10551**
Temple Terrace Beacon (Tampa, FL) **10561**
Temple Terrace News (Brandon, FL) **10555**
Tenino Independent (Tenino, WA) **10760**
Teton Valley News (Driggs, ID) **10569**
Texas Observer (Austin, TX) **10736**
Thief River Falls Times (Thief River
 Falls, MN) **10648**
† This Week (Aledo, IL)

This Week (Cherry Hill, NJ) **10665**
This Week In Bexley (Columbus, OH) **10701**
This Week In Clintonville
 (Columbus, OH) **10701**
This Week In Delaware (Columbus, OH) **10701**
This Week In Eastside (Columbus, OH) **10701**
This Week In Grandview
 (Columbus, OH) **10702**
This Week In Hilliard (Columbus, OH) **10702**
This Week In New Albany
 (Columbus, OH) **10702**
This Week In Northland
 (Columbus, OH) **10702**
This Week In Peachtree City (Peachtree
 City, GA) **10567**
This Week In Pickerington
 (Columbus, OH) **10702**
This Week In Powell (Columbus, OH) **10702**
This Week In Reynoldsburg
 (Columbus, OH) **10702**
This Week In Southside
 (Columbus, OH) **10702**
This Week In Union County
 (Columbus, OH) **10702**
This Week In Westerville
 (Columbus, OH) **10702**
This Week In Westside (Columbus, OH) **10702**
This Week In Worthington
 (Columbus, OH) **10702**
Thomaston Times (Thomaston, GA) **10568**
Thomasville Times (Thomasville, NC) **10695**
Thomasville Times, The
 (Thomasville, AL) **10522**
Thompson-Rake Courier
 (Thompson, IA) **10604**
Thorp Courier (Thorp, WI) **10774**
Thousand Islands Sun (Alexandria
 Bay, NY) **10673**
Thousandsticks (Hyden, KY) **10611**
Three Rivers Gazette (McRae, GA) **10567**
Three Star Edition (Philadelphia, PA) **10723**
Three Village Herald (East
 Setauket, NY) **10676**
Three Village Times (Mineola, NY) **10683**
Thrif-T-Nikel Community Shopping Guide
 (Ottawa, IL) **10587**
Thrifty Nickel (Birmingham, AL) **10518**
Thrifty Nickel (Champaign, IL) **10574**
Thrifty Nickel Want Ads (East
 Moline, IL) **10578**
Tidewater News, The (Franklin, VA) **10753**
Tidewater Review (West Point, VA) **10756**
Tigard Times (Tigard, OR) **10715**
Times-Clarion, The (Harlowton, MT) **10659**
Times-Courier (Ellijay, GA) **10565**
Times-Express (Monroeville, PA) **10720**

WEEKLY NEWSPAPERS

Times-Herald (Timonium, MD) **10622**
Times-Indicator (Fremont, MI) **10632**
Times-Journal, The (Condon, OR) **10712**
Times-Leader (Union City, PA) **10724**
Times-Press (Hartford, WI) **10767**
Times-Press (Seymour, WI) **10773**
Times-Record, The (Denton, MD) **10621**
Times-Sentinel, The (Cheney, KS) **10606**
Times-Sun, The (West Newton, PA) **10725**
Times Chronicle (Jenkintown, PA) **10719**
Times Citizen (Iowa Falls, IA) **10602**
Times Dispatch (Walnut Ridge, AR) **10529**
Times Guthrian (Guthrie Center, IA) **10601**
Times Journal (Cobleskill, NY) **10675**
Times Journal-Spotlight (Eastman, GA) **10565**
Times Journal, The (Russell Springs, KY) **10614**
Times Leader, The (Princeton, KY) **10614**
Times Newsweekly (Ridgewood, NY) **10685**
Times of Fountain Hills & Rio Verde (Fountain Hills, AZ) **10525**
Times of Nesconset, The (Setauket, NY) **10686**
Times of Northeast Benton County (Pea Ridge, AR) **10529**
Times of Scotch Plains & Fanwood, The (Westfield, NJ) **10671**
Times of Smithtown (Setauket, NY) **10686**
Times of St. James (Setauket, NY) **10686**
Times of Ti (Ticonderoga, NY) **10688**
Times Post, The (Houston, MS) **10649**
Times Record (Fayette, AL) **10519**
Times Record (Aledo, IL) **10571**
Times Record (Spencer, WV) **10763**
Times, The (North Little Rock, AR) **10528**
Times, The (Melbourne, FL) **10558**
† Times, The (Augusta, KY)
Times, The (Forest Lake, MN) **10642**
Times, The (Columbus, OH) **10702**
Times, The (Port Royal, PA) **10723**
Times, The (Waitsburg, WA) **10760**
Times, The (Westby, WI) **10775**
† Tioga County Gazette & Times (Owego, NY)
Tipp City Herald (Tipp City, OH) **10707**
Tipton Conservative & Advertiser (Tipton, IA) **10604**
† Tipton News Leader (Altus, OK)
Today (Orange Park, FL) **10560**
Today's News (Bountiful, UT) **10748**
Todd County Standard (Elkton, KY) **10610**
Tomahawk Leader (Tomahawk, WI) **10774**
Tomahawk, The (Mountain City, TN) **10734**
Tomah Journal (Tomah, WI) **10774**
Tomah Monitor-Herald (Tomah, WI) **10774**
Tombstone Epitaph, The (Tombstone, AZ) **10526**

Tomorrow (New Rochelle, NY) **10683**
Tompkinsville News (Tompkinsville, KY) **10614**
Tonkawa News, The (Tonkawa, OK) **10711**
Tonopah Times-Bonanza & Goldfield News (Tonopah, NV) **10662**
Tooele Transcript-Bulletin (Tooele, UT) **10749**
Topics Sun Wave (Los Angeles, CA) **10538**
Toppenish Review (Toppenish, WA) **10760**
Torrington Telegram (Torrington, WY) **10776**
† Total, The (Heflin, AL)
† Town & Country (Bradford, PA)
Town & Country (Pennsburg, PA) **10722**
Town & Country Weekly (Ottawa, IL) **10587**
Town-Crier (West Palm Beach, FL) **10562**
Town 'n Country News (Tampa, FL) **10561**
Town Crier (Stockbridge, MI) **10638**
Town Crier, The (La Porte, IN) **10595**
† Towne & Country Shopper (Columbus, KS)
Towne Courier (East Lansing, MI) **10632**
Town of Paradise Valley Independent (Scottsdale, AZ) **10526**
Townsend Times (Ayer, MA) **10623**
Township Times (Saginaw, MI) **10637**
Town Talk (Holmes, PA) **10718**
Town Talk (Media, PA) **10719**
Town Topics (Princeton, NJ) **10669**
Towson Times (Towson, MD) **10623**
Tracy Headlight-Herald (Tracy, MN) **10648**
Tradewinds (St. John, VI) **10750**
Traer Star-Clipper (Traer, IA) **10605**
† Transcript-Telegram (Holyoke, MA)
Transcript, The (Morrisville, VT) **10750**
Transylvania Times, The (Brevard, NC) **10691**
Traveler/Watchman (Southold, NY) **10686**
Trenton Sun, The (Trenton, IL) **10590**
Trenton Tribune (Trenton, TX) **10747**
† Tri-City Independent (Margate, FL)
Tri-City Ledger (Flomaton, AL) **10519**
Tri-City News (Cumberland, KY) **10610**
Tri-City Record, The (Watervliet, MI) **10639**
Tri-City Reporter (Dyer, TN) **10732**
† Tri-City Times (Geraldine, AL)
Tri-City Times (Imlay City, MI) **10634**
Tri-City Trib (Cozad, NE) **10660**
Tri-City Tribune (Marked Tree, AR) **10528**
Tri-County Advertiser (Brockport, NY) **10674**
Tri-County Banner (Knightstown, IN) **10595**
Tri-County Citizen (Chesaning, MI) **10631**
Tri-County Journal (Pacific, MO) **10655**
Tri-County News (Elmwood, IL) **10578**
Tri-County News (Edinburgh, IN) **10593**
Tri-County News (South Bend, IN) **10598**
Tri-County News (Lockport, NY) **10680**
Tri-County News (Knoxville, TN) **10732**
Tri-County News (Osseo, WI) **10772**
Tri-County Press (Cincinnati, OH) **10700**

Tri-County Press (Cuba City, WI) **10766**
Tri-County Record (Rushford, MN) **10646**
Tri-County Times, The (Slater, IA) **10604**
Tri-County Trader (Waldron, AR) **10529**
Tri-State Advertiser (Bullhead City, AZ) **10524**
Tri-Town News (Sidney, NY) **10686**
Tri-Town Transcript (Danvers, MA) **10624**
Tri-Town Transcript, The (Dover, NH) **10663**
Tri-Village News (Columbus, OH) **10702**
Tribune (Deer Park, WA) **10757**
Tribune-Courier (Ontario, OH) **10706**
Tribune-Times (Fountain Inn, SC) **10727**
Tribune Courier (Benton, KY) **10609**
Tribune Plus (Royal Oak, MI) **10637**
Tribune Press Reporter (Glenwood City, WI) **10767**
Tribune Shopping News (New Lexington, OH) **10706**
Tribune, The (Monument, CO) **10550**
Tribune, The (Melbourne, FL) **10558**
Tribune, The (Greenbush, MN) **10642**
Tribune, The (Elkin, NC) **10692**
Tribune, The (Tabor City, NC) **10695**
Tribune, The (Bethany, OK) **10709**
Tri City Register (Riverton, IL) **10588**
Trinity Journal (Weaverville, CA) **10546**
Troy-Somerset Gazette (Troy, MI) **10638**
Troy Eccentric (Rochester Hills, MI) **10637**
Troy Free Press & Silex Index (Troy, MO) **10658**
Troy Progress (Troy, AL) **10522**
True Citizen, The (Waynesboro, GA) **10568**
True Dakotan, The (Wessington Springs, SD) **10730**
Trumann Democrat (Trumann, AR) **10529**
Trumansburg Free Press (Trumansburg, NY) **10688**
Trumbull Times (Monroe, CT) **10553**
Tucker-DeKalb Neighbor, The (Atlanta, GA) **10563**
Tullahoma News (Tullahoma, TN) **10735**
Tundra Drums (Bethel, AK) **10523**
Tundra Times (Anchorage, AK) **10522**
Tunkhannock New Age-Examiner (Tunkhannock, PA) **10724**
Tupper Lake Free Press & Herald (Tupper Lake, NY) **10688**
Turtle Lake Times, The (Turtle Lake, WI) **10774**
Turtle Mountain Star, The (Rolla, ND) **10697**
Tuscola County Advertiser (Caro, MI) **10631**
Tuscola Review (Tuscola, IL) **10590**
Tuskegee News (Tuskegee, AL) **10522**
Tustin News (Santa Ana, CA) **10544**
Twin-City News, The (Batesburg-Leesville, SC) **10726**

Twin Cities Reader (Minneapolis, MN) **10644**
Twin Cities Times (Corte Madera, CA) **10533**
Twin City News, The (Chattahoochee, FL) **10556**
Twinsburg Sun, The (Cleveland, OH) **10700**
Tyler County Booster (Woodville, TX) **10748**
Tyler Star News (Sistersville, WV) **10763**
Tylertown Times (Tylertown, MS) **10651**
Tyler Tribune (Tyler, MN) **10648**
UA This Week (Columbus, OH) **10702**
Uinta County Herald (Evanston, WY) **10776**
Uintah Basin Standard (Roosevelt, UT) **10749**
Ulster County Townsman (Woodstock, NY) **10690**
Ulysses News (Ulysses, KS) **10609**
Umpqua Free Press (Myrtle Creek, OR) **10714**
Underwood News (Underwood, ND) **10697**
Union City Reporter (Hoboken, NJ) **10667**
Union County Advocate (Morganfield, KY) **10613**
Uniondale Beacon (Hicksville, NY) **10679**
Union Enterprise (Plainwell, MI) **10637**
Union Leader (Union, NJ) **10671**
Union Press-Courier (Patton, PA) **10722**
† Union Shopper, The (Arcata, CA)
Union Springs Herald (Union Springs, AL) **10522**
Union Star (Brookneal, VA) **10751**
† Union, The (Arcata, CA)
Unionville Republican, The (Unionville, MO) **10658**
University Herald (Seattle, WA) **10759**
Upper Arlington News (Columbus, OH) **10702**
Upper Country News-Reporter (Cambridge, ID) **10569**
Upper Darby Press (Drexel Hill, PA) **10717**
Upper Dauphin Sentinel (Millersburg, PA) **10720**
Upper Rogue Independent (Eagle Point, OR) **10713**
Uptown San Diego Examiner (San Diego, CA) **10542**
Utica Herald (Utica, OH) **10708**
Uvalde Leader-News (Uvalde, TX) **10747**
Vadnais Heights Press (St. Paul, MN) **10647**
Vailsburg Leader (Maplewood, NJ) **10668**
Vail Trail (Eagle-Vail, CO) **10548**
Valders Journal (Valders, WI) **10774**
Valdese News (Morganton, NC) **10693**
Valdez Vanguard (Valdez, AK) **10523**
Valencia County News-Bulletin (Belen, NM) **10672**
Valley Advocate (Hatfield, MA) **10625**
Valley Banner, The (Elkton, VA) **10752**
Valley Falls Vindicator (Valley Falls, KS) **10609**
Valley Farmer, The (Bay City, MI) **10630**

WEEKLY NEWSPAPERS   Wahkiakum County Eagle, The   10923

Valley Gazette (Shelton, CT) **10553**
Valley Gazette (Lansford, PA) **10719**
Valley Journal (Carbondale, CO) **10547**
Valley Log, The (Orbisonia, PA) **10721**
Valley News (Meridian, ID) **10570**
Valley News (Elizabethtown, NY) **10677**
Valley News (Fulton, NY) **10678**
Valley News Herald (Spokane, WA) **10760**
Valley News, The (Endwell, NY) **10677**
Valley News, The (Jefferson, OH) **10704**
Valley Post (Anderson, CA) **10530**
Valley Reporter, The (Waitsfield, VT) **10750**
Valley Roadrunner (Valley Center, CA) **10546**
Valley Stream Courier (Freeport, NY) **10677**
Valley Stream Herald (Lawrence, NY) **10680**
Valley Stream Maileader (Mineola, NY) **10683**
Valley Sun (Wasilla, AK) **10523**
Valley Sun, The (Scottsboro, AL) **10522**
Valley Times-Star (Newville, PA) **10721**
Valley Times, The (Moreno Valley, CA) **10539**
Valley Town Crier (McAllen, TX) **10744**
Valley Trader (Lewisburg, PA) **10719**
Valley Value Shopper (Spring Valley, WI) **10773**
Valley Vantage (Woodland Hills, CA) **10547**
Valparaiso Guide (Maryville, IN) **10596**
Van Buren County Advertiser (Gobles, MI) **10633**
Vandalia Leader-Union (Vandalia, IL) **10590**
Vandergrift News (Vandergrift, PA) **10724**
Van Horn Advocate (Van Horn, TX) **10747**
Vashon-Maury Island Beachcomber (Vashon, WA) **10760**
Vassar Pioneer Times (Vassar, MI) **10639**
Vega Enterprise, The (Vega, TX) **10747**
Venice-Marina News (Santa Monica, CA) **10544**
Venice Gondolier (Venice, FL) **10561**
† Ventura Bulletin, The (Los Angeles, CA)
Ventura County & Coast Reporter (Ventura, CA) **10546**
Verde Independent (Cottonwood, AZ) **10525**
Vermilion Photojournal (Vermilion, OH) **10708**
Vermont News Guide (Manchester Village, VT) **10750**
Vermont Standard (Woodstock, VT) **10750**
Vermont Times (Shelburne, VT) **10750**
Vernal Express (Vernal, UT) **10749**
Vernon County Broadcaster (Viroqua, WI) **10774**
Vernon Hills News (Grayslake, IL) **10581**
Vernon Hills Review (Bannockburn, IL) **10572**
Verona-Cedar Grove Times (Verona, NJ) **10671**
Verona Press (Verona, WI) **10774**

Versailles Leader-Statesman (Versailles, MO) **10658**
Versailles Policy, The (Versailles, OH) **10708**
Versailles Republican (Versailles, IN) **10598**
Vestal Town Crier (Conklin, NY) **10676**
Vevay Reveille-Enterprise (Vevay, IN) **10598**
† Victor-Farmington Herald (Webster, NY)
Victor Valley Advertiser (San Bernardino, CA) **10542**
† Victor Valley Living (Hesperia, CA)
Vidorian, The (Vidor, TX) **10747**
Vienna Times (Reston, VA) **10755**
Vienna Times, The (Vienna, IL) **10590**
Vilas County News-Review (Eagle River, WI) **10766**
Village Advocate (Chapel Hill, NC) **10691**
Village Beacon-Record, The (Setauket, NY) **10686**
Village Gazette of Ridgewood (Franklin Lakes, NJ) **10666**
Village Herald (Lawrence, NY) **10680**
† Village Journal (Osterville, MA)
Village News (Montgomery Village, MD) **10622**
Villager (St. Paul, MN) **10647**
Villager Newspaper (Austin, TX) **10736**
Villager, The (New York, NY) **10683**
Villager, The (Syracuse, NY) **10687**
Villager, The (Moscow, PA) **10720**
Village Times, The (Setauket, NY) **10686**
Village Voice, The (New York, NY) **10683**
Villa Park Argus (Elmhurst, IL) **10578**
Villa Rican, The (Villa Rica, GA) **10568**
Ville Platte Gazette (Ville Platte, LA) **10618**
† Vincennes Valley Advance (Vincennes, IN)
Vindicator, The (Liberty, TX) **10743**
Vineyard Gazette (Edgartown, MA) **10625**
† Vinton County Courier (McArthur, OH)
Vinton Messenger (Vinton, VA) **10756**
Virginia Beach Sun (Chesapeake, VA) **10752**
Virginia Gazette (Beardstown, IL) **10573**
Virginia Gazette (Williamsburg, VA) **10756**
Virginia Mountaineer (Grundy, VA) **10753**
Virginian-Leader (Pearisburg, VA) **10754**
† Vista Press (Kansas City, MO)
Vistas (King City, CA) **10535**
Voice-Tribune, The (Louisville, KY) **10612**
Voice Ledger, The (Millbrook, NY) **10682**
Voice of the Valley (Maple Valley, WA) **10758**
Voices (Southbury, CT) **10553**
Voice, The (Phoenixville, PA) **10723**
Waco Citizen, The (Waco, TX) **10747**
Waconia Patriot, The (Waconia, MN) **10648**
Wadena Pioneer Journal (Wadena, MN) **10648**
Wagoner Tribune, The (Wagoner, OK) **10712**
Wahkiakum County Eagle, The (Cathlamet, WA) **10757**

Weeklies Index

ULRICH'S INTERNATIONAL PERIODICALS DIRECTORY 1998

Wahoo Newspaper (Wahoo, NE) **10662**
Wake Weekly, The (Wake Forest, NC) **10695**
Wakulla News (Crawfordville, FL) **10556**
Walker-Westside Advance (Jenison, MI) **10634**
Walker County Messenger (La
  Fayette, GA) **10566**
Wallace Enterprise (Wallace, NC) **10695**
† Wallace Miner (Kellogg, ID)
Waller County News-Citizen
  (Hempstead, TX) **10741**
Wallis News-Review (Wallis, TX) **10747**
Wallkill Valley Times, The (Walden, NY) **10688**
Walpole Times, The (Walpole, MA) **10629**
Walsh County Press (Park River, ND) **10697**
Walsh County Record, The
  (Grafton, ND) **10696**
Walton Reporter, The (Walton, NY) **10688**
Walton Tribune (Monroe, GA) **10567**
Walworth Times, The (Walworth, WI) **10774**
Wampum Saver (Show Low, AZ) **10526**
Wantagh-Seaford Citizen (Bellmore, NY) **10673**
Wapato Independent (Wapato, WA) **10760**
Wareham Courier (Marion, MA) **10625**
Ware River News (Ware, MA) **10629**
Warner Center News (Woodland
  Hills, CA) **10547**
Warren-Newport Press (Grayslake, IL) **10581**
Warren Record, The (Warrenton, NC) **10695**
Warrensburg-Lake George News
  (Elizabethtown, NY) **10677**
Warren Sentinel, The (Front Royal, VA) **10753**
Warren Sheaf (Warren, MN) **10648**
Warren Times Gazette (Warren, RI) **10726**
† Warrenton Banner (Warrenton, MO)
Warrenton Journal (Warrenton, MO) **10658**
Warrenville Free Press (West
  Chicago, IL) **10590**
Warroad Pioneer (Greenbush, MN) **10642**
Warsaw-Faison News (Wallace, NC) **10695**
Warsaw Benton County Enterprise
  (Warsaw, MO) **10658**
Warwick Advertiser, The (Warwick, NY) **10688**
Warwick Beacon (Warwick, RI) **10726**
Warwick Valley Dispatch (Warwick, NY) **10688**
Wasco Tribune (Wasco, CA) **10546**
Waseca County News (Waseca, MN) **10648**
Washburn County Register (Shell
  Lake, WI) **10773**
Washburn Leader (Metamora, IL) **10585**
Washington City Paper
  (Washington, DC) **10555**
Washington County Edition (Salem, IN) **10597**
Washington County News (Chatom, AL) **10518**
Washington County News
  (Washington, KS) **10609**
Washington County News
  (Abingdon, VA) **10750**
Washington Courier (Washington, IL) **10590**
Washington Missourian
  (Washington, MO) **10658**
Washington News-Reporter
  (Washington, GA) **10568**
Washington Reporter (Morton, IL) **10586**
Waterford News (Winton, CA) **10546**
Waterford Post (Waterford, WI) **10775**
Waterloo Republic-Times (Waterloo, IL) **10590**
Watertown Tab & Press
  (Somerville, MA) **10628**
Watkins Review & Express (Watkins
  Glen, NY) **10689**
Watonga Republican, The
  (Watonga, OK) **10712**
Wauconda Leader (Grayslake, IL) **10581**
Waukon Standard (Waukon, IA) **10605**
Waunakee Tribune (Waunakee, WI) **10775**
Waushara Argus (Wautoma, WI) **10775**
Wauwatosa News-Times
  (Newverland, WI) **10771**
Waverly Democrat (Waverly, IA) **10605**
Waverly Journal (Waverly, IL) **10590**
Wayland-Weston Town Crier
  (Needham, MA) **10627**
Wayne County Journal-Banner
  (Piedmont, MO) **10656**
Wayne County Mail (Webster, NY) **10689**
Wayne County News (Waynesboro, MS) **10651**
Wayne County News (Waynesboro, TN) **10735**
Wayne County News (Wayne, WV) **10763**
Wayne County Outlook (Monticello, KY) **10612**
Wayne County Star (Lyons, NY) **10680**
Wayne Eagle (Wayne, MI) **10639**
Wayne Herald (Wayne, NE) **10662**
Wayne Today (Butler, NJ) **10665**
Wayne Wilson News Leader
  (Fremont, NC) **10692**
Wayzata/Orono/Long Lake Sun-Sailor
  (Minnetonka, MN) **10644**
Weakley County Press (Martin, TN) **10733**
Webster County Citizen (Seymour, MO) **10656**
Webster Echo (Webster Springs, WV) **10763**
Webster Herald (Webster, NY) **10689**
Webster Post, The (Webster, NY) **10689**
Webster Progress-Times (Eupora, MS) **10649**
Webster Reporter & Farmer
  (Webster, SD) **10730**
Webster Republican (Webster
  Springs, WV) **10763**
Webster Times, The (Webster, MA) **10629**
Wednesday Journal of Oak Park & River Forest
  (Oak Park, IL) **10587**

WEEKLY NEWSPAPERS

West Roxbury Transcript 10925

Wednesday Magazine (Kansas City, MO) **10654**
Weed Press (Weed, CA) **10546**
Weehawken Reporter (Hoboken, NJ) **10667**
† Weekender Enquirer (Boonville, IN)
Weekender, The (Whitinsville, MA) **10629**
† Weekender, The (Bronx, NY)
Weekender, The (Lexington, VA) **10753**
Weekend Flyer, The (Plainfield, IN) **10597**
Weekend News (Montrose, PA) **10720**
Weekly Almanac, The (Honesdale, PA) **10718**
Weekly Calistogan (Calistoga, CA) **10532**
Weekly Challenger (St. Petersburg, FL) **10561**
Weekly News (Marksville, LA) **10617**
Weekly Observer, The (Hemingway, SC) **10727**
Weekly Packet (Blue Hill, ME) **10618**
Weekly Planet (Tampa, FL) **10561**
Weekly Post (Rainsville, AL) **10521**
Weekly Press (Baton Rouge, LA) **10615**
Weekly Recorder, The (Claysville, PA) **10716**
Weekly Reminder (Paulding, OH) **10706**
† Weekly Territorial (Tucson, AZ)
Weimar Mercury (Weimar, TX) **10747**
Weisbeck, The (Alden, NY) **10673**
Weiser Signal American (Weiser, ID) **10571**
Wellesley Townsman (Wellesley, MA) **10629**
Wellington Royal Palm Beach Forum (Wellington, FL) **10562**
Wellsboro Gazette (Wellsboro, PA) **10724**
Wells Mirror, The (Wells, MN) **10648**
† Wellston Sentry (Wellston, OH)
Wellston Telegram, The (Wellston, OH) **10708**
Wenona Index (Henry, IL) **10581**
Wentzville Journal (Wentzville, MO) **10658**
West Alabama Gazette (Millport, AL) **10521**
West Allis Star (New Berlin, WI) **10771**
West Boca Times (Deerfield Beach, FL) **10556**
West Bridgewater Star (Middleboro, MA) **10626**
Westbury Times (Mineola, NY) **10683**
West Carroll Gazette (Oak Grove, LA) **10617**
Westchester Herald (Oak Park, IL) **10587**
Westchester Observer (Santa Monica, CA) **10544**
Westchester Star (Los Angeles, CA) **10538**
West Chicago Press (West Chicago, IL) **10590**
West Columbia Brazoria County News (West Columbia, TX) **10747**
West Cook County Press (Elmhurst, IL) **10578**
West County Journal (St. Louis, MO) **10658**
Western Breeze (Cut Bank, MT) **10659**
Western Edition (San Francisco, CA) **10543**
Western Express (Des Moines, IA) **10600**
Western Hills Press (Cincinnati, OH) **10700**
Western News (Libby, MT) **10659**
Western Springs Doings (Hinsdale, IL) **10582**

Western Star (Bessemer, AL) **10517**
Western Star (Lebanon, OH) **10704**
Western Wayne News (Cambridge City, IN) **10592**
Western World (Bandon, OR) **10712**
Westerville News & Public Opinion (Westerville, OH) **10708**
West Essex Tribune (Livingston, NJ) **10667**
West Fargo Pioneer (West Fargo, ND) **10698**
Westfield Enterprise (Fishers, IN) **10593**
Westfield Leader (Westfield, NJ) **10671**
Westfield Republican (Westfield, NY) **10689**
Westford Eagle (Chelmsford, MA) **10624**
West Geauga Sun (Beachwood, OH) **10699**
West Hartford News (Bristol, CT) **10551**
West Haven News (Milford, CT) **10553**
West Hempstead Beacon (Hicksville, NY) **10679**
Westine Report (Union Grove, WI) **10774**
West Kentucky News (Paducah, KY) **10613**
Westlake Picayune (Austin, TX) **10736**
Westlaker Times, The (Rocky River, OH) **10707**
Westland Eagle (Wayne, MI) **10639**
Westland Observer (Livonia, MI) **10635**
West Liberty Index (West Liberty, IA) **10605**
West Life (West Lake, OH) **10708**
West Linn Tidings (Lake Oswego, OR) **10713**
West Los Angeles Independent (Santa Monica, CA) **10544**
West Martin Weekly News (Sherburn, MN) **10646**
West Milton Record (West Milton, OH) **10708**
Westminster Window (Westminster, CO) **10551**
Westmont Progress (Downers Grove, IL) **10577**
Westmoreland News (Montross, VA) **10754**
Westmore News (Port Chester, NY) **10685**
West Morris Star-Journal (Ledgewood, NJ) **10667**
West News (West, TX) **10747**
West New York Reporter (Hoboken, NJ) **10667**
Weston Democrat, The (Weston, WV) **10763**
Weston Forum, The (Georetown, CT) **10552**
West Orange Chronicle (Orange, NJ) **10669**
West Orange Times (Winter Garden, FL) **10562**
Westosha Report (Twin Lakes, WI) **10774**
† West Plains Tribune (Spokane, WA)
West Point News (West Point, NE) **10662**
Westport News (Westport, CT) **10554**
West Proviso Herald (Oak Park, IL) **10587**
West Roxbury Transcript (Dedham, MA) **10624**

West Sacramento News-Ledger (West Sacramento, CA) **10546**
West San Bernardino Advertiser (San Bernardino, CA) **10542**
West Schuylkill Herald (Tower City, PA) **10724**
West Seattle Herald (Seattle, WA) **10759**
West Seneca Bee (Williamsville, NY) **10689**
West Side Advance (Kerman, CA) **10535**
Westside Enterprise (Greenfield, IN) **10594**
Westside Flyer (Indianapolis, IN) **10595**
West Side Journal (Port Allen, LA) **10617**
Westside Messenger (Speedway, IN) **10598**
Westside Record-Journal (Ferndale, WA) **10758**
Westsider, The (New York, NY) **10683**
West Side Sun News (North Olmsted, OH) **10706**
West Side Times (Buffalo, NY) **10675**
West Springfield Record (West Springfield, MA) **10629**
West St. Paul/Mendota Heights Sun-Current (Burnsville, MN) **10640**
West Suburban Post (Chicago, IL) **10575**
West Toledo Herald (Toledo, OH) **10708**
West Valley Courier (Hillsboro, OR) **10713**
West Valley Eagle (Bountiful, UT) **10748**
West Valley News (Magna, UT) **10749**
West Valley News/Sunday Advance (Flint, MI) **10632**
West Valley View (Avondale, AZ) **10524**
Westville Indicator (Westville, IN) **10598**
West Virginia Hillbilly (Richwood, WV) **10763**
Westword (Denver, CO) **10548**
Wethersfield Post (Bristol, CT) **10552**
Wet Mountain Tribune (Westcliffe, CO) **10551**
Wetumpka Herald (Wetumpka, AL) **10522**
Wetzel Chronicle (New Martinsville, WV) **10762**
Wewoka Times (Wewoka, OK) **10712**
Weymouth News (Marshfield, MA) **10626**
Weymouth News & Gazette (Braintree, MA) **10624**
Wharton Journal-Spectator (Wharton, TX) **10748**
What Cheer Paper (What Cheer, IA) **10605**
Wheaton Leader (Glen Ellyn, IL) **10580**
Wheaton Press (Bloomingdale, IL) **10573**
Wheaton Sun (Naperville, IL) **10586**
† Wheat Ridge Sentinel (Lakewood, CO)
Wheels 'N Deals (Columbia, MO) **10653**
Whidbey News-Times (Oak Harbor, WA) **10758**
White Bear Press (St. Paul, MN) **10647**
Whitefish Bay Herald (New Berlin, WI) **10771**
Whitefish Pilot (Whitefish, MT) **10659**
White Hall Journal (Pine Bluff, AR) **10529**
Whitehall News (Columbus, OH) **10702**
Whitehall Times (Whitehall, NY) **10689**
Whitehall Times (Whitehall, WI) **10775**
White Lake Beacon (Whitehall, MI) **10639**
White Mountain Independent (Show Low, AZ) **10526**
White Oak Independent (White Oak, TX) **10748**
White River Current (Calico Rock, AR) **10527**
▼White River Gazette (Fishers, IN) **10593**
White River Journal (Des Arc, AR) **10527**
White Settlement News (Fort Worth, TX) **10740**
Whiteside Shopper (Fulton, IL) **10579**
Whitestone Times, The (Bayside, NY) **10673**
Whitewright Sun, The (Whitewright, TX) **1074**
Whitley Republican News Journal (Williamsburg, KY) **10615**
Whitman County Gazette (Colfax, WA) **10757**
Whitman Times (Stoughton, MA) **10628**
Whitney Point Reporter (Greene, NY) **10678**
Wick-Qua-Boag Weekly (Spencer, MA) **10628**
Wickenburg Sun, The (Wickenburg, AZ) **1052**
Wiggins Courier, The (Wiggins, CO) **10551**
Wilcox Progressive Era (Camden, AL) **10518**
Wildwood Leader (Wildwood, NJ) **10672**
† Wilkes-Barre Sunday Independent (Wilkes Barre, PA)
Willamette Week (Portland, OR) **10714**
Willapa Harbor Herald (Raymond, WA) **10759**
Willard Times-Junction (Willard, OH) **10708**
Williams Grand Canyon News (Williams, AZ) **10526**
Williamson County Sun (Georgetown, TX) **10740**
Williamson Leader, The (Franklin, TN) **10732**
Williamston Enterprise (Williamston, NC) **10696**
Williamsville Sun (Riverton, IL) **10589**
Williston Plains Reporter (Williston, ND) **1069**
Willowbrook Doings (Hinsdale, IL) **10582**
Willowbrook Progress (Downers Grove, IL) **10577**
Willow Grove Guide (Fort Washington, PA) **10718**
Willows Journal (Willows, CA) **10546**
Wilmette Life (Glenview, IL) **10580**
Wilmington-Tewksbury Town Crier (Wilmington, MA) **10629**
Wilmington Advocate, The (Wilmington, IL) **10591**
Wilmington Beacon (Compton, CA) **10533**
Wilmington Defender (Wilmington, DE) **10554**
Wilmington Express (Wilmington, IL) **10591**
Wilmington Free Press (Wilmington, IL) **10591**
Wilmington Journal (Wilmington, NC) **10696**
Wilson County Citizen (Fredonia, KS) **10606**

Wilson World, The (Lebanon, TN) **10733**
Wilton Bulletin (Wilton, CT) **10554**
Wimberley Valley-News (Wimberley, TX) **10748**
Winchendon Chronicle
  (Winchendon, MA) **10629**
Winchendon Courier (Winchendon, MA) **10629**
Winchester Star (Woburn, MA) **10629**
Winder News (Winder, GA) **10568**
Windham Journal (Windham, NY) **10689**
Windom Cottonwood County Citizen
  (Windom, MN) **10648**
Wind River News (Lander, WY) **10776**
Windsor Journal (Bristol, CT) **10552**
Windsor Locks Journal (Bristol, CT) **10552**
Windsor Review (Windsor, MO) **10658**
Windsor Standard (Conklin, NY) **10676**
Winfield Estate (Glen Ellyn, IL) **10580**
Winfield Press (West Chicago, IL) **10590**
Winkler County News (Kermit, TX) **10742**
Winneconne News (Winneconne, WI) **10775**
Winner Advocate (Winner, SD) **10731**
Winnetka Talk (Glenview, IL) **10580**
Winn Parish Enterprise (Winnfield, LA) **10618**
Winnsboro News (Winnsboro, TX) **10748**
Winona Times (Winona, MS) **10651**
Winslow Mail (Winslow, AZ) **10526**
Winsted Journal (Winsted, CT) **10554**
Winter Park-Maitland Observer (Winter
  Park, FL) **10562**
Winter Park Manifest (Winter Park, CO) **10551**
Winterset Madisonian (Winterset, IA) **10605**
† Winter Visitor Independent (Mesa, AZ)
Winton Times (Winton, CA) **10546**
Wisconsin Dells Events (Wisconsin
  Dells, WI) **10775**
Wisconsin State Farmer (Waupaca, WI) **10775**
Wise County Messenger (Decatur, TX) **10738**
Wittenberg Enterprise News
  (Wittenberg, WI) **10775**
Woburn Advocate (Woburn, MA) **10629**
Woodbury-South Maplewood Review (St.
  Paul, MN) **10647**
Wood County Democrat (Quitman, TX) **10745**
Wood Dale Press (Elmhurst, IL) **10578**
Woodford County Journal (Eureka, IL) **10578**
Woodford Sun (Versailles, KY) **10615**
Woodridge Progress (Downers
  Grove, IL) **10577**
Wood River Journal (Hailey, ID) **10569**
Woodruff County Monitor Leader Advocate
  (McCrory, AR) **10528**
Woodside Herald (Sunnyside, NY) **10687**
Woodstock Independent, The
  (Woodstock, IL) **10591**

Worcester County Messenger (Pocomoke
  City, MD) **10622**
Worcester Magazine (Worcester, MA) **10630**
Worth Citizen (Midlothian, IL) **10586**
Worthington Suburbia News
  (Columbus, OH) **10702**
Worthington Times, The
  (Worthington, IN) **10598**
Wrangell Sentinel (Wrangell, AK) **10524**
Wray Gazette (Wray, CO) **10551**
Wright County Journal-Press
  (Buffalo, MN) **10640**
Wrightsville Headlight, The
  (Wrightsville, GA) **10568**
† Wrova Reporter (Galva, IL)
Wyandotte West (Kansas City, KS) **10607**
Wyckoff Gazette (Franklin Lakes, NJ) **10666**
Wylie News, The (Wylie, TX) **10748**
Wynne Progress (Wynne, AR) **10530**
Wyoming Advance (Jenison, MI) **10634**
Wyoming State Journal (Lander, WY) **10776**
Yadkin Ripple, The (Yadkinville, NC) **10696**
Yale News, The (Yale, OK) **10712**
Yancey Common Times Journal
  (Burnsville, NC) **10691**
Yankee Trader (Coram, NY) **10676**
Yardley News (Yardley, PA) **10725**
† Yarmouth Sun (Yarmouth Port, MA)
Yazoo Herald (Yazoo City, MS) **10651**
Yoakum Herald-Times (Yoakum, TX) **10748**
Yonkers Home News & Times
  (Yonkers, NY) **10690**
York County Coast Star
  (Kennebunk, ME) **10619**
York Town Crier (Yorktown, VA) **10757**
Yorkville Enquirer (York, SC) **10729**
Your Paper (Roebuck, SC) **10729**
Yucaipa & Calimesa News-Mirror
  (Yucaipa, CA) **10547**
Yucca Valley Hi-Desert Star (Yucca
  Valley, CA) **10547**
Yukon Review (Yukon, OK) **10712**
Yuma Pioneer (Yuma, CO) **10551**
Zachary Plainsman-News (Zachary, LA) **10618**
Zanesville Muskingum Advertiser
  (Zanesville, OH) **10709**
Zebulon Record, The (Zebulon, NC) **10696**
Zephyrhills News (Zephyrhills, FL) **10562**
Zion-Benton News (Zion, IL) **10591**
† Zionsville Eagle (Indianapolis, IN)
Zionsville Times Sentinel (Zionsville, IN) **10598**
1590 Broadcaster (Nashua, NH) **10663**

Geographic Index

ALABAMA

Abbeville Herald (Abbeville) **10517**
Advertiser-Gleam (Guntersville) **10520**
† Alabama Journal (Montgomery)
Alabama Messenger (Birmingham) **10518**
Alexander City Outlook (Alexander City) **10415**
Andalusia Star News (Andalusia) **10415**
Anniston Star (Anniston) **10415**
Arab Tribune (Arab) **10517**
Atmore Advance (Atmore) **10517**
† Azalea City News & Review (Bayou Labatre)
Baldwin Times (Bay Minette) **10517**
† Birmingham Free Press (Birmingham)
Birmingham News (Birmingham) **10415**
Birmingham Post-Herald (Birmingham) **10415**
Birmingham World (Birmingham) **10518**
Blount Countian, The (Oneonta) **10521**
Brewton Standard, The (Brewton) **10518**
Butler County News (Georgiana) **10519**
Centreville Press (Centreville) **10518**
Cherokee County Herald (Centre) **10518**
Choctaw Advocate (Butler) **10518**
Clanton Advertiser (Clanton) **10518**
Clarke County Democrat (Grove Hill) **10519**
Clay Times Journal (Lineville) **10520**
Clayton Record (Clayton) **10518**
Cleburne News (Heflin) **10520**
Colbert County Reporter (Tuscumbia) **10522**
Community News, The (Dora) **10518**
Community Press, The (Millbrook) **10520**
Community Shopper (Birmingham) **10518**
County Reporter, The (Andalusia) **10517**
Courier Journal (Florence) **10519**
Cullman Times (Cullman) **10415**
Cullman Tribune (Cullman) **10518**
Dadeville Record (Alexander City) **10517**
Daily Home (Talladega) **10416**
Daily Sentinel, The (Scottsboro) **10416**
Decatur Daily (Decatur) **10416**
Democrat-Reporter, The (Linden) **10520**
Demopolis Times (Demopolis) **10518**
Dothan Eagle (Dothan) **10416**
East Lauderdale News (Rogersville) **10521**
Elba Clipper, The (Elba) **10519**
Enterprise Ledger (Enterprise) **10416**
Eufaula Tribune (Eufaula) **10519**
Evergreen Courant, The (Evergreen) **10519**
Fairhope Courier, The (Fairhope) **10519**
Florala News, The (Florala) **10519**
Franklin County Plus (Russellville) **10522**
Franklin County Times (Russellville) **10522**
Gadsden Times (Gadsden) **10416**
Geneva County Reaper (Geneva) **10519**
Greene County Independent (Eutaw) **10519**
Greensboro Watchman, The (Greensboro) **10519**
Greenville Advocate, The (Greenville) **10519**
Hanceville Herald (Hanceville) **10520**
Hartselle Enquirer (Hartselle) **10520**

ULRICH'S INTERNATIONAL PERIODICALS DIRECTORY 1998

Headland Observer (Headland) **10520**
† Huntsville News (Huntsville)
Huntsville Times, The (Huntsville) **10416**
Independent, The (Robertsdale) **10521**
Islander, The (Gulf Shores) **10519**
Jacksonville News (Jacksonville) **10520**
Jasper Daily Mountain Eagle (Jasper) **10416**
Journal Record (Hamilton) **10520**
Lafayette Sun, The (Lafayette) **10520**
Lamar Democrat (Vernon) **10522**
Lamar Leader (Sulligent) **10522**
Lee County Eagle, The (Auburn) **10517**
Leeds News (Leeds) **10520**
Luverne Journal & News (Luverne) **10520**
Madison County Record (Madison) **10520**
Marion Times-Standard (Marion) **10520**
Messenger, The (Troy) **10417**
Mobile Beacon (Mobile) **10521**
† Mobile Press (Mobile)
Mobile Register, The (Mobile) **10416**
Monroe Journal (Monroeville) **10521**
Montgomery Advertiser (Montgomery) **10416**
Montgomery Independent (Montgomery) **10521**
Moulton Advertiser (Moulton) **10521**
Moundville Times (Moundville) **10521**
News-Courier (Athens) **10415**
† News Herald, The (Mobile)
North Jackson Progress (Stevenson) **10522**
North Jefferson News (Gardendale) **10519**
Northwest Alabamian (Haleyville) **10520**
Onlooker, The (Foley) **10519**
Opelika-Auburn News (Opelika) **10416**
Opp News (Opp) **10521**
Over the Mountain Journal (Birmingham) **10518**
Phenix-Citizen (Phenix City) **10521**
Pickens County Herald (Carrollton) **10518**
Piedmont Journal-Independent (Piedmont) **10521**
Prattville Progress (Prattville) **10521**
Randolph Leader (Roanoke) **10521**
Red Bay News (Red Bay) **10521**
Samford Crimson (Birmingham) **10518**
Samson Ledger (Geneva) **10519**
Sand Mountain Reporter (Albertville) **10517**
Selma Times-Journal (Selma) **10416**
Shelby County Reporter (Columbiana) **10518**
South Alabamian (Jackson) **10520**
Southern Star (Ozark) **10521**
Standard & Times (Tuscumbia) **10522**
St. Clair News-Aegis (Pell City) **10521**
Sumter County Record-Journal, The (Livingston) **10520**
Tallassee Tribune (Tallassee) **10522**
Thomasville Times, The (Thomasville) **10522**
Thrifty Nickel (Birmingham) **10518**
Times-Journal, The (Fort Payne) **10416**
Times Daily (Florence) **10416**
Times Record (Fayette) **10519**
† Total, The (Heflin)
Tri-City Ledger (Flomaton) **10519**
† Tri-City Times (Geraldine)
Troy Progress (Troy) **10522**
Tuscaloosa News, The (Tuscaloosa) **10417**
Tuskegee News (Tuskegee) **10522**
Union Springs Herald (Union Springs) **10522**
Valley Sun, The (Scottsboro) **10522**
Valley Times-News (Lanett) **10416**
Washington County News (Chatom) **10518**
Weekly Post (Rainsville) **10521**
West Alabama Gazette (Millport) **10521**
Western Star (Bessemer) **10517**
Wetumpka Herald (Wetumpka) **10522**
Wilcox Progressive Era (Camden) **10518**

ALASKA

Alaska Star (Eagle River) **10523**
Anchorage Daily News (Anchorage) **10417**
Arctic Sounder, The (Barrow) **10522**
Bering Strait Record (None) **10523**
Bristol Bay Times, The (Dillingham) **10523**
Capital City Weekly (Juneau) **10523**
Chilkat Valley News (Haines) **10523**
Cordova Times (Cordova) **10523**
Daily Sitka Sentinel (Sitka) **10417**
† Delta Paper (Delta Jct)
Delta Wind, The (Delta Junction) **10523**
Dutch Harbor Fisherman, The (Dutch Harbor) **10523**
Fairbanks Daily News-Miner (Fairbanks) **10417**
Frontiersman, The (Wasilla) **10523**
Great Lander Bush Mailer (Anchorage) **10522**
Homer News (Homer) **10523**
Juneau Empire (Juneau) **10417**
Ketchikan Daily News (Ketchikan) **10417**
Kodiak Daily Mirror (Kodiak) **10417**
† New Alaskan (Ketchikan)
Nome Nugget (Nome) **10523**
Peninsula Clarion (Kenai) **10417**
Petersburg Pilot (Petersburg) **10523**
Seward Phoenix Log (Seward) **10523**
Tundra Drums (Bethel) **10523**
Tundra Times (Anchorage) **10522**
Valdez Vanguard (Valdez) **10523**
Valley Sun (Wasilla) **10523**
Wrangell Sentinel (Wrangell) **10524**

AMERICAN SAMOA

Samoa News (Pago Pago) **10417**

ARIZONA

Ajo Copper News (Ajo) **10524**
Apache Junction Independent (Apache Junction) **10524**
Arizona City Independent (Arizona City) **10524**
Arizona Daily Star (Tucson) **10418**
Arizona Daily Sun (Flagstaff) **10418**
Arizona Republic (Phoenix) **10418**
Arizona Silver Belt (Globe) **10525**
▼ Arrowhead Ranch Independent (Sun City) **10526**
Arrow, The (Glendale) **10525**
Bisbee Daily Review (Bisbee) **10417**
▼ Bisbee News, The (Bisbee) **10524**
Bisbee Observer, The (Bisbee) **10524**
† Brewery Gulch Gazette (Bisbee)
Buckeye Valley News (Buckeye) **10524**
Casa Grande Dispatch (Casa Grande) **10417**
Chandler Arizonan Tribune (Chandler) **10418**
Chandler Independent (Chandler) **10524**
Chino Valley Review (Chino Valley) **10524**
Coolidge Examiner (Coolidge) **10524**
Copper Country News (Globe) **10525**
Copper Era (Clifton) **10524**
Cottonwood Journal Extra (Cottonwood) **10524**
Daily Courier, The (Prescott) **10418**
Daily Dispatch (Douglas) **10418**
Daily News-Sun (Sun City) **10418**
Desert Winds, The (Cave Creek) **10524**
Eastern Arizona Courier (Safford) **10526**
East Mesa Independent (Apache Junction) **10524**
Eloy Enterprise (Eloy) **10525**
Florence Reminder & Blade-Tribune (Florence) **10525**
Foothills Sentinel (Cave Creek) **10524**
Gilbert Independent (Scottsdale) **10526**
Gilbert Tribune (Chandler) **10418**
Glendale Star, The (Glendale) **10525**
Green Valley News & Sun (Green Valley) **10525**
Holbrook Tribune News & Snowflake Herald (Holbrook) **10525**
Kingman Daily Miner (Kingman) **10418**
Lake Havasu City Advertiser (Lake Havasu City) **10525**
Lake Havasu City Herald (Lake Havasu City) **10418**
Lake Powell Chronicle (Page) **10525**
Mesa Tribune (Mesa) **10418**
Mohave Valley Daily News (Bullhead City) **10417**

New Times (Phoenix) **10525**
† North Scottsdale Independent (Scottsdale)
Paradise Valley Independent (Scottsdale) **10526**
Parker Advertiser (Parker) **10525**
Parker Pioneer (Parker) **10525**
Payson Roundup (Payson) **10525**
Peoria Times (Glendale) **10525**
† Phoenix Gazette (Phoenix)
Prescott Valley Tribune, The (Prescott Valley) **10526**
Round Valley Paper, The (Eagar) **10525**
San Carlos Apache Moccasin (Globe) **10525**
San Pedro Valley News-Sun (Benson) **10524**
Scottsdale Progress Tribune (Scottsdale) **10418**
Sedona Red Rock News (Sedona) **10526**
Sierra Vista Herald (Sierra Vista) **10418**
Sun Cities Independent (Sun City) **10526**
Sun City/Youngtown (Sun City) **10526**
Sun City West (Sun City) **10526**
Tempe Daily News Tribune (Tempe) **10418**
Times of Fountain Hills & Rio Verde (Fountain Hills) **10525**
Today's News-Herald (Lake Havasu City) **10418**
Tombstone Epitaph, The (Tombstone) **10526**
Town of Paradise Valley Independent (Scottsdale) **10526**
Tri-State Advertiser (Bullhead City) **10524**
Tribune (Chandler) **10418**
Tucson Citizen (Tucson) **10419**
Verde Independent (Cottonwood) **10525**
Wampum Saver (Show Low) **10526**
† Weekly Territorial (Tucson)
West Valley View (Avondale) **10524**
White Mountain Independent (Show Low) **10526**
Wickenburg Sun, The (Wickenburg) **10526**
Williams Grand Canyon News (Williams) **10526**
Winslow Mail (Winslow) **10526**
† Winter Visitor Independent (Mesa)
Yuma Daily Sun (Yuma) **10419**

ARKANSAS

Advance-Monticellonian (Monticello) **10528**
Advertiser, The (Van Buren) **10529**
Arkadelphia Daily Siftings Herald (Arkadelphia) **10419**
Arkansas Democrat-Gazette (Little Rock) **10420**
Ashley County Shoppers Guide (Crossett) **10527**
Ashley News Observer (Crossett) **10527**

Atkins Chronicle, The (Atkins) **10526**
Banner-News (Magnolia) **10420**
Batesville Guard (Batesville) **10419**
Baxter Bulletin (Mountain Home) **10420**
Beebe News (Beebe) **10526**
Benton County Daily Record (Bentonville) **10419**
Benton Courier (Benton) **10419**
Brinkley Argus (Brinkley) **10527**
Camden News (Camden) **10419**
Citizen, The (Mansfield) **10528**
Clinton Van Buren County Democrat (Clinton) **10527**
Conway County Petit Jean Country Headlight (Morrilton) **10528**
Courier News (Blytheville) **10419**
Courier, The (Russellville) **10420**
Daily Citizen (Searcy) **10420**
Daily News (Mountain Home) **10420**
Decatur Herald (Gentry) **10527**
De Queen Bee (De Queen) **10527**
De Queen Daily Citizen (De Queen) **10419**
Dumas Clarion (Dumas) **10527**
El Dorado News-Times (El Dorado) **10419**
England Democrat (England) **10527**
Eureka Springs Times-Echo (Berryville) **10527**
Evening Times (West Memphis) **10421**
Forrest City Times-Herald (Forrest City) **10419**
Gentry Courier-Journal (Gentry) **10527**
Glenwood Herald (Glenwood) **10527**
Gravette News Herald (Gravette) **10527**
Green Forest Tribune (Berryville) **10527**
Greenwood Democrat (Greenwood) **10527**
Harrison Daily Times (Harrison) **10419**
Helena West Helena Daily World (Helena) **10420**
Herald-Leader (Siloam Springs) **10529**
Hope Star, The (Hope) **10420**
Jacksonville Patriot (Jacksonville) **10420**
Johnson County Graphic (Clarksville) **10527**
Jonesboro Sun (Jonesboro) **10420**
LaVilla News (Hot Springs Village) **10528**
Lincoln Ledger (Star City) **10529**
Log Cabin Democrat (Conway) **10419**
Madison County Record (Huntsville) **10528**
Malvern Daily Record (Malvern) **10420**
Marianna Courier Index (Marianna) **10528**
Marshall Mountain Wave (Marshall) **10528**
Mena Star (Mena) **10528**
Modern News (Harrisburg) **10527**
Morning News of Northwest Arkansas (Springdale) **10421**
Mountain Echo (Yellville) **10530**
Murfreesboro Diamond (Murfreesboro) **10528**
Nashville News (Nashville) **10528**
Nevada County Picayune (Prescott) **10529**

Newport Daily Independent (Newport) **10420**
News, The (Salem) **10529**
Northwest Arkansas Times (Fayetteville) **10419**
Osceola Times (Osceola) **10529**
Ozark Journal (Imboden) **10528**
Paragould Daily Press (Paragould) **10420**
Paris Express (Paris) **10529**
Perry County Petit Jean Country Headlight (Morrilton) **10528**
Piggott Times, The (Piggott) **10529**
Pine Bluff Commercial (Pine Bluff) **10420**
Pine Bluff News (Pine Bluff) **10529**
Pocahontas Star Herald (Pocahontas) **10529**
Press Argus-Courier (Van Buren) **10529**
Scott County Advertiser (Waldron) **10529**
Sentinel-Record, The (Hot Springs) **10420**
Sheridan Headlight (Sheridan) **10529**
Southwest Times Record (Fort Smith) **10419**
Star-Progress, The (Berryville) **10527**
Stone County Citizen (Mountain View) **10528**
Stone County Leader (Mountain View) **10528**
Stuttgart Daily Leader (Stuttgart) **10421**
Sun Times (Heber Springs) **10528**
Times Dispatch (Walnut Ridge) **10529**
Times of Northeast Benton County (Pea Ridge) **10529**
Times, The (North Little Rock) **10528**
Tri-City Tribune (Marked Tree) **10528**
Tri-County Trader (Waldron) **10529**
Trumann Democrat (Trumann) **10529**
White Hall Journal (Pine Bluff) **10529**
White River Current (Calico Rock) **10527**
White River Journal (Des Arc) **10527**
Woodruff County Monitor Leader Advocate (McCrory) **10528**
Wynne Progress (Wynne) **10530**

CALIFORNIA

Acorn, The (Agoura Hills) **10530**
† Adelanto Bulletin, The (Adelanto)
Alameda Times Star (Oakland) **10423**
Alhambra Post Advocate (Los Angeles) **10537**
Aliso Viejo News (Lake Forest) **10536**
† Alvin Tiller (Lamont)
Amador/Calavaras Ledger Dispatch (Jackson) **10535**
Anaheim Bulletin (Anaheim) **10530**
Anaheim Hills News (Anaheim) **10530**
Antelope Valley Press (Palmdale) **10423**
Appeal-Democrat (Marysville) **10423**
Apple Valley News (Apple Valley) **10530**
† Arcadia Tribune (Arcadia)
Argonaut, The (Los Angeles) **10537**
Argus, The (Fremont) **10422**

Ark, The (Bel Tiburon) **10531**
Atascadero News (Atascadero) **10530**
Atwater Times (Winton) **10546**
Auburn Journal (Auburn) **10421**
Avalon Bay News, The (Avalon) **10530**
Avenal Progress (Avenal) **10531**
Azusa Herald (West Covina) **10546**
Bakersfield Californian (Bakersfield) **10421**
Banning Record Gazette (Banning) **10421**
Bay Area Press (Oakland) **10540**
Beach & Bay Press (San Diego) **10542**
Beach Reporter, The (Manhattan Beach) **10539**
Belevedere Citizen (Los Angeles) **10537**
Bell Gardens Review (Los Angeles) **10537**
Bell Maywood Cudahy Industrial Post (Los Angeles) **10537**
Benicia Herald (Benicia) **10421**
Berryessa Sun (Milpitas) **10539**
Beverly Hills Courier (Beverly Hills) **10531**
Beverly Hills Independent (Santa Monica) **10544**
Big Bear Life (Big Bear Lake) **10531**
Blythe Advertiser (Palm Desert) **10540**
Boutique & Villager (Burlingame) **10531**
Brawley Advertiser (El Centro) **10533**
Brea Progress (Anaheim) **10530**
Brentwood Westwood Press (Santa Monica) **10544**
† Buyer's Guide (Napa)
Calexico Advertiser (El Centro) **10533**
California Advocate, The (Fresno) **10534**
California Courier (Glendale) **10534**
Californian, The (Salinas) **10425**
Californian, The (Temecula) **10426**
Camarillo Star (Camarillo) **10421**
Capistrano Valley News (Lake Forest) **10536**
Carlsbad Sun (Carlsbad) **10532**
Carmel Pine Cone (Carmel) **10532**
Carmichael Times (Carmichael) **10532**
† Carpinteria Herald (Goleta)
Carson Bulletin (Compton) **10532**
Carson Wave (Los Angeles) **10537**
Catalina Islander, The (Avalon) **10530**
Central Coast Sun-Bulletin (Morro Bay) **10539**
† Central Coast Times (Paso Robles)
Ceres Courier (Ceres) **10532**
Chico Enterprise-Record (Chico) **10421**
Chronicle, The (Atwater) **10530**
City Terrace Comet (City of Commerce) **10532**
Civic Center NEWSource (Los Angeles) **10537**
Claremont Courier (Claremont) **10532**
Classified Gazette (San Rafael) **10544**
Clear Lake Observer-American (Clearlake) **10532**
Cloverdale Reveille (Cloverdale) **10532**

Clovis Independent (Clovis) **10532**
Coalinga Record (Coalinga) **10532**
Coastal Post (Bolinas) **10531**
Coastside Chronicle (San Mateo) **10543**
Colusa County Sun-Herald (Colusa) **10532**
Community Adviser (Beaumont) **10531**
Compton Bulletin (Compton) **10533**
Compton Wave (Los Angeles) **10537**
Contra Costa Sun (Lafayette) **10535**
Contra Costa Times (Walnut Creek) **10427**
Corning Observer (Corning) **10533**
Corona-Norco Independent (Corona) **10533**
Coronado Journal (Coronado) **10533**
Corridor News (Poway) **10541**
Country Almanac (Menlo Park) **10539**
Country News-Press (Paso Robles) **10424**
Crestline Courier-News (Crestline) **10533**
Culver City-Ladera Independent (Santa Monica) **10544**
Culver City Star (Los Angeles) **10537**
Cupertino Courier (Cupertino) **10533**
Daily Breeze (Torrance) **10426**
Daily Californian, The (El Cajon) **10421**
Daily Democrat (Woodland) **10427**
Daily Independent, The (Ridgecrest) **10424**
Daily Midway Driller (Taft) **10426**
Daily News (Woodland Hills) **10427**
Daily Pilot, The (Costa Mesa) **10421**
Daily Press (Victorville) **10427**
Daily Republic (Fairfield) **10422**
Daily Review (Hayward) **10422**
Daly City Record (San Mateo) **10543**
Dana Point News (Lake Forest) **10536**
Davis Enterprise (Davis) **10421**
Delano Record (Delano) **10533**
Delhi Express (Winton) **10546**
Del Mar, Solana Beach, Carmel Valley, Rancho Santa Fe Sun (Carlsbad) **10532**
Del Norte Triplicate (Crescent City) **10421**
Denair Dispatch (Winton) **10546**
Desert Dispatch (Barstow) **10421**
Desert Mailer News (Lancaster) **10536**
Desert Mobile Home News (Palm Desert) **10540**
† Desert Mountain Express (Hesperia)
Desert Sentinel, The (Desert Hot Springs) **10533**
Desert Sun, The (Palm Springs) **10424**
Digger Shopper & News, The (Oroville) **10540**
Dispatch, The (Gilroy) **10422**
Downey Herald American (Los Angeles) **10537**
Downtown Gazette (Long Beach) **10537**
Eagle Rock Sentinel (Los Angeles) **10537**
East Bay Express (Berkeley) **10531**
East L.A./Commerce Tribune (Los Angeles) **10537**

† East Los Angeles Gazette (South Gate)
† East Los Angeles Tribune (South Gate)
East Riverside Advertiser (Palm Desert) **10540**
Eastside Journal (Los Angeles) **10537**
Eastside Sun (City of Commerce) **10532**
Easy Reader (Hermosa Beach) **10535**
Ebbtide (Sausalito) **10544**
El Centro Advertiser (El Centro) **10533**
Elk Grove Citizen (Elk Grove) **10533**
El Segundo Herald (El Segundo) **10534**
El Sereno Star (Los Angeles) **10537**
Encinitas Sun (Encinitas) **10534**
Enquirer Bulletin (Burlingame) **10531**
† Enterprise News (Pixley)
Enterprise, The (Fallbrook) **10534**
Escondido News-Reporter (Escondido) **10534**
Exeter Sun, The (Exeter) **10534**
Fillmore Herald (Fillmore) **10534**
Firebaugh/Mendota Journal (Kerman) **10535**
Five Cities Times-Press-Recorder (Arroyo Grande) **10530**
Folsom Telegraph (Folsom) **10534**
Fontana Herald News (Fontana) **10534**
Fort Bragg Advocate-News (Fort Bragg) **10534**
Foster City Progress (Burlingame) **10531**
Free Lance (Hollister) **10422**
Fresno Bee, The (Fresno) **10422**
Galt Herald (Galt) **10534**
Gardena Valley News (Gardena) **10534**
Glendale News-Press (Glendale) **10422**
Glendora Press (West Covina) **10546**
Gold River News (Sacramento) **10542**
† Goleta Review (Goleta)
† Goleta Sun (Santa Barbara)
Gonzales Tribune (Soledad) **10545**
Good Times (Santa Cruz) **10544**
Greenfield News (Greenfield) **10534**
Green Sheet, The (San Bernardino) **10542**
Gridley Herald, The (Gridley) **10534**
Grizzly, The (Big Bear Lake) **10531**
Grunion Gazette (Long Beach) **10537**
Half Moon Bay Review (Half Moon Bay) **10534**
Hanford Sentinel, The (Hanford) **10422**
Harte-Hanks Pennysaver (Brea) **10531**
Healdsburg Tribune (Healdsburg) **10535**
Hemet News, The (San Jacinto) **10425**
Hesperia Resorter (Hesperia) **10535**
Highlander (West Covina) **10546**
Highland Park News/Herald/Journal (Los Angeles) **10537**
Hilmar Times (Hilmar) **10535**
† Hollywood Citizen News (Los Angeles)
Holtville Tribune (Holtville) **10535**
Hughson Chronicle (Winton) **10546**
Humboldt Beacon (Fortuna) **10534**

Huntington Beach/Fountain Valley Independent (Huntington Beach) **10535**
Huntington Harbour Sun (Seal Beach) **10545**
Imperial Valley Press (El Centro) **10422**
Independent, The (Livermore) **10536**
Indio Advertiser (Palm Desert) **10540**
Indio Post (Indio) **10535**
Inglewood/Hawthorne Wave (Los Angeles) **10537**
Inglewood Tribune (Compton) **10533**
Inland Valley Daily Bulletin (Ontario) **10423**
Intermountain News (Burney) **10531**
Inyo Register (Bishop) **10531**
Irvine World News (Irvine) **10535**
Jewish Journal of Greater Los Angeles, The (Los Angeles) **10537**
Kerman News (Kerman) **10535**
Kern Valley Sun (Lake Isabella) **10536**
King City Rustler (King City) **10535**
Kingsburg Recorder (Kingsburg) **10535**
La Canada Valley Sun (La Canada) **10535**
Laguna News Post (Lake Forest) **10536**
Laguna Niguel News (Lake Forest) **10536**
La Habra Star (Anaheim) **10530**
La Jolla Light (La Jolla) **10536**
La Jolla Village News/Golden Triange News (San Diego) **10542**
Lake County Record-Bee (Lakeport) **10422**
Lake Elsinore Valley Sun-Tribune (Lake Elsinore) **10536**
La Mesa Forum (Lemon Grove) **10536**
Lamont Reporter (Lamont) **10536**
Las Virgenes Enterprise (Woodland Hills) **10547**
L.A. Weekly (Los Angeles) **10538**
Ledger Dispatch & Sunday Times, The (Antioch) **10421**
Leisure World Golden Rain News (Seal Beach) **10545**
Leisure World News (Laguna Hills) **10536**
Lemon Grove Review (Lemon Grove) **10536**
Lincoln Heights Bulletin-News (Los Angeles) **10538**
Linden Herald (Linden) **10536**
Lindsay Gazette (Lindsay) **10536**
Lockeford-Clements News (Lockeford) **10537**
Lodi News-Sentinel (Lodi) **10422**
Lompoc Record (Lompoc) **10422**
† Long Beach Community News (Long Beach)
Los Altos Town Crier (Los Altos) **10537**
Los Angeles Bulletin (Los Angeles) **10422**
Los Angeles Independent (Los Angeles) **10538**
Los Angeles Log (San Diego) **10542**
Los Angeles Times (Los Angeles) **10423**
Los Banos Enterprise (Los Banos) **10538**
Los Gatos Weekly-Times (Los Gatos) **10539**

Lynwood Journal (Compton) **10533**
Lynwood Press (Los Angeles) **10538**
Madera Tribune (Madera) **10423**
Malibu Surfside News (Malibu) **10539**
Malibu Times (Malibu) **10539**
- Mammoth Lakes Review/Mono Herald (Mammoth Lakes)
Mammoth Times (Mammoth Lakes) **10539**
Manteca Bulletin (Manteca) **10423**
- Marin County Daily Recording (San Rafael)
Marin Independent Journal (Novato) **10423**
Marin Scope (Sausalito) **10544**
Mariposa Gazette (Mariposa) **10539**
Market Shopper, The (Delano) **10533**
Martinez News Gazette (Martinez) **10539**
Mendocino Beacon, The (Mendocino) **10539**
Menifee Valley News (Sun City) **10545**
Merced County Times (Winton) **10546**
Merced Sun-Star (Merced) **10423**
Mesa Tribune Wave (Los Angeles) **10538**
Metro (San Jose) **10543**
Mid Valley News (El Monte) **10533**
Milbrae Recorder-Progress (San Mateo) **10543**
Millbrae & San Bruno Sun (Burlingame) **10531**
Mill Valley Herald (Sausalito) **10544**
Milpitas Post (Milpitas) **10539**
Mira Mesa/Scripps Ranch Sentinel (San Diego) **10542**
Modesto Bee, The (Modesto) **10423**
Modoc County Record (Alturas) **10530**
Mojave Desert News, The (California City) **10531**
Montclarion (Oakland) **10540**
Montebello News (Los Angeles) **10538**
Montecito Life (Goleta)
Monterey County Herald, The (Monterey) **10423**
Monterey Park Progress (Los Angeles) **10538**
Moorpark Star (Moorpark) **10423**
Morgan Hill Times (Morgan Hill) **10539**
Morongo Basin (Palm Desert) **10540**
Morongo Basin Advertiser (Yucca Valley) **10547**
Mountain Democrat (Placerville) **10424**
Mountain Life (Mariposa) **10539**
Mountain Messenger (Downieville) **10533**
Mountain News, The (Lake Arrowhead) **10536**
Mountain Press (Prather) **10541**
Mount Shasta Herald (Mt. Shasta) **10539**
Mt. Washington Star Review (Los Angeles) **10538**
Napa County Record (Napa) **10540**
Napa Valley Register (Napa) **10423**
Needles Desert Star (Needles) **10540**
Newman News, The (Newman)
News-Ledger, The (West Sacramento) **10546**

News-Pilot, The (San Pedro) **10425**
News Enterprise, The (Los Alamitos) **10537**
News Pointer (Sausalito) **10544**
News Press, The (Paso Robles) **10424**
News Review (Ridgecrest) **10541**
New Times (San Luis Obispo) **10543**
North/South Beach Now (San Francisco) **10543**
North County Shopping News (Atascadero) **10530**
North County Times (Escondido) **10422**
Northeast Sun (City of Commerce) **10532**
North Shore Shopper (Pacific Palisades) **10540**
North Tahoe/Truckee Week (Carnelian Bay) **10532**
Norwalk Herald American (Los Angeles) **10538**
Novato Advance (Novato) **10540**
Oakdale Leader (Oakdale) **10540**
Oakland Tribune, The (Oakland) **10423**
▼OC Weekly (Los Angeles) **10538**
Ojai Valley News (Ojai) **10540**
Ontario Advertiser (San Bernardino) **10542**
Orange County Log (San Diego) **10542**
Orange County News (Garden Grove) **10534**
Orange County Register, The (Santa Ana) **10425**
Orange Cove Mountain Times (Reedley) **10541**
† Orangevale News (Folsom)
Orland Press-Register (Orland) **10540**
Oroville Mercury-Register (Oroville) **10423**
Outlook Mail (Santa Monica) **10544**
Outlook, The (Santa Monica) **10426**
† Oxnard Press-Courier (Oxnard)
Pacifica Tribune (Pacifica) **10540**
Pacific Sun (Mill Valley) **10539**
Palisadian-Post (Pacific Palisades) **10540**
Palm Desert Advertiser (Palm Desert) **10540**
Palm Desert Post (Indio) **10535**
Palm Spring Advertiser (Palm Desert) **10540**
▼Palo Alto Daily News (Palo Alto) **10424**
Palo Alto Weekly (Palo Alto) **10541**
Palos Verdes Peninsula News (Palos Verdes Peninsula) **10541**
Palo Verde Valley Times (Blythe) **10531**
Paradise Post (Paradise) **10541**
Park LaBrea News/Beverly Press (Los Angeles) **10538**
Parlier Post (Sanger) **10543**
Pasadena Star-News, The (Pasadena) **10424**
Pasadena Weekly (Pasadena) **10541**
Peninsula Beacon, The (San Diego) **10542**
Peninsula Independent (Burlingame) **10531**
† Peninsula Review, The (Carmel)
† Pennysaver (Vista)
Petaluma Argus-Courier (Petaluma) **10541**

Pico Rivera News (Los Angeles) **10538**
Piedmonter, The (Oakland) **10540**
Pinnacle, The (Hollister) **10535**
Placentia News-Times (Anaheim) **10530**
Placer Herald (Rocklin) **10541**
Point Reyes Light (Point Reyes Station) **10541**
Porterville Recorder (Porterville) **10424**
Post News (San Clemente) **10542**
Poway News Chieftain (Poway) **10541**
Press-Enterprise, The (Riverside) **10424**
Press-Telegram (Long Beach) **10422**
Press, The (Los Angeles) **10538**
Ramona Sentinel (Ramona) **10541**
Rancho Bernardo News Journal (San Diego) **10542**
Rancho Santa Margarita News (Lake Forest) **10536**
Random Lengths News (San Pedro) **10544**
Record Ledger (San Fernando) **10543**
Record Searchlight (Redding) **10424**
Record, The (Stockton) **10426**
Red Bluff Daily News (Red Bluff) **10424**
Redlands Advertiser (Redlands) **10541**
Redlands Daily Facts (Redlands) **10424**
Redwood City Tribune (Redwood City) **10541**
Reedley Exponent (Reedley) **10541**
Register-Pajaronian (Watsonville) **10427**
Reporter, The (Vacaville) **10426**
Review Herald, The (Mammoth Lakes) **10539**
Rialto Record (San Bernardino) **10542**
Riverside Advertiser (San Bernardino) **10542**
Riverside Bulletin, The (Los Angeles) **10538**
† Rohnert Park Cotati Clarion (Cotati)
Rosamond News (Rosamond) **10541**
Roseville Press-Tribune (Roseville) **10542**
Rossmoor News (Walnut Creek) **10546**
Ross Valley Reporter (Sausalito) **10544**
Sacramento Bee (Sacramento) **10425**
Sacramento Bulletin, The (Sacramento) **10542**
† Sacramento Union (Sacramento)
Saddleback Valley News (Lake Forest) **10536**
San Bernardino Advertiser (San Bernardino) **10542**
San Bernardino Bulletin, The (Los Angeles) **10538**
San Bernardino County Sun (San Bernardino) **10425**
San Bruno Herald (San Mateo) **10543**
† San Clemente News (San Clemente)
† San Diego Bulletin (Los Angeles)
San Diego Log (San Diego) **10542**
San Diego Reader (San Diego) **10542**
San Diego Review (San Diego) **10542**
San Diego Union-Tribune (San Diego) **10425**
San Fernando Valley Sun (San Fernando) **10543**

San Francisco Bay Guardian (San Francisco) **10543**
San Francisco Chronicle (San Francisco) **10425**
San Francisco Examiner (San Francisco) **10425**
San Francisco Independent (San Francisco) **10543**
San Francisco Metro Reporter (San Francisco) **10543**
San Francisco Sentinel (San Francisco) **1054**
San Gabriel Progress (Los Angeles) **10538**
San Gabriel Valley Tribune (West Covina) **10427**
Sanger Herald (Sanger) **10543**
San Jacinto Valley Register (San Jacinto) **10543**
San Jose Mercury News (San Jose) **10425**
San Luis Obispo County Telegram-Tribune (San Luis Obisopo) **10425**
San Marcos News Reporter (San Marcos) **10543**
San Marino Tribune (San Marino) **10543**
San Mateo County Times (San Mateo) **10425**
San Mateo Weekly (Burlingame) **10531**
San Rafael News Pointer (Sausalito) **10545**
San Ramon Valley Times, The (Danville) **1042**
Santa Barbara Independent (Santa Barbara) **10544**
Santa Barbara News Press (Santa Barbara) **10425**
Santa Cruz County Sentinel (Santa Cruz) **10425**
Santa Fe Springs News (Los Angeles) **10538**
Santa Maria Times (Santa Maria) **10425**
† Santa Monica Life (Santa Monica)
Santa Paula Times (Santa Paula) **10544**
Santa Rosa Press Democrat (Santa Rosa) **10426**
Saratoga News (Saratoga) **10544**
Selma Enterprise (Selma) **10545**
Sentinel, The (Auburn) **10530**
SF Weekly (San Francisco) **10543**
Shafter Press (Shafter) **10545**
Sierra Madre News (Sierra Madre) **10545**
Sierra Sun (Truckee) **10546**
Signal, The (Valencia) **10427**
Signal, The (Atwater) **10530**
Simi Valley Star (Simi Valley) **10426**
Siskiyou Daily News (Yreka) **10427**
Soledad Bee (Soledad) **10545**
Solvang Santa Ynez Valley News (Solvang) **10545**
Sonoma County Independent (Santa Rosa) **10544**
Sonoma Index Tribune (Sonoma) **10545**

Sonoma West Times & News (Sebastopal) **10545**
South Coast Shoppers/Penny Savers (Laguna Hills) **10536**
South Gate Press (Los Angeles) **10538**
South of the Boulevard (Woodland Hills) **10547**
† South Pasadena Journal (Los Angeles)
South Pasadena Review (South Pasadena) **10545**
South San Francisco Enterprise-Journal (San Mateo) **10544**
South San Gabriel/Rosemead Progress (Los Angeles) **10538**
Southside Journal (Los Angeles) **10538**
Southwest Wave/News (Los Angeles) **10538**
Spring Valley Bulletin (Lemon Grove) **10536**
Star News, The (Chula Vista) **10532**
St. Helena Star (St. Helena) **10545**
Sun City News (Sun City) **10545**
Sun Newspaper, The (Seal Beach) **10545**
Sun Reporter (San Francisco) **10543**
Swap Sheet (Ridgecrest) **10541**
Tahoe Daily Tribune (South Lake Tahoe) **10426**
Tahoe World (Tahoe City) **10545**
Tehachapi News (Tehachapi) **10545**
Thousand Oaks Star (Thousand Oaks) **10426**
Times-Standard (Eureka) **10422**
† Times Tribune (Palo Alto)
Topics Sun Wave (Los Angeles) **10538**
Tracy Press (Tracy) **10426**
Tri-Valley Herald (Pleasanton) **10424**
Trinity Journal (Weaverville) **10546**
Tulare Advance-Register (Tulare) **10426**
Turlock Journal (Turlock) **10426**
Tustin News (Santa Ana) **10544**
Twin Cities Times (Corte Madera) **10533**
Ukiah Daily Journal (Ukiah) **10426**
Union Democrat, The (Sonora) **10426**
† Union Shopper, The (Arcata)
Union, The (Grass Valley) **10422**
† Union, The (Arcata)
Uptown San Diego Examiner (San Diego) **10542**
Vallejo Times-Herald (Vallejo) **10427**
Valley Post (Anderson) **10530**
Valley Roadrunner (Valley Center) **10546**
Valley Times (Pleasanton) **10424**
Valley Times, The (Moreno Valley) **10539**
Valley Vantage (Woodland Hills) **10547**
Venice-Marina News (Santa Monica) **10544**
† Ventura Bulletin, The (Los Angeles)
Ventura County & Coast Reporter (Ventura) **10546**
Ventura County Star (Ventura) **10427**

Victor Valley Advertiser (San Bernardino) **10542**
† Victor Valley Living (Hesperia)
Visalia Times-Delta (Visalia) **10427**
Vistas (King City) **10535**
Warner Center News (Woodland Hills) **10547**
Wasco Tribune (Wasco) **10546**
Waterford News (Winton) **10546**
Weed Press (Weed) **10546**
Weekly Calistogan (Calistoga) **10532**
Westchester Observer (Santa Monica) **10544**
Westchester Star (Los Angeles) **10538**
West County Times (Richmond) **10424**
Western Edition (San Francisco) **10543**
West Los Angeles Independent (Santa Monica) **10544**
West Sacramento News-Ledger (West Sacramento) **10546**
West San Bernardino Advertiser (San Bernardino) **10542**
West Side Advance (Kerman) **10535**
Whittier Daily News (Whittier) **10427**
Willows Journal (Willows) **10546**
Wilmington Beacon (Compton) **10533**
Winton Times (Winton) **10546**
Yucaipa & Calimesa News-Mirror (Yucaipa) **10547**
Yucca Valley Hi-Desert Star (Yucca Valley) **10547**

COLORADO

AG Journal (La Junta) **10549**
Akron News Reporter (Akron) **10547**
† Applewood/Wheat Ridge Transcript (Golden)
Arvada Jefferson Sentinel (Lakewood) **10549**
Aspen Daily News (Aspen) **10427**
Aspen Times, The (Aspen) **10427**
Aurora Sentinel (Aurora) **10547**
Black Forest News (Colorado Springs) **10547**
Brighton Standard Blade (Brighton) **10547**
Broomfield Enterprise (Broomfield) **10547**
Brush News-Tribune (Brush) **10547**
Canyon Courier (Evergreen) **10548**
Center Post Dispatch (Monte Vista) **10550**
Cheyenne Mountain Journal (Manitou Springs) **10550**
Chronicle News, The (Trinidad) **10429**
Citizen Telegram, The (Rifle) **10551**
Clear Creek Courant (Idaho Springs) **10549**
Colorado Statesman (Denver) **10548**
Conejos County Citizen, The (Monte Vista) **10550**
Cortez Montezuma Valley Journal (Cortez) **10548**
Cortez Sentinel (Cortez) **10548**

10938 Boulder, CO

Daily Camera (Boulder) **10428**
Daily Record (Canon City) **10428**
Daily Sentinel, The (Grand Junction) **10428**
Daily Times-Call (Longmont) **10429**
Del Norte Prospector (Monte Vista) **10550**
Delta County Independent (Delta) **10548**
Denver Herald-Dispatch (Denver) **10548**
Denver Post (Denver) **10428**
Douglas County News Press (Castle Rock) **10547**
Dove Creek Press (Dove Creek) **10548**
Durango Herald (Durango) **10428**
Eagle Valley Enterprise (Eagle) **10548**
Eastern Colorado News (Strasburg) **10551**
Eastern Colorado Plainsman (Hugo) **10549**
Elbert County News (Castle Rock) **10547**
Englewood Herald (Littleton) **10549**
Estes Park Trail-Gazette (Estes Park) **10548**
Farmer & Miner (Frederick) **10549**
Florence Citizen (Florence) **10548**
Fort Collins Coloradoan (Fort Collins) **10428**
Fort Lupton Press (Fort Lupton) **10548**
Fort Morgan Times, The (Fort Morgan) **10428**
Fountain Valley News & El Paso County News (Fountain) **10548**
Fowler Tribune, The (Fowler) **10548**
Fruita Times, The (Fruita) **10549**
Garden of the Gods Journal (Manitou Springs) **10550**
Gazette, The (Colorado Springs) **10428**
Glenwood Post (Glenwood Springs) **10428**
Golden Transcript (Golden) **10549**
Greeley Tribune (Greeley) **10428**
Greenhorn Valley News (Colorado City) **10547**
Gunnison Country Times (Gunnison) **10428**
Haxtun-Fleming Herald, The (Haxtun) **10549**
Hayden Valley Press (Craig) **10548**
Herald-Democrat (Leadville) **10549**
Highlands Ranch Herald (Littleton) **10549**
High Timber Times (Pine) **10550**
Jackson County Star (Walden) **10551**
Jefferson County Transcript (Golden) **10549**
Jefferson Sentinel (Lakewood) **10549**
Julesburg Advocate (Julesburg) **10549**
Kiowa County Press (Eads) **10548**
La Junta Tribune-Democrat (La Junta) **10429**
Lamar Daily News (Lamar) **10429**
Life at Ken-Caryl (Littleton) **10549**
Littleton Independent (Littleton) **10549**
† Littleton Times (Littleton)
Loveland Daily Reporter-Herald (Loveland) **10429**
Mancos Times-Tribune (Mancos) **10550**
Meeker Herald, The (Meeker) **10550**
Mesa County Mail (Fruita) **10549**
Mineral County Miner (Monte Vista) **10550**

Monte Vista Journal (Monte Vista) **10550**
Montrose Daily Press (Montrose) **10429**
▼Montrose Morning Sun (Montrose) **10429**
Mountain Mail (Salida) **10429**
Northglenn-Thornton Sentinel (Westminster) **10551**
Northwest Colorado Daily Press (Craig) **10428**
Old Lyons Recorder, The (Lyons) **10550**
Ouray County Plaindealer (Ouray) **10550**
Palisade Tribune (Palisade) **10550**
Pikes Peak Journal (Manitou Springs) **10550**
Pine River Times (Bayfield) **10547**
Pueblo Chieftain (Pueblo) **10429**
Ridgway Sun (Ridgway) **10550**
Rockrimmon Journal (Manitou Springs) **10550**
Rocky Ford Daily Gazette (Rocky Ford) **10429**
Rocky Mountain News (Denver) **10428**
Saturday Advantage, The (Monte Vista) **10550**
Saturday Northwest (Craig) **10548**
† Sentinel/Altitudes (Frisco)
Silverton Standard & The Miner (Silverton) **10551**
† Snake River Press (Craig)
South Fork Times (Monte Vista) **10550**
Steamboat Pilot (Steamboat Springs) **10551**
Steamboat Today (Steamboat Springs) **10429**
Sterling Journal-Advocate (Sterling) **10429**
Summit County Journal (Frisco) **10549**
Summit Daily News (Frisco) **10428**
Telluride Daily Planet (Telluride) **10429**
Telluride Times-Journal (Telluride) **10551**
Tribune, The (Monument) **10550**
Vail Daily (Avon) **10428**
Vail Trail (Eagle-Vail) **10548**
Valley Courier (Alamosa) **10427**
Valley Journal (Carbondale) **10547**
Westminster Window (Westminster) **10551**
Westword (Denver) **10548**
Wet Mountain Tribune (Westcliffe) **10551**
† Wheat Ridge Sentinel (Lakewood)
Wiggins Courier, The (Wiggins) **10551**
Winter Park Manifest (Winter Park) **10551**
Wray Gazette (Wray) **10551**
Yuma Pioneer (Yuma) **10551**

CONNECTICUT

Advocate, The (Stamford) **10430**
▼Bethel Beacon (Bethel) **10551**
Bloomfield Journal (Bristol) **10551**
Branford Review (Branford) **10551**
Bristol Press, The (Bristol) **10429**
Brookfield Journal (Brookfield) **10552**
Cheshire Herald (Cheshire) **10552**
Chronicle, The (Willimantic) **10431**
Clinton Recorder (Clinton) **10552**

Connecticut Post (Bridgeport) **10429**
Cromwell Chronicle (Cromwell) **10552**
† Daily Milford Citizen (Milford)
Darien News Review (Darien) **10552**
Day, The (New London) **10430**
East Hartford Gazette, The (East Hartford) **10552**
East Haven Advertiser (Milford) **10553**
Enfield Press (Enfield) **10552**
† Evening Sentinel (Ansonia)
Fairfield Citizen News (Fairfield) **10552**
Fairfield County Weekly (Stamford) **10554**
† Farmington Valley Herald (Simsbury)
Glastonbury Citizen (Glastonbury) **10552**
† Greenwich News (Greenwich)
▼ Greenwich Post (Greenwich) **10552**
Greenwich Time (Greenwich) **10430**
Hamden Chronicle, The (Milford) **10553**
Hartford Advocate (Hartford) **10552**
Hartford Courant (Hartford) **10430**
Herald, The (New Britain) **10430**
Hour, The (Norwalk) **10430**
Housatonic Weekend (New Milford) **10553**
Journal Inquirer (Manchester) **10430**
Kent Good Times Dispatch (Kent) **10552**
Lakeville Journal, The (Lakeville) **10553**
Lewisboro Ledger, The (Ridgefield) **10553**
Litchfield Enquirer (Litchfield) **10553**
Middletown Press (Middletown) **10430**
† Milford Citizen (Milford)
Monroe Courier (Monroe) **10553**
Naugatuck Daily News (Naugatuck) **10430**
New Canaan Advertiser (New Canaan) **10553**
New Haven Advocate (New Haven) **10553**
New Haven Register (New Haven) **10430**
Newington Town Crier (Bristol) **10551**
New Milford Times (New Milford) **10553**
News-Times, The (Danbury) **10429**
Newtown Bee, The (Newtown) **10553**
† Niantic News (East Lyme)
North Haven Post, The (Milford) **10553**
† Norwalk News (Westport)
Norwich Bulletin (Norwich) **10430**
† Observer-Patriot (Putnam)
Orange Bulletin (Milford) **10553**
Pictorial Gazette (Old Saybrook) **10553**
Record-Journal (Meriden) **10430**
Redding Pilot, The (Georgetown) **10552**
Register Citizen (Torrington) **10430**
Reminder, The (Vernon) **10554**
Ridgefield Press, The (Ridgefield) **10553**
River East News Bulletin (Glastonbury) **10552**
Southington Observer (Southington) **10554**
Stratford Bard (Milford) **10553**
Trumbull Times (Monroe) **10553**
Valley Gazette (Shelton) **10553**

Voices (Southbury) **10553**
Waterbury Republican-American (Waterbury) **10430**
West Hartford News (Bristol) **10551**
West Haven News (Milford) **10553**
Weston Forum, The (Georetown) **10552**
Westport News (Westport) **10554**
Wethersfield Post (Bristol) **10552**
Wilton Bulletin (Wilton) **10554**
Windsor Journal (Bristol) **10552**
Windsor Locks Journal (Bristol) **10552**
Winsted Journal (Winsted) **10554**

DELAWARE

Chronicle, The (Milford) **10554**
Daily Whale, The (Rehoboth Beach) **10431**
Delaware Beachcomber (Rehoboth Beach) **10554**
Delaware Coast Press (Rehoboth Beach) **10554**
Delaware State News (Dover) **10431**
Delaware Wave (Bethany Beach) **10554**
Harrington Journal, The (Harrington) **10554**
Leader-State Register, The (Seaford) **10554**
Newark Post (Newark) **10554**
News Journal, The (New Castle) **10431**
Sussex Countian (Georgetown) **10554**
Sussex Post, The (Rehoboth) **10554**
Wilmington Defender (Wilmington) **10554**

DISTRICT OF COLUMBIA

Georgetown Current, The (Washington) **10554**
Georgetowner, The (Washington) **10555**
Northwest Current, The (Washington) **10555**
Rock Creek Current, The (Washington) **10555**
Spotlight, The (Washington) **10555**
Washington City Paper (Washington) **10555**
Washington Post, The (Washington) **10431**
Washington Times (Washington) **10431**

FEDERATED STATES OF MICRONESIA

National Union (Eastern Caroline Islands) **10555**

FLORIDA

Arcadian, The (Arcadia) **10555**
Aventura News (South Miami) **10561**
Baker County Press, The (MacClenny) **10558**
† Bal Harbor/Bay Harbour News (South Miami)
Bay Beacon, The (Niceville) **10559**
Bay Bulletin (Melbourne) **10558**

Beach Bulletin (Fort Myers Beach) **10557**
Beaches Leader (Jacksonville Beach) **10557**
Belleview Voice of South Marion (Belleview) **10555**
Boca Monday (Deerfield Beach) **10556**
Boca Raton News (Boca Raton) **10431**
Bonita Banner (Bonita Springs) **10555**
Boynton Beach Times (Deerfield Beach) **10556**
Bradenton Herald, The (Bradenton) **10431**
Bradford County Telegraph (Starke) **10561**
Brandon News, The (Brandon) **10555**
Brevard Reporter, The (Merritt Island) **10559**
† Brooksville Sun Journal (Brooksville)
Broward News (Margate) **10558**
Broward Times, The (Coral Springs) **10556**
Bulletin, The (Crestview) **10556**
Caloosa Belle (La Belle) **10558**
Canada News (Auburndale) **10555**
Cape Coral Daily Breeze, The (Cape Coral) **10431**
Carol City/Opa-Locka News (Miami) **10559**
Carrollwood News (Tampa) **10561**
Cedar Key Beacon (Cedar) **10556**
Charlotte Sun Herald (Charlotte Harbor) **10431**
Citrus County Chronicle (Crystal River) **10431**
† Clay Countian (Orange Park)
† Clay County Crescent (Orange Park)
Clay Today (Orange Park) **10559**
Clewiston News (Clewiston) **10556**
Coral Gables News (Miami) **10559**
Courier, The (Plant City) **10560**
† Crestview Okaloosa-News Journal (Crestview)
Daily Commercial (Leesburg) **10432**
Daily News (Palatka) **10433**
Daily Okeechobee News, The (Okeechobee) **10433**
Daytona Pennysaver (Ormond Beach) **10560**
Deerfield Beach Observer (Deerfield Beach) **10556**
Deerfield Beach Thursday Times (Deerfield Beach) **10556**
DeLand Beacon, The (DeLand) **10557**
Delray Times (Deerfield Beach) **10556**
Destin Log (Destin) **10557**
Digest, The (Hallandale) **10557**
Downtown News (South Miami) **10561**
East Bay Breeze (Sun City Center) **10561**
Englewood Sun Herald (Englewood) **10432**
Escambia Sun Press (Pensacola) **10560**
Eustis Lake Region News (Mt. Dora) **10559**
Florida Keys Keynoter (Marathon) **10558**
Florida Times-Union (Jacksonville) **10432**
Florida Today (Melbourne) **10432**
Floridian, The (Marianna) **10558**
Fort Meade Leader, The (Fort Meade) **10557**

Fort Myers Beach Observer (Fort Myers Beach) **10557**
† Fort Myers Observer (Fort Myers)
Free Press, The (Tampa) **10561**
Frostproof News (Frostproof) **10557**
Gadsden County Times (Quincy) **10560**
Gainesville Buyers Guide (Orange Park) **10559**
Gainesville Sun, The (Gainesville) **10432**
Glades County Democrat (Clewiston) **10556**
Graceville News (Graceville) **10557**
† Haines City Herald (Haines City)
Herald-Advocate (Wauchula) **10561**
† Herald, The (Tarpon Springs)
Hernando Today (Brooksville) **10431**
Hi-Riser (Deerfield Beach) **10556**
Hialeah/Opa-Lacka News (Miami) **10559**
† Highlands Press (Mulberry)
High Springs Herald, The (High Springs) **10557**
† Hollywood Sun (Hollywood)
Holmes County Advertiser (Bonifay) **10555**
† Homestead/Florida City News (Miami)
Home Times (West Palm Beach) **10562**
Islander, The (Gulf Breeze) **10557**
Island Reporter (Sanibel) **10560**
Jackson County Floridan (Marianna) **10432**
Jacksonville Shopping Guide (Jacksonville) **10557**
Jasper News (Jasper) **10557**
Jupiter Courier (Jupiter) **10558**
Kendall News-Gazette (Miami) **10559**
Key West Citizen (Key West) **10432**
† Lake Alfred Press (Mulberry)
Lake Area News (Land O' Lakes) **10558**
Lake City Reporter (Lake City) **10432**
Lake News (Fruitland Park) **10557**
Lake Placid Journal (Lake Placid) **10558**
† Lake Wales Highlander (Winter Haven)
Lake Wales News (Lake Wales) **10558**
Lake Worth Herald Coastal Observer (Lake Worth) **10558**
Ledger, The (Lakeland) **10432**
Little Paper, The (Melbourne) **10558**
Lutz Community News (Tampa) **10561**
Madison County Carrier (Madison) **10558**
Madison Enterprise Recorder (Madison) **10558**
Marco Island Eagle, The (Marco Island) **10558**
† Martin County News (Stuart)
Miami Beach News (South Miami) **10561**
Miami Herald (Miami) **10432**
Miami Laker (Miami Lakes) **10559**
† Miami Shores News (Miami)
Miami Today (Miami) **10559**
Monticello News (Monticello) **10559**
Mulberry Press (Mulberry) **10559**
Naples Daily News (Naples) **10433**

Nassau County Record (Callahan) **10556**
News-Journal, The (Daytona Beach) **10432**
News-Press, The (Fort Myers) **10432**
News-Star (Lehigh Acres) **10558**
News Chief (Winter Haven) **10434**
News Herald, The (Panama City) **10433**
News Leader (Fernandina) **10557**
New Smyrna Beach Observer (New Smyrna) **10433**
News Sun, The (Sebring) **10560**
North Bay Village News (South Miami) **10561**
North Miami Beach News (South Miami) **10561**
North Miami News (Miami) **10559**
North Port Sun Herald (North Port) **10433**
Northwest Florida Daily News (Fort Walton Beach) **10432**
Observer, The (New Smyrna) **10433**
Observer, The (Royal Palm Beach) **10560**
Ocala Star Banner (Ocala) **10433**
Orlando Sentinel (Orlando) **10433**
Orlando Weekly, The (Winter Park) **10562**
Osceola News-Gazette (Kissimmee) **10558**
Oviedo Voice, The (Oviedo) **10560**
Palm Beach Daily News (Palm Beach) **10433**
Palm Beach Post (West Palm Beach) **10434**
Pasco News (Dade City) **10556**
Pelican Press (Sarasota) **10560**
Pensacola News Journal (Pensacola) **10433**
Pensacola Voice (Pensacola) **10560**
Perdido Pelican (Pensacola) **10560**
Perry News-Herald (Perry) **10560**
Perry Taco Times (Perry) **10560**
Pine Island Eagle (Bokeelia) **10555**
Plant City Shopper (Plant City) **10560**
Polk City Press (Mulberry) **10559**
Polk County Democrat, The (Bartow) **10555**
Pompano Ledger, The (Pompano Beach) **10560**
Press-Journal (Vero Beach) **10434**
Record, The (Gainesville) **10557**
† Reporter, The (Tampa)
Sanford Herald (Sanford) **10433**
Sanibel-Captiva Islander (Sanibel) **10560**
Santa Rosa Free Press (Milton) **10559**
Santa Rosa Press Gazette (Milton) **10559**
Sarasota Herald Tribune (Sarasota) **10433**
Sebastian Sun (Vero Beach) **10561**
† Seminole Outlook (Oviedo)
Sentinel, The (Gulf Breeze) **10557**
Shopper Observer News (Ruskin) **10560**
Shopper, The (Pensacola) **10560**
South Dade News (South Miami) **10561**
South Dade News Leader (Homestead) **10557**
South Miami News (Miami) **10559**
South Tampa News (Brandon) **10555**

† Southwest News (South Miami)
Star-Advocate (Titusville) **10561**
St. Augustine Record (St. Augustine) **10433**
St. Petersburg Times (St. Petersburg) **10433**
Stuart News (Stuart) **10434**
Sumter County Times (Bushnell) **10556**
Sun-Sentinel (Fort Lauderdale) **10432**
Sun Coast News (New Port Richey) **10559**
† Sunday Glades Trend (Clewiston)
Sun Post, The (Miami) **10559**
Sunrise Times (Coral Springs) **10556**
Sun, The (Sun City Center) **10561**
† Surfside News (South Miami)
Tallahassean (Tallahassee) **10561**
Tallahassee Democrat (Tallahassee) **10434**
Tamarac Forum (Coral Springs) **10556**
Tampa Tribune, The (Tampa) **10434**
Tavares Citizen (Mt. Dora) **10559**
Temple Terrace Beacon (Tampa) **10561**
Temple Terrace News (Brandon) **10555**
Times, The (Melbourne) **10558**
Today (Orange Park) **10560**
Town-Crier (West Palm Beach) **10562**
Town 'n Country News (Tampa) **10561**
† Tri-City Independent (Margate)
Tribune, The (Fort Pierce) **10432**
Tribune, The (Melbourne) **10558**
Twin City News, The (Chattahoochee) **10556**
Venice Gondolier (Venice) **10561**
Wakulla News (Crawfordville) **10556**
Weekly Challenger (St. Petersburg) **10561**
Weekly Planet (Tampa) **10561**
Wellington Royal Palm Beach Forum (Wellington) **10562**
West Boca Times (Deerfield Beach) **10556**
West Orange Times (Winter Garden) **10562**
Winter Park-Maitland Observer (Winter Park) **10562**
Zephyrhills News (Zephyrhills) **10562**

GEORGIA

Acworth Neighbor (Marietta) **10566**
Adel News-Tribune (Adel) **10562**
Albany Herald, The (Albany) **10434**
Albany Journal (Albany) **10562**
Alpharetta Revue (Alpharetta) **10562**
Americus Times-Recorder (Americus) **10434**
Athens Banner Herald (Athens) **10434**
Athens Daily News (Athens) **10434**
Athens Observer, The (Athens) **10562**
Atlanta Bulletin (Atlanta) **10562**
Atlanta Daily World (Atlanta) **10562**
Atlanta Journal-Constitution (Atlanta) **10434**
Augusta Chronicle, The (Augusta) **10434**
† Augusta Herald (Augusta)

Austell Neighbor (Marietta) **10566**
Bainbridge Post-Searchlight
 (Bainbridge) **10563**
Bartow Neighbor, The (Cartersville) **10563**
Baxley News-Banner (Baxley) **10563**
Benning Leader, The (Columbus) **10564**
Berrien Press (Nashville) **10567**
Blade, The (Swainsboro) **10568**
Brantley Enterprise (Nahunta) **10567**
Brunswick News, The (Brunswick) **10434**
Bryan County Times (Pembroke) **10567**
Business Post, The (Alpharetta) **10562**
Cairo Messenger (Cairo) **10563**
Calhoun Times (Calhoun) **10563**
Camden County Tribune (St. Marys) **10567**
Camilla Enterprise (Camilla) **10563**
Cartersville Daily Tribune News
 (Cartersville) **10434**
Catoosa County News (Ringgold) **10567**
Cedartown Standard (Cedartown) **10564**
Chamblee-DeKalb Neighbor (Atlanta) **10562**
Charlton County Herald (Folkston) **10565**
Chatsworth Times, The (Chatsworth) **10564**
Chattooga Press (Summerville) **10568**
Cherokee Tribune, The (Canton) **10563**
Chieftain & Toccoa Record (Toccoa) **10568**
Clayton Neighbor (Forest Park) **10565**
Clayton News Daily (Jonesboro) **10435**
† Clayton Sun (Atlanta)
Clayton Tribune, The (Clayton) **10564**
Clinch County News (Homerville) **10565**
Coastal Courier (Hinesville) **10565**
Columbia News Times, The (Martinez) **10566**
Columbus Ledger-Enquirer (Columbus) **10435**
Commerce News (Commerce) **10564**
Cordele Dispatch (Cordele) **10435**
Courier Herald, The (Dublin) **10435**
† Courier, The (Thomasville)
Covington News (Covington) **10564**
Daily Citizen News (Dalton) **10435**
Daily Sun, The (Warner Robins) **10436**
Daily Tribune News (Cartersville) **10435**
Dallas New Era (Dallas) **10564**
Darien News (Darien) **10564**
Dawson News, The (Dawson) **10564**
Decatur-DeKalb News/Era (Decatur) **10564**
† DeKalb News/Sun (Decatur)
Dodge County News, The (Eastman) **10565**
Donalsonville News (Donalsonville) **10564**
Doraville-DeKalb Neighbor (Atlanta) **10562**
Douglas County Sentinel (Douglasville) **10435**
Douglas Enterprise (Douglas) **10564**
Douglas Neighbor, The (Marietta) **10566**
Dunwoody-DeKalb Neighbor, The
 (Atlanta) **10562**
Dunwoody Crier (Atlanta) **10562**

Elberton Star (Elberton) **10565**
Fayette County News (Fayetteville) **10565**
Fayette Neighbor, The (Fayetteville) **10565**
† Fayette Sun (Fayetteville)
Forsyth County News (Cumming) **10564**
Franklin County Citizen (Lavonia) **10566**
Georgia Times-Union (Brunswick) **10434**
Georgis's Coastal Illustrated (St. Simons
 Island) **10567**
Glennville Sentinel (Glennville) **10565**
Glynco Observer (Brunswick) **10563**
Griffin Daily News (Griffin) **10435**
† Gwinnett Daily News (Lawrenceville)
Gwinnett Daily Post (Lawrenceville) **10435**
Haralson Gateway-Beacon, The
 (Bremen) **10563**
Harbor Sound (Brunswick) **10563**
Hartwell Sun, The (Hartwell) **10565**
Henry Herald, The (McDonough) **10566**
Herald-Gazette, The (Barnesville) **10563**
Herald-Leader, The (Fitzgerald) **10565**
Herald-Tribune, The (Cartersville) **10564**
Herald, The (Rincon) **10567**
Houston Times-Journal (Perry) **10567**
Islander, The (St. Simons Island) **10568**
Jackson Herald (Jefferson) **10566**
Jackson Progress-Argus (Jackson) **10565**
Jeff Davis Ledger (Hazlehurst) **10565**
Jekyll's Golden Islander (Brunswick) **10563**
Kennesaw Neighbor, The (Marietta) **10566**
La Grange Daily News (La Grange) **10435**
▼Lakeside Ledger, The (Woodstock) **10568**
Leader-Tribune, The (Fort Valley) **10565**
Ludowici News (Ludowici) **10566**
Mableton Neighbor, The (Marietta) **10566**
Macon Telegraph (Macon) **10435**
Madisonian, The (Madison) **10566**
Manchester Star-Mercury (Manchester) **10566**
Marietta Daily Journal (Marietta) **10435**
McDuffie Progress, The (Thomson) **10568**
Meriwether Free Press (Greenville) **10565**
Meriwether Vindicator (Manchester) **10566**
Miller County Liberal (Colquitt) **10564**
Newnan Times-Herald (Newnan) **10567**
News Leader, The (Royston) **10567**
North Bartow News (Adairsville) **10562**
Northeast Georgian, The (Cornelia) **10564**
North Georgia News (Blairsville) **10563**
Northside Neighbor, The (Atlanta) **10563**
Observer, The (Moultrie) **10435**
Oconee Breeze (Madison) **10566**
Paulding Neighbor, The (Marietta) **10566**
Pelham Journal (Pelham) **10567**
Powder Springs Neighbor, The
 (Marietta) **10566**
Press-Sentinel, The (Jesup) **10566**

Rockdale Citizen (Conyers) **10435**
Rockdale Neighbor, The (Conyers) **10564**
Rockmart Journal (Rockmart) **10567**
Rome News-Tribune (Rome) **10436**
Roswell-Alpharetta Neighbor (Roswell) **10567**
Roswell/Alpharetta Crier (Atlanta) **10563**
Sandersville Progress (Sandersville) **10567**
Sandy Springs Neighbor, The (Atlanta) **10563**
Savannah Morning News (Savannah) **10436**
South Dekalb Neighbor, The (Atlanta) **10563**
South Fulton Neighbor, The (Forest Park) **10565**
† Southside Sun (East Point)
Sparta Ishmaelite (Sparta) **10567**
Star Express (Covington) **10564**
Statesboro Herald (Statesboro) **10436**
Summerville News (Summerville) **10568**
Sylvester Local News (Sylvester) **10568**
Telfair Enterprise (McRae) **10566**
This Week In Peachtree City (Peachtree City) **10567**
Thomaston Times (Thomaston) **10568**
Thomasville Times-Enterprise (Thomasville) **10436**
Three Rivers Gazette (McRae) **10567**
Tifton Gazette (Tifton) **10436**
Times-Courier (Ellijay) **10565**
Times-Georgian (Carrollton) **10434**
Times Journal-Spotlight (Eastman) **10565**
Times, The (Gainesville) **10435**
True Citizen, The (Waynesboro) **10568**
Tucker-DeKalb Neighbor, The (Atlanta) **10563**
Union-Recorder (Milledgeville) **10435**
Valdosta Daily Times (Valdosta) **10436**
Villa Rican, The (Villa Rica) **10568**
Walker County Messenger (La Fayette) **10566**
Walton Tribune (Monroe) **10567**
Washington News-Reporter (Washington) **10568**
Waycross Journal Herald (Waycross) **10436**
Winder News (Winder) **10568**
Wrightsville Headlight, The (Wrightsville) **10568**

GUAM

Pacific Daily News (Agana) **10436**

HAWAII

Garden Island Extra (Lihue) **10568**
Hawaii Tribune-Herald (Hilo) **10436**
Honolulu Advertiser (Honolulu) **10436**
Honolulu Star-Bulletin (Honolulu) **10436**
Island Times (Lihue) **10436**
Maui News (Wailuku) **10437**
MidWeek (Kaneohe) **10568**
Sun Press (Kaneohe) **10568**
West Hawaii Today (Kailua Kona) **10436**

IDAHO

Aberdeen Times (Aberdeen) **10568**
† Adams County Leader (Council)
Arco Advertiser (Arco) **10569**
Blackfoot Morning News (Blackfoot) **10437**
Bonner County Daily Bee (Sandpoint) **10437**
Bonners Ferry Herald (Bonners Ferry) **10569**
Buhl Herald (Buhl) **10569**
Cable Scene (Idaho Falls) **10569**
Caribou County Sun (Soda Springs) **10571**
Challis Messenger (Challis) **10569**
Clearwater Tribune (Orofino) **10570**
Coeur d'Alene Press (Coeur d'Alene) **10437**
Cottonwood Chronicle (Cottonwood) **10569**
† East County Chronicle (Kimberly)
Fremont County Herald-Chronicle (St. Anthony) **10571**
Gooding County Leader (Gooding) **10569**
† Grace Citizen (Preston)
Idaho County Free Press (Grangeville) **10569**
Idaho Enterprise (Malad City) **10570**
Idaho Falls Post Register (Idaho Falls) **10437**
Idaho Mountain Express (Ketchum) **10570**
Idaho Press-Tribune (Nampa) **10437**
Idaho State Journal (Pocatello) **10437**
Idaho Statesman, The (Boise) **10437**
Independent Enterprise (Payette) **10570**
Jefferson Star, The (Rigby) **10570**
Kendrick-Gazette (Kendrick) **10569**
Kuna-Melba News (Kuna) **10570**
Lewis County Herald (Nezperce) **10570**
Lewiston Morning Tribune (Lewiston) **10437**
Lincoln County Journal (Shoshone) **10571**
Long Valley Advocate, The (Cascade) **10569**
Messenger Index (Emmett) **10569**
Middleton Gazette (Middleton) **10570**
Minidoka County News (Rupert) **10570**
Moscow/Pullman Daily News (Moscow) **10437**
Mountain Home News (Mountain Home) **10570**
News-Examiner (Montpelier) **10570**
North Side News (Jerome) **10569**
Owyhee Avalanche (Homedale) **10569**
Post Falls Tribune (Post Falls) **10570**
Power County Press (American Falls) **10569**
Preston Citizen (Preston) **10570**
Priest River Times (Priest River) **10570**
Recorder-Herald (Salmon) **10570**
Record, The (Council) **10569**
† Sandpoint News-Bulletin (Sandpoint)

Shelley Pioneer (Shelley) **10571**
Shoshone News-Press (Kellogg) **10437**
South Idaho Press (Burley) **10437**
Standard Journal (Rexburg) **10570**
Star-News, The (McCall) **10570**
St. Maries Gazette Record (St. Maries) **10571**
Teton Valley News (Driggs) **10569**
Twin Falls Times-News (Twin Falls) **10437**
Upper Country News-Reporter (Cambridge) **10569**
Valley News (Meridian) **10570**
† Wallace Miner (Kellogg)
Weiser Signal American (Weiser) **10571**
Wood River Journal (Hailey) **10569**

ILLINOIS

Abingdon Argus (Abingdon) **10571**
Addison Press (Elmhurst) **10578**
Advertiser, The (Worden) **10591**
Advocate, The (Clifton) **10576**
Algonquin Countryside (Barrington) **10572**
Alsip Express (Midlothian) **10585**
Altamont News, The (Altamont) **10571**
Amboy News, The (Amboy) **10571**
Antioch News-Reporter (Grayslake) **10580**
Arcola Record Herald (Arcola) **10571**
Arlington Heights Journal & Topics (Des Plaines) **10576**
Arthur Graphic Clarion (Arthur) **10571**
Ashton Gazette (Ashton) **10572**
Astoria South Fulton Argus (Astoria) **10572**
Atwood Herald (Atwood) **10572**
Auburn Citizen (Auburn) **10572**
Austin Weekly News (Oak Park) **10587**
Avon Sentinel (Abingdon) **10571**
Back of the Yards Journal (Chicago) **10574**
Barrington Courier Review (Barrington) **10572**
Beacon News (Aurora) **10438**
Beardstown Illinoian-Star (Beardstown) **10572**
Beecher City Journal (Beecher City) **10573**
Belleville Journal (Belleville) **10573**
Belleville News-Democrat (Belleville) **10438**
Belvidere Daily Republican (Belvidere) **10438**
Bensenville Press (Elmhurst) **10578**
Berwyn/Cicero Life (Berwyn) **10573**
Beverly News (Midlothian) **10585**
Beverly Review (Chicago) **10574**
Blandinsville Star Gazette (Abingdon) **10571**
Bloomingdale Press (Bloomingdale) **10573**
Blue Mound Leader (Blue Mound) **10573**
Bolingbrook Metropolitan (Lemont) **10583**
Bolingbrook Sun (Bolingbrook) **10573**
Braceville Express (Wilmington) **10590**
Braidwood Index (Wilmington) **10591**
Braidwood Journal, The (Braidwood) **10573**
Breese Journal (Breese) **10573**
Bridgeport Leader (Bridgeport) **10573**
Bridgeport News (Chicago) **10574**
Bridgeview Independent (Midlothian) **10585**
Brighton Park-McKinley Park Life (Chicago) **10574**
Buffalo Grove Countryside (Arlington Heights) **10571**
Buffalo Grove Journal & Topics (Des Plaines) **10576**
Bugle, The (Niles) **10586**
Bunker Hill Gazette News (Bunker Hill) **10573**
Burbank-Stickney Independent (Midlothian) **10585**
Bureau County Republican (Princeton) **10588**
Burr Ridge Doings (Hinsdale) **10582**
Cahokia Journal (Columbia) **10576**
Cairo Citizen (Cairo) **10574**
Calhoun News (Hardin) **10581**
Cambridge Chronicle (Cambridge) **10574**
Carlinville Democrat (Carlinville) **10574**
Carlyle Union Banner (Carlyle) **10574**
Carmi Times (Carmi) **10438**
Carol Stream Press (Bloomingdale) **10573**
Carroll County Review (Thomson) **10590**
Carrollton Gazette Patriot (Carrollton) **10574**
Cary-Grove Countryside (Barrington) **10572**
Centralia Sentinel (Centralia) **10438**
Champaign News Gazette (Champaign) **10438**
Charleston Times-Courier (Charleston) **10438**
Chatham Clarion (Auburn) **10572**
Chicago-Lawndale News (Chicago) **10574**
Chicago's N.W. Side Press (Chicago) **10574**
Chicago Defender (Chicago) **10438**
Chicago Near North News (Chicago) **10575**
Chicago Near West Gazette (Chicago) **10575**
Chicago Post (Chicago) **10575**
Chicago Reader (Chicago) **10575**
Chicago Ridge Citizen (Midlothian) **10585**
Chicago Sun Times (Chicago) **10438**
Chicago Tribune (Chicago) **10438**
Chicago West Side Times (Chicago) **10575**
Chillicothe Bulletin (Chillicothe) **10576**
Chrisman Leader (Chrisman) **10576**
Cissna Park News (Cissna Park) **10576**
Clarendon Hills Doings, The (Hinsdale) **10582**
Clarendon Hills Progress (Downers Grove) **10577**
Clarion Journal, The (Columbia) **10576**
Clear-Ridge Reporter (Chicago) **10575**
Clinton County News (Mascoutah) **10584**
Clinton Daily Journal (Clinton) **10438**
Coal City Courant (Coal City) **10576**
Coal City Express (Wilmington) **10591**
Colchester Chronicle (Colchester) **10576**
Collinsville Herald (Collinsville) **10576**

Collinsville Journal (Collinsville) **10576**
Commercial-News (Danville) **10439**
County Journal (Belleville) **10573**
County Journal (Percy) **10588**
Courier-News, The (Elgin) **10439**
† Cuba Journal (Cuba)
Daily American (West Frankfort) **10442**
Daily Chronicle (De Kalb) **10439**
Daily Clay County Advocate-Press (Flora) **10439**
Daily Gazette (Sterling) **10441**
Daily Herald (Arlington Heights) **10437**
Daily Journal (Kankakee) **10440**
Daily Ledger (Canton) **10438**
Daily Review Atlas (Monmouth) **10440**
Daily Southtown (Tinley Park) **10441**
Daily Times (Ottawa) **10441**
Dallas City Enterprise (Dallas City) **10576**
Darien Doings (Hinsdale) **10582**
Darien Metropolitan (Lemont) **10583**
Darien Progress (Downers Grove) **10577**
Decatur Tribune (Decatur) **10576**
Deerfield Review (Bannockburn) **10572**
Delavan Times, The (Delavan) **10576**
Democrat-Message (Mt. Sterling) **10586**
Des Plaines Journal (Des Plaines) **10439**
Des Plaines Times (Park Ridge) **10587**
Divernon News (Auburn) **10572**
Downers Grove Reporter (Downers Grove) **10577**
† DuPage Press Service (Wheaton)
Du Quoin Evening Call (Du Quoin) **10439**
Durand-Dakota Volunteer (Durand) **10577**
Durand Gazette (Love Park) **10584**
Earlville Leader (Earlville) **10578**
East Peoria Courier (Morton) **10586**
East St. Louis Monitor (East St. Louis) **10578**
East St. Louis News Journal (Columbia) **10576**
Edgebrook Times Review (Park Ridge) **10587**
Edison-Norwood Times Review (Park Ridge) **10588**
Edwardsville Intelligencer (Edwardsville) **10439**
Edwardsville Journal (Edwardsville) **10578**
Effingham Daily News (Effingham) **10439**
Elburn Herald (Elburn) **10578**
Eldorado Daily Journal (Eldorado) **10439**
Elmhurst Press (Elmhurst) **10578**
Elm Leaves (Oak Park) **10587**
Elmwood Park-River Grove Times (Lincolnwood) **10583**
El Paso Journal (El Paso) **10578**
Elwood Express (Wilmington) **10591**
Enterprise, The (Plainfield) **10588**
Evanston Review (Evanston) **10579**
Evening News (Benton) **10438**
Evergreen Park Courier (Midlothian) **10585**

Fairfield Wayne County Press (Fairfield) **10579**
Fairview Heights Journal (Belleville) **10573**
Fairview Heights Tribune (Mascoutah) **10584**
Farina News, The (Farina) **10579**
Farmer's Weekly Review (Joliet) **10583**
Farmer City Journal (Farmer City) **10579**
Fisher Reporter (Fisher) **10579**
Flanagan Home Times (Pontiac) **10588**
Ford County Press (Melvin) **10585**
Forest Leaves (Oak Park) **10587**
Forreston Journal (Forreston) **10579**
Fox Lake Press (Grayslake) **10580**
Fox Valley Shopping News, The (Yorkville) **10591**
Fox Valley Villages (Plainfield) **10588**
Franklin Park Herald-Journal, The (Oak Park) **10587**
Franklin Park Star-Sentinel (Melrose Park) **10585**
Freeport Advertiser Shopping News (Freeport) **10579**
Freeport Journal-Standard (Freeport) **10439**
Fulton Democrat (Lewistown) **10583**
Fulton Journal (Fulton) **10579**
Galena Gazette (Galena) **10579**
Galesburg Post, The (Galesburg) **10579**
Galva News (Galva) **10579**
Gardner South Wilmington Post (Wilmington) **10591**
Gazette-Democrat (Anna) **10571**
Geneseo Republic (Geneseo) **10579**
Geneseo Shopper (Geneseo) **10579**
Geneva Republican (Geneva) **10579**
Genoa-Kingston-Kirkland News (Sycamore) **10589**
Gibson City Courier (Gibson City) **10580**
Gillespie Area News (Gillespie) **10580**
Gilman Star (Gilman) **10580**
Glasford Gazette, The (Glasford) **10580**
Glencoe News (Glenview) **10580**
Glendale Heights Press (Elmhurst) **10578**
Glen Ellyn News (Glen Ellyn) **10580**
Glen Ellyn Press (Bloomingdale) **10573**
Glenview Announcements (Glenview) **10580**
Golden Prairie News (Assumption) **10572**
Golfmill Journal (Des Plaines) **10577**
Good News Shopper (Coal City) **10576**
Granite City Press Journal (Granite City) **10580**
Grayslake Times (Grayslake) **10580**
Greene Prairie Press (White Hall) **10590**
Greenup Press (Greenup) **10581**
Greenville Advocate, The (Greenville) **10581**
Gurnee Press (Grayslake) **10580**
Hampshire Register News (Sycamore) **10590**

Hancock County Journal-Pilot (Carthage) **10574**
Hancock County Quill (La Harpe) **10583**
† Hanover Park Township Times (Carol Stream)
Hardin Calhoun Herald (Hardin) **10581**
Hardin County Independent (Elizabethtown) **10578**
Harlem-Foster-Norwood Park-Edison Park Times (Lincolnwood) **10583**
Harlem-Irving Times (Lincolnwood) **10583**
Harrisburg Daily Register (Harrisburg) **10439**
† Harwood Heights News (Park Ridge)
Havana Mason County Democrat (Havana) **10581**
Henderson County Quill (Stronghurst) **10589**
Henry News Republican (Henry) **10581**
Herald & Review (Decatur) **10439**
Herald-News, The (Joliet) **10440**
Herald-Star, The (Edinburg) **10578**
Herald/Country Market, The (Bourbonnais) **10573**
Herald Enterprise (Golconda) **10580**
Herald, The (Cahokia) **10574**
Herrin Spokesman (Herrin) **10581**
Herscher Pilot (Herscher) **10581**
Hickory Hills Citizen (Midlothian) **10585**
Highland News Leader (Highland) **10581**
Highland Park News (Bannockburn) **10572**
Hillsboro Journal (Hillsboro) **10582**
Hinsdale Doings (Hinsdale) **10582**
† Hodgkins Citizen (La Grange)
Hoopeston Chronicle (Hoopeston) **10582**
Huntley Farmside, The (Huntley) **10582**
Hyde Park Herald (Chicago) **10575**
Illinois Times (Springfield) **10589**
Illiopolis Sentinel (Illiopolis) **10582**
Independent News (Georgetown) **10579**
Indian Head Park (Hinsdale) **10582**
Indian Head Park Citizen (Oak Brook) **10586**
Inside (Chicago) **10575**
† Inside Ravenswood (Chicago)
Iroquois County Times Republic (Watseka) **10442**
Jacksonville Journal-Courier (Jacksonville) **10440**
Jefferson Park/Portage Park/Bel Cragin Times (Lincolnwood) **10584**
Journal, The (Chicago) **10575**
Kane County Chronicle (Geneva) **10439**
Kendall County Record (Yorkville) **10591**
Kewanee Star-Courier (Kewanee) **10440**
Kinmundy Express (Kinmundy) **10583**
Knoxville Journal, The (Galesburg) **10579**
Lacon Home Journal (Lacon) **10583**
Lake Forester (Bannockburn) **10572**
Lakeland Press (Grayslake) **10580**

Lake Villa Record (Grayslake) **10580**
Lake Zurich Enterprise (Grayslake) **10581**
Lawrence County News (Lawrenceville) **10583**
Lawrenceville Daily Record (Lawrenceville) **10440**
▼Lebanon Herald (Mascoutah) **10584**
Lemont Metropolitan (Lemont) **10583**
Lemont Reporter (Lemont) **10583**
Libertyville News (Grayslake) **10581**
Libertyville Review (Bannockburn) **10572**
Limestone Independent News (Bartonville) **10572**
† Lincoln-Belmont Booster (Chicago)
Lincoln Courier (Lincoln) **10440**
Lincolnwood Life (Lincolnwood) **10584**
Lincolnwood Review (Evanston) **10579**
Lindenhurst News (Grayslake) **10581**
Lisle Sun (Downers Grove) **10577**
Lisle Sun (Naperville) **10586**
Litchfield News-Herald (Litchfield) **10440**
Loda Times (Paxton) **10588**
Lombardian, The (Lombard) **10584**
Lombardian Villa Park Review (Lombard) **10584**
Lombard Spectator (Elmhurst) **10578**
† London Mills Times (Roseville)
M & M Journal (Hillsboro) **10582**
Macomb Journal (Macomb) **10440**
Macoupin & Montgomery County Journal (Hillsboro) **10582**
Macoupin County Enquirer (Carlinville) **10574**
Macoupin County Shopper (Hillsboro) **10582**
Madison County Chronicle (Worden) **10591**
Marion Daily Republican (Marion) **10440**
Mascoutah Herald (Mascoutah) **10584**
Mattoon Journal Gazette (Mattoon) **10440**
Maywood Herald (Oak Park) **10587**
McDonough-Democrat (Bushnell) **10573**
McLeansboro Times-Leader (McLeansboro) **10584**
Melrose Park Herald (Oak Park) **10587**
Melrose Park Star-Sentinel (Melrose Park) **10585**
Menard County Review (Greenview) **10581**
Mendota Reporter (Mendota) **10585**
Metropolis Planet (Metropolis) **10585**
Midlothian-Bremen Messenger (Midlothian) **10585**
MidWeek, The (DeKalb) **10576**
Millstadt Enterprise (Columbia) **10576**
Minonk News Dispatch (Minonk) **10586**
Mississippi Eagle News, The (Warsaw) **10590**
Monroe County Clarion (Columbia) **10576**
Montgomery County News, The (Hillsboro) **10582**
Morris Daily Herald (Morris) **10440**

Morton Grove-Niles Life (Lincolnwood) **10584**
Morton Grove Champion (Evanston) **10579**
Mount Carmel Daily Republican-Register (Mt. Carmel) **10440**
Mount Greenwood Express (Midlothian) **10585**
Mount Prospect Journal (Des Plaines) **10577**
Mount Prospect Times (Park Ridge) **10588**
Mt. Olive Herald, The (Mt. Olive) **10586**
Mundelein News (Grayslake) **10581**
Mundelein Review (Bannockburn) **10572**
Naperville Metropolitan (Lemont) **10583**
Naperville Sun (Naperville) **10586**
Nashville News, The (Nashville) **10586**
† Near South Herald (Chicago)
New City (Chicago) **10575**
News-Progress (Sullivan) **10589**
News-Record, The (Cerro Gordo) **10574**
News-Sun, The (Waukegan) **10442**
News-Tribune (La Salle) **10440**
News Gazette, The (Love Park) **10584**
NewsMarketer, The (Tinley Park) **10590**
News Star (Lincolnwood) **10584**
Newton Press-Mentor (Newton) **10586**
Niantic-Harristown County Line Observer (Illiopolis) **10582**
Niles Herald Spectator (Park Ridge) **10588**
Niles Journal (Des Plaines) **10577**
Niles Life (Lincolnwood) **10584**
Nokomis Free Press-Progress (Nokomis) **10586**
Norridge-Harwood Heights News (Park Ridge) **10588**
Norridge-Harwood Heights Times (Lincolnwood) **10584**
Northbrook Star (Glenview) **10580**
North Center-Lincoln Belmont-Lake View Booster (Lincolnwood) **10584**
North County News (Red Bud) **10588**
Northern Ogle County Tempo (Byron) **10574**
Northlake Star-Sentinel (Melrose Park) **10585**
North Loop News (Chicago) **10575**
North Suburban Herald (Love Park) **10584**
Northwestern Illinois Dispatch (Savanna) **10589**
Northwestern Illinois Farmer (Lena) **10583**
Northwest Herald (Crystal Lake) **10438**
Northwest Journal & Topics (Des Plaines) **10577**
Northwest Leader (Chicago) **10575**
Northwest Side Press (Chicago) **10575**
O'Fallon Progress (O'Fallon) **10586**
Oak Brook Doings (Hinsdale) **10582**
Oak Brook Press (Elmhurst) **10578**
Oak Brook Terrace Doings (Hinsdale) **10582**
Oak Lawn Independent (Midlothian) **10585**
Oak Leaves, The (Oak Park) **10587**
Ogle County Life (Oregon) **10587**
Olney Daily Mail (Olney) **10441**
Olympia Review (Minier) **10586**
Orion Gazette (Orion) **10587**
† Orion Times (Orion)
Orland Metropolitan (Lemont) **10583**
Orland Township Messenger (Midlothian) **10585**
Palatine Countryside (Arlington Heights) **10571**
Palatine Journal & Topics (Des Plaines) **10577**
Palos Citizen (Midlothian) **10585**
Palos Hills-Hickory Hills (Palos Heights) **10587**
Pana News-Palladium (Pana) **10587**
Pantagraph, The (Bloomington) **10438**
Paper, The (Barry) **10572**
Paris Beacon News (Paris) **10441**
Park Ridge Herald Advocate (Park Ridge) **10588**
Park Ridge Journal (Des Plaines) **10577**
Pawnee Post (Auburn) **10572**
Paxton Daily Record (Paxton) **10441**
Pekin Daily Times (Pekin) **10441**
Penny Saver (Tinley Park) **10590**
Peoria Journal Star (Peoria) **10441**
Peoria Observer (Peoria) **10588**
Petersburg Observer (Petersburg) **10588**
Piatt County Journal-Republican (Monticello) **10586**
▼Plainfield Sun (Plainfield) **10588**
Pontiac Daily Leader (Pontiac) **10441**
Prairie Shopper, The (La Fayette) **10583**
Prairie Times, The (La Fayette) **10583**
Prospect Heights Journal (Des Plaines) **10577**
Proviso Star-Sentinel (Melrose Park) **10585**
Pulaski Enterprise (Mounds) **10586**
Putnam County Record (Granville) **10580**
Quad County Edition, The (Jerseyville) **10583**
Quincy Herald-Whig (Quincy) **10441**
Randolph County Herald Tribune (Chester) **10574**
Rankin Independent (Cissna Park) **10576**
† Rantoul Pacesetter (Rantoul)
Rantoul Press (Rantoul) **10588**
Record Times, The (Paxton) **10588**
Regional News (Palos Heights) **10587**
Register-Mail (Galesburg) **10439**
Register-News (Mt. Vernon) **10440**
Register Star (Rockford) **10441**
Reporter Newspaper, The (Palos Heights) **10587**
Reporter, The (Casey) **10574**
Reporter, The (Chicago) **10575**
Review, The (Erie) **10578**
Review, The (Marion) **10584**
River North News (Chicago) **10575**

Riverton Register (Riverton) **10588**
Roanoke Review (Roanoke) **10589**
Robinson Daily News (Robinson) **10441**
Rochelle News Leader (Rochelle) **10589**
Rochester Times (Auburn) **10572**
Rock Island Argus & The Dispatch (Moline) **10440**
Rogers Park/Edgewater News/Uptown News Star (Lincolnwood) **10584**
Rolling Meadows Journal & Topics (Des Plaines) **10577**
Romeoville Metropolitan (Lemont) **10583**
Romeoville Sun (Bolingbrook) **10573**
† Roselle Record (Carol Stream)
Rosemont Journal (Des Plaines) **10577**
Rosemont Times (Park Ridge) **10588**
Roseville Independent (Roseville) **10589**
Round Lake News (Grayslake) **10581**
Rushville Times, The (Rushville) **10589**
Saint Elmo Banner (St. Elmo) **10589**
Salem Times-Commoner (Salem) **10589**
Savanna Times Journal (Savanna) **10589**
Scottsdale-Ashburn Independent (Midlothian) **10586**
† Sentinel, The (Chicago)
Shelbyville Daily Union (Shelbyville) **10441**
Shopper, The (South Holland) **10589**
Skokie Life (Lincolnwood) **10584**
Skokie Review (Evanston) **10579**
Skyline (Lincolnwood) **10584**
Sorento News (Hillsboro) **10582**
South County Express (Auburn) **10572**
Southern Illinoisan (Carbondale) **10438**
Southwest Beacon (Chicago) **10575**
Southwest Courier (Chicago) **10575**
Southwestern Journal News (Brighton) **10573**
Southwest News-Herald (Chicago) **10575**
Southwest Shopper (Chicago) **10575**
Sparta News Plaindealer (Sparta) **10589**
Springfield Shopper (Springfield) **10589**
Star, The (Tinley Park) **10590**
State Journal-Register (Springfield) **10441**
Staunton Star-Times (Staunton) **10589**
Stockton/Warren Gazette (Stockton) **10589**
Streator Times-Press (Streator) **10441**
Suburban Journal (Des Plaines) **10577**
Suburban Leader (Chicago) **10575**
Suburban Life Citizen (Oak Brook) **10586**
Suburban Life Graphic (Oak Brook) **10587**
Sumner Press (Sumner) **10589**
Sycamore News (Sycamore) **10590**
Taylorville Breeze-Courier (Taylorville) **10441**
Tazewell News (Morton) **10586**
Telegraph-County Edition (Jerseyville) **10583**
Telegraph, The (Alton) **10437**
Telegraph, The (Dixon) **10439**
† This Week (Aledo)
Thrif-T-Nikel Community Shopping Guide (Ottawa) **10587**
Thrifty Nickel (Champaign) **10574**
Thrifty Nickel Want Ads (East Moline) **10578**
Times Record (Aledo) **10571**
Town & Country Weekly (Ottawa) **10587**
Trenton Sun, The (Trenton) **10590**
Tri-County News (Elmwood) **10578**
Tri City Register (Riverton) **10588**
Tuscola Review (Tuscola) **10590**
Vandalia Leader-Union (Vandalia) **10590**
Vernon Hills News (Grayslake) **10581**
Vernon Hills Review (Bannockburn) **10572**
Vienna Times, The (Vienna) **10590**
Villa Park Argus (Elmhurst) **10578**
Virginia Gazette (Beardstown) **10573**
Warren-Newport Press (Grayslake) **10581**
Warrenville Free Press (West Chicago) **10590**
Washburn Leader (Metamora) **10585**
Washington Courier (Washington) **10590**
Washington Reporter (Morton) **10586**
Waterloo Republic-Times (Waterloo) **10590**
Wauconda Leader (Grayslake) **10581**
Waverly Journal (Waverly) **10590**
Wednesday Journal of Oak Park & River Forest (Oak Park) **10587**
Wenona Index (Henry) **10581**
Westchester Herald (Oak Park) **10587**
West Chicago Press (West Chicago) **10590**
West Cook County Press (Elmhurst) **10578**
Western Springs Doings (Hinsdale) **10582**
Westmont Progress (Downers Grove) **10577**
West Proviso Herald (Oak Park) **10587**
West Suburban Post (Chicago) **10575**
Wheaton Leader (Glen Ellyn) **10580**
Wheaton Press (Bloomingdale) **10573**
Wheaton Sun (Naperville) **10586**
Whiteside Shopper (Fulton) **10579**
Williamsville Sun (Riverton) **10589**
Willowbrook Doings (Hinsdale) **10582**
Willowbrook Progress (Downers Grove) **10577**
Wilmette Life (Glenview) **10580**
Wilmington Advocate, The (Wilmington) **10591**
Wilmington Express (Wilmington) **10591**
Wilmington Free Press (Wilmington) **10591**
Winfield Estate (Glen Ellyn) **10580**
Winfield Press (West Chicago) **10590**
Winnetka Talk (Glenview) **10580**
Wood Dale Press (Elmhurst) **10578**
Woodford County Journal (Eureka) **10578**
Woodridge Progress (Downers Grove) **10577**
Woodstock Independent, The (Woodstock) **10591**
Worth Citizen (Midlothian) **10586**
† Wrova Reporter (Galva)

INDIANA

Zion-Benton News (Zion) **10591**

Ad-News (Greenfield) **10594**
Advertiser, The (Ligonier) **10595**
Alexandria Times-Tribune (Alexandria) **10591**
Allen County Times (New Haven) **10596**
Auctioner, The (Pekin) **10597**
Banner-Gazette (Pekin) **10597**
Banner-Graphic (Greencastle) **10443**
Benton Review, The (Fowler) **10594**
Berne Tri-Weekly News (Berne) **10592**
Bluffton News-Banner (Bluffton) **10442**
Boonville Standard (Boonville) **10592**
Brazil Times (Brazil) **10442**
Brookville American-Democrat (Brookville) **10592**
Brown County Democrat (Nashville) **10596**
Call-Leader (Elwood) **10443**
Calumet Press, The (Highland) **10594**
Carmel News Tribune (Fishers) **10593**
Carroll County Comet (Flora) **10594**
Castleton Banner (Fishers) **10593**
Cedar Lake Journal (Lowell) **10595**
Centerville Crusader (Centerville) **10592**
† Chandler Post (Boonville)
Chesterton Guide (Maryville) **10595**
Chesterton Town Crier (Chesterton) **10592**
Chesterton Tribune (Chesterton) **10442**
Chronicle-Tribune (Marion) **10444**
Clarion News (Corydon) **10592**
Connersville News-Examiner (Connersville) **10442**
Corydon Democrat (Corydon) **10592**
Courier, The (Rensselaer) **10597**
Crawfordsville Journal Review (Crawfordsville) **10443**
Crothersville Times (Crothersville) **10592**
Culver Citizen (Culver) **10592**
Cumberland Courier (Lawrence) **10595**
Daily Clintonian (Clinton) **10442**
Daily Journal (Franklin) **10443**
Daily Ledger (Fisher) **10443**
Daily Reporter (Greenfield) **10443**
Dearborn County Register (Lawrenceburg) **10595**
Decatur Daily Democrat (Decatur) **10443**
East Side Herald (Indianapolis) **10594**
Elkhart Truth, The (Elkhart) **10443**
Evansville Courier (Evansville) **10443**
Evansville Press (Evansville) **10443**
Evening Star (Auburn) **10442**
Evening Star Plus, The (Auburn) **10591**
Evening World (Bloomfield) **10442**
Farmweek (Knightstown) **10595**
Ferdinand News, The (Ferdinand) **10593**
Fishers Sun-Herald (Fishers) **10593**
Fort Wayne News-Sentinel (Fort Wayne) **10443**
Fountain County Neighbor (Attica) **10591**
Frankfort Times (Frankfort) **10443**
Franklin Challenger (Greenwood) **10594**
Gary Crusader (Gary) **10594**
Gary Info (Gary) **10594**
Geist Gazette (Fishers) **10593**
Giveaway, The (Scottsburg) **10597**
Goshen News, The (Goshen) **10443**
Greensburg Daily News (Greensburg) **10443**
Greenwood & Southside Challenger (Greenwood) **10594**
Greenwood Gazette, The (Fishers) **10593**
Griffith Guide (Maryville) **10595**
Hagerstown Exponent, The (Hagerstown) **10594**
Heights Herald (Fishers) **10593**
Hendricks County Flyer (Plainfield) **10597**
† Hendricks County Guide Gazette (Plainfield)
Herald-Journal, The (Monticello) **10445**
Herald-Press (Huntington) **10444**
Herald-Republican (Angola) **10591**
Herald-Times (Bloomington) **10442**
Herald-Tribune (Batesville) **10592**
Herald Bulletin (Anderson) **10442**
Herald, The (Jasper) **10444**
Highland Guide (Maryville) **10595**
Hobart Gazette (Merriville) **10596**
Holbert Lake Station Community Shopping Guide (Merrillville) **10596**
Hoosier Express (Washington) **10598**
Independent, The (Winamac) **10598**
Indianapolis News (Indianapolis) **10444**
Indianapolis Recorder (Indianapolis) **10594**
Indianapolis Star (Indianapolis) **10444**
Indianapolis Westside Enterprise (Greenfield) **10594**
Indy Suburban Newspapers (Greenfield) **10594**
Jackson County Banner (Brownstown) **10592**
Jeffersonville Evening News (Jeffersonville) **10444**
Journal & Austin Chronicle (Scottsburg) **10597**
Journal & Courier (Lafayette) **10444**
Journal-Gazette, The (Fort Wayne) **10443**
Journal Press (Lawrenceburg) **10595**
Journal, The (Ellettsville) **10593**
Kendallville News-Sun (Kendallville) **10444**
Kokomo Tribune, The (Kokomo) **10444**
Lafayette Leader (Lafayette) **10595**
La Grange Standard News (La Grange) **10595**
Lake County Star (Crown Point) **10592**
La Porte Herald-Argus (La Porte) **10444**

Lawrence Times (Fishers) **10593**
Lawrence Township Journal (Lawrence) **10595**
Leader, The (Charlestown) **10592**
Ledger Tribune, The (New Albany) **10445**
Ligonier Advance-Leader (Ligonier) **10595**
Linton Daily Citizen (Linton) **10444**
Lowell Tribune (Lowell) **10595**
Madison Courier (Madison) **10444**
Mail-Journal, The (Milford) **10596**
† Marshall County Life (Culver)
Martinsville Daily Reporter (Martinsville) **10445**
Merrillville Herald Community Shopping Guide (Merrillville) **10596**
Messenger, The (Attica) **10591**
Michigan City News-Dispatch (Michigan City) **10445**
Middletown News, The (Middletown) **10596**
Mishawaka Enterprise (Mishawaka) **10596**
Mooresville Times, The (Mooresville) **10596**
Mount Vernon Democrat (Mt. Vernon) **10596**
Munster Guide (Maryville) **10595**
Newburgh-Chandler Register (Newburgh) **10596**
New Castle Courier-Times (New Castle) **10445**
New Prairie Town Crier (New Carlisle) **10596**
News-Gazette, The (Winchester) **10446**
News-Journal (North Manchester) **10596**
News-Sun (Fairmount) **10593**
News-Times (Hartford City) **10444**
News, The (Clay City) **10592**
Nora News Dispatch (Fisherspolis) **10593**
Northeast Reporter (Indianapolis) **10594**
North Knox News (Bicknell) **10592**
North Meridian Observer (Fishers) **10593**
North Side Topics (Fishers) **10593**
North Vernon Plain Dealer (North Vernon) **10596**
North Vernon Sun (North Vernon) **10596**
Northwest Press (Speedway) **10598**
NUVO Newsweekly (Indianapolis) **10594**
Ohio County News (Rising Sun) **10597**
Orange Countian (Paoli) **10597**
Osgood Journal (Versailles) **10598**
Ossian Journal (Ossian) **10596**
Paoli News (Paoli) **10597**
Paoli Republican (Paoli) **10597**
Paper of Wabash County, The (Wabash) **10598**
Paper, The (Elkhart) **10593**
Paper, The (Goshen) **10594**
Paper, The (Warsaw) **10598**
Perry County News, The (Tell City) **10598**
Perry Township Weekly (Beech Grove) **10592**
Peru Tribune (Peru) **10445**
Pharos-Tribune (Logansport) **10444**

Pike Register (Fishers) **10593**
Pilot-News (Plymouth) **10445**
Portage Community Shopping Guide (Merrillville) **10596**
Portland Commercial Review (Portland) **10445**
Post & Mail, The (Columbia City) **10442**
Post-Tribune (Gary) **10443**
Press-Dispatch (Petersburg) **10597**
Princeton Daily Clarion (Princeton) **10445**
Pulaski County Journal (Winamac) **10598**
Regional News, The (La Crosse) **10595**
Remington Press (Rensselaer) **10597**
Rensselaer Republican (Rensselaer) **10445**
Reporter, The (Lebanon) **10444**
Republican, The (Danville) **10592**
Republic, The (Columbus) **10442**
Richmond Palladium-Item (Richmond) **10445**
Rising Sun Recorder (Rising Sun) **10597**
Rochester Sentinel, The (Rochester) **10445**
Rockville Parke County Sentinel (Rockville) **10597**
Rushville Republican (Rushville) **10445**
Salem Democrat, The (Salem) **10597**
Salem Leader (Salem) **10597**
Schererville Guide (Maryville) **10596**
Shelbyville News (Shelbyville) **10446**
Sheridan News (Fishers) **10593**
South Bend Tribune (South Bend) **10446**
South Lake Advertiser (Lowell) **10595**
Speedway Town Press (Speedway) **10598**
Spencer County Journal Democrat (Rockport) **10597**
Spencer County Leader/Dale News (Ferdinand) **10593**
Spencer Evening World (Spencer) **10446**
Spotlight, The (Indianapolis) **10594**
Springs Valley Herald (French Lick) **10594**
Star Journal (Hope) **10594**
Star Press, The (Muncie) **10445**
Sullivan Daily Times (Sullivan) **10446**
Sunriser News (Ossian) **10597**
Switzerland Democrat (Vevay) **10598**
Times-Mail (Bedford) **10442**
Times-Union (Warsaw) **10446**
Times, The (Munster) **10445**
Tipton Tribune (Tipton) **10446**
Town Crier, The (La Porte) **10595**
Tri-County Banner (Knightstown) **10595**
Tri-County News (Edinburgh) **10593**
Tri-County News (South Bend) **10598**
Tribune-Star (Terre Haute) **10446**
Tribune, The (Seymour) **10446**
Valparaiso Guide (Maryville) **10596**
Valparaiso Vidette-Times (Valparaiso) **10446**
Versailles Republican (Versailles) **10598**
Vevay Reveille-Enterprise (Vevay) **10598**

Vincennes Sun-Commercial (Vincennes) **10446**
† Vincennes Valley Advance (Vincennes)
Wabash Plain Dealer (Wabash) **10446**
Washington County Edition (Salem) **10597**
Washington Times-Herald (Washington) **10446**
† Weekender Enquirer (Boonville)
Weekend Flyer, The (Plainfield) **10597**
Western Wayne News (Cambridge City) **10592**
Westfield Enterprise (Fishers) **10593**
Westside Enterprise (Greenfield) **10594**
Westside Flyer (Indianapolis) **10595**
Westside Messenger (Speedway) **10598**
Westville Indicator (Westville) **10598**
▼White River Gazette (Fishers) **10593**
Worthington Times, The (Worthington) **10598**
† Zionsville Eagle (Indianapolis)
Zionsville Times Sentinel (Zionsville) **10598**

IOWA

Adair County Free Press (Greenfield) **10601**
Ad Express & Daily Iowegian (Centerville) **10447**
Afton Star-Enterprise (Afton) **10598**
Albia Union-Republican (Albia) **10599**
Algona Upper Des Moines (Algona) **10599**
Altoona Herald, The (Altoona) **10599**
Anamosa Journal-Eureka (Anamosa) **10599**
Ankeny Press Citizen (Ankeny) **10599**
Atlantic News-Telegraph (Atlantic) **10446**
Beacon-Forum (Eldon) **10600**
Bettendorf News (Bettendorf) **10599**
Boone News-Republican (Boone) **10447**
Bremer County Independent (Waverly) **10605**
Britt News-Tribune (Britt) **10599**
Cedar Rapids Gazette (Cedar Rapids) **10447**
Cedar Valley Daily Times (Vinton) **10449**
Central Shopper (Des Moines) **10600**
Chariton Herald-Patriot (Chariton) **10599**
Chariton Leader (Chariton) **10599**
Charles City Press (Charles City) **10447**
Cherokee Daily Times (Cherokee) **10447**
Clayton County Register (Elkader) **10600**
Clinton Herald (Clinton) **10447**
Community Shopper (Des Moines) **10600**
Corydon Times-Republican (Corydon) **10599**
Cresco Times-Plain Dealer (Cresco) **10599**
Creston News Advertiser (Creston) **10447**
Daily Freeman Journal (Webster City) **10449**
Daily Nonpareil (Council Bluffs) **10447**
Daily Times Herald (Carroll) **10447**
Daily Tribune, The (Ames) **10446**
Decorah Public Opinion & Journal (Decorah) **10599**
Denison Bulletin & Review (Denison) **10600**

Des Moines County News, The (West Burlington) **10605**
Des Moines Register (Des Moines) **10447**
Diamond Trail News (Sully) **10604**
Doon Press (Doon) **10600**
Dyersville Commercial (Dyersville) **10600**
Eagle Grove Eagle (Eagle Grove) **10600**
Eddyville Tribune (Eddyville) **10600**
Edgewood Reminder (Edgewood) **10600**
Eldora Herald-Leader (Eldora) **10600**
Emmetsburg Democrat (Emmetsburg) **10600**
Emmetsburg Reporter (Emmetsburg) **10601**
Essex Independent, The (Essex) **10601**
Estherville Daily News (Estherville) **10447**
Fairfield Daily Ledger (Fairfield) **10447**
Farm Monthly (Atlantic) **10599**
Fayette County Union (West Union) **10605**
Forest City Summit (Forest City) **10601**
Fort Dodge Messenger (Fort Dodge) **10447**
Fort Madison Daily Democrat (Fort Madison) **10448**
Freemont Gazette (Fremont) **10601**
Gateway Express, The (Clinton) **10599**
Glenwood Opinion-Tribune (Glenwood) **10601**
Globe-Gazette (Mason City) **10448**
Greene Recorder, The (Greene) **10601**
Grinnell Herald-Register (Grinnell) **10601**
Grundy Register (Grundy Center) **10601**
Guttenberg Press (Guttenberg) **10601**
Hampton Chronicle & Times (Hampton) **10601**
Hardin County Index (Eldora) **10600**
Harlan News Advertiser (Harlan) **10601**
Harlan Tribune (Harlan) **10601**
Hawk Eye, The (Burlington) **10447**
Herald Journal (Clarinda) **10599**
Hudson Herald, The (Hudson) **10601**
Humboldt Independent (Humboldt) **10601**
† Humboldt Republican (Humboldt)
Humeston New Era (Humeston) **10601**
Independence Bulletin-Journal (Independence) **10601**
Iowa City Press-Citizen (Iowa City) **10448**
Jefferson Bee (Jefferson) **10602**
Jefferson Herald (Jefferson) **10602**
Jones County Town Crier (Anamosa) **10599**
Journal/Express (Knoxville) **10602**
Journal Tribune (Williamsburg) **10605**
Kalona News, The (Kalona) **10602**
Keokuk Daily Gate City (Keokuk) **10448**
† Kossuth County Advance (Algona)
Laurens Sun, The (Laurens) **10602**
Leader, The (Davenport) **10599**
Leader, The (Solon) **10604**
Lee Town Shopper (Des Moines) **10600**
Le Mars Daily Sentinel (Le Mars) **10448**
Leon Journal-Reporter (Leon) **10602**

Lime Springs Herald (Lime Springs) **10602**
Logan Herald Observer (Logan) **10602**
Lone Tree Reporter, The (Lone Tree) **10602**
Lyon-Sioux Press (Rock Rapids) **10603**
Malvern Leader, The (Malvern) **10602**
Manchester Press (Manchester) **10602**
Maquoketa Sentinel-Press (Maquoketa) **10602**
Marshalltown Times-Republican (Marshalltown) **10448**
Missouri Valley Times-News (Missouri Valley) **10602**
Mitchell County Press-News (Osage) **10603**
Monroe News (Albia) **10599**
Montezuma Republican, The (Montezuma) **10602**
Monticello Express (Monticello) **10602**
Mount Ayr Record-News (Mt. Ayr) **10603**
Mount Pleasant News (Mt. Pleasant) **10448**
Muscatine Journal (Muscatine) **10448**
N'West Iowa Review (Sheldon) **10604**
Nashua Reporter (Nashua) **10603**
Nevada Journal (Nevada) **10603**
† New Hampton Economist (New Hampton)
New Hampton Tribune (New Hampton) **10603**
New Sharon Star (New Sharon) **10603**
Newton Daily News (Newton) **10448**
Nishna Valley Tribune (Audubon) **10599**
Northcentral Shopper (Des Moines) **10600**
Northeast Shopper (Des Moines) **10600**
North Scott Press, The (Eldridge) **10600**
Northwest Iowa Shopper (Spencer) **10604**
Northwest Shopper (Des Moines) **10600**
Observer, The (DeWitt) **10600**
Oelwein Daily Register (Oelwein) **10448**
Onawa Democrat (Onawa) **10603**
Onawa Sentinel (Onawa) **10603**
Osceola County Gazette-Tribune (Sibley) **10604**
Osceola Sentinel-Tribune (Osceola) **10603**
Oskaloosa Herald (Oskaloosa) **10448**
Ossian Bee, The (Ossian) **10603**
Ottumwa Courier (Ottumwa) **10448**
Paullina Times (Paullina) **10603**
Pella Chronicle (Pella) **10603**
Perry Chief (Perry) **10603**
Pioneer Republican, The (Marengo) **10602**
Pocahontas Record-Democrat (Pocahontas) **10603**
Prairie City News (Prairie City) **10603**
Quad-City Times (Davenport) **10447**
Record-Herald & Indianola Tribune (Indianola) **10602**
Red Oak Express (Red Oak) **10603**
Schaller Herald (Schaller) **10604**
Sheldon Mail-Sun (Sheldon) **10604**
Shopper Spree (Burlington) **10599**

Sigourney News-Review (Sigourney) **10604**
Sioux City Journal, The (Sioux City) **10448**
Southern County News (Thornton) **10604**
Southside Shopper (Des Moines) **10600**
Spencer Daily Reporter (Spencer) **10448**
Spirit Lake Beacon (Spirit Lake) **10604**
State Center Enterprise-Record (State Center) **10604**
Storm Lake Pilot Tribune (Storm Lake) **10448**
Storm Lake Times (Storm Lake) **10604**
Story City Herald (Story City) **10604**
Sumner Gazette (Sumner) **10604**
Sun, The (Mt. Vernon) **10603**
Tama News-Herald (Tama) **10604**
Telegraph Herald (Dubuque) **10447**
Thompson-Rake Courier (Thompson) **10604**
Times Citizen (Iowa Falls) **10602**
Times Guthrian (Guthrie Center) **10601**
Tipton Conservative & Advertiser (Tipton) **10604**
Traer Star-Clipper (Traer) **10605**
Tri-County Times, The (Slater) **10604**
Valley News Today-Daily Sentinel (Shenandoah) **10448**
Washington Evening Journal (Washington) **10449**
Waterloo Courier (Waterloo) **10449**
Waukon Standard (Waukon) **10605**
Waverly Democrat (Waverly) **10605**
Western Express (Des Moines) **10600**
West Liberty Index (West Liberty) **10605**
What Cheer Paper (What Cheer) **10605**
Winterset Madisonian (Winterset) **10605**

KANSAS

Abilene Reflector-Chronicle (Abilene) **10449**
† Anderson Countian (Garnett)
Anthony Republican, The (Anthony) **10605**
Arkansas City Traveler (Arkansas City) **10449**
Atchison Daily Globe (Atchison) **10449**
Augusta Daily Gazette (Augusta) **10449**
Baldwin City Ledger (Lawrence) **10607**
Baxter Springs Citizen (Baxter Springs) **10605**
Belle Plaine News, The (Belle Plaine) **10605**
Belleville Telescope (Belleville) **10605**
Beloit Daily Call (Beloit) **10449**
Bird City Times (Bird City) **10605**
Bonner Springs-Edwardsville Chieftain (Bonner Springs) **10605**
Capital-Journal (Topeka) **10452**
Chanute Tribune (Chanute) **10449**
Chase County Leader-News (Cottonwood Falls) **10606**
Clay Center Dispatch (Clay Center) **10449**
Coffey County Today (Burlington) **10606**

Coffeyville Journal, The (Coffeyville) **10449**
Colby Free Press (Colby) **10449**
Columbus Daily Advocate (Columbus) **10449**
Concordia Blade-Empire (Concordia) **10449**
Council Grove Republican (Council Grove) **10449**
Courtland Journal-Empire (Courtland) **10606**
Daily Reporter, The (Derby) **10449**
Dodge City Daily Globe (Dodge City) **10450**
El Dorado Times (El Dorado) **10450**
Ellsworth Reporter, The (Ellsworth) **10606**
Emporia Gazette (Emporia) **10450**
Eureka Herald (Eureka) **10606**
Fort Riley Post (Junction City) **10607**
Fort Scott Tribune, The (Fort Scott) **10450**
Garden City Telegram (Garden City) **10450**
† Garnett Review (Garnett)
Girard Press (Girard) **10606**
Goodland Daily News (Goodland) **10450**
Great Bend Tribune (Great Bend) **10450**
Hays Daily News (Hays) **10450**
Hiawatha Daily World (Hiawatha) **10450**
High Plains Journal (Dodge City) **10606**
Hill City Times, The (Hill City) **10606**
Hillsboro Star-Journal (Hillsboro) **10606**
Hoisington Dispatch (Hoisington) **10606**
Holton Recorder (Holton) **10606**
Hutchinson News (Hutchinson) **10450**
Independence Daily Reporter (Independence) **10450**
Independence News, The (Independence) **10606**
Iola Register (Iola) **10450**
Jetmore Republican (Jetmore) **10606**
Johnson County Sun (Shawnee Mission) **10608**
Johnson Pioneer (Johnson) **10606**
Journal-World, The (Lawrence) **10451**
Journal Herald, The (Shawnee) **10608**
Junction City Daily Union (Junction City) **10450**
† Kansas Business News (Augusta)
† Kansas City Evening News (Shawnee Mission)
Kansas City Kansan (Kansas City) **10450**
Kingman Journal (Kingman) **10607**
Leader-Courier (Kingman) **10607**
† Leader, The (Lansing)
Leavenworth Times (Leavenworth) **10451**
Leawood Sun (Shawnee Mission) **10608**
Lebanon Times, The (Lebanon) **10607**
Ledger, The (Moundridge) **10607**
Lenexa Sun (Shawnee Mission) **10608**
Liberal Southwest Daily Times (Liberal) **10451**
Lyons Daily News (Lyons) **10451**
Madison News Inc., The (Madison) **10607**
Manhattan Mercury (Manhattan) **10451**
Marion County Record (Marion) **10607**
Marysville Advocate, The (Marysville) **10607**
McPherson Sentinel (McPherson) **10451**
Miami County Republic (Paola) **10608**
Miltonvale Record (Miltonvale) **10607**
Neodesha Derrick (Neodesha) **10607**
Ness County News, The (Ness City) **10607**
Newton Kansan (Newton) **10451**
Northeast Johnson County (Shawnee Mission) **10608**
Norton Daily Telegram (Norton) **10451**
Oakley Graphic (Oakley) **10607**
Oberlin Herald, The (Oberlin) **10607**
Olathe Daily News (Olathe) **10451**
Olathe Sun (Overland Park) **10608**
Osage County Chronicle (Burlingame) **10606**
Osawatomie Graphic (Osawatomie) **10608**
Osborne County Farmer (Osborne) **10608**
Oskaloosa Independent (Oskaloosa) **10608**
Ottawa Herald (Ottawa) **10451**
Ottawa Times (Ottawa) **10608**
Ottawa Times Shopper (Ottawa) **10608**
Overland Park Sun (Shawnee Mission) **10608**
Oxford Register, The (Belle Plaine) **10605**
Parsons News (Parsons) **10608**
Parsons Sun (Parsons) **10451**
Phillips County Review (Phillipsburg) **10608**
Pittsburg Morning Sun (Pittsburg) **10451**
Prairie Village Sun (Shawnee Mission) **10608**
Pratt Tribune (Pratt) **10451**
Record, The (Kansas City) **10607**
Rush County News (La Crosse) **10607**
Russell Daily News (Russell) **10451**
Russell Record (Russell) **10608**
Salina Journal (Salina) **10451**
Shawnee/Merriam Sun (Shawnee Mission) **10608**
Sherman County Star, The (Goodland) **10606**
Smith County Pioneer (Smith Center) **10609**
Squires, The (Overland) **10608**
† Squire, The (Prairie Village)
St. Francis Herald, The (St. Francis) **10609**
St. John News (St. John) **10609**
St. Marys Star (St. Marys) **10609**
Tiller & Toiler (Larned) **10450**
Times-Sentinel, The (Cheney) **10606**
† Towne & Country Shopper (Columbus)
Ulysses News (Ulysses) **10609**
Valley Falls Vindicator (Valley Falls) **10609**
Washington County News (Washington) **10609**
Wellington Daily News (Wellington) **10452**
Wichita Eagle (Wichita) **10452**
Wilson County Citizen (Fredonia) **10606**
Winfield Daily Courier (Winfield) **10452**

Wyandotte West (Kansas City) **10607**

KENTUCKY

Adair Progress, The (Columbia) **10610**
Adair Russell Shopper, The (Columbia) **10610**
Advance-Yeoman (Lacenter) **10612**
Advertiser, The (Louisa) **10612**
Advertiser, The (Mount Sterling) **10613**
Advertiser, The (Paris) **10613**
Advocate-Messenger (Danville) **10452**
Anderson News, The (Lawrenceburg) **10612**
Appalachian News-Express (Pikeville) **10613**
Barbourville Mountain Advocate (Barbourville) **10609**
Bath County News-Outlook (Owingsville) **10613**
Beaver Dam Ohio County Messenger (Beaver Dam) **10609**
Big Sandy News, The (Louisa) **10612**
Boone County Recorder (Florence) **10610**
Bourbon County Citizen (Paris) **10613**
Breckinridge County Herald-News (Hardinsburg) **10611**
Butler County & Green River Republican Banner, The (Morgantown) **10613**
Cadiz Record, The (Cadiz) **10609**
Campbell County Recorder (Fort Thomas) **10611**
Carlisle Mercury, The (Carlisle) **10610**
Casey County News (Liberty) **10612**
Casey County Shopper, The (Columbia) **10610**
Central City Times-Argus (Central City) **10610**
Central Kentucky News-Journal (Campbellsville) **10609**
Citizen Voice & Times (Irvine) **10612**
Clay City Times, The (Stanton) **10614**
Clinton County News (Albany) **10609**
Columbia News, The (Columbia) **10610**
Commonwealth Journal (Somerset) **10453**
Corbin Times-Tribune (Corbin) **10452**
Courier-Journal, The (Louisville) **10453**
Crittenden Press (Marion) **10612**
Cumberland County News (Burkesville) **10609**
Cumberland Trading Post, The (Middlesboro) **10612**
Cynthiana Democrat (Cynthiana) **10610**
Daily Independent, The (Ashland) **10452**
Daily News (Bowling Green) **10452**
Dawson Springs Progress (Dawson Springs) **10610**
Dixie News (Florence) **10610**
Eastern Kentucky Shopper (Paintsville) **10613**
Estill County Tribune, The (Irvine) **10612**
Floyd County Times (Prestonsburg) **10613**
Franklin Favorite (Franklin) **10611**

Fulton Leader (Fulton) **10611**
Fulton Shopper (Fulton) **10611**
Georgetown News Graphic (Georgetown) **10611**
Glasgow Daily Times (Glasgow) **10452**
Glasgow Republican (Glasgow) **10611**
Grant County News (Williamstown) **10615**
Grayson Advertiser (Leitchfield) **10612**
Grayson County News-Gazette (Leitchfield) **10612**
Grayson Journal-Enquirer (Grayson) **10611**
† Green River Republican (Morgantown)
Greenup County News-Times (Greenup) **10611**
Hancock Clarion (Hawesville) **10611**
Harlan Daily Enterprise (Harlan) **10452**
Harrodsburg Herald (Harrodsburg) **10611**
Hart County News-Herald (Munfordville) **10613**
Hazard Herald-Voice (Hazard) **10611**
Henderson Gleaner (Henderson) **10452**
Henry County Local (New Castle) **10613**
Herald Ledger (Eddyville) **10610**
Interior Journal (Stanford) **10614**
Jessamine Journal (Nicholasville) **10613**
Journal-Enterprise (Providence) **10614**
Kenton County Recorder (Florence) **10610**
Kentucky New Era (Hopkinsville) **10452**
Kentucky Post, The (Covington) **10452**
Kentucky Standard (Bardstown) **10609**
LaRue County Herald-News (Hodgenville) **10611**
Leader-News (Central City) **10610**
Lebanon Enterprise (Lebanon) **10612**
Ledger-Independent (Maysville) **10453**
Leslie County News (Hyden) **10611**
Letcher County Community News-Press (Cromona) **10610**
Lexington Herald-Leader (Lexington) **10453**
Licking Valley Courier (West Liberty) **10615**
Manchester Enterprise (Manchester) **10612**
Mayfield Messenger (Mayfield) **10453**
McCreary County Record (Whitley City) **10615**
Meade County Messenger (Brandenburg) **10609**
Messenger, The (Madisonville) **10453**
Middlesboro Daily News (Middlesboro) **10453**
Minifee County News (Morehead) **10613**
Morehead News (Morehead) **10613**
Mountain Citizen, The (Inez) **10611**
Mountain Eagle, The (Whitesburg) **10615**
Mount Sterling Advocate (Mount Sterling) **10613**
Murray Ledger & Times (Murray) **10453**
News-Democrat, The (Carrollton) **10610**
News-Enterprise (Elizabethtown) **10452**
News-Journal Shopper (Campbellsville) **10610**

News Democrat & Leader (Russellville) **10614**
Ohio County Times News (Hartford) **10611**
Oldham Era, The (La Grange) **10612**
Olive Hill Times (Olive Hill) **10613**
Oliveville Times (Morehead) **10613**
Owensboro Messenger-Inquirer
 (Owensboro) **10453**
Paducah Sun, The (Paducah) **10453**
Paintsville Herald, The (Paintsville) **10613**
Pineville Sun-Cumberland Courier
 (Pineville) **10613**
Pioneer-News (Shepherdsville) **10614**
Progress, The (Cave City) **10610**
Richmond Register (Richmond) **10453**
Russell County News, The (Russell
 Springs) **10614**
Salyersville Independent (Salyersville) **10614**
Scottsville Citizen-Times (Scottsville) **10614**
Sentinel-Echo (London) **10612**
Sentinel, The (Radcliff) **10614**
Shelbyville Sentinel-News (Shelbyville) **10614**
Shopper/PLUS (Shelbyville) **10614**
Shopper's Guide (Bardstown) **10609**
Southwest Newsweek, The (Louisville) **10612**
Spencer Magnet (Taylorsville) **10614**
Springfield Sun (Springfield) **10614**
State Journal (Frankfort) **10452**
Sturgis News (Sturgis) **10614**
T-Ville News Trader (Tompkinsville) **10614**
Thousandsticks (Hyden) **10611**
Times Journal, The (Russell Springs) **10614**
Times Leader, The (Princeton) **10614**
† Times, The (Augusta)
Todd County Standard (Elkton) **10610**
Tompkinsville News (Tompkinsville) **10614**
Tri-City News (Cumberland) **10610**
Tribune Courier (Benton) **10609**
Union County Advocate (Morganfield) **10613**
Voice-Tribune, The (Louisville) **10612**
Wayne County Outlook (Monticello) **10612**
West Kentucky News (Paducah) **10613**
Whitley Republican News Journal
 (Williamsburg) **10615**
Winchester Sun (Winchester) **10453**
Woodford Sun (Versailles) **10615**

LOUISIANA

Abbeville Meridional (Abbeville) **10453**
Advocate, The (Baton Rouge) **10454**
Alexandria Daily Town Talk (Alexandria) **10453**
Alexandria News Weekly (Alexandria) **10615**
Amite Tangi Digest (Amite) **10615**
Avoyelles Journal (Marksville) **10617**
Baker Observer (Baker) **10615**
Bastrop Daily Enterprise (Bastrop) **10453**
Baton Rouge Shopper (Baton Rouge) **10615**
Beauregard Daily News (De Ridder) **10454**
Bienville Democrat & Ringgold Record
 (Arcadia) **10615**
Bogalusa Daily News & Sunday News
 (Bogalusa) **10454**
Bossier Banner-Progress (Bossier City) **10616**
Bossier Press-Tribune (Bossier City) **10616**
Caddo Citizen (Vivian) **10618**
Church Point News (Church Point) **10616**
Community Mirror (Gonzales) **10616**
Concordia Sentinel (Ferriday) **10616**
Consumers' Edge (Baton Rouge) **10615**
Courier, The (Houma) **10454**
Coushatta Citizen (Coushatta) **10616**
Covington St. Tammany Farmer
 (Covington) **10616**
Crowley Post-Signal (Crowley) **10454**
Daily Comet (Thibodaux) **10455**
Daily Iberian (New Iberia) **10455**
Daily Review, The (Morgan City) **10454**
Daily World (Opelousas) **10455**
Denham Springs-Livingston Parish News
 (Denham Springs) **10616**
De Quincy News (De Quincy) **10616**
Donaldsonville Chief (Donaldsonville) **10616**
East Feliciana Watchman (Clinton) **10616**
Enterprise, The (Ponchatoula) **10617**
Eunice News (Eunice) **10616**
Franklin Banner-Tribune (Franklin) **10454**
Franklin Sun, The (Winnsboro) **10618**
Gonzales Weekly (Gonzales) **10616**
Greater Baton Rouge Business Report (Baton
 Rouge) **10615**
Hammond Daily Star (Hammond) **10454**
Jackson Independent, The (Jonesboro) **10616**
Jeanerette Enterprise (Jeanerette) **10616**
Jena Times Olla-Tullos Signal (Jena) **10616**
Jennings Daily News (Jennings) **10454**
Kentwood News-Ledger (Kentwood) **10617**
L'Observateur (La Place) **10617**
Lafayette Advertiser (Lafayette) **10454**
Lake Charles American Press (Lake
 Charles) **10454**
Leesville Daily Leader (Leesville) **10454**
Livingston Leader (Denham Springs) **10616**
Madison Journal (Tallulah) **10618**
Mamou Acadian Press (Mamou) **10617**
Mansfield Enterprise (Mansfield) **10617**
Minden Press-Herald (Minden) **10454**
Natchitoches Times (Natchitoches) **10454**
News-Banner, The (Covington) **10616**
News-Star, The (Monroe) **10454**
News Examiner, The (Lutcher) **10617**
Oakdale Journal (Oakdale) **10617**
Ouachita Citizen (West Monroe) **10618**

Plaquemines Gazette (Belle Chasse) **10615**
Plaquemines Watchman (Belle Chasse) **10615**
Pointe Coupee Banner (New Roads) **10617**
Ponchatoula Times, The (Ponchatoula) **10617**
Post South (Plaquemine) **10617**
Rayne Acadian-Tribune (Rayne) **10617**
Rayne Independent (Rayne) **10617**
Richland Beacon-News (Rayville) **10618**
Ruston Daily Leader (Ruston) **10455**
Sabine Banner (Many) **10617**
Sabine Index (Many) **10617**
† Shreveport Journal (Shreveport)
Slidell Sentry-News (Slidell) **10455**
Southwest Daily News (Sulphur) **10455**
Springhill Press (Springhill) **10618**
St. Bernard Voice, The (Arabi) **10615**
St. Martinville Teche News (St. Martinville) **10618**
St. Mary Journal (Morgan City) **10617**
Times-Picayune (New Orleans) **10455**
Times, The (Shreveport) **10455**
Ville Platte Gazette (Ville Platte) **10618**
Weekly News (Marksville) **10617**
Weekly Press (Baton Rouge) **10615**
West Carroll Gazette (Oak Grove) **10617**
West Side Journal (Port Allen) **10617**
Winn Parish Enterprise (Winnfield) **10618**
Zachary Plainsman-News (Zachary) **10618**

MAINE

American Journal (Westbrook) **10620**
Aroostook Republican & News (Caribou) **10619**
Bangor Daily News (Bangor) **10455**
Bar Harbor Times (Bar Harbor) **10618**
Biddeford-Saco-OOB Courier (Biddeford) **10618**
Boothbay Register (Boothbay Harbor) **10618**
Bridgton News (Bridgton) **10618**
Calais Advertiser (Calais) **10618**
▼Capital Weekly (Augusta) **10618**
Central Maine Morning Sentinel (Waterville) **10456**
Community Advertiser (Farmingdale) **10619**
County Wide (Dover-Foxcroft) **10619**
Courier-Gazette (Rockland) **10620**
Eastern Gazette, The (Dexter) **10619**
Ellsworth American, The (Ellsworth) **10619**
† Evening Express (Portland)
Fort Fairfield Review (Fort Fairfield) **10619**
Franklin Journal & Farmington Chronicle (Farmington) **10619**
Guilford American (Dover-Foxcroft) **10619**
Houlton Pioneer Times (Houlton) **10619**
Island Ad-Vantages (Stonington) **10620**

Islesboro Island News (Islesboro) **10619**
Journal Tribune (Biddeford) **10455**
Katahdin Times (Millinocket) **10619**
Kennebec Journal (Augusta) **10455**
Lincoln County News (Newcastle) **10620**
Lincoln News (Lincoln) **10619**
Livermore Falls Advertiser (Livermore Falls) **10619**
Machias Valley News Observer (Machias) **10619**
Maine Times (Portland) **10620**
Norway Advertiser-Democrat (Norway) **10620**
Penobscot Times (Old Town) **10620**
Piscataquis Observer, The (Dover-Foxcroft) **10619**
Portland Press Herald (Portland) **10455**
Quoddy Tides (Eastport) **10619**
Republican Journal (Belfast) **10618**
Rumford Falls Times (Rumford) **10620**
Sanford News (Sanford) **10620**
Star-Herald, The (Presque Isle) **10620**
St. John Valley Times (Madawaska) **10619**
Suburban News, The (Windham) **10620**
Sun-Journal (Lewiston) **10455**
Times-Record (Brunswick) **10455**
Weekly Packet (Blue Hill) **10618**
York County Coast Star (Kennebunk) **10619**

MARYLAND

Aegis, The (Bel Air) **10621**
Arbutus Times (Baltimore) **10620**
Avenue News (Baltimore) **10620**
Baltimore Chronicle (Baltimore) **10620**
Baltimore Messenger (Baltimore) **10620**
Baltimore Sun (Baltimore) **10456**
Bay Times (Stevensville) **10622**
Bethesda/Chevy Chase Almanac (Potomac) **10622**
Bowie Blade-News (Bowie) **10621**
Brunswick Citizen (Brunswick) **10621**
Calvert Independent (Prince Fredrick) **10622**
Capital, The (Annapolis) **10456**
Carroll County Sun (Westminster) **10456**
Carroll County Times (Westminster) **10457**
Catonsville Times (Baltimore) **10620**
Cecil Whig (Elkton) **10456**
City Paper (Baltimore) **10620**
Columbia Flier (Columbia) **10621**
Community Times (Westminster) **10623**
† Countywide News (Westminster)
Crofton News-Crier (Bowie) **10621**
Cumberland Times-News (Cumberland) **10456**
Daily Banner (Cambridge) **10456**
Daily Mail, The (Hagerstown) **10456**

Daily Times (Salisbury) **10456**
Damascus Gazette (Gatorsburg) **10621**
Dorchester Star (Cambridge) **10621**
Dundalk Eagle, The (Baltimore) **10620**
East Baltimore Guide (Baltimore) **10620**
Enquirer-Gazette (Upper Marlboro) **10623**
Enterprise & Inner Harbor News (Baltimore) **10621**
Enterprise, The (Lexington Park) **10622**
Frederick Post, The (Frederick) **10456**
Gaithersburg Gazette (Gaithersburg) **10621**
Greenbelt News Review (Greenbelt) **10622**
Hancock News (Hancock) **10622**
Herald-Mail, The (Hagerstown) **10456**
Howard County Times (Columbia) **10621**
Jeffersonian, The (Baltimore) **10621**
Kent County News (Chestertown) **10621**
Labor Herald (Baltimore) **10621**
Laurel Leader (Laurel) **10622**
Maryland Gazette (Glen Burnie) **10621**
Maryland Independent (Waldorf) **10623**
Maryland Times-Press (Ocean City) **10622**
Middletown Valley Citizen (Brunswick) **10621**
Montgomery County Sentinel (Gaithersburg) **10621**
Montgomery Journal, The (Rockville) **10456**
News, The (Frederick) **10456**
Northeast Reporter (Towson) **10623**
Owings Mills Times (Baltimore) **10621**
Potomac Almanac (Potomac) **10622**
Prince Georges Journal (Lanham) **10456**
Prince Georges Sentinel (Seabrook) **10622**
Queen Anne's Record-Observer (Centreville) **10621**
Recorder, The (Prince Frederick) **10622**
Record, The (Havre De Grace) **10622**
Republican, The (Oakland) **10622**
Salisbury News & Advertiser, The (Salisbury) **10622**
Silver Spring Gazette (Gaithersburg) **10621**
Somerset Herald (Princess Anne) **10622**
Star-Democrat, The (Easton) **10456**
Times-Herald (Timonium) **10622**
Times-Record, The (Denton) **10621**
Towson Times (Towson) **10623**
Village News (Montgomery Village) **10622**
Worcester County Messenger (Pocomoke City) **10622**

MASSACHUSETTS

Advocate/South Advocate, The (Williamstown) **10629**
Amesbury News (Amesbury) **10623**
Andover Townsman (Andover) **10623**
Arlington Advocate (Arlington) **10623**
Associated Newspaper (Stoughton) **10628**
Athol Daily News (Athol) **10457**
Auburn News (Auburn) **10623**
Barnstable Patriot, The (Hyannis) **10625**
Bay State Banner (Boston) **10623**
Beacon, The (Concord) **10624**
Bedford Minuteman (Concord) **10624**
Belchertown Sentinel (Belchertown) **10623**
Belmont Citizen-Herald (Arlington) **10623**
† Berkshire Courier (Great Barrington)
Berkshire Eagle (Pittsfield) **10458**
Berkshire Penny Saver (Lee) **10625**
Berkshire Record (Great Barrington) **10625**
Billerica Minuteman (North Billerica) **10627**
Blackstone Valley Tribune (Whitinsville) **10629**
Bolton Common (Bolton) **10623**
Boston Globe (Boston) **10457**
Boston Herald (Boston) **10457**
Boston Phoenix (Boston) **10623**
Bourne Courier (Yarmouthport) **10630**
Braintree Forum (Marshfield) **10625**
Bridgewater Independent (Middleboro) **10626**
† Bridgewater Townsman (Bridgewater)
Burlington Union (Woburn) **10629**
Cambridge Chronicle (Somerville) **10628**
Canton Journal (Canton) **10624**
Cape Codder (Orleans) **10627**
† Cape Cod News (Yarmouth Port)
Cape Cod Times (Hyannis) **10457**
Capeway News (Middleboro) **10626**
Carver Reporter (Plymouth) **10627**
† Charlestown Citizen (Brookline)
Chelmsford Independent (Chelmsford) **10624**
Chelsea Record (Revere) **10628**
Chicopee Herald Weekly, The (Chicopee) **10624**
Chronicle, The (North Dartmouth) **10627**
Cohasset Mariner (Marshfield) **10625**
Concord Journal (Concord) **10624**
Daily Evening Item (Lynn) **10458**
Daily Hampshire Gazette (Northampton) **10458**
Daily News of Newburyport, The (Newburyport) **10458**
Daily Times & Chronicle (Reading) **10458**
Daily Times Chronicle (Woburn) **10459**
Daily Transcript (Dedham) **10457**
Danvers Herald (Danvers) **10624**
† Dennis Bulletin (South Yarmouth)
Dover-Sherborn Suburban Press (Needham) **10626**
Dracut Dispatch, The (Dracut) **10624**
Duxbury Reporter (Plymouth) **10627**
Eagle Tribune, The (North Andover) **10458**
East Bridgewater Star (East Bridgewater) **10624**

Easton Bulletin (Stoughton) **10628**
† Enterprise Sun (Marlborough)
Enterprise, The (Brockton) **10457**
Enterprise, The (Falmouth) **10625**
Foxboro Reporter, The (Foxboro) **10625**
Gardner News (Gardner) **10457**
Georgetown Record (Ipswich) **10625**
Gloucester Daily Times (Gloucester) **10457**
Groton Landmark (Ayer) **10623**
Halifax Reporter (Plymouth) **10627**
Hamilton-Wenham Chronicle (Ipswich) **10625**
Hanover Mariner (Marshfield) **10625**
Harvard Spirit (Ayer) **10623**
Harwich Oracle (Orleans) **10627**
Haverhill Gazette (Haverhill) **10457**
Herald News, The (Fall River) **10457**
Hingham Journal & Mariner (Marshfield) **10626**
Holbrook Sun (Marshfield) **10626**
Holbrook Times (Stoughton) **10628**
Improper Bostonian, The (Boston) **10624**
Inquirer & Mirror, The (Nantucket) **10626**
Ipswich Chronicle (Ipswich) **10625**
Item (Clinton) **10624**
Journal Register (Palmer) **10627**
Kingston Independent (Marshfield) **10626**
Kingston Reporter (Plymouth) **10627**
Lakeville Independent (Middleboro) **10626**
Lexington Minuteman (Woburn) **10629**
Littleton Independent (Concord) **10624**
Longmeadow News (Westfield) **10629**
Lowell Sun (Lowell) **10458**
Ludlow Register (Palmer) **10627**
Main Street Trilogy (Townsend) **10629**
Malden Evening News (Malden) **10458**
Mansfield News (Mansfield) **10625**
Marblehead Reporter (Marblehead) **10625**
Marshfield Mariner (Marshfield) **10626**
Marshfield Reporter (Plymouth) **10627**
Mashpee Messenger (Yarmouth) **10630**
Maynard Beacon (Concord) **10624**
Medfield Suburban Press (Needham) **10627**
Medford Daily Mercury (Malden) **10458**
Melrose Free Press (Melrose) **10626**
† Melrose Shoppers News (Stoneham)
Merrimack Valley Sunday (Amesbury) **10623**
Middleboro Gazette (Middleboro) **10626**
Middlesex News (Framingham) **10457**
Milford Daily News (Milford) **10458**
Millbury/Sutton Chronicle (Millbury) **10626**
Milton Record Transcript (Milton Village) **10626**
Nantucket Beacon (Nantucket) **10626**
Natick Bulletin (Needham) **10627**
New Leader (Spencer) **10628**
News-Tribune (Framingham) **10457**

News, The (Southbridge) **10458**
Newton Graphic (Waltham) **10629**
North Shore Sunday (Danvers) **10624**
Norton Courier (Stoughton) **10628**
Norwell Mariner (Marshfield) **10626**
Old Colony Memorial (Plymouth) **10627**
Parkway Transcript (Dedham) **10624**
Patriot Ledger (Quincy) **10458**
† Peabody Times (Peabody)
Pembroke Mariner (Marshfield) **10626**
Pembroke Reporter (Plymouth) **10628**
Pennysaver, The (Yarmouthport) **10630**
Pepperell Free Press (Ayer) **10623**
Pittsfield Gazette, The (Pittsfield) **10627**
Provincetown Advocate (Provincetown) **10628**
Public Spirit (Ayer) **10623**
Quincy Sun (Quincy) **10628**
† Randolph Mariner (Marshfield)
Raynham Journal (Stoughton) **10628**
Recorder, The (Greenfield) **10457**
Register, The (Yarmouthport) **10630**
Revere Journal (Revere) **10628**
Salem Evening News (Beverly) **10457**
Sandwich Broadsider (Orleans) **10627**
Saugus Advertiser (Melrose) **10626**
Sentinel & Enterprise (Fitchburg) **10457**
Sentinel, The (Marion) **10625**
Sharon Advocate (Sharon) **10628**
Somerville Journal (West Somerville) **10629**
South Boston Tribune (Boston) **10624**
South County Weekender (Webster) **10629**
South Shore News (Rockland) **10628**
Spectator, The (Somerset) **10628**
Springfield Advocate (Springfield) **10628**
Standard-Times, The (New Bedford) **10458**
State Line Shopping Guide (Palmer) **10627**
† Stoneham Weekender News (Stoneham)
Stoughton Chronicle (Stoughton) **10628**
† Suburban News (Reading)
Sudbury Town Crier (Needham) **10627**
Sun Chronicle (Attleboro) **10457**
Sunday Post (Lynn) **10625**
Swampscott Reporter (Marblehead) **10625**
Tab, The (Needham) **10627**
Taunton Daily Gazette (Taunton) **10458**
Taunton Independent (Middleboro) **10626**
Telegram & Gazette (Worcester) **10459**
Townsend Times (Ayer) **10623**
† Transcript-Telegram (Holyoke)
Transcript, The (North Adams) **10458**
Tri-Town Transcript (Danvers) **10624**
Union-News (Springfield) **10458**
Valley Advocate (Hatfield) **10625**
† Village Journal (Osterville)
Vineyard Gazette (Edgartown) **10625**
Wakefield Item (Wakefield) **10459**

Walpole Times, The (Walpole) **10629**
Wareham Courier (Marion) **10625**
Ware River News (Ware) **10629**
Watertown Tab & Press (Somerville) **10628**
Wayland-Weston Town Crier (Needham) **10627**
Webster Times, The (Webster) **10629**
Weekender, The (Whitinsville) **10629**
Wellesley Townsman (Wellesley) **10629**
West Bridgewater Star (Middleboro) **10626**
Westfield Evening News (Westfield) **10459**
Westford Eagle (Chelmsford) **10624**
West Roxbury Transcript (Dedham) **10624**
West Springfield Record (West Springfield) **10629**
Weymouth News (Marshfield) **10626**
Weymouth News & Gazette (Braintree) **10624**
Whitman Times (Stoughton) **10628**
Wick-Qua-Boag Weekly (Spencer) **10628**
Wilmington-Tewksbury Town Crier (Wilmington) **10629**
Winchendon Chronicle (Winchendon) **10629**
Winchendon Courier (Winchendon) **10629**
Winchester Star (Woburn) **10629**
Woburn Advocate (Woburn) **10629**
Worcester Magazine (Worcester) **10630**
† Yarmouth Sun (Yarmouth Port)

MICHIGAN

Ad-Visor (Beulah) **10630**
Ad-Visor (Lansing) **10635**
Ada/Cascade/Forest Hills Advance (Jenison) **10634**
Advertiser, The (Iron Mountain) **10634**
Advisor/Source (Utica) **10638**
Albion Recorder (Albion) **10459**
† Algonac Courier Journal (Marine City)
Allegan County News (Allegan) **10630**
Alpena News (Alpena) **10459**
Alpena Star (Alpena) **10630**
† Anchor Bay Beacon (New Baltimore)
Ann Arbor News (Ann Arbor) **10459**
Arenac County Independent (Standish) **10638**
Argus-Press, The (Owosso) **10461**
Battle Creek Enquirer (Battle Creek) **10459**
Battle Creek Shopper (Battle Creek) **10630**
Bay City Times (Bay City) **10459**
Bay Voice (New Baltimore) **10636**
Belleville Enterprise (Wayne) **10639**
Berrien County Record (Buchanan) **10631**
Big Rapids Pioneer (Big Rapids) **10459**
Birmingham Eccentric, The (Birmingham) **10630**
Blazer News (Jackson) **10634**
Blissfield Advance (Blissfield) **10630**
Bloomfield Eccentric, The (Birmingham) **10630**
Blue Water Voice (New Baltimore) **10636**
Brighton Argus (Brighton) **10630**
† Byron Center/Dorr Advance (Jenison)
Cadillac Evening News (Cadillac) **10459**
Caledonia/Gaines Advance (Jenison) **10634**
Canton Eagle (Wayne) **10639**
Canton Observer (Plymouth) **10637**
Cass City Chronicle (Cass City) **10631**
Charlevoix County Star (Gaylord) **10632**
Charlevoix Courier (Charlevoix) **10631**
Charlotte Shopping Guide (Charlotte) **10631**
Cheboygan Daily Tribune (Cheboygan) **10459**
Chelsea Standard, The (Chelsea) **10631**
Citizen, The (Boyne City) **10630**
Citizen, The (Hamtramck) **10633**
Clare Sentinel (Clare) **10631**
Clarkston News (Clarkston) **10631**
Clinton County News (St. Johns) **10638**
Clio Messenger, The (Flint) **10632**
Commercial-Express (Vicksburg) **10639**
Commercial Record (Saugatuck) **10638**
Community Advisor (Marshall) **10635**
Connection, The (Grosse Point) **10633**
County Line Reminder (Ortonville) **10636**
County Press (Parma) **10636**
County Press, The (Lapeer) **10635**
Daily Mining Gazette (Houghton) **10460**
Daily News (Greenville) **10460**
Daily News (Iron Mountain) **10460**
Daily Press, The (Escanaba) **10460**
Daily Reporter, The (Coldwater) **10459**
Daily Telegraph (Adrian) **10459**
Daily Tribune, The (Royal Oak) **10462**
Davison Flagstaff (Swartz Creek) **10638**
Davison Index, The (Davison) **10631**
Dearborn Press & Guide (Dearborn) **10631**
Dearborn Times-Herald (Dearborn) **10632**
Delta Waverly Community News (Grand Ledge) **10633**
Detroit Free Press (Detroit) **10460**
Detroit News (Detroit) **10460**
DeWitt Bath Review (St. Johns) **10638**
† Diamond Drill, The (Crystal Falls)
Dowagiac Daily News (Dowagiac) **10460**
Downriver Voice (New Baltimore) **10636**
Durand Express, The (Durand) **10632**
East Grand Rapids Cadence (Jenison) **10634**
Eaton County News (Charlotte) **10631**
Enterprise, The (Mason) **10635**
Evart Review, The (Evart) **10632**
Exponent, The (Brooklyn) **10630**
Farmers' Advance (Camden) **10631**
Farmington Observer (Farmington) **10632**
Flint Journal (Flint) **10460**
Flushing Observer (Flint) **10632**

Fowlerville Review Shopping Guide (Howell) **10634**
Frankenmuth News (Frankenmuth) **10632**
Garden City Observer (Livonia) **10635**
Gaylord Herald Times (Gaylord) **10632**
† Gladstone Delta Reporter (Escanaba)
Gladwin County Record & Beaverton Clarion (Gladwin) **10633**
Grand Blanc News, The (Flint) **10632**
Grand Haven Tribune (Grand Haven) **10460**
Grand Ledge Independent, The (Grand Ledge) **10633**
Grand Rapids Advance (Jenison) **10634**
Grand Rapids Press, The (Grand Rapids) **10460**
Grand Valley Advance (Jenison) **10634**
Gratiot County Herald (Ithaca) **10634**
Great Lakes Pilot, The (Grand Marais) **10633**
Grosse Pointe News (Grosse Pointe Farms) **10633**
Harbor Beach Times (Harbor Beach) **10633**
† Harper Woods Herald (Birmingham)
Hartland Herald Shopping Guide (Howell) **10634**
Hastings Banner (Hastings) **10633**
Hastings Reminder (Hastings) **10633**
Heights Times-Herald (Dearborn) **10632**
Herald-Palladium (St. Joseph) **10462**
Herald News, The (Reed City) **10637**
Hillsdale Daily News (Hillsdale) **10460**
Holland Sentinel (Holland) **10460**
Holt Community News (Holt) **10634**
Houghton Lake Resorter (Houghton Lake) **10634**
Huron Daily Tribune (Bad Axe) **10459**
Ile Camera, The (Grosse Ile) **10633**
† Independent Press (Marine City)
Independent, The (Flint) **10632**
Ingham County News (Mason) **10635**
Inkster Ledger-Star (Wayne) **10639**
In Your Community/Oakland Press (Pontiac) **10637**
Ionia Sentinel-Standard (Ionia) **10460**
Iosco County News Herald (East Tawas) **10632**
Iron River Reporter (Iron River) **10634**
Ironwood Daily Globe (Ironwood) **10460**
Jackson Citizen Patriot (Jackson) **10460**
Jeffersonian, The (Croswell) **10631**
Kalamazoo Gazette (Kalamazoo) **10461**
Kentwood Advance (Jenison) **10634**
L'Anse Sentinel (L'Anse) **10635**
† Lake Country Chronicle (Buchanan)
Lake County Star (Big Rapids) **10630**
Lake Michigan Examiner, The (Muskegon) **10636**
Lakeview Enterprise (Big Rapids) **10630**
Lansing State Journal (Lansing) **10461**
Leelanau Enterprise (Leland) **10635**
Leslie Local Independent (Leslie) **10635**
Livonia Observer (Livonia) **10635**
Lowell Ledger (Lowell) **10635**
Ludington Daily News (Ludington) **10461**
Macomb Daily (Mt. Clemens) **10461**
Macomb Voice, The (New Baltimore) **10636**
Manistee News-Advocate (Manistee) **10461**
Manistee Observer (Manistee) **10635**
Manistique Pioneer-Tribune (Manistique) **10635**
Maple Valley News (Hastings) **10633**
Marshall Chronicle (Marshall) **10461**
Mayville Monitor (Mayville) **10635**
Metro Times (Detroit) **10632**
Michigan Chronicle (Detroit) **10632**
Midland Daily News (Midland) **10461**
Milan Area Leader (Milan) **10635**
Milford Times (Milford) **10635**
Mining Journal (Marquette) **10461**
Monroe Evening News (Monroe) **10461**
Morenci Observer (Morenci) **10636**
Morning Sun (Mt. Pleasant) **10461**
Munising News (Munising) **10636**
Muskegon Chronicle, The (Muskegon) **10461**
New Buffalo Times (New Buffalo) **10636**
News-Herald, The (Southgate) **10638**
Newsweekly, The (Sebewaing) **10638**
Niles Daily Star (Niles) **10461**
North Country Sun (Ironwood) **10634**
† Northeast Detroiter (Detroit)
Northern Michigan News (Cadillac) **10631**
Northern Star (Gaylord) **10633**
Northfield Advance (Jenison) **10634**
North Macomb Voice (New Baltimore) **10636**
Northville Record (Northville) **10636**
North Woods Call (Charlevoix) **10631**
Norway Current (Norway) **10636**
Novi News (Northville) **10636**
Oakland Press, The (Pontiac) **10461**
Oceana's Herald-Journal (Hart) **10633**
Ogemaw County Herald (West Branch) **10639**
Onaway Outlook (Onaway) **10636**
Ontonagon Herald (Ontonagon) **10636**
Oscoda Press (Oscoda) **10636**
Ottawa Advance (Jenison) **10634**
Our Home Town (Vanderbilt) **10638**
Paw Paw Courier-Leader (Paw Paw) **10636**
Penny Saver (Three Rivers) **10638**
Petoskey News-Review (Petoskey) **10461**
Petosky Star Ad-Vertiser (Gaylord) **10633**
Pinckney Post Shopping Guide (Pinckney) **10637**
Plymouth Observer (Plymouth) **10637**

Porcupine Press (Chatham) **10631**
Portland Review & Observer (Grand Ledge) **10633**
Presque Isle Advance (Rogers City) **10637**
Presque Isle Star (Gaylord) **10633**
Redford Observer (Livonia) **10635**
Richmond Review, The (Richmond) **10637**
Rochester Clarion (Rochester) **10637**
Rochester Eccentric (Rochester Hills) **10637**
Rockford/Cedar Springs Advance (Jenison) **10634**
Rockford Squire (Rockford) **10637**
Romeo Observer (Romeo) **10637**
Romulus Roman (Wayne) **10639**
Roscommon County Herald-News (Roscommon) **10637**
Saginaw News (Saginaw) **10462**
Saginaw Press, The (Saginaw) **10637**
Saline Reporter (Saline) **10637**
Sanilac County News (Sandusky) **10638**
Sault Ste. Marie Evening News (Sault Ste. Marie) **10462**
Shiawassee County Journal (Perry) **10637**
Southfield Eccentric (Birmingham) **10630**
South Haven Daily Tribune (South Haven) **10462**
South Lyon Herald (South Lyon) **10638**
Sparta/Kent City Advance (Sparta) **10638**
Spinal Column Newsweekly (Waterford) **10639**
Star Advertiser (Kalkaska) **10635**
Star Buyers Guide (West Branch) **10639**
St. Clair Shores Herald (Birmingham) **10630**
St. Ignace News, The (St. Ignace) **10638**
St. Johns Reminder (St. Johns) **10638**
Straits Area Star (Cheboygan) **10631**
Sturgis Journal (Sturgis) **10462**
Suburban News, The (Flint) **10632**
Sun & News, The (Hastings) **10633**
Sunday Independent, The (Owosso) **10636**
Tecumseh Herald (Tecumseh) **10638**
Three Rivers Commercial-News (Three Rivers) **10462**
Times-Indicator (Fremont) **10632**
Times Herald (Port Huron) **10462**
Town Crier (Stockbridge) **10638**
Towne Courier (East Lansing) **10632**
Township Times (Saginaw) **10637**
Traverse City Record-Eagle (Traverse City) **10462**
Tri-City Record, The (Watervliet) **10639**
Tri-City Times (Imlay City) **10634**
Tri-County Citizen (Chesaning) **10631**
Tribune Plus (Royal Oak) **10637**
Troy-Somerset Gazette (Troy) **10638**
Troy Eccentric (Rochester Hills) **10637**
Tuscola County Advertiser (Caro) **10631**

Union Enterprise (Plainwell) **10637**
Valley Farmer, The (Bay City) **10630**
Van Buren County Advertiser (Gobles) **10633**
Vassar Pioneer Times (Vassar) **10639**
Walker-Westside Advance (Jenison) **10634**
Wayne Eagle (Wayne) **10639**
Westland Eagle (Wayne) **10639**
Westland Observer (Livonia) **10635**
West Valley News/Sunday Advance (Flint) **10632**
White Lake Beacon (Whitehall) **10639**
Wyoming Advance (Jenison) **10634**

MINNESOTA

Ada Norman County Index (Ada) **10639**
Advertiser, The (Bemidji) **10640**
Aitkin Independent Age (Aitkin) **10639**
Albert Lea Tribune (Albert Lea) **10462**
Anoka County Union (Coon Rapids) **10641**
Apple Valley/Rosemont Sun-Current (Burnsville) **10640**
Austin Daily Herald (Austin) **10462**
Baudette Region, The (Baudette) **10640**
Becker County Record (Detroit Lakes) **10641**
Bird Island Union (Bird Island) **10640**
Blaine-Spring Lake Park Life (Coon Rapids) **10641**
Blaine Banner (Blaine) **10640**
Bloomington Sun-Current (Bloomington) **10640**
Brainerd Daily Dispatch (Brainerd) **10462**
Brooklyn Center Sun Post (Minneapolis) **10643**
Brooklyn Park Sun Post (Minneapolis) **10643**
Budgeteer Press (Duluth) **10641**
Buffalo Ridge Gazette, The (Ruthton) **10646**
Burnsville/Savage Sun-Current (Burnsville) **10640**
Canby News (Canby) **10640**
Chanhassen Villager (Chanhassen) **10641**
Chaska Herald (Chaska) **10641**
Chicago County Press (Lindstrom) **10643**
Chisholm Tribune Press (Chisholm) **10641**
City Pages (Minnepolis) **10644**
Cloquet Billboard Shopper (Cloquet) **10641**
Cloquet Pine Knot (Cloquet) **10641**
Coon Rapids Herald (Coon Rapids) **10641**
Crookston Daily Times (Crookston) **10462**
Daily Journal, The (Fergus Falls) **10463**
Daily Journal, The (International Falls) **10463**
Dakota County Tribune (Burnsville) **10640**
Detroit Lakes Tribune (Detroit Lakes) **10641**
Duluth News-Tribune (Duluth) **10462**
Eagan Sun-Current (Burnsville) **10640**
East Side Review (North St. Paul) **10645**
Echo Press, The (Alexandria) **10639**

ECM Post-Review (North Branch) **10644**
Eden Prairie Sun-Current (Bloomington) **10640**
Edgerton Enterprise, The (Edgerton) **10641**
Edina Sun-Current (Minneapolis) **10644**
Ely Echo (Ely) **10641**
Erskine Echo, The (Erskine) **10641**
Excelsior/Shorewood/Chanhassen Sun-Sailor (Minnetonka) **10644**
Exponent, The (Greenbush) **10642**
Fairmont Photo Press (Fairmont) **10641**
Fairmont Sentinel (Fairmont) **10463**
Faribault County Register (Blue Earth) **10640**
Faribault Daily News (Faribault) **10463**
Farmers Independent (Bagley) **10639**
Focus News (Roseville) **10646**
Forest Lake Press (St. Paul) **10647**
Fosston Thirteen Towns (Fosston) **10642**
† Freeborn County Register (Albert Lea)
Free Press (Mankato) **10463**
Fridley Focus (Roseville) **10646**
Glencoe Enterprise (Glencoe) **10642**
Grand Gazette (St. Paul) **10647**
Grand Rapids/Herald-Review (Grand Rapids) **10642**
Granite Falls/Clerkfield Advocate Tribune (Granite Falls) **10642**
Grygla Eagle (Grygla) **10642**
Hastings Star Gazette (Hastings) **10642**
Hawley Herald (Hawley) **10642**
Hiawatha Valley Shopper (Red Wing) **10646**
Hibbing Daily Tribune (Hibbing) **10463**
Hopkins Sun-Sailor (Minnetonka) **10644**
Hutchinson Leader (Hutchinson) **10642**
Independent News Herald (Clarissa) **10641**
Jackson County Livewire (Jackson) **10642**
Jasper Journal (Jasper) **10643**
Journal, The (New Ulm) **10463**
Kanabec County Times (Mora) **10644**
Kenyon Leader (Kenyon) **10643**
Lake County News-Chronicle (Two Harbors) **10648**
Lakefield Standard (Lakefield) **10643**
Lakeshore Weekly News (Wayzata) **10648**
Lakeville Life & Times (Lakeville) **10643**
Lakeville Sun-Current (Burnsville) **10640**
Lamberton News (Lamberton) **10643**
Leader-Record (Gonvick) **10642**
Le Center Leader (Le Center) **10643**
Lewiston Journal (Lewiston) **10643**
Lillie Suburban Shopping Review (St. Paul) **10647**
Litchfield Independent Review (Litchfield) **10643**
† Little Falls Transcript (Little Falls)
Long Prairie Leader (Long Prairie) **10643**
Madison Western Guard, The (Madison) **10643**
Mahnomen Pioneer, The (Mahnomen) **10643**
Maplewood Review (St. Paul) **10647**
Marshall Independent (Marshall) **10463**
McIntosh Times (McIntosh) **10643**
Melrose Beacon (Melrose) **10643**
Mesabi Daily News (Virginia) **10464**
Mille Lacs County Times (Milaca) **10643**
Minnetonka/Deephaven Sun-Sailor (Minnetonka) **10644**
Montevideo American-News (Montevideo) **10644**
Moose Lake Star-Gazette (Moose Lake) **10644**
Morris Sun (Morris) **10644**
Morris Tribune (Morris) **10644**
Mounds View-New Brighton-St. Anthony Focus (Roseville) **10646**
Murray County Wheel Herald (Slayton) **10646**
New Brighton-Mounds View Bulletin (St. Paul) **10647**
New Hope-Golden Valley Sun Post (Minneapolis) **10644**
New Prague Times (New Prague) **10644**
New River Record (Greenbush) **10642**
Northern Light, The (Greenbush) **10642**
Northern Star, The (Clinton) **10641**
Northern Watch (Thief River Falls) **10647**
Northfield News (Northfield) **10645**
North Minneapolis Sun Post (Minneapolis) **10644**
Northome Record & Mizpah Message (Northome) **10645**
North Star News (Greenbush) **10642**
Oakdale-Lake Elmo Review (St. Paul) **10647**
Oakdale Clarion (Oakdale) **10645**
Observer, The (Belgrade) **10640**
Oklee Herald (Oklee) **10645**
Olivia Times Journal (Olivia) **10645**
Ortonville Independent (Ortonville) **10645**
Osakis Review, The (Osakis) **10645**
Owatonna People's Press (Owatonna) **10463**
Owatonna Weekly Shopper (Owatonna) **10645**
Park Rapids Enterprise (Park Rapids) **10645**
Paynesville Press, The (Paynesville) **10645**
Pelican Rapids Press (Pelican Rapids) **10645**
Perham Enterprise-Bulletin (Perham) **10645**
Pioneer, The (Bemidji) **10462**
Pipestone County Star (Pipestone) **10645**
Plainview News (Plainview) **10645**
Plymouth Sun-Sailor (Minnetonka) **10644**
Pope County Tribune (Glenwood) **10642**
Post-Bulletin (Rochester) **10463**
† Press, The (Alexandria)
Princeton Union-Eagle (Princeton) **10645**
Proctor Journal (Proctor) **10646**
Quad Community Press (White Bear Lake) **10648**

Ramsey County Review (St. Paul) **10647**
Red Wing Republican Eagle (Red Wing) **10463**
Redwood Gazette, The (Redwood Falls) **10646**
Renville County Shopper (Olivia) **10645**
Richfield Sun-Current (Bloomington) **10640**
River Valley Shopper (Spring Valley) **10646**
Rock County Star Herald (Luverne) **10643**
Roosevelt Review (St. Paul) **10647**
Roseau Times-Region (Roseau) **10646**
Roseville Review (St. Paul) **10647**
Sauk Centre Herald (Sauk Centre) **10646**
Sebeka/Menahga Review Messenger (Sebeka) **10646**
Shakopee Valley News (Shakopee) **10646**
Shoreview-Arden Hills Bulletin (St. Paul) **10647**
Shoreview Press (St. Paul) **10647**
Skyworld Duluth News (Duluth) **10641**
South-West Review (St. Paul) **10647**
† South East Metro Shopper (Cottage Grove)
South St. Paul/Inver Grove Heights Sun-Current (Burnsville) **10640**
Springfield Advance-Press (Springfield) **10646**
Spring Valley Tribune (Spring Valley) **10646**
St. Anthony Bulletin (North St. Paul) **10645**
Staples World (Staples) **10646**
Star Tribune (Minneapolis) **10463**
St. Charles Press (St. Charles) **10647**
St. Cloud Times (St. Cloud) **10463**
St. Croix Valley Peach (Forest Lake) **10642**
St. Croix Valley Press (St. Paul) **10647**
Stillwater Gazette (Stillwater) **10463**
St. James Plaindealer (St. James) **10647**
St. Louis Park Sun-Sailor (Minnetonka) **10644**
St. Paul Pioneer Press (St. Paul) **10463**
St. Peter Herald (St. Peter) **10647**
Swift County Monitor-News (Benson) **10640**
Thief River Falls Times (Thief River Falls) **10648**
Times, The (Forest Lake) **10642**
Tracy Headlight-Herald (Tracy) **10648**
Tri-County Record (Rushford) **10646**
Tribune, The (Greenbush) **10642**
Twin Cities Reader (Minneapolis) **10644**
Tyler Tribune (Tyler) **10648**
Vadnais Heights Press (St. Paul) **10647**
Villager (St. Paul) **10647**
Waconia Patriot, The (Waconia) **10648**
Wadena Pioneer Journal (Wadena) **10648**
Warren Sheaf (Warren) **10648**
Warroad Pioneer (Greenbush) **10642**
Waseca County News (Waseca) **10648**
Wayzata/Orono/Long Lake Sun-Sailor (Minnetonka) **10644**
Wells Mirror, The (Wells) **10648**
West Central Tribune (Willmar) **10464**

West Martin Weekly News (Sherburn) **10646**
West St. Paul/Mendota Heights Sun-Current (Burnsville) **10640**
White Bear Press (St. Paul) **10647**
Windom Cottonwood County Citizen (Windom) **10648**
Winona Daily News (Winona) **10464**
Woodbury-South Maplewood Review (St. Paul) **10647**
Worthington Daily Globe (Worthington) **10464**
Wright County Journal-Press (Buffalo) **10640**

MISSISSIPPI

Aberdeen Examiner (Aberdeen) **10648**
Amory Advertiser, The (Amory) **10648**
Bay St. Louis Sea Coast Echo (Bay St. Louis) **10649**
Biloxi-D'Iberville Press (D'Iberville) **10649**
Booneville Banner-Independent (Booneville) **10649**
Brookhaven Daily Leader (Brookhaven) **10464**
Bruce Calhoun County Journal (Bruce) **10649**
Carthaginian, The (Carthage) **10649**
Clarion-Ledger, The (Jackson) **10464**
Clarke County Tribune (Quitman) **10651**
Clarksdale Press Register (Clarksdale) **10464**
Cleveland Bolivar Commercial (Cleveland) **10464**
Columbian-Progress (Columbia) **10649**
Commercial Dispatch, The (Columbus) **10464**
Conservative, The (Carrollton) **10649**
Copiah County Courier (Hazlehurst) **10649**
Daily Corinthian (Corinth) **10464**
Daily Sentinel-Star, The (Grenada) **10464**
Daily Times Leader (West Point) **10465**
Delta Democrat-Times (Greenville) **10464**
Democrat, The (Senatobia) **10651**
De Soto Times (Southaven) **10651**
George County Times (Lucedale) **10650**
Golden Triangle Shopper (Columbus) **10649**
Greenwood Commonwealth (Greenwood) **10464**
Hattiesburg American (Hattiesburg) **10464**
Impact of Laurel (Laurel) **10650**
Itawamba County Times, The (Fulton) **10649**
Iuka Tishomingo County News (Iuka) **10650**
Jasper County News, The (Bay Springs) **10649**
Kemper County Messenger (DeKalb) **10649**
Laurel Leader-Call (Laurel) **10465**
Louisville Winston County Journal (Louisville) **10650**
Macon Beacon, The (Macon) **10650**
Madison County Herald (Canton) **10649**
Magee Courier (Magee) **10650**
Magnolia Gazette, The (Magnolia) **10650**

McComb Enterprise-Journal (McComb) **10465**
Meridian Star (Meridian) **10465**
Mississippi Press (Pascagoula) **10465**
Natchez Democrat (Natchez) **10465**
Neshoba Democrat, The (Philadelphia) **10650**
New Albany Gazette (New Albany) **10650**
Newton Record (Newton) **10650**
Northeast Mississippi Daily Journal (Tupelo) **10465**
Northside Sun, The (Jackson) **10650**
Ocean Springs Record (Ocean Springs) **10650**
Oxford Eagle (Oxford) **10465**
▼Panolian Advantage, The (Batesville) **10648**
Panolian, The (Batesville) **10648**
Picayune Item (Picayune) **10465**
Pontotoc Progress (Pontotoc) **10650**
Port Gibson Reveille (Port Gibson) **10650**
Rankin County News, The (Brandon) **10649**
Richton Dispatch, The (Richton) **10651**
Ripley Southern Sentinel (Ripley) **10651**
Scott County Times (Forest) **10649**
Shopper's Guide, The (Louisville) **10650**
Shopping News, The (Newton) **10650**
Smith County Reformer (Raleigh) **10651**
Southern Herald, The (Liberty) **10650**
South Reporter, The (Holly Springs) **10649**
Star-Herald, The (Kosciusko) **10650**
Starkville Daily News (Starkville) **10465**
Stone County Enterprise (Wiggins) **10651**
Sun Herald, The (Gulfport) **10464**
Times Post, The (Houston) **10649**
Tylertown Times (Tylertown) **10651**
Vicksburg Post (Vicksburg) **10465**
Wayne County News (Waynesboro) **10651**
Webster Progress-Times (Eupora) **10649**
Winona Times (Winona) **10651**
Yazoo Herald (Yazoo City) **10651**

MISSOURI

Albany Ledger, The (Albany) **10651**
Atchison County Mail, The (Rock Port) **10656**
Aurora Advertiser (Aurora) **10651**
Barry County Advertiser (Cassville) **10652**
Belle Banner (Belle) **10651**
Bethany Republican-Clipper (Bethany) **10652**
Bland Courier (Belle) **10651**
Blue Springs Examiner (Blue Springs) **10465**
Bolivar Herald-Free Press (Bolivar) **10652**
Bollinger County Banner-Press (Marble Hill) **10655**
Boone County Journal (Ashland) **10651**
Boonville Daily News (Boonville) **10465**
Bowling Green Times (Bowling Green) **10652**
Branson Daily News (Hollister) **10466**
Buffalo Reflex (Buffalo) **10652**

California Democrat (California) **10652**
Callaway Courier (Holts Summit) **10654**
Cameron Citizen Observer (Cameron) **10652**
Carrollton Democrat (Carrollton) **10652**
Carthage Press (Carthage) **10466**
Cash-Book Journal (Jackson) **10654**
Cassville Democrat (Cassville) **10652**
Cedar County Republican (Stockton) **10658**
Centralia Fireside Guard (Centralia) **10652**
Central Missouri News (Sedalia) **10656**
Central West End Journal (St. Louis) **10657**
Charleston Enterprise-Courier (Charleston) **10652**
Chesterfield Journal (St. Louis) **10657**
Chillicothe Constitution-Tribune (Chillicothe) **10466**
Christian County Headliner News (Ozark) **10655**
Citizen Journal (St. Louis) **10657**
Clay Dispatch-Tribune (Kansas City) **10654**
Clinton Daily Democrat (Clinton) **10466**
Clinton Eye, The (Clinton) **10652**
Columbia Daily Tribune (Columbia) **10466**
Columbia Missourian (Columbia) **10466**
Community News (St. Louis) **10657**
County Star Journal East (St. Louis) **10657**
County Star Journal West (St. Louis) **10657**
Courier-Post, The (St. Charles) **10468**
Cuba Free Press (Cuba) **10653**
Daily American Republic (Poplar Bluff) **10467**
Daily Dunklin Democrat (Kennett) **10467**
Daily Guide (St. Robert) **10468**
Daily Journal (Park Hills) **10467**
Daily Mail & Sunday Herald (Nevada) **10467**
Daily News (Richmond) **10467**
Daily News-Bulletin, The (Brookfield) **10465**
Daily Standard (Excelsior Springs) **10466**
Daily Star-Journal, The (Warrensburg) **10468**
Daily Statesman (Dexter) **10466**
Democrat-Argus, The (Caruthersville) **10652**
Democrat-Leader (Fayette) **10653**
Democrat-News (Fredericktown) **10653**
Dexter Daily Statesman (Dexter) **10466**
Dixon Pilot (Dixon) **10653**
Douglas County Herald (Ava) **10651**
Eldon Advertiser (Eldon) **10653**
Fayette Advertiser, The (Fayette) **10653**
† Flat River Lead Belt News (Flat River)
Florissant Valley Reporter (Florissant) **10653**
Fulton Sun Gazette, The (Fulton) **10466**
Gasconade County Republican (Owensville) **10655**
† Good Times News (Fayette)
Green Hills Weekly (Trenton) **10658**
Hannibal Courier-Post (Hannibal) **10466**
Harrison County Advisor (Bethany) **10652**

Harrisonville Cass County Democrat Missourian (Harrisonville) **10653**
Hermann Advertiser-Courier (Hermann) **10653**
Hermitage Index (Hermitage) **10653**
Holden Image-Progress, The (Holden) **10654**
Hopkins Journal, The (Hopkins) **10654**
Houston Herald & Republican (Houston) **10654**
Independence Examiner, The (Independence) **10466**
Independent-Journal, The (Potosi) **10656**
Jefferson County Journal (Arnold) **10651**
† Jefferson Republic, The (De Soto)
Joplin Globe, The (Joplin) **10467**
Kansas City Star (Kansas City) **10467**
Kayo, The (Clinton) **10652**
Kirksville Daily Express (Kirksville) **10467**
Lake Sun Leader (Camdenton) **10465**
Lamar Democrat (Lamar) **10654**
Lawrence County Record (Mt. Vernon) **10655**
Lebanon Daily Record (Lebanon) **10467**
Lee's Summit Journal (Lee's Summit) **10654**
Lexington News (Lexington) **10654**
Liberty Tribune (Kansas City) **10654**
Linn Unterrified Democrat (Linn) **10654**
Louisiana Press-Journal (Louisiana) **10654**
Macon Chronicle-Herald (Macon) **10467**
† Malden Press-Merit (Malden)
Marceline Press (Marceline) **10655**
Maries County Gazette (Vienna) **10658**
Marshall Democrat-News (Marshall) **10467**
Marshfield Mail (Marshfield) **10655**
Marthasville Record, The (Marthasville) **10655**
Maryville Daily Forum (Maryville) **10467**
Mexico Ledger (Mexico) **10467**
Mid-County Journal (St. Louis) **10657**
Milan Standard, The (Milan) **10655**
Missouri Press News (Columbia) **10652**
Moberly Monitor Index (Moberly) **10467**
Monett Times (Monett) **10467**
Monroe County Appeal (Paris) **10655**
Montgomery Standard (Montgomery City) **10655**
Mound City News (Mound City) **10655**
Mountain Echo (Ironton) **10654**
Mountain Grove News-Journal (Mountain Grove) **10655**
Neosho Daily News (Neosho) **10467**
News-X Press (Butler) **10652**
News Democrat Journal (Festus) **10653**
New Times, The (Kansas City) **10654**
North County Journal East (St. Louis) **10657**
North County Journal West (St. Louis) **10657**
North Missourian (Gallatin) **10653**
Northside Journal (St. Louis) **10657**
O'Fallon Journal (O'Fallon) **10655**

Oakville-Mehville Journal (St. Louis) **10657**
Ozark County Times (Gainesville) **10653**
Palmyra Spectator (Palmyra) **10655**
Perry County Republic-Monitor, The (Perryville) **10656**
Pierce City Leader-Journal (Pierce City) **10656**
Pitch Weekly (Kansas City) **10654**
Plainsman Weekly News (Sedalia) **10656**
Platte County Gazette (Parkville) **10655**
Platte Dispatch Tribune (Kansas City) **10654**
Post-Tribune (Jefferson City) **10466**
Press-News Journal (Canton) **10652**
Press Dispatch (Kansas City) **10654**
Press Journal (St. Louis) **10657**
Press Leader, The (Farmington) **10466**
Prospect-News, The (Doniphan) **10653**
Prospector, The (Doniphan) **10653**
Quad River News (Sheridan) **10656**
† Randolph County Times-Herald (Moberly)
Raytown Dispatch Tribune (Raytown) **10656**
Record, The (Boonville) **10652**
Reynolds County Courier (Ellington) **10653**
Rolla Daily News (Rolla) **10468**
Salem News (Salem) **10656**
Sarcoxie Record, The (Sarcoxie) **10656**
Savannah Reporter & Andrew County Democrat (Savannah) **10656**
Sedalia Democrat, The (Sedalia) **10468**
Shelby County Herald (Shelbyville) **10656**
Sikeston Standard Democrat, The (Sikeston) **10468**
Smithville Lake Herald, The (Smithville) **10656**
South City Journal (St. Louis) **10657**
South County Journal (St. Louis) **10657**
Southeast Missourian (Cape Girardeau) **10466**
South Missourian News (Thayer) **10658**
Southside Journal (St. Louis) **10657**
Southwest City Journal (St. Louis) **10657**
Southwest County Journal (St. Louis) **10658**
Springfield News-Leader, The (Springfield) **10468**
Star-Herald (Belton) **10651**
St. Charles Journal (St. Charles) **10656**
St. Clair Missourian (St. Clair) **10656**
Steele Enterprise (Steel) **10657**
Steelville Star/Crawford Mirror (Steelville) **10657**
Ste. Genevieve Herald (Ste. Genevieve) **10657**
St. James Leader Journal (St. James) **10657**
St. Joseph News-Press (St. Joseph) **10468**
St. Joseph Telegraph, The (St. Joseph) **10657**
St. Louis American Newspaper (St. Louis) **10658**
† St. Louis Naborhood Link News (St. Louis)
St. Louis Post-Dispatch (St. Louis) **10468**

† St. Louis South St. Louis County News (St. Louis)
Sullivan Independent News (Sullivan) **10658**
Sun Times (Perryville) **10656**
Table Rock Gazette (Kimberling City) **10654**
▼Taney County Times (Forsyth) **10653**
Tarkio Avalanche (Tarkio) **10658**
Trenton Republican Times (Trenton) **10468**
Tri-County Journal (Pacific) **10655**
Troy Free Press & Silex Index (Troy) **10658**
Unionville Republican, The (Unionville) **10658**
Versailles Leader-Statesman (Versailles) **10658**
† Vista Press (Kansas City)
† Warrenton Banner (Warrenton)
Warrenton Journal (Warrenton) **10658**
Warsaw Benton County Enterprise (Warsaw) **10658**
Washington Missourian (Washington) **10658**
Wayne County Journal-Banner (Piedmont) **10656**
Webster County Citizen (Seymour) **10656**
Wednesday Magazine (Kansas City) **10654**
Wentzville Journal (Wentzville) **10658**
West County Journal (St. Louis) **10658**
West Plains Daily Quill (West Plains) **10468**
Wheels 'N Deals (Columbia) **10653**
Windsor Review (Windsor) **10658**

MONTANA

Anaconda Leader (Anaconda) **10658**
Bigfork Eagle (Bigfork) **10659**
Billings Gazette (Billings) **10468**
Bozeman Daily Chronicle (Bozeman) **10468**
Daily Inter Lake, The (Kalispell) **10469**
Glasgow Courier, The (Glasgow) **10659**
Glendive Ranger-Review (Glendive) **10659**
Great Falls Tribune (Great Falls) **10468**
Havre Daily News (Havre) **10469**
Herald-News (Wolf Point) **10659**
Hungry Horse News (Columbia Falls) **10659**
Independent Record (Helena) **10469**
Lake County Leader (Ronan) **10659**
Lewistown News-Argus (Lewistown) **10659**
Livingston Enterprise (Livingston) **10469**
Miles City Star (Miles City) **10469**
Missoulian, The (Missoula) **10469**
Montana Standard (Butte) **10468**
Mountaineer, The (Big Sandy) **10659**
Philipsburg Mail, The (Philipsburg) **10659**
Ravalli Republic (Hamilton) **10469**
River Press, The (Fort Benton) **10659**
Sidney Herald-Leader (Sidney) **10659**
Times-Clarion, The (Harlowton) **10659**
Western Breeze (Cut Bank) **10659**
Western News (Libby) **10659**

Whitefish Pilot (Whitefish) **10659**

NEBRASKA

Albion News (Albion) **10659**
Alliance Times-Herald (Alliance) **10469**
Arapahoe Public Mirror (Arapahoe) **10659**
Arlington Citizen (Blair) **10660**
Arthur Enterprise, The (Arthur) **10660**
Atkinson Graphic, The (Atkinson) **10660**
Auburn Press Tribune (Auburn) **10660**
Aurora News-Register (Aurora) **10660**
Beacon Observer, The (Overton) **10661**
Beatrice Daily Sun (Beatrice) **10469**
Bellevue Leader (Bellevue) **10660**
Blair Enterprise (Blair) **10660**
Blair Pilot-Tribune (Blair) **10660**
Burwell Tribune, The (Burwell) **10660**
Central City Republican Nonpareil (Central City) **10660**
Clipper-Herald (Lexington) **10661**
Columbus Telegram (Columbus) **10469**
Courier-Times (Sutherland) **10662**
Crete News, The (Crete) **10660**
Custer County Chief (Broken Bow) **10660**
David City Banner-Press, The (David City) **10660**
Deshler Rustler, The (Deshler) **10660**
Douglas County Post Gazette (Elkhorn) **10660**
Fairbury Journal-News, The (Fairbury) **10661**
Falls City Journal (Falls City) **10661**
Fremont Tribune (Fremont) **10469**
Frontier & Holt County Independent (O'Neill) **10661**
Gering Courier (Gering) **10661**
Grand Island Independent (Grand Island) **10469**
Harlan County Journal (Alma) **10659**
Hastings Daily Tribune (Hastings) **10469**
Holdrege Daily Citizen (Holdrege) **10469**
Kearney Hub (Kearney) **10469**
Keith County News (Ogallala) **10661**
Lincoln Journal Star (Lincoln) **10470**
Lyons Mirror-Sun (Lyons) **10661**
McCook Daily Gazette (McCook) **10470**
Minden Courier, The (Minden) **10661**
Nebraska City News-Press (Nebraska City) **10470**
Nebraska Signal (Geneva) **10661**
Nemaha County Herald (Auburn) **10660**
Norfolk Daily News (Norfolk) **10470**
Oakland Independent (Oakland) **10661**
Omaha Star (Omaha) **10661**
Omaha World-Herald (Omaha) **10470**
Ord Quiz (Ord) **10661**

GEOGRAPHIC   Brick, NJ 10967

Papillion Times (Papillion) **10661**
Plainview News (Plainview) **10661**
Plattsmouth Journal (Plattsmouth) **10661**
Sargent Leader (Burwell) **10660**
Schuyler Sun (Schuyler) **10661**
Seward County Independent (Seward) **10661**
Sidney Telegraph (Sidney) **10662**
South Sioux City Star (South Sioux City) **10662**
Springview Herald (Springview) **10662**
Star-Herald (Scottsbluff) **10470**
Superior Express, The (Superior) **10662**
Syracuse Journal-Democrat (Syracuse) **10662**
Telegraph, The (North Platte) **10470**
Tri-City Trib (Cozad) **10660**
Wahoo Newspaper (Wahoo) **10662**
Wayne Herald (Wayne) **10662**
West Point News (West Point) **10662**
York News-Times (York) **10470**

NEVADA

Boulder City News (Boulder City) **10662**
Chronicle, The (Carson City) **10662**
† Communicator Community News (Reno)
Daily Sparks Tribune, The (Sparks) **10471**
Elko Daily Free Press (Elko) **10470**
Ely Daily Times (Ely) **10470**
Eureka Sentinel (Tonopah) **10662**
† Fallon Eagle Standard (Fallon)
Fernley Leader-Dayton Courier (Yerington) **10662**
Humboldt Sun (Winnemucca) **10471**
Lahontan Valley News (Fallon) **10470**
Las Vegas Review-Journal (Las Vegas) **10470**
Las Vegas Sun (Las Vegas) **10470**
Las Vegas Today (Las Vegas) **10662**
Lovelock Review-Miner (Lovelock) **10662**
Mason Valley News (Yerington) **10663**
Mineral County Independent-News (Hawthorne) **10662**
Nevada Appeal (Carson City) **10470**
North Lake Tahoe Bonanza (Incline Village) **10662**
Reno Gazette-Journal (Reno) **10470**
Tonopah Times-Bonanza & Goldfield News (Tonopah) **10662**

NEW HAMPSHIRE

Argus-Champion, The (Newport) **10663**
Berlin Daily Sun (Berlin) **10471**
Berlin Reporter, The (Berlin) **10471**
Carroll County Independent (Center Ossipee) **10663**
Citizen, The (Laconia) **10471**
Concord Monitor (Concord) **10471**
Conway Daily Sun, The (North Conway) **10471**
Coos County Democrat (Lancaster) **10663**
Courier, The (Littleton) **10663**
Derry News (Derry) **10663**
Eagle-Times (Claremont) **10471**
Exeter News-Letter (Stratham) **10664**
Foster's Daily Democrat (Dover) **10471**
Granite State News (Wolfeboro) **10664**
Hampton Union (Stratham) **10664**
Hudson-Litchfield News (Hudson) **10663**
† Journal Transcript (Franklin)
Keene Sentinel (Keene) **10471**
† Lebanon Connecticut Valley Reporter (Lebanon)
Milford Cabinet & Wilton Journal (Milford) **10663**
Monadnock Ledger (Peterborough) **10663**
Mt. Washington Valley Mountain Ear (Conway) **10663**
New Hampshire Week in Review (Hillsborough) **10663**
News & Sentinel, The (Colebrook) **10663**
Peterborough Transcript (Peterborough) **10663**
Portsmouth Herald (Portsmouth) **10471**
Record Enterprise, The (Plymouth) **10663**
† Rochester Courier (Rochester)
Rochester Times, The (Rochester) **10663**
Salem Observer (Salem) **10664**
Telegraph, The (Hudson) **10471**
Tri-Town Transcript, The (Dover) **10663**
Union Leader/New Hampshire Sunday News (Manchester) **10471**
Valley News (West Lebanon) **10471**
1590 Broadcaster (Nashua) **10663**

NEW JERSEY

Advance News (Lakehurst) **10667**
Asbury Park Press (Neptune) **10472**
Atlantic County Record (Hammonton) **10666**
Bayonne Community News (Bayonne) **10664**
Beachcomber, The (Surf City) **10670**
Beach Haven Times (Manahawkin) **10667**
Beacon, The (Hopewell) **10667**
Beacon, The (Manahawkin) **10667**
Belleville Post (Bloomfield) **10664**
Belleville Times News (Nutley) **10668**
Bergen News, The (Palisades Park) **10669**
Bernardsville News (Bernardsville) **10664**
Blairstown Press (Blairstown) **10664**
Bloomfield Life (Nutley) **10668**
Bound Brook Chronicle (Somerville) **10670**
Brick Township Town News (Brick) **10664**

ULRICH'S INTERNATIONAL PERIODICALS DIRECTORY 1998

Bridgeton Evening News (Bridgeton) **10471**
Burlington County Times (Willingboro) **10473**
Camden County Record (Camden) **10665**
Cape May County Gazette Leader (Wildwood) **10671**
Cape May Herald Dispatch (Rio Grande) **10670**
Cape May Star & Wave (Cape May) **10665**
Central Post (Dayton) **10665**
Chatham Courier (Madison) **10667**
† Cherry Hill News (Cherry Hill)
Citizen of Morris County, The (Denville) **10665**
Clark Eagle (Union) **10670**
Clark Patriot (Rahway) **10669**
Community Forum (Hackettstown) **10666**
Courier-News, The (Bridgewater) **10472**
Courier-Post, The (Cherry Hill) **10472**
Cranbury Press (Dayton) **10665**
Cranford Chronicle (Cranford) **10665**
Daily Journal (Vineland) **10473**
† Daily Journal (Elizabeth)
Daily Record (Parsippany) **10472**
Delaware Valley News (Frenchtown) **10666**
Dispatch, The (New Providence) **10668**
East Orange Record (Orange) **10668**
Echoes-Sentinel (Stirling) **10670**
Egg Harbor News (Hammonton) **10666**
Elizabeth Gazette (Union) **10670**
Fairfield Chronicle, The (West Caldwell) **10671**
Florham Park Eagle (Madison) **10667**
Franklin News-Record (Princeton) **10669**
Franklin Township Sentinel (Franklinville) **10666**
Free Time (Wildwood) **10671**
Gazette, The (Mt. Holly) **10668**
Glen Ridge Paper, The (Bloomfield) **10664**
Glen Rock Gazette (Franklin Lakes) **10666**
Gloucester City News (Gloucester City) **10666**
Gloucester County Times (Woodbury) **10473**
† Haddon Gazette (Cherry Hill)
Hammonton News (Hammonton) **10666**
Hanover Eagle & Regional News (Madison) **10667**
Hawthorne Press (Hawthorne) **10666**
Hillsborough Beacon (Somerville) **10670**
Hillside Leader (Union) **10670**
Hoboken Reporter (Hoboken) **10666**
Home & Store News (Ramsey) **10670**
Home News & Tribune, The (East Brunswick) **10472**
Hudson Current (Hoboken) **10666**
Hunterdon County Democrat (Flemington) **10666**
Hunterdon Review (Lebanon) **10667**
Independent Press (New Providence) **10668**
Independent Press of Bloomfield, The (Bloomfield) **10664**
Independent, The (Morganville) **10668**
Jersey City Reporter (Hoboken) **10666**
Jersey Journal, The (Jersey City) **10472**
Journal, The (Voorhees) **10671**
Kenilworth Leader (Union) **10670**
Lakeland Today (Butler) **10665**
Lawrence Ledger (Pennington) **10669**
Leader, The (Point Pleasant Beach) **10669**
Linden Leader (Union) **10671**
Lower Township Lantern (Rio Grande) **10670**
Madison Eagle (Madison) **10667**
Mainland Journal (Hammonton) **10666**
Manville News (Somerville) **10670**
Maple Shade Progress (Maple Shade) **10667**
Messenger-Press (Hightstown) **10666**
Messenger, The (Garfield) **10666**
Middlesex-Dunellen Chronicle (Somerville) **10670**
Middletown Courier (Middletown) **10668**
Millburn & Short Hills Item (Millburn) **10668**
Milville News (Bridgeton) **10472**
Montclair Times, The (Montclair) **10668**
Morris News Bee (Madison) **10667**
Morristown News, The (West Caldwell) **10671**
Mountainside Echo (Union) **10671**
Mt. Laurel Progress Press (Maple Shade) **10667**
Mt. Olive Chronicle (Budd Lake) **10664**
Netcong News-Leader (Netcong) **10668**
New Jersey Herald (Newton) **10472**
News-Record of Maplewood & South Orange (Maplewood) **10668**
News Beacon (Fair Lawn) **10666**
† News of Paterson (Passaic)
News Report (Blackwood) **10664**
News, The (Belvidere) **10664**
News Transcript (Morganville) **10668**
News Weekly (Mt. Laurel) **10668**
North Bergen Reporter (Hoboken) **10667**
North Brunswick Post (Dayton) **10665**
North Jersey Herald & News, The (Passaic) **10472**
North Jersey Prospector (Clifton) **10665**
Nutley Journal (Bloomfield) **10664**
Nutley Sun, The (Nutley) **10668**
Observer-Tribune (Chester) **10665**
Observer, The (Kearny) **10667**
† Observer, The (Blackwood)
Ocean County's Observer (Toms River) **10472**
Ocean County Reporter (Toms River) **10670**
Orange Transcript (Orange) **10669**
Our Town (Maywood) **10668**
† Parsippany Focus (Morris Plains)
Parsippany News, The (West Caldwell) **10671**

Pascack Valley Community Life (Westwood) **10671**
Passaic Valley Today (Butler) **10665**
Phillipsburg Free Press (Phillipsburg) **10669**
Plain Dealer (Blackwood) **10664**
Post Review, The (Paramus) **10669**
Press Journal, The (Palisades Park) **10669**
Press of Atlantic City, The (Pleasantville) **10472**
Princeton Packet, The (Princeton) **10669**
Progress, The (Caldwell) **10665**
Rahway News-Record (Rahway) **10669**
Rahway Progress (Union) **10671**
Ramsey-Mahwah Reporter (Palisades Park) **10669**
Randolph Reporter (Bernardsville) **10664**
Record-Breeze (Blackwood) **10664**
Record, The (Hackensack) **10472**
Register-News (Bordentown) **10664**
† Register, The (Shrewsbury)
Reporter, The (Franklin Lakes) **10666**
Retrospect, The (Collingswood) **10665**
† Review-Enterprise (Blackwood)
Review, The (Paramus) **10669**
Review, The (Point Pleasant Beach) **10669**
Ridgewood News (Paramus) **10669**
Roselle Park Leader (Union) **10671**
Roselle Spectator (Union) **10671**
Salem County Record (Salem) **10670**
Secaucus Home News (Secaucus) **10670**
Secaucus Reporter (Hoboken) **10667**
Sentinel-Ledger, The (Ocean City) **10668**
Somerset Messenger Gazette (Somerville) **10670**
Somerset Spectator (Somerset) **10670**
South Bergenite (Rutherford) **10670**
South Jersey Advisor (Cologne) **10665**
Sparta Independent (Sparta) **10670**
Springfield Leader (Union) **10671**
Star-Ledger (Newark) **10472**
Star Gazette (Hackettstown) **10666**
Suburbanite, The (Closter) **10665**
Suburban Life (Butler) **10665**
Suburban Town News (Paramus) **10669**
Suburban Trends (Butler) **10665**
Summit Observer (Union) **10671**
Sun-Bulletin, The (Palisades Park) **10669**
Sussex County Chronicle (Byram) **10665**
This Week (Cherry Hill) **10665**
Times of Scotch Plains & Fanwood, The (Westfield) **10671**
Times, The (Trenton) **10472**
Today's Sunbeam (Salem) **10472**
Town Topics (Princeton) **10669**
Trentonian, The (Trenton) **10473**
Union City Reporter (Hoboken) **10667**

Union Leader (Union) **10671**
Vailsburg Leader (Maplewood) **10668**
Verona-Cedar Grove Times (Verona) **10671**
Village Gazette of Ridgewood (Franklin Lakes) **10666**
Wayne Today (Butler) **10665**
Weehawken Reporter (Hoboken) **10667**
West Essex Tribune (Livingston) **10667**
Westfield Leader (Westfield) **10671**
West Morris Star-Journal (Ledgewood) **10667**
West New York Reporter (Hoboken) **10667**
West Orange Chronicle (Orange) **10669**
Wildwood Leader (Wildwood) **10672**
Wyckoff Gazette (Franklin Lakes) **10666**

NEW MEXICO

Alamogordo Daily News (Alamogordo) **10473**
Albuquerque Journal (Albuquerque) **10473**
Albuquerque Street News (Albuquerque) **10672**
Albuquerque Tribune, The (Albuquerque) **10473**
Artesia Daily Press (Artesia) **10473**
Carlsbad Current-Argus (Carlsbad) **10473**
Cibola County Beacon (Grants) **10672**
Clovis News Journal (Clovis) **10473**
Daily Times (Farmington) **10473**
Defensor Chieftain (Socorro) **10672**
Deming Headlight (Deming) **10473**
Estancia Valley Citizen (Estancia) **10672**
Herald, The (Truth or Consequences) **10672**
Hobbs Daily News-Sun (Hobbs) **10473**
Hobbs Flare (Hobbs) **10672**
Las Cruces Sun-News (Las Cruces) **10473**
Las Vegas Daily Optic (Las Vegas) **10473**
Lovington Daily Leader (Lovington) **10474**
Monitor, The (Los Alamos) **10474**
Observer, The (Rio Rancho) **10672**
Portales News-Tribune (Portales) **10474**
Quay County Sun (Tucumcari) **10672**
† Quik Quarter Want Ads (Hobbs)
Raton Range, The (Raton) **10672**
Rio Grande Sun (Espanola) **10672**
Roswell Daily Record (Roswell) **10474**
Ruidoso News, The (Ruidoso) **10672**
Santa Fe New Mexican (Santa Fe) **10474**
Santa Fe Reporter, The (Santa Fe) **10672**
Sierra County Sentinel (Truth or Consequences) **10672**
Silver City Daily Press & Independent (Silver City) **10474**
Taos News (Taos) **10672**

10970   Belen, NM

Valencia County News-Bulletin (Belen) **10672**

NEW YORK

Adirondack Daily Enterprise (Saranac Lake) **10477**
Advance, The (Ogdensburg) **10684**
Albion Advertiser (Albion) **10673**
Altamont Enterprise, The (Altamont) **10673**
Amherst Bee (Williamsville) **10689**
Amityville Record (Amityville) **10673**
† Amsterdam Star, The (Albany)
† Ausable Forks Adirondack Record Post (Elizabethtown)
Baldwin Citizen (Mineola) **10682**
Baldwin Herald (Lawrence) **10680**
Baldwinsville Messenger (Syracuse) **10687**
Ballston Journal (Ballston Spa) **10673**
Batavia Daily News (Batavia) **10474**
Bay News (Brooklyn) **10674**
Bay Ridge Courier (Brooklyn) **10674**
Bayside Times, The (Bayside) **10673**
Beacon Free Press (Wappingers Falls) **10688**
Beacon Light (Mahopac) **10680**
Beacon Newspaper (Babylon) **10673**
Bellmore-Merrick Observer (Bellmore) **10673**
Bellmore Life (Bellmore) **10673**
Boonville Herald & Adirondack Tourist (Boonville) **10673**
Brewster Times (Mahopac) **10681**
Brighton-Pittsford Post, The (Fishers) **10677**
Brockport/Holley Suburban News (Spencerport) **10687**
Brockport Post, The (Brockport) **10674**
Bronx News (Bronx) **10674**
Bronx Press-Review (Bronx) **10674**
Brookhaven Review (Smithtown) **10686**
Brooklyn Daily Eagle & Daily Bulletin (Brooklyn) **10474**
Brooklyn Graphic (Brooklyn) **10674**
Brooklyn Heights Courier (Brooklyn) **10674**
Brooklyn Heights Press (Brooklyn) **10674**
Brooklyn Home Reporter & Sunset News (Brooklyn) **10674**
Brooklyn Record (Brooklyn) **10674**
Brooklyn Spectator (Brooklyn) **10674**
† Brooklyn Times (Brooklyn)
Broome Pennysaver (Johnson City) **10679**
Buffalo News, The (Buffalo) **10474**
Buffalo Rocket (Buffalo) **10675**
Camillus Advocate (Syracuse) **10687**
Canandaigua Daily Messenger (Canandaigua) **10474**
Canarsie Courier (Brooklyn) **10674**
Canarsie Digest (Brooklyn) **10674**
Canastota Bee-Journal (Canastota) **10675**

Candor Chronicle (Trumansburg) **10688**
Carmel Times (Mahopac) **10681**
Carroll Gardens/Cobble Hill Courier (Brooklyn) **10674**
Carthage Republican Tribune (Carthage) **10675**
† Cato Citizen (Red Creek)
Cazenovia Republican (Cazenovia) **10675**
† Chateaugay Record (Chateaugay)
Chatham Courier (Chatham) **10675**
Cheektowaga Bee (Williamsville) **10689**
Cheektowaga Times (Cheektowaga) **10675**
Chelsea Clinton News (New York) **10683**
Chemung Valley Reporter (Horseheads) **10679**
Chenango American (Greene) **10678**
Chittenango-Bridgeport Times (Syracuse) **10687**
Chronicle-Express (Penn Yan) **10684**
Chronicle, The (Glens Falls) **10678**
Citizen Outlet (Mexico) **10681**
Citizen Register (Yorktown Heights) **10478**
Citizen, The (Auburn) **10474**
City News (Bronx) **10674**
Clarence Bee (Williamsville) **10689**
Clarkson Integrator (Potsdam) **10685**
Clarkstown Courier, The (Pearl River) **10684**
Clinton Courier (Clinton) **10675**
Colonie Spotlight (Delmar) **10676**
Commack News (Smithtown) **10686**
Community Journal (Wading River) **10688**
Community News (Clifton Park) **10675**
Cortland Democrat (Marathon) **10681**
Cortland Standard (Cortland) **10475**
Country Courier, The (Conklin) **10676**
Country Shopper (Pound Ridge) **10685**
Courier-Journal (Palmyra) **10684**
Courier-Standard-Enterprise (Fort Plain) **10677**
Courier Gazette (Newark) **10683**
† Current (Potsdam)
Daily & Sunday Freeman (Kingston) **10475**
Daily & Sunday Sentinel (Rome) **10477**
Daily Courier Observer, The (Massena) **10476**
Daily Gazette (Schenectady) **10477**
Daily Item, The (New Rochelle) **10476**
Daily Mail (Catskill) **10474**
Daily Star, The (Oneonta) **10476**
Daily Times, The (New Rochelle) **10476**
Dan's Papers (Bridgehampton) **10673**
Dansville Genesee Country Express (Dansville) **10676**
Delaware County Times (Delhi) **10676**
Depew Bee (Williamsville) **10689**
Deposit Courier (Deposit) **10676**
DeWitt Times (Syracuse) **10687**
Downtown Express (New York) **10683**
Dundee Observer (Dundee) **10676**

GEOGRAPHIC

Eagle Bulletin (Syracuse) **10687**
Eagle, The (Cambridge) **10675**
East Aurora Advertiser (East Aurora) **10676**
East Aurora Bee (Williamsville) **10689**
Eastchester Record (Yonkers) **10690**
East Fishkill Record (Mahopac) **10681**
East Hampton Star (East Hampton) **10676**
East Meadow Beacon (Hicksville) **10679**
East Rochester Post-Herald (Victor) **10688**
East Rockaway Observer (Mineola) **10682**
† Echo, The (Berlin)
Ellenville Press (Ellenville) **10677**
Elma Review (East Aurora) **10676**
Elmont Herald (Elmont) **10677**
Enterprise, The (Hastings-on-Hudson) **10679**
Evening-Observer (Dunkirk) **10475**
Evening Sun, The (Norwich) **10476**
Evening Telegram (Herkimer) **10475**
Evening Times, The (Little Falls) **10475**
Fairfield-Penfield Community News (Rochester) **10685**
† Fair Haven Register (Red Creek)
† Fairport-Perinton Herald-Mail (Webster)
Farmingdale Observer (Mineola) **10682**
Finger Lakes Times, The (Geneva) **10475**
Fire Island Tide (Sayville) **10685**
Fishkill Standard (Mahopac) **10681**
Flatbush Life (Brooklyn) **10674**
Floral Park Bulletin (Floral Park) **10677**
Flushing Times, The (Bayside) **10673**
▼Forest Hills/Rego Park Times (Maspeth) **10681**
Forum of Queens (Ozone Park) **10684**
Franklin Square Bulletin (Floral Park) **10677**
Freeport Baldwin Leader, The (Freeport) **10677**
Free Trader (Massena) **10681**
Fresh Meadows Times, The (Flushing) **10677**
Front Page (Lackawanna) **10680**
Fulton Patriot (Fulton) **10678**
Gates-Chili News (Rochester) **10685**
Gateway, The (Floral Park) **10677**
Gazette-Advertiser (Rhinebeck) **10685**
Gazette, The (Port Jervis) **10685**
Glen Cove Record Pilot (Mineola) **10682**
Glendale Register (Maspeth) **10681**
Glen Oaks Ledger, The (Bayside) **10673**
Golden Times (Rochester) **10685**
Gouverneur Tribune Press (Gouverneur) **10678**
Gowanda Pennysaver News (Gowanda) **10678**
Grand Island Pennysaver (Grand Island) **10678**
Granville Sentinel (Granville) **10678**
Great Neck News (Great Neck) **10678**
Great Neck Record (Mineola) **10682**

Flushing, NY 10971

Greece Post, The (Fishers) **10677**
Greenpoint Gazette/Advertiser (Brooklyn) **10674**
Greenville Local (Ravena) **10685**
Greenwich Journal & Salem Press (Greenwich) **10678**
Greenwood Lake & West Milford News (Greenwood Lake) **10678**
Hamilton County News (Speculator) **10687**
† Hamilton County News (Elizabethtown)
Hamilton Mid-York Weekly (Hamilton) **10679**
▼Hamilton Tribune (Hamilton) **10679**
Hamlin-Clarkson Herald (Spencerport) **10687**
Harborwatch (Brooklyn) **10674**
Harlem Valley Times (Amenia) **10673**
Harrison Independent (Yonkers) **10690**
Hempstead Beacon (Hicksville) **10679**
Henrietta Post (Fishers) **10677**
Herald-Journal (Syracuse) **10477**
Herald Statesman (Yonkers) **10478**
Hicksville Illustrated News (Mineola) **10682**
Hornell Evening Tribune (Hornell) **10475**
▼Howard Beach Resident (Maspeth) **10681**
Hyde Park Townsman (Hyde Park) **10679**
Independent Mirror (Mexico) **10681**
Independent Republican (Goshen) **10678**
Interlaken Review (Trumansburg) **10688**
Irondequoit Press (Rochester) **10685**
Irvington Viewpoint, The (Irvington) **10679**
Island Dispatch (Grand Island) **10678**
Islip Bulletin (Sayville) **10685**
Islip News (Smithtown) **10686**
Ithaca Journal, The (Ithaca) **10475**
Ithaca Times (Ithaca) **10679**
Jackson Heights News (Maspeth) **10681**
▼Jamaica Times, The (Flushing) **10677**
Jefferson County Journal (Adams) **10672**
Journal & Republican (Lowville) **10680**
Journal-Register (Medina) **10476**
† Journal Courier (Moravia)
Journal, The (Ogdensburg) **10476**
Ken-Ton Bee (Williamsville) **10689**
Kings County News (Brooklyn) **10674**
Kings Courier (Brooklyn) **10675**
La Grange Independent (Mahopac) **10681**
Lake Placid News (Lake Placid) **10680**
Lakes Region Free Press, The (Granville) **10678**
Lancaster Bee (Williamsville) **10689**
Leader-Herald, The (Gloversville) **10475**
Leader Observer (Maspeth) **10681**
Leader, The (Corning) **10474**
Leader, The (Freeport) **10677**
Levittown Tribune (Mineola) **10682**
Lewiston-Porter Sentinel (Grand Island) **10678**
Little Neck Ledger, The (Flushing) **10677**

ULRICH'S INTERNATIONAL PERIODICALS DIRECTORY 1998

Liverpool Review (Syracuse) **10687**
Locust Valley Leader (Locust Valley) **10680**
Long Beach Herald (Long Beach) **10680**
Long Beach Independent Voice (Mineola) **10682**
Long Island Advance (Patchogue) **10684**
Long Island City/Astoria Journal (Maspeth) **10681**
Long Island Graphic-Roosevelt Press (Lawrence) **10680**
† Long Island Journal Newspaper Group (Long Beach)
▼Long Island Voice (Mineola) **10682**
Loudenville Weekly (Delmar) **10676**
Lynbrook USA (Mineola) **10682**
Mahopac Press (Mahopac) **10681**
Malone Telegram (Malone) **10475**
Malta Messenger (Ballston Spa) **10673**
Malverne Community Times (Mineola) **10682**
Manhasset Press (Mineola) **10682**
† Marathon Independent Newspaper (Marathon)
Marcellus Observer (Skaneateles) **10686**
Massapequan Observer (Mineola) **10682**
Massapequa Post (Massapequa Park) **10681**
Mayville Sentinel/Chautauqua News (Westfield) **10689**
Meadowbrook Times (Lawrence) **10680**
Merrick Beacon (Hicksville) **10679**
Merrick Life (Merrick) **10681**
Metropolitan News (Brooklyn) **10675**
Mid-Island Times (Hicksville) **10679**
Mid Hudson Times (Walden) **10688**
Millbrook Round Table (Millbrook) **10682**
Millerton News, The (Millerton) **10682**
Mineola American (Mineola) **10682**
† Mirror-Recorder (Stamford)
Moneysaver, The (Ballston Spa) **10673**
Montauk Pioneer (Bridgehampton) **10674**
Moravia Republican Register (Moravia) **10683**
Mountain Eagle (Tannersville) **10688**
Mount Vernon Independent (Yonkers) **10690**
Mt. Vernon Argus (Yonkers) **10478**
Naples Record, The (Naples) **10683**
Nassau Herald (Lawrence) **10680**
† Newburgh Evening News (Newburgh)
Newfield News (Trumansburg) **10688**
News-Review, The (Mattituck) **10681**
Newsday (Melville) **10476**
News of the Highlands (Highland Falls) **10679**
† New York City Tribune (New York)
New York Daily Challenge (Brooklyn) **10474**
New York Daily News, The (New York) **10476**
New York Metropolitan News (Brooklyn) **10675**
† New York Newsday (New York)
New York Observer (New York) **10683**

New York Post (New York) **10476**
New York Press (New York) **10683**
New York Times, The (New York) **10476**
Niagara/Wheatfield Tribune (Grand Island) **10678**
Niagara Gazette (Niagara Falls) **10476**
North Castle News (Yonkers) **10690**
North Country Free Press (Granville) **10678**
North Countryman, The (Elizabethtown) **1067**
North County News (Yorktown Heights) **1069(**
Northshire Free Press, The (Granville) **10678**
North Syracuse Star-News (Syracuse) **10687**
Observer-Dispatch (Utica) **10477**
Observer, The (Northport) **10683**
Oceanside/Island Park Herald (Long Beach) **10680**
Oceanside Centre Beacon (Mineola) **10682**
Olean Times Herald (Olean) **10476**
Oneida Daily Dispatch (Oneida) **10476**
Onondaga Valley News (Syracuse) **10687**
Orchard Park Bee (Williamsville) **10689**
Our Town (New York) **10683**
Our Town (Pearl River) **10684**
Ovid Gazette (Trumansburg) **10688**
Owego Pennysaver (Owego) **10684**
Oxford Review-Times (Greene) **10678**
Oyster Bay-Syosset Guardian (Oyster Bay) **10684**
Oyster Bay Enterprise Pilot (Mineola) **10682**
Palladium-Times, The (Oswego) **10476**
Parkchester News (Bronx) **10674**
Park Slope Courier (Brooklyn) **10675**
Patent Trader (Cross River) **10676**
Patriot & Free Press (Cuba) **10676**
Pawling News Chronicle (Pawling) **10684**
Peekskill Herald (Peekskill) **10684**
Peekskill Star (Yorktown Heights) **10478**
Pelham Sun (Yonkers) **10690**
Penfield Post-Republican, The (Fishers) **10677**
Pennysaver (Elmsford) **10677**
Pennysaver (Yorktown Heights) **10690**
People's Weekly World (New York) **10683**
Perinton-Fairport Post, The (Pittsford) **10684**
Phoenix Newspaper, The (Brooklyn) **10675**
Phoenix Register (Phoenix) **10684**
Photo News (Monroe) **10683**
Pine Plains Register-Herald (Pine Plains) **10684**
Port Times-Record, The (Setauket) **10686**
Port Washington News (Port Washington) **10685**
Post-Herald (Red Creek) **10685**
Post-Journal, The (Jamestown) **10475**
Post-Standard (Syracuse) **10477**
Post-Star (Glens Falls) **10475**
Poughkeepsie Journal (Poughkeepsie) **10477**

Press & Sun-Bulletin (Vestal) **10477**
Press-Republican (Plattsburgh) **10477**
PrimeTime (Lawrence) **10680**
Putnam Courier-Trader, The (Carmel) **10675**
Queens Chronicle (Rego Park) **10685**
Queens Ledger (Maspeth) **10681**
Queens Tribune (Fresh Meadows) **10678**
Queens Village Times, The (Flushing) **10677**
Ravena News Herald (Ravena) **10685**
Record-Advertiser (North Tonawanda) **10684**
Recorder, The (Amsterdam) **10474**
Record, The (Troy) **10477**
Record, The (Huntington) **10679**
Register-Star (Hudson) **10475**
Reporter Dispatch, The (White Plains) **10478**
▼Resident Community News (New York)
Reveille/Between the Lakes (Seneca Falls) **10686**
Review Press Reporter (Yonkers) **10690**
Riverdale Press (Bronx) **10674**
River Reporter, The (Narrowsburg) **10683**
Riverside Review (Buffalo) **10675**
Rochester Democrat & Chronicle (Rochester) **10477**
Rockaway Journal (Lawrence) **10680**
Rockland County Times (Haverstraw) **10679**
Rockland Independent, The (Pearl River) **10684**
Rockland Journal-News (West Nyack) **10478**
Rockville Centre Herald (Lawrence) **10680**
Rockville Centre News & Owl (Mineola) **10682**
Ronkonkoma Review (Smithtown) **10686**
Rye Chronicle (Yonkers) **10690**
Salamanca Press (Salamanca) **10477**
Salmon River News (Pulaski) **10685**
Saratogian, The (Saratoga Springs) **10477**
† Saturday Post-Star (Saugerties)
Saugerties Post Star (Saugerties) **10685**
Scarsdale Inquirer, The (Scarsdale) **10686**
Scotsman Press, The (Syracuse) **10687**
Shelter Island Reporter (Shelter Island Heights) **10686**
Skaneateles Press (Skaneateles) **10686**
Smithtown Messenger (Smithtown) **10686**
Smithtown News, The (Smithtown) **10686**
Sound View News (Yonkers) **10690**
Southampton Press (Southampton) **10686**
South Bay's Newspaper (Lindenhurst) **10680**
† South Bay's Shopper (Lindenhurst)
South Buffalo News (Lackawanna) **10680**
Southern Cayuga Tribune (Moravia) **10683**
Southern Dutchess News (Wappingers Falls) **10688**
Southhampton Press, The/Western Edition (Westhampton Beach) **10689**
South Shore Record (Woodmere) **10689**

Southtowns Citizen (Orchard Park) **10684**
Spackenkill Sentinel (Wappingers Falls) **10688**
Spencer Random Harvest Weekly (Trumansburg) **10688**
Spotlight, The (Delmar) **10676**
Springville Journal (Springville) **10687**
Standard-Star (New Rochelle) **10476**
Star-Gazette (Elmira) **10475**
Star-News, The (North Syracuse) **10684**
Staten Island Advance (Staten Island) **10477**
Staten Island Register (Staten Island) **10687**
Steuben Courier-Advocate (Bath) **10673**
St. Lawrence Plaindealer (Canton) **10675**
Suburban News (Spencerport) **10687**
Suburban Street News (White Plains) **10689**
Suffolk County News (Sayville) **10686**
Suffolk Times (Mattituck) **10681**
Sun & Erie County Independent, The (Hamburg) **10679**
Sunday Spectator (Hornell) **10679**
Syosset Jericho Tribune (Mineola) **10683**
Syracuse New Times (Syracuse) **10687**
Tarrytown Daily News (White Plains) **10478**
Thousand Islands Sun (Alexandria Bay) **10673**
Three Village Herald (East Setauket) **10676**
Three Village Times (Mineola) **10683**
† Times-Union (Rochester)
Times Herald-Record (Middletown) **10476**
Times Journal (Cobleskill) **10675**
Times Newsweekly (Ridgewood) **10685**
Times of Nesconset, The (Setauket) **10686**
Times of Smithtown (Setauket) **10686**
Times of St. James (Setauket) **10686**
Times of Ti (Ticonderoga) **10688**
Times Union (Albany) **10474**
† Tioga County Gazette & Times (Owego)
Tomorrow (New Rochelle) **10683**
Tonawanda News (North Tonawanda) **10476**
Traveler/Watchman (Southold) **10686**
Tri-County Advertiser (Brockport) **10674**
Tri-County News (Lockport) **10680**
Tri-Town News (Sidney) **10686**
Trumansburg Free Press (Trumansburg) **10688**
Tupper Lake Free Press & Herald (Tupper Lake) **10688**
Ulster County Townsman (Woodstock) **10690**
Union-Sun & Journal (Lockport) **10475**
Uniondale Beacon (Hicksville) **10679**
Valley News (Elizabethtown) **10677**
Valley News (Fulton) **10678**
Valley News, The (Endwell) **10677**
Valley Stream Courier (Freeport) **10677**
Valley Stream Herald (Lawrence) **10680**
Valley Stream Maileader (Mineola) **10683**
Vestal Town Crier (Conklin) **10676**

† Victor-Farmington Herald (Webster)
Village Beacon-Record, The (Setauket) **10686**
Village Herald (Lawrence) **10680**
Villager, The (New York) **10683**
Villager, The (Syracuse) **10687**
Village Times, The (Setauket) **10686**
Village Voice, The (New York) **10683**
Voice Ledger, The (Millbrook) **10682**
Wallkill Valley Times, The (Walden) **10688**
Walton Reporter, The (Walton) **10688**
Wantagh-Seaford Citizen (Bellmore) **10673**
Warrensburg-Lake George News (Elizabethtown) **10677**
Warwick Advertiser, The (Warwick) **10688**
Warwick Valley Dispatch (Warwick) **10688**
Watertown Daily Times (Watertown) **10477**
Watkins Review & Express (Watkins Glen) **10689**
Wayne County Mail (Webster) **10689**
Wayne County Star (Lyons) **10680**
Webster Herald (Webster) **10689**
Webster Post, The (Webster) **10689**
† Weekender, The (Bronx)
Weisbeck, The (Alden) **10673**
Wellsville Daily Reporter (Wellsville) **10478**
Westbury Times (Mineola) **10683**
Westfield Republican (Westfield) **10689**
West Hempstead Beacon (Hicksville) **10679**
Westmore News (Port Chester) **10685**
West Seneca Bee (Williamsville) **10689**
Westsider, The (New York) **10683**
West Side Times (Buffalo) **10675**
Whitehall Times (Whitehall) **10689**
Whitestone Times, The (Bayside) **10673**
Whitney Point Reporter (Greene) **10678**
Windham Journal (Windham) **10689**
Windsor Standard (Conklin) **10676**
Woodside Herald (Sunnyside) **10687**
Yankee Trader (Coram) **10676**
Yonkers Home News & Times (Yonkers) **10690**

NORTH CAROLINA

Alamance News (Graham) **10692**
Angier Independent (Angier) **10690**
Anson Record, The (Wadesboro) **10695**
Apex Herald, The (Apex) **10690**
Asheboro Courier-Tribune (Asheboro) **10478**
Asheville Citizen-Times (Asheville) **10478**
Belmont Banner (Belmont) **10690**
Bertie Ledger-Advance (Windsor) **10696**
Bessemer City Record (Kings Mountain) **10692**
Black Mountain News (Black Mountain) **10691**
Bladen Journal (Elizabethtown) **10479**
Blowing Rocket, The (Blowing Rock) **10691**
Boone Watauga Democrat (Boone) **10691**
Brunswick Beacon, The (Shallotte) **10694**
Burke County Observer (Morganton) **10693**
Butner-Creedmoor News, The (Creedmoor) **10691**
Carolina Times, The (Durham) **10692**
Carolinian, The (Raleigh) **10694**
Carteret County News-Times (Morehead City) **10693**
Cary News (Cary) **10691**
Caswell Messenger (Yanceyville) **10696**
Chapel Hill Herald (Chapel Hill) **10478**
Chapel Hill News (Chapel Hill) **10691**
Charlotte Observer (Charlotte) **10478**
Chatham News, The (Siler City) **10694**
Cherokee Scout (Murphy) **10693**
Cherryville Eagle (Cherryville) **10691**
Clayton News-Star (Clayton) **10691**
Clemmons Courier (Clemmons) **10691**
Cleveland Times (Shelby) **10694**
Coastland Times (Manteo) **10693**
Commonwealth Progress (Scotland Neck) **10694**
County News Enterprise (Forest City) **10692**
Courier-Times, The (Roxboro) **10694**
Daily Advance (Elizabeth City) **10479**
Daily Courier (Forest City) **10479**
Daily Dispatch, The (Henderson) **10479**
Daily News (Jacksonville) **10479**
Daily News, The (Eden) **10479**
Daily Southerner, The (Tarboro) **10481**
Danbury Reporter (Walnut Cove) **10695**
Davie County Enterprise-Record (Mocksville) **10693**
Dispatch, The (Lexington) **10480**
Dunn Daily Record (Dunn) **10478**
Eastern Carolina Times-Inquirer (Goldsboro) **10692**
Enquirer-Journal, The (Monroe) **10480**
Enterprise Mountaineer, The (Canton) **10691**
Enterprise, The (Williamston) **10696**
Fayetteville Observer-Times (Fayetteville) **10479**
Four Oaks-Benson News in Review (Benson) **10691**
Franklin Press (Franklin) **10692**
Franklin Times (Louisburg) **10693**
Garner News (Garner) **10692**
Gaston Gazette (Gastonia) **10479**
Gates County Index (Gatesville) **10692**
Gold Leaf Farmer, The (Wendell) **10695**
Goldsboro News-Argus (Goldsboro) **10479**
Greenville Daily Reflector (Greenville) **10479**
Hendersonville Times-News (Hendersonville) **10479**
Herald-Sun, The (Durham) **10478**

Hickory Daily Record (Hickory) **10479**
Hickory News/Extra, The (Hickory) **10692**
High Point Enterprise (High Point) **10479**
Home News, The (Marshville) **10693**
Independent, The (Durham) **10692**
Independent Tribune (Kannapolis) **10479**
Jefferson Post (West Jefferson) **10695**
Journal-Patriot (North Wilkesboro) **10693**
Kenly News (Kenly) **10692**
Kernersville News (Kernersville) **10692**
Kings Mountain Herald (Kings Mountain) **10692**
King Times News (King) **10692**
Kinston Daily Free Press (Kinston) **10480**
Laurinburg Exchange (Laurinburg) **10480**
Lenoir News-Topic (Lenoir) **10480**
Lincoln Times-News (Lincolnton) **10693**
Littleton Observer (Littleton) **10693**
Madison Messenger, The (Madison) **10693**
† Matthews News (Matthews)
McDowell News, The (Marion) **10480**
Mebane Enterprise (Mebane) **10693**
Mecklenburg Gazette (Davidson) **10691**
Mitchell News Journal (Spruce Pine) **10695**
Montgomery Herald (Troy) **10695**
Mooresville Tribune (Mooresville) **10693**
† Mountaineer, The (Waynesville)
▼Mountain Xpress (Asheville) **10690**
Mount Airy News (Mt. Airy) **10480**
Mount Holly News (Belmont) **10691**
Mount Olive Tribune (Mt. Olive) **10693**
Nashville Graphic (Nashville) **10693**
News & Observer (Raleigh) **10480**
News & Record, The (Greensboro) **10479**
† News-Messenger, The (Rockingham)
News Bulletin of McDowell County, The (Old Fort) **10693**
News Herald, The (Morganton) **10480**
News of Orange County, The (Hillsborough) **10692**
† News Outlook (Aberdeen)
News Reporter, The (Whiteville) **10695**
Observer News (Newton) **10480**
Oxford Public Ledger (Oxford) **10694**
Pender Chronicle (Burgaw) **10691**
Pender Post (Burgaw) **10691**
Perquimans Weekly (Hertford) **10692**
Princeton News Leader (Princeton) **10694**
Raeford News-Journal, The (Raeford) **10694**
Randleman Reporter (Randleman) **10694**
Randolph Guide, The (Asheboro) **10690**
Reidsville Review (Reidsville) **10480**
Richlands-Beulaville Advertiser-News (Richlands) **10694**
Richmond County Daily Journal (Rockingham) **10481**

Roanoke-Chowan News-Herald, The (Ahoskie) **10690**
Roanoke Beacon (Plymouth) **10694**
Roanoke Rapids Daily & Sunday Herald (Roanoke Rapids) **10480**
Robersonville Weekly Herald (Williamston) **10696**
Robesonian, The (Lumberton) **10480**
Rocky Mount Telegram (Rocky Mount) **10481**
Salisbury Post (Salisbury) **10481**
Sampson Independent, The (Clinton) **10478**
† ▼Sandhills Living (Southern Pines)
Sanford Herald, The (Sanford) **10481**
Shelby Star (Shelby) **10481**
Smithfield-Selma Sun (Selma) **10694**
Smithfield Herald (Smithfield) **10694**
Southern Pines Pilot (Southern Pines) **10694**
Spectator Magazine (Raleigh) **10694**
Spring Hope Enterprise (Spring Hope) **10695**
Stanly News & Press (Albemarle) **10690**
State Port Pilot, The (Southport) **10695**
Statesville Record & Landmark (Statesville) **10481**
Sun-Journal (New Bern) **10480**
Surry Scene, The (Mount Airy) **10693**
Sylva Herald & Ruralite (Sylva) **10695**
Taylorsville Times, The (Taylorsville) **10695**
Thomasville Times (Thomasville) **10695**
Times-News, The (Burlington) **10478**
Transylvania Times, The (Brevard) **10691**
Tribune, The (Elkin) **10692**
Tribune, The (Tabor City) **10695**
Tryon Daily Bulletin (Tryon) **10481**
Valdese News (Morganton) **10693**
Village Advocate (Chapel Hill) **10691**
Virginian Pilot (Nags Head) **10480**
Wake Weekly, The (Wake Forest) **10695**
Wallace Enterprise (Wallace) **10695**
Warren Record, The (Warrenton) **10695**
Warsaw-Faison News (Wallace) **10695**
Washington Daily News (Washington) **10481**
Wayne Wilson News Leader (Fremont) **10692**
Williamston Enterprise (Williamston) **10696**
Wilmington Journal (Wilmington) **10696**
Wilmington Morning Star (Wilmington) **10481**
Wilson Daily Times (Wilson) **10481**
Winston-Salem Journal (Winston-Salem) **10481**
Yadkin Ripple, The (Yadkinville) **10696**
Yancey Common Times Journal (Burnsville) **10691**
Zebulon Record, The (Zebulon) **10696**

NORTH DAKOTA

Benson County Farmers Press (Minnewaukan) **10697**

Beulah Beacon (Beulah) **10696**
Bismarck Tribune (Bismarck) **10481**
Bowman Finder (Bowman) **10696**
Carson Press (Elgin) **10696**
Cass County Reporter (Casselton) **10696**
Cavalier County Republican (Langdon) **10697**
Center Republican (Washburn) **10697**
Courant, The (Bottineau) **10696**
Daily News (Wahpeton) **10482**
Devil's Lake Daily Journal (Devil's Lake) **10481**
Dickinson Press, The (Dickinson) **10481**
Enderlin Independent (Enderlin) **10696**
Finder, The (Mandan) **10697**
Forum, The (Fargo) **10482**
Grand Forks Herald (Grand Forks) **10482**
Grant County News (Elgin) **10696**
Hazen Star (Hazen) **10697**
Herald-Press (Harvey) **10697**
Jamestown Sun, The (Jamestown) **10482**
Journal, The (Crosby) **10696**
Larimore Pioneer (Northwood) **10697**
Leader-News (Washburn) **10697**
Leader, The (Northwood) **10697**
Linton Emmons County Record (Linton) **10697**
Lisbon Ransom County Gazette & Enterprise (Lisbon) **10697**
Mandan News (Mandan) **10697**
McLean County Independent (Garrison) **10696**
McLean County Journal (Turtle Lake) **10697**
Midweek Eagle (West Fargo) **10698**
Midweek Plus (West Fargo) **10698**
Minot Daily News (Minot) **10482**
Northwood Gleaner (Northwood) **10697**
Pierce County Tribune (Rugby) **10697**
Prairie Post (Jamestown) **10697**
Turtle Mountain Star, The (Rolla) **10697**
Underwood News (Underwood) **10697**
Valley City Times-Record (Valley City) **10482**
Walsh County Press (Park River) **10697**
Walsh County Record, The (Grafton) **10696**
West Fargo Pioneer (West Fargo) **10698**
Williston Herald (Williston) **10482**
Williston Plains Reporter (Williston) **10698**

NORTHERN MARIANA ISLANDS

Marianas Variety News & Views (Saipan) **10482**
Saipan Tribune (Saipan) **10482**

OHIO

Ace News, The (Heath) **10703**
Advertiser-Tribune (Tiffin) **10487**
Advertiser, The (Chillicothe) **10700**
Advocate, The (Newark) **10486**
Akron Beacon Journal (Akron) **10482**
Alliance Review (Alliance) **10482**
Archbold Buckeye (Archbold) **10698**
Ashland Times-Gazette (Ashland) **10482**
Ashtabula Star-Beacon (Ashtabula) **10482**
Athens Messenger, The (Athens) **10482**
Athens News (Athens) **10698**
Attica Hub (Attica) **10698**
Aurora Advocate (Stow) **10707**
† Austintown Leader (Niles)
Barberton Herald (Barberton) **10698**
Barnesville Enterprise (Barnesville) **10698**
Beacon, The (Port Clinton) **10707**
Beavercreek News-Current (Dayton) **10484**
Bedford Sun Banner (Beachwood) **10698**
Bedford Time Register (Bedford) **10699**
Bellefontaine Examiner (Bellefontaine) **10482**
Bellevue Gazette (Bellevue) **10483**
Bethel Journal, The (Loveland) **10704**
Bexley News (Columbus) **10701**
Big Walnut/Sunbury (Columbus) **10701**
Bloomville Gazette (Attica) **10698**
Bluffton News, The (Bluffton) **10699**
Boardman News (Boardman) **10699**
Booster, The (Columbus) **10701**
Brecksville Gazette (Cleveland) **10700**
Brooklyn Sun Journal (Cleveland) **10700**
Brown County Press (Mt. Orab) **10705**
Brunswick Sun Times (Medina) **10705**
Bryan Times (Bryan) **10483**
Buckeye Review, The (Youngstown) **10709**
Bucyrus Telegraph-Forum (Bucyrus) **10483**
Bulletin, The (Bedford) **10699**
Centerville-Bellbrook Times (Kettering) **10704**
Chagrin Herald Sun (Beachwood) **10698**
Chagrin Valley Times (Chagrin Falls) **10700**
Chesterland News (Chesterland) **10700**
Chillicothe Gazette (Chillicothe) **10483**
Cincinnati Enquirer, The (Cincinnati) **10483**
Cincinnati Post (Cincinnati) **10483**
Circleville Herald (Circleville) **10483**
† Clermont County Review (Cincinnati)
† Clermont Courier (Cincinnati)
Clermont Sun (Batavia) **10698**
Cleveland Plain Dealer (Cleveland) **10483**
Clinton County Shoppers Guide (Wilmington) **10708**
Clyde Enterprise (Clyde) **10701**
Columbus Alive (Columbus) **10701**
Columbus Dispatch (Columbus) **10483**
Columbus Messenger (Columbus) **10701**
Community Booster, The (Granville) **10703**
Community Journal, South (Loveland) **10704**
Community Press, Mason (Loveland) **10704**
† Community Press, West Chester (Loveland)

* Conneaut News-Herald (Conneaut)
Coshocton Tribune (Coshocton) **10483**
Countyline, The (Bryan) **10699**
Courier, The (Findlay) **10484**
Courier, The (Conneaut) **10703**
Crescent-News (Defiance) **10484**
Crestline Advocate (Crestline) **10703**
Cuyahoga Falls News-Press (Stow) **10707**
Daily Advocate (Greenville) **10484**
Daily Herald (Delphos) **10484**
Daily Jeffersonian, The (Cambridge) **10483**
Daily News (Wapakoneta) **10487**
Daily Reporter (Columbus) **10483**
Daily Sentinel, The (Pomeroy) **10486**
Daily Standard (Celina) **10483**
Dalton Gazette & Kidron News (Dalton) **10703**
Darke County Early Bird, The (Greenville) **10703**
Dayton Daily News (Dayton) **10484**
Delaware Gazette (Delaware) **10484**
Delhi Press (Cincinnati) **10700**
Delta Atlas (Delta) **10703**
Dublin Suburbia News (Columbus) **10701**
Dublin Villager (Worthington) **10709**
Eastern Hills Journal (Loveland) **10704**
* East Palestine Heritage, The (Columbiana)
Elyria Chronicle-Telegram (Elyria) **10484**
† Erie County Reporter (Huron)
Euclid Sun Journal (Beachwood) **10698**
Evening Leader, The (St. Marys) **10487**
Everybody's News (Cincinnati) **10700**
Extra Merchandiser (St. Marys) **10707**
Fairborn Daily Herald (Fairborn) **10484**
Fairfield Echo (Fairfield) **10703**
Farmland News (Archbold) **10698**
Fayette Review, The (Fayette) **10703**
Forest Hills Journal (Loveland) **10704**
Franklin Chronicle (Franklin) **10703**
Free Press Standard (Carrollton) **10700**
Free Press, The (Canton) **10699**
Free Times, The (Cleveland) **10700**
Fulton County Expositor (Wauseon) **10708**
Galion Inquirer (Galion) **10484**
Gallipolis Daily Tribune (Gallipolis) **10484**
Garfield Maple-Sun (Cleveland) **10700**
Gateway News, The (Streetsboro) **10707**
Gazette Shopper (Cleveland) **10700**
Gazette, The (Jefferson) **10704**
† Geauga Times-Leader (Chardon)
† Girard News (Niles)
Granville Sentinel, The (Granville) **10703**
Greenville Daily Advocate (Greenville) **10484**
Grove City Record (Columbus) **10701**
Harrison News-Herald, The (Cadiz) **10699**
Hartville News (Hartville) **10703**
Herald-Star (Steubenville) **10487**

Hilliard Northwest News (Hilliard) **10703**
Hilltop News-Press (Cincinnati) **10700**
Hocking Valley Advertiser (Logan) **10704**
Holmes County Hub (Millersburg) **10705**
† Hubbard News (Niles)
Huber Heights Courier (Dayton) **10703**
Hudson Hub-Times (Stow) **10707**
Independent, The (Massillon) **10486**
Ironton Tribune (Ironton) **10485**
Jackson-Vinton Journal-Herald (Jackson) **10703**
Johnstown Independent (Columbus) **10701**
Journal-Leader (Caldwell) **10699**
Journal News (Hamilton) **10485**
Journal News (Spencerville) **10707**
Journal, The (Struthers) **10707**
Kent-Ravenna Record-Courier (Ravenna) **10486**
Kenton Times (Kenton) **10485**
Kettering-Oakwood Times (Kettering) **10704**
† Kirtland Enterprise (Willoughby)
Lakewood Sun Post (North Olmsted) **10706**
Lancaster Eagle-Gazette (Lancaster) **10485**
Lancaster Fairfield Advertiser (Carroll) **10699**
Leader Enterprise (Montpelier) **10705**
Leader, The (Cleveland) **10700**
† Leader, The (East Palestine)
† Liberty News (Niles)
Liberty Press, The (Liberty Center) **10704**
† Licking Countian (Newark)
Lima News (Lima) **10485**
Logan Daily News (Logan) **10485**
Lorain County Times, The (Rocky River) **10707**
Loudonville Times, The (Loudonville) **10704**
Louisville Herald, The (Louisville) **10704**
Loveland Herald Press (Loveland) **10704**
Madison Press, The (London) **10485**
† Madison Tribune (Ontario)
Malvern Community News (Minerva) **10705**
Manchester Signal (Manchester) **10705**
Maple Heights Press (Bedford) **10699**
Marietta Times (Marietta) **10485**
Marion Star (Marion) **10485**
Marysville Journal-Tribune (Marysville) **10485**
† Maumee Valley Herald (Toledo)
Medina County Gazette (Medina) **10486**
▼Medina Sun, The (Medina) **10705**
Mercer County Chronicle (Coldwater) **10701**
Metro Press (Millbury) **10705**
Miamisburg News (Miamisburg) **10705**
Middletown Journal (Middletown) **10486**
Milford Advertiser (Loveland) **10704**
Minerva Leader (Minerva) **10705**
Monroe County Beacon (Woodsfield) **10709**
† Monroe County Sentinel (Woodsfield)
Morgan County Herald (McConnelsville) **10705**

Morning Journal (Lisbon) **10485**
Morning Journal (Lorain) **10485**
Morrow County Advertiser (Mt. Gilead) **10705**
Morrow County Independent (Cardington) **10699**
Morrow County Sentinel (Mt. Gilead) **10705**
Mount Vernon News (Mt. Vernon) **10486**
† Mt. Washington Press (Cincinnati)
Newark/Licking Advertiser (Newark) **10705**
New Carlisle Sun (New Carlisle) **10706**
Newcomerstown News (Newcomerstown) **10706**
News-Herald (Port Clinton) **10486**
News-Herald (Willoughby) **10487**
News-Messenger (Fremont) **10484**
† NewsEAST (Columbus)
News Journal (Mansfield) **10485**
News Leader (Stow) **10707**
News Sun, The (Cleveland) **10700**
News Times (Amherst) **10698**
News Watchman, The (Waverly) **10708**
Nordonia Hills Sun (Cleveland) **10700**
North Clermont Community Journal (Loveland) **10704**
Northeast Suburban Life Press (Loveland) **10705**
Northland News (Columbus) **10701**
Northwest Columbus News (Columbus) **10701**
Northwest Press (Cincinnati) **10700**
Northwest Signal (Napoleon) **10486**
Norwalk Reflector (Norwalk) **10486**
† Orrville Courier-Crescent (Orrville)
Other Paper, The (Columbus) **10701**
Ottawa County Exponent, The (Oak Harbor) **10706**
Oxford Press (Oxford) **10706**
Parma Sun Post (Berea) **10699**
Pataskala Standard (Pataskala) **10706**
Paulding Progress (Paulding) **10706**
Penny Saver (Covington) **10703**
People's Defender, The (West Union) **10708**
Perry County Tribune (New Lexington) **10706**
Perrysburg Messenger-Journal (Perrysburg) **10706**
Photo Star (Willshire) **10708**
Pickerington Times-Sun (Columbus) **10701**
Pike County News Watchman (Waverly) **10708**
Piqua Daily Call (Piqua) **10486**
Point & Shoreland Journal (Toledo) **10707**
† Poland Leader (Niles)
Portsmouth Daily Times (Portsmouth) **10486**
Press & Light (West Lake) **10708**
Press-News, The (Minerva) **10705**
Press Review (London) **10704**
Press, The (Avon Lake) **10698**
Press, The (Millbury) **10705**

Price Hill Press (Cincinnati) **10700**
Progressor-Times, The (Carey) **10699**
Pulse-Journal (Mason) **10705**
Putnam County Sentinel (Ottawa) **10706**
Putnam County Vidette (Columbus Grove) **10702**
Pymatuning Area News (Andover) **10698**
Record Herald (Washington Court House) **10487**
Register-Herald (Eaton) **10703**
Repository, The (Canton) **10483**
Review, The (East Liverpool) **10484**
Review Times (Fostoria) **10484**
RFD News, The (Bellevue) **10699**
Rocky Fork Enterprise (Columbus) **10701**
Rocky Fork Enterprise (Gahanna) **10703**
Rossford Record-Journal (Perrysburg) **10706**
Rural-Urban Record (Columbia Station) **10701**
Sabina Advertiser (Sabina) **10707**
Salem News (Salem) **10486**
Sandusky Register (Sandusky) **10486**
Scioto Voice (Wheelersburg) **10708**
Sebring Times (Sebring) **10707**
Sentinel-Tribune (Bowling Green) **10483**
Sentinel, The (Jefferson) **10704**
† Shawnee-Cridersville Press (Wapakoneta)
Shelby Globe (Shelby) **10487**
Shelby Review (Wapakoneta) **10708**
Sidney Daily News (Sidney) **10487**
† Signal, The (Canal Fulton)
Solon Herald Sun (Beachwood) **10699**
Solon Times, The (Chagrin Falls) **10700**
Springfield News-Sun (Springfield) **10487**
Star Press (Springboro) **10707**
Star Republican (Wilmington) **10709**
Stillwater Valley Advertiser (Covington) **10703**
Stow Sentry (Stow) **10707**
Suburbanite, The (Akron) **10698**
Suburban Life (Loveland) **10705**
Sun Banner Pride (Medina) **10705**
Sunbury News (Sunbury) **10707**
Sun Courier, The (Cleveland) **10700**
Sun Herald, The (North Olmsted) **10706**
Sun Journal, The (North Canton) **10706**
Sun Messenger, The (Beachwood) **10699**
Sun Press, The (Beachwood) **10699**
Sun Scoop Journal (Beachwood) **10699**
Sun Star, The (Berea) **10699**
Sun, The (North Olmsted) **10706**
Swanton Enterprise (Swanton) **10707**
† Sycamore Messenger (Cincinnati)
Sylvania Herald (Toledo) **10708**
Tallmadge Express (Stow) **10707**
This Week In Bexley (Columbus) **10701**
This Week In Clintonville (Columbus) **10701**
This Week In Delaware (Columbus) **10701**

This Week In Eastside (Columbus) **10701**
This Week In Grandview (Columbus) **10702**
This Week In Hilliard (Columbus) **10702**
This Week In New Albany (Columbus) **10702**
This Week In Northland (Columbus) **10702**
This Week In Pickerington (Columbus) **10702**
This Week In Powell (Columbus) **10702**
This Week In Reynoldsburg (Columbus) **10702**
This Week In Southside (Columbus) **10702**
This Week In Union County (Columbus) **10702**
This Week In Westerville (Columbus) **10702**
This Week In Westside (Columbus) **10702**
This Week In Worthington (Columbus) **10702**
Times-Bulletin (Van Wert) **10487**
Times-Gazette (Greenfield) **10484**
Times-Reporter, The (New Philadelphia) **10486**
Times Gazette, The (Hillsboro) **10485**
Times Leader (Martins Ferry) **10485**
Times Recorder, The (Zanesville) **10488**
Times, The (Columbus) **10702**
Tipp City Herald (Tipp City) **10707**
Toledo Blade (Toledo) **10487**
Tri-County Press (Cincinnati) **10700**
Tri-Village News (Columbus) **10702**
Tribune-Courier (Ontario) **10706**
Tribune Chronicle, The (Warren) **10487**
Tribune Shopping News (New Lexington) **10706**
Troy Daily News (Troy) **10487**
Twinsburg Sun, The (Cleveland) **10700**
UA This Week (Columbus) **10702**
Upper Arlington News (Columbus) **10702**
Upper Sandusky Daily Chief-Union (Upper Sandusky) **10487**
Urbana Daily Citizen (Urbana) **10487**
Utica Herald (Utica) **10708**
Valley News, The (Jefferson) **10704**
Vermilion Photojournal (Vermilion) **10708**
Versailles Policy, The (Versailles) **10708**
Vindicator, The (Youngstown) **10488**
† Vinton County Courier (McArthur)
Weekly Reminder (Paulding) **10706**
† Wellston Sentry (Wellston)
Wellston Telegram, The (Wellston) **10708**
Western Hills Press (Cincinnati) **10700**
Western Star (Lebanon) **10704**
Westerville News & Public Opinion (Westerville) **10708**
West Geauga Sun (Beachwood) **10699**
Westlaker Times, The (Rocky River) **10707**
West Life (West Lake) **10708**
West Milton Record (West Milton) **10708**
West Side Sun News (North Olmsted) **10706**
West Toledo Herald (Toledo) **10708**
Whitehall News (Columbus) **10702**
Willard Times-Junction (Willard) **10708**

Wilmington News-Journal (Wilmington) **10488**
Wooster Daily Record (Wooster) **10488**
Worthington Suburbia News (Columbus) **10702**
Xenia Daily Gazette (Xenia) **10488**
Zanesville Muskingum Advertiser (Zanesville) **10709**

OKLAHOMA

Ada Evening News (Ada) **10488**
Altus Times (Altus) **10488**
Alva Review-Courier (Alva) **10488**
Anadarko Daily News (Anadarko) **10488**
Atoka County Times (Atoka) **10709**
Bartlesville Examiner-Enterprise (Bartlesville) **10488**
Bixby Bulletin (Tulsa) **10711**
Blackwell Journal-Tribune (Blackwell) **10488**
Boise City News, The (Boise City) **10709**
Bristow News (Bristow) **10709**
Broken Arrow Ledger (Broken Arrow) **10709**
† Broken Arrow Scout (Broken Arrow)
Bryan County Star (Durant) **10710**
Canadian County Chronicle (Yukon) **10712**
Capitol Hill Beacon (Oklahoma City) **10711**
Catoosa Times Herald (Catoosa) **10709**
Cherokee Messenger & Republican (Cherokee) **10709**
Chickasha Daily Express (Chickasha) **10488**
Claremore Progress (Claremore) **10488**
Clinton Daily News (Clinton) **10489**
Collinsville News (Tulsa) **10711**
Cordell Beacon, The (Cordell) **10709**
Country Connection News (Eakly) **10710**
Country Star (Stigler) **10711**
Covington Record (Covington) **10709**
Coweta American (Coweta) **10710**
Cushing Daily Citizen (Cushing) **10489**
Daily Ardmoreite (Ardmore) **10488**
Daily Oklahoman (Oklahoma City) **10490**
Duncan Banner (Duncan) **10489**
Durant Daily Democrat (Durant) **10489**
† Eastside Times (Tulsa)
Edmond Evening Sun (Edmond) **10489**
Elk City Daily News (Elk City) **10489**
El Reno Tribune (El Reno) **10710**
Enid News & Eagle (Enid) **10489**
Fairview Republican (Fairview) **10710**
Frederick Leader (Frederick) **10710**
▼Grove Daily News (Grove) **10489**
Grove Sun (Grove) **10710**
Guthrie News Leader (Guthrie) **10489**
Guymon Daily Herald (Guymon) **10489**
Harrah News, The (Harrah) **10710**
Henryetta Daily Free-Lance (Henryetta) **10489**

Hobart Democrat-Chief (Hobart) **10710**
Holdenville Daily News (Holdenville) **10489**
Hominy News-Progress (Hominy) **10710**
Hughes County Times (Wetumka) **10712**
Hugo Daily News (Hugo) **10489**
Jenks Journal (Tulsa) **10711**
† Jet Visitor (Cherokee)
Johnston County Capital-Democrat (Tishomingo) **10711**
Kingfisher Times & Free Press (Kingfisher) **10710**
Konawa Leader (Konawa) **10710**
Lawton Constitution (Lawton) **10489**
Lincoln County News (Chandler) **10709**
Madill Record (Madill) **10710**
McCurtain Daily Gazette (Idabel) **10489**
Miami News-Record (Miami) **10490**
Moore American (Moore) **10710**
Muskogee Daily Phoenix & Times-Democrat (Muskogee) **10490**
Newcastle Pacer, The (Newcastle) **10710**
News-Capital & Democrat (McAlester) **10490**
Norman Transcript (Norman) **10490**
Nowata Star (Nowata) **10710**
Oklahoma City Friday (Oklahoma City) **10711**
Oklahoma Eagle (Tulsa) **10712**
Oklahoma Gazette (Oklahoma City) **10711**
Okmulgee Times (Okmulgee) **10490**
Oologah Lake Leader (Oologah) **10711**
Oryor Jeffersonian (Pryor) **10711**
Owasso Reporter (Owasso) **10711**
Pauls Valley Daily Democrat (Pauls Valley) **10490**
Pawhuska Journal-Capital (Pawhuska) **10711**
Perry Daily Journal (Perry) **10490**
† Pictorial Press (Tahlequah)
Ponca City News (Ponca City) **10490**
Poteau Daily News & Sun (Poteau) **10490**
Pryor Daily Times (Pryor) **10490**
Purcell Register (Purcell) **10711**
Record-Citizen, The (Bristow) **10709**
Sand Springs Leader (Sand Springs) **10711**
Sapulpa Daily Herald (Sapulpa) **10490**
Sayre Journal (Sayre) **10711**
Seminole Daily Producer (Seminole) **10490**
Sequoyah County Times (Sallisaw) **10711**
Shawnee News-Star (Shawnee) **10490**
Shopper Zone I (Durant) **10710**
Skiatook Journal (Skiatook) **10711**
Southern Oklahoma Leader (Durant) **10710**
South Oklahoma City Leader (Moore) **10710**
Southwest Tulsa News (Tulsa) **10712**
Stigler News-Sentinel (Stigler) **10711**
Stillwater News-Press (Stillwater) **10490**
Stilwell Democrat-Journal (Stilwell) **10711**
Stratford Star (Konawa) **10710**

Tahlequah Daily Press (Tahlequah) **10491**
† Tipton News Leader (Altus)
Tonkawa News, The (Tonkawa) **10711**
Tribune, The (Bethany) **10709**
Tulsa World (Tulsa) **10491**
Vinita Daily Journal (Vinita) **10491**
Wagoner Tribune, The (Wagoner) **10712**
Watonga Republican, The (Watonga) **10712**
Weatherford Daily News (Weatherford) **10491**
Wewoka Times (Wewoka) **10712**
Woodward News (Woodward) **10491**
Yale News, The (Yale) **10712**
Yukon Review (Yukon) **10712**

OREGON

Albany Democrat-Herald (Albany) **10491**
Aloha Breeze (Hillsboro) **10713**
Argus Observer (Ontario) **10492**
Ashland Daily Tidings (Ashland) **10491**
Baker City Herald (Baker City) **10491**
Baker Record-Courier (Baker City) **10712**
Beaverton Valley Times (Tigard) **10715**
Bee, The (Portland) **10714**
Benton Bulletin (Philomath) **10714**
Bulletin, The (Bend) **10491**
Burns Times-Herald (Burns) **10712**
Butte Valley Star (Merrill) **10714**
Canby Herald (Canby) **10712**
Central Oregonian, The (Prineville) **10714**
Central Valley Times (Grants Pass) **10713**
Chronicle, The (Creswell) **10712**
Clackamas Review (Milwaukee) **10714**
Coquille Valley Sentinel (Coquille) **10712**
Corvallis Gazette-Times (Corvallis) **10491**
Cottage Grove Sentinel (Cottage Grove) **1071**
Country Weekly (Grants Pass) **10713**
Courier, The (Reedsport) **10714**
Curry Coastal Pilot (Brookings) **10712**
Daily Astorian (Astoria) **10491**
Dallas Polk County Itemizer-Observer (Dallas) **10712**
Dayton Tribune (Dayton) **10713**
Drain Enterprise (Drain) **10713**
East Oregonian, The (Pendleton) **10492**
Eugene Weekly (Eugene) **10713**
Gold Beach Curry County Reporter (Gold Beach) **10713**
Grants Pass Daily Courier (Grants Pass) **10491**
Gresham Outlook (Gresham) **10713**
Headlight-Herald (Tillamook) **10715**
Herald & News (Klamath Falls) **10492**
Hermiston Herald (Hermiston) **10713**
Hillsboro Argus (Hillsboro) **10713**
Hood River News (Hood River) **10713**

Island Connection (Portland) **10714**
Lake County Examiner (Lakeview) **10713**
Lake Oswego Review (Lake Oswego) **10713**
Lebanon Express (Lebanon) **10713**
Lost River Star (Merrill) **10714**
Madras Pioneer, The (Madras) **10714**
Mail Tribune (Medford) **10492**
Malheur Enterprise (Vale) **10715**
Newberg Graphic (Newberg) **10714**
New Era, The (Sweet Home) **10715**
News-Register (McMinnville) **10714**
News-Review (Roseburg) **10492**
News-Times (Newport) **10714**
News Guard, The (Lincoln City) **10713**
News Times (Forest Grove) **10713**
Observer, The (La Grande) **10492**
Oregonian, The (Portland) **10492**
Pendleton Record, The (Pendleton) **10714**
Redmond Spokesman (Redmond) **10714**
Register-Guard (Eugene) **10491**
Rogue River Press (Rogue River) **10714**
Sandy Post (Sandy) **10715**
Seaside Signal (Seaside) **10715**
Silverton Appeal-Tribune/Mt. Angel News
   (Silverton) **10715**
Siuslaw News, The (Florence) **10713**
Springfield News, The (Springfield) **10715**
Statesman Journal (Salem) **10492**
Stayton Mail (Stayton) **10715**
St. Helens Chronicle (St. Helens) **10715**
St. Johns Review (Portland) **10714**
The Dalles Daily Chronicle (The Dalles) **10492**
Tigard Times (Tigard) **10715**
Times-Journal, The (Condon) **10712**
Umpqua Free Press (Myrtle Creek) **10714**
Upper Rogue Independent (Eagle Point) **10713**
Western World (Bandon) **10712**
West Linn Tidings (Lake Oswego) **10713**
West Valley Courier (Hillsboro) **10713**
Willamette Week (Portland) **10714**
World, The (Coos Bay) **10491**

PALAU

Palau Gazette (Koror) **10715**

PENNSYLVANIA

Abington Journal (Clarks Summit) **10716**
Advance Leader (Monroeville) **10720**
Advance of Bucks County (Newtown) **10721**
Advertiser, The (McMurray) **10719**
Advisor, The (Mt. Pleasant) **10721**
Albion News, The (Albion) **10715**
Alleghany Times (Moon Township) **10495**
Allied News (Grove City) **10718**
Almanac, The (McMurray) **10719**
Altoona Mirror (Altoona) **10492**
Ambler Gazette (Fort Washington) **10717**
Area Shopper (Conneautville) **10716**
Barnesboro Star, The (Barnesboro) **10716**
Beaver County Times (Beaver) **10492**
Bedford Gazette/Gazette Sunday
   (Bedford) **10492**
Bennetts Valley News (Weedville) **10724**
† Biz (Oxford)
Boyertown Area Times (Boyertown) **10716**
Bradford Era, The (Bradford) **10492**
Bradford Journal/Miner (Bradford) **10716**
Brandywine Chronicle (Oxford) **10721**
† Breeze Herald (Conneut Lake Park)
Breeze, The (Rockledge) **10723**
Bridgeville Area News (Monroeville) **10720**
Bristol Pilot (Bristol) **10716**
Broad Top Bulletin (Saxton) **10724**
† Brookville American (Brookville)
Bucks County Courier Times
   (Levittown) **10495**
Bucks County Tribune (Horsham) **10718**
Butler Eagle (Butler) **10493**
Call, The (Schuylkill Haven) **10724**
Cameron County Echo (Emporium) **10717**
Canton Independent-Sentinel (Canton) **10716**
Carbondale News (Carbondale) **10716**
Carlisle Sentinel (Carlisle) **10493**
Centre Daily Times (State College) **10496**
Chester County Press (Oxford) **10721**
Chestnut Hill Local (Philadelphia) **10722**
Citizen-Standard, The (Valley View) **10724**
Clarion News (Clarion) **10716**
Colonial, The (Fort Washington) **10717**
Conneautville Courier (Conneautville) **10716**
Corry Journal (Corry) **10493**
Cosmopolite-Herald (Girard) **10718**
County Neighbors (Punxsutawney) **10723**
County Observer (Yeagertown) **10725**
County Press (Newtown Square) **10721**
County Transcript (Susquehanna) **10724**
Courier-Express (Du Bois) **10493**
Cresson-Gallitzin Mainliner, The
   (Cresson) **10717**
Daily American (Somerset) **10496**
Daily Courier, The (Connellsville) **10493**
Daily Herald, The (Tyrone) **10497**
Daily Item, The (Sunbury) **10497**
Daily Local News (West Chester) **10497**
Daily News (Huntingdon) **10494**
Daily Press, The (St. Marys) **10496**
† Daily Record, The (Westchester)
Daily Review & Sunday Review
   (Towanda) **10497**

Dallas Post (Dallas) **10717**
Danville News (Danville) **10493**
Delaware County Daily-Sunday Times (Clifton Heights) **10493**
Delaware County Journal (Holmes) **10718**
Derrick, The (Oil City) **10495**
Drexel Hill Press (Newtown Square) **10721**
Duncannon Record (New Bloomfield) **10721**
East Penn Press (Allentown) **10715**
Ebensburg News Leader, The (Ebensburg) **10717**
Elizabethtown Chronicle (Elizabethtown) **10717**
Elizabethtown Mount Joy Merchandiser (Mt. Joy) **10721**
Ellwood City Ledger (Ellwood City) **10493**
Ephrata Review (Ephrata) **10717**
Erie Daily Times/Sunday Times News (Erie) **10493**
Erie Morning News (Erie) **10493**
Evening Sun (Hanover) **10494**
Evening Times (Sayre) **10496**
Express (Lock Haven) **10495**
Express-Times, The (Easton) **10493**
Fishtown Star (Philadelphia) **10722**
Forest Press (Tionesta) **10724**
Free Press-Courier (Westfield) **10725**
Free Press, The (Braddock) **10716**
Germantown Courier (Philadelphia) **10722**
Germantown Paper (Philadelphia) **10722**
Gettysburg Times (Gettysburg) **10493**
Girard Home News (Philadelphia) **10722**
Glenside News (Jenkintown) **10718**
Globe, The (Jenkintown) **10718**
Greenville Record-Argus (Greenville) **10494**
Hamburg Item (Hamburg) **10718**
Haverford Press (Newtown Square) **10721**
Hazleton Standard Speaker (Hazleton) **10494**
Herald Standard (Uniontown) **10497**
Herald, The (Sharon) **10496**
Herald, The (Pittsburgh) **10723**
Hershey Chronicle, The (Hershey) **10718**
Independent Observer, The (Scottdale) **10724**
Independent, The (Collegeville) **10716**
Independent, The (Montrose) **10720**
Indiana Gazette (Indiana) **10494**
In Pittsburgh Newsweekly (Pittsburgh) **10723**
Intelligencer/Record, The (Doylestown) **10493**
Intelligencer Journal (Lancaster) **10494**
† Interboro News (Prospect Park)
Jeannette Spirit (Jeannette) **10718**
Jeffersonian Democrat (Brookville) **10716**
Johnsonburg Press, Inc., The (Johnsonburg) **10719**
Journal-Herald, The (White Haven) **10725**
Journal/Valley Views (White Haven) **10725**
Juniata News (Philadelphia) **10722**

Juniata Sentinel (Mifflintown) **10720**
Kane Republican (Kane) **10494**
King of Prussia Courier (King of Prussia) **10719**
Lancaster Intelligencer Journal (Lancaster) **10494**
Lancaster New Era (Lancaster) **10494**
Latrobe Bulletin (Latrobe) **10494**
Leader-Vindicator, The (New Bethlehem) **10721**
Leader, The (Philadelphia) **10722**
Leader Times (Kittanning) **10494**
Lebanon Daily News (Lebanon) **10495**
Lewisburg Daily Journal (Milton) **10495**
Ligonier Echo (Ligonier) **10719**
Ligonier Free Gazette, The (Ligonier) **10719**
† Linesville Herald (Conneaut Lake)
Lititz Record Express, The (Lititz) **10719**
† Main Line Chronicle (West Chester)
Main Line Life (Ardmore) **10716**
Main Line Times (Ardmore) **10716**
Marcus Hook Press (Drexel Hill) **10717**
† Market Place (Vandergrift)
McConnellsburg Fulton County News (McConnellsburg) **10719**
McKeesport Daily News (McKeesport) **10495**
Meadville Tribune, The (Meadville) **10495**
Mercury, The (Pottstown) **10496**
† MidMon Observer (Washington)
Mifflinburg Telegraph, The (Mifflinburg) **10720**
Millcreek Sun (Erie) **10717**
Milton Daily Standard (Milton) **10495**
Montgomery County Progress (Horsham) **10718**
Montgomery Post, The (Norristown) **10721**
Montgomeryville Spirit (Fort Washington) **10717**
Morning Call, The (Allentown) **10492**
Morrisons Cove Herald (Martinsburg) **10719**
Mountaineer-Herald, The (Ebensburg) **10717**
Mountaintop Eagle (Mountain Top) **10720**
Mount Pleasant Journal (Mt. Pleasant) **10721**
Mt. Airy Times (Philadelphia) **10722**
Murrysville Area Star (Monroeville) **10720**
Nanty Glo Journal, The (Nanty Glo) **10721**
New Castle News (New Castle) **10495**
New Hope Gazette (New Hope) **10721**
News-Herald (Oil City) **10495**
News-Item (Shamokin) **10496**
News-Sun, The (New Bloomfield) **10721**
News Eagle (Hawley) **10718**
News Gleaner Publications (Philadelphia) **10722**
News of Delaware County (Havertown) **10718**
News of Southern Berks, The (Boyertown) **10716**

News, The (Aliquippa) **10715**
North East Breeze (North East) **10721**
Northeast Times (Philadelphia) **10722**
North Hills News Record (Warrendale) **10497**
North Star (Philadelphia) **10722**
Observer-Reporter (Waynesburg) **10497**
Observer-Reporter, Washington County Edition (Washington) **10497**
Olney Times (Philadelphia) **10722**
Park News (Library) **10719**
Patriot-News (Harrisburg) **10494**
Patriot, The (Kutztown) **10719**
Perkasie News-Herald (Perkasie) **10722**
Perry County Times (New Bloomfield) **10721**
Philadelphia City Paper (Philadelphia) **10722**
Philadelphia Daily News (Philadelphia) **10495**
Philadelphia Guide Newspaper (Philadelphia) **10722**
Philadelphia Inquirer (Philadelphia) **10495**
Philadelphia Weekly (Philadelphia) **10722**
Phoenix, The (Phoenixville) **10496**
Pike County Dispatch (Milford) **10720**
Pittsburgh City Paper (Pittsburgh) **10723**
Pittsburgh Post-Gazette (Pittsburgh) **10496**
Pittsburgh Press (Pittsburgh)
Pittsburgh Renaissance News (Pittsburgh) **10723**
Pocono Record (Stroudsburg) **10497**
Pocono Shopper (East Stroudsburg) **10717**
Portage Dispatch, The (Portage) **10723**
Port Richmond Star (Philadelphia) **10722**
Post, The (Middleburg) **10720**
Potter Leader-Enterprise (Coudersport) **10717**
Pottsville Republican & Evening Herald (Pottsville) **10496**
Press & Journal, The (Middletown) **10720**
Press Enterprise, The (Bloomsburg) **10492**
Press Herald (Pine Grove) **10723**
Progress, The (Monroeville) **10720**
Progress, The (Clearfield)
Public Opinion, The (Chambersburg) **10493**
Punxsutawney Spirit (Punxsutawney) **10496**
Quakertown Free Press (Quakertown) **10723**
Reading Eagle & Reading Times (Reading) **10496**
Record-Enterprise (McDonald) **10719**
Recorder, The (Conshohocken) **10717**
Record Herald (Waynesboro) **10497**
Record, The (Horsham) **10494**
Record, The (Coraopolis) **10717**
Reporter of the Spring-Ford Area (Royersford) **10723**
Reporter, The (Lansdale) **10494**
Ridgway Record (Ridgway) **10496**
Ridley Press (Drexel Hill) **10717**
Roxborough Review (Philadelphia) **10722**
Scranton Times/Sunday Times (Scranton) **10496**
Sentinel, The (Lewistown) **10495**
Sewickley Herald (Monroeville) **10720**
Shippensburg News-Chronicle (Shippensburg) **10724**
Signal-Item (Monroeville) **10720**
Slatebelt Hometown News, The (Bangor) **10716**
Souderton Independent (Souderton) **10724**
South Hills Record (Pittsburgh) **10723**
South Philadelphia Chronicle (Philadelphia) **10723**
South Philadelphia Review (Philadelphia) **10723**
South Pittsburgh Reporter (Pittsburgh) **10723**
Southwestern Pennsylvania Scene (Scottdale) **10724**
Southwest Globe Times (Philadelphia) **10723**
† Spirit of Bucks County (Hatboro)
Springfield Press (Springfield) **10724**
Springfield Sun (Fort Washington) **10718**
Standard-Observer (Greensburg) **10493**
Suburban & Wayne Times (Wayne) **10724**
Suburban Advertiser (Wayne) **10724**
Suburban Gazette (McKees Rocks) **10719**
Sullivan Review (Dushore) **10717**
Sunday Bucks County Telegraph (Horsham) **10718**
Sunday Dispatch (Pittston) **10723**
Sunday News (Lancaster) **10719**
† Sunday Sun (Scranton)
Sun, The (Hummelstown) **10718**
Susquehanna County Independent (Montrose) **10720**
Three Star Edition (Philadelphia) **10723**
Times-Express (Monroeville) **10720**
Times-Leader (Union City) **10724**
Times-Sun, The (West Newton) **10725**
Times Chronicle (Jenkintown) **10719**
Times Herald, The (Norristown) **10495**
Times Leader, The (Wilkes Barre) **10497**
Times News (Lehighton) **10495**
Times, The (Port Royal) **10723**
Titusville Herald (Titusville) **10497**
Town & Country (Pennsburg) **10722**
† Town & Country (Bradford)
Town Talk (Holmes) **10718**
Town Talk (Media) **10719**
Tribune-Democrat, The (Johnstown) **10494**
Tribune-Review (Greensburg) **10493**
Tribune, The/Sunday Times (Scranton) **10496**
Tunkhannock New Age-Examiner (Tunkhannock) **10724**
Union Press-Courier (Patton) **10722**
Upper Darby Press (Drexel Hill) **10717**

Upper Dauphin Sentinel (Millersburg) **10720**
Valley Gazette (Lansford) **10719**
Valley Independent (Monessen) **10495**
Valley Log, The (Orbisonia) **10721**
Valley News Dispatch (Tarentum) **10497**
Valley Times-Star (Newville) **10721**
Valley Trader (Lewisburg) **10719**
Vandergrift News (Vandergrift) **10724**
Villager, The (Moscow) **10720**
Voice, The (Phoenixville) **10723**
Warren Times Observer (Warren) **10497**
Wayne Independent, The (Honesdale) **10494**
Weekend News (Montrose) **10720**
Weekly Almanac, The (Honesdale) **10718**
Weekly Recorder, The (Claysville) **10716**
Wellsboro Gazette (Wellsboro) **10724**
West Schuylkill Herald (Tower City) **10724**
Wilkes-Barre Citizens' Voice (Wilkes Barre) **10497**
† Wilkes-Barre Sunday Independent (Wilkes Barre)
Williamsport Sun-Gazette (Williamsport) **10498**
Willow Grove Guide (Fort Washington) **10718**
Yardley News (Yardley) **10725**
York Daily Record (York) **10498**
York Dispatch/York Sunday News (York) **10498**

RHODE ISLAND

Barrington Times (Warren) **10726**
Bristol Phoenix (Bristol) **10725**
Call, The (Woonsocket) **10498**
Cranston Herald (Cranston) **10725**
East Greenwich Pendulum (East Greenwich) **10725**
East Providence Post (East Providence) **10725**
Eastside Monthly (Providence) **10726**
Jamestown Press, The (Jamestown) **10725**
Kent County Daily Times (West Warwick) **10498**
Narragansett Times, The (Wakefield) **10726**
Newport Daily News, The (Newport) **10498**
Newport Mercury (Newport) **10725**
Newport This Week (Newport) **10725**
Observer, The (Greenville) **10725**
Providence Journal-Bulletin (Providence) **10498**
Providence Phoenix (Providence) **10726**
Sakonnet Times (Portsmouth) **10725**
Seekonk Star (East Providence) **10725**
Standard-Times (North Kingstown) **10725**
Times, The (Pawtucket) **10498**
Warren Times Gazette (Warren) **10726**
Warwick Beacon (Warwick) **10726**

Westerly Sun (Westerly) **10498**

SOUTH CAROLINA

Aiken Standard (Aiken) **10498**
Alternatives News Magazine (Myrtle Beach) **10728**
Anderson Independent-Mail (Anderson) **10498**
Bamberg Advertizer-Herald, The (Bamberg) **10726**
Beaufort Gazette (Beaufort) **10498**
Beaufort Shopper (Beaufort) **10726**
Berkeley Independent (Moncks Corner) **10728**
Charleston Post & Courier (Charleston) **10498**
Cheraw Chronicle, The (Cheraw) **10726**
Chester News & Reporter (Chester) **10726**
Chronicle-Independent (Camden) **10726**
Clinton Chronicle, The (Clinton) **10727**
Clover Herald (Clover) **10727**
Coastal Times (Charleston) **10726**
† Conway Field & Herald (Conway)
Darco News & Buyers Guide (Hartsville) **10727**
Dillon Herald, The (Dillon) **10727**
Dispatch-News, The (Lexington) **10728**
Dorchester Eagle Record (St. George) **10729**
Easley Progress (Easley) **10727**
Florence Morning News (Florence) **10498**
Fort Mill Times (Fort Mill) **10727**
Gaffney Ledger, The (Gaffney) **10727**
Georgetown Times, The (Georgetown) **10727**
Goose Creek Gazette (Ladson) **10727**
Greenville News (Greenville) **10499**
† Greenville Piedmont (Greenville)
Greer Citizen, The (Greer) **10727**
Hanahan News (North Charleston) **10728**
Hartsville Messenger, The (Hartsville) **10727**
Herald-Independent, The (Winnsboro) **10729**
Herald-Journal (Spartanburg) **10499**
Herald, The (Rock Hill) **10499**
Hilton Head Island Packet (Hilton Head) **10499**
Holly Hill Observer, The (Holly Hill) **10727**
Horry Independent (Conway) **10727**
Index-Journal (Greenwood) **10499**
Item, The (Sumter) **10499**
Jasper County Sun (Ridgeland) **10728**
Journal, The (Mt. Pleasant) **10728**
Journal, The (Williamston) **10729**
Journal Tribune (Seneca) **10729**
Lake Edition, The (Lexington) **10728**
Lancaster News (Lancaster) **10728**
Laurens County Advertiser (Laurens) **10728**
Lee County Observer (Bishopville) **10726**
Loris Times (Loris) **10728**

Marion Star & Mullins Enterprise
(Marion) **10728**
Marlboro Herald-Advocate
(Bennettsville) **10726**
Marlboro Shopper (Bennettsville) **10726**
Messenger, The (Clemson) **10727**
Moultrie News, The (Mt. Pleasant) **10728**
Newberry Observer, The (Newberry) **10728**
News & Press, The (Darlington) **10727**
News Leader, The (Landrum) **10728**
News, The (Kingstree) **10727**
North Myrtle Beach Times (North Myrtle
Beach) **10728**
Pageland Progressive-Journal, The
(Pageland) **10728**
† Paper, The (Spartanburg)
People-Sentinel (Barnwell) **10726**
Pickens Sentinel (Pickens) **10728**
Press & Standard, The (Walterboro) **10729**
Saluda Standard Sentinel (Saluda) **10729**
State, The (Columbia) **10498**
Summerville Journal Scene
(Summerville) **10729**
Sun News, The (Myrtle Beach) **10499**
Times & Democrat, The (Orangeburg) **10499**
Tribune-Times (Fountain Inn) **10727**
Twin-City News, The
(Batesburg-Leesville) **10726**
Union Daily Times (Union) **10499**
Weekly Observer, The (Hemingway) **10727**
Yorkville Enquirer (York) **10729**
Your Paper (Roebuck) **10729**

SOUTH DAKOTA

Aberdeen American News (Aberdeen) **10499**
† Alpena Journal (Wessington Springs)
Argus Leader (Sioux Falls) **10500**
Baltic Beacon (Dell Rapids) **10729**
Belle Fourche Post (Belle Fourche) **10729**
Black Hills Pioneer (Spearfish) **10500**
Black Hills Press (Sturgis) **10730**
Brandon Valley Challenger (Dell Rapids) **10729**
Brookings Register (Brookings) **10499**
Butte County Valley Irrigator (Newell) **10730**
Canistota Clipper (Canistota) **10729**
Canova Herald (Canistota) **10729**
Capital Journal (Pierre) **10499**
Daily Republic (Mitchell) **10499**
Dell Rapids Tribune (Dell Rapids) **10729**
Grant County Review (Milbank) **10730**
Hartford Area News (Canistota) **10729**
Humbolt Journal (Canistota) **10729**
Hutchinson Herald, The (Menno) **10730**
Ipswich Tribune (Ipswich) **10730**
Lawrence County Centennial
(Deadwood) **10729**
† Lead Call (Lead)
Madison Daily Leader (Madison) **10499**
Meade County Times-Tribune (Sturgis) **10730**
Montrose Herald (Canistota) **10729**
Moody County Enterprise (Flandreau) **10730**
Nation's Center News (Buffalo) **10729**
Northwest Blade, The (Eureka) **10730**
Pennington County Prevailer-News (Hill
City) **10730**
Pierre Times, The (Pierre) **10730**
Plainsman, The (Huron) **10499**
Pratt Tribune (Vermillion) **10730**
Rapid City Journal (Rapid City) **10499**
Redfield Press (Redfield) **10730**
Roscoe Hosmer Independent (Ipswich) **10730**
Selby Record (Selby) **10730**
Sisseton Courier (Sisseton) **10730**
True Dakotan, The (Wessington
Springs) **10730**
Watertown Public Opinion (Watertown) **10500**
Webster Reporter & Farmer (Webster) **10730**
Winner Advocate (Winner) **10731**
Yankton Daily Press & Dakotan
(Yankton) **10500**

TENNESSEE

Advocate Democrat (Madisonville) **10733**
Advocate Penny Saver (Sweetwater) **10735**
Athens Daily Post (Athens) **10500**
Bolivar Bulletin-Times (Bolivar) **10731**
Brentwood Journal (Brentwood) **10731**
Brownsville States-Graphic
(Brownsville) **10731**
Buffalo River Review (Linden) **10733**
Camden Chronicle, The (Camden) **10731**
Carroll County News-Leader
(Huntingdon) **10732**
Carthage Courier (Carthage) **10731**
Chattanooga Free Press (Chattanooga) **10500**
Chattanooga Times (Chattanooga) **10500**
Chronicle, The (Humboldt) **10732**
Citizen/Press Plus (Pulaski) **10734**
Citizen Tribune (Morristown) **10501**
Claiborne Progress (Tazewell) **10735**
Cleveland Daily Banner (Cleveland) **10500**
Collierville Herald, The (Collierville) **10731**
Commercial Appeal, The (Memphis) **10501**
Courier-News (Clinton) **10731**
Courier, The (Savannah) **10734**
Cover Story, The (Murfreesboro) **10734**
Covington Leader (Covington) **10731**
Crockett Times, The (Alamo) **10731**
Crossville Chronicle (Crossville) **10731**

† Cumberland Times (Crossville)
Daily Herald (Columbia) **10500**
Daily Times (Maryville) **10501**
Democrat-Union (Lawrenceburg) **10733**
Dickson Herald, The (Dickson) **10731**
† Dispatch, The (Cookeville)
Dresden Enterprise (Dresden) **10731**
Dyer County Tennessean (Newbern) **10734**
East Shelby Review (Somerville) **10735**
Elizabethton Star (Elizabethton) **10500**
Elk Valley Times (Fayetteville) **10732**
Erwin Record (Erwin) **10732**
Fayette County Review (Somerville) **10735**
Fayette Falcon, The (Somerville) **10735**
Germantown News, The (Germantown) **10732**
Grainger County News (Rutledge) **10734**
Greeneville Sun (Greeneville) **10500**
Grundy County Herald (Tracy City) **10735**
Halls Graphic (Ripley) **10734**
Harriman Record (Kingston) **10732**
Hartsville Vidette, The (Hartsville) **10732**
† Hendersonville Free Press (Hendersonville)
Hendersonville Star News (Hendersonville) **10732**
Herald & Tribune (Jonesborough) **10732**
Herald-Chronicle, The (Winchester) **10735**
Herald-Citizen (Cookeville) **10500**
Herald-News (Dayton) **10731**
Herald Gazette, The (Trenton) **10735**
† Huntingdon Carroll Leader (Huntingdon)
Hustler, The (South Pittsburg) **10735**
Independent (Collierville) **10731**
Independent Appeal (Selmer) **10735**
Jackson Sun, The (Jackson) **10500**
Jasper Journal (Jasper) **10732**
Jellico Advance Sentinel (La Follette) **10733**
Johnson City Press (Johnson City) **10501**
Kingsport Daily News (Kingsport) **10501**
Kingsport Times-News (Kingsport) **10501**
Knoxville News-Sentinel (Knoxville) **10501**
La Follette Press (La Follette) **10733**
Lake City Town Crier (La Follette) **10733**
Lauderdale County Enterprise (Ripley) **10734**
Leaf-Chronicle, The (Clarksville) **10500**
Lebanon Democrat, The (Lebanon) **10501**
Lewisburg Tribune (Lewisburg) **10733**
Lexington Progress (Lexington) **10733**
Livingston Enterprise (Livingston) **10733**
Macon County Times (Lafayette) **10733**
Magic Valley Shopper's News (Camden) **10731**
Manchester Times (Manchester) **10733**
Marshall Gazette (Lewisburg) **10733**
McKenzie Banner (McKenzie) **10733**
Memphis Flyer (Memphis) **10734**
Messenger, The (Madison) **10733**
Mid-South Horse Review (Somerville) **10735**
Millington Star, The (Millington) **10734**
Mirror-Exchange (Milan) **10734**
Morgan County News (Wartburg) **10735**
Mountain Press, The (Sevierville) **10501**
† Mountain Visitor (Sevierville)
Murfreesboro Daily News Journal (Murfreesboro) **10501**
Nashville Banner (Nashville) **10501**
Nashville Scene, The (Nashville) **10734**
Newport Plaintalk (Newport) **10734**
News-Examiner (Gallatin) **10732**
News Herald (Lenoir City) **10733**
News Leader, The (Parsons) **10734**
Oak Ridger, The (Oak Ridge) **10501**
Paris Post-Intelligencer, The (Paris) **10501**
Pickett County Press (Byrdstown) **10731**
Pulaski Citizen (Pulaski) **10734**
Pulaski Giles Free Press (Pulaski) **10734**
Roane County News, The (Kingston) **10732**
Robertson County Times (Springfield) **10735**
Rockwood Times (Kingston) **10732**
Rogersville Review (Rogersville) **10734**
Rutherford Courier, The (Smyrna) **10735**
Scott County News (Oneida) **10734**
Shelby Sun Times (Germantown) **10732**
Shelbyville Times-Gazette (Shelbyville) **10501**
Smithville Review (Smithville) **10735**
Southern Standard (McMinnville) **10733**
Sparta Expositor (Sparta) **10735**
Standard Banner (Jefferson) **10732**
State Gazette (Dyersburg) **10500**
Sullivan County News (Blountville) **10731**
Tennessean, The (Nashville) **10501**
Tomahawk, The (Mountain City) **10734**
Tri-City Reporter (Dyer) **10732**
Tri-County News (Knoxville) **10732**
Tullahoma News (Tullahoma) **10735**
Union City Daily Messenger (Union City) **10502**
Wayne County News (Waynesboro) **10735**
Weakley County Press (Martin) **10733**
Williamson Leader, The (Franklin) **10732**
Wilson World, The (Lebanon) **10733**

TEXAS

Abernathy Weekly Review (Abernathy) **10735**
Abilene Reporter-News (Abilene) **10502**
Alice Echo-News (Alice) **10502**
Alpine Avalanche (Alpine) **10736**
Alvarado Post (Alvarado) **10736**
Alvin Advertiser (Alvin) **10736**
Alvin Sun (Alvin) **10736**
Amarillo Daily News/Sunday News Globe (Amarillo) **10502**
Amarillo Globe Times (Amarillo) **10502**

Andrews County News (Andrews) **10736**
Angelina Free Press (Diboll) **10739**
Angleton Times (Angleton) **10736**
Argyle Sun, The (Lake Dallas) **10743**
▼ Arlington Morning News (Arlington) **10502**
Arlington Star Telegram (Arlington) **10502**
Athens Daily Review (Athens) **10502**
Atlanta Citizens Journal (Atlanta) **10736**
Austin American-Statesman (Austin) **10502**
Austin Chronicle (Austin) **10736**
Azle News (Azle) **10736**
Banner Press Newspaper, The (Columbus) **10738**
Baylor County Banner (Seymour) **10746**
Bayshore Sun (La Porte) **10743**
Baytown Sun (Baytown) **10502**
Beaumont Enterprise (Beaumont) **10502**
Beeville Bee-Picayune (Beeville) **10736**
Bellville Times (Bellville) **10736**
Benbrook News (Fort Worth) **10740**
Big Spring Herald (Big Spring) **10502**
Blanco County News (Blanco) **10737**
Bonham Daily Favorite (Bonham) **10502**
Booker News, The (Booker) **10737**
Borden Star (Gail) **10740**
Borger News-Herald (Borger) **10502**
Bosque County News (Meridian) **10744**
Bowie News (Bowie) **10737**
Brackett News The (Brackettville) **10737**
Brady Standard (Brady) **10737**
Brazosport Facts, The (Clute) **10503**
Brenham Banner-Press (Brenham) **10503**
Bridgeport Index (Bridgeport) **10737**
Brownfield News (Brownfield) **10737**
Brownsville Herald (Brownsville) **10503**
Brownwood Bulletin (Brownwood) **10503**
Bryan College Station Eagle (Bryan) **10503**
Bryan College Station Press (Bryan) **10737**
Bulletin, The (Santa Fe) **10746**
Burleson County Citizen Tribune (Caldwell) **10737**
Burleson Star (Burleson) **10737**
Burnet Bulletin (Burnet) **10737**
Callahan County Star (Baird) **10736**
Cameron Herald (Cameron) **10737**
Canyon News (Canyon) **10737**
 Carrollton Chronicle (Carrollton)
Cedar Creek Pilot (Gun Barrel City) **10741**
Cedar Hill Today (DeSoto) **10739**
Childress Index (Childress) **10737**
Cisco Press (Cisco) **10738**
Citizens' Advocate Newspaper (Coppell) **10738**
Citizen, The (Houston) **10741**
Clarksville Times, The (Clarksville) **10738**
Cleveland Advocate (Cleveland) **10738**

Coastal Current, The (South Padre Island) **10747**
Coleman Chronicle & Democrat Voice (Coleman) **10738**
Comanche Chief (Comanche) **10738**
Commerce Journal (Commerce) **10738**
Conroe Courier, The (Conroe) **10503**
Coppell Gazette (Lewisville) **10743**
Copperas Cove Leader Press (Copperas Cove) **10738**
Corpus Christi Caller-Times (Corpus Christi) **10503**
Corrigan Times, The (Corrigan) **10738**
Corsicana Daily Sun (Corsicana) **10503**
Crane News (Crane) **10738**
Crowley Review (Burleson) **10737**
Cuero Record (Cuero) **10738**
D/FW People (Euless) **10739**
Daily Sentinel, The (Nacogdoches) **10505**
Daily Tribune, The (Bay City) **10502**
Dalhart Daily Texan (Dalhart) **10503**
Dallas Morning News, The (Dallas) **10503**
Dallas Park Cities News (Dallas) **10738**
Dallas White Rocker News (Dallas) **10738**
Deer Park Broadcaster, The (Deer Park) **10738**
Deer Park Progress, The (Deer Park) **10739**
Del Rio News-Herald (Del Rio) **10503**
Denton County Express (Lake Dallas) **10743**
Denton Record-Chronicle (Denton) **10503**
DeSoto Today (DeSoto) **10739**
Dripping Springs Dispatch (Dripping Springs) **10739**
Duncanville Today (DeSoto) **10739**
Eagle Lake Headlight (Eagle Lake) **10739**
Eagle Pass News Guide/Brief (Eagle Pass) **10739**
Eastland Telegram (Eastland) **10739**
Edgewood Enterprise (Edgewood) **10739**
Edinburg Daily Review (Edinburg) **10503**
El Campo Leader-News (El Campo) **10739**
El Paso Herald-Post (El Paso) **10504**
El Paso Times (El Paso) **10504**
Ennis Daily News (Ennis) **10504**
Everman Times (Everman) **10739**
Exchange, The (Houston) **10742**
Falfurrias Facts (Falfurrias) **10740**
† Farmers Branch Times (Carrollton)
Fayette County Record, The (La Grange) **10743**
Floresville Chronicle-Journal (Floresville) **10740**
Floyd County Hesperian-Beacon (Floydada) **10740**
Forest Hill News (Everman) **10740**
Fort Bend Mirror (Rosenberg) **10746**

Fort Bend Sun (Sugar Land) **10747**
Fort San Antonio News Leader (San Antonio) **10746**
Fort Stockton Pioneer (Fort Stockton) **10740**
Fort Worth Star-Telegram (Fort Worth) **10504**
Fredericksburg Standard/Radio Post (Fredericksburg) **10740**
Friendswood & Pearland Reporter News (Pearland) **10745**
Gainesville Daily Register (Gainesville) **10504**
Galveston County Daily News, The (Galveston) **10504**
Garland News (Garland) **10740**
Gatesville Messenger (Gatesville) **10740**
Giddings Times & News (Giddings) **10740**
Gilmer Mirror (Gilmer) **10740**
Gladewater Mirror (Gladewater) **10741**
Glen Rose Reporter (Glen Rose) **10741**
Gonzales Inquirer (Gonzales) **10741**
Gorman Progress, The (Gorman) **10741**
Grand Prairie News (Arlington) **10736**
Grand Saline Sun (Grand Saline) **10741**
Grayson County Shopper (Denison) **10739**
Greenville Herald Banner (Greenville) **10504**
Groesbeck Journal (Groesbeck) **10741**
Gulf Coast Tribune, The (West Columbia) **10747**
Hallettsville Tribune-Herald (Hallettsville) **10741**
Hamilton Herald-News (Hamilton) **10741**
Hansford County Reporter-Statesman (Spearman) **10747**
Haskell Free Press (Haskell) **10741**
Henderson Daily News (Henderson) **10504**
Herald-Democrat (Denison) **10503**
Herald Coaster (Rosenberg) **10506**
Hereford Brand (Hereford) **10504**
Hondo Anvil Herald (Hondo) **10741**
Hood County News (Granbury) **10741**
Houston Chronicle (Houston) **10504**
Houston County Courier (Crockett) **10738**
Houston Forward Times (Houston) **10742**
Houston Informer (Houston) **10742**
† Houston Post (Houston)
Howe Enterprise (Howe) **10742**
Hubbard City News (Mexia) **10744**
Humble Sun (Humble) **10742**
Hunt County Shopper (Greenville) **10741**
Huntsville Item (Huntsville) **10504**
Idalou Beacon (Idalou) **10742**
Iowa Park Leader (Iowa Park) **10742**
Irving News (Arlington) **10736**
Jackson County Herald/Tribune (Edna) **10739**
Jacksonville Daily Progress (Jacksonville) **10504**
Jasper NewsBoy (Jasper) **10742**
Jasper NewsBoy Shopper (Jasper) **10742**
Jefferson Jimplecute (Jefferson) **10742**
† Jet Gazette (Austin)
Junction Eagle, The (Junction) **10742**
Karnes Citation (Karnes City) **10742**
Kaufman Herald, The (Kaufman) **10742**
Keller Citizen, The (Keller) **10742**
Kelly Observer (San Antonio) **10746**
Kennedale News (Everman) **10740**
Kennedy Advanced Times (Karnes City) **10742**
Kerrville Daily Times (Kerrville) **10504**
Kilgore News Herald (Kilgore) **10504**
Killeen Daily Herald (Killeen) **10504**
Kingsville Record, The (Kingsville) **10743**
Kingwood Sun (Humble) **10742**
Lackland Tale Spinner (San Antonio) **10746**
La Feria News (La Feria) **10743**
Lake Cities Sun, The (Lake Dallas) **10743**
La Marque Times (La Marque) **10743**
Lamb County Leader-News (Littlefield) **10743**
Lamesa Press-Reporter (Lamesa) **10743**
Lancaster Today (DeSoto) **10739**
Laredo Morning Times (Laredo) **10505**
Levelland Hockley County News-Press (Levelland) **10743**
Lewisville Leader (Lewisville) **10743**
Liberty Gazette (Liberty) **10743**
Light & Champion (Center) **10737**
† Livingston East Texas Eye (Livingston)
Llano News (Llano) **10744**
Lockhart Post Register (Lockhart) **10744**
Longview News Journal (Longview) **10505**
Lorenzo Examiner (Lorenzo) **10744**
Lubbock Avalanche-Journal (Lubbock) **10505**
Lufkin Daily News (Lufkin) **10505**
Luling Newsboy & Signal (Luling) **10744**
Mansfield News-Mirror (Mansfield) **10744**
Marble Falls Highlander (Marble Falls) **10744**
† Mart Herald (Mart)
Mason County News (Mason) **10744**
Mathis News (Mathis) **10744**
McAllen Monitor (McAllen) **10505**
McKinney Courier Gazette (McKinney) **10505**
Menard News & Messenger, The (Menard) **10744**
Mesquite News (Mesquite) **10744**
Metrocom Herald, The (San Antonio) **10746**
Mexia Daily News (Mexia) **10505**
Miami Chief, The (Miami) **10744**
† Mid-Cities News (Arlington)
Midcounty Chronicle (Nederland) **10745**
Midland Reporter-Telegram (Midland) **10505**
Midlothian Mirror (Midlothian) **10744**
Midlothian Today (DeSoto) **10739**
Mid Valley Town Crier (Weslaco) **10747**
Mineral Wells Index (Mineral Wells) **10505**

Monahans News (Monahans) **10744**
Monitor, The (Mabank) **10744**
Montague County Shopper, The (Bowie) **10737**
Moody Courier, The (Moody) **10745**
Moore County News-Press (Dumas) **10739**
Motley County Tribune (Matador) **10744**
Mountain Sun, The (Kerrville) **10742**
Mount Pleasant Daily Tribune (Mt. Pleasant) **10505**
Munday Courier, The (Munday) **10745**
Navasota Examiner Review (Navasota) **10745**
New Braunfels Herald & Zeitung (New Braunfels) **10505**
News Messenger (Marshall) **10505**
New Ulm Enterprise (New Ulm) **10745**
North San Antonio Times (San Antonio) **10746**
Northside Recorder Times, The (San Antonio) **10746**
Nueces County Record Star (Robstown) **10746**
Oak Cliff Tribune (Dallas) **10738**
Odem-Edroy Times (Sinton) **10746**
Odessa American (Odessa) **10505**
Olney Enterprise, The (Olney) **10745**
Orange Leader (Orange) **10505**
Palacios Beacon (Palacios) **10745**
Palestine Herald-Press (Palestine) **10506**
Pampa News (Pampa) **10506**
Panola Watchman (Carthage) **10737**
Paris News, The (Paris) **10506**
Pasadena Citizen (Pasadena) **10506**
Pecos Enterprise (Pecos) **10506**
Pittsburg Gazette (Pittsburg) **10745**
Plainview Daily Herald (Plainview) **10506**
Plano Star Courier (Plano) **10506**
Pleasanton Express (Pleasanton) **10745**
Polk County Enterprise (Livingston) **10743**
Pony Express Mail (Liberty) **10743**
Port Arthur News (Port Arthur) **10506**
Porter/New Caney Sun (Humble) **10742**
Port Isabel-South Padre Item Press (Port Isabel) **10745**
Portland News (Portland) **10745**
Port Lavaca Wave (Port Lavaca) **10745**
Pottsboro Press (Pottsboro) **10745**
Progress, The (Anahuac) **10736**
Ranger Times (Ranger) **10745**
Real American (Leakey) **10743**
Richardson News (Richardson) **10745**
Rising Star, The (Rising Star) **10745**
River Oaks News (Fort Worth) **10740**
Rockdale Reporter (Rockdale) **10746**
Round Rock Leader (Round Rock) **10746**
Sabinal Sampler (Hondo) **10741**
Sabine County Reporter-Rambler (Hemphill) **10741**

San Angelo Standard-Times (San Angelo) **10506**
San Antonio Express-News (San Antonio) **10506**
† San Antonio Light (San Antonio)
San Augustine Tribune (San Augustine) **10746**
San Benito News (San Benito) **10746**
San Marcos Daily Record (San Marcos) **10506**
San Patricio County News (Sinton) **10746**
Sealy News (Sealy) **10746**
Seguin Gazette-Enterprise (Seguin) **10506**
Shopper Zone II (Denison) **10739**
Silsbee Bee (Silsbee) **10746**
Snyder Daily News (Snyder) **10506**
South County News & Advertiser (Fort Worth) **10740**
Southside Reporter (San Antonio) **10746**
Southwest Sun (Sugar Land) **10747**
Springtown Epigraph, The (Springtown) **10747**
Stamford American (Stamford) **10747**
Stephenville Empire-Tribune (Stephenville) **10506**
Suburban Tribune (Balch Springs) **10736**
Sulphur Springs News-Telegram (Sulphur Springs) **10507**
Sunday Sun (Georgetown) **10740**
Sweetwater Reporter (Sweetwater) **10507**
Taft Tribune (Taft) **10747**
Taylor Daily Press (Taylor) **10507**
Temple Daily Telegram (Temple) **10507**
Terrell Tribune (Terrell) **10507**
Texarkana Gazette (Texarkana) **10507**
Texas City Sun (Texas City) **10507**
Texas Observer (Austin) **10736**
Times-Review (Cleburne) **10503**
Times Record News (Wichita Falls) **10507**
Trenton Tribune (Trenton) **10747**
Tyler County Booster (Woodville) **10748**
Tyler Morning Telegraph (Tyler) **10507**
Uvalde Leader-News (Uvalde) **10747**
Valley Morning Star (Harlingen) **10504**
Valley Town Crier (McAllen) **10744**
Van Horn Advocate (Van Horn) **10747**
Vega Enterprise, The (Vega) **10747**
Vernon Daily Record (Vernon) **10507**
Victoria Advocate (Victoria) **10507**
Vidorian, The (Vidor) **10747**
Villager Newspaper (Austin) **10736**
Vindicator, The (Liberty) **10743**
Waco Citizen, The (Waco) **10747**
Waco Tribune Herald (Waco) **10507**
Waller County News-Citizen (Hempstead) **10741**
Wallis News-Review (Wallis) **10747**
Waxahachie Daily Light (Waxahachie) **10507**
Weatherford Democrat (Weatherford) **10507**

Weimar Mercury (Weimar) **10747**
West Columbia Brazoria County News (West Columbia) **10747**
Westlake Picayune (Austin) **10736**
West News (West) **10747**
Wharton Journal-Spectator (Wharton) **10748**
White Oak Independent (White Oak) **10748**
White Settlement News (Fort Worth) **10740**
Whitewright Sun, The (Whitewright) **10748**
Williamson County Sun (Georgetown) **10740**
Wimberley Valley-News (Wimberley) **10748**
Winkler County News (Kermit) **10742**
Winnsboro News (Winnsboro) **10748**
Wise County Messenger (Decatur) **10738**
Wood County Democrat (Quitman) **10745**
Wylie News, The (Wylie) **10748**
Yoakum Herald-Times (Yoakum) **10748**

UTAH

Box Elder News Journal (Brigham City) **10748**
Citizen (American Fork) **10748**
Daily Herald, The (Provo) **10508**
Davis County Clipper (Bountiful) **10748**
Eagle News (Bountiful) **10748**
Emery County Progress (Castle Dale) **10748**
Herald Journal, The (Logan) **10507**
Leader, The (Tremonton) **10749**
Lehi Free Press (American Fork) **10748**
Magna Times (Magna) **10749**
Millard County Gazette (Delta) **10748**
† Murray Eagle (Salt Lake City)
North Utah County Shopper (American Fork) **10748**
Orem-Geneva Times (Orem) **10749**
Park Record, The (Park City) **10749**
Pleasant Grove Review (American Fork) **10748**
Private Eye Weekly (Salt Lake City) **10749**
Pyramid, The (Mt. Pleasant) **10749**
Richfield Reaper (Richfield) **10749**
Salt Lake City Deseret News (Salt Lake City) **10508**
Salt Lake Tribune (Salt Lake City) **10508**
† South Valley Eagle (Salt Lake City)
Spectrum, The (St. George) **10508**
Standard-Examiner (Ogden) **10508**
Sun Advocate (Price) **10749**
Today's News (Bountiful) **10748**
Tooele Transcript-Bulletin (Tooele) **10749**
Uintah Basin Standard (Roosevelt) **10749**
Vernal Express (Vernal) **10749**
West Valley Eagle (Bountiful) **10748**
West Valley News (Magna) **10749**

VERMONT

Addison County Independent (Middlebury) **10750**
Bellows Falls Town Crier (Bellows Falls) **10749**
Bennington Banner (Bennington) **10508**
Brattleboro Reformer (Brattleboro) **10508**
Burlington Free Press (Burlington) **10508**
Caledonian-Record, The (St. Johnsbury) **10508**
County Courier (Enosburg Falls) **10749**
Hardwick Gazette (Hardwick) **10750**
Herald of Randolph (Randolph) **10750**
Islander, The (South Hero) **10750**
Journal Opinion (Bradford) **10749**
Manchester Journal (Manchester Center) **10750**
Message for the Week (Chester) **10749**
Mountain Times (Killington) **10750**
Newport Daily Express (Newport) **10508**
Pennysaver Press (Bennington) **10749**
† ▼Poultney News, The (Rutland)
Rutland Herald (Rutland) **10508**
Rutland Tribune, The (Rutland) **10750**
Springfield Reporter, The (Springfield) **10750**
St. Albans Messenger (St. Albans) **10508**
Stowe Reporter (Stowe) **10750**
Times Argus (Barre) **10508**
Transcript, The (Morrisville) **10750**
Valley Reporter, The (Waitsfield) **10750**
Vermont News Guide (Manchester Village) **10750**
Vermont Standard (Woodstock) **10750**
Vermont Times (Shelburne) **10750**

VIRGIN ISLANDS

St. Croix Avis (St. Croix) **10508**
Tradewinds (St. John) **10750**
Virgin Islands Daily News (St. Thomas) **10509**

VIRGINIA

Abingdon Virginian (Abingdon) **10750**
Alexandria Gazette Packet (Alexandria) **10750**
Alexandria Journal (Fairfax) **10509**
Altavista Journal (Altavista) **10751**
Amelia Bulletin Monitor, The (Amelia Court House) **10751**
Amherst New Era-Progress (Amherst) **10751**
Appomattox Times-Virginian (Appomattox) **10751**
Arlington Courier, The (Arlington) **10751**
Arlington Journal (Fairfax) **10509**
Bedford Bulletin (Bedford) **10751**
Blacksburg Sentinel (Christiansburg) **10752**
Blackstone Courier-Record (Blackstone) **10751**
Bland Messenger (Wytheville) **10756**

Blue Ridge Leader, The (Purcellville) **10754**
Bristol Herald-Courier, The (Bristol) **10509**
Brunswick Times-Gazette
  (Lawrenceville) **10753**
Burke Times, The (Reston) **10754**
Caroline Progress, The (Bowling Green) **10751**
Carroll News, The (Hillsville) **10753**
Central Virginian, The (Louisa) **10754**
Centreville Times (Reston) **10755**
Chantilly Times (Reston) **10755**
Charlotte Gazette (Drakes Branch) **10752**
Charlottesville-Albemarle Tribune
  (Charlottesville) **10751**
Chesapeake Post (Chesapeake) **10752**
Clark Courier (Berryville) **10751**
Clinch Valley News (Tazewell) **10756**
Coalfield Progress (Norton) **10754**
Crewe-Burkeville Journal (Crewe) **10752**
Culpeper News (Culpeper) **10752**
Culpeper Star Exponent (Culpeper) **10509**
Daily News-Record (Harrisonburg) **10509**
Daily News Leader, The (Staunton) **10510**
Daily Press, The (Newport News) **10510**
Daily Progress (Charlottesville) **10509**
Danville Register & Bee (Danville) **10509**
Declaration, The (Independence) **10753**
Denbigh Gazette (Yorktown) **10756**
Dickenson Star/Cumberland Times, The
  (Clintwood) **10752**
Enterprise Buyer's Catalogue
  (Wytheville) **10756**
Enterprise, The (Stuart) **10756**
Fairfax Connection (McLean) **10754**
Fairfax Journal (Fairfax) **10509**
Fairfax Station Times (Reston) **10755**
Fairfax Times (Reston) **10755**
Falls Church News-Press (Falls Church) **10752**
Farmville Herald, The (Farmville) **10752**
Fauquier Citizen (Warrenton) **10756**
Fauquier Times-Democrat (Warrenton) **10756**
Fincastle Herald, The (Fincastle) **10752**
Floyd Press (Floyd) **10753**
Franklin News-Post (Rocky Mount) **10755**
Fredericksburg Free Lance-Star
  (Fredericksburg) **10509**
Free News, The (Farmville) **10752**
Galax Gazette, The (Galax) **10753**
Gloucester-Mathews Gazette Journal
  (Gloucester) **10753**
Goochland Gazette (Goochland) **10753**
Great Falls Times (Reston) **10755**
Greene County Record (Stanardsville) **10755**
† Henrico Gazette (Richmond)
Herald-Progress (Ashland) **10751**
Herndon Times (Reston) **10755**
Hopewell News (Hopewell) **10509**

Independent-Messenger (Emporia) **10752**
Journal Messenger (Manassas) **10509**
Journal, The (King George) **10753**
Kenbridge-Victoria Dispatch (Victoria) **10756**
Lebanon News (Lebanon) **10753**
† Ledger-Star (Norfolk)
Leesburg Today (Leesburg) **10753**
Loudoun Times-Mirror (Leesburg) **10753**
Madison County Eagle (Madison) **10754**
Martinsville Bulletin (Martinsville) **10509**
McLean Providence Journal (Reston) **10755**
Mechanicsville Local (Mechanicsville) **10754**
Mecklenburg Sun (Clarksville) **10752**
Metro Weekenders, The (Norfolk) **10754**
Mountain Advisor (Richlands) **10755**
Mount Vernon Gazette (Alexandria) **10751**
Nelson County Times (Amherst) **10751**
New Castle Record (New Castle) **10754**
News & Advance (Lynchburg) **10509**
News-Gazette (Lexington) **10753**
News-Progress, The (Chase City) **10751**
News-Virginian (Waynesboro) **10510**
News Buyer's Catalogue (Wytheville) **10756**
News Buyers Catalog (Marion) **10754**
News Messenger, The (Christiansburg) **10752**
Northern Piedmont Express (Culpeper) **10752**
Northern Virginia Daily (Strasburg) **10510**
Northern Virginia Sun, The (Fairfax) **10752**
Northumberland Echo (Heathsville) **10753**
Orange County Review (Orange) **10754**
Page News & Courier (Luray) **10754**
Poquoson Post (Yorktown) **10756**
Portsmouth Times (Chesapeake) **10752**
Post, The (Big Stone Gap) **10751**
Potomac News (Woodbridge) **10510**
Powell Valley News (Pennington Gap) **10754**
▼Prince William Journal (Manassas) **10509**
Progress-Index (Petersburg) **10510**
Radford News Journal (Christiansburg) **10752**
Rappahannock News (Washington) **10756**
Rappahannock Record (Kilmarnock) **10753**
Recorder, The (Monterey) **10754**
Reston Times (Reston) **10755**
Richlands News Press (Richlands) **10755**
Richmond Times-Dispatch (Richmond) **10510**
Roanoke Times, The (Roanoke) **10510**
Rockbridge Weekly (Lexington) **10753**
Rural Virginian (Charlottesville) **10751**
Salem Times-Register (Salem) **10755**
Shenandoah Valley-Herald, The
  (Woodstock) **10756**
Smith Mountain Eagle (Moneta) **10754**
Smyth County News & Messenger
  (Marion) **10754**
South Boston Gazette-Virginian (South
  Boston) **10755**

South Boston News & Record (South Boston) **10755**
South Hill Enterprise (South Hill) **10755**
Southside Sentinel (Urbanna) **10756**
Southwest Times, The (Pulaski) **10510**
Southwest Virginia Enterprise (Wytheville) **10756**
Springfield Times Courier (Reston) **10755**
Star-Tribune (Chatham) **10751**
Suffolk News-Herald (Suffolk) **10510**
Sussex-Surry Dispatch (Wakefield) **10756**
Tazewell County Free Press (Richlands) **10755**
Tidewater News, The (Franklin) **10753**
Tidewater Review (West Point) **10756**
Union Star (Brookneal) **10751**
Valley Banner, The (Elkton) **10752**
Vienna Times (Reston) **10755**
Vinton Messenger (Vinton) **10756**
Virginia Beach Sun (Chesapeake) **10752**
Virginia Gazette (Williamsburg) **10756**
Virginia Mountaineer (Grundy) **10753**
Virginian-Leader (Pearisburg) **10754**
Virginian-Pilot, The (Norfolk) **10510**
Virginian Review (Covington) **10509**
Warren Sentinel, The (Front Royal) **10753**
Washington County News (Abingdon) **10750**
Weekender, The (Lexington) **10753**
Westmoreland News (Montross) **10754**
Winchester Star (Winchester) **10510**
York Town Crier (Yorktown) **10757**

WASHINGTON

Anacortes American (Anacortes) **10757**
Bainbridge Review (Bainbridge Island) **10757**
Beacon Hill News, The/South District Journal (Seattle) **10759**
Bellingham Herald (Bellingham) **10510**
Business Examiner (Gig Harbor) **10758**
Camas/Washougal Post Record (Camas) **10757**
Capitol Hill Times (Seattle) **10759**
Cashmere Valley Record (Cashmere) **10757**
Cheney Free Press (Cheney) **10757**
Chronicle, The (Centralia) **10511**
Columbia Basin Herald (Moses Lake) **10511**
Columbian, The (Vancouver) **10512**
Daily News (Longview) **10511**
Daily Record (Ellensburg) **10511**
Daily Sun-News (Sunnyside) **10512**
Daily World, The (Aberdeen) **10510**
Dayton Chronicle (Dayton) **10757**
Des Moines News (Seattle) **10759**
Eastside Journal (Bellevue) **10510**
Enterprise, The (Lynnwood) **10758**
Enumclaw Courier-Herald (Enumclaw) **10757**
† Fairchild Strikehawk (Spokane)
Federal Way News (Federal Way) **10758**
Franklin County Graphic (Connell) **10757**
Gem State Miner (Newport) **10758**
Goldendale Sentinel (Goldendale) **10758**
Grandview Herald (Grandview) **10758**
Grant County Journal (Ephrata) **10757**
Herald, The (Everett) **10511**
Highline News (Seatac) **10759**
Issaquah Press (Issaquah) **10758**
Leavenworth Echo (Leavenworth) **10758**
Lewis River News (Woodland) **10760**
Long Beach Chinook Observer (Long Beach) **10758**
Lynden Tribune (Lynden) **10758**
Madison Park Times (Seattle) **10759**
Mercer Island Reporter (Mercer Island) **10758**
Newport Miner (Newport) **10758**
News Tribune, The (Tacoma) **10512**
Nisqually Valley News (Yelm) **10760**
North Central Outlook (Seattle) **10759**
North Kitsap Herald (Poulsbo) **10759**
Northshore Citizen (Bothell) **10757**
North Snohomish Weekly (Arlington) **10757**
Olympian, The (Olympia) **10511**
Omak-Okanogan County Chronicle (Omak) **10758**
Outlook, The (Othello) **10758**
Peninsula Daily News (Port Angeles) **10511**
Peninsula Gateway (Gig Harbor) **10758**
Pierce County Herald (Puyallup) **10759**
Port Orchard Independent (Port Orchard) **10759**
Port Townsend/Jefferson County Leader (Port Townsend) **10759**
Queen Anne-Magnolia News (Seattle) **10759**
Redmond Sammamish Valley News (Redmond) **10759**
Reflector, The (Battle Ground) **10757**
Rochester Sun News, The (Tenino) **10760**
Royal Review (Royal City) **10759**
Seattle Daily Journal of Commerce (Seattle) **10511**
Seattle Facts (Seattle) **10759**
Seattle Post-Intelligencer (Seattle) **10511**
Seattle Skanner, The (Seattle) **10759**
Seattle Times, The (Seattle) **10511**
Seattle Weekly (Seattle) **10759**
Sequim Gazette (Sequim) **10760**
Shelton-Mason County Journal (Shelton) **10760**
Skagit Valley Herald (Mt. Vernon) **10511**
Snohomish County Tribune (Snohomish) **10760**
South County Journal (Kent) **10511**
South District Journal (Seattle) **10759**

Spokesman-Review, The (Spokane) **10511**
Sprague Advocate, The (Sprague) **10760**
Statesman-Examiner (Colville) **10757**
Sun, The (Bremerton) **10511**
Tacoma City Paper (Tacoma) **10760**
Tenino Independent (Tenino) **10760**
Times, The (Waitsburg) **10760**
Toppenish Review (Toppenish) **10760**
Tri-City Herald (Kennewick) **10511**
Tribune (Deer Park) **10757**
University Herald (Seattle) **10759**
Valley News Herald (Spokane) **10760**
Vashon-Maury Island Beachcomber (Vashon) **10760**
Voice of the Valley (Maple Valley) **10758**
Wahkiakum County Eagle, The (Cathlamet) **10757**
Walla Walla Union-Bulletin (Walla Walla) **10512**
Wapato Independent (Wapato) **10760**
Wenatchee World (Wenatchee) **10512**
West Plains Tribune (Spokane)
West Seattle Herald (Seattle) **10759**
Westside Record-Journal (Ferndale) **10758**
Whidbey News-Times (Oak Harbor) **10758**
Whitman County Gazette (Colfax) **10757**
Willapa Harbor Herald (Raymond) **10759**
Yakima Herald-Republic (Yakima) **10512**

WEST VIRGINIA

Barbour Democrat, The (Philippi) **10762**
Bluefield Daily Telegraph (Bluefield) **10512**
Braxton Citizen's News (Sutton) **10763**
Braxton Democrat-Central (Sutton) **10763**
Brooke County Review (Wellsburg) **10763**
Cabell Record (Culloden) **10761**
Calhoun Chronicle (Grantsville) **10761**
Charleston Daily Mail (Charleston) **10512**
Charleston Gazette, The (Charleston) **10512**
Clarksburg Exponent (Clarksburg) **10512**
Clarksburg Telegram (Clarksburg) **10512**
Clay County Free Press (Clay) **10761**
Coal Valley News (Danville) **10761**
Daily Times (Weirton) **10513**
Dominion Post, The (Morgantown) **10513**
Fayette Tribune (Oak Hill) **10762**
Franklin Pendleton Times (Franklin) **10761**
Glenville Democrat, The (Glenville) **10761**
Glenville Pathfinder (Glenville) **10761**
Grant County Press (Petersburg) **10762**
Greenbrier Valley Ranger (Lewisburg) **10762**
Green Tab (Moundsville) **10762**
Hampshire Review (Romney) **10763**
Herald Record (West Union) **10764**
Hinton News (Hinton) **10761**
Hometown News (Madison) **10762**
Huntington Herald-Dispatch (Huntington) **10512**
Hurricane Breeze (Hurricane) **10761**
Independent Herald, The (Pineville) **10762**
Intelligencer, The (Wheeling) **10513**
Inter-Mountain, The (Elkins) **10512**
Jackson Herald (Ripley) **10763**
Jackson Star News (Ravenswood) **10762**
Journal, The (Martinsburg) **10513**
Lincoln Journal (Hamlin) **10761**
Lincoln Times, The (Hamlin) **10761**
Lincoln Weekly News Sentinel (Hamlin) **10761**
Logan Banner (Logan) **10513**
Mineral Daily Tribune (Keyser) **10513**
Monroe Watchman (Union) **10763**
Montgomery Herald (Montgomery) **10762**
Moorefield Examiner (Moorefield) **10762**
Morgan Messenger, The (Berkeley Springs) **10760**
Moundsville Daily Echo (Moundsville) **10513**
Mountain Messenger (Lewisburg) **10762**
Mountain Statesman (Grafton) **10761**
Mullens Advocate (Mullen) **10762**
News Leader (Richwood) **10763**
Nicholas Chronicle (Summersville) **10763**
† Panhandle Press (Chester)
Parkersburg Sentinel (Parkersburg) **10513**
Parsons Advocate (Parsons) **10762**
Pennsboro News (Pennsboro) **10762**
Piedmont Herald (Piedmont) **10762**
Pocahontas Times (Marlinton) **10762**
Point Pleasant Register (Point Pleasant) **10513**
Post Report, The (Beckley) **10760**
Preston County Journal (Kingwood) **10761**
Preston County News (Kingwood) **10761**
Princeton Times (Princeton) **10762**
Putnam-Cabell Post (Culloden) **10761**
Record-Delta, The (Buckhannon) **10760**
Register/Herald (Beckley) **10512**
Ritchie Gazette (Harrisville) **10761**
Roane County Reporter (Spencer) **10763**
Shepherdstown Chronicle (Shepherdstown) **10763**
Spirit of Jefferson-Advocate (Charles Town) **10761**
Star Herald (Ripley) **10763**
Times Record (Spencer) **10763**
Times West Virginian (Fairmont) **10512**
Tyler Star News (Sistersville) **10763**
Wayne County News (Wayne) **10763**
Webster Echo (Webster Springs) **10763**
Webster Republican (Webster Springs) **10763**
Welch Daily News (Welch) **10513**
Weston Democrat, The (Weston) **10763**
West Virginia Daily News (Lewisburg) **10513**
West Virginia Hillbilly (Richwood) **10763**

Wetzel Chronicle (New Martinsville) **10762**
Wheeling News-Register (Wheeling) **10513**
Williamson Daily News (Williamson) **10513**

WISCONSIN

Abbotsford Tribune-Phonograph (Abbotsford) **10764**
Action Advertiser (Fond Du Lac) **10767**
Adams County Times (Adams) **10764**
Algoma Record Herald (Algoma) **10764**
Amery Free Press (Amery) **10764**
Antigo Area Shoppers Guide (Antigo) **10764**
Antigo Daily Journal (Antigo) **10513**
Arcadia News-Leader (Arcadia) **10764**
Argyle Agenda (Argyle) **10764**
Augusta Area Times (Augusta) **10764**
Baldwin Bulletin (Baldwin) **10764**
Banner Journal (Black River Falls) **10764**
Baraboo News-Republic (Baraboo) **10514**
Bargain Express Newspaper (Milwaukee) **10769**
Barron News Shield (Barron) **10764**
Bay Viewer (New Berlin) **10770**
Beaver Dam Daily Citizen (Beaver Dam) **10514**
Bee, The (Phillips) **10772**
Belleville Recorder (Belleville) **10764**
Beloit Daily News (Beloit) **10514**
Berlin Buyers' Guide (Berlin) **10764**
Berlin Journal (Berlin) **10764**
Billboard, The (Berlin) **10764**
Blade Atlas (Blanchardville) **10765**
Blair Press (Blair) **10765**
Bloomer Advance (Bloomer) **10765**
Boscobel Dial (Boscobel) **10765**
Brillion News (Brillion) **10765**
Brookfield News (New Berlin) **10770**
Brown Deer Herald (New Berlin) **10770**
Buffalo County Journal (Cochrane) **10765**
Bulletin, The (Kenosha) **10768**
Burlington Standard Press (Burlington) **10765**
Burnett County Sentinel (Grantsburg) **10767**
Buyer's Guide Cent Saver (Mauston) **10769**
Cadott Sentinel (Cadott) **10765**
Cambridge News (Cambridge) **10765**
Campbellsport News (Campbellsport) **10765**
Capital Times, The (Madison) **10514**
Cashton Record (Cashton) **10765**
Central Saint Croix News (Hammond) **10767**
Chetek Alert, The (Chetek) **10765**
Chilton Times-Journal (Chilton) **10765**
Chippewa Herald-Telegram (Chippewa Falls) **10514**
Clark County Press (Neillsville) **10770**
Clinton Topper (Clinton) **10765**
Clintonville Tribune-Gazette (Clintonville) **10765**
Colfax Messenger (Colfax) **10766**
Columbus Journal (Columbus) **10766**
Community Herald (Monona) **10770**
Cornell & Lake Holcombe Courier (Cornell) **10766**
County Journal, The (Washburn) **10775**
County Ledger-Press (Balsam Lake) **10764**
Courier-Wedge (Durand) **10766**
Courier Hub (Stoughton) **10774**
Courier Press (Prairie du Chien) **10772**
Courier, The (Sun Prairie) **10774**
Crawford County Independent-Kickapoo Scout (Gay Mills) **10767**
Cudahy Reminder-Enterprise (New Berlin) **10770**
Cumberland Advocate (Cumberland) **10766**
Daily Jefferson County Union (Fort Atkinson) **10514**
Daily News (West Bend) **10516**
Daily Press, The (Ashland) **10513**
Daily Register, The (Portage) **10515**
Daily Tribune, The (Wisconsin Rapids) **10516**
Delavan Enterprise (Delavan) **10766**
Democrat Tribune, The (Mineral Point) **10769**
Denmark Press (Denmark) **10766**
De Pere Journal (De Pere) **10766**
Dodge County Independent-News (Juneau) **10768**
Dodgeville Chronicle, Inc. (Dodgeville) **10766**
Door County Advocate (Sturgeon Bay) **10774**
Dunn County News (Menomonie) **10769**
Eagle-Herald (Marinette) **10515**
East Troy News (East Troy) **10766**
Edgerton Reporter (Edgerton) **10766**
Elkhorn Independent (Elkhorn) **10766**
Elm Grove Elm Leaves (New Berlin) **10770**
Evergreen Shopping Guide (Spooner) **10773**
Fennimore Times (Fennimore) **10767**
Fitchburg Star (Verona) **10774**
Five County/Buyer's Guide (Ripon) **10773**
Florence Mining News (Florence) **10767**
Forest Republican, The (Crandon) **10766**
Forest Times-Tribune (De Forest) **10766**
Foto News (Merrill) **10769**
Fox Lake Representative (Fox Lake) **10767**
Fox Point, Bayside, River Hills Herald (New Berlin) **10770**
Foxxy Shopper (Sparta) **10773**
Franklin-Hales Corner Hub (New Berlin) **1077**
Freeman, The (Waukesha) **10515**
Galesville Republican (Galesville) **10767**
Germantown Banner-Press (New Berlin) **1077**
Glendale Herald (New Berlin) **10770**
Glidden Enterprise (Glidden) **10767**

Good News (Monona) **10770**
Grant County Herald Independent (Lancaster) **10768**
Green Bay News-Chronicle (Green Bay) **10514**
Green Bay Press-Gazette (Green Bay) **10514**
Greendale Village Life (New Berlin) **10770**
Greenfield Observer (New Berlin) **10770**
Green Lake County Reporter (Berlin) **10764**
Herald-Times Reporter (Manitowoc) **10514**
Hillsboro Sentry-Enterprise (Hillsboro) **10768**
Horicon Reporter (Horicon) **10768**
Hudson Star-Observer (Hudson) **10768**
Independence News-Wave (Independence) **10768**
Independent (Deerfield) **10766**
Independent-Register, The (Brodhead) **10765**
Indianhead Advertiser (Frederic) **10767**
Inter-County Leader (Frederic) **10767**
Iola Herald (Iola) **10768**
Iron County Miner (Hurley) **10768**
Isthmus (Madison) **10769**
Janesville Gazette (Janesville) **10514**
Journal & Monitor Herald (Tomah) **10774**
Journal Times (Racine) **10515**
Juneau County Star-Times (Mauston) **10769**
Kaukauna Times (Kaukauna) **10768**
Kenosha News (Kenosha) **10514**
Kettle Moraine Index (Hartland) **10767**
Kewaskum Statesman (Kewaskum) **10768**
Kewaunee Enterprise (Kewaunee) **10768**
Keystone Reporter (Elroy) **10767**
Kiel Tri-County Record (Kiel) **10768**
La Crosse County Countryman (West Salem) **10775**
La Crosse Tribune (La Crosse) **10514**
Ladysmith News (Ladysmith) **10768**
Lake Country Reporter (Hartland) **10767**
Lake Geneva Regional News (Lake Geneva) **10768**
Lakeland Times (Minocqua) **10770**
Lake Mills Leader (Lake Mills) **10768**
Lakeshore Chronicle (Manitowoc) **10769**
Leader-Telegram (Eau Claire) **10514**
Lodi Enterprise (Lodi) **10768**
Loyal Tribune-Record-Gleaner (Loyal) **10769**
Luxemburg News (Luxemburg) **10769**
Marion Advertiser (Marion) **10769**
Marquette County Tribune (Montello) **10770**
Marshfield News-Herald (Marshfield) **10515**
Mayville News, The (Mayville) **10769**
McFarland Community Life (Monona) **10770**
† McFarland Leader (Monona)
Melrose Chronicle (Melrose) **10769**
Menomonee Falls News (New Berlin) **10771**
Mequon-Thiensville Courant (New Berlin) **10771**
† Mid-County Times (Pardeeville)
Middleton Times-Tribune (Middleton) **10769**
Milton Courier (Milton) **10769**
Milwaukee Journal Sentinel (Milwaukee) **10515**
Milwaukee Star (Milwaukee) **10769**
Mondovi Herald News (Mondovi) **10770**
Monroe County Democrat (Sparta) **10773**
Monroe Times, The (Monroe) **10515**
Mosinee Times, The (Mosinee) **10770**
Mukwonago Chief (Mukwonago) **10770**
Muskego Sun (New Berlin) **10771**
Neighbors (Hillsboro) **10768**
Neighbors (Markesan) **10769**
▼Neighbors (Waupun) **10775**
New Berlin Citizen (New Berlin) **10771**
New Holstein Reporter (New Holstein) **10771**
New Richmond News (New Richmond) **10771**
North Star Journal (Presque Isle) **10772**
O-W Enterprise (Withee) **10775**
Oak Creek Pictorial (New Berlin) **10771**
Oconomowoc Enterprise (Oconomowoc) **10771**
Oconto County Times-Herald (Oconto Falls) **10771**
Omro Herald (Omro) **10771**
Oregon Observer (Oregon) **10771**
Orfordville Journal & Footville News (Orfordville) **10772**
Osceola Sun (Osceola) **10772**
Oshkosh Buyers Guide (Oshkosh) **10772**
Oshkosh Northwestern (Oshkosh) **10515**
Ozaukee County News Graphic (Cedarburg) **10765**
Ozaukee Guide (Cedarburg) **10765**
Ozaukee Press (Port Washington) **10772**
Park Falls Herald (Park Falls) **10772**
Peshtigo Times (Peshtigo) **10772**
Picture Post (Waupaca) **10775**
Pierce County Herald (Ellsworth) **10767**
Platteville Journal (Platteville) **10772**
Post-Crescent, The (Appleton) **10513**
Poynette Press (Poynette) **10772**
Prescott Journal (Prescott) **10772**
Press-Star (New London) **10771**
Princeton Times-Republic (Princeton) **10772**
Record-Review, The (Abbotsford) **10764**
Reedsburg Times-Press (Reedsburg) **10772**
Reporter, The (Fond Du Lac) **10514**
Republican-Journal (Darlington) **10766**
Review, The (Plymouth) **10772**
Rhinelander Daily News (Rhinelander) **10515**
Rice Lake Chronotype (Rice Lake) **10773**
Richland Observer (Richland Center) **10773**
Ripon Commonwealth Press (Ripon) **10773**
River Falls Journal (River Falls) **10773**
Sauk-Prairie Star (Sauk City) **10773**
Sawyer County Gazette (Winter) **10775**

Sawyer County Record (Hayward) **10767**
Sharon Reporter, The (Sharon) **10773**
Shawano Leader (Shawano) **10515**
Sheboygan Falls News (Sheboygan Falls) **10773**
Sheboygan Press, The (Sheboygan) **10515**
Shopper Stopper (Merrimac) **10769**
Shopping News (Platteville) **10772**
Shoreline Chronicle (Sheboygan) **10773**
Shorewood Herald (New Berlin) **10771**
Sounder, The (Random Lake) **10772**
South Milwaukee Voice Graphic (New Berlin) **10771**
Sparta Herald (Sparta) **10773**
Spooner Advocate (Spooner) **10773**
Spring Valley Sun (Spring Valley) **10773**
Stanley Republican (Stanley) **10773**
Star News, The (Medford) **10769**
Star, The (Sun Prairie) **10774**
Stevens Point Journal (Stevens Point) **10515**
St. Francis Reminder-Enterprise (New Berlin) **10771**
Stratford Journal (Stratford) **10774**
Superior Daily Telegram (Superior) **10515**
Sussex-Lannon-Lisbon News (New Berlin) **10771**
Sussex Sun (Hartland) **10767**
Thorp Courier (Thorp) **10774**
Times-Press (Hartford) **10767**
Times-Press (Seymour) **10773**
Times, The (Westby) **10775**
Tomahawk Leader (Tomahawk) **10774**
Tomah Journal (Tomah) **10774**
Tomah Monitor-Herald (Tomah) **10774**
Tri-County News (Osseo) **10772**
Tri-County Press (Cuba City) **10766**
Tribune Press Reporter (Glenwood City) **10767**
Turtle Lake Times, The (Turtle Lake) **10774**
Valders Journal (Valders) **10774**
Valley Value Shopper (Spring Valley) **10773**
Vernon County Broadcaster (Viroqua) **10774**
Verona Press (Verona) **10774**
Vilas County News-Review (Eagle River) **10766**
Walworth Times, The (Walworth) **10774**
Washburn County Register (Shell Lake) **10773**
Waterford Post (Waterford) **10775**
Watertown Daily Times (Watertown) **10515**
Waunakee Tribune (Waunakee) **10775**
Wausau Daily Herald (Wausau) **10515**

Waushara Argus (Wautoma) **10775**
Wauwatosa News-Times (Newverland) **10771**
West Allis Star (New Berlin) **10771**
Westine Report (Union Grove) **10774**
Westosha Report (Twin Lakes) **10774**
Whitefish Bay Herald (New Berlin) **10771**
Whitehall Times (Whitehall) **10775**
Winneconne News (Winneconne) **10775**
Wisconsin Dells Events (Wisconsin Dells) **10775**
Wisconsin State Farmer (Waupaca) **10775**
Wisconsin State Journal (Madison) **10514**
Wittenberg Enterprise News (Wittenberg) **10775**

WYOMING

Bridger Valley Pioneer (Lyman) **10776**
Buffalo Bulletin (Buffalo) **10775**
Casper Star Tribune (Casper) **10516**
Cody Enterprise (Cody) **10776**
Daily Times, The (Rawlins) **10516**
Guernsey Gazette/Lingle Guide (Guernsey) **10776**
Jackson Hole Guide (Jackson) **10776**
Jackson Hole News (Jackson) **10776**
Kemmerer Gazette (Kemmerer) **10776**
Lander Wyoming State Journal (Lander) **1077**
Laramie Daily Boomerang (Laramie) **10516**
Lovell Chronicle, The (Lovell) **10776**
Lusk Herald (Lusk) **10776**
Moorcroft Leader (Moorcroft) **10776**
News-Record (Gillette) **10516**
News Letter Journal (Newcastle) **10776**
Northern Wyoming Daily News (Worland) **10516**
Platte County Record-Times (Wheatland) **10776**
Riverton Ranger (Riverton) **10516**
Rock Springs Daily Rocket-Miner (Rock Springs) **10516**
Saratoga Sun (Saratoga) **10776**
Sentinel (Cheyenne) **10775**
Sheridan Press (Sheridan) **10516**
Torrington Telegram (Torrington) **10776**
Uinta County Herald (Evanston) **10776**
Wind River News (Lander) **10776**
Wyoming State Journal (Lander) **10776**
Wyoming Tribune-Eagle (Cheyenne) **10516**

Cessations

Adams County Leader (Council, ID).
Adelanto Bulletin, The (Adelanto, CA).
Alabama Journal (Montgomery, AL).
Algonac Courier Journal (Marine City, MI).
Alpena Journal (Wessington Springs, SD).
Alvin Tiller (Lamont, CA).
Amsterdam Star, The (Albany, NY).
Anchor Bay Beacon (New Baltimore, MI).
Anderson Countian (Garnett, KS).
Applewood/Wheat Ridge Transcript
  (Golden, CO).
Arcadia Tribune (Arcadia, CA).
Augusta Herald (Augusta, GA).
Ausable Forks Adirondack Record Post
  (Elizabethtown, NY).
Austintown Leader (Niles, OH).
Azalea City News & Review (Bayou Labatre, AL).
Bal Harbor/Bay Harbour News (South
  Miami, FL).
Berkshire Courier (Great Barrington, MA).
Birmingham Free Press (Birmingham, AL).
Biz (Oxford, PA).
Breeze Herald (Conneut Lake Park, PA).
Brewery Gulch Gazette (Bisbee, AZ).
Bridgewater Townsman (Bridgewater, MA).
Broken Arrow Scout (Broken Arrow, OK).
Brooklyn Times (Brooklyn, NY).
Brooksville Sun Journal (Brooksville, FL).
Brookville American (Brookville, PA).
Buyer's Guide (Napa, CA).

Byron Center/Dorr Advance (Jenison, MI).
Cape Cod News (Yarmouth Port, MA).
Carpinteria Herald (Goleta, CA).
Carrollton Chronicle (Carrollton, TX).
Cato Citizen (Red Creek, NY).
Central Coast Times (Paso Robles, CA).
Chandler Post (Boonville, IN).
Charlestown Citizen (Brookline, MA).
Chateaugay Record (Chateaugay, NY).
Cherry Hill News (Cherry Hill, NJ).
Clay Countian (Orange Park, FL).
Clay County Crescent (Orange Park, FL).
Clayton Sun (Atlanta, GA).
Clermont County Review (Cincinnati, OH).
Clermont Courier (Cincinnati, OH).
Communicator Community News (Reno, NV).
Community Press, West Chester (Loveland, OH).
Conneaut News-Herald (Conneaut, OH).
Conway Field & Herald (Conway, SC).
Countywide News (Westminster, MD).
Courier, The (Thomasville, GA).
Crestview Okaloosa-News Journal
  (Crestview, FL).
Cuba Journal (Cuba, IL).
Cumberland Times (Crossville, TN).
Current (Potsdam, NY).
Daily Journal (Elizabeth, NJ).
Daily Milford Citizen (Milford, CT).
Daily Record, The (Westchester, PA).
DeKalb News/Sun (Decatur, GA).

Delta Paper (Delta Jct, AK).
Dennis Bulletin (South Yarmouth, MA).
Desert Mountain Express (Hesperia, CA).
Diamond Drill, The (Crystal Falls, MI).
Dispatch, The (Cookeville, TN).
DuPage Press Service (Wheaton, IL).
East County Chronicle (Kimberly, ID).
East Los Angeles Gazette (South Gate, CA).
East Los Angeles Tribune (South Gate, CA).
East Palestine Heritage, The (Columbiana, OH).
Eastside Times (Tulsa, OK).
Echo, The (Berlin, NY).
Enterprise News (Pixley, CA).
Enterprise Sun (Marlborough, MA).
Erie County Reporter (Huron, OH).
Evening Express (Portland, ME).
Evening Sentinel (Ansonia, CT).
Fairchild Strikehawk (Spokane, WA).
Fair Haven Register (Red Creek, NY).
Fairport-Perinton Herald-Mail (Webster, NY).
Fallon Eagle Standard (Fallon, NV).
Farmers Branch Times (Carrollton, TX).
Farmington Valley Herald (Simsbury, CT).
Fayette Sun (Fayetteville, GA).
Flat River Lead Belt News (Flat River, MO).
Fort Myers Observer (Fort Myers, FL).
Freeborn County Register (Albert Lea, MN).
Garnett Review (Garnett, KS).
Geauga Times-Leader (Chardon, OH).
Girard News (Niles, OH).
Gladstone Delta Reporter (Escanaba, MI).
Goleta Review (Goleta, CA).
Goleta Sun (Santa Barbara, CA).
Good Times News (Fayette, MO).
Grace Citizen (Preston, ID).
Green River Republican (Morgantown, KY).
Greenville Piedmont (Greenville, SC).
Greenwich News (Greenwich, CT).
Gwinnett Daily News (Lawrenceville, GA).
Haddon Gazette (Cherry Hill, NJ).
Haines City Herald (Haines City, FL).
Hamilton County News (Elizabethtown, NY).
Hanover Park Township Times (Carol Stream, IL).
Harper Woods Herald (Birmingham, MI).
Harwood Heights News (Park Ridge, IL).
Hendersonville Free Press (Hendersonville, TN).
Hendricks County Guide Gazette (Plainfield, IN).
Henrico Gazette (Richmond, VA).
Herald, The (Tarpon Springs, FL).
Highlands Press (Mulberry, FL).
Hodgkins Citizen (La Grange, IL).
Hollywood Citizen News (Los Angeles, CA).
Hollywood Sun (Hollywood, FL).
Homestead/Florida City News (Miami, FL).
Houston Post (Houston, TX).
Hubbard News (Niles, OH).
Humboldt Republican (Humboldt, IA).
Huntingdon Carroll Leader (Huntingdon, TN).
Huntsville News (Huntsville, AL).
Independent Press (Marine City, MI).
Inside Ravenswood (Chicago, IL).
Interboro News (Prospect Park, PA).
Jefferson Republic, The (De Soto, MO).
Jet Gazette (Austin, TX).
Jet Visitor (Cherokee, OK).
Journal Courier (Moravia, NY).
Journal Transcript (Franklin, NH).
Kansas Business News (Augusta, KS).
Kansas City Evening News (Shawnee Mission, KS).
Kirtland Enterprise (Willoughby, OH).
Kossuth County Advance (Algona, IA).
Lake Alfred Press (Mulberry, FL).
Lake Country Chronicle (Buchanan, MI).
Lake Wales Highlander (Winter Haven, FL).
Lead Call (Lead, SD).
Leader, The (Lansing, KS).
Leader, The (East Palestine, OH).
Lebanon Connecticut Valley Reporter (Lebanon, NH).
Ledger-Star (Norfolk, VA).
Liberty News (Niles, OH).
Licking Countian (Newark, OH).
Lincoln-Belmont Booster (Chicago, IL).
Linesville Herald (Conneaut Lake, PA).
Little Falls Transcript (Little Falls, MN).
Littleton Times (Littleton, CO).
Livingston East Texas Eye (Livingston, TX).
London Mills Times (Roseville, IL).
Long Beach Community News (Long Beach, CA).
Long Island Journal Newspaper Group (Long Beach, NY).
Madison Tribune (Ontario, OH).
Main Line Chronicle (West Chester, PA).
Malden Press-Merit (Malden, MO).
Mammoth Lakes Review/Mono Herald (Mammoth Lakes, CA).
Marathon Independent Newspaper (Marathon, NY).
Marin County Daily Recording (San Rafael, CA).
Market Place (Vandergrift, PA).
Marshall County Life (Culver, IN).
Mart Herald (Mart, TX).
Martin County News (Stuart, FL).
Matthews News (Matthews, NC).
Maumee Valley Herald (Toledo, OH).
McFarland Leader (Monona, WI).
Melrose Shoppers News (Stoneham, MA).
Miami Shores News (Miami, FL).
Mid-Cities News (Arlington, TX).
Mid-County Times (Pardeeville, WI).

CESSATIONS

MidMon Observer (Washington, PA).
Milford Citizen (Milford, CT).
Mirror-Recorder (Stamford, NY).
Mobile Press (Mobile, AL).
Monroe County Sentinel (Woodsfield, OH).
Montecito Life (Goleta, CA).
Mountaineer, The (Waynesville, NC).
Mountain Visitor (Sevierville, TN).
Mt. Washington Press (Cincinnati, OH).
Murray Eagle (Salt Lake City, UT).
Near South Herald (Chicago, IL).
New Alaskan (Ketchikan, AK).
Newburgh Evening News (Newburgh, NY).
New Hampton Economist (New Hampton, IA).
Newman News, The (Newman, CA).
News-Messenger, The (Rockingham, NC).
NewsEAST (Columbus, OH).
News Herald, The (Mobile, AL).
News of Paterson (Passaic, NJ).
News Outlook (Aberdeen, NC).
New York City Tribune (New York, NY).
New York Newsday (New York, NY).
Niantic News (East Lyme, CT).
Northeast Detroiter (Detroit, MI).
North Scottsdale Independent (Scottsdale, AZ).
Norwalk News (Westport, CT).
Observer-Patriot (Putnam, CT).
Observer, The (Blackwood, NJ).
Orangevale News (Folsom, CA).
Orion Times (Orion, IL).
Orrville Courier-Crescent (Orrville, OH).
Oxnard Press-Courier (Oxnard, CA).
Panhandle Press (Chester, WV).
Paper, The (Spartanburg, SC).
Parsippany Focus (Morris Plains, NJ).
Peabody Times (Peabody, MA).
Peninsula Review, The (Carmel, CA).
Pennysaver (Vista, CA).
Phoenix Gazette (Phoenix, AZ).
Pictorial Press (Tahlequah, OK).
Pittsburgh Press (Pittsburgh, PA).
Poland Leader (Niles, OH).
Poultney News, The (Rutland, VT).
Press, The (Alexandria, MN).
Progress, The (Clearfield, PA).
Quik Quarter Want Ads (Hobbs, NM).
Randolph County Times-Herald (Moberly, MO).
Randolph Mariner (Marshfield, MA).
Rantoul Pacesetter (Rantoul, IL).
Register, The (Shrewsbury, NJ).
Reporter, The (Tampa, FL).
Resident Community News (New York, NY).
Review-Enterprise (Blackwood, NJ).
Rochester Courier (Rochester, NH).
Rohnert Park Cotati Clarion (Cotati, CA).
Roselle Record (Carol Stream, IL).

Sacramento Union (Sacramento, CA).
San Antonio Light (San Antonio, TX).
San Clemente News (San Clemente, CA).
Sandhills Living (Southern Pines, NC).
San Diego Bulletin (Los Angeles, CA).
Sandpoint News-Bulletin (Sandpoint, ID).
Santa Monica Life (Santa Monica, CA).
Saturday Post-Star (Saugerties, NY).
Seminole Outlook (Oviedo, FL).
Sentinel/Altitudes (Frisco, CO).
Sentinel, The (Chicago, IL).
Shawnee-Cridersville Press (Wapakoneta, OH).
Shreveport Journal (Shreveport, LA).
Signal, The (Canal Fulton, OH).
Snake River Press (Craig, CO).
South Bay's Shopper (Lindenhurst, NY).
South East Metro Shopper (Cottage Grove, MN).
South Pasadena Journal (Los Angeles, CA).
Southside Sun (East Point, GA).
South Valley Eagle (Salt Lake City, UT).
Southwest News (South Miami, FL).
Spirit of Bucks County (Hatboro, PA).
Squire, The (Prairie Village, KS).
St. Louis Naborhood Link News (St. Louis, MO).
St. Louis South St. Louis County News (St. Louis, MO).
Stoneham Weekender News (Stoneham, MA).
Suburban News (Reading, MA).
Sunday Glades Trend (Clewiston, FL).
Sunday Sun (Scranton, PA).
Surfside News (South Miami, FL).
Sycamore Messenger (Cincinnati, OH).
This Week (Aledo, IL).
Times-Union (Rochester, NY).
Times, The (Augusta, KY).
Times Tribune (Palo Alto, CA).
Tioga County Gazette & Times (Owego, NY).
Tipton News Leader (Altus, OK).
Total, The (Heflin, AL).
Town & Country (Bradford, PA).
Towne & Country Shopper (Columbus, KS).
Transcript-Telegram (Holyoke, MA).
Tri-City Independent (Margate, FL).
Tri-City Times (Geraldine, AL).
Union Shopper, The (Arcata, CA).
Union, The (Arcata, CA).
Ventura Bulletin, The (Los Angeles, CA).
Victor-Farmington Herald (Webster, NY).
Victor Valley Living (Hesperia, CA).
Village Journal (Osterville, MA).
Vincennes Valley Advance (Vincennes, IN).
Vinton County Courier (McArthur, OH).
Vista Press (Kansas City, MO).
Wallace Miner (Kellogg, ID).
Warrenton Banner (Warrenton, MO).
Weekender Enquirer (Boonville, IN).

Weekender, The (Bronx, NY).
Weekly Territorial (Tucson, AZ).
Wellston Sentry (Wellston, OH).
West Plains Tribune (Spokane, WA).
Wheat Ridge Sentinel (Lakewood, CO).
Wilkes-Barre Sunday Independent (Wilkes Barre, PA).
Winter Visitor Independent (Mesa, AZ).
Wrova Reporter (Galva, IL).
Yarmouth Sun (Yarmouth Port, MA).
Zionsville Eagle (Indianapolis, IN).